Oxford Spanish
Desk Dictionary

Oxford Spanish Desk Dictionary

Second edition, revised

Spanish ----> English
English ----> Spanish

Chief editors
Carol Styles Carvajal
Jane Horwood

OXFORD
UNIVERSITY PRESS

OXFORD
UNIVERSITY PRESS

Great Clarendon Street, Oxford ox2 6DP

Oxford University Press is a department of the University of Oxford.
It furthers the University's objective of excellence in research, scholarship,
and education by publishing worldwide in

Oxford New York

Auckland Bangkok Buenos Aires Cape Town Chennai
Dar es Salaam Delhi Hong Kong Istanbul Karachi Kolkata
Kuala Lumpur Madrid Melbourne Mexico City Mumbai Nairobi
São Paulo Shanghai Taipei Tokyo Toronto

Oxford is a registered trade mark of Oxford University Press
in the UK and in certain other countries

Published in the United States
by Oxford University Press Inc., New York

British Library Cataloguing in Publication Data
Data available

Library of Congress Cataloging in Publication Data
Data available
ISBN 0–19–860723–7

10 9 8 7 6 5 4 3 2 1

Designed by Information Design Unit, Newport Pagnell
Typeset in Nimrod, Arial and Meta by Tradespools
Printed in Great Britain by Clays Ltd, Bungay, Suffolk

Preface / Prólogo

This major new edition of the *Oxford Spanish Desk Dictionary* has been enlarged and extensively revised and updated to meet the needs of both the general and school user. New words and phrases reflect scientific and technological innovations, as well as changes in politics, culture, and society.

Combining the authority of the *Oxford Spanish Dictionary* with the convenience of a smaller format and quick-access layout, this easy-to-use pocket dictionary is the ideal reference tool for all those requiring quick and reliable answers to their translation questions. It provides clear guidance on selecting the most appropriate translation, numerous examples to help with problems of usage and construction, and precise information on grammar, style, and pronunciation.

For this edition the principal changes to the use of accents in Spanish recently introduced by the *Real Academia de la Lengua Española* have been adopted, and **ch** and **ll** are alphabetized within the letters **c** and **l** rather than treated as separate letters.

Included as special features are an A–Z of Spanish-speaking countries, a calendar of traditions, festivals, and holidays, and a guide to letter writing, including sample letters and practical tips about key differences between Spanish and English letter styles and layout, and a glossary explaining grammatical terms used in the dictionary.

Geared to the needs of a wide range of users, from the student at intermediate level and above to the enthusiastic tourist or business professional, the *Oxford Spanish Desk Dictionary* is an invaluable practical resource for learners of Spanish at the start of the twenty-first century.

Esta importante nueva edición del *Diccionario Oxford Compact* ha sido ampliada, exhaustivamente revisada y actualizada a fin de satisfacer las necesidades tanto del usuario en general como del escolar. Nuevas palabras y frases reflejan las novedades producidas en el campo científico y técnico como también los cambios que se han experimentado en el plano político, cultural y social.

Al combinarse la autoridad del *Diccionario Oxford* con la comodidad del formato más pequeño y un diseño de acceso rápido, este diccionario compacto y fácil de usar es un instrumento ideal de referencia para todos aquellos que necesiten una respuesta rápida y fiable para las preguntas que surjan al traducir. Proporciona una guía clara para seleccionar la traducción más apropiada, incluye numerosos ejemplos que ayudan con los problemas de uso y construcción, como también información precisa sobre gramática, estilo y pronunciación.

En esta edición se han adoptado las principales modificaciones sobre acentuación introducidas últimamente por la Real Academia de la Lengua Española, asimismo la **ch** y **ll** ya no aparecen como letras independientes dentro del orden alfabético.

Como característica relevante, se incluye información enciclopédica y cultural sobre España y Latinoamérica, una lista desde la A a la Z con las diferentes instituciones, organismos, etc., de la vida y cultura británicas y estadounidenses, y un calendario con los días festivos, fiestas y tradiciones en Gran Bretaña y Estados Unidos. Además contiene una guía para la redacción de cartas, con ejemplos y datos prácticos sobre las diferencias fundamentales entre el español y el inglés en cuanto al estilo y composición de una carta, y también un glosario con los términos gramaticales usados en el diccionario.

El *Diccionario Compact Oxford* ha sido preparado teniendo en cuenta las necesidades de una gran variedad de usuarios, desde el estudiante de un nivel intermedio y superior, al turista entusiasta o el profesional de los negocios, y es un inapreciable instrumento práctico de trabajo para los que aprenden el español moderno e idiomático a comienzos del siglo veintiuno.

List of contributors / Lista de colaboradores

Chief Editors/Dirección editorial
Carol Styles Carvajal
Jane Horwood

Data input/Entrada de datos
Anne McConnell
Marianne Selby-Smith
Anna Cotgreave
Sarah Hawker

Días festivos, fiestas y tradiciones en Gran Bretaña y EEUU
La vida y cultura británicas y estadounidenses desde la 'A' a la 'Z'

Ella Associates
Valerie Grundy

Ana Cristina Llompart
Mónica Bossons

Calendar of traditions, festivals, and holidays in Spanish-speaking countries

Ella Associates
Valerie Grundy

Josephine Grundy

Spanish Grammar
John Butt

Gramática inglesa
Nicholas Rollin
Carmen Fernández Marsden

Contents / Índice

Proprietary names / Marcas registradas

This dictionary includes some words which have, or are asserted to have, proprietary status as trademarks or otherwise. Their inclusion does not imply that they have acquired for legal purposes a non-proprietary or general significance, nor is any other judgment implied concerning their legal status. In cases where the editorial staff have some evidence that a word has proprietary status this is indicated in the entry for that word by the symbol ®, but no judgment concerning the legal status of such words is made or implied thereby.

Este diccionario incluye palabras que constituyen, o se afirma que constituyen, marcas registradas o nombres comerciales. Su inclusión no significa que a efectos legales hayan dejado de tener ese carácter, ni supone un pronunciamiento respecto de su situación legal.

Cuando al editor le consta que una palabra es una marca registrada o un nombre comercial, esto se indica por medio del símbolo ®, lo que tampoco supone un pronunciamiento acerca de la situación legal de esa palabra.

Structure of a Spanish–English entry

Headword
Vocablo cabeza de
artículo

acertijo *m* riddle, puzzle

Variant form of
headword
Variante del vocablo
cabeza de artículo

achichincle, achichinque *mf* (Méx fam &
pey) hanger-on (colloq & pej)

acomodar [A1] *vt* **1** (adaptar, amoldar) to adapt
2 ⟨*huésped*⟩ to put ... up **3** **(a)** (AmL) (arreglar) to
arrange; (poner) to put **(b)** (fam) ⟨*persona*⟩ (en
puesto): **su tío lo acomodó en su sección** his uncle
fixed him up with a job in his department

Sense divisions
Divisiones
correspondientes a las
distintas acepciones

acomplejado -da *adj*: **es muy ~** he's full of
complexes; **está ~ por su gordura** he has a
complex about being fat

A change of part of
speech within an entry
is marked by a box ■
Todo cambio de categoría
gramatical dentro de una
entrada se indica con el
símbolo ■

■ *m,f*: **es un ~** he's a mass of complexes
acomplejar [A1] *vt* to give ... a complex
■ **acomplejarse** *v pron* to get a complex

acondicionar [A1] *vt* **(a)** ⟨*vivienda/local*⟩ to
equip, fit out **(b)** (Col) ⟨*carro*⟩ to soup up
aconsejable *adj* advisable

Part of speech
Función gramatical

Irregular plural form
Plurales irregulares

acusetas *mf* (*pl* ~), **acusete -ta** *m,f* (fam)
tattletale (AmE colloq), telltale (BrE colloq)

adecuar [A1] *or* [A18] *vt* ~ **algo A algo** to
adapt sth ᴛᴏ sth

Every verb has a
reference to the verb
tables on p. 971
Cada verbo se remite a
la tabla de
conjugaciones en la
página 971

The use of ser or estar
with adjectives is
marked when necessary
El uso de ser o estar con
adjetivos se indica donde
es necesario

agarrado¹ -da *adj* **(a)** [ꜱᴇʀ] (fam) ⟨*tacaño*⟩
tightfisted (colloq) **(b)** [ᴇꜱᴛᴀʀ] (CS fam) ⟨*enamorado*⟩
in love
■ *m,f* (fam) ⟨*tacaño*⟩ skinflint (colloq), tightwad (AmE
colloq)

águila *f‡* **(a)** (ave) eagle; **ser un ~** to be very
sharp **(b)** (Méx) (de moneda) ≈ heads (*pl*); **¿~ o**
sol? heads or tails?

The part of speech *f‡*
indicates a feminine
noun that takes the
masculine article in
the singular
La función gramatical
f‡ indica un sustantivo
femenino usado con el
artículo masculino en el
singular

Structure of a Spanish–English entry

x

Pronominal verb •——— ■ **apretujarse** *v pron* to squash *o* squeeze
Verbo pronominal   together

aprobación *f* (de proyecto de ley, moción)
passing; (de préstamo, acuerdo, plan) approval,
endorsement; (de actuación, conducta) approval

•— **Sense indicators**
   Indicadores semánticos

Field labels •——— **arco** *m* ⓵ (Arquit) arch; (Anat) arch; (Mat) arc; ∼
Indicadores de campo   **de triunfo** triumphal arch; ∼ **iris** rainbow
semántico   ⓶ (AmL) (en fútbol) goal ⓷ (a) (Arm, Dep) bow (b)
                        (de violín) bow

arete *m* (Col, Méx) earring
armario *m* (a) (para ropa — mueble) wardrobe;
(— empotrado) closet (AmE), wardrobe (BrE) (b) (de
cocina) cupboard; (de cuarto de baño) cabinet

•— **Regional labels**
   Indicadores de uso
   regional

Stylistic labels •——— **armatoste** *m* (fam) huge great thing (colloq)
Indicadores de estilo

ascendencia *f* (a) (linaje) descent, ancestry;
es de ∼ francesa he is of French descent **(b)**
(origen) origin(s); **su ∼ humilde** her humble
origins

•— **Examples**
   Ejemplos

Idioms and proverbs •——— **ascua** *fḭ* ember; *estar en/tener a algn en ∼s*
appear in bold italics   (fam) to be on/to keep sb on tenterhooks
Los modismos y los   **aspereza** *f* ⓵ (a) (de superficie, piel) roughness
proverbios aparecen en **(b)** (de sabor) sharpness; (de voz, clima) harshness
negritas cursivas   ⓶ (parte áspera): **usar papel de lija para quitar las
                        ∼s** use sandpaper to remove any roughness;
                        limar ∼s to smooth things over

aviso *m* ⓵ (a) (notificación) notice; Ⓢ **aviso al
público** notice to the public; **dio ∼ a la policía** he
notified *o* informed the police ...

•— Ⓢ **indicates the use of
   the headword in
   signs, notices,
   warnings, etc**
   El símbolo Ⓢ indica el
   uso del vocablo cabeza
   de artículo en letreros,
   anuncios, advertencias,
   etc.

balancín *m* (de niños) seesaw, teeter-totter (AmE)

balompié *m* soccer, football (BrE)

Universally valid translation(s) followed by regional alternative(s)
Traducción universalmente válida seguida de alternativas regionales

bancario -ria *adj* ‹*interés/préstamo*› bank (*before n*); ‹*sector*› banking (*before n*)

bañar [A1] *vt* 1 ‹*niño/enfermo*› to bath, give … a bath 2 ‹*pulsera/cubierto*› to plate

bifurcarse [A2] *v pron* «*camino*» to fork, diverge (frml); «*vía férrea*» to diverge

Words often used with the headword, shown to help select the correct translation for each context
Palabras que suelen acompañar al vocablo cabeza de artículo y que ayudan a elegir la traducción que corresponde a cada contexto

bancario -ria *adj* ‹*interés/préstamo*› bank (*before n*); ‹*sector*› banking (*before n*)

Nouns modified by an adjective
Sustantivos calificados por un adjetivo

bañar [A1] *vt* 1 ‹*niño/enfermo*› to bath, give … a bath 2 ‹*pulsera/cubierto*› to plate

Objects of a verb
Complementos de un verbo

bifurcarse [A2] *v pron* «*camino*» to fork, diverge (frml); «*vía férrea*» to diverge

Subjects of a verb appear in double angled parentheses
Los posibles sujetos de un verbo aparecen entre paréntesis angulares dobles

The sign ≈ is used to indicate approximate equivalence
El símbolo ≈ indica un equivalente aproximado en la lengua de destino

canciller *m* (a) (jefe de estado) chancellor (b) (AmS) (ministro) ≈ Secretary of State (*in US*), ≈ Foreign Secretary (*in UK*)

Structure of a Spanish–English entry

Grammatical constructions in which the headword commonly occurs are indicated by small capitals
Las construcciones gramaticales en las que suele aparecer el vocablo cabeza de artículo se destacan mediante versalitas

■ **cansarse** *v pron* **(a)** (fatigarse) to tire oneself out; **se le cansa la vista** her eyes get tired **(b)** (aburrirse) to get bored; **~se DE algo/algn** to get tired OF sth/sb, get bored WITH sth/sb, **~se DE hacer algo** to get tired OF doing sth

carnet /kar'ne/ *m* (*pl* **-nets**) ▶ CARNÉ

ceder [E1] *vt* **1** **(a)** ⟨derecho⟩ to transfer, assign; ⟨territorio⟩ to cede; ⟨puesto/título⟩ (voluntariamente) to hand over; (a la fuerza) to give up; **~ el poder** to hand over power; **me cedió el asiento** he let me have his seat; ▶ PASO 1B **(b)** ⟨balón/pelota⟩ to pass

An arrow directs the user to another entry with the same meaning or to where a compound, idiomatic expression, or other useful expression is to be found
Se utiliza una flecha para remitir al usuario a una variante sinónima o a otro artículo donde aparece un compuesto, un modismo u otro uso de interés

'ver tb' directs the user to a headword where additional information is to be found
'ver tb' remite al usuario a otro artículo donde se hallará información complementaria

chiva *f* **1** (AmL) (barba) goatee **2** (Col) (bus) rural *o* country bus **3** (Col period) (primicia) scoop, exclusive **4** (Chi fam) (mentira) cock-and-bull story (colloq); *ver tb* CHIVO **5** **chivas** *fpl* (Méx fam) (cachivaches) junk (colloq)

Estructura del artículo Inglés–Español

Vocablo cabeza de artículo
Headword

alligator /'æləgeɪtər ‖'ælɪgeɪtə(r)/ *n* aligátor *m*

all: **~-important** /'ɔːlɪm'pɔːrtŋt ‖,ɔːlɪm'pɔːtŋt/ *adj* de suma importancia; **~-night** /'ɔːl'naɪt/ *adj* ⟨party/show⟩ que dura toda la noche; ⟨café/store⟩ que está abierto toda la noche

Nombres compuestos
Compounds

La transcripción fonética aparece inmediatamente después del vocablo cabeza de artículo [ver página xxi]
Pronunciation is shown immediately after the headword [see p. xxi]

allocate /'æləkeɪt/ *vt* asignar; (distribute) repartir; **$3 million has been ~d for research** se han destinado tres millones de dólares a la investigación

Variante del vocablo •— **amoeba**, (AmE also) **ameba** /əˈmiːbə/ *n* ameba
cabeza de artículo *f*, amiba *f*
Variant form of a
headword

answer¹ /ˈænsər ‖ˈɑːnsə(r)/ *n* **1** **(a)** (reply) —• **Divisiones**
respuesta *f*, contestación *f*; **in** ~ **to your question** **correspondientes a**
para contestar tu pregunta **(b)** (response): **her** ~ **las distintas**
to his rudeness was to ignore it respondió a su **acepciones**
grosería ignorándola; **Britain's** ~ **to Elvis Presley** Sense divisions
el Elvis Presley británico **2** **(a)** (in exam, test,
quiz) respuesta *f* **(b)** (solution) solución *f*; ~ **to sth**
solución DE algo

Los verbos con •— **answer²** *vt* **1** **(a)** (reply to) ⟨*person/letter*⟩
partícula aparecen al contestar …
final del artículo ■ **answer back** **1** [*v + adv*] (rudely) contestar
correspondiente **2** [*v + o + adv*] **to** ~ **sb back** contestarle mal *or*
Phrasal verbs appear at de mala manera a algn
the end of the root word ■ **answer for** [*v + prep + o*] (accept responsibility
entry for) ⟨*conduct/consequences*⟩ responder de; **his**
parents have a lot to ~ **for** sus padres tienen
mucha culpa

appreciate /əˈpriːʃieɪt/ *vt* **(a)** (value) ⟨*food/* —• **Todo cambio de**
novel⟩ apreciar **(b)** (be grateful for) agradecer* **(c)** **categoría gramatical**
(understand) ⟨*danger/difficulties*⟩ darse* cuenta de; **de un verbo se indica**
I ~ **that, but …** lo comprendo, pero … **con el símbolo ■**
■ ~ *vi* «*shares/property*» (re)valorizarse* A change of part of
speech of a verb is
marked by a box ■

Función gramatical •— **approximate** /əˈprɑːksəmət ‖əˈprɒksɪmət/
Part of speech *adj* aproximado
approximately /əˈprɑːksəmətli
‖əˈprɒksɪmətli/ *adv* aproximadamente

artery /ˈɑːrtəri ‖ˈɑːtəri/ *n* (*pl* **-ries**) arteria *f* —• **Inflexiones**
auditorium /ˌɔːdəˈtɔːriəm ‖ˌɔːdɪˈtɔːriəm/ *n* (*pl* **irregulares**
-riums *or* **-ria** /-riə/) auditorio *m* Irregular inflections

El comparativo y el •— **baggy** /ˈbægi/ *adj* **-gier, -giest** ancho, guango
superlativo del adjetivo (Méx)
Comparative and
superlative forms of an
adjective

Estructura del artículo Inglés–Español

bang² *vt* (a) (strike) golpear (b) (slam): he ~ed the door dio un portazo (fam)
■ ~ *vi* (a) (strike) to ~ **ON** sth golpear algo; to ~ **INTO** sth darse* CONTRA algo (b) (slam) «*door*» cerrarse* de un golpe

● **Las construcciones gramaticales en las que suele aparecer el vocablo cabeza de artículo se destacan mediante versalitas**
Grammatical constructions in which the headword commonly occurs are indicated by small capitals

Fórmulas que ●──── demuestran el comportamiento sintáctico de cada verbo con partícula. Señalan las posibles combinaciones de verbo [v], adverbio [adv], preposición [prep] y complemento [o]
Syntactical pattern of phrasal verbs, showing the possible combinations of verb [v], adverb [adv], preposition [prep], and object [o]

■ **bear out** [v + o + adv, v + adv + o] «*theory*» confirmar
■ **bear up** [v + adv]: she bore up well under the strain sobrellevó muy bien la situación

beg /beg/ **-gg-** *vt* ⓵ «*money/food*» pedir*, mendigar* ⓶ (frml) (a) (entreat) «*person*» suplicarle* a, rogarle* a (b) (ask for) «*forgiveness*» suplicar*, rogar*
■ ~ *vi* «*beggar*» pedir*, mendigar*; to ~ for mercy pedir* *or* suplicar* clemencia

● **Un asterisco señala los verbos de conjugación irregular en la traducción al español**
An asterisk indicates an irregular verb in the translation

Indicadores ●──── semánticos
Sense indicators

belief /bə'li:f ‖ bɪ'li:f/ *n* (a) (conviction, opinion) creencia *f* (b) (confidence) ~ **IN** sb/sth confianza *f* *or* fe *f* EN algn/algo (c) (Relig) fe *f*

belt¹ /belt/ *n* ⓵ (Clothing) cinturón *m* ⓶ (Mech Eng) correa *f*

● **Indicadores de campo semántico**
Field labels

Indicadores de uso ●──── regional
Regional labels

Biro®, biro /'baɪrəʊ ‖ 'baɪərəʊ/ *n* (*pl* **biros**) (BrE) bolígrafo *m*, birome *f* (RPl), esfero *m* (Col), lápiz *m* de pasta (Chi), boli *m* (Esp fam)

bitch /bɪtʃ/ *n* [1] (female dog) perra *f* [2] (spiteful woman) (AmE vulg, BrE sl) bruja *f* (fam), arpía *f* (fam), cabrona *f* (Esp, Méx vulg)

- **Indicadores de estilo**
  Stylistic labels

Ejemplos
Examples

bounce² *n* (a) (action) rebote *m*, pique *m* (AmL) (b) (springiness, vitality): **this shampoo puts the ~ back into your hair** este champú les da nueva vida a sus cabellos; **she's full of ~** es una persona llena de vida

breath /breθ/ *n* aliento *m*; **to have bad ~** tener* mal aliento; **to take a ~** aspirar, inspirar; **take a deep ~** respire hondo; **out of ~** sin aliento; *to hold one's ~* contener* la respiración; *to take sb's ~ away* dejar a algn sin habla

- **Los modismos y los proverbios aparecen en negritas cursivas**
  Idioms and proverbs appear in bold italics

El símbolo Ⓢ indica el uso del vocablo cabeza de artículo en letreros, anuncios, advertencias, etc.
Ⓢ indicates the use of the headword in signs, notices, warnings, etc

customer /ˈkʌstəmər ‖ ˈkʌstəmə(r)/ *n* cliente, -ta *m,f*; *(before n)* Ⓢ **customer services** información y reclamaciones

dump¹ /dʌmp/ *n* [1] (place for waste) vertedero *m* (de basura), basural *m* (AmL), tiradero *m* (Méx) …

- **Traducción universalmente válida seguida de alternativas regionales**
  Universal Spanish translation followed by regional alternatives

Palabras que suelen acompañar al vocablo cabeza de artículo y que ayudan a elegir la traducción que corresponde a cada contexto
Words often used with the headword, shown to help select the correct translation for each context

ease² *vt* [1] (a) (relieve) ⟨*pain*⟩ calmar, aliviar; ⟨*tension*⟩ hacer* disminuir, aliviar; ⟨*burden*⟩ aligerar; **to ~ sb's mind** tranquilizar* a algn (b) (make easier) ⟨*situation*⟩ paliar; ⟨*transition*⟩ facilitar; **to ~ the way for sth** preparar el terreno para algo
■ **ease off** [*v + adv*] «*rain*» amainar; «*pain*» aliviarse, calmarse; «*pressure/traffic*» disminuir*

efficient /ɪˈfɪʃənt/ *adj* ⟨*person/system*⟩ eficiente; ⟨*machine/engine*⟩ de buen rendimiento

ease² *vt* [1] (a) (relieve) ⟨*pain*⟩ calmar, aliviar; ⟨*tension*⟩ hacer* disminuir, aliviar; ⟨*burden*⟩ aligerar; **to ~ sb's mind** tranquilizar* a algn (b) (make easier) ⟨*situation*⟩ paliar; ⟨*transition*⟩ facilitar; **to ~ the way for sth** preparar el terreno para algo

- **Complementos de un verbo**
  Objects of a verb

■ **ease off** [*v + adv*] «*rain*» amainar; «*pain*» aliviarse, calmarse; «*pressure/traffic*» disminuir*

- **Los posibles sujetos de un verbo aparecen entre paréntesis angulares dobles**
  Subjects of a verb appear in double angled brackets

efficient /ɪˈfɪʃənt/ *adj* ⟨*person/system*⟩ eficiente; ⟨*machine/engine*⟩ de buen rendimiento

- **Sustantivos calificados por un adjetivo**
  Nouns modified by an adjective

Inland Revenue /'mlənd/ *n* (in UK) **the ~ ~**
≈ Hacienda, ≈ la Dirección General Impositiva
(*en RPl*), ≈ Impuestos Internos (*en Chi*)

El símbolo ≈ indica
un equivalente
aproximado en la
lengua de destino
The sign ≈ is used to
indicate approximate
equivalence

inmost /'ɪnməʊst/ *adj* ▶ INNERMOST

jersey /'dʒərzi ‖ 'dʒɜːzi/ *n* (*pl* **-seys**) ① (a)
(sports shirt) camiseta *f* **(b)** (Tex) jersey *m* **(c)** (BrE)
▶ SWEATER ② **Jersey** (la isla de) Jersey

Se utiliza una flecha
para remitir al usuario a
una variante sinónima o
a otro artículo donde
aparece un compuesto,
un modismo u otro uso
de interés
An arrow directs the user
to another entry with the
same meaning or to
where a compound,
idiomatic expression, or
other useful expression is
to be found

jetsam /'dʒetsəm/ *n* echazón *f; see also* FLOTSAM

'see also' remite al
usuario a otro artículo
donde se hallará
información
complementaria
'see also' directs the
user to a headword
where additional
information is to be
found

The pronunciation of Spanish

Symbols used in this dictionary

The pronunciation of Spanish words is directly represented by their written form and therefore phonetic transcriptions have only been supplied for loan words which retain their original spelling.

Consonants and semi-vowels

Symbol	Example	Approximation
/b/	boca /'boka/ vaso /'baso/	English *b* in bin but without the aspiration that follows it.
/β/	cabo /'kaβo/ ave /'aβe/	Very soft *b*, produced with the lips hardly meeting.
/d/	dolor /do'lor/	English *d* in *den*.
/ð/	cada /'kaða/	English *th* in *rather*.
/f/	fino /'fino/	English *f* in *feat*.
/g/	gota /'gota/	English *g* in *goat*.
/ɣ/	pago /'paɣo/ largo /'larɣo/	Very soft continuous sound, not punctuated like /g/.
/ʝ/	mayo /'maʝo/ llave /'ʝaβe/	English *y* in *yet*. For regional variants see points 7 and 14 of **General Rules of Spanish Pronunciation** on page xviii.
/j/	tiene /'tjene/	English *y* in *yet*.
/k/	cama /'kama/ cuna /'kuna/ quiso /'kiso/ kilo /'kilo/	English *c* in *cap* but without the aspiration that follows it.
/l/	lago /'laɣo/	English *l* in *lid*.

Symbol	Example	Approximation
/m/	mono /'mono/	English *m* in *most*.
/n/	no /no/	English *n* in *nib*.
/ŋ/	banco /'baŋko/	English *ng* in *song*.
/ɲ/	año /'aɲo/	Like *gn* in French *soigné*, similar to the *ni* in *onion*.
/p/	peso /'peso/	English *p* in *spin*.
/r/	aro /'aro/ árbol /'arβol/	A single flap with a curved tongue against the palate.
/rr/	rato /'rrato/ parra /'parra/	A rolled '*r*' as found in some Scottish accents.
/s/	asa /'asa/ celo /'selo/	Latin-American Spanish	English *s* in *stop*.
	cinco /'siŋko/ azote /a'sote/		
/θ/	celo /'θelo/ cinco /'θiŋko/ azote /a'θote/	European Spanish	English *th* in *thin*.
/t/	todo /'toðo/	English *t* in *step*.
/tʃ/	chapa /'tʃapa/	English *ch* in *church*.
/w/	cuatro /'kwatro/	English *w*.
/x/	jota /'xota/ general /xene'ral/ gigante /xi'ɣante/	*ch* in *Scottish loch*.
/z/	desde /'dezðe/	English *s* in *is*.

The pronunciation of Spanish

Vowels

None of the five Spanish vowels corresponds exactly to an English vowel.

Symbol	Example	Approximation
/a/	**casa** /'kasa/	Shorter than *a* in *father*.
/e/	**seco** /'seko/	English *e* in *pen*.
/i/	**fin** /fin/	Between English *ee* in *seen* and *i* in *sin*.
/o/	**oro** /'oro/	Shorter than English *o* in *rose*.
/u/	**uña** /'uɲa/	Between English *oo* in *boot* and *oo* in *foot*.

The stress mark

When phonetic transcriptions of Spanish headwords are given in the dictionary, the symbol ' precedes the syllable that carries the stress:

footing /'futin/

For information about where other words should be stressed, see the section **Stress** on the next page.

General rules of Spanish pronunciation

Consonants

1 The letters *b* and *v* are pronounced in exactly the same way: /b/ when at the beginning of an utterance or after *m* or *n* (**barco** /'barko/, **vaca** /'baka/, **ambos** /'ambos/), and /β/ in all other contexts (**rabo** /'rraβo/, **ave** /'aβe/, **árbol** /'arβol/).

2 *C* is pronounced /k/ when followed by a consonant other than *h* or by *a*, *o* or *u* (**acto** /'akto/, **casa** /'kasa/, **coma** /'koma/). When it is followed by *e* or

i, it is pronounced /s/ in Latin America and parts of southern Spain and /θ/ in the rest of Spain (**cero** /'sero/, /'θero/; **cinco** /'siŋko/, /'θiŋko/).

3 *D* is pronounced /d/ when it occurs at the beginning of an utterance or after *n* or *l* (**digo** /'diɣo/, **anda** /'anda/) and /ð/ in all other contexts (**hada** /'aða/, **arde** /'arðe/). It is often not pronounced at all at the end of a word (**libertad** /liβer'ta(ð)/, **Madrid** /ma'ðri(ð)/).

4 *G* is pronounced /x/ when followed by *e* or *i* (**gitano** /xi'tano/, **auge** /'awxe/). When followed by *a*, *o*, *u*, *ue* or *ui* it is pronounced /g/ if at the beginning of an utterance or after *n* (**gato** /'gato/, **gula** /'gula/, **tango** /'taŋgo/, **guiso** /'giso/) and /ɣ/ in all other contexts (**hago** /'aɣo/, **trague** /'traɣe/). Note that the *u* is not pronounced in the combinations *gue* and *gui*, unless it is written with a diaeresis (**paragüero** /para'ɣwero/, **agüita** /a'ɣwita/).

5 *H* is mute in Spanish, (**huevo** /'weβo/, **almohada** /almo'aða/) except in the combination *ch*, which is pronounced /tʃ/ (**chico** /'tʃiko/, **leche** /'letʃe/).

6 *J* is always pronounced /x/ (**jamón** /xa'mon/, **jefe** /'xefe/).

7 The pronunciation of *ll* varies greatly throughout the Spanish-speaking world.

a It is pronounced rather like the *y* in English *yes* by the majority of speakers, who do not distinguish between the pronunciation of *ll* and that of *y* (e.g. between *haya* and *halla*). The sound is pronounced slightly more emphatically when at the beginning of an utterance.

b In some areas, particularly Bolivia, parts of Chile, Peru and Castile in Spain, the distinction between *ll* and *y* has been preserved. In these areas *ll* is pronounced similarly to *lli* in *million*.

c In the River Plate area *ll* is pronounced /ʒ/ (as in English *measure*), sometimes tending toward /ʃ/ (as in *shop*).

8 *Ñ* is always pronounced /ɲ/.

9 *Q* is pronounced /k/, and the *u* that always follows it is silent (**quema** /'kema/, **quiso** /'kiso/).

10 *R* is pronounced /r/ when it occurs between vowels or in syllable-final position (**aro** /'aro/, **barco** /'barko/, **cantar** /kan'tar/). It is pronounced /rr/ when in initial position (**rama** /'rrama/). The double consonant *rr* is always pronounced /rr/.

11 *S* is pronounced /s/ but it is aspirated by speakers in many regions when it occurs in syllable-final position (**hasta** /'ahta/, **los cuatro** /loh'kwatro/). In other regions it is voiced when followed by a voiced consonant (**mismo** /'mɪzmo/, **los dos** /loz'ðos/).

12 *V* see 1 above.

13 *X* is pronounced /ks/, although there is a marked tendency to render it as /s/ before consonants (**extra** /'ekstra/, /'estra/).

In some words derived from Nahuatl and other Indian languages it is pronounced /x/ (**México** /'mexiko/) and in others it is pronounced /s/ (**Xochimilco** /sotʃi'milko/).

14 When followed by a vowel within the same syllable *y* is pronounced rather like the *y* in English *yes* (slightly more emphatically when at the beginning of an utterance). In the River Plate area it is pronounced /ʒ/ (as in English *measure*), sometimes tending toward /ʃ/ (as in *shop*).

As the conjunction *y* and in syllable-final position, *y* is pronounced /i/.

15 *Z* is pronounced /s/ in Latin America and parts of southern Spain and /θ/ in the rest of Spain.

Stress

When no phonetic transcription is given for a Spanish headword, the following rules determine where it should be stressed:

1 If there is no written accent:

a a word is stressed on the penultimate syllable if it ends in a vowel, or in *n* or *s*:
arma /'arma/
ponen /'ponen/
mariposas /mari'posas/

b words which end in a consonant other than *n* or *s* are stressed on the last syllable:
cantar /kan'tar/
delantal /delan'tal/
maguey /ma'ɣei/

2 If a word is not stressed in accordance with the above rules, the written accent indicates the syllable where the emphasis is to be placed:
balcón /bal'kon/
salí /sa'li/
carácter /ka'rakter/

It should be noted that unstressed vowels have the same quality as stressed vowels and are not noticeably weakened as they are in

English. For example, there is no perceptible difference between any of the e's in *entenderé* or between the a's in *Panamá*.

Combinations of vowels

A combination of a strong vowel (*a*, *e* or *o*) and a weak vowel (*i* or *u*) or of two weak vowels forms a diphthong and is therefore pronounced as one syllable. The stress falls on the strong vowel if there is one. In a combination of two weak vowels, it falls on the second element:

cuando /'kwando/ *stressed on the* /a/
aula /'awla/ *stressed on the* /a/
viudo /'bjuðo/ *stressed on the* /u/

A combination of two strong vowels does not form a diphthong and the vowels retain their separate values. They count as two separate syllables for the purposes of applying the above rules on stress:

faena /fa'ena/ *stressed on the* /e/
polea /po'lea/ *stressed on the* /e/

La pronunciación del inglés

La transcripción fonética que sigue a cada palabra cabeza de artículo corresponde a la pronunciación norteamericana de uso más extendido en los Estados Unidos. Se ha incluido la pronunciación británica (precedida por el símbolo ‖) únicamente en aquellos casos en que esta difiere sustancialmente de la pronunciación norteamericana. Ejemplo:

address[1] /ˈædres ‖ əˈdres/
induce /ɪnˈduːs ‖ ɪnˈdjuːs/

Se reconoce la validez de muchas variantes regionales, tanto norteamericanas como británicas, pero estas no se han incluido por razones de espacio.

Los símbolos empleados en las transcripciones son los del Alfabeto Fonético Internacional (AFI). Estos se enumeran a continuación, seguidos de un ejemplo y una breve aproximación o descripción del sonido que representan. Estas descripciones no siguen criterios fonéticos estrictos.

Consonantes y semivocales

Símbolo	Ejemplo	Aproximación
/b/	**bat** /bæt/	Sonido más explosivo que el de una *b* inicial española.
/d/	**dig** /dɪg/	Sonido más explosivo que el de una *d* inicial española.
/dʒ/	**jam** /dʒæm/	Similar a una *ch* pero más cercano al sonido inicial de *Giuseppe* en italiano.
/f/	**fit** /fɪt/	Como la *f* española.
/g/	**good** /gʊd/	Sonido más explosivo que el de una *g* inicial española.

Símbolo	Ejemplo	Aproximación
/h/	**hat** /hæt/	Sonido de aspiración más suave que la *j* española, articulado como si se estuviera intentando empañar un espejo con el aliento.
/hw/	**wheel** /hwiːl/	Una /w/ con la aspiración de la /h/ (muchos hablantes no distinguen entre /hw/ y /w/ y pronuncian *whale* de la misma manera que *wail*).
/j/	**yes** /jes/	Como la *y* española en *yema* y *yo* (excepto en el español rioplatense).

La pronunciación del inglés

Símbolo	Ejemplo	Aproximación
/k/	cat /kæt/	Sonido más explosivo que el de una c española en cama o acto.
/l/	lid /lɪd/	Como la l española.
/l̩/	tidal /'taɪdl̩/	l alargada y resonante.
/m/	mat /mæt/	Como la m española.
/n/	nib /nɪb/	Como la n española.
/n̩/	threaten /'θretn̩/	n alargada y resonante.
/ŋ/	sing /sɪŋ/	Como la n española en banco o anca.
/p/	pet /pet/	Sonido más explosivo que el de una p española.
/r/	rat /ræt/	Entre la r y la rr españolas, pronunciado con la punta de la lengua curvada hacia atrás y sin llegar a tocar el paladar.
/s/	sip /sɪp/	Como la s española.
/ʃ/	ship /ʃɪp/	Sonido similar al de la interjección ¡sh!, utilizada para pedir silencio (ver también /tʃ/).
/t/	tip /tɪp/	Sonido más explosivo que el de una t española.
/tʃ/	chin /tʃɪn/	Como la ch española.
/θ/	thin /θɪn/	Como la c o la z del español europeo en cinco o zapato.

Símbolo	Ejemplo	Aproximación
/ð/	the /ðə/	Sonido similar a una d intervocálica española como la de cada o modo.
/v/	van /væn/	Sonido sonoro que se produce con los incisivos superiores sobre el labio inferior.
/w/	win /wɪn/	Similar al sonido inicial de huevo.
/x/	loch /lɑːx/	Como la j española.
/z/	zip /zɪp/	s sonora (con zumbido).
/ʒ/	vision /'vɪʒən/	Sonido similar al de la y o la ll del español rioplatense en yo o llave, o al de la j francesa en je (ver también /dʒ/).

Vocales y diptongos

El símbolo : indica que la vocal precedente es larga

Símbolo	Ejemplo	Aproximación
/ɑː/	father /'fɑːðər/	Sonido más largo que el de una a española.
/æ/	fat /fæt/	Sonido que se obtiene al pronunciar una a española con los labios en la posición de pronunciar una e.
/ʌ/	cup /kʌp/	Sonido más breve que la a española y que se pronuncia en la parte posterior de la boca.

La pronunciación del inglés

Símbolo	Ejemplo	Aproximación
/e/	met /met/	Sonido parecido a la *e* española en *mesa*.
/ə/	abet /ə'bet/	Sonido similar al de la *e* francesa en *je* (ver también /əʊ/).
/ɜ:/	fur /fɜ:r/	Sonido que se obtiene al pronunciar una *e* española con los labios en la posición de pronunciar una *o*.
/ɪ/	bit /bɪt/	Sonido más breve que el de la *i* española.
/i:/	beat /bi:t/	Sonido más largo que el de la *i* española.
/i/	very /'veri/	Sonido similar al de la *i* española en *papi*.
/ɔ:/	paw /pɔ:/	Sonido más largo que el de la *o* española.
/u:/	boot /bu:t/	Sonido más largo que el de una *u* española.
/ʊ/	book /bʊk/	Sonido más breve que el de la *u* española.
/aɪ/	fine /faɪn/	Como *ai* en las palabras españolas *aire*, *baile*.
/aʊ/	now /naʊ/	Como *au* en las palabras españolas *pausa*, *flauta*.
/eɪ/	fate /feɪt/	Como *ei* en las palabras españolas *peine*, *aceite*.

Símbolo	Ejemplo	Aproximación
/əʊ/	goat /gəʊt/	Como una *o* pronunciada sin redondear demasiado los labios.
/ɔɪ/	boil /bɔɪl/	Como *oy* en *voy*, *coypu*.
/uə/	sexual /'sekʃuəl/	Como una *u* pronunciada sin redondear demasiado los labios y seguida de una /ə/.

Símbolos adicionales utilizados en la transcripción de sonidos vocálicos británicos

Símbolo	Ejemplo	Aproximación
/ɒ/	dog /dɒg/	Similar a una *o* española.
/eə/	fair /feə(r)/	Como una *e* española seguida de /ə/.
/ɪə/	near /nɪə(r)/	Como una *i* española seguida de /ə/.
/ʊə/	tour /tʊə(r)/	Como una *u* española pronunciada sin redondear demasiado los labios y seguida de /ə/.

Acentuación

El símbolo ' precede a la sílaba sobre la cual recae el acento tónico primario:
ago /ə'gəʊ/
dinosaur /'daɪnəsɔ:r/

El símbolo , precede a la sílaba sobre la cual recae el acento tónico secundario:
blackmailer /'blæk,meɪlər/

Abbreviations and labels / Abreviaturas e indicadores

adjetivo	**adj**	adjective
adjetivo invariable	**adj inv**	invariable adjective
Administración	**Adm**	Administration
adverbio	**adv**	adverb
Espacio	**Aerosp**	Aerospace
Agricultura	**Agr**	Agriculture
América Central	**AmC**	Central America
inglés norteamericano	**AmE**	American English
América Latina	**AmL**	Latin America
América del Sur	**AmS**	South America
Anatomía	**Anat**	Anatomy
Andes	**Andes**	Andes
anticuado	**ant**	dated
Antropología	**Anthrop**	Anthropology
arcaico	**arc, arch**	archaic
Arqueología	**Archeol**	Archeology
Arquitectura	**Archit**	Architecture
argot	**arg**	slang
Argentina	**Arg**	Argentina
Armas	**Arm**	Arms
Arqueología	**Arqueol**	Archeology
Arquitectura	**Arquit**	Architecture
artículo	**art**	article
Arte	**Arte, Art**	Art
Astrología	**Astrol**	Astrology
Astronomía	**Astron**	Astronomy
Audio	**Audio**	Audio
Automovilismo	**Auto**	Cars
Aviación	**Aviac, Aviat**	Aviation
Biblia	**Bib**	Bible
Biología	**Biol**	Biology
Bolivia	**Bol**	Bolivia
Botánica	**Bot**	Botany
inglés británico	**BrE**	British English
causativo	**caus**	causative
Química	**Chem**	Chemistry
Chile	**Chi**	Chile
Cine	**Cin**	Cinema
Ingeniería civil	**Civil Eng**	Civil Engineering
Indumentaria	**Clothing**	Clothing
Cocina	**Coc**	Cookery
Colombia	**Col**	Colombia
familiar	**colloq**	colloquial
Comercio	**Com**	Business
Informática	**Comput**	Computing
conjunción	**conj**	conjunction
Construcción	**Const**	Building

Correspondencia	**Corresp**	Correspondence
numerable	**count**	countable
Costa Rica	**CR**	Costa Rica
uso criticado	**crit**	criticized usage
Cono Sur	**CS**	Southern Cone
Cuba	**Cu**	Cuba
Cocina	**Culin**	Cookery
anticuado	**dated**	dated
artículo definido	**def art**	definite article
Odontología	**Dent**	Dentistry
Deporte	**Dep**	Sport
Derecho	**Der**	Law
dialecto	**dial**	dialect
Ecuador	**Ec**	Ecuador
Comunidad Europea	**EC**	European Community
Ecología	**Ecol**	Ecology
Economía	**Econ**	Economics
Educación	**Educ**	Education
Electricidad	**Elec**	Electricity
Electrónica	**Electrón, Electron**	Electronics
enfático	**enf**	emphatic
Ingeniería	**Eng**	Engineering
Equitación	**Equ**	Equestrianism
especialmente	**esp**	especially
España	**Esp**	Spain
Espacio	**Espac**	Aerospace
Espectáculos	**Espec**	Entertainment
eufemismo	**euf, euph**	euphemism
excepto	**exc**	excluding
femenino	**f**	feminine
véase página ix	**f‡**	*see page ix*
familiar	**fam**	colloquial
Farmacología	**Farm**	Pharmacology
Ferrocarriles	**Ferr**	Railways
Filosofía	**Fil**	Philosophy
Finanzas	**Fin**	Finance
Física	**Fis**	Physics
Fisco	**Fisco**	Tax
Fisiología	**Fisiol**	Physiology
Fotografía	**Fot**	Photography
femenino plural	**fpl**	feminine plural
frase hecha	**fr hecha**	set phrase
formal	**frml**	formal
Juegos	**Games**	Games
generalmente	**gen**	generally
Geografía	**Geog**	Geography
Geología	**Geol**	Geology
gerundio	**ger**	gerund

Gobierno	Gob, Govt	Government
Historia	Hist	History
Horticultura	Hort	Horticulture
humorístico	hum	humorous
Imprenta e Industria editorial	Impr	Printing and Publishing
artículo indefinido	indef art	indefinite article
Indumentaria	Indum	Clothing
Informática	Inf	Computing
Ingeniería	Ing	Engineering
interjección	interj	exclamation
irónico	iró, iro	ironical
lenguaje periodístico	journ	journalese
Periodismo	Journ	Journalism
Juegos	Jueg	Games
Relaciones Laborales	Lab Rel	Labor Relations
Derecho	Law	Law
Ocio	Leisure	Leisure
lenguaje infantil	leng infantil	used to or by children
Lingüística	Ling	Linguistics
Literatura	Lit	Literature
literario	liter	literary
locución	loc	phrase
locución adjetiva	loc adj	adjectival phrase
locución adverbial	loc adv	adverbial phrase
locución preposicional	loc prep	prepositional phrase
masculino	m	masculine
Márketing	Marketing	Marketing
Matemáticas	Mat, Math	Mathematics
Mecánica	Mec, Mech Eng	Mechanical Engineering
Medicina	Med	Medicine
Metalurgia	Metal, Metall	Metallurgy
Meteorología	Meteo	Meteorology
México	Méx	Mexico
masculino y femenino	mf	masculine and feminine
masculino, femenino	m, f	masculine, feminine
Militar	Mil	Military
Minería	Min	Mining
Mitología	Mit	Mythology
masculino plural	mpl	masculine plural
Música	Mús, Mus	Music
Mitología	Myth	Mythology
nombre, sustantivo	n	noun
Náutica	Náut, Naut	Nautical
negativo	neg	negative
Ocultismo	Occult	Occult
Ocio	Ocio	Leisure

Odontología	Odont	Dentistry
Óptica	Ópt, Opt	Optics
Panamá	Pan	Panama
Paraguay	Par	Paraguay
participio pasado	past p	past participle
peyorativo	pej	pejorative
Perú	Per	Peru
lenguaje periodístico	period	journalese
Periodismo	Period	Journalism
peyorativo	pey	pejorative
Farmacología	Pharm	Pharmacology
Filosofía	Phil	Philosophy
Fotografía	Phot	Photography
Física	Phys	Physics
Fisiología	Physiol	Physiology
plural	pl	plural
sustantivo plural	pl n	plural noun
poético	poet	poetic
Política	Pol	Politics
Correo	Post	Post
participio pasado	pp	past participle
prefijo	pref	prefix
preposición	prep	preposition
participio presente	pres p	present participle
Imprenta	Print	Printing
pronombre	pron	pronoun
pronombre demostrativo	pron dem	demonstrative pronoun
pronombre personal	pron pers	personal pronoun
pronombre relativo	pron rel	relative pronoun
Psicología	Psic, Psych	Psychology
Industria editorial	Publ	Publishing
Química	Quím	Chemistry
marca registrada	®	registered trademark
Radio	Rad	Radio
Ferrocarriles	Rail	Railways
recíproco	recipr	reciprocal
reflexivo	refl	reflexive
Religión	Relig	Religion
Relaciones Laborales	Rels Labs	Labor Relations
Río de la Plata	RPI	River Plate area
inglés de Escocia	Scot	Scottish English
Servicios Sociales	Servs Socs	Social Administration
singular	sing	singular
argot	sl	slang
Servicios Sociales	Soc Adm	Social Administration
Sociología	Sociol	Sociology
Deporte	Sport	Sport

Abbreviations and labels /Abreviaturas e indicadores

sufijo	suf, suff	suffix	Uruguay	Ur	Uruguay
Tauromaquia	Taur	Bullfighting	verbo	v	verb
Fisco	Tax	Tax	verbo auxiliar	v aux	auxiliary verb
también	tb	also	verbo	vb	verb
Teatro	Teatr	Theater	Venezuela	Ven	Venezuela
Tecnología	Tec, Tech	Technology	Veterinaria	Vet, Vet Sci	Veterinary Science
lenguaje técnico	téc, tech	technical language	verbo intransitivo	vi	intransitive verb
Telecomunica-ciones	Telec	Telecommunica-tions	Video	Video	Video
Textiles	Tex	Textiles	verbo impersonal	v impers	impersonal verb
Teatro	Theat	Theater	Vinicultura	Vin	Wine
Turismo	Tourism	Tourism	verbo modal	v mod	modal verb
Transporte	Transp	Transport	verbo pronominal	v pron	pronominal verb
Televisión	TV	Television	verbo transitivo	vt	transitive verb
no numerable	uncount	uncountable	vulgar	vulg	vulgar
			Zoología	Zool	Zoology

Aa

A, a *f* (*pl* **aes**) (*read as* /a/) *the letter* A, a

a *prep*

■ **Nota** La preposición *a* suele emplearse precedida de ciertos verbos como *empezar, ir, oler, sonar* etc, en cuyo caso ver bajo el respectivo verbo. No se traduce cuando introduce el complemento directo de persona (ser humano, pronombres personales que lo representan, como *quien, alguien, algún* etc) o un nombre con un objeto o animal personalizado: *amo a mi patria* = I love my country, *paseo a mi perro* = I walk my dog. En los casos en que precede al artículo definido *el* para formar la contracción *al*, ver bajo la siguiente entrada, donde también se encontrarán otros ejemplos y usos de *a*.

1 (a) (indicando dirección) to; **voy a México/la tienda** I'm going to Mexico/to the shop; **voy a casa** I'm going home; **se cayó al río** she fell into the river **(b)** (indicando posición): **estaban sentados a la mesa** they were sitting at the table; **a orillas del Ebro** on the banks of the Ebro; **se sentó al sol** he sat in the sun; **se sentó a mi derecha** he sat down on my right **(c)** (indicando distancia): **a diez kilómetros de aquí** ten kilometers from here **2 (a)** (señalando hora, momento) at; **a las ocho** at eight o'clock; **a la hora de comer** at lunch time; **¿a qué hora vengo?** what time shall I come?; **a mediados de abril** in mid-April; **al día siguiente** the next *o* following day **(b)** (señalando fecha): **hoy estamos a lunes/a 20** today is Monday/it's the 20th today **(c) al + INF**: **se cayó al bajar del tren** she fell as she was getting off the train; **al enterarse de la noticia** when he learnt *o* on learning the news **(d)** (indicando distancia en el tiempo): **a escasos minutos de su llegada** (después) a few minutes after she arrived; (antes) a few minutes before she arrived; **de lunes a viernes** (from) Monday to Friday **3** (en relaciones de proporción, equivalencia): **tres veces al día** three times a day; **sale a 100 euros cada uno** it works out at 100 euros each; **a 100 kilómetros por hora** (at) 100 kilometers per hour; **nos ganaron cinco a tres** they beat us five three *o* (AmE) five to three **4** (indicando modo, medio, estilo): **a pie/a caballo** on foot/on horseback; **a crédito** on credit; **funciona a pilas** it runs on batteries; **a mano** by hand; **a rayas** striped; **vestirse a lo punk** to wear punk clothes **5 (a)** (introduciendo el complemento directo de persona): **¿viste a José?** did you see José?; **no he leído a Freud** I haven't read (any) Freud **(b)** (introduciendo el complemento indirecto) to; **le escribió una carta a su padre** he wrote a letter to his father, he wrote his father a letter; **dáselo a ella** give it to her; **le enseña inglés a mis hijos** she teaches my children English; **le echó (la) llave a la puerta** she locked the door **(c)** (indicando procedencia): **se lo compré a una gitana** I bought it from *o* (colloq) off a gipsy

abadía *f* (monasterio) abbey; (dignidad) abbacy

abajo *adv* **1 (a)** (lugar, parte): **aquí** ∼ down here; **en el estante de** ∼ (el siguiente) on the shelf below; (el último) on the bottom shelf; **más** ∼ further down; **por** ∼ underneath; **la parte de** ∼ the bottom (part) **(b)** (en un edificio) downstairs; **los vecinos de** ∼ the people downstairs **(c)** (en una escala, jerarquía): **del jefe para** ∼ from the boss down *o* downward(s); **de 20 años para** ∼ 20 or under **2** (expresando dirección, movimiento) down; **calle/escaleras** ∼ down the street/stairs; **tire hacia** ∼ pull down *o* downward(s); **desde** ∼ from below **3 abajo de** (AmL) under; ∼ **de la cama** under the bed **4** (en interjecciones) down with; **¡**∼ **la dictadura!** down with the dictatorship!

abalanzarse [A4] *v pron*: **se abalanzaron hacia las salidas** they rushed toward(s) the exits; ∼ **SOBRE algn/algo** to leap ON sb/sth

abandonado -da *adj* **1** [ESTAR] (deshabitado) deserted **2** [ESTAR] ‹niño/perro/coche› abandoned **3** [ESTAR] (desatendido, descuidado) ‹jardín/parque› neglected

abandonar [A1] *vt* **1 (a)** (frml) ‹lugar› to leave **(b)** ‹familia/bebé› to leave, abandon; ‹marido/amante› to leave; ‹coche/barco› to abandon; **los abandonó a su suerte** he abandoned them to their fate **2** ‹fuerzas› to desert **3 (a)** ‹actividad/propósito/esperanza› to give up; ∼ **los estudios** to drop out of school/college **(b)** (Dep) ‹carrera/partido› to retire from, pull out of ■ ∼ *vi* (Dep) **(a)** (en carrera, competición) to pull out **(b)** (en ajedrez) to resign; (en boxeo, lucha) to concede defeat ■ **abandonarse** *v pron* **1** (entregarse) ∼**se A algo** ‹a vicios/placeres› to abandon oneself TO sth **2** (en el aspecto personal) to let oneself go

abandono *m* **1 (a)** (de una persona) abandonment; ∼ **del hogar** desertion **2** (Dep) (antes de la carrera, competición) withdrawal; (iniciada la carrera, competición) retirement; (en ajedrez) resignation **3** (descuido, desatención) neglect

abanicar [A2] *vt/vi* to fan ■ **abanicarse** *v pron* to fan oneself

abanico *m* (utensilio) fan

abaratar [A1] *vt* ‹precios/costos› to reduce; ‹producto› to make ... cheaper, reduce the price of ■ **abaratarse** *v pron* ‹costos› to drop, come down; ‹producto› to become cheaper, come down in price

abarcar [A2] *vt* **(a)** ‹temas/materias› to cover; ‹superficie/territorio› span, cover; ‹siglos/generaciones› to span; **la conversación abarcó varios temas** the conversation ranged over many topics **(b)** (dar abasto con) ‹trabajos/actividades› to cope with; **quien mucho abarca poco aprieta** you shouldn't bite off more than you can chew **(c)** (con los brazos, la mano) to encircle

abarrotado -da *adj* crammed, packed; ∼ **DE**
algo ⟨*de gente*⟩ packed o crammed **WITH** sth
abarrotar [A1] *vt* ⟨*sala/teatro*⟩ to pack
abarrotería *f* (Méx) grocery store (AmE),
grocer's (shop) (BrE)
abarrotero -ra *m,f* (Chi, Méx) ⟨*tendero*⟩
storekeeper (AmE), shopkeeper (BrE)
abarrotes *mpl* (AmL exc RPI) ⟨*comestibles*⟩
groceries (*pl*); ⟨*tienda*⟩ grocery store (AmE),
grocer's (shop) (BrE)
abastecedor -dora *m,f* supplier
abastecer [E3] *vt* to supply; ∼ **a** algn **DE** algo
to supply sb **WITH** sth
■ **abastecerse** *v pron* ∼se **DE** algo (obtener) to
obtain sth; (almacenar) to stock up **WITH** sth
abastecimiento *m* supply
abasto *m* (a) (aprovisionamiento) supply; *no dar*
∼: no dan ∼ con el trabajo they can't cope with
all the work (b) (provisiones) *tb* ∼s *mpl* basic
provisions (*pl esp foodstuffs*)
abatible *adj* ⟨*respaldo*⟩ reclining (*before n*);
(hacia adelante) folding (*before n*)
abatido -da *adj* [ESTAR] (deprimido, triste)
depressed; (desanimado) downhearted, dispirited
abatir [I1] *vt* ① (derribar) ⟨*pájaro/avión*⟩ to bring
down; ⟨*muro/edificio*⟩ to knock down; ⟨*árbol*⟩ to
fell; **fue abatido a tiros** he was gunned down
② (deprimir, entristecer): **la enfermedad lo abatió**
mucho his illness made him feel very low; **no te**
dejes ∼ **por las preocupaciones** don't let your
worries get you down ③ ⟨*asiento*⟩ to recline
■ **abatirse** *v pron* ① (deprimirse) to get depressed
② (frml) ∼se **SOBRE** algo/algn «*pájaro/avión*» to
swoop down **ON** sth/sb; «*desgracia*» to befall sth/
sb (frml); **el caos se abatió sobre el país** the
country was plunged into chaos
abdicación *f* abdication
abdicar [A2] *vi* «*soberano*» to abdicate; ∼ **EN**
algn to abdicate **IN FAVOR OF** sb
■ ∼ *vt* ⟨*trono/corona*⟩ to give up, abdicate
abdomen *m* abdomen
abdominal *adj* abdominal
■ *m* sit-up
abecedario *m* alphabet
abedul *m* birch
abeja *f* bee; ∼ **obrera/reina** worker/queen bee
abejorro *m* bumblebee
aberración *f* (disparate, extravío) outrage; **robarle**
a un ciego es una ∼ stealing from sb who's blind
is outrageous
abertura *f* (en general) opening; (agujero) hole;
(rendija) gap; (corte, tajo) slit
abeto *m* fir (tree)
abierto¹ -ta *adj* ① (a) ⟨*ventana/boca*⟩ open;
está ∼ it's open; **con los ojos muy** ∼s with eyes
wide open; **un sobre** ∼ an unsealed envelope; **los**
espacios ∼s **de la ciudad** the city's open spaces
(b) [ESTAR] ⟨*válvula*⟩ open; **dejaste la llave** ∼ you
left the faucet (AmE) o (BrE) tap running (c)
(desabrochado) undone (d) ⟨*herida*⟩ open; ⟨*madera/*
costura⟩ split ② [ESTAR] ⟨*comercio/museo*⟩ open

③ (Ling) ⟨*vocal*⟩ open ④ (a) [SER] (espontáneo)
open (b) (receptivo) open-minded; ∼ **A** algo open
TO sth ⑤ (manifiesto, directo) open
abierto² *m* (Dep) (tournament) open
abismante *adj* (Andes) ⟨*valentía*⟩
extraordinary; ⟨*belleza*⟩ breathtaking; ⟨*cifra/*
cantidad⟩ staggering
abismo *m* abyss; **hay un profundo** ∼ **entre ellos**
there's a deep rift between them
ablandar [A1] *vt* (a) ⟨*cera/cuero*⟩ to soften;
⟨*carne*⟩ to tenderize (b) ⟨*persona*⟩ to soften;
⟨*corazón*⟩ to melt
■ **ablandarse** *v pron* (a) «*cera/cuero*» to soften
(b) «*persona*» to soften up; «*mirada*» to soften
abnegación *f* self-denial, abnegation (frml)
abnegado -da *adj* self-sacrificing, selfless
abofetear [A1] *vt* to slap
abogacía *f* law; **ejercer la** ∼ to practice law
abogado -da *m,f* (en general) lawyer, solicitor
(in UK); (ante un tribunal superior) attorney (in US),
barrister (in UK); ∼ **defensor** defense lawyer
(AmE), defence counsel (BrE); ∼ **del diablo** devil's
advocate
abolición *f* abolition
abolir [I32] *vt* to abolish
abolladura *f* dent
abollar [A1] *vt* ⟨*coche/cacerola*⟩ to dent
■ **abollarse** *v pron* to get dented
abombado -da *adj* ① ⟨*superficie*⟩ convex;
⟨*techo*⟩ domed ② (AmL fam) (atontado) dopey
(colloq), dozy (colloq) ③ (AmS) (en mal estado)
⟨*alimento*⟩: **esta carne está abombada** this meat
has gone bad o (BrE) is off
abombarse [A1] *v pron* (AmS) to go bad, go off
abominable *adj* abominable
abominar [A1] *vt* to detest, abominate (frml)
abonado -da *m,f* (del teléfono, a revista)
subscriber; (del gas) consumer, customer; (a
espectáculo, transporte) season-ticket holder
abonar [A1] *vt* ① ⟨*tierra/campo*⟩ to fertilize
② (a) (frml) (pagar) ⟨*cantidad/honorarios*⟩ to pay;
el cheque se lo ∼**án en caja** you can cash the
check at the cash desk (b) (depositar) to credit;
hemos abonado la cantidad en su cuenta we have
credited your account with the amount (c)
(Andes, Méx) (dar a cuenta) to give ... on account
■ **abonarse** *v pron* ∼se **a** algo ⟨*a espectáculo*⟩ to
buy a season ticket **FOR** sth; ⟨*a revista*⟩ to
subscribe **TO** sth
abono *m* ① (Agr) fertilizer ② (para espectáculos,
transporte) season ticket ③ (frml) (a) (pago)
payment (b) (en una cuenta) credit (c) (Andes, Méx)
(cuota) installment*
abordar [A1] *vt* ① (a) (encarar) ⟨*problema*⟩ to
tackle, deal with (b) (plantear) ⟨*tema/asunto*⟩ to
raise ② ⟨*persona*⟩ to approach; (agresivamente) to
accost ③ (Méx) «*pasajero*» ⟨*barco/avión*⟩ to
board; ⟨*automóvil*⟩ to get into
■ ∼ *vi* (Méx) (subir a bordo) to board
aborigen *adj* aboriginal, indigenous
■ *mf* aborigine, aboriginal

aborrecer [E3] vt (a) ⟨persona/actividad⟩ to detest, loathe (b) ⟨crías⟩ to reject

aborrecible adj loathsome, detestable

abortar [A1] vi (Med) (de forma espontánea) to have a miscarriage, miscarry; (de forma provocada) to have an abortion, abort
■ ~ vt ⟨maniobra/aterrizaje⟩ to abort

aborto m (Med) (espontáneo) miscarriage; (provocado) abortion

abotagado -da adj ⟨cara⟩ swollen; ⟨cuerpo⟩ bloated

abotonar [A1] vt to button up, do up
■ **abotonarse** v pron ⟨chaqueta/camisa⟩ to button up, do up

abrasador -dora adj burning (before n)

abrasar [A1] vt (a) (quemar) to burn; **murieron abrasados** they were burned to death (b) «bebida» to scald, burn; «comida» to burn
■ ~ vi «sol» to burn, scorch
■ **abrasarse** v pron «bosque» to be burned (down); «planta» to get scorched; **nos abrasábamos bajo el sol** we were sweltering under the sun

abrasivo -va adj/m abrasive

abrazar [A4] vt ⟨persona⟩ to hug; (con más sentimiento) to embrace; **abrázame fuerte** hold me tight
■ **abrazarse** v pron (recípr) to hug each other; (con más sentimiento) to embrace each other; ~**se A algn/algo** to hold on o cling TO sb/sth

abrazo m hug; (con más sentimiento) embrace; **me dio un** ~ he gave me a hug, he hugged/embraced me; **dale un** ~ **de mi parte** give my love to her; **un** ~, **Miguel** (en cartas) best wishes, Miguel, regards, Miguel; (más íntimo) love, Miguel

abrebotellas m (pl ~) bottle opener

abrecartas m (pl ~) letter opener

abrelatas m (pl ~) can opener, tin opener (BrE)

abreviar [A1] vt ⟨permanencia/visita⟩ to cut short; ⟨plazo⟩ to shorten; ⟨texto/artículo⟩ to abridge; ⟨palabra⟩ to abbreviate
■ ~ vi: **abreviando** ... in short ...

abreviatura f abbreviation

abridor m (de botellas) bottle opener; (de latas) can opener, tin opener (BrE)

abrigado -da adj (a) [ESTAR] ⟨lugar⟩ sheltered (b) [ESTAR] ⟨persona⟩: **¿estás bien** ~ **con esas mantas?** are you warm enough with those blankets?; **está demasiado** ~ he has too many clothes on; **iba bien** ~ he was wrapped up warm (c) [SER] (RPl, Ven) ⟨ropa⟩ warm

abrigador -dora adj [SER] (Andes, Méx) ⟨ropa⟩ warm

abrigar [A3] vt **1** (con ropa) to wrap ... up warm; **el pañuelo me abriga el cuello** the scarf keeps my neck warm **2** ⟨idea/esperanza⟩ to cherish; ⟨sospecha/duda⟩ to harbor*, entertain
■ ~ vi «ropa» to be warm
■ **abrigarse** v pron (refl) to wrap up warm

abrigo m **1** (a) (prenda) coat (b) (calor que brinda la ropa): **necesita más** ~ she needs to be wrapped up more warmly; **con una manta no tengo suficiente** ~ I'm not warm enough with one blanket; **ropa de** ~ warm clothes **2** (refugio,

protección) shelter; **al** ~ **de la lluvia/los árboles** sheltered from the rain/under the trees; **al** ~ **de la lumbre** by the fireside

abril m April; para ejemplos ver ENERO

abrillantar [A1] vt to polish

abrir [I33] vt **1** (en general) to open; ⟨paraguas⟩ to open, put up; ⟨mapa⟩ to open out, unfold; ⟨cortinas⟩ to open, draw back; ⟨persianas⟩ to raise, pull up; ⟨cremallera⟩ to undo **2** ⟨llave/gas⟩ to turn on; ⟨válvula⟩ to open; ⟨cerradura⟩ to unlock **3** (a) ⟨zanja/túnel⟩ to dig; ⟨agujero⟩ to make (b) (fam) ⟨paciente⟩ to open ... up (colloq) **4** (a) ⟨comercio/museo⟩ (para el quehacer diario) to open; (inaugurar) to open (up); **¿a qué hora abren la taquilla?** what time does the box office open? (b) ⟨carretera/aeropuerto⟩ to open; ⟨frontera⟩ to open (up) **5** (a) (iniciar) ⟨cuenta bancaria⟩ to open; ⟨negocio⟩ to start, set up; ⟨suscripción⟩ to take out; ⟨investigación⟩ to begin, set up; **no han abierto la matrícula aún** registration hasn't begun yet; ~ **fuego** to open fire (b) ⟨acto/debate/baile⟩ to open (c) ⟨desfile/cortejo⟩ to head, lead (d) ⟨paréntesis/comillas⟩ to open **6** ⟨apetito⟩ to whet
■ **abrirse** v pron **1** (a) «puerta/ventana» to open; ~**se A algo** ⟨a jardín/corredor⟩ to open ONTO sth (b) «flor/almeja» to open; «paracaídas» to open **2** (refl) ⟨chaqueta/cremallera⟩ to undo **3** (a) «porvenir» to lie ahead; «perspectivas» to open up; **con este descubrimiento se abren nuevos horizontes** this discovery opens up new horizons (b) «período/era» to begin

abrochar [A1] vt ⟨chaqueta/botón⟩ to fasten, do up; ⟨collar/cinturón de seguridad⟩ to fasten
■ **abrocharse** v pron ⟨chaqueta/botón⟩ to fasten, do up; ⟨collar/cinturón de seguridad⟩ to fasten

abrumador -dora adj (a) ⟨victoria/mayoría⟩ overwhelming (b) ⟨trabajo/tarea⟩ exhausting

abrumar [A1] vt to overwhelm; ~ **a algn CON algo** ⟨con problemas/quejas⟩ to wear sb out WITH sth; **la** ~**on con sus atenciones** she was overwhelmed by their kindness

abrupto -ta adj (a) ⟨camino/pendiente⟩ steep; ⟨terreno⟩ rough (b) ⟨tono⟩ abrupt (c) ⟨cambio/descenso⟩ abrupt, sudden

absentismo m (Esp) absenteeism; ~ **escolar** (Esp) truancy, absenteeism

absolución f (a) (Relig) absolution (b) (Der) acquittal

absolutamente adv totally, absolutely; **no se ve** ~ **nada** you can't see a thing; ~ **nadie** not a soul; **¿estás segura? —** ~ are you sure? — absolutely o I'm positive

absoluto -ta adj **1** ⟨monarca/poder⟩ absolute **2** (a) (total) total, absolute, complete; **tengo la absoluta certeza** I am absolutely convinced (b) **en absoluto** (loc adv): **¿te gustó? — en** ~ **did you like it? —** no, not at all; **no lo consentiré en** ~ there is absolutely no way I will agree to it

absolver [E11] vt (a) (Relig) to absolve (b) (Der) ⟨acusado⟩ to acquit, find ... not guilty

absorbente adj (a) ⟨esponja/papel⟩ absorbent **2** ⟨persona⟩ demanding; ⟨hobby/tarea⟩ time-consuming; ⟨profesión⟩ demanding

absorber [E1] vt **(a)** ‹líquido/ruido/calor› to absorb **(b)** ‹tiempo› to occupy, take up; ‹recursos/energía› to absorb

absorción f (de líquido, calor, ruido) absorption

absorto -ta adj engrossed, absorbed

abstemio -mia adj teetotal
■ m,f teetotaler*

abstención f abstention

abstencionismo m abstentionism

abstenerse [E27] v pron **(a)** (en votación) to abstain **(b)** (frml) (no hacer): ~ DE hacer algo to refrain FROM doing sth **(c)** (privarse de): ~ del alcohol to avoid alcohol

abstinencia f abstinence

abstracto -ta adj abstract

abstraerse [E23] v pron ~se DE algo ‹de pensamiento/preocupación› to block out FROM sth

abstraído -da adj: estar ~ en algo to be absorbed in sth; lo noté como ~ he seemed rather preoccupied

absuelto -ta pp: ▶ ABSOLVER

absurdo -da adj absurd, ridiculous

abuchear [A1] vt to boo

abucheo m booing

abuelito -ta m,f (m) grandpa (colloq), granddad (colloq); (f) grandma (colloq), granny (colloq)

abuelo -la m,f [1] (pariente) (m) grandfather; (f) grandmother; mis ~s my grandparents; ¡cuéntaselo a tu abuela! (fam) pull the other one! (colloq) [2] (fam) (persona mayor) (m) old man, old guy (colloq); (f) old woman, old lady; ¡oiga ~! hey, granddad! (colloq)

abultado -da adj **(a)** ‹ojos/vientre› bulging; ‹labios› thick; ‹cartera› bulging **(b)** (abundante) ‹deuda/suma› enormous, huge **(c)** (exagerado) ‹cifra/cantidad› inflated

abultar [A1] vi **(a)** (formar un bulto) to make a bulge **(b)** (ocupar lugar) to be bulky
■ ~ vt ‹cifras/resultados› to inflate

abundancia f [1] (gran cantidad) abundance; la ~ de peces the abundance of fish; hay comida en ~ there's an abundance of food; darse en ~ to be plentiful [2] (riqueza): tiempos de ~ times of plenty; viven en la ~ they're well-off; nadar en la ~ to be rolling in money (colloq)

abundante adj ‹reservas/cosecha› plentiful, abundant; la pesca es ~ the fishing is good; aguas ~s en especies marinas waters which abound in marine life

abundar [A1] vi **(a)** (existir en gran número o cantidad) ‹especie/mineral› to be abundant **(b)** (tener mucho) ~ EN algo to abound o be rich IN sth

aburrido -da adj [1] [ESTAR] ‹persona› **(a)** (sin entretenimiento) bored; estoy muy ~ I'm bored stiff **(b)** (harto) fed up; ~ DE algo tired OF sth, fed up WITH sth; ~ DE hacer algo tired OF doing sth [2] [SER] ‹película/persona› boring; ‹trabajo› boring, tedious
■ m,f bore

aburridor -dora adj (AmL) ▶ ABURRIDO 2

aburrimiento m **(a)** (estado) boredom **(b)** (cosa aburrida): ¡qué ~! what a bore!

aburrir [I1] vt to bore
■ **aburrirse** v pron **(a)** (por falta de entretenimiento)

to get bored **(b)** (hartarse) ~se DE algo/algn to get tired OF o fed up WITH sth/sb; ~se DE hacer algo to get tired OF doing sth

abusador -dora adj (aprovechado) ‹comerciante› opportunist; ¡qué ~ eres! you really take advantage of the situation!
■ m,f: estos comerciantes son unos ~es these shopkeepers really take advantage; es un ~ con sus padres he takes advantage of his parents

abusar [A1] vi [1] **(a)** (aprovecharse): es muy hospitalaria pero no abuses she's very hospitable but don't take advantage of her; ~ DE algo ‹de autoridad/posición/generosidad› to abuse sth; no quisiera ~ de su amabilidad I don't want to impose (on you); ~ DE algn ‹de padres/amigo› to take advantage OF sb **(b)** (sexualmente) ~ DE algn to sexually abuse sb [2] (usar en exceso): abusa de los tranquilizantes he takes too many tranquilizers; no se debe ~ del alcohol alcohol should be drunk in moderation

abusivo -va adj ‹precio/interés› outrageous

abuso m **(a)** (uso excesivo) abuse; ~ de autoridad abuse of authority; el ~ en la bebida excessive drinking; ~s deshonestos indecent assault; ~ sexual infantil child abuse **(b)** (de hospitalidad, generosidad): espero no lo considere un ~ I hope you don't think it an imposition; ¡qué ~ de confianza! (fam) what a nerve! (colloq) **(c)** (injusticia) outrage; ¡esto es un ~! this is outrageous!; prestarse a ~s to lay itself open to abuse

abusón -sona adj/m,f (Esp, Méx fam) ▶ ABUSADOR

acá adv [1] (en el espacio) here; ¡ven ~! come here!; ya viene para ~ he's on his way over; nos pasamos el día de ~ para allá we spent the whole day going to and fro; un poquito más ~ a little closer o nearer (to me) [2] (en el tiempo): del verano (para) ~ since the summer

acabado¹ -da adj [ESTAR] **(a)** ‹trabajo› finished; son todos productos muy bien ~s they are all well-finished products **(b)** ‹persona› finished

acabado² m finish

acabar [A1] vi [1] **(a)** «reunión/película» to finish, end; «persona» to finish; «novios» to split up; ya casi acabo I've nearly finished **(b)** (en un estado, situación) to end up; acabó en la cárcel he ended up in jail; (+ compl) acabamos cansadísimos by the end we were exhausted; ese chico va a ~ mal that boy will come to no good; la película acabó bien the movie had a happy ending; ~án aceptándolo o por aceptarlo they'll end up accepting it; ~ DE algo to end up AS sth; acabó de camarero he ended up (working) as a waiter **(c)** (rematar) ~ EN algo to end IN sth [2] acabar con algo ~ CON algo (terminar) ‹con libro/tarea› to finish WITH sth; ‹con bombones/bebidas› to finish off sth; ‹con salud/carrera› to ruin sth; ‹con sueldo/herencia› to fritter AWAY sth; ‹con abuso/problema› to put an end TO sth **(b)** (fam) ~ CON algn (pelearse) to finish WITH sb; (matar) to do away WITH sb (colloq); este niño va a ~ conmigo this child will be the death of me [3] acabar de **(a)** (terminar) ~ DE hacer algo to finish doing sth; cuando acabes de leerlo when you've finished reading it **(b)** (para referirse a acción reciente): acaba de salir she's just gone out; acababa de meterme en la cama cuando … I had

just got into bed when … **(c)** (llegar a): **no acabo de entenderlo** I just don't understand; **no acababa de gustarle** she wasn't totally happy about it
■ ∼ *vt* ⟨*trabajo/libro*⟩ to finish; ⟨*curso/carrera*⟩ to finish, complete

■ **acabarse** *v pron* **1** (terminarse) «*provisiones/comida*» to run out; «*problema*» to be over; «*reunión/fiesta/curso*» to end; «*proyecto*» to finish, come to an end; «*año*» to come to an end; **se nos acabó el café** we ran out of coffee; **se le ∼on las fuerzas** he ran out of energy; **un trabajo que no se acaba nunca** a never-ending *o* an endless task; **¡esto se acabó!** that's it! **2** (*enf*) (comer) to finish (up)

acabose *m* (fam): **¡esto es el ∼!** this is the end *o* limit! (colloq)

academia *f* **(a)** (sociedad) academy **(b)** (Educ) school; **∼ de conductores** *or* (AmL) **choferes** driving school; **∼ de idiomas** language school

académico -ca *adj* ⟨*estudios/año*⟩ academic (*before n*); ⟨*estilo/lenguaje*⟩ academic
■ *m,f* academician

acalorado -da *adj* **1** [SER] ⟨*discusión/riña*⟩ heated **2** [ESTAR] ⟨*persona*⟩ (enfadado) worked up; (con calor) hot

acalorarse [A1] *v pron* (enfadarse) to get worked up; (sofocarse) to get hot

acampada *f* camp; **ir de ∼** to go camping

acampanado -da *adj* ⟨*falda/pantalones*⟩ flared

acampante *mf* camper

acampar [A1] *vi* to camp

acantilado *m* cliff

acaparador -dora *adj* (egoísta) selfish, greedy; (posesivo) possessive
■ *m,f* **(a)** (de productos) hoarder **(b)** (persona egoísta) selfish person

acaparar [A1] *vt* **(a)** ⟨*productos/existencias*⟩ to hoard, stockpile **(b)** ⟨*interés/atención*⟩ to capture; **el trabajo acapara todo su tiempo** work takes up all his time

acaramelado -da *adj* **(a)** ⟨*pareja*⟩: **estaban ∼s** they were hugging and kissing **(b)** ⟨*voz*⟩ sugary **(c)** (Coc) toffee-coated; ⟨*molde*⟩ coated with caramel

acariciar [A1] *vt* ⟨*persona*⟩ to caress; ⟨*mejilla/pelo*⟩ to stroke, caress; ⟨*perro/gato*⟩ to stroke

acarrear [A1] *vt* **(a)** ⟨*problema*⟩ to give rise to, lead to; **esto le acarreó problemas** this caused her problems **(b)** ⟨*materiales/paquetes*⟩ to carry

acaso *adv* **1** (en preguntas): **¿∼ no te lo dije?** I told you, didn't I?; **¿∼ tengo yo la culpa?** is it my fault? **2** (*en locs*) **por si acaso** just in case; **si acaso** (quizás) maybe, perhaps; (en caso de que) if

acatar [A1] *vt* ⟨*leyes/orden*⟩ to obey, comply with

acatarrado -da *adj*: **estar ∼** to have a cold

acatarrarse [A1] *v pron* (resfriarse) to catch a cold

acceder [E1] *vi* **1** (consentir) to agree; **∼ A algo** to agree TO sth **2** (entrar) **∼ A algo** gain access TO sth; (Inf) to access sth

accesible *adj* ⟨*a*⟩ ⟨*lugar*⟩ accessible; ⟨*persona*⟩ approachable; ⟨*precio*⟩ affordable **(b)** ⟨*novela/lenguaje*⟩ accessible

acceso *m* **1** **(a)** (a un lugar) access; **rutas de ∼**

approach roads **(b)** (a persona, información) access **(c)** (Inf) access **2** (a curso) entrance; **pruebas de ∼** entrance examinations; **curso de ∼** preparatory course

accesorio *m* accessory (Cin, Teatr) prop; **∼s del vestir** accessories; **∼s de baño** bathroom fittings

accidentado -da *adj* **1** **(a)** ⟨*viaje*⟩ eventful; ⟨*historia*⟩ turbulent; ⟨*carrera/pasado*⟩ checkered* (*before n*); ⟨*vida*⟩ troubled **(b)** ⟨*terreno*⟩ rough, rugged; ⟨*costa*⟩ broken **2** ⟨*persona*⟩ hurt, injured
■ *m,f*: **llevaron a los ∼s al hospital** those injured *o* hurt in the accident were taken to hospital

accidental *adj* ⟨*encuentro*⟩ chance (*before n*), accidental; ⟨*circunstancias*⟩ coincidental

accidente *m* **1** **(a)** (percance) accident; **tener** *or* **sufrir un ∼** to have an accident; **∼ aéreo** plane crash; **∼ de circulación/tráfico** traffic *o* road accident; **∼ laboral** industrial accident **2** (hecho fortuito) coincidence; **por ∼** by chance **3** (del terreno) unevenness; **∼ geográfico** geographical feature

acción *f* **1** (acto, hecho) act; **acciones dignas de elogio** praiseworthy acts *o* actions; **hacer una buena ∼** to do a good deed; **∼ de gracias** thanksgiving **2** **(a)** (actividad) action; **poner algo en ∼** to put sth into action; **novela de ∼** adventure story; **una película llena de ∼** an action-packed movie *o* (BrE) film **(b)** (Mil) action **(c)** (Cin, Lit) (trama) action, plot **3** **(a)** (Der) action, lawsuit **(b)** (Fin) share; **acciones** shares, stock **4** (Per) (de una rifa) ticket

accionar [A1] *vt* ⟨*palanca*⟩ to pull; ⟨*mecanismo/dispositivo*⟩ activate, trigger

accionista *mf* stockholder, shareholder

acebo *m* holly; (árbol) holly tree

acechar [A1] *vt* ⟨*enemigo/presa*⟩ to lie in wait for; **el peligro que nos acecha** the danger that lies ahead of us

acecho *m*: **al ∼** lying in wait

aceite *m* oil; **∼ lubricante** lubricating oil; **∼ de oliva/girasol** olive/sunflower oil; **∼ de ricino** castor oil

aceitera *f* (Tec) oilcan; (Coc) cruet

aceitoso -sa *adj* oily

aceituna *f* olive; **∼s rellenas/sin hueso** stuffed/pitted olives

aceitunado -da *adj* olive (*before n*)

aceleración *f* acceleration

acelerado -da *adj* ⟨*curso*⟩ intensive, crash (*before n*); **a paso ∼** at a brisk pace

acelerador *m* (Auto) accelerator

acelerar [A1] *vt* **(a)** ⟨*coche/motor*⟩: **aceleró el coche** (en marcha) he accelerated; (sin desplazarse) he revved the engine *o* car (up) **(b)** ⟨*proceso/cambio*⟩ to speed up; ⟨*paso*⟩ to quicken
■ **∼** *vi* **(a)** (Auto) to accelerate **(b)** (fam) (darse prisa) to hurry (up)

acelgas *fpl* Swiss chard

acento *m* **(a)** (Ling) (tilde) accent; (de intensidad) stress, accent **(b)** (énfasis) emphasis **(c)** (dejo, pronunciación) accent; **tiene ∼ francés** he has a French accent

acentuado -da *adj* **(a)** ⟨*palabra/sílaba*⟩ accented **(b)** ⟨*diferencia/cambio*⟩ marked, distinct

acentuar [A18] *vt* **(a)** (Ling) (al hablar) to stress, accent; (al escribir) to accent **(b)** (intensificar, hacer resaltar) to accentuate, emphasize
■ **acentuarse** *v pron* ‹*diferencias/problemas*› to become accentuated

acepción *f* sense, meaning

aceptable *adj* acceptable, passable

aceptación *f* (a) (éxito) success; **de gran ~ entre los jóvenes** very popular *o* successful with young people **(b)** (acción) acceptance

aceptar [A1] *vt* ‹*excusas/invitación/cargo*› to accept; ‹*términos/condiciones*› to agree to; **aceptan cheques** they take checks; **aceptó venir** she agreed to come; **no acepto que me digas eso** I won't have you saying that to me

acequia *f* irrigation ditch *o* channel

acera *f* sidewalk (AmE), pavement (BrE)

acerca de *loc prep* about

acercamiento *m* (entre posturas, países) rapprochement; (entre personas): **ese incidente produjo un ~ entre ellos** that incident brought them closer together

acercar [A2] *vt* ⓵ **(a)** (aproximar) to bring ... closer *o* nearer; **~on la mesa a la puerta** they moved the table closer *o* nearer to the door; **acercó las manos al fuego** he held his hands closer to the fire; **¿puedes ~me ese libro?** can you pass *o* give me that book? **(b)** (unir) ‹*posturas/países*› to bring ... closer
⓶ (llevar): **me acercó a la parada** she gave me a ride (AmE) *o* (BrE) lift to the bus stop
■ **acercarse** *v pron* **(a)** (aproximarse) to approach, to get closer *o* nearer; **acércate más** (acercándose al hablante) come *o* get closer *o* nearer; (alejándose del hablante) go *o* get closer *o* nearer; **se le ~on dos policías** two policemen came up to *o* approached him **(b)** «*amigos/países*» to draw *o* come closer together **(c)** «*hora/momento*» to draw near, approach; **ahora que se acerca la Navidad** now that Christmas is coming

acero *m* (Metal) steel; **~ inoxidable** stainless steel

acérrimo -ma *adj* ‹*partidario/defensor*› staunch; ‹*enemigo*› bitter

acertado -da *adj* ‹*comentario*› pertinent; ‹*solución/elección*› good

acertante *adj* winning (*before n*)
■ *m,f* winner

acertar [A5] *vt* ‹*respuesta/resultado*› to get ... right; **a ver si aciertas quién es** see if you can guess who it is
■ ~ *vi* ⓵ **(a)** (dar, pegar): **~le ⋀ algo** to hit sth; **tiró pero no le acertó** he shot at it but (he) missed **(b)** (atinar) to be right; **acertaste con el regalo** your present was perfect ⓶ (lograr) **~ ⋀ hacer algo** to manage to do sth

acertijo *m* riddle, puzzle

acetona *f* (Quím) acetone; (quitaesmaltes) nail-polish remover

achacar [A2] *vt*: **~le la culpa a algn** to lay *o* put the blame on sb

achaques *mpl* ailments (*pl*); **mis acostumbrados ~** my usual aches and pains

achatar [A1] *vt* to flatten

achicar [A2] *vt* ⓵ **(a)** ‹*chaqueta/vestido*› to take in **(b)** ‹*persona*› to intimidate, daunt ⓶ ‹*agua*› to bail out
■ **achicarse** *v pron* **(a)** (de tamaño) to shrink **(b)** (amilanarse) to be intimidated, be daunted

achicharrante *adj* (fam) ‹*sol*› scorching; **hizo un calor ~** it was scorching

achicharrar [A1] *vt* (fam) **(a)** ‹*carne/comida*› to burn ... to a cinder (colloq) **(b)** «*sol*» ‹*planta*› to scorch; **hace un sol que te achicharra** the sun is scorching hot
■ **achicharrarse** *v pron* (fam) **(a)** «*persona*» to fry (colloq); «*planta*» to get scorched **(b)** «*carne/comida*» to be burned to a crisp (colloq)

achichincle, achichinque *mf* (Méx fam & pey) hanger-on (colloq & pej)

achicopalar [A1] *vt* (Col, Méx fam) to intimidate
■ **achicopalarse** *v pron* (Col, Méx fam) to feel intimidated

achicoria *f* chicory

achinado -da *adj* ‹*ojos*› slanting

achiote *m* (AmL) annatto

achispado -da *adj* (fam) tipsy (colloq)

achuras *fpl* (RPI) offal

acicalarse [A1] *v pron* to dress up, get dressed up

acicate *m* **(a)** (estímulo) incentive **(b)** (espuela) spur

acidez *f* (Quím) acidity; (Med) (en el estómago) acidity; (en el esófago) heartburn

ácido¹ -da *adj* **(a)** ‹*sabor*› acid; ‹*fruta*› acid, tart, sharp; ‹*vino*› sharp **(b)** ‹*carácter/tono*› acid, caustic

ácido² *m* **(a)** (Quím) acid **(b)** (arg) (droga) acid (sl)

acierta, aciertas, etc ▶ ACERTAR

acierto *m* **(a)** (decisión correcta) good decision, good *o* wise move **(b)** (respuesta correcta) correct answer

acitronar [A1] *vt* (Méx) to fry ... until golden brown

aclamación *f* acclaim

aclamar [A1] *vt* to acclaim, applaud

aclaración *f* explanation; **quisiera hacer una ~** I'd like to make one thing clear

aclarado *m* (Esp) rinse

aclarar [A1] *v impers* **(a)** (amanecer): **aclara temprano** it gets light early; **cuando nos levantamos estaba aclarando** dawn *o* day was breaking when we got up **(b)** (escampar) to clear up
■ ~ *vi* **(a)** «*día*» (empezar) to break, dawn **(b)** «*tiempo/día*» (escampar) to clear up
■ ~ *vt* ⓵ (quitar color a) to lighten

---

2 ⟨ideas⟩ to get ... straight; ⟨duda⟩ to clear up, clarify; **quiero ∼ que ...** I want to make it clear that ...

3 (Esp) ⟨ropa/vajilla⟩ to rinse
■ **aclararse** v pron 1 ∼**se la voz** to clear one's throat
2 (Esp fam) (entender) to understand; *a ver si nos aclaramos* let's see if we can sort things out o get things straight

aclimatarse [A1] v pron to acclimatize, get o become acclimatized

acné m or f acne

acobardar [A1] vt ⟨persona⟩ to unnerve, intimidate
■ **acobardarse** v pron to lose one's nerve; ∼**se ante el peligro** to lose one's nerve in the face of danger

acogedor -dora adj ⟨casa/habitación⟩ cozy*, welcoming; ⟨ambiente⟩ warm, friendly

acoger [E6] vt (a) ⟨huérfano/anciano⟩ to take in; ⟨refugiado⟩ to accept, admit (b) ⟨propuesta/persona⟩ to receive; **acogieron la noticia con satisfacción** the news was well received
■ **acogerse** v pron ∼**se A algo** ⟨a la ley⟩ to have recourse TO sth; ⟨a un régimen⟩ to opt FOR sth

acogida f (a) (de persona) welcome; (de noticia, propuesta) reception (b) (de huérfano) taking in; (de refugiado) acceptance

acolchar, acolchonar [A1] vt ⟨bata/tela⟩ to quilt; ⟨pared/puerta⟩ to pad

acomedido -da adj (Chi, Méx, Per) obliging, helpful

acomedirse [I14] v pron (Méx) to offer to help

acometer [E1] vi to attack; ∼ **CONTRA algo/algn** to attack sth/sb

acomodado -da adj 1 ⟨familia/gente⟩ well-off, well-to-do; **de posición acomodada** well-off, well-to-do 2 (CS, Méx fam) (que tiene palanca): **estar ∼** to have contacts o connections

acomodador -dora m,f (m) usher; (f) usherette

acomodar [A1] vt 1 (adaptar, amoldar) to adapt 2 ⟨huésped⟩ to put ... up 3 (a) (AmL) (arreglar) to arrange; (poner) to put (b) (fam) ⟨persona⟩ (en puesto): **su tío lo acomodó en su sección** his uncle fixed him up with a job in his department
■ **acomodarse** v pron (a) (ponerse cómodo) to make oneself comfortable (b) (adaptarse, amoldarse) ∼**se A algo** to adapt TO sth (c) (AmL) (arreglarse) ⟨ropa/anteojos⟩ to adjust

acompañado -da adj accompanied; **bien/mal ∼** in good/bad company; **vino ∼ de un amigo** he came with a friend

acompañamiento m (a) (Mús) accompaniment (b) (Coc) accompaniment; **¿con qué ∼ lo quiere?** what would you like it served with?

acompañar [A1] vt 1 (a) (a un lugar) to go with, accompany (frml); **acompáñalo hasta la puerta** see him to the door, see him out; **la acompañé a su casa** I walked her home; **¿me acompañas?** will you come with me? (b) (hacer compañía) to keep ... company (c) (Mús) to accompany (d) (frml) (adjuntar) to enclose; **acompañado de un certificado médico** accompanied by a medical certificate

acomplejado -da adj: **es muy ∼** he's full of complexes; **está ∼ por su gordura** he has a complex about being fat
■ m,f: **es un ∼** he's a mass of complexes

acomplejar [A1] vt to give ... a complex
■ **acomplejarse** v pron to get a complex

acondicionador m (a) tb ∼ **de pelo** (hair) conditioner (b) ∼ **de aire** air conditioner

acondicionamiento m fitting-out

acondicionar [A1] vt (a) ⟨vivienda/local⟩ to equip, fit out (b) (Col) ⟨carro⟩ to soup up

aconsejable adj advisable

aconsejar [A1] vt to advise; ∼**le a algn hacer algo/que haga algo** to advise sb to do sth; **has sido mal aconsejado** you've been given bad advice; **necesito que alguien me aconseje** I need some advice

acontecer [E3] vi (en 3ª pers) (frml) to take place, occur (frml); **los sucesos acontecidos ayer** the events which took place o occurred yesterday;
■ m: **el diario ∼** everyday events o occurrences

acontecimiento m event; **adelantarse a los ∼s** to jump the gun

acoplar [A1] vt (a) ⟨piezas⟩ to fit o put together (b) (Elec) to connect (c) (Ferr) to couple

acorazado m battleship

acordar [A10] vt ⟨términos⟩ to agree; ⟨precio/fecha⟩ to agree (on)
■ ∼ vi (Andes) (recordar) ∼**le a algn DE hacer algo/que haga algo** to remind sb to do sth
■ **acordarse** v pron to remember; **si mal no me acuerdo** if I remember right; ∼**se DE algn/algo** to remember sb/sth; **no quiero ni ∼me** I don't even want to think about it; ∼**se DE hacer algo** (de una acción que hay/había que realizar) to remember to do sth; (de una acción que ya se realizó) to remember o recall doing sth; **se acordó de haberlo visto allí** she remembered o recalled seeing him there; ∼**se (DE) QUE ...** to remember THAT ...

acorde adj (en armonía) ⟨sonidos⟩ harmonious; **colores ∼s** colors that go o blend well together; **con un salario ∼** with a salary to match; ∼ **CON** or **A algo** appropriate TO sth, in keeping WITH sth
■ m (Mús) chord

acordeón m 1 (Mús) accordion 2 (Méx fam) (para un examen) crib

acordeonista mf accordionist

acordonar [A1] vt (a) ⟨lugar⟩ to cordon off (b) ⟨zapatos⟩ to lace (up)

acorralar [A1] vt (a) ⟨animal/fugitivo⟩ to corner (b) ⟨ganado⟩ to round up

acortar [A1] vt ⟨falda/vestido⟩ to shorten; ⟨texto/artículo⟩ to cut, shorten; ⟨vacaciones/permanencia⟩ to cut short; ⟨película/carrera⟩ to reduce the length of; ⟨distancia⟩ to reduce; ∼ **camino** to take a short cut
■ **acortarse** v pron to get shorter

acosar [A1] vt (a) ⟨persona⟩ to hound; (sexualmente) to harass; **me ∼on con preguntas** they plagued o bombarded me with questions (b) ⟨presa⟩ to hound, pursue relentlessly

acosijar [A1] vt (Méx) to badger, pester

acoso m (a) (de persona) hounding, harassment; ∼ **sexual** sexual harassment (b) (de presa) hounding, relentless pursuit

acostar [A10] vt ‹persona› to put ... to bed
■ **acostarse** v pron (a) (irse a dormir) to go to bed
(b) (tenderse, tumbarse) to lie down; **~se boca
abajo** to lie face down (c) (tener relaciones sexuales)
to go to bed together, sleep together; **~se CON
algn** to go to bed WITH sb, sleep WITH sb

acostumbrado -da adj (a) (habituado): **está
mal ~** he's got into bad habits; **~ A algo/hacer
algo** used TO sth/doing sth; **estamos ~s a cenar
temprano** we're used to having dinner early; **está
~ a que le sirvan** he's used to being served (b)
(habitual) customary, usual

acostumbrar [A1] vt **~ a algn A algo/hacer
algo** to get sb used TO sth/doing sth
■ **~** vi: **~ A hacer algo** to be accustomed TO doing
sth, be in the habit OF doing sth
■ **acostumbrarse** v pron **~se A algo/algn** to
get used TO sth/sb; **~se A hacer algo** to get used
TO doing sth

acotación f (en texto) marginal note,
annotation

acotamiento m (Méx) shoulder (AmE), hard
shoulder (BrE)

acrecentar [A5] vt to increase
■ **acrecentarse** v pron to increase, grow

acreditado -da adj (a) ‹establecimiento/
marca› reputable, well-known (b) ‹diplomático/
periodista› accredited; ‹agente/representante›
authorized, official

acreditar [A1] vt **1** ‹diplomático/periodista› to
accredit; ‹representante› to authorize **2** (frml) (a)
(probar, avalar) ‹pago› to prove; **este libro lo
acredita como un gran pensador** this book
confirms him as a great thinker (b) (dar renombre):
con la calidad que lo acredita with the quality for
which it's renowned **3** (Fin) to credit

acreedor -dora m,f creditor

acribillar [A1] vt (a) (llenar de agujeros): **lo ~on
a balazos** they riddled him with bullets (b)
(asediar): **me ~on a preguntas** they fired a barrage
of questions at me

acrílico m acrylic

acristalar [A1] vt to glaze

acrobacia f (arte) acrobatics; **hacer ~s** to
perform acrobatics; **~ aérea** aerobatics

acróbata mf acrobat

acta f: (de reunión) minutes (pl); **levantar (el) ~**
to take (the) minutes; **~ de defunción** (Col, Méx,
Ven) entry in the register of deaths; **~ de
matrimonio/nacimiento** (Méx) marriage/birth
certificate; **~ notarial** notarial deed

actitud f (disposición) attitude; **adoptar una ~
firme (con algn)** to be firm (with sb)

activar [A1] vt (a) (agilizar) ‹proceso/crecimiento›
to speed up; ‹economía/producción› to stimulate;
‹circulación› to stimulate; ‹negociaciones› to give
fresh impetus to (b) (poner en funcionamiento)
‹alarma› to activate, trigger; ‹dispositivo› to
activate; ‹máquina› to set ... in motion
■ **activarse** v pron «alarma» to go off;
«dispositivo» to start working

actividad f activity; **un volcán en ~** an active
volcano

activista mf activist

activo¹ -va adj active

activo² m assets (pl)

acto m **1** (a) (acción) act; **morir en ~ de
servicio** «soldado» to die on active service;
«policía/bombero» to die in the course of one's
duty; **~ sexual** sexual act (frml) (b) (en locs) **acto
seguido** immediately after; **en el acto** ‹morir›
instantly; ‹acudir› immediately; **lo despidieron
en el ~** he was fired on the spot **2** (a)
(ceremonia) ceremony (b) (Teatr) act

actor m actor

actriz f actress

actuación f (a) (acción) action (b) (Cin, Dep,
Teatr) performance; **la ~ es pésima** the acting is
appalling (c) (conducta) conduct (d) (recital, sesión)
performance, concert

actual adj ‹ley/situación/dirección› present,
current; **en el Chile ~** in present-day Chile; **en el
mundo ~** in the modern world, in today's world

actualidad f (a) (tiempo presente): **en la ~**
currently, at present; **la ~ cubana** the current
situation in Cuba (b) (de tema, noticia) topicality;
las noticias de ~ today's (o this week's etc) news;
un tema de ~ (period) a topical subject; **sucesos
de ~** current affairs

actualizar [A4] vt ‹salarios/pensiones/
legislación› to bring ... up to date; ‹información/
manual› to update; (Inf) ‹software› to upgrade

actualmente adv (hoy en día) nowadays; (en
este momento) at present; **se encuentra ~ en
Suecia** she is currently in Sweden, she is in
Sweden at present

actuar [A18] vi (a) «persona» (obrar) to act;
forma de ~ behavior* (b) ‹medicamento› to
work, act (c) «actor» to act; «torero» to
perform; **¿quién actúa en esa película?** who's in
the movie?

acuarela f watercolor*

acuario m aquarium

Acuario m (signo) Aquarius; **es (de) ~** he's an
Aquarius o Aquarian
■ mf (persona) tb **acuario** Aquarian, Aquarius

acuático -ca adj aquatic

acuatizaje m: landing on water

acuatizar [A4] vi to land on water

acuchillar [A1] vt ‹persona› to stab

acudir [I1] vi **1** (frml) (ir) to go; (venir) to come;
nadie acudió en su ayuda nobody went/came to
his aid; **~ A algo** ‹a cita› to arrive FOR sth; ‹a
reunión› to attend sth; **la policía acudió al lugar
de los hechos** the police arrived at the scene (of
the incident) **2** (recurrir) **~ A algn** to turn TO sb;
no tenía a quien ~ he had nobody to turn to

acueducto m aqueduct

acuerdo m (a) (arreglo, pacto) agreement; **llegar
a un ~** to reach an agreement; **~ de paz** peace
agreement o (frml) accord (b) **estar de ~** to agree;
ponerse de ~ to come to o reach an agreement;
estar de ~ EN algo to agree ON something; **estar
de ~ CON algn/algo** to agree WITH sb/sth;
¿mañana a las ocho? — de ~ (indep) tomorrow
at eight? — OK o all right (c) **de ~ con** or **a in**
accordance with

acuesta, acuestas, etc ▶ ACOSTAR

acumulación f accumulation

acumular [A1] vt ‹riquezas/poder› to
accumulate; ‹experiencia› to gain

■ **acumularse** *v pron* «*trabajo*» to pile up, mount up; «*intereses*» to accumulate; «*deudas*» to mount up; «*polvo*» to accumulate

acunar [A1] *vt* to rock

acuñar [A1] *vt* ⟨*moneda*⟩ to mint; ⟨*frase/ palabra*⟩ to coin

acuoso -sa *adj* watery

acupuntura *f* acupuncture

acupunturista *mf* acupuncturist

acurrucarse [A2] *v pron* to curl up

acusación *f* **(a)** (imputación) accusation **(b)** (Der) charge

acusado -da *m,f*: **el/la ~** the accused, the defendant

acusador -dora *adj* accusing, accusatory (frml); **una mirada ~a** an accusing look
■ *m,f* prosecuting attorney (AmE), prosecuting counsel (BrE)

acusar [A1] *vt* **1** **(a)** (culpar) to accuse; **~ a algn DE algo** to accuse sb OF sth; **me acusan de haber mentido** they accuse me of lying **(b)** (Der) **~ a algn DE algo** to chargé sb WITH sth **(c)** (fam) (delatar) to tell on (colloq) **2** (reconocer): **~ recibo de algo** (Corresp) to acknowledge receipt of sth

acusetas *mf* (*pl* **~**), **acusete -ta** *m,f* (fam) tattletale (AmE colloq), telltale (BrE colloq)

acústica *f* (ciencia) acoustics; (de local) acoustics (*pl*)

acústico -ca *adj* acoustic

adaptable *adj* adaptable

adaptación *f* **(a)** (proceso) adaptation, adjustment **(b)** (cosa adaptada) adaptation; **la ~ cinematográfica** the screen version

adaptador *m* adaptor

adaptar [A1] *vt* ⟨*cortinas/vestido*⟩ to alter; ⟨*habitación*⟩ to convert; ⟨*pieza/motor*⟩ to adapt; ⟨*obra/novela*⟩ to adapt; (Inf) to convert
■ **adaptarse** *v pron* to adapt; **~se a algo/hacer algo** to adapt TO sth/doing sth; **un coche que se adapta a cualquier terreno** a car which is well suited to any terrain

a. de C. (= **antes de Cristo**) BC, before Christ

adecentar [A1] *vt* ⟨*habitación*⟩ to tidy up

adecuado -da *adj* **(a)** (apropiado) ⟨*vestido/ regalo*⟩ suitable; ⟨*momento*⟩ right; ⟨*medios*⟩ adequate; **la persona adecuada para el cargo** the right person for the job **(b)** (aceptable) adequate

adecuar [A1] *or* [A18] *vt* **~ algo A algo** to adapt sth TO sth

adefesio *m* (cosa) eyesore; (persona): **es un ~** he's so ugly; **ir hecho un ~** to look a sight *o* fright (colloq)

adelantado -da *adj* **1** **(a)** (desarrollado) ⟨*país*⟩ advanced **(b)** (aventajado): **va muy ~ en sus estudios** he is doing very well in his studies; **va ~ para su edad** he's advanced for his age **2** [ESTAR] ⟨*reloj*⟩ fast **3** (Com, Fin): **pago ~** payment in advance; **por ~** in advance **4** (avanzado): **las obras están muy adelantadas** construction is already well underway; **vamos bastante ~s** we're quite far ahead with it **5** (Dep) ⟨*pase*⟩ forward

adelantamiento *m* passing maneuver (AmE), overtaking manoeuvre (BrE)

adelantar [A1] *vt* **1** **(a)** ⟨*fecha/viaje*⟩ to bring forward **(b)** ⟨*pieza/ficha*⟩ to move ... forward **2** (sobrepasar) to overtake, pass **3** **(a)** ⟨*reloj*⟩ to put ... forward **(b)** ⟨*balón*⟩ to pass ... forward **(c)** ⟨*trabajo*⟩ to get on with **4** (conseguir) to gain; **con llorar no adelantas nada** crying won't get you anywhere
■ **~** *vi* **1** **(a)** (avanzar) to make progress **(b)** «*reloj*» to gain **2** (Auto) to pass, overtake (BrE)
■ **adelantarse** *v pron* **1** **(a)** (avanzar) to move forward **(b)** (ir delante) to go ahead; **se adelantó para comprar las entradas** she went (on) ahead to buy the tickets **2** **(a)** «*cosecha*» to be early; «*verano/frío*» to arrive early **(b)** «*reloj*» to gain **3** (anticiparse): **se adelantó a su época** he was ahead of his time; **~se a los acontecimientos** to jump the gun; **yo iba a pagar, pero él se me adelantó** I was going to pay, but he beat me to it

adelante *adv* **1** (en el espacio) **(a)** (expresando dirección, movimiento) forward; **para/hacia ~** forward; **seguir ~** to go on; **¡~!** (*como interj*) (autorizando la entrada) come in!; (ordenando marchar) forward! **(b)** (lugar, posición): **se sentó ~** (en coche) she sat in front; (en clase, cine) she sat at the front; **más ~ la calle se bifurca** further on, the road forks; **la parte de ~** the front **2** (en el tiempo): **más ~** later; **(de ahora) en ~** from now on; **de hoy en ~** as of *o* from today **3** **adelante de** (*loc prep*) (AmL) in front of

adelanto *m* **1** (avance) step forward; **los ~s de la ciencia** the advances of science **2** (del sueldo) advance; (depósito) deposit **3** (en el tiempo): **llegó con un poco de ~** he/she/it arrived slightly early

adelgazamiento *m* slimming

adelgazante *adj* weight-reducing (*before n*), slimming (*before n*) (BrE)

adelgazar [A4] *vt* ⟨*caderas/cintura*⟩ to slim down; ⟨*kilos*⟩ to lose
■ **~** *vi* to lose weight

ademán *m* (expresión) expression; (movimiento, gesto) gesture; **hizo ~ de levantarse** he made as if to get up

además *adv* **1** **(a)** (también) as well, too; **~ habla ruso** she speaks Russian as well *o* too **(b)** (lo que es más) what's more **(c)** (por otra parte) anyway, besides; **~ ¿a mí qué me importa?** anyway, what do I care? **2** **además de** besides, apart from; **~ de hacerte mal, engorda** besides *o* apart from being bad for you, it's also fattening; **~ de hacerlos, los diseña** he designs them as well as making them

adentro *adv* **1** **(a)** (expresando dirección, movimiento): **vamos para ~** let's go in *o* inside; **ven aquí ~** come in here **(b)** (lugar, parte) inside; [*European Spanish prefers* DENTRO *in many of these examples*] **¡qué calor hace aquí ~!** it's so hot in here!; **¿comemos ~?** shall we eat indoors *o* inside?; **la parte de ~** the inside **2** **adentro de** (AmL) in, inside

adentros *mpl*: **dije para mis ~** I said to myself; **se rió para sus ~s** he chuckled to himself

adepto -ta *adj*: **ser ~ A algo** ⟨*a secta*⟩ to be a follower OF sth; ⟨*a partido*⟩ to be a supporter OF sth
■ *m,f* (de secta) follower; (de partido) supporter

aderezar [A4] vt ⟨guiso⟩ to season; ⟨ensalada⟩ to dress

aderezo m (de guiso) seasoning; (de ensalada) dressing

adherencia f (a) (acción) adherence (b) (Auto) grip, roadholding (c) (Med) adhesion

adherente adj adhesive

adherir [I11] vt to stick
■ **adherirse** v pron (a) (pegarse) to stick (b) (unirse) ~**se A algo** ⟨a propuesta/causa⟩ to give one's support TO sth; ⟨a movimiento/partido⟩ to join sth

adhesión f (a) (a una superficie) adhesion (b) (apoyo) support (c) (a una organización) joining

adhesivo¹ -va adj adhesive, sticky

adhesivo² m (sustancia) adhesive; (lámina, estampa) sticker

adicción f addiction; ~ **a la heroína** heroin addiction

adición f (a) (Mat) addition (b) (RPI) (cuenta) check (AmE), bill (BrE)

adicional adj additional; **una cantidad** ~ a supplement

adicto -ta adj (a la bebida, la droga) addicted; ~ **A algo** addicted TO sth
■ m,f addict; **los** ~**s a la cocaína** cocaine addicts

adiestrar [A1] vt to train

adinerado -da adj wealthy, moneyed

adiós m/interj (al despedirse) goodbye, bye (colloq); (al pasar) hello; ▶ DECIR² vt 3B

aditivo m additive

adivinanza f riddle; **jugar a las** ~**s** to play at guessing riddles

adivinar [A1] vt (a) (por conjeturas, al azar) to guess (b) (por magia) to foretell, predict
■ ~ vi to guess

adivino -na m,f fortune-teller

adjetivo¹ -va adj adjectival

adjetivo² m adjective

adjudicación f (a) (de premio, contrato) awarding; (de viviendas) allocation (b) (en subasta) sale

adjudicar [A2] vt (a) ⟨premio/contrato⟩ to award; ⟨vivienda⟩ to allot, allocate (b) (en subasta): **le** ~**on la alfombra al anticuario the** carpet was sold to o went to the antique dealer; **¡adjudicado!** sold!

adjuntar [A1] vt to enclose

adjunto -ta adj (a) ⟨director⟩ deputy (before n); **profesor** ~ associate professor (AmE), senior lecturer (BrE) (b) ⟨lista/copia⟩ enclosed, attached

administración f 1 (a) (de empresa, bienes) management (b) (Pol) administration; ~ **pública** civil service 2 (a) (conjunto de personas) management (b) (oficina, departamento) administration

administrador -dora m,f (de empresa) manager, administrator; (de bienes) administrator

administrar [A1] vt (a) ⟨empresa/bienes⟩ to manage, administer (frml) (b) (frml) (dar) ⟨sacramentos/medicamento⟩ to give
■ **administrarse** v pron: ~**se bien/mal** to manage one's money well/badly

administrativo -va adj administrative
■ m,f administrative assistant (o officer etc); (con funciones más rutinarias) clerk

admirable adj admirable

admiración f (a) (respeto) admiration (b) (sorpresa) amazement

admirador -dora m,f (a) (de persona) admirer, fan (b) (hum) (pretendiente) admirer (hum)

admirar [A1] vt (a) (respetar) ⟨persona/cualidad⟩ to admire (b) (contemplar) to admire (c) (sorprender) to amaze
■ **admirarse** v pron ~**se DE algo** to be amazed AT o ABOUT sth

admisible adj ⟨comportamiento⟩ admissible, acceptable; ⟨excusa⟩ acceptable

admisión f admission; **examen** or **prueba de** ~ entrance examination o test

admitir [I1] vt 1 (a) (aceptar) to accept; ⓢ **se admiten tarjetas de crédito** we take o accept credit cards (b) (permitir) to allow (c) (reconocer) to admit 2 (dar cabida a) «local» to hold

ADN m (= **ácido desoxirribonucleico**) DNA

adobar [A1] vt ⟨carne/pescado⟩ (condimentar) to marinade; (para conservar) to pickle; (para curar) to cure

adobe m adobe

adobo m (condimento) marinade; (para conservar) pickle

adoctrinar [A1] vt to indoctrinate

adolecer [E3] vi ~ **DE algo** ⟨de enfermedad/defecto⟩ to suffer FROM sth

adolescencia f adolescence; **durante su** ~ (when he was) in his teens, in adolescence (frml)

adolescente adj adolescent; **tiene dos hijos** ~**s** she has two teenage o adolescent children
■ mf (en contextos no técnicos) teenager; (Med, Psic) adolescent

adolorido -da adj (esp AmL) ▶ DOLORIDO A

adonde adv where; **el lugar** ~ **se dirigían** the place where o to which they were going

adónde adv where

adondequiera adv: ~ **que vayas** wherever you go

adopción f adoption

adoptar [A1] vt (a) ⟨actitud/costumbre⟩ to adopt; ⟨decisión/medida/posición⟩ to take (b) ⟨niño/nacionalidad⟩ to adopt

adoptivo -va adj (a) ⟨hijo⟩ adopted; ⟨padres⟩ adoptive (b) ⟨patria/país⟩ adopted

adoquín m (a) (de piedra) paving stone; (ovalado) cobblestone (b) (Per) (helado) Popsicle® (AmE), ice lolly (BrE)

adorable adj adorable

adoración _f_ **(a)** (de persona) adoration **(b)** (de deidad) adoration, worship

adorar [A1] _vt_ **(a)** ⟨persona/cosa⟩ to adore **(b)** ⟨deidad⟩ to worship, adore

adormecer [E3] _vt_ **(a)** ⟨persona⟩ to make ... sleepy _o_ drowsy; ⟨sentidos⟩ to numb, dull **(b)** ⟨pierna/mano⟩ to numb
■ **adormecerse** _v pron_ to fall asleep, doze off

adormecimiento _m_ **(a)** (somnolencia) sleepiness, drowsiness **(b)** (de un miembro) numbness

adormilarse [A1] _v pron_ to doze

adornar [A1] _vt_ **(a)** ⟨habitación/sombrero/comida⟩ to decorate **(b)** ⟨relato/discurso⟩ to embellish **(c)** «⟨flores/banderas⟩» to adorn
■ **adornarse** _v pron_ (refl) ⟨cabeza/pelo⟩ to adorn

adorno _m_ **(a)** (objeto) ornament; **los ~s de Navidad** the Christmas decorations **(b)** (decoración) adornment; **de ~** for decoration

adosado -da _adj_ **~ A algo** fixed TO sth; ▶ CASA 1A

adosar [A1] _vt_ **(a)** ⟨armario/escritorio⟩ **~ algo A algo** to fix sth TO sth **(b)** (Méx) ⟨documento⟩ to enclose, attach

adquiera, adquirió, etc ▶ ADQUIRIR

adquirir [I13] _vt_ ⟨casa/coche⟩ to acquire, obtain; (comprar) to purchase, buy; ⟨conocimientos/colección/fortuna⟩ to acquire; ⟨fama⟩ to attain, achieve; ⟨experiencia⟩ to gain; **~ malas costumbres** to get into bad habits

adquisición _f_ acquisition; (compra) purchase

adquisitivo -va _adj_ purchasing

adrede _adv_ on purpose, deliberately

adrenalina _f_ adrenaline

aduana _f_ customs; **libre de derechos de ~** duty free

aduanero -ra _adj_ customs (before n)
■ _m,f_ customs officer

adulación _f_ flattery

adulador -dora _adj_ flattering
■ _m,f_ flatterer

adular [A1] _vt_ to flatter

adulterar [A1] _vt_ ⟨alimento/vino⟩ to adulterate; ⟨información⟩ to falsify

adulterio _m_ adultery

adulto -ta _adj_ **(a)** ⟨persona/animal⟩ adult (before n) **(b)** ⟨reacción/opinión⟩ adult
■ _m,f_ adult

adusto -ta _adj_ ⟨persona/expresión⟩ austere, severe; ⟨paisaje⟩ bleak, harsh

advenedizo -za _adj_ upstart (before n)
■ _m,f_ social climber

adverbio _m_ adverb

adversario -ria _adj_ opposing (before n)
■ _m,f_ opponent, adversary

adversidad _f_ adversity; **en la ~** in adversity

adverso -sa _adj_ ⟨circunstancias/resultado⟩ adverse

advertencia _f_ warning; **que les sirva de ~** let it be a warning to them

advertir [I11] _vt_ **(a)** (avisar) to warn; **¡te lo advierto!** I'm warning you!; **~le A algn DE algo** to warn sb ABOUT sth; **le advertí que tuviera cuidado**

I warned him to be careful; **te advierto que no me sorprendió nada** I must say I wasn't at all surprised **(b)** (notar) to notice

adviento _m_ Advent

advierta, advirtió, etc ▶ ADVERTIR

adyacente _adj_ adjacent

aéreo -rea _adj_ ⟨vista⟩ aerial; ⟨tráfico⟩ air (before n)

aerobic /e'roβik/ _m_, (Méx) **aerobics** _mpl_ aerobics

aerodeslizador _m_ (Náut) hovercraft

aerodinámica _f_ aerodynamics

aerodinámico -ca _adj_ aerodynamic

aeródromo _m_ aerodrome, airfield

aeroespacial _adj_ aerospace (before n)

aerograma _m_ aerogram, air (mail) letter

aerolínea _f_ airline

aeromodelismo _m_ model airplane making

aeromozo -za _m,f_ (AmL) flight attendant

aeronáutica _f_ **(a)** (ciencia) aeronautics **(b)** (RPl) (aviación militar) air force

aeronáutico -ca _adj_ aeronautic, aeronautical

aeronave _f_ **(a)** (globo dirigible) airship **(b)** (frml) (avión) airliner, aircraft

aeroplano _m_ (ant) airplane, aeroplane (BrE)

aeropuerto _m_ airport

aerosol _m_ aerosol, spray can

afable _adj_ affable

afán _m_ ⟨1⟩ **(a)** (anhelo) eagerness; **su ~ de aventuras** his thirst for adventure; **~ DE hacer algo** eagerness TO do sth; **su ~ de agradar** their eagerness to please; **tiene ~ de aprender** she's eager to learn **(b)** (empeño) effort ⟨2⟩ (Col fam) (prisa) hurry

afanado -da _adj_ ⟨1⟩ [ESTAR] ⟨persona⟩ busy ⟨2⟩ [ESTAR] (Col, Per fam) (con prisa) in a hurry

afanarse [A1] _v pron_ (esforzarse) to work, toil; **~se EN** _or_ **POR hacer algo** to strive TO do sth

afear [A1] _vt_ **(a)** ⟨persona⟩ to make ... look ugly; ⟨paisaje⟩ to spoil **(b)** ⟨conducta⟩ to criticize
■ **afearse** _v pron_ to lose one's looks

afectación _f_ affectation

afectado -da _adj_ **(a)** ⟨gestos/acento⟩ affected **(b)** ⟨área/órgano⟩ affected; **está afectado de una grave enfermedad** (frml) he is suffering from a serious disease

afectar [A1] _vt_ **(a)** (tener efecto en) to affect; **esto nos afecta a todos** this affects us all **(b)** (afligir) to affect (frml); **la noticia lo afectó mucho** the news upset him terribly ⟨2⟩ (fingir) ⟨admiración/indiferencia⟩ to affect, feign

afectísimo -ma _adj_ (Corresp) (frml): **suyo ~** yours truly

afectivo -va _adj_ emotional

afecto _m_ (cariño) affection; **tenerle ~ a algn** to be fond of sb; **tomarle ~ a algn** to grow fond of sb

afectuoso -sa _adj_ ⟨persona⟩ affectionate; **recibe un ~ saludo** (Corresp) with warm _o_ kind regards

afeitadora _f_ shaver, electric razor

afeitar [A1] _vt_ ⟨persona/cabeza⟩ to shave; ⟨barba⟩ to shave off
■ **afeitarse** _v pron_ (refl) to shave; **se afeitó la barba** he shaved off his beard

afeminado -da adj effeminate

aferrarse [A1] v pron: ~se A algo/algn to cling (ON) TO sth/sb

affmo. affma. (Corresp) (frml) = **afectísimo, -ma**

Afganistán m Afghanistan

afgano -na adj/m,f Afghan

afianzar [A4] vt ⟨posición/postura⟩ to consolidate

■ **afianzarse** v pron «prestigio/sistema» to become consolidated

afiche m (esp AmL) poster

afición f (a) (inclinación, gusto) love, liking; ~ a la lectura/música love of reading/music (b) (pasatiempo) hobby (c) (Dep, Taur): la ~ the fans (pl)

aficionado -da adj [SER] (a) (entusiasta) ~ A algo fond OF o keen ON sth (b) (no profesional) amateur

■ m,f (a) (entusiasta) enthusiast; para los ~s al bricolaje for do-it-yourself enthusiasts; un ~ a la música a music lover; los ~s al tenis/fútbol tennis/football fans (b) (no profesional) amateur

aficionarse [A1] v pron: ~se A algo to become interested IN sth

afilado -da adj ⚀ (a) ⟨borde/cuchillo⟩ sharp (b) ⟨nariz⟩ pointed; ⟨rasgos⟩ sharp; ⟨dedos⟩ long ⚁ ⟨mordaz⟩ ⟨lengua⟩ sharp; ⟨pluma⟩ biting

afilar [A1] vt ⟨navaja/cuchillo⟩ to sharpen, hone

afiliación f affiliation

afiliado -da m,f member

afiliarse [A1] v pron ~se A algo ⟨a partido/sindicato⟩ to become a member OF sth, to join sth; ⟨a sistema⟩ to join sth

afín adj ⟨temas/lenguas⟩ related; ⟨culturas/ideologías⟩ similar; ⟨intereses⟩ common; ideas afines a las nuestras ideas which have a lot in common with our own

afinación f tuning

afinar [A1] vt ⚀ (a) ⟨instrumento⟩ to tune (b) ⟨coche⟩ to tune up; ⟨motor⟩ to tune ⚁ ⟨punta⟩ to sharpen

■ ~ vi: afirmó con la cabeza he nodded

afinidad f (entre personas, caracteres) affinity; no tengo ninguna ~ con él I have nothing in common with him

afirmación f ⟨declaración⟩ statement, assertion; ⟨respuesta positiva⟩ affirmation

afirmar [A1] vt ⚀ (a) (aseverar) to state, declare, assert (frml); no lo afirmó ni lo negó he neither confirmed nor denied it ⚁ ⟨escalera⟩ to steady

■ ~ vi: afirmó con la cabeza he nodded

■ **afirmarse** v pron (físicamente) to steady oneself; ~se EN algo/algn to hold ON to sth/sb

afirmativo -va adj ⟨respuesta/frase⟩ affirmative

afligido -da adj distressed

afligir [I7] vt (a) (afectar) to afflict (b) (apenar) to upset

■ **afligirse** v pron to get upset

aflojar [A1] vt ⚀ ⟨cinturón/tornillo⟩ to loosen; ⟨cuerda/riendas⟩ to slacken; ⟨presión/tensión⟩ to ease; ⟨marcha/paso⟩ to slow ⚁ (fam) ⟨dinero⟩ to hand over ⚂ (AmL) ⟨motor⟩ to run in

■ ~ vi ⟨tormenta⟩ to ease off; ⟨fiebre/viento⟩ to drop; «calor» to let up; «tensión/presión» to ease off

■ **aflojarse** v pron (a) (refl) ⟨cinturón⟩ to loosen (b) «tornillo/tuerca» to come o work loose

afónico -ca adj: estar ~ to have lost one's voice; quedarse ~ to lose one's voice

afortunadamente adv fortunately, luckily

afortunado adj ⟨persona⟩ lucky, fortunate; ⟨encuentro/coincidencia⟩ happy, fortunate; una elección poco afortunada a rather unfortunate choice

África f: tb el ~ Africa

África del Sur f: South Africa

africano -na adj/m,f African

afrikaans m Afrikaans

afrikaner adj/mf (pl -ners) Afrikaner

afrodisíaco¹ -ca adj aphrodisiac

afrodisíaco² m aphrodisiac

afrontar [A1] vt ⟨problema/responsabilidad⟩ to face up to; ⟨desafío/peligro⟩ to face

afuera adv ⚀ (a) (expresando dirección, movimiento) outside; ven aquí ~ come out here; ¡~! get out of here! (b) (lugar, parte) outside; [European Spanish prefers FUERA in many of these examples] aquí ~ se está muy bien it's really nice out here; comimos ~ (en el jardín) we ate outside o outdoors; (en un restaurante) we ate out; por ~ es rojo it's red on the outside ⚁ afuera de (AmL): ¿qué haces ~ de la cama? what are you doing out of bed?; ~ del edificio outside the building

afueras fpl: las ~ the outskirts

agachar [A1] vt ⟨cabeza⟩ to lower

■ **agacharse** v pron (a) (ponerse en cuclillas) to crouch down; (inclinarse) to bend down (b) (AmL fam) (rebajarse) to eat humble pie o (AmE) crow (colloq)

agallas fpl (fam) (valor) guts (pl) (colloq); con ~s gutsy (colloq); hay que tener ~s it takes guts (colloq)

agarrado¹ -da adj [SER] (fam) (tacaño) tightfisted (colloq) (b) [ESTAR] (CS fam) (enamorado) in love

■ m,f (fam) (tacaño) skinflint (colloq), tightwad (AmE colloq)

agarrado² adv: bailar ~ to dance closely

agarrar [A1] vt ⚀ (sujetar) to grab, get hold of; me agarró del brazo (para apoyar) she took hold of my arm; (con violencia, rapidez) she grabbed me by the arm

⚁ (esp AmL) ⟨objeto⟩ (tomar) to take; (atajar) to catch; agarra un papel y toma nota get a piece of paper and take this down

⚂ (AmL) (pescar, atrapar) to catch; si lo agarro, lo mato if I get o lay my hands on him, I'll kill him

⚃ (esp AmL) (adquirir) ⟨resfriado/pulmonía⟩ to catch; ⟨costumbre/vicio⟩ to pick up; ⟨ritmo⟩ to get into; ⟨velocidad⟩ to gather, pick up; ~le cariño a algn to grow fond of sb; le agarró asco he got sick of it; le he agarrado odio I've come to hate him

⚄ (AmL) (entender) ⟨indirecta/chiste⟩ to get

■ ~ vi ⚀ (asir, sujetar): toma, agarra here, hold this; agarra por ahí take hold of that part ⚁ ⟨planta/injerto⟩ to take; «tornillo» to grip, catch; «ruedas» to grip; «tinte» to take

■ **agarrarse** v pron ⚀ (asirse) to hold on; agárrate bien or fuerte hold on tight; ~se A or DE algo to hold on TO sth; iban agarrados del brazo they were walking along arm in arm

2 ⟨dedo/manga⟩ to catch; **me agarré el dedo en el cajón** I caught my finger in the drawer **3** (esp AmL) ⟨resfriado/pulmonía⟩ to catch; ∼**se una borrachera** to get drunk; ∼**se un disgusto/una rabieta** to get upset/into a temper **4** (AmL fam) (pelearse) to get into a fight; **se** ∼**on a patadas** they started kicking each other; ∼**se CON algn** to have a set-to WITH sb (colloq)

agarre *m* (de neumático) grip; (de coche) roadholding

agarrotar [A1] *vt* ⟨piernas/músculos⟩ to make … stiff
■ **agarrotarse** *v pron* **(a)** «manos/músculos» to stiffen up; **tengo las manos agarrotadas** my hands are stiff **(b)** «motor/máquina» to seize up

agazaparse [A1] *v pron* «animal» to crouch; «persona» to crouch (down)

agencia *f* (oficina) office; (sucursal) branch; ∼ **de colocaciones** employment agency *o* bureau (*generally for domestic staff*); ∼ **de prensa** *or* **de noticias** press *o* news agency; ∼ **de viajes** travel agent's, travel agency; ∼ **matrimonial** marriage bureau

agenda *f* (libreta) appointment book (AmE), diary (BrE); (programa) agenda; ∼ **de bolsillo** pocket diary; ∼ **de trabajo** engagement book

agente *mf* **1** (Com, Fin) agent; ∼ **de bolsa** stockbroker; ∼ **de publicidad** advertising agent; ∼ **de seguros** insurance broker; ∼ **de viajes** travel agent **2** (fml) (funcionario) employee; ∼ **de policía** police officer; ∼ **de tráfico** (Arg, Méx) **de tránsito** ≈ traffic policeman (*in US*), ≈ traffic warden (*in UK*); ∼ **secreto** secret agent

ágil *adj* ⟨persona/movimiento⟩ agile; ⟨estilo/programa⟩ lively

agilidad *f* (de persona) agility; (de estilo) liveliness

agilizar [A4] *vt* ⟨gestiones/proceso⟩ to speed up; ⟨pensamiento⟩ to sharpen; ⟨ritmo/presentación⟩ to make … livelier *o* more dynamic

agitación *f* **(a)** (nerviosismo) agitation **(b)** (de calle, ciudad) bustle

agitado -da *adj* **(a)** ⟨mar⟩ rough, choppy **(b)** ⟨día/vida⟩ hectic, busy **(c)** ⟨persona⟩ worked up, agitated

agitador -dora *m,f* (persona) agitator

agitar [A1] *vt* **(a)** ⟨líquido/botella⟩ to shake **(b)** ⟨brazo/pañuelo⟩ to wave; ⟨alas⟩ to flap
■ **agitarse** *v pron* **(a)** «mar» to get rough; «barca» to toss; «toldo» to flap **(b)** (inquietarse) to get worked up

aglomeración *f* **(a)** (de gente): **se produjo una** ∼ **a la entrada** people crowded at the entrance; **para evitar las aglomeraciones** to avoid crowding; **las aglomeraciones urbanas** the built-up urban areas **(b)** (de tráfico) buildup

aglomerarse [A1] *v pron* to crowd (together)

agnóstico -ca *adj/m,f* agnostic

agobiado -da *adj* [ESTAR] ∼ **DE algo** ⟨de trabajo⟩ snowed under WITH sth; ⟨de deudas⟩ overwhelmed WITH sth; **estaba agobiada con tantos problemas** she was weighed down by all those problems

agobiante, agobiador -dora *adj* ⟨trabajo/día⟩ exhausting; ⟨calor⟩ stifling; **es una carga** ∼ **para él** it's/he's/she's a terrible burden on him

agobiar [A1] *vt* «problemas/responsabilidad»

to weigh *o* get … down; «calor» to oppress, get … down; **te agobia con tanta amabilidad** she smothers you with kindness; **este niño me agobia** this child is too much for me

agobio *m*: **una sensación de** ∼ a sense of oppression

agonía *f* **(a)** (de moribundo) death throes (*pl*) **(b)** (sufrimiento) suffering

agonizar [A4] *vi* «persona» to be dying, be in the throes of death; «imperio/régimen» to be in its death throes

agosto *m* August; *para ejemplos ver* ENERO; **hacer su** ∼ to make a fortune, to make a killing (colloq)

agotado -da *adj* **(a)** [ESTAR] ⟨recursos⟩ exhausted; ⟨edición⟩ sold out; ⟨pila⟩ dead, flat; ❺ **agotadas todas las localidades** sold out **(b)** [ESTAR] ⟨persona⟩ exhausted

agotador -dora *adj* exhausting

agotamiento *m* exhaustion

agotar [A1] *vt* **(a)** ⟨recursos⟩ to exhaust, use up; ⟨pila⟩ to wear out, run down; ⟨mina/tierra⟩ to exhaust **(b)** (cansar) ⟨persona⟩ to tire … out, wear … out
■ **agotarse** *v pron* **(a)** «existencias/reservas» to run out, be used up; «pila» to run down; «mina/tierra» to become exhausted; «edición» to sell out; **se me está agotando la paciencia** my patience is running out **(b)** «persona» to wear *o* tire oneself out

agraciado -da *adj* ⟨persona/figura⟩ attractive; **es muy poco** ∼ he's not very attractive

agradable *adj* ⟨persona⟩ pleasant, nice; ⟨carácter⟩ pleasant; ⟨día/velada⟩ enjoyable, nice; ⟨sensación/efecto⟩ pleasant, pleasing; ⟨sabor/olor⟩ pleasant, nice; ∼ **a la vista** pleasing to the eye

agradar [A1] *vi* (fml): **¿Le agrada este, señora?** is this one to your liking, madam? (fml); **la idea no me agrada** the idea doesn't appeal to me; **le agrada verlo contento** it gives her pleasure to see him happy; **me** ∼**ía mucho verlos allí** I would be very pleased to see you there
■ ∼ *vt* to please

agradecer [E3] *vt* **(a)** (sentir gratitud por) ⟨ayuda/amabilidad⟩ to appreciate, to be grateful for; ∼**le algo A algn** to be grateful TO sb for sth; **le** ∼**ía (que) me llamara** (fml) I would appreciate it if you would call me (fml) **(b)** (dar las gracias por) to thank; ∼**le algo A algn** to thank sb for sth; **¡y así es como me lo agradece!** and this is all the thanks I get!

agradecido -da *adj* ⟨persona⟩ grateful; **estar** ∼ to be grateful; **¡qué poco** ∼ **eres!** you're so ungrateful!

agradecimiento *m* gratitude; **demostrar** ∼ to show gratitude; **en** ∼ **por todo lo que ha hecho** in appreciation of all you have done

agradezca, agradezcas, etc ▶ AGRADECER

agrado *m* (fml): **espero que sea de su** ∼ I hope this is to your liking; **con sumo** ∼ gladly; **tuve el** ∼ **de verla** I had the pleasure of seeing her

agrandar [A1] *vt* **(a)** ⟨casa⟩ to extend; ⟨agujero/pozo⟩ to make … larger *o* bigger; ⟨fotocopia⟩ to enlarge, blow up; ⟨vestido⟩ to let out **(b)** (exagerar) to exaggerate
■ **agrandarse** *v pron* «agujero/bulto» to grow larger, get bigger

agrario -ria *adj* ‹sector/política› agricultural (*before* n); ‹sociedad› agrarian

agravante *adj* aggravating

■ *f or m* (Der) aggravating factor *o* circumstance; **con la ~ de que estaba borracho** what makes it even worse is that he was drunk

agravar [A1] *vt* to make ... worse, aggravate

■ **agravarse** *v pron* «problema/situación» to become worse, worsen; «enfermo» to deteriorate, get worse

agredir [I32] *vt* (frml) to attack, assault

agregar [A3] *vt* (añadir) to add; **~ algo A algo** to add sth ᴛᴏ sth

agresión *f* aggression; **una ~ brutal** a brutal attack

agresividad *f* aggressiveness

agresivo -va *adj* aggressive

agresor -sora *adj* ‹ejército› attacking (*before* n); ‹país› aggressor (*before* n)

■ *m,f* (país, ejército) aggressor; (persona) attacker, assailant (frml)

agreste *adj* ‹terreno/camino› rough; ‹paisaje› rugged; ‹vegetación/animal› wild

agriarse [A1 *or* A17] *v pron* «leche/vino» to turn *o* go sour; «persona» to become bitter *o* embittered

agrícola *adj* ‹técnicas› agricultural, farming (*before* n)

agricultor -tora *m,f* farmer

agricultura *f* agriculture

agridulce *adj* bittersweet; (Coc) sweet-and-sour

agrietarse [A1] *v pron* «tierra/pared» to crack; «piel» to chap, become chapped

agringado -da *adj* (AmL fam & pey) ‹persona› Americanized; ‹acento/costumbres› (norteamericanizado) Americanized; (extranjero) foreign

agrio, agria *adj* (a) ‹manzana› sour, tart; ‹naranja/limón› sour, sharp (b) ‹tono/persona› sour, sharp; ‹disputa› bitter

agriparse [A1] *v pron* (Andes) to get the flu (AmE), to get flu (BrE); **está agripado** he has (the) flu

agronomía *f* agronomy

agrónomo -ma *m,f* agronomist

agrupación *f* [1] (grupo) group; (asociación) association; **~ coral** choral group, choir [2] (acción) grouping (together)

agrupar [A1] *vt* (a) (formar grupos) to put ... into groups, to group (b) (reunir) ‹organizaciones/partidos› to bring together

■ **agruparse** *v pron* (a) (formar un grupo) «niños/policías» to gather; «partidos» to come together (b) (dividirse en grupos) to get into groups

agua *f* ♪ [1] water; **~ de lluvia/mar** rainwater/seawater; **~ corriente/destilada** running/distilled water; **~ de colonia** eau de cologne; **~ dulce** fresh water; **~ mineral** mineral water; **~ mineral con gas/sin gas** sparkling/still mineral water; **~ oxigenada** peroxide, hydrogen peroxide (tech); **~ potable/salada** drinking/salt water; **como ~ para chocolate** (Méx fam) furious; **estar con el ~ al cuello** to be up to one's neck; **estar más claro que el ~** to be (patently) obvious; **hacérsele ~ la boca a algn** (AmL): **se me hizo ~ la boca** it made my mouth water; **ser ~ pasada** to be a thing of the past; **~ que no has de beber déjala correr** if you're not interested, don't spoil things for me/for other people; **nunca digas de esta ~ no beberé** you never know when the same thing might happen to you [2] (lluvia) rain [3] (AmC, Andes) (infusión) herb tea (AmE), herbal tea (BrE); **~ de menta** mint tea [4] **aguas** *fpl* (a) (de mar, río) waters (*pl*) (b) (de balneario, manantial) waters (*pl*); **tomar las ~s** to take the waters; **~s termales** thermal waters (*pl*)

aguacate *m* (árbol) avocado; (fruto) avocado (pear)

aguacero *m* downpour

aguado -da *adj* [1] ‹leche/vino› watered-down; ‹sopa› watery, thin; ‹café› weak; ‹salsa› thin [2] (AmC, Méx fam) (aburrido) [ᴇsᴛᴀʀ] ‹fiesta/película› boring, dull; [sᴇʀ] ‹persona› boring, dull

aguafiestas *mf* (*pl* ~) (fam) wet blanket (colloq), party pooper (AmE colloq)

aguafuerte *m* (grabado) etching

aguaitar [A1] *vt* (AmS fam) (espiar) to spy on; (vigilar) to keep an eye on

■ *vi* (AmS fam) (espiar) to snoop (colloq); (mirar) to have a look

aguanieve *f* sleet

aguantador -dora *adj* (AmL) [1] (fam) (resistente) ‹tela/ropa/zapatos› hard-wearing; ‹coche› sturdy [2] (fam) (a) (paciente, tolerante): **es muy ~** he puts up with a lot (colloq) (b) (del dolor, sufrimiento) tough (colloq)

aguantar [A1] *vt* [1] ‹dolor/sufrimiento› to bear, endure; **aguanto bien el calor** I can take the heat; **no tengo por qué ~ esto** I don't have to put up with this; **este calor no hay quien lo aguante** this heat is unbearable; **no sabes ~ una broma** you can't take a joke; **no los aguanto** I can't stand them; **no puedo ~ este dolor de muelas** this toothache's unbearable [2] (a) ‹peso/carga› to support, bear; ‹presión› to withstand (b) (durar): **estas botas ~án otro invierno** these boots will last (me/you/him) another winter [3] (sostener) to hold [4] (contener, reprimir) ‹risa/lágrimas› to hold back; **~ la respiración** to hold one's breath

■ **~** *vi*: **¡ya no aguanto más!** I can't take any more!; **no creo que este clavo aguante** I don't think this nail will hold

■ **aguantarse** *v pron* [1] (conformarse, resignarse): **me tendré que ~** I'll just have to put up with it; **si no le gusta, que se aguante** if he doesn't like it, he can lump it (colloq) [2] (euf) (reprimirse, contenerse): **no me pude ~ y me puse a llorar** I couldn't contain myself and burst into tears; **aguántate un poquito que ya llegamos** just hold *o* hang on a minute, we'll soon be there

3 (AmL fam) (esperarse) to hang on (colloq)

aguar [A16] vt **(a)** ⟨leche/vino⟩ to water down **(b)** (fam) (estropear) to put a damper on (colloq)
■ **aguarse** v pron (fam) to be spoiled

aguardar [A1] vt ⟨persona⟩ to wait for; ⟨acontecimiento⟩ to await
■ ~ vi «noticia/destino» to await; **les aguardaba una sorpresa** there was a surprise in store for them

aguardiente m eau-de-vie (clear brandy distilled from fermented fruit juice)

aguarrás m turpentine, turps (colloq)

aguayo m (Bol) multicolored cloth

agudeza f **1** **(a)** (de voz, sonido) high pitch **(b)** (de dolor — duradero) intensity; (— momentáneo) sharpness **2** (perspicacia) sharpness; (de sentido, instinto) keenness, sharpness **3** (comentario ingenioso) witty comment

agudizar [A4] vt ⟨sensación⟩ to heighten; ⟨crisis/conflicto⟩ to make worse; ⟨instinto⟩ to heighten; ⟨sentido⟩ to sharpen
■ **agudizarse** v pron ⟨sensación⟩ to heighten; «dolor» to get worse; «crisis» to worsen; «instinto» to become heightened; «sentido» to become sharper

agudo -da adj **1** **(a)** ⟨filo/punta⟩ sharp **(b)** ⟨ángulo⟩ acute **2** **(a)** ⟨voz/sonido⟩ high-pitched; ⟨nota⟩ high **(b)** ⟨dolor⟩ (duradero) intense, acute; (momentáneo) sharp **(c)** ⟨crisis⟩ severe **(d)** ⟨aumento/descenso⟩ sharp **3** **(a)** (perspicaz) ⟨persona⟩ quick-witted, sharp; ⟨comentario⟩ shrewd **(b)** (gracioso) ⟨comentario/persona⟩ witty **(c)** ⟨sentido/instinto⟩ sharp

agüero m: **ser de mal/buen** ~ (presagio) to be a bad/good omen; (causa) to bring bad/good luck

agüevado -da adj (AmC fam) [ESTAR] upset

aguijón m **(a)** (vara) goad **(b)** (Zool) sting

águila f ⚥ **(a)** (ave) eagle; **ser un** ~ to be very sharp **(b)** (Méx) (de moneda) ≈ heads (pl); **¿~ o sol?** heads or tails?

aguileño -ña adj ⟨nariz⟩ aquiline

aguinaldo m **1** **(a)** (propina) Christmas bonus (AmE), Christmas box (BrE) **(b)** (paga extra) extra month's salary paid at Christmas, Christmas bonus (AmE) **2** (Col, Ven) (canción) ≈ Christmas carol

aguja f **(a)** (de coser, tejer) needle; (para inyecciones) needle; (de tocadiscos) stylus, needle; (de instrumento) needle; (de balanza) pointer, needle; (de reloj) hand; **buscar una** ~ **en un pajar** to look for a needle in a haystack **(b)** (Inf) pin

agujereado -da adj: **está** ~ it has holes in it

agujerear [A1] vt (hacer agujeros en) to make holes in; (atravesar) to pierce

agujero m hole; **hacerse** ~s **en las orejas** to have one's ears pierced

agujeta f **1** (Méx) (de zapato) (shoe) lace **2** **agujetas** fpl (Esp) stiffness; **tengo** ~s **en las piernas** my legs are stiff

aguzar [A4] vt to sharpen; **aguzó el oído** he pricked up his ears

ah interj (expresando sorpresa, lástima, asentimiento) oh!

ahí adv **1** **(a)** (en el espacio) there; ~ **está/viene** there he is/here he comes; ~ **arriba/abajo** up/down there; ~ **mismo** or (AmL) **nomás** or (Méx)

mero right o just there **(b)** **por ahí** somewhere; **debe estar por** ~ it must be around somewhere; **fue a dar una vuelta por** ~ she went off for a walk; **se fue por** ~ she went that way; **yo he estado por** ~ I've been around there; **tendrá unos 35 años o por** ~ he must be 35 or thereabouts **2** **(a)** (refiriéndose a un lugar figurado): ~ **está el truco/problema** that's the secret/problem; **de** ~ **a la drogadicción solo hay un paso** from there it's just a short step to becoming a drug addict; **hasta** ~ **llego yo** that's as far as I'm prepared to go **(b)** **de ahí** hence; **de** ~ **mi sorpresa** hence my surprise; **de** ~ **que hayan fracasado** that is why they failed; **de** ~ **a que venga es otra cosa** whether or not he actually comes is another matter **3** (en el tiempo) then; **de** ~ **en adelante** from then on; ~ **mismo** there and then

ahijado -da m,f (por bautizo) (m) godson; (f) goddaughter; **mis** ~s my godchildren

ahogado -da adj **1** (en agua): **dos niños resultaron** ~s two children were drowned; **morir** ~ (en agua) to drown; (asfixiarse) to suffocate; (atragantarse) to choke to death **2** ⟨llanto/grito⟩ stifled **3** (Méx fam) (borracho) blind o rolling drunk (colloq)

ahogador m (Chi, Méx) (Auto) choke

ahogar [A3] vt **1** **(a)** ⟨persona/animal⟩ (en agua) to drown; (asfixiar) to suffocate; (b) ⟨motor⟩ to flood **2** **(a)** ⟨palabras/voz⟩ to drown (out); ⟨llanto/grito⟩ to stifle **(b)** ⟨penas⟩ to drown
■ **ahogarse** v pron **(a)** ⟨persona/animal⟩⟩ (en agua) to drown; (asfixiarse) to suffocate; (atragantarse) to choke **(b)** «motor» to flood

ahogo m breathlessness; **tiene** ~s he gets out of breath

ahora adv **1** **(a)** (en el momento presente) now; ~ **que lo pienso** now I come to think of it; **la juventud de** ~ young people today; **hasta** ~ so far, up to now; **de** ~ **en adelante** from now on; **por** ~ for the time being; **por** ~ **va todo bien** everything's going all right so far **(b)** (inmediatamente, pronto): ~ **mismo** right now o away; ~ **te lo muestro** I'll show it to you in a minute o second o moment; **¡**~ **voy!** I'm coming!; **¡hasta** ~! (esp Esp) see you soon! **(c)** (hace un momento) a moment ago
2 **ahora bien** (indep) however

ahorcar [A2] vt to hang
■ **ahorcarse** v pron (refl) to hang oneself

ahorita adv (esp AmL fam) **(a)** (en este momento) just o right now **(b)** (inmediatamente, pronto): ~ **te lo doy** I'll give it to you in a second o moment **(c)** (hace un momento) a moment ago

ahorrador -dora adj thrifty; **no soy muy** ~a I'm not very good at saving (money)
■ m,f saver, investor

ahorrante mf (Chi) saver, investor

ahorrar [A1] vt **1** ⟨dinero/energía/agua⟩ to save; ⟨tiempo⟩ to save **2** (evitar) ⟨molestia/viaje⟩ (+ me/te/le etc) to save, spare
■ ~ vi to save
■ **ahorrarse** v pron (enf) **(a)** ⟨dinero⟩ to save (oneself) **(b)** (evitarse) ⟨molestia/viaje⟩ to save oneself

ahorrista mf (RPl, Ven) saver, investor

ahorro m **(a)** (acción) saving **(b)** **ahorros** mpl (cantidad) savings (pl)

ahuecar [A2] vt (a) ⟨tronco/calabaza⟩ to hollow out; ⟨mano⟩ to cup (b) ⟨almohadón⟩ to plump up; ⟨pelo⟩ to give volume to

ahumado adj (a) (Coc) smoked (b) ⟨cristal⟩ smoked; ⟨gafas⟩ tinted

ahumar [A23] vt (a) ⟨jamón/pescado⟩ to smoke (b) ⟨paredes/techo⟩ to blacken

ahuyentar [A1] vt (a) (hacer huir) ⟨ladrón/animal⟩ to frighten off or away (b) (mantener a distancia) ⟨fiera/mosquitos⟩ to keep ... away

aimará adj Aymara
■ mf Aymara Indian

airbag /'erbag/ f airbag

aire m **1** air; sintió que le faltaba el ~ she felt as if she was going to suffocate; salir a tomar el ~ to go outside for a breath of fresh air; al ~ libre outdoors, in the open air; ~ acondicionado air-conditioning; con ~ acondicionado air-conditioned; a mi/tu/su ~: ellos salen en grupo, yo prefiero ir a mi ~ they go out in a group, I prefer doing my own thing (colloq); quedar en el ~: todo quedó en el ~ everything was left up in the air; saltar or volar por los ~s to explode, blow up; **2** (viento) wind; (corriente) draft (AmE), draught (BrE) **3** (Rad, TV): salir al ~ to go on the air **4** (a) (aspecto) air; tiene un ~ aristocrático she has an aristocratic air; la protesta tomó ~s de revuelta the protest began to look like a revolt; darse ~s (de grandeza) to put on o give oneself airs (b) (parecido) resemblance; tienen un ~ they look a bit alike; ~ de familia family resemblance

airear [A1] vt (a) (ventilar) to air (b) (hacer público) ⟨asunto⟩ to air (c) ⟨masa/tierra⟩ to aerate
■ **airearse** v pron (a) «persona» to get some (fresh) air (b) «manta/abrigo» to air; para que se airee el cuarto to let some air into the room

aislado -da adj (a) (alejado) remote, isolated (b) (sin comunicación) cut off; quedar ~ to be cut off; vive ~ del mundo he's cut himself off from the world (c) ⟨caso⟩ isolated (d) (Elec) insulated

aislamiento m (a) (en general) isolation (b) (Elec) insulation

aislante adj insulating, insulation (before n)
■ m insulator

aislar [A19] vt (a) (apartar, separar) ⟨enfermo⟩ to isolate, keep in isolation; ⟨preso⟩ to place ... in solitary confinement; ⟨virus⟩ to isolate (b) (dejar sin comunicación) ⟨lugar⟩ to cut off (c) (Elec) to insulate
■ **aislarse** v pron (refl) to cut oneself off

ajado -da adj ⟨ropa⟩ worn; ⟨manos⟩ wrinkly; ⟨piel⟩ wrinkled

ajedrecista mf chess player

ajedrez m (juego) chess; (tablero y fichas) chess set

ajeno -na adj [SER] (a) (que no corresponde, pertenece): mis ideales le son totalmente ~s my ideals are completely alien to him; aquel ambiente me era ~ that environment was alien o foreign to me; por razones ajenas a nuestra voluntad for reasons beyond our control (b) (que pertenece, corresponde a otro): conduce un coche ~ he drives someone else's car; por el bien ~ for the good of others; las desgracias ajenas other people's misfortunes

ajetreado -da adj hectic, busy

ajetreo m hustle and bustle; un día de mucho ~ a hectic day

ají m (a) (chile) chili* (b) (Andes) (salsa) chili* sauce (c) (RPl) (pimiento) pepper

ajo m (Coc) garlic; un diente de ~ a clove of garlic

ajonjolí m sesame

ajuar m (de novia) trousseau; (de bebé) layette

ajustado -da adj (a) (ceñido) tight; me queda muy ~ it's too tight (for me) (b) ⟨presupuesto⟩ tight

ajustar [A1] vt **1** (a) (apretar) to tighten (up) (b) ⟨volumen/temperatura⟩ to adjust; ~ la entrada de agua to regulate the flow of water (c) ⟨retrovisor/asiento/cinturón de seguridad⟩ to adjust (d) (encajar) ⟨piezas⟩ to fit **2** (en costura) to take in **3** (a) ⟨gastos/horarios⟩ ~ algo A algo to adapt sth TO sth (b) ⟨sueldos/precios⟩ to adjust **4** (concertar) to fix, set **5** ⟨cuentas⟩ (sacar el resultado de) to balance; (saldar) to settle
■ ~ vi to fit
■ **ajustarse** v pron **1** (refl) ⟨cinturón de seguridad⟩ to adjust **2** «piezas» to fit

al contraction of A and EL

ala f‡ **1** (de ave, de avión) wing; ~ delta (deporte) hang gliding; (aparato) hang glider; cortarle las ~s a algn to clip sb's wings; darle ~s a algn: si le das ~s, luego no podrás controlarlo if you let him have his own way, you won't be able to control him later **2** (de sombrero) brim **3** (a) (de edificio) wing (b) (facción) wing (c) (flanco) flank, wing (d) (Dep) (posición) wing
■ mf‡ (jugador) wing, winger

alabanza f praise; digno de ~ praiseworthy

alabar [A1] vt to praise

alacena f larder

alacrán m scorpion

alambrada f (valla) wire fence; (material) wire fencing

alambrado m (AmL) (a) (acción) fencing in/off (b) (valla) wire fence

alambrar [A1] vt to fence in/off

alambre m (hilo metálico) wire; ~ de púas barbed wire, barbwire (AmE)

alameda f (avenida) tree-lined avenue; (terreno con álamos) poplar grove

álamo m poplar

alarde m show, display; hacer ~ de fuerza to show off strength

alardear [A1] vi ~ DE algo to boast ABOUT o OF sth; alardea de tener dinero she boasts about being well-off

alargado -da adj ⟨forma⟩ elongated; ⟨hoja⟩ elongate

alargador m extension cord (AmE), extension lead (BrE)

alargar [A3] vt **1** (a) ⟨vestido/pantalón⟩ to let down, lengthen; ⟨manguera/cable⟩ to lengthen, extend; ⟨riendas/soga⟩ to let out; ⟨paso⟩ to lengthen (b) ⟨cuento/discurso⟩ to drag out; ⟨vacaciones/plazo⟩ to extend; puede ~le la vida it could prolong her life **2** (a) (extender) ⟨mano/brazo⟩ to hold out (b) (alcanzar) ~le algo A algn to hand o give o pass sth TO sb

■ **alargarse** v pron «cara/sombra» to get longer; «días» to grow longer; «reunión/fiesta» to go on

alarido m (de miedo) shriek; (de dolor) scream

alarma f ⊡ (ante peligro) alarm; **dar la voz de** ∼ to sound o raise the alarm ⊡ (dispositivo) alarm; ∼ **contra robos/incendios** burglar/fire alarm

alarmante adj alarming

alarmar [A1] vt to alarm

■ **alarmarse** v pron to be alarmed

alba f꞉ (del día) dawn, daybreak; **al rayar el** ∼ (liter) at the break of day (liter); **al** or **con el** ∼ at the crack of dawn

albacora f (atún) albacore; (pez espada) (Chi) swordfish

albahaca f basil

albanés[1] **-nesa** adj/m,f Albanian

albanés[2] m (idioma) Albanian

Albania f Albania

albañil m (constructor) builder; (que coloca ladrillos) bricklayer

albaricoque m (Esp) apricot

albaricoquero m (Esp) apricot tree

albedrío m (free) will; **lo hizo a su** ∼ he did it of his own free will; **lo dejo a tu libre** ∼ I leave it entirely up to you

alberca f (a) (embalse) reservoir (b) (Méx) (piscina) swimming pool (c) (Col) (lavadero) sink (for washing clothes) (d) (Bol, Per) (comedero) trough

albergar [A3] vt ⟨personas⟩ to house, accommodate; ⟨biblioteca/exposición⟩ to house

■ **albergarse** v pron (a) (hospedarse) to lodge (b) (refugiarse) to shelter, take refuge

albergue m (a) (alojamiento) lodging, accommodations (pl) (AmE); **darle** ∼ **a algn** to take sb in (b) (hostal) hostel; ∼ **juvenil** youth hostel (c) (en la montaña) refuge, shelter; (para vagabundos, mendigos) shelter

albino -na adj/m,f albino

albóndiga f meatball

albornoz m bathrobe

alborotado -da adj ⊡ (a) (nervioso) agitated; (animado, excitado) excited (b) (ruidoso) noisy, rowdy; (amotinado) riotous ⊡ ⟨mar⟩ rough; ⟨pelo⟩ untidy, disheveled*

alborotador -dora adj rowdy, noisy

■ m,f troublemaker

alborotar [A1] vi to make a racket

■ ∼ vt (a) (agitar) to agitate, get ... agitated; (excitar) to get ... excited (b) ⟨muchedumbre⟩ to stir up

■ **alborotarse** v pron (a) (agitarse) to get agitated o upset; (excitarse) to get excited (b) (amotinarse) to riot

alboroto m (a) (agitación, nerviosismo) agitation; (excitación) excitement (b) (ruido) racket (c) (disturbio, jaleo) disturbance, commotion; (motín) riot

álbum m (a) (de fotos, sellos) album; (libro de historietas) comic book (b) (disco) album

alcachofa f (a) (Bot, Coc) artichoke (b) (de ducha) shower head; (de regadera) sprinkler (AmE), rose (BrE)

alcahuete -ta m,f (a) (ant) (mediador) procurer (arch) (b) (CS fam) (chismoso) gossip (colloq); (soplón) tattletale (AmE colloq), telltale (BrE colloq)

alcahuetear [A1] vi (a) (hacer de mediador) to act as a go-between, to procure (b) (Andes fam) (tapar): **les alcahuetea las travesuras** he lets them get away with all kinds of things; **le alcahuetea las mentiras** she covers up for him when he lies (c) (CS fam) (chismear) to gossip (colloq)

■ ∼ vt (fam) (delatar) to tell o snitch on (colloq)

alcalde -desa m,f ⊡ (Gob) mayor

⊡ **alcaldesa** f (mujer del alcalde) mayoress

alcance m (a) (de persona) reach; **fuera del** ∼ **de los niños** out of reach of children; **está fuera de mi** ∼ it is beyond my means (b) (de arma, emisora) range; **misiles de largo** ∼ long-range missiles (c) (de ley, proyecto) scope; (de declaración, noticia) implications (pl) (d) (en locs) **al alcance de** within reach of; **precios al** ∼ **de su bolsillo** prices to suit your pocket; **un lujo que no está a mi** ∼ a luxury I can't afford

alcancía f (AmL) (de niño) piggy bank; (para colectas) collection box

alcanfor m camphor

alcantarilla f (cloaca) sewer; (sumidero) drain

alcantarillado m sewer system, drains (pl)

alcanzar [A4] vt ⊡ (a) ⟨persona⟩ (llegar a la altura de) to catch up with, to catch ... up (BrE); (pillar, agarrar) to catch; **lo alcancé en la curva** I caught up with him on the bend; **¡a que no me alcanzas!** I bet you can't catch me! (colloq) (b) (en tarea, estatura) to catch up with

⊡ (llegar a) ⟨lugar⟩ to reach, get to; ⟨temperatura/nivel/edad⟩ to reach; **casi no alcanzo el tren** I almost missed the train; **estos árboles alcanzan una gran altura** these trees can reach o grow to a great height; ∼ **la mayoría de edad** to come of age

⊡ (conseguir, obtener) ⟨objetivo/éxito⟩ to achieve; ⟨acuerdo⟩ to reach

⊡ (acercar, pasar) ∼**le algo A algn** to pass sb sth, to pass sth TO sb

■ ∼ vi ⊡ (llegar con la mano) to reach; **hasta donde alcanzaba la vista** as far as the eye could see; ∼ **A hacer algo** to manage to do sth

⊡ (ser suficiente) «comida/provisiones» to be enough; **el sueldo no le alcanza** he can't manage on his salary

alcaparra f caper

alcaucil m (RPl) artichoke

alcázar m (fortaleza) fortress; (palacio) palace

alcista adj ⟨tendencia⟩ upward; ⟨mercado⟩ bull (before n)

alcoba f bedroom, bedchamber (liter)

alcohol m ⊡ (Quím) alcohol; (Farm) tb ∼ **de 90 (grados)** rubbing alcohol (AmE), surgical spirit (BrE) ⊡ (bebida) alcohol, drink

alcoholemia f: **hacerle la prueba de la** ∼ **a algn** to breathalyze sb

alcohólico -ca adj alcoholic; **bebida no alcohólica** nonalcoholic drink

■ m,f alcoholic

alcoholímetro m Breathalyzer®, drunkometer (AmE)

alcoholismo m alcoholism

alcornoque m (a) (árbol) cork oak (b) (fam) (persona) idiot

aldaba f (llamador) doorknocker; (cerrojo) latch

aldea f small village, hamlet

aldeano -na adj village (before n)
■ m,f villager

alebrestarse [A1] v pron (a) (Col, Méx) (alterarse, agitarse) to get worked up, agitated (b) (Ven fam) (animarse) to get excited; (excesivamente) to get overexcited

alegación f declaration, statement

alegar [A3] vt ‹motivos/causas› to cite; ‹razones› to put forward; ‹ignorancia/defensa propia›to plead; ‹inmunidad diplomática› to claim; **alegó que no lo sabía** she claimed not to know
■ ~ vi (AmL) (a) (discutir) to argue; ~ **DE algo** to argue ABOUT sth (b) (Der) (protestar) to complain; ~ **POR algo** to complain ABOUT sth

alegata f (Méx) argument

alegato m (a) (exposición) statement, declaration (b) (Der) (escrito) submission (c) (Andes) (discusión) argument

alegrar [A1] vt (a) (hacer feliz) ‹persona› to make ... happy; **me alegra saberlo** I'm glad o pleased to hear it (b) (animar) ‹persona› to cheer up; ‹fiesta› to liven up; ‹habitación› to brighten up; **¡alegra esa cara!** cheer up!
■ **alegrarse** v pron (a) (ponerse feliz, contento): **me alegro mucho por ti** I'm really happy for you; **se alegró muchísimo cuando lo vio** she was really happy when she saw him; **¡cuánto me alegro!** I'm so happy o pleased!; **está mucho mejor — me alegro** she's much better — I'm glad (to hear that); **~se CON algo** to be glad o pleased ABOUT sth; **me alegro de verte** it's good o nice to see you; **me alegro de que todo haya salido bien** I'm glad o pleased that everything went well (b) (animarse) to cheer up (c) (por el alcohol) to get tipsy (colloq)

alegre adj (a) ‹persona/carácter› happy, cheerful; ‹color› bright; ‹fiesta/música› lively; **su habitación es muy ~** her room is nice and bright; **es muy ~** she's very cheerful, she's a very happy person (b) [ESTAR] (por el alcohol) tipsy (colloq)

alegría f (dicha, felicidad) happiness, joy; **¡qué ~ verte!** it's great to see you!; **saltar de ~** to jump for joy

alejado -da adj (a) ‹lugar› remote (b) (distanciado) ‹persona›: **hace tiempo que está ~ de la política** he's been away from o out of politics for some time; **está ~ de su familia** he's estranged from his family

alejar [A1] vt (a) (poner lejos, más lejos) to move ... (further) away; ~ **algo/a algn DE algo/algn** to move sth/sb away FROM sth/sb (b) (distanciar) ~ **a algn DE algn** to distance sb FROM sb (c) ‹dudas/temores› to dispel
■ **alejarse** v pron to move away; (caminando) to walk away; **no se alejen demasiado** don't go too far; **se alejó de su familia** he drifted apart from his family; **necesito ~me de todo** I need to get away from everything

aleluya interj halleluja!

alemán¹ -mana adj/m,f German

alemán² m (idioma) German

Alemania f Germany

alentador -dora adj encouraging

alentar [A5] vt (a) ‹persona› to encourage; ‹jugador/equipo› to cheer ... on (b) ‹esperanza/ilusión› to cherish

alergia f allergy; **le produce ~** she's allergic to it; ~ **A algo** allergy TO sth; **tiene ~ a la penicilina** he's allergic to penicillin

alérgico -ca adj (a) [SER] ‹persona› allergic; ~ **A algo** allergic TO sth (b) ‹afección/reacción› allergic

alerta adj alert; **estar ~** (tener cuidado) to be alert; (estar en guardia) to be on the alert; **mantener el oído ~** to keep one's ears open
■ f: **dar la (voz de) ~** to raise the alarm; **en estado de ~** on alert

alertar [A1] vt ~ **a algn DE algo** to alert sb TO sth

aleta f (a) (de pez) fin; (de foca) flipper (b) (para natación) flipper (c) (de la nariz) wing

aletargado -da adj lethargic, drowsy

aletargar [A3] vt ‹persona› to make ... feel lethargic o drowsy

aletear [A1] vi «pájaro/gallina» to flap its wings; «mariposa» to flutter its wings

alfabético -ca adj alphabetical

alfabetización f teaching of basic literacy; **campaña de ~** literacy campaign

alfabetizar [A4] vt (a) (Educ) to teach ... to read and write (b) ‹sistema/fichero› to put ... in alphabetical order, to alphabetize (frml)

alfabeto m alphabet

alfajor m: type of candy or cake varying from region to region

alfalfa f alfalfa, lucerne (BrE)

alfarería f pottery

alfarero -ra m,f potter

alféizar m sill; **el ~ de la ventana** the windowsill

alférez m second lieutenant

alfil m bishop

alfiler m (en costura) pin; (broche) brooch, pin; ~ **de corbata** tiepin; ~ **de gancho** (CS, Ven) or (Col) **de nodriza** safety pin

alfombra f (a) (suelta) rug; (más grande) carpet (b) (AmL) (de pared a pared) carpet

alfombrado -da adj carpeted

alfombrar [A1] vt to carpet

alfombrilla f **1** (de coche) mat; (de baño) bath mat; ~ **para ratón** (Inf) mouse mat **2** (Med) type of measles

alforja f (para caballerías) saddlebag; (sobre el hombro) knapsack

alga f: (en el mar) seaweed; (en agua dulce) weed, waterweed; (nombre genérico) alga

algarroba f carob (bean)

algarrobo m carob (tree)

álgebra f: algebra

álgido -da adj ⟨punto/momento⟩ culminating (before n), decisive

algo¹ pron **(a)** something; (en frases interrogativas, condicionales, etc) anything; (esperando respuesta afirmativa) something; **quiero decirte ~** I want to tell you something; **si llegara a pasarle ~** if anything happened to her; **¿quieres ~ de beber?** do you want something o anything to drink?; **por ~ será** there must be some o a reason; **le va a dar ~** he'll have a fit; **o ~ así** or something like that; **eso ya es ~** at least that's something; **sé ~ de francés** I know some French; **¿queda ~ de pan?** is there any bread left? **(b)** (en aproximaciones): **serán las once y ~** it must be some time after eleven; **pesa tres kilos y ~** it weighs three kilos and a bit

algo² adv a little, slightly; **está ~ nublado** it's a bit cloudy; **es ~ grande para ti** it's a bit too big for you

algodón m ① (Bot, Tex) cotton **(a)** (material) tb **~ hidrófilo** cotton (AmE), cotton wool (BrE) **(b)** (trozo) piece of cotton (AmE), piece of cotton wool (BrE); **~ de azúcar** cotton candy (AmE), candy floss (BrE)

algodonal, algodonar m cotton field

algodonero -ra adj cotton (before n)

■ m,f (agricultor) cotton planter o farmer; (vendedor) cotton dealer

alguacil -cila m,f **(a)** (agente de autoridad) sheriff **(b)** (de tribunal de justicia) bailiff (AmE), constable (BrE)

alguien pron somebody, someone; (en frases interrogativas, condicionales, etc) anybody, anyone; (esperando respuesta afirmativa) somebody, someone; **~ con experiencia** somebody o someone with experience; **¿ha llamado ~?** has anybody o anyone called?; **si ~ preguntara** if anybody o anyone should ask

algún adj: apocopated form of ALGUNO used before masculine singular nouns

alguno¹ -na adj ① (delante del n) **(a)** (indicando uno indeterminado) some; **algún día** some o one day; **en algún lugar** somewhere **(b)** (en frases interrogativas, condicionales, etc) any; **¿tocas algún instrumento?** do you play any instruments?; **si tienes algún problema** if there's any problem, if you have any problems **(c)** (indicando cantidad indeterminada): **esto tiene alguna importancia** this is of some importance; **hace ~s años** some years ago, a few years ago; **me quedan tres tazas y algún plato** I have three cups and one or two plates; **escribió algún que otro artículo** he wrote one or two articles ② (detrás del n) (con valor negativo): **esto no lo afectará en modo ~** this won't affect it in the slightest o at all

alguno² -na pron **(a)** (cosa, persona indeterminada) one; **~ de nosotros** one of us; **siempre hay ~ que no está conforme** there's always someone who doesn't agree **(b)** (en frases interrogativas, condicionales, etc): **buscaba una guía ¿tiene alguna?** I was looking for a guide, do you have one o any?; **si tuviera ~** if I had one **(c)** (una cantidad indeterminada — de personas) some (people); (— de cosas) some; **~s creen que fue así** some (people) believe that was the case; **he visto algunas** I've seen some; **he tenido ~ que otro** I've had one or two

alhaja f **(a)** (joya) piece of jewelry*; **(b)** (persona) gem, treasure

alhajero m, **alhajera** f (AmL) jewel case

alharaca f fuss; **hacer ~s** to make a fuss

alhelí m wallflower

aliado -da adj allied

■ m,f (Hist, Pol) ally; **los A~s** the Allies

alianza f **(a)** (pacto, unión) alliance; **la A~ Atlántica** the Atlantic Alliance **(b)** (anillo) wedding ring

aliarse [A17] v pron to join forces; **~se CON algn** to form an alliance WITH sb, ally oneself WITH sb

alias adv alias

■ m (pl ~) alias

alicaído -da adj low, down in the dumps (colloq)

alicate m, **alicates** mpl (Tec) pliers (pl); (para uñas) nail clippers (pl); (para cutícula) cuticle clippers (pl)

aliciente m incentive

aliento m ① **(a)** (respiración, aire) breath; **sin ~** out of breath, breathless **(b)** (aire espirado) breath; **mal ~** bad breath ② (ánimo, valor): **dar ~ a algn** to encourage sb

aligerar [A1] vt **(a)** ⟨carga⟩ to lighten; **~ a algn DE algo** to relieve sb of sth **(b)** (acelerar): **~ el paso** to quicken one's pace

alijo m consignment

alimaña f pest; **~s** vermin

alimentación f **(a)** (nutrición, comida) diet; **la ~ integral va ganando adeptos** health food o (BrE) wholefood is growing in popularity **(b)** (de máquina, motor) fuel supply

alimentar [A1] vt ① ⟨persona/animal⟩ to feed ② **(a)** ⟨ilusión/esperanza⟩ to nurture, cherish; ⟨ego⟩ to boost **(b)** ⟨odio/pasión⟩ to fuel ③ ⟨máquina/motor⟩ to feed; ⟨caldera⟩ to stoke

■ ~ vi to be nourishing

■ **alimentarse** v pron «persona/animal» to feed oneself; **~se CON** or **DE algo** to live ON sth

alimenticio -cia, alimentario -ria adj **(a)** ⟨industria⟩ food (before n); **productos ~s** foodstuffs; **hábitos ~s** eating habits **(b)** ⟨valor⟩ nutritional; ⟨comida/plato⟩ nutritious, nourishing

alimento m ① (frml) (comida) food, nourishment; **la leche es un ~ completo** milk is a complete food; **~s naturales** health food ② (valor nutritivo): **no tiene ~ ninguno** it has no nutritional value; **de mucho ~** very nutritious

alineación f ① **(a)** (Dep) (de equipo) lineup; (de jugador) selection **(b)** (puesta en fila) lining up ② (Pol, Tec) alignment

alinear [A1] vt ① ⟨equipo/jugador⟩ to select, pick ② **(a)** (poner en fila, linea) to line up **(b)** (Tec) to align, line up

■ **alinearse** v pron «tropa» to fall in; «niños/presos» to line up

aliñar [A1] vt ⟨ensalada⟩ to dress; ⟨carne/pescado⟩ to season

aliño m (para ensalada) dressing; (para otros alimentos) seasoning

alioli m (mayonesa) garlic mayonnaise; (salsa) garlic and olive oil vinaigrette

alisar [A1] vt ⟨colcha/papel⟩ to smooth out; ⟨pared/superficie⟩ to smooth down ⋯⟫

■ **alisarse** *v pron* (*refl*) **(a)** ⟨*vestido/falda*⟩ to smooth out **(b)** ⟨*pelo*⟩ (con la mano) to smooth down; (quitar los rizos) to straighten

alistamiento *m* (acción) enlistment, recruitment; (soldados alistados) call-up, draft (AmE)

alistarse [A1] *v pron* **(a)** (Mil) to enlist, join up; ∼ **en el ejército** to join the army **(b)** (AmL) (prepararse) to get ready

alivianar *vt* [A1] (AmL) to lighten

aliviar [A1] *vt* ⟨*dolor*⟩ to relieve, soothe; ⟨*síntomas*⟩ to relieve; ⟨*tristeza/pena*⟩ to alleviate; ⟨*persona*⟩ to make ... feel better

■ **aliviarse** *v pron* **(a)** «*dolor*» to let up **(b)** «*persona*» to get better

alivio *m* relief; ¡**qué** ∼! what a relief!

aljibe *m* **(a)** (pozo) well; (depósito de agua) cistern, tank **(b)** (Per) (cárcel) dungeon

allá *adv* ⊡ **(a)** (en el espacio): **ya vamos para** ∼ we're on our way (over); ∼ **en América** over in America; **lo pusiste muy** ∼ you've put it too far away; ¡∼ **voy!** here I come/go! **(b)** (*en locs*) **más allá** further away; **más allá de** (más lejos que) beyond; (aparte de) over and above; ∼ **tú/él** that's your/his lookout *o* problem (colloq) ⊡ (en el tiempo): ∼ **por los años 40** back in the forties; ∼ **para enero** sometime in January

allanamiento *m* **(a)** (AmL) (con autorización judicial) raid; **orden de** ∼ search warrant **(b)** (Esp, Méx) (sin autorización judicial) breaking and entering

allanar [A1] *vt* ⊡ **(a)** (AmL) «*autoridad/ policía*» to raid **(b)** (Esp, Méx) «*delincuente*» to break into ⊡ ⟨*problemas*⟩ to solve, resolve; ⟨*obstáculo*⟩ to remove, overcome; ⟨*terreno*⟩ to level out; ∼(**le**) **el terreno a algn** to smooth the way *o* path for sb

allegado -da *adj* close; **mis amigos y parientes más** ∼**s** my close family and friends

■ *m,f* (amigo, pariente): **los** ∼**s del difunto** those closest to the deceased; **un** ∼ **de la familia** a close friend of the family

allí *adv* there; ∼ **arriba/dentro** up/in there; ∼ **donde estés/vayas** wherever you are/go

alma *f* ⊡ (espíritu) soul; **tener** ∼ **de niño** to be a child at heart; ∼ **mía** *or* **mi** ∼ (*como apelativo*) my love; **con toda el** *or* **mi/tu/su** ∼ with all my/ your/his/ heart; **del** ∼: **su amigo del** ∼ his bosom friend; **en el** ∼: **lo siento en el** ∼ I'm really *o* terribly sorry; **te lo agradezco en el** ∼ I can't tell you how grateful I am; **llegarle a algn al** ∼: **aquellas palabras me llegaron al** ∼ (me conmovieron) I was deeply touched by those words; (me dolieron) I was deeply hurt by those words; **me/le parte el** ∼ it breaks my/his heart ⊡ (persona) soul; **ni un** ∼ **viviente** not a living soul; **ser** ∼**s gemelas** to be soul mates; **ser un** ∼ **bendita** *or* **de Dios** to be a kind soul

almacén *m* **(a)** (depósito) warehouse **(b)** (CS) (de comestibles) grocery store (AmE), grocer's (shop) (BrE) **(c)** (AmC, Col, Ven) (de ropa, etc) store (AmE), shop (BrE) **(d)** (de mayorista) wholesaler's **(e) almacenes** *mpl* department store

almacenamiento *m* storage; ∼ **de datos** data storage

almacenar [A1] *vt* ⟨*mercancías/datos*⟩ to store

almanaque *m* (calendario — de escritorio) almanac, desk calendar; (— de pared) calendar

almeja *f* clam

almendra *f* **(a)** (fruta) almond **(b)** (centro) kernel

almendro *m* almond tree

almíbar *m* syrup

almibarar [A1] *vt* ⟨*fruta*⟩ to preserve ... in syrup; ⟨*pastel*⟩ to soak ... in syrup

almidón *m* starch

almidonar [A1] *vt* to starch

almirante *m* admiral

almohada *f* pillow; **consultarlo con la** ∼ to sleep on it

almohadilla *f* ⊡ (para alfileres) pincushion; (para entintar) ink pad; (para sellos) damper ⊡ (para sentarse) cushion; (en béisbol) bag

almohadón *m* (cuadrado, redondo) cushion; (cilíndrico) bolster; (en la iglesia) kneeler

almorranas *fpl* (fam) piles (*pl*)

almorzar [A11] *vi* **(a)** (a mediodía) to have lunch **(b)** (en algunas regiones) (a media mañana) to have a mid-morning snack

■ ∼ *vt* **(a)** (a mediodía) to have ... for lunch **(b)** (en algunas regiones) (a media mañana) to have ... mid-morning

almuerza, almuerzas, etc ▶ ALMORZAR

almuerzo *m* **(a)** (a mediodía) lunch **(b)** (en algunas regiones) (a media mañana) mid-morning snack

aló *interj* (AmS excl RPI) (al contestar el teléfono) hello?

alocado -da *adj* (irresponsable, imprudente) crazy, wild; (irreflexivo, impetuoso) rash, impetuous; (despistado) scatterbrained

■ *m,f* (imprudente) crazy *o* reckless fool; (irreflexivo) rash fool; (despistado) scatterbrain

alojado -da *m,f* (Chi) guest; **pieza de** ∼**s** guestroom

alojamiento *m* accommodations (*pl*) (AmE), accommodation (BrE); **nos dio** ∼ he put us up

alojar [A1] *vt* ⊡ **(a)** (en hotel): **los hemos alojado en el hotel Plaza** we've booked them into the Plaza Hotel; **el hotel en el que estaban alojados** the hotel where they were staying **(b)** (en casa particular) to put ... up ⊡ (albergar) ⟨*evacuados/refugiados*⟩ to house

■ **alojarse** *v pron* **(a)** (hospedarse) to stay **(b)** «*proyectil/bala*» to lodge

alondra *f* lark

alpaca *f* ⊡ (Zool, Tex) alpaca; **lana de** ∼ alpaca (wool) ⊡ (Metal) nickel silver, German silver

alpargata *f* espadrille

Alpes *mpl*: **los** ∼ the Alps

alpinismo *m* mountaineering, (mountain) climbing

alpinista *mf* mountaineer, (mountain) climber

alpino -na *adj* Alpine

alpiste *m* (semillas) birdseed

alquilar [A1] *vt* ⊡ (dar en alquiler) ⟨*casa/local*⟩ to rent (out), let (BrE); ⟨*televisor*⟩ to rent; ⟨*coche/ bicicleta*⟩ to rent (out) (AmE), to hire out (BrE) ⊡ (tomar en alquiler) ⟨*casa/local/televisor*⟩ to rent; ⟨*coche/bicicleta/disfraz*⟩ to rent (AmE), to hire (BrE)

alquiler *m* **(a)** (renta — de apartamento) rent; (— de televisor, bicicleta) rental **(b)** (acción de alquilar — una casa) renting, letting (BrE); (— un televisor) rental; (— un coche, disfraz) rental (AmE), hire (BrE);

se dedica al ~ de coches he's in the car-rental (AmE) o (BrE) car-hire business; contrato de ~ tenancy agreement; coches de ~ rental (AmE) o (BrE) hire cars

alquitrán m tar

alrededor adv (a) (en torno) around; a mi ~ around me (b) alrededor de (loc prep) (en torno a) around; (aproximadamente) around, about

alrededores mpl (a) (barrios periféricos, extrarradio de ciudad) outskirts (pl); (otras localidades): surroundings (pl) (b) (de edificio, calle) surrounding area; en los ~ de la iglesia in the area around the church

alta f: [1] (Med) discharge; dar el ~ a o dar de ~ a un enfermo to discharge a patient [2] (Fisco, Servs Socs): los dieron de ~ en la Seguridad Social they registered them with Social Security

altanero -ra adj arrogant, haughty

altar m altar

altavoz m (Audio) loudspeaker; (megáfono) megaphone

alteración f (a) (de plan, texto) change, alteration (b) (de hechos, verdad) distortion (c) (del orden, de la paz) disturbance; (agitación) agitation ; ~ del orden público breach of the peace

alterado -da adj [ESTAR] ‹persona› upset

alterar [A1] vt [1] (a) ‹plan/texto› to change, alter (b) ‹hechos/verdad› to distort (c) ‹alimento› to make ... go off, turn ... bad [2] (perturbar) (a) ‹paz› to disturb; ~ el orden público to cause a breach of the peace (b) ‹persona› to upset
■ **alterarse** v pron [1] «alimentos» to go off, go bad [2] «pulso/respiración» to become irregular; «color» to change [3] «persona» to get upset

altercado m argument

alternar [A1] vt ~ algo CON algo to alternate sth WITH sth; alternamos la gimnasia con el tenis we alternate gymnastics with tennis
■ ~ vi «persona» to socialize; ~ CON algn to mix WITH sb
■ **alternarse** v pron to take turns

alternativa f (opción) alternative; la ~ es clara the choice is clear

alternativo -va adj ‹medicina/prensa/música› alternative

Alteza mf (tratamiento) Highness; sí, (su) ~ yes, your Highness

altibajos mpl (a) (cambios bruscos) ups and downs (pl) (b) (del terreno) undulations (pl)

altillo m (desván) attic; (en habitación) (sleeping) loft

altiplanicie f, **altiplano** m high plateau, high plain; el altiplano boliviano the Bolivian altiplano

altiro adv (Chi fam) right away, immediately

altitud f altitude

altivo -va adj (arrogante) arrogant, haughty; (noble, orgulloso) proud

alto¹ -ta adj [1] (a) [SER] ‹persona/edificio/árbol› tall; ‹pared/montaña› high; una blusa de cuello ~ a high-necked blouse (b) [ESTAR]: ¡qué ~ estás! haven't you grown!; está tan alta como yo she's as tall as me now
[2] (indicando posición, nivel) (a) [SER] high; los techos eran muy ~s the rooms had very high ceilings (b) [ESTAR]: el río está muy ~ the river

is very high; la marea está alta it's high tide; los pisos más ~s the top floors; salgan con los brazos en ~ come out with your hands in the air; con la moral bastante alta in pretty high spirits; en lo ~ de la montaña high up on the mountainside; en lo ~ del árbol high up in the tree; por todo lo ~ in style
[3] (en cantidad, calidad) high; el alto nivel de contaminación the high level of pollution; productos de alta calidad high-quality products; tirando por lo ~ at the most
[4] (a) (en intensidad) ‹volumen/televisión› loud; pon la radio más alta turn the radio up (b) en alto or en voz alta aloud, out loud
[5] ‹delante del n› (a) (en importancia, trascendencia) ‹ejecutivo/funcionario› high-ranking, top; conversaciones de ~ nivel high-level talks (b) ‹ideales/opinión› high; un ~ sentido del deber a strong sense of duty (c) (en nombres compuestos) alta burguesía f upper-middle classes (pl); alta costura f haute couture; alta fidelidad f high fidelity, hi-fi; alta mar f: en alta mar on the high seas; flota/pesca de alta mar deep-sea fleet/fishing; alta sociedad f high society; alta tensión f high tension o voltage; ~ cargo m (puesto) high-ranking position; (persona) high-ranking official; ~ mando m high-ranking officer

alto² adv [1] ‹volar/subir› high [2] ‹hablar› loud, loudly; habla más ~ speak up a little

alto³ interj halt!; ¡~ el fuego! cease fire!

alto⁴ m [1] (a) (altura) de alto high; tiene tres metros de ~ it's three meters high (b) (en el terreno) high ground; construido en un ~ built on high ground [2] (a) (parada, interrupción): hacer un ~ to stop; ~ el fuego (Esp) (Mil) cease-fire (b) (Méx) (Auto): pasarse el ~ (un semáforo) to run the red light (AmE), to jump the lights (BrE); (un stop) to go through the stop sign

altoparlante m (AmL) ▶ ALTAVOZ

altruismo m altruism

altruista adj altruistic
■ mf altruist

altura f [1] (de persona, edificio, techo) height; el muro tiene un metro de ~ the wall is one meter high
[2] (indicando posición) height; ponlos a la misma ~ put them at the same height; a la ~ de los ojos at eye level; estar/ponerse a la ~ de algo/algn: para ponernos a la ~ de la competencia to put ourselves on a par with our competitors; estar a la ~ de las circunstancias to rise to the occasion; no está a la ~ de su predecesor he doesn't match up to his predecessor
[3] (a) (Aviac, Geog) (altitud) altitude; a 2.240 metros de ~ at an altitude of 2,240 meters (b) de altura ‹pesquero/flota› deep-sea (before n); ‹remolcador› oceangoing (before n)
[4] (en sentido horizontal): ¿a qué ~ de Serrano vive? how far up Serrano do you live?; cuando llegamos a la ~ de la plaza when we reached the square
[5] (en sentido temporal): a estas ~s ya debe haber llegado he should have arrived by now; ¡a estas ~s me vienes con eso! you wait till now to bring this to me!; a estas ~s del año this late on in the year; a esas ~s ya no me importaba by that stage I didn't mind
[6] (Mús) pitch

alturado -da *adj* (Per) calm

alubia *f* (haricot) bean

alucinación *f* hallucination

alucinado -da *adj* (fam): **los dejó a todos ∼s** she left everybody stunned

alucinante *adj* (a) (Med) hallucinatory (b) (Esp, Méx fam) ‹increíble› amazing (colloq), mind-boggling (colloq)

alucinar [A1] *vi* to hallucinate

alud *m* (de nieve) avalanche; (de tierra) landslide, landslip

aludir [I1] *vi* (a) (sin nombrar) ∼ **A** algn/algo to refer TO sb/sth, allude TO sb/sth; **se sintió aludido** he thought we were referring to him; **no se dio por aludido** he didn't take the hint (b) (mencionar) ∼ **A** algn/algo to refer TO sb/sth, mention sb/sth

alumbrado *m* lighting

alumbramiento *m* (frml) birth

alumbrar [A1] *vt* (iluminar) to light, illuminate; **está muy mal alumbrado** it's very poorly lit; **alumbra este rincón** shine the light in this corner ■ ∼ *vi* «sol» to be bright; «lámpara/bombilla» to give off light

aluminio *m* aluminum (AmE), aluminium (BrE)

alumnado *m* (de colegio) students (*pl*) (AmE), pupils (*pl*) (BrE); (de universidad) students (*pl*)

alumno -na *m,f* (de colegio) pupil; (de universidad) student; ∼ **interno** boarder

alunizar [A4] *vi* to land on the moon

alusión *f* ∼ (**A** algo/algn) allusion *o* reference (TO sth/sb); **hacer** ∼ **a algo/a algn** to make reference *o* an allusion to sth/sb

alverjilla *f* (AmL) sweet pea

alza *f*⁺ rise; **el** ∼ **de los precios** the rise in prices; **en** ∼ ‹intereses/precios› rising (*before n*); **una escritora en** ∼ an up-and-coming writer; **estar en** ∼ to be on the rise

alzado -da *adj* (a) (Andes, Ven fam) (levantisco): **la servidumbre anda medio alzada** the servants have been rather uppity lately (colloq); **un chiquillo** ∼ **a** cocky little brat (colloq) (b) (Méx, Ven fam) (altivo) stuck-up (colloq)

alzamiento *m* uprising

alzar [A4] *vt* **1** (levantar) (a) ‹brazo/cabeza/voz› to raise; **alzó al niño para que viera el desfile** she lifted the little boy up so he could see the parade; **alzó la mirada** she looked up (b) (AmL) ‹bebé› to pick up **2** ‹edificio/monumento› to erect **3** (Méx) (poner en orden) ‹juguetes› to pick up; ‹cuarto/casa› to clean (up)
■ **alzarse** *v pron* (sublevarse) to rise up; ∼**se en armas** to take up arms

ama *f*⁺ (a) (de bebé) *tb* ∼ **de leche** *or* **de cría** wet nurse (b) (de niño mayor) nanny (c) ∼ **de casa/de llaves** housewife/housekeeper; *ver tb* AMO

amabilidad *f* (a) (cualidad) kindness (b) (gesto): **tuvo la** ∼ **de invitarnos** she was kind enough to invite us; **¿tendría la** ∼ **de cerrar la puerta?** would you be so kind as to close the door?; **tenga la** ∼ **de esperar aquí** would you mind waiting here?

amable *adj* (a) ‹persona/gesto› kind; **es muy** ∼ **de su parte** that's very kind of you; **¿sería tan** ∼ **de ...?** would you be so kind as to ...? (b) (AmS) ‹rato/velada› pleasant

amablemente *adv* kindly

amado -da *adj* dear, beloved ■ *m,f* love, sweetheart

amadrinar [A1] *vt* ‹niño› to be godmother to; ‹boda› to act as MADRINA at; ‹barco› to launch, christen

amaestrar [A1] *vt* ‹animales› to train

amago *m*: **tuvo un** ∼ **de infarto** he had a mild heart attack; **un** ∼ **de revuelta** a threat of revolt; **hacer un** ∼ (Dep) to make a feint

amainar [A1] *vi* ‹lluvia› to ease up *o* off, abate; ‹temporal/viento› to die down, abate

amamantar [A1] *vt/vi* ‹mujer› to breastfeed; ‹animal› to suckle

amanecer¹ [E3] *v impers*: **¿a qué hora amanece?** what time does it get light?; **amanecía cuando partieron** dawn was breaking when they left
■ ∼ *vi* (+ compl) (a) «persona»: **amaneció con fiebre** he woke up with a temperature; **amanecieron bailando** they were still dancing at dawn (b) (aparecer por la mañana): **amaneció nublado** it was cloudy first thing in the morning; **todo amaneció cubierto de nieve** in the morning everything was covered in snow
■ **amanecerse** *v pron* (Chi, Méx) to stay up all night

amanecer² *m* dawn, daybreak; **al** ∼ at dawn *o* at daybreak

amanerado -da *adj* (afectado) affected, mannered; (afeminado) (fam) mannered, camp (colloq)

amansar [A1] *vt* ‹caballo› to break in; ‹fiera› to tame
■ **amansarse** *v pron* «fiera» to become tame; «caballo» to quiet (AmE) *o* (BrE) quieten down

amante *mf* lover

amañar [A1] *vt* (fam) ‹elecciones› to rig; ‹partido/pelea› to fix; ‹carnet/documento› to tamper with; ‹informe› to alter, doctor (pej); ‹excusa/historia› to dream *o* cook up, concoct
■ **amañarse** *v pron* **1** *tb* **amañárselas** (ingeniarse) to manage **2** (Col, Ven) (acostumbrarse) to settle in

amapola *f* poppy

amar [A1] *vt* to love
■ **amarse** *v pron* (recípr) to love each other

amarga *f* (Col) beer

amargado -da *adj* bitter, embittered ■ *m,f* bitter *o* embittered person

amargar [A3] *vt* ‹ocasión/día› to spoil; ‹persona› to make ... bitter
■ **amargarse** *v pron* to become bitter; **no te amargues la existencia** (fam) don't get all uptight about it

amargo -ga *adj* **1** (a) ‹fruta/sabor› bitter (b) (sin azúcar) unsweetened, without sugar **2** ‹experiencia/recuerdo› bitter, painful

amargor m bitterness

amargura f bitterness; **con** ~ bitterly

amarillento -ta adj yellowish

amarillista adj (Period) (pey): **prensa** ~ sensationalist o yellow press

amarillo¹ -lla adj ⓵ ⟨color/blusa⟩ yellow; **el semáforo estaba (en)** ~ the light was yellow (AmE), the lights were (on) amber (BrE) ⓶ **(a)** ⟨piel⟩ (de raza oriental) yellow **(b)** ⟨piel/cara⟩ (por enfermedad) yellow, jaundiced

amarillo² m yellow

amarra f mooring rope; ~**s** moorings (pl); **echar (las)** ~**s** to moor

amarradero m **(a)** (poste) bollard; (argolla) mooring ring **(b)** (lugar) berth, slip (AmE)

amarrado -da adj (Col, Méx, Ven fam) stingy (colloq), tightfisted (colloq)

amarrar [A1] vt **(a)** ⟨embarcación⟩ to moor; ⟨animal/persona⟩ to tie up; **le** ~**on las manos** they tied his hands together; ~ **algo/a algn A algo** to tie sth/sb TO sth **(b)** (AmL exc RPl) ⟨zapatos/cordones⟩ to tie; ⟨paquete⟩ to tie ... up
■ **amarrarse** v pron (AmL exc RPl) ⟨zapatos/cordones⟩ to tie up, do up; ⟨pelo⟩ to tie up

amarrete -ta adj (AmS fam) stingy (colloq), tightfisted (colloq)
■ m,f (AmS fam) scrooge (colloq), skinflint (colloq)

amasar [A1] vt ⓵ ⟨pan⟩ to knead; ⟨yeso/argamasa⟩ to mix ⓶ ⟨fortuna/riquezas⟩ to amass

amateur /ama'ter/ adj/mf (pl **-teurs**) amateur

amazona f (Mit) Amazon; (Equ) horsewoman

Amazonas m: **el** ~ the Amazon

amazónico -ca adj Amazonian, Amazon (before n)

ámbar m **(a)** (piedra) amber **(b)** (color) amber

ambición f ambition

ambicionar [A1] vt to aspire to

ambicioso -sa adj ambitious; (codicioso) overambitious

ambidextro -tra adj ambidextrous
■ m,f ambidextrous person

ambientación f **(a)** (de obra, película) atmosphere **(b)** (de persona) adjustment

ambientador m air freshener

ambiental adj environmental

ambientar [A1] vt **(a)** ⟨obra/película⟩ to set **(b)** ⟨fiesta/local⟩ to give ... some atmosphere
■ **ambientarse** v pron to adjust, adapt

ambiente m **(a)** (entorno físico, social, cultural) environment; **creci en un** ~ **rural** I grew up in a rural environment; **se encuentra realmente en su** ~ he's really in his element; **había una cierta tensión en el** ~ there was a feeling of tension in the air **(b)** (creado por la decoración, arquitectura, la gente) atmosphere; **un** ~ **de camaradería/de fiesta** a friendly/festive atmosphere **(c)** (animación) life

ambigüedad f ambiguity

ambiguo -gua adj ambiguous

ámbito m **(a)** (campo, círculo) sphere, field **(b)** (alcance) scope, range; **el** ~ **(de aplicación) de la ley** the scope of the law

ambo m (CS) (two-piece) suit

ambos -bas adj pl both; **a** ~ **lados** on both sides

■ pron pl both; ~ **aceptaron la propuesta** they both accepted the proposal; ~ **me gustan** I like both of them

ambulancia f ambulance

ambulanciero -ra m,f (m) ambulance man; (f) ambulance woman; **los** ~**s** the ambulance crew

ambulante adj traveling* (before n); **biblioteca** ~ bookmobile (AmE), mobile library (BrE)

ambulatorio¹ -ria adj outpatient (before n)

ambulatorio² m (Esp) outpatients' department

ameba f amoeba

amén m amen; ~ **de ...** as well as ...

amenaza f threat; **no me vengas con** ~**s** don't threaten me; ~ **de bomba/muerte** bomb/death threat

amenazador -dora, amenazante adj threatening, menacing

amenazar [A4] vt **(a)** «persona» to threaten; **nos amenazó con llamar a la policía** he threatened to call the police **(b)** (dar indicios de): **esas nubes amenazan lluvia** those clouds look threatening
■ ~ vi: ~ CON hacer algo to threaten to do sth
■ ~ v impers (Meteo): **amenaza tormenta** there's a storm brewing; **amenaza lluvia** it's threatening to rain

amenizar [A4] vt ⟨conversación/discurso⟩ to make ... more enjoyable; **la fiesta fue amenizada por un payaso** a clown provided the entertainment for the party

ameno -na adj pleasant, enjoyable

América f ⓵ (continente) America; **hacerse la** ~ to make a fortune, get rich; ~ **Central** Central America; ~ **del Norte** or **Septentrional** North America; ~ **del Sur** or **Meridional** South America; ~ **Latina** Latin America ⓶ (Esp) (Estados Unidos) America, the States (pl)

americana f jacket

americanismo m Americanism

americano -na adj/m,f American

amerindio -dia adj/m,f American Indian, Amerindian

ameritado -da adj (AmL) meritorious (fml)

ameritar [A1] vt (AmL) to deserve

ametralladora f machine gun

ametrallar [A1] vt to machine-gun

amianto m asbestos

amiba f amoeba

amigable adj ⟨persona⟩ friendly; ⟨trato⟩ friendly, amicable; **un tono poco** ~ a rather unfriendly manner

amígdalas fpl tonsils (pl)

amigdalitis f tonsillitis

amigo -ga adj: **son/se hicieron muy** ~**s** they are/they became good friends; **hacerse** ~ **de algn** to become friends with sb; **es muy** ~ **mío** he's a close friend of mine; **un país** ~ a friendly country; **es muy** ~ **de contradecir** he's a great one for contradicting people (colloq); **no es amiga de las fiestas** she's not keen on parties
■ m,f friend; **un** ~ **mío** a friend of mine; **somos íntimos** ~**s** we're very close friends; **¡un momento,** ~**!** now, just a minute, pal o buddy (AmE) o (BrE) mate! (colloq)

amigote *m* (fam) crony (colloq & pej), buddy (AmE colloq), mate (BrE colloq)

amilanar [A1] *vt* to daunt
- **amilanarse** *v pron* to be daunted

amistad *f* **(a)** (entre personas, países) friendship; entabló *or* hizo ~ con ella he struck up a friendship with her **(b) amistades** *fpl* (amigos) friends (*pl*)

amistoso -sa *adj* ⟨consejo/palmadita/charla⟩ friendly; ⟨partido⟩ friendly (*before n*)

amnesia *f* amnesia

amnistía *f* amnesty

amnistiado -da *m,f*: person pardoned under an amnesty

amnistiar [A17] *vt* ⟨persona⟩ to grant an amnesty to; ⟨delito⟩ to amnesty

amo, ama *m,f* (de animal, criado) (*m*) master; (*f*) mistress; son los ~s del pueblo they own the whole village; *ver tb* AMA

amoblar [A10] *vt* (CS) ▶ AMUEBLAR

amoldable *adj* adaptable

amoldar [A1] *vt* to adjust
- **amoldarse** *v pron* to adapt; ~se A algo ⟨a un trabajo/una situación⟩ to adjust TO sth; estos zapatos todavía no se me han amoldado al pie I haven't broken these shoes in yet

amonestación *f* (reprimenda) warning; (en fútbol) caution, booking

amonestar [A1] *vt* (reprender) to reprimand, admonish (frml); (en fútbol) to caution, book

amoníaco *m* ammonia

amontonar [A1] *vt* **(a)** (apilar) to pile ... up **(b)** (juntar) to accumulate
- **amontonarse** *v pron* «personas» to gather *o* crowd together; «objetos/trabajo» to pile up

amor *m* ⓵ **(a)** (sentimiento) love; ~ no correspondido unrequited love; ~ a primera vista love at first sight; ~ al prójimo/a la patria love for one's neighbor/one's country; ~ propio pride, self-esteem; un gran ~ a la vida/a los animales a great love of life/animals; por ~ al arte (fam) just for the fun of it; por (el) ~ de Dios (mendigando) for the love of God; (expresando irritación) for God's sake! **(b)** (el acto sexual): hacer el ~ a/con algn to make love to/with sb **(c)** (persona, cosa amada) love; ~ mío *or* mi ~ my darling, my love **(d)** (esmero, dedicación): hacer algo con ~ to do sth lovingly
⓶ (fam) (persona encantadora) darling (colloq), dear (colloq)

amoral *adj* amoral

amoratado -da *adj* (de frío) blue; (por un golpe) ⟨piernas/brazos⟩ bruised; ojo ~ black eye

amordazar [A4] *vt* ⟨persona⟩ to gag; ⟨perro⟩ to muzzle

amorío *m* love affair

amoroso -sa *adj* **(a)** (AmL) ⟨persona/casa⟩ lovely **(b)** ⟨vida⟩ love (*before n*); sus relaciones amorosas his relationships

amortajar [A1] *vt* to shroud

amortiguador *m* shock absorber

amortiguar [A16] *vt* ⟨golpe⟩ to cushion, absorb; ⟨sonido⟩ to muffle

amortizable *adj* redeemable

amortización *f* (de inversión) recovery; (de préstamo) repayment; (de bonos, hipoteca) redemption

amortizar [A4] *vt* **(a)** ⟨compra⟩ to recoup the cost of **(b)** (recuperar) ⟨inversión⟩ to recoup, recover **(c)** (pagar) ⟨deuda⟩ to repay, amortize (frml); ⟨valores/hipoteca⟩ to redeem

amotinado -da *adj* ⟨soldado/ejército⟩ rebel (*before n*), insurgent (*before n*); ⟨pueblo/ciudadanos⟩ rebellious, insurgent (*before n*)
- *m,f* insurgent

amotinar [A1] *vt* ⟨tropa⟩ to incite ... to mutiny *o* rebellion; ⟨población/pueblo⟩ to incite ... to rebellion
- **amotinarse** *v pron* ⟨soldados/oficiales⟩ to mutiny, rebel; «población civil» to rise up

amparar [A1] *vt* **(a)** (proteger) to protect; ¡que Dios nos ampare! may the Lord help us! **(b)** (ofrecer refugio) to shelter, give shelter to
- **ampararse** *v pron* **(a)** ~se EN algo ⟨en la ley⟩ to seek protection IN sth; se amparó en su inmunidad diplomática he used his diplomatic immunity to protect himself **(b)** (resguardarse) ~se DE *or* CONTRA algo to shelter FROM sth

amparo *m* **(a)** (protección) protection **(b)** (refugio) refuge; dar ~ A algn to give sb refuge

amperio *m* amp, ampere (frml)

ampliación *f* **(a)** (de local, carretera) extension; (de negocio) expansion **(b)** (Com, Fin): una ~ de capital/de personal an increase in capital/in the number of staff **(c)** (de conocimientos, vocabulario) widening **(d)** (de plazo, período) extension **(e)** (Fot) enlargement

ampliar [A17] *vt* **(a)** ⟨local/carretera⟩ to extend; ⟨negocio⟩ to expand **(b)** ⟨capital/personal⟩ to increase **(c)** ⟨conocimientos/vocabulario⟩ to increase; ⟨explicación⟩ to expand (on); ⟨campo de acción⟩ to widen, broaden; para ~ sus estudios to further her studies **(d)** ⟨plazo/período⟩ to extend **(e)** ⟨fotografía⟩ to enlarge, blow up

amplificador *m* amplifier

amplificar [A2] *vt* to amplify

amplio -plia *adj* **(a)** ⟨calle/valle/margen⟩ wide; ⟨casa⟩ spacious; ⟨vestido/abrigo⟩ loose-fitting; ⟨sonrisa⟩ broad **(b)** ⟨criterio/sentido⟩ broad; por amplia mayoría by a large majority; una amplia gama de colores a wide range of colors **(c)** ⟨garantías/programa⟩ comprehensive

amplitud *f* **(a)** (de calle, margen) width; (de casa) spaciousness; (de vestido) looseness **(b)** (de miras, criterios) range; (de facultades, garantías) extent; la ~ de sus conocimientos the breadth *o* depth of his knowledge **(c)** (Fís) amplitude

ampolla *f* ⓵ (por quemadura, rozamiento) blister ⓶ (con medicamento) ampoule (frml), vial (AmE), phial (BrE)

ampolleta *f* (Chi) light bulb

amputar [A1] *vt* ⟨brazo/pierna⟩ to amputate

amueblar [A1] *vt* to furnish; casa amueblada/sin ~ furnished/unfurnished house

amuleto *m* charm, amulet

anacardo *m* cashew (nut)

anaconda *f* anaconda

anacrónico -ca *adj* anachronistic

anacronismo *m* anachronism

ánade *mf* duck

anafe, anafre *m* (Chi, Méx) portable stove
anagrama *m* anagram
anal *adj* anal
anales *mpl* annals (*pl*)
analfabetismo *m* illiteracy
analfabeto -ta *adj* illiterate
■ *m,f* **(a)** (que no sabe leer) illiterate (person) **(b)** (fam & pey) (ignorante) ignoramus (colloq & pej)
analgésico *m* analgesic, painkiller
análisis *m* (*pl* ∼) analysis; **hacerse un ∼ de sangre** to have a blood test
analista *mf* analyst
analítico -ca *adj* analytic
analizar [A4] *vt* **(a)** (examinar) to analyze*, examine **(b)** (Med, Quím) to analyze* **(c)** (Ling) to parse
■ **analizarse** *v pron* to undergo *o* have analysis
analogía *f* analogy
ananá *m* (*pl* **-nás**) (RPl) pineapple
anaquel *m* shelf
anaranjado -da *adj* orangish (AmE), orangey (BrE)
anarquía *f* anarchy
anárquico -ca *adj* anarchic
anarquismo *m* anarchism
anarquista *adj* anarchist (*before n*)
■ *mf* anarchist
anarquizar [A4] *vt* to cause chaos *o* anarchy in
anatomía *f* anatomy
anatómico -ca *adj* **(a)** (Anat) anatomical **(b)** ⟨asiento/respaldo⟩ anatomically designed
anca *f‡* (de animal) haunch; **∼s de rana** frogs' legs; **llevar a algn en ∼s** (AmL) to take sb on the crupper
ancestral *adj* ⟨costumbre⟩ ancient; ⟨temor⟩ primitive, ancient
ancestro *m* ancestor
ancho¹ -cha *adj* **1 (a)** ⟨camino/río/mueble⟩ wide; **a todo lo ∼ de la carretera** right across the road; **a lo ∼** breadthways *o* (BrE) widthways **(b)** ⟨manos/cara/espalda⟩ broad; **es ∼ de espaldas** he's broad-shouldered **(c)** ⟨ropa⟩ loose-fitting, loose; **me queda ∼ de cintura** it's too big around the waist for me **2** (cómodo, tranquilo): **allí estaremos más ∼s** (Esp) we'll have more room there; **estar/sentirse/ponerse a sus anchas** to be/feel/make oneself at home
ancho² *m* width; **¿cuánto mide de ∼?** how wide is it?; **tiene 6 metros de ∼** it's 6 meters wide
anchoa *f* anchovy
anchura *f* **(a)** (de camino, río, mueble) width **(b)** (medida): **∼ de caderas** hip measurement
ancianato *m* (Col, Ven) old people's home
anciano -na *adj* elderly
■ *m,f* **(m)** elderly man; **(f)** elderly woman
ancla *f‡* anchor; **echar el ∼** to drop anchor; **levar ∼s** to weigh anchor
anclar [A1] *vt/vi* to anchor
andadera *f* (Méx, Ven) ▶ ANDADOR 1
andador *m* **1** (a) (con ruedas) baby walker **(b) andadores** *mpl* (arnés) baby harness, reins (*pl*) **2** (para ancianos) Zimmer® frame
Andalucía *f* Andalusia

andaluz -luza *adj/m,f* Andalusian
andamio *m*: *tb* **∼s** scaffolding
andanzas *fpl* adventures (*pl*)
andar¹ [A24] *vi* **1 (a)** (esp Esp) (caminar) to walk; **¿has venido andando?** did you come on foot?, did you walk? **(b)** (AmL): **∼ a caballo/en bicicleta** to ride (a horse/a bicycle) **(c)** (*en imperativo*) (AmS) (ir): **anda a comprar el periódico** go and buy the newspaper
2 (marchar, funcionar) to work; **el coche anda de maravilla** the car's running *o* (BrE) going like a dream
3 (+ *compl*) **(a)** (estar) to be; **¿cómo andas?** how are you?, how's it going? (colloq); **¿quién anda por ahí?** who's there?; **anda en Londres** he's in London; **anda buscando pelea** he's out for *o* he's looking for a fight; **me anda molestando** (AmL fam) he keeps bothering me **(b)** **∼ CON algn** (juntarse) to mix WITH sb; (salir con) to go out WITH sb; **dime con quién andas y te diré quién eres** a man is known by the company he keeps **(c)** **∼ DETRÁS DE** *or* **TRAS algn/algo** (buscar, perseguir) to be AFTER sb/sth
4 (rondar): **∼á por los 60 (años)** he must be around *o* about 60
5 **∼ CON algo** (esp AmL fam) ⟨con revólver/dinero⟩ to carry sth; ⟨con traje/sombrero⟩ to wear sth
6 (en exclamaciones) **(a)** (expresando sorpresa, incredulidad): **¡anda! ¡qué casualidad!** good heavens! what a coincidence!; **¡anda! ¡mira quién está aquí!** well, well! look who's here! **(b)** (expresando irritación, rechazo): **¡anda! ¡déjame en paz!** oh, leave me alone!; **¡anda! ¡se me ha vuelto a olvidar!** damn! I've forgotten it again! (colloq) **(c)** (instando a hacer algo): **préstamelo, ¡anda!** go on, lend it to me!; **¡ándale** (Méx) *or* (Col) **ándele que llegames tarde!** come on, we'll be late! (colloq)
■ **∼** *vt* **1** (caminar) to walk
2 (AmC) (llevar): **no ando dinero** I don't have any money on me; **siempre ando shorts** I always wear shorts
■ **andarse** *v pron* **1 ∼se CON algo**: **ese no se anda con bromas** he's not one to joke; **ándate con cuidado** take care, be careful
2 (*en imperativo*) (AmL) (irse): **ándate de aquí** get out of here; **ándate luego** get going, get a move on (colloq)
andar² *m*, **andares** *mpl* gait, walk
andarivel *m* **(a)** (AmL) (cable) ferry cable **(b)** (AmS) (en una piscina — carril) lane; (— soga) lane divider
andas *fpl* portable platform (*used in religious processions*); **llevar a algn en ∼** (CS) to carry sb on one's shoulders
ándele, ándale *interj*: ▶ ANDAR¹ 6B, C
andén *m* **(a)** (en estación) platform **(b)** (AmC, Col) (acera) sidewalk (AmE), pavement (BrE)
Andes *mpl*: **los ∼** the Andes
andinismo *m* (AmL) mountaineering, mountain climbing, climbing
andinista *mf* (AmL) mountaineer, mountain climber, climber
andino -na *adj* (AmL) Andean
andrajo *m* rag
andrajoso -sa *adj* ragged
anduve, anduviste, etc ▶ ANDAR
anécdota *f* anecdote

anecdótico -ca adj (a) ‹relato› anecdotal (b) ‹interés/valor› incidental

anegar [A3] vt to flood
■ **anegarse** v pron «campo/terreno» to be flooded

anemia f anemia*

anémico -ca adj anemic*
■ m,f anemic person

anestesia f (proceso) anesthesia*; (droga) anesthetic*; **bajo los efectos de la** ~ under (the) anesthetic; **lo operaron con** ~ he was operated on under (an) anesthetic; **sin** ~ without an anesthetic

anestesiar [A1] vt ‹encía/dedo› to anesthetize*; **me** ~**on** they gave me an anesthetic

anestesista mf anesthetist*

anexo¹ -xa adj (a) ‹edificio/local› joined, annexed (b) ‹cláusula› added, appended (frml); ‹documento› (en informe) attached; (en carta) enclosed

anexo² m (a) (edificio) annex* (b) (documento — en informe) appendix; (— en carta) enclosure (c) (Chi) (del teléfono) extension

anfetamina f amphetamine

anfibio¹ -bia adj amphibious; **avión** ~ seaplane

anfibio² m amphibian

anfiteatro m (Arquit) amphitheater*; (Geol) natural amphitheater*; (en la universidad) lecture hall

anfitrión -triona m,f (m) host; (f) hostess

ánfora f: (cántaro) amphora

angas (Andes, Méx fam): **por** ~ **o por mangas, nunca estás trabajando** for one reason or another, you're never working; **por** ~ **o por mangas tengo que salir** I have to go out whether I like it or not

ángel m (a) (Relig) angel; ~ **guardián** or **de la guarda** guardian angel; **que sueñes con los angelitos** sweet dreams; **pobre angelito** poor little darling (b) (encanto) charm; **tener** ~ to be charming

angelical adj angelic

angelito m (AmL) dead child; ver tb ÁNGEL

angina f [1] (Arg, Col, Ven) (de la garganta) inflammation of the palate, tonsils and/or pharynx [2] tb ~ **de pecho** angina (pectoris)

anginas fpl (a) (Esp, Méx) (inflamación) throat infection (b) (Méx, Ven) (amígdalas) tonsils (pl)

anglicano -na adj/m,f Episcopalian (in US and Scotland), Anglican (in UK)

anglicismo m Anglicism

angloparlante adj English-speaking

Angola f Angola

angoleño -leña adj/m,f Angolan

angora f angora

angosto -ta adj ‹calle/cama› narrow; ‹falda› tight

anguila f eel

angular adj angular

ángulo m (Mat) angle; (rincón, esquina) corner; (punto de vista) angle; ~ **recto** right angle

anguloso -sa adj angular

angustia f (a) (congoja) anguish, distress; **gritos de** ~ anguished cries (b) (desasosiego) anxiety; **vive con la** ~ **de que…** she's constantly worried that… (c) (Psic) anxiety

angustiado -da adj (a) (acongojado) distressed (b) (preocupado) worried, anxious; **vive angustiada** she lives in a constant state of anxiety

angustiar [A1] vt (a) (acongojar) to distress (b) (preocupar) to worry, make … anxious
■ **angustiarse** v pron (acongojarse) to get distressed, get upset; (preocuparse) to get worried, become anxious

angustioso -sa adj ‹situación› distressing; ‹mirada/grito› anguished

anhelante adj (liter) ‹mirada› longing (before n); **esperaba** ~ **su regreso** she longed o she yearned for his return; **con voz** ~ in a voice full of longing

anhelar [A1] vt (liter) ‹fama/poder› to yearn for, to long for; ~ **hacer algo** to long to do sth, yearn to do sth; **anhelaba que su hijo fuera feliz** his greatest wish was for his son to be happy

anhelo m (liter) wish, desire; **mi mayor** ~ my greatest wish

anhídrido m anhydride; ~ **carbónico** carbon dioxide

anidar [A1] vi «aves» to nest

aniego m (Per) flood

anilla f (a) (de cortina, llavero) ring; (de puro) band; (de lata) ringpull; (de ave) ring (b) **anillas** fpl (Dep) rings (pl)

anillo m [1] (sortija) ring; ~ **de boda/compromiso** wedding/engagement ring; **como** ~ **al dedo** (fam) ‹sentar/quedar› to suit down to the ground; ‹venir› to come in very handy (colloq) [2] (aro, arandela) ring; (de columna) annulet; (en árbol) ring

ánima f: (liter) (alma) soul

animación f [1] (bullicio, actividad) activity; **un bar con mucha** ~ a very lively bar [2] (de una velada) entertainment [3] (Cin) animation

animado -da adj [1] (a) ‹fiesta/ambiente› lively; ‹conversación/discusión› lively, animated (b) (optimista, con ánimo) cheerful, in good spirits [2] (impulsado) ~ **DE** or **POR algo** inspired o motivated **BY** sth

animador -dora m,f (a) (de programa) (m) presenter, host; (f) presenter, hostess (b) **animadora** f (de equipo) cheerleader

animal adj [1] ‹instinto› animal (before n) [2] (fam) (a) (estúpido) stupid (b) (grosero) rude, uncouth
■ m (a) (Zool) animal; ~ **doméstico** (de granja) domestic animal; (mascota) pet (b) (fam) (persona — violenta) brute, animal; (— grosera) lout

animar [A1] vt [1] (a) (alentar) to encourage; (levantar el espíritu) to cheer … up; **tu visita lo animó mucho** your visit cheered him up a lot; ~ **a algn A hacer algo** or **A que haga algo** to encourage sb to do sth **(b)** ⟨*fiesta/reunión*⟩ to liven up; **el vino empezaba a ∼los** the wine was beginning to liven them up **(c)** (con luces, colores) to brighten up

2 ⟨*programa*⟩ to present, host

3 (impulsar) to inspire

■ **animarse** *v pron* **(a)** (alegrarse, cobrar vida) «*fiesta/reunión*» to liven up, warm up; «*persona*» to liven up **(b)** (cobrar ánimos) to cheer up; **si me animo a salir te llamo** if I feel like going out, I'll call you **(c)** (atreverse): **¿quién se anima a decírselo?** who's going to be brave enough to tell him?; **no me animo a saltar** I can't bring myself to jump; **al final me animé a confesárselo** I finally plucked up the courage to tell her

anímicamente *adv* emotionally

anímico -ca *adj*: **su estado ∼** her state of mind

ánimo *m* **1** **(a)** (espíritu): **no estoy con el ∼ para bromas** I'm not in the mood for jokes; **tu visita le levantó el ∼** your visit cheered her up; **con el ∼ por el suelo** in very low spirits, feeling very down-hearted; **apaciguar los ∼s** to calm everyone down; **hacerse el ∼ de hacer algo** to bring oneself to do sth **(b)** (aliento, coraje) encouragement; **darle ∼(s) a algn** (animar) to encourage sb; (con aplausos, gritos) to cheer sb on; **¡∼, que ya falta poco para llegar!** come on! it's not far now!; **no tengo ∼(s) de** *or* **para nada** I don't feel up to anything

2 **(a)** (intención, propósito) intention; **lo dije sin ∼ de ofender** I meant no offense, no offense intended **(b)** (mente, pensamiento) mind

animosidad *f* animosity, hostility; **∼ CONTRA algn** animosity *o* hostility TOWARD(S) sb

aniquilar [A1] *vt* ⟨*enemigo/población*⟩ to annihilate, wipe out; ⟨*defensas/instalaciones*⟩ to destroy

anís *m* **(a)** (Bot) (planta) anise; (semilla) aniseed **(b)** (licor) anisette

aniversario *m* anniversary

ano *m* anus

anoche *adv* last night

anochecer¹ [E3] *v impers* to get dark

■ **anochecerse** *v pron* (Chi, Méx) to stay up till really late

anochecer² *m* nightfall; **al ∼** at nightfall

anomalía *f* anomaly

anonadado -da *adj* dumbfounded, speechless

anonimato *m* anonymity; **salir del ∼** to rise from obscurity

anónimo -ma *adj* anonymous

anorak /ano'rak/ *m* parka (AmE), anorak (BrE)

anorexia *f* anorexia

anoréxico -ca *adj/m,f* anorexic

anormal *adj* abnormal

■ *mf* (fam) idiot

anormalidad *f* abnormality

anotación *f* **(a)** (nota) note **(b)** (AmL) (en fútbol) goal; (en fútbol americano) touchdown; (en básquetbol) point

anotador -dora *m,f* (AmL) (en fútbol) scorer, goalscorer; (en fútbol americano, básquetbol) scorer

anotar [A1] *vt* **1** **(a)** (tomar nota de) ⟨*dirección/ nombre*⟩ to make a note of **(b)** ⟨*texto*⟩ to annotate **(c)** (RPl) ▶ APUNTAR *vt* 1B **2** (aml) ⟨*gol/tanto*⟩ to score

■ **anotarse** *v pron* **1** (AmL) ⟨*gol/tanto*⟩ to score **2** (RPl) (inscribirse) ▶ APUNTARSE A

anquilosado -da *adj* **(a)** ⟨*articulación*⟩ (atrofiado) ankylosed; (entumecido) stiff **(b)** ⟨*ideas/ economía*⟩ stagnant

anquilosarse [A1] *v pron* **(a)** «*miembro/ articulación*» (atrofiarse) to ankylose; (entumecerse) to get stiff **(b)** ⟨*ideas/economía*⟩ to stagnate

ansia *f* **(a)** (avidez, deseo): **con ∼** ⟨*comer/beber*⟩ eagerly; **∼ DE algo** ⟨*de paz/libertad*⟩ longing FOR sth, yearning FOR sth; ⟨*de poder*⟩ thirst FOR sth, craving FOR sth; **sentir ∼ de hacer algo** to long *o* yearn to do sth; **sus ∼s de aprender** her eagerness to learn **(b)** (Psic) anxiety **(c) ansias** *fpl* (Col, Ven fam) (náuseas) nausea

ansiar [A17] *vt* (liter) ⟨*libertad/poder*⟩ to long for, yearn for; **∼ hacer algo** to long to do sth

ansiedad *f* **(a)** (preocupación) anxiety; **con ∼** anxiously **(b)** (Med, Psic) anxiety

ansioso -sa *adj* **(a)** (deseoso) eager; **está ∼ por saberlo** he's eager *o* (colloq) dying to know; **estoy ∼ de verlos** I can't wait to see them **(b)** [SER] (fam) (voraz) greedy

antagónico -ca *adj* conflicting

antagonismo *m* antagonism

antagonista *adj* antagonistic

■ *mf* antagonist

antártico -ca *adj* Antarctic

Antártida *f*: **la ∼** Antarctica, the Antarctic

ante *prep* **1** **(a)** (frml) (delante de) before; **ante el juez** before the judge **(b)** (frente a): **∼ la gravedad de la situación** in view of the seriousness of the situation; **iguales ∼ la ley** equal in the eyes of the law; **nos hallamos ∼ un problema** we are faced with a problem **2** **ante todo** (primero) first and foremost; (sobre todo) above all

■ *m* (cuero) suede

anteanoche *adv* the night before last

anteayer *adv* the day before yesterday

antebrazo *m* forearm

antecedente *m* **1** **(a)** (precedente) precedent; **no hay ningún ∼ de la enfermedad en mi familia** there's no history of the illness in my family **(b)** (causa) cause; **estar/poner a algn en ∼s** to be/put sb in the picture **2** (Fil, Ling) antecedent **3** **antecedentes** *mpl* (historial) background, record; **∼s penales** (criminal) record

anteceder [E1] *vt* to precede, come before; **∼ A algo** to come BEFORE sth, precede sth

antecesor -sora *m,f* (predecesor) predecessor; (antepasado) ancestor

antecomedor *m* (Méx) breakfast room

antelación *f*: **con ∼** ⟨*reservar/pagar*⟩ in advance; ⟨*avisar/salir*⟩ in plenty of time; **saqué la entrada con un mes de ∼** I got the ticket one month in advance; **llegó con dos días de ∼** she arrived two days early; **con ∼ a su boda** prior to her wedding

antemano: **de ∼** ⟨*loc adv*⟩ in advance

antena *f* **1** (de radio, televisión, coche) antenna (AmE), aerial (BrE); **en ∼** on the air; **∼ colectiva** ⋯⊹

communal antenna *o* aerial; ~ **de radar** radar
dish; ~ **parabólica** satellite dish; ~ **repetidora**
relay mast ② (Zool) antenna

antenoche *adv* (AmL) the night before last

anteojo *m* (a) (telescopio) telescope (b)
anteojos *mpl* (esp AmL) ▶ GAFAS

antepasado -da *adj* ‹año/semana› before last
■ *m,f* ancestor

antepenúltimo -ma *adj* ‹delante del n› third
from last, antepenultimate (frml)
■ *m,f*: **fue el ~ en la carrera** he came third from
last on the race; **es el ~ en la lista** he's third
from bottom on the list

anteponer [E22] *vt* ~ **algo** A **algo** (poner
delante) to put sth BEFORE *o* IN FRONT OF sth; (dar
preferencia) to put sth BEFORE sth

anteproyecto *m* draft; ~ **de ley** bill

anterior *adj* (a) (en el tiempo) previous; **el día** ~
the previous day, the day before; **en épocas** ~**es**
in earlier times; ~ A **algo** prior TO sth (b) (en un
orden) previous, preceding; **el capítulo** ~ **a este**
the previous chapter (c) (en el espacio) front
(before n); **la parte** ~ the front (part); **las patas**
~**es** the forelegs *o* front legs

anterioridad *f* (frml) anteriority (frml); **con** ~
(antes) before, previously; (con antelación)
beforehand, in advance; **con** ~ **a algo** before sth,
prior to sth

antes *adv* ① (a) (con anterioridad) before; **lo**
compré el día ~ I bought it the day before; **lo** ~
posible as soon as possible (b) (más temprano)
earlier; **no pude llegar** ~ I couldn't arrive earlier
(c) (en locs) antes de before; ~ **de Jesucristo**
before Christ, BC; **no van a llegar** ~ **de dos horas**
they won't be here for two hours; **le daré la**
respuesta ~ **de una semana** I will give you my
reply within a week; ~ **de lo esperado** earlier
than expected; ~ DE **hacer algo** before doing sth;
~ **(de) que me olvide** before I forget; **no se lo des**
~ **(de) que yo lo vea** don't give it to him until
I've seen it (d) (en el espacio) before
② (en tiempos pasados) before, in the past; **ya no**
es el mismo de ~ he's not the same person any
more
③ (a) (indicando orden, prioridad) first; ~ **que nada**
first of all; **yo estaba** ~ I was here first (b)
(indicando preferencia): **¡**~ **me muero!** I'd rather *o*
sooner die!; **cualquier cosa** ~ **que eso** anything
but that

antiabortista *mf* antiabortionist

antiaborto *adj inv* antiabortion (before n)

antiaéreo -rea *adj* antiaircraft (before n)

antialérgico -ca *adj* antiallergenic

antibalas *adj inv* bulletproof

antibiótico *m* antibiotic

anticiclón *m* anticyclone

anticipación *f* (antelación): **con (mucha)** ~
(well) in advance; **con un mes de** ~ a month in
advance

anticipado -da *adj* ‹pago› advance (before n);
‹elecciones› early; **por** ~ in advance

anticipar [A1] *vt* (a) ‹viaje/elecciones› to move
up (AmE), to bring forward (BrE) (b) ‹dinero/
sueldo› to advance; **¿nos podría** ~ **de qué se**
trata? could you give us an idea of what it is
about?
■ **anticiparse** *v pron* (a) «verano/lluvias» to be

o come early (b) (adelantarse): **se anticipó a su**
tiempo he was ahead of his time; **no nos**
anticipemos a los acontecimientos let's not jump
the gun

anticipo *m* (a) (del sueldo, dinero) advance (b)
(pago inicial) down payment

anticoncepción *f* contraception, birth
control

anticonceptivo¹ -va *adj* contraceptive
(before n); **métodos** ~**s** methods of contraception

anticonceptivo² *m* contraceptive

anticongelante *adj/m* antifreeze

anticuado -da *adj* old-fashioned
■ *m,f*: **eres un** ~ you're so old-fashioned

anticuario -ria *m,f* (a) (persona) antique
dealer (b) **anticuario** *m* (tienda) antique shop

anticucho *m* (Bol, Chi, Per) kebab

anticuerpo *m* antibody

antidemocrático -ca *adj* (poco democrático)
undemocratic; (opuesto a la democracia)
antidemocratic

antideportivo -va *adj* unsportsmanlike

antideslizante *adj* ‹superficie/suela› nonslip;
‹neumático/freno› antiskid (before n)

antidisturbios *adj inv* riot (before n)

antídoto *m* antidote

antiestético -ca *adj* unsightly

antifaz *m* mask

antigripal *adj* ‹vacuna› flu (before n)
■ *m* flu remedy

antiguamente *adv* in the past, in the old
days

antigüedad *f* (a) (de monumento, objeto) age;
esas ruinas tienen varios siglos de ~ those ruins
are several centuries old (b) (en el trabajo)
seniority (c) (objeto) antique; **tienda de** ~**es**
antique shop (d) (época): **en la** ~ in ancient times

antiguo -gua *adj* ① (a) (viejo) ‹ciudad/libro›
old; ‹ruinas/civilización› ancient; ‹mueble/
lámpara› antique, old; ‹coche› vintage, old;
‹costumbre/tradición› old; **el A**~ **Testamento** the
Old Testament (b) (veterano) old, long-standing (c)
(en locs) **a la antigua** in an old-fashioned way;
chapado a la antigua old-fashioned; **de** *or* **desde**
antiguo from time immemorial ② ‹delante del n›
(de antes) old (before n), former (before n); **la**
antigua capital del Brasil the former capital of
Brazil ③ (anticuado) old-fashioned

antiguos *mpl*: **los** ~ the ancients

antihéroe *m* antihero

antihigiénico -ca *adj* unhygienic

antiincendios *adj inv* firefighting (before n)

antiinflamatorio *m* anti-inflammatory

antillano -na *adj/m,f* West Indian

Antillas *fpl*: **las** ~ the West Indies

antílope *m* antelope

antimanchas *adj inv* stain-resistant

antimisil *adj* antiballistic (before n)
■ *m* antiballistic missile

antimonárquico -ca *adj* antimonarchical,
antimonarchist (before n)
■ *m,f* antimonarchist

antinatural *adj* unnatural

antioxidante *adj* (Quím) antioxidant (before
n); ‹pintura› antirust (before n)

antipatía f dislike, antipathy; **tomarle ~ a algo/algn** to take a dislike to sth/sb

antipático -ca adj (a) ⟨persona⟩ unpleasant; **¡qué tipo más ~!** what a horrible man! (b) (fam) ⟨tarea⟩: **esto de planchar es de lo más ~** ironing is such a drag (colloq) ▪ m,f: **es un ~** he's really unpleasant

antipatriótico -ca adj unpatriotic

antipedagógico -ca adj pedagogically unsound

antiperspirante m antiperspirant

antípodas fpl: **las ~** the antipodes

antirreglamentario -ria adj (Dep): **una jugada antirreglamentaria** a foul; **estaba en posición antirreglamentaria** (period) he was offside

antirrobo m antitheft device

antisemita adj anti-Semitic ▪ mf anti-Semite

antiséptico m antiseptic

antisocial adj antisocial ▪ mf (Andes period) delinquent

antiterrorista adj antiterrorist (before n)

antítesis f (pl ~) antithesis

antojarse [A1] v pron (+ me/te/le etc): **se me antojó una cerveza** I felt like (having) a beer; **de embarazada se me antojaban las uvas** when I was pregnant, I had a craving for grapes; **hace lo que se le antoja** he does as he pleases; **porque no se me antoja** because I don't feel like it

antojitos mpl (Méx) typical Mexican snacks, usually bought at street stands

antojo m (a) (capricho) whim; **tiene que hacerlo todo a su ~** she has to do everything her own way; **maneja al marido a su ~** she has her husband twisted around her little finger (b) (de embarazada) craving (c) (en la piel) birthmark

antología f anthology; **de ~** (muy bueno) excellent, fantastic (colloq); (muy malo) terrible

antorcha f torch

antro m (local sórdido) dive (colloq); **~ de perdición** den of iniquity

antropología f anthropology

antropólogo -ga m,f anthropologist

anual adj (a) ⟨cuota/asamblea⟩ annual, yearly; ⟨interés/dividendo⟩ annual; **cinco mil euros ~es** five thousand euros a year (b) ⟨planta⟩ annual

anualidad f (inversión) annuity; (cuota anual) annual payment (o subscription etc)

anuario m yearbook

anudar [A1] vt ⟨cordón/corbata⟩ to tie ▪ **anudarse** v pron (refl) ⟨corbata/pañuelo⟩ to tie

anulación f (de contrato, viaje) cancellation; (de matrimonio) annulment; (de sentencia) quashing, overturning; **protestó la ~ del gol** he protested when the goal was disallowed

anular vt (a) ⟨contrato/viaje⟩ to cancel; ⟨matrimonio⟩ to annul; ⟨fallo/sentencia⟩ to quash, overturn; ⟨resultado⟩ to declare ... null and void; ⟨tanto/gol⟩ to disallow (b) ⟨cheque⟩ (destruir) to cancel; (dar orden de no pagar) to stop ▪ m finger ring

anunciador -dora m,f, **anunciante** mf advertiser

anunciar [A1] vt (a) ⟨noticia/decisión⟩ to announce, make ... public; ⟨lluvias/tormentas⟩ to forecast (b) (frml) ⟨persona⟩ to announce (c) ⟨producto⟩ to advertise, promote

anuncio m (a) (de noticia) announcement; (presagio) sign, omen (b) (en periódico) advertisement, ad (colloq); (en televisión) commercial; **~s clasificados** or **por palabras** classified advertisements (pl)

anverso m obverse

anzuelo m hook; **morder** or **tragarse el ~** to swallow o take the bait

añadir [I1] vt to add

añejo -ja adj ⟨vino/queso⟩ mature; ⟨costumbre⟩ old, ancient

añicos mpl: **hacerse ~** to shatter; **tiró el florero y lo hizo ~** he knocked the vase over and smashed it to smithereens

año m [1] (período) year; **los ~s 50** the 50s; **el ~ pasado** last year; **una vez al ~** once a year; **hace ~s que no lo veo** I haven't seen him for o in years; **el ~ de la pera** or **de Maricastaña** (fam): **ese peinado es del ~ de la pera** that hairstyle went out with the ark (colloq), that hairstyle is really old-fashioned; **un disco del ~ de la pera** a record that's really ancient; **~ bisiesto** leap year; **~ fiscal** fiscal year (AmE), tax year (BrE); **~ luz** light year; **A~ Nuevo** New Year
[2] (indicando edad): **soltero, de 30 ~s de edad** single, 30 years old o (frml) 30 years of age; **¿cuántos ~s tienes?** how old are you?; **tengo 14 ~s** I'm 14 (years old); **hoy cumple 29 ~s** she's 29 today; **ya debe de tener sus añitos** he must be getting on (a bit); **quitarse ~s:** **se quita ~s** she's older than she admits o says
[3] (curso) year; **~ académico/escolar** academic/ school year

añoranza f yearning; **siente ~ de** or **por su país** he yearns for his country

añorar [A1] vt ⟨patria/tranquilidad⟩ to yearn for; ⟨persona⟩ to miss

aorta f aorta

apabullante adj ⟨victoria/éxito⟩ resounding (before n), overwhelming; ⟨rapidez/habilidad⟩ incredible, extraordinary; ⟨personalidad⟩ overpowering

apabullar [A1] vt (vencer) to overwhelm, crush; (dejar confuso) to overwhelm

apache adj Apache (before n) ▪ mf Apache

apachurrar [A1] vt (AmL fam) to squash

apacible adj ⟨carácter/persona⟩ calm, placid; ⟨vida⟩ quiet, peaceful; ⟨clima⟩ mild; ⟨mar⟩ calm; ⟨viento⟩ gentle

apaciguar [A16] vt ⟨ánimos⟩ to pacify; ⟨persona⟩ to calm ... down, to pacify ▪ **apaciguarse** v pron ⟨persona⟩ to calm down; «mar» to become calm; «temporal/ viento» to abate, die down

apadrinar [A1] vt ⟨niño⟩ to be godfather/ godparent to; ⟨boda⟩ to act as PADRINO at; ⟨artista/novillero⟩ to sponsor, be patron to; ⟨político/idea/candidatura⟩ to support, back; ⟨barco⟩ to launch, christen

apagado -da adj [1] ⟨persona⟩ [SER] spiritless, lifeless; [ESTAR] subdued [2] (a) ⟨sonido⟩ muffled (b) ⟨color⟩ muted, dull [3] (a) (no encendido): **la** ⋯⋙

televisión/luz está apagada the TV/light is off; **el horno está ~** the oven is switched off; **con el motor ~** with the engine off **(b)** ‹*volcán*› extinct

apagar [A3] *vt* ‹*luz/televisión/motor*› to turn off, switch off; ‹*cigarrillo/fuego*› to put out; ‹*vela/cerilla*› to put out; (soplando) to blow out
■ **apagarse** *v pron* «*luz/fuego/vela*» to go out

apagón *m* power cut, blackout

apalabrar [A1] *vt*: **lo había apalabrado pero no llegué a firmar nada** it was all arranged *o* fixed but I never actually signed anything; **ya tengo apalabrado a un albañil** (fam) I've already fixed up with a builder

apalancar [A2] *vt* **(a)** (para levantar) to jack up (AmE), to lever up (BrE) **(b)** (para abrir) to force open

apalear [A1] *vt* **(a)** ‹*persona/alfombra*› to beat; ‹*árbol*› to beat the branches of **(b)** ‹*arena/carbón*› to shovel

apanar [A1] *vt* (Andes) ▶ EMPANAR

apantallar [A1] *vt* [1] (Méx) (impresionar) to impress [2] (RPl) (abanicar) to fan

apañar [A1] *vt* [1] (fam) ‹*elecciones*› to fix (colloq), to rig [2] (AmS fam) (encubrir) to cover up for
■ **apañarse** *v pron* (Esp fam) ▶ ARREGLARSE 4

apapachar [A1] *vt* (Cu, Méx fam) (abrazar) to cuddle; (acariciar) to stroke, caress

apapacho *m* (Cu, Méx fam) (abrazo) cuddle; (caricia) caress

aparador *m* **(a)** (mueble) sideboard **(b)** (AmL exc CS) (vitrina) store window (AmE), shop window (BrE)

aparato *m* [1] **(a)** (máquina): **uno de esos ~s para hacer pasta** one of those pasta machines; **~s eléctricos** electrical appliances **(b)** (de televisión) set; (de radio) receiver **(c)** (dispositivo) device; **~ ortopédico** surgical appliance; **~ auditivo** hearing aid **(d)** (Odont) *tb* **~** braces (*pl*) **(e)** (teléfono) telephone; **ponerse al ~** to come to the phone [2] (para gimnasia) piece of apparatus; **los ~s** the apparatus, the equipment [3] (fml) (avión) aircraft [4] (estructura, sistema) machine; **el ~ del partido** the party machine; **~ circulatorio/digestivo/respiratorio** circulatory/digestive/respiratory system

aparatoso -sa *adj* ‹*gesto*› flamboyant; ‹*sombrero*› showy, flamboyant; ‹*caída/accidente*› spectacular, dramatic

aparcamiento *m* (Esp) **(a)** (acción) parking **(b)** (lugar — en ciudad) parking lot (AmE), car park (BrE); (— en carretera) rest area *o* stop (AmE), lay-by (BrE)

aparcar [A2] *vt/vi* (Esp) to park; **~ en doble fila** to double-park

aparear [A1] *vt* ‹*animales*› to mate; ‹*objetos*› to match, pair up
■ **aparearse** *v pron* to mate

aparecer [E3] *vi* [1] **(a)** «*síntoma/mancha*» to appear **(b)** ‹*objeto perdido*› to turn up; **hizo ~ un ramo de flores** he produced a bouquet of

flowers **(c)** (en documento) to appear; **mi nombre aparece en la lista** my name appears on the list **(d)** «*revista/libro*» to come out [2] «*persona*» **(a)** (fam) (llegar) to appear, turn up **(b)** (fam) (dejarse ver) to appear, show up (colloq) **(c)** (en película, televisión) to appear
■ **aparecerse** *v pron* **(a)** «*fantasma/aparición*» **~se A** algn to appear TO sb **(b)** (AmL fam) «*persona*» to turn up; **¡no te vuelvas a ~ por aquí!** don't you dare show your face round here again!

aparejar [A1] *vt* ‹*caballos*› (para montar) to saddle; (a carro) to harness

aparejo *m* (de caballo) tack; (de pesca) tackle; (polea) block and tackle

aparentar [A1] *vt* **(a)** (fingir) ‹*indiferencia/interés*› to feign; **quiere ~ que no le importa** he's trying to make out he's not bothered about it **(b)** (parecer): **no aparentas la edad que tienes** you don't look your age
■ **~** *vi* **(a)** «*persona*» to show off; **solo por ~** just for show **(b)** «*regalo/joya*» to look impressive

aparente *adj* [1] (que parece real) ‹*timidez/interés*› apparent (*before n*); **la ~ victoria se tornó en derrota** what had seemed like victory turned into defeat [2] (obvio, palpable) apparent, obvious

apariencia *f* appearance; **un hombre de ~ fuerte** a strong-looking man; **a juzgar por las ~s** judging by appearances; **guardar las ~s** to keep up appearances; **las ~s engañan** appearances can be deceptive

apartado¹ -da *adj* **(a)** ‹*zona/lugar*› isolated **(b)** «*persona*»: **se mantuvo ~ de la vida pública** he stayed out of public life; **vive ~ de la familia** he has little to do with his family

apartado² *m* [1] (Corresp) *tb* **~ de correos** *or* **~ postal** post office box, P.O. Box [2] (de artículo, capítulo) section

apartamento *m* apartment

apartar [A1] *vt* [1] **(a)** (alejar) to move ... away; **sus amigos lo ~on del buen camino** his friends led him astray; **apartó los ojos** he averted his eyes **(b)** ‹*obstáculo*› to move, move ... out of the way **(c)** (fml) (de un cargo) to remove **(d)** (separar) to separate [2] (guardar, reservar) to set aside; **aparta un poco de comida para él** put a bit of food aside for him
■ **apartarse** *v pron* (refl) **(a)** (despejar el camino) to stand aside **(b)** (alejarse, separarse): **apártate de ahí** get/come away from there; **no se aparta de su lado** he never leaves her side; **¡apártate de mi vista!** get out of my sight!; **se apartó de su familia** she drifted away from her family; **nos estamos apartando del tema** we're getting off the subject

aparte *adv* [1] (a un lado, por separado): **pon las verduras ~** put the vegetables to *o* on one side; **¿me lo podría envolver ~?** could you wrap it separately?; **lo llamó ~ y lo reprendió** he called him aside and reprimanded him; **bromas ~** joking aside; **~ de** (excepto) apart from; (además de) as well as; **~ de eso me encuentro bien** apart from that I'm all right; **~ de hacerlos, los diseña** she designs them as well as making them ⟨**2**⟩ (además) as well; (por otra parte) anyway, besides

■ *adj inv:* **esto merece un capítulo ~** this deserves a separate chapter; **es un caso ~** he's a special case

apasionado -da *adj* ⟨*amor/persona*⟩ passionate; ⟨*discurso*⟩ impassioned
■ *m,f* enthusiast

apasionante *adj* ⟨*obra*⟩ exciting, enthralling; ⟨*tema*⟩ fascinating

apasionar [A1] *vi:* **le apasiona la música** she has a passion for music; **no es un tema que me apasione** the subject doesn't exactly fascinate me

apatía *f* apathy

apático -ca *adj* apathetic

apátrida *mf* (a) (sin patria) stateless person (b) (RPI) (que no ama a su país) unpatriotic person

apearse [A1] *v pron* (frml) (bajarse) to get off, alight (frml); **~ DE algo** ⟨*de un tren/caballo/una bicicleta*⟩ to get OFF sth

apechugar [A3] *vi* (fam) to grin and bear it (colloq), to put up with it (colloq); **~ con las consecuencias** to put up with *o* suffer the consequences

apedrear [A1] *vt* (a) (tirar piedras a) to throw stones at (b) (matar a pedradas) to stone (to death)

apego *m* **~ A algo/algn** attachment TO sth/sb; **tenerle ~ a algn/algo** to be attached to sb/sth; **les tiene poco ~ a las cosas materiales** he attaches little importance to material things

apelación *f* appeal

apelar [A1] *vi* (a) (Der) to appeal; **~ ante el Tribunal Supremo** to appeal to the Supreme Court (b) (invocar, recurrir a) **~ A algo/algn** to appeal TO sth/sb

apelativo *m* (a) (sobrenombre) name (b) (Ling) form of address; **un ~ cariñoso** a term of endearment

apellido *m* surname, last name (AmE); **~ de soltera/de casada** maiden/married name

apelmazarse [A4] *v pron* (a) ⟨*arroz/pasta*⟩ to stick together (b) ⟨*colchón/cojín*⟩ to go lumpy; ⟨*lana*⟩ to get *o* become matted

apenar [A1] *vt* to sadden
■ **apenarse** *v pron* ⟨**1**⟩ (entristecerse): **se sintió apenado por su muerte** he was saddened by her death; **se apenó mucho cuando lo supo** he was very upset *o* sad when he learned of it ⟨**2**⟩ (AmL exc CS) (sentir vergüenza) to be embarrassed

apenas *adv* (a) (a duras penas) hardly; **~ podíamos oírlo** we could hardly hear him; **hace ~ dos horas** only two hours ago (b) (no bien): **~ había llegado cuando ...** no sooner had he arrived than ... (c) (Méx, Ven fam) (recién): **~ el lunes la podré ir a ver** I won't be able to go and see her until Monday; **~ va por la página 10** he's only on page 10
■ *conj* (esp AmL) (en cuanto) as soon as

apendejarse [A1] *v pron* (AmL exc CS fam) (volverse estúpido) to go soft in the head (colloq)

apéndice *m* (a) (del intestino) appendix; (de otro miembro) appendage; **lo operaron del ~** his appendix was removed (b) (de texto, documento) appendix

apendicitis *f* appendicitis

apergaminado -da *adj* ⟨*papel*⟩ parchment-like; ⟨*piel*⟩ leathery; ⟨*cara*⟩ wizened

aperitivo *m* (a) (bebida) aperitif; **nos invitaron a tomar el ~** they invited us for drinks before lunch (*o* dinner *etc*) (b) (comida) snack, appetizer

apersonarse [A1] *v pron* (a) (comparecer) to appear (b) (Col) (encargarse) **~ DE algo** to take charge OF sth, take sth in hand (c) (CS, Ven fam) (presentarse) to appear in person

apertura *f* ⟨**1**⟩ (de caja, sobre, cuenta) opening (b) (inauguración) opening; **la sesión de ~** the opening session (c) (de curso, año académico) beginning, start (d) (Fot) aperture ⟨**2**⟩ (actitud abierta) openness; (proceso) opening-up

apestado -da *adj* (a) (con la peste): **gente apestada** plague victims (b) ⟨*lugar*⟩: **~ de turistas** crawling *o* infested with tourists

apestar [A1] *vi* (fam) to stink (colloq); **~ A algo** to stink *o* reek OF sth (colloq)
■ **~** *vt* (fam) to stink out (colloq)

apetecer [E3] *vi* (esp Esp): **me apetece un helado/pasear** I feel like an ice-cream/going for a walk; **haz lo que te apetezca** do whatever you like

apetecible *adj* ⟨*manjar*⟩ appetizing, mouthwatering; ⟨*puesto*⟩ desirable

apetito *m* appetite; **no tengo ~** I don't feel hungry, I'm not hungry; **tiene buen ~** he has a good appetite; **esta caminata me ha abierto el ~** this walk has given me an appetite

apetitoso -sa *adj* ⟨*plato/manjar*⟩ appetizing, mouthwatering

apiadarse [A1] *v pron* **~ DE algn** to take pity ON sb

apiario *m* (AmL) apiary

apicultura *f* beekeeping, apiculture (tech)

apilar [A1] *vt* to pile up, put ... into a pile

apiñarse [A1] *v pron* «*gente*» to crowd together

apio *m* celery

apiolarse [A1] *v pron* (RPI fam) to wise up (colloq)

apisonadora *f* road roller, steamroller

apisonar [A1] *vt* (con apisonadora) to roll, steamroll; (con pisón) to tamp

aplacar [A2] *vt* (a) ⟨*ira*⟩ to soothe; **supo ~ los ánimos** she was able to calm people down (b) ⟨*sed*⟩ to quench; ⟨*hambre*⟩ to satisfy; ⟨*dolor*⟩ to soothe

aplanadora *f* (AmL) road roller, steamroller

aplanar [A1] *vt* (con niveladora) to level; (con apisonadora) to roll

aplastante *adj* ⟨*mayoría*⟩ overwhelming; ⟨*victoria/derrota*⟩ overwhelming, crushing; ⟨*lógica*⟩ devastating

aplastar [A1] *vt* ⟨**1**⟩ (a) (algo blando) to squash; (algo duro) to crush (b) (hacer puré) ⟨*plátanos/papas*⟩ to mash ⟨**2**⟩ (a) ⟨*rebelión*⟩ to crush, quash (b) ⟨*rival*⟩ to crush, overwhelm; (moralmente) to devastate

aplaudir [I1] *vt* to applaud
■ **~** *vi* to applaud, clap

aplauso *m* (a) (ovación) applause; **un ~ para ...** ⋯⋗

a round of applause for ...; **fuertes ~s** loud applause **(b)** (elogio) praise; **ser digno de ~** to be commendable *o* praiseworthy

aplazamiento *m* **(a)** (de reunión — antes de iniciarse) postponement; (— una vez iniciada) adjournment **(b)** (de pago) deferment

aplazar [A4] *vt* **1 (a)** ⟨viaje⟩ to postpone, put off **(b)** ⟨juicio/reunión⟩ (antes de iniciarse) to postpone; (una vez iniciado) to adjourn **(c)** ⟨pago⟩ to defer **2** (RPl, Ven) ⟨estudiante⟩ to fail

aplazo *m* (RPl) fail

aplicable *adj* applicable

aplicación *f* **1 (a)** (frml) (de crema) application (frml); (de pintura, barniz) coat, application (frml) **(b)** (de sanción) imposition; (de técnica, método) application; (de plan, medida) implementation **2** (uso práctico) application, use **3** (Col, Ven) (solicitud) application **4** (Inf) application

aplicado -da *adj* ⟨ciencias/tecnología⟩ applied (*before n*); ⟨estudiante⟩ diligent, hard-working

aplicar [A2] *vt* **1** (frml) ⟨pomada/maquillaje/barniz⟩ to apply (frml) **2** ⟨sanción⟩ to impose; ⟨descuento⟩ to allow; **el acuerdo se aplica solo a los afiliados** the agreement only applies to members **3** ⟨método/sistema⟩ to put into practice
■ **~** *vi* (Col, Ven) to apply; **~ a un puesto/una beca** to apply for a job/a scholarship
■ **aplicarse** *v pron* to apply oneself

aplique, appliqué *m* **(a)** (lámpara) wall light **(b)** (adorno — en mueble) overlay; (— en prenda) appliqué

aplomo *m* composure

apocado -da *adj* **(a)** [SER] (de poco carácter) timid **(b)** [ESTAR] (deprimido) depressed, down (colloq)

apocalipsis *m* apocalypse

apocarse [A2] *v pron:* **se apocó** she lost all her self-confidence; **no se apoca ante** *or* **por nada** nothing intimidates *o* daunts him

apócope *f or m* apocope; (vocablo) apocopated form

apodar [A1] *vt* to nickname, call

apoderado -da *m,f* **(a)** (Der) proxy, representative; **nombrar a algn ~** to give sb power of attorney **(b)** (de deportista) agent, manager

apoderarse [A1] *v pron* **~ DE algo** ⟨de ciudad/fortaleza⟩ to seize sth, take sth; **se apoderó del control de la empresa** he took control of the company

apodo *m* nickname

apogeo *m* height

apolillado -da *adj* ⟨ropa⟩ moth-eaten; ⟨madera⟩ worm-eaten; ⟨ideas⟩ antiquated, fusty

apolillarse [A1] *v pron* ⟨ropa⟩ to get moth-eaten; ⟨madera⟩ to get infested with woodworm

apolítico -ca *adj* apolitical

apología *f* apologia (frml); **hizo ~ del terrorismo** he made a statement (*o* speech *etc*) justifying terrorism

apoltronarse [A1] *v pron* (en asiento) to settle oneself

aporrear [A1] *vt* ⟨puerta/mesa⟩ to bang *o* hammer on; ⟨persona⟩ (fam) to beat

aportación *f* **(a)** (contribución) contribution **(b)** (de socio) investment

aportar [A1] *vt* **(a)** (contribuir) ⟨dinero/tiempo/idea⟩ to contribute **(b)** ⟨socio⟩ to invest
■ **~** *vi* (RPl) (a la seguridad social) to pay contributions

aporte *m* **(a)** (esp AmL) ▶ APORTACIÓN **(b)** (RPl) (a la seguridad social) social security contribution, ≈National Insurance contribution (*in UK*)

aposento *m* (arc *o* hum) (habitación) chamber (dated)

apostar [A10] *vt* to bet; **te apuesto una cerveza** I bet you a beer; **~ algo POR algo/algn** to bet sth ON sth/sb
■ **~** *vi* to bet; **~ a las carreras** to bet on the horses; **te apuesto (a) que gana** I bet (you) he wins
■ **apostarse** *v pron* **(a)** (recípr): **se ~on una comida** they bet a meal on it **(b)** (enf) to bet

apóstol *m* (Relig) apostle

apostolado *m* (Relig) ministry, preaching

apostólico -ca *adj* apostolic

apóstrofo *m* apostrophe

apoteósico -ca *adj* tremendous

apoteosis *f* **(a)** (exaltación) apotheosis; **cuando salió en escena aquello fue la ~** (fam) the audience went wild when she came on stage (colloq) **(b)** (Teatr) finale

apoyabrazos *m* (*pl* **~**) armrest

apoyacabezas *m* (*pl* **~**) headrest

apoyar [A1] *vt* **1** (hacer descansar) **~ ⟨algo EN algo⟩** to rest (sth ON sth); **apóyalo contra la pared** lean it against the wall **2 (a)** ⟨respaldar⟩ ⟨propuesta/persona⟩ to back, support **(b)** ⟨teoría⟩ to support, bear out
■ **apoyarse** *v pron* **1** (para sostenerse, descansar) **~se EN algo** to lean ON sth **2** (basarse, fundarse) **~se EN algo** to be based ON sth

apoyo *m* support; **~ A algo** support FOR sth

apreciable *adj* ⟨cambio/mejoría⟩ appreciable, substantial; ⟨suma/cantidad⟩ considerable, substantial

apreciación *f* **1 (a)** (percepción, enfoque) interpretation **(b)** (juicio) appraisal, assessment **2** (aprecio, valoración) appreciation; **~ musical** musical appreciation

apreciado -da *adj* ⟨amigo⟩ valued; **su piel es muy apreciada** its fur is highly prized

apreciar [A1] *vt* **1** ⟨persona⟩ to be fond of **2** ⟨interés/ayuda/arte⟩ to appreciate **3** (percibir, observar) to see; **para ~ la magnitud de los daños** in order to appreciate the extent of the damage

aprecio *m* (estima) esteem; **siente gran ~ por él** she holds him in great esteem; **goza del ~ de sus compañeros** she is highly regarded by her colleagues

apremiante *adj* ⟨necesidad⟩ pressing, urgent

apremiar [A1] *vt* (presionar): **me están apremiando para que lo termine** they are putting pressure on me to get it finished; **estamos apremiados de tiempo** we are pushed for *o* short of time
■ **~** *vi* to be urgent; **el tiempo apremia** time is getting on *o* is pressing

aprender [E1] *vi/vt* to learn; **~ A hacer algo** to learn to do sth

■ **aprenderse** v pron (enf) ⟨lección/parte⟩ to learn; **me la aprendí de memoria** I learnt it by heart

aprendiz -diza m,f apprentice, trainee; **es ~ de mecánico** he's an apprentice mechanic

aprendizaje m (a) (proceso) learning (b) (periodo como aprendiz) apprenticeship, training period

aprensión f (a) (preocupación, miedo) apprehension (b) (asco) squeamishness; **me da ~ ver sangre** I get squeamish at the sight of blood

aprensivo -va adj: **es muy ~** he's such a worrier

apresar [A1] vt (a) ⟨nave⟩ to seize, arrest; ⟨delincuente⟩ to capture, catch (b) «animal» ⟨presa⟩ to capture, catch

aprestarse [A1] v pron (refl) **~se PARA algo/ A hacer algo** to prepare o get ready FOR sth/to do sth

apresurado -da adj (a) ⟨despedida⟩ quick, hurried; ⟨visita⟩ rushed, hurried (b) ⟨decisión⟩ rushed, hasty; ⟨respuesta/comentario⟩ hasty

apresurar [A1] vt (a) (meter prisa a) to hurry (b) (acelerar) ⟨proceso/cambio⟩ to speed up; ⟨paso⟩ to quicken

■ **apresurarse** v pron: **¡apresúrate!** hurry up!; **no nos apresuremos demasiado** let's not be hasty; **se apresuró a defenderla** he hastened o rushed to her defense

apretado -da adj **1** (a) (ajustado) tight; **me queda muy ~** it is too tight for me (b) (sin dinero): **andamos** or **estamos algo ~s** we're a little short of money (colloq) (c) (apretujado) cramped **2** ⟨calendario/programa⟩ tight; ⟨victoria⟩ narrow **3** (fam) (tacaño) tight (colloq), tightfisted (colloq)

apretar [A5] vt **1** (a) ⟨botón⟩ to press, push; ⟨acelerador⟩ to put one's foot on, press; ⟨gatillo⟩ to pull, squeeze (b) ⟨nudo/tapa/tornillo⟩ to tighten; ⟨puño/mandíbulas⟩ to clench; **apreté los dientes** I gritted my teeth **2** (a) (apretujar): **apretó al niño contra su pecho** he clasped o clutched the child to his breast; **me apretó el brazo con fuerza** he squeezed o gripped my arm firmly (b) (presionar) to put pressure on

■ **~** vi **1** «ropa/zapatos» (+ me/te/le etc) to be too tight; **el vestido le aprieta** the dress is too tight for her **2** (hacer presión) to press down (o in etc)

■ **apretarse** v pron to squeeze o squash together

apretón m (abrazo) hug; **se dieron un ~ de manos** they shook hands

apretujado -da adj cramped; **tuvimos que comer todos ~s** we had to eat all squashed together round the table

apretujar [A1] vt (fam): **no me apretujes, que me haces daño** don't squeeze me so hard, you're hurting me; **me ~on mucho en el tren** I got squashed on the train

■ **apretujarse** v pron to squash o squeeze together

aprieta, aprietas, etc ▶ APRETAR

aprieto m ▶ APURO 2

aprisa adv ▶ DEPRISA

aprisionar [A1] vt to trap

aprobación f (de proyecto de ley, moción) passing; (de préstamo, acuerdo, plan) approval, endorsement; (de actuación, conducta) approval

aprobado m (Educ) pass

aprobar [A10] vt **1** ⟨proyecto de ley/moción⟩ to pass; ⟨préstamo/acuerdo/plan⟩ to approve, sanction; ⟨actuación/conducta⟩ to approve of **2** (Educ) to pass

■ **~** vi «estudiante» to pass

aprontar [A1] v pron (CS) (refl) to get ready

apropiado -da adj suitable; **el discurso fue muy ~ a la ocasión** the speech was very fitting for the occasion; **no era el momento ~** it wasn't the right moment

apropiarse [A1] v pron **~ (de) algo** to take o (frml) appropriate sth

aprovechable adj usable

aprovechado -da adj **1** (oportunista) opportunistic; **no seas ~** don't take advantage (of the situation) **2** ⟨estudiante⟩ hardworking

■ m,f opportunist

aprovechar [A1] vt (a) ⟨tiempo/espacio/ talento⟩ to make the most of; **dinero/tiempo bien aprovechado** money/time well spent; **es espacio mal aprovechado** it's a waste of space (b) ⟨oportunidad⟩ to take advantage of; **aprovecho la ocasión para decirles que ...** I would like to take this opportunity to tell you that ... (c) (usar) to use; **no tira nada, todo lo aprovecha** she doesn't throw anything away, she makes use of everything

■ **~** vi: **aproveché para venir a verte** I thought I'd take the opportunity to come and see you; **¡que aproveche!** enjoy your meal, bon appétit; **aprovechen ahora, que son jóvenes** make the most of it now, while you're young

■ **aprovecharse** v pron (a) (abusar) **~se DE algo/algn** to take advantage OF sth/sb, to exploit sth/sb (b) (abusar sexualmente) **~se DE algn** ⟨de una mujer⟩ to take advantage OF sb; ⟨de un niño⟩ to abuse sb

aprovisionar [A1] vt ⟨buque/tropas⟩ to provision, to supply ... with provisions

■ **aprovisionarse** v pron **~se DE algo** to stock up WITH sth

aproximado -da adj ⟨cálculo/traducción/idea⟩ rough (before n); ⟨costo/velocidad⟩ estimated (before n)

aproximar [A1] vt (a) (acercar): **aproximó la mesa a la ventana** he moved (o brought etc) the table over to the window (b) ⟨países⟩ to bring ... closer together

■ **aproximarse** v pron (a) (acercarse) «fecha/ persona/vehículo» to approach; **se aproximó a mí** she came up to me (b) **~se A algo** ⟨a la realidad/ una cifra⟩ to come close to sth

aprueba, apruebas, etc ▶ APROBAR

aptitud f flair; **tener ~ para los idiomas** to have a flair for languages; **carece de ~es para el ballet** she shows no talent for ballet

apto -ta adj [SER] **~ PARA algo** suitable FOR sth; **no es ~ para el cargo** he's not suitable o right for the job; **~ para el servicio militar** fit for military service; **no ~ para el consumo** not fit for consumption

apuesta f bet; **le hice una ~** I had a bet with him

apuesta, apuestas, etc ▶ APOSTAR

apuesto -ta adj (liter) ⟨hombre/figura⟩ handsome

apunamiento *m* (AmS) altitude *o* mountain sickness

apunarse [A1] *v pron* (AmS) to get altitude *o* mountain sickness

apuntalar [A1] *vt* ⟨*edificio/túnel*⟩ to shore up, brace; ⟨*cimientos*⟩ to underpin

apuntar [A1] *vt* **1** **(a)** (tomar nota de) to make a note of, note down **(b)** (para excursión, actividad) to put ... down
2 (señalar, indicar) to point at; **no la apuntes con el dedo** don't point (your finger) at her
■ ~ *vi* **(a)** (con arma) to aim; **preparen ... apunten ... ¡fuego!** ready ... take aim ... fire!; **le apuntó con una pistola** she pointed/aimed a gun at him **(b)** (indicar, señalar) to point
■ **apuntarse** *v pron* **(a)** (inscribirse) ~**se A** *or* **EN algo** ⟨*a curso*⟩ to enroll* ON sth; ⟨*a clase*⟩ to sign up FOR sth; **me apunté para ir a la excursión** I put my name down for the outing; ~**se al paro** (Esp) to register as unemployed, to sign on (BrE colloq) **(b)** (obtener) ⟨*tanto*⟩ to score; ⟨*victoria*⟩ to chalk up, achieve

apunte *m* **1** **(a)** (nota) note **(b)** **apuntes** *mpl* (Educ) notes (*pl*); (texto preparado) handout; **tomar** *or* (CS) **sacar** ~**s** to take notes **2** **(a)** (Art) sketch; (Lit) outline **(b)** (AmL) (Teatr, TV) sketch **3** (Com) entry

apuñalar [A1] *vt* to stab

apurado -da *adj* **1** (avergonzado) embarrassed **2** (AmL) (con prisa) in a hurry; **andaba** ~ he was in a hurry; **a las apuradas** (RPl fam) in a rush **3** (en apuros): **se vio muy** ~ **para contestar las preguntas** he was hard put to answer the questions; **si te encuentras** ~, **dímelo** if you run into any difficulties, let me know **4** **(a)** (agobiado) ~ **de trabajo** overwhelmed with work **(b)** (escaso) ~ DE **algo** ⟨*de dinero/tiempo*⟩ short OF sth

apurar [A1] *vt* **1** ⟨*copa/botella*⟩: **apuró la cerveza y se fue** he finished (off) his beer and left **2** (meter prisa): **nos están apurando para que lo terminemos** they're pushing us to finish it; **no me apures** (AmL) don't hurry *o* rush me
■ ~ *vi* (Chi) (+ *me/te/le etc*) (urgir): **no me apura** I'm not in a hurry for it
■ **apurarse** *v pron* **1** (preocuparse) to worry **2** (AmL) (darse prisa) to hurry; **¡apúrate!** hurry up!

apuro *m* **1** (vergüenza): **¡qué** ~! how embarrassing!; **me daba** ~ **pedirle dinero** I was too embarrassed to ask him for money **2** (aprieto, dificultad) predicament; **estar/verse en** ~**s** to be/find oneself in a predicament *o* tight spot; **me sacó del** ~ he got me out of trouble; **me puso en un** ~ she put me in a real predicament; **pasaron muchos** ~**s** they had an uphill struggle *o* they went through a lot **3** (AmL) (prisa) rush; **esto tiene** ~ this is urgent

aquel, aquella *adj dem* (*pl* **aquellos, aquellas**) that; (*pl*) those

aquél, aquélla *pron dem* (*pl* **aquéllos, aquéllas**) [The written accent may be omitted when there is no risk of confusion with the adjective] **(a)** (refiriéndose a cosa) that one; (*pl*) those; **ese no,** ~ *or* **aquel** not that one, the *o* that other one **(b)** (refiriéndose a persona): **todo** ~ *or* **aquel que lo necesite** (frml) anyone *o* (frml) any person needing it; **el cuento de** ~ *or* **aquel que ...** the story about the man who ...

aquello *pron dem* (*neutro*) **¿qué es** ~ **que se ve allá?** what's that over there?; ~ **que te dije el otro día** what I told you the other day

aquí *adv* **1** (en el espacio) here; **está** ~ **dentro** it's in here; ~ **mismo** right here; **no soy de** ~ I'm not from these parts *o* from around here; **pase por** ~ come this way; **viven por** ~ they live around here; **el agua me llegaba hasta** ~ the water came up to here; **dando vueltas de** ~ **para allá** going to and fro *o* from one place to another **2** (en el tiempo): **de** ~ **al 2015** from now until 2015; **de** ~ **en adelante** from now on; **de** ~ **a un año** a year from now

ara *f* ‡ (altar) altar; (piedra consagrada) altar stone

árabe *adj* **(a)** ⟨*país/plato*⟩ Arab; ⟨*escritura/manuscritos*⟩ Arabic **(b)** (Hist) (de Arabia) Arabian; (de los moros) Moorish
■ *mf* **(a)** (de país árabe) Arab **(b)** (Hist) (de Arabia) Arabian; (moro) Moor
■ *m* (idioma) Arabic

Arabia Saudí, Arabia Saudita *f* Saudi Arabia

arado *m* plow* (AmE), plough (BrE)

arancel *m* (tarifa) tariff; (impuesto) duty

arancelario -ria *adj* ⟨*derecho/tarifa/barrera*⟩ customs (*before n*)

arandela *f* washer

araña *f* (Zool) spider

arañar [A1] *vt/vi* to scratch

arañazo *m* scratch

arar [A1] *vt/vi* to plow (AmE), to plough (BrE)

araucano -na *adj/m,f* Araucanian

arbitraje *m* **(a)** (en fútbol, boxeo) refereeing; (en tenis, béisbol) umpiring **(b)** (Der, Rels Labs) (acción) arbitration; (resolución) decision, judgment

arbitrar [A1] *vt/vi* **(a)** (en fútbol, boxeo) to referee; (en tenis, béisbol) to umpire **(b)** (en conflicto, disputa) to arbitrate

arbitrario -ria *adj* arbitrary

árbitro -tra *m,f* **(a)** (en fútbol, boxeo) referee; (en tenis, béisbol) umpire; **los** ~**s de la moda** the arbiters of fashion **(b)** (en conflicto) arbitrator

árbol *m* (Bot) tree; ~ **de Navidad** *or* (Andes) **de Pascua** Christmas tree; ~ **genealógico** family tree; **los** ~**es no dejan ver el bosque** you can't see the forest (AmE) *o* (BrE) wood for the trees

arbolado -da *adj* ⟨*terreno*⟩ wooded; ⟨*calle*⟩ tree-lined (*before n*)

arboleda *f* grove

arbusto *m* shrub, bush

arca *f* ‡ **1** (cofre) chest; **el A**~ **de Noé** Noah's Ark **2 arcas** *fpl* (de institución) coffers (*pl*)

arcada f 1 (Med): **tener ~s** to retch; **me provocó ~s** it made me retch 2 (Arquit) arcade; (de puente) arch

arcaico -ca adj archaic

arcángel m archangel

arce m maple

arcén m shoulder (AmE), hard shoulder (BrE)

archidiócesis f (pl ~) archdiocese

archiduque -quesa m,f (m) archduke; (f) archduchess

archipiélago m archipelago

archivador m (mueble) filing cabinet; (carpeta) ring binder, file

archivar [A1] vt ‹documentos› to file; ‹investigación/asunto› (por un tiempo) to shelve; (para siempre) to close the file on

archivo m (a) (local) archive; (conjunto de documentos) tb ~s archives (pl), archive; **los ~s de la policía** the police files o records (b) (Inf) file

arcilla f clay

arco m 1 (Arquit) arch; (Anat) arch; (Mat) arc; ~ **de triunfo** triumphal arch; ~ **iris** rainbow 2 (AmL) (en fútbol) goal 3 (a) (Arm, Dep) bow (b) (de violín) bow

arcón m large chest

arder [E1] vi 1 (quemarse) to burn 2 (estar muy caliente) to be boiling (hot); **estar que arde** «persona» to be fuming; **la cosa está que arde** things have reached boiling point 3 (escocer) «herida/ojos» to sting, smart

ardid m trick, ruse

ardiente adj ‹defensor› ardent; ‹deseo› ardent, burning; ‹amante› passionate

ardilla f squirrel

ardor m (dolor) burning; (escozor) smarting; ~ **de estómago** heartburn

ardoroso -sa adj ardent

arduo -dua adj arduous

área f⁺ area; ~ **chica** or **pequeña** goal area; ~ **de castigo** penalty area; ~ **de servicio** service area, services (pl)

arena f 1 (Const, Geol) sand; ~ **movediza** quicksand 2 (palestra) arena; **en la ~ política** in the political arena

arenoso -sa adj ‹playa/terreno› sandy

arenque m herring; ~ **ahumado** kipper

arepa f: cornmeal roll

arete m (Col, Méx) earring

argamasa f mortar

Argel m Algiers

Argelia f Algeria

argelino -na adj/m,f Algerian

Argentina f: tb **la ~** Argentina

argentino -na adj ‹gobierno/presidente› Argentine (before n); ‹escritor/música› Argentinian
■ m,f Argentinian

argolla f ring; ~ **de compromiso/de matrimonio** (AmL) engagement/wedding ring; **tener ~** (AmC fam) to have contacts (colloq)

argot m (pl **-gots**) slang

argüendero -ra m,f (Méx fam) gossip

argumentación f line of argument (frml)

argumentar [A1] vt to argue

argumento m (a) (razón) argument (b) (Cin, Lit) plot, story line

aria f⁺ aria

aridez f aridity, dryness

árido -da adj arid, dry

Aries m (signo, constelación) Aries; **es (de) ~** she's an Aries o an Arian
■ mf (pl ~) (persona) tb **aries** Aries, person born under (the sign of) Aries

arisco -ca adj (a) [SER] (huraño) ‹persona› unfriendly, unsociable; ‹animal› unfriendly (b) [ESTAR] (Méx fam) (enojado) upset, angry

arista f (Mat) edge; (de viga) arris; (de bóveda) groin; (en montañismo) arête, ridge

aristocracia f aristocracy

aristócrata mf aristocrat

aristocrático -ca adj aristocratic

aritmética f arithmetic

aritmético -ca adj arithmetic

arma f⁺ (a) (Arm, Mil) weapon; ~ **nuclear** nuclear weapon; ~ **blanca** any sharp instrument used as a weapon; ~ **de fuego** firearm; **deponer las ~s** to lay down one's arms; **tomar (las) ~s** to take up arms; **no llevaba ~s** he wasn't carrying a weapon; **de ~s tomar** formidable; **ser un ~ de doble filo** to be a double-edged sword (b) (instrumento, medio) weapon

armada f navy

armadillo m armadillo

armado -da adj ‹lucha/persona› armed; ~ **DE** or **CON algo** armed WITH sth

armador -dora m,f shipowner

armadura f 1 (Hist, Mil) armor* 2 (Const) framework

armamentista adj arms (before n)

armamento m armaments (pl)

armar [A1] vt 1 (a) (Mil) ‹ciudadanos/país› to arm, supply … with arms (b) (equipar) ‹embarcación› to fit out, equip 2 (a) ‹estantería/reloj› to assemble; ‹tienda/carpa› to pitch, put up (b) (AmL) ‹rompecabezas› to do, piece together (c) (Col, RPl) ‹cigarro› to roll 3 (fam) ‹alboroto/ruido/lío› to make; ~ **jaleo** to kick up o make a racket (colloq); ~ **un escándalo** to kick up a fuss; ~**la** (fam): **¡buena la has armado!** you've really done it now! (colloq); **la que me armó porque llegué tarde** you should have seen the way he went on because I was late
■ **armarse** v pron 1 (a) (Mil) to arm oneself (b) ~**se DE algo** ‹de armas/herramientas› to arm oneself WITH sth; ~**se de paciencia** to be patient; ~**se de valor** to pluck up courage 2 (a) (fam) «pelea/discusión» to break out; **¡qué jaleo se armó!** there was a real commotion (b) (fam) «persona»: **me armé un lío/una confusión** I got into a mess (colloq)

armario m (a) (para ropa — mueble) wardrobe; (— empotrado) closet (AmE), wardrobe (BrE) (b) (de cocina) cupboard; (de cuarto de baño) cabinet

armatoste m (fam) huge great thing (colloq)

armazón m or f 1 (Const) skeleton; (de avión) airframe; (de barco, mueble) frame; (de gafas) frames (pl) 2 (de obra literaria) framework, outline

Armenia f Armenia

armenio¹ -nia adj/m,f Armenian

armenio² m (idioma) Armenian

armisticio *m* armistice

armonía *f* harmony

armónica *f* harmonica, mouth organ

armónico -ca *adj* **(a)** (Mús) harmonic **(b)** (armonioso) harmonious

armonioso -sa *adj* harmonious

armonizar [A4] *vt* **(a)** (Mús) to harmonize **(b)** ‹*tendencias/opiniones*› to reconcile, harmonize; ‹*diferencias*› to reconcile
■ ~ *vi* «*estilos/colores*» to blend in, harmonize; ~ CON algo «*color/estilo*» to blend (in) WITH sth

arnés *m* (para niño) baby reins (*pl*); (Dep) harness; (arreos) harness

aro *m* **(a)** (Jueg) hoop **(b)** (Arg, Chi) (para el lóbulo) earring; (en forma de aro) hooped earring **(c)** (de servilleta) napkin ring

aroma *m* (de flores) scent, perfume; (del café, de hierbas) aroma; (del vino) bouquet

aromaterapia *f* aromatherapy

aromático -ca *adj* aromatic

arpa *f*⚥ harp

arpegio *m* arpeggio

arpillera *f* sacking, hessian, burlap (AmE)

arpista *mf* harpist

arpón *m* harpoon; ~ **submarino** speargun

arquear [A1] *vt* ‹*espalda*› to arch; ‹*cejas*› to raise, arch; ‹*estante*› to bow, bend
■ **arquearse** *v pron* ‹*estante*› to sag, bend; «*persona*» to arch one's back

arqueología *f* archaeology

arqueológico -ca *adj* archaeological

arqueólogo -ga *m,f* archaeologist

arquero *m* **1** (Hist, Mil) archer **2** (AmL) (en fútbol) goalkeeper

arquetipo *m* archetype

arquitecto -ta *m,f* architect

arquitectónico -ca *adj* architectural

arquitectura *f* architecture

arrabal *m* poor quarter *o* area

arraigado -da *adj* ‹*costumbre*› deeply rooted, deep-rooted; ‹*vicio*› deeply entrenched

arraigar [A3] *vi* «*costumbre*» to become rooted, take root; «*vicio*» to become entrenched; «*planta*» to take root
■ **arraigarse** *v pron* «*costumbres/ideas*» to take root; «*persona*» to settle

arrancar [A2] *vt* **1** ‹*hoja de papel*› to tear out; ‹*etiqueta*› to tear off; ‹*botón/venda*› to pull off; ‹*planta*› to pull up; ‹*flor*› to pick; ‹*diente/pelo*› to pull out; **le arrancó el bolso** he snatched her bag **2** ‹*confesión/declaración*› to extract **3** ‹*motor/coche*› to start
■ ~ *vi* «*motor/vehículo*» to start
■ **arrancarse** *v pron* **1** (*refl*) ‹*pelo/diente*› to pull out; ‹*piel/botón*› to pull off **2** (Chi fam) (huir) to run away

arranque *m* **(a)** (Auto, Mec) starting mechanism; **tengo problemas con el** ~ I have problems starting the car **(b)** (arrebato) ~ DE algo fit *o* sth

arrasar [A1] *vi* ~ CON algn ‹*con contrincante*› to demolish sb; ‹*con enemigo*› to destroy sb; **nuestro equipo volvió a** ~ our team swept to victory again; ~ CON algo: **la inundación arrasó** **con las cosechas** the flood devastated the crops; ~**on con toda la comida** they polished off all the food (colloq)
■ ~ *vt* ‹*zona*› to devastate; ‹*edificio*› to destroy

arrastrar [A1] *vt* **1** **(a)** (por el suelo) to drag **(b)** ‹*remolque/caravana*› to tow **(c)** (llevar consigo): **arrastró todo a su paso** it swept away everything in its path; **la corriente lo arrastraba mar adentro** the current was carrying him out to sea **2** ‹*problema/enfermedad*›: **arrastra esa tos desde el invierno** that cough of hers has been dragging on since the winter; **vienen arrastrando el problema desde hace años** they've been dragging out the problem for years **(b)** (atraer) to draw; **se dejan** ~ **por la moda** they are slaves to fashion
■ ~ *vi* ‹*mantel/cortina*› to trail along the ground
■ **arrastrarse** *v pron* **(a)** (por el suelo) «*persona*» to crawl; «*culebra*» to slither **(b)** (humillarse) to grovel, crawl

arrastre *m* **(a)** (acción) dragging; **estar para el** ~ (fam) to be done in (colloq) **(b)** (CS fam) (atractivo) appeal

arre *interj* (a un caballo) gee up!, giddy up!

arrear [A1] *vt* **(a)** ‹*ganado*› to drive, herd; ‹*caballerías*› to spur, urge on **(b)** (AmL fam) ‹*gente*› to chivy* (colloq), to hurry ... along **(c)** (AmL fam) (llevar) ~ CON algo/algn to cart sth/sb off (colloq)

arrebatador -dora *adj* ‹*belleza*› breathtaking; ‹*sonrisa*› dazzling; ‹*mirada*› captivating

arrebatar [A1] *vt* (quitar) to snatch

arrebato *m* **(a)** (arranque) ~ DE algo fit OF sth; **le dio un** ~ he flew into a rage **(b)** (éxtasis) ecstasy, rapture

arrechar [A1] *vt* **(a)** (AmL vulg) (excitar sexualmente) to turn ... on (colloq) **(b)** (AmL fam) (enojar) to bug (colloq)
■ **arrecharse** *v pron* **(a)** (AmL vulg) (sexualmente) «*persona*» to get horny (sl); «*animal*» to come in (AmE) *o* (BrE) on heat **(b)** (AmL fam) (enfurecerse) to get furious

arrecho -cha *adj* **1** **(a)** (AmL vulg) (sexualmente excitado) ‹*persona*› horny (sl), turned-on (colloq); ‹*animal*› in heat (AmE), on heat (BrE) **(b)** (Col, Ven fam) (valiente) gutsy (colloq) **2** (AmL fam) (enojado) furious, mad (AmE colloq) **3** (AmC, Ven fam) (difícil) tough

arrecife *m* reef

arreglado -da *adj* **1** **(a)** (limpio, ordenado) tidy **(b)** (ataviado) smartly turned out, smart **2** (AmL fam) ‹*partido/elecciones*› fixed (colloq)

arreglar [A1] *vt* **1** ‹*aparato/reloj*› to mend, fix; ‹*zapatos*› to mend, repair; ‹*falda/vestido*› to alter; ‹*calle*› to repair; **el dentista me está arreglando la boca** the dentist is fixing my teeth (colloq); **esto te** ~**á el estómago** (fam) this'll sort your stomach out (colloq) **2** **(a)** ‹*casa/habitación*› (ordenar) to straighten up, to tidy (up) (BrE); (hacer arreglos en) to do up (colloq) **(b)** (preparar, organizar): **ve arreglando a los niños ¿quieres?** can you start getting the children ready?; **tengo todo arreglado para el viaje** I've got everything ready for the trip; **un amigo me está arreglando los papeles** a friend is sorting out the papers for me; ~ **una entrevista** to arrange an interview **(c)** (disponer) ⟨*flores/muebles*⟩ to arrange

3 (solucionar) ⟨*situación*⟩ to sort out; ⟨*asunto*⟩ to settle, sort out; **lo quiso ~ diciendo que …** she tried to put things right by saying that …

■ **arreglarse** *v pron* **1** (*refl*) (ataviarse): **tarda horas en ~se** she takes hours to get ready; **no te arregles tanto** you don't need to get so dressed up; **sabe ~se** she knows how to make herself look good

2 ⟨*pelo/manos*⟩ **(a)** (*refl*) to do **(b)** (*caus*): **tengo que ir a ~me el pelo** I must go and have my hair done

3 (solucionarse) «*situación/asunto*» to get sorted out

4 (fam) (amañarse): **ya me ~é para volver a casa** I'll make my own way home; **la casa es pequeña pero nos arreglamos** it's a small house, but we manage; **arreglárselas** (fam) to manage; **no sé cómo se las arreglan** I don't know how they manage; **arréglatelas como puedas** sort *o* work it out as best you can; **ya me las ~é** I'll manage, I'll be OK

5 «*día/tiempo*» to get better, clear up

arreglo *m* **1 (a)** (reparación) repair; **hacerle ~s a algo** to carry out repairs on sth; **la casa necesita algunos ~s** the house needs some work done on it; **no tiene ~** «*reloj/máquina*» it's beyond repair; «*persona*» he/she is a hopeless case **(b)** (de ropa) alteration **(c)** (Mús) *tb* ~ **musical** musical arrangement **2** (acuerdo) arrangement, agreement

arrellanarse [A1] *v pron*: **se arrellanó en el sofá** he settled himself into the sofa

arremangarse [A3] *v pron* ▶ REMANGARSE

arremeter [E1] *vi* (embestir) to charge; (atacar) to attack; ~ **CONTRA algo/algn** (acometer) to charge AT sth/sb; (atacar, criticar) to attack sth/sb

arremolinarse [A1] *v pron* ⟨*agua/hojas*⟩ to swirl; «*personas/animales*» to mill around

arrendador -dora *m,f* (*m*) landlord, lessor (frml); (*f*) landlady, lessor (frml)

arrendamiento *m* **(a)** (de casa) renting, letting (BrE); (de tierras, local) renting, leasing; **contrato de ~** tenancy agreement **(b)** (de otra cosa — por el propietario) renting (out); (— por el que la recibe) renting **(c)** (precio — de casa, local) rent; (— de otra cosa) rental

arrendar [A5] *vt* **1** (Der) **(a)** (dar en arriendo) ⟨*casa*⟩ to rent (out), let (BrE); ⟨*local/tierras*⟩ to rent (out), lease **(b)** (tomar en arriendo) ⟨*casa*⟩ to rent; ⟨*local/tierras*⟩ to rent, lease **(c)** (contratar) ⟨*servicios*⟩ to hire **2** (Andes) ⟨*coche/bicicleta*⟩ (dar en arriendo) to rent (out); (tomar en arriendo) to rent (AmE), to hire (BrE); **❾ se arriendan coches** cars for rent (AmE), car hire (BrE)

arrendatario -ria *m,f* (de propiedad) lessee, tenant; (de contrata) contractor

arrepentido -da *adj* ⟨*pecador*⟩ repentant; **estaba ~ de lo que había hecho** he was sorry for *o* feeling remorse for what he had done; **estoy ~ de haberlo dicho** I regret having said it

arrepentimiento *m* remorse, repentance

arrepentirse [I11] *v pron* **(a)** (lamentar) to be

sorry; ~ **DE algo** to regret sth; ~ **DE hacer algo** to regret doing sth **(b)** (cambiar de idea) to change one's mind

arrepienta, arrepintió, etc ▶
ARREPENTIRSE

arrestar [A1] *vt* to arrest

arresto *m* (Der, Mil) **(a)** (detención) arrest; **bajo ~** under arrest **(b)** (prisión) detention

arriar [A17] *vt* ⟨*bandera/vela*⟩ to lower

arriba *adv* **1 (a)** (lugar, parte): **ahí/aquí ~** up there/here; **en el estante de ~** (el siguiente) on the shelf above; (el último) on the top shelf; **ponlo un poco más ~** put it a little higher up; **la parte de ~** the top (part); ~ **del ropero** (AmL) on top of the wardrobe; ~ **de la cocina está el baño** (AmL) the bathroom is above the kitchen; **de ~ abajo: me miró de ~ abajo** he looked me up and down; **limpiar la casa de ~ abajo** to clean the house from top to bottom **(b)** (en edificio) upstairs; **los vecinos de ~** the people upstairs **(c)** (en escala, jerarquía) above; **órdenes de ~** orders from above; **las puntuaciones de 80 para ~** scores of 80 or over

2 (expresando dirección, movimiento): **corrió escaleras ~** he ran upstairs; **calle ~** up the street; **miró hacia ~** he looked up

3 (en interjecciones) **(a)** (expresando aprobación): **¡~ la democracia!** long live democracy! **(b)** (expresando estímulo) come on!; (llamando a levantarse) get up!

arribista *adj* socially ambitious
■ *mf* arriviste, social climber

arriendo *m* (esp Andes) ▶ ARRENDAMIENTO

arriesgado -da *adj* ⟨*acción/empresa*⟩ risky, hazardous; ⟨*persona*⟩ brave, daring

arriesgar [A3] *vt* **(a)** ⟨*vida/dinero*⟩ to risk **(b)** ⟨*opinión*⟩ to venture
■ **arriesgarse** *v pron*: **¿nos arriesgamos?** shall we risk it *o* take a chance?; **~se a hacer algo** to risk doing sth

arrimar [A1] *vt* (acercar) to move/bring … closer; **arrimó la cama a** *or* **contra la pared** he pushed *o* moved the bed up against the wall
■ **arrimarse** *v pron* **1** (*refl*) (acercarse): **se arrimó mucho a la orilla** he went too close to the edge; **arrímate al fuego** come (up) closer to the fire; **se arrimó a** *or* **contra la pared** he moved up against the wall; **~se A algn** to move closer TO sb; (buscando calor, abrigo) to snuggle up TO sb **2** (Méx, Ven fam) (en casa de algn): **se ~on en mi casa** they came to live *o* stay with me, they dumped themselves on me (pey)

arrinconado -da *adj* **(a)** (bloqueado) blocked in, boxed in **(b)** (acorralado, acosado) cornered **(c)** (arrumbado) lying around

arrinconar [A1] *vt* **(a)** (poner en rincón) to put … in a corner **(b)** (acosar, acorralar) to corner **(c)** (marginar) to exclude **(d)** (arrumbar) to leave, dump (colloq)

arrocero -ra *adj* ⟨*cultivo/producción*⟩ rice (*before n*); ⟨*región*⟩ rice-growing (*before n*)
■ *m,f* rice grower

arrodillarse [A1] *v pron* to kneel (down)

arrogancia *f* arrogance; **con ~** arrogantly

arrogante *adj* arrogant, haughty

arrojar [A1] *vt* **1 (a)** (tirar) to throw; (AV)   ···⟶

⟨bomba⟩ to drop **(b)** ⟨lava⟩ to spew (out); ⟨humo⟩ to belch out; ⟨luz⟩ to shed **2** (vomitar) to bring up, throw up

■ **arrojarse** v pron (refl) to throw oneself; ~se SOBRE algo/algn «persona» to throw oneself ONTO sth/sb; «perro/tigre» to pounce ON sth/sb

arrollador -dora adj **(a)** ⟨éxito/mayoría/ victoria⟩ overwhelming **(b)** ⟨fuerza/ataque⟩ devastating **(c)** ⟨personalidad/elocuencia⟩ overpowering

arrollar [A1] vt **(a)** «vehículo» to run over; «muchedumbre/agua/viento» to sweep o carry away **(b)** (derrotar, vencer) to crush, overwhelm

arropar [A1] vt ⟨niño/enfermo⟩ (abrigar) to wrap ... up; (en la cama) to tuck ... in

■ **arroparse** v pron (abrigarse) to wrap up warm; (en la cama) to pull the covers up

arroyo m **(a)** (riachuelo) stream **(b)** (cuneta) gutter **(c)** (AmC) (torrentera) gully **(d)** (Méx) (Auto) slow lane

arroz m rice; ~ a la cubana rice with fried egg, plantain and tomato sauce; ~ con leche rice pudding; ~ integral brown rice

arrozal m ricefield, paddy

arruga f (en piel) wrinkle, line; (en tela, papel) crease

arrugado -da adj ⟨persona/manos/piel⟩ wrinkled; ⟨ropa⟩ wrinkled (AmE), creased (BrE); ⟨papel⟩ crumpled

arrugar [A3] vt ⟨piel⟩ to wrinkle; ⟨tela⟩ to wrinkle (AmE), to crease (BrE); ⟨papel⟩ to crumple; ⟨ceño⟩ to knit; ⟨nariz⟩ to wrinkle; ⟨cara⟩ to screw up; **arrugó el entrecejo** he frowned

■ **arrugarse** v pron **(a)** «persona/piel» to become wrinkled **(b)** (por acción del agua) «piel/ manos» to shrivel up, go wrinkled **(c)** «tela» to wrinkle o get wrinkled (AmE), to crease o get creased (BrE); «papel» to crumple

arruinar [A1] vt to ruin

■ **arruinarse** v pron to be ruined

arrullo m (de palomas) cooing; (para adormecer) lullaby

arrumbar [A1] vt ▶ ARRINCONAR C, D

arsenal m **(a)** (Mil) arsenal; un ~ de datos a mine of information **(b)** (Esp) (Náut) navy yard (AmE), naval dockyard (BrE)

arsénico m arsenic

arte (gen m en el singular y f en el plural) **1** (Art) art; **el ~ por el ~** art for art's sake; **no trabajo por amor al ~** (hum) I'm not working for the good of my health (hum); ~s gráficas graphic arts; (como) por ~ de magia as if by magic **2** (habilidad, destreza) art; **el ~ de la conversación** the art of conversation; **tiene ~ para arreglar flores** she has a flair o gift for flower arranging

artefacto m (instrumento) artifact; (dispositivo) device; ~s de baño (CS) bathroom fixtures (pl), sanitary ware (frml); **un raro ~** a contraption

arteria f artery

arterial adj arterial

artesa f trough

artesanal adj: de fabricación ~ ⟨muebles⟩ handcrafted; ⟨queso⟩ farmhouse; **productos** ~es handicrafts, craftwork

artesanía f **(a)** (actividad) handicraft; **una ~** a piece of craftwork; **objetos de ~** craftwork, handicrafts **(b)** **artesanías** fpl (AmL) (productos) crafts (pl), craftwork; **mercado de ~s** craft market

artesano -na m,f (m) craftsman, artisan; (f) craftswoman, artisan

ártico -ca adj Arctic

Ártico m: **el ~** (región) the Arctic; (océano) the Arctic Ocean

articulación f **1** **(a)** (Anat, Mec) joint **(b)** (organización) organization, coordination **2** (Ling) articulation

articulado -da adj articulated

articular [A1] vt (Tec, Ling) to articulate

articulista mf feature writer, columnist

artículo m **1** (Com): ~s del hogar/de consumo household/consumer goods; ~ de primera necesidad essential item, essential; ~s de escritorio stationery; ~s de tocador toiletries; ~s de punto knitwear **2** **(a)** (en periódico, revista) article; ~ de fondo editorial, leader (BrE) **(b)** (de ley) article **3** (Ling) article

artífice mf **(a)** (responsable, autor): **fue el ~ del secuestro** he planned the kidnapping; **el ~ de esta victoria** the architect of this victory **(b)** (artista) (m) craftsman, artisan; (f) craftswoman, artisan

artificial adj ⟨flor/satélite/sonrisa⟩ artificial; ⟨fibra⟩ man-made, artificial

artificio m **(a)** (artimaña) trick, artful device **(b)** (afectación) affectation **(c)** (artilugio) device

artillería f artillery

artilugio m **(a)** (aparato) device, contraption **(b)** **artilugios** mpl (de oficio) equipment

artimaña f trick

artista mf **(a)** (Arte) artist **(b)** (actor) actor; (actriz) actress; (cantante, músico) artist; **una ~ de cine** a movie star (AmE) o (BrE) film star

artístico -ca adj artistic

artritis f arthritis

arveja f (AmL) pea

arvejilla, arverjilla f (RPl) sweet pea

arzobispado m archbishopric

arzobispal adj ⟨sede/comisión⟩ archiepiscopal (frml)

arzobispo m archbishop

as m ace

asa f‡ (asidero) handle

asadera f (RPl) roasting pan o dish o tin

asadero m (Coc) griddle

asado¹ -da adj **1** **(a)** ⟨carne/pollo⟩ (en horno) roast (before n); (con espetón) spit-roast (before n); (a la parrilla) barbecued, grilled **(b)** ⟨castaña/papa⟩ roast (before n); ⟨papa con piel⟩ baked **2** (fam) [ESTAR] (acalorado) roasting (colloq)

asado² *m* **(a)** (al horno) roast; ~ **de cordero** roast lamb **(b)** (AmL) (a la parrilla) barbecued meat **(c)** (AmL) (reunión) barbecue

asador¹ *m* (espetón) spit; (aparato — de espetones) rotisserie; (— de parrilla) barbecue

asador² -dora *m,f* (RPl) cook (*person who cooks the meat at a barbecue*)

asalariado -da *adj* wage-earning (*before n*)
■ *m,f* wage *o* salary earner

asaltante *mf* **(a)** (ladrón) robber **(b)** (atacante) attacker; **los ~s de la embajada** those who stormed the embassy

asaltar [A1] *vt* **(a)** (atracar) ⟨banco/tienda⟩ to hold up, rob; ⟨persona⟩ to rob, mug **(b)** (tomar por asalto) ⟨ciudad/embajada⟩ to storm **(c)** (atacar) to attack, assault **(d)** «idea» to strike; **me asaltó una duda** I was struck *o* seized by a sudden doubt

asalto *m* ⟦1⟧ **(a)** (atraco — a banco, tienda) holdup, robbery; (— a persona) mugging; **un ~ a mano armada** an armed robbery *o* raid **(b)** (ataque) attack, assault; **tomar algo por ~** to take sth by storm ⟦2⟧ (en boxeo) round; (en esgrima) bout

asamblea *f* **(a)** (reunión) meeting **(b)** (cuerpo) assembly

asar [A1] *vt* **(a)** ⟨carne/pollo⟩ (en horno) to roast; (a la parrilla) to grill; (con espetón) to spit-roast **(b)** ⟨castaña/papa⟩ to roast; ⟨papa con piel⟩ to bake
■ **asarse** *v pron* **(a)** (en horno) to roast **(b)** (fam) (de calor) to roast (colloq)

asbesto *m* asbestos

ascendencia *f* **(a)** (linaje) descent, ancestry; **es de ~ francesa** he is of French descent **(b)** (origen) origin(s); **su ~ humilde** her humble origins

ascendente *adj* ⟨movimiento/tendencia⟩ upward; ⟨astro/marea⟩ rising

ascender [E8] *vi* ⟦1⟧ (frml) «temperatura/precios» to rise; «globo» to rise, ascend (frml); «escalador/alpinista» to climb, to ascend (frml) ⟦2⟧ (frml) «gastos/pérdidas» ~ **A algo** to amount TO sth ⟦3⟧ «empleado/oficial» to be promoted; **ascendió rápidamente en su carrera** he advanced rapidly in his career; ~ **al trono** to ascend the throne
■ ~ *vt* «empleado/oficial» to promote

ascendiente *mf* (antepasado) ancestor

Ascensión *f*: **la ~** the Ascension

ascenso *m* **(a)** (de temperatura, precios) rise **(b)** (a montaña) ascent; **una industria en ~** a growing industry **(c)** (de empleado, equipo, oficial) promotion

ascensor *m* elevator (AmE), lift (BrE)

ascensorista *mf* elevator operator (AmE), lift attendant (BrE)

asco *m* **(a)** (repugnancia): **¡qué ~!** how revolting!, how disgusting!; **me dio ~** it made me feel sick; **poner cara de ~** to make *o* (BrE) pull a face; **tanta corrupción da ~** all this corruption is sickening **(b)** (fam) (cosa repugnante, molesta): **tienen la casa que es un ~** their house is like a pigsty; **el parque está hecho un ~** the park is in a real state (colloq); **¡qué ~ de tiempo!** what foul *o* lousy weather!

ascua *f*‡ ember; **estar en/tener a algn en ~s** (fam) to be on/to keep sb on tenterhooks

aseado -da *adj* (limpio) clean; (arreglado) neat, tidy

asear [A1] *vt* (limpiar) to clean; (arreglar) to straighten (up), to tidy up (BrE)
■ **asearse** *v pron* (refl) (lavarse) to wash; (arreglarse) to straighten *o* (BrE) tidy oneself up

asediar [A1] *vt* **(a)** (Mil) ⟨ciudad⟩ to lay siege to, besiege; ⟨ejército⟩ to surround, besiege **(b)** (acosar) ⟨persona⟩ to besiege

asegurado -da *adj* insured; **tengo el coche ~ a todo riesgo** I have fully comprehensive insurance for the car
■ *m,f* (persona que contrata el seguro) policy-holder; (persona asegurada): **el ~/la asegurada** the insured

asegurador -dora *adj* ⟨compañía⟩ insurance (*before n*)
■ *mf* **(a)** (persona) insurer **(b)** **aseguradora** *f* (compañía) insurance company

asegurar [A1] *vt* ⟦1⟧ **(a)** (prometer) to assure; **te lo aseguro** I assure you; **asegura no haberlo visto** she maintains that she did not see **(b)** (garantizar) ⟨funcionamiento/servicio⟩ to guarantee ⟦2⟧ (Com, Fin) ⟨persona/casa⟩ to insure; **aseguró el coche a todo riesgo** she took out fully comprehensive insurance for *o* on the car ⟦3⟧ **(a)** (sujetar, fijar) ⟨puerta/estante⟩ to secure **(b)** ⟨edificio/entrada⟩ to secure, make ... secure
■ **asegurarse** *v pron* ⟦1⟧ **(a)** (cerciorarse) to make sure **(b)** (garantizarse, procurarse): **con ese gol se ~on el triunfo** by scoring that goal they guaranteed themselves victory ⟦2⟧ (Com, Fin) to insure oneself

asemejar [A1] *vt* **(a)** (hacer parecido) to make ... (look) like **(b)** (comparar) to compare, liken
■ **asemejarse** *v pron* «personas» to be *o* look alike; «objetos» to be similar; **~se A algo/algn** to resemble sth/sb, look like sth/sb

asentado -da *adj* **(a)** [ESTAR] (situado): **el pueblo está ~ a orillas de un río** the village lies *o* is situated on the banks of a river **(b)** [ESTAR] (establecido) ⟨creencia/tradición⟩ deep-rooted, deeply rooted; ⟨persona⟩ settled (in) **(c)** [SER] (esp AmL) (maduro, juicioso) mature

asentamiento *m* settlement

asentar [A5] *vt* ⟦1⟧ ⟨campamento⟩ to set up; ⟨damnificados/refugiados⟩ to place ⟦2⟧ **(a)** ⟨objeto⟩ to place carefully (*o* firmly *etc*) **(b)** ⟨conocimientos/postura⟩ to consolidate ⟦3⟧ (Com, Fin) to enter
■ **asentarse** *v pron* ⟦1⟧ «café/polvo/terreno» to settle ⟦2⟧ (estar situado) «ciudad/edificio» to be situated, be built ⟦3⟧ **(a)** (establecerse) to settle **(b)** (esp AmL) (adquirir madurez) to settle down

asentir [I11] *vi* to agree, consent; **asintió con la cabeza** she nodded

aseo *m* (limpieza) cleanliness; ~ **personal** personal hygiene; Ⓢ **aseos** rest room (AmE), toilets (BrE)

asequible *adj* ⟨precio⟩ affordable, reasonable; ⟨meta⟩ attainable, achievable; ⟨proyecto⟩ feasible; ⟨persona⟩ approachable; ⟨obra/estilo⟩ accessible

aserradero *m* sawmill

aserrar [A5] *vt* to saw

aserrín *m* (esp AmL) sawdust

aserrío *m* (Col, Ec) sawmill

aserruchar [A1] *vt* (Chi) to saw

asesinar [A1] *vt* to murder; (por razones políticas) to assassinate

asesinato *m* murder; (por razones políticas) assassination

asesino -na *adj* ⟨instinto/odio⟩ murderous, homicidal; ⟨animal⟩ killer (*before n*)
■ *m,f* murderer; (por razones políticas) assassin; ∼ **a sueldo** hired killer; ∼ **en serie** serial killer

asesor -sora *adj* ⟨consejo⟩ advisory; ⟨arquitecto/ingeniero⟩ consultant (*before n*)
■ *m,f* advisor*, consultant

asesoramiento *m* advice

asesorar [A1] *vt* to advise
■ **asesorarse** *v pron* ∼**se CON algn** to consult sb

asesoría *f* consultancy; ∼ **fiscal/jurídica** tax/legal consultancy

asestar [A1] *vt*: **me asestó una puñalada/un puñetazo** he stabbed/punched me

asexuado -da *adj* asexual

asfaltado -da *adj* asphalt (*before n*), asphalted

asfaltar [A1] *vt* to asphalt

asfalto *m* asphalt

asfixia *f* (a) (Med) asphyxia, suffocation (b) (fam) (agobio) suffocation

asfixiante *adj* (a) ⟨gas/humo⟩ asphyxiating (*before n*) (b) (fam) ⟨calor⟩ suffocating, stifling; ⟨ambiente/relación⟩ oppressive, stifling

asfixiar [A1] *vt* (a) (ahogar) to asphyxiate, suffocate; **murió asfixiado** he died of asphyxiation *o* suffocation (b) (agobiar) to suffocate, stifle
■ **asfixiarse** *v pron* (a) (ahogarse) to be asphyxiated, to suffocate; (por obstrucción de la tráquea) to choke to death; **me asfixiaba de calor** (fam) I was suffocating in the heat (b) (fam) (agobiarse) to suffocate, feel stifled

así¹ *adj inv* like that; **no seas ∼** don't be like that; **con gente ∼ yo no me meto** I don't mix with people like that; **yo soy ∼** that's the way I am; **∼ es la vida** (fr hecha) that's life; **es un tanto ∼ de hojas** it's about that many pages; **esperamos horas ¿no es ∼?** we waited for hours, didn't we?; **tanto es ∼ que ...** so much so that ...

así² *adv* [1] (de este modo) like this; (de ese modo) like that; **¿por qué me tratas ∼?** why are you treating me like this?; **no le hables ∼** don't talk to him like that; **¡∼ cualquiera!** that's cheating! (colloq & hum); **∼ es como pasó** this is how it happens; **no te pongas ∼** don't get so worked up; **∼ me podré comprar lo que quiera** that way I'll be able to buy whatever I want; **∼ es** that's right; **¿está bien ∼ o quieres más?** is that enough, or do you want some more?; **y ∼ sucesivamente** and so on
[2] **¡∼ de fácil!** it's as easy as that; **∼ de alto/grueso** this high/thick
[3] (en locs) **así así** (fam) so-so; **así como así** just like that; **¡así me gusta!** (fr hecha) that's what I like to see!; **así nomás** (AmL) just like that; **así pues** so; **así que** (por lo tanto) so; **así y todo** even so; **por así decirlo** so to speak

Asia *f⁺* Asia

asiático -ca *adj/m,f* Asian, Asiatic

asidero *m* (a) (asa) handle (b) (punto de sujeción) hand (hold); **sin ∼s en la realidad** with no grip on reality

asiduo -dua *adj* (a) (persistente) ⟨estudiante/lector⟩ assiduous; ⟨admirador⟩ devoted (b) (frecuente) ⟨cliente⟩ regular, frequent
■ *m,f* regular

asiento *m* [1] (a) (para sentarse) seat; ∼ **anatómico** anatomically designed seat; **por favor, tome ∼** (frml) please take a seat (frml) (b) (de bicicleta) saddle (c) (de silla) seat (d) (base, estabilidad) base [2] (en contabilidad) entry

asignación *f* [1] (a) (de tarea, función) assignment (b) (de fondos, renta) allocation, assignment [2] (sueldo) wages (pl); (paga) allowance [3] (AmC) (Educ) homework

asignar [A1] *vt* (a) (dar, adjudicar) ⟨renta/función/tarea⟩ to assign; ⟨valor⟩ to ascribe; ⟨fondos/parcela⟩ to allocate; **me ∼on la vacante** I was appointed to the post; **le ∼on una beca** he was awarded a grant (b) (destinar) ⟨persona⟩ to assign; ∼ **a algn A algo** to assign sb TO sth

asignatura *f* subject; ∼ **pendiente** (Educ) subject which one has to retake; (asunto sin resolver) unresolved matter

asilado -da *m,f* inmate; ∼ **político** political refugee (*who has been granted asylum*)

asilar [A1] *vt* (a) (acoger) ⟨anciano/huérfano⟩ to take ... into care; ⟨refugiado⟩ to grant ... asylum (b) (internar) to put ... in a home
■ **asilarse** *v pron* «anciano/huérfano» to take refuge; «refugiado» to seek asylum

asilo *m* [1] (Servs Socs) home, institution; (para vagabundos, mujeres maltratadas) shelter; ∼ **de ancianos** *or* **de la tercera edad** old people's home [2] (Pol) asylum; **pedir ∼ político** to seek political asylum

asimétrico -ca *adj* asymmetric

asimilación *f* assimilation

asimilar [A1] *vt* [1] ⟨alimentos/ideas/cultura⟩ to assimilate [2] (en boxeo) ⟨golpes⟩ to take, soak up (colloq)

asimismo *adv* (a) (también) also (b) (igualmente) likewise

asir [I10] *vt* (liter) to seize, grasp; ∼ **a algn DE** *or* **POR algo: la asió de un brazo** he seized *o* grasped her arm
■ **asirse** *v pron* (liter) ∼**se DE** *or* **A algo: se asió a la cuerda** she grabbed (hold of) *o* seized the rope; **caminaban asidos de la mano** they walked hand in hand

asistencia *f* [1] (presencia) attendance; ∼ **A algo** attendance AT sth [2] (frml) (ayuda) assistance; **prestarle ∼ a algn** to give sb assistance; ∼ **en carretera** breakdown service; ∼ **médica** (servicio) medical care; (atención médica) medical attention; ∼ **pública** (en CS) municipal health service (*esp for emergencies*); ∼ **técnica** after-sales service [3] (Dep) assist

asistencial *adj* welfare (*before n*)

asistenta *f* (Esp) cleaning lady *o* woman

asistente *mf* [1] (ayudante) assistant; ∼ **social** social worker [2] (frml) **los ∼s** (a una reunión) those present; (a un espectáculo) the audience

asistido -da *adj* assisted

asistir [I1] *vi* (estar presente) ∼ **A algo** ⟨a reunión/acto/clases⟩ to attend sth; **asistió a una sola clase** he only came/went to one class; ∼ **a misa** to go *o* attend Mass
■ ∼ *vt* (frml) (ayudar): **en el consulado lo ∼án** you will receive assistance at the consulate (frml); ∼ **a los pobres** to care for the poor

asma *f⁺* asthma

asmático -ca *adj/m,f* asthmatic

asno m (Zool) donkey; (tonto) (fam) dimwit (colloq)

asociación f association; ~ **de ideas** association of ideas

asociado -da adj associate (before n)
■ m,f (Com) associate; (de club, asociación) member

asociar [A1] vt ‹ideas/palabras› to associate; ~ **algo/a algn CON algo/algn** to associate sth/sb WITH sth/sb; **no logro ~la con nada** I can't place her
■ **asociarse** v pron (a) «empresas/comerciantes» to collaborate; **~se CON algn** to go into partnership WITH sb (b) «hechos/factores» to combine (c) (a grupo, club) **~se A algo** to become a member OF sth

asolar [A1 or A10] vt «guerra/huracán/sequía» to devastate

asoleada f (Andes) (de una persona): **pegarse una ~** (fam) to sunbathe

asoleado -da adj sunny

asolear [A1] vt (exponer al sol) ‹ropa› to hang ... out in the sun; ‹uvas› to dry ... in the sun
■ **asolearse** v pron (AmL) to sunbathe

asomar [A1] vi to show; **empiezan a ~ los primeros brotes** the first shoots begin to show o appear
■ ~ vt ‹cabeza›: **asomó la cabeza por la ventanilla** she stuck her head out of the window; **abrió la puerta y asomó la cabeza** she opened the door and stuck her head out/in
■ **asomarse** v pron: **~se POR algo** to lean out OF sth; **se asomó a la ventana** she looked out of the window; **se ~on al balcón** they came out onto the balcony

asombrar [A1] vt to amaze, astonish; **me asombró su reacción** I was astonished o taken aback by his reaction
■ **asombrarse** v pron to be astonished o amazed; **se asombró con los resultados** she was amazed o astonished at the results; **yo ya no me asombro por nada** nothing surprises me any more

asombro m astonishment; **no salía de su ~** he couldn't get over his surprise

asombroso -sa adj amazing, astonishing

asonante adj assonant

asorocharse [A1] v pron (a) (Chi, Per) (por la altura) to get mountain o altitude sickness (b) (Chi) (por calor, vergüenza) to flush

aspa f⁎ (de molino) sail; (de ventilador) blade; (cruz) cross

aspaviento m: **deja de hacer ~s** stop getting in such a flap

aspecto m ① (a) (de persona, lugar) look, appearance; **un hombre de ~ distinguido** a distinguished-looking man; **¿qué ~ tiene?** what does he look like?; **a juzgar por su ~** judging by the look of her; **tiene mal ~** «persona» she doesn't look well; «cosa» it doesn't look nice (b) (de problema, asunto): **no me gusta el ~ que van tomando las cosas** I don't like the way things are going o looking ② (rasgo, faceta) aspect; **en ese ~ tienes razón** in that respect you're right

aspereza f ① (a) (de superficie, piel) roughness (b) (de sabor) sharpness; (de voz, clima) harshness ② (parte áspera): **usar papel de lija para quitar las ~s** use sandpaper to remove any roughness; **limar ~s** to smooth things over

áspero -ra adj ① ‹superficie/piel› rough; ‹tela› coarse ② (a) ‹sabor› sharp (b) ‹voz/sonido/clima› harsh ③ (a) (en el trato) abrupt, surly (b) ‹discusión› acrimonious

aspersor m sprinkler

aspiración f ① (deseo, ambición) aspiration ② (Fisiol) inhalation; (Ling) aspiration; (Mús) breath

aspiradora f, **aspirador** m (electrodoméstico) vacuum cleaner; **pasé la ~ por la habitación** I vacuumed o (BrE) hoovered the bedroom

aspirante mf: **las ~s al título** the contenders for the title; **ocho ~s al puesto de redactor** eight candidates o applicants for the post of editor

aspirar [A1] vi ① (desear, pretender) **~ A algo/hacer algo** to aspire TO sth/do sth ② (a) ‹aparato› to suck up (b) (Fisiol) to breathe in (c) (AmL) (pasar la aspiradora) to vacuum, hoover (BrE)
■ ~ vt (a) ‹aparato› to suck up o in; ‹aspiradora› to pick up (b) (Fisiol) to inhale (c) (Ling) to aspirate

aspirina f aspirin

asqueante adj sickening, nauseating

asquear [A1] vt (dar asco a) to sicken; (aburrir, hartar): **está asqueado de todo** he's fed up with everything (colloq)

asqueroso -sa adj ① (a) ‹libro/película› disgusting, filthy (b) ‹olor/comida/costumbre› disgusting, revolting (c) (sucio) filthy ② (lascivo): **¡viejo ~!** you dirty old man!

asquiento -ta adj (AmL) ▶ ASQUEROSO 1

asta f⁎ (a) (de bandera) flagpole; **con la bandera a media ~** with the flag at half-mast (b) (cuerno) horn (c) (de lanza, flecha) shaft

astabandera f (Méx) flagpole

asterisco m asterisk

asteroide m asteroid

astigmatismo m astigmatism

astilla f (a) (fragmento) chip; (de madera, hueso) splinter; **se me metió una ~ en el dedo** I have a splinter in my finger (b) **astillas** fpl (para el fuego) kindling

astillarse [A1] v pron «madera/hueso» to splinter; «piedra» to chip

astillero m shipyard

astracán m astrakhan

astringente adj ‹loción› astringent; ‹alimento/medicamento› binding (before n)
■ m astringent

astro m (Astrol, Astron) heavenly body; (Espec) star

astrología f astrology

astrólogo -ga m,f astrologist

astronauta mf astronaut

astronomía f astronomy

astronómico -ca adj astronomical

astrónomo -ma m,f astronomer

astucia f (a) (cualidad — de sagaz) astuteness, shrewdness; (— de ladino) (pey) craftiness, cunning; **la ~ del zorro** the slyness of a fox (b) (ardid) trick, ploy

astuto -ta adj (sagaz) shrewd, astute; (ladino) (pey) crafty, sly, cunning

asueto _m_ time off; **tomarse un día de** ~ to take a day off

asumir [I1] _vt_ **1** (a) ⟨cargo/tarea/responsabilidad⟩ to take on, assume (fml); ⟨riesgo⟩ to take (b) (adoptar) ⟨actitud⟩ to assume (fml) (c) (aceptar) to come to terms with **2** (AmL) (suponer) to assume

asunceno -na, asunceño -ña _adj_ of/from Asunción
■ _m,f_ person from Asunción

Asunción _f_ (Geog) Asunción

asunto _m_ (a) (cuestión, problema) matter; ~s de negocios business matters; ~s exteriores (Esp) foreign affairs; un ~ muy delicado a very delicate matter _o_ issue; está implicado en un ~ de drogas he's mixed up in something to do with drugs; no es ~ mío/tuyo it's none of my/your business (b) (pey) (relación amorosa) affair

asustado -da _adj_ (atemorizado) frightened; (preocupado) worried

asustar [A1] _vt_ to frighten; **me asustó cuando se puso tan serio** he gave me a fright when he went all serious
■ **asustarse** _v pron_ to get frightened; **me asusté cuando vi que no estaba allí** I got a fright _o_ I got worried when I saw he wasn't there; **no se asuste, no es nada grave** there's no need to worry, it's nothing serious

atacante _mf_ attacker, assailant (fml)

atacar [A2] _vt_ to attack

atado _m_ (a) (de ropa) bundle (b) (CS) (de espinacas, zanahorias) bunch; **ser un ~ de nervios** (CS) to be a bundle of nerves (c) (RPl) (de cigarrillos) pack (AmE), packet (BrE)

ataduras _fpl_ ties (_pl_)

atajada _f_ (CS) save

atajador -dora _m,f_ (Méx) (_m_) ballboy; (_f_) ballgirl

atajar [A1] _vt_ **1** (a) (AmL) (agarrar) ⟨pelota⟩ to catch (b) (Esp) (interceptar) ⟨pase/pelota⟩ to intercept **2** (a) ⟨golpe/puñetazo⟩ to parry, block (b) ⟨persona⟩ (agarrar) to stop, catch; (interrumpir, detener) to stop **3** ⟨enfermedad/problema⟩ to keep … in check; ⟨incendio⟩ to contain; ⟨rumor⟩ to quell

atajo _m_ short cut

atañer [E7] _vi_ (en 3ª pers) to concern; **por lo que a mi atañe** as far as I'm concerned

ataque _m_ **1** (a) (Dep, Mil) attack; ~ **aéreo** air strike (b) (verbal) attack **2** (Med) attack; ~ **de asma** asthma attack; ~ **al corazón** heart attack; ~ **epiléptico** epileptic fit; **me dio un ~ de nervios** I got into a panic; **un ~ de risa** a fit of hysterics

atar [A1] _vt_ **1** (a) ⟨caja/paquete⟩ to tie; **le até el pelo con una cinta** I tied her hair back with a ribbon (b) ⟨persona/caballo⟩ to tie … up; ⟨cabra⟩ to tether; **lo ~on de pies y manos** they bound him hand and foot; **ató al perro a un poste** she tied the dog to a lamppost **2** ⟨trabajo/hijos⟩ to tie … down

■ **atarse** _v pron_ (refl) ⟨zapatos/cordones⟩ to tie up, do up; ⟨pelo⟩ to tie up

atarantado -da _adj_ (a) (Col, Méx, Per fam) (por golpe) dazed, stunned (b) (Méx, Per fam) (confundido) in a spin, dazed (c) (Chi fam) (precipitado) harum-scarum (colloq)

atarantar [A1] _vt_ (Col, Méx, Per fam): **con tantas preguntas me ~on** they made my head spin with all their questions; **el golpe lo atarantó** the blow left him dazed
■ **atarantarse** _v pron_ (a) (Col, Méx, Per fam) (aturdirse, confundirse) to get flustered, get in a dither (b) (Chi fam) (precipitarse): **no te atarantes** don't rush into it (colloq)

atardecer¹ [E3] _v impers_ to get dark

atardecer² _m_ dusk; **al** ~ at dusk

atareado -da _adj_ busy

atascar [A2] _vt_ ⟨cañería⟩ to block (b) (Méx) ⟨motor⟩ to stall
■ **atascarse** _v pron_ **1** (a) «cañería/fregadero» to block, get blocked (b) «tráfico» to get snarled up **2** (a) «mecanismo» to jam, seize up (b) (Méx) «motor» to stall

atasco _m_ (a) (de tráfico) traffic jam; (en proceso) holdup, delay (b) (en tubería) blockage

ataúd _m_ coffin

ateísmo _m_ atheism

atemorizar [A4] _vt_ (liter) ⟨persona⟩ to frighten, intimidate; ⟨barrio/población⟩ to terrorize

Atenas _f_ Athens

atención¹ _f_ **1** (a) (concentración) attention; **pon/presta ~ a esto** pay attention to this; **con** ~ attentively (b) **llamar la ~: se viste así para llamar la ~** he dresses like that to attract attention to himself); **una chica que llama la ~** a very striking girl; **me llamó la ~ que estuviera sola** I was surprised she was alone; **llamarle la ~ a algn** (reprenderlo) to reprimand sb (fml), to give sb a talking to **2** (a) (en hotel, tienda) service; ❺ **horario de atención al público** (en banco) hours of business; (en oficina pública) opening hours (b) (cortesía): **nos colmaron de atenciones** we were showered with attention _o_ (BrE) attentions; **no tuvo ninguna ~ con ella a pesar de su hospitalidad** he didn't show the slightest appreciation despite her hospitality

atención² _interj_ (a) (para que se atienda) attention; **¡~, por favor!** (your) attention, please! (b) (para avisar de peligro) look out!, watch out!

atender [E8] _vi_ (a) (prestar atención) to pay attention; ~ **A algo/algn** to pay attention TO sth/sb (b) (cumplir con) ~ **A algo** ⟨a compromisos/gastos/obligaciones⟩ to meet sth (c) (prestar un servicio): **el doctor no atiende los martes** the doctor does not see anyone on Tuesdays; **en esa tienda atienden muy mal** the service is very bad in that store
■ ~ _vt_ **1** (a) ⟨paciente⟩: **¿qué médico la atiende?** which doctor usually sees you?; **los atendieron enseguida en el hospital** they were seen immediately at the hospital; **no tiene quien lo**

atienda he has no one to look after him **(b)** ‹*cliente*› to attend to, see to; (en tienda) to serve; **¿la están atendiendo?** are you being served? **(c)** ‹*asunto*› to deal with; ‹*llamada*› to answer; ‹*demanda*› to meet

2 ‹*consejo/advertencia*› to listen to

■ **atenderse** *v pron* (AmL): **¿con qué médico se atiende?** which doctor usually sees you?

atenerse [E27] *v pron* **(a)** (ajustarse, someterse) ~ **A algo** (a las órdenes) to obey sth; (a las consecuencias) to live WITH *o* abide BY sth; **no sé a qué atenerme** I don't know where I stand **(b)** (limitarse): **si nos atenemos a lo que dijeron ellos** ... if we go by what they said ...; **aténgase a los hechos** confine yourself to the facts

atentado *m* **(a)** (ataque): **un ~ terrorista** a terrorist attack; **un ~ contra el presidente** an assassination attempt on the president **(b)** (afrenta) ~ **CONTRA** *or* **A algo** ‹*a honor/dignidad*› affront TO sth; **un ~ contra la moral** an offense against decency

atentamente *adv* **(a)** ‹*escuchar/mirar*› attentively, carefully **(b)** (amablemente) thoughtfully, kindly; **lo saluda ~** (Corresp) sincerely (AmE), yours faithfully/sincerely (BrE)

atentar [A1] *vi*: **~on contra su vida** they made an attempt on her life; **~ contra la seguridad del Estado** to threaten national security

atento -ta *adj* 1 **(a)** (que presta atención) ‹*alumno/público*› attentive; **estar ~ (A algo)** to pay attention (TO sth) **(b)** (alerta): **estáte ~ y avísame si viene alguien** stay alert and let me know if anyone comes; **estar ~ A algo** to be on the alert FOR sth 2 **(a)** (amable) ‹*esposo/anfitrión/camarero*› attentive; **ser ~ CON algn** to be kind TO sb **(b)** (cortés) courteous

atenuante *adj* extenuating

■ *m or f* mitigating factor, extenuating circumstance

atenuar [A18] *vt* **(a)** (disminuir, moderar) ‹*luz*› to dim; ‹*color*› to tone down; **deberías ~ el tono de tus críticas** you should tone down your criticism **(b)** (Der) ‹*responsabilidad*› to reduce, lessen

ateo, atea *adj* atheistic

■ *m,f* atheist

aterrador -dora *adj* terrifying

aterrar [A1] *vt* ‹*persona*› to terrify; **le aterra la idea** she's terrified at the thought

aterrizaje *m* landing; **un ~ forzoso** an emergency landing

aterrizar [A4] *vi* to land, touch down

aterrorizado -da *adj* terrified

aterrorizar [A4] *vt* to terrorize

atesorar [A1] *vt* ‹*dinero*› to amass

atestado -da *adj* packed, crammed; **~ DE algo** packed *o* crammed full OF sth; **el salón estaba ~ (de gente)** the hall was packed *o* crammed (with people)

atestiguar [A16] *vt* **(a)** (Der) to testify **(b)** (probar) to bear witness to

atiborrar [A1] *vt* **~ algo/a algn DE algo** to stuff sth/sb WITH sth; **atiborrado de gente** packed *o* jam-packed with people

■ **atiborrarse** *v pron* **~se DE algo** to stuff oneself WITH sth

ático *m* **(a)** (apartamento) top-floor apartment *o* (BrE) flat; (de lujo) penthouse; (de techo bajo) garret (AmE), attic flat (BrE) **(b)** (desván) attic, loft (BrE)

atienda, atiendas, etc ▶ ATENDER

atinado -da *adj* ‹*respuesta/comentario*› pertinent, spot-on (colloq); ‹*decisión/medida*› sensible, wise; ‹*solución*› sensible

atinar [A1] *vi*: **~ en el blanco** to hit the target; **¡atinaste!** you're dead right!; **no atiné a decir nada** I couldn't say a word; **~ CON algo** ‹*con solución/respuesta*› to hit ON *o* UPON sth, come up WITH sth; **atinaste con el regalo** the gift you got him/her was perfect; **no atinaba con la calle** I couldn't find the street

atizador *m* poker

atizar [A4] *vt* ‹*fuego*› to poke

Atlántico *m*: **el (océano) ~** the Atlantic (Ocean)

Atlántida *f*: **la ~** Atlantis

atlas *m* (*pl* **~**) atlas

atleta *mf* athlete

atlético -ca *adj* **(a)** ‹*club/competición*› athletics (*before n*) **(b)** ‹*figura*› athletic

atletismo *m* athletics

atmósfera *f* atmosphere

atmosférico -ca *adj* atmospheric

atole *m* (Méx) hot corn *o* maize drink

atolladero *m* **(a)** (lugar cenagoso) mire **(b)** (aprieto, apuro) predicament, awkward situation

atolondrado -da *adj* **(a)** [SER] (impetuoso) rash, impetuous; (despistado) scatterbrained **(b)** [ESTAR] (por golpe) dazed, stunned

■ *m,f* scatterbrain

atolondrar [A1] *vt* **(a)** (confundir) to fluster **(b)** ‹*golpe*› to daze, stun

■ **atolondrarse** *v pron* **(a)** (confundirse) to get flustered **(b)** (precipitarse): **no te atolondres, piénsalo bien** don't rush into it, think it over carefully

atómico -ca *adj* atomic

atomizador *m* spray, atomizer

átomo *m* atom

atónito -ta *adj* astonished, amazed; **se quedó mirándola ~** he stared at her in amazement

atontado -da *adj* (por golpe, asombro) stunned, dazed; (distraído): **contesta, que estás medio ~** answer me, you're in a daze; **ver tb ATONTAR**

atontar [A1] *vt* ‹*golpe*› to stun, daze; **estas pastillas me atontan** these pills make me groggy; **la televisión los atonta** television turns them into vegetables *o* zombies

atorar [A1] *vt* 1 (esp AmL) ‹*cañería*› to block (up) 2 (Méx) (sujetar): **atoramos la puerta con una silla** we jammed the door shut/open with a chair; **atóralo con este alambre** secure it with this bit of wire

■ **atorarse** *v pron* (esp AmL) **(a)** (atragantarse) to choke **(b)** ‹*cañería*› to get blocked; ‹*puerta/cajón*› to jam; (+ *me/te/le etc*) **se me atoró el cierre** my zipper got stuck; **se le atoró el chicle en la garganta** the chewing gum got stuck in her throat

atormentar [A1] *vt* ‹*persona*› (físicamente) to torture; (mentalmente) to torment

■ **atormentarse** *v pron* (*refl*) to torment oneself

atornillar [A1] *vt* to screw on (*o* down *etc*)

atorrante *adj* (a) (Andes, CS fam) (holgazán) lazy; (desaseado) scruffy (b) (Bol, RPI fam) (sinvergüenza) crooked (c) (Col, Per fam) (pesado, cargante): **no seas ~** don't be such a pain in the neck (colloq)
■ *mf* (a) (Andes, CS fam) (vagabundo) tramp; (holgazán) good-for-nothing, layabout; (desaseado) slob (colloq) (b) (Bol, RPI fam) (sinvergüenza): **es un ~** he's a bit of a crook (colloq) (c) (Col, Per fam) (pesado, cargante) pain in the neck (colloq)

atosigar [A3] *vt* (importunar) to pester, hassle (colloq); (presionar) to pressure (AmE), to pressurize (BrE)

atrabancado -da *adj* (Méx fam) (precipitado) rash, reckless

atracador -dora *m,f* (de banco) bank robber, raider (journ); (de persona) mugger

atracar [A2] *vi* «*barco*» to dock, berth
■ **~** *vt* (asaltar) «*banco*» to hold up; «*persona*» to mug

atracción *f* attraction; **la ~ más concurrida** the most popular attraction; **una ~ turística** a tourist attraction; **las atracciones están en la playa** the funfair is on the beach; **siente una gran ~ por ella** he feels strongly attracted to her

atraco *m* (a banco) robbery, raid (journ); (a persona) mugging; **~ a mano armada** armed robbery *o* (journ) raid

atracón *m* (fam): **se dio un ~ de paella** he stuffed himself with paella (colloq)

atractivo¹ -va *adj* attractive

atractivo² *m* (a) (encanto) charm, attractiveness; **tiene mucho ~** she's very charming; **el mayor ~ de la ciudad** the city's main attraction *o* appeal (b) (interés) appeal; **para mí viajar no tiene ningún ~** travel holds no appeal to me

atraer [E23] *vt* (a) (Fís) to attract (b) (traer, hacer venir) to attract; **un truco para ~ al público** a gimmick to attract the public (c) (cautivar, gustar): **se siente atraído por ella** he feels attracted to her; **no me atrae la idea** the idea doesn't attract me *o* appeal to me (d) (atención/miradas) to attract
■ **atraerse** *v pron* (a) (ganarse) (amistad) to gain; (interés) to attract (b) (recípr) to attract (each other)

atragantarse [A1] *v pron* (al tragar) to choke; **se le atragantó una espina** he choked on a fish bone

atraiga, atrajo, etc ▶ ATRAER

atrancar [A2] *vt* (cañería) to block (up); (puerta/ventana) to bar
■ **atrancarse** *v pron* (a) «cañería» to get blocked (b) (fam) «persona» (en tarea) to get stuck

atrapar [A1] *vt* to catch

atrás *adv* **1** (en el espacio) (a) (expresando dirección) back; **muévelo para** *or* **hacia ~** move it back; **da un paso ~** take one step back (b) **¡~!** (como interj) get back! (c) (lugar, parte): **está allí ~** it's back there; **me senté ~** (en coche) I sat in the back; (en clase, cine) I sat at the back; **la parte de ~** the back; **me estaba quedando ~** I was getting left behind; **dejamos ~ la ciudad** we left the city behind us; **estar hasta ~** (Méx fam) to be as high as a kite (colloq)

2 (en el tiempo): **sucedió tres años ~** it happened three years ago; **había sucedido tres años ~** it had happened three years earlier *o* before
3 **atrás de** (loc prep) (AmE) behind

atrasado -da *adj* **1** (a) [ESTAR] (reloj) slow (b) (con respecto a lo esperado): **está muy ~ en los estudios** he's really behind in his studies; **el proyecto está ~** the project is behind schedule; **el tren llegó/salió ~** (AmL) the train arrived/left late; **apúrate que voy ~** (AmL) hurry up, I'm late
2 (acumulado, pasado): **tengo mucho sueño ~** I have a lot of sleep to catch up on; **tengo trabajo ~** I'm behind with my work; **todas las cuotas atrasadas** all outstanding payments; **un ejemplar ~** a back number *o* issue
3 (a) (anticuado, desfasado) (ideas/persona) old-fashioned (b) (país/pueblo) backward

atrasar [A1] *vt* (a) (reloj) to put back (b) (reunión/viaje) to postpone, put back
■ **~** *vi* (reloj) to lose time
■ **atrasarse** *v pron* **1** (a) «reloj» to lose time; **se me ha atrasado 15 minutos** it's 15 minutes slow (b) (esp AmL) (llegar tarde) «avión/tren» to be late, be delayed; «persona» to be late **2** (a) (en estudios, trabajo, pagos) to fall behind, get behind (b) «país/industria» to fall behind

atraso *m* (a) (de país, ideas) backwardness (b) (esp AmL) (retraso) delay; **perdona el ~** I'm sorry about the delay; **salió con unos minutos de ~** it left a few minutes late; **viene con una hora de ~** it's (running) an hour late

atravesado -da *adj* (cruzado): **el piano estaba ~ en el pasillo** the piano was stuck (*o* placed *etc*) across the corridor; **un árbol/camión ~ en la carretera** a tree lying across/a truck blocking the road

atravesar [A5] *vt* **1** (a) (río/frontera) to cross; **atravesó el río a nado** she swam across the river (b) «bala/espada» to go through; **le atravesó la pierna** it went through his leg (c) (crisis/período) to go through **2** (colocar) to put ... across
■ **atravesarse** *v pron*: **se nos atravesó un camión** a truck crossed right in front of us; **se me atravesó una espina en la garganta** I got a fish bone stuck in my throat

atraviesa, atraviesas, etc ▶ ATRAVESAR

atrayente *adj* appealing

atreverse [E1] *v pron* to dare; **¡anda, atrévete!** go on then, I dare you (to); **no me atrevo a decírselo** I daren't tell him; **¿cómo te atreves a pegarle?** how dare you hit him?; **¿a que conmigo no te atreves?** I bet you wouldn't dare take me on

atrevido -da *adj* (a) (insolente) sassy (AmE colloq), cheeky (BrE colloq) (b) (osado) (escote/persona) daring; (chiste) risqué; (diseño) bold (c) (valiente) brave

atrevimiento *m* nerve

atribuir [I20] *vt* (a) **~ algo A algn/algo** to attribute sth TO sb/sth; **le atribuyen algo que no dijo** they attribute words to him which he did not say; **le atribuyen propiedades curativas** it is held *o* believed to have healing powers (b) (funciones/poder) to confer
■ **atribuirse** *v pron* (refl) (a) (éxito/autoría) to claim (b) (poderes/responsabilidad) to assume

atributo *m* (cualidad) attribute, quality; (símbolo) insignia

atril *m* (para partituras) music stand; (para libros) lectern

atrincherar [A1] *vt* to entrench
■ **atrincherarse** *v pron* to entrench oneself

atrocidad *f* (cualidad) barbarity; (acto) atrocity; ¡qué ∼! how atrocious! *o* how awful!

atrofiarse [A1] *v pron* to atrophy

atropellado -da *adj*: ¡qué ∼ eres! you always do things in such a rush!

atropellar [A1] *vt* **(a)** «coche/camión» to knock … down; (pasando por encima) to run … over **(b)** ‹libertades/derechos› to violate, ride roughshod over
■ **atropellarse** *v pron* **(a)** (al hablar, actuar) to rush **(b)** (recípr) (empujarse): **salieron corriendo, atropellándose unos a otros** they came running out, pushing and shoving as they went

atropello *m* (abuso) outrage; ∼ DE *or* A algo violation *of* sth

atroz *adj* atrocious

atte. (Corresp) (= **atentamente**): **lo saluda** ∼ sincerely yours (AmE), yours sincerely/faithfully (BrE)

atuendo *m* (frml) outfit

atún *m* (fish)

aturdimiento *m* (perplejidad) bewilderment; (por golpe, noticia) daze

aturdir [I1] *vt* **(a)** «música/ruido»: **la música te aturdía** the music was deafening; **este ruido me aturde** I can't think straight with this noise **(b)** (dejar perplejo) to bewilder, confuse **(c)** «golpe/ noticia/suceso» to stun, daze
■ **aturdirse** *v pron* (confundirse) to get confused *o* flustered; (por golpe, noticia) to be stunned *o* dazed

audacia *f* (valor) courage, daring; (osadía) boldness, audacity

audaz *adj* (valiente) brave, courageous; (osado) daring, bold

audición *f* **1** (facultad de oír) hearing **2** (prueba) audition **3** (RPl) (Rad) program*

audiencia *f* **1** (cita) audience; **pedir** ∼ to seek an audience **2** (Der) **(a)** (tribunal) court **(b)** (sesión) hearing **3** (espectadores, oyentes) audience; **un programa de mucha** ∼ a program with a large audience; **horas de máxima/mayor** ∼ peak viewing/prime time

audífono *m* **(a)** (para sordos) hearing aid, deaf-aid (BrE) **(b)** (de radio) earphone **(c) audífonos** *mpl* (AmL) headphones (*pl*)

audiolibro *m* audiobook

audiomensajería *f* voice mail

audiovisual *adj* audiovisual
■ *m* audiovisual presentation

auditar [A1] *vt* to audit

auditivo -va *adj* **(a)** ‹nervio/conducto› auditory **(b)** ‹problemas› hearing (before n)

auditor -tora *m,f* **(a)** (persona) auditor **(b) auditora** *f* (empresa) auditors (*pl*), firm of auditors

auditoría *f* audit

auditorio *m* (público) audience; (sala) auditorium

auge *m* **(a)** (punto culminante) peak; **en el** ∼ **de su carrera** at the peak *o* height of his career **(b)**

(aumento): **la comida vegetariana está en** ∼ vegetarian food is on the increase; **un período de** ∼ **económico** a period of economic growth

augurar [A1] *vt* ‹futuro› to predict, foretell

augurio *m* (presagio): **sus** ∼**s no se cumplieron** his predictions did not come true; **es un** ∼ **de mala suerte** it's (a sign of) bad luck *o* a bad omen

aula *f̲* **(a)** (en escuela) classroom **(b)** (en universidad) lecture (*o* seminar *etc*) room; ∼ **magna** main lecture theater* *o* hall

aullar [A23] *vi* «lobo/viento» to howl

aullido *m* howl; **los** ∼**s del perro** the howling of the dog

aumentar [A1] *vt* **(a)** (en general) to increase; ‹precio/sueldo› to increase, raise **(b)** (Opt) to magnify
■ ∼ *vi* «temperatura/presión» to rise; «velocidad» to increase; «precio/producción/ valor» to increase, rise; ∼**á el frío** it will become colder; ∼ DE algo ‹de volumen/tamaño› to increase IN sth; **aumentó de peso** he put on *o* gained weight

aumento *m* **(a)** (incremento) rise, increase; ∼ **de peso** increase in weight; ∼ **de temperatura** rise in temperature; ∼ **de precio** price rise *o* increase; ∼ **de sueldo** salary increase, pay raise (AmE), pay rise (BrE) **(b)** (Opt) magnification; **lentes de mucho** ∼ glasses with very strong lenses

aun *adv* even; **ni** ∼ **trabajando 12 horas al día** (not) even if we worked 12 hours a day; ∼ **así, creo que … even** so, I think …; **ni** ∼ **así me quedaría** even then I wouldn't stay

aún *adv* **1** (todavía) **(a)** (en frases afirmativas o interrogativas) still; ∼ **falta un mes** there's still a month to go; ¿∼ **estás aquí?** are you still here? **(b)** (en frases negativas) yet; ∼ **no ha llamado** she hasn't called yet **2** (en comparaciones) even

aunar [A23] *vt* ‹ideas› to combine
■ **aunarse** *v pron* to unite, come together

aunque *conj* **1** (a pesar de que) **(a)** (refiriéndose a hechos) although; ∼ **no estaba bien fue a trabajar** although he wasn't well he went to work **(b)** (respondiendo a una objeción) (+ *subjuntivo*): **es millonario,** ∼ **no lo parezca** he's a millionaire though he may not look it; ∼ **no lo creas …** believe it or not … **2** (refiriéndose a posibilidades, hipótesis) (+ *subjuntivo*) even if; **iré** ∼ **llueva** I'll go even if it rains

au pair /o'per/ *mf* (*pl* -**pairs**) au pair

aura *f̲* (halo) aura

aureola *f* **(a)** (Relig) halo, aureole (liter) **(b)** (de gloria, fama) aura **(c)** (Astron) aureole, corona **(d)** (CS) (de mancha) ring

auricular *m* **(a)** (del teléfono) receiver **(b) auriculares** *mpl* (Audio) headphones (*pl*), earphones (*pl*)

aurora *f* dawn

auscultar [A1] *vt* to auscultate (tech); **el médico me auscultó** the doctor listened to my chest (with a stethoscope)

ausencia *f* **(a)** (de persona) absence; **brillar por su** ∼ to be conspicuous by one's absence; **el orden brilla por su** ∼ there's a distinct lack of order **(b)** (no existencia) lack, absence **(c)** (frml) (inasistencia) absence

ausentarse [A1] *v pron* (fml) to go away; **pidió permiso para ~ un momento** he asked to leave the room (*o class etc*)

ausente *adj* [ESTAR] **(a)** (no presente) absent; **todos los alumnos ~s** all those pupils who are absent **(b)** (distraído) ⟨*persona*⟩ distracted; ⟨*mirada/expresión*⟩ absent (*before n*)

ausentismo *m* absenteeism; **~ escolar** absenteeism, truancy

auspiciar [A1] *vt* **(a)** (patrocinar) ⟨*exposición/función*⟩ to back, sponsor **(b)** (propiciar, facilitar) to foster, promote

austeridad *f* austerity

austero -ra *adj* ⟨*vida/costumbres/estilo*⟩ austere; **es ~ en el comer** he is frugal in his eating habits

austral *adj* southern

Australia *f* Australia

australiano -na *adj/m,f* Australian

Austria *f* Austria

austriaco -ca, austríaco -ca *adj/m,f* Austrian

autenticar [A2] *vt* **(a)** ⟨*firma/documento*⟩ to authenticate **(b)** (RPl) ⟨*fotocopia*⟩ to attest

autenticidad *f* authenticity

auténtico -ca *adj* **(a)** ⟨*cuadro*⟩ genuine, authentic; ⟨*perla/piel*⟩ real; ⟨*documento*⟩ authentic **(b)** ⟨*interés/cariño/persona*⟩ genuine **(c)** ⟨*pesadilla/catástrofe*⟩ ⟨*delante del n*⟩ real (*before n*)

autista *adj* autistic

auto *m* **1** (esp CS) (Auto) car, automobile (AmE); **~ de carrera** (CS) racing car; **autitos chocadores** (RPl) bumper cars **2** (Lit, Teatr) play

autoabastecerse [E3] *v pron* to be self-sufficient; **~ DE** *or* **EN algo** to be self-sufficient IN sth

autoadhesivo -va *adj* self-adhesive

autobiografía *f* autobiography

autobomba *m* (RPl) fire engine, fire truck (AmE)

autobús *m* bus; **~ de dos pisos** double-decker bus; **~ de línea** (inter-city) bus

autocar *m* (Esp) bus, coach (BrE)

autocine *m* drive-in

autocross *m* autocross

autóctono -na *adj* ⟨*flora/fauna*⟩ indigenous, native; **el elefante es ~ de la India** the elephant is indigenous *o* native to India

autodefensa *f* self-defence

autodeterminación *f* self-determination

autodidacta *mf* self-taught person, autodidact (fml)

autodisciplina *f* self-discipline

auto-escuela, autoescuela *f* driving school

autoestop *m* ▶ AUTOSTOP

autoestopista *mf* hitchhiker

autogol *m* own goal

autografiar [A17] *vt* to autograph

autógrafo *m* autograph

autómata *m* automaton

automático¹ -ca *adj* automatic; **es ~, se sienta a ver la tele y se queda dormido** (fam) it happens every time, he sits down in front of the TV and falls asleep

automático² *m* **(a)** (Fot) self-timer; (Elec) circuit breaker, trip switch **(b)** (cierre) snap fastener (AmE), press stud (BrE)

automatizado -da *adj* automated

automatizar [A4] *vt* to automate

automedicación *f* self-medication

automercado *m* (AmC) supermarket

automotor¹ -triz *or* **-tora** *adj* (fml) ⟨*vehículo/industria*⟩ motor (*before n*)

automotor² *m* (Ferr) railcar ⟨*diesel or electric motor unit*⟩

automóvil *m* car, automobile (AmE)

automovilismo *m* motoring; **~ deportivo** motor racing

automovilista *mf* motorist

automovilístico -ca *adj* ⟨*carrera*⟩ motor (*before n*); ⟨*accidente*⟩ car (*before n*)

autonomía *f* **1** **(a)** (independencia) autonomy; (Pol) autonomy, self-government; **obran con ~** they act autonomously **(b)** (en Esp, comunidad autónoma) autonomous *or* self-governing region **2** (Aviac, Náut) range

autonómico -ca *adj* **(a)** (independiente) autonomous **(b)** ⟨*presidente/elecciones*⟩ (en Esp) regional

autónomo -ma *adj* **(a)** ⟨*departamento/entidad*⟩ autonomous **(b)** (Pol) (en Esp) ⟨*región*⟩ autonomous **(c)** ⟨*trabajador*⟩ self-employed; ⟨*fotógrafo/periodista*⟩ freelance
■ *m,f* (trabajador) self-employed worker *o* person; (fotógrafo, periodista) freelancer

autopista *f* expressway (AmE), motorway (BrE); **~ de peaje** *or* (Méx) **de cuota** turnpike (road) (AmE), toll motorway (BrE); **la ~ de la información** (Inf) the information superhighway

autopsia *f* autopsy, post mortem; **hacerle la ~ a algn** to perform an autopsy *o* a post mortem on sb

autor -tora *m,f* **(a)** (de libro, poema) author, writer; (de canción) writer; (de obra teatral) playwright **(b)** (de delito) perpetrator (fml); **el ~ del gol** the goalscorer

autoridad *f* **1** **(a)** (poder, competencia) authority **(b)** (persona, institución): **la máxima ~ en el ministerio** the top official in the ministry; **se entregó a las ~es** she gave herself up to the authorities **2** (experto) authority; **una ~ en la materia** an authority on the subject

autoritario -ria *adj* authoritarian

autorización *f* authorization (fml); **los menores necesitan la ~ paterna** minors need their parents' consent; **no tiene ~ de sus padres** he doesn't have his parents' permission

autorizado -da *adj* ⟨*fuente/portavoz*⟩ official; ⟨*distribuidor*⟩ authorized, official; ⟨*opinión*⟩ expert (*before n*)

autorizar [A4] *vt* (a) ⟨*manifestación/ documento/firma*⟩ to authorize; ⟨*aumento/pago/ obra*⟩ to authorize, approve (b) ⟨*persona*⟩: **¿quién te autorizó?** who gave you permission?; **lo autoricé para recibir el pago** I authorized him to receive the payment; **me autorizó para salir** he gave me permission to go out; **eso no te autoriza a** *or* **para hablarme así** that doesn't give you the right to talk to me like that

autorretrato *m* self-portrait

autoservicio *m* (*tienda*) supermarket; (*restaurante*) self-service restaurant, cafeteria

autostop, auto-stop /auto(e)stop/ *m* hitchhiking; **hacer ~** to hitchhike

autosuficiencia *f* self-sufficiency

autosuficiente *adj* (a) (Econ) self-sufficient (b) (*presumido*) smug, self-satisfied

autovagón *m* (Per) railcar

autovía *f* divided highway (AmE), dual carriageway (BrE)

auxiliar¹ *adj* (a) ⟨*profesor*⟩ assistant (*before n*); ⟨*personal/elementos*⟩ auxiliary (*before n*) (b) ⟨*servicios*⟩ auxiliary (c) (Tec) auxiliary (d) (Inf) peripheral
■ *mf* (a) (*persona*) assistant; **~ de vuelo** flight attendant (b) **auxiliar** *f* (RPI) (Auto) spare tire

auxiliar² [A1] *vt* to help

auxilio *m* (a) (*ayuda*) help; **pedir ~** to ask for help; **~ en carretera** breakdown *o* recovery service; **acudieron en ~ de las víctimas** they went to the aid of the victims (b) (RPI) (*grúa*) recovery *o* breakdown truck

Av. *f* (= **Avenida**) Ave.

aval *m* (Com, Fin) guarantee; (*respaldo*) backing, support; (*recomendación*) reference

avalancha *f* avalanche

avalar [A1] *vt* (Com, Fin) ⟨*documento*⟩ to guarantee; ⟨*persona/préstamo*⟩ to guarantee, act as guarantor for

avaluar [A18] *vt* (AmL) to value

avalúo *m* (AmL) valuation

avance *m* (a) (*adelanto*) advance; **un ~ en este campo** an advance *o* a step forward in this field (b) (*movimiento*) advance; (Mil) advance; (Dep) move forward

avanzado -da *adj* advanced; **de avanzada edad** of advanced years, advanced in years; **a horas tan avanzadas** at such a late hour

avanzar [A4] *vi* (a) «*persona/tráfico*» to advance, move forward (b) «*ciencia/medicina*» to advance (c) «*cinta/rollo*» to wind on (d) «*persona*» (en los estudios, el trabajo) to make progress; «*negociaciones/proyecto*» to progress (e) «*tiempo*» to draw on
■ **~** *vt* (a) (*adelantarse*) to move forward, advance (b) (*mover*) to move ... forward, advance

avaricia *f* avarice; **la ~ rompe el saco** if you're too greedy you end up with nothing

avaricioso -sa, avariento -ta *adj* greedy, avaricious
■ *m,f* greedy *o* avaricious person

avaro -ra *adj* miserly
■ *m,f* miser

avasallador -dora, avasallante *adj* (a) ⟨*persona/actitud*⟩ domineering, overbearing (b) ⟨*triunfo*⟩ resounding (*before n*)

Avda. *f* (= **Avenida**) Ave.

ave *f*♀ bird; **~ de corral** fowl; **~ de mal agüero** bird of ill omen; **~ rapaz** *or* **de rapiña** (Zool) bird of prey; (*persona*) shark

AVE *m* (= **Alta Velocidad Española**) high-speed train

avecinarse [A1] *v pron* to approach

avejentado -da *adj*: **está muy ~** he's aged a lot; **un rostro ~** an old face

avejentar [A1] *vt* to age, make ... look older

avellana *f* hazelnut

avellano *m* hazel

Avemaría *f*♀ (Relig) Hail Mary; (Mús) Ave Maria

avena *f* oats (*pl*)

avenida *f* (a) (*calle*) avenue, boulevard (b) (de río) freshet, flood

avenido -da *adj*: **bien ~** well-matched; **es una pareja mal avenida** they don't get on well as a couple

avenirse [I31] *v pron* (a) (ponerse de acuerdo) **~se EN algo** to agree ON sth (b) (llevarse bien) **~se CON algn** to get on with sb

aventajado -da *adj* outstanding, excellent

aventajar [A1] *vt* (estar por delante de) to be ahead of; (adelantarse) to overtake, get ahead of

aventar [A5] *vt* (a) (Col, Méx, Per) ⟨*pelota/ piedra*⟩ to throw; **le aventé un sopapo** (fam) I smacked *o* (BrE) thumped him (colloq) (b) (Méx) (empujar) to push
■ **aventarse** *v pron* (a) (Méx fam) (atreverse) to dare; **~se A hacer algo** to dare to do sth (b) (*refl*) (Col, Méx) (arrojarse, tirarse) to throw oneself; **se aventó al agua** he dived into the water

aventón *m* (Méx) (fam) lift; **darle ~ a algn** to give sb a lift *o* ride; **pedir ~** to hitch *o* thumb a lift; **ir de ~** to go hitching

aventura *f* (a) (suceso extraordinario) adventure (b) (empresa arriesgada) venture (c) (relación amorosa — pasajera) fling; (— ilícita) affair

aventurado -da *adj* risky, hazardous

aventurar [A1] *vt* ⟨*opinión*⟩ to venture, put forward; ⟨*conjetura*⟩ to hazard
■ **aventurarse** *v pron* to venture; **me ~ía a decir que ...** I would go so far as to say that ...

aventurero -ra *adj* adventurous
■ *m,f* adventurer

avergonzado -da *adj* (a) (por algo reprensible) ashamed; **~ POR** *or* **DE algo** ashamed OF sth (b) (en situación embarazosa) embarrassed

avergonzar [A13] *vt* (a) (por algo reprensible): **¿no te avergüenza salir así a la calle?** aren't you ashamed to go out looking like that? (b) (en situación embarazosa) to embarrass; **me avergüenza decírselo** I'm embarrassed to tell him
■ **avergonzarse** *v pron* to be ashamed (of oneself); **~se DE algo** to be ashamed *o* of sth; **se avergonzó de haberle mentido** she was ashamed of herself for having lied to him

avergüenza, avergüenzas, etc ▶ AVERGONZAR

avería *f* (Auto, Mec) breakdown

averiado -da *adj* [ESTAR] ⟨*coche/máquina*⟩ broken down; ⟨*ascensor/teléfono*⟩ out of order

averiarse [A17] *v pron* to break down

averiguación *f* inquiry

averiguar [A16] *vt* to find out
■ ~ *vi* (Méx) to quarrel, argue; *averiguárselas* (Méx) to manage

aversión *f* aversion

avestruz *m* ostrich

aviación *f* (civil) aviation; (Mil) air force

aviador -dora *m,f* (Aviac, Mil) pilot

avícola *adj* poultry (*before n*)

avicultura *f* poultry farming

avidez *f* eagerness, avidity; **lee con** ~ he reads avidly

ávido -da *adj* ~ DE algo ⟨*de noticias/aventuras*⟩ eager FOR sth; ⟨*de poder*⟩ hungry FOR sth

avinagrar [A1] *vt* ⟨*vino*⟩ to make ... taste vinegary; ⟨*carácter*⟩ to make ... sour *o* bitter
■ **avinagrarse** *v pron* «*vino*» to turn *o* go vinegary; «*persona*» to become bitter *o* sour

avión *m* (Aviac) plane, aircraft (frml), airplane (AmE), aeroplane (BrE); **viajar en** ~ to fly; Ⓢ **por avión** (Corresp) air mail; ~ **a chorro** *o* **a reacción** jet (plane); ~ **de combate/de pasajeros** fighter/passenger plane

avionazo *m* (Méx) plane crash

avioneta *f* light aircraft

avisar [A1] *vt* (a) (notificar): **¿por qué no me avisaste que venías?** why didn't you let me know you were coming?; **nos han avisado que...** they've notified us that... (b) (Esp, Méx) (llamar) to call; ~ **al médico** to call the doctor (c) (advertir) to warn; **quedas** *or* **estás avisado** you've been warned
■ ~ *vi*: **llegó sin** ~ she showed up without any prior warning *o* unexpectedly; **avísame cuando acabes** let me know when you've finished; ~ **a algn** DE **algo** to let sb know ABOUT sth

aviso *m* ① (a) (notificación) notice; Ⓢ **aviso al público** notice to the public; **dio** ~ **a la policía** he notified *o* informed the police; **sin previo** ~ without prior warning; **último** ~ **para los pasajeros** ... last call for passengers ... (b) (advertencia) warning; **poner sobre** ~ **a algn** to warn sb (c) (Cin, Teatr) bell (d) (Taur) warning ② (AmL) (anuncio, cartel) advertisement, ad

avispa *f* wasp

avispado -da *adj* (fam) sharp, bright

avispero *m* (nido) wasps' nest

avivar [A1] *vt* ⟨*fuego*⟩ to get ... going; ⟨*color*⟩ to make ... brighter; ⟨*pasión/deseo*⟩ to arouse; ⟨*dolor*⟩ to intensify
■ **avivarse** *v pron* (a) «*fuego*» to revive, flare up; «*debate*» to come alive, liven up (b) (AmL fam) (despabilarse) to wise up (colloq)

axila *f* (Anat) armpit, axilla (tech)

axilar *adj* underarm (*before n*)

ay *interj* (a) (expresando — dolor) ow!, ouch!; (— susto, sobresalto) oh! (b) (expresando aflicción) oh dear! (c) (expresando amenaza): **¡~ del que se atreva!** woe betide anyone who tries it!

ayer *adv* (refiriéndose al día anterior) yesterday; ~ **hizo un mes** a month ago yesterday; ~ **por** *or* (esp AmL) **en la mañana** yesterday morning; **antes de** ~ the day before yesterday; **el periódico de** ~ yesterday's paper

ayuda *f* (asistencia) help; **nadie acudió en su** ~

nobody went to his aid; ~**s para la inversión** incentives for investment; **ha sido de gran** ~ it has been a great help

ayudante *mf* assistant; ~ **de cátedra** assistant professor (AmE), (junior) lecturer (BrE); ~ **de cocina** kitchen assistant

ayudar [A1] *vt* to help; ~ **al prójimo** to help one's neighbor; **¿te ayudo?** do you need any help?; **vino a** ~**me** she came to help me out; **ayúdame a poner la mesa** help me (to) set the table
■ ~ *vi* to help; **¿puedo** ~ **en algo?** can I do anything to help?

ayunar [A1] *vi* to fast

ayunas: en ~ (*loc adv*): **estoy en** ~ I haven't eaten anything; **debe tomarse en** ~ it should be taken on an empty stomach

ayuno *m* fast, fasting

ayuntamiento *m* (corporación) town/city council; (edificio) town/city hall

azabache *m* jet; **negro como el** ~ jet black

azada *f* hoe

azadón *m* mattock

azafata *f* ① (a) (en avión) flight attendant, air hostess; ~ **de tierra** ground stewardess (b) (en programa, concurso) hostess; ~ **de congresos** conference hostess ② (Per) (bandeja) tray

azafate *m* (AmS) tray

azafrán *m* saffron

azahar *m* (del naranjo) orange blossom; (del limonero) lemon blossom

azar *m* (a) (casualidad) chance; **dejar algo al** ~ to trust sth to chance; **al** ~ at random (b) **azares** *mpl* (vicisitudes) ups and downs (*pl*), vicissitudes (*pl*)

azaroso -sa *adj* ⟨*viaje*⟩ hazardous; ⟨*proyecto*⟩ risky; ⟨*vida*⟩ eventful

Azerbaiyán, Azerbaiján *m* Azerbaijan, Azerbaidzhan

azerbaiyaní *adj/mf* Azerbaijani, Azeri
■ *m* (idioma) Azerbaijani

azorado -da *adj* (a) (turbado) embarrassed (b) (Col, Méx, RPl) (asombrado) amazed, astonished

azorar [A1] *vt* (turbar) to embarrass
■ **azorarse** *v pron* to get embarrassed

azotador *m* (Méx) caterpillar

azotaina *f* (fam) spanking

azotar [A1] *vt* ① (con látigo) to whip, flog ② (Méx) ⟨*puerta*⟩ to slam

azote *m* ① (a) (látigo) whip, lash; (latigazo) lash (b) (fam) (a un niño): **te voy a dar unos** ~**s** I'm going to spank you ② (calamidad) scourge

azotea *f* terrace roof, flat roof

azteca *adj/mf* Aztec

azúcar *m or f* sugar; **el nivel de** ~ **en la sangre** the blood-sugar level; **chicle sin** ~ sugar-free gum; ~ **blanca** white sugar; ~ **en terrones** *or* (RPl) **pancitos** sugar lumps *o* cubes (*pl*); ~ **glasé** *or* (Méx) **glas** confectioners sugar (AmE), icing sugar (BrE); ~ **lustre/morena** castor*/brown sugar

azucarar [A1] *vt* ⟨*café/leche*⟩ to add sugar to; ⟨*fruta*⟩ to sprinkle ... with sugar

azucarera *f* (a) (AmL) (recipiente) sugar bowl (b) (fábrica) sugar refinery

azucarero¹ -ra *adj* ‹*industria*› sugar (*before n*); ‹*zona*› sugar-producing (*before n*)

azucarero² *m* sugar bowl

azucena *f* Madonna lily, Annunciation lily

azufre *m* sulfur*

azul *adj/m* blue; **de un ~ intenso** deep blue; **~ verdoso (a)** greenish blue **(b)** *adj inv* (*before n*) greenish-blue; **~ cielo** *or* **celeste (a)** *m* sky blue **(b)** *adj inv* sky-blue (*before n*); **~ marino (a)** *m* navy blue **(b)** *adj inv* navy blue, navy-blue (*before n*)

azulado -da *adj* bluish

azulejo *m* (glazed ceramic) tile

azuzar [A4] *vt* **(a)** ‹*perros*› to sic; **~le los perros a algn** to set the dogs on sb **(b)** ‹*persona*› to egg ... on

Bb

B, b *f* (*read as* /be ('larva)/) *the letter* B, b

baba *f* **(a)** (de niño) dribble, drool (AmE) **(b)** (de adulto) saliva; **caérsele a algn la ~ por** *or* **con algn** to drool over sb **(c)** (de perro, caballo) slobber; (de caracol) slime

babear [A1] *vi* **(a)** «*persona*» to dribble, drool (AmE) **(b)** «*animal*» to slaver, slobber

babero *m* bib

babor *m* port; **a ~** to port

babosa *f* slug

babosada *f* (AmL fam) drivel; **decir ~s** to talk drivel

baboso -sa *adj* **1** (con babas) slimy **2** (AmL fam) (estúpido) ‹*persona*› dim (colloq); ‹*libro/ espectáculo*› ridiculous ■ *m,f* (AmL fam) (tonto) dimwit (colloq)

babucha *f* (zapatilla) slipper

baca *f* roof-rack, luggage-rack

bacalao *m* cod, codfish (AmE); **~ seco** salt cod

bacenilla *f* (Col, Ven) chamber pot

bache *m* **(a)** (Auto) pothole **(b)** (Aviac) air pocket **(c)** (mal momento) bad time *o* (BrE) patch

bachillerato *m* **(a)** (educación secundaria) *secondary education and the qualification obtained,* ≈ high school diploma (*in US*) **(b)** (Per) (licenciatura) bachelor's degree

bacinica *f* (AmL exc RPl fam) chamber pot, potty (colloq)

bacteria *f* bacterium; **~s** bacteria (*pl*)

badén *m* **(a)** (vado) ford **(b)** (montículo) road hump **(c)** (depresión) dip

bádminton /'baðminton/ *m* badminton

baffle /'bafle/, **bafle** *m* (altavoz) speaker, loudspeaker

bagaje *m*: **~ cultural** (de persona) cultural knowledge; (de un pueblo) cultural heritage

bagatela *f* (alhaja) trinket; (adorno) knickknack

bah *interj* (expresando — desprecio) huh!, bah!; (— conformidad) oh well!

bahía *f* bay

bailaor -laora *m,f* flamenco dancer

bailar [A1] *vi* **1** (Mús) to dance; **salir a ~** to go out dancing; **la sacó a ~** he asked her to dance **2** «*trompo/peonza*» to spin **3** (fam) (quedar grande) (+ *me/te/le etc*): **estos zapatos me bailan** these shoes are too big for me (colloq) ■ **~** *vt* to dance; **~ un tango** to (dance a) tango

bailarín -rina *m,f* dancer; **primer ~** leading dancer; **primera bailarina** prima ballerina

baile *m* **(a)** (acción) dancing; **abrir el ~** to start the dancing **(b)** (arte, composición, fiesta) dance; **~ de disfraces/máscaras** fancy-dress/masked ball

baja *f* **1** (descenso) fall, drop; **una ~ en los precios** a fall *o* drop in prices; **la ~ de las tasas de interés** the cut in interest rates; **tendencia a la ~** downward trend **2** **(a)** (Esp) (Rels Labs) (permiso) sick leave; (certificado) medical certificate; **está (dado) de ~** he's off sick *o* on sick leave; **~ por maternidad** (Esp) maternity leave **(b)** (Dep): **el equipo tiene varias ~s** the team is missing several regulars **(c)** (Mil) (muerte) loss, casualty **3** (en entidad): **darse de ~** (en club) to cancel one's membership, leave; (en partido) to resign, leave; (Mil) (cese) discharge; **dar de ~** to discharge

bajada *f* **1** (acción) descent; **durante la ~** on the way down; **tuvo una ~ de tensión** his blood pressure dropped; **~ de bandera** (en taxi) minimum fare **2** **(a)** (pendiente) slope; **una ~ muy empinada** a very steep slope **(b)** (camino): **la ~ a la playa es muy empinada** the path (*o* road *etc*) down to the beach is very steep

bajamar *f* low tide

bajar [A1] *vi* **1** **(a)** «*ascensor/persona*» (alejándose) to go down; (acercándose) to come down; **~ por las escaleras** to go/come down the stairs; **ya bajo** I'll be right down **(b)** (apearse) **~ DE algo** ‹*de tren/avión*› to get off sth; ‹*de coche*› to get out OF sth; ‹*de caballo/bicicleta*› to get off sth **(c)** (Dep) «*equipo*» to go down **2** **(a)** «*marea*» to go out **(b)** «*fiebre/tensión*» to go down, drop; «*hinchazón*» to go down; «*temperatura*» to fall, drop **(c)** «*precio/valor*» to fall, drop; «*calidad*» to deteriorate; «*popularidad*» to diminish; **~ de precio** to go down in price ■ **~** *vt* **1** ‹*escalera/cuesta*› to go down **2** ‹*brazo/mano*› to put down, lower **3** **(a)** **~ algo** (DE algo) ‹*de armario/estante*› to get sth down (FROM sth); ‹*del piso de arriba*› (traer) to bring sth down (FROM sth); (llevar) to take sth down (TO sth) **(b)** **~ a algn** DE algo ‹*de mesa/ caballo*› to get sb off sth **4** **(a)** ‹*persiana/telón*› to lower; ‹*ventanilla*› to open **(b)** ‹*cremallera*› to undo **5** ‹*precio*› to lower; ‹*fiebre*› to bring down; ‹*volumen*› to turn down; ‹*voz*› to lower ⋯▸

■ **bajarse** v pron ⟦1⟧ (apearse) ~**se DE algo** ⟨de tren/autobús⟩ to get off sth; ⟨de coche⟩ to get out OF sth; ⟨de caballo/bicicleta⟩ to get off sth; ⟨de pared/árbol⟩ to get down off sth ⟦2⟧ ⟨pantalones⟩ to take down; ⟨falda⟩ to pull down

bajativo m (CS) liqueur, digestif

bajío m (a) (zona poco profunda) shallows (pl); (banco de arena) sandbank (b) (AmL) (terreno bajo) low-lying area

bajista mf bass player, bassist

bajo¹ -ja adj ⟦1⟧ [SER] ⟨persona⟩ short ⟦2⟧ (a) [SER] ⟨techo⟩ low; ⟨tierras⟩ low-lying (b) [ESTAR] ⟨lámpara/cuadro/nivel⟩ low; **la marea está baja** the tide is out; **están ~s de moral** their morale is low; **está ~ de defensas** his defenses are low ⟦3⟧ (a) ⟨calificación/precio/temperatura⟩ low; **~ en nicotina y alquitrán** low in nicotine and tar; **~ en calorías** low-calorie; **de baja calidad** poor-quality (b) ⟨volumen/luz⟩ low; **en voz baja** quietly, in a low voice ⟦4⟧ (grave) ⟨tono/voz⟩ deep, low ⟦5⟧ (vil) ⟨acción/instinto⟩ low, base; **los ~s fondos** the underworld

bajo² adv (a) ⟨volar/pasar⟩ low (b) ⟨hablar/cantar⟩ softly, quietly; **¡habla más ~!** keep your voice down!
■ m ⟦1⟧ (a) (planta baja) first (AmE) o (BrE) ground floor (b) **los bajos** (CS) the first (AmE) o (BrE) ground floor ⟦2⟧ (contrabajo) (double) bass
■ prep under; **~ techo** under cover, indoors; **tres grados ~ cero** three degrees below zero; **~ juramento** under oath

bajón m (fam) (a) (descenso fuerte) sharp drop o fall (b) (de ánimo) depression

bajorrelieve m bas-relief

bala f ⟦1⟧ (Arm) (de pistola, rifle) bullet; (de cañón) cannon ball; **~ de fogueo** blank (round o cartridge); **~ de goma/plástico** rubber/plastic bullet; **a prueba de ~s** bulletproof; **una ~ perdida** a stray bullet; **como (una) ~** ⟨salir/entrar⟩ like a shot (colloq) ⟦2⟧ (AmL) (Dep) shot; **lanzamiento de ~** shot put

balaca f (Col) (a) (Indum) hair-band (b) (Dep) sweatband, headband

balacera f (AmL) shooting

balada f ballad

balance m ⟦1⟧ (a) (resumen, valoración) assessment, evaluation; **hacer ~ DE algo** to take stock OF sth, to evaluate sth (b) (resultado) result, outcome ⟦2⟧ (Com, Fin) (cálculo, cómputo) balance; (documento) balance sheet; (de cuenta) balance

balancear [A1] vt ⟦1⟧ ⟨paquetes/carga⟩ to balance ⟦2⟧ ⟨pierna/brazo⟩ to swing; ⟨barco⟩ to rock
■ **balancearse** v pron (a) «árbol/ramas» to sway; «objeto colgante» to swing (b) «barco» to rock

balanceo m (de hamaca) swinging; (de árboles) swaying; (de barco) rocking

balancín m (de niños) seesaw, teeter-totter (AmE)

balanza f scales (pl); (de dos platillos) scales (pl),

balance; **~ comercial/de pagos** balance of trade/of payments; **poner en la ~** to weigh (AmE), to weigh up (BrE)

balar [A1] vi to bleat, baa

balazo m (Arm) (tiro) shot; (herida) bullet wound; **recibió un ~** he was shot

balboa m balboa (Panamanian unit of currency)

balbucear [A1] vt to stammer
■ ~ vi «adulto» to mutter, mumble; «bebé» to babble

balbuceo m (de adulto) mumbling, muttering; (de bebé) babble

balcón m balcony

balde m ⟦1⟧ (cubo) bucket, pail; **caer como un ~ de agua fría** to come as a complete shock ⟦2⟧ (en locs) **de balde** ⟨trabajar/viajar⟩ for nothing, for free; **en balde** in vain

baldío¹ -día adj (a) (sin cultivar): **terreno ~** waste land (b) ⟨esfuerzo⟩ vain, useless

baldío² m (a) (terreno sin cultivar) area of waste land (b) (Bol, Méx, RPI) (solar) piece o plot of land, vacant lot (AmE)

baldosa f floor tile; **suelo de ~s** tiled floor

baldosín m tile

balear [A1] vt (AmL) to shoot; **murió baleado** he was shot dead

baleo m (AmL) shooting

balero m (Méx, RPI) (juguete) cup-and-ball toy

balido m bleat, baa

balín m (perdigón) pellet; (bala pequeña) shot

balística f ballistics

baliza f (a) (boya) buoy; (señal fija) marker (b) (Aviac) beacon

ballena f (Zool) whale

ballenato m whale calf

ballenero -ra m,f (a) (persona) whaler (b) **ballenero** m (barco) whaleboat, whaler

ballet /ba'le/ m (pl -**llets**) ballet

balneario m ⟦1⟧ (de baños medicinales) spa ⟦2⟧ (AmL) (núcleo residencial) seaside resort, (holiday) resort

balompié m soccer, football (BrE)

balón m (a) (Dep) ball (b) (recipiente) cylinder; **~ de oxígeno** oxygen cylinder

baloncesto m basketball

balonmano m handball

balonvolea m volleyball

balsa f (embarcación) raft; **~ inflable/salvavidas** inflatable/life raft

bálsamo m (a) (Farm, Med) balsam, balm (b) (Chi) (para el pelo) conditioner

baluarte m bastion

bambalina f (Teatr) drop (curtain); **entre ~s** behind the scenes

bambolearse v pron «persona/árbol/torre» to sway; «objeto colgante» to swing; «barco/tren» to rock; «avión/ascensor» to lurch

bambú m (pl -**búes** or -**bús**) bamboo

banal adj banal

banana f (Per, RPI) banana

bananal, bananar m (AmL) banana plantation

bananero¹ -ra adj (AmL) banana (before n)

bananero² m (AmL) banana tree

banano m (árbol) banana tree; (fruta) (AmC, Col) banana

banca f ⚊1⚊ **la ~** (sector) banking; (bancos) the banks ⚊2⚊ (AmL) **(a)** (asiento) bench; (pupitre) desk **(b)** (Dep) (asiento) bench; (jugadores) substitutes (pl)

bancario -ria adj ‹interés/préstamo› bank (before n); ‹sector› banking (before n)

bancarrota f bankruptcy; **en ~** bankrupt; **ir a la ~** to go bankrupt

banco m ⚊1⚊ **(a)** (de parque) bench; (de iglesia) pew; (de barca) thwart; (pupitre) (Chi) desk **(b)** (de carpintero) workbench ⚊2⚊ (Com, Fin) bank; (de órganos, sangre) bank; (de información) bank; **~ de datos** data base o bank; **~ de esperma** or **semen** sperm bank ⚊3⚊ (de peces) shoal; (bajío) bar, bank; **~ de arena** sandbank

banda f ⚊1⚊ (en la cintura, cruzando el pecho) sash; (franja, lista) band; (para pelo) (Méx) hair-band; (en brazo) armband; **~ de frecuencias** frequency band; **~ sonora** (Cin) sound track; **~ transportadora** (Méx) conveyor belt ⚊2⚊ (de barco) side; (en billar) cushion; (en fútbol, rugby) touchline; **saque de ~** (en fútbol) throw-in; (en rugby) put-in ⚊3⚊ **(a)** (de delincuentes) gang; **(b)** (Mús) band

bandada f (de pájaros) flock; (de peces) shoal

bandazo m: **dar ~s** «equipaje» to move about; «coche» to swerve about

bandeja f tray; **servirle algo a algn en ~** to hand sb sth on a platter (AmE) o (BrE) plate

bandera f **(a)** (de nación, club) flag; (de regimiento) colors* (pl); **izar la ~** to run up o raise the flag; **arriar la ~** to lower o strike the flag **(b)** (para señales) flag, pennant; **~ ajedrezada** or **a cuadros** checkered* flag **(c)** (de taxi): **bajar la ~** to start the meter **(d)** (Inf) flag

banderilla f (Taur) banderilla (barbed dart stuck into the bull's neck)

banderillero m banderillero (person who sticks the banderillas into the bull's neck)

banderín m (banderita triangular) pennant; (Dep) flag

banderola f (enseña) banderole

bandido -da m,f (delincuente) bandit; (granuja) crook; (pícaro) rascal

bando m ⚊1⚊ (edicto) edict ⚊2⚊ (facción) side, camp; **están en ~s contrarios** they're on opposing sides

bandolera f (cinturón) Sam Browne (belt); (para cartuchos) bandolier; **en ~** slung across one's shoulder

bandolero -ra m,f bandit

bandoneón m: type of accordion

banjo /'bandʒo/ m banjo

banquero -ra m,f banker

banqueta f **(a)** (taburete) stool; (para los pies) footstool **(b)** (Méx) (acera) sidewalk (AmE), pavement (BrE)

banquete m banquet; **~ de bodas/de gala** wedding/gala reception

banquillo m **(a)** (Der): **el ~ (de los acusados)** the dock **(b)** (Dep) bench

banquina f (RPI) (en autopista) shoulder (AmE), hard shoulder (BrE); (cuneta) ditch

bañado -da adj (Bol, RPI) **~ EN algo** (en sangre/ sudor) covered WITH sth; ‹en lágrimas› bathed IN sth; **~ en oro/plata** gold-plated/silver-plated

bañador m (Esp) (de mujer) bathing suit (esp AmE), swimming costume (BrE); (de hombre) swimming trunks

bañar [A1] vt ⚊1⚊ ‹niño/enfermo› to bath, give ... a bath ⚊2⚊ ‹pulsera/cubierto› to plate
■ **bañarse** v pron (refl) **(a)** (en bañera) to have o take a bath, to bathe (AmE) **(b)** (en mar, río) to swim, bathe

bañera f bath, bathtub

bañero -ra m,f (RPI) lifeguard

bañista mf bather

baño m

■ **Nota** Con referencia al cuarto de baño de una casa particular, el inglés americano emplea normalmente bathroom. El inglés británico emplea toilet, lavatory o (coloquialmente) loo. Cuando se habla de los servicios de un edificio público, el inglés americano utiliza washroom, restroom, men's room o ladies' room. El inglés británico emplea the Gents, the ladies, o the toilets. En la calle y en los parques públicos se emplea public toilets, o en inglés británico más formal, public conveniences.

⚊1⚊ (en bañera) bath; (en mar, río) swim; **darse un ~** to have a bath/to go for a swim; **~ de sangre** bloodbath; **~s públicos** public baths (pl); **~ turco** Turkish bath ⚊2⚊ **(a)** (bañera) bath **(b)** (esp AmL) (en casa privada) bathroom (AmE), toilet (BrE); (en edificio público) restroom (AmE), toilet (BrE); **~ público** (AmL) public toilet ⚊3⚊ (de metal) plating

baptista adj Baptist (before n)
■ mf Baptist

baqueta f **(a)** (Arm) ramrod **(b)** (Mús) drumstick

baquiano -na m,f (AmL) guide

bar m (local) bar; (mueble) liquor cabinet (AmE), drinks cabinet (BrE)

baraja f deck o (BrE) pack (of cards)

barajar [A1] vt ⚊1⚊ ‹cartas› to shuffle ⚊2⚊ ‹nombres/posibilidades› to consider, look at; ‹cifras› to talk about, mention

baranda, (Esp) barandilla f (de balcón) rail; (de escalera) handrail, banister

barata f ⚊1⚊ (Chi) (cucaracha) cockroach ⚊2⚊ (Méx) (liquidación) sale

baratija f (alhaja) trinket; (adorno) knickknack

barato¹ -ta adj **(a)** ‹vestido/restaurante/viaje› cheap, low-priced **(b)** ‹como adv› ‹costar/comprar› cheap

barato² adv ‹comer/vivir› cheaply; **se compra más ~ en el mercado** you can get things cheaper in the market

barba f **(a)** (de quien se la afeita) stubble; **una ~ de dos días** two days' growth of stubble **(b)** (de quien se la deja) beard; **dejarse (la) ~** to grow a beard; **un hombre con ~** a man with a beard; **hacerle la ~ a algn** (Méx fam) to suck up to sb (colloq) **(c)** (mentón, barbilla) chin

barbacoa f (a) (parrilla) barbecue; (carne) barbecued meat (b) (Méx) meat roasted in an oven dug in the earth

barbaridad f (a) (acto atroz) atrocity (b) (disparate): **pagar tanto es una ~** it's madness to pay that much; **lo que hiciste/dijiste es una ~** what you did/said is outrageous; **es capaz de cualquier ~** he's quite capable of doing something really terrible o stupid; **¡qué ~!** good heavens!; **una ~** (fam) ⟨comer⟩ like a horse; ⟨fumar⟩ like a chimney; ⟨pagar/costar⟩ a fortune

barbarie f (de tribu, pueblo) barbarism, savagery; (brutalidad) barbarity

barbarismo m (extranjerismo) loan word, borrowing; (solecismo) barbarism

bárbaro¹ -ra adj **1** (Hist) barbarian **2** (bruto): **el muy ~ la hizo llorar** the brute made her cry; **no seas ~, no se lo digas** don't be crass o cruel, don't tell him **3** (fam) (como intensificador) ⟨casa/coche⟩ fantastic; **tengo un hambre bárbara** I'm starving

bárbaro² adv (fam): **lo pasamos ~** we had a fantastic time (colloq)

bárbaro³ -ra m,f **1** (Hist) Barbarian **2** (fam) (bruto) lout, thug

barbecho m (estado): **dejar la tierra en ~** to leave the land fallow; **estar en ~** (CS) to be in preparation

barbería f barber's (shop)

barbero¹ m barber

barbero² -ra m,f (Méx fam) toady

barbilampiño adj: **un hombre ~** a man with a light beard

barbilla f chin

barbitúrico m barbiturate

barbudo m bearded man, man with a beard

barca f boat; **~ de remos** rowboat (AmE), rowing boat (BrE)

barcaza f (en canales, ríos) barge; (entre barco y tierra) lighter

barco m (Náut) boat; (grande) ship, vessel (frml); **un viaje en ~** a journey by sea (o river etc); **ir/viajar en ~** to go/travel by boat/ship; **~ de guerra** warship; **~ de vapor** steamboat, steamer; **~ de vela** sailing boat, sailboat (AmE)

barda f (Méx) (de cemento) wall; (de madera) fence

barítono -na adj/m baritone

barman /'barman/ m (pl **-mans**) barman, bartender (AmE)

barniz m (a) (para madera) varnish (b) (de cultura, educación) veneer; **~ de** or **para las uñas** nail polish, nail varnish (esp BrE)

barnizar [A4] vt to varnish

barómetro m barometer

barón m (título nobiliario) baron; (de organización) influential member

baronesa f baroness

barquero -ra (m) boatman; (f) boatwoman

barquilla f (de globo) basket, carriage; (Náut) log

barquillo m (galleta) wafer; (cono) ice-cream cone o (BrE) cornet

barra f **1** (a) (de armario) rail; (para cortinas) rod, pole; (de bicicleta) crossbar (b) (de oro, jabón, chocolate) bar; (de turrón, helado) block; (de desodorante) stick; (de pan) (Esp, Méx) stick, French loaf; **~ de labios** lipstick **2** (a) (banda, franja) bar (b) (Mús) bar (line) (c) (signo de puntuación) oblique, slash **3** (para ballet, gimnasia) bar; **~ fija** horizontal bar; **~s asimétricas/paralelas** asymmetric/parallel bars (pl) **4** (de bar, cafetería) bar **5** (AmL fam) (a) (de hinchas, seguidores) supporters (pl) (b) (de amigos) gang (colloq) **6** (Inf): **~ de herramientas** toolbar

barrabasada f (fam) prank; **hacer ~s** to play pranks

barraca f (a) (puesto) stall; (caseta) booth (b) (Mil) barrack hut (c) (casa) adobe house (typical of Valencia and Murcia) (d) (CS) (de materiales de construcción) builders merchant o yard

barranca f, **barranco** m gully; (más profundo) ravine

barrena f (punzón) gimlet; (taladro, perforadora) drill

barrenar [A1] vt (perforar) to drill; (volar) ⟨roca⟩ to blast

barrendero -ra m,f road sweeper, street cleaner

barreno m (barrena) drill; (para explosivo) shot hole

barrer [E1] vt **1** ⟨suelo/cocina⟩ to sweep **2** (a) (arrastrar) to sweep away (b) ⟨rival⟩ to thrash, trounce
■ **~** vi **1** (con escoba) to sweep **2** (arrasar) «equipo/candidato» to sweep to victory; **~ con algo** ⟨con premios/medallas⟩ to walk off with sth; **la inundación barrió con todo** the flood swept everything away; **barrió con todos los premios** she walked off with all the prizes
■ **barrerse** v pron (Méx) «vehículo» to skid; (en fútbol, béisbol) to slide

barrera f barrier; **~ de peaje** toll barrier; **~ generacional** generation gap; **~ idiomática** language barrier

barriada f (a) (barrio) area, district (often poor or working-class) (b) (AmL) (barrio marginal) slum area, shantytown

barrial m (AmL) quagmire

barricada f barricade

barriga f (fam) (vientre) belly (colloq), tummy (colloq); **dolor de ~** bellyache (colloq), tummy ache (colloq); **echar ~** to develop a paunch o (colloq) gut

barrigón -gona adj (fam): **se está volviendo barrigona** she's getting a bit of a belly o tummy (colloq); **un viejo ~** an old man with a paunch

barril m barrel; (de pólvora, cerveza) keg; **ser un ~ sin fondo** (AmL fam) to be a bottomless pit (colloq)

barrio m (a) (zona) neighborhood*; **la gente del ~** people in the neighborhood, local people; **el mercado del ~** the local market; **~ alto** (Chi) smart neighborhood; **~ chino** (Esp) red-light district; **~ espontáneo** (AmC) shantytown; **~s bajos** poor neighborhoods (pl); **~ de invasión** (Col) shantytown (b) (de las afueras) suburb

barriobajero -ra adj (pey) common (pej)

barrizal m quagmire, muddy area

barro m (lodo) mud; (Art) clay, earthenware (before n)

barroco -ca adj ⟨estilo⟩ baroque; (recargado) overelaborate

barrote m (de celda, ventana) bar; (en carpintería) crosspiece

bartola *f*: **echarse a la ~** (fam) (estar sin trabajar) to laze about

bártulos *mpl* (fam) gear (colloq), stuff (colloq)

barullo *m* (alboroto) racket (colloq), ruckus (AmE); (desorden) muddle, mess

basar [A1] *vt* ⟨teoría/idea⟩ **~ algo EN algo** to base sth ON sth

■ **basarse** *v pron* (a) «persona» **~se EN algo**: ¿en qué te basas para decir eso? and what basis o grounds do you have for saying that?; **se basó en esos datos** he based his argument (o theory etc) on that information (b) «teoría/creencia/idea/opinión» **~se EN algo** to be based ON sth

báscula *f* scales (pl); **~ de baño** bathroom scales

base *f* **1** (a) (parte inferior) base (b) tb **~ de maquillaje** foundation

2 (a) (fundamento) basis; **la ~ de una buena salud** the basis of good health; **tengo suficiente ~ para asegurar eso** I have sufficient grounds to claim that; **sentar las ~s de algo** to lay the foundations of sth; **tomar algo como ~** to take sth as a starting point (b) (conocimientos básicos): **tiene una sólida ~ científica** he has a sound grounding in science; **llegó al curso sin ninguna ~** he didn't have the basics when he began the course; **~ de datos** database

3 (en locs) **a base de: un régimen a ~ de verdura** a vegetable-based diet; **vive a ~ de pastillas** he lives on pills

4 (centro de operaciones) base; **~ aérea/naval/militar** air/naval/military base

5 bases *fpl* (de concurso) rules (pl)

6 (a) (en béisbol) base (b) **base** *mf* (en baloncesto) guard

básica *f* (Esp) primary o elementary education

básico -ca *adj* (a) (fundamental, esencial) basic; **alimento ~** staple food (b) ⟨requisito⟩ essential, fundamental

basílica *f* basilica

basket, básquet *m* basketball

básquetbol, basquetbol *m* (AmL) basketball

basquetbolista *mf* (AmL) basketball player

bastante *adj* (a) (suficiente) enough; **~s vasos/~ vino** enough glasses/wine (b) (cantidad considerable) plenty of, quite a lot of; **había ~ gente/~s coches** there were plenty of people/cars

■ *pron* **1** (suficiente) enough; **ya tenemos ~s** we already have enough **2** (demasiado): **deja ~ que desear** it leaves rather a lot to be desired

■ *adv* **1** (suficientemente) enough; **no te has esforzado ~** you haven't tried hard enough **2** (considerablemente) (con verbos) quite a lot; (con adjetivos, adverbios) quite; **le gusta bastante** she likes him quite a lot; **me pareció ~ agradable/aburrido** I thought he was quite pleasant/rather boring

bastar [A1] *vi* to be enough; **¿basta con esto?** will this be enough?; **basta con marcar el 101** just dial 101; **¡basta ya!** that's enough!; (+ me/te/le etc) **me basta con tu palabra** your word is good enough for me

bastardilla *f* italic type, italics (pl)

bastardo -da *adj* (a) (ilegítimo) illegitimate (b) (innoble) base

■ *m,f* bastard

bastidor *m* (Teatr) wing; **entre ~es** behind the scenes

basto -ta *adj* coarse

bastón *m* (para caminar) walking stick, cane; (en desfiles) baton; (de esquí) ski stick o pole

basura *f* (a) (recipiente) garbage o trash can (AmE), dustbin (BrE); **echar o tirar algo a la ~** to throw sth in the garbage o trash (can) o dustbin (b) (desechos) garbage (AmE), trash (AmE), rubbish (BrE); (en sitios públicos) litter; **sacar la ~** to take out the garbage o trash o rubbish (c) (fam) (porquería) trash (AmE colloq), rubbish (BrE colloq)

basural *m* (AmL) ▶ BASURERO B

basurero -ra *m,f* **1** (persona) garbage collector (AmE), dustman (BrE) **2** (a) **basurero** *m* (vertedero) garbage dump (AmE), rubbish dump o tip (BrE) (b) (recipiente) (Chi, Méx) trash can (AmE), dustbin (BrE)

bata *f* (para estar en casa) dressing gown, robe; (de médico) white coat; (de colegio) work coat (AmE), overall (BrE)

batahola *f* (esp AmL fam) racket, din, ruckus (AmE)

batalla *f* battle; **librar ~** to do battle; **~ campal** pitched battle; **de ~** (fam) ⟨zapatos/abrigo⟩ everyday (before n)

batallar [A1] *vi* (a) (luchar) to battle; **~ CON algn/algo** (lidiar) to battle WITH sb/sth (b) (Mil) to fight

batallón *m* (Mil) battalion

batata *f* sweet potato, yam

bate *m* (en béisbol, cricket) bat

batea *f* (a) (bandeja) tray (b) (AmL) (recipiente) shallow pan o tray (for washing)

bateador -dora *m,f* (en béisbol, softbol) batter; (en cricket) batsman

batear [A1] *vi* to bat

■ **~** *vt* to hit

batería *f* **1** (Auto) battery; **se me descargó la ~** my battery went dead (AmE) o (BrE) flat **2** (a) (Mús) drums (pl), drum kit (b) **batería** *mf* drummer

baterista *mf* (AmL) drummer

batido *m* (de leche) (milk) shake; (para panqueues) (AmL) batter

batidor *m* (a) (manual) whisk, beater; (eléctrico) mixer, blender (b) **batidora** *f* (máquina eléctrica) mixer, blender

batir [I1] *vt* **1** ⟨huevos⟩ to beat, whisk; ⟨crema/nata⟩ to whip; ⟨mantequilla⟩ to churn **2** ⟨marca/récord⟩ to break; ⟨enemigo/rival⟩ to beat **3** (a) ⟨ala⟩ to beat, flap (b) **~ palmas** to clap

■ **batirse** *v pron* **1** (enfrentarse): **~se a** o **en duelo** to fight a duel **2** (Méx) (ensuciarse) to get dirty; **llegó todo batido de lodo** he arrived all covered in mud

batracio *m* batrachian

batuta *f* baton; **llevar la ~** (fam) to be the boss (colloq)

baúl *m* (arca) chest; (de viaje) trunk; (del coche, carro) (Col, Ven, RPl) trunk (AmE), boot (BrE)

bautismo *m* (de bebé) baptism, christening; (de adulto) baptism

bautizar [A4] *vt* (a) (Relig) ⟨bebé⟩ to baptize, ····⟶

christen; (*adulto*) to baptize; **la ~ron con el nombre de Ana** she was christened Ana **(b)** (*barco*) to name

bautizo *m* **(a)** (de bebé) christening, baptism; (de adulto) baptism; (fiesta) christening party **(b)** (de barco) naming, launching

bayeta *f* **(a)** (para limpiar) cloth **(b)** (Bol, Col) (tela) baize

bayoneta *f* bayonet

bazar *m* **(a)** (mercado oriental) bazaar **(b)** (tienda) hardware store (*often selling a wide range of electrical goods and toys*)

bazo *m* spleen

bazofia *f* (fam) (comida) crap (colloq); (libro, película) garbage (AmE colloq), rubbish (BrE colloq)

bazooka /ba'suka, ba'θuka/, **bazuca** *f* bazooka

be *f. name of the letter* b, *often called* BE LARGA*or* GRANDE *to distinguish it from* v

beato -ta *adj* (Relig) blessed; (piadoso) pious; (santurrón) (pey) excessively devout

bebe -ba *m,f* (RPl, Per) baby

bebé *m* baby; **~ probeta** test-tube baby

bebedero *m* (paraje) watering hole; (recipiente) trough; (para personas) (CS, Méx) drinking fountain

bebedor -dora *m,f* drinker; **un ~ empedernido** a hardened drinker

beber [E1] *vt/vi* to drink; **¿quieres ~ algo?** do you want something to drink?; **~ a sorbos** to sip; **si bebes no conduzcas** don't drink and drive; **~ a la salud de algn** to drink sb's *o* (BrE) to sb's health; **~ POR algn/algo** to drink TO sb/sth
■ **beberse** *v pron* (enf) to drink up; **nos bebimos la botella entera** we drank the whole bottle

bebida *f* (líquido) drink, beverage (frml); (vicio) drink

bebido -da *adj* [ESTAR] (borracho) drunk

beca *f* (ayuda económica) grant; (que se otorga por méritos) scholarship

becado -da *m,f* (AmL) ▶ BECARIO

becar [A2] *vt* (dar ayuda económica) to give *o* (frml) award a grant to; (dar beca por méritos) to give *o* (frml) award a scholarship to

becario -ria *m,f* recipient of a grant; (por méritos) scholarship holder, scholar

becerro -rra *m,f* calf, young bull; (piel) calfskin

bedel *mf* ≈ porter

beduino -na *adj/m,f* bedouin

beige, (Esp) **beis** /beʒ, beis/ *adj inv/m* beige

béisbol, (Méx) **beisbol** *m* baseball

belén *m* nativity scene, crib, crèche (AmE)

Belén *m* Bethlehem

belga *adj/mf* Belgian

Bélgica *f* Belgium

bélico -ca *adj* (conflicto/material) military; **preparativos ~s** preparations for war

belicosidad *f* aggressiveness

belicoso -sa *adj* (pueblo) warlike; (persona/carácter) bellicose, belligerent

beligerante *adj* belligerent; **los países ~s** the belligerent *o* warring nations

bellaco -ca *m,f* (fam & hum) rogue (colloq & hum)

belleza *f* **(a)** (cualidad) beauty **(b)** (mujer bella) beauty **(c)** (cosa bella): **este paisaje es una ~** this is beautiful countryside

bello -lla *adj* **(a)** (mujer/paisaje/poema) (liter) beautiful; **ser una bella persona** to be a good person **(b)** (Art) **bellas artes** fine art

bellota *f* acorn

bemba *f* (AmL fam) thick lips (*pl*)

bemol *adj* flat; **si ~** B flat

bencina *f* **(a)** (Quím) benzine, petroleum ether **(b)** (Andes) (gasolina) gasoline (AmE), petrol (BrE)

bencinera *f* (Andes) filling station, gas station (AmE), petrol station (BrE)

bencinero -ra *m,f* (Andes) filling station attendant

bendecir [I25] *vt* to bless; **¡que Dios te bendiga!** God bless you!; **~ la mesa** to say grace

bendice, etc ▶ BENDECIR

bendición *f* **(a)** (Relig) blessing, benediction **(b)** (aprobación) blessing; (regalo divino) godsend

bendiga, bendijo, etc ▶ BENDECIR

bendito -ta *adj* **(a)** (Relig) blessed; **¡~ sea Dios!** (expresando contrariedad) good God *o* grief!; (expresando alivio) thank God! **(b)** (agua/pan) holy
■ *m,f* simple soul

benedictino -na *adj/m,f* Benedictine

benefactor -tora *m,f* benefactor

beneficencia *f* (caridad) charity; **asociación/obra de ~** charitable organization/work

beneficiar [A1] *vt* (favorecer) to benefit, to be of benefit to; **esto beneficia a ambas partes** this benefits both sides; **salir beneficiado con algo** to be better off with sth
■ **beneficiarse** *v pron* to benefit; **~se CON/DE algo** to benefit FROM sth

beneficiario -ria *m,f* beneficiary; (de cheque) payee

beneficio *m* **(a)** (Com, Fin) profit; **producir** *or* **reportar ~s** to yield *o* bring returns *o* profits **(b)** (ventaja, bien) benefit; **a ~ de** in aid of; **en ~ de todos** in the interests of everyone

beneficioso -sa *adj* beneficial

benéfico -ca *adj* (influencia) benign, beneficial; (espectáculo) charity (*before n*), benefit (*before n*)

beneplácito *m* approval

benevolencia *f* (indulgencia) leniency, indulgence; (bondad) kindness, benevolence (frml)

benevolente, benévolo -la *adj* (indulgente) lenient, indulgent; (bondadoso) kind, benevolent (frml)

bengala *f* flare

benignidad *f* (del clima) mildness; (de tumor) benignancy

benigno -na adj ‹clima/invierno› mild; ‹tumor›
benign

benjamín -mina m,f (m) youngest son, (f)
youngest daughter

beodo -da adj (frml o hum) inebriated (frml or
hum)
■ m,f (frml o hum) drunkard, toper (liter o hum)

berberecho m cockle

berenjena f eggplant (AmE), aubergine (BrE)

Berlín m Berlin

berlinés -nesa adj of/from Berlin
■ m,f Berliner

berma f (Andes) (de asfalto) shoulder (AmE), hard
shoulder (BrE); (de tierra) verge

bermudas fpl or mpl Bermuda shorts (pl)

Bermudas fpl: las ∼ Bermuda; el triángulo de
las ∼ the Bermuda Triangle

berrear [A1] vi «becerro/ciervo» to bellow

berrido m (de becerro, ciervo) bellow

berrinche m (fam) tantrum; le dio un ∼ (Méx)
hizo un ∼ he threw o had a tantrum

berro m watercress

besar [A1] vt to kiss
■ **besarse** v pron (recípr) to kiss (each other)

beso m kiss; darle un ∼ a algn to give sb a kiss

bestia adj (fam) (a) (grosero) rude (b) (violento,
brusco): ¡qué hombre más ∼! ha vuelto a pegarle
what a brute o an animal! he's hit her again
■ f beast; ∼ salvaje or feroz wild animal
■ mf (persona violenta) animal, brute

bestial adj (fam) (muy grande): tengo un hambre
∼ I'm starving; hace un frío ∼ it's incredibly
cold

best-seller /bes'seler/ m (pl **-llers**)
best-seller

besugo m (Coc, Zool) red bream

besuquear [A1] vt (fam) to smother ... with
kisses
■ **besuquearse** v pron (recípr) (fam) to neck
(colloq)

betabel m (Méx) beet, beetroot (BrE)

betún m (para calzado) shoe polish; dales ∼ a
esos zapatos give those shoes a polish

bianual adj biannual

biberón m (baby's o feeding) bottle; hay que
darle el ∼ I have to give the baby his bottle o
feed

biblia f bible; La B∼ the Bible

bíblico -ca adj biblical

bibliografía f (en libro, informe) bibliography;
(para curso) booklist

biblioteca f (a) (institución, lugar) library; ∼
pública/de consulta public/reference library (b)
(colección) book collection (c) (mueble) bookshelves
(pl), bookcase

bibliotecario -ria m,f librarian

bicameral adj bicameral (frml)

bicampeón -peona m,f twice champion

bicarbonato m bicarbonate

bicentenario m bicentenary

bíceps m (pl ∼) biceps

bicho m [1] (fam) (a) (insecto) bug (colloq),
creepy-crawly (colloq) (b) (animal) animal,
creature; me picó or (Esp) ha picado un ∼ I've

been bitten by something [2] (fam) (persona) nasty
piece of work (colloq); ∼ raro weirdo (colloq); todo
∼ viviente everyone

bici f (fam) bike (colloq)

bicicleta f bicycle; va en ∼ al trabajo she
cycles to work; ¿sabes montar or (AmL) andar en
∼? can you ride a bicycle?; ∼ de carreras/
ejercicio/montaña racing/exercise/mountain bike

bicimoto m (Méx) moped

bicolor adj two-colored*

bidé, bidet /bi'ðe/ m bidet

bidón m (a) (para gasolina, agua) can; (más grande)
jerry can (b) (barril) barrel

bien¹ adj inv [1] [ESTAR] (de salud, en general)
well; sentirse or encontrarse ∼ to feel well;
¿cómo estás? — muy ∼, gracias how are you? —
(I'm) very well, thank you; ¡qué ∼ estás! you
look really well!; ¡tú no estás ∼ de la cabeza!
you are not right in the head
[2] [ESTAR] (a) (cómodo, agradable): ¿vas ∼ ahí
atrás? are you all right in the back?; se está ∼ a
la sombra it's nice in the shade; la casa está muy
∼ the house is very nice (b) [ESTAR] (correcto,
adecuado) right; la fecha/el reloj está ∼ the date/
the clock is right; ¿está ∼ así? is this all right?;
si te parece ∼ if that's all right with you; el
cuadro no queda ∼ ahí the picture doesn't look
right there (c) (suficiente): estar or andar ∼ de
algo to be all right for sth; ¿estamos ∼ de
aceite? are we all right for oil?; ya está ∼ that's
enough
[3] [ESTAR] (a) (en calidad) good; ¿lo has leído?
está muy ∼ have you read it? it's very good (b)
(fam) (sexualmente atractivo) good-looking, attractive
[4] (fam) (a) (de buena posición social) ‹familia/gente›
well-to-do (b) ‹barrio› well-to-do, posh (BrE)

bien² adv [1] (a) (de manera satisfactoria) ‹dormir/
funcionar/cantar› well; no le fue ∼ en Alemania
things didn't work out for her in Germany (b)
(correctamente) well; habla muy ∼ inglés she
speaks English very well o very good English; ¡∼
hecho/dicho! well done/said!; pórtate ∼ behave
yourself; hiciste ∼ en decírselo you were right to
tell him; siéntate ∼ sit properly (c) (de manera
agradable) ‹oler/saber› good
[2] (a) (a fondo, completamente) well, properly; ∼
cocido well o properly cooked; ¿cerraste ∼? did
you lock the door properly?; ∼ sabes que ... you
know perfectly well that ... (b) (con cuidado,
atención) ‹escuchar/mirar› carefully
[3] (a) (como intensificador) (muy) very; canta ∼ mal
he sings really badly; ∼ entrada la noche very
late at night; ¿estás ∼ seguro? are you positive?
(b) (en locs) más bien rather; no bien as soon as;
si bien although
■ interj: ¡(muy) ∼! well done!, (very) good!; ¡qué
∼! great!
■ conj: ∼ ... o ... either ... or ...; se puede subir ∼
a pie o a caballo you can go up either on foot or
on horseback

bien³ m [1] (Fil) good; el ∼ y el mal good and
evil; hacer el ∼ to do good deeds; un hombre de
∼ a good man
[2] (a) (beneficio, bienestar) good; es por mi/tu ∼ it's
for my/your own good (b) hacer bien (+ me/te/le
etc): esto te hará ∼ this will do you good
[3] (en calificaciones escolares) grade of between 6 and
6.9 on a scale of 1-10 ···⟶

b

④ **bienes** *mpl* (a) (Com) goods; ~**es de consumo** consumer goods (b) (Der) property; **le dejó todos sus** ~**es** she left him everything she owned; ~**es inmuebles** *or* **raíces** real estate, property (BrE); ~**es muebles** personal property, goods and chattels; ~**es públicos** public property

bienal *adj* biennial

bienaventurado -da *adj* blessed

bienestar *m* well-being, welfare; **estado de** ~ social welfare state; ~ **social** social welfare

bienhablado -da *adj* well-spoken

bienintencionado -da *adj* well-meaning, well-intentioned

bienvenida *f* welcome; **darle la** ~ **a algn** to welcome sb; **un discurso de** ~ a welcoming speech

bienvenido -da *adj* welcome; **ser** ~ to be welcome

bies *m*: **al** ~ on the cross

bife *m* (CS) (Coc) steak

bifocal *adj* bifocal

bifurcación *f* (en carretera) fork; (en la vía férrea) junction

bifurcarse [A2] *v pron* «camino» to fork, diverge (frml); «vía férrea» to diverge

bigamia *f* bigamy

bígamo -ma *adj* bigamous
■ *m,f* bigamist

bigote *m* ① (de persona) *tb* ~**s** mustache* ② (de gato, ratón) whisker

bigotudo -da, (Méx) **bigotón -tona** *adj* (fam): **un hombre** ~ a man with a big mustache*

bigudí *m* (*pl* **-díes** **-dís**) curler, roller

bikini *m or* (RPl) *f* bikini

bilateral *adj* bilateral

bilingüe *adj* bilingual

bilis *f* (Fisiol) bile

billar *m* (con tres bolas) billiards; (con 16 bolas) pool; (con 22 bolas) snooker

billete *m* ① (Fin) bill (esp AmE), note (BrE) ② (de lotería, rifa, de transporte) ticket; **sacar/pagar un** ~ to get/pay for a ticket; ~ **de ida y vuelta** (Esp) round-trip ticket (AmE), return (ticket) (BrE); ~ **sencillo** *or* **de ida** (Esp) one-way ticket, single (ticket) (BrE)

billetera *f*, **billetero** *m* wallet, billfold (AmE); (con monedero) change purse (AmE), purse (BrE)

billetero -ra *m,f* (Méx, Ven) lottery ticket vendor

billón *m* trillion

bimensual *adj* (dos veces al mes) twice-monthly, fortnightly (BrE)

bimestral *adj* (cada dos meses) bimonthly; (que dura dos meses) two-month (*before n*)

bimestre *m* (period of) two months; (pago) bimonthly payment

bimotor *m* twin-engined aircraft

binario -ria *adj* binary

bingo *m* (juego) bingo; (sala) bingo hall

binoculares (Col, Ven) **binóculos** *mpl* binoculars (*pl*)

biodegradable *adj* biodegradable

biografía *f* biography

biográfico -ca *adj* biographical

biógrafo -fa *m,f* biographer

biología *f* biology

biológico -ca *adj* (Biol) biological; «verduras» organic

biólogo -ga *m,f* biologist

biombo *m* folding screen

biopsia *f* biopsy

bioquímica *f* biochemistry

bioquímico -ca *adj* biochemical
■ *m,f* biochemist

bióxido *m* dioxide

bip *m* (a) (sonido) pip, beep (b) (Méx) (aparato) pager, beeper, bleeper (BrE)

bipartidismo *m* two-party system

bípedo *m* biped

biplaza *m* two-seater

biquini *m* bikini

birlar [A1] *vt* (fam) to swipe (colloq), to pinch (BrE colloq)

Birmania *f* Burma

birmano¹ -na *adj/m,f* Burmese; **los** ~**s** the Burmese

birmano² *m* (idioma) Burmese

birome *f* (RPl) ballpoint pen, Biro®

birrete *m* (a) cap (*worn by lawyers, professors, etc*) (b) (birreta) biretta

bis *m* encore

bisabuelo -la *m, f (m)* great-grandfather; *(f)* great-grandmother; **mis** ~**s** my great-grandparents

bisagra *f* hinge

biselar [A1] *vt* to bevel

bisexual *adj/mf* bisexual

bisexualidad *f* bisexuality

bisiesto *adj*: **1992 fue (año)** ~ 1992 was a leap year

bisne *m* (AmC fam) hustling (colloq), black marketeering

bisnieto -ta *m, f (m)* great-grandson; *(f)* great-granddaughter; **mis** ~**s** my great-grandchildren

bisonte *m* bison

bisoñé *m* toupee, hairpiece

bisoño -ña *adj* inexperienced; **soldados** ~**s** raw recruits

bistec /bi'stek/ *m* (*pl* **-tecs**) steak, beefsteak

bisturí *m* scalpel

bisutería *f* costume *o* imitation jewelry*

bit *m* (*pl* **bits**) (Inf) bit

bividí /biβi'ði/ *m* (Per) undershirt (AmE), vest (BrE)

bizantino -na *adj* (Hist) Byzantine

bizco -ca *adj* cross-eyed
■ *m,f* cross-eyed person

bizcocho *m* (pastel) sponge (cake); (galleta) sponge finger

blanca *f* ① (Mús) half note (AmE), minim (BrE) ② (en dominó) blank; (en ajedrez) white piece ③ (Esp fam) (dinero): **estar sin** *or* **no tener** ~ to be broke (colloq)

Blancanieves Snow White

blanco¹ -ca *adj* ① (a) «color/vestido/pelo» white; **en** ~ «cheque/página» blank; **rellenar los espacios en** ~ fill in the blanks; **me quedé en** ~

my mind went blank **(b)** (pálido) [SER] fair-skinned, pale-skinned; [ESTAR] white; **estoy muy ~** I'm very white *o* pale **2** ⟨*persona/raza*⟩ white **3** ⟨*vino*⟩ white
■ *m,f* white person

blanco² *m* **1** (color) white; **en ~ y negro** black and white **2** (Dep, Jueg) (objeto) target; (centro) bullseye; **tirar al ~** to shoot at the target; **dar en el ~** to hit the target/bullseye **3** (vino) white (wine)

blancura *f* whiteness

blandir [I1] *vt* to brandish, wave

blando -da *adj* **1** **(a)** ⟨*carne*⟩ tender; ⟨*queso/ mantequilla*⟩ soft; **ponerse ~** to go soft **(b)** ⟨*cama/madera/agua*⟩ soft; **un cepillo de cerdas blandas** a soft brush **2** ⟨*carácter*⟩ (débil) weak; (poco severo) soft

blandura *f* **1** (en general) softness; (de la carne) tenderness **2** (falta de severidad) leniency; **trata a sus alumnos con demasiada ~** she's too lenient with *o* too soft on her pupils

blanqueador *m* (para visillos) whitener; (lejía) (Col, Méx) bleach

blanquear [A1] *vt* **(a)** ⟨*ropa*⟩ to bleach; ⟨*pared*⟩ to whitewash **(b)** ⟨*dinero*⟩ to launder

blanqueo *m* **(a)** (de paredes) whitewashing **(b)** (de dinero) laundering

blasfemia *f* blasphemy

blindado -da *adj* ⟨*coche*⟩ armor-plated*, armored*; ⟨*puerta*⟩ reinforced

blindar [A1] *vt* ⟨*barco/coche*⟩ to armor-plate*; ⟨*puerta*⟩ to reinforce

bloc *m* (*pl* **blocs**) (de papel) pad; **~ de notas** note *o* writing pad

blof *m* (Col, Méx) bluff

blofear [A1] *vi* (Col, Méx) **(a)** (en el juego) to bluff **(b)** (fam) (alardear) to show off

bloque *m* **1** (de piedra, hormigón) block **2** (edificio) block; **un ~ de departamentos** (AmL) *or* (Esp) **pisos** an apartment block, a block of flats (BrE) **3** (Inf) block **4** (fuerza política) bloc; **en ~** (*loc adv*) en bloc, en masse

bloquear [A1] *vt* **1** **(a)** ⟨*camino/entrada/ salida*⟩ to block; **estamos bloqueados por un camión** there's a truck blocking our way **(b)** (Mil) to blockade **2** ⟨*cuenta/fondos*⟩ to freeze, block
■ **bloquearse** *v pron* **1** «*mecanismo*» to jam; «*frenos*» to jam, lock on; «*ruedas*» to lock **2** «*negociaciones*» to reach deadlock

bloqueo *m* (de ciudad) blockade, siege; (de puerto) blockade; (Dep) block

bluff /bluf/ *m* (*pl* **bluffs**) **(a)** (Jueg) bluff **(b)** (fam) (fanfarronería): **es puro ~** he's all talk (colloq)

blusa *f* blouse

blusón *m* loose shirt *o* blouse

blvar. *m* (= **bulevar**) Blvd (*in US*)

Bº = **Banco**

boa *f* (Zool) boa

bobada *f* (cosa boba) silly thing; **deja de hacer ~s** stop being so stupid *o* silly; **deja de decir ~s** stop talking nonsense

bobina *f* **(a)** (de hilo) reel **(b)** (Auto, Elec) coil

bobo -ba *adj* (fam) silly
■ *m,f* (fam) fool

boca *f* **1** **(a)** (Anat, Zool) mouth **(b)** (*en locs*) **boca abajo/arriba** ⟨*dormir/echarse*⟩ on one's

stomach/back; **puso los naipes ~ arriba** she laid the cards face up; **en boca de: la pregunta que anda en ~ de todos los niños** the question which is on every child's lips; **el escándalo andaba en ~ de todos** the scandal was common knowledge; **por boca de from; lo supe por ~ de su hermana** I heard it from his sister; *a pedir de ~* just fine; **hacerle el ~ a ~ a algn** to give sb the kiss of life; **hacérsele a algn agua a algn** (Esp): **se le hacía la ~ agua mirando los pasteles** looking at the cakes made her mouth water; **quedarse con la ~ abierta** to be dumbfounded *o* (colloq) flabbergasted **2** (de buzón) slot; (de túnel) mouth, entrance; (de puerto) entrance; (de vasija, botella) rim; **~ de incendios** fire hydrant, fireplug (AmE); **~ del estómago** (fam) pit of the stomach; **~ de metro** *or* (RPl) **subte** subway entrance (AmE), underground *o* tube station entrance (BrE)

bocacalle *f*: entrance to a street; **la primera ~ a la derecha** the first turning on the right

bocadillo *m* **1** (Esp) (emparedado) roll **2** (Col, Ven) (dulce) guava jelly

bocado *m* **(a)** (de comida) bite; **de un ~** in one bite; **no ha probado ~** she hasn't had a bite to eat **(b)** (comida ligera) snack

bocajarro: a ~ (*loc adv*) **(a)** ⟨*disparar*⟩ at point-blank range **(b)** ⟨*decir/preguntar*⟩ point-blank

bocamanga *f* cuff

bocanada *f* (de humo, aliento) puff, mouthful; (ráfaga) gust, blast

bocatoma *f* (Andes) water inlet

boceto *m* (dibujo) sketch; (de proyecto) outline

bochar [A1] *vt* **(a)** (RPl fam) ⟨*sugerencia/ propuesta*⟩ to squash (colloq) **(b)** (RPl arg) (en examen) ⟨*estudiante*⟩ to fail, to flunk (AmE colloq)

bochas *fpl* (RPl) (Jueg) bowls

bochinche *m* (esp AmL fam) **(a)** (riña, pelea) fight, brawl **(b)** (barullo, alboroto) racket (colloq), ruckus (AmE colloq), row (BrE colloq) **(c)** (confusión, lío) muddle, mess (colloq)

bochinchear [A1] *vi* (AmL fam) to fight

bochinchero -ra *adj* (AmL fam) rowdy

bochorno *m* **1** (calor) sultry *o* muggy weather **2** (vergüenza) embarrassment; **¡qué ~!** how embarrassing!

bochornoso -sa *adj* **1** ⟨*tiempo*⟩ sultry, muggy; ⟨*calor*⟩ sticky; **hacía un día ~** it was a close *o* muggy day **2** ⟨*espectáculo/situación*⟩ embarrassing

bocina *f* **1** (de coche) horn; (de fábrica) hooter, siren; (de faro) foghorn **2** (AmL) (auricular) receiver **3** (Méx) (Audio) loudspeaker

bocio *m* goiter*

boda *f* wedding; **~s de oro/plata** (de matrimonio) golden/silver wedding anniversary; (de organización) golden/silver jubilee

bodega *f* **1** **(a)** (Vin) (fábrica) winery; (almacén) wine cellar; (tienda) wine merchant's, wine shop **(b)** (taberna) bar **(c)** (en casa) cellar **2** **(a)** (AmC, Per, Ven) (tienda de comestibles) grocery store (AmE), grocer's (BrE) **(b)** (AmL exc RPl) (depósito) store, warehouse

bodegón *m* **1** (Art) still life **2** (casa de comidas) inn

bodeguero -ra *m,f* **1** (Vin) (productor) ····⊹

wine-producer **2** **(a)** (AmC, Per, Ven) (tendero)
shopkeeper **(b)** (AmL exc RPI) (de un depósito)
warehouseman

bodrio *m* (fam): **es un ~** it is garbage (AmE)
(BrE) rubbish (colloq)

bofetada *f*, **bofetón** *m* slap; **le di** *or* **pegué
una ~** I slapped him (in the face)

boga *f*: **estar en ~** to be in fashion *o* in vogue

Bogotá *m* Bogotá

bogotano -na *adj* of/from Bogotá

bohemio -mia *adj* **(a)** ⟨*vida/artista*⟩ bohemian
(b) (de Bohemia) Bohemian
■ *m,f* bohemian

bohío *m* (AmC, Col, Ven) hut

boicot /boj'kot/ *m* (*pl* **-cots**) boycott

boicotear [A1] *vt* to boycott

boina *f* beret

boite /bwat/ *f* night club

bol *m* bowl

bola *f* **1** (cuerpo redondo) ball; (de helado) scoop;
(Dep) ball; (de petanca) boule; (canica) (Col, Per)
marble; **~ de cristal** crystal ball; **~ de nieve**
snowball; **~ de partido/de set** match/set point
2 **bolas** *fpl* (fam: en algunas regiones vulg)
(testículos) balls (*pl*) (colloq *o* vulg); **estar en ~s**
(fam *or* vulg) to be stark naked (colloq); **hacerse ~s
con algo** (Méx) to get in a mess over sth
3 (fam) (mentira) lie, fib (colloq); **me metió una ~**
he told me a fib; **contar/decir ~s** to fib (colloq), to
tell fibs (colloq)
4 (Méx fam) (montón): **una ~ de** loads of (colloq)

bolchevique *adj/mf* Bolshevik

boleador -dora *m,f* **1** (Méx) (lustrabotas)
bootblack **2** (en las pampas) *person who uses bolas
to catch cattle*

boleadoras *fpl* bolas

bolear [A1] *vi* (Col) to knock up, knock a ball
about
■ **~** *vt* (Méx) to polish, shine

bolera *f* bowling alley

bolero¹ *m* **1** (Mús) bolero **2** (Indum) bolero
jacket/top

bolero² -ra *m,f* (Méx) bootblack

boleta *f* **(a)** (AmL) (en rifa) ticket **(b)** (CS) (de
multa) ticket **(c)** (CS) (recibo) receipt **(d)** (Col)
(entrada) ticket; **~ de calificaciones** (Méx) school
report, report card (AmE); **~ de depósito** (RPI)
deposit slip (AmE), paying-in slip (BrE); **~
electoral** (Méx, RPI) ballot paper

boletaje *m* (Méx, Per) tickets (*pl*)

boletería *f* (AmL) (de teatro, cine) box office; (de
estación, estadio) ticket office

boletín *m* bulletin; **~ de calificaciones** *or* **notas**
school report, report card (AmE)

boleto *m* (de lotería, rifa) ticket; (de quinielas) (Esp)
coupon; (de tren, autobús) (AmL) ticket; **~ de ida**
(AmL) one-way ticket, single (ticket) (BrE); **~ de
ida y vuelta** (AmL) round trip (ticket) (AmE),
return (ticket) (BrE); **~ de viaje redondo** (Méx)
round trip (ticket) (AmE), return (ticket) (BrE)

boli *m* (Esp fam) ballpoint pen, Biro® (BrE)

boliche *m* **1** **(a)** (en petanca) jack **(b)** (juguete)
cup-and-ball toy **(c)** (Col) (bolo) tenpin **2** (Méx)
(juego) bowling, ten pin bowling (BrE); (lugar)
bowling alley **3** **(a)** (CS) (tienda pequeña) (fam)
small store (AmE), small shop (BrE) **(b)** (Bol, RPI)
(taberna) bar

bolígrafo *m* ballpoint pen, Biro®

bolillo *m* (en pasamanería) bobbin; **encaje de ~s**
bobbin lace

bolita *f* (AmS) (Jueg) marble; **jugar a las ~s** to
play marbles

bolívar *m* bolivar (*Venezuelan unit of currency*)

Bolivia *f* Bolivia

boliviano -na *adj/m,f* Bolivian

bollo *m* (Coc) bun; **ser un ~** (RPI fam) to be a
piece of cake (colloq)

bolo *m* **(a)** (palo) skittle, tenpin **(b)** **bolos** *mpl*
(juego) bowling, ten pin bowling (BrE); **jugar a los
~s** to play skittles, to go bowling

bolsa *f* **1** **(a)** (en general) bag; **~ de plástico/de
la compra** plastic/shopping bag; **~ de (la) basura**
garbage *o* trash bag (AmE), rubbish bag *o* bin
liner (BrE); **una ~ de patatas fritas** (Esp) a bag of
chips (AmE), a packet *o* bag of crisps (BrE); **~ de
agua caliente** hot-water bottle **(b)** (Méx) (bolso)
handbag, purse (AmE)
2 **(a)** (de marsupial) pouch **(b)** scrotum **(c)** (Méx)
(bolsillo) pocket
3 (de aire, gas, agua) pocket
4 (Econ, Fin) *tb* **B~** *or* **~ de valores** stock
exchange, stock market; **jugar a la ~** to play the
market; **se cotizará en ~** it will be listed on the
stock exchange; **~ de empleo** (Col) employment
agency; **~ de trabajo** *job vacancies and place
where they are advertised*

bolsear [A1] *vt* **(a)** (Méx fam) (robar): **me ~on en
el camión** I had my pocket picked on the bus **(b)**
(Chi fam) ⟨*comida/cigarillos*⟩ **~le algo ʌ algn** to
scrounge sth FROM *o* OFF sb

bolsillo *m* pocket; **de ~** ⟨*calculadora/
diccionario*⟩ pocket (*before n*); **meterse a algn en
el ~** to get sb eating out of one's hand

bolso *m* (de mujer) (Esp) handbag, purse (AmE); **~
de mano** (de viaje) (overnight) bag; (de mujer) (Esp)
handbag, purse (AmE); **~ de viaje** (overnight) bag

boludo -da *adj* (Col, RPI, Ven vulg) (imbécil): **es tan
~** he's such a jerk (colloq) *o* (vulg) prick
■ *m,f* (Col, RPI, Ven vulg) asshole (AmE vulg),
dickhead (BrE vulg)

bomba *f* **1** **(a)** (Arm, Mil) bomb; **lanzar/arrojar
~s** to drop bombs; **poner una ~** to plant a bomb;
~ atómica atom *o* atomic bomb; **~ de tiempo**
time bomb; **~ lacrimógena** tear gas canister; **caer
como una ~** «*noticia*» to come as a bombshell
(b) (notición) big news **(c)** (en fútbol americano) bomb
2 (Tec) pump; **~ de aire** pump; **~ de agua** water
pump **3** (Andes, Ven) (gasolinera) gas station (AmE),
petrol station (BrE) **4** (Chi) (vehículo) fire engine,
fire truck (AmE); (estación) fire station

bombacha *f* (a) (CS) (de gaucho) baggy trousers (*pl*) (b) (RPl) (de mujer) panties (*pl*), knickers (*pl*) (BrE)

bombardear [A1] *vt* (desde avión) to bomb; (con artillería) to bombard, shell; **me ∼o a preguntas** they bombarded me with questions

bombardeo *m* (desde aviones) bombing; (con artillería) bombardment, shelling

bombardero *m* bomber

bombazo *m* ⓵ (Méx) (explosión) bomb explosion ⓶ (fam) (noticia) bombshell

bombear [A1] *vt* to pump

bombero *mf*, **bombero -ra** *m,f* (de incendios) (*m*) firefighter, fireman; (*f*) firefighter; **llamar a los ∼s** to call the fire department (AmE) *o* (BrE) brigade; **cuerpo de ∼s** fire department (AmE) *o* (BrE) brigade

bombilla *f* ⓵ (Esp) (Elec) light bulb ⓶ (para el mate) *tube through which mate tea is drunk*

bombillo *m* (AmC, Col, Ven) light bulb

bombín *m* ⓵ (Indum) derby (AmE), bowler hat (BrE) ⓶ (para inflar) pump

bombita *f* (RPl) (Elec) light bulb

bombo *m* ⓵ (Mús) (instrumento) bass drum; (músico) bass drummer; **tengo la cabeza como un ∼** my head's about to explode; **con ∼s y platillos** *or* (Esp) **a ∼ y platillo** with a great fanfare; **darle ∼ a algo** to give sth a lot of hype (colloq) ⓶ (de sorteo) drum

bombón *m* (a) (confite) chocolate (b) (fam) (persona) stunner (colloq) (c) (Méx) (malvavisco) marshmallow

bombona *f* gas cylinder *o* canister

bombonería *f* candy store (AmE), sweet shop (BrE)

bonachón -chona *adj* (fam) (amable) good-natured, kind
■ *m,f* (fam) (persona amable) good-natured *o* kind person

bonaerense *adj*: *of/from the province of Buenos Aires*

bonche *m* ⓵ (AmC, Col fam) (riña) fight; (contienda) contest ⓶ (Ven fam) (fiesta) party, rave-up (BrE sl)

bondad *f* (a) (afabilidad, generosidad) goodness, kindness; **¿tendría la ∼ de cerrar la puerta?** (frml) would you mind closing the door? (b) (del clima) mildness

bondadoso -sa *adj* kind, kindhearted, kindly

bongó, bongo *m* bongo

boniato *m* sweet potato

bonificación *f* (a) (aumento, beneficio) bonus (b) (descuento) discount

bonito¹ -ta *adj* pretty; ⟨canción/apartamento⟩ nice, lovely

bonito² *m* tuna, bonito

bono *m* (vale) voucher; (Econ, Fin) bond

boquera *f* cold sore

boquerón *m* anchovy

boquete *m* hole

boquiabierto -ta *adj*: **quedarse ∼** to be speechless *o* dumbfounded

boquilla *f* (de instrumento musical) mouthpiece; (de pipa) stem; (para cigarrillos) cigarette holder

borbotón *m* gush; **a borbotones** ⟨hervir⟩ fiercely; ⟨salir⟩ «sangre/agua» to gush out

borda *f* gunwale, rail; **echar** *or* **tirar algo por la ∼** to throw sth overboard

bordado¹ -da *adj* ⟨mantel/sábana⟩ embroidered

bordado² *m* embroidery

bordar [A1] *vt* ⟨sábana/blusa⟩ to embroider; **lo bordó a mano** she embroidered it by hand

borde *m* (de mesa, cama, acantilado) edge; (de moneda, taza, vaso) rim; **llenó el vaso hasta el ∼** she filled the glass to the brim; **al ∼ de algo** ⟨de la guerra/locura⟩ on the brink of sth; ⟨de las lágrimas/del caos/de la ruina⟩ on the verge of sth; **al ∼ de la muerte** on the point of death

bordear [A1] *vt* (a) (seguir el borde de) ⟨costa⟩ to go along; ⟨isla⟩ to go around (b) (estar a lo largo del borde): **un camino bordeado de álamos** a road lined with poplars

bordillo *m* curb (AmE), kerb (BrE)

bordo *m*: **a ∼** on board; **subir a ∼** to go aboard *o* on board

borgoña *m* (Vin) Burgundy, burgundy

borra *f* (sedimento — del café) dregs; (— del vino) lees (*pl*), sediment

borrachera *f*: **pegarse** *or* (Esp) **cogerse** *or* (esp AmL) **agarrarse una ∼** to get drunk

borracho -cha *adj* (a) [ESTAR] drunk (b) [SER]: **es muy ∼** he is a drunkard *o* a heavy drinker
■ *m,f* drunk; (habitual) drunkard, drunk

borrador *m* ⓵ (de redacción, carta) rough draft; (de contrato, proyecto) draft; (de dibujo) sketch; **lo hice en ∼** I did a rough draft ⓶ (para la pizarra) eraser (AmE), board rubber (BrE)

borraja *f* borage

borrar [A1] *vt* (a) ⟨palabra/dibujo⟩ (con goma) to rub out, erase; (con líquido corrector) to white out, tippex out (BrE); ⟨pizarra⟩ to clean; ⟨huellas digitales⟩ to wipe off (b) ⟨cassette/disquete⟩ to erase, wipe (c) (Inf) ⟨archivo⟩ delete; ⟨pantalla⟩ to clear (d) ⟨recuerdos/imagen⟩ to blot out
■ **borrarse** *v pron* «inscripción/letrero» to fade; **se borró con la lluvia** the rain washed it away *o* off

borrasca *f* (a) (área de bajas presiones) area of low pressure (b) (tormenta) squall

borrascoso -sa *adj* ⟨viento⟩ squally; ⟨tiempo⟩ stormy, squally

borrego -ga *m,f* (cordero) lamb; (oveja) sheep

borrón *m* (mancha) inkblot; (mancha borroneada) smudge; **∼ y cuenta nueva** let's make a fresh start

borronear [A1] *vt* to smudge

borroso -sa *adj* ⟨foto/imagen⟩ blurred; ⟨inscripción⟩ worn; ⟨contorno⟩ indistinct, blurred

boscoso -sa *adj* wooded

bosque *m* wood; (más grande) forest, woods (*pl*); (terreno) woodland; **∼ ecuatorial** *or* **pluvial** (equatorial) rainforest

bosquejar [A1] *vt* (Art) to sketch, make a sketch of; ⟨idea/proyecto⟩ to outline, sketch out

bosquejo *m* (Art) sketch; (de novela) outline

bostezar [A4] *vi* to yawn

bostezo *m* yawn

bota *f* ⓵ (calzado) boot; **∼s de caña alta/de** ⋯∴

media caña knee-high/calf-length boots; ~s de
agua rubber boots, wellingtons (BrE); ~s de
esquí/montar ski/riding boots [2] (para vino) small
wineskin

botadero *m* (Andes) *tb* ~ **de basura** garbage
dump (AmE), rubbish dump *o* tip (BrE)

botado -da *adj* [ESTAR] (AmS exc RPl fam) **(a)**
(barato) dirt cheap (colloq) **(b)** (fácil) dead easy
(colloq)

botadura *f* launching

botana *f* (Méx) snack, appetizer

botánico -ca *adj* botanical

botar [A1] *vt* [1] ‹barco› to launch
[2] ‹pelota› to bounce
[3] (AmL exc RPl) (tirar) to throw ... out; **no lo botes
al suelo** don't throw it on the ground; **bótalo a la
basura** chuck *o* throw it out (colloq); ~ **el dinero**
to throw your money away
[4] (AmL exc RPl fam) **(a)** (echar — de lugar) to throw
... out (colloq); (— de trabajo) to fire (colloq), to sack
(BrE colloq) **(b)** (abandonar) ‹novio/novia› to chuck
(colloq), to ditch (colloq); ‹marido/esposa› to leave;
el tren nos dejó botados we missed the train
[5] (AmL exc RPl fam) (derribar) ‹puerta/árbol› to
knock down; ‹botella/taza› to knock over; **no
empujes que me botas** stop pushing, you're going
to knock me over
[6] (AmL exc RPl) (perder) ‹aceite/gasolina› to leak
■ ~ *vi* (Esp) ‹pelota› to bounce
■ **botarse** *v pron* (AmL exc CS fam) **(a)** (apresurarse)
to rush **(b)** (arrojarse) to jump

botarate *mf* **(a)** (fam) (irresponsable)
irresponsible fool **(b)** (AmL exc RPl) (derrochador)
spendthrift

bote *m* [1] (Náut) boat; ~ **de** *or* **a remos** rowboat
(AmE), rowing boat (BrE); ~ **salvavidas** lifeboat
[2] (recipiente — de lata) tin; (— de vidrio, plástico)
storage jar; (— de cerveza) (Esp) can; (— de
mermelada) (Esp) jar; **el** ~ **de la basura** (Méx) the
trash can (AmE), the rubbish bin (BrE); **de** ~ **en**
~ packed [3] (de pelota) bounce; **dio dos** ~**s** it
bounced twice

botella *f* bottle; **una** ~ **de vino** (recipiente) a wine
bottle; (con contenido) a bottle of wine; **cerveza de
or en ~ bottled beer

botica *f* (en algunas regiones ant) (farmacia)
pharmacy

botijo *m*: *drinking jug with spout*

botillería *f* (Chi) liquor store (AmE), off licence
(BrE)

botín *m* [1] (bota corta) ankle boot; (de bebé)
bootee; (de futbolista) (CS) boot [2] (de guerra)
plunder, booty; (de ladrones) haul, loot

botiquín *m* **(a)** (armario — para medicinas)
medicine chest *o* cabinet; (— para colonias, jabón,
etc) bathroom cabinet **(b)** (maletín) *tb* ~ **de
primeros auxilios** first-aid kit

botón *m* [1] (Indum) button; ~ **de presión** (AmL)
snap fastener, press stud (BrE) [2] (de
mecanismo) button; **el** ~ **del volumen** the volume
control [3] (AmL) (insignia) badge, button (AmE)
[4] (de flor) bud

botones *mf* (*pl* ~) (de hotel) bellboy; (de oficina)
(*m*) office boy; (*f*) office girl

bouquet /bu'ke/ *m* (*pl* **-quets**) **(a)** (del vino)
bouquet **(b)** (ramillete) bouquet

boutique /bu'tik/ *f* boutique

bóveda *f* [1] (Arquit) vault; ~ **de seguridad** (AmL)
bank vault [2] (RPl) (sepulcro) tomb

bovino -na *adj* bovine

bowling /'boulin/ *m* **(a)** (deporte) tenpins (AmE),
tenpin bowling (BrE) **(b)** (lugar) bowling alley

box /boks/ *m* (AmL) (boxeo) boxing

boxeador -dora *m,f* boxer

boxear [A1] *vi* to box

boxeo *m* boxing

boya *f* (Náut) buoy; (en pesca) float

boyante *adj* ‹situación/economía› buoyant

bozal *m* (de perro) muzzle; (de caballo) halter

bozo *m* down (on upper lip)

bracero -ra *m,f* temporary farm worker

bragas *fpl* (Esp) (de mujer) panties (*pl*), knickers
(*pl*) (BrE)

braguero *m* truss

bragueta *f* fly, flies (*pl*)

braille /'brajle/ *adj* braille (before *n*)
■ *m* braille

bramante *m* twine, string

bramar [A1] *vi* «toro/ciervo» to bellow;
«elefante» to trumpet

bramido *m* (de toro, ciervo) bellowing; (de elefante)
trumpeting; **dio un** ~ it bellowed/trumpeted

branquia *f* gill

brasa *f* ember; **carne/pescado a la(s)** ~**(s)**
charcoal-grilled meat/fish

brasero *m* (de carbón — para interiores) small
brazier; (— para la intemperie) brazier; (eléctrico)
electric heater

brasier *m* (Col, Méx, Ven) bra

Brasil *m*: *tb* **el** ~ Brazil

brasileño -ña, (AmL) **brasilero -ra** *adj/m,f*
Brazilian

bravío -vía *adj* ‹toro› fierce, wild; ‹potro› wild,
unmanageable

bravo¹ -va *adj* **(a)** [SER] ‹toro/perro› fierce; *ver
tb* TORO **(b)** [ESTAR] ‹mar› rough **(c)** [ESTAR]
(AmL fam) (enojado) angry

**bravo² ** *interj* (expresando aprobación) well done!,
good job! (AmE); (tras actuación) bravo!

bravucón -cona *adj* (fam) bragging (before *n*)

bravuconada *f* piece of bravado; ~**s** bravado

braza *f* (Esp) (en natación) breaststroke; **nadar a
**~ to swim (the) breaststroke

brazada *f* (al nadar) stroke

brazalete *m* **(a)** (pulsera — de una pieza) bangle,
bracelet; (— de eslabones) bracelet **(b)** (de tela)
armband

brazo *m* [1] (Anat) arm; (parte superior) upper
arm; **llevaba una cesta al** ~ she had a basket on
one arm; **caminar/ir del** ~ to walk arm in arm;
llevaba al niño en ~**s** he was carrying the child
in his arms; **cruzado de** ~**s: no te quedes ahí
cruzado de** ~**s** don't just stand/sit there (doing
nothing); **dar el** ~ **a torcer** to give in; **no dio el** *or*
su ~ **a torcer** he didn't let them/her twist his
arm
[2] (de sillón) arm; (de tocadiscos) arm; (de grúa) jib;
(de río) branch, channel; ~ **de gitano** (Coc) jelly
roll (AmE), swiss roll (BrE); ~ **de mar** inlet, sound
[3] **brazos** *mpl* (trabajadores) hands (*pl*)

brea *f* pitch, tar

brebaje *m* potion; **un** ~ **mágico** a magic potion

brecha f (en muro) breach, opening; (en la frente, cabeza) gash; ~ **generacional** generation gap

bretel m (CS) strap

bretón¹ -tona adj/m,f Breton

bretón² m (idioma) Breton

breva f (Bot) early fig, black fig

breve adj (frml) brief, short; ⟨viaje/distancia⟩ short; **dentro de ~s momentos** in a few moments; **sea usted ~, por favor** please be brief; **en ~** shortly, soon

brevedad f (a) (de discurso, texto) brevity (b) (frml) (prontitud): **con la mayor ~** or **a la ~ posible** as soon as possible o (frml) at your earliest convenience

brevete m (Per) driver's license (AmE), driving licence (BrE)

bribón -bona m,f (fam) rascal (colloq), scamp (colloq)

bricolaje, bricolage m do-it-yourself, DIY

brida f bridle

briega f (Col) hard work, struggle

brigada f (Mil) brigade; (de policía) squad; ~ **de explosivos** bomb squad; ~ **antidroga** or **de estupefacientes** drug squad; ~ **de salvamento** rescue team

brillante adj (a) ⟨luz/estrella/color⟩ bright; ⟨zapatos/metal/pelo⟩ shiny; ⟨pintura⟩ gloss (before n); ⟨papel⟩ glossy; ⟨tela⟩ with a sheen (b) ⟨escritor/porvenir⟩ brilliant; ⟨mente⟩ great; **su actuación fue ~** she performed brilliantly
■ m (diamante) diamond; **un anillo de ~s** a diamond ring

brillar [A1] vi (a) «sol/luz» to shine; «estrella» to shine, sparkle; «zapatos/suelo/metal» to shine, gleam; «diamante/ojos» to sparkle (b) (destacarse) «persona» to shine
■ ~ vt (Col) to polish

brillo m (a) (en general) shine; (de estrella) brightness, brilliance; (de diamante, ojos) sparkle; (de tela) sheen; **darle ~ al suelo** to polish the floor; **fotos con ~** gloss finish photos; **dale un poco de ~** (TV) turn the brightness up a bit (b) (esplendor, lucimiento) splendor*; **sin ~** ⟨discurso/interpretación⟩ dull (c) (para labios) lip gloss; (para uñas) clear nail polish

brilloso -sa adj (AmL) shiny

brincar [A2] vi «niño» to jump up and down; «cordero» to gambol, skip around; «liebre» to hop; ~ **de alegría** to jump for joy
■ ~ vt (Méx) ⟨valla/obstáculo⟩ to jump

brinco m jump, leap, bound; **pegó** or **dio un ~ del susto** (fam) he jumped with fright

brindar [A1] vi to drink a toast; ~ **POR algn/ algo** to drink a toast TO sb/sth
■ ~ vt (frml) (proporcionar) to give; **le brindó su apoyo** she gave him her support
■ **brindarse** v pron (frml) ~**se ʌ hacer algo** to offer o volunteer to do sth; **se brindó a acompañarme** he offered o volunteered to accompany me

brindis m (pl ~) toast; **hacer un ~ por algn** to drink a toast to sb

brío m (a) (ánimo, energía) spirit; **luchó con ~** he fought with great spirit o determination (b) (de caballo) spirit

brioso -sa adj ⟨caballo⟩ spirited

brisa f breeze

británico -ca adj British
■ m,f British person, Briton; **los ~s** the British, British people

brizna f (hebra) strand; (de hierba) blade

briznar [A1] v impers (Ven) to drizzle

broca f (drill) bit

brocado m brocade

brocha f (de pintor) paintbrush, brush; (de afeitar) shaving brush; (en cosmética) blusher brush

broche m (a) (joya) brooch (b) (de collar, monedero) clasp; ~ **de presión** (AmL) snap fastener (AmE), press stud (BrE) (c) (Méx, Ur) (para el pelo) barrette (AmE), hair slide (BrE) (d) (Arg) (grapa) staple

brocheta f (aguja) brochette, skewer; (plato) kebab

brócoli m broccoli

broma f joke; **hacerle** or **gastarle una ~ a algn** to play a (practical) joke on sb; **déjate de ~s** stop kidding around (colloq); **no estoy para ~s** I'm not in the mood for jokes; ~**s aparte** joking apart; **lo dije de** or **en ~** I was joking; **ni en ~** no way (colloq)

bromear [A1] vi to joke

bromista adj: **es muy ~** he's always joking; **¡qué ~ eres!** you're such a joker
■ mf joker

bromuro m bromide

bronca f ① (a) (fam) (disputa, lío) row; **armar** or **montar una ~** to kick up a fuss (colloq); **buscar ~** to look for trouble o a fight (b) (alboroto, bullicio) racket (colloq) ② (esp Esp fam) (regañina) scolding, telling off (colloq); **echarle la ~ a algn** to tell sb off ③ (AmL fam) (rabia): **está con una ~** he's furious; **me da mucha ~** it really gets to o bugs me (colloq); **tenerle ~ a algn** to have it in for sb (colloq)

bronce m (a) (para estatuas, cañones) bronze; **una medalla de ~** a bronze medal (b) (AmL) (para llamadores, placas) brass

bronceado¹ -da adj tanned, suntanned

bronceado² m (de la piel) tan, suntan; (Metal) bronzing

bronceador m suntan lotion

broncear [A1] vt «piel» to tan
■ **broncearse** v pron to get a tan o a suntan

bronconeumonía f bronchopneumonia

bronquio m bronchial tube

bronquitis f bronchitis

brotar [A1] vi (a) «planta» to sprout, come up; «hoja» to appear, sprout; «flor» to come out (b) «sarampión/grano» to appear
■ **brotarse** v pron (AmL) to come out in spots

brote m (a) (Bot) shoot; **echar ~s** to sprout, put out shoots (b) (de violencia, enfermedad) outbreak (c) (Col) (sarpullido) rash

bruces: de ~ (loc adv) face down; **se cayó de ~** he fell flat on his face

brujería f witchcraft

brujo -ja adj (a) ⟨ojos/amor⟩ bewitching (b) (AmC, Méx fam) (sin dinero) broke (colloq)
■ m,f (m) warlock; (f) witch

brújula f compass

bruma f (marina) (sea) mist; (del alba) mist

b

brumoso -sa adj misty

bruñir [I9] vt to polish

brusco -ca adj (a) ‹movimiento/cambio› abrupt, sudden; ‹subida/descenso› sharp, sudden (b) ‹carácter/modales› rough; ‹tono/gesto› brusque, abrupt; ‹respuesta› curt, brusque

Bruselas f Brussels

brusquedad f (a) (en el trato) roughness; con ~ ‹hablar/actuar› abruptly (b) (de movimiento) abruptness, suddenness; **frenó con** ~ he braked sharply

brutal adj ‹crimen› brutal; ‹atentado› savage

brutalidad f brutality, savageness

bruto -ta adj [1] ‹persona› (a) (ignorante) ignorant (b) (violento, brusco); **¡qué** ~**!** what a brute! [2] ‹peso/sueldo› gross; **en** ~ ‹diamante› uncut; ‹mineral› crude
■ m,f (a) (ignorante) ignorant person (b) (persona violenta) brute, animal

bucal adj ‹lesión› mouth (before n); ‹antiséptico/higiene› oral (before n)

buceador -dora m,f diver

bucear [A1] vi to swim underwater, to dive

buceo m underwater swimming, diving

buchaca f (Col) pocket

buche m [1] (a) (de aves) crop (b) (de otros animales) maw [2] (Med, Odont): **hacer** ~**s con algo** to rinse one's mouth out with sth

bucle m (a) (en el pelo) ringlet (b) (Inf) loop

bucólico -ca adj bucolic, pastoral

budín m (a) (dulce) pudding (b) (salado) pie

budismo m Buddhism

budista adj/mf Buddhist

buen adj ▶ BUENO¹

buenaventura f (a) (buena suerte) good fortune (b) (futuro): **me dijo/leyó la** ~ she told my fortune

buen mozo, -na moza adj ‹hombre› good-looking, handsome; ‹mujer› attractive, good-looking

bueno¹ -na adj [BUEN is used before masculine singular nouns]
[1] [SER] (a) ‹hotel/producto/trabajo› good; **ropa buena** good-quality clothes; **la buena mesa** good cooking (b) ‹remedio/método› good; **es** ~ **para la gripe/los dolores de cabeza** it's good for the flu/headaches (c) ‹médico/alumno› good; **un buen padre/amigo** he's a good father/friend; **es muy buena en francés** she's very good at French; **es buena para los negocios** she's got a good head for business (d) (amable, bondadoso) good, kind; **fueron muy** ~**s conmigo** they were very good o kind to me (e) (conveniente, correcto) good; **no es buena hora** it's not a good time; **no es** ~ **comer tanto** it isn't good to eat so much; **es** ~ **para la salud** it's good for your health; **su inglés es** ~ her English is good
[2] (a) (agradable) nice; **hace muy buen tiempo** the weather is nice (b) ‹comida› (en general) **ser** ~ to be good, be nice; (en particular) **estar** ~ to be good, be nice; **el guacamole es buenísimo** guacamole is

really good; **esta sopa está muy buena** this soup is very good (c) (favorable) ‹oferta/crítica› good; **una buena noticia** a piece of good news
[3] [ESTAR] (a) (en buen estado) ‹leche/pescado› fresh; **esta leche no está buena** this milk is off o sour (b) (fam) (sexualmente atractivo): **está buenísimo** he's really gorgeous
[4] (saludable, sano) ‹costumbre/alimentación› good; **estar en buena forma** to be in good shape
[5] (a) (en fórmulas, saludos) good; **¡**~**s días!** good morning; **¡buenas tardes!** (temprano) good afternoon; (más tarde) good evening; **¡buenas noches!** (al llegar) good evening; (al despedirse) good night; **¡buen viaje!** have a good trip!; **¡buen provecho!** enjoy your meal (b) (delante del n) (uso enfático) ‹susto› terrible; **una buena cantidad** a fair amount; **un buen día** one day (c) **¡qué** ~**!** (AmL) great (d) **de buenas a primeras** suddenly; **por las buenas** willingly
■ m,f (a) (hum o leng infantil) (en películas, cuentos) goody (colloq); **los** ~**s y los malos** the good guys and the bad guys (colloq) (b) (bonachón, buenazo): **el** ~ **de Juan/la buena de Pilar** good old Juan/Pilar

bueno² interj [1] (a) (expresando — duda) well; (— conformidad) OK (colloq), all right; **¿un café? — bueno** coffee? — OK o all right (b) (expresando resignación): ~, **otra vez será** never mind, maybe next time (c) (expresando irritación): ~, **se acabó ¡a la cama!** right, that's it, bed!; **¡y** ~**! ¿qué querías que hiciera?** (RPl) well, what did you expect me to do? [2] (Méx) (al contestar el teléfono) **¡**~**!** hello

Buenos Aires m Buenos Aires

buey m (Agr, Zool) ox
■ adj (Méx fam) dumb (colloq)

búfalo¹ -la adj (AmC fam) great (colloq), fantastic (colloq)

búfalo² m buffalo

bufanda f scarf

bufar [A1] vi to snort

bufet /buˈfe/, **bufé** m [1] (Coc) buffet [2] (Andes) (aparador) sideboard

bufete m (Der) (despacho) lawyer's office; (negocio) legal practice, law firm

bufido m snort

bufón m (Hist) jester; (gracioso) (fam) clown (colloq)

buhardilla f (a) (desván) attic (b) (apartamento) attic apartment (AmE) o (BrE) room (c) (ventana) dormer window

búho m owl

buitre m vulture

bujía f (a) (Auto) spark plug (b) (AmC) (Elec) light bulb

bula f (Relig) bull; ~ **papal** papal bull

bulbo m bulb

bulevar m boulevard

Bulgaria f Bulgaria

búlgaro¹ -ra adj/m,f Bulgarian

búlgaro² m (idioma) Bulgarian

bulín m [1] (RPl fam) (a) (de soltero) bachelor pad

(b) (vivienda): **se compraron un bulincito** they bought a little place of their own (colloq) **2** (Per) (burdel) brothel

bulla *f* (ruido) racket (colloq), ruckus (AmE colloq); (actividad) bustle; **armar** *or* **meter** ~ to make a racket, to create a ruckus

bullanguero -ra *adj* (fam) ⟨*persona*⟩ fun-loving; ⟨*música/ambiente*⟩ lively

bullicio *m* **(a)** (ruido) noise, racket (colloq) **(b)** (actividad) **el** ~ **de la gran ciudad** the hustle and bustle of the city

bullicioso -sa *adj* noisy

bullir [I9] *vi*: **la calle bullía de gente** the street was teeming *o* swarming with people; **el lugar bullía de actividad** the place was a hive of activity

bulto *m* **1** **(a)** (cuerpo, forma) shape; **vi un** ~ **que se movía** I saw a shape moving; **escurrir el** ~ (fam) (en el trabajo) to duck out; (en entrevista) to dodge the issue **(b)** (volumen): **hace mucho/poco** ~ it is/isn't very bulky **2** (Med) lump **3** **(a)** (maleta, bolsa) piece of luggage; ~ **de mano** piece *o* item of hand baggage *o* luggage; **cargada de** ~**s** laden with packages (*o* bags *etc*) **(b)** (Col, Méx) (saco) sack

búnker /'buŋker/ *m* (*pl* **-kers**) bunker

buñuelo *m* fritter

BUP /bup/ *m* (en Esp) = **Bachillerato Unificado Polivalente**

buque *m* ship, vessel; ~ **cisterna/de guerra** tanker/warship

burbuja *f* (de gas, aire) bubble; **una bebida con/ sin** ~**s** a fizzy/still drink

burbujear [A1] *vi* **(a)** («champán/agua mineral») to fizz **(b)** (al hervir) to bubble

burdel *m* brothel

burdeos *adj inv* (color) burgundy

burdo -da *adj* **(a)** ⟨*persona/modales*⟩ coarse **(b)** ⟨*mentira*⟩ blatant; ⟨*imitación*⟩ crude; ⟨*excusa*⟩ flimsy **(c)** ⟨*paño/tela*⟩ rough, coarse

burgués -guesa *adj* (Hist) bourgeois; (de clase media) middle-class; (pey) bourgeois (pej)
■ *m,f* **(a)** (Hist) bourgeois **(b)** (persona de clase media) member of the middle class; (pey) bourgeois

burguesía *f* (Hist) bourgeoisie; (clase media) middle class, middle classes (*pl*); (pey) bourgeoisie

burla *f* **(a)** (mofa): **hacerle** ~ **a algn** to make fun of sb, to mock sb **(b)** (atropello): **esto es una** ~ **del reglamento** this makes a mockery of the regulations

burladero *m*: *barrier behind which the bullfighter takes refuge*

burlar [A1] *vt* **(a)** ⟨*medidas de seguridad*⟩ to evade, get around; ~**on la vigilancia de la policía** they slipped past the police **(b)** ⟨*enemigo*⟩ to outwit
■ **burlarse** *v pron* ~**se** DE **algo/algn** to make fun *o*F sth/sb

burlesco -ca *adj* ⟨*género*⟩ burlesque; ⟨*espectáculo*⟩ comic

burlete *m* draft* excluder

burlón -lona *adj* **(a)** (de mofa) ⟨*actitud/tono*⟩ mocking; ⟨*risa*⟩ sardonic, derisive **(b)** (de broma) ⟨*actitud*⟩ joking, teasing

buró *m* **(a)** (escritorio) writing desk, bureau (BrE) **(b)** (Méx) (mesa de noche) bedside table

burocracia *f* bureaucracy

burócrata *mf* **(a)** (pey) bureaucrat (pej) **(b)** (Méx) (funcionario) civil servant, official

burocrático -ca *adj* **(a)** (pey) ⟨*trámite/ proceso*⟩ bureaucratic **(b)** (Méx) ⟨*empleado/ jerarquía*⟩ government (*before n*), state (*before n*)

burrada *f* (fam) (necedad, barbaridad): **decir** ~**s** to talk nonsense *o* drivel; **¿cómo pudiste hacer semejante** ~**?** how could you do such a stupid thing?

burro[1] -rra *adj* **(a)** (fam) (ignorante) stupid, dumb (AmE colloq), thick (BrE colloq) **(b)** (fam) (obstinado, cabezón) pigheaded (colloq)
■ *m,f* **1** (Zool) (asno) (*m*) donkey; (*f*) female donkey, jenny; **trabajar como un** ~ to slog one's guts out **2** (fam) **(a)** (ignorante) idiot **(b)** (cabezón, obstinado) stubborn mule, obstinate pig (colloq)

burro[2] *m* **(a)** (en carpintería) sawhorse; (en herrería) workbench **(b)** (Méx) (para planchar) ironing board; (caballete) trestle; (escalera) stepladder

bursátil *adj* stock market *o* exchange (*before n*)

bus *m* (Auto, Transp) bus; (Inf) bus

busca *f* (búsqueda) search; **en** ~ **de algo** in search of sth; **salieron en su** ~ they set out to look for him
■ *m* (Esp fam) pager, beeper (AmE), bleeper (BrE)

buscador[1] -dora *m,f*: ~ **de oro** gold prospector; ~ **de tesoros** treasure hunter

buscador[2] *m* (Inf) search engine

buscapleitos *mf* (*pl* ~) (fam) troublemaker

buscar [A2] *vt* **1** (intentar encontrar) to look for; ⟨*fama/fortuna*⟩ to seek; **te buscan en la portería** someone is asking for you at reception **(b)** (en libro, lista) to look up; **busca el número en la guía** look up the number in the directory **2** **(a)** (recoger) to collect, pick up; **fui a** ~**lo al aeropuerto** (para traerlo — en coche) I went to pick him up from the airport; (— en tren, a pie) I went to meet him at the airport; **vengo a** ~ **mis cosas** I've come to collect *o* pick up my things **(b)** (conseguir) to get; **yo le busqué trabajo** I found him a job; **fue a** ~ **un médico/un taxi** he went to get a doctor/a taxi; **¿qué buscas con eso?** what are you trying to achieve by that?
■ ~ *vi* to look; **busca en el cajón** look *o* have a look in the drawer
■ **buscarse** *v pron* **1** (intentar encontrar) to look for **2** ⟨*problemas*⟩ to ask for; **no quiero** ~**me complicaciones/problemas** I don't want any trouble; **tú te lo has buscado** you've brought it on yourself, it serves you right; **buscársela(s)** (fam): **te la estás buscando** you're asking for trouble, you're asking for it (colloq)

buseta *f* (Col, Ven) small bus

búsqueda *f* ~ (DE algo/algn) search (FOR sth/ sb)

busto *m* bust

butaca *f* **(a)** (con respaldo) (esp Esp) armchair; (sin respaldo) (esp AmL) stool **(b)** (en teatro, cine) seat; ~ **de patio** (Esp) orchestra (AmE) *o* (BrE) stall seat

buzo *m* **1** (Náut) diver **2** (Indum) **(a)** (Chi, Per) (para hacer ejercicio) track suit **(b)** (Col) (suéter de ⋯

cuello alto) turtleneck sweater (AmE), polo-neck
jumper (BrE) **(c)** (Arg, Col) (camiseta) sweatshirt **(d)**
(Ur) (jersey) sweater, jumper (BrE)
buzón *m* (en la calle) postbox, mailbox (AmE),

letter-box (BrE); (en una casa) mailbox (AmE),
letter-box (BrE); **echar una carta al** *or* **en el** ∼ to
mail (AmE) *o* (BrE) post a letter
byte *m* /'bait/ byte

Cc

C, c *f* (read as /se/ or (Esp) /θe/) the letter C, c
c/ (= **calle**) St, Rd
C *m* (= **centígrado** *or* **Celsius**) C, Centigrade,
Celsius
cabales *mpl*: **no está en sus** ∼ he's not in his
right mind
cabalgar [A3] *vi* (liter) «*jinete*» to ride
cabalgata *f* (desfile) parade; **la** ∼ **de los Reyes
Magos** the Epiphany parade *o* procession
caballa *f* mackerel
caballerango *m* (Méx) groom
caballería *f* (Mil) cavalry
caballeriza *f* (edificio) stable; (caballos) stable,
stables (*pl*)
caballero *m* **(a)** (en general) gentleman; **es todo
un** ∼ he's a perfect gentleman; **sección de** ∼**s**
men's department; **¿en qué puedo servirle,** ∼?
how can I help you, sir?; **❾ caballeros** Men *o*
Gentlemen *o* Gents **(b)** (Hist) knight
caballeroso -sa *adj* gentlemanly, gallant
caballete *m* (para mesa) trestle; (para lienzo,
pizarra) easel; (de moto) kickstand; (del tejado) ridge
caballito *m* **(a)** (juguete — que se mece) rocking
horse; (— con palo) hobbyhorse; ∼ **de mar** sea
horse; *ver tb* CABALLO **(b) caballitos** *mpl*
(carrusel) carousel, merry-go-round
caballo¹ -lla *adj* (AmC fam) (estúpido) stupid
caballo² *m* **1 (a)** (Equ, Zool) horse; **montar** *or*
(AmL) **andar a** ∼ to ride (a horse); **dieron un
paseo a** ∼ they went for a ride (on horseback);
∼ **de carga/de tiro** packhorse/carthorse; ∼ **de
carreras** racehorse; *a* ∼ *entre* ... halfway between
...; *llevar a algn a* ∼ to give sb a piggyback **(b)**
(en ajedrez) knight; (en naipes) ≈queen (*in a
Spanish pack of cards*) **(c)** (Méx) (en gimnasia)
horse **2** (Auto, Fís, Mec) *tb* ∼ **de vapor** (metric)
horsepower
cabaña *f* (choza) cabin, shack
cabaré, cabaret /kaβa're/ *m* (*pl* **-rets**)
cabaret
cabeceada *f* **(a)** (AmL) ▶ CABEZADA **(b)** (CS)
(Dep) header
cabecear [A1] *vi* **(a)** «*persona*» to nod off **(b)**
«*caballo*» to toss its head; «*barco*» to pitch
■ *vt* ‹*balón*› to head
cabecera *f* **(a)** (de la cama) headboard **(b)** (de
una mesa) head, top **(c)** (de una manifestación) head,
front
cabecero *m* headboard
cabecilla *mf* ringleader
cabellera *f* **(a)** (melena) hair **(b)** (de un cometa)
tail

cabello *m* hair; ∼**s de ángel** (fideos) vermicelli
caber [E15] *vi* **1 (a)** (en un lugar) to fit; **no cabe
en la caja** it won't fit in the box; **no cabemos los
cuatro** there isn't room for all four of us; **en esta
botella caben diez litros** this bottle holds ten
liters; **no** ∼ **en sí de alegría** to be beside oneself
with joy **(b)** (pasar) to fit, go; ∼ **POR algo** to go
THROUGH sth **(c)** ‹*falda/zapatos*› to fit; **estos
pantalones ya no me caben** these trousers don't
fit me any more
2 (en 3ª pers) (frml) (ser posible): **cabe la
posibilidad de que haya perdido el tren** he may
have missed the train; **no cabe duda de que** ...
there is no doubt that ...; **cabría decir que** ... it
could be said that ...; **es, si cabe, aún mejor** it is
even better, if such a thing is possible; **dentro de
lo que cabe** all things considered
3 (Mat): **17 entre 5 cabe a 3 y sobran 2** 5 into 17
goes 3 times and 2 over
cabestrillo *m* sling; **llevaba el brazo en** ∼ he
had his arm in a sling
cabeza *f* **1 (a)** (Anat) head; **de la** ∼ **a los pies**
from head to toe *o* foot; **me duele la** ∼ I've got a
headache; **marcó de** ∼ he scored with a header;
pararse la *or* **de** ∼ (AmL) to do a handstand; ∼
rapada skinhead **(b)** (medida) head; **me saca una**
∼ he's a head taller than me **(c)** (pelo) hair; **me
lavé la** ∼ I washed my hair **(d)** (inteligencia): **usa la**
∼ use your head; **¡qué poca** ∼**!** have you/has he
no sense? **(e)** (mente): **¡que** ∼ **la mía!** what a
memory!; **tú estás mal de la** ∼ you're out of your
mind; **se me ha ido de la** ∼ it's gone right out of
my head; **se le ha metido en la** ∼ **que** ... she's got
it into her head that ...; **no se me pasó por la** ∼
it didn't cross my mind; ∼ **de chorlito** *mf* (fam)
scatterbrain (colloq); **írsele a algn la** ∼ to feel
dizzy; **levantar** ∼ (fam) (superar problemas) to get
back on one's feet; **perder la** ∼: **no perdamos la**
∼ let's not panic *o* lose our heads; **perdió la** ∼
por esa mujer he lost his head over that woman;
quitarle a algn algo de la ∼ to get sth out of sb's
head; **romperse la** ∼ (fam) (preocuparse) to rack
one's brains; (lastimarse) to break one's neck
(colloq); **subírsele a algn a la** ∼ «*vino/éxito*» to go
to one's head; **tener la** ∼ **llena de pájaros** (fam) to
have one's head in the clouds
2 (a) (individuo): **por** ∼ each, a head **(b)** (de
ganado): **50** ∼**s de ganado** 50 head of cattle
3 (primer lugar, delantera): **estamos a la** ∼ **del
sector** we are the leading company in this sector;
a la ∼ **de la manifestación** at the front *o* head of
the demonstration; **el equipo va en** ∼ **de la
clasificación** the team is at the top of the
division; ∼ **de familia** head of the family; ∼ **de
serie** seed

4 (a) (de alfiler, clavo, fósforo) head (b) (de misil) warhead **5** (Audio, Video) head **6** (de plátanos) hand, bunch; ~ **de ajo** bulb of garlic

cabezada f (movimiento) nod; **iba dormido, dando ~s** his head kept nodding in his sleep; *dar or echar una ~* (fam) to have a nap (colloq)

cabezal m **1** (a) (almohada) bolster (b) (de sillón) headrest (c) (AmL) (de cama) headboard/footboard **2** (AmL) (terminal) terminal **3** (Audio, Video) head

cabezazo m (a) (golpe): **se dio un ~ en el estante** he hit o banged his head on the shelf (b) (Dep) header

cabezón -zona adj (a) (fam) (terco) pigheaded (colloq) (b) (fam) (de cabeza grande): **¡qué ~ es!** what a big head he has! (c) ⟨vino⟩ heady
■ m,f (fam): **¡eres un ~!** you're so pigheaded! (colloq)

cabezota adj/mf ► CABEZÓN A, B

cabezudo¹ -da adj (de cabeza grande): **es ~** he has a very big head

cabezudo² m: *carnival figure with a large head*

cabida f (capacidad de recipiente, estadio, teatro) capacity; **solo hay ~ para diez pasajeros** there's only room o space for ten passengers; **el estadio puede dar ~ a 100.000 personas** the stadium can hold 100,000 people

cabina f **1** (a) (vestuario) cubicle, stall (AmE) (b) (de laboratorio de idiomas, estudio de radio) booth; ~ **telefónica** telephone booth o (BrE) box **2** (a) (de camión, grúa) cab (b) (Aviac) (para pilotos — en avión grande) flight deck; (— en avión pequeño) cockpit; (para pasajeros) cabin

cabizbajo -ja adj (alicaído) downcast; **caminaba ~** he walked along, head bowed

cable m (Elec, Telec) cable

cablevisión f (esp AmL) cable television

cabo m **1** (Geog) cape **2** (a) (Mil) corporal (b) (en remo) stroke **3** (extremo) end; **al ~ de** after; *de ~ a rabo* (fam) from beginning to end; **llevar a ~** ⟨*misión*⟩ to carry out; **lleva a ~ una excelente labor** he does an excellent job

cabra f goat; **estar como una ~** (fam) to be completely nuts (colloq)

cabrá, cabré, etc ► CABER

cabreado -da adj (fam) furious, mad (colloq)

cabrear [A1] vt (fam) (enfadar) to make ... mad (colloq), to piss ... off (sl)
■ **cabrearse** v pron (fam) (enojarse) to get mad (colloq)

cabreo m (fam) (enojo, irritación): **¡qué ~ tiene!** he's in a foul o a terrible mood! (colloq); **agarrarse un ~** to get mad (colloq), to hit the roof (colloq)

cabría, etc ► CABER

cabriola f: **hacer ~s** ⟨*niño*⟩ to caper o jump around; ⟨*caballo*⟩ to buck, prance around

cabritas fpl (Chi) popcorn

cabrito m (Zool) kid

cabro -bra adj (Chi fam): **es muy ~ para eso** he's too young for that
■ m,f (Chi fam) (niño) kid (colloq)

cabrón¹ -brona adj (Esp, Méx vulg): **el muy ~/la muy cabrona** the bastard o (AmE) son of a bitch (vulg)/the bitch (vulg)
■ m,f (Esp, Méx vulg) (m) bastard (vulg), son of a bitch (AmE vulg); (f) bitch (vulg)

cabrón² m (vulg) (cornudo) cuckold; (proxeneta) (Andes fam o vulg) pimp, ponce (BrE)

cabús m (Méx) caboose (AmE), guard's van (BrE)

caca f (fam o leng infantil): **hacer ~** to go to the bathroom (AmE) o (BrE) toilet (euph), to do a poop (AmE) o (BrE) pooh (used to or by children); **hacerse ~** to mess oneself; **el niño se hizo ~** the baby dirtied his diaper (AmE) o (BrE) nappy (colloq); ~ **de perro** dog mess; **¡no toques eso! ¡~!** don't touch that, it's dirty!

cacahuete, cacahuate m peanut, monkey nut; **me/te/le importa un** ⟨*reverendo*⟩ ~ (Méx fam) I/you/he couldn't give a damn (colloq)

cacao m **1** (a) (Coc) (polvo, bebida) cocoa (b) (Bot) (planta) cacao; (semillas) cocoa beans (pl) (c) (Esp) (para los labios) lipsalve **2** (fam) (jaleo) ruckus (AmE), to-do (BrE); **¡qué ~ se armó!** all hell broke loose (colloq)

cacarear [A1] vi (a) ⟨*gallo*⟩ to crow; ⟨*gallina*⟩ to cluck (b) (fam) (presumir) to brag

cacatúa f (Zool) cockatoo

cacería f (de zorro, jabalí) hunt; (de conejo, perdiz) shoot; **ir de ~** to go hunting/shooting

cacerola f saucepan, pan

cachalote m sperm whale

cachapa f (Ven) corn-based pancake

cachar [A1] vt (a) (AmL fam) ⟨*pelota*⟩ to catch; ⟨*persona*⟩: **la caché del brazo** I caught o grabbed her by the arm (b) (AmL fam) (sorprender, pillar) to catch (c) (RPl fam) (gastar una broma) to kid (colloq) (d) (Andes fam) (enterarse) to get (colloq)

cacharrería f (Col) hardware store, ironmonger's (BrE)

cacharro m (a) (de cocina) pot (b) (fam) (cachivache) thing; (coche viejo) jalopy (AmE), old banger (BrE colloq); (aparato) gadget

cachaza f (bebida) type of rum

cachear [A1] vt **1** (fam) (registrar) to frisk, search **2** (AmL) (Taur) to gore

cachemir m, **cachemira** f cashmere

cachetada f (AmL) slap

cachete m **1** (mejilla) (esp AmL) cheek; (nalga) (CS fam) cheek **2** (esp Esp) (bofetada) slap

cachetear [A1] vt (AmL) to slap

cachetón -tona adj (Andes, Méx fam) (carrilludo) chubby-cheeked

cachimba f pipe; **fumar ~** to smoke a pipe

cachiporra f (palo) billy club (AmE), truncheon (BrE)

cachito m **1** (Méx) (de lotería) one twentieth of a lottery ticket; ver tb CACHO 1 **2** (Ven) (Coc) croissant

cachivache m (fam) (trasto inútil) piece of junk; **tiró todos los ~s que tenía** she threw out all her old junk (colloq)

cacho m **1** (fam) (pedazo) bit **2** (a) (AmS) (cuerno) horn (b) (Andes) (juego) poker dice; (cubilete) shaker

cachondearse [A1] v pron (Esp fam) ~ **DE algn/algo** to make OR fun of sb/sth

cachondeo m (Esp fam): **estar de ~** to be joking; **se lo toma a ~** he treats it as a joke

cachondo -da adj (fam) **(a)** (Esp) (divertido) funny **(b)** (Esp, Méx) (sexualmente) hot (colloq), horny (sl)

cachorro -rra m,f (de perro) puppy, pup; (de león) cub

cachucha f (Col, Méx, Ven) (Indum) cap

cacillo m (cacerola) small saucepan; (cucharón) ladle

cacique m (Hist) chief, cacique; (Pol) local political boss; (hombre poderoso) tyrant

caco m (fam) burglar

cactus (pl ~), **cacto** m cactus

cada adj inv **1 (a)** (con énfasis en el individuo o cosa particular) each; (con énfasis en la totalidad del conjunto) every; **los ganadores de ~ grupo** the winners from each group; **hay un bar en ~ esquina** ther's a bar in every corner; **~ día** every day, each day; **¿~ cuánto viene?** how often does she come?; **hay cinco para ~ uno** there are five each; **cuestan $25 ~ uno** they cost $25 each; **~ uno** or **cual sabe qué es lo que más le conviene** everyone o each individual knows what's best for him or her; **~ vez que viene** every time o whenever he comes (delante de numeral) every; **~ dos días** every two days, every other day; **siete de ~ diez** seven out of (every) ten **2** (indicando progresión): **~ vez más rápido** faster and faster; **lo hace ~ vez mejor** she's getting better all the time; **~ vez más gente** more and more people; **~ vez menos tiempo** less and less time

cadalso m (patíbulo) scaffold; (horca) gallows (pl)

cadáver m (de persona) corpse; (de animal) carcass

cadavérico -ca adj cadaverous, ghastly

caddie, caddy /'kaði/ mf (pl **-dies**) caddy

cadena f **1 (a)** (de eslabones) chain; (para la nieve) (snow) chain; **~ antirrobo** bicycle lock; **~ perpetua** life imprisonment **(b)** (del váter) chain; **tirar de la ~** to flush the toilet **2 (a)** (de hechos, fenómenos) **una larga ~ de atentados** a long series of attacks; **~ de fabricación** or **producción** production line; **~ de montañas** mountain range o chain; **en ~ (transmisión)** simultaneous; **una choque en ~** a pileup **(b)** (de hoteles, supermercados) chain; **~ de radiodifusión** radio network **3** (TV) channel

cadencia f cadence

cadeneta f (labor) chain stitch; (de papel) paper chain

cadera f hip

cadete m (Mil, Náut) cadet

caducar [A2] vi **(a)** «carné/pasaporte» to expire; **el plazo caduca el 17 de enero** the closing date (for enrollment, etc) is January 17; **estar caducado** to be out of date; «yogurt» to be past

its sell-by date/use-by date **(b)** «medicamento» to expire (frml); **S caduca a los tres meses** use within three months

caduco -ca adj **(a)** ⟨hoja⟩ deciduous **(b)** ⟨teoría/costumbres/valores⟩ outdated

caer [E16] vi **1 (a)** (de una altura) to fall; (de posición vertical) to fall over; **el coche cayó por un precipicio** the car went over a cliff; **cayó muerto allí mismo** he dropped down dead on the spot; **cayó en el mar** it came down in the sea; **~ parado** (AmL) to land on one's feet; **dejar ~ algo** ⟨objeto⟩ to drop sth; ⟨indirecta⟩ to drop sth; **dejó ~ la noticia que ...** she let drop the news that ... **2 (a)** «chaparrón/nevada»: **cayó un chaparrón** it poured down; **cayó una fuerte nevada** it snowed heavily; **el rayo cayó cerca** the lightning struck nearby **(b)** «noche» to fall; **al ~ la tarde/noche** at sunset o dusk/nightfall **3 (a)** (pender) «cortinas/falda» to hang **(b)** «terreno» to drop; **~ en pendiente** to slope down **4** (en error, trampa): **no caigas en ese error** don't make that mistake; **todos caímos (en la trampa)** we all fell for it; **cayó en la tentación de mirar** she succumbed to the temptation to look; **~ muy bajo** to stoop very low **5** (fam) (entender, darse cuenta): **¡ah, ya caigo!** (ya entiendo) oh, now I get it! (colloq); (ya recuerdo) oh, now I remember; **no caigo** I'm not sure what (o who etc) you mean; **no caí en que tú no tenías llave** I didn't realize o (fam) I didn't click that you didn't have keys **6** (en un estado): **~ en el olvido** to sink into oblivion; **~ enfermo** to fall ill **7** «gobierno/ciudad» to fall; «soldado» (morir) to fall, die **8** «precios/temperatura» to fall, drop **9 (a)** (sentar): **el pescado me cayó mal** the fish didn't agree with me; **le cayó muy mal que no la invitaran** she was very upset about not being invited **(b)** «persona»: **tu primo me cae muy bien** I really like your cousin; **me cae muy mal** (fam) I can't stand him (colloq); **¿qué tal te cayó?** what did you think of him? **10** «cumpleaños/festividad» to fall on; **¿el 27 en qué (día) cae?** what day's the 27th?

■ **caerse** v pron **(a)** (de una altura) to fall; (de posición vertical) to fall, to fall over; **me caí por las escaleras** I fell down the stairs; **~se del caballo/de la cama** to fall off one's horse/out of bed; **está que se cae de cansancio** (fam) she's dead on her feet (colloq) **(b)** **caérsele algo A algn**: oiga, se le cayó un guante excuse me, you dropped your glove; **no se te vaya a ~** don't drop it; **se me cayó de las manos** it slipped out of my hands; **se me están cayendo las medias** my stockings are falling down **(c)** (desprenderse) «diente» to fall out; «hojas» to fall off; «botón» to come off, fall off; **se le empieza a ~ el pelo** he's started to lose his hair

café adj (gen inv) (AmC, Chi, Méx) (marrón) brown; **ojos ~(s)** brown eyes
■ m **1** (cultivo, bebida) coffee; **me sirvió un ~** he gave me a cup of coffee, he gave me a coffee

(BrE); ∼ **cerrero** (Col) large strong black coffee; ∼ **con leche** (bebida) regular coffee (AmE), white coffee (BrE); ∼ **cortado** *coffee with a dash of milk*; ∼ **expreso** espresso; ∼ **instantáneo** *o* **soluble** instant coffee; ∼ **natural/torrefacto** light roast/ high roast coffee; ∼ **negro** (AmL) *or* (Chi) **puro** *or* (Col) **tinto** *or* (Esp) **solo** black coffee   **2** (cafetería) café; ∼ **bar** café   **3** (AmC, Chi, Méx) (marrón) brown

cafeína *f* caffeine

cafetal *m* coffee plantation

cafetera *f* (a) (para hacer café) coffee maker; (para servir café) coffeepot; ***estar como una*** ∼ (fam) to be off one's rocker *o* head (colloq) **(b)** (fam) (coche viejo) old heap (colloq)

cafetería *f* (café) café; (en museo, fábrica) cafeteria

cafetero -ra *adj* ⟨*industria/finca*⟩ coffee (*before n*); ⟨*país*⟩ coffee-producing (*before n*), coffee-growing (*before n*); **ser muy** ∼ to be a real coffee addict
■ *m,f* coffee planter *o* grower

cafeto *m* coffee tree

caficultor -tora *m,f* (Col) coffee grower

cagar [A3] *vi* (vulg) (defecar) to have a shit (vulg)
■ **cagarse** *v pron* (vulg) to shit oneself (vulg)

caída *f* **1** (en general) fall; sufrir una ∼ «*persona*» to have a fall; ∼ **libre** free fall; **la** ∼ **del gobierno** the fall of the government; **la** ∼ **del cabello** hair loss **2** (de tela, falda): **necesitas una tela con más** ∼ you need a heavier material; **tiene buena** ∼ it hangs well **3** (descenso) ∼ **DE** algo ⟨*del dólar/de los precios/de la demanda*⟩ fall IN sth; ⟨*de temperatura/voltaje*⟩ drop IN sth; ∼ **de agua** waterfall

caído¹ -da *adj* **1** **(a)** (en el suelo) fallen **(b)** ⟨*pechos*⟩ drooping, sagging; **tener los hombros** ∼**s** to be round-shouldered **(c)** (en la guerra): **soldados** ∼**s en combate** soldiers who fell in combat **2** (Col) ⟨*vivienda*⟩ dilapidated, run-down

caído² *m*: **los** ∼**s** the fallen

caiga, caigas, etc ▶ CAER

caimán *m* (Zool) caiman, cayman, alligator

Cairo *m*: **el** ∼ Cairo

caja *f* **1** **(a)** (recipiente) box; **una** ∼ **de fósforos** (con fósforos) a box of matches; (vacía) a matchbox; **una** ∼ **de vino** a crate of wine; ∼ **de cambios** gearbox; ∼ **de herramientas** toolbox; ∼ **de música** music box; ∼ **de resonancia** (Mús) soundbox; ∼ **de seguridad** safe-deposit box, safety deposit box; ∼ **fuerte** safe, strongbox; ∼ **tonta** (fam) goggle box (colloq) **(b)** (de reloj) case, casing **(c)** (Mús) (de violín, guitarra) soundbox; (tambor) drum **(d)** (fam) (ataúd) coffin
2 (Com) **(a)** (lugar — en banco) window; (— en supermercado) checkout; (— en tienda, restaurante) cash desk, till **(b)** (máquina) *tb* ∼ **registradora** till, cash register **(c)** (dinero) cash; **hicimos una** ∼ **de medio millón** we took half a million pesos (*etc*); ∼ **de ahorros** savings bank; **hacer (la)** ∼ to cash up

cajero -ra *m,f* (en tienda) cashier; (en banco) teller, cashier; (en supermercado) check out operator; ∼ **automático** *or* **permanente** cash dispenser, automated teller machine (AmE), ATM (AmE)

cajeta *f* (Méx) caramel topping/filling

cajetilla *f* pack (AmE), packet (BrE)

cajón *m* **1** **(a)** (en mueble) drawer **(b)** (caja grande) *tb* ∼ **de embalaje** crate; (para mudanzas) packing case **(c)** (AmL) (ataúd) coffin, casket (AmE) **2** (Méx) (en un estacionamiento) parking space

cajuela *f* (Méx) trunk (AmE), boot (BrE)

cal *f* lime

cala *f* **(a)** (ensenada) cove **(b)** (Náut) hold

calabacín *m*, (Méx) **calabacita** *f* zucchini (AmE), courgette (BrE)

calabaza *f* (fruto — redondo) pumpkin; (— alargado) squash

calabozo *m* (en comisaría, cárcel) cell; (en cuartel) guardroom; (Hist) dungeon

calada *f* (Esp fam) (de cigarro) drag (sl), puff (colloq)

caladero *m* fishing ground

calado -da *adj* **1** (empapado) [ESTAR] soaked, drenched **2** ⟨*jersey/tela*⟩ openwork (*before n*)

calamar *m* squid; ∼**es a la romana** squid fried in batter

calambre *m* **(a)** (espasmo) cramp; **me ha dado un** ∼ **en el pie** I have a cramp (AmE) *o* (BrE) I've got cramp in my foot **(b)** (sacudida eléctrica) electric shock; **me dio un** ∼ I got an electric shock

calamidad *f* **(a)** (desastre, desgracia) disaster, calamity; **¡las** ∼**es que ha pasado!** the terrible things he's gone through! **(b)** (persona inútil) disaster (colloq)

calar [A1] *vt* **1** «*líquido*» (empapar) to soak; (atravesar) to soak through; **el agua me caló los calcetines** water soaked through my socks **2** (fam) ⟨*persona/intenciones*⟩ to rumble (colloq), to suss ... out (BrE colloq) **3** «*barco*» to draw **4** (Esp) ⟨*coche/motor*⟩ to stall
■ ∼ *vi* **1** «*moda*» to catch on; «*costumbre/ filosofía*» to take root **2** ⟨*zapatos/tienda de campaña*⟩ to leak, let water in
■ **calarse** *v pron* **1** (empaparse) to get soaked, get drenched **2** (Esp) ⟨*coche/motor*⟩ to stall

calavera¹ *f* **1** (Anat) skull **2** (Méx) (Auto) taillight

calavera² *m* (fam) rake

calcado -da *adj* **(a)** [SER] (fam): **ser** ∼ **a algn** to be the spitting image of sb (colloq); **ser** ∼ **a algo** to be exactly the same as sth **(b)** [ESTAR] (fam): **están** ∼**s** one is a carbon copy of the other; **está** ∼ **del de Serra** it's a straight copy of Serra's

calcar [A2] *vt* **(a)** ⟨*dibujo/mapa*⟩ to trace **(b)** (plagiar) to copy

calceta *f* (labor) knitting; **hacer** ∼ to knit

calcetín *m* sock

calcinar [A1] *vt* **(a)** (abrasar) «*fuego*» to burn; **cadáveres calcinados** charred bodies **(b)** (Quím) to calcine

calcio *m* calcium

calco *m* (copia) exact replica

calcomanía *f* transfer, decal (AmE)

calculador -dora *adj* calculating

calculadora *f* calculator

calcular [A1] *vt* **1** **(a)** (Mat) to calculate, work out; **calculé mal la distancia** I miscalculated the distance **(b)** (evaluar) ⟨*pérdidas/gastos*⟩ to estimate **(c)** (conjeturar) to reckon, to guess (esp AmE); **yo le calculo unos sesenta años** I reckon *o* guess he's ⋯⋰

about sixty **(d)** (imaginar) to imagine **2** (planear) to work out; **lo tenía todo calculado** he had it all worked out

cálculo *m* **1** (Mat) **(a)** (operación) calculation; **según mis ~s** according to my calculations; **hizo un ~ aproximado** she made a rough estimate; **~ mental** mental arithmetic **(b)** (disciplina) calculus **2** (plan): **eso no entraba en mis ~s** I hadn't allowed for that in my plans *o* calculations; **le fallaron los ~s** things didn't work out as he had planned; **un error de ~** a miscalculation **3** (Med) stone, calculus (tech)

caldear [A1] *vt* ⟨habitación/local⟩ to heat, heat ... up
■ **caldearse** *v pron* **(a)** «habitación/local» to warm up, heat up **(b)** (enardecerse): **se estaban empezando a ~ los ánimos** feelings started to run high

caldera *f* **(a)** (industrial, de calefacción) boiler **(b)** (caldero) caldron*, copper (BrE)

calderilla *f* change, small *o* loose change

caldero *m* caldron*, copper (BrE)

caldo *m* (Coc) clear soup; (con arroz, etc) soup; (para cocinar) stock; (salsa de asado, etc) juices (*pl*); **~ de pollo** chicken stock

calé *adj* gypsy (*before n*)
■ *mf* gypsy

calefacción *f* heating; **~ a gas** gas heating; **~ central** central heating

caleidoscopio *m* kaleidoscope

calendario *m* **(a)** (en general) calendar; **~ de taco** tear-off calendar; **~ escolar** school calendar **(b)** (programa) schedule; **tiene un ~ muy apretado** she has a very tight schedule

calentador *m* **(a)** (para agua) (water) heater; (estufa) heater **(b) calentadores** *mpl* (Dep, Indum) legwarmers (*pl*)

calentamiento *m* **(a)** (Dep) warm-up **(b)** (Fís) warming; **~ global** *or* **del planeta** global warming

calentar [A5] *vt* **1** **(a)** ⟨agua/comida⟩ to heat (up); ⟨habitación⟩ to heat **(b)** ⟨motor/coche⟩ to warm up **(c)** (Dep): **~ los músculos** to warm up **2** (AmL fam) (enojar) to make ... mad (colloq)
■ **~** *vi*: **¡cómo calienta hoy el sol!** the sun's really hot today!; **esta estufa casi no calienta** this heater is hardly giving off any heat
■ **calentarse** *v pron* **1** **(a)** «horno/plancha» to heat up; «habitación» to warm up, get warm **(b)** «motor/coche» (al arrancar) to warm up; (en exceso) to overheat
2 (vulg) (excitarse sexualmente) to get turned on (colloq)
3 «debate» to become heated; **los ánimos se ~on** tempers flared
4 (AmL fam) (enojarse) to get mad (colloq)

calentura *f* **(a)** (fiebre) temperature **(b)** (en la boca) cold sore

calesita *f* (Per, RPl) merry-go-round, carousel

caleta *f* (ensenada) cove

calibrar [A1] *vt* **(a)** ⟨arma/tubo⟩ to calibrate **(b)** ⟨consecuencias/situación⟩ to weigh up

calibre *m* caliber*; **de ~ 22** 22 caliber; **de grueso ~** ⟨arma/proyectil⟩ large-bore; ⟨error⟩ (AmL) serious

calidad *f* **1** (de producto, servicio) quality; **un artículo de primera ~** a top-quality product; **productos de mala ~** poor-quality products; **~ de**

vida quality of life **2** (condición): **asistió en ~ de observador** he attended as an observer; **en su ~ de presidente** in his capacity as president

cálido -da *adj* **(a)** (Meteo) hot **(b)** ⟨acogida/bienvenida⟩ warm **(c)** ⟨color/tono⟩ warm

calidoscopio *m* kaleidoscope

calienta, etc ▶ CALENTAR

caliente *adj* **1** ⟨agua/comida/horno⟩ hot; **aquí estaremos más calentitas** we'll be warmer here; **tomó la decisión en ~** she made the decision in the heat of the moment **2** (fam) (sexualmente) hot (colloq), horny (sl)

caliento ▶ CALENTAR

califa *m* caliph

calificación *f* **(a)** (Educ) grade (AmE), mark (BrE) **(b)** (descripción) description **(c)** (de película) rating

calificado -da *adj* (esp AmL) ⟨mano de obra⟩ skilled; ⟨profesional⟩ qualified

calificar [A2] *vt* **1** **~ algo/a algn DE algo** (describir) to describe sth/sb as sth; (categorizar) to label sth/sb as sth **2** (Educ) **(a)** ⟨examen⟩ to grade (AmE), to mark (BrE); ⟨alumno⟩ to give a grade (AmE) *o* (BrE) mark to **(b)** (habilitar) «título/diploma»: **~ a algn PARA hacer algo** to qualify sb TO do sth **3** (Ling) to qualify

California *f* California

californiano -na *adj/m,f* Californian

caligrafía *f* (arte) calligraphy; (de persona) writing, handwriting

calipso *m* **(a)** (Mús) calypso **(b) de color ~** deep turquoise

cáliz *m* **(a)** (Relig) chalice **(b)** (Bot) calyx

caliza *f* limestone

calizo -za *adj* ⟨tierra⟩ limy; **piedra caliza** limestone

callado -da *adj* **[ESTAR]** (silencioso) quiet; **estuvo ~ durante toda la reunión** he kept quiet throughout the whole meeting; **lo escucharon ~s** they listened to him quietly **(b)** **[SER]** (poco hablador) quiet

callampa *f* (Chi) **(a)** (hongo) mushroom **(b)** (vivienda) shanty (dwelling) **(c) callampas** *fpl* (poblaciones marginales) shantytown

callar [A1] *vi* to be quiet, shut up (colloq); **no pude hacerlo ~** I couldn't get him to be quiet; **hacer ~ a la oposición** to silence the opposition
■ **~** *vt* **(a)** ⟨secreto/información⟩ to keep ... quiet **(b)** (AmL) ⟨persona⟩ to get ... to be quiet, to shut ... up (colloq)
■ **callarse** *v pron* **(a)** (guardar silencio) to be quiet; **¡cállate!** be quiet!, shut up! (colloq); **cuando entró todos se ~on** when he walked in everyone went quiet *o* stopped talking; **la próxima vez no me ~é** next time I'll say something **(b)** (no decir) ⟨noticia⟩ to keep ... quiet, keep ... to oneself

calle *f* **1** (vía) street; **~ ciega** (Andes, Ven) dead end, cul-de-sac (BrE); **~ de dirección única** *or* (Col) **de una vía** one-way street; **~ peatonal** pedestrian street; **hoy no he salido a la ~** I haven't been out today; **el libro saldrá a la ~ mañana** the book comes out tomorrow; **el hombre de la ~** the man in the street; **el lenguaje de la ~** colloquial language; **echar a algn a la ~** to throw sb out (on the street); **en la ~** ⟨estar/quedar⟩ (en la ruina) penniless; (sin vivienda) homeless; (sin trabajo) out of work

2 (Esp) (en atletismo, natación) lane; (en golf) fairway

callejear [A1] *vi* to hang around the streets (colloq)

callejero¹ -ra *adj* ⟨riña/venta/músico⟩ street (*before n*); ⟨perro⟩ stray (*before n*)

callejero² *m* (Esp) street map *o* plan

callejón *m* alley, narrow street; ∼ **sin salida** (calle) dead end, blind alley; (situación) dead end

callejuela *f* narrow street

callista *mf* chiropodist

callo *m* **(a)** (en los dedos del pie) corn; (en la planta del pie, en las manos) callus; (en una fractura) callus **(b) callos** *mpl* (Esp) (Coc) tripe

callosidad *f* callus

calma *f* calm; **con ∼** calmly; **mantener la ∼** to keep calm; **tómatelo con ∼** take it easy; **no hay que perder la ∼** the thing is not to lose your cool; **el mar está en ∼** the sea is calm; **¡∼, por favor!** (en situación peligrosa) please, keep calm! *o* don't panic!; (en discusión acalorada) calm down, please!

calmante *m* (para dolores) painkiller; (para los nervios) tranquilizer

calmar [A1] *vt* **(a)** (tranquilizar) ⟨persona⟩ to calm … down; ⟨nervios⟩ to calm; **esto calmó los ánimos** this eased the tension **(b)** (aliviar) ⟨dolor⟩ to relieve, ease; ⟨sed⟩ to quench; ⟨hambre⟩ to take the edge off

■ **calmarse** *v pron* **(a)** «persona» to calm down **(b)** «mar» to become calm

calmo -ma *adj* (esp AmL) calm

caló *m* gypsy slang

calor *m* [*Use of the feminine gender, although common in some areas, is generally considered to be archaic or non-standard*] **1** **(a)** (Fis, Meteo) heat; **hace ∼** it's hot; **hacía un ∼ agobiante** the heat was stifling *o* suffocating **(b)** (sensación): **tener ∼** to be hot; **pasamos un ∼ horrible** it was terribly hot; **entrar en ∼** to get warm; **esta chaqueta me da mucho ∼** I feel very hot in this jacket; **al ∼ del fuego** by the fireside **2** (afecto) warmth **3 calores** *mpl* (de la menopausia) hot flashes (*pl*) (AmE), hot flushes (*pl*) (BrE)

caloría *f* calorie

calumnia *f* (oral) defamation, slander; (escrita) libel; **levantaron ∼s contra la institución** they spread slanderous rumors about the institution

calumniar [A1] *vt* (por escrito) to libel; (oralmente) to slander

caluroso -sa *adj* **(a)** ⟨día/clima⟩ hot **(b)** ⟨acogida/aplauso⟩ warm; **recibe un ∼ saludo** (Corresp) best wishes

calva *f* (cabeza sin pelo) bald head; (parte sin pelo) bald patch

calvicie *f* baldness

calvo -va *adj* ⟨persona⟩ bald; **quedarse ∼** to go bald

■ *m,f* bald person

calza *f* **1** **(a)** (cuña) chock **(b)** (Col) (en una muela) filling; **2 calzas** *fpl* (Ind, arc) hose (*pl*), breeches (*pl*)

calzada *f* (camino) road; (de calle) road; (de autopista) side, carriageway

calzado *m* (frml) footwear (frml)

calzador *m* shoehorn

calzar [A4] *vt* **1** **(a)** ⟨persona⟩ (proveerla de

calzado) to provide … with shoes; (ponerle los zapatos): **calzó a los niños** she put the children's shoes on **(b)** (llevar): **calzo (un) 39** I take (a) size 39, I'm a 39; **calzaba zapatillas de deporte** he was wearing training shoes **2** ⟨rueda⟩ to chock, wedge a block under **3** (Col) ⟨muela⟩ to fill

■ **calzarse** *v pron* (refl) **(a)** (ponerse los zapatos) to put one's shoes on **(b)** ⟨zapato⟩ to put on

calzoncillos *mpl*, **calzoncillo** *m* underpants, shorts (*pl*) (AmE), pants (*pl*) (BrE); ∼ **largos** long underwear, long johns (*pl*) (colloq)

calzones *mpl*, **calzón** *m* **1** **(a)** (antiguos) long underwear, long johns (*pl*) (colloq) **(b)** (AmS) (modernos) panties (*pl*), knickers (*pl*) (BrE) **2 calzón** *m* (Esp) (para deporte) shorts (*pl*)

cama *f* (para dormir) bed; **hacer** *or* (AmL) **tender la ∼** to make the bed; **¡métete en la ∼!** get into bed!; **guardar ∼** to stay in bed; **está en ∼** she's in bed; ∼ **camarote** (AmL) bunk bed; ∼ **doble** *or* **de matrimonio** *or* (AmL) **de dos plazas** double bed; ∼ **individual** *or* (AmL) **de una plaza** single bed; ∼ **solar** sunbed; **caer en ∼** to fall ill

camada *f* (Zool) litter; (de ladrones, sinvergüenzas) (pey) gang

camaleón *m* chameleon

cámara *f* **1** **(a)** (arc) (aposento) chamber (frml) **(b)** (recinto): ∼ **acorazada** *or* **blindada** strongroom, vault; ∼ **de descompresión** decompression chamber; ∼ **de gas** gas chamber; ∼ **frigorífica** cold store **2** (Gob, Pol): **C∼ de los Diputados** Chamber of Deputies; **C∼ de los Comunes/de los Lores** House of Commons/of Lords; **C∼ de Representantes** House of Representatives **3** (Com, Fin) association; ∼ **de comercio** chamber of commerce **4** (aparato) camera; **en** *or* (Esp) **a ∼ lenta** in slow motion; ∼ **de cine** film camera; ∼ **de video** *or* (Esp) **vídeo** video camera; ∼ **fotográfica** camera

camarada *mf* **(a)** (de partido político) comrade **(b)** (de colegio) school friend; (de trabajo) colleague

camaradería *f* camaraderie, comradeship

camarero -ra *m,f* **1** (esp Esp) (en bar, restaurante) (*m*) waiter; (*f*) waitress; (detrás de mostrador) (*m*) barman, bartender (AmE); (*f*) barmaid, bartender (AmE) **2** **(a)** (en hotel) (*m*) bellboy; (*f*) maid **(b)** (Transp) (*m*) steward; (*f*) stewardess

camarín *m* (CS) **(a)** (Teatr) dressing room **(b)** (en vestuarios) changing cubicle **(c) camarines** *mpl* (Chi) (Dep) changing rooms (*pl*), locker rooms (*pl*)

camarógrafo -fa *m,f* (*m*) cameraman; (*f*) camerawoman

camarón *m* (crustáceo — pequeño) shrimp; (— más grande) shrimp (AmE), prawn (BrE)

camarote *m* cabin

cambalache *m* **(a)** (fam) (trueque) swap (colloq); **hacer ∼s** to swap (colloq) **(b)** (RPl fam & pey) (tienda) thrift store (AmE), junk shop (BrE)

cambiante *adj* ⟨tiempo⟩ changeable, unsettled; ⟨persona/carácter⟩ moody, temperamental

cambiar [A1] *vt* **1** **(a)** (alterar, modificar) ⟨horario/imagen/persona⟩ to change **(b)** (de lugar, posición): ∼ **los muebles de lugar** to move the furniture around; **cambié las flores de florero** I put the flowers in a different vase **(c)** (reemplazar) ⋯⋗

〈*pieza/fecha/sábanas*〉 to change; **le cambió la pila al reloj** she changed the battery in the clock; **~le el nombre a algo** to change the name of sth **(d)** 〈*niño/bebé*〉 to change **(e)** (Fin) to change; **cambié 100 libras a** *or* (Esp) **en dólares** I changed 100 pounds into dollars

2 (canjear) 〈*sellos/estampas*〉 to swap, to trade (esp AmE); **~ algo POR algo** 〈*sellos/estampas*〉 to swap *o* (esp AmE) trade sth POR sth; 〈*compra*〉 to exchange *o* change sth FOR sth; **¿quieres que te cambie el lugar?** do you want me to swap *o* change places with you?

■ **~ vi (a)** 〈*ciudad/persona*〉 to change; **~ para peor** to change for the worse; **le está cambiando la voz** his voice is breaking **(b)** (Auto) to change gear **(c)** (hacer transbordo) to change; **~ de avión/ tren** to change planes/train **(d)** **~ DE algo** 〈*de tema/canal/color*〉 to change sth; **~ de idea** to change one's mind; **~ de sentido** to make (AmE) *o* (BrE) do a U-turn

■ **cambiarse** *v pron* **(a)** (*refl*) (de ropa) to change, get changed **(b)** (*refl*) 〈*camisa/nombre/ peinado*〉 to change; **~se DE algo** 〈*de camisa/ zapatos*〉 to change sth; **me cambié de silla** I changed places; **~se de casa** to move house; **cámbiate de camisa** change your shirt **(c)** **~se POR algn** to change places WITH sb **(d)** (*recípr*) 〈*sellos/estampas*〉 to swap, to trade (esp AmE) **(e)** (CS) (mudarse de casa) to move

cambio *m* **1** **(a)** (alteración) change; **~ DE algo** 〈*de planes/domicilio*〉 change OF sth; **un ~ de aire(s)** *or* **ambiente** a change of scene **(b)** (Auto) gearshift (AmE), gear change (BrE); **un coche con cinco ~s** (AmL) a car with a five-speed gearbox; **~ de sentido** U-turn

2 (a) (canje) exchange; **Ⓢ no se admiten cambios** goods cannot be exchanged **(b)** (*en locs*) **a cambio (de)** in exchange (for), in return (for); **en cambio: el viaje en autobús es agotador, en ~ en tren es muy agradable** the bus journey is exhausting; by train however *o* on the other hand is very pleasant

3 (a) (Fin) (de moneda extranjera) exchange; **~ de divisas** foreign exchange; **¿a cómo está el ~?** what's the exchange rate?; **Ⓢ cambio** bureau de change, change **(b)** (diferencia) change; **me ha dado mal el ~** he's given me the wrong change **(c)** (dinero suelto) change

cambista *mf* moneychanger

cambur *m* (Ven) (fruta) banana

camelia *f* camellia

camello *m* **1** (Zool) camel **2** **camello** *mf* (arg) (traficante) pusher (sl), dealer (colloq)

camellón *m* (Méx) (en la calle) traffic island

camelo *m* (fam) (timo) con (colloq); (mentira) lie

camerino *m* **(a)** (Teatr) dressing room **(b)** **camerinos** *mpl* (Col) (Dep) changing rooms (*pl*)

camilla *f* (de lona) stretcher; (con ruedas) trolley, gurney (AmE); (en un consultorio) couch

camillero -ra *m,f* stretcher-bearer

caminante *mf* hiker; (liter) traveler*

caminar [A1] *vi* **1** (andar) to walk; **salieron a**

~ they went out for a walk; podemos ir caminando we can walk, we can go on foot; **~ HACIA algo** 〈*hacia meta/fin*〉 to move TOWARD(S) sth **2** (AmL) 〈*reloj/motor*〉 to work; **el asunto va caminando** (fam) things are moving (colloq)

■ **~ vt** 〈*distancia*〉 to walk

caminata *f* long walk; (en el campo) long walk, hike; **después de darme semejante ~** after walking *o* (colloq) trekking all that way

camino *m* **1** (en general) road; (de tierra) track; (sendero) path; **~ vecinal** minor road (*built and maintained by local council*)

2 (a) (ruta, dirección) way; **saberse el ~** to know the way; **me salieron al ~** 〈*asaltantes*〉 they blocked my path *o* way; 〈*amigos*〉 they came out to meet me; **este es el mejor ~ a seguir** this is the best course to follow; **el ~ a la fama** the road *o* path to fame; **se abrió ~ entre la espesura** she made her way through the dense thickets; **abrirse ~ en la vida** to get on in life; **buen/mal ~: este niño va por mal ~** this boy's heading for trouble; **ibas por buen ~ pero te equivocaste** you were on the right track but you made a mistake; **llevar a algn por mal ~** to lead sb astray **(b)** (trayecto, viaje): **el de regreso fue muy largo** the return journey; **se pusieron en ~** they set off; **todavía nos quedan dos horas de ~** we still have two hours to go **(c)** (*en locs*) **camino de/a ...** on my/his/her way to ...; **ir ~ de algo**: **una tradición que va ~ de desaparecer** a tradition which looks set to disappear; **de camino on the way; pilla de ~** it's on the way; **me queda de ~** I pass it on my way; **de ~ a la estación** on the way to the station; **en camino on the way; deben estar ya en ~** they must be on their way already; **por el camino** on the way; **a mitad de** *or* **a medio ~** halfway through

camión *m* **(a)** (de carga) truck, lorry (BrE); (contenido) truckload; **~ cisterna** tanker; **~ de la basura** garbage truck (AmE), dustcart (BrE); **~ de mudanzas** moving van (AmE), removal van (BrE) **(b)** (AmC, Méx) (autobús) bus

camionero -ra *m,f* truck driver, lorry driver (BrE); (conductor de autobús) (AmC, Méx) bus driver

camioneta *f* **(a)** (furgoneta) van; (camión pequeño) light truck, pickup truck **(b)** (AmL) (coche familiar) station wagon (AmE), estate car (BrE)

camisa *f* shirt; **en mangas de ~** in shirtsleeves; **~ de fuerza** straitjacket; **cambiar de ~** to change sides

camiseta *f* **(a)** (prenda interior) undershirt (AmE), vest (BrE) **(b)** (prenda exterior) T-shirt; (de fútbol) shirt, jersey (AmE); (sin mangas) jersey (AmE), vest (BrE)

camisón *m* nightdress

camomila *f* camomile, chamomile

camorra *f* (fam) (bronca, riña) fight; **armar ~** to start a fight; **buscar ~** to look for a fight (colloq)

camorrero -ra *adj/mf* (Col, CS) ► CAMORRISTA

camorrista *adj* (fam) (pendenciero): **no seas ~** stop being a troublemaker

■ *mf* troublemaker (colloq)

camote *m* (Bot) (Andes, Méx) (batata) sweet potato; *hacerse* ~ (Méx fam) to get in a muddle (colloq)

campamento *m* camp; **nos fuimos a Bariloche de** ~ we went camping in Bariloche

campana *f* **(a)** (de iglesia, colegio) bell; **oía las** ~**s** I could hear the bells ringing; **tocar la** ~ to ring the bell; **¿ya ha sonado la** ~**?** has the bell gone yet? **(b)** (de chimenea) hood; (de cocina) extractor hood

campanada *f* **(a)** (de campana) chime, stroke; (de reloj) stroke; **el reloj dio 12** ~**s** the clock struck 12 **(b)** (fam) (sorpresa): **la noticia fue una** ~ the news came like a bolt from the blue (colloq); **dar la** ~ to cause a stir

campanario *m* bell tower, belfry

campanazo *m* (AmL) ▶ CAMPANADA

campanilla *f* **(a)** (campana pequeña) small bell, hand bell **(b)** (Anat) uvula **(c)** (Bot) campanula, bellflower

campante *adj*: **se quedó tan** ~ he didn't bat an eyelash (AmE) o (BrE) eyelid; **nosotros muertos de miedo y él tan** ~ we were scared stiff but he was as cool as a cucumber

campaña *f* campaign; ~ **electoral** electoral o election campaign; ~ **publicitaria** advertising campaign; **hacer una** ~ to run o conduct a campaign

campechano -na *adj* (sin complicaciones) straightforward; (bondadoso) good-natured

campeón -peona *adj* champion (*before n*)
■ *m,f* champion; **el** ~ **del mundo** the world champion

campeonato *m* championship

cámper *f* (Chi, Méx) camper (van)

campera *f* **(a)** (RPI) (chaqueta) jacket **(b) camperas** *fpl* (botas) cowboy boots

campero *m* (Col) (Auto) jeep

campesino -na *adj* ⟨vida/costumbre⟩ rural, country (*before n*); ⟨modales/aspecto⟩ peasant-like
■ *m,f* (persona del campo) country person; (con connotaciones de pobreza) peasant; **son** ~**s** they are country people o folk; **los obreros y los** ~**s** the manual workers and the agricultural workers

campestre *adj* ⟨escena/vida⟩ rural, country (*before n*); ⟨casa/club⟩ country (*before n*)

camping /'kampin/ *m* (*pl* **-pings**) **(a)** (actividad) camping; **irse de** ~ to go camping **(b)** (lugar) campsite, campground (AmE)

campiña *f* countryside; **la** ~ **inglesa** the English countryside

campista *mf* camper

campo *m* **⟨1⟩** (zona no urbana) country; (paisaje) countryside; **la gente del** ~ the country people; **el** ~ **se ve precioso** the countryside looks beautiful; ~ **a través** or **a** ~ **traviesa** ⟨caminar/ir⟩ cross-country **⟨2⟩** (zona agraria) land; (terreno) field; **trabajar el** ~ to work the land; **las faenas del** ~ farm work; **los** ~**s de cebada** the field of barley; ~ **de aterrizaje** landing field; ~ **de batalla** battlefield; ~ **de minas** minefield; ~ **petrolífero** oilfield **⟨3⟩** (Dep) (de fútbol) field, pitch (BrE); (de golf) course; **jugar en** ~ **propio/contrario** to play at home/away; ~ **a través** cross-country running; ~ **de tiro** firing range

⟨4⟩ (ámbito, área de acción) field; **el** ~ **de la informática** the field of computing **⟨5⟩** (campamento) camp; ~ **de concentración/de refugiados** concentration/refugee camp

camposanto *m* (liter) graveyard, cemetery

campus *m* (*pl* ~) campus

camuflaje *m* camouflage

camuflar [A1] *vt* ⟨tanques/contrabando⟩ to camouflage; ⟨intenciones⟩ to disguise
■ **camuflarse** *v pron* «persona» to camouflage oneself; «animal» to camouflage itself

cana¹ *f* **⟨1⟩** (pelo) gray* hair, white hair; *echar una* ~ *al aire* to let one's hair down (colloq) **⟨2⟩** (AmS arg) (cárcel) slammer (sl), nick (BrE colloq) **⟨3⟩** (RPI arg) (cuerpo de policía): **la** ~ the cops (*pl*) (colloq)

cana² *mf* (RPI arg) (agente) cop (colloq)

Canadá *m*: *tb* **el** ~ Canada

canadiense *adj/mf* Canadian

canal *m* **⟨1⟩** (Náut) (cauce artificial) canal; (Agr, Ing) channel; ~ **de la Mancha** English Channel; ~ **de Panamá** Panama Canal; ~ **de San Lorenzo** St Lawrence Seaway **⟨2⟩ (a)** (Rad, Telec, TV) channel; **cambia de** ~ change o switch channels **(b)** (medio) channel
■ *f or m* (canalón) gutter; (ranura) groove

canalizar [A4] *vt* to channel

canalla *mf* (fam) (bribón, granuja) swine (colloq)

canallada *f* (fam): **¡qué** ~**!** what a rotten o mean thing to do (colloq)

canalón *m* (Esp) gutter

canapé *m* **⟨1⟩** (Coc) canapé **⟨2⟩** (sofá) couch

Canarias *fpl*: *tb* **las (Islas)** ~ the Canaries, the Canary Islands

canario¹ -ria *adj* of/from the Canary Islands
■ *m,f* (de las Canarias) person from the Canary Islands

canario² *m* (Zool) canary

canasta *f* **(a)** (para la compra) basket **(b)** (AmL) (en rifa) hamper **(c)** (en baloncesto) basket; **meter una** ~ to make o score a basket **(d)** (Jueg) canasta

canastilla *f* layette

canasto *m* basket (*gen large and with a lid*)

cancel *m* (contrapuerta) inner door; (tabique) (Col, Méx) partition; (biombo) (Méx) folding screen

cancelación *f* **⟨1⟩** (suspensión) cancellation **⟨2⟩** (liquidación) payment

cancelar [A1] *vt* **(a)** ⟨reunión/viaje/pedido⟩ to cancel **(b)** ⟨deuda⟩ to settle, pay off; ⟨cuenta⟩ to pay

cáncer *m* (Med) cancer; **tiene (un)** ~ **de mama** she has breast cancer

Cáncer *m* (signo) Cancer; **es (de)** ~ he's a Cancer o Cancerian
■ *mf* (persona) *tb* **cáncer** Cancerian, Cancer

cancha *f* **⟨1⟩ (a)** (Dep) (de baloncesto, frontón, squash, tenis) court; (de fútbol, rugby) (AmL) field, pitch; (BrE) (de golf) course; (CS) course; (de polo) (AmL) field; (de esquí) (CS) slope **(b)** (Chi) (Aviac) *tb* ~ **de aterrizaje** runway **⟨2⟩** (AmL fam) (desenvoltura): **un político con mucha** ~ a politician with a great deal of experience, a seasoned politician

canchita *f* (Per) popcorn

canciller *m* (a) (jefe de estado) chancellor (b) (AmS) (ministro) ≈ Secretary of State (*in US*), ≈ Foreign Secretary (*in UK*)

cancillería *f* (a) (de embajada) chancery, chancellery (b) (AmS) (ministerio) ≈ State Department (*in US*), ≈ Foreign Office (*in UK*)

canción *f* song; ~ **de cuna** lullaby; ~ **nacional** (Chi) national anthem

candado *m* (cerradura) padlock; **está cerrada con** ~ it is padlocked

candela *f* (a) (fuego) fire; **¿tienes** ~? (fam) have you got a light? (b) (vela) candle

candelabro *m* candelabra

candelero *m* candlestick; **estar en el** ~ to be in the limelight

candente *adj* (a) ⟨*hierro*⟩ red-hot (b) ⟨*tema*⟩ burning

candidato -ta *m,f* candidate; ~ **a la presidencia** presidential candidate; **los** ~**s al puesto de** ... the applicants for the post of ...; **presentarse como** ~ **para algo** (Pol) to run (AmE) *o* (BrE) stand for sth

candidatura *f* (a) (propuesta) candidacy, candidature (b) (Esp) (lista) list of candidates

cándido -da *adj* naive

candil *m* oil lamp

candilejas *fpl* footlights (*pl*)

candor *m* innocence, naivety

caneca *f* (Col) (papelera) wastebasket, waste-paper basket (BrE); (cubo de la basura) garbage *o* trash can (AmE), dustbin (BrE)

canela *f* (Bot, Coc) cinnamon; ~ **en polvo/en rama** ground/stick cinnamon

canelón *m* (a) (Const) gutter (b) **canelones** *mpl* cannelloni

cangrejo *m* (de mar) crab; (de río) crayfish

canguro *m* [1] (Zool) kangaroo [2] (a) (anorak) cagoule (b) (para llevar a un niño) sling [3] (Esp)
canguro *mf* babysitter; **hacer de** ~ to babysit

caníbal *mf* (antropófago) cannibal

canica *f* marble

caniche *mf* /ka'nitʃe, ka'niʃ/ poodle

canijo -ja *adj* [1] (fam) (pequeño) tiny, puny (hum *or* pej) [2] (Méx fam) (terco) stubborn, pig-headed (colloq)

canilla *f* (a) (RPl) (grifo) faucet (AmE), tap (BrE); **cerrar la** ~ to turn off the faucet *o* tap (b) (bobina) bobbin

canillita *mf* (Bol, CS) newspaper vendor *o* seller

canino *m* (Odont) canine (tooth); (Zool) canine

canjear [A1] *vt* to exchange

cannabis *m* cannabis

cano -na *adj* white

canoa *f* canoe

canódromo *m* greyhound stadium, dog track (colloq)

canon *m* [1] (norma) rule, canon (frml) [2] (Mús) canon

canónico -ca *adj* canonical, canonic

canonizar [A4] *vt* to canonize

canoso -sa *adj* ⟨*persona*⟩ gray-haired*, white-haired; ⟨*pelo/barba*⟩ gray*, white

cansado -da *adj* [1] [ESTAR] (a) (fatigado) tired; ~**s de tanto caminar** tired from so much walking; **tienes cara de** ~ you look tired; **en un tono** ~ in a weary tone of voice (b) (aburrido) ~ **DE algo/ hacer algo** tired OF sth/doing sth [2] [SER] ⟨*viaje/ trabajo*⟩ tiring

cansador -dora *adj* (AmS) tiring

cansancio *m* tiredness; **me caigo de** ~ I'm absolutely worn out *o* exhausted

cansar [A1] *vt* (a) (fatigar) to tire, tire ... out; **le cansa la vista** it makes her eyes tired, it strains her eyes (b) (aburrir): **¿no te cansa oír la misma música?** don't you get tired of listening to the same music?
■ ~ *vi* (a) (fatigar) to be tiring (b) (aburrir) to get tiresome
■ **cansarse** *v pron* (a) (fatigarse) to tire oneself out; **se le cansa la vista** her eyes get tired (b) (aburrirse) to get bored; ~**se DE algo/algn** to get tired of sth/sb, get bored WITH sth/sb, ~**se DE hacer algo** to get tired OF doing sth

cantábrico -ca *adj* Cantabrian

Cantábrico *m*: **el (mar)** ~ the Bay of Biscay

cantante *adj* singing (*before n*)
■ *mf* singer

cantar [A1] *vt* ⟨*canción*⟩ to sing
■ ~ *vi* [1] (a) (Mús) to sing (b) ⟨*pájaro*⟩ to sing; ⟨*gallo*⟩ to crow; ⟨*cigarra/grillo*⟩ to chirp, chirrup [2] (fam) (confesar) to talk (colloq)
■ *m* poem (*gen set to music*)

cántara *f* churn

cantarín -rina, (CS) **cantarino -na** *adj* ⟨*voz/ tono/risa*⟩ singsong; ⟨*fuente/aguas*⟩ (liter) babbling

cántaro *m* pitcher, jug; **llover a** ~**s** to pour with rain

cantautor -tora *m,f* singer-songwriter

cante *m* (Mús) Andalusian folk song; ~ **flamenco** flamenco (singing)

cantera *f* (de piedra) quarry

cántico *m* canticle

cantidad *f* (a) (volumen) quantity, amount (b) (suma de dinero) sum, amount (c) (número) number; **la** ~ **de cartas recibidas** the number of letters received (d) (volumen impresionante): **había** ~ **de turistas** there were lots of tourists; **¡qué** ~ **de gente/de comida había!** there were so many people/there was so much food!; **tenemos** ~ *or* ~**es** (fam) we have lots *o* tons (colloq); **cualquier** ~ **de** (AmS) lots of, loads of (colloq)

cantimplora *f* water bottle, canteen

cantina *f* [1] (a) (en estación) buffet, cafeteria; (en universidad) refectory; (en fábrica) canteen (b) (AmL exc RPl) (bar) bar (c) (RPl) (restaurante italiano) trattoria [2] (Col) (para la leche) churn

cantinela *f*: **siempre la misma** ~ always the same old story (*o* thing *etc*)

cantinflear [A1] *vi* (fam) to babble

canto *m* [1] (Mús) (acción, arte) singing; (canción) chant [2] (de pájaro) song; (del gallo) crowing [3] (Lit) (canción) hymn [4] (borde, filo) edge; **colocó el ladrillo de** ~ he lay the brick on its side [5] (Geol) *tb* ~ **rodado** (roca) boulder; (guijarro) pebble

cantor -tora *adj* singing (*before n*)
■ *m,f* (cantante) singer

canturrear [A1] *vi* to sing softly to oneself
■ ~ *vt* to sing ... softly to oneself

canuto *m* (tubo) document tube

caña *f* (a) (planta) reed (b) (tallo del bambú, azúcar) cane; **muebles de** ∼ cane furniture; ∼ **de azúcar** sugar cane **(c)** (de pescar) rod **(d)** (de la bota) leg; **botas de media** ∼ calf-length boots

cañada *f* **(a)** (Geog) gully; (más profunda) ravine **(b)** (AmL) (arroyo) stream

cáñamo *m* (planta) cannabis plant, hemp; (tela) canvas

cañaveral *m* (de juncos) reedbed; (de cañas de azúcar) (Col) sugar-cane plantation

cañería *f* (tubo) pipe; (conjunto de tubos) piping, pipes (*pl*)

cañero -ra *adj* (AmL) (Agr) sugarcane (*before n*)

cañizal *m* reedbed

caño *m* (conducto) pipe; (de una fuente) spout; (grifo) (Per) faucet (AmE), tap (BrE)

cañón *m* **(a)** (Arm) (arma) cannon; (de una escopeta, pistola) barrel **(b)** (valle) canyon; **el Gran C**∼ **del Colorado** the Grand Canyon **(c)** (de pluma) quill

cañonazo *m* (Arm, Mil) cannonshot; **una salva de 21** ∼**s** a 21-gun salute

caoba *f* **(a)** (árbol) mahogany tree (madera) mahogany **(b)** (de) color ∼ mahogany

caos *m* chaos; **será un verdadero** ∼ there'll be absolute chaos

caótico -ca *adj* chaotic

capa *f* ⟨1⟩ **(a)** (en general) layer; **una** ∼ **de nieve** a layer *o* carpet of snow; **la** ∼ **de ozono** the ozone layer; **lleva el pelo cortado en** *or* (Esp) **a** ∼**s** she has layered hair **(b)** (de barniz, pintura) coat **(c)** (estrato) stratum; **las** ∼**s de la sociedad** the social strata ⟨2⟩ **(a)** (Indum) cloak, cape; ∼ **de agua** raincape **(b)** (Taur) cape

capacidad *f* ⟨1⟩ **(a)** (competencia) ability **(b)** (potencial) capacity; **su gran** ∼ **de trabajo** her great capacity for work; ∼ **DE** *or* **PARA hacer algo** ability *o* capacity to do sth **(c)** (Der) capacity ⟨2⟩ (cupo) capacity

capacitado -da *adj* ∼ **PARA** algo/hacer algo qualified FOR sth/to do sth

capacitar [A1] *vt* (formar) to prepare; (profesionalmente) ∼ **a** algn **PARA** algo to qualify sb FOR sth; ∼ **a** algn **PARA hacer algo** to qualify *o* entitle sb to do sth

■ **capacitarse** *v pron* (formarse) to train; (obtener un título) to qualify, become qualified

capar [A1] *vt* ⟨1⟩ (castrar) to castrate ⟨2⟩ (Col fam) ∼ **clase** to play hooky (esp AmE colloq), to skive off (school) (BrE colloq)

caparazón *m or f* shell

capataz *mf* (m) foreman; (f) forewoman

capaz *adj* **(a)** (competente) capable, able **(b)** (de una hazaña) capable; **es** ∼ **de grandes logros** he's capable of great things; **¿te sientes** ∼ **de enfrentarte con ella?** do you feel able to face her?; **¿a qué no eres** ∼ **de saltar esto?** I bet you can't jump over this; **es (muy)** ∼ **de irse sin pagar** he's quite capable of leaving without paying

capazo *m* (cesta) basket; (para un niño) portacrib® (AmE), carrycot (BrE)

capea *f*: amateur bullfight using young bulls

capear [A1] *vt* ⟨1⟩ (Taur) to make passes at (*with the cape*) ⟨2⟩ (Chi fam) ⟨trabajo⟩ to skip, to skive off (BrE colloq); ∼ **clase** to play hooky (esp AmE colloq), to skive off (school) (BrE colloq)

capellán *m* chaplain

Caperucita Roja Little Red Riding Hood

caperuza *f* **(a)** (Indum) pointed hood **(b)** (de un bolígrafo) top, cap

capicúa *adj* palindromic (frml); **era un número** ∼ the number read the same both ways

capilar *adj* **(a)** ⟨loción⟩ hair (*before n*) **(b)** ⟨vaso/tubo⟩ capillary (*before n*)
■ *m* capillary

capilla *f* chapel; ∼ **ardiente** funeral chapel

capital *adj* ⟨importancia⟩ cardinal, prime; ⟨influencia⟩ seminal (frml); ⟨obra⟩ key, seminal (frml)
■ *m* **(a)** (Com, Fin) capital **(b)** (recursos, riqueza) resources (*pl*)
■ *f* (de país) capital; (de provincia) provincial capital, ≈ county seat (*in US*), ≈ county town (*in UK*); **Valencia** ∼ the city of Valencia

capitalino -na *adj* (AmL) of/from the capital
■ *m,f* (AmL) inhabitant of the capital

capitalismo *m* capitalism

capitalista *adj* capitalist (*before n*)
■ *mf* capitalist

capitán -tana *m,f* ⟨1⟩ **(a)** (del ejército) captain; (de la Fuerza Aérea) captain (AmE), flight lieutenant (BrE) **(b)** (Náut) (de transatlántico, carguero) captain, master; (de buque de pesca) skipper **(c)** (Aviac) captain ⟨2⟩ (Dep) captain

capitel *m* capital

capítulo *m* (de libro) chapter; (de serie) episode

capó *m* hood (AmE), bonnet (BrE)

capón *adj* castrated
■ *m* (gallo) capon

caporal *m* (Méx) foreman, charge hand (BrE)

capot /ka'po/ *m* hood (AmE), bonnet (BrE)

capota *f* (de automóvil) convertible top; (de cochecito de bebé) canopy, hood

capote *m* ⟨1⟩ (capa) cloak; (de militar, torero) cape ⟨2⟩ (Méx) (Auto) hood (AmE), bonnet (BrE)

capricho *m* ⟨1⟩ (antojo) whim, caprice (liter); **le consienten todos los** ∼**s** they indulge his every whim; **se lo compró por puro** ∼ he bought it on a whim; **entran y salen a** ∼ they come in and go out at will *o* as they please ⟨2⟩ (Mús) capriccio

caprichoso -sa *adj* **(a)** (inconstante) ⟨carácter/ persona⟩ capricious; ⟨tiempo/moda⟩ changeable **(b)** (difícil, exigente) fussy
■ *m,f*: **es un** ∼ (es inconstante) he's always changing his mind; (es difícil, exigente) he's so fussy

Capricornio *m* (signo, constelación) Capricorn; **es (de)** ∼ she's a Capricorn
■ *mf* (persona) *tb* **capricornio** Capricornean, Capricorn

cápsula *f* **(a)** (Farm, Espac) capsule **(b)** (Audio) cartridge

captar [A1] *vt* **(a)** ⟨atención/interés⟩ to capture; ⟨clientes⟩ to win, gain; ⟨partidarios/empleados⟩ to attract, recruit **(b)** ⟨sentido/matiz⟩ to grasp; ⟨significado/indirecta⟩ to get **(c)** ⟨emisora/señal⟩ to pick up, receive

captura *f* (de delincuente, enemigo, animal) capture; (de un alijo) seizure; (en pesca) catch

capturar [A1] *vt* ⟨delincuente/enemigo/animal⟩ to capture; ⟨alijo⟩ to seize, confiscate; ⟨peces⟩ to catch

capucha *f* hood

capuchón m (de pluma, bolígrafo) top, cap; (Indum) hood

capullo m (a) (Bot) bud (b) (Zool) cocoon

caqui adj inv/m khaki

cara f **1** (a) (Anat) face; **dímelo a la ~** say it to my face; **se le rio en la ~** she laughed in his face; **mírame a la ~** look at me (b) (en locs) **cara a cara** face to face; **de cara: el sol me da de ~** the sun is in my eyes; **se puso de ~ a la pared** she turned to face the wall, she turned her face to the wall; **dar la ~:** **nunca da la ~** he never does his own dirty work; **dar la ~ por algn** to stand up for sb; **echarle algo en ~ a algn** to throw sth back in sb's face; **romperle la ~ a algn** (fam) to smash sb's face in (colloq)

2 (a) (expresión): **no pongas esa ~ que no es para tanto** don't look like that, it's not that bad; **alegra esa ~** cheer up; **le cambió la ~ cuando ...** her face changed when ...; **poner ~ de bueno** to play o act the innocent; **poner ~ de asco** to make o (BrE) pull a face; **andaba con/puso ~ larga** (fam) he had/he pulled a long face (b) (aspecto) look; **tiene ~ de cansado** he looks tired; **tienes mala ~** you don't look well; **¡qué buena ~ tiene la comida!** the food looks delicious!

3 (a) (Mat) face (b) (de disco, papel) side; **~ o cruz** or (Arg) **ceca** or (Andes, Ven) **sello** heads or tails; **lo echaron a ~ o cruz** they tossed for it **4** (fam) (frescura, descaro) nerve (colloq), cheek (BrE colloq); **¡qué ~ (más dura) tienes!** you have some nerve!

■ mf: tb ~ **dura** (fam) (persona) sassy devil (AmE colloq), cheeky swine (BrE colloq)

carabina f (a) (Arm) carbine (b) (Esp fam) (acompañante): **ir de ~** to play gooseberry (colloq)

carabinero -ra m,f (a) (policía) (m) police officer, policeman; (f) police officer, policewoman (b) (agente fronterizo) border guard (c) **carabineros** mpl (institución) police (force); (policía fronteriza) border police

Caracas m Caracas

caracol m (a) (Zool) (de mar) winkle; (de tierra) snail (b) (AmL) (concha) conch

caracola f conch

carácter m (pl -racteres) (a) (en general) character; **tenemos un ~ muy distinto** we have very different characters; **el restaurante tiene mucho ~** the restaurant has lots of character; **una persona de ~ fuerte** a person of strong character; **una persona de buen ~** a good-natured person; **un ~ abierto** an open nature; **tener mal ~** to have a (bad) temper (b) (índole, naturaleza) nature; **una visita de ~ oficial** a visit of an official nature; **heridas de ~ leve** (period) minor wounds (c) (Biol) characteristic (d) (Col, Méx) (personaje) character

característica f (a) (rasgo) feature, characteristic (b) (RPI) (Telec) exchange code

característico -ca adj characteristic

caracterizar [A4] vt **1** (distinguir) to characterize; **con la franqueza que lo caracteriza** with his characteristic frankness **2** (describir) to portray, depict **3** (Teatr) (encarnar) to play, portray

■ **caracterizarse** v pron: **~se POR algo** «enfermedad/región/raza» to be characterized BY sth; «persona» to be noted FOR sth

caradura adj (fam) sassy (AmE colloq), cheeky (BrE colloq)

■ mf (fam) sassy devil (AmE colloq), cheeky swine (BrE colloq)

■ f (fam) nerve (colloq), cheek (BrE colloq)

carajillo m (café) coffee with brandy or similar

carajito -ta m,f (Ven fam) (niño) kid (colloq)

caramba interj (expresando — sorpresa) good heavens!; (— disgusto) dammit! (colloq)

carámbano m icicle

carambola f (a) (en billar) carom (AmE), cannon (BrE) (b) (fam) (casualidad): **fue de ~** it was pure chance (c) (Méx) (choque múltiple) pileup

caramelo m (a) (golosina) candy (AmE), sweet (BrE); **un ~ de menta** a mint (b) (azúcar fundida) caramel

carantoña f (Esp fam) caress

caraota f (Ven) bean

caraqueño -ña adj of/from Caracas

carátula f (a) (de disco) jacket (AmE), sleeve (BrE); (de video) case (b) (Méx) (de reloj) face, dial (c) (máscara) mask

caravana f **1** (a) (de tráfico — retención) backup (AmE) tailback (BrE); (— hilera) convoy; **ir en ~** to drive in a convoy (b) (remolque) trailer (AmE), caravan (BrE) **2** (Méx) (reverencia) bow

carbohidrato m carbohydrate

carbón m (a) (mineral) coal; **negro como el ~** as black as coal (b) (vegetal) charcoal

carboncillo m charcoal; **dibujo al ~** charcoal drawing

carbonilla f (a) (polvo de carbón) cinders (pl) (b) (RPI) (Art) charcoal

carbonizarse [A4] v pron (a) «edificio/muebles» to be reduced to ashes; **los cuerpos carbonizados de las víctimas** the victims' charred remains (b) (Quím) to carbonize

carbono m carbon

carburador m carburetor*

carburante m fuel

carburar [A1] vi (a) «motor» to carburet (b) (fam) (funcionar) «electrodoméstico/coche» to work

■ ~ vt (Andes) ‹motor› to tune

carca adj (fam) old-fashioned, fuddy-duddy (colloq)

■ mf old fogey (colloq)

carcacha f (Andes, Méx fam) (auto viejo) wreck (colloq), old heap (colloq); (otro aparato) contraption (colloq)

carcajada f guffaw; **soltar una ~** to give a guffaw, to burst out laughing; **reírse a ~s** to roar with laughter

carcasa *f* **(a)** (armazón, estructura) frame; (de aparato) casing; (de barca) hulk **(b)** (esqueleto de animal) skeleton

cárcel *f* (prisión) prison, jail; **la metieron en la** ∼ she was put in prison

carcelero -ra *m,f* jailer

carcoma *f* (Zool) woodworm

carcomer [E1] *vt* **(a)** «*carcoma*» to eat away (at); **el marco está carcomido** the frame is worm-eaten **(b)** ⟨*salud*⟩ to undermine; **la envidia lo carcomía** he was eaten up with envy

cardar [A1] *vt* **(a)** ⟨*lana*⟩ to card **(b)** ⟨*pelo*⟩ to backcomb, tease

■ **cardarse** *v pron* (*refl*) to backcomb

cardenal *m* **1** (Relig) cardinal **2** (fam) (moretón) bruise

cardíaco, cardiaco -ca *adj* heart (*before n*), cardiac (tech); **enfermos** ∼**s** heart patients

cárdigan *m* (*pl* **-gans**) cardigan

cardiólogo -ga *m,f* cardiologist

cardo *m* (Bot) thistle

carecer [E3] *vi* (frml) ∼ **DE algo** to lack sth; **carece de interés** it is lacking in interest, it lacks interest; **carece de valor** it has no value, it is worthless

carencia *f* **(a)** (escasez) lack, shortage; ∼ **de recursos financieros** lack of financial resources **(b)** (Med) deficiency; ∼ **de vitamina A** vitamin A deficiency

carente *adj* (frml): **lugares** ∼**s de interés** places which are of no interest; **niños** ∼**s de cariño** children lacking affection

carero -ra *adj* (fam) ⟨*comerciante*⟩ pricey (colloq)

carestía *f* (costo elevado) high cost; **la** ∼ **de la vida** the high cost of living

careta *f* mask

carey *m* (Zool) hawksbill turtle; (material) tortoiseshell

carga *f* **1** **(a)** (de barco, avión) cargo; (de camión) load; (de tren) freight; ⓢ **zona de carga y descarga** loading and unloading only **(b)** (peso) load; **no lleves tanta** ∼ don't carry such a heavy load **2** **(a)** (de escopeta, cañón) charge **(b)** (de bolígrafo, pluma) refill; (de lavadora) load **3** (Elec) (de cuerpo) charge; (de circuito) load **4** (responsabilidad) burden; **es una** ∼ **para la familia** he is a burden to his family **5** **(a)** (de tropas, policía) charge; **¡a la** ∼**!** charge! **(b)** (Dep) *tb* ∼ **defensiva** blitz

cargada *f* (RPI fam) practical joke

cargaderas *fpl* (Col) suspenders (*pl*) (AmE), braces (*pl*) (BrE)

cargado -da *adj* **1** **(a)** (con peso): **iba muy cargada** she had a lot to carry; ∼ **DE algo** ⟨*de regalos*⟩ laden WITH sth; ⟨*de paquetes/maletas*⟩ loaded down WITH sth; ∼ **de deudas** heavily in debt; **un árbol** ∼ **de fruta** a tree laden with fruit; ∼ **de trabajo** overloaded with work **(b)** ⟨*ambiente/atmósfera*⟩ (bochornoso) heavy, close; (con humo, olores desagradables) stuffy; (tenso) strained, tense **(c)** ⟨*café*⟩ strong **2** ∼ **de hombros** *or* **de espaldas** with bowed shoulders

cargador *m* **(a)** (Arm) clip, magazine **(b)** (de pilas, baterías) battery charger

cargamento *m* (de camión) load; (de barco, avión) cargo; (de tren) freight

cargante *adj* **(a)** (CS fam) (antipático) unpleasant, horrible (colloq) **(b)** (Esp fam) annoying

cargar [A3] *vt* **1** **(a)** ⟨*barco/avión/camión*⟩ to load; ∼**on la camioneta de cajas** they loaded the van with boxes; **no cargues tanto el coche** don't put so much in the car **(b)** ⟨*pistola/escopeta*⟩ to load; ⟨*pluma/encendedor*⟩ to fill; ⟨*cámara*⟩ to load, put a film in **(c)** (Elec) to charge **2** **(a)** ⟨*mercancías*⟩ to load **(b)** ⟨*combustible*⟩ to fuel; **tengo que** ∼ **nafta** (RPI) I have to fill up with gasoline (AmE) *o* (BrE) petrol **(c)** (Inf) to load **3** (de obligaciones) ∼ **a algn DE algo** to burden sb WITH sth; **me** ∼**on la culpa** they put *o* laid the blame on me **4** **(a)** ⟨*paquetes/bolsas*⟩ to carry; ⟨*niño*⟩ (AmL) to carry **(b)** (AmL exc RPI) ⟨*armas*⟩ to carry **(c)** (Ven fam) (llevar puesto) to wear; (tener consigo): **cargo las llaves** I have the keys **5** (a una cuenta) to charge **6** (Méx fam) (matar) to kill

■ ∼ *vi* **1** ∼ **CON algo** ⟨*con bulto*⟩ to carry sth; **tiene que** ∼ **con todo el peso de la casa** she has to shoulder all the responsibility for the household **2** ∼ **CONTRA algn** «*tropas/policía*» to charge ON *o* AT sb **3** ⟨*batería*⟩ to charge **4** (fam) (fastidiar): **me cargan los fanfarrones** I can't stand show-offs

■ **cargarse** *v pron* **1** **(a)** «*pilas/flash*» to charge; «*partícula*» to become charged **(b)** ∼**se DE algo** ⟨*de bolsas/equipaje*⟩ to load oneself down WITH sth; ⟨*de responsabilidades*⟩ to take on a lot OF sth; ⟨*de deudas*⟩ to saddle oneself WITH sth **2** **(a)** (fam) (matar) to kill **(b)** (Esp fam) ⟨*motor*⟩ to wreck; ⟨*jarrón*⟩ to smash

cargo *m* **1** (puesto) post, position (frml); (de presidente, ministro) office; **tener un** ∼ **público** to hold public office; **un** ∼ **de responsabilidad** a responsible job *o* post **2** (responsabilidad, cuidado): **los niños están a mi** ∼ the children are in my care; **estar a** ∼ **de algo** to be in charge of sth; **los gastos corren a** ∼ **de la empresa** expenses will be paid *o* met by the company; **hacerse** ∼ **de algo** ⟨*de puesto/tarea*⟩ to take charge of sth; ⟨*de gastos*⟩ to take care of sth; **me da** ∼ **de conciencia** I feel guilty **3** **(a)** (Com, Fin) charge; **sin** ∼ free of charge **(b)** (Der) charge

cargoso -sa *adj* (CS, Per fam) annoying

cargue *m* (Col, Ven) loading; ⓢ **zona de cargue y descargue** loading and unloading only

carguero *m* freighter, cargo ship

Caribe *m*: **el** (mar) ∼ the Caribbean (Sea)

caribeño -ña *adj* Caribbean
■ *m,f*: person from the Caribbean region

caribú *m* caribou

caricatura *f* (dibujo) caricature

caricaturizar [A4] *vt* to caricature

caricia *f* caress; **hacer** ∼**s** to caress; **le hizo una** ∼ **al perro** she stroked the dog

caridad *f* charity; **vivir de la** ∼ to live on charity; **por** ∼ for pity's sake

caries *f* (*pl* ∼) **(a)** (proceso) tooth decay, caries (*pl*) (tech) **(b)** (cavidad) cavity

cariño *m* **(a)** (afecto) affection; **les tengo mucho** ···⫶⟶

∼ I am very fond of them; **te ha tomado mucho** ∼ he's become very fond of you; **∼s por tu casa/ a tu mujer** (AmL) (send my) love to your family/ your wife; **∼s, Beatriz** (en cartas) (AmL) love, Beatriz **(b)** (caricia): **le hice un cariñito al niño** I gave the little boy a cuddle (*o kiss etc*) **(c)** (como apelativo) dear, honey, love (BrE)

cariñoso -sa *adj* ⟨*persona*⟩ affectionate; ⟨*bienvenida*⟩ warm; **un ∼ saludo de mi parte** regards

carioca *adj* of/from Rio de Janeiro

carisma *m* charisma

carismático -ca *adj* charismatic

caritativo -va *adj* charitable; **una organización con fines ∼s** a charitable organization

cariz *m*: **el ∼ que están tomando las cosas** the way things are going *o* developing; **la situación está tomando mal ∼** the situation is beginning to look bad

carmín *adj inv* carmine
■ *m* **(a)** (para labios) lipstick **(b)** (color) carmine

carnada *f* bait

carnal *adj* ⟨*amor/deseo*⟩ carnal
■ *m* (Méx arg) pal (colloq), buddy (AmE colloq), mate (BrE colloq)

carnaval *m* (fiesta) carnival

carne *f* **1** **(a)** (de mamífero, ave) meat; (de pescado, flesh; **∼ de cerdo** *or* (Chi, Per) **chancho** *or* (Ven) **cochino** *or* (Méx) **puerco** pork; **∼ de cordero** lamb; **∼ de ternera** veal; **∼ de vaca** *or* (AmC, Col, Méx, Ven) **res** beef; **∼ molida** *or* (Esp, RPI) **picada** ground beef (AmE), mince (BrE) **(b)** (de fruta) flesh **2** (de una persona) flesh; **es ∼ de mi** ∼ he's my flesh and blood; **tenía la herida en ∼ viva** her wound was raw; **(de) color ∼** flesh-colored*; **en ∼ y hueso** in the flesh; **me pone la ∼ de gallina** it gives me goose pimples (colloq)

carné *m* identity card; **sacar el ∼** to have one's identity (*o* membership *etc*) card issued; **∼ de conducir** driver's license (AmE), driving licence (BrE); **∼ de estudiante** student card; **∼ de identidad** identity card; **∼ de socio** (de club, mutual) membership card; (de biblioteca) library card

carnear [A1] *vt* (CS) to slaughter
■ ∼ *vi* (CS) to slaughter a cow (*o* lamb *etc*)

carnecería *f* butcher's shop (*o* stall *etc*)

cárneo -nea *adj* (CS) meat (*before n*)

carnero *m* ram

carnet /kar'ne/ *m* (*pl* **-nets**) ▶ CARNÉ

carnicería *f* **(a)** (tienda) butcher's shop (*o* stall *etc*) **(b)** (fam) (matanza) slaughter

carnicero -ra *m,f* **(a)** (vendedor) butcher **(b)** (fam & pey) (cirujano) butcher (colloq & pej)

carnitas *fpl* (Méx) pieces of barbecued pork (*pl*)

carnívoro¹ -ra *adj* carnivorous, meat-eating

carnívoro² *m* carnivore

caro¹ -ra *adj* **(a)** ⟨*coche/entrada/ciudad*⟩ expensive; **la vida está muy cara** everything costs so much nowadays **(b)** (*como adv*): **me costó muy** ∼ I had to pay a lot of money for it; **pagarás** ∼ **tu error** you'll pay dearly for your mistake

caro² *adv*: **vender** ∼ to charge a lot; *ver tb* CARO¹ B

carpa *f* **1** **(a)** (de circo) big top; (para actuaciones) marquee **(b)** (AmL) (para acampar) tent **2** (Zool) carp

carpeta *f* (para documentos, dibujos) folder; **∼ de anillos** *or* (Esp) **anillas** *or* (RPI) **ganchos** ring binder

carpintería *f* **(a)** (taller) carpenter's workshop; (actividad) carpentry **(b)** (de construcción, casa) woodwork; **∼ metálica** metalwork

carpintero -ra *m,f* carpenter

carraca *f* **(a)** (matraca) rattle **(b)** (fam) (trasto) wreck (colloq))

carraspear [A1] *vi* to clear one's throat

carraspera *f*: **tener** ∼ to have a rough throat

carrasposo -sa *adj* **(a)** ⟨*garganta*⟩ rough **(b)** (Col) ⟨*superficie*⟩ rough

carrera *f* **1** (Dep) (competición) race; **∼ de caballos** horse race; **la ∼ de los 100 metros vallas** the 100 meters hurdles; **te echo una** ∼ I'll race you; **∼ de armamentos** arms race; **∼ contra reloj** (Dep) time trial; **∼ de fondo** long-distance race; **∼ de postas** *o* **relevos** relay race
2 (fam) (corrida): **darse** *or* **pegarse una** ∼ to run as fast as one can; **me fui de una** ∼ **a su casa** I raced *o* rushed round to her house (colloq); **a la(s) ∼(s)** in a rush
3 **(a)** (Educ) degree course; **está haciendo la** ∼ **de Derecho** he's doing a degree in law **(b)** (profesión, trayectoria) career; **un diplomático de** ∼ a career diplomat; **∼ media/superior** *three-year/ five-year university course*
4 (en la media) run, ladder (BrE); (en el pelo) (Col, Ven) part (AmE), parting (BrE)

carrerear [A1] *vt* (Méx fam) to push (colloq)

carrerilla *f*: **se lo saben de** ∼ they know it (off) by heart; **me lo dijo de** ∼ he reeled it off parrot-fashion; **coger** ∼ (Esp) to take a run-up

carreta *f* (con toldo) wagon; (sin toldo) cart

carrete *m* (de hilo, cinta) spool, reel (BrE); (de película) film; (de caña de pescar) reel

carretear [A1] *vi* (AmL) (Aviac) to taxi

carretela *f* (Chi) cart

carretera *f* road; **∼ de circunvalación** bypass, beltway (AmE), ring road (BrE); **∼ nacional** ≈highway (*in US*), ≈A-road (*in UK*)

carretilla *f* **1** (de mano) wheelbarrow **2** (CS) (quijada) jaw, jawbone

carricoche *m* covered wagon

carril *m* **(a)** (Auto) lane; **∼ bus** bus lane; **∼ de adelantamiento** overtaking lane, fast lane; **∼ de bicicletas** cycleway, cycle path **(b)** (Ferr) rail **(c)** (AmL) (Dep) lane

carrillo *m* cheek

carriola *f* (Méx) baby carriage (AmE), baby buggy (BrE)

carrito *m* **(a)** (para el equipaje) trolley; (en supermercado) shopping cart (AmE), trolley (BrE); (de la compra) shopping trolley *o* (AmE) cart; **∼ chocón** (Méx, Ven) bumper car **(b)** (mesita de servir) trolley

carro *m* **1** **(a)** (carreta) cart; **un ∼ de tierra** a cartload of earth; **∼ de combate** tank **(b)** (AmL exc CS) (Auto) car, automobile (AmE); **∼ bomba** (Col) car bomb; **∼ loco** (Andes) bumper car; **∼ sport** (AmL exc CS) sports car; **∼ de bomberos** (Andes, Méx) fire engine **(c)** (Chi, Méx) (vagón) coach, carriage (BrE); ~ **comedor/dormitorio** (Méx) dining/sleeping car **(d)** (Hist) (romano) chariot [2] (de máquina de escribir) carriage

carrocería *f* (de automóvil) bodywork

carroña *f* **(a)** (de animal muerto) carrion **(b)** (gente despreciable) riffraff (+ *sing or pl vb*)

carroza *f* **(a)** (coche de caballos) carriage **(b)** (de carnaval) float **(c)** (Chi, Ur) (coche fúnebre) hearse

carruaje *m* carriage

carrusel *m* **(a)** (para diapositivas) carousel, slide tray **(b)** (para niños) merry-go-round, carousel (AmE)

carta *f* [1] (Corresp) letter; ¿hay ~ **para mí?** are there any letters for me?; **echar una** ~ **al correo** to mail (esp AmE) *o* (esp BrE) post a letter; ~ **adjunta** *or* **explicatoria** covering letter; ~ **blanca** carte blanche; ~ **certificada** registered letter; ~ **de amor** love letter; ~ **de recomendación** reference, letter of recommendation; ~ **urgente** special-delivery letter
[2] (naipe) card; **jugar a las** ~**s** to play cards; **dar las** ~**s** to deal the cards; *echarle las* ~*s a algn* to tell sb's fortune; *poner las* ~*s sobre la mesa* to put *o* lay one's cards on the table
[3] (en restaurante) menu; **comer a la** ~ to eat à la carte; ~ **de vinos** wine list

cartearse [A1] *v pron:* **nos carteamos durante años** we wrote to each other *o* corresponded for years; ~ **CON algn** to correspond WITH sb

cartel *m* (de publicidad, propaganda) poster; (letrero) sign; ~ **luminoso** neon sign; **lleva dos meses en** ~ *«obra/película»* it has been on for two months; **de** ~ *«cantante/actor»* famous; *«torero»* star (*before n*)

cartelera *f* **(a)** (Cin, Teatr) publicity board; **la película sigue en** ~ the movie is still on *o* still showing; **la obra estuvo en** ~ **durante cuatro años** the play ran for four years **(b)** (en el periódico) listings (*pl*); ~ **de espectáculos** entertainment guide **(c)** (AmL) (tablón de anuncios) bulletin board (AmE), notice board (BrE)

cárter *m* (del cigüeñal) crankcase, sump; (del embrague) housing

cartera *f* [1] **(a)** (billetera) wallet, billfold (AmE) **(b)** (para documentos) document case, briefcase; (de colegial) satchel; (de cobrador) money bag; (de cartero) sack, bag **(c)** (AmS) (bolso de mujer) purse (AmE), handbag (BrE) **(d)** (Com, Fin) portfolio

carterear [A1] *vt* (Chi): **me** ~**on en la micro** my handbag was picked on the bus

carterista *mf* pickpocket

cartero (*m*) mailman (AmE), postman (BrE); (*f*) mailwoman (AmE), postwoman (BrE)

cartílago *m* cartilage

cartilla *f* **(a)** (para aprender a leer) reader, primer **(b)** (libreta) book; ~ **de ahorros** passbook, savings book; ~ **de racionamiento** ration book

cartón *m* **(a)** (material) cardboard; ~ **ondulado** corrugated cardboard; ~ **piedra** papier-mâché **(b)** (de cigarrillos, leche) carton; (de huevos) tray

cartoné *m*: **en** ~ hardback

cartuchera *f* [1] **(a)** (estuche — para cartuchos) cartridge clip; (— para pistola) holster **(b)** (cinturón — para cartuchos) cartridge belt; (— para pistola) gun belt [2] (RPl) (de escolar) pencil case

cartucho *m* cartridge

cartuja *f* charterhouse, monastery

cartulina *f* card

casa *f* [1] **(a)** (vivienda) house; **cambiarse de** ~ to move house; **casita del perro** kennel; ~ **adosada** *or* **pareada** semi-detached *o* terraced house; **C**~ **Blanca** White House; ~ **de acogida** refuge; ~ **de huéspedes** boardinghouse; ~ **de socorro** first-aid post; ~ **de vecinos** *or* (Méx) **de vecindad** tenement house; **C**~ **Real** Royal Household; ~ **refugio** refuge *o* hostel for battered women; ~ **rodante** (CS) trailer (AmE), caravan (BrE) **(b)** (hogar) home; **a los 18 años se fue de** ~ *or* (AmL) **de la** ~ she left home at 18; **no está nunca en** ~ *or* (AmL) **en la** ~ he's never (at) home; **está en casa de Ana** she's (over) at Ana's (house); **¿por qué no pasas por** ~ *or* (AmL) **por la** ~**?** why don't you drop in?; **de** *or* **para andar por** ~ *«vestido»* for wearing around the house; *«definición/terminología»* crude, rough; **echar** *or* **tirar la** ~ **por la ventana** to push the boat out
[2] **(a)** (empresa) company, firm (BrE); **una** ~ **de discos** a record company; ~ **de cambios** bureau de change **(b)** (bar, restaurante): **especialidad de la** ~ house specialty (AmE), speciality of the house (BrE); **invita la** ~ it's on the house
[3] (Dep): **perdieron en** ~ they lost at home

casabe *m* (Col, Ven) cassava bread

casaca *f* (chaqueta) jacket; (Equ) riding jacket

casado -da *adj* married; **está** ~ **con una japonesa** he's married to a Japanese woman
■ *m,f* (*m*) married man; (*f*) married woman; **los recién** ~**s** the newlyweds

casamiento *m* (unión) marriage; (boda) wedding

casar [A1] *vt* «*cura/juez*» to marry
■ ~ *vi* **(a)** (encajar) *«dibujos»* to match up; *«piezas»* to fit together; *«cuentas»* to match, tally **(b)** (armonizar) *«colores/estilos»* to go together; ~ **CON algo** to go well WITH sth
■ **casarse** *v pron* to get married; ~**se por la Iglesia** to get married in church; **se casó con un abogado** she married a lawyer; ~**se en segundas nupcias** to marry again, to remarry

cascabel *m* **(a)** (campanita) bell **(b)** (Chi) (sonajero) rattle
■ *f* (Zool) rattlesnake

cascada *f* (Geog) waterfall, cascade

cascajo *m* (fam) [1] (trasto viejo) wreck (colloq) [2] (Col) (Const) piece of gravel

cascanueces *m* (*pl* ~) (a pair of) nutcrackers

cascar [A2] *vt* *«nuez/huevo»* to crack; *«taza»* to chip
■ **cascarse** *v pron* *«huevo»* to crack; *«taza»* to chip

cáscara *f* (de huevo, nuez) shell; (del queso) rind; (de naranja, limón) peel, rind; (de plátano, papa) skin; (de manzana) peel

cascarilla *f* (de cacao) roasted cacao husks (*pl*) (*used in infusions*); (de cereal) husk

cascarón *m* (de huevo, nuez) shell

cascarrabias *adj inv* (fam) cantankerous, grumpy
■ *mf* (*pl* ~) grouch (colloq)

casco *m* [1] **(a)** (para la cabeza) helmet; ~ **protector** (de obrero) safety helmet; (de motorista) crash helmet **(b) cascos** *mpl* (Audio)

headphones (*pl*) **2** (Equ, Zool) hoof **3** (Náut) hull **4** (a) (de ciudad): ~ **antiguo** old quarter; ~ **urbano** urban area, built-up area **(b)** (RPl) (de estancia) farmhouse and surrounding buildings **5** (Col) (gajo) segment **6** (Esp, Méx) (envase) bottle

cascote *m* piece of rubble; ~s rubble

caserío *m* (poblado) hamlet; (finca) (Esp) farmhouse

casero -ra *adj* **(a)** ⟨*vino/flan*⟩ homemade; ⟨*reparación*⟩ amateur; ⟨*trabajo*⟩ domestic **(b)** ⟨*persona*⟩ home-loving
■ *m,f* **1** **(a)** (propietario) (*m*) landlord; (*f*) landlady **(b)** (cuidador) caretaker **2** (Chi) (cliente) customer; (vendedor) storekeeper (AmE), stallholder

caseta *f* **(a)** (en la playa, de guardia etc) hut **(b)** (en exposición) stand **(c)** (para perro) kennel **(d)** (en fútbol) dugout

casete *m or f* (cinta) cassette; ~ **digital** digital audio tape
■ *m* (Esp) (grabador) cassette recorder/player

casi *adv* **1** (cerca de) almost, nearly; ~ **me caigo** I nearly fell over **2** (en frases negativas): ~ **no se le oía** you could hardly hear him; ~ **nunca** hardly ever; **no nos queda** ~ **nada de pan** there's hardly any bread left; **¿pudiste dormir?** — ~ **nada** did you manage to sleep? — hardly at all; ~ **no vengo** I almost didn't come **3** (expresando una opinión tentativa): ~ **sería mejor venderlo** maybe it would be better to sell it

casilla *f* **1** (para cartas, llaves) pigeonhole; ~ **postal** *or* **de correo** (CS, Per) post office box, P.O. Box **2** (en ajedrez, crucigrama) square; (en formulario) box **3** **(a)** (de guardia, sereno) hut **(b)** (de perro) kennel **(c)** (Méx) (de votación) polling booth

casillero *m* **(a)** (mueble) set of pigeonholes; (compartimento) pigeonhole **(b)** (CS) (en formulario) box

casino *m* **1** (de juego) casino **2** (club social) club

casitas *fpl* (Chi fam & euf) (baño) bathroom (euph)

caso *m* **1** (situación, coyuntura) case; **en esos** ~s in cases like that; **yo en tu caso** ... if I were you ...; **en último** ~ if it comes to it, if the worst comes to the worst; **en el mejor de los** ~s at (the very) best; **en el peor de los** ~s **te multarán** the worst they can do is fine you; **eso no venía al** ~ that had nothing to do with what we were talking about; **pongamos por** ~ **que** ... let's assume that ...; **en** ~ **de incendio** in case of fire; **en** ~ **contrario** otherwise; **en cualquier** ~ in any case; **en tal** ~ in that case, in such a case (frml); **en todo** ~ **dijo que llamaría** in any case she said she'd ring; **llegado el** ~ if it comes to it; **según el** ~ as appropriate; **no hay/hubo caso** (AmL fam) it is no good *o* no use/it was no good *o* no use **2** (Der, Med) case; **ser un** ~ **perdido** (fam) to be a hopeless case (colloq) **3** (atención): **hacerle** ~ A algn to pay attention TO sb, take notice OF sb; **hacer** ~ DE algo to pay attention TO sth, to take notice OF sth; **hacer** ~ **omiso de algo** to ignore sth

caspa *f* dandruff

casquillo *m* **(a)** (de bala, cartucho) case **(b)** (portalámparas) lampholder, bulbholder; (de bombilla): ~ **de rosca/bayoneta** screw-in/bayonet fitting

cassette /ka'set/ *m or f* ▶ CASETE

casta *f* caste; **de** ~ ⟨*toro*⟩ thoroughbred; ⟨*torero*⟩ top-class

castaña *f* (fruto) chestnut; ~ **de Indias** horse chestnut; ~ **de Pará** (RPl) Brazil nut; ~ **pilonga** dried chestnut

castañetear [A1] *vi*: **me castañetean los dientes** my teeth are chattering

castaño¹ -ña *adj* ⟨*pelo*⟩ chestnut; ⟨*ojos*⟩ brown

castaño² *m* **(a)** (Bot) chestnut tree; ~ **de Indias** horse chestnut **(b)** (color) chestnut

castañuela *f* castanet

castellano¹ -na *adj* (de Castilla) Castilian; (español) Spanish
■ *m,f* (persona) Castilian

castellano² *m* (idioma — de Castilla) Castilian; (— español) Spanish

castidad *f* chastity

castigar [A3] *vt* **(a)** (en general) to punish; **fueron castigados con la pena máxima** they received the maximum sentence **(b)** ⟨*niño*⟩ (a quedarse en el colegio) to keep ... in detention; (a quedarse en casa) to keep ... in as a punishment, to ground (esp AmE colloq); **lo** ~**on sin postre** as a punishment he was made to go without dessert

castigo *m* punishment; ~ **corporal** corporal punishment; **les impusieron** ~s **severos** they were severely punished; **levantar un** ~ to lift a punishment

Castilla *f* Castile

castillo *m* castle; ~ **de arena** sandcastle; **construir** ~s **en el aire** to build castles in the air

castizo -za *adj* **(a)** (puro, tradicional) ⟨*estilo/ costumbre*⟩ traditional **(b)** (típicamente castellano): **un lenguaje muy** ~ very pure Castilian/Spanish

casto -ta *adj* chaste

castor *m* beaver

castrar [A1] *vt* ⟨*caballo*⟩ to geld; ⟨*toro/hombre*⟩ to castrate; ⟨*gato*⟩ to neuter

casual *adj* chance (*before n*)

casualidad *f* chance; **por (pura)** ~ by (sheer) chance; **si por** ~ **la ves** if you happen to see her; **¿no tendrás su dirección por** ~**?** you wouldn't (happen to) have her address by any chance?; **¡qué** ~**!** what a coincidence!; **da la** ~ **de que** ... as it happens ...

cataclismo *m* natural disaster, cataclysm (frml)

catacumbas *fpl* catacombs (*pl*)

catador -dora *m,f* taster

catalán¹ -lana *adj/m,f* Catalan

catalán² *m* (idioma) Catalan

catalejo *m* (ant) telescope, spyglass

catalizador *m* (Auto) catalytic converter

AmC	Central America	Arg	Argentina	Cu	Cuba
AmL	Latin America	Bol	Bolivia	Ec	Ecuador
AmS	South America	Chi	Chile	Esp	Spain
Andes	Andean Region	CS	Southern Cone	Méx	Mexico

Per	Peru
RPl	River Plate Area
Ur	Uruguay
Ven	Venezuela

catalogar [A3] *vt* **(a)** (en un catálogo) to catalog (AmE), to catalogue (BrE); (en una lista) to record, list **(b)** (considerar) to class

catálogo *m* (Art, Com) catalog (AmE), catalogue (BrE); **compra por** ∼ mail-order shopping

Cataluña *f* Catalonia

catamarán *m* catamaran

cataplasma *f* poultice, cataplasm (tech)

catapulta *f* catapult

catapultar [A1] *vt* to catapult

catar [A1] *vt* ⟨vino⟩ to taste

catarata *f* **(a)** (Geog) waterfall; **las** ∼**s del Iguazú** Iguaçú Falls **(b)** (Med) cataract

catarro *m* **(a)** (resfriado) cold; **pescarse** *or* (esp Esp) **coger un** ∼ to catch a cold **(b)** (inflamación) catarrh

catastro *m* (censo) cadastre, land registry; (impuesto) property tax

catástrofe *f* catastrophe, disaster

catastrófico -ca *adj* catastrophic, disastrous

catear [A1] *vt* **1** (Esp arg) (suspender) to fail **2 (a)** (Chi) (Min) to prospect **(b)** (Méx) (registrar) ⟨persona⟩ to frisk; ⟨vivienda⟩ to search

catecismo *m* catechism

cátedra *f* (en universidad) professorship, chair; (en colegio) post of head of department

catedral *f* cathedral

catedrático -ca *m,f* (de universidad) professor; (en colegio) head of department

categoría *f* **(a)** (grupo) category; ∼ **gramatical** part of speech; **hotel de primera** ∼ first-class hotel **(b)** (calidad): **de** ∼ ⟨actor/espectáculo/revista⟩ first-rate; **un periódico de poca** ∼ a second-rate newspaper; **el hotel de más** ∼ the finest *o* best hotel **(c)** (estatus): **tiene** ∼ **de embajador** he has ambassadorial status; **gente de cierta** ∼ people of some standing

categórico -ca *adj* ⟨respuesta⟩ categorical

cateo *m* (Chi, Méx) (cacheo) body search

catequesis *f. teaching of the catechism*

catire -ra *adj* (Ven) (de piel blanca) fair-skinned; (de pelo rubio) fair, fair-haired
■ *m,f* (Ven) (de piel blanca) fair-skinned person; (de pelo rubio) fair-haired person

catita *f* (CS) budgerigar

catolicismo *m* Catholicism

católico -ca *adj* **(a)** (Relig) Catholic; **es** ∼ he's a Catholic **(b)** (ortodoxo) orthodox
■ *m,f* Catholic

catorce *adj inv/m/pron* fourteen; *para ejemplos ver* CINCO

catre *m* **(a)** (cama — plegable) folding bed; (— de campaña) camp bed **(b)** (CS) (armazón) bedstead

catsup *m* ketchup, catsup (AmE)

cauce *m* **(a)** (Geog) bed; **el río se salió de su** ∼ the river burst its banks; **desviaron el** ∼ **del arroyo** they changed the course of the stream **(b)** (rumbo, vía): **desvió la conversación hacia otros** ∼**s** he steered the conversation onto another tack; **seguir los** ∼**s establecidos** to go through the normal channels

cauchera *f* (Col) (tirachinas) (fam) slingshot (AmE), catapult (BrE)

caucho *m* **(a)** (sustancia) rubber; (árbol) (Col) rubber tree **(b)** (neumático) (Ven) tire*; (gomita) (Col) rubber band, elastic band (BrE)

caudal *m* **(a)** (de un fluido) volume of flow; **el río tiene muy poco** ∼ the water level is very low **(b)** (riqueza) fortune **(c)** (abundancia) wealth; **un** ∼ **de conocimientos** a wealth of knowledge

caudaloso -sa *adj* ⟨río⟩ large

caudillo *m* (líder) leader; **el C**∼ *title used to refer to General Franco*

causa *f* **1** (motivo) cause; **la** ∼ **de todas mis desgracias** the cause of *o* the reason for all my misfortunes; **se enfadó sin** ∼ **alguna** she got annoyed for no reason at all *o* for no good reason; **a** *or* **por** ∼ **de** because of **2** (ideal) cause; **una** ∼ **perdida** a lost cause **3** (Der) (pleito) lawsuit; (proceso) trial

causante *adj*: **los factores** ∼**s de la crisis** the factors which caused the crisis
■ *mf* (causa) cause; **la** ∼ **de todas mis desgracias** the cause of all my misfortunes

causar [A1] *vt* ⟨daños/problema/sufrimiento⟩ to cause; ⟨indignación⟩ to cause, arouse; ⟨alarma⟩ to cause, provoke; ⟨placer⟩ to give; **le causó mucha pena** it made him very sad; **me causó muy buena impresión** I was very impressed with her

cautela *f* caution; **con** ∼ cautiously

cauteloso -sa *adj* [SER] ⟨persona⟩ cautious

cautivador -dora *adj* captivating

cautivar [A1] *vt* (atraer) to captivate

cautiverio *m* captivity

cautivo -va *adj/m,f* captive

cauto -ta *adj* careful, cautious

cava *f* cellar
■ *m* cava (*sparkling wine*)

cavar [A1] *vt* ⟨fosa/zanja⟩ to dig; ⟨pozo⟩ to sink **(b)** ⟨tierra⟩ to hoe

caverna *f* cave, cavern

cavernícola *adj* (Hist) cave-dwelling; **un hombre** ∼ a caveman
■ *mf* (Hist) cave dweller

caviar *m* caviar

cavidad *f* cavity

cavilar [A1] *vi* to ponder, think deeply; **después de mucho** ∼ after much thought *o* deliberation

cayena *f* cayenne (pepper)

cayera, cayese, etc ▶ CAER

caza *f* **(a)** (para subsistir) hunting; (como deporte — caza mayor) hunting; (— caza menor) shooting; **ir de** ∼ to go hunting/shooting; ∼ **del tesoro** treasure hunt; ∼ **furtiva** poaching; **salieron a la** ∼ **del ladrón** they set off in pursuit of the thief; **dar** ∼ **a algn** (perseguir) to pursue *o* chase sb; (alcanzar) to catch sb **(b)** (animales) game
■ *m* fighter

cazabombardero *m* fighter-bomber

cazador -dora *m,f* hunter; ∼ **furtivo** poacher

cazadora *f* (Esp) (Indum) jacket

cazamariposas *m* (*pl* ∼) butterfly net

cazar [A4] *vt* **(a)** (para subsistir) to hunt; (como deporte—caza mayor) to hunt; (— caza menor) to shoot **(b)** ⟨mariposas⟩ to catch **(c)** (fam) (conseguir, atrapar): **ha cazado un millonario/buen empleo** she's landed herself a millionaire/good job ⋯❖

■ ~ *vi* to hunt; (con fusil) to shoot; **salimos a ~** we went out hunting/shooting

cazo *m* (cacerola) small saucepan; (cucharón) ladle

cazuela *f* casserole

cazurro -rra *adj* (fam) (huraño) sullen, surly; (obstinado) stubborn, pig-headed (colloq)
■ *m,f* (fam) (huraño) sullen *o* surly person; (obstinado) stubborn *o* (colloq) pig-headed person

c.c. (= **centímetros cúbicos**) cc

CD *m* (= **compact disc**) CD

CD-ROM *m* (= **compact disc read-only memory**) CD-ROM

ce *f*: name of the letter c

cebada *f* barley

cebar [A1] *vt* **1** ⟨animal⟩ to fatten ... up **2** ⟨anzuelo/cepo⟩ to bait **3** (CS) ⟨mate⟩ to prepare (and serve)

cebo *m* (a) (en pesca, caza) bait (b) (Arm) primer

cebolla *f* onion

cebolleta *f*, **cebollino** *m* (a) (con tallo verde) scallion (AmE), spring onion (BrE) (b) (hierba) chive

cebra *f* zebra

cebú *m* (pl **-bús** or **-búes**) zebu

cecear [A1] *vi* (a) (Ling) to pronounce the Spanish [/s/] as [θ] (b) (como defecto) to lisp

ceceo *m* (a) (Ling) pronunciation of the Spanish [/s/] as [θ] (b) (como defecto) lisp

cedazo *m* sieve

ceder [E1] *vt* **1** (a) ⟨derecho⟩ to transfer, assign; ⟨territorio⟩ to cede; ⟨puesto/título⟩ (voluntariamente) to hand over; (a la fuerza) to give up; ~ **el poder** to hand over power; **me cedió el asiento** he let me have his seat; ▶ PASO 1B (b) ⟨balón/pelota⟩ to pass **2** (prestar) ⟨jugador⟩ to loan
■ ~ *vi* **1** (cejar) to give way; **no cedió ni un ápice** she didn't give *o* yield an inch; **cedió en su empeño** she gave up the undertaking; ~ **A** algo to give in *to* sth **2** «fiebre/lluvia/viento» to ease off; «dolor» to ease **3** «muro/puente/cuerda» to give way; «zapatos/muelle» to give

cedro *m* cedar

cédula *f* (Fin) bond, warrant; ~ **de identidad** identity card

cegador -dora *adj* blinding

cegar [A7] *vt* **1** (a) (deslumbrar) to blind (b) (ofuscar) to blind; **cegado por los celos** blinded by jealousy **2** ⟨conducto/cañería⟩ to block

ceguera *f* blindness

ceja *f* (a) (Anat) eyebrow; **arquear las ~s** to raise one's eyebrows (b) (Mús) capo

cejilla *f* capo

celador -dora *m,f* (a) (en museo, biblioteca) security guard (b) (AmL) (en la cárcel) prison guard (AmE), prison warder (BrE) (c) (en hospital) orderly, porter

celda *f* cell

celebración *f* celebration

celebrar [A1] *vt* **1** (a) ⟨éxito/cumpleaños/festividad⟩ to celebrate (b) (liter) ⟨belleza/valor/hazaña⟩ to celebrate (liter) (c) ⟨chiste/ocurrencia⟩ to laugh at **2** (frml) (alegrarse) to be delighted at,

be very pleased at; **celebro su éxito** I'm delighted to hear about your success **3** (a) (frml) ⟨reunión/elecciones/juicio⟩ to hold; ⟨partido⟩ to play (b) ⟨misa⟩ to say, celebrate; ⟨boda⟩ to perform
■ ~ *vi* «sacerdote» to say *o* celebrate mass

célebre *adj* (a) (famoso) famous, celebrated (b) (Col) ⟨mujer⟩ elegant

celebridad *f* (fama) fame; (persona) celebrity

celeste *adj* **1** (del cielo) heavenly, celestial **2** ⟨ojos⟩ blue; ⟨pintura/vestido⟩ (claro) light *o* pale blue; (intenso) sky-blue (before n)
■ *m* (claro) light *o* pale blue; (intenso) sky blue

celestial *adj* (a) (Relig) celestial (b) ⟨placer⟩ heavenly

célibe *adj/mf* celibate

celo *m* **1** (esmero, fervor) zeal **2** (Zool) (a) (de los machos) rut (b) (de las hembras) heat; **estar en ~** to be in season, to be in heat (AmE) *o* (BrE) on heat **3** **celos** *mpl* jealousy; **tener ~s DE algn** to be jealous of sb; **darle ~s a algn** to make sb jealous **4** (Esp) (cinta adhesiva) Scotch® tape (AmE), Sellotape® (BrE)

celofán *m* cellophane

celoso -sa *adj* (a) ⟨marido/novia⟩ jealous; **estar ~ DE algn** to be jealous of sb (b) (diligente, esmerado) conscientious, zealous

celta *adj* Celtic
■ *mf* (persona) Celt
■ *m* (Ling) Celtic

célula *f* cell

celular *adj* cellular
■ *m* (a) (AmL) (teléfono) mobile phone (b) (Esp) (furgoneta para presos) patrol wagon (AmE), police van (BrE)

celulitis *f* (gordura) cellulite; (inflamación) cellulitis

cementerio *m* cemetery; (junto a una iglesia) graveyard; ~ **de coches** salvage *o* wrecker's yard (AmE), scrapyard (BrE)

cemento *m* (a) (Const, Odont) cement; ~ **armado** reinforced concrete (b) (AmL) (pegamento) glue, adhesive

cena *f* dinner, supper; (en algunas regiones del Reino Unido) tea; (formal, fuera de casa) dinner; **¿qué hay de ~?** what's for dinner *o* supper?; ~ **de gala** banquet

cenagal *m* (barrizal) bog, mire

cenar [A1] *vi* to have dinner *o* supper; (en algunas regiones del Reino Unido) to have tea; **nos invitaron a ~** they invited us for *o* to dinner; **salimos a ~** we went out for dinner
■ ~ *vt* ⟨tortilla/pescado⟩ to have ... for dinner *o* supper

cencerro *m* cowbell

cenefa *f* (en ropa, sábanas) border; (en techos, muros) frieze

cenicero *m* ashtray

cenicienta *f* drudge; **la C~** Cinderella

cenit *m* zenith

ceniza *f* ash

censo *m* **1** (a) (de población) census (b) (Esp) *tb* ~ **electoral** electoral roll *o* register **2** (Der, Fin) charge; (sobre una finca) ground rent

censor -sora *m,f* (a) (Cin, Period) censor (b) (crítico) critic (c) (Der, Fin) *tb* ~ **de cuentas** auditor

censura f **(a)** (reprobación) censure (frml), condemnation **(b)** (de libros, películas) censorship

censurar [A1] vt **(a)** (reprobar) to censure (frml), to condemn **(b)** ⟨libro/película⟩ to censor, ⟨escena/párrafo⟩ to cut, censor

centavo m **(a)** (en AmL) hundredth part of many currencies; **estar sin un ~** to be penniless **(b)** (del dólar) cent

centella f (rayo) flash of lightning; (chispa) spark; **como una ~** like greased lightning

centelleante adj ⟨estrella⟩ twinkling; ⟨luz/joya⟩ sparkling; ⟨ojos⟩ blazing

centellear [A1] vi ⟨luz/joya⟩ to sparkle, ⟨estrella⟩ to twinkle

centena f: **una ~** a hundred; **unidades, decenas y ~s** units, tens and hundreds

centenar m: **un ~ de personas** a hundred or so people; **~es de cartas** hundreds of letters

centenario m centenary, centennial (AmE)

centeno m rye

centésima f hundredth; **en una ~ de segundo** in a fraction of a second

centésimo m (Fís, Mat) hundredth

centígrado -da adj centigrade, Celsius

centigramo m centigram

centímetro m centimeter*

céntimo m: hundredth part of the euro, the former Spanish peseta, the Venezuelan bolívar and the Paraguayan guaraní; **no tener un ~** to be penniless o (colloq) broke; **no vale ni un ~** it's totally worthless

centinela mf (Mil) guard, sentry; (no militar) lookout; **estar de ~** (Mil) to be on sentry duty

centolla f, **centollo** m spider crab

centrado -da adj (equilibrado) stable, well-balanced; (en un trabajo, lugar) settled

central adj central
■ f head office; **~ telefónica** telephone exchange; **~ hidroeléctrica/nuclear** hydroelectric/nuclear power station

centralista adj/mf centralist

centralita f switchboard

centralizar [A4] vt to centralize

centrar [A1] vt **(a)** ⟨imagen⟩ to center* **(b)** (Dep) to center* **(c)** ⟨atención/investigación/esfuerzos⟩ **~ algo EN algo** to focus sth ON sth
■ ~ vi (Dep) to center*, cross
■ **centrarse** v pron **~se EN algo** «investigación/atención/esfuerzos» to focus o center* ON sth

céntrico -ca adj ⟨área/calle⟩ central; **un bar ~** a downtown bar (AmE), a bar in the centre of town (BrE)

centrifugado m spin

centrifugar [A3] vt **(a)** ⟨ropa⟩ to spin **(b)** (Tec) to centrifuge

centrista adj/mf centrist

centro m **(a)** (en general) center*; **~ ciudad/urbano** downtown (AmE), city/town centre (BrE); **ser el ~ de atención** to be the center of attention; **se convirtió en el ~ de interés** it became the focus of attention; **~ turístico** tourist resort o center; **~ comercial** shopping mall (AmE), shopping centre (BrE); **~ de planificación familiar** family planning clinic **(b)** (en fútbol) cross, center*
■ mf (jugador) center*; **~ delantero** center* forward

Centroamérica f Central America

centroamericano -na adj/m,f Central American

centrocampista mf midfield player

ceñido -da adj tight; **me queda muy ~** it's very tight on me

ceñir [I15] vt: **esa falda te ciñe demasiado** that skirt is too tight for you; **el vestido le ceñía el talle** the dress clung to her waist
■ **ceñirse** v pron **~se A algo** ⟨a las reglas⟩ to adhere TO o (colloq) stick TO sth; **~se al tema** to keep to the subject

ceño m: **arrugó el ~** he frowned; **me miró con el ~ fruncido** she frowned at me

cepa f (Bot) stump; (Vin) stock (of a vine)

cepillar [A1] vt **(a)** ⟨ropa/dientes/pelo⟩ to brush **(b)** ⟨madera⟩ to plane
■ **cepillarse** v pron (refl) ⟨ropa⟩ to brush; ⟨dientes⟩ to brush, clean

cepillo m ⟨1⟩ (para ropa, zapatos, pelo) brush; (para suelo) scrubbing brush; **lleva el pelo cortado al ~** he has a crew cut; **~ de dientes/uñas** toothbrush/nailbrush ⟨2⟩ (de carpintería) plane ⟨3⟩ (en la iglesia) collection box (o plate etc)

cepo m (trampa) trap; (Auto) wheel clamp; (Hist) stocks (pl)

cera f (para velas) wax; (para pisos, muebles) wax polish; (de abejas) beeswax; (de los oídos) wax; **le di ~ al suelo** I polished the floor

cerámica f (arte) ceramics, pottery; (pieza) piece of pottery

cerca adv **(a)** (en el espacio) near, close; **~ DE algo/algn** near sth/sb; **¿hay algún banco ~?** is there a bank nearby o close by?; **está por aquí ~** it's near here (somewhere); **mirar algo/a algn de ~** to look at sth/sb close up o close to; **seguir algo de ~** to follow sth closely **(b)** (en el tiempo) close; **los exámenes estaban ~** the exams were close; **estás tan ~ de lograrlo** you're so close to achieving it; **serán ~ de las dos** it must be nearly 2 o'clock **(c)** (indicando aproximación): **~ de** almost, nearly
■ f (de alambre, madera) fence; (de piedra) wall

cercado m **(a)** (de alambre, madera) fence; (de piedra) wall **(b)** (terreno) enclosure **(c)** (Per) (distrito) district

cercanía f ⟨1⟩ (en el espacio) closeness, proximity; (en el tiempo) proximity, imminence ⟨2⟩ **cercanías** fpl: **Madrid y sus ~s** Madrid and its environs; **en las ~s del aeropuerto** in the vicinity of the airport

cercano -na adj ⟨1⟩ **(a)** (en el espacio) nearby, neighboring*; **~ A algo** near sth, close to sth; **el C~ Oriente** the Near East **(b)** (en el tiempo) close, near; **en fecha cercana** soon; **~ A algo** close TO sth ⟨2⟩ ⟨pariente/amigo⟩ close

cercar [A2] vt **(a)** ⟨campo/terreno⟩ to enclose, surround; (con valla) to fence in **(b)** ⟨persona⟩ to surround **(c)** (Mil) ⟨ciudad⟩ to besiege; ⟨enemigo⟩ to surround

cerciorarse v pron **~se DE algo** to make certain OF sth

cerco m **(a)** (asedio) siege **(b)** (de una mancha) ring **(c)** (AmL) (valla) fence; (seto) hedge

cerda f **(a)** (animal) sow **(b)** (fam) (mujer — sucia) slob (colloq); (— despreciable) bitch (sl) **(c)** (pelo) bristle

cerdo m (a) (animal) pig, hog (AmE) (b) (carne) pork (c) (fam) (hombre — sucio) slob (colloq); (— despreciable) bastard (sl), swine (colloq)

cereal m cereal

cereales mpl (Esp) (para desayunar) cereal

cerebral adj ‹actividad/tumor/derrame› brain (before n); ‹persona› cerebral

cerebro m (a) (Anat) brain; **lavarle el ~ a algn** to brainwash sb (b) (persona) brains; **el ~ de la operación** the brains behind the operation

ceremonia f ceremony; **no andemos con ~s** let's not stand on ceremony

cereza f (fruta) cherry

cerezo m cherry tree

cerilla f ① (esp Esp) (fósforo) match ② (de los oídos) wax

cerillo m (esp AmC, Méx) match

cernícalo m (Zool) kestrel

cero m (a) (Fís, Mat) zero; (en números de teléfono) zero (AmE), oh (n, BrE); (n, BrE); **~ coma cinco** zero point five; **empezar** or **partir de ~** to start from scratch; **ser un ~ a la izquierda** to be useless (b) (en fútbol, rugby) zero (AmE), nil (BrE); (en tenis) love; **ganan por tres a ~** they're winning three-zero (AmE) o (BrE) three-nil (c) (Educ) zero, nought (BrE)

cerquillo m (AmL) (flequillo) bangs (pl) (AmE), fringe (BrE)

cerrado -da adj ① (a) ‹puerta/ventana/ojos/ boca› closed, shut; ‹mejillones/almejas› closed; ‹sobre/carta› sealed; ‹puño› clenched; ‹cortinas› drawn, closed; **estaba ~ con llave** it was locked (b) ‹válvula› closed, shut off; ‹grifo/llave› turned off ② ‹tienda/restaurante/museo› closed, shut ③ ‹espacio/recinto› enclosed; ‹curva› sharp ④ ‹acento/dialecto› broad ⑤ ‹persona› (poco comunicativo) uncommunicative; **está ~ a todo cambio** his mind is closed to change; **~ a influencias externas** shut off from outside influence

cerradura f lock; ▶ OJO

cerrajería f locksmith's shop

cerrajero -ra m,f locksmith

cerrar [A5] vt ① (a) ‹puerta/ventana› to close, shut; ‹ojos/boca› to shut, close; **cierra la puerta con llave** lock the door (b) ‹botella› to put the top on/cork in; ‹frasco› to put the lid on; ‹sobre› to seal (c) ‹paraguas/abanico/mano› to close; ‹libro› to close, shut; ‹puño› to clench (d) ‹cortinas› to close, draw; ‹persianas› to lower, pull down; ‹abrigo› to fasten, button up; ‹cremallera› to do ... up (e) ‹grifo/agua/gas› to turn off; ‹válvula› to close, shut off ② (a) ‹fábrica/comercio/oficina› (en el quehacer diario) to close; (definitivamente) to close (down) (b) ‹aeropuerto/carretera/frontera› to close ③ (a) ‹cuenta bancaria› to close (b) ‹caso/juicio› to close (c) ‹acuerdo/negociación› to finalize (d) ‹acto/debate› to bring ... to an end

■ **~** vi ① (hablando de puerta, ventana): **cierra, que hace frío** close o shut the door (o window etc), it's cold; **¿cerraste con llave?** did you lock up?

② ‹puerta/ventana/cajón› to close, shut ③ ‹comercio/oficina› (en el quehacer diario) to close, shut; (definitivamente) to close (down)

■ **cerrarse** v pron ① (a) ‹puerta/ventana› to shut, close; **la puerta se cerró de golpe** the door slammed shut (b) ‹ojos› to close; **se le cerraban los ojos** his eyes were closing (c) ‹flor/almeja› to close up (d) ‹herida› to heal (up) ② (refl) ‹abrigo› to fasten, button up; ‹cremallera› to do ... up ③ ‹acto/debate/jornada› to end

cerrazón m (terquedad) stubbornness; (mentalidad poco flexible) blinkered attitude

cerro m (Geog) hill

cerrojo m bolt; **echar el ~** to bolt the door

certamen m competition, contest

certero -ra adj (a) ‹tiro› accurate; ‹golpe› well-aimed (b) ‹juicio› sound; ‹respuesta› good

certeza, certidumbre f certainty; **no lo sé con ~** I'm not sure, I don't know for sure

certificado¹ -da adj ‹paquete/carta› registered; **mandé la carta certificada** I sent the letter by registered mail

certificado² m certificate

certificar [A2] vt to certify

cervatillo m fawn

cerveza f beer; **~ tirada** o **de barril** draft beer (AmE), draught beer (BrE); **~ rubia** lager; **~ negra** dark beer

cesante adj [ESTAR] (Chi) (sin empleo) unemployed; **quedó ~** he lost his job

■ mf (Chi) (sin empleo) unemployed person

cesantía f (desempleo) (Chi) unemployment; (despido) (RPI frml) dismissal; (pago) (Col) severance pay

cesar [A1] vi ① (parar) to stop; **~ DE hacer algo** to stop doing sth; **sin ~** incessantly ② (frml o period) (dimitir): **cesó en su cargo** she left her post, she resigned

cesárea f cesarean* (section); **le tuvieron que hacer una ~** she had to have a cesarean

cese m (frml o period) (a) (interrupción) cessation (frml); **el ~ de hostilidades** the cessation of hostilities; **~ del fuego** (AmL) ceasefire (b) (renuncia) resignation

césped m (a) (planta) grass; (extensión) lawn, grass; ❾ **prohibido pisar el césped** keep off the grass (b) (Dep) field, pitch (BrE); (en tenis) (AmL) grass

cesta f (a) (recipiente) basket; **~ de Navidad** Christmas hamper; **~ punta** (deporte) pelota; (canasta) basket (for playing pelota) (b) (esp AmL) (en baloncesto) basket

cesto m (a) (esp Esp) (recipiente) basket; **el ~ de la ropa sucia** the laundry basket (b) (esp AmL) (en baloncesto) basket

cetro m scepter*

CFC m (= clorofluorocarbono) CFC

cg. (= centigramo) cg

AmC	América Central	Arg	Argentina	Cu	Cuba
AmL	América Latina	Bol	Bolivia	Ec	Ecuador
AmS	América del Sur	Chi	Chile	Esp	España
Andes	Región andina	CS	Cono Sur	Méx	México

Per	Perú
RPI	Río de la Plata
Ur	Uruguay
Ven	Venezuela

Ch, ch *f* ⟨*read as* /tʃe/ *or* /se 'atʃe/ *or* (Esp) /θe 'atʃe/⟩ *combination traditionally considered as a separate letter in the Spanish alphabet*

chabacano¹ -na *adj* ⟨ropa/decoración⟩ gaudy, tasteless; ⟨espectáculo/persona⟩ vulgar; ⟨chiste/cuento⟩ coarse, tasteless

chabacano² *m* (Méx) (árbol) apricot tree; (fruta) apricot

chabola *f* (Esp) **(a)** (en los suburbios) shack, shanty dwelling **(b) chabolas** *fpl* shantytown

chabolismo *m* (Esp): **para resolver la cuestión del ~** in order to find a solution to the shanty town problem

chacal *m* jackal

chacarero -ra *m,f* (CS, Per) farmer ⟨*who works a* CHACRA⟩

cháchara *f* **1** (fam) (conversación) chatter; **se pasa la mañana de ~** she spends the whole morning chattering **2** (Méx) (objeto de poca importancia) piece of junk; **un cajón lleno de ~s** a drawer's full of junk

chacharear [A1] *vi* (fam) to chatter

Chaco *m*: *tb* **el Gran ~** *region of scrub and swamp plains covering parts of Paraguay, Bolivia and Argentina*

chacra *f* (CS, Per) (granja) small farm; (casa) farmhouse

chafar [A1] *vt* (fam) **(a)** ⟨peinado⟩ to flatten; ⟨plátano/pulpa⟩ to mash; ⟨huevos⟩ to break; ⟨ajo⟩ to crush **(b)** ⟨vestido/falda⟩ to wrinkle (AmE), to crumple (BrE)
■ **chafarse** *v pron* to get squashed

chal *m* shawl, wrap

chala *f* **(a)** (RPl) (Bot) corn husk **(b)** (Chi) (Indum) sandal

chalado -da *adj* (fam) [ESTAR] crazy (colloq), nuts (colloq)
■ *m,f* nutter (colloq)

chale *interj* (Méx fam) you're kidding! (colloq)

chalé *m* ▶ CHALET

chaleca *f* (Chi) cardigan

chaleco *m* (de traje) vest (AmE), waistcoat (BrE); (jersey sin mangas) sleeveless sweater; (acolchado) body warmer; (chaqueta de punto) (CS) cardigan; **~ antibalas** bulletproof vest; **~ de fuerza** straitjacket; **~ salvavidas** lifejacket; **a ~** (Méx) no matter what

chalet /tʃa'le/ *m* (*pl* **-lets**) (en urbanización) house; (en el campo) cottage; (en la montaña) chalet; (en la playa) villa

chalote *m*, **chalota** *f* shallot, scallion (AmE)

chalupa *f* **1** (barca) skiff; (canoa) (AmL) small canoe **2** (Méx) (Coc) stuffed tortilla

chamaco -ca *m,f* (Méx fam) (muchacho) kid (colloq), youngster (colloq)

chamagoso -sa *adj* (Méx fam) dirty, filthy

chamarra *f* (chaqueta) jacket

chamba *f* **1** (Méx, Per, Ven fam) (trabajo) work; (empleo) job; (lugar) work **2** (Col) **(a)** (zanja) ditch **(b)** (herida) wound, gash

chambear [A1] *vi* (Méx, Per fam) to work

chambón -bona *adj* (AmL fam) clumsy, klutzy (AmE colloq)

chambonada *f* (AmL fam) botch (colloq)

chamizo *m* **1 (a)** (leña quemada) charred log **(b)** (Col) (ramas secas) *tb* **~s** brushwood **2** (choza) thatched hut

chamo -ma *m,f* (Ven fam) (niño, muchacho) kid (colloq)

champán *m*, **champaña** *m or f* champagne

champiñón *m* mushroom

champú *m* (*pl* **-pús** *or* **-púes**) shampoo

champurrear [A1] *vt* (CS) ▶ CHAPURREAR

chamuscar [A2] *vt* to scorch, singe; **madera chamuscada** charred wood
■ **chamuscarse** *v pron*: **~se el pelo** to singe one's hair

chamuyar [A1] *vi* (RPl fam) to chatter
■ *~ vt* (RPl fam) to mutter

chan *m* (AmC) mountain guide

chancaca *f* **(a)** (Andes) (melaza) brown sugarloaf **(b)** (Per) (dulce de maíz) maize cake

chancar [A2] *vt* **1** (Andes) (triturar) to crush, grind **2** (Per arg) (estudiar) to cram (colloq)

chance *f or m* (AmL) (oportunidad) chance; **dar ~ a algn** to give sb the chance; **tiene pocas ~s de ganar** he doesn't have *o* stand much chance of winning

chancear [A1] *vi* (Col fam) to joke, kid around (colloq)
■ **chancearse** *v pron* **~se DE algn** to make fun OF sb

chanchada *f* (AmL fam) **(a)** (porquería, suciedad) mess **(b)** (acción indigna) dirty trick (colloq); **hacerle una ~ a algn** to play a dirty trick on sb

chanchería *f* (AmL) pork butcher's shop

chanchito *m* (fam) **1** (Andes, CS) (Zool) woodlouse **2** (CS) (alcancía) piggy bank

chancho¹ -cha *adj* (AmL fam) (sucio) filthy, gross (colloq); (miserable, ruin) mean
■ *m,f* (AmL) **(a)** (Zool) pig **(b)** (fam) (persona sucia) dirty *o* filthy pig (colloq)

chancho² *m* (Chi, Per) (Coc) *tb* **carne de ~** pork

chanchullero -ra *adj* (fam) shady (colloq), crooked (colloq)
■ *m,f* (fam) racket (colloq)

chanchullo *m* (fam) racket (colloq), fiddle (BrE colloq)

chancla *f* (sandalia) thong (AmE), flip-flop (BrE); (pantufla) (Col) slipper

chancleta *f* (sandalia) thong (AmE), flip-flop (BrE)

chándal *m* (*pl* **-dals**) (Esp) tracksuit

changador *m* (RPl) porter

changarro *m* (Méx) small store

chango -ga *m,f* (Méx) monkey

changuito® *m* (Arg) (para las compras) shopping cart (AmE), shopping trolley (BrE); (para el bebé) stroller (AmE), pushchair (BrE)

chanquetes *mpl* whitebait (*pl*)

chanta *adj* (RPl arg) (informal) unreliable; (mentiroso) deceitful
■ *mf* (RPl arg) (informal) unreliable person; (mentiroso) liar

chantaje *m* blackmail; **le hacen ~** he is being blackmailed

chantajear [A1] *vt* to blackmail

chantajista *mf* blackmailer

chantillí, chantilly /ʃantiˈʝi, tʃantiˈʝi/ *m: tb*
crema ~ *f* whipped cream, chantilly

chao *interj* (fam) (colloq), bye-bye (colloq)

chapa *f* 1 (a) (plancha — de metal) sheet; (— de
madera) panel (b) (lámina de madera) veneer (c)
(carrocería) bodywork 2 (a) (distintivo) badge; (de
policía) shield (AmE), badge (BrE); (con el nombre)
nameplate; (de perro) identification disc *o* tag (b)
(RPl) (de matrícula) license plate (AmE),
numberplate (BrE) 3 (de botella) cap, top 4 (AmL)
(cerradura) lock 5 **chapas** *fpl* (AmL fam) (en las
mejillas): **le salieron** ~**s** (por vergüenza) her cheeks
flushed (red); (por el aire fresco) her cheeks were
red 6 (AmC fam) (joya) earring; (dentadura postiza)
false teeth (*pl*)

chapado -da *adj* ⟨metal⟩ plated; **un reloj** ~ **en
oro** a gold-plated watch

chaparrastroso -sa *adj* (Méx fam) scruffy

chaparro -rra *adj* (AmL fam) short, squat;
quedarse ~ to stop growing
■ *m,f* (AmL fam) shorty (colloq), titch (colloq)

chaparrón *m* (Meteo) downpour, cloudburst

chape *m* (Chi) (trenza) braid (AmE), plait (BrE);
(pelo atado) bunch

chapetes *mpl* (Méx) ▶ CHAPA 5

chapista *mf* panel beater

chapopote *m* (Méx) (alquitrán) tar; (asfalto)
asphalt

chapotear [A1] *vi* (en agua) splash (around);
(en barro) squelch (around)

chapucero -ra *adj* ⟨persona⟩ sloppy, slapdash;
⟨trabajo/reparación⟩ botched
■ *m,f*: **es un** ~ his work is very slapdash

chapulín *m* (AmC, Méx) (Zool) locust

chapurrear [A1] *vt* (fam): ~ **el inglés** to speak
broken *o* poor English

chapuza *f* (fam) (trabajo mal hecho) botched job
(colloq), botch (colloq)

chapuzón *m* dip; **darse un** ~ to have a dip

chaquet (*pl* -**quets**), **chaqué** *m* morning
coat

chaqueta *f* 1 (Indum) jacket; ~ **de punto**
cardigan 2 (Col) (Odont) crown

chaquetón *m* three-quarter length coat

charanga *f* brass band; (militar) military band

charango *m* small five-stringed guitar

charca *f* pond, pool

charco *m* (a) puddle, pool (b) **el** ~ (fam) (océano
Atlántico) the Atlantic, the Pond (colloq & hum)

charcutería *f* delicatessen, charcuterie (AmE)

charla *f* (a) (conversación) chat; **estábamos de** ~
we were having a chat (b) (conferencia) talk

charlar [A1] *vi* to chat, talk

charlatán -tana *adj* (fam) talkative
■ *m,f* (fam) (a) (parlanchín) chatterbox (colloq) (b)
(vendedor) dishonest hawker; (curandero) charlatan

charlestón *m* charleston

charme /ˈʃarm/ *m* charm

charol *m* 1 (barniz) lacquer; (cuero) patent
leather; **zapatos de** ~ patent leather shoes
2 (Col, Per) (bandeja) tray

charola *f* (Bol, Méx, Per) tray

charqui *m* (AmS) charqui, jerked beef

charrasquear [A1] *vt* 1 (AmL) ⟨guitarra⟩ to
strum 2 (Méx) ⟨persona⟩ to stab

charrería *f* (Méx) *the culture of horsemanship
and rodeo riding*

charretera *f* epaulette

charro -rra *adj* 1 (fam) (de mal gusto) gaudy,
garish 2 (en Méx) ⟨tradiciones/música⟩ of/
relating to the CHARRO
■ *m* (en Méx) (jinete) (*m*) horseman, cowboy; (*f*)
horsewoman, cowgirl

chárter *adj inv* charter (*before n*)
■ *m* charter (flight)

chasco *m* (decepción) disappointment, let-down
(colloq); **me llevé un** ~ I felt let down *o*
disappointed

chasis, chasís *m* (*pl* ~) (Auto) chassis; (Fot)
plateholder

chasquear [A1] *vt* (a) ⟨lengua⟩ to click;
⟨dedos⟩ to click, snap (b) ⟨látigo⟩ to crack

chasquido *m* (a) (de la lengua) click; (de los
dedos) click, snap (b) (de látigo) crack; (de rama
seca) crack, snap

chasquilla *f* (Chi) bangs (*pl*) (AmE), fringe
(BrE)

chatarra *adj inv* (Méx): **comida** ~ junk food;
productos ~ cheap goods
■ *f* (Metal) scrap (metal); **el coche es pura** ~ the
car is just a heap of scrap

chatarrero -ra *m,f* scrap merchant

chatel -tela *m,f* (AmC fam) (*m*) little boy; (*f*)
little girl

chato -ta *adj* (a) ⟨nariz⟩ snub (*before n*) (b)
(Per fam) (bajo) short (c) (AmS) ⟨nivel⟩ low; ⟨obra⟩
pedestrian

chaucha *f* (RPl) (Bot, Coc) French bean

chauvinismo /tʃoβiˈnismo/ *m* chauvinism

chauvinista /tʃoβiˈnista/ *adj* chauvinistic
■ *mf* chauvinist

chaval -vala *m,f* (esp Esp fam) (niño) kid (colloq),
youngster

chavalo -la *m,f* (AmC, Méx) ▶ CHAVAL

chavo -va *adj* (Méx fam) young
■ *m,f* (Méx) (a) (fam) (muchacho) guy (colloq);
(muchacha) girl (b) (como apelativo) kid (colloq)

chayote *m* (planta, fruto) chayote, mirliton

che *interj* (RPl fam): **no te hagas el bobo,** ~ come
on, don't act the innocent; ~, **Marta, ¿qué tal?**
hey Marta, how are you?; **¡pero** ~! **¡cómo le
dijiste eso!** for Heaven's sake! whatever made
you tell him that?

checar [A2] *vt* (Méx) (a) (revisar, mirar) to check;
me chequé la presión (Med) I had my blood
pressure checked; **¿por qué no vas a que te
chequen?** why don't you go for a checkup? (b)
(verificar) to check (c) (vigilar) to check up on

checo¹ -ca *adj/m,f* Czech

checo² *m* (idioma) Czech

checoslovaco -ca *adj/m,f* (Hist)
Czechoslovakian, Czechoslovak

Checoslovaquia *f* (Hist) Czechoslovakia

chef /ʃef, tʃef/ *m* chef

chele -la *adj* (AmC) (de piel) light-skinned; (de
pelo) blond-haired

chelín *m* shilling

chelista *mf* cellist

chelo *m* cello

cheque *m* check (AmE), cheque (BrE); **pagar con**

~ to pay by check; **un ~ a nombre de** ... a check made out to *o* made payable to ...; **~ bancario** *o* (AmL) **de gerencia** banker's draft; **~ cruzado/en blanco** crossed/blank check*; **~ de viaje** *or* **de viajero** traveler's check (AmE), traveller's cheque (BrE); **~ sin fondos** bad *o* (frml) dishonored* check*

chequear [A1] *vt* ⌐1⌐ (revisar, verificar) to check; **~ algo** CON **algo** to check sth AGAINST sth ⌐2⌐ (AmL) ⟨equipaje⟩ to check in
■ **chequearse** *v pron* **(a)** (Col, Ven) (Aviac) to check in **(b)** (Ven) (Med) to have a checkup

chequeo *m* **(a)** (Med) checkup; (*para entrar en el ejército, a trabajar*) medical; **someterse a un ~ médico** to have a medical/a checkup **(b)** (control, inspección) check; **mostradores de ~ de tiquetes** (Col) check-in desks

chequera *f* checkbook (AmE), chequebook (BrE)

chévere *adj* (AmL exc CS fam) great (colloq), fantastic (colloq); **¡qué ~!** that's great!

chic /ʃik, tʃik/ *adj inv* chic, fashionable
■ *m* chic; **tiene ~** she's very chic

chica *f* (fam) maid; *ver tb* CHICO

chicanero -ra *adj* (Andes, Méx) tricky, crafty

chicano -na *adj/m,f* Chicano

chicha *f* ⌐1⌐ **(a)** (bebida alcohólica) alcoholic drink made from fermented maize, also called CHICHA BRUJA; **~ andina** alcoholic drink made with corn flour and pineapple juice; **~ de manzana/uva** alcoholic drink made from apple/grape juice **(b)** (bebida sin alcohol) cold drink made with maize or fruit ⌐2⌐ (AmC vulg) (teta) tit (sl)

chícharo *m* (esp Méx) pea

chicharra *f* **(a)** (Zool) cicada **(b)** (timbre) buzzer

chicharrón *m* piece of crackling; **chicharrones** cracklings (*pl*) (AmE), pork scratchings (*pl*) (BrE)

chiche *adj* (AmC fam) dead easy (colloq)
■ *m* ⌐1⌐ (juguete) (CS fam) toy; (adorno) (Chi) trinket ⌐2⌐ (AmC fam) (pecho) tit (sl)

chichi *f* (Méx fam) (de mujer) tit (sl); (de animal) teat

chicho -cha *adj* (Méx fam) **(a)** (bonito) nice, neat (AmE colloq) **(b)** ⟨persona⟩: **es muy chicha para los deportes** she's brilliant at sport (colloq)

chichón *m* swelling *o* bump on the head

chicle, chiclé *m* chewing gum

chiclero -ra *m,f* ⌐1⌐ (Méx) (vendedor) street vendor (selling chewing gum, candy, etc) ⌐2⌐ (AmC) (Agr) rubber tapper

chico -ca *adj* (esp AmL) **(a)** (joven) young; **cuando éramos ~s** when we were little (colloq) **(b)** (bajo) small **(c)** (pequeño) small
■ *m,f* ⌐1⌐ **(a)** (niño) (*m*) boy; (*f*) girl **(b)** (hijo) (*m*) son, boy; (*f*) daughter, girl **(c)** (joven) (*m*) guy (colloq), boy (colloq), bloke (BrE colloq); (*f*) girl; **unos ~s** (varones) some boys; (varones y hembras) some boys and girls **(d)** (empleado joven) (*m*) boy; (*f*) girl **(e)** (como apelativo): **¡~! ¿tú por aquí?** well, well! what brings *you* here? ⌐2⌐ **chico** *m* (AmL) (en billar) frame; (en bolos) game

chicoria *f* chicory

chicotazo *m* (AmL) whipping

chicote *m* (fam) (AmL) (látigo) whip

chicotear [A1] *vt* (AmL) to whip

chifa *m* (Per fam) Chinese (restaurant)

chifla *f* whistling, catcalls (*pl*)

chiflado -da *adj* (fam) crazy (colloq), mad (BrE); **estar ~** POR **algo/algn** to be crazy *o* mad ABOUT sth/sb (colloq)
■ *m,f* (fam) nutter (colloq)

chiflar [A1] *vt* ⟨actor/cantante⟩ to whistle at (*as sign of disapproval*), ≈to boo
■ **~** *vi* ⌐1⌐ (silbar) to whistle ⌐2⌐ (fam) (gustar mucho): **le chiflan los coches** he's crazy about cars (colloq)
■ **chiflarse** *v pron* (fam) **~se** POR **algo/algn** to be crazy ABOUT sth/sb (colloq)

chihuahua *mf* chihuahua

chilaba *f* djellaba

chilango -ga *adj* (Méx) of/from Mexico City

chilaquiles *mpl* (Méx) corn tortilla in tomato and chili sauce

chile *m* ⌐1⌐ (AmC, Méx) (Bot, Coc) chili, hot pepper; **~ con carne** chili con carne ⌐2⌐ (AmC fam) (chiste) joke

Chile *m* Chile

chilear [A1] *vi* (AmC fam) to tell jokes

chileno -na *adj/m,f* Chilean

chilicote *m* (AmS) cricket

chillar [A1] *vi* **(a)** «pájaro» to screech; «cerdo» to squeal; «ratón» to squeak **(b)** «persona» to shout, yell (colloq); (de dolor, miedo) to scream; **~le** A **algn** to yell *o* shout AT sb **(c)** «bebé/niño» (llorar) to scream

chillido *m* **(a)** (de ave) screech; (de cerdo) squeal; (de ratón) squeak **(b)** (grito) shout, yell; (de dolor, miedo) scream, shriek; **dar ~s** *o* **un ~** (fam) to shout, to yell

chillón -llona *adj* (fam) ⟨voz⟩ shrill, piercing; ⟨color⟩ loud

chilote *m* (AmC) baby sweetcorn

chiltoma *f* (AmC) sweet pepper

chimbo -ba *adj* **(a)** (Col fam) (falsificado) ⟨perfume⟩ fake (before n); ⟨whisky/grabación⟩ bootleg (before n); **un cheque ~** a dud check (colloq) **(b)** (Ven arg) (malo) lousy (colloq)

chimbomba *f* (AmC) balloon

chimenea *f* ⌐1⌐ **(a)** (de casa) chimney; (de locomotora, fábrica) smokestack (AmE), chimney (BrE) **(b)** (de volcán) vent ⌐2⌐ (hogar) fireplace, hearth

chimpancé *mf* chimpanzee

chimpún *m* (Per) football boot

china *f* **(a)** (piedra) pebble, small stone **(b)** (Esp) (porcelana) porcelain

China *f*: *tb* **la ~** China

chinamo *m* (AmC fam) (en feria) stall; (bar) small bar

chinchar [A1] *vt* (fam) to pester (colloq)

chinche *adj* (fam) (pesado) irritating; (quisquilloso): **es muy ~** he's a real nit-picker
■ *f or m* ⌐1⌐ (insecto) bedbug ⌐2⌐ (RPl fam) (mal humor) bad mood
■ *mf* **(a)** (fam) (pesado) nuisance, pain in the neck (colloq) **(b)** (fam) (quisquilloso) nit-picker (colloq)
■ *f* (en algunas regiones m) (clavito) thumbtack (AmE), drawing pin (BrE)

chincheta *f* (Esp) thumbtack (AmE), drawing pin (BrE)

chinchilla *f* chinchilla

chin-chin *interj* (fam) cheers!

chinchorro *m* (Col, Ven) (hamaca) hammock

chinchulines *mpl* (Bol, RPI) chitterlings (*pl*)

chincol *m* (Chi) (pájaro) crown sparrow

chinela *f* (pantufla) slipper; (chancla) (AmC) thong (AmE), flip-flop (BrE)

chingada *f* (Méx vulg): **está pa' la** ∼ he's/she's had it (colloq); **¡vete a la** ∼**!** screw you! (vulg); **la casa estaba en la** ∼ the house was in the middle of nowhere (colloq); **¡hijo de la** ∼**!** you son-of-a-bitch! (sl)

chingadera *f* (Méx vulg) trash (colloq), crap (sl)

chingar [A3] *vi* **(a)** (esp Méx vulg) (copular) to screw (vulg), to fuck (vulg) **(b)** (Méx vulg) (molestar): **te lo dijo para** ∼ **nada más** he only said it to annoy you; **¡deja de** ∼**!** stop being such a pain in the ass! (vulg); **¡no chingues!** (no digas) you're kidding! (colloq)
■ ∼ *vt* **(a)** (AmL vulg) (en sentido sexual) to fuck (vulg), to screw (vulg) **(b)** (Méx vulg) (jorobar) to screw (vulg); ∼**la**: **¡no la chingues!** (Méx vulg) shit! (vulg)
■ **chingarse** *v pron* ⟨1⟩ **(a)** (*enf*) (AmL vulg) (en sentido sexual) to fuck (vulg), to screw (vulg) **(b)** (esp Méx vulg) (jorobarse): **creyó que ganaría pero se chingó** he thought he'd win but he got a shock; **se chingó el motor** the engine's had it (colloq); **estamos chingados** we're in deep shit (vulg) ⟨2⟩ (Méx vulg) **(a)** (aguantarse): **si no te gusta, te chingas** if you don't like it, tough (colloq) **(b)** (robar) to rip ... off (colloq)

chingaste *m* (AmC) coffee grounds (*pl*)

chingo¹ -ga *adj* (AmC fam) (desnudo) stark naked (colloq)
■ *m,f* (Ven fam) snub-nosed person

chingo² *m* (Méx fam o vulg): **un** ∼ **de** loads of (colloq); **me costó un** ∼ it cost me a bundle *o* (BrE) packet (colloq)

chingón -gona *adj* (Méx vulg) ⟨partido/película⟩ fantastic (colloq); ⟨persona⟩ cool (sl)

chingue *m* (Chi) **(a)** (Zool) skunk **(b)** (fam) (persona hedionda) smelly person

chinguear [A1] *vi/vt* (AmC) ▶ CHINGAR

chinita *f* (Chi) ladybug (AmE), ladybird (BrE)

chino¹ -na *adj* ⟨1⟩ (de la China) Chinese ⟨2⟩ (Méx) ⟨pelo⟩ curly
■ *m,f* ⟨1⟩ (de la China) (*m*) Chinese man; (*f*) Chinese woman; **los** ∼**s** the Chinese ⟨2⟩ **(a)** (Arg, Per) (mestizo) person of mixed Amerindian and European parentage **(b)** (Col fam) (joven) kid (colloq)

chino² *m* ⟨1⟩ (idioma) Chinese; **me suena a** ∼ it's all Greek to me ⟨2⟩ (Méx) (pelo rizado) curly hair; (para rizar el pelo) curler, roller ⟨3⟩ (Per fam) (tienda) convenience store, corner shop (BrE)

chip *m* (*pl* **chips**) **(a)** (Inf) chip **(b)** (papa frita) potato chip (AmE), crisp (BrE) **(c)** (Arg) (pancito) bridge roll

chipirón *m* small cuttlefish

chipote *m* (Méx fam) bump, lump

Chipre *f* Cyprus

chipriota *adj/mf* Cypriot

chiqueado *adj* (Méx fam) spoilt

chiquear [A1] *ut* (Méx fam) to spoil

chiquero *m* (AmL) (pocilga) pigpen (AmE), pigsty (BrE)

chiquilín -lina *adj* (AmL fam) (infantil) childish; **ser** ∼ to be childish, to act like a kid (colloq)
■ *m,f* (fam) (persona infantil) (AmL) big kid (colloq); (niño) (Ur) kid (colloq)

chiquillada *f*: **se pelearon por una** ∼ they fought over something really silly

chiquillo -lla *adj*: **no seas** ∼ don't be childish
■ *m,f* kid (colloq)

chiquito¹ -ta, chiquitito -ta *adj* (esp AmL fam) small

chiquito² -ta *m,f* (esp AmL fam) (niño) (*m*) little boy; (*f*) little girl

chiribita *f* **(a)** (chispa) spark **(b)** **chiribitas** *fpl* (en la vista) spots in front of the eyes; **los ojos le hacían** ∼**s** his eyes glowed

chirigota *f* (fam) (broma) joke; **estar de** ∼ to be kidding around (colloq)

chirimiri *m* fine drizzle

chirimoya *f* custard apple

chiripa *f* ⟨1⟩ (fam) (casualidad) fluke; **de** *or* **por** ∼ (fam) by sheer luck, by a fluke ⟨2⟩ (Ven) **(a)** (insecto) cockroach **(b)** (palmera) palm

chirla *f* (Coc, Zool) baby clam

chirona *f* (Esp fam) can (AmE sl), nick (BrE sl)

chiros *mpl* (Col) rags (*pl*)

chirriar [A17] *vi* «*puerta/gozne*» to squeak, creak; «*frenos/neumáticos*» to screech

chirrido *m* (de puerta) squeaking, creaking; (de frenos, neumáticos) screech, screeching

chis, chist *interj* shush!, ssh!

chisme *m* **(a)** (chismorreo) piece of gossip; ∼**s** gossip, tittle-tattle (colloq); **contar** ∼**s** to gossip **(b)** (Esp, Méx fam) (trasto, cacharro) thing, thingamajig (colloq); **un cuarto lleno de** ∼**s** a room full of junk *o* stuff (colloq)

chismear, chismorrear [A1] *vi* (fam) to gossip

chismorreo *m* (fam) gossip, tittle-tattle (colloq)

chismoso -sa *adj* gossipy (colloq)
■ *m,f* gossip, scandalmonger (colloq)

chispa *f* ⟨1⟩ **(a)** (del fuego) spark; **está/están que echa/echan** ∼ (fam) he's/they're hopping mad (colloq) **(b)** (Auto, Elec) spark ⟨2⟩ (fam) (pizca) little bit ⟨3⟩ (gracia, ingenio) wit; **tener** ∼ to be witty
■ *adj inv* (fam) (Esp fam) tipsy (colloq)

chisparse [A1] *v pron* (Méx) to come loose

chispazo *m* (Elec, Tec) spark

chispeante *adj* **(a)** ⟨leña/fuego⟩ crackling **(b)** ⟨lenguaje/personalidad⟩ witty; ⟨ingenio⟩ lively, sparkling **(c)** ⟨ojos⟩ (de alegría) sparkling; (de ira) flashing

chispear [A1] *vi* **(a)** «*leña*» to spark **(b)** (Elec) to spark, give off sparks
■ ∼ *v impers* (fam) (lloviznar) to spit, spot

chispero *m* (AmC) (encendedor) (fam) lighter; (Auto) spark plug

chisporrotear [A1] vi «leña/fuego» to spark, crackle; «aceite» to spit, splutter; «carne/pescado» to sizzle

chistar [A1] vi: ¡y sin ~! and not another word!; **no chistó** he didn't say a word

chiste m (a) (cuento gracioso) joke; **contar** or (Col) **echar un** ~ to tell a joke; ~ **picante** or **verde** or (Bol, Méx) **colorado** dirty joke (b) (Bol, CS, Méx) (broma) joke; **hacerle un** ~ **a algn** to play a joke o trick on sb; **me lo dijo en** ~ he was joking (c) (Col, Méx fam) (gracia): **el** ~ **está en hacerlo rápido** the idea o point is to do it quickly; **tener su** ~ (Méx) to be tricky (d) **chistes** mpl (RPl) (historietas) comic strips (pl), funnies (pl) (AmE colloq)

chistera f top hat

chistoso -sa adj funny, amusing
■ m,f comic, joker

chiva f ①(AmL) (barba) goatee ②(Col) (bus) rural o country bus ③(Col period) (primicia) scoop, exclusive ④(Chi fam) (mentira) cock-and-bull story (colloq); **ver tb** CHIVO ⑤ **chivas** fpl (Méx fam) (cachivaches) junk (colloq)

chivarse [A1] v pron (Esp fam) to tell; (a la policía) to squeal (sl)

chivatazo m (Esp fam) tip-off (colloq); **les dieron el** ~ they were tipped off

chivato¹ -ta m,f (Esp, Ven fam) (a) (informador) informer, stool pigeon (colloq) (b) (acusetas) tattletale (AmE colloq), telltale (BrE colloq)

chivato² m (Esp fam) (dispositivo sonoro) bleeper (colloq); (luz piloto) pilot light

chivearse [A1] v pron (Méx) (fam) (turbarse) to get embarrassed

chivo -va m,f ①(a) (cría de la cabra) kid (b) (Ven) (cabra) goat; **ver tb** CHIVA ②(a) **chivo** m (AmL) (macho cabrío) billy goat (b) ~ **expiatorio** scapegoat

chocado -da adj (AmL fam) smashed up (colloq); (superficialmente) dented

chocante adj (a) (que causa impresión): **su reacción me pareció** ~ I was shocked o taken aback by his reaction, his reaction shocked me (b) (en cuestiones morales) shocking (c) (Col, Méx, Ven) (desagradable) unpleasant

chocar [A2] vi ①(a) (colisionar) to crash; (entre sí) to collide; ~ **de frente** to collide o crash head-on; ~ **CON** or **CONTRA algo** «vehículo» to crash o run INTO sth; (con otro en marcha) to collide **WITH** sth; **el balón chocó contra el poste** the ball hit the goalpost; ~ **CON algn** «persona» to run INTO sb; (con otra en movimiento) to collide **WITH** sb (b) (entrar en conflicto) ~ **CON algn** to clash **WITH** sb (c) ~ **CON algo** «con problema/obstáculo» to come up AGAINST sth ②(a) (extrañar): **me chocó que no me lo dijera** I was surprised that he hadn't told me (b) (escandalizar) to shock; **me chocó su lenguaje** I was shocked by her language ③(Col, Méx, Ven fam) (irritar, molestar) to annoy, bug (colloq)
■ ~ vt (a) «copas» to clink; ¡**chócala!** (fam) put it there! (colloq), give me five! (colloq) (b) (AmL) «vehículo» (que se conduce) to crash; (de otra persona) to run into
■ **chocarse** v pron (Col) ①(en vehículo) to have a crash o an accident

②(fam) (molestarse) to get annoyed

chochada f (AmC fam) silly little thing (colloq)

chochear [A1] vi (fam) (a) «anciano» to be gaga (colloq) (b) (sentir adoración) ~ **POR algn** to dote ON sb

chocho -cha adj (fam) (a) «viejo» gaga (colloq) (b) (fam) (encantado): **está** ~ **con su hijita** he dotes on his daughter; **se quedó** ~ **con el regalo** he was delighted with his present

choclo m ①(CS, Per) (mazorca) corn cob; (granos) sweet corn; (cultivo) corn (AmE), maize (BrE) ②(Méx fam) (Indum) brogue

chocolate m ①(a) (para comer) chocolate; ~ **blanco/con leche** white/milk chocolate; ~ **negro** plain chocolate, dark chocolate; (b) (AmL) (chocolate): **sirvieron unos** ~**s con el café** they gave us chocolates with our coffee (c) (bebida) hot chocolate ②(Esp arg) (hachís) dope (sl), pot (colloq)

chocolatería f (cafetería) café serving hot chocolate as a speciality

chocolatina f, (RPl) **chocolatín** m chocolate bar

chocoyo m (AmC) parakeet

chofer, (Esp) **chófer** mf (a) (asalariado — de coche particular) chauffeur; (— de transporte colectivo) driver (b) (persona que maneja) driver

cholga f (Chi) mussel

chollo m (Esp fam) (trabajo fácil) cushy job o number (colloq); (ganga) steal (colloq), bargain

chomba f (sin botones) (Chi) sweater; (con botones) (Arg) polo shirt

chompa f (chaqueta) (Col, Ec) jacket; (suéter) (Bol, Per) sweater

chompipe m (AmC, Méx) turkey

choncho -cha adj (Méx fam) (a) «problema/situación» serious (b) «persona» hefty (colloq), big

chongo m (Méx) (moño) bun

chopo m (Bot) black poplar

choque m (a) (de vehículos) crash, collision; ~ **múltiple** pile-up; ~ **frontal** (Auto) head-on collision; (enfrentamiento) head-on confrontation (b) (conflicto) clash (c) (sorpresa, golpe) shock

chorear [A1] vt (fam) ①(CS, Per) (robar) to swipe (colloq) ②(Chi) (a) (aburrir): **esto me choreó** I'm fed up with this (colloq) (b) (molestar, enojar) to annoy
■ **chorearse** v pron (fam) ①(CS) (robarse) to swipe (colloq) ②(Chi) (a) (fam) (aburrirse) to get bored, get fed up (b) (molestarse, enojarse) to get annoyed

choreto -ta adj (Ven fam) crooked

chorito m (Chi) baby mussel

chorizar [A4] vt (Esp fam) to swipe

chorizo m (embutido curado) chorizo (highly-seasoned pork sausage); (salchicha) (RPl) sausage

chorlito m plover

choro m (Chi, Per) ①(Coc, Zool) mussel ②(fam) (delincuente) crook (colloq)

chorrada f (Esp fam) (a) (estupidez): **decir** ~**s** to talk drivel o twaddle (colloq) (b) (cosa insignificante) little thing

chorrear [A1] vi to drip; **estaba chorreando** (muy mojado) it was dripping wet; **chorreando de sudor** dripping with sweat; **la sangre le chorreaba de la nariz** blood was pouring from his nose ⋯⋮

■ ~ *vt* **1** (AmL fam) (manchar): **chorreado de café** covered in coffee stains **2** (Col, RPl arg) (robar) to swipe (colloq)

■ **chorrearse** *v pron* (refl) (CS, Per fam) (mancharse): **cuidado con** ~**te** mind you don't get it all over yourself

chorrillo *m* (Méx fam) diarrhea*, the runs (colloq)

chorro *m* **1** (de agua) stream, jet; (de vapor, gas) jet; **un chorrito de agua** a trickle of water; **a** ~ ‹motor/avión› jet (before n); **el agua salía a** ~**s** water gushed out **2** (AmC, Ven) (llave) faucet (AmE), tap (BrE) **3** (Méx fam) (cantidad): **¡qué** ~ **de gente!** what a lot of people!; ~**s de dinero** loads of money (colloq); **me gusta un** ~ **salir** I really love going out

chotis *m* schottische

chovinismo *m* chauvinism

chovinista *adj/mf* chauvinist

choza *f* hut, shack

christmas /'krismas/ *m* (pl ~) (Esp) Christmas card

chubasco *m* heavy shower

chubasquero *m* slicker (AmE), cagoule (BrE)

chuchería *f* **(a)** (alhaja) trinket; (adorno) knickknack **(b)** (dulce) tidbit (AmE), titbit (BrE)

chucho -cha *m,f* **1** (Esp fam) (perro) mongrel **2** **chucho** *m* (RPl fam) (escalofrío) shiver; **tengo** ~**s de frío** I have the shivers (colloq)

chueca *f* (Chi) (juego) *game similar to hockey, and the stick with which it's played*

chueco¹ -ca *adj* **1** (AmL) (torcido) crooked, askew **2** (Chi, Méx fam) (deshonesto) ‹persona› crooked (colloq); ‹documento› false; ‹elecciones› rigged

■ *m,f* (Chi, Méx fam) (deshonesto): **es un** ~ he's crooked (colloq)

chueco² *adv* (AmL fam) **(a)** (torcido): **camina/ escribe** ~ he can't walk/write straight **(b)** ‹jugar/pelear› dirty (colloq)

chufa *f* tiger nut, earth almond

chuico *m* (Chi) demijohn

chulear [A1] *vt* **1** (Arg fam) (provocar) to needle (colloq) **2** (Méx fam) (piropear) to compliment; ‹vestido/peinado› to make nice comments about **3** (Col) (con un signo) to check (AmE), to tick (BrE)

chuleta *f* **1** (Coc) chop; ~ **de cordero** lamb chop **2** (Esp arg) (para copiar) crib (colloq) **3** (Chi fam) (patilla) sideburn

chulla *mf* (Ec) (quiteño) *person from Quito*

chulo¹ -la *adj* **1** (fam) (bonito) **(a)** (Esp, Méx) ‹vestido/casa› neat (AmE colloq), lovely (BrE) **(b)** (Méx) ‹hombre› good-looking, cute (esp AmE); ‹mujer› pretty, cute (esp AmE) **2** (Esp fam) (bravucón) nervy (AmE colloq), cocky (BrE colloq) **3** (Chi fam) (de mal gusto) tacky (colloq)

■ *m,f* (Esp fam) (bravucón) flashy type

chulo² *m* (Esp fam) **1** (proxeneta) pimp **2** (Col) (Zool) black vulture **3** (Col) (signo) check mark (AmE), tick (BrE)

chumero -ra *m,f* (AmC) apprentice

chunche *m* (AmC) (fam) (cosa) thing, thingamajig (colloq)

chuño *m* (CS) (fécula de papa) potato flour

chupachups® *m* (pl ~) (Esp) lollipop

chupada *f* (fam) (de helado) lick; (de cigarrillo) puff; **le dio unas** ~**s a la pipa** he puffed on his pipe a few times

chupado -da *adj* **1** [ESTAR] (fam) (flaco) skinny **2** [ESTAR] (Esp fam) (fácil) dead easy (colloq) **3** [ESTAR] (AmL fam) (borracho) plastered (colloq) **4** **(a)** [ESTAR] (Chi, Per) (inhibido) withdrawn **(b)** [SER] (Chi, Per fam) (tímido) shy

chupalla *f* (Chi) straw hat

chupamedias *mf* (pl ~) (CS, Ven fam) bootlicker (colloq)

chupar [A1] *vt* **(a)** (extraer) ‹sangre/savia› to suck **(b)** ‹biberón/chupete› to suck (on); ‹naranja/caramelo› to suck; ‹pipa/cigarrillo› to puff on **(c)** (AmL fam) (beber) to drink

■ ~ *vi* **(a)** «bebé/cría» to suckle **(b)** (AmL fam) (beber) to booze (colloq)

■ **chuparse** *v pron* ‹dedo› to suck

chupeta *f* (Col) lollipop

chupete *m* **1** **(a)** (de bebé) pacifier (AmE), dummy (BrE) **(b)** (CS) (del biberón) nipple (AmE), teat (BrE) **2** (Chi, Per) (golosina) lollipop **3** (Chi) (Auto) choke

chupetín *m* (RPl) lollipop

chupón *m* **(a)** (AmL) ▶ CHUPETE 1A **(b)** (Méx) (del biberón) nipple (AmE), teat (BrE) **(c)** (Col) (chupada) lick

churrasquería *f* (AmS) steak house

churro *m* **1** (Coc) *strip of fried dough* **2** (Esp fam) (chapuza) botched job

churrusco *m* (Col) (Zool) caterpillar; (cepillo) bottle brush

chusco -ca *adj* **1** (gracioso) ‹persona/humor› earthy **2** (Chi, Per fam & pey) **(a)** (ordinario) ‹persona› common (pej); ‹perro› mongrel; ‹barrio/lugar› plebeian (pej) **(b)** ‹mujer› loose (colloq)

chusma *f* rabble (pl), plebs (pl) (colloq)

chuspa *f* (Col) (para lápices) pencil case; (para gafas) glasses case

chutar [A1] *vi* (Dep) to shoot

chute *m* (Dep) shot

chutear [A1] *vt/vi* (CS) to shoot

chuza *f* (Méx) (Dep) (jugada) strike; (marca) mark

chuzo *adj* (CS fam) ‹pelo› dead straight (colloq); ‹persona› hopeless (colloq)

■ *m*: **llover a** ~**s** (fam) to pour (down with rain)

Cía. *f* (= **Compañía**) Co

cianuro *m* cyanide

ciática *f* sciatica

cibercafé *m* cybercafe

ciberespacio *m* (Inf) cyberspace

cibernética *f* cybernetics

cicatero -ra *adj* (fam) tightfisted (colloq)

■ *m,f* skinflint (colloq)

cicatriz *f* scar; **la herida le dejó** ~ the wound left her with a scar

cicatrizar [A4] *vi*, **cicatrizarse** [A4] *v pron* to heal (up), cicatrize (tech)

cicerone *mf* (liter) guide, cicerone (liter)

ciclismo *m* cycling, biking (colloq)

ciclista *adj* cycle (before n)

■ *mf* cyclist

ciclo *m* **(a)** (de fenómenos, sucesos) cycle **(b)** (de películas) season; (de conferencias) series **(c)** (Educ): **el primer ∼** primary school

ciclocross *m* cyclo-cross; **bicicleta de ∼** mountain bike

ciclomotor *m* moped

ciclón *m* cyclone

ciclovía *f* (Col) cycle path

cicuta *f* hemlock

ciego -ga *adj* ⓵ **(a)** (invidente) blind; **es ∼ de nacimiento** he was born blind; **se quedó ∼** he went blind; **anduvimos a ciegas por el pasillo** we groped our way along the corridor **(b)** (ante una realidad) **estar ∼ A algo** to be blind TO sth **(c)** (ofuscado) blind; **∼ de ira** blind with fury ⓶ ⟨fe/obediencia⟩ blind ⓷ ⟨conducto/cañería⟩ blocked; ■ *m,f* (invidente) (*m*) blind man; (*f*) blind woman; **los ∼s** the blind

cielo *m* ⓵ (firmamento) sky; **∼ cubierto** overcast sky; **a ∼ abierto** (Min) opencast (*before n*); **este dinero me viene como caído del ∼** this money is a godsend ⓶ (Relig) heaven; **el ∼** (Paraíso) heaven; **ir al ∼** to go to heaven; **ganarse el ∼** to earn oneself a place in heaven **(b)** (*como interj*): **¡∼s!** (good) heavens! ⓷ (techo) ceiling **∼ raso** ceiling ⓸ **(a)** (aplicado a personas) angel **(b)** (como apelativo) sweetheart, darling; **¡mi ∼!** my darling

ciempiés *m* (*pl* **∼**) centipede

cien *adj inv/pron* a/one hundred; **∼ mil** a/one hundred thousand; **es ∼ por ∼ algodón** (esp Esp) it's a hundred percent cotton
■ *m*: **el ∼** (number) one hundred

ciénaga *f* swamp

ciencia *f* **(a)** (rama del saber) science; (saber, conocimiento) knowledge, learning; **∼ ficción** science fiction; **a ∼ cierta** for sure, for certain **(b)** **ciencias** *fpl* (Educ) science; **C∼s Empresariales/de la Información** Business/Media Studies; **C∼s Políticas/de la Educación** Politics/Education

cieno *m* silt, mud

científico -ca *adj* scientific
■ *m,f* scientist

ciento *adj/pron* (*delante de otro número*) a/one hundred; **∼ dos** a/one hundred and two; *para ejemplos ver* QUINIENTOS
■ *m* **(a)** (número): **∼s de libros** hundreds of books; **vinieron a ∼s** they came in the (AmE) *o* (BrE) in their hundreds **(b) por ciento** percent; **cien por ∼** a hundred percent

cierra, cierras, etc ▶ CERRAR

cierre *m* ⓵ (acción) **(a)** (de fábrica, empresa, hospital) closure **(b)** (de establecimiento) closing **(c)** (de frontera) closing **(d)** (de emisión) end, close **(e)** (Fin) close ⓶ **(a)** (de bolso, pulsera) clasp, fastener; (de puerta, ventana) lock **(b)** (cremallera) zipper (AmE), zip (BrE); **∼ metálico** (en tienda) metal shutter *o* grille; **∼ relámpago** (CS, Per) zipper (AmE), zip (BrE)

cierro ▶ CERRAR

cierto -ta *adj* ⓵ (verdadero) true; **no hay nada de ∼ en ello** there is no truth in it; **una cosa es cierta** one thing's certain; **¡ah!, es ∼** oh yes, of course; **parece más joven, ¿no es ∼?** he looks younger, doesn't he *o* don't you think?; **estabas en lo ∼** you were right; **lo ∼ es que ...** the fact is

that ...; **si bien es ∼ que ...** while *o* although it's true to say that ...; **por ∼** (a propósito) by the way, incidentally
⓶ (*delante del n*) (que no se especifica, define) certain; **cierta clase de gente** a certain kind of people; **de cierta edad** of a certain age; **en cierta ocasión** on one occasion; **en ∼ modo** in some ways; **hasta ∼ punto** up to a point; **durante un ∼ tiempo** for a while

ciervo -va *m,f* (especie) deer; (macho) stag; (hembra) hind

cifra *f* ⓵ **(a)** (dígito) figure; **un número de cinco ∼s** a five-figure number **(b)** (número, cantidad) number; **la ∼ de muertos** the number of dead, the death toll (period) **(c)** (de dinero) figure, sum ⓶ (clave) code, cipher; **en ∼** in code

cifrar [A1] *vt* ⓵ **(a)** ⟨mensaje/carta⟩ to write ... in code, encode **(b)** (Inf) to encrypt ⓶ ⟨esperanza⟩ to place, pin

cigala *f* crawfish, crayfish

cigarra *f* cicada

cigarrería *f* (Andes) tobacco shop (AmE), tobacconist's (BrE)

cigarrillo *m* cigarette; **∼ con filtro** filter tipped cigarette

cigarro *m* (puro) cigar; (cigarrillo) cigarette

cigüeña *f* stork

cigüeñal *m* crankshaft

cilantro *m* coriander

cilindrada *f*, **cilindraje** *m* cubic capacity

cilíndrico -ca *adj* cylindrical

cilindro *m* cylinder; **un motor de cuatro ∼s** a four-cylinder engine

cima *f* (de montaña) top, summit; (de árbol) top; (de profesión) top; (de carrera) peak, height; **está en la ∼ de su carrera** she is at the peak of her career

cimarra *f* (Chi): **hacer la ∼** to play hooky (esp AmE colloq); to skive off (school) (BrE colloq)

cimentar [A1] *or* [A5] *vt* **(a)** ⟨edificio⟩ to lay the foundations of **(b)** (consolidar) to consolidate, strengthen **(c)** (basar) **∼ algo EN algo** to base sth ON sth

cimientos *mpl* foundations (*pl*); **poner los ∼ de algo** to lay the foundations of sth

cinc *m* ▶ ZINC

cincel *m* (de escultor, albañil) chisel; (de orfebre) graver

cincelar [A1] *vt* ⟨piedra⟩ to chisel, carve; ⟨metal⟩ to engrave

cinco *adj inv/pron* five; [*nótese que algunas frases requieren el uso del número ordinal 'fifth' en inglés*] **noventa y ∼** ninety-five; **quinientos ∼** five hundred and five; **la fila ∼** row five, the fifth row; **vinimos los ∼** the five of us came; **somos ∼** there are five of us; **entraron de ∼ en ∼** they went in five at a time; **tiene ∼ años** she's five (years old); **son las ∼ de la mañana** it's five (o'clock) in the morning; **las ocho y ∼** five after (AmE) *o* (BrE) past eight; **∼ para las dos** (AmL exc RPl) five to two; *ver tb* MENOS *prep* 2 B; **hoy estamos a ∼** today is the fifth
■ *m* ⓵ (número) (number) five; **el ∼ de corazones** the five of hearts ⓶ (Per) (momento) moment

cincuenta *adj inv/m/pron* fifty; **los (años) ∼** *or* **la década de los ∼** the fifties; **tiene unos ∼** ···◈

años she's about 50 years old; **~ y tantos/pico** fifty-odd, fifty something; **la página ~** page fifty; **el ~ aniversario** the fiftieth anniversary

cincuentón -tona adj (fam): **es ~** he's in his fifties

■ m,f (fam): **una cincuentona** a woman in her fifties

cine m **(a)** (arte, actividad) cinema; **el ~ francés** French cinema; **actor de ~** movie o film actor; **hacer ~** to make movies o films **(b)** (local) movie house o theater (AmE), cinema (BrE); **¿vamos al ~?** shall we go to the movies (AmE) o (BrE) cinema?; **~ de barrio** local movie theater (AmE), local cinema (BrE); **~ de estreno** *movie theater where new releases are shown*

cineasta mf filmmaker, moviemaker (AmE)

cineclub, cine-club m film club

cinéfilo -la m,f movie buff, cinema buff (BrE)

cinematografía f cinematography

cinematográfico -ca adj movie (before n), film (BrE) (before n)

cínico -ca adj cynical

■ m,f cynic

cinismo m cynicism

cinta f **(a)** (para adornar, envolver) ribbon; **~ adhesiva** (en papelería) adhesive tape; (Med) sticking plaster; **~ durex®** (AmL excl CS) or (AmL) **scotch®** or (Col) **pegante** Scotch tape® (AmE), Sellotape® (BrE); **~ métrica** tape measure; **~ negra** (Méx) mf (Dep) black belt; **~ transportadora** conveyor belt **(b)** (en gimnasia rítmica) ribbon; (en carreras) tape **(c)** (Audio, Video) tape; **~ virgen** blank tape; **~ de video** or (Esp) **vídeo** videotape

cintura f (de persona, prenda) waist; **me tomó de la ~** he grabbed me round the waist; **me queda grande de ~** it's too big for me round the waist

cinturilla f waistband

cinturón m **(a)** (Indum) belt; **~ de castidad** chastity belt; **~ de seguridad** seat belt, safety belt; **~ negro/verde** (Dep) black/green belt **(b)** (de ciudad) belt; **el ~ industrial** the industrial belt

ciprés m cypress

circo m (Espec, Hist) circus

circuito m **(a)** (pista) track, circuit; (de circo, exposición) circuit **(b)** (Elec, Electrón) circuit

circulación f **(a)** (en general) circulation; **tener mala ~** to have poor circulation **(b)** (movimiento) movement; (Auto) traffic

circular¹ adj circular; **de forma ~** circular

■ f circular

circular² [A1] vi **(a)** «*sangre/savia*» circulate, flow; «*agua/corriente*» to flow **(b)** «*transeúnte/peatón*» to walk; (referido al tráfico): **circulan por la izquierda** they drive on the left **(c)** «*autobús/tren*» (estar de servicio) to run, operate **(d)** «*dinero/billete/sello*» to be in circulation **(e)** «*noticia/rumor/memo*» to circulate, go around

■ ~ vt to circulate

circulatorio -ria adj circulation (before n)

círculo m **(a)** (en general) circle; **coloca las mesas en ~** arrange the tables in a circle; **en**

(los) ~s teatrales in theatrical circles; **C~ Polar Antártico/Ártico** Antarctic/Arctic Circle; **~ vicioso** vicious circle **(b)** (asociación) society; **~ de Bellas Artes** Fine Arts Association o Society

circuncisión f circumcision

circundante adj surrounding (before n)

circunferencia f **(a)** (Mat) circle; **dibujar una ~** to draw a circle **(b)** (perímetro) circumference; **tiene 1 km de ~** it has a circumference of 1 km

circunscripción f (distrito) district

circunstancia f 1 (particularidad): **si por alguna ~ no puede ir** if for any reason you cannot go; **se da la ~ de que ...** as it happens ...; **bajo ninguna ~** under no circumstances 2 **circunstancias** fpl (situación) circumstances (pl); **dadas las ~s** given the circumstances; **debido a sus ~s familiares** due to her family situation

cirio m candle

cirrosis f cirrhosis

ciruela f (Bot, Coc) plum; **~ pasa** or (CS) **seca** prune

ciruelo m plum tree

cirugía f surgery; **hacerse la ~ estética/plástica** to have cosmetic/plastic surgery

cirujano -na m,f surgeon; **~ dentista** dental surgeon

Cisjordania f the West Bank

cisma m (Rel) schism; (en partido) split

cisne m (Zool) swan

cisterna f (depósito) tank; (subterránea) cistern; (del retrete) cistern

cistitis f cystitis

cita f 1 (con profesional) appointment; **pedir ~** to make an appointment; **concertar una ~** to arrange an appointment **(b)** (con novio, amigo): **tengo una ~ con mi novio/con un amigo** I have a date with my boyfriend/I'm going out with a friend; **faltó a la ~** he didn't show up (colloq); **~s por computadora** or (Esp) **ordenador** computer dating 2 (en texto, discurso) quote; **una ~ de Cervantes** a quotation o quote from Cervantes

citadino -na adj (AmL) urban, city (before n)

■ m,f **(a)** (AmL) (ciudadano) city dweller **(b)** (Méx) (defeño) inhabitant of México City

citar [A1] vt 1 **(a)** (dar una cita) «*doctor/jefe de personal*» to give ... an appointment; **estar citado con algn** to have an appointment with sb **(b)** (convocar): **nos citó a todos a una reunión** she called us all to a meeting **(c)** (Der) to summon; **~ a algn como testigo** to call sb as a witness 2 **(a)** (mencionar) to mention **(b)** «*escritor/pasaje*» to quote

■ **citarse** v pron **~se con algn** to arrange to meet sb; **se ~on en la plaza** (recípr) they arranged to meet in the square

citófono m (Andes) internal phone system

citología f (análisis) smear test

cítrico¹ -ca adj citrus (before n)

cítrico² m citrus

AmC	América Central	Arg	Argentina	Cu	Cuba	Per	Perú
AmL	América Latina	Bol	Bolivia	Ec	Ecuador	RPI	Río de la Plata
AmS	América del Sur	Chi	Chile	Esp	España	Ur	Uruguay
Andes	Región andina	CS	Cono Sur	Méx	México	Ven	Venezuela

ciudad *f* town; (de mayor tamaño) city; **❺ centro ciudad** town *o* city center; **~ balneario** (AmL) coastal resort; **C~ del Vaticano/de México** Vatican/Mexico City; **~ dormitorio** bedroom community (AmE), dormitory town (BrE); **~ perdida** (Méx) shantytown; **~ satélite** satellite town; **~ universitaria** university campus

ciudadanía *f* **(a)** (nacionalidad) citizenship **(b)** (conjunto de ciudadanos) citizenry (frml), citizens (*pl*)

ciudadano -na *adj* ⟨vida⟩ city (*before n*); **la inseguridad ciudadana** the lack of safety in towns *o* cities; **es un deber ~** it's the duty of every citizen
■ *m,f* (habitante) citizen

cívico -ca *adj* **(a)** ⟨deberes/derechos⟩ civic **(b)** ⟨acto⟩ public-spirited, civic-minded

civil *adj* **(a)** ⟨derechos/responsabilidades⟩ civil **(b)** (no religioso) civil; **casarse por lo ~** *or* (Per, RPl, Ven) **sólo por ~** *or* (Chi, Méx) **por el ~** to be married in a civil ceremony (AmE), to have a registry office wedding (BrE) **(c)** (no militar) civilian (*before n*); **iba (vestido) de ~** he was in civilian clothes
■ *mf* **(a)** (persona no militar) civilian **(b)** (Esp) (guardia civil) Civil Guard

civilización *f* civilization

civilizado -da *adj* civilized

civilizar [A4] *vt* ⟨país/pueblo⟩ to civilize; ⟨persona⟩ to teach ... to behave properly
■ **civilizarse** *v pron* ⟨pueblo⟩ to become civilized; ⟨persona⟩ to learn to behave properly

civismo *m* public-spiritedness

cizaña *f* darnel

clamar [A1] *vi* **~ CONTRA algo** to protest AGAINST sth; **~ POR algo** to clamor* FOR sth, cry out FOR sth
■ *vt:* **~ venganza** to cry out for vengeance

clamor *m* clamor*

clamoroso -sa *adj* ⟨acogida⟩ rousing (*before n*); ⟨ovación⟩ rapturous, thunderous; ⟨éxito⟩ resounding (*before n*)

clan *m* clan

clandestinidad *f* secrecy, secret nature; **trabajar en la ~** to work underground; **pasar a la ~** to go underground

clandestino -na *adj* ⟨reunión/relación⟩ clandestine, secret; ⟨periódico⟩ underground
■ *m,f* (fam) illegal immigrant

claqué *m* tap (dancing); **bailar ~** to tap dance

claqueta *f* clapperboard

clara *f* **(a)** *tb* **~ de huevo** (egg) white **(b)** (Esp) (bebida) shandy

claraboya *f* skylight

clarear [A1] *v impers* **(a)** (amanecer): **estaba clareando** it was getting light *o* day was breaking **(b)** (Meteo): **comenzó a ~** the sky/the clouds began to clear
■ *vi* ⟨pelo⟩ to go gray*/white

clarete *m* (rosado) rosé; (tinto) claret

claridad *f* **(a)** (luz) light **(b)** (luminosidad) brightness **(c)** (de explicación, imagen, sonido) clarity; **con ~** clearly

clarificar [A2] *vt* to clarify

clarín *m* bugle

clarinete *m* clarinet

clarinetista *mf* clarinetist

clarividente *adj* (que adivina el futuro) clairvoyant; (perspicaz) discerning, clear-sighted
■ *mf* clairvoyant

claro¹ -ra *adj* **(a)** (luminoso) ⟨cielo/habitación⟩ bright **(b)** (pálido) ⟨color/verde/azul⟩ light, pale; ⟨piel⟩ fair; **tiene los ojos ~s** she has blue/green/gray eyes **(c)** ⟨salsa/sopa⟩ thin **(d)** ⟨agua/sonido⟩ clear; ⟨ideas/explicación/instrucciones⟩ clear; ⟨situación/postura⟩ clear; **tener algo ~** to be clear about sth; **¿está ~?** is that clear?; **quiero dejar (en) ~ que ...** I want to make it clear that ...; **sacar algo en ~ de algo** to make sense of sth **(e)** (evidente) clear, obvious; **está ~ que ...** it is clear *o* obvious that ...; **a no ser, ~ está, que esté mintiendo** unless, of course, he's lying

claro² *adv* 1 ⟨ver⟩ clearly; **voy a hablarte ~** I'm not going to beat around *o* about the bush; **me lo dijo muy ~** he made it very quite clear (to me) 2 (indep) (en exclamaciones de asentimiento) of course
■ *m* **(a)** (en bosque) clearing; (en pelo, barba) bald patch **(b)** (Meteo) sunny spell *o* period

clase *f* 1 (tipo) kind, sort, type; **distintas ~s de arroz** different kinds of rice
2 (Transp, Sociol) class; **viajar en segunda ~** to travel (in) second class; **~ económica** *or* **turista** economy *o* tourist class; **~ ejecutiva** *or* **preferente** business class; **~ alta/baja/media** upper/lower/middle class; **~ dirigente** *or* **dominante** ruling class; **~ obrera** working class
3 **(a)** (distinción, elegancia) class; **tiene ~** she has class **(b)** (categoría): **productos de primera ~** top-quality products
4 (Educ) **(a)** (lección) class; **~s de conducir** *or* **manejar** driving lessons; **dictar ~s** (AmL frml) *or* **dar ~** *or* (Chi) **hacer ~s** (DE algo) ⟨profesor⟩ to teach (sth); **da ~s de piano** (Esp) she has piano lessons; **~ particular** private class *o* lesson **(b)** (grupo de alumnos) class **(c)** (aula — en escuela) classroom; (— en universidad) lecture hall *o* room

clásico¹ -ca *adj* **(a)** ⟨lengua/mundo⟩ classical; ⟨decoración/estilo/ropa⟩ classical **(b)** ⟨método⟩ standard, traditional; ⟨error/malentendido/caso⟩ classic

clásico² *m* **(a)** (obra) classic **(b)** (AmL) (Dep) traditional big game

clasificación *f* 1 (de documentos, animales, plantas) classification; (de cartas) sorting 2 (de película) certificate 3 **(a)** (Dep) (para una etapa posterior) qualification; **partido de ~** qualifying match **(b)** (tabla) placings (*pl*); (puesto) position, place; **quinto en la ~ final del rally** fifth in the final placings for the rally

clasificador *m* **(a)** (carpeta) ring binder **(b)** (de una máquina) sorter **(c)** (mueble) filing cabinet

clasificar [A2] *vt* **(a)** ⟨documentos/datos⟩ to sort, put in order; ⟨cartas⟩ to sort **(b)** ⟨planta/animal/elemento⟩ to classify **(c)** ⟨hotel⟩ to class, rank; ⟨fruta⟩ to class; ⟨persona⟩ to class, rank
■ **clasificarse** *v pron* (Dep) **(a)** (para etapa posterior) to qualify; **~ para la final** to qualify for the final **(b)** (en tabla, carrera): **se clasificó en sexto lugar** he finished in sixth place

clasista *adj* ⟨actitud/sociedad⟩ classist; ⟨persona⟩ class-conscious

claustro m (a) (Arquit, Relig) cloister (b) (Educ) (de universidad) senate; (de colegio) staff; (reunión) senate/staff meeting

claustrofobia f claustrophobia; **siento ~ allí dentro** I get claustrophobia in there

cláusula f clause

clausura f (a) (de congreso, festival) closing ceremony; **de ~** ⟨ceremonia/discurso⟩ closing (before n) (b) (de local) closure

clausurar [A1] vt (a) ⟨congreso/sesión⟩ «acto/discurso» to bring ... to a close; «persona» to close (b) ⟨local/estadio⟩ to close ... down

clavada f (Méx) (en natación) dive

clavadista mf (Méx) diver

clavado¹ -da adj ① (a) **~ en algo** ⟨puñal/tachuela/espina⟩ stuck IN sth; ⟨estaca⟩ driven INTO sth (b) (fijo): **con la vista clavada en un punto** staring at a point, with his gaze fixed on a point; **se quedó ~ en el lugar** he was rooted to the spot ② (fam) (a) (idéntico) **ser ~ A algn** «persona» to be the spitting image of sb (colloq); **ser ~ A algo** «objeto» to be identical TO sth (b) (en punto): **llegó a las cinco clavadas** he arrived on the dot of five (colloq)

clavado² m (AmL) dive

clavar [A1] vt ① (a) **~ algo EN algo** ⟨clavo⟩ to hammer sth INTO sth; ⟨puñal/cuchillo⟩ to stick sth IN sth; ⟨estaca⟩ to drive sth INTO sth; **me clavó los dientes/las uñas** he sank his teeth/dug his nails into me (b) ⟨cartel/estante⟩ to put up (with nails, etc) (c) ⟨ojos/vista⟩ to fix ... on ② (fam) (a) (cobrar caro) to rip ... off (colloq); **nos ~on $10,000** they stung us for $10,000 (b) (CS) (engañar) to cheat (c) (Méx) (robar) to swipe (colloq), to filch (colloq)

■ **clavarse** v pron ① (a) ⟨aguja⟩ to stick ... into one's finger (o thumb etc); **me clavé una espina en el dedo** I got a thorn in my finger (b) (refl) ⟨cuchillo/puñal⟩: **se clavó el puñal en el pecho** he plunged the dagger into his chest ② (CS fam) **~se CON algo** (por no poder venderlo) to get stuck WITH sth (colloq); (por ser mala compra): **se clavó con el auto que compró** the car turned out to be a bad buy ③ (Méx) (Dep) to dive

clave adj (pl **~ or -ves**) key (before n); **un factor ~** a key factor
■ f (a) (código) code; **en ~** in code; **~ de acceso** (Inf) password (b) (de problema, misterio) key (c) (Mús) clef; **~ de fa/sol** bass/treble clef
■ m harpsichord

clavel m carnation

clavicordio m clavichord

clavícula f collarbone, clavicle (tech)

clavija f (a) (Mec) pin (b) (Elec) (enchufe) plug; (de enchufe) pin (c) (de guitarra) tuning peg

clavo m (a) (Tec) nail; **dar en el ~** to hit the nail on the head (b) (Med) pin (c) (en montañismo) piton (d) (Bot, Coc) tb **~ de olor** clove

claxon /'klakson/ m (pl **-xons**) horn; **tocar el ~** to sound o blow one's horn, to honk

clemencia f mercy, clemency (frml)

clementina f clementine

cleptómano -na m,f kleptomaniac

clérigo -ga m,f ① (en el clero protestante) (m) clergyman, cleric; (f) clergywoman, cleric ② **clérigo** m (en el clero católico) clergyman, priest

clero m clergy

clic m (pl **clics**) click; (al romperse algo) snap; **hacer doble ~** (Inf) to double-click

cliché m (a) (expresión, idea) cliché (b) (de multicopista) stencil; (Impr) plate; (Fot) negative

cliente -ta m,f (de tienda, restaurante) customer; (de empresa, abogado) client; (de hotel) guest; (en taxi) fare, customer; **~ habitual** regular customer (o client etc)

clientela f (de tienda, restaurante) clientele, customers (pl); (de hotel) guests (pl); (de abogado) clients (pl)

clima m (a) (Meteo) climate (b) (ambiente) atmosphere; **un ~ festivo** a festive atmosphere; **el ~ económico** the economic climate

climatizado -da adj ⟨local/casa⟩ air-conditioned; ⟨piscina⟩ heated

clímax m (pl **~**) climax

clínica f private hospital o clinic; **~ dental** dental office (AmE), dental surgery (BrE); **~ de reposo** convalescent o rest home

clínico -ca adj ⟨ensayo⟩ clinical (before n); ▶ HOSPITAL
■ m,f (RPl) general practitioner

clip m (pl **clips**) ① (a) (sujetapapeles) paperclip (b) (para el pelo) bobby pin (AmE), hairgrip (BrE) (c) (cierre) clip; **aretes or pendientes de ~** clip-on earrings ② (Video) (pop) video

cloaca f ① (alcantarilla) sewer ② (de ave, reptil) cloaca

clon m clone

clonar [A1] vt to clone

cloro m (Quím) chlorine; (lejía) (AmC, Chi) bleach

clorofila f chlorophyll

clorofluorocarbono m chlorofluorocarbon, CFC

cloroformo m chloroform

clóset m (pl **-sets**) (AmL exc RPl) (en dormitorio) built-in closet (AmE), fitted o built-in wardrobe (BrE)

clotch /'klotʃ/ m ▶ CLUTCH

clown /'klaun/ m (pl **clowns**) clown

club m (pl **clubs or -es**) club; **~ juvenil** youth club; **~ nocturno** nightclub

clueca adj broody

clutch /'klotʃ/ m (AmC, Col, Méx, Ven) clutch

cm. (= **centímetro**) cm.

coacción f coercion; **bajo ~** under duress

coaccionar [A1] vt to coerce

coagular [A1] vt to clot, coagulate
■ **coagularse** v pron to clot, coagulate

coágulo m clot

coalición f coalition; **gobierno de ~** coalition government

coartada f alibi

coartar [A1] vt ⟨persona⟩ to inhibit; ⟨libertad/voluntad⟩ to restrict

coba f (Ven arg) (mentira, engaño) lie; **darle ~ a algn** (adular) (Esp, Méx, Ven fam) to suck up to sb (colloq)

cobarde adj cowardly
■ mf coward

cobardía *f* cowardice; **fue una** ~ it was an act of cowardice

cobaya *f*, **cobayo** *m* guinea pig

cobertizo *m* shed

cobertura *f* **(a)** (de seguro) cover **(b)** (Period, Rad, TV) coverage; ~ **informativa** news coverage

cobija *f* (AmL) **(a)** (manta) blanket **(b) cobijas** *fpl* (ropa de cama) bedclothes (*pl*)

cobijar [A1] *vt* ‹*persona*› (proteger) to shelter; (hospedar) to give ... shelter, take ... in
■ **cobijarse** *v pron* to shelter, take shelter

cobijo *m* shelter; **darle** ~ **a algn** to shelter sb

cobra *f* cobra

cobrador -dora *m,f* (a domicilio) collector; (de autobús) bus conductor

cobrar [A1] *vt* ① **(a)** ‹*precio/suma/intereses*› to charge; **nos cobran 30.000 pesos de alquiler** they charge us 30,000 pesos in rent; ~ **algo POR algo/hacer algo** to charge sb FOR sth/doing sth; **vino a** ~ **el alquiler** she came for the rent *o* to collect the rent; **¿me cobra estas cervezas?** can I pay for these beers, please?; **me cobró el vino dos veces** he charged me twice for the wine **(b)** ‹*sueldo*› to earn; ‹*pensión*› to draw; **cobra 2.000 euros al mes** he earns/draws 2,000 euros a month; **todavía no hemos cobrado junio** we still haven't been paid for June **(c)** ‹*deuda*› to recover; **nunca llegó a** ~ **esas facturas** he never received payment for those bills **(d)** ‹*cheque*› to cash
② **(a)** (Chi) (pedir): **le cobré los libros que le presté** I asked him to give back the books I'd lent him **(b)** (Chi) ‹*gol/falta*› to give
③ (adquirir) ‹*fuerzas*› to gather; ~ **fama/importancia** become famous/important
④ (period) ‹*vidas/víctimas*› to claim
■ ~ *vi* **(a)** ~ **POR algo/hacer algo** to charge FOR sth/doing sth; **¿me cobra, por favor?** can you take for this, please?, can I pay, please?; **llámame por** ~ (Chi, Méx) call collect (AmE), reverse the charges (BrE) **(b)** (recibir el sueldo) to be paid
■ **cobrarse** *v pron* **(a)** (recibir dinero): **tenga, cóbrese** here you are; **cóbrese las cervezas** can you take for the beers, please? **(b)** (period) ‹*vidas/víctimas*› to claim

cobre *m* (Metal, Quím) copper

cobrizo -za *adj* coppery, copper-colored*

cobro *m* **(a)** (de cheque) cashing; (de sueldo, pensión): **para el** ~ **de la pensión** in order to collect your pension **(b)** (Telec): **llamó a** ~ **revertido** she called collect (AmE), she reversed the charges (BrE)

coca *f* (Bot) coca; (cocaína) (arg) coke (sl)

cocaína *f* cocaine

cocainómano -na *m,f* cocaine addict

cocaví *m* (Chi) things to eat

cocer [E10] *vt* **(a)** (Coc) (cocinar) to cook; (hervir) to boil; ~ **algo a fuego lento** to simmer sth, cook sth over a low heat **(b)** ‹*ladrillos/cerámica*› to fire
■ **cocerse** *v pron* ① «*verduras/arroz*» (hacerse) to cook; (hervir) to boil; **tardan unos 15 minutos en** ~**se** they take about 15 minutes to cook ② (Chi) «*bebé*» to have a diaper (AmE) *o* (BrE) nappy rash

coche *m* **(a)** (Auto) car, auto (AmE), automobile (AmE); **nos llevó en** ~ **a la estación** he drove us to the station; ~ **bomba** car bomb; ~ **de bomberos** fire engine, fire truck (AmE); ~ **de carreras** racing car; ~ **de choque** bumper car; ~ **fúnebre** hearse **(b)** (Ferr) car (AmE), carriage (BrE); ~ **cama** *or* (CS) **dormitorio** sleeper, sleeping car **(c)** (de bebé) baby carriage (AmE), pram (BrE); (en forma de sillita) stroller (AmE), pushchair (BrE) **(d)** (carruaje) coach, carriage; ~ **de caballos** carriage

cochera *f* **(a)** (para autobuses) depot, garage; **las** ~**s** the depot **(b)** (garaje) (Esp, Méx) garage

cochinada *f* (fam) **(a)** (suciedad) filth **(b)** (palabra, acción): **¡no digas esas** ~**s!** don't use such filthy language!; **eso es una** ~ that's a disgusting thing to do **(c)** (mala pasada) dirty trick

cochino -na *adj* **(a)** (fam) (sucio) ‹*persona/manos*› filthy **(b)** (fam) (indecoroso) ‹*persona*› disgusting; ‹*revista/película*› dirty (colloq) **(c)** (Chi) (Dep, Jueg) (violento) dirty (colloq); (tramposo): **es muy** ~ he's a terrible cheat
■ *m,f* **(a)** (Zool) pig, hog (AmE) **(b)** (fam) (persona sucia) filthy pig (colloq), slob (colloq)

cocido¹ -da *adj* **(a)** (hervido) ‹*huevos/verduras*› boiled **(b)** (CS) (no crudo) cooked; **muy/poco** ~ well done/rare **(c)** ‹*arcilla*› fired

cocido² *m* **(a)** (Esp) stew (*made with meat and chickpeas*) **(b)** (Col, Ven) stew (*made with meat, plantains and cassava*)

cociente *m* quotient

cocina *f* **(a)** (habitación) kitchen **(b)** (aparato) stove, cooker (BrE); ~ **de** *or* **a gas** gas stove *o* (BrE) cooker; ~ **eléctrica** electric stove *o* (BrE) cooker **(c)** (arte) cookery; (gastronomía) cuisine; **libro de** ~ cookbook, cookery book (BrE); **la** ~ **casera** home cooking

cocinar [A1] *vt/vi* to cook; **¿quién cocina en tu casa?** who does the cooking in your house?

cocinero -ra *m,f* cook

cocineta *f* (Méx) (cocina) kitchenette

cocinilla *f* camp stove (AmE), camping stove (BrE)

cocktail /'koktel/ *m* (*pl* **-tails**) ▶ CÓCTEL

coco *m* **(a)** (Bot, Coc) coconut **(b)** (fam) (cabeza) head; **está mal del** ~ he's off his head (colloq) **(c)** (fam) (fantasma, espantajo) boogeyman (AmE), bogeyman (BrE)

cocoa *f* (AmL) cocoa

cocodrilo *m* crocodile

cocol *m* (Méx) (bizcocho) cookie (*covered in sesame seeds*)

cocotero *m* coconut palm

cóctel *m* (*pl* **-teles** *or* **-tels**) **(a)** (bebida) cocktail; ~ **de frutas** (AmC, Col) fruit salad, fruit cocktail; ~ **de gambas** (Esp) shrimp (AmE) *o* (BrE) prawn cocktail; ~ **Molotov** Molotov cocktail **(b)** (fiesta) cocktail party

cocuyo *m* **(a)** (AmL) (insecto) firefly **(b)** (Col, Ven) (Auto) parking light (AmE), sidelight (BrE)

codazo *m*: **darle un** ~ **a algn** (leve) to nudge sb; (fuerte) to elbow sb; **se abrió camino a** ~**s** he elbowed his way through

codearse [A1] *v pron* ~ **CON algn** to rub shoulders WITH sb

codera *f* (Indum) elbow patch

codicia *f* (avaricia) greed, avarice

codiciar [A1] *vt* to covet

codicioso -sa *adj* ‹*persona/mirada*› covetous, greedy
■ *m,f* covetous *o* greedy person

· · · **codificar ⋯⃗ cola**

codificar [A2] vt (a) ⟨leyes/normas⟩ to codify (b) (Inf) ⟨información⟩ to code (c) (Ling) ⟨mensaje⟩ to encode

código m (a) (de signos) code; ~ **barrado** or **de barras** bar code; ~ **postal** zipcode (AmE), postcode (BrE) (b) (de leyes, normas) code; ~ **de la circulación** Highway Code

codillo m (a) (Zool) elbow (b) (Coc) knuckle

codo¹ -da adj (Méx fam) tightfisted (colloq)

codo² m elbow; ~ **con** or **a** ~ side by side; **empinar el** ~ (fam) to prop up the bar; **hablar (hasta) por los** ~s (fam) to talk nineteen to the dozen (colloq)

codorniz f quail

coeficiente m (Mat) coefficient; ~ **intelectual** or **de inteligencia** IQ, intelligence quotient

coexistir [I1] vi to coexist

cofia f cap

cofradía f (Relig) brotherhood

cofre m (a) (joyero) jewel case, jewelry* box (b) (arcón) chest (c) (Méx) (capó) hood (AmE), bonnet (BrE)

coger [E6] vt **1** (esp Esp) (a) (tomar) to take; **lo cogió del brazo** she took him by the arm; **coge un folleto** pick up o take a leaflet (b) (quitar) to take; **siempre me está cogiendo los lápices** she's always taking my pencils (c) ⟨flores/fruta⟩ to pick (d) (levantar) to pick up; **coge esa revista del suelo** pick that magazine up off the floor; **no cogen el teléfono** (Esp) they're not answering the phone

2 (atrapar) (esp Esp) (a) ⟨ladrón/pelota⟩ to catch (b) ⟨pescado/liebre⟩ to catch (c) (descubrir) to catch; **lo cogieron robando** he was caught stealing (d) ⟨toro⟩ to gore

3 (a) ⟨tren/autobús/taxi⟩ to catch, take (b) ⟨calle/camino⟩ to take

4 (Esp fam) (a) (obtener) ⟨billete/entrada⟩ to get; ~ **hora para el médico** to make an appointment to see the doctor; ~ **sitio** to save a place (b) (aceptar) ⟨dinero/trabajo/casa⟩ to take (c) (admitir) ⟨alumnos/solicitudes⟩ to take

5 (esp Esp) (adquirir) (a) ⟨enfermedad⟩ to catch; ⟨insolación⟩ to get; **vas a** ~ **frío** you'll catch cold (b) ⟨acento⟩ to pick up; ⟨costumbre/vicio⟩ to pick up; **le cogí cariño** I got quite fond of him

6 (esp Esp) (captar) ⟨sentido/significado⟩ to get (b) ⟨emisora⟩ to pick up, get

7 (Méx, RPI, Ven vulg) to screw (vulg), to fuck (vulg)
■ ~ vi **1** (esp Esp) ⟨planta⟩ to take; ⟨tinte/permanente⟩ to take

2 (Méx, RPI, Ven vulg) to screw (vulg), to fuck (vulg)
■ **cogerse** v pron (esp Esp) (a) (agarrarse, sujetarse) to hold on; **cógete a la barandilla** hold on to the railing (b) (recípr): **se cogieron de la mano** they held hands

cogida f (Taur) goring; **sufrió una** ~ he was gored

cognac m brandy

cogollo m (de lechuga, col) heart; (de hinojo) bulb

cogote m (fam) (nuca) scruff of the neck; (cuello) (AmL) neck

cohabitar [A1] vi (frml) to cohabit (frml), to live together

coherencia f (a) (congruencia) coherence, logic; **con** ~ coherently o logically (b) (consecuencia) consistency; **actuar con** ~ to be consistent (c) (Fís) coherence

coherente adj (a) (congruente) ⟨discurso/razonamiento⟩ coherent, logical (b) (consecuente) ⟨actitud⟩ consistent; **una mujer** ~ a woman who acts according to her beliefs

cohesión f (a) (de ideas, pensamientos) coherence (b) (en grupo) cohesion, unity

cohete m **1** (Espac, Mil) rocket **2 cohetes** mpl fireworks (pl)

cohibido -da adj (tímido) shy; (inhibido) inhibited; (incómodo) awkward

cohibir [I22] vt (a) (inhibir) to inhibit; **su presencia me cohíbe** I feel inhibited in front of him (b) (hacer sentir incómodo): **hablar en público lo cohíbe** he feels awkward about speaking in public
■ **cohibirse** v pron (a) (inhibirse) to feel inhibited (b) (sentirse incómodo) to feel awkward

coincidencia f (a) (casualidad) coincidence; **se dio la** ~ **de que él también estaba allá** by coincidence o chance he was there too; **¡que** ~**!** what a coincidence! (b) (de opiniones) agreement

coincidir [I1] vi (a) ⟨fechas/sucesos/líneas⟩ to coincide; ⟨dibujos⟩ to match up; ⟨versiones/resultados⟩ to coincide, match up, tally; ~ **con algo** to coincide (o match up etc) with sth (b) (en opiniones, gustos): **coinciden en sus gustos** they share the same tastes; **todos coincidieron en que ...** everyone agreed that ...; ~ **con algn** to agree with sb (c) (en un lugar): **a veces coincidimos en el supermercado** we sometimes see each other in the supermarket

coito m intercourse, coitus (frml)

cojear [A1] vi (a) (por herida, dolor) to limp; (permanentemente) to be lame; **entró cojeando** he limped o hobbled in (b) ⟨silla/mesa⟩ to wobble (c) (fam) ⟨explicación/definición⟩ to fall short

cojera f limp

cojín m cushion

cojo -ja adj (a) ⟨persona/animal⟩ lame; **está** ~ **del pie derecho** he's lame in his right leg; **andar a la pata coja** or (Méx) **brincar de cojito** (fam) to hop (b) ⟨mesa/silla⟩ wobbly (c) (fam) ⟨razonamiento⟩ shaky, weak
■ m,f lame person

cojones mpl (vulg) (testículos) balls (pl) (sl o vulg); **estar hasta los** ~ (vulg) to be pissed off (sl); **tener** ~ (vulg) to have guts (colloq), to have balls (sl)

col f (Esp, Méx) cabbage; ~ **de Bruselas** Brussels sprout

cola f **1** (a) (Zool) tail; ~ **de caballo** (en el pelo) ponytail (b) (de vestido) train; (de frac) tails (pl) (c) (de avión, cometa) tail (d) (RPI fam) (nalgas) bottom (colloq)

2 (fila) line (AmE), queue (BrE); **hacer** ~ to line up (AmE), to queue (up) (BrE); **pónganse a la** ~

AmC Central America	Arg	Argentina	Cu	Cuba	Per	Peru
AmL Latin America	Bol	Bolivia	Ec	Ecuador	RPI	River Plate Area
AmS South America	Chi	Chile	Esp	Spain	Ur	Uruguay
Andes Andean Region	CS	Southern Cone	Méx	Mexico	Ven	Venezuela

por favor please join the (end of the) line *o* queue; **brincarse la ~** (Méx) to jump the line *o* queue; **a la ~ del pelotón** at the tail end of the group

⟨3⟩ **(a)** (pegamento) glue; **~ de contacto** superglue **(b)** (bebida) Coke®, cola

⟨4⟩ (Ven) (Auto): **pedir ~** to hitchhike; **darle la ~ a algn** to give sb a lift *o* a ride

colaboración *f* collaboration; **en ~ con algn/ algo** in collaboration with sb/sth

colaborador -dora *m,f* (en revista) contributor; (en tarea) collaborator

colaborar [A1] *vi* to collaborate; **~ CON algn** to collaborate WITH sb; **~ con dinero** to contribute some money; **~ EN algo** ⟨en proyecto/ tarea⟩ to collaborate ON sth; ⟨en revista⟩ to contribute TO sth

colada *f* (Esp) (lavado) laundry, washing

coladera *f* **(a)** (Méx) (sumidero) drain **(b)** (Col) ▶ COLADOR

colador *m* (para té) tea strainer; (para pastas, verduras) colander

colapso *m* **(a)** (Med) collapse; **sufrió un ~** he collapsed **(b)** (paralización) standstill

colar [A10] *vt* **(a)** ⟨verdura/pasta⟩ to strain, drain; ⟨caldo/té⟩ to strain **(b)** ⟨billete falso⟩ to pass

■ **~** *vi* (fam) «cuento/historia»: **no va a ~** it won't wash (colloq)

■ **colarse** *v pron* (fam) **(a)** (en cola) to jump the line (AmE) *o* (BrE) queue **(b)** (entrar a hurtadillas) to sneak in; (en cine, autobús) to sneak in without paying (colloq); (en fiesta) to gatecrash

colcha *f* bedspread

colchón *m* (de cama) mattress; **~ de muelles** sprung mattress

colchoneta *f* (de playa) air bed, Lilo® (BrE); (de gimnasia) mat; (de cama) (Méx) comforter (AmE), duvet (BrE)

colección *f* collection

coleccionar [A1] *vt* to collect

coleccionista *mf* collector

colecta *f* (de donativos) collection; **hacer una ~** (para comprar un regalo) to have a collection; (con fines caritativos) to collect

colectar [A1] *vt* to collect

colectivero -ra *m,f* (de autobús) (Arg) bus driver

colectividad *f* group, community; **en ~** collectively

colectivo¹ -va *adj* collective

colectivo² *m* **(a)** (period) (agrupación) group **(b)** (Andes) (taxi) collective taxi ⟨with a fixed route and fare⟩ **(c)** (Arg) (autobús) bus **(d)** (Per, Ur) (para regalo) collection

colega *mf* **(a)** (de profesión) colleague **(b)** (homólogo) counterpart **(c)** (fam) (amigo) buddy (AmE), mate (BrE colloq)

colegiado -da *m,f* (profesional) member (*of a professional association*)

colegial -giala *m,f* (de colegio) (*m*) schoolboy; (*f*) schoolgirl; **los ~es** (the) schoolchildren

colegiatura *f* (Méx) school fees (*pl*)

colegio *m* **(a)** (Educ) school; **los niños están en el ~** the children are at school; **un ~ de monjas** convent school; **un ~ de curas** a Catholic boys'

school; **~ privado** *or* **de pago** fee-paying *o* private school; **~ electoral** electoral college; **~ estatal** *or* **público** public school (AmE), state school (BrE) **(b)** (de profesionales): **C~ de Abogados** ≈ Bar Association; **C~ Oficial de Médicos** ≈ Medical Association

colegir [I8] *vt* to deduce

cólera *m* cholera

■ *f* rage, anger

colérico -ca *adj* **(a)** [ESTAR] (furioso) furious **(b)** [SER] (malhumorado) quick-tempered

colesterol *m* cholesterol

coleta *f* ponytail; (de torero) braid (AmE), ponytail (BrE)

coletazo *m* **(a)** (con la cola) thrash of the tail; **dar ~s** to thrash about **(b)** (Auto): **el coche dio un ~** the rear of the car skidded

coletilla *f* tag

colgado -da *adj*: **dejar a algn ~** (dejarlo en la estacada) to leave sb in the lurch; *ver tb* COLGAR

colgante *adj* hanging; ▶ PUENTE 1

■ *m* pendant

colgar [A8] *vt* **(a)** ⟨cuadro⟩ to hang, put up; ⟨lámpara⟩ to put up; ⟨ropa lavada⟩ to hang (out); **~ algo DE algo** to hang sth on sth; **el abrigo estaba colgado de un gancho** the coat was hanging on a hook **(b)** (ahorcar) to hang **(c)** ⟨teléfono/auricular⟩ to put down; **tienen el teléfono mal colgado** their phone is off the hook

■ *~ vi* **(a)** (pender) to hang; **colgaba del techo** it was hanging from the ceiling; **el vestido me cuelga de un lado** my dress is hanging down on one side **(b)** (Telec) to hang up; **no cuelgue, por favor** hold the line please, please hold; **me colgó** he hung up on me

■ **colgarse** *v pron* (*refl*) ⟨1⟩ **(a)** (ahorcarse) to hang oneself **(b)** (agarrarse, suspenderse): **no te cuelgues de ahí** don't hang off there; **no te cuelgues de mí** don't cling on to me; **se pasa colgada del teléfono** (fam) she spends her time on the phone

⟨2⟩ (Chi, Méx) (Elec): **~se del suministro eléctrico** to tap into the electricity supply

colibrí *m* hummingbird

cólico *m* colic

coliflor *f or* (RPI) *m* cauliflower

colilla *f* (de cigarrillo) cigarette end *o* butt

colina *f* hill

colirio *m* eye drops (*pl*)

colisión *f* **(a)** (de trenes, aviones) collision, crash; **~ en cadena** pileup **(b)** (conflicto) conflict, clash

colitis *f* colitis

collado *m* (colina) hill; (entre montañas) pass

collage /ko'laʒ/ *m* (*pl* **-llages**) collage

collar *m* **(a)** (alhaja) necklace; **~ de perlas** string of pearls **(b)** (para animales) collar **(c)** (plumaje) collar, ruff

colleras *fpl* (Chi) (gemelos) cuff links (*pl*)

colmado -da *adj* ⟨cucharada⟩ heaped; *ver tb* COLMAR

colmar [A1] *vt* **(a)** ⟨vaso/cesta⟩ to fill ... to the brim **(b)** ⟨deseos/aspiraciones⟩ to fulfill* **(c)** ⟨paciencia⟩ to stretch ... to the limit; **~ a algn DE algo** ⟨de atenciones⟩ to lavish sth on sb; ⟨de regalos⟩ to shower sb WITH sth

colmena *f* beehive

colmillo m (de persona) eyetooth, canine (tech); (de elefante, jabalí, morsa) tusk; (de perro, lobo) fang, canine

colmo m: el ∼ **de la vagancia** the height of laziness; **para ∼ de desgracias** to top o cap it all; **sería el ∼ que** ... it would be too much if ...; **¡esto es el ∼!** this is the limit o the last straw!

colocación f (a) (empleo) job; **buscar ∼** to look for a job (b) (acción) positioning, placing; (de losas, alfombra) laying

colocado -da adj [1] (en un trabajo): **está muy bien ∼** he has a very good job; **ya está ∼** he's found a job [2] (Esp) (a) (fam) (borracho) plastered (colloq) (b) (arg) (con drogas) stoned (colloq)

colocar [A2] vt [1] (a) (en lugar) to place, put; ⟨losas/alfombra⟩ to lay; ⟨cuadro⟩ to hang; ⟨bomba⟩ to plant (b) (Com, Fin) ⟨acciones⟩ to place; ⟨dinero⟩ to place, invest [2] ⟨persona⟩ (a) (en lugar) to put (b) (en trabajo) to get ... a job ■ **colocarse** v pron (a) (situarse, ponerse): **se colocó a mi lado** she stood/sat beside me (b) (en trabajo) to get a job

colocho -cha m,f (AmC) (a) (persona) curly-haired person (b) **colocho** m (rizo) curl

Colombia f Colombia

colombiano -na adj/m,f Colombian

colón m colon (*Costa Rican and Salvadoran unit of currency*)

Colón (Hist) Columbus; **Cristóbal ∼** Christopher Columbus

colonia f [1] (a) (Hist, Pol, Zool, Biol) colony (b) (de viviendas) residential development; **∼ militar** housing estate (*for service families*); **∼ penal** (Per) penal colony (c) (Méx) (barrio) quarter, district (d) (campamento) camp; **∼ de vacaciones** holiday camp [2] (perfume) (eau de) cologne

colonial adj colonial

colonialismo m colonialism

colonización f colonization

colonizador -dora m,f colonizer

colonizar [A4] vt to colonize

colono m (a) (inmigrante) colonist (b) (Agr) (en tierras baldías) settler; (en tierras arrendadas) tenant farmer

coloquial adj colloquial

coloquio m (a) (debate) discussion, talk; (simposio) (AmL) colloquium, symposium; **conferencia ∼** talk (*followed by discussion*) (b) (Lit) dialogue

color m (a) color*; **¿de qué ∼ es?** what color is it?; **cambiar de ∼** to change color; **un sombrero de un ∼ oscuro/claro** a dark/light hat; **las de ∼ amarillo** the yellow ones; **ilustraciones a todo ∼** full color illustrations; **cintas de ∼es** colored ribbons; **fotos en ∼es** or (Esp) **en ∼** color photos; **sin distinción de credo ni ∼** regardless of creed or color; **una chica de ∼** (euf) a colored girl (dated); **tomar ∼** ⟨pollo⟩ to brown; ⟨cebolla frita/pastel⟩ to turn golden-brown; ⟨fruta⟩ to ripen; ⟨piel⟩ to become tanned; **∼ de hormiga** (AmL) to start looking pretty grim; **subido de ∼** (chiste) risqué (b) **colores** mpl (lápices) colored* pencils (pl), crayons (pl)

colorado¹ -da adj (a) red; **ponerse ∼** to blush, turn red, go red (BrE) (b) (Méx fam) ⟨chiste⟩ risqué

colorado² m red

colorante m coloring*; **❺ no contiene colorantes** no artificial colors

colorear [A1] vt (Art) to color*; **∼ algo DE algo** to color* sth IN sth

colorete m blusher, rouge

colorido m colors* (pl); **un desfile de gran ∼** a very colorful parade

colosal adj ⟨estatua/obra/fortuna⟩ colossal; ⟨ambiente/idea⟩ (fam) great (colloq)

coloso m (estatua) colossus; (gigante) giant

columna f (a) (Arquit) column, pillar (b) (Anat) tb **∼ VERTEBRAL** spine, backbone (c) (Impr, Period, Mil) column

columnista mf columnist

columpiar [A1] vt to push (*on a swing*) ■ **columpiarse** v pron (refl) to swing

columpio m (a) (Jueg, Ocio) swing (b) (sofá de jardín) couch hammock

colza f rape, colza; **aceite de ∼** rapeseed oil

coma m (Med) coma; **entrar en (estado de) ∼** to go into a coma
■ f (Ling) comma; ▶ PUNTO 1B (c) (Mat) point

comadre f: godmother of one's child or mother of one's godchild

comadreja f (mustélido) weasel

comadrona f midwife

comal m (Méx) ceramic dish or metal hotplate for cooking TORTILLAS 2

comandante mf (a) (en el ejército) major; (en las fuerzas aéreas) major (AmE), squadron leader (BrE); **∼ en jefe** commander in chief (b) (oficial al mando) commanding officer (c) (Aviac) captain

comando m [1] (grupo de combate) commando group; **∼ terrorista** terrorist cell o squad (b) (AmL) (mando militar) command [2] (Inf) command

comarca f region

comarcal adj regional

comba f (a) (de viga, cable) sag; (de pared) bulge (b) (Esp) (Jueg) jump rope (AmE), skipping rope (BrE); **saltar la ∼** to jump rope (AmE), to skip (BrE)

combarse [A1] v pron «viga/cable» to sag; «pared» to bulge; «disco» to warp

combate m (a) (Mil) combat; **zona de ∼** combat zone; **avión de ∼** fighter plane (b) (en boxeo) fight

combatiente mf combatant (frml); **antiguo** or **ex ∼** veteran

combatir [I1] vi «soldado/ejército» to fight
■ **∼** vt ⟨enemigo/enfermedad/fuego⟩ to fight, to combat (frml); ⟨proyecto/propuesta⟩ to fight; ⟨frío⟩ to fight off

combativo -va adj (a) (luchador) spirited, combative; **espíritu ∼** fighting spirit (b) (agresivo) combative

combi® f (Méx, Per, RPl) VW® van, combi (van) (BrE)

combinación f (a) (de colores, sabores) combination (b) (de caja fuerte) combination (c) (Mat) permutation (d) (Indum) slip (e) (Transp) connection

combinado m (a) (bebida) cocktail (b) (Andes period) (Dep) team, line-up (journ)

combinar [A1] vt (a) (en general) to combine

(b) ⟨colores⟩ to put together; ⟨ropa⟩ to coordinate; ~ **el rojo con el violeta** to put red and purple together
■ ~ vi ⟨⟨colores/ropa⟩⟩ to go together; ~ **CON algo** to go **WITH** sth

combustible adj combustible
■ m (Fís, Quím) combustible; (Transp) (carburante) fuel

combustión f combustion

comedero m (Agr) (para el ganado) feeding trough

comedia f **(a)** (Teatr) ⟨obra⟩ play; ⟨cómica⟩ comedy; ~ **musical** musical **(b)** (serie cómica) comedy series **(c)** (AmL) (telenovela) soap (opera); (radionovela) radio serial

comediante -ta m,f **(a)** (Teatr) (m) actor; (f) actress **(b)** (farsante) fraud

comedido -da adj **(a)** (moderado) moderate, restrained **(b)** (AmL) (atento) obliging, well-meaning

comedor m **(a)** (sala — en casa, hotel) dining room; (— en colegio, universidad) dining hall, refectory; (— en fábrica, empresa) canteen, cafeteria **(b)** (muebles) dining-room furniture

comedura de coco f (Esp fam) **(a)** (lavado de cerebro): **la tele es una ~ de ~** TV just tries to brainwash you **(b)** (preocupación): **tener una ~ de ~** to worry nonstop

comentar [A1] vt **(a)** ⟨suceso/película⟩ to talk about, discuss; ⟨obra/poema⟩ to comment on **(b)** (mencionar) to mention; (hacer una observación) to remark on; **comentó que ...** he remarked that ... **(c)** (CS) (Rad, TV) ⟨partido⟩ to commentate on

comentario m ⒈ **(a)** (observación) comment; **hacer un ~** to make a comment; **fue un ~ de mal gusto** it was a tasteless remark; **sin ~(s)** no comment **(b)** (mención): **no hagas ningún ~ sobre esto** don't mention this **(c)** (análisis) commentary; **~ de texto** textual analysis ⒉ (Rad, TV) commentary

comentarista mf commentator

comenzar [A6] vt to begin, commence (frml)
■ ~ vi to begin; **al ~ el día** at the beginning of the day; **~ haciendo algo/POR hacer algo** to begin BY doing sth; **~ A hacer algo** to start doing o to do sth; **~on a disparar** they started firing o to fire; **~ POR algo** to begin WITH sth

comer [E1] vi **(a)** (en general) to eat; **no tengo ganas de ~** I'm not hungry; **este niño no me come nada** (fam) this child won't eat anything (colloq); **dar(le) de ~ a algn** (en la boca) to spoonfeed sb; **darle de ~ al gato/al niño** to feed the cat/the kid; **salir a ~ (fuera)** to go out for a meal, to eat out; **¿qué hay de ~?** (a mediodía) what's for lunch?; (por la noche) what's for dinner o supper? **(b)** (esp Esp, Méx) (almorzar) to have lunch; **nos invitaron a ~** they asked us to lunch **(c)** (esp AmL) (cenar) to have dinner
■ ~ vt **(a)** ⟨fruta/verdura/carne⟩ to eat; **¿puedo ~ otro?** can I have another one?; **no tienen qué ~** they don't have anything to eat **(b)** (fam) (hacer desaparecer) ▶ COMERSE 3 **(c)** (en ajedrez, damas) to take
■ **comerse** v pron ⒈ **(a)** (al escribir) ⟨acento/palabra⟩ to leave off; ⟨línea/párrafo⟩ to miss out **(b)** (al hablar) ⟨letra⟩ to leave off; ⟨palabra⟩ to swallow
⒉ (enf) ⟨comida⟩ to eat; **cómetelo todo** eat it all up; **~se las uñas** to bite one's nails

⒊ (fam) (hacer desaparecer) **(a)** ⟨⟨acido/óxido⟩⟩ to eat away (at); ⟨⟨polilla/ratón⟩⟩ to eat away (at) **(b)** ⟨⟨inflación/alquiler⟩⟩ ⟨sueldo/ahorros⟩ to eat away at

comercial adj **(a)** ⟨zona/operación/carta⟩ business (before n); **una firma ~** a company; **el déficit ~** the trade deficit; ▶ GALERÍA, CENTRO **(b)** ⟨película/arte⟩ commercial
■ m **(a)** (anuncio) commercial, advert (BrE) **(b)** (CS) (Educ) business school

comercializar [A4] vt ⟨producto⟩ to market; ⟨lugar/deporte⟩ to commercialize
■ **comercializarse** v pron to become commercialized

comerciante mf **(a)** (dueño de tienda) storekeeper (AmE), shopkeeper (BrE); (negociante) dealer, trader **(b)** (mercenario) money-grubber (colloq)

comerciar [A1] vi to trade, do business; ~ **EN algo** to trade o deal in sth

comercio m **(a)** (actividad) trade; **el ~ de armas** the arms trade; **el mundo del ~** the world of commerce **(b)** (tiendas): **hoy cierra el ~** the stores (AmE) o (BrE) shops are closed today **(c)** (tienda) store (AmE), shop (BrE)

comestible adj edible

comestibles mpl food; **tienda de ~** grocery store (AmE), grocer's (shop) (BrE)

cometa m comet
■ f kite; **hacer volar una ~** or (RPl) **remontar una ~** to fly a kite

cometer [E1] vt ⟨crimen/delito/pecado⟩ to commit; ⟨error/falta⟩ to make

cometido m **(a)** (tarea, deber) task, mission **(b)** (Chi) (actuación) performance

comezón f (Med) itching, itch; **tenía ~ en la espalda** his back was itching

comic /'komik/, **cómic** m (pl **-mics**) (esp Esp) (tira ilustrada) comic strip; (revista) comic

comicios mpl elections (pl)

cómico -ca adj ⟨actor/género/obra⟩ comedy (before n); ⟨situación/mueca⟩ comical, funny
■ m,f (actor) comedy actor, comic actor; (humorista) comedian, comic

comida f **(a)** (en general) food; **~ para perros** dog food; **~ basura/rápida** junk/fast food **(b)** (ocasión en que se come) meal; **la ~ fuerte del día** the main meal of the day; **¿quién hace la ~ en tu casa?** who does the cooking in your house?; **todavía no he hecho la ~** I still haven't cooked the meal **(c)** (esp Esp, Méx) (almuerzo) lunch **(d)** (esp AmL) (cena) dinner, supper; (en algunas regiones del Reino Unido) tea

comidilla f: **ser la ~ del pueblo** to be the talk of the town

comience, comienza, etc ▶ COMENZAR

comienzo m beginning; **al ~** at first, in the beginning; **dar ~** to begin; **dar ~ a algo** ⟨⟨persona⟩⟩ to begin sth; ⟨⟨ceremonia/acto⟩⟩ to mark the beginning of sth; **el proyecto está en sus ~s** the project is still in its early stages

comillas fpl quotation marks (pl), inverted commas (BrE) (pl); **poner algo entre ~** to put sth in quotation marks o in inverted commas

comilona f (fam) feast (colloq); **nos dimos una ~** we had a blowout

comino m (Bot, Coc) cumin

comisaría f (edificio) tb ~ **de policía** (police) station

comisario m (a) (de policía) captain (AmE), superintendent (BrE) (b) (delegado) commissioner

comisión f (a) (delegación, organismo) committee; **C~ Europea** European Commission (b) (Com) commission; **trabajar a ~** to work on a commission basis

comisionado -da m,f commissioner

comisionista mf commission agent

comiso m (Col) packed lunch

comisura f (de los labios) corner

comité m (junta) committee; ~ **de redacción** editorial board o committee

comitiva f (a) (séquito) procession; ~ **fúnebre** funeral procession, cortège (b) (grupo) delegation

como prep (a) (en calidad de) as; **quiero hablarte ~ amigo** I want to speak to you as a friend (b) (con el nombre de) as; **se la conoce ~ 'flor de luz'** it's known as 'flor de luz' (c) (en comparaciones, contrastes) like; **uno ~ el tuyo** one like yours; **¡no hay nada ~ un buen coñac!** there's nothing like a good brandy!; **es ~ para echarse a llorar** it's enough to make you want to cry (d) (en locs) **así como** (frml) as well as; **como mucho/poco** at (the) most/at least; **como ser** (CS) such as, for example; **como si** (+ subj) as if, as though
■ conj (a) (de la manera que) as; **tal ~ había prometido** just as he had promised; **~ era de esperar** as was to be expected; **no me gustó ~ lo dijo** I didn't like the way she said it; **(tal y) ~ están las cosas** as things stand; **hazlo ~ quieras/~ mejor puedas** do it any way you like/as best as you can; **no voy — ~ quieras** I'm not going — please yourself (b) (puesto que) as, since; **~ era temprano, fui a dar una vuelta** as it was early, I went for a walk (c) (si) (+ subj) if; **~ te pille ... si** I catch you ...
■ adv (expresando aproximación) about; **está ~ a cincuenta kilómetros** it's about fifty kilometers away; **un sabor ~ a almendras** a kind of almondy taste

cómo adv (a) (de qué manera) how; **¿~ estás?** how are you?; **¿~ es tu novia?** what's your girlfriend like?; **¿~ es de grande?** how big is it?; **¿~ te llamas?** what's your name? (b) (por qué) why, how come (colloq); **¿~ no me lo dijiste antes?** why didn't you tell me before? (c) (al solicitar que se repita algo) sorry?, pardon?; **¿~ dijo?** sorry, what did you say? (d) (en exclamaciones): **¡~ llueve!** it's really raining!; **¡~ comes!** the amount you eat!; **¡~! ¿no te lo han dicho?** what! haven't they told you? (e) (en locs) **¿a cómo ...?: ¿a ~ están los tomates?** (fam) how much are the tomatoes?; **¿a ~ estamos hoy?** (AmL) what's the date today?; **¡cómo no!** of course!; **¿cómo que ...?: ¿~ que no fuiste tú?** what do you mean it wasn't you?; **aquí no está — ¿~ que no?** it isn't here — what do you mean it isn't there?

cómoda f chest of drawers

comodidad f [1] (a) (confort) comfort; **la ~ del** hogar the comfort of home (b) (conveniencia) convenience; **por ~** for the sake of convenience (c) (holgazanería): **no lo hace por ~** he doesn't do it because he's lazy [2] **comodidades** fpl (aparatos, servicios) comforts (pl)

comodín m (a) (Jueg) (mono) joker; (otra carta) wild card (b) (Inf) wild card

cómodo -da adj (a) (confortable) comfortable, comfy (colloq); **ponte ~** make yourself comfortable (b) (conveniente, fácil) ⟨horario/sistema⟩ convenient; **esa es una actitud muy cómoda** that's a very easy attitude to take (c) (holgazán) lazy, idle

compact disc /kompak'ðis(k)/ m (pl **-discs**) (disco) compact disc, CD; (aparato) compact disc player, CD player

compacto -ta adj (a) ⟨tejido⟩ close; ⟨estructura/coche⟩ compact (b) ⟨muchedumbre⟩ dense

compadecer [E3] vt to feel sorry for
■ **compadecerse** v pron (apiadarse) **~se DE algn** to take pity ON sb; **~se de sí mismo** to feel sorry for oneself

compadre m (a) (padrino) godfather of one's child or father of one's godchild (b) (esp AmL fam) (amigo) buddy (AmE colloq), mate (BrE colloq)

compaginar [A1] vt ⟨actividades/soluciones⟩ to combine; **compagina el trabajo con los estudios** she combines work with studying
■ **~** vi (a) (combinar) to go together (b) (llevarse bien) to get on; **~ CON algn** to get on well WITH sb

compañerismo m comradeship

compañero -ra m,f (a) (en actividad): **un ~ de equipo** a fellow team member; **fuimos ~s de universidad** we were at college together; **~ de clase/de trabajo** classmate/workmate (b) (pareja sentimental, en juegos) partner; (de guante, calcetín) (fam) pair (c) (Pol) comrade

compañía f [1] (acompañamiento) company; **llegó en ~ de sus abogados** he arrived accompanied by his lawyers; **hacerle ~ a algn** to keep sb company; **andar en malas ~s** to keep bad company [2] (empresa) company, firm; **~ de seguros** insurance company; **~ de teatro** theater* company; **Ⓢ Muñoz y Compañía** Muñoz and Co. [3] (Mil) company

comparable adj comparable; **~ A** or **CON** comparable TO o WITH

comparación f comparison; **hacer una ~** to make a comparison; **en ~ a** or **con el año pasado** compared to o with last year; **no tienen ni punto de ~** you cannot even begin to compare them

comparar [A1] vt to compare; **~ algo/a algn A** or **CON algo/algn** to compare sth/sb TO o WITH sth/sb; **no puede ni ~se al otro** it doesn't even compare at all to o with the other one
■ **~** vi to make a comparison, to compare

comparecer [E3] vi to appear (in court)

compartimento, compartimiento m compartment

compartir [I1] vt to share; **~ algo CON algn** to share sth WITH sb

compás *m* ⓵ (Mús) **(a)** (ritmo) time, meter (esp AmE); **marcar/llevar el ~** to beat/keep time; **perder el ~** to get out of time; **se movía al ~ de la música** she moved in time to the music **(b)** (división) measure (AmE), bar (BrE); **~ de dos por cuatro** two-four time; **~ mayor/menor** four-four/ two-four time ⓶ (Mat, Náut) (instrumento) compass

compasión *f* pity, compassion; **lo hace por ~** he does it out of compassion

compasivo -va *adj* compassionate

compatible *adj* compatible

compatriota *m,f* *(m)* fellow countryman, compatriot; *(f)* fellow countrywoman, compatriot

compendio *m* (libro) textbook, coursebook; (resumen) summary, compendium (BrE)

compenetrarse [A1] *v pron* **~ con algo** ‹con ideas/objetivos› to identify with sth; **~ con algn** to have a good relationship with sb; (en trabajo) to work well with sb; **se han compenetrado a la perfección** they understand each other perfectly

compensación *f* (contapartida) compensation; **en ~** by way of compensation; **en ~ por algo** in compensation for sth

compensar [A1] *vi*: **no compensa hacer un viaje tan largo** it's not worth making such a long journey; **no me compensa** it's not worth my while
■ **~** *vt* ⓵ **(a)** (contrarrestar) ‹pérdida/deficiencia› to compensate for, make up for; ‹efecto› to offset; **su entusiasmo compensa su falta de experiencia** his enthusiasm makes up for his lack of experience **(b)** ‹persona› **~ a algn por algo** ‹por pérdidas/ retraso› to compensate sb for sth; **lo ~on con $2.000 por los daños** he was awarded $2,000 compensation in damages ⓶ ‹cheque› to clear
■ **compensarse** *v pron* «‹fuerzas›» (recípr) to compensate each other, cancel each other out

competencia *f* ⓵ **(a)** (pugna) competition, rivalry; **hacerse la ~** to be rivals *o* in competition; **hacerle la ~ a algn** to compete with sb **(b)** (persona, entidad) competition; **la ~ se nos adelantó** the competition got in first **(c)** (AmL) (certamen) competition ⓶ **(a)** (de juez, tribunal) competence; **este asunto no es de mi ~** I have no authority *o* say in this matter **(b)** (habilidad, aptitud) competence, ability; **falta de ~** incompetence

competente *adj* competent

competición *f* (Esp) **(a)** (rivalidad): **espíritu de ~** competitive spirit **(b)** (certamen) competition

competidor -dora *m,f* competitor, rival

competir [I14] *vi* **(a)** (pugnar, luchar) to compete; **~ con** *or* **contra algn** (**por algo**) to compete with *o* against sb (for sth) **(b)** (estar al mismo nivel): **los dos modelos compiten en calidad** the two models rival each other in quality

competitividad *f* competitiveness

competitivo -va *adj* competitive

compilar [A1] *vt* to compile

compinche *m,f* (compañero) (fam) buddy (AmE colloq), mate (BrE colloq); (cómplice en crimen) partner in crime

complacer [E3] *vt* to please
■ **complacerse** *v pron* **~se en algo** to take pleasure in sth

complaciente *adj* indulgent

complejidad *f* complexity

complejo¹ -ja *adj* complex

complejo² *m* **(a)** (de edificios) complex; **~ deportivo/industrial** sports/industrial complex **(b)** (Psic) complex; **tiene ~ porque es bajito** he's got a complex about being short; **~ de culpa** *or* **culpabilidad** guilt complex; **~ de inferioridad/ superioridad** inferiority/superiority complex

complementar [A1] *vt* to complement
■ **complementarse** *v pron* (recípr) to complement each other

complementario -ria *adj* **(a)** ‹personalidades/ángulos/colores› complementary **(b)** (adicional) additional

complemento *m* **(a)** (Ling, Mat) complement; **~ directo/indirecto** direct/indirect object **(b)** (acompañamiento) accompaniment **(c)** **complementos** *mpl* (Auto, Indum) accessories *(pl)*

completar [A1] *vt* **(a)** (terminar) to finish, complete **(b)** (AmL) ‹cuestionario/impreso› to complete, fill out *o* in

completo -ta *adj* ⓵ **(a)** (entero) complete; **las obras completas de Neruda** the complete works of Neruda **(b)** (total, absoluto) complete, total; **lo olvidé por ~** I completely forgot about it **(c)** (exhaustivo) ‹explicación› detailed; ‹obra/ diccionario› comprehensive; ‹tesis/ensayo› thorough **(d)** ‹deportista/actor› complete, very versatile ⓶ (lleno) ‹vagón/hotel› full; **❺ completo** (en hostal) no vacancies; (en taquilla) sold out

complexión *f* constitution

complicación *f* **(a)** (contratiempo, dificultad) complication **(b)** (cualidad) complexity **(c)** (esp AmL) (implicación) involvement

complicado -da *adj* **(a)** ‹problema/sistema/ situación› complicated, complex **(b)** ‹carácter› complex; ‹persona› complicated **(c)** ‹diseño/ adorno› elaborate

complicar [A2] *vt* ‹situación/problema/ asunto› to complicate, make ... complicated **(b)** (implicar) ‹persona› to involve, get ... involved
■ **complicarse** *v pron* **(a)** «‹situación/problema/ asunto›» to get complicated; «‹enfermedad›»: **se le complicó con un problema respiratorio** he developed respiratory complications; ▶ VIDA 2 **(b)** (implicarse) **~se en algo** to get involved in sth

cómplice *m,f* accomplice; **~ en algo** accomplice to sth

complicidad *f* complicity

compló, complot *m* (*pl* **-plots**) plot, conspiracy

compondré, compondría, etc ▶ COMPONER

componente *m* **(a)** (de sustancia) constituent (part), component (part); (de equipo, comisión) member **(b)** (Tec) component

componer [E22] *vt* **(a)** (constituir) ‹jurado/ equipo/plantilla› to make up; **el tren estaba compuesto por ocho vagones** the train was made up of eight cars **(b)** ‹sinfonía/canción/verso› to compose **(c)** (esp AmL) (arreglar) ‹reloj/radio/ zapatos› to repair **(d)** (AmL) ‹hueso› to set
■ **~** *vi* to compose
■ **componerse** *v pron* ⓵ (estar formado) **~se de algo** to be made up of sth, to consist of sth; **un** ···✥

conjunto compuesto de falda y chaqueta an outfit consisting of a skirt and a jacket **2** (esp AmL fam) «*persona*» to get better

comportamiento *m* (a) (conducta) behavior*; **mal ~** bad behavior (b) (Mec) performance

comportarse [A1] *v pron* to behave; **~ mal** to behave badly, misbehave

composición *f* composition

compositor -tora *m,f* composer

compostura *f* (a) (circunspección) composure; **guardar la ~** to maintain *o* keep one's composure (b) (CS) (arreglo) repair

compota *f* compote

compra *f* (a) (acción): **ir de ~s** to go shopping; **hacer las ~s** *or* (Esp) **la ~** to do the shopping; **~ por teléfono** teleshopping (b) (cosa comprada) buy, purchase (frml); **fue una buena ~** it was a good buy

comprador -dora *m,f* buyer, purchaser (frml)

comprar [A1] *vt* ‹*casa/regalo/comida*› to buy, purchase (frml); **~le algo ʌ algn** (a quien lo vende) to buy sth FROM sb; (a quien lo recibe) to buy sth FOR sb (b) (fam) (sobornar) to buy (colloq)

comprender [E1] *vt* **1** (a) (entender) to understand, comprehend (frml); **nadie me comprende** nobody understands me (b) (darse cuenta) to realize, understand; **comprendió que lo habían engañado** he realized that he had been tricked **2** (abarcar, contener) «*libro*» to cover; «*factura/precio*» to include

■ **~** *vi* (entender) to understand; **hacerse ~** to make oneself understood

comprensible *adj* understandable

comprensión *f* understanding; **capacidad de ~** comprehension; **~ auditiva** listening comprehension

comprensivo -va *adj* understanding

compresa *f* (a) (Med) compress (b) (Esp) *tb* **~ higiénica** sanitary napkin (AmE) *o* (BrE) towel

comprimido *m* (Farm) pill, tablet

comprimir [I1] *vt* to compress

comprobación *f* (a) (acción) verification, checking (b) (Col) (examen) test

comprobante *m* proof; **~ de pago** proof of payment

comprobar [A10] *vt* (a) (verificar) ‹*operación/resultado/funcionamiento*› to check (b) (demostrar) to prove (c) (darse cuenta) to realize (d) «*hecho*» (confirmar) to confirm

comprometedor -dora *adj* compromising

comprometer [E1] *vt* (a) (poner en un apuro) to compromise (b) ‹*vida/libertad*› to jeopardize, threaten (c) (obligar): **~ a algn ʌ algo** to commit sb TO sth; **esto no me compromete a nada** this does not commit me to anything

■ **comprometerse** *v pron* (a) (dar su palabra): **~se ʌ hacer algo** to promise to do sth; **me he comprometido para salir esta noche** I've arranged to go out tonight (b) «*autor/artista*» to commit oneself politically (c) «*novios*» to get engaged; **~se CON algn** to get engaged TO sb

comprometido -da *adj* (a) [SER] ‹*asunto/situación*› awkward, delicate (b) [SER] ‹*cine/escritor*› politically committed (c) [ESTAR] (para casarse) engaged; **~ CON algn** engaged TO sb

compromiso *m* (a) (moral, financiero) commitment; **adquirir un ~ con algn** to make a commitment to sb; **sin ~ alguno** without obligation; **los invitó por ~** she felt obliged to invite them; **yo con ellos no tengo ningún ~** I'm under no obligation to them (b) (cita) engagement; **~s sociales** social engagements *o* commitments (c) (de matrimonio) engagement (d) (acuerdo) agreement; (con concesiones recíprocas) compromise; **llegaron a un ~** they came to *o* reached an agreement/a compromise (e) (apuro) awkward situation; **me puso en un ~** he put me in an awkward situation

compuesto -ta *adj* ‹*oración/número/flor*› compound (*before n*); *ver tb* COMPONER

compungido -da *adj* (arrepentido) remorseful, contrite; (triste) sad

compuse, compuso, etc ▶ COMPONER

computadora *f*, **computador** *m* (esp AmL) computer; **~ personal/de escritorio** *or* **mesa** personal/desktop computer

computerizar [A4] *vt* to computerize

comulgar [A3] *vi* (Relig) to receive *o* take communion

común *adj* (a) ‹*intereses/características*› common (*before n*); ‹*amigo*› mutual (b) (en locs) **de común acuerdo** by common consent; **de ~ acuerdo con algn** in agreement with sb; **en común** ‹*esfuerzo/regalo*› joint (*before n*); **no tenemos nada en ~** we have nothing in common (c) (corriente, frecuente) common; **es un nombre muy ~** it's a very common name; **un modelo fuera de lo ~** a very unusual model; **~ y corriente** (normal, nada especial) ordinary

comuna *f* (a) (de convivencia) commune (b) (CS, Per) (municipio) town, municipality (frml)

comunal *adj* (a) (de todos) communal (b) (CS, Per) (del municipio) town (*before n*), municipal

comunicación *f* (a) (enlace) link; **~ vía satélite** satellite link (b) (contacto) contact; **ponerse en ~ con algn** to get in contact *o* in touch with sb (c) (por teléfono): **se ha cortado la ~** I've/we've been cut off (d) (entendimiento, relación) communication (e) **comunicaciones** *fpl* (por carretera, teléfono, etc) communications (*pl*)

comunicado *m* communiqué; **~ de prensa** press release

comunicar [A2] *vt* **1** (frml) (a) (informar) to inform; **~le algo ʌ algn** to inform sb of sth (b) (AmL) (por teléfono) ‹*persona*› to put ... through **2** (transmitir) (a) ‹*entusiasmo/miedo*› to convey, communicate (b) ‹*conocimientos*› to impart, pass on; ‹*información*› to convey, communicate; ‹*idea*› to put across (c) ‹*fuerza/calor*› to transmit **3** ‹*habitaciones/ciudades*› to connect, link; **un barrio bien comunicado** an area easily accessible by road/well served by public transport; **~ algo CON algo** to connect sth WITH sth

■ **~** *vi* **1** «*habitaciones*» to be connected **2** (Esp) «*teléfono*» to be busy (AmE) *o* (BrE) engaged; **está comunicando** it's busy *o* engaged

■ **comunicarse** *v pron* **1** (a) (recípr) (relacionarse) to communicate; **~ por señas** to communicate using sign language; **~se CON algn** to communicate WITH sb (b) (ponerse en contacto) **~se con algn** to get in touch *o* in contact WITH sb **2** «*habitaciones/ciudades/lagos*» (recípr) to be connected; **~se con algo** to be connected TO sth

comunicativo -va *adj* communicative

comunidad *f* community; **C~** (Económica) Europea European (Economic) Community

comunión *f* (Relig) communion; **hacer la primera ~** to make one's first Holy Communion

comunismo *m* communism

comunista *adj/mf* communist

comunitario -ria *adj* **(a)** ⟨*bienes*⟩ communal; ⟨*espíritu/trabajo*⟩ community (*before n*) **(b)** (de la CE) EC (*before n*), Community (*before n*)

con *prep* **(a)** (en general) with; **vive ~ su novio** she lives with her boyfriend; **¡~ mucho gusto!** with pleasure!; **córtalo ~ la tijera** cut it with the scissor; **amaneció ~ fiebre** he woke up with a temperature; **hablar ~ algn** to talk to sb; **está casada ~ mi primo** she's married to my cousin; **portarse mal ~ algn** to behave badly toward(s) sb; **tener paciencia ~ algn** to be patient with sb; **pan ~ mantequilla** bread and butter; **¿vas a ir ~ ese vestido?** are you going in that dress? **(b)** (indicando una relación de causa): **¿cómo vamos a ir ~ esta lluvia?** how can we go in this rain?; **ella se lo ofreció, ~ lo que** *or* **lo cual me puso a mí en un aprieto** she offered it to him, which put me in an awkward position; **~ lo tarde que es, ya se debe haber ido** it's really late, he should have gone by now **(c) ~ + INF:** **~ llorar no se arregla nada** crying won't solve anything; **~ llamarlo por teléfono ya cumples** as long as you call him, that should do; **me contento ~ que apruebes** as long as you pass I'll be happy; ▶ TAL *adv* 2 **(d)** (AmL) (indicando el agente, destinatario): **me peino ~ Gerardo** Gerardo does my hair; **se estuvo quejando ~migo** she was complaining to me

cóncavo -va *adj* concave

concebir [I14] *vt* **1** (Biol) to conceive **2** ⟨*plan/idea*⟩ to conceive **3** (entender, imaginar): **no concibe la vida sin él** she can't conceive of life without him; **yo concibo la amistad de modo distinto** I have a different conception of friendship
■ **~** *vi* to conceive

conceder [E1] *vt* **1 (a)** ⟨*premio/beca*⟩ to give, award; ⟨*descuento/préstamo*⟩ to give; ⟨*privilegio/favor/permiso*⟩ to grant; **nos concedió una entrevista** she agreed to give us an interview; **¿me podría ~ unos minutos?** could you spare me a few minutes? **(b)** ⟨*importancia/valor*⟩ to give **2** (admitir, reconocer) to admit, acknowledge

concejal -jala *m,f* town/city councilor*

concejero -ra *m,f* (AmL) town/city councilor*

concejo *m* council

concentración *f* **(a)** (Psic, Quím) concentration; **falta de ~** lack of concentration **(b)** (acumulación) concentration **(c)** (Pol) rally, mass meeting

concentrado¹ -da *adj* concentrated (*before n*)

concentrado² *m* (de verdura, tomate) concentrate; **~ de carne** meat extract

concentrar [A1] *vt* **(a)** ⟨*solución/caldo*⟩ to make ... more concentrated **(b)** ⟨*esfuerzos*⟩ to concentrate; ⟨*atención*⟩ to focus **(c)** (congregar) ⟨*multitud/tropas*⟩ to assemble, bring ... together
■ **concentrarse** *v pron* **(a)** (Psic) to concentrate; **~se EN algo** to concentrate ON sth **(b)** (reunirse) to assemble, gather together

concéntrico -ca *adj* concentric

concepción *f* (Biol) conception

concepto *m* **(a)** (idea): **el ~ de la libertad** the concept of freedom; **tener un ~ equivocado de algo/algn** to have a mistaken idea of sth/sb; **tengo (un) mal ~ de su trabajo** I have a very low opinion of her work; **bajo** *or* **por ningún ~** on no account **(b)** (Com, Fin): **en** *or* **por ~ de** in respect of

conceptuoso -sa *adj* (CS) (amable, elogioso): **una conceptuosa felicitación** warm congratulations

concerniente *adj* **~ A algo** concerning sth; **en lo ~ a este problema** as far as this problem is concerned

concernir [I12] *vi* (en *3ª pers*) to concern; **~ A algn** to concern sb; **por lo que a mí concierne** as far as I'm concerned; **en lo que concierne a su pedido** with regard to your order

concertar [A5] *vt* ⟨*cita/entrevista*⟩ to arrange, set up; ⟨*plan*⟩ to arrange; ⟨*precio*⟩ to agree (on)

concertista *mf* soloist; **~ de piano** concert pianist

concesión *f* **(a)** (de premios) awarding; (de préstamo) granting **(b)** (en una postura) concession; **hacer concesiones** to make concessions **(c)** (Com) dealership, concession, franchise

concesionario *m* dealer, concessionaire

concha *f* **(a)** (de moluscos) shell; **~ nácar** (Méx) *or* (Chi) **de perla** mother-of-pearl **(b)** (carey) tortoise shell **(c)** (Teatr) prompt box **(d)** (Ven) (cáscara — de verduras, fruta) skin; (— del queso) rind; (— del pan) crust; (— de nueces) shell

cónchale *interj* (Ven fam) good heavens!

concho *m* (Chi) **(a)** (del vino) lees (*pl*); (del café) dregs (*pl*) **(b)** (fam) (parte final) end, last bit **(c)** **conchos** *mpl* (restos) leftovers (*pl*)

conciencia *f* **(a)** (en moral) conscience; **tener la ~ tranquila** to have a clear *o* clean conscience; **tener la ~ sucia** to have a bad *o* guilty conscience; **me remuerde la ~** my conscience is pricking me; **no siente ningún cargo de ~** she feels no remorse; **hacer algo a ~** to do something conscientiously **(b)** (conocimiento) awareness; **tener/tomar ~ de algo** to be/become aware of sth

concienciar [A1] *vt* (Esp) ▶ CONCIENTIZAR

concientizar [A4] *vt* (esp AmL) ⟨*población/sociedad*⟩ to make ... aware; **~ a algn DE algo** to raise sb's consciousness ABOUT *o* awareness OF sth
■ **concientizarse** *v pron* (esp AmL) **~se DE algo** to become aware OF sth

concienzudo -da *adj* ⟨*trabajador/estudiante*⟩ conscientious; ⟨*estudio/repaso/análisis*⟩ thorough, painstaking

concierto *m* (Mús) **(a)** (obra) concerto **(b)** (función) concert, recital

conciliación *f* conciliation

conciliar [A1] *vt* **1 (a)** ⟨*personas*⟩ to conciliate **(b)** ⟨*ideas*⟩ to reconcile; ⟨*actividades*⟩ to combine **2** ⟨*sueño*⟩: **~ el sueño** to get to sleep

concilio *m* council

conciso -sa *adj* concise

conciudadano -na *m,f* fellow citizen

concluir [I20] *vt* **(a)** (frml) (terminar) ⟨*obras*⟩ to complete, finish; ⟨*trámite*⟩ to complete; ⟨*acuerdo/* ⋯⋮

tratado⟩ to conclude **(b)** (frml) (deducir) to conclude, come to the conclusion; ∼ **algo DE algo** to conclude sth FROM sth

■ ∼ *vi* (frml) **(a)** «*congreso/negociaciones*» to end, conclude; **el plazo concluyó el día 17** the time limit expired on the 17th **(b)** «*persona*» ∼ **DE hacer algo** to finish doing sth

conclusión *f* **(a)** (terminación) completion **(b)** (deducción) conclusion; **saqué la ∼ de que ...** I came to the conclusion that ...; **tú saca tus propias conclusiones** you can draw your own conclusions; **en ∼** (en suma) in short; (en consecuencia) so

concluyente *adj* ⟨*razón/respuesta/prueba*⟩ conclusive; **fue ∼ al responder** he answered categorically

concordante *adj* concordant (frml), concurrent

concordar [A10] *vi* **(a)** (Ling) to agree; ∼ **CON algo** to agree WITH sth **(b)** ⟨*cifras*⟩ «*versiones*» to agree, coincide; ∼ **CON algo** ⟨*con documento/versión*⟩ to coincide WITH sth; **su comportamiento no concuerda con sus principios** his behavior is not in keeping with his principles

concordato *m* concordat

concretamente *adv* (específicamente) specifically; **vive en Wisconsin, ∼ en Madison** he lives in Wisconsin, in Madison to be precise

concretar [A1] *vt* **(a)** (concertar) ⟨*fecha/precio*⟩ to fix, set **(b)** (precisar, definir) to be specific about; **no concretamos nada** we didn't settle on anything definite

■ ∼ *vi*: **a ver si concretas** try and be more specific; **llámame para ∼** give me a call to arrange the details

■ **concretarse** *v pron* to become a reality

concreto¹ -ta *adj* **(a)** (específico) ⟨*política/solución/acusación*⟩ concrete, specific; ⟨*motivo/ejemplo/pregunta*⟩ specific; ⟨*fecha/hora*⟩ definite; ⟨*caso*⟩ particular; ⟨*lugar*⟩ specific, particular; **en tu caso ∼** in your particular case; **en ∼** specifically; **en una zona en ∼** in a particular *o* specific area; **no sé nada en ∼** I don't know anything definite **(b)** (no abstracto) concrete

concreto² *m* (AmL) concrete; ∼ **armado** reinforced concrete

concubina *f* concubine

concuñado -da *m,f*: **mi ∼** my wife's brother-in-law; **mi concuñada** my husband's sister-in-law

concurrido -da *adj* **(a)** [ESTAR] (con mucha gente) ⟨*discoteca/local*⟩ busy, crowded; ⟨*concierto/exposición*⟩ well-attended **(b)** [SER] (frecuentado) popular

concursante *mf* (en concurso) competitor, contestant; (para empleo) candidate

concursar [A1] *vi* (en concurso) to take part; (para puesto) to compete (*through interviews and competitive examinations*)

concurso *m* **(a)** (certamen) competition; **presentarse a un ∼** to take part in a competition; ∼ **de belleza** beauty contest *o* (esp AmE) pageant;

∼ **hípico** show jumping competition **(b)** (para puestos, vacantes) *selection process involving interviews and competitive examinations* **(c)** (TV) (de preguntas y respuestas) quiz show; (de juegos y pruebas) game show **(d)** (licitación) tender; **sacar algo a ∼** to put sth out to tender

condado *m* (división territorial) county

conde -desa *m,f* (en Gran Bretaña) (*m*) earl; (*f*) countess; (en otros países) (*m*) count; (*f*) countess

condecoración *f* decoration

condecorar [A1] *vt* to decorate

condena *f* **(a)** (Der) sentence; **está cumpliendo su ∼** he is serving his sentence **(b)** (reprobación) ∼ **DE** *or* **A algo** condemnation OF sth

condenado -da *adj* **(a)** (destinado) ∼ **A algo** doomed TO sth **(b)** (obligado) ∼ **A hacer algo** condemned *o* forced to do sth **(c)** (fam) (expresando irritación) wretched (colloq), damn (colloq)

■ *m,f* **(a)** (Der) convicted person; **el ∼ a muerte** the condemned man **(b)** (Relig): **los ∼s** the damned; **como** (un) ∼ (fam) ⟨*correr*⟩ like hell (colloq); ⟨*work*⟩ like mad

condenar [A1] *vt* **(a)** (Der) to sentence, condemn; ∼ **a algn A algo** to sentence sb TO sth; ∼ **a algn a muerte** to sentence sb to death; **lo ∼on por robo** he was convicted *o* found guilty of robbery **(b)** (reprobar, censurar) to condemn

condensación *f* condensation

condensar [A1] *vt* to condense

■ **condensarse** *v pron* to condense

condesa *f* countess

condescendiente *adj* **(a)** ⟨*actitud/respuesta*⟩ (con aires de superioridad) condescending **(b)** (comprensivo) understanding

condición *f* ① (requisito) condition; **sin condiciones** unconditionally; **a ∼** *or* **con la ∼ de que** on condition (that); **acepto con una ∼** I accept on one condition; **me puso una ∼** she made one condition

② **(a)** (calidad, situación): **en su ∼ de sacerdote** as a priest; **en su ∼ de jefe de la delegación** in his capacity as head of the delegation **(b)** (naturaleza) condition; **la ∼ humana** the human condition

③ **condiciones** *fpl* (estado, circunstancias) conditions (*pl*); **condiciones de trabajo/de vida** working/living conditions; **estar en perfectas condiciones** «*coche/mueble*» to be in perfect condition; «*persona*» to be in good shape; **estar en condiciones de hacer algo** (de ayudar, exigir) to be in a position to do sth; (de correr, viajar, jugar) to be fit to do sth **(b)** (aptitudes) talent; **tener condiciones para algo** (para la música, el arte) to have a talent for sth; (para un trabajo) to be suited for sth

condicional *adj* conditional

condicionar [A1] *vt* **(a)** (determinar) to condition, determine **(b)** (supeditar) ∼ **algo A algo** to make sth conditional ON sth

condimentar [A1] *vt* to season

condimento *m*: **el comino es un ∼** cumin is a

condiment; **le falta ~** it needs some seasoning; **los ~s usados en la cocina india** the herbs and spices used in Indian cooking

condominio *m* **(a)** (propiedad) joint ownership, joint control **(b)** (Pol) (territorio) condominium **(c)** (AmL) (edificio) condominium (esp AmE), block of flats (BrE)

condón *m* condom

cóndor *m* condor

conducción *f* **(a)** (Elec, Fís) conduction **(b)** (esp Esp) (Auto) driving **(c)** (AmL) (de programa) presentation; **está a cargo de la ~ del programa** he's in charge of presenting the program **(d)** (Arg) (cúpula) leadership

conducir [I6] *vi* **(a)** (llevar) **~ A algo** «*camino/ sendero*» to lead TO sth; **esa actitud no conduce a nada** that attitude won't achieve anything *o* (colloq) won't get us anywhere; **a qué conduce eso?** what's the point of that? **(b)** (esp Esp) (Auto) to drive; **~ por la izquierda** to drive on the left
■ **~** *vt* **(a)** (guiar, dirigir) to lead; **~ a algn A algo** to lead sb TO sth; **~ a algn ANTE algn** to take sb BEFORE sb **(b)** (AmL) (*programa*) to host, present; (*debate*) to chair **(c)** (esp Esp) (*vehículo*) to drive **(d)** (*electricidad/calor*) to conduct

conducta *f* behavior*, conduct; **mala ~** bad behavior, misconduct (fml)

conducto *m* **(a)** (Anat) duct, tube **(b)** (Tec) (canal, tubo) pipe, tube

conductor¹ -tora *adj* conductive; **materiales ~es de la electricidad** materials which conduct electricity
■ *m,f* **(a)** (de vehículo) driver **(b)** (AmL) (de programa) host

conductor² *m* (Elec, Fís) conductor

conduje, condujiste, etc ▶ CONDUCIR

conduzca, conduzcas, etc ▶ CONDUCIR

conectar [A1] *vt* **(a)** (*cables/aparatos*) to connect (up); (*luz/gas/teléfono*) to connect **(b)** (relacionar) (*hechos/sucesos*) to connect, link **(c)** (AmL) (poner en contacto) **~ a algn CON algn** to put sb in touch *o* in contact WITH sb
■ **~** *vi* **(a)** (Rad, TV) **~ CON algn/algo** to go over TO sb/sth **(b)** (empalmar) to connect, link up **(c)** (llevarse bien, entenderse) to get along *o* on well **(d)** (AmL) **~ CON algo** «*vuelo/tren*» to connect WITH sth; **conectamos con el vuelo a Lima** we took a connecting flight to Lima

conecte *mf* **(a)** (Méx arg) (traficante) (drug) dealer **(b)** (AmC fam) (contacto) friend on the inside (colloq)

conector *m* connector

conejera *f* (madriguera) burrow; (para crianza) (rabbit) hutch

conejillo de Indias *m* guinea pig

conejo -ja *m,f* (Zool) rabbit

conexión *f* **(a)** (Elec) connection; **~ a tierra** ground (AmE), earth (BrE); **~ a la red** connection to the mains **(b)** (relación entre hechos, etc) connection **(c)** (Transp) connection; **perdí la ~ con Roma** I missed my connection to Rome **(d) conexiones** *fpl* (AmL) (amistades) connections (*pl*), contacts (*pl*)

confabularse [A1] *v pron* **~ (CONTRA algn)** to plot *o* conspire (AGAINST sb)

confección *f* **(a)** (de trajes) tailoring; (de vestidos) dressmaking; **industria de la ~** clothing industry; **de ~** ready-to-wear, off-the-peg **(b)** (de lista) drawing-up

confeccionar [A1] *vt* (*falda/vestido*) to make (up); (*artefactos*) to make; (*lista*) to draw up

confederación *f* confederation

conferencia *f* **(a)** (charla — formal) lecture; (— más informal) talk; **dar una ~ SOBRE algo** to give a lecture/talk ON sth **(b)** (reunión) conference; **~ de prensa** press conference **(c)** (Esp) (Telec) long distance call; **poner una ~** to make *o* (AmE) place a long-distance call; **~ a cobro revertido** collect call (AmE), reverse charge call (BrE)

conferenciante, (AmL) **conferencista** *mf* lecturer

conferir [I11] *vt* (frml *o* liter) **(a)** (*honor/ dignidad/responsabilidad*) to confer **(b)** (*prestigio*) to confer; (*encanto*) to lend; **la barba le confería un aire distinguido** the beard lent him an air of distinction

confesar [A5] *vt* **(a)** (Relig) (*pecado*) to confess; **el cura que la confiesa** the priest who hears her confession **(b)** (*sentimiento/ignorancia/delito*) to confess; (*error*) to admit
■ **~** *vi* **(a)** (Relig) to hear confession **(b)** (admitir culpabilidad) to confess, make a confession
■ **confesarse** *v pron* **(a)** (Relig) to go to confession; **~se DE algo** to confess sth; **~se CON algn** (Relig) to go to sb for confession; (hacer confidencias) to open up one's heart to sb **(b)** (declararse) (+ *compl*) to confess to being, admit to being

confesión *f* confession

confesionario *m* confessional

confesor *m* confessor

confeti *m* confetti

confiable *adj* (esp AmL) **(a)** (*estadísticas*) reliable **(b)** (*persona*) (cumplidor) reliable, dependable; (honesto) trustworthy

confiado -da *adj* **(a)** [SER] (crédulo) trusting **[ESTAR]** (seguro): **está muy ~ en que lo van a llevar** he's convinced they're going to take him; **no estés tan ~** don't get over-confident

confianza *f* **(a)** (fe) confidence; **ella me inspira ~** I feel I can trust her; **lo considero digno de toda ~** he has my complete trust; **~ EN algn/algo** confidence IN sb/sth; **tiene ~ en sí misma** she is self-confident; **había puesto toda mi ~ en él** I had put all my trust *o* faith in him; **de ~** (*persona*) trustworthy, reliable; (*producto*) reliable; (*puesto/ posición*) of trust; **nombró a alguien de su ~** he appointed someone he trusted **(b)** (intimidad): **tenemos mucha ~** we are close friends; **no les des tanta(s) ~(s)** don't let them be so familiar with you; **estamos en ~** we're among friends; **te lo digo en ~** I'm telling you in confidence; **tratar a algn con ~** to be friendly with sb

confianzudo -da *adj* (esp AmL fam) forward

confiar [A17] *vi* **(a)** (tener fe) **~ EN algn/algo** to trust sb/sth; **no confío en ella** I don't trust her; **confiamos en su discreción** we rely *o* depend on your discretion **(b)** (estar seguro) **~ EN algo** to be confident OF sth; **~ en la victoria** to be confident of victory; **confiamos en poder llevarlo a cabo** we are confident that we can do it; **confiemos en que venga** let's hope she comes

                          ⋯❖

■ ~ *vt* ~**le algo** A **algn** ⟨*secreto*⟩ to confide sth TO sb; ⟨*trabajo/responsabilidad*⟩ to entrust sb with sth

■ **confiarse** *v pron* **(a)** (hacerse ilusiones) to be overconfident; **no te confíes demasiado** don't get overconfident *o* too confident **(b)** (desahogarse, abrirse) ~**se** A **algn** to confide IN sb

confidencia *f* secret, confidence (frml); **hacer una ~ a algn** to tell sb a secret

confidencial *adj* confidential

confidente *mf* **(a)** (amigo) (*m*) confidant; (*f*) confidante **(b)** (de la policía) informer

confinamiento *m* confinement

confinar [A1] *vt* **(a)** ~ **a algn** A **algo** ⟨*a hospital/a calabozo*⟩ to put sb INTO sth; ⟨*a casa*⟩ to confine sb TO sth; ⟨*a isla*⟩ to banish sb TO sth; **la parálisis lo confinó a una silla de ruedas** he was confined to a wheelchair because of paralysis

confirmación *f* ⟨**1**⟩ (de noticia, de pasaje) confirmation ⟨**2**⟩ (Relig) confirmation; **hacer la ~** to be confirmed

confirmar [A1] *vt* to confirm; **la excepción que confirma la regla** the exception that proves the rule

confiscar [A2] *vt* **(a)** ⟨*contrabando/armas*⟩ to confiscate, seize **(b)** (para uso del estado) to requisition

confitería *f* **(a)** (tienda) patisserie, cake shop (*also selling sweets*) **(b)** (Bol, RPl) (salón de té) tearoom

confitura *f* preserve, jam

conflictivo -va *adj* **(a)** (problemático) ⟨*situación*⟩ difficult; ⟨*época*⟩ troubled; **una zona conflictiva** a trouble spot **(b)** (polémico) ⟨*tema/persona*⟩ controversial

conflicto *m* **(a)** (enfrentamiento) conflict; **estar en ~** to be in conflict; **entrar en ~ con algn/algo** to come into conflict with sb/sth **(b)** (Psic) conflict **(c)** (apuro) difficult situation

confluir [I20] *vi* **(a)** ⟨*calles/ríos*⟩ to converge, meet; ⟨⟨*corrientes/ideologías*⟩⟩ to come together, merge **(b)** ⟨⟨*grupos/personas*⟩⟩ to congregate, come together

conformar [A1] *vt* **(a)** (contentar) ⟨*persona*⟩ to satisfy **(b)** ⟨*cheque*⟩ to authorize payment of

■ **conformarse** *v pron* **(a)** (contentarse) ~**se con algo** to be satisfied WITH sth; **no se conforma con nada** he's never satisfied; **tuvo que ~se con lo que tenía** he had to make do with what he had **(b)** (esp AmL) (resignarse): **no tienes más remedio que ~te** you'll just have to accept it *o* to resign yourself to it; **no se puede ~** she can't get over it

conforme *adj* [ESTAR] **(a)** (satisfecho) satisfied, happy; ~ **con algo/algn** satisfied *o* happy WITH sth/sb **(b)** (de acuerdo): **¡~!** agreed!, fine!; **estoy en que se haga así** I agree that it should be done like that; ~ A **algo** in accordance WITH sth (frml) **(c)** (en regla) in order

■ *conj* as; ~ **se entra, está a mano izquierda** it's on the left as you go in

conformidad *f* **(a)** (aprobación) consent, approval **(b)** (esp AmL) (resignación) resignation

conformista *adj/mf* conformist

confort /kom'for/ *m* comfort; **apartamento todo ~** well-appointed *o* fully equipped apartment

confortable *adj* comfortable

confortar [A1] *vt* to reassure, comfort

confrontación *f* **(a)** (enfrentamiento) confrontation **(b)** (de textos) comparison

confrontar [A1] *vt* **(a)** ⟨*textos/versiones*⟩ to compare **(b)** ⟨*testigos/equipos*⟩ to bring ... face to face; ⟨*ejércitos*⟩ to bring ... into conflict **(c)** ⟨*dificultad/peligro*⟩ to confront, face

■ **confrontarse** *v pron* ~**se con algo** to face up to sth

confundir [I1] *vt* **(a)** (por error) ⟨*fechas/datos*⟩ to confuse, get ... mixed *o* muddled up; ⟨*personas*⟩ to confuse, mix up; ~ **algo/a algn con algo/algn** to mistake sth/sb FOR sth/sb; **me confundió con mi hermana** he mistook me for my sister **(b)** (desconcertar) to confuse **(c)** (turbar) to embarrass

■ **confundirse** *v pron* **(a)** (equivocarse) to make mistakes/a mistake; **me confundí de calle** I got the wrong street **(b)** (desconcertarse) to get confused

confusión *f* **(a)** (en general) confusion; **para que no haya confusiones** to avoid any confusion **(b)** (turbación) embarrassment, confusion

confuso -sa *adj* **(a)** ⟨*idea/texto/explicación*⟩ confused; ⟨*recuerdo*⟩ confused, hazy; ⟨*imagen*⟩ blurred, hazy; ⟨*información*⟩ confused **(b)** (turbado) embarrassed, confused

congelado -da *adj* **(a)** ⟨*alimentos*⟩ frozen **(b)** (Med) frostbitten; *ver tb* CONGELAR

congelador *m* (en el refrigerador) freezer compartment; (independiente) freezer, deepfreeze

congelar [A1] *vt* to freeze

■ **congelarse** *v pron* **(a)** ⟨⟨*agua/lago*⟩⟩ to freeze **(b)** (Med): **se le congeló el pie** he got frostbite in his foot **(c)** (tener mucho frío) to be freezing; **me estoy congelando** I'm freezing!

congeniar [A1] *vi* to get along (esp AmE), to get on (esp BrE); ~ **con algn** to get along *o* on WITH sb

congénito -ta *adj* congenital

congestión *f* congestion

congestionado -da *adj* **(a)** (Med) congested **(b)** ⟨*cara*⟩ flushed **(c)** ⟨*calle/área*⟩ congested

congestionarse [A1] *v pron* **(a)** ⟨*cara*⟩ to become flushed **(b)** (Med) to become congested *o* blocked **(c)** ⟨⟨*calle/área*⟩⟩ to become congested

conglomerado *m* conglomeration

conglomerarse [A1] *v pron* to conglomerate

congratular [A1] *vt* (frml) to congratulate; ~ **a algn POR algo** to congratulate sb ON sth

■ **congratularse** *v pron* ~**se DE** *or* **POR algo** (alegrarse) to be pleased ABOUT sth, congratulate oneself ON sth (frml)

congregar [A3] *vt* to bring together

■ **congregarse** *v pron* to assemble, gather

congreso *m* ⟨**1**⟩ (reunión) conference, congress ⟨**2**⟩ **Congreso** (Gob, Pol) **(a)** (asamblea) Parliament; (in US) Congress; **C~ de los Diputados** (Esp) Chamber of Deputies (*lower chamber of Spanish Parliament*) **(b)** (edificio) Parliament (*o* Congress *etc*) building

congrio *m* (Coc, Zool) conger eel

congruente *adj* (coherente) coherent; **ser ~ con algo** to be consistent with sth

cónico -ca *adj* ⟨*pieza/forma*⟩ conical, conic (tech); ⟨*sección*⟩ conic

conífera *f* conifer

conjetura *f* conjecture, speculation; **hacer ~s** to surmise, conjecture (frml); **son simples ~s** that's pure conjecture *o* speculation

conjugar [A3] *vt* (Ling) to conjugate

conjunción *f* **(a)** (Ling, Astron) conjunction **(b)** (unión) combination; **en ~ con** in conjunction with

conjuntivitis *f* conjunctivitis

conjunto¹ -ta *adj* ‹esfuerzo/acción› joint *before n*

conjunto² ** *m* **(a) (de objetos, obras) collection; (de personas) group; **en su ~** (referido a — obra, exposición) as a whole; (— comité, partido) as a group; **~ residencial** residential complex **(b)** (Mús) *tb* **~ musical** (de música clásica) ensemble; (de música popular) pop group **(c)** (Indum) (de pulóver y chaqueta) twinset; (de prendas en general) outfit; **un ~ de chaqueta y pantalón** matching jacket and trousers; **hacer ~ con algo** to go well with sth **(d)** (Mat) set

conjura, conjuración *f* conspiracy, plot

conjurar [A1] *vi* to conspire, plot

conjuro *m* (fórmula mágica) spell

conllevar [A1] *vt* **(a)** (*en 3ª pers*) (comportar, implicar) to entail; **conlleva mucha responsabilidad** it entails a great deal of responsibility **(b)** ‹desgracia/enfermedad› to bear
■ ~ *vi* (Ven) **~ A algo** to lead TO sth

conmemoración *f* commemoration; **en ~ de** in commemoration of

conmemorar [A1] *vt* to commemorate

conmemorativo *adj* commemorative; **un monumento ~** a memorial

conmigo *pron pers* with me; **vino ~** she came with me; **estoy furiosa ~ misma** I'm furious with myself; **ha sido muy bueno ~** he's been very good to me

conmoción *f* **(a)** (Med) *tb* **~ cerebral** concussion **(b)** (trastorno, agitación): **la noticia produjo una ~ familiar** the news shocked the whole family **(c)** (Geol) shock

conmocionar [A1] *vt* to shake

conmovedor -dora *adj* moving, touching

conmover [E9] *vt* **(a)** (emocionar) to move **(b)** (inducir a piedad) to move … to pity
■ **conmoverse** *v pron* (enternecerse, emocionarse) to be moved

conmutar [A1] *vt* (Der) ‹pena› to commute

connotación *f* connotation

cono *m* (figura) cone; **el C~ Sur** the Southern Cone (*Argentina, Chile, Paraguay and Uruguay*)

conocedor -dora *m,f* connoisseur, expert

conocer [E3] *vt* **1** ‹persona› to know; (por primera vez) to meet; ‹ciudad/país› to know; **¿conoces a Juan?** do you know/have you met Juan?; **te conocía de oídas** he'd heard of you; **lo conozco de nombre** I know the name; **~ a algn de vista** to know sb by sight; **es de todos conocido** he's well known; **quiero que conozcas a mi novio** I want you to meet my boyfriend; **nunca llegué a ~lo bien** I never really got to know him; **¿conoces Irlanda?** do you know Ireland? *o* have you been to Ireland?; **quiere ~ mundo** she wants to see the world; **me encantaría ~ tu país** I'd love to visit your country

2 (estar familiarizado con, dominar) ‹tema/autor/obra› to know, be familiar with; ‹lengua› to speak, know

3 (a) (saber de la existencia de) to know, know of; **conocían sus actividades** they knew of *o* about his activities **(b)** **dar a ~** (frml) ‹noticia/resultado› to announce; ‹identidad/intenciones› to reveal; **darse a ~** «persona» to make oneself known; **intentó no darse a ~** he tried to keep his identity a secret

4 (reconocer) to recognize*; **te conocí por la voz** I knew it was you by your voice

5 (impers) (notar): **se conoce que no están en casa** they don't seem to be in; **se conoce que ya llevaba algún tiempo enfermo** apparently he'd been ill for some time
■ **~ *vi*** (saber) **~ DE algo** ‹de tema/materia› to know ABOUT sth
■ **conocerse** *v pron* **1** (recípr) (tener cierta relación con) to know each other; (por primera vez) to meet; (aprender cómo es) to get to know each other

2 (refl) **(a)** (aprender cómo es) to get to know oneself **(b)** (saber cómo es) to know oneself

conocido -da *adj* **(a)** (famoso) ‹actor/cantante› famous, well-known **(b)** ‹cara/voz› familiar **(c)** ‹hecho/nombre› well-known; **más ~ como …** better known as …
■ *m,f* acquaintance

conocimiento *m* **(a)** (saber) knowledge; **tiene algunos ~s de inglés** he has some knowledge of English; **poner algo en ~ de algn** to inform sb of sth; **tener ~ de algo** to be aware of sth **(b)** (sentido) consciousness; **perder/recobrar el ~** to lose/regain consciousness; **estar sin ~** to be unconscious

conozca, conozco, etc ▶ CONOCER

conque *conj* so; **~ ya lo sabes** so now you know

conquista *f* **(a)** (de territorio, pueblo) conquest; **la C~** (Hist) the Spanish conquest (*of America*) **(b)** (logro) achievement **(c)** (fam) (amorosa) conquest

conquistador -dora *adj* ‹ejército› conquering
■ *m,f* **(a)** (Hist) conqueror; (en la conquista de América) conquistador **(b)** (fam) (en el amor) (*m*) lady-killer; (*f*) femme fatale

conquistar [A1] *vt* **(a)** ‹territorio/pueblo/montaña› to conquer; ‹mercado› to capture **(b)** ‹victoria/título› to win; ‹éxito/fama› to achieve **(c)** ‹simpatía/respeto› to win; ‹persona/público› to captivate; ‹corazón› to capture; **acabó conquistándola** he won her heart in the end

consagrado -da *adj* **(a)** (Relig) consecrated **(b)** ‹artista› acclaimed **(c)** ‹costumbre/procedimiento› established

consagrar [A1] *vt* **(a)** (Relig) to consecrate **(b)** **~ algo A algo/algn** ‹monumento/edificio› to dedicate sth TO sth/sb; ‹vida/esfuerzo› to dedicate *o* devote sth TO sth/sb; ‹programa/publicación› to devote sth TO sth/sb **(c)** (establecer) ‹artista/profesional› to establish; **la película que la consagró como actriz** the movie that established her as an actress
■ **consagrarse** *v pron* (refl) (dedicarse) **~se A algo/algn** to devote oneself TO sth/sb

consciencia *f* **▶** CONCIENCIA B

consciente *adj* **(a)** [ESTAR] (Med) conscious ⋯⋛

(c) (de problema, hecho) ser *or* (Chi, Méx) estar ~ DE algo to be aware *o* conscious OF sth **(c)** [SER] (sensato) sensible; (responsable) responsible

conscripto *m* (AmL) conscript

consecuencia *f* consequence; **atenerse a las** ~**s** to accept the consequences; **esto trajo como** ~ **su renuncia** this resulted in his resignation; **a** ~ **de** as a result of; **en** ~ (frml) (por consiguiente) consequently, as a result; ⟨actuar/obrar⟩ accordingly

consecuente *adj* consistent; **hay que ser** ~ you have to be consistent; **es** ~ **con sus ideas** she acts according to her beliefs (o principles *etc*)

consecutivo -va *adj* consecutive

conseguir [I30] *vt* ⟨objetivo/fin/resultado⟩ to achieve, obtain; ⟨entrada/permiso/empleo⟩ to get; ⟨medalla/título⟩ to win; **si lo intentas, al final lo** ~**ás** if you try, you'll succeed in the end; **la película consiguió un gran éxito** the film was a great success; ~ **hacer algo** to manage to do sth; **no consigo entenderlo** I can't work it out; **conseguí que me lo prestara** I got him to lend it to me

consejero -ra *m,f* **(a)** (asesor) adviser **(b)** (Adm, Com) director **(c)** (en embajada) counselor*

consejo *m* **(a)** (recomendación) piece of advice; **te voy a dar un** ~ let me give you some advice *o* a piece of advice; **me pidió** ~ he asked me for advice *o* asked (for) my advice; **sus** ~**s son siempre acertados** she always gives good advice **(b)** (organismo) council, board; ~ **de administración** board of directors; ~ **de guerra** court-martial; ~ **de ministros** (grupo) cabinet; (reunión) cabinet meeting; **C**~ **de Europa** Council of Europe; **C**~ **de Seguridad** Security Council

consenso *m* consensus; **por** ~ by general consent *o* assent

consentido -da *adj* spoiled
■ *m,f*: **es un** ~ he's spoiled

consentimiento *m* (autorización) consent

consentir [I11] *vt* **(a)** (permitir, tolerar) to allow; **¡no te consiento que me hables así!** I won't have you speak to me like that; **se lo consienten todo** he's allowed to do whatever he likes **(b)** (mimar) ⟨niño⟩ to spoil
■ ~ *vi*: ~ EN algo to consent *o* agree TO sth

conserje *mf* **(a)** (de establecimiento público) superintendent (AmE), caretaker (BrE) **(b)** (de colegio) custodian (AmE), caretaker (BrE) **(c)** (de hotel) receptionist

conserjería *f* reception

conserva *f*: **latas de** ~ cans *o* (BrE) tins of food; **piña en** ~ canned *o* (BrE) tinned pineapple; ~**s** canned *o* (BrE) tinned food

conservación *f* **(a)** (de alimentos) preserving **(b)** (Ecol) conservation **(c)** (de monumentos, obras de arte) preservation

conservador -dora *adj* conservative
■ *m,f* **(a)** (Pol) conservative **(b)** (de museo) curator

conservante *m* preservative

conservar [A1] *vt* **(a)** (mantener, preservar)

⟨alimentos⟩ to preserve; ⟨sabor/calor⟩ to retain; ⟨tradiciones/costumbres⟩ to preserve; ⟨amigo/cargo⟩ to keep; ⟨naturaleza⟩ to conserve; **conservo buenos recuerdos suyos** I have good memories of him; ~ **la calma** to keep calm; ~ **la línea** to keep one's figure **(b)** (guardar) ⟨cartas/fotografías⟩ to keep
■ **conservarse** *v pron* **(a)** ⟨alimentos⟩ to keep **(b)** (perdurar) ⟨restos/tradiciones⟩ to survive **(c)** ⟨persona⟩ (+ compl) to keep; **se conserva joven** she keeps herself young; **está muy bien conservada** she's very well preserved

conservatorio *m* conservatory, conservatoire

considerable *adj* considerable

consideración *f* consideration; **tomar algo en** ~ to take sth into consideration *o* account; **por** ~ **a su familia** out of consideration for his family; **en** ~ **a sus méritos** in recognition of her merits; **la trataron sin ninguna** ~ they treated her most inconsiderately; **¡qué falta de** ~! how thoughtless!; **de** ~ serious

considerado -da *adj* considerate; **ser** ~ CON algn to be considerate TOWARD(s) sb

considerar [A1] *vt* ⟨asunto/posibilidad/oferta⟩ to consider; ⟨ventajas/consecuencias⟩ to weigh up, consider; **considerando que ha estado enfermo** considering (that) he's been ill; **tenemos que** ~ **que ...** we must take into account that ...; **eso se considera de mala educación** that's considered bad manners; **está muy bien considerado** he is very highly regarded
■ **considerarse** *v pron* ⟨persona⟩ (juzgarse) to consider oneself; **se considera afortunado** he considers himself (to be) lucky

consiga, consigas, etc ▶ CONSEGUIR

consigna *f* **(a)** (eslogan) slogan **(b)** (para equipaje) baggage room (AmE), left-luggage (office) (BrE); ~ **automática** (coin-operated *o* automatic) luggage locker (AmE) *o* (BrE) left-luggage locker

consignar [A1] *vt* **1** (depositar) **(a)** ⟨mercancías⟩ to consign **(b)** ⟨equipaje⟩ to check (AmE), to place *o* deposit ... in left luggage (BrE) **(c)** (Der) to pay ... into court **(d)** (Col) ⟨dinero/cheques⟩ to deposit **2** (frml) ⟨hecho/dato⟩ to record **3** (frml) (enviar) ⟨paquete/carga⟩ to dispatch **4** (frml) (asignar) to allocate **5** (Méx) (Der) ⟨presunto delincuente⟩ to bring ... before the authorities

consigo *pron pers* (con él) with him; (con ella) with her; (con uno) with you *o* one; (con usted, ustedes) with you; **no está satisfecho** ~ **mismo** he's not happy with himself; **traigan** ~ **todo lo necesario** bring everything you'll need with you; **hablaba** ~ **misma** she was talking to herself

consigo, consigues, etc ▶ CONSEGUIR

consiguiente *adj* resulting (before n), consequent (before n) (frml); **por** ~ consequently

consistencia *f* **(a)** (de mezcla, masa) consistency; **tomar** ~ to thicken **(b)** (de teoría, argumento) soundness; **un argumento sin** ~ a flimsy argument

---

consistente *adj* **(a)** ‹*salsa/líquido*› thick; ‹*masa*› solid **(b)** ‹*argumentación/tesis*› sound **(c)** (Andes, Méx) ‹*conducta*› consistent; ‹*persona*› ▶ CONSECUENTE

consistir [I1] *vi* **(a)** (expresando composición) ~ EN algo to consist OF sth; **el mobiliario consistía en una cama y una silla** the furniture consisted of a bed and a chair **(b)** (expresando naturaleza): **¿en qué consiste el juego?** what does the game involve?; ~ EN hacer algo to involve *o* entail doing sth **(c)** (radicar) ~ EN algo to lie IN sth; **en eso consiste su gracia** that is where its charm lies

consola *f* **(a)** (mueble) console table **(b)** (panel de controles) console

consolar [A10] *vt* to console, comfort; **si en algo te consuela** if it's any consolation to you
■ **consolarse** *v pron* (*refl*): **me consuelo pensando que ...** I take comfort *o* I find some consolation in the thought that ...

consolidar [A1] *vt* **(a)** ‹*situación/posición/acuerdo*› to consolidate; ‹*amistad*› to strengthen **(b)** ‹*deuda/préstamo*› to consolidate
■ **consolidarse** *v pron* «*situación/acuerdo*» to be consolidated; «*amistad/relación*» to grow stronger

consomé *m* consommé

consonante *f* consonant

conspiración *f* conspiracy, plot

conspirador -dora *m,f* conspirator

conspirar [A1] *vi* to conspire, plot

constancia *f* **1** (perseverancia) perseverance **2** (prueba) proof; **dejar ~ DE algo** (en registro, acta) to record sth (in writing); (verbalmente) to state sth; (atestiguar) to prove sth

constante *adj* **(a)** (continuo) constant **(b)** (perseverante) ‹*persona*› persevering
■ *f* **(a)** (Mat) constant **(b)** (característica) constant feature **(c) constantes** *fpl* (Med) *tb* ~s **vitales** vital signs (*pl*)

constar [A1] *vi* **(a)** (figurar) ~ EN algo ‹*en acta/documento*› to be stated *o* recorded IN sth; ‹*en archivo/catálogo*› to be listed IN sth; ‹*en libro/texto*› to appear IN sth **(b)** (quedar claro): **(que) conste que yo no fui** it certainly wasn't me; **yo nunca dije eso, que conste** just to set the record straight, I never actually said that; **eso me consta** I am sure of that **(c) hacer ~ algo** (manifestar) to state sth; (por escrito) to register sth, to put sth on record **(d)** (estar compuesto de) ~ **DE algo** to consist OF sth

constelación *f* constellation

consternación *f* consternation, dismay

consternar [A1] *vt* to fill ... with dismay

constipación *f* (esp AmL) constipation

constipado¹ -da *adj* **(a)** (resfriado) **está muy ~** he has a bad cold **(b)** (AmL) (estreñido) constipated

constipado² *m* cold

constiparse [A1] *v pron* to catch a cold

constitución *f* **(a)** (establecimiento) setting-up **(b)** (Pol) (de país) constitution **(c)** (complexión) constitution; **un hombre de ~ fuerte** a man with a strong constitution

constitucional *adj* constitutional

constituir [I20] *vt* (frml) **(a)** (componer, formar) to make up, constitute, constitute (frml) **(b)** (ser, representar) to represent, constitute (frml); **esta acción no constituye delito** this action does not constitute a crime **(c)** (crear) ‹*comisión/compañía*› to set up, establish

construcción *f* **(a)** (acción) construction, building; **en ~** under construction; **obrero de la ~** building *o* construction worker **(b)** (edificio, estructura) construction **(c)** (Ling) construction

constructivo -va *adj* constructive

constructor -tora *m,f* **(a)** (Const) builder, building contractor **(b) constructora** *f* construction company, building firm

construir [I20] *vt* **(a)** ‹*edificio/barco/sociedad*› to build **(b)** ‹*figura/frases/oraciones*› to construct

construya, etc ▶ CONSTRUIR

consuegro -gra *m,f* *(m)* father-in-law of one's son or daughter; *(f)* mother-in-law of one's son or daughter

consuelo *m* consolation, comfort

cónsul *mf* consul

consulado *m* (oficina) consulate; (cargo) consulship

consulta *f* **(a)** (pregunta, averiguación): **¿te puedo hacer una ~?** can I ask you something?; **de ~** ‹*biblioteca/libro*› reference (*before n*) **(b)** (Med) (entrevista) consultation; (consultorio) office (AmE), practice (AmE), surgery (BrE); **¿a qué horas tiene ~s el Dr. Sosa?** what are Dr Sosa's office hours (AmE) *o* (BrE) surgery times?; **~ a domicilio** home *o* house visit

consultar [A1] *vt* ‹*persona/obra*› to consult; ‹*dato/duda*› to look up; **~ algo CON algn** to consult sb ABOUT sth
■ **~** *vi*: **~ CON algn** to consult sb

consultor -tora *m,f* consultant

consultorio *m* **(a)** (de médico, dentista) office (AmE), practice (AmE), surgery (BrE); (de abogado) office **(b)** (consultoría) consultancy; **~ sentimental** (en revista) problem page; (en la radio) phone-in (*about personal problems*)

consumición *f* (esp Esp) (bebida) drink; **~ mínima** minimum charge

consumido -da *adj* [ESTAR] (por enfermedad, hambre) emaciated; *ver tb* CONSUMIR

consumidor -dora *m,f* consumer

consumir [I1] *vt* **(a)** (frml) ‹*comida/bebida*› to eat/drink, consume (frml) **(b)** ‹*gasolina/energía/producto*› to consume, use; ‹*tiempo*› to take up **(c)** ‹*salud*› to ruin **(d)** (destruir) ‹*fuego/llamas*› to consume; «*envidia/celos*»: **la envidia la consumía** she was consumed by *o* with envy
■ **consumirse** *v pron* **(a)** ‹*enfermo/anciano*› to waste away; **se consumía de pena** she was being consumed by grief **(b)** «*vela/cigarrillo*» to burn down **(c)** «*líquido*» to reduce

consumismo *m* consumerism

consumo *m* consumption; **~ mínimo** (AmL) minimum charge; **el ~ de drogas** drug-taking

contabilidad *f* **(a)** (ciencia) accounting **(b)** (profesión) accountancy **(c)** (cuentas) accounts (*pl*), books (*pl*); **lleva la ~** she does the accounts *o* the books

contabilizar [A4] *vt* (en contabilidad) to enter; (contar) to count

contable *mf* (Esp) accountant

contactar [A1] *vi* ~ **con algn** to contact sb, get in touch WITH sb
■ ~ *vt* to contact

contacto *m* **(a)** (entre dos cuerpos) contact; **entrar en** ~ to come into contact; **hacer** ~ to make contact **(b)** (comunicación) contact; **estar/ponerse en** ~ **con algn** to be/get in touch *o* contact with sb **(c)** (entrevista, reunión) encounter **(d)** (persona, conocido) contact **(e)** (Auto) ignition **(f)** (Méx) (Elec) socket, power point

contado¹ -da *adj* few; **en contadas ocasiones** on (a) very few occasions; **salimos con los minutos** ~**s** we left with only a few minutes to spare

contado² *m* **(a) al** ~ *or* (Col) **de** ~ ⟨pago/precio⟩ cash (before n); ⟨pagar⟩ (in) cash; **lo compré al** ~ I paid cash for it, I paid for it in cash **(b)** (Col) (cuota, plazo) installment*

contador¹ *m* **(a)** (de luz, de gas) meter; (taxímetro) meter, taximeter **(b)** (AmL) (ábaco) abacus

contador² -dora *m,f* (AmL) accountant; ~ **público** (AmL) certified public (AmE) *o* (BrE) chartered accountant

contagiar [A1] *vt* ⟨enfermedad⟩ to pass on, transmit (tech); ⟨persona⟩ to infect; **me contagió la gripe** she passed her flu on to me; **no te acerques que te voy a** ~ don't come near or I'll give it to you
■ **contagiarse** *v pron* **(a)** «persona/animal» to become infected; **se ha contagiado de mí** she has caught it from me **(b)** «enfermedad» to be transmitted; «manía/miedo» to spread; **se contagia con facilidad** it is very contagious; **se contagió de la enfermedad** she caught the disease

contagioso -sa *adj* **(a)** (por contacto — directo) contagious; (— indirecto) infectious **(b)** ⟨risa/alegría⟩ infectious

contaminación *f* (del mar, aire) pollution; (de agua potable, comida) contamination; (por radiactividad) contamination; ~ **acústica** noise pollution

contaminante *m* pollutant, contaminant

contaminar [A1] *vt* ⟨mar/atmósfera⟩ to pollute; ⟨agua potable/comida⟩ to contaminate; (por radiactividad) to contaminate

contar [A10] *vt* **1** ⟨dinero/votos/días⟩ to count; **eran 6 sin** ~ **al conductor** there were 6 of them not counting the driver; **y eso sin** ~ **las horas extras** and that's without including overtime; **lo cuento entre mis amigos** I consider him (to be) one of my friends
2 ⟨cuento/chiste/secreto⟩ to tell; **no se lo cuentes a nadie** don't tell anyone; **es muy largo de** ~ it's a long story; **¿qué cuentas (de nuevo)?** (fam) how's things? (colloq)
■ ~ *vi* **1** (en general) to count; ~ **con los dedos** to count on one's fingers; **¿este trabajo cuenta para la nota final?** does this piece of work count toward(s) the final grade?; **ella no cuenta para nada** what she says (*o* thinks *etc*) doesn't count for anything
2 contar con (a) ⟨persona/ayuda/discreción⟩ to count on, rely on; **cuento contigo para la fiesta** I'm counting *o* relying on you being at the party; **sin** ~ **con que ...** without taking into account that ... **(b)** (prever) to expect; **no contaba con que hiciera tan mal tiempo** I wasn't expecting the

weather to be so bad **(c)** (frml) (tener) to have; **cuenta con 10 años de experiencia** she has 10 years of experience
■ **contarse** *v pron* **(a)** (frml) (estar incluido): **me cuento entre sus partidarios** I count myself as one of their supporters; **su novela se cuenta entre las mejores** his novel is among the best **(b)** **¿qué te cuentas?** how's it going? (colloq)

contemplación *f* **1** (observación) contemplation **2 contemplaciones** *fpl* (miramientos): **tienes demasiadas contemplaciones con él** you're too soft on him; **lo echaron sin contemplaciones** they threw him out without ceremony

contemplar [A1] *vt* **(a)** ⟨paisaje/cuadro⟩ to gaze at, contemplate **(b)** ⟨posibilidad/idea⟩ to consider, contemplate

contemporáneo -nea *adj* contemporary; **ser** ~ **de algn** to be a contemporary OF sb, be contemporary WITH sb
■ *m,f* contemporary

contenedor *m* container; (para basuras) bin, container; (para escombros) Dumpster® (AmE), skip (BrE); ~ **de recogida de vidrio** bottle bank

contener [E27] *vt* **(a)** «recipiente/producto/libro» to contain **(b)** (parar, controlar) ⟨infección/epidemia⟩ to contain; ⟨tendencia⟩ to curb; ⟨respiración⟩ to hold; ⟨risa/lágrimas⟩ to contain (frml), to hold back; ⟨invasión/revuelta⟩ to contain
■ **contenerse** *v pron* (refl) to contain oneself; **no se pudo** ~ **más** he could contain himself no longer

contenido *m* (de recipiente, producto, mezcla) contents; (de libro, carta) content

contentar [A1] *vt* to please; **¡qué difícil de** ~ **eres!** you're so hard to please!
■ **contentarse** *v pron* ~**se con algo** to be satisfied WITH sth; **se contenta con muy poco** he's easy to please

contento -ta *adj* [ESTAR] **(a)** (feliz, alegre) happy; **se puso muy** ~ **al oír que venías** he was very happy to hear you were coming; ~ **con algo/algn** happy WITH sth/sb **(b)** (satisfecho) pleased; **estamos** ~**s con la nueva secretaria** we're pleased with the new secretary; **no** ~ **con que le prestara el coche ...** not content *o* satisfied with me lending him the car ...

conteo *m* (Andes, Ven) count

contestación *f* (respuesta) answer, reply

contestador -dora *adj* (CS fam) ▶ CONTESTÓN

contestador automático *m* answering machine

contestar [A1] *vt* ⟨pregunta/teléfono⟩ to answer; ⟨carta⟩ to answer, reply to; **me contestó que no** he said no
■ ~ *vi* **(a)** (a pregunta, al teléfono) to answer; (a carta, a invitación) to answer, reply; **no contesta nadie** (Telec) there's no answer **(b)** (insolentarse) to answer back

contestón -tona *adj* (fam): **es muy** ~ he's always answering back

contexto *m* context

contigo *pron pers* with you; **¿puedo ir** ~**?** can I go with you?; **en paz** ~ **misma** at peace with yourself; **ha sido muy amable** ~ she's been very kind to you

contiguo -gua *adj* adjoining

continental *adj* continental

continente *m* (Geog) continent

continuación *f* (a) (acción) continuation (b) (de calle) continuation (c) (de novela) sequel; (de serie) next para *o* episode (d) **a continuación** next, then; **a ~ de** after, following

continuamente *adv* (con frecuencia, repetidamente) continually, constantly; (sin interrupción) continuously

continuar [A18] *vt* to continue
■ ~ *vi* «*guerra/espectáculo/vida*» to continue; **si las cosas continúan así** if things go on *o* continue like this; ⊗ **continuará** to be continued; **la película continúa en cartelera** the movie is still showing; **~ CON algo** to continue WITH sth; **continuó diciendo que ...** she went on to say that ...

continuidad *f* continuity

continuo -nua *adj* (a) (sin interrupción) «*dolor*» constant; «*movimiento/sonido*» continuous, constant; «*lucha*» continual (b) (frecuente) «*llamadas/viajes*» continual, constant

contonearse [A1] *v pron* to swing one's hips

contorno *m* (a) (forma) outline (b) (de árbol, columna) girth; **medir el ~ de cintura** to take the waist measurement (c) (de ciudad) surrounding area

contorsión *f* contortion; **hacer contorsiones** to contort one's body

contorsionista *mf* contortionist

contra *prep* against; **lo puso ~ la pared** he put it against the wall; **nos estrellamos ~ un árbol** we crashed into a tree; **dos ~ uno** two against one; **yo estoy en ~** I'm against it; **40 votos en ~** 40 votes against; **en ~ de** (opuesto a) against; (contrariamente a) contrary to
■ *f* (a) (esp AmL fam) (dificultad) snag; **llevarle la ~ a algn** to contradict sb (b) (Col) (antídoto) antidote (c) (Pol, Hist) (grupo): **la ~ the Contras** (*pl*)
■ *mf* (individuo) Contra rebel
■ *m* ▶ PRO

contraatacar [A2] *vi* to counterattack

contraataque *m* counterattack

contrabajo *m* (instrumento) double bass; (cantante) basso profundo
■ *mf* double-bass player

contrabandista *mf* smuggler

contrabando *m* (a) (actividad) smuggling; **~ de armas** gunrunning; **pasaba relojes de ~** he smuggled watches (b) (mercancías) smuggled goods (*pl*), contraband

contracción *f* contraction

contracorriente *f* crosscurrent; **ir a ~** «*barco*» to go against the current; «*nadador*» to swim against the current; «*diseñador/escritor*» to go *o* swim against the tide

contradecir [I24] *vt* «*persona/argumento*» to contradict
■ **contradecirse** *v pron* (a) «*persona*» to contradict oneself (b) (recípr) «*afirmaciones/órdenes*» to contradict each other, be contradictory; **~se CON algo** to conflict WITH sth, contradict sth

contradicción *f* contradiction; **eso está en ~ con lo que predica** that is a contradiction of what he advocates

contradictorio -ria *adj* contradictory

contraer [E23] *vt* ① (fml) (a) «*enfermedad*» to contract (fml), to catch (b) «*obligación/deudas*» to contract (fml); «*compromiso*» to make; **~ matrimonio con algn** to marry sb ② (a) «*músculo*» to contract, tighten; «*facciones/cara*» to contort (b) «*metal/material*» to cause ... to contract
■ **contraerse** *v pron* to contract

contrafuerte *m* (Arquit) buttress

contraincendios *adj inv* fire-prevention (before n)

contraindicado -da *adj* «*remedio/preparado*» contraindicated (tech)

contralto *m,f* (*f*) (en coro) alto; (solista) contralto; (*m*) countertenor

contraluz *m or f* back light; **a ~** against the light

contramano: **el coche venía a ~** (en calle de dirección única) the car was coming the wrong way down the street; (por el lado contrario) the car was on the wrong side of the road

contraofensiva *f* counteroffensive

contraparte *f* (Andes) opposing party

contrapartida *f* (a) (compensación) compensation; (contraste) contrast; **como ~** in contrast (b) (Com) balancing entry

contrapelo: **cepillar a ~** «*tela*» to brush ... against the nap; «*pelo*» to brush ... the wrong way

contrapesar [A1] *vt* to counterbalance

contrapeso *m* (del ascensor) counterweight; (de equilibrista) balancing pole; **siéntate al otro lado para hacer ~** sit on the other side to balance it

contraportada *f* (de libro, revista) back cover; (de periódico) back page

contraposición *f* comparison; **en ~ a** *or* **con algo** in comparison to *o* with sth

contraproducente *adj* counterproductive

contrapunto *m* counterpoint

contrariado -da *adj* (disgustado) upset; (enojado) annoyed

contrariar [A17] *vt* (disgustar) to upset; (enojar) to annoy

contrariedad *f* (a) (dificultad, problema) setback, hitch; **nos surgió una ~** something came up; **¡qué ~!** how annoying! (b) (disgusto) annoyance, vexation (fml)

contrario -ria *adj* ① (opuesto) «*opiniones/intereses*» conflicting; «*dirección/lado*» opposite; «*equipo*» opposing; «*bando*» opposite; **yo pienso lo ~** I think the opposite; **mientras no se demuestre lo ~** until proven otherwise; **sería ~ a mis intereses** it would be against *o* (fml) contrary to my interests; ▶ SENTIDO² 4
② (en locs) **al contrario** on the contrary; **al ~ de su hermano ...** unlike his brother, ...; **de lo contrario** or else, otherwise; **por el contrario** on the contrary; **en el sur, por el ~, el clima es seco** the south, on the other hand, has a dry climate; **todo lo contrario** quite the opposite; **llevarle la contraria a algn** to contradict sb
■ *m,f* opponent

contrarreloj *adj* «*carrera/etapa*» timed; **a ~** against the clock

contrarrestar [A1] *vt* to counteract

contrasentido *m* contradiction in terms

contraseña f (Mil) watchword, password; (Teatr, Cin) stub; (Inf) password

contrastar [A1] *vi* ~ CON algo to contrast WITH sth
■ ~ *vt* ~ algo CON algo to contrast sth WITH sth

contraste m contrast; hacer ~ con algo to contrast with sth; en ~ con algo in contrast to sth

contrata f contract

contratar [A1] *vt* (a) ⟨empleado/obrero⟩ to hire, take on; ⟨artista/deportista⟩ to sign up; ⟨servicios⟩ to contract (b) (Const) ⟨ejecución de una obra⟩ to put ... out to contract

contratiempo m (problema) setback, hitch; (accidente) mishap; sufrir or tener un ~ to have a setback/a mishap

contratista mf contractor

contrato m contract; ~ de alquiler rental agreement; ~ de compraventa/de trabajo contract of sale and purchase/of employment

contravenir [I31] *vt* to contravene

contraventana f shutter

contravía (Col): ir en ~ to drive the wrong way down the road; un carro que venía en ~ an oncoming car

contribución f (colaboración, donación) contribution; (Fisco) tax

contribuir [I20] *vi* (a) (en general) to contribute; contribuyó con 10 euros he contributed 10 euros; ~ A algo to contribute TO sth (b) (Fisco) to pay taxes

contribuyente mf taxpayer

contrincante mf opponent

control m ⟨1⟩ (en general) control; bajo ~ under control; sin ~ out of control; perdí el ~ I lost control (of myself); hacerse con el ~ de algo to gain control of sth; lleva el ~ de los gastos she keeps a check on the money that is spent; ~ de (la) natalidad birth control; ~ de calidad quality control o check; ~ de pasaportes passport control; ~ remoto remote control ⟨2⟩ (en carretera, rally) checkpoint ⟨3⟩ (a) (Educ) test (b) (Med) check-up; ~ antidoping dope test, drug test

controlador -dora m,f controller; ~ aéreo or de vuelo air traffic controller

controlar [A1] *vt* ⟨1⟩ ⟨nervios/impulsos/persona⟩ to control; ⟨incendio⟩ to bring ... under control; controlamos la situación we are in control of the situation; pasaron a ~ la empresa they took control of the company ⟨2⟩ ⟨inflación/proceso⟩ to monitor; ⟨persona⟩ to keep a check on; ~ el peso/la línea to watch one's weight/one's waistline; controlé el tiempo que me llevó I timed how long it took me ⟨3⟩ (regular) ⟨presión/inflación⟩ to control
■ **controlarse** *v pron* (dominarse) to control oneself; (vigilar) ⟨peso/colesterol⟩ to check, monitor

controversia f controversy

controversial adj (Ven) ▶ CONTROVERTIDO

controvertido -da adj [SER] ⟨persona/tema⟩ controversial

contundente adj (a) ⟨objeto/instrumento⟩ blunt; ⟨golpe⟩ severe, heavy (b) ⟨argumento/respuesta⟩ forceful; ⟨prueba⟩ convincing; ⟨fracaso/victoria⟩ resounding (before n); fue ~ en sus declaraciones he was categorical in his statements

conurbano m (Arg): el ~ the suburbs (pl)

convalecencia f convalescence

convaleciente adj convalescent

convalidar [A1] *vt* ⟨estudios/título⟩ to validate, recognize

convencer [E2] *vt* (a) (de hecho, idea) to convince; no se dejó ~ she wouldn't be convinced; la convencí de que estaba equivocada I convinced her that she was wrong (b) (para hacer algo) to persuade; no pude ~lo de que or para que me prestara dinero I couldn't persuade him to lend me any money (c) (en frases negativas) (satisfacer): no me convence del todo la idea I'm not absolutely sure about the idea; su explicación no convenció a nadie his explanation wasn't at all convincing
■ **convencerse** *v pron* to be convinced; ¿te convenciste? are you convinced?; ~se DE algo to accept sth; ¿te convences de que tenía razón? do you believe o accept I was right?

convención f convention

convencional adj conventional

convenenciero -ra m,f (Méx fam) user (colloq)

convenible adj ⟨solución⟩ suitable; ⟨precio⟩ reasonable

conveniencia f (a) (interés, provecho): solo piensa en su propia ~ he only thinks of his own interests; lo hizo por ~ she only did it because it was in her own interest; se casó por ~ it was a marriage of convenience (b) (comodidad) convenience (c) (de proyecto, acción) advisability

conveniente adj (a) (cómodo) convenient (b) (aconsejable, provechoso) advisable; sería ~ que guardaras cama it would be advisable for you to stay in bed

convenio m agreement

convenir [I31] *vi* ⟨1⟩ (a) (ser aconsejable): no conviene que nos vean juntos we'd better not be seen together; convendría que descansaras it would be a good idea if you rest; no te conviene venderlo it's not worth your while selling it; no le conviene que eso se sepa it's not in his interest for anybody to know that (b) (venir bien): el jueves no me conviene Thursday's no good for me; te convendría tomarte unas vacaciones it would do you good to take a vacation ⟨2⟩ (acordar) ~ EN algo ⟨en fecha/precio⟩ to agree (on) sth
■ ~ *vt* ⟨precio/fecha⟩ to agree (on); a la hora convenida at the agreed o (frml) appointed time

conventillo m (CS) tenement; esta oficina es un ~ (fam) this office is a hotbed of gossip

convento m convent

convergente adj convergent

conversación f (a) (charla) conversation;

trabar ∼ con algn to strike up a conversation with sb; **no tiene** ∼ she has no conversation **(b) conversaciones** *fpl* (negociaciones) talks (*pl*)

conversador -dora *adj* chatty
■ *m,f* conversationalist

conversar [A1] *vi* **(a)** (hablar) to talk **(b)** (esp AmL) (charlar) to chat, gab (AmE colloq); **conversé largo rato con ella** I had a long talk *o* chat with her

conversión *f* conversion

convertible *m* (AmL) convertible

convertir [I11] *vt* **1** **(a)** (transformar) ∼ algo/a algn EN algo to turn sth/sb INTO sth **(b)** (a una religión) to convert; ∼ **a algn** A algo to convert sb TO sth **(c)** ⟨*medida/peso*⟩ ∼ **algo** A algo *or* (Esp) EN algo to convert sth INTO sth **2** (period) (Dep) to score
■ **convertirse** *v pron* **(a)** (transformarse) ∼se EN algo to turn INTO sth **(b)** (a una religión) to convert, be converted; ∼se A algo to convert TO sth

convicción *f* **(a)** (convencimiento) conviction; **tengo la** ∼ **de que lo sabe** I'm certain *o* convinced he knows it **(b)** (persuasión) persuasion; **poder de** ∼ powers of persuasion **(c) convicciones** *fpl* (ideas, creencias) convictions (*pl*)

convicto -ta *m,f* prisoner, convict

convidado -da *m,f* guest

convidar [A1] *vt* **(a)** (invitar) to invite; ∼ **a algn** A algo ⟨a una boda/fiesta⟩ to invite sb TO sth; **nos** ∼**on a unas copas** they invited us for a few drinks; ∼ **a algn a cenar** to invite sb to *o* for dinner **(b)** (AmL) (ofrecer) to offer; ∼ **a algn** CON algo *or* (Chi, Méx) ∼ **algo** A algn to offer sth TO sb, offer sb sth

convincente *adj* convincing

convivencia *f* (de etnias, sectas) coexistence; (de individuos): **la** ∼ **pone el amor a prueba** living together puts love to the test

convivir [I1] *vi* ⟨*personas*⟩ to live together; ⟨*ideologías/etnias*⟩ to coexist; ∼ CON algn to live WITH sb

convocar [A2] *vt* ⟨*huelga/elecciones*⟩ to call; ⟨*manifestación*⟩ to organize; ⟨*concurso/certamen*⟩ to announce; ⟨*reunión/asamblea*⟩ to call, convene (frml); ∼ **a algn** A algo to summon sb TO sth

convocatoria *f* **(a)** (llamamiento a huelga, elecciones) call; **la** ∼ **de huelga** the strike call **(b)** (anuncio — para una reunión) notification; (— de exámenes, concursos) official announcement **(c)** (Esp) (Educ) (período de exámenes): **la** ∼ **de junio** the June exams

convoy *m* (de barcos, camiones) convoy; (Ferr) (period) train

convulsión *f* (Med) convulsion

convulsionar [A1] *vt* to throw ... into confusion

conyugal *adj* (frml) marital, conjugal (frml); **problemas** ∼**es** marital problems

cónyuge *mf* (frml) spouse (frml); **los** ∼**s** the married couple

coñac, coñá *m* brandy, cognac

coñazo *m* **(a)** (Esp fam *o* vulg) (persona o cosa pesada) pain (in the neck) (colloq); **dar el** ∼ (fam) to be a pain (colloq) **(b)** (Col, Ven fam) (golpe) blow

coño *m* (vulg) (de la mujer) cunt (vulg), beaver (AmE sl), fanny (BrE sl)

cooperación *f* cooperation

cooperador -dora *adj* cooperative, helpful

cooperar [A1] *vi* to cooperate; ∼ CON algn to cooperate WITH sb; ∼ **en la lucha contra el cáncer** to work together in the fight against cancer

cooperativa *f* (asociación) cooperative; (tienda) company store

coordinación *f* coordination

coordinado -da *adj* coordinate

coordinador -dora *m,f* **(a)** (organizador) coordinator **(b) coordinadora** *f* coordinating committee

coordinar [A1] *vt* ⟨*movimientos/actividades/ropa*⟩ to coordinate; **no lograba** ∼ **las ideas** he couldn't speak/think coherently
■ ∼ *vi* ⟨*colores*⟩ to match, go together

copa *f* **1** **(a)** (para vino) glass (*with a stem*); (para postres) parfait dish; (para helado) sundae dish; ∼ **de champán/coñac** champagne/brandy glass; ∼ **de vino** wineglass **(b)** (contenido) drink; **vamos a tomar una(s)** ∼**(s)** let's go for a drink **2** (Dep) cup **3** **(a)** (de árbol) top, crown **(b)** (de un sostén) cup **(c)** (de sombrero) crown **4 copas** *fpl* (en naipes) *one of the suits in a Spanish pack of cards*

Copenhague *m* Copenhagen

copeo *m* (fam): **ir/estar de** ∼ to go/be out drinking; **fuimos de** ∼ **por los pubs del barrio** we went barhopping around the area (AmE), we went on a pub crawl around the area (BrE colloq)

copera *f* (AmS) hostess

coperacha *f* (Méx fam) (recaudación) kitty (colloq), collection; (contribución) contribution; **hacer una** ∼ to get up a collection (AmE colloq), to have a whip round (BrE colloq)

copetín *m* (RPl) aperitif

copia *f* copy; **saqué dos** ∼**s** I made two copies

copiadora *f* photocopier, copier

copiar [A1] *vt* to copy; **copió el artículo a máquina** he typed out a copy of the article; **le copia todo al hermano** he copies his brother in everything; **le copié la respuesta a Ana** I copied the answer from Ana
■ ∼ *vi* to copy

copihue *m* Chile-bells (*national flower of Chile*)

copiloto *mf* (Aviac) copilot; (Auto) co-driver

copión -piona *m,f* (fam) copycat (colloq)

copioso -sa *adj* ⟨*cosecha/comida*⟩ abundant, plentiful; ⟨*nevada/lluvia*⟩ heavy; ⟨*información/ejemplos*⟩ copious; ⟨*llamadas*⟩ numerous

copla *f* **(a)** (Lit) stanza **(b)** (Mús) popular folk song

copo *m* (de nieve) flake, snowflake; (de algodón) ball; ∼**s de avena** rolled oats (*pl*); ∼**s de maíz** cornflakes (*pl*)

coproducción *f* coproduction, joint production

copucha *f* (Chi fam) (rumor, chisme) rumor*; (curiosidad) nosiness (colloq)

copuchar [A1] *vi* (Chi fam) (conversar) to chat (colloq); (curiosear) to nose around (colloq)

cópula *f* **(a)** (Biol, Zool) copulation **(b)** (Ling) copula

copular [A1] *vi* to copulate

copulativo -va *adj* copulative

copyright /kopi'rraj(t)/ *m* (*pl* **-rights**) copyright

coqueta *f* **(a)** (chica que flirtea) flirt, coquette (liter); (presumida) vain girl/woman; **eres una ~** you are so vain **(b)** (mueble) dressing table

coquetear [A1] *vi* to flirt; **~ con** algn to flirt WITH sb

coqueto -ta *adj* **(a)** (en el arreglo personal): **es muy coqueta** she's very concerned about her appearance **(b)** (casa/dormitorio) cute, sweet **(c)** (sonrisa/mirada/mujer) flirtatious, coquettish (liter)

coraje *m* **(a)** (valor) courage **(b)** (fam) (desfachatez) nerve; **¡qué ~!** what a lot of nerve! (AmE), what a nerve! (BrE)

coral *adj* choral
■ *m* (Zool) coral; **color ~** coral (*before n*), coral-colored*
■ *f* (Mús) (coro) choir

Corán *m*: **el ~** the Koran

coraza *f* **(a)** (armadura) cuirasse **(b)** (de tortuga) shell

corazón *m* **1** **(a)** (en general) heart; **sufre del ~** she has heart trouble; **es un hombre de buen/ gran~** he's very kind-hearted/big-hearted; **no tener ~** to be heartless (colloq); **con todo mi ~** with all my heart; **de (todo) ~** sincerely; **le partió el ~** it broke her heart; **tener un ~ de oro/de piedra** to have a heart of gold/of stone **(b)** (apelativo cariñoso) (fam) sweetheart (colloq) **2** **(a)** (de manzana, pera) core; (de alcachofa) heart **(b)** (de ciudad, área) heart **3** (en naipes) **(a)** (carta) heart **(b) corazones** *mpl* (palo) hearts (*pl*)

corazonada *f* hunch; **tuve la ~ de que ibas a venir** I had a hunch o feeling you'd come

corbata *f* (Indum) tie, necktie (AmE); **hay que ir de ~** you have to wear a tie; **~ de lazo** *or* (AmL) **de moño** *or* (Chi) **de humita** bow tie

corbatín *m* bow tie

corchete *m* **(a)** (Impr) square bracket **(b)** (en costura) hook and eye **(c)** (Chi) (para sujetar papeles) staple

corchetear [A1] *vt* (Chi) to staple

corchetera *f* (Chi) stapler

corcho *m* cork; (para pescar, nadar) float

corcholata *f* (Méx) bottle top

corcovear [A1] *vi* to buck

cordel *m* **(a)** (fino) cord, string **(b)** (Chi) (cuerda) rope; **saltar al ~** to jump rope (AmE), to skip (BrE)

cordero *m* **(a)** (cría) lamb **(b)** (carne — de cordero) lamb; (— de oveja) mutton **(c)** (piel) lambskin **(d)** (fam) (persona dócil): **ser un corderito** to be as good as gold

corderoy *m* (AmS) corduroy

cordial *adj* (frml) (amistoso) cordial, friendly; (ambiente) congenial; **recibe un ~ saludo** (Corresp) (kindest) regards

cordialidad *f* (frml) cordiality

cordillera *f* (mountain) range; **la ~ de los Andes** the Andes

cordillerano -na *adj* (AmL) Andean, mountain (*before n*)

córdoba *m* cordoba (*Nicaraguan unit of currency*)

cordón *m* **1** **(a)** (cuerda) cord; **~ umbilical**

umbilical cord **(b)** (de zapatos) shoelace, lace **(c)** (Elec) cord **(d)** (de personas) cordon; **~ policial** police cordon **2** **(a)** (CS) (de cerros) chain **(b)** (RPl) (de la vereda) curb (AmE), kerb (BrE)

cordura *f* (Psic) sanity; (sensatez) good sense; **obrar con ~** to act sensibly

Corea *f* Korea

coreano -na *adj/m,f* Korean

corear [A1] *vt* (consignas/insultos) to chant, chorus; (marcha/estrofa) to sing ... in unison

coreografía *f* choreography

coreógrafo -fa *m,f* choreographer

corista *f* (en revista musical) chorus girl

cornada *f* (golpe) thrust (*with the horns*); (herida) wound (*caused by a bull's horn*); **darle una ~ a** algn to gore sb

córnea *f* cornea

córner *m* (*pl* **-ners**) corner (kick); **lanzar un ~** to take a corner

corneta *f* **(a)** (Mús) (sin llaves) bugle; (con llaves) cornet **(b)** (Ven) (Auto) horn

cornetista *mf* (de corneta sin llaves) bugler; (de corneta con llaves) cornet player

cornisa *f* (Arquit) cornice

corno *m* (Mús) horn; **~ inglés** English horn (AmE), cor anglais (BrE)

cornudo -da *m,f* (fam) (*m*) deceived husband; (*f*) deceived wife

coro *m* **(a)** (conjunto vocal) choir; (en revista musical) chorus line; **a ~** (repetir) together, in unison; (cantar) in chorus, together **(b)** (composición) chorus **(c)** (Arquit) choir

corola *f* corolla

corona *f* **1** **(a)** (de soberano) crown **(b)** (institución): **la ~** the Crown **(c)** (de flores) crown, wreath; (para funerales) wreath **(d)** (Astron) corona **2** (moneda) crown **3** (Odont) crown

coronación *f* **(a)** (de soberano) coronation **(b)** (culminación) culmination

coronar [A1] *vt* **(a)** (soberano) to crown; **lo ~on rey** he was crowned king **(b)** (montaña/ cima) to reach the top of **(c)** (en damas) to crown

coronel -nela *m,f* (en el ejército) colonel; (en las fuerzas aéreas) ≈ Colonel (*in US*), ≈ Group Captain (*in UK*)

coronilla *f* crown (of the head); **estar hasta la ~ (de algo/algn)** (fam) to be fed up to the back teeth (with sth/sb) (colloq)

coronta *f* (Chi, Per) *tb* **~ de choclo** stripped corn cob

coroto *m* **(a)** (Col, Ven fam) (trasto) piece of junk (colloq); **recoge tus ~s** get your things o stuff together **(b)** (Ven) (poder político) (political) power

corpiño *m* (chaleco) bodice; (del vestido) bodice; (prenda interior) (RPl) brassière

corporación *f* (Com, Fin) corporation

corporal *adj* (trabajo) physical; (necesidades) bodily (*before n*); (castigo) corporal (*before n*)

corpulento -ta *adj* (persona/animal) hefty, burly; (árbol) solid, sturdy

corpus *m* (*pl* **~**) corpus

Corpus, Corpus Christi Corpus Christi

corral *m* **(a)** (en granja) yard, farmyard **(b)** (para ganado) corral **(c)** *tb* **corralito** (para niños) playpen

corralón *m* **(a)** (Méx) (de la policía) car pound

(b) (Per) (terreno baldío) piece of waste land (*sometimes with shanty dwellings*) **(c)** (Arg) (Const) lumberyard

correa *f* **(a)** (tira) strap; (cinturón) belt; (de perro) leash; ~ **de reloj** watchband (AmE), watchstrap (BrE) **(b)** (Mec) belt; ~ **del ventilador** fan belt

corrección *f* ⟨1⟩ **(a)** (buenos modales): **es un hombre de una gran** ~ he is very well-mannered *o* correct; **vestir con** ~ to dress correctly *o* properly **(b)** (honestidad) correctness **(c)** (propiedad): **habla el francés con** ~ he speaks French well *o* correctly ⟨2⟩ (de exámenes, errores) correction; ~ **de pruebas** proofreading

correccional *f or* (Esp) *m*: *tb* ~ **de menores** reformatory (AmE), detention centre (BrE)

correctamente *adv* **(a)** (sin errores) correctly **(b)** (con cortesía) politely **(c)** (honestamente) honorably

correcto -ta *adj* **(a)** (educado) correct, polite; (honesto) honest **(b)** ⟨respuesta/solución⟩ correct, right **(c)** ⟨funcionamiento/procedimiento⟩ correct

corrector¹ -tora *m,f* (de exámenes) marker; ~ **de pruebas** proofreader

corrector² *m*: ~ **ortográfico** (Inf) spell checker

corredor¹ -dora *m,f* ⟨1⟩ **(a)** (Dep) runner; (ciclista) cyclist; ~ **de coches** racing driver; ~ **de fondo** long-distance runner ⟨2⟩ **(a)** (agente) agent; ~ **de Bolsa** stockbroker; ~ **de bienes raíces** *or* (Esp) **de fincas** real estate broker (AmE), estate agent (BrE) **(b)** (RPl) (viajante) sales representative

corredor² *m* (Arquit, Geog, Pol) corridor

corregir [I8] *vt* (en general) to correct; ⟨modales⟩ to improve, mend; ⟨examen/prueba⟩ to correct; (puntuar) to grade (AmE), to mark (BrE)
■ **corregirse** *v pron* **(a)** (en el comportamiento) to change *o* mend one's ways **(b)** (*refl*) (al hablar) to correct oneself; **un defecto físico que se corrige solo** a defect which corrects itself

correlación *f* correlation

correntoso -sa *adj* (CS) fast-flowing

correo *m* **(a)** mail, post (BrE); **envíamelo por** ~ mail (AmE) *o* (BrE) post it to me; **echar una carta al** ~ to mail (AmE) *o* (BrE) post a letter; ~ **aéreo** air mail; ~ **certificado** *o* (Col, Ur) **recomendado** registered mail; ~ **electrónico** e-mail, electronic mail; ~ **urgente** special delivery; **de** ~**s** ⟨servicio/huelga⟩ postal (*before n*) **(b)** (tren) mail train **(c)** (oficina) *tb* **C**~**s** (Esp) post office **(d)** (mensajero) messenger

correoso -sa *adj* tough, leathery

correr [E1] *vi* ⟨1⟩ **(a)** (en general) to run; **bajó/subió las escaleras corriendo** she ran down/up the stairs; **salieron corriendo del banco** they ran out of the bank; **echó a** ~ he started to run **(b)** (Auto, Dep) ⟨piloto/conductor⟩ to race ⟨2⟩ **(a)** (apresurarse): **¡corre, ponte los zapatos!** hurry *o* quick, put your shoes on!; **no corras tanto que te equivocarás** don't do it so quickly, you'll only make mistakes ; **corrí a llamarte** I rushed to call you; **me tengo que ir corriendo** I have to rush off **(b)** (fam) ⟨vehículo⟩ to go fast; ⟨conductor⟩ to drive fast ⟨3⟩ **(a)** ⟨carretera/río⟩ to run; ⟨agua⟩ to run; ⟨sangre⟩ to flow; **corría una brisa suave** there was a gentle breeze **(b)** ⟨rumor⟩: **corre el rumor/la voz de que ...** there is a rumor going around that ...

⟨4⟩ (pasar, transcurrir): **corría el año 1973 cuando ...** it was 1973 when ...; **con el** ~ **de los años** as time went/goes by; **¡cómo corre el tiempo!** how time flies!
⟨5⟩ (hacerse cargo) ~ **CON** algo ⟨con gastos⟩ to pay sth; ⟨con organización⟩ to be responsible FOR sth
■ ~ *vt* ⟨1⟩ **(a)** (Dep) ⟨maratón⟩ to run **(b)** (Auto, Dep) ⟨prueba/gran premio⟩ to race in ⟨2⟩ (exponerse a): **corres el riesgo de perderlo** you run the risk of losing it; **aquí no corres peligro** you're safe here ⟨3⟩ **(a)** ⟨botón/ficha/silla⟩ to move; ⟨cortina⟩ (cerrar) to draw, close; (abrir) to open, pull back; **corre el cerrojo** bolt the door **(b)** (Inf) ⟨texto⟩ to scroll
■ **correrse** *v pron* ⟨1⟩ **(a)** ⟨silla/cama⟩ to move; ⟨pieza/carga⟩ to shift **(b)** (fam) ⟨persona⟩ to move up *o* over ⟨2⟩ **(a)** ⟨tinta⟩ to run; ⟨rímel/maquillaje⟩ to run, smudge; **se me corrió el rímel** my mascara ran **(b)** (AmL) ⟨media⟩ to ladder

correspondencia *f* **(a)** (relación por correo) correspondence; (cartas) mail, post (BrE); **mantener** ~ **con algn** to correspond with sb **(b)** (equivalencia) correspondence

corresponder [E1] *vi* ⟨1⟩ **(a)** (en un reparto): **le corresponde la mitad de la herencia** he's entitled to half the inheritance; **la parte que te corresponde** your part *o* share **(b)** (incumbir): **te corresponde a ti preparar el informe** it's your job to prepare the report; **el lugar que le corresponde** his rightful place **(c)** (en 3ª pers) (ser adecuado): **debe disculparse, como corresponde** he must apologize, as is right and proper (frml); **según corresponda** as appropriate ⟨2⟩ (encajar, cuadrar): **su aspecto corresponde a la descripción** his appearance fits *o* matches the description; **el texto no corresponde a la foto** the text doesn't belong with *o* match the photograph ⟨3⟩ ~ **A** algo ⟨a un favor⟩ to return sth; ⟨a amabilidad/generosidad⟩ to repay sth
■ ~ *vt* ⟨favor/atención⟩ to return; **un amor no correspondido** an unrequited love

correspondiente *adj* **(a)** (en general) corresponding (*before n*); **la etiqueta** ~ the corresponding label; **los números** ~**s a cada página** the numbers corresponding to each page **(b)** (propio) own; **viene con su** ~ **caja** it comes with its own box **(c)** (pertinente) relevant; **rellene el impreso** ~ complete the relevant form

corresponsal *mf* (Period, Rad, TV) correspondent; ~ **extranjero/de guerra** foreign/war correspondent

corretear [A1] *vi* (correr) to run around
■ ~ *vt* ⟨1⟩ (esp AmL) (perseguir) to chase, pursue ⟨2⟩ (RPl) (Com) to wholesale

corrida *f* ⟨1⟩ (Taur) bullfight ⟨2⟩ (Chi) (serie) series; (fila) row; (de bebidas) round

corrido *m*: Mexican folk song

corriente *adj* ⟨1⟩ (que se da con frecuencia) common; (normal, no extraño) usual, normal; **es un error muy** ~ it's a very common mistake; **lo** ~ **es pagar al contado** the normal thing is to pay cash; **un tipo normal y** ~ an ordinary guy; ~ **y moliente** (fam) ordinary, run-of-the-mill ⟨2⟩ **(a)** (en curso) ⟨mes/año⟩ current **(b)** **al corriente**: **estoy al** ~ **en los pagos** I'm up to date with the payments; **empezó con retraso pero se** ···▷

ha puesto al ∼ she started late but she has caught up; **mantener a algn al ∼ de algo** to keep sb informed about sth

■ *f* **(a)** (de agua) current; **∼s marinas** ocean currents; **dejarse llevar por la ∼** to go along with the crowd; **seguirle la ∼ a algn** to humor* sb **(b)** (de aire) draft (AmE), draught (BrE) **(c)** (Elec) current; **me dio (la) ∼** I got a shock *o* an electric shock; **se cortó la ∼** there was a power cut

corro *m* **(a)** (círculo) circle, ring; **hacer un ∼** to stand/sit in a circle; **se formó un ∼ a su alrededor** a circle of people formed around her **(b)** (Jueg): **jugar al ∼** to play a singing game standing in a ring

corroborar [A1] *vt* to corroborate

corroer [E13] *vt* ⟨metal⟩ to corrode; ⟨mármol⟩ to erode

corromper [E1] *vt* **(a)** ⟨persona/lengua/ sociedad⟩ to corrupt **(b)** ⟨materia orgánica⟩ to rot
■ **corromperse** *v pron* **(a)** «costumbres/ persona/lengua» to become corrupted **(b)** «materia orgánica» to rot

corrompido -da *adj* **(a)** ⟨persona/sociedad⟩ corrupt **(b)** ⟨materia orgánica⟩ rotten

corrosión *f* corrosion

corrosivo -va *adj* ⟨sustancia/acción⟩ corrosive

corrupción *f* **(a)** (de moral, persona, lengua) corruption; **∼ de menores** corruption of minors **(b)** (de materia) decay

corrupto -ta *adj* corrupt

corsé, corset /kor'se/ *m* (*pl* **-sets**) corset

cortacésped *m* lawnmower

cortada *f* **(a)** (Col, Méx) (herida) cut; **hacerse una ∼** to cut oneself **(b)** (RPl) (calle sin salida) no through road

cortado¹ -da *adj* **1** ⟨persona⟩ **(a)** [ESTAR] (Chi, Esp) (turbado, avergonzado) embarrassed **(b)** [ESTAR] (Esp, CS) (aturdido) stunned; **me quedé ∼ con su respuesta** I was stunned by her reply **(c)** [SER] (Esp) (tímido) shy **2** [ESTAR] **(a)** ⟨calle/carretera⟩ closed, closed off **(b)** ⟨película⟩ cut **3** **(a)** [ESTAR] ⟨mayonesa/salsa⟩ separated; **la leche está cortada** the milk is curdled *o* off **(b)** ⟨café⟩ with a dash of milk

cortado² *m* espresso with a dash of milk

cortante *adj* **(a)** ⟨instrumento/objeto⟩ sharp **(b)** ⟨viento⟩ biting **(c)** ⟨respuesta/tono⟩ sharp

cortaplumas *m or f* (*pl* ∼) penknife

cortar [A1] *vt* **1** (dividir) ⟨cuerda/pastel⟩ to cut, chop; ⟨asado⟩ to carve; ⟨leña/madera⟩ to chop; ⟨baraja⟩ to cut; **∼ algo por la mitad** to cut sth in half *o* in two; **∼ algo en rodajas/en cuadritos** to slice/dice sth; **∼ algo en trozos** to cut sth into pieces **2** (quitar, separar) ⟨rama/punta/pierna⟩ to cut off; ⟨árbol⟩ to cut down, chop down; ⟨flores⟩ (CS) to pick; **me cortó un trozo de melón** she cut me a piece of melon **3** (hacer más corto) ⟨pelo/uñas⟩ to cut; ⟨césped/ pasto⟩ to mow; ⟨seto⟩ to cut; ⟨rosal⟩ to cut back; ⟨texto⟩ to cut down

4 (en costura) ⟨falda/vestido⟩ to cut out **5** (interrumpir) **(a)** ⟨agua/gas/luz/teléfono⟩ to cut off; ⟨película/programa⟩ to interrupt **(b)** ⟨calle⟩ «policía/obreros» to close, block off; «manifestantes» to block; **me cortó el paso** he stood in my way **6** (censurar, editar) ⟨película⟩ to cut; ⟨escena/ diálogo⟩ to cut (out) **7** «frío»: **el frío me cortó los labios** my lips were chapped *o* cracked from the cold weather

■ **∼** *vi* **1** ⟨cuchillo/tijeras⟩ to cut **2** **(a)** (Cin): **¡corten!** cut! **(b)** (CS) (por teléfono) to hang up; **no me cortes** don't hang up on me **(c)** (en naipes) to cut

■ **cortarse** *v pron* **1** (interrumpirse) «proyección/ película» to stop; «llamada/gas» to get cut off; **se cortó la luz** there was a power cut; **se me cortó la respiración** I could hardly breathe **2** **(a)** (refl) (hacerse un corte) to cut oneself; ⟨brazo/cara⟩ to cut; **me corté un dedo** I cut my finger **(b)** (refl) ⟨uñas/pelo⟩ to cut; **se corta el pelo ella misma** she cuts her own hair **(c)** (caus) ⟨pelo⟩ to have ... cut; **tengo que ∼me el pelo** I have to have my hair cut **(d)** ⟨piel/labios⟩ to crack, become chapped **3** (cruzarse) «líneas/calles» to cross **4** «leche» to curdle; «mayonesa/salsa» to separate **5** (Chi, Esp) «persona» (turbarse, aturdirse) to get embarrassed

cortaúñas *m* (*pl* ∼) nail clippers (*pl*)

corte *m* **1** (en general) cut; **se hizo un ∼ en la cabeza** he cut his head; **∼ de pelo** haircut; **∼ a (la) navaja** razor cut; **un ∼ de luz** a power cut; **tuvimos varios ∼s de agua** the water was cut off several times; **∼ de digestión** stomach cramp; **∼ publicitario** (RPl) commercial break **2** **(a)** (de tela) length, length of material **(b)** (en costura) cut; **un traje de buen ∼** a well-made *o* well-cut suit; **∼ y confección** dressmaking **3** (Esp fam) (vergüenza) embarrassment; **me da ∼ ir sola** I'm embarrassed to go by myself; **¡qué ∼!** how embarrassing! **4** (RPl fam) (atención): **darle ∼ a algn** to take notice of sb

■ *f* **(a)** (del rey) court **(b)** (esp AmL) (Der) Court of Appeal; **C∼ Suprema (de Justicia)** (AmL) Supreme Court **(c)** **las Cortes** *fpl* (Pol) (en Esp) Parliament, the legislative assembly

cortejo *m* (de rey) retinue, entourage; (de ministro) entourage; **∼ fúnebre** funeral procession *o* (frml) cortege

cortés *adj* polite, courteous

cortesía *f* **(a)** (urbanidad, amabilidad) courtesy, politeness; **la trató con ∼** he was polite to her; **tuvo la ∼ de invitarnos** she was kind enough to invite us **(b)** de cortesía ⟨entrada⟩ complimentary; ⟨visita⟩ courtesy (*before n*)

corteza *f* (de árbol) bark; (del pan) crust; (del queso) rind; (de naranja, limón) peel, rind; **la ∼ terrestre** the earth's crust

cortijo *m* (en Esp) (finca) country estate; (casa) country house

cortina *f* curtain, drape (AmE); ~ **de ducha** shower curtain; ~ **de humo** smokescreen

cortisona *f* cortisone

corto¹ -ta *adj* 1 (a) (en longitud) ‹calle/río› short; **de manga corta** short-sleeved; **el vestido le quedó** ~ the dress is too short for her now; **iba vestida de** ~ she was wearing a short dress/skirt (b) (en duración) ‹película/curso/viaje› short; ‹visita/conversación› short, brief; *a la corta o a la larga* sooner or later 2 (escaso, insuficiente): **un niño de corta edad** a very young child; ~ **de vista** near-sighted, shortsighted (BrE); **andar** ~ **de tiempo** to be pressed for time 3 (fam) (poco inteligente) stupid; ~ **de entendederas** *or* **alcances** dim, dense (colloq)

corto² *m* (Cin) (a) (cortometraje) short (movie *o* film) (b) **cortos** *mpl* (Col, Méx, Ven) (de película) trailer

cortocircuito *m* short circuit; **hacer** ~ to short-circuit

cortometraje *m* short (movie *o* film)

cosa *f* 1 (en general) thing; **cualquier** ~ anything; **¿alguna otra** ~? anything else?; **pon cada** ~ **en su lugar** put everything in its place; **entre una(s)** ~(s) **y otra(s) ...** what with one thing and another ...; **¡qué** ~**s dices!** really, what a thing to say!; **dime una** ~ **...** tell me something ...; **tengo que contarte una** ~ there's something I have to tell you; **fue** ~ **fácil** it was easy; **se enfada por cualquier** ~ he gets angry over the slightest thing; **si por cualquier** ~ **no puedes venir** if you can't come for any reason; **por una** ~ **o por otra** for one reason or another; **esto no es** ~ **de risa/broma** this is no laughing matter/no joke
2 **cosas** *fpl* (pertenencias) things (*pl*); **mis** ~**s de deporte** my sports things 3 (situación, suceso): **así están las** ~**s** that's how things are *o* stand; **la** ~ **se pone fea** things are starting to get unpleasant; **¿cómo** (**te**) **van las** ~**s?** how are things?; **son** ~**s de la vida** that's life!; **¡qué** ~ **más extraña!** how strange *o* funny! 4 (a) (fam) (ocurrencia): **¡tienes cada** ~**!** the things you come up (AmE) *o* (BrE) out with!; **esto es** ~ **de tu padre** this is your father's doing *o* idea (b) (comportamiento típico): **son** ~**s de niños** children are like that; **son** ~**s de Ana** that's one of Ana's little ways 5 (asunto): **no es** ~ **tuya** it's none of your business; **no te preocupes, eso es** ~ **mía** don't worry, I'll handle it 6 (en locs) **cosa de** (AmS fam) so as to; ~ **de terminarlo** so as to finish it; **cosa que** (AmS fam) so that; ~ **que no me olvide** so that I don't forget; **no sea cosa que: llévate el paraguas, no sea** ~ **que llueva** take your umbrella just in case; **átalo, no sea** ~ **que se escape** tie it up so that it doesn't get away; *ser* ~ *de* **...** (fam): **es** ~ **de unos minutos** it'll (only) take a couple of minutes; **es** ~ **de intentarlo** you just have to give it a go

cosecha *f* (a) (acción, época) harvest; **un vino de la** ~ **del 70** a 1970 vintage wine (b) (producto) crop

cosechador -dora *m,f* (a) (persona) harvester (b) **cosechadora** *f* (máquina) combine (harvester)

cosechar [A1] *vt* (a) (recoger) ‹cereales› to

harvest; ‹legumbres› to pick (b) (Esp) (cultivar) ‹cereales/patatas› to grow (c) ‹aplausos/premios/honores› to win; ‹éxitos› to achieve
■ ~ *vi* to harvest

coser [E1] *vt* (a) ‹dobladillo› to sew; ‹botón› to sew on; ‹agujero› to sew (up); **cóselo a máquina** sew it on the machine (b) ‹herida› to stitch
■ ~ *vi* to sew

cosmético¹ -ca *adj* cosmetic (*before n*)

cosmético² *m* cosmetic

cósmico -ca *adj* cosmic

cosmopolita *adj/mf* cosmopolitan

cosmos *m* cosmos

cosquillas *fpl*: **hacerle** ~ **a algn** to tickle sb; **tener** ~ to be ticklish

costa *f* 1 (Geog) (del mar — área) coast; (— perfil) coastline; **una** ~ **muy accidentada** a very rugged coastline; **la** ~ **atlántica** the Atlantic coast 2 (en locs) **a costa de: lo terminó a** ~ **de muchos sacrificios** he had to make a lot of sacrifices to finish it; **a** ~ **mía/de los demás** at my/other people's expense; **a toda costa** at all costs 3 **costas** *fpl* (Der) costs (*pl*)

costado *m* side; **pasar de** ~ to go through sideways; **duerme de** ~ she sleeps on her side

costal *m* sack, bag

costanera *f* (CS) (de río) riverside path (*o* road *etc*); (del mar) promenade; (de lago) lakeside path (*o* road *etc*)

costar [A10] *vt* (a) (en dinero) to cost; **¿cuánto me** ~**á arreglarlo?** how much will it cost to fix it? (b) (en perjuicios): **el atentado que le costó la vida** the attack in which he lost his life; **le costó el puesto** it cost him his job (c) (en esfuerzo): **me costó mucho trabajo** it took me a lot of hard work; **cuesta abrirlo** it's hard to open; **me cuesta trabajo creerlo** I find it hard *o* difficult to believe
■ ~ *vi* (a) (en dinero) to cost; **el reloj me costó caro** the watch cost a lot (b) (resultar perjudicial): **esto te va a** ~ **caro** you're going to pay dearly for this (c) (resultar difícil): **cuesta un poco acostumbrarse** it's not easy to get used to; **no te cuesta nada intentarlo** it won't do you any harm to give it a try; **la física le cuesta** he finds physics difficult; **me costó dormirme** I had trouble getting to sleep

Costa Rica *f* Costa Rica

costarricense *adj/mf* Costa Rican

costarriqueño -ña *adj/m,f* Costa Rican

coste *m* (Esp) ▶ COSTO

costear [A1] *vt* (financiar) to finance
■ **costearse** *v pron* (refl) (financiarse): **yo me costeé el viaje** I paid for the trip myself

costeño -ña *adj* coastal
■ *m,f*: **los** ~**s** people from coastal regions

costero -ra *adj* ‹camino/pueblo› coastal

costilla *f* (a) (Anat) rib (b) (AmS) (chuleta — de vaca) T-bone steak; (— de cerdo, cordero) chop

costipado -da *adj/m* ▶ CONSTIPADO

costo *m* (Com, Econ, Fin) cost; **de bajo** ~ low-cost, budget; **precio de** ~ cost price; **al** ~ at cost price; ~ **de (la) vida** cost of living

costoso -sa *adj* (a) ‹casa/coche/joya› expensive (b) ‹error› costly (c) ‹trabajo/tarea› difficult

costra *f* (a) (de herida) scab (b) (de suciedad) layer, coating

costumbre f (a) (de individuo) habit; **tenía (la)** ~ **de madrugar** he was in the habit of getting up early; **agarró la** ~ **de …** she got into the habit of …; **hacer algo por** ~ to do sth out of habit; **a la hora de** ~ at the usual time; **como de** ~ as usual; **se quejó menos que de** ~ he complained less than he usually does **(b)** (de país, pueblo) custom

costura f (a) (acción) sewing **(b)** (puntadas) seam

costurera f seamstress

costurero m (caja, estuche) workbox; (canasta) sewing basket; ~ **de viaje** sewing kit

cotejar [A1] vt ‹documentos› to compare; ‹información/respuesta› to collate; ~ **algo CON algo** to check sth AGAINST sth

cotelé m (Chi) corduroy

cotidiano -na adj daily; ‹vida› everyday, daily

cotilla mf (Esp fam) gossip (colloq)

cotillear [A1] vi (Esp fam) to gossip

cotilleo m (Esp fam) gossip

cotización f (a) (de moneda) value; (de acciones, valores, producto) price; **su** ~ **llegó a 500 pesos** it reached 500 pesos **(b)** (Andes) (evaluación) valuation; (presupuesto) estimate

cotizado -da adj sought-after

cotizar [A4] vt (a) (Fin) ‹acciones› to quote; **las acciones se cotizan a 525 pesos** the shares are quoted at 525 pesos; **la libra se cotizó a 1,58 euros** the pound stood at 1.58 euros **(b)** (Andes) ‹cuadro/joyas› to value; ‹obra/reparación› to give an estimate for

coto m (Dep, Ecol) reserve; ~ **de caza/pesca** game/fishing preserve

cotorra f (a) (Zool) (loro) parrot **(b)** (fam) (persona) chatterbox (colloq)

cototo m (Chi fam) bump (on the head)

cottolengo /koto'leŋgo/ m (RPl) (para ancianos) old people's home; (para niños) children's home; (para drogadictos, desamparados, etc) shelter, refuge

cotufas fpl (Ven) (maíz tostado) popcorn

COU /kou/ m (en Esp) = **Curso de Orientación Universitaria**

courier /ku'rje(r)/ mf courier

coya mf: indian from the Andean region of Bolivia, Peru and the NW of Argentina

coyote m (Zool) coyote

coyuntura f (Anat) joint

coz f kick; **dar coces** to kick

crac m (pl **cracs**) (a) (sonido) crack, snap **(b)** (Fin) crash

crack m (pl **cracks**) (droga) crack

cráneo m skull, cranium (tech)

cráter m crater

crawl /krol/ m: tb **estilo** ~ crawl, front crawl

crayón m (Méx, RPl) wax crayon

creación f (a) (en general) creation **(b)** (Relig) **la C~** the Creation

creador -dora adj creative
■ m,f (a) (en general) creator; ~**es de moda** fashion designers **(b)** (Relig) **el C~** the Creator

crear [A1] vt to create; ‹producto› to develop; ‹institución/comisión/fondo› to set up; ‹fama/prestigio› to bring; ‹reputación› to earn; **crea**

muchos problemas it causes o creates a lot of problems; **no quiero** ~ **falsas expectativas** I don't want to raise false hopes
■ **crearse** v pron ‹problema› to create … for oneself; ‹enemigos› to make

creatividad f creativity

creativo -va adj creative

crecer [E3] vi 1 (a) ‹ser vivo/pelo/uñas› to grow; **dejarse** ~ **la barba** to grow a beard **(b)** (criarse) to grow up; **crecieron en un pueblo** they grew up in a village 2 (a) ‹río› to rise; ‹ciudad› to grow; ‹luna› to wax **(b)** ‹sentimiento/interés› to grow; ‹rumor› to spread **(c)** ‹economía› to grow; **el número de desempleados ha crecido** the number of unemployed has risen **(d)** (en importancia, sabiduría) ~ **EN algo** to grow in sth

creces: **pagar con** ~ **un error** to pay dearly for a mistake; **superar algo con** ~ ‹nivel/previsiones› to far exceed sth

crecida f (a) (subida de nivel): **el río experimentó una fuerte** ~ the river level rose sharply **(b)** (desbordamiento): **las** ~**s del Paraná** the flooding of the Paraná

creciente adj (a) ‹interés/necesidad› increasing **(b)** (Astron): **luna** ~ waxing moon

crecimiento m growth; **una industria en** ~ a growth industry; **durante el** ~ while they are growing

credibilidad f credibility

crédito m 1 (a) (en negocio) credit; **tengo** ~ **aquí** they let me have credit here; **a** ~ on credit **(b)** (cuenta) account **(c)** (préstamo) loan; ~ **hipotecario** mortgage loan 2 (credibilidad): **fuentes dignas de** ~ reliable sources; **no di** ~ **a sus palabras** I doubted his words (frml) 3 (Cin, TV, Educ) credit

credo m creed

crédulo -la adj credulous, gullible

creencia f belief

creer [E13] vi (a) (tener fe, aceptar como verdad) to believe; ~ **EN algo/algn** to believe IN sth/sb; **¿me crees?** do you believe me? **(b)** (pensar, juzgar) to think; **¿tú crees?** do you think so?; **no creo** I don't think so; **no creas, es bastante difícil** believe me, it's quite hard
■ ~ vt (a) (dar por cierto) to believe; **hay que verlo para** ~**lo** it has to be seen to be believed; **aunque no lo creas** believe it or not; **¡no lo puedo** ~**!** I don't believe it!; **¡ya lo creo!** of course! **(b)** (pensar, juzgar) to think; **creo que sí/creo que no** I think so/I don't think so; **creo que va a llover** I think it's going to rain; **no la creo capaz** I do not think she is capable; **se cree que el incendio fue provocado** the fire is thought to have been started deliberately; **no lo creí necesario** I didn't think it necessary; **no creo que pueda ir** I doubt if o I don't think I'll be able to go; **creí oír un ruido** I thought I heard a noise; **creo recordar que …** I seem to remember that …
■ **creerse** v pron (a) (enf) (con ingenuidad) to believe; **eso nadie se lo cree** no one believes that **(b)** (con arrogancia) to think; **se cree muy listo** he thinks he's really clever; **¿quién se** ~**á que es?** who does he think he is? **(c)** (CS fam) (estimarse superior) to think one is special (o great etc) **(d)** (Méx) (fiarse): ~**se DE algn** to trust sb

creído -da adj [SER] (engreído) conceited

crema f (a) (plato dulce) type of custard (b) (esp AmL) (de la leche) cream; ~ **batida** whipped cream; ~ **agria** or **ácida** (AmL) sour o soured cream; ~ **chantilly** or **chantillí** (AmL) whipped cream (with sugar, vanilla and egg white); ~ **doble/líquida** (AmL) double/single cream; ~ **pastelera** crème pâtissière, confectioner's custard (c) (sopa) cream (d) (en cosmética) cream; ~ **bronceadora** suntan lotion o cream; ~ **de afeitar** shaving cream; ~ **de calzado** (Esp) shoe cream; ~ **hidratante** moisturizer, moisturizing cream

■ adj inv cream; (de) **color** ~ cream, cream-colored

cremallera f (a) (Indum) zipper (AmE), zip (BrE) (b) (Mec, Tec) rack

cremar [A1] vt to cremate

crematorio m crematorium

cremoso -sa adj ⟨salsa⟩ creamy; ⟨queso⟩ soft, creamy

crep m (pl **creps**), (Méx) **crepa** f crepe

crepe /krep/ m or f (Coc) crepe

crepé m (Tex) crepe

crepería f creperie

crepúsculo m (del anochecer) twilight; (del amanecer) dawn light

crespo¹ -pa adj (rizado) (AmL) curly; (muy rizado) frizzy

crespo² m (AmL) curl

cresta f (a) (Zool) crest; (de gallo) comb (b) (de ola, monte) crest

cretino -na adj cretinous

■ m,f cretin

creyente adj: **es muy** ~ she has a strong faith

■ mf believer; **los no** ~**s** the nonbelievers

creyera, creyese, etc ▶ CREER

cría f (a) (crianza) rearing, raising; (para la reproducción) breeding (b) (Zool) (camada) litter; (nidada) brood (c) (animal): **una** ~ **de ciervo** a baby deer

criadero m farm; ~ **de pollos/de truchas** poultry/trout farm; ~ **de perros** kennel (AmE), kennels (BrE); ~ **de ostras** oyster bed

criado -da m,f (m) servant; (f) servant, maid

criador -dora m,f breeder

crianza f ① (Agr) raising, rearing; (para la reproducción) breeding ② (de niños) upbringing

criar [A17] vt ① ⟨niño⟩ (a) (cuidar, educar) to bring up, raise (b) (amamantar) to breast-feed; **criado con biberón** bottle-fed ② (a) ⟨ganado⟩ to raise, rear; (para la reproducción) to breed (b) ⟨pollos/pavos⟩ to breed

■ **criarse** v pron to grow up; **me crie en el campo** I grew up in the country; **me crie con mi abuela** I was brought up by my grandmother

criatura f (a) (niño — pequeño) child; (— recién nacido) baby (b) (cosa creada) creature

criba f (a) (instrumento) sieve (b) (proceso de selección): **la primera** ~ the first stage of the selection process; **hicimos una** ~ **de las solicitudes** we went through the applications

cribar [A1] vt to sieve, sift

cricket /'krike(t)/ m cricket

crimen m (delito grave) serious crime; (asesinato) murder; ~ **de guerra** war crime; ~ **pasional**

crime of passion; **es un** ~ **tirar esta comida** it's a crime to throw away this food; **¡qué** ~! it's wicked o criminal

criminal adj/mf criminal

criminalidad f (a) (cualidad) criminality (b) (número de crímenes) crime

criminalista adj criminal (before n)

■ mf criminal lawyer

crin f (a) (del caballo) tb ~**es** mane (b) (pelo de caballo) horsehair (c) (esparto) esparto grass

crío, cría (esp Esp fam) m,f kid (colloq)

criollo -lla adj (a) (Hist) Creole (b) (AmL) (por oposición a extranjero) Venezuelan (o Peruvian etc); ⟨plato/artesanía/cocina⟩ national

■ m,f (a) (Hist) Creole (of European descent born in a Spanish American colony) (b) (AmL) (nativo) Venezuelan (o Peruvian etc)

cripta f crypt

criquet m (Dep) cricket

crisantemo m chrysanthemum

crisis f (pl ~) (a) (en general) crisis; ~ **nerviosa** nervous breakdown (b) (period) (remodelación ministerial) tb ~ **de Gobierno** cabinet reshuffle

crismas m (pl ~) (Esp) Christmas card

crispar [A1] vt (a) (contraer): **con la expresión crispada por el dolor** his face tensed/contorted with pain (b) (exasperar) to infuriate; **me crispa los nervios** it really irritates me o gets on my nerves

■ **crisparse** v pron «rostro/expresión» to tense up; «persona» to get irritated

cristal m ① (a) (vidrio fino) crystal; ~ **de roca** rock crystal; ~ **tallado** or (AmL) **cortado** cut glass (b) (lente) lens ② (Esp) (vidrio) glass; (trozo) piece of glass; (de ventana) pane; **puerta de** ~ glass door; ~**es rotos** pieces of glass; **limpiar los** ~**s** to clean the windows; ~ **delantero** (Esp) windshield (AmE), windscreen (BrE); ~ **trasero** (Esp) rear windshield (AmE), rear windscreen (BrE)

cristalera f (Esp) (a) (mueble) display cabinet, dresser (b) (escaparate) shop window (c) (puertas) French windows (pl), French doors (pl) (AmE); (ventanas) windows (pl)

cristalería f (objetos) glassware; (juego) set of glasses

cristalero -ra m,f (Esp) (persona que instala) glazier

cristalino -na adj crystalline

cristalizar [A4] vi/vt to crystallize

cristiandad f Christendom

cristianismo m Christianity

cristianizar [A4] vt to Christianize

cristiano -na adj/m,f Christian; **¿eres** ~? are you a Christian?

Cristo Christ; **antes/después de** ~ before Christ o BC/AD

criterio m (a) (norma, principio) criterion; **tenemos que unificar** ~**s** we have to agree on our criteria (b) (capacidad para juzgar, discernir) discernment (fml); judgment*; **lo dejo a tu** ~ I leave that to your discretion o judgment; **no tiene** ~ he has no common sense (c) (opinión, juicio) opinion

crítica f (a) (ataque, censura) criticism; **fue objeto de numerosas** ~**s** she was the object of a lot of criticism (b) (reseña) review; (ensayo) critique; **la** ···⟶

película recibió muy buenas ∼s the movie had very good reviews; **la** ∼ **(los críticos)** the critics (*pl*); ∼ **literaria** literary criticism

criticar [A2] *vt* **(a)** (censurar) to criticize **(b)** (Art, Espec, Lit) ⟨*libro/película*⟩ to review
■ ∼ *vi* to gossip, backbite

crítico -ca *adj* critical
■ *m,f* critic

criticón -cona *adj* (fam & pey) critical, hypercritical
■ *m,f* (fam & pey) faultfinder

Croacia *f* Croatia

croar [A1] *vi* to croak

croata *adj* Croatian, Croat
■ *mf* Croat; **los** ∼**s** the Croats, Croatian people

crochet /kro't∫e/ *m* crochet; **hacer** ∼ to crochet

croissant /krwa'san/ *m* (*pl* **-ssants**) croissant

crol *m* (Dep) crawl

cromo *m* **(a)** (metal) chromium, chrome **(b)** (Esp) (estampa) picture card, sticker

cromosoma *m* chromosome

crónica *f* **(a)** (Period) report, article; (Rad, TV) report; ∼ **deportiva/de sociedad** sport(s)/society page (*o* section *etc*) **(b)** (Hist) chronicle

crónico -ca *adj* chronic

cronista *mf* **(a)** (esp AmL) (periodista) journalist, reporter; ∼ **de radio** radio broadcaster **(b)** (Hist) chronicler

cronología *f* chronology

cronológico -ca *adj* chronological

cronometrar [A1] *vt* to time

cronómetro *m* (Tec) chronometer; (Dep) stopwatch

croqueta *f* croquette

croquis *m* (*pl* ∼) sketch

cross /kros/ *m* **(a)** (deporte — en atletismo) cross-country running; (— en motociclismo) motocross **(b)** (carrera — a pie) cross country, cross-country race; (— en moto) motocross race

cruce *m* **1 (a)** (acción) crossing **(b)** (de calles) crossroads; ⊕ **cruce peligroso** dangerous junction; ∼ **peatonal** *or* **de peatones** pedestrian crossing **(c)** (Telec): **hay un** ∼ **en las líneas** there's a crossed line **2** (Agr, Biol) cross

cruceiro *m* (unidad monetaria) cruzeiro (*former Brazilian unit of currency*)

crucero *m* **(a)** (viaje) cruise; **hizo un** ∼ **por el Caribe** he went on a Caribbean cruise **(b)** (barco de guerra) cruiser **(c)** (Méx) (de carreteras) crossroads; (Ferr) grade crossing (AmE), level crossing (BrE)

crucial *adj* crucial

crucificar [A2] *vt* to crucify

crucifijo *m* crucifix

crucigrama *m* crossword, crossword puzzle

cruda *f* (AmC, Méx fam) hangover

crudeza *f* harshness; (del clima) severity, harshness

crudo -da *adj* **1** [ESTAR] ⟨*carne/verduras/pescado*⟩ (sin cocinar) raw; (poco hecho) underdone **2** [SER] **(a)** ⟨*invierno/clima*⟩ severe, harsh **(b)** ⟨*lenguaje/imágenes/realidad*⟩ harsh

cruel *adj* cruel; **ser** ∼ **con algn** to be cruel to sb

crueldad *f* cruelty; **eso es una** ∼ that's cruel; ∼ **mental** mental cruelty

crujido *m* **(a)** (de tablas, muelles, ramas) creaking **(b)** (de papel, hojas secas) rustling; (de seda) rustle **(c)** (de los nudillos, las rodillas) cracking **(d)** (de la grava, nieve) crunching **(e)** (de los dientes) grinding

crujiente *adj* ⟨*galletas/tostadas*⟩ crunchy; ⟨*pan*⟩ crusty

crujir [I1] *vi* **(a)** «*tabla/muelles/ramas*» to creak; «*hojas secas*» to rustle **(b)** «*nudillos/rodillas*» to crack **(c)** «*grava/nieve*» to crunch **(d)** «*galletas/tostadas*» to be crunchy **(e)** «*dientes*»: **le crujen los dientes** he grinds his teeth

crustáceo *m* crustacean

cruz *f* **1 (a)** (figura) cross; **ponte con los brazos en** ∼ stand with your arms stretched out to the sides; **la C**∼ (Relig) the Cross; ∼ **gamada** swastika; **la C**∼ **Roja** the Red Cross **(b)** (ornamento, condecoración) cross **2** (de moneda) reverse; **cara o** ∼ heads or tails

cruzada *f* crusade

cruzado -da *adj* **1 (a)** (atravesado): **había un árbol** ∼ **en la carretera** there was a tree lying across the road **(b)** ⟨*abrigo/chaqueta*⟩ double-breasted **2** ⟨*cheque*⟩ crossed; *ver tb* CRUZAR

cruzar [A4] *vt* **1** (atravesar) ⟨*calle/mar/puente*⟩ to cross
2 ⟨*piernas*⟩ to cross; ⟨*brazos*⟩ to cross, fold **3 (a)** ⟨*cheque*⟩ to cross **(b)** (tachar) to cross out **(c)** ⟨*palabras/saludos*⟩ to exchange **4** (llevar al otro lado) to take (*o* carry *etc*) ... across **5** ⟨*animales/plantas*⟩ to cross
■ ∼ *vi* (atravesar) to cross; ∼**on por el puente** they went across the bridge
■ **cruzarse** *v pron* **1** (*recípr*) **(a)** «*caminos/líneas*» to intersect, meet **(b)** (en viaje, camino): **nos cruzamos en el camino** we met *o* passed each other on the way; **nuestras cartas se han debido de** ∼ our letters must have crossed in the post; ∼**se CON algn** to see *o* pass sb
2 (interponerse): **se me cruzó una moto** a motorcycle pulled out in front of him; **se me cruzó otro corredor** another runner cut in front of me

cta. (= **cuenta**) a/c

cuaderno *m* (de ejercicios) exercise book; (de notas) notebook; ∼ **(de) borrador** rough notebook; ∼ **de espiral** *o* (Chi) **de anillos** spiral-bound notebook

cuadra *f* **(a)** (Equ) stable, stables (*pl*) **(b)** (AmL) (distancia entre dos esquinas) block

cuadrado¹ -da *adj* **1 (a)** (de forma) square **(b)** (Mat) ⟨*metro/centímetro*⟩ square (*before n*); **2 m²** ∼**s** (*read as: dos metros cuadrados*) m² (*léase:*

two square meters) **2** [ESTAR] (fam) (fornido)
well-built, big, hefty (colloq) **3** [SER] (AmL fam)
(cerrado de mente) inflexible

cuadrado² m square; **25 elevado al ∼ 25**
squared

cuadrar [A1] vi **(a)** «cuentas» to tally, balance
(b) «declaraciones/testimonios» to tally; ∼ **CON**
algo to fit in WITH sth, tally WITH sth **(c)** (Ven)
(para una cita) ∼ **CON algn** to arrange to meet sb;
∼ **PARA hacer algo** to arrange to do sth
■ **cuadrarse** v pron **(a)** «soldado» to stand to
attention **(b)** «caballo/toro» to stand stock-still
(c) (Col, Ven fam) (estacionarse) to park

cuadriculado -da adj «papel» squared; **mapa**
∼ grid map

cuadrilátero m **(a)** (Mat) quadrilateral **(b)**
(period) (de boxeo) ring

cuadrilla f **(a)** (Taur) cuadrilla (team of
matador's assistants) **(b)** (de obreros) team, gang;
(de soldados) squad; (de maleantes) gang

cuadro m **1** **(a)** (Art) (pintura) painting; (grabado,
reproducción) picture **(b)** (Teatr) scene **(c)** (gráfico)
table, chart **2** **(a)** (cuadrado) square, check; **tela a**
∼**s** checked material; **zanahorias cortadas en
cuadritos** diced carrots **(b)** (tablero) board, panel;
∼ **de mandos** or **instrumentos** (Auto) dashboard;
(Aviac) instrument panel **(c)** (de bicicleta) frame
3 (en organización): **los** ∼**s directivos del partido**
the top party officials; **los** ∼**s superiores de la
empresa** the company's senior management; ∼**s
de mando** (Mil) commanders (pl)

cuadrúpedo -da adj/m quadruped (before n)

cuádruple, cuádruplo m: **esta cifra es el** ∼
de la que esperábamos this figure is four times
what we expected

cuajada f junket, curd

cuajar [A1] vi **1** **(a)** «leche» to curdle; «flan/
yogur» to set **(b)** «nieve» to settle **2** **(a)**
«ideología» to be accepted; «plan/proyecto» to
come off; «moda» to catch on, take off **(b)**
«persona» to fit in
■ ∼ vt «leche» to curdle

cuajo m **1** (sustancia) rennet **2** (raíz): **arrancar
algo de** ∼ «planta» to pull sth out by the roots;
«vicio/corrupción» to root out (completely)

cual pron **1** **(a)** **el/la** ∼**/los/las** ∼**es** (hablando de
personas) (sujeto) who; (complemento) who, whom
(frml); (hablando de cosas) which; **mis vecinos, a los**
∼**es no conocía** my neighbors who I didn't know
o (frml) whom I did not know; **el motivo por el** ∼
lo hizo the reason why he did it; **según lo** ∼ ...
by which ...; **dos de los** ∼**es** two of whom/which
(b) lo ∼ which; **por lo** ∼ as a result, therefore;
con lo ∼ so **2** (en locs) **cada cual** everyone,
everybody; **sea cual sea** or **fuera** or **fuere**
whatever

cuál pron (uno en particular) which; (uno en general)
what; ¿∼ **quieres?** which (one) do you want?; ¿**y**
∼ **es el problema?** so, what's the problem?
■ adj (esp AmL): ¿**a** ∼ **colegio vas?** what o which
school do you go to?

cualidad f quality

cualificado -da adj (Esp) ▶ CALIFICADO

cualificar [A2] vt (Esp) ▶ CALIFICAR 2 B

cualquier adj: apocopated form of CUALQUIERA
used before nouns

cualquiera¹ (pl **cualesquiera** or (crit)

cualquiera) adj [see also note under CUALQUIER]
any; **en cualquier momento** (at) any time;
cualquier cosa/persona anything/anyone; **en
cualquier lado** anywhere; **de cualquier forma que
se haga** whichever way you do it; **lo voy a hacer
de** ∼ **forma** I'm going to do it anyway; **es un
mercenario** ∼ he's nothing but a mercenary
■ pron (refiriéndose — a dos personas o cosas) either
(of them); (— a más de dos personas) anybody,
anyone; (— a más de dos cosas) any one; ¿**cuál de
los dos? — cualquiera** which one? — either (of
them); **pregúntaselo a** ∼ ask anybody o anyone
(you like); ∼ **que elijas estará bien** whichever
(one) you choose o any one you choose will be
fine

cualquiera² mf: **un** ∼ a nobody; **una** ∼ a
floozy o (BrE) tart (colloq & pey)

cuando conj **(a)** (con valor temporal) when; **ven** ∼
quieras come when o whenever you like; ∼ **se
mejore** when she gets better; **ahora es** ∼ **me
viene mejor** now is the best time for me **(b)** (si)
if; **será verdad** ∼ **él lo dice** it must be true if he
says so **(c)** (en locs) **cada cuando** (esp AmL) every
so often; **de vez en cuando** from time to time,
every so often

cuándo adv when; ¿**de** ∼ **es esa foto?** when
was that photo taken?; ¿**desde** ∼ **lo sabes?** how
long have you known?; ¿**desde** ∼? since when?;
¡∼ no! (AmL) as usual!

cuantificar [A2] vt «valor/daños/pérdidas» to
quantify, assess

cuantioso -sa adj substantial

cuanto¹ adv **(a)** (tanto como) as much as; **grita**
∼ **quieras** shout as much as you like **(b)** (como
conj): ∼**s más/menos seamos, mejor** the more/
the fewer of us there are the better; ∼ **antes
empecemos, más pronto terminaremos** the sooner
we begin, the sooner we'll finish **(c)** (en locs)
cuanto antes as soon as possible; **en cuanto** (tan
pronto como) as soon as; **en cuanto a** (en lo que
concierne) as for, as regards

cuanto² -ta adj: **llévate** ∼**s discos quieras** take
as many records as you want o like; **unos** ∼**s
amigos** a few friends; **tiene** ∼ **libro hay sobre el
tema** she has every book there is on the subject
■ pron: **le di todo** ∼ **tenía** I gave her everything I
had; **fuimos solo unos** ∼**s** only a few of us went

cuánto¹ adv **(a)** (en preguntas) how much **(b)**
(uso indirecto): **si supieras** ∼ **la quiero/lo siento** if
you knew how much I love her/how sorry I am

cuánto² -ta adj **(a)** (en preguntas) (sing) how
much; (pl) how many; ¿∼ **café queda?** how
much coffee is there left?; ¿∼**s alumnos tienes?**
how many students do you have?; ¿∼**s años
tienes?** how old are you?; ¿∼ **tiempo tardarás?**
how long will you take? **(b)** (uso indirecto) (sing)
how much; (pl) how many; **no sé** ∼ **dinero/**∼**s
libros tengo** I don't know how much money/how
many books I have **(c)** (en exclamaciones): **¡**∼ **vino!**
what a lot of wine!; **¡**∼ **tiempo sin verte!** I haven't
seen you for ages! (colloq)
■ pron **1** (en preguntas) **(a)** (sing) how much; (pl)
how many; ¿∼ **pesas?** how much do you weigh?;
¿∼ **mides?** how tall are you?; ¿∼**s quieres?** how
many do you want? **(b)** (referido a tiempo): **¿a** ∼
estamos hoy? what's the date today? **(b)** (referido a tiempo) how long; ¿∼
falta para llegar? how long before we get there? ⋯⟡

(c) (referido a precios, dinero) how much; ¿~ **cuesta?** how much is it?; ¿~ **es?** how much is that (altogether)?

2 (uso indirecto): **pregúntale ~ va a demorar** ask her how long she'll be; **no sé ~ puede costar/~s tiene** I don't know how much it might cost/how many she has

3 (en exclamaciones): ¡~ **has tardado!** it's taken you a long time!

cuarenta *adj inv/pron/m* forty; *para ejemplos ver* CINCUENTA; **cantarle las ~ a algn** to give sb a piece of one's mind

cuarentena *f* (aislamiento) quarantine

cuarentón -tona *m,f* (fam) person in his/her forties

Cuaresma *f* Lent

cuarta *f* (Auto) fourth (gear); **mete la ~** put it in fourth

cuartel *m* **(a)** (Mil) barracks (*sing o pl*); ~ **de bomberos** (RPl) fire station, fire house (AmE); ~ **general** headquarters (*sing o pl*) **(b)** (tregua): **no dieron ~ a los rebeldes** they showed no mercy to the rebels; **una lucha sin ~** a merciless fight

cuartelada *f*, **cuartelazo** *m* putsch, military uprising

cuarteto *m* (Mús) quartet

cuarto¹ -ta *adj/pron* fourth; **la cuarta parte** a quarter; *para ejemplos ver* QUINTO

cuarto² *m* **1** (habitación) room; (dormitorio) room, bedroom; ~ **de baño** bathroom; ~ **de estar** living room, parlor (AmE), sitting room (BrE); ~ **de (los) huéspedes** guest room, spare room; ~ **trastero** lumber room, junk room

2 (a) (cuarta parte) quarter; **un ~ de kilo** a quarter (of a) kilo; **un ~ de pollo** a quarter chicken; ~ **creciente/menguante** first/last quarter; ~**s de final** quarterfinals (*pl*) **(b)** (en expresiones de tiempo) quarter; **un ~ de hora** a quarter of an hour; **la una y ~ (a)** quarter after (AmE) *o* (BrE) past one, one fifteen; **es un ~ para las dos** *or* (Esp, RPl) **son las dos menos ~** it is a quarter to two

cuarzo *m* quartz

cuate *mf* (Méx) **(a)** (mellizo) twin **(b)** (fam) (amigo) pal (colloq) **(c)** (fam) (tipo, tipa) (*m*) guy (colloq); (*f*) woman

cuatrapearse [A1] *v pron* (Méx) «*aparato*» to break; «*planes*» to fall through

cuatrero -ra *m,f* rustler

cuatrillizo -za *m,f* quadruplet, quad

cuatro *adj inv/pron* four; ¿**llueve?** — **no, solo son ~ gotas** is it raining? no, it's just a drop or two; **le escribí ~ líneas** I wrote him a couple of lines; *para más ejemplos ver tb* CINCO

■ *m* **(a)** (número) (number) four; *para ejemplos ver* CINCO **(b)** (Ven) (guitarra) four-stringed guitar

cuatrocientos -tas *adj/pron* four hundred; *para ejemplos ver* QUINIENTOS

cuba *f* **(a)** (barril) barrel, cask; **estar como una ~** (fam) to be plastered (colloq) **(b)** (tina) tub, vat

Cuba *f* Cuba

cubalibre *m* (de ron) rum and coke; (de ginebra) gin and coke

cubano -na *adj/m,f* Cuban

cubertería *f* cutlery; **una ~ de plata** a set of silver cutlery

cubeta *f* **(a)** (Fot, Quím) tray; (de paredes más altas) tank **(b)** (para hielo) ice tray **(c)** (barril) keg, small cask **(d)** (Méx) (balde) bucket

cúbico -ca *adj* cubic; **2m³** (*read as:* dos metros cúbicos) 2m³ (*léase: two cubic meters*)

cubierta *f* **1 (a)** (funda) cover; (de libro) cover, sleeve **(b)** (Auto) tire* **2** (Náut) (en barco) deck; **salir a ~** to go up on deck

cubierto¹ -ta *adj* ‹cielo› overcast, cloudy; *ver tb* CUBRIR

cubierto² *m* **1 (a)** (pieza) piece of cutlery; **los ~s de plata** the silver cutlery **(b)** (servicio de mesa) place setting; **pon otro ~** can you set another place? **2** (*en locs*) **a cubierto: ponerse a ~ de la lluvia** to take cover *o* to shelter from the rain

cubilete *m* **(a)** (vaso) beaker; (para dados) shaker, cup **(b)** (Col) (sombrero) top hat

cubitera *f* (bandeja) ice tray; (cubo) ice bucket

cubo *m* **1** (Esp) bucket; ~ **de (la) basura** (de la cocina) garbage can (AmE), (kitchen) bin (BrE); (de edificio) garbage can (AmE), rubbish bin (BrE) **2 (a)** (cuerpo geométrico) cube; **cubito de hielo** ice cube; **cubito de caldo** stock cube **(b)** (Mat) cube; **elevar un número al ~** to cube a number

cubrecama *m* bedspread

cubrir [I33] *vt* **(a)** (en general) to cover; ~ **algo DE algo** to cover sth WITH sth; **cubrí al niño con una manta** I covered the child with a blanket **(b)** ‹demanda/necesidad› to meet **(c)** ‹plaza/vacante› to fill

■ **cubrirse** *v pron* **1 (a)** (refl) (taparse) to cover oneself; ‹cara› to cover **(b)** (ponerse el sombrero) to put one's hat on **(c)** (protegerse) to take cover **(d)** (contra riesgo) to cover oneself **2** (llenarse): **las calles se habían cubierto de nieve** the streets were covered with snow

cucaracha *f* (Zool) cockroach

cuchara *f* spoon; ~ **de postre** dessertspoon; ~ **sopera** *or* **de sopa** soup spoon

cucharada *f* spoonful; ~ **sopera** ≈tablespoonful

cucharadita *f* teaspoon, teaspoonful

cucharilla, cucharita *f* (Coc) teaspoon

cucharón *m* ladle

cucheta *f* (RPl) trundle bed, truckle bed

cuchichear [A1] *vi* (fam) to whisper

cuchilla *f* **(a)** (de segadora, batidora, cuchillo) blade; (de arado) coulter, share **(b)** *tb* ~ **de afeitar** (hoja) razor blade; (maquinilla) razor

cuchillada *f*, **cuchillazo** *m* **(a)** (golpe) stab; **le dio una ~** she stabbed him **(b)** (herida) stab wound

cuchillo *m* knife; ~ **de cocina** kitchen knife

cuchitril *m* hole (colloq), hovel

cucho -cha *m,f* **1** (Col fam) **(a)** (padre) dad (colloq); (madre) mom (AmE colloq), mum (BrE colloq) **(b)** (profesor) teacher **(c)** (viejecito) (*m*) old guy (colloq); (*f*) old girl (colloq) **2** (Chi fam) (gato) puss (colloq)

cuclillas *fpl*: **en ~** squatting, crouching; **ponerse en ~** to squat

cuco *m* **1** (Zool) cuckoo **2** (Esp) (de bebé) Moses basket **3** (CS, Per leng infantil) bogeyman

cucú *m* cuckoo

cucurucho *m* **(a)** (de papel, cartón) cone; (de barquillo) cone **(b)** (helado) cone, cornet (BrE) **(c)** (capirote) hood, pointed hat

cuece, cuecen, etc ▸ COCER

cuello *m* **(a)** (Anat) neck; **le cortaron el** ~ they slit *o* cut his throat **(b)** (de botella) neck; ~ **de botella** (Auto) bottleneck **(c)** (de prenda de vestir) collar; **sin** ~ collarless **(d)** (escote) neck; ~ **alto** *or* **vuelto** *or* (AmL) **tortuga** turtleneck (AmE), polo neck (BrE); ~ **de pico** V neck; ~ **redondo** round neck

cuenca *f* **(a)** (Geog, Geol) basin **(b)** (del ojo) socket

cuenco *m* (recipiente) bowl

cuenta *f*

■ **Nota** Cuando la frase *darse cuenta* va seguida de una oración subordinada introducida por *de que*, en el español latinoamericano existe cierta tendencia a omitir la preposición *de* en el lenguaje coloquial: *se dio cuenta que no iba a convencerla* = he realized (that) he wasn't going to convince her

1 (a) (operación, cálculo) calculation, sum; **hacer una** ~ to do a calculation *o* sum; **saca la** ~ add it up, work it out; **hacer** *or* **sacar** ~**s** to do some calculations; **a fin de** ~**s** after all **(b) cuentas** *fpl* (contabilidad) accounts: **yo llevo las** ~**s del negocio** I do the accounts for the business, I handle the money side of the business (colloq); **ella se ocupa de las** ~**s de la casa** she pays all the bills and looks after the money **(c)** (cómputo) count; **llevar/perder la** ~ to keep/lose count; ~ **atrás** countdown; **más de la** ~ too much

2 (a) (factura) bill; **¿nos trae la** ~**, por favor?** could we have the check (AmE) *o* (BrE) bill, please?; **la** ~ **del gas** the gas bill; **a cuenta** on account; **entregó $2.000 a** ~ she gave me/him/them $2,000 on account; **este dinero es a** ~ **de lo que te debo** this money is to go toward(s) what I owe you **(b)** (Com, Fin) (en banco, comercio) account; **abrir/cerrar/liquidar una** ~ to open/close/to settle an account; ~ **corriente/de ahorro(s)** current/savings account

3 cuentas *fpl* (explicaciones): **no tengo por qué darte** ~**s** I don't have to explain *o* justify myself to you; **dar** *or* **rendir** ~**s de algo** to account for sth; **en resumidas** ~**s** in short

4 (cargo, responsabilidad): **los gastos corren por** ~ **de la empresa** the expenses are covered *o* paid by the company; **se instaló por su** ~ she set up (in business) on her own; **trabaja por** ~ **propia** she's self-employed

5 darse ~ **(de algo)** (comprender) to realize (sth); (notar) to notice (sth); **se da** ~ **de todo** she's aware of everything that's going on (around her); **date** ~ **de que es imposible** you must realize (that) it's impossible; **tener algo en** ~ to bear sth in mind; **ten en** ~ **que es joven** bear in mind that he's young; **sin tener en** ~ **los gastos** without taking the expenses into account; **tomar algo en** ~ to take sth into consideration

6 (de collar, rosario) bead

cuenta, cuentas, etc ▸ CONTAR

cuentagotas *m* (*pl* ~) dropper

cuentakilómetros *m* (*pl* ~) (de distancia recorrida) odometer (AmE), mileometer (BrE); (de velocidad) speedometer

cuentero -ra *adj* (Méx, RPl fam) **(a)** (mentiroso): **ser** ~ to be a fibber (colloq) **(b)** (chismoso) gossipy

cuentista *adj* **(a)** (fam) (exagerado): **no seas** ~**, que no duele tanto** don't exaggerate, it doesn't hurt that much **(b)** (fantasioso): **ser** ~ to be a fibber (colloq)

■ *mf* **(a)** (Lit) short-story writer **(b)** (fam) (exagerado): **no te fíes de ese** ~**, es puro teatro** don't fall for his playacting, he's just putting it on **(c)** (fantasioso) fibber (colloq)

cuento *m* **(a)** (narración corta) short story; (para niños) story, tale; **cuéntame un** ~ tell me a story; ~ **de hadas** fairy story, fairy tale; **venir a** ~: **eso no viene a** ~ that doesn't come into it; **sin venir a** ~ for no reason at all **(b)** (chiste) joke, story **(c)** (fam) (mentira, excusa) story (colloq); **no me vengas con** ~**s** I'm not interested in your excuses *o* stories **(d)** (fam) (exageración): **todo ese llanto es puro** ~ all that crying is just put on; **eso es un** ~ **chino** what a load of baloney; **el** ~ **del tío** a con trick

cuento ▸ CONTAR

cuerda *f* **1 (a)** (gruesa) rope; (delgada) string; ~ **floja** (Espec) tightrope **(b)** (Jueg) jump rope (AmE), skipping rope (BrE); **saltar a la** ~ to jump rope (AmE), to skip (BrE) **(c)** (para tender ropa) washing line, clothes line **(d)** (de arco) bowstring **2** (Mús) **(a)** (de guitarra, violín) string **(b) cuerdas** *fpl* (instrumentos) strings (*pl*); ~**s vocales** vocal chords (*pl*) **3** (de reloj, juguete): **un juguete de** ~ a clockwork toy; **le dio** ~ **al despertador** she wound up the alarm clock

cuerdo -da *adj* [ESTAR] sane; **no está** ~ he is insane

cuerno *m* **(a)** (de toro) horn; (de caracol) feeler; (de ciervo) antler; **irse al** ~ (fam) «*plan*» to fall through; «*fiesta*» to be ruined *o* spoiled; **ponerle los** ~**s a algn** (fam) to be unfaithful to sb **(b)** (Mús) horn

cuero *adj* (Méx fam) gorgeous (colloq)

■ *m* (piel) leather; (sin curtir) skin, hide; **chaqueta de** ~ leather jacket; ~ **de chancho** (AmL) pigskin; ~ **de vaca** cowhide; **en** ~**s** (*vivos*) (fam) (desnudo) stark naked (colloq); **ser un** ~ (Chi, Méx fam) «*mujer*» she's a real stunner (colloq); «*hombre*» he's a real hunk (colloq)

cuerpo *m* **1 (a)** (Anat) body; **el** ~ **humano** the human body; **retrato/espejo de** ~ **entero** full-length portrait/mirror; ~ **a** ~ hand-to-hand **(b)** (cadáver) body, corpse **(c)** (Fís) (objeto) body, object **2** (conjunto de personas, de ideas, normas) body; ~ **de bomberos** fire department (AmE), fire brigade (BrE); ~ **de policía** police force; ~ **diplomático** diplomatic corps **3** (consistencia, densidad) body; **de mucho** ~ ‹*tela*› heavy; ‹*vino*› full-bodied

cuervo *m* raven; (como nombre genérico) crow

cuesco *m* (Bot) stone

cuesta *f* **(a)** (pendiente) slope; **una** ~ **muy pronunciada** a very steep slope **ir** ~ **arriba** to go uphill; **iba corriendo** ~ **abajo** I was running downhill **(b) a cuestas: llevar algo a** ~**s** to carry sth on one's shoulders/back; **echarse algo a** ~**s** ‹*carga/bulto*› to put sth on one's back; ‹*problema*› to burden oneself with sth

cuesta, cuestan, etc ▸ COSTAR

cuestión *f* **(a)** (tema, problema) question, matter; **cuestiones de derecho internacional** matters *o* ⋯⊹

questions of international law; **llegar al fondo de la** ∼ to get to the heart of the matter **(b)** (*en locs*) **en cuestión** in question; **en cuestión de** in a matter of; **la cuestión es …** the thing is …; **la** ∼ **es divertirnos** the main thing is to enjoy ourselves; **ser cuestión de** to be a matter of; **todo es** ∼ **de …** it's just a question of …

cuestionar [A1] *vt* to question

cuestionario *m* (*encuesta*) questionnaire; (*Educ*) question paper, questions (*pl*)

cuete *m* ⓵ (Méx, RPI *fam*) (*borrachera*): **agarrar un** ∼ to get plastered (*colloq*) ⓶ (AmL *fam*) (*petardo*) firecracker ⓷ (Per *fam*) (*pistola*) shooter (*colloq*), rod (sl) ⓸ (Méx) (Coc) braising steak

cueva *f* cave

cueza, cuezan, etc ▶ COCER

cuidado¹ -da *adj* ⟨*presentación*⟩ meticulous, careful; ⟨*aspecto*⟩ impeccable; ⟨*dicción*⟩ precise

cuidado² ** *m* **(a) (*precaución*): **tener** ∼ to be careful; **lo envolvió con mucho** ∼ she wrapped it very carefully; **¡**∼ **con el escalón!** mind the step!; ∼ **con lo que haces** watch *o* be careful what you do ; **de** ∼ (*fam*) ⟨*problema/herida*⟩ serious **(b)** (*atención*) care; **pone mucho** ∼ **en su trabajo** he takes a great deal of care over his work **(c)** (*de niños, enfermos*): **no tiene experiencia en el** ∼ **de los niños** he has no experience of looking after children; **estar al** ∼ **de algn/algo** (cuidar) to look after sb/sth; (ser cuidado por) to be in sb's care **(d)** **cuidados** *mpl* (Med) attention, care, treatment; **necesita los** ∼**s de una enfermera** she needs to be looked after by a nurse; ∼**s intensivos** intensive care **(e)** (*preocupación*): **pierde** ∼ (AmL) don't worry; **me tiene sin** ∼ it doesn't matter to me in the slightest
■ *interj* be careful!, watch out!

cuidador -dora *m,f* (de niños) baby sitter (AmE), childminder (BrE); (de animales) zookeeper

cuidadoso -sa *adj* **(a)** ⟨*persona*⟩ careful; ∼ **CON algo** careful WITH sth **(b)** ⟨*búsqueda/investigación*⟩ careful, thorough

cuidar [A1] *vt* **(a)** ⟨*juguetes/plantas/casa*⟩ to look after; ⟨*niño*⟩ to look after, take care of; ⟨*enfermo*⟩ to care for, look after **(b)** ⟨*estilo/apariencia*⟩ to take care over; **debes** ∼ **la ortografía** you must take care over your spelling
■ ∼ *vi* ∼ **DE algo/algn** to take care OF sth/sb; ∼**ré de que no les falte nada** I'll make sure they have everything they need
■ **cuidarse** *v pron* (*refl*) to take care of oneself, look after oneself; **¡cuídate!** take care!; **se cuidó bien de no volver por ahí** he made very sure he didn't go back there; **cuídate de decir algo que te comprometa** take care not to say something which might compromise you

cuije *mf* (Méx) office junior

culantro *m* (*fam*) coriander

culata *f* **(a)** (de escopeta, revólver) butt; (de cañón) breech **(b)** (de motor) cylinder head

culebra *f* (Zool) snake

culebrón *m* (*fam*) soap opera, soap (colloq)

culinario -ria *adj* culinary (*frml*)

culminación *f* **(a)** (de carrera, negociaciones) culmination; (de fiesta) climax **(b)** (realización) fulfillment*

culminante *adj*: **punto** ∼ (de carrera) peak, high point; (de historia, película) climax; (de negociaciones) crucial stage

culminar [A1] *vi* (llegar al clímax): **la novela culmina cuando …** the novel reaches its climax when …; ∼ **EN** *or* **CON algo** to culminate IN sth

culo *m* (*fam*: en algunas regiones *vulg*) **(a)** (*nalgas*) backside (colloq), butt (AmE colloq), bum (BrE colloq), ass (AmE *vulg*), arse (BrE *vulg*); **te voy a pegar en el** ∼ I'm going to spank *o* smack you **(b)** (de vaso, botella) bottom

culpa *f* **(a)** (*responsabilidad*) fault; **yo no tengo la** ∼ it's not my fault; **echarle la** ∼ **a algn** (de algo) to blame sb *o* put the blame on sb (for sth); **llegó tarde por** ∼ **del tráfico** he arrived late because of the traffic **(b)** (*falta, pecado*) sin

culpabilidad *f* (Der,Psic) guilt

culpable *adj* [SER] ⟨*persona*⟩ guilty; **sentirse** ∼ **de algo** to feel guilty about sth; **ser** ∼ **de algo** to be to blame for sth; (Der) to be guilty of sth
■ *mf* **(a)** (de delito) culprit **(b)** (de problema, situación): **tú eres el** ∼ **de todo esto** this is all your fault, you're to blame for all this

culpar [A1] *vt* to blame; ∼ **a algn DE algo** to blame sb FOR sth, blame sth ON sb

cultivable *adj* cultivable

cultivado -da *adj* cultivated

cultivar [A1] *vt* **(a)** ⟨*campo/tierras*⟩ to cultivate, farm; ⟨*plantas*⟩ to grow, cultivate **(b)** ⟨*bacterias/perlas*⟩ to culture **(c)** ⟨*amistad*⟩ to cultivate; ⟨*inteligencia/memoria*⟩ to develop; ⟨*artes/interés*⟩ to encourage

cultivo *m* **(a)** (de tierra) farming, cultivation; (de plantas, frutas) growing, cultivation; ∼ **intensivo** intensive farming **(b)** (cosa cultivada) crop; ∼**s de secano** dry-farmed crops **(c)** (Biol, Med) (acción) culturing; (producto) culture **(d)** (de las artes) promotion, encouragement

culto¹ -ta *adj* **(a)** ⟨*persona/pueblo*⟩ educated, cultured **(b)** (Ling) ⟨*palabra*⟩ learned; ⟨*literatura/música*⟩ highbrow

culto² ** *m* **(a) (adoración, creencia) worship; **rendir** ∼ **a algo/algn** to worship sth/sb; **libertad de** ∼**(s)** freedom of worship **(b)** (interés obsesivo) cult; **el** ∼ **del dinero** the cult of money

cultura *f* **(a)** (civilización) culture **(b)** (conocimientos, ilustración): **una persona de gran** ∼ a very well-educated *o* cultured person; ∼ **general/musical** general/musical knowledge; **la** ∼ **popular** popular culture

cultural *adj* cultural; **un acto** ∼ a cultural event; **bajo nivel** ∼ low standard of general education

culturismo *m* bodybuilding

cumbre *f* **(a)** (de montaña) top **(b)** (apogeo) height; **en la** ∼ **del éxito** at the height of his success **(c)** (Pol) summit (meeting)

AmC	América Central	Arg	Argentina
AmL	América Latina	Bol	Bolivia
AmS	América del Sur	Chi	Chile
Andes	Región andina	CS	Cono Sur

Cu	Cuba	Per	Perú
Ec	Ecuador	RPI	Río de la Plata
Esp	España	Ur	Uruguay
Méx	México	Ven	Venezuela

cumpleañero -ra *m,f* (fam) (*m*) birthday boy (colloq); (*f*) birthday girl (colloq)

cumpleaños *m* (*pl* ~) **(a)** (aniversario) birthday; **¡feliz ~!** happy birthday!; **¿qué vas a hacer el día de tu ~?** what are you going to do on your birthday? **(b)** (fiesta) birthday party

cumplido¹ -da *adj* [SER] **(a)** (atento, cortés) polite **(b)** (considerado) thoughtful **(c)** (Col) (puntual) punctual; *ver tb* CUMPLIR

cumplido² *m*: **hacerle un ~ a algn** to pay sb a compliment; **una visita de ~** a duty *o* courtesy call; **la invitó por ~** he invited her because he felt he ought to

cumplidor -dora *adj* reliable

cumplimiento *m* ⬚1⬚ **(a)** (de ley, norma) performance; **falleció en el ~ del deber** he died in the line of duty; **en ~ con lo dispuesto por la legislación vigente** in compliance with current legislation; **la ley es de obligado ~ para todas las empresas** the law is binding on all companies (frml) **(b)** (logro): **esto favorecerá el ~ de nuestros objetivos** this will help to achieve our objectives ⬚2⬚ (elogio, piropo) ▶ CUMPLIDO²

cumplir [I1] *vt* ⬚1⬚ **(a)** (ejecutar) ⟨*orden*⟩ to carry out; ⟨*ley*⟩ to obey; **la satisfacción del deber cumplido** the satisfaction of having done one's duty **(b)** ⟨*promesa/palabra*⟩ to keep; ⟨*compromiso*⟩ to honor*, fulfill*; ⟨*obligación/contrato*⟩ to fulfill* **(c)** (alcanzar) ⟨*objetivo/ambición*⟩ to achieve; ⟨*requisitos*⟩ fulfill*; **¡misión cumplida!** mission accomplished **(d)** (desempeñar) ⟨*papel*⟩ to perform, fulfill*
⬚2⬚ ⟨*condena/sentencia*⟩ to serve; ⟨*servicio militar*⟩ to do
⬚3⬚ ⟨*años/meses*⟩: **mañana cumple 20 años** she'll be 20 tomorrow; **¡que cumplas muchos más!** many happy returns!; **mañana cumplimos 20 años de casados** (AmL) tomorrow we'll have been married 20 years

■ **~** *vi* **(a)** **~ CON algo** ⟨*con obligación*⟩ to fulfill* sth, satisfy sth; ⟨*con tarea*⟩ to carry out sth; ⟨*con trámite*⟩ to comply WITH sth; ⟨*con requisito/condición*⟩ to fulfill* sth; **cumple con su deber** he does his duty **(b)** (con una obligación social): **nos invitó solo por ~** she only invited us because she felt she ought to; **con los Lara ya hemos cumplido** we've done our bit as far as the Laras are concerned (colloq)

■ **cumplirse** *v pron* **(a)** «*deseo/predicción*» to come true; «*ambición*» to be realized, be fulfilled **(b)** «*plazo*»: **mañana se cumple el plazo para pagar el impuesto** tomorrow is the last day for paying the tax; **hoy se cumple el primer aniversario de** ... today marks the first anniversary of ...

cuna *f* **(a)** (tradicional) cradle; (cama con barandas) crib (AmE), cot (BrE); (portabebé) portacrib (AmE), carrycot (BrE) **(b)** (liter) (lugar de nacimiento) birthplace

cuncho *m* (Col) (poso — del café) grounds (*pl*); (— del vino) lees (*pl*)

cuncuna *f* (Chi) (Zool) caterpillar

cundir [I1] *vi* **(a)** «*rumor*» to spread; «*miedo*» to grow; **¡que no cunda el pánico!** don't panic!; **cundió la alarma** there was widespread alarm **(b)** (rendir) «*detergente/lana*» to go a long way; **hoy no me ha cundido el trabajo** I haven't got much work done today

cuneta *f* **(a)** (en carretera) ditch **(b)** (Chi) (de calle) curb (AmE), kerb (BrE)

cuña *f* ⬚1⬚ **(a)** (pieza triangular) wedge; **en ~** in a V-formation *o* wedge formation **(b)** (Col) (muesca) groove ⬚2⬚ (CS fam) ▶ PALANCA 2

cuñado -da *m,f* **(a)** (pariente político) (*m*) brother-in-law; (*f*) sister-in-law; **mis ~s** (solo varones) my brothers-in-law; (varones y mujeres) my brothers and sisters-in-law **(b)** (Per fam) (compañero) buddy (AmE colloq), mate (BrE colloq)

cuño *m* (troquel) die; (sello) stamp; **de nuevo ~** ⟨*palabra*⟩ newly-coined (*before n*)

cuota *f* **(a)** (de club, asociación) membership fees (*pl*); (de sindicato) dues (*pl*); **~ inicial** deposit, down payment **(b)** (AmL) (plazo) installment*, payment; (parte proporcional) quota; **~s de producción** production quotas **(c)** (Méx) (Auto) toll

cupe ▶ CABER

Cupido *m* Cupid

cupiera, cupiese, etc ▶ CABER

cupimos, cupisteis, etc ▶ CABER

cupo *m* **(a)** (cantidad establecida) quota **(b)** (AmL) (capacidad) room; **una sala con ~ para 300 personas** a hall with room for 300 people **(c)** (AmL) (plaza) place

cupo, cupiste, etc ▶ CABER

cupón *m* **(a)** (vale) coupon, voucher **(b)** (Esp) (de lotería) ticket

cúpula *f* (Arquit) dome, cupola

cura *m* (sacerdote) priest; **se metió de** *or* **a ~** he became a priest

■ *f* **(a)** (curación, tratamiento) cure; **tener/no tener ~** to be curable/incurable; **~ de urgencias** first aid **(b)** (vendaje) dressing; (curita) (Col) Band-Aid® (AmE), (sticking) plaster (BrE)

curable *adj* curable

curación *f* **(a)** (tratamiento) treatment **(b)** (recuperación—de enfermo) recovery; (— de herida) healing

curado -da *adj* ⬚1⬚ ⟨*jamón/carne*⟩ cured; ⟨*cuero/piel*⟩ tanned ⬚2⬚ (fam) (borracho) plastered (colloq)

curandero -ra *m,f* (en medicina popular) folk healer; (hechicero) witch doctor; (charlatán) (pey) quack doctor (pej)

curar [A1] *vt* ⬚1⬚ **(a)** (poner bien) ⟨*enfermo/enfermedad*⟩ to cure; ⟨*herida*⟩ to heal **(b)** (tratar) ⟨*enfermo/enfermedad*⟩ to treat; ⟨*herida*⟩ (desinfectar) to clean; (vendar) to dress ⬚2⬚ ⟨*jamón/pescado*⟩ to cure; ⟨*cuero/piel*⟩ to tan

■ **curarse** *v pron* «*enfermo*» to recover, get better; «*herida*» to heal up; **~se DE algo** to get over sth

curda *mf* (RPl fam) (borracho) soak (colloq)

curiosear [A1] *vi* **(a)** (fisgonear) to pry; **~ en la vida ajena** to pry into other people's affairs; **estaba curioseando en mis cajones** he was going *o* looking through my drawers **(b)** (por las tiendas, en una biblioteca) to browse

curiosidad *f* (cualidad) curiosity; **por ~** out of curiosity; **siente mucha ~** he is very curious; **tengo ~ por saberlo** I'm curious to know; **están muertos de ~** they are dying to see him (*o* to know *etc*)

curioso -sa *adj* ⬚1⬚ (interesante, extraño) curious, ···⟐

strange, odd **2** (a) [SER] (inquisitivo) inquisitive; (entrometido) (pey) nosy* (colloq) (b) [ESTAR] (interesado) curious
■ *m,f* (a) (espectador) onlooker (b) (fam) (fisgón) busybody (colloq)

curita *f* (AmL) Band-Aid® (AmE), (sticking) plaster (BrE)

currículo *m* (Educ) curriculum

curriculum, currículum *m* (*pl* **-lums**) (a) (antecedentes) *tb* ~ **vitae** curriculum vitae, CV (b) (Educ) curriculum

curry /'kurri/ *m* (*pl* **-rries**) (polvo) curry powder; (plato) curry; **pollo al** ~ curried chicken

cursar [A1] *vt* (estudiar): **cursa segundo** (año) she is in her second year; **cursó estudios de Derecho** she did *o* studied *o* (BrE) read Law

cursi *adj* (fam) ⟨objeto⟩ corny, twee (BrE); ⟨idea⟩ sentimental, twee (BrE); ⟨decoración⟩ chichi; ⟨persona⟩ affected;
■ *mf* (fam): **es un** ~ he's so affected *o* (BrE) twee

cursillo *m* (a) (curso corto) short course; ~ **de natación** swimming lessons (b) (ciclo de conferencias) series of lectures

cursiva *f* italics (*pl*)

curso *m* **1** (Educ) (a) (año académico) year; **está en (el) tercer** ~ he's in the third year; **el** ~ **escolar/universitario** the academic year (b) (de inglés, mecanografía) course; ~ **intensivo** crash *o* intensive course; **C**~ **de Orientación Universitaria** (en Esp) pre-university course; ~ **por correspondencia** correspondence course **2** (a) (transcurso, desarrollo) course; **dejar que algo siga su** ~ to let sth take its course (b) (de río) course **3** (circulación): **monedas de** ~ **legal** legal tender, legal currency

cursor *m* cursor

curtido -da *adj* ⟨rostro/piel⟩ weather-beaten; ⟨manos⟩ hardened

curul *f* (Col, Méx) (Pol) seat

curva *f* (a) (línea) curve (b) (en camino, carretera) curve; (más pronunciada) bend; **una** ~ **cerrada** a sharp bend (c) (Dep) curveball (c) **curvas** *fpl* (de una mujer) curves (*pl*); **con** ~**s** curvaceous

curvo -va *adj* curved

cúspide *f* (a) (de montaña) top, summit; (de pirámide) top, apex (b) (de fama, poder) height, pinnacle (c) (de organización) leadership

custodia *f* custody; **le otorgaron la** ~ **de los hijos** she was granted custody of the children

cusuco *m* (AmC) armadillo

cutáneo -nea *adj* skin (before n), cutaneous (tech)

cutícula *f* cuticle

cutis *m* (*pl* ~) skin

cuy *m* (AmS) guinea pig

cuye *m* (Chi) guinea pig

cuyo -ya *adj* whose; **un amigo** ~**s hijos van a ese colegio** a friend whose children go to that school; **vocablos** ~ **uso es extendido** words which are in widespread use, **en** ~ **caso** in which case

C.V. *m* (= **curriculum vitae**) CV

Dd

D, d *f* (read as /de/) the letter D, d

D. = **Don**

dactilar *adj* finger (before n); ▶ HUELLA A

dactilografía *f* typing, typewriting

dactilógrafo -fa *m,f* typist

dado¹ -da *adj* **1** (determinado) given; **en un momento** ~ at a given moment **2** (como conj) given; **dadas las circunstancias** given *o* in view of the circumstances; ~ **que** given that **3** [SER] (proclive) ~ **A algo/hacer algo** given TO sth/doing sth

dado² *m* **1** (Jueg) dice, die (frml); **jugar a los** ~**s** to play dice **2** (Arquit) dado

daga *f* dagger

dalia *f* dahlia

daltónico -ca *adj* color-blind*
■ *m,f*: **los** ~**s** people suffering from color-blindness*

daltonismo *m* color-blindness*

dama *f* **1** (frml) (señora) lady; ~**s y caballeros** ladies and gentlemen; ~ **de honor** (de novia) bridesmaid; (de reina) lady-in-waiting **2** (figura — en damas) king; (— en ajedrez, en naipes) queen **3 damas** *fpl* (juego) checkers (AmE), draughts (BrE); **jugar a las** ~**s** to play checkers *o* draughts

damasco *m* **1** (Tex) damask **2** (AmS) (fruta) apricot; (árbol) apricot tree

Damasco *m* Damascus

damnificado -da *m,f* (frml) victim

danés -nesa *adj* Danish
■ *m,f* (a) (persona) (*m*) Dane, Danish man; (*f*) Dane, Danish woman (b) **danés** *m* (idioma) Danish

danza *f* dance; ~ **moderna** modern dance

danzar [A4] *vi* (frml) (bailar) to dance

danzarín -rina *adj*: **es muy** ~ he loves dancing
■ *m,f* dancer

dañar [A1] *vt* (en general) to damage; ⟨salud/organismo⟩ to be bad for
■ **dañarse** *v pron* **1** (en general) to be/get damaged; ⟨salud⟩ to damage **2** (Col, Ven) (a) «carne/comida» to rot, go bad (b) «carro» to break down; «aparato» to break

dañino -na *adj* [SER] ⟨planta/sustancia⟩ harmful; ~ **PARA algo** harmful TO sth

daño *m* **(a)** (dolor físico): **hacerse** ~ to hurt oneself; **me he hecho** ~ **en la espalda** I've hurt my back; **hacerle** ~ **a algn** «*persona*» to hurt sb; **el picante me hace** ~ hot, spicy food doesn't agree with me **(b)** (destrozo) damage; **sufrir** ~**s** to be damaged, to suffer damage **(c)** ~**s y perjuicios** damages (*pl*)

dar [A25] *vt*

I ⓵ **(a)** (entregar) to give; **dale las llaves a Pedro** give the keys to Pedro; **déme un kilo de peras** can I have a kilo of pears?; ▶ CONOCER *vt* 3 B, ENTENDER *vt* **(b)** ⟨*cartas/mano*⟩ to give

⓶ **(a)** (donar, regalar) ⟨*sangre/limosna*⟩ to give; **me dio su reloj** she gave me her watch **(b)** (proporcionar) ⟨*fuerzas/valor/esperanza*⟩ to give; ⟨*información/idea*⟩ to give

⓷ **(a)** (conferir, aportar) ⟨*sabor/color/forma*⟩ to give **(b)** (aplicar) ⟨*mano de pintura/barniz*⟩ to give **(c)** ⟨*sedante/masaje*⟩ to give

⓸ (conceder) ⟨*prórroga/permiso*⟩ to give; **el dentista me dio hora para el miércoles** I have an appointment with the dentist on Wednesday; **nos dieron un premio** we won *o* got a prize

⓹ **(a)** (expresar, decir) ⟨*parecer/opinón*⟩ to give; **¿le diste las gracias?** did you thank him?, did you say thank you?; **dales saludos** give/send them my regards; **tuve que** ~**le la noticia** I was the one who had to break the news to him **(b)** (señalar, indicar): **me da ocupado** *or* (Esp) **comunicando** the line's busy *o* (BrE) engaged; **el reloj dio las cinco** the clock struck five

II ⓵ **(a)** (producir) ⟨*fruto/flor*⟩ to bear; ⟨*dividendos*⟩ to pay; **un negocio que da mucho dinero** a business which makes a lot of money **(b)** (AmL) (alcanzar hasta): **da 150 kilómetros por hora** it can do *o* go 150 kilometres an hour; **venía a toda lo que daba** it was travelling at full speed; **ponen la radio a todo lo que da** they turn the radio on full blast

⓶ (causar, provocar) ⟨*placer/susto*⟩ to give; ⟨*problemas*⟩ to cause; ~ **trabajo** to be hard work; **el calor le dio sueño/sed** the heat made him sleepy/thirsty

III ⓵ (presentar) ⟨*concierto*⟩ to give; **¿qué dan esta noche en la tele?** what's on TV tonight? (colloq): **¿dónde están dando esa película?** where's that film showing?

⓶ **(a)** ⟨*fiesta/conferencia*⟩ to give; ⟨*baile/banquete*⟩ to hold; ⟨*discurso*⟩ (AmL) to make **(b)** ⟨*examen*⟩ (CS) to take *o* (BrE) sit; *ver tb* CLASE 4

IV (realizar la acción que se indica) ⟨*grito*⟩ to give; ~ **un paso atrás** to take a step back; **dame un beso** give me a kiss; *ver tb* GOLPE, PASEO, VUELTA, ETC

V (considerar) ~ **algo/a algn POR algo**: **lo dieron por muerto** they gave him up for dead; **ese tema lo doy por sabido** I'm assuming you've already covered that topic; **¡dalo por hecho!** consider it done!

■ ~ *vi*

I ⓵ **dar a** «*puerta*» to give onto, open onto; «*ventana/balcón*» to look onto, give onto; «*fachada/frente*» to face

⓶ (ser suficiente, alcanzar) ~ **PARA algo/algn** to be enough FOR sth/sb; **no me dio (el) tiempo** I didn't have time; ~ **de sí** ⟨*zapatos/jersey*⟩ to stretch

⓷ (arrojar un resultado): **el análisis le dio positivo** her test was positive; **¿cuánto da la cuenta?** what does it come to?; **a mí me dio 247** I made it (to be) 247

⓸ (importar): **da lo mismo** it doesn't matter; **¡qué más da!** what does it matter!; **¿qué más da?** what difference does it make?; **me da igual** I don't mind

⓹ (en naipes) to deal

II ⓵ **(a)** (pegar, golpear): ~**le A algn** to hit sb; (como castigo) to smack sb; **dale al balón** kick the ball; **el balón dio en el poste** the ball hit the post **(b)** (acertar) to hit; ~ **en el blanco** to hit the target

⓶ (accionar, mover) ~**le A algo** ⟨*a botón/tecla*⟩ to press sth; ⟨*a interruptor*⟩ to flick sth; ⟨*a manivela/volante*⟩ to turn sth

⓷ **dar con** (encontrar) ⟨*persona*⟩ to find; ⟨*solución*⟩ to hit upon, find; ⟨*palabra*⟩ to come up with

⓸ (hablando de manías, ocurrencias) ~**le a algn POR hacer algo** ⟨*por pintar/cocinar*⟩ to take to doing sth; **le ha dado por decir que …** he's started saying that …

⓹ «*sol/luz*»: **aquí da el sol toda la mañana** you get the sun all morning here; **la luz le daba de lleno en los ojos** the light was shining right in his eyes

■ **darse** *v pron*

I ⓵ (producirse) «*fruta/trigo*» to grow

⓶ (presentarse) «*oportunidad/ocasión*» to arise

⓷ (resultar) (+ *me/te/le etc*): **se le dan los idiomas** she's good at languages

II (a) (*refl*) (realizar lo que se indica) ⟨*ducha/banquete*⟩ to have; **dárselas de valiente/de que sabe mucho** he likes to make out he's brave/he knows a lot; **dárselas de listo** to act smart **(b)** (golpearse, pegarse): **se dio con el martillo en el dedo** he hit his finger with the hammer; **se dieron contra un árbol** they crashed into a tree; **se dio** ~ **un golpe en la rodilla** he hit his knee

III (considerarse) ~**se POR algo**: **con eso me** ~**ía por satisfecha** I'd be quite happy with that; *ver tb* ALUDIR A, ENTERADO 1

dardo *m* **(a)** (Jueg) dart; **jugar a los** ~**s** to play darts **(b)** (arma) small spear

datar [A1] *vi* to date; **data del siglo XII** it dates from the 12th century; **data de hace muchos años** it goes back many years

dátil *m* (Bot) date

dativo *m* (Ling) dative

dato *m* **(a)** (elemento de información) piece of information; **no dispongo de todos los** ~**s** I don't have all the information; ~**s personales** personal details (*pl*) **(b) datos** *mpl* (Inf) data (*pl*), information

d. de C. (= **después de Jesucristo**) AD

de¹ *prep* ⓵ **(a)** (pertenencia, posesión): **la casa** ~ ~ **mis padres** my parents' house; **el rey** ~ **Francia** the king of France; **no es** ~ **él** it isn't his; **es un amigo** ~ **mi hijo** he's a friend of my son's; **un estudiante** ~ **quinto año** a fifth-year student; **la tapa** ~ **la cacerola** the saucepan lid; **un avión** ~ **Mexair** a Mexair plane **(b)** (con un nombre en aposición) of; **la ciudad** ~ **Lima** the city of Lima; **el aeropuerto** ~ **Barajas** Barajas airport; **el mes** ~ **enero** the month of January

⓶ **(a)** (procedencia, origen, razón) from; **es** ~ **Bogotá** she's/he comes from Bogotá; **una carta** ~ **Julia** a letter from Julia; **un amigo** ~ **la infancia** a childhood friend; **la literatura** ~ **ese período** the literature of *o* from that period; ~ **aquí a tu casa** from here to your house **(b)** (material, contenido, composición): **son** ~ **plástico** they're (made of)

⋯⊹

plastic; **una mesa ∼ caoba** a mahogany table; **un vaso ∼ agua** a glass of water; **un millón ∼ dólares** a million dollars **(c)** (causa, modo): **murió ∼ viejo** he died of old age; **∼ tanto gritar** from shouting so much; **verde ∼ envidia** green with envy; **temblando ∼ miedo** trembling with fear; **∼ memoria** by heart; **lo tumbó ∼ un golpe** he knocked him down with one blow **(d)** (en oraciones pasivas) by; **un poema ∼ Neruda** a poem by Neruda; **rodeada ∼ árboles** surrounded by trees **3 (a)** (cualidades, características): **de gran inteligencia** of great intelligence; **objetos ∼ mucho valor** objects of great value; **¿∼ qué color lo quiere?** what color do you want it?; **tiene cara ∼ aburrido** he looks bored; **una botella ∼ un litro** a liter bottle; **la chica ∼ azul** the girl in blue **(b)** (al definir, especificar): **el botón ∼ abajo** the bottom button; **tiene dos metros ∼ ancho** it's two meters wide; **es fácil de pronunciar** it's easy to pronounce; **uno ∼ los míos** one of mine; **el mayor ∼ los Soto** the eldest of the Soto children **4 (a)** (con cifras): **pagan un interés ∼l 15%** they pay 15% interest o interest at 15% **(b)** (en comparaciones de cantidad) than; **más ∼ £100** more than o over £100; **pesa menos ∼ un kilo** it weighs less than o under a kilo; **un número mayor/menor ∼ 29** a number over/under 29 **(c)** (con un superlativo): **es el más caro ∼ todos** it's the most expensive one; **la ciudad más grande ∼l mundo** the biggest city in the world **(d)** (refiriéndose a una parte del día): **∼ día/noche** during the day/at night; **∼ madrugada** early in the morning **5 (a)** (en calidad de) as; **trabaja ∼ secretaria** she works as a secretary; **hace ∼ rey en la obra** he plays (the part of) a king in the play **(b)** (en expresiones de estado, actividad): **∼ mal humor** in a bad mood; **estamos ∼ fiesta** we're having a party **(c)** (indicando uso, destino, finalidad): **el cepillo ∼ la ropa** the clothes brush; **copas ∼ vino** wine glasses; **ropa ∼ cama** bed clothes; **dales algo ∼ comer** give them something to eat; **¿qué hay ∼ postre?** what's for dessert? **6** (con sentido condicional): **∼ haberlo sabido** if I had known, had I known; **∼ no ser así** otherwise

de² *f*: name of the letter d

dé ▶ DAR

deambular [A1] *vi* to wander around o about

debajo *adv* **1** [*Latin American Spanish also uses* ABAJO *in many of these examples*] underneath; **no hay nada ∼** there's nothing underneath; **el que está ∼** the one below, the next one down **2 debajo de** (*loc prep*) under, underneath; **∼ del coche** under o underneath the car; **∼ del agua** underwater; **por ∼ de la puerta** under the door; **temperaturas por ∼ de lo normal** temperatures below average

debate *m* debate; (*más informal*) discussion

debatir [I1] *vt* to debate; (*más informal*) to discuss

debe *m* debit

deber¹ [E1] *vt* ⟨*dinero/favor/explicación*⟩ to owe; **te debo las entradas de ayer** I owe you for the tickets from yesterday

■ *v aux* **1** (expresando obligación): **debemos trabajar más** we must work harder; **no debes usarlo** you must not use it; **∼ías** or **debías habérselo dicho** you ought to have o you should have told her; **no se debe mentir** you mustn't tell lies; **no ∼ías haberlo dejado solo** you shouldn't have left him alone **2** (expresando suposición, probabilidad): **deben (de) ser más de las cinco** it must be after five o'clock; **deben (de) haber salido** they must have gone out; **debe (de) estar enamorado** she/he must be in love; **no deben (de) saber la dirección** they probably don't know the address; **no les debe (de) interesar** they can't be interested

■ **deberse** *v pron* **1** (tener su causa en) **∼se A algo** to be due TO sth; **se debe a que no estudia** it's due to the fact that she doesn't study; **¿a qué se debe este escándalo?** what's all this racket about? **2** (*persona*) (tener obligaciones hacia) **∼se A algn** to have a duty TO sb

deber² *m* **1** (obligación) duty; **cumplió con su ∼** he carried out o did his duty **2 deberes** *mpl* (tarea escolar) homework, assignment (AmE)

debido -da *adj* **(a)** (apropiado): **a su ∼ tiempo** in due course; **tratar a algn con el ∼ respeto** to show due respect to sb; **tomó las debidas precauciones** she took the necessary precautions; **como es** ⟨*sentarse/comer*⟩ properly; ⟨*comida/ regalo*⟩ proper; **más de lo ∼** too much **(b)** (*en locs*) **debido a** owing to, on account of; **debido a que** owing to the fact that

débil *adj* **(a)** ⟨*persona/economía/gobierno*⟩ weak **(b)** ⟨*sonido/voz*⟩ faint; ⟨*moneda/argumento*⟩ weak; ⟨*excusa*⟩ feeble, lame; ⟨*luz*⟩ dim, faint; ⟨*sílaba/ vocal*⟩ unstressed, weak

debilidad *f* weakness; **siento una gran ∼** I feel terribly debilitated o weak; **se aprovechan de su ∼** they take advantage of his weak character; **tener ∼ por algn/algo** to have a soft spot for sb/a weakness for sth

debilitar [A1] *vt* to weaken

■ **debilitarse** *v pron* **(a)** «*persona*» to become weak; «*salud*» to deteriorate; «*voluntad*» to weaken **(b)** «*sonido*» to get o become faint/ fainter **(c)** «*economía*» to grow o become weak/ weaker

débito *m* debit; **∼ bancario** (AmL) direct debit, direct billing (AmE)

debutante *mf* (Dep, Espec) player or artist making his/her public debut

debutar [A1] *vi* to make one's debut

década *f* decade; **la ∼ de los ochenta** the eighties

decadencia *f* **(a)** (proceso) decline **(b)** (estado) decadence

decadente *adj* **(a)** ⟨*moral/costumbres*⟩ decadent **(b)** ⟨*salud*⟩ declining

decaer [E16] *vi* **(a)** «*ánimo/fuerzas*» to flag; «*enfermo*» to deteriorate; «*interés/popularidad*» to wane **(b)** «*barrio/restaurante*» to go downhill; «*calidad/prestigio*» to decline **(c)** «*imperio/ civilización*» to decay, decline

decaído -da *adj* [ESTAR] low, down (colloq)

decálogo *m* decalogue

decano -na *m,f* (de una facultad) dean; (de una profesión, un grupo) senior member

decapitar [A1] *vt* to behead, decapitate

decatlón *m* decathlon

decena *f*: unidades, ~s y centenas (Mat) units, tens and hundreds; **una ~ de personas** about ten people; **~s de personas lo presenciaron** dozens *o* scores of people witnessed it

decencia *f* decency

decenio *m* decade

decente *adj* **(a)** (honrado, decoroso) decent, respectable **(b)** (aceptable) ⟨sueldo/vivienda⟩ decent, reasonable **(c)** [ESTAR] (de apariencia aceptable) respectable

decepción *f* disappointment, letdown (colloq); **me llevé una gran ~** I was very disappointed

decepcionado -da *adj* disappointed; **estar ~ con algo/de algn** to be disappointed with sth/sb

decepcionante *adj* disappointing

decepcionar [A1] *vt* to disappoint; **la película me decepcionó** I was disappointed with the movie

decidido -da *adj* **(a)** [SER] ⟨persona/tono⟩ (resuelto, enérgico) decisive, determined **(b)** [ESTAR] **~ A hacer algo** determined *o* resolved to do sth

decidir [I1] *vt* **1 (a)** (tomar una determinación) to decide; **decidí comprarlo** I decided to buy it **(b)** ⟨persona⟩ to make ... decide; **lo que me decidió** what made me decide **2** ⟨asunto⟩ to settle; ⟨resultado⟩ to decide
■ **~** *vi* to decide; **tiene que ~ entre los dos** she has to choose *o* decide between the two; **~ SOBRE algo** to decide ON sth
■ **decidirse** *v pron* to decide, to make up one's mind; **~se A hacer algo** to decide to do sth; **~se POR algo** to decide ON sth

décima *f* (de segundo, grado) tenth; **tiene 39 y tres ~s** his temperature is 39.3 (degrees)

decimal *m* (número) decimal (number)

décimo¹ -ma *adj/pron* tenth; *para ejemplos ver* QUINTO; **la décima parte** a tenth

décimo² *m* **(a)** (partitivo) tenth **(b)** (de lotería) *tenth share in a lottery ticket*

decir¹ *m*: **¿cientos de personas? — bueno, es un ~** hundreds of people? — well, figuratively speaking

decir² [I24] *vt* **1 (a)** ⟨palabra/frase/poema⟩ to say; ⟨mentira/verdad⟩ to tell; [*para ejemplos con complemento indirecto ver división 2*] **no digas estupideces** don't talk nonsense!; **¿eso lo dices por mí?** are you referring to me?; **¡no lo dirás en serio!** you can't be serious!; **dijo que sí con la cabeza** he nodded; **no se dice 'andé', se dice 'anduve'** it isn't 'andé', it's 'anduve'; **¡eso no se dice!** you mustn't say that!; **¿cómo se dice 'amor' en ruso?** how do you say 'love' in Russian?; **¿lo encontró? — dice que sí/no** did he find it? — he says he did/he didn't **(b)** **decir misa** to say mass **2 ~le algo A algn** to tell sb sth; **voy a ~le a papá que ...** I'm going to tell Dad ...; **¡ya te lo decía yo!** I told you so! **3 (a)** (expresando órdenes, deseos, advertencias): **¡porque lo digo yo!** because I say so!; **harás lo que yo diga** you'll do as I say; **dice que llames**

cuando llegues she says (you are) to phone when you get there; **dijo que tuviéramos cuidado** she said to be careful; **diles que empiecen** tell them to start; **le dije que no lo hiciera** I told him not to do it **(b)** **~(le) adiós (a algn)** to say goodbye (to sb)
4 (a) (opinar, pensar) to think; **¿y los padres qué dicen?** what do her parents think of it?, how do her parents feel about it?; **¡quién lo hubiera dicho!** who would have thought *o* believed it?; **es muy fácil — si tú lo dices ...** it's very easy — if you say so ... **(b)** (sugerir, comunicar): **el tiempo lo dirá** time will tell; **¿te dice algo ese nombre?** does that name mean anything to you?
5 querer decir «palabra/persona» to mean; **¿qué quieres ~ con eso?** what do you mean by that?
6 (*en locs*) **a decir verdad** to tell you the truth, to be honest; **como quien dice** so to speak; **es decir** that is; **¡he dicho!** that's that *o* final!; **ni que decir tiene que ...** it goes without saying that ...; **¡no me digas!** no!, you're kidding *o* joking! (colloq); **por así decirlo** so to speak; **el qué dirán** (fam) what other people (might) think; *ver tb* DICHO¹
■ **~** *vi* **(a)** (invitando a hablar): **papá — dime, hijo** dad — yes, son?; **quería pedirle un favor — usted dirá** I wanted to ask you a favor — certainly, go ahead **(b)** (Esp) (al contestar el teléfono): **¿diga?** *or* **¿dígame?** hello?
■ **decirse** *v pron* **(a)** (*refl*) to say ... to oneself **(b)** (*recípr*) to say .... to each other; **se decían secretos al oído** they were whispering secrets to each other

decisión *f* **(a)** (acción) decision; **tomar una ~** to make a decision; **su ~ de marcharse** her decision to leave **(b)** (cualidad) decisiveness, decision; **una mujer con ~** a woman of decision **(c)** (AmL) (en boxeo): **ganó por ~** he won on points *o* by a decision

decisivo -va *adj* ⟨fecha/voto/resultado⟩ crucial, decisive; ⟨prueba⟩ conclusive; ⟨papel⟩ decisive

declaración *f* **1 (a)** (afirmación) declaration; **una ~ de amor** a declaration of love **(a la prensa, en público)** statement; **hacer una ~** to issue a statement **(c)** (proclamación) declaration; **~ de guerra** declaration of war **2** (Der) statement, testimony; **el policía me tomó ~** the policeman took my statement; **prestar ~ como testigo** to give evidence, to testify; **~ del impuesto sobre la renta** income tax return

declarado -da *adj* declared, professed

declarar [A1] *vt* **1 (a)** (manifestar) ⟨apoyo/oposición/intención⟩ to declare, state; **le declaró su amor** he declared his love to her **(b)** (proclamar) ⟨guerra/independencia⟩ to declare; **el jurado lo declaró inocente** the jury found him not guilty **2 (a)** (en la aduana) to declare **(b)** (Fisco) ⟨bienes/ingresos⟩ to declare
■ **~** *vi* to give evidence, testify; **~ como testigo** to give evidence, to testify
■ **declararse** *v pron* **1 (a)** (manifestarse) to declare oneself; **~se en quiebra** to declare oneself bankrupt; **~se culpable/inocente** to plead guilty/not guilty; **~se en huelga** to go on strike **(b)** (confesar amor): **se le declaró** he declared himself *o* his love to her **2** «incendio/epidemia» to break out

declinación f (Ling) declension

declinar [A1] vt (a) ⟨invitación/oferta/honor⟩ to turn down, decline (frml) (b) (Ling) to decline

declive m (a) (de una superficie) slope, incline (frml); terreno en ~ sloping ground (b) (decadencia) decline

decolaje m (AmL) take-off

decolar [A1] vi (AmL) to take off

decoración f (a) (de pasteles, platos) decoration; (de habitación) decor; (de árbol de Navidad) (AmL) decoration (b) (interiorismo) tb ~ de interiores interior decoration

decorado m set

decorador -dora m,f. tb ~ de interiores interior decorator

decorar [A1] vt to decorate

decorativo -va adj decorative

decoro m (pudor, respeto) decorum

decoroso -sa adj decent, respectable

decrecer [E3] vi (a) «afición/interés» to wane, decrease; «importancia» to decline (b) «número/cantidad» to decline, fall (c) «aguas» to drop, fall

decreciente adj decreasing (before n)

decrépito -ta adj decrepit

decretar [A1] vt to order, decree (frml)

decreto m decree

dedal m thimble

dedicación f dedication

dedicar [A2] vt (a) (consagrar) ~ algo A algo/ hacer algo ⟨tiempo/esfuerzos⟩ to devote sth TO sth/doing sth; dedicó su vida a la ciencia/ayudar a los pobres she devoted her life to science/to helping the poor (b) (ofrendar, ofrecer) ⟨obra/ canción⟩ to dedicate
  ■ **dedicarse** v pron (a) (consagrarse) ~se A algo/ hacer algo to devote oneself TO sth/doing sth (b) (tener cierta ocupación, profesión): ¿a qué se dedica tu padre? what does your father do?; se dedica a la investigación she does research; se dedica a pintar en sus ratos libres she spends her free time painting

dedicatoria f dedication

dedillo m: conocer algo al ~ to know sth like the back of one's hand; sabía la lección al ~ I knew the lesson (off) by heart

dedo m (de mano, guante) finger; (del pie) toe; señalar con el ~ to point; ~ anular/(del) corazón ring/middle finger; ~ gordo (fam) (de la mano) thumb, (del pie) big toe; (de la mano) thumb; ~ índice forefinger, index finger; ~ meñique little finger; ~ pulgar thumb; a ~ (fam): ir a ~ to hitchhike, hitch (colloq); recorrió Europa a ~ she hitchhiked around Europe; hacer ~ (fam) to hitchhike, hitch (colloq); poner el ~ en la llaga to hit o touch a raw nerve; señalar a algn con el ~ (literal) to point at sb; (culpar) to point the finger at sb

deducción f deduction

deducible adj ① (que se puede inferir) deducible ② (Com, Fin) deductible

deducir [I6] vt ① (inferir) to deduce; ~ algo DE algo to deduce sth FROM sth ② (descontar) to deduct

deduje, deduzca, etc ▶ DEDUCIR

defecto m (a) (en un sistema) fault, flaw, defect;

~ de fábrica manufacturing fault o defect (b) (de una persona) fault, shortcoming; ~ físico physical handicap

defectuoso -sa adj faulty, defective

defender [E8] vt to defend; ⟨intereses⟩ to protect; ~ a algo/algn DE algo/algn to defend sth/ sb AGAINST sth/sb
  ■ **defenderse** v pron (a) (refl) (contra una agresión) to defend o protect oneself; (Der) to defend oneself; ~se DE algo/algn to defend oneself AGAINST sth/sb (b) (fam) (arreglárselas) to get by (colloq); me defiendo bastante bien en francés I can get by quite well in French

defensa f ① (a) (protección) defense*; salir en ~ de algn to come to sb's defense; actuó en ~ propia he acted in self-defense; ~ DE algo/algn defense* OF sth/sb; ~ personal self-defense* (b) (Dep) defense* ② (a) **Defensa** f the Defense Department (AmE), the Ministry of Defence (BrE) (b) **defensas** fpl (Biol, Med) defenses* (pl) (c) **defensa** mf (jugador) defender

defensivo -va adj ⟨arma/actitud/táctica⟩ defensive; estar/ponerse a la defensiva to be/get on the defensive

defensor -sora adj (a) ⟨ejército⟩ defending (before n) (b) (Der) ⟨abogado⟩ defense* (before n)
  ■ m,f (a) (Mil) defender (b) (de una causa) champion (c) (Der) defense counsel (AmE), defence lawyer (BrE)

defeño -ña m,f (Méx) person from the DISTRITO FEDERAL

deferencia f (frml) deference; por o a ~ a algn/ algo out of o in deference to sb/sth

deficiencia f (a) (defecto) fault (b) (insuficiencia alimentaria, inmunológica) deficiency

deficiente adj poor, inadequate; ⟨salud⟩ poor; ~ EN algo deficient IN sth
  ■ mf (persona) tb ~ mental mentally subnormal person
  ■ m (calificación) poor

déficit m (pl ~ o -cits) (a) (Com, Fin) deficit (b) (en la producción) shortfall; (de lluvias) shortage

defienda, defiendas, etc ▶ DEFENDER

definición f (de palabra, postura) definition

definido -da adj clearly-defined

definir [I1] vt to define

definitivamente adv ⟨resolver/rechazar⟩ once and for all; ⟨quedarse/instalarse⟩ permanently, for good

definitivo -va adj ⟨texto/solución/respuesta⟩ definitive; ⟨cierre⟩ permanent, definitive; ya es ~ que no viene he's definitely not coming

deforestación f deforestation

deforestar [A1] vt to deforest

deformación f (a) (en general) distortion (b) (Anat, Med) deformity

deformar [A1] vt (a) (en general) to distort (b) (Anat, Med) to deform
  ■ **deformarse** v pron (a) (en general) to become distorted (b) (Anat, Med) to become deformed

deforme adj deformed

defraudar [A1] vt (a) (decepcionar) to disappoint (b) (estafar) to defraud; defraudó al fisco he evaded his taxes

defunción f (frml) death; ⑤ cerrado por defunción closed owing to bereavement

degenerado -da *adj/m,f* degenerate

degenerar [A1] *vi* to degenerate; ~ EN algo to degenerate INTO sth

degollar [A12] *vt* ⟨*persona/animal*⟩: lo ~on they slit his/its throat

degradante *adj* degrading

degradar [A1] *vt* (a) (Mil) to demote (b) (envilecer) to degrade (c) (empeorar) ⟨*calidad/valor*⟩ to diminish

■ **degradarse** *v pron* «*persona*» to demean oneself, degrade oneself

dehesa *f* (a) (terreno) meadow, pasture (b) (hacienda) farm

dejación *f* (AmC, Chi) ▶ DEJADEZ

dejadez *f* (a) (en el aseo personal) slovenliness (b) (en tarea, trabajo) laziness, slackness

dejado -da *adj* (a) (en aseo personal, aspecto) slovenly (b) (en tarea, trabajo) slack, lazy

dejar [A1] *vt*

I ⬚1 (a) (en lugar determinado) to leave; **lo dejé en recepción** I left it in reception; **dejó a los niños en el colegio** she dropped the children (off) at school; ~ **un recado** to leave a message; ~ **propina** to leave a tip; **deja ese cuchillo** put that knife down; **déjala, ella no tuvo la culpa** leave her alone, it wasn't her fault; ~ **mucho que desear** to leave a great deal to be desired (b) (olvidar) ⟨*dinero/objeto*⟩to leave; **¡déjalo!** forget it! (c) (como herencia) to leave

⬚2 (a) ⟨*mancha/huella/sabor*⟩ to leave (b) ⟨*ganancia*⟩ to produce; **el negocio dejó pérdidas** the business made a loss

⬚3 (abandonar) ⟨*novia/marido*⟩ to leave; ⟨*familia*⟩ to leave, abandon; ⟨*trabajo*⟩ to give up, leave; ⟨*lugar*⟩ to leave; **quiere** ~ **el ballet** he wants to give up ballet dancing

⬚4 (+ *compl*) (en cierto estado) to leave; **dejé la ventana abierta** I left the window open; **me dejó esperando afuera** she left me waiting outside; **¡déjame en paz!** leave me alone!; **me lo dejó en 1.000 pesos** he let me have it for 1,000 pesos; ▶ LADO 3

⬚5 (a) (posponer) leave; **no lo dejes para después, hazlo ahora** don't put it off *o* leave it until later, do it now (b) (reservar, guardar) ⟨*espacio/margen/comida*⟩ to leave

II (permitir) ~algo/algn hacer algo to let sth/sb do sth; **déjalo entrar** let it/him in; **deja correr el agua** let the water run; **¿me dejas ir?** will you let me go?; ~ **que algo/algn haga algo** to let sb/sth do sth; **déjame que te ayude** let me help you; ▶ CAER 1, PASO 1B

■ ~ *vi* ~ DE hacer algo to stop doing sth; ~ **de fumar** to give up *o* to stop smoking; **no dejes de escribirme** make sure you write to me

■ **dejarse** *v pron* ⬚1 (a) (abandonarse) to let oneself go (b) ~se **hacer algo: se deja dominar por la envidia** he lets his feelings of envy get the better of him; **se deja influir fácilmente** he's easily influenced; ~se **llevar por la música** to let oneself be carried along by the music; ~se **estar** (AmL); (descuidarse) to be careless; (abandonarse) to let oneself go

⬚2 ⟨*barba/bigote*⟩ to grow

⬚3 ~se DE hacer algo to stop doing sth; **déjate de lamentarte** stop complaining

⬚4 (esp Esp fam) (olvidar) to leave

deje *m* ▶ DEJO A

dejo *m* (a) (acento) (slight) accent, lilt (b) (de una bebida, comida) aftertaste; ~ A algo slight taste OF sth (c) (de arrogancia, ironía) touch, hint (d) (impresión, sensación): **me quedó un** ~ **triste** I was left with a feeling of sadness

del: *contraction of* DE *and* EL

delantal *m* (para cocinar) apron; (de escolar) pinafore

delante *adv* ⬚1 (lugar, parte) [*Latin American Spanish also uses* ADELANTE *in many of these examples*]: **yo voy** ~ I'll go ahead *o* in front; **no te pongas** ~ don't stand in front of me; **lo tengo aquí** ~ I have it right here; **el asiento de** ~ the front seat; **la parte de** ~ the front; **el pasajero de** ~ the passenger in the front ⬚2 **delante de** (*loc prep*) in front of

delantera *f* (a) (en general) lead; **llevar/tomar la** ~ to be in/to take the lead (b) (Dep) (de equipo) forwards (*pl*), forward line

delantero -ra *adj* (a) ⟨*asiento/rueda*⟩ front (*before n*) (b) (Dep) ⟨*línea/posición*⟩ forward (*before n*), offensive (*before n*) (AmE)

■ *m,f* (Dep) forward; ~ **forward** center* forward

delatar [A1] *vt* «*persona*» (acusar) to denounce, inform on

■ **delatarse** *v pron* (*refl*) to give oneself away

delator -tora *adj* (a) ⟨*prueba/arma*⟩ incriminating (b) ⟨*mirada/sonrisa*⟩ revealing

■ *m,f* informer

delegación *f* ⬚1 (grupo) delegation ⬚2 (de poderes) delegation ⬚3 (a) (Méx) (comisaría) police station (b) (Esp) (oficina local) regional *o* local office

delegado *m,f* (representante) delegate; ~ **de curso** student representative

delegar [A3] *vt* to delegate; ~ **algo** EN **algn** to delegate sth TO sb

■ ~ *vi* to delegate

deleitar [A1] *vt* to delight

■ **deleitarse** *v pron* ~se **haciendo algo** to delight IN doing sth, enjoy doing sth

deleite *m* delight

deletrear [A1] *vt* to spell

delfín *m* (Zool) dolphin

delgado -da *adj* (a) ⟨*persona/piernas*⟩ (esbelto) slim; (flaco) thin (b) ⟨*tela/lámina/pared*⟩ thin; ⟨*hilo*⟩ fine, thin

deliberado -da *adj* deliberate

delicadeza *f* ⬚1 (cuidado, suavidad) gentleness; **con mucha** ~ very gently ⬚2 (a) (tacto, discreción) tact; **fue una falta de** ~ it was tactless of him (*o* you *etc*) (b) (gesto amable): **fue una** ~ **de su parte traerme** it was very kind of him to bring me; **ni siquiera tuvo la** ~ **de informarme** he didn't even have the courtesy to inform me

delicado -da *adj* ⬚1 (fino) ⟨*rasgos/manos*⟩ delicate; ⟨*sabor*⟩ delicate, subtle; ⟨*lenguaje/modales*⟩ refined ⬚2 (a) (que requiere cuidados) ⟨*cerámica/cristal*⟩ fragile; ⟨*tela*⟩ delicate; ⟨*piel*⟩ sensitive (b) ⟨*salud/estómago*⟩ delicate; ⟨*corazón*⟩ weak ⬚3 ⟨*asunto/cuestión/tema*⟩ delicate, sensitive; ⟨*situación*⟩ delicate, tricky ⬚4 (a) (melindroso) delicate, fussy (b) (susceptible) touchy

delicia *f* delight; **ser una** ~ to be delicious

delicioso -sa *adj* ⟨*comida/bebida/sabor*⟩ delicious; ⟨*tiempo*⟩ delightful

delimitar [A1] vt (a) ⟨terreno/espacio⟩ to demarcate (frml), to delimit (frml) (b) ⟨poderes/responsabilidades⟩ to define, specify

delincuencia f crime, delinquency (frml); ~ juvenil juvenile delinquency

delincuente mf criminal; ~ común common criminal; ~ juvenil juvenile delinquent

delinear [A1] vt (a) ⟨dibujo/plano⟩ to outline, draft; ⟨contorno⟩ to delineate (b) ⟨programa/proyecto⟩ to formulate, draw up

delinquir [I3] vi to commit a criminal offense*

delirar [A1] vi (Med) to be delirious; **la fiebre lo hacía** ~ the fever made him delirious

delirio m (Med) delirium; ~s de grandeza mpl delusions of grandeur (pl)

delito m crime, offense*; ~ ambiental environmental crime; ~ informático computer crime

delta m (Geog) delta
■ f (letra griega) delta

demacrado -da adj (pálido) haggard, drawn; (delgado) emaciated

demagogia f demagogy, demagoguery

demagogo -ga m,f demagogue, demagog (AmE)

demanda f ① (Com) demand; **tiene mucha** ~ it's in great demand ② (a) (Der) lawsuit; **presentar una** ~ **contra algn** to bring a lawsuit against sb (b) (petición) request; **accedí a su** ~ I agreed to his request

demandado -da m,f defendant

demandante mf plaintiff

demandar [A1] vt ① (Der) to sue ② (AmL) (requerir) to require

demarcar [A2] to demarcate

demás adj inv (delante del n): **los** ~ **estudiantes** the rest of the o the remaining students
■ pron ① (a) **lo** ~ the rest; **todo lo** ~ everything else (b) (en locs) **por lo demás** apart from that, otherwise; **por demás** extremely ② **los/las** ~ (referido a cosas) the rest, the others; (referido a personas) the rest, everybody else; **me dio uno y se quedó con los** ~ he gave me one and kept the rest o the others; **los** ~ **han terminado** the rest (of them) have finished, everybody else has finished

demasía: **en** ~ ⟨beber/comer⟩ to excess; **todo alimento, tomado en** ~, **es perjudicial** any food, when eaten in excess, can be harmful

demasiado¹ -da adj (delante del n): ~ **dinero** too much money; **había** ~s **coches** there were too many cars; **hace** ~ **calor** it's too hot
■ pron: **es** ~ it's too much; **somos** ~s there are too many of us; **hizo** ~ she made too many

demasiado² adv ① ⟨pequeño/caliente/caro⟩ too; **fue un esfuerzo** ~ **grande para él** it was too much of an effort for him ② ⟨comer/hablar/preocuparse⟩ too much; ⟨trabajar⟩ too hard

demencia f dementia

demente adj insane

■ mf insane person

democracia f democracy

demócrata mf democrat

democratacristiano -na adj/m,f Christian Democrat

democrático -ca adj democratic

demografía f demography

demográfico -ca adj demographic, population (before n)

demoledor -dora adj (a) ⟨máquina⟩ demolition (before n) (b) ⟨ataque/crítica⟩ devastating

demoler [E9] vt (a) ⟨edificio⟩ to demolish, pull down (b) ⟨mito/teoría⟩ (fam) to debunk, demolish

demonio m ① (diablo) devil ② (fam) (uso expletivo): **¡cómo** ~s **lo hizo!** how on earth did he do it?; **¿qué** ~s ... ?** what the hell ... ? (colloq); **¡~(s)!** (expresando enfado) damn! (colloq); (expresando sorpresa) goodness!, heavens!

demora f ① (esp AmL) (retraso) delay; **perdón por la** ~ I'm sorry I'm late; ~ **EN hacer algo** delay in doing sth; **sin** ~ without delay ② (Náut) bearing

demorar [A1] vt (a) (AmL) (tardar): **demoró tres horas en llegar** he took o it took him three hours to arrive (b) (AmL) (retrasar) ⟨viaje/decisión⟩ to delay
■ ~ vi (AmL): **¡no demores!** don't be long!
■ **demorarse** v pron (AmL) (a) (tardar cierto tiempo): **¡qué poco te demoraste!** that didn't take you very long; **me demoro 3 horas** it takes me 3 hours (b) (tardar demasiado) to be o take too long; ~**se EN hacer algo** to take a long time TO do sth

demoroso -sa adj (Bol, Chi) ⟨persona/vehículo⟩ slow; ⟨trabajo⟩ time-consuming

demostración f demonstration; (de teorema) proof

demostrar [A10] vt ① ⟨verdad/teorema⟩ to prove, demonstrate; ⟨ignorancia⟩ to show, prove; **ha demostrado ser muy capaz** he's shown himself to be very able; ~ **que algo es/no es cierto** to prove sth right/wrong ② (a) ⟨interés/sentimiento⟩ to show (b) ⟨funcionamiento/método⟩ to demonstrate

demostrativo -va adj (a) ⟨ejemplo⟩ illustrative (b) ⟨adjetivo/pronombre⟩ demonstrative (c) (AmL) ⟨persona/carácter⟩ demonstrative

denantes adv (Chi fam) a moment ago, just now

denegar [A7] vt (frml) ⟨permiso/autorización⟩ to refuse; ⟨petición⟩ to turn down; ⟨recurso⟩ (Der) to refuse

dengue m (Med) dengue fever

denigrante adj degrading, humiliating

denigrar [A1] vt (a) (hablar mal de) to denigrate (b) (degradar) to degrade

denominar [A1] vt (frml) (a) (dar nombre a) to call; **el denominado efecto invernadero** the so-called greenhouse effect (b) (con carácter oficial) to designate

AmC	América Central	Arg	Argentina	Cu	Cuba	Per	Perú
AmL	América Latina	Bol	Bolivia	Ec	Ecuador	RPI	Río de la Plata
AmS	América del Sur	Chi	Chile	Esp	España	Ur	Uruguay
Andes	Región andina	CS	Cono Sur	Méx	México	Ven	Venezuela

denotar [A1] *vt* **(a)** (frml) (demostrar, indicar) to show, denote (frml); **sus modales denotan una esmerada educación** her manners are the sign of an impeccable upbringing **(b)** (Ling) to denote

densidad *f* density; (de vegetación, niebla) thickness, denseness

denso -sa *adj* dense

dentado -da *adj* ‹filo› serrated; **una rueda dentada** a gearwheel, a cogwheel

dentadura *f* teeth (*pl*); ~ **postiza** false teeth (*pl*), dentures (*pl*)

dental *adj* dental

dentera *f* (sensación): **darle** ~ **a algn** to set sb's teeth on edge

dentífrico *m* toothpaste

dentista *mf* dentist

dentística *f* (Chi) dentistry, dental surgery

dentro *adv* ⊡ (lugar, parte) [*Latin American Spanish also uses* ADENTRO *in this sense*] inside; **aquí/ahí** ~ in here/there; **el perro duerme** ~ **the** dog sleeps indoors; **por** ~ on the inside; **la parte de** ~ the inside ⊡ **dentro de (a)** (en el espacio) in, inside; ~ **del edificio** in *o* inside the building **(b)** (en el tiempo) in; ~ **de dos semanas** in two weeks' time **(c)** (de límites, posibilidades) within; ~ **de nuestras posibilidades** within our means

denuncia *f* ⊡ (de robo, asesinato) report; **hizo la** ~ **del robo del coche** he reported the theft of his car; **presentar una** ~ to make a formal complaint ⊡ (crítica pública) denunciation

denunciar [A1] *vt* ⊡ ‹robo/asesinato/persona› to report ⊡ (condenar públicamente) to denounce, condemn

Dep., Dept. (= **Departamento**) Dept

departamento *m* ⊡ **(a)** (de empresa, institución) department **(b)** (provincia, distrito) department ⊡ (AmL) (apartamento) apartment (esp AmE), flat (BrE)

dependencia *f* ⊡ (condición) dependence; ~ DE **algo** dependence ON sth ⊡ **dependencias** *fpl* (edificios) buildings (*pl*); (salas) rooms (*pl*)

depender [E1] *vi* **(a)** «resultado/solución» to depend; ~ DE **algo/algn** to depend ON sth/sb **(b)** «persona» ~ DE **algn** to be dependent ON sb/sth

dependiente -ta *m,f* salesclerk (AmE), shop assistant (BrE)

depilación *f* (con cera) waxing; (con crema) hair-removal, depilation (frml); (de cejas) plucking

depilar [A1] *vt* ‹piernas/axilas› to wax (*o* shave *etc*); ‹cejas› to pluck
■ **depilarse** *v pron*: ~**se las piernas** to shave (*o* wax *etc*) one's legs; (*caus*) to have one's legs waxed

deplorable *adj* deplorable

deportar [A1] *vt* to deport

deporte *m* sport; **no practican ningún** ~ they don't play *o* do any sport(s); **hace** ~ **para estar en forma** she does sports (AmE) *o* (BrE) some sport to keep fit; ~ **acuático/de invierno** water/winter sport

deportista *adj* sporty; **fue muy** ~ **en su juventud** he was a keen sportsman in his youth;
■ *mf* (*m*) sportsman (*f*) sportswoman

deportividad *f* sportsmanship

deportivo¹ -va *adj* ‹club/centro› sports (*before n*) **(b)** ‹ropa› (para deporte) sports (*before n*); (informal) sporty, casual

deportivo² *m* sports car

depositar [A1] *vt* ⊡ **(a)** (frml) (colocar) to place, deposit (frml) **(b)** (dejar) to leave, deposit (frml) ⊡ (Fin) ‹dinero› to deposit; (en cuenta corriente) (AmL) to deposit, pay in (BrE)

depósito *m* ⊡ **(a)** (almacén) warehouse; ~ **de armas** arms depot; ~ **de cadáveres** morgue, mortuary (BrE) **(b)** (tanque) tank; ~ **de gasolina** gas tank (AmE), petrol tank (BrE) ⊡ (sedimento) deposit, sediment; (yacimiento) deposit ⊡ (Fin) **(a)** (AmL) (en una cuenta) deposit **(b)** (garantía) deposit

depravado -da *m,f* degenerate

depreciarse [A1] *v pron* to depreciate, fall in value

depredador¹ -dora *adj* (Zool) ‹animal/ave› predatory

depredador² *m* predator

depresión *f* depression

deprimente *adj* depressing

deprimido -da *adj* depressed

deprimir [I1] *vt* to depress
■ **deprimirse** *v pron* to get/become depressed

deprisa *adv* fast; **trabajar más** ~ to work faster; **¡~! escóndelo** quick! hide it

depurado -da *adj* ‹lenguaje/estilo› polished, refined; ‹gusto› refined

depuradora *f* **(a)** (de aguas residuales) sewage treatment plant **(b)** (en piscina) filter system

depurar [A1] *vt* ⊡ **(a)** ‹agua› to purify, treat; ‹aguas residuales› to treat **(b)** ‹sangre› to cleanse ⊡ **(a)** ‹organización/partido› to purge **(b)** ‹lenguaje/estilo› to polish, refine

derecha *f* ⊡ **(a)** (lado derecho) right; **la primera calle a la** ~ the first street on the right; **dobla a la** ~ turn right; **por la** ~ ‹conducir/caminar› on the right; **mantenga su** ~ keep to the right **(b)** (mano derecha) right hand ⊡ (Pol): **la** ~ **the** Right; **un político de** ~ *or* (Esp) ~**s** a right-wing politician

derecho¹ -cha *adj* ⊡ ‹mano/ojo/zapato› right; ‹lado› right, right-hand; **el ángulo superior** ~ the top right-hand corner; **queda a mano derecha** it's on the right-hand side *o* on the right ⊡ **(a)** (recto) straight; **ese cuadro no está** ~ that picture isn't straight; **siéntate** ~ sit up straight **(b)** (fam) (justo, honesto) honest, straight

derecho² *adv* straight; **siga todo** ~ go *o* keep straight on

derecho³ *m* ⊡ **(a)** (facultad, privilegio) right; ~**s humanos** human rights (*pl*); **estás en tu** ~ you're within your rights; ~ A **algo** right TO sth; **el** ~ **al voto** the right to vote; **tengo** ~ **a saber** I have a *o* the right to know; **esto da** ~ **a participar** this entitles you to participate; **¡no hay** ~**!** (fam) it's not fair! **(b)** (Com, Fin) tax; ~**s de aduana** customs duties (*pl*); ~**s de autor** royalties; ~ **de matrícula** registration fee; ~ **de reproducción** copyright ⊡ (Der) law ⊡ (de prenda) right side, outside; (de tela) right side, face; **póntelo al** ~ put it on properly *o* right side out

deriva *f*: **a la** ~ adrift

derivar [A1] *vi* **(a)** (proceder) ~ DE **algo** ⋯≯

«*palabra*» to derive FROM sth, come FROM sth; «*problema/situación*» to arise FROM sth **(b)** (traer como consecuencia) ~ EN algo to result IN sth, lead TO sth
■ ~ *vt* (Med) (AmL) ~ **a algn a un especialista** to refer sb to a specialist
■ **derivarse** *v pron* (proceder) ~se DE algo «*palabra*» to be derived FROM sth, come FROM sth; «*problema/situación*» to arise FROM sth

dermatólogo -ga *m,f* dermatologist

derogar [A3] *vt* to abolish, repeal

derramar [A1] *vt* **(a)** ⟨*agua/leche/azúcar*⟩ to spill; ⟨*cuentas/sangre*⟩ to shed **(b)** ⟨*lentejas/ botones*⟩ to spill, scatter
■ **derramarse** *v pron* **(a)** «*tinta/leche*» to spill; «*corriente*» to pour out **(b)** «*cuentas/botones*» to scatter, spread

derrame *m* **(a)** (Med): **tengo un ~ en el ojo** I have a burst blood vessel in my eye; **~ cerebral** brain hemorrhage* **(b)** (de líquido) spillage

derrapar [A1] *vi* ⟨*vehículo*⟩ to skid; «*embrague*» to slip; «*llantas*» to spin

derredor: **al/en ~** (*loc adv*) around

derretir [I14] *vt* ⟨*mantequilla/helado*⟩ to melt; ⟨*hielo/nieve*⟩ to melt, thaw
■ **derretirse** *v pron* «*mantequilla/helado*» to melt; «*nieve/hielo*» to thaw, melt

derribar [A1] *vt* **(a)** ⟨*edificio/muro*⟩ to demolish, knock down; ⟨*puerta*⟩ to break down **(b)** ⟨*avión*⟩ to shoot down, bring down **(c)** ⟨*persona*⟩ to floor, knock ... down; ⟨*novillo*⟩ to knock ... over **(d)** «*viento*» to bring down **(e)** ⟨*gobierno*⟩ to overthrow, topple

derrocar [A2] *vt* to overthrow, topple

derrochador -dora *adj*: **es muy ~** he's a real spendthrift
■ *m,f* squanderer, spendthrift

derrochar [A1] *vt* (malgastar) ⟨*dinero*⟩ to squander, waste; ⟨*electricidad/agua*⟩ to waste
■ ~ *vi* to throw money away, to squander money

derroche *m* (de dinero, bienes) waste

derrota *f* (Dep, Mil) defeat

derrotado -da *adj* **(a)** ⟨*ejército*⟩ defeated; ⟨*equipo/contrincante*⟩ defeated, beaten **(b)** (desesperanzado) despondent

derrotar [A1] *vt* ⟨*ejército/partido*⟩ to defeat; ⟨*equipo/contrincante*⟩ to defeat, beat

derrotista *adj/mf* defeatist

derruido -da *adj* ⟨*casa*⟩ ruined; **medio ~** virtually in ruins

derrumbamiento *m* collapse

derrumbar [A1] *vt* ⟨*casa/edificio*⟩ to demolish, pull down
■ **derrumbarse** *v pron* **(a)** «*edificio*» to collapse **(b)** «*persona*» to go to pieces; «*esperanzas/ilusiones*» to be shattered, collapse

desabastecimiento, (Méx) **desabasto** *m* shortage of supplies (o food etc)

desabotonarse [A1] *v pron* **(a)** «*prenda*» to come undone **(b)** (*refl*) «*persona*» ⟨*camisa/ abrigo*⟩ to unbutton, undo

desabrido -da *adj* (comida) tasteless, bland

desabrigado -da *adj* ⟨*lugar*⟩ exposed; **estás muy ~** you're not wearing warm enough clothes

desabrochar [A1] *vt* ⟨*prenda/zapatos/ pulsera*⟩ to undo; **¿me desabrochas?** can you undo me? (colloq)
■ **desabrocharse** *v pron* **(a)** «*prenda*» to come undone **(b)** (*refl*) «*persona*» ⟨*camisa/abrigo*⟩ to undo

desaconsejar [A1] *vt* to advise against

desacostumbrarse [A1] *v pron* to get out of the habit; **~ A hacer algo** to get out of the habit OF doing sth; **se desacostumbró al tráfico de la ciudad** she forgot what city traffic was like

desacreditar [A1] *vt* to discredit
■ **desacreditarse** *v pron* (*refl*) to discredit oneself, damage one's reputation

desactivar [A1] *vt* ⟨*bomba/explosivo*⟩ to defuse, deactivate

desacuerdo *m* disagreement; **~ CON algo/ algn** disagreement WITH sth/sb

desadaptado -da *adj*: **un niño ~** a child who has problems settling in o adjusting; **sentirse ~** to feel unsettled

desafiante *adj* ⟨*gesto/palabras*⟩ defiant

desafiar [A17] *vt* **(a)** ⟨*persona*⟩ to challenge; **~ a algn A algo/hacer algo** to challenge sb TO sth/do sth **(b)** ⟨*peligro/muerte*⟩ to defy

desafilado -da *adj* blunt

desafinado -da *adj* out of tune

desafinar [A1] *vi* «*instrumento*» to be out of tune; «*músico/cantante*» to be off key o out of tune

desafío *m* (reto) challenge; (al peligro, a la muerte) defiance

desaforado -da *m,f*: **como un ~** ⟨*correr*⟩ hell for leather; ⟨*gritar*⟩ at the top of one's voice

desafortunado -da *adj* **(a)** (desdichado) ⟨*persona*⟩ unlucky; ⟨*suceso*⟩ unfortunate **(b)** (desacertado) ⟨*medidas/actuación*⟩ unfortunate

desagradable *adj* unpleasant; ⟨*respuesta/ comentario*⟩ unkind

desagradar [A1] *vt*: **me desagrada el calor/ tener que decírselo** I don't like the heat/having to tell her

desagradecido -da *adj* ⟨*persona*⟩ ungrateful; ⟨*trabajo/tarea*⟩ thankless

desagrado *m* displeasure; **lo hizo con ~** she did it reluctantly o unwillingly

desagüe *m* **(a)** (de lavabo, lavadora) wastepipe; (de patio, azotea) drain **(b)** (acción) drainage

desahogado -da *adj* ⟨*posición económica/ vida*⟩ comfortable; ⟨*casa/habitación*⟩ uncluttered, spacious

desahogar [A3] *vt* ⟨*penas/ira*⟩ to give vent to
■ **desahogarse** *v pron* to let off steam ; **se desahogó dándole patadas a la rueda** he vented his anger (o frustration etc) by kicking the wheel; **~se CON algn** to pour one's heart out to sb

desahogo *m* **(a)** (alivio) relief; **llorar le servirá de ~** crying will make him feel better **(b)** (en ~ dinero): **vivir con ~** to be comfortably off

desahuciar [A1] *vt* ① ⟨*enfermo*⟩ to declare ... terminally ill ② **(a)** ⟨*inquilino*⟩ to evict **(b)** (Chi) ⟨*empleado*⟩ (despedir) to dismiss; (notificar el despido) to give ... notice

desaire *m* snub, slight; **hacerle un ~ a algn** to snub o slight sb

desalentador -dora *adj* disheartening, discouraging

desalentar [A5] *vt* to discourage, dishearten

desaliento *m* dejection, despondency

desaliñado -da *adj* slovenly

desalojar [A1] *vt* (a) ⟨*edificio/recinto*⟩ «*ocupantes*» to vacate; ⟨*policía/juez*⟩ to clear (b) ⟨*residentes*⟩ to evacuate; ⟨*inquilino*⟩ (esp AmL) to evict

desamarrar [A1] *vt* (AmL exc RPl) ⟨*embarcación*⟩ to cast off; ⟨*zapatos/paquete*⟩ to undo, untie; ⟨*animal/persona*⟩ to untie
■ **desamarrarse** *v pron* (AmL exc RPl) **1** «*paquete/zapatos*» to come undone; «*bultos/barco*» to come untied **2** (*refl*) «*persona*» to get free; «*animal*» to get loose *o* free

desamparado -da *adj* ⟨*niño/anciano*⟩ defenseless*; ⟨*lugar*⟩ bleak, unprotected

desamparo *m* neglect

desangrarse *v pron* to bleed to death

desanimado -da *adj* discouraged, dispirited

desanimar [A1] *vt* to discourage
■ **desanimarse** *v pron* to become disheartened *o* discouraged

desánimo *m* dejection, despondency

desaparecer [E3] *vi* «*persona/objeto*» to disappear; «*dolor/síntoma/cicatriz*» to disappear, go; «*costumbre*» to disappear, die out; «*mancha*» to come out
■ **desaparecerse** *v pron* (Andes) to disappear

desaparecido -da *adj* (a) (que no se encuentra) missing (b) ⟨*period*⟩ ⟨*muerto*⟩ late (*before n*), deceased (fml)
■ *m,f* (a) (en un accidente) missing person (b) (Pol): **los ~s** the disappeared *o* those who have disappeared

desaparición *f* disappearance; **una especie en vías de ~** an endangered species

desapercibido -da *adj*: **pasar ~** to go unnoticed

desaprovechar [A1] *vt* ⟨*oportunidad*⟩ to waste; ⟨*tiempo/comida*⟩ to waste

desarmable *adj* ⟨*mueble/mecanismo*⟩ which can be dismantled *o* taken apart

desarmado -da *adj* ⟨*policía/criminal*⟩ unarmed

desarmador *m* (Méx) (a) (herramienta) screwdriver (b) (bebida) screwdriver

desarmar [A1] *vt* **1** ⟨*mueble/mecanismo*⟩ to dismantle; ⟨*carpa*⟩ (AmL) to take down; ⟨*rifle/motor*⟩ to strip (down); ⟨*rompecabezas*⟩ to take ... to pieces, break up; ⟨*juguete/maqueta*⟩ to take ... apart **2** (a) (quitar armas) to disarm (b) (dejar sin argumentos) to disarm

desarme *m* disarmament

desarrollado -da *adj* developed; **un niño muy/poco ~a** well-developed/an underdeveloped child

desarrollar [A1] *vt* **1** (en general) to develop **2** (a) (exponer) ⟨*teoría/tema*⟩ to explain (b) (llevar a cabo) ⟨*actividad/labor*⟩ to carry out
■ **desarrollarse** *v pron* **1** (en general) to develop **2** ⟨*acto/entrevista/escena*⟩ to take place

desarrollo *m* development; **países en vías de ~** developing countries; **según el ~ de los acontecimientos** according to how things develop

desastrado -da *adj* ⟨*persona*⟩ scruffy, untidy; ⟨*habitación/trabajo*⟩ untidy

desastre *m* disaster; **como cantante es un ~** he's a hopeless singer; **tienes la habitación hecha un ~** your room is a shambles; **vas hecha un ~** you look a real mess (colloq)

desastroso -sa *adj* disastrous

desatado -da *adj*: **estar ~** ⟨*perro*⟩ to be loose; ⟨*cordón/nudo*⟩ to be undone

desatar [A1] *vt* (a) ⟨*nudo/lazo*⟩ to untie, undo (b) ⟨*persona*⟩ to let ... loose
■ **desatarse** *v pron* (a) «*nudo/cordones*» to come undone *o* untied; «*perro/caballo*» to get loose (b) (*refl*) «*persona*» to untie oneself; ⟨*cordones/zapatos*⟩ to untie, undo

desatascador *m* (instrumento) plunger; (producto) nitric acid (o caustic soda *etc*) (*used to clear blocked drains*)

desatascar [A2] *vt* ⟨*cañería/fregadero*⟩ to unblock, clear
■ **desatascarse** *v pron* «*cañería/fregadero*» to unblock; «*carretera*» to clear

desatender [E8] *vt* (a) ⟨*trabajo/familia*⟩ to neglect (b) ⟨*tienda/mostrador*⟩ to leave ... unattended

desatento -ta *adj* (a) [SER] (desconsiderado) thoughtless, inconsiderate (b) [ESTAR] (distraído) inattentive

desatornillador *m* (AmC, Chi) screwdriver

desatornillar [A1] *vt* to unscrew

desautorizar [A4] *vt* (a) (restar autoridad a) ⟨*persona*⟩ to undermine the authority of; ⟨*declaraciones*⟩ to disavow (fml) (b) (retirar la autorización para) ⟨*marcha/huelga*⟩ to ban

desayunar [A1] *vt* to have ... for breakfast; **¿qué desayunaste?** what did you have for breakfast?
■ **~** *vi* to have breakfast
■ **desayunarse** *v pron* (AmL) (tomar el desayuno) to have breakfast; **~se CON algo** to have sth FOR breakfast

desayuno *m* breakfast; **tomar el ~** to have breakfast

desbarajuste *m* (fam) mess; **un ~ económico** an economic mess *o* chaos

desbaratar [A1] *vt* (a) ⟨*planes*⟩ to spoil, ruin; ⟨*sistema*⟩ to disrupt (b) (Méx) ⟨*papeles*⟩ to jumble (up), muddle (up); ⟨*mecanismo*⟩ to ruin, destroy
■ **desbaratarse** *v pron* (a) «*plan*» to be ruined, be spoiled; «*sistema*» to be disrupted, break down (b) (Méx) «*papeles*» to get jumbled up, get muddled (up); «*mecanismo*» to break, get broken

desbarrancarse [A2] *v pron* to go over a sheer drop

desbloquear [A1] *vt* (a) ⟨*carretera/entrada*⟩ to clear; ⟨*mecanismo*⟩ to release, free (b) ⟨*negociaciones/diálogo*⟩ to break the deadlock in (c) (Com, Fin) ⟨*cuenta*⟩ to unfreeze

desbocado -da *adj* (a) ⟨*caballo*⟩ runaway (*before n*) (b) ⟨*cuello/escote*⟩ loose, wide

desbocarse [A2] *v pron* «*caballo*» to bolt

desbordante *adj* ⟨*entusiasmo/júbilo*⟩ boundless; **está ~ de entusiasmo** he's bursting with enthusiasm

desbordarse [A1] *v pron* (a) «*río/canal*» to burst its banks (b) «*vaso/cubo*» to overflow (c) «*multitud*» to get out of hand, get out of control

descabellado -da *adj* crazy, ridiculous

descafeinado -da *adj* decaffeinated

descalabro *m* (a) (desastre) disaster (b) (Mil) defeat

descalificación *f* (Dep) disqualification

descalificar [A2] *vt* ⟨*deportista/equipo*⟩ to disqualify

descalzarse [A4] *v pron* to take off one's shoes

descalzo -za *adj* ⟨*pie*⟩ bear; ⟨*persona*⟩ barefoot

descaminado -da *adj*: **andar** ~ to be on the wrong track

descampado *m* (a) (terreno) area *o* piece of open ground *o* land (b) **al descampado** (AmS) ⟨*dormir*⟩ in the open (air)

descansado -da *adj* (a) [ESTAR] ⟨*persona*⟩ rested, refreshed (b) [SER] ⟨*actividad/trabajo*⟩ easy, undemanding; ⟨*vida*⟩ quiet, peaceful

descansar [A1] *vi* (a) (de actividad, trabajo) to rest, have a rest; **sin** ~ without a break; ~ **DE algo** to have a rest *o* break FROM sth (b) (yacer) to lie; **que en paz descanse** God rest his soul ■ ~ *vt* ~ **la vista** to rest one's eyes, to give one's eyes a rest; ~ **la mente** to give one's mind a break *o* rest

descansillo *m* (Esp) landing

descanso *m* 1 (a) (reposo) rest (b) (en trabajo, colegio) break; **sin** ~ without a break (c) (Mil): **estar en posición de** ~ to be standing at ease 2 (intervalo) (Dep) half time; (Teatr) interval 3 (alivio, tranquilidad) relief 4 (AmL) (rellano) landing

descapotable *adj/m* convertible

descarado -da *adj* ⟨*persona/actitud*⟩ brazen, shameless; **es muy** ~ he has a lot of nerve

descarga *f* 1 (de mercancías) unloading 2 (Elec) discharge; **una** ~ **eléctrica** an electric shock 3 (de arma) shot, discharge (frml); (de conjunto de armas) volley

descargar [A3] *vt* 1 ⟨*vehículo/mercancías*⟩ to unload 2 (a) ⟨*pistola*⟩ (extraer las balas) to unload; (disparar) to fire, discharge (frml); **la pistola está descargada** the pistol is not loaded (b) ⟨*tiro*⟩ to fire; ⟨*golpe*⟩ to deal, land 3 ⟨*ira/agresividad*⟩ to vent; ⟨*preocupaciones/tensiones*⟩ to relieve ■ ~ *v impers* «*aguacero*» to pour down; «*temporal*» to break ■ **descargarse** *v pron* 1 (Elec) «*pila*» to run down; «*batería*» to go dead *o* flat 2 «*tormenta*» to break; «*lluvias*» to come down, fall

descaro *m* audacity, nerve (colloq); **¡qué** ~! what a nerve!

descarriado -da *adj*: **hoy día la juventud anda descarriada** the youth of today has lost its way; ▶ OVEJA

descarrilamiento *m* derailment

descarrilar [A1] *vi* to derail, be derailed

■ **descarrilarse** *v pron* (AmL) to derail, be derailed

descartar [A1] *vt* to rule out

descascararse [A1] *vpron* «*pared/pintura*» to peel; «*taza/plato*» to chip

descendencia *f* descendants (*pl*)

descendente *adj* ⟨*curva/línea*⟩ downward; ⟨*escala*⟩ descending

descender [E8] *vi* 1 (a) «*temperatura/nivel*» to fall, drop (b) (frml) (desde una altura) «*avión*» to descend; «*persona*» to descend (frml), to come/go down 2 (en clasificación) to go down 3 (proceder) ~ **DE** algn to be descended FROM sb

descendiente *mf* descendant

descenso *m* 1 (a) (de temperatura, nivel) fall, drop; (de precios) fall (b) (desde una altura) descent 2 (Dep) relegation

descentrado -da *adj* (a) ⟨*eje/rueda*⟩ off-center* (b) ⟨*persona*⟩ disoriented, disorientated (BrE)

descentralizar [A4] *vt* to decentralize

descifrar [A1] *vt* (a) ⟨*mensaje*⟩ to decode, decipher; ⟨*escritura/jeroglífico/código*⟩ to decipher (b) ⟨*misterio/enigma*⟩ to work out, figure out

descodificador *m* decoder

descolgar [A8] *vt* (a) ⟨*cuadro/cortina*⟩ to take down (b) ⟨*teléfono*⟩ to pick up; **dejar el teléfono descolgado** to leave the phone off the hook ■ **descolgarse** *v pron* 1 (por una cuerda) to lower oneself 2 (en carrera) to pull away, break away

descollar [A10] *vi* to be outstanding

descolorido -da *adj* ⟨*tela/papel*⟩ faded

descomponer [E22] *vt* 1 ⟨*alimento/cadáver*⟩ to rot, cause ... to decompose *o* rot 2 (esp AmL) ⟨*máquina/aparato*⟩ to break; ⟨*peinado*⟩ to mess up 3 ⟨*persona*⟩ (a) (producir malestar) «*olor*» to make ... queasy (b) (producir diarrea) to give ... diarrhea* ■ **descomponerse** *v pron* 1 «*luz*» to split; «*sustancia*» to break down, separate 2 «*cadáver/alimento*» to rot, decompose (frml) 3 (esp AmL) «*máquina/aparato*» to break down 4 «*persona*» (sentir malestar) to feel sick; (del estómago) to have an attack of diarrhea* 6 (CS) «*tiempo*» to become unsettled; «*día*» to cloud over

descompuesto -ta *adj* 1 ⟨*alimento*⟩ rotten, decomposed (frml); ⟨*cadáver*⟩ decomposed 2 ⟨*expresión*⟩ changed, altered 3 (esp AmL) [ESTAR] ⟨*máquina/aparato*⟩ broken; ⟨*teléfono*⟩ out of order 4 **estar** ~ (indispuesto) to feel sick; (del estómago) to have diarrhea*/an upset stomach

descompuse, descompuso, etc ▶ DESCOMPONER

desconcertado -da *adj* disconcerted; **quedarse** ~ to be taken aback

desconcertante *adj* disconcerting

desconcertar [A5] *vt* to disconcert; **su respuesta me desconcertó** I was disconcerted by her reply

desconchado *m* (en taza, plato) chip; (en pared) *place where plaster or paint has come off*

desconcharse [A1] *v pron* «*taza/plato*» to chip, get chipped; «*pared/piel*» to peel

desconcierto *m*: su llamada los llenó de ~ they were disconcerted by his call; **el ~ reinante** the prevailing atmosphere of uncertainty

desconectar [A1] *vt* ⟨*alarma/teléfono*⟩ to disconnect; ⟨*calefacción*⟩ to switch off, turn off; ~ **algo DE algo** to disconnect sth FROM sth
■ **desconectarse** *v pron* «*aparato*» to switch *o* turn off

desconfiado -da *adj* (receloso) distrustful; (suspicaz) suspicious

desconfianza *f* distrust, suspicion

desconfiar [A17] *vi* ~ **DE algn** to mistrust sb, to distrust sb; ~ **DE algo** ⟨*de motivos*⟩ to mistrust sth; ⟨*de honestidad*⟩ to doubt sth

descongelante *m* deicer

descongelar [A1] *vt* ⟨*refrigerador*⟩ to defrost; ⟨*alimentos*⟩ to defrost, thaw
■ **descongelarse** *v pron* «*refrigerador*» to defrost; «*alimentos*» to defrost, thaw

descongestionar [A1] *vt* to clear

desconocer [E3] *vt* (a) (no conocer): **por razones que desconocemos** for reasons unknown to us; **desconocía este hecho** I was unaware of this fact (b) (no reconocer): **te desconocí** I didn't recognize you

desconocido -da *adj* (en general) unknown; **un cantante ~** an unknown singer; **una persona desconocida** a stranger
■ *m,f* (no conocido) stranger

desconocimiento *m* ignorance

desconsiderado -da *adj* thoughtless, inconsiderate

desconsolado -da *adj* **estar ~ POR algo** to be heartbroken OVER sth; **lloraba ~** he cried inconsolably

desconsuelo *m* grief, despair

descontado *adj*: **eso dalo por ~** you can be sure of that; **doy por ~ que vendrás a cenar** I'm assuming that you're coming to dinner

descontaminar [A1] *vt* ⟨*alimentos/cultivos*⟩ to decontaminate; ⟨*atmósfera*⟩ to clean up

descontar [A10] *vt* **1** (a) (rebajar): **me descontó el 15%** he gave me a 15% discount (b) (restar) ⟨*gastos/impuestos*⟩ to deduct, take off; ⟨*horas*⟩ to deduct **2** (exceptuar): **si descontamos a Pedro/los domingos ...** if we don't count Pedro/ Sundays ... **3** ⟨*letra/pagaré*⟩ to discount

descontento¹ -ta *adj* [ESTAR] dissatisfied; ~ **CON algo/algn** unhappy *o* dissatisfied WITH sth/sb

descontento² *m* discontent

descontrolado -da *adj* out of control

descontrolarse [A1] *v pron* to get out of control

desconvocar [A2] *vt* to call off

descorazonar [A1] *vt* to dishearten, discourage

descorchar [A1] *vt* to uncork, open

descorrer [E1] *vt* ⟨*cortinas*⟩ to draw (back); ⟨*cerrojo*⟩ to draw back

descortés *adj* ⟨*persona*⟩ impolite, ill-mannered; ⟨*comportamiento*⟩ rude, impolite

descortesía *f* (a) (acto descortés) discourtesy (b) (cualidad) rudeness, impoliteness

descoserse [E1] *v pron* «*prenda/costura*» to come unstitched

descosido -da *adj* ⟨*dobladillo/costura*⟩ unstitched

descremado -da *adj* skimmed

describir [I34] *vt* to describe

descripción *f* description

descriptivo -va *adj* descriptive

descrito -ta *pp*: ▶ DESCRIBIR

descuartizar [A4] *vt* ⟨*res*⟩ to quarter (b) «*asesino*» to chop ... (up) into pieces

descubierto -ta *adj* **1** ⟨*piscina/terraza*⟩ open-air, outdoor (*before n*); ⟨*carroza*⟩ open-top **2** ⟨*cielos*⟩ clear **3** **al descubierto: quedar al ~** «*planes/escándalo*» to come to light; **han puesto al ~ sus chanchullos** his shady dealings have been exposed; **girar al** *or* **en ~** (Com, Fin) to overdraw

descubridor -dora *m,f* discoverer

descubrimiento *m* discovery

descubrir [I33] *vt* **1** ⟨*tierras/oro/artista*⟩ to discover **2** (a) (enterarse de, averiguar) ⟨*razón/ solución*⟩ to discover, find out; ⟨*complot/engaño*⟩ to uncover; ⟨*fraude*⟩ to detect (b) ⟨*persona escondida*⟩ to find, track down (c) ⟨*culpable*⟩ find ... out (d) (delatar) to give ... away **3** (a) ⟨*estatua/placa*⟩ to unveil (b) (revelar) ⟨*planes/ intenciones*⟩ to reveal

descuento *m* **1** (a) (rebaja) discount; **hacen un ~ del 15%** they give a 15% discount (b) (del sueldo) deduction **2** (Dep) injury time **3** (de letra, pagaré) discount

descuidado -da *adj* **1** [SER] (negligente) careless; (en el vestir) sloppy (b) [ESTAR] (desatendido) neglected

descuidar [A1] *vt* ⟨*negocio/jardín*⟩ to neglect
■ ~ *vi*: **descuide, yo me ocuparé de eso** don't worry, I'll see to that
■ **descuidarse** *v pron* (a) (no prestar atención, distraerse): **se descuidó un momento y el perro se le escapó** his attention strayed for a moment and the dog ran off; **si te descuidas, te roban** if you don't watch out, they'll rob you; **como te descuides, te van a quitar el puesto** if you don't look out, they'll take your job from you (b) (en el aspecto físico) to neglect one's appearance

descuido *m* (a) (distracción): **en un ~ el niño se le escapó** she took her eyes off the child for a moment and he ran off; **basta el más pequeño ~** the smallest lapse of concentration is enough (b) (error) slip; (omisión) oversight

desde *prep* **1** (en el tiempo) since; ~ **entonces/ ~ que se casó** since then/since he got married; **¿~ cuándo trabajas aquí?** how long have you been working here?; ~ **el primer momento** right from the start; **no los veo ~ hace meses** I haven't seen them for months; ~ **el 15 hasta el 30** from the 15th to *o* until the 30th **2** (en el espacio) from; ~ **aquí/allá** from here/ there; **¿~ dónde tengo que leer?** where do I have to read from?; ~ **la página 12 hasta la 20** from page 12 (up) to page 20 **3** (en escalas, jerarquías) from; **blusas ~ 12 euros** blouses from 12 euros.

desdén *m* disdain, scorn

desdeñable *adj* insignificant

desdeñar [A1] *vt* **(a)** (menospreciar) to scorn **(b)** ⟨*pretendiente*⟩ to spurn

desdeñoso -sa *adj* disdainful

desdicha *f* (desgracia) misfortune; (infelicidad) unhappiness

desdichado -da *adj* **(a)** (infeliz) unhappy **(b)** [SER] ⟨*día*⟩ ill-fated; **ser ~ en amores** to be unlucky in love
■ *m,f*: **es un pobre ~** he's a poor unfortunate wretch

desdoblar [A1] *vt* ⟨*servilleta/pañuelo*⟩ to unfold
■ **desdoblarse** *v pron* to divide into two, split into two

deseable *adj* desirable

desear [A1] *vt* **1** ⟨*suerte/éxito/felicidad*⟩ to wish; **te deseo un feliz viaje** I hope you have a good trip **2** (querer): **un embarazo no deseado** an unwanted pregnancy; **las tan deseadas vacaciones** the long-awaited holidays; **lo que más deseo es …** my greatest wish is …; **si tú lo deseas** if you want to; **~ía una respuesta ahora** I would like a reply now; **está deseando verte** he's really looking forward to seeing you; **¿desea que se lo envuelva?** (frml) would you like me to wrap it for you? **3** ⟨*persona*⟩ to desire, want

desechable *adj* disposable

desechar [A1] *vt* **(a)** ⟨*ayuda/propuesta*⟩ to reject; ⟨*idea/plan*⟩ (rechazar) to reject; (renunciar a) to drop, give up **(b)** ⟨*restos/residuos*⟩ to throw away *o* out; ⟨*ropa*⟩ to throw out

desecho *m* waste

desembarcar [A2] *vi* (de barco, avión) «*pasajeros*» to disembark; «*tropas*» to land, disembark
■ **~** *vt* ⟨*mercancías*⟩ to unload; ⟨*pasajeros*⟩ to disembark; (en emergencia) to evacuate

desembocadura *f* mouth, estuary

desembocar [A2] *vi* **~ EN algo** ⟨*en mar/río*⟩ to flow INTO algo; ⟨*en calle*⟩ to come out ONTO sth; ⟨*en plaza*⟩ to come out INTO sth

desembolsar [A1] *vt* to spend, pay out

desembolso *m* expenditure; (gasto inicial) outlay

desempacar [A2] *vt/vi* (esp AmL) to unpack

desempaquetar [A1] *vt* to unwrap

desempatar [A1] *vi* **(a)** (Dep) to break the tie (AmE), to break the deadlock (BrE) **(b)** (en una votación) to break the deadlock

desempate *m* **(a)** (Dep): **el ~ se produjo en el minuto 36** the breakthrough came in the 36th minute; **un partido de ~** a decider; **~ a penaltys** penalty shoot-out **(b)** (en concurso) tiebreak, tiebreaker; (en una votación) run-off

desempeñar [A1] *vt* **(a)** (Teatr) ⟨*papel*⟩ to play **(b)** ⟨*funciones*⟩ to carry out, perform; ⟨*cargo*⟩ to hold
■ **desempeñarse** *v pron* (AmL): **se desempeña bien en su trabajo** she does her job well; **se desempeñó muy bien** she did *o* managed very well

desempleado -da *m,f*: **un ~** someone who is out of work *o* unemployed; **los ~s** the unemployed

desempleo *m* **(a)** (situación) unemployment **(b)** (subsidio) unemployment benefit

desencadenar [A1] *vt* **(a)** ⟨*crisis/protesta/reacción*⟩ to trigger **(b)** ⟨*perro*⟩ to unleash; ⟨*preso*⟩ to unchain
■ **desencadenarse** *v pron* «*explosión/reacción*» to be triggered off; «*guerra*» to break out; «*tempestad*» to break

desencajado -da *adj* **(a)** ⟨*pieza*⟩ out of position **(b)** ⟨*mandíbula/rótula*⟩ dislocated **(c)** (alterado) shaken

desencajar [A1] *vt* **(a)** (Mec) to knock out of position **(b)** ⟨*mandíbula/rótula*⟩ to dislocate
■ **desencajarse** *v pron* **(a)** (Mec) to be knocked *o* come out of position **(b)** «*mandíbula/rótula*» to become/get dislocated

desencaminado -da *adj* (AmL) ▶ DESCAMINADO

desencanto *m* disillusionment, disenchantment

desenchufar [A1] *vt* to unplug, disconnect

desenfadado -da *adj* **(a)** (seguro de sí mismo) self-assured, confident; (sin inhibiciones) uninhibited **(b)** ⟨*estilo/moda/actitud*⟩ free-and-easy, carefree

desenfocado -da *adj* out of focus

desenganchar [A1] *vt* ⟨*caballos/remolque*⟩ to unhitch; ⟨*vagones*⟩ to uncouple

desengañar [A1] *vt* (decepcionar) to disillusion; (sacar del engaño, error) to get … to face the facts
■ **desengañarse** *v pron* **(a)** (decepcionarse) **~se DE algo** to become disillusioned WITH *o* ABOUT sth **(b)** (salir del engaño, error) to stop fooling oneself

desengaño *m* disappointment; **llevarse un ~** to be disappointed; **un ~ amoroso** an unhappy love affair

desenlace *m* (de película, libro) ending; (de aventura) outcome

desenredar [A1] *vt* ⟨*pelo/lana*⟩ to untangle, disentangle; ⟨*lío*⟩ to straighten out, sort out
■ **desenredarse** *v pron* (refl) ⟨*pelo*⟩ to get the knots out of

desenrollar [A1] *vt* ⟨*alfombra/póster*⟩ to unroll; ⟨*persiana*⟩ to let down; ⟨*ovillo/cuerda*⟩ to unwind

desenroscar [A2] *vt* to unscrew

desentenderse [E8] *v pron* **~ DE algo** ⟨*de un asunto*⟩ to wash one's hands OF sth; **se desentiende de los hijos** he doesn't take an interest in the children

desenterrar [A5] *vt* ⟨*cadáver*⟩ to exhume, dig up; ⟨*ruinas/tesoro*⟩ to unearth, dig up

desentonar [A1] *vi* **(a)** (Mús) to go out of tune *o* off key **(b)** «*color*» to clash **(c)** ⟨*atuendo/comentario*⟩ to be out of place

desentrenado -da *adj* out of condition *o* training

desenvoltura *f* self-assurance

desenvolver [E11] *vt* to unwrap, open
■ **desenvolverse** *v pron* **(a)** (manejarse) to get by, manage; **se desenvuelve muy bien en inglés** she gets by very well in English; **se desenvolvió bien en la entrevista** she managed the interview all right **(b)** (en situaciones difíciles) to cope **(c)** «*hechos/sucesos*» to develop

desenvuelto -ta *adj* ⟨*persona*⟩ self-assured, confident

deseo *m* (a) (anhelo) wish; **formular un** ∼ to make a wish (b) (apetito sexual) desire

desequilibrado -da *adj* ⟨*rueda/mecanismo*⟩ out of balance; ⟨*persona*⟩ unbalanced

desequilibrar [A1] *vt* (a) ⟨*embarcación/ vehículo*⟩ to unbalance, make ... unbalanced; ⟨*persona*⟩ (físicamente) to throw ... off balance; (mentalmente) to unbalance (b) ⟨*fuerzas/poder*⟩ to upset the balance of
■ **desequilibrarse** *v pron* «*ruedas/mecanismo*» to get out of balance

desequilibrio *m* (a) (desigualdad) imbalances (b) (Psic) unbalanced state of mind

desertar [A1] *vi* (Mil) to desert; (de partido) to defect

desértico -ca *adj* ⟨*zona/clima*⟩ desert (*before n*)

desertización *f* desertification

desertor -tora *m,f* (Mil) deserter; (de un partido) defector

desesperación *f* (a) (angustia) desperation; **con** ∼ ⟨*luchar/gritar*⟩ desperately; ⟨*mirar/ suplicar*⟩ despairingly; ⟨*llorar*⟩ bitterly; **de** ∼ out of desperation (b) (desesperanza) despair

desesperado -da *adj* desperate

desesperante *adj* (a) (exasperante) exasperating (b) (angustioso) distressing

desesperar [A1] *vt* to drive ... to distraction *o* despair
■ ∼ *vi* to despair, give up hope
■ **desesperarse** *v pron* to become exasperated

desestabilizar [A4] *vt* to destabilize

desfachatez *f* audacity, nerve (colloq)

desfalco *m* embezzlement

desfallecer [E3] *vi* (a) (flaquear) «*persona*» to become weak; «*fuerzas*» to fade, fail; «*ánimos*» to flag; **lucharon sin** ∼ they fought tirelessly (b) (desmayarse) to faint, pass out

desfasado -da *adj* ⟨*ideas/persona*⟩ old-fashioned

desfase *m* (falta de correspondencia): **hay un** ∼ **entre su madurez física y su desarollo mental** his physical maturity is out of step with his intellectual development; ∼ **de horario** jetlag

desfavorable *adj* unfavorable*; **el tiempo nos ha sido** ∼ we had unfavorable weather conditions

desfigurado -da *adj* disfigured

desfigurar [A1] *vt* **1** «*quemaduras/cicatriz*» ⟨*persona*⟩ to disfigure **2** ⟨*hechos*⟩ to distort, twist; ⟨*realidad*⟩ to distort

desfiladero *m* (barranco) ravine, narrow gorge; (puerto) narrow pass

desfilar [A1] *vi* (a) «*soldados*» to parade (b) «*manifestantes*» to march; **la manifestación desfiló por la Gran Vía** the demonstration passed along the Gran Vía (c) «*modelo*» to parade up and down the catwalk

desfile *m* (de carrozas) parade, procession; (Mil) parade, march past; ∼ **de modelos** fashion show

desgajar [A1] *vt* ∼ **algo DE algo** ⟨*rama*⟩ to break *o* snap sth OFF sth; ⟨*páginas*⟩ to tear *o* rip sth OUT OF sth

■ **desgajarse** *v pron* «*rama*» to break off, snap off

desgana *f* (a) (inapetencia) lack of appetite (b) (falta de entusiasmo): **con** *or* **a** ∼ ⟨*trabajar*⟩ half-heartedly; ⟨*obedecer*⟩ reluctantly

desganado -da *adj* (a) (inapetente): **me siento** ∼ I'm not hungry (b) (apático) lethargic

desgano *m* (AmL) ▶ DESGANA

desgarbado -da *adj* ⟨*persona/aspecto*⟩ gangling, gawky; ⟨*movimientos/andar*⟩ ungainly

desgarrador -dora *adj* heartbreaking, heartrending

desgarrar [A1] *vt* (a) ⟨*vestido/papel*⟩ to tear, rip (b) ⟨*corazón*⟩ to break
■ **desgarrarse** *v pron* (a) «*vestido/camisa*» to tear, rip (b) (Med) to tear

desgarro *m* (de ligamento, músculo): **sufrió un** ∼ she tore a muscle

desgastar [A1] *vt* (a) (gastar) ⟨*suelas/ropa*⟩ to wear out; ⟨*roca*⟩ to wear away, erode (b) (debilitar) to wear ... down
■ **desgastarse** *v pron* (a) (gastarse) «*ropa*» to wear out; «*roca*» to wear away; «*tacón*» to wear down (b) «*persona*» to wear oneself out; «*relación*» to grow stale

desgaste *m* (a) (de ropa, suelas) wear; (de rocas) erosion, wearing away (b) (debilitamiento físico) debilitation

desgracia *f* (a) (desdicha, infortunio) misfortune; **tiene la** ∼ **de ser ciego** he has the misfortune to be blind; **caer en** ∼ to fall from favor (b) **por desgracia** (indep) unfortunately

desgraciado -da *adj* (a) [SER] (infeliz) unhappy (b) [SER] (desafortunado) ⟨*viaje*⟩ ill-fated (c) (desacertado) ⟨*elección/coincidencia*⟩ unfortunate, unwise
■ *m,f* **1** (desdichado) wretch **2** (persona vil) swine (colloq)

desgravación *f* tax exemption (AmE), tax relief (BrE)

desgravar [A1] *vt* (a) ⟨*gastos/suma*⟩ to claim tax exemption on (AmE), to claim tax relief on (BrE) (b) ⟨*producto/importación*⟩ to eliminate the tax *o* duty on
■ ∼ *vi* to be tax-deductible

desguazar [A4] *vt* to scrap

deshabitado -da *adj* ⟨*región*⟩ uninhabited; ⟨*edificio*⟩ empty, unoccupied

deshacer [E18] *vt* **1** (a) ⟨*costura/bordado*⟩ to unpick (b) ⟨*nudo/lazo/trenza*⟩ to undo; ⟨*ovillo*⟩ to unwind
2 (a) (desarmar, desmontar) ⟨*maqueta/mecanismo*⟩ to take ... apart; ⟨*paquete*⟩ to undo, unwrap (b) ⟨*cama*⟩ (para cambiarla) to strip; (desordenar) to mess up; ⟨*maleta*⟩ to unpack
3 (a) (derretir) ⟨*nieve/helado*⟩ to melt (b) (desmenuzar) to break up (c) (en líquido) to dissolve
4 ⟨*acuerdo/trato*⟩ to break; ⟨*noviazgo*⟩ to break off; ⟨*planes/compromiso*⟩ to cancel
■ **deshacerse** *v pron* **1** «*dobladillo/costura*» to come undone *o* unstitched; «*nudo/trenza/ moño*» to come undone; «*peinado*» to get messed up, be ruined
2 (a) (desintegrarse) to disintegrate (b) «*nieve/ helado*» to melt (c) (en líquido) to dissolve

3 ~se EN algo: ~se en llanto to dissolve into tears; **me deshice en cumplidos** I went out of my way to be complimentary

4 deshacerse de (a) (librarse de) to get rid of (b) (desprenderse de) to part with

deshaga, deshagas, etc ▶ DESHACER

deshecho -cha adj [ESTAR] (a) (cansado, agotado) exhausted (b) (destrozado moralmente) shattered, devastated (c) (estropeado) ruined

deshelar [A5] vt ‹cañería› to thaw out, unfreeze; ‹nevera/congelador› to defrost; ‹parabrisas› to deice
■ **deshelarse** v pron «nieves» to thaw, melt; «río/lago» to thaw; «relaciones» to thaw

desheredar [A1] vt to disinherit

deshice, deshiciera, etc ▶ DESHACER

deshidratarse [A1] v pron to become dehydrated

deshielo m (a) (de ríos, nieves) thaw; **agua de ~** meltwater (b) (de relaciones) thaw, thawing-out

deshizo ▶ DESHACER

deshojar [A1] vt ‹flor› to pull the petals off; ‹cuaderno› to tear o rip the pages out of

deshonesto -ta adj (a) (tramposo, mentiroso) dishonest (b) (indecente) ‹proposiciones› improper, indecent

deshonor m ▶ DESHONRA A

deshonra f (a) (vergüenza) disgrace; **ese chico es una ~ para su familia** that boy is a disgrace to his family (b) (pérdida de la honra) dishonor*

deshonrar [A1] vt ‹familia/patria› to dishonor*, disgrace; ‹mujer› to dishonor*

deshonroso -sa adj dishonorable*, disgraceful

deshora: **a ~(s)** off hours (AmE), out of hours (BrE)

deshuesar [A1] vt **1** (a) ‹aceitunas› to pit (b) ‹pollo› to bone **2** (Méx) ‹coche/barco› to scrap

desidia f (a) (apatía) slackness, indolence (frml) (b) (desaseo) slovenliness

desierto¹ -ta adj ‹lugar› deserted

desierto² m desert

designar [A1] vt **1** (frml) (elegir) (a) ‹persona› to appoint, designate (frml) (b) ‹lugar/fecha› to fix, set; (con carácter oficial) to designate **2** (frml) (denominar) to designate (frml)

designio m plan

desigual adj **1** (a) (diferente) uneven; **las mangas quedaron ~es** one sleeve turned out longer (o wider etc) than the other (b) (desequilibrado) ‹lucha› unequal; ‹fuerzas› unevenly-matched **2** (irregular) ‹terreno/superficie› uneven; ‹letra› uneven, irregular; ‹calidad› variable, varying (before n); ‹rendimiento› inconsistent, erratic

desigualdad f **1** (a) (diferencia) inequality (b) (desequilibrio) inequality, disparity **2** (de superficie) unevenness

desilusión f (decepción) disappointment; **se llevó una ~** she was disappointed

desilusionado -da adj (decepcionado) disappointed

desilusionar [A1] vt to disappoint
■ **desilusionarse** v pron (decepcionarse) to be disappointed; (perder las ilusiones) to become disillusioned

desinfectante m disinfectant

desinfectar [A1] vt to disinfect

desinflar [A1] vt ‹globo/balón/neumático› to let the air out of, to deflate, let down (esp BrE)
■ **desinflarse** v pron «globo/balón/neumático» to deflate, go down

desinformación f disinformation, misleading information

desinformar [A1] vt to misinform

desinhibido -da adj uninhibited

desintegrarse [A1] v pron to disintegrate, break up; «familia» to break up

desinterés m (falta de interés) lack of interest; (altruismo) unselfishness

desinteresado -da adj ‹consejo/ayuda› disinterested; ‹persona› selfless

desintoxicación f detoxification

desintoxicarse [A2] v pron to undergo detoxification

desistir [I1] vi to give up; **~ DE algo** (de propósito) to give up sth, desist FROM sth (frml); (de demanda/derecho) to relinquish sth; **~ DE hacer algo** to give up doing sth, desist FROM doing sth (frml)

desleal adj [SER] disloyal; **~ CON** or **A algn/ algo** disloyal TO sb/sth

desligarse [A3] v pron (a) (librarse) **~se DE algo** ‹de obligaciones› to free oneself OF sth; ‹de compromiso› to get out OF sth (b) (apartarse) **~se DE algo/algn** to cut oneself off FROM sth/sb

desliz m (error, falta) slip; (al hablar) gaffe, faux pas

deslizador m (Méx) (ala delta) hang glider

deslizar [A4] vt (hacer resbalar) to slip, slide
■ **deslizarse** v pron (a) «patinador/bailarines» to glide; «esquiador» to ski, slide; «serpiente» to slither, glide; **~se POR algo** to slide down sth; **se deslizó por la cuerda** he slid down the rope (b) «barco/cisne» to glide; **~se SOBRE algo** to glide OVER sth (c) ‹cajón/argollas de cortina› to slide (d) «agua/arroyo» to flow gently (e) (escurrirse, escaparse) to slip away

deslucido -da adj ‹actuación/desfile› dull, lackluster*; ‹colores/paredes› faded, drab; ‹plata› tarnished

deslumbrante, deslumbrador -dora adj ‹luz› blinding; ‹belleza› dazzling, stunning

deslumbrar [A1] vt to dazzle

desmadrarse [A1] v pron (fam) «persona» to go wild (colloq)

desmán m (exceso, abuso) outrage, excess

desmanchar [A1] vt (AmL) to get the stains out of

desmandarse [A1] *v pron* «*niños/tropas*» to get out of control *o* hand

desmano: a ~ (*loc adv*) «*estar/quedar*» out of the way; **me pilla a** ~ it's out of my way

desmantelar [A1] *vt* to dismantle; «*coche*» to strip

desmarcarse [A2] *v pron* (Dep) to slip the coverage (AmE), to slip one's marker (BrE)

desmayado -da *adj* «*persona*» unconscious (*from having fainted*)

desmayarse [A1] *v pron* to faint

desmayo *m* (a) (Med) faint; **sufrir un** ~ to faint (b) **sin** ~ «*luchar/trabajar*» resolutely, tirelessly

desmedido -da *adj* excessive; **le han dado una importancia desmedida** they have attributed too much importance to it

desmejorado -da *adj* (a) (de salud): **lo encontré muy** ~ he didn't look at all well to me (b) (de atractivo): **está desmejorada** she's lost her looks

desmemoriado -da *adj* forgetful, absent-minded

desmentir [I11] *vt* «*noticia/rumor*» to deny; «*acusación*» to deny, refute

desmenuzar [A4] *vt* «*pescado*» to flake; «*pollo*» to shred; «*pan*» to crumble

desmigajarse [A1] *v pron* to crumble

desmilitarizar [A4] *vt* to demilitarize

desmontable *adj* (a) (desarmable) «*mecanismo/mueble*» which can be dismantled *o* taken apart (b) (separable) «*forro/pieza*» detachable, removable

desmontar [A1] *vt* (a) (desarmar) «*mueble/ mecanismo*» to dismantle, take apart; «*tienda de campaña*» to take down (b) (separar) «*forro/pieza*» to detach, remove
■ ~ *vi* «*jinete*» to dismount

desmoralizar [A4] *vt* to demoralize, dishearten
■ **desmoralizarse** *v pron* to get demoralized *o* disheartened, to lose heart

desmoronarse [A1] *v pron* (a) «*muro/ edificio*» to collapse; «*imperio/sociedad*» to crumble, collapse (b) «*fe/moral*» to crumble; «*persona*» to go to pieces

desnatado -da *adj* (Esp) skimmed

desnaturalizado -da *adj* (a) «*aceite/vino*» denatured (b) «*madre*» unnatural

desnivel *m* [1] (en superficie) (a) (irregularidad) unevenness, irregularity; **es un terreno lleno de** ~**es** it is a very uneven piece of land; **un** ~ **entre la cocina y el comedor** a difference in floor level between the kitchen and the dining room (b) (inclinación, pendiente) slope, incline (frml) (c) (depresión) drop (*in the level of the ground*) [2] (diferencia) difference, disparity

desnivelado -da *adj* (a) (irregular) «*terreno*» uneven (b) (fuera de nivel): **la mesa está desnivelada** the table isn't level

desnucarse [A2] *v pron* to break one's neck

desnuclearizar [A4] *vt* to denuclearize; **zona desnuclearizada** nuclear-free zone

desnudar [A1] *vt* (desvestir) to undress
■ **desnudarse** *v pron* (*refl*) (desvestirse) to undress, take one's clothes off; ~**se de (la) cintura para arriba** to strip to the waist

desnudez *f* (de persona) nakedness, nudity

desnudo¹ -da *adj* (a) (sin ropa) «*persona*» naked; **nadar** ~ to swim in the nude; **totalmente** ~ stark naked; ~ **de la cintura para arriba** naked to the waist (b) (descubierto) «*hombros/brazos/ torso*» bare

desnudo² *m* (Art) nude

desnutrido -da *adj* malnourished, undernourished

desobedecer [E3] *vt/vi* to disobey

desobediente *adj* disobedient

desocupado -da *adj* [1] (vacío, libre) «*casa/ habitación*» unoccupied, vacant; «*asiento/baño*» free [2] (desempleado) unemployed

desodorante *m* deodorant; ~ **en barra** stick deodorant; ~ **ambiental** (CS) air freshener

desolado -da *adj* [1] «*paisaje/campos*» desolate; «*ciudad*» devastated [2] (afligido) desolated, devastated

desolador -dora *adj* [1] (devastador) «*tormenta/ epidemia*» devastating [2] (triste, penoso) «*noticia*» devastating; «*espectáculo*» distressing

desollar [A10] *vt* «*animal*» to skin, flay

desorbitado -da *adj* (a) «*precios*» exorbitant, astronomical (b) **con los ojos** ~**s** with her/his eyes popping out of her/his head (colloq)

desorden *m* [1] (a) (de persona, cuarto, cajón) untidiness, mess (colloq); **perdona el** ~ sorry about the mess; **en** ~ «*salir/entrar*» in a disorderly fashion; **todo estaba en** ~ everything was in disorder *o* in a mess (b) (confusión) disorder [2] **desórdenes** *mpl* (disturbios) disturbances (*pl*), disorder

desordenado -da *adj* [1] (a) «*persona/ habitación*» untidy, messy (colloq); **tengo la casa toda desordenada** my house is in a mess *o* is very untidy (b) [ESTAR] «*naipes/hojas*» out of order [2] «*vida*» disorganized

desordenar [A1] *vt* «*mesa/habitación*» to make ... untidy, mess up (colloq); «*naipes/hojas*» to get ... out of order

desorganización *f* lack of organization

desorganizado -da *adj* disorganized

desorientado -da *adj* disoriented, disorientated (BrE)

desorientar [A1] *vt* to confuse
■ **desorientarse** *v pron* to lose one's bearings, become disoriented

despabilado -da *adj* ▶ ESPABILADO

despabilar [A1] *vt* ▶ ESPABILAR

despachar [A1] *vt* [1] (a) «*asunto/tarea/*» to take care of, deal with; «*correspondencia*» to deal with, attend to (b) «*carta/paquete*» to send; «*mercancías*» (por barco) to ship; (por avión, tren) to send, dispatch [2] (Com) (en tienda) to serve, deal with
■ ~ *vi* (Com) «*dependiente*» to serve

despacho *m* [1] (a) (oficina) office; (estudio) study (b) (mobiliario) office furniture [2] (envío) dispatch, despatch [3] (comunicado) communiqué; (Mil) dispatch; (Period) report

despacio *adv* [1] (lentamente) slowly [2] (CS) (en voz baja) quietly, softly; (sin hacer ruido) quietly

despampanante *adj* (fam) stunning (colloq)

desparpajo *m* (desenvoltura) self-confidence; (desfachatez) audacity, nerve (colloq)

desparramado -da adj (esparcido) scattered; (derramado) spilt

desparramar [A1] vt ⟨líquido/azúcar⟩ to spill; ⟨botones/monedas⟩ to spill, scatter; ⟨papeles/ juguetes⟩ to scatter

■ **desparramarse** v pron «líquido/azúcar» to spill; «botones/monedas» to scatter, spill

despavorido -da adj terrified, petrified

despecho m spite; **por ~** out of spite

despectivo -va adj ⟨trato/gesto/actitud⟩ contemptuous; ⟨tono⟩ disparaging; ⟨término⟩ pejorative, derogatory

despedazar [A4] vt **(a)** (cortar en trozos) to cut ... into pieces **(b)** ⟨presa⟩ to tear ... to pieces o shreds

despedida f **(a)** (acción) goodbye, farewell (liter) **(b)** (celebración) farewell party; **regalo de ~** a farewell gift; **~ de soltera/soltero** hen/stag night o party

despedir [I14] vt **1** (decir adiós): **vinieron a ~me al aeropuerto** they came to see me off at the airport **2** (del trabajo) to dismiss, fire (colloq); (por reducción de personal) to lay off **3** ⟨olor⟩ to give off; ⟨humo/vapor⟩ to emit, give off; **salir despedido** «corcho/pelota» to shoot out; **el conductor salió despedido del asiento** the driver was thrown out of his seat

■ **despedirse** v pron (decir adiós) to say goodbye; **~se DE algn** to say goodbye TO sb

despegar [A3] vt ⟨etiqueta/esparadrapo⟩ to remove, peel off; ⟨piezas/ensambladura⟩ to get ... unstuck o apart; **no despegó los labios** she didn't say a word

■ **~** vi «avión» to take off; «cohete» to lift off, be launched

■ **despegarse** v pron «sello/etiqueta» to come unstuck, peel off; «esparadrapo/empapelado» to come off

despegue m (de avión) takeoff; (de cohete) launch, lift-off

despeinado -da adj ⟨pelo/melena⟩ unkempt, disheveled*; **estar ~** to have one's hair in a mess

despeinar [A1] vt: **~ a algn** to mess up sb's hair

■ **despeinarse** v pron to mess one's hair up

despejado -da adj **1** (Meteo) ⟨día/cielo⟩ clear **2** (libre, vacío) ⟨carretera/camino⟩ clear **3** **(a)** ⟨persona⟩ clearheaded; ⟨mente⟩ clear **(b)** [ESTAR] (sobrio) sober

despejar [A1] vt **1** **(a)** (desocupar, desalojar) to clear **(b)** ⟨nariz⟩ to unblock, clear; **el paseo me despejó** the walk cleared my head **2** ⟨balón⟩ (en fútbol) to clear; (en fútbol americano) to punt

■ **~** vi (en fútbol) to clear; (en fútbol americano) to punt

■ **~** v impers (Meteo) to clear up

■ **despejarse** v pron (espabilarse) to wake (oneself) up; (desembotarse) to clear one's head; «borracho» to sober up

despellejar [A1] vt ⟨animal⟩ to skin

■ **despellejarse** v pron to peel; **se me despellejó la nariz** my nose peeled

despelote m (AmL fam) (caos, lío) shambles (colloq)

despenalizar [A4] vt to legalize, decriminalize

despensa f larder, pantry

despeñadero m cliff, precipice

despeñarse [A1] v pron to go over a cliff (o precipice etc)

desperdiciar [A1] vt ⟨comida/papel/tela⟩ to waste; ⟨oportunidad⟩ to miss, waste

desperdicio m **(a)** (de comida, papel) waste **(b)** **desperdicios** mpl (residuos) scraps (pl)

desperdigado -da adj scattered

desperezarse [A4] v pron to stretch

desperfecto m **(a)** (daño) damage **(b)** (defecto) flaw

despertador m alarm clock; **poner ~** to set the alarm

despertar [A5] vt ⟨persona⟩ to wake, wake ... up **(b)** ⟨sentimientos/pasiones⟩ to arouse; ⟨apetito⟩ to whet; ⟨recuerdos⟩ to evoke; ⟨interés⟩ to awaken, stir up

■ **~** vi (del sueño) to wake (up); (de la anestesia) to come round

■ **despertarse** v pron (del sueño) to wake (up)

despiadado -da adj ⟨persona⟩ ruthless, heartless; ⟨ataque/crítica⟩ savage, merciless

despida, despidas, etc ▶ DESPEDIR

despido m dismissal; (por falta de trabajo) redundancy, layoff

despierta, despiertas, etc ▶ DESPERTAR

despierto -ta adj **(a)** [ESTAR] (del sueño) awake **(b)** [SER] ⟨persona/mente⟩ bright, alert

despilfarrar [A1] vi to waste o squander money

■ **~** vt to squander, waste

despilfarro m waste

despistado -da adj **(a)** [SER] vague, absentminded; **soy muy ~ para los nombres** I never remember names **(b)** **estar ~** to be miles away (colloq) o daydreaming; (desorientado, confuso) to be bewildered o lost

■ m,f scatterbrain (colloq)

despistar [A1] vt **(a)** (desorientar, confundir) to confuse **(b)** ⟨perseguidor⟩ to shake off; ⟨sabueso⟩ to throw ... off the scent

■ **despistarse** v pron (confundirse) to get confused o muddled; (distraerse) to lose concentration

despiste m **(a)** (distracción) absentmindedness; **fue un ~** it was a lapse of concentration **(b)** (equivocación) slip, mistake

desplazamiento m **1** (movimiento) movement, displacement (fml) **2** (fml) (traslado, viaje) trip; **gastos de ~** traveling expenses

desplazar [A4] vt **1** (fml) (mover, correr) to move; (Inf) to scroll **2** (suplantar, relegar) ⟨persona⟩ to displace; **~ A algo** to take the place OF sth

■ **desplazarse** v pron (fml) (trasladarse, moverse) «animal» to move around; «avión/barco» to travel, go; «persona» to get around

desplegar [A7] vt **1** **(a)** ⟨alas⟩ to spread; ⟨mapa⟩ to open out, spread out; ⟨velas⟩ to unfurl **(b)** (demostrar) ⟨talento/ingenio⟩ to display; (emplear) ⟨encantos/poder⟩ to use **(c)** (llevar a cabo) ⟨campaña⟩ to mount; ⟨esfuerzo⟩ to make **2** (Mil) ⟨tropas/misiles⟩ to deploy

■ **desplegarse** v pron (Mil) to deploy

despliegue m **1** (de tropas, recursos) deployment **2** (de riqueza, sabiduría) display

desplomarse [A1] *v pron* «*persona/edificio*»
to collapse

desplumar [A1] *vt* (a) ‹*ave*› to pluck (b) (fam)
‹*persona*› to fleece (colloq)

despoblación *f* depopulation; ~ **forestal**
(Esp) deforestation

despoblado -da *adj* ⓵ (sin habitantes)
deserted, uninhabited; (subpoblado)
underpopulated, sparsely populated ⓶ ‹*cejas*›
thin, sparse

despojar [A1] *vt* (frml) ~ **A algn DE algo** ‹*de
privilegios/poderes*› to divest sb OF sth (frml); ‹*de
título/posesiones*› to dispossess (frml) o strip sb OF
sth
■ **despojarse** *v pron* (frml o liter) ~**se DE algo** ‹*de
ropa*› to remove sth; ‹*de bienes*› to relinquish sth

despojos *mpl* (a) (restos) remains (*pl*) (b)
(presa, botín) spoils (*pl*), loot (c) (de aves) head,
wings, feet and giblets; (de reses) head, feet and
offal

desportillado -da *adj* chipped

desposeído -da *m,f*: **los ~s** the destitute, the
dispossessed

déspota *mf* tyrant, despot

despótico -ca *adj* despotic, tyrannical

despotricar [A2] *vi* (fam) ~ (**CONTRA algo/
algn**) to rant and rave (ABOUT sth/sb)

despreciable *adj* (a) ‹*persona/conducta*›
despicable, contemptible (b) **no/nada ~** ‹*suma/
número*› not inconsiderable, significant

despreciar [A1] *vt* (a) (menospreciar) ‹*persona*›
to look down on; (profundamente) to despise (b)
(rechazar) ‹*oferta/ayuda*› to reject

despreciativo -va *adj* disdainful

desprecio *m* (a) (menosprecio) disdain; (más
intenso) contempt; **me miró con ~** she gave me a
disdainful o scornful look (b) (indiferencia por el
peligro, la vida) disregard (c) (desaire) snub, slight;
hacerle un ~ a algn to snub o slight sb

desprender [E1] *vt* (soltar, separar) ‹*teja*› to
dislodge; ‹*etiqueta*› to detach
■ **desprenderse** *v pron* ⓵ «*teja*» to come
loose; «*botón*» to come off; «*retina*» to become
detached; ~**se DE algo** to come away FROM sth
⓶ (renunciar, entregar) ~**se DE algo** ‹*de posesiones*›
to part WITH sth

desprendido -da *adj* [SER] generous,
open-handed; *ver tb* DESPRENDER

desprendimiento *m* detachment; ~ **de
retina** detachment of the retina; ~ **de tierras**
landslide

despreocupado -da *adj* (a) (sin
preocupaciones) ‹*vida*› carefree (b) (descuidado)
negligent (c) (indiferente) unworried

despreocuparse [A1] *v pron* (a) ▶
DESENTENDERSE (b) (dejar de preocuparse):
despreocúpate de todo don't worry about
anything

desprestigiar [A1] *vt* to discredit
■ **desprestigiarse** *v pron* «*persona/producto/
empresa*» to lose prestige

desprestigio *m* (a) (pérdida de prestigio) loss of
prestige; **ir en ~ de algo/algn** to bring discredit
on o upon sth/sb (b) (falta de prestigio) bad
reputation

desprevenido -da *adj*: **estar ~** to be

---

unprepared o unready; **pillar a algn ~**
«*pregunta*» to catch sb unawares o off guard;
«*lluvia*» to catch sb by surprise

desprolijo -ja *adj* (CS) (a) [ESTAR] ‹*trabajo*›
untidy, messy (b) [SER] ‹*persona*› careless

desproporción *f* disparity, disproportion

desproporcionado -da *adj* out of
proportion

desprovisto -ta *adj* ~ **DE algo** lacking IN sth

después *adv* ⓵ (a) (más tarde) later; **para ~**
for later (b) (en una serie de sucesos) then,
afterward(s); ~ **no lo he vuelto a ver** I haven't
seen him since then (c) (en locs) **después de**
after; ~ **de Cristo** AD; ~ **DE hacer algo** after
doing sth; **después de todo** after all; **después (de)
que** after; (refiriéndose al futuro) once, when; ~ **(de)
que todos se hayan ido** once o when everybody
has left; **después que** after
⓶ (en el espacio): **bájate dos paradas ~** get off two
stops further on; **hay una casa y ~ está el
colegio** there is a house and then you come to
the school; **está justo ~ del puente** it's just past
the bridge

despuntado -da *adj* blunt

despuntar [A1] *vt* to blunt
■ ~ *vi* (a) «*día*» to break, dawn; **al ~ el día** at
daybreak (b) «*flor*» to bud; «*plantas*» to sprout
(c) ‹*persona*› ~ **EN algo** to excel AT o IN sth

desquiciado -da *adj* ‹*mundo/persona*› crazy;
tengo los nervios ~s my nerves are in tatters

desquiciante *adj* maddening, infuriating

desquicio *m* (RPl fam) chaos

desquitarse [A1] *v pron* to get even; **lo hizo
para ~ de él** she did it to get even with him; ~
CON algn/algo to take it out on sb/sth

destacado -da *adj* ⓵ ‹*profesional/artista*›
prominent, distinguished; ‹*actuación*›
outstanding ⓶ [ESTAR] ‹*tropas*› stationed

destacar [A2] *vt* ⓵ (recalcar, subrayar) to
emphasize, stress ⓶ (realzar) ‹*belleza/figura*› to
enhance; ‹*color/plano*› to bring out ⓷ (a) (Mil)
‹*tropas*› to post (b) ‹*periodista/fotógrafo*› to send
■ ~ *vi* to stand out; ~ **EN algo** to excel AT o IN sth

destajo *m* (Com, Rels Labs) piecework; **trabajar a
~** to do piecework

destapado -da *adj* (a) (sin tapa) ‹*olla*›
uncovered; **dejó la botella destapada** he left the
top off the bottle (b) (en la cama): **siempre duerme
~** he always sleeps with the covers thrown back

destapador *m* (AmL) bottle opener

destapar [A1] *vt* ⓵ (a) ‹*botella/caja*› to open,
take the top/lid off; ‹*olla*› to uncover, take the lid
off (b) (descubrir) ‹*mueble*› to uncover; ‹*escándalo*›
to uncover (c) (en la cama) to pull the covers off
⓶ (AmL) ‹*cañería/inodoro*› to unblock
■ **destaparse** *v pron* (refl) ⓵ (en la cama) to
throw the covers o bedclothes off ⓶ «*nariz/
oídos*» to unblock

destaponar [A1] *vt* ‹*cañería*› to unblock

destartalado -da *adj* (fam) ‹*coche*› beat-up
(AmE colloq), clapped-out (BrE colloq); ‹*mueble*›
shabby; ‹*casa*› ramshackle, rundown

destellar [A1] *vi* ‹*brillante/joya*› to sparkle,
glitter; «*estrella*» to twinkle, sparkle

destello *m* (de estrella) twinkle, sparkle; (de
brillante, joya) sparkle, glitter

destemplado -da adj **1** ⟨persona⟩: estoy ∼ (con fiebre) I have a slight fever; (indispuesto) I'm feeling off-color* **2 (a)** ⟨instrumento/voz/tono⟩ discordant **(b)** ⟨nervios⟩ frayed

destemplar [A1] vt **1** ⟨guitarra/violín⟩ to make ... go out of tune **2** ⟨ánimos/nervios⟩ to fray **3** (AmL) ⟨dientes⟩ to set ... on edge

desteñir [I15] vi «prenda/color» to run; (decolorarse) to fade
■ **desteñirse** v pron to run; (decolorarse) to fade

desternillarse [A1] v pron (fam): ∼ **de risa** to split one's sides (laughing) (colloq)

desterrado -da m,f exile

desterrar [A5] vt ⟨persona⟩ to exile, banish (liter)

destiempo: **a** ∼ ⟨marchar⟩ out of step; ⟨tocar⟩ out of time; **habló a** ∼ she picked the wrong moment to say it

destierro m exile, banishment

destilar [A1] vt **(a)** ⟨alcohol/petróleo⟩ to distill*; ⟨hulla/madera⟩ to char **(b)** (rezumar) to ooze

destilería f distillery

destinado -da adj **1 (a)** (predestinado): ∼ **a triunfar/al fracaso** destined to succeed/to fail **(b)** (dirigido, asignado): ∼ **A algn** ⟨carta/paquete⟩ addressed TO sb; ⟨víveres⟩ intended FOR sb; ⟨libro/novela⟩ aimed AT sb; **las cajas destinadas a Montevideo** the boxes destined for Montevideo; **los aviones ∼s a este fin** the planes used for this purpose **2 (a)** ⟨militar⟩: ∼ **en Ceuta** stationed in Ceuta **(b)** ⟨funcionario/diplomático⟩: **ahora está** ∼ **en Lima** now he's been posted to Lima

destinar [A1] vt **1** ⟨funcionario/militar⟩ to post, send, assign **2** (asignar un fin): **destinó todos sus ahorros a pagar las deudas** she used all her savings to pay her debts; **∼on el dinero a la investigación** the money was used for research; **∼on parte de los fondos a este fin** they earmarked part of the funds for this purpose

destinatario -ria m,f (de carta, paquete) addressee; (de giro, transferencia) payee

destino m **1** (sino) fate **2 (a)** (de avión, autobús) destination; **con** ∼ **a Roma** ⟨vuelo/tren⟩ to Rome; ⟨pasajero⟩ traveling to Rome; ⟨carga⟩ destined for Rome; **salieron con** ∼ **a Lima** they set off for Lima **(b)** (puesto) posting, assignment **3** (uso, fin) use

destituir [I20] vt (frml) (despedir) to dismiss

destornillador m screwdriver

destornillar [A1] vt to unscrew

destreza f skill; **con gran** ∼ very skillfully

destronar [A1] vt ⟨rey⟩ to dethrone, depose; ⟨líder/campeón⟩ to depose, topple

destrozar [A1] vt **(a)** (romper, deteriorar) ⟨zapatos⟩ to ruin; ⟨cristal/jarrón⟩ to smash; ⟨juguete⟩ to pull ... apart; ⟨coche⟩ to wreck; ⟨libro⟩ to pull apart **(b)** ⟨felicidad/matrimonio/vida⟩ to wreck, destroy; ⟨corazón⟩ to break; **tiene los nervios destrozados** he's a nervous wreck

■ **destrozarse** v pron **(a)** (romperse) «zapatos» to be ruined; «jarrón/cristal» to smash **(b)** ⟨estómago/hígado⟩ to ruin

destrozo m: tb ∼**s** damage

destrucción f destruction

destructivo -va adj destructive

destructor m destroyer

destruir [I20] vt **(a)** ⟨documentos/pruebas⟩ to destroy; ⟨ciudad⟩ to destroy; ⟨medio ambiente⟩ to damage **(b)** (echar por tierra) ⟨reputación⟩ to ruin; ⟨plan⟩ to wreck; ⟨esperanzas⟩ to dash, shatter

desubicado -da adj (AmS) **(a)** [ESTAR] (desplazado) out of position **(b)** [ESTAR] (desorientado) confused, disoriented **(c)** [SER] (en cuestiones sociales): **es tan** ∼ he just doesn't have a clue (colloq)

desuso m disuse; **caer en** ∼ to fall into disuse

desvaído -da adj ⟨color⟩ faded, washed-out; ⟨persona⟩ colorless*, insipid

desvalido -da m,f helpless person

desvalijar [A1] vt **(a)** ⟨casa/tienda⟩ to strip ... bare **(b)** ⟨persona⟩ (robar) to rob; (en juego) (fam) to clean ... out (colloq)

desván m attic, loft

desvanecerse [E3] v pron **(a)** «humo/nubes/niebla» to clear, disperse; ⟨dudas/temores/sospechas⟩ to vanish, be dispelled; «fantasma/visión» to disappear, vanish **(b)** «color» to fade

desvariar [A17] vi (Med) to be delirious; (decir tonterías) to talk nonsense, rave

desvelado -da adj: estoy ∼ I can't sleep

desvelar [A1] vt **1** ⟨persona⟩ to keep ... awake, stop ... from sleeping **2** (Esp) ▶ DEVELAR
■ **desvelarse** v pron (perder el sueño): **me desvelé anoche** I couldn't sleep last night

desvelo m **1** (insomnio) sleeplessness **2 desvelos** mpl (esfuerzos) efforts (pl), pains (pl)

desvencijado -da adj ⟨silla/cama⟩ rickety; ⟨coche⟩ dilapidated, beat-up (AmE colloq), clapped-out (BrE colloq)

desventaja f disadvantage; **en** ∼ at a disadvantage

desvergonzado -da m,f: **ser un** ∼ (impúdico) to have no shame; (descarado) to be very impertinent

desvestir [I14] vt to undress
■ **desvestirse** v pron to undress, get undressed; **∼se de la cintura para arriba** to strip to the waist

desviación f **(a)** (en general) diversion **(b)** (Med) curvature **(c)** (alejamiento) ∼ DE algo deviation FROM sth

desviar [A17] vt ⟨tráfico/vuelo/fondos⟩ to divert; ⟨río⟩ to alter the course of; ⟨golpe/pelota⟩ to deflect, parry; ∼ **la conversación** to change the subject; **desvió la mirada** he looked away
■ **desviarse** v pron **1** «carretera» to branch off; «vehículo» to turn off; **la conversación se desvió hacia otros temas** the conversation turned to other things **2** «persona» **∼se DE algo** ⟨de ruta⟩ to deviate FROM sth; ⟨de tema⟩ to get off sth

AmC	Central America	Arg	Argentina	Cu	Cuba	Per	Peru
AmL	Latin America	Bol	Bolivia	Ec	Ecuador	RPI	River Plate Area
AmS	South America	Chi	Chile	Esp	Spain	Ur	Uruguay
Andes	Andean Region	CS	Southern Cone	Méx	Mexico	Ven	Venezuela

desvincularse [A1] *v pron* ~se DE algn/algo to dissociate oneself FROM sth/sb; **está desvinculado de la política** he is no longer involved in politics

desvío *m* **(a)** (por obras) diversion, detour (AmE); **tomar un** ~ to make a detour **(b)** (Esp) (salida, carretera) exit

desvivirse [I1] *v pron* ~ POR algn to be completely devoted TO sb; ~ POR hacer algo to go out of one's way to do sth

detallado -da *adj* ‹factura/cuenta› itemized; ‹estudio/descripción› detailed

detallar [A1] *vt* to detail

detalle *m* [1] **(a)** (pormenor) detail; **entrar en** ~s to go into details; **describir algo con todo** ~ to describe sth in great detail **(b)** (elemento decorativo) detail [2] **(a)** (pequeño regalo) little gift **(b)** (Esp, Méx) (atención, gesto) nice (*o* thoughtful *etc*) gesture; **tener un** ~ CON algn to do sth nice FOR sb [3] (Com) **al detalle** retail

detallista *adj* (minucioso) precise, meticulous

detectar [A1] *vt* to detect

detective *mf* detective

detector *m* detector; ~ **de mentiras/metales** lie/metal detector

detención *f* [1] (arresto) arrest; (encarcelamiento) detention [2] ▶ DETENIMIENTO

detener [E27] *vt* [1] (parar) ‹vehículo/máquina› to stop; ‹trámite/proceso› to halt; ‹hemorragia› to stop, staunch [2] (arrestar) to arrest; (encarcelar) to detain; **¡queda usted detenido!** you're under arrest!

■ **detenerse** *v pron* **(a)** (pararse) «vehículo/ persona» to stop; ~se A hacer algo to stop to do sth **(b)** (tomar mucho tiempo) ~se EN algo: **no nos detengamos demasiado en los detalles** let's not spend too much time discussing the details

detenido -da *adj* **(a)** ‹vehículo/tráfico› held up **(b)** ‹investigación/estudio› detailed, thorough **(c)** [ESTAR] ‹persona› under arrest; (por período más largo) in custody

■ *m,f* person under arrest; (durante un período más largo) detainee, person held in custody

detenimiento *m*: **con** ~ carefully *o* in detail

detergente *m* **(a)** (para ropa) laundry detergent (AmE), washing powder (BrE) **(b)** (Bol, CS) (para vajilla) dishwashing liquid (AmE), washing-up liquid (BrE)

deteriorado -da *adj* ‹mercancías› damaged; ‹edificio› dilapidated, run down; ‹mueble/cuadro› in bad condition

deteriorar [A1] *vt* ‹relaciones/salud/situación› to cause ... to deteriorate

■ **deteriorarse** *v pron* «relaciones/salud/ situación» to deteriorate, worsen; «mercancías» to get damaged

deterioro *m* **(a)** (de edificio, muebles) deterioration, wear **(b)** (empeoramiento) deterioration, worsening

determinación *f* (cualidad) determination, resolve; (decisión) decision; **tomar una** ~ to make a decision

determinado -da *adj* ‹fecha/lugar› certain; **en determinadas circunstancias** in certain circumstances; **una determinada dosis** a particular dosage

determinante *adj* ‹causa› main (*before n*); ‹factor› deciding (*before n*)

determinar [A1] *vt* [1] (establecer, precisar) **(a)** «ley/contrato» to state; «persona» to determine **(b)** (por deducción) to establish, determine [2] (motivar) to cause, bring about

detestar [A1] *vt* to hate, detest

detiene, detienes, etc ▶ DETENER

detonación *f* **(a)** (ruido) explosion; (acción) detonation **(b)** (Auto) (de motor) backfire

detonador *m* detonator

detonar [A1] *vi* to detonate, explode

detrás *adv* [1] (lugar, parte) [*Latin American Spanish also uses* ATRÁS *in this sense*]: **iba corriendo** ~ he ran along behind; **las cajas de** ~ the boxes at the back; **por** ~ ‹abrocharse› at the back; ‹atacar› from behind [2] **detrás de** (*loc prep*) behind; ~ **de la puerta** behind the door; ~ **de mí/ti** behind me/you; **un cigarrillo** ~ **de otro** one cigarette after another

detuve, detuvo, etc ▶ DETENER

deuda *f* **(a)** (Com, Fin) debt; **pagar una** ~ to pay (off) a debt; **contraer una** ~ to run up *o* (frml) contract a debt; ~ **pública** public debt (AmE), national debt (BrE) **(b)** (compromiso moral): **estoy en** ~ **con usted** I am indebted to you

deudor -dora *adj* debtor (*before n*)

■ *m,f* debtor

devaluación *f* devaluation

devaluar [A18] *vt* to devalue

■ **devaluarse** *v pron* «moneda» to fall; «terrenos/propiedad» to depreciate, fall in value

devanar [A1] *vt* ‹hilo/lana/alambre› to wind

devaneo *m* **(a)** (amorío) affair; (pasajero) fling **(b)** (pasatiempo frívolo) idle pursuit

devastador -dora *adj* devastating

devastar [A1] *vt* to devastate

develar [A1] *vt* (AmL) ‹secreto› to reveal, disclose; ‹misterio› to uncover; ‹monumento/ placa› to unveil

devoción *f* devotion; **siente** ~ **por sus hijos** she's devoted to her children

devolución *f* (de artículo) return; (de dinero) refund

devolver [E11] *vt* [1] **(a)** (restituir) ‹objeto prestado› to return, give back; ‹dinero› to give back, pay back; ‹envase› to return; ‹objeto comprado› to bring/take ... back; **devuélvelo a su lugar** put it back in its place; ~**le algo** A algn to return sth to sb; ‹dinero› to give *o* pay sth back TO sb; **me devolvieron los documentos** I got my papers back; **el teléfono me devolvía las monedas** the telephone kept rejecting my coins; **la operación le devolvió la vista** the operation restored his sight **(b)** ‹refugiado› to return, send back **(c)** (Fin) ‹letra› to return [2] (corresponder) ‹visita/favor› to return [3] (vomitar) to bring up, throw up (colloq)

■ ~ *vi* to bring up; **tengo ganas de** ~ I feel sick

■ **devolverse** *v pron* (AmL exc RPI) (regresar) to go/come/turn back

devorar [A1] *vt* «animal» to devour; «persona» to devour, wolf down (colloq); ~ **a algn con los ojos** *or* **la mirada** to devour sb with one's eyes (colloq); **fue devorado por las llamas** it was consumed by the flames

d

devoto -ta *adj* ⟨*persona*⟩ devout; ⟨*lugar/obra*⟩ devotional
■ *m,f* **(a)** (Relig) ∼ **DE algn** devotee OF sb **(b)** (aficionado) ∼ **DE algo/algn** devotee OF sth/admirer of sb

devuelva, devuelvas, etc ▶ DEVOLVER

DF *m* (en Méx) = **Distrito Federal**

di ▶ DAR, DECIR

día *m* **1** **(a)** (en general) day; **todos los** ∼**s** every day; ∼ **a** ∼ day by day; **de** *or* **durante el** ∼ during the day; **el** ∼ **anterior** the day before, the previous day; **el** ∼ **siguiente** the next *o* the following day; **trabaja doce horas por** ∼ she works twelve hours a day; **un** ∼ **sí y otro no** *or* (AmL) ∼ **(de) por medio** every other day, on alternate days; **dentro de quince** ∼**s** in two weeks *o* (BrE) a fortnight; **cada** ∼ every day; **buenos** ∼**s** *or* (RPI) **buen** ∼ good morning; **al** ∼: **una vez al** ∼ once a day; **estoy al** ∼ **en los pagos** I'm up to date with the payments; **poner algo al** ∼ to bring sth up to date; **ponerse al** ∼ **con algo** (con noticias) to get up to date with sth; (con trabajo) to catch up on sth; **mantenerse al** ∼ to keep up to date; **de un** ∼ **para otro** overnight; **hoy en** ∼ nowadays, these days **(b)** (fecha): **¿qué** ∼ **es hoy?** what day is it today?; **empieza el** ∼ **dos** it starts on the second; **el** ∼ **de Año Nuevo** New Year's Day; ∼ **de los enamorados** (St) Valentine's Day; ∼ **de los inocentes** December 28, ≈ April Fool's Day; ∼ **de Reyes** Epiphany; ∼ **festivo** *or* (AmL) **feriado** public holiday; ∼ **laborable** working day; ∼ **libre** (sin trabajo) day off; (sin compromisos) free day
2 **(a)** (tiempo indeterminado) day; **algún** ∼ one day; **lo haremos otro** ∼ we'll do it some other time; **un** ∼ **de estos** one of these days; **¡hasta otro** ∼**!** so long!, see you!; **el** ∼ **menos pensado** when you least expect it **(b)** **días** *mpl* (vida, tiempo) days (*pl*); **tiene los** ∼**s contados** his days are numbered; **hasta nuestros** ∼**s** (up) to the present day

diabetes *f* diabetes

diabético -ca *adj/m,f* diabetic

diablo *m* **1** (demonio) devil; **como (el** *or* **un)** ∼ like crazy *o* mad (colloq); **del** ∼ *or* **de mil** ∼**s** (fam) devilish (colloq); **está de un humor de mil** ∼**s** she's in a devil of a mood (colloq); **donde el** ∼ **perdió el poncho** (AmS fam) (en un lugar — aislado) in the back of beyond; (— lejano) miles away (colloq); **mandar algo/a algn al** ∼ (fam) to pack sth in/to tell sb to go to hell (colloq) **2** (fam) (uso expletivo): **¿cómo/dónde/qué/quién** ... **?** how/where/what/who the hell ... ? (colloq)

diablura *f* (fam) prank

diabólico -ca *adj* (del diablo) diabolic, satanic; ⟨*persona*⟩ evil; ⟨*plan/intenciones*⟩ devilish, fiendish

diadema *f* (para el pelo) hair-band; (corona) crown, diadem; (media corona) tiara

diafragma *m* (Anat, Fot, Med) diaphragm

diagnosticar [A2] *vt* to diagnose

diagnóstico *m* diagnosis

diagonal *f* **(a)** (Mat) diagonal **(b)** (en fútbol americano) endzone

diagrama *m* diagram

dial *m* (Rad, Tec) dial; (del teléfono) dial

dialecto *m* dialect

dialogar [A3] *vi* to talk; ∼ **CON algn** to talk TO sb

diálogo *m* **(a)** (conversación) conversation; (Lit) dialogue, dialog (AmE) **(b)** (Pol, Rels Labs) talks (*pl*), negotiations (*pl*)

diamante *m* **(a)** (piedra) diamond; **un anillo de** ∼**s** a diamond ring **(b)** (Dep) diamond **(c)** **diamantes** *mpl* (en naipes) diamonds (*pl*)

diámetro *m* diameter

diana *f* **1** (Mil) reveille **2** (Dep, Jueg) (objeto) target; (para dardos) dartboard; (centro) bull's-eye

diapasón *m* (para afinar) tuning fork; (de instrumento de cuerda) fingerboard

diapositiva *f* slide, transparency

diariero -ra *m,f* (CS) newspaper vendor

diario -ria *adj* **(a)** (de todos los días) ⟨*tarea/clases*⟩ daily; ⟨*gastos*⟩ everyday, day-to-day **(b)** (por día): **trabaja cuatro horas diarias** she works four hours a day **(c)** (en locs) **a diario** every day; **de diario** ⟨*ropa/vajilla*⟩ everyday (before n); **para diario** for everyday (use)
■ *m* **1** (periódico) newspaper; ∼ **mural** (Chi) bulletin board (AmE), notice board (BrE) **2** (libro personal) diary, journal (AmE) **3** (Méx, Col, Ven) (gastos cotidianos): **el** ∼ day-to-day expenses

diarrea *f* diarrhea*

dibujante *mf* (*m*) draftsman*; (*f*) draftswoman*; (de cómics) comic book artist, strip cartoonist

dibujar [A1] *vt/vi* to draw; ∼ **a mano alzada** to draw freehand

dibujo *m* **(a)** (arte) drawing; **clase de** ∼ drawing class; ∼ **lineal** line drawing **(b)** (representación) drawing; **un** ∼ **al carboncillo** a charcoal drawing; ∼**s animados** cartoons (*pl*) **(c)** (estampado) pattern

diccionario *m* dictionary; ∼ **bilingüe** bilingual dictionary; ∼ **de sinónimos** dictionary of synonyms, ≈ thesaurus

dice, dices, etc ▶ DECIR

dicha *f* **(a)** (felicidad) happiness; **¡qué** ∼ **verlos a todos reunidos!** what a joy to see you all together!; **¡qué** ∼**! dejó de llover** (AmL fam) fantastic *o* wonderful! it's stopped raining! **(b)** (suerte) good luck, good fortune; **nunca es tarde si la** ∼ **es buena** better late than never

dicharachero -ra *adj* (que habla mucho) chatty (colloq), talkative; (gracioso) witty

dicho¹ -cha *pp* [*ver tb* DECIR²]: ∼ **esto, se fue** having said this, he left; **con eso queda todo** ∼ that says it all; ∼ **de otro modo** to put it another way, in other words; ∼ **sea de paso** incidentally, by the way; **y ¡**∼**! y hecho!** and in diez minutos estaba **listo** and, sure enough, ten minutes later there it was
■ *adj dem* (frml): **en dichas cuidades** ... in these cities ...; **dicha información** that information; ∼**s documentos** (en escrito, documento) the above *o* (frml) said documents

dicho² *m* saying

dichoso -sa *adj* **1** (feliz) happy; (afortunado) fortunate, lucky **2** (*delante del n*) (fam) (maldito) blessed (colloq), damn (sl)

diciembre *m* December; *para ejemplos ver* ENERO

diciendo ▶ DECIR

dictado *m* dictation; **nos hizo un** ~ she gave us a dictation; **escribir al** ~ to take dictation

dictador -dora *m,f* dictator

dictadura *f* dictatorship

dictar [A1] *vt* **(a)** ⟨*carta/texto*⟩ to dictate **(b)** ⟨*leyes/medidas*⟩ to announce; ⟨*sentencia*⟩ to pronounce, pass **(c)** ⟨*acción/tendencia/moda*⟩ to dictate **(d)** (AmL) ⟨*clase/curso/conferencia*⟩ to give ■ ~ *vi* to dictate

didáctico -ca *adj* ⟨*juguete/programa*⟩ educational; ⟨*poema/exposición*⟩ didactic

diecinueve *adj inv/m/pron* nineteen; *para ejemplos ver* CINCO

dieciocho *adj inv/m/pron* eighteen; *para ejemplos ver* CINCO

dieciséis *adj inv/m/pron* sixteen; *para ejemplos ver* CINCO

diecisiete *adj inv/m/pron* seventeen; *para ejemplos ver* CINCO

diente *m* **(a)** (Anat, Zool) tooth; **lavarse** *or* **cepillarse los** ~**s** to clean *o* brush one's teeth; ~ **de leche** milk tooth; **daba** ~ **con** ~ my/his teeth were chattering; **hablar** *or* **murmurar entre** ~**s** to mutter (under one's breath) **(b)** (de engranaje, sierra) tooth; (de tenedor) prong, tine; ~ **de ajo** clove of garlic

diera, dieras, etc ▶ DAR

diéresis *f* (*pl* ~) diaeresis

diese, dieses, etc ▶ DAR

diestra *f* (liter *o* period) right hand; *a* ~ *y* *siniestra* left and right (AmE), left, right and centre (BrE)

diestro¹ -tra *adj* **(a)** (frml) ⟨*mano*⟩ right; ⟨*persona*⟩ right-handed **(b)** (hábil) ⟨*persona/jugada*⟩ skillful*

diestro² *m* matador, bullfighter; *a* ~ *y* *siniestro* (Esp) left and right (AmE), left, right and centre (BrE)

dieta *f* ⟦1⟧ (alimentación, régimen) diet; **ponerse a** ~ to go on a diet ⟦2⟧ **(a)** (para viajes) allowance **(b)** (de parlamentario) salary

diez *adj inv/m/pron* ten; *para ejemplos ver* CINCO

difamar [A1] *vt* (por escrito) to libel, defame (frml); (oralmente) to slander, defame (frml)

difamatorio -ria *adj* ⟨*palabras/discurso*⟩ slanderous; ⟨*artículo/carta*⟩ libelous*

diferencia *f* **(a)** (disparidad) difference; **la** ~ **de precio** the difference in price; **a** ~ **del marido, ella es encantadora** unlike her husband, she's really charming **(b)** (distinción) distinction; **hacer una** ~ to make a distinction **(c)** (desacuerdo) difference; **resolver sus** (*or* **mis** *etc*) ~**s** to resolve one's differences **(d)** (resto) difference, **yo pagué la** ~ I paid the difference

diferenciar [A1] *vt* ⟨*colores/sonidos*⟩ to tell the difference between, differentiate **■ diferenciarse** *v pron*: **¿en qué se diferencia esta especie?** what makes this species different?; **no se diferencian en nada** there's no difference between them; ~**se** DE **algo/algn** to differ FROM sth/sb; **solo se diferencia del otro en** *or* **por el precio** the only difference between this one and the other one is the price

diferente *adj* **(a)** (distinto) different; **ser** ~ A *or* DE **algn/algo** to be different FROM sb/sth **(b)** (en

pl, delante del n) ⟨*motivos/soluciones/maneras*⟩ various; **nos vimos en** ~**s ocasiones** we've met on several occasions

diferido: **una transmisión en** ~ a prerecorded broadcast

difícil *adj* ⟦1⟧ **(a)** ⟨*problema/situación*⟩ difficult; ⟨*examen*⟩ hard, difficult; **me fue muy** ~ **decírselo** it was very hard *o* difficult for me to tell him; **es** ~ **de hacer/entender** it's difficult *o* hard to do/understand **(b)** ⟨*persona/carácter*⟩ difficult ⟦2⟧ (poco probable) unlikely; **va a ser** ~ **que acepte** it's unlikely that he'll accept; **veo** ~ **que gane** I doubt if she'll win

dificultad *f* difficulty; **respira con** ~ he has difficulty breathing; **tiene** ~**es en hacerse entender** she has difficulty in making herself understood; **me pusieron muchas** ~**es para entrar** they made it very hard for me to get in; **meterse en** ~**es** to get into difficulties

dificultar [A1] *vt* to make ... difficult

dificultoso -sa *adj* difficult, problematic

difteria *f* diphtheria

difundir [I1] *vt* ⟨*noticia/rumor*⟩ to spread; ⟨*ideas/doctrina*⟩ to spread, disseminate; ⟨*cultura*⟩ to disseminate; ⟨*comunicado*⟩ to issue; (por radio) to disseminate; **muy difundidas** very widespread

difunto -ta *adj* (frml) late (*before n*), deceased (frml); **su** ~ **marido** her late husband **■** *m,f* (frml) deceased (frml)

difusión *f* (de noticia, rumor) spreading; (de ideas, doctrina, cultura) spreading, diffusion (frml); **los medios de** ~ the media

difuso -sa *adj* ⟨*luz*⟩ dim, diffused; ⟨*idea/conocimientos*⟩ vague

diga, digas, etc ▶ DECIR

digerir [I11] *vt* to digest

digestión *f* digestion; **hacer la** ~ to let one's food go down

digestivo -va *adj* ⟨*aparato*⟩ digestive

digital *adj* **(a)** (dactilar) finger (*before n*), digital (frml) **(b)** ⟨*aparato/sonido*⟩ digital

dignarse [A1] *v pron* ~ (A) **hacer algo** to condescend *o* deign TO sth

dignatario -ria *m,f* dignitary

dignidad *f* **(a)** (cualidad) dignity **(b)** (título) rank; (cargo) position

digno -na *adj* ⟦1⟧ **(a)** ⟨*persona/actitud*⟩ honorable*; **(b)** ⟨*sueldo*⟩ decent, living (*before n*); ⟨*vivienda*⟩ decent ⟦2⟧ ~ **de algo/algn** worthy OF sth/sb; **una persona digna de admiración** a person worthy of admiration; **una medida digna de elogio** a praiseworthy measure; **un espectáculo** ~ **de verse** a show worth seeing

dije *adj* (Chi fam) **(a)** (agradable) nice, lovely **(b)** (bondadoso) kind **■** *m* charm

dije, dijera, etc ▶ DECIR

dilapidar [A1] *vt* to squander

dilatado -da *adj* ⟨*pupila/conducto*⟩ dilated

dilatarse [A1] *v pron* ⟦1⟧ «*cuerpo/metal*» to expand; «*corazón*» to expand, dilate; «*pupila*» to dilate; «*embarazada*» to dilate ⟦2⟧ **(a)** (prolongarse) to be prolonged **(b)** (diferirse) to be postponed, be put off ⟦3⟧ (Méx, Ven) ▶ DEMORARSE B

dilema *m* (disyuntiva) dilemma

diligencia *f* **(a)** (aplicación) diligence, ···⟶

conscientiousness; **con ~** diligently **(b)** (gestión): **tengo que hacer unas ~s** I have some business to attend to

diligente *adj* (trabajador) diligent, conscientious

diluir [I20] *vt* ‹*líquido*› to dilute; ‹*pintura*› to thin (down); ‹*sólido*› to dissolve

diluviar [A1] *vi* to pour (with rain)

diluvio *m* (lluvia) heavy rain, deluge; (inundación) flood; **el D~ Universal** the Flood

diluyente *m* thinner

dimensión *f* **1** **(a)** (Fís, Mat) dimension; **una figura en tres dimensiones** a three-dimensional figure **(b) dimensiones** *fpl* (tamaño) dimensions (*pl*); **de enormes dimensiones** huge, enormous **2** (alcance, magnitud — de problema) magnitude, scale; (— de tragedia) scale

diminutivo *m* diminutive

diminuto -ta *adj* tiny, minute

división *f* resignation

dimitir [I1] *vi* to resign; **~ DE algo** to resign FROM sth

dimos ▶ DAR

Dinamarca *f* Denmark

dinamarqués -quesa *adj/m,f* ▶ DANÉS

dinámico -ca *adj* dynamic

dinamita *f* dynamite

dinamitar [A1] *vt* to dynamite

dínamo, dinamo *m or* (Esp) *f* dynamo

dinastía *f* dynasty

dineral *m* fortune, huge amount of money

dinero *m* money; **estar escaso de ~** to be short of money; **gente de ~** well-off *o* wealthy people; **hacer ~** to make money; **~ de bolsillo** pocket money; **~ (en) efectivo** cash; **~ suelto** change; **~ contante y sonante** (fam) hard cash

dinosaurio *m* dinosaur

dio ▶ DAR

diócesis *f* diocese

dioptría *f* diopter*; **¿cuántas ~s tiene?** what's your correction *o* gradation?

dios, diosa *m,f* **1** (Mit) (*m*) god; (*f*) goddess **2 Dios** *m* (Relig) God; **el D~ de los musulmanes** the Muslim God; **gracias a D~** thank God *o* heaven; **si D~ quiere** God willing; **te lo juro por D~** I swear to God; **¡por (el) amor de D~!** for God's sake *o* for heaven's sake!; **que D~ te bendiga** God bless you; **¡D~ me libre!** God *o* heaven forbid!; **¡sabe D~!** God knows!; **¡vaya por D~!** oh dear!; **¡por D~!** for God's *o* heaven's sake!; **¡D~ mío!** *or* **¡D~ santo!** (expresando angustia) my God!, oh God!; (expresando sorpresa) (good) God!; *como* **D~ manda**: **un coche como D~ manda** a real *o* a proper car; **pórtate como D~ manda** behave properly; **hacer algo a la buena de D~** to do sth any which way (AmE) *o* (BrE) any old how

diploma *m* diploma, certificate

diplomacia *f* **1** (Pol) (carrera) diplomacy; (cuerpo) diplomatic corps **2** (tacto) diplomacy, tact

diplomado -da *adj* qualified; **~ en peluquería** qualified hairdresser

diplomarse [A1] *v pron* **(a)** (AmL) (obtener un título universitario) to graduate; **~ DE/EN algo** to graduate AS/IN sth **(b)** (obtener otro título) to obtain a diploma (*o* certificate *etc*)

diplomático -ca *adj* **1** (Pol) ‹*carrera/pasaporte*› diplomatic **2** (en el trato) diplomatic, tactful
■ *m,f* diplomat

diptongo *m* diphthong

diputación *f* **(a)** (delegación) deputation, delegation **(b)** (Gob) (en Esp) council

diputado -da *m,f* deputy, ≈ representative (*in US*), ≈ member of parliament (*in UK*)

dique *m* dike*

diré, dirá, etc ▶ DECIR

dirección *f* **1** (señas) address **2** (sentido, rumbo) direction; **ellos venían en ~ contraria** they were coming the other way *o* from the opposite direction; **¿en qué ~ iba?** which way was he heading *o* going?; **señal de ~ prohibida** no-entry sign; **~ obligatoria** one way only **3** (Auto) (mecanismo) steering; **~ asistida** power-assisted steering, power steering **4** (Adm) **(a)** (cargo — en escuela) principalship (AmE), headship (BrE); (— en empresa) post *o* position of manager **(b)** (cuerpo directivo — de empresa) management; (— de periódico) editorial board; (— de prisión) authorities (*pl*); (— de partido) leadership **(c)** (oficina — en escuela) principal's office (AmE), headmaster's/headmistress's office (BrE); (— en empresa) manager's/director's office; (— en periódico) editorial office

direccional *f* (Col, Méx) turn signal (AmE), indicator (BrE)

directamente *adv* (derecho) straight; (sin intermediarios) directly

directiva *f* **1** (de empresa) board (of directors); (de partido) executive committee, leadership **2** (directriz) guideline

directo -ta *adj* **1** ‹*vuelo*› direct, nonstop; ‹*ruta/acceso*› direct; ‹*tren*› direct, through (*before n*) **2** (Rad, TV): **en ~** live **3** ‹*lenguaje/pregunta*› direct; ‹*respuesta*› straight; ‹*persona*› direct, straightforward

director -tora *m,f* **(a)** (de escuela) (*m*) head teacher, principal (AmE), headmaster (BrE); (*f*) head teacher, principal (AmE), headmistress (BrE); (de periódico, revista) editor (in chief); (de hospital) administrator; (de prisión) warden (AmE), governor (BrE) **(b)** (Com) (gerente) manager; (miembro de junta directiva) director, executive; **~ gerente** managing director **(c)** (Cin, Teatr) director; **~ de orquesta** conductor

directorio *m* (AmL exc CS) (guía telefónica) telephone directory, directory

directriz *f* (Mat) directrix; (guía) guideline, principle; (instrucción) directive

dirigente *mf* (de partido, país) leader

dirigible *m* airship, dirigible

dirigir [I7] *vt* ⊡ **(a)** ⟨*empresa*⟩ to manage, run; ⟨*periódico/revista*⟩ to run, edit; ⟨*investigación/tesis*⟩ to supervise; ⟨*debate*⟩ to lead, chair; ⟨*tráfico*⟩ to direct **(b)** ⟨*obra/película*⟩ to direct; ⟨*orquesta*⟩ to conduct

⊡ **(a)** ~ algo A algn ⟨*mensaje/carta*⟩ to address sth TO sb; ⟨*críticas*⟩ to direct sth TO sb; **la pregunta iba dirigida a usted** the question was meant for you; **no me dirigió la palabra** he didn't say a word to me **(b)** ~ algo HACIA *or* A algo/algn ⟨*telescopio*⟩ to point sth TOWARD(s) sth/sb; ⟨*pistola*⟩ to point sth TOWARD(s) sth/sb; ~ **la mirada hacia** *or* **a algo/algn** to look at sth/sb; **dirigió sus pasos hacia la esquina** he walked toward(s) the corner

⊡ (encaminar) ~ algo A hacer algo ⟨*esfuerzos*⟩ to channel sth INTO doing sth; ⟨*energía/atención*⟩ to direct sth TOWARD(s) doing sth

■ **dirigirse** *v pron* ⊡ (encaminarse): ~**se HACIA algo** to head FOR sth

⊡ ~**se A algn** (oralmente) to speak *o* talk TO sb; (por escrito) to write TO sb

discado *m* (AmL) dialing*; ~ **automático** *or* **directo** (AmL) direct dialing*

discapacitado -da *m,f* disabled person, handicapped person

discar [A2] *vt/vi* (AmL) to dial

disciplina *f* discipline; **mantener la** ~ to keep *o* maintain discipline

discípulo -la *m,f* disciple

disco *m* ⊡ **(a)** (Audio) record; **grabar un** ~ to make a record; **poner un** ~ to put on a record; ~ **compacto** CD, compact disc; ~ **de larga duración** album, LP; ~ **volador** (CS) flying saucer **(b)** (Inf) disk; ~ **duro** hard disk; ~ **flexible** *or* **floppy** floppy disk ⊡ **(a)** (Dep) discus **(b)** (Anat) disk*; (Auto, Mec) disk **(c)** (del teléfono) dial ⊡ (señal de tráfico) (road) sign

disconforme *adj* **(a)** (no satisfecho) dissatisfied; ~ **CON algo/algn** dissatisfied WITH sth/sb **(b)** (en desacuerdo) ~ **CON algo** in disagreement WITH sth

discontinuo -nua *adj* ⟨*línea*⟩ broken; ⟨*sonido*⟩ intermittent

discordante *adj* (Mús) discordant; ⟨*opiniones/versiones*⟩ conflicting

discordia *f* discord

discoteca *f* **(a)** (local) discotheque **(b)** (colección de discos) record collection **(c)** (AmC) (tienda) record store *o* shop

discreción *f* ⊡ **(a)** (tacto, mesura) tact, discretion **(b)** (reserva) discretion ⊡ **a discreción** ⟨*comer/beber*⟩ as much as you (*o* we *etc*) like; **esto queda a ~ del juez** this is left to the discretion of the judge

discreto -ta *adj* **(a)** ⟨*persona/carácter/comportamiento*⟩ discreet **(b)** ⟨*color/vestido*⟩ discreet **(c)** ⟨*cantidad/sueldo/actuación*⟩ modest

discriminación *f* discrimination

discriminar [A1] *vt* **(a)** ⟨*persona/colectividad*⟩ to discriminate against **(b)** (distinguir) to differentiate, distinguish

disculpa *f* apology; **me debe una** ~ she owes me an apology; **un error que no tiene** ~ an inexcusable error; **pedir(le)** ~**s (a algn) por algo** to apologize (to sb) for sth

disculpar [A1] *vt* **(a)** ⟨*error/falta/comportamiento*⟩ to forgive, excuse; **le disculpó la indiscreción** he forgave her her indiscretion; **disculpa mi tardanza** I am sorry I'm late **(b)** ⟨*persona*⟩ to make excuses for; **su madre siempre lo está disculpando** his mother's always making excuses for him

■ ~ *vi*: **disculpe, no lo volveré a hacer** I'm sorry *o* (frml) I apologize, I won't do it again

■ **disculparse** *v pron* to apologize; ~**se CON algn** to apologize TO sb

discurso *m* speech; **pronunciar un** ~ to give *o* make a speech

discusión *f* **(a)** (de asunto, tema) discussion **(b)** (altercado, disputa) argument

discutible *adj* debatable

discutido -da *adj* controversial

discutir [I1] *vt* **(a)** (debatir) ⟨*problema/asunto*⟩ to discuss; ⟨*proyecto de ley*⟩ to debate, discuss **(b)** (cuestionar) ⟨*derecho/afirmación*⟩ to question, challenge

■ ~ *vi* to argue, quarrel; **discutió de política con su padre** he argued with his father about politics; ~ **POR algo** to argue ABOUT sth; ~**le A algn** to argue WITH sb

disecar [A2] *vt* **(a)** ⟨*animal muerto*⟩ (para estudiarlo) to dissect; (para conservarlo) to stuff **(b)** ⟨*planta*⟩ to preserve

disección *f* dissection

diseccionar [A1] *vt* to dissect

diseminado -da *adj* scattered; **los pueblos** ~**s por la región** the villages scattered throughout the region; **los hoteles están muy** ~**s** the hotels are very spread out

diseminarse [A1] *v pron* ⟨*personas*⟩ to scatter, disperse; ⟨*ideas/cultura*⟩ to spread

diseñador -dora *m,f* designer; ~ **de moda(s)** fashion designer

diseñar [A1] *vt* ⟨*moda/mueble/máquina*⟩ to design; ⟨*parque/edificio*⟩ to design, plan

diseño *m* design; ~ **de moda** fashion design; **blusas de** ~ **francés** French-designed blouses; **ropa de** ~ designer clothes

disforzarse [A11] *v pron* (Per fam) to clown around

disfraz *m* **(a)** (Indum) (para jugar, fiestas) costume, fancy dress outfit (BrE); (para engañar) disguise; **una fiesta de disfraces** a costume *o* (BrE) fancy dress party **(b)** (simulación) front

disfrazar [A4] *vt* **(a)** ~ **a algn DE algo** (para fiesta) to dress sb up AS sth; (para engañar) to disguise sb AS sth **(b)** (disimular, ocultar) ⟨*sentimiento/verdad*⟩ to conceal, hide; ⟨*voz/escritura/intención*⟩ to disguise

■ **disfrazarse** *v pron* **(a)** (por diversión) to dress up; ~**se DE algo/algn** to dress up AS sth/sb **(b)** (para engañar) to disguise oneself; ~**se DE algo/algn** to disguise oneself AS sth/sb, dress up AS sth/sb

disfrutar [A1] *vi* **(a)** (divertirse) to enjoy oneself, have fun; ~ **CON/DE algo** to enjoy sth; ~ **haciendo algo** to enjoy doing sth **(b)** (tener) ~ **DE algo** ⟨*de privilegio/derecho/buena salud*⟩ to enjoy, have

■ ~ *vt* ⟨*viaje/espectáculo*⟩ to enjoy; ⟨*beneficio/derecho*⟩ to have, enjoy

disgregarse [A3] *v pron* **(a)** «*grupo/familia*» to break up, split up; «*multitud/manifestaciones*» to break up, disperse **(b)** (Tec) to disintegrate

disgustado -da *adj* [ESTAR] upset

disgustar [A1] *vt*: **me disgustó mucho que me mintiera** I was very upset that he lied to me; **me disgusta tener que decírselo** I don't like having to tell her
■ **disgustarse** *v pron* to get upset

disgusto *m* ① (sufrimiento, pesar): **tiene un ~ tremendo** he's very upset; **me ha dado muchos ~s** he's given me lots of upset *o* heartache; **lo hizo a ~** she did it reluctantly ② (discusión) argument, quarrel

disidente *mf* (que discrepa) dissident; (escindido) member of a splinter *o* breakaway group

disimulado -da *adj* **(a)** (disfrazado, oculto) disguised; **un mal ~ descontento** ill-concealed displeasure **(b)** (discreto) discreet; **sé más ~** be more discreet
■ *m,f*: **me vio pero se hizo el ~** he saw me but he pretended he hadn't

disimular [A1] *vt* **(a)** «*alegría/rabia/dolor*» to hide, conceal **(b)** «*defecto/imperfección*» to hide, disguise

disimulo *m*: **con ~** without anyone noticing; **sin ~** openly

disiparse [A1] *v pron* «*nubes/niebla*» to clear; «*temores/sospechas*» to be dispelled; «*ilusiones*» to vanish, disappear

dislexia *f* dyslexia

disléxico -ca *adj/m,f* dyslexic

dislocado -da *adj* «*articulación*» dislocated

dislocarse [A2] *v pron* «*articulación*» to dislocate

disminución *f* decrease, fall; (de temperatura) drop; (de tarifa) reduction

disminuido -da *m,f*: **~ psíquico/físico** mentally/physically handicapped person

disminuir [I20] *vi* (menguar) «*número/cantidad*» to decrease, fall; «*precios/temperaturas*» to drop, fall; «*dolor*» to diminish, lessen
■ **~** *vt* (reducir) «*gastos/producción*» to cut back on; «*impuestos*» to cut; «*velocidad/número/cantidad*» to reduce

disolución *f* **(a)** (de contrato, matrimonio) annulment; (de organización, del parlamento) dissolution **(b)** (de manifestación) breaking up **(c)** (Quím) (acción) dissolving

disolvente *m* solvent; (de pintura) thinner

disolver [E11] *vt* **(a)** «*matrimonio/contrato*» to annul; «*parlamento/organización*» to dissolve **(b)** «*manifestación/reunión*» to break up **(c)** (en líquido) to dissolve **(d)** (Med) to dissolve, break up
■ **disolverse** *v pron* «*manifestación/reunión*» to break up; «*azúcar/aspirina*» to dissolve

disonante *adj* (Mús) dissonant; «*voz*» discordant; «*colores*» clashing

dispar *adj* **(a)** (irregular) uneven **(b)** (diferente) different, disparate (frml)

disparado -da *adj* (fam): **salir ~** (irse de prisa) to shoot off (colloq); **con el choque salió ~ del asiento** the impact catapulted him from his seat; *ver tb* DISPARAR

disparador *m* (de arma) trigger; (Fot) shutter release; (de reloj) escapement

disparar [A1] *vi* **(a)** (con arma) to shoot, fire; **~ al aire** to fire *o* shoot into the air; **~ a matar** to shoot to kill; **le disparó por la espalda** he shot him in the back; **~ a quemarropa** *or* **a bocajarro** to fire at point-blank range; **~ CONTRA algn** to shoot *o* fire AT sb **(b)** (Dep) to shoot
■ **~** *vt* ① **(a)** «*arma/flecha*» to shoot, fire; «*tiro/proyectil*» to fire; **le ~on un tiro en la nuca** they shot him in the back of the head **(b)** (Dep): **disparó el balón a portería** he shot at goal ② (Méx fam) (pagar) to pay
■ **dispararse** *v pron* ① **(a)** «*arma*» to go off **(b)** (*refl*): **se disparó un tiro en la sien** he shot himself in the head ② (fam) «*precio*» to shoot up, rocket

disparatado -da *adj* «*acto/proyecto/idea*» crazy, ludicrous; «*gasto/precio*» outrageous, ridiculous

disparate *m* **(a)** (acción insensata, cosa absurda): **hacer ~s** to do stupid things; **decir ~s** to make foolish remarks; **es un ~ casarse tan joven** it's crazy to get married so young; **temo que haga algún ~** I'm afraid he might do something crazy **(b)** (fam) (cantidad exagerada) ridiculous (*o* crazy *etc*) amount

disparo *m* shot

dispensar [A1] *vt* ① «*honor*» to give, accord (frml); «*acogida*» to give, extend (frml); «*ayuda/protección*» to give, afford (frml); «*asistencia médica*» to give; «*medicamentos*» to dispense; **le ~on un caluroso recibimiento** he was given *o* (frml) extended a warm reception ② **(a)** (eximir) **~ a algn DE algo** to exempt sb FROM sth; **la ~on de asistir a misa** she was excused from attending mass **(b)** (perdonar) to forgive
■ **~** *vi* to forgive; **dispense, por favor** excuse me

dispersar [A1] *vt* **(a)** «*manifestantes/multitud/enemigo*» to disperse **(b)** «*rayos*» to scatter, diffuse; «*niebla/humo*» to clear, disperse
■ **dispersarse** *v pron* **(a)** «*manifestantes/manifestación/multitud*» to disperse **(b)** «*rayos*» to diffuse, scatter; «*niebla/humo*» to disperse, clear

disperso -sa *adj* (diseminado) scattered, dispersed (frml)

displicente *adj* (indiferente) indifferent, blasé; (frío) disdainful

disponer [E22] *vt* ① (frml) (establecer, ordenar) «*ley*» to provide (frml), to stipulate (frml); «*rey*» to decree; «*general/juez*» to order ② (frml) (colocar, arreglar) to arrange, set out, lay out
■ **~** *vi*: **~ DE algo** «*de tiempo/ayuda*» to have sth; **con los recursos de que dispongo** with the means available to me *o* at my disposal
■ **disponerse** *v pron* (frml) **mientras se disponían a tomar el tren** as they were about to catch the train; **la tropa se dispuso a atacar** the troops prepared to attack

disponible *adj* available; «*tiempo*» free (*before* n), available; **cuando estés ~** when you're free

disposición *f* ① (norma) regulation ② **(a)** (actitud) disposition **(b)** (talento) aptitude **(c)** (inclinación, voluntad) willingness ③ **(a)** (de un bien) disposal **(b)** **a ~ de algn** «*coche/chofer*» at sb's disposal; **estoy a tu ~ para lo que sea** I'm here to help if you need anything; **será puesto a ~ del juez** he will appear before the judge; **puso su casa a mi ~** he offered me his house

dispositivo *m* **1** (mecanismo) mechanism; (aparato) device **2** (frml) (destacamento): **un fuerte ~ policial/militar** a large police/military presence

dispuesto -ta *adj* (a) (preparado) ready (b) (con voluntad) willing; **~ A hacer algo** prepared to do sth

dispuse, dispuso, etc ▶ DISPONER

disputa *f* (a) (discusión, pelea) quarrel, argument (b) (combate) fight (c) (controversia) dispute

disputar [A1] *vt* (a) **~le algo A algn** ⟨*título*⟩ to challenge sb for sth; **le disputaban su derecho a la herencia** they contested his right to the inheritance (b) ⟨*partido*⟩ to play; ⟨*combate*⟩ to fight

■ **disputarse** *v pron*: **se disputan el primer puesto** they are competing for first place

disquete, disquette /dis'kete/ *m* diskette, floppy disk

distancia *f* (a) distance; **la ~ que separa dos puntos** the distance between two points; **¿a qué ~ está Londres?** how far is it to London?, **se situó a una ~ de un metro** she stood a meter away; ▶ LLAMADA (b) (*en locs*) **a distancia: se situó a ~ para verlo en conjunto** she stood back to see it as a whole; **se veía a ~** one could see it from a distance; **mantenerse a ~** to keep at a distance; **en la distancia** in the distance; ▶ EDUCACIÓN 1, ENSEÑANZA B

distanciado -da *adj* (afectivamente): **estamos algo distanciadas** we're not as close as we were

distanciar [A1] *vt* (a) (espaciar) to space ... out (b) (en lo afectivo) ⟨*amigos/familiares*⟩ to make ... drift apart; **~ a algn DE algn** to distance sb FROM sb

■ **distanciarse** *v pron* (a) (en el espacio) **~se DE algo** to get far FROM sth (b) (en lo afectivo) (*recípr*) to grow *o* drift apart; (*refl*) **~se DE algn** to distance oneself FROM sb

distante *adj* distant

distar [A1] *vi* (en 3ª *pers*) (estar a): **el colegio dista unos dos kilómetros de su casa** the school is about two kilometers from her house

diste, etc ▶ DAR

distinción *f* (a) (diferencia) distinction; **hacer una ~** to make a distinction; **sin ~ de raza o credo** regardless of race or creed; **no hago distinciones con nadie** I don't give anyone preferential treatment (b) (elegancia) distinction, elegance (c) (honor, condecoración) award

distinguido -da *adj* ⟨*escritor/actor/aire*⟩ distinguished; ⟨*alumno*⟩ outstanding

distinguir [I2] *vt* **1** (a) (diferenciar) to distinguish (b) (caracterizar) to characterize **2** (percibir) ⟨*figura/sonido*⟩ to make out **3** (con medalla, honor) to honor*

■ **distinguirse** *v pron* (destacarse): **~se POR algo** «*persona*» to distinguish oneself BY sth; «*producto*» to be distinguished BY sth

distintivo¹ -va *adj* ⟨*rasgo/característica*⟩ distinctive

distintivo² *m* (insignia) emblem; (símbolo) sign

distinto -ta *adj* **1** (diferente) different; **ser ~ A** *or* DE **algo/algn** to be different FROM *o* TO *o* (AmE)

THAN **sth/sb; estas/te encuentro ~** you look different **2** (*en pl, delante del n*) (varios) several, various

distorsionar [A1] *vt* to distort

distracción *f* (a) (entretenimiento) entertainment (b) (descuido): **en un momento de ~se la robaron** she took her eye off it for a moment and someone stole it; **la más mínima ~ puede ser fatal** the slightest lapse of concentration could be fatal (c) (de fondos) embezzlement

distraer [E23] *vt* (a) ⟨*persona/atención*⟩ to distract; **~ a algn DE algo** ⟨*de trabajo/estudios*⟩ to distract sb FROM sth ⟨*de preocupaciones*⟩ to take sb's mind OFF sth (b) (entretener) ⟨*persona*⟩ to keep ... entertained

■ **distraerse** *v pron* (a) (despistarse, descuidarse) to get distracted (b) (entretenerse): **se distraen viendo la televisión** they pass the time watching television; **se distrae con cualquier cosa** she doesn't need much to keep amused

distraído -da *adj* (a) [SER] ⟨*persona*⟩ absentminded, vague (b) **estaba/iba ~** he was miles away (colloq)

distribución *f* (a) (reparto — de dinero, víveres) distribution; (— de tareas) allocation (b) (de producto, película) distribution (c) (disposición, división) layout, arrangement (d) (Auto) valve-operating gear

distribuidor¹ -dora *m,f* (Com) distributor

distribuidor² *m* (Auto, Mec) distributor

distribuidora *f* (empresa) distributor, distribution company

distribuir [I20] *vt* (a) ⟨*dinero/víveres/panfletos*⟩ to hand out, distribute; ⟨*ganancias*⟩ to distribute; ⟨*tareas*⟩ to allocate, assign; ⟨*carga/peso*⟩ to distribute, spread (b) ⟨*producto/película*⟩ to distribute (c) ⟨*canal/conducto*⟩ ⟨*agua*⟩ to distribute (d) (disponer) to lay out (e) (dividir) to divide ... up; **los distribuyeron en tres grupos** they divided them (up) into three groups

■ **distribuirse** *v pron* (*refl*) to divide up

distrito *m* district

Distrito Federal *m* Federal District (*including Mexico City*)

disturbio *m* (a) (perturbación del orden) disturbance (b) **disturbios** *mpl* (motín) riot, disturbances (journ)

disuadir [I1] *vt* to deter, discourage; **~ A algn DE algo/DE que haga algo** to dissuade sb FROM sth/doing sth

disuasión *f* (Mil, Pol) deterrence

disuasivo -va, disuasorio -ria *adj* ⟨*tono/ palabras*⟩ dissuasive, discouraging; ⟨*efecto*⟩ deterrent; ⟨*medida*⟩ designed to act as a deterrent

disuelto -ta *pp*: ▶ DISOLVER

diurético *m* diuretic

diurno -na *adj* day (*before n*); **clases diurnas** daytime classes

diva *f* diva, prima donna; *ver tb* DIVO

divagación *f* digression

divagar [A3] *vi* (a) (desviarse del tema) to digress (b) (hablar sin sentido) to ramble

diván *m* couch

diversidad *f* diversity

diversificar [A2] vt ‹actividades/métodos› to diversify; ‹inversión/producción› to diversify
■ **diversificarse** v pron to diversify

diversión f (a) (esparcimiento) fun (b) (espectáculo, juego): **aquí hay pocas diversiones** there isn't much to do here

diverso -sa adj [1] (variado, diferente): **su obra es muy diversa** his work is very diverse; **seres de diversa naturaleza** various types of creatures; **ha desempeñado las más diversas actividades** she has engaged in a very wide range of activities [2] (pl) (varios) various, several

divertido -da adj (a) (que interesa, divierte) ‹espectáculo/fiesta› fun, enjoyable; ‹momento/situación› entertaining; **es un tipo muy ~** he's a really fun guy, he's really fun to be with (b) (gracioso) funny

divertir [I11] vt to amuse
■ **divertirse** v pron (entretenerse) to amuse oneself; (pasarlo bien) to have fun, enjoy oneself; **¡que te diviertas!** have fun!, enjoy yourself!; **nos divertimos mucho en la fiesta** we had a really good time at the party

dividendo m dividend

dividir [I1] vt (a) (partir) to divide; **lo dividió en partes iguales** he divided it (up) into equal portions (b) (repartir) to divide, share (out) (c) (enemistar) ‹partido/familia› to divide
■ ~ vi (Mat) to divide
■ **dividirse** v pron (a) «célula» to split; «grupo/partido» to split up; «camino/río» to divide (b) ~ **EN algo** «obra/período» to divide INTO sth (c) (repartirse) to divide up, share out

divierta, divirtió, etc ▶ DIVERTIR

divinidad f (a) (deidad) deity, god (b) (cualidad) divinity (c) (fam) (preciosidad) delight

divinizar [A4] vt to deify

divino -na adj divine

divisa f [1] (Com, Fin) currency; **la fuga de ~s** the flight of capital; **una fuente de ~s** a source of foreign currency [2] (emblema) emblem, insignia

divisar [A1] vt ‹tierra/barco› to sight, make out; **a lo lejos se divisaba un poblado** they (or he etc) could make out a village in the distance

divisible adj ~ **POR algo** divisible BY sth

división f (en general) division; **hacer una ~** (Mat) to do a division

divisor m divisor

divisorio -ria adj dividing (before n)

divo -va m,f (estrella) celebrity, star; (con actitud soberbia) prima donna; ver tb DIVA

divorciado -da adj divorced
■ m,f (m) divorcé (esp AmE), divorcee (esp BrE); (f) divorcée (esp AmE), divorcee (esp BrE)

divorciarse [A1] v pron to get divorced; ~se DE algn to divorce sb, get divorced FROM sb

divorcio m (Der) divorce

divulgar [A3] vt ‹noticia/información› to spread, circulate; ‹secreto/plan› to divulge; ‹cultura› to spread, disseminate
■ **divulgarse** v pron to spread

dizque, diz que adv (AmL) (a) (según parece) apparently (b) (expresando escepticismo): **esta ~ democracia** this so-called democracy; **estaban allí, ~ trabajando** they were there, supposedly working

Dn. = **Don**

Dña. = **Doña**

do m (nota) C; (en solfeo) do, doh (BrE); ~ **de pecho** high C, top C

dobladillo m hem

doblar [A1] vt [1] ‹camisa/papel› to fold; ‹brazo/vara› to bend [2] ‹esquina› to turn, go around; ‹cabo› to round [3] (aumentar al doble) ‹oferta/apuesta/capital› to double; (tener el doble que): **la dobla en edad** he's twice her age [4] ‹actor› (en banda sonora) to dub; (en escena) to double for; ‹película› to dub; **doblada al castellano** dubbed into Spanish
■ ~ vi [1] (torcer, girar) «persona» to turn; «camino» to bend, turn; **dobla a la izquierda** turn left [2] «campanas» to toll
■ **doblarse** v pron [1] «rama/alambre» to bend [2] «precios/población» to double

doble¹ adj [1] ‹whisky/flor/puerta› double; ‹café› large; ‹costura/hilo/consonante› double; **lo veo todo ~** I'm seeing double; **cerrar con ~ llave** to double-lock; **tiene ~ sentido** it has a double meaning; **calle de ~ sentido** two-way street; ~ **crema** f (Méx) double cream; ~ **fondo** m false bottom; ~ **ve** or ~ **u** f: name of the letter W; ~ **ventana** f double glazing [2] (Andes, Ven fam) ‹persona› two-faced

doble² m [1] (Mat): **los precios aumentaron el ~** prices doubled; **tardó el ~** she took twice as long; **el ~ de tres es seis** two threes are six; **el ~ QUE algn/algo** twice as much AS sb/sth; **el ~ de largo/rápido** twice as long/quick [2] (a) (en béisbol) double (b) **dobles** mpl (en tenis) doubles [3] **doble** mf (actor, actriz) stand-in, double; (en escenas peligrosas) (m) stuntman; (f) stuntwoman; (persona parecida) (fam) double

doblez m [1] (en tela, papel) fold [2] **doblez** m or f (falsedad) deceitfulness

doce adj inv/m/pron twelve; **son las ~ de la noche** it's twelve o'clock, it's midnight; para más ejemplos ver tb CINCO

docena f dozen; **una ~ de huevos** a dozen eggs; **media ~** half a dozen

dócil adj ‹niño/comportamiento› meek, docile; ‹perro/caballo› docile, well-trained; ‹pelo› manageable

doctor -tora m,f doctor; ~ **en derecho** Doctor of Law

doctorado m doctorate, PhD

doctorarse [A1] v pron to earn o get one's doctorate, do one's PhD

doctrina f (ideología) doctrine; (enseñanza) teaching

documentación f [1] (de persona) papers (pl); (de vehículo, envío) documents (pl), documentation (frml) [2] (información) information, data (pl)

AmC Central America	Arg Argentina	Cu Cuba	Per Peru
AmL Latin America	Bol Bolivia	Ec Ecuador	RPI River Plate Area
AmS South America	Chi Chile	Esp Spain	Ur Uruguay
Andes Andean Region	CS Southern Cone	Méx Mexico	Ven Venezuela

documental _adj_ **(a)** (Cin, TV) ‹_programa/serie_› documentary (_before n_) **(b)** (Der) ‹_prueba_› documentary
■ _m_ documentary

documentar [A1] _vt_ ①‹_trabajo/hipótesis/ solicitud_› to document ② (Méx) ‹_equipaje_› to check in
■ **documentarse** _v pron_ ① (informarse) to do research ② (Méx) ‹_pasajero_› to check in

documento _m_ (Adm, Der, Inf) document; ~ **adjunto** (Corresp) enclosed document; (Inf) attachment

dogma _m_ dogma

dogmático -ca _adj_ dogmatic

dólar _m_ dollar

dolencia _f_ ailment, complaint

doler [E9] _vi_ **(a)** ‹_inyección/herida/brazo_› to hurt; **no duele nada** it doesn't hurt at all; (+ _me/ te/le etc_) **le dolió mucho** it hurt a lot; **le duele una muela/la cabeza** she has (a) toothache/a headache; **me dolía el estómago** I had (a) stomachache; **me duele la garganta** I have a sore throat; **me duelen los pies** my feet ache; **me duele todo (el cuerpo)** I ache all over **(b)** (apenar) (+ _me/ te/le etc_): **me duele tener que decirte esto** I'm sorry to have to tell you this; **me dolió muchísimo lo que me dijo** I was deeply hurt by what he said

dolido -da _adj_ hurt; **estar ~ POR algo** to be hurt AT sth

dolor _m_ **(a)** (físico) pain; **sentía mucho ~** he was in a lot of pain; **tener ~ de muelas/cabeza/ garganta** to have a toothache/a headache/a sore throat **(b)** (pena, tristeza) pain, grief

dolorido -da _adj_ **(a)** (físicamente): **estoy toda dolorida** I'm aching all over; **tengo el brazo muy ~** I've got a very sore arm **(b)** (afligido) hurt

doloroso -sa _adj_ **(a)** ‹_tratamiento/enfermedad_› painful **(b)** ‹_decisión/momento/recuerdo_› painful; ‹_separación/espectáculo_› distressing, upsetting

domador -dora _m,f_ (de fieras) tamer; (de caballos) horsebreaker, broncobuster (AmE)

domar [A1] _vt_ **(a)** ‹_fieras_› to tame; ‹_caballo_› to break in **(b)** (fam) ‹_niño_› to bring _o_ get ... under control **(c)** (fam) ‹_zapatos_› to break in

domesticado -da _adj_ tame, domesticated

domesticar [A2] _vt_ to domesticate

doméstico -ca _adj_ ①‹_vida/problemas/ servicio_› domestic; ‹_gastos_› household; **tareas domésticas** housework ②‹_vuelo_› domestic

domiciliar [A1] _vt_ (Esp) ‹_pago/letras_› to pay ... by direct debit _o_ (AmE) direct billing; ‹_sueldo_› to have ... paid direct into one's bank account
■ **domiciliarse** _v pron_ (frml) (residir) to reside (frml), to be domiciled (frml)

domicilio _m_ (frml) address; **en su ~ particular** at his home address; **sin ~ fijo** of no fixed abode (frml); **Pat Lee, con ~ en Londres** Pat Lee currently living in London

dominante _adj_ ①‹_color/tendencia_› predominant, dominant; ‹_opinión_› prevailing (_before n_); ‹_cultura_› dominant **(b)** (Biol, Mús, Astrol) dominant ②‹_persona_› domineering

dominar [A1] _vt_ **(a)** (controlar) ‹_nación/territorio/ persona_› to dominate; ‹_pasión/cólera_› to control; ‹_vehículo/caballo_› to control; **dominado por la ambición/los celos** ruled by ambition/consumed

by jealousy **(b)** ‹_idioma_› to have a good command of; ‹_tema/asignatura_› to know ... very well **(c)** (abarcar con la vista): **desde allí se domina toda la bahía** there's a view over the whole bay from there
■ ~ _vi_ ‹_color/tendencia_› to predominate; ‹_opinión_› to prevail; ‹_equipo_› to dominate
■ **dominarse** _v pron_ ‹_persona_› to restrain _o_ control oneself

domingo _m_ (día) Sunday; (Relig) Sabbath; **traje de ~** Sunday best; **~ de Pascua** _or_ **de Resurrección** Easter Sunday; **~ de Ramos** Palm Sunday; _para más ejemplos ver_ LUNES

dominicano -na _adj/m,f_ (Geog) Dominican

dominio _m_ ① **(a)** (control) control; **perdió el ~ de sí mismo** he lost his self-control **(b)** (de idioma, tema) command; **ser del ~ público** to be public knowledge ② **(a)** (Hist, Pol) dominion **(b)** **dominios** _mpl_ (colonias) dominions (_pl_) ③ (Inf) domain

dominó _m_ (_pl_ **-nós**) **(a)** (juego) dominoes; **jugar** _or_ (Esp, RPl) **al ~** to play dominoes **(b)** (ficha) domino

don _m_ ① **(a)** (liter) (dádiva) gift **(b)** (talento) talent, gift; **el ~ de la palabra** the gift of speech; **~ de gentes** ability to get on well with people; **~ de mando** leadership qualities (_pl_) ② (tratamiento de cortesía) ≈ Mr; **buenos días ~ Miguel** good morning Mr López; **ser un ~ nadie** to be a nobody

dona _f_ (Méx) (Coc) doughnut, donut (AmE)

donación _f_ donation

donador -dora _m,f_, **donante** _mf_ donor

donar [A1] _vt_ ‹_bienes/dinero_› to donate, give; ‹_sangre_› to give, donate; ‹_órganos_› to donate

donativo _m_ donation

doncella _f_ **(a)** (arc) (virgen) maiden (liter) **(b)** (ant) (criada) maid

donde _conj_ where; **la ciudad ~ se conocieron** the city where they met; **siéntate ~ quieras** sit wherever _o_ where you like; **déjalo ~ sea** leave it anywhere; **de ~ se deduce que ...** from which it can be deduced that ...; **la ventana por ~ había entrado** the window through which he had got in
■ _prep_ (esp AmL, en algunas regiones crít): **ve ~ tu hermana y dile que ...** (a su casa) go over to your sister's and tell her ...; (al lugar donde está ella) go and tell your sister ...

dónde _adv_ ① where; **¿~ está?** where is it?; **¿de ~ es?** where is he from?; **¿por ~ quieres ir?** which way do you want to go? ② (Chi, Méx, Per) (cómo) how; **¡~ íbamos a imaginar que ...!** how were we to imagine that ...!

dondequiera _adv_: **~ QUE** wherever

donjuán _m_ (tenorio) womanizer, Don Juan

doña _f_ (tratamiento de cortesía) ≈ Mrs/Ms; **~ Cristina Fuentes** Mrs/Ms Cristina Fuentes

dopado -da _adj_ [ESTAR] drugged

dopar [A1] _vt_ ‹_enfermo_› to drug, dope (colloq); ‹_caballo_› to dope
■ **doparse** _v pron_ (refl) to take drugs

doping _m_ (Equ) doping; (Dep) drug-taking

dorada _f_ gilthead (bream)

dorado¹ -da _adj_ **(a)** ‹_botón/galones_› gold; ‹_pintura_› gold, gold-colored*; ‹_cabello_› (liter) golden **(b)** ‹_época_› golden

dorado² *m* (acción) gilding; (capa) gilt

dorar [A1] *vt* ⟨*marco/porcelana*⟩ to gild; (Coc) ⟨*cebolla/papas*⟩ to brown
■ **dorarse** *v pron* (Coc) to brown

dormida *f* (AmL) sleep

dormido -da *adj* **(a)** (durmiendo) asleep; **estar/ quedarse** ∼ to be/to fall asleep **(b)** (sin sensibilidad): **tengo la pierna dormida** my leg's gone to sleep (colloq); *ver tb* DORMIR

dormilón -lona *adj* (fam): **es muy** ∼ he's a real sleepyhead (colloq)
■ *m,f* (fam) (persona) sleepyhead (colloq)

dormir [I16] *vi* to sleep; **no dormí nada** I didn't sleep a wink; **dormimos en un hotel** we spent the night in a hotel; **durmió de un tirón** she slept right through (the night); **se fue a** ∼ **temprano** he went off to bed early, he had an early night; ∼ **a pierna suelta** (fam) to sleep the sleep of the dead; ∼ **como un lirón o tronco** to sleep like a log (colloq)
■ ∼ *vt* **(a)** (hacer dormir) ⟨*niño/bebé*⟩ to get ... off to sleep; **sus clases me duermen** his classes send *o* put me to sleep **(b)** (anestesiar) ⟨*persona*⟩ to put to sleep, put out (colloq); **todavía tengo este lado dormido** this side is still numb **(c)** ∼ **la siesta** to have a siesta *o* nap
■ **dormirse** *v pron* **(a)** (conciliar el sueño) to fall asleep; (lograr conciliar el sueño) to get to sleep; **casi me duermo en la clase** I almost fell asleep *o* (colloq) dropped off in class **(b)** (no despertarse) to oversleep, sleep in (AmE) **(c)** «*pierna/brazo*» (+ *me/te/le etc*) to go to sleep (colloq); **se me durmió el pie** my foot went to sleep **(d)** (fam) (distraerse, descuidarse): **no te duermas** don't waste any time

dormitar [A1] *vi* to doze, snooze (colloq)

dormitorio *m* (en casa) bedroom; (en colegio, cuartel) dormitory

dorso *m* **(a)** (de un papel) back; **al** ∼ ⟨*ver*⟩ overleaf; ⟨*escribir*⟩ on the back **(b)** (de la mano, animal) back

dos *adj inv/m/pron* two; **lo hicimos entre los** ∼ we did it between the two of us; **sujétalo con las** ∼ **manos** hold it with both hands; **llamó** ∼ **veces** he called twice; **caminaban de** ∼ **en** ∼ they walked in pairs; **entraron de** ∼ **en** ∼ they came in two at a time *o* two by two; ∼ **puntos** colon; **en un** ∼ **por tres** in a flash; *para más ejemplos ver* CINCO

doscientos¹ -tas *adj/pron* two hundred; *para ejemplos ver* QUINIENTOS

doscientos² *m* (number) two hundred

dosel *m* (de cama) canopy; (de trono, púlpito) baldachin

dosificar [A2] *vt* ⟨*medicamento*⟩ to dose

dosis *f* (*pl* ∼) dose

dotado -da *adj* ⟨*persona*⟩ gifted; **estar** ∼ **DE algo** ⟨*persona*⟩ to be blessed WITH sth; «*cocina/ oficina*» to be equipped WITH sth

dotar [A1] *vt* **(a)** (frml) ⟨*institución/organismo*⟩ ∼ **(A) algo DE** *or* **CON algo** ⟨*de fondos*⟩ to provide sth WITH sth; ⟨*de técnica/maquinaria*⟩ to equip sth WITH sth; ⟨*de poderes*⟩ to invest sth WITH sth **(b)** «*naturaleza/Dios*» ∼ **a algn DE** *or* **CON algo** to endow sb WITH sth

dote *f* ⟨1⟩ (de novia) dowry ⟨2⟩ **dotes** *fpl*: ∼**s para el canto** a talent for singing; ∼**s de mando** leadership qualities

doy ▶ DAR

Dr. *m* (= **Doctor**) Dr

Dra. *f* (= **Doctora**) Dr

dracma *m* drachma

dragar [A3] *vt* ⟨*río*⟩ to dredge; ⟨*minas*⟩ to sweep for

dragón *m* (Mit) dragon

drama *m* drama; **hacer un** ∼ **de algo** (fam) to make a big deal out of sth

dramático -ca *adj* dramatic; **un autor** ∼ a playwright *o* dramatist

dramatismo *m* dramatic quality *o* character

dramatización *f* dramatization

dramaturgo -ga *m,f* dramatist, playwright

drástico -ca *adj* drastic

driblar, driblear [A1] *vt* to dribble past *o* around

drible *m* dribble

droga *f* drug; ∼**s duras/blandas** hard/soft drugs

drogadicción *f* (drug) addiction

drogadicto -ta *adj* addicted to drugs
■ *m,f* drug addict

drogar [A3] *vt* to drug
■ **drogarse** *v pron* (*refl*) to take drugs

drogata *mf* (fam) junkie (colloq)

drogodependiente *adj* (frml) drug-dependent
■ *mf* (frml) drug addict

droguería *f* **(a)** (Esp) (tienda) *store selling cleaning materials and other household goods* **(b)** (Col) (farmacia) drugstore (AmE), chemist's (BrE) **(c)** (RPl) (de productos químicos) *pharmaceutical wholesaler's*

dromedario *m* dromedary

dual *adj/m* dual

Dublín *m* Dublin

dublinés -nesa *m,f* Dubliner

ducado *m* (título) dukedom; (territorio) duchy, dukedom

ducha *f* shower; **darse una** ∼ to take *o* (BrE) have a shower

ducharse [A1] *v pron* (*refl*) to take *o* (BrE) have a shower

ducto *m* **(a)** (Méx) (de gas, petróleo) pipeline **(b)** (Ur) (para la basura) garbage chute (AmE), rubbish chute (BrE) **(c)** (Col, Ven) (de ventilación) duct, shaft

duda *f* ⟨1⟩ (interrogante, sospecha) doubt; **expuso sus** ∼**s sobre** ... he expressed his reservations about ...; **tengo unas** ∼**s para consultar** I have a few points I'd like to check; **me ha surgido una** ∼ there's something I'm not sure about; **¿tienen alguna** ∼**?** are there any queries *o* questions?; **nunca tuve la menor** ∼ **de que tenía razón** I never doubted that he was right; **fuera de (toda)** ∼ beyond (all) doubt; **de eso no cabe la menor** ∼ there's absolutely no doubt about that; **lo pongo en** ∼ I doubt it; **sin** ∼ *or* **sin lugar a** ∼**s** undoubtedly; **sin** ∼ **ya te lo habrás preguntado** no doubt you'll have already asked yourself that question; **para salir de** ∼**s** just to be doubly sure ⟨2⟩ (estado de incertidumbre, indecisión): **ahora me has hecho entrar en (la)** ∼ now you've made me wonder; **a ver si puedes sacarme de la** ∼ do you think you can clear something up for me?; **si estás en (la) ~ no lo compres** if you're not sure don't buy it

dudar [A1] *vt* to doubt; **dudo que lo haya terminado** I doubt if *o* whether he's finished it
■ **~** *vi*: **duda entre comprar y alquilar** she can't make up her mind whether to buy or rent; **~ EN hacer algo** to hesitate to do sth; **~ DE algo/algn** to doubt sth/sb

dudoso -sa *adj* **(a)** (incierto) doubtful; **lo veo ~** I doubt it **(b)** (cuestionable) dubious **(c)** (indeciso) hesitant, undecided

duela *f* (Méx) (del suelo) floorboard

duele, duelen, etc ▶ DOLER

duelo *m* 1 (dolor) sorrow, grief; (luto) mourning; **estar de ~** to be in mourning 2 (desafío) duel; **retar a ~** to challenge ... to a duel; **batirse en ~** to fight a duel; **~ a muerte** duel to the death

duende *m* **(a)** (en cuentos) goblin, imp **(b)** (espíritu) spirit (*which inhabits a house or room*)

dueño -ña *adj* 1 [SER] (libre) **~ DE hacer algo** free to do sth, at liberty to do sth (frml) 2 [SER] (indicando control): **ser ~ DE algo** to be in control OF sth; **hacerse ~ DE algo** to gain control OF sth
■ *m,f* **(a)** (de casa, pensión) (*m*) owner, landlord; (*f*) owner, landlady; (de negocio) (*m*) owner, proprietor; (*f*) owner, proprietress; **~ de casa** (AmL) (propietario) householder; (en fiesta) (*m*) host; (*f*) hostess **(b)** (de perro) owner

duerma, duermas, etc ▶ DORMIR

dulce *adj* **(a)** 〈fruta/vino〉 sweet; **prefiero lo ~** I prefer sweet things **(b)** 〈agua〉 fresh; **pez de agua ~** freshwater fish **(c)** 〈persona〉 gentle, kind; 〈sonrisa/voz〉 sweet; 〈música〉 soft, sweet
■ *m* **(a)** (AmL exc RPl) (golosina) candy (AmE), sweet (BrE) **(b)** (RPl) (mermelada) jam; **~ de leche** caramel spread (*made by boiling down milk and sugar*) **(c)** (AmC) (azúcar) type of sugarloaf **(d) dulces** *mpl* (cosas dulces) sweet things (*pl*)

dulcificar [A2] *vt* 〈persona〉 to mellow; 〈vejez〉 to make ... more pleasant
■ **dulcificarse** *v pron* 〈carácter/persona〉 to mellow, soften

dulzor *m* sweetness, sweet taste

dulzura *f* sweetness; **habló con ~** she spoke kindly *o* gently; **los trata con mucha ~** she's very sweet *o* gentle with them

duna *f* dune

dúo *m* **(a)** (composición) duet, duo **(b)** (de músicos, instrumentos) duo; **a ~** 〈contestar〉 in unison; **lo cantaron a ~** they sang it as a duet

duodécimo -ma *adj/pron* twelfth

dúplex *m* (*pl* **~**) **(a)** (apartamento) duplex apartment, maisonette (BrE) **(b)** (Méx) (casa) semi-detached house

duplicado¹ -da *adj* duplicated; **por ~** in duplicate

duplicado² *m* copy, duplicate

duplicar [A2] *vt* 〈documento/llave〉 to copy, duplicate
■ **duplicarse** *v pron* 〈número〉 to double

duplo *m*: **el ~ de dos es cuatro** two times two is four

duque *m* duke

duquesa *f* duchess

duración *f* **(a)** (de película, acto, curso) length, duration **(b)** (de pila, bombilla) life; **pila de larga ~** long-life battery; ▶ DISCO 1A

duradero -ra *adj* 〈amistad/recuerdo〉 lasting (*before n*); 〈ropa/zapatos〉 hardwearing, longwearing (AmE)

durante *prep* (en el transcurso de) during; (cuando se especifica la duración) for; **~ 1980** during *o* in 1980; **gobernó el país ~ casi dos décadas** she governed the country for almost two decades; **los precios aumentaron un 0,3% ~ el mes de diciembre** prices rose by 0.3% in December; **~ todo el invierno** throughout the winter

durar [A1] *vi* 〈reunión/guerra/relación〉 to last; **¿cuánto dura la película?** how long is the film? **(b)** 〈coche/zapatos〉 to last **(c)** (Col, Ven) ▶ DEMORAR A
■ **durarse** *v pron* (Ven) ▶ DEMORARSE

durazno *m* (esp AmL) (fruto) peach; (árbol) peach tree

durex® *m* (AmL) Scotch tape® (AmE), Sellotape® (BrE)

dureza *f* 1 (en general) hardness; (de la carne) toughness 2 **(a)** (severidad, inflexibilidad) harshness; **nos trataban con ~** they treated us harshly; **fue castigado con ~** he was severely punished **(b)** (en el deporte) roughness

durmiera, durmió, etc ▶ DORMIR

duro¹ -ra *adj* 1 (en general) hard; 〈carne〉 tough; 〈pan〉 stale; **las peras están duras** the pears aren't ripe 2 〈luz/voz〉 harsh; 〈acciones〉 hard, harsh 3 **(a)** (severo, riguroso) harsh; 〈juego〉 rough, hard; **fuiste demasiado ~ con él** you were too hard on him; **una postura más dura** a tougher line **(b)** (difícil, penoso) 〈trabajo/vida〉 hard, tough; **fue un golpe muy ~** it was a very hard blow

duro² *adv* (esp AmL) 〈trabajar/estudiar/llover〉 hard; 〈hablar〉 (Col, Ven) loudly

duro³ *m* (en España) (Hist) five-peseta coin

Ee

E, e *f* (*pl* **es**) (*read as* /e/) the letter E, e

e *conj* [*used instead of* Y *before* I- *or* HI-] and

E. (= **Este**) E, East

EAU *mpl* (= **Emiratos Árabes Unidos**) UAE

ebanista *mf* cabinetmaker

ébano *m* ebony

ebrio, ebria *adj* (frml) inebriated (frml), drunk

ebullición *f* (a) (Coc, Fís): **entrar en** ~ to come to the boil; **punto de** ~ boiling point (b) (agitación) turmoil

eccema *m* eczema

echado -da *adj* (acostado): **está** ~ **en el sofá** he's lying down on the sofa

echador -dora *adj* (Méx fam) boastful
■ *m,f* (Méx fam) boaster (colloq)

echar [A1] *vt*
I 1 (a) (lanzar, tirar) to throw; **lo eché a la basura** I threw it out *o* away; **echó la moneda al aire** he tossed the coin; ~**on el ancla/la red** they cast anchor/their net; **echó la cabeza hacia atrás** she threw her head back; ~ **algo** *a* **perder** to ruin sth; ~ *de* **menos** *algo/a* **algn** to miss sth/sb (b) **echar abajo** ⟨*edificio*⟩ to pull down; ⟨*gobierno*⟩ to bring down; ⟨*proyecto*⟩ to destroy; ⟨*esperanzas*⟩ to dash; ⟨*moral*⟩ to undermine; ⟨*puerta/valla*⟩ to break ... down
2 (expulsar) ⟨*persona*⟩ (de trabajo) to fire (colloq), to sack (BrE colloq); (de bar, casa) to throw ... out; (de colegio) to expel
3 ⟨*carta*⟩ to mail (AmE), to post (BrE)
4 (a) (pasar, correr) ⟨*cortinas*⟩ to pull, draw; **échale (la) llave** lock it; **¿echaste el cerrojo?** did you bolt the door? (b) (mover): **lo echó para atrás/a un lado** she pushed (*o* moved *etc*) it backward(s)/to one side
5 (a) (expeler, despedir) ⟨*color/humo/chispas*⟩ to give off (b) (producir) ⟨*hojas*⟩ to sprout; **ya está echando flores** it's flowering already
II 1 (a) (poner) ⟨*gasolina*⟩ to put in; **¿le echas azúcar al café?** do you take sugar in your coffee? (b) (servir, dar) to give; **échame un poco de vino** can you give me a little wine? (c) ⟨*trago*⟩ to have
2 (a) ⟨*sermón/discurso*⟩ (fam) (+ *me/te/le etc*) to give; **le echó una maldición** she put a curse on him (b) (fam) ⟨*condena/multa*⟩ (+ *me/te/le etc*) to give; ~**le la culpa a algn** to put *o* lay the blame on sb
3 (fam) (calcular) (+ *me/te/le etc*): **¿cuántos años me echas?** how old do you think I am?; **de aquí a tu casa échale una hora** it's *o* it takes about an hour from here to your house
4 (Esp fam) (dar, exhibir) ⟨*programa/película*⟩ to show
■ **echarse** *v pron* 1 (a) (tirarse, arrojarse) to throw oneself; **me eché al suelo** I threw myself to the ground; ~**se de cabeza al agua** to dive into the water; ~**se a perder** «*comida*» to go bad, go off (BrE); «*cosecha/proyecto/plan*» to be ruined (b) (tumbarse, acostarse) to lie down (c) (apartarse, moverse) (+ *compl*): **se echó a un lado** she moved to one side; **échate un poco para allá** move over that way a bit; ~**se atrás** to back out
2 (a) (ponerse) ⟨*crema/bronceador*⟩ to put on (b) ⟨*cigarrillo*⟩ to have (c) (Esp fam) ⟨*novio/novia*⟩: **se ha echado novia** he's found *o* got himself a girlfriend (d) (Méx fam) (beberse) to drink
3 (Méx fam) (romper) to break
4 (Col fam) (tardar) ⟨*horas/días*⟩ to take
5 (empezar) ~**se** A to start *o* begin to, start *o*

begin; **se echó a correr** he started to run *o* started running; **las palomas se** ~**on a volar** the doves flew off

echarpe *m* shawl, stole

ecléctico -ca *adj/m,f* eclectic

eclesiástico -ca *adj* ecclesiastical, church (*before n*)

eclipse *m* eclipse

eco *m* (Fís) echo; **la cueva tiene** ~ there's an echo in the cave; **hacer** ~ to echo

ecografía *f* ultrasound scan

ecología *f* ecology

ecológico -ca *adj* ⟨*problema/estudio*⟩ ecological; ⟨*daño/desastre*⟩ environmental; ⟨*producto*⟩ eco-friendly, environmentally friendly; ⟨*cultivo/agricultura*⟩ organic

ecologismo *m* environmentalism, conservationism

ecologista *adj* ecology (*before n*), environmentalist (*before n*)
■ *mf* ecologist, environmentalist

economato *m* (a) (de empresa) company store (b) (Mil) PX (AmE), NAAFI shop (BrE)

economía *f* (a) (ciencia) economics (b) (de país) economy; ~ **de (libre) mercado** (free) market economy (c) (ahorro): **hacer** ~**s** to economize (d) (de persona, familia) finances (*pl*)

económico -ca *adj* 1 ⟨*crisis/situación*⟩ economic (*before n*); ⟨*problema/independencia*⟩ financial 2 (a) ⟨*piso/comida*⟩ cheap; ⟨*restaurante/hotel*⟩ cheap, inexpensive (b) (que gasta poco) ⟨*motor*⟩ economical; ⟨*persona*⟩ thrifty

economista *mf* economist

economizar [A4] *vt* ⟨*tiempo*⟩ to save; ⟨*combustible/recursos*⟩ to economize on, save
■ ~ *vi* to economize, save money

ecosistema *m* ecosystem

ecu, ECU /'eku/ *m* (= Unidad Monetaria Europea) ECU

ecuación *f* equation

ecuador *m* 1 (línea) equator 2 **Ecuador** (país) Ecuador

ecuatorial *adj* equatorial

ecuatoriano -na *adj/m,f* Ecuadorean

eczema *m* eczema

edad *f* 1 (de persona, árbol) age; **tienen la misma** ~ they are the same age; **un joven de unos quince años de** ~ a boy of about fifteen; **¿qué** ~ **tiene?** how old is he?; **aún no tiene la** ~ **suficiente** he's still not old enough ...; **de** ~ **madura** *o* **de mediana** ~ middle-aged; **una persona de** ~ an elderly person; **niños en** ~ **escolar** children of school age; **estar en la** ~ **del pavo** to be at that awkward age 2 (Hist) (época) age, period; **la E**~ **de bronce/de hierro/de piedra** the Bronze/Iron/Stone Age; **la E**~ **media** the Middle Ages (*pl*)

edema *m* edema*

Edén *m*: **el** ~ (the Garden of) Eden

edición *f* 1 (Impr, Period) (tirada) edition; (acción)

publication; ∼ **de bolsillo** pocket edition; **Ediciones Rivera** Rivera Publications **2** (Rad, TV) program*, edition

edificado -da adj built-up

edificar [A2] vt/vi to build

edificio m building

Edimburgo m Edinburgh

editar [A1] vt **1** (publicar) ⟨libro/revista⟩ to publish **2** (modificar) ⟨película/grabación/texto⟩ to edit; (Inf) to edit

editor -tora adj publishing (before n)
■ m,f (que publica) publisher; (que revisa, modifica) editor

editorial adj ⟨casa/actividad⟩ publishing (before n); ⟨puesto/decisión⟩ editorial
■ f (empresa) publishing company o house
■ m (en periódico) editorial, leading article

edredón m eiderdown, comforter (AmE); (que se usa sin mantas) duvet, continental quilt (BrE)

educación f **1** (enseñanza) education; (para la convivencia) upbringing; ∼ **a distancia** correspondence courses (pl), distance learning; ∼ **física** physical education; ∼ **general básica** (en Esp) primary education; ∼ **para adultos** adult education; ∼ **primaria/secundaria/superior** primary/secondary/higher education; ∼ **universitaria** university education, college education (AmE); ∼ **vocacional** (AmS) careers guidance **2** (modales) manners (pl); **es una falta de** ∼ it's rude, it's bad manners

educado -da adj polite, well-mannered

educador -dora m,f (frml) teacher, educator (frml)

educar [A2] vt **1** (a) (Educ) to educate, teach (b) (para la convivencia) ⟨hijos⟩ to bring up; ⟨ciudadanos⟩ to educate **2** ⟨oído/voz⟩ to train
■ **educarse** v pron (hacer los estudios) to be educated

educativo -va adj ⟨programa/juego⟩ educational; ⟨establecimiento⟩ educational, teaching (before n); ⟨sistema⟩ education (before n)

edulcorante m sweetener

EEUU or **EE.UU.** (= **Estados Unidos**) USA

efe f: name of the letter f

efectista adj theatrical, dramatic

efectividad f (eficacia) effectiveness

efectivo¹ -va adj ⟨remedio/medio/castigo⟩ effective; **hacer** ∼ ⟨cheque⟩ to cash; ⟨pago⟩ to make

efectivo² m (Fin) cash; **pagar en** ∼ to pay cash

efecto m **1** (a) (resultado, consecuencia) effect; **hacer** ∼ to take effect; **un calmante de** ∼ **inmediato** a fast-acting painkiller; **mecanismo de** ∼ **retardado** delayed-action mechanism; **bajo los** ∼**s del alcohol** under the influence of alcohol; ∼ **dos mil** (Inf) millennium bug; ∼ **invernadero** greenhouse effect; ∼ **óptico** optical illusion; ∼ **secundario** side effect; ∼**s especiales** special effects; ∼**s sonoros** sound effects **(b) en efecto** in fact; (así es) indeed
2 (impresión): **su conducta causó mal** ∼ his behavior made a bad impression o (colloq) didn't go down well; **no sé qué** ∼ **le causaron mis palabras** I don't know what effect my words had on him

3 (Dep) (desvío) swerve; (movimiento rotatorio) spin; **le dio a la bola con** ∼ she put some spin on the ball

4 ∼**s personales** personal effects (pl)

efectuar [A18] vt (frml) ⟨maniobra/redada⟩ to carry out, execute (frml); ⟨pago⟩ to make; ⟨viaje/cambio⟩ to make; ⟨disparo⟩ to fire; **el tren** ∼**á su salida a las 10.50** the train will depart at 10:50

efervescente adj ⟨pastilla⟩ effervescent; ⟨bebida⟩ sparkling, fizzy (colloq)

eficacia f (a) (de acción, remedio) effectiveness, efficacy (frml) (b) (eficiencia) efficiency

eficaz adj (a) ⟨fórmula/remedio⟩ effective, efficacious (frml) (b) ⟨eficiente⟩ efficient

eficiencia f efficiency

eficiente adj efficient

efigie f (cuadro) image, picture; (estatua) statue, effigy

efímero -ra adj ephemeral

efusivo -va adj ⟨temperamento/recibimiento⟩ effusive; ⟨persona⟩ demonstrative; ⟨recibimiento⟩ warm

EGB f (en Esp) = **Educación General Básica**

egipcio -cia adj/m,f Egyptian

Egipto m Egypt

ego m ego

egocéntrico -ca adj egocentric, self-centered*

egoísmo m selfishness, egotism

egoísta adj selfish, egotistic
■ mf (Psic) egotist; **es una** ∼ she is very selfish

egresado -da adj (AmL): **los alumnos** ∼**s** (de universidad) the graduates; (de colegio) the high school graduates (AmE), the school leavers (BrE)
■ m,f (AmL) (de universidad) graduate; (de colegio) high school graduate (AmE), school leaver (BrE)

egresar [A1] vi (AmL) (de universidad) to graduate; (de colegio) to graduate from high school (AmE), to leave school (o college etc) (BrE)
■ ∼ vt (Andes) (Fin) to withdraw, take out

egreso m (AmL) (de universidad) graduation; (de colegio) graduation (AmE)

eh interj (a) (para llamar la atención) hey! (b) (expresando amenaza, advertencia) eh?, huh?, OK? (c) (contestando una pregunta) eh?, what?

Ej., ej. (read as **por ejemplo**) eg

eje m **1** (a) (Astron, Fís, Mat) axis (b) (Auto, Mec) (barra) axle **2** (de asunto, política) core, central theme

ejecución f **1** (de persona) execution **2** (a) (de plan) implementation; (de orden) carrying out (b) (Mús) performance

ejecutar [A1] vt **1** ⟨condenado/reo⟩ to execute **2** ⟨plan⟩ to implement, carry out; ⟨orden/trabajo⟩ to carry out; ⟨sentencia⟩ to execute, enforce; ⟨ejercicio/salto⟩ to perform; ⟨sinfonía/himno nacional⟩ to play, perform

ejecutivo¹ -va adj ⟨función/comisión⟩ executive
■ m,f (Bot, Com) executive

ejecutivo² m (Gob) executive

ejemplar adj ⟨conducta/vida/castigo⟩ exemplary; ⟨trabajador/padre⟩ model (before n)
■ m (a) (de libro, documento) copy (b) (Bot, Zool) specimen

ejemplarizador -dora adj (Chi, Per) exemplary

ejemplo m example; **dar (el) ~** to set an example; **pongamos por ~ el caso de Elena** let's take Elena's case as an example; **por ejemplo** for example

ejercer [E2] vt [1] (a) ‹profesión› to practice*; **~ la abogacía** to practice law (b) ‹derecho› to exercise [2] ‹influencia/poder/presión› to exert ■ **~** vi «abogado/médico» to practice*; **es maestra pero no ejerce** she's a teacher but she doesn't practice her profession

ejercicio m [1] (actividad física) exercise; **hacer ~** to exercise [2] (Educ) (a) (trabajo de práctica) exercise (b) (prueba, examen) test, exam [3] (de profesión) practice [4] (Mil) exercise, maneuver*

ejercitar [A1] vt [1] ‹músculo/dedos/memoria› to exercise [2] ‹caballos› to train; ‹tropa› to drill, train; ‹alumnos› to train

ejército m army; **~ del aire** air force; **~ de tierra** army

ejidal adj (en Méx) cooperative (before n)

ejidatario -ria m,f (en Méx) member of a cooperative

ejido m (en Méx) (sistema) system of communal or cooperative farming; (sociedad) cooperative; (terreno) land belonging to a cooperative

ejote m (Méx) green bean

el (pl **los**), **la** (pl **las**) art [the masculine article EL is also used before feminine nouns which begin with accented A or HA, e.g. EL AGUA PURA, EL HADA MADRINA] [1] (a) (en general) the; **la Tierra** the Earth (b) (con sustantivos en sentido genérico): **odio el pescado** I hate fish; **así es la vida** that's life; **(nosotros) los mexicanos** we Mexicans; **¿ya vas a la escuela?** do you go to school yet? (c) (refiriéndose a algo que se conoce o se está definiendo): **en la calle Solís** in Solís street; **las tuyas** yours; **el último** the last one; **el estúpido del marido** that stupid husband of hers [2] (a) **el + DE: la del sombrero** the one with the hat; **el de las nueve** the nine o'clock one; **el de mi hijo** my son's (b) **el + QUE: las que yo vi** the ones I saw; **los que estén cansados**; those who are tired, anyone who's tired; **la que te guste** whichever you like [3] (en expresiones de tiempo): **ocurrió el domingo** it happened last Sunday; **mi cumpleaños es el 28 de mayo** my birthday's on May 28; **el mes pasado** last month; **toda la mañana** all morning; **a las ocho** at eight o'clock [4] (cada): **$80 el metro/kilo** $80 a meter/a kilo, $80 per kilo/meter [5] (con fracciones, porcentajes, números): **la mitad/la cuarta parte del dinero** half the money/a quarter of the money; **el 20% de ...** 20% of ... [6] (con partes del cuerpo, prendas de vestir, artículos personales, etc): **tenía las manos en los bolsillos** she had her hands in her pockets; **¡te cortaste el pelo!** you've had your hair cut!; **tiene los ojos azules** he has blue eyes [7] (a) (con apellidos acompañados de título, adjetivos, etc): **el señor Ortiz/la doctora Vidal** Mr Ortiz/ Doctor Vidal; **los Ortega** the Ortegas (b) (con algunos nombres geográficos): **en la India** in India; ▶ ÁFRICA, ARGENTINA, ETC

él pron pers (a) (como sujeto) he; **¿quién se lo va a decir? — él** who's going to tell her? — he is; **lo**

hizo ~ mismo he did it himself; **fue ~** it was him (b) (en comparaciones, con preposiciones) him; (refiriéndose a cosas) it; **llegué antes que ~** I arrived before him o before he did; **con/para ~** with/for him; **son de ~** they're his

elaboración f (de producto, vino) production, making; (de pan) baking, making

elaborado -da adj elaborate

elaborar [A1] vt [1] ‹producto/vino› to produce, make; ‹pan› to bake, make [2] ‹plan/teoría› to devise, draw up; ‹informe/estudio› to prepare, write

elasticidad f (de material) elasticity; (de horario) flexibility

elástico¹ -ca adj ‹membrana/cinta› elastic; ‹medias/venda› elastic, stretch (before n); ‹horario› flexible

elástico² m (a) (material) elastic; (cordón) piece of elastic; (en géneros de punto) rib, ribbing (b) (Chi) (goma) rubber band

ele f. name of the letter l

elección f (a) (acción de escoger) choice; **llévate tres, a tu ~** take o choose any three (b) (Pol) (de candidato) election (c) **elecciones** fpl (Pol) election; **convocar elecciones** to call an election

elector -tora m,f (Pol) voter, elector

electorado m electorate

electoral adj ‹campaña/discurso› election (before n)

electricidad f electricity

electricista mf electrician

eléctrico -ca adj ‹tren/motor/luz› electric; ‹instalación/aparato› electrical; ‹carga› electrical, electric

electrocardiograma m electrocardiogram

electrocutar [A1] vt to electrocute ■ **electrocutarse** v pron to be electrocuted

electrodoméstico m electrical appliance

electrón m electron

electrónica f electronics

electrónico -ca adj electronic

elefante -ta m,f elephant

elegancia f (a) (en el vestir) smartness, elegance; (garbo, gracialidad) elegance; (de barrio, restaurante) smartness (b) (de estilo) elegance

elegante adj [1] (a) ‹moda/vestido› elegant, smart; **iba muy ~** he was very well o very smartly dressed (b) ‹barrio/restaurante/fiesta› smart [2] ‹estilo/frase› elegant, polished

elegir [I8] vt (a) (escoger) to choose; **me dieron a ~** I was given a o the choice (b) (por votación) to elect

elemental adj (a) (esencial) ‹norma/principio› fundamental (b) (básico) ‹curso/nivel/texto› elementary; ‹conocimientos/nociones› rudimentary, basic

elemento m (a) (en general) element; **se siente en su ~** he's in his element; **los ~s** (fuerzas naturales) the elements (b) (persona): **un ~ pernicioso** a bad influence; **~s subversivos** subversive elements; **es un ~ de cuidado** (Esp fam & pey) he's a nasty piece of work (c) (RPI) (tipo de gente) crowd

elepé m album, LP

elevado -da adj [1] ‹terreno/montaña› high; ‹edificio› tall, high [2] (a) ‹cantidad› large;

⟨*precio/impuestos*⟩ high; ⟨*pérdidas*⟩ heavy, substantial **(b)** ⟨*categoría/calidad/posición*⟩ high **(c)** ⟨*ideas/pensamientos*⟩ noble, elevated; ⟨*estilo*⟩ lofty, elevated

elevador *m* (montacargas) hoist; (ascensor) (Méx) elevator (AmE), lift (BrE)

elevar [A1] *vt* ⟨1⟩ (frml) **(a)** (levantar) ⟨*objeto*⟩ to raise, lift **(b)** ⟨*espíritu/mente*⟩ to uplift **(c)** ⟨*muro/nivel*⟩ to raise, make ... higher ⟨2⟩ (frml) **(a)** (aumentar) ⟨*precios/impuestos*⟩ to raise, increase; ⟨*nivel de vida*⟩ to raise **(b)** ⟨*voz/tono*⟩ to raise

■ **elevarse** *v pron* ⟨1⟩ (tomar altura) «*avión/cometa*» to climb, gain height; «*globo*» to rise, gain height ⟨2⟩ (frml) (aumentar) «*temperatura*» to rise; «*precios/impuestos*» to rise, increase; «*tono/voz*» to rise ⟨3⟩ (frml) (ascender): **la cifra se elevaba ya al 13%** the figure had already reached 13%

elige, elija, etc ▶ ELEGIR

eliminación *f* elimination; (de residuos) disposal

eliminar [A1] *vt* **(a)** ⟨*obstáculo*⟩ to remove; ⟨*párrafo*⟩ to delete, remove **(b)** ⟨*candidato*⟩ to eliminate; (Dep) to eliminate, knock out **(c)** (euf) (matar) to eliminate (euph), to get rid of (euph) **(d)** ⟨*residuos*⟩ to dispose of **(e)** ⟨*toxinas/grasas*⟩ to eliminate

eliminatoria *f* (en torneo) qualifying round; (para carrera) heat; (certamen) qualifying competition

eliminatorio -ria *adj* ⟨*examen/fase*⟩ qualifying (*before n*), preliminary (*before n*)

elite /e'lit/, **élite** /'elite e'lit/ *f* elite, élite

elitista *adj* ⟨*sociedad/actitud*⟩ elitist; ⟨*colegio/club*⟩ exclusive

elixir *m* **(a)** (Mit) elixir **(b)** (Esp) (Farm) mouthwash

ella *pron pers* **(a)** (como sujeto) she; **¿quién lo va a hacer? — ella** who's going to do it? — she is; **lo hizo ~ misma** she did it herself; **fue ~** it was her **(b)** (en comparaciones, con preposiciones) her; (referido a cosas) it; **salí después que ~** I left after her *o* after she did; **con/para ~** with/for her; **son de ~** they're hers

ello *pron pers* it; **ya que estamos en ~** while we're at it; **todo ~ exquisitamente presentado** all beautifully presented; **para ello hay que obtener un permiso** (frml) you need a permit for this

ellos, ellas *pron pers pl* **(a)** (como sujeto) they; **lo hicieron ~ mismos** they did it themselves; **fueron ellas** it was them **(b)** (en comparaciones, con preposiciones) them; **llegué antes que ~** I arrived before them *o* before they did; **con/para ~/ellas** with/for them; **son de ~** they're theirs, they belong to them

elocuencia *f* eloquence; **con ~** eloquently

elocuente *adj* eloquent

elogiar [A1] *vt* to praise

elogio *m* praise; **digno de ~** praiseworthy

elote *m* (mazorca) (AmC, Méx) corncob, ear of corn (AmE); (granos) (Méx) corn (AmE), sweetcorn (BrE)

El Salvador *m* El Salvador

eludir [I1] *vt* **(a)** ⟨*problema/compromiso/pago*⟩ to evade, avoid **(b)** ⟨*persona*⟩ to avoid

emancipación *f* emancipation

emancipado -da *adj* emancipated

embadurnar [A1] *vt* **~ algo DE algo** to smear sth with sth

■ **embadurnarse** *v pron* (refl) **~se DE algo** to plaster *o* smear oneself with sth

embajada *f* (sede, delegación) embassy; (cargo) ambassadorship

embajador -dora *m,f* (Adm, Pol) ambassador

embalaje *m* ⟨1⟩ (acción) packing; (envoltura) packaging, wrapping ⟨2⟩ (Col) (Dep) sprint

embalar [A1] *vt* to pack

embaldosar [A1] *vt* to tile

embalsamar [A1] *vt* to embalm

embalse *m* (depósito) reservoir

embarazada *adj* pregnant; **(se) quedó ~** she got *o* became pregnant; **está ~ de dos meses** she's two months pregnant; **la dejó ~** he got her pregnant

■ *f* pregnant woman

embarazo *m* (Med) pregnancy

embarazoso -sa *adj* embarrassing, awkward

embarcación *f* (frml) vessel (frml), craft (frml)

embarcadero *m* (atracadero) jetty; (para mercancías) wharf

embarcar [A2] *vi* (Aviac) to board; (Náut) to embark, board

■ **~** *vt* ⟨1⟩ ⟨*mercancías/equipaje*⟩ to load ⟨2⟩ (Ven) to let ... down

■ **embarcarse** *v pron* **(a)** ⟨*pasajero*⟩ (en barco) to board, embark; (en tren, avión) to board, get on; **se ~on para América** they set sail for America **(b)** (en asunto, negocio) **~se EN algo** to embark on sth

embargar [A3] *vt* ⟨*bienes*⟩ to seize, to sequestrate (frml); ⟨*vehículo*⟩ to impound

embargo *m* ⟨1⟩ **(a)** (Der) (incautación, decomiso) seizure, sequestration (frml) **(b)** (Mil, Pol) embargo ⟨2⟩ **sin embargo: sin ~, tiene algunas desventajas** however *o* nevertheless, it has some disadvantages; **sin ~, ayer no decías eso** you weren't saying that yesterday, though; **tiene de todo y sin embargo se queja** he has everything and yet he still complains

embarrada *f* (AmS fam) (metida de pata) blunder, boo-boo (colloq)

embarrar [A1] *vt* to cover ... in mud; **~la** (AmS fam) to mess up (AmE colloq), to mess things up (BrE colloq)

■ **embarrarse** *v pron* «*persona*» to get covered in mud; ⟨*prenda/ropa*⟩ to get...muddy

embaucador -dora *adj* deceitful

■ *m,f* trickster

embaucar [A2] *vt* to trick, con (colloq)

embeber [E1] *vt* **(a)** (en líquido) ⟨*bizcocho/esponja*⟩ to soak **(b)** «*secante/toalla*» ⟨*líquido*⟩ to soak up **(c)** ⟨*tela*⟩ to gather in

■ **~** *vi* to shrink

■ **embeberse** *v pron* **(a)** (enfrascarse) **~se EN algo** to become wrapped up *o* absorbed in sth **(b)** (imbuirse) **~se DE algo** to become imbued with sth (frml)

embelesado -da *adj* spellbound

embelesar [A1] *vt* to captivate

embellecer [E3] *vt* ⟨*persona*⟩ to make ... beautiful; ⟨*campiña/ciudad*⟩ to beautify, improve the appearance of

embestida f charge

embestir [I14] vi to charge; ∼ **CONTRA** algo/algn to charge AT sth/sb
■ ∼ vt «*toro*» to charge (at)

embetunar [A1] vt ☐1 ⟨*zapatos*⟩ to polish, put polish on ☐2 (CS) (*ensuciar*) to get ... dirty

emblema m emblem

embobado -da adj spellbound; **la miraban** ∼**s** they were watching her open-mouthed; **está** ∼ **con ella** he's besotted with her

embolador -dora m,f (Col) bootblack

embolar [A1] vt ☐1 (RPl arg) (*fastidiar*) to bug (colloq), to piss ... off (sl) ☐2 (Col) ⟨*zapatos*⟩ to shine, polish
■ **embolarse** v pron (AmC fam) to get plastered (colloq)

embolia f embolism

embolsarse [A1] v pron ⟨*dinero ajeno*⟩ to pocket; ⟨*premio*⟩ to collect, receive; ⟨*ganancia*⟩ to make

embonar [A1] vi (Méx) ⟨*tubos/ventana/piezas*⟩ to fit; ∼ **CON algo** to fit in WITH sth

emborrachar [A1] vt «*bebida*» to make ... drunk; «*persona*» to get ... drunk
■ **emborracharse** v pron to get drunk

emborronar [A1] vt (*manchar*) to smudge; (con tinta) to make blots on, to blot
■ **emborronarse** v pron to smudge, get smudged

emboscada f ambush

emboscar [A2] vt to ambush

embotado -da adj ⟨*punta/filo*⟩ dull, blunt; **estoy totalmente** ∼ my brain's seized up, I can't take in any more

embotar [A1] vt ⟨*mente/sentidos*⟩ to dull

embotellado -da adj (a) ⟨*agua/vino*⟩ bottled (b) ⟨*calle/tráfico*⟩ jammed solid

embotellamiento m (del tráfico) traffic jam

embotellar [A1] vt to bottle

embragar [A3] vi to engage the clutch

embrague m clutch

embriagado -da adj (frml) (borracho) inebriated (frml)

embriagador -dora adj ⟨*vino*⟩ heady; ⟨*sensación*⟩ (liter) intoxicating (liter)

embriagarse [A3] v pron (frml) (con alcohol) to become intoxicated (frml)

embriaguez f (borrachera) drunkness

embrión m (Biol) embryo

embrollar [A1] vt (a) ⟨*hilo/madeja*⟩ to tangle (up) (b) (confundir) ⟨*situación*⟩ to complicate; ⟨*persona*⟩ to muddle, confuse (c) (implicar) ∼ **a** algn **EN algo** to embroil sb IN sth, get sb involved IN sth
■ **embrollarse** v pron «*hilo/madeja*» to get tangled; «*situación*» to get confused o muddled; «*persona*» to get muddled, to get mixed up (colloq)

embrollo m (de hilos, cables) tangle; (de callejuelas,

pasillos) maze; (situación confusa) muddle, mess; **el argumento es un** ∼ the plot is extremely involved o complicated

embromado -da adj ☐1 [ESTAR] (AmS fam) (enfermo, delicado) in a bad way; **tiene un pie** ∼ she has a bad foot ☐2 (AmS fam) ⟨*situación*⟩ tricky; ⟨*problema*⟩ thorny

embromar [A1] vt (AmS fam) (a) (*molestar*) to pester (b) (estropear) ⟨*aparato*⟩ to ruin (colloq); ⟨*plan*⟩ to ruin, spoil (c) (perjudicar): **la guerra nos embromó a todos** we all suffered because of the war; **¡me embromaste!** now you've really landed me in it! (colloq)
■ **embromarse** v pron (AmS fam) (a) (*jorobarse*): **que se embrome por estúpido** it serves him right for being so stupid; **si no te gusta, te embromas** if you don't like it, tough! (b) (hacerse daño) to hurt oneself; ⟨*rodilla/hígado*⟩ to screw up (AmE colloq), to do ... in (BrE colloq) (c) (enfermarse) to get ill (colloq) (d) «*aparato/frenos*» to go wrong

embrujado -da adj [ESTAR] ⟨*persona*⟩ bewitched; ⟨*casa/lugar*⟩ haunted

embrujar [A1] vt (a) (hechizar) to bewitch, put ... under a spell (b) (fascinar, enamorar) to bewitch

embrujo m (a) (hechizo) spell; (maleficio) curse (b) (encanto, atractivo) magic, enchantment

embrutecer [E3] vt «*trabajo*» to stultify; «*televisión*» to make ... mindless

embudo m funnel

embuste m tall story, story (colloq)

embustero -ra adj: **¡qué niño más** ∼**!** what a little fibber (colloq)
■ m,f fibber (colloq), liar

embutido m (salchicha) sausage; (fiambre) cold meat

eme f: name of the letter m

emergencia f emergency

emerger [E6] vi (a) «*submarino*» to surface (b) «*persona*» to emerge (c) (sobresalir) to emerge

emigración f (de personas) emigration; (de animales) migration

emigrante adj/mf emigrant

emigrar [A1] vi «*persona*» to emigrate; «*animal*» to migrate

eminencia f (a) (personalidad) expert (b) (frml) (Relig) Eminence (frml)

eminente adj eminent

Emiratos Árabes Unidos mpl United Arab Emirates

emisario -ria m,f emissary

emisión f (a) (Tec) emission (b) (Fin) issue (c) (Rad, TV) (acción) broadcasting; (programa) (frml) program*, broadcast

emisor m (aparato) transmitter

emisora f (Rad) radio station

emitir [I1] vt ⟨*sonido/luz/señal*⟩ to emit, give out; ⟨*acciones/sellos/comunicado*⟩ to issue; ⟨*programa*⟩ to broadcast; ⟨*película*⟩ to show; ⟨*veredicto*⟩ to deliver, announce; ⟨*voto*⟩ to cast

AmC	Central America	Arg	Argentina	Cu	Cuba	Per	Peru
AmL	Latin America	Bol	Bolivia	Ec	Ecuador	RPl	River Plate Area
AmS	South America	Chi	Chile	Esp	Spain	Ur	Uruguay
Andes	Andean Region	CS	Southern Cone	Méx	Mexico	Ven	Venezuela

emoción *f* (sentimiento) emotion; (expectación, excitación) excitement; **¡qué ~!** how exciting!

emocionado -da *adj* (conmovido) moved; (entusiasmado) excited

emocional *adj* emotional

emocionante *adj* (conmovedor) moving; (excitante, apasionante) exciting

emocionar [A1] *vt* to move, affect
■ **emocionarse** *v pron* (conmoverse) to be moved; (entusiasmarse) to get excited

emotivo -va *adj* ⟨desarrollo/mundo/persona⟩ emotional; ⟨acto/discurso⟩ moving, emotional

empacar [A2] *vt* **(a)** (empaquetar) to pack **(b)** ⟨algodón/heno⟩ to bale **(c)** (AmL) ⟨maleta⟩ to pack
■ ~ *vi* to pack

empachar [A1] *vt* (fam) (indigestar) to give ... an upset stomach
■ **empacharse** *v pron* (fam) (indigestarse) **~se DE algo** to get an upset stomach FROM sth

empacho *m* (fam) (indigestión): **agarrarse un ~** to get *o* have an upset stomach

empadronarse [A1] *v pron* to register

empalagar [A3] *vt*: **los bombones me empalagan** chocolates are too sweet *o* sickly for my taste
■ ~ *vi* «licor/dulce» to be too sweet *o* sickly; «estilo/sentimentalismo» to be cloying

empalagoso -sa *adj* ⟨tarta/licor⟩ sickly; ⟨persona/sonrisa⟩ sickly sweet, cloying

empalizada *f* palisade

empalmar [A1] *vt* ⟨cuerdas/películas/cintas⟩ to splice; ⟨cables⟩ to connect
■ ~ *vi* «líneas/carreteras» to converge, meet

empalme *m* (de cables) connection; (de cuerdas) splice; (de carreteras, líneas) junction

empanada *f* **(a)** (AmL) (individual) pasty, pie **(b)** (Esp) (grande) pie

empanadilla *f* (Esp) tuna/meat pasty

empanar [A1], (Méx) **empanizar** [A4] *vt* to coat ... in breadcrumbs

empantanado -da *adj* ⟨camino/campo⟩ swampy

empantanarse [A1] *v pron* «camino/campo» to become swamped; «coche» to get bogged down

empañar [A1] *vt* ⟨vidrio/espejo⟩ to steam *o* mist up
■ **empañarse** *v pron* «vidrio/espejo» to steam *o* mist up

empapar [A1] *vt* **(a)** (embeber) ⟨esponja/toalla/galleta⟩ to soak **(b)** (mojar mucho) ⟨persona⟩ to soak, drench
■ **empaparse** *v pron* (mojarse mucho) «persona/zapatos/ropa» to get soaking wet

empapelar [A1] *vt* ⟨habitación/pared⟩ to wallpaper, paper

empaque *m* **1** (Col, Méx, Ven) (Tec) seal; (de llave de agua) washer **2** (Col) (acción de empaquetar) packing; (de regalo) wrapping

empaquetar [A1] *vt* (embalar) to pack

emparedado *m* sandwich

emparejar [A1] *vt* **1** ⟨personas⟩ to pair ... off; ⟨calcetines/zapatos⟩ to pair up **2** (nivelar) ⟨pelo⟩ to make ... even; ⟨dobladillo⟩ to even up; ⟨pared/suelo⟩ to level, make ... level; ⟨montones/pilas⟩ to make ... the same height

■ **emparejarse** *v pron* **(a)** (formar parejas) to pair off **(b)** (nivelarse) to level off, even up

emparentado -da *adj* [ESTAR] related; **~ con algn** related TO sb

empastar [A1] *vt* ⟨diente/muela⟩ to fill

empaste *m* (Odont) filling; (Chi) (pasta) filler

empatar [A1] *vi* **1** **(a)** (durante un partido) to draw level, equalize; (como resultado) to tie, draw (BrE); **~on a dos** they tied two-two (AmE), it was a two-all draw (BrE); **van empatados** they're equal *o* level at the moment **(b)** (en una votación) to tie **2** (Col, Ven) «listones/piezas» to fit together
■ ~ *vt* **(a)** (Ven) (amarrar) to tie *o* join ... together **(b)** (Col, Per, Ven) ⟨cables/tubos⟩ to connect
■ **empatarse** *v pron* (Ven) **(a)** (unirse) «calles/líneas» to join, meet (up); «huesos» to knit together **(b)** (fam) «pareja» to get together (colloq), to start going out together

empate *m* **1** **(a)** (en partido, certamen) tie (AmE), draw (BrE); **terminó con ~ a cero** it finished in a scoreless tie (AmE) *o* (BrE) goalless draw; **el gol del ~** the equalizer *o* (AmE) the tying goal **(b)** (en una votación) tie **2** (Col, Per, Ven) (unión — en carpintería) joint; (— de tubos, cables) connection **3** (Ven fam) (novio) boyfriend; (novia) girlfriend

empecinado -da *adj* (esp AmL) (terco) stubborn; (determinado) determined

empecinarse [A1] *v pron* (obstinarse) to get an idea into one's head; (empeñarse) to persist

empedernido -da *adj* ⟨bebedor/fumador⟩ hardened, inveterate; ⟨jugador⟩ compulsive; ⟨solterón⟩ confirmed

empedrado *m* (de adoquines) paving; (de piedras irregulares) cobbled paving

empedrar [A5] *vt* to pave

empeine *m* instep

empellón *m* shove; **se abrió paso a empellones** she shoved her way through

empeñado -da *adj* **1** **(a)** (resuelto) determined; **está ~ en hacerlo** he's determined to do it **(b)** (obstinado): **está ~ en que nos quedemos** he's insistent that we should stay **2** (endeudado) in debt

empeñar [A1] *vt* **(a)** ⟨joyas/pertenencias⟩ to pawn, hock (colloq) **(b)** ⟨palabra⟩ to pledge
■ **empeñarse** *v pron* **1** (endeudarse) to get *o* go into debt **2** **~se EN hacer algo** (esforzarse) to strive to do sth, to make an effort to do sth; (proponerse) to be determined to do sth; (obstinarse) to insist ON doing sth

empeño *m* **(a)** (afán) determination; (esfuerzo) effort; **estudiar con ~** to study hard; **pondré todo mi ~** I will do my best **(b)** (obstinación) **~ EN algo** insistence ON sth **(c)** (intento, empresa) undertaking, endeavor*

empeñoso -sa *adj* (AmL) hard-working

empeoramiento *m* (de la salud) deterioration, worsening; (del tiempo, de una situación) worsening

empeorar [A1] *vi* ⟨salud⟩ to deteriorate, get worse; «tiempo/situación» to get worse, worsen
■ ~ *vt* to make ... worse

emperador *m* (soberano) emperor

emperatriz *f* empress

empezar [A6] *vi* 1 «*película/conferencia/ invierno*» to begin, start; **empezó a nevar** it started to snow *o* snowing

2 «*persona*» to start; **volver a ~** to start again; **todo es cuestión de ~** it'll be fine once we/you get started; **no sé por dónde ~** I don't know where to begin; **vamos a ~ por ti** let's start with you; **~ A hacer algo** to start doing sth, start to do sth; **empezó diciendo que ...** she started *o* began by saying that ...; **empezó trabajando de mecánico** he started out as a mechanic; **empecemos por estudiar el contexto histórico** let's begin *o* start by looking at the historical context

3 **para empezar** first of all, to start with
■ ~ *vt* (a) «*tarea/actividad*» to start (b) «*frasco/ mermelada*» to start, open

empiece, empieza *etc* ▶ EMPEZAR

empinado -da *adj* «*calle/pendiente*» steep

empinar [A1] *vt* «*bota/botella/vaso*» to raise
■ **empinarse** *v pron* (de puntillas) to stand on tiptoe

emplasto *m* (a) (Farm, Med) dressing (b) (fam) (cosa blanda, pegajosa) sticky mess (colloq)

empleada *f* maid; **~ de planta** (Méx) live-in maid; **~ doméstica** *or* **de servicio** (frml) maid, domestic servant (frml); *ver tb* EMPLEADO

empleado -da *m,f* (a) (trabajador) employee; **una nómina de 300 ~s** a staff of 300; **~ público** civil servant (b) (en oficina) office *o* clerical worker; (en banco) bank clerk, teller; (en tienda) (AmL) clerk (AmE), shop assistant (BrE)

empleador -dora *m,f* employer

emplear [A1] *vt* 1 (a) «*empresa/ organización*» to employ (b) (colocar) «*hijo/ sobrino*» to fix ... up with a job 2 (usar) «*energía/ imaginación/material*» to use
■ **emplearse** *v pron* (esp AmL) to get a job

empleo *m* 1 (a) (trabajo) employment; **la creación de ~** job creation (b) (puesto) job; **está sin ~** she's out of work 2 (uso) use; **⊝ modo de empleo** instructions for use

emplomadura *f* (RPl) filling

emplomar [A1] *vt* (RPl) to fill

empobrecer [E3] *vt* «*población/tierra/ lenguaje*» to impoverish
■ **empobrecerse** *v pron* «*país/lenguaje/ vocabulario*» to become impoverished

empobrecimiento *m* impoverishment

empollar [A1] *vt* 1 «*gallina*» to brood 2 (Esp fam) «*estudiante*» to cram (colloq), to swot (BrE colloq)
■ ~ *vt* 1 «*huevos*» to hatch, sit on 2 (Esp fam) «*lección*» to cram (colloq), to swot up (on) (BrE colloq)

empollón -llona *m,f* (Esp fam & pey) grind (AmE colloq), swot (BrE colloq & pej)

empolvarse [A1] *v pron* (refl) «*nariz/cara*» to powder

empotrado -da *adj* built-in, fitted (*before n*)

empotrarse [A1] *v pron*: **el coche se empotró en el muro** the car crashed into the wall

emprendedor -dora *adj* enterprising

emprender [E1] *vt* «*viaje*» to embark on; «*proyecto/aventura*» to undertake; «*ataque/ ofensiva*» to launch; **~ la marcha** to set out; **~ el regreso** to begin one's return journey

empresa *f* 1 (compañía) company, firm (BrE); **~ pública** public sector company 2 (tarea, labor) venture, undertaking

empresario -ria *m,f* (a) (Com, Fin) (*m*) businessman; (*f*) businesswoman; **~ de pompas fúnebres** undertaker (b) (Teatr) impresario (c) (en boxeo) promoter

empujar [A1] *vt* (a) «*coche/columpio*» to push; **¡empújame!** give me a push! (b) (incitar, presionar) to spur ... on; (obligar) to force (c) (Tec) to drive
■ ~ *vi* (a) (hacer presión) to push (b) (dar empellones) to push, shove

empuje *m* (dinamismo) drive

empujón *m* (a) (empellón) shove, push; **abrió la puerta de un ~** he pushed the door open; **abrirse paso a (los) empujones** to shove one's way through (b) (fam) (para animar, incitar) prod (colloq); **voy a darle un ~ al asunto** I'm going to push things along a bit (colloq)

empuñadura *f* (de espada) hilt; (de daga, navaja) handle; (de bastón, paraguas) handle

empuñar [A1] *vt* «*arma/espada*» to take up; «*bastón/palo*» to brandish

en *prep* 1 (en expresiones de lugar) (a) (refiriéndose a ciudad, edificio) **viven ~ París** they live in Paris; **el número diez/~ un hotel** they live in Paris/at number ten/in a hotel; **~ el último piso** on the top floor; **está ~ la calle Goya** it's on *o* (BrE) in Goya Street; **~ casa** at home (b) (dentro de) in; **~ una caja** in a box (c) (sobre) on; **~ una silla** on a chair; **se le nota ~ la cara** you can see it in his face

2 (expresando circunstancias, ambiente) in; **~ peligro** in danger

3 (a) (indicando tema, especialidad): **un experto ~ la materia** an expert on the subject; **doctor ~ derecho** Doctor of Law (b) (indicando proporción, precio): **~ un diez por ciento** by ten per cent; **~ dólares** in dollars

4 (a) (indicando estado, manera) in; **~ malas condiciones** in bad condition; **~ llamas** in flames, on fire (b) (en forma de): **termina ~ punta** it's pointed; **colóquense ~ círculo** get into *o* in a circle (c) (con medios de transporte) by; **ir ~ taxi** to go by taxi; **fueron ~ bicicleta** they cycled, they went on their bikes; **dimos una vuelta ~ coche** we went for a ride in the car

5 (a) (indicando el material): **seda natural** in natural silk; **una escultura ~ bronce** a bronze (sculpture) (b) (indicando el modo de presentación o expresión) in; **~ azul/ruso** in blue/Russian

6 (con expresiones de tiempo): **~ verano** in (the) summer; **~ varias ocasiones** on several occasions; **~ la mañana/noche** (esp AmL) in the morning/at night

7 (a) (seguido de construcción verbal): **no hay nada de malo ~ lo que hacen** there's nothing wrong in what they're doing; **fui el último ~ salir** I was the last to leave (b) (con complementos de persona) in; **no sé qué ve ~ ella** I don't know what he sees in her

enagua *f*, **enaguas** *fpl* (a) (prenda interior) petticoat, underskirt (b) (AmC) (falda) skirt

enamorado -da *adj* [ESTAR] in love; **~ DE algn** in love WITH sb; **están muy ~s** they are very much in love
■ *m,f* lover; **una pareja de ~s** two lovers; **vino con su ~** (Bol, Per) she came with her boyfriend; **es un ~ de su profesión** he loves his work

enamoramiento *m* infatuation

enamorar [A1] *vt* to make ... fall in love, get ... to fall in love

■ **enamorarse** *v pron* to fall in love; ~se DE algo/algn to fall in love WITH sth/sb

enano -na *m,f* (de proporciones normales) midget; (de cabeza más grande) dwarf
■ *adj* ⟨especie/planta⟩ dwarf (*before n*); ⟨ración⟩ (fam) minute, tiny

encabezado *m* (Chi, Méx) headline

encabezamiento *m* (a) (en carta — saludo) opening; (— dirección, fecha) heading (b) (en ficha, documento) heading

encabezar [A4] *vt* [1] ⟨artículo/escrito⟩ to head [2] (a) ⟨liga/clasificación/lista⟩ to head, be at the top of; ⟨carrera/movimento/revolución⟩ to lead (b) ⟨delegación/comité⟩ to head, lead

encabritarse [A1] *v pron* «caballo» to rear up

encachado -da *adj* (Chi fam) (a) (bonito) ⟨ropa/lugar⟩ lovely, nice; ⟨persona⟩ attractive (b) (arreglado) well-dressed (c) (entretenido) ⟨historia⟩ entertaining

encadenar [A1] *vt* ⟨prisionero/bicicleta⟩ to chain (up)

encajar [A1] *vt* [1] (meter, colocar) to fit [2] (esp AmL fam) (endilgar): me ~on a mí el trabajito I got saddled o landed with the job (colloq); le encaja los hijos a la suegra she dumps the kids on her mother-in-law (colloq); les ~on tres goles they put three goals past them
■ ~ *vi* (a) «pieza/cajón» to fit; no encaja bien it doesn't fit properly; las piezas ~on the pieces fitted together (b) (corresponder, cuadrar) «hechos/descripción» to fit; no encaja con la decoración it doesn't fit in with the decor

encaje *m* (Indum) lace; pañuelo de ~ lace handkerchief

encajonar [A1] *vt* (en lugar estrecho) ~ algo/a algn EN algo to cram o pack sth/sb INTO sth; me ~on el coche my car o I got boxed in

encalar [A1] *vt* to whitewash

encalillarse [A1] *v pron* (Chi fam) to get into debt

encallar [A1] *vi* to run aground

encallecido -da *adj* ⟨manos⟩ callused

encamar [A1] *vt* (Méx) to confine ... to bed

encaminado -da *adj*: el proyecto va bien ~ the project is shaping up well o is going well; iba bien ~ he was on the right track; medidas encaminadas a reducir ... measures designed to reduce o aimed at reducing ...

encaminar [A1] *vt* (a) ⟨intereses/esfuerzos⟩ to direct, channel (b) ⟨estudiante/niño⟩ to point ... in the right direction
■ **encaminarse** *v pron* (liter) ~se HACIA algo (a) «persona» (dirigirse a) to head FOR/TOWARD(s) sth; (emprender el camino) to set off FOR/TOWARD(s) sth (b) «esfuerzos» to be aimed AT sth, be directed TOWARD(s) sth

encandilar [A1] *vt* (a) «luz» to dazzle (b) (asombrar, pasmar) to dazzle

encanecer [E3] *vi* to (go) gray*

encantado -da *adj* [1] (a) (muy contento) delighted; estoy ~ de haber venido I am delighted o very glad that I came (b) (en fórmulas de cortesía): ~ de conocerla pleased to meet you; le presento al Señor Ruiz — encantado let me introduce you to Mr Ruiz — how do you do; ~ de poder ayudarte I'm glad to be/to have been of help [2] ⟨bosque/castillo⟩ enchanted

encantador -dora *adj* ⟨persona/lugar⟩ charming, delightful
■ *m,f* magician; ~ de serpientes snake charmer

encantar [A1] *vi* (+ me/te/le etc): me encantó la obra I loved o I really enjoyed the play; me ~ía que me acompañaras I'd love you to come with me
■ ~ *vt* to cast o put a spell on, bewitch

encanto *m* [1] (a) (atractivo) charm; sabe utilizar sus ~s she knows how to use her charms; su sencillez es su mayor ~ its most appealing feature is its simplicity (b) (fam) (maravilla): ¡qué ~ de hombre! what a lovely o charming man!; tienen un jardín que es un ~ they have a lovely garden [2] (a) (hechizo) spell; como por ~ as if by magic (b) (Ven fam) (fantasma) ghost

encapotado -da *adj* overcast, cloudy

encapricharse [A1] *v pron*: se ha encaprichado con esa moto he's really taken a liking o (BrE) a fancy to that motorbike; ~ CON or (Esp) DE algn to fall for sb (colloq)

encarado -da *adj* (Esp, Méx): mal ~ (enojado) bad-tempered; (de mal aspecto) nasty-looking

encaramarse [A1] *v pron* ~ A or EN algo ⟨a árbol/valla⟩ to climb up; ⟨a taburete⟩ to climb on to

encarar [A1] *vt* [1] (enfocar) ⟨tarea⟩ to approach; (afrontar) ⟨desgracia/problema⟩ to face up to; ⟨futuro⟩ to face [2] (AmL) ⟨persona⟩ to stand up to
■ **encararse** *v pron* ~se CON algn to face up to o stand up to sb

encarcelar [A1] *vt* to imprison, jail

encarecer [E3] *vt* (hacer más caro): el envase encarece el producto the packaging makes the product more expensive; ~á los alquileres it will push rents up
■ **encarecerse** *v pron* «precios» to increase, rise; «productos/vida» to become more expensive

encargado -da *adj* ~ DE algo/hacer algo responsible FOR sth/doing sth, in charge OF sth/doing sth
■ *m,f* (a) (de negocio) manager, person in charge (b) (de tarea): tú serás el ~ de avisarles it will be your responsibility to tell them

encargar [A3] *vt* [1] (a) ~le algo A algn ⟨tarea⟩ to entrust sb WITH sth; me encargó una botella de whisky escocés she asked me to buy o get her a bottle of Scotch (b) ~ a algn QUE haga algo to ask sb to do sth [2] ⟨mueble/paella/libro⟩ to order; ⟨informe/cuadro⟩ to commission
■ **encargarse** *v pron* ~se DE algo/algn to take care OF sth/sb; me tuve que ~ del asunto I had to take charge of the matter

encargo *m* (a) (recado, pedido): ¿te puedo hacer unos ~s? could you buy o get a few things for me?; mi hijo está haciendo un ~ my son is out on o is running an errand (b) (Com) order; los hacemos por ~ we make them to order (c) (cargo, misión) job, assignment

encariñarse [A1] *v pron* ~ CON algo/algn to grow fond OF sth/sb

encarnación *f* incarnation

encarnado -da *adj* ⒈ ⟨*color/vestido*⟩ red ⒉ ⟨*uña*⟩ ingrowing

encarnarse [A1] *v pron* (a) (Relig) to become incarnate (b) ⟨*uña*⟩ to become ingrown

encarrilar [A1] *vt* ⟨*trabajo/asunto*⟩ to direct; ⟨*persona*⟩ to guide, give guidance to

encasillar [A1] *vt* to class, categorize, pigeonhole

encauzar [A4] *vt* to channel; ~ algo HACIA algo to channel sth INTO sth

encefalograma *m* encephalogram

enceguecedor -dora *adj* (AmL) blinding

enceguecer [E3] *vt* (AmL) to blind
■ **enceguecerse** *v pron* (AmL) (por la luz) to be blinded; (de ira) to become furious

encendedor *m* lighter

encender [E8] *vt* (a) ⟨*cigarrillo/hoguera/vela*⟩ to light; ⟨*fósforo*⟩ to strike, light (b) ⟨*luz/ calefacción*⟩ to switch on, turn on; ⟨*motor*⟩ to start; no dejes el televisor encendido don't leave the television on
■ ~ *vi* ⟨*fósforo*⟩ to light; «*leña*» to catch light; «*luz/radio*» to come on
■ **encenderse** *v pron* ⟨*aparato/luz*⟩ to come on; ⟨*fósforo/piloto*⟩ to light; «*leña*» to catch light

encendido *m* ignition

enceradora *f* polisher

encerar [A1] *vt* to polish, wax

encerrado -da *adj*: está ~ en su habitación he's shut away *o* shut up in his room; se quedó ~ en el cuarto de baño he got locked in the bathroom; siguen ~s en la universidad they are still occupying the university; oler a ~ (AmL) to be stuffy

encerrar [A5] *vt* ⒈ ⟨*ganado*⟩ to shut up, pen; ⟨*perro*⟩ to shut ... in; ⟨*persona*⟩ (en cárcel, calabozo) to lock up; me encerró en mi habitación he shut me *o* locked me in my room; me dejaron encerrada en la oficina I got locked in the office ⒉ (conllevar) ⟨*peligro/riesgo*⟩ to involve, entail
■ **encerrarse** *v pron* (refl) (en habitación) to shut oneself in; (en fábrica, universidad) «*obreros/ estudiantes*» to lock oneself in

encerrona *f* (trampa) trap

encestar [A1] *vi* to score (a basket)

enchapar [A1] *vt* (de metal) to plate; (de madera) to veneer

encharcarse [A2] *v pron* «*terreno/zona*» to become waterlogged *o* flooded; «*agua*» to form a pool/pools

enchastrar [A1] *vt* (RPl fam) ⟨*ropa/cocina*⟩ to make a mess of
■ **enchastrarse** *v pron* (RPl fam) to get dirty

enchastre *m* (RPl fam) mess

enchilada *f* enchilada (*tortilla with a meat or cheese filling, served with a tomato and chili sauce*)

enchilado¹ -da *adj* (Méx) (Coc) seasoned with chili

enchilado² *m* stew (*with chili*)

enchilar [A1] *vt* (Méx) (Coc) to add chili to
■ **enchilarse** *v pron* (Méx) (comiendo): ya me enchilé my mouth's burning; con este plato me enchilo this dish is too hot for me

enchinar [A1] *vt* (Méx) to perm
■ **enchinarse** *v pron* (Méx): se me enchina la piel I come out in goose bumps *o* goose pimples

enchuecar [A2] *vt* (AmL fam) ⟨*metal*⟩ to bend; ⟨*madera/lámina*⟩ to warp; ⟨*cara/boca*⟩ to twist; ⟨*cuadro*⟩ to tilt
■ **enchuecarse** *v pron* (Chi fam) ⟨*metal*⟩ to bend, get bent; «*madera/lámina*» to warp; «*cara/boca*» to become twisted

enchufado -da *adj* (fam): está ~ he knows all the right people; estar ~ con ... to be well in with ... (colloq)

enchufar [A1] *vt* ⒈ (fam) ⟨*radio/televisión*⟩ to plug in ⒉ (fam) ⟨*persona*⟩: me enchufó en la empresa he set me up with a job in the company (colloq)

enchufe *m* ⒈ (a) (Elec) (macho) plug; (hembra) socket, power point (BrE) (b) (del teléfono) socket, point (BrE) ⒉ (Esp fam) (influencia): necesitas algún ~ you need to have connections; por ~ by pulling some strings

encía *f* gum

enciclopedia *f* encyclopedia

encienda, enciendas, etc ▶ ENCENDER

encierra, encierras, etc ▶ ENCERRAR

encierro *m* (a) (en fábrica, universidad) sit-in (b) (reclusión): salió de su ~ después de ocho meses she emerged after being holed up for eight months (c) (Taur) (conducción) *running of bulls through the streets*; (toros) *bulls to be used in a bullfight*

encima *adv* ⒈ (en el espacio): le puso una piedra ~ he put a stone on it; no llevo dinero ~ I don't have any money on me; se tiró el café ~ she spilled the coffee over herself; se me vino el armario ~ the cupboard came down on top of me ⒉ (además): ¡y ~ se queja! and then she goes and complains!; y ~ no me lo devolvió and on top of that, he didn't give it back! ⒊ (en locs) encima de: ~ de la mesa on the table; ~ del armario on top of the cupboard; llevaba un chal ~ de la chaqueta she wore a shawl over her jacket; viven ~ de la tienda they live over *o* above the shop; ~ de caro es feo not only is it expensive, it's also ugly; por encima over; saltó por ~ he jumped over; le eché un vistazo por ~ I just looked over it quickly; una limpieza por ~ a quick clean; por encima de above; por ~ de la media above average; por ~ de todo above everything; volaban por ~ de las nubes/del pueblo they flew above the clouds/over the town; está por ~ del jefe de sección she's above the head of department; quitarse algo de ~ ⟨*problema/tarea*⟩ to get sth out of the way; quitarse a algn de ~ to get rid of sb

AmC	América Central	Arg	Argentina
AmL	América Latina	Bol	Bolivia
AmS	América del Sur	Chi	Chile
Andes	Región andina	CS	Cono Sur

Cu	Cuba	Per	Perú
Ec	Ecuador	RPl	Río de la Plata
Esp	España	Ur	Uruguay
Méx	México	Ven	Venezuela

encimar [A1] *vt* **(a)** (Col) (regalar): **me encimó dos más** she gave me two extra **(b)** (Méx, RPl) ⟨*cajas/libros*⟩ to stack up

encina *f* holm oak, ilex

encinta *adj* ▶ EMBARAZADA

enclenque *adj* **(a)** ⟨*persona*⟩ (enfermizo) sickly; (delgado) weak, weedy (colloq) **(b)** ⟨*estructura*⟩ rickety

encoger [E6] *vi* to shrink
■ ~ *vt* **(a)** ⟨*ropa*⟩ to shrink **(b)** ⟨*piernas*⟩ to tuck ... in; **encogió el cuerpo de miedo** he shrank back in fear
■ **encogerse** *v pron* ⌐1⌐ «*ropa/tela*» to shrink ⌐2⌐ «*persona*» **(a)** (físicamente): **~se de hombros** to shrug one's shoulders; **caminar encogido** to walk with one's shoulders hunched **(b)** (por la edad) to shrink, get shorter **(c)** (acobardarse) to be intimidated

encomendería *f* (Per) grocery store (AmE), grocer's shop (BrE)

encomendero *m* (Per) (tendero) grocer

encomienda *f* (AmL) (Corresp) package (AmE), parcel (BrE)

encontrar [A10] *vt* ⌐1⌐ **(a)** (buscando) ⟨*casa/trabajo/persona*⟩ to find; **no encontré entradas para el teatro** I couldn't get tickets for the theater; **no le encuentro lógica** I can't see the logic in it **(b)** (casualmente) ⟨*cartera/billete*⟩ to find, come across **(c)** (descubrir) ⟨*falta/error*⟩ to find, spot; ⟨*cáncer/quiste*⟩ to find, discover **(d)** ⟨*obstáculo/dificultad*⟩ to meet (with), encounter ⌐2⌐ (+ *compl*): **te encuentro muy cambiado** you look very different; **lo encuentro ridículo** I find it ridiculous; **¿cómo encontraste el país?** how did the country seem to you?
■ **encontrarse** *v pron* ⌐1⌐ (por casualidad) **~se con algn** to meet sb, bump INTO sb (colloq) ⌐2⌐ (*recípr*) **(a)** (reunirse) to meet; (por casualidad) to meet, bump into each other (colloq) **(b)** «*carreteras/líneas*» to meet ⌐3⌐ (*enf*) (inesperadamente) ⟨*billete/cartera*⟩ to find, come across; **me encontré con que todos se habían ido** I found they had all gone ⌐4⌐ (*frml*) (estar) to be; **me encuentro mejor** I am feeling better; **el hotel se encuentra cerca de la estación** the hotel is (located) near the station

encorvado -da *adj*: **anda ~** he walks with a stoop

encorvarse [A1] *v pron* to develop a stoop

encrespar [A1] *vt* ⟨*pelo*⟩ to make ... go curly; ⟨*mar*⟩ to make ... rough o choppy
■ **encresparse** *v pron* «*pelo*» to curl, go curly; «*mar*» to get rough o choppy

encrucijada *f* crossroads

encuadernación *f* **(a)** (cubierta) binding **(b)** (acción) book binding

encuadernador -dora *m,f* bookbinder

encuadernar [A1] *vt* to bind

encuadrar [A1] *vt* **(a)** (clasificar) to class, classify **(b)** (Cin, Fot, TV) to frame, center*

encubrir [I33] *vt* **(a)** ⟨*delincuente*⟩ to harbor* **(b)** ⟨*delito*⟩ to cover up; **siempre lo está encubriendo** she's always covering up for him **(c)** ⟨*temor/verdad/problema*⟩ to mask

encuclillarse [A1] *v pron* to squat (down)

encuentra, encuentras, etc ▶ ENCONTRAR

encuentro *m* **(a)** (acción) meeting, encounter; **una secretaria le salió al ~** he was met by a secretary **(b)** (Dep) (period) game

encuerarse [A1] *v pron* (*refl*) (AmL fam) (desnudarse) to strip off (colloq), get undressed; (en el escenario) to strip

encuesta *f* **(a)** (sondeo) survey; **~ de opinión** opinion poll **(b)** (investigación) inquiry

encuestado -da *m,f*: **el 50% de los ~s** 50% of those polled

encumbrar [A1] *vt* (Chi) ⟨*volantín*⟩ to fly

endeble *adj* weak; ⟨*salud*⟩ delicate, poor

endemoniado -da *adj* **(a)** (inaguantable) ⟨*niño/asunto*⟩ wretched (*before n*); ⟨*genio/humor*⟩ foul, wicked **(b)** (poseído del demonio) possessed (by the devil)

enderezar [A4] *vt* **(a)** (destorcer) ⟨*clavo*⟩ to straighten **(b)** (poner vertical) ⟨*poste/espalda*⟩ to straighten; ⟨*planta*⟩ to stake; ⟨*barco*⟩ to right **(c)** ⟨*persona*⟩ to straighten ... out
■ **enderezarse** *v pron* (ponerse derecho) «*persona*» to stand up straight, straighten up; «*árbol*» to straighten up

endeudado -da *adj* in debt; **~ CON algn** indebted TO sb

endeudarse [A1] *v pron* to get (oneself) into debt; **~ CON algn** to get into debt WITH sb

endiablado -da *adj* **(a)** (malo) ⟨*carácter/genio*⟩ terrible; **¡este ~ niño!** this wretched child! **(b)** (peligroso) ⟨*velocidad*⟩ reckless, dangerous

endibia *f* endive, chicory (BrE)

endilgar [A3] *vt* (fam): **nos endilgó un sermón** he lectured us; **me ~on el trabajito** I got saddled o landed with the job (colloq); **me endilgó a los niños** she dumped the kids on me (colloq)

endivia *f* endive, chicory (BrE)

endrogarse [A3] *v pron* (Méx) to get into debt

endulzar [A4] *vt* **(a)** ⟨*café*⟩ to sweeten **(b)** ⟨*tono/respuesta*⟩ to soften; ⟨*vida/vejez*⟩ to brighten up; ⟨*carácter*⟩ to mellow

endurecer [E3] *vt* ⌐1⌐ (en general) to harden ⌐2⌐ ⟨*persona/carácter*⟩ (volver insensible) to harden; (fortalecer) to toughen ... up; **ese corte te endurece las facciones** that haircut makes you look harsher
■ **endurecerse** *v pron* **(a)** (en general) to harden; «*pan*» to go stale **(b)** «*persona/carácter*» (volverse insensible) to harden; (fortalecerse) to toughen up **(c)** «*facciones*» to become harder o harsher

ene *f. name of the letter* n

eneldo *m* dill

enemigo -ga *adj* **(a)** ⟨*tropas/soldados/país*⟩ enemy (*before n*) **(b)** **ser ~ DE algo** to be against sth; **era enemiga de pegarles a los niños** she was against hitting children
■ *m,f* enemy

enemistad *f* enmity

enemistado -da *adj*: **están ~s** they're at odds (with each other); **quedó ~ con ellos** she fell out with them

enemistar [A1] *vt* ⟨*dos facciones/países*⟩ to make enemies of; **~ un país con otro** to turn one country against the other; **ella los enemistó** she turned them against each other ⋯⟶

■ **enemistarse** *v pron* to fall out; ~**se CON** algn
(**POR** algo) to fall out **WITH** sb (**OVER** sth)

energético -ca *adj* ⟨*crisis/política/recursos*⟩
energy (*before n*); ⟨*alimento*⟩ energy-giving, fuel
(*before n*) (AmE)

energía *f* **1** (Fís) energy; ~ **nuclear/solar**
nuclear/solar power **2** (vigor, empuje) energy;
protestar con ~ to protest vigorously; **está lleno
de** ~ he's very energetic **(b)** (firmeza) firmness

enérgico -ca *adj* **(a)** (físicamente) energetic **(b)**
(firme, resuelto) ⟨*carácter*⟩ forceful; ⟨*protesta/
ataque*⟩ vigorous; ⟨*medidas*⟩ firm, strong;
⟨*negativa/rechazo*⟩ flat, firm

enero *m* January; **a principios de** ~ at the
beginning of January; **a mediados de** ~ in the
middle of January, in mid-January; **el tres de** ~
the third of January, January the third, January
third (AmE); **en (el mes de)** ~ in (the month of)
January; **Lima, 8 de** ~ **de 1987** (Corresp) Lima,
January 8 *o* January 8th, 1987

enfadado -da *adj* (esp Esp) angry; (en menor
grado) annoyed; **están** ~**s** they've fallen out; **está**
~ **contigo** he's angry/annoyed with you

enfadar [A1] *vt* (esp Esp) (enojar) to anger, make
... angry; (en menor grado) to annoy

■ **enfadarse** *v pron* (esp Esp) **(a)** (enojarse) to get
angry, get mad (esp AmE colloq); (en menor grado)
get annoyed, get cross (BrE colloq); ~**se CON** algn
to get angry/annoyed **WITH** sb **(b)** «*novios*» to
fall out

enfado *m* (esp Esp) anger; (menos serio)
annoyance

énfasis *m* emphasis; **poner** ~ **en algo** to stress
o emphasize sth

enfático -ca *adj* emphatic

enfatizar [A4] *vt* to emphasize, stress

enfermar [A1] *vi* to fall ill, get sick (AmE)

■ **enfermarse** *v pron* **(a)** (esp AmL) (caer enfermo)
to fall ill, get sick (AmE); ~**se del estómago** to
develop stomach trouble **(b)** (CS euf) (menstruar) to
get one's period

enfermedad *f* illness; **contraer una** ~ to
contract an illness/a disease (frml); **después de
una larga** ~ after a long illness; **está con permiso
por** ~ he's off sick; ~**es de la piel** skin diseases;
~ **mental** mental illness; ~ **nerviosa** nervous
disorder

enfermería *f* **1** (sala) infirmary, sickbay
2 (carrera) nursing

enfermero -ra *m,f* nurse; ~ **jefe** ≈ head nurse
(AmE), ≈ charge nurse (BrE)

enfermizo -za *adj* unhealthy, sickly; **de
aspecto** ~ unhealthy-looking

enfermo -ma *adj* **(a)** (Med) ill, sick;
gravemente ~ seriously ill; **está** ~ **del corazón**
he has heart trouble; **está enferma de los nervios**
she suffers with her nerves; **se puso** ~ he fell *o*
got ill, he got sick (AmE); **poner** ~ **a algn** (fam) to
get on sb's nerves (colloq), to get sb (colloq) **(b)** (CS
euf) (con la menstruación): **estoy enferma** I've got my
period, it's the time of the month (euph)

■ *m,f* (en hospital) patient; **quiere cuidar** ~**s** she
wants to care for sick people *o* the sick; ~**s del
corazón** people with heart trouble; ~**s de cáncer**
cancer sufferers

enfocar [A2] *vt* **1** ⟨*objeto/persona*⟩ (con cámara,
prismáticos) to focus on; **los** ~**on con la linterna**

they shone the torch on them **2** **(a)** (Fot, Ópt)
⟨*telescopio/cámara*⟩ to focus **(b)** ⟨*tema/asunto*⟩ to
approach, look at

enfoque *m* **(a)** (Fot, Ópt) (acción) focusing*;
(efecto) focus **(b)** (de asunto) approach; **todo
depende del** ~ **que se le dé** everything depends
on the way you look at it; ~ **DE algo** approach **TO**
sth

enfrentamiento *m* clash; ~ **bélico** military
confrontation

enfrentar [A1] *vt* **1** ⟨*problema/peligro/
realidad*⟩ to confront, face up to; ⟨*futuro*⟩ to face
2 **(a)** ⟨*contrincantes/opositores*⟩ to bring ... face
to face **(b)** (enemistar) to bring ... into conflict

■ **enfrentarse** *v pron* **(a)** (hacer frente a) ~**se CON**
algn ⟨*con rival/enemigo*⟩ to confront sb; ~**se A**
algo ⟨*a dificultades/peligros*⟩ to face sth; ⟨*a
realidad/responsabilidad*⟩ to face up to sth **(b)**
(recípr) «*equipos/atletas*» to meet; «*tropas/
oponentes*» to clash

enfrente *adv* **1** (al otro lado de una calle, etc)
opposite; ~ **de mí/del parque** opposite me/the
park **2** (delante) in front; ~ **DE algo** in front of
sth

enfriamiento *m* **(a)** (catarro) chill **(b)** (de amor,
entusiasmo, relaciones) cooling (off)

enfriar [A17] *vt* **(a)** ⟨*alimento*⟩ to cool; (en el
refrigerador) to chill, cool **(b)** ⟨*entusiasmo/relación*⟩
to cool, cause ... to cool

■ ~ *vi*: **no dejes** ~ **el café** don't let your coffee go
o get cold; **deja** ~ **el motor** let the engine cool
down; **ponlo a** ~ put it in the refrigerator to chill

■ **enfriarse** *v pron* **1** **(a)** «*comida/bebida*»
(ponerse — demasiado frío) to get cold, go cold; (— lo
suficientemente frío) to cool down **(b)** «*manos*» to
get cold **(c)** «*entusiasmo/relaciones*» to cool (off)
2 (tomar frío) to catch *o* get cold; (resfriarse) to
catch a cold, catch a chill

enfurecer [E3] *vt* to infuriate, make ... furious

■ **enfurecerse** *v pron* to fly into a rage, get
furious

enfurecido -da *adj* [ESTAR] ⟨*persona*⟩ furious

enfurruñarse [A1] *v pron* (fam) to go into a
sulk (colloq), to get into a huff (colloq)

enganchar [A1] *vt* **(a)** ⟨*cable/cadena*⟩ to hook
(b) ⟨*remolque*⟩ to hitch up, attach; ⟨*caballos*⟩ to
harness; ⟨*vagón*⟩ to couple, attach **(c)** ⟨*pez*⟩ to
hook

■ **engancharse** *v pron* **(a)** (quedar prendido) to get
caught; **se me enganchó la media en el clavo** my
tights got caught on the nail **(b)** (fam) (hacerse
adicto) ~**se (A** algo) to get hooked (**ON** sth)

enganche *m* **1** (pieza, mecanismo) (Auto) towing
hook; (Ferr) coupling **2** (Esp) (de la luz, del teléfono)
connection **3** (Méx) (Fin) down payment

engañar [A1] *vt* **(a)** (hacer errar en el juicio) to
deceive, mislead; **me engañó la vista** my eyes
deceived me; **tú a mí no me engañas** you can't
fool me; **lo engañó haciéndole creer que** ... she
deceived him into thinking that ...; ~ **a algn
PARA QUE haga algo** to trick sb **INTO** doing sth
(b) (estafar, timar) to cheat, con (colloq) **(c)** (ser infiel
a) to be unfaithful to, cheat on

■ **engañarse** *v pron* (refl) (mentirse) to deceive
oneself, kid oneself (colloq)

engaño *m* **(a)** (mentira) deception **(b)** (timo,
estafa) swindle, con (colloq) **(c)** (ardid) ploy, trick

engañoso -sa *adj* ⟨*palabras*⟩ deceitful; ⟨*apariencias*⟩ deceptive

engarce *m* setting

engarzar [A4] *vt* ⟨1⟩ ⟨*piedra/brillante*⟩ to set ⟨2⟩ (Col, Ven) (enganchar) to hook

■ **engarzarse** *v pron* (Col) (engancharse) to get caught

engatusar [A1] *vt* to sweet-talk; ~ **a algn** PARA QUE **haga algo** to sweet-talk sb INTO doing sth

engendrar [A1] *vt* ⟨*hijos*⟩ to father; ⟨*odio/sospecha*⟩ to breed, engender (frml)

engendro *m* (a) (feto) fetus* **(b)** (criatura malformada) malformed creature **(c)** (creación monstruosa) freak, monster

engentado -da *adj* (Méx) dazed, confused

engomado -da *adj* ⟨*etiqueta*⟩ gummed, self-adhesive; ⟨*sobre*⟩ gummed, self-sealing

engordar [A1] *vt* (a) (aumentar) to put on, gain **(b)** (cebar) to fatten (up) **(c)** ⟨*cifras/estadísticas*⟩ to swell

■ ~ *vi* (a) «*persona*» to put on *o* gain weight; «*animales*» to fatten **(b)** «*alimentos*» to be fattening

engorroso -sa *adj* ⟨*problema*⟩ complicated, thorny; ⟨*situación*⟩ awkward, difficult; ⟨*asunto*⟩ trying, tiresome

engranaje *m* ⟨1⟩ (Mec) gear assembly (*o* mechanism *etc*), gears (*pl*); **el ~ del reloj** the cogs of the watch ⟨2⟩ (de partido, sociedad) machinery

engrandecer [E3] *vt* (ennoblecer) to ennoble (frml)

engrapadora *f* (AmL) stapler

engrapar [A1] *vt* (AmL) to staple

engrasado *m* lubrication, greasing

engrasar [A1] *vt* (a) (Auto, Mec) (con grasa) to grease, lubricate; (con aceite) to oil, lubricate **(b)** (Coc) ⟨*molde*⟩ to grease

engreído -da *adj* (a) (vanidoso) conceited, bigheaded (colloq) **(b)** (Per) (mimado) spoiled*

■ *m,f* (a) (vanidoso) bighead (colloq) **(b)** (Per) (mimado) spoiled brat

engrupir [I1] *vt* (CS fam) to fool (colloq)

engullir [I9] *vt* to bolt (down)

enhebrar [A1] *vt* ⟨*aguja*⟩ to thread; ⟨*perlas*⟩ to string

enhorabuena *f* congratulations (*pl*); **darle la ~ a algn** to congratulate sb

■ *interj* congratulations!

enigma *m* enigma, mystery

enigmático -ca *adj* enigmatic, mysterious

enjabonar [A1] *vt* to soap

■ **enjabonarse** *v pron* (refl) to soap oneself; **~se las manos** to soap one's hands

enjambre *m* (Zool) swarm

enjaular [A1] *vt* ⟨*pájaro/fiera*⟩ to cage, put ... in a cage

enjuagar [A3] *vt* ⟨*boca/ropa/vajilla*⟩ to rinse; ⟨*palangana/cubo*⟩ to swill out

■ **enjuagarse** *v pron* (refl) to wash off the soap; **~se el pelo** to rinse one's hair

enjuague *m* (a) (acción de enjuagar) rinse **(b)** (AmL) (para el pelo) conditioner **(c)** **~ bucal** mouthwash

enjugar [A3] *vt* (liter) ⟨*lágrimas/sudor*⟩ to wipe away

■ **enjugarse** *v pron* (refl) (liter) ⟨*lágrimas*⟩ to wipe away; ⟨*frente*⟩ to mop, wipe

enlace *m* (a) (conexión, unión) link **(b)** (de vías, carreteras) intersection, junction **(c)** *tb* ~ **matrimonial** marriage **(d)** (persona) liaison; **~ sindical** (Esp) shop steward, union rep

enlatado¹ -da *adj* (a) ⟨*alimentos*⟩ canned, tinned (BrE) **(b)** ⟨*música/programa*⟩ canned **(c)** (Inf) ⟨*programa*⟩ stored

enlatado² *m* ⟨1⟩ (proceso) canning ⟨2⟩ (AmL pey) (TV) programming

enlazar [A4] *vt* ⟨1⟩ (a) ⟨*ciudades*⟩ to link (up); ⟨*ideas/temas*⟩ to link, connect **(b)** ⟨*cintas*⟩ to tie ... together ⟨2⟩ (Col, RPl) ⟨*res/caballo*⟩ to lasso, rope (AmE) ⟨3⟩ (Méx frml) (casar) to marry

■ ~ *vi* ~ CON **algo** «*tren/vuelo*» to connect WITH sth; «*carretera*» to link up WITH sth

enlistarse [A1] *v pron* (AmC, Col, Ven) to enlist, join up

enloquecedor -dora *adj* ⟨*dolor*⟩ excruciating; **el ruido era** ~ the noise was enough to drive you crazy

enloquecer [E3] *vt* to drive ... crazy *o* mad

■ ~ *vi* (perder el juicio) to go crazy *o* mad; **enloqueció de celos** he was driven crazy *o* insane with jealousy

enlozado -da *adj* (AmL) ⟨*cacerola*⟩ enameled*; ⟨*fuente*⟩ glazed

enmarañado -da *adj* (a) ⟨*pelo/lana*⟩ tangled **(b)** (complicado, confuso) complicated, involved

enmarcar [A2] *vt* ⟨*lámina/foto*⟩ to frame

enmascarado -da *adj* masked

■ *m,f* (*m*) masked man; (*f*) masked woman

enmendar [A5] *vt* ⟨*conducta*⟩ to improve, amend (frml); ⟨*actitud*⟩ to change; ⟨*error*⟩ to amend, rectify

■ **enmendarse** *v pron* (refl) to mend one's ways

enmienda *f* amendment

enmohecer [E3] *vt* ⟨*ropa*⟩ to make ... moldy*; ⟨*metal*⟩ to rust

■ **enmohecerse** *v pron* «*ropa/pan/queso*» to become moldy*; «*metal*» to rust, become rusty

enmoquetar [A1] *vt* (Esp) to carpet

enmudecer [E3] *vi* to fall silent

ennegrecer [E3] *vt* (poner negro) to blacken; (oscurecer) to darken

■ **ennegrecerse** *v pron* (a) (ponerse negro) to go black **(b)** (ponerse oscuro) ⟨*cielo/nubes*⟩ to darken, go dark; «*plata*» to tarnish

enojadizo -za *adj* (esp AmL) irritable, touchy

enojado -da *adj* (esp AmL) angry, mad (esp AmE colloq); (en menor grado) annoyed, cross (BrE colloq); **está ~ contigo** he's angry/annoyed with you; **están ~s** they've fallen out

enojar [A1] *vt* (esp AmL) to make ... angry; (en menor grado) to annoy

■ **enojarse** *v pron* (esp AmL) to get angry, get mad (esp AmE colloq); (en menor grado) to get annoyed, get cross (BrE colloq); **~se CON algn** to get angry/annoyed WITH sb

enojo *m* (esp AmL) anger; (menos serio) annoyance; **¿ya se te pasó el ~?** are you still angry/annoyed?

enojón -jona *adj* (Chi, Méx fam) irritable, touchy

enojoso -sa adj (esp AmL) (violento) awkward; (aburrido) tedious, tiresome

enorgullecer [E3] vt: **mi hijo me enorgullece** I am proud of my son
■ **enorgullecerse** v pron to be proud; **no es para ~se** it's nothing to be proud of; **~se DE algo** to take pride in sth

enorme adj ⟨edificio/animal/suma⟩ huge, enormous; ⟨zona⟩ vast, huge; **sentí una pena ~** I felt tremendously sad

enraizado -da adj ⟨prejuicio⟩ deep-seated, deep-rooted; ⟨tradición⟩ deeply rooted

enrarecido -da adj **(a)** ⟨atmósfera/aire⟩ rarefied **(b)** ⟨ambiente/relaciones⟩ strained, tense

enredadera f creeper, climbing plant

enredado -da adj ⟨1⟩ ⟨lana/cuerda⟩ tangled; ⟨pelo⟩ tangled, knotted; ⟨asunto/idea⟩ complicated ⟨2⟩ **(a)** (involucrado) **~ EN algo** mixed up IN sth **(b)** (fam) (en lío amoroso) **~ CON algn** involved WITH sb

enredar [A1] vt **(a)** ⟨cuerdas/cables⟩ to get ... tangled up, tangle up **(b)** (embarullar) ⟨persona⟩ to muddle ... up, confuse; ⟨asunto/situación⟩ to complicate **(c)** (fam) (involucrar) **~ a algn EN algo** to get sb mixed up o caught up IN sth
■ **~** vi (fam) **(a)** (intrigar) to make trouble, stir up trouble **(b)** (Esp) (molestar) to fidget; **~ CON algo** to fiddle (around) WITH sth
■ **enredarse** v pron ⟨1⟩ «lana/cuerda» to get tangled, become entangled; «pelo» to get tangled o knotted; «planta» to twist itself around ⟨2⟩ (fam) **(a)** (en lío amoroso) **~se CON algn** to get involved WITH sb **(b)** (involucrarse) **~se EN algo** to get mixed up o involved IN sth **(c)** (fam) (embarullarse) to get mixed up, get muddled up

enredo m **(a)** (de hilos) tangle; (en el pelo) tangle, knot **(b)** (embrollo) mess; **tengo un ~ en las cuentas** ... my accounts are in a terrible mess **(c)** (fam) (lío amoroso) affair

enrejado m (de verja, balcón) railing, railings (pl); (rejilla) grating, grille; (para plantas) trellis

enrevesado -da adj complicated

enrielar [A1] vt ▶ ENCARRILAR

enriquecer [E3] vt ⟨1⟩ ⟨país/población⟩ to make ... rich ⟨2⟩ ⟨espíritu/lengua/alimento⟩ to enrich
■ **enriquecerse** v pron ⟨1⟩ (hacerse rico) to get rich ⟨2⟩ «cultura/relación/lengua» to be enriched

enrojecer [E3] vt ⟨rostro/mejillas⟩ to redden, make ... go red; ⟨pelo⟩ to turn ... red, make ... go red
■ **~** vi (liter) (ruborizarse) to redden, blush; (de ira, rabia) to go red in the face
■ **enrojecerse** v pron «rostro/mejillas» to redden, blush; «pelo» to go o turn red; «cielo» to turn red

enrolarse [A1] v pron to enlist, join up; **~ en la marina** to enlist in o join the navy; **~ en un partido** to join a party

enrollado -da adj ⟨1⟩ **(a)** ⟨papel⟩ rolled up **(b)** ⟨cable⟩ coiled (up) ⟨2⟩ (Esp) **(a)** (fam) **estar ~ CON algn** to have a thing (going) WITH sb (colloq); **están ~s** they've got sth going between them (colloq)

(c) estar ~ CON algo ⟨con exámenes/preparativos⟩ wrapped up IN sth **(c)** (arg) (en la onda) ⟨persona/música/coche⟩ cool (sl) ⟨3⟩ (Ven fam) (preocupado) uptight (colloq), freaked out (sl)

enrollar [A1] vt ⟨1⟩ ⟨papel/persiana⟩ to roll up; ⟨cable/manguera⟩ to coil; **~ el hilo en el carrete** wind the thread onto the spool
⟨2⟩ (Esp arg) ⟨persona⟩ (confundir) to confuse, get ... confused; (en asunto) to involve, get ... involved
■ **enrollarse** v pron ⟨1⟩ «papel» to roll up; «cuerda/cable» to coil up; **la cadena se enrolló en la rueda** the chain wound itself around the wheel
⟨2⟩ (Esp fam) **(a)** (hablar mucho): **no te enrolles** stop jabbering on (colloq); **se ~on hablando** they got deep into conversation **(b)** (tener relaciones amorosas): **se ~on en la discoteca** they made out (AmE colloq) o (BrE colloq) they got off together in a disco; **~se CON algn** to make out WITH sb (AmE colloq), to get off WITH sb (BrE colloq)

enroque m (en ajedrez) castling

enroscar [A2] vt ⟨tornillo⟩ to screw in; ⟨cable/cuerda⟩ to coil; **~ algo EN algo** to wind sth AROUND o ONTO sth
■ **enroscarse** v pron **(a)** «víbora» to coil up **(b)** «gato/persona» to curl up

enrular [A1] vt (Col, CS) to curl

ensalada f (Coc) salad; **~ de fruta** fruit salad

ensaladera f salad bowl

ensalzar [A4] vt ⟨virtudes⟩ to extol; ⟨persona⟩ to praise, sing the praises of

ensamblar [A1] vt to assemble

ensanchar [A1] vt **(a)** ⟨calle⟩ to widen; ⟨vestido⟩ to let out **(b)** ⟨horizontes/posibilidades⟩ to expand
■ **ensancharse** v pron **(a)** «calle/acera» to widen, get wider; «jersey» to stretch **(b)** «horizontes» to expand

ensangrentado -da adj bloodstained

ensangrentar [A5] vt to stain ... with blood

ensañarse [A1] v pron: **se ensañaron con los prisioneros** they showed the prisoners no mercy o pity; **no te ensañes con él** don't take it out on him (colloq)

ensartar [A1] vt **(a)** ⟨perlas/cuentas⟩ to string **(b)** (con pincho) to skewer **(c)** (enhebrar) to thread **(d)** (clavar) **~ algo EN algo** to stick sth IN(TO) sth

ensayar [A1] vt **(a)** ⟨obra/baile⟩ to rehearse **(b)** ⟨método⟩ to test, try out
■ **~** vi to rehearse

ensayo m ⟨1⟩ **(a)** (Espec) rehearsal; **~ general** (de obra teatral) dress rehearsal; (de concierto) final rehearsal **(b)** (prueba) trial, test; (intento) attempt ⟨2⟩ (Lit) essay ⟨3⟩ (en rugby) try

enseguida adv at once, immediately, right away; **¡~ voy!** I'll be right with you; **~ de almorzar** (esp AmL) right o straight after lunch

enseñado -da adj: **bien/mal ~** ⟨niño⟩ well/badly brought up; ⟨animal⟩ well/badly trained

enseñanza f **(a)** (docencia) teaching **(b)** (educación) education; **~ a distancia** distance learning; ~ **media** or **secundaria** high school (AmE) o (BrE) secondary education; ~ **primaria** elementary (AmE) o (BrE) primary education; ~ **universitaria** college (AmE) o (BrE) university education

enseñar [A1] vt 1 (a) ‹asignatura/niño› to teach; ‹animal› to train; ~**le a algn A hacer algo** to teach sb to do sth (b) (dar escarmiento) to teach 2 (mostrar) ‹camino/procedimiento› to show
■ **enseñarse** v pron (Méx fam) ~**se A hacer algo** (aprender) to learn to do sth; (acostumbrarse) to get used TO doing sth

ensillar [A1] vt to saddle (up)

ensimismado -da adj [ESTAR] lost in thought; ~ **EN algo** engrossed IN sth, absorbed IN sth

ensordecedor -dora adj deafening

ensuciar [A1] vt (a) ‹ropa/mantel› to get … dirty, dirty; **lo vas a ~ todo de barro** you'll get mud everywhere (b) (liter) ‹honor/nombre› to sully, tarnish
■ **ensuciarse** v pron (a) (refl) «persona» to get dirty; **no te ensucies los dedos** don't get your fingers dirty (b) «falda/suelo» to get dirty; **que no se te ensucie** don't get it dirty; **se me ensució el vestido de grasa** I got grease on my dress

entablar [A1] vt (a) (iniciar) ‹conversación/amistad› to strike up; ‹negociaciones› to enter into (b) ‹partida› to set up

entablillar [A1] vt to splint, put … in a splint

entallado -da adj ‹chaqueta/vestido› waisted; ‹camisa› tailored, fitted

ente m (a) (ser) being, entity (b) (organismo, institución) body

entender [E8] vt to understand; ‹chiste› to understand, get (colloq); **no te entiendo la letra** I can't read your writing; **no entendí su nombre** I didn't get his name; **lo entendió todo al revés** he got it all completely wrong; **tú ya me entiendes** you know what I mean; **me has entendido mal** you've misunderstood me; **se hace ~** or (AmL) **se da a ~** he makes himself understood; **me dio a ~ que …** she gave me to understand that …; **dar algo a ~** to imply sth
■ **~** vi (a) (comprender) to understand (b) (saber) ~ **DE algo** to know ABOUT sth
■ **entenderse** v pron 1 (a) (comunicarse) to communicate; **se entienden por señas** they communicate using sign language; ~**se CON algn** to communicate WITH sb; **a ver si nos entendemos ¿quién te pegó?** let's get this straight, who hit you? (b) (llevarse bien); **lo que pasa es que no nos entendemos** the thing is we just don't get on very well; ~**se CON algn** to get along o on WITH sb
2 (refl): **déjame, yo me entiendo** leave me alone, I know what I'm doing

entendido -da adj 1 [ESTAR] (comprendido) understood; **según tengo ~** as I understand it; **tenía ~ que …** I was under the impression that …; **eso se da por ~** that goes without saying 2 [SER] (experto): **no soy muy ~ en estos temas** I'm not very well up on these subjects; **es muy ~ en política** he's very knowledgeable about politics
■ m,f expert

entendimiento m (a) (acuerdo)

understanding (b) (capacidad para entender) mind; **todavía no tiene suficiente ~** he's not old enough to understand

enterado -da adj 1 (de hecho, suceso): **¿estás ~ de lo ocurrido?** have you heard what's happened?; **no estoy enterada de nada** I have no idea what's going on; **darse por ~** to get the message, take the hint 2 (Esp) (que sabe mucho) knowledgeable, well-informed

enterarse [A1] v pron 1 (de suceso, noticia): **ahora me entero** this is the first I've heard of it; **me enteré por tus padres** I found out from your parents; **le robaron el reloj y ni se enteró** they stole her watch and she didn't even notice o realize; **me enteré de la noticia por la radio** I heard the news on the radio; **si papá se entera de esto …** if Dad finds out about this … 2 (averiguar) to find out; ~ **DE algo** to find out ABOUT sth 3 (esp Esp fam) (entender): **te voy a castigar ¿te enteras?** I'll punish you, have I made myself clear?; **¡para que te enteres!** (fam) so there! (colloq)

entereza f (serenidad, fortaleza) fortitude; (rectitud) integrity; (firmeza) determination, strength of mind

enternecedor -dora adj moving, touching

enternecer [E3] vt to move, touch
■ **enternecerse** v pron to be moved o touched

entero¹ -ra adj (a) (en su totalidad) whole; **una caja entera de bombones** a whole o an entire box of chocolates; **en el mundo ~** all over the world; **por ~** completely, entirely (b) (intacto) intact (c) ‹número› whole

entero² m (a) (Fin) point (b) (Mat) whole number, integer (c) (de lotería) (whole) lottery ticket

enterrador -dora m,f gravedigger

enterrar [A5] vt to bury; **lo entierran mañana** the funeral is tomorrow

entibiar [A1] vt ‹líquido› (enfriar) to cool; (calentar) to warm (up)

entidad f (frml) (organización, institución) entity, body; ~ **deportiva** sporting body

entienda, entiendas, etc ▶ ENTENDER

entierro m (acto) burial; (ceremonia) funeral; (procesión) funeral procession; **ir a un ~** to attend a funeral

entoldado m (marquesina) awning; (carpa) marquee

entonación f intonation

entonado -da adj 1 (Mús) in tune 2 [ESTAR] (fam) (por el alcohol) tipsy (colloq), merry (BrE colloq)

entonar [A1] vt 1 ‹canción› to intone, sing; ‹voz› to modulate; ‹nota› to sing, give 2 (animar) «café/sopa» ‹persona› to perk … up
■ **~** vi (Mús) to sing in tune

entonces adv 1 (en aquel momento) then; **por** or **en aquel ~** in those days 2 (a) (introduciendo conclusiones) so; **¿~ vienes o te quedas?** so are you coming with us or staying here? (b) (uso expletivo) well, anyway; ~**, como te iba diciendo …** well o anyway, as I was saying …

entornado -da adj ‹puerta› ajar, half-open; ‹ventana› slightly open; ‹ojos› half-closed

entorno m (a) (situación) environment (b) (Lit) setting (c) (Inf) environment

entorpecer [E3] *vt* **(a)** (dificultar) ⟨*tráfico*⟩ to hold up, slow down; ⟨*planes/movimiento*⟩ to hinder; **estas cajas entorpecen el paso** these boxes are (getting) in the way **(b)** ⟨*entendimiento/reacciones*⟩ to dull

■ **entorpecerse** *v pron* «*entendimiento/reacciones*» to become dulled

entrada *f* **1** (acción) entrance; **la ~ es gratuita** admission *o* entrance is free; **vigilaban sus ~s y salidas** they watched his comings and goings; ⑤ **prohibida la entrada** no entry; ⑤ **entrada libre** admission free; **la ~ de divisas** the inflow of foreign currency; **~ EN** *or* (esp AmL) **A algo** entry INTO sth; **forzaron su ~ en el** *or* **al edificio** they forced an entry into the building; **de ~** right from the start

2 (a) (en etapa, estado): **la ~ en vigor del nuevo impuesto** the coming into effect of the new tax **(b)** (ingreso, incorporación) entry; **la ~ de Prusia en la alianza** Prussia's entry into the alliance; **esto le facilitó la ~ a la universidad** that made it easier for him to get into university **(c)** (lugar de acceso) entrance; **espérame en** *or* **a la ~** wait for me at the entrance; **repartían folletos a la ~** they were handing out leaflets at the door **(d)** (vestíbulo) hall

3 (Espec) ticket; **los niños pagan media ~** it's half-price for children

4 (Com, Fin) **(a)** (Esp) (depósito) deposit **(b)** (ingreso) income; **~s y salidas** income and expenditure, receipts and outgoings

5 (de comida) starter

6 (Dep) **(a)** (en fútbol) tackle; **hacerle una ~ a algn** to tackle sb **(b)** (en béisbol) inning

7 (en el pelo): **tiene ~s** he has a receding hairline

entrado -da *adj*: **era entrada la noche** it was dark *o* night-time; **duró hasta bien entrada la tarde** it went on well into the evening

entrador -dora *adj* (AmL fam) (lanzado) daring, forward

entrante *adj* **(a)** (próximo): **el año ~** next year, the coming year **(b)** (nuevo) ⟨*gobierno/presidente*⟩ new, incoming (*before n*)

entrañable *adj* **(a)** ⟨*amistad*⟩ close, intimate; ⟨*amigo*⟩ very close, bosom (*before n*); ⟨*recuerdo*⟩ fond (*before n*) **(b)** ⟨*persona*⟩ pleasant, likable*

entrañar [A1] *vt* to entail, involve

entrañas *fpl* (vísceras) entrails (*pl*)

entrar [A1] *vi* **1** (acercándose) to come in; (alejándose) to go in; **déjame ~** let me in; **hazla ~** tell her to come in, show her in; **entró corriendo** he ran in, he came running in; **¿se puede ~ con el coche?** can you drive in?; **había gente entrando y saliendo** there were people coming and going; **¿cómo entró?** how did he get in?; **~ EN** *or* (esp AmL) **A algo** ⟨*a edificio/habitación*⟩ to go INTO sth; **entró en el** *or* **al banco** she went into the bank

2 (en etapa, estado) **~ EN algo** ⟨*a periodo/guerra/negociaciones*⟩ to enter sth; **~ en calor** to get warm; **entró en coma** he went into a coma

3 (a) (introducirse, meterse): **cierra la puerta, que entra frío** close the door, you're letting the cold in; **me entró arena en los zapatos** I've got sand in my shoes **(b)** (poderse meter): **¿entrará por la puerta?** will it get through the door?; (+ *me/te/le etc*): **estos vaqueros no me entran** I can't get into

these jeans; **el zapato no le entra** he can't get his shoe on; **no me entra la segunda** (Auto) I can't get it into second (gear)

4 «*hambre*» (+ *me/te/le etc*): **le entró hambre** she felt *o* got hungry; **me ha entrado la duda** I'm beginning to have my doubts; **me entró sueño** I got *o* began to feel sleepy

5 (empezar) to start, begin; **entró de aprendiz** he started *o* began as an apprentice

6 (incorporarse) **~ EN** *or* (esp AmL) **A algo** ⟨*en empresa/ejército/club*⟩ to join sth; ⟨*en convento*⟩ to enter sth; **el año que entré en** *or* **a la universidad** the year I started college I've just joined the association

7 (estar incluido): **el postre no entra en el precio** dessert is not included in the price; **¿cuántas entran en un kilo?** how many do you get in a kilo?

■ **~** *vt* (traer) to bring in; (llevar) to take in; **¿cómo van a ~ el sofá?** how are they going to get the sofa in?

entre *prep* **1 (a)** (dos personas, cosas) between; **lo decidieron ~ ellos dos** they decided it between the two of them; **está ~ las dos casas** it's between the two houses; **~ paréntesis** in brackets; **cuando hablan ~ los dos** when they talk to each other **(b)** (más de dos personas, cosas) among; **los alumnos hablaban ~ ellos** the pupils were talking among themselves; **~ otras cosas** among other things; **se perdió ~ la muchedumbre** he disappeared into the crowd; **~ estas cuatro paredes** within these walls **(c)** (indicando cooperación, distribución): **~ los tres logramos levantarlo** we managed to lift it between the three of us; **le hicimos un regalo ~ todos** we all got together and brought him a present; **repártelos ~ los niños/~ todos** share them out among the children/between everybody

2 (en expresiones de tiempo): **abierto ~ semana** open during the week; **llegaré ~ las tres y las cuatro** I'll be arriving between three and four; **cualquier semana ~ julio y agosto** any week in July or August

3 entre tanto meanwhile, in the meantime

■ *adv* (esp AmL): **~ más come más/menos engorda** the more he eats the more/less he puts on weight

entreabierto -ta *adj* ⟨*puerta*⟩ ajar, half-open; ⟨*ventana/ojos/boca*⟩ half-open

entreabrir [I33] *vt* to half-open

entrecejo *m* space between the eyebrows; **fruncir el ~** to frown

entrecortado -da *adj* ⟨*respiración*⟩ difficult, labored*; **con la voz entrecortada por la emoción** in a voice choked with emotion

entrecruzar [A4] *vt* to intertwine, interweave

entredicho *m* **1** (duda): **estar en ~** to be in doubt *o* question; **poner algo en ~** «*persona*» to question sth **2** (CS, Per) (entre dos personas) argument; (entre dos países) dispute

entrega *f* **1** (de pedido, paquete, carta) delivery; (de premio) presentation; **~ de premios** prize-giving; **la ~ de los documentos** the handing over of the documents; **el plazo para la ~ de solicitudes** the deadline for handing in *o* (frml) submitting applications; **servicio de ~ a domicilio** delivery service **2 (a)** (partida) delivery, shipment **(b)** (plazo, cuota) installment*

(c) (de enciclopedia) installment*, fascicle; (de revista) issue **3** (dedicación) dedication, devotion; (abandono) surrender

entregar [A3] *vt* **1** (llevar) ⟨*pedido/paquete/carta*⟩ to deliver
2 (a) (dar) to give; **me entregó un cuestionario** she gave me *o* handed me a questionnaire; **no quiso entregármelo** he refused to hand it over to me **(b)** ⟨*premio/trofeo*⟩ to present; ∼**le algo a algn** to present sb WITH sth **(c)** ⟨*trabajo/deberes/informe*⟩ to hand in, give in; ⟨*solicitud/impreso*⟩ to hand in, submit (fml)
3 (a) ⟨*ciudad/armas*⟩ to surrender; ⟨*poder/control*⟩ to hand over **(b)** ⟨*delincuente/prófugo*⟩ to turn in, hand over; ⟨*rehén*⟩ to hand over **(c)** ⟨*novia*⟩ to give away **(d)** (dedicar) to devote
■ **entregarse** *v pron* **1** (dedicarse) ∼**se a algo/algn** to devote oneself TO sth/sb
2 (a) (rendirse) to surrender, give oneself up; ∼**se a algo/algn** ⟨*al enemigo/a la policía*⟩ to give oneself up *o* surrender TO sth/sb **(b)** (abandonarse): **se entregó a la bebida** he gave himself over to drink

entrelazar [A4] *vt* ⟨*cintas/hilos*⟩ to interweave, intertwine; **con las manos entrelazadas** hand in hand
■ **entrelazarse** *v pron* to intertwine, interweave

entremedias, entremedio *adv* **(a)** (entre dos cosas) in between; **son muy caros o muy baratos, no hay nada** ∼ they're very expensive or very cheap, there's nothing in between; **lo metí** ∼ I put it in between **(b)** (mezclado con) ∼ **de algo** among; ∼ **de mis papeles/de la gente** among my papers/the people **(c)** (en el tiempo) in between

entremés *m* (Coc) hors d'oeuvre, starter

entremezclar [A1] *vt* to intermingle
■ **entremezclarse** *v pron* «*recuerdos*» to intermingle, become intermingled; «*culturas*» to mix, intermingle

entrenador -dora *m,f* (manager) coach, manager; (preparador físico) trainer

entrenamiento *m* **(a)** (por el entrenador) coaching, training **(b)** (ejercicios) training **(c)** (sesión) training session

entrenar [A1] *vt/vi* to train
■ **entrenarse** *v pron* to train

entrepierna *f* (Anat) crotch; (medida) inside leg measurement

entrepiso *m* (AmL) mezzanine

entreplanta *f* mezzanine

entretanto *adv* meanwhile, in the meantime

entretejer [E1] *vt* ⟨*hilos*⟩ (en tela) to weave; (entrelazar) to interweave

entretelones *mpl* (CS, Per) (de un caso) ins and outs (*pl*)

entretención *f* (AmL) ▶ ENTRETENIMIENTO

entretener [E27] *vt* **1** «*crucigrama/libro*» to keep ... amused; «*obra/payaso*» to entertain; **pintar me entretiene** I enjoy painting **2 (a)** (distraer, apartar de una tarea) to distract **(b)** (retener) to keep, detain; **no te entretengo más** I won't keep *o* detain you any longer
■ **entretenerse** *v pron* **1 (a)** (divertirse) to amuse oneself; **se entretiene con cualquier cosa** «*adulto*» she's easily amused; «*niño*» she's

happy playing with anything **(b)** (pasar el tiempo) to keep (oneself) busy *o* occupied **2** (demorarse) to hang around, dally about

entretenido -da *adj* **1** [SER] ⟨*película/conversación*⟩ entertaining, enjoyable; ⟨*persona*⟩ entertaining **2** [ESTAR] ⟨*persona*⟩ (ocupado) busy

entretenimiento *m* entertainment; **lo hace por** ∼ he does it for pleasure *o* for fun

entretiempo *m* **(a)** (período entre estaciones): **de** ∼ ⟨*abrigo*⟩ lightweight; ⟨*ropa*⟩ spring/autumn (*before n*) **(b)** (Chi) (Dep) halftime

entrever [E29] *vt* **(a)** (ver confusamente) to make out **(b)** ⟨*solución/acuerdo*⟩ to begin to see; **ha dejado** ∼ **que ...** she has hinted *o* suggested that ...

entreverado -da *adj* **(a)** (intercalado) interspersed **(b)** (fam) (desordenado, mezclado) muddled up, mixed up

entrevista *f* **(a)** (para trabajo, en periódico) interview **(b)** (period) (reunión) meeting

entrevistador -dora *m,f* interviewer

entrevistar [A1] *vt* to interview

entristecer [E3] *vt* to sadden
■ **entristecerse** *v pron* to grow sad

entrometerse [E1] *v pron* to meddle

entrometido -da *adj* meddling (*before n*), interfering (*before n*)
■ *m,f* meddler, busybody (colloq)

entronque *m* (AmL) (Ferr) junction

entumecerse [E3] *v pron* (perder la sensibilidad) to go numb; (perder la flexibilidad) to get stiff; **estar entumecido de frío** to be numb with cold

entusiasmado -da *adj* excited, enthusiastic; **está** ∼ **con la idea** he's excited *o* enthusiastic about the idea

entusiasmar [A1] *vt* (apasionar): **lo entusiasma el fútbol** he's crazy about football; **no me entusiasma mucho la idea** I'm not very enthusiastic about the idea
■ **entusiasmarse** *v pron* ∼**se con algo** to get excited *o* enthusiastic ABOUT sth

entusiasmo *m* enthusiasm

entusiasta *adj* enthusiastic
■ *mf* enthusiast

enumerar [A1] *vt* to list, enumerate (fml)

enunciar [A1] *vt* ⟨*idea/teoría*⟩ to state, enunciate (fml); ⟨*problema/teorema*⟩ to formulate

envainar [A1] *vt* ⟨*espada*⟩ to sheathe

envalentonar [A1] *vt* to make ... bolder, encourage
■ **envalentonarse** *v pron* (ponerse valiente) to become bolder *o* more daring; (insolentarse) to become defiant

envasar [A1] *vt* (en botellas) to bottle; (en latas) to can; (en paquetes, cajas) to pack

envase *m* (en general) container; (botella) bottle; (lata) can, tin (BrE)

envejecer [E3] *vi* **(a)** «*persona*» (hacerse más viejo) to age, grow old; (parecer más viejo) to age **(b)** «*vino/queso*» to mature, age
■ ∼ *vt* **(a)** ⟨*persona*⟩ ⟨*tragedia/experiencia*⟩ to age; ⟨*ropa/peinado*⟩ to make ... look older **(b)** ⟨*madera*⟩ to make ... look old; ⟨*vaqueros*⟩ to give ... a worn look

envejecido -da *adj* (a) ⟨*persona*⟩: está tan ~ he's aged so much, he looks so old (b) ⟨*cuero/madera*⟩ distressed

envenenamiento *m* poisoning

envenenar [A1] *vt* to poison

■ **envenenarse** *v pron* (involuntariamente) to be poisoned; (voluntariamente) to poison oneself

envergadura *f* (importancia) magnitude (frml), importance; **de cierta** ~ of some importance

enviado -da *m,f* (Pol) envoy; (Period) reporter, correspondent

enviar [A17] *vt* (a) ⟨*carta/paquete*⟩ to send; ⟨*pedido/mercancías*⟩ to send, dispatch (b) ⟨*persona*⟩ to send; **me envió por pan** she sent me out for bread

enviciarse [A1] *v pron* to become addicted, get hooked (colloq); ~ **CON algo** to become addicted TO sth *o* (colloq) hooked ON sth

envidia *f* envy, jealousy; **le da** ~ **que yo vaya** he's envious *o* jealous because I'm going; **le tienes** ~ you are jealous of him; **me muero de** ~ I'm green with envy; **¡qué** ~**!** I'm so jealous!

envidiable *adj* enviable

envidiar [A1] *vt* to envy; ~**le algo A algn** to envy sb sth

envidioso -sa *adj* envious

envío *m* [1] (acción): **el** ~ **de los fondos** the remittance *o* sending of the money; **fecha de** ~ date of dispatch, date sent; ~ **contra reembolso** COD, cash on delivery [2] (partida — de mercancías) consignment, shipment; (— de dinero) remittance

enviudar [A1] *vi* to be widowed

envoltorio *m* (a) (de paquete, regalo) wrapping; (de caramelo) wrapper (b) (bulto) bundle

envolver [E11] *vt* [1] ⟨*paquete/regalo*⟩ to wrap (up); **¿me lo puede** ~ **para regalo?** could you gift wrap it?; ~ **algo/a algn EN algo** to wrap sth/sb (up) IN sth [2] (rodear) «*membrana/capa*» to surround; «*humo/tristeza*» to envelop [3] (involucrar) to involve

■ **envolverse** *v pron* (a) (*refl*) (en manta) to wrap oneself (up) (b) (en delito, asunto) to become involved

envuelto -ta *adj* [1] ⟨*paquete/regalo*⟩ wrapped; ~ **para regalo** gift-wrapped [2] (rodeado) ~ **EN algo** ⟨*en humo/niebla*⟩ enveloped IN sth; ⟨*en misterio*⟩ cloaked *o* shrouded IN sth; ⟨*en una manta*⟩ wrapped (up) IN sth [3] (involucrado) ~ **EN algo** involved IN sth

enyesar [A1] *vt* (a) (Const) to plaster (b) ⟨*brazo/pierna*⟩ to put ... in a plaster cast, put ... in plaster (BrE)

enzarzarse [A4] *v pron* ~ **EN algo** to get involved IN sth

eñe *f. name of the letter* ñ

épica *f* (a) (género) epic poetry (b) (poema) epic

epicentro *m* epicenter*

épico -ca *adj* epic

epidemia *f* epidemic

epilepsia *f* epilepsy

epiléptico -ca *adj/m,f* epileptic

epílogo *m* (Lit) epilogue; (de suceso) conclusion

episodio *m* (Cin, Rad, TV) episode; (suceso) episode, incident

epístola *f* (frml *o* hum) epistle (frml *or* hum)

epitafio *m* epitaph

época *f* (a) (período de tiempo) time, period; **en la** ~ **de Franco** in Franco's time; **la** ~ **de los Tudor** the Tudor period; **muebles de** ~ period furniture; **en aquella** ~ in those days *o* at that time; **esa** ~ **de mi vida** that period of my life; **es música de mi** ~ it's music from my time (b) (parte del año) time of year; **la** ~ **de lluvias** the rainy season

epopeya *f* (a) (Lit) (poema) epic, epic poem (b) (empresa difícil): **el viaje fue toda una** ~ the journey turned out to be a real ordeal

equilátero -ra *adj* equilateral

equilibrado -da *adj* ⟨*persona/dieta*⟩ well-balanced, balanced; ⟨*lucha/partido*⟩ close

equilibrar [A1] *vt* ⟨*peso/carga/ruedas*⟩ to balance; ~ **las diferencias económicas** to redress economic imbalances

■ **equilibrarse** *v pron* «*fuerzas*» to even up; «*balanza de pagos*» to be restored; «*platillos de la balanza*» to balance out

equilibrio *m* (de fuerzas, estabilidad) balance; **perdió el** ~ he lost his balance; **en estado de** ~ in equilibrium

equilibrista *mf* (Espec) tightrope walker

equinoccio *m* equinox; ~ **de primavera/de otoño** vernal/autumnal equinox

equipaje *m* baggage (esp AmE), luggage (BrE); **facturar el** ~ to check in one's baggage *o* luggage; ~ **de mano** hand baggage *o* luggage; **viaja con poco** ~ he travels light

equipar [A1] *vt* (a) ⟨*persona*⟩ to equip, fit ... out; ~ **a algn CON** *or* **DE algo** to equip sb WITH sth (b) ⟨*casa*⟩ to furnish; ⟨*local/barco*⟩ to fit out; (de víveres) to provision; **una cocina bien equipada** a well-equipped kitchen

equiparable *adj* comparable

equiparar [A1] *vt* (a) (poner al mismo nivel) ~ **algo/a algn A** *or* **CON algo/algn** to put sth/sb on a level WITH sth/sb (b) (comparar) ~ **algo CON algo** to compare sth TO *o* WITH sth

equipo *m* [1] (de trabajadores, jugadores) team; **el** ~ **local/visitante** the home/visiting team; **trabajo de** ~ team work; **trabajar en** ~ to work as a team; ~ **de filmación** film crew [2] (de materiales, utensilios) equipment; ~ **de pesca** fishing tackle; ~ **de gimnasia** gym kit; ~ **de alta fidelidad** hi-fi system

equis *f. name of the letter* x

equitación *f* riding, horseback riding (AmE), horse riding (BrE); **practica (la)** ~ he rides

equitativo -va *adj* ⟨*persona*⟩ fair; ⟨*reparto*⟩ equitable

equivalente *adj* equivalent; ~ **A algo** equivalent TO sth

■ *m* equivalent; ~ **A** *or* **DE algo** equivalent OF sth

equivaler [E28] *vi* ~ **A algo** to be equivalent

TO sth; **¿a cuánto equivalen mil euros en libras?** how much is a thousand euros equivalent to *o* worth in pounds?

equivocación *f* mistake; **por ~** by mistake, in error (fml)

equivocado -da *adj* **(a)** ⟨*dato/número/ respuesta*⟩ wrong **(b)** [ESTAR] ⟨*persona*⟩ mistaken, wrong

equivocar [A2] *vt* ⟨*persona*⟩ to make … make a mistake, to make … go wrong

■ **equivocarse** *v pron* (cometer un error) to make a mistake; (estar en un error) to be wrong *o* mistaken; **me equivoqué con él** I was wrong about him; **me equivoqué de autobús** I took the wrong bus; **no te equivoques de fecha** don't get the date wrong; **se equivocó de camino** he went the wrong way

era *f* (período, época) era, age

era, éramos, etc ▶ SER

eras ▶ SER

erección *f* erection

erecto -ta *adj* erect

eres ▶ SER

erguido -da *adj* upright

erguir [I26] *vt* (liter) ⟨*cabeza*⟩ to raise, lift; ⟨*cuello*⟩ to straighten

■ **erguirse** *v pron* (liter) «*persona*» to stand up; «*edificio/torre*» to rise

erigir [I7] *vt* **(a)** (fml) ⟨*edificio*⟩ to build, erect (fml); ⟨*monumento*⟩ to erect (fml), to raise (fml) **(b)** (fml) (convertir, elevar) **~ algo/a algn EN algo** to set sth/sb up AS sth

■ **erigirse** *v pron* (llegar a ser) **~se EN algo** to become sth; (atribuirse funciones de) to set oneself up AS sth

erizado -da *adj* (de punta): **tenía el pelo ~** her hair was standing on end

erizar [A4] *vt* ⟨*pelo/vello*⟩ to make … stand on end

■ **erizarse** *v pron* «*pelo*» to stand on end

erizo *m* hedgehog; **~ de mar** sea urchin

ermita *f* chapel

ermitaño -ña *m,f* (asceta) hermit

erosión *f* erosion

erosionar [A1] *vt* to erode

■ **erosionarse** *v pron* to be/become eroded

erótico -ca *adj* erotic

erotismo *m* eroticism

erradicar [A2] *vt* (fml) to eradicate

errado -da *adj* **1** (desacertado): **cinco tiros ~s** five misses **2** (esp AmL) **(a)** [ESTAR] ⟨*persona*⟩ mistaken, wrong; **están muy ~s en estos cálculos** they're way off the mark with these calculations **(b)** [SER] ⟨*decisión*⟩ wrong; ⟨*política*⟩ misguided

errante *adj* **(a)** ⟨*persona*⟩ wandering (*before n*), roaming (*before n*); ⟨*pueblo*⟩ wandering (*before n*) **(b)** ⟨*mirada*⟩ faraway, distant; **una vida ~** a nomadic existence

errar [A26] *vt* ⟨*tiro/golpe*⟩ to miss; **erró su vocación** she chose the wrong vocation/career

■ **~** *vi* «*tirador*» to miss; **erró en su decisión** he made the wrong decision

errata *f* (error de imprenta) misprint, printer's error; (error de mecanografía) typing error

erre *f*. name of the letter r

erróneo -nea *adj* (fml) ⟨*decisión/afirmación*⟩ wrong, erroneous (fml)

error *m* mistake; **cometer un ~** to make a mistake *o* an error; **~ de ortografía** spelling mistake; **~ de cálculo** miscalculation; **~ de imprenta** misprint, printer's error; **por ~** by mistake, in error (fml)

eructar [A1] *vi* to belch, burp (colloq)

eructo *m* belch, burp (colloq)

erudición *f* erudition (fml), learning

erudito -ta *adj* ⟨*lenguaje/obra*⟩ erudite; ⟨*persona*⟩ learned, knowledgeable; **~ EN algo** learned IN sth, knowledgeable ABOUT sth

■ *m,f* scholar

erupción *f* **(a)** (de volcán) eruption; **el volcán entró en ~** the volcano erupted **(b)** (en la piel) rash, eruption (fml)

es ▶ SER

esbelto -ta *adj* slender

esbozar [A4] *vt* **(a)** ⟨*figura*⟩ to sketch **(b)** ⟨*idea/tema*⟩ to outline

esbozo *m* **(a)** (Art) sketch **(b)** (de proyecto) outline, rough draft

escabeche *m* pickling brine (*made with oil, vinegar, peppercorns and bay leaves*)

escabroso -sa *adj* **(a)** ⟨*terreno*⟩ rugged, rough **(b)** ⟨*asunto/problema/tema*⟩ thorny, tricky; ⟨*escena/relato*⟩ shocking

escabullirse [I9] *v pron* (escaparse) to slip away; **logró ~ entre la multitud** he managed to slip away into the crowd; **no puedes escabullirte de tus responsabilidades** you can't get away from your responsibilities

escafandra *f* diving suit

escala *f* **1** (en general) scale; **~ centígrada/ Fahrenheit** centigrade *o* Celsius/Fahrenheit scale; **~ de valores** set of values; **~ musical** (musical) scale; **la ~ social** the social scale; **hecho a ~** done to scale; **a gran ~** on a large scale **2** (Aviac, Náut) stopover; **hicimos ~ en Roma** we stopped over in Rome

escalada *f* **1** (Dep) (de montaña) climb, ascent **2** (aumento, subida): **una ~ de la violencia** an escalation of violence; **la ~ de los precios** the increase *o* escalation in prices

escalador -dora *m,f* (de montañas) mountaineer, climber; (de rocas) rock-climber; (en ciclismo) climber, mountain rider

escalafón *m* scale; **subir un puesto en el ~** to go up one step on the promotion ladder

escalar [A1] *vt* ⟨*montaña/pared*⟩ to climb, scale; (en jerarquía, clasificación) to climb (up)

■ **~** *vi* (Dep) to climb, go climbing

escaldar [A1] *vt* **(a)** ⟨*acelgas/tomates*⟩ to blanch, scald **(b)** ⟨*manos/persona*⟩ to scald

■ **escaldarse** *v pron* **(a)** (con agua, vapor) to scald oneself **(b)** «*bebé*» to get diaper (AmE) *o* (BrE) nappy rash

escalera *f* **1** (de edificio) stairs (*pl*), staircase; **bajó las ~s** he came downstairs *o* down the stairs; **el hueco de la ~** the stairwell; **~ (de) caracol** spiral staircase; **~ mecánica** escalator **2** (portátil) *tb* **~ de mano** ladder; (de tijera) stepladder **3** (en naipes) run; (juego de tablero) snakes and ladders

escalfar [A1] *vt* to poach

escalinata *f* staircase, steps (*pl*)

escalofriante *adj* ⟨*crimen/escena*⟩ horrifying; ⟨*cifra*⟩ staggering, incredible

escalofrío *m* shiver; **me da** ~**s** it makes me shiver *o* shudder; **tiene** ~**s** she's shivering

escalón *m* (peldaño) step; (travesaño) rung

escalonar [A1] *vt* ⟨*pagos/vacaciones*⟩ to stagger; ⟨*terreno*⟩ to terrace

escalope *m* escalope

escama *f* **(a)** (Zool) scale **(b)** (en la piel) flake

escamotear [A1] *vt* **(a)** (ocultar) ⟨*naipe*⟩ to palm; ⟨*informe*⟩ to keep … secret; **nos escamoteaban la información** they were keeping the information (secret) from us **(b)** (robar) to swipe

escampar [A1] *v impers* to stop raining, to clear up

■ ~ *vi* (Col) to shelter

escanciar [A1] *vt* (frml) ⟨*vino*⟩ to serve; ⟨*sidra*⟩ to pour (*from a height*)

escandalizar [A4] *vt/vi* to shock

■ **escandalizarse** *v pron* to be shocked

escándalo *m* **1** (hecho, asunto chocante) scandal; **¡qué ~!** **¡qué manera de vestir!** what a shocking *o* an outrageous way to dress! **2** (alboroto, jaleo) fuss; **tanto ~ para nada** all this fuss over nothing; **cuando lo sepa va a armar un ~** when she finds out she'll kick up a fuss; **no armen tanto ~** don't make such a racket *o* row (colloq); **nada de ~s dentro del local** we don't want any trouble in here

escandaloso -sa *adj* **(a)** ⟨*conducta*⟩ shocking, scandalous; ⟨*ropa*⟩ outrageous; ⟨*película*⟩ shocking; ⟨*vida*⟩ scandalous **(b)** (ruidoso) ⟨*persona/griterío*⟩ noisy; ⟨*risa*⟩ loud, uproarious

Escandinavia *f* Scandinavia

escandinavo -va *adj/m,f* Scandinavian

escaño *m* (Esp) (Pol) (cargo, asiento) seat; (banco) bench

escapada *f* **(a)** (huida) breakout, escape **(b)** (de un peligro) escape **(c)** (en ciclismo) breakaway

escapar [A1] *vi* **1** to escape; ~ **DE algo** ⟨*de cárcel/rutina/peligro*⟩ to escape FROM sth; ⟨*de castigo/muerte*⟩ to escape sth **2** **dejar escapar** ⟨*carcajada/suspiro*⟩ to let out, give; ⟨*oportunidad*⟩ to pass up; ⟨*persona/animal*⟩ to let … get away

■ **escaparse** *v pron* **1** «*prisionero*» to escape; «*animal/niño*» to run away; ~**se DE algo** ⟨*de cárcel/jaula*⟩ to escape FROM sth; ⟨*de situación/castigo*⟩ to escape sth; ~**se DE algn** ⟨*de policía/perseguidor*⟩ to escape (FROM) sth; ~**se de casa** to run away from home; **se me escapó el perro** the dog got away from me **2** (+ *me/te/le etc*) (involuntariamente): **se le escapó un grito** he cried out, he let out a cry **(b)** (pasar inadvertido): **no se le escapa nada** he doesn't miss anything; **se me escapó ese detalle** that detail escaped my notice **3** «*gas/aire/agua*» to leak

escaparate *m* **(a)** (esp Esp) (de tienda) shop window **(b)** (Col) (vitrina) display cabinet; (aparador) sideboard **(c)** (Ven) (armario) wardrobe

escapatoria *f* (salida, solución) way out

escape *m* **(a)** (fuga) escape **(b)** (de gas, fluido) leak **(c)** (Auto) exhaust

escapismo *m* escapism

escarabajo *m* beetle

escaramuza *f* (Mil) skirmish; (Dep) scrimmage

escarbadientes *m* (*pl* ~) toothpick

escarbar [A1] *vi* **(a)** (en la tierra — haciendo un hoyo) to dig; (— superficialmente) to scrabble *o* scratch around **(b)** (buscando algo) ~ **EN algo** ⟨*en cajón/armario*⟩ to rummage (about *o* around) IN sth; **perros escarbando en la basura** dogs rummaging through the garbage

■ ~ *vt*: ~ **la tierra** (hacer un hoyo) to dig a hole; (superficialmente) to scratch around in the soil

■ **escarbarse** *v pron* (refl) ⟨*nariz/dientes*⟩ to pick

escarcha *f* frost

escarchar [A1] *vt* to crystallize

escarlata *adj inv/m* scarlet

escarlatina *f* scarlet fever, scarlatina

escarmentar [A5] *vi* to learn one's lesson; **¡para que escarmientes!** that'll teach you!; **no escarmienta** she never learns

■ ~ *vt* to teach … a lesson

escarmiento *m* lesson; **habrá que darle un buen ~** he needs to be taught a good lesson

escarola *f* escarole, endive (BrE)

escarpado -da *adj* ⟨*montaña/terreno*⟩ precipitous; ⟨*pared/acantilado*⟩ sheer, steep

escarpín *m* (AmL) (calcetín — de bebé) bootee; (— de adulto) bed sock

escasear [A1] *vi*: **empiezan a ~ los alimentos** food is running short; **va a ~ el café** there's going to be a coffee shortage

escasez *f* shortage; **hubo ~ de agua** there was a water shortage; **por ~ de medios** owing to a lack of resources

escaso -sa *adj* **(a)** ⟨*recursos económicos*⟩ limited, scant; ⟨*posibilidades*⟩ slim, slender; ⟨*visibilidad*⟩ poor; ⟨*conocimientos/experiencia*⟩ limited **(b)** [ESTAR] (falto) ~ **DE algo** ⟨*de dinero/tiempo*⟩ short OF sth

escatimar [A1] *vt* ⟨*comida/tela*⟩ to skimp on, be sparing with; **no** ~**on esfuerzos** they spared no effort

escayola *f* (Esp) (material) plaster; (Med) plaster cast

escayolar [A1] *vt* (Esp) to put … in a (plaster) cast, to put … in plaster (BrE)

escena *f* **1** **(a)** (de obra) scene; **la ~ del duelo** the duel scene **(b)** (sin art) (escenario): **poner en ~** to stage; **entrar en ~** to come/go on stage **2** **la ~ del accidente** (period) the scene of the accident; **no me hagas una ~** there's no need to make a scene

escenario *m* (Teatr) stage

escenografía *f* (decorado) scenery; (arte) scenography, set design

escenógrafo -fa *m,f* scenographer, set designer

escepticismo *m* skepticism*

escéptico -ca *adj* skeptical*

■ *m,f* skeptic*

esclarecer [E3] *vt* ⟨*situación/hechos*⟩ to clarify, elucidate (frml); ⟨*crimen/misterio*⟩ to clear up

esclavitud *f* slavery

esclavizar [A4] *vt* to enslave; **está esclavizado por el trabajo** he's a slave to his work

esclavo -va *m,f* slave; **es un ~ del trabajo** he is a slave to his work

esclerosis *f* sclerosis; **~ múltiple** multiple sclerosis

esclusa *f* (de canal) lock; (de presa) floodgate

escoba *f* (para barrer) broom; (de bruja) broomstick

escobilla *f* **(a)** (de motor) brush **(b)** (del limpiaparabrisas) wiper-blade, blade **(c)** (del inodoro) toilet brush

escocedura *f* irritation; (de bebé) diaper rash (AmE), nappy rash (BrE)

escocer [E10] *vi* «herida/ojos» to sting, smart

escocés -cesa *adj* **(a)** ‹ciudad/persona› Scottish; ‹dialecto› Scots **(b)** ‹whisky› Scotch; ‹tela/manta› tartan
■ *m,f* (m) Scotsman, Scot; (f) Scotswoman, Scot

Escocia *f* Scotland

escocido -da *adj* ‹cuello/axila› sore, chafed; **tiene las nalgas escocidas** he has diaper rash (AmE) o (BrE) nappy rash

escoger [E6] *vt* to choose; **escoge que quieras** pick o choose whichever (one) you want; **no hay mucho (de) donde ~** there isn't a great deal of choice, there isn't much to choose from

escogido -da *adj* **(a)** (selecto) ‹mercancía/clientela› choice; ‹clientela› select **(b)** (Méx fam) (manoseado) picked over

escolar *adj* school (before n)
■ *m,f* (m) schoolboy, schoolchild; (f) schoolgirl, schoolchild

escolaridad *f* education, schooling

escolarizar [A4] *vt* to educate, provide schooling for; **niños sin ~** children without any (formal) education o schooling

escoleta *f* (Méx) **(a)** (banda) band (of amateur musicians) **(b)** (ensayo) rehearsal

escollo *m* (Náut) reef; (dificultad) obstacle, hurdle

escolta *m,f* (persona) escort; (en baloncesto) guard
■ *f* (grupo) escort

escoltar [A1] *vt* to escort

escombros *mpl* rubble

esconder [E1] *vt* to hide, conceal (frml)
■ **esconderse** *v pron* 1 (refl) «persona» to hide; **~se DE algn** to hide FROM sb 2 (estar oculto) to hide, lie hidden

escondidas *fpl* 1 (AmL) (Jueg): **jugar a las ~** to play hide-and-seek 2 **a escondidas** in secret, secretly; **hacer algo a ~ de algn** to do sth behind sb's back

escondido -da *adj* **(a)** (oculto) hidden **(b)** (lejano) remote

escondite *m* **(a)** (para personas) hideout; (para cosas) hiding place **(b)** (Jueg): **jugar al ~** to play hide-and-seek

escondrijo *m* hidden place, recess (liter)

escopeta *f* shotgun

escoria *f* (de fundición) slag; **la ~ de la sociedad** the dregs of society

Escorpio *m* (signo) Scorpio; **es (de) ~** he's a Scorpio
■ *mf* (pl ~ or -pios) (persona) tb escorpio Scorpio

escorpión *m* scorpion

escotado -da *adj* **(a)** ‹blusa/vestido› low-cut; **~ por detrás** cut low at the back **(b)** (RPl) ‹zapato› strapless

escote *m* (Indum) neck, neckline; (profundo) low-cut neck o neckline; **~ redondo** round neck; (en suéters) crew neck; **~ en pico** V neck; **pagar a ~** (Esp fam) to go Dutch

escotilla *f* hatch, hatchway

escozor *m* **(a)** (Med) stinging, burning sensation **(b)** (resentimiento, amargura) bitterness

escribanía *f* (RPl) (Der) (oficina) notary's office; (profesión): **ejerce la ~** he is a practicing notary (public)

escribano -na *m,f* **(a)** (Hist) (amanuense) scribe **(b)** (RPl) (notario) notary (public)

escribiente *mf* clerk

escribir [I34] *vt* 1 **(a)** (anotar) to write; **escríbelo aquí** write it down here **(b)** (ser autor de) ‹libro/canción/carta› to write
2 (ortográficamente) to write; **la escribió sin acento** she wrote it without an accent; **no sé cómo se escribe** I don't know how you spell it; **se escribe sin acento** it's written without an accent
■ **~** *vi* to write; **nunca le escribe** she never writes him (AmE) o (BrE) writes to him; **~ a máquina** to type
■ **escribirse** *v pron* (recípr): **me escribo con ella** we write to each other; **se escribe con un peruano** she has a Peruvian penfriend o penpal

escrito¹ -ta *adj* ‹examen› written; **por ~** in writing

escrito² *m* (documento) document

escritor -tora *m,f* writer, author

escritorio *m* **(a)** (mueble) desk **(b)** (AmL) (oficina, despacho) office; (en casa particular) study; **~ público** (en Méx) office or stall offering letter writing, form-filling or typing services

escritura *f* 1 (sistema de signos) writing; (letra) writing, handwriting 2 (Der) (documento) deed; **la ~ de la casa** the deeds to o of the house

escrúpulo *m* scruple

escrupuloso -sa *adj* **(a)** (honrado) honest, scrupulous **(b)** (meticuloso) meticulous **(c)** (Esp) (aprensivo) fastidious

escrutinio *m* **(a)** (Pol) count; **los resultados del ~** the results of the ballot **(b)** (inspección) scrutiny

escuadra *f* 1 (instrumento — triangular) set square; (— de carpintero) square 2 (en el ejército) squad; (en la marina) squadron

escuadrón *m* **(a)** (Aviac) squadron **(b)** (de caballería) squadron; (más pequeño) troop

escuálido -da *adj* ‹persona/animal› skinny, scrawny

escuchar [A1] *vt* **(a)** (prestar atención) ‹música/persona› to listen to **(b)** (esp AmL) (oír) to hear
■ **~** *vi* to listen

escudarse [A1] *v pron*: **quiso ~ en su inmunidad diplomática** he tried to hide behind his diplomatic immunity

escudero *m* (Hist, Mil) squire

escudilla *f* bowl

escudo *m* **(a)** (Hist, Mil) shield **(b)** (emblema) tb **~ de armas** coat of arms **(c)** (en la solapa, etc) badge

escudriñar [A1] *vt* **(a)** (liter) (mirar intensamente) ⋯

⟨*horizonte*⟩ to scan **(b)** (examinar) ⟨*persona*⟩ to scrutinize, examine; ⟨*casa/habitación*⟩ to search ... thoroughly

escuela *f* school; ~ **de conductores** *or* **choferes** (AmL) driving school; ~ **primaria** primary school; ~ **militar/naval** military/naval academy; ~ **pública** public (AmE) *o* (BrE) state school; **E~ de Medicina** Medical Faculty *o* School

escueto -ta *adj* ⟨*explicación*⟩ succinct; ⟨*lenguaje/estilo*⟩ concise, plain; **fue muy** ~ he was very succinct

escuincle -cla *m,f* (Méx fam) kid (colloq)

esculcar [A2] *vt* (AmC, Col, Méx, Ven) ⟨*cajones/papeles*⟩ to go through; ⟨*persona/casa*⟩ to search

esculpir [I1] *vt* ⟨*estatua/busto*⟩ to sculpt, sculpture; ⟨*inscripción*⟩ to engrave, carve
■ ~ *vi* to sculpt, sculpture

escultor -tora *m,f* sculptor

escultura *f* sculpture; ~ **en madera** wood carving

escupida *f* (RPl) gob (of spit) (colloq)

escupir [I1] *vi* to spit; ~**le a** algn to spit AT sb; **le escupió en la cara** he spat in her face
■ ~ *vt* **(a)** ⟨*comida*⟩ to spit out; ⟨*sangre*⟩ to spit, cough up **(b)** ⟨*llamas/lava*⟩ to belch out

escupitajo *m* gob (of spit) (colloq)

escupo *m* (Chi, Ven) gob (of spit) (colloq)

escurreplatos *m* (*pl* ~) (mueble) cupboard with built-in plate rack; (rejilla) plate rack

escurridizo -za *adj* ⟨*piel/jabón*⟩ slippery; ⟨*persona/respuesta*⟩ evasive; ⟨*idea/concepto*⟩ elusive

escurrir [I1] *vt* ⟨*ropa*⟩ to wring out, wring; ⟨*verduras/pasta*⟩ to strain, drain; ⟨*líquido*⟩ to drain (off)
■ ~ *vi* to drain; **dejar** ~ ⟨*platos*⟩ to leave ... to drain; ⟨*camisa*⟩ to leave ... to drip-dry
■ **escurrirse** *v pron* ⏎1⏎ **(a)** ⟨*líquido*⟩: **cuelga la camisa para que se escurra el agua** hang the shirt out to drip-dry **(b)** ⟨*verduras/vajilla*⟩ to drain ⏎2⏎ **(a)** (escapar, escabullirse) to slip away; ~**se DE** algo to wriggle *o* get out OF sth **(b)** (resbalarse, deslizarse) to slip

escúter *m* scooter

esdrújula *f* word with the stress on the antepenultimate syllable

ese¹ *f*: name of the letter s

ese², esa *adj dem* (*pl* **esos, esas**) that; (*pl*) those; **en** ~ **país/esos países** in that country/those countries

ése, ésa *pron dem* (*pl* **ésos, ésas**) [*The written accent may be omitted for clarity when there is no confusion with the adjective*] **(a)** that one; (*pl*) those; ~ *or* **ese es el tuyo** that (one) is yours; **prefiero ésos** *or* **esos** I prefer those (ones); [*usually indicates disapproval when used to refer to a person*] **ésa** *or* **esa no sabe lo que dice** (fam) she doesn't know what she's talking about **(b)** **ésas** (fam) (esas cosas, esos asuntos): **¡conque ésas** *or* **esas tenemos!** so that's it!; **¡no me vengas con ésas** *or* **esas!** don't give me that! (colloq)

esencia *f* essence

esencial *adj* (fundamental) essential; **coincidimos en lo** ~ we agree on the essentials *o* on the main points; **lo** ~ **es** ... the main *o* the most important thing is ...

esfera *f* **(a)** (Astron, Mat) sphere **(b)** (de reloj) face **(c)** (ámbito) sphere; **en las altas** ~**s de la política** in the highest political circles

esférico -ca *adj* spherical

esfero *m* (Col fam) ballpoint pen, biro® (BrE)

esfinge *f* sphinx

esforzar [A11] *vt* ⟨*voz/vista*⟩ to strain
■ **esforzarse** *v pron*: **se esforzó mucho** he tried very hard, he put in a lot of effort; **tienes que** ~**te más** you'll have to work harder; ~**se POR** *o* **EN hacer algo** to strive to do sth

esfuerzo *m* effort; **hizo el** ~ **de ser amable** he made an effort *o* tried to be friendly

esfumarse [A1] *v pron* **(a)** ⟨*ilusiones/sueños*⟩ to evaporate; ⟨*temores*⟩ to melt away, be dispelled **(b)** (fam) ⟨*persona/dinero*⟩ to vanish, disappear

esgrima *f* fencing

esgrimista *mf* fencer

esguince *m* sprain; **sufrió un** ~ **en el tobillo** he sprained his ankle

eslabón *m* link

eslálom (*pl* **-loms**), **eslalon** *m* slalom

eslavo -va *adj* Slavic, Slavonic
■ *m,f* Slav

eslogan *m* (*pl* **-lóganes**) slogan

eslovaco¹ -ca *adj* Slovakian
■ *m,f* Slovak

eslovaco² *m* (idioma) Slovak

Eslovaquia *f* Slovakia

esmaltar [A1] *vt* ⟨*metal*⟩ to enamel; ⟨*cerámica*⟩ to glaze

esmalte *m* **(a)** (capa — sobre metales) enamel; (— sobre cerámica) glaze; ~ **de** *or* **para uñas** nail polish *o* (BrE) varnish **(b)** (Odont) enamel **(c)** (Art) enamel

esmerado -da *adj* ⟨*persona*⟩ conscientious, painstaking; ⟨*presentación*⟩ careful, painstaking; ⟨*trabajo*⟩ carefully done

esmeralda *f* emerald

esmerarse [A1] *v pron* to go to a lot of trouble; **se esmera en hacerlo bien** she goes to great pains to do it properly

esmero *m* care

esmirriado -da *adj* (fam) ⟨*persona*⟩ skinny (colloq), scrawny (colloq); ⟨*animal*⟩ scrawny

esmog *m* smog

esmoquin *m* (*pl* **-móquines**) tuxedo (AmE), dinner jacket (BrE)

esnifar [A1] *vt* ⟨*cocaína*⟩ (arg) to snort (sl); ⟨*pegamento*⟩ to sniff (colloq)

esnob *adj* (*pl* **-nobs**) snobbish
■ *mf* (*pl* **-nobs**) snob

esnobismo *m* snobbery, snobbishness

eso *pron dem* **(a)** (*neutro*) that; **no digas ∼** don't say that; **∼ que te contaron** what they told you **(b)** (*en locs*) **a eso de** (at) around *o* about; **en eso: en ∼ llegó su madre** (just) at that moment her mother arrived; **¡eso es!** that's it!; **y eso que …** even though …; **por ∼** that's why **(c)** **¡eso!** (*interj*) exactly!

esófago *m* esophagus*

esos, esas *pron dem:* ► ESE[2]

ésos, ésas *adj dem:* ► ÉSE

espabilado -da *adj* **(a)** (despierto) awake **(b)** (vivo, listo) bright, smart; **tienes que ser más ∼** you have to keep more on the ball
■ *m,f:* **los ∼s de la clase** the smart ones of the class

espabilar [A1] *vt* **(a)** (quitar el sueño) to wake … up **(b)** (avivar) to wise … up (colloq)
■ **∼** *vi* **(a)** (sacudirse el sueño) to wake up **(b)** (darse prisa) to get a move on (colloq) **(c)** (avivarse) to wise up (colloq)
■ **espabilarse** *v pron* **(a)** (sacudirse el sueño) to wake (oneself) up **(b)** (darse prisa) to get a move on (colloq) **(c)** (avivarse) to wise up (colloq)

espaciado -da *adj* **(a)** (en el espacio): **los árboles están muy ∼s** the trees are too far apart **(b)** (en el tiempo): **sus visitas se hicieron más espaciadas** her visits became more infrequent

espacial *adj* **(a)** ⟨cohete/vuelo⟩ space (*before n*) **(b)** (Fís, Mat) spatial

espacio *m* [1] **(a)** (amplitud) space, room; **ocupan demasiado ∼** they take up too much space *o* room **(b)** (entre líneas, palabras) space; (entre objetos) space, gap; **rellenar los ∼s en blanco** fill in the blank spaces *o* the blanks **(c)** (recinto, área) area [2] (Espac): **el ∼** space; **∼ aéreo** airspace [3] (de tiempo): **un corto ∼ de tiempo** a short space of time; **por ∼ de 24 horas** for 24 hours *o* for a period of 24 hours [4] **(a)** (Rad, TV) (programa) program*; **∼ publicitario** advertising slot **(b)** (en periódico, revista) space

espacioso -sa *adj* spacious

espada *f* [1] (arma) sword [2] **(a)** (carta) *any card of the* ESPADAS *suit* **(b)** **espadas** *fpl* (palo) *one of the suits in a Spanish pack of cards*

espagetis, espaguettis *mpl* spaghetti

espalda *f* back; **ancho de ∼** broad-shouldered; **perdona, te estoy dando la ∼** sorry, I've got my back to you; **de ∼s a nosotros** with his/her back to us; **vuélvete de ∼** turn around *o* (BrE) round; **los 100 metros ∼** the 100 meters backstroke; **tenderse de ∼s** to lie on one's back; **lo atacaron por la ∼** he was attacked from behind; **hacer algo a ∼s de algn** to do sth behind sb's back

espantado -da *adj* **(a)** (asustado) frightened, scared; **salieron ∼s** they ran off in fright **(b)** (horrorizado) horrified, appalled

espantapájaros *m* (*pl* ∼) scarecrow

espantar [A1] *vt* [1] **(a)** (ahuyentar) ⟨peces/pájaros⟩ to frighten away *o* scare **(b)** (asustar) ⟨caballo⟩ to frighten, scare [2] (fam) (horrorizar) to horrify, appall*
■ **∼** *vi* **(a)** (fam) (asustar): **es tan feo que espanta** he's absolutely hideous (colloq) **(b)** (Bol, Col, Ven fam) «*fantasma*»: **en esa casa espantan** that house is haunted

■ **espantarse** *v pron* «*pájaro/peces*» to get frightened away; «*caballo*» to take fright, be startled

espanto *m* [1] **(a)** (miedo) fright, horror **(b)** (uso hiperbólico): **la noticia nos llenó de ∼** we were horrified *o* appalled at the news; **hace un frío de ∼** (fam) it's freezing *o* terribly cold (colloq); **ya está curada de ∼** (fam) she's seen/heard it all before [2] (Bol, Col, Ven fam) (espíritu) ghost, spook (colloq)

espantoso -sa *adj* **(a)** ⟨escena/crimen⟩ horrific, appalling **(b)** (fam) (uso hiperbólico) ⟨comida/letra/tiempo⟩ atrocious; ⟨vestido/color⟩ hideous; ⟨ruido/voz⟩ terrible, awful; **pasé un frío ∼** I was absolutely freezing (colloq)

España *f* Spain

español[1] -ñola *adj* Spanish
■ *m,f* (persona) (*m*) Spaniard, Spanish man; (*f*) Spaniard, Spanish woman; **los ∼es** the Spanish, Spaniards, Spanish people

español[2] *m* (idioma) Spanish

esparadrapo *m* surgical tape

esparcir [I4] *vt* **(a)** ⟨libros/juguetes⟩ to scatter **(b)** ⟨rumor⟩ to spread **(c)** (Chi) ⟨mantequilla⟩ to spread
■ **esparcirse** *v pron* **(a)** «*líquido*» to spread; «*papeles/semillas*» to be scattered **(b)** «*noticia/rumor*» to spread

espárrago *m* asparagus; **mandar a algn a freír ∼s** (fam) to tell sb to get lost (colloq)

espasmo *m* spasm

espátula *f* **(a)** (paleta) spatula; (Art) palette knife **(b)** (para quitar pintura, papel) scraper

especia *f* (condimento) spice

especial *adj* **(a)** (en general) special; **en ∼** especially, particularly; **nadie en ∼** nobody in particular; **un día muy ∼ para mí** a very special day for me **(b)** (difícil) ⟨persona/carácter⟩ fussy

especialidad *f* **(a)** (actividad, estudio) specialty (AmE), speciality (BrE); **hizo dos años de ∼** she did two years' specialization **(b)** (de restaurante) specialty (AmE), speciality (BrE)

especialista *adj* specialist (*before n*)
■ *mf* **(a)** (experto) specialist, expert **(b)** (Med) specialist; **un ∼ de(l) corazón** a heart specialist **(c)** (Cin, TV) (*m*) stuntman; (*f*) stuntwoman

especialización *f* specialization

especializado -da *adj* ⟨librería/restaurante⟩ specialty (*before n*) (AmE), specialist (*before n*) (BrE); **∼ EN algo** specializing IN sth **(b)** ⟨lenguaje⟩ technical, specialized **(c)** ⟨obrero⟩ skilled, specialized (*before n*)

especializarse [A4] *v pron* to specialize

especie *f* **(a)** (Biol, Bot, Zool) species **(b)** (clase) kind, sort

especificar [A2] *vt* to specify

específico -ca *adj* specific

espécimen *m* (*pl* **-címenes**) (ejemplar) specimen; (muestra) sample, specimen

espectacular *adj* spectacular

espectáculo *m* [1] (representación) show; **un ∼ de variedades** a variety show; **❺ espectáculos** (en periódicos) entertainment guide; **el mundo del ∼** showbusiness [2] (visión, panorama) sight; **un triste ∼** a sad sight *o* spectacle

espectador -dora *m,f* (Dep) spectator; (Espec) ⋯⋮

member of the audience; **asistieron al estreno dos mil ~es** two thousand people attended the premiere

espectro m [1] (gama) spectrum [2] (fantasma) specter*, ghost; (amenaza) specter*

especulación f speculation

especulador -dora m,f speculator

especular [A1] vi to speculate

espejismo m (fenómeno óptico) mirage; (ilusión) illusion

espejo m mirror; **~ de cuerpo entero** full-length mirror; **lateral/retrovisor** wing/rear-view mirror; **mirarse al ~** to look (at oneself) in the mirror; **la obra es ~ de esa sociedad** the play mirrors that society

espeleología f spelunking, potholing (BrE)

espeluznante adj ‹tragedia/estado/experiencia› horrific, horrifying; ‹grito› terrifying, blood-curdling

espera f [1] (acción, periodo) wait; **una larga ~** a long wait; **estoy a la ~ de una oferta concreta** I am waiting for a concrete offer; **en ~ de su respuesta saluda a Vd. atte.** (frml) I look forward to hearing from you, yours faithfully [2] (Der) respite

esperado -da adj (a) (aguardado) ‹acontecimiento/carta› eagerly awaited (b) (que es de esperar): **no obtuvo los resultados ~s** he didn't get the results he expected

esperanza f hope; **mi única ~** my only hope; **puso todas sus ~s en su hijo** he pinned all his hopes on his son; **hay ~s de éxito** there are hopes that he/it/they will succeed; **perdimos toda ~ de encontrarlos vivos** we gave up o lost hope of finding them alive; **fue con la ~ de que …** he went in the hope that …; **me dio ~s de que el niño mejoraría** he gave me hope that the child would recover; **~ de vida** life expectancy

esperanzado -da adj hopeful

esperanzador -dora adj encouraging

esperar [A1] vt [1] (a) ‹autobús/persona/acontecimiento› to wait for; **¿qué estás esperando para decírselo?** tell him! what are you waiting for? (b) (recibir) to meet; **la fuimos a ~ al aeropuerto** we went to meet her at the airport (c) «sorpresa» to await; **le espera un futuro difícil** he has a difficult future ahead of him [2] (a) (contar con, prever) to expect; **tal como esperábamos** just as we expected; **cuando uno menos lo espera** when you least expect it; **te espero alrededor de las nueve** I'll expect you around nine; **¿esperabas que te felicitara?** did you expect me to congratulate you?; **era de ~ que el proyecto fracasara** the project was bound to fail (b) ‹niño/bebé› to be expecting [3] (con esperanza) to hope; **eso espero** or **espero que sí** I hope so; **espero que no** I hope not; **~ hacer algo** to hope to do sth; **espero que no llueva** I hope it doesn't rain; **esperemos que no sea nada grave** let's hope it's nothing serious
■ **~** vi (a) (aguardar) to wait; **no podemos ~ más** we can't wait any longer; **espera a estar seguro** wait until you're sure; **~on (a) que él se fuera para entrar** they waited for him to go before they went in (b) «embarazada»: **estar esperando** to be expecting

■ **esperarse** v pron [1] (fam) (aguardar) to hang on (colloq), to hold on (colloq) [2] (fam) (prever) to expect; **¡quién se lo iba a ~!** who would have thought it!

esperma m or f (Biol) sperm
■ f (a) (sustancia) spermaceti (b) (Col) (vela) candle

espesar [A1] vt/vi to thicken
■ **espesarse** v pron «salsa» to thicken; «vegetación» to become thick, become dense

espeso -sa adj (a) «salsa» thick; «vegetación/niebla» dense, thick; «nieve» thick, deep; «cabello/barba» bushy, thick (b) (Per fam) (cargoso) annoying

espesor m thickness

espesura f vegetation; **se abrieron paso por entre la ~** they hacked a path through the vegetation

espía adj inv ‹avión/satélite› spy (before n); ‹cámara› hidden (before n), secret (before n)
■ mf (persona) spy

espiar [A17] vt ‹enemigo/movimientos› to spy on, keep watch on
■ vi to spy

espiga f (Agr, Bot) (de trigo) ear, spike; (de flores) spike

espigón m (a) (rompeolas) breakwater (b) (Per, RPl) (en aeropuerto) terminal (building)

espina f (a) (de rosal, zarza) thorn; (de cactus) prickle (b) (de pez) bone (c) (Anat) spine; **~ dorsal** spine, backbone; **darle a algn mala ~** to make sb feel uneasy; **esto me da mala ~** I don't like the look of this

espinaca f spinach

espinazo m spine, backbone

espinilla f [1] (Anat) shin [2] (en la piel) (a) (de cabeza negra) blackhead (b) (AmL) (barrito) pimple, spot

espino m hawthorn

espinoso -sa adj [1] (a) ‹rosal/zarza› thorny; ‹cactus› prickly (b) ‹pescado› bony [2] ‹problema/asunto› thorny, knotty

espionaje m spying, espionage; **novela de ~** spy novel

espiral f (a) (forma, movimiento) spiral; **un cuaderno de ~(es)** a spiral-bound notebook; **escalera de ~** spiral staircase (b) (muelle) hairspring (c) (dispositivo intrauterino) coil

espirar [A1] vi to breathe out, exhale

espiritismo m spiritualism; **sesión de ~** séance

espiritista adj/mf spiritualist

espíritu m (a) (en general) spirit; **un ~ maligno** an evil spirit; **E~ Santo** Holy Ghost o Spirit; **con ~ de sacrificio** in a spirit of self-sacrifice; **el ~ de la ley** the spirit of the law (b) (naturaleza, carácter) nature; **tiene un ~ rebelde** she has a rebellious nature

espiritual adj spiritual
■ m: tb **~ negro** (Negro) spiritual

espita f spigot (AmE), tap (BrE)

espléndido -da adj (a) ‹fiesta/comida› splendid, magnificent; ‹día/tiempo› splendid, marvelous*; ‹regalo/joya/abrigo› magnificent (b) (generoso) ‹persona› generous; ‹regalo› lavish, generous

esplendor m **(a)** (magnificencia) splendor*, magnificence **(b)** (apogeo) splendor*

espolear [A1] vt ‹caballo› to spur (on)

espoleta f (Arm) fuse

espolvorear [A1] vt to sprinkle

esponja f sponge

esponjoso -sa adj ‹masa/bizcocho› spongy, fluffy; ‹tejido› soft; ‹lana› fluffy

espontaneidad f spontaneity

espontáneo -nea adj ‹persona/gesto/ayuda› spontaneous; ‹actuación› impromptu
■ m,f: spectator who jumps into the ring to join in the bullfight

esporádico -ca adj ‹sucesos/visitas› sporadic, intermittent

esposado -da adj handcuffed, in handcuffs

esposas fpl handcuffs (pl)

esposo -sa m,f (m) husband; (f) wife

espray m (pl **-prays**) **(a)** (atomizador) spray **(b)** (pintura) spray paint

esprint m (pl **-prints**) sprint

espuela f spur

espuelear [A1] vt (AmL) to spur (on)

espuma f ① **(a)** (del mar) foam; (al romper las olas) surf; (en agua revuelta) foam, froth **(b)** (del jabón) lather; **este jabón no hace ~** this soap doesn't lather; **un baño de ~** a foam o bubble bath; **~ de afeitar** shaving foam; **~ seca** carpet shampoo **(c)** (de la cerveza) head, froth **(d)** (Coc) (capa) scum ② **(a)** (caucho celular) foam rubber **(b)** (tejido elástico) stretch nylon

espumadera f skimmer, slotted spoon

espumante m sparkling wine

espumillón m tinsel

espumoso¹ -sa adj ‹ola› foaming; ‹cerveza› frothy; ‹vino› sparkling

espumoso² m sparkling wine

esqueje m (para plantar) cutting; (para injertar) scion

esquela f **(a)** (AmL) (carta) note **(b)** (Andes) (papel) stationery set **(c)** (Esp) (aviso fúnebre) tb **~ mortuoria** death notice

esqueleto m **(a)** (Anat) skeleton **(b)** (de edificio, novela) framework

esquema m ① (croquis) sketch, diagram; (sinopsis) outline ② (de ideas): **~ liberal** liberal philosophy o thinking; **no se sale de sus ~s** she doesn't change her way of thinking

esquemático -ca adj schematic; **el libro es algo ~** the book is a little oversimplified

esquematizar [A4] vt/vi to schematize

esquí m (pl **-quís** o **-quíes**) (tabla) ski; (deporte) skiing; **pista de ~** ski run, piste; **~ acuático** or **náutico** waterskiing; **hacer ~ acuático** to water-ski

esquiador -dora m,f skier

esquiar [A17] vi to ski

esquilar [A1] vt to shear, clip

esquimal adj/mf Eskimo

esquina f **(a)** (en calle) corner; **en la calle Vidal, ~ (a) Cádiz** on the corner of Vidal (Street) and Cadiz (Street); **doblar la ~** to go round o turn the corner; **hace ~ con la plaza** it's on the corner of the square **(b)** (Dep): **sacar de ~** to take a corner (kick)

esquinazo m ① (Esp): **darle (el) ~ a algn** (dejar plantado) to stand sb up; (esquivar) to give sb the slip ② (Chi) (serenata) serenade of traditional singing and dancing

esquirol mf (pey) strikebreaker, scab (pej)

esquivar [A1] vt ‹persona/problema/dificultad› to avoid; ‹golpe/pregunta› to dodge, evade; ‹responsabilidad› to avoid, evade

esquivo -va adj **(a)** (difícil de encontrar) elusive; (huraño) aloof, unsociable; (tímido) shy **(b)** ‹respuesta› elusive, evasive

esquizofrenia f schizophrenia

esquizofrénico -ca adj/m,f schizophrenic

estabilidad f stability

estabilizar [A4] vt to stabilize
■ **estabilizarse** v pron to stabilize

estable adj stable; ‹trabajo› steady

establecer [E3] vt ① **(a)** ‹colonia/dictadura› to establish; ‹campamento› to set up; **estableció su residencia en Mónaco** he took up residence in Monaco **(b)** ‹relaciones/contacto› to establish ② (dejar sentado) **(a)** ‹criterios/bases› to establish, lay down; ‹precio› to fix, set; ‹precedente› to establish, set **(b)** (frml) ‹ley/reglamento› (disponer) to state, establish **(c)** ‹récord/marca/moda› to set; ‹uso› to establish ③ (determinar) to establish
■ **establecerse** v pron ‹colono/emigrante› to settle; ‹‹comerciante/empresa›› to set up

establecimiento m establishment

establo m stable

estaca f **(a)** (poste) stake, post **(b)** (para carpa) tent peg **(c)** (garrote) club, stick **(d)** (clavo de madera) peg

estación f ① (de tren, metro, autobús) station; **~ de bomberos** (Col, Méx, Ven) fire station; **~ de policía** (Col, Ven) police station; **~ de esquí** ski resort; **~ de servicio** service station, gas (AmE) o (BrE) petrol station; **~ terminal** or **término** terminal, terminus (BrE) ② (del año) season ③ (AmL) (emisora) radio station

estacionamiento m **(a)** (acción de estacionar) parking **(b)** (espacio para estacionar) parking space; (en recinto cerrado) (AmL) parking lot (AmE), car park (BrE)

estacionar [A1] vt to park
■ **~** vi to park; ⊝ **prohibido estacionar** no parking; **~ en doble fila** to double-park
■ **estacionarse** v pron **(a)** ‹‹crecimiento›› to stop; ‹‹peso›› to stabilize; ‹‹proceso/enfermedad›› to halt **(b)** (Chi, Méx) ‹‹conductor›› to park

estadía f (AmL) (en un lugar) stay

estadio m stadium

estadista mf (m) statesman; (f) stateswoman

estadística f **(a)** (estudio) statistical study **(b)** (cifra) statistic, figure **(c)** (disciplina) statistics

estadístico -ca adj statistical

estado m ① **(a)** (en general) state; **~ de ánimo** state of mind; **~ de cuenta** bank statement; **~ de emergencia** or **excepción** state of emergency; **la casa está en buen ~** the house is in good condition **(b)** (Med) condition; **estar en ~** (euf) to be expecting (colloq); **quedarse en ~** (euf) to get pregnant **(c)** **estado civil** marital status ② (nación, gobierno) state; **la seguridad del E~** national o state security; **~ de bienestar** welfare state

Estados Unidos m: tb los ~ ~ mpl the United States (+ sing or pl vb)

Estados Unidos Mexicanos mpl (frml) United States of Mexico (frml)

estadounidense adj American, US (before n)
■ mf American

estafa f (a) (Der) fraud, criminal deception (b) (fam) (timo) rip-off (colloq), con (colloq)

estafador -dora m,f (a) (Der) fraudster (b) (fam) (timador) swindler (colloq)

estafar [A1] vt (a) (Der) to swindle, defraud; ~le algo A algn to defraud sb OF sth, swindle sb OUT OF sth (b) (fam) (timar) to rip ... off (colloq), to con (colloq)

estafeta f: tb ~ **de correos** mail office (AmE), sub-post office (BrE)

estallar [A1] vi (a) «bomba» to explode; «neumático» to blow out, burst; «globo» to burst; «vidrio» to shatter; **hizo ~ el dispositivo** he detonated the device (b) «guerra/revuelta» to break out; «tormenta/escándalo/crisis» to break (c) «persona» (ponerse furioso) to blow one's top (colloq); ~ **EN algo** «en llanto/carcajadas» to burst INTO sth

estallido m (a) (de bomba) explosion; (de neumático) bursting; (de cristal) shattering (b) (de guerra) outbreak

estamento m (de sociedad) stratum, class

estampado¹ -da adj patterned, printed

estampado² m pattern; **los ~s están de moda** patterned o printed fabrics are in fashion

estampar [A1] vt (imprimir) ⟨tela/diseño⟩ to print; ⟨metal⟩ to stamp; (formando relieve) to emboss

estampida f stampede; **salir en** or **de ~ to** stampede out

estampido m (de pistola) bang, report; (de bomba) bang

estampilla f (a) (AmL) (sello — postal) postage (stamp); (— fiscal) tax stamp (b) (sello de goma) rubber stamp

estampillar [A1] vt (AmL) (con sello fiscal o de correos) to stamp

estancado -da adj (a) ⟨agua⟩ stagnant (b) (detenido): **las negociaciones están estancadas** negotiations are at a standstill (c) (con un problema) stuck, bogged down

estancamiento m stagnation

estancarse [A2] v pron (a) «agua» to become stagnant, to stagnate (b) «negociación/proceso» to come to a halt o standstill (c) (con un problema) to get bogged down o stuck

estancia f [1] (frml) (habitación) large room [2] (Esp, Méx) (permanencia) stay [3] (en el CS) (Agr) farm; (de ganado) ranch

estanciero -ra m,f (en el CS) (Agr) farmer; (de ganado) rancher

estanco m (tienda) tobacconist's

estándar adj/m standard

estandarte m standard, banner

estanque m pond

estanquillo m (Méx) general store (AmE), grocer's shop (BrE)

estante m shelf

estantería f shelves (pl); (para libros) bookcase, bookshelves (pl)

estaño m (elemento) tin; (para soldar) solder; (peltre) pewter

estar¹ [A27] cópula [1] (a) (seguido de adjetivos) [ESTAR denotes a changed condition or state as opposed to identity or nature, which is normally expressed by SER. ESTAR is also used when the emphasis is on the speaker's perception of things, of their appearance, taste, etc. The examples given below should be contrasted with those to be found in SER¹ cópula 1] to be; **estás más gordo** you've put on weight; **estoy cansada** I'm tired; **está muy simpático conmigo** he's being o he's been so nice to me (recently); **¡todo está tan caro!** things are o have become so expensive! (b) (con BIEN, MAL, MEJOR, PEOR): **están todos bien, gracias** they're all fine, thanks; **¡qué bien estás en esta foto!** you look great in this photo!; **está mal que no se lo perdones** it's wrong of you not to forgive him; ver tb BIEN, MAL, MEJOR, PEOR

[2] (hablando de estado civil) to be; **está casada con un primo mío** she's married to a cousin of mine [3] (seguido de participios) ~ **sentado** to be sitting; **estaban abrazados** they had their arms around each other; ver tb v aux 3 [4] (seguido de preposición) to be; (para más ejemplos ver tb la preposición o el nombre correspondiente); **estoy a régimen** I'm on a diet; **¿a cómo está la uva?** how much are the grapes?; **está con el sarampión** she has (the) measles; **estoy de cocinera** I'm doing the cooking; **estamos sin electricidad** the electricity is off at the moment; **está sin pintar** it hasn't been painted yet

■ ~ vi [1] (en un lugar) to be; **¿dónde está Chiapas?** where's Chiapas?; **está a 20 kilómetros de aquí** it's 20 kilometers from here; **¿sabes dónde está Pedro?** do you know where Pedro is?; **¿está Rodrigo?** is Rodrigo in?; **solo ~é unos días** I'll only be staying a few days; **¿cuánto tiempo ~ás en Londres?** how long are you going to be in London (for)?

[2] (en el tiempo): **¿a qué (día) estamos?** what day is it today?; **¿a cuánto estamos hoy?** what's the date today?; **estamos a 28 de mayo** it's May 28th (AmE) o (BrE) the 28th of May; **estamos en primavera** it's spring

[3] (a) (tener como función, cometido): **para eso están los amigos** that's what friends are for; **estamos para ayudarlos** we're here to help them (b) (radicar) to lie; **en eso está el problema** that's where the problem lies

[4] (estar listo, terminado): **la carne todavía no está** the meat's not ready yet; **lo atas con un nudo y ya está** you tie a knot in it and that's it o there you are; **enseguida estoy** I'll be right with you

5 (Esp) (quedar) (+ *me/te/le etc*) (+ *compl*): **te está pequeña** it's too small for you; **la 46 te está mejor** the 46 fits you better

■ ~ *v aux* **1** (con gerundio): **está lloviendo** it's raining; **estoy viendo que va a ser imposible** I'm beginning to see that it's going to be impossible **2** (con participio): **ese asiento está ocupado** that seat is taken; **ya está hecho un hombrecito** he's a proper young man now; *ver tb* ESTAR *cópula* 3

■ **estarse** *v pron* (*enf*) (permanecer) to stay; **¿no te puedes ~ quieto?** can't you stay *o* keep still?; **estese tranquilo** don't worry

estar² *m* (esp AmL) living room

estárter *m* choke

estatal *adj* state (*before n*)

estático -ca *adj* static

estatua *f* statue

estatura *f* height; **mide dos metros de ~** he's two meters (tall); **¿qué ~ tenía?** how tall was she?; **de mediana ~** of medium height

estatus *m* status

estatuto *m* (a) (Der, Pol) statute; (regla) rule (b) **estatutos** *mpl* (de empresa) articles of association (*pl*)

este¹ *adj inv* ⟨región⟩ eastern; **iban en dirección ~** they were heading east *o* eastward(s); **el ala/la costa ~** the east wing/coast

■ *m* (a) (parte, sector): **el ~** the east; **al ~ de Lima** to the east of Lima (b) (punto cardinal) east, East; **vientos del E~** easterly winds; **las ventanas dan al ~** the windows face east (c) **el Este** (Hist, Pol) the East; **los países del E~** the Eastern Bloc countries

este², esta *adj dem* (*pl* **estos, estas**) (a) this; (*pl*) these; **este chico** this boy; **estos dólares** these dollars; [*usually indicates a pejorative or emphatic tone when placed after the noun*] **la estúpida esta no me avisó** (*fam*) this idiot here didn't tell me (b) (como muletilla) well, er

éste, ésta *pron dem* (*pl* **éstos, éstas**) [*The written accent may be omitted when there is no confusion with the adjective*] this one; (*pl*) these; **~ *or* este es el mío** this (one) is mine; **un día de éstos *or* estos** one of these days; **~ *or* este es el que yo quería** this is the one I wanted; **prefiero éstos *or* estos** I prefer these (ones); [*sometimes indicates irritation, emphasis or disapproval*] **¡qué niña ésta!** (*fam*) honestly, this child!; **residente en ésta *or* esta** resident in Seville (*o* Lima *etc*)

estela *f* (de barco) wake; (de avión, cohete) trail

estelar *adj* (a) (Espec) star (b) (Astron) stellar

estelarizar [A4] *vt* (Méx) to star in

estepa *f* steppe

estera *f* mat

estercolero *m* dunghill, dung heap

estéreo *adj inv/m* stereo

estereofónico -ca *adj* stereophonic

estereotipado -da *adj* ⟨frase⟩ clichéd; ⟨idea/personaje⟩ stereotyped

estereotipo *m* stereotype

estéril *adj* (a) ⟨animal/persona⟩ sterile; ⟨terreno⟩ infertile, barren (b) ⟨esfuerzo/discusión⟩ futile (c) ⟨gasa/jeringa⟩ sterile

esterilidad *f* infertility; (de un hombre) sterility

esterilizar [A4] *vt* to sterilize

esterilla *f* (a) (alfombrilla) mat (b) (AmS) (mimbre) wicker

esternón *m* sternum, breastbone

estero *m* (a) (AmS) (laguna, pantano) marsh (b) (Chi) (arroyo) stream

esteroide *m* steroid

estética *f* (a) (Art) aesthetics (b) (Med) cosmetic surgery

esteticien, esteticista *mf* aesthetician, beautician

estético -ca *adj* aesthetic

estetoscopio *m* stethoscope

estiércol *m* (excremento) dung; (abono) manure

estigma *m* stigma

estilar [A1] *vi* (Chi) (gotear) to drip; (escurrir) to drain

■ **estilarse** *v pron* «moda/peinado» to be fashionable

estilista *mf* (a) (Lit) stylist (b) (diseñador de modas) designer (c) (AmL) (peluquero) hairstylist

estilístico -ca *adj* stylistic

estilizado -da *adj* (a) (Art) stylized (b) ⟨cuerpo/figura⟩ slender, slim

estilo *m* (a) (en general) style; **~ barroco** baroque style; **~ de vida** way of life, lifestyle; **ropa ~ deportivo** casual wear; **vestir con ~** to dress stylishly; **al ~ de mi tierra** the way they do it back home; **por el ~:** **son todos por el ~** they are all the same; **algo por el ~** something like that (b) (en natación) stroke, style; **~ libre** freestyle; **~ mariposa** butterfly; **~ pecho** *or* (Esp) **braza** breaststroke

estilográfica *f* fountain pen

estima *f* esteem; **ganarse la ~ de algn** to raise oneself in sb's esteem; **tener(le) ~ a algn** to think highly of sb; **tiene en gran ~ tu amistad** he values your friendship very highly

estimación *f* **1** (cálculo) estimate **2** (aprecio) esteem

estimado -da *adj* dear

estimar [A1] *vt* **1** (a) ⟨persona⟩ (respetar) to respect, hold ... in high esteem (frml); (tener cariño) to be fond of (b) ⟨objeto⟩ to value; **su piel es muy estimada** its skin is highly prized **2** (frml) (considerar) (+ *compl*) to consider, deem (frml)

estimulante *adj* stimulating

estimular [A1] *vt* (a) (en general) to stimulate (b) (alentar) ⟨persona⟩ to encourage

estímulo *m* (a) (incentivo) incentive (b) (Biol, Fisiol) stimulus

estirado -da *adj* (fam) stuck-up (colloq)

estirar [A1] *vt* **1** (a) ⟨goma/elástico/suéter⟩ to stretch; ⟨cable/soga⟩ to pull out, stretch (b) ⟨sábanas/mantel⟩ (con las manos) to smooth out; (con la plancha) to run the iron over **2** ⟨brazos/piernas/músculo⟩ to stretch; **estiró el cuello para poder ver** she craned her neck to be able to see **3** ⟨dinero/comida/recursos⟩ to make ... go further

■ **estirarse** *v pron* to stretch

estirón *m*: **dar** *or* **pegar un ~** (fam) to shoot up (colloq)

estirpe *f* stock, lineage

estítico -ca *adj* (Chi) constipated

estitiquez *f* (Chi) constipation

esto *pron dem* (*neutro*) this; ¿qué es ∼? what's this?; ∼ **es lo que quiero** this is what I want

estofado¹ -da *adj* stewed; (con menos líquido) braised

estofado² *m* stew

estoico -ca *adj* stoic, stoical

estomacal *adj* stomach (*before n*)

estómago *m* (Anat) stomach; **tengo dolor de** ∼ I have a stomachache, my stomach hurts; **beber con el** ∼ **vacío** to drink on an empty stomach; *revolverle el* ∼ *a algn* to turn sb's stomach

estoperol *m* ⊞ (Andes) (en carretera) cat's eye ⊡ (Chi) (Dep) stud

estoque *m* sword (*used for killing bull*)

estorbar [A1] *vi* to be/get in the way
■ ∼ *vt* to obstruct; **el piano estorbaba el paso** the piano was in the way

estorbo *m* (obstáculo) hindrance; (molestia) nuisance

estornudar [A1] *vi* to sneeze

estornudo *m* sneeze

estos -tas *adj dem*: ▶ ESTE²

éstos -tas *pron dem*: ▶ ÉSTE

estoy ▶ ESTAR¹

estrabismo *m* squint, strabismus (tech)

estrado *m* (tarima) platform, dais

estrafalario -ria *adj* ⟨persona/ideas/conducta⟩ eccentric; ⟨vestimenta⟩ outlandish, bizarre
■ *m,f* eccentric

estragón *m* tarragon

estragos *mpl*: **los** ∼ **de la guerra** the ravages of war; *causar/hacer* ∼**s** «*terremoto/inundación*» to wreak havoc; **la epidemia causó** ∼ **entre la población** the epidemic devastated the population

estrambótico -ca *adj* ⟨persona/idea/conducta⟩ eccentric; ⟨vestimenta⟩ outlandish, bizarre

estrangulador -dora *m,f* strangler

estrangular [A1] *vt* (a) ⟨persona/animal⟩ to strangle, throttle (b) ⟨vena/conducto⟩ to strangulate

estraperlo *m* black market

estratagema *f* stratagem

estrategia *f* strategy

estratégico -ca *adj* strategic

estratosfera *f* stratosphere

estrechar [A1] *vt* ⊞ (a) ⟨falda/pantalones⟩ to take ... in; ⟨carretera⟩ to make ... narrower (b) ⟨relaciones/lazos⟩ to strengthen ⊡ (abrazar, apretar): **la estrechó entre sus brazos** he held her tightly in his arms; **me estrechó la mano** he shook my hand
■ **estrecharse** *v pron* ⊞ (a) «carretera/acera» to narrow, get narrower (b) «relaciones/lazos» to strengthen ⊡ (recípr) (apretarse): **se** ∼**on en un abrazo** they embraced; **se** ∼**on la mano** they shook hands

estrecho¹ -cha *adj* ⊞ ⟨calle/pasillo⟩ narrow; ⟨falda⟩ tight; **íbamos muy** ∼**s** it was very cramped ⊡ ⟨amistad/colaboración/vigilancia⟩ close ⊠ (limitado) ⟨criterio⟩ narrow; **es muy** ∼ **de miras** he's very narrow-minded

estrecho² *m* (Geog) strait, straits (*pl*); **el E**∼ **de Gibraltar** the Strait(s) of Gibraltar

estrella *f* (a) (en general) star; ∼ **de mar** starfish; ∼ **fugaz** shooting star; ∼ **polar** Pole Star; **un hotel de tres** ∼**s** a three-star hotel; **una** ∼ **de cine** a movie star (b) (asterisco) asterisk

estrellado -da *adj* (lleno de estrellas) starry; (en forma de estrella) star-shaped

estrellar [A1] *vt*: **estrelló un plato contra la pared** he smashed a plate against the wall; **estrelló el coche contra un árbol** he smashed his car into a tree
■ **estrellarse** *v pron* (chocar) to crash; **se estrelló con la moto** he had a motorcycle accident; ∼**se** CONTRA *algo* «*coche*» to crash INTO sth; «*olas*» to crash AGAINST sth; **se estrelló contra el vidrio** he walked smack into the glass door

estremecedor -dora *adj* ⟨escena/noticia⟩ horrifying; ⟨grito/relato⟩ spine-chilling, hair-raising

estremecer [E3] *vt* to make ... shudder
■ ∼ *vi* to shudder; **hacer** ∼ **a algn** to make sb shudder
■ **estremecerse** *v pron* (a) «persona» ∼**se** DE *algo* ⟨de miedo/horror⟩ to shudder WITH sth; ⟨de frío⟩ to shiver o tremble WITH sth; **se estremeció solo de pensarlo** he shuddered at the mere thought of it (b) «edificio/ventana» to shake

estremecimiento *m* (de miedo) shudder; **tenía** ∼**s de frío** he was shivering with cold

estrenar [A1] *vt* ⊞ (Cin, Teatr): **la película se estrenó en marzo** the movie opened o (journ) had its premiere in March; **acaban de** ∼ **la obra en Madrid** the play's just started showing o just opened in Madrid ⊡ (usar por primera vez): **voy a** ∼ **corbata** I'm going to wear a new tie; **todavía no he estrenado la blusa** I still haven't worn the blouse; **todavía no estrenamos el gimnasio** we still haven't tried out the gymnasium

estreno *m* ⊞ (de película, nueva obra) premiere; (de nueva puesta en escena) opening night ⊡ (primer uso): **ir de** ∼ to be wearing new clothes; **el** ∼ **del local** the opening of the new premises

estreñido -da *adj* constipated

estreñimiento *m* constipation

estreñir [I15] *vi* to cause constipation
■ ∼ *vt* to make ... constipated, bind (colloq)

estrés *m* stress

estresado -da *adj* under stress

estresante *adj* stressful

estría *f* (a) (de la piel) stretch mark (b) (de columna) groove, stria (tech)

estriado -da *adj* (a) ⟨piel⟩ stretch-marked (b) ⟨columna⟩ fluted

estribillo *m* (Lit) refrain; (Mús) chorus

estribo *m* (a) (Equ) stirrup; *perder los* ∼**s** to fly off the handle, lose one's cool; *tomarse la del* ∼ to have one for the road (colloq) (b) (de vehículo) running board; (de moto) footrest

estribor *m* starboard

estricto -ta *adj* strict

estridente *adj* (a) ⟨pitido/chirrido⟩ shrill (b) ⟨voz⟩ (agudo) shrill; (fuerte) strident (c) ⟨color⟩ garish, loud

estrofa *f* stanza, verse

estropajo *m* scourer

estropeado -da *adj*: **estar** ∼ «*zapato/sillón*» to be falling apart; «*motor/coche*» to be broken down; *ver tb* ESTROPEAR

estropear [A1] *vt* ①(a) ⟨*aparato/mecanismo*⟩ to damage, break; ⟨*coche*⟩ to damage (b) (malograr) ⟨*plan/vacaciones*⟩ to spoil, ruin ②(deteriorar, dañar) ⟨*piel*⟩ to damage, ruin; ⟨*juguete*⟩ to break; ⟨*ropa*⟩ to ruin; **el calor estropeó la fruta** the heat made the fruit go bad

■ **estropearse** *v pron* ①(a) (averiarse) «*motor/coche*» to break down; **la lavadora está estropeada** the washing machine is broken (b) «*plan/vacaciones*» to go wrong ②(deteriorarse) «*fruta*» to go bad; «*leche/pescado*» to go off; «*zapatos/chaqueta*» to get ruined

estructura *f* structure

estructurar [A1] *vt* to structure, to organize

estruendo *m* (de las olas) roar; (de cascada, tráfico) thunder, roar; (de maquinaria) din

estrujar [A1] *vt* ①(a) (apretar arrugando) ⟨*papel*⟩ to crumple up, scrunch up; ⟨*tela*⟩ to crumple (up) (b) (para escurrir) to wring (out) (c) ⟨*uvas*⟩ to press ②⟨*persona*⟩ to squeeze, hold ... tightly

estuche *m* (de gafas, lápices, violín) case; (de cubiertos) canteen; (de collar, reloj) box, case

estudiante *mf* (de universidad) student; (de secundaria) (high-school) student (AmE), (secondary school) pupil (BrE)

estudiantil *adj* student (*before n*)

estudiar [A1] *vt* ①(a) ⟨*asignatura*⟩ to study; (en la universidad) to study, read (frml); **¿qué carrera estudió?** what subject did he do at college/university? (b) ⟨*instrumento*⟩ to learn (c) ⟨*lección/tablas*⟩ to learn ②(observar) ⟨*rostro/comportamiento*⟩ to study ③(considerar, analizar) ⟨*mercado/situación/proyecto*⟩ to study; ⟨*propuesta*⟩ to study, consider; ⟨*causas*⟩ to look into, investigate

■ ∼ *vi* to study; **estudia en un colegio privado** he goes to a private school; **debes** ∼ **más** you must work harder; **dejó de** ∼ **a los 15 años** she left school at 15; ∼ **PARA algo** to study to be sth

■ **estudiarse** *v pron* (enf) ⟨*lección*⟩ to study; ⟨*papel*⟩ to learn

estudio *m* ①(a) (Educ) (actividad): **primero está el** ∼ studying *o* your studies *o* work must come first (b) (investigación, análisis) study; ∼ **de mercado** market research (c) (de asunto, caso) consideration; **está en** ∼ it is being considered ②(lugar) (a) (de artista) studio; (de arquitecto) office, studio (b) (Cin, Rad, TV) studio (c) (en casa) study; (apartamento) studio apartment ③**estudios** *mpl* (Educ) education; ∼**s superiores** higher education; **quiso darle** ∼**s a su hijo** she wanted to give her son an education; **tener** ∼**s superiores** to have a degree; **dejar los** ∼**s** to give up one's studies

estudioso -sa *adj* studious
■ *m,f* scholar

estufa *f* (a) (de calefacción) stove; ∼ **eléctrica** electric heater (b) (Col, Méx) (cocina) stove; ∼ **de gas** gas stove *o* (BrE) cooker

estupefaciente *m* narcotic (drug); **tráfico de** ∼**s** drug trafficking

estupefacto -ta *adj* astonished, amazed

estupendo¹ -da *adj* (a) (excelente) marvelous*, fantastic (colloq), great (colloq); ¡∼! great! (b) (guapo) gorgeous

estupendo² *adv* ⟨*cantar*⟩ marvelously*; **lo pasé** ∼ I had a great *o* wonderful time

estupidez *f* (a) (cualidad) stupidity, foolishness (b) (dicho): **no digas estupideces** don't talk nonsense (c) (acto): **eso sería una** ∼ that would be stupid *o* foolish

estúpido -da *adj* ⟨*persona*⟩ stupid; ⟨*argumento*⟩ stupid, silly; **¡ay, qué estúpida soy!** oh, how stupid of me!
■ *m,f* idiot, fool

estupor *m* astonishment

estuve, estuviste, etc ▶ ESTAR¹

esvástica *f* swastika

ETA /'eta/ *f* (= **Euzkadi ta Azkatasuna**) ETA

etapa *f* stage; **por** ∼**s** in stages; **la** ∼ **más feliz de mi vida** the best *o* happiest time of my life

etarra *mf*: member of ETA

etcétera etcetera, and so on (and so forth)

etéreo -rea *adj* ethereal

eternidad *f* eternity

eterno -na *adj* eternal; ⟨*amor*⟩ everlasting

ética *f* ethics

ético -ca *adj* ethical

etimología *f* etymology

etíope, etiope *adj/mf* Ethiopian

Etiopía *f* Ethiopia

etiqueta *f* ①(a) (adherida) label (b) (atada) tag; (en prenda) label ②(protocolo) etiquette; **baile/traje de** ∼ formal ball/dress

etiquetar [A1] *vt* ⟨*producto*⟩ to label; ⟨*persona*⟩ ∼ **a algn DE algo** to label sb (AS) sth

étnico -ca *adj* ethnic

eucalipto *m* eucalyptus

Eucaristía *f* Eucharist

eufemismo *m* euphemism

euforia *f* elation, euphoria

eufórico -ca *adj* ecstatic, euphoric

euro *m* euro

eurocheque *m* eurocheque

eurodiputado -da *m,f* Euro MP, MEP, Member of the European Parliament

Europa *f* Europe

europeísta *adj* pro-European

europeo -pea *adj/m,f* European

Eurotunnel®, eurotúnel *m* Channel Tunnel

Euskadi *f* the Basque Country

euskera, eusquera *adj/m* Basque

eutanasia *f* euthanasia

evacuación *f* (desalojo) evacuation

evacuar [A18] *or* [A1] *vt* ⟨*local/zona/población*⟩ to evacuate

evadir [I1] *vt* (a) ⟨*pregunta/peligro/responsabilidad*⟩ to avoid; ⟨*tema*⟩ to dodge, evade (b) ⟨*impuestos*⟩ to evade
■ **evadirse** *v pron* (a) «*preso*» to escape (b) ∼**se DE algo** ⟨*de responsabilidad/problema*⟩ to run away FROM sth; ⟨*de la realidad*⟩ to escape FROM sth

evaluación *f* (a) (de daños, situación) ⋯⟡

assessment; (de datos, informes) evaluation, assessment **(b)** (Educ) (acción) assessment; (prueba, examen) test

evaluar [A18] *vt* ⟨*pérdidas/situación*⟩ to assess; ⟨*datos*⟩ to evaluate; ⟨*alumno*⟩ to assess

evangélico -ca *adj* **(a)** (del evangelio) evangelical **(b)** (protestante) protestant (*before n*) ■ *m,f* Protestant

evangelio *m* gospel

evaporación *f* evaporation

evaporarse [A1] *v pron* «*líquido*» to evaporate; «*ayuda/dinero*» to evaporate; «*persona*» (fam) to vanish *o* disappear into thin air

evasión *f* escape, breakout; ~ **de impuestos** tax evasion

evasiva *f*: **me contestó con** ~**s** she avoided *o* dodged the issue

evasivo -va *adj* evasive, noncommital

evento *m* **(a)** (period) (suceso) event **(b)** (caso) case; **en este** ~ in such a case

eventual *adj* **1** (posible) ⟨*problema/conflicto*⟩ possible; ⟨*gastos*⟩ incidental; ⟨*riesgos/pasivos*⟩ contingent **2** ⟨*trabajo/trabajador*⟩ casual, temporary; ⟨*cargo*⟩ temporary

evidencia *f* **(a)** (pruebas) evidence, proof; **negar la** ~ to deny the obvious *o* the facts **(b)** (cualidad) obviousness; *dejar or poner a algn en* ~ to show sb up

evidente *adj* obvious, clear

evidentemente *adv* (*indep*) obviously, clearly

evitar [A1] *vt* **(a)** (eludir, huir de) to avoid; ~ **hacer algo** to avoid doing sth **(b)** (impedir) **para** ~ **que sufran** to avoid *o* prevent them suffering **(c)** (remediar): **me puse a llorar, no lo puede** ~ I started to cry, I couldn't help it **(d)** (ahorrar) ~**le algo** ᴀ **algn** ⟨*molestia/preocupación*⟩ to save *o* spare sb sth ■ **evitarse** *v pron* ⟨*problemas*⟩ to save oneself; **evítese la molestia de ir a la tienda** avoid the inconvenience of going to the store

evolución *f* **(a)** (Biol) evolution **(b)** (de ideas, sociedad, enfermedad) development; (de enfermo) progress

evolucionado -da *adj* ⟨*especie*⟩ highly developed *o* evolved; ⟨*sociedad/ideas*⟩ advanced, highly developed

evolucionar [A1] *vi* **(a)** (Biol) to evolve **(b)** «*ideas/sociedad/ciencia*» to develop, evolve **(c)** «*enfermo*» to progress

exactamente *adv* exactly

exactitud *f* **(a)** (precisión) accuracy, precision; **las órdenes se cumplieron con** ~ the orders were carried out to the letter **(b)** (veracidad, rigor) accuracy

exacto -ta *adj* **(a)** ⟨*medida/cantidad*⟩ exact; **40 kilos** ~**s** exactly 40 kilos; **hay que ser muy** ~ **en los cálculos** you have to be very accurate *o*

precise in your calculations **(b)** ⟨*informe/mapa/descripción*⟩ accurate **(c)** ⟨*copia*⟩ exact; ⟨*reproducción*⟩ accurate

exageración *f* exaggeration

exagerado -da *adj* **(a)** ⟨*persona*⟩: **¡qué** ~ **eres!** you do exaggerate! **(b)** ⟨*historia/relato*⟩ exaggerated **(c)** (excesivo) ⟨*precio*⟩ exorbitant; ⟨*cariño/castigo*⟩ excessive; ⟨*moda*⟩ extravagant, way-out (colloq)

exagerar [A1] *vt* ⟨*suceso/noticia*⟩ to exaggerate ■ ~ *vi* (al hablar) to exaggerate; (al hacer algo) to overdo it, go over the top (colloq)

exaltado -da *adj* **(a)** (vehemente) ⟨*discurso*⟩ impassioned **(b)** (excitado): **los ánimos estaban** ~**s** feelings were running high; **estaba muy** ~ he was really worked up **(c)** [SER] ⟨*persona*⟩ hotheaded ■ *m,f* hothead

exaltar [A1] *vt* **1** **(a)** (excitar) ⟨*personas*⟩ to excite; ⟨*pasiones*⟩ to arouse **(b)** (hacer enojar) to anger **2** (fml) (alabar) to extol (fml) ■ **exaltarse** *v pron* to get worked up

exalumno -na *m,f* (de colegio) ex-pupil; (de universidad) ex-student

examen *m* **(a)** (Educ) exam, examination (fml); ~ **de admisión** entrance examination *o* test; ~ **parcial** modular exam *o* test; **hacer** *or* (CS) **dar un** ~ to take an exam; **presentarse a un** ~ to take *o* (BrE) sit an exam; ~ **de ingreso** entrance examination *o* test **(b)** (estudio, investigación) examination; **someter algo a** ~ to examine sth; ~ **médico** medical examination, medical

examinador -dora *adj* examining (*before n*) ■ *m,f* examiner

examinar [A1] *vt* to examine; ⟨*situación/caso*⟩ to study, consider ■ **examinarse** *v pron* (Esp) to take an exam

exangüe *adj* (liter) spent (liter), exhausted

exasperante *adj* exasperating

exasperar [A1] *vt* to exasperate ■ **exasperarse** *v pron* to get worked up *o* exasperated

excavación *f* excavation

excavadora *f* excavator

excavar [A1] *vt* **(a)** ⟨*túnel/fosa*⟩ to dig **(b)** (Arqueol) to excavate ■ ~ *vi* to dig, excavate

excedencia *f* (Esp) extended leave of absence

excedente *adj* **(a)** ⟨*producción*⟩ excess (*before n*), surplus (*before n*) **(b)** (con permiso) (Esp) on extended leave of absence ■ *m* surplus

exceder [E1] *vt* **(a)** ⟨*límite/peso*⟩ to exceed **(b)** (superar, aventajar) ~ ᴀ **algo** to be superior ᴛᴏ sth ■ **excederse** *v pron* (al beber, trabajar) to overdo it; **se excedió en sus críticas** she went too far in her criticism

excelencia *f* **1** (cualidad) excellence **2** (fml) (tratamiento): **Su E**~ **(m)** His Excellency; **(f)** Her Excellency

excelente *adj* excellent

excéntrico -ca *adj/m,f* eccentric

excepción *f* exception; **esta norma tiene una** ∼ there is an exception to this rule; **hacer una** ∼ **(con algn)** to make an exception (for sb); **a excepción de** with the exception of, except for

excepcional *adj* ⟨caso/circunstancia/talento⟩ exceptional; ⟨contribución/labor⟩ outstanding

excepto *prep* except, apart from; **todos** ∼ **yo** everyone but me

exceptuar [A18] *vt* to except (frml); **exceptuando un pequeño incidente** except for *o* with the exception of a minor incident

excesivo *adj* excessive

exceso *m* **(a)** (excedente) excess; ∼ **de equipaje** excess baggage **(b)** (demasía): **un** ∼ **de ejercicio** too much exercise; **me multaron por** ∼ **de velocidad** I was fined for speeding; **en** ∼ ⟨beber/fumar/trabajar⟩ too much **(c) excesos** *mpl* (abusos) excesses (*pl*)

excitabilidad *f* excitability

excitación *f* **(a)** (entusiasmo) excitement **(b)** (sexual) arousal, excitement

excitante *adj* ⟨espectáculo/libro⟩ exciting

excitar [A1] *vt* **(a)** (hacer enojar): **la discusión lo excitó mucho** he got very excited *o* worked up during the argument **(b)** (sobreexcitar) to get ... overexcited; **el café me excita** coffee makes me jumpy **(c)** (en sentido sexual) to arouse, excite **(d)** ⟨deseo/odio/curiosidad⟩ to arouse
■ **excitarse** *v pron* **(a)** (enojarse) to get agitated, get worked up **(b)** (sobreexcitarse) to get overexcited **(c)** (sexualmente) to get aroused, get excited

exclamación *f* exclamation

exclamar [A1] *vt* to exclaim

excluir [I20] *vt* to exclude; ⟨posibilidad⟩ to rule out

exclusión *f* exclusion

exclusiva *f* **(a)** (Period) (derechos) exclusive rights (*pl*); (reportaje) exclusive **(b)** (Esp) (Com) exclusive rights (*pl*); **tendrán la** ∼ **de nuestros productos** they will be sole distributors of our products

exclusive *adj inv* (detrás del n): **del tres al quince, ambos** ∼ from the third to the fifteenth not inclusive

exclusividad *f* **(a)** (de club, colegio, diseño) exclusiveness, exclusivity **(b)** (AmL) (Com) exclusive rights (*pl*), sole rights (*pl*)

exclusivo -va *adj* ⟨club/diseño⟩ exclusive; ⟨distribuidor⟩ sole; ⟨derechos⟩ exclusive, sole

excombatiente *mf* (*m*) veteran (AmE), ex-serviceman (esp BrE); (*f*) veteran (AmE), ex-servicewoman (esp BrE)

excomulgar [A3] *vt* to excommunicate

excomunión *f* excommunication

excremento *m* excrement

excursión *f* (viaje organizado) excursion, day trip; (paseo, salida) trip, excursion; **ir de** ∼ **al campo** to go on a trip to the countryside

excursionismo *m* hiking

excursionista *mf* (que hace una excursión) tripper; (que hace excursionismo) hiker

excusa *f* **(a)** (pretexto) excuse **(b) excusas** *fpl* (disculpas) apologies (*pl*)

excusar [A1] *vt* **(a)** (disculpar) ⟨comportamiento⟩ to excuse **(b)** (eximir) ∼ **a algn DE algo/hacer algo** to excuse sb (FROM) sth/doing sth
■ **excusarse** *v pron* (frml) **(a)** (pedir perdón) to apologize **(b)** (ofrecer excusas) to excuse oneself

exento -ta *adj* (frml) [ESTAR] exempt; ∼ **DE algo** exempt FROM sth; ∼ **de impuestos** tax-exempt, tax-free (BrE)

exfoliador *m* (Col) notepad

exhaustivo -va *adj* exhaustive

exhausto -ta *adj* exhausted

exhibición *f* **(a)** (demostración) display **(b)** (de cuadros, artefactos) exhibition, display; **estar en** ∼ to be on show *o* display

exhibicionista *mf* **(a)** (pervertido) exhibitionist, flasher (colloq) **(b)** (ostentoso) exhibitionist, show-off (colloq)

exhibir [I1] *vt* **(a)** ⟨colección/modelos⟩ to show, display **(b)** ⟨película⟩ to show, screen; ⟨cuadro/obras de arte⟩ to show **(c)** (con orgullo) ⟨regalos/trofeos⟩ to show off
■ ∼ *vi* (period) (Art) to exhibit
■ **exhibirse** *v pron* (mostrarse en público) to show oneself; (hacerse notar) to draw attention to oneself

exhumar [A1] *vt* to exhume, disinter

exigencia *f* **(a)** (pretensión) demand; **¡no me vengas con** ∼**s!** don't start making demands **(b)** (requisito) requirement

exigente *adj* ⟨persona/prueba⟩ demanding; ⟨clientela/paladar⟩ discerning

exigir [I7] *vt* **(a)** ⟨pago/respuesta/disciplina⟩ to demand; **exigió que se retiraran** he demanded that they leave **(b)** (requerir) ⟨concentración/paciencia⟩ to call for, demand **(c)** (esperar de algn) (+ *me/te/le etc*): **le exigen demasiado en ese colegio** they ask too much of him at that school

exiliado -da *adj* exiled, in exile
■ *m,f* exile

exiliarse [A1] *v pron* to go into exile

exilio *m* exile

eximir [I1] *vt* (frml) to exempt; ∼ **a algn DE algo/hacer algo** to exempt sb FROM sth/doing sth; **esto me exime de toda culpa** this relieves *o* absolves me of all responsibility

existencia *f* **1** **(a)** (hecho de existir) existence **(b)** (vida) life; **amargarle la** ∼ **a algn** to make sb's life a misery **2** (Com) stock

existir [I1] *vi* **(a)** (en 3ª pers) (haber): **siempre ha existido rivalidad entre ellos** there has always been rivalry between them; **no existen pruebas** there is no evidence **(b)** (ser) to exist; **ya no existe** it doesn't exist anymore

éxito *m* success; **con** ∼ successfully; **tener** ∼ to be successful; ∼ **de ventas** best-seller; ∼ **de taquilla** a box-office hit

exitoso -sa *adj* (AmL) ⟨campaña/gira⟩ successful

éxodo *m* exodus; **el** ∼ **rural** the drift from the land

exorbitante *adj* exorbitant

exorcismo *m* exorcism

exorcizar [A4] *vt* to exorcize

exótico -ca *adj* exotic

expandirse [I1] *v pron* to expand

expansión *f* expansion; **en** ∼ expanding

expatriado -da *m,f* expatriate

expatriarse [A1] *or* [A17] *v pron* (emigrar) to leave one's country; (exiliarse) to go into exile

expectación *f* sense of expectancy *o* anticipation

expectante *adj* expectant; **esperaba ~** she waited expectantly

expectativa *f* (a) (espera): **estar a la ~ (de algo)** to be waiting (for sth) (b) (esperanza) expectation; **defraudó las ~s de su padre** he failed to live up to his father's expectations (c) **expectativas** *fpl* (perspectivas) prospects (*pl*); **tienen pocas ~s de ganar** they have little hope of winning; **~s de vida** life expectancy

expedición *f* expedition; **~ de salvamento** (misión) rescue mission; (equipo) rescue party

expediente *m* (a) (documentos) file, dossier; **~ académico** student record (b) (investigación) investigation, inquiry (c) (medidas disciplinarias) disciplinary action; **le abrieron ~** disciplinary action was taken against him

expedir [I14] *vt* (pasaporte/visa) to issue

expendio *m* (AmL) (tienda) store (AmE), shop (BrE); (venta) sale; **un ~ de licores** a package store (AmE), an off-licence (BrE)

expensas: **a expensas de algo** (de ideales/salud) at the expense of; **vive a ~ de su familia** he lives off his family

experiencia *f* (a) (conocimiento, suceso) experience; **saber algo por ~** to know sth by *o* from experience; **~ piloto** pilot scheme (b) (experimento) experiment

experimentado -da *adj* experienced

experimental *adj* experimental

experimentar [A1] *vi* **~ CON algo** to experiment ON *o* WITH sth
■ **~** *vt* (a) (sensación) to experience, feel; (tristeza/alegría) to feel (b) (sufrir) (cambio) to undergo; **ha experimentado una leve mejoría** there's been a slight improvement in his condition

experimento *m* experiment

experto -ta *adj*: **es ~ en casos de divorcio** he's an expert on divorce cases; **~ EN hacer algo** very good AT doing sth
■ *m,f* expert

expiar [A17] *vt* to expiate, atone for

explanada *f* (plataforma) raised area, terrace; (delante de un edificio) leveled* area; (al lado del mar) esplanade

explayarse [A1] *v pron* (a) (sobre un tema) to speak at length (b) (desahogarse) to unburden oneself (c) (esparcirse) to relax

explicación *f* explanation

explicar [A2] *vt* to explain; **no sé ~lo** I don't know how to explain it
■ **explicarse** *v pron* (a) (comprender, concebir) to understand; **no me lo explico** I can't understand it *o* (colloq) I just don't get it (b) (hacerse comprender) to express oneself; **explícate** explain what you mean; **¿me explico?** do you understand what I mean?

explícito -ta *adj* explicit

exploración *f* (a) (de territorio) exploration; (de yacimientos) prospecting (b) (Mil) reconnaisance (c) (Med) examination, exploration

explorador -dora *m,f* **1** (expedicionario) explorer; (Mil) scout **2** **exploradora** *f* (Col) (Auto) fog lamp

explorar [A1] *vt* (a) (región) to explore; (yacimientos) to prospect for; (Inf) **~ la web** *or* **Red** to surf the Web (b) (posibilidades) to explore, investigate; (situación) to investigate, examine (c) (Mil) to reconnoiter*, scout; «radar/sonar» to scan

explosión *f* (a) (de bomba) explosion; **la bomba hizo ~** (period) the bomb exploded *o* went off (b) (de cólera, júbilo) outburst (c) (crecimiento brusco) explosion

explosivo¹ -va *adj* explosive; **materiales ~s** explosives

explosivo² *m* explosive

explotación *f* (a) (de tierra, mina) exploitation, working; (de negocio) running, operation (b) (de trabajador) exploitation

explotador -dora *adj* exploitative
■ *m,f* exploiter

explotar [A1] *vt* (a) (tierra) to exploit, work; (mina) to operate, work; (negocio) to run, operate (b) (idea/debilidad) to exploit (c) (trabajador) to exploit
■ *vi* (a) «bomba» to explode, go off; «caldera/máquina» to explode, blow up (b) (fam) «persona» to explode, to blow a fuse (colloq)

exponer [E22] *vt* **1** (a) (en museo) (cuadro/escultura) to exhibit, show (b) (en vitrina) to display **2** (razones/hechos) to set out, state; (ideas/teoría) to put forward; (tema) to present **3** (a) (poner en peligro) to put ... at risk (b) (al aire, sol) **~ algo A algo** to expose sth TO sth
■ **~** *vi* to exhibit, exhibit *o* show one's work
■ **exponerse** *v pron* **~se (A algo)** to expose oneself (TO sth); **te expones a que te multen** you're risking a fine

exportación *f* (a) (acción) exportation, export (b) **exportaciones** *fpl* (mercancías) exports (*pl*)

exportador -dora *adj*: **países ~es de petróleo** oil-exporting countries; **una región ~a de cítricos** a region that exports citrus fruit
■ *m,f* exporter

exportar [A1] *vt* to export

exposición *f* **1** (a) (acción) exhibition, showing (b) (muestra — de cuadros, esculturas) exhibition; (— de productos, maquinaria) show **2** (de hechos, razones) statement; (de tema, teoría) presentation **3** (al aire, sol) exposure; (Fot) exposure

expositor -tora *m,f* **1** (de cuadros, maquinaria) exhibitor **2** (Col, Ven) (conferenciante) speaker

exprés *adj inv* (Esp) (servicio/envío) express (before n)
■ *m* (Esp) (Ferr) express train, fast train

expresar [A1] *vt* to express
■ **expresarse** *v pron* to express oneself

expresión *f* expression

expresividad *f* expressiveness

expresivo -va *adj* (persona/rostro/lenguaje) expressive

expreso¹ -sa *adj* **1** (explícito) express (before n) **2** (tren) express (before n), fast (before n); (carta/envío) express (before n); **por correo ~** express **3** (café) espresso

expreso² *m* **1** (Ferr) express train, fast train **2** (café) espresso

exprimidor *m* (manual) reamer (AmE), lemon squeezer (BrE); (eléctrico) juicer

exprimir [I1] *vt* **(a)** ⟨*naranja/limón*⟩ to squeeze; ⟨*ropa*⟩ to wring **(b)** (explotar) ⟨*trabajadores*⟩ to exploit

expropiación *f* (sin indemnización) expropriation; (con indemnización) compulsory purchase

expropiar [A1] *vt* (sin indemnización) to expropriate; (con indemnización) to acquire ... by compulsory purchase

expulsar [A1] *vt* **1 (a)** (de institución) to expel; (de local) to throw ... out, eject (frml) **(b)** (de territorio) to expel, drive out **(c)** (Dep) to send off **2** ⟨*aire/cálculo*⟩ to expel

expulsión *f* expulsion; (Dep) sending-off

expurgar [A3] *vt* to expurgate

exquisito -ta *adj* ⟨*comida*⟩ delicious; ⟨*tela/poema/música*⟩ exquisite; ⟨*persona*⟩ refined

éxtasis *m* ecstasy

extático -ca *adj* ecstatic

extender [E8] *vt* **1** ⟨*periódico/mapa*⟩ to open ... up *o* out; ⟨*mantel/toalla*⟩ to spread ... out **2** ⟨*brazos*⟩ to stretch out; ⟨*alas*⟩ to spread; **le extendió la mano** he held out his hand to her **3** ⟨*pintura/mantequilla*⟩ to spread **4** (ampliar) ⟨*poderes/plazo/permiso*⟩ to extend **5** (frml) ⟨*factura/cheque/escritura*⟩ to issue; ⟨*receta*⟩ to make out, write

■ **extenderse** *v pron* **1** (en el espacio) **(a)** «*fuego/epidemia/noticia*» to spread **(b)** «*territorio/propiedad*» to stretch; **se extiende hasta el río** it stretches down to the river **(c)** «*influencia/autoridad*» to extend; **~se A algo** to extend ᴛᴏ sth **2** (en el tiempo) **(a)** «*época/debate*» to last **(b)** «*persona*»: **se extendió demasiado en ese tema** he spent too much time on that subject; **¿quisiera ~se sobre ese punto?** would you like to expand on that point?

extendido -da *adj* **(a)** ⟨*costumbre/error*⟩ widespread **(b)** ⟨*brazos/alas*⟩ outstretched

extensión *f* **1 (a)** (superficie): **una gran ~ de terreno** a large expanse *o* stretch of land; **una ~ de 20 hectáreas** an area of 20 hectares **(b)** (longitud) length; **la ~ de la novela** the length of the novel; **por ~** by extension **2** (grado, importancia) extent; **en toda la ~ de la palabra** in every sense of the word **3 (a)** (prolongación) extension; **pidió una ~ del plazo** he asked for an extension on the deadline **(b)** (de cable) extension cord (AmE), extension lead (BrE); (línea telefónica) extension

extenso -sa *adj* extensive

exterior *adj* **1 (a)** ⟨*aspecto*⟩ external (*before n*), outward (*before n*); ⟨*bolsillo/temperatura/mundo*⟩ outside (*before n*); ⟨*revestimiento/capa*⟩ outer (*before n*) **(b)** ⟨*habitación/apartamento*⟩ outward-facing **2** ⟨*comercio/política*⟩ foreign (*before n*)

■ *m* **1** (fachada) outside, exterior; (espacio circundante) outside; **desde el ~ de la iglesia** from outside the church **2 el exterior** (países extranjeros): **la influencia del ~** foreign influence;

las relaciones con el ~ relations with other countries **3 exteriores** *mpl* (Cin) location shots (*pl*); **rodar en ~es** to film on location

exteriorizar [A4] *vt* to externalize, exteriorize

exterminar [A1] *vt* to exterminate

exterminio *m* extermination

externar [A1] *vt* (Méx) to display, show

externo -na *adj* **(a)** ⟨*apariencia/signos*⟩ outward (*before n*), external; ⟨*influencia*⟩ outside, external; ⟨*superficie*⟩ external; ⟨*ángulo*⟩ exterior **(b)** ⟨*alumno*⟩ day (*before n*)

■ *m,f* day pupil

extinción *f* (de especie, volcán) extinction; **una especie en peligro de ~** an endangered species

extinguidor *m* (AmL) fire extinguisher

extinguir [I2] *vt* **(a)** ⟨*especie*⟩ to wipe out; ⟨*violencia/injusticia*⟩ to put an end to **(b)** ⟨*fuego*⟩ to extinguish, put out

■ **extinguirse** *v pron* **(a)** «*especie*» to become extinct, die out **(b)** «*fuego*» to go out; «*volcán*» to become extinct; «*sonido*» to die away **(c)** «*entusiasmo/amor*» to die

extintor *m* (Esp): *tb* **~ de incendios** fire extinguisher

extirpar [A1] *vt* (Med) to remove

extorsión *f* extortion

extorsionar [A1] *vt* to extort money from

extra *adj* **(a)** (Com) top quality, fancy grade (AmE) **(b)** (adicional) ⟨*gastos/ración*⟩ additional, extra; ⟨*edición*⟩ special

■ *adv* extra

■ *mf* (Cin) extra

■ *m* (gasto) extra expense; (paga) bonus

extracción *f* **(a)** (en general) extraction **(b)** *tb* **~ social** background, origins (*pl*); **de ~ humilde** of humble origins

extraconyugal *adj* extramarital

extracto *m* **(a)** (resumen) summary, abstract; **~ de cuenta** (bank) statement **(b)** (esencia) extract

extractor *m* extractor; **~ de aire** extractor fan

extradición *f* extradition

extraer [E23] *vt* (en general) to extract; ⟨*bala*⟩ to remove; ⟨*conclusión*⟩ to draw

extraescolar *adj* extramural, out-of-school (*before n*)

extralimitarse [A1] *v pron* to exceed one's authority

extramatrimonial *adj* extramarital

extranjero -ra *adj* foreign

■ *m,f* **(a)** (persona) foreigner **(b) extranjero** *m*: **al/en el ~** abroad; **noticias del ~** foreign news

extrañar [A1] *vt* (esp AmL) ⟨*amigo/país*⟩ to miss

■ **~** *vi* **1** (sorprender) (+ *me/te/le etc*) to surprise; **me extraña que no lo sepas** I'm surprised you didn't know that; **ya me extrañaba a mí que ...** I thought it was strange that ... **2** (RPl) (tener nostalgia) to be homesick

■ **extrañarse** *v pron* **~se ᴅᴇ algo** to be surprised ᴀᴛ sth

extrañeza *f* surprise; **me miró con ~** she looked at me in surprise

extraño -ña *adj* (raro) strange, odd; **eso no tiene nada de ~** there's nothing unusual about that

■ *m,f* (desconocido) stranger

extraoficial *adj* unofficial

extraordinario -ria adj (en general)
extraordinary; ‹edición› special; ‹contribución›
extra, additional; **la película no fue nada ~** the
movie was nothing special o nothing out of the
ordinary

extraplano -na adj ‹reloj/calculadora›
slimline; ‹compresa› extra-slim

extrarradio m outlying districts (pl),
outskirts (pl)

extrasensorial adj extrasensory

extraterrestre adj/mf alien, extraterrestrial

extravagancia f (acto) outrageous thing (to
do); (cualidad) extravagance

extravagante adj ‹comportamiento/ideas›
outrageous, extravagant; ‹persona/ropa›
flamboyant, outrageous

extraviado -da adj ‹objeto/niño› lost,
missing; ‹perro/gato› stray

extraviar [A17] vt (fml) to mislay (fml), to lose
■ **extraviarse** v pron (fml) «persona/animal» to
get lost; «documento» to go missing

extremado -da adj extreme

extremar [A1] vt (fml) to maximize (fml)
■ **extremarse** v pron ~ (**EN hacer algo**) to make
a great effort (to do sth)

extremaunción f extreme unction

extremidad f (a) (extremo) end (b)
extremidades fpl (Anat) extremities

extremista adj (extremo) extreme; (Pol)
extremist
■ mf (Pol) extremist

extremo¹ -ma adj extreme; **un caso de
extrema gravedad** an extremely serious case; **en
caso ~** as a last resort; **~ derecha/izquierda** (Pol)
extreme right/left; **~ derecho/izquierdo** (Dep)
right/left wing; **E~ Oriente** Far East

extremo² m (a) (de palo, cable) end (b) (postura
extrema) extreme; **va de un ~ a otro** she goes from
one extreme to the other; **son ~s opuestos** they
are complete opposites (c) (límite): **si se llega a
ese ~** ... if it gets that bad o to that point ...; **en
último ~** as a last resort

extrovertido -da adj/m,f extrovert

exuberante adj exuberant; ‹mujer›
voluptuous

exudar [A1] vt to exude

exultar [A1] vi to exult (fml), to rejoice

eyaculación f ejaculation

eyacular [A1] vi to ejaculate

Ff

F, f f (read as /'efe/) the letter F, f

fa m (nota) F; (en solfeo) fa, fah (BrE)

fábrica f factory; **una ~ de zapatos** a shoe
factory; **~ de textiles/papel** textile/paper mill; **~
de cerveza** brewery; **~ de conservas** cannery

fabricación f manufacture; **la ~ de coches**
car manufacture; **de ~ japonesa** made in Japan;
de ~ casera home-made; **~ en serie** mass
production

fabricante mf manufacturer

fabricar [A2] vt to manufacture; **~ en cadena/
serie** to mass-produce; Ⓢ **fabricado en Perú** made
in Peru

fábula f (Lit) fable; (mentira) fabrication

fabuloso -sa adj (maravilloso) (fam) fabulous
(colloq)

facción f (a) (Pol) faction (b) **facciones** fpl
(rasgos) features (pl)

faceta f facet

facha f (fam) (aspecto) look; **no me gustó su ~** I
didn't like the look of him; **¿vas a salir con esa
~?** are you going out looking like that?; **estar
hecho una ~** to be o look a sight (colloq)
■ adj/mf (Chi, Esp fam) fascist

fachada f (a) (de edificio) facade (tech), front (b)
(apariencia) facade

fácil adj ① (a) ‹problema/lección/vida› easy; **~
de entender** easy to understand (b) (pey) (en lo
sexual) easy (pej), loose (pej) ② (probable): **es ~
que se le olvide** he'll probably forget; **no es ~
que me lo den** they are unlikely to let me have it

facilidad f ① (a) (cualidad de fácil) ease; **con ~**
easily (b) (de una tarea) simplicity ② (aptitud):
tener ~ para los idiomas/los números to have a
gift for languages/to be good at figures; **tiene ~
de palabra** he has a way with words
③ **facilidades** fpl (a) (posibilidades,
oportunidades): **se le dieron todas las ~es** they
gave her every chance (b) (Fin) tb **~es de pago**
credit facilities (pl)

facilitar [A1] vt (a) (hacer más fácil) ‹tarea› to
make ... easier, facilitate (fml) (b) (fml)
(proporcionar) ‹datos/información› to provide

factible adj possible, feasible

factor m factor; **el ~ tiempo** the time factor

factoría f (fábrica) factory; (astillero) shipyard;
(fundición) foundry

factura f ① (Com) invoice (fml), bill; **pasarle ~
a algn** (Fin) to invoice sb ② (RPl) (Coc) rolls,
croissants, etc

facturación *f* 1 (Com) (a) (acción) invoicing (b) (volumen) turnover 2 (Ferr) registration; (Aviac) check-in

facturar [A1] *vt* 1 (Com) (a) ‹mercancías/arreglo› to invoice for, bill for (b) (refiriéndose al volumen de ventas) to turn over, have a turnover of 2 (Ferr) to register; (Aviac) to check in
■ ~ *vi* (Ferr) to register; (Aviac) to check in

facultad *f* 1 (capacidad) faculty; **está perdiendo ~es** he's losing his faculties; **~es mentales** (mental) faculties (*pl*) 2 (Educ) faculty; **F~ de Filosofía y Letras** Faculty of Arts

facultar [A1] *vt* (frml) **~ a algn PARA hacer algo** «jefe/presidente» to authorize sb to do sth; «carnet/documento» to entitle sb to do sth; «ley» to allow sb to do sth

faena *f* 1 (tarea) task, job; **es una ~ dura** it's hard work; **~s domésticas** housework; **~s agrícolas** farm work 2 (fam) (a) (mala pasada) dirty trick; **hacerle una ~ a algn** to play a dirty trick on sb (colloq) (b) (contratiempo) drag (colloq), pain (colloq)

fagot /faˈɣo(t)/ *m* (instrumento) bassoon
■ *mf* (músico) bassoonist

faisán *m* pheasant

faja *f* (a) (prenda interior) girdle (b) (cinturón — de traje regional) wide belt; (— de sotana) sash; (— de smoking) cummerbund (c) (franja, zona) strip

fajo *m* (de billetes) wad, roll (AmE); (de papeles) bundle, sheaf

falange *f* 1 (Anat) phalanx, phalange 2 (a) (Mil) phalanx (b) (Hist, Pol) phalanx; **la F~** the Spanish Falangist Movement

falda *f* (a) (Indum) skirt; **~ escocesa** (de mujer) tartan skirt, kilt; (de hombre) kilt; **~ pantalón** split skirt, culottes (*pl*); **se enemistaron por un asunto de ~s** they fell out over a woman (b) (de montaña) side

faldón *m*, **faldones** *mpl* (a) (de camisa) shirttails; (de frac, chaqué) coattails (b) (de bebé) christening robe

falla *f* 1 (a) (de tela, cristal) flaw; **la pieza tenía una ~** the part was defective (b) (Geol) fault 2 (a) (de motor, máquina, sistema — en la composición) defect, fault; (— en el funcionamiento) failure; **~s en el sistema de seguridad** security failures (b) (de persona) mistake; **~ humana** (AmL) human error; **¡qué ~!** what a stupid mistake! (c) (Dep) miss 3 (AmL exc CS fam) (lástima) pity, shame 4 (a) (figura) model, figure (*burned during the* FALLAS) (b) **las Fallas** *fpl* (fiesta) *the festival of San José in Valencia*

fallado -da *adj* (CS) flawed, defective

fallar [A1] *vi* 1 «juez/jurado» **~ a** *or* **en favor/en contra de algn** to rule in favor* of/against sb 2 (a) «frenos/memoria» to fail; «planes» to go wrong; **le falló el corazón** his heart failed; **le falló la puntería** he missed; **a ti te falla** (AmL) (fam) you've a screw loose (colloq) (b) «persona» (+ *me/te/le* etc) to let ... down
■ ~ *vt* (errar) to miss; **fallé el tiro** I missed (the shot)

fallecer [E3] *vi* (frml *o* euf) to pass away (frml *or* euph), to die

fallecimiento *m* (frml) death, passing (frml *or* euph)

fallero -ra *m,f*: *person who takes part in the preparation of the* FALLAS

fallo *m* (a) (en concurso, certamen) decision; (Der) ruling, judgment (b) (Esp) ▶ FALLA 2

falluca *f* (Méx fam) (comercio ilegal) black market (*gen in smuggled goods*); (mercancía) smuggled goods (*pl*)

falsear [A1] *vt* ‹hechos/datos› to falsify; ‹verdad/realidad› to distort

falsedad *f* (a) (de afirmación) falseness; (de persona) insincerity, falseness (b) (mentira) lie

falsificador -dora *m,f* forger

falsificar [A2] *vt* (a) ‹firma/billete/cheque› to forge (b) ‹documento› (copiar) to forge, counterfeit; (alterar) to falsify

falso -sa *adj* (a) ‹billete› counterfeit, forged; ‹cuadro› forged; ‹documento› false, forged; ‹diamante/joya› fake; ‹cajón/techo› false (b) (insincero) ‹persona› insincere, false; ‹sonrisa/promesa› false (c) (no cierto) ‹dato/nombre/declaración› false; **eso es ~** that is not true *o* is untrue; **falsa alarma** false alarm; **~ testimonio** *m* (Der) false testimony, perjury

falta *f* 1 (carencia, ausencia) (de ‹interés/dinero›) lack OF sth; **~ de personal** staff shortage; **es la ~ de costumbre** it's because I'm/you're not used to it; **fue una ~ de respeto** it was very rude of you/him/her/them; **eso es una ~ de educación** that's bad manners; **a ~ de más información** in the absence of more information 2 (inasistencia) *tb* **~ de asistencia** absence; **le pusieron ~** they marked her down as absent 3 (a) **hacer falta**: **no hace ~ que se queden** there's no need for you to stay; **si hace ~ ...** if necessary ...; **hacen ~ dos vasos más** we need two more glasses; **le hace ~ descansar** he/she needs to rest (b) **sin falta** without fail 4 (defecto) fault; **a pesar de todas sus ~s** in spite of all his faults; **sacarle** *or* **encontrarle ~s a algo** to find fault with sth; **~ de ortografía** spelling mistake 5 (Dep) (infracción — en fútbol, baloncesto) foul; (— en tenis) fault (b) (tiro libre — en fútbol) free kick; (— en balonmano) free throw

faltar [A1] *vi* 1 (a) (no estar) to be missing; **¿quién falta?** who's missing?; (en colegio, reunión) who's absent?; **te falta un botón** you have a button missing; **a esta taza le falta el asa** there's no handle on this cup (b) (no haber suficiente): **va a ~ vino** there won't be enough wine; **nos faltó tiempo** we didn't have enough time (c) (hacer falta): **le falta alguien que la aconseje** she needs someone to advise her; **les falta cariño** they need affection
2 (quedar): **yo estoy lista ¿a ti te falta mucho?** I'm ready, will you be long?; **nos falta poco para terminar** we're almost finished; **me faltan tres páginas para terminar el libro** I have three pages to go to to finish the book; **solo me falta pasarlo a máquina** all I have to do is type it out; **falta poco para Navidad** it's not long until Christmas; **faltan cinco minutos para que empiece** there are five minutes to go before it starts; **¡no faltaba más!** (respuesta — a un agradecimiento) don't mention it!; (— a una petición) of course, certainly!; (— a un ofrecimiento) I wouldn't hear of it!
3 (a) (no asistir): **te esperamos, no faltes** we're expecting you, make sure you come; **~ a algo** «al ⋯⟶

colegio) to be absent FROM sth; ⟨*a una cita*⟩ to miss sth; ~ **a clase** to skip lessons; **ha faltado dos veces al trabajo** she's been off work twice **(b)** (*no cumplir*): **faltó a su promesa** he didn't keep his promise; **¡no me faltes al respeto!** don't be rude to me

fama *f* **(a)** (*renombre, celebridad*) fame; **una marca de ~ mundial** a world-famous brand; **dar ~ a algo/algn** to make sb/sth famous **(b)** (*reputación*) reputation; **tener mala ~** to have a bad reputation; **tiene ~ de ser severo** he has a reputation for being strict; **tiene ~ de bromista** he's well known as a joker

familia *f* **(a)** (*parientes*) family; **una ~ numerosa** a large family; **mi ~ política** my wife's/husband's family, my in-laws (colloq); **es de buena ~** *or* **de ~ bien** he's from a good family; **somos como de la ~** we're just like family; **le viene de ~** it runs in the family **(b)** (*hijos*) children; **no tienen ~** they don't have any children

familiar *adj* **(a)** ⟨*vida/vínculo*⟩ family (*before n*); ⟨*envase/coche*⟩ family (*before n*) **(b)** ⟨*trato/tono*⟩ familiar, informal; ⟨*lenguaje/expresión*⟩ colloquial **(c)** (*conocido*) ⟨*cara/lugar*⟩ familiar; **su voz me resulta ~** her voice is familiar
■ *mf* relative, relation

familiaridad *f* familiarity

familiarizarse [A4] *v pron* **~ CON algo** to familiarize oneself WITH sth, become familiar WITH sth

famoso -sa *adj* famous; **~ POR algo** famous FOR sth
■ *m,f* celebrity, famous person

fan *mf* (*pl* **fans**) fan

fanático -ca *adj* fanatical
■ *m,f* (*en general*) fanatic; **es un ~ de la gimnasia** he's a gym fanatic; (*de fútbol*) (AmS period) fan

fanatismo *m* fanaticism

fanfarrón -rrona *adj* (fam) (*al hablar*) loudmouthed (colloq); (*al actuar*): **no seas ~** stop showing off
■ *m,f* (fam) (*al hablar*) loudmouth (colloq); (*al actuar*) show-off (colloq)

fanfarronear [A1] *vi* (fam) **(a)** (*al hablar*) to boast, brag **(b)** (*al actuar*) to show off (colloq)

fango *m* mud

fantasear [A1] *vi* to fantasize

fantasía *f* ⊡ **(a)** (*imaginación*) imagination **(b)** (*ficción*) fantasy; **vive en un mundo de ~** he's living in a fantasy world ⊡ (*bisutería*): **joyas de ~** costume jewelry*; **una pulsera de ~** an imitation diamond (*o* ruby *etc*) bracelet

fantasma *m* **(a)** (*aparición*) ghost **(b)** (*amenaza*) specter*

fantástico -ca *adj* fantastic

fantochear [A1] *vi* (AmL fam) ▶ FANFARRONEAR

faquir *m* fakir

faraón *m* Pharaoh

fardar [A1] *vi* (Esp fam) «*persona*» ▶ FANFARRONEAR

fardo *m* (*de algodón, paja*) bale; (*de ropa*) bundle

faringe *f* pharynx

faringitis *f* pharyngitis

farmacéutico -ca *adj* pharmaceutical
■ *m,f* druggist (AmE), chemist (BrE)

farmacia *f* **(a)** (*tienda*) drugstore (AmE), chemist's (BrE); **~ de guardia** *or* **de turno** duty chemist **(b)** (*disciplina*) pharmacy

faro *m* **(a)** (Náut) lighthouse **(b)** (Auto) headlight, headlamp; **~ antiniebla** fog light *o* (BrE) lamp

farol *m* (*de alumbrado público*) streetlight, streetlamp; (*en jardín, portal*) lantern, lamp; **~ de papel** paper lantern

farola *f* (*luz*) streetlight, streetlamp; (*poste*) lamppost

farolillo *m* (*de papel*) Chinese lantern

farra *f* (fam) ▶ JUERGA

farrear [A1] *vi* (AmL fam) to go out partying (colloq), go out on the town (colloq)
■ **farrearse** *v pron* (AmL fam) ⟨*fortuna/dinero*⟩ to blow (colloq); ⟨*oportunidad*⟩ to throw away

farrero -ra *adj/m,f* (AmL fam) ▶ FARRISTA

farrista *adj* (AmL fam): **estudiantes ~s** students who are always out living it up
■ *mf* (AmL fam): **es un ~** he's always out living it up

farsa *f* (Teatr) farce; (*engaño*) sham, farce

farsante *mf* fraud, fake

fascículo *m* part (*of a serialized publication*), fascicle (tech)

fascinación *f* fascination

fascinante *adj* fascinating

fascinar [A1] *vi* (fam): **me fascinó ese programa** I found that program fascinating; **me fascina viajar** I love travelling
■ **~** *vt* to fascinate, captivate

fascismo *m* fascism

fascista *adj/mf* fascist

fase *f* **(a)** (*etapa*) stage, phase; **la ~ de clasificación** the preliminary round; **está todavía en ~ de negociación** it is still being negotiated **(b)** (Astron, Elec, Fis, Quím) phase

fastidiado -da *adj* (esp Esp fam): **estoy un poco ~** I'm not too good *o* too well; **anda ~ de los riñones** he's having trouble with his kidneys

fastidiar [A1] *vt* **(a)** (*molestar, irritar*) ⟨*persona*⟩ to bother, pester **(b)** (esp Esp fam) (*estropear*) ⟨*mecanismo/plan*⟩ to mess up; ⟨*fiesta/excursión*⟩ to spoil; ⟨*estómago*⟩ to upset
■ **~** *vi*: **me fastidia tener que repetir las cosas** it annoys me to have to repeat things; **¡no fastidies! ¿de veras?** go on! you're kidding! (colloq)
■ **fastidiarse** *v pron* **(a)** (AmL fam) (*molestarse*) to get annoyed **(b)** (fam) (*jorobarse*): **tendré que ~me** I'll have to put up with it (colloq); **¡te fastidias!** (Esp) tough! (colloq) **(c)** (Esp fam) (*estropearse*) «*velada/plan*» to be ruined

fastidio *m* (*molestia*) annoyance; **¡qué ~!** what a nuisance!

fastidioso -sa *adj* **(a)** (*molesto*) ⟨*persona*⟩ tiresome, annoying; ⟨*trabajo*⟩ tiresome, irksome **(b)** (Méx, Per fam) (*quisquilloso*) fussy (colloq)

fastuoso -sa *adj* ⟨*salón*⟩ magnificent; ⟨*banquete*⟩ lavish

fatal *adj* ⊡ ⟨*accidente/enfermedad/consecuencias*⟩ fatal ⊡ (fam) (*muy malo*) terrible, awful; **fue un fin de semana ~** it was a terrible weekend; **me encuentro ~** I feel awful; **su padre está ~** his father's in a really bad way (colloq)
■ *adv* (esp Esp fam): **viste ~** he dresses really badly; **me caen ~** I can't stand them (colloq)

fatiga *f* **(a)** (cansancio) tiredness, fatigue (frml) **(b)** (ahogo) breathlessness

fatigado -da *adj* tired, weary

fatigar [A3] *vt* (físicamente) to tire ... out; (mentalmente) to tire

■ **fatigarse** *v pron* **(a)** (cansarse) to get tired, wear oneself out (colloq) **(b)** (ahogarse) to get breathless

fatigoso -sa *adj* ‹trabajo› tiring, exhausting

faul *m* (*pl* **fauls**) (AmL) foul

faulear [A1] *vt* (AmL) to foul

fauna *f* fauna

favor *m* **(a)** (ayuda, servicio) favor*; ¿me puedes hacer un ∼? can you do me a favor?; **vengo a pedirte un ∼** I've come to ask you (for) a favor; ¿me harías el ∼ **de copiarme esto?** would you copy this for me, please?; **hagan el ∼ de esperar** would you mind waiting, please? **(b)** (*en locs*) a favor in favor*; **dos votos a ∼** two votes in favor; **en ∼ de** in favour of; **estar a ∼ de algo/algn/ hacer algo** to be in favour* of sth/sb/doing sth; **por favor** please

favorable *adj* favorable*

favorecedor -dora *adj* becoming

favorecer [E3] *vt* **(a)** (ayudar, beneficiar) to favor*; **una política para ∼ la agricultura** a policy to help agriculture **(b)** «peinado/color» (sentar bien) to suit

favoritismo *m* favoritism*

favorito -ta *adj/m,f* favorite*

fax *m* fax; **mándaselo por ∼** fax it to him

faxear [A1] *vt* to fax, send ... by fax

Fdo (= **firmado**) (en correspondencia) signed

fe *f* **(a)** (Relig) faith; (creencia, confianza) faith; **tener ∼ en algo/algn** to have faith in sth/sb; **puse toda mi ∼ en ti** I put all my trust in you **(b)** (intención): **no dudo de su buena ∼** I don't doubt his good intentions; **actuar de buena/mala ∼** to act in good/bad faith

febrero *m* February; *para ejemplos ver* ENERO

fecha *f* date; ¿qué ∼ **es hoy?** what's the date today?, what date is it today?; **con ∼ 7 de marzo** (Corresp) dated March 7 *o* (BrE) 7th March; **hasta la ∼** to date; **el año pasado por estas ∼s** this time last year; **en ∼ próxima** soon; **∼ de caducidad** *or* (AmL) **vencimiento** (de medicamento) expiration date (AmE), expiry date (BrE); (de alimento) use-by date; **∼ de consumo preferente** best-before date; **∼ límite** *or* **tope** (para solicitud, suscripción) closing date; (para proyecto, trabajo) deadline

fechar [A1] *vt* to date

fechoría *f* misdeed

fecundación *f* fertilization; **∼ in vitro** in vitro fertilization

fecundar [A1] *vt* ‹óvulo› to fertilize; ‹animal› to inseminate

fecundo -da *adj* **(a)** (Biol) ‹mujer› fertile **(b)** ‹región/tierra› fertile; ‹labor› fruitful

federación *f* federation

federal *adj* federal

felicidad *f* **(a)** (alegría) happiness **(b)** **¡felicidades!** *interj* (por cumpleaños) Happy Birthday!; (en Navidad) Merry Christmas!; (por un logro) congratulations!

felicitación *f* **(a)** (escrito — por un logro) letter of congratulation; (— en Navidad) Christmas card (*or letter wishing sb Merry Christmas*) **(b)**

felicitaciones *fpl* (deseo — por un logro) congratulations (*pl*); (— en Navidad) greetings (*pl*) **(c)** **¡felicitaciones!** *interj* (AmL) congratulations!

felicitar [A1] *vt* **(a)** (por un logro) to congratulate; **¡te felicito!** congratulations!; **me felicitó por el premio** he congratulated me on winning the prize **(b)** (por Navidad) to wish ... (a) Merry Christmas; (por cumpleaños) to wish ... (a) Happy Birthday

feligrés -gresa *m,f* parishioner

feliz *adj* happy; **les deseo que sean muy felices** I wish you every happiness; **¡∼ cumpleaños!** happy birthday!; **¡∼ Navidad!** Merry Christmas!; **¡∼ Año Nuevo!** Happy New Year!; **¡∼ viaje!** have a good trip!

felpa *f* (Tex) (para toallas) toweling*; (en tapicería) plush

felpudo *m* doormat

femenil *adj* (Méx) ‹equipo/moda› ladies' (*before n*), women's (*before n*)

femenino -na *adj* **(a)** ‹equipo/moda› ladies' (*before n*), women's (*before n*); ‹hormona/sexo› female **(b)** ‹vestido/modales/chica› feminine **(c)** (Ling) feminine

femineidad, feminidad *f* femininity

feminismo *m* feminism

feminista *adj/mf* feminist

fenomenal *adj* (fam) great (colloq)

■ *adv* (fam): **lo pasamos ∼** we had a great time (colloq); **me vino ∼** it was exactly *o* just what I needed; **¡∼!** great! (colloq)

fenómeno[1] **-na** *adj/adv* (AmL) ▶ FENOMENAL

fenómeno[2] *m* (suceso) phenomenon

feo[1]**, fea** *adj* **(a)** ‹persona/edificio› ugly; ‹peinado› unflattering; **es fea de cara** she has a very plain face; **es un barrio ∼** it's not a very nice neighborhood **(b)** ‹asunto/situación› unpleasant; ‹olor/sabor› (esp AmL) unpleasant!; **¡qué ∼ está el día!** what an awful day!; **la cosa se está poniendo fea** things are getting nasty *o* ugly; **es** *or* (Esp) **está muy ∼ hablar así** it's not nice to talk like that

feo[2] *adv* (AmL) ‹oler/saber› bad; **me miró ∼** she gave me a dirty look

féretro *m* coffin

feria *f* **1** **(a)** (exposición comercial) fair; **∼ de muestras** trade fair **(b)** (CS, Per) (mercado) (street) market **2** **(a)** (fiesta popular) festival **(b)** (parque de atracciones) fair **3** **(a)** (Méx fam) (cambio, suelto) small change; (dinero) cash (colloq)

feriado *m* (AmL) (public) holiday

fermentar [A1] *vi/vt* to ferment

fermento *m* ferment

feroz *adj* **(a)** ‹animal› ferocious, fierce; ‹ataque/ mirada/odio› fierce, vicious; ‹viento/tempestad› fierce, violent **(b)** (Col, Méx, Ven fam) (feo) horrendous (colloq)

ferretería *f* (tienda) hardware store, ironmonger's (BrE); (mercancías) hardware, ironmongery (BrE)

ferrocarril *m* railroad (AmE), railway (BrE)

ferrocarrilero -ra *adj* (Chi, Méx) rail (*before n*)

ferroviario -ria *adj* rail (*before n*)

ferry /'feri/ *m* (*pl* **-rrys**) ferry

fértil *adj* fertile

fertilización *f* fertilization; ~ **in vitro** in vitro fertilization

fertilizante *m* fertilizer

fertilizar [A4] *vt* to fertilize, put fertilizer on

ferviente *adj* ⟨admiración/creyente⟩ fervent; ⟨deseo⟩ burning; ⟨fe/defensor⟩ passionate

fervor *m* fervor*; **con** ~ fervently

festejado -da *m,f* (CS) *person celebrating his/her birthday* (*o saint's day etc*)

festejar [A1] *vt* (AmL) ⟨celebrar⟩ to celebrate

festejo *m* celebration, festivity

festín *m* feast, banquet

festival *m* festival; ~ **de cine** film festival

festividad *f* **(a)** (fiesta religiosa) feast, festivity **(b) festividades** *fpl* (festejos) festivities (*pl*)

festivo -va *adj* festive; ▶ DÍA 1B

fetidez *f* (cualidad) smelliness; (olor) stench

fétido -da *adj* fetid, foul-smelling

feto *m* fetus*

feúcho -cha *adj* (fam) ⟨mujer⟩ plain, homely (AmE colloq); **es** ~ he's not much to look at

feudalismo *m* feudalism

fiable *adj* reliable

fiaca *adj inv* (RPl fam) bone idle (colloq), lazy ■ *f* (Andes, CS fam) (pereza): **me da** ~ I can't be bothered

fiador -dora *m,f* (Com, Der, Fin) guarantor

fiambre *m* (Coc): *tb* ~**s** cold cuts (*pl*) (AmE), cold meats (*pl*) (BrE)

fiambrería *f* (AmL) delicatessen

fianza *f* **(a)** (Der) bail; **salió bajo** ~ she was released on bail **(b)** (Com) deposit

fiar [A17] *vt* ⟨mercancías⟩ to sell … on credit ■ ~ *vi* **(a)** (dar crédito) to give credit **(b) ser de** ~ «persona» (digno de confianza) to be trustworthy; (responsable) to be reliable; «mecanismo/motor» to be reliable ■ **fiarse** *v pron*: **no me fío de lo que dice** I don't believe what he says; **~se DE** algn to trust sb

fiasco *m* fiasco

fibra *f* fiber*; ~**s artificiales** man-made fibers; ~ **de vidrio** fiberglass*; ~ **óptica** optical fiber*

ficción *f* fiction

ficha *f* **1** (para datos) card; (de fichero) index card; ~ **médica** medical records (*pl*); ~ **policial** police record **2 (a)** (de teléfono, estacionamiento) token **(b)** (Jueg) (de dominó) domino; (de damas) checker(AmE), draught (BrE); (de otros juegos de mesa) counter; (de ruleta, póker) chip

fichaje *m* (Dep) (acción) signing (up); (jugador) signing, trade (AmE)

fichar [A1] *vt* **(a)** «policía» to open a file on **(b)** «equipo/club» to sign (up) ■ ~ *vi* (en fábrica, oficina — a la entrada) to clock in, punch in (AmE); (— a la salida) to clock out *o* (BrE) off, to punch out (AmE)

fichero *m* **(a)** (mueble para carpetas) filing cabinet **(b)** (cajón — de carpetas) filing draw; (— para tarjetas) card index draw **(c)** (caja) index card file (AmE), card index box (BrE) **(d)** (conjunto de fichas) file; (Inf) file

ficticio -cia *adj* ⟨personaje/suceso⟩ fictitious

fidelidad *f* **(a)** (de persona, animal) fidelity, faithfulness **(b)** (de reproducción) faithfulness, fidelity; (de instrumento) accuracy, precision

fideo *m* **(a)** (pasta fina) noodle; (muy finos) vermicelli **(b) fideos** *mpl* (RPl) (pasta en general) pasta

fiebre *f* **(a)** (Med) fever; **tener** ~ to be feverish, to have a fever (esp AmE), to have a temperature (esp BrE); **le bajó la** ~ his fever *o* temperature came down; ~ **del heno** hay fever; ~ **palúdica** malaria **(b)** (furor) obsession; **le dio la** ~ **de la limpieza** he went crazy and started cleaning the whole house (colloq); ~ **del oro** gold fever

fiel *adj* **(a)** ⟨persona/animal⟩ faithful; **serle** ~ **a** algn to be faithful to sb; ~ **al rey** loyal to the king **(b)** ⟨traducción/copia⟩ faithful, accurate ■ *mf* (Relig) **los** ~**es** the faithful

fieltro *m* felt

fiera *f* (animal) wild animal, beast (liter); **ponerse como** *or* **hecho una** ~ to go wild (colloq)

fiero -ra *adj* ⟨animal⟩ fierce, ferocious

fierro *m* **(a)** (AmL) (hierro) iron; (fam) (trozo de metal) piece of metal **(b) fierros** *mpl* (Méx fam) (en los dientes) braces (*pl*) (AmE), brace (esp BrE)

fiesta *f* **(a)** (celebración) party; ~ **de cumpleaños** birthday party; **dieron una gran** ~ they threw *o* had a big party; **estar de** ~ to be having a party; **aguar la** ~ to spoil the fun **(b)** (día festivo) (public) holiday; **el lunes es** ~ Monday is a holiday; ~ **nacional** (día festivo) public holiday; (Taur) bullfighting; ~ **patria** (AmL) independence day **(c) fiestas** *fpl* (festejos) fiesta, festival; (de fin de año, etc) festive season; **¡felices** ~**s!** Merry Christmas!; **¿dónde vas a pasar estas** ~**s?** where are you going to spend the vacation (AmE) *o* (BrE) holidays?

FIFA /'fifa/ *f*: **la** ~ FIFA

figura *f* figure; **tiene buena** ~ she has a good figure; **una** ~ **de las letras** an important literary figure; ~ **paterna** father figure

figuración *f* (imaginación) imagining; **son figuraciones tuyas** it's all in your imagination

figurado -da *adj* figurative; **en sentido** ~ in a figurative sense

figurar [A1] *vi* (en lista, documento) to appear ■ **figurarse** *v pron* to imagine; **me figuro que sí** I imagine so, I figure she (*o* he *etc*) will (AmE); **me figuro que tardaremos una hora** I reckon *o* (AmE) figure that it'll take us one hour; **¡figúrate, tardamos dos horas!** just imagine! it took us two hours; **ya me lo figuraba yo** I thought as much, so I thought

figurita *f* (de adorno) figurine; (lámina) (RPl) picture card

AmC	Central America	Arg	Argentina	Cu	Cuba	Per	Peru
AmL	Latin America	Bol	Bolivia	Ec	Ecuador	RPl	River Plate Area
AmS	South America	Chi	Chile	Esp	Spain	Ur	Uruguay
Andes	Andean Region	CS	Southern Cone	Méx	Mexico	Ven	Venezuela

fijación *f* (Psic) fixation, obsession; ¡que ∼ tienes con ese tema! you're obsessed with that subject!

fijar [A1] *vt* **1** **(a)** (poner, clavar) ‹poste/ estantería› to fix; **⊖ prohibido fijar carteles** stick no bills; **fijó la mirada en el horizonte** she fixed her gaze on the horizon **(b)** ‹atención/mente› to focus
2 **(a)** ‹residencia› to take up, establish (frml) **(b)** ‹fecha/cifra/precio› to set **(c)** «reglamento/ley» to state

■ **fijarse** *v pron* **(a)** (prestar atención): fíjate bien en cómo lo hace watch carefully how she does it; fíjate en lo que haces watch *o* pay attention to what you're doing **(b)** (darse cuenta) to notice; ¿te has fijado en que no discuten nunca? have you noticed that they never quarrel?; ¡fíjate lo que ha crecido! just look how she's grown!

fijo¹ -ja *adj* **(a)** (no movible) fixed; una lámpara fija a la pared a lamp fixed to the wall; con los ojos ∼s en ella with his eyes fixed on her; asegúrate de que la escalera está bien fija make sure the ladder is steady **(b)** ‹sueldo/precios› fixed; ‹trabajo/empleado› permanent; ‹cliente› regular **(c)** (definitivo) ‹fecha› definite, firm

fijo² *adv* (fam): ¿crees que vendrá? — fijo do you think she'll come? — definitely *o* (colloq) sure; ∼ que el domingo llueve it's bound to rain on Sunday

fila *f* **(a)** (hilera) line; formen ∼ aquí line up *o* form a line here; en ∼ india in single file; estacionado en doble ∼ double-parked **(b)** (en teatro, aula) row **(c)** filas *fpl* (Mil) ranks (*pl*); incorporarse a ∼s to join up; lo llamaron a ∼s he was drafted

filamento *m* (Elec) filament; (hilo, fibra) thread

filatelia *f* stamp collecting, philately

filete *m* (de pescado) fillet; (de carne — bistec) steak; (— corte entre las costillas y el lomo) (Chi, Méx) fillet

filiación *f* (afiliación) affiliation; ∼ política political affiliation

filial *adj* **(a)** ‹amor› filial **(b)** ‹compañía/ asociación› affiliate (*before n*), subsidiary
■ *f* subsidiary (company)

Filipinas *fpl*: *tb* las ∼ the Philippines

filipino -na *adj* Philippine, Filipino
■ *m,f* Filipino

film *m* (*pl* films) **(a)** (Cin, TV) movie, film (BrE) **(b)** (Coc) *tb* ∼ transparente Saran wrap® (AmE), clingfilm (BrE)

filmadora *f* (AmL) movie camera (AmE), cinecamera (BrE)

filmar [A1] *vt* ‹película› to shoot; ‹persona/ suceso› to film

filmina *f* slide

filmoteca *f* film library

filo *m* **(a)** (de cuchillo, espada) cutting edge, blade; no tiene mucho ∼ it isn't very sharp; le voy a dar ∼ I'm going to sharpen it **(b)** (borde) edge; el ∼ de la mesa the edge of the table; al ∼ de las siete at seven o'clock sharp

filología *f* philology; una licenciatura en ∼ francesa a degree in French

filólogo -ga *m,f* philologist; soy ∼ I have a degree in languages

filón *m* **(a)** (Min) seam, vein **(b)** (fam) (negocio) gold mine (colloq)

filoso -sa *adj* (AmL) ‹cuchillo/hoja› sharp

filosofía *f* philosophy

filosófico -ca *adj* philosophical

filósofo -fa *m,f* philosopher

filtración *f* (en general) leak ; (de información) leak; la ∼ de un informe the leaking of a report

filtrar [A1] *vt* **(a)** ‹líquido/rayos› to filter **(b)** ‹informaciones/noticias› to leak
■ **filtrarse** *v pron* **(a)** «agua» to leak; «humedad» to seep; la luz se filtraba por entre las persianas light filtered through the shutters **(b)** «noticia» to leak

filtro *m* filter; ∼ solar sunscreen

fin *m* **1** **(a)** (final) end; a ∼es de junio at the end of June; a ∼ de mes at the end of the month; ∼ de año New Year's Eve; ∼ de semana (sábado y domingo) weekend; puso ∼ a la discusión she put an end to the discussion **(b)** (en locs) por *or* al fin at last; en fin (expresando resignación) ah well; en ∼ ¡sigamos! anyway, let's carry on!; a ∼ de cuentas in the end, at the end of the day; al ∼ y al cabo after all
2 **(a)** (objetivo, finalidad) purpose; el ∼ de esta visita the aim *o* purpose of this visit **(b)** (en locs) a fin de que (frml) in order to; con este fin (frml) with this aim (frml), to this end (frml); con el fin *or* a fin de (frml) with the aim *o* purpose of

final *adj* ‹decisión› final; ‹objetivo› ultimate
■ *m* end; a ∼es de junio at the end of June; un ∼ feliz a happy ending; al ∼ de la lista at the bottom of the list; al ∼ tendrá que decidirse he'll have to make his mind up in the end *o* eventually
■ *f* (Dep) **(a)** (en fútbol, tenis etc) final; la ∼ de copa the cup final; pasar a la ∼ to go through to *o* make it to the final **(b)** finales *fpl* (en béisbol, baloncesto, fútbol americano) playoffs (*pl*)

finalidad *f* (propósito, utilidad) purpose, aim

finalista *adj*: los dos equipos ∼s the two teams that reach (*o* reached *etc*) the final
■ *mf* finalist

finalizar [A4] *vt* to finish
■ ∼ *vi* to end; una vez finalizada la reunión once the meeting is/was over

financiación *f*, **financiamiento** *m* financing

financiar [A1] *vt* **(a)** ‹empresa/proyecto› to finance, fund **(b)** (AmL) (vender a plazos) to give credit facilities for

financiero -ra *adj* financial
■ *m,f* financier

financista *mf* (AmL) financier

finanzas *fpl* finances (*pl*)

finca *f* **(a)** (explotación agrícola) farm **(b)** (casa de campo) country estate **(c)** (Esp) (propiedad urbana) building

fincar [A2] *vt* (Méx) to build

fingido -da *adj* hypocritical, false

fingir [I7] *vt* **(a)** ‹alegría/desinterés› to feign, fake; fingió no verme she pretended not to see me **(b)** ‹voz› to imitate
■ ∼ *vi* to pretend
■ **fingirse** *v pron*: se fingió apenado he pretended to be sorry

finlandés¹ -desa adj Finnish
■ m,f (persona) Finn

finlandés² m (idioma) Finnish

Finlandia f Finland

fino¹ -na adj **1** (en grosor) ⟨papel/capa/hilo⟩ fine, thin; ⟨loncha⟩ thin; ⟨arena/pelo/lluvia⟩ fine; ⟨labios⟩ thin; ⟨cintura/dedos⟩ slender; ⟨punta/lápiz⟩ fine **2** (en calidad) ⟨pastelería/bollería⟩ high quality; ⟨porcelana⟩ fine; ⟨lencería⟩ sheer **3** (en modales) refined **4** (a) ⟨oído/olfato⟩ acute (b) ⟨ironía/humor⟩ subtle

fino² m fino, dry sherry

firma f **1** (nombre) signature; (acción) signing **2** (empresa) company, firm (BrE)

firmamento m (liter) firmament (liter)

firmar [A1] vt/vi to sign

firme adj **1** ⟨escalera/silla/mesa⟩ steady; terreno ∼ solid ground; con paso/pulso ∼ with a firm step/steady hand; una oferta en ∼ a firm offer; de ∼ ⟨estudiar/trabajar⟩ hard **2** (Mil): ¡∼s! attention! **3** (a) ⟨persona⟩ firm; mostrarse ∼ con algn to be firm with sb; me mantuve ∼ en mi idea I stuck o kept to my idea (b) (delante del n) ⟨creencia/convicción⟩ firm

firmeza f (a) (de convicciones, carácter) strength; con ∼ firmly (b) (del terreno) firmness

fiscal adj fiscal, tax (before n)
■ mf ≈ district attorney (in US), ≈ public prosecutor (in UK)

fiscalizar [A4] vt to supervise, control

fisco m ≈ Treasury (in US), ≈ Exchequer (in UK)

fisgar [A3] vi (fam) to snoop (colloq); andaba fisgando por las oficinas he was snooping around the offices

fisgón -gona adj (fam) nosy (colloq)
■ m,f (fam) busybody (colloq)

fisgonear [A1] vi (fam) to nose around (colloq)

física f physics; ∼ nuclear nuclear physics

físico¹ -ca adj physical
■ m,f physicist

físico² m (cuerpo — de hombre, atleta) physique; (— de mujer) figure; (apariencia) appearance

fisonomía, fisonomía f (a) (de persona) features (pl) (b) (de objeto, lugar) appearance

fisioterapia f physiotherapy, physical therapy (AmE)

flaccidez f flaccidity

fláccido -da adj flaccid, flabby

flaco -ca adj thin, skinny (colloq)

flagelar [A1] vt to flagellate (frml); (Bib) to scourge
■ **flagelarse** v pron to flagellate oneself (frml), to whip oneself

flagrante adj ⟨mentira⟩ blatant; ⟨injusticia⟩ glaring, flagrant; lo sorprendieron en ∼ delito they caught him red-handed

flama f (Méx) flame

flamable adj (Méx) inflammable, flammable

flamante adj (gen delante del n) (nuevo) brand-new; (vistoso) smart (colloq)

flamenco¹ -ca adj **1** ⟨cante/baile⟩ flamenco (before n) **2** (de Flandes) Flemish
■ m,f Fleming; los ∼s the Flemish

flamenco² m **1** (Mús) flamenco **2** (idioma) Flemish **3** (Zool) flamingo

flan m (a) (dulce) crème caramel (b) (de arroz) mold*; (de pescado, verduras) terrine

flanco m (a) (Mil) flank (b) (de animal) flank, side; (de persona) side

Flandes m Flanders

flaquear [A1] vi ⟨persona/fuerzas⟩ to flag; su voluntad empezó a ∼ she began to lose heart

flaqueza f weakness

flash /'flas/ m (pl **flashes**) (Fot) flash

flato m (a) (Esp) (dolor en el costado): tengo ∼ I have a stitch (b) (Chi fam) (eructo) burp (colloq)

flauta f (Mús) flute; ∼ dulce recorder
■ mf flute player, flutist (AmE), flautist (BrE)

flautín m piccolo
■ mf piccolo (player)

flautista mf flute player, flutist (AmE), flautist (BrE)

flecha f arrow

flechazo m (a) (fam) (enamoramiento): fue un ∼ it was love at first sight (b) (herida) arrow wound

fleco m (Méx) (en el pelo) bangs (pl) (AmE), fringe (BrE)

flecos mpl (a) (adorno) fringe; un chal con ∼ a fringed shawl (b) (borde deshilachado) frayed edge

flema f phlegm

flemático -ca adj phlegmatic

flemón m boil, abscess; (en la encía) gumboil

flequillo m bangs (pl) (AmE), fringe (BrE)

fletar [A1] vt (Com, Transp) ⟨barco/avión⟩ to charter; ⟨autobús/camión⟩ to hire, rent (AmE)

flete m (a) (contratación — de barco, avión) charter; (— de autobús, camión) hire (b) (precio de contratación — de barco, avión) charter fee; (— de autobús, camión) hire charge, rental charge (AmE)

flexibilidad f flexibility

flexible adj flexible

flexión f (Dep) (de brazos) push-up, press-up (BrE); (de piernas) squat; hacer flexiones (de brazos) to do push-ups o press-ups; (de cintura) to touch one's toes

flexionar [A1] vt (Dep) ⟨pierna/rodillas⟩ to bend

flirt /'flirt/ m (pl **flirts**) (a) (relación) fling (b) (hombre) boyfriend; (mujer) girlfriend

flirtear [A1] vi to flirt

flojear [A1] vi (a) (debilitarse) to grow o get weak; me flojean las piernas my legs are getting weak (b) (fam) (holgazanear) to laze around

flojera f (a) (fam) (debilidad) lethargy (b) (fam) (pereza) laziness; me da ∼ I can't be bothered; tengo ∼ I feel lazy

flojo -ja adj **1** (a) ⟨nudo/tornillo/vendaje⟩ loose; ⟨cuerda/goma⟩ slack (b) ⟨débil⟩ weak (c) ⟨vientos⟩ light (d) ⟨café/té⟩ weak **2** (mediocre) ⟨trabajo/examen⟩ poor; ⟨película/vino⟩ second-rate; ⟨estudiante⟩ poor; está ∼ en física he's weak in (AmE) o (BrE) at physics **3** ⟨persona⟩ (fam) (perezoso) lazy
■ m,f (fam) (perezoso) lazybones (colloq)

floppy /'flopi/ m (pl **floppys**) floppy disk, diskette

flor f (de planta) flower; (de árbol frutal) blossom; ∼es secas dried flowers; un vestido de ∼es a flowery dress; **en** ~ in flower o bloom/in blossom; ~ **de azahar** orange/lemon blossom; *la* ~ **y nata** the cream, the crème de la crème

flora f flora

florear [A1] vi **(a)** (Chi, Méx) (Bot) to flower, blossom **(b)** (Méx) (halagar): **le** ~**on mucho su vestido** her dress got a lot of compliments

florecer [E3] vi **(a)** «tulipán/rosa» to flower, bloom; «árbol» to flower, blossom **(b)** (prosperar) to flourish, thrive

floreciente adj flourishing, thriving

Florencia f Florence

florentino -na adj/m,f Florentine

florería f (AmL) florist's, flower shop

florero m vase

florido -da adj **(a)** «campo» full of flowers **(b)** «estilo/lenguaje» flowery

florín m (moneda holandesa) guilder

florista mf florist

floristería f florist's, flower shop

flota f [1] (de barcos, camiones, aviones) fleet [2] (Col) (autobús) bus (AmE), coach (BrE)

flotador m (en general) float; (para la cintura) rubber ring; (para los brazos) armband

flotante adj floating

flotar [A1] vi to float

flote: **a** ~ afloat; **mantenerse a** ~ to stay afloat; **logró mantener el negocio a** ~ he managed to keep the business afloat; **salir a** ~ «cuerpo sumergido» to float to the surface; «país/persona en apuros» to get back on its/one's feet

flotilla f (Náut) flotilla; (Aviac) fleet

fluctuar [A18] vi to fluctuate

fluidez f **(a)** (de expresión) fluency; **habla griego con** ~ she speaks Greek fluently **(b)** (de tráfico) smooth flow **(c)** (Fís, Quím) fluidity

fluido adj «estilo/lenguaje» fluent; «circulación» free-flowing; «movimientos» fluid, fluent ■ m fluid

fluir [I20] vi to flow

flujo m [1] (circulación, corriente) flow; ~ **sanguíneo** blood flow [2] (Med) (secreción) discharge; ~ **menstrual** menstrual flow [3] (Náut) tide; ~ **y reflujo** ebb and flow

fluminense adj of/from Rio de Janeiro

flúor, fluor m (gas) fluorine; (fluoruro) fluoride

fluorescente adj fluorescent

fluvial adj river (before n)

fobia f phobia; **tiene** ~ **a los aviones** he has a phobia about flying

foca f (animal) seal; (piel) sealskin

focal adj focal

foco m [1] **(a)** (Fís, Fot, Mat) focus **(b)** (centro, núcleo) focus; **fue el** ~ **de todas las miradas** everybody's eyes were focused on him **(c)** (de incendio) seat [2] **(a)** (reflector) (Cin, Teatr) spotlight; (en estadio, monumento) floodlight **(b)** (AmL) (Auto) light **(c)** (Ec, Méx, Per) (de lámpara) light bulb **(d)** (AmC) (linterna) flashlight (AmE), torch (BrE)

fogata f bonfire

fogón m (quemador) burner; (fogata) (AmL) bonfire, campfire; (de caldera) firebox

fogonazo m flash, explosion

fogueado -da adj (AmS fam) experienced

fogueo m (Mil): **un cartucho de** ~ a blank (cartridge)

folio m **(a)** (hoja) sheet (of paper); **papel tamaño** ~ A4 paper **(b)** (de un trabajo, una tesis) page

folk /'fo(l)k/ adj folk (before n) ■ m folk (music)

folklore m folklore

folklórico -ca adj **(a)** «danza/música/leyenda» folk (before n) **(b)** (fam) (pintoresco) quaint

follaje m foliage

folletín m (en periódicos, revistas) newspaper serial; (revista mala) rag (colloq); (película, novela mala) melodrama

folleto m (hoja) leaflet, flier (AmE); (librito) brochure, pamphlet; ~ **de viaje** travel brochure

follón m (Esp fam) **(a)** (trifulca) commotion, ruckus; (ruido) racket (colloq), din (AmE colloq); **armó un buen** ~ (montó una trifulca) he kicked up a hell of a fuss (colloq); (hizo ruido) he made such a racket o din (colloq) **(b)** (situación confusa, desorden) mess **(c)** (problema) trouble; **no te metas en follones** don't get into trouble

fomentar [A1] vt «industria/turismo» to promote; «ahorro/inversión» to encourage, boost; «disturbio/odio» to incite, foment (frml); «interés/ afición» to encourage

fonda f **(a)** (esp AmL) (restaurant) cheap restaurant **(b)** (esp Esp) (pensión) boarding house **(c)** (Chi) (puesto) refreshment stand

fondista mf (Dep) long-distance runner

fondo m [1] **(a)** (parte más baja) bottom; **el** ~ **del mar** the bottom of the sea; **llegaré al** ~ **de esta cuestión** I'll get to the bottom of this matter **(b)** (parte de atrás — de pasillo, calle) end; (— de habitación) back; **al** ~ **de la sala** at the back of the room **(c)** (profundidad): **tiene poco** ~ it is not very deep **(d)** (de edificio) depth **(e)** (en cuadro, fotografía) background
[2] (Lit) (contenido) content
[3] (Fin) (de dinero) fund; **hacer un** ~ **común** to start a joint fund o (colloq) a kitty **(b) fondos** mpl (dinero) money, funds (pl); **recaudar** ~**s** to raise money; **un cheque sin** ~**s** a dud o (AmE) rubber check (colloq)
[4] (Dep) (en atletismo): **de** ~ «corredor/carrera/ prueba» long-distance (before n)
[5] (Méx) (Indum) slip, underskirt
[6] (en locs) **a fondo** (loc adj) «estudio/ investigación» in-depth (before n); «limpieza» thorough; (loc adv) «prepararse/entrenar» thoroughly; **conoce el tema a** ~ she knows the subject really well; **de fondo** «ruido/música» background (before n); **en el fondo**: **en el** ~ **nos llevamos bien** we get on all right, really; **en el** ~ **no es malo** deep down he's not a bad person

fonética f phonetics

fonógrafo m phonograph

fontanería f (esp Esp) plumbing

fontanero -ra m,f (esp Esp) plumber

footing /'futin/ m jogging; **hacer** ~ to jog

forajido -da m,f fugitive, outlaw

foráneo -nea adj foreign, strange

forastero -ra m,f stranger, outsider

forcejear [A1] vi to struggle

forcejeo m struggle

fórceps m (pl ~) forceps (pl)

forense *adj* forensic
■ *mf* forensic scientist

forestal *adj* forest (*before n*)

forjar [A1] *vt* **(a)** ⟨*utensilio/pieza*⟩ to forge; ⟨*metal*⟩ to work **(b)** ⟨*porvenir*⟩ to shape, forge; ⟨*plan*⟩ to make; ⟨*ilusiones/esperanzas*⟩ to build up **(c)** ⟨*nación/bases*⟩ to create; ⟨*amistad/alianza*⟩ to forge
■ **forjarse** *v pron* ⟨*porvenir*⟩ to shape, forge; ⟨*ilusiones*⟩ to build up

forma *f* **1** **(a)** (contorno, apariencia) shape; **en ~ de cruz** in the shape of a cross; **tiene la ~ de un platillo** it's the shape of a saucer; **dar ~ a algo** (al barro) to shape sth; (a proyecto) to give shape to sth **(b)** (tipo, modalidad) form; **distintas ~s de vida animal** different forms of animal life; **~ de pago** form *o* method of payment
2 (Dep, Med): **estar en ~** to be fit; **está en baja ~** he's not on form; **en plena ~** on top form; **en ~**: **nos divertimos en ~** we had a really good time
3 (manera, modo) way; **es su ~ de ser** it's just the way he is; **¡vaya ~ de conducir!** what a way to drive!; **~ de vida** way of life; **de ~ distinta** differently; **de cualquier ~** *or* **de todas ~s** anyway, in any case
4 **formas** *fpl* **(a)** (de mujer) figure **(b)** (apariencias) appearances (*pl*); **guardar las ~s** to keep up appearances
5 (Méx) (formulario) form

formación *f* **1** (en general) formation; **la ~ de un gobierno** the formation of a government **2** (educación recibida) education; (para trabajo) training; **~ profesional** *or* (CS) **vocacional** professional *o* vocational training

formal *adj* **1** (en general) formal; ⟨*promesa/oferta*⟩ firm **2** ⟨*persona*⟩ (cumplidora) reliable, dependable; (responsable) responsible

formalidad *f* **1** (de persona) reliability; **no tiene ~** he's so unreliable **2** (requisito) formality

formalizar [A4] *vt* ⟨*noviazgo/relación*⟩ to make ... official; ⟨*transacción/contrato*⟩ to formalize

formar [A1] *vt* **1** **(a)** (crear) ⟨*círculo/figura*⟩ to make, form; ⟨*asociación/gobierno*⟩ to form, set up; ⟨*barricada*⟩ to set up; **¡formen parejas!** (en clase) get into pairs *o* twos!; (en baile) take your partners! **(b)** (Ling) to form **(c)** (Mil) ⟨*tropas*⟩ to have ... fall in
2 (componer) to make up; **un equipo formado por cinco personas** a team made up of five people; **~ parte de algo** to be part of sth, to belong to sth
3 ⟨*carácter/espíritu*⟩ to form, shape
4 (educar) to bring up; (para trabajo) to train
■ **~** *vi* (Mil) to fall in
■ **formarse** *v pron* **1** **(a)** (hacerse, crearse) «*grupo/organismo*» to form; **se formó una cola** a line (AmE) *o* (BrE) queue formed **(b)** (desarrollarse) «*niño/huesos*» to develop **(c)** ⟨*idea/opinión*⟩ to form
2 (educarse) to be educated; (para trabajo) to be trained

formatear [A1] *vt* (Inf) to format

formato *m* **1** **(a)** (tamaño, forma) format **(b)** (Inf) format; **sin ~** unformatted **2** (Méx) (formulario, solicitud) form

formidable *adj/interj* (fam) fantastic (colloq)

fórmula *f* **1** **(a)** (Mat, Quím) formula **(b)** (manera, sistema) way **(c)** (frase, expresión) standard expression, formula; **~s de cortesía** polite expressions **(d)** (Col) (receta médica) prescription
2 (Auto) formula; **un coche de F~ 1** a Formula 1 car

formular [A1] *vt* **1** ⟨*queja*⟩ to make, lodge; ⟨*teoría/plan*⟩ to formulate **2** (Col) «*médico*» to prescribe

formulario *m* form

forrado -da *adj* **1** ⟨*prenda*⟩ lined; ⟨*sillón/libro*⟩ covered; **un abrigo ~ de seda** a coat lined with silk **2** [ESTAR] (fam) (de dinero) loaded (colloq)

forrar [A1] *vt* ⟨*prenda*⟩ to line; ⟨*libro/sillón*⟩ to cover
■ **forrarse** *v pron* (fam) *tb* **~se de dinero** to make a killing *o* mint (colloq)

forro *m* (de abrigo) lining; (de sillón) cover; (de libro) cover, jacket

fortalecer [E3] *vt* ⟨*organismo/músculos/amistad*⟩ to strengthen
■ **fortalecerse** *v pron* «*organismo/músculo*» to get stronger

fortaleza *f* **1** (física) strength; (moral) fortitude, strength of spirit **2** (Mil) fortress

fortificar [A2] *vt* **(a)** (Mil) ⟨*lugar/plaza*⟩ to fortify **(b)** (dar fuerza) to strengthen, make ... stronger

fortín *m* (fuerte pequeño) (small) fort; (emplazamiento) pillbox, bunker

fortuito -ta *adj* ⟨*encuentro/suceso*⟩ chance (*before n*), fortuitous

fortuna *f* **(a)** (riqueza) fortune **(b)** (azar, suerte) fortune; **por ~** fortunately; **probar ~** to try one's luck

forzado -da *adj* forced, unnatural

forzar [A11] *vt* **1** (obligar) to force **2** **(a)** ⟨*vista*⟩ to strain; **estaba forzando la vista** I was straining my eyes **(b)** ⟨*sonrisa*⟩ to force **3** ⟨*puerta/cerradura*⟩ to force

forzoso -sa *adj* ⟨*aterrizaje/anexión/paro*⟩ forced; ⟨*jubilación/liquidación*⟩ compulsory

fosa *f* (zanja) ditch; (hoyo) pit; (tumba) grave; **~ común** common *o* communal grave

fosfato *m* phosphate

fosforescente *adj* **(a)** (Fís) phosphorescent **(b)** ⟨*color/pintura*⟩ fluorescent

fósforo *m* **(a)** (Quím) phosphorus **(b)** (cerilla) match

fósil *adj* fossilized, fossil (*before n*)
■ *m* fossil

foso *m* **(a)** (zanja) ditch; (en fortificaciones) moat; (Equ) water jump **(b)** (Teatr) pit; **~ de la orquesta** orchestra pit **(c)** (Auto) (inspection) pit

foto *f* picture, photo (esp BrE); **me sacó** *or* **tomó una ~** he took a picture *o* photo of me; **~ de carné/pasaporte** passport photo

fotocopia *f* photocopy, Xerox®; **hizo** *or* **sacó una ~ de la carta** he made *o* took a photocopy of the letter

fotocopiadora *f* photocopier, Xerox® machine

fotocopiar [A1] *vt* to photocopy, xerox

fotogénico -ca *adj* photogenic

fotografía *f* (técnica, arte) photography; (retrato, imagen) photograph

fotografiar [A17] *vt* to photograph, take a photograph of

fotográfico -ca *adj* photographic

fotógrafo -fa *m,f* photographer

fotomatón *m* photo booth

fotómetro *m* (Fot) exposure *o* light meter; (Fís) photometer

foul /'faul/ *m* (*pl* **fouls**) (AmL) foul

FP (en Esp) = **Formación Profesional**

frac *m* (*pl* **fracs** *or* **fraques**) (chaqueta) tail coat, tails (*pl*); (traje) morning suit

fracasado -da *adj* failed, unsuccessful
■ *m,f* failure

fracasar [A1] *vi* to fail

fracaso *m* failure

fracción *f* fraction

fractura *f* (a) (Med) fracture (b) (Geol) fault

fracturar [A1] *vt* to fracture
■ **fracturarse** *v pron* to fracture

fragancia *f* fragrance, perfume

fragata *f* frigate

frágil *adj* (a) ⟨cristal/fuente⟩ fragile (b) ⟨salud/constitución⟩ delicate; ⟨persona⟩ frail; ⟨economía⟩ fragile

fragmento *m* (a) (de jarrón) shard; (de hueso) fragment (b) (de conversación) snippet, snatch (c) (extracto de novela, carta) extract, passage

fragua *f* forge

fraguar [A16] *vt* (a) (Metal) to forge (b) ⟨complot/plan⟩ to hatch; ⟨plan⟩ to conceive
■ ~ *vi* «cemento» to set

fraile *m* friar, monk

frailecillo *m* puffin

frambuesa *f* raspberry

francés¹ -cesa *adj* French
■ *m,f* (*m*) Frenchman; (*f*) Frenchwoman; **los franceses** the French, French people

francés² *m* (idioma) French

Francia *f* France

franco¹ -ca *adj* **1** (sincero) ⟨persona⟩ frank; ⟨sonrisa⟩ natural; **para serte ~ ...** to be frank *o* honest ...; **una mirada franca** an honest *o* open expression **2** (delante del *n*) (patente) ⟨mejoría/decadencia⟩ marked; **un clima de franca cordialidad** an atmosphere of genuine warmth **3** (Com) free; **~ de porte** carriage free; **paso ~** free passage; **~ de derechos** duty-free **4** [ESTAR] (a) (Mil) off duty (b) (RPl) (libre de trabajo): **el lunes estoy ~** I have Monday off

franco² *m* (unidad monetaria) franc

francotirador -dora *m,f* sniper

franela *f* (a) (Tex) flannel (b) (Ven) (camiseta) T-shirt (c) (Col) (camiseta de interior) undershirt (AmE), vest (BrE)

franja *f* (banda) stripe, band; (cinta, adorno) border, fringe

franquear [A1] *vt* **1** ⟨paso/entrada⟩ to clear; ⟨puerta⟩ to go through; ⟨umbral/río⟩ to cross **2** ⟨carta⟩ (pagar) to pay the postage on
■ **franquearse** *v pron* **~se CON algn** to confide IN sb

franqueo *m* postage

franqueza *f* frankness, openness; **hablar con (toda) ~** to be (perfectly) frank *o* honest

franquicia *f* **1** (exención) exemption; (en seguros) excess; **~ aduanera** (condición) duty-free status; (cantidad) duty-free allowance **2** (concesión) franchise

franquismo *m* Franco's regime

frasco *m* bottle; (de mermelada) jar

frase *f* (oración) sentence; (sintagma) phrase; **~ hecha** set phrase

fraternal *adj* brotherly, fraternal

fraude *m* fraud; **~ fiscal** tax evasion

fraudulento -ta *adj* ⟨negocio⟩ fraudulent; ⟨elecciones⟩ rigged

fray *m* (delante de n propio) Brother

frazada *f* (AmL) blanket; **~ eléctrica** electric blanket

frecuencia *f* frequency; **con ~** frequently; **~ modulada** frequency modulation, FM

frecuentar [A1] *vt* to frequent

frecuente *adj* ⟨llamada/visita⟩ frequent

freelance /'frilans/ *mf* freelancer; **trabaja de ~** he works freelance

freezer /'friser/ *m* (a) (AmL) (electrodoméstico) freezer, deep freeze (b) (Chi, Ven) (en el refrigerador) freezer (compartment)

fregadero *m* (de la cocina) kitchen sink; (para lavar ropa) (Méx) sink

fregado -da *adj* (AmL exc RPl fam) (a) (molesto) annoying; **¡no seas ~, hombre!** stop being such a pain (colloq) (b) (difícil) ⟨examen/tema⟩ tricky (colloq), tough (colloq); ⟨persona/carácter⟩ difficult (c) [ESTAR] (enfermo, delicado) in a bad way (colloq); (sin dinero) broke (colloq)
■ *m,f* (AmL exc RPl fam) (persona difícil) difficult person

fregar [A7] *vt* **1** (lavar, limpiar) to wash; **fregué el suelo** I washed the floor; (con cepillo) I scrubbed the floor; **~ los platos** to wash the dishes, to do the dishes (colloq) **2** (AmL exc RPl fam) (a) (molestar) to bug (colloq) (b) ⟨planes/vacaciones⟩ to ruin
■ ~ *vi* **1** (lavar los platos) to wash the dishes, to do the dishes (colloq); (limpiar) to clean; (restregar) to scrub **2** (AmL exc RPl fam) (molestar): **¡déjate de ~!** stop being such a pest!; **¡no friegues!** (no digas) you're kidding! (colloq)
■ **fregarse** *v pron* **1** (AmL fam) (embromarse): **¡te friegas!** tough! (colloq); **¡me fregué!** I've really done it now! (colloq) **2** (AmL exc RPl fam) (malograrse): **se ~on nuestros planes** that's ruined *o* messed up our plans (colloq)

fregona *f* (Esp) (utensilio) mop

freidora *f* deep fryer

freír [I35] *vt* to fry
■ **freírse** *v pron* to fry

frenada *f* (esp AmL) ▶ FRENAZO

frenar [A1] *vt* 1 (Transp) to brake 2 ⟨proceso/
deterioro⟩ to slow ... down; ⟨alza/inflación⟩ to
curb, check; ⟨progreso/desarrollo⟩ to hold ... back
■ ~ *vi* to brake, apply the brake(s) (frml)

frenazo *m* (fam): oí el ~ I heard the screeching
of brakes; **dio un ~** she slammed *o* jammed on
her brakes

frenético -ca *adj* frenzied, frenetic; **ponerse
~** (fam) to go crazy *o* wild

frenillos *mpl* (AmL) (para los dientes) braces (*pl*)
(AmE), brace (esp BrE)

freno *m* (a) (Mec, Transp) brake; ~ **de mano**
emergency brake (AmE), handbrake (BrE) (b)
(Equ) bit (c) (contención): **poner** ~ **a algo** ⟨a gastos,
importaciones⟩ to curb sth; ⟨a abusos⟩ to put a stop
to sth (d) **frenos** *mpl* (Méx) ▸ FRENILLOS

frente *f* forehead, brow (liter); **arrugar la** ~ to
frown
■ *m* 1 (a) (de edificio) front, facade (frml); **hacer** (le)
~ **a algo** (a la realidad, una responsabilidad) to face up
to sth; (a gastos, obligaciones) to meet sth; **hacerle** ~
a algn (a enemigo, atacante) to face sb (b) (en locs) **al
frente: dar un paso al** ~ to take a step forward;
vive al ~ (Chi) she lives opposite; **estar al** ~ **de
algo** (de una clasificación) to be at the top of sth; (de
una empresa) to be in charge of sth; **de frente**
⟨chocar⟩ head on; **una foto de** ~ a full-face photo;
de frente a (AmL) facing; **frente a** opposite; **estamos
~ a un grave problema** we are faced with a
serious problem
2 (Meteo, Mil, Pol) front

fresa *f* (planta) strawberry plant; (fruta)
strawberry

fresco¹ -ca *adj* 1 (a) ⟨viento⟩ cool, fresh;
⟨agua⟩ cold; ⟨bebida⟩ cool, cold; **el tiempo está** ~
the weather is a bit chilly (b) ⟨ropa/tela⟩ cool
2 (a) ⟨pescado/fruta⟩ fresh; **trae noticias frescas**
she has the latest news; Ⓢ **pintura fresca** wet
paint (b) ⟨cutis/belleza⟩ fresh, young (c) (no
viciado) ⟨aire⟩ fresh 3 ⟨persona⟩ (a) [SER] (fam)
(descarado): **¡qué tipo más** ~! that guy sure has
some nerve! (colloq) (b) [ESTAR] (descansado)
refreshed; (no cansado) fresh (c) (tranquilo): **él
estaba tan** ~ he was as cool as a cucumber
■ *m,f* (fam) (descarado): **¡eres un** ~! you have a lot
of nerve! (colloq)

fresco² *m* 1 (a) (aire) fresh air; **tomar el** ~ to
get some fresh air (b) (frío moderado): **hace un
fresquito que da gusto** it's lovely and cool; **hace
~** it's chilly 2 (Art) fresco; **pintura al** ~ fresco
painting 3 (AmL) (gaseosa) soda (AmE), fizzy drink
(BrE); (refresco de frutas) fruit drink

frescura *f* (descaro) nerve (colloq)

fresón *m* (long stem) strawberry

frialdad *f* (en general) coldness; **la** ~ **de su
mirada** the coldness in his eyes; **me trató con** ~
he treated me coldly *o* frostily; **la** ~ **del público**
the audience's lack of enthusiasm

friega *f* (fricción) rub; **date una(s)** ~(s) **en el
pecho con esto** rub this on your chest

friega, friegas, etc ▸ FREGAR

frígido -da *adj* frigid

frigorífico *m* (a) (Esp) (nevera) refrigerator,
fridge (b) (en tiendas) cold store (c) (AmS) (de
carne) meat processing plant

frijol *m* (AmL exc CS) (Bot, Coc) bean; ~ **colorado/
negro** kidney/black bean; **ganarse los** ~**es** to
earn a living

frío¹, fría *adj* 1 ⟨comida/agua/motor/viento⟩
cold; **tengo los pies** ~**s** my feet are cold; **dejar** ~
a algn: la noticia lo dejó ~ (indiferente) the news
was quite unmoved by the news; (atónito) he was
staggered by the news; **el jazz me deja fría** jazz
does nothing for me 2 (a) ⟨persona⟩ cold;
⟨público⟩ unresponsive; ⟨recibimineto⟩ cool;
estuvo ~ **conmigo** he was cold towards me (b)
⟨decoración/color⟩ cold

frío² *m* cold; **no salgas con este** ~ don't go out
in this cold; **¡qué** ~ **hace!** it's so cold!; **tener/
pasar** ~ to be cold; **tengo** ~ **en los pies** my feet
are cold; **tomar** *or* (Esp) **coger** ~ to catch cold

friolento -ta *adj* (AmL): **es muy** ~ he really
feels the cold

friolero -ra *adj* (Esp) ▸ FRIOLENTO

friso *m* frieze

fritanga *f* (a) (AmC, Andes, Méx) (alimento frito)
fried snack (b) (pey) (comida frita) greasy fried
food

frito -ta *adj* 1 (Coc) fried 2 (a) (fam) (harto) fed
up (colloq); **me tienes** ~ I'm fed up with you (b)
(CS, Méx fam) (en apuros) done for (colloq)

frivolidad *f* (cualidad) frivolousness, frivolity;
(cosa vana) triviality, frivolous thing

frívolo -la *adj* frivolous

frondoso -sa *adj* ⟨árbol⟩ leafy; ⟨vegetación⟩
lush; ⟨bosque⟩ thick

frontal *adj* ⟨colisión⟩ head-on; ⟨ataque⟩ direct,
frontal (frml); ⟨oposición⟩ direct

frontenis *m* pelota (played with tennis rackets)

frontera *f* border, frontier (frml)

frontón *m* (juego) pelota; (cancha) pelota court;
(pared) fronton

frotar [A1] *vt/vi* to rub
■ **frotarse** *v pron* (refl) ⟨ojos/rodillas⟩ to rub;
⟨manos⟩ to rub ... together

fructífero -ra *adj* fruitful, productive

fruncir [I4] *vt* (a) ⟨tela⟩ to gather (b) ~ **el ceño**
or **entrecejo** to frown

frustración *f* frustration

frustrado -da *adj* (a) ⟨persona⟩ frustrated;
⟨actor/bailarina⟩ frustrated (before n) (b)
⟨atentado/intento⟩ failed (before n)

frustrar [A1] *vt* ⟨persona⟩ to frustrate; ⟨planes⟩
to thwart; ⟨esperanzas⟩ to dash; **me frustra que
no entiendan** I find it frustrating that they don't
understand
■ **frustrarse** *v pron* «planes» to be thwarted,
fail; «esperanzas» to come to nothing

fruta *f* fruit; **una** ~ a piece of fruit; ~ **confitada**
or **escarchada** crystallized fruit, candied fruit; ~
del tiempo *or* **de (la) estación** seasonal fruit

frutal *adj* fruit (before n)
■ *m* fruit tree

frutería *f* fruit store *o* shop, greengrocer's (BrE)

frutero¹ -ra *m,f* (vendedor) fruit seller,
greengrocer (BrE)

frutero² *m* (recipiente) fruit bowl

frutilla *f* (Bol, CS) strawberry

fruto *m* 1 (Bot) fruit; ~**s secos** nuts and dried
fruit (*pl*) 2 (resultado, producto) fruit; **dar** *or* **rendir**
~**s** to bear fruit; ~ **DE algo** ⟨de inversión⟩ return

ON sth; ⟨*de trabajo/investigación*⟩ fruits OF sth;
todo fue ∼ de su imaginación it was all a figment
of his imagination

FTP *m* (= **protocolo de transferencia de archivo**) FTP

fucsia *f* fuchsia
■ *m/adj inv* fuchsia

fue ▶ IR, SER

fuego *m* **(a)** (en general) fire; **¡∼!** fire!; **le prendieron ∼ a la casa** they set the house on fire; **abrieron ∼ sobre los manifestantes** they opened fire on the demonstrators; **∼s artificiales** fireworks (*pl*) **(b)** (para cigarrillo): **¿me da ∼, por favor?** have you got a light, please? **(c)** (Coc): **cocinar a ∼ lento** to cook over a low heat; (apenas hirviendo) to simmer; **poner la sartén al ∼** put the frying pan on to heat

fuel, fuel-oil *m* fuel oil

fuelle *m* bellows (*pl*)

fuente *f* **1 (a)** (manantial) spring; **∼ termal** thermal spring **(b)** (origen) source; **la ∼ del río** the source of the river; **∼ de ingresos** source of income; **información de buena ∼** information from reliable sources **2** (construcción) fountain; **∼ de soda** (Chi, Méx) soda fountain (AmE), (*place where drinks and ice creams are bought and consumed*) **3** (plato) dish; **∼ de horno** ovenproof dish

fuera *adv* **1 (a)** (lugar, parte) [*Latin American Spanish also uses* AFUERA *in this sense*] outside; **comeremos ∼** (en el jardín) we'll eat outside; (en un restaurante) we'll eat out; **por ∼ es rojo** it's red on the outside; **aquí ∼ se está muy bien** it's very nice out here; **se pasa el día ∼** she's out all day **(b)** (en el extranjero) abroad, out of the country; (del lugar de trabajo, la ciudad, etc) away **2 fuera de** (*loc prep*) **(a)** (en el exterior de, más allá de) out of; **está ∼ del país** he's out of the country; **ocurrió ∼ del edificio** it happened outside the building; **∼ de peligro/lugar** out of danger/place; **¡∼ (de aquí)!** get out (of here)! **(b)** (excepto) apart from; **∼ de eso, me encuentro bien** apart *o* (AmE) aside from that, I feel fine **3** (*en otras locs*): **fuera de combate: lo dejó ∼ de combate** (Dep) he knocked him out; **fuera de serie** ⟨*jugador/cantante*⟩ exceptional, outstanding; **fuera de sí: estaba ∼ de sí** he was beside himself; **fuera de temporada** out of season

fuera, fuéramos, etc ▶ IR, SER

fueraborda *m* outboard

fuereño -ña *m,f* (Méx fam): **un ∼** some guy from out of town (colloq)

fuero *m* **(a)** (jurisdicción) jurisdiction **(b)** (privilegio, derecho) privilege; **en mi/su ∼ interno** in my/his heart of hearts, deep down inside

fuerte *adj* **1** (en general) strong; **un equipo/una cuerda ∼** a strong team/rope **2 (a)** ⟨*viento*⟩ strong; ⟨*terremoto*⟩ severe; ⟨*lluvia/nevada*⟩ heavy **(b)** ⟨*dolor*⟩ intense, bad; ⟨*golpe*⟩ heavy; ⟨*resfriado*⟩ bad; ⟨*abrazo/beso*⟩ big **(c)** ⟨*ruido/música*⟩ loud **(d)** ⟨*olor/sabor/medicina*⟩ strong; ⟨*comida/dosis*⟩ heavy **(e)** ⟨*acento*⟩ strong, thick **3** (violento) ⟨*discusión*⟩ violent, heated; ⟨*película/escena*⟩ shocking
■ *adv* **1** ⟨*golpear/empujar*⟩ hard; ⟨*agarrar/apretar*⟩ tightly; ⟨*llover*⟩ heavily **2** ⟨*hablar*⟩ loudly; **pon la radio más ∼** turn the radio up; **habla más ∼** speak up

■ *m* **(a)** (Mil) fort **(b)** (especialidad) strong point, forte

fuerza *f* **1 (a)** (vigor, energía) strength; **tener ∼** to be strong; **no me siento con ∼s** I don't have the strength; **tiene mucha ∼ en los brazos** she has very strong arms; **agárralo con ∼** hold on to it tightly; **empuja con ∼** push hard; **le fallaron las ∼s** his strength failed him; **recuperar ∼s** to get one's strength back; **gritó con todas sus ∼s** she shouted with all her might; **∼ de voluntad** willpower **(b)** (del viento, de olas) strength, force **(c)** (de estructura, material) strength **2** (violencia) force; **recurrir a la ∼** to resort to force; **∼ bruta** brute force **3** (Mil, Pol, Fís) force; **∼s políticas** political forces; **las ∼s armadas** the armed forces; **las ∼s de orden público** (period) the police; **∼ de gravedad** (force of) gravity **4** (*en locs*) **a la fuerza: a la ∼ tuvo que verme** he must have seen me; **lo llevaron a la ∼** they dragged him there; **comí a la ∼** I forced myself to eat; **entraron a la ∼** they forced their way in; **a fuerza de** by; **aprobó a ∼ de estudiar** he managed to pass by studying hard; **por fuerza: por ∼ tiene que saberlo** he <u>must</u> know about it; **por la fuerza** by force

fuerza, fuerzas, etc ▶ FORZAR

fuese, fuésemos, etc ▶ IR, SER

fuete *m* (AmL exc CS) riding crop; (más largo) whip

fuga *f* **1** (huida) escape; **un intento de ∼** an attempted escape; **se dieron a la ∼** they fled; **∼ de capitales** *or* **divisas** flight of capital; **∼ de cerebros** brain drain **2** (de líquido, gas) leak, escape (frml) **3** (Mús) fugue

fugarse [A3] *v pron* **(a)** (huir) to flee, run away; «*preso*» to escape; **∼ DE algo** to escape FROM sth **(b)** «*enamorados*» to run away together

fugaz *adj* ⟨*sonrisa/visión/amor*⟩ fleeting; ⟨*visita/tregua*⟩ brief

fugitivo -va *adj* fugitive; **anda ∼** he is on the run

fui, fuimos, etc ▶ IR, SER

fuiste, etc ▶ IR, SER

fulano -na *m,f* (fam) (persona cualquiera) so-and-so; **don ∼ de tal** Mr so-and-so
■ *m* (fam) (tipo) guy (colloq)

fulminante *adj* ⟨*enfermedad*⟩ sudden and devastating; ⟨*mirada*⟩ withering; **tuvo un efecto ∼** it had an immediate and devastating effect

fulminantes *mpl* (AmL) (Jueg) caps (*pl*); **pistola de ∼** cap gun

fumador -dora *m,f* smoker; **∼ pasivo** passive smoker; **sección de ∼es/no ∼es** smoking/no-smoking section

fumar [A1] *vt* **1** ⟨*cigarrillo/puro*⟩ to smoke **2** (Méx fam) (hacer caso) to take notice of
■ *vi* to smoke; **∼ en pipa** to smoke a pipe

fumigar [A3] *vt* ⟨*campo/cultivo*⟩ to spray, dust; ⟨*local*⟩ to fumigate

función *f* **1 (a)** (cometido, propósito) function; **tiene la ∼ de ...** it performs the function of ...; **salario en ∼ de la experiencia** salary according to experience **(b) funciones** *mpl* duties (*pl*); **en el ejercicio de sus funciones** in the performance of her duties; **el secretario en funciones** the acting secretary; **entrar en funciones** (AmL) «*empleado*» ⋯⟶

to take up one's post; «*presidente*» to assume office **2** (Fisiol, Mat, Ling) function **3** (de teatro, circo) performance; (de cine) showing, performance; ~ **de noche** late night performance

funcionamiento *m*: me explicó su ~ he explained (to me) how it works (*o* worked *etc*); **para el buen** ~ **de la escuela** for the smooth running of the school; **ponerse en** ~ «*hospital/estación/fábrica*» to become operational; «*central nuclear*» to come into operation; «*mecanismo/máquina*» to start up; «*servicio/sistema*» to start; **estar en** ~ to be running; **poner en** ~ «*central/fábrica*» to bring into operation; «*mecanismo/máquina*» to start ... up

funcionar [A1] *vi* «*aparato/máquina*» to work; «*servicio*» to operate; **◉ no funciona** out of order; ~ **con pilas/gasolina** to run off batteries/on gasoline

funcionario -ria *m,f* **(a)** (empleado público) *tb* ~ **público** *or* **del Estado** government employee; **un alto** ~ a senior *o* high-ranking official **(b)** (de organización internacional) member of staff, staff member **(c)** (RPI) (de empresa, banco) employee

funda *f* **(a)** (de libro) dustjacket; (de disco) sleeve **(b)** (de raqueta, cojín, sillón) cover **(c)** *tb* ~ **de almohada** pillowcase, pillowslip **(d)** (Odont) cap

fundación *f* **1** (institución) foundation; **una** ~ **benéfica** a charity **2** (de ciudad, escuela) founding; (de empresa, partido) establishment

fundado -da *adj* «*temor/sospecha*» justified, well founded

fundador -dora *m,f* founder

fundamental *adj* fundamental

fundamento *m* **(a)** (base, sustentación) foundation; **los rumores carecen de** ~ the rumors are totally without foundation **(b)** **fundamentos** *mpl* (nociones básicas) fundamentals (*pl*), basics (*pl*)

fundar [A1] *vt* **(a)** «*ciudad/hospital/escuela*» to found; «*partido/empresa*» to establish **(b)** (basar) «*sospecha/argumento*» ~ **algo** **EN algo** to base sth ON sth

■ **fundarse** *v pron* ~**se EN algo** «*afirmación/sospecha*» to be based ON sth; **¿en qué te fundas para decirlo?** what grounds do you have for saying that?

fundir [I1] *vt* **1 (a)** «*metal/hierro*» to melt; «*mineral*» to smelt **(b)** «*estatua/campana*» to cast **2** (Elec) to blow **3** (fusionar) to merge

■ **fundirse** *v pron* **1** «*metal*» to melt; «*nieve/hielo*» to melt, thaw **2** (Elec): **se ha fundido la bombilla** the bulb has gone (colloq); **se fundieron los fusibles** the fuses blew **3** (fusionarse) «*empresas/partidos*» to merge; ~**se EN algo** to merge sth INTO sth

fundo *m* (Chi) country estate, large farm

fúnebre *adj* «*música/ambiente*» funereal; ▸ COCHE A, CORTEJO, ETC

funeral *m*, **funerales** *mpl* (exequias) funeral; (oficio religioso) funeral service

funeraria *f* undertaker's, funeral parlor*

funesto -ta *adj* disastrous, terrible

fungir [I7] *vi* (Méx, Per) ~ **COMO** *or* **DE algo** to act as sth

funicular *m* (tren) funicular (railway); (teleférico) cable car

furgón *m* (Auto) truck, van; (Ferr) boxcar (AmE), goods van (BrE)

furgoneta *f* (para carga) van; (para pasajeros) van, minibus

furia *f* fury; **estar/ponerse hecho una** ~ (fam) to be/to get furious

furioso -sa *adj* furious; **se puso** ~ he was furious, he flew into a rage

furor *m* **(a)** (rabia) fury, rage **(b)** (de las olas, del viento, de una tempestad) fury **(c)** (entusiasmo) enormous enthusiasm; **causar** *or* **hacer** ~ to be all the rage (colloq)

furtivo -va *adj* **(a)** (ilegal): **la caza/pesca furtiva** poaching; **un cazador** ~ a poacher **(b)** «*mirada/caricia*» furtive

furúnculo *m* boil

fusible *m* (Elec) fuse; **saltaron los** ~**s** the fuses blew

fusil *m* **1** (Arm) rifle **2** (Méx fam) (plagio) plagiarism

fusilar [A1] *vt* **1** (Mil) to shoot; **fue fusilado** he was executed by firing squad **2** (fam) (plagiar) to plagiarize, lift (colloq)

fusión *f* **1** (de empresas, partidos) merger **2 (a)** (de un metal) melting; (de metales, piezas) fusion, fusing together **(b)** (Fís) fusion

fusionar [A1] *vt* **(a)** «*piezas/metales*» to fuse, fuse together **(b)** «*empresas/partidos*» to merge **(c)** (Inf) to merge

■ **fusionarse** *v pron* **(a)** «*piezas/metales*» fuse (together) **(b)** «*empresas/partidos*» to merge; «*ideas*» to fuse

fusta *f* riding crop; (más larga) whip

fustigar [A3] *vt* «*caballo*» to whip

futbito *m* (Esp) five-a-side soccer *o* football, ≈ indoor soccer (AmE)

fútbol, (AmC, Méx) **futbol** *m* soccer, football (esp BrE); ~ **americano** American football; ~ **sala** five-a-side soccer *o* football, ≈ indoor soccer (AmE)

futbolín *m* **(a)** (juego) table football **(b)** **futbolines** *mpl* (local) amusement arcade

futbolista *mf* soccer *o* football player

futuro¹ -ra *adj* future (*before n*); **las futuras generaciones** future generations; **la futura mamá** the mother-to-be

futuro² m **1** (porvenir) future; **¿qué nos deparará el** ~**?** what will the future bring?; **en un** ~ **cercano** *or* **próximo** in the near future; **en el** *or* **en lo** ~ in future; **un empleo con/sin** ~ a job with good prospects/with no prospects; **su relación no tiene** ~ their relationship has no future **2** (Ling) future (tense)

Gg

G, g *f* (*read as* /xe/) *the letter* G, G

gabacho -cha *m,f* **(a)** (Chi, Esp fam & pey) (francés) frog (colloq & pej) **(b)** (Méx fam & pey) (extranjero) foreigner (*of North American or European origin*)

gabán *m* (abrigo — largo) overcoat; (— corto) jacket

gabardina *f* (prenda) raincoat; (tela) gabardine

gabinete *m* **1** (despacho) office; (en una casa) study **2** (conjunto de profesionales) department; (Pol) cabinet **3** (armario —de la cocina) (Méx) kitchen cabinet *o* cupboard; (— del baño) (Col, Ven) bathroom cabinet

gacela *f* gazelle

gacho -cha *adj* **(a)** ‹orejas› drooping (*before n*); **con la cabeza gacha** with his head bowed **(b)** **a gachas** (agachado) crouching; (a gatas) on all fours

gachupín *m* (Méx pey) Spaniard

gaélico¹ -ca *adj* Gaelic

gaélico² *m* (idioma) Gaelic

gafar [A1] *vt* (Esp fam) to jinx

gafas *fpl* **(a)** (anteojos) glasses (*pl*), spectacles (*pl*) (frml); **unas ∼s nuevas** a new pair of glasses; **∼ de sol** sunglasses; **∼ oscuras** dark glasses **(b)** (de protección) goggles (*pl*)

gafe *adj* (Esp fam): **es ∼** she has a jinx on her; **no seas ∼** don't say that, you'll bring us bad luck

gafo -fa *adj* (Ven fam) (estúpido) dumb (colloq)

gagá *adj inv* **1** (fam) (senil) gaga (colloq) **2** (Per fam) (elegante) smart (colloq)

gaita *f tb* **∼ gallega/escocesa** (Galician/ Scottish) bagpipes (*pl*)

gaitero -ra *m,f* (Mús) (bag)piper

gajes *mpl*: **son (los) ∼ del oficio** it's all part of the job

gajo *m* **1** (de naranja, limón) segment **2** (Col) (de pelo) lock

gala *f* **(a)** (cena) gala; **cena de ∼** gala (dinner); (en el teatro) *tb* **función de ∼** gala (evening *o* performance); **vestido de ∼** formal *o* full dress; **hacer ∼ de algo** to display sth **(b)** **galas** *fpl* (ropa) clothes (*pl*); **mis/tus mejores ∼s** my/your best clothes *o* Sunday best

galán *m* **(a)** (actor) hero **(b)** (hum) (novio) young man (hum)

galante *adj* ‹hombre› gallant, attentive

galantería *f* **(a)** (caballerosidad) gallantry **(b)** (piropo) compliment; (gesto cortés) polite gesture, attention

galápago *m* (Zool) (tortuga — gigante) giant turtle; (— europea) terrapin

galaxia *f* galaxy

galera *f* **1** (Hist, Náut) galley **2** (RPI) (sombrero) top hat

galería *f* **(a)** (interior) corridor; (exterior) gallery **(c)** (Teatr) gallery **(c)** **∼ comercial** shopping mall (AmE), shopping arcade (BrE); **∼ de arte** art gallery

Gales *m*: *tb* **el país de ∼** Wales

galés¹ -lesa *adj* Welsh
■ *m,f* (persona) (*m*) Welshman; (*f*) Welshwoman; **los galeses** the Welsh, Welsh people

galés² *m* (idioma) Welsh

galgo *mf* greyhound

galgódromo *m* (Méx) dog track

galicismo *m* gallicism

galimatías *m* (*pl* ∼) (lenguaje incomprensible) gibberish; (de cosas, ideas) jumble

gallada *f* (Andes fam): **la ∼** the crowd

gallego¹ -ga *adj* **(a)** (de Galicia) Galician **(b)** (AmL fam) (español) Spanish
■ *m,f* **(a)** (de Galicia) Galician **(b)** (AmL fam) (español) Spaniard

gallego² *m* (idioma) Galician

galleta *f* (Coc) (dulce) cookie (AmE), biscuit (BrE); (salada) cracker

gallina *f* **1** (Zool) hen; (Coc) chicken; **∼ clueca** (empollando) broody hen; (cuidando la pollada) mother hen; **gallinita ciega** blind man's buff **2** **gallina** *mf* (fam) (cobarde) chicken (colloq)

gallinazo *m* (Zool) (de cabeza roja) turkey buzzard *o* vulture; (de cabeza negra) black vulture

gallinero *m* **(a)** (Zool) (corral) henhouse, coop **(b)** (fam) (sitio ruidoso) madhouse (colloq) **(c)** (fam) (en el cine, teatro): **el ∼** the gods (colloq)

gallito *m* **1** (fam) (persona) tough guy (colloq) **2** (Col, Méx) (Dep) shuttlecock, birdie (AmE)

gallo¹ *m* **1** (Zool) (ave) cockerel; **∼ de pelea** *or* (AmS) **de riña** fighting *o* game cock; (más grande) rooster; **en menos (de lo) que canta un ∼** in no time at all; **otro ∼ cantaría** *or* **otro ∼ me/te/nos cantara** (fam) things would be very different **2** (Méx fam) (bravucón) macho, tough guy (colloq) **3** (fam) **(a)** (de un cantante) false note **(b)** (de adolescente): **soltó un ∼** his voice went squeaky **4** (Méx) (serenata) serenade

gallo² -lla *adj* (AmL fam) tough (colloq)
■ *m,f* (Chi fam) (*m*) guy (colloq); (*f*) woman; **hola ∼** hi, buddy (AmE) *o* (BrE) mate (colloq)

galón *m* **1** (Mil) stripe **2** (medida) gallon

galopante *adj* ‹inflación/tuberculosis› galloping (*before n*)

galopar [A1] *vi* (Equ) to gallop

galope *m* gallop; **a** *or* **al ∼** at a gallop

galpón *m* (AmL) (cobertizo) shed; (almacén) storehouse

gama *f* **(a)** (de colores, productos) range **(b)** (de notas musicales) scale

gamba *f* (esp Esp) (Coc, Zool) shrimp (AmE), prawn (BrE)

gamberrada *f* (Esp) (grosería) loutish act; (acto violento) act of hooliganism

gamberrismo *m* (Esp) (comportamiento — escandaloso) loutishness; (— violento) hooliganism

gamberro -rra *m,f* (Esp) (grosero) lout; (vándalo) hooligan

gamín -mina *m,f* (Col) street urchin

gamo -ma *m,f* fallow deer

gamulán® *m* (CS) (prenda) sheepskin coat/jacket

gamuza *f* (a) (Zool) chamois (b) (piel) chamois (leather); (de otros animales) suede

gana *f* (deseo) ¡con qué ~s me comería un helado! I'd love an ice cream!; **lo hizo sin ~s** he did it very half-heartedly; **siempre hace lo que le da la ~** she always does just as she pleases; **quería ir pero me quedé con las ~s** (fam) I wanted to go, but it wasn't to be; **tener ~s de hacer algo** to feel like doing sth; **(no) tengo ~s de ir** I (don't) feel like going; **tengo ~s de volver a verte** I'm looking forward to seeing you again; **le dieron ~s de reírse** she felt like bursting out laughing; **se me quitaron las ~s de** I don't feel like going any more; **tengo ~s de que llegue el verano** I'm looking forward to the summer; **con ~s:** **llover con ~s** to pour down; **es feo/tonto con ~s** he is so ugly/stupid!; **de buena/mala ~** willingly/reluctantly

ganadería *f* (actividad) ranching, stockbreeding; (ganado) cattle (*pl*), livestock (+ *sing or pl vb*)

ganadero -ra *adj* ranching (*before n*), stockbreeding (*before n*)
■ *m,f* rancher, stockbreeder

ganado *m* cattle (*pl*), livestock (+ *sing or pl vb*); **~ bovino** *or* **vacuno** cattle (*pl*); **~ caballar** *or* **equino** horses (*pl*); **~ en pie** (AmL) cattle on the hoof (*pl*); **~ ovino/porcino** sheep (*pl*)/pigs (*pl*)

ganador -dora *adj* ⟨equipo/caballo⟩ winning (*before n*); **la película ~a del Oscar** the Oscar-winning film
■ *m,f* winner

ganancia *f* (Com, Fin) profit; **~ neta/bruta** net/gross profit; **~ del capital** capital gain

ganar [A1] *vt* **1** (a) ⟨sueldo⟩ to earn; **lo único que quiere es ~ dinero** all he's interested in is making money (b) ⟨tiempo⟩ to gain; **¿qué ganas con eso?** what do you gain by (doing) that? (c) (adquirir) ⟨experiencia⟩ to gain
2 ⟨partido/guerra/premio⟩ to win; **le gané la apuesta** I won my bet with him
■ ~ *vi* (a) (vencer) to win; **van ganando 2 a 1** they're winning 2-1; **~le A algn** to beat sb; **nos ~on por cuatro puntos** they beat us by four points (b) (aventajar) **le ganas en estatura** you're taller than him; **me gana en todo** he beats me on every count; **salir ganando: salió ganando con el trato** he did well out of the deal; **al final salí ganando** in the end I came out of it better off
■ **ganarse** *v pron* **1** (enf) (mediante el trabajo) to earn; **~se la vida** to earn a/one's living
2 (enf) ⟨premio/apuesta⟩ to win
3 ⟨afecto/confianza⟩ to win; **se ganó el respeto de todos** he won *o* earned everyone's respect
4 (descanso) to earn oneself; **te lo has ganado** you've earned it, you deserve it

ganchillo *m* (aguja) crochet hook; (labor) crochet; **hacer ~** to crochet

gancho *m* **1** (a) (garfio) hook (b) (AmL) (para la ropa) hanger (c) (Andes, Ven) (imperdible) safety pin
2 (a) (en boxeo) hook (b) (en baloncesto) hook shot

gandalla *mf* (Méx fam) (persona deshonesta) crook (colloq); (sinvergüenza) swine (colloq)

gandul -dula *m,f* (fam) lazybones (colloq)

ganga *f* (compra ventajosa) bargain; **a precio de ~** at a bargain *o* giveaway price

ganglio *m* (en los vasos linfáticos) gland; (de células nerviosas) ganglion

gangrena *f* gangrene

ganso -sa *m,f* **1** (Zool) (*m*) goose, gander; (*f*) goose **2** (fam) (a) (persona torpe) clumsy oaf (colloq) (b) (tonto) idiot, clown (colloq)

ganzúa *f* picklock

garabatear [A1] *vi/vt* (escribir) to scribble, scrawl; (dibujar) to doodle

garabato *m* **1** (a) (dibujo) doodle (b) **garabatos** *mpl* (escritura) scrawl, scribble **2** (Chi) (palabrota) swearword

garaje /ga'raxe/ *m*, (esp AmL) **garage** /ga'raʒ/ *m* garage

garantía *f* **1** (Com) guarantee, warranty, **estar bajo** *or* **en ~** to be under guarantee *o* warranty **2** (a) (Der) (fianza) surety, guarantee (b) (seguridad) guarantee (c) **~s constitucionales** constitutional rights (*pl*)

garantizar [A4] *vt* **1** (Com) ⟨producto⟩ to guarantee, warrant (AmE) **2** (asegurar) to guarantee

garapiña *f* (Méx) pineapple squash

garbanzo *m* chickpea

garbo *m* (elegancia) poise, grace; (gracia, desenvoltura) jauntiness

garfio *m* hook

gargajo *m* (fam) gob (sl)

garganta *f* **1** (a) (Anat) throat; **me dolía la ~** I had a sore throat (b) (cuello) neck **2** (desfiladero) gorge, ravine; (entre montañas) narrow pass
■ *mf* (Per fam) scrounger (colloq)

gargantilla *f* choker, necklace

gárgara *f* gargle; **hacer ~s** to gargle

garita *f* (de centinela) sentry box; (de portero) lodge

garito *m* gambling den

garra *f* **1** (de animal) claw; (de águila) talon **2** (arrojo, valor) fighting spirit; (personalidad) personality **3** **garras** *fpl* (poder, dominio) clutches (*pl*)

garrafa *f* (a) (para vino) demijohn (b) (RPI) (para gas) cylinder

garrafal *adj* terrible; ⟨error⟩ monumental

garrapata *f* tick

garrapiñada *f* (esp AmL) caramel-coated peanuts/almonds (*pl*)

garrobo *m* (AmC) iguana

garrocha *f* **1** (Taur) lance, goad **2** (AmL) (Dep) pole

garrochista *mf* (AmL) pole-vaulter

garrotazo *m* (golpe) blow (*with a club*)

garrote *m* (palo) club, stick; (método de ejecución) garrotte

garúa *f* (AmL) drizzle

garuar [A18] *v impers* (AmL) to drizzle

garza *f* (Zool) heron

garzón -zona *m,f* (Chi) *(m)* waiter; *(f)* waitress

gas *m* 1 (Fís, Quím) gas; **~es tóxicos** toxic fumes; **~ ciudad** town gas; **~ lacrimógeno/licuado** tear/liquified gas 2 **gases** *mpl* (Fisiol) wind, gas (AmE)

gasa *f* (Med, Tex) gauze

gaseosa *f* (a) (bebida efervescente) soda (AmE), fizzy drink (BrE) (b) (CS) (cualquier refresco) soft drink

gaseoso -sa *adj* (a) ‹cuerpo/estado› gaseous (b) ‹bebida› carbonated, fizzy (BrE)

gásfiter *mf* (*pl* **-ters**) (Chi) plumber

gasfitería *f* (Chi, Per) plumbing

gasfitero -ra *m,f* (Per) plumber

gasoducto *m* gas pipeline

gas-oil, gasóleo *m* (para calefacción) (gas) oil; (para motores) diesel (fuel *o* oil)

gasolina *f* gasoline (AmE), gas (AmE), petrol (BrE); **~ normal** regular gasoline (AmE), two-star petrol (BrE); **~ sin plomo** unleaded gasoline (AmE) *o* (BrE) petrol; **~ super** premium gasoline (AmE), four-star petrol (BrE)

gasolinera *f* gas station (AmE), petrol station (BrE)

gastado -da *adj* ‹ropa/zapatos› worn-out; ‹político/cantante› washed-up (colloq)

gastador -dora *adj/m,f* spendthrift

gastar [A1] *vt* 1 (consumir) (a) ‹dinero› to spend; **~ algo EN algo** to spend sth ON sth (b) ‹gasolina/electricidad› to use 2 (desperdiciar, malgastar) ‹dinero/tiempo/energía› to waste 3 (desgastar) ‹ropa/zapatos› to wear out; ‹tacones› to wear down 4 (fam) (llevar, usar) ‹ropa/gafas› to wear; **gasto el 37** I'm a size 37 5 ‹broma› to play; **le ~on una broma** they played a joke *o* trick on him
■ **gastarse** *v pron* 1 (enf) ‹dinero› to spend 2 ‹pilas/batería› to run down; **se me gastó la tinta** I ran out of ink 3 ‹ropa/zapatos› (desgastarse) to wear out 4 (enf) (fam) (tener) to have; **se gasta un genio …** he has a terrible temper!

gasto *m* expense; **un ~ innecesario** an unnecessary expense; **este mes he tenido muchos ~s** this has been an expensive month for me; **el ~ público** public expenditure; **~s de correo** postage; **~s de envío** postage and handling (AmE) *o* (BrE) packing

gastritis *f* gastritis

gastronomía *f* gastronomy

gata *f* 1 (Chi, Per) (Auto) jack; *ver tb* GATO¹ 2 **a gatas** (*loc adv*) (a cuatro patas): **ir *o* andar a ~s** to crawl; **tuve que entrar a ~s** I had to go in on all fours

gatear [A1] *vi* (andar a gatas) to crawl

gatera *f* cathole (AmE), cat flap (BrE)

gatillero *m* (Méx) gunman

gatillo *m* trigger; **apretar el ~** to pull the trigger

gatito -ta *m,f* kitten

gato¹ -ta *m,f* (Zool) cat; **~ montés** wild cat; **aquí hay ~ encerrado** there's something fishy going

on here; **le dieron ~ por liebre** he was conned *o* had! (colloq); **llevarse el ~ al agua** (fam) to pull it off (colloq)

gato² *m* 1 (Auto) jack 2 (Chi, Méx) (Jueg) ticktacktoe (AmE), noughts and crosses (BrE) 3 (Méx) (signo) hash sign

gauchada *f* (Bol, CS fam) favor*, good turn

gaucho *m* gaucho

gaveta *f* drawer

gavilán *m* sparrowhawk

gavilla *f* (de cereales) sheaf

gaviota *f* seagull, gull

gay /gai, gei/ *adj* (*pl* **~** *or* **gays**) gay
■ *mf* *(m)* gay man, gay; *(f)* gay woman, lesbian

gazmoño -ña *adj* (pudoroso) prudish; (mojigato) sanctimonious

gaznate *m* (garganta) (fam) throat, gullet; **refrescar el ~** (fam) to have a drink

gazpacho *m*: *tb* **~ andaluz** gazpacho (*cold soup made from tomatoes, peppers, etc*)

ge *f*: name of the letter G

gel *m* gel

gelatina *f* (a) (sustancia) gelatin* (b) (postre) Jell-O® (AmE), jelly (BrE)

gelatinoso -sa *adj* gelatinous

gema *f* gem

gemelo¹ -la *adj* twin (*before n*)
■ *m,f* twin

gemelo² *m* (a) (de camisa) cuff link (b) **gemelos** *mpl* (Ópt) binoculars (*pl*)

gemido *m* (a) (de dolor, pena) groan, moan (b) (de animal) whine

Géminis *m* (signo, constelación) Gemini; **es (de) ~** she's (a) Gemini, she's a Geminian
■ *mf* (*pl* **~**) (persona) *tb* **géminis** Geminian, Gemini

gemir [I14] *vi* (a) «persona» to moan, groan (b) «animal» to whine

gen *m* gene

gendarme *mf* gendarme

gendarmería *f* gendarmerie

genealógico -ca *adj* genealogical

generación *f* generation

generacional *adj* generation (*before n*), generational

generador *m* generator

general *adj* (a) (no específico, global) general; **de interés ~** of general interest; **hablando en líneas ~es** broadly speaking; **un panorama ~ de la situación** an overall view of the situation (b) (*en locs*) **en general** on the whole, in general; **el público en ~** the general public; **por lo general** as a (general) rule
■ *mf* (Mil) general

generalidad *f* (vaguedad) general comment, generality; (mayoría) majority

generalizado -da *adj* widespread

generalizar [A4] *vi* to generalize, make generalizations
■ **generalizarse** *v pron* to spread

generalmente *adv* generally

generar [A1] *vt* to generate

género *m* 1 (a) (clase, tipo) kind, type; **el ~** ···>

humano the human race, mankind **(b)** (Biol) genus **(c)** (Lit, Teatr) genre; **el ~ dramático** drama **(d)** (Ling) gender ②(tela) cloth, material

generosidad f generosity

generoso -sa adj generous

genética f genetics

genéticamente adv genetically; **~ modificado** genetically modified, GM

genético -ca adj genetic

genial adj **(a)** ⟨idea/escritor/pintor⟩ brilliant **(b)** (fam) (estupendo) great (colloq), fantastic (colloq); (fam) (ocurrente, gracioso) witty, funny

genialidad f (cualidad) genius; (ocurrencia) brilliant idea, stroke of genius

geniecillo m elf

genio m **(a)** (carácter) temper; **tener buen/mal ~** to be even-tempered/bad-tempered **(b)** (lumbrera) genius **(d)** (ser fantástico) genie

genitales mpl genitals (pl), genital organs (pl)

genocidio m genocide

Génova f Genoa

gente f

■ **Nota** Nótese que en español, cuando el nombre *gente* significa *personas*, se traduce al inglés por *people* con verbo en plural - *allí la gente es muy amable* = people are very nice there. Cuando tiene el sentido de *familia* se traduce al inglés por *family* con el verbo en singular o plural - *mi gente está de vacaciones* = my family is o are on holiday

(a) (personas) people (pl); **la gente está asustada** people are frightened; **había muy poca/tanta ~** there were very few/so many people; **~ bien** (de respeto) respectable people; (adinerada) well-to-do people; **la ~ de a pie** the man in the street; **ser buena ~** to be nice (o kind etc); **ser ~** (AmS) to behave (properly) **(b)** (Méx) (persona) person

■ adj (AmL) (de buenas maneras) respectable; (amable) kind, good

■ adv (Chi, Méx: **se portó muy ~ conmigo** she was very good o kind to me

gentil adj (amable) kind

gentileza f (cualidad) kindness; (atención, gesto): **tuvo la ~ de cederme el asiento** she was kind enough to let me have her seat; **ni siquiera tuvo la ~ de avisarnos** he didn't even have the courtesy to inform us

gentilicio m: *name given to the people from a particular region or country*

gentío m crowd

gentuza f (pey) riffraff (pej), rabble (pej)

genuflexión f genuflection

genuino -na adj genuine

geografía f geography

geográfico -ca adj geographical

geología f geology

geólogo -ga m,f geologist

geometría f geometry

geométrico -ca adj geometric

geranio m geranium

gerencia f **(a)** (cargo) post o position of manager **(b)** (personas) management **(c)** (oficina) manager's office

gerenciar [A1] vt (AmL) to manage

gerente mf manager; **~ comercial** business manager

geriatría f geriatrics

geriátrico -ca adj geriatric

germen m ①(microbio) germ ②**(a)** (embrión) germ **(b)** (origen) seeds (pl)

germicida m germicide

germinar [A1] vi to germinate

gerundio m gerund

gestación f gestation

gesticular [A1] vi to gesticulate

gestión f **(a)** (trámite) step; **la única ~ que había hecho** the only step he had taken; **hizo gestiones para adoptar un niño** he went through the procedure for adopting a child; **su apoyo a las gestiones de paz** their support for the peace process **(b) gestiones** fpl (negociaciones) negotiations (pl)

gestionar [A1] vt ⟨compra/préstamo⟩ to negotiate; **le están gestionando el permiso de trabajo** they are getting his work permit sorted out o arranged

gesto m ①(en general) gesture; **un ~ grosero** a rude gesture; **le hizo un ~ para que se callara** she gestured to him to be quiet ②(expresión) expression; **hacer ~s** to make faces

gestoría f agency (which obtains official documents on clients' behalf)

ghetto /'geto/ m ghetto

Gibraltar m Gibraltar

gibraltareño -ña adj/m,f Gibraltarian

gigabyte /xɪva'βaɪt/ m gigabyte

gigante¹ adj giant (before n)

gigante² -ta m,f (en cuentos) (m) giant; (f) giantess; (persona alta) giant

gigantesco -ca adj huge, gigantic

gil mf (RPl fam o vulg) jerk (sl)

gilipollas adj inv (Esp fam o vulg): **¡qué ~ es ese tío!** that guy's such a jerk! (sl & pej)

■ mf (pl **~**) (Esp fam o vulg) jerk (sl & pej)

gilipollez f (Esp fam o vulg): **decir gilipolleces** to talk garbage (AmE) o (BrE) rubbish; **no discutáis por esa ~** don't argue over a stupid o silly thing like that; **pagar tanto es una ~** it's stupid paying that much

gimnasia f gymnastics; (como asignatura) gym, PE (BrE); **hago ~ todos los días** I do exercises every day; **~ de mantenimiento** keep-fit

gimnasio m gymnasium, gym

gimnasta mf gymnast

gimotear [A1] vi to whine, whimper

ginebra f gin

Ginebra f Geneva

ginecólogo -ga m,f gynecologist*

gira f tour; **de ~** on tour

AmC	América Central	Arg	Argentina	Cu	Cuba
AmL	América Latina	Bol	Bolivia	Ec	Ecuador
AmS	América del Sur	Chi	Chile	Esp	España
Andes	Región andina	CS	Cono Sur	Méx	México

Per	Perú
RPI	Río de la Plata
Ur	Uruguay
Ven	Venezuela

girar [A1] *vi* **1** (a) «*rueda*» to turn, go around; «*disco*» to revolve, go around; «*trompo*» to spin; ∼ ALREDEDOR DE algo/algn to revolve AROUND sth/sb (b) (darse la vuelta) to turn **2** (torcer, desviarse) to turn; ∼on a la derecha they turned right
■ ∼ *vt* **1** ⟨*manivela/volante*⟩ to turn **2** (Com, Fin) ⟨*cheque/letra de cambio*⟩ to draw

girasol *m* sunflower

giratorio -ria *adj* revolving (*before n*)

giro *m* **1** (en general) turn; hizo un ∼ a la derecha she made a right turn; un ∼ de 180 grados a volte-face, an about-turn; el ∼ que estaba tomando la conversación the direction the conversation was taking **2** (Fin): enviar un ∼ (a través de un banco) to transfer money; (por correo) to send a money order; ∼ **bancario** (cheque) bank *o* banker's draft; (transferencia) credit transfer; ∼ **postal** money order

gis *m* (Méx) chalk

gitano -na *adj* gypsy (*before n*)
■ *m,f* gypsy

glacial *adj* (a) ⟨*zona/período*⟩ glacial (b) ⟨*viento/temperatura*⟩ icy

glaciar *m* glacier

gladiador *m* gladiator

gladiolo *m* gladiolus

glamoroso -sa *adj* glamorous

glándula *f* gland

glandular *adj* glandular

glicerina *f* glycerin

global *adj* global; ⟨*informe*⟩ full, comprehensive; ⟨*resultado*⟩ overall; ⟨*precio/cantidad*⟩ total

globo *m* **1** (a) (Aviac, Jueg, Meteo) balloon; ∼ **aerostático/sonda** hot-air/observation balloon (b) (de chicle) bubble (c) (de lámpara) globe (d) ∼ **ocular** eyeball **2** (mundo) world; *tb* ∼**terráqueo** globe

glóbulo *m* (cuerpo esférico) globule; (corpúsculo) corpuscle; ∼ **blanco/rojo** white/red corpuscle

gloria *f* **1** (Relig) glory; *estar/sentirse en la* ∼ to be in seventh heaven (b) (fama, honor) glory; **cubrirse de** ∼ to win glory **2** (personalidad) figure; es una de las ∼s del deporte he is one of the great sporting figures *o* heroes

glorieta *f* (a) (plaza) square; (Auto) traffic circle (AmE), roundabout (BrE) (b) (en el jardín) arbor*

glorioso -sa *adj* ⟨*hecho*⟩ glorious; ⟨*personaje*⟩ great

glotón -tona *adj* gluttonous, greedy
■ *m,f* glutton

glotonería *f* gluttony

glúteo *m* gluteus

gnomo /'nomo/ *m* gnome

gobelino *m* Gobelin

gobernador -dora *m,f* governor

gobernante *adj* ⟨*partido/organismo*⟩ ruling (*before n*), governing (*before n*)
■ *mf* leader, ruler

gobernar [A5] *vt* ⟨*país*⟩ to govern, rule; ⟨*barco*⟩ to steer
■ ∼ *vi* (Gob, Pol) to govern; (Náut) to steer

gobierna, gobiernas ▶ GOBERNAR

gobierno *m* government

goce *m* (a) (de derecho, título) enjoyment; **en pleno** ∼ **de sus facultades** in full possession of her faculties (b) (placer) pleasure

gol *m* goal; **marcar** *or* **meter un** ∼ to score a goal

goleada *f* heavy defeat

goleador -dora *adj* high-scoring
■ *m,f* scorer, goal-scorer

golear [A1] *vt*: el Madrid goleó al Osasuna Real Madrid thrashed Osasuna

golero -ra *m,f* (CS) goalkeeper

golf *m* golf

golfa *f* (fam) (prostituta) whore (colloq)

golfillo -lla *m,f* street urchin

golfista *mf* golfer

golfito *m* (AmL) mini-golf, miniature golf

golfo¹ -fa *m,f* (a) (holgazán) good-for-nothing, layabout (b) (fam) (niño travieso) rascal (colloq), little devil (colloq)

golfo² *m* (Geog, Náut) gulf; G∼ **de México** Gulf of Mexico; G∼ **de Vizcaya** Bay of Biscay

golilla *f* **1** (Indum) (a) (cuello fruncido) ruff (b) (RPI) (pañuelo) neckerchief **2** (arandela) washer

gollete *m* neck (*of a bottle*); **estar hasta el** ∼ (fam) to be fed up to the back teeth (colloq); *no tiene* ∼ (RPI fam) it's the limit

golondrina *f* (Zool) swallow

golosa *f* (Col) hopscotch

golosina *f* (dulce) candy (AmE), sweet (BrE)

goloso -sa *adj* (amante de lo dulce): es muy ∼ he has a really sweet tooth

golpe *m* **1** (choque, impacto) knock; me di un ∼ en la cabeza I got a knock on the head, I hit *o* banged my head; **darse un** ∼ **contra algo** to bang *o* knock into sth; dio unos ∼s en la mesa he tapped on the table; (más fuerte) he knocked on the table; (aún más fuerte) he banged on the table; **a** ∼ **de** (Ven) around; **de** ∼ **(y porrazo)** suddenly; **se abrió/cerró de** ∼ it flew open/slammed shut; **de un** ∼ (de una vez) all at once; (de un trago) in one go *o* gulp
2 (a) (al pegarle a algn) blow; lo derribó de un ∼ he knocked him down with one blow; casi lo matan a ∼s they almost beat him to death; siempre andan a ∼s they're always fighting (b) (marca) bruise, mark
3 (Dep) stroke
4 (a) (desgracia) blow (b) ∼ **de suerte** stroke of luck
5 (fam) (atraco, timo) job (colloq); **dar el** ∼ to do the job
6 (Pol) *tb* ∼ **de estado** coup (d'état)

golpear [A1] *vt* **1** ⟨*objeto/superficie*⟩ to bang; (repetidamente) to beat; **no golpees la puerta al salir** don't slam *o* bang the door as you go out; **la lluvia golpeaba los cristales** the rain beat against the window panes; **golpeó la mesa con el puño** he banged his fist on the table
2 (pegar) to hit; **algo me golpeó en la cara** something hit me in the face; **su marido la golpea** her husband hits her
■ ∼ *vi* (a) (dar, pegar) ∼ CONTRA algo to beat AGAINST sth (AmS) (llamar a la puerta) to knock (c) (en fútbol americano) to scrimmage
■ **golpearse** *v pron* (a) (refl) ⟨*cabeza/codo*⟩ to bang, hit (b) (AmL) «*puerta*» to bang

golpetazo *m* (fam) hard blow

golpeteo m (tamborileo) drumming, tapping; (de la lluvia) patter, pitter-patter; (de una puerta) banging

golpismo m pro-coup tendency

golpista adj ‹minoría/tendencia› in favor of a coup; **los militares ~s** the soldiers who took part in the coup

golpiza f (AmL) beating

goma f 1 (a) (caucho) rubber; **suelas de ~** rubber soles (b) (pegamento) glue, gum; **~ de mascar** chewing gum 2 (a) (para sujetar) rubber band, elastic band (BrE) (b) (de borrar) eraser (c) (RPI) (neumático) tire* 3 (AmC fam) (resaca) hangover; **ando de ~** I've got a hangover

gomina f hair gel

gomita f 1 (RPI) (para sujetar) rubber band, elastic band (BrE) 2 (Chi, Méx, Ven) (dulce) gumdrop, gum (BrE)

góndola f gondola

gondolero m gondolier

gordo[1] **-da** adj 1 ‹persona/piernas› fat; **siempre ha sido ~** he's always been overweight o fat; **estás ~** you've put on weight; **es más bien gordita** she's quite plump 2 (grueso) ‹libro/lana/suéter› thick 3 ‹carne/tocino› fatty
■ m,f (a) (persona) (m) fat man; (f) fat woman (b) (fam) (como apelativo ofensivo) fatso (colloq), fatty (colloq)

gordo[2] m (Jueg) (premio mayor) jackpot (in the state lottery)

gordura f (a) (grasa) fat (b) (exceso de peso) fatness; **me preocupa su ~** I'm worried about how fat he is

gorgorito m trill

gorgotear [A1] vi (en cañería) to gurgle; (al hervir) to bubble

gorila m 1 (Zool) gorilla 2 (fam) (a) (matón) thug (b) (guardaespaldas) heavy (colloq) (c) (reaccionario) fascist (d) (Esp) (en un club) bouncer

gorjear [A1] vi ‹pájaro› to trill, warble; ‹niño› to gurgle

gorra f cap; (con visera) peaked cap; (de bebé) bonnet

gorrear [A1] vt 1 (fam) (pedir) to scrounge (colloq); **me gorreó $20** he scrounged $20 off me 2 (Chi fam) ‹cónyuge› to cheat on (colloq)

gorrero -ra m,f (AmL fam) (aprovechado) scrounger (colloq)

gorrión m sparrow

gorro m cap; **~ de baño** (para nadar) bathing cap; (para la ducha) shower cap; **estar hasta el ~** (fam) to be fed up to the back teeth (colloq)

gorrón -rrona m,f (Esp, Méx fam) scrounger (colloq)

gorronear [A1] vt/vi (Esp, Méx fam) to scrounge (colloq)

gota f 1 (de líquido) drop; **~s de sudor** beads of sweat; **la ~ que colma o rebasa el vaso** the last straw; **parecerse/ser como dos ~s de agua** to be as like as two peas in a pod 2 (enfermedad) gout

gotear [A1] vi ‹líquido/grifo/vela› to drip; ‹cañería› to leak
■ v impers (lloviznar) to spit, drizzle

goteo m dripping

gotera f (a) (filtración) leak (b) (mancha) damp stain

gótico -ca adj Gothic

gourde m gourde (Haitian unit of currency)

gozador -dora adj (AmL) fun-loving

gozar [A4] vi: **~ DE algo** to enjoy sth; **~ de la vida** to enjoy life; **goza viéndolos jugar** she enjoys watching them play; **~ CON algo** to enjoy sth; **goza de perfecta salud** he enjoys perfect health; **goza de una buena posición** he has a good position

gozne m hinge

gozo m 1 (a) (alegría) joy; **no caber en sí de ~** to be beside oneself with joy (b) (placer) pleasure, enjoyment 2 **gozos** mpl (Relig) verses (pl)

gozque mf (Col) mongrel

grabación f recording; **~ en video** video recording

grabado m engraving

grabador -dora m,f 1 (Art) engraver 2 **grabadora** f (a) (casa discográfica) record company (b) (magnetófono) tape recorder

grabar [A1] vt/vi (a) (Audio, TV) to record, tape (b) (Art) to engrave
■ **grabarse** v pron: **sus palabras se me ~on en la memoria** her words are etched on my memory; **su cara se me quedó grabada** I'll never forget her face

gracia f
I 1 (comicidad): **yo no le veo la ~** I don't think it's funny; **tener ~** «chiste/broma» to be funny; **me hace ~ que digas eso** it's funny you should say that; **no me hace ninguna ~ tener que ir** I don't relish the idea of having to go 2 (a) (chiste) joke; (broma) joke, trick (b) (de niño) party piece 3 (encanto, elegancia) grace; **con ~** «moverse/bailar» gracefully; **un vestido sin ~** a very plain dress; **tiene mucha ~ para arreglar flores** she has a real flair for flower arranging
II **gracias** fpl (a) (expresión de agradecimiento): **darle las ~s a algn** to thank sb; **no dieron ni las ~s** they didn't even say thank you (b) (como interj) thank you, thanks (colloq); **muchas ~s** thank you very much, thanks a lot (colloq); **un millón de ~s por ayudarme/tu ayuda** thank you very much for helping me/your help (c) **gracias a** thanks to; **~s a Dios** thank God

gracioso -sa adj 1 (divertido) ‹chiste/persona› funny; **¡qué ~!** how funny!; **hacerse el ~** to play the fool 2 (atractivo) ‹cara/figura› attractive; **las pecas le dan un aspecto muy ~** those freckles make her look really cute o sweet

grada f (a) (peldaño) step (b) **gradas** fpl (Dep) stand, grandstand

gradería f, (Esp) **graderío** m stands (pl)

gradiente f (AmL) (pendiente) slope, gradient

grado m 1 (en general) degree; **estamos a tres ~s bajo cero** it's three degrees below zero; **~ centígrado** or **Celsius/Fahrenheit** degree centigrade o Celsius/Fahrenheit; **el ~ de confusión reinante** the degree of confusion that prevails; **en ~ sumo** extremely 2 (de escalafón) grade; (Mil) rank 3 (disposición): **de buen/mal ~** willingly/unwillingly 4 (a) (esp AmL) (Educ) (curso, año) year (b) (título): **tiene el ~ de licenciado** he has a college (AmE) o (BrE) university degree

graduable adj adjustable

graduación f **(a)** (acción de regular) adjustment **(b)** (de bebida alcohólica) alcohol content **(c)** (Mil) rank **(d)** (Educ) graduation

graduado -da adj **(a)** ⟨gafas/lentes⟩ prescription (before n) **(b)** ⟨termómetro⟩ graduated
■ m,f (Educ) graduate

gradual adj gradual

graduar [A18] vt **(a)** (regular) to adjust **(b)** (marcar) ⟨instrumento/termómetro⟩ to calibrate
■ **graduarse** v pron **(a)** (Educ) to graduate **(b)** (Mil) to take a commission

graffiti /graˈfiti/ mpl graffiti

gráfico¹ -ca adj graphic; ⟨gesto⟩ expressive

gráfico² m **(a)** (Mat) graph **(b)** (Inf) graphic

grafología f graphology

gragea f **(a)** (Farm) tablet **(b)** (Coc) small candy (AmE) o (BrE) sweet

Gral. m (= **General**) Gen.

grama f (AmC, Ven) (césped) lawn

gramática f (disciplina) grammar; (libro) grammar (book)

gramatical adj grammatical

gramo m gram

gran adj: ▶ GRANDE

granada f **1** (Bot) pomegranate **2** (Arm, Mil) grenade; ~ **de mano** hand grenade

Granada f (en España) Granada; (en el Caribe) Grenada

granadilla f (fruta — redonda, oscura) passion fruit; (— más grande, amarilla) granadilla

granate adj inv maroon (before n)
■ m (color) maroon

Gran Bretaña f Great Britain

grande adj [GRAN is used before singular nouns] **1** **(a)** (en dimensiones) ⟨casa/área/nariz⟩ big, large; **un tipo ~ a** big guy; **unos ~ almacenes a** department store **(b)** (en demasía) too big; **me queda ~** it's too big for me **(c)** (en número) ⟨familia⟩ large, big; ⟨clase⟩ big; **la gran parte** or **mayoría** the great majority
2 (a) (alto) tall; **¡qué ~ está Andrés!** isn't Andrés tall! **(b)** (en edad): **cuando sea ~** when I grow up; **ya son ~s** they are all grown up now **3** (Geog): **el G~ Santiago** Greater Santiago **4** (delante del n) **(a)** (notable, excelente) great; **un gran hombre** a great man **(b)** (poderoso) big; **los ~s bancos** the big banks; **a lo ~** in style **5 (a)** (en intensidad, grado) ⟨pena/honor/ventaja⟩ great; ⟨explosión⟩ powerful; **¡me llevé un susto más ~ ... !** I got such a fright!; **una temporada de gran éxito** a very o a highly successful season; **son ~s amigos** they're great friends; **eso es una gran verdad** that is absolutely true; **¡qué mentira más ~!** that's a complete lie! **(b)** (elevado): **a gran velocidad** at high o great speed; **volar a gran altura** to fly at a great height; **un gran número de personas** a large number of people; **objetos de gran valor** objects of great value; **en ~: lo pasamos en ~** we had a great time (colloq)
■ m,f **(a)** (mayor): **la grande ya está casada** their eldest (daughter) is already married **(b)** (adulto): **los ~s** the grown-ups

grandeza f **1** (excelencia, nobleza) nobility; ~ **de alma** (liter) magnanimity; ~ **de ánimo** (liter)

valor* (liter) **2 (a)** (dignidad de Grande) rank of grandee **(b)** (conjunto de Grandes): **la ~ the** (Spanish) nobility o grandees

grandilocuencia f grandiloquence

grandiosidad f grandeur

grandioso -sa adj **(a)** ⟨espectáculo/obra⟩ impressive, magnificent **(b)** (rimbombante) ⟨gesto/ palabras⟩ grandiose

granel: a ~ (a) (loc adj) (en abundancia) ⟨comida/ bebida⟩ stacks of **(b)** (loc adv) **comprar/vender a ~** ⟨vino/aceite⟩ to buy/sell ... by the liter (o pint etc); ⟨galletas/nueces⟩ to buy/sell ... loose; (en grandes cantidades) to buy/sell ... in bulk

granero m granary, barn

granito m (roca) granite

granizado m (bebida) drink served on crushed ice

granizar [A4] v impers to hail

granizo m (grano, bola) hailstone; (conjunto) hail

granja f (Agr) farm; ~ **avícola** poultry farm

granjearse [A1] v pron to earn, win

granjero -ra m,f farmer

grano m **1** (de arena, azúcar, trigo, arroz) grain; (de café) bean; (de mostaza) seed; **~s de pimienta** peppercorns; **ir al ~** (fam) to get (straight) to the point **2** (Med) spot, pimple (esp AmE) **3 (a)** (de la piedra, la madera) grain **(b)** (Fot) grain

granuja mf rascal

grapa f **1 (a)** (para papeles) staple; (para cables) cable clip **(b)** (Arquit) cramp iron **2** (CS) (aguardiente) grappa

grapadora f stapler

grapar [A1] vt to staple

grasa f **1 (a)** (Biol, Coc) fat; **la comida tenía mucha ~** the food was very greasy **(b)** (suciedad) grease; **está lleno de ~** it's all greasy **(c)** (Mec) grease **2** (Méx) (betún) shoe polish

grasiento -ta adj greasy

grasitud f (AmL) greasiness

graso -sa adj **(a)** ⟨pelo/cutis⟩ greasy **(b)** (Coc) greasy, oily, fatty; **queso ~** full fat cheese

grasoso -sa adj (AmL) greasy

gratificación f **(a)** (bonificación) bonus; (recompensa) reward **(b)** (satisfacción) gratification

gratificador -dora adj (AmL) rewarding, gratifying (frml)

gratificante adj rewarding, gratifying (frml)

gratificar [A2] vt **(a)** ⟨persona⟩ to give ... a bonus **(b)** (recompensar) to give ... a reward; **Ⓢ se gratificará** reward offered

gratinado -da adj au gratin

gratinador m grill

gratis adj/adv free; **es ~** it is free (of charge); **entramos ~** we got in free o for nothing

gratitud f gratitude

grato -ta adj pleasant

gratuito -ta adj **(a)** (gratis) free **(b)** (infundado) ⟨afirmaciones⟩ unwarranted; ⟨insulto⟩ gratuitous

grava f gravel

gravamen m (impuesto) tax; (carga) burden; (sobre finca, casa) encumbrance

gravar [A1] vt (con impuesto) ⟨ingresos/productos⟩ to tax

grave adj **1 (a)** [ESTAR] ⟨enfermo⟩ seriously ill ···⟩

(a) [SER] ⟨herida/enfermedad⟩ serious
2 ⟨situación/asunto/error⟩ serious **3 (a)** ⟨tono/
expresión/gesto⟩ grave, solemn **(b)** ⟨voz⟩ deep **(c)**
⟨sonido/nota⟩ low **4** (Ling) ⟨acento⟩ grave;
⟨palabra⟩ paroxytone

gravedad f **1** (en general) seriousness; **está
herido de ∼** he is seriously injured; **es un asunto
de mucha ∼** it is a very serious matter **2** (Fís)
gravity

gravilla f gravel

graznar [A1] vi «cuervo» to caw; «ganso» to
honk; «pato» to quack

graznido m (del cuervo) caw; (del ganso) honk;
(del pato) quack

Grecia f Greece

greda f (para cerámica) clay

grei m (Col) grapefruit

greifrú mf (pl **-frús**) (AmC, Ven fam) grapefruit

gremial adj **(a)** (profesional) ⟨asociación⟩
professional **(b)** (AmL) (sindical) union (before n)

gremialista mf (AmL) trade unionist

gremio m **(a)** (de oficio, profesión) trade **(b)** (CS,
Per) (sindicato) union

greña f **(a)** (enredo) tangle **(b)** en greña (Méx)
⟨trigo⟩ unthreshed; ⟨plata/azúcar⟩ unrefined;
⟨tabaco⟩ leaf (before n) **(c) greñas** fpl untidy
hair

gresca f (fam) (jaleo) rumpus (colloq); (riña) fight

griego¹ -ga adj/m,f Greek

griego² m (idioma) Greek

grieta f (en una pared) crack; (en la tierra) crack,
crevice; (en la piel) crack

grifo¹ m **1** (Esp) (de lavabo, bañera) faucet (AmE),
tap (BrE); **abrir/cerrar el ∼** to turn the faucet o tap
on/off **2** (Per) (gasolinera) filling station **3** (Chi)
(de incendios) fire hydrant, fireplug (AmE)

grifo² -fa m,f (Méx fam) pothead (sl), dopehead
(sl)

grillo m **1** (Zool) cricket **2 grillos** mpl (de los
presos) fetters (pl), shackles (pl)

grima f (Esp fam): **darle ∼ a algn** (repulsión) to
make sb's flesh crawl; (dentera) to set sb's teeth on
edge

gringo -ga adj **(a)** (AmL fam & pey) gringo,
foreign (of or relating to a person from a
non-Spanish speaking country) **(b)** (Andes fam)
(rubio) fair-haired
■ m,f **(a)** (AmL fam & pey) (extranjero) gringo,
foreigner (from a non-Spanish speaking country);
(norteamericano) Yank (colloq & pej), Yankee (colloq &
pej) **(b)** (Andes fam) (rubio) (m) fair-haired boy/
man; (f) fair-haired girl/woman

Gringolandia f (Andes fam & pey) Yankeeland
(colloq & pej)

gripa f (Col, Méx) ▶ GRIPE

gripe f flu; **estar con/tener ∼** to have (the) flu

gris adj/m gray*

gritar [A1] vi to shout; **no hace falta que grites**
there's no need to shout o yell; **∼ de dolor** to

scream with pain; **∼ de alegría** to shout for joy;
∼ pidiendo ayuda to shout for help; **∼le ʌ algn** to
shout ᴀᴛ sb; (para llamarlo) to shout (out) ᴛᴏ sb
■ **∼** vt to shout

griterío m shouting, clamor*

grito m (de dolor, alegría) shout, cry; (de terror)
scream; **un ∼ de socorro** a cry for help; **∼s de
protesta** shouts o cries of protest; **hablar a ∼s** to
talk at the top of one's voice; **ser el último ∼** to
be the last word in fashion **(b)** (de pájaro, animal)
call, cry

groenlandés -desa adj of/from Greenland

Groenlandia f Greenland

grosella f redcurrant

grosería f **(a)** (acción): **fue una ∼ de su parte** it
was very rude of him **(b)** (comentario) rude
comment; **¡qué ∼!** how rude!; **decir ∼s** to swear

grosero -ra adj **(a)** (descortés) ⟨persona/
lenguaje⟩ rude **(b)** (vulgar) crude, vulgar
■ m,f: **es un ∼** (vulgar) he's so vulgar o crude!;
(descortés) he's so rude!

grosor m thickness

grotesco -ca adj ⟨personaje/mueca⟩ grotesque;
⟨espectáculo⟩ hideous, grotesque

grúa f **(a)** (Const) crane **(b)** (Auto) (de taller)
wrecker (AmE), breakdown van (BrE); (de la policía)
tow truck; **se lo llevó la ∼** it was towed (away)

grueso -sa adj thick

grulla f crane

grumete m cabin boy

grumo m lump

grumoso -sa adj lumpy

gruñido m grunt; (del perro) growl

gruñir [I9] vi **(a)** «cerdo» to grunt; «perro» to
growl **(b)** (fam) «persona» to grumble

gruñón -ñona adj (fam) grumpy (colloq)

grupa f rump, hindquarters (pl)

grupo m **(a)** (de personas, empresas, países) group;
(de árboles) clump; **∼ sanguíneo** blood group; **∼s
sociales** social groups; **de ∼** ⟨terapia/trabajo⟩
group (before n); **en ∼** ⟨salir/trabajar⟩ in a
group/in groups **(b)** (Mús) tb **∼ musical** group,
band

gruta f (natural) cave; (artificial) grotto

guaca f (Andes) pre-Columbian tomb

guacal m **(a)** (Col, Méx, Ven) (caja) wooden crate
(b) (Ven) (medida) crate, crateload **(c)** (AmC)
(calabaza) large gourd (used for storing tortillas)

guacamaya f (Méx) **1** (ave) macaw **2** (fam)
(persona) loudmouth (colloq)

guacamayo m macaw

guacamole m guacamole

guachimán m (AmS fam) watchman

guachinango m (Méx) red snapper

guacho¹ -cha adj **1** (fam) ⟨niño⟩ orphaned; ⟨perro⟩ stray **(b)** (fam & pey)
⟨hijo⟩ bastard (before n) (pej) **2** (Chi, Per fam)
⟨calcetín/guante⟩ odd
■ m,f (Andes, RPI) **(a)** (fam) (niño abandonado) orphan,

AmC	Central America	Arg	Argentina	Cu	Cuba
AmL	Latin America	Bol	Bolivia	Ec	Ecuador
AmS	South America	Chi	Chile	Esp	Spain
Andes	Andean Region	CS	Southern Cone	Méx	Mexico

Per	Peru
RPI	River Plate Area
Ur	Uruguay
Ven	Venezuela

waif; (perro) stray **(b)** (fam & pey) (hijo ilegítimo) bastard (vulg) **(c)** (insulto — a un hombre) bastard (pej); (— a una mujer) bitch (sl & pej)

guacho² *m* (Per) (de la lotería) *tenth share in a lottery ticket*

guaco *m* (Andes) pot *(found in pre-Columbian tomb)*

guadaña *f* scythe

guagua *f* (fam) ⓵ (Andes) (bebé) baby ⓶ (Cu) (autobús) bus

guaje -ja *m,f* ⓵ (Méx fam) sucker (colloq); **hacerle ~ a algn** (serle infiel) to cheat on sb (colloq); (engañarlo) to rip sb off (colloq); **hacerse ~** to act dumb (colloq) ⓶ **guaje** *m* (Méx) **(a)** (planta, fruto) bottle gourd **(b)** (vasija) gourd **(c)** (instrumento) maraca *(made from a bottle gourd)*

guajiro -ra *m,f* **(a)** (en Cuba) peasant **(b)** (en Col, Ven) *native of the Guajira peninsula*

guajolote -ta *m,f* (Méx) turkey

guanábana *f* (fruto) soursop; (árbol) soursop tree

guanaco *m* ⓵ (Zool) guanaco ⓶ (Chi fam) (de la policía) water cannon

guanera *f* guano deposit

guanero -ra *adj* guano *(before n)*

guano *m* guano

guante *m* glove; **~s de lana/boxeo** woollen/ boxing gloves; **echarle el ~ a algn** (fam) to nab sb (colloq)

guantera *f* glove compartment

guapetón -tona *adj* (fam) ⟨chico⟩ handsome; ⟨chica⟩ pretty

guapo -pa *adj* ⓵ ⟨hombre⟩ handsome, good-looking; ⟨mujer⟩ attractive, good-looking; ⟨bebé⟩ beautiful; **estás muy ~ con ese traje** you look very nice in that suit ⓶ **(a)** (fam) (bravucón): **ponerse ~** to get cocky (colloq) **(b)** (AmS fam) (valiente) gutsy (colloq)

guarangada *f* (RPl, Ven fam) ▶ GROSERÍA B

guarango -ga *adj* (CS, Ven fam) (grosero) rude, loutish
■ *m,f* (CS, Ven fam) (grosero) lout (colloq)

guaraní *adj/m,f* Guaraní
■ *m* (idioma) Guaraní

guarapear [A1] *vi* (Per fam) to get plastered (colloq)

guarda *mf* (de museo, parque) keeper; (de edificio público) *tb* **~ jurado** security guard

guardabarros *m* (*pl* ~) **(a)** (Auto) fender (AmE), mudguard (BrE) **(b)** (de bicicleta) mudguard

guardabosque *mf* (en parque nacional) forest ranger

guardacostas *mf* (*pl* ~) **(a)** (persona) coastguard **(b) guardacostas** *m* (buque) coastguard vessel

guardaespaldas *mf* (*pl* ~) bodyguard

guardalíneas *mf* (*pl* ~) (Chi) *(m)* linesman; *(f)* lineswoman

guardameta *mf* goalkeeper

guardapelo *m* locket

guardapolvo *m* (bata — de niño) overall; (— de profesor, tendero) workcoat (AmE), overall (BrE)

guardar [A1] *vt* ⓵ (reservar) to save, keep; **guarda algo para después** save *o* keep sth for later

⓶ **(a)** (poner en un lugar) ⟨juguetes/libros⟩ to put ... away; **ya guardé toda la ropa de invierno** I've already put away all my winter clothes **(b)** (conservar, mantener) to keep; **lo guardó durante años** she kept it for years; **~ las apariencias** to keep up appearances **(c)** ⟨secreto⟩ to keep; ⟨rencor⟩ to bear, harbor*; **guardo muy buenos recuerdos de él** I have very good memories of him

■ **guardarse** *v pron* ⓵ **(a)** (quedarse con) to keep **(b)** (reservar) to save, keep
⓶ (poner en un lugar): **se guardó el cheque en el bolsillo** he put the check (away) in his pocket

guardarropa *m* **(a)** (en restaurantes, teatros) cloakroom **(b)** (ropa) wardrobe **(c)** (armario) dressing room

guardavallas *mf* (*pl* ~) (AmL) goalkeeper

guardería *f*: *tb* **~ infantil** nursery

guardia *f* ⓵ **(a)** (vigilancia): **estar de ~** «soldado» to be on guard duty; «médico» to be on duty *o* call; «empleado» to be on duty; «marino» to be on watch; **montar ~** to stand guard; **poner en ~ a algn** to warn sb **(b)** (en esgrima): **en ~** on guard ⓶ (cuerpo militar) guard; **cambio de ~** changing of the guard; **G~ Civil** Civil Guard; **~ municipal** *or* **urbana** police *(mainly involved in traffic duties)* ⓷ **guardia** *mf* *(m)* policeman; *(f)* policewoman

guardiamarina *mf* midshipman

guardián -diana *m,f* **(a)** (de un edificio) security guard, guard **(b)** (protector, defensor) guardian

guarecer [E3] *vt* to shelter, protect
■ **guarecerse** *v pron* (refl) to shelter, take shelter

guarén *m* water rat

guargüero *m* (AmL fam) (garganta) throat

guarida *f* (de animales) den, lair; (de personas) hideout

guarnecer [E3] *vt* (Coc) to garnish

guarrada *f* (Esp fam) **(a)** (porquería, suciedad) mess (colloq) **(b)** (mala pasada) dirty trick (colloq) **(c)** (indecencia, vulgaridad): **no digas ~s** don't be filthy; **esa película es una ~** that's a filthy movie

guarro -rra *m,f* (Esp fam) **(a)** (persona sucia) filthy pig (colloq) **(b)** (indecente, vulgar): **es un ~** he's really disgusting

guarura *m* (Méx) bodyguard

guasa *f* (fam) (broma, burla) joke; **de ~** as a joke; **no te lo tomes a ~** it's no joke, it's no laughing matter

guasca *f* (Chi, Per) (ramal de cuero) strap

guasón -sona *m,f* (fam) (bromista) joker

guata *f* ⓵ (Esp) (algodón) wadding ⓶ (Andes fam) (barriga) paunch; **echar ~** to get a paunch; **me duele la ~** I've got a tummy ache (colloq)

Guatemala *f* Guatemala

guatemalteco -ca *adj/m,f* Guatemalan

guateque *m* (Esp, Méx fam) (fiesta) bash (colloq), party

guatitas *fpl* (Chi) tripe

guatón -tona *adj* (Chi, Per fam): **está muy ~** he has a real paunch (colloq)
■ *m,f* (Chi, Per fam) fatty (colloq)

guau *interj* (del perro) woof!, bow-wow!

guayaba *f* (fruta) guava

guayabera *f: loose lightweight shirt*

guayabo *m* 1 (Bot) guava tree 2 (Col fam) (resaca) hangover

Guayana *f: tb* la ~ **Francesa** French Guiana

gubernatura *f* (Méx) government

güero -ra *adj* (Méx fam) (rubio) blond, fair-haired; (amarillo) yellow
■ *m,f* (Méx fam) (*m*) blond *o* fair-haired man; (*f*) blonde *o* fair-haired woman

guerra *f* 1 (Mil, Pol) war; **nos declararon la** ~ they declared war on us; **estar en** ~ to be at war; **hacerle la** ~ **a algn** to wage war on *o* against sb; ~ **bacteriológica** *or* **biológica** germ *o* biological warfare; ~ **civil** civil war; ~ **fría** cold war; ~ **mundial** world war; ~ **nuclear** nuclear war; ~ **química** chemical warfare 2 (fam) (problemas) trouble, hassle (colloq); **estos niños me dan mucha** ~ these kids give me a lot of hassle

guerrera *f* army jacket

guerrero -ra *adj* ⟨pueblo/espíritu⟩ warlike; **canto** ~ war cry
■ *m,f* warrior

guerrilla *f* (a) (grupo) guerrillas (*pl*) (b) (lucha) guerrilla warfare

guerrillero -ra *m,f* guerrilla

guía *f* 1 (libro, folleto) guide (book); (de calles) map; ~ **turística/de hoteles** tourist/hotel guide; ~ **telefónica** *or* **de teléfonos** telephone directory, phone book 2 **guía** *mf* (persona) guide; ~ **de turismo** tourist guide

guiar [A17] *vt* to guide
■ **guiarse** *v pron* ~**se POR algo** ⟨por mapa/consejo⟩ to follow sth; ~**se por las apariencias** to be led by appearances; ~**se por el instinto** to follow one's instincts

guijarro *m* pebble

guillotina *f* guillotine

guillotinar [A1] *vt* to guillotine

guinda *f* morello cherry; (confitada) glacé cherry

guindar [A1] *vt* 1 (Esp arg) (robar) ⟨novia/trabajo⟩ to steal 2 (a) (Col, Méx, Ven fam) ⟨ropa⟩ to hang up (b) (Col fam) ⟨hamaca⟩ to hang
■ **guindarse** *v pron* (Col, Méx, Ven) (colgarse) to hang

guindilla *f* chili

guindo *m* morello cherry tree

guiñar [A1] *vt* to wink; ~**le el ojo** *or* **un ojo a algn** to wink at sb

guiño *m* wink; **hacerle un** ~ **a algn** to give sb a wink

guion *m* 1 (a) (Cin, TV) script; ~ **cinematográfico** screenplay (b) (esquema) outline, plan 2 (Impr) (en diálogo) dash; (en palabras compuestas) hyphen; **lleva** ~ it's hyphenated

guionista *mf* scriptwriter, screenwriter

güirila *f* (AmC) maize pancake

guirnalda *f* garland

guisante *m* (Esp) pea

guisar [A1] *vi* (Esp) to cook; **guisa muy bien** he's a very good cook
■ ~ *vt* (con bastante líquido) to stew; (con poco líquido) to braise

guiso *m* stew, casserole

guita *f* (arg) cash (colloq), dough (sl)

guitarra *f* guitar; ~ **eléctrica/española/clásica** electric/Spanish/classical guitar

guitarrear [A1] *vi* (Mús) to play the guitar

guitarrista *mf* guitarist

gula *f* greed, gluttony

gusano *m* 1 (a) (como nombre genérico) worm; (lombriz de tierra) earthworm, worm (b) (larva — de mariposa) caterpillar; (— de mosca) maggot; ~ **de luz** glowworm; ~ **de seda** silkworm 2 (pey) (persona despreciable) worm (pej)

gustar [A1] *vi* 1 (+ *me/te/le etc*): **¿te gustó el libro?** did you like *o* enjoy the book?; **me gusta su compañía** I enjoy her company; **los helados no me/te/nos gustan** I/you/we don't like ice cream; **le gusta mucho la música** he likes music very much; **a Juan le gusta María** Juan likes María; **le gusta tocar la guitarra** she likes to play the guitar (AmE), she likes playing the guitar (BrE); **le gusta mucho viajar** she's very fond of traveling (colloq); **nos gusta dar un paseo después de comer** we like to have a walk after lunch; **¿te** ~**ía visitar el castillo?** would you like to visit the castle?; **me** ~**ía que vinieras temprano** I'd like you to come early

2 (en frases de cortesía) to wish (frml); **como guste** as you wish; **cuando usted guste** whenever it is convenient for you
■ ~ *vt* (AmL) (querer) to like; **¿gustan tomar algo?** would you like something to drink?

gusto *m* 1 (a) (sentido, sabor) taste; **resulta amargo al** ~ it has a bitter taste; **tiene un** ~ **medio raro** it has a funny taste to it; **tiene** ~ **a fresa** it tastes of strawberry; **deja un** ~ **a menta** it has a minty aftertaste (b) (sentido estético) taste; **tiene muy buen** ~ **para vestirse** she has very good taste in clothes; **una broma de mal** ~ a tasteless joke; **para todos los** ~**s** to suit all tastes 2 (a) (placer, agrado) pleasure; **tendré mucho** ~ **en acompañarlos** (frml) it will be a pleasure for me to accompany you (frml); **da** ~ **estar aquí** it's so nice (being) here; **me dio mucho** ~ **volverlo a ver** it was lovely to see him again; **por** ~ for fun, for pleasure; **un lugar donde se está a** ~ a place where you feel comfortable *o* at ease (b) (en fórmulas de cortesía): **mucho** ~ **(en conocerla)** pleased *o* nice to meet you; **el** ~ **es mío** the pleasure is mine

gustoso -sa *adj* willingly

gutural *adj* guttural

Hh

H, h *f (read as* /'atʃe/) *the letter* H, h (*ver tb* HACHE)

h. (= **hora**) hr

ha *interj* ah!, ha!

Ha. (= **hectárea**) ha., hectare

haba *f* (Bot) (broad) bean

Habana *f*: **La ∼** Havana

habanero -ra *adj/m,f* Havanan

habano *m* (cigarro) Havana cigar

haber¹ [E17] *v aux* (en tiempos compuestos) to have; **no habían llegado** they hadn't arrived; **de ∼lo sabido** had I known, if I'd known; **¡deberías ∼lo dicho!** you should have said so!

■ **∼** *v impers*

I (existir, estar, darse): **hay una carta/varias cartas para ti** there's a letter/there are several letters for you; **¿hay un banco por aquí?** is there a bank near here?; **hubo dos accidentes** there were two accidents; **¿hay helado?** do you have any ice cream?; **no hay como un buen descanso** there's nothing like a good rest; **hubo varios heridos** several people were injured; **las hay rojas y verdes** there are red ones and green ones; **gracias — no hay de qué** thank you — don't mention it *o* not at all *o* you're welcome; **no hay de qué preocuparse** there's nothing to worry about; **¿qué hay de nuevo?** (fam) what's new?; **hola ¿qué hay?** (fam) hello, how are things?; **¿qué hubo?** (Andes, Méx, Ven fam) how are things?

II (ser necesario) **∼ QUE + INF**: **hay que estudiar** you/we/they must study; **hubo que romperlo** we/ they had to break it; **no hay que lavarlo** (no es necesario) you don't need *o* have to wash it; (no se debe) you mustn't wash it

haber² *m* (a) (bienes) assets (*pl*) (b) (en contabilidad) credit side (c) **haberes** *mpl* (frml) (ingresos) income, earnings (*pl*)

habichuela *f* (a) (semilla) bean (b) (Col) (con vaina) green bean, French bean (BrE)

hábil *adj* **1** (a) (diestro) ⟨*carpintero*⟩ skilled, adept; ⟨*conductor*⟩ good, skillful*; ⟨*juego/táctica*⟩ skillful* (b) (astuto, inteligente) clever, able **2** ⟨*horas/días*⟩ working (*before n*) **3** (Der) competent

habilidad *f* **1** (a) (para actividad manual, física) skill; **tiene ∼ para la carpintería** he is good at carpentry (b) (astucia, inteligencia) skill, cleverness; **con ∼** cleverly, skillfully **2** (Der) competence

habilidoso -sa *adj* [SER] good with one's hands, handy

habilitación *f* **1** (de lugar) fitting out **2** (autorización) authorization **3** (Col) (Educ): **exámenes de ∼** retakes

habilitar [A1] *vt* **1** ⟨*lugar*⟩ to fit out **2** ⟨*persona/institución*⟩ to authorize; «*título*» to qualify, authorize; «*documento*» to authorize, empower **3** (Col) (Educ) to retake, to make up (AmE)

habiloso -sa *adj* (Chi fam) (inteligente) bright, smart (colloq)

habitable *adj* habitable

habitación *f* (cuarto) room; (dormitorio) bedroom; **∼ individual** single room

habitacional *adj* (CS) housing (*before n*)

habitante *mf* (Geog, Sociol) inhabitant; (de barrio) resident

habitar [A1] *vt* ⟨*vivienda*⟩ to live in; ⟨*isla/ planeta*⟩ to inhabit

■ **∼** *vi* (frml) to dwell (frml)

hábitat /'aβita(t)/ *m* (*pl* **-tats**) (Ecol, Zool) habitat; (Geog, Sociol) environment

hábito *m* **1** (costumbre) habit; **adquirir/tener el ∼ DE hacer algo** to get into/have the habit OF doing sth **2** (de religioso) habit

habitual *adj* ⟨*sitio/hora*⟩ usual; ⟨*cliente/lector*⟩ regular

habituar [A18] *vt* **∼ a algn A algo** to get sb used to sth

■ **habituarse** *v pron* **∼se A algo** to get used TO sth, get *o* become accustomed TO sth

habla *f*: **1** (facultad) speech; **perder el ∼** to lose one's powers of speech; **al verla me quedé sin ∼** when I saw her I was speechless **2** (a) (idioma): **países de ∼ hispana** Spanish-speaking countries (b) (manera de hablar): **el ∼ de esta región** the local way of speaking **3** **al habla** (en el teléfono) speaking; **estamos al ∼ con nuestro corresponsal** we have our correspondent on the line

hablado -da *adj* (a) ⟨*lenguaje*⟩ spoken (b) **bien/mal ∼** ⟨*persona*⟩ well-spoken/foul-mouthed

hablador -dora *adj* (a) (charlatán) talkative, chatty (colloq) (b) (chismoso) gossipy (c) (Méx fam) (mentiroso): **es tan ∼** he's such a fibber (colloq);

■ *m,f* (a) (charlatán) chatterbox (colloq) (b) (chismoso) gossip (colloq) (c) (Méx fam) (mentiroso) storyteller, fibber (colloq)

habladurías *fpl* idle gossip *o* talk

hablar [A1] *vi* **1** (a) (articular palabras) to speak; **habla más alto** speak up; **habla más bajo** keep your voice down (b) (expresarse) to speak; **∼ claro** (claramente) to speak clearly; (francamente) to speak frankly; **∼ por señas** to use sign language; **un político que habla muy bien** a politician who is a very good speaker; **∼ por ∼** to talk for the sake of it

2 (a) (conversar) to talk; **habla mucho** he talks a lot; **tenemos que ∼** we must (have a) talk; **∼ CON algn** to speak *o* talk TO sb; **tengo que ∼te** *or* que **∼ contigo** I need to speak to you *o* have a word with you; **está hablando por teléfono** he's on the phone; **¡ni ∼!** no way! (colloq), no chance! (colloq) (b) (bajo coacción) to talk (c) (murmurar) to talk, gossip; **dar que ∼** to start people talking (d) (rumorear): **se habla ya de miles de víctimas** there is already talk of thousands of casualties; **se habla de que va a renunciar** it is said *o* rumored that she's going to resign (e) (al teléfono): **¿con quién hablo?** who am I speaking with (AmE) *o* (BrE) speaking to?

3 (a) (tratar, referirse a) **∼ DE algo/algn** to talk ···❖

ABOUT sth/sb; ~ **de negocios** to talk (about) o discuss business; **siempre habla mal de ella** he never has a good word to say about her; **hablan muy bien de él** people speak very highly of him; **me ha hablado mucho de ti** she's told me a lot about you; **en tren sale caro, y no hablemos ya del avión** going by train is expensive, and as for flying ...; **háblame de tus planes** tell me about your plans; ~ SOBRE or ACERCA DE **algo** to talk ABOUT sth **(b)** (dirigirse a) to speak; **no me hables así** don't speak to me like that; **háblale de tú** use the 'tú' form with him **(c)** (anunciar propósito) ~ DE **hacer algo** to talk OF doing sth; **habla de jubilarse** he's talking of retiring
4 (Méx) (por teléfono) to call, phone
■ ~ *vt* 1 ⟨*idioma*⟩ to speak
2 (tratar): **tenemos que** ~ **las cosas** we must talk things over; **ya lo** ~**emos más adelante** we'll talk about o discuss that later
■ **hablarse** *v pron*: **llevan meses sin** ~**se** they haven't spoken to each other for months; **no se habla con ella** he's not speaking o talking to her, he's not on speaking terms with her

habrá, **habría**, etc ▶ HABER[1]

hacendado -da *adj* landowning (*before n*)
■ *m,f* landowner, owner of a ranch (*o* farm *etc*)

hacendoso -sa *adj* hardworking (*esp referring to housework*)

hacer [E18] *vt*
I 1 (a) (crear) ⟨*mueble/vestido*⟩ to make; ⟨*casa/carretera*⟩ to build; ⟨*nido*⟩ to build, make; ⟨*túnel*⟩ to make, dig; ⟨*dibujo/plano*⟩ to do, draw; ⟨*lista*⟩ to make, draw up; ⟨*resumen*⟩ to do, make; ⟨*película*⟩ to make; ⟨*nudo/lazo*⟩ to tie; ⟨*pan/pastel*⟩ to make, bake; ⟨*vino/café/tortilla*⟩ to make; ⟨*cerveza*⟩ to make, brew; **me hizo un lugar en la mesa** he made room for me at the table; **hacen buena pareja** they make a lovely couple **(b)** (producir, causar) ⟨*ruido*⟩ to make; **los chistes no me hacen gracia** I don't find jokes funny; **estos zapatos me hacen daño** these shoes hurt my feet
2 (a) (efectuar, llevar a cabo) ⟨*sacrificio*⟩ to make; ⟨*milagro*⟩ to work, perform; ⟨*deberes/ejercicios/limpieza*⟩ to do; ⟨*mandado*⟩ to run; ⟨*transacción/investigación*⟩ to carry out; ⟨*experimento*⟩ to do, perform; ⟨*entrevista*⟩ to conduct; ⟨*gira/viaje*⟩ to do; ⟨*regalo*⟩ to give; ⟨*favor*⟩ to do; ⟨*trato*⟩ to make; **me hicieron una visita** they paid me a visit; **aún queda mucho por** ~ there is still a lot (left) to do; **dar que** ~ to make a lot of work **(b)** ⟨*cheque/factura*⟩ to make out, write out
3 (formular, expresar) ⟨*declaración/promesa/oferta*⟩ to make; ⟨*proyecto/plan*⟩ to make, draw up; ⟨*crítica/comentario*⟩ to make, voice; ⟨*pregunta*⟩ to ask; **nadie hizo ninguna objeción** nobody raised any objections
4 (a) (refiriéndose a necesidades fisiológicas): ~ **caca** (fam) to do a poop (AmE) o (BrE) a pooh (colloq); ~ **pis** *or* **pipí** (fam) to have a pee (colloq); ~ **sus necesidades** (euf) to go to the bathroom o toilet (euph) **(b)** (refiriéndose a sonidos onomatopéyicos) to go; **las vacas hacen 'mu'** cows go 'moo'

5 (adquirir) ⟨*dinero/fortuna*⟩ to make; ⟨*amigo*⟩ to make
6 (preparar, arreglar) ⟨*cama*⟩ to make; ⟨*maleta*⟩ to pack; **hice el pescado al horno** I did o cooked the fish in the oven; **tengo que** ~ **la comida** I must make lunch; *ver tb* COMIDA B
7 (recorrer) ⟨*trayecto/distancia*⟩ to do, cover
8 (en cálculos, enumeraciones): **son 180 ... y 320 hacen 500** that's 180 ... and 320 is o makes 500
II 1 (a) (ocuparse en actividad) to do; ~ **la(s) compra(s)** to do the shopping; **¿hacemos algo esta noche?** shall we do something tonight?; ~ **ejercicio** to do (some) exercise; **¿hace algún deporte?** do you play o do any sports?; ▶ AMOR 1B **(b)** (como profesión, ocupación) to do; **¿qué hace tu padre?** what does your father do? **(c)** (estudiar) to do
2 (realizar cierta acción, actuar de cierta manera) to do; **¡eso no se hace!** you shouldn't do that!; **¡qué le vamos a** ~! what can you o (frml) one do?; **toca bien el piano** — **antes lo hacía mejor** she plays the piano well — she used to play better; ~**la buena** (fam): **¡ahora sí que la hice!** now I've really done it!; ▶ TONTO *m,f*
III 1 (transformar en, volver) to make; **ella lo hizo posible** she made it possible; **hizo pedazos la carta** she tore the letter into tiny pieces; **ese vestido te hace más delgada** that dress makes you look thinner; ~ **algo** DE **algo** to turn sth INTO sth; **quiero** ~ **de ti un gran actor** I want to make a great actor of you
2 (a) (obligar a, ser causa de que) ~ **a algn hacer algo** to make sb do sth; **me hizo abrirla** he made me open it; **me hizo llorar** it made me cry; **hágalo pasar** tell him to come in; **me hizo esperar tres horas** she kept me waiting for three hours; ~ **que algo/algn haga algo** to make sth/sb do sth **(b)** **hacer hacer algo** to have o get sth done/made; **hice acortar las cortinas** I had o got the curtains shortened
■ ~ *vi*
I 1 (obrar, actuar): **déjame** ~ **a mí** just let me handle this o take care of this; **¿cómo se hace para que te den la beca?** what do you have to do to get the scholarship?; **hiciste bien en decírmelo** you did o were right to tell me; **haces mal en mentir** it's wrong of you to lie
2 (fingir, simular): **hice como que no oía** I pretended not to hear; **haz como si no lo conocieras** act as if o pretend you don't know him
3 (servir): **esta sábana hará de toldo** this sheet will do for o as an awning; **la escuela hizo de hospital** the school served as o was used as a hospital
4 (interpretar personaje) ~ DE **algo/algn** to play (the part of) sth/sb
II (+ *compl*) (sentar): **tanto sol hace mal** (AmL) too much sun is not good for you; (+ *me/te/le etc*) **el descanso le hizo bien** the rest did him good; **la trucha me hizo mal** (AmL) the trout didn't agree with me
■ ~ *v impers* 1 (refiriéndose al tiempo atmosférico):

hace frío/sol it's cold/sunny; **hace tres grados** it's three degrees; **(nos) hizo un tiempo espantoso** the weather was terrible

2 (expresando tiempo transcurrido): **hace dos años que murió** he's been dead for two years; **hace mucho que lo conozco** I've known him for a long time; **hacía años que no lo veía** I hadn't seen him for o in years; **¿cuánto hace que se fue?** how long ago did she leave?; **hace poco/un año** a short time/a year ago; **hasta hace poco** until recently

■ **hacerse** *v pron*

I **1** (producirse) (+ *me/te/le etc*): **se me hizo un nudo en el hilo** I got a knot in the thread; **se le hizo una ampolla** she got a blister; **hacérsele algo a algn** (Méx): **por fin se le hizo ganar el premio** she finally got to win the award

2 **(a)** (*refl*) (hacer para sí) *‹café/falda›* to make oneself; **se hicieron una casita** they built themselves a little house **(b)** (*caus*) (hacer que otro haga): **se hicieron una casita** they had a little house built; **se hizo la cirugía estética** she had plastic surgery

3 (causarse): **¿qué te hiciste en el brazo?** what did you do to your arm?; **¿te hiciste daño?** did you hurt yourself?

4 (refiriéndose a necesidades fisiológicas): **todavía se hace pis/caca** (fam) she still wets/messes herself

5 (*refl*) (adquirir) to make; **~se un nombre** to make a name for oneself

II **1** **(a)** (volverse, convertirse en) to become; **se hicieron amigos** they became friends; **se están haciendo viejos** they are getting o growing old **(b)** (resultar): **se hace muy pesado** it gets very boring; (+ *me/te/le etc*) **se me hizo interminable** it seemed interminable; **se me hace difícil creerlo** I find it very hard to believe **(c)** (*impers*): **se hace de noche muy pronto** it gets dark very early; **se está haciendo tarde** it's getting late **(d)** (cocinarse) *«pescado/guiso»* to cook **(e)** (AmL) (pasarle a): **¿qué se habrá hecho María?** what can have happened to María?

2 (acostumbrarse) **~se A algo** to get used TO sth

3 (fingirse): **no te hagas el inocente** don't act the innocent; **¿es bobo o se (lo) hace?** (fam) is he stupid or just a good actor? (colloq); **~se pasar por algn** (por periodista, doctor) to pass oneself off as sb

4 (moverse) (+ *compl*) to move; **~se a un lado** to move to one side

5 **hacerse de** (AmL) (de fortuna, dinero) to get; (de amigos) to make

hacha *f⚣* (herramienta) ax (AmE), axe (BrE)

hache *f*: *the name of the letter* h

hachís *m* hashish, hash (colloq)

hacia *prep* **(a)** (dirección) toward (esp AmE), towards (esp BrE): **~ el sur** southward(s), toward(s) the south; **~ adelante** forward(s); **~ adentro/arriba** inward(s)/upward(s); **el centro queda ~ allá** the center is (over) that way; **¿~ dónde tenemos que ir?** which way do we have to go? **(b)** (aproximación) toward(s); **llegaremos ~ las dos** we'll arrive toward(s) o at around two **(c)** (con respecto a) toward(s); **su actitud ~ mí** his attitude toward(s) o to me

hacienda *f* **1** **(a)** (esp AmL) (finca) estate; (dedicada a ganadería) ranch **(b)** (bienes) possessions (*pl*), property **2** **Hacienda (a)** (ministerio) ≈ the Treasury Department (*in US*), ≈ the Treasury (*in*

UK) **(b)** (oficina) tax office; **el dinero que debo a H~** the money I owe the IRS (AmE) o (BrE) the Inland Revenue

hada *f⚣* fairy; **el ~ madrina** the fairy godmother

haga, etc ▶ HACER

hago ▶ HACER

Haití *m* Haiti

haitiano -na *adj/m,f* Haitian

hala *interj* (Esp) **(a)** (para animar) come on! **(b)** (expresando sorpresa) wow!

halagador -dora *adj* flattering

halagar [A3] *vt* to flatter; **me halaga que me lo ofrezcas a mí** I am flattered that you're offering it to me; **le ~on el vestido** they complimented her on her dress

halago *m* praise; **~s** praise, flattery

halagüeño -ña *adj* ‹palabras/frases› flattering, complimentary; ‹situación› promising, encouraging; ‹noticia› encouraging; ‹futuro› promising

halcón *m* (Zool) falcon

hall /'xol/ *m* (*pl* **halls**) (de casa) hall, hallway; (de teatro, cine) foyer

hallaca *f* (Ven) cornmeal, meat and vegetables wrapped in banana leaves

hallar [A1] *vt* **1** (frml) (encontrar) to find; **halló la puerta abierta** she found the door open **2** (esp AmL) (en frases negativas) (saber): **no halla cómo sentarse** she can't find a comfortable position to sit in; **no hallo cómo decírselo** I don't know how to tell her **(b)** (opinar, creer) to find

■ **hallarse** *v pron* **(a)** (frml) (estar, encontrarse) (+ *compl*) to be **(b)** (sentirse) (+ *compl*) to feel

hallazgo *m* find

hallulla *f* **1** (Chi) (pan) *slightly leavened white bread* **2** (Chi) (sombrero) straw boater

halo *m* **(a)** (aureola) halo **(b)** (de inocencia, santidad) aura

halógeno -na *adj* halogen (*before n*)

halterofilia *f* weightlifting

hamaca *f* **(a)** (para colgar) hammock **(b)** (RPI) (mecedora) rocking chair; (columpio) swing **(c)** (Esp) (asiento plegable) deckchair

hamacar [A2] *vt* (columpiar) (RPI) to swing; (mecer) (CS) to rock

■ **hamacarse** *v pron* (columpiarse) to swing; (mecerse) to rock (oneself)

hambre *f⚣* **(a)** (sensación) hunger; **tengo ~** I'm hungry; **pasar ~** to go hungry; **morirse de ~** to starve to death; **me muero de ~** (fam) I'm starving (colloq) **(b)** (como problema) **el ~** hunger

hambreado -da *adj* (Andes, Méx, RPI) hungry, starving

hambriento -ta *adj* [ESTAR] hungry, starving (colloq); **~ DE algo** hungry FOR sth

■ *m,f*: **los ~s** hungry people

hamburguesa *f* (bistec) hamburger, beefburger (BrE); (sandwich) hamburger, burger

hampa *f⚣*: **el ~** criminals (*pl*), the underworld

hámster /'xamster/ *m* (*pl* **-ters**) hamster

handicap /'xandikap/ *m* (*pl* **-caps**) handicap

hangar *m* hangar

haragán -gana *adj* lazy, idle

■ *m,f* shirker, layabout

harapiento -ta *adj* ragged

harapo *m* rag

haré, etc ▶ HACER

harén *m* harem

haría, etc ▶ HACER

harina *f* flour; ~ **de avena/maíz** oatmeal/cornmeal

harinoso -sa *adj* floury

hartar [A1] *vt* 1 (cansar, fastidiar): **me hartó con sus quejas** I got tired of his complaints
2 (fam) (llenar): **nos hartaban a** *or* **de sopa** they fed us on nothing but soup; **lo ~on a palos** they gave him a real beating
■ **hartarse** *v pron* 1 (cansarse, aburrirse) to get fed up; **~se DE algo/algn** to get tired *o* sick of sth/sb, get fed up WITH sth/sb; **~se DE hacer algo** to get tired *o* sick of doing sth, get fed up WITH doing sth
2 (llenarse): **~se (DE algo)** to gorge oneself (ON sth), to stuff oneself (WITH sth) (colloq)

harto¹ -ta *adj* 1 (a) (cansado, aburrido) fed up; **~ DE algo/algn** fed up WITH sth/sb, tired OF sth/sb; **~ DE hacer algo** tired OF doing sth, fed up WITH doing sth; **estaba harta de que le dijeran eso** she was tired of *o* fed up with them telling her that (b) (de comida) full
2 (*delante del n*) (mucho) (AmL exc RPl): **te llamé hartas veces** I phoned you lots of times; **tiene hartas ganas de verte** he really wants to see you
■ *pron* (AmL exc RPl): **tenía ~ que hacer** I had an awful lot to do; **¿tienes amigos allí? — ¡sí, ~s!** do you have friends there? — yes, lots

harto² *adv* (a) (AmL exc RPl) (modificando un adjetivo) very; **es ~ mejor que el hermano** he's much *o* a lot better than his brother (b) (modificando un verbo): **me gustó ~** I really liked it; **bailamos ~** we danced a lot

hasta *prep* 1 (en el tiempo) (a) until; **no descansó ~ terminar** she didn't rest until she'd finished; **~ el momento** so far, up to now (b) **hasta que** until, till; **espera ~ que pare de llover** wait until *o* till it stops raining (c) **hasta tanto** until such time as (d) (AmC, Col, Méx) (con valor negativo): **cierran ~ las nueve** they don't close until *o* till nine (e) (en saludos): **~ mañana** see you tomorrow; **~ luego/pronto** see you (colloq), see you soon
2 (en el espacio) to; **el agua me llegaba ~ los hombros** the water came up to my shoulders; **el pelo le llega ~ la cintura** her hair goes down to her waist; **¿~ dónde llega?** how far does it go?
3 (en cantidades) up to; **~ cierto punto** up to a point
■ *adv* even

hastiante *adj* boring, sickening

hastiarse [A17] *v pron* **~se DE algo** to grow tired *o* weary OF sth; **hastiado de la vida** tired *o* weary of life

Hawai *m* Hawaii

hawaiano -na *adj/m,f* Hawaiian

hay ▶ HABER

haya *f*⚓ (árbol, madera) beech

haya, hayas, etc ▶ HABER

hayaca *f* (Ven) ▶ HALLACA

haz *m* (de leña, paja) bundle; (de trigo) sheaf; (de luz) beam

haz ▶ HACER

hazaña *f* (acción — heróica) great *o* heroic deed, exploit; (— de mucho esfuerzo) feat, achievement

hazmerreír *m* (fam) laughing stock

he ▶ HABER

hebilla *f* (de zapato) buckle; (de cinturón) clasp, buckle

hebra *f* (a) (Tex) thread, strand (b) (fibra vegetal, animal) fiber*; (c) (del gusano de seda) thread (d) (de la madera) grain

hebreo¹ -brea *adj/m,f* Hebrew

hebreo² *m* (idioma) Hebrew

heces *fpl;* ▶ HEZ

hechicero -ra *adj* ⟨persona⟩ enchanting, captivating; ⟨ojos/sonrisa⟩ captivating
■ *m,f* (a) (brujo) (*m*) sorcerer, wizard; (*f*) sorceress, witch (b) (de tribu) witch doctor

hechizar [A4] *vt* (a) ⟨brujo⟩ to cast a spell on, bewitch (b) (cautivar) to captivate

hechizo¹ -za *adj* (Chi, Méx) home-made

hechizo² *m* (a) (maleficio) spell (b) (atractivo, encanto) charm

hecho¹ -cha *pp* [*ver tb* HACER]
1 (manufacturado) made; **~ a mano** handmade; **un traje ~ a (la) medida** a made-to-measure suit; **bien/mal ~** well/badly made
2 (refiriéndose a acción): **¡bien ~!** well done!; **no le avisé — pues mal ~** I didn't let him know — well you should have (done); **lo ~, ~ está** what's done is done
3 (convertido en): **estaba ~ una fiera** he was furious; **tú estás ~ un vago** you've become *o* turned into a lazy devil
■ *adj* (a) ⟨ropa⟩ ready-to-wear (b) (terminado) ⟨trabajo⟩ done (c) (esp Esp) ⟨carne⟩ done; **un filete muy/poco ~** a well-done/rare steak

hecho² *m* 1 (a) (acto, acción): **yo quiero ~s** I want action, I want something done; **demuéstramelo con ~s** prove it to me by doing something about it (b) (suceso, acontecimiento) event; **el lugar de los ~s** the scene of the crime
2 (realidad, verdad) fact; **de hecho** in fact

hechura *f* (a) (de traje, vestido): **no cobran por la ~** they don't charge for making it up (b) (modelo, estilo) style; **la falda tiene una ~ muy simple** the skirt is cut very simply (c) (forma) shape, form

hectárea *f* hectare

hediondez *f* stench, stink

hediondo -da *adj* (fétido) foul-smelling, stinking

hegemonía *f* hegemony, dominance

helada *f* frost

heladera *f* (para hacer helados) ice-cream maker; (nevera) (RPl) refrigerator, fridge; (para picnic) (Arg, Col) cool *o* cold box

heladería *f* ice-cream parlor*

heladero -ra *m,f* (esp AmL) ice-cream vendor *o* seller

helado¹ -da *adj* 1 (a) ⟨persona/manos⟩ freezing (colloq), frozen (colloq); ⟨casa/habitación⟩ freezing (colloq); **quedarse ~** (de asombro) to be stunned (b) ⟨comida⟩ stone-cold; ⟨líquido/bebida⟩ (muy frío) freezing; (que se ha enfriado) stone-cold; **servir el vino bien ~** (AmL) serve the wine well chilled 2 ⟨agua/estanque⟩ frozen

helado² *m* ice cream; ~ **de agua** (Andes) water ice, sherbet (AmE); (con palo) Popsicle® (AmE), ice lolly (BrE)

helar [A5] *vt/vi* to freeze
■ ~ *v impers*: **anoche heló** it went below freezing last night (AmE), there was a frost last night (BrE)
■ **helarse** *v pron* **1** «*río/charco*» to freeze (over); «*agua/plantas/cosecha*» to freeze **2** (fam) **(a)** «*persona*» to freeze **(b)** «*comida/café*» to get *o* go cold

helecho *m* (como nombre genérico) fern; (más específico) bracken

hélice *f* (de barco) propeller, screw; (de avión) propeller

helicóptero *m* helicopter

hematoma *m* (tumor) hematoma*; (moretón) bruise

hembra *adj inv* female
■ *f* **(a)** (Zool) female; **la ~ del faisán** the hen pheasant **(b)** (mujer) female, woman **(c)** (de enchufe, corchete) female (part)

hemisferio *m* **(a)** (Geog, Mat) hemisphere; **el ~ norte** the northern hemisphere **(b)** (Anat) cerebral hemisphere

hemofilia *f* hemophilia*

hemofílico -ca *adj/m,f* hemophiliac*

hemorragia *f* hemorrhage*

hemorroides *fpl* piles, hemorrhoids (tech)

hendidura *f* (en madera) crack; (en roca) fissure, crack

heno *m* hay

hepatitis *f* hepatitis

heráldica *f* heraldry

heraldo *m* herald

herbáceo -cea *adj* herbaceous

herbicida *m* herbicide, weedkiller

herbívoro -ra *adj* herbivorous
■ *m,f* herbivore

herboristería *f* herbalist's

heredar [A1] *vt* «*bienes/título/tradiciones*» to inherit; «*trono*» to succeed to; **heredó los ojos de su madre** he has his mother's eyes

heredero -ra *m,f* (*m*) heir; (*f*) heir, heiress; **príncipe ~** crown prince; **~ DE algo** heir TO sth

hereditario -ria *adj* hereditary

herejía *f* heresy

herencia *f* **(a)** (Der) inheritance; **le dejó en ~ la finca** he bequeathed *o* left her the farm **(b)** (patrimonio cultural, nacional) heritage **(c)** (Biol) heredity

herida *f* **(a)** (en el cuerpo): **sufrir ~s de carácter grave** to suffer serious injuries; **se hizo una ~ en la rodilla** he cut his knee; **curar una ~** to clean/ dress a wound **(b)** (pena, sufrimiento) wound

herido -da *adj* **(a)** (físicamente) injured; **está gravemente ~** (por accidente) he is seriously injured; (por agresión) he has been seriously wounded; **~ de muerte** fatally wounded **(b)** (en sentimiento) «*persona*» hurt
■ *m,f*: **los ~s** the injured/wounded

herir [I11] *vt* **(a)** (físicamente) to wound **(b)** «*orgullo*» to hurt **(c)** «*vista*» to hurt

hermanar [A1] *vt* **(a)** (en sentimiento, propósito) to unite **(b)** «*ciudades*» to twin **(c)** «*calcetines*» to match up, put ... in pairs; «*fichas/naipes*» to match up

hermanastro -tra *m,f* **(a)** (con vínculo sanguíneo) (*m*) half brother; (*f*) half sister **(b)** (sin vínculo sanguíneo) (*m*) stepbrother; (*f*) stepsister

hermandad *f* **(a)** (de hombres) brotherhood, fraternity; (de mujeres) sisterhood **(b)** (asociación) association

hermano -na
■ *m,f* **1** (pariente) (*m*) brother; (*f*) sister; **mis ~s** (solo varones) my brothers; (varones y mujeres) my brothers and sisters; **~ gemelo/hermana gemela** twin brother/twin sister; **~ político/hermana política** brother-in-law/sister-in-law **2** (como apelativo) (Col, Per, Ven fam) buddy (AmE colloq), mate (BrE colloq) **3** **(a)** (religioso) (*m*) brother; (*f*) sister **(b)** (prójimo) (*m*) brother; (*f*) sister **4** (de guante, calcetín) pair
■ *adj* «*buque*» sister (*before n*); «*ciudades*» twin (*before n*)

hermético -ca *adj* **(a)** «*envase/cierre*» airtight, hermetic (tech) **(b)** «*persona/rostro*» inscrutable, secretive

hermoso -sa *adj* **(a)** (bello) beautiful, lovely **(b)** (magnífico) splendid **(c)** (lozano, corpulento) big and healthy, bonny (BrE) **(d)** (noble) noble

hermosura *f* **(a)** (cualidad) beauty, loveliness **(b)** (persona, cosa hermosa): **¡qué ~ de niño/paisaje!** what a beautiful child/landscape!

hernia *f* hernia, rupture; **~ discal** slipped disk*

herniarse [A1] *v pron* to get a hernia, rupture oneself

héroe *m* hero

heroico -ca *adj* heroic

heroína *f* **1** (persona) heroine **2** (droga) heroin

heroinómano -na *m,f* heroin addict

heroísmo *m* heroism

herpes *m* (*pl* ~) (en boca, genitales) herpes; (en cintura) shingles

herradura *f* horseshoe

herramienta *f* tool

herrería *f* blacksmith's, smithy

herrero -ra *m,f* blacksmith

herrumbre *f* rust

hervidero *m* (de moscas) swarm; (de chismes, delincuencia) hotbed; **un ~ de gente** a seething mass of people; **la casa era un ~** the house was buzzing

hervidor *m* (de agua) kettle; (de leche) milk pan

hervir [I11] *vi/vt* to boil; **el café está hirviendo** the coffee is boiling

heterosexual *adj/mf* heterosexual

hez *f* **(a)** (escoria) dregs (*pl*) **(b)** (Vin) *tb* **heces** sediment, lees (*pl*) **(c)** **heces** *fpl* (excrementos) feces* (*pl*)

hibernar [A1] *vi* to hibernate

híbrido¹ -da *adj* hybrid (*before n*)

híbrido² *m* hybrid

hice, hiciera, etc ▶ HACER

hidalgo *m* gentleman, nobleman (*from the lower ranks of the nobility*)

hidratante *adj* moisturizing (*before n*)

hidratar [A1] *vt* «*verduras*» to hydrate; «*piel*» to moisturize

hidrato *m* hydrate; ∼s de carbono carbohydrates

hidráulico -ca *adj* hydraulic

hidroavión *m* seaplane

hidroeléctrico -ca *adj* hydroelectric

hidrofobia *f* hydrophobia (tech), rabies

hidrógeno *m* hydrogen

hiedra *f* ivy

hiel *f* bile

hiela, hielas, etc ▶ HELAR

hielo *m* ice; *romper el* ∼ to break the ice

hiena *f* hyena

hierba *f* ⓵ (césped) grass; ∼ *mala nunca muere* the Devil looks after his own ⓶ (a) (Bot, Coc, Med) herb; *malas* ∼s weeds (b) (arg) (marihuana) grass (colloq)

hierbabuena *f* mint

hierbajo *m* (esp Esp) weed

hierro *m* (a) (Metal) iron; ∼ *forjado* wrought iron; ∼ *fundido* cast iron; *de* ∼ iron *(before n)* (b) (de lanza, flecha) head, tip (c) (en golf) iron; *un* ∼ *cuatro* a four iron

hígado *m* liver

higiene *f* hygiene

higiénico -ca *adj* hygienic

higo *m* (de la higuera) fig; ∼ *chumbo* (Esp) prickly pear

higuera *f* fig tree

hijastro -tra *m,f* (*m*) stepson; (*f*) stepdaughter; *mis* ∼s (varones y mujeres) my stepchildren

hijo -ja *m,f* ⓵ (pariente) (*m*) son; (*f*) daughter; *mis* ∼s (solo varones) my sons; (varones y mujeres) my children; *espera un* ∼ she's expecting a baby; *no tienen* ∼s they don't have any children; ∼ *adoptivo/hija adoptiva* adopted son/daughter; ∼/ *hija de papá* rich kid (colloq); ∼/*hija natural* illegitimate son/daughter; ∼ *político/hija política* son-in-law/daughter-in-law; ∼ *único/hija única* only child; *M. Pérez,* ∼ *M. Pérez Junior;* ∼ *de tigre sale pintado* (AmL fam) he's just like his father/mother ⓶ (apelativo): *¡*∼*, por Dios!* (hablándole a un niño) for heaven's sake, child!; (hablándole a un adulto) for heaven's sake, Pedro (*o* Luis *etc*)!

híjole *interj* (Méx) jeez! (AmE colloq), gosh (colloq)

hilacha *f* loose thread

hilar [A1] *vi* to spin; ∼ *fino* to split hairs
■ ∼ *vt* (a) ⟨algodón/lana⟩ to spin; «araña» to spin (b) ⟨ideas/hechos⟩ to string together

hilera *f* (a) (fila) row, line (b) (Mil) file (frml *or* liter) (c) (de ladrillos) course (d) (de semillas) row, drill

hilo *m* ⓵ (a) (en costura) thread; ∼ *dental* dental floss (b) (lino) linen (c) (de araña) thread (d) (fam) (de las judías) string ⓶ (Elec) wire; ∼ *musical* (Esp) piped music ⓷ (de relato, conversación) thread ⓸ (de sangre, agua) trickle

hilvanar [A1] *vt* ⓵ (coser) to baste (AmE), to tack (BrE) ⓶ ⟨frases/ideas⟩ to put together

himen *m* hymen

himno *m* (a) (religioso) hymn; (de colegio) school song *o* anthem; ∼ *nacional* national anthem (b) (Lit) ode

hincada *f* (Col, Per) sharp pain

hincapié *m*: *hacer* ∼ *en algo* to stress *o* emphasize sth

hincar [A2] *vt* (clavar) ∼ *algo* EN *algo* ⟨estaca⟩ to drive *o* thrust sth INTO sth; *me hincó los dientes en la mano* it buried its teeth *o* sunk its teeth into my hand
■ **hincarse** *v pron tb* ∼se *de rodillas* to kneel

hincha *mf* (fam) (Dep) fan (colloq), supporter

hinchado -da *adj* ⟨vientre/pierna⟩ swollen; ⟨estilo/lenguaje⟩ overblown

hinchar [A1] *vt* (Esp) ⟨globo⟩ to inflate (frml), to blow up; ⟨rueda⟩ to inflate, pump up; ⟨suceso/ noticia⟩ (fam) to blow ... up (colloq)
■ ∼ *vi* (CS fam) (fastidiar) «*persona*» to be a pain in the ass (AmE vulg) *o* (BrE vulg) arse; (+ *me/te/le etc*) *me hincha su actitud* his attitude really pisses me off (sl)
■ **hincharse** *v pron* (a) «*vientre/pierna*» (+ *me/ te/le etc*) to swell up (b) (fam) (enorgullecerse) to swell with pride (c) (Esp fam) (hartarse) ∼se DE *algo* ⟨de pasteles/ostras⟩ to stuff oneself WITH sth

hinchazón *f* swelling

hindú *adj/mf* (a) (Relig) Hindu (b) (crit) (de la India) Indian

hinduismo *m* Hinduism

hinojo *m* (Bot, Coc) fennel

hiperactivo -va *adj* hyperactive

hipermercado *m* large supermarket, hypermarket (BrE)

hipertensión *f* high blood pressure, hypertension

hípica *f* equestrian sports (*pl*); (carreras) horse racing

hípico -ca *adj* ⟨deportes/centro⟩ equestrian *(before n)*

hipnosis *f* hypnosis

hipnotismo *m* hypnotism

hipnotizador -dora *adj* ⟨mirada⟩ hypnotic
■ *m,f* hypnotist

hipnotizar [A4] *vt* (Psic) to hypnotize; (fascinar) to mesmerize

hipo *m* hiccups (*pl*), hiccoughs (*pl*)

hipocondríaco -ca *m,f* hypochondriac

hipocresía *f* hypocrisy

hipócrita *adj* hypocritical
■ *mf* hypocrite

hipodérmico -ca *adj* hypodermic

hipódromo *m* (Equ, Ocio) racecourse, racetrack (AmE); (Hist) hippodrome

hipopótamo *m* hippopotamus

hipoteca *f* mortgage

hipotecar [A2] *vt* to mortgage

hipotecario -ria *adj* mortgage *(before n)*

hipótesis *f* hypothesis

hipotético -ca *adj* hypothetical

hippy, hippie /'xipi/ *adj* (*pl* **hippies**) hippy (*before n*), hippie (*before n*)
■ *mf* hippy, hippie

hiriente *adj* hurtful, wounding (*before n*)

hirviendo ▶ HERVIR

hisopo *m* **(a)** (bastoncillo) cotton swab (AmE), cotton bud (BrE) **(b)** (Chi) (de afeitar) shaving brush

hispánico -ca *adj* **(a)** (de los países de habla hispana) Hispanic **(b)** (relativo a España) Spanish

hispanismo *m* (giro propio del español de España) word/expression peculiar to Spain; (palabra derivada del español) hispanicism; (estudio) Hispanic studies

hispano -na *adj* **(a)** (español) Spanish, Hispanic (frml); **países de habla hispana** Spanish-speaking countries **(b)** (hispanoamericano) Spanish American, Latin American; (en EE UU) Hispanic
■ *m,f* **(a)** (liter) (español) Spaniard **(b)** (hispanoamericano) Spanish American, Latin American; (en EE UU) Hispanic

Hispanoamérica *f* Spanish America

hispanoamericano -na *adj/m,f* Spanish American

hispanohablante, hispanoparlante *mf* Spanish speaker

histeria *f* hysteria; ~ **colectiva** mass hysteria

histérico -ca *adj* (Med, Psic) hysterical; (exaltado): **ponerse** ~ to have hysterics *o* a fit; **me pones** ~ you drive me mad
■ *m,f* (Med, Psic) hysteric; (exaltado): **es un** ~ he gets quite hysterical about things

historia *f* **1** (Hist) history; ~ **antigua** ancient history; ~ **clínica** medical history; *pasar a la* ~ (por ser importante) to go down in history; (perder actualidad) (fam): **aquello ya pasó a la** ~ that's ancient history now (colloq) **2** (relato) story; **la** ~ **de su vida** the story of his life **3** (fam) (cuento, asunto): **me vino con la** ~ **de que ...** he came up with this story *o* tale about ...; **déjate de** ~**s** stop making excuses; **se quejó de no sé qué** ~**s** he complained about something or other (colloq)

historiador -dora *m,f* historian

historial *m* record; ~ **clínico** *or* **médico** medical history; ~ **personal** resumé (AmE), curriculum vitae (BrE)

histórico -ca *adj* (real) historical; (importante) historic

historieta *f* comic strip, cartoon story

hit /'xit/ *m* (*pl* **hits**) hit

hito *m* (hecho trascendental) landmark, milestone

hizo ▶ HACER

Hnos. (= **hermanos**) Bros.

hobby /'xoβi/ *m* (*pl* **-bbies**) hobby

hocico *m* (de cerdo) snout; (de perro, lobo) snout, muzzle

hocicón -cona *m,f* (CS, Méx fam & pey) bigmouth (colloq & pej), blabbermouth (colloq & pej)

hockey /'(x)oki/ *m* hockey; ~ **sobre hielo** ice hockey

hogar *m* home; **formar un** ~ to set up home; **artículos para el** ~ household goods; **las labores del** ~ housework; **quedarse sin** ~ to be left homeless; ~ **de ancianos** residential home for the elderly, old people's home (colloq)

hogareño -ña *adj* ⟨persona⟩ home-loving; ⟨vida/escena⟩ domestic (*before n*)

hoguera *f* bonfire; **murió en la** ~ he was burned at the stake

hoja *f* **1** (Bot) leaf **2 (a)** (folio) sheet; ~ **de vida** (Col, Ven) resumé (AmE), curriculum vitae (BrE) **(b)** (de libro) page, leaf; **pasar las** ~**s** to turn the pages **(c)** (formulario) form, sheet; ~ **electrónica** spreadsheet program **3 (a)** (de puerta, mesa) leaf **(b)** (de madera, metal) sheet **(c)** (de cuchillo) blade; ~ **de afeitar** razor blade

hojalata *f* tinplate

hojalatería *f* (Méx) body work (AmE), panel-beating (BrE)

hojalatero -ra *m,f* (Auto) (Méx) body shop worker (AmE), panel beater (BrE)

hojaldre *m* puff pastry, puff paste (AmE)

hojear [A1] *vt* to leaf *o* glance through

hojilla *f* (Ven) razor blade

hojuela *f* (AmL exc CS) flake

hola *interj* (saludo) hello, hi! (colloq)

holá *interj* (RPl) (por teléfono) hello?

holán *m* (Méx) flounce, frill

Holanda *f* Holland

holandés¹ -desa *adj* Dutch
■ *m,f* (*m*) Dutchman; (*f*) Dutchwoman; **los holandeses** the Dutch, Dutch people

holandés² *m* (idioma) Dutch

holgado -da *adj* **(a)** ⟨prenda⟩ loose-fitting, baggy **(b)** ⟨posición⟩ comfortable; **viven** ~**s** they're comfortably off **(c)** ⟨victoria/mayoría⟩ comfortable **(d)** (de espacio): **así iremos más** ~**s** we'll be more comfortable like that

holgar [A8] *vi* (*en 3ª pers*) (frml) (estar de más): **huelga decir que ...** it goes without saying that ...; **huelgan los comentarios** what can one say?

holgazán -zana *adj* lazy
■ *m,f* idler, lazybones (colloq)

holgazanear [A1] *vi* to idle, laze *o* loaf around

holgura *f* **(a)** (bienestar económico, comodidad): **vivir con** ~ to live comfortably **(b)** (de prenda) fullness, looseness

hollejo *m* skin

hollín *m* soot

hombre *m* **(a)** (varón) man; ~**s, mujeres y niños** men, women and children; **no es lo bastante** ~ **para ...** he's not man enough to ...; **¡**~ **al agua!** man overboard!; **este** ~ **no sabe lo que dice** this guy doesn't know what he's talking about; ~ **de confianza** right-hand man; ~ **del tiempo** weatherman; ~ **de negocios** businessman; ~ **lobo** werewolf; ~ **medio** man in the street; ~ **rana** frogman, diver; ~ *precavido vale por dos* forewarned is forearmed **(b)** (especie humana): **el** ~ **man**
■ *interj*: **¡**~**! ¡qué sorpresa!** well! what a nice surprise!; **¿te gustaría venir? —** **¡**~**! I would you like to come? —** you bet! what do you think?; ~, **no es lo mismo** come off it, it's not the same thing at all (colloq)

hombrera *f* (almohadilla) shoulder pad; (Mil) (de uniformes) epaulet

hombría *f* manliness

hombrillo *m* (Ven) shoulder (AmE), hard shoulder (BrE)

hombro *m* shoulder; **encogerse de** ~**s** to shrug (one's shoulders); **lo llevaron a** ~**s** they ···⊱

carried him on their shoulders *o* shoulder high;
arrimar el ~ to pull one's weight, put one's
shoulder to the wheel; *mirar a algn por encima
del* ~ to look down on sb

hombruno -na *adj* (pey) ⟨*mujer*⟩ mannish,
butch (colloq & pej); ⟨*gestos/modales*⟩ masculine,
mannish

homenaje *m* **(a)** (tributo) tribute; **rendir(le)** ~ **a
algn** to pay tribute *o* homage to sb; **en** ~ **a** in
honor of **(b)** (acto): **le ofrecieron un** ~ they held a
party (*o* reception, *etc*) in his honor

homeópata *mf* homeopath

homeopatía *f* homeopathy

homeopático -ca *adj* (Med) homeopathic

homicida *adj* (frml) ⟨*instinto*⟩ homicidal;
⟨*arma*⟩ murder (*before n*)
■ *mf* (frml) murderer, homicide (frml)

homicidio *m* (frml) homicide

homogéneo -nea *adj* ⟨*grupo*⟩ homogeneous;
⟨*masa/mezcla*⟩ smooth

homologación *f* **1** **(a)** (de un producto —
recomendación) endorsement; (— autorización)
authorization **(b)** (Dep) (de un récord) ratification
2 (equiparación) ~ **con algo: han pedido su** ~ **con
los técnicos** they have asked for parity with the
technicians; **la** ~ **de los títulos australianos con
los europeos** the recognition of Australian
qualifications as equivalent to European ones

homologar [A3] *vt* **(a)** ⟨*producto*⟩ (recomendar)
to approve, endorse; (autorizar) to authorize,
approve **(b)** (Dep) ⟨*récord*⟩ to ratify, recognize **(c)**
⟨*convenio*⟩ to recognize

homólogo -ga *adj* equivalent
■ *m,f* (period) counterpart

homosexual *adj/mf* homosexual

honda *f* (de cuero) sling; (con elástico) slingshot
(AmE), catapult (BrE)

hondo¹ -da *adj* **(a)** ⟨*piscina/río*⟩ deep; **en lo
más** ~ **de mi corazón** in my heart of hearts, deep
down; **en lo** ~ **del valle** at the bottom of the
valley **(b)** (*gen delante del n*) (frml) ⟨*pena/pesar*⟩
profound (frml), deep

hondo² *adv*: **respirar** ~ to breathe deeply

hondonada *f* hollow

Honduras *f* Honduras

hondureño -ña *adj/m,f* Honduran

honestidad *f* integrity, honesty

honesto -ta *adj* (íntegro) honest, honorable*

hongo *m* **(a)** (Bot, Med) fungus **(b)** (AmL) (Coc)
mushroom **(c)** *tb* **sombrero de** ~ derby (AmE),
bowler hat (BrE) **(d)** ~ **atómico** mushroom cloud

honor *m* **(a)** honor*; **tengo el** ~ **de ... it is my
honor** *o* I have the honor to ...; **me hizo el** ~ **de
recibirme** he did me the honor of receiving me;
en ~ **a la verdad** to be truthful; **hacer** ~ **a su
nombre** to live up to one's reputation **(b)**
honores *mpl* (homenaje) honors* (*pl*); **le
rindieron los** ~**es correspondientes a su rango** he
was accorded the honors befitting his rank (frml)

honorable *adj* honorable*

honorario -ria *adj* honorary

honorarios *mpl* fees (*pl*)

honorífico -ca *adj* honorary

honra *f* **(a)** (en general) honor*; **¡y a mucha** ~**!**
and proud of it! **(b)** ~**s fúnebres** *fpl* funeral rites
(*pl*)

honradez *f* (honestidad) honesty; (decencia)
decency

honrado -da *adj* **(a)** (honesto) honest,
honorable* **(b)** ⟨*mujer*⟩ respectable

honrar [A1] *vt* **1** «*comportamiento/actitud*» to
do ... credit *o* honor*; **nos honra hoy con su
presencia** she is honoring us with her presence
here today **2** (respetar) to honor*
■ **honrarse** *v pron* to be honored*

hora *f* **1** (período de tiempo) hour; **media** ~ half
an hour, a half hour (AmE); **las** ~**s de mayor
afluencia** the busiest time; **cobrar por** ~**s** to be
paid by the hour; **45 euros la** ~ 45 euros an
hour; ~ **libre** free period; ~ **pico** (AmL) *or* (Esp)
punta rush hour; ~**s extra(s)** *o* **extraordinaria(s)**
overtime
2 **(a)** (momento puntual) time; **¿tiene** ~**, por favor?**
have you got the time, please?; **¿qué** ~ **es?**
what's the time?, what time is it?; **pon el reloj en**
~ put the clock right; **todavía no es la** ~ it's not
time yet; **nunca llegan a la** ~ they never arrive
on time; **el avión llegó antes de (su)** ~ the plane
arrived early **(b)** (momento sin especificar) time; **es**
~ **de irse a la cama** it's bedtime *o* time for bed; **a
la** ~ **de almorzar** at lunchtime; **ya es** ~ **de irnos**
it's time for us to go; **¡ya era** ~ **de que llamases!**
it's about time you called; **a primera** ~ **de la
mañana** first thing in the morning; **a última** ~ at
the last moment; *a la* ~ *de*: **a la** ~ **de traducirlo**
when it comes to translating it; **a la** ~ **de la
verdad** when it comes down to it; *entre* ~**s**
between meals; **hacer** ~ (Chi) to kill time
3 (cita) appointment; **pedir** ~ to make an
appointment

horadar [A1] *vt* ⟨*roca*⟩ to bore through; ⟨*pared*⟩
to drill a hole in

horario *m* **1** (de trenes, aviones) schedule (AmE);
timetable (BrE); (de clases) timetable; **tiene un** ~
muy flexible his hours are very flexible; **la
empresa ofrece** ~ **flexible** the company offers
flextime *or* (BrE) flexitime; ~ **continuo** *or* (AmL)
corrido *or* (Esp) **intensivo** *continuous working day
(usually from eight to three) with no break for
lunch*; ~ **de visitas** visiting hours (*pl*); ~ **partido**
working day with a long break for lunch **2** (de
reloj) hour hand

horca *f* **1** (patíbulo) gallows (*pl*); (juego): **la** ~
hangman **2** (Agr) pitchfork, hayfork

horcajadas: a ~ (*loc adv*) astride

horchata *f* (de chufas) horchata (*cold drink
made from tiger nuts*); (en Méx) *drink made from
ground melon seeds*

horda *f* horde

horizontal *adj/f* horizontal

horizonte *m* **(a)** (línea) horizon **(b)**
horizontes *mpl* (perspectivas) horizons (*pl*)

horma *f* (para hacer zapatos) last; (para conservar su
forma) shoetree

hormiga *f* ant

hormigón *m* concrete

hormigueo *m* pins and needles (*pl*), tingling

hormiguero *m* **(a)** (Zool) (nido) ant's nest;
(montículo) anthill **(b)** (de personas): **era un** ~ **de
gente** it was swarming with people

hormona *f* hormone

hornada *f* (de pan, pasteles) batch

hornalla *f* (RPl) ▶ HORNILLO 1

hornilla *f* **(a)** (AmL exc CS) ▶ HORNILLO 1 **(b)** (Chi) ▶ HORNILLO 2

hornillo *m* **1 (a)** (Esp) **(a)** (de gas) burner **(b)** (de una cocina eléctrica — espiral) ring; (— placa) hotplate **2** (cocinilla portátil) portable electric stove

horno *m* **(a)** (de cocina) oven; **resistente al ∼** ovenproof; **pollo al ∼** roast chicken; **pescado al ∼** baked fish; **(b)** (Metal, Tec) furnace **(c)** (para cerámica) kiln

horóscopo *m* horoscope

horqueta *f* (Chi) (de jardinero) fork; (de campesino) pitchfork

horquilla *f* **(a)** (para pelo) hairpin **(b)** (Agr) pitchfork **(c)** (en bicicleta) fork

horrendo -da *adj* ▶ HORROROSO

horrible *adj* ⟨accidente/muerte⟩ horrible, horrific **(b)** (feo) ⟨persona⟩ hideous, ugly; ⟨camisa/adorno⟩ horrible, hideous **(c)** ⟨tiempo⟩ terrible, awful **(d)** (inaguantable) unbearable

horripilante *adj* terrifying, horrifying

horror *m* **1 (a)** (miedo, angustia) horror; **me causa ∼ verlo** it horrifies me to see it; **les tengo ∼ a los hospitales** I'm terrified of hospitals **(b)** (fam) (uso hiperbólico): **¡qué ∼!** how awful *o* terrible! **2 horrores** *mpl* (cosas terribles) horrors (*pl*); **los ∼s de la guerra** the horrors of the war

horrorizar [A4] *vt* to horrify, appall ■ **horrorizarse** *v pron* to be horrified, be appalled; **∼se DE algo** to be horrified BY *o* AT sth

horroroso -sa *adj* ⟨crimen⟩ horrific, horrifying; ⟨película/novela⟩ terrible, awful; ⟨persona/vestido⟩ awful, horrific (colloq); **tengo un hambre horrorosa** I'm absolutely starving (colloq)

hortaliza *f* vegetable

hortelano -na *m,f* truck farmer (AmE), market gardener (BrE)

hortensia *f* hydrangea

hortera *adj* (Esp fam) ⟨vestido/canción⟩ tacky (colloq); **es muy ∼** he has very tacky taste

horticultor -ra *m,f* horticulturalist, gardener

horticultura *f* horticulture, gardening

hosco -ca *adj* ⟨persona/semblante⟩ surly, sullen

hospedaje *m* accommodations (AmE), accommodation (BrE)

hospedar [A1] *vt* to provide ... with accommodations (AmE) *o* (BrE) accommodation ■ **hospedarse** *v pron* to stay, put up (AmE colloq)

hospedería *f* (posada) inn; (Rel) hospice

hospicio *m* (para niños huérfanos) orphanage

hospital *m* hospital; **∼ clínico** teaching hospital

hospitalario -ria *adj* **(a)** ⟨pueblo/persona⟩ hospitable, welcoming **(b)** (Med) hospital (*before n*)

hospitalidad *f* hospitality

hospitalizar [A4] *vt* to hospitalize ■ **hospitalizarse** *v pron* (AmL) to go into the hospital (AmE) *o* (BrE) into hospital

hostal *m* cheap hotel; **∼ residencia** guesthouse, boarding house

hostelería *f* (Esp) ▶ HOTELERÍA

hostia *f* **1** (Relig) host **2** (Esp vulg *o* fam) (golpe) slap, smack in the face (*o* mouth *etc*); **se pegó una ∼ con el coche** he smashed his car up badly (colloq) **3** (uso expletivo) (Esp vulg *o* fam) **¡∼(s)!** jeez!

(AmE colloq), bloody hell! (BrE sl); **hace un frío de la ∼** it's goddamn (AmE) *o* (BrE) bloody freezing! (sl); **¡qué ∼s ...!** what the hell ...! (sl)

hostigar [A3] *vt* **1 (a)** (acosar) to bother, pester **(b)** (Mil) to harass **(c)** ⟨caballo⟩ to whip **2** (Andes fam) ⟨comida/bebida⟩ to pall on

hostigoso -sa *adj* (Andes) ⟨comida/bebida⟩ sickly, sickly-sweet; ⟨persona⟩ annoying, irritating

hostil *adj* [SER] ⟨medio/clima⟩ hostile; ⟨gente/actitud⟩ hostile, unfriendly

hostilidad *f* **(a)** (del clima) hostility; (de actitud) hostility, unfriendliness **(b) hostilidades** *fpl* hostilities (*pl*)

hotel *m* hotel; **∼ residencia** guesthouse, boarding house

hotelería *f* (AmL) (negocio, industria) hotel and catering trade *o* business; (profesión) hotel management

hotelero -ra *adj* hotel (*before n*) ■ *m,f* hotel manager, hotelier

hoy *adv* **1** (este día) today; **∼ hace un año** a year ago today; **¿a cuánto estamos ∼?** what's the date today? **2 (a)** (actualmente) today, nowadays **(b)** (en locs) **hoy (en) día** nowadays, these days; **hoy por hoy** at this precise moment, at this moment in time

hoyo *m* (agujero) hole; (depresión) hollow; (fosa) pit; (en golf) hole; (sepultura) (fam) grave

hoyuelo *m* dimple

hoz *f* sickle

huacal *m* (Col, Méx, Ven) (caja) wooden crate

huachafo -fa *adj* (Per fam) **(a)** ⟨persona⟩ pretentious, affected **(b)** ⟨vestido/adorno⟩ tacky (colloq)

huachinango *m* (Méx) red snapper

huacho -cha *adj/m,f* ▶ GUACHO

huarache *m* (Méx) (Indum) sandal

huasca *f* (Chi, Per) ▶ GUASCA

huaso -sa *m,f* (Chi) **(a)** (campesino) peasant **(b)** (fam) (persona — rústica) hick (AmE colloq), country bumpkin (colloq); (—sin modales) uncouth yob (colloq)

hube, hubo, etc ▶ HABER

hucha *f* (Esp) moneybox, piggybank

hueco¹ -ca *adj* **(a)** [ESTAR] ⟨árbol/bola⟩ hollow; ⟨nuez⟩ empty, hollow; **tienes la cabeza hueca** (fam & hum) you've got a head full of sawdust (colloq & hum) **(b)** [SER] (vacío) ⟨palabras⟩ empty; ⟨estilo⟩ superficial; ⟨persona⟩ shallow, superficial **(c)** (esponjoso) ⟨lana⟩ soft; ⟨colchón⟩ soft, spongy **(d)** ⟨sonido/tos⟩ hollow; ⟨voz⟩ resonant

hueco² *m* **(a)** (cavidad en árbol, roca) hollow; (de ascensor) shaft; **suena a ∼** it sounds hollow; **el ∼ de la escalera** the stairwell **(b)** (espacio) space; (entre dos dientes) gap; **un ∼ para aparcar** a parking space; **hazme un ∼** make room for me; **llenar un ∼ en el mercado** to fill a gap in the market **(c)** (concavidad) hollow

huela, huele, etc ▶ OLER

huelga *f* strike; **hacer ∼** to (go on) strike; **estar en ∼** to be on strike

huelga, huelgan, etc ▶ HOLGAR

huelguista *mf* striker

huella *f* **(a)** (pisada — de persona) footprint, ···⫸

footstep; (— de rueda) track; **las ~s del animal** the animal's tracks o pawprints (o hoofmarks *etc*); **~s dactilares** fingerprints **(b)** (vestigio) mark; **sin dejar ~** without (a) trace

huelo ▸ OLER

huemul *m* deer (*native to the Southern Andes*)

huérfano -na *adj*: **un niño ~** an orphan; **quedó ~** he was orphaned; **es ~ de padre** he doesn't have a father
■ *m,f* orphan

huerta *f* **(a)** (huerto grande) (vegetable) garden; (con frutales) orchard **(b)** (explotación agrícola) truck farm (AmE), market garden (BrE)

huerto *m* (para verduras) vegetable garden; (con frutales) orchard

hueso *m* ⚀ **(a)** (Anat) bone; **en los ~s** (fam) nothing but skin and bone(s) (colloq) **(b)** (de) **color ~** off-white, bone-colored ⚁ (de fruta) pit (AmE), stone (BrE)

huésped *mf* (en casa, hotel) guest

huesudo -da *adj* bony

hueva *f* ⚀ *tb* **~s** (Coc) roe; (Zool) spawn ⚁ (Andes vulg) (testículo): **~s** balls (vulg), bollocks (BrE vulg)

huevada *f* (Andes vulg) (estupidez): **¿dónde compraste esa ~?** where did you buy that crap (sl) o (vulg) that shit?; **¡no digas ~s!** don't talk crap! (sl); **déjate de ~s y ponte a trabajar** stop screwing around (AmE) o (BrE) pissing about and get on with some work (vulg)

huevear [A1] *vi* (Chi, Per vulg) (perder el tiempo) to goof off (AmE colloq), to piss around (BrE sl)
■ **~** *vt* (Chi vulg) ⟨persona⟩ (molestar) to bug (colloq), to hassle (colloq); (tomar el pelo a) to kid

hueveo *m* (Chi vulg) (tomadura de pelo) pisstake (vulg); **agarrar a algn para el ~** to make fun of sb, to take the piss out of sb (BrE sl)

huevera *f* ⚀ (para guardar huevos) egg box; (para servir huevos) eggcup ⚁ (Per) (huevas) roe

huevo *m* ⚀ (Biol, Coc, Zool) egg; **~ a la copa** (Chi) boiled egg; **~ de Pascua** Easter egg; **~ duro** or (Ven) **sancochado** hard-boiled egg; **~ escalfado** or (Méx, RPl) **poché** poached egg; **~ estrellado** (frito) fried egg; **~ pasado por agua** or (Col, Méx) **tibio** soft boiled egg; **~s revueltos** or (Col) **pericos** scrambled eggs (*pl*); **a ~: tuve que leer el libro a ~** (Méx vulg) I had no damn o (BrE) bloody choice but to read the book (sl); **comprar/vender a ~** (Andes fam) to buy/sell for peanuts (colloq); **mirar a ~** (Chi fam) to look down on
⚁ (vulg) (testículo) ball (vulg); *para modismos ver* COJONES 1

huevón -vona *adj* **(a)** (Andes, Ven fam o vulg) (tonto, estúpido) (fam) dumb (colloq); **es tan ~** he's so fucking stupid (vulg) **(b)** (Méx vulg) (holgazán) lazy (colloq)
■ *m,f* **(a)** (Andes, Ven vulg) (imbécil) dickhead (vulg), asshole (AmE vulg) **(b)** (Méx vulg) (holgazán) lazy bum (colloq)

huida *f* (fuga) flight; **emprender la ~** to take flight (frml)

huidizo -za *adj* ⟨mirada⟩ evasive, shy; ⟨carácter/persona⟩ elusive; ⟨animal⟩ timid

huila *f* (Chi) rag

huincha *f* **(a)** (Andes) (cinta) ribbon; (en carrera) tape **(b)** (Andes) (para pelo) hair-band **(c)** (Bol, Chi, Per) (para medir) tape measure

huipil *m* (en AmC, Méx) huipil (*traditional embroidered dress worn by Indian women*)

huir [I20] *vi* **(a)** (escapar) to flee (liter *or* journ), escape; **huyó de la cárcel** he escaped from prison; **~ del país** to flee the country **(b)** (tratar de evitar) **~ DE algo** to avoid sth; **~le A algn** to avoid sb

huira *f* (Per) rope

huiro *m* (Chi, Per) seaweed

hule *m* ⚀ (para mantel) oilcloth; (para ropa impermeable) oilskin ⚁ (Méx) (goma) rubber

hule-espuma *m* (Méx) foam rubber

hulera *f* (AmC) slingshot (AmE), catapult (BrE)

hulla *f* coal

humanidad *f* **(a)** (los humanos): **la ~** the human race, humanity, mankind **(b)** (piedad, benevolencia) humanity **(c) humanidades** *fpl* (estudios de letras) humanities (*pl*); (enseñanza secundaria) (Chi) secondary education

humanista *mf* humanist

humanitario -ria *adj* humanitarian

humano¹ -na *adj* **(a)** ⟨naturaleza⟩ human (*before n*) **(b)** (benevolente) humane

humano² *m* human being; **los ~s** humans

humareda *f* cloud of smoke

humeante *adj* ⟨leño/lava⟩ smoking; ⟨sopa/café⟩ steaming (hot), piping hot

humear [A1] *vi* «chimenea/hoguera» to smoke; «sopa/café» to steam

humectante *m* moisturizer

humedad *f* **(a)** (Meteo) dampness; (con calor) humidity **(b)** (en paredes, suelo) damp

humedecer [E3] *vt* to moisten, dampen
■ **humedecerse** *v pron* «paredes/ropa» to get damp

húmedo -da *adj* **(a)** (Meteo) damp; (con calor) humid **(b)** ⟨suelo/casa/ropa⟩ damp **(c)** ⟨labios⟩ moist

humildad *f* **(a)** (sumisión) humility; **con ~** humbly **(b)** (pobreza) humbleness, lowliness

humilde *adj* ⟨carácter/tono⟩ meek; ⟨vivienda/ropa⟩ humble, lowly

humillación *f* humiliation

humillante *adj* humiliating

humillar [A1] *vt* to humiliate
■ **humillarse** *v pron*: **no se humilla ante nadie** she doesn't kowtow to anyone; **no me voy a ~ a pedirle que vuelva** I'm not going to demean myself by begging him to come back

humita *f* ⚀ (CS) (Coc) *flavored corn paste wrapped in corn leaves* ⚁ (Chi) (Indum) bow tie

humo *m* ⚀ (de tabaco, incendio) smoke; (gases) fumes (*pl*); **echaba ~** smoke was pouring out of it; **hacerse ~** (AmL fam) to make oneself scarce

---

AmC	América Central	Arg	Argentina	Cu	Cuba	Per	Perú
AmL	América Latina	Bol	Bolivia	Ec	Ecuador	RPl	Río de la Plata
AmS	América del Sur	Chi	Chile	Esp	España	Ur	Uruguay
Andes	Región andina	CS	Cono Sur	Méx	México	Ven	Venezuela

(colloq) **2 humos** *mpl* (aires) airs (*pl*); **¡qué ∼s se da!** she really gives herself airs (colloq); **bajarle los ∼s a algn** to take sb down a peg or two

humor *m* (a) (estado de ánimo) mood; **estar de buen ∼** to be in a good mood; **no estoy de ∼ para salir** I'm not in the mood to go out (b) (gracia) humor*

humorada *f* (a) (extravagancia): **hacer una ∼** to do something crazy (b) (broma) little joke, witticism

humorista *mf* (autor) humorist, comic writer; (dibujante) cartoonist; (cómico) comic, comedian

humorístico -ca *adj* humorous

hundido -da *adj* (a) ⟨barco⟩ sunken (b) ⟨ojos⟩ deep-set; (por enfermedad) sunken

hundimiento *m* (a) (de barco) sinking (b) (de negocio) collapse (c) (de edificio — bajada de nivel) subsidence; (— derrumbe) collapse

hundir [I1] *vt* ⟨barco⟩ to sink; ⟨persona⟩ to destroy; ⟨negocio/empresa⟩ to drive ... under

■ **hundirse** *v pron* (a) ⟨barco⟩ to sink (b) (en barro, nieve) to sink (c) «empresa/negocio» to fold (d) «edificio» (bajar de nivel) to sink, subside; (derrumbarse) to collapse

húngaro¹ -ra *adj/m,f* Hungarian

húngaro² *m* (idioma) Hungarian

Hungría *f* Hungary

huracán *m* hurricane

huraño -ña *adj* ⟨persona⟩ unsociable; ⟨animal⟩ timid

hurgar [A3] *vi* ∼ **EN algo** ⟨en basura⟩ to rummage o rake THROUGH sth; **∼ en el pasado** to delve into the past

■ **hurgarse** *v pron* (refl): **∼se la nariz** to pick one's nose

hurguetear [A1] *vi* (CS) ∼ **EN algo** ⟨en papeles⟩ to nose THROUGH sth; ⟨en cartera⟩ to rummage o ferret around IN sth

■ ∼ *vt* ⟨cajón/cartera⟩ to rummage around in, rummage through

■ **hurguetearse** *v pron* (refl) (esp AmL) ▶ HURGARSE

hurra, hurrah *interj* hurrah!, hooray!

hurtadillas *fpl*: **entrar/salir a ∼** to sneak in/out

hurtar [A1] *vt* (frml) to purloin (frml), to steal

hurto *m* (frml) (robo) robbery, theft; (en las tiendas) shoplifting

husmear [A1] *vt* to sniff

■ ∼ *vi* (a) «perro» to sniff around (b) (fam) (fisgonear) to snoop, sniff (around) (colloq)

huso *m* spindle

huy *interj* (fam) (para expresar— dolor) ouch!, ow!; (— asombro) wow!; (— alivio) phew!

huya, huyas, etc ▶ HUIR

I i

I, i *f* (*pl* **íes**) (read as /i/) *tb* **i latina** the letter I, i; **i griega** *the letter* Y

iba, íbamos, etc ▶ IR

Iberia *f* Iberia

ibérico -ca *adj* Iberian

Iberoamérica *f* Latin America

iberoamericano -na *adj/m,f* Latin American

icaco *m* (Col, Méx, Ven) coco plum

iceberg /'aısβer, 'iθe'βer/ *m* (*pl* **-bergs**) iceberg

icono, ícono *m* icon

ictericia *f* jaundice

ida *f* (a) (viaje) outward journey; **a la ∼** on the way out; **¿cuánto cuesta la ∼?** how much does it cost one way?; **¿saco de ∼ y vuelta?** shall I buy a round-trip ticket (AmE) o (BrE) return ticket? (b) (partida) departure

idea *f* idea; **la ∼ de libertad** the idea o concept of freedom; **es de ∼s fijas** he has very set ideas about things; **no tiene ∼ de cómo funciona** he has no idea how it works; **no tengo ∼** I don't have a clue; **hacerse una ∼ de la situación** to get an idea of the situation; **se me ocurre una ∼** I've got an idea; **cambió de ∼** she changed her mind; **hacerse (a) la ∼ de algo** to get used to the idea of sth

ideal *adj* ideal

■ *m* (a) (prototipo) ideal (b) (aspiración) dream (c) **ideales** *mpl* (valores, principios) ideals (*pl*)

idealismo *m* idealism

idealista *adj* idealistic

■ *mf* idealist

idealizar [A4] *vt* to idealize

ídem *adv* ditto, idem (frml)

idéntico -ca *adj* identical; **es ∼ al padre** (físicamente) he looks just like his father, he's the spitting image of his father (colloq); (en el carácter) he's exactly like his father; **∼ A algo** identical TO sth

identidad *f* identity

identificar [A2] *vt* to identify

■ **identificarse** *v pron* (a) (compenetrarse, solidarizarse) **∼se CON algo/algn** to identify WITH sth/sb (b) (demostrar la identidad) to identify oneself

ideología *f* ideology

ideológico -ca *adj* ideological

idílico -ca *adj* idyllic

idilio *m* (a) (Lit) idyll (b) (romance) romance

idioma *m* language

idiota *adj* (fam) (tonto) stupid, idiotic; **¡no seas ∼!** don't be such an idiot!

■ *mf* (tonto) (fam) idiot, stupid fool (colloq)

idiotez *f* (fam) (cosa estúpida): **decir idioteces** to talk nonsense; **fue una ∼ hacer eso** that was a stupid thing to do

ido, ida adj (distraído) ⟨mirada⟩ faraway (before n); **estás como ~** you seem miles away

ídolo m idol

idóneo -nea adj suitable; **es la persona idónea para el cargo** he's suitable for the job, he's the right person for the job

iglesia f church; **no van a la ~** they don't go to church; **casarse por la ~** or (Bol, Per, RPl) **por ~** to have a church wedding

iglú m igloo

ignorancia f ignorance; **por ~** out of o through ignorance

ignorante adj (a) (sin instrucción) ignorant (b) (sin información): **estar ~ de algo** to be unaware of sth
■ mf ignoramus, ignorant fool (colloq)

ignorar [A1] vt (a) (desconocer): **lo ignoro** I've no idea; **ignoran las causas del accidente** they do not know what caused the accident; **ignora los peligros que le acechan** he's unaware of the dangers which await him (b) (no hacer caso de) to ignore

igual adj ⟨1⟩ (a) (idéntico): **de ~ peso** of equal o the same weight; **son ~es** they are the same o alike; **de forma son ~es** they're the same shape; **~ A** or **QUE algo/algn** the same AS sth/sb; **es ~ita a or que su madre** (físicamente) she looks just like her mother; (en personalidad) she's exactly the same as o just like her mother; **es ~ a x** (Mat) it equals x; **me/nos es** or **da ~** I/we don't mind, it makes no difference to me/to us (b) (en una jerarquía) equal; **~es ante la ley** equal in the eyes of the law
⟨2⟩ (en tenis): **quince ~es** fifteen all; **van ~es** they're even
■ adv ⟨1⟩ (a) (de la misma manera): **los trato a todos ~** I treat them all the same (b) (en locs) **al igual que** (frml) as, like; **igual que: tiene pecas, ~ que su hermano** she has freckles, (just) like her brother; **se llama ~ que su padre** he's named after his father; **me aburrí — ~ que yo** I got bored — so did I o me too; **opino ~ que tú** I agree with you; **por igual** equally
⟨2⟩ (de todos modos) anyway
⟨3⟩ (expresando posibilidad): **~ llueve y no podemos salir** it might rain and then we won't be able to go out; **~ llamaron y no estábamos** they may have called and we weren't in
■ mf (par) equal; **le habló de ~ a ~** he spoke to him on equal terms; **me trató de ~ a ~** she treated me as an equal; **sin ~** ⟨belleza/talento⟩ unequaled*, matchless (frml); **es un compositor sin ~** he's unrivaled as a composer
■ m (signo) equals sign

igualado -da adj ⟨1⟩ (a) (Dep): **van muy ~s** they're very close, they're neck and neck; **quedaron ~s** they drew; **iban ~s a tres** they were level at three-three (b) ⟨superficie⟩ even, level ⟨2⟩ (Méx fam) (irrespetuoso) sassy (AmE colloq), cheeky (BrE colloq)

igualar [A1] vt ⟨1⟩ (a) ⟨superficie/terreno⟩ to level, level off; ⟨flequillo/dobladillo⟩ to even up, make ... straight (b) ⟨salarios⟩ to make ... equal o the same; **~ algo CON** or **A algo** to make sth the same AS sth ⟨2⟩ ⟨éxito/récord⟩ to equal, match
■ **igualarse** v pron: **nada se le iguala** it has no equal, there's nothing like it; **~se A** or **CON algo** to match o equal sth

igualdad f equality; **~ de oportunidades** equal opportunities; **en ~ de condiciones** on equal terms

igualmente adv (a) (en fórmulas de cortesía): **que lo pases muy bien — igualmente** have a great time — you too o and you (b) ⟨bueno/malo⟩ equally (c) (frml) (también) likewise

iguana f (Zool) iguana

ilegal adj illegal; **de manera ~** illegally

ilegible adj illegible, unreadable

ilegítimo -ma adj ⟨hijo⟩ illegitimate

ileso -sa adj unhurt, unharmed

ilícito -ta adj illicit

ilimitado -da adj unlimited

ilógico -ca adj illogical

iluminación f (de habitación) lighting; (de monumento) illumination; (Teatr) lighting

iluminar [A1] vt (a) ⟨calles⟩ to light, illuminate; ⟨monumento⟩ to illuminate; ⟨escenario⟩ to light (b) (con focos muy potentes) ⟨estadio⟩ to floodlight (c) ⟨rostro/ojos⟩ (liter) to light up

ilusión f ⟨1⟩ (a) (esperanza) hope; **no te hagas ilusiones** don't build your hopes up; **no me hago muchas ilusiones** I'm not very hopeful; **su mayor ~ es ...** her dearest o fondest wish is ... (b) (esp Esp) (alegría, satisfacción): **me hizo mucha ~** I was thrilled; **le hace ~ el viaje** he's looking forward to the trip; **¡qué ~!** isn't it wonderful! ⟨2⟩ (noción falsa) illusion

ilusionar [A1] vt: **me ilusiona mucho** I'm very excited about it; **no la ilusiones** don't raise her hopes
■ **ilusionarse** v pron (a) (hacerse ilusiones) to build one's hopes up (b) (entusiasmarse) **~se CON algo** to get excited ABOUT sth

iluso -sa adj naive
■ m,f dreamer

ilustración f illustration

ilustrado -da adj (a) ⟨revista/libro⟩ illustrated (b) (frml) ⟨persona⟩ erudite, learned

ilustrar [A1] vt to illustrate

ilustre adj illustrious, distinguished

imagen f ⟨1⟩ (a) (Fís, Ópt) image; (TV) picture, image (b) (foto) picture (c) (en espejo) reflection; **ser la viva ~ de algn** to be the image of sb (d) (en la mente) picture ⟨2⟩ (de político, cantante, país) image

imaginación f imagination; **¡ni (se) me pasó por la ~!** it never even crossed my mind!; **son imaginaciones tuyas** you're imagining things

imaginar [A1] vt (a) (suponer, figurarse) ▶ IMAGINARSE (b) (idear) ⟨plan/método⟩ to think up, come up with
■ **imaginarse** v pron to imagine; **me imagino que no querrá ir** I don't imagine o suppose he feels like going; **no te puedes ~ lo mal que nos trató** you've no idea how badly she treated us; **¿quedó contento? — ¡imagínate!** was he pleased? — what do you think!; **me imagino que sí** I suppose so; **me lo imaginaba más alto** I imagined he'd be taller

imaginario -ria adj imaginary

imaginativo -va adj imaginative

imán m magnet

imbécil adj (a) (fam) (tonto) stupid (b) (Med) imbecilic

■ *mf* **(a)** (fam) (tonto) stupid idiot, moron (colloq & pej) **(b)** (Med) imbecile

imberbe *adj*: un joven ~ (sin barba) a beardless youth; (sin experiencia) a callow youth, a fresh-faced youth

imborrable *adj* lasting (*before n*), indelible

imitación *f* **(a)** (acción) imitation **(b)** (parodia) impression **(c)** (copia) imitation; **bolso ~ cuero** imitation-leather bag

imitador -dora *m,f* (Teatr) impressionist, impersonator; (plagiario) imitator

imitar [A1] *vt* **(a)** ‹persona› (copiar) to copy, imitate; (para hacer reír) to do an impression of, mimic; **se sentó y todos lo ~on** he sat down and everyone followed suit **(b)** ‹voz/gesto/estilo› to imitate; (para hacer reír) to imitate, mimic **(c)** (tener el aspecto de) to simulate

impaciencia *f* impatience

impacientarse [A1] *v pron* (por retraso) to get impatient; (exasperarse) to lose (one's) patience, get exasperated

impaciente *adj* **(a)** [SER] impatient **(b)** [ESTAR]: estaba ~ he was (getting) impatient; ~ POR hacer algo impatient to do sth

impactante *adj* ‹noticia› shocking; ‹libro/ imagen› powerful; ‹espectáculo/efecto› stunning, impressive

impactar [A1] *vt* **(a)** (golpear) to hit **(b)** (impresionar) to have a profound impact on
■ ~ *vi* **(a)** (impresionar) to shock **(b)** (chocar) to hit, strike

impacto *m* **(a)** (choque) impact; **recibió un ~ de bala** she was shot **(b)** (huella, señal) hole, mark; **el cadáver tiene varios ~s de bala** there are several bullet wounds in the body **(c)** (en el ánimo, público) impact **(d)** (Inf) hit

impago -ga *adj* (AmL) ‹persona› unpaid; ‹deuda/impuesto› unpaid, outstanding

impalpable *adj* impalpable

impar *adj* ‹número› odd
■ *m* odd number

imparcial *adj* impartial, unbiased

imparcialidad *f* impartiality

impasible *adj* impassive

impecable *adj* impeccable; **va siempre ~** she is always impeccably dressed

impedido -da *adj* disabled
■ *m,f* disabled person

impedimento *m* obstacle, impediment; **si no surge ningún ~** if there are no hitches; **~ físico** physical handicap

impedir [I14] *vt* **(a)** (imposibilitar) to prevent; **nadie te lo impide** nobody's stopping you; **~le a algn hacer algo** to prevent sb FROM doing sth; **quiso ~ que nos viéramos** she tried to stop us seeing each other **(b)** ‹paso/entrada› to block **(c)** (dificultar) to hamper, hinder

impenetrable *adj* **(a)** ‹bosque› impenetrable; ‹fortaleza› impregnable **(b)** ‹persona/expresión› inscrutable; ‹misterio/secreto› unfathomable

impensable *adj* unthinkable, inconceivable

imperante *adj* ‹moda/tendencia/condiciones› prevailing (*before n*); ‹dinastía/régimen› ruling (*before n*)

imperativo¹ -va *adj* **(a)** (Ling) imperative **(b)** ‹voz/tono› commanding, authoritative

imperativo² *m* imperative

imperdible *m* safety pin

imperdonable *adj* ‹error/comportamiento› unforgivable, inexcusable

imperfección *f* **(a)** (en tela) flaw; (en mecanismo) defect **(b)** (cualidad) imperfection

imperfecto¹ -ta *adj* ⟨1⟩ ‹trabajo/tela/ facciones› flawed ⟨2⟩ (Ling) imperfect

imperfecto² *m* imperfect (tense)

imperial *adj* ‹dinastía/corona› imperial

imperialismo *m* imperialism

imperialista *adj/mf* imperialist

imperio *m* empire

impermeable *adj* ‹material/tela› waterproof, impermeable (tech)
■ *m* (Indum) raincoat

impersonal *adj* impersonal

impersonar [A1] *vt* (Méx) to impersonate

impertinencia *f* **(a)** (cualidad) impertinence **(b)** (hecho, dicho): me dijo que me callara — ¡qué ~! he told me to shut up — how impertinent!; me contestó con una ~ she gave me a very cheeky reply

impertinente *adj* ‹persona/pregunta/tono› impertinent; ‹comentario› uncalled-for
■ *mf* (persona): eres una ~ you're extremely impertinent

imperturbable *adj* **(a)** [SER] (sereno) imperturbable **(b)** [ESTAR] (ante un peligro) unperturbed **(c)** ‹rostro/sonrisa› impassive

ímpetu *m* **(a)** (Fís, Mec) impetus, momentum **(b)** (energía, ardor) vigor*, energy **(c)** (violencia) force

impetuoso -sa *adj* impetuous, impulsive

impida, impidas, etc ▶ IMPEDIR

implacable *adj* **(a)** ‹odio/furia› implacable; ‹avance/lucha› relentless; ‹sol› relentless **(b)** ‹juez/crítico› implacable **(c)** ‹enemigo/ contrincante› ruthless

implantar [A1] *vt* ⟨1⟩ ‹método/norma/moda› to introduce; ‹régimen político› to establish; ‹estado de excepción› to impose ⟨2⟩ ‹embrión/cabello› to implant

implante *m* implant

implementar [A1] *vt* ⟨1⟩ ‹medidas/plan› to implement ⟨2⟩ (Ven) (instalar) to install*, set up

implicación *f* ⟨1⟩ (participación) involvement ⟨2⟩ **implicaciones** *fpl* (consecuencias) implications (*pl*)

implicancia *f* (AmL) (consecuencia) implication

implicar [A2] *vt* ⟨1⟩ (significar, conllevar) to entail, involve ⟨2⟩ (envolver, enredar) to involve; **estuvo implicado en un delito** (participó) he was involved in a crime; (estuvo bajo sospecha) he was implicated in a crime
■ **implicarse** *v pron* to get involved

implícito -ta *adj* implicit

implorar [A1] *vt* ‹perdón/ayuda› to beg for; **~le algo A algn** to beg sth OF sb; **~le a algn QUE haga algo** to implore o beg sb TO do sth

imponente *adj* ‹belleza› impressive; ‹edificio/ paisaje› imposing, impressive

imponer [E22] *vt* (frml) **(a)** to impose (frml); **le impusieron una pena de un año de cárcel** he was ⋯⋗

sentenced to one year in prison **(b)** ‹*respeto*› to command; ‹*temor*› to inspire, instill* **(c)** ‹*moda*› to set

■ **imponerse** *v pron* ⟦1⟧ **(a)** (*refl*) ‹*horario/meta*› to set oneself **(b)** «*idea*» to become established **(c)** «*color/estilo*» to come into fashion ⟦2⟧ (hacerse respetar) to assert oneself *o* one's authority ⟦3⟧ (fml) (vencer) to win; **se impondrá el sentido común** common sense will prevail

importación *f* **(a)** (acción) importation; **de** ～ ‹*artículos/mercancías*› imported; ‹*permiso*› import (*before n*) **(b) importaciones** *fpl* (mercancías) imports (*pl*)

importado -da *adj* imported

importador -dora *adj*: **países** ～**es de petróleo** oil-importing countries

■ *m,f* importer

importancia *f* importance; **darle** ～ **a algo** to attach importance to sth; **quitarle** ～ **a algo** to play down the importance of sth; **detalles sin** ～ minor *o* insignificant details; **no tiene** ～ it doesn't matter; ***darse*** ～ to give oneself airs

importante *adj* **(a)** ‹*noticia/persona*› important; ‹*acontecimiento/cambio*› important, significant; **dárselas de** *or* **hacerse el** ～ to give oneself airs **(b)** ‹*pérdidas*› serious, considerable; ‹*daños*› severe, considerable; ‹*cantidad*› considerable, significant

importar [A1] *vi* **(a)** (tener importancia, interés) to matter; **no importa quién lo haga** it doesn't matter *o* it makes no difference who does it; **lo que importa es que te recuperes** the important thing is for you to get better; **no me importa lo que piense** I don't care what he thinks; **¿a mí qué me importa?** what do I care?; **¿a ti qué te importa?** what business is it of yours?; **yo no le importo** I don't mean a thing to him; **me importa un bledo** *or* **un comino** *or* **un pepino** *or* **un rábano** (fam) I couldn't care less, I don't give a damn (colloq); **meterse en lo que no le importa** (fam) to poke one's nose into other people's business (colloq); **no te metas en lo que no te importa** mind your own business! **(b)** (molestar): **no me** ～**ía venir el sábado** I wouldn't mind coming on Saturday; **no me importa que me llame a casa** I don't mind her calling me at home

■ ～ *vt* (Com, Fin) ‹*productos*› to import

importe *m* **(a)** (de factura, letra) amount; **el** ～ **total** the full *o* total amount; **el** ～ **de la compra** the purchase price **(b)** (costo) cost

importunar [A1] *vt* (fml) to inconvenience, disturb

■ *vi*: **espero no** ～ I hope it's not inconvenient, I hope I'm not disturbing you

importuno -na *adj* inopportune

imposibilitado -da *adj* [ESTAR] (Med) disabled

imposibilitar [A1] *vt* **(a)** (hacer imposible) to make ... impossible **(b)** (impedir) to prevent

imposible *adj* ⟦1⟧ [SER] ‹*sueño/amor*› impossible; **me es** ～ **acompañarte** I won't be able to go with you; **es** ～ **que lo sepan** they can't

possibly know; **hicieron lo** ～ they did everything they could ⟦2⟧ (inaguantable) ‹*persona*› impossible; **está** ～ **hoy** he's (being) impossible today

impositivo -va *adj* ‹*sistema/reforma*› tax (*before n*)

impostor -tora *m,f* impostor

impotencia *f* (falta de poder) powerlessness, helplessness; (Med) impotence

impotente *adj* (incapaz, sin poder) powerless, helpless; (Med) impotent

impreciso -sa *adj* vague, imprecise; **un número** ～ **de personas** an indeterminate number of people

impredecible *adj* unpredictable

imprenta *f* (taller) printer's; (aparato) (printing) press

imprescindible *adj* ‹*requisito/herramienta/factor*› essential, indispensable; **lleva lo** ～ take the bare essentials; **es** ～ **hacerlo** it is essential to do it; **es** ～ **que nos acompañe** it is essential that you come with us

impresión *f* **(a)** (idea, sensación) impression; **nos causó** *or* **nos hizo muy buena** ～ he made a very good impression on us; **da la** ～ **de ser demasiado ancho** it looks too wide; **me da/tengo la** ～ **de que me está mintiendo** I have a feeling he's lying to me; **cambiar impresiones** to exchange ideas **(b)** (sensación desagradable): **el accidente me produjo mucha** ～ the accident really shocked me

impresionable *adj* squeamish, easily affected

impresionante *adj* ‹*éxito/cantidad/paisaje*› amazing, incredible; ‹*accidente*› horrific

impresionar [A1] *vt* ⟦1⟧ **(a)** (causar buena impresión): **París me impresionó** I was really taken with Paris **(b)** (afectar) to affect; **verlo llorar me impresionó mucho** seeing him cry really affected *o* moved me **(c)** (alarmar) to shock; **me impresionó verla tan delgada** it shocked me to see her looking so thin **(d)** (sorprender) to strike ⟦2⟧ (Fot) ‹*película*› to expose

■ ～ *vi* to impress

impresionismo *m* impressionism

impresionista *adj* ‹*movimiento/pintor*› Impressionist; ‹*estilo/descripción*› impressionistic

impreso¹ -sa *pp*: ▶ IMPRIMIR

impreso² *m* (formulario) form; ～ **de solicitud** application form

impresora *f* (Inf) printer; ～ **láser** *or* **de láser** laser printer

imprevisible *adj* ‹*hecho/factor*› unforeseeable; ‹*persona*› unpredictable

imprevisión *f* lack of foresight

imprevisto¹ -ta *adj* unforeseen, unexpected; **de modo** ～ unexpectedly

imprevisto² *m* unforeseen event (*o* factor *etc*); **si no surge ningún** ～ if nothing unexpected happens

imprimir [I36] *vt* (Impr) to print; **impreso en Perú** printed in Peru

AmC	Central America	Arg	Argentina	Cu	Cuba	Per	Peru
AmL	Latin America	Bol	Bolivia	Ec	Ecuador	RPI	River Plate Area
AmS	South America	Chi	Chile	Esp	Spain	Ur	Uruguay
Andes	Andean Region	CS	Southern Cone	Méx	Mexico	Ven	Venezuela

improbable ⋯❯ inclinación ⋯

improbable *adj* unlikely, improbable

impropio -pia *adj* (a) ‹actitud/respuesta› inappropriate; **un comportamiento ~ de una persona educada** behavior unbecoming to an educated person (fml) (b) (incorrecto) incorrect

improvisación *f* (acción) improvisation; (actuación) impromptu performance

improvisar [A1] *vt* to improvise; **~ una comida** to rustle up a meal
■ ~ *vi* «actor/músico» to improvise

improviso: **de ~** (*loc adv*) ‹llegar/aparecer› unexpectedly, out of the blue

imprudencia *f* imprudence; **no cometas esa ~** don't be so rash *o* reckless; **su ~ al conducir** his reckless driving

imprudente *adj* (que actúa sin cuidado) imprudent, careless; (temerario) reckless; **fuiste muy ~ al decírselo** it was very rash *o* imprudent of you to tell him

impúdico -ca *adj* (frml *o* hum) (a) (obsceno) indecent (b) (desvergonzado) shameless

impuesto *m* tax; **libre de ~s** tax-free, duty-free; **~ a** *or* **sobre la renta** income tax; **~ de circulación** road tax

impugnar [A1] *vt* ‹decisión/fallo› to contest, challenge

impulsar [A1] *vt* (a) ‹motor/vehículo› to propel, drive (b) ‹persona› to drive (c) ‹comercio, producción› to boost, give a boost to; ‹cultura/relaciones› to promote

impulsivo -va *adj* impulsive

impulso *m* (a) (empuje): **un fuerte ~ para el comercio** a major boost for trade; **dar ~ a algo** (a comercio) to give a boost to sth; (a iniciativa) to give impetus to sth; **tomar** *or* **darse ~** to gather momentum, to get up speed (b) (reacción, deseo) impulse; **mi primer ~ fue …** my first instinct was … (c) (Fís) impulse

impuntualidad *f* unpunctuality

impureza *f* impurity

impuro -ra *adj* impure

impuse, impuso, etc ▶ IMPONER

in *adj inv* ‹discoteca› trendy (colloq); **lo que está muy ~** the in thing (colloq), the trendy thing (colloq)

inaccesible *adj* (a) ‹montaña/persona/concepto› inaccessible (b) (crit) ‹precios› prohibitive; ‹objetivo› unattainable

inaceptable *adj* unacceptable

inactividad *f* inactivity

inactivo -va *adj* inactive

inadaptación *f* failure to adapt

inadaptado -da *adj* maladjusted

inadecuado -da *adj* ‹color/traje› inappropriate, unsuitable; ‹norma/sistema› inadequate

inadmisible *adj* (a) ‹comportamiento/pretensiones› unacceptable, inadmissible (b) (Der) inadmissible

inadvertido -da *adj* (no notado): **pasar ~** to go unnoticed

inagotable *adj* ‹fuente/reservas› inexhaustible, endless

inaguantable *adj* unbearable

inalámbrico -ca *adj* ‹teléfono› cordless; ‹comunicaciones› wireless

inalcanzable *adj* unattainable, unachievable

inanimado -da *adj* inanimate

inapetente *adj* lacking in appetite

inapreciable *adj* ① (muy valioso) ‹ayuda/amistad› invaluable; **un cuadro de un valor ~** a priceless painting ② (insignificante) negligible

inapropiado -da *adj* inappropriate

inaudible *adj* inaudible

inaudito -ta *adj* ‹decisión/suceso› unprecedented

inauguración *f* opening, inauguration (fml)

inaugurar [A1] *vt* ‹teatro/hospital› to open, inaugurate (fml); ‹monumento› to unveil; ‹exposición/sesión› to open

inca *mf* Inca

incaico -ca *adj* Inca, Incaic

incalculable *adj* inestimable, incalculable

incandescente *adj* incandescent

incansable *adj* tireless

incapacidad *f* ① (física) disability, physical handicap; (mental) mental handicap; (Der) incapacity; **~ laboral** invalidity ② (ineptitud) incompetence; (falta de capacidad) inability ③ (Col) (baja) sick leave

incapacitado -da *adj* (físicamente) disabled, physically handicapped; (mentalmente) mentally handicapped

incapacitar [A1] *vt* «enfermedad» to incapacitate; **la lesión lo incapacita para su trabajo** the injury has made him unfit for work

incapaz *adj* [SER] (de un logro, una hazaña): **no lo conseguirá nunca, es ~** he'll never do it, he simply isn't capable; **es ~ de una cosa así** he's incapable of doing something like that; **es ~ de llamarme** he can't even be bothered to phone me
■ *mf* (inútil, inepto) incompetent (fool)

incendiar [A1] *vt* (a) (prender fuego a) to set fire to (b) (quemar) ‹edificio› to burn down; ‹coche› to burn; ‹pueblo/bosque› to burn … to the ground
■ **incendiarse** *v pron* (a) (empezar a arder) to catch fire (b) (destruirse) «edificio» to be burned down; **los bosques que se ~on** the forests that were destroyed by fire

incendiario -ria *m,f* arsonist

incendio *m* fire; **~ provocado** arson attack

incentivo *m* incentive

incertidumbre *f* uncertainty

incesante *adj* incessant

incesto *m* incest

incestuoso -sa *adj* incestuous

incidente *m* incident

incienso *m* incense; (Bib) frankincense

incierto -ta *adj* (dudoso, inseguro) uncertain

incineración *f* (a) (de basura) incineration (b) (de cadáveres) cremation

incinerador *m* incinerator

incinerar [A1] *vt* ‹basura› to incinerate, burn; ‹cadáver› to cremate

incitar [A1] *vt* **~ a algn A algo** to incite sb TO sth; **~ a algn CONTRA algn** to incite sb AGAINST sb

incivilizado -da *adj* uncivilized

inclinación *f* ① (a) (pendiente) slope (b) (ángulo) inclination ② (movimiento del cuerpo) bow; ⋯❯

asintió con una ∼ de la cabeza he nodded (his head) in agreement ③ ⟨interés, tendencia⟩: **tener ∼ por** or **hacia la música** to have a musical bent o musical inclinations; **inclinaciones políticas/ sexuales** political/sexual leanings

inclinado -da adj ① ⟨tejado/terreno⟩ sloping; ⟨torre⟩ leaning ⟨before n⟩; ⟨cuadro⟩ crooked; **una pendiente muy inclinada** a very steep slope o incline ② (predispuesto): **sentirse ∼ a hacer algo** to feel inclined to do sth

inclinar [A1] vt ① ⟨botella/sombrilla/plato⟩ to tilt; **inclinó la cabeza a un lado** she tilted her head to one side; **inclinó la cabeza en señal de asentimiento** he nodded (his head) in agreement; **∼ el cuerpo** to bend over; (en señal de respeto) to bow; **el viento inclinaba los árboles** the wind bent the trees

② (inducir, predisponer) ⟨persona⟩: **ello me inclina a pensar que …** this inclines me to think that … (frml)

■ **inclinarse** v pron ① (tender) **∼se A hacer algo** to be inclined to do sth; **me inclino por su candidato** I'm inclined to go for your candidate; **me ∼ía por esta opción** I would tend to favor this option

② (doblarse) to bend; (en señal de respeto) to bow; **∼se ante algn** to bow to sb; **se inclinó sobre la cuna** she leaned over the cradle; **∼se hacia adelante/atrás** to lean forward/back

incluir [I20] vt ① (comprender) (a) ⟨impuestos/ gastos⟩ to include; **$500 todo incluido** $500 all inclusive o all in (b) ⟨tema/sección⟩ to include, contain ② (poner, agregar) (a) (en un grupo) to include (b) (en una carta) to enclose

inclusive adj inv inclusive; **del 10 al 18, ambos ∼** from 10 to 18 inclusive; **domingos ∼** including Sundays

incluso adv even

incógnita f (a) (Mat) unknown (factor o quantity) (b) (misterio) mystery

incógnito: **de ∼** (loc adv) incognito

incoherente adj incoherent, illogical

incoloro -ra adj colorless*

incomible adj inedible, uneatable

incómodo -da adj (a) (en general) uncomfortable; **¿no estás ∼ en esa silla?** aren't you uncomfortable in that chair?; **se siente muy ∼ en las fiestas** he feels ill at ease o uncomfortable at parties (b) (inconveniente) inconvenient; **es muy ∼ vivir tan lejos** it's very inconvenient living so far away

incompatibilidad f mutual incompatibility; **∼ de caracteres** incompatibility

incompatible adj ⟨personas/caracteres⟩ incompatible; **el horario de clases es ∼ con el de mi trabajo** the times of the classes clash with my work hours

incompetente adj/mf incompetent

incompleto -ta adj incomplete

incomprensible adj incomprehensible

incomprensión f lack of understanding

incomunicado -da adj ⟨prisonero⟩ in solitary confinement; **hay varios pueblos ∼s** several villages have been cut off

inconcebible adj inconceivable

inconcluso -sa adj unfinished

incondicional adj (a) ⟨apoyo⟩ unconditional, wholehearted; ⟨obediencia⟩ absolute; ⟨aliado/ admirador⟩ staunch; ⟨amigo⟩ true, loyal (b) ⟨rendición⟩ unconditional

inconexo -xa adj unconnected

inconfesable adj unmentionable

inconformista adj/mf nonconformist

inconfundible adj unmistakable

incongruente adj ⟨imágenes⟩ unconnected; **decía palabras ∼s** his words didn't make sense

inconsciencia f (a) (Med) unconsciousness (b) (insensatez) irresponsibility

inconsciente adj ① [ESTAR] (Med) unconscious ② [SER] (insensato) irresponsible ③ [SER] (no voluntario) ⟨movimiento/gesto⟩ unwitting, unconscious; **de una manera ∼** unconsciously

■ mf irresponsible person; **son unos ∼s** they are very irresponsible

inconsecuente adj: **ser ∼ con uno mismo** to be inconsistent with one's principles

inconsistente adj (a) ⟨material⟩ flimsy, weak (b) ⟨argumento⟩ (falto de solidez) weak, flimsy; (falto de coherencia) inconsistent, flawed

inconsolable adj inconsolable

inconstante adj (a) (falto de perseverancia) lacking in perseverance (b) (voluble) fickle

inconstitucional adj unconstitutional

incontable adj countless, innumerable

incontrolado -da adj (a) ⟨furia/pasión/ira⟩ uncontrolled, unbridled (liter) (b) ⟨llanto/risa⟩ uncontrollable

inconveniencia f (a) (cualidad) inconvenience (b) (comentario inoportuno) tactless remark

inconveniente adj (incómodo) ⟨hora/fecha⟩ inconvenient

■ m (a) (problema) problem; **si no surge ningún ∼** if everything goes according to plan, if there are no problems; **¿habría algún ∼ en que nos quedemos?** would it be alright if we stayed? (b) (desventaja) drawback; **tiene sus ∼s** it has its disadvantages o drawbacks (c) (objeción) objection; **no tengo ∼** I have no objection; **no tengo ∼ en decírselo** I don't mind telling him; **no veo ningún ∼ en que venga** I see no reason why he shouldn't come

incordiar [A1] vt (Esp fam) to annoy, to pester (colloq)

■ **∼** vi (Esp): **¡no incordies!** don't be such a nuisance!

incordio m (Esp fam) nuisance, pain in the neck (colloq)

incorporación f incorporation

incorporado -da adj integral, built-in

incorporar [A1] vt ① (a) (agregar) to add; **∼ algo A algo** to add sth TO sth (b) (integrar) to incorporate ② ⟨enfermo/niño⟩ to sit … up

■ **incorporarse** v pron (frml) ① (a equipo, puesto) to join; **∼se A algo** to join sth ② (levantarse) to sit up

incorrecto -ta adj (a) ⟨respuesta/ interpretación⟩ incorrect, wrong (b) ⟨comportamiento⟩ impolite, discourteous (frml)

incorregible adj ⟨mentiroso/idealista⟩ incorrigible; ⟨defecto⟩ irremediable, irreparable

incredulidad *f* skepticism*

incrédulo -la *adj* skeptical*
■ *m,f* skeptic*

increíble *adj* incredible, unbelievable

incrementar [A1] *vt* (frml) to increase

incremento *m* (frml) increase

incriminar [A1] *vt* (frml) **(a)** «*pruebas*» to incriminate **(b)** (acusar, inculpar) to charge

incrustación *f* **(a)** (de madera, metal) inlay **(b)** (Col) (Odont) filling

incrustar [A1] *vt* ⟨*piedra preciosa*⟩ ~ **algo EN algo** to set sth in sth
■ **incrustarse** *v pron* ~**se EN algo** «*bala*» to embed itself in sth; «*suciedad*» to get embedded in sth

incubadora *f* incubator

incubar [A1] *vt* to incubate

inculcar [A2] *vt* to instill*, inculcate (frml); **las ideas que les inculcan** the ideas they fill their heads with

inculto -ta *adj* (sin cultura) uncultured, uneducated; (ignorante) ignorant
■ *m,f* **(a)** (persona sin cultura): **es un** ~ he's uneducated **(b)** (persona ignorante) ignorant person

incumplido -da *adj* (AmL exc CS) unreliable

incumplidor -dora *adj* (CS) unreliable

incumplir [I1] *vt* ⟨*ley/promesa*⟩ to break; ⟨*contrato*⟩ to breach
■ ~ *vi* (AmL exc CS): **no me vayas a** ~ don't let me down; **incumplió a la cita** she didn't show *o* turn up

incurable *adj* incurable

indagación *f* (frml) investigation; **hacer indagaciones** to make inquiries, to investigate

indagar [A3] (frml) *vi* to investigate; ~ **SOBRE algo** to investigate sth

indecencia *f* **(a)** (cualidad) indecency **(b)** (cosa, hecho): **presentarse así en público es una** ~ it's indecent to appear in public like that

indecente *adj* ⟨*persona/vestido*⟩ indecent; ⟨*película/lenguaje*⟩ obscene
■ *mf* rude *o* shameless person

indecisión *f* indecision

indeciso -sa *adj* ⟨*persona*⟩ **(a)** [SER] indecisive **(b)** [ESTAR] undecided
■ *m,f* **(a)** (en general) indecisive person **(b)** (sobre un tema): **hay un gran número de** ~**s** there are a lot of people who are as yet undecided

indecoroso -sa *adj* unseemly, indecorous (frml)

indefenso -sa *adj* ⟨*niño/animal*⟩ defenseless*; ⟨*fortaleza*⟩ undefended

indefinido -da *adj* **(a)** ⟨*forma*⟩ undefined, vague; **un color** ~ a difficult color to describe **(b)** (ilimitado) indefinite, unlimited; **por tiempo** ~ for an indefinite *o* unlimited period

indemnización *f* **(a)** (por pérdidas sufridas) compensation, indemnity (frml); (por posibles pérdidas) indemnity (frml); ~ **por daños y perjuicios** damages (*pl*) **(b)** (por despido) severance pay

indemnizar [A4] *vt* **(a)** (por pérdidas sufridas) to compensate, indemnify (frml); (por posibles pérdidas) to indemnify (frml); **fue indemnizado con diez mil**

euros he was given ten thousand euros (in) compensation **(b)** (por despido) to pay severance pay to

independencia *f* independence

independentista *adj* ⟨*político/ideas*⟩ pro-independence (*before n*)
■ *mf* supporter of the independence movement

independiente *adj/mf* independent

independizarse [A4] *v pron* to become independent, gain independence; ~ **DE algn** to become independent OF sb

indescriptible *adj* indescribable

indestructible *adj* indestructible

indeterminado -da *adj* **(a)** (indefinido) indefinite; **por tiempo** ~ indefinitely **(b)** (no establecido) undetermined **(c)** (vago, impreciso) ⟨*contorno/forma*⟩ indeterminate **(d)** (Ling) indefinite

India *f*: **la** ~ India

indicación *f* **(a)** (instrucción) instruction; **me dio indicaciones de cómo llegar** he gave me directions as to how to get there **(b)** (muestra) indication; **no dio ninguna** ~ **de sus intenciones** she gave no indication of her intentions

indicado -da *adj* **(a)** (adecuado) suitable; **es el menos** ~ **para hacerlo** he's the last person who should do it; **lo más** ~ **sería ...** the best thing to do would be ... **(b)** (señalado) ⟨*hora/fecha*⟩ specified

indicador *m* (Auto) **(a)** *tb* ~ **de dirección** indicator **(b)** (señal de tráfico) sign **(c)** (del aceite, la gasolina) gauge; ~ **de velocidad** speedometer

indicar [A2] *vt* to indicate, show; **hay una flecha que indica el camino** there's an arrow indicating the way; **¿me podría** ~ **cómo llegar allí?** could you tell me how to get there?; **me indicó el lugar en el mapa** he showed me *o* pointed out the place on the map; **todo parece** ~ **que ...** there is every indication that ...; **el asterisco indica que ...** the asterisk indicates *o* shows that ...

indicativo *m* (Ling) indicative; **presente de** ~ present indicative

índice *m* [1] (de una publicación) index; (catálogo) catalog* [2] (Anat) index finger, forefinger [3] (tasa, coeficiente) rate; ~ **de natalidad** birth rate

indicio *m* **(a)** (señal, huella) sign, indication **(b)** (vestigio) trace, sign; ~**s de potasio** traces of potassium

Índico *adj*: **el** (Océano) ~ the Indian Ocean

indiferencia *f* indifference

indiferente *adj* **(a)** (poco importante, de poco interés): **es** ~ **que venga hoy o mañana** it doesn't matter *o* it makes no difference whether he comes today or tomorrow; **me es** ~ **su amistad** I'm not concerned *o* (colloq) bothered about his friendship **(b)** (poco interesado) indifferent; ~ **A algo** indifferent TO sth

indígena *adj* indigenous, native (*before n*)
■ *mf* native

indigestión *f* indigestion

indignación *f* indignation, anger; (más fuerte) outrage; **sentí una gran** ~ I was outraged

indignado -da *adj* indignant, angry; (más fuerte) outraged, incensed

indignante *adj* outrageous

indignar [A1] *vt* to make ... angry *o* indignant; (más fuerte) to outrage
■ **indignarse** *v pron* to get angry, become indignant; (más fuerte) to be outraged *o* incensed

indigno -na *adj* (a) (impropio) unworthy; ~ **DE algn** unworthy *o*f sb (b) (no merecedor) unworthy (c) (humillante) degrading, humiliating (d) (vergonzoso) shameful, disgraceful

indio -dia *adj* (a) (de América) (American) Indian, Amerindian (b) (de la India) Indian, of/from India
■ *m,f* (a) (de América) (American) Indian, Amerindian (b) (de la India) Indian

indirecta *f* hint; **lanzar** *or* **soltar una** ~ to drop a hint

indirecto -ta *adj* indirect

indisciplinado -da *adj* ⟨alumno⟩ undisciplined, unruly; ⟨soldado⟩ insubordinate

indiscreción *f* (a) (dicho, declaración — que molesta) indiscreet *o* tactless remark; (— que revela un secreto) indiscreet *o* unguarded remark; **¿su edad, si no es ~?** how old are you, if you don't mind my asking?; **cometió la ~ de preguntárselo** he was indiscreet *o* tactless enough to ask her (b) (cualidad) lack of discretion

indiscreto -ta *adj* (a) (falto de tacto) indiscreet, tactless (b) (que revela un secreto) indiscreet

indiscutible *adj* ⟨pruebas/hecho/verdad⟩ indisputable (b) ⟨líder/campeón⟩ undisputed

indispensable *adj* ⟨persona⟩ indispensable; ⟨objeto⟩ indispensable, essential; **lleva lo** ~ take the bare essentials

indispuesto -ta *adj* (a) (enfermo) unwell, indisposed (frml) (b) (CS euf) ⟨mujer⟩: **está indispuesta** it's the time of the month (euph)

individual *adj* (a) ⟨características/libertades⟩ individual (b) ⟨cama/habitación⟩ single (before n); **mantel** ~ place mat (c) ⟨caso⟩ one-off (before n), isolated (d) (Dep) ⟨prueba/final⟩ singles (before n)
■ *m* (Dep) singles (*pl*); ~ **femenino** women's singles

individualismo *m* individualism

individualista *adj* individualistic
■ *mf* individualist

individuo *m* (a) (persona indeterminada): **un** ~ **alto** a tall man (b) (pey) (tipo) character (colloq), individual (colloq); **ese** ~ **que iba contigo** (fam) that guy you were with (colloq)

indivisible *adj* indivisible

Indochina *f* Indo-China

índole *f* (a) (tipo, clase) kind, nature; **un problema de** ~ **afectiva** a problem of an emotional nature (b) (manera de ser) nature; **ser de buena/mala** ~ to be good-natured/ill-natured

indolente *adj* lazy, slack, indolent

indoloro -ra *adj* painless

indomable *adj* (a) ⟨animal salvaje⟩ untamable*; ⟨caballo⟩ unbreakable (b) ⟨pueblo/tribu⟩ indomitable, unconquerable; ⟨persona⟩ indomitable (c) (fam) ⟨pelo/remolino⟩ unruly, unmanageable

Indonesia *f* Indonesia

indonesio -sia *adj/m,f* Indonesian

indudable *adj* unquestionable; **es** ~ **que** ... there is no doubt that ...

indulgente *adj* (tolerante) indulgent; (para perdonar castigos) lenient; ~ **CON algn** indulgent **WITH**/lenient **TOWARD**(s) sb

indultar [A1] *vt* (Der) to pardon; (la pena de muerte) to reprieve

indulto *m* (Der) pardon; (de la pena de muerte) reprieve

indumentaria *f* clothing, clothes (*pl*), attire (frml)

industria *f* (Com, Econ) industry; ~ **del turismo** tourist industry; ~ **pesquera** fishing industry

industrial *adj* industrial
■ *mf* industrialist

industrialización *f* industrialization

industrializarse [A4] *v pron* to become industrialized

inédito -ta *adj* (a) ⟨obra/autor⟩ unpublished (b) (nuevo, sin precedente) unprecedented; **una técnica inédita en nuestro país** a technique unknown in our country

ineficacia *f* (de medida) ineffectiveness; (de método, persona) inefficiency

ineficaz *adj* (a) ⟨remedio/medida⟩ ineffectual, ineffective (b) ⟨método/sistema/persona⟩ inefficient

ineficiencia *f* inefficiency

ineficiente *adj* inefficient

inepto -ta *adj* inept, incompetent
■ *m,f* incompetent

inercia *f* (a) (Fís) inertia (b) **por** ~ (por rutina) out of habit; (por apatía) out of inertia *o* apathy

inescrutable *adj* inscrutable

inesperado -da *adj* unexpected; **de manera inesperada** unexpectedly

inestabilidad *f* instability

inestable *adj* (a) (en general) unstable (b) ⟨tiempo⟩ changeable, unsettled

inestimable *adj* ⟨ayuda⟩ invaluable

inevitable *adj* (ineludible) inevitable; ⟨cambio/conflicto/controversia⟩ unavoidable; **era** ~ **que empeorase la situación** the situation was bound to get worse

inexcusable *adj* ⟨comportamiento/error⟩ inexcusable, unforgivable; ⟨deber⟩ inescapable, unavoidable

inexistente *adj* nonexistent

inexperiencia *f* inexperience

inexperto -ta *adj* (falto de experiencia) inexperienced; (falto de habilidad) inexpert, unskilled

inexplicable *adj* inexplicable

inexpresivo -va *adj* expressionless, inexpressive

---

infalibilidad *f* infallibility

infalible *adj* ⟨persona/método⟩ infallible; ⟨puntería⟩ unerring

infancia *f* (período) childhood

infante -ta *m,f* (hijo del Rey) (*m*) prince, infante; (*f*) princess, infanta

infantería *f* infantry; ∼ **de marina** marines (*pl*), Marine Corps

infantil *adj* (a) ⟨enfermedad⟩ children's (*before n*), childhood (*before n*); ⟨literatura/programa/moda⟩ children's (*before n*); ⟨rasgos/sonrisa⟩ childlike; ⟨población⟩ child (*before n*) (b) (pey) ⟨persona/actitud/reacción⟩ childish (pej), infantile (pej)

infarto *m* heart attack

infección *f* infection

infeccioso -sa *adj* infectious

infectar [A1] *vt* to infect
■ **infectarse** *v pron* to become infected

infelicidad *f* unhappiness

infeliz *adj* (a) ⟨persona/vida⟩ unhappy (b) ⟨intervención/tentativa⟩ unfortunate
■ *mf* poor wretch, poor devil

inferior *adj* **1** (en el espacio) ⟨piso/planta⟩ lower **2** (en jerarquía) ⟨especie/rango⟩ inferior **3** (en comparaciones) lower; **temperaturas ∼es a los 10°** temperatures lower than *o* below 10°; **un número ∼ al 20** a number below twenty

inferioridad *f* inferiority

infernal *adj* ⟨ruido⟩ infernal, hideous; ⟨música⟩ diabolical; **hacía un calor ∼** it was baking hot (colloq)

infértil *adj* infertile

infertilidad *f* infertility

infestado -da *adj* ∼ **DE algo** ⟨de insectos, parásitos⟩ infested WITH sth; ∼ **de turistas** crawling with tourists

infestar [A1] *vt* to infest

infidelidad *f* infidelity, unfaithfulness

infiel *adj* (a) (desleal) unfaithful; **ser ∼ A algn/algo** to be unfaithful TO sb/sth (b) (Relig) unbelieving (*before n*), infidel (*before n*) (dated)

infiernillo *m* (Esp) kerosene stove, primus® stove (BrE)

infierno *m* (a) (en general) hell; **¡vete al ∼!** (fam) go to hell! (sl); **su vida es un ∼** her life is hell (b) (fam) (lugar — ruidoso) madhouse (colloq), bedlam (colloq); (— horrendo) hellhole (colloq)

infílder *mf* (Col, Ven) infielder

infiltración *f* infiltration

infiltrado -da *m,f* infiltrator

infiltrar [A1] *vt* to infiltrate; ∼ **a algn EN algo** to infiltrate sb INTO sth
■ **infiltrarse** *v pron* to infiltrate; ∼**se EN algo** ⟨en partido/organización⟩ to infiltrate sth

infinidad *f* (gran cantidad): **en ∼ de ocasiones** on countless occasions; ∼ **de veces** innumerable *o* countless times

infinitivo *m* infinitive

infinito¹ -ta *adj* (a) (Fil, Mat) infinite (b) ⟨bondad/sabiduría⟩ infinite; ⟨amor⟩ boundless (c) (delante del n, en pl) (innumerables) innumerable, countless

infinito² -m (a) **el ∼** (Fil) the infinite; **mirar al ∼** to look into the distance (b) (Mat) infinity

inflación *f* inflation

inflador *m* (Bol, Per, RPl) bicycle pump

inflamable *adj* flammable, inflammable

inflamación *f* (Med) inflammation; (Quím) ignition

inflamar [A1] *vt* (a) (Med) to inflame (b) (Quím) to ignite, set ... on fire
■ **inflamarse** *v pron* (a) (Med) to become inflamed (b) (Quím) to ignite

inflar [A1] *vt* (a) ⟨balón/rueda⟩ to inflate; ⟨globo⟩ to blow up (b) ⟨noticia/acontecimiento⟩ to exaggerate
■ **inflarse** *v pron* «velas» to swell, fill

inflexible *adj* inflexible; **se mostró ∼** he refused to give in

inflexión *f* inflection

influencia *f* **1** (influjo) influence; **bajo la ∼ del alcohol** under the influence of alcohol; ∼ **EN** *or* **SOBRE algo** influence ON *o* UPON sth; ∼ **SOBRE algn** influence ON sb **2** **influencias** *fpl* (contactos) contacts (*pl*)

influenciable *adj* easily influenced

influenciar [A1] *vt* to influence

influir [I20] *vi* ∼ **EN algo/algn** to influence sth/sb, have an influence ON sth/sb
■ ∼ *vt* to influence

influyente *adj* influential

infografía *f* computer graphics

información *f* **1** (a) (datos, detalles) information; **el mostrador de ∼** the information desk (b) (Telec) information (AmE), directory enquiries (BrE) **2** (Period, Rad, TV) news; **la ∼ internacional** the foreign news **3** (Inf) data (*pl*)

informado -da *adj* (sobre tema, noticia) informed; **está usted muy mal informada** you have been misinformed *o* wrongly informed; **fuentes bien informadas** reliable sources

informal *adj* **1** (a) ⟨persona⟩ unreliable (b) ⟨ropa/estilo⟩ informal, casual; ⟨cena/ambiente⟩ informal (c) (no oficial) ⟨reunión⟩ informal **2** (AmL) ⟨economía/sector⟩ black (*before n*), informal (*before n*)

informar [A1] *vt* ⟨persona/prensa⟩ to inform; **te han informado mal** you've been misinformed; **¿podría ∼me sobre los cursos de idiomas?** could you give me some information about language courses?
■ ∼ *vi* (dar noticias, información) to report; ∼ **SOBRE algo** to report ON sth, give a report ON sth; ∼ **DE algo** to announce sth
■ **informarse** *v pron* to get information; ∼**se SOBRE algo** to find out *o* inquire ABOUT sth

informática *f* computer science, computing

informático -ca *adj* computer (*before n*)

informativo -va *adj* (a) ⟨servicios/campaña⟩ information (*before n*); **programa ∼** news program*; (b) (instructivo) informative

informatizar [A4] *vt* to computerize

informe *m* **1** (exposición, dictamen) report; ∼ **médico** medical report **2** **informes** *mpl* (a) (datos) information, particulars (*pl*) (b) (de empleado) reference, references (*pl*); **pedir ∼s** to ask for a reference/for references

infovía *f* information highway

infracción *f* offense*, infraction (fml); ∼ **de tráfico** traffic violation (AmE), driving offence (BrE)

infractor -tora *m,f* offender

infraestructura *f* infrastructure

in fraganti *loc adv* red-handed

infrarrojo -ja *adj* infrared

infringir [I7] *vt* to infringe, break

ínfulas *fpl*: **darse** *or* **tener muchas** ∼ to put on *o* give oneself airs

infundado -da *adj* unfounded, groundless

infundir [I1] *vt* ‹*confianza/respeto*› to inspire; ‹*sospechas*› to arouse; **les infundía miedo** it filled them with fear; **para** ∼**les ánimo** to give them encouragement

infusión *f* infusion; ∼ **de manzanilla** chamomile tea

ingeniar [A1] *vt* ‹*método/sistema*› to devise, think up; **ingeniárselas** (fam): **se las ingenió para arreglarlo** he managed to fix it

ingeniería *f* engineering; ∼ **civil** civil engineering

ingeniero -ra *m,f* engineer; ∼ **agrónomo** agriculturist; ∼ **civil/industrial** civil/industrial engineer; ∼ **técnico** engineer (*qualified after a three-year university course*)

ingenio *m* **1** (a) (talento) ingenuity, inventiveness; **aguzar el** ∼ to rack one's brains (b) (chispa, agudeza) wit **2** (aparato) device **3** (AmL) (refinería) *tb* ∼ **azucarero** sugar refinery

ingenioso -sa *adj* (a) (lúcido) ‹*persona/idea*› clever, ingenious (b) (con chispa, agudeza) ‹*persona/dicho/chiste*› witty (c) ‹*aparato/invención*› ingenious

ingenuidad *f* naivety, ingenuousness

ingenuo -nua *adj* naive, ingenuous ∎ *m,f*: **es un** ∼ he's so naive

Inglaterra *f* England

ingle *f* groin

inglés¹ -glesa *adj* (a) (de Inglaterra) English (b) (crit) (británico) British, English (crit) ∎ *m,f* (a) (de Inglaterra) (*m*) Englishman; (*f*) Englishwoman; **los ingleses** the English, English people (b) (crit) ▶ BRITÁNICO

inglés² *m* (idioma) English

ingratitud *f* ingratitude

ingrato -ta *adj* (a) (desagradecido) ‹*persona*› ungrateful; ∼ **con ella** ungrateful to her (b) (desagradable, difícil) ‹*vida*› hard; ‹*trabajo/tarea*› unrewarding ∎ *m,f* ungrateful wretch (*o* swine *etc*) (colloq), ingrate (liter)

ingrediente *m* ingredient

ingresar [A1] *vi* **1** «*persona*» (en organización, club) to join; (en colegio) to enter; (en el ejército) to join; **después de** ∼ **en el hospital** after being admitted to (the) hospital; **ingresó cadáver** (Esp) he was dead on arrival **2** ‹*dinero*› to come in ∎ ∼ *vt* **1** ‹*persona*› (en hospital): **el médico decidió** ∼**lo** the doctor decided to send him to hospital; **hubo que** ∼**lo de urgencia** he had to be admitted as a matter of urgency; **fueron ingresados en esta prisión** they were taken to this prison **2** (Esp) (Fin) ‹*dinero/cheque*› to pay in; ∼ **una cantidad en una cuenta** «*persona*» to pay a sum into an account; «*banco*» to credit an account with a sum

ingreso *m* **1** (a) (en organización): **el año de mi** ∼ **a** *or* **en la universidad/el ejército/la compañía** the year I entered university/joined the army/joined the company; **examen de** ∼ entrance examination (b) (en hospital) admission **2** (Fin) (a) (Esp) (depósito) deposit (b) **ingresos** *mpl* (ganancias) income; ∼**s brutos/netos** gross/net income

íngrimo -ma *adj* (Col, Méx, Ven fam) (a) (sin compañía) all alone, all by oneself (b) ‹*lugar*› lonely, deserted

inhábil *adj* (a) (torpe) unskillful*, clumsy (b) (no apto) ∼ **PARA algo** unsuited to sth

inhabitado -da *adj* uninhabited

inhalación *f* inhalation; **hacer inhalaciones** to inhale; ∼ **de pegamento** *or* (Méx) **cemento** glue sniffing

inhalador *m* inhaler

inhalar [A1] *vt* to inhale; ‹*pegamento*› to sniff

inhibición *f* inhibition

inhibir [I1] *vt* to inhibit ∎ **inhibirse** *v pron* to become inhibited

inhóspito -ta *adj* inhospitable

inhumano -na *adj* (a) (falto de compasión) inhumane (b) (cruel) inhuman

iniciación *f* (a) (fml) (comienzo) beginning, start (b) (introducción) introduction; **curso de** ∼ introductory course (c) (a una secta) initiation

inicial *adj* initial ∎ *f* (a) (letra) initial (b) (en béisbol) first base

iniciar [A1] *vt* (a) (fml) ‹*curso/viaje*› to begin, commence (fml); ‹*negociaciones/diligencias*› to initiate, commence (fml) (b) ∼ **a algn EN algo** ‹*en secta*› to initiate sb INTO sth; ‹*en un arte*› to introduce sb TO sth ∎ **iniciarse** *v pron* (a) «*ceremonia/ negociaciones*» to begin, commence (fml) (b) «*persona*» ∼**se EN algo** ‹*en secta*› to be initiated INTO sth; ‹*en un arte*› to take one's first steps IN sth

iniciativa *f* initiative; **tomó la** ∼ he took the initiative

inicio *m* beginning, start

inigualable *adj* ‹*belleza*› matchless, incomparable; ‹*precios/oferta*› unbeatable

ininteligible *adj* unintelligible, incomprehensible

ininterrumpido -da *adj* ‹*lluvias/trabajo*› continuous, uninterrupted; ‹*sueño*› uninterrupted; ‹*línea*› continuous

injertar [A1] *vt* to graft

injerto *m* (a) (Agr) (acción) grafting; (tallo) graft, scion (b) (Med) graft

injusticia *f* (a) (acto injusto) injustice, act of injustice; **es una** ∼ **que te hayan dicho eso** it's unfair of them to have said that to you (b) (cualidad) unfairness, injustice

injustificable *adj* unjustifiable

injustificado -da *adj* unwarranted, unjustified; **despido** ∼ unfair dismissal

injusto -ta *adj* unfair; **ser** ∼ **CON algn** to be unfair TO *o* ON sb

inmaculado -da *adj* **(a)** ⟨*presentación/vestido/ superficie*⟩ immaculate **(b)** ⟨*fama*⟩ impeccable

inmadurez *f* immaturity, lack of maturity

inmaduro -ra *adj* ⟨*persona/animal*⟩ immature; ⟨*fruta*⟩ unripe

inmediaciones *fpl* vicinity, surrounding area; **el hotel está en las ∼ del aeropuerto** the hotel is in the vicinity of the airport; **en las ∼ de la capital** in the area around the capital

inmediatamente *adv* immediately

inmediato -ta *adj* **(a)** ⟨*efecto/respuesta*⟩ immediate; **de ∼** immediately, right away, straightaway (BrE) **(b)** ⟨*zona*⟩ immediate; ⟨*lugar/ pueblo*⟩ **∼ A algo** close TO sth

inmejorable *adj* ⟨*resultados/posición*⟩ excellent, unbeatable; **está en una situación ∼** it is superbly located

inmenso -sa *adj* ⟨*fortuna/cantidad*⟩ immense, vast, huge; ⟨*casa/camión*⟩ huge, enormous; ⟨*alegría/pena*⟩ great, immense; **¡es ∼!** it's absolutely huge!

inmerecido -da *adj* undeserved, unmerited

inmerso -sa *adj* ⟨*submarino/buzo*⟩ submerged; ⟨*objeto*⟩ immersed

inmigración *f* immigration

inmigrante *mf* immigrant

inmigrar [A1] *vi* to immigrate

inmiscuirse [I20] *v pron* **∼ EN algo** to interfere IN sth, meddle IN sth

inmobiliaria *f* **(a)** (agencia) real estate agency (AmE), estate agent's (BrE) **(b)** (empresa propietaria) real estate company (AmE), property company (BrE) **(c)** (empresa constructora) property developer

inmoral *adj* immoral
■ *mf*: **eres un ∼** you have no morals

inmoralidad *f* immorality

inmortal *adj/mf* immortal

inmortalidad *f* immortality

inmortalizar [A4] *vt* to immortalize
■ **inmortalizarse** *v pron* to achieve immortality, be immortalized

inmovible *adj* immovable

inmóvil *adj* still

inmovilismo *m* resistance to change, immobilism (frml)

inmovilizar [A4] *vt* **1** ⟨*persona/país/vehículo*⟩ to immobilize **2** (Com, Fin) ⟨*capital*⟩ to tie up

inmundo -da *adj* **(a)** ⟨*lugar*⟩ filthy **(b)** ⟨*sabor/ comida*⟩ foul, disgusting **(c)** (repulsivo) ⟨*escena/ película*⟩ filthy, disgusting

inmune *adj* immune; **∼ A algo** immune TO sth

inmunidad *f* immunity

inmunizar [A4] *vt* to immunize; **∼ a algn CONTRA algo** to immunize sb against sth

inmunodeficiencia *f* immunodeficiency

inmunológico -ca *adj* ⟨*tolerancia*⟩ immunological; ⟨*sistema/reacción*⟩ immune (before n)

inmutarse [A1] *v pron* «*persona*»: **cuando se lo dije ni se inmutó** she didn't bat an eyelash *o* (BrE) eyelid when I told her (colloq); **lo escuchó sin ∼se** she listened to him unperturbed

innato -ta *adj* innate, inborn

innavegable *adj* ⟨*río*⟩ unnavigable; ⟨*embarcación*⟩ unseaworthy

innecesario -ria *adj* unnecessary

innegable *adj* undeniable

innovación *f* innovation

innovador -dora *adj* innovative
■ *m,f* innovator

innovar [A1] *vi* to innovate

innumerable *adj* innumerable

inocencia *f* innocence

inocentada *f* ≈ April Fools' joke (*played on 28 December*); **gastarle** *or* **hacerle ∼s a algn** to play practical jokes on sb

inocente *adj* **(a)** (sin culpa) innocent; (Der) innocent, not guilty; **lo declararon ∼** he was found not guilty **(b)** ⟨*broma*⟩ harmless **(c)** (ingenuo) naive, gullible
■ *mf* innocent; **no te hagas el ∼** don't play the innocent

inodoro *m* **(a)** (wáter) toilet, lavatory **(b)** (taza) bowl, pan

inofensivo -va *adj* harmless, inoffensive

inolvidable *adj* unforgettable

inoportuno -na *adj* **(a)** ⟨*visita/llamada*⟩ untimely, inopportune; **llamó en un momento ∼** he phoned at a bad moment **(b)** ⟨*comentario/ crítica*⟩ ill-timed, inopportune

inquebrantable *adj* ⟨*fe*⟩ unshakable, unyielding; ⟨*lealtad*⟩ unswerving; ⟨*voluntad/ salud*⟩ iron (before n)

inquietante *adj* ⟨*noticia/cifras*⟩ disturbing, worrying; ⟨*síntoma*⟩ worrying

inquietarse [A1] *v pron* to worry; **∼ POR algo/algn** to worry ABOUT sth/sb

inquieto -ta *adj* **(a)** [ESTAR] (preocupado) worried **(b)** [SER] (emprendedor) enterprising; (vivo) lively, inquiring (before n) **(c)** (que se mueve mucho) restless

inquietud *f* **(a)** (preocupación) worry; **∼ POR algo** concern ABOUT sth **(b)** (interés): **es una persona sin ∼es** she has no interest in anything; **su ∼ filosófica** his philosophical preoccupations

inquilino -na *m,f* (arrendatario) tenant

Inquisición *f* (Hist): **la ∼** the Inquisition

inquisidor *m* inquisitor

insaciable *adj* insatiable; ⟨*sed*⟩ unquenchable

insalubre *adj* unhealthy

insalvable *adj* insurmountable, insuperable

insatisfacción *f* dissatisfaction

insatisfactorio -ria *adj* unsatisfactory

insatisfecho -cha *adj* **(a)** (descontento) dissatisfied; **∼ CON algo/algn** dissatisfied WITH sth/sb **(b)** ⟨*hambre/deseo*⟩ unsatisfied

inscribir [I34] *vt* (en registro) to register; (en curso, escuela) to register, enroll*
■ **inscribirse** *v pron* «*persona*» (en curso, colegio) to enroll*, register; (en concurso) to enter; (en congreso) to register

inscripción *f* **(a)** (para curso) enrollment*, registration; (para concurso) entry; (en congreso) registration; **la ∼ se cierra el ...** the last day for enrollment is ... **(b)** (de un nacimiento) registration **(c)** (leyenda, lema) inscription

inscrito -ta, (RPl) **inscripto -ta** *pp*: ▶ INSCRIBIR

insecticida *m* insecticide

insecto *m* insect

inseguridad *f* **(a)** (falta de confianza) insecurity **(b)** (falta de firmeza, estabilidad) unsteadiness **(c)** (falta de garantías) insecurity, lack of security **(d)** (en ciudad, barrio): **la ~ ciudadana** the lack of safety on our streets

inseguro -ra *adj* **(a)** (falto de confianza) insecure **(b)** (falto de firmeza, estabilidad) unsteady **(c)** ‹*situación/futuro*› insecure **(d)** ‹*ciudad/barrio*› unsafe, dangerous

inseminación *f* insemination; **~ artificial** artificial insemination

insensatez *f* **(a)** (cualidad) foolishness, senselessness **(b)** (dicho, hecho): **lo que has dicho/ hecho es una ~** that was a stupid thing to say/do

insensato -ta *adj* foolish
■ *m,f* fool

insensible *adj* insensitive; **~ al frío** insensitive to the cold

inseparable *adj* inseparable

insertar [A1] *vt* to insert

inservible *adj* (inútil) useless; (inutilizable) unusable

insignia *f* **(a)** (distintivo, emblema) insignia, emblem; (prendedor) badge, button (AmE) **(b)** (bandera) flag; (estandarte) standard, banner

insignificante *adj* ‹*asunto/detalle/suma*› insignificant, trivial; ‹*objeto/regalo*› small; ‹*persona*› insignificant

insinuación *f* hint; (que ofende) insinuation; **hacerle insinuaciones (amorosas) a algn** ▶ INSINUARSE

insinuante *adj* ‹*mirada/voz*› suggestive; ‹*escote*› provocative

insinuar [A18] *vt* to imply, hint at; (algo ofensivo) to insinuate
■ **insinuarse** *v pron*: **insinuársele a algn** to make advances to sb, to make a pass at sb

insípido -da *adj* insipid, bland

insistencia *f* insistence; **con ~** insistently

insistente *adj* ‹*persona*› insistent; ‹*recomendaciones/pedidos*› repeated (*before n*), persistent; ‹*timbrazos*› insistent, repeated (*before n*)

insistir [I1] *vi* to insist; **ya que insistes** if you insist; **es inútil que insistas** there's no point going on about it; **~ EN hacer algo** to insist ON doing sth; **insiste en que lo hagamos** he insists (that) we do it; **insiste en que es suyo** she is adamant that it's hers; **~ SOBRE** *or* **EN algo** to stress sth

insociable *adj* unsociable

insolación *f* (Med) sunstroke; **agarrar una ~** to get sunstroke

insolencia *f* **(a)** (cualidad) insolence **(b)** (dicho): **no pienso tolerar sus ~s** I don't intend putting up with his insolence *o* his insolent behavior; **contestarle así fue una ~** it was very rude of you to answer him like that

insolente *adj* rude, insolent
■ *mf*: **es una ~** she's so rude *o* insolent

insólito -ta *adj* unusual

insolvencia *f* insolvency

insolvente *adj* insolvent

insomnio *m* insomnia

insonorizado -da *adj* soundproof

insoportable *adj* unbearable, intolerable

insostenible *adj* **(a)** ‹*situación/gasto*› unsustainable **(b)** ‹*posición/tesis*› untenable

inspección *f* inspection

inspeccionar [A1] *vt* to inspect

inspector -tora *m,f* inspector; **~ de Hacienda** revenue agent (AmE), tax inspector (BrE); **~ de policía** (police) inspector

inspiración *f* (Art, Lit, Mús) inspiration

inspirado -da *adj* inspired

inspirar [A1] *vt* ① ‹*confianza*› to inspire; ‹*compasión*› to arouse, inspire; **sabe ~les confianza** she knows how to inspire confidence in them ② «*obra/canción/persona*» to inspire
■ **inspirarse** *v pron* **~se EN algo** «*persona/obra/ ley*» to be inspired BY sth

instalación *f* **(a)** (colocación) installation **(b)** (equipo, dispositivo) system; **la ~ sanitaria** the plumbing **(c)** **instalaciones** *fpl* (dependencias) installations (*pl*); **instalaciones deportivas** sports facilities

instalar [A1] *vt* **(a)** (colocar y conectar) ‹*teléfono/ lavaplatos*› to install; ‹*antena*› to erect, put up; (Inf) ‹*programa*› to install **(b)** (colocar) ‹*archivador/piano*› to put **(c)** ‹*oficina/consultorio*› to open, set up
■ **instalarse** *v pron* to settle, install oneself

instantánea *f* snapshot

instantáneo -nea *adj* **(a)** ‹*resultado/crédito*› instant (*before n*); ‹*reacción*› instantaneous, immediate **(b)** ‹*café*› instant (*before n*)

instante *m* moment; **un ~, por favor** just a second *o* moment, please; **me llama a cada ~** he calls me all the time; **al ~** right away, straightaway (BrE)

instigar [A3] *vt* **~ a algn A algo/hacer algo** to incite sb TO sth/do sth

instintivo -va *adj* instinctive

instinto *m* instinct; **por ~** instinctively; **~ de conservación** survival instinct

institución *f* institution

instituto *m* institute; **~ nacional de bachillerato** (Esp) high school (AmE), secondary school (BrE)

institutriz *f* governess

instrucción *f* ① (educación) education; (práctica) training; **~ militar** military training ② **instrucciones** *fpl* **(a)** (de aparato, juego) instructions (*pl*); (para llegar a un lugar) directions (*pl*) **(b)** (órdenes) instructions

instructor -tora *m,f* instructor

instruir [I20] *vt* (adiestrar, educar) **~ a algn EN algo** to instruct *o* train sb IN sth
■ **instruirse** *v pron* (refl) to broaden one's mind, improve oneself

instrumental *adj* (Mús) instrumental

AmC	Central America	Arg	Argentina	Cu	Cuba	Per	Peru
AmL	Latin America	Bol	Bolivia	Ec	Ecuador	RPI	River Plate Area
AmS	South America	Chi	Chile	Esp	Spain	Ur	Uruguay
Andes	Andean Region	CS	Southern Cone	Méx	Mexico	Ven	Venezuela

■ *m* (Med) equipment, set of instruments

instrumentar *vt* [A1] (Mús) to orchestrate

instrumento *m* **1** (en general) instrument; ~ **de cuerda** string instrument; ~**s de precisión** precision instruments **2** (medio) means

insubordinación *f* insubordination

insubordinarse [A1] *v pron* ~ (CONTRA algn) (desobedecer) to be insubordinate (TO sb); (sublevarse) to rebel (AGAINST sb)

insuficiencia *f* (escasez): ~ **de medios** lack of resources; ~ **de personal** staff shortage

insuficiente *adj* (a) ⟨medios/cantidad⟩ inadequate, insufficient (b) (Educ) ⟨trabajo⟩ poor, unsatisfactory
■ *m* (Esp) fail

insular *adj* insular

insulina *f* insulin

insulso -sa *adj* (a) ⟨comida⟩ insipid, tasteless (b) ⟨persona⟩ insipid, dull; ⟨conversación/libro⟩ dull

insultante *adj* insulting

insultar [A1] *vt* (a) (proferir insultos) to insult (b) (ofender) to insult, offend

insulto *m* insult

insumiso -sa *m,f*: person refusing to do military service

insumos *mpl* (esp AmL) consumables (*pl*)

insuperable *adj* (a) (insalvable) ⟨problema/dificultad⟩ insurmountable, insuperable (b) (inmejorable) ⟨calidad/precio⟩ unbeatable

insurgente *mf* (frml) rebel, insurgent (frml)

insurrección *f* (frml) uprising, insurrection (frml)

intachable *adj* impeccable, irreproachable

intacto -ta *adj* (íntegro, no dañado) intact

integración *f* integration

integrado -da *adj* integrated

integral *adj* (a) (completo, total) comprehensive (b) (incorporado) built-in

integrante *mf* member

integrar [A1] *vt* **1** (formar) ⟨grupo/organización⟩ to make up **2** (incorporar) ⟨idea/plan⟩ to incorporate **3** (Mat, Sociol) to integrate **4** (CS) ⟨suma/cantidad⟩ to pay
■ **integrarse** *v pron* (a) (asimilarse) to integrate, fit in; ~**se A** *or* **EN algo** to integrate INTO sth, fit INTO sth (b) (unirse) ~**se A** *or* **EN algo** to join sth

integridad *f* integrity

íntegro -gra *adj* **1** ⟨texto⟩ unabridged; **se proyectó en versión íntegra** they screened the full-length version **2** ⟨persona⟩ upright

intelecto *m* intellect

intelectual *adj/mf* intellectual

inteligencia *f* **1** (a) (facultad, ser inteligente) intelligence (b) (comprensión) understanding **2** (Mil, Pol) intelligence

inteligente *adj* intelligent; ⟨persona⟩ intelligent, clever

inteligible *adj* intelligible

intemperie *f*: **pasar la noche a la** ~ to spend the night out in the open; **gente sin hogar que duerme a la** ~ people who sleep rough

intención *f* intention; **no fue mi** ~ **ofenderte** I didn't mean to offend you; **tiene buenas/malas intenciones** she's well-intentioned/up to no good;

lo dijo con segunda *or* **doble** ~ she had an ulterior motive for saying it; **con la mejor** ~ with the best of intentions; **lo que cuenta es la** ~ it's the thought that counts; **vine con (la)** ~ **de ayudarte** I came to help you; **tiene (la)** ~ **de abrir un bar** she plans *o* intends to open a bar; **no tengo la menor** ~ **de venderlo** I have no intention whatsoever of selling it

intencionado -da *adj* (hecho a propósito) deliberate, intentional; **mal** ~ malicious, hostile; **bien** ~ well-intentioned

intendencia *f* (a) (Andes) (división territorial) administrative division (b) (RPl) (gobierno municipal) town/city council; (edificio) town/city hall

intendente *mf* (a) (Andes) governor (b) (RPl) mayor

intensidad *f* (a) (de terremoto) intensity, strength; (del viento) strength; (de dolor, sentimiento) intensity (b) (Elec, Fís) intensity

intensivo -va *adj* intensive

intenso -sa *adj* (a) ⟨frío/luz/color⟩ intense (b) ⟨emoción/mirada⟩ intense; ⟨dolor/sentimiento⟩ intense, acute (c) ⟨esfuerzo⟩ strenuous; ⟨negociaciones⟩ intensive

intentar [A1] *vt* to try; **¡inténtalo otra vez!** try again!; ~ **un aterrizaje de emergencia** to attempt an emergency landing; ~ **hacer algo** to try to do sth; **¿has intentado que te lo arreglen?** have you tried getting *o* to get it fixed?

intento *m* (a) (tentativa) attempt (b) (Méx) (propósito) intention, aim

intercalar [A1] *vt* ~ **algo EN algo** ⟨en texto⟩ to insert sth INTO sth; **intercaló algunas citas en su discurso** she interspersed her speech with some quotations; **intercala uno rojo cada dos azules** put a red one between every two blue ones

intercambiable *adj* interchangeable

intercambiar [A1] *vt* ⟨impresiones/ideas⟩ to exchange; ⟨sellos/revistas⟩ to swap

intercambio *m* (a) (de ideas, información, bienes) exchange (b) (de sellos, revistas) swap; (de estudiantes, prisioneros) exchange

interceder [E1] *vi* (frml) to intercede; **intercedió por ellos ante el rey** he interceded for them with the king

interceptar [A1] *vt* (a) ⟨correspondencia/mensaje⟩ to intercept (b) ⟨teléfono⟩ to tap (c) (Dep) ⟨balón/pase⟩ to intercept; ⟨golpe⟩ to block (d) ⟨calzada/carretera⟩ to block; ~ **el paso** to block the way

intercomunicar [A2] *vt* to link (up)

interés *m* **1** (en general) interest; **de** ~ **turístico** of interest to tourists; **pon más** ~ **en tus estudios** take more interest in your schoolwork; **tengo especial** ~ **en que ...** I am particularly concerned *o* keen that ...; **tienen gran** ~ **en verlo** they are very interested in seeing it; **por tu propio** ~ in your own interest, for your own good; **actúa solo por** ~ he acts purely in his own interest *o* out of self-interest; **conflicto de intereses** conflict of interests
2 (Fin) interest; **a** *or* **con un** ~ **del 12%** at 12% interest *o* at an interest rate of 12%; **ganar intereses** to earn interest; **tipo de** ~ rate of interest

interesado -da *adj* (a) [ESTAR] (que muestra   ···⟶

interés) interested; **∼ EN algo** interested IN sth **(b)** [SER] (egoísta) selfish; **actuó de manera interesada** he acted selfishly **(c)** (parcial) biased, biassed
■ *m,f* **(a)** (que tiene interés) interested party (frml); **los ∼s deberán …** all those interested *o* (frml) all interested parties should … **(b)** (que busca su provecho): **es un ∼** he always acts in his own interest *o* out of self-interest

interesante *adj* interesting; **hacerse el ∼** (fam) to try to draw attention to oneself

interesar [A1] *vi* **(a)** (suscitar interés): (+ *me/te/le etc*) **no me interesa la política** I'm not interested in politics; **esto a ti no te interesa** this doesn't concern you, this is no concern of yours **(b)** (convenir): **∼ía comprobar los datos** it would be useful/advisable to check the data; **me interesa este tipo de préstamo** this sort of loan would suit me
■ **∼** *vt* **∼ a algn EN algo** to interest sb IN sth, get sb interested IN sth
■ **interesarse** *v pron* **(a)** (tener interés) to take interest; **∼se EN** *or* **POR algo** to take an interest IN sth **(b)** (preguntar) **∼se POR algo/algn** to ask *o* inquire ABOUT sth/sb

interferencia *f* interference

interferir [I11] *vt* **(a)** (obstaculizar) to interfere in **(b)** (emisión) to jam
■ **∼** *vi* to interfere, meddle; **∼ EN algo** (en asunto) to interfere *o* meddle IN sth
■ **interferirse** *v pron* **∼se EN algo** to interfere *o* meddle IN sth

interfono *m* **(a)** (portero automático) intercom (AmE), entryphone (BrE); (intercomunicador) intercom **(b)** (para bebés) baby alarm

interinato *m* (esp AmL) (cargo) temporary post *o* position

interino -na *adj* (secretario/director) acting (before *n*), (profesor) substitute (AmE) (before *n*), supply (BrE) (before *n*); (gobierno) interim (before *n*); **médico ∼** locum
■ *m,f* (funcionario) temporary clerk (*o* accountant *etc*); (profesor) substitute teacher (AmE), supply teacher (BrE); (médico) locum

interior *adj* **(a)** (patio/escalera) interior, internal, inside (before *n*); (habitación/piso) with windows facing onto a central staircase *o* patio **(b)** (bolsillo/revestimiento) inside (before *n*); **en la parte ∼** inside *o* on the inside **(c)** (vida/mundo) inner **(d)** (política/comercio) domestic, internal
■ *m* **1** **(a)** (de cajón, maleta, coche) inside; (de edificio) interior, inside; (de un país) interior; **en el ∼ de la habitación** inside the room **(b)** (Méx, RPl, Ven) (provincias) provinces (*pl*) **(c)** (de una persona): **en su ∼ estaba muy intranquilo** inside he was very worried; **allá en su ∼ la amaba** deep down he really loved her
2 Interior *m* (period) (Ministerio del Interior) Ministry of the Interior, ≈ Department of the Interior (in US), ≈ Home Office (in UK)
3 interiores *mpl* (Col, Ven) (Indum) underwear

interjección *f* interjection

intermediario -ria *adj* intermediary
■ *m,f* **(a)** (Com) middleman, intermediary **(b)** (mediador) intermediary, mediator, go-between

intermedio¹ -dia *adj* **(a)** (punto/etapa) intermediate; **alumnos de nivel ∼** students at

intermediate level **(b)** (calidad/tamaño) medium (before *n*); **un color ∼ entre el gris y el verde** a color halfway between gray and green

intermedio² *m* (Espec) intermission, interval

interminable *adj* (serie/discusión/espera) interminable, never-ending; (cola/fila) endless, never-ending

intermitente *adj* **(a)** (lluvia) intermittent, sporadic **(b)** (luz) flashing; (señal) intermittent **(c)** (fiebre) intermittent
■ *m* turn signal (AmE), indicator (BrE)

internacional *adj* international; (noticia) foreign (before *n*), international (before *n*); (política) foreign (before *n*); **de fama ∼** internationally famous; **S salidas internacionales** international departures

internado¹ -da *adj* (AmL): **está ∼** he's been admitted to (the) hospital, he's been hospitalized

internado² *m* **(a)** (Educ) boarding school **(b)** (Med) position or term as an intern *or* a houseman *at a* hospital, internship (AmE)

internar [A1] *vt*: **la ∼on en un manicomio** she was put in an asylum; **lo ∼on en el hospital** he was admitted to (the) hospital; **tuvimos que ∼lo** we had to take him to (the) hospital
■ **internarse** *v pron* **(a)** (adentrarse) **∼se EN algo** (en bosque/espesura) to penetrate INTO sth, to go deep INTO sth **(b)** (AmL) (en hospital) to go into the hospital

internauta *mf* Internet user

Internet /inter'ne/ *m* (a veces *f*): **(el) ∼** the Internet

interno¹ -na *adj* **1** (en general) internal **2** **(a)** (Educ): **está ∼ en un colegio inglés** he is a boarder at an English school **(b)** (Med): **médico ∼** ≈ intern (in US), ≈ houseman (in UK)
■ *m,f* **(a)** (Educ) boarder **(b)** (en cárcel) inmate **(c)** (médico) ≈ intern (in US), ≈ houseman (in UK)

interno² *m* (RPl) (Telec) (extensión) extension

interponerse [E22] *v pron*: **se interpuso y paró la pelea** he stepped in and stopped the fight; **nada se interpone en su camino** nothing stands in her way

interpretación *f* **(a)** (de un texto) interpretation **(b)** (Cin, Mús, Teat) interpretation **(c)** (traducción oral) interpreting; **∼ simultánea** simultaneous interpreting

interpretar [A1] *vt* **1** (texto/comentario/ sueño) to interpret; **interpretó mal tus palabras** she misinterpreted what you said **2** **(a)** (papel/ personaje) to play **(b)** (pieza/sinfonía) to play, perform; (canción) to sing

intérprete *mf* **1** (traductor oral) interpreter; **∼ jurado** sworn interpreter **2** (Mús) performer; (cantante) singer

interpuesto -ta *pp*: ▶ INTERPONERSE

interrogación *f* **(a)** (de un sospechoso) interrogation **(b)** (Chi) (Educ) test

interrogar [A3] *vt* (testigo/acusado) to question, examine; (detenido/sospechoso) to interrogate, question; (examinado) to examine

interrogatorio *m* (de acusado, testigo) questioning, examination; (de detenido) interrogation, questioning

interrumpir [I1] *vt* **1** (temporalmente) **(a)** (persona/reunión) to interrupt **(b)** (suministro) to cut off; (servicio) to suspend; (tráfico) to hold up;

las obras no ∼án el paso the work will not block
the road **2** (a) (acortar) ⟨viaje/vacaciones/
reunión⟩ to cut short (b) ⟨embarazo⟩ to terminate
■ ∼ vi to interrupt

interrupción f interruption; ∼ (voluntaria)
del embarazo termination of pregnancy

interruptor m switch

intersección f (a) (en geometría) intersection
(b) (frml) (Transp) intersection, junction

intertanto m: en el ∼ (AmL) in the meantime

interurbano -na adj ⟨transporte/autobús/
llamada⟩ long-distance; ⟨tren⟩ intercity

intervalo m (a) (de tiempo) interval; (entre
clases) recess (AmE), break (BrE) (b) (Mús) interval
(c) (Teatr) (intermedio) intermission (AmE), interval
(BrE) (d) (en el espacio) gap

intervención f (a) (en general) intervention;
se probó su ∼ en el atraco his involvement in
the robbery was proved; una política de no ∼ a
policy of nonintervention; ∼ quirúrgica operation
(b) (de droga, armas) seizure, confiscation

intervenir [I31] vi (a) (en debate, operación) to
take part; (en espectáculo) to appear, perform (b)
(mediar) to intervene, intercede (frml); en mi
decisión intervinieron muchos factores there were
many factors involved in my decision; ∼ en una
pelea to intervene o step in to stop a fight;
(involucrarse) to get involved in a fight
■ ∼ vt **1** (a) ⟨teléfono⟩ to tap (b) (tomar control de)
⟨empresa⟩ to place ... in administration (c)
(inspeccionar) ⟨cuentas⟩ to audit, inspect (d)
⟨armas/droga⟩ to seize, confiscate
2 (operar) to operate on; fue intervenido en una
clínica privada he underwent surgery in a private
clinic

interviú f interview

intestinal adj intestinal

intestino m intestine, gut

inti m inti (former Peruvian unit of currency)

intimar [A1] vi ∼ CON algn to get close TO sb

intimidación f intimidation

intimidad f **1** (a) (ambiente privado) privacy; en
la ∼ del hogar in the privacy of one's home (b)
(relación estrecha) intimacy **2** intimidades fpl
(a) (cosas íntimas) private life, personal o private
affairs (pl) (b) (euf) (partes pudendas) private parts
(pl), privates (pl) (colloq)

intimidante adj intimidating

intimidar [A1] vt (a) (atemorizar) to intimidate
(b) (amenazar) to threaten

íntimo -ma adj (a) ⟨vida/diario/ceremonia⟩
private; ⟨secreto⟩ intimate; ⟨ambiente⟩ intimate;
una cena íntima a small dinner (with a few
friends/members of the family); (en pareja) a
candlelit o romantic dinner (b) ⟨amistad⟩ close;
⟨amigo⟩ close, intimate (before n)

intocable adj (a) (sagrado) sacred, sacrosanct
(b) ⟨tema⟩ taboo (c) ⟨casta⟩ untouchable

intolerable adj intolerable

intolerancia f intolerance

intolerante adj intolerant

intoxicación f (Med) intoxication, poisoning;
∼ alimenticia food poisoning; ∼ etílica (Med)
alcohol poisoning

intoxicar [A2] vt to poison
■ **intoxicarse** v pron to get food poisoning

intranquilizar [A4] vt to worry

intranquilo -la adj (a) [ESTAR] (preocupado)
worried, anxious (b) (agitado) restless

intranscendente adj ▶ INTRASCENDENTE

intransferible adj not transferable,
untransferable

intransigente adj intransigent

intransitivo -va adj intransitive

intrascendente adj ⟨episodio/detalle⟩
insignificant, unimportant; ⟨comentario⟩ trivial

intravenoso -sa adj intravenous

intriga f intrigue; ⟨novela/película de⟩ ∼ thriller

intrigante mf schemer, intriguer (AmE)

intrigar [A3] vt to intrigue
■ ∼ vi to scheme

intrincado -da adj (a) ⟨problema/asunto⟩
intricate, complex; ⟨laberinto/sistema⟩
complicated (b) ⟨nudo⟩ tangled

introducción f introduction; ∼ A algo
introduction TO sth

introducir [I6] vt **1** (en general) to put ... in;
⟨moneda⟩ to insert; ∼ algo EN algo to put sth
INTO sth; ⟨moneda⟩ to insert sth IN sth **2** (a)
⟨cambios/medidas/ley⟩ to introduce, bring in;
⟨producto⟩ to introduce (b) ⟨contrabando/drogas⟩
to bring in, smuggle in **3** (presentar) ⟨acto/
cantante⟩ to introduce
■ **introducirse** v pron (a) (meterse) «ladrón» to
gain access; la moneda se introdujo por una
grieta the coin fell down a crack (b) (entrar en uso)
«moda» to come in; «costumbre» to be
introduced (c) (hacerse conocido) «escritor/actor»
to become known

introductorio -ria adj introductory

introvertido -da adj introverted
■ m,f introvert

intruso -sa m,f intruder; (Inf) cracker (colloq)

intuición f intuition; hacer algo por ∼ to do
sth intuitively; tuve la ∼ de que ... I had a
feeling that ...

intuir [I20] vt to sense; intuía que me iba a llamar
I had a feeling he was going to ring me

intuitivo -va adj intuitive

inundación f (en área limitada, casa) flood; (en
zona más amplia) floods (pl), flooding

inundar [A1] vt (a) «riada/aguas» to flood,
inundate (frml); «turistas/manifestantes» to
inundate, crowd (b) «persona» (con agua) to
flood; (con productos) to flood, swamp; ∼ algo DE
or CON algo to flood sth WITH sth
■ **inundarse** v pron (de agua) to be flooded

inusitado -da adj unusual, rare

inusual adj unusual

inútil adj useless; es ∼ que insistas there's no
point (in) insisting
■ mf: es un ∼ he's useless

invadir [I1] vt (a) «ejército/fuerzas» to invade
(b) «espacio aéreo/aguas» to enter, encroach upon
(c) «tristeza/alegría» to overcome, overwhelm

invalidez f (Med) disability, disablement

inválido -da adj (Med) ⟨persona⟩ disabled,
handicapped
■ m,f invalid, disabled person

invariable adj (a) ⟨precio/estado⟩ constant,
stable (b) (Ling) invariable

invasión f ① (de zona, país) invasion ② (Col) (chabolas) shantytown

invasor -sora m,f invader

invencible adj (a) ⟨luchador/equipo⟩ unbeatable, invincible (b) ⟨miedo/timidez⟩ insuperable, insurmountable

invención f (a) (en general) invention (b) (mentira) fabrication

inventar [A1] vt (a) ⟨aparato/sistema⟩ to invent (b) ⟨juego/palabra⟩ to make up, invent; ⟨cuento/excusa/mentira⟩ to make up

inventario m (de negocio) inventory, stock list; (de casa) inventory

inventiva f inventiveness; **tiene mucha ~** she's very inventive

invento m invention

inventor -tora m,f inventor

invernadero m greenhouse

invernal adj ⟨lluvias⟩ winter (before n); ⟨frío⟩ wintry

inverosímil adj implausible

inversión f ① (de dinero, tiempo, esfuerzos) investment ② (de posiciones, términos) reversal; (de una imagen) inversion; **~ térmica** thermal inversion

inversionista mf investor

inverso -sa adj ⟨sentido/orden⟩ reverse; **puedes ordenarlo así o a la inversa** you can arrange it like this or the other way around

inversor -sora m,f investor

invertido -da adj ⟨posición/orden⟩ reversed; ⟨imagen/figura⟩ inverted, reversed

invertir [I11] vt ① ⟨dinero/capital⟩ to invest; ⟨tiempo⟩ to invest, devote ② ⟨orden/papeles/términos⟩ to reverse; ⟨imagen/figura⟩ to invert, reverse
■ **~** vi to invest; **~ EN algo** to invest IN sth
■ **invertirse** v pron «papeles/funciones» to be reversed

investigación f (a) (de caso, delito) investigation; (por comisión especial) inquiry (b) (Educ, Med, Tec) research; **~ científica** scientific research; **~ de mercados** market research

investigador -dora m,f (a) (que indaga) investigator (b) (Educ, Med, Tec) researcher

investigar [A3] vt (a) ⟨delito/caso⟩ to investigate (b) (Educ, Med, Tec) «persona» to research, do research into
■ **~** vi (a) «policía» to investigate (b) (Educ, Med, Tec) **~ SOBRE algo** to research o do research INTO sth

invierno m winter; (en la zona tropical) rainy season; **en ~** in winter, in wintertime; **ropa de ~** winter clothes

invierta, inviertas, etc ▶ INVERTIR

invirtiera, invirtió, etc ▶ INVERTIR

invisible adj invisible

invitación f invitation

invitado -da m,f guest; **tenemos ~s a cenar** we have people coming to dinner; **los ~s a la boda** the wedding guests

invitar [A1] vt to invite; **~ a algn A algo** to invite sb TO sth; **te invito a una copa** I'll buy o get you a drink; **~ a algn A hacer algo** or **A QUE haga algo** to invite sb to do sth; **me invitó a cenar** (en casa) she invited me (round) to dinner; (en restaurante) she invited me out to dinner
■ **~** vi «persona»: **invito yo** it's on me, I'm buying; **invita la casa** it's on the house

invocar [A2] f (a) ⟨divinidad/santos⟩ to invoke (frml), to call on (b) ⟨auxilio/protección⟩ to appeal for

involucrar [A1] vt (a) (implicar) to involve; **~ a algn EN algo** ⟨en asunto/crimen⟩ to involve sb IN sth (b) (AmL) (conllevar) to involve
■ **involucrarse** v pron «persona» to get involved

involuntario -ria adj ⟨error/movimiento/gesto⟩ involuntary; ⟨testigo/cómplice⟩ unwitting

inyección f (Med) injection; (dosis) injection, shot (colloq); **le puso una ~** she gave him an injection

inyectado -da adj: **ojos ~s en sangre** bloodshot eyes

inyectar [A1] vt to inject; **le ~on morfina** they gave him morphine injections/a shot of morphine
■ **inyectarse** v pron (refl) «persona» to give oneself an injection, inject oneself; **se inyectó heroína** he injected himself with heroin

ion m ion

ir [I27] vi

I ① (a) (trasladarse, desplazarse) to go; **~ en taxi** to go by taxi; **iban a caballo/a pie** they were on horseback/on foot; **~ por mar** to go by sea; **¡Fernando! — ¡voy!** Fernando! — (just) coming! o I'll be right there!; **el ~ y venir de los invitados** the coming and going of the guests; **vamos a casa** let's go home; **¿adónde va este tren?** where's this train going (to)?; **~ de compras/de caza** to go shopping/hunting; **ya vamos para allá** we're on our way; **¿por dónde se va a ...?** how do you get to ...?; **~ por** or (Esp) **a por algo/algn** to go to get sth/sb; **voy a por pan** I'm going to get some bread (b) (asistir) to go to; **voy a clases nocturnas** I go to evening classes; **ya va al colegio** she's already at school

② (expresando propósito) **~ A + INF: ¿has ido a verla?** have you been to see her?; **ve a ayudarla** go and help her; ver tb — **v AUX 1**

③ (al arrojar algo, arrojarse): **tírame la llave — ¡allá va!** throw me the key — here you are o there you go!; **tírate del trampolín — ¡allá voy!** jump off the board! — here I go/come!

④ «comentario»: **no iba con mala intención** it wasn't meant unkindly; **eso va por ti también** that goes for you too, and the same goes for you

II ① (+ compl) (sin énfasis en el movimiento): **iban cantando por el camino** they sang as they went along; **¿van cómodos?** are you comfortable?;

íbamos sentados we were sitting down; **vas muy cargada** you have a lot to carry; **yo iba a la cabeza** I was in the lead

2 (refiriéndose al atuendo): **iban de largo** they wore long dresses; **voy a ~ de Drácula** I'm going to go as Dracula; **iba de verde** she was dressed in green

3 (en calidad de) **~ DE algo** to go (along) AS sth; **yo fui de intérprete** I went along as interpreter

III **1** «*camino/sendero*» (llevar) **~ A algo** to lead TO sth, to go TO sth

2 (extenderse, abarcar): **la autopista va desde Madrid hasta Valencia** the highway goes from Madrid to Valencia; **el período que va desde ... hasta ...** the period from ... to ...

IV **1** (marchar, desarrollarse): **¿cómo va el nuevo trabajo?** how's the new job going?; **va de mal en peor** it's going from bad to worse; **¿cómo te va?** how's it going?, how are things? (colloq), what's up? (AmE colloq); **¿cómo les fue en Italia?** how was Italy?, how did you get on in Italy?; **me fue mal/ bien en el examen** I did badly/well in the exam; **¡que te vaya bien!** all the best!, take care!; **¡que se vaya bien (en) el examen!** good luck in the exam

2 (en competiciones): **¿cómo van? — 3-1** what's the score? — 3-1; **voy ganando yo** I'm ahead, I'm winning

3 (en el desarrollo de algo): **¿por dónde van en historia?** where have you got (up) to in history?; **¿todavía vas por la página 20?** are you still on page 20?

4 (estar en camino): **¡vamos para viejos!** we're getting on o old!; **va para los cincuenta** she's going on fifty; **ya va para dos años que ...** it's getting on for two years since ...

5 (sumar, hacer): **ya van tres veces que te lo digo** this is the third time I've told you; **con este van seis** six, counting this one

6 (haber transcurrido): **en lo que va del** or (Esp) **de año/mes** so far this year/month

V **1** (deber colocarse) to go; **¿dónde van las toallas?** where do the towels go?; **¡qué va!** (fam): **¿has terminado? — ¡qué va!** have you finished? — you must be joking!; **¿se disgustó? — ¡qué va!** did she get upset? — not at all!; **vamos a perder el avión — ¡qué va!** we're going to miss the plane — no way!

2 **(a)** (combinar) **~ CON algo** to go WITH sth **(b)** (sentar bien, convenir) (+ *me/te/le etc*): **el negro no te va bien** black doesn't suit you; **te ~á bien un descanso** a rest will do you good

3 (Méx) (tomar partido por, apoyar) **~le A algo/algn** to support sth/sb; **le va al equipo peruano** he supports the Peruvian team

VI **1** **vamos (a)** (expresando incredulidad, fastidio): **¡vamos! ¿eso quién se lo va a creer?** come off it o come on! who do you think's going to believe that? **(b)** (intentando tranquilizar, animar, dar prisa): **vamos, mujer, dile algo** go on, say something to him; **¡vamos, date prisa!** come on, hurry up! **(c)** (al aclarar, resumir): **eso sería un disparate, vamos, digo yo** that would be a stupid thing to do, well, that's what I think anyway; **vamos, que no es una persona de fiar** basically, he's not very trustworthy; **es mejor que el otro, vamos** it's better than the other one, anyway

2 **vaya (a)** (expresando sorpresa, contrariedad): **¡vaya! ¡tú por aquí!** what a surprise! what are you

doing here?; **¡vaya! ¡se ha vuelto a caer!** oh no o (colloq) damn! it's fallen over again! **(b)** (Esp) (para enfatizar): **¡vaya cochazo!** what a car!

■ **~** *v aux* **~ A + INF**: **1** **(a)** (para expresar tiempo futuro, propósito) to be going to + INF; **voy a estudiar medicina** I'm going to study medicine; **va a hacer dos años que ...** it's getting on for two years since ... **(b)** (en propuestas, sugerencias): **vamos a ver ¿cómo dices que te llamas?** now then, what did you say your name was?; **bueno, vamos a trabajar** all right, let's get to work

2 (al prevenir, hacer recomendaciones): **que no se te vaya a caer** make sure you don't drop it; **cuidado, no te vayas a caer** mind you don't fall (colloq); **lleva el paraguas, no vaya a ser que llueva** take the umbrella, in case it rains

3 (expresando un proceso paulatino): **poco a poco irá aprendiendo** she'll learn little by little; **ya puedes ~ haciéndote a la idea** you'd better get used to the idea; **la situación ha ido empeorando** the situation has been getting worse and worse

■ **irse** *v pron* **1** (marcharse) to leave; **¿por qué te vas tan temprano?** why are you leaving o going so soon?; **vámonos** let's go; **bueno, me voy right** then, I'm taking off (AmE) o (BrE) I'm off; **no te vayas** don't go; **vete a la cama** go to bed; **se fue de casa/de la empresa** she left home/the company; **vete de aquí** get out of here; **se han ido de viaje** they're away, they've gone away

2 (consumirse, gastarse): **¡cómo se va el dinero!** I don't know where the money goes!; **se me va medio sueldo en el alquiler** half my salary goes on the rent

3 (desaparecer) «*mancha/dolor*» to go; **se ha ido la luz** the electricity's gone off; (+ *me/te/le etc*) **¿se te ha ido el dolor de cabeza?** has your headache gone?

4 (salirse, escaparse) «*líquido/gas*» to escape; **se le está yendo el aire al globo** the balloon's losing air o going down

5 (caerse, perder el equilibrio) (+ *compl*): **~se de boca/espaldas** to fall flat on one's face/back; **me iba para atrás** I was falling backwards; **frenó y nos fuimos todos para adelante** he braked and we all went flying forwards

ira *f* rage, anger

Irak, Iraq *m* Iraq

Irán *m* Iran

iraní *adj/mf* Iranian

iraquí *adj/mf* Iraqi

irguieron, irguió, etc ► ERGUIR

iris *m* (*pl* **~**) iris

Irlanda *f* Ireland; **~ del Norte** Northern Ireland

irlandés¹ -desa *adj* Irish
■ *m,f* (persona) (*m*) Irishman; (*f*) Irishwoman; **los irlandeses** the Irish, Irish people

irlandés² *m* (idioma) Irish (Gaelic)

ironía *f* irony

irónico -ca *adj* **(a)** «*situación*» ironic **(b)** «*persona/comentario/tono*» sarcastic; **en tono ~** sarcastically

irracional *adj* irrational

irradiar [A1] *vt* **(a)** «*calor/luz*» to radiate **(b)** «*simpatía/felicidad*» to radiate, irradiate

irrazonable *adj* unreasonable

irreal *adj* unreal

irrealizable *adj* ‹proyecto› unfeasible; ‹deseo› unattainable, unrealizable

irreconocible *adj* unrecognizable

irrecuperable *adj* unrecoverable, irretrievable

irreemplazable *adj* irreplaceable

irregular *adj* (en general) irregular; ‹letra/superficie› irregular, uneven

irregularidad *f* irregularity

irrelevante *adj* irrelevant

irremediable *adj* irreparable

irrepetible *adj* unrepeatable; **una actuación ∼** a once-in-a-lifetime performance

irreprochable *adj* irreproachable

irresistible *adj* **(a)** ‹sonrisa/mujer/hombre› irresistible; ‹deseo/tentación› irresistible **(b)** ‹dolor› unbearable

irrespetar [A1] *vt* (Col, Ven) ‹persona› to be disrespectful o rude to; ‹lugar sagrado› to desecrate

irrespetuoso -sa *adj* disrespectful

irrespirable *adj* unbreathable

irresponsabilidad *f* irresponsibility

irresponsable *adj* irresponsible
■ *mf*: **es un ∼** he's irresponsible, he's an irresponsible person

irreversible *adj* irreversible

irritable *adj* irritable

irritación *f* **(a)** (Med) irritation, inflammation **(b)** (enfado) irritation, annoyance

irritante *adj* ‹situación/actitud› irritating, annoying

irritar [A1] *vt* **(a)** ‹piel/garganta› to irritate; **tiene la garganta irritada** his throat is sore o inflamed **(b)** ‹persona› to annoy, irritate
■ **irritarse** *v pron* **(a)** «piel/ojos» to become irritated **(b)** «persona» to get annoyed, get irritated

irrompible *adj* unbreakable

isla *f* **(a)** (Geog) island, isle (liter) **(b)** (Ven) (en autopistas) median strip (AmE), central reservation (BrE); **∼ peatonal** safety island (AmE), traffic island (BrE)

Isla de Pascua *f*: **la ∼ de ∼** Easter Island

Islam *m*: **el ∼** Islam

islámico -ca *adj* Islamic

islandés¹ -desa *adj* Icelandic
■ *m,f* (persona) Icelander

islandés² *m* (idioma) Icelandic

Islandia *f* Iceland

Islas Británicas *fpl* British Isles (*pl*)

Islas Canarias *fpl* Canary Islands (*pl*), Canaries (*pl*)

Islas Malvinas *fpl* Falkland Islands (*pl*)

isleño -ña *adj* ‹población/productos› island (*before n*)
■ *m,f* (habitante de una isla) islander

islote *m* small island, islet

ISP *m* (= **proveedor de servicios Internet**) ISP

Israel *m* Israel

israelí *adj/mf* Israeli

itacate *m* (Méx) pack, bundle

Italia *f* Italy

italiano¹ -na *adj/m,f* Italian

italiano² *m* (idioma) Italian

ítem *m* (*pl* **ítems**) item

itinerario *m* itinerary, route

IVA /'iβa/ *m* (= **Impuesto al Valor Agregado** *or* **sobre el Valor Añadido**) VAT

izar [A4] *vt* ‹vela/bandera› to hoist, raise, run up

izquierda *f* **1** **(a)** (mano izquierda): **la ∼** the left hand (b) (lado) left; **la puerta de la ∼** the door on the left, the left-hand door; **torció a la ∼** he turned left; **ahí enfrente a la ∼** over there on the left; **conducen por la ∼** they drive on the left **2** (Pol) left; **de ∼** *or* (Esp) **de ∼s** left-wing

izquierdo -da *adj* left (*before n*)

J j

J, j *f* (*read as* /'xota/) *the letter* J, j

ja *interj* ha!

jabalí *m* (*pl* **-íes**) wild boar

jabalina *f* **(a)** (Arm, Dep) javelin **(b)** (Zool) wild sow

jabón *m* (producto) soap; **una barra** *or* **pastilla de ∼** a bar o cake of soap; **∼ de afeitar** shaving soap

jabonada *f* (con jabón): **dale una buena ∼** wash it well in soapy water

jabonar [A1] *vt* ▶ ENJABONAR

jabonera *f* soap dish

jabonoso -sa *adj* soapy

jacal *m* (Méx) hut, small house (*made of adobe or reeds*)

jacarandá *m or f* jacaranda

jacinto *m* (Bot) hyacinth

jactarse [A1] *v pron* to boast, brag; **∼ DE algo** to boast o brag ABOUT sth

Jacuzzi® /dʒə'kuzi/ *m* Jacuzzi®

jade *m* jade

jadeante *adj*: **venía ∼ por la cuesta** he came up the hill (puffing and) panting; **con voz ∼** in a breathless voice

jadear [A1] *vi* to pant

jadeo *m* panting

jaguar *m* jaguar

jagüey, jagüel *m* (AmL) pool

jai *f* (AmS fam) (alta sociedad) high society

jai alai *m* jai alai, pelota

jaiba f (AmL) crab; (de río) freshwater crab

jaibol m (Méx) highball (AmE), whisky and soda (BrE)

jalada f (Méx fam) **1** (tirón) pull, tug **2** (tontería, exageración): **esas son puras ∼s** that's a load of garbage (AmE) o (BrE) rubbish (colloq)

jalado¹ -da adj **1** (AmC, Col, Méx fam) (borracho) tight (colloq) **2** (Méx fam) (descabellado) crazy (colloq) **3** (Per fam) ⟨ojos⟩ slanting
■ m,f (Per fam) oriental-looking person

jalado² m (Per arg) (Educ) fail

jalador -dora adj **1** (Méx fam) (a) (trabajador) hard-working (b) (animoso) willing (c) (que atrae) ⟨oferta⟩ attractive; ⟨cantante/actor⟩ popular **2** (Per arg) ⟨profesor⟩ tough (colloq)

jalapeño m (Méx) jalapeño pepper

jalar [A1] vt **1** (a) (AmL exc CS) (tirar de) to pull; **me jaló la manga** he pulled o tugged at my sleeve (b) (Méx) (agarrar y acercar) ⟨periódico/libro⟩ to pick up, take; ⟨silla⟩ to draw up **2** (Per arg) ⟨alumno⟩ to fail, flunk (esp AmE colloq) **3** (Per fam) (en automóvil, moto) to give ... a lift o ride
■ ∼ vi **1** (AmL exc CS) (tirar) to pull; **∼ DE algo** to pull sth; **∼ con algn** (Méx fam) (llevarse bien) to get on o along well with sb **2** (a) (Méx fam) (apresurarse) to hurry up, get a move on (colloq); **¡jálale!** hurry up! (b) (Col, Méx fam) (ir) to go; **jálale por el pan** go and get the bread **3** (Méx fam) «motor/aparato» to work; **mi coche no jalaba en la mañana** my car wouldn't start this morning; **¿cómo van los negocios?** — **jalando, jalando** how's business? — oh, not so bad (colloq) **4** (AmC fam) «pareja» to date, go out; **«persona» ∼ con algn** to date sb, go out with sb
■ **jalarse** v pron **1** (Méx) (enf) ▶ JALAR vt 1B **2** (Méx) (enf) (a) (irse) to go (b) (venir) to come **3** (Col, Méx fam) (emborracharse) to get tight (colloq)

jalea f jelly; **∼ real** royal jelly

jaleo m (fam) (a) (alboroto, ruido) racket (colloq), row (colloq) (b) (confusión) muddle, mess; (desorden) mess; (problemas) hassle (colloq) (c) (actividad intensa): **hemos tenido mucho ∼ en casa** everything's been very hectic at home; **con todo el ∼ de la mudanza** with all the upheaval of the move (d) (riña) brawl

jallán m (AmC, Col) lout

jalón m (a) (AmL exc CS fam) (tirón) pull, yank; **de un ∼** in one go (b) (Méx) (tramo) stretch

jalonazo m (AmL exc CS fam) tug, yank; **el carro iba a ∼s** the car jerked o lurched along

jalonear [A1] vt (Méx, Per fam) to tug (at)
■ ∼ vi (a) (AmL exc CS fam) (dar tirones) to pull, tug (b) (AmC fam) (regatear) to haggle

jamaica f (Bot) hibiscus

Jamaica f Jamaica

jamaicano -na adj/m,f Jamaican

jamás adv never; **∼ volverá a suceder** it will never happen again; **nunca ∼** never ever; **por** or **para siempre ∼** for ever and ever

jamón m (Coc) ham; **∼ serrano** ≈ Parma ham

jaña f (AmC fam) (compañera) girlfriend; (chica) girl

Japón m: tb **el ∼** Japan

japonés¹ -nesa adj/m,f Japanese

japonés² m (idioma) Japanese

jaque m check; **∼ mate** checkmate

jaqueca f migraine, severe headache

jarabe m **1** (Coc, Farm, Med) syrup; **∼ para la tos** cough mixture o syrup **2** (Mús) Mexican folk dance and music

jarana f **1** (fam) (a) (bromas): **basta de ∼** that's enough fun and games o fooling around (colloq) (b) (juerga): **salir de ∼** to go out on the town o out partying (colloq) **2** (a) (baile) folk dance from south-east Mexico (b) (Per) (fiesta) party (with folk music)

jaranero -ra adj (fam): **es muy ∼** he's always out on the town o out partying (colloq)

jardín m **1** (con plantas) garden; **∼ botánico** botanical garden; **∼ zoológico** zoological garden, zoo; **∼ de infancia** or **de niños** nursery school, kindergarten **2 los jardines** mpl (en béisbol) the outfield; **∼ central** center* field

jardinear [A1] vi **1** (en béisbol) to field **2** (Chi) (en el jardín) to do the gardening

jardinera f (para la ventana) window box; (con pedestal) jardinière

jardinería f gardening

jardinero -ra m,f **1** (persona) gardener **2** (Dep) outfielder

jareta f (a) (para pasar una cinta) casing; (de adorno) tuck (b) (AmC) (bragueta) fly

jaripeo m: Mexican rodeo

jarra f **1** (a) (para servir) pitcher (AmE), jug (BrE) (b) (para beber) stein (AmE), tankard (BrE); **en ∼s**: **con los brazos en ∼s** (with) arms akimbo, hands on hips **2** (Méx fam) bender (colloq); **irse de ∼** to go on a bender

jarro m (a) (para servir) pitcher (AmE), jug (BrE) (b) (AmS) (tazón) mug; (para cerveza) beer mug

jarrón m vase

jaspe m (piedra) jasper; (mármol) veined marble

jaspeado -da adj ⟨mármol⟩ veined; ⟨tela/lana⟩ flecked; ⟨plumaje/huevos⟩ speckled

jauja f (fam): **piensan que la universidad es ∼** they think that university is a bed of roses; **¡esto es ∼!** this is the life!

jaula f cage

jauría f (de perros) pack (of hounds)

jayán -yana adj (AmC fam) foul (colloq); **no seas ∼** don't be a jerk o creep (colloq)

jazmín m jasmine

jazz /(d)ʒas/ m jazz

jebo -ba m,f (Ven arg) (a) (novio) (m) boyfriend; (f) girlfriend (b) **jeba** f (muchacha) chick (AmE colloq), bird (BrE colloq)

Jeep® /(d)ʒip/ m (pl **Jeeps**) Jeep®

jefatura f **1** (sede) headquarters (sing o pl) **2** (de partido) leadership

jefe -fa m,f, **jefe** mf (a) (superior) boss; **∼ de estudios** director of studies; **∼ de personal/ ventas** personnel/sales manager; **∼ de redacción** editor-in-chief (b) (de empresa) manager; (de sección) head; (de tribu) chief (c) (Pol) leader; **∼ de Estado/gobierno** head of state/government

jején m: small mosquito

jengibre m ginger

jeque m sheik, sheikh

jerarca mf leader

jerarquía f (a) (organización) hierarchy (b) (categoría, rango) rank

jerez m sherry

jerga f [1] (a) (de gremio, profesión) jargon; (de los adolescentes) slang (b) (galimatías) mumbo jumbo (colloq) [2] (Méx) (trapo) floorcloth

jergón m straw mattress

jeringa f (Med) syringe

jeringuilla f syringe

jeroglífico m (escritura) hieroglyphic, hieroglyph; (acertijo) rebus

jersey m (pl **-seys**) (a) /'ʒersi/ (AmL) (tela) jersey (b) /xer'sei/ (Esp) (prenda) sweater

Jerusalén m Jerusalem

Jesucristo Jesus Christ

jesuita adj/m Jesuit

Jesús (a) (Relig) Jesus (b) (como interj) ¡∼! (expresando — dolor, fatiga) heavens!; (— susto, sorpresa) good heavens!, good grief!; (cuando alguien estornuda) (Esp) bless you!

jet /'(d)ʒet/ m (pl **jets**) (Aviac) jet

jeta f (fam) (a) (cara) face, mug (colloq) (b) (AmL fam) (boca) trap (sl)

jet lag /'(d)ʒetlav/ m jet lag

jet set /'(d)ʒetset/ m or (Esp) f jet set

jíbaro -ra adj/m,f Jivaro

jibia f cuttlefish

jícama f yam bean

jícara f [1] (Méx) (Bot) calabash [2] (a) (Méx) (taza) (drinking) bowl (b) (Col, Méx) (vasija — de calabaza) gourd, calabash; (— de otro material) pot

jicote m (Méx) wasp

jicotera f (a) (Méx) (nido) wasp's nest (b) (ruido) row (colloq)

jilguero m goldfinch

jinete mf (Equ) (m) horseman, rider; (f) horsewoman, rider

jinetear [A1] vt [1] (Equ) (Chi) (montar) to ride [2] (Méx fam) ⟨dinero⟩ to speculate with

jirafa f (Zool) giraffe

jirón m [1] (de tela) shred; **hecho jirones** in tatters o shreds [2] (Per) (avenida) avenue, street

jitomate m (Méx) tomato

jo interj (Esp fam) (expresando — sorpresa) wow! (colloq); (— enfado, disgusto) damn it! (colloq)

jockey /'(d)ʒoki/ mf (pl **-ckeys**) jockey

jocoso -sa adj humorous, jocular

joda f (AmL fam)(a) (molestia) pain (colloq), drag (colloq) (b) (broma): **en ∼** as a joke

joder¹ [E1] vi [1] (vulg) (copular) to screw (vulg), fuck (vulg)
[2] (fam: en algunas regiones vulg) (molestar) to annoy (sl); **lo hace solo por ∼** he only does it to annoy
■ ∼ vt [1] (vulg) (copular con) to screw (vulg), fuck (vulg)
[2] (fam: en algunas regiones vulg) (a) (molestar) to bug (colloq) (b) (engañar) to rip ... off (colloq)
[3] (fam: en algunas regiones vulg) ⟨televisor/reloj⟩ to

bust (colloq), to fuck up (vulg); ⟨planes⟩ to mess up (colloq), to screw up (vulg); **∼la** (fam) to screw up (vulg)
■ **joderse** v pron (fam: en algunas regiones vulg) (a) (jorobarse): **y si no te gusta, te jodes** and if you don't like it, that's tough! (colloq) (b) ⟨espalda⟩ to do ... in (colloq); ⟨hígado/estómago⟩ to mess up (colloq) (c) «planes» to get screwed up (vulg), fucked up (vulg); **se ha jodido el motor** the engine's had it (colloq)

joder² interj (esp Esp fam: en algunas regiones vulg) (expresando — fastidio) for heaven's sake! (colloq), for fuck's sake! (vulg); (— asombro) good grief!, holy shit! (vulg)

jodido -da adj [1] (fam: en algunas regiones vulg) (a) [SER] (difícil) ⟨trabajo⟩ tricky, tough (colloq); ⟨persona⟩ difficult, pain in the neck (colloq) (b) (delante del n) (maldito) damn (colloq), fucking (vulg) (c) [SER] (AmL) (exigente) demanding, tough (colloq) [2] [ESTAR] (fam: en algunas regiones vulg) (a) (estropeado) ⟨ascensor/radio⟩ bust (colloq), fucked (vulg) (b) (enfermo) in a bad way (colloq) (c) (deprimido) down (colloq) [3] [SER] (Col fam) (astuto) sharp

jogging /(d)ʒovin/ m (a) (Dep, Ocio) jogging; **hacer ∼** to jog, go jogging (b) (RPl) (Indum) jogging suit

jojoto m (Ven) corn (AmE), maize (BrE)

jolgorio m revelry, merrymaking; **irse de ∼** (fam) to go out on the town o out partying (colloq)

jonrón m (AmL) home run

Jordania f Jordan

jordano -na adj/m,f Jordanian

jornada f [1] (a) (period) (día) day (b) (Rels Labs) tb ∼ **laboral** working day; **trabajar ∼ completa/media ∼** to work full-time/part-time; **∼ continuada** or **intensiva** or (Chi) **única** working day with no break for lunch so as to finish earlier; **∼ partida** split shift (working day with long break for lunch) [2] (esp Col) (viaje) journey

jornal m day's wages (pl), day's pay; **trabajar a ∼** to be paid on a daily basis

jornalero -ra m,f day laborer*

joroba f (a) (de persona, camello) hump (b) (fam) (molestia) drag (colloq), pain in the neck (colloq)

jorobado -da adj [1] (giboso) hunchbacked [2] (fam) (a) (enfermo, delicado): **todavía anda algo jorobada** she's still a bit low (colloq); **está ∼ del estómago** his stomach's been playing (him) up (colloq) (b) (sin dinero) broke (colloq) (c) ⟨asunto⟩ tricky
■ m,f hunchback

jorobar [A1] vt (fam) (a) (molestar) to bug (colloq) (b) (malograr) to ruin, spoil
■ ∼ vi (fam) (molestar) to annoy; **lo que más me joroba es ...** what really bugs o gets me is ... (colloq)
■ **jorobarse** v pron (fam) (a) (aguantarse): **y si no te gusta, te jorobas** and if you don't like it, that's tough (colloq) (b) (dañarse) ⟨hígado/estómago⟩ to

---

AmC	Central America		Arg	Argentina		Cu	Cuba		Per	Peru
AmL	Latin America		Bol	Bolivia		Ec	Ecuador		RPl	River Plate Area
AmS	South America		Chi	Chile		Esp	Spain		Ur	Uruguay
Andes	Andean Region		CS	Southern Cone		Méx	Mexico		Ven	Venezuela

mess up (colloq); ‹*espalda*› to do ... in (colloq) **(c)** «*plan*» to be scuppered (colloq); «*fiesta*» to be ruined

jorongo *m* (Méx) poncho

joropo *m*: *Colombian/Venezuelan folk dance*

jota *f* **(a)** (letra) *name of the letter* j; **ni ~** (fam): **no entiendo/no veo ni ~** I don't understand/I can't see a thing; **no sabe ni ~** he doesn't have a clue (colloq) **(b)** (Mús) jota (*Aragonese folk song/dance*) **(c)** (en naipes) jack

joven *adj* young
■ *mf* (*m*) young person, young man; (*f*) young person, young woman; **de aspecto ~** youthful looking; **los jóvenes de hoy** ... young people today ...

jovencito -ta (*m*) young man; (*f*) young lady, young woman; **moda para jovencitas** teenage fashions (*for girls*)

jovial *adj* jovial, cheerful

joya *f* **1** (alhaja) piece of jewelry*; **~s** jewelry *o* jewels; **~ de fantasía** piece *o* item of costume jewelry **2** (persona) gem, treasure; (cosa): **este coche es una ~** this is a real gem of a car

joyería *f* (tienda) jeweler's*

joyero -ra *m,f* **(a)** (persona) jeweler* **(b)** **joyero** *m* (estuche) jewelry* box, jewel case

joystick /'(d)ʒoɪstɪk/ *m* joystick

jr (en Perú) (= **jirón**) street

Jr. (= **Júnior**) Jr

juanete *m* (Med) bunion

jubilación *f* (retiro) retirement; (pensión) pension; **~ anticipada/forzosa** early/compulsory retirement

jubilado -da *adj* retired
■ *m,f* pensioner, retired person (*o* worker *etc*)

jubilar [A1] *vi* (Andes) to retire
■ **jubilarse** *v pron* (del trabajo) to retire

júbilo *m* jubilation

jubiloso -sa *adj* (liter) jubilant

judaísmo *m* Judaism

judía *f* (Esp) bean; **~ verde** green bean

judicial *adj* judicial
■ *m* (Méx) policeman

judío -día *adj* **1** (Relig, Sociol) Jewish **2** (fam & pey) (tacaño) miserly, tightfisted (colloq)
■ *m,f* Jewish person, Jew

judo /'(d)ʒuðo/ *m* judo

juega, juegas, etc ▶ JUGAR

juego *m* **1** **(a)** (en general) play; **entrar en ~** «*jugador*» to come on; «*factores/elementos*» to come into play; **estar en ~** to be at stake; **~ limpio/sucio** fair/foul play; **seguirle el ~ a algn** to go *o* play along with sb **(b)** (por dinero): **el ~** gambling **(c)** (fam) (maniobras, estratagemas) game (colloq) **(d)** (en naipes) hand, cards (*pl*)
2 **(a)** (de mesa, de niños, etc) game; **~ de azar** game of chance; **~ de manos** conjuring trick; **~ de palabras** pun, play on words; **~s malabares** juggling; **J~s Olímpicos** Olympic Games (*pl*), Olympics (*pl*) **(b)** (AmL) (en la feria) fairground attraction, ride **(c)** (en tenis) game **(d)** **juegos** *mpl* (columpios, etc) swings, slide, etc (*in a children's playground*)
3 (conjunto) set; **un ~ de cuchillos/llaves** a set of knives/keys; **un ~ de platos** a dinner service; **~**

de café/té coffee/tea set; **~ de escritorio** desk set; **hacer ~** «*colores/cortinas*» to go together; **te hace ~ con los zapatos** it goes with your shoes

juerga *f* (fam): **ir de ~** to go out on the town *o* out partying (colloq); **organizar una ~** to have *o* throw a party

juerguista *mf* (fam) reveller

jueves *m* (*pl* **~**) Thursday; *para ejemplos ver* LUNES; **J~ Santo** Maundy Thursday

juez *mf*, **juez -za** *m,f* **(a)** (Der) judge **(b)** (Dep) referee; **~ de banda** *o* **línea** (en fútbol, tenis) (*m*) linesman; (*f*) lineswoman; (en fútbol americano, rugby) line judge; **~ de silla** umpire

jugada *f* **(a)** (con pelota — individual) move; (— entre varios) play **(b)** (en ajedrez, damas, etc) move; **hacerle una (mala) ~ a algn** to play a (dirty) trick on sb

jugado -da *adj* (Col, Méx) experienced

jugador -dora *m,f* (Dep) player; (en naipes, juegos de mesa) player; (que juega habitualmente por dinero) gambler

jugar [A15] *vi* **1** **(a)** (en general) to play; **~ A algo** to play sth; **~ a la pelota** to play ball; **~ al fútbol** (Esp, RPI) to play football; **~ a las muñecas** to play with dolls; **~ limpio/sucio** to play fair/dirty **(b)** (en ajedrez, damas) to move; (en naipes) to play; (en otros juegos) to play; **me tocaba ~ a mí** it was my turn/move/go **(c)** (apostar fuerte) to gamble
2 **jugar con (a)** ‹*persona/sentimientos*› to play with, toy with **(b)** (manejar) ‹*colores/luz/palabras*› to play with
■ **~** *vt* **1** **(a)** ‹*partido/carta*› to play **(b)** (AmL exc RPI) ‹*tenis/fútbol/ajedrez*› to play
2 (apostar) **~ algo A algo** to bet sth ON sth
3 ‹*rol/papel*› to play
■ **jugarse** *v pron* **(a)** (gastarse en el juego) ‹*sueldo*› to gamble (away) **(b)** (arriesgar) ‹*reputación/vida*› to risk, put ... at risk; **~se el pellejo** (fam) to risk one's neck (colloq) **(c)** (apostarse) (*recípr*): **nos jugamos una comida** we bet a meal on it

jugarreta *f* (fam) dirty trick (colloq); **hacerle una ~ a algn** to play a dirty trick on sb

juglar *m* minstrel, jongleur

jugo *m* (líquido) juice; **~ de tomate** tomato juice

jugoso -sa *adj* **(a)** ‹*fruta/carne*› juicy **(b)** ‹*historia/anécdota*› colorful*; ‹*chisme*› juicy **(c)** ‹*artículo/guion*› meaty **(d)** ‹*negocio*› lucrative, profitable

juguera *f* (CS) (para hacer jugos) juicer

juguete *m* toy; **un tren de ~** a toy train

juguetear [A1] *vi* to play

juguetería *f* (tienda) toy store; (ramo) toy trade *o* business

juguetón -tona *adj* playful

juicio *m* **1** (facultad) judgment; **no está en su sano ~** he's not in his right mind; **perder el ~** to go out of one's mind **2** (prudencia, sensatez) sense **3** (opinión) opinion; **a mi ~** in my opinion, to my mind; **lo dejo a tu ~** I'll leave it up to you; **~ de valor** value judgment **4** (Der) trial; **llevar a ~ a algn** to take sb to court; **ir a ~** to go to court; **~ civil/criminal** civil/criminal proceedings (*pl*); **el J~ Final** (Relig) the Final Judgment

juicioso -sa *adj* sensible

jul. (= **julio**) Jul

julepe m [1] (Jueg) card game similar to whist [2] (AmS fam) (susto) fright; **le da ~ la oscuridad** she's terrified of the dark

julia f (Méx fam) Black Maria (colloq)

julio m (mes) July; *para ejemplos ver* ENERO

jumbo /'(d)ʒumbo/ m jumbo jet

jun. (= **junio**) Jun

junco m [1] (planta) rush, reed [2] (Náut) *tb* ~ **chino** junk

jungla f jungle

junio m June; *para ejemplos ver* ENERO

júnior /'(d)ʒunjo(r)/ adj inv ‹equipo/categoría› junior (*before n*), youth (*before n*) (BrE)
■ mf (pl ~**s**) (a) (Dep): **los ~s** the juniors (b) (el más joven, el hijo) Junior
■ m (a) (Chi) (en oficina) office junior (b) (Méx) (hijo de papá) rich kid (colloq)

junta f [1] (a) (comité, comisión) board, committee; (de empresa) board; (reunión) meeting; ~ **directiva** board of directors (b) (de militares) junta (c) (gobierno regional) *autonomous government in some regions of Spain* [2] (Mec) (acoplamiento) joint; (para cerrar herméticamente) gasket

juntar [A1] vt (a) (unir) ‹pies/manos/camas› to put ... together (b) (reunir) ‹fichas/piezas› to collect up, gather together; ‹dinero› to save (up); ~ **sellos** (esp AmL) to collect stamps (c) (cerrar) ‹puerta› to push ... to
■ **juntarse** v pron [1] «personas» (a) (acercarse) to move o get closer together (b) (reunirse) to get together; ~**se con algn** to join sb, meet up with sb (c) (como pareja) to live together; **se volvieron a** ~ they got back together again [2] (a) «desgracias/sucesos» to come together (b) «carreteras/conductos» to meet, join

junto -ta adj [1] (a) (unido, reunido) together; **nunca había visto tanto dinero** ~/**tanta gente junta** I'd never seen so much money/so many people in one place (b) (pl) (cercanos, contiguos) together; **están demasiado** ~**s** they're too close together; **bailaban muy** ~**s** they were dancing very close [2] (como adv) (a) ‹estudiar/trabajar/ vivir› together (b) ‹llegar/saltar› at the same time; **¡ahora todos** ~**s!** all together now! [3] (en locs) **junto a** next to; **junto con** (together) with

juntura f join, joint

Júpiter m Jupiter

jurado m (cuerpo) (Der) jury; (de concurso) panel of judges, jury
■ mf (persona) (Der) juror, member of a jury; (de concurso) judge, member of the jury

juramento m oath; **prestar** ~ to take an oath; **tomarle** ~ **a algn** (Der) to swear sb in; **bajo** ~ under o on oath

jurar [A1] vt to swear; **juró su cargo el 22 de julio** he was sworn in on July 22; ~**on** (la) **bandera** or (AmL) **a la bandera** they swore allegiance to the flag; **juró vengarse** he swore to get his revenge; **no lo entiendo, te lo juro** I honestly don't understand

■ ~ vi (a) (maldecir) to curse, swear (b) (prometer): ~ **en falso** or **vano** to commit perjury

jurídico -ca adj legal (*before n*)

jurisdicción f jurisdiction

justicia f (a) (equidad) justice; **pedir** ~ to call for justice; **en** ~ in all fairness, to be fair; **la** ~ **de su decisión** the fairness of her decision; **nunca se le ha hecho** ~ **como escritor** he has never received due recognition as a writer (b) (sistema, leyes): **la** ~ the law; **huir de la** ~ to flee from justice o the law; **tomarse la** ~ **por su mano** to take the law into one's own hands

justificable adj justifiable

justificación f (disculpa, razón) justification; (Der) (prueba) proof

justificante m receipt; ~ **de pago** receipt, proof of payment; ~ **de asistencia** certificate of attendance; ~ **de ausencia** note explaining reasons for one's absence

justificar [A2] vt (a) (en general) to justify; **eso no justifica su actitud** that does not justify her attitude; **sus sospechas no estaban justificadas** his suspicions were not justified; **trabajar por tan poco no se justifica** it isn't worth working for so little (b) (disculpar) ‹persona› to find o make excuses for
■ **justificarse** v pron to justify oneself, excuse oneself

justo¹ -ta adj [1] ‹persona/castigo/sociedad› just, fair; ‹causa› just [2] (a) (exacto) ‹medida/ peso/cantidad› exact; **me dio el dinero** ~ he gave me the right money; **son 40 euros justos** that's 40 euros exactly; **buscaba la palabra justa** he was searching for exactly o just the right word (b) (apenas suficiente): **tener lo** ~ **para vivir** to have just enough to live on; **andan muy** ~**s de dinero** they're very short of money; **teníamos las sillas justas** we had just enough chairs for everybody (c) (ajustado): **estos zapatos me quedan demasiado** ~**s** these shoes are too tight (for me)

justo² adv (a) (exactamente) just; ~ **a tiempo** just in time; **es** ~ **lo que quería** it's just o exactly what I wanted; **vive** ~ **al lado** he lives just o right next door; **y** ~ **hoy que pensaba salir** and today of all days, when I was planning to go out (b) (ajustado): **con el sueldo que gana vive muy** ~ he only just manages to scrape by on what he earns; **me cupo todo, pero muy** ~ I managed to get everything in, but only just

juvenil adj ‹moda› young; ‹aspecto› youthful; ‹categoría/competición› junior (*before n*), youth (*before n*) (BrE)
■ mf junior; **los** ~**es** the juniors

juventud f (edad) youth; (gente joven) youth; **¡esta** ~ **de hoy!** young people today!

juzgado m court

juzgar [A3] vt (a) (Der) ‹acusado› to try; ‹caso› to try, judge (b) (conducta/persona) to judge; ~ **mal a algn** to misjudge sb (c) (considerar) to consider; **a** ~ **por las apariencias** judging by appearances

Kk

K, k *f (read as /ka/) the letter* K, k
ka *f: name of the letter* k
kaleidoscopio *m* kaleidoscope
karate, kárate *m* karate
kárdex *m* (archivo) file; (mueble) filing cabinet
kart *m (pl* **karts**) kart
Kenia, Kenya *f* Kenya
kermesse /ker'mes/f (CS, Méx) charity fair,
kermess (AmE), fête (BrE)
ketchup /'katʃup 'katsup/ *m* ketchup, catsup
(AmE)
Kg. (= **kilogramo**) kg
kilo *m* kilogram, kilo
kilogramo *m* kilogram
kilometraje *m* ≈ mileage
kilométrico -ca *adj* (fam) (pasillo) endless;
una cola kilométrica a line (AmE) *o* (BrE) queue a
mile long
kilómetro *m* kilometer*
kilovatio *m* kilowatt
kimono *m* kimono

kindergarten *m (pl* ∼ *or* **-tens**)
kindergarten
kiosco, kiosko *m* **(a)** (de periódicos) newsstand,
newspaper kiosk; (de refrescos) drinks stand; (de
helados) ice-cream stand; (de caramelos, tabaco)
kiosk **(b)** (para orquesta) bandstand
kiwi /'kiwi/ *m* **(a)** (Bot) kiwifruit, Chinese
gooseeberry **(b)** (Zool) kiwi
klaxon *m* ▶ CLAXON
Kleenex®, kleenex /'klineks/ *m (pl* ∼)
tissue
Km. (= **kilómetro**) km
K.O. /'nokau(t)/ *or* (Esp) /'kao/ *m* KO; **lo dejó** ∼
he knocked him out
koala *m* koala (bear)
kuchen /'kuxen/ *m* (Chi) (Coc) tart
Kurdistán *m* Kurdistan
kurdo -da *adj* Kurdish
■ *m,f* Kurd
Kuwait *m* Kuwait
Kuwaití *adj/mf* Kuwaiti

Ll

L, l *f (read as* /'ele/) *the letter* L, l
l. (= **litro**) l, liter*
la *art: ver* **el**
■ *pron pers* **(a)** (referido — a ella) her; (— a usted)
you; (— a cosa) it; **no** ∼ **conozco** I don't know
her; ¿∼ **atienden?** can I help you?; **yo se** ∼ **llevo**
I'll take it to him **(b)** (impers) you, one (frml)
■ *m* (nota) A; (en solfeo) la
laberinto *m* (de caminos, pasillos) maze,
labyrinth; (en jardín, parque) maze
labia *f* (fam) gift of the gab (colloq)
labio *m* lip; **leer los** ∼**s** to lip-read; **sin dispegar
los** ∼**s** without uttering a single word
labor *f* **(a)** (trabajo) work; **una** ∼ **de equipo**
teamwork; ∼**es domésticas** housework; ∼**es
agrícolas** *or* **del campo** farm work **(b)** (de coser,
bordar) needlework; (de punto) knitting
laborable *adj* **(a)** (día) working (before n) **(b)**
(tierra) arable
laboral *adj* (problemas/conflictos) labor* (before
n), work (before n); ▶ ACCIDENTE
laboratorio *m* laboratory
laborioso -sa *adj* (persona) hardworking,
industrious; (abejas) industrious; (tarea)
laborious
laborista *adj* Labour (before n)
■ *mf* member of the Labour Party

labrador -dora *m,f* (Agr) (propietario) farmer;
(trabajador) farmworker
labrar [A1] *vt* ⨦ (Agr) (tierra) to work
⨧ (madera) to carve; (piedra) to cut; (cuero) to
tool, work; (metales) to work
■ **labrarse** *v pron* (forjarse): ∼**se un porvenir** to
carve out a future for oneself
labriego -ga *m,f* farmworker
laburar [A1] *vi* (CS fam) to work
laca *f* (resina) lac, shellac; (barniz) lacquer; (para el
pelo) hairspray
lacear [A1] *vt* (CS) (ganado) to lasso
lacio -cia *adj* (pelo) straight; (cuerpo) limp,
weak
lacónico -ca *adj* laconic
lacrar [A1] *vt* (con cera) to seal
lacre *adj* (AmL) bright-red; (Chi) red
■ *m* sealing wax
lacrimógeno -na *adj* (fam) (película) weepy
(colloq), tear-jerking (before n) (colloq); ▶ GAS
lactancia *f* (secreción de leche) lactation; **durante
el período de** ∼ while breastfeeding
lácteo -tea *adj* dairy (before n), milk (before n)
ladeado -da *adj*: **el cuadro está** ∼ the picture ···ᑲ

is on a slant *o* is askew; **llevaba el sombrero** ~ he wore his hat at an angle; **con la cabeza ladeada** with his head tilted to one side

ladear [A1] *vt* ⟨*cabeza*⟩ to tilt ... to one side; ⟨*objeto*⟩ to tilt

■ **ladearse** *v pron* (inclinarse) to lean to one side

ladera *f* hillside, mountainside; **la** ~ **norte** the northern slope *o* side

ladino -na *adj* **1** (taimado) sly, cunning **2** (AmC, Méx) **(a)** (mestizo) mestizo, of mixed race **(b)** (hispanohablante) Spanish-speaking (*often used to refer to Indians who adopt Spanish ways*) **3** (Méx fam) (agudo) high-pitched, piercing
■ *m,f* (AmC, Méx) **(a)** (mestizo) mestizo, person of mixed race **(b)** (hispanohablante) Spanish-speaking Indian

lado *m* **1** **(a)** (en general) side; **está en el** ~ **derecho** it is on the right-hand side; **a este/al otro** ~ **del río** on this/on the other side of the river; **hacerse a un** ~ to move to one side; **echarse a un** ~ «*coche*» to swerve; «*persona*» to move over; **ponlas a un** ~ set them aside; **¿de qué** ~ **estás?** whose side are you on?; **cambiar de** ~ (Dep) to change sides (AmE) *o* (BrE) ends; **ver el** ~ **positivo de las cosas** to look on the bright side of things; **por el** ~ **de mi padre** on my father's side (of the family) **(b)** (de papel, moneda, tela) side **2** (sitio, lugar): **a/en/por todos** ~**s** everywhere; **en algún** ~ somewhere; **en cualquier** ~ anywhere; **ir de un** ~ **para otro** to run around **3** (*en locs*) **al lado**: **viven en la casa de al** ~ they live next door; **los vecinos de al** ~ the next-door neighbors; **al lado de algn/algo** (contiguo a) next to sb/sth, beside sb/sth; (en comparación con) compared to sb/sth; **de lado** ⟨*meter/colocar*⟩ sideways; ⟨*tumbarse/dormir*⟩ on one's side; **de** ~ **a** ~ ⟨*extenderse/cruzar*⟩ from one side to the other; **por otro lado** (en cambio) on the other hand; (además) apart from anything else; **por un** ~ **..., pero por otro** ~ **...** on the one hand ..., but on the other hand ...; **dejar algo de** ~ to leave sth aside *o* to one side; **ir cada uno por su** ~: **cada uno se fue por su** ~ they went their separate ways

ladrar [A1] *vi* **(a)** «*perro*» to bark **(b)** (fam) «*persona*» to yell (colloq), to bark (colloq)

ladrido *m* bark; ~**s** barking

ladrillo *m* brick; **(de) color** ~ brick-red

ladrón -drona *m,f* **1** (de bolsos, coches) thief; (de bancos) bank robber; (de casas) burglar **2** **ladrón** *m* (Elec) adaptor

ladronzuelo -la *m,f* petty thief

lagartija *f* wall lizard

lagarto *m* **1** (Zool) lizard **2** (Col fam) (persona) crawler (colloq)

lago *m* lake

lágrima *f* (Fisiol) tear; **le caían las** ~**s** tears were running down her face; **se le saltaron las** ~**s** it brought tears to his eyes; ~**s de cocodrilo** crocodile tears (*pl*); **llorar a** ~ **viva** to cry one's eyes *o* heart out

lagrimal *m* **(a)** (extremo del ojo) corner of the eye **(b)** *tb* **conducto** ~ tear duct

laguna *f* **1** (de agua dulce) lake, pool; (de agua salada) lagoon **2** **(a)** (en estudio, artículo) gap **(b)** (en la memoria) memory lapse

laico -ca *adj* secular, lay (*before n*)
■ *m,f* (*m*) layman, layperson; (*f*) laywoman, layperson

laísmo *m*: use of LA/LAS *instead of* LE/LES (*as in* LA/LAS DIJE QUE NO), *common in certain regions of Spain but not acceptable to most speakers*

laja *f* (AmS) slab

lama *m* lama
■ *f* (AmL) (musgo) moss; (verdín) green slime; (moho) mold*

lambetear [A1] *vt* (Col, Méx, Ven) to lick

lambiscón -cona *m,f* (Méx fam) bootlicker (colloq)

lambisquear [A1] *vt* **(a)** (Col) (lamer) to lick **(b)** (Méx fam) (lisonjear) to suck up to (colloq)

lamentable *adj* ⟨*conducta/error/suceso*⟩ deplorable, terrible **(b)** ⟨*pérdida*⟩ sad; ⟨*estado/aspecto*⟩ pitiful; ⟨*error*⟩ regrettable

lamentación *f* lamentation (liter); **estoy harta de oír tus lamentaciones** (fam) I'm fed up with your complaining *o* grumbling

lamentar [A1] *vt* to regret; **lamento molestarlo** I'm sorry to disturb you; **lamentamos tener que comunicarle que ...** (frml) we regret to have to inform you that ...; **lo lamento mucho** I am very sorry
■ **lamentarse** *v pron* to complain, to grumble (colloq)

lamento *m* **(a)** (quejido — por un dolor físico) groan; (— por tristeza) wail **(b)** (elegía) lament

lamer [E1] *vt* ⟨*persona/animal*⟩ to lick

lámina *f* **1** (hoja, plancha) sheet **2** (Impr) **(a)** (plancha, ilustración) plate; (estampa) picture card **(b)** (Educ) wall chart

laminar [A1] *vt* to laminate

lámpara *f* lamp; ~ **de pie/mesa** standard/table lamp

lamparín *m* (Per) kerosene lamp

lamparita *f* (RPl) (light) bulb

lampiño -ña *adj* (sin barba) smooth-faced; (con poco vello) with little body hair

lana *f* **1** (material) wool; (vellón, pelambre) fleece; ~ **virgen** new wool; **una bufanda de** ~ **a** wool *o* woolen scarf **2** (AmL fam) (dinero) dough (sl); **tienen mucha** ~ they're loaded (colloq)

lanceta *f* **(a)** (Med) lancet **(b)** (Andes, Méx) (aguijón) sting

lancha *f* (barca grande) launch, cutter; (bote) motorboat; ~ **fuera borda** (outboard) launch; ~ **neumática** inflatable (dinghy); ~ **salvavidas** lifeboat

langosta *f* (crustáceo) lobster; (insecto) locust

langostino *m* (grande) king prawn; (pequeño) prawn; ~ **de río** crayfish, crawfish (esp AmE)

langüetear [A1] *vt* (Chi) to lick

languidecer [E3] *vi* «*persona*» to languish (liter); «*entusiasmo/conversación*» to flag

lánguido -da *adj* **(a)** (débil) listless, weak **(b)** ⟨*mirada/aspecto*⟩ languid

lanolina *f* lanolin

lanudo -da *adj* long-haired, shaggy

lanza *f* (arma — en las lides) lance; (— arrojadiza) spear
■ *m* (Chi) (delincuente) pickpocket, thief

lanzacohetes *m* (*pl* ~) rocket launcher

lanzado -da *adj* ⟨1⟩ [SER] (fam) (precipitado) impulsive, impetuous; (decidido, atrevido) forward ⟨2⟩ (fam) (rápido): **ir** ~ to shoot along (colloq); **pasar** ~ to shoot past

lanzador -dora *m,f* (Dep) (de disco, jabalina) thrower; (en béisbol) pitcher; ~ **de bala** *or* (Esp) **de peso** shot-putter

lanzamiento *m* ⟨1⟩ **(a)** (de objetos, pelota) throwing; (de misil, torpedo) launch; (de bomba) dropping **(b)** (de cohete, satélite) launch **(c)** (Dep) (de disco, jabalina) throw; (de bala) put; (en béisbol) pitch; ~ **de bala** *or* (Esp) **de peso** shot put; ~ **de disco/jabalina** discus/javelin throwing ⟨2⟩ (de producto, libro) launch, launching ⟨3⟩ (CS) (Der) *tb* **orden de** ~ eviction order

lanzamisiles *adj inv* missile-launching (*before n*)
■ *m* (*pl* ~) missile launcher

lanzar [A4] *vt* ⟨1⟩ **(a)** ⟨*pelota/objetos/jabalina*⟩ to throw; (en béisbol) to pitch **(b)** ⟨*misil/satélite*⟩ to launch; ⟨*bomba*⟩ to drop ⟨2⟩ ⟨*producto/libro*⟩ to launch ⟨3⟩ **(a)** ⟨*ofensiva/ataque/crítica*⟩ to launch **(b)** ⟨*mirada*⟩ to shoot, give; ⟨*indirecta*⟩ to drop; ⟨*grito*⟩ to give; **lanzó un grito de dolor** he cried out in pain
■ ~ *vi* (en béisbol) to pitch
■ **lanzarse** *v pron* **(a)** (*refl*) (arrojarse) to throw oneself; ~**se al agua/al vacío** to leap into the water/the void; ~**se en paracaídas** to parachute; (en una emergencia) to bale out **(b)** (abalanzarse, precipitarse): ~**se sobre algo/algn** to pounce on sth/sb; ~**se al ataque** to attack

lapa *f* **(a)** (molusco) limpet **(b)** (Ven) (mamífero) paca **(c)** (AmC) (ave) macaw

lapicera *f* (CS) pen; ~ **fuente** *or* **estilográfica** fountain pen

lapicero *m* **(a)** (portaminas) automatic pencil (AmE), propelling pencil (BrE) **(b)** (Esp) (lápiz) pencil **(c)** (AmC, Per) (bolígrafo) ballpoint pen

lápida *f* (en tumba) tombstone, gravestone; (losa conmemorativa) stone plaque

lapislázuli *m* lapis lazuli

lápiz *m* (de madera) pencil; (portaminas) automatic pencil (AmE), propelling pencil (BrE); **con** *or* **a** ~ in pencil; **lápices de colores** crayons (*pl*); ~ **de labios** lipstick; ~ **de ojos** eye pencil; ~ **de pasta** (Chi) ballpoint pen

lapso *m* **(a)** (de tiempo) space **(b)** (error, olvido) ▶ LAPSUS

lapsus *m* (*pl* ~) (error) slip, blunder; (olvido): **tuve un pequeño** ~ it slipped my mind

laptop *m* laptop (computer)

larga *f* (largo plazo): **a la** ~ in the long run; **darle** ~**s a algn/algo** to put sb/sth off **(b)** (Auto) high beam (AmE), full *o* main beam (BrE)

largar [A3] *vt* ⟨1⟩ **(a)** (Náut) ⟨*amarras/cabo*⟩ to let out, pay out **(b)** (RPl) (soltar, dejar caer) to let … go ⟨2⟩ ⟨*discurso/sermón*⟩ to give; ⟨*palabrota/*

insulto⟩ to let fly ⟨3⟩ (fam) (despedir) to fire, to give … the boot (colloq); ⟨*novio*⟩ to ditch ⟨4⟩ (CS, Méx) (Dep) ⟨*pelota*⟩ to throw; ⟨*carrera*⟩ to start
■ **largarse** *v pron* **(a)** (fam) (irse) to beat it (colloq); **¡yo me largo!** I'm taking off! (AmE), I'm off! (BrE) (colloq) **(b)** (CS fam) (empezar) to start, get going (colloq); ~**se A hacer algo** to start to do sth, to start doing sth

largavistas *m* (*pl* ~) (CS) binoculars (*pl*)

largo¹ -ga *adj* **(a)** (en general) long; **me queda largo** it's too long (for me); **es muy** ~ **de contar** it's a long story; **un tren de** ~ **recorrido** a long-distance train **(b)** (*en locs*) **a lo largo** ⟨*cortar/partir*⟩ lengthways; **a lo largo de** (de camino, río) along; (de jornada, novela) throughout; (de una semana, vida) in the course of; **de largo** ⟨*vestirse*⟩ to wear a long skirt/dress; *ver tb* PASAR I 1A; **va para** ~ (fam) it's going to be a while

largo² *m* **(a)** (longitud) length; **¿cuánto mide de** ~**?** how long is it? **(b)** (en natación) lap (AmE), length (BrE)
■ *interj* (fam) *tb* **¡** ~ **de aquí!** get out of here!

largometraje *m* feature film, full-length film

larguero *m* **(a)** (Arquit, Const) (viga) crossbeam; (de puerta) jamb **(b)** (de cama) side **(c)** (Dep) crossbar

larguirucho -cha *adj* (fam) gangling (*before n*)

laringe *f* larynx

laringitis *f* laryngitis

larva *f* larva, grub

lasaña *f* lasagna, lasagne

lascivo -va *adj* lascivious, lustful

láser *m* laser

lástima *f* **(a)** (pena) shame, pity; **¡qué** ~**!** what a shame *o* pity!; **me da** ~ **tirarlo** it seems a pity *o* shame to throw it out **(b)** (compasión): **sentir** ~ **por algn** to feel sorry for sb; **digno de** ~ worthy of compassion

lastimadura *f* (AmL) graze

lastimar [A1] *vt* to hurt
■ **lastimarse** *v pron* (*refl*) (esp AmL) to hurt oneself; ⟨*dedo/rodillas*⟩ to hurt

lastimero -ra *adj* pitiful

lastre *m* **(a)** (de buque, globo) ballast **(b)** (carga, estorbo) burden

lata *f* ⟨1⟩ **(a)** (hojalata) tin **(b)** (envase) can, tin (BrE); **sardinas en** ~ canned *o* tinned sardines **(c)** (para galletas, etc) tin ⟨2⟩ (fam) (pesadez) nuisance, pain (colloq); **¡qué** ~**!** what a nuisance!; **dar (la)** ~ (fam) to be a nuisance; **¡deja ya de darme** ~**!** stop bugging *o* pestering me! (colloq)

latente *adj* latent

lateral *adj* ⟨*puerta/salida/calle*⟩ side (*before n*); ⟨*línea/sucesión*⟩ indirect, lateral
■ *m* (Dep) (poste) goalpost
■ *m or f* (Auto) (calle perpendicular) side street; (calle paralela) service road, frontage road (AmE)
■ *mf* (Dep) (alero) wing, winger; (defensa) left/right back

latido *m* (del corazón) heartbeat; (en la sien, una herida) throbbing

latifundio *m* large estate

latigazo *m* **(a)** (golpe) lash **(b)** (chasquido) crack of the whip

látigo *m* whip

latín *m* Latin

latino -na *adj* **(a)** ⟨*literatura/gramática/pueblo*⟩ Latin **(b)** (fam) (latinoamericano) Latin American
■ *m,f* **(a)** (español, italiano, etc) Latin **(b)** (fam) (latinoamericano) Latin American

Latinoamérica *f* Latin America

latinoamericano -na *adj/m,f* Latin American

latir [I1] *vi* **1** «*corazón*» to beat; «*vena*» to pulsate; «*herida/sien*» to throb **2 (a)** (Chi, Méx fam) (parecer) (+ *me/te/le etc*): **me late que no vendrá** I have a feeling o something tells me he isn't going to come **(b)** (Méx fam) (parecer bien, gustar) (+ *me/te/le etc*): **¿te late ir al cine?** do you feel like going to the movies?

latitud *f* (Astron, Geog) latitude; **la flora de otras ∼es** the flora of other parts of the world

latón *m* **(a)** (Metal) brass **(b)** (RPI) (palangana) metal bowl

latonería *f* (Col) body shop

latoso -sa *adj* **(a)** (fam) (molesto) annoying, tiresome; **no seas ∼** don't be such a pain (colloq) **(b)** (Andes fam) (aburrido) dull, boring
■ *m,f* **(a)** (fam) (pesado) pain (in the neck) (colloq) **(b)** (Andes fam) (aburrido) bore

laucha *f* (CS) mouse

laúd *m* lute

laurel *m* (árbol) laurel; (Coc) bay leaf

lava *f* lava

lavable *adj* washable

lavabo *m* **(a)** (pila) sink (AmE), washbasin (BrE) **(b)** (retrete) toilet, bathroom; ☻ **lavabos** rest rooms (*in US*), toilets (*in UK*)

lavadero *m* **(a)** (habitación) utility room, laundry room; (pila) sink; (al aire libre) washing place **(b)** (RPI) (lavandería) laundry **(c)** (Col) (tina de lavar) washtub

lavado¹ -da *adj* **(a)** ⟨*ropa/manos*⟩ washed **(b)** (RPI fam) ⟨*color*⟩ (descolorido) washed-out; (muy claro) light; ⟨*persona*⟩ pale

lavado² *m* **1 (a)** (de ropa) wash, washing; (de coche) wash; **∼ en seco** dry cleaning; **hacerle un ∼ de cerebro a algn** to brainwash sb; **le hicieron un ∼ de estómago** they pumped his stomach out **(b)** (ropa, tanda) wash **2** (AmL) (de dinero) laundering

lavadora *f* washing machine

lavamanos *m* sink (AmE), washbasin (BrE)

lavanda *f* lavender
■ *m* lavander

lavandería *f* laundry; **∼ automática** Laundromat® (AmE), launderette (BrE)

lavaplatos *mf* (*pl* ∼) (persona) dishwasher
■ *m* (*pl*) **(a)** (máquina) dishwasher **(b)** (Andes) (fregadero) sink

lavar [A1] *vt* **1** ⟨*ropa/coche*⟩ to wash; ⟨*suelo*⟩ to mop; ⟨*fruta/verdura*⟩ to wash; **hay que ∼lo en seco/a mano** it has to be dry-cleaned/hand-washed **2** (AmL) ⟨*dinero*⟩ to launder
■ ∼ *vi* **(a)** (lavar ropa) to do the laundry o (BrE) washing **(b)** (en peluquería): **∼ y marcar** to shampoo and set
■ **lavarse** *v pron* **(a)** (*refl*) to have a wash; ⟨*cara/manos*⟩ to wash; ⟨*dientes*⟩ to clean, brush; **∼se el pelo** or **la cabeza** to wash one's hair **(b)** (Col fam) (empaparse) to get soaked

lavarropas *m* (*pl* ∼) (RPI) washing machine

lavatorio *m* **(a)** (CS) (lavamanos) sink (AmE), washbasin (BrE) **(b)** (Chi, Per) (palangana) washbowl (AmE), washbasin (BrE)

lavavajillas *m* (*pl* ∼) (detergente) dishwashing liquid (AmE), washing-up liquid (BrE); (máquina) dishwasher

laxante *adj* laxative (*before n*)
■ *m* laxative

lazar [A4] *vt* (Méx) to rope, lasso

lazo *m* **1 (a)** (cinta) ribbon; (nudo decorativo) bow; **¿te hago un ∼?** shall I tie it in a bow? **(b)** (Méx) (del matrimonio) *cord with which the couple are symbolically united during the wedding ceremony* **2 (a)** (Agr) lasso **(b)** (cuerda) (Col, Méx) rope; (para saltar) (Col) ▶ CUERDA 1B **(c)** (para cazar) snare, trap **3** (vínculo) bond, tie

le *pron pers* **1** (como objeto indirecto): **∼ dije la verdad** (a él) I told him the truth; (a ella) I told her the truth; (a usted) I told you the truth; **∼ di otra mano de barniz** I gave it another coat of varnish; **∼ robaron el dinero** they stole the money from him; **a este libro ∼ faltan páginas** there are some pages missing from this book **2** (como objeto directo) (esp Esp) (referido — a él) him; (— a usted) you; **¿le conoces?** do you know him?; **hoy no ∼ puedo recibir** I can't see him/you today

leal *adj* loyal, trusty; ⟨*tropas*⟩ loyal

lealtad *f* loyalty

leasing /'lisin/ *m* (contrato) lease; (sistema) leasing

lección *f* lesson; **no me supe la ∼** I hadn't learned the lesson; **eso te servirá de ∼** let that be a lesson to you

lechal *adj* suckling

leche *f* **1** (de madre, de vaca) milk; **∼ descremada** *or* (Esp) **desnatada** skim milk (AmE), skimmed milk (BrE); **∼ en polvo** powdered milk; **∼ entera** whole milk, full-cream milk **2** (en cosmética) milk, lotion **3** (Esp vulg) (mal humor): **tiene una ∼ ...** he's got a foul temper; **hacer algo con mala ∼** to do sth deliberately o to be nasty; **tener mala ∼** to be bad-tempered **4** (Andes fam) (suerte) luck; **estar con** *or* **de ∼** to be lucky

lechera *f* (para transportar) churn; (para servir) milk jug

lechería *f* dairy, creamery

lechero -ra *adj* **1 (a)** ⟨*industria/vaca*⟩ dairy (*before n*) **(b)** ⟨*producción*⟩ milk (*before n*) **2** (Col, Per fam) (afortunado) lucky
■ *m,f* (vendedor) (*m*) milkman; (*f*) milkwoman

lecho *m* **1** (liter) (cama) bed; **en su ∼ de muerte** on her deathbed **2** (de río) bed; (capa, estrato) layer

lechón *m* (Coc) (cochinillo) suckling o sucking pig

lechosa *f* (AmC, Col, Ven) papaya

lechoso -sa *adj* ⟨*líquido*⟩ milky; ⟨*piel*⟩ pale

lechuga *f* lettuce

lechuza *f* owl

lectivo -va *adj* ⟨*día*⟩ school (*before n*); ⟨*año*⟩ academic (*before n*)

lector -tora *m,f* **(a)** (de libros, revistas) reader **(b)** (Esp) (Educ) foreign language assistant

lectura *f* **(a)** (acción) reading; **la ∼ es su**

pasatiempo preferido reading is her favorite pastime **(b)** (texto) reading matter; **∼s para niños** reading material for children

leer [E13] *vt* **(a)** ⟨*libro/texto*⟩ to read; **∼ los labios** to lip-read; **∼le el pensamiento a algn** to read sb's mind **(b)** (Educ) ⟨*tesis doctoral*⟩ to defend **(c)** (Inf) to scan
■ **∼** *vi* to read

legado *m* (Der) bequest, legacy

legal *adj* **1** (Der) **(a)** ⟨*trámite/documentos*⟩ legal **(b)** (lícito, permitido) lawful; **lo haré si es ∼** I'll do it as long as it's within the law **2** (Col, Per arg) (estupendo) great (colloq)

legalización *f* (Der) (de droga, aborto) legalization; (de documento) authentication

legalizar [A4] *vt* (Der) ⟨*droga/aborto*⟩ to legalize; ⟨*documento*⟩ to authenticate

legaña *f* sleep; **tienes ∼s en los ojos** you have (some) sleep in your eyes

legar [A3] *vt* (en testamento) to bequeath, leave

legendario -ria *adj* legendary

legible *adj* legible

legión *f* (Hist, Mil) legion; (multitud) crowd

legionario¹ -ria *adj* legionary

legionario² -ria *m* (romano) legionary; (de otras asociaciones) legionnaire

legislación *f* legislation

legislar [A1] *vi* to legislate

legislatura *f* **(a)** (mandato) term (of office); (año parlamentario) session **(b)** (AmL) (cuerpo) legislature, legislative body

legítimo -ma *adj* **1** ⟨*hijo*⟩ legitimate; ⟨*esposa*⟩ lawful (*before n*); ⟨*heredero*⟩ rightful (*before n*); ⟨*derechos/reclamación/representante*⟩ legitimate; **en legítima defensa** in self-defense **2** ⟨*cuero*⟩ genuine, real; ⟨*oro*⟩ real

lego -ga *adj* **1** (seglar) lay (*before n*) **2** (ignorante): **soy ∼ en la materia** I know nothing at all about the subject
■ *m,f* **(a)** (fiel laico) layperson **(b)** (religioso) (*m*) lay brother; (*f*) lay sister **(c)** (Col) (curandero) quack

legua *f* league

legumbre *f* (garbanzo, lenteja, etc) pulse, legume; (hortaliza) vegetable

leído -da *adj*: **ser muy ∼** to be well-read

leísmo *m*: *use of* LE/LES *instead of* LO/LOS/LA/LAS *(as in* ESTE LIBRO NO TE LE PRESTO*), common in certain regions of Spain but not acceptable to most speakers*

lejanía *f* remoteness; **en la ∼** in the distance

lejano -na *adj* **(a)** ⟨*época/futuro*⟩ distant; ⟨*lugar*⟩ remote, far-off; **el L∼ Oriente** the Far East **(b)** ⟨*pariente*⟩ distant

lejía *f* bleach

lejísimos *adv* ⟨*quedar/estar*⟩ very far (away); **vive ∼** she lives miles away

lejos *adv* **1** **(a)** (en el espacio) far; **no está muy ∼** it isn't very far; **queda ∼ del centro** it's a long way from the center; **estaba ∼ de imaginarme la verdad** I was far from guessing the truth **(b)** (*en locs*) **a lo lejos** in the distance; **de lejos** from a distance; **ir demasiado ∼** to go too far; **sin ir más ∼** for example, for instance **(c)** (fam) (con mucho): **es ∼** (CS) *o* (Col, Méx) **de ∼** by far **2** (en el futuro) a long way off; **las vacaciones aún están ∼s** the holidays are still a long way off

lelo -la *adj* (fam) (tonto) slow on the uptake; (pasmado) speechless

lema *m* (de insignia, de persona) motto; (de partido, anuncio publicitario) slogan

lempira *m* lempira (*Honduran unit of currency*)

lencería *f* lingerie

lengua *f* **1** **(a)** (Anat) tongue; **se me traba la ∼** I get tongue-tied (colloq); **irse de la ∼** *or* **írsele la ∼ a algn** (fam): **no debía haberlo dicho pero se me fue la ∼** I shouldn't have said it but it just slipped out; **no te vayas a ir de la ∼** make sure you don't tell anybody; ▶ MALO 2 **(b)** (Coc) tongue **(c)** (de tierra) spit, tongue; (de fuego) tongue **2** (Ling) language; **∼ materna** mother tongue

lenguado *m* sole

lenguaje *m* language

lengüeta *f* (de zapato) tongue; (Mús) reed

lente *m* [*en algunas regiones f*] lens; **∼ de contacto** contact lens; *ver tb* LENTES

lenteja *f* lentil

lentejuela *f* sequin

lentes *mpl* (esp AmL) ▶ GAFAS A

lentilla *f* (Esp) contact lens

lentitud *f* slowness; **con ∼** slowly

lento¹ -ta *adj* slow

lento² *adv* slowly

leña *f* wood, firewood

leñador -dora *m,f* woodcutter

leño *m* log

Leo *m* (signo) Leo; **es (de) ∼** he's a) Leo;
■ *mf* (*pl* **∼**) (persona) *tb* **leo** Leo

león -ona *m,f* (de África) (*m*) lion; (*f*) lioness

leonera *f* **(a)** (de león) lion's den **(b)** (Esp fam) (lugar desordenado) tip (colloq)

leopardo *m* leopard; **∼ hembra** leopardess

leotardo *m*: *tb* **∼s** (woolen) tights (*pl*)

lépero -ra *adj* (Méx) coarse

lepra *f* leprosy

leproso -sa *adj* leprous
■ *m,f* leper

lerdo -da *adj* (fam) (torpe) clumsy; (tonto) slow

les *pron pers* **1** (como objeto indirecto): **∼ quiero mostrar algo** (a ellos, ellas) I want to show them something; (a ustedes) I want to show you something; **∼ puse fundas a los muebles** I put covers on the furniture **2** (como objeto directo) (esp Esp) (referido — a ellos) them; (— a ustedes) you; **no ∼ reconocí** I didn't recognize them/you; **¿∼ atienden?** can I help you?

lesbiana *f* lesbian

lesear [A1] *vi* (Chi fam) (tontear) to clown *o* fool around (colloq); (bromear) to joke (colloq); (flirtear) to flirt; (perder el tiempo) to laze around

lesera *f* (Chi fam) nonsense, tripe (colloq)

lesión *f* injury; **sufrió una ∼ cerebral** he suffered brain damage

lesionado -da *adj* injured

lesionar [A1] *vt* ⟨*persona*⟩ to injure; **le ∼on la pierna en el partido** his leg was hurt *o* injured in the game
■ **lesionarse** *v pron* «*persona*» to injure oneself; ⟨*pierna/rodilla*⟩ to injure

leso -sa *adj* (Chi fam) dumb (colloq); **hacer ∼ a algn** (fam) to make a monkey out of sb (colloq)

letárgico -ca *adj* lethargic

letargo *m* lethargy

letra *f* ⌐1⌐ (a) (Impr, Ling) letter; ∼ **bastardilla** *or* **cursiva** italic script, italics (*pl*); ∼ **de imprenta** print; ∼ **negrita** boldface, bold type; ∼ **pequeña** *or* (AmS) **chica** small print (b) (caligrafía) writing, handwriting; **no entiendo tu** ∼ I can't read your writing (c) **letras** *fpl* (carta breve): **solo unas** ∼**s para decirte que ...** just a few lines to let you know that ...
⌐2⌐ (Mús) (de canción) words (*pl*), lyrics (*pl*)
⌐3⌐ (Fin) *tb* ∼ **de cambio** bill of exchange, draft; **me quedan tres** ∼**s por pagar** I still have three payments to make
⌐4⌐ **letras** *fpl* (Educ) arts (*pl*), liberal arts (*pl*) (AmE)

letrado -da *adj* learned
■ *m,f* (frml) lawyer

letrero *m* sign, notice; ∼ **luminoso** neon sign

letrina *f* latrine

leucemia *f* leukemia

levadura *f* yeast; **pan sin** ∼ unleavened bread; ∼ **de cerveza** brewer's yeast; ∼ **en polvo** (Esp) baking powder

levantado -da *adj*: **estar** ∼ to be up

levantador -dora *m,f* (Dep) *tb* ∼ **de pesas** weightlifter

levantamiento *m* (a) (sublevación) uprising (b) (de embargo, sanción) lifting; ∼ **de pesas** weightlifting

levantar [A1] *vt* ⌐1⌐ (a) (del suelo) ⟨bulto/peso⟩ to lift, pick up (b) ⟨tapadera/mantel⟩ to lift (up); ⟨cabeza/mano/copa⟩ to raise; ⟨alfombra⟩ to lift up (c) ⟨persiana⟩ to pull up, raise (d) (elevar) ⟨voz⟩ to raise; **sin** ∼ **la vista del libro** without looking up from her book (e) ⟨polvo⟩ to raise (f) (Jueg) ⟨carta⟩ to pick up
⌐2⌐ (a) ⟨ánimo⟩ to boost; ⟨moral⟩ to raise, boost (b) ⟨industria/economía⟩ to help ... to pick up
⌐3⌐ ⟨estatua/muro/edificio⟩ to erect, put up
⌐4⌐ ⟨embargo/sanción⟩ to lift; **le levantó el castigo** he let him off; **se levanta la sesión** the meeting is adjourned
⌐5⌐ ⟨rumor/protestas⟩ to spark (off); ⟨polémica⟩ to cause; ∼ **sospechas** to arouse suspicion
⌐6⌐ ⟨campamento⟩ to strike; ∼ **la mesa** (AmL) to clear the table
⌐7⌐ (en brazos) ⟨persona⟩ to pick up; (de la cama) to get ... out of bed; (poner de pie) to get ... up
⌐8⌐ (AmS) ⟨mujer⟩ to pick up (colloq)
■ **levantarse** *v pron* ⌐1⌐ (a) (de la cama) to get up (b) (ponerse en pie) to stand up, to rise (frml); **¿me puedo** ∼ **de la mesa?** may I leave the table?
⌐2⌐ «polvareda» to rise; «temporal» to brew; «viento» to begin to blow, rise
⌐3⌐ (sublevarse) to rise (up)
⌐4⌐ (refl) ⟨solapas/cuello⟩ to turn up
⌐5⌐ (AmS fam) ⟨mujer⟩ to pick up (colloq)

levante *m* ⌐1⌐ (a) (Geog) (este) east (b) (viento) east wind ⌐2⌐ (AmS fam) (conquista) pick up

levar [A1] *vt*: ∼ **anclas** to weigh anchor

leve *adj* (a) ⟨perfume/gasa⟩ delicate (b) ⟨sospecha/duda⟩ slight; ⟨sonrisa⟩ slight; ⟨brisa⟩ gentle, slight; ⟨golpe⟩ gentle, light; ⟨enfermedad⟩ mild; ⟨herida/lesión⟩ slight; ⟨pecado⟩ venial; ⟨castigo/sanción⟩ light; ⟨infracción⟩ minor

levita *f* (Indum) frock coat

léxico¹ -ca *adj* lexical

léxico² *m* (vocabulario) vocabulary, lexis (tech); (diccionario) lexicon; (glosario) glossary, lexicon

ley *f* ⌐1⌐ (en general) law; **violar la** ∼ to break the law; **iguales ante la** ∼ equal in the eyes of the law; ∼ **de la oferta y la demanda** law of supply and demand; **la** ∼ **del más fuerte** the survival of the fittest; ∼ **pareja no es dura** (CS) a rule isn't unfair if it applies to everyone ⌐2⌐ (de oro, plata) assay value

leyenda *f* (a) (Lit) (narración) legend (b) (de moneda, escudo) legend; (de ilustración) caption, legend

leyeron, leyó, etc ▶ LEER

liado -da *adj* (fam) (a) (ocupado) tied up (b) (relacionado) ∼ **CON algn** involved WITH sb

liana *f* liana

liar [A17] *vt* ⌐1⌐ (a) ⟨cigarrillo⟩ to roll (b) (atar) to tie (up); (envolver) to wrap (up); (en un fardo, manojo) to bundle (up) ⌐2⌐ (fam) (a) ⟨situación/asunto⟩ to complicate (b) (confundir) ⟨persona⟩ to confuse, get ... in a muddle (c) (en un asunto) ⟨persona⟩ to involve
■ **liarse** *v pron* ⌐1⌐ (fam) (a) «asunto» to get complicated (b) «persona» to get confused
⌐2⌐ (Esp fam) (a) (entretenerse): **nos liamos a hablar y ...** we got talking and ... (b) (emprenderla): **se** ∼**on a golpes** they started throwing punches at each other

libanés -nesa *adj/m,f* Lebanese

Líbano *m*: *tb* **el** ∼ Lebanon

libélula *f* dragonfly

liberación *f* (de preso, rehén) release, freeing; (de pueblo, país) liberation; **la** ∼ **de la mujer** Women's Liberation, Women's Lib

liberado -da *adj* ⟨mujer⟩ liberated

liberal *adj* liberal
■ *mf* Liberal

liberalismo *m* liberalism

liberalizar [A4] *vt* ⟨comercio/importaciones⟩ to relax the restrictions on

liberar [A1] *vt* (a) ⟨prisionero/rehén⟩ to release, free; ⟨pueblo/país⟩ to liberate (b) (de una obligación) ∼ **a algn DE algo** to free sb FROM sth
■ **liberarse** *v pron* ∼**se DE algo** ⟨de ataduras/deudas⟩ to free oneself FROM sth

libertad *f* ⌐1⌐ (para actuar) freedom; **queda usted en** ∼ you are free to go; **poner a algn en** ∼ to release sb; ∼ **bajo fianza** bail; ∼ **condicional** parole; ∼ **de expresión/de prensa** freedom of speech/of the press ⌐2⌐ (confianza): **pídelo con toda** ∼ feel free to ask; **habla con toda** ∼ speak freely; **tomarse la** ∼ **de hacer algo** to take the liberty of doing sth

libertador -dora *m,f* liberator

libertinaje *m* licentiousness

libertino -na *adj* dissolute, licentious
■ *m,f* libertine

Libia *f* Libya

libidinoso -sa *adj* lustful

libido, líbido *f* libido

libio -bia *adj/m,f* Libyan

libra *f* pound; ~ **esterlina** pound sterling

Libra *m* (signo) Libra; **es (de)** ~ she's a Libra,
she's a Libran
■ *mf* (*pl* ~ *or* **-bras**) (persona) *tb* **libra** Libran,
Libra

libramiento *m* (Méx) (Transp) beltway (AmE),
relief road (BrE)

librar [A1] *vt* ⊡ (liberar) ~ **a algn DE algo** ⟨*de
peligro*⟩ to save sb FROM sth; ⟨*de obligación/
responsabilidad*⟩ to free sb FROM sth; **¡Dios nos
libre!** God forbid! ⊡ ⟨*batalla/combate*⟩ to fight
■ **librarse** *v pron*: **se libró por poco** he had a
lucky escape; ~**se DE algo** ⟨*de tarea/obligación*⟩
to get out of sth; ~**se de un castigo** to escape
punishment; **se libró de tener que ayudarlo** he
got out of having to help him; **se ~on de morir
asfixiados** they escaped being suffocated; ~**se DE
algn** to get rid of sb

libre *adj* ⊡ ⟨*país/pueblo*⟩ free; **lo dejaron** ~ they
set him free; **eres** ~ **de ir donde quieras** you're
free to go wherever you want; ~ **albedrío** free
will; ~ **cambio** *or* **comercio** free trade; ~
mercado free market ⊡ ⟨*traducción/adaptación*⟩
free; **los 200 metros** ~**s** the 200 meters freestyle
⊡ (no ocupado) ⟨*persona/tiempo/asiento*⟩ free;
¿tienes un rato ~**?** do you have a (spare)
moment?; **en sus ratos** ~**s** in her spare *o* free
time; **tengo el día** ~ I have the day off
⊡ (exento): **artículos** ~**s de impuestos** duty-free
goods

librecambista *adj* free-trade (*before n*)

librería *f* ⊡ (tienda) bookstore (AmE), bookshop
(BrE); ~ **de ocasión** second-hand bookstore
⊡ (Esp) (mueble) bookcase

librero -ra *m,f* (a) (Com) bookseller (b)
librero *m* (Chi, Méx) (mueble) bookcase

libreta *f* notebook; ~ **de ahorro** passbook,
bankbook; ~ **de calificaciones** (AmL) school
report

libretearse [A1] *v pron* (AmC fam) to play
hooky (esp AmE colloq), to skive off (school) (BrE
colloq)

libreto *m* ⊡ (a) (de ópera) libretto (b) (AmL)
(guion) script ⊡ (Chi) *tb* ~ **de cheques**
checkbook*

libro *m* (Impr) book; **un** ~ **de cocina** a cookbook;
llevar los ~**s** (Fin) to do the bookkeeping; ~ **de
bolsillo** paperback; ~ **de consulta** reference book;
~ **de escolaridad** school record; ~ **de familia**
*booklet recording details of one's marriage,
children's birthdates, etc*; ~ **de texto** textbook

liceal *mf* (Ur) high school student (AmE),
secondary school pupil (BrE)

liceano -na *m,f* (Chi) ▶ LICEAL

liceísta *mf* (Ven) ▶ LICEAL

licencia *f* ⊡ (documento) license*; ~ **de caza**
hunting permit; ~ **de conducir** *or* (AmC, Méx, Ven)
de manejar driver's license (AmE), driving licence
(BrE) ⊡ (a) (Mil) leave; **con** ~ on leave (b) (AmL)
(de un trabajo) leave; **estar de** ~ to be on leave

licenciado -da *m,f* (a) (Educ) graduate; ~ **en
Filosofía y Letras** ≈ arts *o* (AmE) liberal arts
graduate (b) (AmC, Méx) (abogado) lawyer

licenciar [A1] *vt* ⟨*soldado*⟩ to discharge
■ **licenciarse** *v pron* «*estudiante*» to graduate

licenciatura *f* degree

licencioso -sa *adj* dissolute

liceo *m* (CS, Ven) high school (AmE), secondary
school (BrE)

licitación *f* (esp AmL) tender; **se llamará a** ~
para la construcción del puente the construction
of the bridge will be put out to tender

licitar [A1] *vt* (esp AmL) (llamar a concurso para) to
invite tenders for; (presentar una propuesta para) to
put in a tender for

lícito -ta *adj* (a) (dentro de la ley) ⟨*acto/conducta*⟩
legal, lawful; ⟨*jugada*⟩ legal (b) (admisible)
justifiable, reasonable

licor *m* (bebida dulce) liqueur; (alcohol) liquor,
spirits (*pl*)

licuado *m* (AmL) (con leche) (milk) shake; (de
frutas) fruit drink

licuadora *f* blender, liquidizer (BrE)

licuar [A18] *vt* (a) (Coc) ⟨*frutas/verduras*⟩ to
blend, liquidize (b) (Fís, Quím) to liquefy

líder¹ *mf* (a) (Com, Dep, Pol) leader (b) (*como adj*)
⟨*equipo/marca/empresa*⟩ leading (*before n*)

líder² lideresa *m,f* (Méx) (Dep, Pol) leader

liderazgo, liderato *m* leadership

lidiar [A1] *vt* ⟨*toro*⟩ to fight
■ ~ *vi*: ~ **CON algn/algo** to battle WITH sb/sth

liebre *f* ⊡ (Zool) hare ⊡ (Chi) (Transp) small bus

liendre *f* nit

lienzo *m* ⊡ (a) (Art) canvas (b) (Tex) cloth
⊡ (Arquit) (pared) wall

lifting /'liftin/ *m* facelift

liga *f* ⊡ (asociación) league; (Dep) league,
conference (esp AmE) ⊡ (a) (Indum) garter (b)
(AmL) (gomita) rubber *o* (BrE) elastic band

ligado *adj* [ESTAR] (conectado) connected, linked;
(apegado) ~ **A algn** attached TO sb; **se siente muy**
~ **a su país** he feels a strong bond with his
country

ligadura *f* (a) (Med) ligature (b) **ligaduras** *fpl*
(ataduras) bonds (*pl*), ties (*pl*)

ligamento *m* ligament

ligar [A3] *vt* (a) (unir) to bind; **los ligaba una
gran amistad** they were bound together by a
strong friendship (b) (atar): **le** ~**on las manos**
they tied his hands together; **un fajo de billetes
ligados con una goma elástica** a bundle of bills
held together with a rubber band (c) ⟨*metales*⟩ to
alloy; ⟨*salsa*⟩ to bind
■ ~ *vi* (fam) (con el sexo opuesto): **salieron a** ~ they
went out on the make *o* (BrE) pull (colloq); ~ **CON
algn** to make out WITH sb (AmE), to get off WITH sb
(BrE)
■ **ligarse** *v pron* (fam) (conquistar) to make out
with (AmE colloq), to get off with (colloq BrE)

ligazón *f* connection, link

ligereza *f* ⊡ (de objeto) lightness ⊡ (a) (de
carácter) flippancy; **con** ~ ⟨*actuar/hablar*⟩
flippantly (b) (acto, dicho irreflexivo): **cometió la** ~
de mencionarlo he thoughtlessly mentioned it
⊡ (agilidad) agility, nimbleness; (rapidez) speed

ligero¹ -ra *adj* ⊡ (liviano) (a) ⟨*paquete/gas/* ⋯⟶

metal⟩ light; ⟨tela⟩ light, thin; **~ de ropa** lightly
dressed; **viajar ~ de equipaje** to travel light **(b)**
⟨comida/masa⟩ light **2** ⟨leve⟩ **(a)** ⟨dolor/sabor/
olor⟩ slight; ⟨inconveniente⟩ slight, minor; ⟨golpe⟩
gentle, slight; **tener el sueño ~** to be a light
sleeper **(b)** ⟨sensación/sospecha⟩ slight **3** ⟨no
serio⟩ ⟨conversación⟩ lighthearted; ⟨película/
lectura⟩ lightweight; **a la ligera** ⟨actuar⟩ without
thinking, hastily; **todo se lo toma a la ligera** he
doesn't take anything seriously **4** ⟨ágil⟩
⟨movimiento⟩ agile, nimble; ⟨rápido⟩ ⟨persona/
animal/vehículo⟩ fast

ligero² *adv* quickly, fast

light /lajt/ *adj inv* ⟨cigarrillos⟩ low-tar;
⟨alimentos⟩ low-calorie; ⟨refresco⟩ diet (*before n*)

ligue *m* (Esp, Méx fam) **(a)** ⟨persona⟩: **el nuevo ~
de Ana** Ana's new man (colloq) **(b)** ⟨acción⟩: **ir de
~** to go out on the make *o* (BrE) pull

liguero *m* garter belt (AmE), suspender belt
(BrE)

lija *f* **(a)** (para madera, metales) *tb* **papel de ~**
sandpaper **(b)** (Ven) ▶ LIMA 1B

lijar [A1] *vt* to sand (down)

lila *f* (Bot) lilac
■ *adj* (gen inv) ⟨color⟩ lilac
■ *m* (color) lilac

lima *f* **1** **(a)** (herramienta) file **(b)** (para uñas — de
metal) nail file; (—de papel) emery board **2** (Bot)
(fruto) lime; (árbol) lime (tree)

Lima *f* Lima

limar [A1] *vt* ⟨uñas/metal⟩ to file
■ **limarse** *v pron* ⟨uñas⟩ to file

limeño -ña *adj* of/from Lima
■ *m,f* person from Lima

limitación *f* **(a)** (restricción) restriction,
limitation **(b)** (carencia) limitation; (defecto)
shortcoming

limitado -da *adj* ⟨poder/número/edición⟩
limited; **estar ~ A/POR algo** to be restricted TO/BY
sth

limitar [A1] *vt* ⟨funciones/derechos⟩ to limit,
restrict
■ **~** *vi* **~ CON algo** «país/finca» to border ON sth
■ **limitarse** *v pron*: **el problema no se limita a las
ciudades** the problem is not confined *o* limited to
cities; **me limité a repetir lo dicho** I just repeated
what was said

límite *m* **1** (Geog, Pol) boundary **2** (tope) limit;
el ~ de velocidad the speed limit; **su ambición no
tiene ~s** his ambition knows no limits; **sin ~s**
unlimited; **¡todo tiene un ~!** enough is enough!
3 (como adj inv): **tiempo ~** time limit; **situación
~** extreme situation; **fecha ~** deadline

limítrofe *adj* ⟨país/provincia⟩ neighboring*
(*before n*); ⟨conflicto⟩ border (*before n*)

limo *m* **1** (barro) mud, slime **2** (Col) (Bot) lime
(tree)

limón *m* **(a)** (fruto amarillo) lemon **(b)** (AmL) (árbol)
lemon tree **(c)** (Méx, Ven) (fruto verde) lime

limonada *f* lemonade

limonero *m* lemon tree

limosna *f* alms (*pl*) (arch); **pedir ~** to beg; **dar
~** to give money to beggars

limosnear [A1] *vi* (AmL) to beg

limosnero -ra *m,f* (AmL) beggar

limpiabotas *mf* (*pl* **~**) bootblack; (niño)
shoeshine boy

limpiacristales *m* (*pl* **~**) (Esp) (líquido)
window cleaner
■ *mf* (persona) window cleaner

limpiador¹ -dora *m,f* (persona) cleaner

limpiador² *m* (Méx) (Auto) ▶ LIMPIAPARABRISAS

limpiamuebles *m* (*pl* **~**) furniture polish

limpiaparabrisas *m* (*pl* **~**) windshield
wipers (*pl*) (AmE), windscreen wipers (*pl*) (BrE)

limpiar [A1] *vt* **1** **(a)** ⟨casa/mueble/zapatos⟩ to
clean; ⟨arroz/lentejas⟩ to wash; ⟨pescado⟩ to
clean; ⟨aire/atmósfera⟩ to clear; **lo limpió con un
trapo** he wiped it with a cloth; **~ algo en seco** to
dry-clean sth **(b)** ⟨nombre⟩ to clear; ⟨honor⟩ to
restore **2** (dejar libre) **~ algo DE algo** to clear sth
OF sth **3** (fam) **(a)** (en el juego) ⟨persona⟩ to clean
... out (colloq) **(b)** «ladrones» ⟨casa⟩ to clean ...
out (colloq)
■ **~** *vi* to clean
■ **limpiarse** *v pron* (refl) ⟨boca/nariz⟩ to wipe; **se
~on los zapatos al entrar** they wiped their shoes
as they came in

limpiavidrios *mf* (*pl* **~**) (esp AmL) (persona)
window cleaner
■ *m* (líquido) window cleaner

limpieza *f* **1** (estado, cualidad) cleanliness
2 (acción) cleaning; **la señora de la ~** the
cleaning lady; **~ de cutis** skin cleansing; **~ en
seco** drycleaning; **~ general** spring-cleaning
(AmE), spring-clean (BrE); **~ étnica** ethnic
cleansing **3** (por la policía) clean-up operation;
(Pol) purge

limpio¹ -pia *adj* **1** **(a)** [ESTAR] ⟨casa/vestido/
vaso⟩ clean **(b)** ⟨aire⟩ clean; ⟨cielo⟩ clear **(c)**
pasar algo en *or* (Esp) **a ~** to make a clean (AmE)
o (BrE) fair copy of sth **2** [SER] **(a)** ⟨persona⟩ clean **(b)** ⟨dinero/
campaña⟩ clean; ⟨elecciones/juego⟩ fair, clean; **un
asunto poco ~** an underhand business **(c)** (libre)
~ DE algo ⟨de impurezas/polvo⟩ free of sth
3 (neto): **saca unos $70 ~s por mes** she makes
$70 a month after deductions; **sacar en ~:** **no
sacó nada en ~ de todo lo que dijo** he didn't
make sense of anything he said; **lo único que
saqué en ~ es que ...** the only thing that I got
clear was that ...

limpio² *adv* ⟨jugar/pelear⟩ fairly, clean

linaje *m* descent, lineage (frml)

linaza *f* linseed

lince *m* (Zool) lynx; (persona): **es un ~ para los
negocios** he's a very shrewd businessman

linchar [A1] *vt* to lynch

lindar [A1] *vi* **~ CON algo** (limitar) to adjoin sth;
(aproximarse a) to border ON sth, verge ON sth

lindo¹ -da *adj* **1** (bonito) ⟨bebé⟩ cute, sweet;
⟨casa/canción⟩ lovely; ⟨cara⟩ pretty **2** (esp AmL)
(agradable) ⟨gesto/detalle⟩ nice; ⟨fiesta/viaje⟩
wonderful; ⟨ceremonia⟩ beautiful; **¡es una
persona tan linda!** she's such a lovely person; **de
lo ~** (fam): **nos divertimos de lo ~** we had a great
time

lindo² *adv* (AmL) ⟨cantar/bailar⟩ beautifully; **se
siente ~** (Méx) it feels wonderful

lindura *f* (AmL) delight; **me pareció una ~** I
thought it was lovely

línea *f* **1** (en general) line; **la ~ de puntos** the dotted line; **escribirle unas ~s a algn** to drop sb a line; **seguir la ~ del partido** to follow the party line; **en ~s generales** broadly speaking; **por ~ materna** on his (*o* her *etc*) mother's side; **~ de montaje** assembly line; **~ de gol** goal line; **~ de llegada** finishing line, wire (AmE); **~ de salida** starting line; *de primera ~* ‹*tecnología*› state-of-the-art; ‹*producto*› top-quality, high-class; ‹*actor/jugador*› first-rate; *leer entre ~s* to read between the lines

2 (Transp, Tele) line; **~ aérea** airline; **final de la ~** end of the line; **no hay ~ directa a Córdoba** there is no direct service to Cordoba; **intenté llamarte pero no había ~** I tried to ring you but the phone *o* the line was dead; **la ~ está ocupada** the line is busy

3 (a) (gama, colección) line, range; **nuestra nueva ~ de cosméticos** our new line *o* range of cosmetics **(b)** (estilo): **una ~ más clásica** a more classic look

4 (figura): **cuidar la ~** to watch one's figure

lineal *adj* linear

lingo *m* (Per) leapfrog

lingote *m* ingot

lingüística *f* linguistics

lingüístico -ca *adj* ‹*fenómeno/aptitud*› linguistic; ‹*barrera*› language (*before n*)

lino *m* (planta) flax; (tela) linen

linóleo *m* lino, linoleum

linterna *f* (fanal) lantern; (de pilas) flashlight (AmE), torch (BrE)

lío *m* **1 (a)** (fam) (embrollo, confusión) mess; **armarse/hacerse un ~** (con algo) to get into a mess (with sth) (colloq) **(b)** (fam) (problema, complicación) trouble; **meterse en un ~** to get oneself into trouble; **tiene ~s con la policía** he's in trouble with the police (colloq); **¡qué ~ se va a armar!** there's going to be hell to pay! (colloq) **(c)** (fam) (amorío) affair **2** (fardo) bundle

lioso -sa *adj* (fam) confusing, muddling

liquidación *f* **1** (en tienda) sale; **~ total** clearance sale **2** (de negocio, activo) liquidation **3 (a)** (de cuenta, deuda) settlement **(b)** (Méx) (compensación por despido) severance pay

liquidar [A1] *vt* **1** ‹*existencias*› to sell off **2** ‹*negocio*› to wind up; ‹*activo*› to liquidate **3 (a)** ‹*deuda/cuenta*› to settle; ‹*sueldo/pago*› to pay **(b)** (Méx) ‹*trabajador*› to pay … off **4** (fam) ‹*persona*› (matar) to do away with (colloq); (destruir) (AmL) to destroy (colloq)

liquidez *f* liquidity

líquido¹ -da *adj* **1** ‹*sustancia*› liquid **2** ‹*sueldo/renta*› net

líquido² *m* **1** (sustancia) liquid; **~ de frenos** brake fluid **2** (dinero) cash

lira *f* **(a)** (Mús) lyre **(b)** (Fin) lira

lírica *f* poetry

lírico -ca *adj* **(a)** (Lit, Mús) lyric **(b)** (Per, RPI fam) ‹*persona*› dreamy, starry-eyed (colloq)

lirio *m* iris

lirón *m* dormouse; ▸ DORMIR *vi*

lis *f* lily

lisiado -da *adj* crippled
■ *m,f* cripple; **un ~ de guerra** a disabled veteran

lisiarse [A1] *v pron* (refl): **se lisió la columna vertebral** he damaged his spine

liso -sa *adj* **1** ‹*piel/superficie*› smooth; ‹*pelo*› straight; ‹*terreno*› flat **2** (sin dibujos) plain **3** (Per fam) (insolente) fresh (AmE colloq), cheeky (BrE colloq)

lisonjero -ra *adj* ‹*palabras*› flattering; **es un hombre muy ~** he's a terrible flatterer

lista *f* **(a)** (de nombres, números) list; **pasar ~** (Educ) to take roll call, to take the register (BrE); **~ de boda** wedding list; **~ de espera** waiting list; **~ de éxitos** (Mús) charts (*pl*); (Lit) best-seller list **(b)** (raya) stripe; **a ~s** striped

listado *m* (Inf) printout; (lista) list; **~ electoral** (RPI) electoral roll *o* register

listar [A1] *vt* to list

listín *m* (Esp) *tb* **~ de teléfonos** telephone directory

listo -ta *adj* **1** [SER] ‹*persona*› clever, bright, smart (colloq); **se pasó de ~** he tried to be too clever; **estar ~** (fam): **ahora sí que estamos ~s** we're in real trouble now (colloq); **está lista si cree eso** if that's what she thinks, she's got another think coming (colloq) **2 (a)** [ESTAR] (preparado) ready; **~ PARA algo/hacer algo** ready FOR sth/to do sth **(b)** [ESTAR] (terminado) finished; **lo doblas así y ~** you fold it like this and that's it (finished) **(c)** (Andes fam) (manifestando acuerdo) okay (colloq)
■ *m,f* (esp Esp) **(a)** (inteligente) clever one; **el ~ de la clase** (pey) the class know-it-all (colloq & pej) **(b)** (vivo, astuto) tricky customer (colloq)

listón *m* **(a)** (de madera) strip; (en salto de altura) bar **(b)** (Méx) (cinta) ribbon

lisura *f* (Per) **(a)** (fam) (grosería) four-letter word (colloq) **(b)** (gracia) gracefulness

litera *f* (en dormitorio) bunk; (en barco) bunk, berth; (en tren) berth, couchette (BrE)

literal *adj* literal

literalmente *adv* ‹*traducir*› literally; ‹*repetir*› word for word

literario -ria *adj* literary

literato -ta *m,f* (*m*) man of letters; (*f*) woman of letters

literatura *f* literature; **~ infantil** juvenile books (AmE), children's books (BrE)

litigar [A3] *vi* to be at law *o* in litigation (frml), to be in dispute

litigio *m* **(a)** (Der) lawsuit **(b)** (disputa) dispute

litografía *f* (sistema) lithography; (grabado) lithograph

litoral *adj* coastal
■ *m* coast; **un largo ~** a long coastline

litro *m* liter*

Lituania *f* Lithuania

lituano¹ -na *adj/m,f* Lithuanian

lituano² *m* (idioma) Lithuanian

liturgia *f* liturgy

liviano -na *adj* (esp AmL) **(a)** ‹*paquete/tela*› light **(b)** ‹*comida*› light; **tiene un sueño muy ~** she's a very light sleeper **(c)** ‹*obra/película*› lightweight

lívido -da *adj* (pálido) pallid; (morado) livid

living /'liβin/ *m* (*pl* **-vings**) (esp AmS) living room

Ll, ll *f* (read as /'eye/) combination traditionally considered as a separate letter in the Spanish alphabet

llaga *f* (Med) sore, ulcer; (Bib) wound

llama f [1] (de fuego) flame; **la casa ardía en** ~**s** the house was in flames; ~ **piloto** pilot light [2] (Zool) llama

llamada f call; **hacer una** ~ to make a phone call; ~ **a cobro revertido** or (Chi, Méx) **por cobrar** collect call (AmE), reverse-charge call (BrE); ~ **de larga distancia** long-distance call; ~ **local** or **urbana** local call; ~ **al orden** call to order

llamado¹ -da adj [1] (por un nombre) called; **un lugar** ~ **La Dehesa** a place called La Dehesa; **el 747, también** ~ **'jumbo'** the 747, also known as the jumbo jet; **el** ~ **'boom' de los sesenta** the so-called 'boom' of the sixties [2] (a la fama, éxito) ▶ DESTINADO 1A

llamado² m (a) (AmL) (al público) ▶ LLAMAMIENTO (b) (Arg) (Telec) ▶ LLAMADA

llamamiento m call; **hacer un** ~ **a la calma** to appeal for calm

llamar [A1] vt [1] ⟨bomberos/policía⟩ to call; ⟨médico⟩ to call (out); ⟨camarero/criada/ascensor⟩ to call; ⟨súbditos/servidores⟩ to summon; ⟨taxi⟩ (por teléfono) to call; (en la calle) to hail; **lo llamó por señas** she beckoned to him; **el sindicato los llamó a la huelga** the union called them out on strike
[2] (por teléfono) to phone, to call; **te llamó Eva** Eva phoned (for you)
[3] (a) (dar el nombre de) to call, name; (dar el título, apodo de) to call (b) (considerar) to call; **eso es lo que yo llamo un amigo** that's what I call a friend
■ ~ vi [1] (con los nudillos) to knock; (tocar el timbre) to ring (the doorbell); **llaman a la puerta** there's someone at the door
[2] (Telec) ⟨persona⟩ to telephone, phone, call; ⟨teléfono⟩ to ring; **¿quién llama?** who's calling?; ver tb COBRO B
■ **llamarse** v pron to be called; **su padre se llama Pedro** his father is called Pedro, his father's name is Pedro; **¿cómo te llamas?** what's your name?

llamarada f (de fuego) sudden blaze, flare-up

llamativo -va adj ⟨color⟩ bright; ⟨mujer/vestido⟩ striking

llanamente adv: **lisa** or **simple y** ~ ⟨explicar/hablar⟩ in straightforward terms; **lisa y** ~, **hay que despedirlos** they should be fired, it's as simple as that

llanero -ra m,f (a) (habitante del llano) (m) plainsman; (f) plainswoman (b) (vaquero) cattle herder, cowboy (of the Colombian/Venezuelan LLANOS)

llaneza f simplicity

llano¹ -na adj (a) ⟨terreno/superficie⟩ (horizontal) flat; (sin desniveles) even; **los 100 metros** ~**s** (RPI) the 100 meters dash o sprint (b) ⟨persona⟩ straightforward (c) ⟨trato⟩ natural; ⟨lenguaje⟩ plain

llano² m (a) (Geog) (llanura) plain (b) (extensión de terreno) area of flat ground

llanta f (a) (de metal) rim (b) (AmL) (neumático) tire*; ~ **de repuesto** or (Méx) **de refacción** spare tire*

llanto m (de niño) crying; (de adulto) crying, weeping (liter)

llanura f (Geog) plain, prairie

llapa f ▶ YAPA

llave f [1] (en general) key; **cierra la puerta con** ~ lock the door; **bajo** ~ under lock and key; **la** ~ **del éxito** the key to success; ~ **de contacto** ignition key; ~ **maestra** master key, passkey
[2] (Mec) (herramienta) wrench (AmE), spanner (BrE); ~ **inglesa** monkey wrench
[3] (a) (interruptor) switch; (en tubería) valve; **la** ~ **del gas** the gas jet (AmE) o (BrE) tap; **cerrar la** ~ **de paso** to turn the water/gas off at the main valve (AmE) o (BrE) at the mains (b) (AmL) (de lavabo, bañera) faucet (AmE), tap (BrE)
[4] (en un texto) brace
[5] (en lucha, judo) hold; **lo inmovilizó con una** ~ **(de brazo)** she got him in an armlock

llavero m key ring

llegada f (a) (de un viaje) arrival; (b) (Dep) (meta) finishing line, wire (AmE); (Equ) winning post

llegar [A3] vi [1] «persona/tren/carta» to arrive; **tienen que estar por** or **al** ~ they'll be arriving any minute now; ~**on cansadísimos** they were exhausted when they arrived; **¿falta mucho para** ~? is it much further (to go)?; **siempre llega tarde** he's always late; **no me llegó el telegrama** I didn't get the telegram; ~ **A algo** ⟨a país/ciudad⟩ to arrive IN sth; ⟨a edificio⟩ to arrive AT sth; ~ **a casa** to arrive o get home; **el rumor llegó a oídos del alcalde** the rumor reached the mayor
[2] «camino/ruta/tren» (ir) ~ **A** or **HASTA** to go all the way to, to go as far as; **solo llega al tercer piso** it only goes (up) to the third floor
[3] «día/invierno» to come, arrive; **ha llegado el momento de ...** the time has come to ...
[4] (a) (alcanzar) to reach; ~ **A algo** ⟨a acuerdo/conclusión⟩ to reach sth, come to sth; ⟨a estante/techo⟩ to reach; **llegué a la conclusión de que...** I reached o came to the conclusion that ...; **los pies no le llegan al suelo** her feet don't touch the floor; **la falda le llegaba a los tobillos** her skirt came down to her ankles; **el agua le llegaba al cuello** the water came up to her neck; **las cosas** ~**on a tal punto que ...** things reached such a point that ... (b) (expresando logro): ~**á lejos** she'll go far o a long way; **así no vas a** ~ **a ningún lado** you'll never get anywhere like that; **llegó a (ser) director** he became director; ~ **a viejo** to live to old age; **llegué a conocerlo mejor** I got to know him better
[5] ~ **A** + **INF** (a) (al extremo de): **llegó a amenazarme** she even threatened me; **no llegó a pegarme** he didn't actually hit me (b) (en oraciones condicionales): **si lo llega a saber, no vengo** if I'd known, I wouldn't have come; **si llega a enterarme de algo, te aviso** if I happen to hear anything, I'll let you know

llenado m filling, filling up

llenador -dora adj (CS) ⟨comida⟩ filling

AmC	América Central	Arg	Argentina	Cu	Cuba
AmL	América Latina	Bol	Bolivia	Ec	Ecuador
AmS	América del Sur	Chi	Chile	Esp	España
Andes	Región andina	CS	Cono Sur	Méx	México

Per	Perú
RPI	Río de la Plata
Ur	Uruguay
Ven	Venezuela

llenar [A1] *vt* **1** **(a)** ⟨*vaso/plato/cajón*⟩ to fill; ⟨*tanque*⟩ to fill (up); ⟨*maleta*⟩ to fill, pack; **no me llenes el vaso** don't fill my glass right up; **∼ algo DE/CON algo** to fill sth WITH sth **(b)** ⟨*formulario*⟩ to fill out, to fill in (esp BrE) **2** **(a)** (cubrir) **∼ algo DE algo** to cover sth WITH sth **(b)** ⟨*vacante*⟩ to fill **3** (colmar) ⟨*persona*⟩: **la noticia nos llenó de alegría** we were overjoyed by the news; **nos llenó de atenciones** he made a real fuss of us **4** (hacer sentirse realizado) ⟨*persona*⟩: **su carrera no la llena** she doesn't find her career fulfilling

■ **∼** *vi* «*comida*» to be filling

■ **llenarse** *v pron* **1** **(a)** ⟨*recipiente/estadio*⟩ to fill (up); **el teatro solo se llenó a la mitad** the theater only filled to half capacity *o* was only half full; **∼se DE algo** to fill WITH sth **(b)** (cubrirse) **∼se DE algo** ⟨*de polvo/pelos*⟩ to be covered IN sth **2** ⟨*bolsillo/boca*⟩ to fill; **∼se algo DE algo** to fill sth WITH sth **3** (colmarse): **su corazón se llenó de alegría** she filled with joy; **se ∼on de deudas** they got heavily into debt **4** ⟨*persona*⟩ (de comida): **con un plato de ensalada ya se llena** one plate of salad and she's full; **me llené** (colloq) I'm full (up) (colloq)

lleno¹ **-na** *adj* **1** **(a)** ⟨*estadio/autobús/copa*⟩ full; **∼ DE algo** full OF sth **(b)** (cubierto) **∼ DE algo** ⟨*de granos/manchas/polvo*⟩ covered IN sth **(c)** (después de comer) full (up) (colloq) **2** de lleno ⟨*consagrarse/dedicarse*⟩ fully; **el sol nos daba de ∼** the sun was shining down on us

lleno² *m* sellout

llevadero -ra *adj* bearable

llevar [A1] *vt*

I **1** **(a)** (de un lugar a otro) to take; **le llevé unas flores** I took her some flowers; **te lo ∼é cuando vaya** I'll bring it when I come; **¿qué llevas en la bolsa?** what have you got in your bag?; **comida para ∼** take out (AmE) *o* (BrE) takeaway meals **(b)** (transportar) ⟨*carga*⟩ to carry; **la ayudé a ∼ las bolsas** I helped her carry her bags **(c)** ⟨*persona*⟩ to take; **nos llevó a cenar** he took us out to dinner; **me llevó (en su coche) hasta la estación** she gave me a lift to the station; **lo llevaba en brazos/de la mano** she was carrying him in her arms/holding her hand **(d)** (tener consigo) ⟨*llaves/dinero/documentación*⟩ to have **2** **(a)** (guiar, conducir) to take; **la llevaba de la mano** I/he was holding her hand; **esto no nos ∼á a ninguna parte** this won't get us anywhere **(b)** (impulsar, inducir) to lead; **esto me lleva a pensar que ...** this leads me to believe that ... **3** **(a)** ⟨*ropa/perfume/reloj*⟩ to wear **(b)** (tener) ⟨*barba/bigote*⟩ to have; **llevaba el pelo corto** she had short hair

II **1** (tener a su cargo) ⟨*negocio/tienda*⟩ to run; ⟨*caso*⟩ to handle; ⟨*contabilidad*⟩ to do **2** (esp Esp) (conducir) ⟨*vehículo*⟩ to drive; ⟨*moto*⟩ to ride **3** ⟨*vida*⟩ to lead; **∼ una vida tranquila** to lead a quiet; **¿cómo llevas el informe?** how are you getting on with the report? **4** (seguir, mantener): **∼ el ritmo** *or* **el compás** to keep time; **¿llevas la cuenta de lo que te debo?** are you keeping track of what I owe you?; **¿qué dirección llevaban?** which direction were they going in?

III **1** **(a)** (requerir) ⟨*tiempo*⟩ to take; **le llevó**

horas aprendérselo it took her hours to learn it **(b)** (aventajar) (+ *me/te/le etc*): **me lleva un año** he's a year older than me; **nos llevan un día de ventaja** they have a one-day lead over us **2** (Esp) (cobrar) to charge

■ **∼** *v aux*: **llevo una hora esperando** I've been waiting for an hour; **lleva tres días sin comer** he hasn't eaten for three days; **el tren lleva una hora de retraso** the train's an hour late; **llevo revisada la mitad** I've already checked half of it

■ **∼** *vi* ⟨*camino/carretera*⟩ to go, lead

■ **llevarse** *v pron* **1** **(a)** (a otro lugar) to take; **la policía se llevó al sospechoso** the police took the suspect away; **¿quién se llevó mi paraguas?** who took my umbrella?; **el agua se llevó las casas** the water swept away the houses **(b)** ⟨*premio/dinero*⟩ to win **(c)** (quedarse con, comprar) to take; **me llevo este** I'll take this one **(d)** (Mat) to carry; **9 y 9 son 18, me llevo una** 9 plus 9 is 18, carry one **(e)** (Arg) ⟨*asignatura*⟩ to carry over **2** ⟨*susto/regañina*⟩ to get; **me llevé una decepción** I was disappointed; **se llevó un buen recuerdo** he left here with pleasant memories **3** **∼se bien con algn** to get along with sb **4** (hablando de modas) to be in fashion; **vuelven a ∼se las faldas cortas** short skirts are back in fashion

llorar [A1] *vi* (derramar lágrimas) **(a)** «*persona*» to cry; **estaba a punto de ∼** she was on the verge of tears; **∼ DE algo** ⟨*de risa/rabia*⟩ to cry WITH sb; ⟨*de emoción*⟩ to weep WITH sth; **∼ POR algo/algn** to cry over sth/sb **(b)** «*ojos*» (+ *me/te/le etc*) to water

lloriquear [A1] *vi* (fam) to whine (colloq)

lloro *m* crying, weeping (liter)

llorón -rona *adj* (fam): **es muy ∼** he cries a lot; **no seas tan ∼** don't be such a crybaby (colloq) ■ *m,f* **(a)** (fam) (que llora mucho) crybaby (colloq) **(b)** (Col, RPl, Ven fam) (quejón) whiner (colloq)

llover [E9] *v impers* to rain; **aquí llueve mucho** it rains a lot here; **llueve a cántaros** *or* **a mares** *or* **a chuzos** it's pouring (with rain)

llovizna *f* drizzle

lloviznar [A1] *v impers* to drizzle

llueva, llueve ▶ LLOVER

lluvia *f* **(a)** (Meteo) rain; **un día de ∼** a rainy day; **zonas de mucha ∼** areas of heavy rainfall; **∼ radiactiva** nuclear fallout **(b)** (de balas) hail; (de críticas) hail, barrage

lluvioso -sa *adj* ⟨*tiempo/día/época*⟩ rainy; ⟨*región*⟩ wet

lo *art* **1**: **prefiero ∼ dulce** I prefer sweet things; **∼ interesante del caso es ...** the interesting thing about the case is ...; **¿estoy en ∼ cierto?** am I right?; **en ∼ alto de la sierra** high up in the mountains; **ser ∼ más objetivo posible** to be as objective as possible; **me dijo ∼ de siempre** he came out with the same old story; **se ha enterado de ∼ nuestro/de ∼ de Pablo** she's found out about us/about Pablo; **voy a ∼ de Eva** (RPl) I'm going to Eva's (place) **2** **(a)** lo cual which; **∼ cual fue desmentido por el gobierno** which was denied by the Government **(b)** lo que what; **no entiendo ∼ que dices** I don't understand what you're saying; **pide ∼ que quieras** ask for whatever you want; **límpialo con un trapo o ∼ que sea** clean it with a cloth or whatever; **¡∼ que debe haber sufrido!** how she

must have suffered!; ¡no te imaginas ~ que fue aquello! you can't imagine what it was like!; ¡~ que es saber idiomas! it sure is something (AmE) o (BrE) what it is to be able speak languages
■ *pron pers* **1** (a) (referido — a él) him; (— a usted) you; (— a cosa, etc) it; ¿~ conozco? do I know you?; ~ compré hoy I bought it today; ya ~ sé I know (b) (*impers*): duele que a uno ~ traten así it hurts when people treat you like that **2** (con estar, ser): ¿que si estoy harta? pues sí, ~ estoy am I fed up? well, yes, I am; si ella es capaz, yo también ~ soy if she can, so can I

loable *adj* commendable, praiseworthy

lobezno -na *m,f* wolf cub

lobo -ba *m,f* (Zool) wolf; ~ marino seal

lóbrego -ga *adj* gloomy

lóbulo *m* lobe

locación *f* (Méx) (lugar): visite el museo Rivera, ~: Calle Altavista visit the Rivera Museum on Altavista Street; ¿en qué ~? whereabouts?

local *adj* local; el equipo ~ the home team
■ *m* premises (*pl*)

localidad *f* **1** (población) town, locality (frml) **2** (Espec) seat, ticket

localizar [A4] *vt* (a) (persona/lugar/tumor) to locate; estoy intentando ~la I am trying to get hold of her (b) (incendio/epidemia) to localize

loción *f* lotion

loco¹ -ca *adj* (a) (Med, Psic) mad, insane (b) (chiflado) crazy (colloq), nuts (colloq); este tipo está medio ~ (fam) the guy's not all there (colloq); eso no lo hago (pero) ni ~ there's no way I'd do that; hacer algo a lo ~ to do sth any which way (AmE) o (BrE) any old how (colloq); estar ~ de remate (fam) to be completely nuts (colloq); tener or (Esp) traer ~ a algn to be driving sb crazy (colloq); volver ~ a algn to drive sb crazy (colloq); volverse ~ to go mad (c) (entusiasmado): está loca por él she's crazy about him (colloq); está ~ por volver he's dying to come back (colloq) (d) (fam) (ajetreado): anda (como) ~ con los preparativos the preparations are driving him mad (colloq) (e) (indicando gran cantidad): tengo unas ganas locas de verla I'm dying to see her (colloq); tuvo una suerte loca she was incredibly lucky (f) estar ~ DE algo: (de entusiasmo/furia/celos) to be wild WITH sth; (de dolor/remordimiento) to be racked WITH sth; estaba loca de alegría she was blissfully happy
■ *m,f* (enfermo mental) (*m*) madman; (*f*) madwoman; se puso como un ~ he went crazy o mad; corrimos como ~s (fam) we ran like crazy o mad (colloq); *hacerse el* ~ to act dumb (colloq)

loco² *m* (Chi) (Zool) abalone

locomoción *f* (a) (acción) locomotion (b) (Chi) (Transp) *tb* ~ colectiva public transport

locomotora *f* (Ferr) locomotive, engine

locuaz *adj* talkative, loquacious (frml)

locución *f* phrase

locura *f* (a) (demencia) madness, insanity; lo que hizo/dijo fue una ~ what he did/said was sheer madness (b) (inclinación exagerada): siente ~ por la pequeña she's absolutely besotted with the little one; la quiero con ~ I'm crazy about her (colloq)

locutor -tora *m,f* (en general) broadcaster

(informativo) newscaster (AmE), newsreader (BrE); (deportivo) sports commentator; (de continuidad) commentator, announcer (BrE)

lodo *m* mud; *para modismos ver* BARRO

logia *f* (a) (de los masones) lodge (b) (Arquit) loggia

lógica *f* logic

lógico¹ -ca *adj* (a) (normal, natural) natural, logical; como es ~ naturally, obviously; es ~ que así sea it's (only) natural that it should be so; lo ~ sería ... the logical thing would be ... (b) (conclusión/consecuencia) logical

lógico² *adv* (*indep*) (fam) of course

logotipo *m* logo, logotype

logrado -da *adj* (satisfactorio) successful; (verosímil) (retrato/personaje) lifelike

lograr [A1] *vt* (objetivo) to attain, achieve; (éxito) to achieve; logró el quinto puesto she managed fifth place; ~ hacer algo to manage to do sth

logro *m* (de un objetivo) achievement; (éxito) success

loísmo *m*: use of LO/LOS *instead of* LE/LES (*as in* LO/LOS DIJE QUE NO), *common in certain regions of Spain but not acceptable to most speakers*

lolo -la *m,f* (Chi fam) teenager

loma *f* hill; (más pequeño) hillock

lombriz *f* (de tierra) worm, earthworm; (en el intestino) (fam) worm (colloq)

lomo *m* (a) (de animal) back; ~ de burro (RPl) or (Chi) de toro (Auto) speed bump (b) (Coc) (de cerdo) loin; (de vaca) (AmL) fillet steak (c) (de libro) spine; (de cuchillo) back

lona *f* canvas

loncha *f* slice

lonche *m* (Per) (merienda) tea

lonchera *f* (AmL) lunch box

londinense *adj* (público/teatro/periódico) London (*before n*); es ~ she's from London, she's a Londoner
■ *mf* Londoner

Londres *m* London

longaniza *f*: spicy pork sausage

longitud *f* (a) (largo) length; de 30 metros de ~ 30 meters long (b) (Astron, Geog) longitude; ~ de onda (Fís, Rad) wavelength

lonja *f* **1** (a) (loncha) slice (b) (RPl) (de cuero) strip **2** (a) (Esp) (mercado de pescado) fish market (b) (institución mercantil) guild; ~ de propiedad raíz (Col) association of realtors (AmE) o (BrE) estate agents

loro¹ -ra *m,f* (Zool) parrot

loro² *m* (fam) (charlatán) chatterbox (colloq), gasbag (colloq)

los, las *art*; *ver* el
■ *pron pers* **1** (referido — a ellos, ellas, cosas, etc) them; (— a ustedes) you; ¿las atienden? can I help you? **2** (con el verbo haber): las hay de muchos tamaños they come in many different sizes; también ~ hay de chocolate we have chocolate ones too

losa *f* (de sepulcro) tombstone; (de suelo) flagstone

lote *m* (a) (de un producto) batch; (en subastas) lot (b) (terreno) plot (of land)

lotería *f* lottery; **me tocó** *or* **me gané la ~** I won the lottery

loto *m* lotus

loza *f* **(a)** ⟨material⟩ china **(b)** ⟨vajilla⟩ crockery; ⟨de mejor calidad⟩ china

lozano -na *adj* ⟨persona⟩ healthy-looking; ⟨cutis⟩ fresh; ⟨verduras⟩ fresh

Ltda (= **Limitada**) Ltd, Limited

lubina *f* sea bass

lubricante *adj* lubricating
■ *m* lubricant

lubricar [A2] *vt* to lubricate

lucero *m* bright star; **~ del alba** morning star

luces *fpl* ▶ LUZ

lucha *f* **(a)** ⟨combate, pelea⟩ fight; ⟨para conseguir algo⟩ struggle; **~ de clases** class struggle; **la ~ contra el cáncer** the fight against cancer **(b)** ⟨Dep⟩ wrestling; **~ libre** all-in wrestling

luchador -dora *m,f* **(a)** ⟨persona esforzada⟩ fighter **(b)** ⟨Dep⟩ wrestler

luchar [A1] *vi* **(a)** ⟨combatir, pelear⟩ to fight **(b)** ⟨para conseguir algo⟩ to struggle, fight; **~ para salir adelante** struggle hard to get on in life; **~ por la paz** to fight for peace **(c)** ⟨batallar⟩ **~ CON algo** ⟨con problema⟩ to wrestle WITH sth **(d)** ⟨Dep⟩ to wrestle

luche *m* ⟨Chi⟩ ⟨Jueg⟩ hopscotch

lucidez *f* lucidity

lucido -da *adj* ⟨fiesta⟩ magnificent, splendid; **su actuación no fue muy lucida** her performance wasn't particularly brilliant

lúcido -da *adj* **(a)** [SER] ⟨mente/análisis⟩ lucid, clear; ⟨persona⟩ clear-thinking **(b)** [ESTAR] ⟨enfermo⟩ lucid

luciente *adj* bright, shining

luciérnaga *f* glowworm; ⟨insecto volador⟩ firefly

lucir [I5] *vi* ⟨aparentar⟩ to look good, look special; **gasta mucho en ropa pero no le luce** she spends a fortune on clothes but it doesn't do much for her
■ **~** *vt* **(a)** ⟨period⟩ ⟨vestido/modelo⟩ to wear, sport ⟨journ⟩; ⟨peinado/collar⟩ to sport ⟨journ⟩ **(b)** ⟨figura/piernas⟩ to show off, flaunt
■ **lucirse** *v pron* **(a)** ⟨destacarse⟩ to excel oneself **(b)** ⟨presumir⟩ to show off

lucrativo -va *adj* lucrative, profitable; **una entidad sin fines ~s** a nonprofit (AmE) *o* (BrE) non-profit-making organization

lucro *m* profit, gain; **sin ánimo de ~** with no profit motive in mind

lúcuma *f* eggfruit

lúdico -ca *adj* ⟨fantasías/diversiones⟩ playful, ludic (before n) ⟨liter⟩

luego *adv* **1** **(a)** ⟨más tarde⟩ later (on); ⟨después de otro suceso — en el futuro⟩ afterwards; ⟨— en el pasado⟩ then, next; **¡hasta ~!** goodbye!, see you!; **~ DE hacer algo** after doing sth **(b)** ⟨Chi, Méx⟩ ⟨pronto⟩ soon, quickly; **~ ~** ⟨Méx⟩ immediately **2** **(a)** ⟨en el espacio⟩: **hay una tienda y ~ está el banco** you come to a shop and the bank is next **(b)** ⟨Méx⟩ ⟨cerca⟩ nearby; **aquí ~** just here **(c)** ⟨indicando orden, prioridad⟩ then; **primero está él y ~ nosotros** he's first and then we're next **3** **desde luego** of course; **desde ~ que no** of course not
■ *conj* ⟨frml⟩ therefore

lugar *m* **1** ⟨en general⟩ place; **este es el ~** this is the place; **en cualquier otro ~** anywhere else; **en algún ~** somewhere; **cambiar los muebles de ~** to move the furniture around; **el ~ del suceso** the scene of the incident; **yo en tu ~ ...** if I were you ...; **ponte en mi ~** put yourself in my place; **se clasificó en primer ~** she finished in first place
2 ⟨localidad, región⟩: **los habitantes del ~** the local people; **~ y fecha de nacimiento** place and date of birth
3 **(a)** ⟨espacio libre⟩ room; **hacer ~ para algn/algo** to make room *o* space for sb/sth; **me hizo un ~** he made me some room **(b)** ⟨asiento⟩ seat
4 **dar lugar a** ⟨a disputa, comentarios⟩ to provoke, give rise to
5 ⟨en locs⟩ **en lugar de** instead of; **ella firmó en mi ~** she signed on my behalf; **en primer lugar** ⟨antes que nada⟩ first of all, firstly; **en último lugar** ⟨finalmente⟩ finally, lastly; **sin ~ a dudas** without doubt, undoubtedly; **tener ~** to take place

lugareño -ña *adj/mf* local

lugarteniente *mf* deputy

lúgubre *adj* gloomy

lujo *m* luxury; **no puedo permitirme el ~ de llegar tarde** I can't afford to be late; **nos dimos el ~ de viajar en primera** we treated ourselves and traveled first class; **a todo ~** in style; **de ~** luxury (before n); **con ~ de detalles** with a wealth of detail

lujoso -sa *adj* luxurious

lujuria *f* ⟨liter⟩ lust, lechery

lumbago *m* lumbago

lumbre *f* ⟨de hoguera, chimenea⟩ fire; ⟨de la cocina⟩: **puso el cazo en la ~** she put the saucepan on the stove

lumbrera *f* ⟨fam⟩ ⟨persona brillante⟩ genius, whiz* ⟨colloq⟩

luminoso -sa *adj* **(a)** ⟨habitación⟩ bright, light; ⟨fuente⟩ luminous; ⟨letrero⟩ illuminated **(b)** ⟨idea⟩ bright, brilliant

luna *f* **1** ⟨Astron⟩ moon; **a la luz de la ~** in the moonlight; **hay ~** the moon's out; **~ creciente/menguante/llena/nueva** waxing/waning/full/new moon; **~ de miel** honeymoon; **estar en la ~** ⟨fam⟩ to have one's head in the clouds **2** ⟨espejo⟩ mirror; ⟨de puerta, ventana⟩ glass; ⟨escaparate⟩ window; ⟨parabrisas⟩ windshield (AmE), windscreen (BrE) **3** ⟨de la uña⟩ half-moon, lunule ⟨tech⟩

lunar *adj* lunar
■ *m* **(a)** ⟨en la piel⟩ mole; ⟨pintado⟩ beauty spot **(b)** ⟨en el pelo⟩ gray* patch **(c)** ⟨en un diseño⟩ polka-dot

lunático -ca *adj* lunatic (before n)
■ *m,f* lunatic

lunes *m* (*pl* **~**) Monday; **el ~ por la mañana/noche** on Monday morning/night; **todos los ~** every Monday; **el próximo ~** next Monday; **el ~ pasado** last Monday; **el ~ es fiesta** Monday is a holiday; **nos vemos el ~** I'll see you on Monday; **los ~ voy a nadar** on Mondays I go swimming

luneta *f* **1** ⟨Auto⟩ window **2** ⟨Col, Méx⟩ ⟨Teatr⟩ orchestra seats (*pl*) (AmE), front stalls (*pl*) (BrE)

lunfardo *m* Buenos Aires slang

lupa *f* magnifying glass

lustrabotas *mf* (*pl* **~**) ▶ LUSTRADOR

lustrada *f* ⟨AmS⟩ polish, shine

lustrador -dora *m,f* (AmS) bootblack; (niño) shoeshine boy

lustrar [A1] *vt* (esp AmL) ⟨*zapatos/muebles*⟩ to polish
■ **lustrarse** *v pron* **1** (esp AmL) ⟨*zapatos*⟩ to polish **2** (AmC) (en una actividad) to excel

lustre *m* **(a)** (brillo) shine, luster*; **darle** or **sacarle ~ a algo** to polish sth **(b)** (distinción) glory, distinction

lustrín *m* (AmS) (cajón) bootblack's box; (puesto) shoeshine stand

lustro *m* period of five years

luterano -na *adj/m,f* Lutheran

luto *m* mourning; **estar de ~** to be in mourning; **~ riguroso** deep mourning; **ir de ~** to wear mourning (clothes); **ponerse de ~** to go into mourning

Luxemburgo *m* Luxembourg

luxemburgués -guesa *adj* of/from Luxembourg

luz *f* **1** (en general) light; **la ~ del sol** the sunlight; **me da la ~ en los ojos** the light's in my eyes; **a plena ~ del día** in broad daylight; **este reflector da mucha ~** this spotlight is very bright; **leer con poca ~** to read in poor light; **a la ~ de los últimos acontecimientos** in the light of recent events; **a todas luces**: whichever way you look at it; **dar a ~** to give birth; **sacar algo a la ~** ⟨*secreto/escándalo*⟩ to bring sth to light; ⟨*publicación*⟩ to bring out; **salir a la ~** «*secreto/escándalo*» to come to light; «*publicación*» to come out
2 (a) (fam) (electricidad) electricity; **les cortaron la ~** their electricity was cut off; **se fue la ~** (en una casa) the electricity went off; (en una zona) there was a power cut **(b)** (dispositivo) light; **encender** or (AmL) **prender** or (Esp) **dar la ~** to turn on o switch on the light; **apagar la ~** to turn off o switch off the light; **cruzar con la luz roja** to cross when the lights are red; **luces de estacionamiento** or (Esp) **de situación** parking lights (*pl*) (AmE), sidelights (*pl*) (BrE); **luces de cruce** or **cortas** or (AmL) **bajas** dipped headlights (*pl*); **poner las luces largas** or **altas** to put the headlights on high (AmE) o (BrE) full beam; **~ de frenado** stoplight, brake light (BrE); **~ de giro** (Arg) indicator

luzca, luzcan, etc ▶ LUCIR

M m

M, m *f* (read as /'eme/) the letter M, m

m (= **metro**) m, meter*

macabro -bra *adj* macabre

macaco -ca *m,f* (Zool) macaque

macana *f* **1** (AmL) (de policía) billy club (AmE), truncheon (BrE) **2 (a)** (CS fam) (tontería, disparate): **decir ~s** to talk nonsense; **no hagas la ~ de renunciar** don't be so stupid as to resign (colloq) **(b)** (CS fam) (problema) trouble, snag; **¡qué ~ que no puedas venir!** what a shame o (colloq) drag you can't come! **(c)** (RPl fam) (mentira) lie

macanear [A1] *vt* (Méx) (golpear) to beat
■ **~** *vi* (RPl fam) (mentir) to lie; (decir tonterías) to talk garbage (AmE) o (BrE) rubbish (colloq)

macanudo -da *adj* (CS, Per fam) great (colloq)

macarrón *m* **(a)** (pasta) piece of macaroni; **macarrones** macaroni **(b)** (galleta) macaroon

macedonia *f* (de frutas) fruit salad, macedoine; (de verduras) mixed vegetables (*pl*), macedoine

macerar [A1] *vt* ⟨*fruta*⟩ to soak, macerate; ⟨*carne*⟩ to marinate, marinade

maceta *f* flowerpot

macetero *m* **(a)** (para tiestos) flowerpot holder **(b)** (AmS) (tiesto) large flowerpot; (jardinera) window box

machacar [A2] *vt* **(a)** ⟨*ajo*⟩ to crush; ⟨*almendras*⟩ to grind, crush; ⟨*piedra*⟩ to crush, pound **(b)** (fam) ⟨*contrincante*⟩ to thrash (colloq)
■ **~** *vi* **(a)** (fam) (insistir): **~ con** or **sobre algo** to go on o harp on about sth (colloq) **(b)** (fam) (para un examen) to cram (colloq)

machacón -cona *adj* (insistente) insistent; (pesado) tiresome

machamartillo: **a ~** (loc adj) ⟨*monárquico/feminista*⟩ ardent, staunch; (loc adv) firmly

machete *m* (cuchillo) machete
■ *adj inv* (Ven fam) great (colloq)

machetero -ra *m,f* (cañero) cane cutter
■ *adj* (Méx fam) persevering

machismo *m* (actitud, ideología) sexism, male chauvinism

machista *adj* sexist, chauvinist
■ *mf* sexist, male chauvinist

macho *m* **1** (Biol, Zool) male; **~ cabrío** billy goat **2** (fam) (hombre fuerte) tough guy (colloq); (pey) macho man (colloq & pej) **3** (Mec, Tec) pin; (Elec) male (plug); (de un corchete) hook; (en carpintería) peg, pin
■ *adj* **1** ⟨*animal/planta*⟩ male; **ballena/elefante ~** bull whale/elephant; **gato ~** tomcat **2** (fam) (valiente, fuerte) tough, brave; (pey) macho (pej) **3** ⟨*pieza*⟩ male

AmC	Central America	Arg	Argentina	Cu	Cuba
AmL	Latin America	Bol	Bolivia	Ec	Ecuador
AmS	South America	Chi	Chile	Esp	Spain
Andes	Andean Region	CS	Southern Cone	Méx	Mexico

Per	Peru
RPl	River Plate Area
Ur	Uruguay
Ven	Venezuela

machote -ta *m,f* **(a)** (fam) (hombre) tough guy (colloq); (pey) macho man (colloq & pej) **(b)** (fam & pey) (mujer) butch woman (colloq & pej)

machucar [A2] *vt* **(a)** ⟨fruta⟩ to bruise **(b)** (fam) ⟨dedo⟩ to crush **(c)** (Méx) ⟨ajo⟩ to crush

machucón *m* (AmL fam) (moretón) bruise

macilento -ta *adj* **(a)** ⟨persona/cara⟩ gaunt, haggard **(b)** ⟨luz⟩ wan (liter)

macillo *m* hammer

macizo¹ -za *adj* **(a)** [SER] (sólido) solid **(b)** [ESTAR] (fam) ⟨persona⟩ (robusto) strapping (colloq)

macizo² *m* (de montañas) massif; (de flores, arbustos) clump

maco *m* (Col) monkey

macramé *m* macramé

macrobiótico -ca *adj* macrobiotic

macroeconomía *f* macroeconomics

macuco -ca *adj* (Chi, Per fam) cute (AmE colloq), sharp (BrE colloq)

macuto *m* back pack, rucksack (BrE)

madalena *f* ≈ cupcake (AmE), ≈ fairycake (BrE)

madeja *f* (de lana, hilo) hank, skein

madera *f* (material) wood; (para construcción, carpintería) lumber (esp AmE), timber (BrE); ~ blanda/dura softwood/hardwood; **es de** ~ it's made of wood, it's wooden; **mesa de** ~ wooden table; ~ **de pino** pine (wood); **tener** ~ **de algo** to have the makings of sth; ***tocar*** ~ to knock (on) wood (AmE), touch wood (BrE)

maderero -ra *adj* timber (*before n*); lumber (*before n*) (esp AmE)
■ *m,f* timber merchant

madero *m* (piece of) timber

madrastra *f* stepmother

madrazo *m* (Méx fam) blow; **darle un** ~ **a algn** to give sb a beating; **películas de** ~ violent movies

madre *f* mother; **ser** ~ to be a mother; ~ **de familia** mother; ~ **política** mother-in-law; ~ **soltera** single o unmarried mother; ~ **superiora** Mother Superior; **¡~ mía!** or **¡mi ~!** (my) goodness!, (good) heavens!; **me vale ~s** (Méx vulg) I don't give a damn (colloq) o (vulg) shit; ***salirse de*** ~ «río» to burst its banks; «situación» to get out of hand

madreperla *f* mother-of-pearl

madreselva *f* honeysuckle

Madrid *m* Madrid

madriguera *f* **(a)** (de conejos) warren, burrow; (de zorros) earth; (de tejones) set **(b)** (de maleantes) den, lair

madrileño -ña *adj* of/from Madrid
■ *m,f* person from Madrid

madrina

■ **Nota** En inglés *godmother* no se usa como apelativo

f **1 (a)** (en bautizo) godmother; (en boda) ≈ matron of honor* **(b)** (de barco) *woman who launches a ship* **2** (Méx fam) paddy wagon (AmE sl), police van (BrE)

madroño *m* (Bot) tree strawberry

madrugada *f* **(a)** (amanecer, alba) dawn, daybreak; **se levantó de** ~ (muy temprano) she got up very early (in the morning); (al amanecer) she got up at dawn o daybreak **(b)** (después de

medianoche) (early) morning; **las tres de la** ~ three o'clock in the morning; **llegó de** ~ he arrived in the early hours of the morning o in the small hours

madrugador -dora *adj*: **ser** ~ to be an early riser

madrugar [A3] *vi* to get up early

maduración *f* **(a)** (de fruta) ripening (process) **(b)** (de persona) maturing (process) **(c)** (de idea) development, maturing

madurar [A1] *vi* **(a)** «fruta» to ripen **(b)** «persona» to mature **(c)** «ideas» to mature, come to fruition
■ ~ *vt* **(a)** ⟨fruta⟩ to ripen **(b)** ⟨plan⟩ to develop, bring to fruition

madurez *f* **(a)** (de fruta) ripeness **(b)** (de persona) maturity

maduro -ra *adj* **1** [ESTAR] ⟨fruta⟩ ripe **2 (a)** [SER] (entrado en años) mature, of mature years **(b)** [SER] (sensato) mature; **es joven pero muy** ~ he's young but very mature for his age

maestría *f* **1** (liter) (habilidad) skill, mastery **2** (esp AmL) (Educ) (postgrado) master's degree, master's

maestro -tra *m,f* **1 (a)** (Educ) teacher, schoolteacher; **maestra jardinera** (Arg, Col) kindergarten teacher, nursery school teacher (BrE) **(b)** (en un arte): **es un** ~ **de la danza española** he is a master of Spanish dance; **un** ~ **de las letras españolas** a leading authority o an expert on Spanish literature **(c)** (en un oficio) master (*before n*); ~ **carpintero** master carpenter **(d)** (Chi) (obrero) builder **2** (Mús) maestro **3** (en ajedrez) master

mafia *f* mafia

mafioso -sa *adj* mafia (*before n*)
■ *m,f* (criminal) gangster, racketeer; (de la Mafia siciliana) mafioso

magdalena *f* (Esp) ≈ cupcake (AmE), ≈ fairycake (BrE)

magia *f* magic; **hacer** ~ to do magic (tricks)

mágico -ca *adj* **(a)** ⟨poderes/número⟩ magic (*before n*) **(b)** ⟨belleza/ambiente⟩ magical

magisterio *m* (enseñanza) teaching; (carrera) teacher training; **estudia** ~ he's training to be a teacher

magistrado -da *m,f* judge

magistral *adj* ⟨actuación/libro⟩ masterly; ⟨tono/actitud⟩ magisterial (frml)

magnánimo -ma *adj* magnanimous

magnate *mf* magnate, tycoon; **los** ~**s de la prensa** the press barons

magnesia *f* magnesia

magnesio *m* magnesium

magnético -ca *adj* magnetic

magnetismo *m* magnetism

magnetófono, magnetófon *m* (reel-to-reel) tape recorder

magnífico -ca *adj* **(a)** (estupendo) ⟨edificio/panorama⟩ magnificent, superb; ⟨espectáculo/escritor/oportunidad⟩ marvelous*, wonderful; **¡~!** excellent! **(b)** (suntuoso) magnificent, splendid

magnitud *f* magnitude; **la** ~ **de la tragedia** the extent o magnitude of the tragedy

magnolia *f* magnolia

m

mago -ga *m,f* **(a)** (prestidigitador) conjurer, magician **(b)** (en cuentos) wizard, magician **(c)** (persona habilidosa) wizard

magro -gra *adj* lean

magulladura *f* bruise

magullar [A1] *vt* to bruise
■ **magullarse** *v pron* to bruise

mahometano -na *adj* Islamic
■ *m,f* follower of Islam

mahonesa *f* mayonnaise

maicena® *f* cornstarch (AmE), cornflour (BrE)

maillot /ma'yo(t)/ *m* **(a)** (traje de baño) swimsuit **(b)** (de ciclista) jersey

maíz *m* (planta) maize, corn (AmE); (Coc) corn (AmE), sweet corn (esp BrE); ~ **tostado** *or* **pira** *or* **tote** (Col) popcorn

maizal *m* cornfield (AmE), maize field (BrE)

maizena® *f* cornstarch (AmE), cornflour (BrE)

majadería *f* (fam) **(a)** (cualidad) stupidity **(b)** (dicho, acto): **no dice más que ~s** he talks a lot of rubbish *o* nonsense (colloq); **fue una ~** it was a stupid thing to do

majadero -ra *adj* (fam) (insensato) stupid
■ *m,f* clown (colloq)

majar [A1] *vt* to crush

maje *mf* [1] (AmC arg) (individuo) (*m*) guy (colloq), bloke (BrE colloq); (*f*) girl [2] (Méx fam) (persona crédula) sucker (colloq)

majestad *f* [1] (aspecto grandioso) majesty [2] **su Majestad** (al referirse — al rey) His Majesty; (— a la reina) Her Majesty; (al dirigirse al rey, a la reina) Your Majesty; **sus M~es los Reyes** Their Majesties the King and Queen

majestuosidad *f* majesty

majestuoso -sa *adj* majestic

majo -ja *adj* (Esp fam) **(a)** (simpático) nice **(b)** (guapo) ‹*hombre*› handsome, good-looking; ‹*mujer*› good-looking, pretty **(c)** ‹*casa/vestido*› lovely, nice

mal *adj*: ▶ MALO
■ *adj inv* [1] [ESTAR] (enfermo) ill; (anímicamente) in a bad way (colloq); (incómodo) uncomfortable; **andar ~ del estómago** to have trouble with one's stomach; **¡este está ~ de la cabeza!** he's not right in the head; **esas cosas me ponen ~** things like that really upset me
[2] (fam) (en frases negativas) (refiriéndose al aspecto): **no está nada ~** she's/he's/it's not at all bad (colloq)
[3] (insatisfactorio): **estoy** *or* **salí muy ~ en esta foto** I look awful in this photograph; **le queda ~ ese color** that color doesn't suit her
[4] [ESTAR] (incorrecto) wrong
[5] (indicando escasez) **estar** *or* **ir ~ DE algo** ‹*de dinero/tiempo*› to be short of sth
■ *adv* [1] (de manera no satisfactoria) ‹*vestir/cantar/jugar*› badly; **le fue ~ en los exámenes** his exams went badly; **te oigo muy ~** I can hardly hear you; **el negocio marcha ~** the business isn't doing well; **de ~ en peor** from bad to worse
[2] (desfavorablemente) badly, ill; **hablar ~ de algn** to speak badly *o* ill of sb
[3] **(a)** (de manera errónea) wrong, wrongly; **te han informado ~** you've been badly *o* wrongly informed; **te entendí ~** I misunderstood you **(b)** (de manera reprensible) ‹*obrar/partarse*› badly;

haces ~ en no ir a verla it's wrong of you not to go and see her; **me contestó muy ~** she answered me very rudely
[4] (desagradable) ‹*oler/saber*› bad; **aquí huele ~** there's a horrible smell *o* it smells in here
[5] (en locs) **hacer mal** (AmL) (a la salud): **esto hace ~ al hígado** this is bad for the liver; **el pescado me hizo ~** the fish didn't agree with me; **menos mal: ¡menos ~!** thank goodness!; **¡menos ~ que le avisaron a tiempo!** it's just as well they told him in time!; **tomarse algo a ~** to take sth to heart
■ *m* [1] (Fil) evil; **el bien y el ~** good and evil, right and wrong
[2] (daño, perjuicio): **el divorcio de sus padres le hizo mucho ~** her parents' divorce did her a lot of harm
[3] (cosa dañina) ill, evil; **los ~es sociales** the social ills; **no hay ~ que por bien no venga** every cloud has a silver lining
[4] (Med) (liter) (enfermedad) illness; **tiene ~ de amores** (fam) he's lovesick; **~ de (las) altura(s)** altitude sickness, mountain sickness
[5] (pena) trouble

malabarismo *m* juggling; **hacer ~s** «*malabarista*» to juggle; (en situación difícil) to do a juggling *o* balancing act

malabarista *mf* juggler

malacostumbrado -da *adj* spoiled*, pampered

malacostumbrar [A1] *vt* to spoil
■ **malacostumbrarse** *v pron* to become spoilt

malacrianza *f* (AmL) rudeness

malaria *f* malaria

Malasia *f* Malaysia

malasio -sia *adj/m,f* Malaysian

malayo¹ -ya *adj/m,f* Malay

malayo² *m* (idioma) Malay

malcriado -da *adj* (mimado) spoiled*; (travieso) bad-mannered, badly brought up

malcriar [A17] *vt* to spoil, bring ... up badly

maldad *f* **(a)** (cualidad) evilness, wickedness **(b)** (acto) evil deed, wicked thing

maldecir [I25] *vt* to curse
■ *vi* **(a)** (renegar) to curse; **~ DE algo/algn** to speak ill OF sth/sb **(b)** (blasfemar) to swear, curse (AmE)

maldición *f* **(a)** (imprecación) curse; **nos echó una ~** she put a curse on us **(b)** (palabrota) swearword; **soltó una ~** he swore

maldiga, maldijo, etc ▶ MALDECIR

maldito -ta *adj* (fam) (expresando irritación) damn (*before n*) (colloq), wretched (*before n*) (colloq); **¡este ~ ruido!** this damn *o* wretched noise!; **¡maldita/~ sea!** damn (it)! (colloq)

maldoso -sa *adj* (Méx) mischievous

malecón *m* **(a)** (rompeolas) breakwater; (embarcadero) jetty **(b)** (AmL) (paseo marítimo) seafront

maleducado -da *adj* rude, bad-mannered

maléfico -ca *adj* ‹*poderes/espíritu*› evil; ‹*influencia*› harmful

malenseñado -da *adj* (CS) (maleducado) rude, bad-mannered; (mimado) spoiled

malenseñar [A1] *vt* (CS) to spoil

malentender [E8] *vt* to misunderstand

malentendido *m* misunderstanding

malestar *m* **(a)** (Med) discomfort **(b)** (desazón, inquietud) unease

maleta *f* **1** (valija) suitcase, case; **hacer la ∼** to pack (one's case) **2** (Chi, Per) ▶ MALETERA

maletera *f* (Chi, Per) trunk (AmE), boot (BrE)

maletero *m* **(a)** (Auto) trunk (AmE), boot (BrE) **(b)** (mozo de estación) porter

maletín *m* (para documentos) briefcase; (maleta pequeña) overnight bag, small case; (de médico) bag

malévolo -la *adj* malevolent, malicious

maleza *f* **1** (espesura) undergrowth; (malas hierbas) weeds (*pl*) **2** (AmL) (mala hierba) weed

malformación *f* malformation

malgastador -dora *adj* wasteful, spendthrift ■ *m,f* squanderer, spendthrift

malgastar [A1] *vt* ⟨tiempo/esfuerzo⟩ to waste; ⟨dinero/herencia⟩ to squander

malhablado -da *adj* foul-mouthed

malhechor -chora *m,f* criminal, delinquent

malhumorado -da *adj* **(a)** [SER] ⟨persona/gesto⟩ bad-tempered **(b)** [ESTAR] ⟨persona⟩ in a bad mood

malicia *f* **(a)** (intención malévola) malice, malevolence **(b)** (picardía) mischief

malicioso -sa *adj* **(a)** (malintencionado) malicious, spiteful **(b)** (pícaro) mischievous

maligno -na *adj* **(a)** ⟨tumor⟩ malignant **(b)** ⟨persona/intención⟩ evil; ⟨influencia⟩ harmful, evil

malinchista *adj* (Méx) *preferring foreign things*

malinformar [A1] *vt* (CS frml) to misinform (frml)

malintencionado -da *adj* ⟨persona/palabras⟩ malicious, spiteful; ⟨golpe⟩ malicious

malinterpretar [A1] *vt* to misinterpret

malla *f* **1** (red) mesh; **una ∼ para los insectos** a screen *o* mesh to stop insects **2** **(a)** (para gimnasia) leotard; **∼ de baño** (RPl) bathing suit, swimsuit **(b)** **mallas** *fpl* (medias) tights (*pl*); (sin pie) leggings (*pl*)

Mallorca *f* Majorca

mallorquín¹ -quina *adj/m,f* Majorcan

mallorquín² *m* (idioma) Majorcan

mallugar [A3] *vt* (Méx, Ven) to bruise

malnutrición *f* malnutrition

malnutrido -da *adj* malnourished

malo -la *adj* [*The form* MAL *is used before masculine singular nouns*] **1** **(a)** [SER] (en general) bad; **una novela mala** a bad novel; **un mal amigo** a bad friend; **una mala caída** a bad fall; **soy muy ∼ para los números** I'm very bad with figures; **¡qué mala suerte** *or* (fam) **pata!** what bad luck!, how unlucky!; **lo ∼ es que …** the thing *o* trouble is that …; **las malas compañías** bad company; **mala hierba** weed; **∼s tratos** ill-treatment; **es ∼ tomar tanto sol** it's not good to sunbathe so much; **tienes mala cara** *or* **mal aspecto** you don't look well **(b)** ⟨calidad/visibilidad⟩ poor; **tiene mala ortografía** her spelling is poor; **estar de malas** (de mal humor) (fam) to be in a bad mood; (con mala suerte) (esp AmL) to be unlucky; **más vale ∼ conocido que bueno por conocer** better the devil you know (than the devil you don't)

2 [SER] ⟨persona⟩ (en sentido ético) nasty; (travieso) naughty; **¡qué ∼ eres con tu hermano!** you're really horrible *o* nasty to your brother; **no seas mala, préstamelo** don't be mean *o* rotten, lend it to me (colloq); **una mala mujer** a loose woman; **una mujer mala** a wicked *o* an evil woman; **lo hizo a** *or* **con mala idea** he did it deliberately *o* to be nasty; **mala palabra** (esp AmL) a dirty word; **dicen las malas lenguas que …** (fam) there's a rumor going around that …, people are saying that …; **hacerse mala sangre** to get upset *ver tb* LECHE 3

3 [ESTAR] **(a)** (en mal estado) ⟨alimento⟩: **el pescado/queso está ∼** the fish/cheese has gone bad, that fish/cheese is off (BrE) **(b)** (Esp, Méx fam) (enfermo) sick (AmE), ill (BrE); **el pobre está malito** the poor thing's not very well (colloq) ■ *m,f* (leng infantil *o* hum) baddy (colloq)

malograr [A1] *vt* ⟨oportunidad⟩ to waste; ⟨trabajo⟩ to ruin, spoil ■ **malograrse** *v pron* **1** «proyecto/cosecha» to fail **2** **(a)** «persona» (morir joven) to die young *o* before one's time **(b)** (Per) «reloj» to stop working; «lavadora» to break down

maloliente *adj* stinking, smelly

malparado -da *adj*: **salir ∼** to come off badly

malpensado -da *adj*: **no seas ∼** why do you always think the worst of people?

malsano -na *adj* ⟨clima/lugar⟩ unhealthy; ⟨influencia⟩ bad, unhealthy

malsonante *adj* rude

malta *f* **(a)** (cereal) malt **(b)** (Chi) (cerveza) stout

malteada *f* (AmL) milk shake

maltratar [A1] *vt* **(a)** ⟨persona/animal⟩ to maltreat, ill-treat, mistreat; (pegar) ⟨niño/mujer⟩ to batter **(b)** ⟨juguete/coche⟩ to mistreat, treat … very roughly

maltrecho -cha *adj*: **lo dejaron muy ∼** they left him in a bad way

malucho -cha *adj* (fam) (algo enfermo): **estar ∼** to be *o* feel under the weather (colloq)

malva *adj inv/m* mauve ■ *f* mallow; **∼ real** hollyhock, rose mallow (AmE)

malvado -da *adj* wicked, evil

malvavisco *m* marshmallow

malvender [E1] *vt* to sell … off cheap, sell … at a loss

malversación *f*: *tb* **∼ de fondos** embezzlement (of funds)

malversar [A1] *vt* to embezzle, misappropriate

Malvinas *fpl*: **las ∼** the Falkland Islands, the Falklands

malvón *m* (RPl, Méx) geranium

mama *f* (Anat) breast; (Zool) mammary gland

mamá *f* (*pl* **-más**) (fam) mom (AmE colloq), mum (BrE colloq); (usado por niños) mommy (AmE colloq), mummy (BrE colloq)

mamadera *f* (CS, Per) (biberón) (feeding) bottle, baby bottle

mamado -da *adj* **(a)** (fam) (borracho) tight (colloq), sloshed (colloq) **(b)** (Col, Ven fam) (cansado) dead beat (colloq), shattered (colloq); (aburrido) bored

mamar [A1] *vi* **1** **(a)** «bebé» to feed; **dar de ∼** to breastfeed **(b)** «gato/cordero» to suckle **2** (fam) (beber alcohol) to booze (colloq)

mameluco *m* (AmL) **(a)** (de niño, bebé) rompers (*pl*), romper suit (BrE) **(b)** (pantalón con peto) overalls (*pl*) (AmE), dungarees (*pl*) (BrE); (de trabajo) coveralls (*pl*) (AmE), overalls (*pl*) (BrE)

mamífero *adj* mammalian
■ *m* mammal

mamila *f* (Méx) (biberón) (feeding) bottle; (tetilla) nipple (AmE), teat (BrE)

mampara *f* **(a)** (biombo, tabique) screen, partition **(b)** (Chi, Per) (puerta) inner door

mampostería *f* masonry

manada *f* **(a)** (Zool) (de elefantes) herd; (de leones) pride; (de lobos) pack **(b)** (fam) (de gente) herd

Managua *f* Managua

managüense *adj* of/from Managua

manantial *m* (de agua) spring

manar [A1] *vi* to pour

manatí *m* manatee

mancha *f* 1 **(a)** (de suciedad) spot, mark; (difícil de quitar) stain; **una ~ de grasa** a grease stain; **~s de humedad** damp patches; **~ de petróleo** oil slick **(b)** (borrón) blot 2 **(a)** (en la piel) mark **(b)** (en el pelaje, las plumas) patch; (del leopardo) spot 3 (liter) (imperfección, mácula) stain; **sin ~** ‹*alma*› pure; ‹*reputación*› spotless 4 (Per fam) (pandilla) gang

manchado -da *adj* ‹*mantel/vestido*› stained; **está ~ de vino** it has wine stains on it; **~ de sangre** blood-stained

manchar [A1] *vt* 1 (ensuciar) to mark, get ... dirty; (de algo difícil de quitar) to stain 2 ‹*reputación/honra/memoria*› to tarnish
■ ~ *vi* to stain
■ **mancharse** *v pron* **(a)** «*ropa/mantel*» to get dirty; (de algo difícil de quitar) to get stained; **~se DE** *or* **CON algo** to get stained WITH sth **(b)** (*refl*) «*persona*» to get dirty; **me manché la blusa de aceite** I got oil stains on my blouse

manchego -ga *adj* of/from La Mancha

manco -ca *adj*: **es ~ de un brazo/una mano** he only has one arm/hand

mancomunidad *f* community, association; **M~ Británica de Naciones** British Commonwealth

mancorna *f* (Col) cufflink

mancuernilla *f* (Méx) cufflink

manda *f* (Chi, Méx) offering, promise

mandadero -ra *m,f* (esp AmL) (*m*) office boy; (*f*) office girl

mandado¹ -da *adj* (Méx fam): **es muy ~** he's a real opportunist; **no seas mandada, solo te ofrecí uno** don't be so greedy, I only offered you one (colloq)
■ *m,f* (esp Esp) (subordinado) minion (hum *or* pej); **no soy más que un ~** I'm just following orders

mandado² *m* **(a)** (esp AmL) (compra): **hacer los ~s** *or* (Méx) **ir al ~** to do the shopping **(b)** (Méx) (cosa comprada): **¿me trajiste el ~?** did you get the shopping *o* things I asked you for? **(c)** (diligencia) errand

mandamiento *m* 1 (Relig) commandment 2 (orden) order; (Der) warrant, order

mandar [A1] *vt* 1 **(a)** (ordenar): **a mí nadie me manda** nobody tells me what to do, nobody orders me about; **haz lo que te mandan** do as you're told; **la mandó callar** he told *o* ordered her to be quiet; **mandó que sirvieran la comida** she ordered lunch to be served **(b)** (recetar) to prescribe; **el médico le mandó descansar** the doctor advised him to rest 2 (enviar) to send; **la mandé por el pan** I sent her out to buy the bread 3 (AmL) (tratándose de encargos): **mis padres me ~on llamar** my parents sent for me; **mandó decir que ...** she sent a message to say that ...; **~ algo a arreglar** to get *o* have sth mended 4 (AmL fam) (arrojar, lanzar): **mandó la pelota fuera de la cancha** he kicked/sent/hit the ball out of play
■ ~ *vi* (ser el jefe) to be in charge, be the boss (colloq); **¿mande?** (Méx) (I'm) sorry?, pardon?; **¡María! — ¿mande?** (Méx) María! — yes?

mandarina *f* (Bot, Coc) mandarin (orange), tangerine

mandatario -ria *m,f* (Pol) *tb* **primer ~/primera mandataria** head of state

mandato *m* 1 **(a)** (período) term of office **(b)** (orden) mandate 2 (Der) mandate

mandíbula *f* jaw

mandil *m* (delantal) leather apron

mandioca *f* (planta) cassava; (fécula) tapioca

mando *m* 1 (en general) command; **entregarle el ~ a algn** to hand over command to sb; **dotes de ~** leadership qualities; **estar al ~ (de algo)** to be in charge (of sth) 2 (Auto, Elec) control; **~ a distancia** remote control

mandolina *f* mandolin

mandón -dona *adj* bossy

mandonear [A1] *vt* (fam) to boss ... around (colloq)

mandril *m* (Zool) mandrill

manearse [A1] *v pron* (Chi fam) to get in a tangle (colloq), to be all fingers and thumbs (colloq)

manecilla *f* hand; **la ~ grande/pequeña** the minute/hour hand

manejable *adj* 1 ‹*coche*› maneuverable*; ‹*máquina*› easy-to-use; ‹*pelo*› manageable 2 ‹*persona*› easily led, easily manipulated

manejar [A1] *vt* 1 (usar) ‹*herramienta/arma/diccionario*› to use; ‹*máquina*› to use, operate 2 (dirigir, llevar) ‹*negocio/empresa*› to manage; ‹*asuntos*› to manage, handle 3 (manipular) to manipulate 4 (AmL) ‹*auto*› to drive
■ ~ *vi* (AmL) to drive
■ **manejarse** *v pron* 1 (desenvolverse) to get by, manage 2 (Col) (comportarse) to behave

manejo *m* 1 (uso): **el ~ de la máquina es muy sencillo** the machine is easy to use *o* operate; **su ~ de la lengua** his use of the language 2 (de asunto, negocio) management 3 (AmL) (Auto) driving

manera *f* 1 (modo, forma) way; **yo lo hago a mi ~** I do it my way; **a ~ de** by way of; **de todas ~s**

anyway; **su ~ de ser** the way she is; **se puede ir vestido de cualquier ~** you can dress however you want; **no lo pongas así, de cualquier ~** don't just put it in any which way (AmE) o (BrE) any old how; **de ninguna ~ lo voy a permitir** there's no way I'm going to allow it; **de alguna ~ tendré que conseguirlo** I'll have to have it somehow (or other); **no hay/hubo ~** it is/it was impossible; **de ~ que** so; **de mala ~** ‹contestar› rudely; ‹tratar› badly

2 **maneras** *fpl* (modales) manners (*pl*)

manga *f* **1** **(a)** (de abrigo, blusa) sleeve; **sin ~s** sleeveless; **de ~ corta/larga** short-sleeved/long-sleeved; **en ~s de camisa** in shirtsleeves; **tener (la) ~ ancha** to be tolerant o lenient **(b)** (capa de jerga) (AmC) poncho **2** (Coc) (filtro) strainer; (para repostería) *tb* **~ pastelera** pastry bag **3** (Dep) round **4** (manguera) hose; **~ de incendio** fire hose; **~ de riego** hosepipe **5** (AmL) (de langostas) swarm

manglar *m* mangrove swamp

mangle *m* mangrove

mango *m* **1** (de cuchillo, paraguas) handle **2** (Bot) (árbol) mango (tree); (fruta) mango **3** (Méx fam & hum) (persona atractiva): **es un ~ «mujer»** she's a real stunner (colloq); «hombre» he's a real hunk (colloq)

mangonear [A1] *vi* (fam) **(a)** (mandonear) to order o (colloq) boss people around **(b)** (entrometerse) to meddle
■ **~** *vt* (fam) to boss ... around (colloq)

mangosta *f* mongoose

manguera *f* (para regar) hose, hosepipe; (de bombero) hose

maní *m* (*pl* **-níes** or (crit) **-níses**) (AmC, AmS) peanut

manía *f* **1** (obsesión, capricho): **tiene sus ~s** he has his funny little ways; **tiene la ~ de la limpieza** she has a mania for cleanliness o (colloq) a thing about cleaning; **le ha dado la ~ de vestirse de negro** she has this fad o craze of dressing in black; **~ persecutoria** or **de persecución** persecution complex o mania **2** (antipatía): **tenerle ~ a algn** to have it in for sb (colloq)

maniaco -ca, maníaco -ca *m,f* **(a)** (Psic) manic **(b)** (fam) (loco) maniac; **~ sexual** sex maniac

maniatar [A1] *vt* **(a)** ‹persona›: **los ladrones lo ~on** the burglars tied his hands **(b)** ‹animal› to hobble

maniático -ca *adj* **(a)** (delicado, difícil) finicky, fussy **(b)** (obsesionado) obsessive

manicero -ra *m,f* (AmC, AmS) peanut seller

manicomio *m* mental hospital, lunatic asylum

manicura *f* manicure; **hacerse la ~** (*refl*) to do one's nails; (*caus*) to have a manicure

manido -da *adj* ‹frase› hackneyed; ‹tema› stale

manifestación *f* **1** (Pol) demonstration **2** (expresión, indicio) sign; **las manifestaciones artísticas culturales de la época** the artistic cultural expression of the era

manifestante *mf* demonstrator

manifestar [A5] *vt* **(a)** (expresar) ‹desaprobación/agradecimiento› to express; **~on su apoyo a esta propuesta** they expressed their support for the proposal **(b)** (demostrar) ‹emociones› to show
■ **manifestarse** *v pron* **1** (hacerse evidente) to become apparent o evident; (ser evidente) to be apparent o evident **2** (Pol) to demonstrate, take part in a demonstration **3** (dar opinión): **~se en contra/a favor de algo** to express one's opposition to/support for sth

manifiesta, manifiestas, etc ▸ MANIFESTAR

manifiesto¹ -ta *adj* (frml) manifest (frml), evident (frml); **poner algo de ~** (Pol) to highlight sth; **quedar de ~** to become plain o obvious o evident

manifiesto² *m* (Pol) manifesto

manija *f* (esp AmL) handle

manilla *f* **(a)** (de reloj) hand **(b)** (de cajón) handle **(c)** (Col) (guante) baseball glove

manillar *m* (esp Esp) handlebars (*pl*)

maniobra *f* maneuver*; **estar de ~s** (Mil) to be on maneuvers

maniobrar [A1] *vi/vt* to maneuver*

manipulador -dora *adj* manipulative
■ *m,f* (aprovechado) manipulator

manipular [A1] *vt* **1** **(a)** ‹mercancías› to handle **(b)** ‹aparato/máquina› to operate, use **2** ‹persona/información/datos› to manipulate; **~ los resultados** to fix o rig the results

maniquí *mf* **(a)** (persona) model **(b)** **maniquí** *m* (de sastre, escaparate) mannequin, dummy

manirroto -ta *adj* **(a)** (fam) extravagant **(b)** (generoso) generous, open-handed
■ *m,f* (fam) spendthrift

manitas *mf* (Esp, Méx fam) handyman (colloq)

manito -ta *m,f:* ▸ MANO²

manivela *f* crank, handle

manjar *m* delicacy; **~ blanco** (Andes) ▸ DULCE DE LECHE

mano¹ *f* **1** **(a)** (Anat) hand; **tengo las ~s sucias** my hands are dirty; **levantar la ~** to raise one's hands, put one's hand up; **¡~s arriba!** or **¡arriba las ~s!** hands up!; **con la ~ en el corazón** hand on heart; **le hizo adiós con la ~** he waved goodbye to her; **su carta pasó de ~ en ~** her letter was passed around; **darle la ~ a algn** (para saludar) to shake hands with sb, to shake sb's hand; (para ayudar, ser ayudado) to give sb one's hand; **dame la ~** hold my hand; **me tendió la ~** he held out his hand to me; **me tomó de la ~** she took me by the hand; **ir (tomados) de la ~** to walk hand in hand; **~ de obra** labor **(b)** (Zool) (de oso, mono) paw; (de mono) hand; (Equ) forefoot, front foot
2 (control, posesión) *gen* **~s** hands (*pl*); **ha cambiado de ~s** it has changed hands; **cayó en ~s del enemigo** it fell into the hands of the enemy; **haré todo lo que esté en mis ~s** I will do everything in my power; **la oportunidad se nos fue de las ~s** we let the opportunity slip through our fingers; **se tomó la justicia por su propia ~** he took the law into his own hands
3 (en fútbol) handball
4 (del mortero) pestle
5 (de pintura, barniz) coat
6 (Jueg) (vuelta, juego) hand; (conjunto de cartas) hand; (jugador): **soy/eres ~** it's my/your lead
7 (en locs) **a mano** (no a máquina) by hand; **hecho** ⋯⋗

a ~ handmade; **escrito a ~** handwritten; **tejido a ~** handwoven; **las tiendas me quedan muy a ~** the shops are very close by o near; **siempre tengo un diccionario a ~** I always keep a dictionary by me; **a la mano** (AmL) close at hand; **de mano** hand (*before n*); **en mano** ‹*lápiz/copa*› in hand; *agarrar or* (esp Esp) *coger a algn con las ~s en la masa* to catch sb red-handed; *agarrarle or tomarle la ~ a algo* (CS fam) to get the hang of sth (colloq); *bajo ~* on the quiet, on the sly (colloq); *con las ~s vacías* empty-handed; *darse la ~* (para saludar) to shake hands; (para cruzar, jugar, etc) to hold hands; *de segunda ~* secondhand; *echar or dar una ~* to give o lend a hand; *echar ~ a algo* (fam) to grab sth; *estar/quedar a ~* (AmL fam) to be even o quits (colloq); *lavarse las ~s* to wash one's hands; *levantarle la ~ a algn* to raise one's hand to sb; *llegar or pasar a las ~s* to come to blows; *pedir la ~ de algn* to ask for sb's hand in marriage; *ser la ~ derecha de algn* to be sb's right-hand man/woman; *tenderle una ~ a algn* to offer sb a (helping) hand; *tener ~ dura* to have a firm hand; *tener ~ para algo* to be good at sth; *traerse algo entre ~s* to be up to sth (colloq)

8 **(a)** (lado) side; **queda de esta ~** it's on this side of the street; **a ~ derecha** on the right **(b)** (Auto) side of the road

mano² **-na** *m,f* (AmL fam) (apelativo) buddy (AmE colloq), mate (BrE colloq)

manojo *m* bunch; **ser un ~ de nervios** to be a bundle of nerves

manoseado -da *adj* **(a)** ‹*libro*› well-thumbed; **fruta manoseada** fruit that has been handled by lots of people **(b)** ‹*tema*› hackneyed, well-worn

manosear [A1] *vt* **(a)** ‹*objeto*› to handle **(b)** (fam) ‹*persona*› to grope (colloq)

manotada *f* (Col) handful

manotazo *m* swipe

mansalva: **a ~** (*loc adv*) ‹*disparar*› at close range

mansión *f* mansion; **~ señorial** stately home

manso -sa *adj* **(a)** ‹*caballo*› tame; ‹*toro*› docile; ‹*perro*› friendly **(b)** (liter) ‹*río*› gently-flowing (liter)

manta *f* **1** (de cama) blanket **2** (Chi) (poncho) poncho **3** (Méx) (tela) *a coarse muslin-like cloth*, calico (BrE)

manteca *f* **(a)** (grasa) fat; (de cerdo) lard **(b)** (mantequilla) (RPl) butter; **~ de cacao** cocoa butter; **~ de maní** (RPl) peanut butter

mantecoso -sa *adj* greasy

mantel *m* (de mesa) tablecloth; (del altar) altar cloth; **~ individual** place mat

mantelería *f* table linen

mantención *f* (CS) maintenance

mantener [E27] *vt* **1** (económicamente) ‹*familia/persona*› to support, maintain; ‹*amante*› to keep **2** (conservar, preservar) to keep; **~ la calma** to keep calm; **~ el equilibrio** to keep one's balance; **~ algo en equilibrio** to balance sth; **para ~ su peso actual** to maintain his present weight **3** **(a)** ‹*conversaciones*› to have; ‹*contactos*› to maintain, keep up; ‹*correspondencia*› to keep up; ‹*relaciones*› to maintain **(b)** (cumplir) ‹*promesa/palabra*› to keep **4** (afirmar, sostener) to maintain

■ **mantenerse** *v pron* **1** (sustentarse económicamente) to support oneself

2 (en cierto estado, cierta situación) to keep; **~se en forma** to keep fit; **la torre aún se mantiene en pie** the tower is still standing; **~se en contacto (con algn)** to keep in touch (with sb) **3** (alimentarse): **~se a base de latas** to live off tinned food

mantenimiento *m* maintenance; **ejercicios de ~** keep-fit exercises

manteña *f* butter; **~ de cacao** (Chi, Per) cocoa butter

mantequillera *f* butter dish

mantiene, mantienes, etc ▶ MANTENER

mantilla *f* **(a)** (de mujer) mantilla **(b)** (de bebé) terry diaper (AmE), terry nappy (BrE)

manto *m* (Indum) cloak

mantón *m* shawl

mantuve, mantuvo, etc ▶ MANTENER

manual *adj* ‹*trabajo/destreza*› manual; **tener habilidad ~** to be good with one's hands
■ *m* manual, handbook

manualidades *fpl* handicrafts (*pl*)

manubrio *m* **(a)** (manivela) crank, handle **(b)** (AmL) (de bicicleta) handlebars (*pl*) **(c)** (Chi, Par) (de auto) steering wheel

manufacturar [A1] *vt* to manufacture

manuscrito¹ -ta *adj* hand-written, manuscript (fml)

manuscrito² *m* manuscript

manutención *f* maintenance

manzana *f* **1** (Bot) apple **2** (de edificios) block; **dar una vuelta a la ~** to go round the block **3** (AmL) (Anat) *tb* **~ de Adán** Adam's apple

manzanar *m* apple orchard

manzanilla *f* (planta) camomile; (infusión) camomile tea
■ *m* manzanilla (*dry sherry*)

manzano *m* apple tree

maña *f* **1** (habilidad) skill, knack (colloq); **tener or darse ~ para algo** to be good at sth; **más vale ~ que fuerza** brain is better than brawn **2** **mañas** *fpl* (artimañas) wiles (*pl*), guile **3** (capricho) bad habit; (manía) (AmL fam): **tiene ~s de viejo** he's like an old man with all his funny little ways (colloq); **tiene la ~ de morderse las uñas** he has the annoying habit of biting his nails

mañana *adv* tomorrow; **pasado ~** the day after tomorrow; **~ por la ~** tomorrow morning; **adiós, hasta ~** goodbye, see you tomorrow; **el día de ~** tomorrow
■ *m* future
■ *f* morning; **a la ~ siguiente** (the) next o the following morning; **a media ~ nos reunimos** we met mid-morning; **a las nueve de la ~** at nine (o'clock) in the morning; **en or** (esp Esp) **por or** (RPl) **a la(s) ~(s)** in the morning; **muy de ~** very early in the morning; **el tren de la ~** the morning train

mañanero -ra *adj* (fam): **soy muy ~** I'm a very early riser

mañanitas *fpl* (en Méx) song often sung on birthdays

mañosear [A1] *vi* (Chi fam) to play o act up (colloq)

mañoso -sa *adj* **1** (habilidoso) good with one's hands **2** (AmL) (caprichoso) difficult

mapa *m* map; ~ **de carreteras** road map; **cambios en el ~ político** changes in the political scene *o* landscape; **desaparecer del ~** to disappear off the face of the earth

mapache *m* racoon

mapamundi *m* map of the world, world map

mapurite *m* (AmC, Ven) skunk

maqueta *f* (de edificio) model, mock-up

maquiladora *f* (Méx) (cross-border) assembly plant

maquillador -dora *m,f* makeup artist

maquillaje *m* makeup; ~ **de fondo** foundation

maquillar [A1] *vt* to make up
■ **maquillarse** *v pron* to put one's makeup on, to make up

máquina *f* [1] **(a)** (aparato) machine; **¿se puede lavar a ~?** can it be machine-washed?; **escribir a ~** to type; ~ **de afeitar** safety razor; (eléctrica) electric razor, shaver; ~ **de coser/lavar** sewing/washing machine; ~ **de escribir** typewriter; ~ **expendedora** vending machine; ~ **tragamonedas** *or* (Esp) **tragaperras** slot machine, fruit machine **(b)** (Jueg) fruit machine; (Fot) camera [2] **(a)** (Ferr, Náut) engine **(b)** (Ven fam) (auto) car

maquinación *f* plot, scheme

maquinar [A1] *vt* to plot, scheme

maquinaria *f* **(a)** (conjunto) machinery **(b)** (mecanismo) mechanism; **la ~ del estado** the state machinery

maquinilla *f* [1] *tb* ~ **de afeitar** safety razor; (eléctrica) electric razor, shaver [2] (AmC) (máquina de escribir) typewriter

maquinista *mf* [1] (operador de una máquina) machine operator [2] (Ferr) engine driver, engineer (AmE); (Náut) engineer

mar *m* (*sometimes f in literary language and in set idiomatic expressions*) [1] (Geog) sea; **a orillas del ~** by the sea; **el fondo del ~** the seabed, the bottom of the sea; ~ **abierto** open sea; **la corriente llevó la barca ~ adentro** the boat was swept out to sea by the current; **hacerse a la ~** (liter) to set sail; **por ~** by sea; ~ **Cantábrico** Bay of Biscay; ~ **de las Antillas** Caribbean Sea; ~ **Mediterráneo** Mediterranean Sea; ~ **gruesa** rough *o* heavy sea [2] (costa): **prefiero el ~ a la montaña** I prefer the seaside to the mountains

maraca *f* maraca

maracuyá *m* passion fruit

maraña *f* tangle; **la ~ burocrática** the tangle of bureaucracy

maratón *m or f* marathon

maravilla *f* [1] (portento, prodigio) wonder; **las ~s de la tecnología moderna** the wonders of modern technology; **mi secretaria es una verdadera ~** my secretary is absolutely wonderful; **a las mil ~s** marvelously; **de ~** wonderfully; **hacer ~s** to work wonders [2] (Bot) marigold

maravillar [A1] *vt* to amaze, astonish
■ **maravillarse** *v pron* to be amazed *o* astonished; ~**se DE algo/algn** to marvel AT sth/sb

maravilloso -sa *adj* marvelous*, wonderful

marca *f* [1] **(a)** (señal, huella) mark **(b)** (en el ganado) brand **(b)** (Com) (de coches, cámaras) make; (de productos alimenticios, cosméticos, etc) brand; **comprar artículos de ~** to buy brand products *o* brand names; **ropa de ~** designer clothes; ~

patentada *or* **registrada** registered trademark [3] (Dep) record; **superar** *or* **batir una ~** to break a record

marcado¹ -da *adj* marked; **un ~ acento escocés** a marked *o* pronounced Scottish accent

marcado² *m* **(a)** (del pelo) set **(b)** (de reses) branding

marcador *m* [1] (Dep) scoreboard; **¿cómo va el ~?** what's the score? [2] **(a)** (para libros) bookmark **(b)** (AmL) (rotulador) felt-tip pen, fiber-tip* pen

marcaje *m* (Dep) coverage, cover

marcapasos *m* (*pl* ~) pacemaker

marcar [A2] *vt* [1] **(a)** (con señal) ⟨ropa/página/baraja⟩ to mark; ⟨ganado⟩ to brand **(b)** «experiencia/suceso» (dejar huella) to mark [2] **(a)** (indicar, señalar) to mark; **el precio va marcado en la tapa** the price is marked on the lid; **el reloj marca las doce en punto** the time is exactly twelve o'clock **(b)** (hacer resaltar) ⟨cintura/busto⟩ to accentuate **(c)** (Mús): ~ **el compás/el ritmo** to beat time/the rhythm [3] ⟨pelo⟩ to set [4] (Telec) to dial [5] (Dep) **(a)** ⟨gol/tanto⟩ to score **(b)** ⟨jugador⟩ to mark
■ ~ *vi* [1] (Dep) to score [2] (Telec) to dial
■ **marcarse** *v pron*: ~**se el pelo** (refl) to mark one's hair; (caus) to have one's hair set

marcha *f* [1] **(a)** (Mil) march; (manifestación) march; (caminata) hike, walk; **ir de ~** to go walking *o* hiking; **recojan todo y ¡en ~!** pick up your things and off you/we go!; **ponerse en ~** to set off **(b)** (en atletismo) *tb* ~ **atlética** walk [2] (paso, velocidad) speed; **el vehículo disminuyó la ~** the car reduced speed *o* slowed down; **acelerar la ~** to speed up; **a toda ~** at full *o* top speed, flat out [3] (Auto) gear; **cambiar de ~** to change gear; **meter la ~ atrás** to put the car into reverse; **dar** *or* **hacer ~ atrás** (Auto) to go into reverse; (arrepentirse, retroceder) to pull out, back out [4] (funcionamiento) running; **estar en ~** «motor» to be running; «proyecto» to be up and running, to be under way; «gestiones» to be under way; **poner en ~** ⟨coche/motor⟩ to start; ⟨plan/sistema⟩ to set ... in motion; **ponerse en ~** «tren» to move off [5] (curso, desarrollo) course; **la ~ de los acontecimientos** the course of events; **sobre la ~:** **hago correciones sobre la ~** I make corrections as I go along; **lo decidiremos sobre la ~** we'll play it by ear [6] (partida) departure [7] (Mús) march; ~ **nupcial** wedding march [8] (Esp fam) (animación, ambiente): **una ciudad con mucha ~** a very lively city; **¡qué ~ tiene!** he's so full of energy

marchante -ta *m,f* [1] (de obras de arte) art dealer [2] (Méx) (en mercado — vendedor) stallholder; (— comprador) customer

marchar [A1] *vi* [1] «coche» to go, run; «reloj/máquina» to work; «negocio/relación/empresa» to work; **su matrimonio no marcha muy bien** his marriage isn't going *o* working very well [2] **(a)** (Mil) to march **(b)** (caminar) to walk

⸱⸱⸱⟐

■ **marcharse** *v pron* (esp Esp) to leave; **se marcha a Roma** he's leaving for *o* going off to Rome

marchitarse [A1] *v pron* (a) ‹*flores*› to wither (b) (liter) «*belleza/juventud*» to fade

marchito -ta *adj* (a) ‹*flores*› withered (b) (liter) ‹*belleza/juventud*› faded

marchoso -sa *adj* (Esp fam) ‹*ambiente/ciudad*› lively; **es un tío** ~ he's really into the night life (colloq), he's really into having a good time (colloq)

marcial *adj* martial

marciano -na *adj/m,f* Martian

marco *m* ⓵ (a) (de cuadro) frame; (de puerta) doorframe (b) (Dep) goalposts (*pl*), goal (c) (Andes) (de bicicleta) frame ⓶ (contexto) framework; **dentro del** ~ **de la ley** within the framework of the law ⓷ (Fin) mark

marea *f* tide; **cuando baja/sube la** ~ when the tide goes out/comes in; ~ **creciente** rising tide, flood tide; ~ **menguante** falling tide, ebb tide; ~ **negra** oil slick

mareado -da *adj* (a) (Med): **está** ~ (con náuseas) he's feeling sick *o* queasy; (con pérdida del equilibrio, etc) he's feeling dizzy *o* giddy; (a punto de desmayarse) he's feeling faint (b) (confundido): **me tienes** ~ **con tanta cháchara** all your chatter is making my head spin

marear [A1] *vt* (a) (Med) (con náuseas) to make … feel sick *o* queasy; (con pérdida de equilibrio) to make … dizzy (b) (confundir) to confuse, get … confused *o* muddled; **me mareas con tantas preguntas** you're confusing me with all these questions

■ **marearse** *v pron* (a) (al viajar — en coche) to get carsick; (— en barco) to get seasick; (— en avión) to get airsick; (perder el equilibrio) to feel dizzy; (con alcohol) to get tipsy (b) (confundirse) to get muddled *o* confused

marejada *f* heavy sea, swell

maremoto *m* (a) (sismo) seaquake (b) (ola) tidal wave

mareo *m* (a) (del estómago) sickness, nausea; (producido por movimiento) motion sickness; (en coche) carsickness; (en avión) airsickness; (en barco) seasickness; (pérdida de equilibrio, etc) dizziness, giddiness; **me dio un** ~ I felt dizzy (b) (confusión) muddle, mess

marfil *m* ivory

margarina *f* margarine

margarita *f* (Bot) (pequeña) daisy; (grande) marguerite

margen *f* (a veces *m*) (de río) bank; (de carretera) side
■ *m* ⓵ (en general) margin; ~ **de beneficio** *or* **ganancias** profit margin; ~ **de error** margin of error; **ver nota al** ~ see margin note; **al margen de** apart from: **al** ~ **de la ley** on the fringes of the law; **mantenerse al** ~ **de algo** to keep out of sth; **dejar a algn al** ~ to leave sb out; ~ **de acción/tiempo** leeway ⓶ **márgenes** *mpl* (límites, parámetros) limits (*pl*); **dentro de ciertos márgenes** within certain limits

marginación *f* (Sociol) marginalization

marginado -da *adj* (a) (Sociol) marginalized (b) (excluido) excluded
■ *m,f* social outcast

marginal *adj* ⓵ (Sociol): **en los barrios** ~**es** in the poor, outlying areas of the city ⓶ (secundario) ‹*posición*› peripheral; ‹*asunto*› marginal, peripheral ⓷ (Impr): **una nota** ~ a note in the margin, a marginal note

marginar [A1] *vt* (en la sociedad) to marginalize; (en un grupo) to ostracize

mariachi *m* mariachi musician

marialuisa *f* (Méx) mount, passe-partout

maricón¹ -cona *adj* (fam & pey) (a) (homosexual) queer (colloq & pej), bent (sl & pej) (b) (como insulto): **el muy** ~ the bastard *o* (AmE) son of a bitch (vulg); **la muy maricona** the bitch (vulg) (c) (AmL) (cobarde) wimpy (colloq), wimpish (colloq)

maricón² *m* (fam & pey) fag (AmE colloq & pej), poof (BrE colloq & pej)

mariconera *f* (fam & hum) (men's) handbag

marido *m* husband

marihuana *f* marijuana

marihuanero -ra *m,f* (fam) dope fiend (colloq)

marimacho *m or f* (fam & pey) (a) (niña) tomboy (colloq) (b) (mujer hombruna) butch woman (colloq)

marimba *f* marimba (*type of xylophone*)

marina *f* ⓵ (organización) navy; (barcos) fleet; ~ **de guerra** navy ⓶ (Art) seascape

marinar [A1] *vt* to marinate, marinade

marinera *f* ⓵ (blusa) sailor top; (chaqueta) (Col) sailor jacket ⓶ (baile) *Andean folk dance*

marinero *m* sailor

marino¹ -na *adj* ‹*brisa/corriente*› sea (*before n*); ‹*fauna/biología*› marine (*before n*)

marino² *m* (marinero) sailor; (oficial) naval officer; ~ **mercante** merchant seaman

marioneta *f* puppet, marionette

mariposa *f* butterfly; ~ **nocturna** moth; **estilo** ~ butterfly; **nadar** ~ *or* (Esp) **a** *o* (Méx) **de** ~ to swim butterfly

mariquita *f* (Zool) ladybug (AmE), ladybird (BrE)
■ *m* (fam & pey) fag (AmE colloq & pej), poof (BrE colloq & pej)

mariscal *m* (Hist, Mil) marshal; ~ **de campo** (Mil) field marshal; (en fútbol americano) quarterback

marisco *m* shellfish (*pl*), seafood

marisma *f* marsh

marisquería *f* seafood *o* shellfish restaurant/bar/shop

marital *adj* ‹*relaciones*› marital (*before n*); ‹*vida*› married (*before n*)

marítimo -ma *adj* ‹*comercio*› maritime; ‹*ruta/agente*› shipping (*before n*); ‹*transporte*› sea (*before n*); ‹*ciudad*› coastal, maritime; **un puerto** ~ a seaport

marketing /'marketin/ *m* marketing

mármol *m* marble

AmC	Central America	Arg	Argentina	Cu	Cuba	Per	Peru
AmL	Latin America	Bol	Bolivia	Ec	Ecuador	RPI	River Plate Area
AmS	South America	Chi	Chile	Esp	Spain	Ur	Uruguay
Andes	Andean Region	CS	Southern Cone	Méx	Mexico	Ven	Venezuela

marmota *f* (a) (Zool) marmot (b) (fam) (persona dormilona) sleepyhead (colloq)

maroma *f* ⒈ (a) (Andes) (acrobacia, malabarismo) trick, stunt; **las ∼s del payaso** the clown's antics (b) (Méx) (voltereta) somersault, tumble; **dar una ∼** to do a somersault

marqués -quesa *m,f* ⒈ (persona) (*m*) marquis, marquess (BrE); (*f*) marquise, marchioness (BrE) ⒉ **marquesa** *f* (Chi) (catre) bed

marquesina *f* (en parada, andén) shelter; (de teatro, hotel) marquee (AmE), canopy (BrE); (en estadio) roof

marquetería *f* marquetry

marranada *f* (fam) (faena) dirty trick

marrano -na *adj* filthy
■ *m,f* (fam) (a) (animal) (*m*) pig, hog; (*f*) pig, sow (b) (Col) (carne) pork (c) (persona grosera) dirty swine (colloq)

marraqueta *f* (Chi) bread roll

marrón *adj/m* brown; **zapatos ∼ oscuro** dark brown shoes

marroquí *adj/mf* Moroccan

marroquinería *f* (a) (artículos de cuero) leather goods (*pl*) (b) (tienda) leather goods shop

marrueco *m* (Chi) fly, flies (*pl*)

Marruecos *m* Morocco

marsupial *adj/m* marsupial

marta *f* (pine) marten; **∼ cibelina** sable

Marte *m* Mars

martes *m* (*pl* ∼) Tuesday; **∼ (y) trece** ≈ Friday the thirteenth; **∼ de carnaval** Shrove Tuesday, Mardi Gras; *para ejemplos ver* LUNES

martillar, martillear [A1] *vt/vi* to hammer

martilleo *m* hammering; **un ∼ terrible en las sienes** a terrible pounding in the temples

martillero -ra *m,f* (CS, Per) auctioneer

martillo *m* hammer; **∼ neumático** jackhammer, pneumatic drill

martín pescador *m* kingfisher

mártir *mf* martyr

martirio *m* (a) (muerte) martyrdom (b) (sufrimiento) torment, ordeal

martirizar [A4] *vt* (a) (matar) to martyr (b) (atormentar) to torment

marxismo *m* Marxism

marxista *adj/mf* Marxist

marzo *m* March; *para ejemplos ver* ENERO

mas *conj* (liter) but

más *adv* ⒈ (a) (comparativo): **¿tiene algo ∼ barato/moderno?** do you have anything cheaper/ more modern?; **duran ∼** they last longer; **me gusta ∼ sin azúcar** I prefer it without sugar; **ahora la vemos ∼** we see more of her now; **tendrás que estudiar ∼** you'll have to study harder; **∼ lejos/atrás** further away/back; **el ∼ allá** the other world; **∼ que nunca** more than ever; **me gusta ∼ el vino seco que el dulce** I prefer dry wine to sweet, I like dry wine better than sweet; **pesa ∼ de lo que parece** it's heavier than it looks; **es ∼ complicado de lo que tú crees** it's more complicated than you think; **eran ∼ de las cinco** it was after five o'clock; **∼ de 30** more than 30, over 30 (b) (especialmente) particularly, especially

⒉ (superlativo): **la ∼ bonita/la ∼ inteligente** the prettiest/the most intelligent; **el que ∼ sabe** the one who knows most; **el que ∼ me gusta** the one I like best; **estuvo de lo ∼ divertido** it was great fun

⒊ (*en frases negativas*): **no tiene ∼ que tres meses** she's only three months old; **nadie ∼ que ella** nobody but her; **no tengo ∼ que esto** this is all I have; **no tuve ∼ remedio** I had no alternative; **no juego ∼** I'm not playing any more; **nunca ∼** never again

⒋ (con valor ponderativo): **¡cantó ∼ bien...!** she sang so well!; **¡qué cosa ∼ rara!** how strange!
■ *adj inv* ⒈ (comparativo) more; **∼ dinero** more money; **una vez ∼** once more; **ni un minuto ∼** not a minute longer; **hoy hace ∼ calor** it's warmer today; **son ∼ que nosotros** there are more of them than us

⒉ (superlativo) most; **el equipo que ganó ∼ partidos** the team that won most games; **las ∼ de las veces** more often than not

⒊ (con valor ponderativo) **¡me da ∼ rabia ...!** it makes me so mad!; **¡tiene ∼ amigos ...!** he has so many friends!

⒋ **¿qué ∼?** what else?; **nada/nadie ∼** nothing/ nobody else; **algo/alguien ∼** something/somebody else; **¿quién ∼ vino?** who else came?; **¿algo ∼?** **— nada ∼ gracias** anything else? — no, that's all, thank you
■ *pron* ⒈ more; **¿te sirvo ∼?** would you like some more?

⒉ (*en locs*) **a lo ∼** at the most; **a ∼ no poder: corrimos a ∼ no poder** we ran as fast *o* hard as we could; **a ∼ tardar** at the latest; **cuanto ∼** at the most; **de ∼: ¿tienes un lápiz de ∼?** do you have a spare pencil?; **me dio cinco dólares de ∼** he gave me five dollars too much; **no está de ∼ repetirlo** there's no harm in repeating it; **es ∼** in fact; **∼ bien** (un poco) rather; **∼ o menos** (aproximadamente) more or less; (no muy bien) so-so; **ni ∼ ni menos** no less; **no ∼ ▶** NOMÁS; **por ∼: por ∼ que llores** however much you cry; **por ∼ que trataba** however hard he tried; **¿qué ∼ da?** what does it matter?; **sin ∼ (ni ∼)** just like that
■ *prep* (a) (Mat) (en sumas) plus; **8+7 =15** (*read as:* **ocho ∼ siete (es) igual (a) quince**) eight plus seven equals fifteen (b) (además de) plus; **mil pesos, ∼ los gastos** a thousand pesos, plus expenses
■ *m* plus sign

masa *f* ⒈ (Coc) (a) (para pan, pasta) dough; (para empanadas, tartas) pastry; (para bizcocho) mixture; (para crepes) batter; **∼ de hojaldre** puff pastry (b) (RPl) (pastelito) pastry, cake ⒉ (Pol, Sociol, Fís) mass; **educar a las ∼s** to educate the masses ⒊ **en masa** (a) (*loc adj*) ⟨fabricación/despidos⟩ mass (*before n*) (b) (*loc adv*) ⟨acudir⟩ en masse

masacrar [A1] *vt* to massacre

masacre *f* massacre

masaje *m* massage; **darle ∼s** *or* **un ∼ a algn** to give sb a massage

masajear [A1] *vt* to massage

masajista *mf* ⒈ (que da masajes) (*m*) masseur; (*f*) masseuse ⒉ (en fútbol) coach, trainer

mascada *f* (a) (Chi) (mordisco) bite (b) (Méx) (pañuelo grande) scarf

mascar [A2] *vt* to chew

máscara *f* mask; ~ **antigás** gas mask; ~ **de oxígeno** oxygen mask; ~ **facial** face pack

mascarilla *f* mask; (en cosmética) face pack

mascota *f* (talismán) mascot; (animal doméstico) pet

masculino¹ -na *adj* **(a)** ‹actitud/hormona› male; ‹mujer/aspecto› masculine, manly **(b)** (Ling) masculine

masculino² *m* masculine

mascullar [A1] *vt* to mumble, mutter

masía *f* (granja) farm; (casa) country house

masificación *f* overcrowding

masificado -da *adj* ‹universidad› overcrowded

masilla *f* (para cristales) putty; (para rellenar grietas) mastic, filler

masivo -va *adj* **(a)** ‹ejecución/migración› mass (*before n*); ‹protesta› large-scale (*before n*), mass (*before n*); ‹concurrencia› massive **(b)** ‹dosis› massive, huge

masón *adj* Masonic
■ *m* Freemason, Mason

masonería *f* Freemasonry

masoquismo *m* masochism

masoquista *adj* masochistic
■ *mf* masochist

máster /'master/ *m* (*pl* **-ters**) **1** (Audio, Vídeo) master **2** (Educ) master's degree

masticar [A2] *vt/vi* to chew

mástil *m* (Náut) mast; (para una bandera) flagpole, flagstaff **(b)** (de guitarra, violín) neck **(c)** (de carpa) centerpole*

mastín *m* mastiff

mastodonte *m* **(a)** (animal prehistórico) mastodon **(b)** (fam) (persona grande) giant

mastuerzo *m* (planta) (garden) cress

masturbación *f* masturbation

masturbarse [A1] *v pron* to masturbate

mata *f* **1** (arbusto) bush, shrub; (planta) (AmL) plant **2** (ramita) sprig; (de hierba) tuft **3** (fam) (de pelo) mane (colloq), mop (colloq)

matadero *m* slaughterhouse, abattoir

matado -da *m,f* (Méx fam & pey) grind (AmE colloq), swot (BrE colloq)

matador *m* matador

matamoscas *m* (*pl* ~) **(a)** (paleta) flyswatter **(b)** (spray) fly spray, fly killer

matanza *f* (acción de matar) killing, slaughter; (de res, cerdo) slaughter; **la** ~ **de gente inocente** the mass killing of innocent people

matapolillas *m* (*pl* ~) moth killer

matar [A1] *vt* **1** **(a)** ‹persona› to kill **(b)** (sacrificar) ‹perro/caballo› to put down, destroy; ‹reses› to slaughter; **lo mató un coche** he was run over and killed by a car **(c)** (en sentido hiperbólico): **la vas a** ~ **a disgustos** you'll be the death of her; **es para** ~**los** I could murder *o* kill them (colloq); **nos mataban de hambre** they used to starve us; **estos zapatos me están matando** these shoes are killing me!
2 (fam) ‹sed› to quench; ‹tiempo› to kill; **compraron fruta para** ~ **el hambre** they bought some fruit to keep them going
■ ~ *vi* to kill
■ **matarse** *v pron* **1** **(a)** (morir violentamente) to be killed; **casi me mato** I almost got killed **(b)** (*refl*) (suicidarse) to kill oneself; **se mató de un tiro** she shot herself
2 (fam) **(a)** (esforzarse): **me maté estudiando** *or* (Esp) **a estudiar** I studied like crazy *o* mad (colloq) **(b)** (Méx fam) (para un examen) to cram (colloq), to swot (BrE colloq)

matarife *m* (en matadero) slaughterman

matarratas *m* (*pl* ~) (veneno) rat poison

matasellos *m* (*pl* ~) **(a)** (marca) postmark **(b)** (instrumento) datestamp, stamp

matazón *f* (Col, Méx, Ven fam) massacre, slaughter

mate *adj or adj inv* ‹pintura/maquillaje› matt; **fotos** ~ photos with a matt finish
■ *m* **1** (en ajedrez) *tb* **jaque** ~ checkmate, mate **2** (infusión) maté; **cebar** ~ to brew maté **(b)** (AmL) (calabaza) gourd

matear [A1] *vi* (CS fam) to drink maté
■ **matearse** *v pron* (Chi fam) to cram (colloq), to swot (Br colloq)

matemáticas *fpl* mathematics, math (AmE), maths (BrE)

matemático -ca *adj* mathematical
■ *m,f* mathematician

mateo -tea *m,f* (Chi fam) grind (AmE colloq), swot (BrE colloq)

materia *f* **1** (sustancia) matter; ~ **gris** gray* matter; ~ **prima** (Econ, Tec) raw material; (Fin) commodity **2** **(a)** (tema, asunto) subject; **en** ~ **de** as regards, with regard to **(b)** (asignatura) subject

material *adj* ‹necesidades/ayuda/valor› material; **daños** ~**es** damage to property, material damage **(b)** ‹autor/causante› actual
■ *m* **1** (en general) material; ~**es para la construcción** building materials **2** (útiles) materials (*pl*); ~ **de oficina** office stationery; ~ **didáctico/escolar** teaching/school materials (*pl*)

materialismo *m* materialism

materialista *adj* materialistic
■ *mf* **1** (persona) materialist **2** (Méx) (constructor) building contractor; (camionero) truck driver, lorry driver (BrE)

maternal *adj* ‹instinto› maternal; ‹amor› motherly, maternal

maternidad *f* **(a)** (estado) motherhood, maternity **(b)** (hospital) maternity hospital; (sala) maternity ward

materno -na *adj* ‹amor› motherly; ‹pariente› maternal; ‹lengua› mother

matinal *adj* morning (*before n*)

matinée, matiné *f* (AmS) (de tarde) matinée **(b)** (Méx) (de mañana) morning performance

matiz *m* **(a)** (de color) shade, hue **(b)** (de palabra, frase) nuance, shade of meaning; **tiene cierto** ~ **peyorativo** it has a slightly pejorative nuance **(c)** (de ironía) touch, hint

matizar [A4] *vt* **1** ‹colores› to blend **2** (concretar, puntualizar) to qualify, clarify

matón *m* (del barrio) thug; (en la escuela) bully; (criminal) thug, heavy (colloq)

matorral *m* **(a)** (conjunto de matas) thicket, bushes (*pl*) **(b)** (terreno) scrubland

matraca *f* **1** (juguete) rattle **2** (Méx fam) (coche) rattletrap (colloq)

matrero -ra adj [1] (Col fam) (basto) shoddy [2] (RPl) (fugitivo): **un gaucho ~ a** gaucho on the run from the law [3] (Col) (traicionero) sly, crafty

matriarcado m matriarchy

matriarcal adj matriarchal

matrícula f [1] (Educ) (inscripción) registration, enrollment*; **derechos** or **tasas de ~** registration fees; **~ de honor** (Esp) ≈ distinction, ≈ magna cum laude [2] (Transp) (número) registration number; (placa) license* plate, number plate (BrE)

matricular [A1] vt (a) ⟨persona⟩ to register, enroll* (b) ⟨coche/barco⟩ to register
■ **matricularse** v pron (refl) to register, enroll*; **~se EN algo** to enroll ON sth

matrimonial adj marital

matrimonio m (a) (institución) marriage, matrimony (frml); **contraer ~** (frml) to marry (b) (pareja) (married) couple; **el ~ Garrido** Mr and Mrs Garrido, the Garridos (c) (AmS exc RPl) (boda) wedding; **~ civil/religioso** civil/church wedding

matriz f (a) (útero) womb, uterus (b) (molde) mold* (c) (de talonario) stub

matrona f (comadrona) midwife

matutino¹ -na adj morning (before n)

matutino² m morning paper

maullar [A23] vi to miaow

maullido m miaow

mausoleo m mausoleum

maxilar m jawbone, maxilla (tech)

máxima f maxim

máxime adv especially

máximo¹ -ma adj ⟨temperatura/velocidad⟩ top (before n), maximum (before n); ⟨carga/altura⟩ maximum (before n); ⟨punto⟩ highest; ⟨esfuerzo/ambición⟩ greatest (before n); **el ~ dirigente francés** the French leader

máximo² m maximum; **como ~** at the most; **aprovechar algo al ~** to make the most of sth; **se esforzó al ~** she did her utmost; **rendir al ~** «persona» to give a hundred percent; «máquina» to work to its full capacity

maya adj Mayan
■ mf Maya, Mayan; **los ~s** the Maya o Mayas

mayo m May; **el primero de ~** May Day; para ejemplos ver ENERO

mayonesa f mayonnaise, mayo (AmE) (colloq)

mayor adj [1] (a) (comparativo de GRANDE) ⟨número/porcentaje⟩ greater, higher; ⟨beneficio⟩ greater; **vuelan a ~ altura** they fly at a greater height; **a ~ escala** on a larger scale; **un número ~ que 40** a number greater than 40 (b) (superlativo de GRANDE): **el ~ número de accidentes** the greatest o highest number of accidents; **su ~ preocupación** her greatest o biggest worry; **a la ~ brevedad posible** as soon as possible; **la ~ parte de los estudiantes** most students, the majority of students
[2] (en edad) (a) (comparativo) older; **~ QUE algn** older THAN sb (b) (superlativo): **es la ~ de las dos** she is the older o elder of the two; **mi hijo ~** my eldest o oldest son (c) (anciano) elderly (d) (adulto): **las personas ~es** adults, grown-ups (colloq); **cuando sea ~** when I grow up; **ser ~ de edad** (Der) to be of age; **soy ~ de edad y haré lo que quiera** I'm over 18 (o 21 etc) and I'll do as I please

[3] (en nombres) (principal) main; **Calle M~** Main Street (in US), High Street (in UK)
[4] (Mús) major
[5] (Com): **(al) por ~** wholesale
■ mf (adulto) adult, grown-up (colloq); **solo para ~es** adults only; **mis/tus ~es** my/your elders; **~ de edad** person who is legally of age

mayoral m (capataz) foreman; (de finca) farm manager, steward

mayordomo m (criado principal) butler, majordomo; (capataz) (CS) foreman; (portero) (Chi) superintendent (AmE), caretaker (BrE)

mayoría f majority; **la gran ~ de ...** the great majority of ...; **ser ~** or **estar en ~** to be in the majority; **gobierno de la ~** majority rule; **~ absoluta/relativa** absolute/simple majority; **llegar a la ~ de edad** to come of age

mayorista adj wholesale
■ mf wholesaler

mayoritario -ria adj (a) ⟨apoyo/decisión/partido⟩ majority (before n) (b) (Fin) ⟨socio/accionista⟩ principal

mayúscula f capital (letter), uppercase letter (tech); **se escribe con ~** it is written with a capital letter; **rellenar en** or **con ~s** write in block capitals o in capital letters

mayúsculo -la adj (a) ⟨letra⟩ capital (before n), upper-case (tech) (b) ⟨susto/error⟩ terrible

maza f (a) (Const) drop hammer (b) (de bombo) drumstick (c) (arma) mace

mazacote m (a) (fam) (Coc): **un ~** a lumpy mess (b) (fam) (obra tosca) eyesore

mazamorra f (a) (AmS) milky pudding made with maize (b) (Per) pudding made with corn starch, sugar and honey (c) (Col) maize soup

mazapán m marzipan

mazmorra f dungeon

mazo m [1] (a) (herramienta) mallet; (del mortero) pestle; (para la carne) meat tenderizer; (porra) club (b) (en croquet, polo) mallet [2] (esp AmL) (manojo) bunch; (de naipes) deck (of cards) (AmE), pack (of cards) (BrE)

mazorca f (Bot, Coc) cob; **~ de maíz** corncob

mazurca f mazurka

me pron pers me; **¿~ lo prestas?** will you lend it to me o lend me it?; **~ arregló el televisor** he fixed the television for me; **~ lo quitó** he took it off me o away from me; **~ robaron el reloj** my watch was stolen; **~ miré en el espejo** (refl) I looked at myself in the mirror; **~ corté el pelo** (refl) I cut my hair; (caus) I had my hair cut; **~ equivoqué** I made a mistake; **~ alegro mucho** I'm very pleased; **se ~ murió el gato** my cat died

mear [A1] vi (vulg) to (have a) piss (vulg)
■ **mearse** v pron (fam) to wet oneself; **me estoy meando** I'm dying for a pee (colloq)

mecánica f mechanics

mecánico -ca adj mechanical
■ m,f (de vehículos) mechanic; (de maquinaria industrial) fitter; (de fotocopiadoras, lavadoras) engineer

mecanismo m mechanism; **~ de defensa** defense* mechanism

mecanizado -da adj mechanized

mecanizar [A4] vt to mechanize

mecanografía f typing

mecanografiar [A17] vt to type

mecanógrafo -fa *m,f* typist

mecate *m* (AmC, Méx, Ven) string, cord; (más grueso) rope

mecedora *f* rocking chair

mecenas *mf* (*pl* ~) patron, sponsor

mecer [E2] *vt* ‹bebé/cuna› to rock; ‹niño› (en columpio) to push
  ■ **mecerse** *v pron* **(a)** (en mecedora) to rock; (en columpio) to swing **(b)** (bambolearse) to sway

mecha *f* **1** (de vela) wick; (de armas, explosivos) fuse **2** **mechas** *fpl* (en peluquería) highlights (*pl*)

mechero *m* **(a)** (Esp) (encendedor) lighter **(b)** (Col) (candil) oil lamp

mechón¹ *m* **(a)** (de pelo) lock **(b)** (de lana) tuft **(c)** **mechones** *mpl* (Col) (en peluquería) highlights (*pl*)

mechón² -chona *m,f* (Chi) (estudiante) freshman, fresher (BrE)

medalla *f* (Dep, Mil) medal; (Relig) medallion (*with religious engraving on it*)

medallón *m* medallion

media *f* **1** (Indum) **(a)** (hasta el muslo) stocking; ~s con/sin costura seamed/seamless stockings **(b)** **medias** *fpl* (hasta la cintura) panty hose (*pl*) (AmE), tights (*pl*) (BrE); ~s bombacha(s) (RPI) *or* (Col, Ven) **pantalón** panty hose (*pl*) (AmE), tights (*pl*) (BrE) **(c)** (AmL) (calcetín) sock **2** (Mat) average; **la ~ de velocidad** the average speed **3** **a medias** (*loc adv*) **(a)** (incompleto): **dejó el trabajo a ~s** he left the work half-finished; **me dijo la verdad a ~s** she didn't tell me the whole truth *o* story **(b)** (entre dos): **pagar a ~s** to pay half each, go halves; **lo hicimos a ~s** we did half (of it) each

mediación *f* mediation; **por ~ de** through

mediador -dora *m,f* mediator

mediados: **a ~ de mes** halfway through the month, in the middle of the month; **a ~ de los años 30** in the mid thirties

mediagua *f* (Andes) hut, shack

medialuna *f* **(a)** (esp RPI) (Coc) croissant (*often with ham and cheese*) **(b)** (Chi) (corral) ring

mediana *f* (Auto) median strip (AmE), central reservation (BrE)

medianero -ra *adj* dividing (*before n*)

mediano -na *adj* **(a)** ‹tamaño/porción› medium; ‹coche› medium-sized; **de mediana estatura/inteligencia** of average height/intelligence; **de mediana edad** middle-aged **(b)** (mediocre) average, mediocre

medianoche *f* midnight; **a ~** at midnight

mediante *prep* through, by means of

mediar [A1] *vi* **(a)** (intervenir) to mediate; **~ EN algo** ‹en conflicto/negociaciones› to mediate IN sth, to act as mediator IN sth **(b)** (interceder) **~ POR algn** to intercede for sb; **~ ANTE algn** to intercede *o* intervene WITH sb

mediasnueves *fpl* (Col) mid-morning snack, elevenses (BrE colloq)

medicamento *m* (frml) medicine, medicament (frml)

medicatura *f* (Ven) first aid post, clinic

medicina *f* medicine

medicinal *adj* ‹aguas/planta› medicinal; ‹champú/jabón› medicated

medición *f* **(a)** (acción) measuring **(b)** (frml) (medida) measurement

médico¹ -ca *adj* medical; **un reconocimiento ~** a medical (examination)

médico² *mf* doctor; **~ de cabecera** family doctor *o* (AmE) physician, general practitioner, GP; **~ de medicina general** general practitioner, GP

medida *f* **1** (Mat) (dimensión) measurement; **tomarle las ~s a algn** to take sb's measurements; **tomar las ~s de algo** to measure something **2** (en locs) **a (la) medida** ‹traje/zapato› custom-made (AmE), made-to-measure (BrE); **a medida que** as; **a ~ que fue creciendo** as he grew up **3** (utensilio) measure; (contenido) measure **4** (grado, proporción): **en gran/cierta ~** to a large/certain extent; **en la ~ de lo posible** as far as possible **5** (disposición) measure; **tomar ~s** to take steps *o* measures

medido -da *adj* (CS) ‹persona/comportamiento› restrained; **es muy ~ con la bebida** he's a very moderate drinker

medidor *m* (AmL) meter

medieval *adj* medieval

medio¹ -dia *adj* **1** (delante del n) (la mitad de): **~ kilo** half a kilo; **media manzana** half an apple; **pagar ~ pasaje** to pay half fare *o* half price; **media hora** half an hour, a half hour (AmE); **dos horas y media** two and a half hours; **a las cinco y media** at half past five; **a media mañana/tarde** in the middle of the morning/afternoon; **a ~ camino** halfway; **media pensión** (en hoteles) half board; **(se) dio ~ vuelta y se fue** she turned on her heel and left; **un jugador de ~ campo** a midfield player; **~ tiempo** (AmL) half-time; *mi media naranja* (fam & hum) my better half (colloq & hum) **2** (mediano, promedio) average; **el ciudadano ~** the average citizen; **a ~ y largo plazo** in the medium and long term

medio² *adv* half; **está ~ loca** she's half crazy; **todo lo deja a ~ terminar** he leaves everything half finished
  ■ *m* **1** (Mat) (mitad) half **2** (centro) middle; **en (el) ~ de la habitación** in the middle *o* center of the room; **quitarse de en ~** *or* **del ~** to get out of the way **3** **(a)** (recurso, manera) means (*pl*); **como ~ de coacción** as a means of coercion; **los ~s de comunicación** the media; **~ de transporte** means of transport **(b)** **medios** *mpl* (recursos económicos) *tb* **~s económicos** means (*pl*), resources (*pl*) **4** (en locs) **en medio de**: **en ~ de tanta gente** (in) among so many people; **en ~ de la confusión** in *o* amid all the confusion; **por medio** (CS, Per): **día/semana por ~** every other day/week; **dos casas**

por ~ every two houses; **por medio de** (de proceso/técnica) by means of; **por** ~ **de tu primo** from *o* through your cousin
5 (a) (círculo, ámbito): **en** ~**s literarios/políticos** in literary/political circles; **no está en su** ~ he's out of his element (b) (Biol) environment; **la adaptación al** ~ adaptation to one's environment; ~ **ambiente** environment; **que no da daña el** ~ **ambiente** eco-friendly, environmentally friendly
mediocampista *mf* midfield player
mediocre *adj* mediocre
mediocridad *f* mediocrity
mediodía *m* (a) (las doce de la mañana) midday, noon; **a** ~ *or* **al** ~ at midday (b) (hora de comer) lunch time
Medio Oriente *m* Middle East, Mid-East (AmE)
medir [I14] *vt* **1** ⟨habitación/distancia/velocidad⟩ to measure **2** (tener ciertas dimensiones) to be, measure; **mido 60 cm de cintura** I measure *o* I'm 60 cm round the waist; **¿cuánto mide de alto/largo?** how tall/long is it?; **mide casi 1,90 m** he's almost 1.90 m (tall) **3** (calcular, considerar) to consider, weigh up; ~ **los pros y contras de algo** to weigh up the pros and cons of sth.
■ **medirse** *v pron* **1** (*refl*) to measure oneself; ⟨caderas/pecho⟩ to measure **2** (Col, Méx, Ven) (probarse) to try on
meditación *f* meditation
meditar [A1] *vi* to meditate; ~ **sobre algo** to reflect *o* meditate on sth
■ ~ *vt* (considerar) to think about; (durante más tiempo) to ponder, meditate on; **una decisión muy meditada** a very carefully thought-out decision
mediterráneo -nea *adj* Mediterranean
Mediterráneo *m*: *tb* **el (mar)** ~ **the** Mediterranean (sea)
médula *f* (Anat) marrow, medulla (tech); ~ **ósea** bone marrow; **británico hasta la** ~ British through and through
medusa *f* jellyfish, medusa
megafonía *f* PA system
megáfono *m* megaphone
mejicano -na *adj/m,f* Mexican
Méjico *m* ▶ MEXICO
mejilla *f* cheek; **poner la otra** ~ to turn the other cheek
mejillón *m* mussel
mejor *adj* **1** (a) (comparativo de BUENO) ⟨producto/profesor⟩ better; ⟨calidad⟩ better, higher, superior; **tanto** ~ so much the better; **cuanto más grande** ~ the bigger the better (b) (comparativo de BIEN) better; **está** ~ **así** it's better like this
2 (a) (superlativo de BUENO) (entre dos) better; (entre varios) best; **mi** ~ **amiga** my best friend; **productos de la** ~ **calidad** products of the highest quality; **lo** ~ **es que se lo digas** the best thing (to do) is to tell her; **le deseo lo** ~ I wish you the very best *o* all the best (b) (superlativo de BIEN): **la que está** ~ **de dinero** the one who has the most money
■ *adv* **1** (comparativo) better; **luego lo pensé** ~ then I thought better of it; **pintas cada vez** ~ your painting is getting better and better; **me lleva dos años,** ~ **dicho, dos y medio** she's two years older than me, or rather, two and a half

2 (superlativo) best; **este es el lugar desde donde se ve** ~ this is where you can see best (from); **la versión** ~ **ambientada de la obra** the best-staged production of the play; **lo hice lo** ~ **que pude** I did it as best I could *o* (frml) to the best of my ability; **a lo** ~ maybe, perhaps; **a lo** ~ **vamos a Italia** we may *o* might go to Italy
3 (esp AmL) (en sugerencias): ~ **lo dejamos para otro día** why don't we leave it for another day?; ~ **me callo** I think I'd better shut up
■ *mf*: **el/la** ~ (de dos) the better; (de varios) the best; **es la** ~ **de la clase** she's the best in the class
mejora *f* improvement
mejorana *f* marjoram
mejorar [A1] *vt* ⟨condiciones/situación/oferta⟩ to improve; ⟨marca⟩ to improve on, beat; **el tratamiento la mejoró** the treatment made her a lot better
■ ~ *vi* ⟨tiempo/calidad/situación⟩ to improve, get better; ⟨persona⟩ (Med) to get better; **ha mejorado de aspecto** he looks a lot better
■ **mejorarse** *v pron* ⟨enfermo⟩ to get better; **que te mejores** get well soon, I hope you get better soon
mejoría *f* improvement; **le deseamos una pronta** ~ we wish you a speedy recovery
melancolía *f* melancholy, sadness
melancólico -ca *adj* melancholy
■ *m,f* melancholic
melaza *f* molasses
melé *f* (Dep) (libre) ruck, maul; (organizada) scrum
melena *f* (a) (pelo suelto) long hair (b) (estilo de corte) bob (c) (del león) mane
melenudo -da *adj* (fam) long-haired
melindroso -sa *adj* (a) (remilgado) affected (b) (Méx) (delicado) choosy, finicky (c) (mojigato) prudish
mellado -da *adj* ⟨diente/taza⟩ chipped; ⟨cuchillo/borde⟩ jagged
mellar [A1] *vt* (a) ⟨cuchillo/hoja⟩ to notch, nick; ⟨diente/porcelana⟩ to chip (b) (esp AmL) ⟨honor/fama⟩ to damage
mellizo -za *adj* twin (*before n*)
■ *m,f* (m) twin (brother); (f) twin (sister); **tuvo** ~**s** she had twins
melocotón *m* (a) (esp Esp) (fruta redonda) peach (b) (AmC) (fruta en forma de estrella) star fruit
melodía *f* melody, tune
melódico -ca *adj* melodic
melodioso -sa *adj* melodious, tuneful
melodrama *m* melodrama
melodramático -ca *adj* melodramatic
melómano -na *m,f* music lover
melón *m* (Bot) melon
meloso -sa *adj* ⟨persona/voz⟩ sickly-sweet; ⟨música/canción⟩ schmaltzy, slushy
membrana *f* membrane
membresía *f* (AmL frml) membership
membrete *m* letterhead; **papel con** ~ headed paper
membrillo *m* (árbol) quince (tree); (fruta) quince; **dulce de** ~ quince jelly
memorable *adj* memorable
memorándum *m* (*pl* **-dums**),
memorando *m* (nota) memorandum, memo

memoria f **1** (en general) memory; **tener buena/mala ~** to have a good/poor memory; **si la ~ no me falla** or **engaña** if my memory serves me right; **desde que tengo ~** for as long as I can remember; **aprender/saber algo de ~** to learn/know sth by heart; **respetar la ~ de algn** to respect the memory of sb; **a la** or **en ~ de algn** in memory of sb **2 memorias** fpl (Lit) memoirs (pl) **3** (a) (Adm, Com) report; **~ anual** annual report (b) (Educ) written paper

memorial m memorial

memorizar [A4] vt to memorize

menaje m: **artículos de ~** household items; **sección de ~ del hogar** household department

mención f mention; **hacer ~ de algo** to mention sth

mencionar [A1] vt to mention; **no quiero oír ~ ese nombre** I don't want to hear that name mentioned

mendicidad f begging

mendigar [A3] vi to beg
■ ~ vt «mendigo» to beg for

mendigo -ga m,f beggar

mendrugo m: tb ~ **de pan** piece of stale bread

menear [A1] vt «rabo» to wag; «cabeza» to shake; «caderas» to wiggle
■ **menearse** v pron (a) (con inquietud) to fidget (b) (provocativamente) to wiggle one's hips

menester m **1 ser ~** (frml) (ser necesario) to be necessary; **es ~ que lo hagamos sin demora** we must do it without delay **2** (frml) (tarea) occupation; **se ganaba la vida en los ~es más diversos** he earned his living from some very diverse activities

menestra f vegetable stew

menguar [A16] vi **1** (frml) «temperatura/nivel» to fall, drop; «cantidad/número/reservas» to diminish **2** (al tejer) to decrease
■ ~ vt **1** (frml) «responsabilidad/influencia» to diminish; «reputación» to damage **2** «puntos» (en tejido) to decrease

meningitis f meningitis

menisco m cartilage, meniscus (tech)

menopausia f menopause

menopáusico -ca adj menopausal

menor adj **1** (a) (comparativo de PEQUEÑO) «número/porcentaje» lower, smaller; **en ~ medida/grado** to a lesser extent o degree; **~ QUE algo** lower THAN sth; **un ingreso ~ que el mío** an income lower than mine (b) (superlativo de PEQUEÑO): **el país con el ~ número de parados** the country with the lowest unemployment figures; **haciendo el ~ ruido posible** making as little noise as possible; **el de ~ tamaño** the smallest one
2 (en edad) (a) (comparativo) younger; **~ QUE algn** younger THAN sb (b) (superlativo): **¿cuál es el ~ de los hermanos?** who's the youngest of the brothers?; **el ~ de los dos niños** the younger of the two boys
3 (secundario) «escritor/obra» minor; **lesiones de ~ importancia** minor injuries
4 (Mús) minor
5 (Com): **(al) por ~** retail
■ mf: tb ~ **de edad** minor; **ser ~ de edad** to be a minor, to be under age; **película no apta para menores** film not suitable for under-18s

menorista mf (Col, Méx, Ven) retailer

menos adv **1** (comparativo) less; **cada vez estudia ~** she's studying less and less; **ya me duele ~** it hurts less now; **ahora lo vemos ~** we don't see him so often now, we don't see so much of him now; **pesa ~ de 50 kilos** it weighs less than o under 50 kilos; **éramos ~ de diez** there were fewer than ten of us; **los niños de ~ de 7 años** children under seven
2 (superlativo) least; **es la ~ complicada** it is the least complicated one; **el que ~ me gusta** the one I like (the) least; **se esfuerza lo ~ posible** he makes as little effort as possible; **cuando ~ lo esperaba** when I was least expecting it
■ adj inv **1** (comparativo) (en cantidad) less; (en número) fewer; **alimentos con ~ fibra/calorías** food with less fiber/fewer calories; **hay ~ errores** there are fewer mistakes; **mide medio metro ~** it's half a meter shorter; **~ estudiantes que el año pasado** fewer students than last year; **tengo ~ tiempo que tú** I haven't as o so much time as you
2 (superlativo) (en cantidad) least; (en número) fewest; **donde hay ~ luz** where there's least light; **el que obtuvo ~ votos** the one who got (the) fewest votes
■ pron **1** (en cantidad) less; (en número) fewer; **sírveme ~** give me less; **ya falta ~** it won't be long now
2 (en locs) **al menos** at least; **a menos que** unless; **cuando menos** at least; **de menos: me dió 100 pesos de ~** he gave me 100 pesos too little; **me cobró de ~** he undercharged me; **lo menos** the least; **menos mal** just as well, thank goodness; **por lo menos** at least; **eso es lo de ~** that's the least of my (o our etc) problems
■ prep **1** (excepto): **todos ~ Alonso** everybody except o but Alonso; **~ estos dos, ...** apart from o with the exception of these two, ...; **tres latas de pintura, ~ la que usé para la puerta** three cans of paint, less what I used on the door
2 (a) (Mat) (en restas, números negativos) minus (b) (Esp, RPl) (en la hora): **son las cinco ~ diez/cuarto** it's ten to five/(a) quarter to five; **son ~ veinte** it's twenty to

menoscabar [A1] vt «autoridad/fortuna» to diminish, reduce; «derechos» to impinge upon, infringe; «honor/fama/salud» to damage, harm

menospreciar [A1] vt (a) (despreciar) «persona/obra» to despise, look down on (b) (subestimar) to underestimate

menosprecio m contempt, scorn

mensaje m (en general) message; (nota) note

mensajero -ra adj messenger (before n)
■ m,f (en general) messenger; (Com) messenger, courier (BrE)

menso -sa adj (AmL fam) stupid
■ m,f (AmL fam) fool

menstruación f menstruation; **estar con la ~** to have one's period

menstruar [A3] vi to menstruate

mensual adj «publicación/sueldo» monthly; **9.000 pesos ~es** 9,000 pesos a month

mensualidad (a) f (sueldo) monthly salary (b) (cuota) monthly payment o installment*

menta f mint; **licor de ~** crème de menthe; **caramelos de ~** mints, peppermints

mentada ⋯⟶ mersa

mentada *f* (Col, Méx, Ven euf) *tb* ~ **de madre** insult (*usually about a person's mother*)

mental *adj* mental

mentalidad *f* mentality; **tener una ~ muy cerrada** a very closed mind

mentalizar [A4] *vt* ~ **a algn DE algo** to make sb aware of sth

■ **mentalizarse** *v pron* **(a)** (*prepararse mentalmente*) to prepare oneself (mentally), get into the right frame of mind **(b)** (*tomar conciencia*): **tuve que ~me de que mi carrera se había acabado** I had to come to terms with the fact that my career was over

mentar [A5] *vt* to mention

mente *f* mind; **tenía la ~ en blanco** my mind was a blank; **de repente me vino a la ~** it suddenly came to me; **tener algo en ~** to have sth in mind

mentecato -ta *m,f* fool

mentir [I11] *vi* to lie; **me mintió** he lied to me

mentira *f* lie; **eso es ~** that's a lie; **¡~! yo no le pegué** that's a lie, I didn't hit him!; **¡parece ~! ¡cómo pasa el tiempo!** isn't it incredible! doesn't time fly!; **~ piadosa** white lie; **una araña de ~** *or* (Méx) **de ~s** (leng infantil) a toy spider; **una ~ como una casa** *or* **un templo** (fam) a whopping great lie (colloq), a whopper (colloq)

mentiroso -sa *adj*: **es muy ~** he's an awful *o* terrible liar; (*dicho sin ánimo de ofender*) he's a real fibber (colloq)

■ *m,f* liar; (*dicho sin ánimo de ofender*) fibber (colloq)

mentolado -da *adj* menthol (*before n*)

mentón *m* chin

menú *m* (*pl* **-nús**) menu; **~ del día** set menu

menudencia *f* **1** (*cosa insignificante*): **eso es una ~** that's not important **2 menudencias** *fpl* (AmL) (Coc) giblets (*pl*)

menudeo *m* (Col, Méx) retail trade; **ventas al ~** retail sales

menudillos *mpl* giblets (*pl*)

menudo¹ -da *adj* **1** **(a)** (*persona*) slight **(b)** (*letra/pie*) small **2** (Esp) (*en exclamaciones*) (*delante del n*): **¡~ lío!** what a mess!; **¡~ cochazo!** that's some car! **3** **a menudo** often

menudo² *m* (Col, Ven) (*dinero suelto*) loose change

meñique *m* little finger

meollo *m* **(a)** (Anat) marrow **(b)** (de un tema) heart

mercadería *f* (esp AmS) merchandise

mercadillo *m* street market

mercado *m* market; **ir al ~** *or* (Col, Méx) **hacer el ~** to go to market; **~ de abastos** market (*selling fresh food*); **~ de (las) pulgas** flea market; **~ persa** (CS) bazaar, street market; **el ~ del petróleo** the oil market; **salir al ~** to come onto the market; **el M~ Común** the Common Market; **~ de divisas** foreign exchange market; **~ de trabajo** job market; **~ negro** black market; **~ paralelo** parallel market

mercancía *f*, **mercancías** *fpl* (Com) goods (*pl*), merchandise

mercante *adj* merchant (*before n*)

mercantil *adj* (*ley/operación*) commercial, mercantile

merced *f* (arc) (favor) favor*; **conceder una ~** to grant a favor; **a (la) ~ de** at the mercy of

mercenario -ria *adj/m,f* (Mil) mercenary

mercería *f* (tienda de hilos, botones) notions store (AmE), haberdashery (BrE); (ferretería) (Chi) hardware store

Mercosur *m*: *economic community comprising Argentina, Brazil, Paraguay and Uruguay*

mercurio *m* mercury

Mercurio *m* Mercury

merecedor -dora *adj* ~ **DE algo** worthy OF sth, deserving OF sth (fml)

merecer [E3] *vt* (*premio/castigo*) to deserve; **merece que le den el puesto** she deserves to get the job

■ **merecerse** *v pron* (enf) (*premio/castigo*) to deserve; **te lo tienes bien merecido** it serves you right; **se merece que la asciendan** she deserves to be promoted

merecido *m*: **recibió** *or* **se llevó su ~** he got what he deserved

merendar [A5] *vi* to have a snack in the afternoon, have tea; **merendamos en el campo** we had a picnic (tea) in the country

■ ~ *vt* to have ... as an afternoon snack

merendero *m* (bar) outdoor bar; (instalaciones para picnics) picnic area

merengada *f* (Ven) milkshake

merengue *m* **1** (pastel) meringue **2** (baile) merengue

meridiano *m* meridian; **~ cero** *or* **de Greenwich** /'grɪnɪtʃ/ Greenwich Meridian

meridional *adj* southern

■ *mf* southerner

merienda *f* afternoon snack, tea; (para la escuela) (RPl) snack; **ir de ~ al campo** to go for a picnic (tea) in the country

mérito *m* merit, worth; **no le veo ningún ~ a eso** I can't see any merit in that; **una persona de ~** a worthy person; **tener ~** to be praiseworthy; **quitarle ~s a algn** to take the credit away from sb; **atribuirse el ~ de algo** to take the credit for sth

meritorio -ria *adj* (SER) (fml) commendable, praiseworthy (fml); **~ DE algo** worthy OF sth

■ *m,f* unpaid trainee

merluza *f* (Coc, Zool) hake

mermar [A1] *vi* (fml) «*viento/frío*» to abate (fml); «*luz*» to fade

■ ~ *vt* (fml) to reduce

mermelada *f* (de cítricos) marmalade; (de otras frutas) jam

mero¹ -ra *adj* (*delante del n*) **1** (solo, simple) mere; **el ~ hecho de ...** the mere *o* simple fact of ...; **es un ~ juego** it's only *o* just a game **2** (AmC, Méx fam) (uso enfático): **¿cuántas quedaron? — una mera** how many were left? — just one; **el ~ día de su boda** the very day of her wedding; **el ~ patrón** the boss himself; **en la mera esquina** right on the corner

mero² *m* grouper; **el ~ ~** (Méx fam) the boss

■ *adv* (Méx fam) **(a)** (casi) nearly, almost **(b)** (uso enfático): **así ~ me gustan los tacos** this is just how I like tacos; **ya ~** right now; **aquí merito** right here

merodear [A1] *vi* to prowl

mersa *adj* (RPl fam & pey) (*ropa/lugar*) tacky (colloq); (*persona*) common (pej)

⋯⟶

■ *mf* (RPl fam & pey) **(a)** ⟨persona⟩: **es un ~** he's so common (pej) **(b) la mersa** *f* the plebs (*pl*) (colloq & pej), the riffraff (hum *or* pej)

mes *m* month; **el ~ pasado/que viene** last/next month; **una vez al ~** once a month; **tiene siete ~es** he's seven months old; **nos deben dos ~es** they owe us two months' rent (*o* pay *etc*)

mesa *f* **1** (mueble) table; **poner/recoger la ~** to lay/clear the table; **bendecir la ~** to say grace; **sentarse a la ~** to sit at the table; **se levantó de la ~** he got up from *o* left the table; **reservar ~** to reserve a table; **~ de centro** coffee table; **~ de noche** *or* (RPl) **de luz** bedside table **2** (conjunto de personas) committee; **~ redonda/de negociaciones** round/negotiating table

mesada *f* (AmL) (dinero) monthly allowance; (para niños) pocket money

mesero -ra *m,f* (AmL) (*m*) waiter; (*f*) waitress

meseta *f* (Geog) plateau

Mesías *m* Messiah

Mesoamérica *f* Middle America (*most of Mexico and Central America*)

mesón *m* **1** (bar) old-style bar/restaurant **2** (Chi) (en tienda) counter; (de bar) bar, counter; **~ de información** information desk

mesonero -ra *m,f* **(a)** (de bar) (*m*) landlord; (*f*) landlady **(b)** (Ven) (camarero) (*m*) waiter; (*f*) waitress

mestizo -za *adj* **(a)** ⟨persona⟩ of mixed race (*particularly of Indian and white parentage*); **de sangre mestiza** of mixed blood **(b)** ⟨animal⟩ crossbred

■ *m,f* mestizo, person of mixed race

meta *f* **1** **(a)** (en atletismo) finishing line; (en ciclismo, automovilismo) finish; (en carreras de caballos) winning post **(b)** (en fútbol) goal **2** **(a)** (propósito) aim; **su única ~ es ganar dinero** his only aim *o* ambition is to earn money **(b)** (objetivo) goal; **trazarse ~s** to set oneself targets *o* goals

metabolismo *m* metabolism

metafísico -ca *adj* metaphysical

metáfora *f* metaphor

metal *m* **(a)** (material, elemento) metal; **~ noble** *or* **precioso** precious metal **(b)** *tb* **metales** (Mús) brass (section)

metálico¹ -ca *adj* **(a)** (de metal) metallic, metal (*before n*) **(b)** ⟨sonido/brillo/color⟩ metallic

metálico² *m*: **pagar en ~** to pay (in) cash; **un premio en ~** a cash prize

metalurgia *f* metallurgy

metalúrgico -ca *adj* metallurgical

■ *m,f* metalworker

metamorfosis, metamórfosis *f* (*pl* **~**) metamorphosis

metate *m* (AmC, Méx) *flat stone used for grinding corn*

metedura de pata *f* (esp Esp fam) blunder, gaffe

metegol *m* (Arg) table football

meteorito *m* meteorite

meteoro *m* meteor

meteorología *f* meteorology

meteorológico -ca *adj* meteorological, weather (*before n*)

meteorólogo -ga *m,f* meteorologist

meter [E1] *vt* **1** **(a)** (introducir, poner) to put; **~ algo EN algo** to put sth IN(TO) sth; **~ la llave en la cerradura** to put the key into the lock; **logró ~ todo en la maleta** he managed to fit everything into the suitcase **(b)** (hacer entrar): **~ a algn en la cárcel** to put sb in prison; **consiguió ~lo en la empresa** she managed to get him a job in the company **(c)** (involucrar): **~ a algn EN algo** to involve sb IN sth, get sb involved IN sth **2** **(a)** (invertir) ⟨ahorros/dinero⟩ to put **(b)** ⟨tanto/gol⟩ to score **(c)** (en costura) ⟨dobladillo⟩ to turn up **(d)** (Auto): **mete (la) tercera** put it into third (gear); **~ la marcha atrás** to get into reverse **3** (provocar, crear): **~le prisa a algn** to rush sb; **~le miedo a algn** to frighten *o* scare sb; **no metas ruido** keep the noise down

■ **meterse** *v pron* **1** **(a)** (entrar): **me metí en el agua** (en la playa) I went into the water; (en la piscina) I got into the water; **nos metimos en un museo** we went into a museum; **~se en la cama/la ducha** to get into bed/the shower; **¿dónde se habrá metido el perro?** where can the dog have got to?; **se me metió algo en el ojo** I got something in my eye **(b)** (introducirse): **me metí el dedo en el ojo** I stuck my finger in my eye; **se metió el dinero en el bolsillo** he put the money in(to) his pocket

2 **(a)** (en trabajo): **se metió de secretaria** she got a job as a secretary; **~se de** *or* **a cura/monja** to become a priest/nun **(b)** (involucrarse) **~se EN algo** to get involved IN sth; **te has metido en un buen lío** you've got yourself into a fine mess; **no te metas en lo que no te importa** mind your own business; **~se con algn** (fam) to pick on sb; **~se por medio** to interfere

metiche *adj* (AmL fam) nosy (colloq)

■ *mf* busybody (colloq)

meticuloso -sa *adj* ⟨trabajo/investigación⟩ meticulous, thorough; ⟨persona⟩ meticulous

metida de pata *f* (AmL fam) blunder, gaffe

metódico -ca *adj* methodical

metodista *adj/mf* Methodist

método *m* method; **con ~** methodically

metodología *f* methodology

metomentodo *mf* (*pl* **~**) (fam) busybody (colloq)

metralla *f* (trozos) shrapnel; (munición) grapeshot

metralleta *f* submachine gun

métrico -ca *adj* metric, metrical

metro *m* **1** **(a)** (medida) meter*; **~ cuadrado/cúbico** square/cubic meter; **vender algo por ~(s)** to sell sth by the meter; **los 100 ~s valla** the 100-meter hurdles **(b)** (cinta métrica) tape measure **2** (Transp) subway (AmE), tube (BrE) **3** (en poesía) meter*

metrónomo *m* metronome

metrópolis (*pl* ∼), **metrópoli** *f* metropolis

metropolitano¹ -na *adj* metropolitan

metropolitano² *m* subway (AmE), underground (BrE)

mexicanismo *m* Mexicanism

mexicano -na *adj/m,f* Mexican

México *m* Mexico; (capital) Mexico City

mexiquense *adj* (Méx) of/from Mexico City

mezcal *m* mescal

mezcla *f* 1 (proceso) **(a)** (en general) mixing **(b)** (de vinos, tabacos, cafés) blending 2 (combinación) **(a)** (de cosas diversas) mixture; (de vinos, tabacos, cafés) blend; (de tejidos) mix; **una ∼ de harina y azúcar** a mixture of flour and sugar **(b)** (de razas, culturas) mix **(c)** (Audio) mix

mezclador -dora *m,f* (persona) *tb* **∼ de sonido** *or* **audio** sound mixer

mezcladora *f* (Const) mixer

mezclar [A1] *vt* 1 **(a)** (combinar) to mix; **∼ algo CON algo** to mix sth WITH sth **(b)** ⟨café/vino/tabaco⟩ to blend 2 ⟨documentos/ropa⟩ to mix up, get ... mixed up; **∼ algo CON algo** to get sth mixed up WITH sth 3 (involucrar) **∼ a algn EN algo** to get sb mixed up *o* involved IN sth

■ **mezclarse** *v pron* 1 **(a)** (involucrarse) **∼se EN algo** to get mixed up *o* involved IN sth **(b)** (tener trato con) **∼se CON algn** to mix WITH sb 2 «razas/culturas» to mix

mezclilla *f* **(a)** (tela de mezcla) cloth of mixed fibers **(b)** (Chi, Méx) (tela de jeans) denim

mezcolanza *f* (pey) hodgepodge (esp AmE), hotchpotch (BrE)

mezquindad *f* **(a)** (cualidad — de tacaño) meanness, stinginess (colloq); (— de vil): smallmindedness, pettiness **(b)** (acción egoísta) mean thing to do

mezquino¹ -na *adj* **(a)** (tacaño) mean, stingy (colloq); (vil) mean, small-minded **(b)** (escaso) ⟨sueldo/ración⟩ paltry, miserable

mezquino² *m* (Col, Méx) wart

mezquita *f* mosque

mezzo-soprano *f* mezzo soprano

mg. (= **miligramo**) mg

mi *adj* (delante del n) my; **∼s libros** my books; **sí, ∼ vida** yes, darling; **sí, ∼ capitán** yes, sir
■ *m* (nota) E; (en solfeo) mi

mí *pron pers* me; **¿es para ∼?** is it for me?; **por ∼ no hay problema** as far as I'm concerned that's fine, that's fine by me; **¿y a ∼ qué?** so what?, what do I care?; **a ∼ no me importa** I couldn't care less; **∼ mismo/misma** (refl) myself

miau *m* miaow; **hacer ∼** to miaow

mica *f* 1 **(a)** (Min) mica **(b)** (AmL) (de un reloj) crystal 2 (Col) (de niño) potty (colloq)

mico -ca *m,f* (Zool) long-tailed monkey; (como término genérico) monkey

micrero -ra *m,f* (Chi) bus driver

micro *m* 1 (fam) (microbús) small bus; (autobús) (Arg) bus, coach (BrE) 2 (fam) (micrófono) mike (colloq)
■ *f* (Chi) bus

microbio *m* microbe

microbiología *f* microbiology

microbús *m* small bus

microchip /mikro'tʃip/ *m* (*pl* **-chips**) microchip

microcomputadora *f* (esp AmL) microcomputer, micro

microcosmos (*pl* ∼), **microcosmo** *m* microcosm

microfilm (*pl* **-films**), **microfilme** *m* microfilm

micrófono *m* microphone; **hablar por el ∼** to speak over the microphone

microondas *m* (*pl* ∼) microwave (oven)

microordenador *m* (Esp) microcomputer, micro

microorganismo *m* microorganism

microscópico -ca *adj* microscopic

microscopio *m* microscope; **mirar algo al** *or* **por el ∼** to look at sth under the microscope

mida, midas, etc ▶ MEDIR

miedo *m* fear; **¡qué ∼ pasamos!** we were so frightened *o* scared!; **temblaba de ∼** he was trembling with fear; **me da ∼ salir de noche** I'm afraid to go *o* of going out at night; **∼ A algo/algn** fear OF sth/sb; **el ∼ a lo desconocido** fear of the unknown; **le tiene ∼ a su padre** he's scared *o* afraid of his father; **∼ a salir a escena** stage fright; **agarrarle** *or* (esp Esp) **cogerle ∼ a algo/algn** to become frightened *o* scared of sth/sb; **por ∼ a** for fear of; **tener ∼** to be afraid *o* frightened *o* scared; **tiene ∼ de caerse** he's afraid he might fall; **tengo ∼ de que se ofenda** I'm afraid he will take offense

miedoso -sa *adj*: **¡no seas ∼!** no te va a hacer daño don't be frightened *o* scared! it won't hurt you; **¡qué ∼ es!** he's such a coward!

miel *f* honey; **∼ de palma** palm syrup

miembro *m* 1 **(a)** (de organización, asociación) member **(b)** (como adj) ⟨estado/países⟩ member (before n) 2 (Anat) limb; **∼s anteriores/posteriores** fore/back limbs

mienta, mientas, etc ▶ MENTIR

mientras *adv* 1 (al mismo tiempo) *tb* **∼ tanto** in the meantime, meanwhile 2 (esp AmL) (cuanto): **∼ más se le da, más pide** the more you give him, the more he wants; **∼ menos coma, mejor** the less I eat the better
■ *conj* 1 (indicando simultaneidad) while; **∼ dormíamos** while we were asleep 2 (con idea de futuro, condición, etc) as long as; **∼ viva/él no se entere** as long as I live/he doesn't find out 3 **mientras que** (con valor adversativo) whereas, while

miércoles *m* (*pl* ∼) Wednesday; **∼ de ceniza** Ash Wednesday; *para ejemplos ver* LUNES

mierda *f* 1 (vulg) (excremento) shit (vulg) 2 (vulg) **(a)** (cosa despreciable): **una ∼ de empleo** a crappy *o* lousy job (colloq); **la película es una ∼** the movie is (a load of) crap (sl) **(b)** (mugre) filth, crap (sl); **¡a la ∼ con ... !** (vulg) to hell with ... ! (colloq); **irse a la ∼** (vulg) «proyecto/empresa» to go to the dogs, go to pot (colloq); **mandar a algn a la ∼** (vulg) to tell sb to go to hell (colloq *o* vulg) to screw himself/herself; **¡vete a la ∼!** (vulg) go to hell! (colloq), fuck off!

mies *f* ripe grain; **∼es** cornfields

miga *f* 1 (de pan) crumb; **hacer buenas/malas ∼s (con algn)** to get on well/badly (with sb)

2 migas *fpl* (Coc) *breadcrumbs fried with garlic, etc* **3** (contenido, sustancia) substance; (dificultad) difficulties (*pl*); **el asunto tiene su** ∼ it has its difficulties *o* it's quite tricky

migajas *fpl* (de pan) breadcrumbs (*pl*); (sobras) leftovers (*pl*), scraps (*pl*)

migración *f* migration

migraña *f* migraine

mijo¹ *m* millet

mijo² -ja *pron* (apelativo) (AmL fam) dear; **¿qué le pasa, mijita?** what's the matter, darling? (colloq)

mil *adj inv/pron* thousand; ∼ **quinientos pesos** fifteen hundred pesos, one thousand five hundred pesos; **20** ∼ **millones** 20 billion (AmE), 20 thousand million (BrE); **tengo** ∼ **cosas que hacer** I have a thousand and one things to do
■ *m* (number) one thousand

milagro *m* miracle; **alcancé el tren de** ∼ by a miracle I caught the train; **escaparon de** ∼ they had a miraculous escape; **hacer** ∼**s** to work wonders

milagroso -sa *adj* miraculous

milanesa *f*. *thin breaded cutlet of meat/chicken*

milano *m* kite

milenio *m* millennium

milésima *f* thousandth

milésimo -ma *adj/pron* thousandth; **la milésima parte** a thousandth

milhojas *f* (*pl* ∼) (Coc) millefeuille

mili *f* (Esp fam) military service; **hacer la** ∼ to do one's military service

milicia *f* militia

miliciano -na *m,f* militiaman

milico *m* (AmL fam & pey) soldier; **los** ∼**s** the military

miligramo *m* milligram

mililitro *m* milliliter*

milímetro *m* millimeter*

militancia *f* (filiación) political affiliation; (militantes) members (*pl*)

militante *adj* politically active
■ *mf* activist

militar¹ *adj* military
■ *mf* soldier, military man; **los** ∼**es** the military

militar² [A1] *vi* to be politically active; ∼ **en un partido político** to be an active member of a political party

milla *f* mile

millar *m* thousand; **un** ∼ **de seguidores** about a thousand supporters

millón *m* million; **15 mil millones** 15 billion (AmE), 15 thousand million (BrE); **un** ∼ **de gracias** thank you very much

millonario -ria *adj*: **es** ∼ he's a millionaire
■ *m,f* millionaire

milonga *f* **1** (Mús) *a type of dance and music from the River Plate region* **2** (RPl arg) **(a)** (fiesta) party, bash (colloq) **(b)** (mujer fácil) slut (colloq & pej)

milonguero -ra *m,f* (RPl arg) reveler, raver (BrE colloq)

milpa *f* (AmC, Méx) (campo) field (*used mainly for the cultivation of maize*); (cultivo) crop

mimado -da *adj* spoiled, pampered
■ *m,f* spoiled child; **este niño es un** ∼ this child is spoiled *o* (pej) is a spoiled brat

mimar [A1] *vt* to spoil, pamper

mimbre *m* (material) wicker; **silla de** ∼ wicker *o* basket chair

mimbrera *f* (arbusto) osier; (sauce) willow

mímica *f* (Teatr) mime; (gestos, señas) sign language, mime

mimo *m* **(a)** (caricia) cuddle; **hacerle** ∼**s a algn** to cuddle sb **(b)** (trato indulgente) pampering; **lo criaron con mucho** ∼ he had a very pampered upbringing
■ *mf* mime

mimosa *f* mimosa

min (= **minuto**) min

mina *f* **1** (yacimiento, excavación) mine; ∼ **de carbón** coalmine; ∼ **a cielo abierto** *or* (Andes) **a tajo abierto** strip mine (AmE), opencast mine (BrE); **es una** ∼ **de información** he's a mine of information **2** (Mil, Náut) mine; **un campo de** ∼**s** a minefield **3** (de lápiz) lead **4** (CS arg) (mujer) broad (AmE sl), bird (BrE sl)

minar [A1] *vt* **(a)** ⟨campo/mar⟩ to mine **(b)** (debilitar) ⟨salud⟩ to damage; ⟨autoridad/moral⟩ to undermine

minarete *m* minaret

mineral *adj* mineral
■ *m* **(a)** (sustancia) mineral **(b)** (de un metal) ore

minería *f* mining industry

minero -ra *adj* mining (*before n*)
■ *m,f* miner

mini *f* (fam) miniskirt, mini (colloq)

miniatura *f* (Art) miniature; **¡qué** ∼ **de pie!** (fam) what a tiny little foot!

minicomputadora *f* (esp AmL) minicomputer

minifalda *f* miniskirt

minifundio *m* (propiedad) smallholding

mini-golf *m* miniature golf

mínima *f* minimum temperature

minimizar [A4] *vt* (reducir al mínimo) to minimize; (quitar importancia) to make light of, play down

mínimo¹ -ma *adj* **(a)** ⟨temperatura/peso⟩ minimum (*before n*); **no le importa lo más** ∼ he couldn't care less; **el trabajo no le interesa en lo más** ∼ he is not in the slightest (bit) interested in his work; **no tengo la más mínima idea** I haven't the faintest idea **(b)** (insignificante) ⟨detalle⟩ minor; ⟨diferencia/beneficios⟩ minimal

mínimo² *m* minimum; **reducir los gastos al** ∼ to keep costs to a minimum; **como** ∼ at least

miniordenador *m* (Esp) minicomputer

ministerial *adj* ⟨reunión⟩ cabinet (*before n*); ⟨orden⟩ ministerial

ministerio *m* **1** (Pol) ministry, department (AmE); **M**∼ **de Hacienda** ≈ Treasury Department (*in US*), ≈ Treasury (*in UK*); **M**∼ **del Interior** ≈ Department of the Interior (*in US*), ≈ Home Office (*in UK*); **M**∼ **de Relaciones** *or* **Asuntos Exteriores** ≈ State Department (*in US*), ≈ Foreign Office (*in UK*) **2** (Relig) ministry

ministro -tra *m,f* minister, government minister; **M**∼ **de Hacienda** ≈ Secretary of the Treasury (*in US*), ≈ Chancellor of the Exchequer (*in UK*); **M**∼ **del Interior** ≈ Secretary of the

Interior (*in US*), ≈Home Secretary (*in UK*); **M∼ de Relaciones** *or* **Asuntos Exteriores** ≈ Secretary of State (*in US*), ≈Foreign Secretary (*in UK*)

minoría *f* minority; **estar en ∼** to be in a/the minority; **∼ de edad** minority

minorista *adj* retail (*before n*)
■ *mf* retailer

minoritario -ria *adj* minority (*before n*)

mintiera, mintió, etc ▶ MENTIR

minucia *f* **(a)** (detalle pequeño) minor detail **(b)** (cualidad) detail; **explicar algo con ∼** to explain sth in detail *o* thoroughly

minuciosidad *f* attention to detail

minucioso -sa *adj* ‹búsqueda/investigación/persona› meticulous, thorough; ‹informe› detailed

minúscula *f* lower case letter, minuscule (tech)

minúsculo -la *adj* **(a)** (diminuto) minute, tiny **(b)** ‹letra› lower case

minusvalía *f* **1** (física) physical handicap *o* disability; (psíquica) mental handicap **2** (Econ) drop *o* fall in value

minusválido -da *adj* (físico) physically handicapped, disabled; (psíquico) mentally handicapped
■ *m,f* (físico) disabled person, physically handicapped person; (psíquico) mentally handicapped person; **coches para ∼s** cars for the disabled

minuta *f* **1** (de abogado, notario) bill **2** (plato rápido) (RPI) quick meal

minutero *m* minute hand

minuto *m* minute; **a tres ∼s de su casa** three minutes (away) from his house

mío, mía *adj* (detrás del n) mine; **un primo ∼** a cousin of mine; **eso es asunto ∼** that's my business; **Muy señor ∼** (Corresp) (frml) Dear Sir
■ *pron:* **el ∼/la/mía,** *etc* mine; **sus hijos y los ∼s** their children and mine; **los idiomas no son lo ∼** languages are not my thing; **los ∼s** my family and friends

miope *adj* **(a)** (Med, Ópt) myopic (tech), nearsighted (AmE), short-sighted (BrE) **(b)** (falto de perspicacia) short-sighted
■ *mf* myopic person (tech), nearsighted person (AmE), short-sighted person (BrE)

miopía *f* **(a)** (Med, Ópt) myopia (tech), nearsightedness (AmE), short-sightedness (BrE) **(b)** (falta de perspicacia) shortsightedness

mira *f* **(a)** (Arm, Ópt) sight; **(b)** (intención, objetivo): **con ∼s a reducir costos** with a view to reducing costs; **con la ∼ puesta en el porvenir** with one's sight set on the future; **es muy estrecho de ∼s** he's very narrow-minded

mirada *f* **(a)** (modo de mirar) look; **una ∼ reprobatoria** a disapproving look; **su ∼ era triste** he had a sad look in his eyes; **lo fulminó con la ∼** she looked daggers at him **(b)** (vistazo, ojeada) glance; **echarle una ∼ por encima a algo** to take a quick glance at sth; **échales una ∼ a los niños** have a look at the children **(c)** (vista): **tenía la ∼ fija en el suelo** she had her eyes fixed on the ground; **recorrió la habitación con la ∼** she cast her eyes over the room; **bajar/levantar la ∼** to look down/up

miradero *m* (Col) viewpoint

mirado -da *adj* (considerado): **eso no está bien ∼**

that's not approved of, that's looked down on; **está muy mal ∼ en el barrio** he is not at all well thought of *o* well regarded in the neighborhood; *ver tb* MIRAR *vt*

mirador *m* viewpoint

miramiento *m*: **tratar a algn sin ningún ∼** to treat sb with a total lack of consideration

mirar [A1] *vt* **1 (a)** (observar, contemplar) to look at; **∼ un cuadro** to look at a picture; **no me mires así** don't look at me like that; **∼ a algn a los ojos** to look sb in the eye; **se me quedó mirando** he just stared at me; **miraba distraída por la ventana** he was gazing absent-mindedly out of the window; **miraba cómo lo hacía** he was watching how she did it; **ir a ∼ escaparates** *or* (AmL) **vidrieras** to go window shopping **(b)** ‹programa/partido/televisión› to watch

2 (fijarse) to look; **¡mira lo que has hecho!** look what you've done!; **mira bien que esté apagado** make sure *o* check it's off; **miré a ver si estaba listo** I had a look to see if he was ready

3 (considerar): **míralo desde otro punto de vista** look at it from another point of view; **lo mires por donde lo mires** whatever *o* whichever way you look at it; **mirándolo bien** (pensándolo detenidamente) all things considered; (pensándolo mejor) on second thoughts; **∼ a algn en menos** to look down on sb; **∼ mal a algn** to disapprove of sb

4 (expresando incredulidad, irritación, etc): **¡mira que poner un plato de plástico en el horno …!** honestly *o* really! imagine putting a plastic dish in the oven …! (colloq); **¡mira que eres tacaño!** boy, you're mean! (colloq); **¡mira las veces que te lo habré dicho …!** the times I've told you!
■ **∼** *vi* **1** (en general) to look; **he mirado por todas partes** I've looked everywhere; **∼ por la ventana** to look out of the window; **¿miraste bien?** did you have a good look?, did you look properly?; **∼ atrás** to look back

2 (estar orientado) **∼ a/HACIA algo** «fachada» to face sth; «terraza/habitación» to look out over sth, overlook sth; **ponte mirando hacia la ventana** stand (o sit *etc*) facing the window

3 mirar por (a) (preocuparse por) to think of **(b)** (Col) (cuidar) to look after
■ **mirarse** *v pron* **(a)** (refl) to look at oneself; **∼se en el espejo** to look at oneself in the mirror **(b)** (recípr) to look at each other

mirilla *f* peephole, spyhole

mirlo *m* blackbird

mirto *m* myrtle

misa *f* mass; **están en ∼** they're at mass; **ir a ∼** to go to mass; **decir ∼** «sacerdote» to say *o* celebrate mass; **∼ de cuerpo presente** funeral mass; **∼ de difuntos** Requiem (mass); **∼ de** *or* **del gallo** midnight mass (on Christmas Eve)

miscelánea *f* **(a)** (variedad) miscellany **(b)** (Méx) (tienda) small general store, corner shop (BrE)

misceláneo -nea *adj* miscellaneous

miserable *adj* **(a)** (pobre) ‹vivienda› miserable, wretched; ‹sueldo› paltry, miserable **(b)** (avaro) mean, stingy (colloq) **(c)** (malvado) malicious, nasty
■ *mf* wretch, scoundrel

miseria *f* **1** (pobreza) poverty, destitution **2** (cantidad insignificante) miserable amount, paltry ⋯⋮⋯

amount; **gana una ～** she earns a pittance
3 (desgracia) misfortune; **las ～s de la guerra** the
miseries of war

misericordia *f* mercy, compassion

misericordioso -sa *adj* merciful

mísero -ra *adj* miserable

misil *m* missile; **～ antiaéreo/balístico**
antiaircraft/ballistic missile

misión *f* **1** (tarea) mission **2** (delegación): **una ～**
científica a team of scientists; **una ～ diplomática**
a diplomatic delegation

misionero -ra *adj* missionary (*before n*)
■ *m,f* missionary

Misisipí *m* (río): **el (río) ～** the Mississippi
(River); (estado) Mississippi

mismo¹ -ma *adj* **1** (a) (*delante del n*)
(expresando identidad) same; **hacer dos cosas al ～**
tiempo to do two things at once *o* at the same time
(b) (*como pron*) same; **Roma ya no es la misma**
Rome isn't the same any more; **el ～ que vimos**
ayer the same one we saw yesterday
2 (uso enfático) **(a)** (refiriéndose a lugares, momentos,
cosas): **en el ～ centro de Lima** right in the center
of Lima; **en este ～ instante** this very minute; **eso**
～ pienso yo that's exactly what I think **(b)**
(refiriéndose a personas): **el mismísimo presidente**
the president himself; **te perjudicas a ti ～** you're
only hurting yourself; **ella misma lo trajo** she
brought it herself
3 lo mismo: **siempre dice lo ～** he always says
the same thing; **lo ～ para mí** the same for me,
please; **nuestra empresa, lo ～ que tantas otras**
our company, like so many others; **los niños**
pueden ir lo ～ que los adultos children can go as
well as adults; **lo que es lo ～** in other words;
da lo ～ it doesn't matter; **me/le da lo ～** I don't
care/he/she doesn't care

mismo² adv (uso enfático): **aquí/ahora ～** right
here/now; **hoy ～ te mando el cheque** I'll send
you the check today; **ayer ～ hablé con él** I spoke
to him only yesterday

miss /mis/ *f* beauty queen; **M～ Universo** Miss
Universe

misterio *m* mystery

misterioso -sa *adj* mysterious

misticismo *m* mysticism

místico -ca *adj* ⟨experiencia⟩ mystic, mystical;
⟨escritor⟩ mystic (*before n*)
■ *m,f* mystic

mitad *f* **1** (parte) half; **la ～ de la población** half
(of) the population; **solo quiero la ～** I only want
half; **a ～ de precio** half price; **lo hizo en la ～ del**
tiempo she did it in half the time; **～ y ～** half
and half
2 (medio, centro): **cortar algo por la ～** to cut sth
in half; **dividir algo por la ～** to halve sth; **a** *or* **en**
(la) ～ de la reunión in the middle of the meeting;
a ～ de camino halfway; **en la ～ de la película/del**
libro halfway through the movie/the book

mítico -ca *adj* mythical

mitigar [A3] *vt* ⟨dolor⟩ to relieve, ease; ⟨pena/
sufrimiento⟩ to alleviate, mitigate (frml); ⟨sed⟩ to
quench

mitin, mitín *m* (Pol) political meeting, rally

mito *m* **(a)** (leyenda) legend **(b)** (invención, mentira)
myth

mitología *f* mythology

mitológico -ca *adj* mythological

mixto¹ -ta *adj* mixed; **educación mixta**
coeducation

mixto² *m* toasted sandwich (*with two different*
fillings)

ml. (= **mililitro**) ml

mm. (= **milímetro**) mm

moaré *m* moiré

mobiliario *m* furniture, furnishings (*pl*);
renovar el ～ del comedor to refurnish the dining
room; **～ de baño** bathroom furnishings (*pl*); **～**
de cocina kitchen fittings *o* units (*pl*)

moca *m*: *tb* **café ～** mocha; **tarta de ～** coffee
cake

mocasín *m* moccasin

mochila *f* (de excursionista, soldado) backpack; (de
escolar) satchel

mochilear [A1] *vi* (CS) to backpack

mochilero -ra *m,f* (CS) backpacker

moción *f* motion; **presentar una ～** to propose *o*
(BrE) table a motion; **～ de censura** vote of
censure *o* no confidence

moco *m* **(a)** (líquido) snot (colloq); **límpiate los ～s**
wipe *o* blow your nose; **le colgaban los ～s** he
had a runny nose (colloq) *o* (sl) snotty nose **(b)**
(seco) booger (AmE colloq), bogey (BrE colloq)

mocoso -sa *m,f* (fam) squirt (colloq), pipsqueak
(colloq)

moda *f* fashion; **la ～ joven** *or* **juvenil** young
fashion; **la ～ de los 30** 30's fashion; **ir a la ～** to
be trendy; **estar de ～** to be in fashion, be in
(colloq); **ponerse/pasar de ～** to come into/go out
of fashion; **seguir la ～** to follow fashion

modal *adj* modal

modales *mpl* manners (*pl*); **tener buenos/**
malos ～ to be well-mannered/bad-mannered

modalidad *f*: **varias ～es de pago** several
methods *o* modes of payment; **la medalla de oro**
en la ～ de esquí alpino the gold medal for
downhill skiing

modelaje *m* (Andes, Ven) modeling*; **hacer ～** to
model

modelar [A1] *vt* (Art) ⟨arcilla⟩ to model;
⟨estatua/figura⟩ to model, sculpt; ⟨carácter⟩ to
mold*
■ **～** *vi* **1** (Art) to model **2** (Andes) (para fotos,
desfiles) to model

modelo *adj inv* **(a)** ⟨niño/estudiante⟩ model
(*before n*); ⟨comportamiento/carácter⟩ exemplary
(b) (de muestra): **visité la casa ～** I visited the
model home (AmE) *o* (BrE) the showhouse
■ *m* **1** (en general) model; **tomar/utilizar algo como**
～ to take/use sth as a model; **tomó a su padre**

como ~ he followed his father's example; ~ **en** *or* **a escala** scale model **2** (Indum) design; **un ~ de Franelli** a Franelli (design); **llegó con un nuevo modelito** (fam) she arrived wearing a little new number

■ *mf* model; **desfile de ~s** fashion show

módem *m* (*pl* **-dems**) modem

moderación *f* moderation; **beber con ~** to drink in moderation

moderado -da *adj* **(a)** ⟨*persona/comportamiento*⟩ restrained **(b)** ⟨*temperatura*⟩ moderate; ⟨*precio*⟩ reasonable; ⟨*ideología/facción*⟩ moderate

■ *m,f* moderate

moderador -dora *m,f* (en debate) moderator, chair; (Rad, TV) presenter

moderar [A1] *vt* **1 (a)** ⟨*impulsos/aspiraciones*⟩ to curb, moderate; **por favor modera tu vocabulario** please mind your language **(b)** ⟨*gasto/consumo*⟩ to curb; ⟨*velocidad*⟩ to reduce **2** ⟨*debate/coloquio*⟩ to moderate, chair

■ **moderarse** *v pron*: **modérate, estás comiendo mucho** restrain yourself *o* (colloq) go easy, you're eating too much; **~se en los gastos** to cut down on spending

modernismo *m* (Arquit, Art, Lit) modernism; (cualidad) modernness, modernity

modernista *adj/mf* modernist

modernizar [A4] *vt* ⟨*fábrica/técnica/sociedad*⟩ to modernize; ⟨*costumbres*⟩ to update; ⟨*vestido/abrigo*⟩ to do up

■ **modernizarse** *v pron*: **debes ~te** you have to keep up with the times

moderno -na *adj* **(a)** (actual) modern; **el hombre ~** modern man; **una edición más ~** a more up-to-date edition **(b)** (a la moda) ⟨*vestido/peinado*⟩ fashionable, trendy **(c)** ⟨*edad/historia*⟩ modern

modestia *f* modesty

modesto -ta *adj* **(a)** (falto de pretensión) modest **(b)** (humilde) ⟨*familia*⟩ humble; ⟨*posición social*⟩ modest, humble **(c)** ⟨*sueldo/ingresos*⟩ modest

módico -ca *adj* reasonable

modificar [A2] *vt* **(a)** ⟨*aparato*⟩ to modify; ⟨*plan*⟩ to change; ⟨*horario/ley*⟩ to change, alter **(b)** (Ling) to modify; **modifica al verbo** it modifies the verb

■ **modificarse** *v pron* to change, alter

modismo *m* idiom

modista *mf* (que diseña) couturier, designer; (que confecciona) dressmaker

modistería *f* (Col) (actividad) dressmaking; (establecimiento) dressmaker's shop/workshop

modisto *m* couturier, designer

modo *m* **1 (a)** (manera, forma) way, manner (frml); **el ~ de hacerlo** the way of doing it; **del siguiente ~** in the following manner; **a mi ~ de ver** to my way of thinking, in my opinion; **no lo digas de ese ~** don't say it like that; **de un ~ u otro** one way or another; **su ~ de ser** the way he is; **ⓢ modo de empleo** instructions for use, directions; **me lo pidió de muy mal ~** (AmL) she asked me (for it) very rudely **(b)** (en locs) **a mi/tu/su modo** (in) my/your/his (own) way; **de cualquier modo** (de todas formas) (indep) in any case, anyway; (sin cuidado) anyhow; **del mismo** *or* **de igual modo que** just as, in the same way

(that); **de modo que** (así que) so; (para que) so that; **de ningún modo** no way; **de ningún ~ puedo aceptar** there's no way I can accept; **de todos modos** anyway, anyhow; **en cierto modo** in a way; **ni modo** (AmL exc CS fam) no way; **traté de persuadirlo pero ni ~** I tried to persuade him but it was no good; **ni ~ que te quedes aquí** there's no way you're staying here (colloq)

2 modos *mpl* (modales) manners (*pl*); **con buenos/malos ~s** politely/rudely *o* impolitely

modulación *f* modulation; **~ de amplitud/frecuencia** amplitude/frequency modulation

modular [A1] *vt/vi* to modulate

módulo *m* **(a)** (de mueble) unit, module **(b)** (de prisión) unit **(c)** (Espac, Educ) module

mofarse [A1] *v pron* — **DE algo/algn** to make fun of sth/sb

mofle *m* (AmC, Méx) muffler (AmE), silencer (BrE)

moflete *m* (fam) chubby cheek

mofletudo -da *adj* (fam) chubby-cheeked

mogolla *f* (Col) bread roll

mohair /mo'er/ *m* mohair

mohín *m* face; **hacer un ~** to make *o* (BrE) pull an angry face

mohíno -na *adj* **(a)** (enfurruñado): **está ~ porque lo regañaron** he's sulking because he's been told off **(b)** (alicaído) depressed

moho *m* **(a)** (en fruta, pan) mold*, mildew; **criar ~** «*fruta/queso*» to go moldy* **(b)** (en cobre) patina, verdigris; (en hierro) rust

moisés *m* (cuna) cradle, Moses basket; (portátil) portacrib (AmE), carrycot (BrE)

mojado -da *adj* wet

■ *m,f* (Méx fam) wetback (colloq & pej)

mojar [A1] *vt* **(a)** ⟨*suelo/papel/pelo*⟩ (accidentalmente) to get *o* make ... wet; (a propósito) to wet; **pasó un coche y me mojó** a car went by and splashed me; **~ la cama** to wet the bed **(b)** (sumergiendo) ⟨*galleta/bizcocho*⟩ to dip, dunk (colloq)

■ **mojarse** *v pron* **(a)** «*persona/ropa/suelo*» to get wet; **se me ~on los zapatos** my shoes got wet; **me mojé toda** I got soaked **(b)** ⟨*pelo/pies*⟩ (a propósito) to wet; (accidentalmente) to get ... wet

mojigatería *f* prudishness

mojigato -ta *adj* prudish

■ *m,f* prude

mojón *m* (señal) marker, boundary stone; (hito) landmark; (Auto) *tb* **~ kilométrico** ≈ milestone

molar *m* molar, back tooth

molcajete *m* (Méx) mortar

molde *m* **(a)** (para hornear) baking pan (AmE), baking tin (BrE); (para flanes, gelatina) mold*; **~ de pan** loaf pan (AmE) *o* (BrE) tin **(b)** (Tec) cast; **un ~ de yeso** (Art) a plaster cast **(c)** (AmL) (para coser) pattern

moldeable *adj* **(a)** ⟨*barro*⟩ moldable*, malleable **(b)** ⟨*persona/carácter*⟩ malleable

moldear [A1] *vt* **(a)** (en bronce) to cast; (en barro) to mold*, model **(b)** ⟨*persona/carácter*⟩ to mold*, shape; ⟨*pelo*⟩ to style

moldura *f* molding*

mole *f* mass; **una ~ de hormigón** a huge mass of concrete ⋯⟶

■ *m* (Méx) (salsa) chili sauce (*with chocolate and peanuts*); (plato) turkey, chicken or pork with MOLE *sauce*

molécula *f* molecule

moler [E9] *vt* ⟨especias/café⟩ to grind; ⟨trigo⟩ to grind, mill; ⟨aceitunas⟩ to crush; ⟨carne⟩ to grind (AmE), to mince (BrE); ⟨plátano⟩ (Chi, Méx) to mash; **café molido** ground coffee

molestar [A1] *vt* **1** (a) (importunar) to bother; **perdone que lo moleste** sorry to trouble *o* bother you (b) (interrumpir) to disturb
2 (ofender, disgustar) to upset
■ ~ *vi* **1** (importunar): **¿le molesta si fumo?** do you mind if I smoke?; **me molesta su arrogancia** her arrogance irritates *o* annoys me; **no me duele, pero me molesta** it doesn't hurt but it's uncomfortable
2 (fastidiar) to be a nuisance; **no quiero** ~ I don't want to be a nuisance *o* to cause any trouble
■ **molestarse** *v pron* **1** (disgustarse) to get upset; ~**se POR algo** to get upset ABOUT sth; ~**se CON algn** to get annoyed WITH sb
2 (tomarse el trabajo) to bother, trouble oneself (frml); **ni se molestó en llamarme** he didn't even bother to call me; **se molestó en venir hasta aquí a avisarnos** she took the trouble to come all this way to tell us

molestia *f* **1** (a) (incomodidad, trastorno): **ser una** ~ to be a nuisance; **siento causarte tantas** ~**s** I'm sorry to cause you so much trouble; **perdona la** ~, **pero ...** sorry to bother you, but ... (b) (trabajo) trouble; **se tomó la** ~ **de escribirnos** she took the trouble to write to us; **¿para qué te tomaste la** ~? why did you bother to do that?; **no es ninguna** ~ it's no trouble *o* bother
2 (malestar): ~**s estomacales** stomach problems *o* upsets; **no es un dolor, solo una** ~ it's not a pain, just a feeling of discomfort

molesto -ta *adj* **1** [SER] (a) (fastidioso) ⟨ruido/tos⟩ annoying, irritating; ⟨sensación/síntoma⟩ unpleasant (b) (violento, embarazoso) awkward, embarrassing **2** [ESTAR] (ofendido) upset; (irritado) annoyed; **está muy** ~ **por lo que hiciste** he's very upset/annoyed about what you did

molestoso -sa *adj* (AmL fam) annoying

molido -da *adj* (a) (fam) (agotado) bushed (AmE colloq), shattered (BrE colloq) (b) (Andes fam) (dolorido) stiff

molinero -ra *m,f* miller

molinillo *m* (a) (de café, especias) grinder, mill; ~ **de carne** grinder (AmE), mincer (BrE) (b) (juguete) pinwheel (AmE), windmill (BrE) (c) (Col, Méx) (para batir) whisk

molino *m* (a) (máquina — para el trigo) mill; (— para la carne) grinder (AmE), mincer (BrE) (b) (fábrica) mill; ~ **de agua** waterwheel; ~ **de viento** windmill; ~ **de papel** paper mill

molleja *f* (de res) sweetbread; (de ave) gizzard

mollera *f* (fam) head; **está mal de la** ~ he's off his head *o* rocker (colloq); **cerrado** *or* **duro de** ~ pigheaded (colloq)

molo *m* (Chi) *tb* ~ **de abrigo** breakwater, mole

molusco *m* mollusk*

momentáneo -nea *adj* (a) (breve) momentary (b) (pasajero) temporary

momento *m* **1** (a) (instante puntual) moment; **justo en ese** ~ just at that moment; **a partir de**

ese ~ from that moment on; **en todo** ~ at all times (b) (lapso breve) minute, moment; **dentro de un** ~ in a minute *o* moment; **¡un momentito!** (por teléfono) just a moment, just a minute; **eso te lo arreglo en un** ~ I'll fix that for you in no time at all (c) (época, período) time, period; **atravesamos** ~**s difíciles** we're going through a difficult time *o* period; **está en su mejor** ~ he is at his peak (d) (ocasión) time; **llegas en buen/mal** ~ you've arrived at the right time/at a bad time; **en ningún** ~ at no time
2 (en locs) **al momento** at once; **de momento** (ahora mismo) right now; (mientras tanto) for the time being; (por ahora) for the moment; **de un momento al otro** (dentro de muy poco) any minute now; **en cualquier momento** at any time; **en el momento** immediately; **en el momento menos pensado** when they (*o* you *etc*) least expect it; **por el momento** for the time being
3 (Fís, Mec) momentum

momia *f* mummy

mona *f* **1** (fam) (borrachera): **agarrar una** ~ to get plastered (colloq); **dormir la** ~ to sleep it off
2 (a) (en naipes) old maid (b) (Col) (para un álbum) picture card; **como la** ~ (CS fam) terrible

monada *f* (fam) (a) (cosa bonita): **¡qué** ~ **de vestido!** what a lovely dress! (b) (persona bonita): **su novia es una** ~ his girlfriend's really pretty; **¡qué** ~ **de niño!** what a lovely *o* (colloq) cute kid (c) (RPl) (persona encantadora) angel (colloq)

monaguillo *m* altar boy, acolyte, server

monarca *mf* monarch

monarquía *f* monarchy

monárquico -ca *adj* ⟨régimen⟩ monarchical; ⟨persona/ideas⟩ monarchist (before n)
■ *m,f* monarchist, royalist

monasterio *m* monastery

monástico -ca *adj* monastic

mondadientes *m* (*pl* ~) toothpick

mondar [A1] *vt* (Esp) ⟨fruta/patatas⟩ to peel
■ **mondarse** *v pron* (refl): **se mondaba los dientes** she was picking her teeth; ~**se de risa** (Esp fam) to die laughing

moneda *f* **1** (a) (pieza) coin; **una** ~ **de cinco pesos** a five-peso coin *o* piece (b) (de país) currency; **acuñar** ~ to mint money **2 la Moneda** (en Chi) Presidential Palace

monedero *m* change purse (AmE), purse (BrE)

monerías *fpl* (fam): **hacer** ~ (tontear) to mess around (colloq); (hacer payasadas) to monkey *o* clown around (colloq)

mongólico -ca *adj* (a) (ant *o* crit) (Med) ⟨rasgos⟩ mongoloid (dated *or* crit); **niños** ~**s** Down's syndrome children (b) (fam & pey) (tonto) moronic (colloq & pej)

mongolismo *m* (ant *o* crit) Down's syndrome

monigote *m* (muñeco) rag doll; (de papel) paper doll; (dibujo) doodle

monitor -tora *m,f* **1** (a) (CS) (Dep): ~ **de esquí/natación** ski/swimming instructor; ~ **de tenis** tennis coach (b) (Educ) (en la escuela) (RPl) monitor; (en la universidad) (Col) *student who acts as an assistant teacher* **2 monitor** *m* (Inf, Med, Tec) monitor

monja *f* nun; **meterse a** *or* **de** ~ to become a nun

monje *m* monk

277

mono¹ -na adj [1] (fam) ⟨mujer⟩ pretty, lovely-looking (colloq); ⟨niño⟩ lovely, cute (colloq); ⟨vestido/piso⟩ gorgeous, lovely [2] (Col) (rubio) ⟨hombre/niño⟩ blond; ⟨mujer/niña⟩ blonde [3] (Audio) mono
■ m,f [1] (Zool) monkey; **ser el último** ~ (fam) to be the lowest of the low [2] m (a) (de mecánico) coveralls (pl) (AmE), overalls (pl) (BrE) (b) (de moda — de cuerpo entero) jumpsuit; (— con peto) overalls (pl) (AmE), dungarees (pl) (BrE) (c) (Méx) (malla de bailarina) leotard

mono² m (monigote) [1] doodle; **una revista de monitos** (Andes, Méx) a comic; ~ **animado** (Chi) cartoon; ~ **de nieve** (Chi) snowman [2] (a) (de mecánico) coveralls (pl) (AmE), overalls (pl) (BrE), boiler suit (BrE) (b) (de moda — de cuerpo entero) jumpsuit; (— con peto) overalls (pl) (AmE), dungarees (pl) (BrE) (c) (Méx) (malla de bailarina) leotard [3] (arg) (síndrome de abstinencia) cold turkey (sl); **está con el** ~ he's gone cold turkey (sl)

monocarril m monorail
monocolor adj one-color* (before n)
monóculo m monocle
monogamia f monogamy
monógamo -ma adj monogamous
■ m,f monogamist
monografía f monograph
monográfico -ca adj monographic
monolingüe adj monolingual
monolítico -ca adj monolithic
monolito m monolith
monólogo m monologue
monoparental adj: **las familias** ~**es** one-parent families
monopatín m (con manillar) (CS) scooter; (sin manillar) (Esp) skateboard
monopolio m monopoly
monopolizar [A4] vt to monopolize
monorriel m (AmL) monorail
monosílabo m monosyllable
monoteísmo m monotheism
monotonía f (de tarea) monotony; (de sonido) monotone
monótono -na adj monotonous
monóxido m monoxide; ~ **de carbono** carbon monoxide
monseñor m Monsignor
monstruo m (a) (en general) monster (b) (fenómeno) phenomenon; **un** ~ **de la música pop** a pop phenomenon
monstruosidad f (a) (cosa fea, grande) monstrosity (b) (atrocidad) atrocity (c) (cualidad) monstrous nature, monstrousness
monstruoso -sa adj (a) ⟨crimen/comportamiento⟩ monstrous, atrocious (b) ⟨ser/facciones⟩ hideous, grotesque
monta f (monto) total (value); **de poca** ~ ⟨asunto⟩ of little importance o note; ⟨escritor⟩ third-rate; ⟨daños⟩ slight, minor
montacargas m (pl ~) freight o service elevator (AmE), service o goods lift (BrE)
montado -da adj ⟨policía⟩ mounted; **iba** ~ **a caballo** he was riding a horse; **estaba montada en su bicicleta** she was sitting on her bicycle; ver tb MONTAR

montador -dora m,f (Mec, Tec) fitter; (Cin, TV) film editor
montaje m (a) (de máquina, mueble) assembly (b) (de obra) staging; (de película) editing; **seguro que todo es un** ~ I bet it's all a big con o a set-up (colloq)
montallantas m (pl ~) (Col) (taller) workshop where tires* are retreaded; (mecánico) person who retreads tires*
montaña f [1] (Geog) mountain; **tienen un chalet en la** ~ they have a chalet in the mountains; ~ **rusa** roller coaster [2] (montón) pile
montañero -ra m,f mountaineer, mountain climber
montañés -ñesa adj mountain (before n), highland (before n)
■ m,f highlander
montañismo m mountaineering, mountain climbing
montañoso -sa adj ⟨cadena⟩ mountain (before n); ⟨terreno/país⟩ mountainous
montar [A1] vt [1] (a) ⟨caballo⟩ (subirse a) to mount, get on; (ir sobre) to ride (b) (subir, colocar): **montó al niño en el poni** he lifted the boy up onto the pony [2] ⟨vaca/yegua⟩ to mount [3] (a) (poner, establecer) ⟨feria/exposición⟩ to set up; ⟨negocio⟩ to start up, set up (b) ⟨máquina/mueble⟩ to assemble; ⟨estantería⟩ to put up; ⟨tienda de campaña⟩ to put up, pitch (c) ⟨piedra preciosa⟩ to set; ⟨diapositiva⟩ to mount (d) (organizar) ⟨obra/producción⟩ to stage [4] (Esp) ⟨nata⟩ to whip; ⟨claras⟩ to whisk
■ ~ vi [1] (a) (ir): ~ **a caballo/en bicicleta** to ride a horse/bicycle (b) (Equ) to mount [2] (cubrir parcialmente) ~ **SOBRE algo** to overlap sth
■ **montarse** v pron (en coche) to get in; (en tren, autobús, bicicleta) to get on; (en caballo) to mount, get on; **¿me dejas** ~**me en tu bicicleta?** can I have a ride on your bicycle?
monte m (Geog) (a) (montaña) mountain (b) (terreno — cubierto de maleza) scrubland, scrub; (— cubierto de árboles) woodland
montera f (gorra) cap; (de torero) bullfighter's hat
montés adj ⟨animal/planta⟩ wild
montevideano -na adj of/from Montevideo
Montevideo m Montevideo
montgomery m (CS) duffle coat
montículo m mound
montón m (a) (pila) pile; **del** ~ (fam) ordinary, average (b) (fam) (gran cantidad): **un** ~ **de gente** loads of people (colloq); **me gusta un** ~ I like her/him/it a lot
montonero -ra m,f (guerrillero) guerrilla
montura f [1] (Equ) (silla) saddle; (animal) mount [2] (a) (de anteojos) frame (b) (engarce) setting, mount
monumental adj (fam) (a) ⟨cocina/jardín⟩ huge, massive (b) ⟨error/esfuerzo⟩ monumental
monumento m [1] (obra conmemorativa) monument; ~ **histórico/nacional** historical/national monument; ~ **a los caídos** war memorial; ~ **funerario** commemorative stone [2] (obra excepcional) masterpiece, classic [3] (fam) (mujer atractiva) stunner (colloq)

monzón *m* monsoon

moña *f* (Taur) ribbon; (lazo) (RPI) bow

moño *m* **(a)** (peinado) bun; **se hizo un ~** she put her hair up in a bun; ***estar hasta el ~*** to be fed up (to the back teeth) (colloq) **(b)** (AmL) (lazo) bow

moñona *f* (Col fam) strike; **hacer ~** to get a strike

moqueta *f* (Esp) wall-to-wall carpet, fitted carpet (BrE)

moquillento -ta *adj* (Andes fam) **(a)** (resfriado) coldy (colloq) **(b)** (con mocos) ⟨*nariz*⟩ runny, snotty (colloq); ⟨*niño*⟩ runny-nosed, snotty-nosed (colloq)

moquillo *m* distemper

mora *f* (de zarzamora) blackberry; (de moral) mulberry; (de morera) white mulberry

morada *f* (frml o liter) dwelling (frml), abode (frml or liter)

morado¹ -da *adj* ⟨*color*⟩ purple; **~ del frío** blue with cold; **ponerle a algn un ojo ~** to give sb a black eye

morado² *m* (Esp, Ven) bruise

moral *adj* moral
■ *f* ⓵ (Fil, Relig) **(a)** (doctrina) moral doctrine **(b)** (moralidad) morality, morals (*pl*) ⓶ (estado de ánimo) morale; **levantarle la ~ a algn** to raise sb's morale, lift sb's spirits; **estar bajo de ~** to be feeling low; **tener la ~ alta** to be in good spirits
■ *m* mulberry (tree)

moraleja *f* moral

moralidad *f* morality, ethics (*pl*)

morar [A1] *vi* (liter) to dwell (liter)

moratón *m* bruise

morboso -sa *adj* ⟨*escena/película*⟩ gruesome; ⟨*persona/mente*⟩ ghoulish; (truculento, retorcido) morbid
■ *m,f* (fam) ghoul

morcilla *f* blood sausage (AmE), black pudding (BrE)

mordaz *adj* ⟨*estilo/lenguaje*⟩ scathing, caustic; ⟨*crítica*⟩ sharp, scathing

mordaza *f* **(a)** (en la boca) gag **(b)** (Tec) clamp

mordedura *f* bite

morder [E9] *vt* ⓵ (con los dientes) to bite; **el perro le mordió la mano** the dog bit her hand ⓶ (Méx fam) ⟨*policía/funcionario*⟩ to extract a bribe from
■ *vi* to bite
■ **morderse** *v pron* (refl) to bite oneself; **~se las uñas** to bite one's nails

mordida *f* ⓵ (CS) (en general) bite; (huella) toothmarks (*pl*) ⓶ (Méx fam) (soborno) bribe, backhander (BrE colloq)

mordisco *m* bite; **le dio un ~ en el brazo** it bit her (on the) arm

mordisquear [A1] *vt* to nibble

moreno -na *adj* **(a)** [SER] ⟨*persona*⟩ (de pelo oscuro) dark, dark-haired; (de tez oscura) dark; (de raza negra) (euf) dark-skinned (euph) **(b)** [ESTAR] (bronceado) brown, tanned **(c)** ⟨*piel*⟩ brown, dark
■ *m,f* **(a)** (de pelo oscuro) (*m*) dark-haired man (o

boy *etc*); (*f*) dark-haired woman (o girl *etc*), brunet* **(b)** (de tez oscura) dark person (o man *etc*); (de raza negra) (euf) dark-skinned person (o man *etc*) (euph), coloured man (o woman *etc*) (BrE euph)

morera *f* white mulberry tree

moretón *m* bruise

morfar [A1] *vi* (RPI arg) to eat

morfina *f* morphine

morgue *f* (AmL) morgue, mortuary

moribundo -da *adj* dying, moribund (frml)
■ *m,f* dying man (o woman *etc*)

morir [I37] *vi* **(a)** «*persona/animal*» to die; **~ ahogado** to drown; **murió asesinada** she was murdered; **~ DE algo** ⟨*de vejez/cáncer*⟩ to die OF sth; **murió de hambre** she starved to death; **¡y allí muere!** (AmC fam) and that's all there is to it! **(b)** (liter) «*civilización/costumbre*» to die out
■ **morirse** *v pron* «*persona/animal/planta*» to die; **se les murió la madre** their mother died; **se me murió la perra** my dog died; **no te vas a ~ por ayudarlo** (fam) it won't kill you to help him (colloq); **como se entere me muero** (fam) I'll die if she finds out (colloq); **~se DE algo** ⟨*de un infarto/ de cáncer*⟩ to die OF sth; **se moría de miedo/ aburrimiento** he was scared stiff/bored stiff; **me muero de frío** I'm freezing; **me estoy muriendo de hambre** I'm starving (colloq); **me muero por una cerveza** I'm dying for a beer (colloq); **se muere por verla** he's dying to see her (colloq)

morisco -ca *adj* Moorish, Morisco

morisqueta *f* (CS): **hacer ~s** to make o (BrE) pull faces

mormado -da *adj* (Méx) ⟨*nariz*⟩ blocked; **estoy ~** I'm all stuffed up (colloq)

mormón -mona *adj/m,f* Mormon

moro -ra *adj* ⓵ (Hist) Moorish ⓶ (Esp) (de África del Norte) (fam & pey) North African; (referido a un hombre machista) (fam) chauvinistic, sexist
■ *m,f* ⓵ **(a)** (Hist) Moor **(b)** (mahometano) Muslim ⓶ (Esp) (de África del Norte) (fam & pey) North African; (hombre machista)
■ *m* (fam) sexist, male chauvinist pig

morocho -cha *adj* (AmS fam) (de pelo oscuro) dark, dark-haired; (de piel oscura) dark
■ *m,f* (de pelo oscuro) dark-haired person (o man *etc*); (de piel oscura) dark person (o man *etc*)

morral *m* **(a)** (al hombro) rucksack, haversack; (a la espalda) backpack, rucksack **(b)** (para el pienso) nosebag

morralla *f* ⓵ (cosas sin valor) junk ⓶ (chusma) riffraff, rabble ⓷ (Méx) (dinero suelto) loose change

morriña *f* (fam) homesickness; **tener ~** to feel o be homesick

morro *m* ⓵ **(a)** (hocico) snout **(b)** (Esp fam) (boca) *tb* **~s** mouth, chops (*pl*) (BrE colloq); ***estar de ~s (con algn)*** (Esp fam) to be in a bad mood (with sb) **(c)** (Esp fam) (descaro) nerve (colloq) **(d)** (Esp fam) (de coche, avión) nose ⓶ (cerro) hill

morrón *m* (CS) (pimiento) red pepper

morsa *f* walrus

mortadela f mortadella

mortaja f **1** (sábana) shroud **2** (Tec) mortise

mortal adj **1** (a) ⟨ser⟩ mortal (b) ⟨herida⟩ fatal, mortal; ⟨dosis⟩ fatal, lethal; ⟨enfermedad/veneno⟩ deadly; **un golpe** ∼ a death blow **2** ⟨odio/enemigo⟩ mortal
■ mf mortal

mortalidad f mortality; **la** ∼ **infantil** infant mortality

mortecino -na adj ⟨luz⟩ weak; ⟨color⟩ pale

mortero m mortar

mortífero -ra adj deadly, lethal

mortificar [A2] vt (a) (atormentar) to torment; **los celos lo mortifican** he's tortured o tormented by jealousy (b) (Relig) to mortify
■ **mortificarse** v pron (refl) (atormentarse) to fret, distress oneself; (Relig) to mortify the flesh

mortuorio -ria adj funeral (before n)

mosaico m (a) (Art) mosaic (b) (Méx, RPl) (baldosa) floor tile; **piso de** ∼ tiled floor (c) (Col) (foto) school/college photograph

mosca f fly; **no se oía ni una** ∼ you could have heard a pin drop (colloq); **por si las** ∼**s** (fam) just in case (colloq)

moscardón m botfly

moscatel adj muscat (before n)
■ m muscatel

moscovita adj/mf Muscovite

Moscú m Moscow

mosqueado -da adj (esp Esp fam) (a) (molesto, disgustado) annoyed, sore (AmE colloq), cross (BrE colloq) (b) (desconfiado, suspicaz) suspicious, wary

mosquearse [A1] v pron (esp Esp fam) (a) (sospechar, desconfiar) to get suspicious, smell a rat (colloq) (b) (disgustarse) to get annoyed, get sore (AmE colloq), to get cross (BrE colloq)

mosquetero m musketeer

mosquitero m, **mosquitera** f (de ventana) mosquito netting; (de tela) mosquito net

mosquito m mosquito

mostaza f mustard; (color) : **(de) color** ∼ mustard, mustard-colored*

mosto m grape juice, must

mostrador m (en tienda) counter; (en bar) bar; (en aeropuerto) check-in desk

mostrar [A10] vt to show; **muéstrame cómo funciona** show me how it works
■ **mostrarse** v pron (+ compl): **se mostró muy atento con nosotros** he was very obliging (to us); **se** ∼**on partidarios de la propuesta** they expressed support for the proposal

mota f **1** (partícula) tiny bit, dot; **una** ∼ **de polvo** a speck of dust **2** (Tex): **una tela a** ∼**s** spotted fabric; **una lana azul con** ∼**s de colores** blue wool with flecks of colors **3** (AmC, Méx arg) (marihuana) grass (colloq), weed (sl) **4** (a) (para empolvarse) powder puff (b) (Méx) (borla) pom-pom

mote m **1** (apodo) nickname; **le pusieron como** ∼ **'el Oso'** they nicknamed him 'the Bear' **2** (Andes) (trigo) boiled wheat; (maíz) boiled corn (AmE) o (BrE) maize

moteado -da adj ⟨tela⟩ (jaspeado) flecked; (a lunares) dotted, spotted; ⟨piel⟩ mottled

motel m motel

motín m (de tropas, tripulación) mutiny; (de prisioneros) riot, rebellion

motivación f (incentivo) motivation; (motivo) motive

motivar [A1] vt **1** (en general) to motivate; **motivado por la venganza** motivated by revenge; **¿qué te motivó a hacerlo?** what made you do it? **2** (causar) to bring about, cause

motivo m **1** (a) (razón, causa) reason, cause; **el** ∼ **de su viaje** the reason for her trip; **por este** ∼ **nos hallamos aquí** that's (the reason) why we're here; **con** ∼ **de algo** on the occasion of sth; **no des** ∼**s para que te critiquen** don't give them cause to criticize you; **hay** ∼**s para preocuparse** there is cause for concern; **el adulterio es** ∼ **suficiente de divorcio** adultery is sufficient grounds for divorce; **sin ningún** ∼ for no reason at all; **¡que sea un** ∼**!** (Col fam) let's drink to that! (colloq) (b) (propósito, finalidad) purpose; **el** ∼ **de esta carta es …** the purpose of this letter is … **2** (Art, Lit, Mús) motif; ∼**s decorativos** decorative motifs

moto f (motocicleta) motorcycle, motorbike (BrE); (motoneta, escúter) (motor) scooter; **fue en** ∼ he went on his motorcycle

motocicleta f motorcycle

motociclismo m motorcycling

motociclista mf motorcyclist

motocross, moto-cross m motocross

motoneta f (AmL) (motor) scooter

motor¹ -triz, motor -tora adj motor (before n)

motor² m **1** (Tec) engine; ∼ **fuera (de) borda** outboard motor **2** (impulsor) driving force

motora f small motorboat, powerboat

motorismo m motorcycling

motorista mf (a) (que va en moto) motorcyclist (b) (Col) (automovilista) motorist (frml), driver

motorizado -da adj ⟨ejército⟩ motorized
■ m,f (Ven) motorcycle messenger o (BrE) courier

motudo -da adj (CS fam) frizzy

mousse /mus/ f or m mousse

mouton /mu'ton/ m sheepskin

movedizo -za adj ⟨niño⟩ restless, fidgety

mover [E9] vt **1** (a) (trasladar, desplazar) to move (b) (Jueg) ⟨ficha/pieza⟩ to move (c) (agitar): **no muevas la cámara** keep the camera still; **el viento movía los árboles** the wind shook the trees; **movió la cabeza** (asintiendo) he nodded (his head); (negando) she shook her head; **mueve la cola** it wags its tail (d) (accionar) to drive **2** (inducir): ∼ **a algn a hacer algo** to move sb to do sth
■ ∼ vi (Jueg) to move
■ **moverse** v pron (a) (en general) to move; **no te muevas de ahí** don't move; **la lámpara se movía con el viento** the lamp was moving o swaying in the wind (b) (apresurarse) to hurry up, get a move on (colloq)

movida f **1** (Jueg) move **2** (Esp) (fam) (a) (asunto, rollo): **no me interesa la** ∼ **ecológica** I'm not into this ecology thing (colloq); **anda en** ∼**s chuecas** (Méx) he's into some shady deals (colloq) (b) (actividad cultural): **la** ∼ **madrileña** the Madrid scene; **donde está la** ∼ where it's all going on

movido -da adj (a) (Fot) blurred (b) (agitado) ⟨mar⟩ rough, choppy; ⟨día/año⟩ hectic, busy; ⟨fiesta⟩ lively

móvil *adj* mobile
■ *m* **1** (frml) (impulso) motive **2** (adorno) mobile
movilidad *f* mobility
movilización *f* **1** (a) (Mil) mobilization (b) (Rels Labs) (manifestación) demonstration; **un calendario de movilizaciones** a program of industrial action **2** (Chi) (Transp) public transportation (AmE), public transport (BrE)
movilizar [A4] *vt* ⟨tropas/población⟩ to mobilize
■ **movilizarse** *v pron* **1** (Mil, Rels Labs) to mobilize **2** (CS) (desplazarse) to move o get around
movimiento *m* **1** (a) (en general) movement; **el menor ∼ de la mano** the slightest movement of the hand; **el ∼ surrealista** the surrealist movement; **∼ pictórico** school of painting; **∼ sísmico** earth tremor (b) (Fís, Tec) motion, movement; **poner algo en ∼** to set sth in motion; **se puso en ∼** it started moving (c) (agitación, actividad) activity; **una calle de mucho ∼** a very busy street **2** (Mús) (parte de obra) movement; (compás) tempo **3** (Jueg) move
mozárabe *adj* Mozarabic
■ *mf* Mozarab
mozo -za *adj*: **en mis años ∼s** in my youth; **sus hijos ya son ∼s** her children are quite grown-up now
■ *m,f* (a) (ant) (joven) (*m*) young boy; (*f*) young girl; **los ∼s del pueblo** the young people in the village (b) (AmS) (camarero) (*m*) waiter; (*f*) waitress (c) (Ferr) *tb* **∼ de equipajes** *or* **de estación** porter
muaré *m* moiré
mucamo -ma (AmL) (*m*) servant; (*f*) maid, servant; **mucama de hotel** chambermaid
muchacha *f*: *tb* **∼ de servicio** maid; *ver tb* MUCHACHO
muchacho -cha *m,f* (*m*) kid (colloq), boy, guy (colloq); (*f*) girl
muchedumbre *f* crowd
mucho¹ *adv* (a) ⟨salir/ayudar⟩ a lot; ⟨trabajar⟩ hard; **no salen ∼** they don't go out much o a lot; **me gusta muchísimo** I like it very much o a lot; **∼ mejor** a lot better; **por ∼ que insistas** no matter how much you insist; **después de ∼ discutir** after much discussion (b) (en respuestas): **¿estás preocupado? — mucho** are you worried? — (yes, I am,) very; **¿te gusta? — sí, ∼** do you like it? — yes, very much
mucho² -cha *adj* (a) (*sing*) a lot of; (en oraciones negativas, interrogativas) much, a lot of; **∼ vino** a lot of wine; **no gano ∼ dinero** I don't earn much o a lot of money; **¿ves mucha televisión?** do you watch much o a lot of television; **tiene mucha hambre** he's very hungry (b) (*pl*) many, a lot of; **había ∼s extranjeros/muchas personas allí** there were many o a lot of foreigners/people there; **hace ∼s años** many years ago
■ *pron* **1** (referido a cantidad) (a) (*sing*) a lot; (en oraciones negativas, interrogativas) much; **∼ de lo dicho** a lot of what was said; **tengo ∼ que hacer** I have a lot to do; **eso no es ∼** that's not much; **no queda mucha** there isn't much left (b) (*pl*) many; **∼s creen que ...** many (people) believe that ...; **∼s de nosotros** many of us
2 mucho (referido a tiempo): **hace ∼ que no la veo** I haven't seen her for a long time; **¿te falta ∼ para terminar?** will it take you long to finish?; **∼ antes** long before; **¿tuviste que esperar ∼?** did you have to wait long? (b) (*en locs*) **como mucho** at (the) most; **con mucho** by far, easily; **ni mucho menos** far from it; **por mucho que ...** however much ...
mucosidad *f* mucus, mucosity
muda *f* (de ropa) change of clothes; (de la piel) shedding, sloughing off
mudanza *f* move, removal (BrE); **camión de ∼s** moving van (AmE) o (BrE) removal van; **estoy de ∼** I'm in the process of moving (house)
mudar [A1] *vi* **1** (cambiar): **las serpientes mudan de piel** snakes slough off o shed their skin; **cuando mudó de voz** when his voice broke **2** (Méx) (cambiar los dientes) to lose one's milk teeth
■ **∼** *vt* **1** ⟨bebé/sábanas⟩ to change **2** (Zool) ⟨piel/plumas⟩ to molt, shed
■ **mudarse** *v pron* (a) (de casa) to move (house); **se ∼on a una casa más grande** they moved to a bigger house (b) (de ropa) to get changed, change (one's) clothes
mudéjar *adj/mf* Mudejar
mudo -da *adj* (a) (Med) dumb, mute; **es ∼ de nacimiento** he was born mute; **se quedó ∼ de asombro** he was dumbfounded (b) ⟨letra⟩ silent, mute
■ *m,f* mute
mueble *m* piece of furniture; **los ∼s del dormitorio** the bedroom furniture; **∼ bar** drinks cabinet, cocktail cabinet; **∼ cama** foldaway bed
mueca *f*: **hacerle ∼s a algn** to make o (BrE) pull faces at sb; **sus graciosísimas ∼s** her funny faces; **una ∼ burlona** a sneer
muela *f* **1** (Odont) molar, back tooth; (como término genérico) tooth; **me sacaron una ∼** I had a tooth taken out; **tengo dolor de ∼s** I have (a) toothache; **∼ del juicio** wisdom tooth **2** (de molino) millstone; (para afilar) whetstone **3** (Col) (en calle) parking bay; (en carretera) rest stop (AmE), lay-by (BrE)
muelle *m* **1** (Náut) (saliente) pier, mole; (rústico, más pequeño) jetty; (sobre la costa) quay, wharf **2** (resorte) spring
muera, mueras, etc ▶ MORIR
muérdago *m* mistletoe
muerte *f* death; **condenado a ∼** sentenced to death; **a la ∼ de su padre** on her father's death; **∼ de cuna** crib death (AmE), cot death (BrE); **me dio un susto de ∼** (fam) she scared me to death (colloq); **dar ∼ a algn** (frml) to kill sb; **de mala ∼** (fam) ⟨pueblo/hotel⟩ grotty (colloq); **ser la ∼** (fam) (ser atroz) to be hell o murder (colloq); (ser estupendo) to be fantastic (colloq)
muerto -ta *adj* **1** [ESTAR] (a) ⟨persona/animal/planta⟩ dead; **lo dieron por ∼** he was given up for dead; **resultaron ∼s 30 mineros** 30 miners died o were killed; **caer ∼** to drop dead (b) (fam) (cansado) dead beat (colloq) (c) (fam) (pasando, padeciendo): **estar ∼ de hambre/frío/sueño** to be starving/freezing/dead-tired (colloq); **estaba ∼ de miedo** he was scared stiff (colloq); **∼ de (la) risa** (fam): **estaba ∼ de risa** he was laughing his head off **2** (a) ⟨pueblo/zona⟩ dead, lifeless (b) (inerte) limp

■ *m,f* **1** (persona muerta): **hubo dos ~s** two people died *o* were killed; **hacerse el ~** to pretend to be dead; **cargar con el ~** (fam) (con un trabajo pesado) to do the dirty work; **cargarle el ~ a algn** (fam) (responsabilizar) to pin the blame on sb; (endilgarle la tarea) to give sb the dirty work (colloq); **hacer el ~** to float on one's back

2 muerto *m* (en naipes) dummy

muesca *f* (a) (hendidura) nick, notch (b) (para encajar) slot, groove

muesli /'musli/ *m* muesli

muestra *f* **1** (a) (de mercancía) sample (b) (de sangre, orina) specimen, sample (c) (en estadísticas) sample **2** (prueba, señal) sign; **una ~ de cansancio/falta de madurez** a sign of tiredness/immaturity; **como *o* en ~ de mi gratitud** as a token of my gratitude **3** (exposición) exhibition, exhibit (AmE); (de teatro, cine) festival

mueva, muevas, etc ▶ MOVER

mufa *f* (RPl fam) (a) (mal humor) bad mood (b) (moho) mold*

mugido *m* moo; **los ~s de las vacas** the mooing of the cows

mugir [I7] *vi* «*vaca*» to moo; «*toro*» to bellow

mugre *f* (suciedad) dirt, filth; (grasa) grime, grease

mugriento -ta *adj* filthy

mugroso -sa *adj* (Chi, Méx fam) filthy

mujer *f* (a) woman; **ser ~** to be a woman; **~ de la limpieza** cleaning lady, cleaner; **~ de mala vida** *or* **de mal vivir** prostitute; **~ de negocios** businesswoman; **hacerse ~** (euf) to reach puberty, become a woman (euph) (b) (esposa) wife

mujeriego *m* womanizer

mújol *m* gray* mullet

mula *f* mule; **~ de carga** pack mule; **terco/ tozudo como una ~** as stubborn as a mule (colloq)
■ *adj* (Méx fam) stubborn

mulato -ta *adj* of mixed race (*black and white*), mulatto (dated *or* pej)
■ *m,f* person of mixed race (*of a black and a white parent*), mulatto (dated *or* pej)

muleta *f* **1** (bastón) crutch; (apoyo) crutch, prop **2** (Taur) red cape (*attached to a stick*)

muletilla *f* tag, filler (tech)

mulita *f* (Per) (de pisco) glass, shot

mullido -da *adj* ‹colchón/sofá› soft; ‹hierba› springy

mulo *m* (male) mule

multa *f* fine; **le pusieron una ~** she was fined

multar [A1] *vt* to fine

multicine *m* multiscreen movie complex (AmE), multiscreen cinema (BrE)

multicolor *adj* multicolored*

multicultural *adj* multicultural

multimillonario -ria *adj*: **es ~** he is a multimillionaire; **un contrato ~** a multi-million dollar (*o* pound *etc*) contract
■ *m,f* multimillionaire

multinacional *adj/f* multinational

múltiple *adj* **1** ‹aplicaciones/causas› many, numerous **2** ‹flor/imagen/fractura› multiple

multiplicación *f* **1** (Biol, Mat) multiplication **2** (incremento) increase

multiplicar [A2] *vt* to multiply; **~ algo POR algo** to multiply sth BY sth
■ *vi* to multiply
■ **multiplicarse** *v pron* **1** «*especie*» to multiply, reproduce **2** (aumentar) to increase several times over

múltiplo *m* multiple

multitud *f* **1** (muchedumbre) crowd **2 ~ DE algo** (muchos): **tengo (una) ~ de cosas que hacer** I have dozens of things to do (colloq); **una ~ de usos** an enormous variety of uses

multitudinario -ria *adj* ‹manifestación/ movilizaciones› mass (*before n*); ‹concierto› with mass audiences

mundano -na *adj* (a) ‹problemas/placeres› worldly (b) ‹fiesta› society (*before n*)

mundial *adj* ‹historia/mercado› world (*before n*); **la marca ~** the world record; **de fama ~** world-famous; **es un problema ~** it's a global *o* worldwide problem
■ *m*: tb **~es** *mpl* World Championship(s); **el ~ de fútbol** the World Cup

mundialmente *adv*: **es ~ famoso** he is world famous; **un producto conocido ~** a product well-known throughout the world

mundo *m* **1** (en general) world; **artistas venidos de todo el ~** artists from all over the world; **el mejor del ~** the best in the world; **me parece lo más normal del ~** it seems perfectly normal to me; **es conocido en todo el ~** he is known worldwide; **el ~ árabe** the Arab world; **el ~ de la droga** the drugs world; **el ~ del espectáculo** showbusiness; **todo el ~ lo sabe** everybody knows it; **el ~ es un pañuelo** it's a small world; **por nada del *or* en el ~**: **yo no me lo pierdo por nada del ~** I wouldn't miss it for the world; **no lo vendería por nada en el ~** I wouldn't sell it for anything in the world *o* (colloq) for all the tea in China; **traer a algn/venir al ~** to bring sb/come into the world; **ver ~** to see the world **2** (planeta, universo) planet, world; **él vive en otro ~** he's on another planet *o* in another world

munición *f* (carga) tb **municiones** ammunition, munitions (*pl*)

municipal *adj* ‹impuesto› local; ‹elecciones/ piscina/mercado› municipal

municipalidad *f* ▶ MUNICIPIO

municipio *m* (territorio) municipality; (entidad) town council; (edificio) town hall

muñeca *f* **1** (a) (Jueg) doll; **~ de trapo** rag doll; **jugar a las ~s** to play with dolls; **ser** *or* **parecer una ~** to be a little doll (b) (fam) (como apelativo) darling, honey (colloq) **2** (Anat) wrist

muñeco *m* **1** (a) (con forma humana) doll; (con forma de animal) toy animal; **~ de peluche** stuffed animal (AmE), soft toy (BrE); **~ de nieve** snowman (b) (de ventrílocuo, sastre, etc) dummy (c) (dibujo) figure **2 muñecos** *mpl* (Per fam): **estar con los ~s** to be very nervous

muñequera *f* (Dep) wristband; (Med) wrist bandage

muñón *m* (de un miembro) stump

mural *adj* wall (*before n*), mural (*before n*)
■ *m* mural

muralista *adj/mf* muralist

muralla f (a) (de ciudad) walls (pl), city wall; (de convento) wall; **la M~ China** the Great Wall of China (b) (Chi) (pared) wall

murciélago m bat

muriera, murió, etc ▶ MORIR

murmullo m (de voces) murmur

murmuraciones fpl gossip

murmurador -dora adj gossipy
■ m,f gossip

murmurar [A1] vt (a) (hablar bajo) to murmur; **le murmuró algo al oído** he whispered something in her ear (b) (con enojo) to mutter; **— no pienso hacerlo —** murmuró I won't do it, she muttered (c) (en son de crítica): **cosas que se murmuran en la oficina** rumors that go around the office
■ ~ vi (criticar) to gossip (maliciously); ~ **DE algn** to gossip ABOUT sb

muro m wall; **M~ de las Lamentaciones** or **los Lamentos** Wailing Wall

mus m: a Spanish card game

musa f (Mit) Muse; (inspiración) muse

muscular adj muscular

musculatura f muscles (pl), musculature (tech)

músculo m muscle; **sacar** ~ to flex one's muscles

musculoso -sa adj muscular

muselina f muslin

museo m museum; ~ **de cera** wax museum, waxworks (pl); ~ **de ciencias naturales** natural science museum

musgo m moss

música f music; **pon algo de** ~ put some music on; ~ **ambiental** background music; (en tienda, fábrica) piped o canned music

musical adj/m musical

músico -ca m,f (compositor) composer; (instrumentista) musician; ~ **callejero** street musician, busker (BrE)

musitar [A1] vt to whisper, murmur

muslera f thighband

muslo m (Anat) thigh (Coc); ~**s de pollo** chicken legs

mustio -tia adj 1 (flor/planta) withered 2 (Méx fam) (hipócrita) two-faced (colloq)

musulmán -mana adj/m,f Muslim, Moslem

mutable adj changeable, mutable (frml)

mutación f mutation

mutilado -da m,f disabled person; **un** ~ **de guerra** a disabled serviceman

mutilar [A1] vt (a) (persona/pierna) to mutilate; **quedó mutilado en el accidente** he was maimed as a result of the accident (b) (árbol/estatua) to vandalize

mutua f benefit society (AmE), friendly society (BrE)

mutual f (CS) (de asistencia económica) benefit society (AmE), friendly society (BrE)

mutuo -tua adj mutual; **de** ~ **acuerdo** by mutual o joint agreement; **redundará en beneficio** ~ it will be to our mutual benefit

muy adv (a) very; ~ **poca gente** very few people; **son** ~ **amigos** they're great friends; ~ **admirado** much admired; ~ **respetado** highly respected; ~ **bien, sigamos adelante** OK o fine, let's go on; **por** ~ **cansado que estés** however o no matter how tired you are (b) (demasiado) too; **quedó** ~ **dulce** it's rather o too sweet

Nn

N, n f (read as /'ene/) the letter N, n

N. (= **norte**) North, N

nabo m turnip

nácar m mother-of-pearl, nacre

nacer [E3] vi 1 (a) (niño/animal) to be born; **¿dónde naciste?** where were you born?; **al** ~ at birth; **nació para (ser) músico** he was born to be a musician (b) (pollito/insecto) to hatch (c) (hoja/rama) to sprout (d) (río) to have its source; (carretera) to start (e) (pelo/plumas) to grow 2 (surgir) (amistad/relación) to spring up; ~ **DE algo** (problema/situación) to arise o spring FROM sth; **nació de ella invitarlo** it was her idea to invite him

nacido -da adj born; **un niño recién** ~ a newborn baby

naciente adj (sol) rising (before n); **el** ~ **interés por la ecología** the new interest in ecology

nacimiento m 1 (de niño, animal) birth; **es argentino de** ~ he's Argentinian by birth; **es sorda de** ~ she was born deaf 2 (de idea, movimiento) birth; **el** ~ **de una amistad duradera** the start o beginning of a lasting friendship 3 (belén) crib

nación f nation; **las Naciones Unidas** the United Nations (pl)

nacional adj (a) (de la nación) (deuda/reservas/industria) national; **en todo el territorio** ~

AmC América Central	Arg Argentina	Cu Cuba	Per Perú
AmL América Latina	Bol Bolivia	Ec Ecuador	RPI Río de la Plata
AmS América del Sur	Chi Chile	Esp España	Ur Uruguay
Andes Región andina	CS Cono Sur	Méx México	Ven Venezuela

throughout the country; **un programa de difusión** ~ a program broadcast nationwide **(b)** ⟨*vuelo*⟩ domestic

■ *mf* (frml) (ciudadano) national

nacionalidad *f* (ciudadanía) nationality

nacionalismo *m* nationalism

nacionalista *adj* nationalist (*before n*)

■ *mf* nationalist

nacionalización *f* (de industria) nationalization; (naturalización) naturalization

nacionalizar [A4] *vt* ⟨*industria*⟩ to nationalize; ⟨*persona*⟩ to naturalize

■ **nacionalizarse** *v pron* «*persona*» to become naturalized

naco -ca *adj* (Méx fam & pey) plebby (colloq & pej)

■ *m, f* pleb (colloq & pej)

nada *pron* ① **(a)** nothing; **es mejor que** ~ it's better than nothing; **de** ~ **sirve que le compres libros** there's no point in buying him books; **antes que** *o* **de** ~ first of all; **no quiere** ~ he doesn't want anything; **¡no sirves para** ~**!** you're useless; **sin decir** ~ without a word **(b)** (*en locs*) **de nada** you're welcome; **nada de nada** (fam) not a thing; **nada más: no hay** ~ **más** there's nothing else; **¿algo más?** — ~ **más** anything else? — no, that's it *o* that's all; ~ **más fui yo** (Méx) I was the only one who went; **salí** ~ **más comer** I went out right *o* straight after lunch; **sacó** (~ **más ni**) ~ **menos que el primer puesto** she came first no less; **para nada: no me gustó para** ~ I didn't like it at all; **por nada: la compraron por** ~ they bought it for next to nothing; **discuten por** ~ they argue over nothing; **llora por** ~ she cries at the slightest little thing

② (Esp) (en tenis) love; **quince-**~ fifteen-love

■ *adv* : **no está** ~ **preocupado** he isn't at all *o* the least bit worried; **esto no me gusta** ~ I don't like this at all *o* (colloq) one bit

nadador -dora *m,f* swimmer

nadar [A1] *vi* **(a)** «*persona/pez*» to swim; **¿sabes** ~**?** can you swim?; ~ (**estilo**) **mariposa/ pecho** to do (the) butterfly/breaststroke; ~ **de espalda** *or* (Méx) **de dorso** to do (the) back stroke **(b)** «*ramas/hojas*» (flotar) to float **(c) nadar en** (tener mucho): ~ **en dinero** to be rolling in money (colloq); **el pollo nadaba en grasa** the chicken was swimming in grease

■ ~ *vt* to swim

nadie *pron* nobody, no one; **no me ayudó** ~ nobody helped me; **no vi a** ~ I didn't see anybody; **sin que** ~ **se diera cuenta** without anyone noticing

nado *m* **(a) a nado: cruzó el río a** ~ he swam across the river **(b)** (Méx, Ven) (natación) swimming

nafta *f* **(a)** (Quím) naphtha **(b)** (RPl) (gasolina) gas (AmE), petrol (BrE)

naftalina *f* (Quím) naphthalene; (para ropa) mothballs (*pl*)

naguas *fpl* (Méx fam) petticoat

náhuatl¹ *adj/mf* (*pl* **nahuas**) Nahuatl

náhuatl² *m* (idioma) Nahuatl

nailon *m* nylon

naipe *m* (playing) card; **juegos de** ~**s** card games

nalga *f* (Anat) buttock; **una inyección en la** ~ an injection in the buttock *o* bottom

nalgada *f* (Méx) smack on the bottom

nana *f* **(a)** (canción de cuna) lullaby **(b)** (fam) (abuela) grandma (colloq), granny (colloq) **(c)** (Andes, Ven) (niñera) nanny

naranja *f* (fruta) orange; ~ **amarga** Seville orange

■ *m* (color) orange

■ *adj* (gen inv) orange

naranjada *f* orangeade

naranjal *m* orange grove

naranjo *m* orange tree

narciso *m* **(a)** (Bot) daffodil; (género) narcissus **(b)** (persona) narcissist

narcótico *m* narcotic

narcotraficante *mf* drug-trafficker

narcotráfico *m* drug trafficking

nardo *m* spikenard, nard

nariz *f* **(a)** (Anat) nose; **sonarse la** ~ to blow one's nose; **no te metas los dedos en la** ~ don't pick your nose; **en mis/sus propias narices** (fam) right under my/his nose; **estar hasta las narices de algo/algn** (fam) to be fed up (to the back teeth) with sth/sb (colloq); **meter las narices** *or* **la** ~ **en algo** (fam) to poke one's nose into sth (colloq) **(b)** (de avión) nose

narizota *f* (fam) schnozzle (AmE colloq), conk (BrE colloq)

narración *f* (relato) story; (acción de contar) account

narrador -dora *m,f* narrator

narrar [A1] *vt* (frml) **(a)** «*película/libro*» ⟨*hazañas/experiencias*⟩ to tell of (frml), to relate; ⟨*historia*⟩ to tell, relate **(b)** «*persona*» ⟨*historia*⟩ to tell, narrate (frml)

narrativa *f* (género) fiction; (narración) narrative

narrativo -va *adj* narrative

nasal *adj* nasal

nata *f* **(a)** (sobre leche hervida) skin **(b)** (Esp) ▶ CREMA B

natación *f* swimming

natal *adj* **(a)** ⟨*país*⟩ native (*before n*); ⟨*ciudad*⟩ home (*before n*) **(b)** (Méx) (originario): **es** ~ **de Chiapas** she was born in Chiapas

natalidad *f* birthrate

natillas *fpl* custard

natividad *f* **(a) la** ~ (nacimiento de Cristo) the Nativity **(b) la N**~ (navidad) Christmas

nativo -va *adj* ⟨*tierra/país/lengua*⟩ native **(b)** ⟨*flora/fauna*⟩ native; ~ **DE algo** native TO sth

■ *m,f* (aborigen) native; (hablante) native speaker

nato -ta *adj* ⟨*artista/deportista*⟩ born (*before n*)

natural *adj* ① **(a)** ⟨*fenómeno/ingrediente*⟩ natural; ⟨*fruta*⟩ fresh; **al** ~ ⟨*mejillones*⟩ in brine **(b)** (a temperatura ambiente) ⟨*cerveza/gaseosa*⟩ unchilled **(c)** (Mús) natural ② **(a)** (espontáneo) ⟨*gesto/persona*⟩ natural **(b)** (inherente) natural, innate **(c)** (normal) natural; **me parece lo más** ~ **del mundo** it seems perfectly natural to me ③ (frml) (nativo) **ser** ~ **DE** to be a native OF, to come FROM

■ *m* **(a)** (carácter) nature **(b)** (nativo) native; **los** ~**es del lugar** people from the area

naturaleza *f* **(a)** (Ecol): **la** ~ nature; ~ **muerta** still life **(b)** (índole) nature

naturalidad *f*: su ～ her natural manner; **con la mayor ～ del mundo** as if it were the most natural thing in the world

naturalización *f* naturalization

naturalizarse [A4] *v pron* to become naturalized

naturismo *m* (estilo de vida) natural lifestyle

naturista *adj* ‹médico/tratamiento› natural

naufragar [A3] *vi* (a) «barco» to be wrecked; «persona» to be shipwrecked (b) «plan/negocio» to go under

naufragio *m* (a) (Náut) shipwreck (b) (fracaso) failure

náufrago -ga *adj* shipwrecked
■ *m,f* (Náut) shipwrecked person

náuseas *fpl* nausea, sickness; **sentir** *or* **tener ～** to feel sick *o* nauseous; **me da ～** it makes me sick

náutico -ca *adj* nautical

navaja *f* (de bolsillo) penknife; (para afeitar) razor

navajazo *m* (herida) knife wound

naval *adj* naval

nave *f* ① (Náut) (arc *o* liter) ship; **～ espacial** spacecraft, spaceship ② (de iglesia) nave

navegabilidad *f* (de río) navigability; (de embarcación) seaworthiness

navegable *adj* ‹río› navigable; ‹barco› seaworthy

navegación *f* (acción de navegar) navigation; (tráfico) shipping; **～ aérea** aerial navigation; **～ fluvial** river navigation

navegador *m* (Inf) browser

navegante *mf* (a) (arc) (marino) mariner (arch) (b) (que determina el rumbo) navigator

navegar [A3] *vi* (a) «nave» to sail (b) «persona» (a vela) to sail (c) (determinar el rumbo) to navigate (d) (Inf): **～ en la web** *or* **Red** to surf the Web
■ **～** *vt* (liter) to sail

Navidad *f* Christmas; **el día de ～** Christmas Day; **¡feliz ～!** happy Christmas!; **en ～** at Christmas (time)

navideño -ña *adj* Christmas (*before n*)

navío *m* ship

nazi *adj/mf* Nazi

nazismo *m* Nazism

NE (= nordeste) NE

neblina *f* mist

nebuloso -sa *adj* (a) (Meteo) misty (b) ‹idea/imagen› hazy, nebulous

necedad *f* (a) (cualidad) crassness (b) (dicho, acto): **decir ～es** to talk nonsense; **es una ～** it's sheer stupidity

necesario -ria *adj* (imprescindible) necessary; **haré lo que sea ～** I'll do whatever's necessary; **si es ～** if necessary, if need be; **no es ～** there's no need, it isn't necessary; **me sentía ～** I felt needed

neceser *m* (estuche) toilet kit (AmE), toilet bag (BrE); (maleta pequeña) overnight bag

necesidad *f* ① (a) (urgencia, falta) need; **no hay ～ de que se entere** there's no need for her to know; **en caso de ～** if necessary, if need be (b) (cosa necesaria) necessity, essential (c) (pobreza) poverty, need ② **necesidades** *fpl* (a) (requerimientos) needs (*pl*), requirements (*pl*) (b)

(privaciones) hardship; **pasar ～es** to suffer hardship (c) **hacer sus ～es** (euf) to relieve oneself (euph)

necesitado -da *adj* (a) (falto) **～ DE algo** ‹de dinero› short OF sth; ‹de afecto› in need OF sth (b) (pobre) in need, needy
■ *m,f* needy person; **los ～s** the needy

necesitar [A1] *vt* to need; **❺ se necesita vendedora** saleswoman required; **necesito verte hoy** I need to see you today
■ **～** *vi* (frml) **～ DE algo** to need sth

necio -cia *adj* (a) (tonto) stupid (b) (AmC, Col, Ven fam) (travieso) naughty

néctar *m* nectar

nectarina *f* nectarine

nefasto -ta *adj* ‹consecuencias› disastrous; ‹influencia› harmful; ‹tiempo/fiesta› (fam) awful (colloq)

negación *f* (acción) denial, negation; (antítesis) antithesis; (Ling) negative

negado -da *adj*: **ser ～ para algo** to be useless *o* hopeless at sth

negar [A7] *vt* (a) ‹acusación/rumor› to deny; **no puedo ～lo** I can't deny it; **niega habértelo dicho** she denies having told you (b) (no conceder) ‹permiso/favor› to refuse; **les ～on la entrada** they were refused entry
■ **～** *vi*: **～ con la cabeza** to shake one's head
■ **negarse** *v pron* (rehusar) to refuse; **～se A hacer algo** to refuse to do sth; **se negó a que llamáramos a un médico** he refused to let us call a doctor

negativa *f* (ante acusación) denial; (a propuesta) refusal

negativo¹ -va *adj* negative

negativo² *m* (Fot) negative

negligé /nevli'ʒe/ *m* negligee

negligencia *f* negligence

negociable *adj* negotiable

negociación *f* ① (Pol, Rels Labs) negotiation ② (Méx) (empresa) business

negociado *m* ① (departamento) department ② (AmS fam) (negocio sucio) shady deal (colloq)

negociador -dora *adj* negotiating (*before n*)
■ *m,f* negotiator

negociante *mf* (a) (Com, Fin) (*m*) businessman; (*f*) businesswoman (b) (pey) (mercenario) money-grubber (colloq & pej)

negociar [A1] *vt/vi* to negotiate

negocio *m* (a) (Com) business; **montar** *or* **poner un ～** to set up a business; **dedicarse a los ～s** to be in business; **hablar de ～s** to talk business; **en el mundo de los ～s** in the business world (b) (transacción) deal; **un buen ～** a good deal (c) (CS) (tienda) store (AmE), shop (BrE) (d) (fam) (asunto) business (colloq)

negra *f* (a) (Mús) crotchet (b) (en ajedrez): **las ～s** the black pieces

negrita *f* boldface, bold type; **en ～(s)** in boldface, in bold (type)

negro¹ -gra *adj* (a) ‹pelo/hombre/raza› black; ‹ojos› dark (b) (fam) (por el sol) tanned (c) (sombrío) black, gloomy; **lo ve todo tan ～** she's always so pessimistic; **pasarlas negras** (fam) to have a rough time of it (colloq)
■ *m,f* (persona de raza negra) black person

negro² *m* (color) black

negrura *f* blackness

nene -na *m,f* (Esp, RPl fam) **(a)** (niño pequeño) (*m*) little boy; (*f*) little girl; **los** ~**s** the kids (colloq) **(b)** (apelativo cariñoso) darling, honey **(c) nena** *f* (arg) (mujer) chick (AmE colloq), bird (BrE colloq)

nené *mf* (Ven fam) (*m*) little boy; (*f*) little girl

neocelandés -desa *adj* of/from New Zealand
■ *m,f* New Zealander

neologismo *m* neologism

neonazi *adj/mf* neonazi

neoyorquino -na *adj* of/from New York
■ *m,f* New Yorker

nepotismo *m* nepotism

Neptuno *m* Neptune

nervio *m* ⒈ **(a)** (Anat) nerve **(b)** (en la carne) sinew; **carne con** ~**s** gristly meat ⒉ **nervios** *mpl* nerves (*pl*); **tiene los** ~**s destrozados** his nerves are in shreds; **está enfermo de los** ~**s** he suffers with his nerves; **tengo unos** ~**s** ... I'm *o* I feel so nervous; **me muero de** ~**s** I'm a nervous wreck (colloq); **ponerle a algn los** ~**s de punta** to get on sb's nerves

nerviosismo *m* nervousness; **el** ~ **que producen los exámenes** the feeling of nervousness *o* nerves that exams produce

nervioso -sa *adj* ⒈ ⟨*persona/animal*⟩ **(a)** [SER] (excitable) nervous **(b)** [ESTAR] (preocupado, tenso) nervous; **estoy muy** ~ **por lo de los exámenes** I'm very nervous about the exams **(c)** [ESTAR] (agitado) agitated; **últimamente se le nota** ~ he's been on edge *o* (colloq) uptight lately; **ese ruido me pone muy nerviosa** that noise is getting on my nerves; **me pongo** ~ **cada vez que la veo** I get flustered every time I see her ⒉ ⟨*trastorno*⟩ nervous; ⟨*célula*⟩ nerve (*before n*)

nervudo -da *adj* sinewy

neto -ta *adj* **(a)** ⟨*sueldo/precio*⟩ net **(b)** (claro) ⟨*silueta/perfil*⟩ distinct, clear

neumático *m* tire (AmE), tyre (BrE)

neumonía *f* pneumonia

neura *adj* (fam): **eso me pone** ~ that drives me crazy *o* (BrE) mad (colloq); **es tan** ~ he's so neurotic
■ *mf* (fam) ⒈ (persona): **es un** ~ he's a complete neurotic (colloq) ⒉ **neura** *f*: **está con la** ~ she's in a real state (colloq)

neurasténico -ca *adj/m,f* **(a)** (Med) neurasthenic **(b)** (fam) ▶ NEURA

neurólogo -ga *m,f* neurologist

neurosis *f* neurosis

neurótico -ca *adj/m,f* neurotic

neutral *adj* neutral

neutralizar [A4] *vt* to neutralize

neutro¹ -tra *adj* **(a)** (Elec, Fís) neutral **(b)** (Biol, Ling) neuter

neutro² *m* **(a)** (Ling) neuter **(b)** (AmL) (Auto) neutral

nevada *f* snowfall

nevado -da *adj* ⟨*cumbres/picos*⟩ snowcapped, snow-covered; ⟨*campos/techos*⟩ covered with snow

nevar [A5] *v impers* to snow

nevasca *f*, (CS) **nevazón** *f* blizzard, snowstorm

nevera *f* **(a)** (refrigerador) refrigerator, fridge, icebox (AmE); ~ **congelador** fridge-freezer **(b)** (para picnic) cooler (AmE), cool bag/box (BrE)

nevoso -sa *adj* snowy

nexo *m* (enlace, vínculo) link

ni *conj* **(a)** (con otro negativo): **no vino él** ~ **su mujer** neither he nor his wife came; **yo no pienso ir** — ~ **yo (tampoco)** I don't intend going — neither do I; ~ **fumo** ~ **bebo** I don't smoke or drink, I neither smoke nor drink; **no nos avisó** ~ **a él** — **a mí** he didn't tell him or me (either); ~ **siquiera** not even; **¿** ~ **siquiera piensas llamarlo?** aren't you even going to call him?; **no vendieron** ~ **un libro** they didn't sell a single book **(b)** (expresando rechazo, enfado): **¡**~ **hablar!** out of the question!; ~ **aunque me lo ruegue** not even if he gets down on his knees

Nicaragua *f* Nicaragua

nicaragüense *adj/mf* Nicaraguan

nicho *m* (Arquit) niche; (en cementerio) *deep recess in a wall used as a tomb*

nicotina *f* nicotine

nidada *f* (de huevos) clutch; (de crías) clutch, brood

nido *m* nest; **un** ~ **de ladrones** a den of thieves; **un** ~ **de amor** a love nest

niebla *f* fog; **había** ~ it was foggy

niega, niegas, etc ▶ NEGAR

nieto -ta *m,f* (*m*) grandson, grandchild; (*f*) granddaughter, grandchild; **mis** ~**s** my grandchildren

nieva ▶ NEVAR

nieve *f* **(a)** (Meteo) snow **(b)** (Coc): **batir las claras a** ⟨**punto de**⟩ ~ whisk the egg whites until stiff **(c)** (Méx) (helado) sorbet, water ice

nimiedad *f* triviality

nimio -mia *adj* trivial, petty

ningún *adj*: apocopated form of NINGUNO *used before masculine singular nouns*

ningunear [A1] *vt* (Méx fam) to treat ... like dirt (colloq)

ninguno -na *adj* (*see note under* NINGÚN) **(a)** (*delante del n*): **no prestó ninguna atención** he didn't pay any attention; **en ningún momento** never; **no lo encuentro por ningún lado** I can't find it anywhere **(b)** (*detrás del n*): **no hay problema** ~ there's absolutely no problem
■ *pron* **(a)** (refiriéndose a dos personas o cosas) neither; (— a más de dos) none; ~ **de los dos vino** neither of them came; **no trajo** ~ **de los dos** she didn't bring either of them; ~ **de nosotros la conoce** none of us know her **(b)** (nadie) nobody, no-one

niña *f* pupil; *ver tb* NIÑO *m,f*

niñera *f* nanny, nursemaid (AmE)

niñería *f* (pey): **déjate de** ~**s** stop being so childish

niñez *f* childhood

niño -ña *adj* (joven) young; (infantil, inmaduro) immature, childish
■ *m,f* **(a)** (*m*) boy, child; (*f*) girl, child; (bebé) baby; **¿te gustan los** ~**s?** do you like children?; **de** ~ as a child; ~ **bien** rich kid (colloq); ~ **de pecho** small *o* young baby; **el** ~ **mimado de la maestra** the teacher's favorite* *o* pet; ~ **prodigio** ⋯⟶

child prodigy **(b)** (con respecto a los padres) (*m*)
son, child; (*f*) daughter, child; **tengo que llevar al
~ al dentista** I have to take my son to the dentist
nipón -pona *adj/m,f* Japanese
níquel *m* nickel
níspero *m* loquat
nitidez *f* (de imagen, del día) clarity; (de recuerdo)
vividness
nítido -da *adj* ⟨foto/imagen⟩ clear
nitrógeno *m* nitrogen
nivel *m* **(a)** (altura) level **(b)** (en escala, jerarquía)
level; **conversaciones de alto ~** high-level talks;
~ de vida standard of living; **no está al ~ de los
demás** he's not up to the same standard as the
others; **el ~ de las universidades mexicanas** the
standard of Mexican universities
nivelar [A1] *vt* **(a)** (Const) ⟨suelo/terreno⟩ to
level; ⟨estante⟩ to get … level **(b)** ⟨presupuesto⟩ to
balance
no *adv* **(a)** (como respuesta) no; (modificando
adverbios, oraciones, verbos) not [*la negación de la
mayoría de los verbos ingleses requiere el uso del
auxiliar 'do'*] **¿te gustó? — no** did you like it? —
no, I didn't; **¿vienes o ~?** are you coming or
not?; **~ te preocupes** don't worry; **¿por qué ~
quieres ir? — porque ~** why don't you want to
go? — I just don't **(b)** (con otro negativo): **~ veo
nada** I can't see a thing *o* anything; **~ viene
nunca** she never comes **(c)** (en coletillas
interrogativas): **está mejor ¿~?** she's better, isn't
she?; **ha dimitido ¿~?** he has resigned, hasn't he?
(d) (expresando incredulidad): **se ganó la lotería —
¡no!** he won the lottery — he didn't! *o* no! **(e)**
(sustituyendo a una cláusula): **creo que ~** I don't
think so; **¿te gustó? a mí ~** did you like it? I
didn't **(f)** (delante de *n*, *adj*, *pp*): **los ~ fumadores**
nonsmokers; **la ~ violencia** non-violence; **un hijo
~ deseado** an unwanted child
■ *m* (*pl* **noes**) no
NO (= **noroeste**) NW
Nobel *m* **(a)** *tb* **Premio ~** Nobel Prize **(b)**
(ganador) Nobel prizewinner
noble *adj* **(a)** (en general) noble; **un caballero de
~ linaje** (liter) a knight of noble lineage (liter) **(b)**
⟨madera⟩ fine
■ *mf* (*m*) nobleman; (*f*) noblewoman; **los ~** the
nobles, the nobility
nobleza *f* nobility
nocaut *adj* (AmL): **lo dejó ~** he/it knocked him
out; **está ~** he's out for the count
■ *m* (*pl* **-cauts**) (AmL) knockout
noche *f* **(a)** night; **la ~ anterior** the night
before, the previous evening; **esta ~** tonight, this
evening; **¡buenas ~s!** (al saludar) good evening!; (al
despedirse) goodnight **(b)** (en locs) **de noche**
⟨trabajar/conducir⟩ at night; ⟨vestido/función⟩
evening (before *n*); **hacerse de ~** to get dark; **en
la** *or* (esp Esp) **por la** *or* (RPl) **a la noche: en la ~
fuimos al teatro** in the evening we went to the
theater; **el lunes en la ~** on Monday evening/
night; **de la ~ a la mañana** overnight
Nochebuena *f* Christmas Eve

Nochevieja *f* New Year's Eve (*in the evening*)
noción *f* **(a)** (idea, concepto) notion, idea; **no
tiene la menor ~ del tema** he doesn't know the
first thing about the subject **(b) nociones** *fpl*
(conocimientos): **tengo nociones de ruso** I have a
smattering of Russian; **las nociones de
electrónica** the basics *o* rudiments of electronics
nocivo -va *adj* ⟨sustancia⟩ harmful;
⟨influencia⟩ damaging
noctámbulo -la *adj*: **siempre ha sido ~** he's
always been a night bird *o* (AmE) nighthawk
(colloq)
nocturno -na *adj* **(a)** ⟨vuelo/tren/vida⟩ night
(before *n*); ⟨clases⟩ evening (before *n*) **(b)**
⟨animal/planta⟩ nocturnal
nodriza *f* (ama de cría) wet nurse; (niñera) (ant)
nursemaid
nogal *m* (árbol) walnut tree; (madera) walnut
nómada *adj* nomadic
■ *mf* nomad
nomás *adv* **(a)** (AmL): **pase ~** come on in; **no lo
vas a convencer así ~** you're not going to
convince him as easily as that; **déjelo aquí ~** just
leave it here; **lo dijo por molestar ~** she only said
it to be difficult **(b) nomás (que)** (Col, Méx fam) as
soon as; **~ (que) tenga dinero** as soon as I have
some money
nombramiento *m* (designación) appointment;
(documento) letter of appointment
nombrar [A1] *vt* **(a)** (citar, mencionar) to mention;
no lo volvió a ~ she never mentioned his name *o*
him again **(b)** (designar) to appoint
nombre *m* **(a)** (de cosa, persona, animal) name; **~
y apellidos** full name, name in full; **~ artístico**
stage name; **~ de pila** first name, christian
name; **~ de soltera** maiden name; **¿qué ~ le
pusieron?** what did they call him?; **lo conozco de
~** I know him by name; **en ~ de** (en representación
de) on behalf of; (apelando a) in the name of; **a ~
de** ⟨paquete/carta⟩ made payable to, made out to;
lo que ha hecho no tiene ~ what she has done is
unspeakable **(b)** (Ling) noun; **~ compuesto**
compound noun **(c)** (fama): **un científico de ~** a
renowned scientist; **hacerse un ~ en la vida** to
make a name for oneself
nómina *f* (lista de empleados) payroll; (hoja de
pago) payslip; (suma de dinero) salary, wages (*pl*)
nominación *f* nomination
nominar [A1] *vt* to nominate
nominativo *adj* (Fin): **un cheque ~ a favor de
…** a check made out to *o* payable to …
nomo *m* gnome
non *adj* odd
■ *m* odd number; **pares y ~es** odds and evens
noqueada *f* knockout
noquear [A1] *vt* to knock out
noratlántico -ca *adj* north-Atlantic (before
n)
nordeste, noreste *adj inv* ⟨región⟩
northeastern; **iban en dirección ~** they were
heading northeast

■ *m* (punto cardinal) northeast, Northeast; **vientos del ~** northeasterly winds

nórdico -ca *adj ⟨país/pueblo⟩* Nordic (*esp Scandinavian*)

noria *f* (a) (para sacar agua) waterwheel (b) (Ocio) Ferris wheel (AmE), big wheel (BrE)

norma *f* (a) (regla) rule, regulation; **~s de conducta** rules of conduct; **~s de seguridad** safety regulations; **tengo por ~ ...** I make it a rule ... (b) (manera común de hacer algo): **la ~ es que acudan los directivos** it is standard practice for the directors to attend

normal *adj* normal; **es ~ que reaccionen así** it's normal for them to react like that; **hoy en día es muy ~** it's very common nowadays; **no es ~ que haga tanto frío** it's unusual *o* it isn't normal for it to be so cold; **superior a lo ~** above-average; **~ y corriente** ordinary
■ *f* (a) (escuela): **la N ~** teacher training college (b) (gasolina) regular gas (AmE), two-star petrol (BrE)

normalidad *f* (a) (cualidad): **con ~** normally (b) (situación) normality, normalcy (AmE); **el país volvió a la ~** the country returned to normal

normalización *f* (a) (de situación) normalization (b) (estandarización) standardization

normalizar [A4] *vt* (a) *⟨situación/relaciones⟩* to normalize (b) (estandarizar) to standardize
■ **normalizarse** *v pron* (a) *«situación/relaciones»* to return to normal (b) (estandarizarse) to become standardized

normalmente *adv* normally, usually

noroeste *adj inv ⟨región⟩* northwestern; **iban en dirección ~** they were heading northwest
■ *m* (punto cardinal) northwest, Northwest; **vientos del ~** northwesterly winds

norte *adj inv ⟨región⟩* northern; *⟨costa/ala⟩* north (*before n*); **iban en dirección ~** they were heading north *o* northward(s)
■ *m* north, North; **al ~ de Matagalpa** to the north of Matagalpa; **vientos del N~** northerly winds; **caminaron hacia el N~** they walked north *o* northward(s); **la casa da al ~** the house faces north

Norteamérica *f* (América del Norte) North America; (EEUU) America, the States (colloq)

norteamericano -na *adj/m,f* (de América del Norte) North American; (estadounidense) American

norteño -ña, (Chi, Per) **nortino -na** *adj* northern
■ *m,f* northerner

Noruega *f* Norway

noruego¹ -ga *adj/m,f* Norwegian

noruego² *m* (idioma) Norwegian

nos *pron pers* (a) (como complemento directo, indirecto) us; **~ ayudaron mucho** they helped us a lot; **escúchanos** listen to us; **~ han robado el coche** our car's been stolen (b) (*refl*) ourselves; **~ hicimos daño** we hurt ourselves; **sentémonos** let's sit down (c) (*recípr*): **~ conocemos desde hace años** we have known each other for years

nosotros -tras *pron pers pl* (a) we; **¿quién lo trajo? — nosotros** who brought it? — we did; **ábrenos, somos nosotras** open the door, it's us; **~ mismos lo arreglamos** we fixed it ourselves (b) (en comparaciones, con preposiciones) us; **antes/después que ~** before/after us; **ven con ~** come with us

nostalgia *f* nostalgia; **siente ~ por su país** he feels homesick

nostálgico -ca *adj* nostalgic

nota *f* 1 (apunte, mensaje) note; **tomar ~ de algo** (apuntar) to make a note of sth; (fijarse) to take note of sth; **tomar ~s** to take notes; **~ a pie de página** footnote 2 (a) (Educ) (calificación) grade (AmE), mark (BrE); **sacar buenas ~s** to get good grades *o* marks (b) (Mús) note 3 (detalle) touch; **una ~ de humor** a touch of humor

notable *adj ⟨diferencia/mejoría⟩* notable; **una actuación ~** an outstanding performance; **posee una ~ inteligencia** she is remarkably *o* extremely intelligent
■ *m* (a) (Educ) *grade between 7 and 8.5 on a scale from 1 to 10* (b) (persona importante) dignitary

notar [A1] *vt* (a) (advertir) to notice; **no noté nada extraño** I didn't notice anything strange; **hacer(le) ~ algo (a algn)** to point sth out (to sb); **te noto muy triste** you look very sad; **se le notaba indeciso** he seemed hesitant (b) (*impers*): **se nota que es novato** you can tell *o* see he's a beginner; **se te nota en la cara** it's written all over your face
■ **notarse** *v pron* (+ *compl*) to feel; **me noto rara con este vestido** I feel funny in this dress

notaría *f* (a) (profesión) profession of notary; (oficina) notary's office (b) (Col) (registro civil) registry office

notarial *adj* notarial

notario -ria *m,f* notary, notary public

noticia *f* (información): **una ~** a piece *o* an item of news; **buenas/malas ~s** good/bad news; **la última ~ del programa** the final item on the news; **una ~ de última hora** a late *o* last-minute news item 2 **noticias** *fpl* (a) (referencias) news; **no hemos tenido ~s suyas** (provenientes de él) we haven't heard from him; (provenientes de otra persona) we haven't had (any) news of him (b) (Rad, TV) news

noticiario *m*, (AmL) **noticiero** *m* (Rad, TV) news; (Cin) newsreel

notificación *f* (frml) notification (frml)

notificar [A2] *vt* (frml) to notify

notorio -ria *adj* (a) (evidente) evident, obvious (b) (conocido) well-known (c) (notable) *⟨descenso/mejora⟩* marked

nov. (= **noviembre**) Nov

novato -ta *adj* inexperienced, new
■ *m,f* novice, beginner

novecientos -tas *adj/pron* nine hundred; *para ejemplos ver* QUINIENTOS

novedad *f* 1 (a) (innovación) innovation; **la última ~ en el campo de la informática** the latest innovation in the field of computing (b) (cualidad, cosa nueva) novelty; **eran una ~ en aquel entonces** they were a novelty then 2 (noticia): **¿alguna ~?** any news?; **eso no es ninguna ~** everybody knows that; **sin ~** *⟨llegar⟩* safely; **¿cómo sigue? — sin ~** how is he? — much the same

novedoso -sa *adj ⟨idea/enfoque⟩* novel, original

novela *f* (Lit) novel; (TV) soap opera; **~ policíaca** detective novel *o* story; **~ rosa** (pey) novelette (pej), romantic novel

novelesco -ca *adj* ⟨*vida/historia*⟩ like something out of a novel; ⟨*viajes/andanzas*⟩ fabulous

novelista *mf* novelist

noveno¹ -na *adj/pron* ninth; **la novena parte** a ninth; *para ejemplos ver* QUINTO

noveno² *m* ninth

noventa *adj inv/pron/m* ninety; *para ejemplos ver* CINCUENTA

noviar [A1] *vi* (AmL fam) to go out together, to date (AmE); ~ **CON algn** to go out WITH sb, to date sb (AmE)

noviazgo *m*: **el** ~ **duró un año** they went out (together) for one year; **~s a larga distancia** long-distance relationships

novicio -cia *m,f* novice

noviembre *m* November; *para ejemplos ver* ENERO

novillo -lla *m,f* (*m*) young bull; (*f*) heifer; **hacer ~s** (fam) to play hooky (esp AmE colloq), to skive off (school) (BrE colloq)

novio -via *m,f* **(a)** (no formal) (*m*) boyfriend; (*f*) girlfriend; (después del compromiso) (*m*) fiancé; (*f*) fiancée **(b)** (el día de la boda) (*m*) groom; (*f*) bride; **los ~s** the bride and groom

nubarrón *m* storm cloud

nube *f* (Meteo) cloud; (de polvo, humo) cloud; (de insectos) cloud, swarm; **un cielo cubierto de ~s** an overcast *o* a cloudy sky; ~ **atómica** mushroom cloud; **estar** *or* **andar en las ~s** (fam) to have one's head in the clouds

nublado -da *adj* ⟨*cielo/día*⟩ cloudy, overcast

nublar [A1] *vt* **(a)** ⟨*vista*⟩ to cloud **(b)** (liter) ⟨*felicidad*⟩ to cloud (liter)

■ **nublarse** *v pron* **(a)** «*cielo*» to cloud over **(b)** «*vista*» to cloud over

nubosidad *f*: **la** ~ **irá en aumento** it will become increasingly cloudy; **un día con mucha** ~ a day with a lot of cloud about

nuboso -sa *adj* cloudy

nuca *f* back *o* nape of the neck

nuclear *adj* nuclear

núcleo *m* **(a)** (Biol, Fís) nucleus **(b)** (Elec) core

nudillo *m* knuckle

nudismo *m* nudism

nudista *adj/mf* nudist

nudo *m* **(a)** (en general) knot; **se hizo un** ~ **en el hilo** the thread got into a knot; **¿me haces el** ~ **de la corbata?** can you do my tie for me?; **tenía un** ~ **en la garganta** I had a lump in my throat **(b)** (de carreteras, vías férreas) junction

nuera *f* daughter-in-law

nuestro -tra *adj* our; ~ **coche** our car; **un amigo** ~ a friend of ours

■ *pron*: **el** ~, **la nuestra** *etc* ours; **es de los ~s** he's one of us; **nosotros a lo** ~ let's just get on with our own business; **sabe lo** ~ he knows about us

Nueva York *f* New York

Nueva Zelandia, Nueva Zelanda *f* New Zealand

nueve *adj inv/pron/m* nine; *para ejemplos ver* CINCO

nuevo -va *adj* **(a)** [SER] ⟨*estilo/coche/novio*⟩ new; **soy** ~ **en la oficina** I'm new in the office; **de** ~ again; **¿qué hay de** ~? what's new? (colloq); ~ **rico** nouveau riche **(b)** (delante del *n*) ⟨*intento/cambio*⟩ further; **ha surgido un** ~ **problema** another *o* a further problem has arisen; **N~ Testamento** New Testament **(c)** [ESTAR] (no desgastado) as good as new

Nuevo México *m* New Mexico

nuez *f* ① **(a)** (del nogal) walnut **(b)** (Méx) (pacana) pecan (nut) **(c)** ~ **moscada** nutmeg ② (Anat) Adam's apple

nulidad *f* ① **(a)** (Der) nullity ② (fam) (calamidad) dead loss (colloq); **soy una** ~ **para los idiomas** I'm useless at languages

nulo -la *adj* **(a)** (Der) ⟨*testamento/votación*⟩ null and void; ⟨*voto*⟩ void **(b)** ⟨*persona*⟩ useless (colloq), hopeless (colloq) **(c)** (inexistente): **mis conocimientos del tema son ~s** my knowledge of the subject is virtually nil

Núm., núm. (= **número**) no.

numerable *adj* countable

numeración *f* (acción) numbering; (números) numbers (*pl*); (sistema) numerals (*pl*)

numeral *adj/m* numeral

numerar [A1] *vt* to number

número *m* ① **(a)** (Mat) number; ~ **de identificación personal** PIN number, Personal Identification Number; ~ **de matrícula** license number (AmE), registration number (BrE); ~ **de serie** serial number; ~ **de teléfono/fax** phone/fax number; **una suma de seis ~s** a six figure sum; **problemas sin** ~ innumerable *o* countless problems **(b)** (de zapatos) size; **¿qué** ~ **calzas?** what size shoe do you take? **(c)** (billete de lotería) lottery ticket ② (Espec) **(a)** (Espec) act **(b)** (de publicación) issue

numeroso -sa *adj* ⟨*clase/grupo*⟩ large; ⟨*ocasiones/ejemplos*⟩ numerous, many

nunca *adv* never; **como** ~ like never before; **casi** ~ hardly ever; **más que** ~ more than ever (before); ~ **más** never again

nuncio *m* (Relig) *tb* ~ **apostólico** papal nuncio

nupcial *adj* ⟨*festejos*⟩ (liter) nuptial (liter); ⟨*ceremonia*⟩ wedding (before *n*)

nupcias *fpl* (liter) nuptials (*pl*) (liter), wedding; **en 1970 se casó en segundas** ~ **con doña Inés Díaz** in 1970 he married his second wife, Inés Díaz

nutria *f* otter

nutrición *f* nutrition

nutrido -da *adj*: **mal** ~ undernourished, malnourished; **bien** ~ well-nourished

nutrir [I1] *vt* ⟨*organismo*⟩ to nourish; ⟨*niño/planta*⟩ to nourish, feed

nutritivo -va *adj* ⟨*alimento*⟩ nutritious; ⟨*valor*⟩ nutritional

nylon /'najlon, ni'lon/ *m* nylon

Ññ

Ñ, ñ f (read as /'eɲe/) the letter Ñ, ñ

ñandú m rhea

ñandutí m nanduti (fine Paraguayan lace)

ñango -ga adj (Méx fam) wimpish (colloq)

ñapa f (AmL fam) small amount of extra goods given free, lagniappe (AmE); **dar algo de ~** to throw sth in (for free) (colloq); **me dio dos de ~** she threw in a couple extra

ñato -ta adj (AmS fam) ⟨persona⟩ snub-nosed; ⟨animal⟩ pug-nosed

ñauca (Chi), (RPl) **ñaupa** f (fam): **es del año de ~** it's really ancient (colloq); **ropa del año de ~** clothes that went out with the ark (colloq)

ñoquis mpl (Coc) gnocchi (pl)

ñorbo m (Ec, Per) passionflower

ñu m gnu, wildebeest

Oo

O, o f (read as /o/) the letter O, o

o conj or; **¿vienes o no?** are you coming or not?; **o … o …** either … or …; **o mañana o el jueves** either tomorrow or Thursday; [between two digits o is written with an accent: **unas 100 ó 120** about 100 or 120]; **o sea ▶** SER vi II

O. (= **oeste**) W, West

oasis m (pl ~) oasis

obcecarse [A2] v pron to become obsessed; **está obcecado con la idea** he's obsessed with the idea

obedecer [E3] vt (a) ⟨orden/norma⟩ to obey, comply with (b) ⟨persona⟩ to obey; **obedece a tu madre** do as your mother tells you
■ **~** vi (a) «persona» to obey; **para que aprendas a ~** to teach you to do as you're told (b) «mecanismo» to respond (c) (frml) (a motivo, causa) **~ A algo** to be due TO sth

obediente adj obedient

obelisco m obelisk

obertura f overture

obesidad f obesity

obeso -sa adj obese

obispo m bishop

objeción f objection; **nadie puso objeciones** nobody objected o made any objection; **~ de conciencia** conscientious objection

objetar [A1] vt to object; **¿tienes algo que ~?** do you have any objection?
■ **~** vi (Esp fam) to declare oneself a conscientious objector

objetividad f objectivity; **con ~** objectively

objetivo¹ -va adj objective

objetivo² ** m **1 (finalidad) objective, aim; (Mil) objective **2** (Fot, Ópt) lens

objeto m **1** (cosa) object; **~s de valor** valuables; **~s de uso personal** items o articles for personal use; **~s perdidos** lost and found (AmE), lost property (BrE); **~ volador no identificado** unidentified flying object, UFO **2** (a) (finalidad) aim, object; **con el ~ de hacer** algo in order to do sth, with the aim of doing sth; **con el ~ de que se conozcan** so that they can get to know each other; **ser ~ de algo** (de admiración/críticas) to be the object of sth; (de investigación/estudio) to be the subject of sth; **ser ~ de malos tratos** to be ill-treated (b) (Ling) object

objetor -tora m,f objector; **~ de conciencia** conscientious objector

oblicuo -cua adj ⟨línea⟩ oblique

obligación f (deber) obligation; **cumplió con sus obligaciones** he fulfilled his obligations; **tiene (la) ~ de …** it is his duty to …, he has an obligation to …; **es mi ~ decírtelo** it is my duty to tell you; **lo hace por ~** she does it out of obligation; **si sus obligaciones se lo permiten** if her commitments permit

obligado -da adj [ESTAR] ⟨persona⟩ obliged; **~ A hacer algo** obliged to do sth; **se vio ~ a acompañarla** he felt obliged to accompany her

obligar [A3] vt (a) **~ a algn A hacer algo** to force sb to do sth, to make sb do sth; **no lo obligues a comer** don't force him to eat; **nos obligan a llevar uniforme** we are required to wear uniform; **~ a algn A QUE haga algo** to make sb do sth (b) «ley/disposición» to bind

obligatorio -ria adj compulsory, obligatory; **no es ~ firmarlo** it doesn't have to be signed

oboe m (instrumento) oboe
■ mf (músico) oboist

obra f **1** (creación artística) work; **sus primeras ~s** her earliest works; **una ~ de artesanía** a piece of craftsmanship; **sus ~s de teatro** her plays; **~ de arte** work of art; **~ maestra** masterpiece **2** (acción): **mi buena ~ del día** my good deed for the day; **~ benéfica** (acto) act of charity; (organización) charity, charitable organization **3** (Arquit, Const) (a) (construcción) building work; **estamos de ~s** we're having some building work done (b) (sitio) building o construction site

obrar [A1] vi (actuar) to act; **~ de buena fe** to act in good faith ⋯⟶

■ ~ *vt* ‹*milagros*› to work

obrera *f* (hormiga) worker (ant); (abeja) worker (bee); *ver tb* OBRERO *m, f*

obrero -ra *adj* ‹*barrio*› working-class; **el movimiento** ~ the workers' movement; **la clase obrera** the working class
■ *m,f* (de fábrica, industria) worker; **los ~s dejaron la arena en el jardín** the workmen left the sand in the garden

obsceno -na *adj* obscene

obscuro, etc ► OSCURO, ETC

obsequio *m* (frml) gift

observación *f* **1** (examen, vigilancia) observation; **tener a algn en** ~ (Med) to keep sb under observation; **tener mucha capacidad de** ~ to be very observant **2** (comentario) observation, remark; (en texto) note

observador -dora *m,f* observer

observar [A1] *vt* **(a)** (en general) to observe; **alguien la observaba** someone was watching *o* (frml) observing her **(b)** (notar) to observe (frml); **¿has observado algún cambio?** have you noticed *o* observed any changes?

observatorio *m* observatory

obsesión *f* obsession

obsesionar [A1] *vt* to obsess; **estaba obsesionado con la idea** he was obsessed with the idea
■ **obsesionarse** *v pron* to become obsessed

obsesivo -va *adj* obsessive

obsidiana *f* obsidian

obsoleto -ta *adj* obsolete

obstaculizar [A4] *vt* ‹*progreso/trabajo*› to hinder, hamper; ‹*tráfico*› to hold up; **no obstaculice el paso** don't stand in the way

obstáculo *m* obstacle

obstante: **no obstante** (sin embargo) nevertheless, nonetheless; (a pesar de) despite, in spite of

obstinado -da *adj* **(a)** (tozudo) obstinate, stubborn **(b)** (tenaz) tenacious, dogged

obstinarse [A1] *v pron* ~ **EN hacer algo** to (obstinately) insist ON doing sth; **se obstinó en no ir** he obstinately refused to go; **se ha obstinado en que hay que terminarlo hoy** he is bent on finishing it today

obstrucción *f* obstruction

obstruir [I20] *vt* **1** (bloquear) ‹*conducto*› to block; ‹*salida*› to block, obstruct **2** (entorpecer) ‹*plan/proceso*› to obstruct; ‹*tráfico*› to obstruct, hold up; ‹*progreso*› to impede **3** (Dep) to obstruct
■ **obstruirse** *v pron* to get blocked (up)

obtener [E27] *vt* ‹*premio*› to win, receive; ‹*resultado/autorización*› to obtain; ‹*calificación*› to obtain, set

obturador *m* (Fot) shutter

obtuve, obtuvo, etc ► OBTENER

obvio -via *adj* obvious

oca *f* (Zool) goose

ocasión *f* **1 (a)** (vez, circunstancia) occasion; **con** ~ **de** on the occasion of; **en alguna** ~ occasionally **(b)** (momento oportuno) opportunity; **no tuve** ~ **de hablarle** I didn't have an opportunity *o* a chance to talk to him **2** (ganga) bargain; **de** ~ ‹*precios*› bargain (*before n*); ‹*muebles*› (usados) secondhand; (baratos) cut-rate *o* (BrE) cut-price; ‹*coches*› secondhand

ocasional *adj* ‹*encuentro*› chance (*before n*); ‹*trabajo*› temporary

ocasionar [A1] *vt* to cause

occidental *adj* ‹*zona*› western; ‹*cultura/países*› Western; **África O**~ West Africa
■ *mf* westerner

occidentalizarse [A4] *v pron* to become westernized

occidente *m* west

Oceanía *f* Oceania

océano *m* ocean

ochenta *adj inv/pron/m* eighty; *para ejemplos ver* CINCUENTA

ocho *adj inv/pron/m* eight; *para ejemplos ver* CINCO

ochocientos -tas *adj/pron* eight hundred; *para ejemplos ver* QUINIENTOS

ocio *m* **(a)** (tiempo libre) spare time, leisure time **(b)** (inactividad, holgazanería) inactivity, idleness

ociosidad *f* inactivity, idleness

ocioso -sa *adj* (inactivo) idle

ocre *m* : **(de) color** ~ ocher-colored*

oct. (= octubre) Oct

octavilla *f* pamphlet

octavo¹ -va *adj/pron* eighth; **la octava parte** an eighth; *para ejemplos ver* QUINTO

octavo² *m* eighth; ~**s de final** *round before the quarter-finals*

octubre *m* October; *para ejemplos ver* ENERO

oculista *mf* ophthalmologist

ocultar [A1] *vt* (en general) to conceal, hide; ‹*persona*› to hide; ~**le algo A algn** to conceal *o* hide sth FROM sb
■ **ocultarse** *v pron* **(a)** «*persona*» to hide **(b)** (estar oculto) to hide, lie hidden **(c)** «*sol*» to disappear

ocultismo *m* occult, occultism

oculto -ta *adj* **(a)** [ESTAR] (escondido) hidden **(b)** [SER] (misterioso) ‹*razón/designio*› mysterious, secret

ocupación *f* (empleo) occupation; (actividad) activity

ocupado -da *adj* **(a)** (atareado) busy **(b)** ‹*línea telefónica*› busy, engaged (BrE); **¿este asiento está** ~**?** is this seat taken? **(c)** ‹*territorio*› occupied

ocupante *mf* occupant; ~ **ilegal** squatter

ocupar [A1] *vt* **1** ‹*espacio/tiempo*› to take up; **me ocupó toda la mañana** it took up my whole morning; **¿en qué ocupas tu tiempo libre?** how do you spend your spare time? **2** «*persona*» **(a)** (situarse en) ‹*asiento*› to take; **volvió a** ~ **su asiento** she returned to her seat, she took her seat again; **ocupaban (todo) un lado**

de la sala they took up one (whole) side of the
room **(b)** (estar en) ‹vivienda› to live in, occupy;
‹habitación› to be in; ‹asiento› to be (sitting) in
(c) (en clasificación): ¿qué lugar ocupan en la liga?
what position are they in the division? **(d)**
‹cargo› to hold, occupy (fml); ‹vacante› to fill
3 ‹fábrica/territorio› to occupy
4 (AmC, Chi, Méx) (usar) to use
■ **ocuparse** v pron **1** ~se DE algo/algn ‹de tarea/
trabajo› to take care OF sth; ‹de problema/asunto›
to deal WITH sth; yo me ~é de eso I'll see to that;
~se DE algn ‹de niño/enfermo› to take care OF sb,
to look after sb

ocurrencia f (comentario gracioso) witty o funny
remark, witticism; (idea disparatada) crazy idea

ocurrente adj (gracioso) witty; (ingenioso) clever

ocurrir [I1] vi (en 3ᵃpers) to happen; ocurra lo
que ocurra whatever happens; lo que ocurre es
que ... the trouble is (that) ...; lamento lo
ocurrido I'm sorry about what happened
■ **ocurrirse** v pron (en 3ᵃpers): se me ha
ocurrido una idea I've had an idea; no se les
ocurría nada they couldn't think of anything; di
lo primero que se te ocurra say the first thing
that comes into your head; ¿cómo se te ocurrió
comprarlo? whatever made you buy it?

odiar [A1] vt to hate; odio planchar I hate
ironing

odio m hate, hatred; tenerle ~ a algn to hate sb

odioso -sa adj ‹trabajo/tema› horrible, hateful;
‹persona› horrible, odious

oeste adj inv ‹región› western; conducían en
dirección ~ they were driving west o
westward(s); la costa ~ the west coast
■ m **1 (a)** (parte, sector): el ~ the west; en el ~
de la provincia in the west of the province; al ~
de Oaxaca to the west of Oaxaca **(b)** (punto
cardinal) west, West; vientos del O~ westerly
winds; caminaron hacia el O~ they walked west
o westward(s) **2** el Oeste (de los Estados Unidos)
the West; una película del O~ a Western

ofender [E1] vt to offend
■ **ofenderse** v pron to take offense*

ofensa f (agravio) insult

ofensiva f offensive

ofensivo -va adj offensive

oferta f **1 (a)** (proposición) offer **(b)** (Econ, Fin)
supply **2** (Com) offer; están de or en ~ they are
on special offer

oficial adj official
■ mf (de policía) police officer (above the rank of
sergeant); (Mil) officer

oficialismo m (AmL): representantes del ~
representatives of the ruling o governing party

oficialista adj (AmL) ‹periódico›
pro-government; ‹candidato› fielded by the party
in power

oficina f (despacho) office; en horas de ~ during
office hours; ~ de empleo/turismo
unemployment/tourist office

oficinista mf office worker

oficio m **1** (trabajo) trade; carpintero de ~
carpenter by trade **2** (Der) de ~ court-appointed
(before n) **3** (Relig) service, office

ofimática f office automation

ofrecer [E3] vt **1 (a)** ‹ayuda/cigarrillo/empleo›

---

to offer **(b)** ‹dinero› to offer; (en una subasta) to
bid **(c)** ‹fiesta› to give; ‹recepción› to lay on **(d)**
‹sacrificio/víctima› to offer
2 (a) ‹oportunidad/posibilidad› to give, provide;
‹dificultad› to present **(b)** «persona»
‹resistencia› to put up, offer
■ **ofrecerse** v pron **1** «persona» to offer,
volunteer; ~se A or PARA hacer algo to offer o
volunteer TO do sth
2 (fml) (querer, necesitar) (gen neg o interrog):
¿qué se le ofrece, señora? what would you like,
madam? (fml); si no se le ofrece nada más if
there's nothing else I can do for you

ofrecimiento m offer

ofrenda f offering

ofuscarse [A2] v pron to get worked up

OGM m (= organismo genéticamente
modificado) GMO

ogro m ogre

oídas: de ~ (loc adv) lo conozco de ~ I've
heard of him, I know of him

oído m **(a)** (Anat) ear; me lo susurró al ~ she
whispered it in my ear **(b)** (sentido) hearing; (para
la música, los idiomas) ear; es duro de ~ he's hard
of hearing; aguzar el ~ to prick up one's ears; no
tiene ~ she's tone-deaf, she has no ear for music;
tocar de ~ (Mús) to play by ear

oiga, oigas, etc ▶ OÍR

oír [I28] vt **1** (percibir sonidos) to hear; no oigo
nada I can't hear anything o a thing; se oyeron
pasos I (or you etc) heard footsteps; he oído
hablar de él I've heard of him **2** (escuchar)
‹música/radio› to listen to **3** oír misa to go to
mass **4** oiga/oye (para llamar la atención) excuse
me; ¡oiga! se le cayó la cartera excuse me, you've
dropped your wallet; oye, si ves a Gustavo dile
que me llame listen, if you see Gustavo tell him
to call me
■ ~ vi to hear

ojal m buttonhole

ojalá interj: seguro que apruebas — ¡~! I'm
sure you'll pass — I hope so!; ¡~ que todo salga
bien! let's hope everything works out all right!; ~
fuera rico! if only I were rich!, I wish I was rich!

ojeada f glance; echar una ~ a algo to have a
quick glance o look at sth

ojear [A1] vt to (have a) look at

ojeras fpl rings under the eyes (pl)

ojeriza f grudge; tenerle ~ a algn to have a
grudge against sb

ojeroso -sa adj: estar ~ to have rings under
one's eyes

ojo m **1 (a)** (en general) eye; un niño de ~s
negros a boy with dark eyes; mirar fijamente a
los ~s to stare straight into sb's eyes; no me
quita los ~s de encima he won't take his eyes off
me; a los ~s de la sociedad in the eyes of
society; ~ de la cerradura keyhole; ~ de buey
porthole; ~ de vidrio or (Esp) cristal glass eye; ~
mágico (AmL) spyhole, peephole; ~ morado or
(Méx) moro or (CS fam) en tinta black eye; costar
un ~ de la cara (fam) to cost an arm and a leg
(colloq); cuatro ~s ven más que dos two heads are
better than one; en un abrir y cerrar de ~s in the
twinkling of an eye; ~ por ~ an eye for an eye
(b) (vista): bajó los ~s avergonzada she lowered
her eyes in shame; sin levantar los ~s del libro ⋯➤

without looking up from her book; **a ~** (*de buen cubero*) or (AmS) **al ~** at a guess; **echar un ~ a algo/algn** (fam) to have o take a (quick) look at sth/sb; **tener ~ de lince** or **de águila** to have eyes like a hawk

2 (perspicacia): **¡vaya ~ que tiene!** he's pretty sharp o on the ball; **tener ~ para los negocios** to have a good eye for business

3 (fam) (cuidado, atención): **hay que andar** or **ir con mucho ~** you have to keep your eyes open; **¡~! que viene un coche** watch out! o be careful! there's a car coming

ojota *f* (CS) (para playa, piscina) thong (AmE), flip-flop (BrE); (calzado rústico) sandal

okey *interj* (esp AmL) OK!, okay!

okupa *mf* (Esp fam) squatter

ola *f* wave; **~ de calor** heat wave; **~ de frío** cold spell

olán *m* (Méx) flounce, frill

olé, ole *interj* olé!, bravo!

oleada *f* wave

oleaje *m* swell

óleo *m* (sustancia) oil; (cuadro) oil painting; **pintura al ~** oil painting

oleoducto *m* (oil) pipeline

oler [E12] *vi* **1** (percibir olores) **~ A algo** to smell sth; **¿no hueles a humo?** can't you smell smoke? **2** (despedir olores) «*comida/perfume*» to smell; **¡qué bien/mal huele!** it smells good/awful!; **le huelen los pies** his feet smell; **~ A algo** ‹*a rosas/ajo*› to smell o*F* sth **3** (fam) (expresando sospecha) (+ *me/te/le etc*): **esto me huele mal** it sounds fishy to me; **me huele que fue ella** I have a feeling it was her

■ **~** *vt* «*persona*» to smell; «*animal*» to smell, sniff

■ **olerse** *v pron* (fam) to suspect; **ya me lo olía** I thought so

olfatear [A1] *vt* (a) (oler con insistencia) to sniff (b) ‹*rastro/presa*› to scent, follow

olfato *m* (sentido) smell; (perspicacia, intuición) nose

oligarquía *f* oligarchy

olimpiada, olimpíada *f*: *tb* **~s** Olympic Games (*pl*), Olympics (*pl*)

olímpico -ca *adj* (a) ‹*campeón/récord*› Olympic (*before n*) (b) (AmL fam) ‹*pase/gol*› fantastic (colloq), sensational (colloq)

olisquear [A1] *vt* to sniff

oliva *f* olive

olivar *m* olive grove

olivo *m* olive (tree)

olla *f* pot; **~ a presión** pressure cooker

olmo *m* elm (tree)

olor *m* smell; **tiene un ~ raro** it has a funny smell; **tomarle el ~ a algo** (AmL) to smell sth; **~ A algo** smell o*F* sth

oloroso -sa *adj* (a) ‹*jabón/flor*› scented, fragrant (b) ‹*queso/pies*› smelly

olote *m* (AmC, Méx) cob, corncob

olvidadizo -za *adj* forgetful

olvidar [A1] *vt* **1** ‹*pasado/nombre*› to forget; **había olvidado que ...** I had forgotten that ...; **~ hacer algo** to forget to do sth **2** (dejar en un lugar) to forget, leave ... behind; **olvidó el pasaporte en casa** she left her passport at home

■ **olvidarse** *v pron* **1** (en general) to forget; **~se**

DE algo to forget sth; **~se DE hacer algo** to forget to do sth; (+ *me/te/le etc*) **¡ah! se me olvidaba ah!** I almost forgot; **se me olvidó decírtelo** I forgot to tell you **2** (dejar en un lugar) to forget, leave ... behind

olvido *m* (a) (abandono, indiferencia) obscurity; **caer en el ~** to fall o sink into obscurity o oblivion (b) (descuido) oversight; **fue un ~** it was an oversight, I forgot

ombligo *m* navel, belly button (colloq)

omisión *f* omission

omitir [I1] *vt* ‹*frase/nombre*› to omit, leave out; **omitió mencionar que ...** he omitted o failed to mention that ...

ómnibus *m* (*pl* **~** or **-buses**) (autobús — urbano) (Per, Ur) bus; (— de larga distancia) (Arg) bus, coach (BrE)

omnipotente *adj* omnipotent

omoplato, omóplato *m* shoulder blade, scapula (tech)

once *adj inv/pron/m* eleven; *para ejemplos ver* CINCO

onces *fpl* (Andes) tea

onda *f* (en general) wave; **~ corta/larga** short/long wave; **~ expansiva** blast, shock wave; **longitud de ~** wavelength; **agarrarle la ~ a algo** (AmL fam) to get the hang of sth (colloq); **estar en la ~** (fam) (a la moda) to be trendy (colloq); (al tanto) to be bang up to date (colloq); **¡qué buena/mala ~!** (AmL fam) that's great/terrible! (colloq); **¿qué ~?** (AmL fam) what's up? (colloq)

ondear [A1] *vi* «*bandera*» to fly

ondulado *adj* ‹*pelo*› wavy; ‹*terreno*› undulating, rolling

ondulante *adj* ‹*movimiento*› undulatory; ‹*terreno*› undulating, rolling

ondularse [A1] *v pron* to go wavy

onix *m* onyx

onomatopeya *f* onomatopoeia

onomatopéyico -ca *adj* onomatopoeic

ONU /'onu/ *f* (= **Organización de las Naciones Unidas**): **la ~** the UN, the United Nations

onza *f* **1** (peso) ounce **2** (de chocolate) square

opaco -ca *adj* (no transparente) opaque; (sin brillo) dull

ópalo *m* opal

opción *f* option; **no tenía ~** I had no option o choice; **con ~ a compra** with option to buy

opcional *adj* optional

open *m* open championship o tournament

ópera *f* (obra musical) opera; (edificio) opera house

operación *f* (a) (Mat) operation (b) (Med) operation; **una ~ a corazón abierto** open-heart surgery (c) (Fin) transaction (d) (misión) operation; **~ de rescate** rescue operation

operador -dora *m,f* (a) (Inf, Tec, Telec) operator (b) (Cin, TV) (de cámara) (*m*) cameraman; (*f*) camerawoman; (de proyección) projectionist (Chi, Méx) (obrero) ▶ OPERARIO (d) **~ turístico** tour operator

operar [A1] *vt* **1** (Med) to operate on; **me van a ~ de la vesícula** I'm having a gallbladder operation; **lo ~on de apendicitis** he had his appendix taken out **2** (fml) ⟨*cambio/ transformación*⟩ to produce, bring about **3** (Chi, Méx) ⟨*máquina*⟩ to operate

■ ~ *vi* **(a)** (Med) to operate **(b)** (fml) «*servicio/ vuelo*» to operate

■ **operarse** *v pron* **1** (Med) (*caus*) to have an operation; ~**se del corazón** to have a heart operation **2** (fml) «*cambio/transformación*» to take place

operario -ria *m,f* (fml) operator; **el ~ de la máquina** the machine operator

opinar [A1] *vi* to express an opinion; **prefiero no ~** I would prefer not to comment

■ ~ *vt* **(a)** (pensar) to think; **¿qué opinas del aborto?** what do you think about abortion?; **¿qué opinas de ella?** what do you think of her?; **no opino lo mismo** I do not share that view *o* opinion; **opino que debería renunciar** in my opinion he should resign **(b)** (expresar un juicio): **opinó que deberían aplazarlo** he expressed the view that it should be postponed

opinión *f* opinion; **en mi ~** in my opinion; **cambió de ~** he changed his mind; **la ~ pública** public opinion

opio *m* (Bot, Farm) opium

oponente *mf* opponent

oponer [E22] *vt* ⟨*resistencia*⟩ to offer, put up; ⟨*objeción*⟩ to raise

■ **oponerse** *v pron* (ser contrario) to object; ~**se A algo** to oppose sth; **nuestros caracteres se oponen** (*recípr*) we are opposites

oporto *m* (vino) port

oportunidad *f* **1** (momento oportuno, posibilidad) chance, opportunity; **a la primera ~** at the earliest opportunity; **tuve ~ (la) de conocerla** I got to meet her; **igualdad de ~es** equal opportunities **2** (AmL) (vez, circunstancia) occasion; **en aquella ~** that time *o* on that occasion

oportunismo *m* opportunism

oportunista *mf* opportunist

oportuno -na *adj* **(a)** ⟨*visita/lluvia*⟩ timely, opportune; **llegó en el momento ~** he arrived at just the right moment **(b)** ⟨*medida/respuesta*⟩ appropriate; **sería ~ avisarle** we ought to inform her; **estuvo muy ~** what he said was very much to the point

oposición *f* **1** (en general) opposition **2** (Esp, Ven) (concurso) (public) competitive examination; **hacer oposiciones** to take *o* (BrE) sit a competitive examination

opresión *f* (de un pueblo) oppression; (en el pecho) tightness

opresivo -va *adj* oppressive

oprimido -da *adj* ⟨*pueblo*⟩ oppressed

oprimir [I1] *vt* **(a)** (apretar, presionar) to press **(b)** (tiranizar) to oppress

optar [A1] *vi* **1** (decidirse) ~ **POR algo** to choose sth, opt **FOR** sth; ~ **POR hacer algo** to choose *o* opt to do sth **2** ~ **A algo** ⟨*a plaza/puesto*⟩ to apply **FOR** sth

optativo -va *adj* optional

óptica *f* (Fís, Ópt) optics; (tienda) optician's

óptico -ca *adj* optical

■ *m,f* optician

optimismo *m* optimism

optimista *adj* optimistic

■ *mf* optimist

óptimo -ma *adj* ⟨*posición*⟩ ideal, optimum; **en condiciones óptimas** ⟨*persona*⟩ in peak condition; ⟨*coche*⟩ in perfect condition; ⟨*alimento*⟩ fresh

opuesto -ta *adj* ⟨*versiones/opiniones*⟩ conflicting; ⟨*extremo/polo/lado*⟩ opposite; **tienen caracteres ~s** they have very different personalities; **venía en dirección opuesta** he was coming from the opposite direction

opulento -ta *adj* opulent, affluent

oración *f* **(a)** (Relig) prayer **(b)** (Ling) sentence

orador -dora *m,f* speaker

oral *adj* oral

órale *interj* (Méx fam) (expresando acuerdo) right!, OK!; (para animar) come on!

orangután *m* orangutan

orar [A1] *vi* (fml) (Relig) to pray

oratorio *m* (Relig) oratory, chapel; (Mús) oratorio

órbita *f* **1** (Astron) orbit; **poner en ~** to put into orbit **2** (Anat) (eye) socket, orbit (tech)

orca *f* killer whale

orden¹ *f* **1** (mandato) order; **deja de darme órdenes** stop ordering me about; **hasta nueva ~** until further notice; **estamos a la ~ para lo que necesite** (AmL) just let us know if there's anything we can do for you; **¡a la ~!** (Mil) yes, sir!; (fórmula de cortesía) (Andes, Méx, Ven) you're welcome, not at all; ~ **de arresto** *or* **de busca y captura** arrest warrant; ~ **de registro** *or* (Chi, Méx) **de cateo** search warrant; ~ **judicial** court order **2** (Fin) order; ~ **bancaria** banker's order **3** (Hist, Mil, Relig) order **4** (AmL) (pedido) order

orden² *m* **1** (en general) order; **en** *or* **por ~ alfabético** in alphabetical order; **por ~ de estatura** according to height; **vayamos por ~** let's begin at the beginning; **poner algo en ~** ⟨*habitación/armario/juguetes*⟩ to straighten sth (up) (esp AmE), to tidy sth (up) (esp BrE); ⟨*asuntos/papeles*⟩ to sort sth up; ⟨*fichas*⟩ to put sth in order; **mantener el ~ en la clase** to keep order in the classroom; ~ **del día** agenda; ~ **público** public order; **alterar el ~ público** to cause a breach of the peace **2** **(a)** (fml) (carácter, índole) nature; **problemas de ~ económico** problems of an economic nature **(b)** (cantidad): **del ~ de** (fml) on the order of (AmE), in *o* of the order of (BrE)

ordenado -da *adj* **(a)** [ESTAR] (en orden) tidy **(b)** [SER] ⟨*persona*⟩ (metódico) organized, orderly; (para la limpieza) tidy

ordenador *m* (Esp) ▸ COMPUTADORA

ordenanza *m* (en oficinas) porter; (Mil) orderly, batman (BrE)

ordenar [A1] *vt* **1** ⟨*habitación/armario/ juguetes*⟩ to straighten (up) (esp AmE), to tidy (up) (BrE); ⟨*fichas*⟩ to put in order; **ordené los libros por materias** I arranged the books according to subject **2** **(a)** (dar una orden) to order; **le ordenó salir de la oficina** she ordered him to leave the office **(b)** (AmL) (pedir) ⟨*taxi/bebida/postre*⟩ to order **3** ⟨*sacerdote*⟩ to ordain

■ **ordenarse** *v pron* to be ordained

ordeñar [A1] *vt* to milk

ordinal *m* ordinal (number)

ordinariez *f* **(a)** (falta de refinamiento) vulgarity; ⋯∴

(grosería) rudeness, bad manners (*pl*); (en la manera de hablar) vulgarity, coarseness **(b)** (comentario — poco refinado) vulgar comment; (— grosero) rude comment

ordinario -ria *adj* **1** (poco refinado) vulgar, common (*pej*); (grosero) rude, bad-mannered; (en el hablar) vulgar, coarse **2** (de mala calidad) poor *o* bad quality **3** (no especial) ordinary; **correo ~** regular (AmE) *o* (BrE) normal delivery **4** **de ordinario** usually, normally; **hay menos gente que de ~** there are fewer people than usual *o* normal
■ *m,f* (persona — poco refinada) vulgar *o* (*pej*) common person; (— grosera) rude *o* bad-mannered person

orégano *m* oregano

oreja *f* (Anat) ear; **el perro puso las ~s tiesas** the dog pricked up its ears; **tirarle a algn de las ~s** *or* (AmL) **tirarle las ~s a algn** to pull sb's ears
■ *mf* (Méx *fam*) (soplón — de la policía) stool pigeon (*colloq*), grass (BrE *colloq*); (que escucha a escondidas) eavesdropper

orfanato, (Méx) **orfanatorio** *m* orphanage

orfelinato *m* orphanage

orgánico -ca *adj* organic

organismo *m* (Biol) organism; (Adm, Pol) organization

organización *f* organization

organizado -da *adj* organized

organizador -dora *m,f* organizer

organizar [A4] *vt* to organize, arrange
■ **organizarse** *v pron* to organize oneself

órgano *m* organ

orgasmo *m* orgasm

orgía *f* orgy

orgullo *m* pride; **con ~** proudly

orgulloso -sa *adj* **(a)** [ESTAR] (satisfecho) proud; **~ DE algn/algo** proud OF sb/sth **(b)** [SER] (soberbio) proud

orientación *f* **(a)** (de habitación, edificio) aspect (*frml*); **¿cuál es la ~ de la casa?** which way does the house face?; **la ~ de la antena** the way the antenna (AmE) *o* (BrE) aerial is pointing **(b)** (enfoque, dirección) orientation **(c)** (guía) guidance, direction; (acción de guiar) orientation; **~ profesional** (para estudiantes) vocational guidance, careers advice; (para desempleados) career guidance *o* advice **(d)** (en un lugar) bearings (*pl*)

oriental *adj* (del este) eastern; (del Lejano Oriente) oriental; (uruguayo) (AmL) Uruguayan
■ *mf* (del Lejano Oriente) oriental; (uruguayo) (AmL) Uruguayan

orientar [A1] *vt* **1** **(a)** ⟨reflector/antena⟩ to position; **la casa está orientada al sur** the house faces south (*frml*) **(b)** (Náut) ⟨velas⟩ to trim **2** (encaminar) ⟨esfuerzos/política⟩ to direct **3** ⟨persona⟩ **(a)** ⟨faro/estrellas⟩ to guide **(b)** (aconsejar) to advise; (mostrar el camino): **una mujer nos orientó** a woman told us the way
■ **orientarse** *v pron* (ubicarse) to get one's bearings, orient oneself; **~se por las estrellas** (Náut) to steer by the stars

oriente *m* (punto cardinal) east; (viento) east wind; **O~ Medio/Próximo** Middle/Near East

orificio *m* (*frml*) (de bala) hole; **los ~s de la nariz** the nostrils

origen *m* origin; **en su ~** originally, in the beginning; **dar ~ a algo** to give rise to sth; **país de ~** country of origin; **de ~ humilde** of humble origin(s)

original *adj/m* original

originalidad *f* (cualidad) originality; (comentario) clever remark

originar [A1] *vt* to start, give rise to
■ **originarse** *v pron* «idea/costumbre» to originate; «movimiento» to start, come into being, originate; «incendio/disputa» to start

originario -ria *adj* (de un lugar) native; **ser ~ de algo** «persona» to come from sth; «especie» to be native to sth

orilla *f* **(a)** (del mar, de lago) shore; (de río) bank; **viven a la ~ del mar** they live by the sea; **un paseo a la ~ del mar** a walk along the seashore **(b)** (de mesa, plato) edge **(c)** (dobladillo) hem

orillar [A1] *vt* **1** **(a)** ⟨muro/costa/zona⟩ to skirt (around) **(b)** (Col, Méx, Ven) (hacer a un lado): **orilló el coche** he pulled over **2** (Méx) (obligar) **~ a algn A algo** to drive sb TO sth
■ **orillarse** *v pron* (Col, Méx, Ven) to move over

orina *f* urine

orinal *m* (de dormitorio) chamber pot; (para niños) pot, potty (*colloq*); (para enfermos) bedpan

orinar [A1] *vi* to urinate
■ **~** *vt*: **~ sangre** to pass blood
■ **orinarse** *v pron* to wet oneself; **se orina en la cama** he wets the bed

Orinoco *m*: **el (río) ~** the Orinoco (River)

oriundo -da *adj* ▶ ORIGINARIO

ornamentación *f* ornamentation

oro *adj inv* gold
■ *m* **1** (metal) gold; **~ (de) 18 quilates** 18-carat gold; **bañado en ~** gold-plated; **~ negro** black gold; **ni por todo el ~ del mundo** not for all the tea in China (*colloq*) **2** (en naipes) **(a)** (carta) *any card of the* OROS *suit* **(b)** **oros** *mpl* (palo) *one of the suits in a Spanish pack of cards*

orquesta *f* orchestra; **~ de jazz** jazz band

orquídea *f* orchid

ortiga *f* (stinging) nettle

ortodoxo -xa *adj* orthodox

ortografía *f* spelling, orthography (*frml*)

ortopédico -ca *adj* orthopedic*; ⟨pierna⟩ artificial

oruga *f* (Zool) caterpillar; (Auto) caterpillar *o* crawler track

orzuela *f* (Méx): **tengo ~** I've got split ends

orzuelo *m* sty*

os *pron pers* (Esp) **(a)** (complemento directo, indirecto) you; **~ veo mañana** I'll see you tomorrow; **~ lo prometió** she promised it to you **(b)** (*refl*) yourselves; **no ~ engañéis** don't kid yourselves **(c)** (*recípr*): **creía que ~ conocíais** I thought you knew each other

osar [A1] *vi* (liter) **~ + INF** to dare to + INF; **no osó decirles la verdad** he dared not tell them the truth (liter)

oscar /'oskar/ *m* (*pl* **~** *or* **-cars**) Oscar

oscilación *f* (movimiento) oscillation; (fluctuación) fluctuation

oscilar [A1] *vi* **1** «*péndulo*» to swing, oscillate (tech); «*aguja*» to oscillate; «*torre/ columna*» to sway **2** (fluctuar) «*cotización/ valores*» to fluctuate; **sus edades oscilaban entre** ... their ages ranged between ...

oscuras: **a ~** (*loc adv*) in darkness

oscurecer [E3] *v impers* to get dark
■ **~** *vt* ⟨*habitación/color*⟩ to darken, make ... darker
■ **oscurecerse** *v pron* to get darker

oscuridad *f* (de la noche, de lugar) darkness, dark; **¡qué ~!** it's so dark in here!

oscuro -ra *adj* **1** **(a)** ⟨*calle/habitación*⟩ dark; **a las seis ya está ~** at six it's already dark **(b)** ⟨*color/ojos/pelo*⟩ dark; **vestía de ~** she was wearing dark clothes **2** **(a)** (dudoso) ⟨*intenciones*⟩ dark; ⟨*asunto*⟩ dubious **(b)** (poco claro) ⟨*significado/asunto*⟩ obscure **(c)** (poco conocido) ⟨*escritor/orígenes*⟩ obscure

oso, osa *m,f* bear; **~ de felpa** *or* **peluche** teddy bear; **~ hormiguero** anteater, ant bear (AmE); **~ panda** panda; **~ polar** polar bear

ostensible *adj* obvious, evident

ostentación *f* ostentation

ostentar [A1] *vt* **1** (fml) (tener) ⟨*cargo/título*⟩ to hold **2** (exhibir) ⟨*alhajas/dinero*⟩ to flaunt
■ **~** *vi* to show off

ostentoso -sa *adj* ostentatious

ostión *m* **(a)** (CS) scallop **(b)** (Méx) oyster

ostra *f* oyster; **aburrirse como una ~** (fam) to get bored stiff *o* to death (colloq)

ostracismo *m* ostracism

OTAN /'otan/ *f* (= **Organización del Tratado del Atlántico Norte**) NATO

otitis *f* inflammation of the ear, otitis (tech)

otoñal *adj* ⟨*colores/paisaje*⟩ autumnal, fall (*before n*) (AmE), autumn (*before n*) (BrE)

otoño *m* fall (AmE), autumn (BrE); **en ~** in the fall, in (the) autumn

otorgar [A3] *vt* (fml) ⟨*premio*⟩ to award; ⟨*favor/ préstamo*⟩ to grant; ⟨*poderes*⟩ to bestow (fml), to give

otro, otra *adj* **1** (con carácter adicional) (*sing*) another; (*pl*) other; (con numerales) another;

¿puedo comer ~ trozo? can I have another piece?; **prueba otra vez** try again; **una y otra vez** time and time again; ▶ TANTO[2] *pron* 2
2 (diferente) (*sing*) another; (*pl*) other; **otra manera de hacerlo** another way of doing it; **¿no sabes ninguna otra canción?** don't you know any other songs?; **en ~ sitio** somewhere else; **en ~ momento** some other time
3 (estableciendo un contraste) other; **queda del ~ lado de la calle** it's on the other side of the street
4 (siguiente, contiguo) next; *ver tb* DÍA
■ *pron* **1** (con carácter adicional) (*sing*) another (one); **¿quieres ~?** would you like another (one)?
2 (diferente): **parece otra** she looks like a different person; **no voy a aceptar ningún ~** I won't accept any other; **lo cambié por ~** I changed it for another one; **¿no tiene ~s?** have you any other ones?; **~s piensan que no es así** others feel that this is not so
3 (estableciendo un contraste): **los ~s no están listos** (hablando — de personas) the others aren't ready; (— de cosas) the others *o* the other ones aren't ready
4 (siguiente, contiguo): **la semana que viene no, la otra** not next week, the week after; **uno detrás del ~** one after the other

ovación *f* (fml) ovation

ovalado -da *adj* oval

óvalo *m* oval

ovario *m* ovary

oveja *f* (nombre genérico) sheep; (hembra) ewe; **un rebaño de ~s** a flock of sheep; **la ~ negra** the black sheep; **la ~ descarriada** (Bib) the lost sheep

overol *m* (AmL) (pantalón con peto) overalls (*pl*) (AmE), dungarees (*pl*) (BrE); (con mangas) coveralls (*pl*) (AmE), overalls (*pl*) (BrE)

ovillo *m* ball (*of yarn*); **hacerse un ~** to curl up (in a ball)

ovni, OVNI /'oβni/ *m* (= **objeto volador** *or* **volante no identificado**) UFO

ovulación *f* ovulation

ovular [A1] *vi* to ovulate

óvulo *m* (Biol) ovule; (Farm) pessary

oxidado -da *adj* rusty

oxidarse [A1] *v pron* «*hierro*» to rust, go rusty, oxidize (tech); «*cobre*» to oxidize, form a patina

óxido *m* (herrumbre) rust; (Quím) oxide

oxígeno *m* oxygen

oye, etc ▶ OÍR

oyente *mf* **(a)** (Educ) occasional student, auditor (AmE) **(b)** (Rad) listener

oyera, oyese, etc ▶ OÍR

ozono *m* ozone; **la capa de ~** the ozone layer

P

Pp

P, p *f* (*read as* /pe/) the letter P, p

pabellón *m* **1** **(a)** (en hospital, cuartel) block,

building; (en feria, exposición) pavilion; (de palacio) pavilion; (en jardín) summerhouse **(b)** (de instrumento de viento) bell **2** (fml) (bandera) flag

paceño -ña *adj* of/from La Paz
■ *m,f* person from La Paz

pacer [E3] *vi* to graze

pacha *f* (AmC) baby's bottle

pachanga *f* (esp AmL fam) ▶ JARANA

pachanguero -ra *adj* (esp AmL fam) ▶
JARANERO

pachón -chona *adj* (Méx) ⟨*suéter*⟩ chunky;
⟨*perro*⟩ wooly*

pachucho -cha *adj* [ESTAR] (Esp fam)
⟨*persona*⟩ poorly (colloq); ⟨*fruta*⟩ overripe

pachuco -ca *m,f* (Méx) *young Mexican
influenced by US culture*

paciencia *f* patience; **perder la** ~ to lose
patience; **ten** ~ be patient, have a little patience

paciente *adj* (tolerante) patient
■ *mf* patient

pacificador -dora *adj* peace (*before n*)
■ *m,f* peacemaker

pacificar [A2] *vt* (Mil) to pacify (frml); (calmar) to
pacify, appease; ~ **los ánimos** to calm people
down

pacífico -ca *adj* **(a)** ⟨*manifestación/medios*⟩
peaceful, pacific (frml) **(b)** ⟨*carácter/persona*⟩
peace-loving, peaceable; ⟨*animal*⟩ peaceful

Pacífico *m*: **el** ⟨*océano*⟩ ~ the Pacific (Ocean)

pacifista *adj/mf* pacifist

paco -ca *m,f* (Andes fam) cop (colloq)

pacotilla *f* trash; **de** ~ ⟨*escritor/novela*⟩
second-rate; ⟨*reloj*⟩ cheap, shoddy

pactar [A1] *vt* ⟨*paz/tregua*⟩ to negotiate, agree
terms for; ⟨*plazo/indemnización*⟩ to agree on
■ ~ *vi* to make a pact, negotiate an agreement

pacto *m* pact, agreement; **cumplir/romper un** ~
to abide by the terms of/to break an agreement;
P~ **de Varsovia** Warsaw Pact

padecer [E3] *vt* ⟨*enfermedad/hambre*⟩ to suffer
from; ⟨*desgracias/injusticias/privaciones*⟩ to
suffer, undergo
■ ~ *vi* to suffer; ~ **DE algo** to suffer FROM sth;
padece del corazón he has heart trouble

padrastro *m* **1** (pariente) stepfather **2** (Anat)
hangnail

padre *m* **1** (pariente) father; **mis** ~**s** my
parents; ~ **de familia** father, family man
2 (Relig) (sacerdote) father
■ *adj* **(a)** (fam) (grande) terrible (colloq) **(b)** [ESTAR]
(Méx fam) ⟨*coche/persona*⟩ great (colloq), fantastic

padrenuestro *m* Lord's Prayer

padrino *m*
■ **Nota** En inglés *godfather* no se usa como
apelativo.Nótese también que cuando el plural
padrinos se refiere al padrino y a la madrina se
traduce por *godparents*.

(a) (en bautizo) godfather; (de boda) *man who gives
away the bride, usually her father* **(b)** (en duelo)
second **(c)** (protector) sponsor, patron

padrón *m* **(a)** (Gob, Pol) register; ~ **electoral**
(AmL) electoral roll *o* register **(b)** (Chi) (Auto)
registration documents (*pl*)

paella *f* paella

pág. *f* (= **página**) p.; **760 págs.** 760 pp.

paga *f* **(a)** (acción de pagar) payment **(b)** (sueldo)

pay; ~ **de Navidad** *extra month's salary paid at
Christmas*; ~ **extra** *or* **extraordinaria** *extra
month's salary gen paid twice a year*

paganismo *m* paganism

pagano -na *adj/m,f* pagan; (pey) heathen

pagar [A3] *vt* **(a)** (abonar) ⟨*cuenta/alquiler*⟩ to
pay; ⟨*deuda*⟩ to pay (off), repay; ⟨*comida/
entradas/mercancías*⟩ to pay for; **¿cuánto pagas
de alquiler?** how much rent do you pay?; **le
pagan los estudios** they are paying for his
education; **no puedo** ~ **tanto** I can't afford (to
pay) that much; ~ **algo POR algo** to pay sth FOR
sth **(b)** ⟨*favor/desvelos*⟩ to repay **(c)** (expiar)
⟨*delito/atrevimiento*⟩ to pay for; ~ **algo CON algo**
to pay FOR sth WITH sth; **¡me las vas a** ~**!** you'll
pay for this!
■ ~ *vi* (Com, Fin) to pay; ~**le a algn** to pay sb

pagaré *m* promissory note, IOU

página *f* page; ~**s amarillas** yellow pages; ~
web (Inf) Web page; ~ **inicial** *or* **frontal** *or*
principal (Inf) home page

pago *m* **(a)** (Com, Fin) payment; ~ **adelantado** *or*
anticipado payment in advance; ~ **inicial** down
payment; ~ **al contado/a plazos/en especie**
payment in cash/by installments/in kind **(b)**
(recompensa) reward; **en** ~ **a algo** as a reward for
sth

pagoda *f* pagoda

pai *m* (AmC, Méx) pie

país *m* **(a)** (unidad política) country; ~ **de origen**
(de persona) home country, native land; (de
producto) country of origin; **los P**~**es Bajos** the
Netherlands; **el P**~ **de Gales** Wales; **el P**~ **Vasco**
the Basque Country **(b)** (ciudadanos) nation **(c)** (en
ficción) land

paisaje *m* **(a)** (panorama) landscape, scenery **(b)**
(Art) landscape

paisanaje *m* civilians (*pl*); civil population

paisano -na *m,f* **1** **(a)** (compatriota) (*m*) fellow
countryman, compatriot; (*f*) fellow
countrywoman, compatriot **(b)** (de la misma zona,
ciudad): **es un** ~ **mío** he's from the same area/
place as I am **2** (Indum): **vestir de** ~ «*soldado*»
to wear civilian clothes *o* (colloq) civvies;
«*policía*» to be in/to wear plain clothes;
«*sacerdote*» to be in/to wear secular dress
3 **(a)** (Per) *mountain-dweller of Indian origin* **(b)**
(RPl) peasant

paja *f* **1** **(a)** (Agr, Bot) straw; **sombrero de** ~
straw hat; **techo de** ~ thatched roof **(b)** (para
beber) (drinking) straw **2** **(a)** (fam) (en texto,
discurso) padding, waffle (BrE colloq) **(b)** (Col fam):
hablar *or* **echar** ~ (decir mentiras) to tell lies;
(charlar) to chat, gab (colloq) **3** (AmC) (grifo) faucet
(AmE), tap (BrE)

pajar *m* (granero) barn; (desván) hayloft

pajarita *f* **(a)** *tb* ~ **de papel** origami bird **(b)**
(Esp) (Indum) bow tie

pajarito *m* (cria) baby bird; (pájaro) (fam) little
bird, birdie (colloq)

pájaro *m* **1** (Zool) bird; ~ **carpintero**
woodpecker; **más vale** ~ **en mano que cien** *or*
ciento volando a bird in the hand is worth two in
the bush **2** (fam) (granuja) nasty piece of work
(colloq)

pajarraco *m* (fam) **(a)** (Zool) big, ugly bird **(b)**
(granuja) rogue

paje m **(a)** (Hist) page **(b)** (en boda) page (boy)

pajita, pajilla f (drinking) straw

pajizo -za adj straw-colored*

pajuerano -na m,f (RPl fam) country bumpkin, hick (AmE colloq)

Pakistán m Pakistan

pakistaní adj/mf Pakistani

pala f ⚊**1** (para cavar, de niño) spade; (para mover arena, carbón) shovel; (para recoger la basura) dustpan ⚊**2** (Coc) (para servir — pescado) slotted spatula (AmE), fish slice (BrE); (— tarta) cake slice ⚊**3** (de remo, hélice) blade; (de frontenis) racket; (de ping-pong) paddle, bat (BrE); (en piragüismo) paddle

palabra f ⚊**1** (vocablo) word; **una ~ de seis letras** a six-letter word; **no son más que ~s** it's all talk; **en pocas ~s, es un cobarde** in a word, he's a coward; **~ por ~** word for word; **yo no sabía ni una ~ del asunto** I didn't know a thing o anything about it; **no entendí (ni) una ~** I didn't understand a (single) word; **sin decir (una) ~** without a word; **~ compuesta** compound word; **tener la última ~** to have the final say ⚊**2** (promesa) word; **~ de honor** word of honor*; **una mujer de ~** a woman of her word; **cumplió con su ~** she kept her word; **nunca falta a su ~** he never breaks o goes back on his word ⚊**3** **(a)** (habla) speech; **el don de la ~** the gift of speech; **un acuerdo de ~** a verbal agreement; **no me dirigió la ~** she didn't speak to me; **dejar a algn con la ~ en la boca** to cut sb off in mid-sentence **(b)** (frml) (en ceremonia, asamblea): **pedir la ~** to ask for permission to speak; **tener/ tomar la ~** to have/to take the floor (frml)

palabrería f, **palabrerío** m talk; **no dice más que ~s** he's full of hot air (colloq)

palabrota f (fam) swearword; **decir ~s** to swear

palacio m **(a)** (residencia) palace; **el personal de ~** the Royal Household; **P~ Episcopal** Bishop's Palace; **P~ Real** Royal Palace **(b)** (edificio público) large public building; **P~ de Justicia** lawcourts (pl)

paladar m palate

paladear [A1] vt to savor*

palanca f ⚊**1** (en general) lever; (para forzar, abrir algo) crowbar; **lo levanté haciendo ~** I lifted it using a lever; **~ de cambios** gearshift (AmE), gear lever o stick (BrE); **~ de mando** joystick ⚊**2** (AmL fam) (influencia) influence; (persona influyente) contact

palangana f **(a)** (para fregar) bowl **(b)** (jofaina) washbowl (AmE), washbasin (BrE)

palanquear [A1] vt ⚊**1** (AmL) ▶ APALANCAR ⚊**2** (AmL fam) (usando influencias): **le ~on un puesto** they pulled some strings to get him a job (colloq) ▪ **~** vi (AmL fam) to pull strings

palapa f (Méx) palm shelter

palco m box

palenque m ⚊**1** (RPl) (poste) tethering post ⚊**2** (Méx) **(a)** (fiesta popular) festival (with cockfights, music, etc) **(b)** (para gallos) cockpit

Palestina f Palestine

palestino -na adj/m,f Palestinian

paleta f ⚊**1** **(a)** (de pintor) palette; (de cocina) spatula; (de ventilador) blade; (de albañil) trowel **(b)** (Dep) (de ping-pong) paddle, bat (BrE); (Jueg) (AmL) beach tennis ⚊**2** (fam) (diente) front tooth ⚊**3** (Coc)

shoulder; (Anat, Zool) (Andes) shoulder blade ⚊**4** **(a)** (Andes, Méx) (helado) Popsicle® (AmE), ice lolly (BrE) **(b)** (Méx) (dulce) lollipop

paletilla f **(a)** (Anat, Zool) shoulder blade **(b)** (Coc) shoulder

paleto -ta m,f (Esp fam & pey) country bumpkin, hick (AmE colloq & pej)

paliacate m (Méx) brightly colored* scarf

palidecer [E3] vi «persona» to turn o go pale

palidez f paleness

pálido -da adj «persona/luz/color» pale; **estás ~** you're very pale; **se puso ~** he went pale

paliducho -cha adj (fam) pale, peaky (colloq)

palillo m **(a)** (mondadientes) tb **~ de dientes** toothpick **(b)** (para comida oriental) chopstick; (de tambor) drumstick; (para tejer) (Chi) knitting needle **(c)** (fam) (persona flaca): **es un ~** he's as thin as a rake

palio m **(a)** (dosel) canopy **(b)** (prenda) pallium

paliza f ⚊**1** **(a)** (zurra) hiding, beating; **su padre le dio una buena ~** his father gave him a good hiding; **los matones le pegaron una ~** the thugs beat him up **(b)** (fam) (derrota) thrashing (colloq) ⚊**2** (fam) **(a)** (esfuerzo): **fue una ~ de viaje** the journey was a real killer; **darse la ~** (fam) (trabajando, estudiando) to work one's butt off (AmE colloq), to slog one's guts out (BrE colloq) **(b)** (aburrimiento) drag (colloq)

palizada f (valla) palisade; (terreno) fenced enclosure

pallar m (Per) (Bot, Coc) butter bean

palma f ⚊**1** (de la mano) palm; **conocer algo como la ~ de la mano** to know sth like the back of one's hand ⚊**2** **(a)** (Bot) (planta) palm; (hoja) palm leaf; **~ de coco** (Col) coconut palm **(b)** (gloria, triunfo) distinction ⚊**3** **palmas** fpl: **dar** or **batir ~s** (aplaudir) to clap (one's hands), applaud; **tocar las ~s** (marcando el ritmo) to clap in time

palmada f **(a)** (golpecito amistoso) pat; **le dio una ~ en la espalda** he gave him a pat on the back; **me dio unas palmaditas en la mejilla** he patted me on the cheek **(b)** (para llamar la atención) clap; **dio unas ~s para pedir silencio** he clapped his hands for silence **(c)** (AmL) (golpe, azote) smack, slap

palmado adj **(a)** (AmC fam) (sin dinero) broke (colloq) **(b)** (Arg fam) (cansado) worn out (colloq)

palmatoria f candlestick

palmera f **(a)** (Bot) palm tree **(b)** (Coc) palmier

palmito m (planta) European fan palm; (tallo) palm heart

palmo m span, handspan; **casi un ~** several inches; **conocer algo ~ a ~** to know sth like the back of one's hand

palo m ⚊**1** **(a)** (trozo de madera) stick; (de valla, portería) post; (de herramienta) handle; (de tienda, carpa) tent pole; **~ de escoba** broomstick, broomhandle; **de tal ~, tal astilla** a chip off the old block, like father like son (o like mother like daughter etc) **(b)** (AmC, Col fam) (árbol) tree **(c)** (Dep) (de golf) (golf) club; (de hockey) hockey stick **(d)** (Náut) mast; **~ mayor** mainmast ⚊**2** (madera) wood; **cuchara de ~** wooden spoon ⚊**3** (fam) (golpe) blow (with a stick); **lo molieron a ~s** they beat him till he was black and blue ⚊**4** (en naipes) suit

paloma f (Zool) pigeon; (blanca) dove; (como ···⧉

símbolo) dove; ∼ **de la paz** dove of peace; ∼ **mensajera** carrier pigeon; ∼ **torcaz** or **torcaza** ringdove, wood pigeon (BrE)

palomar m dovecot, pigeon loft

palomilla f [1] (mariposa nocturna) moth; (crisálida) chrysalis [2] (tuerca) wing nut, butterfly nut; (soporte) wall bracket [3] (Méx fam) (pandilla, grupo) gang
■ mf (Andes fam) (muchacho — callejero) street kid (colloq); (— travieso) little monkey (colloq), little devil (colloq)

palomita f [1] (Méx fam) (marca) check (AmE), tick (BrE) [2] **palomitas** fpl: tb ∼**s de maíz** popcorn

palomo m (ave) cock pigeon

palote m [1] (en caligrafía) line, stroke [2] (RPl) (de amasar) rolling pin

palpable adj (claro, evidente) palpable (frml), obvious; (al tacto) palpable, tangible

palpar [A1] vt (Med) to palpate; (tantear) to touch, feel
■ **palparse** v pron ⟨bolsillo⟩ to feel

palpitación f palpitation

palpitar [A1] vi (a) «corazón» to beat (b) «vena/sien» to throb

pálpito m (AmS fam) feeling (colloq); **me dio el** or **tuve un** ∼ I had a feeling o a hunch

palta f (Bol, CS, Per) (Bot, Coc) avocado (pear)

palto m (Bol, CS, Per) avocado tree

paludismo m malaria

palurdo -da m,f (fam) yokel (pej & hum), hick (AmE colloq & pej)

pamela f picture hat

pampa f pampa, pampas (pl); **la** ∼ **argentina** the Argentinian Pampas; **la** ∼ **salitrera** region of nitrate deposits in northern Chile

pampeano -na adj pampas (before n)

pamplinas fpl (fam) (a) (zalamerías) sweet talk (colloq); **no me vengas con** ∼ don't try to sweet-talk me (colloq) (b) (tonterías) nonsense

pan m (Coc) bread; (pieza) loaf; (panecillo) roll; ¿**quieres** ∼? would you like some bread?; **una rebanada de** ∼ a slice of bread; ∼ **blanco/de centeno/integral** white/rye/whole wheat bread; ∼ **de molde** bread/loaf baked gen in a rectangular tin, tin o pan loaf (BrE); ∼ **de Pascua** (Chi) panettone; ∼ **dulce** (con pasas) (RPl) panettone; (bollo) (AmC, Méx) bun, pastry; ∼ **rallado** breadcrumbs (pl); ∼ **tostado** toast; **un** ∼ **tostado** (Chi, Méx) a piece of toast; **ganarse el** ∼ to earn one's daily bread; **ser** ∼ **comido** (fam) to be a piece of cake (colloq)

pana¹ f [1] (tela) corduroy; **pantalones de** ∼ corduroy trousers [2] (Chi) (avería) breakdown

pana² mf (Ven fam) pal (colloq), buddy (AmE colloq), mate (BrE colloq)

panacea f panacea

panadería f (tienda) bakery, baker's (shop); (fábrica) bakery

panadero -ra m,f baker

panal m honeycomb

panamá m panama hat

Panamá m (a) (país) Panama; **el Canal de** ∼ the Panama Canal (b) (capital) tb **ciudad de** ∼ Panama (City)

panameño -ña adj/m,f Panamanian

Panamericana f: **la** ∼ the Pan-American Highway

pancarta f banner, placard

panceta f (a) (Esp) (sin curar) belly pork (b) (RPl) (curada) streaky bacon

pancho¹ -cha adj (tranquilo) calm; **quedarse tan** ∼ (fam): **se lo dije y se quedó tan** ∼ he didn't bat an eyelash o (BrE) eyelid when I told him

pancho² m (RPl) hot dog

pancito m (AmL) (bread) roll

páncreas m (pl ∼) pancreas

panda mf panda
■ f (Esp fam) gang

pandemónium m pandemonium

pandereta f (Mús) tambourine

pandero m [1] (Mús) tambourine [2] (Per) (Fin) cooperative savings scheme

pandilla f (fam) gang

panecillo m (Esp) bread roll

panecito m (AmL) bread roll

panel m [1] (a) (de puerta, pared) panel (b) (tablero — de anuncios) noticeboard; (— en exposición) exhibition panel; (— en estación) arrivals/departures board (c) (Chi) (de auto) dashboard (d) ∼ **de instrumentos** instrument panel o console [2] (de personas) panel

panela f (Col, Ven) brown sugarloaf

panera f (para servir pan) bread basket; (para guardar pan) bread box (AmE), bread bin (BrE)

pánfilo -la adj (fam) dimwitted (colloq)
■ m,f (fam) dimwit (colloq)

panfleto m pamphlet

pánico m panic; **tenerle** ∼ **a algo** to be terrified of sth; **sembrar el** ∼ to spread panic

panocha f [1] (de maíz, trigo) ear [2] (Méx) (melaza) candy made from molasses

panorama m (a) (vista, paisaje) view, panorama (b) (perspectiva) outlook, prospect

panorámica f (Cin, TV) pan; (perspectiva) outlook

panorámico -ca adj panoramic

panque m (Méx) sponge cake

panqueque m (AmL) pancake, crepe

pantaletas fpl (AmC, Ven) panties (pl), knickers (pl) (BrE)

pantalla f [1] (Cin, Inf, TV) screen; ∼ **de radar** radar screen; **la** ∼ **chica** (AmL) the small screen [2] (a) (de lámpara) shade (b) (de chimenea) fireguard (c) (cobertura) front

pantalones mpl, **pantalón** m pants (pl) (AmE), trousers (pl) (BrE); **unos** ∼ a pair of pants

p

o trousers; **~ cortos** shorts (*pl*); **~ de peto** overalls (*pl*) (AmE), dungarees (*pl*) (BrE); **~ tejanos** *or* **vaqueros** jeans (*pl*)

pantano *m* [1] (natural) marsh, swamp; (artificial) reservoir [2] (dificultad) mess, predicament

pantanoso -sa *adj* [1] ⟨*terreno*⟩ marshy, swampy [2] ⟨*asunto/negocio*⟩ difficult, tricky (colloq)

panteón *m* (a) (monumento) pantheon, mausoleum; **~ familiar** *or* **de familia** family vault (b) (AmL) (cementerio) cemetery

pantera *f* panther

panti *m* (*pl* **-tis**), (Méx) **pantimedia** *f* ▶ PANTY

pantomima *f* pantomime

pantorrilla *f* calf

pants *mpl* (Méx) tracksuit, sweat suit (AmE)

pantufla *f* slipper

panty *m* (*pl* **-tys**) panty hose (*pl*) (AmE), tights (*pl*) (BrE)

panza *f* (a) (fam) (barriga) belly, paunch (colloq); **tener ~** to have a belly *o* paunch (colloq) (b) (de cántaro) belly (c) (de rumiante) rumen

panzada *f* (fam) [1] (en el agua) belly flop (colloq); **se dio una ~** he did a belly flop [2] (comilona): **darse una ~ de algo** to pig out on sth (colloq)

panzón -zona *adj* (fam) potbellied (colloq)

pañal *m* diaper (AmE), nappy (BrE)

pañito *m* doily

paño *m* (a) (Tex) woollen cloth; **abrigo de ~** wool coat; **en ~s menores** (fam & hum) in my/his undies (colloq & hum) (b) (para limpiar) cloth; **~ de cocina** (para limpiar) dishcloth; (para secar) teatowel; **~ higiénico** sanitary napkin (AmE), sanitary towel (BrE) (c) (de adorno) antimacassar

pañolenci *m* (CS) baize, felt

pañoleta *f* (de mujer) shawl; (de torero) neckerchief

pañuelo *m* (para la nariz) handkerchief; (para la cabeza) headscarf, scarf; (para el cuello) scarf, neckerchief

papa¹ *m* pope; **el P~** the Pope

papa² *f* (esp AmL) (Bot) potato; **~ caliente** hot potato; **~ dulce** (AmL) sweet potato; **~s fritas** (esp AmL) (de paquete) potato chips (AmE) *o* (BrE) crisps (*pl*); (de cocina) French fries (*pl*) (AmE), chips (*pl*) (BrE); **ni ~** (fam) not a thing; **no sé ni ~ de coches** I haven't a clue about cars (colloq)

papá *m* (*pl* **-pás**) (fam) daddy (colloq), pop (AmE colloq); **mis ~s** (AmL) my parents, my mom and dad (AmE), my mum and dad (BrE colloq); **P~ Noel** Santa Claus, Father Christmas

papada *f* (de persona) double chin, jowl

papagayo *m* [1] (ave) parrot; **recitar algo como un ~** to recite sth parrot-fashion [2] (Ven) (juguete) kite

papalote *m* (AmC, Méx) (juguete) kite; (ala delta) hang glider

Papanicolau *m* (AmL) smear test

papaya *f* papaya, pawpaw

papel *m* [1] (material) paper; **un ~** a piece of paper; **toalla de ~** paper towel; **~ carbón** carbon paper; **~ cuadriculado/rayado** squared/lined paper; **~ de aluminio** tinfoil, aluminum* foil; **~ de embalar/de envolver/de regalo** wrapping paper; **~ higiénico** *or* **de water** toilet paper; **~ picado** (RPl) confetti

[2] (documento) document, paper; **no tenía los ~es en regla** her papers were not in order [3] (a) (Cin, Teatr) role, part; **hace el ~ de monja** she plays the part of a nun (b) (actuación) performance; **hizo un lamentable ~ en el congreso** his performance at the conference was abysmal (c) (función) role; **juega un ~ importante en ...** it plays an important role in ...

papeleo *m* (fam) red tape, paperwork

papelera *f* (a) (de oficina) wastepaper basket; (en la calle) litter basket (AmE), litter bin (BrE) (b) (fábrica) paper mill

papelería *f* (tienda) stationery store (AmE), stationer's (BrE); **artículos de ~** stationery

papelero -ra *adj* paper (*before n*)
■ *m,f* [1] (fabricante) paper manufacturer; (vendedor) stationer [2] **papelero** *m* (CS) ▶ PAPELERA A

papeleta *f* (a) (de votación) ballot (paper); **~ en blanco** blank ballot (paper) (b) (de rifa) raffle ticket (c) (de calificación) grade slip (d) (de empeño) pawn ticket

papelillo *m* cigarette paper

papelitos *mpl* (Ur) confetti

papelón *m* (fam) (cosa vergonzosa): **hacer un ~** to make a fool of oneself; **¡qué ~!** how embarrassing!

paperas *fpl* mumps

papi *m* (fam) ▶ PAPÁ

papilla *f* (para bebés) baby food, formula (AmE); (para enfermos) puree, pap; **estar hecho ~** ⟨*persona*⟩ to be absolutely shattered (colloq)

papiro *m* papyrus

paprika *f* paprika

paquete¹ -ta *adj* (RPl fam) smart, chic

paquete² *m* [1] (a) (bulto envuelto) package, parcel; **hacer un ~** to wrap up a parcel; **~ bomba** parcel bomb; **~ postal** parcel (*sent by mail*) (b) (de galletas, cigarrillos) pack, packet (BrE); **un ~ de papas fritas** (AmL) a bag of chips (AmE), a packet of crisps (BrE) [2] (conjunto) package; (Inf) package [3] (Méx fam) (problema) headache (colloq)

Paquistán *m* Pakistan

paquistaní *adj/mf* Pakistani

par *adj* ⟨*número*⟩ even; **jugarse algo a ~es o nones** *to decide sth by guessing whether the number of objects held is odd or even*
■ *m* [1] (a) (de guantes, zapatos) pair; **un ~ de preguntas/de veces** a couple of questions/of times; **a ~es** two at a time (b) (comparación) equal; **sin ~** (liter) incomparable, matchless (liter) [2] (Arquit) rafter; ⟨*abierto*⟩ **de ~ en ~** wide open [3] (en golf) par; **sobre/bajo ~** over/under par
■ *f* par; **a la ~** (Fin) at par (value); **sabroso a la ~ que sano** both tasty and healthy; **baila a la ~ que canta** he dances and sings at the same time

para *prep*
I [1] (destino, finalidad, intención) for; **una carta para él** a letter for him; **¿~ qué sirve esto?** what's this (used) for?; **champú ~ bebés** baby shampoo; **~ eso no voy** I might as well not go; **~ + INF:** **ahorra ~ comprarse un coche** he's saving up to buy a car; **tomé un taxi ~ no llegar tarde** I took a taxi so I wouldn't be late; **está listo ~ pintar** it's ready to be painted *o* for painting; **~ aprobar** (in order) to pass; **entró en puntillas para no despertarla** he went in on tiptoe so as not to ⋯►

wake her; **lo dice ∼ que yo me preocupe** he (only) says it to worry me; **cierra ∼ que no nos oigan** close the door so (that) they don't hear us **2** (a) (suficiencia) for; **no hay ∼ todos** there isn't enough for everybody; **no es ∼ tanto** it's not that bad; **soy lo bastante viejo (como) ∼ recordarlo** I'm old enough to remember it **(b)** (en comparaciones, contrastes): **hace demasiado frío ∼ salir** it's too cold to go out; **son altos ∼ su edad** they're tall for their age; **∼ lo que come, no está gordo** considering how much he eats, he's not fat; **¿quién es él ∼ hablarte así?** who does he think he is, speaking to you like that?; **es mucho ∼ que lo haga sola** it's too much for you to do it on your own

II 1 (dirección): **salieron ∼ el aeropuerto** they left for the airport; **empuja ∼ arriba** push up o upward(s); **¿vas ∼ el centro?** are you going to o toward(s) the center?

2 (tiempo) (a) (señalando una fecha, un plazo): **estará listo ∼ el día 15** it'll be ready by o for the 15th; **deberes ∼ el lunes** homework for Monday; **faltan cinco minutos ∼ que termine** there are five minutes to go before the end; **me lo prometió ∼ después de Pascua** he promised me it for after Easter; **¿cuánto te falta ∼ terminar?** how much have you got left to do?; **∼ entonces estaré en Madrid** I'll be in Madrid (by) then; **tengo hora ∼ mañana** I have an appointment (for) tomorrow **(b)** (AmL exc RPl) (al decir la hora) to; **son cinco ∼ las diez** it's five to ten **(c)** (duración): **∼ siempre** forever; **tengo ∼ rato** (fam) I'm going to be a while (yet)

parábola f **(a)** (Relig) parable **(b)** (Mat) parabola

parabrisas m (pl ∼) windshield (AmE), windscreen (BrE)

paracaídas m (pl ∼) (Aviac) parachute; **tirarse** or **lanzarse en ∼** to parachute

paracaidismo m parachuting

paracaidista adj parachute (before n)
■ mf **(a)** (Mil) paratrooper; (Dep) parachutist **(b)** (AmL fam) gatecrasher; **llegar de ∼** to come/go uninvited (to a party)

parachoques m (pl ∼) (Auto) bumper

parada f **1** (Transp) **(a)** (acción) stop **(b)** (lugar) tb **∼ de autobús** (or **de ómnibus** etc) bus stop; **me bajo en la próxima ∼** I'm getting off at the next stop; **∼ de taxi** taxi stand, taxi rank (BrE) **2** (Dep) (en fútbol) save, stop **3** (desfile) parade **4** (Per) (mercado) street market

paradero m **(a)** (frml) (de persona) whereabouts (pl) **(b)** (AmL exc RPl) ▶ PARADA 1B

parado -da adj **1** (detenido): **un coche ∼ en medio de la calle** a car sitting o stopped in the middle of the street; **no te quedes ahí ∼, ven a ayudarme** don't just stand there, come and help me
2 (AmL) **(a)** (de pie): **estar ∼** to stand, be standing **(b)** (erguido): **tengo el pelo todo ∼** my hair's standing on end; **ver tb ▶ PARAR** vt 2B
3 (Esp) (desempleado) unemployed
4 **salir (de algo) bien/mal parado** (de pelea, discusión) to come off well/badly (in sth); **es el que mejor ∼ ha salido** he's the one who's come off best
■ m,f (Esp) unemployed person; **los ∼s** the unemployed

paradoja f paradox

paradójico -ca adj paradoxical

parador m **(a)** (mesón) roadside bar/hotel **(b)** (en Esp) parador, state-owned hotel

parafina f **(a)** (sólida) paraffin (wax); **∼ líquida** mineral oil (AmE), liquid paraffin (BrE) **(b)** (AmL) (combustible) kerosene

paragolpes m (pl ∼) (RPl) bumper

paraguas m (pl ∼) umbrella

Paraguay m: tb **el ∼** Paraguay

paraguayo -ya adj/m,f Paraguayan

paragüero m umbrella stand

paraíso m (Relig) **el ∼** paradise, heaven; **∼ fiscal** tax haven

paraje m spot, place

paralela f **1** (línea) parallel (line) **2 paralelas** fpl (Dep) parallel bars (pl)

paralelismo m parallelism, parallel

paralelo¹ -la adj **(a)** ⟨líneas/planos⟩ parallel; **∼ A algo** TO sth **(b)** (como adv) ⟨marchar/crecer⟩ parallel

paralelo² m parallel

paralelogramo m parallelogram

parálisis f paralysis; **∼ cerebral** cerebral palsy; **∼ infantil** poliomyelitis, infantile paralysis

paralítico -ca adj paralytic (before n); **se quedó ∼** he was paralyzed
■ m,f paralytic

paralizar [A4] vt **(a)** (Med) to paralyze; **se quedó paralizada de un lado** she was paralyzed down one side **(b)** ⟨industria/economía⟩ to paralyze; ⟨circulación/producción⟩ to bring ... to a halt o standstill

paramilitar adj paramilitary

páramo m high plateau, bleak upland o moor

paramuno -na m,f (Col) person from the high plateau

paraninfo m main hall o auditorium

paranoia f paranoia

paranoico -ca adj/m,f paranoid

paranormal adj paranormal

parapente m paragliding

parapetarse [A1] v pron to take cover

parapeto m (Arquit) parapet; (barricada) barricade

paraplejía, paraplejia f paraplegia

parapléjico -ca adj/m,f paraplegic

parapsicología f parapsychology

parar [A1] vi **1** (detenerse) to stop; **paró en seco** she stopped dead; **ir/venir a ∼** to end up; **fue a ∼ a la cárcel** he ended up in prison; **¿a dónde habrá ido a ∼ aquella foto?** what can have happened to that photo?; **¡a dónde iremos a ∼!** I don't know what the world's coming to
2 (cesar) to stop; **para un momento** hang on a minute; **ha estado lloviendo sin ∼** it hasn't stopped raining; **no para quieto ni un momento** he can't keep still for a minute; **no para en casa** she's never at home; **∼ DE + INF** to stop -ING; **paró de llover** it stopped raining
3 (AmL) «obreros/empleados» to go on strike
■ **∼** vt **1** **(a)** ⟨coche/tráfico/persona⟩ to stop; ⟨motor/máquina⟩ to stop, switch off **(b)** ⟨hemorragia⟩ to stanch (AmE), to staunch (BrE) **(c)** ⟨balón/tiro⟩ to save, stop; ⟨golpe⟩ to block, ward off

2 (AmL) **(a)** (poner de pie) to stand **(b)** (poner vertical) ‹vaso/libro› to stand ... up; **el perro paró las orejas** the dog pricked up its ears

■ **pararse** v pron **1** (detenerse) **(a)** «persona» to stop **(b)** «reloj/máquina» to stop; «coche/motor» to stall; **se me paró el reloj** my watch stopped **2 (a)** (AmL) (ponerse de pie) to stand up; **párate derecho** stand up straight; **se paró en una silla** she stood on a chair; **¿te puedes ~ de cabeza/de manos?** can you do headstands/handstands? **(b)** (AmL) «pelo» (hacia arriba) to stick up; (en los lados) to stick out **(c)** (Méx, Ven) (levantarse de la cama) to get up

pararrayos m (pl ~) (en edificio) lightning rod (AmE), lightning conductor (BrE)

parasailing /'parɪseɪlɪŋ/ m parasailing

parásito m parasite

parasol m (sombrilla) parasol, sunshade

parcela f plot (of land), lot (AmE)

parchar [A1] vt (AmL) (arreglar) to repair; (con parche) to patch (up)

parche m patch; **~ de nicotina** nicotine patch

parchís m (Esp, Méx) Parcheesi® (AmE), ludo (BrE)

parcial adj **1** ‹solución/victoria› partial **2** (no equitativo) biased, partial

■ m (examen) assessment examination (taken during the year and counting towards the final grade)

parcialidad f **(a)** (cualidad) partiality, bias **(b)** (seguidores) supporters (pl)

parco -ca adj **(a)** (lacónico) laconic **(b)** (sobrio, moderado) frugal; **ser ~ en palabras** to be sparing with words

pardo -da adj ‹color› dun, brownish-gray*

parecer¹ [E3] vi **1** (aparentar ser): **parece fácil** it looks easy; **no pareces tú en esta foto** this picture doesn't look like you (at all); **parecía de cuero** it looked like leather; **parece ser muy inteligente** she seems to be very clever **2** (expresando opinión) (+ me/te/le etc): **todo le parece mal** he's never happy with anything; **¿qué te parecieron?** what did you think of them?; **vamos a la playa ¿te parece?** what do you think, shall we go to the beach?; **si te parece bien** if that's alright with you; **me parece que sí** I think so; **¿a ti qué te parece?** what do you think?; **me parece importante** I think it's important; **me pareció que no era necesario** I didn't think it necessary; **hazlo como mejor te parezca** do it however o as you think best; **me parece mal que vaya sola** I don't think it's right that she should go on her own **3** (dar la impresión) (en 3ᵃ pers): **así parece** or **parece que sí** it looks like it; **aunque no lo parezca, está limpio** it might not look like it, but it's clean; **parece que va a llover** it looks like (it's going to) rain; **parece que fue ayer** it seems like only yesterday; **parece mentira que tenga 20 años** it's hard to believe o I can't believe that he's 20; **parece que fuera más joven** you'd think she was much younger

■ **parecerse** v pron **(a)** (asemejarse) «~se A algn/algo» (en lo físico) to look o to be like sb/sth; (en el carácter) to be like sb/sth **(b)** (recípr) to be alike; **no se parecen en nada** they're not/they don't look in the least bit alike; **se parecen mucho** they are very similar

parecer² m (opinión) opinion; **a mi ~** in my opinion; **son del mismo ~** they're of the same opinion

parecido¹ -da adj [SER] ‹personas› alike; ‹cosas› similar; **son muy parecidas de cara** they have very similar features; **una especie de capa o algo ~** a cape or something like that; **~ A algo** similar TO sth; **eres muy ~ a tu padre** you're a lot like your father

parecido² m resemblance, similarity; **tiene cierto ~ con su hermano** he bears some o a certain resemblance to his brother; **hay un ~ en sus estilos** there is a resemblance o similarity in their styles

pared f **1 (a)** (Arquit, Const) wall; **viven ~ por medio** they live next door; **las ~es oyen** walls have ears **(b)** (de recipiente) side **(c)** (de montaña) face **2** (en fútbol) one-two

paredón m **(a)** (de roca) rock face, wall of rock **(b)** (pared gruesa) thick wall **(c)** (de fusilamiento) wall

pareja f **1 (a)** (equipo, conjunto) pair; **salieron por ~s** they came out in pairs; **formar ~s** to get into pairs **(b)** (en una relación) couple; **hacen buena ~** they make a good couple **(c)** (en naipes) pair **2 (a)** (compañero) partner **(b)** (de guante, zapato) pair; **no encuentro la ~ de este guante** I can't find the pair for this glove; **un calcetín sin ~** an odd sock

parejo -ja adj **1 (a)** (esp AmL) (sin desniveles) even; **los dos ciclistas van muy ~s** the two cyclists are neck and neck; **el nivel en la clase es muy ~** the class are all at the same level **(b)** (afín, semejante) similar **(c)** (CS, Méx) (equitativo) ‹trato› equal; ‹ley› fair, impartial **2** (Méx fam) **al ~ (a la par):** **trabajan al ~** they all do the same amount of work; **al ~ de los mejores del mundo** on a par with the world's best

parentela f (fam) clan (colloq), tribe (colloq)

parentesco m relationship; **tener ~ con algn** to be related to sb

paréntesis m (pl ~) **(a)** (signo) parenthesis, bracket (BrE); **cerrar el ~** to close parentheses o brackets; **entre ~** (literal) in parentheses o in brackets; (a propósito) by the way **(b)** (digresión) digression, parenthesis

parezca, parezcas, etc ▶ PARECER¹

paria mf pariah

pariente mf, **pariente -ta** m,f (familiar) relative, relation; **~ lejano** distant relative o relation; **~ político** in-law

parir [I1] vi «mujer» to give birth; «vaca» to calve; «yegua/burra» to foal; «oveja» to lamb

■ **~** vt **(a)** «mujer» to give birth to, have **(b)** «mamíferos» to have, bear (frml)

París m Paris

parisiense adj/mf Parisian

parisino -na adj/m,f Parisian

parking /'parkɪn/ m (esp Esp) parking lot (AmE), car park (BrE)

parlamentar [A1] vi **~** (CON algn) to talk (TO sb)

parlamentario -ria m,f member of parliament, parliamentarian

parlamento m (asamblea) parliament; (Lit, Teatr) speech

p

parlanchín -china *adj* (fam) chatty (colloq)
■ *m,f* (fam) chatterbox (colloq)

parlante *m* (AmL) (en lugar público) loudspeaker;
(de equipo de música) speaker

paro *m* 1 (esp AmL) (huelga) strike; **hacer un ~
de 24 horas** to go on a 24-hour strike; **están en** *or*
de ~ (AmL) they're on strike; **~ cívico** (Col)
community protest; **~ general** (esp AmL) general
strike 2 (Esp) **(a)** (desempleo) unemployment;
está en ~ he's unemployed **(b)** (subsidio)
unemployment benefit; **cobrar el ~** to claim
unemployment benefit 3 **~ cardíaco** *or* **cardiaco**
cardiac arrest

parodia *f* parody, send-up (colloq)

parpadear [A1] *vi* **(a)** «*persona/ojo*» to blink
(b) «*luz*» to flicker; «*estrellas*» to twinkle

párpado *m* eyelid

parque *m* 1 (terreno) park; **~ de atracciones** *or*
(Col, RPl) **de diversiones** *or* (Chi) **de entretenciones**
amusement park, funfair; **~ de bomberos** (Esp)
fire station; **~ natural** nature reserve; **~
zoológico** zoo 2 (para niños) playpen

parqué *m* (suelo) parquet (flooring)

parqueadero *m* (Col) parking lot (AmE), car
park (BrE)

parquear [A1] *vt* (Col) to park
■ **parquearse** *v pron* (Col) to park

parquet *m* (*pl* **-quets**) ▶ PARQUÉ

parquímetro *m* parking meter

parra *f* vine

párrafo *m* paragraph; **~ aparte** new paragraph

parral *m* (en un jardín) vine arbor*; (viñedo)
vineyard

parranda *f* (fam): **estar/irse de ~** to be/go out
on the town *o* out partying (colloq)

parrilla *f* 1 **(a)** (Coc) grill, broiler (AmE);
pescado a la ~ grilled *o* (AmE) broiled fish **(b)**
(restaurante) grillroom, grill bar **(c)** (de la chimenea)
grate 2 (AmL) (para el equipaje) luggage rack, roof
rack

parrillada *f* **(a)** (comida) grill, barbecue **(b)**
(RPl) (restaurante) grillroom, grill bar

párroco *m* parish priest

parroquia *f* (iglesia) parish church; (área)
parish; (feligreses) parishioners (*pl*)

parroquiano -na *m,f* **(a)** (Relig) parishioner
(b) (cliente) regular customer *o* (fml) patron

parsimonia *f* **(a)** (calma) calm **(b)** (frugalidad)
parsimony

parsimonioso -sa *adj* **(a)** (tranquilo)
phlegmatic, unhurried **(b)** (frugal) parsimonious

parte *m* 1 (informe, comunicación) report; **dar ~
de un incidente** «*particular*» to report an
incident; «*autoridad*» to file a report about an
incident; **dar ~ de enfermo** to call in sick; **~
meteorológico** weather report
2 (Andes) (multa) ticket (colloq), fine
■ *f* 1 **(a)** (porción, fracción) part; **tres ~s iguales**
three equal parts; **pasa la mayor ~ del tiempo al
teléfono** she spends most of her *o* the time on the
phone; **la mayor ~ de los participantes** the

majority of *o* most of the participants **(b)** (en una
distribución) share; **su ~ de la herencia** his share of
the inheritance **(c)** (de lugar) part; **¿de qué ~ de
México eres?** what part of Mexico are you from?;
en la ~ de atrás at the back
2 (en locs) **en parte** partly; **en gran ~** to a large
extent, largely; **en su mayor ~** for the most part;
de un tiempo a esta parte for some time now; **de
parte de algn** on behalf of sb; **llamo de ~ de
María** I'm ringing on behalf of María; **dale
recuerdos de mi ~** give him my regards; **vengo
de ~ del señor Díaz** Mr Díaz sent me; **¿de ~ de
quién?** (por teléfono) who's calling?, who shall I
say is calling? (fml); **formar parte de algo** «*pieza/
sección*» to be part of sth; «*persona/país*» to
belong to sth; **entrar a formar ~ de algo** to join
sth; **por mi/tu/su parte** as far as I'm/you're/he's
concerned; **por partes: revisémoslo por ~s** let's
go over it section by section; **vayamos por ~s**
let's take it step by step; **por otra parte** (además)
anyway, in any case; (por otro lado) however, on
the other hand; **por una parte ..., por la otra ...** on
the one hand ..., on the other ...
3 (participación) part; **tomar ~** to take part
4 (lugar): **vámonos a otra ~** let's go somewhere
else *o* (AmE) someplace else; **esto no nos lleva a
ninguna ~** this isn't getting *o* leading us
anywhere; **¿adónde vas? — a ninguna ~** where
are you going? — nowhere; **en cualquier ~**
anywhere; **a/en/por todas ~s** everywhere; **en
alguna ~** somewhere
5 (en negociación, contrato, juicio) party
6 (Teatr) part, role
7 (Méx) (repuesto) part, spare (part)

participación *f* 1 (intervención) participation;
la ~ del público audience participation; **~ EN
algo** «*en debate/clase/huelga*» participation in
sth; «*en robo/fraude*» involvement IN sth; «*en
obra/película*» role in sth 2 **(a)** (en ganancias)
share **(b)** (en empresa) stockholding, interest **(c)**
(de lotería) share (*in a lottery ticket*)

participante *adj* participating (*before n*)
■ *mf* (en debate) participant; (en concurso)
contestant; (en carrera) competitor

participar [A1] *vi* (tomar parte) **~ (EN algo)**
to take part (IN sth), participate (IN sth) (fml) **(b)**
~ EN algo (en ganancias) to have a share IN sth;
(en empresas) to have a stockholding IN sth

participio *m* participle; **~ pasado** *or* **pasivo**
past participle

partícula *f* particle

particular *adj* **(a)** (privado) «*clases/profesor*»
private; «*teléfono*» home (*before n*) **(b)** (específico)
«*caso/aspecto*» particular; **en ~** in particular,
particularly **(c)** (especial) «*estilo/gusto*» individual,
personal; **es un tipo muy ~** (fam) he's a very
peculiar guy; **no tiene nada de ~ que vaya**
there's nothing unusual *o* strange in her going; **la
casa no tiene nada de ~** there's nothing special
about the house
■ *m* **(a)** (fml) (asunto) matter, point; **sin otro ~
saluda a usted atentamente** sincerely yours

AmC	Central America	Arg	Argentina	Cu	Cuba	Per	Peru
AmL	Latin America	Bol	Bolivia	Ec	Ecuador	RPl	River Plate Area
AmS	South America	Chi	Chile	Esp	Spain	Ur	Uruguay
Andes	Andean Region	CS	Southern Cone	Méx	Mexico	Ven	Venezuela

(AmE), yours faithfully (BrE) **(b)** (persona)
(private) individual; **viajar como** ∼ to travel on
private *o* personal business

partida *f* **1** (Jueg) game; **una** ∼ **de ajedrez/
cartas** a game of chess/cards; **echar una** ∼ to
have a game **2** (en registro, contabilidad) entry; (en
presupuesto) item **3** (certificado) certificate; ∼ **de
defunción/nacimiento** death/birth certificate
4 (frml) (salida) departure, leaving

partidario -ria *adj* (a favor) ∼ DE **algo/hacer
algo** in favor* OF sth/doing sth
■ *m,f* supporter; **los** ∼**s de Gaztelu** Gaztelu's
supporters; **los** ∼**s de la violencia** those who
favor *o* advocate the use of violence

partido¹ -da *adj* **1** ⟨*labios*⟩ chapped;
⟨*barbilla*⟩ cleft **2** (Mat): **siete** ∼ **por diez** seven
over ten; **nueve** ∼ **por tres da** ... nine divided by
three gives ...

partido² *m* **1** **(a)** (de fútbol) game, match (BrE);
(de tenis) match; **echar un** ∼ to have a game; **un**
∼ **de béisbol** a baseball game; ∼ **amistoso**
friendly game *o* match; ∼ **de desempate** deciding
game, decider; ∼ **en casa/fuera de casa** home/
away match **(b)** (AmL) (partida) game; **un** ∼ **de
ajedrez** a game of chess **2** (Pol) party; ∼ **de la
oposición** opposition party; **tomar** ∼ to take sides
3 (provecho): **sacar** ∼ **de algo** to benefit from sth;
sacarle ∼ **a algo** to make the most of sth **4** (para
casarse): **un buen** ∼ a good catch

partir [I1] *vt* **(a)** (con cuchillo) ⟨*tarta/melón*⟩ to
cut; **lo partió por la mitad** he cut it in half **(b)**
(romper) ⟨*piedra/coco*⟩ to break, smash; ⟨*nuez/
avellana*⟩ to crack; ⟨*rama/palo*⟩ to break **(c)** (con
golpe) ⟨*labio*⟩ to split (open); ⟨*cabeza*⟩ to split open
(d) ⟨*frío*⟩ ⟨*labios*⟩ to chap
■ ∼ *vi* **1** **(a)** (frml) (marcharse) to leave, depart
(frml) **(b)** «*auto*» (Chi) to start
2 **(a)** ∼ DE **algo** ⟨*de una premisa/un supuesto*⟩
to start FROM sth **(b)** **a partir de** from; **a** ∼ **de
ahora/ese momento** from now on/that moment
on; **a** ∼ **de hoy** (as *o* starting) from today
■ **partirse** *v pron* **(a)** ⟨*mármol/roca*⟩ to split,
smash **(b)** (*refl*) ⟨*labio*⟩ to split; ⟨*diente*⟩ to break,
chip

partitura *f* (de obra orquestada) score

parto *m* (Med) labor*; **estar de** ∼ to be in labor;
fue un ∼ **difícil** it was a difficult birth; **provocar
el** ∼ to induce labor; ∼ **sin dolor** pain-free labor*

parvulario *m* kindergarten, nursery school
(BrE)

pasa *f* raisin

pasable *adj* (tolerable) passable

pasabordo *m* (Col) boarding pass

pasada *f* **(a)** (con un trapo) wipe; (de barniz, cera)
coat **(b)** (paso): **trató el tema de** ∼ he dealt with
the subject in passing; **hacerle** *or* **jugarle una
mala** ∼ **a algn** to play a dirty trick on sb

pasadizo *m* passageway, passage

pasado¹ -da *adj* **1** (en expresiones de tiempo): **el
año/sábado** ∼ last year/Saturday; ∼**s dos días**
after two days; **son las cinco pasadas** it's after *o*
past five o'clock; ∼ **mañana** the day after
tomorrow **2** (anticuado) *tb* ∼ **de moda**
old-fashioned **3** ⟨*fruta*⟩ overripe; ⟨*arroz/pastas*⟩
overcooked; ⟨*leche*⟩ sour; **el pescado está** ∼ the
fish is bad; **el filete muy** ∼, **por favor** I'd like my
steak well done

pasado² *m* **(a)** (época pasada) past **(b)** (Ling)
past (tense)

pasador *m* **(a)** (de pelo — decorativo) barrette
(AmE), hair slide (BrE); (— en forma de horquilla)
(Méx) bobby pin (AmE), hair clip (BrE) **(b)** (de
corbata) tiepin **(c)** (Per) (cordón) shoelace

pasaje *m* **1** (esp AmL) (Transp) ticket; **un** ∼ **de
ida/de ida y vuelta** a one-way/round-trip ticket
(AmE), a single/return ticket (BrE) **2** (callejón)
passage, narrow street; (galería comercial) arcade,
mall **3** (Lit, Mús) passage

pasajero -ra *adj* ⟨*capricho/moda*⟩ passing
(*before n*); ⟨*amor*⟩ fleeting (*before n*); ⟨*molestia/
dolor*⟩ temporary
■ *m,f* passenger

pasamanos *m* (*pl* ∼) banister

pasamontañas *m* (*pl* ∼) balaclava

pasapalo *m* (Ven fam) nibble (colloq)

pasaporte *m* passport; **sacar el** ∼ to get a
passport

pasapurés *m* (*pl* ∼) (con manivela) food mill;
(para aplastar) potato masher

pasar [A1] *vi*
I **1** **(a)** (ir por un lugar) to come/go past; **no ha
pasado ni un taxi** not one taxi has come/gone
past; **los otros coches no podían** ∼ the other
cars weren't able to get past; **no dejan a nadie**
they're not letting anyone through; ∼ **de largo** to
go right *o* straight past; ∼ **por la aduana** to go
through customs; **es un vuelo directo, no pasa
por Miami** it's a direct flight, it doesn't go via
Miami; **¿este autobús pasa por el museo?** does
this bus go past the museum?; **pasamos por
delante de su casa** we went past her house;
pasaba por aquí y ... I was just passing by *o* I
was in the area and ... **(b)** (deteniéndose en un
lugar): **¿podríamos** ∼ **por el banco?** can we stop
off at the bank?; **pasa un día por casa** why don't
you drop *o* come by the house sometime?; **puede**
∼ **a recogerlo mañana** you can come and pick it
up tomorrow **(c)** (atravesar) to cross; ∼ **de un lado
a otro** ⟨*persona/barco*⟩ to go *o* cross from one
side to the other; «*humedad*» to go through
from one side to the other **(d)** (caber): **no** ∼**á por
la puerta** it won't go through the door
2 (entrar — acercándose al hablante) to come in; (—
alejándose del hablante) to go in; **pase, por favor**
please, do come in; **¡que pase el siguiente!** next,
please!; **haga** ∼ **al Sr Díaz** show Mr Díaz in please
3 **(a)** (transmitirse, transferirse) ⟨*corona/título*⟩ to
pass; **pasó de mano en mano** it was passed
around (to everyone) **(b)** (comunicar): **te paso con
Javier** (en el mismo teléfono) I'll hand *o* pass you
over to Javier; (en otro teléfono) I'll put you
through to Javier
4 **(a)** (Educ) to pass; ∼ **de curso** to get through
o pass one's end-of-year exams **(b)** (ser aceptable):
no está perfecto, pero puede ∼ it's not perfect,
but it'll do; **por esta vez, (que) pase** I'll let it pass
o go this time
5 **pasar por (a)** (ser tenido por): **podrían** ∼ **por
hermanas** they could pass for sisters; *ver tb*
HACERSE II 3 **(b)** (experimentar) to go through; ∼
por una crisis to go through a crisis
II (suceder) to happen; **cuéntame lo que pasó** tell
me what happened; **la cosa** *o* **el problema es ...**;
pase lo que pase whatever happens, come what may; **siempre pasa** ···⟶

p

igual *or* lo mismo it's always the same; ¿qué
pasa? what's the matter?, what's up? (colloq);
¿qué te pasa? what's the matter with you?; ¿qué
te pasó en el ojo? what happened to your eye?;
¿qué le pasa a la tele? what's wrong with the
TV?; eso le pasa a cualquiera that can happen to
anybody; no le pasó nada nothing happened to
him

III 1 (transcurrir) «*tiempo/años*» to pass, go by;
~on muchos años many years went by *o* passed;
ya han pasado dos horas it's been two hours
now; un año pasa muy rápido a year goes very
quickly; ¡cómo pasa el tiempo! doesn't time fly!

2 (cesar) «*crisis/mal momento*» to be over;
«*efecto*» to wear off; «*dolor*» to go away

3 (arreglárselas) ~ **SIN** algo to manage WITHOUT
sth

■ ~ *vt*

I 1 (a) (cruzar, atravesar) ⟨*frontera*⟩ to cross;
⟨*pueblo/ciudad*⟩ to go through (b) (dejar atrás)
⟨*edificio/calle*⟩ to go past (c) (adelantar, sobrepasar)
to overtake

2 (a) (hacer atravesar) ~ algo **POR** algo to put sth
THROUGH sth; ~ la salsa por un tamiz to put the
sauce through a sieve (b) (por la aduana —
legalmente) to take through; (— ilegalmente) to
smuggle

3 (hacer recorrer): ~ la aspiradora to vacuum, to
hoover (BrE); pásale un trapo al piso give the
floor a quick wipe; hay que ~le una plancha it
needs a quick iron

4 (exhibir, mostrar) ⟨*película/anuncio*⟩ to show

5 ⟨*examen/prueba*⟩ to pass

6 ⟨*página/hoja*⟩ to turn; ~ por alto ⟨*falta/error*⟩
to overlook; ⟨*tema/punto*⟩ to leave out, omit

II 1 (entregar, hacer llegar): pásaselo a Miguel pass
it on to Miguel; ¿me pasas el martillo? can you
pass me the hammer?

2 (contagiar) to give, to pass on

III 1 (a) ⟨*tiempo*⟩ to spend; pasamos las
Navidades en casa we spent Christmas at home;
fuimos a Toledo a ~ el día we went to Toledo for
the day (b) (con idea de continuidad): pasé toda la
noche en vela I was awake all night; pasa todo el
día al teléfono she spends all day on the phone
(c) pasarlo *or* pasarla bien to have a good time;
¿qué tal lo pasaste en la fiesta? did you have a
good time at the party?, did you enjoy the party?;
lo pasé mal I didn't enjoy myself

2 (sufrir, padecer) ⟨*penalidades/desgracias*⟩ to go
through, to suffer; pasé mucho miedo/frío I was
very frightened/cold

■ **pasarse** *v pron*

I 1 (cambiarse): ~se al enemigo to go over to the
enemy

2 (a) (ir demasiado lejos) to go too far; nos
pasamos de estación we went past our station;
esta vez te has pasado (fam) you've gone too far
this time (b) (*enf*) (fam) (ir): pásate por casa come
round; ¿podrías ~te por el mercado? could you
go down to the market?

3 (a) «*peras/tomates*» to go bad, get overripe;
«*carne/pescado*» to go off, go bad; «*leche*» to go
off, go sour (b) (recocerse) «*arroz/pasta*» to get
overcooked

II 1 (a) (desaparecer) «*efecto*» to wear off;
«*dolor*» to go away; (+ *me/te/le etc*) ya se me
pasó el dolor the pain's gone *o* eased now; espera

a que se le pase el enojo wait until he's calmed *o*
cooled down (b) (transcurrir): el año se ha pasado
muy rápido this year has gone very quickly; *ver
tb* PASAR *vt* III 1A, B

2 (+ *me/te/le etc*) (a) (olvidarse): se me pasó su
cumpleaños I forgot his birthday (b) (dejar
escapar): se me pasó la oportunidad I missed the
opportunity

pasarela *f* (a) (en desfiles de modelos) runway
(AmE), catwalk (BrE) (b) (Náut) gangway

pasatiempo *m* (a) (entretenimiento) hobby,
pastime (b) **pasatiempos** *mpl* (en periódico)
puzzles (*pl*)

Pascua *f* (a) (fiesta de Resurrección) Easter (b)
(Navidad) Christmas (c) (fiesta judía) Passover

pase *m* 1 (a) (permiso) pass; ~ de abordar
(Méx) boarding pass; ~ de periodista press pass
(b) (para espectáculo) *tb* ~ de favor complimentary
ticket (c) (Col) (licencia de conducción) license*

2 (a) (Dep) (en fútbol, baloncesto, rugby) pass; (en
esgrima) feint (b) (Taur) pass (c) (en magia) sleight
of hand

pasear [A1] *vi* (a) (a pie) to go for a walk *o*
stroll; salir a ~ to go out for a walk *o* stroll (b)
(en bicicleta) to go for a (bike) ride; (en coche) to go
for a drive

■ ~ *vt* ⟨*perro*⟩ to walk

paseo *m* 1 (a) (caminata) walk; dar un ~ to go
for a walk *o* (colloq) stroll; *mandar a algn a* ~
(fam) to tell sb to get lost (colloq) (b) (en bicicleta)
ride; (en coche) drive; fuimos a dar un ~ en coche
we went for a drive (c) (AmL) (excursión) trip,
outing; no vivo aquí, estoy de ~ I don't live here,
I'm just visiting 2 (en nombres de calles) walk,
avenue; ~ marítimo esplanade, seafront

pasillo *m* (corredor) corridor; (en avión) aisle

pasión *f* passion; tiene ~ por el fútbol he has a
passion for football

pasional *adj*: un crimen ~ a crime of passion

pasito *adv* (Col, Ven) ⟨*hablar*⟩ quietly, softly;
poner ~ la música to turn the music down

pasivo¹ -va *adj* passive

pasivo² *m* (en negocio) liabilities (*pl*); (en cuenta)
debit side

pasmado -da *adj* (fam) ⟨*persona*⟩: la noticia me
dejó pasmada I was stunned by the news (colloq)

pasmar [A1] *vt* (fam) to amaze, stun

paso *m* 1 (a) (acción): el ~ del tren the passing
of the train; el ~ del tiempo the passage of time;
el ~ de la dictadura a la democracia the
transition from dictatorship to democracy; de ~:
están de ~ they're just visiting *o* just passing
through; me pilla de ~ it's on my way; y dicho
sea de ~ ... and incidentally ... (b) (camino,
posibilidad de pasar) way; abrir/dejar ~ (a algn/algo)
to make way (for sth/sb); me cerró el ~ she
blocked my way; dejen el ~ libre leave the way
clear; Ⓢ ceda el paso yield (*in US*), give way (*in
UK*); Ⓢ prohibido el paso no entry; ~ de cebra
zebra crossing; ~ de peatones crosswalk (AmE),
pedestrian crossing (BrE); ~ a nivel grade (AmE) *o*
(BrE) level crossing; ~ elevado *or* (Méx) a desnivel
overpass (AmE), flyover (BrE); ~ subterráneo (para
peatones) underpass, subway (BrE); (para vehículos)
underpass; *abrirse* ~ to make one's way; (a
codazos) to elbow one's way; *salir al* ~ *de algn*
(abordar) to waylay sb; (detener) to stop sb

2 (Geog) (en montaña) pass; *salir del ∼* to get out of a (tight) spot *o* (AmE) crack (colloq) **3** (a) (al andar, bailar) step; *dio un ∼ para atrás* he took a step backward(s); *oyó ∼s* she heard footsteps; *entró con ∼ firme* he came in purposefully; *∼ a ∼* step by step; *seguirle los ∼s a algn* to tail sb; *seguir los ∼s de algn* to follow in sb's footsteps (b) (distancia corta): *vive a dos ∼s de mi casa* he lives a stone's throw (away) from my house; *está a un ∼ de aquí* it's just around the corner/down the road from here (c) (avance) step forward; *eso ya es un ∼ (adelante)* that's a step forward in itself (d) (de gestión) step **4** (ritmo, velocidad): *apretó/aminoró el ∼* he quickened his pace/he slowed down; *a este ∼ ...* at this rate ...; *a ∼ de hormiga* or *tortuga* at a snail's pace; *marcar el ∼* to mark time **5** (en contador) unit

pasodoble *m* paso doble

pasota *mf* (Esp fam): *ese tío es un ∼* that guy couldn't give a damn about anything (colloq)

pasparse [A1] *v pron* (RPl) «*cara/labios*» to get chapped

pasta *f* **1** (Coc) (a) (fideos, macarrones, etc) pasta (b) (Esp) (masa de harina) pastry; (galleta) *tb ∼ de té* cookie (c) (de tomates, anchoas, etc) paste **2** (a) (materia moldeable) paste; *∼ dentífrica* or *de dientes* toothpaste; *un libro en ∼* a book in boards; *libros de ∼ blanda* (Méx) paperback books (b) (Chi) (betún) polish **3** (Esp fam) (dinero) money, dough (sl)

pastar [A1] *vi* to graze

pastel *m* **1** (a) (dulce) cake; *∼ de boda/cumpleaños* wedding/birthday cake (b) (cubierto de masa) pie; *∼ de papas* (CS) shepherd's pie, cottage pie **2** (Art) pastel; *al ∼ pastel* (*before n*) ∎ *adj inv* pastel

pastelería *f* (tienda) cake shop, patisserie (BrE); (actividad) (cake) baking

pastelero -ra *m,f* (fabricante) patissier, pastry cook; (vendedor) cake seller

pasteurizado -da, pasterizado -da *adj* pasteurized

pastilla *f* **1** (a) (Farm, Med) (para tragar) pill, tablet; (para chupar) pastille, lozenge; *∼s para dormir* sleeping tablets *o* pills; *∼s para los nervios* tranquilizers (b) (caramelo) candy (AmE), sweet (BrE); *∼ de menta* mint **2** (de jabón) bar; (de chocolate) bar; (de caldo) cube **3** (Electrón) chip, microchip

pasto *m* (a) (Agr) pasture (b) (AmL) (hierba) grass; (extensión) lawn, grass

pastor -tora *m,f* **1** (Agr) (*m*) shepherd; (*f*) shepherdess; *∼ alemán* German shepherd, Alsatian **2** (Relig) minister

pastoso -sa *adj* (a) «*sustancia/masa*» doughy (b) «*boca/lengua*» furry (c) «*voz/tono*» rich, mellow

pata *f* **1** (Zool) (a) (pierna — de animal, ave) leg; *las ∼s delanteras/traseras* the front/hind legs (b) (pie — de perro, gato) paw; (— de ave) foot **2** (de persona) (fam & hum) (pierna) leg; (pie) (AmL) foot; *∼ de palo* wooden leg; *a ∼* (fam & hum) on foot; *estirar la ∼* (fam) to kick the bucket (colloq); *meter la ∼* (fam) to put one's foot in it (colloq); *∼s*

(para) arriba (fam) upside down; *saltar a (la) ∼ coja* to hop; *tener ∼* (AmL fam) to have contacts; ▶ MALO 1A **3** (de mueble) leg ∎ *m* (Per fam) (a) (tipo) guy (colloq), bloke (BrE colloq) (b) (amigo) buddy (AmE colloq), mate (BrE colloq)

patada *f* **1** (puntapié) kick; *le dio una ∼ al balón* he kicked the ball, he gave the ball a kick; *tiró la puerta abajo de una ∼* he kicked the door down; *dio una ∼ en el suelo* he stamped his foot; *los echaron a ∼s* they were kicked out **2** (AmL) (a) (de arma) kick (b) (fam) (producida por la electricidad) shock (colloq); *me dio tremenda ∼* I got a real shock

Patagonia *f*: *la ∼* Patagonia

patagónico -ca *adj* Patagonian

patalear [A1] *vi* (a) (con enfado) to stamp (one's feet) (b) (en el aire, agua) to kick (one's legs in the air/water) (c) (fam) (protestar) to kick up a fuss (colloq)

pataleta *f* (fam) (de niño pequeño) tantrum; *le dio una ∼* «*niño*» he threw a tantrum; «*adulto*» he had a fit (colloq)

patán *adj* (fam) loutish, uncouth; *no seas ∼* don't be such a lout *o* so uncouth ∎ *m* **1** (fam) (grosero) lout, yob (BrE colloq) **2** (Chi) (holgazán) good-for-nothing

patata *f* (Esp) potato; *∼ frita* (Esp) (de sartén) French fry, chip (BrE); (de bolsita) (potato) chip (AmE), (potato) crisp (BrE)

patatús *m* (fam) fit (colloq)

paté, pâté *m* pâté; *∼ de hígado* liver pâté

patear [A1] *vt* (a) «*persona*» to kick, boot (colloq) (b) «*animal*» to kick ∎ *∼ vi* (a) (dar patadas en el suelo) to stamp (one's feet) (b) (AmL) «*animal*» to kick

patentado -da *adj* «*invento*» patented; «*marca*» registered

patentar [A1] *vt* **1** «*marca*» to register; «*invento*» to patent **2** (CS) «*coche*» to register

patente *adj* clear, evident; *dejó ∼ cuál era su objetivo* he made his aim quite clear ∎ *f* **1** (de invento) patent **2** (Auto) (a) (CS) (impuesto) road tax; (placa) license* plate, numberplate (BrE); *el número de la ∼* the registration number, the license number (AmE) (b) (Col) (carnet de conducir) driving license*

paternal *adj* paternal

paternalismo *m* paternalism

paternalista *adj* paternalistic

paternidad *f* **1** (del padre) (a) (Der) paternity (frml) (b) (circunstancia) fatherhood; *la ∼ lo ha cambiado* fatherhood *o* being a father has changed him **2** (de los padres) parenthood

paterno -na *adj* (a) «*abuelo*» paternal (*before n*) (b) «*autoridad/herencia*» paternal; «*cariño*» paternal, fatherly; *su domicilio ∼* her parents' home

patético -ca *adj* pathetic, moving

patetismo *m* pathos (liter); *imágenes de (un) gran ∼* very moving images

patíbulo *m* (a) (tablado) scaffold (b) (horca) gallows

patilla *f* **1** (a) (barba) sideburn, sideboard (BrE) (b) (de las gafas) sidepiece, arm **2** (fruta) (Col, Ven) watermelon; (esqueje) (Chi) cutting

patín *m* **(a)** (con ruedas) (roller) skate; (para el hielo) (ice) skate; **le regalé unos patines** I gave him a pair of skates; **~ en línea** Rollerblade® **(b)** (tabla) skateboard **(c)** (Esp) (bote) pedalo, pedal boat

pátina *f* patina

patinador -dora *m,f* (Dep) (sobre ruedas) (roller) skater; (sobre hielo) (ice) skater

patinaje *m* (sobre ruedas) roller skating; (sobre hielo) ice skating; **~ artístico/de velocidad** figure/speed skating

patinar [A1] *vi* **1 (a)** (Dep) (con ruedas) to skate, roller-skate; (sobre hielo) to skate, ice-skate **(b)** (resbalar) «*persona*» to slip, slide; «*vehículo*» to skid; «*embrague*» to slip **2** (fam) (equivocarse) to slip up

patinazo *m* **1** (de vehículo) skid; **el coche pegó un ~** the car skidded **2** (fam) (equivocación) blunder, slip-up (colloq)

patineta *f* **(a)** (con manillar) scooter **(b)** (CS, Méx, Ven) (sin manillar) skateboard

patinete *m* scooter

patio *m* **1** (en una casa) courtyard, patio; (de escuela) playground, schoolyard **2** (Esp) (Cin, Teatr) *tb* **~ de butacas** (Esp) orchestra (AmE), stalls (*pl*) (BrE)

patizambo -ba *adj* (con las piernas arqueadas — hacia adentro) knock-kneed; (— hacia afuera) bowlegged

pato¹ -ta *m,f* (Zool) duck

pato² *m* **1** (Esp fam) (persona) clodhopper (colloq) **2** (Andes, Méx) (Med) bedpan

patochada *f* (fam) piece of nonsense; **decir ~s** talk nonsense

patología *f* pathology

patológico -ca *adj* pathological

patón -tona *adj* (AmL fam) ▶ PATUDO 1

patoso -sa *adj* (Esp fam) clumsy
■ *m,f* (Esp fam) clumsy idiot (colloq)

patota *f* (AmL fam) mob, gang

patraña *f* tall story

patria *f* homeland, motherland, fatherland; **luchar por la ~** to fight for one's country

patriarca *m* patriarch

patrimonio *m* patrimony; **~ personal** personal assets (*pl*); **el ~ nacional** national wealth; **~ histórico** heritage; **~ artístico/cultural** artistic/cultural heritage

patriota *adj* patriotic
■ *mf* patriot

patriotero -ra *adj* jingoistic, chauvinistic
■ *m,f* jingoist, chauvinist

patriótico -ca *adj* patriotic

patriotismo *m* patriotism

patrocinador -dora *m,f* (de acto, proyecto) sponsor; (Art) patron

patrocinar [A1] *vt* **1** ‹*acto/proyecto*› to sponsor **2** (Chi, Méx) ‹*abogado*› to represent

patrón -trona *m,f* **1 (a)** (Rels Labs) employer (frml), boss **(b)** (Esp) (de casa de huéspedes) (*m*) landlord; (*f*) landlady **2** (Relig) patron saint **3** (CS fam) (como apelativo) (*m*) sir; (*f*) madam **4 patrón** *m* **(a)** (en costura) pattern **(b)** (para mediciones) standard

patrono -na *m,f* **(a)** (esp AmL) (Relig) patron saint **(b)** (Rels Labs) employer

patrulla *f* patrol; **están de ~** they are on patrol; **la ~ costera** the coastguard (patrol)
■ *m or f* (coche) patrol *o* squad car

patrullar [A1] *vi/vt* to patrol

patrullera *f* (lancha) patrol boat

patrullero *m* (barco) patrol boat; (avión) patrol plane; (coche — militar) patrol car; (— policial) (CS, Per) patrol *o* squad car

patudo -da *adj* **1** (AmL fam) (de pies grandes) with big feet; **¡qué niño tan ~!** what big feet he has! **2** (Chi fam) (descarado) nervy (AmE colloq), cheeky (BrE colloq)

paulatino -na *adj* gradual

paulista *adj* of/from São Paulo

pausa *f* **(a)** (interrupción) pause; (Rad, TV) break; **hacer una ~** to pause/have a break **(b)** (Mús) rest

pauta *f* **1** (guía) guideline; **~s de comportamiento** rules *o* norms of behavior **2** (de un papel) lines (*pl*)

pava *f* **1** (para calentar agua) kettle **2** (Col fam) (de cigarrillo) butt; *ver tb* PAVO

pavada *f* (RPI fam) **(a)** (dicho, acción) silly thing to say/do **(b)** (cosa insignificante) little thing

pavimentar [A1] *vt* (con asfalto) to surface, asphalt; (con cemento, adoquines) to pave

pavimento *m* (de asfalto) road surface; (de cemento, adoquines) paving

pavo -va *m,f* (Coc, Zool) turkey; **~ real** peacock; **de ~** (Chi, Per fam) ‹*viajar/entrar*› without paying
■ *adj* **(a)** (fam) (tonto, bobo) silly, dumb (AmE colloq) **(b)** (Chi fam) (ingenuo) naive (colloq)

pavonearse [A1] *v pron* (fam) to show off; **~ de algo** to brag *o* crow ABOUT sth (colloq)

pavor *m* terror; **me da ~** it terrifies me; **les tiene ~ a los perros** (fam) she's terrified of dogs

pavoroso -sa *adj* terrifying, horrific

paya (Chi), **payada** (RPI) *f.* improvised musical dialogue

payador *m* (CS) singer (*who performs* PAYADAS)

payasada *f* **1** (bufonada) **deja de hacer ~s** stop clowning around *o* acting the clown (colloq) **2** (fam) **(a)** (ridiculez) ridiculous thing to say/do **(b)** (Chi) (tontería) stupid thing to say/do; **son puras ~s** that's utter nonsense **(c)** (Chi) (cosa) thingamajig (colloq)

payasear [A1] *vi* (AmL fam) to clown around (colloq)

payaso -sa *m,f* **(a)** (Espec) clown; **hacer (se) el ~** to clown around (colloq) **(b)** (persona — cómica) clown, comedian; (— poco seria) joker (colloq & pej)

payo -ya *m,f* (Esp) *word used by gypsies to refer to a non-gypsy*

paz *f* **(a)** (Mil, Pol) peace; **firmar la ~** to sign a peace agreement *o* treaty; **en época de ~** in

AmC	América Central	Arg	Argentina	Cu	Cuba	Per	Perú
AmL	América Latina	Bol	Bolivia	Ec	Ecuador	RPI	Río de la Plata
AmS	América del Sur	Chi	Chile	Esp	España	Ur	Uruguay
Andes	Región andina	CS	Cono Sur	Méx	México	Ven	Venezuela

peacetime; *hacer las paces* to make (it) up **(b)** (calma) peace; **no me dejan vivir en** ~ they don't give me a moment's peace; **dejar algo/a algn en** ~ to leave sth/sb alone; **descanse en** ~ (frml) rest in peace (frml)

PC *m or f* personal computer, PC

P.D. (= *post data*) PS

pe *f: name of the letter* P

peaje *m* (dinero) toll; (lugar) toll barrier; **carretera de** ~ toll road

pearse [A1] *v pron* (AmL fam) to fart (sl)

peatón *m* pedestrian

peatonal *adj* pedestrian (*before n*)

pebete -ta,*f,m* (RPl fam) kid (colloq)

pebre *m: sauce made with onion, chili, coriander, parsley and tomato*

peca *f* freckle

pecado *m* **(a)** (Relig) sin; ~ **capital** deadly sin; ~ **mortal** mortal sin **(b)** (lástima) crime, sin

pecador -dora *m,f* sinner

pecaminoso -sa *adj* sinful

pecar [A2] *vi* (Relig) to sin

pecera *f* (redonda) goldfish bowl; (rectangular) fish tank

pechera *f* (de camisa, vestido) front

pecho *m* (tórax) chest; (mama) breast; **dar (el)** ~ **a un niño** to breast-feed *o* suckle a child; *tomarse algo a* ⟨crítica⟩ to take sth to heart; ⟨responsabilidad⟩ to take sth seriously

pechuga *f* (de pollo) breast

pechugona *f* (fam & hum) big-breasted woman

pecoso -sa *adj* freckly

pectoral *adj* **1** ⟨músculos⟩ pectoral (*before n*) **2** (Med): **jarabe** ~ cough mixture *o* syrup

peculiar *adj* **1** (característico) particular; **un rasgo** ~ a particular trait; **con su** ~ **buen humor** with his characteristic good humor **2** (poco común, raro) ⟨sensación⟩ peculiar, unusual

peculiaridad *f* peculiarity

pedagogía *f* pedagogy, teaching

pedagógico -ca *adj* pedagogical, teaching (*before n*)

pedagogo -ga *m,f* (estudioso) educationalist; (educador) educator, teacher, pedagogue (frml)

pedal *m* pedal; ~ **de embrague/de freno** clutch/brake pedal; ~ **de arranque** kickstart

pedalear [A1] *vi* to pedal

pedante *adj* pedantic
■ *mf* pedant

pedantería *f* pedantry

pedazo *m* **1** (trozo) piece; **un** ~ **de pan** a piece of bread; **se hizo** ~s it smashed (to pieces); **el coche saltó** *or* **voló en** ~s the car was blown to pieces; **lo hice** ~s I smashed it; *caerse a* ~s to fall to pieces **2** (fam) (en insultos): **¡** ~ **de idiota!** you idiot! (colloq)

pederasta *m* (homosexual) homosexual; (pedófilo) pederast

pedernal *m* flint

pedestal *m* pedestal

pedestre *adj* prosaic

pediatra *mf* pediatrician*

pediatría *f* pediatrics*

pediátrico -ca *adj* pediatric*

pedicuro -ra *m,f* chiropodist

pedido *m* **1** (Com) order; **hacer un** ~ to place an order **2** (AmL) (solicitud) request; **a** ~ **de** at the request of

pedigree /peðiˈɣri/, **pedigrí** *m* pedigree; **un perro de** *or* **con** ~ a pedigree dog

pedinche *mf* (Méx fam) scrounger (colloq)

pedir [I14] *vt* **1 (a)** ⟨dinero/ayuda⟩ to ask for; **pidieron un préstamo al banco** they asked the bank for a loan; **pidió permiso para salir** she asked permission to leave; **pide limosna** he begs (for money); ~**le algo a algn** to ask sb for sth; **le pidió ayuda** he asked her for help; **me pidió disculpas** *or* **perdón** he apologized (to me); ~ **hora** to make an appointment; ~ **la palabra** to ask for permission to speak; **me pidió que le enseñara** he asked me to teach him; ▶ PRESTADO **(b)** (en bar, restaurante) ⟨plato/bebida⟩ to order; ⟨cuenta⟩ to ask for
2 (Com) **(a)** (como precio) ~ **algo** POR **algo** to ask sth FOR sth; **¿cuánto pide por la casa?** how much is she asking for the house? **(b)** ⟨mercancías⟩ to order
■ ~ *vi* **(a)** (en bar, restaurante) to order **(b)** (mendigar) to beg

pedo *m* **1** (fam) (ventosidad) fart (sl); **tirarse un** ~ to fart (sl), to let off (BrE colloq); **al** ~ (RPl fam) for nothing **2** (arg) (borrachera): **agarró un buen** ~ he got really plastered (colloq); **tenía un** ~ **que no veía** he was blind drunk (colloq) **3** (Méx fam) (problema, lío) hassle (colloq); **hacérsela de** ~ **a algn** (Méx vulg) to give sb hell (colloq)

pedofilia *f* pedophilia*

pedófilo *m* pedophile*

pedorreta *f* (fam) raspberry (colloq)

pedrada *f* **1** (golpe): **me dio una** ~ **en la cabeza** she hit me on the head with a stone **2** (Méx fam) (indirecta) hint

pedrisco *m* hail

pega *f* **1** (Col fam) (broma) trick; **de** ~ (Esp fam) ⟨araña/culebra⟩ joke (*before n*), trick (*before n*); ⟨revólver⟩ dummy (*before n*) **2** (Esp fam) (dificultad, inconveniente) problem, snag (colloq); **te ponen muchas** ~s they make it really difficult for you **3** (Andes fam) **(a)** (trabajo) work; (empleo) work; **está sin** ~ he's out of work **(b)** (lugar) work

pegadizo -za *adj* catchy

pegado -da *adj* [ESTAR] **(a)** (junto) ~ A **algo: su casa está pegada a la mía** her house is right next to mine; **iba muy** ~ **al coche de delante** he was too close to the car in front; **pon la cama pegada a la pared** put the bed right up against the wall **(b)** (adherido) stuck; (con cola, goma) glued; **está** ~ **al suelo** it's stuck to the floor; **las piezas están pegadas** the pieces are glued together

pegajoso -sa *adj* **(a)** ⟨superficie/sustancia⟩ sticky **(b)** ⟨calor⟩ sticky **(c)** (fam) ⟨persona⟩ clinging (colloq) **(d)** (AmL fam) ⟨canción/música⟩ catchy

pegamento *m* glue, adhesive

pegar [A3] *vt* **1 (a)** ⟨bofetada/patada⟩ to give; **le pegó una paliza terrible** he gave him a terrible beating; **le** ~**on un tiro** they shot her **(b)** ⟨grito/chillido⟩ to let out; ~ **un salto de alegría** to jump for joy; ~**le un susto a algn** to give sb a fright ⋯⟶

p

2 (a) (adherir) to stick; (con cola) to glue, stick (b) (coser) ‹mangas/botones› to sew on (c) (arrimar) to move … closer

3 (fam) (contagiar) ‹enfermedad› to give; **me pegó la gripe** he gave me the flu

■ ~ *vi* **1** (a) (golpear): **~le A algn** to hit sb; (a un niño, como castigo) to smack sb; **le pega a su mujer** he beats his wife; **la pelota pegó en el poste** the ball hit the goalpost (b) (fam) (hacerse popular) ‹producto/moda› to take off; ‹artista› to be very popular

2 (a) (adherir) to stick (b) (armonizar) to go together; **~ CON algo** to go WITH sth; **no pega con el vestido** it doesn't go (very well) with the dress

■ **pegarse** *v pron* **1** (a) (golpearse): **me pegué con la mesa** I knocked o hit myself on the table; **me pegué en la cabeza** I banged o knocked my head (b) (recípr) (darse golpes) to hit each other

2 ‹susto› to get; **~se un tiro** to shoot oneself

3 (contagiarse) ‹enfermedad› to be infectious; **eso se pega** you can easily catch it; **se te va a ~ mi catarro** you'll catch my cold; **se le ha pegado el acento mexicano** he's picked up a Mexican accent

pegatina *f* (Esp) sticker

pegoste *mf* (Méx fam) hanger-on (colloq)

peinado¹ -da *adj*: **no estaba peinada** she hadn't combed her hair; **siempre va muy bien peinada** her hair always looks very nice

peinado² **m (arreglo del pelo) hairstyle; **lavado y ~** shampoo and set

peinador -dora *m,f* (Méx, RPl) (persona) hairdresser, stylist

peinar [A1] *vt* **1** (a) ‹melena/flequillo› (con peine) to comb; (con cepillo) to brush (b) ‹peluquero›: **¿quién te peina?** who does your hair? **2** ‹lana› to card **3** ‹period› ‹área/zona› to comb

■ **peinarse** *v pron* (refl) (con peine) to comb one's hair; (con cepillo) to brush one's hair (b) (caus) to have one's hair done; **me peino en esta peluquería** I have my hair done at this salon

peine *m* comb

peineta *f* (a) (para sujetar, adornar) ornamental comb (b) (Chi) (peine) comb

p. ej. (= por ejemplo) eg, for example

Pekín *m* Peking, Beijing

pekinés -nesa *m,f* Pekinese

pela *f* (Esp fam) (peseta) peseta

peladez *f* (Méx) rude word

pelado -da *adj* **1** (a) (con el pelo corto): **lo dejaron ~ o con la cabeza pelada (al rape)** they cropped his hair very short (b) (CS) (calvo) bald **2** (a) ‹manzana› peeled; ‹hueso› clean; ‹almendras› blanched (b) ‹nariz/espalda›: **tengo la nariz/espalda pelada** my nose/back is peeling **3** (Chi fam) ‹pies/trasero› bare; **ir a pie ~** to go barefoot **4** (Méx fam) (grosero) foulmouthed

■ *m,f* (CS fam) (calvo) baldy (colloq)

peladura *f* (a) (de fruta) peel; **~s de papa** potato peelings (b) (Andes) (en la piel) graze

pelaje *m* (de animal) coat, fur

pelar [A1] *vt* (a) ‹fruta/zanahoria› to peel; ‹habas/marisco› to shell; ‹caramelo› to unwrap (b) ‹ave› to pluck **2** (rapar): **lo ~on al cero o al rape** they cropped his hair very short **3** (fam) (en

el juego) to clean … out (colloq) **4** (Chi fam) ‹persona› to badmouth (AmE colloq), to slag off (BrE colloq)

■ **pelarse** *v pron* (a causa del sol) ‹persona› to peel; ‹cara/hombros› (+ me/te/le etc) to peel; **se te está pelando la nariz** your nose is peeling

peldaño *m* (escalón) step, stair; (travesaño) rung

pelea *f* (a) (discusión) quarrel, fight (colloq), argument; **buscar ~** to try to pick a quarrel o fight; **tuvimos una ~** we quarreled o had an argument (b) (en sentido físico) fight; **~ de gallos** cockfight

peleado -da *adj* (a) (enfadado): **están ~s** they've fallen out; **estar ~ con algn** to have fallen out with sb (b) ‹partido/carrera/elecciones› keenly-contested

peleador -dora *adj* (fam) (que discute) argumentative; (que pelea): **es muy ~** he's always fighting

pelear [A1] *vi* (a) (discutir) to quarrel; **~on por una tontería** they quarreled o (colloq) had a fight over a silly little thing (b) ‹novios› (discutir) to quarrel, argue; (terminar) to break up, split up (c) (en sentido físico) to fight; **~ POR algo** to fight OVER sth

■ **pelearse** *v pron* (a) (discutir) to quarrel; (pegarse) to fight; **~se POR algo** to quarrel/fight OVER sth (b) ‹novios› (discutir) to quarrel; (terminar) to break up, split up

pelele *m* (a) (de trapo) rag doll; (de paja) straw doll (b) (persona — manipulada) puppet; (— débil) (fam) wimp (colloq)

peletería *f* (oficio) fur trade; (tienda) furrier's, fur shop; (género) furs (pl)

peliagudo -da *adj* ‹problema› difficult, tricky; ‹asunto› thorny

pelícano *m* pelican

película *f* **1** (a) (Cin, TV) movie, film (BrE); **hoy dan o** (Esp) **echan or ponen una ~** there's a movie o film on today, they're showing a movie o film today; **~ de dibujos animados** cartoon; **~ del Oeste or de vaqueros** Western; **~ de miedo or de terror** horror movie o film; **~ de suspenso or** (Esp) **suspense** thriller; **~ muda** silent movie o film (b) (Fot) film **2** (capa fina — de aceite) film; (— de polvo) thin layer

peligrar [A1] *vi* to be at risk; **hacer ~ algo** to put sth at risk

peligro *m* danger; **estar en or correr ~** ‹persona› to be in danger; ‹vida› to be in danger o at risk; **un ~ para la salud** a health risk; **poner algo/a algn en ~** to put sth/sb at risk; **corren el ~ de perder la final** they're in danger of losing the final; **corres el ~ de que te despidan** you run the risk of being fired; **estar fuera de ~** to be out of danger; **⑨ peligro de incendio** fire hazard

peligrosidad *f* dangerousness

peligroso -sa *adj* dangerous

pelillo *m* small hair

pelirrojo -ja *adj* red-haired, ginger-haired ■ *m,f* redhead

pellejerías *fpl* (Andes fam) hard times (pl)

pellejo *m* (a) (piel — de animal) skin, hide; (— de persona) (fam) skin (colloq); **ponerse en el ~ de**

algn (fam) to put oneself in sb's shoes **(b)** (fam) (vida) neck (colloq); **jugarse** *or* **arriesgar el** ~ to risk one's neck (colloq) **(c)** (odre) wineskin

pellizcar [A2] *vt* ⟨*persona/brazo*⟩ to pinch

pellizco *m* **(a)** (en la piel) pinch; **me dio un** ~ **en la pierna** she pinched my leg **(b)** (fam) (cantidad pequeña) little bit; **un** ~ **de sal** a pinch of salt

pelmazo -a *adj* (fam) boring
■ *m,f* (fam) bore

pelo *m* **①** (de personas) hair; ~ **rizado/liso** *or* **lacio** curly/straight hair; **tiene mucho/poco** ~ he has really thick/thin hair; **llevar el** ~ **suelto** to wear one's hair down *o* loose; **se le está cayendo el** ~ he's losing his hair; **con** ~**s y señales** (fam) down to the last detail; **no tiene** ~**s en la lengua** (fam) he doesn't mince his words; **se me/le ponen los** ~**s de punta** (fam) it sends shivers down my/his spine, it makes my/his hair stand on end; **tomarle el** ~ **a algn** (fam) (bromeando) to pull sb's leg (colloq); (burlándose) to mess around with sb (AmE), to mess sb around (BrE)
② (Zool) (filamento) hair; (pelaje — de perro, gato) hair, fur; (— de conejo, oso) fur; ~ **de camello** camelhair
③ (de alfombra) pile

pelón -lona *adj* (fam) (sin pelo) bald
■ *m,f* **①** (fam) (sin pelo) baldy (colloq) **②** **pelón** *m* (RPI) (duranzo) nectarine

pelota *f* **①** (Dep, Jueg) ball; **una** ~ **de fútbol** (esp AmL) a football; **jugar a la** ~ to play ball; ~ **vasca** jai alai, pelota; **darle** ~ **a algn** (CS fam) to take notice of sb; **hacerle la** ~ **a algn** (Esp fam) to suck up to sb (colloq) **②** **pelotas** *fpl* (vulg) (testículos) balls (*pl*) (colloq *o* vulg); **en** ~**s** (vulg) (sin ropa) stark naked; (sin dinero) flat broke (colloq)
■ *mf* **①** (AmS vulg) (imbécil) jerk (sl) **②** (Esp fam) (adulador) creep (colloq)

pelotari *mf* jai alai *o* pelota player

pelotazo *m* (golpe): **me dio un** ~ he hit me with the ball

pelotera *f* (fam) **(a)** (lío, jaleo) ruckus (AmE colloq), rumpus (BrE colloq) **(b)** (riña) argument, row (colloq)

pelotero -ra *m,f* **(a)** (AmL) (jugador — de béisbol) baseball player; (— de fútbol) soccer *o* football player, footballer **(b)** (Chi) (recogepelotas) (*m*) ballboy; (*f*) ballgirl

pelotón *m* **(a)** (Mil) squad; ~ **de ejecución** *or* **fusilamiento** firing squad **(b)** (en ciclismo) bunch, pack; (en atletismo) pack **(c)** (fam) (de gente) gang (colloq)

pelotudo -da *adj* (AmS vulg): **¡qué** ~**!** what a jerk! (sl)
■ *m,f* (AmS vulg) jerk (sl)

peluca *f* wig

peluche *m* felt, plush; **un juguete de** ~ a cuddly toy; ▶ **oso**

pelucón -cona *adj* (Chi, Per fam) (con mucho pelo) hairy; (de pelo largo) long-haired

peludo -da *adj* ⟨*hombre/brazo*⟩ hairy; ⟨*barba*⟩ bushy; ⟨*animal*⟩ hairy, furry; ⟨*cola*⟩ bushy; ⟨*lana/jersey*⟩ hairy

peluquería *f* **(a)** (establecimiento) hairdresser's, hairdressing salon **(b)** (oficio) hairdressing, hairstyling

peluquero -ra *m,f* hairdresser, hairstylist

peluquín *m* toupee, hairpiece

pelusa¹, pelusilla *f* **①** (en la cara) down, fuzz; (de fruta) down; (en jersey) ball of fluff *o* fuzz; (de suciedad) ball of fluff **②** (Esp fam) (celos) jealousy; **tener** ~ to be jealous

pelusa² *mf* (Chi fam) (niño — callejero) street kid (colloq); (— travieso) little rascal (colloq)

pelvis *f* (*pl* ~) pelvis

pena *f* **①** **(a)** (tristeza): **tenía/sentía mucha** ~ he was *o* felt very sad; **me da** ~ **verlo** it upsets me *o* it makes me sad to see it; **a mí la que me da** ~ **es su mujer** it's his wife I feel sorry for; **está que da** ~ she's in a terrible state **(b)** (lástima) pity, shame; **¡qué** ~**!** what a pity *o* shame!; **es una** ~ **que ...** it's a pity (that) ...; **vale** *or* **merece la** ~ it's worth it; **vale la** ~ **leerlo/visitarlo** it's worth reading/a visit
② **penas** *fpl* **(a)** (problemas) sorrows (*pl*); **ahogar las** ~**s** to drown one's sorrows; **me contó sus** ~**s** he told me his troubles; **a duras** ~**s** (apenas) hardly; (con dificultad) with difficulty **(b)** (penalidades) hardship
③ (Der) sentence; **la** ~ **máxima** the maximum sentence; ~ **capital** *or* **de muerte** death penalty
④ (AmL exc CS) (vergüenza) embarrassment; **¡qué** ~**!** how embarrassing!; **me da mucha** ~ **pedírselo** I'm too embarrassed to ask him

penal *adj* criminal (*before* n)
■ *m* **①** (cárcel) prison, penitentiary (AmE) **②** (AmL period) (Dep) penalty

pénal *m* (Andes) penalty

penalidades *fpl* hardship, suffering

penalizar [A4] *vt* (Der) to penalize

penalty /'penalti, pe'nalti/ *m* (*pl* -**tys**) penalty; **pitar** *or* **señalar** ~ to award *o* give a penalty

penca *f* **(a)** (de hoja) main rib **(b)** (del nopal) stalk **(c)** (Méx) (de bananas) bunch

pendejada *f* **(a)** (AmL exc CS fam) (estupidez) stupid thing to say/do **(b)** (Per vulg) (mala jugada) dirty trick

pendejear [A1] *vi* (Méx fam) to clown around (colloq)

pendejez *f* (Méx vulg) stupidity

pendejo -ja *adj* **(a)** (AmL exc CS fam) (estúpido) dumb (AmE colloq), thick (BrE colloq) **(b)** (Per fam) (listo) sly, sharp (colloq)
■ *m,f* **(a)** (AmL exc CS fam) (estúpido) dummy (colloq), nerd (colloq); **hacerse el** ~ (fam) (hacerse el tonto) to act dumb (colloq); (no hacer nada) to loaf around (colloq) **(b)** (Per fam) (persona lista) sly devil

pendenciero -ra *adj* quarrelsome
■ *m,f* troublemaker

pendiente *adj* **①** ⟨*asunto/problema*⟩ unresolved; ⟨*cuenta*⟩ outstanding **②** (atento): **está** ~ **del niño a todas horas** he devotes every minute of the day to the child; **estoy** ~ **de que me llamen** I'm waiting for them to call me
■ *m* (Esp) earring
■ *f* (de terreno) slope, incline; (de tejado) slope; **una** ~ **muy pronunciada** a very steep slope *o* incline; **tiene mucha** ~ it slopes steeply

péndulo *m* pendulum

pene *m* penis

penetración *f* penetration

penetrante *adj* **①** **(a)** ⟨*mirada/voz*⟩ penetrating, piercing; ⟨*olor*⟩ pungent, penetrating; ⟨*sonido*⟩ piercing **(b)** ⟨*viento/frío*⟩ bitter, biting **②** ⟨*inteligencia/mente/ironía*⟩ sharp

penetrar [A1] *vi* (entrar) ∼ POR algo «*agua/ humedad*» to seep THROUGH sth; «*luz*» to shine THROUGH sth; «*ladrón*» to enter THROUGH sth; ∼ EN algo to penetrate sth

■ ∼ *vt* to penetrate; **la bala le penetró el pulmón** the bullet penetrated *o* entered his lung

penicilina *f* penicillin

península *f* peninsula

peninsular *adj* peninsular

■ *mf*: **los** ∼**es** people from mainland Spain

penique *m* penny

penitencia *f* **1** (Relig) penance; **en** ∼ **as** (a) penance **2** (a) (Andes) (en juegos) forfeit; (b) (RPl fam) (castigo) punishment; **el maestro me puso en** ∼ the teacher punished me

penitenciaría *f* penitentiary

penitente *mf* penitent

penoso -sa *adj* **1** (lamentable) terrible, awful **2** (a) (triste) sad (b) «*viaje*» grueling*; «*trabajo*» laborious, difficult **3** (AmL exc CS fam) (a) «*persona*» shy (b) (embarazoso) embarrassing

pensamiento *m* **1** (a) (facultad) thought (b) (cosa pensada) thought (c) (doctrina) thinking (d) (máxima) thought **2** (Bot) pansy

pensar [A5] *vi* to think; **después de mucho** ∼ ... after much thought ...; **actuó sin** ∼ he did it without thinking; **pensé para mí** *or* **para mis adentros** I thought to myself; ∼ EN algo/algn to think ABOUT sth/sb; **cuando menos se piensa** ... just when you least expect it ...; ∼ **mal/bien de algn** to think ill *o* badly/well of sb; **dar que** *or* **hacer** ∼ **a algn** to make sb think

■ ∼ *vt* **1** (a) (creer, opinar) to think; **pienso que no** I don't think so; **¿qué piensas del divorcio/del jefe?** what do you think about divorce/the boss? (b) (considerar) to think about; **lo** ∼**é** I'll think about it; **piénsalo bien antes de decidir** think it over before you decide; **pensándolo bien,** ... on second thought(s) *o* thinking about it, ...; **¡y** ∼ **que** ...**!** (and) to think that ...!; **¡ni** ∼**lo!** no way! (colloq), not on your life! (colloq) (c) (Col) «*persona*» to think about

2 (tener la intención de): ∼ **hacer algo** to think of doing sth; **pensamos ir al teatro** we're thinking of going to the theater; **no pienso ir** I'm not going

■ **pensarse** *v pron* (enf) (fam) «*decisión/ respuesta*» to think about; *ver tb* PENSAR *vt* 1B

pensativo -va *adj* pensive, thoughtful

pensión *f* **1** (Servs Socs) pension; **cobrar la** ∼ to draw one's pension; ∼ **alimenticia** maintenance; ∼ **de invalidez** disability (allowance) (AmE), invalidity benefit (BrE) **2** (a) (casa — de huéspedes) guesthouse, rooming house (AmE), boarding house (BrE); (— para estudiantes) student hostel; ∼ **completa** full board ▶ MEDIO[1] 1 (b) (alojamiento) accommodations (*pl*) (AmE), lodging, accommodation (BrE) **3** (Col) (mensualidad) tuition (AmE), school fees (*pl*) (BrE

pensionado -da *m,f* **1** (Servs Socs) pensioner **2** **pensionado** *m* (a) (Esp) (internado) boarding school (b) (CS) (pensión para estudiantes) student hostel

pensionarse [A1] *v pron* (Col) to retire

pensionista *mf* **1** (Servs Socs) pensioner **2** (en casa de huéspedes) resident, lodger

pentágono *m* (a) (Mat) pentagon (b) **el Pentágono** the Pentagon

pentagrama *m* (Mús) stave, staff

pentatlón *m* pentathlon

penúltimo -ma *adj* penultimate

■ *m,f*: **ser el** ∼ to be second to last

penumbra *f* (media luz) half-light, semidarkness

penuria *f* (a) (escasez) shortage, dearth; **pasar** ∼**s** to suffer hardship (b) (pobreza) poverty

peña *f* **1** (roca) crag, rock **2** (a) (grupo) circle, group; ∼ **taurina** bullfighting club (b) (AmL) *tb* ∼ **folklórica** folk club

peñasco *m* crag, rocky outcrop

peón *m* **1** (Const) laborer*; (Agr) (esp AmL) agricultural laborer*, farm worker; ∼ **albañil** (building) laborer*; ∼ **caminero** road worker **2** (en ajedrez) pawn; (en damas) piece, checker (AmE), draughtsman (BrE)

peonza *f* spinning top

peor *adj/adv* **1** (uso comparativo) worse; **va a ser** ∼ **para él como no estudie** if he doesn't study so much the worse for him; **y si vienen los dos, tanto** ∼ and it'll be even worse if the two of them come; **cada vez** ∼ worse and worse; **su situación es** ∼ **que la mía** his situation is worse than mine; **está** ∼ **que nunca** it's worse than ever **2** (uso superlativo) worst; **el** ∼ **alumno de la clase** the worst pupil in the class; **lo** ∼ **que puede pasar** the worst (thing) that can happen; **en el** ∼ **de los casos** if the worst comes to the worst; **el lugar donde** ∼ **se come** the worst place to eat in

■ *mf*: **el/la** ∼ (de dos) the worse; (de varios) the worst

pepa *f* (AmS) (semilla — de uva, naranja) pip; (— de durazno, aguacate) stone, pit

Pepe: *diminutive of José*

pepenador -dora *m,f* (Méx) scavenger (*on garbage dumps*)

pepenar [A1] *vt* (Méx fam) (en la basura) to scavenge

pepinillo *m* gherkin

pepino *m* cucumber

pepita *f* (a) (de uva) pip; (de tomate) seed; (de calabaza) (Méx) dried pumpkin seed (b) (de oro) nugget

pepona *f* large doll

pequeño -ña *adj* (a) (de tamaño) small; **me queda** ∼ it's too small for me; **en** ∼ in miniature (b) (de edad) young, small; **mi hermano** ∼ my younger *o* little brother; **cuando era** ∼ when I was small *o* little (c) (de poca importancia) «*distancia*» short; «*retraso*» short, slight; «*cantidad*» small; «*esfuerzo*» slight; «*problema/ diferencia*» slight, small

■ *m,f*: **el** ∼**/la pequeña** the little one (colloq); (edad — de dos) the younger; (— de muchos) the youngest

pera *f* **1** (Bot) pear; ∼ **de agua** dessert pear; **pedirle** ∼**s al olmo** to ask the impossible **2** (de

---

AmC	Central America	Arg	Argentina	Cu	Cuba	Per	Peru
AmL	Latin America	Bol	Bolivia	Ec	Ecuador	RPl	River Plate Area
AmS	South America	Chi	Chile	Esp	Spain	Ur	Uruguay
Andes	Andean Region	CS	Southern Cone	Méx	Mexico	Ven	Venezuela

goma) bulb **3** (en boxeo) punching ball (AmE), punchball (BrE) **4** (CS fam) (mentón) chin; (barba) goatee

peral *m* pear tree

percal *m* percale

percance *m* (contratiempo) mishap; (accidente) minor accidente

percatarse [A1] *v pron* to notice; ∼ **DE algo** to notice sth

percebe *m* (molusco) goose barnacle

percepción *f* (por los sentidos) perception; ∼ **extrasensorial** extrasensory perception, ESP

perceptible *adj* (por los sentidos) perceptible, noticeable

percha *f* **(a)** (para el armario) (coat) hanger **(b)** (gancho) coat hook; (perchero) coat stand

perchero *m* (de pared) coat rack; (de pie) coat stand

percibir [I1] *vt* **1** ⟨sonido/olor⟩ to perceive; ⟨peligro⟩ to sense **2** (frml) ⟨sueldo/cantidad⟩ to receive

percusión *f* percussion

perdedor -dora *adj* losing (before n)
■ *m,f* loser; **es un mal** ∼ he's a bad loser

perder [E8] *vt* **1** (en general) to lose; **perdí el pasaporte** I lost my passport; **quiere** ∼ **peso** he wants to lose weight; **con preguntar no se pierde nada** we've/you've nothing to lose by asking; ∼ **la vida** to lose one's life, to perish; ▶ CABEZA 1E, VISTA 3; **yo no pierdo las esperanzas** I'm not giving up hope; ∼ **la práctica** to get out of practice; ∼ **el equilibrio** to lose one's balance; ∼ **el conocimiento** to lose consciousness, to pass out; ∼ **el ritmo** (Mús) to lose the beat; (en trabajo) to get out of the rhythm **2 (a)** ⟨autobús/tren/avión⟩ to miss **(b)** ⟨ocasión/oportunidad⟩ to miss; **sin** ∼ **detalle** without missing any detail **(c)** ⟨tiempo⟩ to waste; ¡**no me hagas** ∼ (el) **tiempo!** don't waste my time!; **no hay tiempo que** ∼ there's no time to lose **3 (a)** ⟨guerra/pleito/partido⟩ to lose **(b)** ⟨curso/año⟩ to fail; ⟨examen⟩ (Ur) to fail **4** ⟨agua/aceite/aire⟩ to lose
■ ∼ *vi* **1** (ser derrotado) to lose; **perdieron 3 a 1** they lost 3-1; **no sabes** ∼ you're a bad loser; **llevar las de** ∼ to be onto a loser; **la que sale perdiendo soy yo** I'm the one who loses out *o* comes off worst **2** ⟨cafetera/tanque⟩ to leak **3 echar(se) a perder** ▶ ECHAR I 1A, ECHARSE 1A
■ **perderse** *v pron* **1** ⟨persona/objeto⟩ to get lost; **siempre me pierdo en esta ciudad** I always get lost in this town; **se le perdió el dinero** he's lost the money; **cuando se ponen a hablar rápido me pierdo** when they start talking quickly I get lost **2** ⟨fiesta/película/espectáculo⟩ to miss

perdición *f* ruin

pérdida *f* **(a)** (en general) loss; ∼ **de calor/energía** heat/energy loss; **tuvo una** ∼ **de conocimiento** he lost consciousness, he passed out; *no tiene* ∼ (Esp) you can't miss it **(b)** (Fin) loss; **la compañía sufrió grandes** ∼s the company made a huge loss; ∼s **materiales** damage; ∼s **y ganancias** profit and loss **(c)** (desperdicio) waste; **fue una** ∼ **de tiempo** it was a waste of time **(d)** (escape de gas, agua) leak

perdido -da *adj* **1** [ESTAR] **(a)** ⟨objeto/persona⟩ lost; **dar algo por** ∼ to give sth up for lost; *de* ∼ (Méx fam) at least **(b)** (confundido, desorientado) lost, confused **(c)** ⟨bala/perro⟩ stray (before n) **2** [ESTAR] (en un apuro): **si se enteran, estás** ∼ if they find out, you've had it *o* you're done for (colloq) **3** (aislado) ⟨lugar⟩ remote, isolated; ⟨momento⟩ idle, spare **4** ⟨idiota⟩ complete and utter (before n), total (before n); ⟨loco⟩ raving (before n); ⟨borracho⟩ out and out (before n)
■ *m,f* degenerate

perdidoso -sa *m, f* (Méx) loser

perdigón *m* (Arm) pellet

perdiz *f* partridge

perdón *m* (Der) pardon; (Relig) forgiveness; **me pidió** ∼ **por su comportamiento** he apologized to me for his behavior, he said he was sorry about his behavior; *con* ∼ if you'll pardon the expression
■ *interj* (expresando disculpas) I beg your pardon (frml), excuse me (AmE), sorry; (para atraer la atención) excuse me, pardon me (AmE); (al pedir que se repita algo) sorry?, pardon me? (AmE)

perdonar [A1] *vt* **(a)** ⟨persona/falta/pecado⟩ to forgive; **te perdono** I forgive you; **perdona mi curiosidad, pero ...** forgive my asking but ...; **perdone que lo moleste, pero ...** sorry to bother you *o* (AmE) pardon me for bothering you, but ... **(b)** ⟨deuda⟩ to write off; **le perdonó el castigo** she let him off the punishment
■ ∼ *vi*: **perdone ¿me puede decir la hora?** excuse me *o* (AmE) pardon me, can you tell me the time?; **perdone ¿cómo ha dicho?** sorry? what did you say?, excuse *o* pardon me? what did you say? (AmE); **perdona, pero yo no dije eso** I'm sorry but that's not what I said

perdurar [A1] *vi* ⟨duda/sentimiento/recuerdo⟩ to remain, last; ⟨crisis/situación/relación⟩ to last

perecear [A1] *vi* (Col) to laze around

perecedero -ra *adj* ⟨producto⟩ perishable

perecer [E3] *vi* (frml) to die, perish (journ o liter)

peregrinación *f*, **peregrinaje** *m* pilgrimage

peregrino -na *adj* **1** ⟨idea/respuesta⟩ outlandish, peculiar **2 (a)** ⟨ave⟩ migratory **(b)** ⟨monje⟩ wandering (before n)
■ *m,f* pilgrim

perejil *m* (Bot, Coc) parsley

perenne *adj* perennial; **árbol de hoja** ∼ evergreen tree

pereza *f* laziness; **me da** ∼ **ir** I can't be bothered to go; **tengo una** ∼ **horrible** I feel terribly lazy; ¡**qué** ∼ **tener que ir!** what a bind *o* drag having to go! (colloq)

perezosa *f* (Col, Per) deck chair

perezoso -sa *adj* lazy, idle
■ *m,f* **1** (holgazán) lazybones (colloq) **2 perezoso** *m* (Zool) sloth

perfección *f* perfection; **habla francés a la** ∼ she speaks perfect French

perfeccionar [A1] *vt* (mejorar) to improve; (hacer perfecto) to perfect

perfeccionista *mf* perfectionist

perfecto¹ -ta *adj* **(a)** (ideal, excelente) perfect ···⫶

(b) (delante del n) (absoluto): un ∼ caballero a
perfect gentleman; **es un ∼ desconocido** he is
completely unknown

perfecto² interj fine!

perfil m **(a)** (del cuerpo, la cara) profile; **una foto
de ∼** a profile photograph; **visto de ∼** seen from
the side **(b)** (contorno, silueta) profile, silhouette

perfilar [A1] vt ⟨plan/estrategia⟩ to shape
■ **perfilarse** v pron **(a)** «silueta/contorno» to be
outlined **(b)** (tomar forma) «posición/actitud» to
become clear

perforación f **(a)** (en general) drilling, boring;
(pozo) borehole **(b)** (Med) perforation **(c)** (en
papeles, sellos) perforation

perforadora f **1** (Min, Tec) drill **2** (de papeles)
hole puncher; (de sellos) perforator

perforar [A1] vt **1** **(a)** ⟨pozo⟩ to sink, drill,
bore **(b)** ⟨madera⟩ to drill o bore holes/a hole in
(c) «ácido» to perforate; «bala» to pierce
2 ⟨papel/tarjeta⟩ to perforate
■ **perforarse** v pron «úlcera/intestino» to
become perforated

perfumar [A1] vt to perfume
■ **perfumarse** v pron (refl) to put perfume o
scent on

perfume m perfume, scent

perfumería f perfumery

pergamino m (material) parchment; (documento)
scroll

pérgola f pergola

pericia f (destreza) skill

periferia f **(a)** (de círculo) periphery,
circumference **(b)** (de ciudad) outskirts (pl) **(c)**
(Inf) peripherals (pl)

periférico¹ -ca adj ⟨barrio/zona⟩ outlying
(before n)

periférico² m **1** (Inf) peripheral **2** (AmC,
Méx) (carretera) beltway (AmE), ring road (BrE)

perilla f (barba) goatee; **venir de ∼(s)** (fam) to
come in very handy (colloq)

perímetro m perimeter

periódico¹ -ca adj periodic

periódico² m newspaper, paper

periodiquero -ra m,f (Méx) news o newspaper
vendor

periodismo m journalism

periodista mf journalist, reporter; **∼ gráfico**
press photographer

período, periodo m period

peripecia f **(a)** (incidente): **un viaje lleno de ∼s**
an eventful journey; **sus ∼s en el extranjero** her
adventures abroad **(b)** (problema) vicissitude

periquito m (americano) parakeet; (australiano)
budgerigar, budgie (colloq)

periscopio m periscope

peritaje m **(a)** (informe) expert's report; (de casa)
survey (report) **(b)** (Educ) technical studies (pl)

perito -ta m,f (experto) expert; **∼ agrónomo**
agricultural technician; **∼ industrial** engineer; **∼
mercantil** qualified accountant

peritonitis f (pl ∼) peritonitis

perjudicado -da adj: **el que resultó ∼** the
one who lost out o who was worst hit; **los más
∼s** the worst hit, the worst affected
■ m,f: **el ∼ fui yo** I was the one who lost out

perjudicar [A2] vt (dañar) to be detrimental to
(frml), damage; **el tabaco perjudica la salud**
smoking is detrimental to o damages your health;
estas medidas perjudican a los jóvenes these
measures are detrimental to o harm young
people

perjudicial adj [SER] damaging, harmful,
detrimental (frml); **∼ PARA algo/algn** damaging o
harmful o detrimental TO sth/sb

perjuicio m (daño) damage; **no sufrió ningún ∼**
it did him no harm o damage; **le causó un gran
∼** it was very damaging to him; **redunda o va en
∼ de todos** it works against o (frml) is
detrimental to everyone; **sin ∼ para su salud**
without detriment to his health (frml); **sin ∼ de
que cambiemos de opinión** even though we may
change our minds later

perjurio m perjury

perla f (joya) pearl; **∼ cultivada** or **de cultivo**
cultured pearl

permanecer [E3] vi (frml) **(a)** (en lugar) to stay,
remain (frml) **(b)** (en actitud, estado) to remain;
permaneció en silencio he was o remained silent

permanencia f (en lugar) stay; (en organización,
cargo) continuance (frml)

permanente adj permanent
■ f **1** (en el pelo) perm; **hacerse la ∼** to have one's
hair permed, to have a perm **2** (Col) (juzgado)
emergency court (for cases of violent crime)

permisible adj permissible

permisionario -ria m,f (Méx) concessionaire,
official agent

permisivo -va adj permissive

permiso m **1** (autorización) permission;
(documento) permit, license*; **me dio ∼** she gave
me permission; **(con) permiso** (al abrirse paso)
excuse me; (al entrar) may I come in?; **∼ de
conducir** driver's license (AmE), driving licence
(BrE); **∼ de residencia** residence permit, green
card (AmE); **∼ de trabajo** work permit **2** (días
libres) leave; **de ∼** on leave

permitir [I1] vt **(a)** (autorizar) to allow, permit
(frml); **no le permitieron verla** he was not allowed
to see her; **no van a ∼les la entrada** they're not
going to let them in; **¿me permite?** (frml) may I?
(b) (tolerar, consentir): **no te permito que me hables
así** I won't have you speak o I won't tolerate you
speaking to me like that; **si se me permite la
expresión** if you'll pardon the expression **(c)**
(hacer posible) to enable, to make ... possible; **esto
∼á mejores comunicaciones** this will enable
better communications; **si el tiempo lo permite**
weather permitting
■ **permitirse** v pron (refl) to allow oneself;
(económicamente): **puedo/no puedo ∼me ese lujo** I
can/can't afford that luxury

permutación f permutation

pernera f (del pantalón) leg

pero conj but; **ella fue, ∼ yo no** she went, but I
didn't; **¡∼ si queda lejísimos!** but it's miles
(away)!; **¿∼ tú estás loca?** are you crazy?
■ m **(a)** (defecto) defect, bad point; (dificultad,
problema) drawback; **ponerle ∼s a algo/algn** to
find fault with sth/sb **(b)** (excusa) objection; **¡no
hay ∼ que valga!** I don't want any excuses (o
arguments etc)

perogrullada f (fam) platitude, truism

Perogrullo m: **ser de** ~ to be patently obvious

perol m (pequeño) saucepan; (grande) pot

peroné m fibula

perorata f (fam) lecture (colloq)

perpendicular adj/f perpendicular

perpetrar [A1] vt to perpetrate (frml), to carry out

perpetuar [A18] vt to perpetuate

perpetuo -tua adj perpetual

perplejidad f perplexity, puzzlement

perplejo -ja adj perplexed, puzzled; **estar** ~ **con** algo to be puzzled o perplexed by sth

perra f ⒈ (Zool) dog, bitch [BITCH solo se emplea cuando se quiere hacer referencia al sexo del animal] ver tb PERRO ⒉ (Esp fam) (a) (rabieta) tantrum; **coger una** ~ to have o throw a tantrum (b) (manía) obsession; **le ha logido la** ~ **de tener uno** he's obsessed with having one

perrada f (AmL fam) dirty trick

perrera f (a) (lugar) dog pound, dog's home (b) (vehículo) dog catcher's van

perrería f (fam) terrible thing (colloq)

perrero -ra m,f dog catcher, dog warden (BrE)

perrito m ⒈ (Zool) little dog; ver tb PERRO ⒉ (AmL) (Bot) snapdragon

perro -rra m,f (Zool) dog; ~ **callejero** stray (dog); ~ **de compañía** pet dog; ~ **guardián** guard dog; ~ **guía** o **lazarillo** guide dog; ~ **pastor** sheepdog; **perrito caliente** (Coc) hot dog; **perrito faldero** lapdog; ~ **policía** German shepherd, Alsatian (BrE); ~ **rastreador** (para seguir una huella) tracker dog; (para buscar drogas) sniffer dog; ~ **salchicha** dachshund, sausage dog (colloq); **de ~s** (fam) foul; **hace un tiempo de ~s** the weather's foul o horrible; **está de un humor de ~s** he's in a foul mood; **llevarse como (el)** ~ **y (el) gato** to fight like cats and dogs (AmE) o (BrE) cat and dog
■ adj (fam) (a) ⟨vida/suerte⟩ rotten (colloq), lousy (colloq) (b) ⟨persona⟩ nasty

persa adj/mf Persian
■ m (idioma) Persian

persecución f (a) (en sentido físico) pursuit; **salir en** ~ **de algn** to set off in pursuit of sb (b) (por la ideología) persecution; **sufrir persecuciones** to be subjected to persecution, to be persecuted

perseguir [I30] vt ⒈ (a) ⟨fugitivo/delincuente/ presa⟩ to pursue, chase (b) (por la ideología) to persecute ⒉ ⟨objetivo/fin⟩ to pursue; ~ **la fama** to be in pursuit of fame; **me persigue la mala suerte** I'm dogged by bad luck

perseverante adj persevering, persistent

perseverar [A1] vi to persevere

Persia f Persia

persiana f (a) (que se enrolla o levanta) blind; ~ **veneciana** or **de lamas** Venetian blind (b) (AmL) (contraventana, postigo) shutter

persignarse [A1] v pron to cross oneself

persistencia f persistence

persistente adj persistent

persistir [I1] vi: **persiste el temporal** there is still a storm blowing; ~ **EN algo** to persist IN sth

persona f (a) (ser humano) person; **una** ~ **muy educada** a very polite person; **dos o más** ~**s** two or more people; **las** ~**s interesadas** ... all those interested ... (b) (en locs) **en persona** ⟨ir/ presentarse⟩ in person; **no lo conozco en** ~ I

don't know him personally; **por persona** per person; **solo se venden dos entradas por** ~ you can only get two tickets per person; **la comida costó 20 dólares por** ~ the meal cost 20 dollars per o a head (c) (Ling) person

personaje m (a) (Cin, Lit) character (b) (persona importante) important figure, personage (frml); **un** ~ **de la política** an important political figure; **es todo un** ~ **en el pueblo** he's something of a local celebrity

personal adj personal; **objetos de uso** ~ personal effects
■ m (de fábrica, empresa) personnel (pl), staff (sing or pl); **estamos escasos de** ~ we're short-staffed

personalidad f (a) (Psic) personality (b) (persona importante) ▸ PERSONAJE B

personalizar [A4] vi: **no quiero** ~ I don't want to name names o mention any names
■ ~ vt to personalize

personería f (Col, RPl) legal capacity

personero -ra m,f (AmL) (representante) representative; (portavoz) (m) spokesman, spokesperson; (f) spokeswoman, spokesperson

personificar [A2] vt to personify; **es la bondad personificada** she is kindness itself

perspectiva f (a) (Arquit, Art) perspective; **en** ~ in perspective (b) (vista, paisaje) view, perspective (frml) (c) (punto de vista) perspective (d) (posibilidad) prospect; **las** ~**s son buenas** the prospects are good; **no tengo ningún plan en** ~ I've no plans for the immediate future

perspicacia f shrewdness, insight

perspicaz adj shrewd, perceptive

persuadir [I1] vt to persuade; ~ **a algn DE QUE** or **PARA QUE haga algo** to persuade sb to do sth

persuasión f persuasion

persuasivo -va adj persuasive

pertenecer [E3] vi (a) (ser propiedad) ~ **A algn/ algo** to belong TO sb/sth (b) (formar parte) ~ **A algo** to belong TO sth, be a member OF sth

perteneciente adj: **los países** ~**s al grupo** the countries belonging to o which are members of the group

pertenencia f (a) (a grupo, organización) membership (b) (frml) (propiedad): **los objetos de su** ~ his belongings (c) **pertenencias** fpl belongings (pl), possessions (pl)

pértiga f (a) (vara) pole (b) (Esp) (Dep) pole; **salto con** ~ pole vault

pertinente adj (a) (oportuno, adecuado) ⟨medida⟩ appropriate (b) (relevante) ⟨observación/ comentario⟩ relevant, pertinent

perturbación f (alteración) disruption; (Psic) disturbance

perturbado -da adj disturbed
■ m,f: tb ~ **mental** mentally disturbed person

perturbar [A1] vt to disturb

Perú m: tb **el** ~ Peru

peruanismo m Peruvianism, Peruvian word/ expression

peruano -na adj/m,f Peruvian

perversión f (a) (maldad) evil, wickedness (b) (corrupción) perversion

perverso -sa adj evil
■ m,f evil o wicked person

pervertido -da m,f pervert

p

pervertir [I11] *vt* to corrupt, pervert
■ **pervertirse** *v pron* to become corrupted
pesa *f* **(a)** (de balanza, reloj) weight **(b)** (Dep) (grande) weight; (pequeña) dumbbell; **levantamiento de ~s** weightlifting; **hacer ~s** to do weight training **(c)** (balanza) scales (*pl*)
pesadez *f* ⊡ (sensación de cansancio) heaviness ⊠ (fam) **(a)** (aburrimiento, molestia) drag (colloq); **¡qué ~ de conversación!** what a boring conversation! **(b)** (Andes) (broma) tiresome joke; (comentario) nasty remark
pesadilla *f* **(a)** (sueño) nightmare, bad dream **(b)** (situación) nightmare; **de ~** ⟨viaje/visión⟩ nightmare (*before n*)
pesado -da *adj* ⊡ (en general) heavy; ⟨estómago⟩ bloated; ⟨sueño⟩ deep ⊠ **(a)** (fam) (fastidioso, aburrido) ⟨libro/película⟩ tedious; ⟨persona⟩: **¡qué ~ es!** he's such a pain in the neck! (colloq); **no te pongas ~** don't be so annoying *o* (colloq) such a pest! **(b)** (AmL) (difícil, duro) ⟨trabajo/tarea⟩ heavy, hard ⊟ (Andes fam) (antipático) unpleasant; **¡qué tipo tan ~!** what a jerk! (colloq)
■ *m,f* **(a)** (fam) (latoso) pain (colloq), pest (colloq) **(b)** (Andes fam) (antipático) jerk (colloq)
pesadumbre *f* grief, sorrow
pésame *m* condolences (*pl*); **darle el ~ a algn** to offer sb one's condolences; **mi más sentido ~** (fr hecha) my deepest sympathies
pesar¹ *m* ⊡ **(a)** (pena, tristeza) sorrow; **a ~ mío** *or* **muy a mi ~** much to my regret **(b)** (remordimiento) regret, remorse ⊠ **a pesar de** despite, in spite of; **a ~ de todo** in spite of *o* despite everything; **a ~ de que** even though
pesar² [A1] *vi* ⊡ ⟨paquete/maleta⟩ to be heavy; **estas gafas no pesan** these glasses don't weigh much; **no me pesa** it's not heavy ⊠ (causar arrepentimiento) (+ *me/te/le etc*): **ahora me pesa mucho** now I deeply regret it; **me pesa haberlo ofendido** I'm very sorry I offended him ⊟ **pese a** despite, in spite of; **pese a que** even though; **mal que me/le pese** whether I like/he likes it or not
■ ~ *vt* **(a)** ⟨niño/maleta⟩ to weigh; ⟨manzanas⟩ to weigh (out) **(b)** (tener cierto peso) to weigh; **pesa 80 kilos** he weighs 80 kilos
■ **pesarse** *v pron* (refl) to weigh oneself
pesca *f* **(a)** (en general) fishing; **ir** *or* **salir de ~** to go fishing; **~ con caña** angling; **~ con red** net fishing; **~ submarina** underwater fishing **(b)** (peces) fish (*pl*); **aquí hay mucha ~** there are a lot of fish here **(c)** (lo pescado) catch
pescada *f* hake
pescadería *f* fish shop, fishmonger's (BrE)
pescadero -ra *m,f* fish dealer (AmE), fishmonger (BrE)
pescadilla *f* whiting, young hake
pescado *m* (Coc) fish; (pez) (AmL) fish; **~ azul/blanco** blue/white fish
pescador -dora (*m*) fisherman; (*f*) fisherwoman
pescar [A2] *vt* ⊡ ⟨trucha/corvina⟩ to catch;

fuimos a ~ trucha(s) we went trout-fishing, we went fishing for trout ⊠ (fam) **(a)** ⟨catarro/gripe⟩ to catch **(b)** ⟨novio/marido⟩ to get, hook (colloq & hum) **(c)** ⟨chiste/broma⟩ to get (colloq) **(d)** (pillar) to catch; **lo ~on robando** they caught him red-handed (as he was stealing something)
■ ~ *vi* to fish; **~ a mosca** to fly-fish
pescuezo *m* (fam) neck
pese a *loc prep* ▶ PESAR² 3
pesebre *m* (en establo) manger, trough; (de Navidad) crib
pesebrera *f* (Col) stable
pesero *m* (Méx) minibus
peseta *f* peseta (*former Spanish unit of currency*)
pesimismo *m* pessimism
pesimista *adj* pessimistic
■ *mf* pessimist
pésimo -ma *adj* dreadful, terrible, abysmal
peso *m* ⊡ **(a)** (Fís, Tec) weight; **ganar/perder ~** to gain *o* put on/lose weight; **~ bruto/neto** gross/net weight **(b) al peso** by weight ⊠ **(a)** (carga, responsabilidad) weight, burden; **quitarle un ~ de encima a algn** to take a load *o* a weight off sb's mind **(b)** (influencia) weight; **todo el ~ de la ley** the full weight of the law **(c)** de peso ⟨argumento⟩ strong, weighty; ⟨razón⟩ forceful ⊟ (Dep) **(a)** (Esp) (en atletismo) shot; **lanzamiento de ~** shot-put, shot-putting **(b)** (Esp) (en halterofilia) weight; **levantamiento de ~s** weightlifting **(c)** (en boxeo) weight; **~ ligero/mosca/pesado/pluma** lightweight/flyweight/heavyweight/featherweight ⊞ (báscula) scales (*pl*) ⊡ (Fin) peso (*unit of currency in many Latin American countries*)
pespunte *m* backstitch
pesquero -ra *adj* fishing (*before n*)
pesquisa *f* investigation, inquiry
pestaña *f* (Anat) eyelash
pestañear [A1] *vi* to blink; **sin ~** (literal) without blinking; (sin inmutarse) without batting an eyelash (AmE) *o* (BrE) eyelid
peste *f* **(a)** (Med, Vet) plague, epidemic; **~ cristal** (Chi) chickenpox; **~ negra** Black Death **(b)** (AmL fam) (enfermedad contagiosa) bug (colloq); (resfriado) cold **(c)** (fam) (mal olor) stink
pesticida *m* pesticide
pestilente *adj* ⟨olor⟩ foul
pestillo *m* (cerrojo) bolt; (de cerradura) latch, catch; **echó** *or* **corrió el ~** she put the bolt across
petaca *f* **(a)** (cigarrera) cigarette case; (para tabaco — de cuero) tobacco pouch; (— de metal) tobacco tin **(b)** (para bebidas alcohólicas) hipflask
pétalo *m* petal
petanca *f* petanque
petardo *m* firecracker, banger (BrE)
petate *m* ⊡ (Mil) (para dormir) bedroll; (bolsa) knapsack ⊠ (Col, Méx) (estera) matting ⊟ **petates** *mpl* (CS fam) (pertenencias) gear (colloq)

---

petición *f* (a) (acción) request; **a ~ del público** by popular request *o* demand; **a ~ fiscal** at the prosecutor's request (b) (escrito) petition; **~ de divorcio** petition for divorce; **~ de extradición** application for extradition

petirrojo *m* robin

petiso -sa *m,f* ① (AmS fam) (de baja estatura) shorty (colloq) ② **petiso** *m* (CS) (Equ) small horse, pony

peto *m* (a) (de pantalón, delantal) bib; **pantalones de ~** (Esp) overalls (*pl*) (AmE), dungarees (*pl*) (BrE) (b) (de armadura) breastplate (c) (Taur) protective covering (*for picador's horse*) (d) (en béisbol) chest protector

petrificado -da *adj* ⟨madera⟩ petrified; ⟨animal⟩ fossilized; **al oírlo se quedó ~** he was thunderstruck when he heard

petrificar [A2] *vt* to petrify
■ **petrificarse** *v pron* to become petrified, turn to stone

petrodólar *m* petrodollar

petróleo *m* (a) (Min) oil, petroleum; **~ crudo** crude oil (b) (combustible) kerosene, paraffin (BrE)

petrolero¹ -ra *adj* oil (*before n*)

petrolero² *m* oil tanker

petrolífero -ra *adj* oil (*before n*);
▶ YACIMIENTO

petulante *adj* smug, self-satisfied
■ *mf* smug *o* self-satisfied fool

petunia *f* petunia

peyorativo -va *adj* pejorative

pez *m* fish; **~ de río** freshwater fish; **~ de colores** goldfish; **~ espada** swordfish; **~ gordo** (fam) (persona importante) bigwig (colloq); (en delito) big shot (colloq); **~ volador** flying fish; **estar** *or* **sentirse como ~ en el agua** to be in one's element
■ *f* (sustancia) pitch, tar

pezón *m* (Anat) nipple; (Zool) teat

pezuña *f* (Zool) hoof

piadoso -sa *adj* ⟨personas⟩ devout, pious; ⟨obra⟩ kind

pianista *mf* pianist

piano *m* piano; **~ de cola/de media cola** grand piano/baby grand; **~ vertical** upright piano

pianola *f* Pianola®, player piano

piar [A17] *vi* to chirp, tweet

PIB *m* (Esp) (= **Producto Interior Bruto**) GDP

pibe -ba *m,f* (RPl fam) kid (colloq)

pica *f* ① (Arm) pike; (Taur) lance, goad; (para cavar) pick, pickax* ② (Jueg) (a) (carta) spade (b) **picas** *fpl* (palo) spades

picada *f* ① (AmL) (descenso pronunciado): **caer en ~** ⟨avión⟩ to nose-dive; ⟨pájaro⟩ to plunge, to dive; ⟨acciones/valores⟩ to plummet ② (AmL) (aperitivo) nibbles (*pl*)

picadero *m* (para caballos) exercise ring; (escuela) riding school

picado¹ -da *adj* (a) ⟨diente/muela⟩ decayed, bad; ⟨manguera/llanta⟩ perished (b) ⟨ajo/perejil⟩ chopped; ⟨carne⟩ (Esp, RPl) ground (AmE), minced (BrE) (c) ⟨manzana⟩ rotten; ⟨vino⟩ sour (d) (fam) (enfadado, ofendido) put out (colloq), miffed (colloq) (e) ⟨mar⟩ choppy

picado² *m* (Esp) ▶ PICADA 1

picador *m* (a) (Taur) picador (b) (en mina) face worker

picadura *f* ① (de mosquito, serpiente) bite; (de abeja) sting; (de polilla) hole ② (en diente, muela) cavity

picaflor *m* (AmL) (Zool) hummingbird; (donjuán) (fam) womanizer

picana *f* (AmL) (a) (para bueyes) prod, goad (b) *tb* **~ eléctrica** cattle prod

picante *adj* (a) (Coc) ⟨comida⟩ hot (b) ⟨chiste/libro⟩ risqué; ⟨comedia⟩ racy

picaporte *m* (manivela) door handle; (mecanismo) latch

picar [A2] *vt* (a) «mosquito/víbora» to bite; «abeja/avispa» to sting; **me ~on los mosquitos** I got bitten by mosquitoes; **una manta picada por las polillas** a moth-eaten blanket (b) «ave» ⟨comida⟩ to peck at; ⟨enemigo⟩ to peck (c) ⟨anzuelo⟩ to bite (d) (fam) (comer) to eat; **solo quiero ~ algo** I just want a snack *o* a bite to eat (e) ⟨billete/boleto⟩ to punch (f) (Taur) to jab ② (a) (Coc) ⟨carne⟩ (Esp, RPl) to grind (AmE), to mince (BrE); ⟨cebolla/perejil⟩ to chop (up) (b) ⟨hielo⟩ to crush; ⟨pared⟩ to chip; ⟨piedra⟩ to break up, smash ③ ⟨dientes/muelas⟩ to rot, decay
■ **~** *vi* ① (a) (morder el anzuelo) to bite, take the bait (b) (comer) to nibble ② (a) (ser picante) to be hot (b) (producir comezón) «lana/suéter» to itch, be itchy; **me pica la espalda** my back itches *o* is itchy; **me pican los ojos** my eyes sting ③ (AmL) «pelota» to bounce ④ (RPl arg) (irse, largarse) to split (sl); **~le** (Méx fam) to get a move on (colloq)
■ **picarse** *v pron* ① (a) «muelas» to decay, rot; «manguera/llanta» to perish; «cacerola/pava» to rust; «ropa» to get moth-eaten (b) «manzana» to go rotten; «vino» to go sour ② «mar» to get choppy ③ (fam) (enfadarse) to get annoyed; (ofenderse) to take offense

picardía *f* (a) (astucia) craftiness, cunning (b) (malicia) mischief (c) (travesura) prank

picaresco -ca *adj* picaresque

pícaro -ra *adj* (a) (ladino) crafty, cunning (b) (malicioso) ⟨persona⟩ naughty, wicked (colloq); ⟨chiste/comentario⟩ naughty, racy; ⟨mirada/sonrisa⟩ mischievous, cheeky (BrE)
■ *m,f* (a) (Lit) rogue, villain (b) (astuto) cunning *o* crafty devil (colloq)

picatoste *m* (para sopa) crouton

picazón *f* irritation, itch

pichanga *f* (Chi) (partido — improvisado) kickabout, friendly game; (— malo) bad game

pichi *m* (Esp) jumper (AmE), pinafore (BrE)

pichi *m* (CS fam) wee-wee (used to or by children)

pichicatearse [A1] *v pron* (CS, Per fam) to take drugs

pichincha *f* (RPl fam) (ganga) bargain, steal (colloq)

pichirre *mf* (Ven fam) skinflint (colloq)

pichón -chona *m,f* (de paloma) young pigeon; (de otros pájaros) chick

picnic *m* (*pl* **-nics**) picnic

pico *m* ① (a) (de pájaro) beak (b) (fam) (boca) mouth; **¡cierra el ~!** shut up (colloq), keep your ⋯⃗

trap shut! (colloq) **2** **(a)** (cima, montaña) peak **(b)**
(en gráfico) peak **(c)** (en diseños, costura) point;
cuello de ~ V neck **(d)** (de jarra, tetera) spout
3 (fam) (algo): **tiene 50 y ~ de años** she's fifty
odd *o* fifty something (colloq); **son las dos y ~** it's
past *o* gone two; **tres metros y ~** (just) over three
meters **4** **picos** *mpl* (Méx) (zapatillas) spikes (*pl*)
5 (arg) shot

picor *m* irritation, itch

picoso *adj* (Méx) hot, spicy

picotazo *m* peck

picotear [A1] *vt* to peck
■ ~ *vi* (fam) (entre comidas) to nibble, snack

picudo -da *adj* **(a)** ⟨nariz⟩ pointed, sharp **(b)**
⟨ave⟩ long-beaked

pida, pidas, etc ▶ PEDIR

pie¹ *m* **1** **(a)** (Anat) foot; **un dedo del ~** a toe;
tiene (los) ~s planos she has flat feet; **~ de atleta**
athlete's foot **(b)** (*en locs*) **a pie** on foot; **ir a ~** to
go on foot, walk; **hoy ando a ~** (AmL) I'm without
wheels today; **de pie** standing; **ponte de ~** stand
up; **en pie: estoy en ~ desde las siete** I've been
up since seven *o*'clock; **no puedo tenerme en ~** I
can hardly walk/stand; **solo la iglesia quedó en
~** only the church remained standing; **mi oferta
sigue en ~** my offer still stands; **a ~ pelado** (Chi)
barefoot, in one's bare feet; **de a ~** common,
ordinary; **de la cabeza a los ~s** *or* **de ~s a
cabeza** from head to foot *o* toe, from top to toe
(colloq); **en ~ de guerra** on a war footing; **en (un)
~ de igualdad** on an equal footing; **hacer ~** to be
able to touch the bottom; **levantarse con el ~
derecho** to get off to a good start; **no tener ni ~
ni cabeza** to make no sense whatsoever; **por mi/
tu/su (propio) ~** unaided, without any help
2 **(a)** (de calcetín, media) foot **(b)** (de lámpara,
columna) base; (de copa — base) base; (— parte
vertical) stem; (de montaña) foot **(c)** (de página, escrito)
foot, bottom; **una nota a ~** *or* **al ~ de página** a
footnote; **~ de fotografía** caption; **al ~ de la letra**
⟨copiar/repetir⟩ word by word, exactly **(d)** (de
cama) *tb* **~s** foot
3 **(a)** (medida) foot **(b)** (Lit) foot

pie² /paɪ/ *m* (AmL) pie

piedad *f* **(a)** (compasión) mercy; **ten ~ de
nosotros** have mercy on us; **es un hombre sin ~**
he's merciless; **¡por ~!** for pity's sake! **(b)**
(devoción) devotion

piedra *f* **1** (material) stone; (trozo) stone, rock
(esp AmE); **casas de ~** stone houses; **me tiró una
~** he threw a stone *o* rock at me; **~ caliza** *or* **de
cal** limestone; **~ de molino** millstone; **~ pómez**
pumice stone; **~ preciosa** precious stone; **dejar a
algn de ~** (fam) to stun sb; ⟨duro⟩ **como una ~**
⟨pan/asado⟩ rock hard; **tiene el corazón duro
como una ~** he has a heart of stone **2** **(a)** (de
mechero) flint **(b)** (cálculo) stone; **tiene ~s en el
riñón/la vesícula** she has kidney stones/gallstones

piel *f* **1** (Anat, Zool) skin; **~ grasa/seca** oily *o*
greasy/dry skin; **~ roja** *mf* (fam & pey) redskin
(colloq & pey), Red Indian; **se me/te pone la ~ de
gallina** I/you get gooseflesh *o* goose pimples
2 (Indum) **(a)** (Esp, Méx) (cuero) leather; **guantes
de ~** leather gloves; **~ de cocodrilo** crocodile
skin; **~ de serpiente** snakeskin; **~ sintética** (cuero
sintético) (Esp, Méx) synthetic leather; (imitación

nutria, visón, etc) synthetic fur **(b)** (de visón, zorro,
astracán) fur; **abrigo de ~(es)** fur coat **(c)** (sin
tratar) pelt
3 (Bot) (de cítricos, papa) peel; (de manzana) peel,
skin; (de otras frutas) skin

pienso *m* (comida) fodder, feed

pierda, pierdas, etc ▶ PERDER

pierna *f* **(a)** (Anat) leg; **con las ~s cruzadas**
cross-legged; **abrirse de ~s** (en gimnasia) to do the
splits **(b)** (Coc) leg; **~ de cordero** leg of lamb

pieza *f* **1** **(a)** (elemento, parte) piece **(b)** (de motor,
reloj) part; **~ de recambio** *or* **de repuesto** spare
part; **quedarse de una ~** to be dumbfounded; **ser
de una sola ~** (AmL) to be as straight as a die **(c)**
(en ajedrez) piece; (unidad, objeto) piece; **ser una ~
de museo** (fam) to be a museum piece **(d)** (en
caza) piece, specimen **2** (Mús, Teatr) piece **3** (esp
AmL) (dormitorio) bedroom; (en hotel) room

pifia *f* **1** **(a)** (fam) (error) boob (colloq) **(b)** (en
billar) miscue **(c)** (Chi) (defecto) fault **2** (Chi, Per)
(del público) booing and hissing

pifiar [A1] *vt* **1** (fam) (fallar) to fluff (colloq); **~la**
(fam) to blow it (colloq) **2** (Chi, Per) ⟨público⟩ to
boo

pigmentación *f* pigmentation

pigmento *m* pigment

pigmeo -mea *adj/m,f* pygmy

pijama *m* pajamas (*pl*) (AmE), pyjamas (*pl*)
(BrE)

pije *adj/mf* (Chi) ▶ PIJO

pijo -ja *adj* (Esp fam & pey) ⟨persona/moda/lugar⟩
posh (colloq & pej)
■ *m,f* (Esp fam & pey) rich kid (colloq & pej)

pila *f* **1** (Elec, Fís) battery; **funciona a ~(s)** *or*
con ~s it runs on batteries, it's battery-operated
2 (fregadero) sink; (de una fuente) basin, bowl; **~
bautismal** baptismal font **3** (fam) (de libros, platos)
pile, stack

pilar *f* (Arquit) pillar, column; (de puente) pier
■ *mf* (en rugby) prop (forward)

pilchas *fpl* (CS fam) clothes (*pl*), gear (colloq)

píldora *f* (a) (pastilla) pill, tablet **(b)** *tb* **~
anticonceptiva** (contraceptive) pill; **tomar la ~** to
be on the pill; **~ del día siguiente** morning-after
pill

pileta *f* **(a)** (RPI) (fregadero) kitchen sink; (del
baño) washbowl (AmE), washbasin (BrE) **(b)** (RPI)
(piscina) swimming pool **(c)** (Chi) (estanque) pond;
(bebedero) drinking fountain

pillaje *m* pillage

pillar [A1] *vt* **1** (fam) **(a)** (atrapar) to catch; **le
pilló un dedo** it caught *o* trapped her finger; **¡te
pillé!** caught *o* got you! **(b)** ⟨catarro/resfriado⟩ to
catch **2** (Esp fam) ⟨coche⟩ to hit
■ **pillarse** *v pron* (fam) ⟨dedos/manga⟩ to catch

pillo -lla *adj* (fam) (travieso) naughty, wicked
(colloq); (astuto) crafty, cunning
■ *m,f* (fam) (travieso) rascal (colloq); (astuto) crafty *o*
cunning devil (colloq)

pilón *m* **1** **(a)** (de fuente) basin **(b)** (Arquit) pillar;
(de puente) pylon **2** (Méx fam) (en la compra) *small
amount of extra goods given free*; **me dio tres
manzanas de ~** he threw in three extra apples
(for free)

pilotar ⋯⟶ pique ⋯

pilotar [A1] *vt* **(a)** ⟨*avión*⟩ to pilot, fly; ⟨*barco*⟩ to pilot, steer; ⟨*coche*⟩ to drive; ⟨*moto*⟩ to ride **(b)** ⟨*empresa/país*⟩ to guide, steer

pilotear [A1] *vt* (AmL) ▶ PILOTAR

piloto *mf* **1** (Aviac, Náut) pilot; (de coche) driver; (de moto) rider; **~ de carreras** racing driver; **~ de pruebas** test pilot; (de avión) test pilot; (de coche) test driver; (de moto) test rider **2** **piloto** *m* **(a)** (de aparato eléctrico, a gas) pilot light **(b)** (CS) (impermeable) raincoat **3** (*como adj inv*) ⟨*programa/producto*⟩ pilot (*before n*)

piltrafa *f* **(a)** (de comida) scrap **(b)** (cosa inservible) useless thing

pimentón *m* **(a)** (dulce) paprika; (picante) cayenne pepper **(b)** (AmS exc RPI) (fruto) pepper, capsicum

pimienta *f* pepper

pimiento *m* pepper, capsicum; **~ rojo/verde** red/green pepper

pimpón *m* Ping-Pong®, table tennis

pin *m* (broche) pin

PIN *m* PIN

pináculo *m* (Arquit) pinnacle; (apogeo) pinnacle, peak

pinar *m* pine forest

pincel *m* (Art) paintbrush; (para maquillarse) brush

pincelada *f* brushstroke

pinchadiscos *mf* (*pl* **~**) (Esp fam) disc jockey, DJ (colloq)

pinchar [A1] *vt* **1** **(a)** ⟨*globo/balón*⟩ to burst; ⟨*rueda*⟩ to puncture **(b)** (con alfiler, espina) to prick **(c)** (para recoger) to spear
2 (fam) (poner una inyección) to give ... a shot (colloq)
3 ⟨*teléfono*⟩ to tap, bug
4 (Esp fam) ⟨*discos*⟩ to play
■ **~** *vi* **1** «*planta*» to be prickly
2 (Auto) to get a flat (tire*), get a puncture
3 (Chi fam) (con el sexo opuesto) ▶ LIGAR *vi*
■ **pincharse** *v pron* **1** (*refl*) «*persona*» (accidentalmente) to prick oneself; (inyectarse) (fam) to shoot up (sl), to jack up (sl)
2 «*rueda*» to puncture; «*globo/balón*» to burst; **se me pinchó un neumático** I got a flat (tire*) *o* a puncture

pinchazo *m* **(a)** (herida) prick; (inyección) shot (colloq) **(b)** (en una rueda) flat, puncture **(c)** (dolor agudo) sharp pain **(d)** (fam) (de droga) fix (colloq)

pinche *adj* **(a)** (AmL exc CS fam) ⟨*delante del n*⟩ (maldito): **¡~ vida!** what a (lousy *o* rotten) life!; **por unos ~s pesos** for a few measly pesos (colloq); **vámonos de este ~ lugar** let's get out of this damn place! **(b)** (Méx fam) (de poca calidad) lousy (colloq); (despreciable) horrible **(c)** (AmC fam) (tacaño) tightfisted (colloq)
■ *mf* (Coc) kitchen assistant

pincho *m* **1** (de rosa, zarza) thorn, prickle (colloq); (de cactus) spine, prickle (colloq) **2** (Esp) (de aperitivo) bar snack

pingo -ga *m,f* (Méx fam) little scamp *o* rascal (colloq)

Ping-Pong® *m* Ping-Pong®, table tennis

pingüino *m* penguin

pino *m* **1** (Bot) (árbol) pine (tree); (madera) pine **2** (Esp) (en gimnasia): **hacer el ~** to do a handstand **3** (Méx) (en bolos) pin

pinolillo *m* (AmC) (maíz) cornstarch (AmE), maize flour (BrE); (bebida) *drink made with cornstarch and water*

pinta *f* **1** (fam) (aspecto) look; **eso se le da ~ de intelectual** it gives him an intellectual look; **tiene ~ de extranjero** he looks foreign; **¿dónde vas con esa(s) ~(s)?** where are you going looking like that?; **echar** *or* **tirar** (Andes) *or* (RPI) **hacer ~** (fam) to impress **2** (en tela, animal) spot **3** (medida) pint **4** (Méx fam) (de la escuela): **irse de ~** to play hooky* (esp AmE colloq), to skive off (school) (BrE colloq)

pintada *f* piece of graffiti; (Pol) slogan

pintado -da *adj* ⟨*vaca*⟩ spotted; ⟨*caballo*⟩ dappled, pied

pintalabios *m* (*pl* **~**) (fam) lipstick

pintar [A1] *vt* **(a)** (en general) to paint; **pintó la puerta de rojo** she painted the door red; **~ algo al óleo** to paint sth in oils **(b)** (fam) (dibujar) to draw
■ **~** *vi* **1** **(a)** (con pintura) to paint **(b)** (fam) (dibujar) to draw **2** (en naipes) to be trumps
■ **pintarse** *v pron* (*refl*) (maquillarse) to put on one's makeup; **~se los labios** to put on some lipstick; **~se los ojos** to put on eye makeup; **~se las uñas** to paint one's nails

pintarrajear [A1] *vt* to daub

pintor -tora *m,f* (de cuadros) painter, artist; (de paredes) (house) painter; **~ de brocha gorda** (de casas, barcos) painter

pintoresco -ca *adj* picturesque

pintura *f* **(a)** (arte, cuadro) painting; **~ a la acuarela/al óleo** watercolor*/oil painting **(b)** (material) paint; (en cosmética) makeup

pinza *f* **1** **(a)** (para la ropa) clothespin (AmE), clothes peg (BrE) **(b)** (para el pelo) bobby pin (AmE), hairgrip (BrE) **(c)** (de un cangrejo) pincer **(d)** (en costura) dart; **un pantalón con ~s** pleated pants (AmE) *o* (BrE) trousers **2** *tb* **~s (a)** (para depilar) tweezers (*pl*); (de cirujano) forceps (*pl*); (de cocina, chimenea) tongs (*pl*) **(b)** (alicates) pliers (*pl*)

piña *f* (Bot) (fruta) pineapple; (del pino) pine cone

piñata *f. container hung up during festivities and hit with a stick to release candy inside*

piñón *m* **1** (Bot) pine kernel *o* nut **2** (Mec) pinion; (de bicicleta) sprocket wheel

pío¹, pía *adj* devout, pious

pío² *m* peep, tweet; **no decir ni ~** (fam) not to say a word

piojo *m* louse; **~s** lice

piojoso -sa *adj* **(a)** (con piojos) lousy, lice-ridden **(b)** (fam) (sucio) filthy

piola *adj inv* (RPI fam) **(a)** (divertido) fun (*before n*) (colloq) **(b)** (astuto) crafty (colloq) **(c)** ⟨*ropa*⟩ trendy (colloq)
■ *f* (AmL) cord

piolet /pjo'le(t)/ *m* (*pl* **-lets**) ice ax*

pionero -ra *adj* pioneering (*before n*)
■ *m,f* pioneer

pipa *f* **1** (para fumar) pipe; **fumar (en) ~** to smoke a pipe **2** (tonel) cask, barrel **3** (Esp) (de sandía, mandarina) pip; (de girasol, calabaza) seed; **pasarlo ~** (fam) to have a great time **4** (Méx) (camión) tanker

pipí *m* (fam) pee (colloq), wee (BrE colloq); **hacer ~** to have a pee *o* (BrE) wee

pique *m* **1** **a pique: una caída a** *or* (Méx) **en ~** ⋯⟶

hasta el mar a vertical o sheer drop to the sea below; **a pique de** on the point of, about to; **irse a ~** «*barco*» to sink; «*negocio*» to go under ⚁ (fam) **(a)** (enfado, resentimiento): **tener un ~ con algn** to be at odds with sb **(b)** (rivalidad) rivalry, needle ⚂ **(a)** (carta) spade **(b) piques** *fpl* (palo) spades (*pl*)

piqueta *f* pick, pickax*

piquete *m* ⚀ (de huelguistas) picket; (de soldados) squad, picket (arch) ⚁ (Méx fam) **(a)** (herida) prick; (inyección) shot (colloq), jab (colloq) **(b)** (de insecto) sting, bite

pira *f* pyre

piragua *f* (Dep) canoe

piragüismo *m* canoeing

pirámide *f* pyramid

piraña *f* (Zool) piranha

pirarse [A1] *v pron* (Esp fam) to make oneself scarce (colloq)

pirata *adj* **(a)** ⟨*barco*⟩ pirate (*before n*) **(b)** (clandestino) ⟨*casete/copia*⟩ pirate (*before n*), bootleg (*before n*) (colloq) ■ *mf* **(a)** (Náut) pirate; **~ aéreo** hijacker **(b)** (de casetes, videos) pirate

piratear [A1] *vt* ⟨*videos/casetes*⟩ to pirate; ⟨*sistema*⟩ to hack into

piratería *f* piracy; **~ informática** hacking (colloq)

Pirineos *mpl*, **Pirineo** *m*: **los ~** *or* **el Pirineo** the Pyrenees (*pl*)

pirinola *mf* (Andes, Méx) (peonza) spinning top

pirómano -na *m,f* pyromaniac

piropear [A1] *vt* to make flirtatious/flattering comments to

piropo *m* flirtatious/flattering comment

pirueta *f* (en danza) pirouette; (de un caballo) pesade

pis *m* ▶ PIPÍ

pisada *f* (acción) footstep; (huella) footprint

pisapapeles *m* (*pl* ~) paperweight

pisar [A1] *vt* ⚀ **(a)** (con el pie) ⟨*mina/clavo*⟩ to step on; ⟨*charco*⟩ to step in, tread in (esp BrE); **la pisó sin querer** he accidentally stepped o (esp BrE) trod on her foot; ❺ **prohibido pisar el césped** keep off the grass **(b)** (humillar) to trample on, walk all over ⚁ (RPI, Ven) **(a)** (Coc) to mash **(b)** (fam) (atropellar) to run over ■ **~** *vi* to tread; **pisó mal y se cayó** she lost her footing and fell

pisca *f* (Méx) harvest

piscina *f* swimming pool; **~ cubierta/climatizada** covered/heated swimming pool

Piscis *m* (signo, constelación) Pisces; **es (de) ~** he's (a) Pisces, he's a Piscean ■ *mf* (*pl* ~) (persona) *tb* **piscis** Piscean, Pisces

pisco *m* (aguardiente) ≈ grappa

piso *m* ⚀ **(a)** (de edificio) floor, story*; (de autobús) deck; **una casa de seis ~s** a six-story building; **un autobús de dos ~s** a double-decker bus **(b)** (de pastel) layer ⚁ (AmL) **(a)** (suelo) floor

(b) (de carretera) road surface ⚂ (Esp) (apartamento) apartment (esp AmE), flat (BrE); **~ piloto** (Esp) show apartment o (BrE) flat ⚃ (Chi) (taburete) stool; (alfombrita) rug; (felpudo) doormat

pisotear [A1] *vt* **(a)** (con los pies) to trample, stamp on **(b)** ⟨*persona/derecho*⟩ to ride roughshod over

pisotón *m* stamp; **darle un ~ a algn** (intencional) to stamp on sb's foot o toes; (sin querer) to tread o step on sb's foot o toes

pista *f* ⚀ **(a)** (rastro) trail, track; **seguirle la ~ a algn** to be/get on sb's trail **(b)** (indicio) clue ⚁ **(a)** (carretera) road, track **(b)** (Chi) (carril) lane **(c)** (Audio) track ⚂ **(a)** (en el circo) ring; (en el picadero) ring; (en el hipódromo) track (AmE), course (BrE); **~ de aterrizaje** runway, landing strip; **~ de baile** dance floor; **~ de esquí** ski slope, piste; **~ de hielo/de patinaje** ice/skating rink **(b)** (Esp) (de tenis) court

pistacho *m* pistachio (nut)

pistola *f* **(a)** (Arm) pistol; **a punta de ~** at gunpoint **(b)** (para pintar) spray gun

pistolero *m* gunman

pistón *m* **(a)** (émbolo) piston **(b)** (de arma) percussion cap **(c)** (de instrumento) key

pitada *f* ⚀ **(a)** (pitido) beep **(b)** (en espectáculo) ≈ booing and hissing, whistling (*as sign of disapproval*) ⚁ (AmL) (de cigarrillo) puff, drag (colloq)

pitar [A1] *vi* **(a)** «*guardia/árbitro*» to blow one's whistle **(b)** «*vehículo*» to blow the horn, to hoot **(c)** «*público*» (como protesta) to boo and hiss ■ **~** *vt* ⟨*falta*⟩ to blow for, award, call (AmE)

pítcher *mf* pitcher

pitido *m* (sonido agudo) whistle, whistling; (de claxon) beep, hoot, honk

pitillera *f* cigarette case

pitillo *m* ⚀ (fam) (cigarrillo) smoke (colloq), fag (BrE colloq) ⚁ (Col) (para beber) straw

pito *m* ⚀ **(a)** (silbato) whistle; **tocar el ~** to blow the whistle; **tener voz de ~** (fam) to have a squeaky voice **(b)** (fam) (de coche) horn, hooter; (de tren) whistle; **tocar el ~** to hoot, honk ⚁ (Chi fam) (de marihuana) joint (colloq), spliff (sl) ⚂ (fam) (pene) weenie (AmE colloq), willy (BrE colloq)

pitón *f or m* python

pitonisa *f* fortuneteller

pitorrearse [A1] *v pron* (Esp fam) **~ DE algn** to make fun OF sb

pituco -ca *adj* (CS, Per fam) **(a)** (elegante) posh (colloq) **(b)** (engreído) stuck-up (colloq) ■ *m,f* (CS, Per fam) **es un ~** he's stuck-up (colloq)

pituto *m* (Chi fam) (para conseguir algo) contact

pívot *mf* (*pl* **-vots**) (Dep) center*, pivot

piyama *m or f* (AmL) pajamas (*pl*) (AmE), pyjamas (*pl*) (BrE)

pizarra *f* **(a)** (Min) slate **(b)** (en el aula) blackboard, chalkboard; (del alumno) slate **(c)** (Cin) clapperboard **(d)** (en béisbol) scoreboard

pizarrón *m* (AmL) blackboard, chalkboard

pizca f ⓵ (cantidad pequeña): **una ∼ de algo** (de sal, azúcar) a pinch of sth; (de vino, agua) a drop of sth; **no tiene ni ∼ de gracia** it's not the slightest bit funny ⓶ (Méx) (cosecha) harvest

pizcar [A2] vt (Méx) ⟨maíz⟩ to harvest; ⟨algodón⟩ to pick

■ ∼ vi (Méx) to take in the harvest

pizza /'pitsa, 'pisa/ f pizza

pizzería /pitse'ria, pise'ria/ f pizzería

Pl. (= **Plaza**) Sq, Square

placa f ⓵ (lámina, plancha) sheet ⓶ (a) (con inscripción) plaque; **una ∼ con el nombre** a nameplate; **∼ de matrícula** license (AmE) o (BrE) number plate (b) (de policía) badge ⓷ (Chi) (dentadura) dentures (pl), dental plate

placaje m (en fútbol americano) block; (en rugby) tackle

placar [A2] vt (en fútbol americano) to block; (en rugby) to tackle

placard /pla'kar/ m (RPl) built-in closet (AmE), fitted wardrobe (BrE)

placenta f placenta, afterbirth

placentero -ra adj pleasant, agreeable

placer [E4] vi (en 3ªpers) (+ me/te/le etc): **haz lo que te plazca** do as you please; **me place informarle que ...** (frml) it is my pleasure to inform you that ... (frml)

■ m (gusto, satisfacción) pleasure; **ha sido un ∼ conocerla** (frml) it has been a pleasure to meet you; **un viaje de ∼** a pleasure trip

placero m (Per) street vendor

placidez f placidity, placidness, calmness

plácido -da adj placid, calm

plaga f (a) (de insectos, ratas) plague; **las ardillas son consideradas una ∼** squirrels are considered to be a pest (b) (calamidad, azote) plague

plagado -da adj: [ESTAR] **∼ DE algo** ⟨de faltas/errores⟩ riddled WITH sth; ⟨de turistas/insectos⟩ swarming WITH sth

plagiar [A1] vt ⟨idea/libro⟩ to plagiarize

plagio m (copia) plagiarism

plan m ⓵ (proyecto, programa) plan; **hacer ∼es** to make plans; **∼ de estudios** syllabus ⓶ (fam) (cita, compromiso): **si no tienes otros ∼es** if you're not doing anything else; **¿tienes algún ∼ para esta noche?** do you have any plans for tonight? ⓷ (fam) (actitud): **vienen en ∼ de diversión** they're here to have fun; **lo dijo en ∼ de broma** he was only kidding (colloq); **en ∼ económico** cheaply, on the cheap (colloq)

plana f ⓵ (de periódico) page; **aparece en primera ∼** it's on the front page ⓶ (Educ) (ejercicio) handwriting exercise ⓷ **la ∼ mayor** (Mil) the staff officers (pl); (jefes) (fam) the top brass (colloq)

plancha f ⓵ (a) (electrodoméstico) iron (b) (acto) ironing; (ropa para planchar) ironing ⓶ (a) (Const, Tec) sheet (b) (Impr) plate ⓷ (utensilio de cocina) griddle; **filete a la ∼** grilled steak ⓸ (a) (fam) (metedura de pata) boo-boo (colloq), boob (colloq) (b) (Chi fam) (vergüenza) embarrassment

planchar [A1] vt ⟨sábana/mantel⟩ to iron; ⟨pantalones⟩ to press, iron; ⟨traje⟩ to press

■ ∼ vi (con la plancha) to do the ironing

plancton m plankton

planeación f (Méx) planning

planeador m glider

planear [A1] vt to plan

■ ∼ vi (Aviac) to glide; «águila» to soar; (Náut) to plane

planeta m planet

planetario m planetarium

planificación f planning; **∼ familiar** family planning

planificar [A2] vt to plan, draw up a plan for

planilla f ⓵ (a) (tabla) table, chart; (lista) list (b) (AmL) (nómina) payroll; **estar en ∼** to be on the payroll (c) (AmL) (personal) staff ⓶ (a) (Méx) (en elección) list of candidates (b) (Col) (censo electoral) electoral register

plano¹ -na adj ⓵ ⟨superficie/terreno/zapato⟩ flat; **los 100 metros ∼s** (AmL) the hundred meters dash o sprint ⓶ ⟨figura/ángulo⟩ plane

plano² m ⓵ (de edificio) plan; (de ciudad) street plan, map ⓶ (Mat) plane ⓷ (a) (nivel) level; **en el ∼ afectivo** on an emotional level (b) (Cin, Fot) shot ⓸ **de plano** ⟨rechazar/rehusar⟩ flatly

planta f ⓵ (Bot) plant; **∼ de interior** houseplant, indoor plant ⓶ (Arquit) (a) (plano) plan (b) (piso) floor; **una casa de dos ∼s** a two-story house; **∼ baja** first floor (AmE), ground floor (BrE) ⓷ (Tec) (instalación) plant ⓸ (del pie) sole

plantación f (a) (terreno plantado) field; (de árboles) plantation (b) (explotación agrícola) plantation (c) (acción) planting

plantado -da adj **∼ DE algo** planted WITH sth; **dejar ∼ a algn** ▶ PLANTAR 2B

plantar [A1] vt ⓵ (a) ⟨árboles/cebollas⟩ to plant (b) ⟨postes⟩ to put in; ⟨tienda⟩ to pitch, put up ⓶ (fam) (a) (abandonar) ⟨novio⟩ to ditch (colloq), to dump (colloq); ⟨estudios⟩ to give up, to quit (AmE) (b) (dejar plantado) ⟨persona⟩ (en cita) to stand ... up; (el día de la boda) to jilt

■ **plantarse** v pron ⓵ (fam) (quedarse, pararse) to plant oneself (colloq) ⓶ (Jueg) (en cartas, apuesta) to stick

planteamiento m (a) (enfoque) approach (b) (exposición): **no les sabe dar el ∼ adecuado a sus ideas** he doesn't know how to set his ideas out; **ese no es el ∼ que me hicieron** that's not the way they explained the situation to me

plantear [A1] vt ⓵ (a) ⟨teoría/razones⟩ to set out (b) (exponer) ⟨tema/pregunta⟩ to raise; **me lo planteó de la siguiente manera** he explained it to me in the following way; **∼le algo a algn** to raise sth with sb; **le ∼é la cuestión a mi jefe** I'll raise the matter with my boss; **nos ∼on dos opciones** they presented us with o gave us two options; **le planteé la posibilidad de ir a Grecia** I suggested going to Greece ⓶ ⟨problemas/dificultades⟩ to pose

■ **plantearse** v pron ⓵ (considerar) ⟨problema/posibilidad⟩ to think about, consider ⓶ (presentarse) ⟨problema/posibilidad⟩ to arise

plantel m ⓵ (cuerpo) staff ⓶ (Agr) nursery ⓷ (AmL frml) (escuela) educational establishment (frml)

plantilla f ⓵ (de zapato) insole ⓶ (Esp) (personal) staff; (nómina) payroll; **estar en ∼** to be on the staff o payroll ⓷ (para marcar, cortar) template; (para corregir exámenes) mask

plantón m (a) (fam) (espera) long wait; *darle el ∼ a algn* ▶ PLANTAR 2B (b) (Méx) (para protestar) sit-in

plasma m (Biol, Fís) plasma

plasta f (fam) (masa — blanda) soft lump; (— aplastada) flat o shapeless lump

plasticina® f (CS) Plasticine®

plástico¹ -ca adj plastic

plástico² m (a) (material) plastic (b) (explosivo) plastic explosive, plastique (c) (fam) (tarjetas de crédito) credit cards (pl), plastic (colloq)

plastificar [A2] vt ‹tela› to plasticize; ‹carné/documento› to laminate

plata f ⒈ (a) (metal) silver; ∼ **de ley** hallmarked silver (b) (vajilla) silver, silverware ⒉ (AmS fam) (dinero) money; **tiene mucha ∼** she has a lot of money

plataforma f platform; ∼ **de lanzamiento** launchpad

platal m (AmS fam) fortune (colloq)

platanal, platanar m banana plantation

platanera f (empresa) banana company

platanero m (árbol) banana tree

plátano m ⒈ (árbol) tb ∼ **oriental** plane tree ⒉ (a) (fruto que se come crudo) banana; (árbol) banana tree (b) (fruto para cocinar) plantain; (árbol) plantain

platea f (a) (patio de butacas) orchestra (AmE), stalls (pl) (BrE) (b) (localidad) seat (in the orchestra/stalls)

plateado -da adj (a) (del color de la plata) silver (b) (con baño de plata) silver-plated

platería f (a) (arte) silverwork (b) (objetos) silver(ware) (c) (tienda) silversmith's

plática f (a) (conferencia) talk (b) (esp AmL) (conversación) [this noun is widely used in Mexico and Central America but is formal in other areas] talk; **estar de ∼** to talk, to chat (colloq)

platicar [A2] vi (esp AmL) [this verb is widely used in Mexico and Central America but is literary in other areas] to talk, chat (colloq) ■ ∼ vt (Méx) (contar) to tell

platillo m ⒈ (a) (plato pequeño) saucer; (de balanza) pan; (para limosnas) collection plate o bowl; ∼ **volador** or (Esp) **volante** flying saucer (b) (Mús) cymbal (c) (Dep) clay pigeon ⒉ (Méx) (en una comida) course

platino m ⒈ (metal) platinum ⒉ **platinos** mpl (Auto, Mec) (contact breaker) points (pl)

plato m ⒈ (a) (utensilio) plate; **lavar** or **fregar los ∼s** to wash o do the dishes; ∼ **de postre** dessert plate; ∼ **hondo** or **sopero** soup dish; ∼ **llano** or (RPl) **playo** or (Chi) **bajo** or (Méx) **extendido** (dinner) plate (b) (para taza) tb **platito** saucer ⒉ (contenido) plate, plateful ⒊ (a) (receta) dish; ∼ **típico** typical dish (b) (en una comida) course; ∼ **central** (Ven) main course; ∼ **combinado** (Esp) meal served on one plate, eg burger, eggs and fries; ∼ **del día** dish of the day; ∼ **fuerte** or **principal** (Coc) main course ⒋ (a) (de balanza) (scale) pan (b) (de tocadiscos) turntable (c) (Dep) clay pigeon (d) (en béisbol) home plate

plató m set

platónico -ca adj platonic

platudo -da adj (AmS fam) well-heeled (colloq)

playa f (a) (extensión de arena) beach; (lugar de veraneo) seaside (b) ∼ **de estacionamiento** (CS, Per) parking lot (AmE), car park (BrE)

playera f (zapatilla) canvas shoe, beach shoe; (camiseta) (Méx) T-shirt

plaza f ⒈ (espacio abierto) square; ∼ **de armas** (Mil) parade ground; (lugar público) (Andes) main square; ∼ **de toros** bullring; ∼ **mayor** main square ⒉ (a) (esp AmL) (bolsa) market (b) (Esp) (mercado) market (plaza) ⒊ (a) (puesto de trabajo) post, position; (en una clase, universidad) place; **hay varias ∼s vacantes** there are several vacancies (b) (asiento) seat

plazo m ⒈ (de tiempo) period; **dentro de un ∼ de dos meses** within a two-month period; **el ∼ vence el próximo lunes** (para proyecto, trabajo) the deadline is next Monday; (para entrega de solicitudes) next Monday is the closing date; **tenemos un mes de ∼ para pagar** we have one month to pay; **un objetivo a corto/largo ∼** a short-term/long-term objective ⒉ (mensualidad, cuota) installment*; **pagar a ∼s** to pay in installments; **comprar a ∼s** to buy on installments

plazoleta, plazuela f small square

plebe f (a) (Hist) **la ∼** the masses (pl), the populace (b) (pey) (chusma) rabble (pej), plebs (pl) (colloq & pej)

plebeyo -ya adj/m,f plebeian

plebiscito m plebiscite

plegable adj folding (before n)

plegar [A7] vt ‹papel› to fold; ‹silla› to fold up ■ **plegarse** v pron ⒈ (ceder) to yield, submit; ∼**se A algo** to yield TO sth, submit TO sth ⒉ (AmS) (unirse) to join in; ∼**se A algo** to join sth

plegaria f prayer

pleitear [A1] vi (AmL fam) (discutir) to argue

pleito m ⒈ (Der) action, lawsuit ⒉ (AmL) (a) (disputa, discusión) argument, fight (colloq) (b) (de boxeo) fight, boxing match

plenario -ria adj plenary, full

plenitud f: **en la ∼ de algo** (de la vida) in the prime of sth; (de la carrera) at the height o peak of sth; **vivir la vida con ∼** to live life to the full

pleno¹ -na adj (a) (completo, total) full; **en ∼ uso de sus facultades** in full possession of his faculties (b) (uso enfático): **en ∼ verano** in the middle of summer; **le dio una bofetada en plena cara** he slapped her right across the face; **a plena luz del día** in broad daylight; **a ∼ sol** in the full sun

pleno² m ⒈ (reunión) plenary o full meeting/session ⒉ (Jueg) (en bolos) strike; (en lotería, bingo) full house; (en las quinielas) correct forecast o prediction

pliego m (a) (hoja de papel) sheet of paper (b) (Impr) section, signature (c) (documento) document

pliegue m (a) (en papel) fold, crease; (en la piel) fold; (en tela) pleat (b) (Geol) fold

plinto m (en gimnasia) box

plomería f (AmL) plumbing

plomero -ra m,f (AmL) plumber

plomizo -za adj ‹cielo› gray*, leaden (liter)

plomo m ⒈ (a) (metal) lead; **soldado de ∼** tin

soldier **(b)** (arg) (balas) lead (sl) **2** (fam) (persona aburrida): **este profesor es un ~** this teacher is deadly boring (colloq) **3** (Esp) (fusible) fuse

pluma *f* **1** (de aves) feather; (antigua para escribir) quill; (como adorno) plume, feather; **mudar la ~** to molt* **2** (para escribir) pen; **~ atómica** (Méx) ballpoint pen; **~ estilográfica** *or* (AmL) **fuente** fountain pen

plumaje *m* (de ave) plumage; (en un casco) plume, crest

plumero *m* **(a)** (para limpiar) feather duster **(b)** (estuche) pencil case; (recipiente) pen holder

plumilla *f* **1** (para escribir) nib **2** **(a)** (del limpiaparabrisas) blade **(b)** (Mús) brush **(c)** (Dep) shuttlecock

plumón *m* **1** **(a)** (pluma suave) down **(b)** (edredón) down-filled quilt *o* (BrE) duvet **2** (Chi) (rotulador) felt-tip pen

plural *adj/m* plural; **tercera persona del ~** third person plural; **en ~** in the plural

pluralizar [A4] *vi* to generalize

pluscuamperfecto *m* pluperfect, past perfect

Plutón *m* Pluto

plutonio *m* plutonium

pluviosidad *f* rainfall

población *f* **1** (habitantes) population; (Zool) population, colony; **~ activa/pasiva** working/ non-working population **2** (ciudad) town, city; (aldea) town, village; **~ callampa** (Chi) shantytown **3** (acción) settlement

poblado¹ -da *adj* **1** (habitado) populated; **poco ~** sparsely populated **2** ‹barba/cejas› bushy, thick; ‹pestañas› thick

poblado² *m* village

poblador -dora *m,f* **(a)** settler **(b)** (Chi) *inhabitant of a shantytown*

poblar [A10] *vt* **1** ‹territorio/región› **(a)** «colonos/inmigrantes» (ir a ocupar) to settle, populate **(b)** (habitar) to inhabit **2** **~ algo DE algo** ‹bosque› to plant sth with sth; ‹río/colmena› to stock sth with sth
■ **poblarse** *v pron* «tierra/colonia» to be settled

pobre *adj* **1** **(a)** ‹persona/barrio/nación› poor; ‹vestimenta› poor, shabby **(b)** (escaso) ‹vocabulario› poor, limited; **aguas ~s en minerales** water with a low mineral content **(c)** (mediocre) ‹examen/trabajo/actuación› poor; ‹salud› poor, bad; ‹argumento› weak **(d)** ‹tierra› poor **2** (delante del n) (digno de compasión) poor; **~ animal** poor animal; **~, tiene hambre** poor thing, he's hungry; **¡~ de mí!** poor (old) me!
■ *mf* (necesitado) poor person, pauper (arch); **los ~s** the poor

pobreza *f* **(a)** (económica) poverty; **extrema ~** abject poverty **(b)** (mediocridad) poverty, poorness **(c)** (de la tierra) poorness, poor quality

poceta *f* (Ven) toilet bowl *o* pan

pocho -cha *adj* **(a)** (Esp fam) [ESTAR] ‹persona› off-color, peaked (AmE colloq) **(b)** ‹fruta› overripe; ‹flor› withered

pocilga *f* pigsty

pócima *f* (Farm) potion; (bebida) (fam) concoction (colloq)

poción *f* potion

poco¹ *adv*: **habla ~** he doesn't say much *o* a lot;

es muy ~ agradecido he is very ungrateful; **un autor muy ~ conocido** a very little-known author; **viene muy ~ por aquí** he hardly ever comes around; *para locs ver* POCO² 4

poco² -ca *adj* (con sustantivos no numerables) little; (en plural) few; **muy ~ vino** very little wine; **muy ~s niños** very few children; **había poquísimos coches** there were hardly any cars
■ *pron* **1** (poca cantidad, poca cosa): **había ~ que hacer** there was little to do; **por ~ que gane ...** no matter how little *o* however little she earns ...; **se conforma con ~** he's easily satisfied; **todo le parece ~** she is never satisfied; **~s quisieron ayudar** few were willing to help; **~s pueden permitirse ese lujo** not many people can afford to do that
2 poco (refiriéndose a tiempo): **lo vi hace ~** I saw him recently *o* not long ago; **hace muy ~ que lo conoce** she hasn't known him for very long; **tardó ~ en hacerlo** it didn't take him long to do it; **falta ~ para las navidades** it's not long till Christmas; **a ~ de venir él** soon *o* shortly after he came; **dentro de ~** soon; **~ antes de que ...** a short while *o* shortly before ...
3 un poco (a) (refiriéndose a cantidades) a little; (refiriéndose a tiempo) a while; **dame un ~** I'll have some *o* a little; **espera un ~** wait a while **(b)** **un poco de** a little, a bit of **(c)** **un poco + ADJ/ADV**: **un ~ caro/tarde** a bit *o* a little expensive/late
4 (en locs) **a poco** (Méx): **¡a ~ no está fabuloso Acapulco!** isn't Acapulco just fantastic!; **¡a ~ ganaron!** don't tell me they won!; **de a poco** (AmL) gradually, little by little; **poco a poco** gradually; **poco más o menos** approximately, roughly; **por poco** nearly

poda *f* (acción) pruning; (temporada) pruning season

podar [A1] *vt* ‹árbol› to prune

poder¹ [E21] *v aux*
I **1** (tener la capacidad o posibilidad de): **puedo ir ahora o mañana** I can go now or tomorrow; **no puedo pagar tanto** I can't pay that much; **no podía dormir** I couldn't sleep; **no va a ~ venir** he won't be able to come; **no pudo asistir** he was unable to *o* he couldn't attend; **¿pudiste hacerlo sola?** were you able to do it on your own?
2 (a) (expresando idea de permiso): **¿puedo servirme otro?** can *o* may I have another one?; **¿podría irme más temprano hoy?** could I leave earlier today?; **puedes hacer lo que quieras** you can do whatever you like; **no puede comer sal** he isn't allowed to eat salt; **¿se puede? — ¡adelante!** may I? — come in; **aquí no se puede fumar** smoking is not allowed here **(b)** (solicitando un favor): **¿puedes bajar un momento?** can you come down for a moment?; **¿podrías hacerme un favor?** could you do me a favor?
3 (expresando derecho moral): **no podemos hacerle eso** we can't do that to her
4 (en quejas, reproches): **podías** *or* **podrías haberme avisado** you could *o* might have warned me!
II (con idea de esfuerzo) **1** **~ CON algo/algn**: **¿puedes con todo eso?** can you manage all that?; **no puedo con este niño** I can't cope with this child; **estoy que no puedo más** (cansado) I'm exhausted; (lleno) I can't eat anything else; **ya no puedo más** I can't go on like this
2 (con idea de eventualidad, posibilidad): **te podrías** *or* ⸱⸱⸱⟶

podías haber matado you could have killed
yourself!; no podía haber estado más amable she
couldn't have been kinder; podría volver a ocurrir
it could happen again; no pudo ser it wasn't
possible; puede (ser) que tengas razón you may *o*
could be right; puede que sí, puede que no
maybe, maybe not

3 (Méx) (doler): nos pudo mucho la muerte de
Julio we were terribly upset by Julio's death

poder² *m* **1** (a) (control, influencia) power; tiene
mucho ∼ he has a great deal of power; estamos
en su ∼ we are in her power (b) (Pol) el ∼
power; estar en el ∼ to be in power; tomar el ∼
to take *o* seize power

2 (posesión): la carta está en ∼ de ... the letter is
in the hands of ...

3 (a) (derecho, atribución) power; tener amplios
∼es para hacer algo to have wide-ranging powers
to do sth (b) (Der) (documento) letter of
authorization; (hecho ante notario) power of
attorney; casarse por ∼ (AmL) *or* (Esp) por ∼es to
get married by proxy

4 (a) (capacidad, facultad) power; su ∼ de
convicción her power of persuasion; ∼
adquisitivo purchasing power (b) (de motor,
aparato) power

poderío *m* power

poderoso -sa *adj* powerful

poderosos *mpl*: los ∼s (los ricos) the wealthy;
(los que tienen poder) the powerful

podio *m*, **pódium** *m* (*pl* **-diums**) (Dep)
podium; (Mús) podium, rostrum

podólogo -ga *m,f* chiropodist, podiatrist
(AmE)

podré, etc ▶ PODER¹

podría, etc ▶ PODER¹

podrido -da *adj* **1** (a) (descompuesto) rotten;
huele a *or* (AmL) hay olor a ∼ there's a smell of
something rotting *o* rotten (b) (corrompido) rotten,
corrupt; estar ∼ de dinero *or* (AmS) estar ∼ en
plata/oro (fam) to be stinking *o* filthy rich (colloq)
2 (RPI fam) (harto, aburrido) fed up (colloq)

podrir [I38] *vt* ▶ PUDRIR

poema *m* poem

poesía *f* (género) poetry; (poema) poem

poeta -tisa *m,f*, **poeta** *mf* poet

poético -ca *adj* poetic

póker *m* ▶ PÓQUER

polaco -ca *adj* Polish
■ *m,f* **1** (persona) Pole **2** **polaco** *m* (idioma)
Polish

polar *adj* polar

polarizar [A4] *vt* (a) (Fot, Ópt) to polarize (b)
⟨atención⟩ to focus (c) ⟨nación/opiniones⟩ to
polarize

polea *f* (Tec) pulley; (Náut) tackle

polémica *f* controversy, polemic (frml)

polémico -ca *adj* controversial, polemic (frml)

polemizar [A4] *vi* to argue

polen *m* pollen

poleo *m* pennyroyal

polera *f* (suéter) (RPI) polo neck; (Chi) (camiseta)
T-shirt

polichinela *m* (títere) string puppet

policía *f* **1** (cuerpo) police; la ∼ está
investigando el caso the police are investigating
the case; ∼ antidisturbios riot police; ∼ de tráfico
or (AmL) de tránsito traffic police, highway patrol
(AmE); ∼ municipal local *o* city police; ∼ nacional
(state) police **2** **policía** (agente) (*m*) policeman,
police officer; (*f*) policewoman, police officer

policíaco -ca, policiaco -ca *adj* ⟨novela/
serie⟩ crime (before n), detective (before n)

policial *adj* police (before n)

polideportivo *m* sports center*

poliéster *m* polyester

poliestireno *m*: *tb* ∼ expandible polystyrene

polietileno *m* polyethylene (AmE), polythene
(BrE)

polifacético -ca *adj* versatile, multifaceted

poligamia *f* polygamy

polígamo -ma *m,f* polygamist

políglota *mf* polyglot

polígono *m* **1** (Mat) polygon **2** (Esp) (zona)
area, zone; (urbanización) development, housing
estate; ∼ industrial (Esp) industrial area *o* zone

polilla *f* (Zool) moth; ∼ de la madera woodworm

Polinesia *f* Polynesia

polinesio¹ -sia *adj/m,f* Polynesian

polinesio² *m* (idioma) Polynesian

polinización *f* pollination

polio *f* polio

poliomielitis *f* poliomyelitis

politécnico -ca *adj* ⟨universidad⟩ specializing
in technical or practical subjects; escuela
politécnica technical college

politeísmo *m* polytheism

política *f* **1** (Pol) politics **2** (postura) policy; ∼
interior/exterior domestic/foreign policy

político -ca *adj* **1** (Pol) political **2** (diplomático)
diplomatic, tactful **3** (en relaciones de parentesco):
la familia política the in-laws
■ *m,f* politician

politizarse [A4] *v pron* to become politicized

póliza *f* **1** (de seguros) policy **2** (esp Esp) (sello)
fiscal stamp

polizón *mf* stowaway; viajar de ∼ to stow away

polla *f* **1** (Esp vulg) (pene) cock (vulg), prick (vulg)
2 (a) (AmL) (apuesta) bet (b) (Per) (quiniela) ≈
sports lottery (*in US*), ≈ pools (*in UK*) (c) (Chi)
(lotería) lottery; *ver tb* POLLO

pollera *f* (CS) (Indum) skirt

pollería *f* poultry store, poulterer's store

pollito -ta *m,f* chick

pollo -lla *m,f* (Zool) (a) (cría) chick (b) (adulto)
chicken (c) (Coc) chicken; ∼ asado roast chicken

polluelo *m* chick

polo *m* **1** (a) (Geog) pole; P∼ Norte/Sur North/
South Pole (b) (Elec, Fís) pole; ∼ negativo

AmC	América Central		Arg	Argentina		Cu	Cuba		Per	Perú
AmL	América Latina		Bol	Bolivia		Ec	Ecuador		RPI	Río de la Plata
AmS	América del Sur		Chi	Chile		Esp	España		Ur	Uruguay
Andes	Región andina		CS	Cono Sur		Méx	México		Ven	Venezuela

negative pole; **ser ∼s opuestos** (fam) to be poles apart $\boxed{2}$ (centro) center*, focus $\boxed{3}$ **(a)** (Dep) polo **(b)** (Indum) polo shirt $\boxed{4}$ (Esp) (helado) Popsicle® (AmE), ice lolly (BrE)

pololear [A1] *vi* (Chi) to have a boyfriend/ girlfriend; **∼ CON algn** to go out WITH sb

pololo -la *m,f* (Chi fam) (*m*) boyfriend; (*f*) girlfriend

Polonia *f* Poland

poltrona *f* armchair, easy chair

polución *f* pollution; **la ∼ atmosférica** atmospheric pollution

polvareda *f* dust cloud

polvera *f* powder compact

polvo *m* **(a)** (suciedad) dust; **limpiar** *or* **quitar el ∼** to do the dusting, to dust; **estar hecho ∼** (agotado) to be all in (fam); (deprimido) to be devastated; (destruido) to be a wreck **(b)** (Coc, Quím) powder **(c)** **polvos** *mpl* (en cosmética) face powder; **∼s de talco** talcum powder, talc (colloq)

pólvora *f* **(a)** (explosivo) gunpowder **(b)** (fuegos artificiales) fireworks (*pl*)

polvoriento -ta *adj* dusty

polvorín *m* **(a)** (almacén de explosivos) magazine **(b)** (lugar, país peligroso) powder keg

pomada *f* (Farm) ointment, cream; **∼ de zapatos** (RPI) shoe polish

pomelo *m* (fruto) grapefruit; (árbol) grapefruit tree

pomo *m* (de puerta, mueble) handle, knob; (de espada) pommel

pompa *f* $\boxed{1}$ *tb* **∼ de jabón** bubble $\boxed{2}$ (esplendor) pomp, splendor*; **∼s fúnebres** *fpl* (ceremonia) funeral ceremony; (funeraria) funeral parlor*, funeral director's

pomposo -sa *adj* **(a)** ⟨boda/fiesta⟩ magnificent, splendid; ⟨lenguaje/estilo⟩ pompous, high-sounding **(b)** (ostentoso) pompous, ostentatious

pómulo *m* (hueso) cheekbone; (mejilla) cheek

pon ▶ PONER

ponchadura *f* (Méx) flat, puncture

ponchar [A1] *vt* (Méx) ⟨llanta/balón⟩ to puncture

■ **poncharse** *v pron* $\boxed{1}$ (Méx) «balón» to puncture; **se nos ponchó una llanta** we had a flat tire *o* a puncture $\boxed{2}$ (Col, Ven) (en béisbol) to fan (colloq), to strike out

ponche *m* (bebida) punch

poncho *m* poncho

ponderar [A1] *vt* **(a)** ⟨cálculo/índice⟩ to weight, adjust **(b)** (considerar) to weigh up, consider, ponder **(c)** (alabar) to praise, speak highly of

pondré, pondría, etc ▶ PONER

ponedora *f* layer, laying hen

poner [E22] *vt*
I $\boxed{1}$ **(a)** (colocar) to put; **ponlo en el suelo** put it on the floor; **ponle el collar al perro** put the dog's collar on; **∼ una bomba** to plant a bomb **(b)** ⟨anuncio/aviso⟩ to place, put **(c)** ⟨ropa⟩ (+ *me/te/ le etc*): **le puse el sombrero** I put his hat on (for him)
$\boxed{2}$ (agregar) to put
$\boxed{3}$ ⟨inyección/supositorio⟩ to give
$\boxed{4}$ **poner la mesa** to lay *o* set the table

$\boxed{5}$ (instalar, montar) **(a)** ⟨oficina/restaurante⟩ to open **(b)** ⟨cocina/teléfono/calefacción⟩ to install **(c)** ⟨cerradura/armario⟩ to fit
$\boxed{6}$ «ave» ⟨huevo⟩ to lay
$\boxed{7}$ (Esp) (servir, dar): **póngame un café, por favor** I'll have a coffee, please; **¿cuántos le pongo?** how many would you like?

II $\boxed{1}$ ⟨dinero⟩ (contribuir) to put in; **pusimos 500 pesos cada uno** we put in 500 pesos each
$\boxed{2}$ ⟨atención⟩ to pay; ⟨cuidado/interés⟩ to take; **pon más cuidado en la presentación** take more care over the presentation
$\boxed{3}$ **(a)** (imponer) ⟨deberes⟩ to give, set; ⟨examen/ problema⟩ to set; **le pusieron una multa** he was fined **(b)** (oponer) ⟨inconvenientes⟩ to raise; **me pusieron problemas para entrar** they made it difficult for me to get in **(c)** (adjudicar) ⟨nota⟩ to give
$\boxed{4}$ (dar) ⟨nombre/apodo⟩ to give; ⟨ejemplo⟩ to give; **le pusieron Eva** they called her Eva
$\boxed{5}$ (enviar) ⟨telegrama⟩ to send
$\boxed{6}$ (escribir) ⟨dedicatoria/líneas⟩ to write
$\boxed{7}$ (Esp) (exhibir, dar) ⟨película⟩ to show; **¿ponen algo interesante en la tele?** is there anything interesting on TV?; **¿qué ponen en el Royal?** what's on *o* what's showing at the Royal?

III $\boxed{1}$ **(a)** (conectar, encender) ⟨televisión/ calefacción⟩ to turn on, switch on, put on; ⟨programa/canal⟩ to put on; ⟨cinta/disco/música⟩ to put on; **puso el motor en marcha** she switched on *o* started the engine **(b)** (ajustar, graduar) ⟨despertador⟩ to set; **pon la música más alta** turn the music up; **puso el reloj en hora** she put the clock right
$\boxed{2}$ (Esp) (al teléfono): **∼ a algn CON algo/algn** to put sb THROUGH TO sth/sb

IV (en estado, situación) (+ *compl*): **∼ a algn nervioso** to make sb nervous; **∼ a algn en un aprieto** to put sb in an awkward position

■ *vi* «ave» to lay

■ **ponerse** *v pron*
I $\boxed{1}$ (refl) (colocarse): **pongámonos ahí** let's stand (*o* sit *etc*) there; **∼se de pie** to stand (up); **∼se de rodillas** to kneel (down), get down on one's knees
$\boxed{2}$ ⟨sol⟩ to set
$\boxed{3}$ (refl) ⟨calzado/maquillaje/alhaja⟩ to put on; **no tengo nada que ∼me** I don't have a thing to wear

II $\boxed{1}$ (en estado, situación) (+ *compl*): **∼se enfermo** to get sick; **se puso triste** she became sad; **cuando lo vio se puso muy contenta** she was so happy when she saw it; **se puso como loco** he went mad; **∼se cómodo** to make oneself comfortable
$\boxed{2}$ (empezar) **∼se A + INF** to start -ING, to start + INF; **se puso a llover** it started raining, it started to rain

III (Esp): **∼se al teléfono** to come to the phone

ponga, pongas, etc ▶ PONER

poni *m* ▶ PONY

poniente *m* (occidente) west; (viento) west wind

pontífice *m* pontiff, pope

pony /'poni/ *m* (*pl* **-nies** *or* **-nys**) pony

pop *m* $\boxed{1}$ (Mús) pop (music) $\boxed{2}$ (Ur) (Coc) popcorn

popa *f* stern

popis, popoff *adj inv* (Méx fam) posh

popote *m* (Méx) straw

popular *adj* $\boxed{1}$ **(a)** ⟨cultura/tradiciones⟩ ⋯⟩

popular (*before n*); ‹canción/baile/costumbres›
traditional **(b)** (Pol) ‹movimiento/rebelión›
popular (*before n*) **2** (que gusta) ‹actor/programa/
deporte› popular

popularidad *f* popularity

popularizar [A4] *vt* to popularize, make ...
popular
■ **popularizarse** *v pron* to become popular

popurrí *m* (de cosas, colores) potpourri

póquer *m* (*juego — de naipes*) poker; (*— de dados*)
poker dice; **un ~ de ases** four aces

poquísimo *adj* ▶ POCO

por *prep*

I **1** (*causa*) because of; **~ falta de dinero** because
of *o* owing to lack of money; **~ naturaleza** by
nature; **~ necesidad** out of necessity; **~ eso no
dije nada** that's why I didn't say anything; **fue ~
eso que no te llamé** that was why I didn't call
you; **si no fuera ~ mi hijo ...** if it wasn't for my
son ...; **me pidió perdón ~ haberme mentido** he
apologized for lying *o* for having lied to me
2 (*en locs*) **por qué** why; **no dijo ~ qué** he didn't
say why; **¿por qué no vienes conmigo?** why don't
you come with me?; **por si** in case; **~ si no
entiende** in case he doesn't understand; ▶ ACASO
2, MOSCA
3 (*en expresiones concesivas*): **~ más que me
esfuerzo** however hard *o* no matter how hard I
try; **~ (muy) fácil que sea** however easy *o* no
matter how easy it is
4 **(a)** (*modo*): **colócalos ~ orden de tamaño** put
them in order of size; **~ adelantado** in advance;
~ escrito in writing **(b)** (*medio*): **se lo
comunicaron ~ teléfono** they told him over the
phone; **lo dijeron ~ la radio** they said it on the
radio; **~ avión** by air; **la conocí ~ la voz** I
recognized her by her voice; **me enteré ~ un
amigo** I heard from *o* through a friend
5 **(a)** (*proporción*): **cobra $30 ~ clase** he charges
$30 a *o* per class; **120 kilómetros ~ hora** 120
kilometers an *o* per hour; **~ metro/docena** by the
meter/dozen; **tú comes ~ tres** you eat enough for
three people; **tiene tres metros de largo ~ uno de
ancho** it's three meters long by one meter wide;
uno ~ uno one by one; ▶ CIENTO B **(b)** (*en
multiplicaciones*): **tres ~ cuatro (son) doce** three
times four is twelve, three fours are twelve
6 **(a)** (*sustitución*) for; **su secretaria firmó ~ él** his
secretary signed for him *o* on his behalf; **pasa ~
inglesa** she passes for an Englishwoman **(b)**
(*como*): **~ ejemplo** for example
7 (*introduciendo el agente*) by; **compuesto ~ Mozart**
composed by Mozart
II **1** (*finalidad, objetivo*): **pelearse ~ algo** to fight
over sth; **lo hace ~ el dinero** he does it for the
money; **no entré ~ no molestarlo** I didn't go in
because I didn't want to disturb him; **~ QUE +
SUBJ** (*here* POR QUE *can also be written* PORQUE):
estaba ansioso ~ que lo escucharan he was
eager for them to listen to him
2 (*indicando inclinación, elección*): **su amor ~ la
música** her love of music; **no siento nada ~ él** I
don't feel anything for him; **votó ~ ella** he voted
for her
3 (*en busca de*): **salió/fue ~** *or* (Esp) **a ~ pan** he
went (out) for some bread, he went (out) to get
some bread
4 (*en lo que respecta a*): **~ mí que haga lo que quiera**
as far as I'm concerned, he can do what he likes

5 (*esp AmL*) **estar ~ + INF** (*estar a punto de*) to be
about to + INF; **está ~ terminar** he's about to
finish; **deben (de) estar ~ llegar** they should be
arriving any minute
III **1** **(a)** (*lugar*): **entró ~ la ventana** he came in
through the window; **sal ~ aquí** go out this way;
se cayó ~ la escalera he fell down the stairs; **¿el
121 va ~ (la) Avenida Rosas?** does the 121 go
along Rosas Avenue?; **¿~ dónde has venido?**
which way did you come?; **está ~ ahí** he's over
there somewhere; **¿~ dónde está el hotel?**
whereabouts is the hotel?; **viven ~ mi barrio** they
live around my area; **voy ~ la página 15** I'm up to
o I'm on page 15; **empieza ~ el principio** start at
the beginning; **agárralo ~ el mango** hold it by the
handle **(b)** (*indicando extensión*): **~ todos lados** *or* **~
todas partes** everywhere; **viajamos ~ el norte de
Francia** we traveled around *o* in the North of
France; *ver tb* DENTRO, FUERA, ENCIMA, ETC
2 (*tiempo*) for; **~ un mes** for a month; **~ el
momento** *or* **~ ahora** for the time being, for now;
ver tb MAÑANA, TARDE, NOCHE
3 (Esp) (*ocasión*) for; **me lo regaló ~ mi
cumpleaños** she gave it to me for my birthday

porcelana *f* **(a)** (*material*) china; (*de mejor
calidad*) porcelain **(b)** (*objeto*) piece of china/
porcelain

porcentaje *m* percentage

porche *m* (de casa) porch; (soportal) arcade

porción *f* (de un todo) portion; (en reparto) share;
(de comida) portion, helping, serving

pordiosero -ra *m,f* beggar

porfiado -da *adj* stubborn, pig-headed (colloq)
■ *m,f* (*persona*) stubborn creature (colloq)

porfiar [A17] *vi* (insistir) to insist; **no me porfíes,
ya te dije que no** don't keep on *o* go on about it, I
said no

pormenor *m* detail; **los ~es del incidente** the
details of the incident; **entrar en ~es** to go into
detail

pornografía *f* pornography

pornográfico -ca *adj* pornographic

poro *m* **1** (Anat, Biol) pore **2** (Méx) (puerro) leek

pororó *m* (RPl) popcorn

poroso -sa *adj* porous

poroto *m* (CS) bean; **~ verde** (Chi) green bean

porque *conj* **(a)** (*indicando causa*) because; **¿por
qué no vas a ir?** — **~ no** why don't you go? —
because I don't want to **(b)** (*indicando finalidad*) ▶
POR II 1

porqué *m* reason; **quiero saber el ~** I want to
know the reason

porquería *f* **1** **(a)** (*suciedad*) dirt **(b)**
(*cochinada*): **no hagas ~s** don't do disgusting *o*
filthy things like that; **la casa está hecha una ~**
(fam) the house is in such a state (colloq) **2** (*cosa
de mala calidad*): **el libro es una ~** the book's a
piece of junk; **la comida es una ~** the food is
dreadful *o* terrible

porra *f* **1** (de guardia, policía) nightstick (AmE),
truncheon (BrE) **2** (fam) (*expresando disgusto, enojo*):
mandar a algn a la ~ (colloq) to tell sb to get lost
(colloq); **¡vete** *or* **ándate a la ~!** go to hell! (colloq),
get lost!; **mandar algo a la ~** (colloq)
‹trabajo› to chuck sth in (colloq) **3** (Jueg) draw,
lottery **4** (Col, Méx fam) **(a)** (seguidores, hinchas)
fans (*pl*) **(b)** (canto, grito): **¡una ~ para Villalva!**

three cheers for Villalva!; **la ∼ de la universidad** the college chant; *echarle* **∼s a algn** (Méx fam) ⟨*a equipo/corredor*⟩ to cheer sb (on)

porrista *mf* **(a)** (Col, Méx) (seguidor) fan **(b)**

porrista *f* (Col, Méx) (animadora) cheerleader

porro *m* (Esp arg) (de hachís) joint (colloq), spliff (sl)

porrón *m* **1 (a)** (de vino) wine bottle (*with a long spout for drinking from*) **(b)** (Arg) (de cerveza) bottle of beer **2** (CS) (pimiento) green pepper; (puerro) leek

portabebés *m* (*pl* ∼) portacrib® (AmE), carrycot (BrE)

portada *f* **1 (a)** (de libro) title page; (de periódico) front page; (de revista) cover **2** (de iglesia) front, facade

portadocumentos *m* (*pl* ∼) (AmL) (grande) briefcase, attaché case; (pequeño) document wallet

portador -dora *m,f* **1** (Med) (de virus, germen) carrier **2** (Com, Fin) bearer; **páguese al ∼** pay the bearer

portaequipajes *m* (*pl* ∼) **(a)** (Auto) (para el techo) roofrack; (maletero) trunk (AmE), boot (BrE) **(b)** (en tren, autobús) luggage rack

portafolios *m* (*pl* ∼) (maletín) briefcase

portal *m* **(a)** (de casa — entrada) doorway; (— vestíbulo) hall **(b)** (de iglesia, palacio) portal **(c)** (en muralla) gate

portar [A1] *vt* (fml) ⟨*arma/bandera*⟩ to carry, bear (fml)

■ **portarse** *v pron* **(a)** (comportarse): **∼se bien** to behave (oneself); **∼se mal** to behave badly; **∼se bien/mal CON algn** to treat sb well/badly **(b)** (cumplir): **el Zaragoza se portó en la final** Zaragoza delivered the goods in the final; **hoy te portaste** you've really excelled today

portátil *adj* portable

portaviones *m* (*pl* ∼) aircraft carrier

portavoz *mf* (*m*) spokesperson, spokesman; (*f*) spokesperson, spokeswoman

portazo *m* slam, bang; **dar un ∼** to slam the door

porte *m* **1** (tamaño) size; **es de este ∼** (AmL) it's about this big **2** (acción de portar) carrying; (costo) carriage; **∼s pagados** freight/postage paid

porteño -ña *adj* of/from the city of Buenos Aires

portería *f* **1 (a)** (de edificio) desk/area *from where the super/caretaker supervises the building* **(b)** (vivienda) super's *o* superintendent's apartment (AmE), caretaker's flat (*o* house *etc*) (BrE) **2** (Dep) goal

portero -ra *m,f* **1** (que abre la puerta) doorman, porter; (que cuida el edificio) super (AmE), superintendent (AmE), caretaker (BrE); **∼ eléctrico** *or* (Esp) **automático** *m* entryphone **2** (Dep) goalkeeper

portezuela *f* door

pórtico *m* (entrada) portico, porch; (galería) arcade

portón *m* (puerta grande) large door; (puerta principal) front door; (en cerca) gate

portorriqueño -ña *adj/m,f* Puerto Rican

Portugal *m* Portugal

portugués¹ -guesa *adj/m,f* Portuguese

portugués² *m* (idioma) Portuguese

porvenir *m* future; **un joven sin ∼** a young man with no future *o* no prospects

posada *f* **(a)** (arc) (taberna) inn (arch) **(b)** (cobijo) hospitality

posaderas *fpl* (fam) backside (colloq), butt (AmE colloq), bum (BrE colloq)

posar [A1] *vi* to pose

■ **posarse** *v pron* «*pájaro/insecto*» to alight, land; «*avión/helicóptero*» to land

posavasos *m* (*pl* ∼) coaster; (de cartón) beermat

pose *f* **(a)** (para foto) pose **(b)** (pey) (afectación) pose

poseedor -dora *m,f* (fml) (de título, récord, billete) holder

poseer [E13] *vt* **(a)** ⟨*tierras/fortuna*⟩ to own **(b)** ⟨*conocimientos*⟩ to have **(c)** ⟨*récord/título*⟩ to hold

posesión *f* possession; **tomar ∼ de algo** (de casa) to take possession of sth; (de cargo) to take up sth; **está en ∼ de todas sus facultades** he is in full possession of his faculties

posesivo -va *adj* possessive

posguerra *f* postwar period

posibilidad *f* **1** (circunstancia) possibility; **tener la ∼ de hacer algo** to have the chance of doing sth; **tiene muchas ∼es de salir elegido** he has a good chance of being elected; **existe la ∼ de que estés equivocado** you might just be wrong **2** **posibilidades** *fpl* **(a)** (medios económicos) means (*pl*); **vivo de acuerdo a mis ∼es** I live within my means; **la casa está por encima de mis ∼es** I can't afford the house **(b)** (potencial) potential; **un cantante con muchas ∼es** a singer of great potential

posibilitar [A1] *vt* to make ... possible

posible *adj* possible; **es ∼** it's possible; **a ser ∼** *or* **si es ∼** if possible; **hicieron todo lo ∼** they did everything possible *o* everything they could; **prometió ayudarlo dentro de lo ∼** *or* **en lo ∼** she promised to do what she could to help (him); **¡no es ∼!** that can't be true! (colloq); **en cuanto te sea ∼** as soon as you can; **no creo que me sea ∼** I don't think I'll be able to; **es ∼ hacerlo más rápido** it's possible to do it more quickly; **no me fue ∼ terminarlo** I wasn't able to finish it; **es ∼ que sea cierto** it might *o* may *o* could be true

■ *adv*: **lo más pronto ∼** as soon as possible; **lo mejor ∼** the best you can

posición *f* **(a)** (en general) position; **en ∼ vertical** in an upright position **(b)** (en la sociedad) social standing; **gente de buena ∼** people of high social standing **(c)** (actitud) position, stance; **adoptar una ∼ intransigente** to take a tough stand *o* stance

positivo -va *adj* positive

poso *m* (del vino) sediment, lees (*pl*), dregs (*pl*); (del café) dregs (*pl*), grounds (*pl*)

posponer [E22] *vt* (aplazar) to postpone, put off

posta *f* **1** (AmL) (Dep) relay (race) **2** (AmC) (Mil) sentry post **3** (Esp) **a posta** on purpose, deliberately **4** (Chi) (centro médico) accident and emergency center*

postal *adj* ⟨*distrito/servicio*⟩ postal

■ *f* postcard

postdata *f* postscript

poste *m* **(a)** (de alambrado) (fence) post; (de teléfono, telégrafo) pole **(b)** (Dep) post, upright

postemilla *f* (AmL) gumboil, abscess

póster *m* (*pl* **-ters**) poster

postergar [A3] *vt* **1** (esp AmL) (aplazar) ⟨juicio/reunión⟩ to postpone, put back **2** (relegar) ⟨empleado⟩ to pass over

posteridad *f* posterity

posterior *adj* **1 (a)** (en el tiempo) later, subsequent; **en años ∼es** in later *o* subsequent years; **ese incidente fue ∼ a su llegada** that incident happened after his arrival **(b)** (en orden) subsequent **2** (trasero) ⟨patas⟩ back (*before n*), rear (*before n*); **la parte ∼** the back *o* rear

posterioridad *f*: **con ∼** subsequently, later

postgrado *m* postgraduate course

postgraduado -da *adj/m,f* postgraduate

postguerra *f* postwar period

postigo *m* shutter

postizo¹ -za *adj* **(a)** ⟨pestañas⟩ false; **dentadura postiza** dentures, false teeth **(b)** ⟨manga/cuello⟩ detachable

postizo² *m* hairpiece

postor *m* bidder

postrarse [A1] *v pron* (frml) (arrodillarse) to kneel

postre *m* dessert, pudding (BrE)
■ *f*: **a la ∼** (*loc adv*) (frml) in the end

postulante -ta *m,f* **(a)** (AmL) (Pol) (candidato) candidate **(b)** (CS) (para puesto) applicant

postular [A1] *vt* (AmL) (Pol) ⟨candidato⟩ to nominate, propose
■ *vi* **∼ PARA algo** (CS) ⟨para puesto⟩ to apply FOR sth
■ **postularse** *v pron* (AmL) to stand, run

póstumo -ma *adj* posthumous

postura *f* **1** (del cuerpo) position **2 (a)** (actitud) stance, stand; **adoptar una ∼ firme con respecto a algo** to take a tough stance *o* stand on sth **(b)** (opinión) opinion; **tomar ∼** to take a stand **3** (AmL) (de ropa, zapatos): **se le rompieron a la primera ∼** they broke the first time she wore them; **∼ de argollas** (Chi) (acción) exchange of rings (*to seal one's engagement*); (fiesta) engagement party

potable *adj* ⟨agua⟩ drinkable, potable (frml); Ⓢ **agua no potable** not drinking water

potaje *m* (Coc) vegetable stew/soup (*gen with pulses*)

potasio *m* potassium

pote *m* (olla) pot; (de crema, maquillaje) (CS) pot, jar

potencia *f* power; **∼ militar/nuclear** military/nuclear power; **este niño es un artista en ∼** this child has the makings of an artist

potencial *adj* (posible) potential; (Ling) conditional
■ *m* (capacidad, posibilidades) potential

potenciar [A1] *vt* (period) **(a)** ⟨desarrollo/investigación/exportaciones⟩ to boost; ⟨relaciones/unidad/talento⟩ to foster; ⟨cultura⟩ to promote **(b)** (mejorar) ⟨seguridad⟩ to improve

potentado -da *m,f* tycoon

potente *adj* **(a)** (en general) powerful **(b)** ⟨hombre⟩ virile

potestad *f* legal authority

potingue *m* (fam) cream, lotion

poto *m* (Andes fam) (de persona) butt (AmE colloq), bum (BrE colloq); (de botella) bottom

potpourri /popu'rri/ *m* medley

potrero *m* (AmL) (terreno cercado) field; (para pastar) pasture

potrillo -lla *m,f* (Zool) foal

potro -tra *m,f* **1** (caballo joven) (*m*) colt; (*f*) filly **2 potro** *m* (instrumento de tortura) rack; (cepo) stocks (*pl*); (en gimnasia) vaulting horse, buck

pozo *m* **(a)** (de agua) well; **∼ ciego** *or* **negro** *or* **séptico** septic tank, cesspool, cesspit; **∼ de petróleo** oil well **(b)** (en mina) shaft **(c)** (en río) deep pool

práctica *f* **1 (a)** (en actividad) practice; (en trabajo) experience; **perder la ∼** to be out of practice **(b)** (de profesión) practicing* **2** (aplicación) practice; **en la ∼** in practice; **poner algo en ∼** *or* **llevar algo a la ∼** to put sth into practice **3 prácticas** *fpl* (de Anatomía, Química) practicals (*pl*); (de maestro) teaching practice; **∼s de tiro** target practice **4** (costumbre) practice

practicante *adj* (Rel) practicing* (*before n*)
■ *mf* (Med) nurse (*specializing in giving injections, dressing wounds, etc*)

practicar [A2] *vt* **1 (a)** ⟨idioma/pieza musical⟩ to practice*; ⟨tenis⟩ to play; **∼ la natación** to swim; **no practica ningún deporte** he doesn't play *o* do any sport(s) **(b)** ⟨profesión⟩ to practice* **2** (frml) (llevar a cabo, realizar) ⟨corte/incisión⟩ to make; ⟨autopsia/operación⟩ to perform, do; ⟨redada/actividad⟩ to carry out; ⟨detenciones⟩ to make
■ *vi* (repetir) to practice*; (ejercer) to practice*

práctico -ca *adj* **1** ⟨envase/cuchillo⟩ useful, handy; ⟨falda/diseño⟩ practical; **es muy ∼ tener el coche para hacer la compra** it's very handy *o* convenient having the car to do the shopping **2** (no teórico) practical **3** ⟨persona⟩ [SER] (desenvuelto) practical

pradera *f* meadow; **las ∼s de los Estados Unidos** the prairies of the United States

prado *m* **(a)** (Agr) meadow, field **(b)** (lugar de paseo) park (*with lawns*) **(c)** (Col) (jardín) garden, yard (AmE)

Praga *f* Prague

pragmático -ca *adj* pragmatic
■ *m,f* pragmatist

pragmatismo *m* pragmatism

preámbulo *m* **(a)** (de obra) introduction; (de constitución) preamble **(b)** (rodeo): **sin más ∼s** without further ado; **dímelo sin tanto ∼** stop beating about the bush and tell me **(c)** (de curso, negociaciones) preliminary

preaviso *m* notice

precalentamiento *m* **(a)** (Dep) warm-up **(b)** (del horno) preheating **(c)** (de motor) warming up

precalentar [A5] *vt* ⟨*horno*⟩ to preheat; ⟨*motor*⟩ to warm up

precario -ria *adj* ⟨*vivienda*⟩ poor; ⟨*medios*⟩ scarce, meager*; ⟨*salud/situación*⟩ precarious, unstable; ⟨*gobierno/puesto*⟩ unstable

precaución *f* **1** (medida) precaution **2** (prudencia): **medida de ∼** precautionary measure; **actuar con ∼** to act with caution

precaverse [E1] *v pron* to take precautions

precavido -da *adj* cautious, prudent

precedencia *f* precedence, priority

precedente *adj* previous
■ *m* precedent; **sentar (un) ∼** to set a precedent

preceder [E1] *vt* to precede

precepto *m* rule, precept (fml)

preciado -da *adj* ⟨*bien/objeto*⟩ prized, valued; ⟨*don*⟩ valuable

preciarse [A1] *v pron* (a) (estimarse): **un abogado que se precie no haría eso no** self-respecting lawyer would do that (b) (jactarse) **∼ DE algo** to pride oneself ON sth

precintar [A1] *vt* (a) ⟨*paquete/botella*⟩ to seal (b) ⟨*local*⟩ (tras crimen) to seal; (clausurar) to close down (*often on health or safety grounds*)

precinto *m* seal

precio *m* **1** (de producto) price; **∼ al contado/a plazos** cash/credit price; **¿qué ∼ tiene este vestido?** how much is this dress?; **∼ de costo** *or* (Esp) **coste** cost price; **∼ de venta al público** (de alimento, medicamento) recommended retail price; (de libro) published price; **no tener ∼** to be priceless **2** (sacrificio, costo) price, cost; **a cualquier ∼** at any price, whatever the cost

preciosidad *f*: **ser una ∼** to be absolutely beautiful

precioso -sa *adj* (hermoso) beautiful, gorgeous, lovely; (de gran valor) precious, valuable

preciosura *f* (AmL) ▶ PRECIOSIDAD

precipicio *m* (despeñadero) precipice

precipitación *f* **1** (prisa) rush, hurry; **lo hizo con mucha ∼** she did it in a rush *o* hurry **2** (Meteo) rainfall; **la ∼ mensual** the monthly rainfall; **habrá precipitaciones débiles** there will be some light rain

precipitado -da *adj* ⟨*decisión/actuación*⟩ hasty; ⟨*juicio*⟩ snap (*before n*)

precipitarse [A1] *v pron* **1** (en decisión, juicio) to be hasty; **te precipitaste juzgándolo así** you were rash to judge him like that **2** (apresurarse) to rush; **∼se A hacer algo** to rush to do sth **3** (a) (caer) to plunge (b) (*refl*) (arrojarse) to throw oneself

precisado -da *adj* (AmL fml): **verse ∼ a hacer algo** to be forced *o* obliged to do sth

precisar [A1] *vt* **1** (determinar con exactitud) to specify **2** (necesitar) to need

precisión *f* (a) (exactitud) precision; **no puedo decírtelo con ∼** I can't tell you exactly; **de ∼** ⟨*instrumento/máquina*⟩ precision (*before n*) (b) (claridad, concisión) precision

preciso -sa *adj* **1** (a) (exacto, claro) precise (b) (*delante del n*) (como intensificador) very; **en este ∼ momento** this very minute, right now; **en el ∼ momento en que salía** just as he was going out; **en este ∼ lugar** in this very spot **2** (necesario) necessary; **si es ∼** if necessary, if need be; **ser ∼**

hacer algo to be necessary to do sth; **es ∼ que la veas** you must see her; **no es ∼ que vayamos todos** there's no need for all of us to go

preconcebido -da *adj* preconceived

precoz *adj* ⟨*niño/desarrollo*⟩ precocious; ⟨*diagnóstico/fruto/helada*⟩ early

precursor -sora *m,f* precursor, forerunner

predecesor -sora *m,f* predecessor

predecir [I25] *vt* to predict, foretell (fml)

predestinación *f* predestination

predestinar [A1] *vt* to predestine; **estar ∼ a algo/hacer algo** to be predestined to sth/to do sth

predeterminar [A1] *vt* to predetermine

predicado *m* predicate

predicador -dora *m,f* preacher

predicamento *m* (AmL) (situación difícil) predicament

predicar [A2] *vt/vi* to preach

predicativo -va *adj* predicative

predicción *f* prediction, forecast

predecible *adj* (Andes) predictable

predilección *f* predilection; **tiene/siente ∼ por su hijo** she's especially fond of her son

predilecto -ta *adj/m,f* favorite*

predisponer [E22] *vt* **1** (Med) to predispose **2** (influir en) to prejudice; **lo predispusieron en contra mía** they prejudiced him against me

predisposición *f* **1** (Med) predisposition **2** (inclinación): **tener ∼ contra algn** to be prejudiced against sb

predispuesto -ta *adj* (a) [SER] (propenso) **∼ A algo** prone TO sth (b) [ESTAR] (prejuiciado) **∼ A FAVOR/EN CONTRA DE algo/algn** biased TOWARDS/ AGAINST sth/sb

predominante *adj* predominant

predominar [A1] *vi* «*actitud/opinión*» to prevail; **∼ EN algo** to dominate sth; **el tema predominó en el congreso** the subject dominated the conference; **∼ SOBRE algo** to be predominant OVER sth

predominio *m* predominance

preescolar *adj* ⟨*edad/educación*⟩ preschool (*before n*); **centro de educación ∼** kindergarten, nursery school (BrE)

preestreno *m* preview

prefabricado -da *adj* prefabricated

prefacio *m* preface

prefecto *m* (a) (Relig) prefect (b) (Gob) (en Francia) prefect (c) (Per) (gobernador) civil governor (d) (Col) (Educ) teacher responsible for discipline

preferencia *f* (a) (prioridad) priority, precedence; (Auto) right of way, priority (BrE) (b) (predilección) preference; **tiene ∼ por el más pequeño** the youngest one is her favorite (c) (Espec) (localidad) grandstand

preferente *adj* (especial) special

preferible *adj* preferable, better; **es ∼ quedarse callado** it's better to stay quiet; **es ∼ a uno de plástico** it's better than *o* preferable to a plastic one; **es ∼ que no vayas** you'd better not go

preferido -da *adj/m,f* favorite*

preferir [I11] *vt* to prefer; **prefiero esperar aquí** ⋯⋗

p

I'd rather wait here, I'd prefer to wait here; ∼ algo A algo to prefer sth TO sth; **prefiero que te quedes** I'd rather you stayed, I prefer you to stay
prefiera, prefieras, etc ▶ PREFERIR
prefijo *m* (Ling) prefix; (de teléfono) (dialing*) code
prefiriera, prefirió, etc ▶ PREFERIR
pregonar [A1] *vt* (a) ⟨noticia/secreto⟩ to make ... public (b) ⟨virtudes/méritos⟩ to extol (c) ⟨mercancía⟩ to hawk, cry
pregunta *f* question; **hacer/contestar una** ∼ to ask/answer a question
preguntar [A1] *vt* to ask; **eso no se pregunta** you shouldn't ask things like that; **la maestra me preguntó la lección** the teacher tested me on the lesson
■ ∼ *vi* to ask; **le preguntó sobre** *or* **acerca de lo ocurrido** he asked her (about) what had happened; ∼ **POR algo/algn** to ask ABOUT sth/sb; **preguntaban por un tal Mario** they were looking for *o* asking for someone called Mario
■ **preguntarse** *v pron* (*refl*) to wonder
prehistoria *f* prehistory
prehistórico -ca *adj* prehistoric
prejuiciado -da *adj* (AmL) prejudiced
prejuicio *m* prejudice; **tener** ∼**s raciales** to be racially prejudiced
prejuzgar [A3] *vt/vi* to prejudge
prelavado *m* prewash
preliminar *adj* preliminary
preludio *m* prelude
premamá *adj inv* (Esp fam) maternity (*before n*)
prematrimonial *adj* ⟨relaciones⟩ premarital
prematuro -ra *adj* premature
premeditación *f* premeditation
premeditado -da *adj* premeditated
premeditar [A1] *vt* to premeditate
premenstrual *adj* premenstrual
premiación *f* (AmL) (acción) awarding of prizes; (ceremonia) awards ceremony, prize-giving (BrE)
premiado -da *adj* ⟨número/boleto⟩ winning; ⟨novela/película/escritor⟩ prizewinning (*before n*); *ver tb* PREMIAR
premiar [A1] *vt* (a) ⟨actor/escritor⟩ to award a/ the prize to, award ... a/the prize (b) ⟨generosidad/sacrificio⟩ to reward
premio *m* (a) (en general) prize; **conceder** *or* **dar un** ∼ to award *o* give a prize; **ganar** *or* **llevarse un** ∼ to win a prize; **el** ∼ **a la mejor película** the award *o* prize for the best movie; ∼ **de consolación** *or* (CS) **(de) consuelo** consolation prize; ∼ **gordo** jackpot; **P**∼ **Nobel** (galardón) Nobel Prize; (galardonado) Nobel Prize winner (b) (a esfuerzos, sacrificios) reward; **como** ∼ **a su dedicación** as a reward for your dedication
premisa *f* premise
premonición *f* premonition
prenatal *adj* prenatal (AmE), antenatal (BrE)
prenda *f* [1] (de vestir) garment; ∼ **íntima** undergarment, item of underwear [2] (señal, garantía) security, surety [3] (Jueg) forfeit
prendarse [A1] *v pron* (liter) ∼ **DE algn** to fall in love WITH sb
prender [E1] *vt* [1] ⟨persona⟩ to catch, seize [2] (sujetar) to pin; ⟨bajo/dobladillo⟩ to pin up

[3] (a) ⟨cigarrillo/cerilla⟩ to light; ∼**(le) fuego a algo** to set fire to sth (b) (AmL) ⟨gas⟩ to light; ⟨estufa/horno⟩ to turn on; ⟨radio/luz/televisión⟩ to turn on, switch on
■ ∼ *vi* [1] «rama/planta» to take [2] (a) «fósforo/ piloto» to light; «leña» to catch (light) (b) (AmL) «luz/radio/televisión» to come on; **la televisión no prende** the TV won't come on [3] «idea/ moda» to catch on
■ **prenderse** *v pron* (a) (con fuego) to catch fire (b) (AmL) «luz/radio/televisión» to come on
prensa *f* (a) (Impr, Period, Tec) press; **la** ∼ **oral** radio and television; **estar en** ∼ to be in *o* at the press (b) (periodistas) **la** ∼ the press; ∼ **amarilla** gutter press, yellow press; ∼ **del corazón** gossip magazines (*pl*); ∼ **roja** (CS) sensationalist press (*specializing in crime stories*)
preñado -da *adj* ⟨animal⟩ pregnant
preocupación *f* (a) (problema) worry; **les causa muchas preocupaciones** she causes them a lot of worry *o* problems (b) (inquietud) concern
preocupado -da *adj* worried; ∼ **POR algo** worried ABOUT sth
preocupante *adj* worrying
preocupar [A1] *vt* to worry; **no quiero** ∼**lo** I don't want to worry him; **le preocupa el futuro** she's worried *o* concerned about her future; **me preocupa que no haya llamado** it worries me that she hasn't phoned; **no me preocupa** it doesn't bother *o* worry me
■ **preocuparse** *v pron* [1] (inquietarse) to worry; ∼**se POR algo/algn** to worry ABOUT sth/sb [2] (ocuparse) ∼**se DE algo: me preocupé de que no faltara nada** I made sure *o* I saw to it that we had everything; **no se preocupó más del asunto** he gave the matter no further thought
preparación *f* [1] (de examen, discurso) preparation [2] (a) (conocimientos, educación) education; (para trabajo) training (b) (de deportista) training; **su** ∼ **física es muy buena** he's in peak condition [3] (Farm, Med) preparation
preparado -da *adj* [1] [ESTAR] (listo, dispuesto) ready; ∼ **PARA algo** ready FOR sth; **¡**∼**s, listos, ya!** get ready, get set, go! (AmE), on your marks, get set, go! (BrE) [2] [SER] (instruido, culto) educated; **un profesional muy bien** ∼ a highly-trained professional
preparar [A1] *vt* [1] ⟨plato⟩ to make, prepare; ⟨comida⟩ to prepare, get ... ready; ⟨medicamento⟩ to prepare, make up; ⟨habitación⟩ to prepare, get ... ready; ⟨cuenta⟩ to draw up (AmE), make up (BrE) [2] ⟨examen/prueba⟩ to prepare [3] ⟨persona⟩ (para examen) to tutor, coach (BrE); (para partido) to train, coach, prepare; (para tarea, reto) to prepare
■ **prepararse** *v pron* [1] (*refl*) (disponerse): ∼**se PARA algo** to get ready FOR sth [2] (*refl*) (formarse) to prepare; ∼**se PARA algo** ⟨para examen/ competición⟩ to prepare FOR sth
preparativos *mpl* preparations (*pl*)
preparatoria *f* (Méx) three-year pre-university course and college where this is taught
preparatorio -ria *adj* ⟨curso⟩ preparatory; ⟨ejercicios⟩ warm-up (*before n*)
preponderante *adj* predominant, preponderant (frml)
preposición *f* preposition
prepotencia *f* arrogance

prepotente *adj* ⟨*persona*⟩ arrogant, overbearing; ⟨*actitud*⟩ high-handed

prepucio *m* foreskin, prepuce (tech)

presa *f* **1** (en caza) prey; **ser ∼ de algo** (de terror, pánico) to be seized with sth **2** (dique) dam; (embalse) reservoir, lake **3** (AmS) (de pollo) piece

presagio *m* **(a)** (señal) omen **(b)** (premonición) premonition

prescindir [I1] *vi* **1** (arreglárselas sin) **∼ DE algo/algn** to do WITHOUT sth/sb **2** (omitir) **∼ DE algo** ⟨*de detalles/formalidades*⟩ to dispense WITH sth

prescribir [I34] *vt* to prescribe

prescripción *f* prescription; **por ∼ facultativa** *or* **médica** on doctor's orders

prescrito -ta, prescripto -ta *pp* ▶ PRESCRIBIR

preselección *f*: **hacer una ∼ de los candidatos** to draw up a shortlist of candidates; **una vez terminada la ∼** once the initial selection process is/was complete

preseleccionar [A1] *vt* ⟨*candidatos/ solicitantes*⟩ to shortlist

presencia *f* **(a)** (en lugar, acto) presence; **su ∼ me cohíbe** I feel awkward in his presence; **en ∼ de algn** in the presence of sb **(b)** (euf) (aspecto físico) appearance; **se requiere buena ∼** good *o* (BrE) smart appearance required **(c)** **∼ de ánimo** (serenidad) presence of mind; (valor) courage, strength

presenciar [A1] *vt* ⟨*suceso/asesinato*⟩ to witness; ⟨*acto/espectáculo*⟩ to be present at, to attend

presentable *adj* presentable

presentación *f* (en general) presentation; (de personas) introduction

presentador -dora *m,f* presenter

presentar [A1] *vt* **1** **(a)** (mostrar) to present **(b)** (exponer por primera vez) ⟨*libro/disco*⟩ to launch; ⟨*obra de arte*⟩ to present; ⟨*colección de moda*⟩ to present, exhibit **(c)** (entregar) ⟨*informe/solicitud*⟩ to submit; ⟨*trabajo*⟩ to hand in; ⟨*renuncia*⟩ to hand in, submit **(d)** (enseñar) ⟨*carnet/pasaporte*⟩ to show **(e)** ⟨*disculpas/excusas*⟩ to make; ⟨*queja*⟩ to file, make; ⟨*cargos*⟩ to bring; **∼on una denuncia** they reported the matter (to the police), they made an official complaint; **∼ pruebas** to present evidence **(f)** (Mil): **∼ armas** to present arms

2 (TV) ⟨*programa*⟩ to present, introduce

3 ⟨*persona*⟩ to introduce; **te presento a mi hermana** I'd like you to meet my sister, this is my sister

4 ⟨*novedad/ventaja*⟩ to offer; ⟨*síntoma*⟩ to show

■ **presentarse** *v pron* **1** **(a)** (en lugar) to turn up, appear; **∼se (como) voluntario** to volunteer **(b)** **∼se A algo** ⟨*a examen*⟩ to take sth; ⟨*a concurso*⟩ to enter sth; ⟨*a elecciones*⟩ to take part IN sth; **se presenta como candidato independiente** he's running (AmE) *o* (BrE) he's standing as an independent; **∼se para un cargo** to apply for a post

2 ⟨⟨*dificultad/problema*⟩⟩ to arise, come up; ⟨⟨*oportunidad*⟩⟩ to arise

3 (darse a conocer) to introduce oneself

presente *adj* **1** (en un lugar) [ESTAR] present; **❺** **Presente** (CS) (Corresp) ≈ by hand; **tener algo**

∼ to bear sth in mind 2 (actual) present; **hasta el momento ∼** up to the present time; **el día 15 del ∼ mes** the 15th of this month; **en su atenta carta del 3 ∼** (Méx frml) (Corresp) in your letter of the 3rd of this month *o* (frml) of the 3rd inst.

■ *m* **1** **(a)** (en el tiempo) **el ∼ the** present **(b)** (Ling) present (tense) **2** **los presentes** *mpl* (asistentes) those present

presentimiento *m* premonition; **tengo el ∼ de que ...** I have a feeling that ...

presentir [I11] *vt* ⟨*desgracia*⟩ to have a premonition of; **presiento que ...** I have a feeling that ...

preservar [A1] *vt* **(a)** (proteger) to preserve **(b)** (AmL) (conservar, mantener) to maintain

preservativo *m* **1** (condón) condom **2** (Andes) (conservante) preservative

presidencia *f* **(a)** (Gob, Pol) (cargo) presidency; **∼ municipal** (Méx) town hall **(b)** (de compañía, banco) presidency (esp AmE), chairmanship (BrE); (de reunión, comité) chairmanship, chair

presidente -ta *m,f* **(a)** (Gob, Pol) president; **el ∼ del gobierno** the premier, the prime minister **(b)** (de compañía, banco) president (AmE), chairman (BrE) **(c)** (de reunión, comité, acto) chairperson, chair **(d)** (Der) (de tribunal) presiding judge/magistrate **(e)** (de jurado) chairman/chairwoman

presidiario -ria *m,f* convict, inmate, prisoner

presidio *m* (lugar) prison; (pena) prison sentence; **condenado a cinco años de ∼** sentenced to five years imprisonment

presidir [I1] *vt* ⟨*país*⟩ to be president of; ⟨*reunión*⟩ to chair, preside at *o* over; ⟨*comité*⟩ to chair; ⟨*tribunal/cortes/jurado*⟩ to preside over; ⟨*compañía*⟩ to be president of (AmE), to be chairman of (BrE)

presilla *f* (para abrochar) eye; (lazo) loop

presión *f* **(a)** (Fís, Med, Meteo) pressure; **∼ arterial** *or* **sanguínea** blood pressure **(b)** (coacción) pressure; **bajo ∼** under pressure

presionar [A1] *vt* **(a)** (coaccionar) to put pressure on, to pressure (esp AmE), to pressurize (esp BrE) **(b)** ⟨*botón/timbre*⟩ to press ■ **∼** *vi* (Dep) to put on the pressure

preso -sa *adj*: **estuvo ∼ diez años** he was in prison for ten years; **llevarse a algn ∼** to take sb prisoner

■ *m,f* prisoner

prestaciones *fpl* (Servs Socs) benefits (*pl*), assistance

prestado -da *adj*: **el libro está ∼** the book is on loan *o* (colloq) is already out; **esta chaqueta es prestada** this jacket is borrowed; **pedir algo ∼** to borrow sth; **me pidió el coche ∼** she asked if she could borrow my car; **pídeselo ∼** ask (him) if you can borrow it

prestamista *mf* moneylender

préstamo *m* (Econ, Fin) (acción — de prestar) lending; (— de tomar prestado) borrowing; (cosa prestada) loan

prestar [A1] *vt* **1** ⟨*dinero/libro*⟩ to lend; **¿me prestas el coche?** will you lend me your car?, can I borrow your car? **2** **(a)** ⟨*ayuda*⟩ to give; ⟨*servicio*⟩ to render; ⟨*servicio militar*⟩ to do **(b)** ⟨*atención*⟩ to pay **3** ⟨*juramento*⟩ to swear

■ **prestarse** *v pron* **1** (dar ocasión) **∼se A algo** ⟨*a críticas/malentendidos/abusos*⟩ to be open TO sth ···❖

2 (ser apto, idóneo) **~se PARA algo** to be suitable FOR sth **3** (*refl*) **(a)** (ofrecerse) **~se a hacer algo** to offer to do dth **(b)** (en frases negativas): **no me presto a negocios sucios** I won't take part in anything underhand

prestidigitador -dora *m,f* conjurer

prestigio *m* prestige; **de ~** prestigious

prestigioso -sa *adj* famous, prestigious

presumido -da *adj* **(a)** (engreído) conceited, full of oneself; (arrogante) arrogant **(b)** (coqueto) vain

presumir [I1] *vi* to show off; **~ DE algo** ⟨*de dinero*⟩ (hablando) to boast *o* brag ABOUT sth; (enseñándolo) to flash sth around; **presume de guapo** he thinks he's good-looking
■ **~** *vt*: **se presume una reacción violenta** there is likely to be a violent reaction; **era de ~ lo que ocurriría** it was quite predictable what would happen

presunto -ta *adj* (*delante del n*) (frml) ⟨*asesino/terrorista*⟩ alleged (*before n*)

presuntuoso -sa *adj* conceited, vain

presuponer [E22] *vt* to presuppose (frml), assume

presupuesto *m* **1 (a)** (Fin) budget **(b)** (precio estimado) estimate; **hacer un ~** to give an estimate **2** (supuesto) assumption, supposition

pretencioso -sa *adj* ⟨*casa/película*⟩ pretentious

pretender [E1] *vt*: **¿qué pretendes con esa actitud?** what do you hope to gain with that attitude?; **pretendía entrar sin pagar** he was trying to get in without paying; **no pretendo saberlo todo** I don't claim to know everything; **lo único que pretendía era ayudar** I was only trying to help; **¿pretendes que te crea?** do you expect me to believe you?

pretendido -da *adj* (*delante del n*) ⟨*interés/amabilidad*⟩ feigned; **el ~ duque** the so-called duke; **con ~ interés** with false interest

pretendiente *mf* **1** (al trono) pretender; (a un puesto) applicant **2 pretendiente** *m* (de una mujer) suitor

pretensión *f* **1** (a trono, herencia) claim **2 pretensiones** *fpl* (ínfulas): **tener pretensiones** to be pretentious; **una película sin pretensiones** an unpretentious film

pretensioso -sa *adj* (AmL) vain

pretérito *m* preterit*; **~ indefinido** simple past, preterit*; **~ perfecto/pluscuamperfecto** present/past perfect

pretexto *m* pretext; **volvió con el ~ de recoger el paraguas** he went back on the pretext of getting his umbrella; **siempre sale con algún ~** she always comes out with some excuse; **bajo ningún ~** under no circumstances

prevalecer [E3] *vi* to prevail

prevención *f* **(a)** (de un mal, problema) prevention **(b)** (medida) precaution; **tomar prevenciones** to take precautionary measures

prevenido -da *adj* **(a)** (SER) (precavido)

well-prepared, well-organized; **es muy prevenida** she likes to be prepared *o* ready for all eventualities **(b)** (ESTAR) (advertido) forewarned; **ahora ya estás ~** you've been warned

prevenir [I31] *vt* **(a)** ⟨*enfermedad/accidente*⟩ to prevent **(b)** (advertir, alertar) to warn
■ **prevenirse** *v pron* **~se CONTRA algo** to take preventive *o* preventative measures AGAINST sth, take precautions AGAINST sth

preventiva *f* (Méx) yellow (AmE) *o* (BrE) amber light

preventivo -va *adj* preventive, preventative

prever [E29] *vt* **(a)** (anticipar) ⟨*acontecimiento/consecuencias*⟩ to foresee, anticipate; ⟨*tiempo*⟩ to forecast; **se prevé un aumento de precios** a rise in prices has been predicted **(b)** (proyectar, planear): **medidas previstas por el gobierno** measures planned by the government; **tiene prevista su llegada a las 11 horas** it is due *o* scheduled to arrive at 11 o'clock; **todo salió tal como estaba previsto** everything turned out just as planned **(c)** ⟨*ley*⟩ to envisage
■ **~** *vi*: **como era de ~** as was to be expected

previo -via *adj* **(a)** (anterior) ⟨*experiencia/conocimientos*⟩ previous; **sin ~ aviso** without (prior) warning **(b)** ⟨*reunión/asunto*⟩ preliminary

previsible *adj* foreseeable

previsión *f* **(a)** (precaución) precaution; **en ~ de ...** as a precaution against ...; **por falta de ~** owing to a lack of foresight **(b)** (predicción) forecast

previsor -sora *adj* (con visión de futuro) farsighted; (precavido) well-prepared

prieta *f* (Chi) blood sausage, black pudding (BrE)

prieto -ta *adj* (Méx fam) (oscuro) dark; (de piel oscura) dark-skinned

prima *f* **(a)** (de seguro) premium **(b)** (pago extra) bonus; **~ de** *or* **por peligrosidad** danger money

primar [A1] *vi*: **debería ~ el interés público** the public interest should be (a) top priority; **~ SOBRE algo** to take precedence *o* priority OVER sth

primaria *f* **1** (Educ) elementary *o* (BrE) primary education **2** (Pol) (en EEUU) primary

primario -ria *adj* **(a)** (básico) ⟨*necesidades/objetivo*⟩ primary, basic **(b)** (primitivo) ⟨*instintos*⟩ primitive

primavera *f* **1** (estación) spring; **en ~** in spring, in springtime **2** (Bot) primrose

primaveral *adj* ⟨*tiempo/moda*⟩ spring (*before n*); ⟨*ambiente*⟩ spring-like

primer ▶ PRIMERO

primera *f* **(a)** (Auto) first (gear) **(b)** (Transp) (clase) first class; **viajar en ~** to travel first class; *ver tb* PRIMERO

primerizo -za *m,f* **(a)** novice, beginner **(b) primeriza** *f* first-time mother

primero -ra *adj/pron* [PRIMER *is used before masculine singular nouns*] **1** (en el espacio, el tiempo) first; **el primer piso** the second (AmE) *o* (BrE) first floor; **en primer lugar ...** first (of all), ..., firstly, ...; **1° de julio** (*read as: primero de julio*)

1st July, July 1st (*léase: July the first*); **Olaf I** (*read as: Olaf primero*) Olaf I (*léase: Olaf the First*); **a primeras horas de la madrugada** in the early hours of the morning; **primera plana** front page; **∼s auxilios** *mpl* first aid; **primer plano** (Fot) close-up (shot)

2 (en calidad, jerarquía): **un artículo de primera calidad** a top-quality product; **de primera** (categoría) first-class, first-rate; **es el ∼ de la clase** he is top of the class; **primer ministro** Prime Minister

3 (básico, fundamental): **nuestro primer objetivo** our primary objective; **artículos de primera necesidad** basic necessities; **lo ∼ es ...** the most important thing is ...

■ *adv* **1** (en el tiempo) first
2 (en importancia): **estar ∼** to come first

primicia *f* (Period): **conseguimos la ∼ del reportaje** we were the first to carry the report; **una ∼ informativa** a scoop

primitivo -va *adj* primitive

primo -ma *adj* ⟨*número*⟩ prime; ⟨*materia*⟩ raw;
■ *m,f* **(a)** (pariente) cousin; **∼ hermano** first cousin **(b)** (Esp fam) (bobo) sucker (AmE colloq), mug (BrE colloq); **hacer el ∼** (Esp fam) to be taken for a ride

primogénito -ta *m,f* first *o* firstborn child

primordial *adj* ⟨*objetivo*⟩ fundamental, prime (*before n*); ⟨*interés/importancia*⟩ paramount

prímula *f* primula; (amarilla) primrose

princesa *f* princess

principal *adj* main; ⟨*papel*⟩ leading (*before n*); **lo ∼ es que...** the main thing is that...

príncipe *m* prince; **∼ heredero** crown prince

principiante *mf* beginner; **un error de ∼** a basic mistake

principio *m* **1** (comienzo) beginning; **a ∼s de temporada** at the beginning of the season; **empieza por el ∼** start at the beginning; **eso es un buen ∼** that's a good start; **en un** *or* **al ∼** at first, in the beginning **2** **(a)** (postulado, norma moral) principle; **es una mujer de ∼s** she's a woman of principle; **por ∼** on principle

pringar [A3] *vt* (fam) (ensuciar) to get ... dirty (with grease, oil etc)
■ **pringarse** *v pron* (fam) (ensuciarse) **∼se DE algo** ⟨*de grasa/mermelada*⟩ to get covered IN sth

pringoso -sa *adj* greasy

prioridad *f* priority

prisa *f* **1** (rapidez, urgencia) rush, hurry; **¿a qué viene tanta ∼?** what's the rush *o* hurry?; **con las ∼s olvidé decírselo** in the rush I forgot to tell her; **tenía ∼ por llegar a casa** he was in a rush to get home; **no me metas ∼** don't rush *o* hurry me; **tengo ∼** (Esp, Méx) I'm in a rush *o* a hurry; **darse ∼** to hurry (up) **2** (*en locs*) **a** *or* **de prisa ▶** DEPRISA; **a toda prisa** as fast as possible; **correr prisa: estos no (me) corren ∼** there's no rush for these

prisco *m* (CS) *type of peach*

prisión *f* **1** (edificio) prison, jail, penitentiary (AmE) **2** (pena) prison sentence; **seis años de ∼** six years' imprisonment

prisionero -ra *m,f* prisoner; **lo hicieron ∼** he was taken prisoner *o* captured

prisma *m* (Fís, Ópt) prism; (perspectiva) perspective

prismáticos *mpl* binoculars (*pl*), field-glasses (*pl*); **unos ∼** a pair of binoculars

privacidad *f* privacy

privación *f* **(a)** (acción) deprivation; **la ∼ de libertad** deprivation of liberty **(b)** (falta, carencia) privation, deprivation; **pasar privaciones** to suffer privations *o* deprivations

privada *f* (Méx) private road (*with security control*)

privado -da *adj* **(a)** ⟨*reunión/vida*⟩ private; **en ∼** in private **(b)** (Col, Méx) (desmayado) unconscious **(c)** (Méx) ⟨*teléfono/número*⟩ unlisted (AmE), ex-directory (BrE)

privar [A1] *vt* **1 ∼ a algn DE algo** ⟨*de derecho/ libertad*⟩ to deprive sb OF sth **2** (Col, Méx) (dejar inconsciente) to knock ... unconscious
■ **privarse** *v pron* **1 ∼se DE algo** ⟨*de lujos/ placeres*⟩ to deprive oneself OF sth **2** (Col, Méx) (desmayarse) to lose consciousness, pass out

privatización *f* privatization

privatizar [A4] *vt* to privatize

privilegiado -da *adj* **(a)** ⟨*persona/clase*⟩ privileged **(b)** (excelente) ⟨*posición*⟩ privileged; ⟨*clima/inteligencia/memoria*⟩ exceptional
■ *m,f*: **unos pocos ∼s** a privileged few

privilegio *m* privilege

pro *m* (ventaja) advantage; **sopesar los ∼s y los contras de algo** to weigh up the pros and cons of sth
■ *prep*: **los sectores ∼ amnistía** the sectors in favor of an amnesty

proa *f* bow, prow

probabilidad *f* (Mat) probability; **con toda ∼** in all probability *o* likelihood; **¿qué ∼es tiene de ganar?** what are her chances of winning?

probable *adj* (posible) probable; **es ∼** probably; **es ∼ que llegue hoy** he will probably arrive today

probado -da *adj* (delante del n) proven

probador *m* fitting room, changing room (BrE)

probar [A10] *vt* **1** (demostrar) ⟨*teoría/inocencia*⟩ to prove **2** **(a)** ⟨*vino/sopa*⟩ to taste; (por primera vez) to try **(b)** ⟨*método*⟩ to try; ⟨*coche/mecanismo*⟩ to try out **(c)** ⟨*ropa*⟩ to try on; **∼le algo A algn** to try sth ON sb **(d)** (poner a prueba) ⟨*empleado/ honradez*⟩ to test; ⟨*arma/vehículo*⟩ to test (out)
■ **∼** *vi* (intentar) to try; **∼ A hacer algo** to try doing sth
■ **probarse** *v pron* ⟨*ropa/zapatos*⟩ to try on

probeta *f* test tube
■ *adj inv* ⟨*gemelos/hijos*⟩ test-tube (before n)

problema *m* problem; **resolver/solucionar un ∼** to solve a problem; **los coches viejos dan muchos ∼s** old cars give a lot of trouble; **no te hagas ∼** (AmL) don't worry about it

problemático -ca *adj* problematic, difficult

procaz *adj* ⟨*comentario/chiste*⟩ indecent, lewd; ⟨*lenguaje*⟩ obscene

procedencia *f* **(a)** (origen) origin **(b)** (de barco) port of origin

procedente *adj*: **el vuelo/tren ∼ de París** the flight/train from Paris

proceder [E1] *vi* **1** (provenir) **∼ DE algo** to come FROM sth **2** (actuar) to act, to proceed (frml); **procedió con mucha corrección** he behaved very correctly; **∼ contra algn** (Der) to iniciate

p

proceedings against sb **3** (frml) (iniciar) ~ A algo to proceed TO sth **4** (ser conveniente): **procede actuar rápidamente** it would be wise to act swiftly; **rellenar lo que proceda** complete as appropriate

procedimiento m **1** (método) procedure; (Tec) process **2** (Der) proceedings (pl)

prócer m national hero (esp of a struggle for independence)

procesado -da m,f (Der) accused, defendant

procesador m processor; ~ **de textos** word processor

procesamiento m **1** (Der) prosecution, trial **2** (Tec, Inf) processing; ~ **de textos** word processing

procesar [A1] vt **1** (Der) to try, prosecute **2** ‹materia prima/datos/solicitud› to process

procesión f procession

proceso m **1** (serie de acciones, sucesos) process **2** (Der) trial **3** (Inf) processing; ~ **de datos/textos** data/word processing **4** (transcurso) course

proclamación f proclamation, declaration

proclamar [A1] vt to proclaim
■ **proclamarse** v pron to proclaim oneself

procrear [A1] vi to procreate, breed

procurador -dora m,f (Der) (abogado) attorney, lawyer; (asistente) ≈ paralegal (in US), ≈ clerk (in UK)

procurar [A1] vt (intentar) ~ **hacer algo** to try to do sth; **procura que no te vea** try not to let him see you

prodigio m (a) (maravilla) wonder (b) (milagro) miracle

prodigioso -sa adj prodigious, phenomenal; ‹éxito/jugador/músico› phenomenal

producción f **1** (Com, Econ) (proceso, acción) production; (cantidad) output, production; ~ **en cadena** or **serie** mass production **2** (Cin, Teatr, TV) production

producir [I6] vt **1** (a) (en general) to produce (b) ‹sonido› to cause, generate **2** (causar) ‹conmoción/reacción/explosión› to cause; **le produjo una gran alegría** it made her very happy
■ **producirse** v pron **1** (frml) (tener lugar) «accidente/explosión» to occur (frml), to take place; «cambio» to occur (frml), to happen; **se produjeron 85 muertes** there were 85 deaths, 85 people died o were killed **2** (refl) (frml) ‹heridas› to inflict ... on oneself (frml)

productividad f (cualidad) productivity; (rendimiento) productivity, output

productivo -va adj productive; ‹empresa/ negocio› lucrative

producto m (a) (artículo producido) product; ~**s agrícolas/de granja** agricultural/farm produce; ~ **alimenticio** foodstuff; ~ **lácteo** dairy product (b) (resultado) result, product

productor -tora adj producing (before n)
■ m,f (a) (en general) producer (b) **productora** f (empresa) production company

produje, produzca, etc ▶ PRODUCIR

proeza f (logro) feat, exploit; (Mil) heroic deed o exploit

profanar [A1] vt ‹templo/sepultura› to desecrate, defile

profano -na adj **1** (a) (no sagrado) ‹escritor/

música› secular, profane (frml); ‹fiesta› secular (b) (antirreligioso) profane (frml), irreverent **2** (no especializado): **soy ~ en la materia** I'm not an expert on the subject
■ m,f **1** (Relig) (m) layman; (f) laywoman **2** (no especialista) non-specialist

profecía f prophecy

proferir [I11] vt ‹palabras/amenazas› to utter; ‹insultos› to hurl

profesar [A1] vt (a) (declarar) ‹religión/doctrina› to profess (b) (sentir) ‹cariño› to feel; ‹respeto› to have

profesión f (ocupación) profession; (en formularios) occupation; ~ **liberal** profession

profesional adj ‹fotógrafo/deportista› professional (before n)
■ mf professional

profesionalidad f professionalism

profesionista mf (Méx) professional

profesor -sora m,f (de escuela secundaria) teacher, schoolteacher; (de universidad) professor (AmE), lecturer (BrE); **tiene un ~ particular** he has a private tutor

profesorado m (cuerpo) faculty (AmE), teaching staff (BrE); (actividad) teaching profession

profeta m prophet

profetizar [A4] vt to prophesy

prófugo -ga m,f (Der) fugitive; (Mil) deserter

profundidad f (a) (de pozo, río, mar) depth; **tiene 20 metros de ~** it's 20 meters deep (b) (de conocimientos, ideas) depth; **en ~** ‹analizar› in depth; ‹reformar› radically

profundizar [A4] vi ~ **EN algo** ‹en tema› to go into sth in depth

profundo -da adj (a) ‹herida/pozo/raíz› deep; **un río poco ~** a shallow river (b) ‹pensamiento› profound, deep; ‹respeto/desprecio› profound; ‹lazos› strong; ‹desengaño› grave, terrible (c) ‹misterio› profound; ‹silencio› deep, profound (d) ‹voz/suspiro› deep (e) ‹sueño› deep, sound

progenitor -tora m,f (a) (antepasado) ancestor (b) (frml) (m) (padre) father; (f) (madre) mother

programa m **1** (a) (Rad, TV) program*; ~ **concurso** quiz show; ~ **de entrevistas** chat show (b) (folleto) program* **2** (programación, plan) program* **3** (a) (político) program*; **su ~ electoral** their election manifesto (b) (Educ) (de asignatura) syllabus; (de curso) curriculum, syllabus **4** (Inf, Elec) program*

programación f **1** (a) (Rad, TV) programs* (pl) (b) (de festejos, visitas — lista) program*; (— organización) organization, planning **2** (Inf) programming

programador -dora m,f programmer

programar [A1] vt **1** (a) (Rad, TV) to schedule (b) ‹actividades/eventos› to plan, draw up a program* for; ‹horario/fecha› to schedule, program*; ‹viaje› to organize (c) (Transp) ‹llegadas/salidas› to schedule, timetable (BrE) **2** (Inf) to program

progresar [A1] vi «persona» to make progress, to progress; «negociaciones/proyecto» to progress

progresión f (Mat, Mús) progression

progresista adj/mf progressive

progresivo -va adj progressive

progreso *m* (a) (adelanto): **supuso un gran ~** it was a great step forward; **hacer ~s** to make progress (b) (evolución, desarrollo) progress

prohibición *f* (acción) prohibition, banning; (orden) ban

prohibir [I22] *vt* (a) (acto/venta) to ban, prohibit (frml); **iba en dirección prohibida** I was going the wrong way up a one-way street; **Ⓢ prohibido el paso** *or* **prohibida la entrada** no entry; **Ⓢ prohibido fumar** no smoking; **Ⓢ se prohíbe la entrada a menores de 16 años** over 16s only, no admission to persons under 16 years of age (b) **~le algo A algn** to ban sb FROM sth; **~le A algn hacer algo** to forbid sb to do sth, prohibit sb FROM doing sth (frml); **~ A algn QUE haga algo** to forbid sb to do sth

prohibitivo -va *adj* prohibitive

prójimo *m* (semejante) fellow man; **amar al ~** to love one's neighbor

prole *f* kids (*pl*) (colloq), offspring (hum)

proletario -ria *adj/m,f* proletarian

proliferar [A1] *vi* to proliferate, spread

prolífico -ca *adj* prolific

prolijo -ja *adj* ① (extenso) protracted, long-winded; (minucioso) detailed ② (RPl) (ordenado, aseado) (persona/casa) tidy; (cuaderno) neat

prólogo *m* (de libro) preface, foreword; (de acto) prelude

prolongación *f* extension

prolongado -da *adj* prolonged, lengthy

prolongar [A3] *vt* (a) (contrato/plazo) to extend; (vacaciones/visita) to prolong, extend; **~le la vida a algn** to prolong sb's life (b) (línea/calle) to extend
■ **prolongarse** *v pron* (a) (en el tiempo) «debate/fiesta» to go on, carry on (b) (en el espacio) «carretera/línea» to extend

promedio *m* (a) (Mat) average; **el ~ de mis ingresos** my average earnings; **como ~** on average (b) (nota media) average grade *o* (BrE) mark (c) (punto medio) mid-point

promesa *f* (a) (palabra) promise; **cumplí (con) mi ~** I kept my promise *o* word; **romper una ~** to break a promise (b) (persona) hope

prometedor -dora *adj* promising

prometer [E1] *vt* (a) (dar su palabra) to promise; **te lo prometo** I promise (b) (augurar) to promise
■ ~ *vi* «persona/negocio» to show *o* have promise
■ **prometerse** *v pron* (a) (en matrimonio) to get engaged (b) (refl) (viaje/descanso) to promise oneself

prometido -da *adj* (a) (para casarse) engaged (b) (aumento/regalo) promised; **cumplir con lo ~** to keep one's promise *o* word
■ *m, f (m)* fiancé; (f) fiancée

prominente *adj* prominent

promiscuidad *f* promiscuity

promiscuo -cua *adj* promiscuous

promoción *f* ① (a) (de actividad, producto) promotion; **hacer ~ de un producto** to promote a product (b) (ascenso) promotion ② (Educ): **somos de la misma ~** we graduated at the same time

promocionar [A1] *vt* to promote

promontorio *m* (en tierra) hill, rise; (en el mar) promontory, headland

promotor -tora *m,f* (persona) (a) (Const) developer (b) (Espec) promoter (c) (de rebelión, huelga) instigator

promover [E9] *vt* (ahorro/turismo) to promote; (conflicto/enfrentamientos) to provoke; (querella/pleito) to bring

promulgar [A3] *vt* to enact, to promulgate (frml)

pronombre *m* pronoun

pronosticar [A2] *vt* (tiempo/resultado) to forecast; (victoria/muerte) to predict

pronóstico *m* (a) (predicción) forecast, prediction; **el ~ del tiempo** the weather forecast (b) (Med) prognosis (c) (en carreras de caballos) tip

prontitud *f* promptness

pronto¹ -ta *adj* (a) (rápido) (entrega/respuesta) prompt (b) (RPl) (preparado) ready

pronto² *adv* ① (a) (en poco tiempo) soon; **¡hasta ~!** see you soon!; **lo más ~ posible** as soon as possible (b) (Esp) (temprano) early ② (en locs) **de pronto** (repentinamente) suddenly; **por lo pronto** *or* **por de pronto** for the moment, for now; **tan pronto como** as soon as

pronunciación *f* pronunciation

pronunciado -da *adj* (a) (curva) sharp, pronounced; (pendiente) steep, pronounced (b) (facciones/rasgos) pronounced, marked; (tendencia) marked, noticeable

pronunciamiento *m* rebellion, military uprising

pronunciar [A1] *vt* ① (a) (Ling) to pronounce (b) (discurso) to deliver, give ② (resaltar) to accentuate
■ **pronunciarse** *v pron* ① (dar una opinión) **~se A FAVOR/EN CONTRA DE algo** to declare oneself to be in FAVOR OF/AGAINST sth ② (acentuarse) to become more marked, become more pronounced

propaganda *f* (a) (Pol) propaganda (b) (Com, Marketing) advertising; **hacer ~ de un producto** to advertise a product (c) (material publicitario) advertisements (*pl*); **no trae más que ~** it has nothing but advertisements in it; **repartir ~** to hand out advertising leaflets

propagar [A3] *vt* (a) (doctrina/rumores/enfermedad) to spread, propagate (b) (especie) to propagate
■ **propagarse** *v pron* to spread; «especie/sonido/luz» to propagate

propasarse [A1] *v pron* (a) (excederse) to go too far, overstep the mark (b) (en sentido sexual) **~ CON algn** to make a pass AT sb

propenso -sa *adj* **~ A algo** prone TO sth

propiamente *adv* exactly; **no vive en Londres ~ dicho** he doesn't live in London proper

propiciar [A1] *vt* (favorecer) to favor*; (causar) to bring about

propicio -cia *adj* (momento) opportune, propitious (frml); (condiciones) favorable*, propitious (frml)

propiedad *f* ① (a) (pertenencia) property; **son ~ del museo** they are the property of the museum; **la casa es ~ de mi hijo** the house belongs to my son (b) (lo poseído) property; **~ intelectual** copyright; **~ privada/pública** private/public property ② (cualidad) property; (corrección): **con ~** (hablar) correctly; (comportarse) with decorum

propietario -ria *m,f* **(a)** (de comercio) owner, proprietor **(b)** (de casa) owner **(c)** (de tierras) landowner

propina *f* **(a)** (a camarero, empleado) tip, gratuity (frml); **dejó 25 pesos de** ～ she left a 25 peso tip; **darle** ～ **a algn** to tip sb **(b)** (Per) (de niño) pocket money

propio -pia *adj* **1 (a)** (indicando posesión) own; **¿es** ～ **o alquilado?** is it your own or is it rented?; **tienen piscina propia** they have their own swimming pool **(b)** (de uno mismo) own; **por tu** ～ **bien** for your own good; **todo lo hace en beneficio** ～ everything he does is for his own gain; **lo vi con mis** ～**s ojos** I saw it with my own two eyes *o* with my (very) own eyes
2 (característico, típico): **esa actitud es muy propia de él** that kind of attitude is very typical of him; **una enfermedad propia de la vejez** an illness common among old people; **no es un comportamiento** ～ **de una señorita** it's not ladylike behaviour
3 (delante del n) (mismo): **fue el** ～ **presidente** it was the president himself; **debe ser el** ～ **interesado quien lo pida** it must be the person concerned who makes the request

proponer [E22] *vt* **(a)** ⟨idea⟩ to propose, suggest; ⟨brindis⟩ to propose; **nos propuso ir al campo** she suggested we go to the countryside; **te voy a** ～ **un trato** I'm going to make you a proposition **(b)** ⟨persona⟩ (para cargo) to put forward, nominate; (para premio) to nominate **(c)** ⟨moción⟩ to propose **(d)** ⟨teoría⟩ to propound
■ **proponerse** *v pron*: ～**se hacer algo** to set out to do sth; **me lo propuse como meta** I set myself that goal; **me propuse decírselo** I made up my mind *o* I decided to tell her

proporción *f* **1** (relación) proportion; **en** ～ **a los ingresos** in proportion to income
2 proporciones *fpl* (dimensiones) proportions (pl)

proporcionado -da *adj*: ～ **a la figura humana** in proportion to the human body; **mal** ～ ⟨dibujo⟩ poorly proportioned; **es bajo pero bien** ～ he's short but he's well-proportioned

proporcional *adj* proportional, proportionate

proporcionar [A1] *vt* ⟨materiales/información/comida⟩ to provide; ～ **algo A algn** to provide sb WITH sth

proposición *f* proposal, proposition; ～ **de matrimonio** proposal of marriage

propósito *m* **(a)** (intención) intention, purpose; **con el** ～ **de verla** with the intention *o* purpose of seeing her; **tiene el firme** ～ **de dejar de fumar** she's determined to give up smoking; **buenos** ～**s** good intentions **(b) a propósito** (adrede) deliberately, on purpose; (por cierto) by the way

propuesta *f* **(a)** (sugerencia) proposal **(b)** (oferta) offer

propulsar [A1] *vt* ⟨desarrollo/actividad⟩ to promote, stimulate; ⟨avión/cohete⟩ to propel; ⟨vehículo⟩ to drive, propel

propulsión *f* propulsion; ～ **a chorro** jet propulsion

propulsor -sora *adj* ⟨mecanismo⟩ driving (before n), propulsion (before n); ⟨cohete⟩ propulsion (before n)
■ *m,f* **(a)** (de actividad, idea) promoter **(b)** *m* (Tec) propellant

propulsor *m* (Tec) propellant

propuse, propuso, etc ▸ PROPONER

prórroga *f* **(a)** (extensión) extension; (Dep) overtime (AmE), extra time (BrE) **(b)** (aplazamiento) deferral, deferment

prorrogar [A3] *vt* **(a)** (alargar) to extend **(b)** (aplazar) ⟨fecha⟩ to postpone, put back

prosa *f* prose

prosaico -ca *adj* ⟨existencia/vida⟩ mundane, prosaic

proseguir [I30] *vi/vt* (frml) to continue

prospecto *m* **(a)** (de fármaco) directions for use (pl), patient information leaflet **(b)** (de propaganda) pamphlet, leaflet

prosperar [A1] *vi* **(a)** «negocio/país» to prosper, thrive; «persona» to do well, make good **(b)** «iniciativa/proyecto» (aceptarse) to be accepted, prosper

prosperidad *f* prosperity

próspero -ra *adj* prosperous

próstata *f* prostate (gland)

prostíbulo *m* brothel

prostitución *f* prostitution

prostituir [I20] *vt* to prostitute
■ **prostituirse** *v pron* to prostitute oneself

prostituto -ta *m,f* (m) male prostitute; (f) prostitute

protagonista *mf* **(a)** (personaje principal) main character **(b)** (actor) **el** ～ **de la nueva serie** the actor who is playing the leading role in the new series; **los principales** ～**s de nuestra historia** the major figures of our history

protagonizar [A4] *vt* **(a)** (Cin, Teatr) to star in, play the lead *o* leading role in **(b)** ⟨tiroteo⟩ to be involved in; ⟨debate⟩ to take part in; ⟨disturbios⟩ to be responsible for

protección *f* protection

proteccionismo *m* protectionism

proteccionista *adj/mf* protectionist

protector -tora *adj* protective; **sociedad** ～**a de animales** society for the prevention of cruelty to animals
■ *m,f* (defensor) protector; (benefactor) patron

protectorado *m* protectorate

proteger [E6] *vt* **(a)** (en general) to protect; ～ **algo/a algn DE** *o* **CONTRA algo/algn** to protect sth/sb FROM *o* AGAINST sth/sb **(b)** ⟨artes⟩ to champion, patronize; ⟨pintor/poeta⟩ to act as patron to
■ **protegerse** *v pron* (refl) ～**se DE** *o* **CONTRA algo** to protect oneself FROM *o* AGAINST sth; ～**se de la lluvia** to shelter from the rain

protegido -da *adj* **(a)** ⟨especie⟩ protected **(b)** ⟨vivienda⟩ subsidized **(c)** (Inf) write-protected

AmC Central America	Arg	Argentina	Cu	Cuba	Per Peru
AmL Latin America	Bol	Bolivia	Ec	Ecuador	RPI River Plate Area
AmS South America	Chi	Chile	Esp	Spain	Ur Uruguay
Andes Andean Region	CS	Southern Cone	Méx	Mexico	Ven Venezuela

■ *m,f* (*m*) protegé; (*f*) protegée

proteína *f* protein

prótesis *f* prosthesis

protesta *f* **1** **(a)** (queja) protest; **en señal de ~** in protest **(b)** (manifestación) demonstration, protest march (*o* rally *etc*) **2** (Méx) **(a)** (promesa) promise; **cumplieron con su ~** they kept their promise *o* word **(b)** ▶ JURAMENTO

protestante *adj/mf* Protestant

protestantismo *m* Protestantism

protestar [A1] *vi* **(a)** (mostrar desacuerdo) to protest; **~ CONTRA algo** to protest AGAINST *o* ABOUT sth **(b)** (quejarse) to complain; **~ POR** *or* **DE algo** to complain ABOUT sth

protocolo *m* **(a)** (ceremonial, etiqueta) protocol; **(b)** (Inf) protocol

prototipo *m* **(a)** (de especie) archetype, prototype **(b)** (Tec) prototype

protuberancia *f* bulge, protuberance (frml)

provecho *m* **(a)** (beneficio, utilidad) benefit; **no sacó mucho ~ de la experiencia** she didn't benefit much from the experience; **le sacó mucho ~ a su estancia** she got a lot out of her stay; **solo piensa en su propio ~** he's only out for himself (colloq); **de ~** ⟨*estudiante*⟩ hardworking; ⟨*experiencia/visita*⟩ worthwhile **(b)** (en la mesa): **¡buen ~!** (dicho por uno mismo) bon appetit!; (dicho por camarero) enjoy your meal!

provechoso -sa *adj* profitable, fruitful

proveedor -dora *m,f* supplier, purveyor (frml); **~ de servicios Internet** Internet service provider

proveer [E14] *vt* (suministrar) to provide; **~ a algn DE algo** to provide sb WITH sth; **iban provistos de botes salvavidas** they were equipped with *o* they carried lifeboats

■ **proveerse** *v pron* (*refl*): **~se DE algo** ⟨*de herramientas/armas*⟩ to equip oneself WITH sth; ⟨*de comida*⟩ to get sth

provenir [I31] *vi* **~ DE algo/algn** to come FROM sth/sb

proverbio *m* proverb

providencia *f* (Relig): **la** (**divina**) **P~** (divine) Providence

providencial *adj* **(a)** (oportuno) fortunate, lucky, providential (frml); **fue ~ que ...** it was fortunate that ... **(b)** (Relig) providential

provincia *f* **1** (Gob, Relig) province **2** **provincias** *fpl* (por oposición a la capital) provinces (*pl*); **la vida de ~s** provincial life

provinciano -na *adj* **(a)** (de provincias) provincial **(b)** (pey) (estrecho de miras) provincial, parochial

■ *m,f* **(a)** (de provincias): **los ~s** people from the provinces **(b)** (pey) (de mentalidad estrecha) provincial **(c)** (paleto) country bumpkin, hick (AmE colloq)

provisional *adj* provisional

provisiones *fpl* (víveres) provisions (*pl*)

provisto -ta *pp* ▶ PROVEER

provocación *f* provocation

provocador -dora *adj* provocative

■ *m,f* agitator

provocar [A2] *vt* **1** **(a)** ⟨*explosión*⟩ to cause; ⟨*incendio*⟩ to start; ⟨*polémica*⟩ to spark off,

prompt; ⟨*reacción*⟩ to cause **(b)** (Med) ⟨*parto*⟩ to induce **2** ⟨*persona*⟩ (al enfado) to provoke; (sexualmente) to lead ... on

■ **~** *vi* (Andes) (apetecer): **¿le provoca un traguito?** do you want a drink?, do you fancy a drink? (BrE colloq)

provocativo -va *adj* **1** (insinuante) provocative **2** (Col, Ven) (apetecible) tempting, mouthwatering

proxeneta *mf* (*m*) procurer (frml), pimp (colloq); (*f*) procuress (frml), pimp (colloq)

proximidad *f* **(a)** (en el tiempo, espacio) closeness, proximity (frml) **(b)** **proximidades** *fpl* (cercanías) vicinity

próximo -ma *adj* **1** **(a)** (siguiente) next; **el ~ jueves** next Thursday **(b)** (*como pron*): **esto lo dejamos para la próxima** we'll leave this for next time; **tome la próxima a la derecha** take the next (on the) right **2** [ESTAR] (cercano) **(a)** (en el tiempo) close; **la fecha ya está próxima** the day is close; **en fecha próxima** in the near future **(b)** (en el espacio) near, close; **~ A algo** close *o* near TO sth

proyección *f* **(a)** (Cin) showing **(b)** (de sombra) casting; (de luz) throwing

proyectar [A1] *vt* **1** (planear) to plan; **~ hacer algo** to plan to do sth **2** **(a)** ⟨*película*⟩ to show, screen; ⟨*diapositivas*⟩ to project, show **(b)** ⟨*sombra*⟩ to cast; ⟨*luz*⟩ to throw, project

proyectil *m* projectile, missile

proyecto *m* **(a)** (plan) plan; **¿qué ~s tienes para el próximo año?** what are your plans for next year?; **tiene un viaje en ~** she's planning a trip; **~ de ley** bill **(b)** (trabajo) project **(c)** (Arquit, Ing) plans and costing

proyector *m* **1** (Cin, Fot) projector **2** (Teatr) spotlight; (para monumentos) floodlight; (Mil) searchlight

prudencia *f* (cuidado) caution; (sabiduría) wisdom, prudence; **conduce con ~** drive carefully

prudente *adj* (sensato. responsable) prudent, sensible; (cauto, precavido) cautious, prudent

prueba *f* **1** **(a)** (demostración, testimonio) proof; **no hay ~s de que eso sea verdad** there's no proof that that's true; **eso es ~ de que le caes bien** that proves he likes you; **en** *or* **como ~ de mi agradecimiento** as a token of my gratitude **(b)** (Der) piece of evidence **2** (Educ) test; (Cin) screen test, audition; (Teatr) audition **3** **(a)** (ensayo, experimento) test; **vamos a hacer la ~** let's try; **~ de la alcoholemia** Breathalyzer® test, sobriety test (AmE), drunkometer test (AmE); **~ del embarazo** pregnancy test **(b)** (*en locs*) **a prueba: tomar a algn a ~** to take sb on for a trial period; **tener algo a ~** to have sth on trial; **poner algo a ~** to put sth to the test; **a ~ de golpes/de balas** shockproof/bulletproof **(c)** (en costura) fitting **4** (Fot, Impr) proof; **corregir ~s** to proofread **5** (Dep): **en las ~s de clasificación** in the qualifying heats; **la ~ de los 1.500 metros** the 1,500 meters (event *o* race)

prueba, pruebas, etc ▶ PROBAR

PSI *m* (= **provedor de sevicios Internet**) ISP

psicoanálisis *m* psychoanalysis

p

psicoanalista *mf* psychoanalyst

psicodélico -ca *adj* psychedelic

psicología *f* psychology

psicológico -ca *adj* psychological

psicólogo -ga *m,f* psychologist

psicópata *mf* psychopath

psicosis *f* (*pl* ∼) psychosis

psicosomático -ca *adj* psychosomatic

psicoterapia *f* psychotherapy

psiquiatra *mf* psychiatrist

psiquiatría *f* psychiatry

psiquiátrico¹ -ca *adj* psychiatric (*before n*)

psiquiátrico² *m* psychiatric hospital, mental hospital

psíquico -ca *adj* psychic

ptas, pts = **pesetas**

púa *f* **1** (a) (de erizo) spine, quill; (de alambre) barb; (de peine) tooth **(b)** (Chi, Ven) (en zapatos de atletismo) spike **2** (para guitarra) plectrum, pick; (de tocadiscos) (RPI) needle

pub /puβ, pʌβ/ *m* (*pl* **pubs** *or* **pubes**) bar (*gen with music, open late at night*)

pubertad *f* puberty

pubis *m* (*pl* ∼) pubis

publicación *f* publication

publicar [A2] *vt* (a) (artículo/noticia) to publish **(b)** (divulgar) to divulge, disclose

publicidad *f* (a) (de tema, suceso) publicity **(b)** (Com, Marketing) advertising; **hacer ∼ de algo** to advertise sth

publicista *mf* (a) (AmL) (Com) advertising executive *o* agent, publicist **(b)** (Period) publicist

publicitario -ria *adj* (campaña/espacio) advertising (*before n*); (truco/montaje) publicity (*before n*)

público¹ -ca *adj* public; **hacer ∼ algo** to announce sth; **es un peligro ∼** he's a danger to the public

público² *m* (en teatro) audience, public; (Dep) spectators (*pl*); **⊜ horario de atención al público** (en oficinas públicas) opening hours; (en bancos) hours of business; **película apta para todo(s) (los) ∼(s)** 'G' movie (AmE), 'U' film (BrE); **el ∼ en general** the general public; **en ∼** (hablar) in public; (cantar/bailar) in front of an audience; **salir al ∼** (Andes) (periódico/revista) to come out, appear; (noticia/información) to be published

pucherazo *m* (fam) electoral rigging; **hubo ∼** the election was fixed *o* rigged

puchero *m* **1** (Coc) (recipiente) pot, stewpot; (cocido) stew **2** (mueca) pout; **hacer ∼s** to pout

pucho *m* (AmS fam) (a) (cigarrillo — de tabaco) smoke (colloq), fag (BrE colloq); (— de marihuana) joint (colloq) **(b)** (resto — de cigarrillo) butt, fag end (BrE colloq); (— de comida) scrap; (— de bebida) drop

pude ▶ PODER

púdico -ca *adj* (ropa) modest; (comportamiento/beso) chaste

pudiera, pudiese, etc ▶ PODER

pudín *m* ▶ BUDÍN

pudiste, etc ▶ PODER

pudor *m* (a) (recato sexual) modesty; **no se desnudó por ∼** she was too embarrassed *o* shy to take her clothes off; **es una falta de ∼** it shows a lack of (a sense of) decency **(b)** (reserva) reserve; **nos habló sin ∼** he talked to us very openly

pudoroso -sa *adj* ▶ PÚDICO

pudrir [I38] *vt* (descomponer) (carne/fruta/madera) to rot, decay

■ **pudrirse** *v pron* **1** (descomponerse) «fruta/carne» to rot, decay; «madera/tela» to rot; «cadáver» to decompose, rot **2** (fam) (por el abandono); **∼se en la cárcel** to rot in jail

pueblerino -na *adj* (aire) provincial; **¡qué ∼ eres!** you're such a country bumpkin *o* (AmE colloq) hick!

pueblo *m* **1** (poblado) village; (más grande) small town; **∼ joven** (Per) shantytown **2** (a) (comunidad) people; **un ∼ nómada** a nomadic people **(b)** (ciudadanos, nación) people; **el ∼ vasco** the Basque people

pueda, puedas, etc ▶ PODER

puente *m* **1** (Ing) bridge; **∼ colgante/giratorio** suspension/swing bridge; **∼ levadizo** (en castillo) drawbridge; (en carretera) lifting bridge; **∼ aéreo** (servicio frecuente) shuttle (service); (Mil) airlift **2** (Mús, Odont) bridge; (de anteojos) bridge **3** (Elec) bridge (circuit) **4** (vacación) ≈ long weekend (*linked to a public holiday by an extra day's holiday in between*) **5** (Náut) *tb* **∼ de mando** bridge

puerco -ca *adj* (fam & pey) (sucio) dirty; (despreciable) low-down (colloq)

■ *m,f* **1** (a) (animal) (*m*) pig, hog, boar; (*f*) pig, hog, sow; **∼ espín** porcupine **(b)** (Méx) (carne) pork **2** (fam) (persona — sucia) pig (colloq); (— despreciable) swine (colloq)

puericultor -tora *m,f*: nurse or doctor who specializes in babycare/childcare

puericultura *f* babycare, childcare

pueril *adj* (a) (infantil) childish, puerile (frml) **(b)** (ingenuo) naive

puerro *m* leek

puerta *f* (de casa, coche, horno) door; (en jardín, valla) gate; **llamar a la ∼** to ring the doorbell/knock on the door; **te espero en la ∼ del teatro** I'll meet you at the entrance of the theater; **te acompaño a la ∼** I'll see *o* show you out; **servicio ∼ a ∼** door-to-door service; **un coche de dos ∼s** a two-door car; **∼ de embarque** gate; **∼ principal** *or* **de la calle** (de casa) front door; (de edificio público) main door *or* entrance; **∼ trasera** back door

puerto *m* **1** (Náut) port, harbor*; **entrar a ∼** to enter port *o* harbor; **∼ deportivo** marina; **∼ franco** *or* **libre** free port; **∼ pesquero** fishing port **2** (Geog) *tb* **∼ de montaña** (mountain) pass

Puerto Príncipe *m* Port-au-Prince

Puerto Rico *m* Puerto Rico

pues *conj* (a) (en general) well **(b)** (indicando consecuencia) then; **∼ si te gusta tanto, cómpralo** if you like it that much, then buy it

puesta *f* **1** (acción de poner): **hasta la ∼ en servicio de los autobuses** until the buses come into service; **la ∼ en libertad de los prisioneros** the freeing *o* release of the prisoners; **∼ a punto** (de vehículo) tune-up; (de máquina) adjustment; **∼ de sol** sunset; **∼ en escena** production; **∼ en marcha** (de vehículo, motor) starting (up); **∼ al día** updating **2** (de huevos) lay

puestero -ra *m,f* (AmL) **(a)** (vendedor) stallholder, market vendor **(b)** (en una estancia) farmer (*responsible for the running of part of a large ranch*)

puesto¹ -ta *adj*: ¿qué haces con el abrigo ∼? what are you doing with your coat on?; **tenía las botas puestas** she was wearing her boots; **la mesa estaba puesta** the table was laid; *ver tb* PONER

puesto² *m* **1 (a)** (lugar, sitio) place; **se sentó en mi** ∼ he sat in my place **(b)** (en una clasificación) place, position; **sacó el primer** ∼ **de la clase** she came top *o* (AmE) came out top of the class **2** (empleo) position, job; ∼ **de trabajo** (empleo) job; (Inf) workstation **3 (a)** (Com) (en mercado) stall; (quiosco) kiosk; (tienda) stand, stall **(b)** (de la policía, del ejército) post; ∼ **de socorro** first-aid post/ station **4 puesto que** (*conj*) (frml) since

puf *m* (*pl* **pufs**) hassock (AmE), pouffe (BrE) ■ *interj* (expresando — repugnancia) ugh! (colloq), pee-yoo! (AmE); (— cansancio, sofoco) whew!, oof!

púgil *m* (period) boxer, pugilist (frml)

pugna *f* **(a)** (lucha) struggle **(b)** (conflicto): **tendencias/intereses en** ∼ conflicting trends/ interests; **entrar en** ∼ **con algo/algn** to clash *o* come into conflict **with** sth/sb

pugnar [A1] *vi* (liter) (luchar) ∼ POR + INF to strive to + INF (frml)

pujante *adj* booming (before n)

pujanza *f* vigor*, strength

pujar [A1] *vi* **1** (luchar) ∼ POR algo/hacer algo to struggle POR sth/to do sth **2** (Esp) (en subasta) to bid **3** (Méx fam) (gemir) to moan, whimper

pulcro -cra *adj* ⟨persona/aspecto⟩ immaculate, neat and tidy; ⟨informe/trabajo⟩ meticulous

pulga *f* (Zool) flea; **tener malas** ∼**s** (fam) to be bad-tempered

pulgada *f* inch

pulgar *m* (de la mano) thumb; (del pie) big toe

pulgón *m* aphid, plant louse

pulir [I1] *vt* **1 (a)** ⟨metal/piedra/vidrio⟩ to polish **(b)** ⟨madera⟩ to sand **(c)** (lustrar) to polish **2** (refinar) ⟨estilo/trabajo⟩ to polish up; ⟨persona⟩ to make ... more refined; ⟨idioma⟩ to brush up

pulla *f* gibe

pulmón *m* lung; ∼ **de acero** iron lung

pulmonía *f* pneumonia; ∼ **doble** double pneumonia

pulóver *m* (*pl* **-vers**) (suéter) pullover, sweater, jumper (BrE)

pulpa *f* (de fruta, vegetal) pulp; (de madera) (wood) pulp

pulpería *f* (AmL) local store

pulpero -ra *m,f* (AmL) local storekeeper

púlpito *m* pulpit

pulpo *m* (Zool) octopus

pulque *m* pulque (*drink made from fermented cactus sap*)

pulquería *f* (Méx) bar, restaurant (*serving pulque*)

pulquero -ra *m,f* (Méx) owner of a PULQUERÍA

pulsación *f* **1** (latido) beat **2** (en mecanografía) keystroke; ¿**cuántas pulsaciones piden por minuto?** ≈ how many words a minute do they want?

pulsar [A1] *vt* **1 (a)** (Mús) ⟨cuerda⟩ to pluck; ⟨tecla⟩ to press **(b)** ⟨botón⟩ to push, press; ⟨timbre⟩ press, ring **2** ⟨opinión/situación⟩ to gauge, assess

pulsera *f* bracelet; ∼ **de tobillo** ankle bracelet, anklet

pulso *m* **(a)** (Med) pulse; **tomarle el** ∼ **a algn** to take sb's pulse; **tomarle el** ∼ **a algo** to gauge sth **(b)** (firmeza en la mano): **tengo muy mal** ∼ I have a very unsteady hand; **me temblaba el** ∼ my hand was shaking; **a** ∼ ⟨levantar⟩ with one's bare hands; ⟨dibujar⟩ freehand

pulular [A1] *vi* **(a)** (bullir) «muchedumbre» to mill around **(b)** (abundar): **aquí pululan los mosquitos** there are swarms of mosquitos here

pulverizador *m* (de perfume) atomizer, spray; (de pintura) spray gun; (del carburador) jet

pulverizar [A4] *vt* ⟨líquido⟩ to atomize, spray; ⟨sólido⟩ to pulverize, crush

puma *m* (animal) cougar, mountain lion, puma

puna *f* **(a)** (páramo) high Andean plateau **(b)** (Andes) (soroche) mountain *o* altitude sickness

punki /'puŋki, 'pʌŋki/ *adj/mf* (fam) punk

punta *f* **1 (a)** (de lengua, dedos) tip; (de nariz) end, tip; (de pan) end; (de pincel) tip; **vivo en la otra** ∼ **de la ciudad** I live on the other side *o* at the other end of town; **con la** ∼ **del pie** with the print of one's foot; **la** ∼ **del iceberg** the tip of the iceberg; **tener algo en la** ∼ **de la lengua** to have sth on the tip of one's tongue **(b) puntas** *fpl* (del pelo) ends (*pl*) **2 (a)** (de aguja, clavo, cuchillo, lápiz) point; (de flecha, lanza) tip; ∼ **de lanza** spearhead; **sácale** ∼ **al lápiz** sharpen the pencil; **de** ∼ point first; **en** ∼ pointed; **por un extremo acaba en** ∼ it's pointed at one end **(b) a punta de** (AmL fam): **a** ∼ **de repetírselo mil veces** by telling him it a thousand times; **a** ∼ **de palos lo hicieron obedecer** they beat him until he did as he was told **3** (de pañuelo) corner ■ *adj inv*: **la hora** ∼ the rush hour

puntabola *f* (Bol) ballpoint pen, Biro® (BrE)

puntada *f* **1** (en costura) stitch **2** (CS) (de dolor) stab of pain, sharp pain **3** (Méx fam) (comentario ingenioso) quip, witticism

puntaje *m* (AmL) (en competencia, prueba) score; (Educ) grades (*pl*) (AmE), marks (BrE)

puntal *m* **(a)** (Const) prop **(b)** (sostén, apoyo) mainstay

puntapié *m* kick; **darle** *or* **pegarle un** ∼ **a algo/ algn** to kick sth/sb, to give sth/sb a kick; **para modismos** *ver* PATADA

puntear [A1] *vt* **1** (Mús) to pluck **2** (AmL) (Dep) to lead

punteo *m* plucking

puntería *f* aim; **tener buena/mala** ∼ to have a good/poor aim; **afinar la** ∼ to take careful aim; **¡qué** ∼**!** what a shot!

puntero *m* **1** (para señalar) pointer; (Inf) cursor; (de reloj) (Andes) hand **2** (Dep) **(a)** (equipo) leader, leaders (*pl*) **(b)** (Andes, RPl) (en fútbol) winger

puntiagudo -da *adj* (acabado en punta) pointed; (afilado) sharp

P

puntilla f [1] (Taur) dagger (*used to administer the coup de grâce in a bullfight*); **dar la ~** (Taur) to administer the coup de grâce [2] (*punta del pie*): **de ~s** or (AmL) **en ~s** on tiptoe; **entró de ~s** she tiptoed into the room [3] (*encaje*) lace edging

puntilloso -sa *adj* particular, punctilious

punto m [1] (a) (*señal, marca*) dot (b) (Ling) (*sobre la 'i', la 'j'*) dot; (*signo de puntuación*) period (AmE), full stop (BrE); **~ decimal** decimal point ; **~ final** period (AmE), full stop (BrE); **~s suspensivos** ellipsis (tech), suspension points (*pl*) (AmE), dot, dot, dot; **~ y aparte** period (AmE) o (BrE) full stop, new paragraph; **~ y coma** semicolon; **~ com** (Com, Inf) dot com; **a ~ fijo** exactly, for certain; **... y punto** ... and that's that, ... period (AmE); ▶ DOS

[2] (a) (*momento, lugar*) point; **en ese ~ de la conversación** at that point in the conversation; **el ~ donde ocurrió el accidente** the spot o place where the accident happened; **~ cardinal** cardinal point ; **~ ciego** blind spot; **~ de apoyo** (*de palanca*) fulcrum; **no hay ningún ~ de apoyo para la escalera** there is nowhere to lean the ladder; **~ de vista** (*perspectiva*) viewpoint, point of view; (*opinión*) views; **~ flaco/fuerte** weak/strong point; **~ muerto** (Auto) neutral; (*en negociaciones*) deadlock (b) (*en geometría*) point

[3] (*grado*) point, extent; **hasta cierto ~ tiene razón** she's right, up to a point; **hasta tal ~ que ...** so much so that ...

[4] (*asunto, aspecto*) point; **analizar algo ~ por ~** to analyze sth point by point; **los ~s a tratar en la reunión** the matters o items on the agenda for the meeting

[5] (*en locs*) **a punto** (a tiempo) just in time; **estábamos a ~ de cenar** we were about to have dinner; **estuvo a ~ de caerse** he almost fell over; **batir las claras a ~ de nieve** beat the egg whites until they form stiff peaks; **en su punto** just right; **en punto:** **las 12 en ~** at 12 o'clock sharp; **son las tres en ~** it's exactly three o'clock; **llegaron en ~** they arrived exactly on time

[6] (a) (*en costura, labores*) stitch; **artículos de ~** knitwear; **hacer ~** (Esp) to knit; **~ (de) cruz** cross-stitch (b) (*en cirugía*) *tb* **~ de sutura** stitch

[7] (*unidad*) (a) (Dep, Jueg) point; **~ para partido/set** (Méx) match/set point (b) (Educ) point, mark; (Fin) point

puntuación f [1] (Impr, Ling) punctuation [2] (a) (*acción*) (Educ) grading (AmE), marking (BrE); (Dep) scoring (b) (esp Esp) (Educ) grade (AmE), mark (BrE); (Dep) score

puntual *adj* [1] (a) (*persona*) punctual (b) (*como adv*) (*llegar*) punctually, on time [2] (*detallado*) detailed; (*exacto*) precise

puntualidad f punctuality

puntualizar [A4] *vt* (a) (*especificar*) to state (b) (*señalar*) to point out

puntuar [A18] *vt* [1] (*examen/prueba*) to grade (AmE), to mark (BrE) [2] (*texto*) to punctuate ∎ ~ *vi* (a) (*partido/prueba*) **~ PARA algo** to count TOWARD(s) sth (b) (*deportista*) to score (points)

puntudo -da *adj* (Andes, RPI) ▶ PUNTIAGUDO

punzada f sharp pain, stab of pain; **me dio una ~ en el costado** I felt a sharp pain o a stab of pain in my side

punzante *adj* (*objeto*) sharp; (*dolor*) sharp, stabbing (*before n*); (*palabras/comentario*) biting, incisive; (*estilo*) caustic

punzón m (*para hacer agujeros*) bradawl, awl; (*para hacer ojetes*) hole punch; (*de grabador, escultor*) burin

puñado m handful

puñal m dagger

puñalada f (a) (*navajazo*) stab; **lo mató a ~s** she stabbed him to death (b) (*herida*) stab wound

puñeta f (Esp fam): **hacerle la ~ a algn** to mess things up for sb; **mandar a algn a hacer ~s** to tell sb to go to hell; **¡vete a hacer ~s!** go to hell! (colloq)

puñetazo m punch; **darle** or **pegarle un ~ a algn** to punch sb; **pegó un ~ en la mesa** he thumped the table with his fist; **le rompió la cara de un ~** he smashed his face in (colloq)

puñetero -ra *adj* (Esp fam) (a) (*delante del n*) (*uso enfático*) damn, blasted (b) [SER] (*persona*): **no seas ~** don't be a swine (colloq), don't be a jerk (colloq)

puño m [1] (Anat) fist; **apretar los ~s** to clench one's fists [2] (*de camisa*) cuff [3] (*de espada*) hilt; (*de bastón*) handle, haft; (*de moto*) grip

pupa f (a) (fam) (*en los labios*) cold sore (b) (Esp leng infantil) (*dolor, daño*): **mamá, (tengo) ~** mummy, it hurts; **¿te has hecho ~?** have you hurt yourself?

pupila f pupil

pupilo -la m,f (*de maestro*) pupil; (*de tutor*) ward, charge (b) (RPI) (*alumno interno*) boarder

pupitre m desk

purasangre mf thoroughbred

puré m: **~ de verduras** puréed vegetables; **~ de tomates** tomato purée o paste; **~ de papas** or (Esp) **patatas** mashed o creamed potatoes

pureza f purity

purgante *adj/m* purgative, laxative

purgatorio m purgatory

purificador m purifier; **~ de ambientes** (Col) air freshener

purificadora f *tb* **~ de agua** water treatment plant, waterworks (*sing or pl*)

purificar [A2] *vt* to purify

puritanismo m puritanism

puritano -na *adj* (Relig) Puritanical, Puritan (*before n*); (*mojigato*) puritanical ∎ m,f (Relig) Puritan; (*mojigato*) puritan

puro¹ -ra *adj* [1] (a) (*sin mezcla*) pure; (*limpio*) (*aire*) fresh, clean (b) (*casto, inocente*) (*mujer*) chaste, pure; (*niño*) innocent; (*mirada/amor*) innocent, pure [2] (*delante del n*) (a) (*mero, simple*) (*verdad*) plain, honest (colloq); (*casualidad/coincidencia*) pure, sheer; **lo hizo por ~ capricho** she did it purely on a whim; **de ~ cansancio**

from sheer exhaustion **(b)** (AmL fam) (sólo): **a ese bar van ~s viejos** only old men go to that bar; **son puras mentiras** it's just a pack of lies (colloq)

puro² *adv* (fam) (muy, tan): **se murió de ~ vieja** she just died of old age; **lo hizo de ~ egoísta** he did it out of sheer selfishness
■ *m* cigar

púrpura *f*: **(de) color ~** purple

purpurina *f* (en pinturas) metallic powder; (para adornar) glitter

pus *m* pus

puse, pusiera, etc ▶ PONER

pusilánime *adj* fainthearted, pusillanimous (frml)

pusiste, etc ▶ PONER

puso ▶ PONER

puta *f* (vulg & pey) (prostituta) whore (colloq & pej), hooker (colloq); **hijo (de) ~** son of a bitch (vulg), bastard (vulg)

putada *f* (vulg): **hacerle una ~ a algn** to play a dirty trick on sb (colloq)

putrefacción *f* putrefaction

putrefacto -ta, pútrido -da *adj* putrid

puya *f* **(a)** (Taur) point (*of the picador's lance*) **(b)** (comentario irónico) gibe; **lanzar** *or* **echar una ~** to make a gibe

puzzle /'pusle, 'pu∂le/ *m* (rompecabezas) (jigsaw) puzzle

Pza. *f* (= **Plaza**) Sq

Qq

Q, q *f* (*read as* /ku/) *the letter* Q, q

que *conj* **1** (oraciones subordinadas) **(a)** that; **creemos ~ esta es la solución** we believe that this is the solution; **estoy seguro de ~ vendrá** I'm sure (that) she'll come; **¿cuántos años crees ~ tiene?** how old do you think she is?; **eso de ~ estaba enfermo es mentira** (fam) this business about him being ill is a lie; **quiero ~ vengas** I want you to come; **dice ~ no vayas** she says you're not to go; **es importante ~ quede claro** it's important that it should be clear; **sería una lástima ~ no vinieras** it would be a shame if you didn't come **(b)** es que: **es ~ hoy no voy a poder** I'm afraid (that) I won't be able to today; **es ~ no tengo dinero** the trouble is I don't have any money **2 (a)** (en expresiones de deseo): **¡~ te mejores!** I hope you feel better soon; **¡~ se diviertan!** have a good time!; *ver tb* IR *v aux* 2 **(b)** (en expresiones de mandato): **¡~ te calles!** shut up! (colloq); **¡~ no!** I said no! **(c)** (en expresiones de sorpresa): **¿~ se casa?** she's getting married?; **¿cómo ~ no vas a ir?** what do you mean, you're not going? **(d)** (indicando persistencia): **se pasa dale ~ dale con lo mismo** he goes on and on about the same old thing; **y aquí llueve ~ llueve** and over here it just rains and rains **3** (introduciendo una consecuencia) that; **se parecen tanto ~ apenas los distingo** they're so alike (that) I can hardly tell them apart **4** (en comparaciones): **su casa es más grande ~ la mía** his house is bigger than mine; **tengo la misma edad ~ tú** I'm the same age as you **5** (fam) (en oraciones condicionales) if; **yo ~ tú** if I were you
■ *pron* **1** (refiriéndose a personas) **(a)** (sujeto) who; **los ~ estén cansados** those who are tired; **es la ~ manda aquí** she's the one who gives the orders here **(b)** (complemento): **la mujer ~ amo** the woman (that) I love; **las chicas ~ entrevistamos** the girls (that *o* who) we interviewed; **el único al ~ no le han pagado** the only one who hasn't been paid; **la persona de la ~ te hablé** the person (that *o* who) I spoke to you about **2** (refiriéndose a cosas, asuntos, etc) **(a)** (sujeto) that, which; **la pieza ~ se rompió** the part that *o* which broke; **eso es lo ~ me preocupa** that's what worries me **(b)** (complemento): **el disco ~ le regalé** the record (which *o* that) I gave her; **la casa en ~ vivo** the house (that) I live in; **¿sabes lo difícil ~ fue?** do you know how hard it was?; *ver tb* LO *art* 2B

qué *pron* **1** (interrogativo) **(a)** what; **¿~ es eso?** what's that?; **¿y ~?** so what?; **¿de ~ habló?** what did she talk about?; **¿sabes ~?** you know what *o* something?; **no sé ~ hacer** I don't know what to do **(b)** (al pedir que se nos repita algo) what; **¿qué?** what? **(c)** (en saludos): **¿~ tal?** how are you?; **¿~ es de tu vida?** how's life?
2 (en exclamaciones): **¡~ va a ser abogado ese!** him, a lawyer?; *ver tb* IR V1
■ *adj* **1** (interrogativo) what, which; **¿~ color quieres?** what *o* which color do you want?
2 (en exclamaciones) what; **¡~ noche!** what a night!
■ *adv*: **¡~ lindo!** how lovely!; **¡~ inteligente eres!** aren't you clever!; **¡~ bien (que) se está aquí!** it's so nice here!; **¡~ bien!** great!, good!

quebrada *f* **(a)** (despeñadero) gully; (más profunda) ravine **(b)** (AmS) (arroyo) stream

quebradero de cabeza *m* problem, headache (colloq)

quebradizo -za *adj* **(a)** (frágil) fragile; ⟨uña/hueso⟩ brittle **(b)** (que se desmenuza con facilidad) crumbly

quebrado¹ -da *adj* **1 (a)** ⟨hueso⟩ broken; ⟨vaso/huevo⟩ (roto) broken; (rajado) cracked **(b)** ⟨voz⟩ faltering **2** ⟨empresa/comerciante⟩ bankrupt **3 (a)** ⟨línea⟩ crooked, zigzag (*before n*) **(b)** (Mat): **número ~** fraction

quebrado² *m* fraction

quebradura *f* (esp AmL) crack

quebrar [A5] *vt* **1** (esp AmL) ⟨lápiz/rama⟩ to snap; ⟨vaso/plato⟩ (romper) to break; (rajar) to crack **2** (Méx fam) (matar) to kill
■ **~** *vi* **1** (Com) «empresa/persona» to go bankrupt **2** (AmC) (romper una relación) to break up
■ **quebrarse** *v pron* **1** (esp AmL) **(a)** «lápiz/ ···⟶

rama» to snap; «*vaso/plato*» (romperse) to break; (rajarse) to crack **(b)** *⟨pierna/brazo⟩* to break; *⟨diente⟩* **2** (Col) (arruinarse) to go bankrupt

quechua *adj* Quechua
■ *mf* (persona) Quechuan
■ *m* (idioma) Quechua

quedar [A1] *vi*
I **1** (en un estado, una situación): ~ **viudo/huérfano** to be widowed/orphaned; **quedó paralítico** he was left paralyzed; **el coche quedó como nuevo** the car is as good as new (now); **y que esto quede bien claro** and I want to make this quite clear; **¿quién quedó en primer lugar?** who was *o* came first?

2 (en la opinión de los demás): **si no voy** ~**é mal con ellos** it won't go down very well *o* it'll look bad if I don't turn up; **lo hice para** ~ **bien con el jefe** I did it to get in the boss's good books; **quedé muy bien con el regalo** I made a very good impression with my present; **me hiciste** ~ **muy mal diciendo eso** you really showed me up by saying that; **nos hizo** ~ **mal a todos** he embarrassed us all; **quedó en ridículo** (*por culpa propia*) he made a fool of himself; (*por culpa ajena*) he was made to look a fool

3 (permanecer): **¿queda alguien adentro?** is there anyone left inside?; **le quedó la cicatriz** she was left with a scar; **esto no puede** ~ **así** we can't leave things like this; **nuestros planes** ~**on en nada** our plans came to nothing; ~ **atrás** «*persona*» to fall behind; «*rencillas/problemas*» to be in the past

4 (*+ me/te/le etc*) **(a)** «*tamaño/talla*»: **me queda largo** it's too long for me; **la talla 12 le queda bien** the size 12 fits (you/him) fine **(b)** (sentar): **el azul le queda bien/mal** blue suits her/doesn't suit her

II (a) (acordar, convenir): **¿en qué** ~**on?** what did you decide?; **¿entonces en qué quedamos?** so, what's happening, then?; ~**on en** *or* (AmL) **de no decirle nada** they agreed *o* decided not to tell him anything; **quedó en** *or* (AmL) **de venir a las nueve** she said she would come at nine **(b)** (citarse): **¿a qué hora quedamos?** what time shall we meet?; **quedé con unos amigos para cenar** I arranged to meet some friends for dinner

III (estar situado): **queda justo enfrente de la estación** it's right opposite the station; **me queda muy lejos** it's very far from where I live (*o* work *etc*)

IV (en *3ª pers*) **1 (a)** (haber todavía) to be left; **¿te queda algo de dinero?** do you have any money left?; **¿queda café?** is there any coffee left?; **solo quedan las ruinas** only the ruins remain; **no nos queda más remedio que ir** we have no choice but to go **(b)** (sobrar) «*comida/vino*» to be left (over)

2 (faltar): **queda poco para que acabe la clase** it's not long till the end of the class; **¿cuántos kilómetros quedan?** how many kilometers are there to go?; **todavía le quedan dos años** he still has two years to go *o* do; **queda mucho por ver** there is still a lot to see; **aún me queda todo esto por hacer** I still have all this to do; **no me/le queda otra** (fam) I have/he has no choice

■ **quedarse** *v pron*
I **1 (a)** (en un lugar, país) to stay; ~**se en la cama** to stay in bed **(b)** (en un estado, una situación)

(*+ compl*): **te estás quedando calvo** you're going bald; ~**se dormido** to fall asleep; ~**se sin trabajo** to lose one's job

2 (*+ me/te/le etc*) **(a)** (permanecer): ~**se soltera** to stay single; **no me gusta** ~**me sola en casa** I don't like being alone in the house; **¡no te quedes ahí parado!** don't just stand there!; **nos quedamos charlando hasta tarde** we went on chatting until late in the evening; **se me quedó mirando** he sat/stood there staring at me; **de repente el motor se quedó** (AmL) the engine suddenly died on me **(b)** (Andes) (olvidarse): **se me quedó el paraguas** I left my umbrella behind **(c)** (Esp) (llegar a ser): **la casa se les está quedando pequeña** the house is getting (to be) too small for them

II *⟨cambio/lápiz⟩* to keep; **se quedó con mi libro** she kept my book; **me quedo con este** I'll take this one

quehacer *m* (actividad, tarea) work; ~**es domésticos** housework, household chores; **el** ~ **diario** the daily routine

queja *f* (protesta) complaint; **presentar una** ~ to make a complaint

quejarse [A1] *v pron* **(a)** (protestar) to complain; (refunfuñar) to grumble; ~ **DE algo/algn** to complain ABOUT sth/sb **(b)** (de una afección, un dolor) ~ **DE algo** to complain OF sth **(c)** (gemir) to moan, groan

quejica *adj/mf* (Esp fam) ▶ QUEJÓN

quejido *m* groan, moan; (más agudo) whine; **un** ~ **de dolor** a cry of pain

quejón -jona *adj* (fam) whining (*before n*) (colloq)
■ *m,f* (fam) crybaby (colloq)

quemada *f* **(a)** (Andes, Ven fam) (del sol): **pegarse una** ~ to get sunburned **(b)** (Méx) ▶ QUEMADURA

quemado -da *adj* **1** [ESTAR] **(a)** *⟨comida/tostada⟩* burnt; **esto sabe a** ~ this tastes burnt; **huele a** ~ I can smell burning **(b)** (rojo) *⟨cara/espalda⟩* burnt **(c)** (AmL) (bronceado) tanned, brown **2** [ESTAR] (desgastado, agotado) burned-out

quemador *m* burner

quemadura *f* **(a)** (herida causada — por fuego, ácido) burn; (— por líquido caliente) scald; ~ **de sol** sunburn **(b)** (en prenda — de cigarrillo) cigarette burn; (— al planchar) scorch mark; (en mueble) burn mark

quemar [A1] *vt* **1** *⟨basura/documentos/leña⟩* to burn **(b)** *⟨herejes/brujas⟩* to burn ... at the stake

2 *⟨calorías⟩* to burn up; *⟨grasa⟩* to burn off **3 (a)** *⟨comida/mesa/mantel⟩* to burn; (con la plancha) to scorch **(b)** «*líquido/vapor*» to scald **(c)** *⟨ácido⟩* *⟨ropa/piel⟩* to burn **(d)** *⟨motor⟩* to burn ... out; *⟨fusible⟩* to blow **(e)** *⟨sol⟩* *⟨plantas⟩* to scorch; *⟨piel⟩* to burn; (broncear) (AmL) to tan
■ ~ *vi* **(a)** «*plato/sartén*» to be very hot; «*café/sopa*» to be boiling (hot) (colloq) **(b)** «*sol*» to burn

■ **quemarse** *v pron* **1 (a)** (*refl*) (con fuego, calor) to burn oneself; (con líquido, vapor) to scald oneself; *⟨mano/lengua⟩* to burn; *⟨pelo/cejas⟩* to singe **(b)** (al sol — ponerse rojo) to get burned; (— broncearse) (AmL) to tan

2 (a) (destruirse) «*papeles*» to get burned; «*edificio*» to burn down **(b)** (sufrir daños) «*alfombra/vestido*» to get burned; «*comida*» to burn; **se me** ~**on las tostadas** I burned the toast

3 «*persona*» (desgastarse) to burn oneself out

quemarropa: **a ~** (*loc adv*) ⟨*disparar*⟩ at point-blank range; ⟨*preguntar*⟩ point-blank

quemazón *f* (sensación de ardor) burning

quena *f* reed flute (*used in Andean music*)

quepa, etc ▶ CABER

quepo ▶ CABER

querella *f* **(a)** (Der) private prosecution; **presentar ~ contra algn** to bring a private prosecution against sb **(b)** (disputa) dispute

querendón -dona *adj* (AmL fam) (cariñoso) affectionate; (enamoradizo) flighty

querer [E24] *vt*
I (amar) to love; **te querré siempre** I'll always love you; **sus alumnos lo quieren mucho** his pupils are very fond of him; **¡por lo que más quieras!** for pity's sake!, for God's sake!

II **1** **(a)** (expresando deseo, intención, voluntad): **no sabe lo que quiere** she doesn't know what she wants; **quisiera una habitación doble** I'd like a double room; **¿qué más quieres?** what more do you want?; **hazlo cuando/como quieras** do it whenever/however you like; **iba a hacerlo pero él no quiso** I was going to do it but he didn't want me to; **tráemelo mañana ¿quieres?** bring it tomorrow, will you?; **no quiero** I don't want to; **quiero ir** I want to go; **quisiera reservar una mesa** I'd like to book a table; **quisiera poder ayudarte** I wish I could help you; **no quiso comer nada** she wouldn't eat anything; **quiero que estudies más** I want you to study harder; **¡qué quieres que te diga ...!** quite honestly *o* frankly ...; **el destino así lo quiso** it was destined to be; **~ es poder** where there's a will there's a way **(b)** (al ofrecer algo): **¿quieres un café?** would you like a coffee?; (menos formal) do you want a coffee? **(c)** (introduciendo un pedido): **¿querrías hacerme un favor?** could you do me a favor?; **¿te quieres callar?** be quiet, will you?

2 (*en locs*) **cuando quiera que** whenever; **donde quiera que** wherever; **queriendo** (adrede) on purpose, deliberately; **sin querer** accidentally; **fue sin ~** it was an accident; **querer decir** to mean; **¿qué quieres decir con eso?** what do you mean by that?

3 (como precio): **¿cuánto quieres por el coche?** how much do you want *o* are you asking for the car?

■ **quererse** *v pron* (*recípr*): **se quieren mucho** they love each other very much

querido -da *adj* **(a)** (amado) ⟨*patria*⟩ beloved; **mis recuerdos más ~s** my fondest memories; **seres ~s** loved ones; **un profesor muy ~ por todos** a well-liked teacher **(b)** (Corresp) Dear **(c)** (Col fam) (simpático) nice
■ *m,f* **(a)** (como apelativo) darling, dear, sweetheart **(b)** (amante) (*m*) fancy man; (*f*) fancy woman

querré, querría, etc ▶ QUERER

querubín *m* cherub

quesadilla *f* **(a)** (Méx) (tortilla): *tortilla filled with a savory mixture and topped with melted cheese* **(b)** (Ven) (panecillo) small roll (*flavored with cheese*)

quesera *f* cheese dish

queso *m* (Coc) cheese; **~ crema** (AmL) cream cheese; **~ fundido** processed cheese; **~ para untar** cheese spread

quetzal *m* (Fin) quetzal (*Guatemalan unit of currency*)

quicio *m* doorjamb; **sacar de ~ a algn** to drive sb crazy (colloq)

quid *m*: **el ~ de la cuestión** the crux of the matter

quiebra *f* (Com, Fin) (de empresa, individuo) bankruptcy; **declarse en ~** to go into liquidation

quiebra, quiebras, etc ▶ QUEBRAR

quien *pron* **1** **(a)** (*sujeto*) who, that; (*complemento*) who, that, whom (fml); **tienes que ser tú misma ~ lo decida** you are the one who *o* that has to decide; **es a él a ~ debemos agradecérselo** he's the one (who) we must thank; **la chica con ~ salía** the girl (who) I was going out with **(b)** (fml *o* liter) (en frases explicativas) who, whom (fml); **su hermano, a ~ no había visto, ...** her brother, who *o* whom she had not seen, ...
2 (la persona que): **~es hayan terminado** those who have finished; **~ lo haya encontrado** the person who found it; **~ se lo haya dicho** whoever told him

quién *pron* who; **¿~es eran?** who were they?; **¿~ de ustedes se atrevería?** which of you would dare?; **¿con ~es fuiste?** who did you go with?; **¿de ~ es esto?** whose is this?; **llegó una postal — ¿de ~?** there's a postcard — who's it from?

quienquiera *pron* (*pl* **quienesquiera**) whoever

quiera, quieras, etc ▶ QUERER

quieto -ta *adj* still; **¡estte ~!** keep still!

quietud *f* (ausencia de movimiento) stillness; (tranquilidad, sosiego) calm, peace

quihubo *interj* (Chi, Méx fam) hi! (colloq), how's it going? (colloq)

quihúbole *interj* (Méx fam) ▶ QUIHUBO

quijada *f* jaw (bone)

Quijote *m*: **Don ~** Don Quixote

quilate *m* karat (AmE), carat (BrE); **oro de 18 ~s** 18-karat gold

quilla *f* keel

quilombo *m* (Bol, RPl arg) (lío, jaleo) mess

quiltro -tra *m,f* (Chi fam) mongrel

quimera *f* (ilusión) illusion, chimera (liter)

química *f* chemistry

químico -ca *adj* chemical
■ *m,f* chemist

quimioterapia *f* chemotherapy

quince *adj inv/pron/m* fifteen; **dentro de ~ días** in two weeks' time, in a fortnight's time (BrE); *para ejemplos ver tb* CINCO

quinceañero -ra *m,f* (de quince años) fifteen-year-old; (menos específico) teenager

quincena *f* (dos semanas) two weeks (*pl*), fortnight (BrE); **la primera ~ de marzo** the first two weeks in March

quincenal *adj* bimonthly (AmE), fortnightly (BrE)

quiniela *f* (Esp) (boleto) sports lottery ticket (AmE), pools coupon (BrE); (juego): **las ~s** the sports lottery (AmE), the football pools (BrE)

quinientos -tas *adj/pron* five hundred; **~ cinco** five hundred and five; **~ y pico** five hundred odd; **el ~ aniversario** the five hundredth anniversary

q

quinqué *m* oil lamp

quinquenal *adj* ‹revisión/censo› five-yearly, quinquennial (fml); **un plan ~** a five-year plan

quinta *f* **1** **(a)** (casa) *house in its own grounds, usually in the country* **(b)** (Agr) estate, farm **2** (Esp) (Mil) draft, call up

quintaesencia *f* quintessence (fml)

quinteto *m* quintet

quintillizo -za *m,f* quintuplet

quinto¹ -ta *adj/pron* fifth; **llegó en ~ lugar** he came fifth; **Carlos V** *(read as: Carlos quinto)* Charles V *(read as: Charles the fifth)*; **vive en el ~ (piso)** she lives on the sixth (AmE) *o* (BrE) fifth floor; **la quinta parte** a fifth

quinto² *m* **1** **(a)** (partitivo) fifth; **tres ~s** three-fifths **(b)** (en Méx) (moneda) five centavo coin; **estar sin un ~** (Méx fam) to be broke (colloq) **2** (Esp) (Mil) conscript

quíntuple *m* quintuple ■ *mf* (Chi, Ven) quintuplet

quíntuplo¹ -pla *adj* quintuple, fivefold

quíntuplo² *m* quintuple

quiosco *m* ▶ KIOSCO

quirófano *m* operating room (AmE), operating theatre (BrE)

quiromancia *f* palmistry, chiromancy (fml)

quirúrgico -ca *adj* surgical; **fue sometido a una intervención quirúrgica** (fml) he underwent surgery (fml)

quise, quisiera, etc ▶ QUERER

quisquilloso -sa *adj* (meticuloso, exigente) fussy, picky (colloq); (susceptible) touchy

quiste *m* cyst

quitaesmalte *m* nail polish remover

quitamanchas *m* (*pl* **~**) stain remover

quitar [A1] *vt* **1** (apartar, retirar): **¡quítalo de aquí!** get it out of here!; **quité la silla de en medio** I got the chair out of the way; **quita tus cosas de mi escritorio** take your things off my desk; **~ la mesa** (Esp) to clear the table; **¡quítame las manos**

de encima! take your hands off me!; **no le puedo ~ la tapa** I can't get the top off; **le quitó los zapatos** she took his shoes off **2** (+ *me/te/le etc*) **(a)** (de las manos): **le quitó la pistola al ladrón** he got *o* took the gun off the thief; **le quité el cuchillo** I took the knife (away) from her **(b)** (privar de) ‹pasaporte/carnet de conducir› to take away **(c)** ‹cartera/dinero› to take, steal; ‹asiento/lugar› to take **3** (restar) (+ *me/te/le etc*): **me quita mucho tiempo** it takes up a lot of my time; **~le años a algn** to take years off sb; **~le importancia a algo** to play sth down; **le quita valor** it detracts from its value **4** (hacer desaparecer) ‹mancha› to remove, get ... out; ‹dolor› to relieve, get rid of; ‹sed› to quench; ‹apetito› to take away; (+ *me/te/le etc*) **eso te ~á el hambre** that will stop you feeling hungry; **hay que ~le esa idea de la cabeza** we must get that idea out of his head **5** **quitando** (*ger*) (fam) except for ■ **~** *vi* **1** (Esp fam): **¡quita (de ahí)!** get out of the way! **2** (en locs) **de quita y pon** ‹funda/etiqueta› removable; **eso no quita que ...** that doesn't mean that ... ■ **quitarse** *v pron* **1** (desaparecer) «mancha» to come out; «dolor» to go (away); **ya se me ~on las ganas** I don't feel like it any more **2** (apartarse, retirarse) to get out of the way; **¡quítate de mi vista!** get out of my sight! **3** (refl) **(a)** ‹prenda/alhaja/maquillaje› to take off **(b)** ‹dolor/resfriado› to get rid of; ‹miedo› to overcome, get over; **se quita la edad** she lies about her age; **~se algo/a algn de encima** to get rid of sth/sb

quitasol *m* sunshade

quiteño -ña *adj* of/from Quito

Quito *m* Quito

quiubo *interj* (Chi, Méx fam) ▶ QUIHUBO

quizá, quizás *adv* maybe, perhaps

quórum /'kworum/ *m* (*pl* **-rums**) quorum

Rr

R, r *f* (read as /'ere/) the letter R

rábano *m* radish; ▶ IMPORTAR

rabia *f* **1** (enfermedad) rabies **2** **(a)** (expresando fastidio): **no sabes la ~ que me da** you've no idea how much it annoys *o* irritates me; **¡qué ~!** how annoying! **(b)** (furor, ira) anger, fury; **tener ~** to be angry; **con ~** angrily, in a rage **(c)** (antipatía, manía): **tenerle ~ a algn** to have it in for sb (colloq)

rabiar [A1] *vi* (de furor, envidia): **el jefe está que rabia contigo** the boss is furious with you; **no lo hagas ~** don't annoy him

rabieta *f* tantrum; **le dio una ~** he threw a tantrum

rabino -na *m,f* rabbi

rabioso -sa *adj* **1** (Med, Vet) rabid **2** (furioso) furious

rabo *m* **(a)** (Zool) tail **(b)** (de letra) tail **(c)** (Bot) stem, stalk

AmC	Central America	Arg	Argentina	Cu	Cuba	Per	Peru
AmL	Latin America	Bol	Bolivia	Ec	Ecuador	RPI	River Plate Area
AmS	South America	Chi	Chile	Esp	Spain	Ur	Uruguay
Andes	Andean Region	CS	Southern Cone	Méx	Mexico	Ven	Venezuela

racha *f* **(a)** (secuencia) una ∼ DE algo ‹de buena/ mala suerte› a run *o* spell *o* sth; ‹de enfermedades/éxitos› a string OF sth; **pasar una mala ∼** to go through bad times *o* (BrE) a bad patch; **tengo una buena ∼ , voy a seguir jugando** I'm on a winning streak so I'm going to carry on playing; **va/viene por ∼s** it goes/comes in phases **(b)** (Meteo) gust of wind

racial *adj* racial; ‹disturbio› race (*before n*)

racimo *m* bunch

raciocinio *m* (facultad) reason; (argumento) reasoning

ración *f* **(a)** (parte) share **(b)** (porción de comida) portion, helping; **una ∼ de calamares** a portion *o* plate of squid **(c)** (Mil) ration

racional *adj* rational

racionalizar [A4] *vt* to rationalize

racionamiento *m* rationing

racionar [A1] *vt* to ration

racismo *m* racism

racista *adj/mf* racist

radar *m* radar

radiación *f* radiation

radiactividad *f* radioactivity

radiactivo -va *adj* radioactive

radiador *m* radiator

radiante *adj* **(a)** (brillante) brilliant; **hace un sol ∼** it's brilliantly *o* beautifully sunny; **un día ∼** a bright, sunny day **(b)** [ESTAR] ‹persona› radiant; **∼ de alegría** radiant with happiness

radical *adj/mf* radical

radicar [A2] *vi* «problema/dificultad» to lie ■ **radicarse** *v pron* to settle

radio *m* **(a)** (Mat) radius **(b)** (distancia) range, radius; **en un ∼ de diez kilómetros** within a ten kilometer radius **(c)** (de rueda) spoke; **∼ de acción** (de avión, barco) operational range; (de organización) area of operations
■ *f or* (AmL exc CS) *m* **(a)** (medio de comunicación) radio; **por (la) ∼** on the radio; **escuchar la ∼** to listen to the radio **(b)** (aparato) radio **(c)** (emisora) radio station

radioactividad *f* radioactivity

radioactivo -va *adj* radioactive

radioaficionado -da *m,f* radio ham

radiocassette /rraðioka'set/, **radiocasete** *m* radio cassette player

radiodifusión *f* broadcasting

radiodifusora *f* (AmL fml) radio station

radiofónico -ca *adj* radio (*before n*)

radiografía *f* X-ray; **hacerse una ∼** to have an X-ray taken

radiólogo -ga *m,f* radiologist

radionovela *f* radio serial

radiooperador -dora *m,f* (AmL) radio operator

radiopatrulla *m* radio patrol car

radioterapia *f* radiotherapy

radioyente *mf* listener

raer [E16] *vt* ‹superficie› to scrape; ‹barniz/ pintura› to scrape off

ráfaga *f* (de viento) gust; (de ametralladora) burst

raid *m* (AmC) (en carro) ride; **pedir ∼** to hitch a ride *o* lift

raído -da *adj* worn-out, threadbare

raíz *f* (en general) root; **arrancar de ∼** ‹planta› to uproot; ‹vello› to remove ... at the roots; **cuadrada** (Mat) square root; **a ∼ de** as a result of; **echar raíces** «planta/costumbre/ideología» to take root; «persona» to put down roots

raja *f* **(a)** (en pared, cerámica) crack **(b)** (rotura — en costura) split; (— en tela) tear, rip **(c)** (abertura — en falda) slit; (— en chaqueta) vent **(d)** (de melón, salami) slice

rajar [A1] *vt* ☐1 **(a)** (agrietar) to crack, cause ... to crack **(b)** (con cuchillo, navaja) ‹neumático/persona› to slash ☐2 **(a)** (CS fam) (criticar) to run ... down **(b)** (Andes) (en examen) (fam) to fail, flunk (AmE colloq)
■ **rajarse** *v pron* ☐1 «pared/cerámica» to crack; «tela» to split, tear, rip ☐2 (fam) (acobardarse) to back off

rajatabla: a ∼ (*loc adv*) to the letter

rallador *m* grater

ralladura *f*: **∼ de limón** grated lemon rind

rallar [A1] *vt* to grate

ralo -la *adj* ‹bosque› sparse; ‹monte› bare; ‹pelo/ barba› thin, sparse

rama *f* branch; **una ramita de perejil** a sprig of parsley; **andarse/irse por las ∼s** to beat about the bush

ramada *f* **(a)** (AmS) (cobertizo) shelter (*made from branches*) **(b)** (Chi) (pérgola) arbor, arbour (BrE)

ramal *m* (Ferr) branch line; (Geog) branch; (cuerda) strap

rambla *f* **(a)** (RPI) (paseo marítimo) esplanade, promenade **(b)** (avenida) boulevard

ramera *f* prostitute

ramificación *f* ramification

ramificarse [A2] *v pron* **(a)** «árbol/plantas/ nervios» to branch **(b)** «carretera/ciencia» to branch **(c)** «problema» to ramify (fml), to become complex

ramillete *m* **(a)** (de flores) posy **(b)** (iró) (grupo selecto) bunch (colloq)

ramo *m* ☐1 (de flores) bunch; (para novia, dignatario) bouquet ☐2 **(a)** (en industria) industry **(b)** (Chi) (Educ) subject

rampa *f* (pendiente) ramp; **∼ de lanzamiento** launch pad

rana *f* (Zool) frog

ranchera *f* (Mús) *Mexican folk song*

ranchería *f* **(a)** (Col) ▶ RANCHERÍO **(b)** (Méx) dairy

rancherío *m* (CS) (poblado) settlement; (en suburbios) shantytown

ranchero -ra *adj* (Méx fam) shy
■ *m,f* (Méx) rancher

rancho *m* ☐1 (comida) food (*for a group of soldiers, workers, etc*) ☐2 **(a)** (AmL) (choza) hut; (casucha) hovel; (chabola) shack, shanty **(b)** (Méx) (hacienda) ranch

rancio -cia *adj* ☐1 ‹mantequilla/tocino› rancid ☐2 **(a)** ‹vino› mellow **(b)** (delante del n) ‹abolengo/tradición› ancient, long-established

rango *m* ☐1 **(a)** (Mil) rank **(b)** (categoría, nivel) level ☐2 (Chi) (lujo, pompa) luxury; (de persona) high social status

rangoso -sa *adj* (Chi) ‹fiesta/casa› lavish; ‹persona› of high social status

r

ranura *f* **(a)** (para monedas, tarjetas, cartas) slot; **por la ~ de la puerta** through the chink *o* gap in the door **(b)** (en ensambladura, tornillo) groove

rapapolvo *m* (Esp) telling-off (colloq), talking-to (colloq)

rapar [A1] *vt* ⟨*cabeza*⟩ to shave; ⟨*pelo*⟩ to crop

rapaz *adj* (Zool) predatory; **ave ~** bird of prey

rape *m* **(a)** (Coc, Zool) monkfish, goosefish (AmE) **(b) al rape: tiene el pelo cortado al ~** he has closely-cropped hair

rápidamente *adv* quickly

rapidez *f* speed; **con ~** quickly; **¡qué ~!** that was quick!

rápido[1] *adv* ⟨*hablar/trabajar*⟩ quickly, fast; ⟨*conducir/ir*⟩ fast; **tráemelo ¡~!** bring it to me, quick!

rápido[2] **-da** *adj* ⟨*aumento*⟩ rapid; ⟨*cambio*⟩ quick, rapid, swift; ⟨*desarrollo*⟩ rapid, swift; **a paso ~** quickly, swiftly; **comida rápida** fast food
■ *m* (Ferr) express train, fast train
■ *m* [1] (Ferr) fast train [2] **rápidos** *mpl* (Geog) rapids (*pl*)

rapiña *f* robbery, pillage

raptar [A1] *vt* ⟨*secuestrar*⟩ to kidnap, abduct (frml)

rapto *m* (secuestro) kidnapping, abduction (frml)

raptor -tora *m,f* kidnapper

raqueta *f* (de tenis, squash) racket; (para nieve) snowshoe

raquítico -ca *adj* ⟨*niño/animal*⟩ rickety, rachitic (tech); ⟨*árbol*⟩ stunted

rareza *f* **(a)** (de persona) peculiarity, quirk **(b)** (cosa poco común) rarity **(c)** (cualidad) rareness

raro -ra *adj* **(a)** (extraño) strange, odd, funny (colloq); **es ~ que …** it's strange *o* odd *o* funny that …; **¡qué ~!** how odd *o* strange!; **te noto muy ~ hoy** you're acting very strangely today **(b)** (poco frecuente) rare; **salvo raras excepciones** with a few rare exceptions; **aquí es ~ que nieve** it's very unusual *o* rare for it to snow here

ras: a ras de (*loc prep*): **llega a ~ del suelo** it reaches down to the floor; **volar a ~ de tierra** to fly very low

rasca *adj* (CS fam) **(a)** ⟨*persona*⟩ vulgar, common (pej); ⟨*lugar/canción*⟩ tacky (colloq) **(b)** (de mala calidad) trashy (colloq)

rascacielos *m* (*pl* ~) skyscraper

rascar [A2] *vt* **(a)** (con las uñas) to scratch **(b)** (con cuchillo) ⟨*superficie*⟩ to scrape; ⟨*pintura*⟩ to scrape off
■ **rascarse** *v pron* (refl) to scratch (oneself)

rasgado -da *adj* ⟨*ojos*⟩ almond (*before n*), almond-shaped

rasgar [A3] *vt* to tear, rip
■ **rasgarse** *v pron* to tear, rip

rasgo *m* [1] **(a)** (característica) characteristic, feature **(b)** (gesto) gesture **(c)** (de la pluma) stroke; (en pintura) brushstroke; **a grandes ~s** in outline, broadly speaking [2] **rasgos** *mpl* (facciones) features (*pl*)

rasguear [A1] *vt* to strum

rasguñar [A1] *vt* to scratch
■ **rasguñarse** *v pron* (refl) (con uña, púa) to scratch oneself; (con algo áspero) to graze oneself; **me rasguñé la rodilla** I grazed my knee

rasguño *m* scratch

rasmillarse [A1] *v pron* (Chi fam) to graze oneself

raso[1] **-sa** *adj* [1] ⟨*taza/cucharada*⟩ level (*before n*) [2] (exterior) open country; **dormir al ~** to sleep out in the open

raso[2] *m* satin

raspado *m* (Col, Méx) ▶ GRANIZADO

raspadura *f* (arañazo) scratch; (ralladura de metal, chocolate) shavings (*pl*)

raspar [A1] *vt* **(a)** (con espátula) ⟨*superficie*⟩ to scrape; ⟨*pintura*⟩ to scrape off **(b)** (limar) to file, rasp **(c)** ⟨*piel*⟩ to scrape, graze
■ ~ *vi* **(a)** ⟨*toalla/manos*⟩ to be rough; «*barba*» to scratch, be scratchy **(b)** «*garganta*» (+ *me/te/le etc*) to feel rough
■ **rasparse** *v pron* ⟨*rodillas/codos*⟩ (con algo puntiagudo) to scratch; (con algo áspero) to scrape, graze

raspón *m* (AmL) (por algo puntiagudo) scratch; (por algo áspero) graze, scrape; **hay un ~ en la puerta** the door is scratched

rastra: a rastras (*loc adv*): **llevar algo/a algn a ~s** to drag sth/sb; **fue a ~s hasta la puerta** she dragged herself to the door

rastreador -dora *m,f* tracker

rastrear [A1] *vt* **(a)** ⟨*zona*⟩ to comb **(b)** ⟨*persona/satélite*⟩ to track **(c)** ⟨*río/lago*⟩ «*pescadores*» to trawl; «*policías*» to drag, dredge

rastrero -ra *adj* **(a)** (despreciable) despicable, contemptible **(b)** ⟨*tallo*⟩ creeping (*before n*); ⟨*animal*⟩ crawling (*before n*)

rastrillo *m* [1] (Agr) rake [2] (Méx) (para afeitarse) safety razor

rastro *m* [1] (pista, huella) trail; (señal, vestigio) trace, sign; **sin dejar ~** without (a) trace [2] (mercado) flea market

rasurador *m*, **rasuradora** *f* (AmC, Méx) electric razor *o* shaver

rasurar [A1] *vt* (AmL) to shave
■ **rasurarse** *v pron* (AmL) to shave

rata *f* [1] (Zool) rat; **hacerse la ~** (RPl fam) to play hooky (esp AmE colloq), to skive off (school) (BrE colloq) [2] (Col) (Econ, Mat) (tasa) rate; (razón) ratio; (porcentaje) percentage
■ *mf* (fam) (tacaño) miser, stingy devil (colloq), tightwad (AmE colloq)

ratán *m* rattan

ratero -ra *m,f* (fam) (carterista) pickpocket; (ladrón) petty thief

ratificar [A2] *vt* ⟨*tratado/contrato*⟩ to ratify; ⟨*persona*⟩ (en un puesto) to confirm; ⟨*noticia*⟩ to confirm

rato *m* **(a)** (tiempo breve) while; **hace un ~** a while ago; **espera un ratito** wait a minute (colloq); **en mis ~s libres** in my spare time; **pasé un mal ~** it was terrible; **iré dentro de un ~** I'll go shortly **(b)** (*en locs*) **a cada rato** (AmL): **me interrumpe a cada ~** he keeps interrupting me; **al (poco) rato** shortly afterwards; **al poco ~ de irte tú** shortly *o* just after you left; **a ratos** from time to time; **para ~** (fam): **tengo para ~** I'll be a while, I'll be some time; **todavía hay para ~** there's still a long way to go; **pasar el ~** to while away the time

ratón[1] **-tona** *m,f* (Zool) mouse; **~ de biblioteca** (fam) bookworm

ratón² *m* **1** (Inf) mouse; ~ **de bola** trackball **2** (AmC) **(a)** (Coc) *sinewy cut of meat* **(b)** (fam) (bíceps) biceps **3** (Ven fam) (resaca) hangover

ratonera *f* (trampa) mousetrap; (madriguera) mousehole

raudal *m* (de agua) torrent; **el agua entraba a ~es** the water poured in in torrents

ravioles, raviolis *mpl* ravioli

raya *f* **1** **(a)** (línea) line; (lista) stripe; **a** *or* **de ~s** ‹tela/vestido› striped; **pasarse de la ~** to overstep the mark, to go too far; **tener a algn a ~** to keep a tight rein on sb **(b)** (del pantalón) crease **(c)** (del pelo) part (AmE), parting (BrE); **hacerse la ~** to part one's hair **(d)** (Impr) dash **2** (Zool) ray, skate

rayado -da *adj* **1** ‹papel› lined, ruled (frml); ‹tela/vestido› striped, stripy (colloq) **2** [ESTAR] (AmS fam) (loco) screwy (colloq), nutty (colloq)

rayar [A1] *vt* **(a)** ‹pintura/mesa› to scratch **(b)** (garabatear) to scrawl
■ ~ *vi* **1** (dejar marca) to scratch **2** (aproximarse) ~ **EN algo** to border ON sth, verge ON sth **3** (Méx) «obreros» to get one's wages, get paid
■ **rayarse** *v pron* **1** «superficie» to get scratched **2** (AmS fam) (volverse loco) to crack up (colloq)

rayo *m* **1** (en general) ray; **un ~ de luz** a ray *o* beam (of light); **un ~ de luna** a moonbeam; ~ **láser** laser beam; ~**s ultravioleta** ultraviolet rays (*pl*); ~**s X** X-rays (*pl*) **2** (Meteo) bolt (of lightning); **como un ~** (fam) ‹salir› like greased lightning (colloq) **3** (AmL) (de rueda) spoke

rayuela *f* **(a)** (juego de adultos) *game similar to pitch-and-toss* **(b)** (RPI) (juego de niños) hopscotch

raza *f* (etnia) race; (Agr, Zool) breed; **un perro de ~** a pedigree dog

razón *f* **1** (motivo, causa) reason; **la ~ por la que te lo digo** the reason (that) I'm telling you; **se enojó y con ~** she got angry and rightly so; **con ~ o sin ella** rightly *or* wrongly; **se quejan sin ~/ con ~** they're complaining for no good reason/ they have good reason to complain; **¡con ~ no contestaban!** no wonder they didn't answer!; ~ **de más para …** all the more reason to … **2** (verdad, acierto): **tener** *or* **llevar ~** to be right; **tuve que darle la ~** I had to admit she was right; **tienes toda la ~** (fam) you're absolutely right **3** (habilidad para razonar) reason; **actuó guiado por la ~** he was guided by reason; **desde que tengo uso de ~** for as long as I can remember; **entrar en ~** to see reason *o* sense; **perder la ~** to go out of one's mind; (en sentido hiperbólico) to take leave of one's senses

razonable *adj* reasonable

razonamiento *m* reasoning

razonar [A1] *vi* to reason

re *m* (nota) D; (en solfeo) re, ray

reacción *f* **1** (en general) reaction **2** (Pol) (AmL) right wing

reaccionar [A1] *vi* to react; ~ **A** *or* **FRENTE A** *or* **ANTE algo** to react TO sth

reaccionario -ria *adj/m,f* reactionary

reacio -cia *adj* reluctant

reactor *m* (a) (Fís) reactor; ~ **nuclear** nuclear reactor **(b)** (Aviac) (motor) jet engine; (avión) jet (plane)

readmitir [I1] *vt* ‹trabajador› to reemploy; ‹alumno› to readmit

reafirmar [A1] *vt* to reaffirm, reassert

reajuste *m* adjustment; ~ **ministerial** cabinet reshuffle; ~ **salarial** wage settlement

real *adj* **(a)** (verdadero, no ficticio): **un hecho ~** a true story; **en la vida ~** in real life; **historias de la vida ~** real-life *o* true-life stories **(b)** (de la realeza) royal; **porque me da la ~ gana** (fam) because I damn well want to (colloq)
■ *m* **(a)** (Hist) real (*old Spanish coin*); **no valer un ~** (fam) to be worth nothing **(b)** (Fin) real (*Brazilian unit of currency*) **(c)** **reales** *mpl* (AmC fam) (dinero) cash (colloq)

realce *m*: **dar ~ A algo** ‹a belleza/figura› to enhance sth; ‹a ocasión› to add luster TO sth

realeza *f* royalty; **la ~** (personas) the royal family

realidad *f* reality; **la ~ paraguaya** the reality of life *o* of the situation in Paraguay; **esa es la dura ~** those are the harsh facts; **en ~** in reality, actually

realismo *m* realism

realista *adj* (pragmático) realistic; (Art, Lit, Fil) realist
■ *mf* realist

realizable *adj* feasible, practicable

realización *f* **1** (de tarea) carrying out, execution (frml); (de sueños, deseos) fulfillment*, realization **2** (Cin, TV) production

realizado -da *adj* fulfilled*

realizador -dora *m,f* producer

realizar [A4] *vt* **(a)** ‹tarea› to carry out, execute (frml); ‹viaje/visita› to make; ‹entrevista/ pruebas› to conduct; ‹encuesta/investigación› to carry out; ‹experimento› to perform, do; ‹compra/ inversión› to make; **realizó una magnífica labor** she did a magnificent job **(b)** ‹ambiciones/ ilusiones› to fulfill*, realize
■ **realizarse** *v pron* «sueños/ilusiones» to come true, be realized; «persona» to fulfill* oneself

realmente *adv* really, in fact

realzar [A4] *vt* ‹belleza/figura› to enhance, set off; ‹color› to highlight, bring out

reanimar [A1] *vt* to revive
■ **reanimarse** *v pron* (recobrar fuerzas) to revive; (recobrar el conocimiento) to come to *o* around

reanudar [A1] *vt* (frml) ‹conversaciones/ negociaciones/viaje› to resume; ‹hostilidades› to renew, resume; ‹amistad/relación› to renew, revive
■ **reanudarse** *v pron* to resume

reaparición *f* (de publicación, persona) reappearance; (de artista) comeback

reapertura *f* reopening

rearme *m* rearmament

reata *f* **(a)** (Méx) (cuerda) rope; (Agr) lasso **(b)** (Col) (correa) cartridge belt

reavivar [A1] *vt* to revive
■ **reavivarse** *v pron* to be revived

rebaja *f* **(a)** (descuento) discount, reduction; **nos hicieron una ~ del 10%** they gave us a 10% discount *o* reduction; **de ~** reduced **(b)** **rebajas** *fpl* (saldos) sale, sales (*pl*); **están de ~s** there's a sale on, they're having a sale

rebajar [A1] *vt* **1** ‹precio› to lower, bring … down; ‹artículo› to reduce; **me rebajó $200** he took $200 off **2** ‹peso/kilos› to lose ····⊱

r

■ ~ *vi* (humillar) to degrade, be degrading

■ **rebajarse** *v pron* ~se A hacer algo to lower oneself TO doing sth; ~se ANTE algn to humble oneself BEFORE sb

rebalsarse [A1] *v pron* (CS) «*agua/cauce/ vaso*» to overflow; **se rebalsó el río** the river burst its banks

rebanada *f* slice

rebanar [A1] *vt* to slice, cut

rebaño *m* (de ovejas) flock; (de cabras) herd

rebasar [A1] *vt* (a) (sobrepasar) ⟨*límite de velocidad*⟩ to exceed, go over; ⟨*cifras previstas*⟩ to exceed; ⟨*punto*⟩ to go beyond; **el agua ha rebasado el límite** the water has risen above the limit (b) (Méx) (Auto) to pass, overtake

■ ~ *vi* (Méx) to pass, overtake (BrE)

rebatir [I1] *vt* to refute

rebeca *f* (Esp) cardigan

rebelarse [A1] *v pron* to rebel

rebelde *adj* (a) ⟨*tropas/ejército*⟩ rebel (*before n*) (b) ⟨*niño/carácter*⟩ unruly, rebellious (c) ⟨*tos*⟩ persistent; ⟨*mancha*⟩ stubborn

■ *mf* (Mil, Pol) rebel

rebeldía *f* (cualidad) rebelliousness

rebelión *f* rebellion, uprising

reblandecer [E3] *vt* to soften

■ **reblandecerse** *v pron* to become o go soft

rebobinar [A1] *vt* to rewind

rebosante *adj* ~ DE algo ⟨*de alegría/ optimismo*⟩ brimming WITH sth; ⟨*de vino/agua*⟩ filled to the brim WITH sth

rebosar [A1] *vi* (a) ~ DE algo ⟨*de felicidad/ entusiasmo*⟩ to be brimming o bubbling over WITH sth; ⟨*de salud*⟩ to be bursting o brimming WITH sth (b) ⟨*agua/embalse*⟩ to overflow

■ ~ *vt* ⟨*alegría/felicidad*⟩: **rebosaba felicidad** she was radiant with happiness

rebotar [A1] *vi* «*pelota/piedra*» to bounce; «*bala*» to ricochet

rebote *m* (a) (al golpear algo): **la pelota dio un ~ en el poste** the ball bounced off the post; **de ~** «*pelota*» ⟨*pegar/entrar*⟩ on the rebound; **la bala le dio de ~** he was hit by a ricochet (b) (en baloncesto) rebound

rebozar [A4] *vt* to coat ... in batter (o in egg and breadcrumbs *etc*)

rebozo *m* (AmL) (Indum) shawl, wrap

rebuscado -da *adj* ⟨*explicación*⟩ over-elaborate, overcomplicated; ⟨*ejemplo/ argumento*⟩ far-fetched; ⟨*estilo*⟩ affected

rebuscar [A2] *vi*: **rebuscó entre los papeles** he searched through the papers; **rebuscaba en la basura** he was rummaging about in the garbage

rebuznar [A1] *vi* to bray

recadero -ra *m, f* messenger, runner

recado *m* (a) (mensaje) message; **le mandó ~ de que volviera** she sent word that he should return (b) (Esp) (encargo, diligencia) errand; **hacer un ~** to run an errand

recaer [E16] *vi* [1] «*enfermo*» to have o suffer a

relapse [2] (a) «*sospechas/responsabilidad*» ~ SOBRE algn to fall ON sb (b) «*premio/ nombramiento*» ~ EN algn to go TO sb

recaída *f* relapse

recalcar [A2] *vt* to stress, emphasize

recalentamiento *m* overheating; ~ **global** global warming

recalentar [A5] *vt* (a) ⟨*motor*⟩ to cause ... to overheat (b) ⟨*comida*⟩ to heat up, warm up; **me dio un guiso recalentado** he gave me some reheated stew

■ **recalentarse** *v pron* to overheat, become overheated

recámara *f* (Méx) (dormitorio) bedroom; (muebles) bedroom furniture

recamarera *f* (Méx) chambermaid

recambio *m* (a) (Auto, Mec) spare (part); **rueda de ~** spare wheel (b) (de bolígrafo) refill

recapacitar [A1] *vi* to reconsider, think again; ~ SOBRE algo to reconsider sth

recargable *adj* ⟨*batería/pila*⟩ rechargeable; ⟨*encendedor/pluma*⟩ refillable

recargado -da *adj* ⟨*decoración*⟩ overelaborate; ⟨*texto*⟩ overwritten

recargar [A3] *vt* ⟨*batería*⟩ to recharge; ⟨*encendedor/estilográfica*⟩ to refill; ⟨*arma/ programa*⟩ to reload

■ **recargarse** *v pron* (Col, Méx, Ven) (apoyarse) ~se CONTRA algo to lean AGAINST sth

recargo *m* surcharge; **sin ~** at no extra charge

recatado -da *adj* (pudoroso) demure, modest

recato *m* (pudor) modesty

recauchar, (Esp) recauchutar [A1] *vt* to retread, remold*

recaudación *f* (a) (acción) collection (b) (ganancia — en tienda) takings (*pl*); (— en cine) box office receipts (*pl*); (— en estadio) gate

recaudador -dora *m,f*: **tb ~ de impuestos** tax collector

recaudar [A1] *vt* to collect

recelo *m* suspicion, distrust; **con ~** distrustfully

recepción *f* (en general) reception; (de mercancías) receipt (frml)

recepcionista *mf* receptionist

receptivo -va *adj* receptive

receptor -tora *m,f* [1] (Med, Ling) recipient [2] (Dep) (en fútbol americano) receiver; (en béisbol) catcher [3] **receptor** *m* (Rad) radio, receiver; (TV) television (receiver o set)

recesión *f* recession

receso *m* (AmL) recess

receta *f* (Coc) recipe; (Med) prescription

recetar [A1] *vt* to prescribe

rechazar [A4] *vt* (a) ⟨*invitación/propuesta/ individuo*⟩ to reject; ⟨*moción/enmienda*⟩ to defeat; ⟨*oferta/trabajo*⟩ to turn down (b) ⟨*ataque/ enemigo*⟩ to repel, repulse (c) (Med) ⟨*órgano*⟩ to reject

rechazo *m* (de invitación, individuo, órgano) rejection; (de moción, enmienda) defeat

rechifla *f* whistling (*as a sign of disapproval*), ≈booing

rechinar [A1] *vi* «*polea/bisagra*» to creak, squeak; **le rechinan los dientes** he grinds his teeth

rechinón *m* (Méx) screech

rechistar [A1] *vi* ▶ CHISTAR

rechoncho -cha *adj* (fam) dumpy (colloq), short and fat

rechupete (fam): **de rechupete** (*loc adj*) ‹*comida*› delicious, scrumptious (colloq)

recibidor *m* entrance hall

recibimiento *m* reception

recibir [I1] *vt* (en general) to receive; **recibió muchos regalos** she got lots of gifts; **reciba un atento saludo de ...** (Corresp) sincerely yours (AmE), yours faithfully/sincerely (BrE); **~ a algn con los brazos abiertos** to welcome sb with open arms; **van a ir a ~lo** they are going to meet him; **el encargado la ~á enseguida** the manager will see you right away

■ **recibirse** *v pron* (AmL) (Educ) to graduate; **~se DE algo** to qualify AS sth

recibo *m* (en general) receipt; (de luz, teléfono) bill

reciclado, reciclaje *m* **(a)** (de papel, vidrio) recycling **(b)** (de persona) retraining

reciclar [A1] *vt* ‹*papel/vidrio*› to recycle

recién *adv* ⌐1⌐ (con participio): **pan ~ hecho** freshly baked bread; **está ~ pintado** it's just been painted; **tiene un año ~ cumplido** he's just one; **los ~ casados** the newlyweds; **un ~ nacido** a newborn baby ⌐2⌐ (AmL) (hace poco tiempo) just; **~ llegaron** they have just arrived **(b)** (solo ahora) only just; **~ me entero** I've only just found out **(c)** (sólo) only; **~ voy por la página 20** I'm only on page 20; **~ el lunes iré** the first day I'll be able to go is Monday

reciente *adj* ‹*acontecimiento/foto*› recent; ‹*huella*› fresh; **en fecha ~** recently

recinto *m* enclosure; **el público abandonó el ~** the public left the premises/building; **~ ferial** (de muestras) showground, exhibition site; (de atracciones) fairground

recio -cia *adj* ‹*hombre/aspecto*› robust, sturdy

recipiente *m* (utensilio) container, receptacle (frml)

recíproco -ca *adj* reciprocal

recital *m* recital

recitar [A1] *vt* to recite

reclamación *f* **(a)** (petición, demanda) claim **(b)** (queja) complaint

reclamar [A1] *vt* **(a)** «*persona*» ‹*derecho/indemnización*› to claim; (con insistencia) to demand **(b)** «*situación/problema*» to require, demand

■ **~** *vi* to complain; **reclamó ante los tribunales** she took the matter to court

réclame *m or f* (AmL) commercial, advertisement; **~ publicitario** advertising

reclamo *m* **(a)** (de pájaro) call **(b)** (esp AmL) (para atraer la atención, provocar interés) lure **(c)** (AmL) (queja) complaint

reclinable *adj* reclining (*before n*)

reclinar [A1] *vt* to rest, lean

■ **reclinarse** *v pron* to lean back; **reclinado contra la pared** leaning against the wall

recluir [I20] *vt* (en prisión) to imprison; (en hospital psiquiátrico), to intern (frml)

reclusión *f* imprisonment; **~ perpetua** life imprisonment

recluso -sa *m,f* prisoner, inmate

recluta *mf* (Mil) recruit; (en servicio militar) conscript, recruit

reclutar [A1] *vt* to recruit

recobrar [A1] *vt* **(a)** ‹*confianza/conocimiento*› to regain; ‹*salud/vista*› to recover; **~ las fuerzas** to recover one's strength **(b)** ‹*dinero/botín/joyas*› to recover, retrieve **(c)** ‹*ciudad/plaza fuerte*› to recapture

■ **recobrarse** *v pron* **~se DE algo** ‹*de enfermedad/susto*› to recover FROM sth, get over sth; ‹*de pérdidas económicas*› to recoup sth

recogedor *m* dustpan

recogepelotas *mf* (*pl* **~**) (*m*) ball boy; (*f*) ball girl

recoger [E6] *vt* ⌐1⌐ **(a)** (levantar) ‹*objeto/papeles*› to pick up; **recogí el agua con un trapo** I mopped the water up **(b)** ‹*casa/habitación*› to straighten (up) (AmE), to tidy (up) (BrE); ‹*platos*› to clear away; **~ la mesa** to clear the table ⌐2⌐ **(a)** ‹*dinero/firmas*› to collect **(b)** ‹*deberes/cuadernos*› to collect, take in ‹*trigo/maíz*› to harvest, gather in; ‹*fruta*› to pick; ‹*flores/hongos*› to pick, gather **(d)** ‹*tienda de campaña/vela*› to take down **(e)** ‹*pelo*› to tie ... back; **le recogió el pelo en una cola** he tied her hair back in a ponytail ⌐3⌐ (ir a buscar) ‹*persona*› to pick up, fetch, collect; ‹*paquete*› to collect, pick up; ‹*basura*› to collect; ‹*equipaje*› to reclaim

■ **~** *vi* to clear up, to straighten up (AmE), to tidy up (BrE)

■ **recogerse** *v pron* ‹*pelo*› to tie up; ‹*falda*› to gather up

recogida *f* **(a)** (de basura, correo) collection **(b)** (Agr) harvest

recolección *f* **(a)** (Agr) harvest **(b)** (de fondos, dinero) collection

recolectar [A1] *vt* ‹*trigo*› to harvest, gather in; ‹*fruta*› to pick, harvest **(b)** ‹*dinero*› to collect

recomendación *f* **(a)** (consejo) advice **(b)** (para empleo) reference, recommendation

recomendado -da *adj* ⌐1⌐ **(a)** ‹*método/producto*› recommended **(b)** (apropiado) suitable; **no recomendada para menores de 15 años** not suitable for under-15s ⌐2⌐ (Col, Ur) ‹*carta*› registered

recomendar [A5] *vt* **(a)** ‹*libro/restaurante/persona*› to recommend **(b)** (aconsejar) to advise; **no te lo recomiendo** I wouldn't advise it

recomienda, recomiendas, etc ▶ RECOMENDAR

recompensa *f* reward

recompensar [A1] *vt* to reward

reconciliación *f* reconciliation

reconciliar [A1] *vt* to reconcile

■ **reconciliarse** *v pron* **(a)** **~se** (CON algn) to make (it) up (WITH sb) **(b)** **~se** CON algo ‹*con idea/postura*› to reconcile oneself TO sth

r

reconfortante *adj* ⟨*palabras/pensamientos*⟩ comforting; ⟨*baño*⟩ relaxing

reconfortar [A1] *vt* to comfort

reconocer [E3] *vt* **1** (a) ⟨*hecho/error*⟩ to admit; ⟨*verdad/autoridad*⟩ to acknowledge (b) ⟨*hijo/gobierno/derecho*⟩ to recognize **2** (identificar) ⟨*persona/letra/voz*⟩ to recognize **3** ⟨*terreno*⟩ to reconnoiter*

reconocimiento *m* (a) (en general) recognition (b) (Med) *tb* ~ **médico** medical (examination) (c) (de territorio) reconnaissance

reconquista *f* reconquest; **la R**~ the Reconquest

reconquistar [A1] *vt* ⟨*territorio*⟩ to reconquer, regain; ⟨*cariño/afecto*⟩ to win back

reconstituyente *m* tonic, restorative

reconstruir [I20] *vt* to reconstruct

reconversión *f* (a) (reestructuración) restructuring, rationalization (b) (de un trabajador) *tb* ~ **profesional** retraining

reconvertir [I11] *vt* (a) ⟨*industria*⟩ to rationalize, restructure (b) ⟨*profesional*⟩ to retrain
■ **reconvertirse** *v pron* (a) «*industria*» to be rationalized *o* restructured (b) «*profesional*» to retrain

recopilación *f* compilation, collection

recopilar [A1] *vt* to compile, gather together

récord, record *adj inv* record (*before n*)
■ *m* (*pl* -**cords**) record; **batir un** ~ to break a record; **posee el** ~ **mundial** she is the world record holder

recordar [A10] *vt* **1** (a) ⟨*nombre/fecha*⟩ to remember, recall; **recuerdo que lo puse ahí** I remember *o* recall putting it there (b) (rememorar) ⟨*niñez/pasado*⟩ to remember **2** (a) (traer a la memoria) ~**le A** algn algo/QUE haga algo to remind sb ABOUT sth/to do sth; **les recuerdo que ...** I would like to remind you that ... (b) (por asociación, parecido) to remind; **me recuerdas a tu hermano** you remind me of your brother
■ ~ *vi* (acordarse) to remember; **si mal no recuerdo** if I remember right

recorrer [E1] *vt* (a) (viajar por): **recorrí toda España** I traveled all over Spain; (como turista) I toured all over Spain; ~ **mundo** to travel all around the world; **recorrimos toda la costa** we traveled the whole length of the coast (b) ⟨*distancia/trayecto*⟩ to cover, do (c) (con la mirada): **recorrió la sala con la mirada** he looked around the hall

recorrido *m* (a) (viaje): **un** ~ **por Perú** a trip around Peru; (turístico) a tour around Peru (b) (trayecto) route; **cubrir el** ~ to cover the route (c) (de proyectil) trajectory; (de balón) path (d) (en golf) round; (en esquí) run

recortable *adj* cutout (*before n*)

recortar [A1] *vt* **1** (a) ⟨*figura/artículo/anuncio*⟩ to cut out (b) ⟨*pelo/puntas*⟩ to trim **2** ⟨*gastos/plantilla*⟩ to reduce

recorte *m* **1** (de periódico, revista) cutting, clipping **2** (Fin) (acción) cutting; (efecto) cut, reduction

recostar [A10] *vt* (apoyar) to lean
■ **recostarse** *v pron* (a) (acostarse) to lie down; **recuéstate en el almohadón** lie back on the pillow

(b) (apoyarse) to lean; **recostados en el escritorio** leaning on the desk; **estaba recostado en un sillón** he was sitting back in an armchair

recoveco *m*: **un camino lleno de** ~**s** a road full of twists and turns; **en todos los** ~**s de la casa** in every nook and cranny of the house

recreativo -va *adj* recreational

recreo *m* (a) (diversión): **nos servía de** ~ it served as entertainment; **viaje de** ~ pleasure trip (b) (en el colegio) recess (AmE), break (BrE)

recriminar [A1] *vt* to reproach

recta *f* (Mat) straight line; (Dep) straight; ~ **final** (Dep) home stretch

rectángulo *m* rectangle

rectificar [A2] *vt* to correct
■ ~ *vi* (corregirse) to correct oneself

rectitud *f* rectitude (frml), honesty

recto¹ -ta *adj* (a) ⟨*línea/nariz/falda*⟩ straight (b) (honrado) honest, upright

recto² *m* (Anat) rectum
■ *adv* straight; **todo** ~ straight on

rector -tora *m,f* (de universidad) rector (AmE), vice-chancellor (BrE)

recuadro *m* box

recubrir [I33] *vt* ~ **algo DE** *or* **CON algo** to cover sth WITH sth

recuento *m* (de votos) recount

recuerdo *m* **1** (a) (reminiscencia) memory (b) (souvenir) souvenir; (regalo) memento, keepsake; **un** ~ **de familia** a family heirloom **2** **recuerdos** *mpl* regards (*pl*), best wishes (*pl*); **dale** ~**s** give him my regards

recuperación *f* (a) (en general) recovery (b) (Esp) (Educ) *tb* **examen de** ~ retake, makeup (exam) (AmE)

recuperar [A1] *vt* (a) ⟨*dinero/joyas/botín*⟩ to recover, get back; ⟨*pérdidas*⟩ to recoup (b) ⟨*vista/salud*⟩ to recover; ⟨*confianza*⟩ to regain; ~ **fuerzas** to get one's strength back (c) (compensar) ⟨*tiempo perdido*⟩ to make up for; **tienes que** ~ **esas tres horas** you have to make up those three hours (d) ⟨*examen/asignatura*⟩ to retake, make up (AmE)
■ **recuperarse** *v pron* ~**se DE algo** ⟨*de enfermedad*⟩ to recover FROM sth, recuperate FROM sth (frml); ⟨*de sorpresa/desgracia*⟩ to get over sth, recover FROM sth

recurrir [I1] *vi* (frente a problema) ~ **A** algn to turn TO sb; ~ **A algo** to resort TO sth

recursivo *adj* (Col) resourceful

recurso *m* **1** (medio): **agoté todos los** ~**s** I exhausted all the options; **como último** ~ as a last resort; **un hombre de** ~**s** a resourceful man **2** **recursos** *mpl* (medios económicos — de país) resources (*pl*); (— de persona) means (*pl*); ~**s energéticos** energy resources (*pl*); ~**s humanos** human resources (*pl*); ~**s naturales** natural resources (*pl*)

red *f* **1** (a) (para pescar) net (b) (Dep) net (c) (para pelo) hairnet (d) (en tren) (luggage) rack **2** (de comunicaciones, emisoras, transportes) network; (de comercios, empresas) chain, network; (de espionaje, contrabando) ring **3** (de electricidad) power supply, mains; (de gas) mains **4** **la Red** (Inf) the Net

redacción *f* **1** (a) (de carta) writing; (de

borrador) drafting; (de tratado) drawing-up, drafting **(b)** (lenguaje, estilo) wording, phrasing **2** (Educ) composition, essay **3** (Period) **(a)** (acción) writing **(b)** (equipo) editorial staff *o* team **(c)** (oficina) editorial department *o* office

redactar [A1] *vt* ‹informe/artículo/composición› to write; ‹acuerdo/tratado› to draw up
■ ~ *vi*: **redacta muy bien** she writes very well

redactor -tora *m,f* editor; ~ **jefe** editor in chief

redada *f* raid

redentor -tora *adj* redeeming
■ *m,f* redeemer

redimir [I1] *vt* to redeem

redoblar [A1] *vt* (aumentar) ‹esfuerzos/críticas› to redouble; ‹vigilancia› to step up, tighten
■ ~ *vi* «*tambor*» to roll

redoble *m* drumroll

redoma *f* (Ven) (Auto) traffic circle (AmE), roundabout (BrE)

redomado -da *adj* utter, out-and-out

redonda *f* **1** (Mús) semibreve **2** **a la redonda**: **en diez metros a la ~** within a ten meter radius; **se oyó a varios kilómetros a la ~** it could be heard for miles around

redondear [A1] *vt* **(a)** (dar forma curva) to round (off) **(b)** ‹cifra/número› to round off; (por lo alto) to round up; (por lo bajo) to round down
■ ~ *vi*: **digamos 200, para ~** let's make it a round 200

redondel *m* (figura circular) ring

redondela *f* (Andes) ▶ REDONDEL

redondo -da *adj* **1** ‹cara/espejo› round; **caer (se) ~** (desplomarse) to collapse; **en ~** ‹girar› (right) around **2** ‹cifra/número› round **3** (perfecto): **un negocio ~** a great *o* excellent deal; **nos salió todo ~** everything turned out perfectly for us **4** (Méx) ‹boleto/pasaje› return (before *n*), round-trip (before *n*) (AmE)

reducción *f* reduction; ~ **de impuestos** tax cuts, reduction in taxes; **una ~ de personal** a reduction *o* cutback in the workforce

reducido -da *adj* **(a)** (pequeño) ‹espacio/presupuesto› limited; ‹tamaño› small **(b)** (rebajado, achicado) ‹precio/fotografía› reduced; **un número ~ de personas** a small number of people; **trabaja jornada reducida** she is on short-time (working)

reducidor -dora *m,f* (AmS) (de objetos robados) receiver, fence (colloq)

reducir [I6] *vt* **1** **(a)** ‹gastos/costos› to cut, reduce; ‹velocidad/producción/consumo› to reduce; **debería ~ el consumo de sal** you should cut down on salt; ~ **algo A algo** to reduce sth *o* sth; ~ **algo EN algo** to reduce sth by sth **(b)** ‹fotocopia/fotografía› to reduce **2** **(a)** (transformar): ~ **los gramos a miligramos** to convert the grams to milligrams; **quedaron reducidos a cenizas** they were reduced to ashes **(b)** (AmS) ‹objeto robado› to receive, fence (colloq) **3** (dominar) ‹enemigo/rebeldes› to subdue; ‹ladrón› to overpower
■ **reducirse** *v pron*: **todo se reduce a tener tacto** it all comes down to being tactful

redundancia *f* (Ling) tautology, redundancy; **valga la ~** if you'll forgive the repetition

redundante *adj* redundant

reedición *f* reissue, reprint

reeditar [A1] *vt* to reprint, reissue

reelegir [I8] *vt* to reelect

reembolsar [A1] *vt* ‹gastos› to refund, reimburse (fml); ‹depósito› to refund; ‹préstamo› to repay

reembolso *m* (de gastos) refund, reimbursement (fml); (de depósito) refund; (de préstamo) repayment; **contra ~** cash on delivery, COD

reemplazar [A4] *vt* ‹persona› (durante período limitado) to substitute for, stand in for; (durante más tiempo) to replace; ‹aparato/pieza› to replace; ~ **algo/a algn POR** *o* **CON algo/algn** to replace sth/sb WITH *o* BY sth/sb

reemplazo *m* (durante período limitado) substitution; (durante más tiempo) replacement; **entró en ~ del jugador lesionado** he came on as a substitute for the injured player

reencarnación *f* reincarnation

reencarnarse [A1] *v pron* to be reincarnated; ~ **EN algn/algo** to be reincarnated AS sb/sth

reencuentro *m* reunion

reestreno *m* (de película) rerelease; (de obra teatral) revival

reestructurar [A1] *vt* to restructure

refacción *f* **1** (AmS) (para ampliar, mejorar) refurbishment **2** (Méx) (pieza de repuesto) spare part; **llanta de ~** spare tire

refaccionar [A1] *vt* (AmS) to refurbish

refaccionaria *f* (Méx) (tienda) auto spares store; (taller) garage

referencia *f* reference; **hacer ~ a algo** to refer to *o* mention sth; **con ~ a ...** with reference to ...; **número de ~** reference number; **tener buenas ~s** to have good references

referéndum *m* (pl **-dums**) referendum; **someter algo a ~** to hold a referendum on sth

referente *adj*: **las noticias ~s al accidente** the news about the accident; **en lo ~ a ...** regarding ...

réferi, referí *mf* (AmL) referee

referirse [I11] *v pron* **(a)** (aludir) ~**se A algo/algn** to refer TO sth/sb **(b)** (estar relacionado con): **por lo que se refiere a este asunto ...** with regard to this matter ..., as far as this matter is concerned ...

refilón: **de refilón** (loc adv): **lo miré de ~** I gave him a sidelong glance; **la vi solo de ~** I just caught a glimpse of her

refinado -da *adj* ‹persona/modales› refined; ‹ironía› subtle

refinar [A1] *vt* to refine; ‹estilo› to polish

refinería *f* refinery

reflector *m* **(a)** (pantalla reflectante) reflector **(b)** (foco) (Teatr) spotlight; (Dep) floodlight; (Mil) searchlight; (en monumento) floodlight

reflejar [A1] *vt* to reflect
■ **reflejarse** *v pron* **(a)** «*imagen*» to be reflected **(b)** «*emoción/cansancio/duda*» to show

reflejo¹ -ja *adj* reflex (before *n*)

reflejo² ** *m* **1 **(a)** (en general) reflection; (luz reflejada) reflected light **(b)** **reflejos** *mpl* (en peluquería) highlights (*pl*) **2** (Fisiol) reflex

reflexionar [A1] *vi* to reflect (fml); **¿has** ⋯⟫

reflexionado bien? have you thought it over *o* through carefully?; ~ **SOBRE algo** to think ABOUT sth, reflect ON sth (frml)

reflexivo -va *adj* **(a)** (Ling, Mat) reflexive **(b)** ⟨*persona*⟩ thoughtful, reflective

reflujo *m* (de marea) ebb (tide)

reforestación *f* reforestation

reforestar [A1] *vt* to reforest

reforma *f* **(a)** (en general) reform; **la R~** (Relig) the Reformation **(b)** (en edificio, traje) alteration

reformar [A1] *vt* **(a)** (en general) to reform **(b)** ⟨*casa/edificio*⟩ to make alterations to

■ **reformarse** *v pron* to mend one's ways

reformatorio *m* reformatory

reforzar [A11] *vt* ⟨*puerta/costura*⟩ to reinforce; ⟨*guardia*⟩ to increase, strengthen; ⟨*relaciones*⟩ to reinforce; ⟨*medidas de seguridad*⟩ to step up, tighten

refrán *m* saying, proverb; **como dice el ~** as the saying goes

refregar [A7] *vt* ⟨*puños/cuello*⟩ to scrub

refrendar [A1] *vt* (Col, Méx) ⟨*pasaporte*⟩ to renew

refrescante *adj* refreshing

refrescar [A2] *vt* **(a)** ⟨*bebida*⟩ to cool; ⟨*ambiente*⟩ to make … fresher *o* cooler **(b)** ⟨*conocimientos*⟩ to brush up (on)

■ ~ *v impers* to turn cooler

refresco *m* soft drink, soda (AmE)

refrigerador *m* **(a)** (nevera) refrigerator, fridge **(b)** (del aire acondicionado) cooling unit

refrigeradora *f* (Col, Per) refrigerator, fridge

refrigerar [A1] *vt* **(a)** ⟨*alimentos/bebidas*⟩ to refrigerate **(b)** ⟨*motor*⟩ to cool; ⟨*cine/bar*⟩ to air-condition; ⑤ **local refrigerado** air-conditioned premises

refrito *m* (Coc): **un ~ de tomate y cebolla** fried onions and tomato

refuerzo *m* **(a)** (para puerta, pared, costura) reinforcement **(b)** (de vacuna) booster **(c)** **refuerzos** *mpl* (Mil) reinforcements (*pl*)

refugiado -da *adj* refugee (*before n*)

■ *m,f* refugee

refugiar [A1] *vt* to give … refuge

■ **refugiarse** *v pron* to take refuge; **~se DE algo** ⟨*de bombardeo/ataque*⟩ to take refuge FROM sth; ⟨*de lluvia/tormenta*⟩ to take shelter FROM sth

refugio *m* **(a)** (de la lluvia, bombardeo) shelter; (en montaña) refuge, shelter **(b)** (de un ataque, perseguidores) refuge; **buscar ~** to seek refuge **(c)** (en calzada) traffic island

refunfuñar [A1] *vi* (fam) to grumble, grouch (colloq)

refunfuñón -ñona *adj* (fam) grouchy (colloq), grumpy (colloq)

regadera *f* **(a)** (para jardín) watering can **(b)** (Col, Méx, Ven) (de ducha) rose, shower head (AmE); (ducha) shower

regadío *m* (sistema) irrigation; **tierras de ~** irrigated land

regalado -da *adj* **(a)** (fam) (muy barato): **precios ~s** giveaway prices (colloq); **esos zapatos están ~s** those shoes are dirt cheap *o* are a steal (colloq) **(b)** (Chi, Méx, Ven fam) (muy fácil) easy

regalar [A1] *vt* **(a)** (obsequiar): **¿qué te ~on para tu cumpleaños?** what did you get for your birthday?; **le ~on un reloj de oro** he was given a gold watch **(b)** (vender muy barato) to sell … at bargain prices

regaliz *m* licorice (AmE), liquorice (BrE)

regalo *m* **(a)** (obsequio) gift, present **(b)** (cosa barata) steal (colloq) **(c)** (deleite, festín) treat

regalón -lona *adj* (CS fam) spoiled

■ *m,f* (CS fam) spoilt brat (colloq)

regalonear [A1] *vt* (CS fam) to spoil

■ ~ *vi* (CS fam): **le encanta ~ con su abuela** she loves being made a fuss of by her grandmother

regañadientes: **a regañadientes** (*loc adv*) reluctantly, unwillingly

regañar [A1] *vt* (esp AmL) to scold, to tell … off (colloq)

■ ~ *vi* (Esp) (pelearse) to quarrel

regañina, (Méx) **regañiza** *f* (fam) scolding, talking-to (colloq), telling-off (colloq)

regaño *m* (AmL fam) scolding, telling-off (colloq)

regar [A7] *vt* **(a)** ⟨*planta/jardín*⟩ to water; ⟨*tierra/campo*⟩ to irrigate; ⟨*calle*⟩ to hose down **(b)** «*río*» to water **(c)** (AmC, Ven) ⟨*noticia/versión*⟩ to spread

regata *f* (carrera) yacht race; (serie de carreras) regatta

regate *m* (Esp) (en fútbol) feint

regatear [A1] *vi* (Com) to bargain, haggle

■ ~ *vt* **①** (escatimar): **no han regateado esfuerzos para …** no efforts have been spared to …; **sin ~ medios** whatever it takes **②** (Esp) (Dep) to get past, swerve past

regencia *f* (en lugar del soberano) regency

regenerar [A1] *vt* to regenerate

■ **regenerarse** *v pron* **(a)** (Biol, Tec) to be regenerated **(b)** «*persona*» to be reformed

regente *mf* regent

régimen *m* **①** (dieta) diet; **hacer ~** to be on a diet; **ponerse a ~** to go on a diet **②** (Pol) regime

regimiento *m* (Mil) regiment

regio -gia *adj* **(a)** (majestuoso) regal **(b)** (Col, CS fam) (estupendo) great (colloq); **te queda ~** it looks fantastic on you (colloq); **me viene ~** it suits you fine

región *f* region

regional *adj* regional

regir [I8] *vt* to govern

■ ~ *vi* «*ley/disposición*» to be in force, be valid; **ese horario ya no rige** that timetable is no longer valid

■ **regirse** *v pron* **~se POR algo** «*sociedad*» to be governed BY sth; «*economía/mercado*» to be controlled BY sth *o* subject TO sth

registrar [A1] *vt* **①** **(a)** ⟨*nacimiento/defunción/patente*⟩ to register **(b)** ⟨*sonido/temperatura*⟩ to record; ⟨*temblor*⟩ to register **②** ⟨*equipaje/lugar/*

persona⟩ to search; **estaba registrando mis cajones** (fam) he was going through my drawers **3** (Méx) ⟨*carta*⟩ to register
■ **registrarse** *v pron* (inscribirse) to register; (en hotel) to register, check in

registro *m* **1** (libro) register; (acción de anotar) registration; (cosa anotada) record, entry; ~ **civil** (oficina) registry, registry office (BrE) **2** (por la policía) search; **orden de** ~ search warrant

regla *f* **(a)** (utensilio) ruler **(b)** (norma) rule; **todo está en** ~ everything is in order; **por** ~ **general** as a (general) rule **(c)** (menstruación) period; **tengo la** ~ I have my period

reglamentario -ria *adj* ⟨*horario*⟩ set (*before n*); ⟨*uniforme/arma*⟩ regulation (*before n*)

reglamento *m* rules (*pl*), regulations (*pl*)

regocijarse [A1] *v pron* to rejoice; ~ **DE** *or* **POR algo** (por buena noticia) to rejoice AT sth; (por mal ajeno) to take delight IN sth, delight IN sth

regocijo *m* **(a)** (júbilo, alborozo) rejoicing; (alegría) joy, delight; **sintió gran** ~ **al verla** he was delighted to see her **(b)** (ante el mal ajeno) pleasure

regodearse [A1] *v pron* **(a)** (complacerse) to delight in, take great delight in; **se regodea haciéndome sufrir** he delights in making me suffer; ~ **EN** *or* **CON algo** to delight IN sth, gloat OVER sth **(b)** (Chi) (al elegir) to hesitate

regordete -ta *adj* (fam) chubby

regresar [A1] *vi* to return, come/go back; **no sé cuándo va a** ~ I don't know when he'll be back
■ ~ *vt* (AmL exc CS) **(a)** ⟨*libro/llaves*⟩ to return, give back **(b)** ⟨*persona*⟩ to send ... back
■ **regresarse** *v pron* (AmL exc RPl) to return, go/come back; **ya se regresó** she's back now

regreso *m* **(a)** (vuelta) return; **emprendió el** ~ she set off on the return journey o trip; **de** ~ **paramos en León** on the way back we stopped in León **(b)** (AmL) (devolución) return

reguero *m* (rastro) trail

regulable *adj* adjustable

regulador *m* regulator

regular¹ *adj* **1** (en general) regular **2** **(a)** (no muy bien): **¿qué tal te va?** — **regular** how's it going? — so-so; **¿qué tal la película?** — **regular** how was the movie? — nothing special **(b)** (de tamaño) medium-sized, middling
■ *m* (calificación) fair

regular² [A1] *vt* **1** **(a)** ⟨*espejo/asiento*⟩ to adjust **(b)** ⟨*caudal/temperatura/velocidad*⟩ to regulate, control **2** «*ley/norma*» to regulate

regularidad *f* regularity; **con** ~ regularly

regusto *m* aftertaste

rehabilitación *f* **(a)** (de enfermo, delincuente) rehabilitation **(b)** (en cargo) reinstatement **(c)** (de vivienda) renovation, restoration

rehabilitar [A1] *vt* **(a)** ⟨*paciente/delincuente*⟩ to rehabilitate **(b)** (en cargo) to reinstate **(c)** ⟨*vivienda/local*⟩ to renovate, restore

rehacer [E18] *vt* (volver a hacer) to redo; **trató de** ~ **su vida** she tried to rebuild her life
■ **rehacerse** *v pron* ~**se DE algo** to get over sth

rehén *m* hostage

rehogar [A3] *vt* to fry ... lightly

rehuir [I21] *vt* to shy away from

rehusar [A23] *vt/vi* to refuse

■ **rehusarse** *v pron* (esp AmL) to refuse

reilón -lona *adj* (Per, Ven fam) smiley (colloq)

reimpresión *f* **(a)** (acción) reprinting **(b)** (obra) reprint

reimprimir [I36] *vt* to reprint

reina *f* queen; ~ **de belleza** beauty queen

reinado *m* reign

reinante *adj* **(a)** ⟨*casa/dinastía*⟩ reigning **(b)** ⟨*frío/lluvias*⟩ prevailing; **el malestar** ~ **en el partido** the unease prevailing in the party

reinar [A1] *vi* **(a)** «*monarca/dinastía*» to reign **(b)** «*silencio/paz*» to reign; «*terror/buen tiempo*» to prevail

reincidente *mf* reoffender

reincidir [I1] *vi* (Der) to reoffend

reincorporarse [A1] *v pron* to return; ~ **a filas** to rejoin the army

reiniciar [A1] *vt* to resume; (Inf) to reboot

reino *m* kingdom; ~ **animal** animal kingdom; **el** ~ **de la fantasía** the realm of fantasy

Reino Unido *m*: **el** ~~ the United Kingdom

reinserción *f*: *tb* ~ **social** social rehabilitation, reintegration into society

reintegrar [A1] *vt* **1** ⟨*persona*⟩ (a cargo) to reinstate; (a la comunidad) to reintegrate; ~ **a algn A** *or* **EN algo** ⟨*a cargo*⟩ to reinstate sb IN sth; ⟨*a la comunidad*⟩ to reintegrate sb INTO sth **2** (fml) ⟨*depósito*⟩ to refund, return; ⟨*gastos*⟩ to reimburse; ⟨*préstamo*⟩ to repay
■ **reintegrarse** *v pron* to return; ~**se A algo** ⟨*a trabajo/equipo*⟩ to return TO sth; ~**se en la comunidad** to reintegrate into the community

reintegro *m* **(a)** (en banco) withdrawal; (de depósito) refund; (de gastos) reimbursement; (de préstamo) repayment **(b)** (en lotería) refund (*of the ticket price*)

reír [I18] *vi* to laugh; **se echaron a** ~ they burst out laughing
■ ~ *vt* ⟨*gracia/chiste*⟩ to laugh at
■ **reírse** *v pron* to laugh; ~**se a carcajadas** to guffaw; ~**se DE algo/algn** to laugh AT sth/sb

reivindicación *f* **(a)** (demanda) demand, claim **(b)** (reconocimiento) recognition **(c)** (rehabilitación): **luchó por la** ~ **de su buen nombre** she fought to vindicate her good name **(d)** (de atentado): **la** ~ **del atentado** the claiming of responsibility for the attack

reivindicar [A2] *vt* **(a)** ⟨*derecho*⟩ to demand; ⟨*tierras*⟩ to claim **(b)** (rehabilitar) ⟨*imagen/reputación*⟩ to restore **(c)** ⟨*atentado*⟩ to claim responsibility for

reja *f* **(a)** (de ventana) grille **(b)** (para cercar) railing

rejego *adj* (Méx fam) ⟨*persona*⟩ mouthy (AmE), cheeky (BrE)

rejilla *f* **(a)** (de ventilación) grille; (Auto) grille; (del confesionario) screen; (del desagüe) grating **(b)** (para equipajes) luggage rack; (de horno) rack; (base de chimenea) grate

rejuntar [A1] *vt* (Méx fam) ⟨*reses*⟩ to round up; ⟨*borregos*⟩ to gather

rejuvenecer [E3] *vt* to rejuvenate
■ **rejuvenecerse** *v pron* to be rejuvenated

relación *f* **1** **(a)** (conexión) connection; **con** ~ **a** *or* **en** ~ **con** (con respecto a) in connection with; (en comparación con) relative to; **en** ~ **con su carta** ···⟶

... with regard to o regarding your letter ... **(b)**
(correspondencia): **en una ~ de diez a uno** (Mat) in a
ratio of ten to one; **una ~ causa-efecto** a
relationship of cause and effect
2 **(a)** (entre personas) relationship; **las relaciones
entre padres e hijos** the relationship between
parents and their children; **estoy en buenas
relaciones con él** I'm on good terms with him **(b)**
relaciones *fpl* (influencias) contacts (*pl*),
connections (*pl*); (trato comercial, diplomático)
relations (*pl*); (trato carnal) sex; **relaciones
exteriores** foreign affairs; **relaciones
prematrimoniales** premarital sex; **relaciones
públicas** (actividad) public relations (*pl*); (persona)
public relations officer; (de cantante, artista) PR;
relaciones sexuales sexual relations
3 **(a)** (exposición) account **(b)** (lista) list

relacionado -da *adj* **(a)** [ESTAR] 〈*temas/
ideas/hechos*〉 related, connected **(b)** 〈*persona*〉:
está muy bien ~ he is very well connected; **estar
~ CON algn/algo** to be connected WITH sb/sth

relacionar [A1] *vt* (conectar) to relate, connect;
~ algo A *o* **CON algo** to relate *o* connect sth TO
sth
■ **relacionarse** *v pron* **(a)** **~se CON algo** 〈*con
tema/asunto*〉 to be related TO sth **(b)** «*persona*»
~se CON algn to mix WITH sb

relajación *f* (de músculos, mente) relaxation

relajado -da *adj* **(a)** (tranquilo) relaxed **(b)**
〈*costumbres*〉 dissolute, lax

relajante *adj* **1** 〈*música/baño*〉 relaxing
2 (CS fam) (empalagoso) sickly-sweet (pej)

relajar [A1] *vt* 〈*músculo/persona/mente*〉 to relax
■ **~** *vi* 〈*ejercicio/música*〉 to be relaxing
■ **relajarse** *v pron* **1** **(a)** (físicamente, mentalmente)
to relax; (tras período de tensión, mucho trabajo) to
relax, unwind **(b)** «*tensión*» to ease;
«*ambiente*» to become more relaxed
2 (degenerar) «*costumbres/moral*» to decline

relajo *m* **1** (en la moral) decline **2** (esp Esp fam)
(relax): **¡qué ~!** how relaxing! **3** **(a)** (Méx fam)
(persona divertida) laugh (colloq) **(b)** (persona
problemática) troublemaker

relamerse [E1] *v pron* (por algo sabroso) to lick
one's lips; (de satisfacción) to smack one's lips

relámpago *m* (Meteo) bolt *o* flash of lightning;
como un ~ 〈*salir/pasar*〉 like greased lightning

relatar [A1] *vt* 〈*historia/aventura*〉 to recount,
relate

relativo -va *adj* **1** (no absoluto) relative; **eso es
muy ~** that depends; **una enfermedad de relativa
gravedad** a relatively serious illness
2 (concerniente) **~ A algo** relating TO sth; **todo lo
~ a la política** anything to do with *o* related to
politics; **en lo ~ a este problema** with regard to
this problem

relato *m* **(a)** (historia, cuento) story, tale **(b)**
(relación) account

relax *m* relaxation

relegar [A3] *vt*: **se siente relegado** he feels left
out; **el problema quedó relegado a un segundo
plano** the matter was pushed into the
background; **relegado al olvido** consigned to
oblivion

relevante *adj* notable, outstanding

relevar [A1] *vt* **(a)** (sustituir) 〈*guarda/enfermera*〉

to relieve; 〈*jugador*〉 to replace, take over from;
~ la guardia (Mil) to change the guard **(b)**
(destituir) to remove
■ **relevarse** *v pron* to take turns, take it in
turn(s)

relevo *m* **(a)** de ~ 〈*conductor/equipo*〉 relief
(*before n*) **(b)** (Dep) *tb* **~s** relay (race)

relieve *m* **1** **(a)** (Art, Geog) relief; **la costa tiene
un ~ muy accidentado** the coast is very rugged;
letras en ~ embossed letters **(b)** (parte que
sobresale): **el marco tiene un centímetro de ~** the
frame protrudes by a centimeter **2** (importancia)
prominence; **personas de ~** prominent people;
dar ~ a algo to lend (special) importance to sth;
poner de ~ to highlight

religión *f* religion

religiosidad *f* religiousness, religiosity

religioso -sa *adj* religious
■ *m,f* member of a religious order

relinchar [A1] *vi* to neigh, whinny

reliquia *f* relic; **una ~ de familia** a family
heirloom

rellano *m* (de escalera) landing; (de ladera,
montaña) shelf

rellenar [A1] *vt* **1** **(a)** 〈*pavo/pimientos/cojín*〉
to stuff; 〈*pastel*〉 to fill; **~ algo DE** *or* **CON algo** to
stuff/fill sth WITH sth **(b)** 〈*agujero/grieta*〉 to fill
2 (volver a llenar) to refill **3** 〈*impreso/formulario*〉
to fill out *o* in; 〈*examen/discurso*〉 to pad out

relleno¹ -na *adj* 〈*pavo/pimientos*〉 stuffed;
caramelos ~s de chocolate candies with a
chocolate filling

relleno² *m* (para pasteles, tortas) filling; (para
pavo, pimientos, cojín) stuffing; (de ropa interior)
padding; (para agujeros, grietas) filler

reloj *m* (de pared, mesa) clock; (de pulsera, bolsillo)
watch; **funciona como un ~** it's going like
clockwork; **contra ~** against the clock; **~ de
arena** hourglass; **~ de pie** grandfather clock;
~ de sol sundial; **~ despertador** alarm clock

relojería *f* (tienda, taller) clockmaker's,
watchmaker's; (actividad) watchmaking

relojero -ra *m,f* (de relojes — de pulsera)
watchmaker; (— de pared, mesa) clockmaker

reluciente *adj* 〈*dientes/coche*〉 gleaming;
〈*metal/suelo*〉 shiny, shining; **una mañana ~** a
bright, sunny morning

relucir [I5] *vi* «*sol*» to shine; «*estrellas*» to
twinkle, glitter; «*plata/zapatos*» to shine, gleam;
salir/sacar a ~ to come to the surface/to bring up

relumbrante *adj* brilliant, dazzling

relumbrar [A1] *vi* to shine brightly

remachar [A1] *vt* **(a)** 〈*clavo*〉 to clinch; 〈*perno/
chapas*〉 to rivet **(b)** (recalcar) to repeat, reiterate;
(finalizar) to round off, finish off
■ **~** *vi* (en tenis) to smash; (en vóleibol) to spike

remache *m* **1** (perno) rivet **2** (en tenis) smash;
(en vóleibol) spike

remangarse [A3] *v pron* (refl) 〈*pantalones/
manga*〉 to roll up; **se remangó para lavar los
platos** he rolled up his sleeves to wash the dishes

remanso *m* pool; **un ~ de paz** a haven of
peace (liter)

remar [A1] *vi* (en bote) to row; (en canoa) to
paddle

remarcar [A2] *vt* (hacer notar) to stress, emphasize

rematado -da *adj* complete, absolute; **es un loco** ~ he's a raving lunatic

rematar [A1] *vt* **1 (a)** ⟨*actuación/intervención*⟩ to round off, finish off; ⟨*negocio*⟩ to conclude, close; ⟨*torre/bastón*⟩ to top, crown; **y para ~la** (fam) and to crown *o* cap it all (colloq) **(b)** ⟨*costura*⟩ to finish off **(c)** ⟨*animal/persona*⟩ to finish off
2 (en tenis) to smash; (en vóleibol) to spike; (en fútbol): **remató el centro a la portería** he hit the cross straight into the goal
3 (AmL) **(a)** (en subasta — vender) to auction; (— comprar) to buy ... at an auction **(b)** (liquidar) to sell ... off cheaply
■ ~ *vi* **1** (terminar) ~ **EN algo** to end **IN** sth
2 (en tenis) to smash; (en vóleibol) to spike; (en fútbol) to shoot; ~ **de cabeza** to head the ball

remate *m* **1 (a)** (de actividades, esfuerzos) culmination; **y como** ~ (fam) and to crown *o* cap it all (colloq) **(b)** (en costura) double stitch (*to finish off*) **2** (en tenis) smash; (en vóleibol) spike; (en fútbol) shot; ~ **de cabeza** header **3** (AmL) (subasta) auction

remedar [A1] *vt* to mimic, ape

remediar [A1] *vt* **1** ⟨*situación/problema*⟩ to remedy; ⟨*daño*⟩ to repair; **¿qué piensas hacer para ~lo?** what are you going to do to put things right?; **con llorar no remedias nada** crying won't solve anything **2** (evitar): **no lo puedo/pude** ~ I can't/couldn't help it

remedio *m* **1 (a)** (Med) (cura) remedy, cure **(b)** (esp AmL) (Farm) medicine **2** (solución) solution; **ya no tiene** ~ there's nothing we (*or* you *etc*) can do now; **su matrimonio no tiene** ~ her marriage is beyond hope; **un caso sin** ~ a hopeless case **3** (alternativa, recurso) option; **no queda más** ~ **que ...** we have no alternative *o* choice but ...; **iré si no hay otro** ~ I'll go if I really have to *o* if I must

remendar [A5] *vt* to mend

remera *f* (RPl) (camiseta) T-shirt

remero -ra *m,f* (*m*) rower, oarsman; (*f*) rower, oarswoman

remesa *f* (de mercancías) consignment, shipment; (de dinero) remittance

remezón *m* (Andes) (temblor) earth tremor; (sacudida brusca) shake; (suceso inesperado) shake-up

remiendo *m* (pedazo de tela, cuero) patch; **le hizo un** ~ she mended *o* patched it

remilgado -da *adj* fussy

remilgón -gona, remilgoso -sa *adj* (delicado) (Andes, Méx) fussy; (difícil) (Méx) difficult

remisión *f* **1** (en texto) reference; ~ **A algo** reference **TO** sth **2** (de enfermedad) remission **3** (Relig, Der) remission

remite *m* (persona) sender; (dirección) return address

remitente *mf* sender

remitir [I1] *vt* **(a)** (frml) (mandar) to send **(b)** ⟨*lector/estudiante*⟩ ~ **A algn A algo** to refer sb **TO** sth
■ ~ *vi* ⟨«*fiebre*»⟩ to drop, go down; ⟨«*tormenta*»⟩ to abate, subside
■ **remitirse** *v pron* ~**se A algo** ⟨*a obra*⟩ to refer **TO** sth

remo *m* (con soporte) oar; (sin soporte) paddle

remodelación *f* (Arquit) remodeling*, redesigning; (de organización) reorganization, restructuring; (del gabinete) (Pol) reshuffle

remodelar [A1] *vt* ⟨*plaza/barrio*⟩ to remodel, redesign; ⟨*organización*⟩ to reorganize; ⟨*gabinete*⟩ to reshuffle

remojar [A1] *vt* ⟨*ropa/lentejas*⟩ to soak

remojo *m* (en agua): **poner algo a** *or* **en** ~ to put sth to soak; **dejar algo en** ~ to leave sth to soak

remojón *m* **1** (fam) (en agua) soaking, drenching; **¿quién quiere darse un** ~? who's for a dip? (colloq) **2** (Méx fam) (de algo nuevo): **nos dio el** ~ (en el coche) he took us for a spin in his new car; (en la casa) he had us over for a housewarming party

remolacha *f* beet (AmE), beetroot (BrE); ~ **azucarera** sugar beet

remolcador *m* (Náut) tug; (Auto) tow truck (AmE), breakdown van (BrE)

remolcar [A2] *vt* ⟨*barco*⟩ to tug; ⟨*coche*⟩ to tow

remolino *m* **(a)** (de viento) eddy, whirl **(b)** (de agua) eddy; (más violento) whirlpool **(c)** (en el pelo) cowlick

remolón -lona *adj* (fam) idle, lazy
■ *m,f* (fam) slacker (colloq)

remolque *m* **(a)** (vehículo) trailer **(b)** (acción) towing; **ir a** ~ (Auto) to be in tow **(c)** (AmS) (grúa) tow truck (AmE), breakdown van (BrE)

remontar [A1] *vt* **1** ⟨*dificultad/problema*⟩ to overcome, surmount (frml) **2 (a)** ~ **el vuelo** «*avión*» to gain height; «*pájaro*» to fly *o* soar up **(b)** ~ **el río** to go upriver **(c)** (RPl) ⟨*barrilete*⟩ to fly
■ **remontarse** *v pron* **1** «*avión*» to gain height; «*pájaro*» to soar up **2** (en el tiempo) to go back

remorder [E9] *vi* (+ *me/te/le etc*): **me remuerde haberlo dicho** I feel guilty for having said it; **¿no te remuerde la conciencia?** don't you feel guilty?

remordimiento *m* remorse; **sentir** *o* **tener** ~**s de conciencia** to suffer pangs of conscience

remoto -ta *adj* **(a)** ⟨*tiempo/época*⟩ distant, far-off (*before n*) **(b)** ⟨*lugar/mares/tierras*⟩ remote, far-off **(c)** ⟨*posibilidad*⟩ remote, slim; ⟨*esperanza*⟩ faint; **no tengo (ni) la más remota idea** I haven't the remotest *o* faintest idea

remover [E9] *vt* **1 (a)** ⟨*líquido/salsa*⟩ to stir; ⟨*ensalada*⟩ to toss; ⟨*tierra/piedras*⟩ to turn over; ⟨*escombros*⟩ to dig about in; ⟨*brasas*⟩ to poke, stir **(b)** ⟨*asunto*⟩ to bring ... up again; ⟨*pasado*⟩ to revive, stir up **2** (frml) **(a)** ⟨*impedimento/obstáculo*⟩ to remove **(b)** (esp AmL) (destituir) ~ **A algn DE algo** to remove sb **FROM** sth

remunerar [A1] *vt* to pay, remunerate (frml)

renacentista *adj* Renaissance (*before n*)

renacer [E3] *vi* to be reborn; **sentí** ~ **la esperanza** I felt renewed hope

renacimiento *m* **(a)** (acción) revival, rebirth **(b)** (Art, Hist) **el R**~ the Renaissance

renacuajo *m* (Zool) tadpole; (niño, persona baja) (fam) shrimp (colloq)

rencilla *f* quarrel, row

rencor *m* resentment; **con el corazón lleno de** ···⫶

∼ with his heart full of resentment; **no te guardo** ∼ I don't bear you any grudge; **siento** ∼ **por lo que me hizo** I feel bitter about what he did to me

rencoroso -sa *adj* [SER] resentful

rendición *f* surrender

rendido -da *adj* [ESTAR] (exhausto) exhausted; **cayó** ∼ **(de cansancio)** he collapsed from exhaustion; *ver tb* RENDIR

rendidor -dora *adj* (AmL) ⟨*tierra*⟩ productive; **un detergente** ∼ a detergent that goes a long way

rendija *f* (grieta) crack, crevice; (hueco) gap

rendimiento *m* **(a)** (de persona, coche) performance **(b)** (de máquina, factoría) output; **funciona a pleno** ∼ it is working at full capacity **(c)** (de terreno) yield **(d)** (Fin) return

rendir [I14] *vt* **1** ⟨*homenaje/tributo*⟩ to pay; ∼**le culto a algn** to worship sb **2** (Fin) to yield; (producir) to produce **3** ⟨*persona*⟩: **me rindió el sueño** I was overcome by sleep; **tanto trabajo rinde a cualquiera** working that hard is enough to exhaust anyone **4** (CS) (Educ) ⟨*examen*⟩ to take, sit (BrE)
■ ∼ *vi* **(a)** (cundir) (+ *me/te/le etc*): **me rindió mucho la mañana** I had a lot done this morning; **trabaja mucho pero no le rinde** he works hard but he doesn't make much headway **(b)** «*alumno/obrero/empleado*» to perform well **(c)** «*tela/arroz/jabón*» to go a long way
■ **rendirse** *v pron* (en pelea, guerra) to surrender; (en tarea, adivinanza) to give up

renegado -da *m,f* renegade

renegar [A7] *vi* **(a)** (Relig) to apostatize; ∼ **DE algo** ⟨*de creencias/principios*⟩ to renounce sth **(b)** (maldecir) to swear, curse; (blasfemar) to blaspheme **(c)** (refunfuñar) to grumble; ∼ **DE algo ABOUT** sth **(d)** (AmL) (enojarse) to get annoyed

RENFE /ˈrrenfe/ *f* = **Red Nacional de los Ferrocarriles Españoles**

renglón *m* (línea) line

rengo -ga *adj* (AmL) lame
■ *m,f* (AmL) lame person, cripple (pej)

renguear [A1] *vi* (AmL) to limp

renguera *f* (AmL) limp

reno *m* reindeer

renombrado -da *adj* well-known, renowned

renombre *m* renown; **de** ∼ renowned

renovación *f* **(a)** (de pasaporte, contrato) renewal **(b)** (del mobiliario) complete change; (de edificio, barrio) renovation **(c)** (de organización, sistema) updating **(d)** (reanudación) renewal

renovar [A10] *vt* **(a)** ⟨*pasaporte/contrato*⟩ to renew **(b)** ⟨*mobiliario*⟩ to change; ⟨*edificio/barrio*⟩ to renovate **(c)** ⟨*organización/sistema*⟩ to update, bring up to date **(d)** ⟨*ataque/esperanza/promesa*⟩ to renew
■ **renovarse** *v pron* **(a)** «*sospechas/dolor/interés*» to be renewed **(b)** «*persona*» to be revitalized

renta *f* **(a)** (beneficio) income; **inversiones de** ∼

fija fixed interest investments; **vivir de las** ∼**s** (de dinero) to live off the interest; (de propiedades) to live off the rent **(b)** (esp Méx) (alquiler) rent

rentabilidad *f* profitability

rentable *adj* ⟨*inversión/negocio*⟩ profitable

rentar [A1] *vt* (Méx) **(a)** ⟨*departamento*⟩ «*propietario*» to rent out, let (BrE); «*usuario*» to rent **(b)** ⟨*coche*⟩ to rent, hire (BrE)

renuncia *f* **1** (dimisión) resignation; **presentar la** ∼ to resign, tender one's resignation (frml) **2** (abandono) ∼ **A algo** renunciation OF sth **3** (abnegación) self-sacrifice

renunciar [A1] *vi* (dimitir) to resign; ∼ **A algo** ⟨*a puesto*⟩ to resign sth; ⟨*a derecho*⟩ to relinquish sth, renounce sth (frml); ⟨*a título*⟩ to give up sth, relinquish sth (frml); ⟨*a trono*⟩ to renounce sth

reñido -da *adj* **1** ⟨*partido/batalla*⟩ hard-fought, tough **2** [ESTAR] **(a)** (peleado): **está** ∼ **con su novia** he has fallen out with his girlfriend (colloq) **(b)** (en contradicción) ∼ **CON algo** ⟨*con principios*⟩ against sth

reñir [I15] *vi* (esp Esp) **(a)** (discutir) to argue, quarrel **(b)** ∼ **CON algn** (pelearse) to quarrel *o* have a row WITH sb; (enemistarse) to fall out WITH sb
■ ∼ *vt* (Esp) (regañar) to scold, tell ... off (colloq)

reo *mf* (en lo penal — acusado) accused, defendant; (— condenado) convicted offender; (en lo civil) (Méx) defendant

reojo: **de reojo** (loc adv): **mirar a algn de** ∼ to look at sb out of the corner of one's eye

reorganizar [A4] *vt* to reorganize

reparación *f* **(a)** (arreglo) repair; **taller de reparaciones** repair shop **(b)** (de daño, ofensa) redress, reparation

reparador -dora *adj* ⟨*sueño/descanso*⟩ refreshing

reparar [A1] *vt* ⟨*coche*⟩ to repair, fix; ⟨*gotera/avería*⟩ to mend, fix **(b)** ⟨*error*⟩ to correct, put right; ⟨*ofensa/agravio*⟩ to make amends for, make up for; ⟨*daño/perjuicio*⟩ to make good, compensate for
■ ∼ *vi* **1** ∼ **EN algo** (darse cuenta) to notice sth; (considerar): **no repara en gastos** she spares no expense **2** (Méx) «*caballo/toro*» to rear, shy

reparo *m* **(a)** (inconveniente, objeción): **pone** ∼**s a todo** she finds fault with everything; **no tengo ningún** ∼ **en decírselo** I have no qualms about telling him **(b)** (duda) reservation

repartición *f* **(a)** (división) distribution, share-out **(b)** (CS) (departamento, sección) department; (del ejército) division

repartidor -dora *m,f* (m) delivery man; (f) delivery woman; (de periódicos) newspaper man (*o* boy etc)

repartir [I1] *vt* ⟨*ganancias/trabajo*⟩ to distribute, share out **(b)** ⟨*panfletos/propaganda*⟩ to hand out, give out; ⟨*periódicos/correo*⟩ to deliver; ⟨*naipes/fichas*⟩ to deal **(c)** (esparcir) to spread, distribute
■ ∼ *vi* (Jueg) to deal

AmC	América Central	Arg	Argentina	Cu	Cuba	Per	Perú
AmL	América Latina	Bol	Bolivia	Ec	Ecuador	RPI	Río de la Plata
AmS	América del Sur	Chi	Chile	Esp	España	Ur	Uruguay
Andes	Región andina	CS	Cono Sur	Méx	México	Ven	Venezuela

reparto *m* 1 (a) (distribución) distribution; (entre socios, herederos) share-out; ~ **de premios** prize-giving (b) (servicio de entrega) delivery; ~ **a domicilio** delivery service 2 (Cin, Teatr) cast

repasador *m* (RPl) dish towel (AmE), tea towel (BrE)

repasar [A1] *vt* ‹lección/tema› to review (AmE), to revise (BrE); ‹lista/cuenta/carta› to go over, check
■ ~ *vi* to review (AmE), to revise (BrE)

repaso *m* (revisión — para aprender algo) review (AmE), revision (BrE); (— para detectar errores) check; **dio un ~ a sus apuntes** she went *o* looked over her notes

repatriado -da *m,f* repatriate

repatriar [A1 *or* A17] *vt* to repatriate

repelar [A1] *vi* (Méx fam) to grumble, to moan (BrE colloq)

repelente *adj* ‹persona› repulsive, repellent; ‹niño› obnoxious
■ *m* insect repellent

repeler [E1] *vt* ‹ataque/agresión› to repel, repulse (frml)
■ ~ *vi* (+ *me/te/le etc*): **las serpientes me repelen** I find snakes repellent *o* repulsive

repente: **de repente** (*loc adv*) (a) (de pronto) suddenly (b) (RPl, Per) (quizás) maybe, perhaps

repentino -na *adj* sudden

repentizar [A4] *vt/vi* to sight-read

repercusión *f* (consecuencia) repercussion

repercutir [I1] *vi* (a) «sonido» to reverberate (b) (afectar) ~ **EN algo** to have an effect *o* an impact ON sth

repertorio *m* repertoire

repetición *f* (a) (de experimento, palabra) repetition; (de un sueño, fenómeno) recurrence (b) (de programa) repeat, rerun

repetido *adj* (a) ‹sello/disco›: **este lo tengo ~** I have two of these (b) (delante del n) ‹casos/avisos/intentos› repeated (before n)

repetir [I14] *vt* (a) ‹pregunta/explicación› to repeat; **¿me lo puedes ~?** could you repeat it, please?; **¡que no te lo tenga que volver a ~!** don't let me have to tell you again! (b) ‹tarea› to do ... again; ‹programa› to repeat, rerun; ‹experimento/curso/asignatura› to repeat (c) ‹plato› to have a second helping of, to have seconds of (colloq)
■ ~ *vi* 1 (volver a comer) to have a second helping, to have seconds (colloq)
2 «pimientos/pepinos» to repeat; **el ajo me repite** garlic repeats on me
3 (Educ) to repeat a year/course
■ **repetirse** *v pron* (a) «fenómeno/incidente/sueño» to recur, happen again; «persona» to repeat oneself (b) (Chi) (volver a comer) to have a second helping, have seconds (colloq)

repetitivo -va *adj* repetitive

repicar [A2] *vi* to ring out, peal

repiquetear [A1] *vi* (a) «campanas» to peal, ring out (b) (golpear) «lluvia» to patter; ~ **con los dedos en la mesa** to drum *o* tap one's fingers on the table

repiqueteo *m* (a) (de campanas) ringing, pealing (b) (de lluvia) pattering, pitter-patter (colloq); (con los dedos) drumming, tapping

repisa *f* (estante) shelf; (de chimenea) mantelpiece

repita, repitas, etc ▶ REPETIR

repleto -ta *adj* (a) ‹calle/vehículo/sala› ~ **DE algo** full *o* sth, packed WITH sth; **el tren iba ~** the train was packed *o* (colloq) jam-packed (b) ‹persona› replete (frml *or* hum), full

réplica *f* (a) (copia) replica (b) (Chi, Méx) (de terremoto) aftershock

replicar [A2] *vt* (frml) to retort, reply
■ ~ *vi* 1 (argumentar) to argue 2 (Der) to reply

repoblar [A10] *vt* (a) ‹río/lago› to restock (b) (de árboles) to reforest (c) (de personas) to repopulate, resettle

repollo *m* cabbage

reponer [E22] *vt* (a) (reemplazar) ‹existencias› to replace; ‹dinero› to put back, repay; ~ **fuerzas** to get one's strength back (b) ‹funcionario/trabajador› to reinstate (c) ‹obra› to put ... on again, revive; ‹serie› to repeat, rerun; ‹película› to show ... again
■ **reponerse** *v pron* to recover

reportaje *m* (en periódico, revista) article, feature; (en televisión) report, item; (entrevista) (AmL) interview

reportar [A1] *vt* 1 ‹beneficios/pérdidas› to produce, yield; **solo me reportó disgustos** it brought *o* caused me nothing but trouble 2 (AmL) (denunciar, dar cuenta de) to report 3 (Méx) ▶ REPORTEAR
■ **reportarse** *v pron* (AmL) (presentarse) to report

reporte *m* (Méx) (informe) report; (queja) complaint

reportear [A1] *vt* (Andes) to cover, report on
■ ~ *vi* (Andes) to report

reportero -ra *m,f* reporter; ~ **gráfico** press photographer

reposacabezas *m* (*pl* ~) headrest

reposado -da *adj* [SER] ‹persona/temperamento› calm; ‹ademanes/habla› unhurried

reposar [A1] *vi* (a) (descansar) «persona» to rest; «restos mortales» to lie (b) «líquido/solución» to settle; **dejar ~ la masa** let the dough stand

reposición *f* (a) (reemplazo) replacement (b) (de serie) repeat, rerun; (de obra) revival; (de película) reshowing

reposo *m* (a) (descanso) rest (b) (Coc): **dejar en ~** leave to stand

repostar [A1] *vt* ‹gasolina› to fill up with; ‹provisiones› to stock up with
■ ~ *vi* (Auto) to fill up, to get some gas (AmE) *o* (BrE) petrol; (Aviac, Náut) to refuel

repostería *f* confectionery, baking (*of pastries, desserts*)

repostero -ra *m,f* (persona) confectioner, pastrycook

reprender [E1] *vt* to scold, tell ... off (colloq)

represa *f* (a) (en río — dique) dam; (— embalse) reservoir (b) (de molino) millpond

represalia *f* reprisal; **como *o* por ...** in retaliation for ...

representación *f* 1 (acción) representation; ~ **legal** legal representation; **asistió en ~ del Rey** she attended as the King's representative; **en ~** ····>

de mis compañeros on behalf of my companions [2] (delegación) delegation [3] (Teatr) performance, production [4] (símbolo) representation

representante *mf* representative; (de artista, cantante) agent; **es ~ de una editorial** she represents a publishing house

representar [A1] *vt* [1] ⟨*persona/ organización/país*⟩ to represent [2] ⟨*obra*⟩ to perform, put on; ⟨*papel*⟩ to play [3] (aparentar) to look; **no representa su edad** he doesn't look his age [4] (simbolizar) to represent, symbolize [5] (reproducir) «*dibujo/fotografía/escena*» to show, depict; «*obra/novela*» to portray, depict [6] (equivaler a, significar) to represent; **esto representa un aumento del 5%** this represents a 5% increase; **eso ~ía tres días de trabajo** that would mean *o* involve three days' work

representativo -va *adj* representative

represión *f* repression

reprimenda *f* reprimand

reprimido -da *adj* repressed
∎ *m,f*: **es un ~** he's repressed

reprimir [I1] *vt* **(a)** ⟨*rebelión*⟩ to suppress, crush **(b)** ⟨*risa/llanto/bostezo*⟩ to suppress, stifle **(c)** (Psic) to repress
∎ **reprimirse** *v pron* (*refl*) to control oneself

reprobar [A10] *vt* **(a)** ⟨*actitud/conducta*⟩ to condemn **(b)** (AmL) ⟨*estudiante/materia/curso*⟩ to fail; **me ~on en física** I failed physics

reprochar [A1] *vt* to reproach; **~le algo a algn** to reproach sb for sth

reproche *m* reproach; **hacerle ~s a algn** to reproach sb

reproducción *f* reproduction

reproducir [I6] *vt* to reproduce
∎ **reproducirse** *v pron* **(a)** (Biol, Bot) to reproduce, breed **(b)** «*fenómeno*» to recur, happen again

reproductor -tora *adj* ⟨*animal*⟩ breeding (*before n*); ⟨*órgano*⟩ reproductive

reptar [A1] *vi* «*serpiente*» to slither; «*cocodrilo*» to crawl, slide

reptil *m* reptile

república *f* republic

República Dominicana *f* Dominican Republic

republicano -na *adj/m,f* republican

República Oriental del Uruguay *f* (fml) *official name of Uruguay*

repudiar [A1] *vt* [1] ⟨*atentado/violencia*⟩ to condemn [2] (Der) ⟨*mujer*⟩ to disown, repudiate (fml); ⟨*herencia*⟩ to repudiate

repuesto *m* (pieza) (spare) part; **de ~** spare (*before n*)

repugnancia *f*: **me causa ~** I find him repulsive *o* repugnant; **siento ~ hacia las culebras** I find snakes repulsive

repugnante *adj* ⟨*olor*⟩ disgusting, revolting; ⟨*crimen*⟩ abhorrent, repugnant; ⟨*persona*⟩ (físicamente) repulsive, revolting; (moralmente) repugnant

repugnar [A1] *vi*: **me repugna beber de un vaso sucio** I find having to drink out of a dirty glass disgusting; **me repugna su comportamiento** I find his behavior disgusting *o* repulsive

repulsa *f* (condena) condemnation; (rechazo) rejection

repulsivo -va *adj* ⟨*persona*⟩ (físicamente) repulsive, revolting; (moralmente) repugnant; ⟨*olor*⟩ disgusting, revolting

reputación *f* reputation; **~ de algo** reputation as sth

requerir [I11] *vt* **(a)** (necesitar) to require **(b)** ⟨*documento*⟩ to require **(c)** ⟨*persona*⟩ to summon

requesón *m* curd (cheese)

requisar [A1] *vt* **(a)** (expropiar) ⟨*vehículo/ suministros*⟩ to requisition; (confiscar) ⟨*drogas/ objetos robados*⟩ to seize **(b)** (Col, Ven) (registrar) to search

requisito *m* requirement; **reunir los ~s** to fulfill *o* meet the requirements; **~ previo** prerequisite

res *f* **(a)** (animal) animal **(b)** (Col, Méx, Ven) (Coc) *tb* **carne de ~** beef

resaca *f* [1] (de las olas) undertow [2] (después de beber) hangover

resaltador *m* (Col) highlighter

resaltante *adj* (AmL) outstanding

resaltar [A1] *vi* (sobresalir, destacarse) to stand out; **hacer ~** ⟨*color*⟩ to bring out; ⟨*importancia/ necesidad*⟩ to highlight, stress
∎ ~ *vt* ⟨*cualidad/importancia/necesidad*⟩ to highlight

resarcir [I4] *vt* **~ a algn DE algo** ⟨*de daños/ inconvenientes*⟩ to compensate sb FOR sth; ⟨*de gastos*⟩ to reimburse sb FOR sth
∎ **resarcirse** *v pron* **~se DE algo** (desquitarse) to get one's own back FOR sth; (compensar) to make up FOR sth

resbalada *f* (AmL) slip

resbaladilla *f* (Méx) slide, chute

resbaladizo -za *adj* **(a)** ⟨*superficie/carretera*⟩ slippery **(b)** ⟨*asunto/tema*⟩ delicate, tricky (colloq)

resbalar [A1] *vi* [1] (caerse) to slip; **las lágrimas le resbalaban por las mejillas** the tears ran *o* trickled down his cheeks [2] (fam) (ser indiferente): **todo lo que le digas le resbala** anything you say to him is just like water off a duck's back (colloq); **todo le resbala** he couldn't care less about anything (colloq)
∎ **resbalarse** *v pron* (caerse) to slip

resbalín *m* (Chi) slide, chute

resbalón *m* slip

resbaloso -sa *adj* (AmL) ⟨*superficie*⟩ slippery

rescatar [A1] *vt* **(a)** (salvar) to rescue **(b)** ⟨*dinero/pulsera*⟩ to recover, get back

rescate *m* **(a)** (salvamento) rescue; **equipo de ~** rescue team **(b)** (precio) ransom **(c)** (de dinero, joya) recovery

rescoldo *m* embers (*pl*)

resecar [A2] *vt* ⟨*piel/ambiente*⟩ to make ... very dry
∎ **resecarse** *v pron* to dry up, get very dry

reseco -ca *adj* ⟨*planta*⟩ dried-up; ⟨*pan*⟩ dry; ⟨*tierra/garganta*⟩ parched

resentido -da *adj* (dolorido) painful **(b)** (disgustado) upset, hurt; (con rencor) resentful
∎ *m,f*: **es un ~** he has a chip on his shoulder

resentimiento *m* resentment, bitterness

resentirse [I11] *v pron* **(a)** (sentir dolor): **aún se resiente de la lesión** he is still suffering the effects of the injury; **aún se resienten de la derrota** they're still smarting from the defeat **(b)** (sufrir las consecuencias) «*salud/trabajo*» to suffer **(c)** (ofenderse, molestarse) to get upset

reseña *f* **(a)** (de congreso, reunión) summary, report; (de libro) review; **una ∼ biográfica** a biographical outline **(b)** (descripción) description; (sobre escritor, deportista) profile

reserva *f* **1** (de habitación, pasaje) reservation; (de mesa) booking, reservation; **¿tiene ∼?** do you have a reservation?, have you booked?
2 (cantidad guardada) reserve; **tengo otro par de ∼** I have a spare pair
3 (a) (Dep) (equipo) reserves (*pl*), reserve team; (conjunto de suplentes) substitutes (*pl*) **(b)** (de indígenas) reservation; (de animales) reserve; **∼ natural** nature reserve
4 (secreto, discreción): **en la más absoluta ∼** in the strictest confidence
5 reservas *fpl* **(a)** (dudas) reservations (*pl*) **(b)** (reparos): **habló sin ∼s** he talked openly *o* freely
6 (Méx): **a ∼ de que (no) llueva** as long as *o* provided (that) it doesn't rain
■ *mf* (Dep) reserve

reservación *f* (AmL) ▶ RESERVA 1

reservado -da *adj* «*persona/actitud*» reserved; «*asunto/tema*» confidential; *ver tb* RESERVAR

reservar [A1] *vt* **(a)** «*asiento/habitación/mesa*» to reserve, book; «*pasaje/billete*» to book
2 (guardar) «*porción de comida/dinero*» to set aside; **nos reservaba una sorpresa** he had a surprise in store for us; **reservó lo mejor para el final** she kept the best till last
■ **reservarse** *v pron* **(a)** (para sí mismo) «*porción/ porcentaje*» to keep ... for oneself; **∼se la opinión** to reserve judgment **(b)** (*refl*) (para otra tarea) to save oneself

resfriado¹ -da *adj*: **estoy (algo) ∼** I have a (slight) cold

resfriado² *m* cold

resfriarse [A17] *v pron* to catch a cold

resfrío *m* (esp AmS) cold

resguardar [A1] *vt* **∼ algo/a algn DE algo** «*de peligro/frío*» to protect sth/sb FROM sth
■ **resguardarse** *v pron* (de peligro) to protect oneself; (de la lluvia, el frío) to shelter, take shelter

resguardo *m* **1** (Esp) (de depósito) deposit slip; (en tintorería, zapatería) slip, ticket **2** (Col) (reserva) reservation, reserve **3** (Méx) (control, vigilancia) control

residencia *f* **1 (a)** (en país, ciudad) residence; **fijar ∼** to take up residence **(b)** (documento) *tb* **permiso de ∼** residence permit **2 (a)** (casa) residence **(b)** (de estudiantes) dormitory (AmE), hall of residence (BrE); (de enfermeras) hostel, home; **∼ de ancianos** old people's home **(c)** (hostal, fonda) boarding house, guest house (*not providing meals*) **3** (AmL) (Med) residency (AmE), time spent as a houseman (BrE)

residencial *adj* residential
■ *f* (CS) guest house, boarding house

residente *adj* resident
■ *m,f* **(a)** (en país) resident **(b)** (médico) resident (AmE), houseman (BrE)

residir [I1] *vi* **(a)** «*persona*» to live, reside (frml) **(b)** «*encanto/interés*» (radicar) **∼ EN algo** to lie IN sth

residuo *m* **(a)** (Mat) remainder; (Quím) residue **(b) residuos** *mpl* (desperdicios) waste, waste materials *o* products (*pl*); **∼s radiactivos** radioactive waste

resignación *f* resignation

resignado -da *adj* resigned; **∼ A algo** resigned TO sth

resignarse [A1] *v pron* to resign oneself; **∼ a hacer algo** to resign oneself to doing sth

resina *f* resin

resistencia *f* **1 (a)** (en general) resistance **(b)** (aguante físico) stamina; **prueba de ∼** endurance test **2** (componente de circuito) resistor; (de secador, calentador) element

resistente *adj* «*material/metal*» resistant, tough; «*tela*» tough, hard-wearing; «*persona/ animal/planta*» tough, hardy; **∼ al calor** heat-resistant

resistir [I1] *vt* **(a)** (aguantar) «*dolor/calor/ presión*» to withstand, take; **no la resisto** (Col, Per fam) I can't stand her **(b)** «*tentación/impulso*» to resist «*ataque/enemigo*» to resist
■ **∼** *vi* **(a)** (aguantar) «*cuerda/puerta*» to hold; **ya no resisto más** I can't take (it) any more **(b)** «*ejército*» to hold out, resist
■ **resistirse** *v pron* **(a)** (oponer resistencia) to resist **(b)** (tener reticencia): **se resiste a aceptarlo** she's unwilling *o* reluctant to agree to it; **me resisto a creerlo** I find it hard to believe

resolución *f* **1** (de problema) solution; (de conflicto) settlement, resolution **2** (decisión) decision; **tomar una ∼** to make a decision; **tomaron la ∼ de emigrar** they decided to emigrate **3** (determinación) determination, resolve

resolver [E11] *vt* **(a)** «*crimen/problema/ misterio*» to solve, clear up; «*asunto/conflicto*» to resolve, settle; «*duda*» to clear up; **tiene resuelto su futuro** his future is sorted out **(b)** (decidir) to decide

resonancia *f* (Mús, Fís) resonance; (eco) echo; (de noticia, suceso) impact

resonante *adj* «*sonido*» resonant; «*éxito*» resounding, tremendous

resonar [A10] *vi* **(a)** (hacer eco) to echo, resound **(b)** «*gritos/risas*» to ring (out)

resoplar [A1] *vi* (por cansancio) to puff; (por enfado) to snort

resoplido *m* **(a)** (de enfado) snort **(b)** (cansancio): **dando ∼s** puffing and panting **(c)** (de caballo) snort

resorte *m* **(a)** (muelle) spring **(b)** (AmC, Col, Méx) (elástico) elastic

resortera *f* (Méx) slingshot (AmE), catapult (BrE)

respaldar [A1] *vt* «*persona*» (apoyar) to support, back; (en discusión) to back up; «*propuesta/plan*» to support, back; «*versión/teoría*» to support, back up

respaldo *m* **(a)** (de asiento) back **(b)** (apoyo) support, backing; **en ∼ de** in support of **(c)** (Fin) backing

respectar [A1] *vi* (en *3ª pers*): **en** *o* **por lo que a mí respecta** as far as I'm concerned

respectivo -va *adj* (correspondiente) respective

respecto *m*: **a este ∼** on this respect, in this regard (frml); **(con) ∼ a algo** regarding sth, with regard to sth

r

respetable adj ⟨digno de respeto⟩ respectable; (considerable) considerable

respetar [A1] vt (a) ⟨persona⟩ to respect; **se hizo ∼ por todos** he won o gained everyone's respect (b) ⟨opinión/tradiciones⟩ to respect; ⟨señal/luz roja⟩ to obey; ⟨ley/norma⟩ to observe

respeto m (a) (consideración, deferencia) respect; **con ∼** respectfully, with respect; **por ∼ a algn/algo** out of consideration o respect for sb/sth; **faltarle al** or (CS) **el ∼ a algn** to be rude o disrespectful to sb; **presentaron sus ∼s a ...** they paid their repects to ... (frml) (b) (temor): **su presencia impone ∼** her presence commands (a feeling of) respect; **les tengo mucho ∼ a los perros** I have a healthy respect for dogs

respetuoso -sa adj ⟨persona/silencio⟩ respectful

respingado -da adj (AmL) ⟨nariz⟩ turned-up

respingo m start; **dio un ∼** he gave a start

respingón -gona adj (a) ⟨nariz⟩ turned-up (b) (Méx fam) ⟨persona⟩ touchy

respiración f (Fisiol) breathing, respiration (frml); **me quedé sin ∼** I was out of breath; **contener la ∼** to hold one's breath; **∼ boca a boca** mouth-to-mouth resuscitation, kiss of life

respirar [A1] vi to breathe; **respire hondo** take a deep breath
■ ∼ vt (a) ⟨aire⟩ to breathe; ⟨humo/gases⟩ to breathe in (b) ⟨tranquilidad⟩: **la paz que se respira aquí** the feeling of peace that you get here

respiratorio -ria adj respiratory

respiro m (descanso) break; **tomarse un ∼** to take a break o (colloq) have a breather

resplandecer [E3] vi «sol» to shine; «luna/metal/cristal» to gleam; «hoguera» to blaze

resplandeciente adj (a) ⟨luna/metal/cristal⟩ gleaming (b) (limpio) ⟨sol⟩ dazzling ⟨cocina/coche⟩ sparkling clean

resplandor m (del sol) glare, brightness; (de luna, metal, cristal) gleam; (de relámpago, explosión) flash

responder [E1] vi ① (a) (contestar) to reply, answer, respond (frml); **respondió con una evasiva** he gave an evasive reply (b) (replicar) to answer back
② (reaccionar) to respond; **∼ A algo** ⟨a amenaza/estímulo⟩ to respond TO sth
③ (corresponder): **no responden a la descripción** they do not answer the description; **las cifras no responden a la realidad** the figures do not reflect the true situation
④ (responsabilizarse): **si ocurre algo, yo no respondo** if anything happens I will not be held responsible; **∼ ante la justicia** to answer for one's acts in a court of law; **yo respondo de su integridad** I will vouch for his integrity; **no respondo de lo que hizo** I am not responsible for what he did; **∼ POR algn** to vouch FOR sb
■ ∼ vt (a) (contestar) to reply, answer (b) ⟨pregunta⟩ to answer (c) ⟨llamada/carta⟩ to answer, reply to

respondón -dona adj (fam) ⟨niño⟩ mouthy (AmE colloq), cheeky (BrE colloq)
■ m,f (fam): **es un ∼** he's always answering back

responsabilidad f responsibility; **un puesto de mucha ∼** a post which involves a great deal of responsibility; **tener sentido de la ∼** to have a sense of responsibility; **cargó con toda la ∼** she took full responsibility

responsabilizar [A4] vt **∼ a algn DE algo** to hold sb responsible o accountable FOR sth
■ **responsabilizarse** v pron to take responsibility; **∼se DE algo** ⟨de tarea/error/accidente⟩ to take responsibility FOR sth; ⟨de atentado⟩ to claim responsibility FOR sth; ⟨de delito⟩ to admit responsibility FOR sth

responsable adj [SER] (concienzudo) responsible; **∼ DE algo** ⟨de tarea/error⟩ responsible FOR sth; (culpable) responsible FOR sth; ⟨de accidente/delito⟩ liable FOR sth; **nadie se ha hecho ∼ del atentado** no one has claimed responsibility for the attack
■ mf: **el ∼ de ventas** the person responsible for sales; **los ∼s serán castigados** those responsible will be punished

respuesta f (a) (a carta, mensaje) reply, answer, response (frml) (b) (reacción) response (c) (solución) answer, solution

resquebrajar [A1] vt ⟨loza/roca⟩ to crack; ⟨madera⟩ to split
■ **resquebrajarse** v pron «loza/roca» to crack; «madera» to split

resquicio m ① (grieta) crack; (abertura) gap ② (huella, resto) trace

resta f subtraction

restablecer [E3] vt ⟨relaciones/comunicaciones⟩ to re-establish; ⟨orden/democracia/normalidad⟩ to restore
■ **restablecerse** v pron to recover

restablecimiento m (de relaciones, comunicaciones) re-establishment; (de orden, paz) restoration; (de enfermo) recovery

restante adj remaining

restantes mpl/fpl: **los ∼s** the rest, the remainder

restar [A1] vt (a) (Mat) ⟨número⟩ to subtract, take away; **∼ algo DE algo** to take (away) o subtract sth FROM sth (b) ⟨gastos/cantidad⟩ to deduct, take away (c) (quitar): **∼le importancia a algo** to minimize o play down the importance of sth
■ ∼ vi ① (Mat) to subtract, take away ② (Esp) (Dep) to return (service)

restauración f restoration

restaurante m restaurant

restaurar [A1] vt to restore

resto m ① (a) (lo demás, lo que queda) **el ∼** the rest (b) (Mat) remainder ② **restos** mpl (humanos, arqueológicos) remains (pl); (de avión, barco siniestrado) wreckage; (de comida) leftovers (pl) ③ (Esp) (Dep) return (of service)

restregar [A7] *vt* ⟨*suelo*⟩ to scrub; ⟨*ropa*⟩ to rub, scrub
■ **restregarse** *v pron* (*refl*) ⟨*ojos/mejilla*⟩ to rub

restricción *f* restriction

restringido -da *adj* ⟨*libertad*⟩ restricted, limited; ⟨*posibilidades/cantidad*⟩ limited

restringir [I7] *vt* to restrict

resucitar [A1] *vt* **(a)** (Relig) to raise ... from the dead, to bring ... back to life **(b)** (Med) to resuscitate, revive **(c)** ⟨*costumbres/rencores*⟩ to revive, resurrect
■ ~ *vi* «*persona*» to rise (from the dead); «*costumbre/grupo*» to take on a new lease of life

resuelto -ta *adj* **(a)** [SER] ⟨*persona*⟩ decisive; **en tono** ~ decisively **(b)** [ESTAR] (decidido) determined, resolved (frml); *ver tb* RESOLVER

resultado *m* result; **como** ~ **de** as a result of; **mi idea dio** ~ my idea worked; **intentó convencerlo, pero sin** ~ she tried to persuade him, but without success *o* to no avail; ~ **final** (Dep) final score

resultar [A1] *vi* **1** (dar resultado) to work; **su idea no resultó** his idea didn't work (out) **2** (+ *compl*): **resulta más barato así** it works out cheaper this way; **me resulta simpático** I think he's very nice; **resultó ser un malentendido** it turned out to be *o* proved to be a misunderstanding; **resultó tal como lo planeamos** it turned out *o* worked out just as we planned **3** (en *3ª pers*): **ahora resulta que era periodista** now it turns out that he was a journalist **4** (derivar) ~ **EN algo** to result IN sth, lead TO sth

resumen *m* summary; **hacer un** ~ **de un texto** to summarize a text; **en** ~ in short

resumidero *m* (AmL) drain

resumir [I1] *vt* **(a)** (condensar) ⟨*texto/libro*⟩ to summarize **(b)** (recapitular) ⟨*discurso/argumento*⟩ to sum up
■ ~ *vi*: **resumiendo ... in short ..., to sum up ...

resurgir [I7] *vi* to reemerge

resurrección *f* resurrection

retachar [A1] *vt* (Méx fam) **(a)** ⟨*carta/trabajo*⟩ to reject, refuse to accept **(b)** (no dejar entrar): **nos** ~**on** they turned us away
■ ~ *vi* (Méx) «*bala*» to ricochet

retador -dora *m,f* (AmL) challenger

retaguardia *f* (Mil) rearguard

retahíla *f* string

retaliación *f* (AmL) retaliation

retar [A1] *vt* **(a)** (desafiar) to challenge **(b)** (CS) (regañar) to tell ... off (colloq), to scold

retardado -da *adj* **1** (Tec) delayed; **de apertura retardada** with time-delay lock **2** ⟨*persona*⟩ mentally handicapped *o* retarded

retardar [A1] *vt* (frenar) to delay, hold up, retard (tech); (posponer) to postpone

retén *m* **(a)** (patrulla) patrol; (pelotón) squad; (puesto de policía) police post **(b)** (Ven) (correccional) reformatory (AmE), remand home (BrE)

retener [E27] *vt* **1** **(a)** ⟨*datos/información*⟩ to keep back, withhold **(b)** ⟨*pasaporte/tarjeta*⟩ to retain **(c)** (Fin, Fisco) ⟨*dinero/cuota*⟩ to deduct, withhold **2** **(a)** «*policía*» ⟨*persona*⟩ to detain, hold **(b)** (hacer permanecer): **no te retendré mucho I**

won't keep you long **3** ⟨*calor/carga/líquidos*⟩ to retain **4** ⟨*atención/interés*⟩ to keep, retain **5** (recordar) to retain, keep ... in one's head

reticencia *f* **(a)** (renuencia) reluctance; **con** ~ reluctantly **(b)** (reserva) reticence

reticente *adj* **(a)** (reacio) reluctant **(b)** (reservado) reticent

retina *f* retina

retintín *m* (fam) (tonillo sarcástico) sarcastic tone of voice; **con** ~ sarcastically

retirada *f* **(a)** (en general) withdrawal **(b)** (Mil) retreat; **batirse en** ~ to retreat **(c)** (de actividad profesional) retirement **(d)** (de competición — antes de iniciarse) withdrawal; (— una vez iniciada) retirement

retirado -da *adj* **1** **(a)** ⟨*lugar/casa*⟩ remote, out-of-the-way; **una casa retirada de la calle** a house set back from the road; **un barrio** ~ **del centro** an outlying district **(b)** ⟨*vida*⟩ secluded, quiet **2** (jubilado) retired

retirar [A1] *vt* **1** **(a)** (quitar) to remove, take away; (apartar) to move away; **retiró la cacerola del fuego** he removed the saucepan from the heat; ~ **de la circulación** to withdraw from circulation **(b)** ⟨*cabeza/mano*⟩ to pull ... back **(c)** ⟨*embajador/tropas*⟩ to withdraw, pull out **(d)** (+ *me/te/le etc*) ⟨*apoyo*⟩ to withdraw; ⟨*pasaporte/carnet*⟩ to withdraw, take away **2** ⟨*afirmaciones/propuesta*⟩ to withdraw; **retiro lo dicho** I take back what I said **3** (de cuenta) ⟨*dinero*⟩ to withdraw
■ **retirarse** *v pron* **1** **(a)** (apartarse) to move back *o* away; (irse) to leave, withdraw **(b)** «*ejército/tropas*» to withdraw, pull out **(c)** (irse a dormir) to go to bed, retire (frml) **2** (jubilarse) to retire; (de competición — antes de iniciarse) to withdraw, pull out; (— una vez iniciada) to pull out

retiro *m* **(a)** (jubilación) retirement; (pensión) (retirement) pension **(b)** (AmL) (de fuerzas, empleados) withdrawal; (de apoyo, fondos) withdrawal

reto *m* **(a)** (desafío) challenge **(b)** (CS) (regañina) telling-off (colloq), scolding

retobar [A1] *vi* (Méx fam) to answer back

retocar [A2] *vt* ⟨*fotografía/maquillaje*⟩ to touch up, retouch

retoño *m* (Bot) shoot

retoque *m*: **dar los últimos** ~**s a algo** to put the final *o* the finishing touches to sth

retorcer [E10] *vt* to twist
■ **retorcerse** *v pron* **1** **(a)** (enrollarse) to become tangled (up) **(b)** «*serpiente*» to writhe **(c)** «*persona*»: ~**se de dolor** to writhe in agony; ▸ RISA **2** (*refl*) ⟨*manos*⟩ to wring

retorcido -da *adj* ⟨*persona/mente*⟩ twisted, devious; ⟨*estilo/argumento*⟩ convoluted, involved

retorcijón *m* (AmL) sharp pain (*in the stomach or gut*); **retorcijones de tripas** stomach cramps

retórico -ca *adj* rhetorical

retornable *adj* returnable; **no** ~ non-returnable

retornar [A1] *vi/vt* (frml *o* liter) to return

retorno *m* (frml *o* liter) (regreso, devolución) return; (viaje de regreso) return journey

retortijón *m* (Esp, Méx) ▸ RETORCIJÓN

retraído -da *adj* withdrawn, retiring (*before n*)

retransmisión *f* (a) (transmisión) transmission; ∼ **en directo** live broadcast *o* transmission (b) (repetición) repeat

retransmitir [I1] *vt* (a) (repetir) to repeat, rebroadcast (frml) (b) (Esp period) (Rad, TV) to broadcast

retrasado -da *adj* (a) [SER] (Med, Psic) mentally handicapped (b) [ESTAR] (en tarea, actividad): **está muy** ∼ **con respecto a los demás** he lags a long way behind the others; **están** ∼**s en los pagos** they are behind in their payments; **tengo trabajo** ∼ I have work to catch up on (c) ⟨país/sociedad⟩ backward (d) ⟨reloj⟩ slow
■ *m,f*: *tb* ∼ **mental** mentally handicapped person, (mentally) retarded person

retrasar [A1] *vt* (a) ⟨persona⟩ to make ... late; **el tráfico nos retrasó** we got held up in the traffic (b) ⟨producción/proceso⟩ to delay, hold up; **la niebla retrasó la salida del avión** the departure (of the plane) was delayed by fog (c) ⟨partida/fecha⟩ to postpone (d) ⟨reloj⟩ to put back
■ **retrasarse** *v pron* (a) (llegar tarde) to be late (b) «producción/trámite» to be delayed, be held up (c) (en trabajo, estudios, pagos) to fall behind; **se retrasó en presentarlo** she was late (in) submitting it (d) «reloj» to run slow

retraso *m* (a) (demora) delay; **viene con media hora de** ∼ it's (running) half an hour late; **llevamos un** ∼ **de dos meses sobre lo previsto** we're two months behind schedule (b) (de país) backwardness

retratar [A1] *vt* (a) (pintar) to paint a portrait of; (fotografiar) to photograph (b) ⟨realidad/costumbres⟩ to portray, depict

retrato *m* (Art, Fot) portrait; **ser el vivo** ∼ **de algn** to be the (spitting) image of sb (colloq) (descripción) depiction, portrayal

retreta *f* [1] (Mil) (toque) retreat [2] (AmL) (concierto) open-air concert

retribuir [I20] *vt* (a) ⟨esfuerzos/trabajo⟩ to pay (b) (recompensar) to reward (c) (AmL) ⟨favor⟩ to return

retroactivo -va *adj* retrospective, retroactive; **un aumento con efecto** ∼ **desde enero** an increase backdated to January

retroceder [E1] *vi* (a) «persona/coche» to go back, move back; «ejército» to withdraw, retreat (b) (volverse atrás) to back down

retroceso *m* (a) (movimiento hacia atrás) backward movement; (en plan, desarrollo) backward step (b) (de ejército) withdrawal, retreat (c) (Arm) recoil (d) (Ven) (Auto) reverse

retrógrado -da *adj* ⟨persona/actitud⟩ reactionary; ⟨planteamiento/idea⟩ retrograde
■ *m,f* reactionary

retroproyector *m* overhead projector

retrospectiva *f* retrospective

retrospectivo -va *adj* retrospective

retrovisor *m* (interior) (rear-view) mirror; (lateral) (wing) mirror

retumbar [A1] *vi* «voz/explosión» to boom; «eco» to resound; «paso» to echo; «trueno» to roll, boom; «habitación» to resound

reubicar [A2] *vt* (AmL) (a) ⟨trabajadores⟩ to relocate, redeploy; ⟨empresas⟩ to relocate;

⟨pobladores/damnificados⟩ to resettle (b) (cambiar de lugar) to put ... in a different place, change the position of

reuma, reúma *m or f* rheumatism

reumático -ca *adj* rheumatic

reunido -da *adj*: **estuvieron** ∼**s tres horas** the meeting lasted three hours; **está reunida** (Esp) she's in a meeting; *ver tb* REUNIR

reunificar [A2] *vt* ⟨nación⟩ to reunify; ⟨familia⟩ to reunite, bring together

reunión *f* (a) (para discutir algo) meeting; (de carácter social) gathering; (reencuentro) reunion (b) (de datos, información) gathering, collecting

reunir [I23] *vt* [1] ⟨cualidades/características⟩ to have; ⟨requisitos⟩ to satisfy, meet; ⟨condiciones⟩ to fulfill, satisfy [2] ⟨datos⟩ to gather; ⟨dinero/fondos⟩ to raise; ⟨información⟩ to gather together, collect [3] ⟨amigos/familia⟩ to get ... together; **reunió a los jefes de sección** he called a meeting of the heads of department
■ **reunirse** *v pron* «consejo/junta» to meet; «amigos/parientes» to get together; ∼**se con algn** (encontrarse) to meet up WITH sb; (tener una reunión) to have a meeting WITH sb, meet WITH sb (AmE)

reutilizable *adj* reusable

reutilización *f* reuse, recycling

reutilizar [A4] *vt* to reuse

reválida *f* (RPl) validation

revalidación *f* (a) (Chi, Méx) (convalidación) validation (b) (Col, Ven) (del pasaporte) renewal

revalidar [A1] *vt* [1] ⟨campeonato/título⟩ to defend, win ... again; ⟨victoria⟩ to repeat [2] (a) (Chi, Méx) (convalidar) to validate (b) (Col, Ven) ⟨pasaporte⟩ to renew

revalorización *f* (a) (de una divisa) revaluation; (de una pensión) increase, adjustment (b) (de un activo) appreciation (frml), increase in value

revalorizar [A4] *vt* (a) ⟨moneda⟩ to revalue; ⟨pensiones⟩ to increase, adjust (b) ⟨sistema/situación⟩ to reassess
■ **revalorizarse** *v pron* «acciones/propiedad» to appreciate; «moneda» to gain in value

revancha *f* (a) (Dep, Jueg) return game (b) (desquite): **¡me tomaré la** ∼**!** I'll get my own back! (colloq)

revelación *f* [1] (de secreto, noticia) revelation, disclosure [2] (éxito, figura) revelation

revelado *m* developing

revelador -dora *adj* revealing

revelar [A1] *vt* (a) ⟨secreto/verdad⟩ to reveal (b) (Cin, Fot) to develop

revendedor -dora *m,f* (de entradas) scalper (AmE), ticket tout (BrE)

revender [E1] *vt* ⟨alimentos/artículos⟩ to resell; ⟨entradas⟩ to scalp (AmE), to tout (BrE); ⟨acciones⟩ to sell off

reventa *f* (de alimentos, artículos) resale; (de entradas) scalping (AmE), touting (BrE)

reventar [A5] *vi* [1] «globo» to burst, pop; «neumático» to blow out, burst; «ampolla/tubería» to burst; «ola» to break [2] (a) «persona» (uso hiperbólico): **si sigue comiendo así,**

va a ∼ if he carries on eating like that, he'll burst! **(b)** (fam) (irritar) to rile (colloq), to make ... mad (colloq); **me revienta cocinar** I hate cooking
■ ∼ *vt* ‹globo/neumático› to burst
■ **reventarse** *v pron* **(a)** «globo/tubería» ▶ REVENTAR *vi* 1 **(b)** (refl) ‹grano› to squeeze; ‹ampolla› to burst

reventón *m* **1** (de neumático) blowout; (de tubería) burst **2** (Méx fam) (fiesta) party

reverencia *f* (de hombre, niño) bow; (de mujer, niña) curtsy; **hacer una** ∼ «hombre» to bow; «mujer» to curtsy

reverendo -da *adj* **(a)** (Relig) reverend (*before n*) **(b)** (esp AmL fam) (como intensificador) (*delante del n*) ▶ SOBERANO 2

reversa *f* (Col, Méx) reverse; **meter** ∼ to put the car into reverse

reversible *adj* reversible

reverso *m* **(a)** (de papel, cuadro) back **(b)** (de moneda, medalla) reverse

revés *m* **1** **(a)** **el** ∼ (de prenda) the inside; (de tela) the back, the wrong side; (de papel, documento) the back **(b) al revés** (*loc adv*) (con lo de adelante atrás) back to front; (con lo de arriba abajo) upside down; (con lo de dentro fuera) inside out; **así no, va al** ∼ not that way, it goes the other way around *o* (BrE) round; **se puso los zapatos al** ∼ he put his shoes on the wrong feet; **todo lo entiende al** ∼ she's always getting the wrong end of the stick; **todo me sale al** ∼ nothing goes right for me; **saberse algo al** ∼ **y al derecho** to know sth (off) by heart **2** (Dep) backhand **3** (contratiempo) setback

revestir [I14] *vt* (cubrir) ‹pared/suelo› to cover; ‹cable› to sheathe, cover; ‹tubería› (con material aislante) to lag; **paredes revestidas de madera** wood-paneled walls

revienta, revientas, etc ▶ REVENTAR

revisación *f* (RPl) (Med, Odont) examination; (periódica) checkup

revisar [A1] *vt* **(a)** ‹documento› to go through, look through; ‹traducción/cuenta› to check, go through **(b)** ‹criterio/doctrina/edición› to revise **(c)** ‹máquina/instalación/frenos› to check; ‹coche› (hacer revisión periódica) (Esp) to service **(d)** (AmL) ‹equipaje/bolsillos› to search, go through **(e)** (AmL) ‹paciente› to examine; ‹dentadura› to check; **se hizo** ∼ **la dentadura** he had a dental checkup

revisión *f* **(a)** (de trabajo, documento) checking, check **(b)** (de criterio, doctrina) revision **(c)** (de instalación) inspection; (de frenos) check; (de coche) (Esp) service **(d)** (AmL) (de equipaje) inspection **(e)** (Med, Odont) checkup; ∼ **médica** (Esp) (periódica) checkup; (para trabajo) medical examination

revisor -sora *m,f* (Esp) ticket inspector

revista *f* **(a)** (publicación ilustrada) magazine; (de profesión) journal; ∼ **del corazón** real-life *o* true-romance magazine **(b)** (Espec, Teatr) revue; **teatro de** ∼ variety theater **(c)** (inspección) review; **pasar** ∼ **a las tropas** to inspect *o* review the troops

revistero *m* magazine rack

revitalizar [A4] *vt* to revitalize

revivir [I1] *vi* to revive
■ ∼ *vt* to relive

revocar [A2] *vt* **1** (Der) ‹consentimiento/ testamento› to revoke; ‹fallo› to reverse, revoke **2** (Const) ‹pared interior› to plaster; ‹pared exterior› to render

revolcar [A9] *vt*: **lo** ∼**on por el suelo** they knocked him to the ground and pushed him around
■ **revolcarse** *v pron* to roll around; (en lodo) to wallow, roll around

revolcón *m* (caída) tumble; (vuelta) roll

revolotear [A1] *vi* «mariposa» to flutter; «polilla» to flit; «pájaro» to flutter around; «papeles/hojas» to swirl around

revoltijo, revoltillo *m* (fam) **(a)** (desorden) mess, jumble **(b)** (comida, bebida) mixture, concoction

revoltoso -sa *adj* ‹niño› naughty; ‹soldados/ estudiantes› rebellious

revolución *f* revolution

revolucionar [A1] *vt* **(a)** ‹costumbres/ industria› to revolutionize **(b)** ‹niños› to get ... excited; ‹estudiantes/obreros› to stir up

revolucionario -ria *adj/m,f* revolutionary

revolver [E11] *vt* **(a)** ‹salsa/guiso› to stir; **me revuelve el estómago** it turns my stomach **(b)** (AmL) ‹dados› to shake **(c)** ‹cajones/papeles› to rummage through, go through; «ladrones» ‹casa› to turn ... upside down
■ ∼ *vi*: **revolvió en mis cosas** he rummaged through my things

revólver *m* revolver

revuelo *m* (conmoción) stir

revuelta *f* **(a)** (de civiles) uprising; (de tropas) uprising, revolt; (de estudiantes, presos) riot **(b)** (jaleo) commotion, row (colloq)

revuelto¹ -ta *adj* **(a)** (desordenado) in a mess; ‹pelo› disheveled*; **tener el estómago** ∼ to feel sick *o* nauseous **(b)** ‹mar› rough; ‹tiempo› unsettled

revuelto² *m* vegetables sautéed with egg

rey *m* **1** **(a)** (monarca) king; **los R**∼**es de Suecia** the King and Queen of Sweden; **los R**∼**es y sus hijos** the royal couple and their children **(b)** (en ajedrez, naipes) king **(c)** (como apelativo) pet (colloq), precious (colloq) **2** **Reyes** Epiphany, January 6th; **Los R**∼**es Magos** the Three Wise Men, The Three Kings

rezagado -da *adj*: **quedar(se)** ∼ to fall *o* drop behind; **iban** ∼**s** they were lagging behind; **los alumnos más** ∼**s** the slower students

rezar [A4] *vi* (Relig) to pray; ∼ **POR algn/algo** to pray FOR sb/sth; **reza por que todo salga bien** pray that everything turns out all right
■ ∼ *vt* ‹oración/rosario› to say

rezo *m* prayer

rezongar [A3] *vi* to grumble
■ ∼ *vt* (AmC, Ur fam) (regañar) to tell ... off (colloq)

rezumar [A1] *vt/vi* to ooze

RFA *f* (= **República Federal de Alemania**) FRG

ría *f* ria (long, narrow, tidal inlet)

ría, rías, etc ▶ REÍR

riachuelo *m* stream, brook

riada *f* flood; (en área más extensa) flooding

ribera *f* **(a)** (orilla — de río) bank; (— de lago, mar) shore **(b)** (vega) strand, riverside

ribete m (adorno) trimming, edging

rico -ca adj 1 (a) ⟨persona/país⟩ rich, wealthy
(b) ⟨tierra⟩ rich; ⟨vegetación⟩ lush; ⟨lenguaje/
historia⟩ rich; ~ EN algo rich IN sth 2 (a)
⟨comida⟩ good, nice; ¡esto está riquísimo! this is
delicious! (b) (esp CS) ⟨perfume⟩ nice, lovely; ¡qué
~ olor tiene! what a lovely smell! (c) (fam) (mono)
⟨niño/chica⟩ lovely, cute (d) (AmL exc RPl)
(agradable) lovely, wonderful
■ m,f (a) (m) rich o wealthy man; (f) rich o
wealthy woman; los ~s rich people, the rich (b)
(como apelativo) (fam & iró) sweetie (colloq & iro),
honey (colloq & iro)

ricura f (fam): tiene un bebé que es una ~ she
has the cutest little baby (colloq); ven, ~ come
here, darling (colloq)

ridiculez f (a) (tontería, insignificancia): lo que dijo
fue una ~ what he said was ridiculous; ¡qué ~!
that's ridiculous!; pagué una ~ por esto I paid
next to nothing for this (b) (cualidad)
ridiculousness

ridiculizar [A4] vt to ridicule

ridículo¹ -la adj (a) ⟨persona/comentario/
vestimenta⟩ ridiculous; lo ~ de la situación era
que ... the ridiculous thing about the situation
was that ...; eso es ~ it's absurd o ridiculous (b)
⟨cantidad/precios⟩ ridiculous, ludicrous; ⟨sueldo⟩
ridiculous, laughable

ridículo² m: sentido del ~ sense of the
ridiculous o absurd; dejar or poner a algn en ~
to make a fool of sb; hacer el ~ to make a fool of
oneself

ríe, etc ▶ REÍR

riega, riegas, etc ▶ REGAR

riego m (a) (Agr) irrigation (b) falta de ~
sanguíneo insufficient blood supply

riel m rail

rienda f rein; aflojar las ~s to slacken the
reins; llevar las ~s to be in charge o control;
tomar las ~s to take charge

riesgo m risk; un ~ para la salud a health
hazard; a ~ de perder su amistad at the risk of
losing his friendship; ~s que hay que correr
risks you have to take; corres el ~ de perderlo
you run the risk of losing it; un seguro a or
contra todo ~ an all-risks o a comprehensive
insurance policy

riesgoso -sa adj (AmL) risky

rifa f (sorteo) raffle, draw

rifar [A1] vt to raffle

rifle m rifle

rigidez f (a) (de material) stiffness, rigidity; (de
un miembro) stiffness (b) (de ley, doctrina, horario)
inflexibility; (de educación, dieta) strictness

rígido -da adj (a) ⟨material⟩ rigid, stiff (b)
⟨educación/dieta⟩ strict; ⟨regla/horario/carácter⟩
inflexible; ⟨actitud⟩ rigid, inflexible; ⟨moral/
principios⟩ strict

rigor m (en general) rigor*; (de medidas, castigo)
harshness, severity; con todo el ~ de la ley with

the full rigor of the law; el ~ del invierno the
rigors of winter; con ~ rigorously, strictly; los
saludos de ~ the usual greetings

riguroso -sa adj (a) ⟨método⟩ rigorous; ⟨dieta/
control/orden⟩ strict; ⟨examen⟩ thorough;
rigurosas medidas de seguridad tight security (b)
⟨juez⟩ harsh; ⟨maestro⟩ strict; ⟨castigo⟩ severe,
harsh (c) ⟨invierno⟩ hard; ⟨clima⟩ harsh

rima f (de sonidos) rhyme

rimar [A1] vi to rhyme

rimbombante adj ⟨estilo⟩ grandiose,
overblown; ⟨palabras⟩ high-flown; ⟨boda/fiesta⟩
ostentatious, showy

rímel m mascara

rin m 1 (Col, Méx) (rueda) wheel; (llanta) rim
2 (Per) (teléfono) public telephone; (ficha)
(telephone) token

rincón m 1 (de habitación, armario) corner
2 (lugar) spot, place; bellos rincones de Perú
beautiful places o spots in Peru; registraron hasta
el último ~ de la casa they searched every nook
and cranny of the house

ring /rrin/ m (pl rings) (Dep) ring

rinoceronte m rhinoceros

riña f (a) (pelea) fight; ~ de gallos (AmS)
cockfight (b) (discusión) quarrel, argument, row
(colloq)

riñón m (a) (Anat) kidney (b) (Coc) kidney (c)
riñones mpl (fam) (espalda baja) lower part of the
back, kidneys (pl)

río m river; ~ abajo/arriba downstream/
upstream; el R~ de la Plata the River Plate

río, rio, etc ▶ REÍR

Río de Janeiro m Rio de Janeiro

rioplatense adj of/from the River Plate

riqueza f (a) (bienes) wealth; las ~s del museo
the treasures of the museum (b) (recursos): las ~s
del suelo the earth's riches; las ~s naturales de
un país a country's natural resources (c)
(variedad, abundancia) richness

risa f laugh; una risita nerviosa a nervous giggle
o laugh; ¡qué ~! what a laugh!, how funny!; entre
las ~s del público amid laughter from the
audience; me entró la ~ I got the giggles; da ~
oírla hablar it's very funny hearing her talk;
morirse de (la) ~ (fam) to die laughing (colloq);
estábamos muertos de (la) ~ we were killing
ourselves laughing (colloq); retorcerse de la ~ to
double up with laughter; tomarse algo a ~ (fam)
to treat sth as a joke

risotada f guffaw

risueño -ña adj ⟨cara/expresión⟩ smiling;
⟨persona⟩ cheerful; ⟨porvenir/perspectivas⟩ bright

rítmico -ca adj rhythmic, rhythmical

ritmo m (a) (compás) rhythm; al ~ de la música
to the rhythm of the music, in time to the music;
llevaba el ~ con los pies he kept time with his
feet; seguir el ~ to keep in time, follow the beat
(b) (velocidad) pace, speed; llevan un buen ~ de

trabajo they work at a steady pace *o* speed; **a este ∼ no terminaremos nunca** at this rate we'll never finish; **el ∼ de crecimiento** the rate of growth

rito *m* (Relig) rite; (costumbre) ritual

ritual *adj/m* ritual

rival *adj* rival (*before n*)
■ *mf* rival; **sin ∼** unrivaled

rivalidad *f* rivalry

rizado -da *adj* ⟨pelo⟩ curly; ⟨mar⟩ slightly choppy

rizar [A4] *vt* ⟨pelo/melena⟩ to curl, perm
■ **rizarse** *v pron* (a) «pelo» (con la humedad) to frizz, go frizzy (b) (*refl*) ⟨pelo⟩ to curl

rizo *m* (a) (de pelo) curl (b) (Tex) bouclé (c) (Aviac) loop

róbalo *m* sea bass

robar [A1] *vt* 1 (a) ⟨dinero/bolso⟩ to steal; ⟨banco⟩ to rob; **∼le algo A algn** to steal sth FROM sb; **le robó dinero a su jefe** he stole some money from his boss; **le robaron el bolso** she had her bag stolen; ⟨raptar⟩ ⟨niño⟩ to abduct, kidnap 2 (estafar) to cheat, rip off (colloq) 3 (Jueg) (en naipes, dominó) to draw, pick up (colloq)
■ ∼ *vi* to steal; **∼on en la casa de al lado** the house next door was broken into; **¡me han robado!** I've been robbed!

roble *m* (árbol) oak (tree); (madera) oak

robo *m* (a) (en banco, museo) robbery; (hurto de dinero, objeto) theft; **∼ a mano armada** armed robbery (b) (en vivienda) burglary; (forzando la entrada) break-in (c) (fam) (estafa) rip-off (colloq)

robot *m* (*pl* **-bots**) robot

robustecer [E3] *vt* to strengthen
■ **robustecerse** *v pron* to become *o* grow stronger

robustez *f* robustness, sturdiness

robusto -ta *adj* ⟨árbol⟩ robust, strong; ⟨persona⟩ robust, sturdy; ⟨construcción⟩ sturdy

roca *f* rock

roce *m* (a) (contacto) rubbing; (fricción) friction; **no soporta el ∼ de la sábana** he can't bear the sheet rubbing against his skin; **el ∼ de su mejilla** the brush of her cheek; **tiene los puños gastados por el ∼** his cuffs are worn (b) (trato frecuente) regular contact (c) (desacuerdo): **∼s dentro del partido** friction within the party; **tener un ∼ con algn** to have a brush with sb

rociar [A17] *vt* (con pulverizador) to spray; **lo ∼on de keroseno** they doused it with kerosene; **rocíelo con limón** sprinkle with lemon

rocío *m* dew; **una gota de ∼** a dewdrop

rock *adj inv* rock (*before n*)
■ *m* rock music; **∼ duro** *or* (AmL) **pesado** hard rock

rockero -ra *adj* ⟨grupo/ambiente⟩ rock (*before n*)
■ *m,f* rock artist *o* musician, rocker (colloq)

rocola *f* (AmL) jukebox

rocoso -sa *adj* rocky

rocote, rocoto *m* (AmS) hot pepper

rodaballo *m* turbot

rodachina *f* (Col) caster, roller

rodaja *f* slice; **en ∼s** sliced

rodaje *m* (a) (Cin) filming, shooting (b) (Auto) breaking-in (AmE), running-in (BrE); **estar en ∼** to be breaking in (AmE) *o* (BrE) running in

rodapié *m* baseboard (AmE), skirting board (BrE)

rodar [A10] *vi* 1 «moneda/pelota» to roll; «rueda» to go round, turn; **la moneda rodó por la mesa** the coin rolled across the table; **rodó escaleras abajo** she went tumbling down the stairs 2 (Cin) to film, shoot; **¡se rueda!** action!
■ ∼ *vt* (Cin) to shoot, film

rodeado -da *adj* **∼ DE algo** surrounded BY sth

rodear [A1] *vt* (a) ⟨edificio/persona⟩ to surround; **∼ algo DE algo** to surround sth WITH sth; **las circunstancias que ∼on su muerte** the circumstances surrounding his death; **le rodeó la cintura con los brazos** he put his arms around her waist (b) (AmL) ⟨ganado⟩ to round up 2 (estar alrededor de) to surround; **todos los que lo rodean** everyone who works with him/knows him
■ **rodearse** *v pron* **∼se DE algo/algn** to surround oneself WITH sth/sb

rodeo *m* (a) (desvío) detour; **dar un ∼** to make a detour; **andarse con ∼s** to beat about the bush (b) (Espec) rodeo

rodilla *f* knee; **ponerse de ∼s** to kneel down, to get down on one's knees

rodillera *f* (a) (Dep) kneepad; (Med) knee bandage (b) (remiendo) knee patch

rodillo *m* (de cocina) rolling pin; (para pintar) paint roller; (de máquina de escribir) roller, platen

roedor -dora *m,f* rodent

roer [E13] *vt* ⟨hueso/cable⟩ to gnaw (at)

rogar [A8] *vt*: **te lo ruego** I beg you; **se ruega no fumar** you are kindly requested not to smoke; **te ruego que me perdones** please forgive me; **le rogó que tuviera misericordia** she begged him to have mercy
■ ∼ *vi* (Relig) to pray; **roguemos al Señor** let us pray; **hacerse (de)** *or* (Méx) **(del) ∼** to play hard to get; **aceptó sin hacerse (de) ∼** he accepted immediately, without any persuading

rojizo -za *adj* reddish

rojo¹ -ja *adj* 1 (a) ⟨color/vestido⟩ red; **ponerse ∼** «persona» to blush, turn red; «semáforo» to turn red, go red (BrE); **ponerse ∼ de ira** to turn *o* (BrE) go red with anger (b) ⟨piel⟩ (por el sol) sunburnt, red 2 (pey *o* hum) (Pol) (a) (de izquierda) red (pej *or* hum), commie (pej *or* hum) (b) (en la Guerra Civil española) Republican
■ *m,f* (pey *o* hum) (a) (izquierdista) red (pej *or* hum), commie (pej *or* hum) (b) (en la Guerra Civil española) Republican

rojo² *m* red; **al ∼ vivo** ⟨metal⟩ red-hot

rol *m* (a) (lista) roll, list (b) (papel) role

rolar [A1] *vi* (Méx fam) (dar vueltas) to wander around
■ ∼ *vt* (Méx fam) ⟨persona⟩ to move
■ **rolarse** *v pron* (recípr) (Méx fam) (turnarse) to take turns; **tenemos que ∼nos el libro** we have to take turns with the book *o* pass the book around

rollizo -za *adj* chubby

rollo *m* 1 (a) (de papel, tela, película) roll (b) (de cable, cuerda) reel (c) (fam) (de gordura) roll of fat 2 (a) (Esp fam) (cosa aburrida) bore; **¡qué ∼ de conferencia!** what a boring lecture! (b) (Esp, Méx fam) (lata) nuisance, pain (colloq); **¡qué ∼!** what a nuisance *o* pain! 3 (fam) (a) (perorata) speech (colloq), lecture   ⋯▷

(colloq); **siempre nos suelta el mismo ~** he always gives us the same speech; **bueno, corta el ~ ya** OK, can it, will you? (AmE colloq), OK, put a sock in it, will you? (BrE colloq) **(b)** (mentira) story ④ (Esp, Méx fam) (asunto) business
■ *adj inv* (Esp fam) boring; **¡qué tío más ~!** that guy's such a pain o bore! (colloq)

Roma *f* Rome

romance *m* romance

románico -ca *adj* ⟨arquitectura/columna⟩ Romanesque; ⟨lengua⟩ Romance (*before n*)

romano -na *adj* (Hist) Roman; (de la ciudad) of/ from Rome, Roman
■ *m,f* (Hist) Roman; (de la ciudad) person from Rome

romanticismo *m* (Art, Lit, Mús) Romanticism; (sentimentalismo) romanticism

romántico -ca *adj/m,f* (Art, Lit, Mús) Romantic; (sentimental) romantic

rombo *m* **(a)** (Mat) rhombus **(b)** (carta) diamond **(c) rombos** *mpl* (palo) diamonds (*pl*)

romería *f* **(a)** (Relig) procession (*to a local shrine, gen followed by festivities*) **(b)** (AmL fam) (multitud) mass, crowd

romero *m* (Bot, Coc) rosemary

rompecabezas *m* (*pl* ~) puzzle

rompehielos *m* (*pl* ~) icebreaker

rompeolas *m* (*pl* ~) breakwater

romper [E30] *vt* ① **(a)** ⟨loza/mueble⟩ to break; ⟨ventana⟩ break, smash; ⟨lápiz/cuerda⟩ to break, snap **(b)** ⟨hoja/póster⟩ (rasgar) to tear; (en varios pedazos) to tear up **(c)** ⟨camisa⟩ to tear, split ② **(a)** ⟨silencio/monotonía⟩ to break; ⟨tranquilidad⟩ to disturb **(b)** ⟨promesa/pacto⟩ to break; ⟨relaciones/compromiso⟩ to break off
■ ~ *vi* ① **(a)** ⟨olas⟩ to break **(b)** (liter) «alba» to break; **al ~ el día** at daybreak, at the crack of dawn **(c)** (empezar): **rompió a llorar/reír** she burst into tears/burst out laughing
② «novios» to break up, split up; **~ CON algn** ⟨con novio⟩ to split o break up WITH sb; **~ CON algo** ⟨con el pasado⟩ to break WITH sth; ⟨con tradición⟩ to break away FROM sth
■ **romperse** *v pron* **(a)** «vaso/plato» to break, smash, get broken o smashed; «papel» to tear, rip, get torn o ripped; «televisor/ascensor» (RPl) to break down **(b)** «pantalones/zapatos» to wear out **(c)** (refl) ⟨brazo/pierna⟩ to break

rompevientos *m* (*pl* ~) (Méx, RPl) (pulóver) sweater; (anorak) windbreaker (AmE), windcheater (BrE)

ron *m* **(a)** (bebida) rum **(b)** (Per) (combustible) methanol

roncar [A2] *vi* (al dormir) to snore; (dormir) (fam) to sleep

roncha *f* (Med) (por picadura de insecto) bump; **se llenó de ~s** she came out in a rash

ronco -ca *adj* **(a)** ⟨persona⟩ hoarse; **se quedó ~ de tanto gritar** he shouted himself hoarse **(b)** ⟨voz⟩ husky

ronda *f* ① (de soldado, guarda) patrol; (de enfermera) round; (de policía) patrol, beat; **hacer la ~** «policía» to patrol one's beat; «soldado/ guarda» to be on patrol; «repartidor» to do one's round ② (vuelta, etapa) round; (de bebidas) round ③ (CS, Per) (de niños): **formaron una ~**

tomándose de la mano they held hands in a circle; **danzaban en ~** they were dancing around in a circle ④ (Esp, Méx) (serenata) serenade

rondar [A1] *vt* **(a)** «vigilante/patrulla» to patrol **(b)** «pensamiento»: **hace días que me ronda esa idea** that idea has been going round and round in my head for days **(c)** ⟨lugar⟩ to hang around **(d)** (acercarse a): **debe estar rondando los 60** she must be getting on for 60
■ ~ *vi* (merodear) to hang around

ronquido *m* snore

ronronear [A1] *vi* to purr

roña *f* ① **(a)** (mugre) dirt, grime; **lleno de ~** covered in dirt o grime **(b)** (en metal) rust **(c)** (Vet) mange ② (Méx) (juego) tag; **jugar a la ~** to play tag

roñoso -sa *adj* ① [ESTAR] **(a)** (mugriento) grubby **(b)** (oxidado) rusty **(c)** (Vet) mangy ② [SER] (fam) (tacaño) tight-fisted (colloq), stingy (colloq)
■ *m,f* (fam) scrooge (colloq), skinflint (colloq)

ropa *f* clothes (*pl*); **cambiarse de ~** to get changed, to change (one's clothes); **la ~ sucia** the dirty laundry; **tengo un montón de ~ para planchar** I've got a stack of ironing to do; **~ interior** underwear, underclothes (*pl*)

ropero *m* wardrobe

roquero -ra *adj/m,f* ▶ ROCKERO

rosa *f* **(a)** (flor) rose **(b)** (rosal) rosebush **(c)** (Chi) (nudo) bow
■ *adj* (gen inv) pink; **un vestido (de color) ~** a pink dress; **verlo todo de color ~** to see things through rose-colored glasses o (BrE) rose-tinted spectacles
■ *m* pink

rosado -da *adj* **(a)** ⟨color/vestido⟩ pink **(b)** ⟨mejillas⟩ rosy; ⟨vino⟩ rosé
■ *m* **(a)** (color) pink **(b)** (vino) rosé

rosal *m* (árbol) rosetree; (arbusto) rosebush

rosario *m* **(a)** (Relig) (rezo) rosary; (cuentas) rosary (beads) **(b)** (serie, sarta) string

rosca *f* **(a)** (de tornillo, tuerca) thread; **tapón de ~** screw top; **pasarse de ~: el tornillo se pasó de ~** the screw isn't biting; **te has pasado de ~** (fam) you've gone too far **(b)** (Bol, Col) (círculo, grupo) clique, set

rosedal *m* (CS, Méx) rose garden

roseta *f* (Arquit) rose, rosette; (de ducha) showerhead; (de regadera) spinkler (AmE), rose (BrE)

rosetón *m* (ventana) rose window, rosette; (en el techo) ceiling rose

rosquilla *f. type of doughnut*

rosticería *f* (Méx) ▶ ROTISERÍA

rostizar [A4] *vt* (Méx) to roast; **pollo rostizado** roast chicken

rostro *m* **(a)** (cara) face **(b)** (Esp fam) (desfachatez) nerve (colloq), cheek (BrE colloq)

rotación *f* rotation

rotar [A1] *vt/vi* to rotate
■ **rotarse** *v pron* (en trabajo) to work on a rota system; **~se para hacer algo** to take it in turns to do sth

rotativo *m* **(a)** (period) (diario) newspaper **(b)** (Chi) (Cin) movie theater (AmE), cinema (BrE) (*showing a continuous performance*)

rotería f (Chi) (fam) (hecho): **fue una ~ no invitarlo** it was incredibly rude not to invite him; **me hizo una ~** he was rude to me

rotisería f (CS) delicatessen selling spit-roast chickens

roto¹ -ta adj **1** (a) ‹camisa› torn, ripped; ‹zapato› worn-out (b) ‹vaso/plato/brazo› broken (c) ‹papel› torn; **me devolvió el libro ~** the book was falling apart when he gave it back to me (d) (RPl) ‹televisor/heladera› broken; ‹coche› broken down **2** (Chi fam & pey) (a) ‹barrio/gente› lower-class (pej), plebby (colloq & pej) (b) (mal educado) rude

■ m,f **1** (Chi) (a) (fam & pey) (de clase baja) pleb (colloq & pej) (b) (fam & pey) (mal educado): **es una rota, nunca saluda** she's so rude, she doesn't even say hello **2** (Per fam) (chileno) Chilean

roto² m (Esp) (agujero) hole

rotonda f (glorieta) traffic circle (AmE), roundabout (BrE)

rotoso -sa adj (a) (CS, Per fam) ‹persona/ropa› scruffy (b) (Chi fam & pey) ‹barrio/gente› lower-class (pej)

rótula f (Anat) kneecap

rotulador m (Esp) felt-tip pen

rótulo m (a) (Impr) (título) title; (encabezamiento) heading (b) (etiqueta) label (c) (letrero) sign

rotundo -da adj (a) ‹respuesta› categorical, emphatic; ‹negativa› categorical, outright (before n); **me contestó con un 'no' ~** his answer was an emphatic 'no' (b) ‹éxito/fracaso› resounding

rotura f: **hay una ~ en la cañería** there's a burst in the pipe; **sufrió ~ de cadera** she fractured her hip; **tiene ~ de ligamentos** she has torn ligaments; **tiene una ~ en la manga** (CS) it has a rip in the sleeve

round /rraun/ m (Dep) round

rozado -da adj (gastado) worn; (sucio) grubby

rozadura f scratch; **le hizo una ~ al coche** he scratched the car; **los zapatos nuevos le hicieron una ~** her new shoes rubbed

rozagante adj (AmL) healthy

rozamiento m friction

rozar [A4] vt (tocar ligeramente): **el gato me rozó la pierna** the cat brushed against my leg; **sus labios ~on mi frente** her lips brushed my forehead; **las sillas rozan la pared** the chairs rub o scrape against the wall; **la bala le rozó el brazo** the bullet grazed his arm; **me roza el zapato** my shoe's rubbing

■ **rozarse** v pron (a) (recípr) ‹cables/piezas› to chafe; ‹‹manos/labios›› to touch (b) (refl) ‹brazo/ rodillas› to graze (c) ‹‹cuello/puños›› to wear (d) (Méx) ‹‹bebé›› to get diaper rash (AmE), get nappy rash (BrE); **el bebé está rozado** the baby has diaper (AmE) o (BrE) nappy rash

Rte. (= **remite** or **remitente**) sender

ruana f (Colombian, Venezuelan poncho)

rubeola f German measles

rubí m (a) (Min) ruby (b) (de reloj) jewel (c) (color) : **de color ~** ruby red

rubio -bia adj ‹pelo› fair, blonde; ‹hombre› fair-haired, blond; ‹mujer› fair-haired, blonde
■ m,f (m) blond o fair-haired man; (f) blonde o fair-haired woman, blonde (colloq)

rublo m ruble*

rubor m (a) (liter) (sonrojo) flush; **el ~ de sus mejillas la delató** her flushed cheeks betrayed her (b) (Méx, RPl) (cosmética) rouge, blusher

ruborizarse [A4] v pron to blush, to turn red (in the face), to flush

rúbrica f (de firma) flourish; (firma) signing

rubro m (esp AmL) (a) (área) area; **nuestro ~ de peletería** our line in furs; **trabaja en el ~ de la computación** he works in computers (b) (en contabilidad — apartado) heading; (— renglón) item

rucio -cia adj (a) ‹caballo› gray* (b) (Chi fam) ‹pelo› fair, blonde; ‹hombre› fair-haired, blond; ‹mujer› fair-haired, blonde

ruco -ca adj (Méx fam) old

rudimentario -ria adj rudimentary

rudimento m rudiment

rudo -da adj (tosco) rough, rude (arch)

rueca f distaff

rueda f (a) (de vehículo, mecanismo) wheel; **~ de molino** millstone; **~ dentada** gear wheel, cogwheel; **~ de recambio** or **repuesto** or (RPl) **de auxilio** spare wheel; **patinar sobre ~s** to roller-skate; **ir sobre ~s** to go o run smoothly (b) (neumático) tire*; **se me pinchó una ~** I got a flat tire o a puncture (c) (de mueble) caster, roller (d) (corro) ring, circle; **~ de prensa** press conference (e) (en gimnasia) cartwheel

ruedo m (a) (Taur) bullring (b) (esp AmL) (de falda, pantalón) hem

ruego m (a) (súplica) plea; **de nada te servirán tus ~s** your pleading will get you nowhere (b) (petición) request; **en respuesta a un ~ de sus oyentes** in response to a request from his listeners

rufián m (granuja) rogue, scoundrel (dated); (chulo) pimp

rugby /'rruvbi/ m rugby

rugido m roar

rugir [I7] vi ‹león/mar/viento› to roar

rugoso -sa adj rough, bumpy

ruibarbo m rhubarb

ruido m noise; **sin hacer ~** quietly; **no hagas tanto ~** don't make so much noise

ruidoso -sa adj ‹calle/máquina/persona› noisy

ruin adj (mezquino, vil) despicable, contemptible; (avaro) miserly, mean (BrE)

ruina f (a) (bancarrota) ruin; **dejar a algn en la ~** to ruin sb; **estar en la ~** ‹empresario› to be ruined; ‹país› to be in financial ruin; **la compañía está en la ~** the company has collapsed (b) (perdición) downfall; **el juego fue su ~** gambling was his downfall (c) (hundimiento) collapse; **la casa amenaza ~** the house is on the point of collapse (d) **ruinas** fpl (de edificio, ciudad) ruins (pl); **en ~s** in ruins

ruiseñor m nightingale

rulero m (Per, RPl) curler

ruleta f roulette

ruletero -ra m,f (Méx fam) cab o taxi driver, cabbie (colloq)

rulo m (para el pelo) curler, roller; (rizo) (CS, Per) curl

rulot f (Esp) trailer (AmE), caravan (BrE)

ruma f (Chi) pile, heap

Rumania, Rumanía f Romania

rumano¹ -na adj/m,f Romanian, Rumanian

rumano² m (idioma) Romanian, Rumanian

rumba f rumba

rumbo m (dirección) direction, course; (Náut) course; **caminar sin ~ fijo** to wander aimlessly; **partió (con) ~ a Toluca** he set off for Toluca; **navegar con ~ norte** to sail a northerly course; **los acontecimientos tomaron un ~ trágico** events took a tragic turn

rumiante m ruminant

rumiar [A1] vi «vaca» to chew the cud, ruminate

rumor m (a) (murmuración) rumor*; **circulan ~es de que ...** rumors are circulating that ..., rumor has it that ... (b) (sonido) murmur

rumorear [A1] vt: **se rumorea que ...** rumor has it that ...

rupestre adj ⟨pintura/dibujo⟩ cave (before n); ⟨planta⟩ rock (before n)

rupia f rupee

ruptura f (a) (de relaciones, negaciones) breaking-off; (de contrato) breach, breaking; (de matrimonio) breakup; (con pasado, tradición) break; **esa fue la causa de la ~ de las negociaciones** that was what caused the negotiations to be broken off (b) (Dep) (en tenis) service break

rural adj rural

Rusia f Russia

ruso¹ -sa adj/m,f Russian

ruso² m (idioma) Russian

rústica (esp Esp): **en rústica** (loc adj) ⟨edición⟩ paperback (before n); **un libro en ~** a paperback

rústico -ca adj (del campo) rustic; (basto) coarse

ruta f (a) (itinerario) route (b) (RPl) (carretera) road

rutina f routine; **inspección de ~** routine inspection; **por pura ~** out of habit

rutinario -ria adj (a) ⟨trabajo/vida⟩ monotonous (b) ⟨inspección/procedimiento⟩ routine (before n)

Ss

S, s f (read as /'ese/) the letter S, s

s. m (= **siglo**) C; **s.XX** C20

S (= **sur**) S, South

S. (= **santo**) St

S.A. (= **Sociedad Anónima**) ≈ Inc (in US), ≈ Ltd (in UK), ≈ PLC (in UK)

sábado m Saturday; (Relig) Sabbath; **S~ de Gloria** or **Santo** Easter Saturday; **~ inglés** (CS) non-working Saturday

sabana f (Geog) savanna*, grassland

sábana f sheet; **~ ajustable** or (Méx) **de cajón** fitted sheet; **~ bajera/encimera** bottom/top sheet

sabandija f **1** (insecto) creepy-crawly (colloq), bug; (reptil) creepy-crawly (colloq) **2 sabandija** mf (AmL fam) (pícaro) rascal (colloq)

sabañón m chilblain

sabático -ca adj sabbatical

sabelotodo mf (fam) know-it-all (AmE colloq), know-all (BrE colloq)

saber¹ m knowledge; **una persona de gran ~** a person of great learning

saber² [E25] vt **1** (a) ⟨nombre/dirección/canción⟩ to know; **ya lo sé** I know; **no lo sé** I don't know; **no sé cómo se llama** I don't know his name; **¡yo qué sé!** how (on earth) should I know! (colloq); **que yo sepa** as far as I know; **~ algo DE algo** to know sth ABOUT sth; **sé muy poco de ese tema** I know very little about the subject; **no sabe lo que dice** he doesn't know what he's talking about (b) (enterarse) to find out; **lo supe**

por mi hermana I found out about it through my sister; **sin que lo supiéramos** without our knowing; **¡si yo lo hubiera sabido antes!** if I had only known before!; **¡cómo iba yo a ~ que ...!** how was I to know that ...!

2 (ser capaz de): **~ hacer algo** to know how to do sth; **¿sabes nadar?** can you swim?, do you know how to swim?; **sabe escuchar** she's a good listener; **sabe hablar varios idiomas** she can speak several languages

■ **~ vi**

I (a) (tener conocimiento) to know; **¿quién sabe?** who knows?; **~ DE algo/algn** to know OF sth/sb; **yo sé de un lugar donde te lo pueden arreglar** I know of a place where you can get it fixed (b) (tener noticias, enterarse): **no sé nada de ella desde hace más de un mes** I haven't heard from her for over a month; **yo supe del accidente por la radio** I heard about the accident on the radio

II (a) (tener sabor) (+ compl) to taste; **sabe dulce/bien** it tastes sweet/nice; **~ A algo** to taste OF sth; **no sabe a nada** it doesn't taste of anything; **sabe a podrido** it tastes rotten (b) (causar cierta impresión): **me sabe mal** or **no me sabe bien tener que decírselo** I don't like having to tell him

■ **saberse** v pron (enf) ⟨lección/poema⟩ to know

sabido -da adj [SER] well-known; **como es ~** as everybody knows

sabiduría f wisdom

sabiendas: **a sabiendas** (loc adv): **lo hizo a ~ de que me molestaba** he did it full well o perfectly well that I found it annoying

sabihondo -da *m,f* (fam) know-it-all (AmE colloq), know-all (BrE colloq)

sabio -bia *adj* (con grandes conocimientos) learned, wise; (sensato) ⟨*persona/medida*⟩ wise; ⟨*consejo*⟩ sound, wise

■ *m,f* (*m*) wise man, sage (liter); (*f*) wise woman

sable *m* **1** (Arm) saber*; (Náut) batten **2** (en heráldica) sable

sabor *m* (a) (de comida, bebida, etc) taste, flavor*; con ∼ a menta mint-flavoured; viene en tres ∼es it comes in three flavors; no tiene ∼ it has no taste to it (b) (carácter) flavor*

saborear [A1] *vt* to savor*; ⟨*éxito/triunfo*⟩ to relish

sabotaje *m* sabotage

saboteador -dora *m,f* saboteur

sabotear [A1] *vt* to sabotage

sabré, sabría, etc ▶ SABER

sabroso -sa *adj* **1** ⟨*comida*⟩ tasty, delicious; ⟨*chisme/historia*⟩ spicy (colloq), juicy (colloq) **2** (AmL fam) (agradable) ⟨*música/ritmo*⟩ pleasant, nice; ⟨*clima/agua*⟩ beautiful

sabrosón -sona *adj* (a) (AmL fam) ⟨*guiso*⟩ tasty, delicious; ⟨*fruta*⟩ delicious (b) (AmL fam) ⟨*clima*⟩ mild (c) (Col, Méx, Ven fam) ⟨*música*⟩ pleasant

sabueso *m* (Zool) bloodhound

sacacorchos *m* (*pl* ∼) corkscrew

sacapuntas *m* (*pl* ∼) pencil sharpener

sacar [A2] *vt*
I **1** (extraer) (a) ⟨*billetera/lápiz*⟩ to take out, get out; ⟨*pistola/espada*⟩ to draw; ∼ algo DE algo to take *o* get sth OUT OF sth; lo saqué del cajón I took *o* got it out of the drawer (b) ⟨*muela*⟩ to pull out, take out; ⟨*riñón/cálculo*⟩ to remove; me ∼on sangre they took some blood (c) ⟨*diamantes/cobre/petróleo*⟩ to extract (d) ⟨*carta/ficha*⟩ to draw
2 (poner, llevar fuera) (a) ⟨*maceta/mesa/basura*⟩ to take out; sácalo aquí al sol bring it out here into the sun; tuvimos que ∼lo por la ventana we had to get it out through the window; ∼ el perro a pasear to take the dog out for a walk; ∼ el coche del garaje to get the car out of the garage (b) (invitar): el marido no la saca nunca her husband never takes her out; ∼ a algn a bailar to ask sb to dance (c) ⟨*parte del cuerpo*⟩ to put out; me sacó la lengua he stuck *o* put his tongue out at me
3 (retirar) to take out; ∼ dinero del banco to take out *o* withdraw money from the bank
4 (de una situación difícil) ∼ a algn DE algo ⟨*de apuro/atolladero*⟩ to get sb OUT OF sth
5 (Esp) ⟨*dobladillo*⟩ to let down; ⟨*pantalón/falda*⟩ (alargar) to let down; (ensanchar) to let out
II (obtener) **1** ⟨*pasaporte/permiso*⟩ to get; ⟨*entrada/billete*⟩ to get, buy
2 (a) ⟨*votos/puntos/calificación*⟩ to get (b) ⟨*premio*⟩ to get, win (c) ⟨*conclusión*⟩ to draw (d) ⟨*suma/cuenta*⟩ to do, work out
3 ⟨*beneficio*⟩ to get; ⟨*ganancia*⟩ to make; ¿qué sacas con eso? what do you gain by doing that?; no sacó ningún provecho del curso she didn't get anything out of the course
4 ∼ algo DE algo ⟨*idea/información*⟩ to get sth FROM sth; ⟨*porciones/unidades*⟩ to get sth OUT OF sth; ∼le algo A algn ⟨*dinero/información*⟩ to get sth OUT OF sb

5 ⟨*brillo*⟩ to bring out; ∼le brillo a algo to polish sth to a shine
III **1** (a) ⟨*libro*⟩ to publish, bring out; ⟨*disco*⟩ to bring out, release; ⟨*modelo/producto*⟩ to bring out (b) ⟨*tema*⟩ to bring up (c) ⟨*foto*⟩ to take; ⟨*copia*⟩ to make, take; ⟨*apuntes*⟩ to make, take; ∼le una foto a algn to take a photo of sb (d) (Esp) ⟨*defecto/falta*⟩ (+ me/te/le etc) to find; a todo le tiene que ∼ faltas he always has to find fault with everything
2 sacar adelante ⟨*proyecto*⟩ (poner en marcha) to get sth off the ground; (salvar de la crisis) to keep sth going; luché tanto para ∼ adelante a mis hijos I fought so hard to give my children a good start in life
3 (Dep) ⟨*tiro libre/falta*⟩ to take
IV (quitar) **1** (esp AmL) (a) ∼le algo A algn ⟨*botas/gorro*⟩ to take sth OFF sb (b) ∼le algo A algo ⟨*tapa/cubierta*⟩ to take sth OFF sth (c) (retirar): saca esto de aquí take this away; saquen los libros de la mesa take the books off the table (d) (hacer desaparecer) ⟨*mancha*⟩ to remove, get ... out

■ ∼ *vi* (Dep) (en tenis, vóleibol) to serve; (en fútbol) to kick off

■ **sacarse** *v pron* (refl) **1** (extraer) ⟨*astilla/púa*⟩ to take ... out; ⟨*ojo*⟩ to poke ... out; me tengo que ∼ una muela (caus) I have to have a tooth out; ∼se algo DE algo to take sth OUT OF sth; sácate las manos de los bolsillos take your hands out of your pockets
2 (AmL) (quitarse) ⟨*ropa/zapatos*⟩ to take off; ⟨*maquillaje*⟩ to remove, take off
3 (a) (caus) ⟨*foto*⟩: tengo que ∼me una foto I have to have my photo taken (b) (AmL) ⟨*calificación/nota*⟩ to get

sacarina *f* saccharin

sacerdote *m* priest

sacerdotisa *f* priestess

saciar [A1] *vt* ⟨*hambre*⟩ to satisfy; ⟨*sed*⟩ to quench; ⟨*deseo*⟩ (liter) to satiate (liter); ⟨*ambición*⟩ to fulfill*, realize

■ **saciarse** *v pron*: comer/beber hasta ∼se to eat/drink one's fill

saco *m* **1** (continente) sack; (contenido) sack, sackful; ∼ de dormir sleeping bag **2** (AmL) (de tela) jacket; ∼ sport (AmL) sports coat (AmE), sports jacket (BrE)

sacramento *m* sacrament; los últimos ∼s the last rites

sacrificado -da *adj* ⟨*persona*⟩ selfless, self-sacrificing

sacrificar [A2] *vt* (a) (Relig) ⟨*cordero/víctimas*⟩ to sacrifice (b) ⟨*res/ganado*⟩ to slaughter; ⟨*perro/gato*⟩ (euf) to put ... to sleep (euph) (c) ⟨*carrera/juventud*⟩ to sacrifice

■ **sacrificarse** *v pron* to make sacrifices

sacrificio *m* (a) (privación, renuncia) sacrifice (b) (inmolación) sacrifice (c) (de res) slaughter

sacrilegio *m* sacrilege

sacrílego -ga *adj* sacrilegious

sacristán *m* sacristan, verger

sacristía *f* vestry, sacristy

sacudida *f* (a) (agitando) shake, shaking; (golpeando) beating (b) (de terremoto) tremor; (de explosión) blast; (de tren, coche) jerk, jolt (c) (fam) (descarga) electric shock

S

sacudir [I1] *vt* **1** (a) (agitar) ‹*toalla/alfombra*› to shake; (golpear) ‹*alfombra/colchón*› to beat; **sacudió la arena de la toalla** he shook the sand out of the towel (b) (fam) ‹*niño*› to clobber (colloq); ~ **la cabeza** (para negar) to shake one's head; (para afirmar) to nod (one's head) (c) (hacer temblar) to shake (d) (CS, Méx) (limpiar) to dust, do the dusting **2** (conmover, afectar) to shake
■ ~ *vi* (CS, Méx) to dust
■ **sacudirse** *v pron* (refl) (quitarse) ‹*arena/polvo*› to shake off

sádico -ca *adj* sadistic
■ *m,f* sadist

sadismo *m* sadism

sadomasoquismo *m* sadomasochism

sadomasoquista *mf* sadomasochist

safari *m* (a) (gira, viaje) safari; **ir de** ~ to go on safari (b) (zoológico) safari park

sagaz *adj* shrewd, astute

Sagitario *m* (signo, constelación) Sagittarius; **es (de)** ~ she's (a) Sagittarian
■ *mf* (pl ~ or **-rios**) (persona) *tb* **sagitario** Sagittarian, Sagittarius

sagrado -da *adj* **1** (Relig) ‹*altar*› holy; ‹*lugar*› holy, sacred **2** (fundamental, intocable) sacred

Sahara /sa'ara/ *m*: **el (desierto del)** ~ the Sahara (Desert)

sajón -jona *adj/m,f* Saxon

sal *f* **1** (Coc) salt; **mantequilla sin** ~ unsalted butter; *echarle la* ~ *a algn* (Méx fam) to put a jinx on sb **2** (Quím) salt; ~ **de fruta** liver salts (pl); ~**es de baño** bath salts (pl)

sal ▶ SALIR

sala *f* (a) (de casa) *tb* ~ **de estar** living room, lounge (BrE) (b) (de hotel) lounge; (en hospital) ward; (para reuniones, conferencias) hall; (Teatr) theater*; (Cin) movie theater (AmE), cinema (BrE); ~ **cuna** (Chi) day nursery, creche; ~ **de clases** (CS frml) classroom; ~ **de conciertos** concert hall; ~ **de embarque** departure lounge; ~ **de espera** waiting room; ~ **de exposiciones** gallery, exhibition hall; ~ **de fiestas** night club (*usually featuring dancing and cabaret*); ~ **de profesores** staff room (c) (sede de tribunal) courtroom, court

salado -da *adj* **1** (Coc) (a) (con sal) ‹*almendras/bacalao*› salted; ‹*gusto*› salty; **está demasiado** ~ it's too salty (b) [SER] (no dulce) ‹*plato/comida*› savory* **2** (a) (fam) ‹*persona*› (gracioso) funny, witty (b) (fam) ‹*chiste*› risqué; ‹*anécdota*› spicy **3** (Méx fam) (que trae mala suerte) jinxed (colloq)

salamandra *f* (Zool) salamander; (estufa) salamander stove

salame *m* (a) (CS) (Coc) salami (b) (RPl fam) (tonto) idiot

salar¹ [A1] *vt* (a) (para conservar) ‹*carne/pescado*› to salt (down); ‹*pieles*› to salt (b) (para condimentar) to salt, add salt to
■ **salarse** *v pron* (Méx fam) (echarse a perder) «*planes*» to fall through; «*negocio*» to go bust

salar² *m* (Chi) salt pan, salt flat

salario *m* (frml) wage, salary

salchicha *f* sausage

salchichón *m*: spiced sausage similar to salami

salchichonería *f* (Méx) delicatessen

saldar [A1] *vt* (a) ‹*cuenta*› to settle; ‹*deuda*› to settle, pay (off) (b) ‹*mercancías/productos*› to sell off

saldo *m* **1** (de cuenta) balance; ~ **a su/nuestro favor** credit/debit balance **2** (a) (artículo): **los** ~**s no se cambian** sale goods cannot be exchanged; **precios de** ~ sale prices; **S venta de saldos** clearance sale (b) **saldos** *mpl* (rebajas) sales (pl)

saldré, saldría, etc ▶ SALIR

salero *m* **1** (recipiente) salt shaker (AmE), saltcellar (BrE) **2** (fam) (gracia): **tener** ~ (contando chistes) to be funny; (bailando) to be stylish

salga, salgas, etc ▶ SALIR

salida *f*
I (hacia el exterior) **1** (a) (lugar, puerta) exit; ~ **de emergencia/incendios** emergency/fire exit; **todas las** ~**s de Bilbao** all the roads out of Bilbao; **es una calle sin** ~ it's a dead end (b) (de tubería) outlet, outflow; (de circuito) outlet
2 (a) (acción): **me lo encontré a la** ~ I met him on my way out; **nos encontramos a la** ~ **del concierto** we met at the door after the concert; **una** ~ **al campo** an outing *o* a trip to the country (b) (de líquido, gas, electricidad) output (c) **la** ~ **del sol** sunrise
II (partida) **1** (de tren, avión) departure; **el tren efectuará su** ~ **por la vía cinco** the train will leave from track five; **S salidas nacionales/internacionales** domestic/international departures **2** (Dep) (en una carrera) start
III **1** (solución): **no le veo ninguna** ~ **a esta situación** I can see no way out of this situation; **no nos queda otra** ~ we have no other option **2** (Com, Fin) (gasto) payment

salido -da *adj* ‹*ojos/dientes*› protruding; ‹*frente/mentón*› prominent

saliente *adj* ‹*pómulo/hueso*› prominent; ‹*cornisa/balcón*› projecting
■ *f or* (Esp) *m* (de edificio, muro) projection; (de precipicio) ledge

salir [I29] *vi*
I **1** (partir) to leave; **¿a qué hora sale el tren?** what time does the train leave?; **el jefe había salido de viaje** the boss was away; **salió corriendo** (fam) she was off like a shot (colloq); ~ DE **algo** to leave FROM sth; **¿de qué andén sale el tren?** what platform does the train leave from?; **salgo de casa a las siete** I leave home at seven; ~ PARA **algo** to leave FOR sth
2 (al exterior — acercándose al hablante) to come out; (— alejándose del hablante) to go out; **no salgas sin abrigo** don't go out without a coat; **no puedo** ~, **me he quedado encerrado** I can't get out, I'm trapped in here; ~ DE **algo** to come out/get out OF sth; **¡sal de ahí/de aquí!** come out of there/get out of here!; **¿de dónde salió este dinero?** where did this money come from?; **nunca ha salido de España** he's never been out of Spain; ~ **por la ventana/por la puerta** to get out through the window/leave by the door; **salieron al balcón/al jardín** they went out onto the balcony/into the garden; **¿por aquí se sale a la carretera?** can I get on to the road this way?; **salió a hacer las compras** she's gone out (to do the) shopping
3 (habiendo terminado algo) to leave; **¿a qué hora sales de clase?** what time do you get out of class *o* finish your class?; **¿cuándo sale del hospital?** when is he coming out of (the) hospital?

4 **(a)** (como entretenimiento) to go out; ~ **a cenar** to go out for dinner **(b)** (tener una relación) to go out; ~ **CON algn** to go out WITH sb
5 «*clavo/tapón/mancha*» to come out; «*anillo*» to come off
II **1** (aparecer, manifestarse) **(a)** «*cana/sarpullido*» to appear; (+ *me/te/le etc*) **me empiezan a ~ canas** I'm starting to go gray; **le están saliendo los dientes** she's teething; **me salió una ampolla** I've got a blister; **le salió un sarpullido** he came out in a rash; **me salieron granos** I broke out *o* (BrE) came out in spots; **me sale sangre de la nariz** my nose is bleeding; **a la planta le están saliendo hojas nuevas** the plant's putting out new leaves **(b)** «*sol*» (por la mañana) to rise, come up; (de detrás de una nube) to come out **(c)** (surgir) «*tema/ idea*» to come up **(d)** «*carta*» (en naipes) to come up
2 **(a)** «*revista/novela*» to come out; «*disco*» to come out, be released; ~ **al mercado** to come on to the market **(b)** (en televisión, en el periódico) to appear **(c)** (en una foto) to appear; (+ *compl*) **saliste muy bien en la foto** you came out very well in the photo
III **1** (expresando logro) (+ *me/te/le etc*): **no me sale esta ecuación** I can't do this equation; **ahora mismo no me sale su nombre** (fam) I can't think of her name right now; **no le salían las palabras** he couldn't get his words out
2 **(a)** (costar) to work out; **sale más barato/caro** it works out less/more expensive **(b)** (resultar): **todo salió bien** everything turned out *o* worked out well; **salió tal como lo planeamos** it turned out just as we planned; **no salió ninguna de las fotos** none of the photographs came out; **¿qué número salió premiado?** what was the winning number?; ~ **bien/mal en un examen** (Chi fam) to pass/fail an exam; (+ *me/te/le etc*) **el postre no me salió bien** the dessert didn't come out right
3 (de situación, estado) ~ **DE algo** ‹*de apuro*› to get out of sth; ‹*de depresión*› to get over sth; **salieron ilesos del accidente** they were not hurt in the accident; ~ **adelante** «*negocio*» to stay afloat, survive; «*propuesta*» to prosper; **lograron ~ adelante** they managed to get through it
4 (con preposición) **(a)** **salir a** (parecerse a) to take after **(b)** **salir con** (Col) (combinar con) to go with
■ **salirse** *v pron* **1** **(a)** (de borde, límite) «*agua*» to overflow; «*leche*» to boil over; ~**se DE algo** ‹*de carretera*› to come/go off sth; ‹*de tema*› to get off sth; **el río se salió de su cauce** the river overflowed its banks; **procura no ~te del presupuesto** try to keep within the budget **(b)** (por orificio, grieta) «*agua/tinta*» to leak (out), come out; «*gas*» to escape, come out
2 (soltarse) «*pedazo/pieza*» to come off; (+ *me/te/ le etc*) **estos zapatos se me salen** these shoes are too big for me
3 (irse) to leave; ~**se DE algo** ‹*de asociación*› to leave sth; ~**se con la suya** to get one's (own) way
saliva *f* saliva, spit (colloq)
salivar [A1] *vi* to salivate
salmo *m* psalm
salmón *m* salmon
■ *adj inv* salmon-pink, salmon, salmon-colored*
salmonete *m* red mullet, surmullet (AmE)
salmuera *f* brine
salón *m* **(a)** (en casa particular) living room,

sitting room (BrE), lounge (BrE) **(b)** (en hotel) reception room, function room **(c)** (en palacio) hall **(d)** (de clases) classroom; ~ **de actos** auditorium (AmE), assembly hall (BrE); ~ **de baile** ballroom; ~ **de belleza** beauty salon, beauty parlor; ~ **de fiestas** (AmL) function room, reception room; ~ **náutico/del automóvil** boat/motor show
salpicadera *f* (Méx) (de coche, bicicleta) fender (AmE), mudguard (BrE)
salpicadero *m* (Esp) dashboard
salpicadura *f* splash
salpicar [A2] *vt* (de agua) to splash; (de barro, aceite) to splash, spatter
salpicón *m* (de pescado, ave) *chopped seafood or meat with onion, tomato and peppers*
salsa *f* **1** (Coc) sauce; (de jugo de carne) gravy; ~ **bechamel** *or* **blanca** bechamel (sauce); ~ **de tomate** (sofrito) tomato sauce; (catsup) (Col) ketchup, catsup (AmE) **2** (Mús) salsa
saltamontes *m* (*pl* ~) grasshopper
saltar [A1] *vi* **1** **(a)** (brincar) to jump; (más alto, más lejos) to leap; ~ **a la cuerda** *or* (Esp) **comba** to jump rope (AmE), to skip (BrE); ~ **de alegría** to jump for joy; ~ **con** *or* **en una pierna** to hop; ~ **de la cama/silla** to jump out of bed/one's chair **(b)** (en atletismo) to jump **(c)** «*pelota*» to bounce **(d)** (lanzarse) to jump; ~ **al agua** to jump into the water; ~ **en paracaídas** to parachute; **¿sabes ~ del trampolín?** can you dive off the springboard?; **saltó al vacío** he leapt into space; ~ **SOBRE algo/ algn** to jump ON sth/sb
2 (pasar) ~ **DE algo A algo** to jump FROM sth TO sth; **saltaba de una idea a otra** she kept jumping from one idea to the next
3 «*botón*» to come off, pop off; «*chispas*» to fly; «*aceite*» to spit; «*corcho*» to pop out; «*fusibles*» to blow; **la bomba hizo ~ el coche por los aires** the bomb blew the car into the air
■ ~ *vt* ‹*obstáculo/valla/zanja*› to jump (over); (apoyándose) to vault (over)
■ **saltarse** *v pron* **1** **(a)** (omitir) ‹*línea/página/ nombre*› to skip, miss out; ‹*comida*› to miss, skip **(b)** ‹*semáforo/stop*› to jump
2 «*botón*» to come off, pop off; «*pintura*» to chip; **se le ~on las lágrimas** her eyes filled with tears
3 (Chi) «*diente/loza*» to chip
salteado -da *adj*: **¿se pueden contestar las preguntas salteadas?** can we answer the questions in any order?; **leí unos capítulos ~s** I read a few odd chapters
saltear [A1] *vt* (Coc) to sauté
saltimbanqui *m* (Espec, Hist) tumbler, acrobat
salto *m* **1** **(a)** (brinco) jump; **se levantó de un ~** (de la cama) he leapt *o* sprang out of bed; (del suelo) he leapt *o* jumped up from the floor; **se puso en pie de un ~** she leapt *o* sprang to her feet; **los pájaros se acercaban dando saltitos** the birds were hopping closer to me/us; **dar** *or* **pegar un ~** (dar un brinco) to jump; (de susto) to start, jump; **daban ~s de alegría** they were jumping for joy **(b)** (Dep) (en atletismo, esquí, paracaidismo) jump; (en natación) dive; ~ **con pértiga** *or* (AmL) **garrocha** pole vault; ~ **de altura/longitud** high/long jump; ~ (**en**) **alto/(en) largo** (AmL) high/long jump; ~ **mortal** somersault
2 (Geog) *tb* ~ **de agua** waterfall
saltón -tona *adj* ‹*ojos*› bulging

salud f [1] (Med) health; **estar bien de** ~ to be in good health; **gozar de buena** ~ to enjoy good health [2] ¡~! (al brindar) cheers!; (cuando alguien estornuda) (AmL) bless you!

saludable adj ‹clima/alimentación› healthy; ‹experiencia› salutary

saludar [A1] vt (a) ‹persona› to greet, say hello to; **saluda a tu hermano de mi parte** give my regards to your brother; **lo saluda atentamente** (Corresp) Sincerely (yours) (AmE), Yours sincerely (BrE); **los saludó con la mano** she waved at them (b) (Mil) to salute
■ ~ vi (a) (de palabra) to say hello (o good morning etc) (b) (con la mano) to wave (c) (Mil) to salute
■ **saludarse** v pron (recípr) to say hello to o greet each other

saludo m (a) greeting; **te mandan** ~s they send (you) their regards o best wishes; ~s (Corresp) best wishes; **le hice un** ~ **con la mano** I gave him a wave, I waved to him (b) (Mil) salute

salva f: **una** ~ **de 21 cañonazos** a 21-gun salute o salvo; **una** ~ **de aplausos** a burst o round of applause

salvación f salvation

salvado m bran

salvador -dora m,f savior*

Salvador ▶ EL SALVADOR

salvadoreño -ña adj/m,f Salvadoran, Salvadorean

salvaguardar [A1] vt to safeguard

salvaguardia f safeguard, defense*

salvaje adj [1] (a) ‹animal› wild (b) ‹primitivo› ‹tribu› savage (c) ‹vegetación/terreno› wild [2] (cruel) ‹persona/tortura› brutal; ‹ataque/matanza› savage
■ mf (primitivo) savage; (bruto) (pey) animal, savage

salvamanteles m (pl ~) (para platos, fuentes) tablemat; (para vasos) coaster

salvamento m rescue; **equipo de** ~ rescue team

salvar [A1] vt [1] (en general) to save; ~ **algo/a algn DE algo** to save sth/sb FROM sth [2] (a) ‹dificultad/obstáculo› to overcome (b) ‹distancia› to cover (c) (Per, Ur) ‹examen› to pass
■ **salvarse** v pron to survive; **¡sálvese quien pueda!** every man for himself!; ~**se DE algo** ‹de accidente/incendio› to survive sth; **se** ~**on de una muerte segura** they escaped certain death

salvavidas mf (pl ~) (a) (persona) lifeguard (b) **salvavidas** m (flotador) life jacket, life preserver (frml)

salvia f sage

salvo: **a salvo** (loc adv) **poner algo a** ~ to put sth in a safe place; **los niños están a** ~ the children are safe o unharmed; **ponerse a** ~ to reach safety; **a** ~ **de** safe from
■ prep (excepto) except, apart from; ~ **que** unless

salvoconducto m safe-conduct

samba m or f samba

San adj (apócope de SANTO usado delante de nombres de varón excepto Domingo, Tomás y Tomé) St, Saint

sanar [A1] vi ‹enfermo› to get well, recover; ‹herida› to heal; ~ **DE algo** to recover FROM sth

sanatorio m (a) (para convalecientes) nursing home, sanitarium (AmE), sanatorium (BrE) (b) (hospital) clinic, hospital (usually private) (c) (Col, Ven) (hospital psiquiátrico) psychiatric hospital

sanción f [1] (castigo a empleado, obrero) disciplinary measure; (Der) sanction, penalty; **una** ~ **de tres partidos** a three-game ban o suspension; ~ **económica** (multa) fine; **sanciones económicas** (a país) economic sanctions [2] (de ley) sanction; (de costumbre) sanction (frml), authorization

sancionar [A1] vt [1] (multar) to fine; (castigar) ‹empleado/obrero› to discipline; ‹jugador› to penalize [2] ‹ley/disposición/acuerdo/huelga› to sanction; ‹costumbre› to approve, sanction

sancochar [A1] vt (AmL) (cocer a medias) to parboil

sandalia f sandal

sándalo m sandalwood

sandez f (fam) silly o stupid thing to say; **¡no digas sandeces!** don't talk nonsense!

sandía f watermelon

sándwich /'saŋgwitʃ/ m, **sándwiche** /'saŋgwitʃe/ m (esp AmL) (de pan de molde) sandwich; (de pancito) (filled) roll

sanfermines mpl: festival in Pamplona in which bulls are run through the streets

sangrar [A1] vi ‹persona/herida/nariz› to bleed

sangre f [1] (Biol) blood; **una transfusión de** ~ a blood transfusion; **no me salió** ~ it didn't bleed; **te sale** ~ **de** or **por la nariz** your nose is bleeding; **los ojos inyectados en** ~ bloodshot eyes; **animales de** ~ **fría/caliente** cold-blooded/warm-blooded animals; ~ **fría** calmness and courage; **a** ~ **fría** (matar) in cold blood; ▶ MALO 2 [2] (linaje) blood; **era de** ~ **noble** he was of noble blood o birth; **es de** ~ **mestiza** he is of mixed race; **no son de la misma** ~ they are not from the same family; ~ **azul** blue blood

sangría f [1] (bebida) sangria (type of red wine punch) [2] (a) (Med) bleeding (b) (de capital, recursos) outflow, drain [3] (Impr) indentation

sangriento -ta adj bloody

sangrón -grona adj (Méx fam) annoying
■ m,f (Méx fam) nuisance

sanguijuela f (a) (Zool) leech (b) (fam) (persona) leech, bloodsucker

sanguinario -ria adj ‹persona› cruel, bloodthirsty; ‹animal› vicious, ferocious

sanidad f [1] (calidad de sano) health, healthiness [2] (a) (salud pública) public health (b) **Sanidad** (sin art) (departamento) Department of Health

sanitario¹ -ria adj ‹medidas› public health

(before n); ⟨*condiciones*⟩ sanitary *(before n)*;
servicios ~s sanitation; **asistencia sanitaria**
health-care

sanitario² *m* **(a)** (retrete) toilet, lavatory **(b)**
sanitarios *mpl* (para cuarto de baño) bathroom
fittings (*pl*)

sano -na *adj* ⟦1⟧ ⟨*persona/planta/cabello*⟩
healthy; ⟨*clima/vida*⟩ healthy; ⟨*alimentación*⟩
healthy, wholesome; **~ y salvo** safe and sound
⟦2⟧ (en sentido moral) ⟨*lecturas/ideas*⟩ wholesome;
⟨*ambiente*⟩ healthy; ⟨*persona*⟩ good

San Salvador *m* San Salvador

sánscrito *m* Sanskrit

Santa Sede *f*: **la ~ ~** the Vatican, the Holy
See (frml)

Santiago (de Chile) *m* Santiago

Santiago (de Compostela) *m* Santiago
(de Compostela)

santiaguino -na *adj* of/from Santiago *(Chile)*

santiamén *m*: **en un ~** (fam) in no time at all

santiguarse [A16] *v pron* (*refl*) to cross
oneself, make the sign of the cross

santo -ta *adj* ⟦1⟧ (Relig) **(a)** ⟨*lugar/mujer/vida*⟩
holy **(b)** (con nombre propio) St, Saint; **Santa Teresa**
Saint Theresa; *ver tb* SAN ⟦2⟧ (fam) (uso enfático)
blessed; **llovió todo el ~ día** it rained the whole
blessed day (colloq)
■ *m,f* ⟦1⟧ (persona) saint; **una paciencia de ~** the
patience of a saint; **no te hagas el ~** don't come
over all virtuous; **~ y seña** password ⟦2⟧ **santo**
m (festividad) name day, saint's day; (cumpleaños)
(esp AmL) birthday

Santo Domingo *m* (Geog) Santo Domingo;
(Relig) Saint Dominic

santuario *m* (Relig) sanctuary, shrine; (refugio)
sanctuary

saña *f* viciousness, brutality; **con ~** brutally,
viciously

São Paulo *m* São Paulo

sapo *m* (Zool) toad

saque *m* **(a)** (en tenis, vóleibol) serve, service **(b)**
(en fútbol) kickoff; **~ de banda** (en fútbol) throw-in;
(en rugby) line-out; **~ de esquina** corner (kick); **~**
de puerta *or* (CS) **valla** goal kick; **~ inicial** kickoff

saquear [A1] *vt* ⟨*ciudad/población*⟩ to sack,
plunder; ⟨*tienda/establecimiento*⟩ to loot

sarampión *m* measles

sarape *m* (Méx) ▶ ZARAPE

sarcasmo *m* **(a)** (cualidad) sarcasm; **con ~**
sarcastically **(b)** (comentario) sarcastic remark

sarcástico -ca *adj* sarcastic

sarcófago *m* sarcophagus

sardina *f* sardine

sardinel *m* (Col) **(a)** (de la acera) curb (AmE),
kerb (BrE) **(b)** (de ventana) windowsill

sargento *mf* (Mil) (en el ejército) sergeant; (en las
fuerzas aéreas) ≈ staff sergeant *(in US)*, ≈ sergeant
(in UK)

sari *m* sari

sarita *f* (Per) straw hat

sarna *f* (Med) scabies; (Vet) mange

sarpullido *m* rash, hives (*pl*)

sarro *m* (en los dientes) plaque, tartar; (en la
lengua) fur; (en tetera eléctrica, cañería) scale

sarta *f* string

sartén *f*, (AmL) *m or f* frying pan, fry pan (AmE),
skillet

sastre *mf* (persona) tailor

sastrería *f* tailor's shop

Satanás, Satán *m* Satan

satánico -ca *adj* (del diablo) satanic; (malvado)
evil, satanic

satélite *m* satellite; **~ artificial** artificial
satellite

satén, (AmL) **satín** *m* satin

sátira *f* satire

satírico -ca *adj* satirical

satirizar [A4] *vt* to satirize

satisfacción *f* satisfaction; **la ~ del deber**
cumplido the satisfaction of a job well done; **es**
una ~ para mí estar aquí it is a pleasure to be
here

satisfacer [E20] *vt* to satisfy; **su respuesta no**
me satisface I am not satisfied *o* happy with your
reply
■ **satisfacerse** *v pron* **(a)** (contentarse) to be
satisfied **(b)** (de agravio) to obtain satisfaction

satisfactorio -ria *adj* satisfactory

satisfaga, satisfará, etc ▶ SATISFACER

satisfecho -cha *adj* ⟦1⟧ [ESTAR] (complacido,
contento) satisfied, pleased ⟦2⟧ [ESTAR] (saciado,
lleno): **estoy ~** I've had plenty; **no queda nunca ~**
he never seems to be full

saturado -da *adj* (en general) saturated; ⟨*líneas*
telefónicas⟩ busy, engaged (BrE)

saturar [A1] *vt* to saturate

Saturno *m* Saturn

sauce *m* willow; **~ llorón** weeping willow

saudí, saudita *adj/mf* (Saudi) Arabian

sauna *f or* (AmL) *m* sauna

savia *f* (Bot) sap

sávila *f* (Méx) aloe vera

saxo *m* (fam) **(a)** (instrumento) sax (colloq)
(b) saxo *mf* (persona) sax player (colloq)

saxofón, saxófono *m* saxophone

saxofonista *mf* saxophonist

sazón *f* ⟦1⟧ **(a)** (condimento) seasoning; (sabor)
flavor*; **(b)** (de la fruta) ripeness; **estar en ~** to be
ripe ⟦2⟧ **a la sazón** (liter) at that time

sazonar [A1] *vt* to season

schop /ʃop/ *m* (Chi) (vaso) beer mug; (cerveza)
keg beer

Scotch® /(e)sˈkotʃ/ *m* (Andes) Scotch® tape
(AmE), Sellotape® (BrE)

scout /(e)sˈkau̯t/ *mf* scout

se *pron pers* ⟦1⟧ [seguido de otro pronombre:
sustituyendo a LE, LES]: **ya ~ lo he dicho** (a él)
I've already told him; (a ella) I've already told
her; (a usted, ustedes) I've already told you; (a ellos)
I've already told them; **el vestido tenía cuello**
pero ~ lo quité the dress had a collar but I took
it off
⟦2⟧ (en verbos pronominales): **¿no ~ arrepienten?**
«*ellos/ellas*» aren't they sorry?; «*ustedes*» aren't
you sorry?; **el barco ~ hundió** the ship sank; **~**
secó/secaron (*refl*) he dried himself/they dried
themselves; **~ secó el pelo** (*refl*) she dried her
hair; **~ hizo un vestido** (*refl*) she made herself a
dress; (*caus*) she had a dress made; **no ~ hablan** ⋯⟶

S

(*recípr*) they're not on speaking terms, they're not speaking to each other; **~ lo comió todo** (*enf*) he ate it all

3 (a) (*voz pasiva*): **~ oyeron unos gritos** there were shouts, I (*o* we *etc*) heard some shouts; **~ publicó el año pasado** it was published last year (b) (*impersonal*): **aquí ~ está muy bien** it's very nice here; **~ castigará a los culpables** those responsible will be punished (c) (*en normas, instrucciones*): **¿cómo ~ escribe tu nombre?** how is your name spelled?, how do you spell your name?; **~ pica la cebolla bien menuda** chop the onion finely

sé ▶ SABER, SER

sea, seas, etc ▶ SER

sebo *m* (grasa) grease, fat; (para jabón, velas) tallow; (Coc) suet

secador *m* **1** *tb* **~ de pelo** hairdryer **2** (Per) (paño) dishtowel (AmE), tea towel (BrE); (toalla) towel

secadora *f* (de ropa, tabaco) dryer; (para el pelo) (Méx) hairdryer

secano *m*: **de secano** ⟨*campo/tierra*⟩ dry, unirrigated

secar [A2] *vt* (a) ⟨*ropa/pelo/platos*⟩ to dry; ⟨*pintura/arcilla*⟩ to dry (b) ⟨*tierra/plantas/hierba*⟩ to dry up; ⟨*piel*⟩ to make ... dry
■ **~** *vi* to dry

■ **secarse** *v pron* **1** (a) «*ropa/pintura/pelo*» to dry; «*piel*» to get dry; **se me seca mucho la piel** my skin gets very dry (b) «*herida*» to heal (up) (c) «*tierra/planta/hierba*» to dry up (d) «*río/pozo/fuente*» to dry up (e) «*arroz/guiso*» to go dry **2** (*refl*) «*persona*» to dry oneself; ⟨*manos/pelo*⟩ to dry; ⟨*lágrimas*⟩ to dry, wipe away

sección *f* **1** (corte) section **2** (a) (división, área — en general) section; (— de empresa, en grandes almacenes) department (b) (de periódico, orquesta) section **3** (Mil) platoon

seccionar [A1] *vt* (cortar) to cut off; (dividir en secciones) to section

seco -ca *adj* **1** (a) [ESTAR] ⟨*ropa/platos/pintura*⟩ dry; ⟨*boca/garganta*⟩ dry (b) [ESTAR] ⟨*planta/río/comida*⟩ dry (c) [SER] ⟨*clima/región*⟩ dry **2** ⟨*higos/flores*⟩ dried; **bacalao ~** stockfish, dried salt cod **3** [SER] (no graso) ⟨*piel/pelo*⟩ dry **4** [SER] (no dulce) ⟨*vino/licor/vermut*⟩ dry **5** ⟨*golpe/sonido*⟩ sharp; ⟨*tos*⟩ dry **6** ⟨*respuesta/carácter*⟩ dry; **estuvo muy ~ conmigo** he was very short with me **7** (*en locs*) **en seco** ⟨*frenar/parar*⟩ sharply, suddenly; **limpieza en ~** dry cleaning

secreción *f* (de glándula) secretion; (de herida) discharge

secretaría *f* **1** (a) (cargo) office of secretary (b) (oficina) secretary's office (c) (departamento administrativo) secretariat **2** (Méx) (ministerio) department, ministry (BrE)

secretariado *m* secretarial work; **estudia ~** she's doing a secretarial course

secretario -ria *m,f* **1** (a) (trabajador administrativo) secretary (b) (de asociación, sociedad) secretary; **~ de dirección** secretary to the director; **~ general** secretary general **2** (Méx) (Gob, Pol) secretary of state, minister; **S~ de Gobernación** (en Méx) Minister of the Interior, ≈ Home Secretary (*in UK*)

secretear [A1] *vi* (AmL fam) to whisper
■ **secretearse** *v pron* (AmL fam) to whisper

secreter *m* writing desk

secreto¹ -ta *adj* secret

secreto² *m* (a) (información confidencial) secret; **los preparamos en ~** we prepared them secretly *o* in secret; **~ a voces** open secret (b) (truco) secret; **el ~ está en ...** the secret is in ...

secta *f* sect

sectario -ria *adj* sectarian

sector *m* (a) (grupo) sector, group (b) (Mat) sector (c) (de ciudad) area (d) (Com, Econ) sector

secuela *f* consequence

secuencia *f* sequence, series

secuestrador -dora *m,f* (de persona) kidnapper; (de avión) hijacker

secuestrar [A1] *vt* ⟨*persona*⟩ to kidnap; ⟨*avión*⟩ to hijack

secuestro *m* (de persona) kidnapping; (de avión) hijack(ing)

secundaria *f* (a) (enseñanza media) secondary education, high school (AmE) (b) (Méx) (instituto) middle school

secundario -ria *adj* ⟨*factor/problema*⟩ secondary; ⟨*actor/actriz*⟩ supporting (*before n*)

sed *f* thirst; **el agua le quitó la ~** the water quenched his thirst; **tengo ~** I'm thirsty; **me da ~** it makes me (feel) thirsty; **su ~ de venganza/riqueza** her thirst for vengeance/riches

seda *f* (Tex) silk; (Odont) **~ dental** dental floss

sedal *m* fishing line

sedante *adj/m* (Med) sedative

sede *f* (a) (del gobierno) seat (b) (Relig) see (c) (de organización internacional) headquarters (*sing or pl*); (de compañía) headquarters (*sing or pl*), head office (d) (de congreso, feria) venue; **la ~ de los Juegos Olímpicos** the venue for the Olympic Games

sedentario -ria *adj* sedentary

sediento -ta *adj* thirsty

sedimento *m* sediment, deposit

sedoso -sa *adj* silky

seducción *f* seduction

seducir [I6] *vt* (a) (en sentido sexual) to seduce (b) (fascinar, cautivar) to captivate (c) ⟨*idea/proposición*⟩ (atraer) to attract, tempt; **no me seduce la idea** the idea doesn't appeal to me at all

seductor -tora *adj* (a) (en sentido sexual) seductive (b) (que cautiva, fascina) enchanting, charming (c) ⟨*idea/proposición*⟩ attractive, tempting
■ *m,f* (*m*) seducer; (*f*) seducer, seductress

seg. *m* (= **segundo/segundos**) sec.

segar [A7] *vt* ⟨*mies*⟩ to reap (liter), to cut

seglar *adj* lay (*before n*)
■ *mf* (*m*) layman; (*f*) laywoman

segmento *m* (Mat) segment; (Zool) segment; (Com) sector

segregación *f* segregation; **~ racial** racial segregation

segregar [A3] *vt* ⟨*personas/grupos*⟩ to segregate

seguida: **en seguida** (*loc adv*) immediately,

right *o* (BrE) straight away; **vinieron en ~** they came at once *o* right away; **en ~ voy/vuelvo** I'll be right there/back

seguido¹ -da *adj* consecutive, in a row; **faltó tres días ~s** she was absent three days running *o* in a row; **pasaron tres autobuses ~s** three buses went by one after the other; **~ DE algo/algn** followed BY sth/sb

seguido² ** *adv* 1 (recto, sin desviarse) straight on; **vaya todo ~ go straight on 2 (AmL) (a menudo) often

seguidor -dora *m,f* (de teoría, filósofo) follower; (Dep) supporter, fan

seguir [I30] *vt* 1 ⟨persona/vehículo/presa⟩ to follow; **camina muy rápido, no la puedo ~** she walks very fast, I can't keep up with her 2 ⟨camino/ruta⟩ to follow, go along; **siga esta carretera hasta llegar al puente** go along *o* follow this road as far as the bridge; **la saludé y seguí mi camino** I said hello to her and went on (my way); **la enfermedad sigue su curso normal** the illness is running its normal course 3 (a) ⟨instrucciones/consejo/flecha⟩ to follow (b) ⟨autor/método/tradición/moda⟩ to follow; **~ los pasos de algn** to follow in sb's footsteps 4 (a) ⟨trámite/procedimiento⟩ to follow; ⟨tratamiento⟩ to undergo (b) (Educ) ⟨curso⟩ to do, take 5 ⟨explicaciones/profesor⟩ to follow; **dicta demasiado rápido, no la puedo ~** she dictates too quickly, I can't keep up
■ **~** *vi* 1 (a) (por un camino) to go on; **siga derecho** *or* **todo recto** keep *o* go straight on; **sigue por esta calle** go on down this street; **~ de largo** (AmL) to go straight past (b) seguir adelante to carry on; **resolvieron ~ adelante con los planes** they decided to go ahead with their plans (c) (Col, Ven) (entrar): **siga por favor** come in, please 2 (en lugar, estado): **¿tus padres siguen en Ginebra?** are your parents still in Geneva?; **espero que sigan todos bien** I hope you're all keeping well; **sigue soltera** she's still single; **si las cosas siguen así ...** if things carry on like this ... 3 «tareas/buen tiempo/lluvia» to continue; «rumores» to persist; **sigo pensando que deberíamos haber ido** I still think we ought to have gone; **~é haciéndolo a mi manera** I'll go on *o* carry on doing it my way 4 (a) (venir después): **lee lo que sigue** read what comes next; **el capítulo que sigue** the next chapter (b) «historia/poema» to continue, go on

según *prep* 1 (de acuerdo con) according to; **~ Elena** according to Elena; **~ parece** apparently 2 (dependiendo de): **~ cómo lo hagas** depending (on) how you do it; **¿me llevas a casa? — ~ dónde vivas** will you take me home? — (it) depends where you live
■ *adv* it depends; **puede resultar o no, ~** it may or may not work, it depends
■ *conj* (a medida que) as; **~ van entrando** as they come in

segunda *f* 1 (a) (Auto) (marcha) second (gear); **mete (la) ~** put it in second (gear) (b) (Transp) (clase) second class; **viajar en ~** to travel second class 2 **segundas** *fpl*: **todo lo dice con ~s** there's a hidden meaning to everything he says

segundero *m* second hand

segundo¹ -da *adj/pron* (a) (ordinal) second; **relegar a algn a un ~ plano** to push sb into the background; *para ejemplos ver* QUINTO (b) ⟨categoría/clase⟩ second
■ *m,f* deputy, second-in-command

segundo² *m* second; **un ~, ahora te atiendo** just a second, I'll be right with you

seguridad *f* 1 (ausencia de peligro) safety; (protección contra robos, atentados) security; **medidas de ~** (contra accidentes, incendios) safety measures; (contra robos, atentados) security measures; **una prisión de alta ~** a high security prison; **~ ciudadana** public safety; **~ social** social security 3 (a) (certeza) certainty; **podemos decir con ~ que ...** we can say for sure *o* with certainty that ... (b) (confianza, aplomo) confidence, self-confidence

seguro¹ -ra *adj* 1 (a) [SER] (exento de riesgo) safe; **en un lugar ~** in a safe place (b) (estable) secure; **un trabajo ~** a secure job; **esa escalera no está segura** that ladder isn't safe *o* steady (c) [SER] (fiable) ⟨test/método⟩ reliable; ⟨anticonceptivo⟩ safe; **el cierre de la pulsera es muy ~** the fastener on the bracelet is very secure (d) [ESTAR] (a salvo) safe 2 (a) [ESTAR] (convencido) sure; **no estoy ~** I'm not sure; **~ DE algo** sure *o* certain OF sth (b) [SER] (que no admite duda) ⟨muerte/victoria⟩ certain; ⟨fecha⟩ definite; **todavía no es ~** it's not definite yet; **no te preocupes, ~ que no es nada** don't worry, I'm sure it's nothing; **~ que se le olvida** he's sure *o* bound to forget (c) (con confianza en sí mismo) self-assured, self-confident

seguro² *m* 1 (a) (mecanismo — de armas) safety catch; (— de pulsera, collar) clasp, fastener; **echó el ~ antes de acostarse** he locked the door before going to bed (b) (Méx) (imperdible) safety pin 2 (a) (contrato) insurance; **~ contra** *or* **a todo riesgo** comprehensive insurance, all-risks insurance; **~ contra** *or* **de incendios** fire insurance; **~ de desempleo** unemployment benefit; **~ de viaje** travel insurance; **~ de vida** life assurance, life insurance (b) (Seguridad Social): **el ~** *or* **el S~** the state health care system, ≈ Medicaid (*in US*), ≈ the National Health Service (*in UK*)
■ *adv*: **dijo que llegaría mañana ~** she said she'd definitely be arriving tomorrow; **no lo sabe ~** she doesn't know for sure *o* certain; **~ que sospecha lo nuestro** I'm sure he suspects we're up to something

seis *adj inv/pron/m* six; *para ejemplos ver* CINCO

seiscientos -tas *adj/pron* six hundred

seísmo *m* (Esp) (temblor) tremor; (terremoto) earthquake

selección *f* selection; **hizo una ~ de los mejores** she selected the best ones; **la ~ mexicana** (Dep) the Mexican national team

seleccionador -dora *m,f* (Dep) (a) (entrenador) coach (AmE), manager (BrE) (b) (miembro de una junta) selector

seleccionar [A1] *vt* to select, choose

selectividad *f* (a) (cualidad) selectivity (b) (Educ) (en Esp) *university entrance examination*

selectivo -va *adj* selective

selecto -ta adj ⟨fruta/vino⟩ select, choice; ⟨ambiente/club⟩ select, exclusive

sellar [A1] vt ⟦1⟧ (a) ⟨pasaporte⟩ to stamp (b) ⟨plata/oro⟩ to hallmark ⟦2⟧ (cerrar) to seal

sello m ⟦1⟧ (de correos) (postage) stamp; (útil de oficina) rubber stamp; (marca) stamp ⟦2⟧ (a) (en el oro, la plata) hallmark (b) (AmL) (de una moneda) reverse; ¿cara o ∼? (Andes, Ven) heads or tails? (c) (anillo) signet ring, seal ring (d) (distintivo) hallmark (e) (Mús) tb ∼ discográfico record label ⟦3⟧ (precinto) seal

selva f (bosque) forest; (de vegetación tropical) jungle; S∼ **Negra** Black Forest; ∼ **tropical** tropical rainforest, selva

semáforo m (a) (Auto) traffic lights (pl); **se pasó un ∼ en rojo** she went through o (AmE) ran a red light (b) (Ferr) stop signal (c) (Náut) semaphore

semana f ⟦1⟧ (periodo) week; ∼ **laboral** workweek (AmE), working week (BrE); S∼ **Santa** Easter ⟦2⟧ (Col) (dinero) allowance, pocket money

semanal adj weekly

semanario m (Period) weekly magazine (o newspaper etc), weekly

semántico -ca adj semantic

sembrado1 m sown field

sembrado2 -da m,f (Méx) (Dep) seed

sembrar [A5] vt ⟨terreno/campo⟩ to sow; ⟨trigo/hortalizas⟩ to sow, plant; ∼ **algo DE algo** to plant sth WITH sth

semejante adj (a) (similar) similar; ∼ A **algo** similar TO sth (b) ⟨delante del n⟩ (para énfasis): **¡cómo puedes decir ∼ cosa!** how can you say such a thing!; **nunca había oído ∼ estupidez** I'd never heard such nonsense o anything so stupid ∎ m: **nuestros ∼s** our fellow men

semejanza f similarity; **a ∼ de sus antepasados** like his ancestors

semen m semen

semental m (caballo) stud horse; (toro) stud bull

semestral adj (a) (en frecuencia) ⟨exámenes/reuniones⟩ half-yearly, six-monthly (b) (en duración) ⟨curso⟩ six-month (before n)

semestre m (a) (seis meses): **cada curso dura un ∼** each course lasts six months (b) (Educ) (en algunos países latinoamericanos) tb ∼ **lectivo** semester (AmE), term (BrE)

semicírculo m semicircle

semicorchea f sixteenth note (AmE), semiquaver (BrE)

semidesnatado -da adj (Esp) semi-skimmed, half-cream (before n)

semifinal f semifinal

semifinalista mf semifinalist

semilla f seed

semillero m (a) (Agr, Bot) seedbed (b) (de discordias) source; (de delincuencia) hotbed, breeding ground

seminario m (a) (Relig) seminary (b) (Educ) seminar

seminarista m seminarian

semita adj Semitic
∎ mf Semite

sémola f semolina; ∼ **de arroz** ground rice

Sena m: **el ∼** the Seine

senado m senate

senador -dora m,f senator

sencillez f simplicity; **con ∼** ⟨vestir⟩ simply; ⟨comportarse⟩ with modesty; **habla con ∼** she uses plain language

sencillo1 -lla adj ⟦1⟧ (a) ⟨ejercicio/problema⟩ simple, straightforward; **no fue ∼ hacerlos entrar** it wasn't easy getting them in (b) ⟨persona⟩ modest, unassuming; ⟨vestido/estilo⟩ simple, plain; ⟨casa/comida⟩ simple, modest ⟦2⟧ (Esp, Méx) (Transp) one-way (AmE), single (BrE)

sencillo2 m ⟦1⟧ (disco) single ⟦2⟧ (AmL) (dinero suelto) change ⟦3⟧ (Esp, Méx) (Transp) one-way ticket (AmE), single (ticket) (BrE)

senda f (a) (camino) path (b) (Ur) (de carretera) lane

sendero m path, track

sendos -das adj pl (cada uno): **llevaban sendas pistolas** each of them was carrying o they were each carrying a gun; **con sendas fiestas en Madrid y Barcelona** with parties in both Madrid and Barcelona

Senegal m Senegal

senilidad f senility

seno m (a) (mama) breast; (pecho) bosom; **los ∼s** the breasts; **dar el ∼** (Ven) to breastfeed (b) (de organización, empresa) heart

sensación f ⟦1⟧ (percepción, impresión) feeling; **una ∼ de tristeza/impotencia** a feeling of sadness/impotence; **una vaga ∼ de placer** a vague sensation of pleasure; **una ∼ de pérdida/espacio** a sense of loss/space; **tengo** or **me da la ∼ de que no vamos a ganar** I have a feeling we're not going to win ⟦2⟧ (furor, éxito) sensation; **ser una ∼** to be a sensation

sensacional adj sensational

sensacionalismo m sensationalism

sensacionalista adj ⟨prensa⟩ sensationalist (before n); ⟨artículo/foto⟩ sensationalistic

sensatez f sense; **tuvo la ∼ de ...** she had the (good) sense to ...; **obró con ∼** she acted sensibly

sensato -ta adj sensible

sensibilidad f (a) (en general) sensitivity (b) (en brazo, pierna) feeling

sensibilizar [A4] vt to raise ... awareness

sensible adj ⟦1⟧ (en general) sensitive; ∼ A **algo** sensitive TO sth ⟦2⟧ (gen delante del n) (frml) (ostensible) ⟨cambio/diferencia⟩ appreciable; ⟨mejoría⟩ noticeable; ⟨aumento/pérdida⟩ considerable

sensiblero -ra adj (pey) mawkish

sensitivo -va adj sensory

sensorial adj sensory

sensual adj ⟨boca/cuerpo⟩ sensual, sensuous; ⟨placeres/gesto⟩ sensual; ⟨descripción⟩ sensuous

S

sensualidad *f* (de boca, gesto) sensuality; (de descripción) sensuousness

sentada *f* (a) (protesta) sit-in, sit-down protest (b) de *or* en una sentada in one go

sentado -da *adj* sitting, seated (frml); **estaban ∼s a la mesa** they were (sitting) at the table; *dar algo por ∼* to assume sth

sentador -dora *adj* (AmL) flattering, fetching

sentar [A5] *vi* (+ *me/te/le etc*) (a) «*ropa/color*» (+ *compl*): **ese vestido le sienta de maravilla** that dress really suits her (b) «*comida/bebida/clima*» (+ *compl*): **el café no le sienta bien** coffee doesn't agree with her; **me sentó bien el descanso** the rest did me a lot of good (c) «*actitud/comentario*» (+ *compl*): **me sentó mal que no me invitaran** I was rather put out that they didn't ask me (colloq)
■ ∼ *vt* [1] ‹*niño/muñeca*› to sit; ‹*invitado*› to seat, sit
[2] (establecer) to establish
■ **sentarse** *v pron* to sit; **∼se a la mesa** to sit at (the) table; **siéntese, por favor** please (do) sit down

sentencia *f* (Der) judgment, ruling

sentenciar [A1] *vt* to sentence; **la ∼on a muerte** (Der) she was sentenced to death

sentido¹ -da *adj* [1] ‹*palabras/carta*› heartfelt; ‹*anhelo/dolor*› deep; **mi más ∼ pésame** my deepest sympathy [2] [ESTAR] (AmL) (ofendido) hurt, offended

sentido² m [1] (a) (Fisiol) sense (b) (noción, idea) **∼ DE algo** sense OF sth; **su ∼ del deber** her sense of duty; **∼ común** common sense; **∼ del humor** sense of humor*
[2] (conocimiento) consciousness; **perder el ∼** to lose consciousness; **el golpe lo dejó sin ∼** he was knocked unconscious by the blow
[3] (significado) sense; **en el buen ∼ de la palabra** in the nicest sense of the word; **en ∼ literal** in a literal sense; **lo dijo con doble ∼** he was intentionally ambiguous; **el ∼ de la vida** the meaning of life; **en cierto ∼ … in a sense …; no le encuentro ∼ a lo que haces** I can't see any sense *o* point in what you're doing; **esa política ya no tiene ∼** that policy doesn't make sense anymore *o* is meaningless now; **palabras sin ∼** meaningless words
[4] (dirección) direction; **gírese en ∼ contrario al de las agujas del reloj** turn (round) in a counterclockwise (AmE) *o* (BrE) an anticlockwise direction; **venían en ∼ contrario al nuestro** they were coming in the opposite direction to us; **calle de ∼ único** *or* (Méx) **de un solo ∼** one-way street

sentimental *adj* (a) (relativo a los sentimientos) sentimental (b) ‹*persona/canción/novela*› sentimental; **ponerse ∼** to get sentimental (c) ‹*aventura/vida*› love (*before n*)

sentimentalismo *m* sentimentalism

sentimiento *m* [1] (a) (emoción) feeling; **ser de buenos ∼s** to be a caring person; **no se deja llevar por los ∼s** she doesn't let herself get carried away by her emotions (b) (pesar): **les acompaño en el ∼** my commiserations
[2] **sentimientos** *mpl* feelings (*pl*); **herir los ∼s de algn** to hurt sb's feelings

sentir [I11] *vt* [1] (a) ‹*dolor/pinchazo*› to feel; **∼**

hambre/frío/sed to feel hungry/cold/thirsty (b) ‹*emoción*› to feel; **sentimos una gran alegría** we were overjoyed; **∼ celos** to feel jealous
[2] (a) (oír) ‹*ruido/disparo*› to hear (b) (esp AmL) (percibir): **siento olor a gas** I can smell gas; **le siento gusto a vainilla** I can taste vanilla
[3] (lamentar): **lo siento mucho** I'm really sorry; **sentí mucho no poder ayudarla** I was very sorry not to be able to help her; **ha sentido mucho la pérdida de su madre** she has been very affected by her mother's death
■ **sentirse** *v pron* (+ *compl*) to feel; **me siento mal** I don't feel well, I'm not feeling well; **no me siento con ánimos** I don't feel up to it
[2] (Chi, Méx) (ofenderse) to be offended *o* hurt; **∼se CON algn** to be offended *o* upset WITH sb

seña *f* [1] (gesto) sign; **hacer una ∼** to make a sign, to signal; **les hice ∼s de que se callaran** I gestured *o* motioned to them to keep quiet
[2] **señas** *fpl* (dirección) address [3] **señas** *fpl* (indicios): **dar ∼s DE algo** to show signs OF sth
[4] (RPl) ▶ SEÑAL 5

señal *f* [1] (a) (aviso, letrero) sign; **∼es de tráfico** traffic signs; **S∼ de la Cruz** sign of the cross (b) (signo) signal; **nos hacía ∼es para que nos acercáramos** she was signaling *o* gesturing for us to come nearer; **∼ de auxilio** *or* **socorro** distress signal (c) (Ferr) signal
[2] (marca, huella): **pon una ∼ en la página** mark the page; **∼es de violencia** signs of violence
[3] (Rad, TV) signal (b) (Telec): **la ∼ para marcar** the dial (AmE) *o* (BrE) dialling tone; **la ∼ de ocupado** *or* (Esp) **comunicando** the busy signal (AmE), the engaged tone (BrE)
[4] (indicio) sign; **eso es mala ∼** that's a bad sign; **no daba ∼es de vida** he showed no signs of life; **en ∼ de respeto/amor** as a token of respect/love
[5] (Esp) (Com) (depósito) deposit, down payment

señalar [A1] *vt* [1] (indicar) ‹*ruta/camino*› to show; **el reloj señalaba las doce** the clock showed twelve; **me señaló con el dedo** he pointed at me (with his finger); **∼le algo A algn** to show sb sth, point sth out TO sb; **me señaló con el dedo qué pasteles quería** he pointed out (to me) which cakes he wanted
[2] (marcar con lápiz, rotulador) to mark
[3] (afirmar) to point out; **señaló que …** she pointed out that …
[4] (fijar) ‹*fecha*› to fix, set; **en el lugar señalado** in the appointed *o* agreed place
[5] (anunciar) to mark
■ **∼** *vi* to point

señalización *f* (a) (en carretera, calle) signposting; (en edificio, centro comercial) signs (*pl*) (b) (Ferr) signaling*

señalizar [A4] *vt* (a) ‹*carretera/calle/ciudad*› to signpost; ‹*edificio/centro comercial*› to put up directions on/in (b) (Ferr) ‹*tramo/vía*› to install signals on

señor -ñora *m,f* [1] (a) (persona adulta) (*m*) man, gentleman; (*f*) lady; **peluquería de ∼as** ladies' hairdresser's (b) (persona distinguida) (*m*) gentleman; (*f*) lady; **es todo un ∼** he's a real gentleman
[2] (dueño, amo): **el ∼/la ∼a de la casa** the gentleman/the lady of the house (frml)
[3] (Relig) (a) **Señor** *m* Lord (b) **Señora** *f*: **Nuestra S∼a de Montserrat** Our Lady of Montserrat

4 señora *f* (esposa) wife
5 (tratamiento de cortesía) **(a)** (con apellidos) *(m)* Mr; *(f)* Mrs; los ~es de Paz Mr and Mrs Paz **(b)** (frml) (con otros sustantivos): la ~a directora está ocupada the director is busy; S~ Director (Corresp) Dear Sir, Sir (frml) **(c)** (frml) (sin mencionar el nombre): perdón, ~ ¿tiene hora? excuse me, could you tell me the time?; muy ~ mío/~es míos (Corresp) Dear Sir/Sirs; Teresa Chaves — ¿~a o ~ita? Teresa Chaves — Miss, Mrs or Ms?; los ~es han salido Mr and Mrs Paz (*o* López *etc*) are not at home

señorial *adj* ‹casa› stately; ‹ciudad› noble

señorita *f* **1 (a)** (mujer joven) young lady **(b)** (joven distinguida) young lady **(c)** (maestra) teacher **2** (tratamiento de cortesía) (con apellidos) Miss **(b)** (con nombres de pila): ~ Teresa ¿puede atender a la señora? Teresa/Miss Chaves (*o* López *etc*), could you serve this lady please? **(c)** (maestra) Miss **(d)** (sin mencionar el nombre) (frml) Miss

señorito *m* (pey) rich young man, rich kid (colloq)

señuelo *m* (persona) bait; (para aves) decoy

sepa, sepas, etc ▶ SABER

separación *f* **1 (a)** (división) separation; la ~ de la Iglesia y del Estado the separation of the Church and the State **(b)** (espacio) gap, separation **2** (del matrimonio) separation

separado -da *adj* **1** ‹persona› separated **2 (a)** ‹camas› separate **(b)** por separado separately
■ *m,f*: es hijo de ~s his parents are separated

separador *m* **1** (de carpeta) divider **2** (Col) (Auto) median strip (AmE), central reservation (BrE)

separar [A1] *vt* **1 (a)** (apartar, alejar) to separate; ~ los machos de las hembras to separate the males from the females; separa la cama de la pared move the bed away from the wall **(b)** (dividir un todo) to divide **(c)** (guardar, reservar) to put *o* set aside
2 (a) (actuar de división) «valla/línea» to separate; los Andes separan a Chile de Argentina the Andes separate Chile from Argentina **(b)** (despegar): no puedo ~ estas dos fotos I can't get these two photographs apart
■ **separarse** *v pron* **(a)** «matrimonio» to separate; ~se DE algn to separate FROM sb **(b)** (seguir direcciones distintas) to split up; a mitad de camino nos separamos we split up half way **(c)** (apartarse, alejarse): no se separen, que los pequeños se pueden perder please stay together in case the children get lost; no me he separado nunca de mis hijos I've never been away *o* apart from my children

separatismo *m* separatism

separatista *mf* separatist

separo *m* (Méx) cell

sepia *f* **(a)** (Coc, Zool) cuttlefish, sepia (tech) **(b)** (en pintura) sepia
■ *m* (color) sepia

septentrional *adj* northern

septiembre *m* September; *para ejemplos ver* ENERO

séptimo¹ -ma *adj/pron* seventh; la séptima parte a seventh; el ~ arte the movies (*pl*) (AmE), the cinema (BrE); *para ejemplos ver* QUINTO

séptimo² *m* seventh

sepulcral *adj* (liter) ‹silencio› deathly

sepulcro *m* tomb, sepulcher* (liter)

sepultar [A1] *vt* **(a)** (frml) ‹muerto› to inter (frml), to bury **(b)** (period) (cubrir): fue sepultado por un alud de nieve he was buried by an avalanche

sepultura *f* **(a)** (acción) burial **(b)** (tumba) tomb, grave

sepulturero -ra *m,f* gravedigger

sequedad *f* **(a)** (de terreno, región, piel) dryness **(b)** (de respuesta, tono) curtness

sequía *f* drought

séquito *m* (de rey) retinue, entourage

ser [E26] *cópula* **1** (seguido de adjetivos) to be [SER *expresses identity or nature as opposed to condition or state, which is normally conveyed by* ESTAR. *The examples given below should be contrasted with those to be found in* ESTAR¹ *cópula* 1] es bajo/muy callado he's short/very quiet; es sorda de nacimiento she was born deaf; es inglés/católico he's English/(a) Catholic; era cierto it was true; sé bueno, estate quieto be a good boy and keep still; que seas muy feliz I hope you'll be very happy; (+ *me/te/le etc*) siempre le he sido fiel I've always been faithful to her; *ver tb* IMPOSIBLE, DIFÍCIL *etc*
2 (hablando de estado civil) to be; el mayor es casado the oldest is married; es viuda she's a widow; *ver tb* ESTAR¹ *cópula* 2
3 (seguido de nombre, pronombre) to be; soy abogada I'm a lawyer; ábreme, soy yo open the door, it's me
4 (con predicado introducido por 'de'): esos zapatos son de plástico those shoes are (made of) plastic; soy de Córdoba I'm from Cordoba; es de los vecinos it belongs to the neighbors, it's the neighbors'; no soy de aquí I'm not from around here
5 (hipótesis, futuro): será un error it must be a mistake; ¿será cierto? can it be true?
■ ~ *vi*
I 1 (a) (existir) to be **(b)** (liter) (en cuentos): érase una vez ... once upon a time there was ...
2 (a) (tener lugar, ocurrir): la fiesta va a ~ en su casa the party is going to be (held) at her house; ¿dónde fue el accidente? where did the accident happen? **(b)** (en preguntas): ¿qué habrá sido de él? I wonder what happened to *o* what became of him; ¿qué es de Marisa? (fam) what's Marisa up to (these days)? (colloq); ¿qué va a ser de nosotros? what will become of us?
3 (sumar): ¿cuánto es (todo)? how much is that (altogether)?; son 3.000 pesos that'll be *o* that's 3,000 pesos; somos diez en total there are ten of us altogether
4 (indicando finalidad, adecuación) ~ PARA algo to be FOR sth; este agua es para beber this water is for drinking
II (en locs) a no ser que (+ *subj*) unless; ¿cómo es eso? why is that?, how come? (colloq); como/ cuando/donde sea: tengo que conseguir ese trabajo como sea I have to get that job no matter what; hazlo como sea, pero hazlo do it any way *o* however you want but get it done; el lunes *o* cuando sea next Monday or whenever; puedo dormir en el sillón *o* donde sea I can sleep in the armchair or wherever you like *o* anywhere you like; de ser así (frml) should this be so *o* the case (frml); ¡eso es! that's it!, that's right!; es que ...:

¿es que no lo saben? do you mean to say they don't know?; **es que no sé nadar** the thing is I can't swim; **lo que sea: cómete una manzana, o lo que sea** have an apple or something; **estoy dispuesta a hacer lo que sea** I'm prepared to do whatever it takes; **o sea: en febrero, o sea hace un mes** in February, that is to say a month ago; **o sea que no te interesa** in other words, you're not interested; **(ya) sea ..., (ya) sea ...** either ..., or ...; **sea como sea** at all costs; **sea cuando sea** whenever it is; **sea donde sea** no matter where; **sea quien sea** whoever it is; **si no fuera/hubiera sido por ...** if it wasn't o weren't/hadn't been for ...

III (en el tiempo) to be; **¿qué fecha es hoy?** what's the date today?, what's today's date; **serían las cuatro cuando llegó** it must have been (about) four (o'clock) when she arrived; *ver tb v impers*

■ ~ *v impers* to be; **era primavera** it was spring(time)

■ ~ *v aux* (en la voz pasiva) to be; **fue construido en 1900** it was built in 1900

■ *m* **1** **(a)** (ente) being; ~ **humano/vivo** human/living being **(b)** (individuo, persona): **un ~ querido** a loved one

2 (naturaleza): **desde lo más profundo de mi ~** from the bottom of my heart

Serbia *f* Serbia

serbio¹ -bia *adj/m,f* Serbian

serbio² *m* (idioma) Serbian

serbocroata *adj/mf* Serbo-Croat, Serbo-Croatian

■ *m* (idioma) Serbo-Croat

seré, seremos, etc ▶ SER

serenarse [A1] *v pron* (calmarse) to calm down

serenata *f* serenade; **dar una** *or* (Méx) **llevar ~** to serenade

serenidad *f* calmness, serenity; **no pierdas la ~** keep calm

sereno¹ -na *adj* **(a)** ‹rostro/expresión/belleza› serene; ‹persona› serene, calm **(b)** ‹cielo› cloudless, clear; ‹tarde› still; ‹mar› calm, tranquil (liter)

sereno² *m* (vigilante nocturno) night watchman

sería, etc ▶ SER

serial *m*, (CS) *f* ▶ SERIE 2

serie *f* **1** **(a)** (sucesión) series; **una ~ de pueblos** a series of villages **(b)** (clase) series; **coches de ~** production cars; **fabricación en ~** mass production; **producir/fabricar en ~** to mass produce; **fuera de ~** (fam) out of this world (colloq) **(c)** (Dep) heat **2** (Rad, TV) series; (historia continua) serial

seriedad *f* **(a)** (en general) seriousness **(b)** (sensatez, responsabilidad): **se comportó con mucha ~** she behaved very sensibly o responsibly; **¡un poco de ~!** come on, let's be serious now!

serio -ria *adj* **1** (poco sonriente) serious **2** ‹empleado› responsible, reliable; ‹empresa› reputable **3** **(a)** ‹cine/tema› serious **(b)** ‹grave› ‹enfermedad/problema› serious; **tengo serias dudas acerca de él** I have serious doubts about him **(c)** **en serio** ‹hablar› seriously, in earnest; **¿lo dices en ~?** are you (being) serious?, do you really mean it?; **tomarse algo en ~** to take sth seriously

sermón *m* sermon; **me echó un ~** (fam) he gave me a lecture

seropositivo -va *adj* (en general) seropositive; (con el VIH) HIV positive

serpentear [A1] *vi* «río» to meander, wind; «camino» to wind, twist

serpentina *f* streamer

serpiente *f* snake, serpent; ~ **(de) cascabel** rattlesnake; ~ **pitón** python

serrar [A5] *vt* to saw (up)

serrín *m* sawdust

serruchar [A1] *vt* (AmL) to saw

serrucho *m* handsaw

servicentro *m* (Andes) service station

servicial *adj* helpful, obliging

servicio *m* **1** **(a)** (acción de servir) service; **estamos a su ~** we are at your service; **estar de ~** «policía/bombero» to be on duty; ~ **público** public service; ~**s informativos** broadcasting services (*pl*) **(b)** (favor) favor*, service **(c)** **servicios** *mpl* (asistencia) services (*pl*); **me ofreció sus ~s** he offered me his services **2** (funcionamiento) service, use; **está fuera de ~** it's out of service; **han puesto en ~ el nuevo andén** the new platform is now in use o is now open **3** (en hospital) department; ~ **de urgencias** casualty department **4** (en restaurante, hotel) **(a)** (atención al cliente) service **(b)** (propina) service (charge) **5** (servidumbre): **entrada de ~** tradesman's entrance; **cuarto de ~** servant's quarters (frml), maid's room; ~ **doméstico** (actividad) domestic service; (personas) servants (*pl*), domestic staff **6** (Mil) service; ~ **militar** military service **7** (retrete) restroom (AmE), bathroom (esp AmE), toilet (esp BrE) **8** (en tenis) service, serve **9** (Relig) service **10** (AmL) (Auto) service

servidor -dora *m,f* **1** **(a)** (sirviente) servant **(b)** (frml) (Corresp): **su (atento y) seguro ~** your humble servant (frml) **2** **servidor** *m* (Inf) server

servidumbre *f* **1** (esclavitud) servitude **2** (conjunto de criados) domestic staff, servants (*pl*)

servil *adj* **(a)** ‹persona/actitud› servile, obsequious (frml) **(b)** ‹trabajo› menial

servilleta *f* napkin, serviette (esp BrE)

servilletero *m* napkin ring, serviette ring (BrE)

servir [I14] *vi* **1** (ser útil): **esta caja no sirve** this box won't do o is no good; **ya no me sirve** it's (of) no use to me anymore; **¿para qué sirve este aparato?** what's this device for?; **no lo tires, puede ~ para algo** don't throw it away, it might come in useful for something; **este cuchillo no sirve para cortar pan** this knife is no good for cutting bread; **no sirves para nada** you're useless; **no creo que sirva para este trabajo** I don't think he's right o suitable for this job; ~ **DE algo: de nada sirve llorar** it's no use o good crying; **¿de qué sirve?** what's the point o the use?; **esto te puede ~ de mesa** you can use this as a table **2** **(a)** (en la mesa) to serve **(b)** (trabajar de criado) to be in (domestic) service **(c)** (Mil) to serve (frml) **3** (Dep) (en tenis) to serve ···⋗

■ ~ *vt* **1** ⟨*comida*⟩ to serve; ⟨*bebida*⟩ to serve, pour
2 (estar al servicio de) ⟨*persona/a la patria*⟩ to serve; **¿en qué puedo ~la?** (frml) how can I help you?

■ **servirse** *v pron* (*refl*) ⟨*comida*⟩ to help oneself to; ⟨*bebida*⟩ to pour oneself, help oneself to

sésamo *m* sesame

sesear [A1] *vi*: to pronounce the Spanish [θ] as [s], *eg* /ser'βesa/ *instead of* /θer'βeθa/ *for* CERVEZA

sesenta *adj inv/m/pron* sixty; *para ejemplos ver* CINCUENTA

seseo *m*: pronunciation of the Spanish /θ/ as /s/, *eg* /ser'βesa/ *instead of* /θer'βeθa/ *for* CERVEZA

sesión *f* **(a)** (reunión) session; ~ **de clausura** closing session **(b)** (de tratamiento, actividad) session; (de fotografía, pintura) sitting **(c)** (de cine) showing, performance; (de teatro) show, performance; ~ **de noche** late evening performance

sesionar [A1] *vi* (AmL) to be in session

seso *m* **(a)** (Anat, Zool) brain **(b) sesos** *mpl* (Coc) brains (*pl*)

set *m* (*pl* **sets**) set

seta *f* (comestible) mushroom; (venenosa) toadstool

setecientos -tas *adj/pron* seven hundred; *para ejemplos ver* QUINIENTOS

setenta *adj inv/m/pron* seventy; *para ejemplos ver* CINCUENTA

setiembre *m* ▶ SEPTIEMBRE

seto *m* hedge

seudónimo *m* pseudonym; (de escritor) pen name, pseudonym

severidad *f* (de castigo, pena) severity, harshness; (de padre, educador) strictness; (de clima) harshness

severo -ra *adj* ⟨*padre/profesor*⟩ strict; ⟨*castigo*⟩ severe, harsh; ⟨*invierno*⟩ hard, severe; ⟨*dieta/régimen*⟩ strict

Sevilla *f* Seville

sexismo *m* sexism

sexista *adj/mf* sexist

sexo *m* sex; **el ~ débil** the weaker sex; ~ **seguro** safe sex

sexto¹ -ta *adj/pron* sixth; *para ejemplos ver* QUINTO; **la sexta parte** a sixth; ~ **sentido** sixth sense

sexto² *m* sixth

sexual *adj* ⟨*relaciones/órganos/comportamiento*⟩ sexual; ⟨*educación/vida*⟩ sex (*before n*)

sexualidad *f* sexuality

sexy /'seksi, 'sesi/ *adj* (fam) sexy

sh, shh *interj* shush!, ssh!, hush!

sha, shah *m* shah

sheriff /'ʃerif/ *mf* sheriff

shock /ʃok/ *m* **(a)** (Med) shock; **en estado de ~** in (a state of) shock **(b)** (sorpresa desagradable) shock

show /ʃou, tʃou/ *m* (*pl* **shows**) show

si *conj* **1 (a)** (en general) if; ~ **pudiera** if I could;

~ **lo hubiera** *or* **hubiese sabido ...** if I'd known ..., had I known ...; **empezó a decir que ~ esto, que ~ lo otro** he said this, that and the other **(b)** (en frases que expresan deseo) if only; **¡~ yo lo supiera!** if only I knew! **(c)** (en frases que expresan protesta, indignación, sorpresa): **¡pero ~ te avisé ...!** but I warned you ...! **(d)** (planteando eventualidades, sugerencias): **y ~ no quiere hacerlo ¿qué?** and if she doesn't want to do it, what then?; **¿y ~ lo probáramos?** why don't we give it a try? **(e)** (en *locs*) **si no** otherwise

2 (en interrogativas indirectas) whether; **no sé ~ marcharme o quedarme** I don't know whether to go or to stay

■ *m* (nota) B; (en solfeo) ti, te (BrE); ~ **bemol/sostenido** B flat/sharp

sí *adv* **1** (respuesta afirmativa) yes; **¿has terminado? — sí** have you finished? — yes (I have); **decir que ~ con la cabeza** to nod

2 (uso enfático): **ahora ~ que lo has hecho bien** now you've really done it! (colloq); **tú ~ que sabes vivir** you certainly know how to live!; **eso ~ que es caro** that is expensive; **no puedo — ¡~ que puedes!** I can't — yes, you can! o of course, you can!; **que ~ cabe** it does fit; **es de muy buena calidad — eso ~** it's very good quality — (yes,) that's true

3 (sustituyendo a una cláusula): **creo que ~** I think so; **me temo que ~** I'm afraid so; **¿lloverá? — puede que ~** do you think it will rain? — it might; **un día ~ y otro no** every other day; **no puedo ir pero ella ~** I can't go but she can

■ *m* yes

■ *pron pers* **1 (a)** (*refl*) (él) himself; (ella) herself; (ellos, ellas) themselves; **solo piensa en ~ (mismo)** he only thinks of himself; **parece muy segura de ~ (misma)** she seems very sure of herself; **fueron para convencerse a ~ mismos/mismas** they went to convince themselves **(b)** (*refl*) (usted) yourself; (ustedes) yourselves; **descríbase a ~ mismo** describe yourself; **léanlo para ~ (mismos)** read it (to) yourselves **(c)** (*impers*): **hay cosas que uno tiene que ver por ~ mismo** there are some things you have to see for yourself

2 (en *locs*) **entre sí** (entre dos) between themselves; (entre varios) among themselves; **lo discutieron entre ~** they discussed it between/among themselves; **no se respetan entre ~** they don't respect each other; **de por sí: es de por ~ nervioso** he is nervous by nature; **el sistema es de por ~ complicado** the system is in itself complicated; **en sí (mismo): el hecho en ~ (mismo) no tenía demasiada importancia** this in itself was not so important

siamés -mesa *adj* Siamese
■ *m,f* (gemelo) Siamese twins

sibarita *mf* (amante de los lujos) lover of luxury, sybarite (frml); (en cuestiones de comida) gourmet, epicure (frml)

Siberia *f* Siberia

Sicilia *f* Sicily

siciliano -na *adj/m,f* Sicilian

AmC	América Central	Arg	Argentina	Cu	Cuba
AmL	América Latina	Bol	Bolivia	Ec	Ecuador
AmS	América del Sur	Chi	Chile	Esp	España
Andes	Región andina	CS	Cono Sur	Méx	México

Per	Perú
RPI	Río de la Plata
Ur	Uruguay
Ven	Venezuela

sida *m* (= **Síndrome de Inmunodeficiencia Adquirida**) AIDS

sidecar /siðe'kar, 'saikar/ *m* (*pl* **-cares** *or* **-cars**) sidecar

sideral *adj* (Astron) sidereal

siderurgia *f* iron and steel industry

sidra *f* hard cider (AmE), cider (BrE)

siempre *adv* **1** always; ~ **se sale con la suya** he always gets his own way; **como** ~ as usual; **lo de** ~ the usual thing; **a la hora de** ~ at the usual time; **los conozco desde** ~ I've known them for as long as I can remember; **para** ~ (definitivamente) ‹*regresar/quedarse*› for good; (eternamente) ‹*durar/vivir*› for ever **2** (en todo caso) always; ~ **podemos modificarlo después** we can always modify it later **3** (AmL) (todavía) still; ¿~ **viven en Malvín?** do they still live in Malvín? **4** (*en locs*) **siempre que** (cada vez que) whenever; (a condición de que) (+ *subj*) provided (that), providing (that) **5** (Méx) (en definitiva) after all; ~ **no se va** he's not leaving after all

sien *f* temple

sienta, sientas, etc ▶ SENTAR, SENTIR

sierra *f* **1** (Tec) saw; ~ **de mano** handsaw; ~ **mecánica** power saw **2** (Geog) (cordillera) mountain range; (zona montañosa): **fuimos a la** ~ we went to the mountains

Sierra Leona *f* Sierra Leone

sierraleonés -nesa *adj* of/from Sierra Leone

siervo -va *m,f* serf, slave

siesta *f* siesta, nap; **dormir la** ~ *or* **echar una** ~ to have a siesta *o* nap

siete *adj inv/pron* seven; *para ejemplos ver* CINCO
■ *m* **(a)** (cardinal) (number) seven; *para ejemplos ver* CINCO **(b)** (rotura) tear (*L-shaped*)

sietemesino -na *m,f* premature baby (*esp when born two months early*)

sífilis *f* syphilis

sifilítico -ca *m,f* person with *o* suffering from syphilis, syphilitic

sifón *m* **1 (a)** (botella) siphon* **(b)** (Esp fam) (soda) soda (water) **(c)** (Col) (cerveza) draft* beer **2** (para trasvasar líquidos) siphon; (en fontanería) U-bend, trap

siga, sigas, etc ▶ SEGUIR

sigilo *m* stealth; **con** ~ stealthily

sigiloso -sa *adj* stealthy

sigla *f* abbreviation; (pronunciado como una palabra) acronym

siglo *m* (período) century; **hace** ~**s** *or* **un** ~ **que no le escribo** (fam) I haven't written to her for ages (colloq)

significación *f* (importancia) significance, importance

significado *m* **1** (de palabra) meaning; (de símbolo) meaning, significance **2** (importancia) ▶ SIGNIFICACIÓN

significar [A2] *vt* **(a)** (querer decir) to mean **(b)** (suponer, representar) ‹*mejora/ruina*› to represent; ‹*esfuerzo/riesgo*› to involve **(c)** (valer, importar) to mean

significativo -va *adj* **1** ‹*cambio/detalle*› significant **2** ‹*gesto/sonrisa*› meaningful

signo *m* **1** (en general) sign; ~ **de admiración** exclamation point (AmE), exclamation mark (BrE); ~ **de interrogación** question mark; ~ **de la victoria** V-sign; ~ **de puntuación** punctuation mark **2** (Astrol) *tb* ~ **del zodiaco** sign; ¿**de qué** ~ **eres?** what sign are you?

sigo, sigue, etc ▶ SEGUIR

siguiente *adj* **1 (a)** (en el tiempo) following (*before n*); **al día** ~ the next *o* the following day **(b)** (en secuencia) next; **en el capítulo** ~ in the next *o* following chapter **(c)** (*como n*): **serán los** ~**s en entrar** they'll be the next to go; ¡**(que pase) el** ~! next please! **2** (que se va a nombrar) following (*before n*); **la carta decía lo** ~ ... the letter said the following ...

sílaba *f* syllable

silbar [A1] *vt* **(a)** ‹*melodía*› to whistle **(b)** ‹*cantante/obra*› (en señal de desaprobación) to whistle at, catcall
■ ~ *vi* **(a)** (Mús) to whistle **(b)** «*viento*» to whistle **(c)** «*oídos*»: **me silban los oídos** I've got a ringing *o* whistling in my ears

silbato *m* **(a)** (pito) whistle; **tocar el** ~ to blow the whistle **(b)** (Col period) (árbitro) referee

silbido *m* **(a)** (con la boca, un silbato) whistle; **dio un** ~ he whistled **(b)** (del viento, balas) whistling; (de respiración) wheezing **(c)** (en los oídos) ringing, whistling **(d)** **silbidos** *mpl* (en señal de desaprobacion) catcalls (*pl*)

silenciador *m* **(a)** (Auto) muffler (AmE), silencer (BrE) **(b)** (de arma) silencer

silencio *m* **1** (en general) silence; **deben guardar** ~ you must remain silent; **en el** ~ **más absoluto** in dead *o* total silence **2** (Mús) rest

silenciosamente *adv* silently, quietly

silencioso -sa *adj* **1** ‹*máquina/motor*› quiet, silent, noiseless; ‹*persona*› silent, quiet **2** ‹*calle/barrio*› quiet

silicona *f* silicone

silicosis *f* silicosis

silla *f* **(a)** (mueble) chair; ~ **de ruedas** wheelchair; ~ **eléctrica** electric chair; ~ **plegable** *or* **de tijera** folding chair **(b)** (Equ) *tb* ~ **de montar** saddle

sillín *m* (de bicicleta) saddle

sillón *m* armchair, easy chair

silogismo *m* syllogism

silueta *f* **(a)** (cuerpo) figure **(b)** (contorno) silhouette

silvestre *adj* wild

simbólico -ca *adj* symbolic

simbolizar [A4] *vt* to symbolize, represent

símbolo *m* symbol

simetría *f* symmetry

simétrico -ca *adj* symmetric, symmetrical

símil *m* **(a)** (comparación) comparison **(b)** (Lit) simile

similar *adj* similar; ~ **A algo** similar TO sth

similitud *f* similarity, resemblance

simio *m* ape, simian (tech)

simpatía *f* **(a)** (de una persona) friendliness **(b)** ···>

S

(sentimiento): **se ganó la(s) ~(s) de todos** everyone came to like him; **no le tengo mucha ~** I don't really like him

simpático -ca *adj* **(a)** ⟨*persona*⟩ nice; **me cae** *or* **me resulta muy ~** I really like him **(b)** ⟨*gesto/detalle*⟩ nice, lovely **(c)** ⟨*ambiente*⟩ pleasant, congenial; ⟨*paseo*⟩ pleasant, nice

simpatizante *mf* (de partido) sympathizer, supporter

simpatizar [A4] *vi* **(a)** (caerse bien) **~ (CON algn)** to get on well (WITH sb); **~on desde el primer momento** they took to each other right from the start **(b)** (Pol) **~ con algo** to be sympathetic TO sth, to sympathize WITH sth

simple *adj* [1] (sencillo, fácil) simple; ▶ LLANAMENTE [2] ⟨*delante del n*⟩ (mero) simple; **el ~ hecho de ...** the simple fact of ...; **es un ~ resfriado** it's just a common cold; **un ~ soldado** an ordinary soldier [3] (tonto) simple, simple-minded
■ *mf* simpleton

simpleza *f* **(a)** (falta de inteligencia) simpleness; (ingenuidad) gullibility **(b)** (tontería): **deja de hacer/decir ~s** stop being silly; **discutieron por una ~** they argued over a trifling matter

simplicidad *f* simplicity

simplificar [A2] *vt* to simplify

simplista *adj* simplistic

simposio, simposium *m* symposium

simulacro *m* **(a)** (cosa fingida): **no era de verdad, solo fue un ~** it wasn't for real, they (*o* he *etc*) were (*o* was *etc*) just pretending **(b)** (farsa) sham; **~ de ataque** mock attack; **~ de incendio** fire drill, fire practice

simular [A1] *vt* ⟨*sentimiento*⟩ to feign; ⟨*accidente*⟩ to fake; ⟨*efecto/sonido*⟩ to simulate

simultánea *f* (en ajedrez) simultaneous match

simultáneo -nea *adj* simultaneous

sin *prep* [1] without; **~ azúcar** without sugar; **seguimos ~ noticias** we still haven't had any news; **agua mineral ~ gas** still mineral water; **cerveza ~ alcohol** non-alcoholic beer, alcohol-free beer; **me quedé ~ pan** I ran out of bread [2] **(a)** (con significado activo) without; **se fue ~ pagar** he left without paying; **estuvo una semana ~ hablarme** she didn't speak to me for a week; **sigo ~ entender** I still don't understand; **la pisé ~ querer** I accidentally trod on her foot **(b)** (con significado pasivo): **preguntas ~ contestar** unanswered questions; **esto está aún ~ terminar** it still isn't finished
[3] **~ QUE + SUBJ**: **no voy a ir ~ que me inviten** I'm not going if I haven't been invited; **quítaselo ~ que se dé cuenta** get it off him without his *o* without him noticing; ▶ EMBARGO 2

sinagoga *f* synagogue

sinceridad *f* sincerity; **te voy a contestar con toda ~** I'm going to be quite honest *o* frank with you

sincero -ra *adj* sincere

sincronía *f* synchrony

sincronizar [A4] *vt* **(a)** ⟨*frecuencias/relojes*⟩ to synchronize; **~ algo CON algo** to synchronize sth WITH sth **(b)** (Col) ⟨*carro*⟩ to tune

sindical *adj* union (*before n*), labor union (*before n*) (AmE), trade union (*before n*) (BrE)

sindicalismo *m* **(a)** (movimiento) labor union movement (AmE), trade union movement (BrE) **(b)** (sistema, ideología) unionism, trade unionism (BrE)

sindicalista *mf* **(a)** (Rels Labs) member of the unions, trade unionist (BrE) **(b)** (Pol) syndicalist

sindicalizarse [A4] *v pron* (formar un sindicato) to unionize, form a union; (afiliarse a un sindicato) to join a union

sindicato *m* (Rels Labs) union, labor union (AmE), trade union (BrE)

síndrome *m* syndrome; **~ de abstinencia** withdrawal symptoms (*pl*); **~ de inmunodeficiencia adquirida** Acquired Immune Deficiency Syndrome, AIDS; **el ~ premenstrual** premenstrual syndrome *o* (BrE) tension, PMS, PMT (BrE); **~ de Down** Down's syndrome

sinfín *m*: **un ~ de** a great many

sinfonía *f* symphony

sinfónico -ca *adj* ⟨*música*⟩ symphonic; ⟨*orquesta*⟩ symphony (*before n*)

Singapur *m* Singapore

single /'siŋgel/ *m* [1] (Mús) single [2] (en tenis) **(a)** (CS) (partido) singles (match) **(b) singles** *mpl* (AmL) (partido) singles (match)

singular *adj* singular
■ *m* singular; **en ~** (Ling) in the singular

siniestro¹ -tra *adj* ⟨*mirada/aspecto*⟩ sinister; ⟨*intenciones*⟩ sinister, evil

siniestro² *m* (frml) (accidente) accident; (causado por una fuerza natural) disaster, catastrophe

sinnúmero *m* ▶ SINFÍN

sino *conj* but; **se comió no uno, ~ tres** he ate not one, but three; **no hace ~ criticar a los demás** he does nothing but criticize everybody else; **no vino, ~ que llamó** he didn't come, he telephoned; **no solo ... ~ que ...** not only ... but ...
■ *m* (liter) fate

sínodo *m* synod

sinónimo¹ -ma *adj* synonymous; **~ DE algo** synonymous WITH sth

sinónimo² *m* synonym; **~ DE algo** synonym FOR sth

sinsabores *mpl* (problemas) troubles (*pl*); (experiencias tristes) heartaches (*pl*)

sintáctico -ca *adj* syntactic

sintagma *m* syntagm, syntagma

sintaxis *f* syntax

síntesis *f* (*pl* **~**) **(a)** (resumen) summary **(b)** (deducción) synthesis; (combinación) synthesis, combination

sintético -ca *adj* ⟨*fibra*⟩ synthetic, man-made; ⟨*suelas*⟩ man-made

sintetizador *m* synthesizer

sintetizar [A4] *vt* **(a)** (resumir) to summarize **(b)** (combinar) to synthesize, combine

sintiera, sintió, etc ▶ SENTIR

síntoma *m* (Med) symptom; (señal) sign, indication

sintonía *f* **(a)** (Rad, TV): **están ustedes en la ~ de Radio Victoria** you are listening to Radio Victoria; **para una mejor ~** for better reception **(b)** (armonía): **en ~ con el pueblo** in tune with the people

sintonizador *m* tuner

sintonizar [A4] *vt* ⟨*emisora*⟩ to tune (in) to

■ ~ *vi* (Rad, TV) to tune in

sinvergüenza *adj* (a) (canalla): ¡qué tipo más ~! what a swine! (colloq) (b) (hum) (pícaro) naughty

■ *mf* (a) (canalla) swine (colloq); (estafador, ladrón) crook (colloq) (b) (hum) (pícaro) rascal (hum)

síper *m* (Méx) zipper (AmE), zip (BrE)

siquiera *adv* 1 (por lo menos) at least; **dile ~ adiós** at least say goodbye to her; **¡si (tan) ~ me hubiera avisado …!** if only you'd warned me …! 2 (en frases negativas) even; **ni ~ nos saludó** he didn't even say hello to us

sirena *f* 1 (Mit) mermaid; (en mitología clásica) siren 2 (de fábrica, ambulancia, alarma) siren 3 (Col) (en pirotecnia) rocket

Siria *f* Syria

sirope *m* syrup

sirviente -ta *m,f* (*m*) servant; (*f*) maid, servant

sísmico -ca *adj* seismic

sismo *m* (terremoto) earthquake; (temblor) earth tremor

sismógrafo *m* seismograph

sistema *m* 1 (método) system; **trabajar con ~** to work systematically *o* methodically 2 (conjunto organizado) system; **~ nervioso** nervous system; **~ solar** solar system; **S~ Monetario Europeo** European Monetary System 3 (Inf) system; **entrar en el/salir del ~** to log on/off

sistemático -ca *adj* (*persona*) systematic, methodical; (*método*) systematic

sistematizar [A4] *vt* to systematize

sitiar [A1] *vt* (a) (Mil) to besiege; **estamos sitiados** we are under siege (b) (acorralar) to corner

sitio *m* 1 (a) (lugar) place; **pon ese libro en su ~** put that book back in its place; **cambié la tele de ~** I moved the TV; **déjalo en cualquier ~** leave it anywhere; **tiene que estar en algún ~** it must be around somewhere (b) (espacio) room, space; **¿hay ~ para todos?** is there (enough) room for everyone?; **hacer ~** to make room (c) (plaza, asiento): **guárdame el ~** keep my seat *o* place; **le cambié el ~** I changed places with him (d) (Inf); *tb* **~ web** Web site (e) (Méx) (parada de taxis) taxi stand *o* rank (f) (Chi) (terreno urbano) vacant lot 2 (Mil) siege

situación *f* 1 (a) (coyuntura) situation (b) (en la sociedad) position, standing 2 (emplazamiento) position, situation (frml), location (frml)

situado -da *adj* (a) (ubicado) situated (b) (*persona*): **estar bien ~** to have a good position in society

situar [A18] *vt* (a) (colocar, ubicar) (*fábrica/aeropuerto*) to site, to locate (frml) (b) (Lit) (*obra/acción*) to set (c) (*soldados*) to post, station

■ **situarse** *v pron* (a) (colocarse, ubicarse): **con esta victoria se sitúan en primer lugar** this victory puts them in first place; **se situó entre los cinco mejores** she got a place among the top five (b) (socialmente): **se ha situado muy bien** he has done very well for himself

siútico -ca *adj/m,f* (Chi) ▶ CURSI

skai®, **skay**® /(e)s'kai/ *m* imitation leather

S.L. *f* = **Sociedad Limitada**

slalom /(e)s'lalom/ *m* (*pl* **-loms**) slalom

slip /(e)s'lip/ (*pl* **slips**) *m* 1 (prenda interior) (a) (de hombre) underpants (*pl*), pants (*pl*) (BrE) (b) (de mujer) panties (*pl*), knickers (*pl*) (BrE) 2 (bañador) swimming trunks (*pl*)

SME *m* (= **Sistema Monetario Europeo**) EMS

smog /(e)s'moɣ/ *m* (AmL) smog

snowboard /es'nobor(d)/ *m* snowboard

sobaco *m* armpit

sobado -da *adj* (*tapizado/cortinas/prenda*) worn, shabby; (*libro*) dog-eared, well-thumbed

sobajear [A1] *vt* (AmL fam) ▶ SOBAR 1A, B

sobar [A1] *vt* 1 (a) (manosear) (*tela/ropa/tapizado*) to handle, finger (b) (fam) (*chica*) to feel up (colloq), to grope (esp BrE colloq) (c) (Col, Per fam) (adular) to suck up to (colloq) 2 (Col, Ven) (dar masajes) to massage

soberanía *f* sovereignty

soberano -na *adj* 1 (*estado/pueblo/poder*) sovereign 2 (fam) (enorme) tremendous; **eso es una soberana estupidez** that's an absolutely ridiculous thing to say/do

■ *m,f* (Gob, Pol) sovereign

soberbia *f* (orgullo) pride; (altivez) arrogance, haughtiness

soberbio -bia *adj* 1 (*persona/carácter*) (orgulloso) proud; (altivo) arrogant, haughty 2 (magnífico) superb, magnificent

sobornar [A1] *vt* to bribe, suborn (frml)

soborno *m* (acción) bribery; (dinero, regalo) bribe

sobra *f* 1 **de sobra** (a) (mucho): **hay comida de ~** there's plenty of food (b) (de más): **tengo una entrada de ~** I have a spare *o* an extra ticket; **tú aquí estás de ~** you're not wanted/needed here (c) (muy bien): **saber de ~ que …** to know full well *o* perfectly well that … 2 **sobras** *fpl* (de comida) leftovers (*pl*)

sobrado -da *adj* 1 (a) (*experiencia*) ample, more than enough; **tengo ~s motivos para sospechar** I have every reason to be suspicious (b) (*persona*): **estar ~ de algo** to have plenty of sth; **no ando muy ~ de tiempo** I'm a bit short of time 2 (Andes fam) (engreído) full of oneself (colloq)

sobrar [A1] *vi* (a) (quedar, restar): **sobró mucha comida** there was a lot of food left over; **¿te ha sobrado dinero?** do you have any money left? (b) (estar de más): **ya veo que sobro aquí** I can see I'm not wanted/needed here; **a mí no me sobra el dinero** I don't have money to throw around (colloq); **sobra un cubierto** there's an extra place

sobre *m* 1 (Corresp) envelope 2 (AmL) (cartera) clutch bag

■ *prep* 1 (indicando posición) (a) (encima de) on; **lo dejé ~ la mesa** I left it on the table; **los puso uno ~ otro** she placed them one on top of the other; **estamos ~ su pista** we're on their trail (b) (por encima de) over; **volamos ~ Lima** we flew over Lima; **en el techo, justo ~ la mesa** on the ceiling right above *o* over the table; **4.000 metros ~ el nivel del mar** 4,000 meters above sea level (c) (alrededor de) on; **gira ~ su eje** it spins on its axis 2 (en relaciones de jerarquía): **amar a Dios ~ todas las cosas** to love God above all else 3 (acerca de) on; about; **hay muchos libros ~ el tema** there are many books on *o* about the subject ⋯⋗

4 (Esp) (con cantidades, fechas, horas) around, about (BrE); ~ **unos 70 kilos** around *o* about 70 kilos **5 sobre todo** above all

sobrecama *f or m* (AmL exc CS) bedspread, counterpane

sobrecarga *f* **(a)** (en vehículo) excess load *o* weight **(b)** (de circuito, motor) overload; (de batería) overcharging

sobrecargar [A3] *vt* **(a)** ⟨*vehículo/animal*⟩ to overload **(b)** ⟨*circuito/motor*⟩ to overload; ⟨*batería*⟩ to overcharge **(c)** ⟨*persona*⟩ ~ **a algn DE algo** ⟨*de trabajo/responsabilidad*⟩ to overburden sb WITH sth

sobrecargo *mf* **(a)** (Aviac) (supervisor) purser, chief flight attendant; (auxiliar de vuelo) flight attendant **(b)** (Náut) purser

sobrecogedor -dora *adj* shocking, horrific

sobrecoger [E6] *vt* **(a)** (conmover) to move **(b)** (asustar) to strike fear into

sobredosis *f* (*pl* ~) overdose

sobregirado -da *adj* (esp AmL) overdrawn

sobregirar [A1] *vt* (esp AmL) to overdraw (on) ■ **sobregirarse** *v pron* to overdraw

sobregiro *m* (esp AmL) overdraft

sobrehumano -na *adj* superhuman

sobrellevar [A1] *vt* ⟨*dolor/enfermedad*⟩ to endure, bear; ⟨*tragedia*⟩ to bear; ⟨*soledad*⟩ to endure

sobremesa *f* (conversación) after-lunch/ after-dinner conversation; **estuvimos de ~** we sat around the table chatting

sobrenatural *adj* supernatural

sobrenombre *m* nickname

sobrepasar [A1] *vt* **(a)** ⟨*nivel/cantidad*⟩ to exceed, go above; ~ **el límite de velocidad** to exceed *o* go over the speed limit **(b)** ⟨*persona*⟩ (en capacidad) to outstrip; (en altura) to overtake

sobrepeso *m* (AmL) (exceso — de equipaje) excess (baggage); (— de carga) excess load *o* weight

sobreponerse [E22] *v pron* (recuperarse) to pull oneself together; **~se A algo** to get over sth, recover FROM sth

sobrepuesto *pp* ▶ SOBREPONER

sobresaliente *adj* ⟨*actuación*⟩ outstanding; ⟨*noticia/hecho*⟩ most significant *o* important ■ *m* (Educ) *grade between 8.5 and 10 on a scale of 10*

sobresalir [I29] *vi* **(a)** ⟨*alero/viga*⟩ to project, overhang; ⟨*borde*⟩ to protrude **(b)** (destacarse, resaltar) to stand out; **sobresale entre los demás** it/ she stands out from the rest; ~ **EN algo** ⟨*en deportes/idiomas*⟩ to excel *o* shine AT sth

sobresaltar [A1] *vt* to startle, make … jump ■ **sobresaltarse** *v pron* to jump, be startled

sobresalto *m* fright

sobretiempo *m* (Chi, Per) **(a)** (horas extra, pago) overtime **(b)** (Dep) overtime (AmE), extra time (BrE)

sobretodo *m* overcoat

sobrevenir [I31] *vi* ⟨*desgracia/accidente*⟩ to strike

sobrevivencia *f* survival

sobreviviente *adj/mf* ▶ SUPERVIVIENTE

sobrevivir [I1] *vi* to survive; ~ **A algo** to survive sth

sobrevolar [A10] *vt* to fly over

sobrino -na *m,f* (*m*) nephew; (*f*) niece; **mis ~s** (solo varones) my nephews; (varones y mujeres) my nephews and nieces

sobrio -bria *adj* **1** [SER] **(a)** ⟨*persona*⟩ sober, restrained; ⟨*hábitos*⟩ frugal **(b)** ⟨*decoración/estilo/ color*⟩ sober **2** [ESTAR] (no borracho) sober

sobros *mpl* (AmC) leftovers (*pl*)

socarrón -rrona *adj* (sarcástico) sarcastic, snide; (taimado) sly, crafty

socavón *m* (hoyo) hole; (excavación) shaft, tunnel; (cueva) cave

sociable *adj* sociable

social *adj* social

socialdemocracia *f* social democracy

socialdemócrata *adj* social democratic ■ *mf* social democrat

socialismo *m* socialism

socialista *adj/mf* socialist

socializar [A4] *vt* to socialize

sociedad *f* **1** (Sociol) society; ~ **de consumo** consumer society **2** (asociación, club) society **3** (Der, Fin) company; ~ **anónima** ≈ public corporation (*in US*), ≈ public limited company (*in UK*); ~ **de responsabilidad limitada** limited corporation (*in US*), (private) limited company (*in UK*); ~ **inmobiliaria** (Esp) (que construye) construction company; (que administra) real estate (AmE) *o* (BrE) property management company; ~ **mercantil** trading company **4** (clase alta) (high) society

socio -cia *m,f* **1** (miembro) member; **hacerse ~ de un club** to join a club **2** (Der, Fin) partner; ~ **accionista** shareholder **3** (fam) (camarada) buddy (AmE colloq), mate (BrE colloq)

sociología *f* sociology

sociológico -ca *adj* sociological

sociólogo -ga *m,f* sociologist

socorrer [E1] *vt* to help, come to the aid of

socorrido -da *adj* ⟨*excusa/recurso*⟩ handy, useful

socorrismo *m* (en el agua) lifesaving; (en la montaña) mountain rescue; (primeros auxilios) first aid

socorrista *mf* (en el agua) lifeguard, lifesaver; (en la montaña) mountain rescue worker; (de primeros auxilios) first-aider

socorro *m* help; **pedir ~** to ask for help; **¡~!** help!; **un grito de ~** a cry for help

soda *f* **(a)** (bebida) soda water, soda (AmE) **(b)** (AmC) (cafetería) coffee bar

sodio *m* sodium

sofá *m* sofa, settee, couch

sofá-cama *m* sofa bed

AmC	Central America	Arg	Argentina	Cu	Cuba	Per	Peru
AmL	Latin America	Bol	Bolivia	Ec	Ecuador	RPI	River Plate Area
AmS	South America	Chi	Chile	Esp	Spain	Ur	Uruguay
Andes	Andean Region	CS	Southern Cone	Méx	Mexico	Ven	Venezuela

sofisticado -da *adj* sophisticated

sofocante *adj* stifling

sofocar [A2] *vt* ⟨*fuego*⟩ to smother, put out; ⟨*motín/revolución*⟩ to stifle, put down
■ **sofocarse** *v pron* (acalorarse) to get upset *o* (colloq) worked up

sofoco *f* (a) (mal) (disgusto): **estaba con un ∼ terrible** I was so upset **(b)** (por el calor) suffocation; (en la menopausia) hot flash (AmE), hot flush (BrE)

sofreír [I35] *vt* to sauté, fry lightly

sofrito *m: lightly fried tomatoes, onion, garlic, etc*

software /'sofwer/ *m* software

soga *f* (cuerda) rope

sois ▶ SER

soja *f* (Esp) soy (AmE), soya (BrE)

sol *m* [1] (Astron, Meteo) sun; **brillaba el ∼** the sun was shining; **al salir/ponerse el ∼** at sunrise/ sunset; **ayer hizo** *or* **hubo ∼** it was sunny yesterday; **un día de ∼** a sunny day; **en esa habitación no da el ∼** that room doesn't get any sunlight *o* sun; **ayer hubo siete horas de ∼** we had seven hours of sunshine yesterday; **tomar el ∼** *or* (CS) **tomar ∼** to sunbathe
[2] (fam) (persona encantadora): **es un ∼** she's an angel (colloq)
[3] (Mús) (nota) G; (en solfeo) so*, sol; **∼ bemol/ sostenido** G flat/sharp
[4] (moneda) sol (*Peruvian unit of currency*)

solamente *adv* ▶ SÓLO

solapa *f* (de chaqueta) lapel; (de bolsillo, libro, sobre) flap

solapado -da *adj* ⟨*persona*⟩ sly, underhand (BrE); ⟨*maniobra*⟩ surreptitious, sly

solar *adj* ⟨*energía/año/placa*⟩ solar; **los rayos ∼es** the sun's rays
■ *m* [1] (terreno) piece of land, site [2] (a) (casa solariega) ancestral home **(b)** (linaje) lineage [3] (Per) (casa de vecindad) tenement building

solario, solárium *m* solarium

soldado *mf* soldier; **∼ de caballería** cavalryman; **∼ de infantería** infantryman; ; **∼ raso** private; **∼** *or* **soldadito de plomo** tin soldier

soldar [A10] *vt* (con estaño) to solder; (sin estaño) to weld

soleado -da *adj* sunny

soledad *f*: **en la ∼ de su cuarto** in the solitude of his room; **bebe para olvidar su ∼** she drinks to forget her loneliness; **no soporta la ∼** he can't stand being alone; **pasó sus últimos años en ∼** she spent her last years alone

solemne *adj* [1] (en general) solemn [2] (delante del n) (fam) ⟨*mentira*⟩ complete, downright

solemnidad *f* solemnity

soler [E9] *vi*: **suele venir una vez a la semana** she usually comes once a week; **no suele retrasarse** he's not usually late; **solía correr todos los días** he used to go for a run every day

solera *f* [1] (tradición, calidad): **una familia con ∼ a** family with a long pedigree, a long-established family [2] (CS) (Indum) sundress

solfear [A1] *vt* to sol-fa

solfeo *m* (asignatura) music theory, sol-fa

solicitado -da *adj* ⟨*persona*⟩ in demand; ⟨*canción*⟩ popular

solicitante *mf* applicant

solicitar [A1] *vt* ⟨*empleo/plaza*⟩ to apply for; ⟨*permiso/entrevista/información, servicios/apoyo/ cooperación*⟩ to request, ask for

solícito -ta *adj* (dispuesto a ayudar) attentive; (amable) thoughtful, kind

solicitud *f* (a) (para trabajo) application; (para licencia) application, request; (para información, ayuda) request **(b)** (formulario) application form

solidaridad *f* solidarity; **en** *o* **por ∼ con algn** in solidarity with *o* in sympathy with sb

solidario -ria *adj* (fraterno) supportive; **un gesto ∼** a gesture of solidarity

solidarizar [A4] *vi* **∼ CON algn** to support sb
■ **solidarizarse** *v pron* **∼se CON algn** to support sb; **∼se CON algo** to support sth, to back sth

solidez *f* (de muro, edificio) solidity; (de argumento, empresa) soundness; (de relación) strength

sólido -da *adj* [1] (en sentido físico) solid [2] (a) ⟨*argumento/razonamiento*⟩ solid, sound; ⟨*preparación/principios*⟩ sound **(b)** ⟨*empresa*⟩ sound; ⟨*relación*⟩ steady, strong

sólido² *m* (a) (Fís, Mat) solid **(b)** **sólidos** *mpl* (Med) solids (*pl*)

solista *mf* soloist

solitaria *f* tapeworm

solitario -ria *adj* (a) ⟨*persona/animal*⟩ solitary; ⟨*vejez/niñez*⟩ lonely; **(b)** ⟨*calles*⟩ empty, deserted; ⟨*paraje/lugar*⟩ lonely, solitary
■ *m,f* [1] (persona) loner [2] **solitario** *m* solitaire (AmE), patience (BrE)

sollozar [A4] *vi* to sob

sollozo *m* sob

solo¹ -la *adj* (a) (sin compañía): **estar/sentirse ∼** to be/feel lonely; **lo dejaron ∼** (sin compañía) they left him on his own *o* by himself; (para no molestar) they left him alone; **el niño ya camina ∼** the baby's walking on his own now; **hacen los deberes ∼s** they do their homework by themselves; **hablar ∼** to talk to oneself; **a solas** alone, by oneself **(b)** ⟨*café/té*⟩ black; ⟨*whisky*⟩ straight, neat; ⟨*pan*⟩ dry **(c)** (delante del n) (único): **lo haré con una sola condición** I'll do it on one condition; **hay un ∼ problema** there's just one problem

solo² *m* (Mús) solo

sólo *adv* [*The written accent may be omitted if there is no confusion with the adjective*] only; **∼** *or* **solo quería ayudarte** I only wanted to help, I was only *o* just trying to help; **∼** *or* **solo de pensarlo me dan escalofríos** just *o* merely thinking about it makes me shudder; **canto ∼ porque me gusta** I sing just for pleasure

solomillo *m* fillet/tenderloin/sirloin steak

solsticio *m* solstice

soltar [A10] *vt* [1] (dejar ir) ⟨*persona*⟩ to release, to let ... go; **soltó al perro** he let the dog off the leash
[2] (dejar de tener agarrado) to let go of; **no lo sueltes** don't let go of it; **soltó el dinero y huyó** he dropped/let go of the money and ran; **¡suelta la pistola!** drop the gun!
[3] (a) (desatar) ⟨*cuerda/cable*⟩ to undo, untie; **∼ amarras** to cast off **(b)** (aflojar): **suelta la cuerda poco a poco** let *o* pay out the rope gradually **(c)** ···❖

⟨*freno*⟩ to release; ⟨*embrague*⟩ to let out **(d)** (desatascar) ⟨*cable/cuerda*⟩ to free; ⟨*tuerca*⟩ to undo, get ... undone

4 (desprender) ⟨*calor/vapor*⟩ to give off; ⟨*pelo*⟩ to shed

5 ⟨*carcajada*⟩ to let out; ⟨*palabrotas/disparates*⟩ to come out with; ⟨*grito*⟩ to let out

■ **soltarse** *v pron* **1** (*refl*) «*perro*» to get loose; **no te sueltes de la mano** don't let go of my hand **2** (desatarse) «*nudo*» to come undone, come loose; (aflojarse) «*nudo*» to loosen, come loose; «*tornillo*» to come loose

soltería *f: the fact or state of being unmarried*; (en hombre) bachelorhood (frml); (en mujer) spinsterhood (frml)

soltero -ra *adj* single; **soy** *or* (esp Esp) **estoy soltera** I'm single, I'm not married

■ *m,f* (*m*) single man, bachelor; (*f*) single woman, spinster (dated *o* pej)

solterón -rona *m,f* (pey) (*m*) old *o* confirmed bachelor; (*f*) old maid (pej)

soltura *f:* **habla dos idiomas con ∼** he speaks two languages fluently; **se desenvuelve con ∼ en cualquier situación** she is at ease in any situation

soluble *adj* **1** (Quím) soluble; **∼ en agua** water-soluble **2** ⟨*problema*⟩ soluble, solvable

solución *f* solution; **encontrar una ∼ a algo** to find a solution to sth

solucionar [A1] *vt* ⟨*problema*⟩ to solve; ⟨*asunto/conflicto*⟩ to settle, resolve

■ **solucionarse** *v pron* «*problema*» to be resolved; **al final todo se solucionó** everything worked out in the end

somalí *adj/mf* Somali

Somalia *f* Somalia

sombra *f* (lugar sin sol) shade; (proyección) shadow; **las ∼s de los árboles** the shadows of the trees; **sentarse a** *or* **en la ∼** to sit in the shade; **este árbol casi no da ∼** this tree gives hardly any shade; **∼ de** *or* **para ojos** eyeshadow

sombrero *m* hat; **∼ de copa** top hat; **∼ de jipijapa** Panama (hat); **∼ hongo** derby (AmE), bowler (hat) (BrE); **∼ jarano** Mexican sombrero

sombrilla *f* **(a)** (de mano) parasol; (de playa) sunshade **(b)** (Col, Ven) (paraguas) lady's umbrella

sombrío -bría *adj* (liter) ⟨*lugar*⟩ (umbrío) dark **(b)** (lúgubre) cheerless, dismal; ⟨*persona*⟩ gloomy

someter [E1] *vt* **1** (dominar) ⟨*país*⟩ to subjugate; **fue necesario usar la fuerza para ∼lo** they had to use force to subdue him **2** (a torturas, presiones, prueba) to subject; **lo sometieron a un interrogatorio** they subjected him to an interrogation; **∼ algo a votación** to put sth to the vote

■ **someterse** *v pron* **(a)** (a autoridad) to submit to, yield to; (a capricho) to give in to; (a ley) to comply with **(b)** (a prueba, examen, operación) to undergo

somier /so'mje(r)/ *m* (*pl* **-miers** *or* **-mieres**) sprung bed base

somnífero *m* sleeping pill, soporific (frml)

somnolencia *f* drowsiness, sleepiness

somnoliento -ta *adj* sleepy, drowsy

somos ▶ SER

son *m* **1** **(a)** (sonido) sound; **al ∼ del violín** to the strains *o* to the sound of the violin **(b)** **en son de:** **lo dijo en ∼ de burla** she said it mockingly; **venimos en ∼ de paz** we come in peace **2** (canción latinoamericana) *song with a lively, danceable beat*

son ▶ SER

sonado -da *adj* **1** ⟨*boda/suceso/noticia*⟩ much-talked-about **2** **(a)** ⟨*boxeador*⟩ punch-drunk **(b)** (fam) (torpe) stupid (colloq) **3** (AmL fam) (en dificultades) [ESTAR] in a mess (colloq), in trouble (colloq)

sonaja *f* (Méx) rattle

sonajero *m* rattle

sonámbulo -la *adj* somnambulistic (frml); **es ∼** he sleepwalks, he walks in his sleep

■ *m,f* sleepwalker, somnambulist (frml)

sonar [A10] *vi* **1** ⟨*teléfono*⟩ to ring; «*disparo*» to ring out; **el despertador sonó a las cinco** the alarm went off at five o'clock; **∼on las doce en el reloj** the clock struck twelve; **me suenan las tripas** (fam) my tummy's rumbling (colloq)

2 (+ *compl*) **(a)** «*motor/instrumento*» to sound; «*persona*» to sound; **suena raro** it sounds funny; **sonaba preocupada** she sounded worried; **suena a hueco** it sounds hollow **(b)** «*palabra/ expresión*» to sound

3 **(a)** (resultar conocido) (+ *me/te/le* etc): **me suena tu cara** your face is *o* looks familiar; **¿te suena este refrán?** does this proverb ring a bell (with you) *o* sound familiar to you? **(b)** (parecer) **∼ a algo** to sound like sth

4 (AmL fam) (fracasar): **soné en el examen** I blew it in the exam (colloq); **sonamos** we've blown it now (colloq)

■ ∼ *vt* **1** **(a)** (+ *me/te/le* etc) ⟨*nariz*⟩ to wipe **(b)** ⟨*trompeta*⟩ to play **2** (Méx fam) **(a)** (pegar) ⟨*persona*⟩ to thump (colloq), to clobber (colloq) **(b)** (en competición) to beat, thrash (colloq)

■ **sonarse** *v pron*: *tb* **∼se la nariz** to blow one's nose

sonata *f* sonata

sonda *f* **(a)** (Med) catheter **(b)** (para perforar) drill **(c)** (Náut) sounding line, lead line **(d)** (Espac, Meteo) probe

sondeo *m* **1** (encuesta) poll, survey **2** (perforación) test drilling; (Náut) sounding; (Espac, Meteo) exploration

soneto *m* sonnet

sonido *m* sound

sonoro -ra *adj* ⟨*golpe*⟩ resounding (*before n*), loud; ⟨*voz/lenguaje*⟩ sonorous, resonant; (Ling) voiced

sonreír [I18] *vi* **(a)** «*persona*» to smile; **∼(le) a algn** to smile AT sb **(b)** «*vida/fortuna*» (+ *me/te/ le* etc) to smile on

sonriente *adj* ⟨*ojos/expresión*⟩ smiling (*before n*); ⟨*persona*⟩ cheerful

sonrisa *f* smile

sonrojarse [A1] *v pron* to blush

sonsacar [A2] *vt*: **me costó trabajo ∼le la verdad** I had a hard time getting the truth out of her

soñado -da *adj* (AmL fam) divine (colloq), heavenly (colloq); *ver tb* SOÑAR

soñador -dora *adj* ⟨*mirada*⟩ dreamy, faraway; **soy muy ∼** I'm a real dreamer

■ *m,f* dreamer

soñar [A10] vt **(a)** (durmiendo) to dream **(b)** (fantasear) to dream; **la casa soñada** her/his/their dream house

■ ~ vi **(a)** (durmiendo) to dream; ~ **CON algo/algn** to dream ABOUT sth/sb; **que sueñes con los angelitos** (fr hecha) sweet dreams **(b)** (fantasear) to dream; ~ **despierto** to daydream; ~ **CON algo** to dream OF sth

sopa f (caldo) soup; ~ **de sobre** packaged soup (AmE), packet soup (BrE)

sopapo m (fam) (bofetón) slap, smack (colloq)

sope m (Méx) fried tortilla topped with refried beans, onion and hot sauce

sopera f soup tureen

sopesar [A1] vt ⟨situación/ventajas⟩ to weigh up; ⟨palabras⟩ to weigh

soplar [A1] vi **1 (a)** (con la boca) to blow **(b)** «viento» to blow **2** (fam) (en examen) to whisper (answers in an exam)

■ ~ vt **1 (a)** ⟨vela⟩ to blow out; ⟨fuego/brasas⟩ to blow on **(b)** ⟨vidrio⟩ to blow **2** (fam) ⟨respuesta⟩ (en examen) to whisper **3** (fam) (robar) to swipe (colloq), to pinch (BrE colloq); (cobrar) to sting (colloq)

■ **soplarse** v pron (Méx, Per fam) (aguantar) ⟨persona⟩ to put up with; ⟨discurso/película⟩ to sit through, suffer

soplete m (para soldar) gas welding torch; (para quitar pintura) blowtorch

soplido m puff

soplo m **1 (a)** (soplido) puff; **de un** ~ with one puff, in one go **(b)** (de aire) puff; (más fuerte) blast **(c)** (de viento) puff; (más fuerte) gust **2** (fam) (chivatazo): **alguien dio el** ~ **a la policía** someone tipped off the police (colloq) **3** (Med) heart murmur

soplón -plona m,f **(a)** (fam) (en colegio) tattletale (AmE colloq), telltale (BrE colloq) **(b)** (fam) (a la policía) informer, stoolie (AmE colloq), grass (BrE colloq)

soponcio m (fam) **(a)** (desmayo): **le dio un** ~ she fainted **(b)** (ataque de nervios) fit (colloq)

sopor m **(a)** (somnolencia) drowsiness, sleepiness **(b)** (letargo) torpor

soporífero -ra adj ⟨efecto/discurso/clase⟩ soporific

soportable adj bearable

soportal m **(a)** (de casa) porch **(b)** **soportales** mpl (de calle) arcade, colonnade

soportar [A1] vt **1 (a)** ⟨situación/frío/dolor⟩ to put up with, bear, endure (frml); ⟨persona⟩ to put up with; **no soporto este calor/la gente así I** can't stand this heat/people like that **2** ⟨peso/carga⟩ to support, withstand; ⟨presión⟩ to withstand

soporte m **(a)** (de estante) bracket; (de viga) support; (de maceta, portarretratos) stand **(b)** (Inf) medium

soprano mf soprano

soquete m **1** (CS) (Indum) ankle sock **2** (Chi) (Elec) lampholder, socket **3** (Col, Méx, RPI fam) (tonto) fool, idiot

sor f (Relig) sister

sorber [E1] vt **(a)** (beber) to suck in o up; (tomar poco a poco) to sip **(b)** «esponja» to absorb, soak up

sorbete m sherbet (AmE), sorbet (esp BrE)

sorbo m **(a)** (cantidad pequeña) sip; **bébetelo a sorbitos** sip it **(b)** (trago grande) gulp; **de un** ~ in one gulp

sordera f deafness

sórdido -da adj ⟨lugar/ambiente⟩ squalid; ⟨asunto/libro⟩ sordid

sordina f (de trompeta, violín) mute; (de piano) damper

sordo -da adj **1** (Med) deaf; **se quedó** ~ he went deaf; **es** ~ **de nacimiento** he was born deaf **2** ⟨ruido/golpe⟩ dull, muffled; ⟨dolor⟩ dull; (Ling) voiceless

■ m,f deaf person; **hacerse el** ~ to pretend not to hear

sordomudo -da adj deaf-mute (before n), deaf and dumb (BrE)

■ m,f deaf-mute

soroche m (Andes) (en la montaña) mountain sickness, altitude sickness

sorprendente adj surprising

sorprender [E1] vi to surprise; **me sorprende que no lo sepas** I'm surprised you don't know

■ ~ vt (coger desprevenido) to surprise, catch ... unawares; **nos sorprendió la lluvia** we got caught in the rain

■ **sorprenderse** v pron to be surprised

sorprendido -da adj surprised; **me miró** ~ he looked at me in surprise; **ver tb** SORPRENDER

sorpresa f **(a)** (emoción) surprise; **se va a llevar una** ~ she's going to be surprised, she's in for a surprise (colloq); **tomar** or (esp Esp) **coger a algn de** ~ to take sb by surprise **(b)** (regalo) surprise

■ adj inv ⟨fiesta/ataque⟩ surprise (before n)

sorpresivo -va adj (AmL) surprise (before n), unexpected

sortear [A1] vt **1** ⟨premio/puesto⟩ to draw lots for; **se** ~**á un coche** there will be a prize draw for a car **2 (a)** ⟨bache/obstáculo⟩ to avoid, negotiate **(b)** ⟨problema/dificultad⟩ to get around

sorteo m draw; **por** ~ by drawing lots

sortija f **(a)** (anillo) ring **(b)** (en el pelo) ringlet

sortilegio m (embrujo) spell, charm; (brujería) sorcery; (adivinación) fortune-telling

SOS: equivalent of 'eres' in Central America and the River Plate area

SOS m SOS, distress call

sosa f soda

soslayo: **de soslayo** ⟨mirada⟩ sidelong (before n), sideways; ⟨mirar⟩ sideways

soso -sa adj **(a)** ⟨comida⟩ (sin sabor) bland, tasteless; **está** ~ (sin sabor) it's bland o tasteless; (sin sal) it needs more salt **(b)** ⟨persona/película⟩ boring, dull; ⟨estilo⟩ flat, drab

sospecha f suspicion; **tengo la** ~ **de que ...** I suspect o I have a feeling that ...

sospechar [A1] vt to suspect

■ ~ vi ~ **DE algn** to suspect sb, have one's suspicions ABOUT sb

sospechoso -sa adj ⟨movimiento/comportamiento⟩ suspicious; ⟨paquete⟩ suspicious, suspect; **tres hombres de aspecto** ~ three suspicious-looking men

■ m,f suspect

sostén m **(a)** (físico) support; (económico) means of support **(b)** (Indum) bra, brassiere

S

sostener [E27] vt **1** (apoyar) **(a)** ⟨estructura/
techo⟩ to hold up, support; ⟨carga/peso⟩ to bear
(b) (sustentar) ⟨familia⟩ to support, maintain
2 (sujetar, tener cogido) ⟨paquete⟩ to hold; **no
tengas miedo, yo te sostengo** don't be afraid, I've
got you o I'm holding you
3 ⟨conversación/relación/reunión⟩ to have
4 **(a)** (opinar) to hold **(b)** ⟨argumento/afirmación⟩
to support, back up
5 **(a)** ⟨lucha/ritmo/resistencia⟩ to keep up,
sustain; **ella sostuvo mi mirada** she held my gaze
(b) (Mús) ⟨nota⟩ to hold, sustain
■ **sostenerse** v pron **(a)** (no caerse): **la estructura
se sostiene sola** the structure stays up without
support; **apenas se sostenía en pie** he could
hardly stand **(b)** (en un estado) to remain; **se
sostuvo en el poder** she managed to remain in
power

sostenido -da adj sharp; **re ∼ D** sharp

sostuve, sostuvo, etc ▶ SOSTENER

sota f jack (in Spanish pack of cards)

sotana f cassock, soutane

sótano m (habitable) basement; (para
almacenamiento) cellar, basement

souvenir /suβe'nir/ m (pl **-nirs**) souvenir

soviético -ca adj/m,f (Hist) Soviet

soy ▶ SER

soya f (AmL) soy (AmE), soya (BrE)

sport /(e)s'por/ m: **ropa (de) ∼** leisure wear,
casual clothes (pl); **vestido de ∼** casually dressed

spot /(e)s'pot/ m (pl **spots**) tb ∼ **publicitario**
(espacio) slot; (anuncio) commercial, advertisement
(BrE)

spray /(e)s'prai/ m (pl **sprays**) spray

Sr. m (= **señor**) Mr

Sra. f (= **señora**) Mrs

Sres. mpl = **señores**

Srta. f (= **señorita**) Miss

SS.MM. = **Sus Majestades**

Sta. (= **Santa**) St

status /(e)s'tatus/ m (pl ∼) status

Sto. (= **Santo**) St

stop /(e)s'top/ m (disco) stop sign

su adj (delante del n) (de él) his; (de ella) her; (de
usted, ustedes) your; (de ellos, ellas) their; (de animal,
cosa) its

suave adj **1** ⟨piel/cutis⟩ smooth, soft; ⟨pelo⟩
soft; ⟨superficie/pasta⟩ smooth **2** **(a)** ⟨tono⟩
gentle; ⟨acento/música⟩ soft **(b)** ⟨color⟩ soft, pale
(c) ⟨sabor⟩ (no fuerte) delicate, mild; (sin acidez)
smooth **3** **(a)** ⟨movimiento/gesto⟩ gentle, slight
(b) ⟨temperaturas/clima⟩ mild; ⟨brisa⟩ gentle **(c)**
⟨modales/carácter/reprimenda⟩ mild, gentle **(d)**
⟨cuesta/curva⟩ gentle, gradual **(e)** ⟨jabón/
champú⟩ gentle, mild **(f)** ⟨laxante/sedante⟩ mild
4 (Méx fam) (fantástico): **¡qué ∼!** great! (colloq),
fantastic! (colloq)

suavidad f (de la piel) smoothness, softness; (de
jabón, champú, clima) mildness; (de tono, acento)

gentleness, softness; (de color) softness, paleness;
(de movimiento) gentleness; (de carácter) mildness,
gentleness

suavizante m (para el pelo) (Esp) conditioner;
(para la ropa) (fabric) softener o conditioner

suavizar [A4] vt ⟨piel⟩ to leave ... smooth/soft;
⟨color⟩ to soften, tone down; ⟨sabor⟩ to tone
down; ⟨carácter⟩ to mellow, make ... gentler;
⟨dureza/severidad⟩ to soften, temper; ⟨situación⟩
to calm, ease
■ **suavizarse** v pron ⟨piel⟩ to become
smoother/softer; ⟨carácter⟩ to mellow, become
gentler; ⟨situación⟩ to calm down, ease

subalterno -na m,f **(a)** (en jerarquía)
subordinate **(b)** (Taur) member of a matador's
support team

subarrendar [A5] vt to sublease, sublet

subasta f **(a)** (venta) auction; **sacar algo a ∼** to
put sth up for auction **(b)** (de obras) invitation to
tender

subastar [A1] vt ⟨cuadro⟩ to auction, sell ... at
auction; ⟨contrato/obra pública⟩ to put ... out to
tender

subcampeón -peona m,f (en liga) runner-up;
(en torneo eliminatorio) losing finalist

subcomisión f subcommittee

subcomité m subcommittee

subconsciente adj/m subconscious

subcontratar [A1] vt to subcontract

subdesarrollado -da adj underdeveloped

subdesarrollo m underdevelopment

subdirector -ra m,f (de organización) deputy
director; (de comercio) assistant manager, deputy
manager

súbdito -ta m,f subject

subdividir [I1] vt to subdivide

subestimar [A1] vt to underestimate

subida f **(a)** (pendiente) rise, slope **(b)** (a
montaña) ascent, climb; (al poder) rise **(c)** (de
temperatura, precios, salarios) rise, increase

subido -da adj ⟨color⟩ intense, deep

subir [I1] vi **1** **(a)** ⟨ascensor/persona/coche⟩ (ir
arriba) to go up; (venir arriba) to come up; **hay que
∼ a pie** you have to walk up; **ahora subo** I'll be
right up; **el camino sube hasta la cima** the path
goes up to o leads to the top of the hill **(b)** ∼ A
algo ⟨a autobús/tren/avión⟩ to get ON o ONTO sth;
⟨a coche⟩ to get in o INTO sth; ⟨a caballo/bicicleta⟩
to get ON o ONTO sth, to mount sth (frml); ∼ **a
bordo** to go o get on board **(c)** (de categoría) to go
up; (en el escalafón) to be promoted
2 **(a)** «marea» to come in; «aguas/río» to rise
(b) «fiebre/tensión» to go up, rise;
«temperatura» to rise
3 «precio/valor/cotización/salario» to rise, go
up
■ ∼ vt **1** ⟨montaña⟩ to climb; ⟨escaleras/cuesta⟩ to
go up, climb
2 **(a)** ⟨objeto/niño⟩ (traer arriba) to bring up; (llevar
arriba) to take up; **tengo que ∼ unas cajas al
desván** I have to put some boxes up in the attic

AmC	América Central	Arg	Argentina	Cu	Cuba	Per	Perú
AmL	América Latina	Bol	Bolivia	Ec	Ecuador	RPI	Río de la Plata
AmS	América del Sur	Chi	Chile	Esp	España	Ur	Uruguay
Andes	Región andina	CS	Cono Sur	Méx	México	Ven	Venezuela

(b) (poner más alto) ‹*objeto*› to put up ... (higher); ‹*cuello de prenda*› to turn up: **sube al niño al caballo** lift the child onto the horse **(c)** ‹*persiana/telón/ventanilla*› to raise; ‹*pantalones*› to pull up; **¿me subes la cremallera?** will you zip me up?, will you fasten my zipper (AmE) *o* (BrE) zip? **(d)** ‹*dobladillo*› to take up; ‹*falda*› to take *o* turn up

3 (a) ‹*precios/salarios*› to raise, put up **(b)** ‹*volumen/radio/calefacción*› to turn up

■ **subirse** *v pron* **1 (a)** (a coche, autobús, etc) ▸ **~** *vi* 1B **(b)** (trepar) to climb; **se subió al árbol/al muro** she climbed up the tree/(up) onto the wall; **estaba subido a un árbol** he was up a tree **(c)** (a la cabeza) (+ *me/te/le etc*): **el éxito se le subió a la cabeza** the success went to his head

2 (*refl*) ‹*calcetines/pantalones*› to pull up; ‹*cuello*› to turn up

súbitamente *adv* suddenly

súbito -ta *adj* **(a)** (repentino) sudden; **de ~** suddenly, all of a sudden **(b)** (precipitado) hasty

subjetivo -va *adj* subjective

subjuntivo *m* subjunctive

sublevarse [A1] *v pron* to revolt, rise up, rebel

sublime *adj* ‹*acción/sacrificio*› noble; ‹*cuadro/música*› sublime

submarinismo *m* scuba diving

submarinista *mf* (buzo) scuba diver; (tripulante de submarino) submariner

submarino¹ -na *adj* underwater (*before n*), submarine (*before n*)

submarino² *m* submarine

subnormal *adj* **(a)** (Psic) mentally handicapped, subnormal **(b)** (fam & pey) (como insulto) moronic (colloq & pej)

■ *mf* **(a)** (Psic) mentally handicapped person **(b)** (fam & pey) (cretino) moron (colloq & pej), cretin (colloq & pej)

subordinado -da *adj/mf* subordinate

subordinar [A1] *vt* to subordinate; **~ algo A algo** to subordinate sth TO sth

subrayar [A1] *vt* **(a)** ‹*texto*› to underline, underscore **(b)** (poner énfasis en) to underline, emphasize, stress

subsanar [A1] *vt* ‹*error*› to rectify, correct; ‹*carencia*› to make up for; ‹*obstáculo/dificultad*› to overcome

subscribirse *etc* ▸ SUSCRIBIRSE, ETC

subsidio *m* subsidy; **~ de enfermedad** sickness benefit; **~ de desempleo** unemployment compensation (AmE), unemployment benefit (BrE)

subsistencia *f* subsistence, survival

subsistir [I1] *vi* «*persona/planta*» to survive, subsist (fml); «*creencia/tradición*» to persist, survive

subte *m* (RPl fam) subway (AmE), tube (BrE colloq)

subterráneo¹ -nea *adj* underground, subterranean

subterráneo² *m* **(a)** (pasaje) subway, tunnel **(b)** (RPl) (Transp) subway (AmE), underground (BrE)

subtitular [A1] *vt* to subtitle; **versión original subtitulada** original version with subtitles

subtítulo *m* subtitle

suburbano -na *adj* suburban

suburbio *m* (extrarradio) suburb; (barrio pobre) depressed area (*on the outskirts of town*)

subvención *f* subsidy, subvention (fml)

subvencionar [A1] *vt* to subsidize

subversivo -va *adj* subversive

subyacer [E5] *vi* **~ (EN algo)** to underlie (sth)

succionar [A1] *vt* to suck (up)

sucedáneo *m* substitute

suceder [E1] *vi* **1** (ocurrir) to happen; **¿le ha sucedido algo?** has something happened to him?; **le expliqué lo sucedido** I explained to him what had happened; **por lo que pueda ~** just in case **2** (en el tiempo) «*hecho/época*» **~ A algo** to follow sth

■ **~** *vt* (en trono, cargo) to succeed

sucesión *f* **1 (a)** (al trono, en un cargo) succession **(b)** (herederos) heirs (*pl*), issue (fml) **(c)** (Der) (herencia) estate, inheritance **2** (serie) succession, series

sucesivo -va *adj* consecutive; **~s gobiernos lo han intentado** successive governments have tried it; **en lo ~** from now on, in future

suceso *m* **(a)** (acontecimiento) event **(b)** (accidente, crimen): **el lugar del ~** the scene of the incident/crime/accident; **sección de ~s** accident and crime reports

sucesor -sora *m,f* (al trono, en un puesto) successor; (heredero) heir, successor (fml)

suciedad *f* **(a)** (mugre) dirt **(b)** (estado) dirtiness

sucio -cia *adj* **1 (a)** [ESTAR] ‹*ropa/casa/vaso*› dirty; **hacer algo en ~** to do a rough draft of sth (AmE), do sth in rough (BrE) **(b)** ‹*lengua*› furred, coated **2** [SER] **(a)** ‹*trabajo*› dirty; ‹*dinero/negocio/juego*› dirty **(b)** ‹*lenguaje*› filthy; ‹*mente*› dirty; **una jugada sucia** a dirty trick

sucre *m* sucre (*Ecuadorean unit of currency*)

sucursal *f* (de banco, comercio) branch; (de empresa) office

sudadera *f* (Dep, Indum) (suéter) sweatshirt; (conjunto) (Col, Ven) tracksuit

Sudáfrica *f* South Africa

sudafricano -na *adj/m,f* South African

Sudamérica *f* South America

sudamericano -na *adj/m,f* South American

Sudán *m*: *tb* **el ~** (the) Sudan

sudanés -nesa *adj/m,f* Sudanese

sudar [A1] *vi* to sweat, perspire (fml)

sudario *m* shroud

sudeste *adj inv* ‹*región*› southeastern; **iban en dirección ~** they were heading southeast

■ *m* **(a)** (parte, sector): **el ~** the southeast, the Southeast **(b)** (punto cardinal) southeast, Southeast

sudoeste *adj inv* ‹*región*› southwestern; **iban en dirección ~** they were heading southwest

■ *m* **(a)** (parte, sector): **el ~** the southwest, the Southwest **(b)** (punto cardinal) southwest, Southwest

sudor *m* sweat, perspiration (fml)

sudoroso -sa *adj* sweaty

Suecia *f* Sweden

sueco¹ -ca *adj* Swedish

■ *m,f* (persona) Swede

S

sueco² *m* (idioma) Swedish; **me hice/se hizo el ~** (fam) I/he pretended not to have heard (o seen etc)

suegro -gra *m,f* (*m*) father-in-law; (*f*) mother-in-law; **mis ~s** my in-laws, my mother-and father-in-law

suela *f* sole

sueldo *m* (de funcionario, oficinista) salary; (de obrero) wage; **~ base** base salary (AmE), basic salary (BrE)

suelo *m* (a) (tierra) ground; **se cayó al ~** she fell over (b) (en casa) floor (c) (en calle, carretera) road (surface) (d) (Agr) land (e) (territorio) soil; **el ~ patrio** one's native soil *o* land

suelta, sueltas, etc ▶ SOLTAR

suelto¹ -ta *adj* ⓵ (a) ⟨tornillo/tabla/hoja⟩ loose; ⟨cordones⟩ loose, untied (b) (libre): **el perro está ~ en el jardín** the dog's loose in the garden; **el asesino anda ~** the murderer is on the loose (c) ⟨vestido/abrigo⟩ loose; **déjate el pelo ~** leave your hair loose *o* down (d) (separado): **ejemplares ~s** individual *o* single issues; **no los vendemos ~s** ⟨yogures/sobres⟩ we don't sell them individually *o* separately; ⟨caramelos/tornillos⟩ we don't sell them loose ⓶ (a) (fraccionado): **dinero ~** loose change; **diez euros sueltas** ten euros in change (b) ⟨lenguaje/estilo⟩ fluent; ⟨movimientos⟩ fluid (c) (euf) ⟨vientre⟩ loose

suelto² *m* (Esp, Méx) (monedas) (small) change

suena, suenan, etc ▶ SONAR

sueño *m* ⓵ (a) (estado) sleep; **oyó un ruido entre ~s** she heard a noise in her sleep; **tener el ~ ligero/pesado** to be a light/heavy sleeper; **perder el ~ (por algo)** to lose sleep (over sth) (b) (ganas de dormir): **¿tienes ~?** are you tired/sleepy?; **el vino me dio ~** the wine made me sleepy; **me empezó a entrar ~** I started feeling sleepy; **se me quitó el ~** I don't feel sleepy any more ⓶ (a) (cosa soñada) dream; **un mal ~** a bad dream (b) (ilusión) dream; **la mujer de sus ~s** the woman of his dreams; **su ~ dorado es llegar a ser actriz** her (greatest) dream is to become an actress

suero *m* (a) (Med) (para alimentar) saline solution; (para inmunizar) serum (b) (de la sangre) blood serum (c) (de la leche) whey

suerte *f* (a) (fortuna) luck; **buena/mala ~** good/bad luck; **ha sido una ~ que vinieras** it was lucky you came; **¡qué mala ~!** how unlucky!; **¡qué ~ tienes!** you're so lucky!; **no tengo ~** I'm not a lucky person; **hombre de ~** lucky man; **por ~ no estaba sola** luckily *o* fortunately I wasn't alone; **¡(que tengas) buena ~!** good luck!; **probar ~** to try one's luck; **traer** *or* **dar mala ~** to bring bad luck (b) (azar) chance; **echar algo a ~s** (con monedas) to toss for sth; (con pajitas) to draw straws for sth (c) (destino) fate

suertero -tera *m,f* (Per) lottery ticket seller

suéter *m* sweater, pullover, jersey (BrE), jumper (BrE)

suficiencia *f* (a) (aptitud) aptitude (b) (presunción) self-satisfaction, smugness; **aire de ~** air of self-satisfaction

suficiente *adj* (a) (bastante) enough; **con esto hay más que ~** there's more than enough here (b) ⟨persona⟩ self-satisfied, smug

■ *m* pass (*equivalent to a grade of 5 on a scale from 0-10*)

sufijo *m* suffix

suflé *m* soufflé

sufragio *m* (sistema) suffrage; (voto) (frml) vote

sufrido -da *adj* ⟨persona⟩ long-suffering, uncomplaining; ⟨ropa/tejido⟩ hard-wearing; **un color ~** a color that doesn't show the dirt

sufrimiento *m* suffering; **pasar ~s** to suffer

sufrir [I1] *vt* (a) ⟨dolores/molestias⟩ to suffer; **sufre lesiones de gravedad** he has serious injuries (b) ⟨derrota/persecución/consecuencias⟩ to suffer; ⟨cambio⟩ to undergo; ⟨accidente⟩ to have; **sufrió un atentado** there was an attempt on his life; **el coche sufrió una avería** the car broke down
■ **~** *vi* to suffer; **~ DE algo** to suffer FROM sth

sugerencia *f* suggestion

sugerente *adj* ⟨mirada/pose⟩ suggestive; ⟨vestido/blusa⟩ sexy

sugerir [I11] *vt* to suggest; **me sugirió que lo probara** he suggested that I (should) try it; **¿qué te sugiere este cuadro?** what does this picture make you think of?

sugestión *f* (convencimiento): **es pura ~** it's all in your (*o* his *etc*) mind; **tiene gran poder de ~** he is very persuasive

sugestionarse [A1] *v pron* to get ideas into one's head

sugestivo -va *adj* ⟨mirada⟩ suggestive; ⟨escote⟩ sexy; ⟨libro/idea⟩ stimulating

suicida *adj* suicidal
■ *mf* suicide victim

suicidarse [A1] *v pron* to commit suicide

suicidio *m* suicide

suite /swit/ *f* (Mús) suite

Suiza *f* Switzerland

suizo -za *adj,m,f* Swiss

sujetador *m* (Esp) bra, brassiere

sujetar [A1] *vt* ⓵ (a) (mantener sujeto) to hold; **sujétalo bien, que no se escape** hold it tight, don't let it go; **tuvimos que ~los para que no se pegaran** we had to hold them back to stop them hitting each other (b) (sostener) to hold; **sujétame los paquetes** hold on to the packages for me (c) (fijar, trabar — con clip) to fasten ... together; (— con alfileres) to pin ... together ⓶ (dominar) to subdue, conquer
■ **sujetarse** *v pron* ⓵ (a) (agarrarse) **~se A algo** to hold on TO sth (b) (trabar, sostener): **se sujetaba los pantalones con la mano** he held his trousers up with his hand; **se sujetó la falda con un imperdible** she fastened her skirt with a safety pin ⓶ (someterse) **~se A algo** ⟨a ley/reglas⟩ to abide BY sth

sujeto¹ -ta *adj* ⓵ (sometido) **~ A algo** ⟨a cambios/revisión⟩ subject TO sth ⓶ (fijo) secure

sujeto² *m* ⓵ (individuo) character, individual ⓶ (Fil, Ling) subject

sultán *m* sultan

suma *f* ⓵ (cantidad) sum ⓶ (Mat) addition; **hacer ~s** to do addition, to do sums (BrE)

sumamente *adv* extremely, exceedingly (frml)

S

sumar [A1] *vt* **(a)** ⟨*cantidades*⟩ to add (up) **(b)** (totalizar) to add up to; **8 y 5 suman 13** 8 and 5 add up to *o* make 13
■ ~ *vi* to add up

■ **sumarse** *v pron* **(a)** (agregarse) ~**se A algo: esto se suma a los problemas ya existentes** this comes on top of *o* is in addition to any already existing problems **(b)** (adherirse) ~**se A algo** ⟨*a protesta/celebración*⟩ to join sth

sumario *m* ⓵ (Der) **(a)** (en lo penal) indictment **(b)** (juicio administrativo) disciplinary action ⓶ (índice) (table of) contents

sumergible *adj* ⟨*reloj*⟩ waterproof; ⟨*nave*⟩ submersible

sumergido -da *adj* ⟨*submarino*⟩ submerged; ⟨*ciudad*⟩ submerged, sunken

sumergir [I7] *vt* (en líquido) to immerse, submerge

■ **sumergirse** *v pron* **(a)** «*submarino/buzo*» to dive, submerge oneself **(b)** (en ambiente) to immerse oneself

sumidero *m* drain

suministrar [A1] *vt* (frml) to supply; ~ **algo A algn** to supply sb WITH sth

suministro *m* supply; **el ~ de gas** the gas supply

sumir [I1] *vt* ⓵ (sumergir) ~ **algo/a algn EN algo** ⟨*en tristeza/desesperación*⟩ to plunge sth/sb INTO sth ⓶ (Col, Méx) (abollar) to dent, make a dent in

■ **sumirse** *v pron* ⓵ (hundirse) ~**se EN algo** ⟨*en tristeza*⟩ to plunge INTO sth; ⟨*en pensamientos*⟩ to become lost IN sth ⓶ (Col, Méx) (abollarse) to get dented

sumisión *f* (acción) submission; (actitud dócil) submissiveness

sumiso -sa *adj* submissive

sumo -ma *adj* utmost (*before n*); **de suma importancia** of the utmost importance; **con ~ cuidado** with great *o* the utmost care; **a lo ~** at the most

suntuoso -sa *adj* sumptuous; ⟨*palacio*⟩ magnificent

supe ▶ SABER

súper *adv* (fam): **lo pasamos ~ bien** we had a great *o* fantastic time (colloq); **es ~ bueno** it's great *o* fantastic (colloq); **lo hizo ~ rápido** he did it incredibly quickly
■ *f* ≈ premium grade gasoline (*in US*), ≈ four-star petrol (*in UK*)

superación *f* (de problema) surmounting, overcoming; (de récord) breaking, beating; (de teoría) superseding

superar [A1] *vt* ⓵ **(a)** (ser superior a) to exceed; **superó todas las expectativas** she exceeded all expectations; **nadie lo supera en experiencia** no one has more experience than him; **supera en estatura a su hermano** he's taller than his brother **(b)** (mejorar) ⟨*marca*⟩ to beat ⓶ **(a)** (vencer, sobreponerse a) ⟨*timidez/dificultad/etapa*⟩ to overcome; ⟨*trauma*⟩ to get over **(b)** (frml) ⟨*examen/prueba*⟩ to pass

■ **superarse** *v pron* to better oneself

superbloque *m* (Ven) large apartment building

superdotado -da *adj* highly gifted
■ *m,f* highly-gifted person

superficial *adj* ⓵ (frívolo) ⟨*persona*⟩

superficial, shallow; ⟨*charla/comentario*⟩ superficial ⓶ ⟨*herida*⟩ superficial; ⟨*marca/grieta*⟩ surface (*before n*)

superficie *f* ⓵ (parte expuesta, aparente) surface; **salir a la ~** to surface, come to the surface ⓶ (Mat) (área) area

superfluo -flua *adj* superfluous, unnecessary; ⟨*gastos*⟩ unnecessary

superior¹ *adj* ⓵ (en posición) ⟨*parte/piso*⟩ top (*before n*), upper (*before n*); ⟨*nivel*⟩ higher; ⟨*labio/mandíbula*⟩ upper (*before n*) ⓶ **(a)** (en calidad) superior; ~ **A algo/algn** superior TO sth/sb; **se siente ~ a los demás** he thinks he's better than everyone else; **una inteligencia ~ a la media** above-average intelligence **(b)** (en jerarquía) ⟨*oficial*⟩ superior; ⟨*clase social*⟩ higher **(c)** (en cantidad, número): **los atacantes eran ~es en número** the attackers were greater *o* more in number; ~ **A algo** above sth; **un número ~ a 9** a number greater than *o* higher than *o* above 9

superior² -riora *m,f* **(a)** (Relig) (*m*) Superior; (*f*) Mother Superior **(b) superior** *m* (en rango) superior

superioridad *f* superiority

superlativo *m* superlative

supermercado *m* supermarket

superpoblación *f* (de una región) overpopulation; (de una ciudad) overcrowding

superpoblado -da *adj* ⟨*mundo/país*⟩ overpopulated; ⟨*barrio/ciudad*⟩ overcrowded

superpotencia *f* superpower

superstición *f* superstition

supersticioso -sa *adj* superstitious

supervisar [A1] *vt* to supervise

supervisor -sora *m,f* supervisor

supervivencia *f* survival

superviviente *adj* surviving (*before n*)
■ *mf* survivor

supiera, supiste, etc ▶ SABER

suplantar [A1] *vt* ⟨*persona*⟩ to impersonate, pass oneself off as

suplementario -ria *adj* ⟨*información/ingresos*⟩ additional, supplementary; ⟨*trabajo*⟩ extra

suplemento *m* supplement

suplencia *f* **(a)** (sustitución): **hacer una ~** «*profesor*» to do substitute (AmE) *o* (BrE) supply teaching **(b)** (trabajo) temporary job

suplente *mf* **(a)** (de médico) covering doctor (AmE), locum (BrE) **(b)** (de actor) understudy **(c)** (Dep) substitute **(d)** (de profesor) substitute (teacher) (AmE), supply teacher (BrE)

supletorio -ria *adj* ⟨*cama*⟩ extra, additional; **teléfono ~** extension

súplica *f* (ruego) entreaty, plea; (Der) petition

suplicante *adj* imploring (*before n*)

suplicar [A2] *vt* (rogar) to beg; ~**le a algn que haga algo** to beg *o* implore *o* (liter) beseech sb to do sth

suplicio *m* **(a)** (tortura) torture **(b)** (castigo) punishment

suplir [I1] *vt* ⓵ (compensar) ⟨*falta/deficiencia*⟩ to make up for ⓶ (reemplazar) ⟨*profesor/médico*⟩ to stand in for, substitute for; ⟨*jugador*⟩ to replace, substitute ⓷ (Chi, Col, Ven) (suministrar) to provide, supply

S

suponer [E22] vt **1** (a) (tomar como hipótesis) to suppose, assume; **supongamos que lo que dice es cierto** let's suppose o assume what he says is true; **suponiendo que todo salga bien** assuming everything goes OK (b) (imaginar): **supongo que tienes razón** I suppose you're right; **¿va a venir hoy? — supongo que sí** is she coming today? — I should think so o I suppose so; **es de ~ que se lo habrán dicho** presumably o I should think he's been told; **se supone que empieza a las nueve** it's supposed to start at nine **2** (significar, implicar) to mean; **eso supondría tener que repetirlo** that would mean having to do it again

suposición f supposition

supositorio m suppository

supremacía f supremacy

supremo -ma adj supreme

suprimir [I1] vt (a) ⟨impuesto/ley/costumbre⟩ to abolish; ⟨restricción⟩ to lift; ⟨servicio⟩ to withdraw; ⟨gasto/ruido/alcohol⟩ to cut out (b) (Impr) ⟨párrafo/capítulo⟩ to delete (c) ⟨noticia/detalles⟩ to suppress

supuesto¹ -ta adj (a) (falso) false; **un nombre ~** a false name; **el ~ mendigo** the supposed beggar (b) (que se rumorea) ⟨milagro⟩ alleged (before n) (c) **por supuesto** of course; **dar algo por ~** to take sth for granted

supuesto² m supposition

supuse, supuso, etc ▶ SUPONER

sur adj inv ⟨región⟩ southern; **conducían en dirección ~** they were driving south o southward(s); **la costa ~** the south coast
■ m (a) (parte, sector): **el ~** the south; **al ~ de Cartagena** to the south of Cartagena (b) (punto cardinal) south, South; **vientos del ~** southerly winds; **viajábamos hacia el ~** we were travelling south o southward(s)

Suráfrica f South Africa

surafricano -na adj/m,f South African

Suramérica f South America

suramericano -na adj/m,f South American

surco m **1** (a) (en la tierra) furrow (b) (en el agua) wake, track (c) (en disco) groove; (en superficie) groove, line; (marca de rueda) ruts, track **2** (Col) (de flores) flowerbed

sureño -ña adj southern
■ m,f southerner

sureste adj inv/m ▶ SUDESTE

surf /'surf/, **surfing** /'surfin/ m surfing

surfista mf surfer

surgir [I7] vi «manantial» to rise; «problema/dificultad» to arise, come up, emerge; «interés/sentimiento» to develop, emerge; «idea» to emerge, come up; «tema» to come up, crop up; «movimiento/partido» to come into being, arise

suroeste adj inv/m ▶ SUDOESTE

surrealismo m surrealism

surrealista adj ⟨artista/exposición⟩ surrealist (before n); ⟨estilo/efecto⟩ surrealistic

surtido¹ -da adj ⟨bombones/galletas⟩ assorted (b) (provisto) stocked; **una tienda bien/mal surtida** a well-stocked/poorly-stocked shop

surtido² m (de bombones, galletas) assortment; (de herramientas, ropa) range, selection, assortment

surtidor m (aparato) gas pump (AmE), petrol pump (BrE); (estación de servicio) gas station (AmE), petrol station (BrE)

surtir [I1] vt (a) (proveer) **~ a algn DE algo** to supply sb WITH sth (b) **surtir efecto** to take effect
■ **surtirse** v pron **~se DE algo** ⟨de provisiones⟩ to stock up WITH sth

susceptibilidad f sensitivity, touchiness

susceptible adj ⟨persona⟩ sensitive, touchy; **~ A algo** sensitive TO sth

suscribirse [I34] v pron (refl) **~ A algo** to take out a subscription TO sth

suscripción f (a una publicación) subscription

suscriptor -tora m,f subscriber

suspender [E1] vt **1** (a) ⟨pagos⟩ to suspend; ⟨garantía/derecho⟩ to suspend, withdraw; ⟨sesión⟩ to adjourn; ⟨vuelo⟩ to cancel; (aplazar) to postpone; ⟨viaje/reunión⟩ to call off; (aplazar) to put off; ⟨tratamiento⟩ to stop, suspend; ⟨servicio⟩ to suspend, discontinue; ⟨programa⟩ to cancel (b) ⟨empleado/jugador⟩ to suspend; ⟨alumno⟩ (AmL) to suspend **2** (colgar) **~ algo DE algo** to hang sth FROM sth **3** (Esp) ⟨asignatura/examen/alumno⟩ to fail
■ **~** vi (Esp) to fail

suspense m (Esp) ▶ SUSPENSO 1

suspensión f suspension

suspenso m **1** (AmL) (Cin, Lit) suspense; **película/novela de ~** thriller **2** (Esp) (Educ) fail, failure; **no he tenido ningún ~** I haven't failed anything

suspensores mpl (Chi) (tirantes) suspenders (pl) (AmE), braces (pl) (BrE)

suspicacia f suspicion

suspicaz adj suspicious

suspirar [I1] vi (a) (de pena, alivio) to sigh (b) (anhelar) **~ POR algo** to yearn o long FOR sth

suspiro m sigh; **un ~ de alivio** a sigh of relief

sustancia f substance

sustantivo m noun, substantive (frml)

sustentar [I1] vt (a) ⟨peso⟩ to support (b) ⟨persona/familia⟩ to support, maintain

sustento m (a) (apoyo) means of support (b) (alimento) sustenance

sustitución f (a) (permanente) replacement (b) (transitoria) substitution

sustituir [I20] vt (a) (permanentemente) to replace; **~ A algo** to replace sth; **~ algo/a algn POR algo/algn** to replace sth/sb WITH sth/sb (b) (transitoriamente) ⟨trabajador/profesor⟩ to stand in for; ⟨deportista⟩ to come on as a substitute for

sustituto -ta m,f (a) (permanente) replacement (b) (transitorio) substitute; (de médico) covering

AmC Central America	Arg	Argentina	Cu	Cuba	Per	Peru
AmL Latin America	Bol	Bolivia	Ec	Ecuador	RPI	River Plate Area
AmS South America	Chi	Chile	Esp	Spain	Ur	Uruguay
Andes Andean Region	CS	Southern Cone	Méx	Mexico	Ven	Venezuela

doctor (AmE), locum (BrE); (de actor) understudy; **el ~ de la profesora de alemán** the substitute (AmE) o (BrE) stand-in for the German teacher

susto m (impresión momentánea) fright; **darle un ~ a algn** to give sb a fright; **darse** or **llevarse un ~** to get a fright (colloq)

susurrar [A1] vi (a) «persona» to whisper (b) (liter) «agua» to murmur; «viento» to sigh; «hojas» to rustle
■ ~ vt to whisper; **le susurró algo al oído** she whispered something in his ear

susurro m (a) (murmullo) whisper (b) (liter) (del agua) murmuring; (del viento) sighing; (de las hojas) rustling

sutil adj (a) ‹diferencia› subtle, fine; ‹ironía› subtle; ‹mente/inteligencia› keen, sharp (b) ‹gasa/velo› fine; ‹fragancia› subtle, delicate

sutileza f subtlety

suyo -ya adj (de él) his; (de ella) hers; (de usted, ustedes) yours; (de ellos, ellas) theirs; **Marta y un amigo ~** Marta and a friend of hers
■ pron **el ~, la suya,** etc (de él) his; (de ella) hers; (de usted, ustedes) yours; (de ellos, ellas) theirs; **él me prestó el ~** he lent me his

svástica f swastika

switch /'(e)switʃ/ m (a) (Col, Ven, Méx) (interruptor) light switch (b) (Méx) (Auto) ignition switch

Tt

T, t f (read as /te/) the letter T, t

tabaco m (a) (planta, producto) tobacco; **~ de hebra/de pipa** loose/pipe tobacco; **~ negro/rubio** dark/Virginia tobacco (b) (Esp) (cigarrillos) cigarettes (pl) (c) (Col) (puro) cigar

tábano m horsefly

tabaquismo m nicotine poisoning; **~ pasivo** passive smoking

tabasco m Tabasco® (sauce)

taberna f bar, tavern (arch), pub (BrE)

tabernáculo m tabernacle

tabernero -ra m,f (propietario) (m) bar owner, landlord (BrE); (f) bar owner, landlady (BrE); (camarero) (m) bartender; (f) barmaid

tabique m (a) (pared) partition (b) (Méx) (ladrillo) brick

tabla f [1] (de madera) plank; **las ~s del suelo** the floorboards; **~ de picar/planchar** chopping/ironing board; **tener ~s** «actor/cantante» (fam) to be an old hand o an expert [2] (de surfing) surfboard; (de windsurf) sailboard, windsurfer; (para natación) float [3] (gráfico, listado) table; (Mat) tb **~ de multiplicar** multiplication table [4] (de falda) pleat; **una falda de ~s** a pleated skirt [5] **tablas** fpl (en ajedrez): **acabar** or **quedar en ~s** to end in a draw; **estar ~s** (Méx fam) to be even o quits (colloq)

tablado m (para discursos) platform; (para espectáculos) stage

tablao m: tb **~ flamenco** bar or club where flamenco is performed

tablero m (a) (en estación, aeropuerto) board; (para anuncios) bulletin board (AmE), noticeboard (BrE); **~ de dibujo** drawing board; **~ de instrumentos** or **de mandos** instrument panel (b) (Jueg) board; **un ~ de ajedrez** a chessboard; **un ~ de damas** a checkerboard (AmE), a draughtboard (BrE) (c) (pizarra) blackboard (d) (de mesa) top

tableta f (a) (Farm) tablet, pill (b) (de chocolate) bar

tablilla f (Méx) (de chocolate) bar

tablón m (a) (de madera) plank (b) tb **~ de anuncios** (Esp) bulletin board (AmE), noticeboard (BrE)

tabú adj inv taboo
■ m (pl **-búes** or **-bús**) taboo

tabulador m tabulator, tab

taburete m stool

tacañería f stinginess, meanness (colloq)

tacaño -ña adj stingy, mean
■ m,f miser, tightwad (AmE colloq)

tacha f stain, blemish; **sin ~** ‹reputación› unblemished, spotless; ‹conducta› irreproachable

tachadura f crossing out, correction

tachar [A1] vt [1] (en escrito) to cross out [2] (tildar): **~ a algn DE algo** to brand o label sb AS sth

tacho m (a) (CS) (recipiente) (metal) container (b) (CS, Per) (papelero) wastebasket (AmE), wastepaper basket (BrE); **~ de la basura** (en la cocina) garbage can (AmE), rubbish bin (BrE); (en la calle) garbage o trash can (AmE), dustbin (BrE)

tachón m (en escrito) crossing out

tachuela f (clavo) tack; (en cinturón) stud

tácito -ta adj ‹acuerdo› tacit, unspoken

taciturno -na adj (a) [SER] (callado, silencioso) taciturn, uncommunicative (b) [ESTAR] (triste) glum, gloomy

taco m [1] (a) (de madera) plug; (para tornillo) Rawl® (AmE), Rawlplug® (BrE) (b) (de billetes) book; (de folletos) wad; (de queso, jamón) (Esp) cube [2] (a) (en billar) cue (b) (Col) (de golf) tee [3] (a) (de botas de deporte) cleat (AmE), stud (BrE) (b) (CS, Per) (tacón) heel; **zapatos de ~ alto/bajo** high-heeled/low-heeled o flat shoes [4] (a) (Coc) taco (b) (Méx) (comida ligera) snack, bite to eat (colloq) [5] (Esp fam) (palabrota) swearword; **soltar ~s** to swear [6] (Chi) (embotellamiento) traffic jam

tacón m heel; **zapatos de ~ alto/bajo** high-heeled/low-heeled o flat shoes; **~ de aguja** spike heel

táctica f tactic, strategy

táctico -ca adj tactical

táctil *adj* tactile

tacto *m* ☐1 (a) (sentido) sense of touch (b) (acción) touch; **áspero al ~** rough to the touch (c) (cualidad) feel ☐2 (delicadeza) tact; **¡qué falta de ~!** how tactless!; **tiene mucho ~** he's very tactful

Tahití *m* Tahiti

tailandés¹ -desa *adj/m,f* Thai

tailandés² *m* (idioma) Thai

Tailandia *f* Thailand

taimado -da *adj* ☐1 (astuto) crafty, cunning ☐2 (Chi) (malhumorado) sulky, huffy

taimarse [A1] *v pron* (Chi fam) (a) «*persona*» to get into a huff (colloq) (b) «*mula*» to balk

tajada *f* (a) (de melón, queso) slice (b) (Ven) (de plátano frito) slice of fried plantain

tajante *adj* ‹*respuesta*› categorical, unequivocal; ‹*tono*› sharp; **un 'no' ~** an emphatic *o* categorical 'no'

tajear [A1] *vt* (AmL) to slash

tajo *m* ☐1 (corte) cut ☐2 (a) (Geol) gorge, ravine (b) (Min) face

tal *adj* ☐1 (dicho) such; **en ~es casos** in such cases; **nunca dije ~ cosa** I never said anything of the kind *o* such a thing
☐2 (seguido de consecuencia): **se llevó ~ disgusto que ...** she was so upset (that) ...; **había ~ cantidad de gente que ...** there were so many people that ...
☐3 (con valor indeterminado) such-and-such; **~ día, en ~ lugar** such-and-such a day, at such-and-such a place; **llamó un ~ Méndez** a Mr Méndez phoned
■ *pron*: **eres un adulto, compórtate como ~** you're an adult, behave like one; **que si ~ y que si cual** and so on and so forth; **son ~ para cual** they're as bad as each other
■ *adv* ☐1 (fam) (en preguntas): **hola ¿qué ~?** hello, how are you?; **¿qué ~ es Marisa?** what's Marisa like?; **¿qué ~ lo pasaron?** how did it go?
☐2 (en locs) **con tal de: hace cualquier cosa con ~ de llamar la atención** he'll do anything to get attention; **con ~ de no tener que volver** as long as I don't have to come back; **tal (y) como: ~ (y) como están las cosas** the way things are; **hazlo ~ (y) como te indicó** do it exactly as she told you; **tal cual: lo dejé todo ~ cual** I left everything exactly as it was; **tal vez** maybe

talacha *f* (a) (Méx) (reparación de llantas) flat *o* puncture repair (b) (Méx fam) (trabajo manual) work

taladradora *f* pneumatic drill

taladrar [A1] *vt* ‹*pared/madera*› to drill (through)

taladro *m* (a) (mecánico) hand drill; (eléctrico) electric *o* power drill (b) (agujero) drill hole

talante *m* (humor) mood; **estar de buen ~** to be in a good mood

talar [A1] *vt* ‹*árbol*› to fell, cut down

talco *m* talc; **polvos de ~** talcum powder

talento *m* (a) (aptitud) talent; **tiene ~ para la música** he has a talent *o* gift for music; **un joven de ~** a talented young man (b) (persona) talented person

talentoso -sa *adj* talented, gifted

TALGO /'talvo/ *m* (= **Tren Articulado Ligero Goicoechea Oriol**) air-conditioned express train

talismán *m* talisman, lucky charm

talla *f* (a) (Indum) size; **¿cuál es su ~?** what size are you?; **de *o* en todas las ~s** in all sizes (b) (estatura) size, height; **de ~ mediana** of medium height

tallado *m* (de madera) carving; (de piedras preciosas) cutting

tallar [A1] *vt* ☐1 ‹*madera*› to carve; ‹*escultura/ mármol*› to sculpt; ‹*piedras preciosas*› to cut ☐2 (Méx) (a) (para limpiar) to scrub (b) (para aliviar) to rub
■ **~** *vi* (Col) «*zapatos*» to be too tight
■ **tallarse** *v pron* (Méx) (a) (para limpiarse) to scrub oneself (b) (para aliviar) to rub oneself; ‹*ojos*› to rub

tallarín *m* noodle

talle *m* (a) (cintura) waist (b) (figura) figure (c) (en costura) trunk measurement; **es corta de ~** she's short-waisted

taller *m* ☐1 (a) (Auto) *tb* **~ mecánico** garage, repair shop (AmE) (b) (de carpintero, técnico) workshop ☐2 (Educ) workshop

tallo *m* stem, stalk

talón *m* ☐1 (a) (del pie, zapato, calcetín) heel; **~ de Aquiles** Achilles' heel (b) (de zapato, calcetín) heel ☐2 (a) (AmL) (matriz) stub, counterfoil (b) (Esp) (cheque) check (AmE), cheque (BrE); (vale) chit; **~ de compra** receipt

talonario *m* (de cheques) checkbook (AmE), chequebook (BrE); (de recibos) receipt book; (de volantes) book of vouchers

talonear [A1] *vt* (AmL) ‹*caballo*› to spur (on)

tamal *m* tamale

tamaño *m* size; **pañuelos de todos los ~s** handkerchiefs in all sizes; **de ~ bolsillo** pocket-size; **un busto ~ natural** a life-size bust

tamarindo *m* (a) (Bot) tamarind (b) (Méx fam) (agente) traffic cop (colloq)

tambache *m* (Méx fam) (bulto) bundle; (montón) pile

tambalearse [A1] *v pron vi* «*silla/botella*» to wobble; «*persona*» to stagger; **caminaba tambaleándose** he was staggering; **todo empezó a ~** everything began to shake

también *adv* too, as well **~ habla ruso** she speaks Russian too *o* as well; **que te diviertas — tú ~** have fun! — you too *o* and you; **Pilar fuma — yo ~** Pilar smokes — so do I *o* (colloq) me too

tambo *m* ☐1 (Méx) (a) (recipiente) can (AmE), bin (BrE) (b) (fam) (cárcel) slammer (sl), can (AmE sl) ☐2 (Per) (tienda) wayside stall

tambor *m* ☐1 (a) (instrumento) drum; **un redoble de ~es** a drum roll (b) (persona) drummer ☐2 (a) (del freno) drum (b) (AmL) (barril) drum

tamborilear [A1] *vi* to drum, tap

Támesis *m*: **el ~** the (River) Thames

tamiz *m* sieve; **pasar algo por el ~** ‹*harina*› to sift sth; ‹*salsa*› to sieve sth

tamizar [A4] *vt* ‹*harina*› to sift; ‹*salsa*› to sieve

tampoco *adv* not ... either; **yo ~ entendí** I didn't understand either; **él no va, ni yo ~** he isn't going and neither am I; **no he estado en Roma ni ~ en París** I've never been to Rome or Paris

tampón *m* (a) (para entintar) ink pad (b) (Farm, Med) tampon

tan *adv: apocopated form of* TANTO *used before adjectives (except some comparatives), adverbs, and adjectival or adverbial phrases*

tanda *f* **1** (grupo) batch, lot; **cada dos minutos hay una ∼ de avisos** (AmL) every couple of minutes there's another lot of commercials; **los horneamos en dos ∼s** we baked them in two batches **2** (AmC, Méx fam) (función — de teatro) performance; (— de cine) showing, performance **3** (Col, Méx) (ronda) round (of drinks)

tándem *m* (bicicleta) tandem

tanga *f or m* tanga

tangente *f* tangent; *irse or salirse por la* ∼ to go off at a tangent

tangerina *f* tangerine

tango *m* tango; **bailar el** ∼ to tango

tano -na *adj/m,f* (RPl fam & pey) Italian

tanque *m* **1** (Arm) (carro) tank **2** (de agua, gasolina) tank; (de gas, oxígeno) cylinder, bottle

tantear [A1] *vt* **(a)** (con el tacto) to feel **(b)** ‹situación› to weigh up, size up; ‹persona› to sound out **(c)** (calcular aproximadamente) to estimate ■ ∼ *vi* to feel one's way

tanteo *m* (Dep) score

tantito *adv* (Méx fam) a bit; **espérame ∼, ya voy** just wait a bit, I'm coming

tanto¹ *adv* **1** [*see note under* TAN] (aplicado a adjetivo o adverbio) so; (aplicado a verbo) so much; **es tan bonito** it's so beautiful; **¡es una chica tan amable!** she's such a nice girl!; **∼ mejor** so much the better; **tan solo** only; **∼ es así que** ... so much so that ...; **ya no salimos ∼** we don't go out so often *o* so much now; **llegó tan tarde que** ... he arrived so late (that) ...; **no es tan tímida como parece** she's not as shy as she looks; **sale ∼ como tú** he goes out as much as you do; **tan pronto como puedas** as soon as you can; **∼ Suárez como Vargas votaron en contra** both Suárez and Vargas voted against

2 (AmL exc RPl) **qué tanto/qué tan: ¿qué ∼ te duele?** how much does it hurt?; **¿qué tan alto es?** how tall is he?

■ *m* **1** (cantidad): **un ∼ por ciento** a percentage; **hay que dejar un ∼ de depósito** you have to put down a certain amount as a deposit **2** (punto — en fútbol) goal; (— en fútbol americano, tenis, juegos) point **3** (en locs) **al tanto: me puso al ∼** she put me in the picture; **mantenerse al ∼ de algo** to keep up to date with sth; **estar al ∼** ‹pendiente, alerta› to be on the ball (colloq); **está al ∼ de lo ocurrido** he knows what's happened; **un tanto** somewhat, rather; **un ∼ triste** somewhat sad

tanto² -ta *adj* **(a)** (sing) so much; (pl) so many; **había ∼ espacio/∼s niños** there was so much space/there were so many children; **¡∼ tiempo sin verte!** it's been so long!; **∼ dinero/∼s turistas como** ... as much money/as many tourists as ... **(b)** (expresando cantidades indeterminadas): **tenía setenta y ∼s años** he was seventy something, he was seventy-odd (colloq)

■ *pron* **1 (a)** (sing) so much; (pl) so many; **¡tengo ∼ que hacer!** I've so much to do!; **vinieron ∼s que** ... so many people came (that) ...; **¿de verdad gana ∼?** does he really earn that much?; **no ser para ∼** (fam): **duele, pero no es para ∼** it hurts, but it's not *that* bad **(b)** (fam) (expresando cantidades indeterminadas): **hasta las tantas de la**

madrugada until the early hours of the morning; **treinta y tantas** thirty or so **(c)** (refiriéndose a tiempo): **hace ∼ que no me llama** it's been so long since she called me; **aún faltan dos horas — ¿tanto?** there's still two hours to go — what? that long?

2 (en locs) **en tanto** while; **entre tanto** meanwhile, in the meantime; **otro tanto** as much again; **me queda otro ∼ por hacer** I have as much again still to do; **por (lo) tanto** therefore

tañer [E7] *vt* (liter) ‹arpa› to strum ■ ∼ *vi* «campana» to peal, ring out

tapa *f* **1 (a)** (de caja, cacerola) lid; (de botella, frasco) top; **∼ de rosca** screw top **(b)** (de lente, bolígrafo) cap; **la ∼ del tanque de gasolina** the gas (AmE) *o* (BrE) petrol cap **2 (a)** (de libro, revista) cover; (de disco) sleeve **(b)** (de tacón) heelpiece **(c)** (de bolsillo) flap **(d)** (Auto) head **3** (Esp) (para acompañar la bebida) tapa, bar snack

tapabarros *m* (*pl* ∼) (Chi, Per) (de coche) fender (AmE), wing (BrE); (de bicicleta) splashguard (AmE), mudguard (BrE)

tapadera *f* **(a)** (de cazo) lid **(b)** (de fraude, engaño) cover, front **(c)** (Méx) (de botella) cap, top

tapado *m* **1** (RPl, Ven) (abrigo) (winter) coat **2** (Méx) (Pol) potential candidate (*with official support*)

tapadura *f* (Andes, Méx) filling

tapar [A1] *vt* **1** (cubrir) ‹caja› to put the lid on; ‹botella/frasco› to put the top on; ‹olla› to cover, put the lid on; ‹bebé/enfermo/cara› to cover **2 (a)** ‹agujero/hueco› to fill in; ‹puerta/ventana› to block up **(b)** (Andes, Méx) ‹muela› to fill; **me ∼on dos muelas** I had two fillings **(c)** ‹defecto/error› to cover up **3 (a)** ‹vista/luz› to block **(b)** ‹salida/entrada› to block; ‹excusado/cañería› (AmL) to block ■ **taparse** *v pron* **1** (refl) (cubrirse) to cover oneself up; ‹cara› to cover **2 (a)** «oídos/nariz» to get *o* become blocked; **tengo la nariz tapada** my nose is blocked **(b)** (AmL) «cañería/excusado» to get blocked

taparrabos *m* (*pl* ∼) loincloth

tapatío -tía *adj* of/from Guadalajara (*in Mexico*)

tapeo *m* (Esp fam): **ir de ∼** to go for a drink and a few tapas *o* bar snacks; **bares de ∼** tapas bars

tapete *m* **1** (para mesa) decorative table cloth; (para sofá) antimacassar **2** (Col, Méx, Ven) (alfombra) rug

tapia *f* (muro) wall; (cerca) fence; **ser/estar más sordo que una ∼** (fam) to be as deaf as a post (colloq)

tapiar [A1] *vt* **(a)** ‹espacio› to wall in **(b)** ‹puerta/ventana› to brick up

tapicería *f* **(a)** (de coches, muebles) upholstery **(b)** (arte) tapestry making; (tapiz) tapestry

tapicero -ra *m,f* (de muebles) upholsterer

tapilla *f* (Chi) heelpiece

tapir *m* tapir

tapiz *m* (para pared) tapestry; (para suelo) carpet

tapizado *m* upholstery

tapizar [A4] *vt* ‹sillón› to upholster; ‹pared› to line

tapón *m* **1 (a)** (de vidrio, goma) stopper; (de corcho) cork; (del lavabo) plug; (de botella) (Esp) top ⋯⟶

(b) (para los oídos) earplug; (de cerumen) plug **2** **(a)** (fam) (atasco) traffic jam, tailback (BrE) **(b)** (en baloncesto) block **3** (CS) (Elec) fuse

taponar [A1] vt «agujero» to block
■ **taponarse** v pron **(a)** «oídos/nariz» to get blocked **(b)** «cañería» to get blocked **(c)** (Col, RPl) «ciudad/zona» to block

taquigrafía f shorthand, stenography (AmE)

taquilla f **(a)** (de cine) box office; (en estación, estadio) ticket office **(b)** (cantidad recaudada) takings (pl) **(c)** (casillero) rack, pigeonholes (pl)

taquillero -ra m,f box-office clerk

tara f **1** (peso) tare **2** (defecto) defect

tarántula f tarantula

tararear [A1] vt to la-la-la

tardado -da adj (Méx) ‹proceso/tarea› time-consuming; ‹persona› slow

tardanza f delay; sin ~ without delay; perdona la ~ en contestar forgive my delay in replying; me preocupa su ~ I'm worried that he's so late; su ~ se debió a ... his lateness was due to ...

tardar [A1] vt (emplear cierto tiempo): está tardando mucho she's taking a long time; tarda una hora en hacerse it takes about an hour to cook; tardó un mes en contestar it took him a month to reply; no tardo ni un minuto I won't be a minute; ¿cuánto se tarda en coche? how long does it take by car?
■ ~ vi (retrasarse) to be late; (emplear demasiado tiempo) to take a long time; empieza a las seis, no tardes it starts at six, don't be late; parece que tarda he seems to be taking a long time; ¡no tardo! I won't be long!; aún ~á en llegar it'll be a while yet before he gets here; no ~on en detenerlo it didn't take them long to arrest him
■ **tardarse** v pron (Méx, Ven) ▶ TARDAR vt, vi

tarde adv late; llegar ~ to be late; se está haciendo ~ it's getting late; ~ o temprano sooner or later
■ f (temprano) afternoon; (hacia el anochecer) evening; a las seis de la ~ at six in the evening; ¡buenas ~s! (temprano) good afternoon!; (hacia el anochecer) good evening!; en la or (esp Esp) por la or (RPl) a la ~ in the afternoon/evening

tardón -dona adj (fam) slow
■ m,f (fam) slowpoke (AmE colloq), slowcoach (BrE colloq)

tarea f **(a)** (trabajo) task, job; las ~s de la casa the housework **(b)** (deberes escolares) homework

tarifa f **(a)** (baremo, escala) rate; ~s postales postal rates **(b)** (Transp) fare **(c)** (lista de precios) price list **(d)** (arancel) tariff

tarima f (plataforma) dais

tarjar [A1] vt (Andes) to cross out, delete (fml)

tarjeta f card; marcar (AmL) or (Méx) checar ~ to clock in/out, punch in/out (AmE); ~ amarilla/ roja yellow/red card; ~ de crédito credit card; ~ de embarque boarding pass o card; ~ de Navidad Christmas card; ~ de visita or (Méx) de

presentación (personal) visiting card; (de negocios) business card; ~ postal/telefónica postcard/ phonecard

tarro m **1** (recipiente— de vidrio) jar; (— de cerámica) pot; (— de metal) (Chi) can, tin (BrE) **2** (Méx, Ven) (taza) mug

tarta f (Esp) cake; (de hojaldre — descubierta) tart; (— cubierta) pie

tartamudear [A1] vi to stutter, stammer

tartamudo -da adj stuttering (before n), stammering (before n); es ~ he has a stutter o stammer
■ m,f: hay un ~ en mi clase one of the boys in my class has a stutter o stammer

tartera f (para cocinar) cake tin

tarumba adj crazy (colloq); me vuelve ~ he drives me crazy (colloq)

tasa f **(a)** (valoración) valuation **(b)** (impuesto) tax **(c)** (índice) rate; ~ de desempleo rate of unemployment; ~ de mortalidad/natalidad mortality rate/birthrate

tasación f valuation

tasajear [A1] vt (Méx, Per) to slash

tasar [A1] vt ‹objeto/coche› to value

tasca f (taberna) bar, tavern

tata m (AmL fam) **(a)** (padre) dad (colloq), pop (AmE colloq) **(b)** (abuelo) grandpa (colloq)

tatarabuelo -la m,f (m) great-great-grandfather; (f) great-great-grandmother; mis ~s my great-great-grandparents

tataranieto -ta m,f (m) great-great-grandson; (f) great-great-granddaughter; sus ~s his great-great-grandchildren

ta-te-ti m (RPl) tic-tac-toe (AmE), noughts and crosses (BrE)

tatuaje m (acción) tattooing; (dibujo) tattoo

tatuar [A18] vt to tattoo

taurino -na adj ‹temporada/afición› bullfighting (before n), taurine (fml)

Tauro m (signo, constelación) Taurus; es (de) ~ he's (a) Taurus, he's a Taurean
■ mf (pl -ros) (persona) tb **tauro** Taurean, Taurus

taxi m taxi, cab; ~ colectivo (Col) minibus

taxímetro m taximeter

taxista mf taxi driver, cabdriver

taza f **(a)** (recipiente) cup; ~ de café/té coffee cup/teacup **(b)** (contenido) cupful; una ~ de azúcar a cupful of sugar; tomar una ~ de té to have a cup of tea **(c)** (del retrete) (toilet) bowl **(d)** (de fuente) basin

tazón m bowl

te pron pers **(a)** you; no ~ lo quiero prestar I don't want to lend it to you; ¿~ lo paso a máquina? shall I type it for you?; voy a serte sincera I'll be frank with you; cuídate (refl) look after yourself; ¿~ has cortado el pelo? (caus) have you had your hair cut?; ¿~ sientes bien?

are you feeling all right?; **no ~ muevas** don't move **(b)** (*impers*): **cuando ~ pasa eso ...** when that happens ...

■ *f*: *name of the letter* t

té *m* **(a)** (infusión, planta) tea; **¿quieres un ~?** do you want a cup of tea? **(b)** (AmL) (reunión) tea party

tea *f* torch

teatral *adj* **(a)** (Teatr) ⟨grupo/temporada⟩ theater* (*before n*); **una obra ~** a play; **un autor ~** a playwright **(b)** ⟨persona/gesto/tono⟩ theatrical

teatro *m* **1** (Teatr) **(a)** (arte, actividad) theater*; **una obra de ~** a play; **actor de ~** stage actor; **~ de guiñol** puppet theater*; **~ de variedades** vaudeville (AmE), music hall (BrE) **(b)** (local) theater*; **un ~ al aire libre** an open-air theater **2** (fam) (exageración): **es puro ~** it's all an act

tebeo *m* (Esp) comic (*for children*)

techo *m* **(a)** (cielo raso) ceiling **(b)** (AmL) (tejado, cubierta) roof; **~ corredizo** sunroof **(c)** (hogar, casa) house; **sin ~** homeless; **bajo el mismo ~** under the same roof

techumbre *f* roof

tecla *f* key

teclado *m* keyboard; **~ numérico** numeric keypad

teclear [A1] *vt* ⟨palabra/texto⟩ to key in, type in

■ ~ *vi* (en máquina de escribir) to type; (en ordenador) to key

técnica *f* **1** **(a)** (método) technique **(b)** (destreza) skill **2** (tecnología) technology **3** (en baloncesto) technical foul

tecnicismo *m* (cualidad) technical nature; (palabra) technical term

técnico -ca *adj* technical

■ *m,f* **(a)** (en fábrica) technician **(b)** (de lavadoras, etc) repairman (AmE), engineer (BrE) **(c)** (Dep) trainer, coach (AmE), manager (BrE)

tecnicolor *m* Technicolor®

tecnología *f* technology; **~ punta** state-of-the-art technology

tecnológico -ca *adj* technological

tecolote *m* (Méx) (Zool) owl

tedio *m* boredom, tedium

teja *f* tile; **~s de pizarra** slates

tejado *m* (esp Esp) roof

tejano -na *adj/m,f* Texan

Tejas *m* Texas

tejaván *m* (Méx) shed

tejedor -dora *m,f* **(a)** (con telar) weaver **(b)** (con agujas, máquina) knitter

tejer [E1] *vt* **(a)** (en telar) to weave; **tejido a mano** hand-woven **(b)** (con agujas, a máquina) to knit; (con ganchillo) to crochet; **máquina de ~** knitting machine **(c)** «araña» to spin

■ ~ *vi* (en telar) to weave; (con agujas, a máquina) to knit; (con ganchillo) to crochet

tejido *m* **1** **(a)** (tela) fabric; **~s sintéticos** synthetic fabrics **(b)** (AmL) (con agujas, máquina) knitting; (con ganchillo) crochet **2** (Anat) tissue

tejo *m* **(a)** (disco) disco disc **(b)** (juego – de niños) hopscotch; (– de adultos) *game similar to pitch-and-toss*

tejolote *m* (Méx) pestle

tejón *m* badger

tela *f* **1** (Tex) (material) material, fabric; **~ de lana** wool (fabric); **~ de araña** ▶ TELARAÑA; **~ metálica** wire mesh **2** (Art) (cuadro) canvas, painting **3** (membrana) skin, film

telar *m* **(a)** (máquina) loom **(b)** **telares** *mpl* (fábrica) textile mill

telaraña *f* spiderweb (AmE), spider's web (BrE); (polvorienta) cobweb; **~ mundial** (Inf) World Wide Web

tele *f* (fam) TV (colloq), telly (BrE colloq)

telebanca *f* telebanking

telebanco *m* cash dispenser

telecomunicación *f* telecommunication

teleculebra *f* (Ven fam) soap opera (colloq)

telediario *m* (Esp) (television) news

teledirigido -da *adj* ⟨coche⟩ radio-controlled, remote-controlled; **misiles ~s** guided missiles

teleférico *m* cable railway

telefonazo *m* (fam) buzz (colloq); **darle** *or* (Méx) **echarle un ~ a algn** to give sb a buzz (colloq)

telefonear [A1] *vt* to telephone, phone, call; **¿puedo ~ a Londres?** can I make a (telephone) call to London?

■ ~ *vi* to telephone, phone

telefónico -ca *adj* telephone (*before n*)

telefonista *mf* telephone operator

teléfono *m* **1** (Telec) telephone, phone; **número de ~** phone number; **contestar el ~** to answer *o* (colloq) get the phone; **me colgó el ~** she hung up on me; **hablé por ~ con ella** I spoke to her on the phone; **está hablando por ~** he's on the phone; **llamar a algn por ~** to call sb (up), phone sb; **~ celular** *or* (Esp) **móvil** mobile telephone; **~ rojo** hotline **2** (de la ducha) shower head

telegrafiar [A17] *vi/vt* to telegraph

telégrafo *m* telegraph

telegrama *m* telegram

telemarketing /teleˈmarketin/ *m* telemarketing

telenovela *f* soap opera

telepatía *f* telepathy

telescopio *m* telescope

telespectador -dora *m,f* viewer

telesquí *m* ski lift

teletexto, teletex *m* teletext, videotex

televentas *fpl* telesales

televidente *mf* viewer

televisar [A1] *vt* to televise

televisión *f* **(a)** (sistema) television; **¿qué hay en (la) ~?** what's on television?; **lo transmitieron por ~** it was broadcast on television; **~ a** *or* **en color(es)** color* television; **~ de alta definición** high definition television, HDTV; **~ en blanco y negro** black and white television; **~ en circuito cerrado** closed circuit television; **~ por cable/por satélite** cable/satellite television; **~ matinal** breakfast television **(b)** (programación) television; **ver (la) ~** to watch television **(c)** (televisor) television (set)

televisor *m* television (set)

télex *m* (*pl* ~) telex

telón *m* curtain; **~ de fondo** (Teatr) backdrop

tema *m* **(a)** (asunto, cuestión) matter; (de conferencia, composición) topic; (de examen) subject; ···›

(Art, Cin, Lit) subject; **es un ~ delicado** it's a delicate matter; **~ de conversación** topic of conversation; **cambiar de ~** to change the subject **(b)** (Mús) (motivo) theme

temario *m* **(a)** (para examen) syllabus, list of topics **(b)** (en congreso) agenda

temblar [A5] *vi* **(a)** «*persona*» (de frío) to shiver; (por nervios, miedo) to shake, tremble; (+ me/te/le etc) «*párpado*» to twitch; «*mano*» to shake; «*voz*» to tremble; **la voz le temblaba de emoción** her voice was trembling with emotion **(b)** «*edificio/tierra*» to shake
■ **~** *v impers*: **¡está temblando!** (AmL) it's an earthquake!; **tembló ayer** there was an (earth) tremor yesterday

temblor *m* **(a)** (de frío, fiebre) shivering; (de miedo, nervios) trembling, shaking; **con un ligero ~ en la voz** in a tremulous voice **(b)** *tb* **~ de tierra** (earth) tremor

tembloroso -sa *adj* **(a)** «*manos*» trembling, shaking; «*voz*» trembling, tremulous; **~ de frío** shivering with cold **(b)** «*llama/luz*» flickering, quivering

temer [E1] *vt* «*castigo/reacción*» to fear, dread; «*persona*» to be afraid of; **sus hijos le temen** her children are afraid of her; **temo ofenderlo** I'm afraid of offending him
■ **~** *vi* to be afraid; **no temas** don't be afraid
■ **temerse** *v pron* (sospechar) to fear; **ya me lo temía** I knew this would happen; **me temo que tenía razón** I fear that he was right **(b)** (en fórmulas de cortesía) to be afraid; **me temo que no ha llegado** I'm afraid he hasn't arrived

temeridad *f* **(a)** (acción): **eso fue una ~** that was a very rash *o* bold thing to do **(b)** (cualidad) temerity; **conduce con ~** she drives recklessly

temible *adj* fearsome, fearful

temor *m* fear; **no dije nada por ~ a ofenderlo** I didn't say anything for fear of offending him

témpano *m* ice floe

témpera *f* tempera

temperamental *adj* (irascible, cambiable) temperamental; (de mucho carácter) spirited

temperamento *m* **(a)** (manera de ser) temperament; **son ~s muy diferentes** they have very different temperaments **(b)** (vigor de carácter): **un chico con mucho ~** a boy with a lot of spirit

temperatura *f* temperature; **tomarle la ~ a algn** to take sb's temperature; **tiene ~** (CS) she has a fever (AmE) *o* (BrE) a temperature; **~ ambiente** room temperature

tempestad *f* storm, tempest (liter); **~ de arena** sandstorm

tempestuoso -sa *adj* stormy, tempestuous

templado -da *adj* **(a)** «*clima*» mild, temperate; «*zona*» temperate; «*día*» warm **(b)** «*agua/comida*» lukewarm

templo *m* temple

temporada *f* **(a)** (época establecida) season; **verduras de ~** seasonal vegetables; **fuera de/en ~** out of/in season; **~ alta/baja** high/low season **(b)** (período de tiempo) spell; **una ~ de mucho trabajo** a very busy spell *o* period

temporal *adj* **1** (transitorio) temporary **2** (relativo al tiempo) temporal
■ *m* (Meteo) storm; **~ de nieve** snowstorm, blizzard

temporalero -ra *m,f* (Méx) seasonal worker

temporario -ria *adj* (AmL) temporary

temprano *adv* early; **levantarse ~** to get up early; **por la mañana ~** in the morning

ten ▶ TENER

tenacidad *f* (perseverancia) tenacity

tenacillas *fpl* hair crimper

tenaz *adj* **(a)** «*persona*» tenacious **(b)** «*dolor*» persistent; «*mancha*» stubborn

tenaza *f*, **tenazas** *fpl* **(a)** (Mec, Tec) pliers (*pl*) **(b)** (de chimenea, cocina) tongs (*pl*) **(c)** (del cangrejo) pincer **(d)** (Méx) (de pelo) curling iron (AmE), hair crimper (BrE)

tendajón *m* (Méx) shack (*serving as a store or stall*)

tendal *m* (AmL) (para el café) drying area

tendedero *m* (cuerda) clothes-line; (caballete) clotheshorse

tendencia *f* tendency; **~s homosexuales** homosexual tendencies *o* leanings; **~ A algo** trend TOWARD(s) sth; **tiene ~ a exagerar** she has a tendency to exaggerate; **existe una ~ a la centralización** there is a trend toward centralization

tender [E8] *vt* **1** «*ropa*» (afuera) to hang out; (dentro de la casa) to hang (up); **tengo ropa tendida** I have some washing on the line
2 (a) (extender) «*manta*» to spread out, lay out; «*mantel*» to spread; **le tendió la mano** he held out his hand to him **(b)** (AmL) «*cama*» to make; «*mesa*» to lay, set **(c)** «*persona*» to lay
3 (a) «*cable*» (sobre superficie) to lay; (suspendido) to hang **(b)** «*vía férrea*» to lay
4 «*emboscada*» to lay, set; «*trampa*» to set
■ **~** *vi* (inclinarse): **~ A hacer algo** to tend to do sth; **tiende a encoger** it tends to shrink
■ **tenderse** *v pron* (tumbarse) to lie down

tendero -ra *m,f* storekeeper (esp AmE), shopkeeper (esp BrE)

tendido *m* **1** (Elec) (cables) cables (*pl*), wires (*pl*) **2** (Col, Ven) (ropa de cama) bedclothes (*pl*)

tendón *m* tendon

tendré, tendría, etc ▶ TENER

tenebroso -sa *adj* «*lugar*» dark, gloomy; «*asunto/maquinaciones*» sinister; «*porvenir*» dismal, gloomy

tenedor *m* (cubierto) fork

tenencia *f* (Méx) (Auto) road tax

tener [E27] *vt* [*El uso de 'got' en frases como 'I've got a new dress' está mucho más extendido en el inglés británico que en el americano. Este prefiere la forma 'I have a new dress'*] **1 (a)** (poseer, disponer de) «*dinero/trabajo/tiempo*» to have; **¿tienen hijos?** do they have any children?, have they got any children?; **no tenemos pan** we don't have any bread, we haven't got any bread; **tiene el pelo largo** she has *o* she's got long hair **(b)** (llevar encima) «*lápiz/cambio*» to have; **¿tiene hora?** have you got the time? **(c)** (hablando de actividades, obligaciones) to have; **tengo invitados a cenar** I have *o* I've got some people coming to dinner; **tengo cosas que hacer** I have *o* I've got things to do **(d)** (dar a luz) «*bebé/gemelos*» to have
2 (a) (señalando características, tamaño) to be; **la casa tiene mucha luz** the house is very light; **tiene un metro de largo** it is one meter long; **le lleva 15 años — ¿y eso qué tiene?** (AmL fam) she's

15 years older than he is — so what does that matter? **(b)** (señalando edad) to be; ¿cuántos años tienes? how old are you?; tengo veinte años I'm twenty (years old)

3 (a) (sujetar, sostener) to hold; tenlo derecho hold it upright **(b)** (tomar): ten la llave take o here's the key

4 (a) (sentir): tengo hambre/frío I'm hungry/cold; le tengo mucho cariño I'm very fond of him; tengo el placer de … it gives me great pleasure to … **(b)** (refiriéndose a enfermedades) ‹gripe/cáncer› to have; tengo dolor de cabeza I have o I've got a headache **(c)** (refiriéndose a experiencias) ‹discusión/accidente› to have; que tengas buen viaje have a good trip

5 (refiriéndose a actitudes): ten más respeto have a little more respect; ten paciencia/cuidado be patient/careful; tiene mucho tacto he's very tactful

6 (indicando estado, situación): la mesa tiene una pata rota one of the table legs is broken; tengo las manos sucias my hands are dirty; tienes el cinturón desabrochado your belt's undone; me tiene muy preocupada I'm very worried about it

■ ~ v aux **1** ~ QUE hacer algo **(a)** (expresando obligación, necesidad) to have (got) to do sth; tengo que estudiar hoy I have to o I must study today; tienes que comer más you ought to eat more **(b)** (expresando propósito, recomendación): tenemos que ir a ver esa película we must go and see that movie; tendrías que llamarlo you should ring him **(c)** (expresando certeza): tiene que estar en este cajón it must be in this drawer; ¡tú tenías que ser! it had to be you!

2 (con participio pasado): tengo entendido que sí viene I understand he is coming; te lo tengo dicho que … I've told you before (that) …; teníamos pensado irnos hoy we intended leaving today **3** (AmL) (en expresiones de tiempo): tienen tres años de casados they've been married for three years; tenía un año sin verlo she hadn't seen him for a year

■ **tenerse** v pron (sostenerse): no podía ~se en pie he couldn't stand; no ~se de sueño to be dead on one's feet

tenga, tengas, etc ▶ TENER

tenia f (Med) tapeworm, taenia (tech)

tenida f (Chi) outfit

teniente mf **(a)** (en ejército) lieutenant **(b)** (en fuerzas aéreas) ≈first lieutenant (in US), ≈flying officer (in UK)

tenis m (pl ~) tennis; ~ de mesa table tennis

tenista mf tennis player

tenor m (Mús) tenor

tensar [A1] vt ‹músculo› to tense; ‹cuerda/cable› to tighten; ‹arco› to draw; ‹relaciones/lazos› to strain

tensión f **1 (a)** (de cuerda, músculo) tension **(b)** tb ~ arterial blood pressure; tomarle la ~ a algn to take sb's blood pressure; ~ nerviosa nervous tension **2** (estrés) strain, stress; (en relaciones, situación) tension **3** (Elec) voltage

tenso -sa adj **1** ‹cuerda/cable› taut, tight; ‹músculo› tense **2** ‹persona/situación› tense; ‹relación› strained, tense

tentación f **(a)** (impulso) temptation; no resistió la ~ de comérselo he couldn't resist the

temptation to eat it **(b)** (cosa, persona): los bombones son mi ~ I can't resist chocolates (colloq)

tentáculo m tentacle

tentador -dora adj tempting

tentar [A5] vt **1 (a)** (atraer, seducir) «plan/idea» to tempt; «persona» to tempt; me tienta tu propuesta I am very tempted by your proposal; estuve tentado de decírselo I was tempted to tell him; ~ a algn A hacer algo to tempt sb to do sth **2** (probar) **(a)** ‹cuerda/tabla› to test **(b)** (palpar) to feel

tentativa f attempt

tentempié m (bocado) snack

tenue adj **(a)** ‹luz› faint, weak; ‹voz/sonido/sonrisa› faint; ‹neblina/llovizna› light; ‹línea› faint, fine **(b)** ‹color› subdued, pale

teñir [I15] vt **(a)** ‹ropa/zapatos/pelo› to dye **(b)** (manchar) to stain; la tinta le tiñó los dedos de rojo the ink stained his fingers red

■ **teñirse** v pron (refl) ‹pelo/zapatos› to dye

teología f theology

teoría f theory; en ~ in theory

teórico -ca adj ‹existencia/valor/curso› theoretical; examen ~ theory (exam)

tequila m tequila

terapeuta mf therapist

terapéutico -ca adj therapeutic

terapia f therapy; ~ de pareja marriage counseling*; ~ intensiva (Méx, RPI) intensive care

tercer ▶ TERCERO[1]

tercera f (Auto) third (gear); mete (la) ~ put it into third (gear)

tercermundista adj third-world (before n)

tercero[1] -ra adj/pron [TERCER is used before masculine singular nouns] third; en el tercer piso on the third floor; el Tercer Mundo the Third World; personas de la tercera edad senior citizens; la tercera parte a third; para ejemplos ver QUINTO

tercero[2] m third party; seguro contra ~s third party insurance

tercio m **(a)** (tercera parte) third **(b)** (Taur) each of the three main stages of a bullfight

terciopelo m velvet

terco -ca adj stubborn, obstinate

tergiversar [A1] vt to distort, twist

termas fpl (baños) o thermal baths (pl); (manantial) hot o thermal springs (pl)

térmico -ca adj thermal

terminación f **(a)** (finalización) termination (frml) **(b)** (acabado) finish **(c)** (Ling) ending

terminal adj ‹enfermedad/caso› terminal; los enfermos ~es the terminally ill
■ m (Elec, Inf) terminal
■ f (de autobuses) terminus, bus station; (Aviac, Inf) terminal

terminante adj ‹respuesta› categorical; ‹orden› strict

terminar [A1] vt ‹trabajo/estudio› to finish; ‹casa/obras› to finish, complete; ‹discusión/conflicto› to put an end to; termina esa sopa finish up that soup; ~ la comida con un café to end the meal with a cup of coffee
■ ~ vi **1** «persona» **(a)** (de hacer algo) to finish; ⋯⋗

~ **DE hacer algo** to finish doing sth; **déjame ~ de hablar** let me finish (speaking) **(b)** (en estado, situación) to end up; **terminé muy cansada** I ended up feeling very tired; **va a ~ mal** he's going to come to a bad end; **terminó marchándose** or **por marcharse** he ended up leaving
2 (a) «*reunión/situación*» to end, come to an end; **al ~ la clase** when the class ended; **esto va a ~ mal** this is going to turn out o end badly **(b)** (rematar) ~ **EN algo** to end IN sth; **termina en consonante** it ends in a consonant **(c)** (llegar a): **no termina de convencerme** I'm not totally convinced; **no terminaba de gustarle** she wasn't totally happy about it
3 terminar con (a) (acabar) ~ **CON algo** «*con libro/tarea*» to finish WITH sth; «*con problema/abuso*» to put an end to sth **(b)** ~ **CON algn** (pelearse) to finish WITH sb; (matar) to kill sb
■ **terminarse** v pron **1** «*azúcar/pan*» to run out; **se me terminó la lana** I've run out of wool **2** «*curso/reunión*» to come to an end, be over **3** (enf) «*libro/comida*» to finish, polish off

término m **1** (posición, instancia): **en primer ~** first, first of all; ~ **medio** happy medium; **por ~ medio** on average **2** (Ling) term; **en ~s reales** in real terms **3 términos** mpl (condiciones, especificaciones) terms (pl) **4** (Col, Méx, Ven) (Coc): **¿qué ~ quiere la carne?** how would you like your meat (done)?

termita f termite
termo® m (recipiente) Thermos®, vacuum flask
termómetro m thermometer
termostato m thermostat
ternera f veal
ternero -ra m,f calf
terno m (AmS) suit (*in some countries specifically a three-piece suit*)
ternura f tenderness; **con ~** tenderly
terquedad f obstinacy, stubbornness
terracería f (Méx) (camino) rough dirt track
terracota f terra-cotta
terrateniente mf landowner
terraza f **(a)** (balcón) balcony **(b)** (azotea) terrace **(c)** (de bar) *area outside a bar or café where tables are placed*; **sentémonos en la ~** let's sit outside **(d)** (Agr) terrace
terregal m (Méx) loose topsoil
terremoto m earthquake
terrenal adj worldly, earthly
terreno¹ -na adj (Relig) earthly
terreno² m 1 (a) (lote, parcela) plot of land, lot (AmE); **heredó unos ~s en Sonora** she inherited some land in Sonora; **un ~ plantado de viñas** a field planted with vines; ~ **de juego** field, pitch **(b)** (extensión de tierra) land; **una casa con mucho ~** a house with a lot of land **2** (Geog) (refiriéndose al relieve) terrain; (refiriéndose a la composición) land, soil; **un ~ fértil** fertile land **3** (esfera, campo de acción) sphere, field; **en el ~ político** within the field of politics
terrestre adj **(a)** «*transportes/comunicaciones*»

land (*before n*), terrestrial (frml); **por vía ~** overland, by land; **fuerzas ~s** ground o land forces; **la superficie ~** the earth's surface **(b)** (Relig) «*vida*» earthly

terrible adj **(a)** «*tortura/experiencia*» terrible, horrific **(b)** (uso hiperbólico) terrible; **tengo un sueño ~** I'm terribly tired
territorial adj territorial
territorio m territory
terrón m (de azúcar) lump; (de tierra) clod, lump
terror m **(a)** (miedo) terror; **le tengo ~** it terrifies me, I find it terrifying; **de ~** «*novela/relato*» horror (*before n*) **(b)** (persona) terror
terrorífico -ca adj horrific
terrorismo m terrorism
terrorista adj/mf terrorist
terso -sa adj smooth
tertulia f (reunión) gathering (*to discuss philosophy, politics, art, etc*)
tertuliano -na m,f participant in a TERTULIA
tesina f dissertation (*submitted as part of a first degree*)
tesis f (pl ~) **(a)** (Educ, Fil) thesis; ~ **doctoral** doctoral thesis **(b)** (opinión): **los dos sostienen la misma ~** they are both of the same opinion; **esto confirma la ~ inicial** this confirms the initial theory
tesón m tenacity, determination
tesorería f (oficina) treasury; (cargo) post of treasurer
tesorero -ra m,f treasurer
tesoro m **(a)** (cosa valiosa) treasure **(b)** (persona) treasure, gem (colloq); **¿qué te pasa, ~?** what's the matter, darling?
test m (pl **tests**) test; **un examen tipo ~** a multiple-choice exam
testamento m will, testament (frml); **hacer ~** to make one's will
testarudo -da adj stubborn, pigheaded
testículo m testicle
testificar [A2] vt/vi to testify, give evidence
testigo mf witness; **ser ~ de algo** to witness sth, be a witness to sth
testimonio m **(a)** (Der) (declaración) testimony, statement **(b)** (prueba) proof, testimony (frml); **dar ~ de algo** to bear witness to sth
tétanos, tétano m tetanus
tetera f **(a)** (para servir té) teapot **(b)** (Andes, Méx) (para hervir agua) kettle **(c)** (Méx) (biberón) baby's bottle
tetero m (Col, Ven) baby's bottle
tetilla f **(a)** (Anat) nipple; (Zool) teat **(b)** (del biberón) teat
tetina f teat
tétrico -ca adj dismal, gloomy
textil adj textile (*before n*)
texto m text
textual adj «*traducción*» literal; «*palabras*» exact; «*cita*» direct

textura *f* texture

tez *f* complexion

ti *pron pers* **(a)** you; **para ~** for you; **delante de ~** in front of you; **a mí me gusta ¿y a ~?** I like it, do you? **(b)** *(refl)*: **~ mismo/misma** yourself; **piensa un poco en ~ mismo** just think of yourself a little **(c)** *(impers)* you; **si a ~ te cuentan que …** if someone tells you that …

tianguis *m* (Méx) street market

tibio -bia *adj* **(a)** *(agua/baño)* lukewarm, tepid **(b)** *(atmósfera/ambiente)* warm **(c)** *(relación)* lukewarm; *(acogida)* unenthusiastic, cool

tiburón *m* **(a)** (Zool) shark **(b)** (fam) *(persona)* shark **(c)** (Fin) raider

tic *m* **1** (movimiento) *tb* **~ nervioso** nervous tic **2** (marca en escrito) tick

tico -ca *adj/m,f* (AmL fam) Costa Rican

tiempo *m* **1** **(a)** (en general) time; **¡cómo pasa el ~!** how time flies!; **te acostumbrarás con el ~** you'll get used to it in time; **perder el ~** to waste time; **¡no hay ~ que perder!** there's no time to lose!; **para ganar ~** (in order) to gain time; **~ libre** spare time, free time; **¿cuánto ~ hace que no lo ves?** how long is it since you last saw him?; **hace ~ que no sé de él** I haven't heard from him for a long time; **ya hace ~ que se marchó** he left quite some time ago; **¡cuánto ~ sin verte!** I haven't seen you for ages; **la mayor parte del ~** most of the time; **me llevó mucho ~** it took me a long time; **no pude quedarme más ~** I couldn't stay any longer; **poco ~ después** a short time after; **de un ~ a esta parte** for some time (now); **a ~ completo/parcial** full time/part time; **no vamos a llegar a ~** we won't get there in time; **al mismo ~** at the same time; **avísame con ~** let me know in good time; **¡qué ~s aquellos!** those were the days!; **en aquellos ~s** at that time, in those days **(b)** (temporada) season; **fruta del ~** fruits in season **(c)** (momento propio, oportuno): **a su (debido) ~** in due course; **cada cosa a su ~** everything in (its own) good time **(d)** (edad de bebé): **¿cuánto ~ tiene?** how old is he?

2 (Dep) (en partido) half; **primer ~** first half

3 (Mús) (compás) tempo, time; (de sinfonía) movement

4 (Ling) tense

5 (Meteo) weather; **hace buen/mal ~** the weather's good/bad; **del** *or* (Méx) **al ~** *(bebida)* at room temperature

tienda *f* **1** (Com) (en general) store (esp AmE), shop (esp BrE); **ir de ~s** to go shopping; **~ de comestibles** *or* (AmC, Andes, Méx) **abarrotes** grocery store (AmE), grocer's (shop) (BrE) **2** (Dep, Mil, Ocio) *tb* **~ de campaña** tent; **poner** *or* **montar una ~** to put up *o* pitch a tent; **desmontar una ~** to take down a tent

tiene, tienes, etc ▶ TENER

tienta *f*: **a tientas** *(loc adv)*: **andar** *or* **ir a ~s** to feel one's way; **buscó el timbre a ~s** he fumbled *o* felt around for the bell

tierno -na *adj* **1** *(carne)* tender; *(pan)* fresh; *(brote/planta)* young, tender **2** *(persona)* affectionate, loving; *(mirada/corazón)* tender

tierra *f* **1** **(a)** (campo, terreno) land; **~s fértiles** fertile land; **~ de cultivo** arable land

2 (suelo, superficie) ground; (materia, arena) earth; **cavar la ~** to dig the ground; **un camión de ~** a truckload of soil *o* earth; **no juegues con ~** don't play in the dirt; **un camino de ~** a dirt road *o* track; **echar algo por ~** *(planes)* to wreck, ruin; *(argumentos)* to demolish, destroy; *(esperanzas)* to dash

3 (AmL) (polvo) dust

4 (Elec) ground (AmE), earth (BrE); **estar conectado a ~** *or* (AmL) **hacer ~** to be grounded *o* earthed

5 (por oposición al mar, al aire) land; **viajar por ~** to travel overland *o* by land; **~ firme** solid ground; **tomar ~** to land, touch down

6 (país, lugar): **su ~ (natal)** his homeland, his native land; **costumbres de aquellas ~s** customs in those places *o* countries; **la T~** Santa the Holy Land

7 (planeta) **la T~** (the) Earth

tieso -sa *adj* **1** **(a)** (rígido) stiff; **con las orejas tiesas** with ears pricked up **(b)** (Col, Ven) (duro) *(pan)* hard; *(carne)* tough **2** *(persona)* (erguido) upright, erect; (orgulloso) stiff; **quedarse ~** (fam) (helarse) to get frozen stiff (colloq)

tiesto *m* **(a)** (para plantas) flowerpot **(b)** (Chi) (palangana) basin

tifón *m* typhoon

tifus *m* **(a)** (transmitido por parásitos) typhus (fever) **(b)** (fiebre tifoidea) typhoid

tigre -gresa *m,f* (animal asiático) *(m)* tiger; *(f)* tigress

tijeras *fpl*, **tijera** *f* (para cortar papel, tela) scissors *(pl)*; (para uñas) nail scissors *(pl)*; (para césped) shears *(pl)*; **unas ~s** a pair of scissors; **~ de podar** pruning shears *(pl)*; **de ~** *(silla/cama)* folding *(before n)*; **escalera de ~** stepladder

tila *f* (infusión) lime (blossom) tea

tilde *f* (acento) accent; (sobre la ñ) tilde, swung dash

tiliches *mpl* (Méx fam) stuff (colloq)

tilo *m* **(a)** (árbol) lime (tree) **(b)** (Chi) ▶ TILA

timador -dora *m,f* swindler, cheat

timar [A1] *vt* to swindle, cheat

timbal *m* (Mús) kettledrum; **los ~es** the timpani, the timps (colloq)

timbrar [A1] *vt* *(documento)* to stamp; *(carta)* to frank

■ **~** *vi* (Col, Méx) to ring the bell

timbre *m* **1** (para llamar) (door)bell; **tocar el ~** to ring the bell; **~ de alarma** alarm bell **2** (de sonido, voz) tone, timbre **3** **(a)** (sello) fiscal stamp **(b)** (Méx) (sello postal) (postage) stamp

timidez *f* (retraimiento) shyness; (falta de decisión, coraje) timidity

tímido -da *adj* (retraído) shy; (falto de decisión, coraje) timid

timo *m* (fam) con (colloq), scam (colloq)

timón *m* **(a)** (Aviac, Náut) rudder **(b)** (Col, Per) (volante) steering wheel; **ir al ~** to be at the wheel

timonel *mf* *(m)* helmsman; *(f)* helmswoman

tímpano *m* (Anat) eardrum

tinaco *m* (Méx) water tank

tinaja *f* large earthenware jar

tinca *f* (Andes) (fam) (empeño) effort

tincada *f* (Andes fam) feeling, hunch (colloq)

tincar [A2] *vi* (Andes fam) **(a)** (parecer): **me tinca que ya no viene** I get the feeling she's not coming ⋯∴

(b) (parecer bien, gustar): **ese pescado me tinca** I like the look of that fish; **¿te tinca ir al cine?** do you feel like going to the movies?

tinieblas *fpl* darkness

tino *m* **(a)** (sentido común) sound judgment, good sense **(b)** (tacto) tact, sensitivity

tinta *f* ink; ~ **China** India ink; **escribir con** ~ to write in ink (AmE), Indian ink (BrE); **saber algo de buena** ~ to have sth on good authority

tinte *m* **1** (acción) dyeing; (sustancia) dye **2** (Esp) (establecimiento) dry cleaner's

tintero *m* inkwell

tintín *m* (de campanilla) tinkling, jingling; (de copa) clinking

tinto¹ -ta *adj* ⟨vino/uva⟩ red

tinto² *m* **1** (Vin) red wine **2** (Col) (café) black coffee

tintorería *f* dry cleaner's

tiña *f* (Med) ringworm

tiñoso -sa *adj* (Med) scabby, mangy

tío, tía *m,f* **1** (pariente) (*m*) uncle; (*f*) aunt; **mis** ~**s** (varones) my uncles; (varones y mujeres) my aunts and uncles **2** (Esp) (individuo) (fam) ▶ TIPO¹

tiovivo *m* (Esp) merry-go-round, carousel (AmE)

tipear [A1] *vt* (AmS) to type

típico -ca *adj* typical; ⟨plato/traje⟩ typical, traditional; **¡eso es ~ de él!** that's typical of him!

tipo¹ -pa *m,f* (fam) (*m*) guy (colloq), bloke (BrE colloq); (*f*) woman

tipo² *m* **1** (clase) kind, type, sort; **todo ~ de plantas** all kinds of plants; **no es mi ~** he's not my type **2** (figura — de mujer) figure; (— de hombre) physique **3** (como adv) (CS fam) around, about; **vénganse ~ cuatro** come around about four o'clock

tique, tíquet (*pl* ~**ts**) *m* **(a)** (de tren, bus) ticket **(b)** (recibo) receipt, sales slip (AmE)

tiquete *m* (Col) ▶ TIQUE

tira *f* (de papel, tela) strip; (de zapato) strap; ~ **cómica** comic strip, strip cartoon

■ *mf* **(a)** (Chi, Méx fam) (agente) cop (colloq) **(b)** (Per, RPI arg) (detective infiltrado) police plant (colloq), undercover cop (colloq) **(c) la tira** *f* (Méx fam) (cuerpo) the cops (colloq)

tirabuzón *m* **1** (sacacorchos) corkscrew **2** (rizo, bucle) ringlet **3** (en béisbol) screwball

tirada *f* **1** (Jueg) (en juegos de mesa) throw **2** (Impr) print run; **un periódico con una ~ de 300.000 ejemplares diarios** a newspaper with a daily circulation of 300,000 copies

tiradero *m* (Méx) (basurero) garbage (AmE) *o* (BrE) rubbish dump; (casa, habitación) mess, pigsty

tirado -da *adj* **1** (en desorden): **lo dejan todo ~** they leave everything lying around **2** (fam) [ESTAR] **(a)** (muy fácil) dead easy (colloq) **(b)** (muy barato) dirt cheap (colloq)

tirador¹ *m* **(a)** (de cajón, puerta) knob, handle **(b)** (tirachinas) slingshot (AmE), catapult (BrE) **(c) tiradores** *mpl* (Arg, Bol) (de pantalón) suspenders (*pl*) (AmE), braces (*pl*) (BrE)

tirador² -dora *m,f* (*m*) marksman; (*f*) markswoman; **es un buen ~** he's a good shot

tiraje *m* **(a)** (AmL) (Impr) ▶ TIRADA 2 **(b)** (CS) (de la chimenea) damper

tiranía *f* tyranny

tirano -na *adj* tyrannical

■ *m,f* tyrant

tirantas *fpl* (Col) suspenders (*pl*) (AmE), braces (*pl*) (BrE)

tirante *adj* **(a)** ⟨piel/costura/cuerda⟩ taut **(b)** ⟨situación⟩ tense; ⟨relaciones⟩ tense, strained

■ *m* **1** (Const) strut, brace **2** (Indum) **(a)** (de prenda) strap, shoulder strap; **pantalones de ~s** overalls (*pl*) (AmE), dungarees (*pl*) (BrE) **(b) tirantes** *mpl* (Esp, Méx, Ven) (de pantalón) suspenders (*pl*) (AmE), braces (*pl*) (BrE)

tirar [A1] *vt* **1 (a)** (lanzar) to throw; **tiró la pelota al aire** he threw the ball up in the air; ~**le algo A algn** (para que lo agarre) to throw sb sth; (con agresividad) to throw sth AT sb **(b)** (desechar) to throw out *o* away **(c)** (desperdiciar) to waste; **¡qué manera de ~ el dinero!** what a waste of money! **2 (a)** (hacer caer) ⟨jarrón/silla⟩ to knock over; **el perro me tiró al suelo** the dog knocked me over **(b)** (derribar) ⟨pared/puerta⟩ to knock down **3 (a)** ⟨bomba⟩ to drop; ⟨cohete⟩ to fire, launch; ⟨flecha⟩ to shoot **(b)** ⟨foto⟩ to take **4** (AmL) (atrayendo hacia sí) to pull; **tiró la cadena** he pulled the chain

■ ~ *vi* **1** (atrayendo hacia sí) to pull; ~ **DE algo** to pull sth; **no le tires del pelo** don't pull her hair **2 (a)** (disparar) to shoot; ~ **a matar** to shoot to kill **(b)** (Dep) to shoot; ~ **al arco** (AmL) *or* (Esp) **a puerta** to shoot at goal **(c)** (Jueg) (descartarse) (en juegos de dados) to throw; (en dardos) to throw; (en bolos) to bowl **3 (a)** «chimenea/cigarro» to draw **(b)** «coche/motor» to pull **4 tirando** *ger* (fam): **gano poco pero vamos tirando** I don't earn much but we're managing; **¿qué tal andas? — tirando** how are things? — not too bad **5 tirar a** (tender a): **tira más bien a azul** it's more of a bluish color; **ella tira más a la madre** she takes after her mother more

■ **tirarse** *v pron* **1 (a)** (lanzarse, arrojarse) to throw oneself; **se tiró por la ventana** he threw himself out of the window; ~**se en paracaídas** to parachute; (en emergencia) to bale out; ~**se al agua** to jump into the water; ~**se de cabeza** to dive in, to jump in headfirst **(b)** (AmL) (tumbarse) to lie down **2** (fam) ⟨horas/días⟩ to spend; **se tiró dos años escribiéndolo** he spent two years writing it **3** (fam) (expulsar): ~**se un pedo** to fart (sl)

tirita *f* (Esp) Band-Aid® (AmE), sticking plaster (BrE)

tiritar [A1] *vi* to shiver, tremble; ~ **de frío** to shiver with cold

tiro *m* **1** (disparo) shot; **le dispararon un ~** they shot him; **lo mató de un ~** she shot him dead; **al ~** (Chi fam) right away, straightaway (BrE); **errar el ~** (literal) to miss; (equivocarse) to get it wrong **2** (en fútbol, baloncesto) shot; (deporte) shooting; ~ **al arco** (deporte) archery; (en fútbol) (AmL) shot at goal; ~ **al blanco** (deporte) target shooting; (lugar) shooting gallery; ~ **al plato** skeet shooting (AmE), clay-pigeon shooting (BrE); ~ **de esquina** (AmL) corner (kick); ~ **libre** (en fútbol) free kick; (en baloncesto) free shot *o* throw **3** (de chimenea) flue; **tiene muy buen ~** it draws well **4 animal/caballo de ~** draught animal/horse

tirón *m* **(a)** (movimiento) tug, pull; **me dio un ∼ de pelo** he pulled my hair; **dale un ∼ de orejas** tweak his ears for him (colloq); **el autobús avanzaba a tirones** the bus jerked along; **de un ∼: me arrancó la cadena de un ∼** he ripped the chain from my neck; **lo leyó/bebió de un ∼** (fam) she read/downed it in one go **(b)** (de músculo): **sufrió un ∼ en la pierna** he pulled a muscle in his leg **(c)** (forma de robo): **le dieron un** *or* **el ∼** they snatched her bag

tironear [A1] *vi* (AmL fam) to tug, pull
■ **∼** *vt* (AmL fam) to tug (at)

tiroteo *m* (tiros) shooting; (intercambio de tiros) shoot-out

tirria *f* (fam) grudge; **tenerle ∼ a algn** to have a grudge against sb

tisú *m* (*pl* **-sús** *or* **-súes**) (pañuelo) tissue; (tela) lamé

titánico -ca *adj* huge, colossal (*before n*)

títere *m* **(a)** (marioneta, persona) puppet **(b) títeres** *mpl* (función) puppet show

titiritar [A1] *vi* to shiver, tremble

titiritero -ra *m,f* (de marionetas) puppeteer; (acróbata) acrobat

titubeante *adj* ⟨voz/respuesta⟩ faltering, halting; ⟨actitud⟩ hesitant

titubear [A1] *vi* **(a)** (dudar, vacilar) to hesitate; **sin ∼** without hesitation **(b)** (balbucear) to stutter

titubeo *m* (duda, vacilación) hesitancy, hesitation

titulación *f* qualifications (*pl*); **personas con ∼ universitaria** university graduates, college graduates (AmE)

titulado -da *adj* qualified
■ *m,f* graduate; **∼ medio** *graduate with a qualification obtained after a three-year degree course as opposed to a five-year course*; **∼ superior** *or* **universitario** university graduate, college graduate (AmE)

titular¹ *adj* ⟨médico/profesor⟩ permanent
■ *mf* (de pasaporte, cuenta, cargo) holder
■ *m* **(a)** (en periódico) headline **(b)** (Rad, TV) main story; **los ∼es** the main stories, the news headlines

titular² [A1] *vt* ⟨obra⟩: **su novela titulada 'Julia'** his novel called *o* (frml) entitled 'Julia'
■ **titularse** *v pron* **1** ⟨obra/película⟩ to be called, be entitled (frml) **2** (Educ) to graduate, get one's degree; **∼se EN/DE algo** to graduate IN/AS sth

título *m* **1** (en general) title; **un poema que lleva por ∼ ...** a poem called *o* (frml) entitled ...; **el ∼ de campeón juvenil** the junior title; **∼ nobiliario** title; **a ∼ de: a ∼ de introducción** by way of introduction; **asiste a ∼ de observador** he's attending as an observer **2** (Educ) degree; (diploma) certificate; **∼ académico** academic qualification; **∼ universitario** university degree, college degree (AmE)

tiza *f* (material) chalk; (barra) (piece of) chalk; (en billar) chalk

tizón *m* (leño) charred stick/log

toalla *f* **(a)** (tejido) toweling*; **(b)** (para secarse) towel; **∼ higiénica** sanitary napkin (AmE), sanitary towel (BrE); **tirar** *or* **arrojar la ∼** to throw in the towel

toallero *m* (barra) towel rail; (aro) towel ring

tobillera *f* **(a)** (Med) ankle support **(b)** (de ciclista) cycle clip

tobillo *m* ankle

tobogán *m* **(a)** (en parque) slide; (en piscina) water chute **(b)** (Aviac) escape chute **(c)** (trineo) toboggan

toca *f* (de religiosa) wimple; (de tocado) circlet

tocadiscos *m* (*pl* **∼**) record player

tocador *m* (mueble) dressing table

tocar [A2] *vt* **1** **(a)** (en general) to touch; (palpar) to feel; (manosear) to handle; **¡no vayas a ∼ ese cable!** don't touch that cable!; **mis ahorros no los quiero ∼** I don't want to touch my savings; **la planta ya toca el techo** the plant is already touching the ceiling **(b)** (hacer sonar) ⟨timbre/campana⟩ to ring; ⟨claxon⟩ to blow, sound **(c)** (Mús) ⟨instrumento/pieza⟩ to play **2** ⟨tema⟩ (tratar) to touch on, refer to; (sacar) to bring up **3** (atañer, concernir) to affect; **un problema que nos toca de cerca** a problem which affects us directly
■ **∼** *vi* **1** **(a)** (AmL) (llamar) «*persona*» to knock at the door; **alguien está tocando** (a la puerta) there's somebody at the door **(b)** «*campana/timbre*» to ring; **las campanas tocaban a misa** the bells were ringing for mass **(c)** (Mús) to play **2** **(a)** (corresponder en reparto, concurso, sorteo): **a ella le toca la mitad de la herencia** she gets half of the inheritance; **le tocó el primer premio** she won the first prize; **me tocó la maestra más antipática del colegio** I got the most horrible teacher in the school **(b)** (ser el turno): **te toca a ti** it's your turn; **¿a quién le toca cocinar?** whose turn is it to do the cooking?
■ **tocarse** *v pron* **(a)** (refl) ⟨herida/grano⟩ to touch; ⟨barba⟩ to play with **(b)** (recípr) «*personas*» to touch each other; «*cables*» to touch

tocayo -ya *m,f* namesake

tocino *m* (para guisar) pork fat; (con vetas de carne) fatty salt pork; (para freír) bacon

tocología *f* obstetrics

tocólogo -ga *m,f* obstetrician

todavía *adv* **1** **(a)** (aún) still; **¿∼ estás aquí?** are you still here? **(b)** (en frases negativas) yet; **∼ no está lista** she isn't ready yet **2** (en comparaciones) even, still; **sus primos son ∼ más ricos** her cousins are even richer *o* richer still **3** (fam) (encima) still; **¡y ∼ se queja!** and he still complains!

todo¹ -da *adj* **1** (la totalidad de) all; **nos comimos ∼ el pan** we ate all the bread; **toda la mañana** all morning, the whole morning; **invitó a toda la clase** she invited the whole class; **por ∼s lados** all over the place; **∼s ustedes lo sabían** you all knew; ▶ MUNDO 1 **2** (cualquier, cada): **∼ artículo importado** all imported items, any imported item; **∼ aquel que quiera** anyone who wishes to; **∼s los días** every day **3** (uso enfático): **a toda velocidad** at top speed; **con toda inocencia** in all innocence; **le dieron ∼ tipo de facilidades** they gave him all kind of facilities; **a ∼ esto** (mientras tanto) meanwhile, in the meantime; (a propósito) incidentally, by the way
■ *pron* **1** **(a)** (sin excluir nada) everything; **lo perdieron ∼** they lost everything; **∼ le parece** ···⟶

t

poco he's never satisfied; **come ~ lo que quieras**
eat as much as you like; **~ o nada** all or nothing
(b) ~**s/todas** (referido a — cosas) all; (— a personas)
all, everybody; **los compró** ~**s** she bought all of
them; **vinieron** ~**s** they all came, everybody
came; **buena suerte a** ~**s** good luck to everybody;
es el más alto de ~**s** he's the tallest of the lot *o*
of them all; **¿están** ~**s?** is everyone *o* everybody
here?; ~**s y cada uno** each and every one
2 (*en locs*) **con todo (y eso)** (*fam*) (*aun así*) all the
same, even so; **de todo: come de** ~ she'll eat
anything; **venden de** ~**s** they sell everything *o* all
sorts of things; **hace de** ~ **un poco** he does a bit
of everything; **del todo** totally
3 (*como adv*) **(a)** (*completamente*) all; **está** ~
mojado it's all wet **(b)** (en frases ponderativas) quite;
fue ~ **un espectáculo** it was quite a show!

todo² *m*: **el/un** ~ the/a whole; **jugarse el** ~ **por**
el ~ to risk *o* gamble everything on one throw

todopoderoso -sa *adj* all-powerful

Todopoderoso *m*: **el** ~ the Almighty

todoterreno *m* (Auto) four-wheel-drive
vehicle, 4 x 4 (*léase: four by four*)

Tokio *m* Tokyo

toldo *m* **(a)** (de terraza) canopy; (de tienda)
awning; (en la playa) awning; (en camión) tarpaulin
(b) (para fiestas) tent (AmE), marquee (BrE) **(c)**
(RPl) (de los indios) hut

tolerable *adj* tolerable

tolerancia *f* tolerance

tolerante *adj* tolerant

tolerar [A1] *vt* to tolerate; **¡eso no se puede** ~**!**
that's intolerable!; **🄢 tolerada (para menores de**
14 años) (Esp) ≈PG; **le toleras demasiado** you're
too lenient with him

toma *f* **1 (a)** (Mil) capture, taking **(b)** (de
universidad, fábrica) occupation; (de tierras) seizure
2 (Cin, Fot — imagen) shot; (— acción de filmar) take
3 (de medicamento) dose **4** (de datos) gathering;
(de muestras) taking; **la** ~ **de decisiones** the
decision-making **5** (AmL) (acequia) irrigation
channel **6 (a)** ~ **de tierra** (Elec) ground (wire)
(AmE), earth (wire) (BrE) **(b)** (Aviac) landing,
touchdown

tomado -da *adj* **1** (*voz*): **tengo la voz tomada**
I'm hoarse **2** (AmL fam) (*persona*) drunk

tomadura de pelo *f* **(a)** (broma, chiste) joke
(b) (burla): **esto es una** ~ **de** ~ they're just
messing around with us (AmE) *o* (BrE) messing us
around

tomar [A1] *vt* **1** (en general) to take; **tomé un**
libro de la estantería I took a book from the shelf;
la tomé de la mano I took her by the hand; **toma**
lo que te debo here's what I owe you; **¿lo puedo**
~ **prestado?** can I borrow it?; **tomó el asunto en**
sus manos she took charge of the matter; ~
precauciones/el tren/una foto to take
precautions/the train/a picture; ~**le la**
temperatura a algn to take sb's temperature; ~
algo por escrito to write sth down; ~ **algo/a algn**
POR algo/algn to take sth/sb FOR sth/sb; **¿por**
quién me has tomado? who *o* what do you take

me for?; **lo tomó a mal/a broma** he took it the
wrong way/as a joke; **eso toma demasiado tiempo**
that takes up too much time
2 (a) (beber) to drink; **el niño toma (el) pecho**
the baby's being breast-fed **(b)** (servirse, consumir)
to have; **¿qué vas a** ~**?** what are you going to
have?
3 (esp AmL) **(a)** (contratar) to take on **(b)**
«*profesor*» «*alumnos/clases*» to take on **(c)**
«*colegio*» «*niño*» to take
4 (apoderarse de) (*fortaleza/tierras*) to seize;
(*universidad/fábrica*) to occupy
5 (adquirir) (*forma*) to take; (*aspecto*) to take on;
(*velocidad/altura*) to gain; (*costumbre*) to get into
6 (cobrar): **le he tomado cariño a esta casa/la**
niña I've become quite attached to this house/
quite fond of the girl
7 (exponerse a): ~ **el aire** to get some (fresh) air;
~ **(el) sol** to sunbathe; **vas a** ~ **frío** (CS) you'll
get *o* catch cold
■ ~ *vi* **1** (asir): **toma, aquí tienes tus tijeras** here
are your scissors; **tome, yo no lo necesito** take it,
I don't need it
2 (esp AmL) (beber alcohol) to drink
3 (AmL) (ir) to go; ~**on para el norte** they went
north; ~ **a la derecha** to turn *o* go right
4 «*injerto*» to take
■ **tomarse** *v pron* **1** (*vacaciones/tiempo*) to take;
se tomó el día libre he took the day off
2 (*molestia/libertad*) to take; ~**se la molestia/**
libertad de hacer algo to take the trouble to do
sth/the liberty of doing sth
3 (*enf*) **(a)** (*café/vino*) to drink **(b)**
(*medicamento/vitaminas*) to take **(c)** (*desayuno/*
merienda/sopa) to eat, have; (*helado/yogur*) to
have
4 (*autobús/tren/taxi*) to take
5 (Med) **(a)** (*refl*) to take; **se tomó la temperatura**
she took her temperature **(b)** (*caus*): ~**se la**
tensión to have one's blood pressure taken
6 (*caus*) (esp AmL) (*foto*) to have ... taken
7 (*enf*) (reaccionar frente a) (*comentario/noticia*) to
take; **no te lo tomes a mal** don't take it the wrong
way
8 (Chi) (*universidad/fábrica*) to occupy

tomate *m* tomato; **estar/ponerse (colorado)**
como un ~ (de vergüenza) to be/turn as red as a
beet (AmE), to be/go as red as a beetroot (BrE);
(por el sol) to be/turn as red as a lobster

tomavistas *m* (*pl* ~) movie camera

toma y daca *m* give-and-take

tómbola *f* tombola

tomillo *m* thyme

tomo *m* volume

ton *m*: **hacer algo sin** ~ **ni son** to do sth for no
reason

tonada *f* **(a)** (melodía) tune; (canción) ballad, song
(b) (AmL) (acento) accent

tonel *m* barrel

tonelada *f* ton

tongo *m* (*fam*) (en partido, pelea) fix (colloq); **hubo**
~ it was fixed (colloq)

tónica *f* $\boxed{1}$ (bebida) tonic (water) $\boxed{2}$ (tendencia, tono) trend, tendency

tónico¹ -ca *adj* $\boxed{1}$ (Med) tonic (*before n*) $\boxed{2}$ (a) ⟨*sílaba/vocal*⟩ tonic (*before n*), stressed (b) (Mús) tonic

tónico² *m* (Med) tonic; (en cosmética) toner

tono *m* $\boxed{1}$ (a) (en general) tone; **en ~ cariñoso** in an affectionate tone of voice; **en ~ de reproche** reproachfully; **el ~ en que lo dijo** the way he said it; **el ~ general de la conversación** the general tone of the conversation (b) (Rad, Telec, TV) tone; **este teléfono no da** *or* **tiene ~** I can't get a dial tone (AmE) *o* (BrE) dialling tone on this phone; **~ de marcar** *or* (AmL) **de discado** *or* (AmS) **de discar** dial tone (AmE), dialling tone (BrE); **~ de ocupado** busy signal (AmE), engaged tone (BrE); **no venir a ~** to be out of place $\boxed{2}$ (de color) shade; **subido de ~** risqué $\boxed{3}$ (Mús) key

tontear [A1] *vi* (a) (hacer el tonto) to play the fool; (decir tonterías) to talk nonsense (b) (flirtear) to fool around (colloq)

tontería *f* (a) (cosa tonta) silly *o* stupid thing; (dicho tonto) silly remark; **¡déjate de ~s!** stop fooling around; **¡~s!** nonsense! (b) (cosa insignificante) silly thing, small thing; **se enoja por cualquier ~** she gets angry over the slightest little thing (c) (cualidad) stupidity

tonto -ta *adj* $\boxed{1}$ (a) [SER] (falto de inteligencia) stupid, dumb (colloq); (ingenuo) silly (b) [ESTAR] (intratable) difficult, silly; (disgustado) upset $\boxed{2}$ ⟨*excusa/error/historia*⟩ silly
■ *m,f* (falto de inteligencia) idiot, dummy (colloq); (ingenuo) idiot, fool; **hacer el ~** (hacer payasadas) to play *o* act the fool; (actuar con necedad) to make a fool of oneself; **hacerse el ~** to act dumb

topacio *m* topaz

toparse [A1] *v pron* **~se CON algn** (tropezarse) to bump INTO sb; (encontrarse) to bump *o* run INTO sb; **~se CON algo** (tropezarse) to bump INTO sth; (encontrarse) to come across sth

tope *m* $\boxed{1}$ (a) (límite) limit; **han establecido un ~ máximo** an upper limit has been set (b) (como adj inv) ⟨*edad/precio*⟩ maximum (*before n*); **fecha ~** deadline $\boxed{2}$ (a) (para las puertas) doorstop; (Ferr) buffer (b) (Auto) speed bump $\boxed{3}$ (Andes) (cima) top $\boxed{4}$ (a) (Andes) (golpe, choque) bump (b) (Méx fam) (cabezazo): **me di un ~** I bumped my head

tópico¹ -ca *adj* $\boxed{1}$ ⟨*comentario/afirmación*⟩ trite $\boxed{2}$ (Farm): ⓢ **uso tópico** for external use only

tópico² *m* (a) (tema, asunto) topic, subject (b) (tema trillado) hackneyed subject; (expresión) cliché

top-less, topless /'toples/ *m*: **el ~ es habitual aquí** it is quite normal for people to go topless here

topo *m* (a) (Zool) mole (b) (Col) (pendiente) earring

topografía *f* topography, surveying

toque *m* $\boxed{1}$ (a) (de timbre) ring; (de campana) stroke, chime; **al ~ de las doce** on the stroke of twelve; **~ de queda** curfew (b) (Esp fam) (llamada) call, ring (BrE colloq) $\boxed{2}$ (en béisbol) bunt $\boxed{3}$ (detalle) touch; **falta darle los últimos ~s** we have to put the finishing touches to it $\boxed{4}$ (Méx fam) (descarga) electric shock

toquetear [A1] *vt* (fam) to touch; (sexualmente) to touch up

toquilla *f* shawl

tórax *m* thorax

torbellino *m* (a) (de viento) whirlwind; (de polvo) dust storm (b) (de actividad) whirl (c) (persona inquieta) bundle of energy

torcedura *f* sprain

torcer [E10] *vt* $\boxed{1}$ ⟨*cuerpo*⟩ to twist; ⟨*cabeza*⟩ to turn; **me torció el brazo** she twisted my arm $\boxed{2}$ ⟨*esquina*⟩ to turn $\boxed{3}$ ⟨*curso/rumbo*⟩ to change
■ **~** *vi* (girar) ⟨*persona/vehículo*⟩ to turn; ⟨*camino*⟩ to bend, curve
■ **torcerse** *v pron* $\boxed{1}$ ⟨*tobillo/muñeca*⟩ to sprain $\boxed{2}$ ⟨*madera/viga*⟩ to warp

torcido -da *adj* $\boxed{1}$ [ESTAR] (a) (con respecto a otra cosa) crooked; **tiene la nariz torcida** he has a crooked nose; **llevas la falda torcida** your skirt's twisted (b) (curvo) bent; **una rama torcida** a bent branch; **tiene las piernas torcidas** (para adentro) he is knock-kneed; (para afuera) he is bowlegged $\boxed{2}$ ⟨*intenciones*⟩ devious, crooked

torcijón *m* stomach cramp

tordo -da *m,f* (a) (caballo) dapple, dapple-gray* (b) (pájaro) thrush

torear [A1] *vi* to fight; **quiere ~** he wants to be a bullfighter
■ **~** *vt* $\boxed{1}$ ⟨*toro/novillo*⟩ to fight $\boxed{2}$ (fam) (a) ⟨*perseguidor/pregunta*⟩ to dodge (b) (AmL) (provocar) to torment, needle

toreo *m* bullfighting

torero -ra *m,f* bullfighter, matador

tormenta *f* $\boxed{1}$ (Meteo) storm; **~ de nieve** snowstorm; (con viento) blizzard; **hacer frente a la ~** to weather the storm $\boxed{2}$ (de pasiones) storm; (de celos) frenzy

tormentoso -sa *adj* stormy

tornado *m* tornado

tornamesa *f or m* (Col, Méx) (plato giratorio) turntable

tornar [A1] *vi* (liter) (a) (regresar) to return; **tornó a nevar** it snowed again (b) (volver, hacer) to make, render
■ **tornarse** *v pron* (liter) to become; **~se EN algo** to turn INTO sth

torneo *m* tournament

tornero -ra *m,f* lathe operator

tornillo *m* (Tec) screw; **te/le falta un ~** you have/he has a screw loose (colloq)

torniquete *m* (Med) tourniquet

torno *m* $\boxed{1}$ (a) (de carpintero) lathe; **~ de alfarero** potter's wheel (b) (Odont) drill (c) (para alzar pesos) winch $\boxed{2}$ **en torno a** around

toro *m* (animal) bull; **~ bravo** *or* **de lidia** fighting bull; **los ~s** (el espectáculo) bullfighting; **ir a los ~s** to go to a bullfight

toronja *f* (AmL) grapefruit

torpe *adj* (a) (en las acciones) clumsy (b) (de entendimiento) slow (colloq) (c) (sin tacto) ⟨*persona/comentario*⟩ clumsy; **de manera ~** clumsily

torpedo *m* $\boxed{1}$ (Arm) torpedo $\boxed{2}$ (Chi fam) (de estudiante) crib (note) (colloq)

torpeza *f* $\boxed{1}$ (cualidad) (a) (en las acciones) clumsiness (b) (falta de inteligencia) stupidity; **perdona mi ~, pero no entiendo** I'm sorry to be ⋯⟶

so stupid o dim, but I don't understand **(c)** (falta de tacto) clumsiness **2** (dicho desacertado) gaffe; (acción desacertada) blunder

torrar [A1] *vt* to roast

torre *f* **(a)** (de castillo, iglesia) tower; (en punta) steeple, spire **(b)** (de cables de alta tensión) pylon; (de pozo de petróleo) derrick **(c)** (en ajedrez) rook, castle **(d)** (edificio alto) apartment block (AmE), tower block (BrE)

torreja *f* **1** (AmL) (pan frito) ▶ TORRIJA **2** (Chi) (rodaja) slice

torrencial *adj* torrential

torrente *m* (Geog) torrent

torrentoso -sa *adj* (AmL) fast-flowing

torreón *m* tower

torrija *f* piece o slice of French toast; ~s French toast

torsión *f* torsion

torso *m* (Anat) torso, trunk; (Art) bust

torta *f* **1** (CS, Ven) (de cumpleaños, etc) cake; (decorada, con crema, etc) gateau **2** (Méx) (bocadillo) sandwich **3** (fam) (golpe): **darle una ~ a** algn to hit o wallop sb (colloq); **pegarse una ~** to bang one's head (o arm *etc*); **liarse a ~s** to come to blows

tortazo *m* (fam) ▶ TORTA 3

tortícolis *f* stiff neck, torticollis (tech)

tortilla *f* **1** (de huevos) omelet*; **~ de papas** or (Esp) **de patatas** Spanish omelet* (*made with potatoes and sometimes onion*) **2** (de maíz) tortilla

tortillero -ra *m,f* tortilla seller

tórtola *f* turtledove

tortuga *f* (Zool) (de tierra) tortoise, turtle (AmE); (de mar) turtle

tortuoso -sa *adj* **(a)** ⟨sendero⟩ tortuous, winding **(b)** ⟨maquinaciones/conducta⟩ devious; ⟨mente⟩ devious, twisted

tortura *f* torture

torturar [A1] *vt* (con violencia física) to torture; (angustiar) to torment, torture

tos *f* cough; **tener ~** to have a cough; **~ convulsa** or **convulsiva** whooping cough

tosco -ca *adj* **(a)** ⟨utensilio/mueble/ construcción⟩ crude, basic; ⟨tela⟩ coarse, rough **(b)** ⟨persona/manos⟩ rough; ⟨lenguaje⟩ unrefined; ⟨modales⟩ coarse; ⟨facciones⟩ coarse

toser [E1] *vi* to cough

tostada *f* **(a)** (de pan) piece o slice of toast; **desayuno café con ~s** I have coffee and toast for breakfast **(b)** (Méx) (de tortilla) tostada (*fried maize tortilla*)

tostado -da *adj* ⟨pan/almendras⟩ toasted; ⟨café⟩ roasted; ⟨piel⟩ tanned

tostadora *f*, **tostador** *m* (para pan) toaster; (para café) roaster

tostar [A10] *vt* **(a)** ⟨pan/almendras⟩ to toast; ⟨café⟩ to roast **(b)** ⟨piel/persona⟩ to tan ■ **tostarse** *v pron* (broncearse) to tan

tostón *m* **1** **(a)** (Esp) (pan frito) crouton **(b)** (Ven) (plátano frito) fried plantain **2** (Esp fam) (cosa fastidiosa) drag (colloq); **darle el ~ a** algn (Esp fam) to pester somebody **3** (Méx fam) (moneda) fifty-cent coin

total *adj* **(a)** (absoluto) ⟨desastre/destrucción⟩ total; ⟨éxito⟩ resounding (*before n*), total; ⟨cambio⟩ complete **(b)** (global) ⟨costo/importe⟩ total ■ *m* total; **en ~** altogether ■ *adv* (*indep*) (fam) (al resumir una narración) so, in the end; **~, que me di por vencida** so in the end I gave up

totalidad *f*: **la ~ de la población** the whole o entire population; **fue destruido en su ~** it was totally destroyed; **se pagó en su ~** it was paid in full

totalitario -ria *adj* totalitarian

totalitarismo *m* totalitarianism

totogol *m* (Col) sports lottery (AmE), football pools (*pl*) (BrE)

totopo *m* (Méx) tortilla chip

totora *f* reed mace, bulrush

tóxico¹ -ca *adj* toxic

tóxico² *m* poison, toxin

toxicómano -na *m,f* drug addict

tozudo -da *adj* obstinate, stubborn ■ *m,f*: **es un ~** he's extremely stubborn o obstinate

traba *f* **1** (en ventana) catch; (de cinturón) belt loop **2** (dificultad, impedimento) obstacle; **me puso muchas ~s** he made things really difficult for me

trabajado -da *adj* ⟨diseño/bordado/plan⟩ elaborate

trabajador -dora *adj* (que trabaja mucho) hard-working ■ *m,f* worker; **un ~ no calificado** (AmL) or (Esp) **cualificado** an unskilled worker o laborer; **~ autónomo** self-employed worker o person; **~ de medio tiempo** (AmL) or (Esp) **a tiempo parcial** part-time worker; **~a social** (Méx) social worker

trabajar [A1] *vi* **1** (en general) to work; **~ por cuenta propia** to be self-employed; **~ jornada completa** or **a tiempo completo** to work full-time; **~ media jornada** to work part-time; **~ mucho** to work hard; **¿en qué trabajas?** what do you do (for a living)?; **estoy trabajando en una novela** I'm working on a novel; **~ DE** or **COMO algo** to work AS sth **2** (actuar) to act, perform; **¿quién trabaja en la película** who's in the movie? ■ *vt* **1** **(a)** ⟨campo/tierra/madera⟩ to work **(b)** ⟨masa⟩ (con las manos) to knead, work **2** (perfeccionar, pulir) to work on

trabajo *m* **1** **(a)** (empleo) job; **buscar ~** to look for work o for a job; **quedarse sin ~** to lose one's job; **un ~ fijo** a steady job; **un ~ de media jornada** a part-time job; **un ~ de jornada completa** or **a tiempo completo** a full-time job **(b)** (lugar) work; **está en el ~** she's at work; **ir al ~** to go to work **2** (actividad, labor) work; **~ en equipo** teamwork; **el ~ de la casa** housework; **los niños dan mucho ~** children give work; **¡buen ~!** well done!; **~ de campo** fieldwork; **~s forzados** hard labor*; **~s manuales** handicrafts (*pl*); **~ voluntario** voluntary o (AmE) volunteer work **3** **(a)** (tarea): **limpiar el horno es un ~ que odio** cleaning the oven is a job I hate **(b)** (obra escrita) piece of work; (en universidad, escuela) essay **4** (esfuerzo): **con mucho ~ consiguió levantarse** with great effort she managed to get up; **me cuesta ~ creerlo** I find it hard to believe

trabajoso -sa adj ‹subida› arduous; ‹tarea› laborious

trabalenguas m (pl ~) tongue twister

trabar [A1] vt **1** (a) ‹puerta/ventana› (para que no se abra) to hold … shut; (para que no se cierre) to hold … back o open (b) ‹caballo› to hobble **2** (a) ‹conversación/amistad/relación› to strike up (b) ‹historia› to weave together **3** ‹proceso/ negociaciones› to hamper the progress of
■ **trabarse** v pron ‹cajón/cierre› to get jammed o stuck; **se le traba la lengua** he gets tongue-tied

trabilla f (de pantalón) stirrup; (para cinturón) belt loop

trácala m (Méx, Ven fam) cheat
■ f (Méx, Ven fam) trick, swindle; **se la pasa haciendo ~** he's always cheating people

tracalada f (Andes fam) bunch (colloq)

tracalear [A1] vt (Méx, Ven fam) to cheat, swindle

tracalero -ra adj (Méx, Ven fam) dishonest

tracción f (Auto, Mec) traction, drive; **un vehículo con** or **de ~ a cuatro ruedas** a four-wheel-drive vehicle

tractor m tractor

tradición f (costumbre) tradition

tradicional adj traditional

tradicionalista adj/mf traditionalist

traducción f translation; **~ del inglés al español** translation from English into Spanish

traducir [I6] vt ‹texto/escritor› to translate; **~ DE algo A algo** to translate FROM sth INTO sth

traductor -tora m,f translator

traer [E23] vt **1** (de un lugar a otro) to bring; **me trajo en la moto** he brought me on his motorbike; **¿qué te trae por aquí?** what brings you here? **2** (ocasionar, causar) ‹problemas/dificultades› to cause; **~ buena suerte** to bring good luck **3** «libro/artículo» ‹artículo/capítulo› to have; **este diccionario no lo trae** it's not in this dictionary **4** (a) ‹ropa/sombrero› to wear (b) (tener consigo) to bring; **traje poco dinero** I didn't bring much money (with me)
■ **traerse** v pron **1** (enf) (a un sitio) to bring (along); **lo invité a él y se trajo a toda la familia** I invited him and he brought the whole family along **2** (fam) (tramar) to be up to (colloq); **¿qué se ~án esas dos?** what are those two up to?

traficante mf dealer, trafficker; **~ de drogas** drug dealer o trafficker; **~ de esclavos** slave trader

traficar [A2] vi **~ EN** or **CON algo** to deal IN sth

tráfico m **1** (de vehículos) traffic; **accidente de ~** road accident **2** (de mercancías) trade; **~ de armas** arms trade; **~ de drogas** drug dealing o trafficking

tragaluz m (en el techo) skylight; (en una puerta, ventana) fanlight

traganíqueles m (pl ~) (AmC) slot machine

tragaperras m or f (pl ~) (Esp fam) slot machine

tragar [A3] vt **1** ‹comida/agua/medicina› to swallow **2** (fam) (aguantar): **no lo trago** I can't stand him

■ **~** vi **1** (Fisiol) to swallow **2** (RPl fam) (estudiar) to cram
■ **tragarse** v pron **1** (enf) (a) ‹comida› to swallow; **~se el humo** to inhale (b) ‹lágrimas› to choke back; ‹orgullo› to swallow (c) «máquina» ‹dinero/tarjeta› to swallow up **2** (fam) (a) (soportar) ‹obra/recital› to sit through (b) (creerse) ‹excusa/cuento› to swallow, fall for (colloq)

tragedia f tragedy

trágico -ca adj (a) ‹actriz/obra› tragic (before n) (b) ‹vida/final/consecuencia› tragic; **no te pongas ~** don't be so melodramatic

tragicomedia f tragicomedy

trago m **1** (a) (de líquido) drink, swig; **un ~ de agua** a drink of water; **de un ~** in one gulp (b) (esp AmL fam) (bebida alcohólica) drink; **¿vamos a tomar un ~?** shall we go for a drink? **2** (experiencia): **pasar un ~ amargo** to have a rough time

traición f (a) (delito) treason (b) (acto desleal) treachery, betrayal; **lo mataron a ~** they killed him by treachery

traicionar [A1] vt (a) ‹patria/amigo› to betray (b) (delatar) «mirada/nerviosismo» to give … away

traicionero -ra adj (a) ‹persona/acción› treacherous (b) ‹mar/carretera› treacherous, dangerous

traidor -dora adj traitorous, treacherous
■ m,f traitor; **~ A algo** traitor TO sth

traiga, traigas, etc ▶ TRAER

trailer /'trailer/ m (pl ~s) **1** (a) (AmL) (casa rodante) trailer (AmE), caravan (BrE) (b) (para caballos) horsebox **2** (Méx) (camión) semitrailer (AmE), articulated lorry (BrE)

tráiler m (pl ~s) **1** (Esp) (Cin) trailer **2 ▶** TRAILER

trailero -ra m,f (Méx) truck driver

traje m (de dos, tres piezas) suit; (vestido de mujer) dress; (Teatr) costume; (de país, región) dress; **~ de baño** (de hombre) swimming trunks (pl); (de mujer) bathing suit, swimsuit; **~ de etiqueta/gala** formal/evening dress; **~ largo** evening dress

traje, etc ▶ TRAER

trajera, trajese, etc ▶ TRAER

trajimos, trajiste, etc ▶ TRAER

trajín m: **un día de mucho ~** a very hectic day; **con todo este ~ …** with all this coming and going…; **el ~ de las grandes ciudades** the hustle and bustle of big cities

trajinar [A1] vi (fam) to rush about (colloq)

trajiste, etc ▶ TRAER

trama f **1** (de tejido) weave, weft **2** (de película, novela) plot

tramar [A1] vt ‹engaño› to devise; ‹venganza› to plot; ‹complot› to hatch, lay; **¿qué andan tramando?** what are they up to? (colloq)

tramitación f processing; **la ~ del divorcio tardó años** the divorce proceedings took years

tramitar [A1] vt ‹préstamo› «funcionario» to deal with; «interesado» to arrange; **están tramitando el divorcio** «cónyuges» they have started divorce proceedings; **~ un permiso de trabajo** «organismo» to deal with a work permit application; «interesado» to apply for one's work permit

t

trámite m (proceso) procedure; (etapa) step, stage; **simplificar los ∼s aduaneros** to simplify customs procedures; **el préstamo está en ∼** the loan application is being processed; **tengo que hacer unos ∼s en el centro** I have some business to attend to in the centre

tramo m (de carretera, vía) stretch; (de escalera) flight

tramoyista mf (Teatr) sceneshifter, stagehand

trampa f **(a)** (para animales) trap; (de lazo) snare **(b)** (ardid) trap; **le tendieron una ∼** they laid o set a trap for him **(c)** (en el juego): **hacer ∼(s)** to cheat; **eso es ∼** that's cheating

trampilla f trapdoor

trampolín m (en natación — flexible) springboard; (— rígido) diving board; (en gimnasia) trampoline; (en esquí) ski jump

tramposo -sa adj: **ser ∼** to be a cheat ■ m,f cheat

tranca f ⓵ **(a)** (de puerta, ventana) bar **(b)** (palo) cudgel, club ⓶ **(a)** (esp AmL fam) (borrachera) bender (colloq); **agarrarse una ∼** to get plastered o smashed (colloq) ⓷ (Ven fam) (Auto) holdup, tailback

trancar [A1] vt ⟨puerta/ventana⟩ to bar

trance m (Psic, Relig) trance; **estar en ∼** to be in a trance

tranque m (CS) reservoir

tranquilidad f **(a)** (calma) peace; **ni un minuto de ∼** not a moment's peace; **con ∼** (sin prisas) at my (o your etc) leisure; (sin nerviosismo) calmly **(b)** (falta de preocupación): **llámame a la hora que sea, con toda ∼** feel free to call me at any time; **lo hice para mi propia ∼** I did it for my own peace of mind

tranquilizante adj **(a)** ⟨noticia⟩ reassuring; ⟨música⟩ soothing **(b)** (Med) tranquilizing* ■ m tranquilizer*

tranquilizar [A4] vt **(a)** (apaciguar) to calm … down; **intenté ∼lo** I tried to calm him down; **sus palabras la ∼on** his words reassured her **(b)** (atenuar la preocupación): **eso me tranquiliza mucho** that makes me feel a lot better
■ **tranquilizarse** v pron (calmarse) to calm down; (dejar de preocuparse): **al oír su voz me tranquilicé** when I heard his voice I felt reassured

tranquilo¹ -la adj ⓵ **(a)** [SER] ⟨persona⟩ (pacífico) calm **(b)** ⟨mar/ambiente⟩ calm; ⟨lugar⟩ quiet, peaceful, tranquil
⓶ [ESTAR] **(a)** (libre de preocupacion) ⟨conciencia⟩ clear; ⟨persona⟩: **ahora que trabaja estoy más ∼** I feel better now that he's found a job; **¡tranquilo!** relax!; **tú, ∼, de eso me encargo yo** there's no need for you to worry, I'll take care of that; **lo hice para quedarme ∼** I did it for my own peace of mind; **déjalo ∼** leave him alone **(b)** (sin inmutarse): **su hermano en el hospital y él tan ∼** his brother's in hospital and he doesn't seem at all bothered; **…y se quedó tan tranquila** …and she didn't bat an eyelash (AmE) o (BrE) eyelid

tranquilo² adv (Méx fam): **te cuesta ∼ unas 2,000 libras** it costs 2,000 pounds easily (colloq)

tranquiza f (Méx fam) hiding (colloq)

transa adj/mf (Méx fam) ▶ TRANZA

transacción f (Com, Fin) transaction, deal

transandino¹ -na adj trans-Andean

transandino² m trans-Andean railroad o railway

transar [A1] vi (AmL) **(a)** (hacer concesiones) ▶ TRANSIGIR A **(b)** (llegar a un acuerdo) to reach an agreement o a compromise; **∼ EN algo** to settle FOR sth

transatlántico¹ -ca adj transatlantic

transatlántico² m ocean liner

transbordador m ferry

transbordar [A1] vt ⟨mercancías/equipajes⟩ to transfer
■ ∼ vi «pasajeros» to change

transbordo m **(a)** (de viajeros) change; **hacer ∼** to change **(b)** (de equipaje, mercancías) transfer

transcribir [I34] vt to transcribe

transcurrir [I1] vi **(a)** «tiempo/años» to pass, go by **(b)** «acontecimiento/acto» to take place

transcurso m course; **en el ∼ del año** during the course of the year; **con el ∼ del tiempo** as time goes/went by

transeúnte mf (peatón) passer-by; (no residente) non-resident

transexual adj/mf transsexual

transferencia f transfer; **∼ bancaria** credit o bank transfer

transferir [I11] vt to transfer

transformación f **(a)** (cambio) transformation, change **(b)** (en rugby) conversion **(c)** (Ling) transformation

transformador m transformer

transformar [A1] vt **(a)** (convertir) to convert; **∼ algo EN algo** to convert sth INTO sth **(b)** (cambiar radicalmente) ⟨persona/situación/país⟩ to transform, change o alter … radically **(c)** (en rugby) to convert
■ **transformarse** v pron **(a)** (convertirse) **∼se EN algo** to turn INTO sth **(b)** (cambiar radicalmente) «persona/país» to change completely, be transformed

transfusión f transfusion; **le hicieron una ∼ de sangre** they gave him a blood transfusion

transgénico¹ -ca adj genetically modified

transgénico² m genetically modified organism (o product etc)

transgredir [I1] vt (frml) to transgress (frml)

transgresión f (frml) transgression (frml)

transgresor -sora m,f transgressor

transición f transition; **∼ DE algo A algo** transition FROM sth TO sth

transigente adj accommodating

transigir [I7] vi **(a)** (hacer concesiones) to compromise, give way; **∼ EN algo** to compromise ON sth **(b)** (tolerar) **∼ CON algo** to tolerate sth, put up WITH sth

transistor m transistor

AmC	Central America	Arg	Argentina	Cu	Cuba	Per	Peru
AmL	Latin America	Bol	Bolivia	Ec	Ecuador	RPI	River Plate Area
AmS	South America	Chi	Chile	Esp	Spain	Ur	Uruguay
Andes	Andean Region	CS	Southern Cone	Méx	Mexico	Ven	Venezuela

transitar [A1] *vi* «*vehículo*» to travel; «*peatón*» to walk

transitivo -va *adj* transitive

tránsito *m* [1] (tráfico) traffic; ~ **rodado** vehicular traffic; **una calle de mucho** ~ a very busy road; **un accidente de** ~ (AmL) a road accident; **infracción de** ~ (AmL) traffic violation (AmE), motoring offense (BrE) [2] (paso) movement; **el** ~ **de turistas en los meses de verano** the movement of tourists during the summer months; **pasajeros en** ~ passengers in transit

transitorio -ria *adj* (a) ⟨*medida*⟩ provisional; ⟨*situación*⟩ temporary; ⟨*período*⟩ transitional (b) ⟨*efímero*⟩ transitory, fleeting

transmisión *f* (a) (acción) transmission (b) (Rad, TV) (señal) transmission; (programa) broadcast; **una** ~ **en directo/en diferido** a live/ prerecorded broadcast; ~ **de pensamiento** thought transference

transmisor *m* transmitter

transmitir [I1] *vt* [1] (Rad, TV) ⟨*señal*⟩ to transmit; ⟨*programa*⟩ to broadcast [2] (a) ⟨*sonido/movimiento*⟩ to transmit (b) ⟨*enfermedad/ lengua/costumbres*⟩ to transmit, pass on; ⟨*conocimientos*⟩ to pass on (c) ⟨*saludos/ felicidades*⟩ to pass on
■ ~ *vi* (Rad, TV) to transmit

transparentarse [A1] *v pron* (a) «*blusa/ falda*»: **una blusa que se transparenta** a see-through blouse; **con ese vestido se le transparenta la enagua** her petticoat shows through that dress (b) «*intenciones*» to be evident, be apparent

transparente *adj* (a) ⟨*cristal/agua*⟩ transparent, clear; ⟨*aire*⟩ clear (b) ⟨*tela/papel*⟩ transparent; ⟨*blusa*⟩ see-through (c) ⟨*persona/ carácter*⟩ transparent; ⟨*intenciones*⟩ clear, plain

transpirar [A1] *vi* (Fisiol) to perspire, sweat; (Bot) to transpire

transportador *m* (Mec) conveyor

transportar [A1] *vt* (a) ⟨*personas/mercancías*⟩ to transport; ~ **algo por aire** to ship sth by air (b) ⟨*energía/sonido*⟩ to transmit

transporte *m* [1] (de pasajeros, mercancías) transportation (esp AmE), transport (esp BrE); ~ **aéreo** airfreight; ~ **público** public transportation (AmE), public transport (BrE) [2] (medio, vehículo) means of transport [3] (gastos de viaje) traveling expenses

transportista *mf* haulage contractor

transversal *adj* ⟨*eje/línea*⟩ transverse; **una calle** ~ **al Paseo de Recoletos** a street which crosses the Paseo de Recoletos; **un corte** ~ a cross section
■ *f* (Mat) transversal

tranvía *m* (a) (vehículo urbano) streetcar (AmE), tram (BrE) (b) (Esp) (Ferr) local train

tranza *adj* (Méx fam) crooked
■ *mf* (Méx fam) (persona) con artist (colloq), shark (colloq)
■ *f* (Méx fam) (engaño, fraude) scam (colloq)

tranzar [A4] *vt* (Méx fam) ⟨*persona*⟩ to con (colloq)

trapear [A1] *vt* (AmL) to mop

trapecio *m* (a) (Mat) trapezoid (AmE), trapezium (BrE) (b) (Espec) trapeze

trapecista *mf* trapeze artist

trapero -ra *m,f* [1] (ropavejero) junkman (AmE), rag and bone man (BrE) [2] **trapero** *m* (AmL) (para el suelo) floorcloth

trapo *m* (para limpiar) cloth; **pásale un** ~ **a la mesa** wipe the table; ~ **de cocina** dishtowel (AmE), tea towel (BrE); ~ **de sacudir** dust cloth (AmE), duster (BrE)

tráquea *f* windpipe, trachea

traquetear [A1] *vi* «*tren/carreta*» (hacer ruido) to clatter; (moverse) to jolt

traqueteo *m* (de tren, carreta — movimiento) jolting; (— ruido) clatter, clattering

tras *prep* [1] (a) (frml) (después de) after; ~ **interrogarlo lo pusieron en libertad** after questioning him they released him (b) (indicando repetición) after; **día** ~ **día** day after day [2] (a) (detrás de) behind; **la puerta se cerró** ~ **él** the door closed behind him; **la policía anda** ~ **él** the police are after him (b) (más allá de) beyond

trascendental *adj* (a) (importante) ⟨*noticia/ ocasión*⟩ momentous; (de gran alcance) ⟨*decisión/ cambio/efecto*⟩ far-reaching (b) (Fil) transcendental

trascendente *adj* (a) (importante) ⟨*hecho/ suceso*⟩ significant, important (b) (Fil) transcendent

trascender [E8] *vi* (ir más allá) ~ **DE algo** to transcend sth (frml), to go beyond sth
■ ~ *vt* to go beyond, transcend (frml)

trasero¹ -ra *adj* ⟨*puerta/habitación/asiento*⟩ back (*before n*); ⟨*rueda/pata/asiento*⟩ rear (*before n*), back (*before n*); ⟨*motor*⟩ rear-mounted

trasero² *m* (fam) (de persona) bottom, backside (colloq); (de animal) hindquarters (*pl*)

trasladar [A1] *vt* [1] (cambiar de sitio) ⟨*objeto/ oficina/tienda*⟩ to move; ⟨*preso/enfermo*⟩ to move, transfer; ⟨*información*⟩ to transfer; **los heridos fueron trasladados al hospital** the injured were taken to hospital [2] (cambiar de destino) ⟨*empleado/ funcionario*⟩ to transfer
■ **trasladarse** *v pron* (mudarse) to move

traslado *m* (de prisioneros) transferal; (de oficina) removal; (de empleados) transfer; (de objeto): **el** ~ **del cuadro se llevó a cabo ayer** the picture was moved yesterday; **gastos de** ~ relocation expenses

traslúcido -da *adj* translucent

trasluz *m*: **al** ~ against the light

trasmano: **a trasmano** (*loc adv*) out of the way; **vive muy a** ~ she lives in a very out-of-the-way place

trasnochar [A1] *vi* (no acostarse) to be up all night; (acostarse de madrugada) to stay up late
■ **trasnocharse** *v pron* (Col, Per, Ven) ▶ TRASNOCHAR

traspasar [A1] *vt* [1] (a) «*bala/espada*» to pierce, go through; «*líquido*» to go through, soak through (b) (sobrepasar) to go beyond [2] ⟨*bar/farmacia*⟩ (vender) to sell; (arrendar) to let, lease [3] ⟨*poderes/fondos/negocio*⟩ to transfer [4] (Dep) ⟨*jugador*⟩ to transfer, trade (AmE)

traspaso *m* [1] (a) (de bar, farmacia — venta) sale; (— arrendamiento) leasing, letting (b) (suma) premium [2] (de poderes, fondos, negocio) transfer [3] (Dep) (a) (de jugador) transfer, trade (AmE) (b) (suma) transfer fee

traspié *m* (tropezón) stumble; **dar un ~** to stumble

trasplantar [A1] *vt* (Bot, Med) to transplant

trasplante *m* (Bot, Med) transplant

trasquilar [A1] *vt* **(a)** ‹ovejas› to shear, clip **(b)** (fam) ‹pelo› to hack … about (colloq); ‹persona› to scalp (colloq)

trastada *f* **(a)** (fam) (mala pasada) dirty trick; **hacerle una ~ a algn** to play a dirty trick on sb **(b)** (travesura) prank

traste *m* **1** (Mús) fret **2** (fam) (trasero) backside (colloq) **3** (AmC, Méx) ‹utensilio› utensil; **lavar los ~s** to do the dishes *o* (BrE) the washing-up

trastero *m* junk room, lumber room (AmE)

trastienda *f* back room (*of a shop*)

trasto *m* (fam) (cosa inservible) piece of junk (colloq); **el cuarto de los ~s** the junk room

trastornado -da *adj* ‹persona/mente› disturbed; **su muerte lo dejó ~** he was deeply disturbed *o* traumatized by his death

trastornar [A1] *vt* **1** (Psic) to disturb; **la muerte de su hijo la trastornó** her son's death left her deeply disturbed; **esa chica lo ha trastornado** (fam) he's lost his head over that girl (colloq) **2** (alterar la normalidad) to upset, disrupt

■ **trastornarse** *v pron* (Psic) to become disturbed

trastorno *m* **1** (Med, Psic) disorder **2** (alteración de la normalidad) disruption; **los ~s provocados por la huelga** the disruption caused by the strike; **me ocasionó muchos ~s** it caused me a great deal of inconvenience

trastrocar [A9] *vt* to alter, change; **~ algo EN algo** to transform *o* change sth INTO sth

trasvasar [A1] *vt* **(a)** ‹vino/aceite› to decant **(b)** (Inf) to download

tratado *m* **1** (Der, Pol) treaty; **~ de paz** peace treaty **2** (libro) treatise

tratamiento *m* **1** **(a)** (en general) treatment; **estoy en ~ médico** I am undergoing medical treatment; **no me quejo del ~ que recibí** I can't complain about the treatment I received **(b)** (Inf) (de información, datos) processing; **~ de textos** word processing **2** (título de cortesía) form of address

tratar [A1] *vi* **1** (intentar) to try; **traten de llegar temprano** try to arrive early; **~é de que no vuelva a suceder** I'll try to make sure it doesn't happen again **2** «obra/libro/película» **~ DE algo** to be ABOUT sth; **~ SOBRE algo** to deal WITH sth; **la conferencia ~á sobre medicina alternativa** the lecture will deal with alternative medicine **3** (tener contacto, relaciones) **~ CON algn** to deal WITH sb; **en mi trabajo trato con gente de todo tipo** in my job I deal with all kinds of people

■ **~** *vt* **1** ‹persona/animal/instrumento› to treat; **me tratan muy bien** they treat me very well **2** (frecuentar) **lo trataba cuando era joven** I saw quite a lot of him when I was young **3** ‹tema/asunto› to discuss, to deal with **4** **(a)** (Med) to treat **(b)** ‹sustancia/metal› to treat

■ **tratarse** *v pron* **1** **~se CON algn** (ser amigo de) to be friendly with sb; (alternar) to socialize *o* mix WITH sb; **no nos tratamos mucho** (recíp) we don't have much to do with each other

2 (+ compl) (recípr): **se tratan sin ningún respeto** they show no respect for each other **3** (Med) to have *o* undergo treatment **4 tratarse de** (en 3ª pers) **(a)** (ser acerca de) to be about; **¿de qué se trata?** what's it about? **(b)** (ser cuestión de) to be a question of; **se trata de participar, no de ganar** it's a question of taking part, not of winning; **solo porque se trata de ti** just because it's you

trato *m* **1** **(a)** (acuerdo) deal; **cerrar un ~** to finalize a deal; **¡~ hecho!** it's a deal! **(b) tratos** *mpl* (negociaciones): **estamos en ~s con otra compañía** we are talking to *o* negotiating with another company **2** **(a)** (relación): **no tiene ~ con los vecinos** he doesn't have much to do with his neighbors; **tengo poco ~ con ella** I don't really have much contact with her *o* much to do with her **(b)** (manera de tratar) treatment; **le dan un ~ preferente** they give him preferential treatment

trauma *m* trauma

traumatizado -da *adj* traumatized

traumatizar [A4] *vt* to traumatize

■ **traumatizarse** *v pron* (fam) to be traumatized

través **(a) a través de** (loc prep) (de lado a lado) across; (por medio de) through; **pusieron barricadas a ~ de la calle** they erected barricades across the street; **se enteró a ~ de un amigo** he heard about it through a friend **(b) al** *or* (Méx) **de través** (loc adv) diagonally

travesaño *m* **(a)** (Const) crossbeam **(b)** (Dep) crossbar

travesía *f* **1** (viaje) crossing **2** (Esp) (callejuela) alleyway, side street

travesti, travestí *m* transvestite

travesura *f* prank; **hacer ~s** to play pranks

travieso -sa *adj* naughty, mischievous

trayecto *m* **(a)** (viaje) journey; **charlamos todo el ~** we chatted the whole journey **(b)** (ruta) route; **¿qué ~ hace este autobús?** which route does this bus take? **(c)** (trayectoria) trajectory, path

trayectoria *f* **(a)** (de proyectil, pelota) trajectory, path **(b)** (de persona, institución): **una brillante ~ profesional** a brilliant career; **una larga ~ democrática** a long democratic tradition

trayendo ▸ TRAER

trazar [A4] *vt* **1** **(a)** ‹línea› to trace, draw; ‹plano› to draw; **~on la ruta a seguir** they traced out the route to be followed; **~ el contorno de algo** to outline sth **(b)** (Arquit) ‹puente/edificio› to design **2** ‹plan/proyecto/estrategia› to draw up, devise

trazo *m* stroke

trébol *m* **1** (Bot) clover **2** (Jueg) **(a)** (carta) club **(b) tréboles** *mpl* (palo) clubs (*pl*)

trece *adj inv/m/pron* thirteen; *para ejemplos ver* CINCO; **mantenerse** *or* **seguir en sus ~** to stand one's ground

trecho *m* **(a)** (tramo) stretch **(b)** (distancia) distance; **aún nos queda un buen ~** we still have a good distance *o* a fair way to go

tregua *f* **(a)** (Mil) truce; **acordar una ~** to agree to a truce **(b)** (interrupción): **sin ~** relentlessly

treinta *adj inv/m/pron* thirty; *para ejemplos ver* CINCO, CINCUENTA

tremendo -da *adj* **1** **(a)** (muy grande, extraordinario) ‹diferencia/cambio› tremendous, enormous; ⟨velocidad/éxito⟩ tremendous; ⟨chichón⟩ huge; **hace un frío ∼** it's incredibly cold! (colloq); **me dio (una) tremenda patada** he kicked me really hard **(b)** ⟨terrible⟩ ⟨ruido/dolor/situación⟩ terrible; **la película tiene unas escenas tremendas** (AmL) the film has some horrific scenes **2** (fam) ⟨persona⟩ terrible

trémulo -la adj (liter) ⟨manos⟩ trembling; ⟨voz⟩ tremulous; ⟨llama/luz⟩ flickering; **trémula de gozo** (liter) trembling with pleasure

tren m **1** (Ferr) train; **tomar** or (esp Esp) **coger el ∼** to take o catch the train; **ir en ∼** to go by train; **cambiar de ∼** to change trains; **∼ correo** or **postal** mail train; **∼ de alta velocidad** high-speed train; **∼ de cercanías** local o suburban train; **∼ directo** through train; **∼ expreso** or **rápido** express train **2** (fam) ⟨ritmo⟩ rate; **a este ∼** at this rate (colloq); **∼ de vida** lifestyle

trenazo m (Méx) train crash

trenca f (Esp) duffle o duffel coat

trenza f ⟨de cintas, fibras⟩ plait; ⟨de pelo⟩ braid (AmE), plait (BrE)

trepador -dora m,f **1** (Col, CS, Ven) social climber **2 trepadora** f (Bot) climber

trepar [A1] vi to climb; **∼ a un árbol** to climb (up) a tree

tres adj inv/m/pron three; **∼ en raya** tic-tac-toe (AmE), noughts and crosses (BrE); para ejemplos ver CINCO

trescientos -tas adj/pron three hundred; para ejemplos ver QUINIENTOS

tresillo m (Esp) ⟨sofá⟩ three-seater sofa; ⟨juego de muebles⟩ suite

treta f **(a)** ⟨ardid⟩ trick, ruse **(b)** ⟨en esgrima⟩ feint

trial m motocross

triangular adj triangular

triángulo m **1** (Mat) triangle; **∼ rectángulo** right-angled triangle **2 (a)** ⟨en relaciones amorosas⟩ (love) triangle **(b)** (Mús) triangle **(c)** (Auto) tb **∼ reflectante** advance-warning triangle

tribu f tribe

tribuna f **(a)** ⟨para orador⟩ platform, rostrum **(b)** ⟨para autoridades⟩ platform; ⟨para espectadores⟩ grandstand, stand; **la ∼ de la prensa** the press box **(c)** ⟨de iglesia⟩ gallery

tribunal m **1** (Der) **(a)** ⟨lugar⟩ court; ⟨jueces⟩ judges (pl); **∼ militar** court martial, military court; **∼ supremo** ≈ supreme court (in US), ≈ high court (in UK); **∼ (tutelar) de menores** juvenile court **(b) tribunales** mpl ⟨justicia⟩: **acudir a los ∼es** to go to court **2** ⟨en examen⟩ examining board; ⟨en concurso⟩ panel of judges

tributar [A1] vt **(a)** (Fisco) to pay **(b)** ⟨rendir, ofrecer⟩: **∼ un homenaje a algn** to pay tribute to sb

tributo m **(a)** (Fisco) tax **(b)** ⟨ofrenda, homenaje⟩ tribute; **rendirle ∼ a algn/algo** to pay tribute to sb/sth

triciclo m tricycle

tricotar [A1] vt (Esp) to knit

tridimensional adj three-dimensional

trifulca f (fam) rumpus, commotion

trigal m wheat field

trigo m wheat

trigueño -ña adj ⟨pelo⟩ light brown; ⟨persona⟩ dark; **una niña de tez trigueña** an olive-skinned girl

trillar [A1] vt to thresh

trillizo -za m,f triplet

trilogía f trilogy

trimestral adj ⟨publicación/pago⟩ quarterly; **examen ∼** end-of-semester examination (AmE), end-of-term examination (BrE)

trimestre m **(a)** quarter, three-month period; **pago por ∼s** I pay quarterly **(b)** (Educ) term, ≈ semester (in US)

trinar [A1] vi ⟨pájaro⟩ to sing

trinchar [A1] vt to carve

trinchera f **(a)** (Mil) trench **(b)** (Indum) trench coat

trineo m **(a)** (Dep, Jueg) sled (AmE), sledge (BrE) **(b)** ⟨tirado por perros, caballos⟩ sleigh

trinidad f trinity; **La (Santísima) T∼** (Relig) the Trinity

trino m trill

trío m trio

tripa f **1 (a)** tb **tripas** fpl ⟨intestino⟩ intestine, gut; ⟨vísceras⟩ (fam) innards (pl) (colloq); **se me revuelven las ∼s de solo verlo** just looking at it turns my stomach **(b)** ⟨material⟩ gut **2** (Esp fam) ⟨barriga⟩ belly (colloq)

triple adj triple
■ m **1** (Mat): **el precio aumentó al ∼** the price tripled o trebled; **tardó el ∼** it took three times as long; **el ∼ de tres es nueve** three times three equals nine **2** (Elec) three-way adapter o adaptor

triplicado: **por triplicado** (loc adv) in triplicate

triplicar [A2] vt ⟨capacidad/precio/ventas⟩ to treble; ⟨longitud/cifra⟩ to triple
■ **triplicarse** v pron to treble, triple

trípode m tripod

tripulación f crew

tripulante mf crew member; **los ∼s** the crew

tripular [A1] vt to crew, man

triquiñuela f (fam) trick, dodge (colloq)

trisílabo -ba adj trisyllabic

triste adj **1 (a)** [ESTAR] ⟨persona⟩ sad; **esa música me pone ∼** that music makes me sad **(b)** ⟨expresión/mirada⟩ sad, sorrowful **(c)** [SER] ⟨que causa tristeza⟩ ⟨historia/película/noticia⟩ sad; ⟨paisaje/color⟩ dismal, gloomy; ⟨lugar/ambiente⟩ gloomy **2** ⟨delante del n⟩ ⟨miserable, insignificante⟩ miserable; **por cuatro ∼s pesos** for a few miserable pesos; **es la ∼ realidad** it's the sad truth

tristeza f ⟨de mirada, persona⟩ sadness, sorrow; ⟨de lugar, ambiente⟩ gloominess

triturador m: **∼ de basura** garbage disposal unit (AmE), waste disposal unit (BrE); **∼ de ajos** garlic press

trituradora f crushing machine, crusher

triturar [A1] vt ⟨almendras/ajo⟩ to crush; ⟨minerales⟩ to grind, crush

triunfador -dora adj ⟨ejército⟩ triumphant; ⟨equipo⟩ winning (before n), triumphant
■ m,f winner

triunfal adj ⟨marcha/arco⟩ triumphal; ⟨gesto/sonrisa/entrada⟩ triumphant

t

triunfalismo *m* triumphalism

triunfar [A1] *vi* (a) (ganar) ~ **sobre** algo/algn to triumph over sth/sb; **triunfó en el concurso** she won the competition (b) (tener éxito) to succeed, be successful (c) «*justicia/verdad/razón*» (prevalecer) to prevail, win out (AmE) *o* (BrE) through

triunfo *m* ⊡ (a) (victoria) victory; **el ~ del equipo irlandés** the Irish team's victory (b) (logro) triumph; **uno de los ~s de la ciencia** one of the triumphs of science (c) (éxito) success ⊡ (en naipes) trump; **palo del ~** trumps (*pl*)

trivial *adj* trivial

trivialidad *f* (a) (cualidad) triviality (b) (dicho) trivial *o* trite remark; (cosa) triviality

trivializar [A4] *vt* (asunto) to trivialize; (éxito) to play down

trizarse [A4] *v pron* (Chi) (rajarse) «*anteojos/vaso*» to crack; «*diente*» to chip

trizas *fpl*: **hacer ~ algo** (tela/carta) to tear sth to shreds; **el jarrón se cayó y se hizo ~** the vase fell and smashed (to bits *o* smithereens); **tengo los nervios hechos ~** my nerves are in shreds *o* tatters

trofeo *m* (premio) trophy

troglodita *mf* (a) (cavernícola) troglodyte (b) (fam) (bruto) lout

trolebús *m* trolleybus

tromba *f* (terrestre) whirlwind, tornado; (marina) waterspout; ~ **de agua** downpour

trombón *m* ⊡ (instrumento) trombone ⊡ **trombón** *mf* (músico) trombonist

trombonista *mf* trombonist

trombosis *f* thrombosis

trompa *f* ⊡ (de elefante) trunk; (de insecto) proboscis ⊡ (boca) (AmL fam) lips (*pl*), mouth ⊡ (instrumento) horn ⊡ (Esp fam) (borrachera): **coger una ~** to get plastered (colloq) ⊡ **trompa** *mf* (músico) horn-player

trompada *f* (AmS fam) (puñetazo) punch; **darle** *or* **pegarle una ~ a algn** to punch sb

trompazo *m* (fam): **me di un ~ con la puerta** I walked (*o* ran *etc*) smack into the door (colloq)

trompear [A1] *vt* (AmL fam) to thump (colloq), to punch

trompeta *f* ⊡ (instrumento) trumpet ⊡ **trompeta** *mf* (persona) trumpet player; (Mil) trumpeter

trompetista *mf* trumpet player

trompicón *m*: **iba dando trompicones** he was staggering; **a trompicones** in fits and starts

trompo *m* (a) (Jueg) (spinning) top (b) (Auto) spin

trona *f* (Esp) high chair

tronar [A10] *v impers* to thunder
■ ~ *vi* ⊡ «*cañones/voz*» to thunder ⊡ (Méx fam) (a) (en relación) to split up (colloq) (b) (fracasar) to flop (colloq); (en examen) to fail
■ ~ *vt* ⊡ (AmC, Méx fam) (fusilar) to shoot ⊡ (Méx fam) (examen/alumno) to fail, flunk (AmE colloq)

tronchar [A1] *vt* (tallo/rama) to snap
■ **troncharse** *v pron* «*tallo/rama*» to break *o* snap off; ~**se de (la) risa** (Esp fam) to die laughing (colloq)

tronco *m* ⊡ (Bot) trunk; (leño) log ⊡ (en genealogía) stock ⊡ (Anat) trunk, torso

tronera *f* (en billar) pocket

trono *m* throne; **subir al ~** to come to the throne

tropa *f* (a) (soldados rasos): **la ~** the troops (*pl*) (b) **tropas** *fpl* (ejército, soldados) troops

tropel *m* (de personas) mob; **entraron al estadio en ~** they poured into the stadium

tropezar [A6] *vi* (al caminar, correr) to stumble, trip; ~ **con algo** (con piedra/escalón) to trip over sth; (con árbol/muro) to walk (*o* run *etc*) into sth (b) (encontrarse) ~ **con algo** (con dificultad/problema) to come up against sth; ~ **con algn** to run *o* bump into sb (colloq)
■ **tropezarse** *v pron* (encontrarse) ~**se con algn** to run *o* bump into sb

tropezón *m* (a) (acción de tropezar) stumble; **dio un ~ y cayó** he stumbled and fell; **a tropezones** (fam) in fits and starts (b) (equivocación) mistake, slip

tropical *adj* tropical

trópico *m* tropic

tropiece, tropieces, etc ▶ TROPEZAR

tropieza, tropiezas, etc ▶ TROPEZAR

tropiezo *m* (contratiempo) setback, hitch; (equivocación) mistake, slip

trotar [A1] *vi* (a) (caballo/jinete) to trot (b) (fam) (ir de un lado a otro) to rush around (c) (CS, Méx) (como ejercicio) to jog

trote *m* ⊡ (Equ) trot; **al ~** at a trot ⊡ (fam) (ajetreo): **¡qué ~ he tenido hoy!** it's been so hectic today (colloq); **ya no estoy para esos ~s** I'm not up to that sort of thing any more

trovador *m* troubadour, minstrel

trozar [A4] *vt* (AmL) to cut ... into pieces, cut up

trozo *m* (a) (de pan, pastel) piece, bit, slice; (de madera, papel, tela) piece, bit; (de vidrio, cerámica) piece, fragment; **cortar la zanahoria en trocitos** dice the carrot (b) (Lit, Mús) passage

trucar [A2] *vt* (a) (dados/juego/elecciones) to fix, rig (b) (fotografía) to touch up

trucha *f* (Coc, Zool) trout

truco *m* trick; **el ~ está en...** the trick *o* secret is...; **pillarle el ~ a algo** to get the hang of sth

trueno *m* (a) (Meteo) thunderclap, clap of thunder; ~**s** thunder (b) (de cañones) thunder

trueque *m* (cambio) barter

trufa *f* truffle

truncar [A2] *vt* (a) (frase/discurso/texto) to cut short (b) (vida) to cut short; (planes) to frustrate, thwart; (ilusiones) to shatter

tu *adj* (delante del *n*) your; ~**s amigos** your friends

tú *pron pers* [*familiar form of address*] ⊡ (como sujeto, en comparaciones, con preposición) you; **¿quién**

lo va a hacer? — tú who's going to do it? — you are; **llegó después que** ~ he arrived after you (did); **entre** ~ **y yo** between you and me; **tratar de** ~ **a algn** to address sb using the familiar **TÚ** form ⟨2⟩ (uno) you; **te dan varias opciones y** ~ **eliges una** you're given several options and you choose one

tuba f tuba

tubérculo m (Bot) tuber

tuberculosis f tuberculosis

tuberculoso -sa m,f tuberculosis sufferer (o patient etc)

tubería f ⟨cañería⟩ pipe; ⟨conjunto de tubos⟩ piping, pipes (pl)

tubo m ⟨1⟩ **(a)** ⟨cilindro hueco⟩ tube; ~ **de escape** exhaust (pipe) **(b)** ⟨del órgano⟩ pipe **(c)** (Chi, Méx) ⟨para el pelo⟩ roller, curler ⟨2⟩ (RPI) ⟨del teléfono⟩ receiver

tuco m (Per, RPI) (Coc) tomato sauce

tuerca f nut

tuerce, tuerces, etc ▶ TORCER

tuerto -ta adj one-eyed; **es** ~ (sin un ojo) he only has one eye; (ciego de un ojo) he's blind in one eye

■ m,f: person blind in one eye or with only one eye

tuerza, tuerzas, etc ▶ TORCER

tuétano m marrow

tufo m (fam) ⟨olor — a sucio, podrido⟩ stink (colloq); ⟨— a cerrado⟩: **aquí dentro hay un** ~ **horrible** it smells really stuffy in here

tugurio m ⟨vivienda⟩ hovel; ⟨bar⟩ dive

tul m tulle

tulipa f lampshade

tulipán m tulip

tullido -da adj crippled

■ m,f cripple

tumba f ⟨excavada⟩ grave; ⟨construida⟩ tomb

tumbar [A1] vt **(a)** (hacer caer) to knock down; **lo tumbó en el primer asalto** he knocked him down in the first round; **un olor que te tumbaba** a smell that knocked you backward(s) **(b)** (AmL) ⟨árbol⟩ to fell, cut down; ⟨muro/casa⟩ to demolish, knock down

■ **tumbarse** v pron to lie down

tumbo m ⟨1⟩ (vaivén): **salió del bar dando** ~**s** he staggered out of the bar; **la carreta iba dando** ~**s por el camino** the cart jolted along the path ⟨2⟩ (Bol) (fruta) passion fruit

tumbona f (Esp) sun lounger, deck chair

tumor m tumor*

tumulto m ⟨multitud⟩ crowd; ⟨alboroto⟩ commotion, tumult

tumultuoso -sa adj tumultuous

tuna f ⟨1⟩ (Bot, Coc) ⟨planta, fruto⟩ prickly pear ⟨2⟩ (Mús) tuna (musical group made up of university students)

tundra f tundra

túnel m tunnel; ~ **de lavado** car wash

túnica f (Hist) tunic; (Relig) robe

tuntún m (fam): **al** ~ ⟨elegir⟩ at random; **contestó al** ~ he just said the first thing that came into his head

tupé m ⟨1⟩ (fam) (descaro) nerve ⟨2⟩ (Esp) (peluquín) toupee; (mechón de pelo) forelock

tupido¹ -da adj ⟨follaje/vegetación⟩ dense; ⟨tela⟩ closely-woven; ⟨cejas⟩ bushy; ⟨niebla⟩ thick

tupido² adv (Méx) intensely

turbante m turban

turbar [A1] vt ⟨1⟩ (liter o period) ⟨orden/silencio⟩ to disturb ⟨2⟩ (liter o period) **(a)** (aturdir, confundir): **sus insistentes miradas la** ~**on** the way he kept looking at her embarrassed and confused her; **su presencia lo turbó** her presence made him uncomfortable

■ **turbarse** v pron (liter o period) **(a)** (aturdirse, confundirse): **la besó en la mejilla y se turbó** he kissed her on the cheek and she was covered with confusion (liter); **se turbó ante tantos elogios** such praise confused and embarrassed him

turbina f turbine

turbio -bia adj **(a)** ⟨agua⟩ cloudy; ⟨río⟩ muddy **(b)** ⟨visión/ojos⟩ blurred, misty **(c)** ⟨asunto/negocio⟩ shady, murky

turbo adj inv turbocharged

■ m (turbocompresor) turbocharger; (automóvil) turbo

turbulencia f turbulence

turbulento -ta adj turbulent

turco¹ -ca adj (Geog) Turkish

■ m,f **(a)** (Geog) ⟨persona⟩ Turk **(b)** (AmL) ⟨árabe⟩ term used (often pejoratively) to refer to someone of Middle Eastern origin

turco² m (idioma) Turkish

turismo m (Com, Ocio) tourism; **los ingresos del** ~ income from tourism o from the tourist industry; **dependen del** ~ **alemán** they rely on German tourists; **oficina de** ~ tourist office; **hacer** ~ to travel (around)

turista adj tourist (before n); **clase** ~ tourist o economy class

■ mf tourist

turistear [A1] vi (Andes, Méx) (en país) to tour around; (en ciudad) to do some sightseeing

turístico -ca adj ⟨información/folleto⟩ tourist (before n); ⟨viaje⟩ sightseeing (before n); ⟨empresa⟩ travel (before n); ⟨atracción/actividad/lugar⟩ tourist (before n)

turnarse [A1] v pron to take turns

turnio -nia adj (Chi fam) ⟨persona⟩ cross-eyed; ⟨ojos⟩ squint

turno m **(a)** (horario de trabajo): **hacer el** ~ **de noche** to work the night shift; **estar de** ~ to be on duty **(b)** (personas) shift **(c)** (en un orden): **cuando te toque el** ~ when your turn comes; **cuidémoslo por** ~**s** let's take turns looking after him; **pedir** ~ (Esp) to ask who is last in the line (AmE) o (BrE) queue

turquesa f (Min) turquoise

■ m/adj inv turquoise

Turquía f Turkey

turrón m: type of candy traditionally eaten at Christmas

tute m: card game in which the object is to win all the kings or queens

tutear [A1] vt: to address sb using the familiar **TÚ** form

■ **tutearse** v pron: to address each other using the familiar **TÚ** form

tutela f **(a)** (Der) guardianship, tutelage **(b)** (protección) protection

tuteo m: use of the familiar **TÚ** form

tutor -tora *m,f* **1** (Educ) (encargado de curso) course tutor, class teacher; (en la universidad) tutor **2** (Der) guardian

tutoría *f* **1** (Educ) tutorship **2** (Der) guardianship, tutelage

tutú *m* (Indum) tutu

tuve, tuviera, etc ▶ TENER

tuyo -ya *adj* yours; **esto es** ∼ this is yours; **¿es amigo** ∼? is he a friend of yours?; **fue idea tuya** it was your idea
■ *pron*: **el** ∼, **la tuya etc** yours; **la música no es lo** ∼ music isn't your strong point *o* your forte; **los** ∼**s** (tu familia) your family and friends

twist /twis(t)/ *m* twist

U u

U, u *f* (*pl* **úes**) (*read as* /u/) *the letter* U, u

u *conj* [*used instead of* o *before* o- *or* ho-] or; **siete u ocho** seven or eight

ubicación *f* **(a)** (esp AmL) (situación, posición) location **(b)** (AmL) (localización): **se hizo difícil la** ∼ **del avión** locating the airplane was very difficult

ubicar [A2] *vt* (AmL) **(a)** (colocar, situar): **me** ∼**on a su lado** they placed me next to him; ∼**on las sillas para la reunión** they arranged the chairs for the meeting **(b)** (localizar) ⟨persona/lugar⟩ to find, locate **(c)** (identificar): **la ubico solo de nombre** I only know her by name; **lo ubiqué por el color** I recognized it by the color; **me suena el nombre, pero no lo ubico** the name rings a bell, but I can't quite place him
■ **ubicarse** *v pron* **1** (AmL) **(a)** (colocarse, situarse): **se ubicó en la primera fila** he sat in the front row **(b)** (en empleo) to get oneself a good job **(c)** (orientarse) to find one's way around; **¿te ubicas?** have you got your bearings?
2 (esp AmL) (estar situado) to be, be situated *o* located

ud. = **usted**

uds. = **ustedes**

UE *f* (= **Unión Europea**) EU

uf *interj* (expresando — cansancio, sofocación) whew! (colloq); (— repugnancia) yuck (colloq)

ufano -na *adj* **(a)** (satisfecho, orgulloso) proud **(b)** (engreído) self-satisfied, smug

ujier *m* uniformed doorman; (en tribunales) usher

úlcera *f* ulcer

ulpo *m* (Chi) *cold drink made with roasted flour and sugar*

ultimar [A1] *vt* **1** ⟨preparativos⟩ to complete; ⟨detalles⟩ to finalize **2** (AmL frml) (matar) to kill, murder

ultimátum *m* (*pl* ∼ *or* **-tums**) ultimatum

último -ma *adj* (*delante del n*) **1** (en el tiempo) last; **a última hora** at the last minute *o* moment; **su** ∼ **libro** his latest book; **en los** ∼**s tiempos** recently; **¿cuándo fue la última vez que lo usaste?** when did you last use it?
2 (a) (en una serie) last; **estar en** ∼ **lugar** to be last; **por última vez** for the last time; **como** ∼ **recurso** as a last resort; **última voluntad** last wishes (*pl*) **(b)** (*como adv*) (CS) ⟨salir/terminar⟩ last
3 (en el espacio): **el** ∼ **piso** the top floor; **la última fila** the back row
4 (definitivo): **es mi última oferta** it's my final offer

■ *m,f* last one; **era el** ∼ **que me quedaba** it was my last one; **es el** ∼ **de la clase** he's bottom of the class; **a** ∼**s de** (Esp) toward(s) the end of; **por** ∼ finally, lastly

ultra *mf* (Esp) right-wing extremist

ultraderecha *f*: **la** ∼ **the far** *o* **extreme right**

ultraderechista *adj* extreme right-wing
■ *mf* right-wing extremist

ultrafino -na *adj* ultrafine, superfine

ultrajar [A1] *vt* (frml) ⟨persona⟩ to outrage, offend ... deeply; ⟨bandera⟩ to insult; ⟨honor⟩ to offend against

ultraje *m* outrage, insult

ultramarinos *mpl* (comestibles) groceries; **tienda de** ∼ grocery store (AmE), grocer's shop (BrE)

ultrasónico -ca *adj* ultrasonic

ultravioleta *adj* (*pl* ∼ *or* **-tas**) ultraviolet

umbilical *adj* umbilical

umbral *m* **(a)** (de puerta) threshold **(b)** (borde, frontera) *tb* ∼**es** threshold; **en los** ∼**es de la muerte** at death's door; **en los** ∼**es de la civilización** at the dawn of civilization

un (*pl* **unos**), **una** (*pl* **unas**) *art* [*the masculine article* UN *is also used before feminine nouns which begin with stressed* A *or* HA *e.g.* UN ARMA PODEROSA, UN HAMBRE FEROZ] **1** (*sing*) a; (*delante de sonido vocálico*) an; (*pl*) some; **una nueva droga** a new drug; **un asunto importante** an important matter; **hay unas cartas para ti** there are some letters for you; **tiene unos ojos preciosos** he has lovely eyes
2 (con valor ponderativo): **tú haces unas preguntas** ... you go ask some questions!
3 (con nombres propios) a; **es un Miró** it's a Miró
4 (*pl*) (expresando aproximación) about; **tiene unos 30 años** she's about 30

una *pron* (*ver tb* UN, UNO): **a la** ∼, **a las dos, ¡a las tres!** ready, steady, go!

unánime *adj* unanimous

unanimidad *f* unanimity; **por** ∼ unanimously

undécimo -ma *adj/pron* eleventh; *para ejemplos ver* QUINTO

UNED /u'neð/ *f* (en Esp) = **Universidad Nacional de Educación a Distancia**

UNESCO /u'nesko/ *f*: **la** ∼ UNESCO

ungüento *m* ointment

únicamente *adv* only

UNICEF /uni'sef, uni'θef/ *f*: **la** ∼ UNICEF

único -ca *adj* ☐**1** (a) (solo) only; **soy hijo ~** I'm an only child; **¡es lo ~ que faltaba!** that's all we needed! (b) ‹*mercado/moneda*› single; **tarifa única** flat rate; **talla única** one size ☐**2** (extraordinario) extraordinary
■ *m,f*: **el ~/las únicas que tengo** the only one/ones I have

unicornio *m* unicorn

unidad *f* ☐**1** (Com, Mat) unit; **costo por ~** unit cost; **~ de peso** unit of weight; **~ de cuidados intensivos** *or* (Esp) **de vigilancia** *or* (Arg, Méx) **terapia intensiva** *or* (Chi) **de tratamiento intensivo** intensive care unit ☐**2** (unión, armonía) unity ☐**3** (Inf): **~ de disco** (Inf) disk drive

unido -da *adj* (a) ‹*familia/amigos*› close (b) (sobre un tema) united

unificación *f* unification

unificar [A2] *vt* ‹*país*› to unify; ‹*precios*› to standardize

uniforme *adj* ‹*velocidad/temperaturas*› constant, uniform; ‹*superficie*› even, uniform; ‹*terreno*› even, level; ‹*paisaje/estilo*› uniform; ‹*criterios/precios*› standard, uniform
■ *m* uniform

unilateral *adj* ‹*desarme/decisión*› unilateral; ‹*criterio/opinión*› one-sided

unión *f* ☐**1** (a) (acción): **la ~ de las dos empresas** the merger of the two companies; **la ~ de estos factores** the combination of these factors (b) (agrupación) association (c) **la U~ Americana** (Méx) (Period) the United States ☐**2** (relación) union, relationship; (matrimonio) union, marriage ☐**3** (juntura) joint

Unión Europea *f*: **la ~ ~** the European Union

Unión Soviética *f* (Hist): **la ~ ~** the Soviet Union

unir [I1] *vt* ☐**1** (a) ‹*cables*› to join; (con cola, pegamento) to stick … together; ‹*esfuerzos*› to combine (b) ‹*sentimientos/intereses*› to unite (c) ‹*características/cualidades/estilos*› to combine; **~ algo A algo** to combine sth WITH sth ☐**2** (comunicar) ‹*lugares*› to link ☐**3** (fusionar) ‹*empresas/organizaciones*› to merge
■ **unirse** *v pron* ☐**1** (aliarse) ‹‹*personas/colectividades*›› to join together; **se unió a nuestra causa** he joined our cause ☐**2** (juntarse) ‹‹*caminos*›› to converge, meet ☐**3** (fusionarse) ‹‹*empresas/organizaciones*›› to merge

universal *adj* universal

universalidad *f* universality

universidad *f* university; **~ a distancia** *or* (Méx) **abierta** open university; **~ laboral** ≈ technical college (*school with emphasis on vocational training*)

universitario -ria *adj* university (*before n*)
■ *m,f* (estudiante) undergraduate, (university) student; (licenciado) (university) graduate

universo *m* universe

uno¹, una *adj* [UNO *becomes* UN *before a masculine noun or noun phrase*] one; **no había ni un asiento libre** there wasn't one empty seat *o* a single empty seat; **treinta y un pasajeros** thirty-one passengers; **el capítulo uno** chapter one

■ *pron* ☐**1** (numeral) one; **uno a** *or* **por uno** one by one; **es la una** it's one o'clock; **más de uno/una** (fam) quite a few
☐**2** (personal) (*sing*) one; (*pl*) some; **uno es mío, el otro no** one's mine, the other isn't; **¿te gustaron? — unos sí, otros no** did you like them? — some I did, others I didn't; **se ayudan los unos a los otros** they help one another
☐**3** (fam) (alguien) (*m*) some guy (colloq); (*f*) some woman (colloq); **les pregunté a unos que estaban allí** I asked some people who were there
☐**4** (uso impersonal) you; **uno no sabe qué decir** you don't *o* (frml) one doesn't know what to say; **nunca le dicen nada a uno** they don't tell you anything

uno² *m* (number) one; *para ejemplos ver* CINCO

untar [A1] *vt* (a) (cubrir): **~ las galletas con miel** spread honey on the cookies; **se unta el molde con mantequilla** grease the cake tin (with butter) (b) (empapar) **~ algo EN algo** to dip sth IN sth
■ **untarse** *v pron* (a) (ensuciarse): **se untó las manos de pintura** he got paint all over his hands (b) (ponerse): **se untó los hombros con bronceador** she rubbed suntan lotion on her shoulders

uña *f* (a) (Anat) (de la mano) nail, fingernail; (del pie) nail, toenail; **arreglarse** *or* **hacerse las ~s** (*refl*) to do one's nails; (*caus*) to have one's nails done (b) (de oso, gato) claw; (de caballo, oveja) hoof

uralita® *f* asbestos

uranio *m* uranium

Urano *m* Uranus

urbanidad *f* courtesy, urbanity (frml)

urbanismo *m* city (AmE) *o* (BrE) town planning

urbanización *f* (acción) urbanization, development; (núcleo residencial) (Esp) (housing) development

urbanizado -da *adj* built-up; **esta zona está muy urbanizada** this area is heavily developed

urbanizar [A4] *vt* ‹*zona/terreno*› to develop, urbanize; **una zona sin ~** an undeveloped area

urbano -na *adj* ‹*núcleo/transporte*› urban, city (*before n*); ‹*población*› urban

urdir [I1] *vt* (a) (en telar) to warp; ‹*puntos*› to cast on (b) ‹*plan*› to devise, hatch

urgencia *f* (a) (cualidad) urgency; **con ~** urgently (b) (Med) emergency; **🅢 urgencias** accident and emergency; **lo operaron de ~** he had an emergency operation

urgente *adj* ‹*asunto*› pressing, urgent; ‹*mensaje*› urgent; ‹*caso/enfermo*› emergency (*before n*); ‹*carta*› express (*before n*)

urgido -da *adj* (AmL): **estaban ~s de dinero** they were in urgent need of money; **estamos ~s de tiempo** we are pressed for time

urgir [I7] *vi* (en *3ª pers*): **urge la finalización del proyecto** the project must be finished as soon as possible; **me urge llegar allí el martes** I absolutely must be there on/by Tuesday; **le urge el préstamo** he needs the loan urgently

urinario *m* urinal

urna *f* ☐**1** (vasija) urn; (de exposición) display case; (para votar) ballot box; **~ cineraria** funerary urn ☐**2** (Chi, Ven) (ataúd) coffin, wooden box (euph)

urólogo -ga *m,f* urologist

urraca *f* magpie

u

URSS /urs/ f (Hist) (= **Unión de Repúblicas Socialistas Soviéticas**) USSR

urubú m black vulture

Uruguay m (a) (país) tb el ~ Uruguay (b) (río): el (río) ~ the Uruguay River

uruguayismo m Uruguayan word (o phrase etc)

uruguayo -ya adj/m,f Uruguayan

USA /'usa/ (fam) USA

usado -da adj (a) (SER) (de segunda mano) secondhand (b) (ESTAR) (gastado, viejo) worn

usar [A1] vt (a) (utilizar) to use; ¿qué champú usas? what shampoo do you use?; ~ algo/a algn DE or COMO algo to use sth/sb AS sth (b) (llevar) ⟨alhajas/ropa/perfume⟩ to wear; **estos zapatos están sin ~** these shoes are unworn, these shoes have never been worn

■ **usarse** v pron (en 3ª pers) (esp AmL) (estar de moda) «color/ropa» to be in fashion, to be popular; **ya no se usa hacer fiestas de compromiso** people don't tend to have engagement parties any more

usina f (AmS) (fábrica) large factory; (industria) industry

uso m (a) (de producto, medicamento, máquina) use; **instrucciones para su ~** instructions for use; **hacer ~ de algo** to use sth (b) (de facultad, derecho): **en pleno ~ de sus facultades mentales** in full possession of his mental faculties; **hacer ~ de un derecho** to exercise a right; **desde que tengo ~ de razón** ever since I can remember; **hacer ~ de la palabra** (frml) to speak (c) (de prenda): **ropa de ~ diario** everyday clothes; **los zapatos ceden con el ~** shoes give with wear

usted pron pers [Polite form of address but also used in some areas, eg Colombia and Chile, instead of the familiar TÚ form] **1** (como sujeto, en comparaciones, con preposición) you; ¿**quién lo va a hacer? — usted** who's going to do it? — you (are); **tratar a algn de ~** to address sb using the USTED form; **muchas gracias — a ~** thank you very much — thank you; **son de ~** they're yours **2** (uso impersonal) you, one (frml); **le dicen eso y ~ no sabe qué contestar** when they say that you just don't know what to say in reply

ustedes pron pers pl [Polite plural form of address also used in Latin American countries as the familiar plural form] you; ¿**quién lo va a hacer? — ustedes** who's going to do it? — you (are); ~ **mismos lo dijeron** you said so yourselves; **son de ~** they're yours

usual adj usual, normal

usuario -ria m,f user

usurero -ra m,f usurer

usurpador -dora m,f usurper

usurpar [A1] vt (frml) ⟨propiedad/título⟩ to misappropriate; ⟨territorio⟩ to seize; ⟨poder⟩ to usurp

utensilio m (instrumento) utensil; (herramienta) tool; ~**s de cocina** kitchen o cooking utensils; ~**s de laboratorio** laboratory apparatus; ~**s de pesca** fishing tackle

útero m womb, uterus (tech)

útil adj useful

utilería f (esp AmL) (Cin, Teatr) props (pl)

utilero -ra m,f (esp AmL) (Cin, Teatr) props manager

útiles mpl (a) (herramientas, instrumentos) tools (pl), implements (pl); ~ **de pesca** fishing tackle; ~ **de jardinería** gardening tools (b) (AmL) (artículos escolares) tb ~ **escolares** pencils, pens, rulers, etc for school

utilidad f (a) (de aparato) usefulness; **un coche me sería de mucha ~** a car would be of great use to me (b) **utilidades** fpl (AmL) (ganancia, beneficio) profits (pl)

utilitario m small (economical) car

utilización f use, utilization (frml)

utilizar [A4] vt to use, utilize (frml)

utopía f Utopia

utópico -ca adj Utopian

uva f grape; ~ **blanca/negra** white/black grape

uve f (Esp) name of the letter v; ~ **doble** (Esp) name of the letter w

uy interj (expresando — asombro) ooh! (colloq); (— malestar, disgusto) oh!; (— emoción súbita) ah!, oh!; (— dolor) ow!, ouch!

Vv

V, v f (read as /be/, /be 'korta/, /be 'tʃika/, /be pe'keɲa/ or /'uβe/) the letter V, v

va, vas, etc ▶ IR

vaca f (a) (Zool) cow; **estar como una ~** (fam) to be very fat; **hacer una ~** (AmL fam) to make a collection (b) (Coc): (carne de) ~ beef; **filete de ~** fillet steak

vacacionar [A1] vi (Méx) to spend one's vacation(s) o holidays

vacaciones fpl vacation(s) (esp AmE), holiday(s) (esp BrE); ~ **de verano** summer vacation o holidays; **irse de ~** to go away on vacation o on holiday; **estamos de ~** we're on

---

AmC	Central America	Arg	Argentina	Cu	Cuba	Per	Peru
AmL	Latin America	Bol	Bolivia	Ec	Ecuador	RPI	River Plate Area
AmS	South America	Chi	Chile	Esp	Spain	Ur	Uruguay
Andes	Andean Region	CS	Southern Cone	Méx	Mexico	Ven	Venezuela

vacation *o* holiday; **tomarse unas** ∼ to take a vacation *o* holiday

vacacionista *mf* (Méx) vacationer (AmE), holidaymaker (BrE)

vacante *adj* ‹puesto/plaza› vacant; ‹piso/asiento› empty, unoccupied
■ *f* vacancy; **cubrir una** ∼ to fill a vacancy

vaciar [A17] *vt* **1** **(a)** ‹vaso/botella› to empty; ‹radiador› to drain; ‹bolsillo/cajón› to empty; ‹armario/habitación› to clean out **(b)** ‹contenido› to empty (out) **2** (ahuecar) to hollow out
■ **vaciarse** *v pron* to empty

vacilación *f* hesitation, vacillation (fml); **tras un momento de** ∼ after a moment's hesitation

vacilante *adj* **(a)** (oscilante) unsteady, shaky; **con paso** ∼ unsteadily **(b)** (dubitativo) ‹expresión› doubtful; ‹voz› hesitant **(c)** ‹luz› flickering

vacilar [A1] *vi* **1** **(a)** (dudar) to hesitate; **sin** ∼ without hesitating; **no vaciló en aceptar** he did not hesitate to accept, he accepted without hesitation **(b)** «fe/determinación» to waver **(c)** «luz» to flicker **2** (oscilar) «persona» to stagger, totter **3** (AmL exc CS fam) (divertirse) to have fun

vacile *m* (fam) (tomadura de pelo) joke; **basta de** ∼ that's enough kidding (colloq)

vacilón *m* (AmL fam) **(a)** (diversión): **le encanta el** ∼ he loves having a good time; **la fiesta fue un** ∼ the party was great fun **(b)** (tomadura de pelo) joke; **es puro** ∼ it's just a joke

vacío¹ -cía *adj* **(a)** ‹botella/caja› empty; ‹calle/ciudad› empty, deserted; ‹casa› empty, unoccupied; ‹palabras/retórica› empty; **con el estómago** ∼ on an empty stomach **(b)** (frívolo) ‹persona› shallow; ‹vida/frase› empty, meaningless

vacío² *m* **(a)** (Fís) vacuum; **envasado al** ∼ vacuum-packed **(b)** (espacio vacío) space; **mirar al** ∼ to gaze into space **(c)** (falta, hueco) gap; **dejó un** ∼ **en su vida** she left a gap *o* a void in his life; **una sensación de** ∼ a feeling of emptiness

vacuna *f* vaccine; **me tengo que poner la** ∼ I have to have my vaccination

vacunación *f* vaccination

vacunar [A1] *vt* to vaccinate; ∼ **a algn CONTRA algo** to vaccinate sb AGAINST sth
■ **vacunarse** *v pron* to get vaccinated; ∼**se CONTRA algo** to get vaccinated AGAINST sth

vacuno -na *adj* bovine; **ganado** ∼ cattle (*pl*)

vado *m* (de río) ford; **⊗ vado permanente** no parking

vagabundear [A1] *vi* to drift (around)

vagabundo -da *adj* ‹perro› stray; **niños** ∼**s** street urchins
■ *m,f* tramp, vagrant

vagar [A3] *vi* to wander, roam

vagina *f* vagina

vago -ga *adj* **1** (fam) ‹persona› lazy, idle **2** ‹recuerdo/idea› vague, hazy; ‹contorno/forma› vague, indistinct; ‹explicación/parecido› vague
■ *m,f* (fam) layabout, slacker (colloq); **deja ya de hacer el** ∼ stop lazing around (colloq)

vagón *m* (de pasajeros) coach, car (AmE), carriage (BrE); ∼ **restaurante** dining *o* (BrE) restaurant car

vagoneta *f* (Méx) (para pasajeros) van, minibus

vaguedad *f* **(a)** (de palabras, ideas) vagueness

(b) (expresión imprecisa) vague remark; **¡déjate de** ∼**es y ve al grano!** stop being so vague *o* stop beating about the bush and get to the point

vaho *m* **(a)** (aliento) breath **(b)** (vapor) steam, vapor* **(c)** (inhalación): **hacer** ∼**s** to inhale

vaina *f* **1** (de espada) scabbard; (de navaja) sheath **2** (Bot) (de habas, etc) pod **3** (Col, Per, Ven fam) **(a)** (problema, contrariedad): **¡qué** ∼**!** what a drag *o* pain (colloq); **la** ∼ **es que no sé cómo the thing *o* problem is that I don't know how; **estoy metida en una** ∼ I'm in a spot of trouble (colloq) **(b)** (cosa, asunto) thing, thingamajig (colloq) **(c)** (comportamiento sospechoso): **tenían una** ∼ they were up to something funny; **¿qué** ∼ **te traes tú?** what are you up to?

vainilla *f* (Bot, Coc) vanilla

vais ► IR

vaivén *m* (de columpio, péndulo) swinging; (de tren) rocking; (de barco) rolling; (de mecedora) rocking; (de gente) toing and froing

vajilla *f* (en general) dishes (*pl*); (juego) dinner service *o* set

valdré, valdría, etc ► VALER

vale *m* **(a)** (para adquirir algo) voucher; (por devolución) credit note *o* slip; ∼ **de descuento** a money-off coupon **(b)** (pagaré) IOU
■ *interj* ► VALER *vi* 4

valenciana *f* (Méx) cuff (AmE), turn-up (BrE)

valenciano¹ -na *adj/m,f* Valencian

valenciano² *m* (Ling) Valencian

valentía *f* bravery, courage; **con** ∼ courageously

valer [E28] *vt* **1** (tener un valor de) to be worth; (costar) to cost; **¿cuánto valen?** how much are they?, what do they cost?
2 (+ *me/te/le etc*) (ganar): **esta obra le valió un premio** this play earned *o* won her a prize
■ ∼ *vi* **1** (+ *compl*) (tener cierto valor) to be worth; (costar) to cost; **vale más, pero es mejor** it costs more but it's better; **cada cupón vale por un regalo** each voucher is worth a gift
2 (tener valor no material): **ha demostrado que vale** he has shown his worth; **como profesor no vale (nada)** as a teacher he's useless; **vales tanto como él** you're as good as he is; **hacerse** ∼ to assert oneself; **hacer** ∼ **algo** ‹derecho› to assert *o* enforce sth
3 (servir): **esta no vale, es muy ancha** this one's no good, it's too wide; **no le valió de nada protestar** protesting got him nowhere; **no** ∼ **PARA algo** to be useless *o* no good AT sth
4 **vale** (Esp fam) (expresando acuerdo) OK; **¿a las ocho? — ¡vale!** at eight o'clock? — sure *o* fine *o* OK?; **¿vale?** OK?, all right? **(b)** (basta): **¿**∼ **así?** is that OK *o* enough?
5 **más vale: más vale así** it's better that way; **más te vale ir** you'd better go
6 **(a)** (ser válido) «entrada/pasaporte» to be valid; «jugada/partido» to count **(b)** (estar permitido): **eso no vale, estás haciendo trampa** that's not fair, you're cheating; **no vale mirar** you're not allowed to look
7 (Méx fam) **(a)** (no importar): **a mí eso me vale** I don't give a damn about that (colloq) **(b)** (no tener valor) to be useless *o* no good (colloq) **(c)** (estropearse): **mi coche ya valió** my car's had it (colloq)

⋯✦

■ **valerse** v pron ⓵ (servirse) ~se DE algo/algn to use sth/sb
⓶ «anciano/enfermo»: ~se por sí mismo to look after oneself
⓷ (estar permitido, ser correcto): no se vale golpear por debajo del cinturón hitting below the belt is not allowed; ¡no se vale! that's not fair!

valeroso -sa adj brave, courageous, valiant (liter)

valga, valgas, etc ▶ VALER

validar [A1] vt to validate

validez f validity

válido -da adj valid

valiente adj «persona» brave, courageous

valija f (RPl) suitcase; ~ diplomática diplomatic bag

valioso -sa adj «joya/consejo/experiencia» valuable; un hombre ~ a man of great worth

valla f (a) (cerca) fence (b) (en atletismo) hurdle; (en fútbol) goal; ~ publicitaria billboard (AmE), hoarding (BrE)

valle m valley

valor m ⓵ (a) (Com, Fin) value; libros por ~ de $150 books to the value of $150; objetos de ~ valuables; ~ adquisitivo purchasing power (b) (importancia, mérito) value; ~ sentimental sentimental value (c) (validez) validity; sin la firma no tiene ningún ~ it's not valid without the signature ⓶ (a) (coraje, valentía) courage; me faltó ~ I didn't have the courage; armarse de ~ to pluck up courage (b) (fam) (descaro, desvergüenza) nerve (colloq); ¡encima tiene el ~ de protestar! and then she has the nerve to complain! ⓷ **valores** mpl (a) (principios morales) values (b) (Fin) securities, stocks, shares

valoración f (a) (de bienes, joyas) valuation; (de pérdidas, daños) assessment (b) (frml) (de suceso, trabajo) assessment, appraisal (frml)

valorar [A1] vt (a) «joya/cuadro» to value; «pérdida/daño» to assess; ~ algo EN algo to value/assess sth AT sth; eso no se puede ~ en dinero you cannot put a value on it (b) (frml) «trabajo/actuación» to assess (c) «amistad/lealtad» to value

valorización f (a) (tasación) ▶ VALORACIÓN A (b) (AmL) (aumento de valor) appreciation

vals m waltz; bailar un ~ to waltz

valuar vt [A18] (AmL) to value

válvula f valve

vamos ▶ IR

vampiresa f femme fatale, vamp (dated)

vampiro m (a) (en historias de horror) vampire; (explotador) vampire, bloodsucker (b) (Zool) vampire (bat)

van ▶ IR

vanagloriarse [A1] v pron ~ DE algo to boast o brag ABOUT sth

vandalismo m vandalism, hooliganism

vándalo -la m,f (gamberro) vandal, hooligan

vanguardia f (Mil) vanguard; (Art, Lit) avant-garde; teatro de ~ avant-garde theater; ir or estar a la ~ (de algo) to be in the vanguard (of sth)

vanguardista adj avant-garde

vanidad f vanity

vanidoso -sa adj (presumido) vain, conceited; (en cuanto al aspecto físico) vain
■ m,f: es un ~ he's so vain o conceited

vano -na adj (a) (ineficaz) «discusión/intento» vain, futile; «esfuerzo» futile; en ~ in vain (b) (falto de realidad) vain; ilusiones vanas wishful thinking (c) «palabra/promesa» empty

vapor m (a) (Fis, Quím) vapor*, steam (b) (Coc): al ~ steamed (c) (Náut) steamer, steamship

vaquero¹ -ra adj ⓵ (a) (Indum) «falda/cazadora» denim; un pantalón ~ a pair of jeans o denims (b) «estilo» cowboy (before n)
■ m,f (Agr) (m) cowboy, cowhand; (f) cowgirl, cowhand

vaquero² m (Indum) tb ~s: unos ~s a pair of jeans o denims

vaquilla f heifer

vara f ⓵ (palo) stick, pole ⓶ (Per fam) (influencia) connections (pl) (colloq)

varado -da adj ⓵ (a) (Náut) «barco» aground (b) (AmL) (detenido): miles de turistas se quedaron ~s thousands of tourists were left stranded; me quedé ~ con el trabajo I got stuck with my work ⓶ (a) (Col, Méx fam) (sin dinero) broke (colloq) (b) (Andes) (sin empleo) out of work

variable adj «carácter/humor» changeable; tiempo ~ unsettled o changeable weather

variación f variation

variado -da adj (a) «programa/vida/trabajo» varied (b) (diverso): ropa de colores ~s clothes in a variety of colors

variante f ⓵ (de palabra) variant ⓶ (carretera) turnoff

variar [A17] vi «precio/temperatura» to vary; las temperaturas varían entre 20°C y 25°C temperatures range o vary between 20°C and 25°C; para ~ (iró) (just) for a change (iro)
■ ~ vt ⓵ (hacer variado) «menú» to vary; «producción» to vary, diversify ⓶ (cambiar) «decoración/rumbo» to change, alter

varicela f chicken pox

várices, (Esp) varices fpl ▶ VARIZ

varicoso -sa adj varicose

variedad f (a) (en general) variety (b) **variedades** fpl (Espec) vaudeville (AmE), variety (BrE)

varilla f (en general) rod; (de abanico, paraguas) rib; (de jaula) bar; (de rueda de bicicleta) spoke; (para medir el aceite) dipstick

vario -ria adj ⓵ ~s/varias (más de dos) several; hace ~s años several years ago ⓶ (variado, diverso) various; asuntos ~s various matters

varios -rias pron several; lo compraron entre ~s several of them got together to buy it

varita f wand; ~ mágica magic wand

variz (pl **várices** or (Esp) **varices**) f varicose vein

varón adj «heredero/descendiente» male; un hijo ~ a son
■ m (niño) boy; (hombre) man, male

varonil adj (a) (viril) manly, masculine; voz ~ masculine voice (b) «mujer» (hombruna) mannish, masculine

vas ▶ IR

vasallo m vassal

vasco¹ -ca adj/m,f Basque

vasco² *m* (idioma) Basque

vasectomía *f* vasectomy

vaselina *f* Vaseline®, petroleum jelly

vasija *f* (Arqueol) vessel (frml)

vaso *m* [1] (recipiente, contenido) glass; **un ~ de vino** (con vino) a glass of wine; (para vino) a wine glass; **~ de papel** paper cup [2] (Anat) vessel; **~ sanguíneo** blood vessel

vasto -ta *adj* (*gen delante del n*) ⟨*mar/llanura*⟩ vast, immense; ⟨*conocimientos/experiencia*⟩ vast, enormous

váter *m* (Esp fam) (inodoro) toilet, lavatory; (cuarto) bathroom (esp AmE), toilet (BrE), loo (BrE colloq)

Vaticano *m*: **el ~** the Vatican

vatio *m* watt

vaya, vayas, etc ▶ IR

Vd. = **usted**

ve *f* (AmL) *tb* **~ corta** *or* **chica** *or* **pequeña** *name of the letter* v

ve ▶ IR, VER²

vea, veas, etc ▶ VER²

vecindad *f* [1] (lugar, barrio) neighborhood*, area; (vecinos) residents (*pl*) [2] (Méx) (edificio) tenement house

vecindario ▶ VECINDAD 1

vecino -na *adj* (a) (contiguo) neighboring*; **los países ~s** the neighboring countries; **~ A algo** bordering ON sth, adjoining sth (b) (cercano) neighboring*, nearby

■ *m,f* (a) (persona que vive cerca) neighbor*; **mi ~ de al lado** my next-door neighbor (b) (habitante — de población, municipio) inhabitant; (— de barrio, edificio) resident

veda *f* (en caza y pesca) closed (AmE) *o* (BrE) close season; **la perdiz está en ~** it is the closed *o* close season for partridge

vedar [A1] *vt* (a) ⟨*caza/pesca*⟩ to prohibit, ban (*during the closed season*) (b) (prohibir) to ban

vedette /be'ðet/ *f* cabaret star

vegetación *f* (a) (Bot) vegetation (b) (Med) **vegetaciones** *fpl* adenoids (*pl*)

vegetal *adj* ⟨*vida*⟩ plant (*before n*); ⟨*aceite/reino*⟩ vegetable (*before n*)

■ *m* plant, vegetable

vegetar [A1] *vi* (a) (Bot) to grow (b) (fam) ⟨*persona*⟩ to vegetate (colloq & pej)

vegetariano -na *adj/m,f* vegetarian

vehemente *adj* vehement

vehículo *m* vehicle

veía, veíamos, etc ▶ VER

veinte *adj inv/m/pron* twenty; *para ejemplos ver* CINCO, CINCUENTA

veintitantos -tas *adj/pron* twenty-odd

veintiuno¹ -na *adj/pron* [VEINTIÚN *is used before masculine nouns and before feminine nouns which begin with accented* A *or* HA] twenty-one; **veintiún años** twenty-one years; *para ejemplos ver tb* CINCO

veintiuno² *m* (number) twenty-one

vejestorio *m* (a) (fam) (persona): **la profesora es un ~** the teacher is ancient (colloq) (b) (AmL fam) (cosa) old relic (colloq), piece of old junk (colloq)

vejez *f* old age

vejiga *f* (Anat) bladder

vela *f* [1] (para alumbrar) candle [2] (vigilia): **pasé la noche en ~** (por preocupación, dolor) I couldn't get to sleep all night; (cuidando a un enfermo) I was up all night [3] (a) (de barco) sail (b) (deporte) sailing; **hacer ~** to go sailing

velado -da *adj* ⟨*película*⟩ fogged; ⟨*amenaza/referencia*⟩ veiled; ⟨*sonido*⟩ muffled

velador¹ *m* (a) (mesa) pedestal table (b) (AmS) (mesilla de noche) bedside table, night stand (AmE)

velador² -dora *m,f* [1] (Méx) (de fábrica) watchman, guard [2] **veladora** *f* (Méx) (vela) candle

velar [A1] *vt* [1] (a) ⟨*difunto*⟩ to hold a wake over (b) ⟨*enfermo*⟩ to watch over [2] ⟨*película*⟩ to fog, expose

■ **~** *vi* [1] (permanecer despierto) to stay up *o* awake [2] (cuidar) **~ POR algo/algn** to watch OVER sth/sb

■ **velarse** *v pron* «*película*» to get fogged *o* exposed

velatorio *m* (a) (reunión) wake, vigil (frml) (b) (establecimiento) funeral parlor*; (sala) chapel of rest

velero *m* (a) (Náut) (grande) sailing ship; (pequeño) sailboat (AmE), sailing boat (BrE) (b) (Aviac) glider

veleta *f* [1] (para el viento) weather vane, weathercock [2] **veleta** *mf* (fam) (persona inconstante) fickle person

vello *m* [1] (pelusa) down; (en las piernas, etc) hair [2] (Bot) bloom

velo *m* veil

velocidad *f* [1] (en general) speed; **cobrar ~** to pick up *o* gather speed; **¿a qué ~ iba?** how fast was he going?; **disminuir la ~** to slow down; **a toda ~** at top speed; **la ~ con que lo hizo** the speed with which he did it [2] (Auto, Mec) gear; **un modelo de cinco ~es** a five-gear model

velocímetro *m* speedometer

velódromo *m* cycle track, velodrome

veloz *adj* ⟨*corredor*⟩ fast; ⟨*movimiento*⟩ swift, quick

ven ▶ VENIR, VER²

vena *f* [1] (Anat) vein; **cortarse las ~s** to slash *o* cut one's wrists [2] (Geol, Min) vein, seam [3] (de madera) grain; (de piedra) vein, stripe

venado *m* (a) (Zool) deer; **pintar ~** (Méx fam) to play hooky (esp AmE colloq), skive off (school) (BrE colloq) (b) (Coc) venison

vencedor -dora *adj* ⟨*ejército/país*⟩ victorious; ⟨*equipo/jugador*⟩ winning (*before n*)

■ *m,f* (en guerra) victor; (en competición) winner

vencer [E2] *vt* (a) ⟨*enemigo*⟩ to defeat, vanquish (liter); ⟨*rival/competidor*⟩ to defeat, beat; **no te dejes ~** don't give in (b) ⟨*miedo/pesimismo/obstáculo*⟩ to overcome (c) (dominar): **me venció el sueño** I was overcome by sleep

■ **~** *vi* [1] ⟨*ejército/equipo*⟩ to win, be victorious; **¡~emos!** we shall overcome! [2] (a) «*pasaporte/garantía*» to expire; **el lunes vence el plazo** Monday is the deadline (b) «*letra*» to be due for payment

■ **vencerse** *v pron* (AmL) «*pasaporte/garantía*» to expire; **se me venció el carnet** my card expired *o* ran out

vencido -da *adj* [1] ⟨*ejército/país*⟩ defeated, vanquished (liter); ⟨*equipo/jugador*⟩ losing (*before n*), ···⊹

beaten; **darse por** ~ to give up *o* in 2 (a) ⟨visa/pasaporte⟩ expired, out-of-date (before n); **estos antibióticos están** ~**s** (AmL) these antibiotics are past their expiration (AmE) *o* (BrE) expiry date (b) ⟨boleto/cheque⟩ out-of-date (before n) (c) ⟨letra/intereses⟩ due for payment
■ *m,f*: **los** ~**s** the defeated, the vanquished (liter)

vencimiento *m* (de letra, pago) due date; (de carnet, licencia) expiration (AmE) *o* (BrE) expiry date

venda *f* bandage; ~ **elástica** elastic bandage

vendaje *m* dressing; **poner un** ~ to put on a dressing

vendar [A1] *vt* to bandage

vendaval *m* gale, strong wind

vendedor -dora *m,f* (a) (en mercado) stallholder, stallkeeper (AmE); (en tienda) salesclerk (AmE), shop assistant (BrE); (viajante, representante) sales representative; ~ **a domicilio** door-to-door sales agent; ~ **ambulante** peddler, hawker; ~ **de periódicos** newspaper vendor *o* seller (b) (Der) ⟨propietario que vende⟩ vendor

vender [E1] *vt* ⟨mercancías/casa⟩ to sell; **le vendí el reloj** I sold him the watch; **vendió la casa muy bien** she got a very good price for her house; **❸ se vende** for sale; **lo venden a $500 el kilo** they sell it at $500 a kilo; **vendí el cuadro en** *or* **por $20.000** I sold the painting for $20,000; **se vende por kilo(s)/unidades** it's sold by the kilo/unit
■ ~ *vi* «producto» to sell
■ **venderse** *v pron* (dejarse sobornar) to sell out

vendimia *f* grape harvest, wine harvest

vendimiar [A1] *vt* to pick, harvest

vendré, vendría, etc ▶ VENIR

venduta *f* (Col) public sale (of household goods)

Venecia *f* Venice

veneno *m* (a) (sustancia tóxica) poison; (de culebra) venom (b) (malevolencia) venom

venenoso -sa *adj* ⟨sustancia/planta⟩ poisonous; ⟨araña/serpiente⟩ poisonous, venomous; ⟨palabras/mirada⟩ venomous

venerable *adj/m,f* venerable

venerar [A1] *vt* (adorar) to revere, worship; (Relig) to venerate

venéreo -rea *adj* venereal

venezolanismo *m* Venezuelan word (*o* phrase *etc*), Venezuelanism

venezolano -na *adj/m,f* Venezuelan

Venezuela *f* Venezuela

venga *interj* (Esp fam) (a) (para animar) come on (b) (expresando insistencia): **y** ~ **a protestar** and they just kept *o* went on (and on) complaining

vengáis, vengamos, etc ▶ VENIR

venganza *f* revenge, vengeance (liter)

vengar [A3] *vt* ⟨insulto/derrota⟩ to take revenge for, to avenge; ⟨persona⟩ to avenge
■ **vengarse** *v pron* to take revenge; ~**se DE** *or* **POR algo** to take revenge FOR sth; ~**se DE/EN algn** to take (one's) revenge ON sb

vengativo -va *adj* vindictive, vengeful (liter)

vengo ▶ VENIR

venia *f* (AmS) (inclinación de cabeza) bow

venial *adj* venial

venida *f* (a) (llegada) arrival (b) (AmL) (vuelta): **a la** *or* **de** ~ on the way back

venidero -ra *adj* future (before n)

venir [I31] *vi* 1 (a) (a un lugar) to come; **vine en tren** I came by train; **¿a qué vino?** what did he come by *o* around for?; **vine dormida todo el tiempo** I slept (for) the whole journey; ~ **POR** *or* (Esp) **A POR algn/algo** to come FOR sb/sth, to come to pick sb/sth up; **la vino a buscar su madre** her mother came to pick her up; **ven a ver esto** come and see this (b) (volver) to come back; **ahora vengo** I'll be back in a moment; **no vengas tarde** don't be late home *o* back (c) (salir): **me vino con un cuento** he came up with some excuse; **no me vengas con exigencias** don't start making demands
2 (a) (tener lugar): **ahora viene esa escena que te conté** that scene I told you about is coming up now; **¿qué viene después de las noticias?** what's on after the news?; **ya vendrán tiempos mejores** things will get better (b) (indicando procedencia) ~ **DE algo** to come FROM sth; **viene de la India** it comes from India; **le viene de familia** it runs in his family; **¿a qué viene eso?** why do you say that? (c) (indicando presentación) to come; **viene en tres tamaños** it comes in three sizes (d) (estar incluido): **viene en primera página** it's on the front page; **no viene nada sobre la huelga** there's nothing about the strike
3 (convenir): **estas cajas me vendrían muy bien** these boxes would come in handy; **el jueves no me viene bien** Thursday's no good for me; **me vendría bien un descanso** I could do with a rest
4 (como aux): **esto viene a confirmar mis sospechas** this confirms my suspicions; **hace mucho que lo venía diciendo** I'd been saying so all along
■ **venirse** *v pron* (enf) (a) (a un lugar) to come; **se vinieron a pie** they came on foot; ~**se abajo** «persona» to go to pieces; «techo» to fall in, collapse; «estante» to collapse; «ilusiones» to go up in smoke; «proyectos» to fall through (b) (volver) to come back

venta *f* (Com) sale; ~ **al contado** cash sale; ~ **al por mayor/menor** wholesale/retail; ~ **a plazos** installment plan (AmE), hire purchase (BrE); ~ **por catálogo** *or* **correo** mail order; **pronto saldrá a la** ~ it will be on sale soon; **estar en** *or* **a la** ~ ⟨coche/bicicleta⟩ to be for sale; «casa» to be (up) for sale

ventaja *f* (a) (beneficio) advantage; **tiene la** ~ **de que está cerca** it has the advantage of being near; **tienes** ~ **por tu experiencia** you have an advantage because of your experience (b) (en carrera): **lleva una** ~ **de diez segundos** she has a ten-second lead; **jugar con** ~ to be at an advantage

ventajero -ra *m,f* (RPI) opportunist

ventajoso -sa *adj* (a) ⟨negocio⟩ profitable; ⟨acuerdo/situación⟩ favorable*, advantageous (b) (Col) ⟨persona⟩ opportunistic

ventana f ❘1❘ (Arquit, Const, Inf) window ❘2❘ (de la nariz) nostril

ventanilla f (a) (de coche, tren) window (b) (en oficinas) window; (en cines, teatros) box office; **horario de ~** opening hours (c) (Inf) window

ventilación f (a) (posibilidad de ventilarse) ventilation (b) (acción de ventilar) airing

ventilador m (aparato) fan; (abertura) ventilator, air vent

ventilar [A1] vt ‹habitación› to air, ventilate; ‹ropa/colchón› to air
■ **ventilarse** v pron ❘1❘ «habitación/ropa» to air ❘2❘ (fam) (tomar el aire) to get a breath of fresh air, get some air

ventisca f snowstorm; (con más viento) blizzard

ventolera f gust of wind

ventosa f (a) (de goma, plástico) suction pad (b) (Zool) sucker

ventosidad f wind, flatulence

ventoso -sa adj windy

ventrículo m ventricle

ventrílocuo -cua m,f ventriloquist

ventura f ❘1❘ (liter) (suerte) fortune; **tiene la ~ de** ... he has the good fortune to ...; **echarle la buena ~ a algn** to tell sb's fortune ❘2❘ (en locs) **a la ventura: viven a la ~** they take each day as it comes; **salieron a la ~** they set out with no fixed plan

Venus m (Astron) Venus
■ f (Art, Mit) Venus

veo ❯ VER 2

ver¹ m ❘1❘ (aspecto): **ser de buen ~** to be good-looking o attractive ❘2❘ (opinión): **a mi/su ~** in my/his view

ver² [E29] vt ❘1❘ (a) (percibir con la vista) to see; **¿ves algo?** can you see anything?; **no se ve nada aquí** you can't see a thing in here; **lo vi hablando con ella** I saw him talking to her (b) (mirar) ‹programa/partido› to watch; **~ (la) televisión** to watch television; **esa película ya la he visto** I've seen that movie before; **no poder (ni) ~ a algn: no la puede ~** he can't stand her ❘2❘ (entender, notar) to see; **¿no ves lo que está pasando?** don't o can't you see what's happening?; **se la ve preocupada** she looks worried; **hacerse ~** (RPl) to show off ❘3❘ (a) (constatar, comprobar) to see; **ve a ~ quién es** go and see who it is; **ya ~ás lo que pasa!** you'll see what happens; **¡ya se ~á!** we'll see (b) (ser testigo de) to see; **¡nunca he visto cosa igual!** I've never seen anything like it!; **¡si vieras lo mal que lo pasé!** you can't imagine how awful it was!; **¡hubieras visto cómo se asustaron!** (AmL) you should have seen the fright they got! ❘4❘ **a ver:** (vamos) **a ~ ¿de qué se trata?** OK o all right, now, what's the problem?; **está aquí, en el periódico — ¿a ~?** it's here in the newspaper — let's see; **apriétalo a ~ qué pasa** press it and see what happens; **a ~ si escribes pronto** make sure you write soon ❘5❘ (a) (estudiar): **esto mejor que lo veas tú** you'd better have a look at this; **tengo que ~ cómo lo arreglo** I have to work out how I can fix it; **ya ~é qué hago** I'll decide what to do later (b) «médico» (examinar) to see; **¿la ha visto un médico?** has she been seen by a doctor yet? ❘6❘ (a) (juzgar, considerar): **yo eso no lo veo bien** I

don't think that's right; **a mi modo or manera de ~** the way I see it (b) (encontrar) to see; **no le veo salida a esto** I can't see any way out of this; **no le veo la gracia** I don't think it's funny ❘7❘ (visitar, entrevistarse con) ‹amigo/pariente› to see, visit; ‹médico/jefe› to see; **¡cuánto tiempo sin ~te!** I haven't seen you for ages! ❘8❘ **tener ... que ver: ¿y eso qué tiene que ~?** and what does that have to do with it?; **no tengo nada que ~ con él** I have nothing to do with him; **¿qué tiene que ~ que sea sábado?** what difference does it make that it's Saturday?
■ **~ vi** ❘1❘ (percibir con la vista) to see; **así no veo** I can't see like this; **no veo bien de lejos/de cerca** I'm shortsighted/longsighted ❘2❘ (constatar): **¿hay cerveza? — no sé, voy a ~** is there any beer? — I don't know, I'll have a look; **pues ~ás, todo empezó cuando ...** well you see, the whole thing began when ... ❘3❘ (pensar) to see; **ya ~é** I'll see; **estar/seguir en ~emos:** ‹todavía está en ~emos› it isn't certain yet; **seguimos en ~emos** we still don't know anything
■ **verse** v pron ❘1❘ (refl) (percibirse, imaginarse) to see oneself ❘2❘ (hallarse) (+ compl) to find oneself; **me vi en un aprieto** I found myself in a tight spot; **me vi obligado a despedirlo** I had no choice but to dismiss him ❘3❘ (esp AmL) (parecer): **se ve bien con esa falda** she looks good in that skirt; **no se ve bien con ese peinado** that hairdo doesn't suit her ❘4❘ (recípr) (encontrarse) to meet; **nos vemos a las siete** I'll meet o see you at seven; **¡nos vemos!** (esp AmL) see you! (b) (visitarse, encontrarse) to see each other; **nos vemos a menudo** we see each other often; **~se CON algn** to see sb

veraneante mf vacationer (AmE), holidaymaker (BrE)

veranear [A1] vi: **solía ~ en un pueblo** she used to spend her summer vacation (AmE) o (BrE) holidays in a small town

veraneo m: **fuimos de ~ al campo** we spent our summer vacation (AmE) o (BrE) holidays in the country; **lugar de ~** summer resort

veraniego -ga adj summer (before n)

verano m summer; (en la zona tropical) dry season; **ropa de ~** summer clothes

veras: **de veras** (loc adv) really; **lo siento de ~** I really am sorry; **¡no lo dirás de ~!** you can't be serious!

verbal adj verbal

verbena f ❘1❘ (Bot) verbena ❘2❘ (fiesta popular) festival; (baile) open-air dance

verbo m (Ling) verb

verdad f (a) (en general) truth; **dime la ~** tell me the truth; **es la pura ~** it's the gospel truth; **a decir ~ ...** to tell you the truth ...; **la ~, no lo sé** I don't honestly know; **¡no es ~!** that's not true!; **eso es una gran ~** that is so true! (b) **de verdad** (loc adv) really; (loc adj) real; **¡de ~ que me gusta!** I really do like it!; **una pistola de ~** a real gun (c) (buscando corroboración): **es guapa ¿~?** she's beautiful, isn't she?; **¿~ que tú me entiendes?** you understand me, don't you?

verdadero -ra adj ❘1❘ (a) ‹premisa/historia› true; ‹caso/nombre› real (b) ‹pieles/joyas› real ···❯

2 (*delante del n*) (uso enfático) real; **se portó como un ~ imbécil** he behaved like a real *o* (colloq) proper idiot

verde *adj* **1** ⟨*color/ojos/vestido*⟩ green; **zapatos ~ oliva** olive-green shoes; **ojos ~ azulado** bluish *o* (BrE) bluey green eyes **2** ⟨*fruta*⟩ green, unripe; ⟨*leña*⟩ green; **estar ~** (fam) (no tener experiencia) to be green (colloq); (en una asignatura): **está ~ en historia** he doesn't know much about history (colloq) **3** (Pol) Green **4** (fam) ⟨*chiste*⟩ dirty, blue (colloq)
■ *m* (color) green; (Bot) greenery
■ *mf* (Pol) Green; **los ~s** the Greens

verdín *m* (a) (musgo) moss (b) (moho) mold*; (en el agua) slime; (en metal) verdigris

verdor *m* greenness

verdoso -sa *adj* greenish

verdugo *m* **1** (a) (en ejecuciones) executioner; (en la horca) hangman (b) (persona cruel) tyrant **2** (Indum) balaclava; (para el esquí) ski mask

verdulería *f* fruit and vegetable store, greengrocer's (BrE)

verdulero -ra *m,f* (persona) greengrocer

verdura *f* (Bot, Coc) vegetable; **sopa de ~(s)** vegetable soup

vereda *f* (a) (senda) path (b) (CS, Per) (acera) sidewalk (AmE), pavement (BrE) (c) (Col) (distrito) district

veredicto *m* (Der) verdict; (dictamen) opinion, verdict

vergonzoso -sa *adj* **1** (tímido) shy, bashful **2** ⟨*asunto/comportamiento*⟩ disgraceful, shameful

vergüenza *f* **1** (turbación) embarrassment; **no lo hagas pasar ~** don't embarrass him; **me da ~ pedírselo otra vez** I'm embarrassed to ask him again; **sentí ~ ajena** I felt embarrassed for him (*o* her *etc*) **2** (sentido del decoro) (sense of) shame; **no tiene ~** he has no (sense of) shame **3** (escándalo, motivo de oprobio) disgrace; **ser una ~ para algo/algn** to be a disgrace to sth/sb; **estos precios son una ~** these prices are outrageous

verídico -ca *adj* true

verificar [A2] *vt* ⟨*hechos*⟩ to establish, verify; ⟨*resultado*⟩ to check; ⟨*pagos/cuentas*⟩ to check, audit; ⟨*máquina/instrumento*⟩ to check, test

verja *f* (cerca) railings (*pl*); (puerta) wrought-iron gate; (de ventana) (wrought-iron) grille

vermut /ber'mu(t)/ *m* (*pl* **-muts**) vermouth
■ *f* (CS) early evening performance

verosímil *adj* ⟨*excusa/versión*⟩ plausible; ⟨*argumento/historia*⟩ realistic

verruga *f* (a) (Med) (en la mano, cara) wart; (en los pies) verruca (b) (Bot) wart

versículo *m* verse

versión *f* (a) (de obra, suceso) version; **~ original** movie in its original language (b) (traducción) translation (c) (modelo) model

verso *m* (Lit) (línea) line, verse; (poema) poem; (género) verse; **en ~** in verse

vértebra *f* vertebra

vertebrado¹ -da *adj* vertebrate

vertebrado² *m* vertebrate; **los ~s** the vertebrates

vertedero *m* **1** (para basura) dump; **un ~ de residuos nucleares** a dumping site for nuclear waste **2** (desagüe) outlet

verter [E31] *or* [E8] *vt* (a) (en un recipiente) ⟨*agua/vino/trigo*⟩ to pour (b) (derramar) ⟨*líquido*⟩ to spill; ⟨*lágrimas/sangre*⟩ (liter) to shed (liter) (c) ⟨*residuos radiactivos*⟩ to dump

vertical *adj* **1** (a) ⟨*línea/madero*⟩ vertical; **en posición ~** in a vertical position (b) (en crucigramas): **el tres ~** three down **2** (Pol, Rels Labs) vertical
■ *f* (a) (Mat, Tec) vertical line, vertical (tech) (b) (Dep) handstand

vértice *m* (de ángulo, figura) vertex, apex; (coronilla) crown

vertiente *f* (a) (de montaña, tejado) slope (b) (faceta, aspecto) aspect (c) (CS) (manantial) spring

vertiginoso -sa *adj* ⟨*velocidad*⟩ dizzy, giddy, vertiginous (frml)

vértigo *m* vertigo; **tener ~** to have vertigo; **me produce ~** it makes me dizzy *o* giddy

ves ▶ VER²

vesícula *f* vesicle; **~ biliar** gallbladder

vespa® *f* Vespa®, scooter

vespertino -na *adj* evening (*before n*); **diario ~** evening newspaper

vespino® *m* moped

vestíbulo *m* (de casa particular) hall; (de edificio público) lobby; (de teatro, cine) foyer

vestido¹ -da *adj* dressed; **bien ~** well/badly dressed; **¿cómo iba ~?** what was he wearing?; **iba vestida de azul** she was wearing blue; **~ de uniforme** in uniform; **¿de qué vas a ir ~?** what are you going to go as?

vestido² *m* (a) (de mujer) dress; **~ de baño** (Col) swimsuit; **~ de noche** evening dress; **~ de novia** wedding dress *o* gown (b) (Col) (de hombre) suit

vestidor *m* (en casa) dressing room; (en club, gimnasio) (Chi, Méx) locker room (AmE), changing room (BrE)

vestier *m* (Col) (en tienda) fitting room; (en club, gimnasio) locker room (AmE), changing room (BrE)

vestigio *m* trace; **no quedan ~s de aquella civilización** no trace remains of that civilization; **~s históricos** historical remains

vestir [I14] *vt* **1** (a) ⟨*niño/muñeca*⟩ to dress (b) (proporcionar ropa a) to clothe (frml) (c) (confeccionar ropa a) ⟨*modisto*⟩ to dress **2** (liter *o* period) (llevar puesto) to wear
■ *vi* **1** «*persona*» to dress; **~ bien** to dress well; **~ DE algo** ⟨*de uniforme/azul*⟩ to wear sth; **~ de etiqueta** to wear formal dress **2** (ser elegante): **no sabe ~** he has no dress sense; **de ~** ⟨*traje/zapatos*⟩ smart
■ **vestirse** *v pron* (refl) (a) (ponerse ropa) to dress, get dressed; **date prisa, vístete** hurry up, get dressed (b) (de cierta manera): **se viste mal** he dresses badly; **se viste a la última moda** she wears the latest styles; **siempre se viste de verde** she always wears green (c) (disfrazarse) **~se DE algo** to dress up AS sth

vestón *m* (CS) jacket

vestuario *m* **1** (conjunto de ropa) wardrobe; (Cin, Teatr) wardrobe **2** (en club, gimnasio) locker room (AmE), changing room (BrE)

veta f 1 (a) (en madera) streak (b) (en la carne) streak (c) (en roca, mármol) vein 2 (inclinación) bent, leanings (pl)

vetar [A1] vt to veto

veteranía f (experiencia) experience; (antigüedad) seniority

veterano -na adj/m,f veteran

veterinaria f (ciencia) veterinary science o medicine; (clínica) veterinary surgery

veterinario -ria adj ‹clínica› veterinary (before n); médico ~ vet, veterinarian (AmE), veterinary surgeon (BrE)
■ m,f vet, veterinarian (AmE), veterinary surgeon (BrE)

veto m veto; poner el ~ a algo to veto sth

vez f 1 (ocasión) time; una ~/dos veces once/twice; una ~ por semana once a week; me acuerdo de una/aquella ~ cuando ... I remember once/that time when ...; la última ~ que lo vi the last time I saw him; mil veces or miles de veces a thousand times, thousands of times; algunas veces sometimes; ¿te has arrepentido alguna ~? have you ever regretted it?; érase una ~ (liter) once upon a time (liter); por primera ~ for the first time; otra ~ again; déjalo para otra ~ leave it for another time o day; otra ~ será maybe next time; una ~ más once again
2 (en locs) a la vez at the same time; a veces sometimes; cada vez every o each time; cada ~ más more and more; lo encuentro cada ~ más viejo he looks older every time I see him; cada ~ menos less and less; de una vez (expresando impaciencia) once and for all; (simultáneamente) in one go; de vez en cuando from time to time, every now and then; en vez de instead of; rara vez seldom, hardly ever; una vez once; una ~ que hayas terminado once o when you have finished
3 (Esp) (turno en una cola): ¿quién tiene or me da la ~? who's last?; pedir la ~ to ask who's last

vi ▶ VER²

vía f 1 (a) (ruta, camino): la ~ rápida the fast route; una ~ al diálogo a channel o an avenue for dialogue; ¡dejen ~ libre! clear the way!; ~ de comunicación road (o rail etc) link; V~ Láctea Milky Way; ~ marítima sea route, seaway (b) (medio de transporte): por ~ aérea/marítima/terrestre by air/by sea/by land; ⑤ vía aérea airmail (c) (medio, procedimiento) channel (pl); por la ~ diplomática/política through diplomatic/political channels
2 en vías de: está en ~s de solucionarse it's in the process of being resolved; países en ~s de desarrollo developing countries; una especie en ~s de extinción an endangered species
3 (Ferr) track; saldrá por la ~ dos it will depart from track (AmE) o (BrE) platform two
4 (Anat, Med): por ~ oral/venosa orally/intravenously; ~s respiratorias/urinarias respiratory/urinary tract
■ prep via; ~ Miami via Miami

viable adj ‹proyecto/plan› viable, feasible; ‹bebé› viable

viaducto m viaduct

viajante mf traveling* salesman/saleswoman

viajar [A1] vi to travel; ~ en avión to travel by plane; ~ en primera clase to travel o go first class

viaje m trip, journey; hacer un ~ to go on a trip o journey; un ~ en tren a train journey; hizo el ~ en coche he drove; estar de ~ to be away; salir de ~ to go on a trip; en el ~ de vuelta on the way back; ¡buen ~! have a good trip!; hicimos un ~ por todo Chile we traveled all around Chile; ~ de negocios business trip; ~ de novios honeymoon; ~ organizado package tour; hice varios ~s para llevarlas todas I made several trips to take them all

viajero -ra m,f traveler*; (pasajero) passenger

vial adj road (before n)

viáticos mpl (esp AmL) travel allowance

víbora f (a) (Zool) viper; ~ de cascabel (Méx) rattlesnake (b) (fam & pey) (persona): es una ~ he has a vicious tongue

vibración f vibration

vibrante adj ‹voz› vibrant, resonant; ‹discurso› vibrant

vibrar [A1] vi «cuerdas/cristales» to vibrate

vicaría f vicariate

vicario -ria m,f (párroco) vicar

vicecampeón -peona m,f runner-up

vicepresidencia f (Gob, Pol) vice presidency; (de empresa) vice presidency (AmE), deputy chairmanship (BrE)

vicepresidente -ta m,f, **vicepresidente** mf (Gob, Pol) vice president; (de empresa) vice president (AmE), deputy chairman/chairwoman (BrE)

vice versa adv vice versa

vichar [A1] vi (RPl fam) to peep (colloq)
■ ~ vt to peep at

viciado -da adj 1 ‹atmósfera› stuffy; aquí dentro el aire está ~ it's very stuffy in here
2 ‹estilo/dicción› marred

viciar [A1] vt ‹persona› to get ... into a bad habit; ‹estilo/lenguaje› to mar
■ **viciarse** v pron (a) «persona»: ~se CON algo to become addicted TO sth (b) «estilo/lenguaje» to deteriorate

vicio m 1 (corrupción) vice; darse al ~ to give oneself over to vice 2 (hábito): el único ~ que tengo my only vice o bad habit; el juego se convirtió en ~ para él his gambling became an addiction; se queja de ~ (fam) she complains for the sake of it

vicioso -sa adj ‹persona› depraved, debauched
■ m,f dissolute person

víctima f victim; ~ DE algo victim OF sth; fue ~ de una emboscada he was the victim of an ambush; ~s del cáncer cancer victims

victoria f victory; (Dep) win; no cantes ~ antes de tiempo don't count your chickens before they're hatched

victorioso -sa adj victorious

vicuña f vicuna

vid f vine

vida f 1 (a) (Biol) life; la ~ marina marine life; una cuestión de ~ o muerte a matter of life and death; quitarse la ~ to take one's (own) life (frml); salir con ~ to escape alive (b) (viveza, vitalidad) life; lleno de ~ full of life; le falta ~ it's/she's/he's not very lively
2 (extensión de tiempo, existencia) life; a lo largo de su ~ throughout his life; toda una ~ a lifetime; ⋯⟶

V

la ~ de un coche the life-span of a car; **un amigo de toda la ~** a lifelong friend; **amargarle la ~ a algn** to make sb's life a misery; **complicarse la ~** to make life difficult for oneself; **de por ~** for life; **hacerle la ~ imposible a algn** to make sb's life impossible
3 (manera de vivir, actividades) life; **lleva una ~ muy ajetreada** she leads a very busy life; **¿qué es de tu ~?** what have you been up to?; **hace** *or* **vive su ~** he lives his own life; **¡esto sí que es ~!** this is the life!; **¡(así) es la ~!** that's life, such is life; **~ privada** private life; **su ~ sentimental** his love life; **una mujer de ~ alegre** a woman of easy virtue; **¡qué ~ de perros!** it's a dog's life; **hacer ~ social** to socialize; **estar encantado de la ~** to be thrilled, to be over the moon (colloq)
4 (necesidades materiales): **la ~ está carísima** the cost of living is very high; **ganarse la ~** to earn one's *o* a living; **tiene la ~ resuelta** he's set up for life
5 (como apelativo) darling; **¡mi ~!** (my) darling!

vidente *mf* (que ve) sighted person; (que adivina) clairvoyant

video, (Esp) **vídeo** *m* **(a)** (medio, sistema) video; **en ~** on video **(b)** (cinta) videocassette, videotape, video (colloq); (grabación) video **(c)** (aparato) video (cassette recorder), VCR

videocámara *f* video camera, camcorder

videoclip *m* video

videoclub *m* (*pl* **-clubs** *or* **-clubes**) videoclub

videodisco *m* video disk

videojuego *m* video game

videoteca *f* video library

videotex *m* videotex(t), teletext

vidriado -da *adj* glazed

vidriera *f* **(a)** (puerta) glazed door; (ventana) window; (en iglesia) *tb* **~ de colores** stained glass window **(b)** (AmL) (escaparate) shop window; **mirar ~s** to window-shop

vidrierista *mf* (AmL) window dresser

vidriero *m* glazier

vidrio *m* **(a)** (material) glass; **una botella de ~** a glass bottle; **fábrica de ~** glassworks **(b)** (esp AmL) (objeto): **limpiar los ~s** to clean the windows; **cambié uno de los ~s** I replaced one of the panes *o* windowpanes; **me corté con un ~** I cut myself on a piece of glass; **hay ~s rotos en la calle** there is broken glass in the street; **pagar los ~s rotos** to take the responsibility *o* the blame **(c)** (de reloj) crystal, glass

vieira *f* (molusco) scallop; (concha) scallop shell

vieja *f* (Col, Méx, Ven fam) (mujer) broad (AmE sl), bird (BrE sl); *ver tb* VIEJO *m,f*

viejo -ja *adj* **1** [SER] ⟨persona/animal⟩ old; ⟨coche/ropa/casa⟩ old; **hacerse ~** to get old
2 (a) [ESTAR] ⟨persona/animal⟩ (envejecido) old; **ya está ~** he's got(ten) old; **¡qué vieja estoy!** I look so old! **(b)** [ESTAR] ⟨zapatos/pantalones⟩ (desgastado) old

3 (delante del n) (antiguo) ⟨costumbre/amigo⟩ old; **los ~s tiempos** the old days; **V~ Testamento** Old Testament
■ *m,f* **1** (*m*) old man; (*f*) old woman; **los ~s** old people, the elderly; **llegar a ~** to reach old age; **se casó de ~** he was an old man when he got married; **se murió de ~** he died of old age; **V~ Pascuero** (Chi) ▶ PAPÁ NOEL; **~ verde** *or* (Méx) **~ rabo verde** (fam) dirty old man
2 (fam) (refiriéndose a los padres): **mi ~/mi vieja** my old man/lady (colloq); **tus ~s** your folks, your Mom and Dad
3 (AmL) (hablándole a un niño, al cónyuge etc) darling (colloq), love (colloq); (a un amigo) buddy (AmE), mate (BrE)
4 (Méx fam) (esposo) (*m*) old man (colloq); (*f*) old woman *o* lady (colloq)

Viena *f* Vienna

viendo ▶ VER²

viene, vienes, etc ▶ VENIR

vienés -nesa *adj/m,f* Viennese

viento *m* **1** (en general) wind; **correr** *or* **hacer ~** to be windy; **un ~ helado** an icy wind; **~ en contra/a favor** *or* **de cola** head/tail wind; **instrumento de ~** wind instrument **2** (de tienda de campaña) guy (rope)

vientre *m* **(a)** (cavidad) abdomen; **el bajo ~** the lower abdomen; **hacer de ~** to have a bowel movement **(b)** (región exterior) stomach, belly (colloq) **(c)** (de mujer embarazada) womb, belly (colloq)

viera, vieras, etc ▶ VER²

viernes *m* (*pl* **~**) Friday; **V~ Santo** Good Friday; *para ejemplos ver* LUNES

viese, vieses, etc ▶ VER²

viga *f* (de madera) joist, beam; (de metal) beam, girder

vigencia *f* validity; **entrar en ~** «ley» to come into force *o* effect

vigente *adj* ⟨pasaporte/contrato⟩ valid; ⟨legislación/precio⟩ current (*before n*); **estar ~** «ley» to be in force

vigésimo -ma *adj/pron* twentieth; **~ primero** twenty-first; **el ~ aniversario** the twentieth anniversary; **la vigésima parte** a twentieth

vigía *mf* (persona) lookout

vigilancia *f* (atención, cuidado) vigilance; (por guardias, la policía) surveillance; **estar bajo ~** to be under surveillance; **servicio de ~** security patrol

vigilante *adj* vigilant, on the alert; **en actitud ~** on the alert
■ *mf* (en tienda) store detective; (en banco, edificio público) security guard; **~ jurado/nocturno** security guard/night watchman

vigilar [A1] *vt* **(a)** (cuidar, atender) to watch, keep an eye on **(b)** ⟨preso/local⟩ to guard, keep watch on; ⟨frontera/zona⟩ to guard, patrol; ⟨examen⟩ to proctor (AmE), to invigilate at (BrE) **(c)** (fam) (espiar) to watch
■ **~** *vi* to keep watch

AmC	Central America	Arg	Argentina	Cu	Cuba	Per	Peru
AmL	Latin America	Bol	Bolivia	Ec	Ecuador	RPI	River Plate Area
AmS	South America	Chi	Chile	Esp	Spain	Ur	Uruguay
Andes	Andean Region	CS	Southern Cone	Méx	Mexico	Ven	Venezuela

vigilia *f* ① (vela) wakefulness; **de ∼** awake ② (Relig) (víspera) vigil; (abstinencia) abstinence; (tiempo de abstinencia) day/period of abstinence

vigor *m* (a) (fuerza, energía) vigor*, energy; **con ∼** vigorously (b) **en vigor** *‹estar›* in force; **entrar en ∼** to come into effect *o* force

vigoroso -sa *adj* *‹persona/movimiento›* vigorous, energetic; *‹esfuerzo›* strenuous

VIH *m* (= **virus de inmunodeficiencia humana**) HIV

vil *adj* (liter) *‹acto/persona›* vile, despicable

villa *f* ① (Hist) (población) town; **∼ miseria** (Arg) shantytown ② (casa) villa

villancico *m* (Christmas) carol

villano -na *m,f* (persona ruin) rogue, scoundrel

vilo: en vilo (*loc adv*): **la levantó en ∼** he lifted her up; **permanecen en ∼ esperando el resultado** they're on tenterhooks awaiting the result

vinagre *m* vinegar

vinagrera *f* (a) (para vinagre) vinegar bottle (b) **vinagreras** *fpl* (para aceite y vinagre) cruet set *o* stand

vinagreta *f* vinaigrette

vinatero -ra *adj* wine (*before n*)
■ *m,f* vintner (AmE), wine merchant (BrE)

vincha *f* (AmS) (elástica, rígida) hair-band; (hebilla del pelo) barrette (AmE), hair slide (BrE)

vinculación *f* (relación) links (*pl*), connections (*pl*); **∼ con** *or* **a algo/algn** links *o* connections WITH sth/sb

vincular [A1] *vt* (a) (conectar, relacionar) **∼ algo/a algn a** *or* **con algo/algn** to link sth/sb TO *o* WITH sth/sb; **están vinculados por lazos de amistad** they are linked by bonds *o* ties of friendship; **grupos estrechamente vinculados** closely linked groups (b) (comprometer) to bind, be binding on

vínculo *m* (unión, relación) tie, bond; **∼s familiares** family ties

vine ▶ VENIR

vinería *f* (AmL) wineshop, liquor store (*specializing in wines*)

vinero -ra *adj* (Chi, Per) wine (*before n*)

vinícola *adj* *‹industria/producción›* wine (*before n*); *‹región›* wine-producing, wine-growing

vinicultor -tora *m,f* wine producer, winegrower

viniera, viniese, etc ▶ VENIR

viniste, etc ▶ VENIR

vino *m* (bebida) wine; **∼ dulce/seco** sweet/dry wine; **∼ blanco/rosado/tinto** white/rosé/red wine; **∼ de la casa** house wine

vino ▶ VENIR

viña *f* vineyard

viñatero -ra *adj* (AmL) wine (*before n*), wine-growing (*before n*)
■ *m,f* (AmL) (a) (propietario) winegrower (b) (trabajador) vineyard worker

viñedo *m* vineyard

viola *f* (a) (instrumento) viola (b) **viola** *mf* (persona) viola player, violist (AmE)

violáceo -cea *adj* purplish

violación *f* (a) (de persona) rape (b) (de ley, acuerdo, derecho) violation; (de templo) violation

violador -dora *m,f* (a) (de persona) rapist (b) (de ley, acuerdo) violator

violar [A1] *vt* (a) *‹persona›* to rape (b) *‹ley›* to violate, break; *‹tratado/derecho›* to violate; *‹templo›* to violate

violencia *f* violence; **recurrir a la ∼** to resort to violence

violentar [A1] *vt* (a) (forzar) *‹cerradura/puerta›* to force; *‹persona›* to rape (b) (poner en situación embarazosa) to make ... feel awkward
■ **violentarse** *v pron* to get embarrassed

violento -ta *adj* ① (en general) violent; **utilizar medios ∼s** to use violent means ② (incómodo) *‹situación›* embarrassing, awkward; **le resulta ∼ hablar del tema** she finds it embarrassing to talk about it; **estaba muy ∼** I felt very awkward

violeta *f* violet
■ *m/adj* violet

violín (a) *m* (instrumento) violin (b) **violín** *mf* (persona) violinist

violinista *mf* violinist

violón (a) *m* (instrumento) double bass (b) **violón** *mf* (persona) double bass player

violonchelista *mf* cellist

violonchelo *m* cello, violoncello

viral *adj* viral

virar [A1] *vi* (a) (Náut) to tack, go about (b) *«vehículo/conductor»* to turn; **viró bruscamente** she swerved (c) *«política/partido»* to veer

virgen *adj* (a) *‹persona›*: **una mujer/un hombre ∼** a virgin; **ser ∼** to be a virgin (b) *‹cinta›* blank; *‹película›* unexposed (c) *‹selva›* virgin
■ *f* virgin; **la V∼** (Relig) the Virgin

virginidad *f* virginity

Virgo *m* (signo) Virgo; **es (de) ∼** she's (a) Virgo, she's a Virgoan
■ *mf* (*pl* **∼** *or* **-gos**) (persona) *tb* **virgo** Virgo, Virgoan

viril *adj* *‹cualidades›* virile, manly

virilidad *f* virility

virreinato *m* viceroyalty

virtual *adj* (a) (potencial) virtual (b) (tácito) implicit

virtud *f* (a) (cualidad) virtue (b) (capacidad) power; **con ∼es curativas** with healing powers

virtuoso -sa *adj* virtuous
■ *m,f* virtuoso

viruela *f* (enfermedad) smallpox; (marca) pockmark

virus *m* (*pl* **∼**) virus

viruta *f* shaving

visa *f*, (Esp) **visado** *m* visa

visar [A1] *vt* *‹documento›* to endorse; *‹pasaporte›* to visa

visceral *adj* (a) (Anat) visceral (b) *‹odio/impresión›* visceral, deep; **un sentimiento ∼** a gut feeling

vísceras *fpl* entrails (*pl*), viscera (*pl*)

visconde -desa *m,f* (*m*) viscount; (*f*) viscountess

viscosa *f* viscose

viscoso -sa *adj* viscous

visera *f* (de casco) visor; (de gorra) peak; (de jugador) eyeshade

visibilidad *f* visibility

visible *adj* (a) [SER] visible (b) (fam) [ESTAR] (presentable) presentable, decent

visillo *m* net curtain, lace curtain

visión *f* **1** (a) (vista) vision, sight; **perdió la ~ de un ojo** she lost the sight of one eye (b) (aparición) vision; **ver visiones** to be seeing things **2** (enfoque, punto de vista) view; **una ~ romántica de la vida** a romantic view of life; **tener ~ de futuro** to be forward-looking

visionario -ria *adj/m,f* visionary

visir *m* vizier

visita *f* (a) (acción) visit; **hacer(le) una ~ (a algn)** to pay (sb) a visit; **ir de ~** to go visiting; **horario de ~** visiting hours *o* times; **~ a domicilio** house call; **~ de cortesía** courtesy call, duty visit; **~ guiada** (AmL) guided tour (b) (visitante) visitor; (invitado) guest; **espera una ~ importante** he's expecting an important visitor; **tener ~** to have visitors/guests

visitador social -dora social *m,f* (AmL) social worker

visitante *adj* visiting (*before n*)
■ *mf* visitor

visitar [A1] *vt* (a) ⟨persona⟩ to visit, visit with (AmE) (b) ⟨lugar⟩ to visit
■ **visitarse** *v pron* (recípr) to visit each other

vislumbrar [A1] *vt* (en la distancia) to make out, discern (frml); (entre los árboles, las nubes) to glimpse; **a lo lejos se vislumbraba una iglesia** a church could just be made out in the distance

viso *m* (Indum) petticoat, underskirt

visón *m* mink

visor *m* (a) (en cámara) viewfinder; (para diapositivas) slide viewer (b) (Arm) sight

víspera *f* (a) (día anterior): **la ~** the day before (b) (tiempo anterior): **~s de fiesta** days prior to public holidays; **en ~s de un viaje** just before a journey

vista *f* **1** (a) (sentido) sight, eyesight; **tener buena ~** to have good eyesight; **ser corto de ~** to be near-sighted; **perdió la ~** he lost his sight; **~ cansada** eyestrain (b) (ojos) eyes; **le hace daño a la ~** it hurts his eyes; **lo operaron de la ~** he had an eye operation **2** (mirada): **alzar/bajar la ~** to look up/down **3** (en locs) **a la vista: ponlo bien a la ~** put it where it can be seen easily; **estar/no estar a la ~** to be within/out of sight; **a la ~ de todos** in full view of everyone; **¿tienes algún proyecto a la ~?** do you have any projects in view?; **a primera** *or* **a simple vista** at first sight *o* glance; **con vistas a** with a view to; **en vista de** in view of; **en ~ de que ...** in view of the fact that ...; **¡hasta la vista!** see you!, so long! (colloq); **perder algo/a algn de ~** to lose sight of sth/sb; **perderse de ~** to disappear from view **4** (panorama) view; **con ~ al mar** with a sea view; **~ aérea** aerial view **5** (Der) hearing

vistazo *m* look; **darle** *or* **echarle un ~ a algo** to have a look at sth

viste, visteis ▶ VER²

viste, vistieron, etc ▶ VESTIR

visto¹ -ta *adj* **1** (a) (claro, evidente) obvious, clear; **está/estaba ~ que ...** it is/was clear *o* obvious that ... (b) **por lo visto** (loc adv) apparently **2** [ESTAR] (común, trillado): **un truco que está muy ~** an old trick; **eso ya está muy ~** that's not very original **3** (considerado): **en ciertos**

círculos **eso no está bien ~** in some circles that is not considered correct; **estaba mal ~ que las mujeres fumaran** it was not the done thing *o* it was frowned upon for women to smoke

visto² *m* (a) (Esp) check (AmE), tick (BrE) (b) **visto bueno** approval; **tiene que dar el ~ bueno** she has to give her approval

visto ▶ VESTIR, VER²

vistoso -sa *adj* bright and colorful*

visual *adj* visual; **campo ~** field of vision

vital *adj* **1** (fundamental) vital; **de ~ importancia** of vital importance **2** (a) (Biol, Med) ⟨órgano⟩ vital (*before n*) (b) ⟨persona⟩ dynamic, full of life

vitalicio -cia *adj* ⟨miembro/presidente⟩ life (*before n*); **cargo ~** post held for life

vitalidad *f* vitality

vitamina *f* vitamin

viticultor -tora *m,f* vine-grower

viticultura *f* vine-growing

vitorear [A1] *vt* to cheer

vitral *m* stained-glass window

vitrina *f* (a) (mueble — en tienda) showcase; (— en casa) glass cabinet, display cabinet (b) (AmL) (escaparate) shop window

vitrinear [A1] *vi* (Andes fam) to window-shop

viudez *f* (de mujer) widowhood; (de hombre) widowerhood

viudo -da *adj*: **su madre es** *or* (Esp) **está viuda** her mother is a widow; **(se) quedó ~ a los 40 años** he lost his wife *o* he was widowed when he was 40
■ *m,f* (*m*) widower; (*f*) widow

viva *m*: **dar ~s** to cheer; **fuera se oían ~s** cheering could be heard outside

vivacidad *f* (de persona) liveliness, vivacity; (de ojos) brightness

vivaracho -cha *adj* (a) ⟨ojos⟩ sparkling; ⟨niño⟩ lively (b) (AmL) (espabilado) crafty

vivaz *adj* ⟨persona⟩ lively, vivacious; ⟨ojos⟩ bright; ⟨imaginación⟩ vivid, lively

vivencia *f* experience

víveres *mpl* provisions (*pl*), supplies (*pl*)

vivero *m* (de plantas) nursery; (de peces) hatchery; (de moluscos) bed

viveza *f* (a) (rapidez, agilidad) liveliness; **~ de ingenio** readiness *o* sharpness of wit (b) (de recuerdo) vividness; **lo describió con gran ~** she described it very vividly (c) (de color) brightness; (de ojos, mirada) liveliness, brightness; (de emoción, deseo) strength, intensity

vividor -dora *m,f* pleasure seeker

vivienda *f*: **el problema de la ~** the housing *o* accommodation problem; **un bloque de ~s** an apartment building, a block of flats (BrE); **la construcción de 50 ~s** the construction of 50 homes *o* (frml) dwellings

vivir [I1] *vi* **1** (en general) to live; **vive solo** he lives alone *o* on his own; **~ para algo/algn** to live for sth/sb; **~ en paz** to live in peace; **la pintura no da para ~** you can't make a living from painting; **el sueldo no le alcanza para ~** his salary isn't enough (for him) to live on; **~ DE algo** ⟨de la caridad⟩ to live on sth; ⟨del arte/de la pesca⟩ to make a living FROM sth; ▶ ver tb RENTA **2** (estar vivo) to be alive

3 (*como interj*): ¡viva el Rey! long live the King!; ¡vivan los novios! three cheers for the bride and groom!; ¡viva! hurray!
■ ~ *vt* **(a)** (pasar por): ~ momentos difíciles to live in difficult times; los que vivimos la guerra those of us who lived through the war **(b)** ⟨*personaje/música*⟩ to live **(c)** ⟨*vida*⟩ to live

vivisección *f* vivisection

vivo -va *adj* **1 (a)** (con vida) alive; no quedó nadie ~ no one was left alive; en ~ ⟨*actuación/transmisión*⟩ live **(b)** ⟨*lengua*⟩ living (*before n*) **2 (a)** ⟨*persona*⟩ (despierto, animado) vivacious, bubbly; ⟨*descripción*⟩ graphic; ⟨*relato/imaginación*⟩ lively **(b)** ⟨*color*⟩ bright, vivid; ⟨*llama/fuego*⟩ bright; ⟨*ojos/mirada*⟩ lively, bright **(c)** ⟨*sentimiento/deseo*⟩ intense, strong **3** (avispado, astuto) sharp; no seas tan ~ don't try to be clever
■ *m,f* (oportunista) sharp *o* smooth operator (colloq); (aprovechado) freeloader

vizconde -desa *m,f* (*m*) viscount; (*f*) viscountess

vocablo *m* (frml) word

vocabulario *m* vocabulary; ¡qué ~! what language!

vocación *f* vocation; tiene ~ de músico he has a vocation for music

vocacional *adj* vocational

vocal *adj* vocal
■ *f* **1** (Ling) vowel **2 vocal** *mf* (de consejo, tribunal) member

vocalista *mf* vocalist, singer

vocalizar [A4] *vi* to vocalize

voceador *m* (Col, Méx) (de periódicos) newspaper vendor

vocear [A1] *vt* **(a)** ⟨*mercancías*⟩ to cry (dated); ⟨*noticias*⟩ to shout out **(b)** (hacer público) to spread **(c)** (corear) to shout **(d)** (Méx) ⟨*persona*⟩ to page

vocerío *m* clamor*, shouting

vocero -ra *m, f* (AmL) (*m*) spokesman, spokesperson; (*f*) spokeswoman, spokesperson

vociferar [A1] *vi* to shout, vociferate (frml)

vodevil *m* vaudeville (AmE), variety (BrE)

vodka *m or f* /'bo(ð)ka/ vodka

volado *m* **(a)** (Méx fam) (con moneda): te lo juego a un ~ I'll toss you for it; echar un ~ to toss *o* flip a coin **(b)** (RPl, Ven) (en costura) flounce

volador¹ -dora *adj* flying (*before n*)

volador² *m* (en pirotecnia) rocket

volanta *f* (RPl) horse-drawn carriage

volantazo *m* (Esp, Méx) swerve; dar un ~ to swerve

volante *m* **1** (Auto) steering wheel; ir/ponerse al ~ to be at/to take the wheel **2 (a)** (AmL) (de propaganda) leaflet, flier **(b)** (Esp) (para el médico) referral note *o* slip **3** (en costura) flounce **4** (Dep) shuttlecock

volantín *m* **1** (Chi) (cometa) kite; encumbrar un ~ to fly a kite **2** (Per) (en gimnasia) somersault

volar [A10] *vi* **1** ⟨*pájaro/avión*⟩ to fly **2 (a)** ⟨*tiempo*⟩ to fly; ¡cómo vuela el tiempo! doesn't time fly!; las malas noticias vuelan bad news travels fast **(b) volando** *ger* ⟨*comer/cambiarse*⟩ in a rush, in a hurry; se fue volando he/she rushed off; sus clases se me pasan volando her classes seem to go so quickly

3 (a) (con el viento) ⟨*sombrero*⟩ to blow off; ~on todos los papeles my papers blew all over the place **(b)** (fam) (desaparecer) ⟨*dinero/pasteles*⟩ to vanish, disappear
■ ~ *vt* **1** ⟨*puente/edificio*⟩ to blow up; ⟨*caja fuerte*⟩ to blow **2** (Méx, Ven fam) (robar) to swipe (colloq), to nick (BrE colloq)
■ **volarse** *v pron* **1 (a)** (Col fam) ⟨*preso*⟩ to escape **(b)** (Col, Méx fam) ⟨*alumno*⟩ to play hooky (esp AmE colloq), to skive off (school) (BrE colloq) **2 (a)** (Méx fam) (coquetear) to flirt **(b)** (Méx, Ven fam) (robar) to swipe (colloq), nick (BrE colloq)

volcán *m* volcano

volcánico -ca *adj* volcanic

volcar [A9] *vt* **1 (a)** (tumbar) to knock over **(b)** ⟨*carga*⟩ to tip, dump **(c)** (vaciar) to empty (out) **(d)** (Inf) to dump
■ ~ *vi* ⟨*automóvil/camión*⟩ to overturn, turn over; ⟨*embarcación*⟩ to capsize
■ **volcarse** *v pron* **1 (a)** ⟨*vaso/botella*⟩ to get knocked *o* tipped over **(b)** ▶ **VOLCAR** *vi* **2** (entregarse, dedicarse) ~se A algo ⟨*a tarea*⟩ to throw oneself INTO sth **3** (desvivirse) ~se PARA *or* POR hacer algo to go out of one's way to do sth; ~se CON algn: se ~on conmigo they bent over backwards to make me feel welcome

volea *f* volley

volear [A1] *vt/vi* (Dep) to volley

vóleibol, voleibol *m* volleyball

voleo *m*: a *or* al ~ (al azar) at random; contesté al ~ I said the first thing that came into my head

volibol *m* (Col, Méx, Ven) volleyball

voltaje *m* voltage

volteado -da *adj* (Col, Méx fam & pey) bent (pej), queer (pej)

voltear [A1] *vt* **1 (a)** ⟨*mies*⟩ to winnow; ⟨*tierra*⟩ to turn (over) **(b)** (por el aire) ⟨*toro*⟩ to toss; ⟨*caballo*⟩ to throw
2 (AmL exc CS) **(a)** ⟨*tortilla/disco*⟩ to turn over; ⟨*cuadro*⟩ to turn ... around; ⟨*copa/jarrón*⟩ (poner — boca arriba) to turn ... the right way up; (— boca abajo) to turn ... upside down **(b)** ⟨*calcetín/manga*⟩ (poner — del revés) to turn ... inside out; (— del derecho) to turn ... the right way round; ~ la página to turn the page
3 (AmL exc CS) (dar la vuelta): me volteó la espalda she turned her back on me; al oír su voz volteó la cara when she heard his voice she turned her head
4 (CS) (tumbar, echar abajo) ⟨*bolos/botella*⟩ to knock over; ⟨*puerta*⟩ to knock down
■ **voltearse** *v pron* (AmL exc CS) (volverse, darse la vuelta) to turn around; (cambiar de ideas) to change one's ideas **(b)** (Méx) ⟨*vehículo*⟩ to overturn, turn over

voltereta *f* somersault

voltio *m* volt

voluble *adj* (inconstante) changeable, fickle

volumen *m* **1 (a)** (en general) volume; ~ de ventas volume of sales, turnover; bajar/subir el ~ to turn the volume down/up; a todo ~ on full volume, at full blast (colloq) **2** (tomo) volume

voluminoso -sa *adj* ⟨*paquete*⟩ sizeable, bulky

voluntad *f* **1 (a)** (facultad) will **(b)** (deseo) wish; por expresa ~ de los familiares by express wish of the family; lo hizo por (su) propia ~ he ···⟩

did it of his own free will; **manifestó su ~ de renunciar** he expressed his wish to resign; **por causas ajenas a su ~** for reasons beyond his control **2** ⟨firmeza de intención⟩ *tb* **fuerza de ~** willpower **3** ⟨disposición, intención⟩: **con la mejor ~** with the best of intentions; **agradezco tu buena ~** I appreciate your willingness to help; **mostrar buena ~ hacia algn** to show goodwill to o toward(s) sb

voluntario -ria *adj* (a) ⟨acto/donación⟩ voluntary; **fue una elección voluntaria** I/he did it of my/his own free will (b) ⟨como adv⟩ voluntarily
■ *m,f* volunteer

voluptuoso -sa *adj* voluptuous

volver [E11] *vi* **1** (regresar — al lugar donde se está) to come back; (— a otro lugar) to go back; **no sé a qué hora ~é** I don't know what time I'll be back; **¿cómo vas a ~?** how are you getting back?; **ha vuelto con su familia** she's gone back to her family; **~ A algo** ⟨a un lugar⟩ to go back TO sth; ⟨a una situación/actividad⟩ to return TO sth; **mañana volvemos a clases** tomorrow we go back to school; **quiere ~ al mundo del espectáculo** he wants to return to show business; **volviendo a lo que decía** ... to get o go back to what I was saying ...; **¿cuándo volviste de las vacaciones?** when did you get back from your vacation?; **ha vuelto de París** she's back from Paris
2 «calma/paz» to return; **~ A algo** to return TO sth
3 **volver en sí** to come to o round
■ ~ *v aux*: **~ a empezar** to start again o (AmE) over; **no ~á a ocurrir** it won't happen again; **lo tuve que ~ a llevar al taller** I had to take it back to the workshop
■ ~ *vt* **1** (dar la vuelta) (a) ⟨colchón/tortilla⟩ to turn (over); ⟨tierra⟩ to turn o dig over; ⟨calcetín/chaqueta⟩ (poner — del revés) to turn ... inside out; (— del derecho) to turn ... the right way round; ⟨cuello⟩ to turn; **~ la página** to turn the page (b) ⟨cabeza⟩ to turn; **volvió la mirada hacia mí** he turned his gaze toward(s) me (c) ⟨esquina⟩ to turn
2 (convertir en, poner): **la ha vuelto muy egoísta** it has made her very selfish; **me está volviendo loca** it's/he's/she's driving me mad
3 (Méx) **~ el estómago** to be sick
■ **volverse** *v pron* **1** (girar) to turn (around); **se volvió hacia él** she turned to face him; **no te vuelvas, que nos están siguiendo** don't look back, we're being followed; **se volvió de espaldas** he turned his back on me (o her etc); **~se boca arriba/abajo** to turn over onto one's back/stomach
2 (convertirse en, ponerse): **se ha vuelto muy antipático** he's become very unpleasant; **se vuelve agrio** it turns o goes sour; **se volvió loca** she went mad

vomitar [A1] *vi* to vomit, be sick; **tengo ganas de ~** I think I'm going to vomit o be sick, I feel sick
■ ~ *vt* ⟨comida⟩ to bring up; ⟨sangre⟩ to cough up

vomitarse *v pron* (Col, Méx, Ven) to vomit, be sick

vómito *m* (a) ⟨acción⟩ vomiting; **¿ha tenido ~s?** have you been vomiting o (BrE) sick? (b) ⟨cosa vomitada⟩ vomit

voraz *adj* ⟨persona/animal/apetito⟩ voracious; ⟨incendio/fuego⟩ fierce

vos *pron pers* [*Familiar form of address which is widely used instead of* tú *mainly in the River Plate area and parts of Central America*] **1** (como sujeto, en comparaciones, con preposición) you; **¿quién lo va a hacer? — vos** who's going to do it? — you (are); **che,** ~ hey, you; **~ misma lo dijiste** you said so yourself; **menos que ~** less than you; **para/sin ~** for/without you **2** (uso impersonal) you; **dan tres opciones y ~ elegís** you're given three options and you choose one

vosear [A1] *vt* to address sb using the vos form

voseo *m* use of the vos form instead of tú

vosotros -tras *pron pers pl* [*Familiar form of address not normally used in Latin America or in certain parts of Spain, where* ustedes *is used instead*] you; **¿quién lo va a hacer? — vosotros** who's going to do it? — you (are); **lo podéis hacer ~ mismos** you can do it yourselves; **más que ~** more than you; **para ~** for you

votación *f* ⟨acción⟩ voting; ⟨método⟩ vote; **decidir por ~** to decide by ballot; **fue elegida por ~** she was elected o voted in; **hagamos una ~** let's vote on it; **una ~ a mano alzada** a vote by a show of hands

votante *mf* voter

votar [A1] *vi* to vote; **~ POR algo/algn** to vote FOR sth/sb; **~ A FAVOR DE/EN CONTRA DE algo** to vote FOR/AGAINST sth
■ ~ *vt* ⟨candidato⟩ to vote for; ⟨reforma/aumento⟩ to approve, vote to approve

voto *m* **1** (en general) vote; **~ secreto** secret ballot o vote; **por ~ a mano alzada** by a show of hands; **~ de confianza/censura** vote of confidence/no confidence; **~ en blanco** blank ballot paper; **~ por correo** postal vote, absentee ballot (AmE) **2** (Relig) vow; **hacer los ~s solemnes** to take solemn vows

voy ▶ IR

voyeurista /bwaje'rista, bojer'ista/ *mf* voyeur

voz *f* **1** (en general) voice; **levantar la ~** to raise one's voice; **tener la ~ tomada** to be hoarse; **hablar en ~ baja** to speak quietly; **en ~ alta** ⟨hablar⟩ loudly; ⟨leer⟩ aloud, out loud; **quedarse sin ~** to lose one's voice; **una pieza a cuatro voces** (Mús) a piece for four voices, a four-part piece; **~ activa/pasiva** (Ling) active/passive voice **2** **voces** *fpl* ⟨gritos⟩ shouting, shouts (*pl*); **hablar a voces** to talk in loud voices

vozarrón *m* booming voice

vudú *m* voodoo

vuela, vuelan, etc ▶ VOLAR

vuelco *m* **1** (sobre sí mismo): **dar un ~** «coche» to overturn, turn over; «embarcación» to capsize **2** (cambio radical): **las cosas pueden dar un ~**

things could change *o* alter drastically; **el mercado dio un ~ favorable** the market registered a favorable upturn **3** (Inf) dump

vuelo *m* **1 (a)** (acción): **el ~ de las gaviotas** the seagulls' flight; **remontar el ~** to soar up; *alzar or levantar el* ~ «*pájaro*» to fly away *o* off; «*avión*» to take off; «*persona*» to fly *o* leave the nest; **a ~ de pájaro** (AmL): **un cálculo a ~ de pájaro** a rough estimate; **lo leí a ~ de pájaro** I just skimmed through it **(b)** (Aviac) flight; **son dos horas de ~** it is a two-hour flight; **~ charter/ regular** charter/schedule flight; **~ internacional/ nacional** international/domestic *o* internal flight; **~ sin motor** gliding, soaring (AmE)
2 (en costura) (amplitud): **la falda tiene mucho ~** it is a very full skirt

vuelo ► VOLAR

vuelta *f*
I 1 (a) (circunvolución): **dar ~s alrededor de algo** to go around sth; **da ~s alrededor de su eje** it spins *o* turns on its axis; **dar la ~ al mundo** to go around the world; **todo/la cabeza me da ~s** everything's/my head's spinning; **dar una ~ a la manzana** to go around the block; **dar toda la ~** to go all the way around **(b)** (Dep) (en golf) round; (en carreras) lap; **~ al ruedo** (Taur) lap of honor; **~ ciclista** cycle race, tour **(c)** (en carretera) bend; **el camino da muchas ~s** the road winds about a lot; **el autobús da muchas ~s** the bus takes a very roundabout route
2 (giro): **darle ~ a algo** ‹*a llave/manivela*› to turn sth; **dale otra ~** give it another turn; **el coche dio una ~ de campana** the car turned (right) over; **~ (de) carnero** (CS) somersault; **~ en redondo** (vuelta completa) 360 degree turn, complete turn; (cambio radical) U-turn
3 (a) **darle la ~ a algo** ‹*a disco/colchón*› to turn ... (over); ‹*a calcetín*› (ponerlo — del derecho) to turn ... the right way out; (— del revés) to turn ... inside out; ‹*a copa*› (ponerla — boca arriba) to turn ... the right way up; **dar la ~ a la página** to turn the page, turn over **(b)** (para cambiar de dirección, posición): **dar la ~** (Auto) to turn (around); **darse la ~** to turn (around)

4 (CS) **dar vuelta algo** ‹*disco/colchón*› to turn sth over; ‹*calcetín*› (ponerlo — del derecho) to turn sth the right way out; (— del revés) to turn sth inside out; ‹*copa*› (ponerla — boca arriba) to turn sth the right way up; (— boca abajo) to turn sth upside down; **dar ~ la página** to turn the page, turn over; **dio ~ la cara** she looked away; **¿damos ~ aquí?** (Auto) shall we turn (around) here?; **darse ~** «*persona*» to turn (around); «*vehículo*» to overturn; «*embarcación*» to capsize
5 (paseo): **dar una ~** (a pie) to go for a walk; (en coche) to go for a drive; (en bicicleta) to go for a ride
6 (a) a la vuelta (de la esquina) (just) around the corner **(b) vuelta y vuelta** (Coc) rare
7 (a) (regreso) return; (viaje de regreso) return journey; **a la ~ paramos para almorzar** on the way back we stopped for lunch; **a la ~ se encontró con una sorpresa** when he got back he found a surprise; **¡hasta la ~!** see you when you get back! **(b)** (a un estado anterior) **~ A algo** return TO sth
8 (a) (Esp) (cambio) change; **quédese con la ~** keep the change **(b) vueltas** (Col) (cambio, dinero suelto) change
9 (a) (en elecciones) round **(b)** (de bebidas) round
10 (Per, RPl fam) (vez) time; **de ~** (de nuevo) again
11 (de collar) strand; (en labores de punto) row; (de pantalones) cuff (AmE), turn-up (BrE)

vuelto -ta *pp* ► VOLVER

vuelto *m* (AmL) change; **quédese con el ~** keep the change

vuelva, vuelvas, etc ► VOLVER

vuestro -tra *adj* **(a)** (Esp) (de vosotros) your; **~s libros** your books; **un amigo ~** a friend of yours **(b)** (frml) your; **Vuestra Majestad** Your Majesty
■ *pron* (Esp): **el ~, la vuestra, *etc*** yours; **sabe lo ~** he knows about the two of you

vulcanizadora *f* (Chi, Méx) tire* repairshop

vulgar *adj* **(a)** (corriente, común) common; **un ~ resfriado** a common cold **(b)** (poco refinado) vulgar, coarse **(c)** (no técnico) common, popular

vulgaridad *f* (cualidad) vulgarity, coarseness

vulnerable *adj* vulnerable

Ww

W, w *f* (*read as* /'doβle βe/, /'doβle u/ *or* (Esp) /'uβe/, 'uβe 'doβle/) *the letter* W, w

w. (= watio) w, watt

walkie-talkie /'wo(l)ki 'to(l)ki/ *m* (*pl* **-kies**) walkie-talkie

walkman® /'wo(l)kman/ *m* (*pl* **-mans**) Walkman®

wáter /'(g)water *or* (Esp) 'bater/ *m* **(a)** (inodoro) toilet **(b)** (cuarto) bathroom (esp AmE), toilet (BrE)

waterpolo /'(g)waterpolo/ *m* water polo

WC /'be θe, 'uβe 'δoβle θe/ *m* WC

web /(g)web/ *f or m*: **la** *or* **el web** the Web

weekend /'wiken/ *m* weekend

western *m* (*pl* **~** *or* **-terns**) western

whisky /'(g)wiski/ *m* (*pl* **-kies** *or* **-kys**) whiskey*; **~ americano** bourbon

windsurf /'winsurf/ *m* (deporte) windsurfing; (tabla) windsurfer, sailboard

windsurfing /'winsurfin/ *m* windsurfing

windsurfista /winsur'fista/ *mf* windsurfer

WWW *m* WWW

Xx

X, x *f* (*read as* /'ekis/) *the letter* X, x
xenofobia *f* xenophobia
xenófobo -ba *adj* xenophobic
■ *m,f* xenophobe

xilofón, xilófono *m* xylophone

Yy

Y, y *f* (*read as* /i 'vrjeva/, /je/ *or* (RPl) /ʒe/) *the letter* Y, y

y *conj* **1** (en general) and; **habla inglés y alemán** he speaks English and German; **¡yo gano el dinero y él lo gasta!** I earn the money and he spends it! **2** (a) (en preguntas): **¿y tu padre? ¿qué tal está?** and how's your father?; **yo no oigo nada ¿y tú?** I can't hear anything, can you? **(b)** (fam) (expresando indiferencia) so (colloq); **¿y qué?** so what?; **¿y a mí qué?** so, what's it to me? **3** (esp RPl fam) (encabezando respuestas) well; **¿fuiste? — y sí, no tuve más remedio** did you go? — well yes, I had no choice; **y bueno** oh well **4** (en números, la hora): **cuarenta y cinco** forty-five; **doscientos treinta y tres** two hundred and thirty-three; **la una y diez** ten after (AmE) *o* (BrE) past one

ya *adv* [*Both the simple past* YA TERMINÉ *and the present perfect* YA HE TERMINADO *are used to refer to the recent indefinite past. The former is the preferred form in Latin America while in Spain there is a tendency to use the latter*] **1** (a) (en frases afirmativas o interrogativas) already; **¿~ te has gastado todo el dinero?** have you spent all the money already?; **~ terminé** I've (already) finished; **¿~ ha llegado Ernesto?** has Ernesto arrived yet?, did Ernesto arrive yet? (AmE); **aprietas este botón ¡y ~ está!** you press this button, and that's it! **(b)** (expresando que se ha comprendido) yes, sure (colloq) **2** (a) (en frases negativas) any more; **ese color ~ no se lleva** nobody wears that color any more **(b)** **no ya ... sino** not (just) ... but **3** (enseguida, ahora) right now; **desde ~ te digo que no puede ser** (esp AmL) I can tell you right now that it's not possible; **~ mismo** (esp AmL) right away, straightaway (BrE); **¡~ voy!** coming!; **preparados listos ¡~!** on your mark(s), get set, go! **4** (con verbo en futuro): **~ te contaré** I'll tell you all about it; **~ lo entenderás** you'll understand one day **5** (uso enfático): **¡~ quisiera yo!** I should be so lucky!; **~ era hora** about time (too)!; **¡~ me tienes harta!** I'm (just about) fed up with you! **6** ya que since, as; **~ que estás aquí** since *o* as you're here

■ *conj*: **se puede solicitar ~ sea en persona o por teléfono** it can be ordered either in person or by telephone

yacer [E5] *vi* (frml) to lie (frml)

yacimiento *m* (a) (de mineral) deposit; **~ petrolífero** oilfield **(b)** (Arqueol) site

yámper *m* (Per) jumper (AmE), pinafore dress (BrE)

yanqui *adj* (*pl* **-quis**) (fam) Yankee (colloq)
■ *mf* Yank (colloq), Yankee (colloq)

yapa *f* (CS, Per fam) *small amount of extra goods given free*, lagniappe (AmE); **dar algo de ~** to throw sth in (for free) (colloq)

yate *m* yacht

yayo -ya *m,f* (fam) (*m*) grandpa (colloq), granddad (colloq); (*f*) granny (colloq), grandma (colloq)

yedra *f* ivy

yegua *f* (Zool) mare

yelmo *m* helmet

yema *f* (a) (de huevo) yolk **(b)** (dulce) *sweet made with egg yolk and sugar* **(c)** (del dedo) fingertip **(d)** (Bot) leaf bud

yen *m* yen

yendo ▶ IR

yerba *f* (a) *tb* **~ mate** maté **(b)** (Andes, Méx, Ven fam) (marihuana) grass (sl) **(c)** (césped) grass

yerbatero -ra *adj* maté (*before n*)
■ *m,f* (Andes) (curandero) witch doctor; (que vende hierbas medicinales) herbalist

yerga, yergue ▶ ERGUIR

yerno *m* son-in-law

yerra, yerras, etc ▶ ERRAR

yeso *m* (a) (Art, Const) plaster **(b)** (AmL) (Med) (plaster) cast; **me quitaron el ~** I had my cast taken off

yesquero *m* (Col, RPl, Ven) cigarette lighter

yo *pron pers* (a) (como sujeto) I; **~ que tú** if I were you; **¿quién quiere más? — ¡yo!** who wants some more? — me! *o* I do!; **soy ~** it's me; **¿quién, ~?** who, me?; **~ misma** myself; **estoy cansada — ~ también** I'm tired — so am I *o* me too **(b)** (en comparaciones, con ciertas preposiciones) me; **come más que** ∼ he eats more than me *o* more than I do; **llegó después que** ∼ she arrived after me

yodo *m* iodine

yoga *m* yoga

yogui *m* yogi

yogurt (*pl* **-gurts, yogur**) *m* yogurt, yoghurt

yonqui *mf* (*pl* **-quis**) (fam) junkie (colloq)

yo-yo *m* (*pl* **-yos**) yo-yo

yuca *f* ⟨tubérculo comestible⟩ cassava, manioc; ⟨planta ornamental⟩ yucca

yudo *m* judo

yudoca *mf* judoka, judoist

yugo *m* yoke

Yugoslavia, Yugoeslavia *f* (Hist) Yugoslavia

yugoslavo -va, yugoeslavo -va *adj/m,f* (Hist) Yugoslavian

yugular *adj/f* jugular

yunque *m* anvil

yunta *f* ⟨de bueyes⟩ yoke

yute *m* jute

yuyo *m* **(a)** (Per, RPI) ⟨hierba⟩ herb; **té de** ∼**s** herbal tea **(b)** (RPI) ⟨mala hierba⟩ weed **(c)** (Per) ⟨alga⟩ seaweed

· ·

Zz

· ·

Z, z *f* ⟨read as /'seta/ *or* (Esp) /'θeta/⟩ *the letter* Z, z

zacate *m* (AmC, Méx) **(a)** ⟨hierba⟩ grass; ⟨heno⟩ hay **(b)** ⟨estropajo⟩ scourer

zafar [A1] *vt* **(a)** (Chi, Méx) ⟨brazo/dedo⟩ to dislocate **(b)** (Col, Ven) ⟨nudo⟩ to untie; ⟨tuerca⟩ to unscrew; ⟨persona/animal⟩ to let ... loose
■ **zafarse** *v pron* **(a)** ⟨de compromiso⟩ ∼**se DE algo** to get *o* wriggle OUT OF sth **(b)** ⟨soltarse⟩ «*persona/animal*» to get loose, get away **(c)** (*refl*) (Chi, Méx) ⟨dislocarse⟩ ∼**se la muñeca** to dislocate one's wrist

zafiro *m* sapphire

zaga *f* **(a)** (Dep) defense* **(b) a la zaga** ⟨*ir/ quedarse*⟩ in the rear, behind

zaguán *m* hallway

zalamería *f*: *tb* ∼**s** sweet talk, flattery; **hacerle** ∼**s a algn** to sweet-talk sb

zalamero -ra *adj* ⟨palabras⟩ flattering; **¡qué** ∼ **estás!** you're being very nice (to me)! (iro)

zamarra *f* ⟨chaqueta⟩ leather/sheepskin jacket; ⟨chaleco⟩ leather/sheepskin jerkin

zamba *f* zamba (*South American folk dance*)

zambo -ba *adj* bowlegged
■ *m,f* (AmL) person of mixed black and Amerindian origin

zambomba *f* (Mús) traditional drum-like instrument

zambullida *f* ⟨salto⟩ dive, plunge; ⟨baño⟩ dip

zambullirse [I9] *v pron* ⟨lanzarse⟩ to dive (in); ⟨sumergirse⟩ to duck *o* dive underwater

zamuro *m* (Ven) turkey vulture

zanahoria *adj* **(a)** (RPI fam) ⟨tonto⟩ stupid **(b)** (Ven fam) ⟨anticuado⟩ square (colloq)
■ *mf* **(a)** (RPI fam) ⟨tonto⟩ idiot, nerd (colloq) **(b)** (Ven fam) ⟨mojigato⟩ straitlaced person; ⟨anticuado⟩ old fogey (colloq)
■ *f* (Bot, Coc) carrot

zanca *f* leg

zancada *f* stride; **bajaba la cuesta a** ∼**s** he came striding down the hill

zancadilla *f* trip; **me hizo** *or* (Esp) **puso una** ∼ he tripped me (up)

zancos *mpl* stilts (*pl*)

zancuda *f* wader, wading bird

zancudo¹ -da *adj* **(a)** ⟨ave⟩ wading (*before n*) **(b)** (fam) ⟨persona⟩ long-legged

zancudo² *m* ⟨típula⟩ crane fly, daddy longlegs; ⟨mosquito⟩ (AmL) mosquito

zángano -na *m,f* **1** (fam) ⟨persona⟩ lazybones (colloq) **2 zángano** *m* ⟨abeja⟩ drone

zanja *f* ⟨para desagüe⟩ ditch; ⟨para cimientos, tuberías⟩ trench; ⟨acequia⟩ irrigation channel

zanjar [A1] *vt* ⟨polémica/diferencias⟩ to settle, resolve; ⟨deuda⟩ to settle, pay off

zapallito *m* (CS): *tb* ∼ **largo** *or* **italiano** zucchini (AmE), courgette (BrE)

zapallo *m* (CS, Per) pumpkin

zapata *f* (Auto, Mec) brake shoe

zapateado *m* **(a)** (en general) ▶ ZAPATEO **(b)** ⟨baile⟩ zapateado (*type of Flamenco dance*)

zapatear [A1] *vi* **(a)** (en danza) to tap one's feet; (más fuerte) to stamp (*in time to the music*) **(b)** (para protestar, vitorear) to stamp (one's feet)

zapateo *m* tapping; (más fuerte) stamping

zapatería *f* **(a)** ⟨tienda⟩ shoe store (AmE), shoe shop (BrE) **(b)** ⟨taller — de fabricación⟩ shoemaker's, cobbler's; ⟨— de reparación⟩ shoe repairer's, cobbler's

zapatero -ra *m,f* shoemaker, cobbler

zapatilla *f* **(a)** ⟨de lona⟩ canvas shoe; ⟨para deportes⟩ sneaker (AmE), trainer (BrE); ⟨alpargata⟩ espadrille; ⟨para ballet⟩ ballet shoe; ⟨pantufla⟩ slipper **(b)** (Méx) ⟨zapato de mujer⟩ lady's shoe; ∼ **de piso** flat shoe

zapato *m* shoe; ∼**s bajos/de tacón** low-heeled/ high-heeled shoes; ∼ **de cordón** lace-up shoe; ∼ **de goma** (Ven) sneaker (AmE), trainer (BrE)

zaperoco *m* (Ven fam) riot

zar *m* tsar, czar

Zaragoza *f* Saragossa

zarandear [A1] *vt* ⟨de un lado a otro⟩ to shake; ⟨para arriba y para abajo⟩ to shake *o* jog up and down
■ **zarandearse** *v pron* (esp AmL) «*tren*» to ⋯⁖

Z

shake around; «*barco*» to toss about; **nos
zarandeamos mucho durante el vuelo** we got
shaken around *o* buffeted a lot during the flight

zarape *m* (en AmC, Méx) serape (*colorful
blanket-like shawl worn esp by men*)

zarcillo *m* [1] (arete) earring [2] (Bot) tendril

zarina *f* czarina

zarpa *f* (a) (Zool) paw (b) (fam) (mano) paw (colloq)

zarpar [A1] *vi* to set sail, weigh anchor

zarpazo *m* (de gato, león) swipe; **me dio un** ∼ it
took a swipe at me (with its paw)

zarza *f* bramble, blackberry bush

zarzamora *f* (fruto) blackberry; (arbusto)
bramble, blackberry bush

zarzo *m* (Col) loft, attic

zarzuela *f* (Espec, Mús) *traditional Spanish
operetta*

zenit *m* zenith

zeppelin /sepeˈlin, θepeˈlin/, **zepelín** *m*
zeppelin, airship

zeta *f*: name of the letter z

zigzag *m* (*pl* **-zags** *or* **-zagues**) zigzag

zigzaguear [A1] *vi* to zigzag

zinc *m* zinc; **techo de chapa de** ∼ corrugated
iron roof

zíper *m* (AmC, Méx, Ven) zipper (AmE), zip (BrE)

zócalo *m* [1] (rodapié) baseboard (AmE), skirting
board (BrE) [2] (Méx) (plaza) main square

zodíaco, zodiaco *m* zodiac

zombi *mf* zombie

zona *f* [1] (área, región) area; **fue declarada** ∼
neutral it was declared a neutral zone; **⑤ zona de
carga y descarga** loading and unloading only; ∼
comercial commercial district; ∼ **de castigo**
penalty area; ∼ **industrial** industrial park; ∼
peatonal pedestrian precinct; ∼ **roja** (AmL) (zona
de prostitución) red-light district; ∼ **verde** park,
green space [2] (en baloncesto) free-throw lane,
three-second area

zonzo -za *m,f* (AmL fam) idiot, fool

zoo *m* zoo

zoología *f* zoology

zoológico *m* zoo, zoological garden (frml)

zoólogo -ga *m,f* zoologist

zoom /sum, θum/ *m* zoom (lens)

zopenco -ca *adj* (fam) stupid, idiotic
■ *m,f* (fam) blockhead (colloq)

zopilote *m* (AmC, Méx) turkey vulture

zoquete *adj* (fam) dim, dense (colloq)
■ *mf* (fam) (persona) dimwit (colloq), blockhead
■ *m* (CS) (Indum) sock, ankle sock

zorra *f* (fam & pey) (prostituta) whore (colloq & pej),
tart (colloq & pej); *ver tb* ZORRO 1A, 2

zorrillo *m* (AmL) (mofeta) skunk

zorro -rra *m,f* [1] (a) (Zool) (*m*) fox; (*f*) vixen
(b) (AmC, Méx fam) (oposum) opossum [2] (fam)
(persona astuta) sly *o* crafty person [3] **zorro** *m*
(piel) fox (fur); *ver tb* ZORRA

zorzal *m* thrush

zozobrar [A1] *vi* [1] «*barco*» (hundirse) to
founder; (volcar) to capsize [2] «*proyecto/negocio*»
to founder

zueco *m* clog

zumbar [A1] *vi* «*insecto*» to buzz; «*motor*» to
hum, whirr; **pasar zumbando** «*bala/coche*» to
whizz by; **me zumbaban los oídos** my ears were
buzzing *o* ringing
■ ∼ *vt* [1] (fam) (persona) to give … a good hiding
(colloq) [2] (Ven fam) (tirar) to chuck (colloq), to throw

zumbido *m* (de insecto) buzzing, droning; (de
motor) humming, whirring

zumo *m* (esp Esp) juice

zurcir [I4] *vt* to darn, mend

zurdo -da *adj* left-handed; (futbolista) left-footed;
(boxeador/lanzador) southpaw (*before n*)
■ *m,f* left-handed person; (tenista) left-hander;
(boxeador) southpaw

zurra *f* (fam) (good) hiding (colloq)

zurrar [A1] *vt* (fam) to wallop (colloq), to give … a
(good) thrashing *o* hiding (colloq)

zurrón *m* (de pastor) leather bag; (de cazador)
hunter's pouch

Calendario / Calendar
The Spanish-speaking world
Vida y cultura
Letters / Cartas

Calendario de días festivos, fiestas y tradiciones en Gran Bretaña y EEUU / Calendar of traditions, festivals, and holidays in Spanish-speaking countries

January

[1]	8	15	22	29
(2)	9	16	23	30
3	10	17	24	31
4	11	18	(25)	
◇5	12	19	26	
[6]	13	◇20	27	
7	14	21	28	

February

1	8	15	22
[2]	9	16	23
◇3	10	17	24
4	11	18	25
5	12	19	◇26
6	13	20	27
7	(14)	◇21	28

March

(1)	8	15	22	29
2	9	16	23	30
3	10	(17)	24	31
4	11	18	25	
5	12	19	26	
6	13	20	27	
7	14	21	28	

April

(1)	8	15	22	29
2	9	16	[23]	30
3	10	17	24	
4	11	18	25	
5	12	19	26	
6	13	20	27	
7	◇14	21	28	

May

[1]	8	15	22	29
2	9	16	23	30
3	10	17	24	31
4	11	18	◇25	
◇5	12	19	26	
6	13	20	27	
7	14	21	28	

June

1	8	15	22	29
2	9	16	23	30
3	10	17	◇24	
4	11	18	25	
5	12	19	26	
6	13	◇20	27	
7	14	21	28	

July

1	8	15	22	29
2	◇9	16	23	30
3	10	17	24	31
(4)	11	18	◇25	
◇5	12	19	26	
6	13	20	27	
7	14	21	◇28	

August

1	8	15	22	29
2	9	16	23	30
3	◇10	◇17	24	31
4	11	18	◇25	
5	12	19	26	
◇6	13	20	27	
7	14	21	28	

September

1	8	◇15	22	29
2	9	16	23	30
3	10	17	24	
4	◇11	◇18	25	
5	12	19	26	
6	◇13	20	27	
7	14	21	28	

October

1	8	15	22	29
2	9	16	23	30
3	10	17	24	[31]
4	11	18	25	
5	[12]	19	26	
6	13	20	27	
7	14	21	28	

November

1	8	15	22	29
2	9	16	23	(30)
3	◇10	17	24	
4	(11)	18	25	
(5)	12	19	26	
6	13	◇20	27	
7	14	21	28	

December

1	8	15	22	29
◇2	9	16	23	30
3	10	17	(24)	[31]
4	11	18	[25]	
5	12	19	(26)	
6	13	20	27	
7	14	21	◇28	

□ Celebrated in Spanish and English-speaking countries / Celebrado en países de habla española e inglesa

◇ Celebrated in Spanish-speaking countries / Celebrado en países de habla española

○ Celebrated in English-speaking countries / Celebrado en países de habla inglesa

1 January Año Nuevo (New Year's Day). A public holiday in all Spanish-speaking countries.

5 January (Mexico) **Día de la Constitución** (Constitution Day). A public holiday.

6 January **Día de Reyes** (Epiphany/Twelfth Night). In many Spanish-speaking countries, this is when presents are given, rather than on Christmas Day.

20 January San Sebastián (Saint Sebastian's Day). Celebrated in Spain with parades, sporting events, and bullfights, it is also a day of celebration and dancing for the people of the Basque city that bears the name of the saint.

2 February La Candelaria (Candlemas). An occasion for celebrations and parades in many Spanish-speaking countries.

3 February Fiesta de San Blas (patron saint of Paraguay). A public holiday.

21 February (Mexico) **Anniversary of the birth of Benito Juárez**, a famous nineteenth-century statesman, who was twice president. A public holiday.

26 February Aberri Eguna - Basque national day and a public holiday in the Basque country of Spain.

12 - 19 March Las Fallas are one of the best known *fiestas* in Spain. They are held in Valencia in eastern Spain. The high point of the celebration is on the last night, when the *cabezudos* (carnival figures with large heads), which have been carefully prepared by the *falleros*, are paraded through the streets and then burned, all this to the accompaniment of an enormous fireworks display.

14 April (Paraguay) **Día de la Independencia**. A public holiday.

23 April San Jordi The feast day of Catalonia's patron saint. According to custom, women give men books and men give women roses on this Catalan version of St Valentine's Day.

1 May **Día del Trabajo** (Labor Day). A public holiday in all Spanish-speaking countries.

5 May (Mexico) The anniversary of the victory of the state of Puebla against the French invasion of 1862. A public holiday.

25 May (Argentina) The anniversary of the May revolution of 1810.

20 June (Argentina) **Día de la Bandera** (Argentinian National Day). A public holiday.

(Colombia) **Día de la Independencia**. A public holiday.

24 June San Juan (Feast of St John). Traditionally fires are lit on the night of San Juan in order to keep away the cold of winter. In some places, people jump over the fires and in others the faithful will try to walk through them barefoot. The custom is slowly dying out, but continues in many parts of the Spanish-speaking world.

5 July (Venezuela) **Día de la Independencia**. A public holiday.

6 - 14 July Sanfermines. The festival of *el encierro* (the 'running of the bulls'), takes place in Pamplona in northern Spain. The animals are released into the barricaded streets and people run in front of them, in honor of the town's patron saint, San Fermín, who was put to death by being dragged by bulls.

9 July (Argentina) **Día de la Independencia**. A public holiday.

25 July Fiesta de Santiago (Feast of St James). The famous *Camino de Santiago*, the pilgrimage of thousands of people from all over Spain and many other parts of Europe to the holy city of Santiago de Compostela, takes place in the week leading up to St James' Day, 25 July. The city also has its *fiestas* around this time. The streets are full of musicians and performers for two weeks of celebrations culminating in the *Festival del Apóstol*.

28 July (Peru) **Día de la Independencia**. A public holiday.

6 August (Bolivia) **Día de la Independencia**. A public holiday.

10 August (Ecuador) **Primer Grito de Independencia**. A public holiday commemorating the first cry of independence in 1809.

17 August (Argentina) A public holiday to celebrate the anniversary of the death of the San Martín who liberated Argentina from Spanish rule in 1816.

25 August (Uruguay) **Día de la Independencia**. A public holiday.

11 September **Día Nacional de Cataluña**. Catalonian National Day and a public holiday in Catalonia.

Calendario / Calendar

13 September (Mexico) Commemoration of the *Niños Héroes* (child heroes) who fell while defending the castle of Chapultepec against European invaders in 1847.

15 September (Mexico) **Conmemoración de la Proclamación de la Independencia**. Throughout the country, at 11 o'clock at night, there is a communal shout, *El Grito*, in memory of Padre Hidalgo's cry of independence from the Spanish in the town of Dolores.

18 September (Chile) **Día de la Independencia**. A public holiday.

12 October **Día de la Hispanidad**. A public holiday, this is also **Columbus Day**, which is celebrated in all Spanish-speaking countries, as well as the US, in commemoration of the discovery of the Americas by Christopher Columbus in 1492. In Spanish-speaking countries of the Americas, it is also called the **Día de la Raza** (literally, Day of the Race) in celebration of the *mestizaje*, the mingling of races, which gave birth to the populations of today.

31 October **Todos los Santos** (All Saints). People all over the Spanish-speaking world flock to the cemeteries on this and the following day *el día de los Difuntos/Muertos* to put flowers on the graves of relatives and friends and to remember the dead. In Mexico this is an important festival in which Catholic traditions are mixed with those of pre-Hispanic religions.

10 November (Argentina) **Fiesta de la Tradición**. This festival takes place throughout the country but is especially important in the town of San Antonio de Areco, near Buenos Aires. The capital also holds a festival in November, the **Semana de Buenos Aires**, in honor of its patron saint San Martín de Tours.

20 November (Mexico) **Día de la Revolución de 1910**. A public holiday to celebrate the revolution of 1910.

2 December (Mexico) **Virgen de Guadalupe**. Celebrations are held in honor of the patron saint of the country, with music and dancers, in particular the *concheros*, who dance, wearing bells around their ankles, to the sound of stringed instruments and conches.

25 December **Navidad** (Christmas Day). A time of great religious celebration in all Spanish-speaking countries. In many places, re-enactments of the nativity are held, with a variety of traditions, parades, and costumes.

28 December **Día de los Inocentes**. This is the equivalent to April Fool's Day. In most Spanish-speaking countries it is a day for playing tricks on people. And if you trick someone into lending you money for that day, you keep it and tell them *que te lo paguen los Santos Inocentes* (let the Holy Innocents pay you back).

31 December **La noche de Fin de Año**. This is often the occasion for parties, and at midnight the New Year is welcomed with much noise and merrymaking. In Spain and in many other Spanish-speaking countries, the families gather together twelve seconds before midnight *para tomar las uvas* (to see the New Year in by eating one grape on each chime of the clock) for good luck.

Movable feasts and holidays

Martes de Carnaval. (Shrove Tuesday). The last Tuesday before the beginning of *Cuaresma* (Lent). *Carnaval* is celebrated in many Spanish-speaking countries just before this date. In many places, there are masked balls and parades. The biggest in Spain are those of Cádiz, on the south coast, and Madrid, where a strange ceremony called *el entierro de la sardina* (literally the burial of the sardine) takes place. In Mexico, the best-known are in Veracruz and Mazatlán.

Pascua (Easter) - **Semana Santa** (Holy Week). The week leading up to Easter Sunday is the most important time of religious celebration throughout the Spanish-speaking world. In many places, there are processions in which statues of Christ or the Virgin Mary, often covered in jewels and flowers, are carried to the church.

Seville's famous **Feria de abril** (April festival) takes place in the week following Easter. The site of the *feria* is decked out with hundreds of *casetas* or small marquees, hired by companies or private individuals, in which people entertain, eat *tapas*, drink *manzanilla* (a pale dry sherry), play music, and dance *sevillanas*, the popular dances of Andalucía. Many people dress up in colorful traditional costumes, some of them on horseback or in horse-drawn carriages.

Corpus Christi - 9 weeks after Easter is celebrated in most Spanish-speaking countries with religious parades.

1 de enero
New Year's Day (día de Año Nuevo).
El primero de enero es festivo y normalmente
es un día tranquilo en el que la gente se
recupera de los festejos de la
noche anterior.

2 de enero
Día festivo en Escocia.

6 de enero
Epiphany o Twelfth night (Día de Reyes).
No hay ninguna costumbre en especial
relacionada con este día, pero
tradicionalmente se guarda el árbol de
Navidad junto con el resto de los adornos
navideños.

25 de enero
Burns Night. Es el aniversario del
nacimiento del poeta escocés Robert Burns en
el siglo XVIII. Los escoceses preparan una
cena llamada *Burns Supper*, cuyo plato
principal se llama *haggis* (estómago de oveja
relleno con una mezcla de avena, hígado y
otras vísceras, cebollas y especias) y que es
acompañado a la mesa por un gaitero (*piper*)
que toca la gaita escocesa.

2 de febrero
Groundhog Day. Según la tradición
estadounidense, la pequeña marmota
(*groundhog*) sale de su madriguera en este día,
luego de su hibernación. Si está soleado y ve
su sombra, regresa a su madriguera, y habrá
otras seis semanas de tiempo invernal. Si no
ve su sombra, la primavera comenzará
temprano.

14 de febrero
St Valentine's Day. En el día de San Valentín
los enamorados se intercambian flores
y regalos.También es tradicional mandarle
una tarjeta anónima a alguien que le guste
a uno.

1 de marzo
St David's Day. San David es el santo patrono
de Gales.

17 de marzo
St Patrick's Day. San Patricio es el santo
patrono de Irlanda, es día festivo y se celebra
por todos los irlandeses con música y bebida
en cantidad.

1 de abril
April Fools' Day (día de los Inocentes).
Se gastan muchas bromas en este día, los
que son objeto de ellas, se llaman *April Fools*.

23 de abril
St George's Day. San Jorge es el santo
patrono de Inglaterra.

4 de julio
Independence Day. Día festivo en los Estados
Unidos para celebrar el Día de la
Independencia con desfiles, fuegos artificiales
y banderas. La gente se reúne haciendo
comidas al aire libre y parrilladas o asados.

12 de octubre
Columbus Day. Día festivo en los Estados
Unidos, en el que se conmemora el
descubrimiento de América por Cristóbal
Colón en 1492.

31 de octubre
Halloween (víspera de Todos Santos).
Ocasión en la que se mezcla la religión con
antiguas creencias paganas. Los niños se
disfrazan de fantasmas y brujas y visitan
casas de la vecindad jugando a la "broma
o golosina" (*trick or treat*). Si los vecinos no les
dan dinero o golosinas, los niños les gastan
una broma. En los Estados Unidos, las
familias suelen hacer una fiesta de disfraces.

5 de noviembre
Bonfire Night/Guy Fawkes. Se conmemora
en Gran Bretaña el intento frustrado por parte
de Guy Fawkes de hacer volar el Parlamento
en 1605. Se tiran fuegos artificiales y se hacen
enormes fogatas en las que se quema una
efigie llamada '*guy*'.

11 de noviembre
Remembrance Day, en Estados Unidos,
Veterans' Day. El día en que se conmemora el
armisticio de 1918, y se recuerdan los caídos en
las dos guerras mundiales y otros conflictos
más recientes. También se lo conoce en Gran
Bretaña como el día de la amapola (*Poppy
Day*), ya que la gente lleva prendida una
amapola roja de papel como signo
recordatorio.

30 de noviembre
St Andrew's Day. San Andrés es el santo
patrono de Escocia.

25 de diciembre
Christmas Day (el día de Navidad). Es
día festivo. Se intercambian regalos alrededor
del árbol de Navidad, y en muchas casas los
niños, al despertar, encuentran en su cama
una media llena de regalitos y golosinas que,
según la tradición, deja *Father Christmas*,
también conocido como *Santa Claus*.

26 de diciembre
Boxing Day en Gran Bretaña, **St Stephen's
Day** en Irlanda. Día festivo en ambos países.

31 de diciembre
New Year's Eve (la noche de Fin de Año)
llamada **Hogmanay** en Escocia, país donde se
acostumbra ir a visitar a amigos y vecinos

a medianoche, para comer y beber hasta las primeras horas de la mañana. Antiguamente era tradicional llevar un pedazo de carbón como símbolo de buena suerte.

Fiestas móviles

El tercer lunes de febrero, es el día de los Presidentes (**Presidents' Day**) en Estados Unidos. Es día festivo en el que se celebran los nacimientos de George Washington y Abraham Lincoln.

Shrove Tuesday (martes de Carnaval) es el último día de carnaval antes del comienzo de la Cuaresma el miércoles de Ceniza. Tradicionalmente se comen creps o panqueques.

El cuarto domingo de la Cuaresma en Gran Bretaña y el segundo domingo de mayo en Estados Unidos, es el día de la Madre (**Mother's Day** o **Mothering Sunday**). Las madres suelen recibir tarjetas y pequeños regalos de sus hijos.

El tercer domingo de junio es el día del Padre (**Fathers' Day**) en el que los padres suelen recibir tarjetas y pequeños regalos de sus hijos.

Good Friday el Viernes Santo. Se celebra en la iglesia, es día festivo.

Easter Sunday (el Domingo de Pascua). La gente religiosa va a la iglesia. A los niños se les dan huevos de Pascua.

Easter Monday. El lunes siguiente al Domingo de Pascua es día festivo en Gran Bretaña e Irlanda.

El primer lunes de mayo (**Early May Bank Holiday**) es día festivo en Gran Bretaña e Irlanda

Whitsun o **Pentecost.** El domingo de Pentecostés es el séptimo después de la Pascua de Resurrección (**Easter Sunday**). Se celebra solamente en la iglesia.

El lunes siguiente solía ser día festivo en Gran Bretaña, pero ha sido reemplazado por el último lunes del mes de mayo (**Spring Bank Holiday**).

El último lunes de agosto (**Late Summer Bank Holiday**) es día festivo en Inglaterra, Gales e Irlanda del Norte.

El primer lunes de septiembre es el día del Trabajo (**Labor Day**) en Estados Unidos. Es día festivo y se celebra con desfiles.

Thanksgiving (el día de Acción de Gracias) en Estados Unidos, es el cuarto jueves de noviembre. Es un día de festejos tanto religiosos como familiares, que culmina con una gran comida consistente en un pavo acompañado con batatas y salsa de arándano, seguido de un pastel de calabaza.

Advent El período que incluye los cuatro domingos previos a la Navidad. Por tradición, los niños tienen calendarios de Adviento (*Advent Calendars*), con pequeñas 'ventanitas' de papel que contienen ilustraciones navideñas y algunas veces golosinas.

A-Z of the Spanish-speaking countries of the world

Argentina

Official Name: The Argentine Republic
Capital: Buenos Aires
Currency: peso
Area: 1,073,809 square miles
(2,780,092 square kilometers)
Population: 35,672,000 (1997 estimate)

The second largest country in South America, Argentina is one of the continent's leading agricultural and industrial nations. Its main exports are meat and grain, and, more recently, minerals.

Colonized by Spain in the sixteenth century, Argentina declared independence in 1816. It has a history of political and economic instability, with periods under military rule. In 1982, Argentina's claim to the Falkland Islands/Malvinas led to an unsuccessful war with Britain. The governing military dictatorship was subsequently ousted, and a democratic government elected in 1983.

Argentina has a directly elected president who can hold office for a maximum of two four-year terms. The legislature (Congreso) consists of a Chamber of Deputies with 257 members who are elected by universal adult suffrage for a period of four years, and a Senate whose members are chosen by legislative elections. Under the amended Constitution of 1994, the Senate will eventually have 72 members who will hold office for 6 years. The country is divided into 22 provinces, the Federal District of Buenos Aires, and the National Territory of Tierra del Fuego. There is an elected governor and legislature for each of these.

The Argentine population is mostly of European origin. A wide number of European languages are spoken in addition to Spanish, including Italian, French, German, and English.

Bolivia

Official Name: Republic of Bolivia
Administrative capital: La Paz
Judicial and legal capital: Sucre
Currency: boliviano
Area: 424,162 square miles
(1,098,580 square kilometers)
Population: 7,767,000 (1997 estimate)

A landlocked country in South America, Bolivia's main topographical feature is the *altiplano*, a plateau between the east and west chains of the Andes. This has a clear atmosphere, and is suited to growing cereals and potatoes, and rearing livestock. Bolivia's major products are petroleum, zinc, tin, silver, gold, and lead; the main cash crops are soya beans, sugar, chestnuts, and coffee. Considerable amounts of coca are also grown illegally.

Bolivia was part of the Inca empire before coming under Spanish rule. It was freed from Spain in 1825, and named after the great Latin American liberator Simón Bolívar.

After independence, Bolivia lost land, including its coastline, to surrounding countries. Since then, it has been plagued by poverty and political instability. Bolivia's President and Congress are elected by universal adult suffrage. The President holds office for five years whilst the 130 members of the Chamber of Deputies, and the 27 members of the Senate, who together comprise the Congress, are elected for a four-year term. The President holds executive power and appoints the Cabinet. Each of the country's nine administrative departments is governed by a prefect appointed by the President.

Bolivia has a very large indigenous population. Aymara and Quechua are spoken in addition to Spanish.

The Spanish-speaking world

Chile

Official Name: The Republic of Chile
Capital: Santiago
Currency: peso
Area: 292,132 square miles
(756,622 square kilometers)
Population: 14,622,000 (1997 estimate)

Chile occupies a long strip down the Pacific coast of South America. Mines in the desert north produce copper, iron ore, and nitrate of soda, while the central region, where most of the country's population lives, is also the main agricultural area, producing grain, fruit, and vegetables. The south is rich in forest and grazing land.

Most of Chile belonged to the Inca empire, becoming part of the Viceroyalty of Peru under Spanish rule. Chilean independence was proclaimed in 1810 by Bernardo O'Higgins, and finally achieved in 1818. The country expanded northward in the War of the Pacific (1879-1883), gaining land from Bolivia and Peru.

In 1973 the government of the Marxist democrat Salvador Allende was overthrown. Chile was then ruled by a military dictatorship until March 1990, when a democratically elected president took office.

Chile's President and Congress are elected by universal adult suffrage. The President holds office for six years. The legislature (Congreso Nacional) consists of a Chamber of Deputies with 120 members and a Senate with 47 members. The President holds executive power and appoints the Cabinet. The country is divided into 12 regions and a metropolitan area.

Colombia

Official Name: The Republic of Colombia
Capital: Bogotá
Currency: peso
Area: 440,365 square miles
(1,140,105 square kilometers)
Population: 40,214,723 (1997 estimate)

Situated in the extreme north-west of South America, Colombia has Pacific and Atlantic coastlines, plus islands in the Pacific and Caribbean. Its chief products are minerals, particularly petroleum, coal, and natural gas, as well as coffee and tobacco. Illegal trading in cocaine is also widespread.

Colombia was conquered by Spain in the early sixteenth century, and became independent in the early nineteenth century, as part of the Republic of Gran Colombia. In 1830 Venezuela, then Ecuador, broke away; the remaining state, New Granada, changed its name to Colombia in 1863.

With a constitution dating from 1886, Colombia is the second oldest democracy in the western hemisphere. However, it suffered civil war between 1949 and 1968, and since then there has been open conflict between its government and drug traffickers who monopolize the world trade in narcotics.

Colombia's President and Congress are elected for four years by universal adult suffrage. The legislature (Congreso) consists of a House of Representatives with 161 members, and a Senate with 102 members. The President holds executive power and appoints the Cabinet. The country is divided into 32 Departments and a Capital District.

Costa Rica

Official Name: The Republic of Costa Rica
Capital: San José
Currency: colón
Area: 19,707 square miles
(51,022 square kilometers)
Population: 3,464,000 (1997 estimate)

Costa Rica, on the Isthmus of Panama, is a heavily forested, mainly agricultural country, whose exports include bananas, coffee, cocoa beans, sugar, and beef. Its coastal regions have a tropical climate, while the central, highland region is more temperate. The population is mostly of European origin.

Colonized by Spain in the early sixteenth century, Costa Rica became independent in 1823, within the Federation of Central America. It emerged as a separate country in 1838. Since then it has been one of Central America's most stable and prosperous states.

Costa Rica's President and Legislative Assembly are elected by universal adult suffrage for four years. The successful presidential candidate must obtain at least 40% of the vote. The unicameral Legislative Assembly has 57 members. The President has executive power and appoints the Cabinet.

Costa Rica has civil and rural guards, but abolished the army in 1948.

Cuba

Official Name: The Republic of Cuba
Capital: Havana/La Habana
Currency: peso
Area: 42,820 square miles
(110,860 square kilometers)
Population: 11,059,000 (1997 estimate)

Cuba is the largest island in the West Indies. It has a tropical climate and a landscape ranging from rolling plains to 2,000-meter high mountains. Its main export is sugar.

One of Spain's first colonies, Cuba became independent in 1898, but was under heavy North American influence. In 1959, after years of political instability including several dictatorships, Communist rebels, led by Fidel Castro, seized power.

The politics of Castro's government, coupled with Cuba's proximity to the USA, antagonized the USA, which made various attempts to oust Castro, and blockaded the island. This made Cuba heavily reliant on the USSR until the break-up of the Soviet Union in 1991. The Communist party is Cuba's only authorized political party. The sole legislative authority is the National Assembly of People's Power, consisting of 601 Deputies elected by direct vote for five years. It in turn elects 31 of its members to form the Council of State, whose President is both Head of State and Head of Government. The National Assembly also appoints, on the proposal of the head of State, the executive and administrative authority, the Council of Ministers. There are also municipal, regional, and provincial assemblies.

Dominican Republic/República Dominicana

Capital: Santo Domingo
Currency: peso
Area: 18,704 square miles
(48,442 square kilometers)
Population: 8,190,000 (1997 estimate)

The Dominican Republic forms the eastern part of the Caribbean island of Hispaniola. It is a mountainous country with a tropical climate. Its main exports are sugar, coffee, cocoa beans, tobacco, meat, ferronickel, gold, and silver. Columbus discovered Hispaniola in 1492, and it became a Spanish colony. In 1697 the island was split when Spain ceded its western third (now Haiti) to France. The eastern part was re-named Santo Domingo. The Dominican Republic was proclaimed in 1844.

The Republic has had a turbulent history, including a 31-year dictatorship from 1930 to 1961. This was followed by civil war and US military intervention, until a new, democratic constitution was introduced in 1966.

The Republic's President and Congress are elected by universal adult suffrage for four years. The legislature (Congreso Nacional) consists of a Chamber of Deputies with 149 members and a Senate with 30 members. The President holds executive power and appoints the Cabinet. The country is divided into 26 provinces, each with its own appointed Governor, and a Distrito Nacional, which contains the capital.

Ecuador

Official Name: The Republic of Ecuador
Capital: Quito
Currency: sucre
Area: 109,484 square miles
(270,670 square kilometers)
Population: 12,174,628 (1998 estimate)

Ecuador, on the Pacific coast of South America, is a largely agricultural country, dependent on exports of coffee, bananas, and shrimp. Its coastal plain, in the west, is separated from the tropical jungles of the Amazon by ranges and plateaux of the Andes.

Originally part of the Inca empire,

The Spanish-speaking world

Ecuador was conquered by Spain in 1534, finally gaining independence in 1822, as part of the Republic of Gran Colombia. In 1830 it became a separate state. It has since lost territory in border disputes with neighbouring Peru and Colombia. In 1832, the Galapagos Islands were added to its territory.

Constitutionally, Ecuador's President and Congress are elected by universal adult suffrage. The President holds office for one four-year term only.

The legislature is the unicameral Congress, 12 members of which are elected nationally for four years, the remaining 65 being elected provincially for one two-year term. The President holds executive power and appoints the Governors of the 21 provinces.

El Salvador

Official Name: The Republic of El Salvador
Capital: San Salvador
Currency: colón
Area: 8,260 square miles (21,393 square kilometers)
Population: 5,118,599 (1992)

El Salvador, on the Pacific coast of Central America, is dominated by volcanic mountain ranges running from east to west. Most of its population lives in the subtropical valleys of the central region. Its economy is mainly agricultural, the chief crops being coffee, cotton, and sugar cane. It also exports shrimp and honey.

Conquered by Spain in 1524, El Salvador became independent in 1821, and joined the Federation of Central America in 1824, emerging as a separate republic in 1839.

For many years El Salvador was ruled by a small number of wealthy landowners; a peasant rebellion in 1932 was brutally suppressed. In 1972, following a military coup, the country dissolved into a vicious civil war, marked by killings by right-wing death squads, and left-wing guerrilla resistance. A peace accord was finally agreed in 1992.

El Salvador's President and National Assembly are elected by universal adult suffrage. The President holds office for five years. The legislature is the unicameral National Assembly whose 84 members are elected for 3 years. The President holds executive power and appoints the Council of Ministers.

Guatemala

Official Name: The Republic of Guatemala
Capital: Guatemala City/Ciudad de Guatemala
Currency: quetzal
Area: 42,056 square miles (108,889 square kilometers)
Population: 10,928,000 (1996 estimate)

Situated in the north of Central America, Guatemala consists of a narrow coastal plain, separating the Pacific from a heavily-populated highland region, and a short Caribbean coastline. The north is densely forested. The main exports are coffee, sugar, bananas, meat, shrimp, and petroleum.

Guatemala has one of the highest indigenous populations in Latin America.

A former center of Mayan civilization, Guatemala was conquered by Spain in 1523-24. After independence it formed the core of the Federation of Central America before becoming a republic in its own right in 1839.

Guatemala's history since then has often been marked by dictatorship and revolution, with conflict since the 1960s between the military and rural guerrilla movements. After a succession of military governments, an elected president took office in 1985.

The President and Congress are elected for four years by universal adult suffrage. The legislature is the unicameral National Congress consisting of 80 members, 16 of whom are elected nationally and the remaining 64 departmentally. The President holds executive power and appoints the Cabinet. The country is divided into 22 Departments.

Honduras

Official Name: The Republic of Honduras
Capital: Tegucigalpa
Currency: lempira
Area: 43,294 square miles
(112,088 square kilometers)
Population: 5,294,000 (1994 estimate)

The landscape of Honduras combines tropical lowlands with more temperate regions in the mountain ranges that cross the country's interior from north to south. Its main exports are bananas, coffee, sugar, fruit, grain, shrimp, and beef. Discovered by Columbus in 1502, Honduras was governed by Spain from 1524 until it became independent in 1821. Since then it has suffered from years of instability, making it one of the most poorly developed countries in Latin America.

Under the 1982 Constitution the President and National Assembly are elected by universal adult suffrage.

The President holds office for a single four-year term. The legislature is the unicameral National Assembly consisting of 128 members.

The President holds executive power. If the amended Constitution of 1997 is adopted, the National Assembly will be reduced to 80 members. The country is divided into 18 Departments.

Mexico/México

Official Name: The United Mexican States
Capital: Mexico City/México
Currency: peso
Area: 756,200 square miles
(1,958,200 square kilometers)
Population: 94,400,000 (1997 provisional estimate)

Bordering the USA, Mexico is by far the largest country in Central America. Its topography ranges from low desert plains and tropical lowlands to high plateaux. The climate varies with altitude, the coastal lowlands and the tropical southern region being hot and wet and the highlands of the central plateau temperate.

Mexico has large reserves of petroleum and many other minerals including zinc, silver, and copper, and fluorite. A large part of its export earnings comes from these; it also exports cotton, coffee, sugar, shrimp, fruit, and vegetables. Tourism is a principal source of foreign exchange with an estimated 10.1 million people visiting Mexico in 1998.

The center of Aztec and Mayan civilization, Mexico was conquered by the Spanish in the early sixteenth century. It became independent in 1821. In 1836 Texas rebelled and broke away; Mexico's remaining territory north of the Río Grande was lost to the USA in the Mexican War of 1846-48. Half a century of political instability followed until the presidency of Porfirio Díaz, which began in 1876, and, with a brief interruption, went on until 1911. Civil war broke out in 1910 leading to partial political reform. Mexican politics since 1946 have been dominated by the PRI (Partido Revolucionario Institucional).

Mexico is a federal republic made up of 31 federal states and a Federal District, which contains the capital.

The President is elected by universal adult suffrage for six years.

The legislature is the Congress which consists of the Chamber of Deputies and the Senate. The Chamber of Deputies has 500 members, directly elected for three years, whilst the Senate has 128 members, directly elected for six years at the same time as the President.

The President has executive power and appoints the Cabinet. Each state has its own constitution, its own governor, elected for six years, and an elected chamber of deputies.

Education, which is free in state schools, is officially compulsory between the ages of six and twelve. Numbers of children enrolled in secondary schools are increasing steadily.

Nicaragua

Official Name: The Republic of Nicaragua
Capital: Managua
Currency: córdoba
Area: 46,448 square miles
(120,254 square kilometers)
Population: 4,357,099 (1995)

Nicaragua in Central America extends over a central mountain range, from the Atlantic to the Pacific coastlines. It has a tropical climate and its chief exports are coffee, cotton, bananas, sugar, meat, and shellfish.

Sighted by Columbus in 1502, and colonized by Spain in the early sixteenth century, Nicaragua gained independence in 1821, becoming a separate republic in 1838 after brief membership of the Federation of Central America.

Since then the country's history has been marked by border disputes, internal disturbances, and resistance to political and economic domination by the USA. In 1979, the left-wing Sandinistas overthrew the dictatorship of Anastasio Somoza, an event that led to a US-sponsored counter-revolutionary campaign.

The Sandinistas were defeated in democratic elections in 1990.

Nicaragua's President is elected by popular vote for five years.

The legislature is the unicameral National Assembly whose members are elected by universal adult suffrage, also for five years. The President holds executive power and appoints the Cabinet.

Panama/Panamá

Official Name: The Republic of Panama
Capital: Panama City/Ciudad de Panamá
Currency: balboa
Area: 29,773 square miles
(77,082 square kilometers)
Population: 2,719,000 (1997 estimate)

Situated on the isthmus connecting North and South America, Panama is mostly agricultural, its chief exports being bananas, coffee, fish, sugar, and clothing. It has tropical lowlands on the coasts, separated by an interior mountain range. The population is mostly of mixed Spanish and Indian stock, with West Indian and indigenous Indian minorities. Colonized by Spain in the early sixteenth century, Panama became independent in 1821 and joined the Republic of Gran Colombia, then became a province of Colombia. It gained full independence in 1903.

Construction of the Panama Canal was completed by the USA in 1914. The surrounding territory, the Canal Zone, was leased to the US until 1977, splitting Panama in two. The Canal was owned and operated by the United States until the Panama treaties, which went into effect in 1979, provided for its operation by the Panama Commission, a US government agency, until 31 December 1999, when the United States transferred ownership of the Canal to Panama.

Panama's President and Legislative Assembly are elected for five years by universal adult suffrage. The unicameral Legislative Assembly has 72 members. The President holds executive power, is assisted by two elected Vice-Presidents, and appoints the Council of Ministers and the Governors of the provinces. The country is divided into nine provinces and three autonomous Indian Reservations.

Paraguay

Official Name: The Republic of Paraguay
Capital: Asunción
Currency: guaraní
Area: 157,108 square miles
(406,752 square kilometers)
Population: 5,085,000 (1997 estimate)

Paraguay is an inland country in South America. The north-west of Paraguay is part of the flat, desolate and sparsely-populated Chaco region, while the south-east is cooler, wetter, and more developed, with farming communities and huge cattle ranches. Its main exports are soy bean seeds, cotton, timber, and meat. Paraguay achieved independence from Spain in 1811. Between 1865 and 1870, it lost over half its population in the war against Brazil, Argentina, and Uruguay. It gained territory from Bolivia in the Chaco War of 1932-35 but the country has remained largely undeveloped, with a low standard of living.

In 1954, General Alfredo Stroessner seized power in a military dictatorship that lasted until 1989, when he was overthrown by a military coup. Since then, Paraguay has had a turbulent history, marked by struggles for power within the democratic system.

Under the 1992 Constitution, the President and Congress are elected by universal adult suffrage. The President holds office for five years as do the 80 members of the Chamber of Deputies, and the 45 members of the Senate, who together comprise Congress, the legislature. The President holds executive power and appoints the Council of Ministers. The country is divided into 17 departments, each with its own elected governor.

Peru/Perú

Official Name: The Republic of Peru
Capital: Lima
Currency: sol
Area: 496,414 square miles
(1,285,216 square kilometers)
Population: 24,371,000 (1997 estimate)

Peru, on the Pacific coast of South America, has a narrow coastal plain with a dry desert climate, separated from the tropical lowlands of the Amazon by the Andes. Sheep, cattle, llamas, and alpacas are bred in mountain districts. Its main exports are fish meal, lead, zinc, copper, iron ore, and silver.
Peru was the center of the Inca empire, and still has a large indigenous population, with Quechua as well as Spanish being an official language. It was conquered for Spain by Pizarro in 1532, liberated between 1820 and 1824, and established as a democratic republic.
The War of the Pacific (1879-83) resulted in the loss of territory to Chile.
In recent years, Peru's stability has been threatened by the activities of guerrilla groups, notably Sendero Luminoso (Shining Path). Cultivation of the coca plant in the valleys of the Andes has also led to problems related to the narcotics trade.
Peru's President and two Vice-Presidents are elected by universal adult suffrage. The President holds office for five years. The legislature is the unicameral Congreso, consisting of 120 members, elected for five years by a single national list system. The President holds executive power and appoints the Council of Ministers. The country is divided into 25 departments.

Puerto Rico

Capital: San Juan
Currency: US dollar
Area: 3,460 square miles
(8,959 square kilometers)
Population: 3,833,000 (1998 estimate)

Puerto Rico is a mountainous island in the West Indies, partly of volcanic origin and partly formed of limestone. Its main exports are chemicals, electronic goods, clothing, fish, rum, and tobacco products. Visited by Columbus in 1493, Puerto Rico was one of the earliest Spanish settlements. In 1898, after the Spanish-American War, it was ceded to the USA. In 1952 it was established as a commonwealth in voluntary association with the USA, with full powers of local government. Since then there has been a great deal of political wrangling, both with the USA and within Puerto Rico, with a number of moves being made towards the island's transition to full statehood within the USA.
Industrialization and progress in social welfare have given Puerto Rico one of the highest standards of living in Latin America. Nevertheless many Puerto Ricans have emigrated to the United States. Spanish and English are the official languages.
According to the present self-governing commonwealth status, the Governor, the Legislative Assembly, and the Resident Commissioner are elected by universal adult suffrage for four years.
The legislature is the Legislative Assembly consisting of the House of Representatives, which has 54 members, and the Senate, which has 28 members. The Resident Commissioner represents Puerto Rico in the US House of Representatives but is allowed to vote only in committees.
Puerto Ricans have American citizenship, but only those resident in the USA can participate in presidential elections.

The Spanish-speaking world

Spain/España

Official Name: The Kingdom of Spain
Capital: Madrid
Currency: peseta
Area: 194,959 square miles
(505,750 square kilometers)
Population: 39,371,147 (1998 estimate)

Mainland Spain comprises the greater part of the Iberian Peninsula in south-west Europe. It is bounded by France to the north and by Portugal to the west. The kingdom also includes the Canary Islands in the Atlantic, the Balearic Islands in the Mediterranean, and Ceuta and Melilla in North Africa. Much of the interior consists of a high plateau (*meseta*). There are also mountain ranges in the north and south. Summers are hot throughout most of the country and particularly in the south. Winters are cold in the mountains and on the central plateau. The principal language is Castilian Spanish, but Catalan is widely spoken in the north-east, Basque in the north, and Galician in the north-west. There is no official state religion, but the vast majority of the population is Catholic.

Spain has industrialized rapidly in recent years and is now one of the world's largest car exporters.

Other important industries are steel, chemicals, shipbuilding, textiles, and footwear. However, the country is still predominantly agricultural, producing grain, citrus fruits, vegetables, olives, and wine. The Spanish fishing fleet is one of the largest in the world.

Conquered successively by the Carthaginians, Romans, Visigoths, and Moors, Spain was reunited as an independent country at the end of the fifteenth century. It emerged as a European and world power in the sixteenth century, but declined thereafter, losing most of its empire in the early nineteenth century.

The Moorish occupation, which lasted for over 700 years, left behind it a rich architectural heritage, particularly to be seen in Andalusia, in the very south of the country, in such celebrated buildings as the Alhambra in Granada, the Alcázar in Seville, and the great *mezquita* (mosque) of Córdoba.

Political instability in the nineteenth and early twentieth century finally led to the Civil War of 1936-39, resulting in the dictatorship of General Francisco Franco.

Democracy followed Franco's death in 1975 and the succession of King Juan Carlos as Head of State. The first democratic elections after the Franco era were held in 1977, and a constitutional hereditary monarchy re-established. Liberalization and decentralization of the state followed. In 1986, Spain joined the European Economic Community. Since then the country has modernized increasingly rapidly. Transportation systems are fast and efficient, and the big cities, notably Barcelona, have seen programmes of architectural redevelopment which are widely regarded as being amongst the most innovative in Europe.

The Franco era, during which the Basque, Catalan, and Galician languages were banned, saw the rise of increasingly vociferous separatist movements.

The process of regional self-government was initiated in 1967, but the first autonomous parliaments, in the Basque Country and Catalonia, were not established until 1980. The Galician parliament was elected in October 1981 and the Andalusian parliament in 1982. The process of devolution was completed in 1983 with the election of the remaining 13 parliaments. However, extreme separatist movements are still active, notably in the Basque country and, to a much lesser extent, in Catalonia. These have the support of only a small minority of the local populations, but ETA, the Basque separatist organization has frequently resorted to violence in its attempt to gain complete independence from Spain.

Under the 1978 Constitution, the King is Head of State and appoints the Prime Minister and, on the latter's recommendation, the other members of the Council of Ministers. The legislature is the Cortes Generales, consisting of the Congress of Deputies, which has 350 members, and the Senate, which has 208 members. In both cases, election is by direct universal adult suffrage for four years. The Senate has in addition 48 regional representatives, elected by the autonomous regional parliaments. These regional parliaments have varying degrees of autonomy, and each is elected by direct universal adult suffrage for four years.

Spain has a comprehensive system of social welfare and National Insurance is compulsory for all employed or self-employed citizens. Education is compulsory between the ages of six and sixteen, with around 30% of children attending private schools, the vast majority of which are administered by the Roman Catholic Church. In some autonomous regions, for example Catalonia, teaching of the regional language is compulsory in all schools.

Uruguay

Official Name: The Oriental Republic of Uruguay
Capital: Montevideo
Currency: peso
Area: 68,063 square miles
(176,215 square kilometers)
Population: 3,221,000 (1997 estimate)

Uruguay, on the Atlantic coast of South America, comprises an extensive range of well-watered grassy plains and low hills. This, together with a temperate climate, makes most of the country suitable for raising livestock. Its chief exports are live animals, meat, hide, wool, and fish. Although Uruguay was not permanently settled by Europeans until the seventeenth century, the Uruguayan population is now predominantly of European origin. Its proximity to Brazil made it a focus of Spanish-Portuguese rivalry. It was liberated from Spain in 1825. It remained relatively backward in the nineteenth century, but emerged in the early twentieth century as South America's first welfare state. Civil unrest beginning in the 1960s, and particularly fighting against the Marxist Tupamaro guerrillas, led to a period of military rule, but civilian government was restored in 1985.

Uruguay's President and Congress are elected by universal adult suffrage. The President holds office for five years, as do the 99 Deputies of the Chamber of Representatives and the 31 members of the Senate, who together comprise the Congress. The President holds executive power and appoints the Council of Ministers. The country is divided into 19 departments.

Venezuela

Official Name: The Republic of Venezuela
Capital: Caracas
Currency: bolivar
Area: 352,279 square miles
(912,050 square kilometers)
Population: 22,777,000 (1997 estimate)

Venezuela is in northern South America, with a Caribbean coastline. It has mountains in the north-west (Cordillera de Mérida) and south-east (the Guyana Highlands), between which lie the extensive plains (*llanos*) of the interior. Its chief exports are oil, iron ore, aluminum, steel, coffee, and cocoa. Visited by Columbus in 1498, Venezuela was given its name, meaning 'little Venice', by early Italian explorers when they saw Amerindian houses built on stilts over water, and were reminded of Venice. It was settled by the Spanish in the sixteenth century, becoming independent in 1821 as part of the Republic of Gran Colombia. It emerged as a separate nation in 1830.

Since then, Venezuela's political history has been characterized by instability, civil war, and dictatorships. It is however now a functioning democracy, with a well-developed social welfare system.

Venezuela is a federal republic made up of 22 states, a Federal District which contains the capital, and 72 Federal Dependencies. The President and the Congress are elected for five years by universal adult suffrage. The legislature is the Congress, consisting of the Chamber of Deputies and the Senate. The President has executive power and appoints the Council of Ministers. Each state has a directly elected governor and an elected legislature.

····································

La vida y cultura británicas y estadounidenses desde la 'A' a la 'Z'

····································

ABC - American Broadcasting Company
Una de las principales cadenas de televisión norteamericanas, actualmente propiedad de la compañía Walt Disney.

ACT - American College Test
Una prueba que los estudiantes de la mayor parte de los estados que forman Estados Unidos tienen que aprobar para ser admitidos en la universidad. Normalmente tiene lugar al final de la **HIGH SCHOOL** y cubre un número de materias principales, que incluye inglés y matemáticas.

African-American
Este es el término de más amplia aceptación hoy en día en Estados Unidos para referirse a americanos de origen africano.

Afro-Caribbean
Este es el término de más amplia aceptación hoy en día, tanto en Gran Bretaña como en Estados Unidos, para referirse a gente con antepasados africanos que procede del Caribe o que vive allí.

A level - Advanced level
Un examen sobre una asignatura en particular que tiene lugar en Inglaterra y Gales, en el último año de la enseñanza secundaria (*secondary school*), cuando el estudiante tiene alrededor de 18 años. Los alumnos que aspiran a avanzar hacia la educación terciaria (*higher education*), se presentan normalmente a 3 ó 4 *A levels*. La nota final (*grade*) se da independientemente para cada materia. Las universidades u otras instituciones seleccionan a los alumnos en razón de las notas que hayan obtenido, especialmente en aquellas materias que tienen relación directa con el área de estudio terciario que se ha elegido.

Alliance Party
Un partido político de Irlanda del Norte que reúne a personas de opiniones moderadas y cuyo objetivo es conseguir la resolución del conflicto existente entre grupos religiosos extremistas.

American Indian ▶ NATIVE AMERICAN.

AS level - Advanced Supplementary level
Un examen sobre una materia particular que muchos estudiantes de Inglaterra y Gales hacen, normalmente a los 18 años, en el último año del colegio secundario (*secondary school*). Este examen se sitúa entre el nivel del **GCSE** y del **A LEVEL**. Vale la mitad de un *A level* a la hora de solicitar una vacante en la universidad.

Asian-American
Este es el término de más amplia aceptación hoy en día para referirse a norteamericanos de origen asiático, especialmente del Extremo Oriente.

BBC - British Broadcasting Corporation
Una de las principales cadenas de televisión y radiodifusión británicas. Se creó por cédula real en 1927. No se financia a través de la publicidad, sino que con los ingresos provenientes del pago de una licencia anual que se debe obtener para poder utilizar un receptor de televisión. Tiene la obligación de informar de un modo imparcial.

• •

bed and breakfast
También puede verse anunciado como *Bed & Breakfast* o *B&B* y se encuentran por toda Gran Bretaña. Es un sistema de alojamiento en casas privadas o pequeños hoteles por el cual se paga un precio, normalmente razonable, por una habitación por persona y por noche, más un desayuno de jugo, cereales, huevos fritos con panceta y tostadas con mermelada de naranja. A veces, también, suele referirse al establecimiento donde se otorga este servicio.

Big Issue - The Big Issue
Una revista que la gente sin hogar vende en las calles de muchas ciudades de Gran Bretaña. Los artículos cubren normalmente temas de carácter social y a menudo son de alta calidad. Los vendedores compran la revista a uno de los centros de la organización que edita la revista, y luego la venden a un precio superior acordado previamente. Se les permite conservar este margen de ganancia para que de esta forma puedan mantenerse sin tener que mendigar.

broadsheet
Es cualquier periódico de formato grande que se publica en Gran Bretaña, a diferencia de un **TABLOID** cuyas páginas son de un formato más pequeño. El formato grande está generalmente asociado a un periódico serio, mientras que el más pequeño es utilizado por periódicos de temática popular.

BT
La compañía telefónica más grande de Gran Bretaña. El servicio telefónico británico fue el primer servicio público que se privatizó (en 1984). Inicialmente conocida como *British Telecom*, cambió su nombre a *BT* en 1991. Actualmente hay varias compañías telefónicas privadas operando en Gran Bretaña.

busking
Es una palabra del inglés coloquial para referirse a la práctica de cantar o tocar un instrumento en la calle y otros lugares públicos como una forma de conseguir dinero. Las personas que lo hacen se llaman *buskers* y es frecuente encontrar a algunos de ellos en las grandes ciudades de Gran Bretaña.

Cabinet
El gabinete (ministerial) del gobierno británico es un cuerpo formado por unos 20 ministros (*ministers*) nombrados por el Primer Ministro (*Prime Minister*) y que se reúne regularmente para discutir asuntos administrativos y de política gubernamental. Cada uno de los ministros es responsable de un área en particular, mientras que a la totalidad del gabinete le atañe decidir acerca de la política a seguir por el gobierno. El líder del principal partido de la oposición también nombra un gabinete, llamado a veces gabinete en la sombra (**SHADOW CABINET**), con el objeto de que pueda gobernar en caso de que el gobierno sea derrotado, normalmente como resultado de unas elecciones generales.

Capitol
La sede del Congreso de Estados Unidos, situada en *Capitol Hill*, en Washington DC.

CBS - Columbia Broadcasting System
Una de las tres primeras compañías de radio y televisión nacionales norteamericanas. Las otras dos son **ABC** y **NBC**.

Channel Five
Un canal de televisión comercial británico que emite programas de entretenimiento de contenido ligero y popular.

Channel Four
Un canal de televisión comercial británico que emite una amplia variedad de programas de interés social y cultural. Su buen prestigio proviene del hecho de que produce documentales de gran calidad y da cobertura a acontecimientos artísticos y culturales.

Vida y cultura

• •

City - The City
Es el área que se encuentra dentro de los límites de la antigua ciudad de Londres.
Hoy en día es el centro financiero y de negocios de la capital, y es el lugar donde tienen sus
oficinas centrales muchos bancos e instituciones financieras. A menudo, cuando se habla
de *The City*, se está refiriendo a estas instituciones y no a la zona propiamente dicha.

City Technology College (CTC)
Un tipo de colegio británico de educación secundaria (*secondary education*) que ha sido el
resultado de una asociación entre el gobierno y diversas compañías. Están situados en
zonas urbanas, normalmente en el centro de ciudades, y dan especial importancia a la
enseñanza de ciencias y tecnología.

CNN - Cable News Network
Una compañía de televisión norteamericana que emite programas de noticias e
información vía satélite, las veinticuatro horas del día.

college of further education (CFE)
Un tipo de colegio universitario (*college*) de Gran Bretaña que ofrece cursos a tiempo
completo y a tiempo parcial para estudiantes de más de 16 años. Su programa incluye
cursos de preparación para los **GCSE**s y **A LEVEL**s así como clases diurnas y nocturnas
en una amplia variedad de materias.

community college
Una clase de universidad norteamericana que ofrece una variedad de cursos de tipo
práctico, especialmente orientados a la población local.

community service
Trabajo organizado y no remunerado que se realiza en beneficio de la comunidad. Puede
consistir en proporcionar ayuda a los ancianos, a las personas discapacitadas o en llevar a
cabo reparaciones en edificios comunitarios u otras instalaciones. En el caso de delitos
menores, este tipo de trabajo se suele dar a delincuentes, en lugar de enviarlos a la cárcel.

comprehensive school
Un colegio británico de educación secundaria con gran número de alumnos de todo nivel,
cuyas edades fluctúan entre 11 y 18 años.

Congress
El Congreso es el organismo nacional legislativo de Estados Unidos. Se reúne en el
CAPITOL y está compuesto por dos cámaras, el Senado (**SENATE**) y la Cámara de
Representantes (**HOUSE OF REPRESENTATIVES**). La función del Congreso es elaborar
leyes. Toda nueva ley debe ser aprobada primero por las dos cámaras y posteriormente por
el Presidente (**PRESIDENT**).

Conservative Party
El Partido Conservador es uno de los principales partidos políticos británicos. Se sitúa a la
derecha del espectro político que apoya el sistema capitalista, la libre empresa y la
privatización de la industria y los servicios públicos. Surgió alrededor de 1830 como
resultado de la evolución del *Tory Party* y a menudo se le denomina aún por este nombre.

council
El ayuntamiento (*council*) es un organismo, elegido por todos los ciudadanos, responsable
del gobierno local en áreas tales como un condado (**COUNTY**), parte de un condado, una
ciudad pequeña o parte de una ciudad grande del Reino Unido. Debe mantener en buen
estado los caminos y las instalaciones de uso comunitario, así como el mantenimiento de
un amplio número de servicios.

council tax
Impuesto que los habitantes de un inmueble deben pagar, en Gran Bretaña, a la
municipalidad local. La cantidad que debe pagarse se calcula tomando como base el valor
estimado de la vivienda, y el número de personas que viven en ella.

. . . .

county
Una región administrativa de Gran Bretaña que agrupa un número de distritos (*districts*). Los condados son las principales unidades administrativas de Gran Bretaña y muchos tienen demarcaciones que se remontan a muchos años atrás. Sin embargo, en las últimas décadas, estas se han cambiado mucho como también sus nombres, y el término '*county*' a menudo ya no se usa.

Democratic Party
El Partido Demócrata es uno de los dos principales partidos políticos de Estados Unidos. El otro es el Partido Republicano (**REPUBLICAN PARTY**). El Partido Demócrata está considerado como el propulsor de políticas más liberales, especialmente referidas a temas que afectan a la sociedad. Por esta razón, consigue el apoyo de sindicatos y grupos minoritarios.

Downing Street
Es el nombre de una calle del barrio de Westminster, en el centro de Londres. El número 10 de Downing Street es la residencia oficial del Primer Ministro y el número 11 la del *Chancellor of the Exchequer* (equivalente al cargo del Ministro de Economía y Hacienda). Los periodistas utilizan a menudo las expresiones *Downing Street* o *Number 10* para referirse al despacho del Primer Ministro.

DUP – Democratic Unionist Party ▶ ULSTER DEMOCRATIC UNIONIST PARTY.

elementary school
En los Estados Unidos, un colegio que imparte una educación formal en los primeros niveles de enseñanza. Es el equivalente a un colegio de enseñanza primaria. Estos colegios están dirigidos a niños de edades comprendidas entre seis y doce o trece años. Este nivel de enseñanza se denomina también *grade school*.

football pools
Juego de apuestas muy popular en Gran Bretaña, similar a las quinielas en España y al prode en Argentina. Consiste en intentar acertar los resultados de los partidos de fútbol, llenando unos cupones (*pools coupons*). El premio, que se junta con el dinero que se paga por cada apuesta, se reparte entre aquellos que más se han acercado al resultado. Puede suceder que una sola persona se lleve todo el premio.

further education
En Gran Bretaña, el término *further education* se utiliza normalmente para referirse cualquier tipo de enseñanza dirigida a personas de edad superior a los 16 años, edad mínima en que se puede dejar la escolaridad obligatoria, y que no están en la universidad, en cuyo caso se habla de *higher education*. Sin embargo, en los Estados Unidos, el término *further education* también se utiliza para referirse a la educación universitaria.

Gaelic
Es la lengua de origen celta que hablan algunas personas en Escocia (e Irlanda). El gaélico escocés solo lo hablan unas 40.000 personas que viven en las *Highlands* y en las islas del oeste de Escocia.

GCSE - General Certificate of Secondary Education
Un examen sobre una materia en particular que tiene lugar, en Inglaterra y Gales, en el quinto año de la enseñanza secundaria (*secondary school*), cuando el estudiante tiene alrededor de 16 años. Todos los alumnos, sea cual sea su nivel de habildad, pueden presentarse a este examen y la mayoría lo hace en varias asignaturas. Las nota final (*grade*) se da en forma independiente para cada materia. Los que deseen seguir estudiando para presentarse más tarde a los exámenes de **A LEVEL**, necesitan tener un cierto número de *GCSE*s. También se pueden presentar a una mezcla de *GCSE*s y de **GNVQ**.

Vida y cultura

· ·

GNVQ - General National Vocational Qualification

Un examen sobre una materia en particular que tiene lugar en Inglaterra y Gales, en el quinto año de la enseñanza secundaria (*secondary school*), cuando el estudiante tiene alrededor de 16 años. Estos exámenes fueron introducidos en 1992, como una alternativa a los del **GCSE,** en un número de materias de orientación más práctica o vocacional. Tiene como objeto preparar a los alumnos para el mundo laboral. Muchos estudiantes se presentan a una mezcla de *GNVQ*s y *GCSE*s.

GP - General Practitioner

Es un médico de medicina general (también llamado a menudo *family doctor*), que trata a todo tipo de pacientes dentro de una localidad de Gran Bretaña. Es el equivalente al médico de cabecera. En un consultorio (*surgery*) suelen atender varios médicos (*group practice*), y los pacientes que están registrados en ese consultorio pueden ser atendidos por el médico de su elección. Los pacientes de la Seguridad Social (**NATIONAL HEALTH SERVICE**) tienen atención gratuita. Cada consultorio tiene financiación directa o indirecta del gobierno. Cuando es necesario, un médico puede remitir a un paciente a un especialista o arreglar su hospitalización.

grade school ▶ ELEMENTARY SCHOOL

graduate school

Especialmente en Estados Unidos, departamento de una universidad que ofrece cursos avanzados para los que quieren seguir estudiando y/o investigando una vez que han obtenido un título, normalmente después de realizar 3 ó 4 años de estudios universitarios.

grammar school

En áreas de Inglaterra y Gales, un tipo de colegio de enseñanza secundaria (*secondary school*) que admite a alumnos de 11 ó 12 años que han aprobado una prueba de aptitud. Desde 1965, estos colegios han sido reemplazados en su mayor parte por los **COMPREHENSIVE SCHOOL**s.

green card

Un documento oficial que autoriza a una persona que no es ciudadana americana a residir y trabajar en Estados Unidos. Este permiso es obligatorio para cualquiera que desee ir a ese país a residir de forma permanente y trabajar.

Greyhound bus

Vehículo que pertenece a la mayor compañía de autobuses de los Estados Unidos (*The Greyhound Lines Company*). Circulan entre ciudades y grandes poblaciones a través de toda la geografía estadounidense y son muy usados por la gente joven y los turistas, quienes a menudo recorren grandes distancias en ellos.

Guardian Angels

Una organización formada por jóvenes en Estados Unidos, creada para proteger a la población de la delincuencia. Sus miembros llevan gorras rojas y camisas que tienen el eslogan *Dare to Care* (que viene a expresar la idea de 'Atrévete a preocuparte por los demás'). Trabajan en colaboración con la policía y no van armados.

high school

El último ciclo del colegio secundario en Estados Unidos, generalmente para alumnos cuyas edades fluctúan entre los 14 y 18 años. En Gran Bretaña, algunos colegios secundarios también se llaman *high schools*.

House of Commons

La Cámara de los Comunes es la cámara baja del Parlamento británico o **HOUSES OF PARLIAMENT**. Los parlamentarios (*Members of Parliament*), que son elegidos por el pueblo, se reúnen aquí para debatir temas de política internacional y nacional de actualidad y para votar a favor o en contra de la nueva legislación.

. . . .

House of Lords

La Cámara de los Lores es la cámara alta del Parlamento británico o **HOUSES OF PARLIAMENT**. Sus miembros no son elegidos por el pueblo, sino que son nombrados por los partidos políticos. Hasta 1999 un número de los cargos eran hereditarios. Su función es discutir y posteriormente aprobar o sugerir cambios a la legislación que ha sido aprobada en la Cámara de los Comunes (**HOUSE OF COMMONS**). Es también el último tribunal de apelación.

House of Representatives

La Cámara de Representantes es la cámara baja del Congreso (**CONGRESS**) de Estados Unidos. Está formada por 435 representantes (**REPRESENTATIVE**s) que son elegidos cada dos años. Cada estado de la unión tiene un número de representantes proporcional a su población. Esta cámara es la encargada de introducir nueva legislación, por lo que toda nueva ley debe ser aprobada por ella.

Houses of Parliament

Son las dos cámaras del Parlamento británico, la Cámara de los Comunes (**HOUSE OF COMMONS**) y la Cámara de los Lores (**HOUSE OF LORDS**). El Palacio de Westminster (*Palace of Westminster*), que es el grupo de edificios situados en el centro de Londres donde se reúnen los miembros de las dos cámaras, también se conoce con este nombre.

independent school

Un colegio de Gran Bretaña que no recibe dinero alguno del estado y se autofinancia mediante el pago de cuotas por parte de los padres. Los **PUBLIC SCHOOL**s y los **PREPARATORY SCHOOL**s están dentro de esta categoría.

infant school

Un colegio de Gran Bretaña que ofrece los tres primeros años de educación formal. A menudo forma parte de un **PRIMARY SCHOOL**, que junto al **JUNIOR SCHOOL** cubren la educación del niño hasta los 11 años. En Gran Bretaña los niños deben empezar la educación a los cinco años.

International Herald Tribune - The International Herald Tribune

Un periódico estadounidense de difusión internacional. Su equipo editorial está basado en París y se publica en 180 países. Tiene una gran reputación por la seriedad y profundidad con la que cubre la información. Es un periódico de formato grande (**BROADSHEET**).

Internet

Algunos sitios Web en inglés :
CNN Interactive http://www.cnn.com; **BBC** http://www.bbc.co.uk; **New York Times** http://www.nytimes.com; **The Times** http://www.the-times.co.uk; **Museum of Modern Art** http://www.moma.org

interstate (highway)

En Estados Unidos, una ruta nacional de larga distancia que cruza de un estado a otro. Están señalizadas con un símbolo rojo y azul que lleva la letra 'I' seguida del número de la ruta. Las que van de norte a sur tienen números impares y las que van de este a oeste tienen números pares. Cada calzada tiene cuatro carriles.

IRA – Irish Republican Army

El IRA (Ejército Republicano Irlandés) es la rama militar del **SINN FEIN**. Su objetivo es la unión de la República de Irlanda e Irlanda del Norte. Declaró el alto el fuego en 1994 y luego en 1997.

ITV - Independent Television

Un grupo de compañías de televisión que emiten en el Canal 3 de la televisión británica. Ofrecen quince programaciones diferentes para quince regiones distintas del Reino Unido. Cada programación incluye sus propios programas y noticias, aunque también efectúan muchas transmisiones en común.

• •

Jobcentre
Es una oficina que proporciona diversos servicios a aquellas personas que están buscando trabajo, servicios tales como anunciar las vacantes de empleo que se producen en un área determinada y concertar entrevistas con los que ofrecen trabajo. Estas oficinas se pueden encontrar en la mayor parte de las poblaciones británicas y están dirigidas por el gobierno a través del *Employment Service*.

junior high school
En Estados Unidos, un colegio que cubre la educación entre el **ELEMENTARY SCHOOL** y el **HIGH SCHOOL** y que tiene normalmente conexiones con este último.

junior school
Un colegio estatal de Gran Bretaña para niños de entre 7 y 11 años.

Labour Party
El Partido Laborista es uno de los tres principales partidos políticos de Gran Bretaña. Accedió por primera vez al poder en 1924 y tiene como objetivo representar los intereses de los trabajadores y sindicatos. En los últimos 20 años, el partido ha abandonado su postura de izquierda en puntos tales como la propiedad pública de la industria y los servicios, por lo que, hoy en día, se le denomina con frecuencia **New Labour**.

L-driver - learner driver
Es el término con el que en Gran Bretaña se denomina a los que están aprendiendo a conducir un coche u otro vehículo. Estas personas cuando están al volante, siempre deben ir acompañadas de otra que tenga una licencia de conducción (*driving license*) en vigencia. También deben llevar una placa de L o de prácticas (*L-plates*), en las partes delantera y trasera del vehículo que conducen, hasta que hayan aprobado el examen de conducir (*driving test*). La placa L es un cuadrado blanco de plástico con una letra 'L' roja.

Liberal Democratic Party
Al Partido Demócrata Liberal también se le conoce informalmente como los **Lib Dems**. Es el tercer partido en importancia en Gran Bretaña. Se formó en 1988 mediante la unión del Partido Liberal (*Liberal Party*) y el Partido Socialdemócrata (*Social Democratic Party*).

Los Angeles Times - The Los Angeles Times
Un diario que se publica en Los Angeles y que está considerado como uno de los mejores periódicos de Estados Unidos. Distribuye sus artículos por todo el mundo y ha ganado más de veinte **PULITZER PRIZE**s.

Mann Booker Prize
Un premio que se otorga, normalmente en octubre, a la mejor novela, escrita por un autor británico o de un país miembro de la *Commonwealth*, que se haya publicado en el año. La selección de una lista de candidatos y la elección final del ganador son objeto de considerable atención y discusión por parte de los medios de comunicación.

Medicaid
Un seguro de enfermedad administrado por el gobierno de Estados Unidos para ciudadanos de menos de 65 años y con bajos ingresos.

Medicare
Un seguro de enfermedad administrado por el gobierno de Estados Unidos para ciudadanos de más de 65 años.

motorway
Gran Bretaña tiene un amplio sistema de autopistas (*motorways*) que normalmente tienen tres carriles por calzada. Están señalizadas con la letra 'M' seguida de un número y tienen un límite de velocidad de 70 millas por hora (112 kms/h). En las autopistas británicas no hay que pagar peaje.

● ●

MP - Member of Parliament

Un miembro de la Cámara de los Comunes (**HOUSE OF COMMONS**) que representa a una de las 659 circunscripciones electorales de Inglaterra, Escocia, Gales e Irlanda del Norte.

National Book Award

Cualquiera de los varios premios otorgados anualmente, por la *Association of American Publishers*, a un libro nuevo que se haya publicado en Estados Unidos. Los premios corresponden a una serie de categorías tales como ficción, ensayo, y poesía.

National Health Service (NHS)

En Gran Bretaña, es el servicio público que proporciona asistencia médica a toda la población. Está financiado en gran parte por el gobierno y la asistencia, por lo general, es gratuita. Se deben pagar la atención dental y las medicinas que el médico haya recetado. Sin embargo, las personas que pertenecen a ciertos grupos, tales como los niños, jóvenes hasta los 18 años de edad y los jubilados, no pagan por estos servicios.

National Insurance (NI)

En Gran Bretaña, sistema de pagos obligatorios, *National Insurance Contributions* (cotizaciones o contribuciones a la Seguridad Social), que los empleados y empleadores deben realizar a fin de que el gobierno pueda financiar los diferentes beneficios sociales que proporciona, tales como **JOBSEEKEERS' ALLOWANCE** y las jubilaciones, así como el **NATIONAL HEALTH SERVICE**. Todo adulto debe tener un número de la seguridad social (*National Insurance Number*).

National Lottery

Una lotería que se sortea en Gran Bretaña, mediante la cual se recauda dinero tanto para una amplia variedad de proyectos culturales o deportivos como para obras benéficas y la conservación del patrimonio nacional.

National Trust

En Gran Bretaña, una fundación que tiene como objetivo la conservación de lugares de interés histórico o de belleza natural. Se financia mediante legados y subvenciones privadas y es la mayor propietaria de tierras en Gran Bretaña. A lo largo del tiempo ha obtenido, mediante compra o cesión, enormes extensiones de tierras, así como pueblos y casas, muchas de las cuales están abiertas al público en ciertas épocas del año.

Native American

Es actualmente el término cuyo uso se acepta para referirse a cualquiera de los pueblos indígenas de América del Norte, América del Sur y el Caribe. Este término se prefiere al de *American Indian*, especialmente en contextos oficiales. Se considera más preciso y positivo ya que el término *Indian* (indio) deriva del hecho de que Cristóbal Colón, cuando llegó a América, creyó que se encontraba en la India. Con todo, *American Indian* todavía se usa ampliamente y los propios indígenas no lo consideran ofensivo.

NBC - National Broadcasting Company

La primera compañía de radiodifusión que se fundó en Estados Unidos (1926). El primer canal de televisión de la NBC empezó a transmitir en 1940.

Newsweek

Una revista estadounidense que se publica semanalmente en Nueva York. Cubre una gran variedad de temas políticos, sociales, culturales y científicos.

New Yorker - The New Yorker

Una revista muy conocida y respetada que se publica semanalmente en Nueva York. Se especializa en artículos largos que analizan, en profundidad, una gran variedad de temas. Ofrece información sobre novelas de ficción y poesía de reciente publicación, artículos y dibujos humorísticos.

• •

NVQ - National Vocational Qualification

Un título que se obtiene en Gran Bretaña mediante planes de educación y formación que se llevan a cabo en el lugar de trabajo o en ciertas universidades y colegios. Las materias guardan una relación directa con el trabajo y se imparten en varios niveles.

pantomime

Un tipo de representación teatral que tiene lugar tradicionalmente, en teatros de toda Gran Bretaña, durante las semanas previas y posteriores a la Navidad. Generalmente está dirigida a los niños. El argumento, a menudo, es una adaptación cómica de un cuento tradicional y cuenta con un número de personajes de características exageradas e increíbles. También requiere de un gran nivel de participación por parte del público. De acuerdo con la tradición, el papel del héroe (*principal boy*) es interpretado por una actriz y el de la *dame*, un personaje femenino grotesco, es interpretado por un actor.

Parliament

El Parlamento británico es el más alto organismo legislativo de Gran Bretaña y está formado por el soberano (el rey o la reina), la Cámara de los Lores (**HOUSE OF LORDS**) y la Cámara de los Comunes (**HOUSE OF COMMONS**).

PBS - Public Broadcasting Service

Un servicio de radiodifusión estadounidense, financiado por el gobierno, famoso por la calidad de sus programas. Consiste en una asociación de emisoras locales que trasmiten sin fines de lucro y sin publicidad.

Pentagon - The Pentagon

Es el edificio de forma pentagonal, situado en Wahington, donde se encuentra la oficina central del Ministerio de Defensa y de las fuerzas armadas de Estados Unidos. A menudo se utiliza el término *'The Pentagon'* para referirse al Estado Mayor, es decir a los generales y jefes militares que trabajan allí.

Plaid Cymru

El partido nacionalista galés. Su objetivo fundamental es conseguir la independencia de Gales del resto del Reino Unido. Gran parte de su esfuerzo se ha visto dirigido a la recuperación de la lengua galesa (**WELSH**) y a la conservación de la cultura de Gales.

preparatory school

En Gran Bretaña, un colegio privado, llamado también *prep school*, para alumnos de edades comprendidas entre siete y trece años. Algunos tienen el régimen de internado y otros no, pero la mayoría son una mezcla de ambos. Normalmente es un colegio no mixto. Los padres pagan por la educación de sus hijos y otros servicios y gran parte de los alumnos pasa, a continuación, a un colegio privado (**PUBLIC SCHOOL**). Los *preparatory schools* y los *public schools* actualmente se llaman a menudo **INDEPENDENT SCHOOL**s.

President

En Estados Unidos el Presidente es la cabeza del Estado, es responsable de la política exterior y es comandante en jefe de las fuerzas armadas. El Presidente puede nombrar a jueces federales y a ministros. A solicitud del Congreso (**CONGRESS**) aprueba las nuevas leyes. Puede gobernar un máximo de dos legislaturas (*terms*) de cuatro años cada una.

primary school

En Gran Bretaña, un colegio estatal para niños cuyas edades fluctúan entre 5 y 11 años.

public school

En Inglaterra y Gales, un colegio privado para alumnos de edades comprendidas entre trece y dieciocho años. La mayor parte de los alumnos que va a estos colegios ha estudiado anteriormente en un **PREPARATORY SCHOOL**. La mayoría de los *public schools* son internados y normalmente no son mixtos. Los padres pagan por la educación de sus hijos y otros servicios. En Escocia y Estados Unidos el término *public school* se utiliza para referirse a un colegio estatal.

· ·

Pulitzer Prize
Es un premio de gran prestigio que se otorga anualmente por los éxitos más destacados en el mundo del periodismo, la literatura y la música norteamericanos.

Queen's Speech
Un discurso preparado por los miembros de gobierno británico para que sea leído por la reina en la Cámara de los Lores (**HOUSE OF LORDS**) en la ceremonia de apertura del Parlamento, que tiene lugar todos los años en otoño. Es una ocasión importante, ya que el discurso esboza los planes del gobierno para el año siguiente.

region
Es la unidad administrativa más grande de Escocia. Existen nueve y cada una tiene su propio ayuntamiento (**COUNCIL**).

Representative
Un miembro de la Cámara de Representantes (**HOUSE OF REPRESENTATIVE**s) de Estados Unidos.

Republican Party
El Partido Republicano es uno de los dos principales partidos políticos de Estados Unidos. El otro es el Partido Demócrata (**DEMOCRATIC PARTY**). Está considerado como más conservador que este último.

SAT
1 - **Scholastic Aptitude Test.** Una prueba de aptitud, que se hace normalmente en el último año del **HIGH SCHOOL** y que los estudiantes deben aprobar para entrar a la mayor parte de las universidades estadounidenses.
2 - **Standard Assessment Test.** Una prueba que se hace a los alumnos de todos los colegios de Inglaterra y Gales, a los 7, 11, y 14 años a fin de evaluar su progreso.

Scottish Certificate of Education
El certificado más importante que se obtiene al terminar el colegio en Escocia, que cuenta con su propio sistema educativo dentro de Gran Bretaña. El examen de nivel inferior (*Standard*) se hace a los 16 años y es el equivalente al **GCSE** de Inglaterra. El de nivel superior (*Higher*) se hace a los 17 años y es el equivalente al **A-LEVEL** de Inglaterra.

Scottish National Party (SNP)
El Partido Nacionalista Escocés tiene como objetivo conseguir un gobierno completamente independiente para Escocia.

Scottish Parliament
El Parlamento escocés, cuyos miembros se reúnen en *Holyrood House*, en Edimburgo, la capital de Escocia. Se inauguró en 1999 después de la celebración de elecciones y da al país un mayor grado de autonomía que el que tenía anteriormente con respecto al Parlamento británico de Londres.

SDLP - Social Democratic and Labour Party
Partido de Irlanda del Norte cuyo objetivo es conseguir la igualdad de derechos para los católicos y la unificación de Irlanda del Norte y de la República de Irlanda. Sin embargo, no aprueba el uso de la violencia como medio para conseguirlo.

Senate
El Senado es la cámara alta del Congreso (**CONGRESS**) de Estados Unidos. Está formado por 100 senadores (**SENATOR**s), dos por cada estado y son elegidos por periodos de seis meses. Toda nueva ley debe ser aprobada por el Senado y la Cámara de Representantes (**HOUSE OF REPRESENTATIVE**s), pero el Senado tiene responsabilidad especial en asuntos relacionados con la política exterior y tiene poder para 'asesorar y aprobar' los nombramientos hechos por el Presidente (**PRESIDENT**).

Vida y cultura

• •

Senator
Un miembro del Senado (**SENATE**) de Estados Unidos.

Shadow Cabinet ▶ CABINET

Silicon Valley
Es el nombre utilizado para referirse al Valle de Santa Clara, en California, donde se concentra un gran número de compañías de electrónica e informática. El nombre deriva del uso del silicio *(silicon)* en la electrónica.

Sinn Fein
Partido político cuyo objetivo es una Irlanda republicana unida. Desde los años 20 empezó a funcionar como la rama política del **IRA**.

soap opera
Nombre con el que se designa, de forma humorística, un tipo de serie televisiva extremadamente popular en Gran Bretaña y Estados Unidos. Trata normalmente de la vida diaria de gente corriente perteneciente a una comunidad particular. Algunas de las series británicas más populares son *Coronation Street*, la más antigua ya que empezó emitirse en 1960, y *Eastenders*. En Estados Unidos las más conocidas son *Dallas* y *Dynasty*, que ya han dejado de filmarse pero cuyos capítulos se repiten a veces en la televisión por satélite. Las primeras *soap operas* (literalmente significa óperas de jabón) que se emitieron en Estados Unidos estaban financiadas por compañías de jabón, y de ahí su nombre.

Stars and Stripes
La bandera de Estados Unidos.

Star-Spangled Banner
El himno de Estados Unidos.

state school
En Gran Bretaña, un colegio que está financiado directa o indirectamente por el gobierno, y que ofrece educación gratuita. La mayor parte de los niños británicos va a este tipo de colegios.

tabloid
En Gran Bretaña, un periódico que se imprime en páginas de formato pequeño, a diferencia de los periódicos de formato grande (**BROADSHEET**s), que se imprimen en páginas de un tamaño dos veces mayor. El formato *tabloid* está normalmente asociado con la prensa popular, representada por periódicos como *The Sun* y *The Mirror*, mientras que el formato grande es el utilizado por la mayor parte de los periódicos de calidad, como por ejemplo *The Guardian* y *The Times*.

The City, The Washington Post, The White House, etc. ▶ CITY, WASHINGTON POST, WHITE HOUSE, etc.

Time
Una revista americana que es famosa en todo el mundo por su cobertura de noticias y sucesos internacionales.

TOEFL – Test of English as a Foreign Language
Un examen que, a la hora de solicitar el ingreso a una universidad americana, evalúa el dominio del inglés de aquellos estudiantes cuya lengua materna no es este idioma.

Tory ▶ CONSERVATIVE PARTY

Ulster Democratic Unionist Party
Partido político de Irlanda del Norte apoyado en su mayor parte por protestantes y que sostiene que Irlanda del Norte debe seguir siendo parte del Reino Unido.

Ulster Unionist Party

Partido político de Irlanda del Norte, que sostiene que Irlanda del Norte debe seguir siendo parte del Reino Unido. Está considerado como más moderado que el **ULSTER DEMOCRATIC UNIONIST PARTY**.

Union Jack

Es el nombre que se le da a la bandera del Reino Unido. Está formada por la cruz de San Jorge representando a Inglaterra, la cruz de San Andrés representando a Escocia, y la cruz de San Patricio representando a Irlanda del Norte.

Wall Street

Es una calle en Manhattan, Nueva York, donde se encuentran la Bolsa de Nueva York y las oficinas centrales de muchas instituciones financieras. A menudo, cuando se habla de *Wall Street,* se estás refiriendo a esta instituciones y no a la calle propiamente dicha.

Washington Post - The Washington Post

Un periódico americano que se publica diariamente en Washington. Es famoso por la amplia cobertura de su información, por el alto nivel de calidad de su periodismo de investigación y por sus opiniones liberales.

Welsh

El galés, de origen céltico, es la lengua oficial de Gales, conjuntamente con el inglés. Para más del 20% de la población sigue siendo la lengua materna y como muchas otras lenguas minoritarias, ha experimentado un resurgimiento durante los últimos cuarenta años. Actualmente se estudia como materia obligatoria en todos los colegios de Gales, los letreros y otras señales de las ciudades aparecen normalmente en inglés y galés.

Welsh Assembly

El parlamento galés, cuyos miembros se reúnen en la capital de Gales, Cardiff. Se inauguró en 1999 después de la celebración de elecciones y da al país un mayor grado de autonomía que el que tenía anteriormente con respecto al Parlamento británico de Londres.

Westminster

Un barrio del centro de Londres en el que se encuentran muchos de los principales edificios del gobierno. Entre estos, los más importantes son el Palacio de Westminster (*Palace of Westminster*), también llamado el Parlamento (**HOUSES OF PARLIAMENT**), donde se reúnen las dos cámaras. En el mismo barrio se encuentra la Abadía de Westminster (*Westminster Abbey*), donde han sido coronados todos los monarcas ingleses, a partir de Guillermo el Conquistador en 1066.

Whitehall

Una calle del centro de Londres donde están situadas una gran parte de las oficinas del gobierno. Los periodistas utilizan a menudo el término para referirse al gobierno y la administración.

White House – The White House

La residencia y el despacho oficial del presidente de Estados Unidos, situada en Washington. Los periodistas utilizan a menudo el término '*the White House*' para referirse al Presidente y a sus consejeros.

Vida y cultura

Letter-writing / Redacción de cartas

Holiday postcard

- *Beginning (quite informal): this formula is used among young people, very close friends, and, generally speaking, when addressee and sender address each other using the familiar form tú. Querido Juan can also be used, or Querida Ana if the addressee is a woman. If addressed to two or more people, males and females or only males, the masculine plural Queridos is always used: Queridos Juan y Ana, Queridos amigos, Queridos Juan y Pedro. Queridas is used if the card or letter is addressed to more than one female: Queridas chicas, Queridas Ana y Conchita*

- *Address: Note that the title (Sr., Sra., Srta.) is always followed by a full stop and stands next to the name.*

  The house number (sometimes also N° ...) comes after the street name. In addresses of apartments in Spain, this is often followed by a floor number and sometimes the apartment's position on the landing: c/ Hermosilla 98, 6° Dcha.

  The zip code comes before the place

Hola Juan

¿Qué tal? Hemos llegado a esta maravilla de ciudad hace dos días y estamos disfrutando muchísimo de todo lo que vemos. ¡a pesar del tiempo! Ya sabes tú como es el clima por aquí.

Hemos visitado los baños romanos (por supuesto), la catedral y sus alrededores. Hicimos un paseo por el río en barca y hemos recorrido la ciudad a pie. Es la mejor forma de apreciar la increíble arquitectura de este lugar.

¡Ah! También tomamos un té inglés como es debido, con sándwichs de pepino incluidos, en la elegante "Pump Room". Mañana regresamos a Londres y luego de vuelta a la dura realidad.

Esperamos que todo te haya ido bien con el cambio de trabajo. Ya nos contarás.

Hasta pronto.

Ana y Eduardo

Bath, 8 de octubre 2003 ①

Sr. Juan Elizalde
P° Pintor Rosales 101
28008 Madrid
Spain

- *Endings (informal):* Un fuerte abrazo, Muchos saludos, Muchos besos y abrazos. *Also in Latin America:* Cariños (NB not between men), Hasta pronto *(See you soon).*

- ① *Not only on postcards, but on most personal letters, Spanish speakers do not put the address at the top, but just the name of the place and the date. The sender's address is recorded on the back of the envelope.*

Postal desde un lugar de vacaciones

- Por tratarse de una postal, el encabezamiento es muy simple, siempre Dear, seguido del primer nombre del destinatario.

- En la dirección, el título (Mr, Mrs, Miss, Ms) precede al nombre del destinatario en la primera línea. Las abreviaturas Mr, Mrs y Ms no van seguidas de punto. En Gran Bretaña muchas casas suelen tener un nombre, el que aparece encima del de la calle. Tanto en Norteamérica como en Gran Bretaña, el número de la casa se coloca antes del nombre de la calle. Debajo le siguen, en Gran Bretaña, el barrio, la ciudad o el condado y el código postal (postcode) cada uno en una línea. En Norteamérica debajo del número de la casa y el nombre de la calle, se incluyen la ciudad, las iniciales del Estado y el código postal (zip code), todo en una línea:

  Mr John Spaline Jr
  100 Irving Palace
  New York, NY 10001
  USA

Dear John

6.8.2003 ①

Greetings from Mexico City! Got here a couple of days ago, but already in love with the place (in spite of the traffic and smog). Everything is so different and the food sometimes a bit too hot for us. Delicious though. We have visited the Archaeological Museum (out of this world). The Zócalo, the Cathedral, an Aztec temple and other places. Last night we went to Plaza Garibaldi to see the mariachis sing. Very atmospheric. Tomorrow we're visiting Tehotihuacán and the pyramids, and then on Thursday we head home. Hope ② your mother is fully recovered by now.

See you soon,

Mark and Juliet.

Mr J. Roberts

The Willows

49 North Terrace

Kings Barton

Nottinghamshire

NG8 42l

England

- Fórmula de despedida informal empleada cuando el destinatario es un amigo íntimo o un pariente cercano. Otras alternativas pueden ser: All the best, With love from, o simplemente Love (from).

① No sólo en postales sino también en la mayoría de las cartas de tipo personal, tanto los norteamericanos como los ingleses colocan la fecha en el ángulo superior derecho.

② Estilo telegrama, típico de una postal, en el que se suprime el pronombre: Got here ... y Hope you're ... en lugar de We got here ... y We hope you're ... respectivamente.

Christmas and New Year Wishes

On a card:

> Feliz Navidad ① y Próspero Año Nuevo ②
>
> Feliz Navidad ① y los mejores deseos para el Año
> Nuevo ③

① *Or:* Felices Pascuas,
Felices Navidades.

② *Or:* Próspero Año 2003.

③ *Or:* para el Año 2003.

In a letter:

- *Beginning: the name on the first line is usually followed by a colon.*

④ *This is a letter to friends who are addressed as* vosotros, *the plural of the familiar form* tú. *However, Latin American Spanish uses the formal plural* ustedes *instead of this form, so would replace the words marked * in the letter as follows:* vosotros *by* ustedes, vuestro *and* vuestra *by* su *or* de ustedes, os *by* les *or* los. *The verbs, marked **, should be replaced by the formal plural form, e.g.* estéis *by* estén.

⑤ *Or (if the children are older):* para vosotros y los chicos (*or* y las chicas *if there are only females*), para vosotros y para toda la familia.

⑥ *Or:* todos muy bien.

> Barcelona, 18 de diciembre de 2003
>
> Queridos Juan y Elsa:
>
> ④ Antes que nada, os* deseamos a vosotros* y a los niños ⑤ unas muy felices Navidades y os* enviamos nuestros mejores deseos para el año 2004. Esperamos que estéis** todos estupendamente ⑥. No sabéis** cómo nos alegramos con el anuncio de vuestro* viaje para enero. Ya tenemos pensado todo lo que podemos hacer durante vuestra* estancia aquí. Os* esperamos.
>
> Conchita hizo los exámenes del último año de su carrera y sacó muy buenas notas. Ahora tiene que hacer su trabajo de práctica. Elena está bien y muy contenta en el colegio. Tiene muchísimos amigos y es muy buena chica. Luis y yo estamos bien también y sumamente felices con la reciente noticia del próximo ascenso de Luis. En definitiva, 2003 ha sido un buen año y no nos podemos quejar. Confiamos en que el próximo será aún mejor.
>
> Decidnos** con antelación la fecha de vuestro* viaje para que podamos ir a esperaros* al aeropuerto.
>
> Recibid** todo nuestro cariño y un fuerte abrazo.
>
> Luis y Ana.

. . . .

Saludos de Navidad y Año Nuevo

En una tarjeta:

[Best wishes for a] Happy ① Christmas and
a Prosperous New Year

Best wishes for Christmas and the New Year

Wishing you every happiness this Christmas
and in the New Year

① O: Merry.

En una carta:

44 Louis Gardens
London NW6 4GM

December 20th 2003

Dear Peter and Claire,

First of all, a very happy Christmas and all the best for the New Year to you
and the children. ② We hope you're all well ③ and that we'll see you again.
It seems ages since we last met up.

We've had a very eventful year. Last summer Gavin came off his bike and
broke his arm and collarbone. Kathy scraped through her A Levels and is
now at Sussex doing European Studies. Poor Tony was made redundant in
October and is still looking for a job.

Do come and see us next time you are over this way. Just give us a ring a
couple of days before so we can fix something.

All best wishes

Tony and Ann

② O (si los hijos son mayores): to you and your family.

③ O (coloquial): flourishing.

Letter-writing / Redacción de cartas

Invitation (informal)

Madrid, 22 de abril del 2003

Querido James:

Te escribo para preguntarte si te apetecería ① pasar las vacaciones de verano con nosostros. A Tito y a Pilar les haría mucha ilusión (y también a Juan y a mí, por supuesto). Pensamos ir al noreste del país a finales de julio o a principios de agosto. Es una región realmente hermosa y nos encantaría que tú también vinieras. Es muy probable que llevemos tiendas de campaña ¡espero que no te importe dormir en el suelo!

Te agradecería que me avisaras lo más pronto posible si puedes venir.

Un cariñoso saludo,

Ana de Salas

① Or (in Latin America and also in Spain): si te gustaría.

Invitation (formal)

Invitations to parties are usually by word of mouth, while for weddings announcements are usually sent out.

Carmen S.de Pérez y Ramón Pérez Arrate, Lucía N.de Salas y Mario Salas Moro Participan a Ud. de la boda de sus hijos

Consuelo y Hernán

Y le invitan a la ceremonia religiosa que se efectuará en la Capilla del Sagrado Corazón, de Mirasierra, Madrid, el sábado 25 de julio del 2003 a las 7 p.m.

Y luego a una recepción en la Sala de Banquetes del Restaurante Galán en C/Los Santos 10 de Majadahonda, Madrid.
S.R.C.②

- In Latin America invitations to the reception are sent to relatives and close friends in a separate smaller card enclosed with the announcement.

- In Spanish-speaking countries, the answer is not usually given in writing.

  ② In Latin America: R.S.V.P.

Invitación (informal)

- *La fecha también se puede escribir de la siguiente manera: April 10, 10 April, 10th April.*

- *La dirección del remitente va en el ángulo superior derecho de la carta y la fecha va inmediatamente debajo.*

35 Winchester Drive
Stoke Gifford
Bristol
BS34 8PD

April 22nd 2003

Dear Luis,

Is there any chance of your coming to stay with us in the summer holidays? Roy and Debbie would be delighted if you could (as well as David and me, of course). We hope to go to North Wales at the end of July/beginning of August, and you'd be very welcome to come too. It's really beautiful up there. We'll probably take tents - I hope that's OK by you.

Let me know as soon as possible if you can manage it.

All best wishes

Rachel Hemmings

Invitación (formal)

Invitación a una boda con recepción:

Mr and Mrs Peter Thompson
request the pleasure of your company
at the marriage of their daughter
Hannah Louise
to
Steven David Warner
at St Mary's Church, Little Bourton
on Saturday 22nd July 2003 at 2 p.m.
And afterwards at the Golden Cross Hotel, Billing

R.S.V.P

23 Santers Lane
Little Bourton
Northampton
NN6 1AZ

Letters / Cartas

Accepting an invitation

Winchester, 2 de mayo del 2003

Estimada Sra. de Salas:

Muchísimas gracias por su amable carta y su invitación ①.

No tengo nada planeado para las vacaciones de verano, así es que me encantaría acompañarles ② al norte. Desgraciadamente, no podré quedarme más de cinco o seis días debido a que mi madre no se encuentra muy bien y no me gustaría estar mucho tiempo fuera de casa.

Por favor dígame lo que tengo que llevar. ¿Hace mucho calor en la región adonde vamos? ¿Hay mar o río donde se pueda nadar? En cuanto a hacer camping, no tengo ningún problema. Nosotros siempre llevamos nuestras tiendas de campaña a todas partes.

Esperando verles ③ pronto otra vez,

Un afectuoso saludo,

James

① Since this is a letter from a younger person writing to the mother of a friend, he uses the formal usted form and the possessive su, and writes to her as Sra. de Salas and Estimada, which is normally used to begin a letter when the relationship is not too close. Querida ... could also be used (Estimado Sr. ... or Querido Sr. ... if the addressee is a man). On the other hand it was quite natural for Sra. de Salas to use the informal tú form to him.

② In Latin America: acompañarlos.

③ In Latin America: verlos.

■ Ending: This is normally used when the relationship is not too close, generally when the person is known to you but the usted form would be used. Un saludo muy afectuoso is also possible.

Aceptación de una invitación (informal)

> Luis Villegas
> Las Acacias 30
> 28020 Madrid
>
> 2 May 2003
>
> Dear Mrs Hemmings ①,
>
> Many thanks for your letter and kind invitation. Since I don't have anything fixed yet for the summer holidays, I'd be delighted to come. However I mustn't be away for more than four or five days since my mother hasn't been very well.
>
> You must let me know what I should bring. How warm is it in North Wales? Can you swim in the sea? Camping is fine as far as I'm concerned, we take our tents everywhere.
>
> Looking forward to seeing you soon.
>
> Yours ②,
>
> Luis

① Este es un encabezamiento relativamente formal, puesto que esta es una carta de una persona joven dirigida a la madre de un amigo.

② Otras alternativas para este tipo de carta: With best wishes, Yours sincerely, Kind/Kindest regards.

Respuesta a una invitación (formal)

> **Aceptando:** Richard Willis has great pleasure in accepting Mr and Mrs Peter Thompson's kind invitation to the marriage of their daughter Hannah Louise to Steven Warner at St Mary's Church, Little Bourton, on Saturday 22nd July.
>
> **No aceptando:** Richard Willis regrets that he is unable to accept Mr and Mrs Peter Thompson's kind invitation to ....

■ Se repiten los datos de la invitación, pero no en forma detallada.

■ Si no se acepta la invitación, es de mejor educación enviar una carta a los padres de la novia, si se conocen personalmente.

Replying to a job advertisement

■ In Spain when the full address is given it is usually written in the top left-hand corner and in Latin America in the bottom left-hand corner, beneath the signature.

■ This is the most commonly used opening for a formal or business letter, or when the addressee is not personally known to you. Alternatively Estimado Sr. and, in Latin America, De mi mayor consideración, can also be used.

■ When the full address is given, the name of the town or city is not repeated in the date.

David Baker
67 Whiteley Avenue
St George
Bristol
BS5 6TW

26 de septiembre de 2003

Gerente del Personal
Renos Software S.A.
Alcalá 52
28014 Madrid

Muy señor mío:

Con referencia al puesto de programador anunciado recientemente en El País del 12 de septiembre del presente, les agradecería me enviaran información más detallada acerca de la plaza vacante ① .

Actualmente estoy trabajando para una empresa de Bristol, pero mi contrato termina a finales de este mes y querría aprovechar esta oportunidad para ② trabajar en Madrid. Como se desprende del currículum vitae que adjunto, viví durante algún tiempo en España, tengo perfecto dominio del idioma español y también las cualificaciones ③ y experiencia requeridas.

Estaré disponible para asistir a una entrevista, en cualquier momento desde el 6 de octubre, fecha a partir de la cual se me puede contactar en la siguiente dirección en Madrid:

C/ Sevilla 25
28020 Madrid
Teléf. 91 429-96-67

Sin otro particular, quedo a la espera de su respuesta, ④

Atentamente, ⑤

① Or if you have enough details and want to apply for the job right away: quisiera solicitar la plaza vacante.

② Or if you are unemployed: Actualmente estoy buscando trabajo y quisiera ...

③ In Latin America: calificaciones.

④ Or: Agradeciendo de antemano su atención or En espera de su respuesta.

⑤ Or: Le (Lo in Latin America) saluda atentamente. Me despido de usted atentamente, Muy atentamente, or Esperando su respuesta, se despide atentamente are also possible.

Respuesta a un anuncio de trabajo

C/Islas Baleares 18. 2º B
FUENCARRAL
28080 Madrid
Spain

13th February 2003

The Personnel Manager ①
Patterson Software plc
Milton State
Bath BA6 8YZ

Dear Sir o Madam ①,

I am interested in the post of programmer advertised in The Guardian of
12 February and would be very grateful if you could send me further
particulars. ②

I am currently working for the Sempo Corporation, but my contract finishes
at the end of the month, and I would like ③ to work in England. As you can
see from my CV (enclosed), I have an excellent command of English and also
the required qualifications and experience.

I will be available for interview any time after 6th October, from which date I
can be contacted at the following address in the UK:

    c/o Lewis
    51 Dexter Road
    London N7 6BW
    Tel. 0181 607 5512

I look forward to hearing from you. ④

Yours sincerely

María Luisa Márquez Blanco

Encl.

① *Otra alternativa puede ser* Ms Angela Summers, ..., *si en el anuncio aparece* Reply to Angela
Summers *o* Dear Ms Summers, Dear Mrs Wright, *si en el anuncio sólo se indica el apellido.*

② *O* and would like to apply for this position, *si en el anuncio se incluye suficiente información
acerca del puesto.*

③ *O si se encuentra desempleado:* I am currently looking for work and I would like ...

④ *También:* Thanking you in anticipation/advance.

Curriculum Vitae (CV), (*AmE*) Resumé

CURRÍCULUM VITAE

Nombre y apellidos	David Baker
Fecha de nacimiento	30/6/71
Lugar	Londres
Estado civil	Soltero ①
Domicilio actual	67 Whiteley Avenue
	St George
	Bristol
	BS5 6TW
	Gran Bretaña
Teléfono	+44 (0)117 945 3421

DATOS ACADÉMICOS

1986-88 GCSE (equivalente a la ESO en España) en 7 asignaturas.

1988-90 A Levels (equivalente al Curso de Orientación Universitaria en España) en Matemáticas, Informática y Español, Croydon Sixth Form College.

1990-91 Trabajos temporales de oficina en España y estudios de Español para los negocios en clases nocturnas.

1991-95 Universidad de Aston, Birmingham, BSc en Informática (equivalente a Licenciatura en Ciencias de la Información).

EXPERIENCIA PROFESIONAL

1995-1996 Trabajo de práctica como programador de software para IBM, desarrollo de programas para la industria, con especialidad en infografía.

1996-al presente Programador para Wondersoft plc, Bristol.

IDIOMAS

Inglés   Lengua materna.

Español   Dominio total, hablado y escrito.

Francés   Bueno.

AFICIONES

Leer, viajar, esquí, tenis.

① Or: Casado (sin hijos *or* con un hijo/dos/tres *etc*, hijos), Divorciado (sin hijos *or* con un hijo/dos/tres *etc*, hijos).

Currículum Vitae

CURRICULUM VITAE ①

Name:	María Luisa Márquez Blanco
Address:	C/Islas Baleares 18. 2ºB FUENCARRAL 28080 Madrid Spain
Telephone:	(+34) 91. 243 53 94
Nationality:	Spanish
Date of Birth:	11/3/73

EDUCATION:

1990-95	Degree Course in Information Technology and English at Universidad Complutense of Madrid.
1987- 1991	BUP (secondary education)/COU (equivalent to A levels) at the Instituto de Enseñanza Media in Fuencarral.

EMPLOYMENT:

1996-present	Program development engineer with Sempo Informática, Madrid, specializing in computer graphics.
1995-1996	Trainee programmer with Oregón-España, Madrid.

FURTHER SKILLS:

Languages:	Spanish (mother tongue),
	English (fluent, spoken and written),
	French (good).
Interests:	Travel, fashion, tennis.

① O: Resumé (*AmE*).

Letters / Cartas

Inquiry to a tourist office

■ *This is a standard formula for starting a business letter addressed to a firm or organization, and not to a particular person. Alternatively,* Estimados señores *and, also in Latin America,* De nuestra mayor consideración, *could be used.*

  ■ *A simple business-style letter. The sender's address is on the top left-hand corner, the date is on the right, and the recipient's address is on the left, beneath the sender's address.*

Sally McGregor
16 Victoria Road
Brixton
London SW2 5HU

4 de mayo del 2003

Oficina de Información y Turismo
Princesa 5
Oviedo

Muy señores míos:

Les agracedería me remitieran a la mayor brevedad una lista de hoteles y pensiones, de precio medio, en Oviedo y los pueblos de la provincia.

También me interesaría obtener información acerca de excursiones en autocar ① a los lugares de interés de la zona durante la segunda mitad de agosto.

Agradeciendo de antemano su atención, les saluda atentamente,

Sally McGregor

■ Les *(*Los *in Latin America)* saluda atentamente *is the standard ending for a formal or business letter. Other possibilities are:* Me despido de ustedes atentamente *or* Reciban un atento saludo de ...

① *In Latin America:* autobús.

Carta a una oficina de turismo

■ *Encabezamiento típico de una carta de negocios cuando no se sabe si el destinatario es hombre o mujer. Otra alternativa sería* Dear Sirs, *si el destinatario fuese una empresa u organización (como por ejemplo si, en este caso, la carta estuviese dirigida a* The Regional Tourist Office *en lugar de a* The Manager).

> C/Antonio Cedaceros 9
> 05002 Ávila
> Spain
>
> 4th May 2003
>
> The Manager
> Regional Tourist Office
> 3 Virgin Road
> Canterbury
> CT1 3AA
>
> Dear Sir or Madam,
>
> Please send me a list of hotels and guesthouses in Canterbury in the medium price range.
>
> I would also like details of coach trips to local sights in the second half of August.
>
> Yours faithfully
>
> Antonio López A.

■ *Fórmula típica de despedida de cartas formales dirigidas a un destinatario a quien no se conoce personalmente. Es la fórmula que debe emplearse cuando el encabezamiento de la carta es* Dear Sir or Madam, Dear Sirs, Dear Sir *or* Dear Madam.

Booking a hotel room

Luis Granados
C/Felipe V 32
Segovia

23 de abril del 2003

Sr. Director
Hotel Los Palomos
C/Piedrabuena 40
Cádiz

Apreciado señor: ①

Su hotel aparece en un folleto turístico sobre la zona para el año 2003 y me ha causado muy buena impresión. Por ello le escribo para reservar una habitación doble con baño y una habitación individual ② para nuestro hijo, desde el 2 hasta 11 de agosto (nueve noches). Preferiblemente ambas habitaciones con vista al mar.

Si tiene disponibilidad para esas fechas, le rogaría que me comunicara el precio y si se requiere depósito.

Sin otro particular le saluda ③ atentamente,

Luis Granados

① *Also:* Estimado Sr.

② *Or:* una habitación doble y una individual para nuestro hijo, ambas con baño.

③ *In Latin America:* lo saluda ...

Booking a campsite

Urbanización El Molino
Chalet 88
Villanueva de la Cañada
Madrid

25 de abril del 2003

Camping Loredo
Sr. Roberto Loredo
Nájera
La Rioja

Muy señor mío:

Un amigo que suele acampar en la zona me ha recomendado su camping ① . por lo que quisiera reservar una plaza para una tienda ② . preferiblemente en un lugar abrigado ③ . Dos amigos y yo queremos pasar una semana allí, desde el 18 al 25 de julio inclusive.

Le agradecería que me confirmara la reserva lo antes posible y que me dijera si se requiere depósito. También le estaría muy agradecido si me enviara indicaciones para llegar al camping desde la carretera.

A la espera de su confirmación, le saluda ④ atentamente.

Pedro Salguedo

① *Or:* Su camping aparece anunciado en la revista Guía del Buen Campista.

② *Other possibility:* para una caravana.

③ *Alternatively:* en un lugar sombreado/ cerca de la playa.

④ *In Latin America:* lo saluda ...

Reserva de habitación en un hotel

The Manager   35 Prince Edward Road
Torbay Hotel   Oxford OX7 3AA
Dawlish
Devon   Tel. 01865 322435
EX37 2LR

23rd April 2003

Dear Sir or Madam,

I saw your hotel listed in the Inns of Devon guide for last year, and wish to reserve a double (or twin-bedded) room with shower ① in a quiet position from August 2nd-11th (nine nights), also a single room for my son.

If you have anything suitable for this period please let me know the price and whether you require a deposit.

Yours faithfully,

Charles Fairhurst

① *Otra alternativa:* with bath/with ensuite.

Reserva de camping

22 Daniel Avenue
Caldwood
Leeds LS8 7RR

Tel. 01132 998767

25th April 2003

Mr Joseph Vale
Lakeside Park
Rydal
Cumbria
LA22 9RZ

Dear Mr Vale,

Your campsite was recommended to me by James Dallas, who knows it from several visits ① . I and two friends would like to come for a week from July 18th to 25th. Could you please reserve us a pitch for one tent ② , preferably close to the shore ③ .

Please confirm the booking and let me know if you require a deposit. Would you also be good enough to send me instructions on how to reach you from the motorway.

Yours sincerely,

Frances Good

① *O si se ha obtenido información de otra fuente:* I found your site in the Tourist Board's list/the Good Camper's Guide *etc.*

② *Otra alternativa:* a pitch for one caravan.

③ *Otra posición:* in a shady/sheltered spot.

Letters / Cartas

Letter-writing / Redacción de cartas

. . . .

Canceling a reservation

Sra. Rosario de Barros
Av. Colonial
San Isidro
Lima

20 de julio de 2003

Estimada señora (de Barros):

Debido a circunstancias ajenas a nuestra voluntad ①, nos hemos visto obligados a cambiar nuestros planes para las vacaciones, por lo que le rogaría cancelara la reserva ② hecha a mi nombre para la semana del 7 al 14 de agosto.

Lamento muchísimo tener que hacer esta cancelación (tan a último momento) y espero que esto no le cause muchos inconvenientes.

La saluda atentamente.

Paul Roberts
2633 Higland Avenue
Urbandale, IA 51019
EEUU

① *Or:* Debido al repentino fallecimiento de mi marido/a la hospitalización de mi hijo/a la enfermedad de mi marido *etc.*

② *Also in Latin America:* reservación.

■ *In Latin America if the full address is given, it is usually written in the bottom left-hand corner, beneath the signature.*

Cancelación de una reserva

Sagasta 45
Santander
Spain

July 20th
2003

Mrs J. Warrington
Downlands
Steyning
West Sussex
BN44 6LZ

Dear Mrs Warrington,

Unfortunately I have to cancel my/our reservation for the week of August 7th ①. Due to unforeseen circumstances ②, I/we have had to abandon my/our holiday plans.

I very much regret having to cancel (at such a late stage) and hope it does not cause you undue inconvenience.

Yours sincerely,

Carlos Rubio García

① *Otra alternativa:* for the period from August 7th to 14th.

② *Otro motivo:* Owing to my father's sudden death/my wife's illness/son's hospitalization *etc.*

Letters / Cartas

Sending an e-mail

The illustration shows a typical interface for sending e-mail.

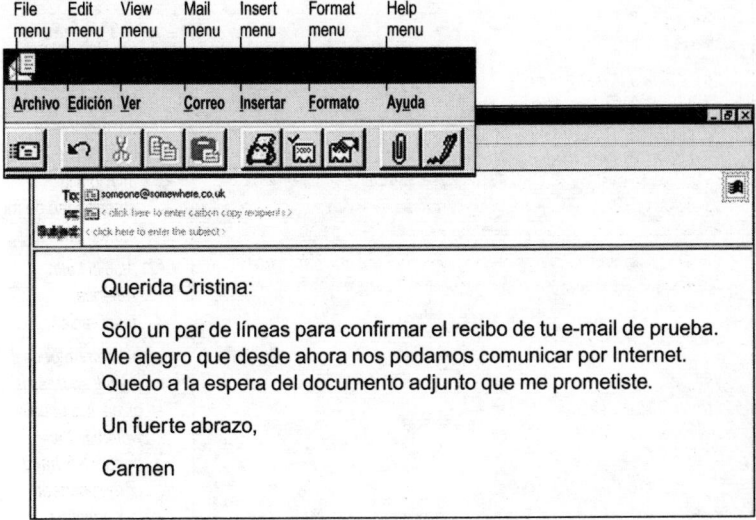

Para enviar correo electrónico

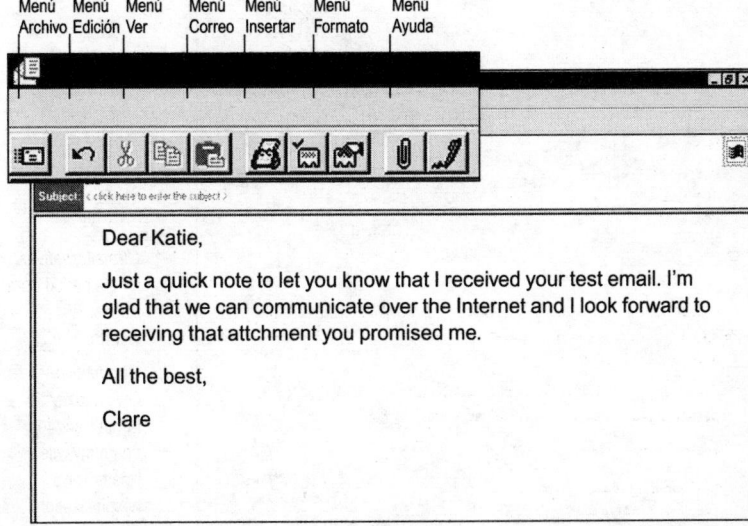

A, a /eɪ/ n **(a)** (letter) A, a f **(b)** (Mus) la m

a /ə, stressed form eɪ/ (before vowel **an**) indef art un, una; **a Mrs Smith called** llamó una tal señora Smith; **have you got a car?** ¿tienes coche?; **he didn't say a word** no dijo ni una palabra; **she's a dentist** es dentista; **what a shock!** ¡qué susto!; **it costs 2 dollars a pound** cuesta 2 dólares la libra

AA n **1** (no art) = **Alcoholics Anonymous** **2** (in US) = **Associate in Arts** **3** (in UK) = **Automobile Association**

AAA n = **American Automobile Association**

aback /ə'bæk/ adv ▶ TAKE ABACK

abacus /'æbəkəs/ n (pl **-cuses** or **-ci** /-saɪ/) ábaco m

abandon¹ /ə'bændən/ vt ⟨home/family⟩ abandonar; ⟨project/idea/search⟩ renunciar a; ⟨hope⟩ perder*; **to ~ ship** abandonar el barco

abandon² n: **they were dancing with gay ~** bailaban desenfrenadamente

abandoned /ə'bændənd/ adj ⟨vehicle/cottage/wife⟩ abandonado

abase /ə'beɪs/ v refl **to ~ oneself** humillarse

abashed /ə'bæʃt/ adj (pred) avergonzado

abate /ə'beɪt/ vi (fml) «storm/wind» amainar; «anger» aplacarse*; «noise/violence» disminuir*; «pain» calmarse

abattoir /'æbətwɑːr ‖'æbətwɑː(r)/ n matadero m

abbey /'æbi/ n (pl **abbeys**) abadía f

abbot /'æbət/ n abad m

abbreviate /ə'briːvieɪt/ vt abreviar

abbreviation /ə,briːvi'eɪʃən/ n abreviatura f

ABC n **1** (alphabet, rudiments) abecé m **2** (in US) (no art) (= **American Broadcasting Company**) la ABC

abdicate /'æbdɪkeɪt/ vt/i abdicar*

abdication /'æbdɪ'keɪʃən/ n abdicación f

abdomen /'æbdəmən/ n abdomen m

abduct /æb'dʌkt ‖əb'dʌkt/ vt (fml) raptar, secuestrar

abduction /æb'dʌkʃən ‖əb'dʌkʃən/ n (fml) rapto m, secuestro m

abet /ə'bet/ vt **-tt-** ▶ AID²

abeyance /ə'beɪəns/ n: **to be in ~** estar* suspendido

abhor /əb'hɔːr ‖əb'hɔː(r)/ vt **-rr-** (fml) detestar

abide /ə'baɪd/ vt tolerar, soportar

■ **abide by** [v + prep + o] ⟨verdict/rules⟩ acatar

ability /ə'bɪləti/ n (pl **-ties**) capacidad f; **to the best of one's ~** lo mejor que uno pueda

abject /'æbdʒekt/ adj (fml) (before n) ⟨slave/flattery⟩ abyecto; **in ~ poverty** en la mayor miseria

ablaze /ə'bleɪz/ adj (pred): **to be ~** arder

able /'eɪbəl/ adj **1** (pred) **to be ~ to + INF** poder* + INF; (referring to particular skills) saber* +

INF; **to be ~ to see/hear** poder* ver/oír **2** **abler** /'eɪblər ‖'eɪblə(r)/, **ablest** /'eɪbləst ‖'eɪblɪst/ (proficient) hábil

able-bodied /'eɪbəl'bɑːdid ‖,eɪbəl'bɒdid/ adj sano, no discapacitado

abnormal /'æb'nɔːrməl ‖æb'nɔːməl/ adj anómalo, anormal

abnormality /'æbnər'mæləti ‖,æbnɔː'mæləti/ n (pl **-ties**) anomalía f, anormalidad f

aboard¹ /ə'bɔːrd ‖ə'bɔːd/ adv (on ship, plane) a bordo

aboard² prep a bordo de; **~ the bus/train** en el autobús/tren

abode /ə'bəʊd/ n (liter o hum) morada f (liter o hum); **of no fixed ~** (Law) sin domicilio fijo

abolish /ə'bɑːlɪʃ ‖ə'bɒlɪʃ/ vt abolir*

abolition /'æbə'lɪʃən/ n abolición f

abominable /ə'bɑːmənəbəl ‖ə'bɒmmənəbəl/ adj **(a)** (horrible) ⟨deed⟩ abominable **(b)** (awful) (colloq) ⟨weather/food⟩ espantoso

abomination /ə'bɑːmə'neɪʃən ‖ə,bɒmɪ'neɪʃən/ n abominación f

aboriginal¹ /'æbə'rɪdʒənl/ adj aborigen

aboriginal² n **(a)** (indigenous inhabitant) aborigen mf **(b)** ▶ ABORIGINE

Aborigine /'æbə'rɪdʒəni/ n aborigen australiano, -na m,f

abortion /ə'bɔːrʃən ‖ə'bɔːʃən/ n aborto m (provocado); **to have an ~** hacerse* un aborto, abortar

abortive /ə'bɔːrtɪv ‖ə'bɔːtɪv/ adj frustrado

abound /ə'baʊnd/ vi abundar; **to ~ IN o WITH sth** abundar EN algo

about¹ /ə'baʊt/ adv **1** (approximately) más o menos, aproximadamente; **she must be ~ 60** debe (de) tener unos 60 años; **at ~ six o'clock** alrededor de or a eso de las seis; **~ a month ago** hace cosa de un mes **2** to be about to + INF estar* a punto de + INF **3** (movement): **she can't get ~ very easily** le cuesta desplazarse; **he was waving a knife ~** blandía un cuchillo **4** (in the vicinity, in circulation) (esp BrE): **is Teresa ~?** ¿Teresa anda por aquí?; **there's a lot of flu ~** hay mucha gente con gripe

about² prep **1 (a)** (concerning) sobre, acerca de; **what's the play ~?** ¿de qué se trata la obra?; **he wants to see you about something** quiere verte acerca de or por algo; **she won — how ~ that!** ganó — ¡pues qué te parece! or ¡pues mira tú! **(b)** (pertaining to): **there's something ~ him that I don't like** tiene un no sé qué que no me gusta **2** (engaged in): **while you're ~ it, could you fetch my book?** ¿ya que estás me traes el libro?

aboutface /ə'baʊtfeɪs/, (BrE also) **about-turn** /-'tɜːrn ‖-'tɜːn/ n cambio m radical de postura

above¹ /ə'bʌv/ prep **1 (a)** (on top of, over) encima de; **~ sea level** sobre el nivel del mar **(b)** (upstream of) más allá or más arriba de **2** (superior ⋯⟩

to) por encima de; **to get ~ oneself** (pej) subirse a la parra **3** (more than): **~ average** por encima de la media; **~ and beyond** más allá de

above² *adv* **1** (on top, higher up) arriba **2** (in text): **as shown ~** como se demostró anteriormente *or* más arriba; **see ~, page 43** véase página 43

above³ *adj* (frml) (*before n*): **for the ~ reasons** por dichas razones, por lo antedicho

above: ~**board** /əˈbʌvˈbɔːrd ‖əˌbʌvˈbɔːd/ *adj* (*pred*) legítimo; **open and ~board** sin tapujos; ~**mentioned** /əˈbʌvˈmentʃənd ‖əˌbʌvˈmenʃənd/ *adj* antedicho (frml)

abrasive /əˈbreɪsɪv/ *adj* (*powder*) abrasivo; (*surface*) áspero; (*tone/manner*) áspero

abreast /əˈbrest/ *adv* **(a)** (side by side): **to march four ~** marchar en columna de cuatro en fondo **(b)** (up to date): **to keep ~ of sth** mantenerse* al día en *or* al corriente de algo

abridge /əˈbrɪdʒ/ *vt* (*book*) compendiar; **~d edition** edición *f* condensada

abroad /əˈbrɔːd/ *adv* (*live/work*) en el extranjero *or* al exterior; (*go*) al extranjero, al exterior; **I've never been ~** nunca he salido del país

abrupt /əˈbrʌpt/ *adj* (*departure/conclusion*) repentino; (*rise/decline*) abrupto; (*manner*) brusco

abruptly /əˈbrʌptli/ *adv* (*end/stop*) repentinamente; (*rise/fall*) bruscamente; (*speak/act*) abruptamente

abscess /ˈæbses/ *n* absceso *m*

abscond /æbˈskɑːnd ‖əbˈskɒnd/ *vi* (fml) fugarse*

absence /ˈæbsəns/ *n* **(a)** (of person) ausencia *f* **(b)** (lack) **~ of sth** falta *f* DE algo

absent /ˈæbsənt/ *adj* ausente; **to be ~ from sth** faltar A algo

absentee /ˌæbsənˈtiː/ *n* (*pl* **-tees**) ausente *mf*

absenteeism /ˌæbsənˈtiːɪzəm/ *n* ausentismo *m or* (Esp) absentismo *m*

absentminded /ˈæbsəntˈmaɪndəd ‖ˌæbsəntˈmaɪndɪd/ *adj* (temporarily) distraído; (habitually) despistado

absolute /ˈæbsəluːt/ *adj* **1** (complete) (*trust/confidence*) absoluto; **it was an ~ disaster** fue un absoluto desastre *or* un desastre total **2** (*right*) incuestionable; (*pardon/freedom*) incondicional; (*guarantee/monarchy/rule*) absoluto

absolutely /ˈæbsəˈluːtli/ *adv* (*deny/reject*) rotundamente; (*impossible*) absolutamente; **I'm ~ certain** estoy segurísima *or* absolutamente segura; **you're ~ right!** ¡tienes toda la razón!

absolution /ˈæbsəˈluːʃən/ *n* absolución *f*

absolve /əbˈzɑːlv ‖əbˈzɒlv/ *vt* **to ~ sb of sth** absolver* a algn DE algo; **to ~ sb from sth** eximir a algn DE algo

absorb /əbˈsɔːrb ‖əbˈzɔːb/ *vt* (*light/energy*) absorber; (*impact/shock*) amortiguar*; (*information*) asimilar; **to be ~ed in sth** estar* absorto EN algo

absorbent /əbˈsɔːrbənt ‖əbˈzɔːbənt/ *adj* absorbente

absorbent cotton *n* (AmE) algodón *m* (hidrófilo)

absorption /əbˈsɔːrpʃən ‖əbˈzɔːpʃən/ *n* absorción *f*

abstain /əbˈsteɪn/ *vi* **1** (in vote) abstenerse* **2** (refrain) **to ~ FROM sth/-ING** abstenerse* DE algo/+ INF

abstract /ˈæbstrækt/ *adj* abstracto

absurd /əbˈsɜːrd ‖əbˈsɜːd/ *adj* absurdo

absurdity /əbˈsɜːrdəti ‖əbˈsɜːdəti/ *n* (*pl* **-ties**) lo absurdo

abundance /əˈbʌndəns/ *n* abundancia *f*

abundant /əˈbʌndənt/ *adj* (*resources*) abundante; (*enthusiasm*) desbordante

abuse¹ /əˈbjuːs/ *n* **1** (insulting language) insultos *mpl*; **a term of ~** un insulto **2** (misuse) abuso *m*; **sexual ~** abusos *mpl* deshonestos; **child ~** malos tratos *mpl* a la infancia; (sexual) abusos *mpl* deshonestos (*a un niño*); **drug ~** consumo *m* de drogas

abuse² /əˈbjuːz/ *vt* **1** **(a)** (use wrongly) (*power/hospitality*) abusar de **(b)** (*child/woman*) maltratar; (sexually) abusar de **2** (insult) insultar

abusive /əˈbjuːsɪv/ *adj* insultante

abysmal /əˈbɪzməl/ *adj* pésimo

abyss /əˈbɪs/ *n* (liter) abismo *m*

a/c (= **account**) cta.

AC /ˈeɪˈsiː/ **(a)** (= **alternating current**) CA **(b)** (esp AmE) = **air conditioning**

A/C = **air conditioning**

academic¹ /ˌækəˈdemɪk/ *adj* **1** **(a)** (*career/record*) académico **(b)** (*child/student*) intelectualmente capaz **2** (abstract) (*question/debate*) puramente teórico

academic² *n* académico, -ca *m,f*

academy /əˈkædəmi/ *n* (*pl* **-mies**) academia *f*; (*before n*) **A~ Award** Oscar *m*

accede /əkˈsiːd/ *vi* (frml) **to ~ TO sth** (grant) acceder A algo

accelerate /əkˈseləreɪt/ *vi* «*vehicle*» acelerar; «*person*» acelerar; (Auto) apretar* el acelerador; «*process/growth*» acelerarse ■ **~** *vt* acelerar

accelerator /əkˈseləreɪtər ‖əkˈseləreɪtə(r)/ *n* acelerador *m*

accent /ˈæksent ‖ˈæksent, ˈæksənt/ *n* **(a)** (Ling, Mus) acento *m* **(b)** (emphasis) énfasis *m*

accentuate /əkˈsentʃueɪt/ *vt* **(a)** (*difference*) hacer* resaltar; (*fact/necessity*) subrayar; (*eyes/features*) realzar*, hacer* resaltar **(b)** (*syllable/word*) acentuar*

accept /əkˈsept/ *vt* aceptar; **do you ~ that you were wrong?** ¿reconoces que estabas equivocado?

acceptable /əkˈseptəbəl/ *adj* (satisfactory) aceptable; (tolerable) admisible

acceptance /əkˈsəptəns/ *n* **1** (of offer, responsibility) aceptación *f* **2** (approval) aprobación *f*

AmC	Central America	Arg	Argentina	Cu	Cuba	Per	Peru
AmL	Latin America	Bol	Bolivia	Ec	Ecuador	RPI	River Plate Area
AmS	South America	Chi	Chile	Esp	Spain	Ur	Uruguay
Andes	Andean Region	CS	Southern Cone	Méx	Mexico	Ven	Venezuela

access¹ /'ækses/ n acceso m; (before n) ∼ **road** carretera f de acceso

access² vt (Comput) obtener* acceso a, entrar a

accessible /ək'sesəbəl/ adj accesible

accession /ək'seʃən, æk'seʃən/ n (frml) (a) (to throne, power) acceso m (b) (acquisition) adquisición f

accessory /ək'sesəri/ n (pl -ries) [1] (a) (extra) accesorio m (b) **accessories** pl (Clothing) accesorios mpl [2] (Law) ∼ (**TO sth**) cómplice mf (**EN** algo)

accident /'æksədənt ‖'æksɪdənt/ n (a) (mishap) accidente m (b) (chance) casualidad f; **by** ∼ (by chance) por casualidad; (unintentionally) sin querer

accidental /ˌæksə'dentl ‖ˌæksɪ'dentl/ adj ⟨discovery/meeting⟩ fortuito; ⟨blow⟩ accidental; ∼ **death** muerte f por caso fortuito

accidentally /ˌæksə'dentli ‖ˌæksɪ'dentəli/ adv (a) (unintentionally) sin querer (b) (by chance) por casualidad, de manera fortuita

accident-prone /'æksədəntprəʊn ‖'æksɪdəntprəʊn/ adj propenso a los accidentes

acclaim¹ /ə'kleɪm/ vt aclamar

acclaim² n aclamación f

acclimate /'ækləmeɪt/ vt (AmE) ▶ ACCLIMATIZE

acclimatize /ə'klaɪmətaɪz/ vt aclimatar; **to become** ∼**d TO sth** aclimatarse A algo

accolade /'ækəleɪd/ n (praise) elogio m; (honor) honor m; (award) galardón m

accommodate /ə'kɑːmədeɪt ‖ə'kɒmədeɪt/ vt [1] (a) (provide lodging for) alojar (b) (have room for) tener* cabida para [2] (cater to) ⟨wish/need⟩ tener* en cuenta

accommodating /ə'kɑːmədeɪtɪŋ ‖ə'kɒmədeɪtɪŋ/ adj complaciente

accommodation /əˌkɑːmə'deɪʃən ‖əˌkɒmə'deɪʃən/ n [1] (a) (AmE also) **accommodations** (lodgings) alojamiento m (b) (seat, berth) (AmE) plaza f [2] (agreement, compromise) acuerdo m

accompaniment /ə'kʌmpənimənt/ n acompañamiento m

accompanist /ə'kʌmpənəst ‖ə'kʌmpənɪst/ n acompañante mf

accompany /ə'kʌmpəni/ vt -nies, -nying, -nied (a) (go with) acompañar (b) (Mus) acompañar

accomplice /ə'kɑːmpləs ‖ə'kʌmplɪs/ n cómplice mf

accomplish /ə'kɑːmplɪʃ ‖ə'kʌmplɪʃ/ vt ⟨task⟩ llevar a cabo; ⟨goal⟩ lograr

accomplished /ə'kɑːmplɪʃt ‖ə'kʌmplɪʃt/ adj ⟨performer/liar/thief⟩ consumado; ⟨performance⟩ logrado

accomplishment /ə'kɑːmplɪʃmənt ‖ə'kʌmplɪʃmənt/ n (a) (of aim) logro m (b) (success) logro m (c) (skill) habilidad f

accord /ə'kɔːrd ‖ə'kɔːd/ n acuerdo m; **of one's own** ∼ (de) motu proprio

accordance /ə'kɔːrdns ‖ə'kɔːdns/ n: **in** ∼ **with** de acuerdo con or a, según

according /ə'kɔːrdɪŋ ‖ə'kɔːdɪŋ/ **according to** prep según

accordion /ə'kɔːrdiən ‖ə'kɔːdiən/ n acordeón m

accost /ə'kɔːst ‖ə'kɒst/ vt abordar

account /ə'kaʊnt/ n

I [1] (explanation) explicación f; (version) versión f; (report) informe m; **by all** ∼**s** a decir de todos [2] (consideration): **to take sth into** ∼ tener* algo en cuenta [3] (in phrases) **on account of** (as prep) debido a; **on no account** de ningún modo, de ninguna manera; **on sb's account** por algn

II [1] (with bank, at shop) cuenta f [2] **accounts** (Busn, Fin) (+ pl vb) contabilidad f ■ **account for** [v + prep + o] [1] (a) (provide record of, justify) ⟨expenditure/time⟩ dar* cuentas de (b) (explain) explicar*; **there's no** ∼**ing for taste** sobre gustos no hay nada escrito [2] (add up to): **wages** ∼ **for 70% of the total** los sueldos representan un or el 70% del total

accountable /ə'kaʊntəbəl/ adj (pred) responsable; **to be** ∼ **TO sb (FOR sth)** ser* responsable **ANTE** algn (**DE** algo)

accountancy /ə'kaʊntnsi/ n contabilidad f

accountant /ə'kaʊntnt/ n contador, -dora m,f (AmL), contable mf (Esp)

accredit /ə'kredət ‖ə'kredɪt/ vt (usu pass) acreditar

accrue /ə'kruː/ vi acumularse ■ ∼ vt acumular

accumulate /ə'kjuːmjələt ‖ə'kjuːmjʊleɪt/ vt ⟨wealth/interest⟩ acumular; ⟨information/evidence⟩ reunir* ■ ∼ vi acumularse

accuracy /'ækjərəsi/ n (of measurement, instrument, description, translation) exactitud f; (of weapon) precisión f; (of aim, blow) lo certero

accurate /'ækjərət/ adj ⟨measurement/instrument/description/translation⟩ exacto; ⟨weapon/aim/blow⟩ certero

accusation /ˌækjə'zeɪʃən ‖ˌækjuː'zeɪʃən/ n acusación f

accuse /ə'kjuːz/ vt acusar

accused /ə'kjuːzd/ n (pl ∼) (Law) **the** ∼ el acusado, la acusada; (pl) los acusados, las acusadas

accusing /ə'kjuːzɪŋ/ adj acusador

accustom /ə'kʌstəm/ vt **to** ∼ **sb TO sth/-ING** acostumbrar a algn A algo/+INF

accustomed /ə'kʌstəmd/ adj (pred) **to be** ∼ **TO sth/-ING** estar* acostumbrado A algo/+ INF; **to become** ∼ **TO sth/-ING** acostumbrarse A algo/+ INF

AC/DC /'eɪsiː'diːsiː/ adj (Elec) CA/CC

ace /eɪs/ n (a) (in cards, dice) as m (b) (expert, champion) as m

ache¹ /eɪk/ vi (a) «tooth/ear/leg» doler*; **my back** ∼**s** me duele la espalda (b) **aching** pres p ⟨shoulders/muscles⟩ dolorido

ache² n dolor m (sordo y continuo); ∼**s and pains** achaques mpl

achieve /ə'tʃiːv/ vt (a) (accomplish) lograr (b) (attain) ⟨success/victory⟩ conseguir*, obtener*; ⟨aim⟩ lograr, conseguir*; ⟨ambition⟩ hacer* realidad

achievement /ə'tʃiːvmənt/ n (a) (feat) logro m (b) (success) éxito m; **a sense of** ∼ la satisfacción de haber logrado algo

Achilles heel /ə'kɪliːz/ n talón m de Aquiles

acid¹ /'æsəd ‖'æsɪd/ n ácido m

acid², **acidic** /ə'sɪdɪk/ adj ácido

acid rain n lluvia f ácida

acknowledge /ək'nɑːlɪdʒ ‖ək'nɒlɪdʒ/ vt **1** (a) (admit) ⟨mistake/failure⟩ admitir (b) (recognize) ⟨skill/authority/right⟩ reconocer*; ⟨quotations/sources⟩ hacer* mención de (c) (express appreciation of) agradecer* **2** ⟨letter/order⟩ acusar recibo de; ⟨greeting⟩ responder a; ⟨person⟩ saludar

acknowledgment, acknowledgement /ək'nɑːlɪdʒmənt ‖ək'nɒlɪdʒmənt/ n (a) (recognition) reconocimiento m (b) (confirmation, response): **I've had no ~ of my letter** no han acusado recibo de mi carta (c) **acknowledgments** pl (in book) lista f de menciones

acne /'ækni/ n acné m or f, acne f‡

acorn /'eɪkɔːrn ‖'eɪkɔːn/ n bellota f

acoustic /ə'kuːstɪk/ adj acústico

acoustics /ə'kuːstɪks/ n (of room) (+ pl vb) acústica f

acquaintance /ə'kweɪntns/ n (a) (person) conocido, -da m,f (b) (with person) relación f; **to make sb's ~** conocer* a algn (c) (knowledge) ~ WITH sth conocimiento m DE algo

acquainted /ə'kweɪntəd ‖ə'kweɪntɪd/ adj (pred) (a) **to be ~ WITH sb** conocer* a algn (b) **to be ~ WITH sth** (be informed of) estar* al corriente DE algo; (be familiar with) estar* familiarizado CON algo

acquiesce /ˌækwi'es/ vi **to ~** (IN sth/-ING) consentir* (algo/EN + INF)

acquire /ə'kwaɪr ‖ə'kwaɪə(r)/ vt ⟨collection/skill⟩ adquirir*; ⟨reputation⟩ hacerse*

acquired /ə'kwaɪrd ‖ə'kwaɪəd/ adj ⟨characteristic⟩ adquirido; **it's an ~ taste** es algo a lo que se le va tomando el gusto con el tiempo

acquisition /ˌækwə'zɪʃən ‖ˌækwɪ'zɪʃən/ n adquisición f

acquit /ə'kwɪt/ vt **-tt- to ~** sb (OF sth) absolver* a algn (DE algo)

acre /'eɪkər ‖'eɪkə(r)/ n acre m (0,405 hectáreas)

acrid /'ækrəd ‖'ækrɪd/ adj acre

acrobat /'ækrəbæt/ n acróbata mf

acrobatic /ˌækrə'bætɪk/ adj acrobático

across¹ /ə'krɔːs ‖ə'krɒs/ adv (a) (indicating movement): **the boatman ferried them ~** el barquero los cruzó (b) (indicating position) del otro lado; **she sat ~ from me** estaba sentada frente a mí (c) (in width, diameter): **it is 20m ~** tiene or mide 20m de ancho

across² prep (a) (from one side to other): **they ran ~ the road** cruzaron la calle corriendo (b) (on the other side of): **they live just ~ the road** viven justo enfrente; **it's ~ the river** está al otro lado del río

acrylic /ə'krɪlɪk/ n acrílico m; (before n) acrílico

act¹ /ækt/ vi **1** (a) (take action, do sth) actuar* (b) ⟨drug/chemical⟩ hacer* efecto (c) (serve) **to ~ AS sth** servir* DE algo; **she will ~ as interpreter** hará de intérprete (d) **acting** pres p ⟨chairman/director⟩ interino **2** (behave) comportarse*; **don't ~ dumb** ¡no te hagas el tonto! **3** (perform) actuar*; (as profession) ser* actor/actriz

■ **~** vt (a) (perform) ⟨role/part⟩ interpretar (b) (behave like, play role of) hacerse*

■ **act for** [v + prep + o] (represent) representar

■ **act on** [v + prep + o] (a) (follow) ⟨advice⟩ seguir*; ⟨orders⟩ cumplir (b) (affect) ⟨⟨drug/chemical⟩⟩ actuar* sobre

■ **act out** [v + o + adv, v + adv + o] representar

act² n **1** (deed) acto m; **to catch sb in the ~** agarrar or (esp Esp) coger* a algn con las manos en la masa **2** (Govt) ley f **3** (a) (division of play) acto m (b) (routine) número m; **to get one's ~ together** organizarse* **4** (pretense): **it was all a big ~** era puro cuento (fam)

acting /'æktɪŋ/ n (performance) interpretación f; **have you done any ~ before?** ¿has hecho teatro/cine alguna vez?

action /'ækʃən/ n **1** (a) (practical measures): **prompt ~ by the police saved several lives** la rápida actuación de la policía salvó varias vidas; **to take ~** (against sb/sth) tomar medidas (contra algn/algo); **~!** (Cin) ¡acción! (b) (in phrases) **to put sth into ~** poner* algo en práctica; **to be out of ~** ⟨⟨car⟩⟩ estar* averiado; ⟨⟨person⟩⟩ estar* fuera de circulación **2** (deed) acto m **3** (Mil) acción f (de guerra) **4** (a) (plot of play, movie) acción f (b) (exciting activity) animación f **5** (a) (movement) movimiento m (b) (operation) funcionamiento m (c) (of drug, chemical) acción f

action: ~-packed adj lleno de acción; **~ replay** n (BrE) repetición f de la jugada

active /'æktɪv/ adj **1** ⟨person/life⟩ activo; ⟨volcano⟩ en actividad **2** (Ling) activo

activist /'æktəvəst ‖'æktɪvɪst/ n activista mf

activity /æk'tɪvəti/ n (pl **-ties**) actividad f

actor /'æktər ‖'æktə(r)/ n actor, actriz m,f

actress /'æktrəs/ n actriz f

actual /'æktʃuəl/ adj (before n) (a) (real) real; **in ~ fact** en realidad (b) (precise, very) mismo; **on the ~ day of the election** el mismo día de las elecciones

actually /'æktʃuəli/ adv en realidad; **~, I'd rather not go** la verdad es que preferiría no ir

acumen /ə'kjuːmən ‖'ækjuːmən/ n sagacidad f, perspicacia f; **business ~** visión f para los negocios

acupuncture /'ækjəˌpʌŋktʃər ‖'ækjʊˌpʌŋktʃə(r)/ n acupuntura f

acute /ə'kjuːt/ adj **1** ⟨condition/pain⟩ agudo; ⟨crisis/shortage⟩ grave; ⟨anxiety⟩ profundo; ⟨sense of smell⟩ fino; ⟨sight/hearing⟩ agudo **2** (Ling) ⟨accent⟩ agudo

ad /æd/ n (colloq) ▶ ADVERTISEMENT

AD (= **Anno Domini**) después de Cristo; (written form) d. de C., d. de J.C.

Adam /'ædəm/ n Adán; **~'s apple** nuez f (de Adán)

adamant /'ædəmənt/ adj ⟨refusal⟩ firme; **she was ~ that she wouldn't go** se mantuvo firme en su decisión de no ir

adapt /ə'dæpt/ vt adaptar

■ **~** vi **to ~** (TO sth/-ING) adaptarse (A algo/+ INF)

adaptable /ə'dæptəbəl/ adj adaptable

adaptation /ˌædæp'teɪʃən/ n adaptación f

adapter, adaptor /ə'dæptər ‖ə'dæptə(r)/ *n* (plug — with several sockets) enchufe *m* múltiple; (— for different sockets) adaptador *m*

add /æd/ *vt* [1] (put in in addition) añadir; **at least I think so, she** ~**ed** —al menos eso creo —añadió [2] (Math) sumar; ~ **the numbers together** suma los números [3] **added** *past p* ‹*bonus/incentive*› adicional; **with** ~**ed vitamins** con vitaminas
■ **add to** [*v + prep + o*] ‹*building*› ampliar*; ‹*confusion/difficulties*› aumentar
■ **add up** [1] [*v + adv*] **(a)** (Math) cuadrar **(b)** (make sense) (colloq) «*story/facts*» cuadrar; **it just doesn't** ~ **up** no tiene sentido [2] [*v + o + adv, v + adv + o*] (Math) ‹*figures*› sumar; ‹*bill*› hacer*, preparar
■ **add up to** [*v + adv + prep + o*] «*figures*» sumar en total; «*total*» ascender* a

adder /'ædər ‖'ædə(r)/ *n* víbora *f*

addict /'ædɪkt/ *n* adicto, -ta *m,f*; **drug** ~ drogadicto, -ta *m,f*

addicted /ə'dɪktəd ‖ə'dɪktɪd/ *adj* **to be** ~ (**TO sth**) ser* adicto (**A** algo)

addiction /ə'dɪkʃən/ *n* adicción *f*

addictive /ə'dɪktɪv/ *adj* ‹*drug*› que crea adicción; ‹*activity*› que crea hábito

addition /ə'dɪʃən/ *n* [1] **(a)** (Math) suma *f*, adición *f* (frml) **(b)** (adding) adición *f* **(c)** (*in phrases*) **in addition** además; **in addition to** además de [2] (extra thing): **the latest** ~**s to our library** las últimas adquisiciones de nuestra biblioteca

additional /ə'dɪʃənəl ‖ə'dɪʃənḷ/ *adj* ‹*cost/weight*› extra, adicional

additive /'ædətɪv ‖'ædɪtɪv/ *n* aditivo *m*

address¹ /'ædres ‖ə'dres/ *n* [1] **(a)** (of house, offices etc) dirección *f*, señas *fpl*; **🅢 address** (on form) domicilio; (*before n*) ~ **book** libreta *f* de direcciones **(b)** (Comput) dirección *f* [2] (speech) discurso *m* [3] **form of** ~ tratamiento *m*

address² /ə'dres/ *vt* [1] (AmE also) /'ædres/ ‹*mail*› ponerle* la dirección a [2] **(a)** (speak to) ‹*person*› dirigirse* a; ‹*assembly*› pronunciar un discurso ante **(b)** (direct) (frml) ‹*question/remark*› dirigir* [3] (deal with, confront) ‹*problem/issue*› tratar
■ *v refl* **(a)** (speak to) **to** ~ **oneself TO sb** dirigirse* **A** algn **(b)** (turn one's attention to) (frml) **to** ~ **oneself TO sth** dedicarse* **A** algo

addressee /ˌædre'si:/ *n* destinatario, -ria *m,f*

adept /ə'dept/ *adj* experto

adequate /'ædɪkwət/ *adj* ‹*help/funding*› suficiente; ‹*standard/explanation*› adecuado

adhere /æd'hɪr ‖əd'hɪə(r)/ *vi* (frml) **(a)** (stick) **to** ~ (**TO sth**) adherirse* (**A** algo) **(b)** **to** ~ **TO sth** ‹*to principles/cause*› adherirse* **A** algo; ‹*to regulations*› observar algo

adhesive¹ /æd'hi:sɪv ‖əd'hi:sɪv/ *adj* adhesivo

adhesive² *n* adhesivo *m*

ad hoc /'æd'hɑːk ‖ˌæd'hɒk/ *adj* ‹*arrangement/measure*› ad hoc; ~ ~ **committee** comisión *f* especial *or* ad hoc

adjacent /ə'dʒeɪsnt/ *adj* ‹*fields*› adyacente; ‹*rooms*› contiguo; ~ **TO sth** «*field*» adyacente **A** algo; «*room*» contiguo **A** algo

adjective /'ædʒɪktɪv/ *n* adjetivo *m*

adjoin /ə'dʒɔɪn/ *vt* (frml) **(a)** (be adjacent to) lindar con **(b) adjoining** *pres p* ‹*houses*› contiguo; **the** ~**ing room** el cuarto de al lado

adjourn /ə'dʒɜːrn ‖ə'dʒɜːn/ *vt* ‹*talks/trial*› suspender; **the meeting was** ~**ed** se levantó la sesión
■ ~ *vi*: **the court** ~**ed** el tribunal levantó la sesión

adjournment /ə'dʒɜːrnmənt ‖ə'dʒɜːnmənt/ *n* suspensión *f*

adjudicate /ə'dʒuːdɪkeɪt/ *vi* (give judgment) arbitrar
■ ~ *vt* (frml) ‹*competition*› juzgar*; ‹*claim*› decidir sobre

adjust /ə'dʒʌst/ *vt* ‹*instrument/prices/wages*› ajustar; ‹*volume/temperature/speed*› regular; **he** ~**ed his tie** se arregló la corbata
■ ~ *vi* **to** ~ (**TO sth/-ING**) adaptarse (**A** algo/+ INF)

adjustable /ə'dʒʌstəbəl/ *adj* ‹*focus/temperature*› regulable

adjustment /ə'dʒʌstmənt/ *n* [1] (to machine, instrument, figures) ajuste *m*; (to clothes) arreglo *m*; (to plan, system) cambio *m* [2] (act, process) **(a)** (of machine, instrument) ajuste *m* **(b)** (of person) adaptación *f*

ad-lib /'æd'lɪb/ *vt/i* **-bb-** improvisar

administer /əd'mɪnəstər ‖əd'mɪnɪstə(r)/ *vt* **(a)** (manage) administrar **(b)** (frml) ‹*punishment/drug*› administrar

administration /ədˌmɪnə'streɪʃən ‖ədˌmɪnɪ'streɪʃən/ *n* **(a)** (of institution, business, estate) administración *f* **(b)** (managing body) administración *f*; (Pol) gobierno *m*, administración *f* **(c)** (of justice, medicine) administración *f*

administrative /əd'mɪnəstreɪtɪv ‖əd'mɪnɪstrətɪv/ *adj* administrativo

administrator /əd'mɪnəstreɪtər ‖əd'mɪnɪstreɪtə(r)/ *n* administrador, -dora *m,f*

admirable /'ædmərəbəl/ *adj* ‹*honesty/work*› digno de admiración; ‹*plan*› excelente

admiral /'ædmərəl/ *n* almirante *mf*

admiration /ˌædmə'reɪʃən/ *n* admiración *f*

admire /əd'maɪr ‖əd'maɪə(r)/ *vt* admirar

admirer /əd'maɪrər ‖əd'maɪərə(r)/ *n* admirador, -dora *m,f*

admission /əd'mɪʃən/ *n* [1] **(a)** (to building, exhibition) entrada *f*; (price) (precio *m* de) entrada *f*; (into college, society) ingreso *m* [5] (into hospital) ingreso *m* [2] (confession) admisión *f*; **he was, by his own** ~, **a poor father** él mismo admitía que no era un buen padre

admit /əd'mɪt/ **-tt-** *vt* [1] **(a)** (allow entry) dejar entrar; ‹*light/air*› permitir entrar; **🅢 admit one** entrada individual **(b)** ‹*patient*› ingresar, internar (CS, Méx) [2] (confess) ‹*crime/mistake*› admitir; **to** ~ **sth TO sb** confesarle* algo **A** algn
■ **admit to** [*v + prep + o*] (confess) ‹*error*› admitir; ‹*crime*› declararse culpable de

admittance /əd'mɪtns/ *n* (frml) ~ (**TO sth**) acceso *m* (**A** algo); **🅢 no admittance** prohibida la entrada

admittedly /əd'mɪtədli ‖əd'mɪtɪdli/ *adv* (*indep*): ~, **it wasn't an easy task, but ...** hay que reconocer que no era una tarea fácil pero ...

admonish /æd'mɑːnɪʃ ‖əd'mɒnɪʃ/ *vt* (frml) **to** ~ **sb** (**FOR sth**) amonestar a algn (**POR** algo)

ado /əˈduː/ n: without further o more ~ sin más (preámbulos)

adolescence /ˌædəˈlesns/ n adolescencia f

adolescent¹ /ˌædəˈlesnt/ n adolescente mf

adolescent² adj adolescente

adopt /əˈdɑːpt ‖əˈdɒpt/ vt (a) ⟨child⟩ adoptar (b) ⟨idea/custom/title⟩ adoptar (c) ⟨recommendation⟩ aprobar*

adopted /əˈdɑːptəd ‖əˈdɒptɪd/ adj ⟨son/country⟩ adoptivo; she's ~ es adoptada

adoption /əˈdɑːpʃən ‖əˈdɒpʃən/ n (a) (of child) adopción f (b) (of approach, custom, title) adopción f (c) (of report, motion) aprobación f

adoptive /əˈdɑːptɪv ‖əˈdɒptɪv/ adj ⟨before n⟩ adoptivo

adorable /əˈdɔːrəbəl/ adj ⟨house/hat⟩ divino; ⟨child⟩ adorable

adoration /ˌædəˈreɪʃən/ n adoración f

adore /əˈdɔːr ‖əˈdɔː(r)/ vt (a) (love, worship) adorar (b) **adoring** pres p ⟨gaze⟩ lleno de adoración; ⟨mother⟩ amantísimo (c) (like, enjoy): I ~ figs me encantan los higos

adorn /əˈdɔːrn ‖əˈdɔːn/ vt (frml or liter) adornar

adornment /əˈdɔːrnmənt ‖əˈdɔːnmənt/ n adorno m

adrenaline /əˈdrenlən ‖əˈdrenəlm/ n adrenalina f

Adriatic /ˌeɪdriˈætɪk/ n the ~ (Sea) el (mar) Adriático

adrift /əˈdrɪft/ adj (pred) (Naut) a la deriva; to come o go ~ «plans» fallar

adroit /əˈdrɔɪt/ adj (a) ⟨answer/speaker⟩ hábil (b) ⟨movement⟩ ágil; ⟨player⟩ diestro

adulation /ˌædʒəˈleɪʃən ‖ˌædjʊˈleɪʃən/ n adulación f

adult¹ /əˈdʌlt, ˈædʌlt/ n adulto, -ta m,f

adult² adj (a) (physically mature) adulto (b) (mature) ⟨behavior/approach⟩ maduro, adulto (c) (suitable for adults) para mayores or adultos

adult education n educación f para adultos; ⟨before n⟩ ⟨class⟩ para adultos

adultery /əˈdʌltəri/ n adulterio m

adulthood /əˈdʌlthʊd , ˈædʌlthʊd/ n edad f adulta, adultez f

advance¹ /ədˈvæns ‖ədˈvɑːns/ vi «person/vehicle» avanzar*; «science/society» avanzar*, progresar
■ ~ vt **1** (a) (move forward) ⟨troops⟩ avanzar* (b) (further) ⟨knowledge⟩ fomentar; ⟨interests/cause⟩ promover* **2** (a) ⟨date/meeting⟩ adelantar (b) ⟨money/wages⟩ anticipar

advance² n **1** (of person, army, vehicle) avance m; (of civilization, science) avance m, progreso m **2** **advances** pl (overtures) insinuaciones fpl **3** (a) (early payment) anticipo m (b) (loan) préstamo m **4** in advance: to pay in ~ pagar* por adelantado; it was planned well in ~ se planeó con mucha antelación

advance³ adj ⟨before n⟩: ~ booking is essential es imprescindible hacer la reserva por anticipado

advanced /ədˈvænst ‖ədˈvɑːnst/ adj ⟨civilization/course/student⟩ avanzado

advantage /ədˈvæntɪdʒ ‖ədˈvɑːntɪdʒ/ n (a) (superior factor) ventaja f (b) (gain): to take ~ of sth aprovechar algo; (pej) aprovecharse de algo; to take ~ of sb (exploit) aprovecharse de algn; to turn sth to one's ~ sacar* provecho de algo (c) (in tennis) (no pl) ventaja f

advantageous /ˌædvænˈteɪdʒəs ‖ˌædvənˈteɪdʒəs/ adj ⟨arrangement⟩ ventajoso; ⟨position/situation⟩ de ventaja

advent /ˈædvent/ n (a) (arrival) llegada f (b) **Advent** (Relig) Adviento m

adventure /ədˈventʃər ‖ədˈventʃə(r)/ n aventura f; ⟨before n⟩ ⟨story/film⟩ de aventuras

adventurous /ədˈventʃərəs/ adj ⟨traveler⟩ intrépido; ⟨spirit/person⟩ aventurero

adverb /ˈædvɜːrb ‖ˈædvɜːb/ n adverbio m

adversary /ˈædvərseri ‖ˈædvəsəri/ n (pl -ries) (frml) adversario, -ria m,f

adverse /ˈædvɜːrs, ædˈvɜːrs ‖ˈædvɜːs/ adj adverso

adversity /ædˈvɜːrsəti ‖ədˈvɜːsəti/ n (pl -ties) adversidad f

advert /ˈædvɜːrt ‖ˈædvɜːt/ n (BrE colloq) ▶ ADVERTISEMENT

advertise /ˈædvərtaɪz ‖ˈædvətaɪz/ vt ⟨product⟩ hacerle* publicidad a, hacerle* réclame a (AmL); I saw it ~d on TV lo vi anunciado en la tele
■ ~ vi hacer* publicidad

advertisement /ˈædvərtaɪzmənt ‖ədˈvɜːtɪsmənt/ n anuncio m, aviso m (AmL)

advertiser /ˈædvərtaɪzər ‖ˈædvətaɪzə(r)/ n anunciante mf

advertising /ˈædvərtaɪzɪŋ ‖ˈædvətaɪzɪŋ/ n (a) (action, business) publicidad f; ⟨before n⟩ ⟨campaign/slot⟩ publicitario; ~ agency agencia f de publicidad (b) (advertisements) propaganda f

advice /ədˈvaɪs/ n (counsel) consejos mpl; (professional) asesoramiento m; a piece of ~ un consejo; to give sb ~ aconsejar a algn; to take sb's ~ seguir* los consejos de algn

advisable /ədˈvaɪzəbəl/ adj aconsejable

advise /ədˈvaɪz/ vt **1** (a) (recommend) aconsejar; to ~ sb to + INF aconsejar(le) A algn QUE (+ subj); they ~d him against marrying so young le aconsejaron que no se casara tan joven (b) (give advice to) aconsejar; (professionally) asesorar **2** (inform) (frml) informar; (in writing) notificar* (frml)
■ ~ vi aconsejar; (professionally) asesorar; to ~ AGAINST sth/-ING desaconsejar algo/+ INF

adviser, advisor /ədˈvaɪzər ‖ədˈvaɪzə(r)/ n consejero, -ra m,f; (professional) asesor, -sora m,f

advisory /ədˈvaɪzəri/ adj ⟨body/service⟩ consultivo; in an ~ capacity en calidad de asesor

advocate¹ /'ædvəkət/ n (a) (supporter, defender) ~ (OF sth) defensor, -sora m,f (DE algo) (b) (in a court of law) abogado, -da m,f

advocate² /'ædvəkeɪt/ vt recomendar*, abogar* por

Aegean /ɪ'dʒiːən/ n the ~ (Sea) el (mar) Egeo

aerial¹ /'eriəl ‖'eəriəl/ adj (before n) aéreo; ~ photograph aerofoto f

aerial² n (esp BrE) antena f

aerobics /e'rəʊbɪks, ə- ‖eə'rəʊbɪks/ n (+ sing or pl vb) aerobic(s) m, aerobismo m (CS)

aerodynamic /'erəʊdaɪˈnæmɪk ‖,eərəʊdaɪˈnæmɪk/ adj aerodinámico

aeroplane /'erəplem ‖'eərəpleɪn/ n (BrE) avión m

aerosol /'erəsɒːl ‖'eərəsɒl/ n aerosol m, spray m

aerospace /'erəʊspeɪs ‖'eərəʊspeɪs/ adj (before n) ⟨research/industry⟩ aeroespacial

aesthetic, (AmE also) **esthetic** /es'θetɪk ‖iːs'θetɪk/ adj estético

afar /ə'faːr ‖ə'faː(r)/ adv (liter) lejos

affable /'æfəbəl/ adj afable

affair /ə'fer ‖ə'feə(r)/ n 1 (a) (case) caso m (b) (event): the wedding was a small, family ~ la boda se celebró en la intimidad; it was a very formal ~ fue una ocasión muy ceremoniosa (c) (business, concern) asunto m (d) affairs pl (matters) asuntos mpl 2 (liaison) affaire m

affect /ə'fekt/ vt (have effect on) afectar a; ⟨organ/nervous system⟩ comprometer

affected /ə'fektəd ‖ə'fektɪd/ adj afectado

affection /ə'fekʃən/ n cariño m

affectionate /ə'fekʃnət/ adj cariñoso

affiliate /ə'fɪliett/ vt (often pass) afiliar

affiliation /ə'fili'eɪʃən/ n afiliación f; her political ~s su filiación política

affinity /ə'fɪnəti/ n (pl -ties) afinidad f

affirm /ə'fɜːrm ‖ə'fɜːm/ vt declarar

affirmative /ə'fɜːrmətɪv ‖ə'fɜːmətɪv/ adj afirmativo

affix /ə'fɪks/ vt (fml) ⟨stamp/seal⟩ poner*; ⟨notice⟩ fijar

afflict /ə'flɪkt/ vt ⟨disease/problem⟩ aquejar

affliction /ə'flɪkʃən/ n (a) (suffering) aflicción f (b) (cause of suffering) desgracia f, (ailment) mal m

affluence /'æfluəns/ n prosperidad f

affluent /'æfluənt/ adj ⟨suburb/country⟩ próspero; ⟨person⟩ acomodado

afford /ə'fɔːrd ‖ə'fɔːd/ vt: I can't ~ a new car no me alcanza el dinero para comprarme un coche nuevo; you can't ~ to miss this opportunity no puedes perderte esta oportunidad

affordable /ə'fɔːrdəbəl ‖ə'fɔːdəbəl/ adj asequible

affront /ə'frʌnt/ n (fml) afrenta f

Afghan¹ /'æfgæn/ adj afgano

Afghan² n afgano, -na m,f

Afghanistan /æf'gænəstæn ‖æf'gænɪstaːn/ n Afganistán m

afield /ə'fiːld/ adv: she travels as far ~ as China viaja a lugares tan distantes como la China; we had to look further ~ for help tuvimos que buscar ayuda en otra parte

afloat /ə'fləʊt/ adj (pred) a flote; to stay ~ mantenerse* a flote

afoot /ə'fʊt/ adj (pred): plans are ~ to create ... hay planes de crear ...; what's ~? ¿qué se está tramando?

aforementioned /ə'fɔːr'mentʃənd ‖ə,fɔː'menʃənd/ adj (fml) (before n) ⟨clause/ statement⟩ anteriormente mencionado, antedicho (fml); the ~ person el susodicho, la susodicha (fml o hum)

afraid /ə'freɪd/ adj (pred) 1 (scared): to be ~ OF sb/sth tenerle* miedo A algn/A algo; there's nothing to be ~ of no tienes nada que temer 2 (sorry): she's not in, I'm ~ lo siento pero no está; I'm ~ not me temo que no

afresh /ə'freʃ/ adv: to start ~ empezar* de nuevo, volver* a empezar

Africa /'æfrɪkə/ n África f‡

African¹ /'æfrɪkən/ adj africano

African² n africano, -na m,f

African-American¹ /'æfrɪkənə'merɪkən/adj norteamericano de origen africano

African-American² n norteamericano, -na m,f de origen africano

Afro-American¹ /'æfrəʊə'merɪkən/ adj afroamericano

Afro-American² n afroamericano, -na m,f

Afro-Caribbean /ˌæfrəʊˌkærɪ'biːən/ adj (BrE) afroantillano, afrocaribeño

after¹ /'æftər ‖'aːftə(r)/ prep 1 (following in time) después de; I'll be at home ~ eight o'clock estaré en casa después de or a partir de las ocho; it's just ~ midnight son las doce pasadas; it's a quarter ~ two (AmE) son las dos y cuarto; the day ~ the party al día siguiente de la fiesta 2 (in sequence, rank) tras; day ~ day día tras día; do go in — ~ you! pase — ¡primero usted! 3 (a) (behind): shut the door ~ you cierra la puerta al salir (b) (in pursuit of) tras; he ran ~ them corrió tras ellos; he's ~ her money anda a la caza de su dinero (fam); see also ASK AFTER 4 after all después de todo

after² conj: it happened ~ you left ocurrió después de que tú te fuiste; ~ examining it después de examinarlo

after³ adv (a) (afterward, following) después; the day ~ al día siguiente (b) (behind) detrás

aftereffect /'æftərɪˌfekt ‖'aːftərɪˌfekt/ n (of drug) efecto m secundario; (of problem) secuela f

aftermath /'æftərmæθ ‖'aːftəmæθ, 'aːftəmaː:θ/ n (a) (subsequent period): in the ~ of the riots tras los disturbios (b) (consequences) repercusiones fpl

afternoon /'æftər'nuːn ‖,aːftə'nuːn/ n 1 (time of day) tarde f; on Friday ~ el viernes por or (AmL) en la tarde; he came in the ~ vino por la tarde, vino en la tarde (AmL); good ~! ¡buenas tardes! 2 afternoons (as adv) por las tardes, en las tardes (AmL)

after: ~shave (lotion) n loción f para después de afeitarse, aftershave m; **~thought** n: it occurred to me as an ~thought que ...; después se me ocurrió qué ...; it was added on as an ~thought fue una idea de último momento

afterward /'æftərwərd ‖'aːftəwəd/, (BrE also) **afterwards** /-z/ adv después

again /ə'gen, ə'geɪn/ *adv* otra vez, de nuevo; **to do sth ~** volver* a hacer algo, hacer* algo otra vez *or* de nuevo; **never ~!** ¡nunca más!

against /ə'genst, ə'geɪnst/ *prep* contra; **I've nothing ~ her** no tengo nada contra ella *or* en contra suya *or* en contra de ella; **I'm ~ capital punishment** estoy en contra de la pena de muerte; **he put a cross ~ my name** puso una cruz al lado de mi nombre

age¹ /eɪdʒ/ *n* **1** (of person, animal, thing) edad *f*; **he is six years of ~** tiene seis años; **to be under ~** ser* menor de edad; *(before n)* **~ group** grupo *m* etario (frml) **2** **(a)** (epoch, period) era *f*; **through the ~s** a través de los tiempos **(b)** (long time) (colloq): **I haven't seen her for ~s** hace siglos que no la veo (fam)

age² *(pres p* **aging** *or* **ageing**; *past p* **aged** /eɪdʒd/) *vi* «*person*» envejecer*; «*cheese*» madurar
■ **~** *vt* ‹*person*› hacer* envejecer; ‹*wine*› añejar

aged *adj* **1** /'eɪdʒəd ‖ 'eɪdʒɪd/ (elderly) anciano **2** /eɪdʒd/ *(pred)*: **he was ~ 20** tenía 20 años de edad

ageing *adj/n* ▶ AGING

ageism /'eɪdʒɪzəm/ *n* discriminación *f* por razones de edad

ageist /'eɪdʒəst ‖ 'eɪdʒɪst/ *adj* que discrimina a las personas en razón de su edad

agency /'eɪdʒənsi/ *n (pl* **-cies) (a)** (office) agencia *f* **(b)** (branch) sucursal *f* **(c)** (department) organismo *m*

agenda /ə'dʒendə/ *n* orden *m* del día, agenda *f*

agent /'eɪdʒənt/ *n* **1** (person) agente *mf* **2** (substance) agente *m*

aggravate /'ægrəveɪt/ *vt* **(a)** (make worse) agravar **(b)** (annoy) (colloq) exasperar

aggression /ə'greʃən/ *n* **(a)** (feeling, attitude) agresividad *f* **(b)** (unprovoked attack) agresión *f*

aggressive /ə'gresɪv/ *adj* ‹*person/country*› agresivo; ‹*tactics/strategy*› de agresión

aghast /ə'gæst ‖ ə'gɑːst/ *adj (pred)* aterrado

agile /'ædʒəl ‖ 'ædʒaɪl/ *adj* ágil

agility /ə'dʒɪləti/ *n* agilidad *f*

aging¹ /'eɪdʒɪŋ/ *adj (before n)* ‹*person*› envejecido

aging² *n* envejecimiento *m*

agitate /'ædʒəteɪt ‖ 'ædʒɪteɪt/ *vt* **(a)** (disturb) ‹*surface/liquid*› agitar **(b)** (upset) inquietar
■ **~** *vi* **to ~ FOR/AGAINST sth** hacer* campaña A FAVOR DE/EN CONTRA DE algo

agitated /'ædʒəteɪtəd ‖ 'ædʒɪteɪtɪd/ *adj* ‹*movements/gestures*› nervioso; **to become/get ~** ponerse* nervioso

agitation /ædʒə'teɪʃən ‖ ,ædʒɪ'teɪʃən/ *n* agitación *f*

AGM *n* (BrE) = **annual general meeting**

agnostic /æg'nɑːstɪk ‖ æg'nɒstɪk/ *n* agnóstico, -ca *m,f*

ago /ə'gəʊ/ *adv*: **five days ~** hace cinco días; **a long time ~** hace mucho (tiempo)

agog /ə'gɑːg ‖ ə'gɒg/ *adj (pred)*: **I was all ~** estaba que me moría de curiosidad

agonize /'ægənaɪz/ *vi*: **stop agonizing, just do it** no le des más vueltas al asunto y hazlo; **he ~d over the decision** le costó muchísimo decidirse

agonizing /'ægənaɪzɪŋ/ *adj* ‹*experience*› angustioso; ‹*pain*› atroz; ‹*decision*› muy difícil

agony /'ægəni/ *n (pl* **-nies)**: **he was in ~** estaba desesperado de dolor; **she's going through agonies of doubt** las dudas la están atormentando; **to prolong the ~** alargar* el martirio

agoraphobia /ægərə'fəʊbiə/ *n* agorafobia *f*

agree /ə'griː/ *vt* **1** **(a)** (be in agreement over) **to ~ (THAT)** estar* de acuerdo (EN QUE); **yes, it must feel odd, he ~d** —sí, debe resultar extraño — asintió **(b)** (reach agreement over) decidir; **it was ~d that he should go on his own** se decidió que fuera él solo; **to ~ WHEN/WHAT/HOW** *etc* ponerse* de acuerdo EN CUÁNDO/EN QUÉ/EN CÓMO *etc*; **to ~ to + INF** quedar EN + INF; **(c)** (decide on) ‹*price*› acordar*
2 **(a)** (consent) **to ~ to + INF** aceptar + INF **(b)** (admit) **to ~ (THAT)** reconocer* (QUE)
■ **~** *vi* **1** (be of same opinion) estar* de acuerdo; **to ~ ABOUT sth** estar* de acuerdo EN algo **2** **(a)** (get on well) congeniar **(b)** (tally) «*statements/figures*» concordar*
■ **agree on** [*v + prep + o*] ‹*date/details*› acordar*; **we ~ on the color** estamos de acuerdo en el color
■ **agree to** [*v + prep + o*] ‹*terms/conditions*› aceptar
■ **agree with** [*v + prep + o*] **(a)** (approve of) estar* de acuerdo con **(b)** **to ~ with sb** «*food/heat/climate*» sentarle* bien a algn

agreeable /ə'griːəbəl/ *adj* **1** (pleasant) agradable **2** (willing) *(pred)*: **bring her along, if she's ~** tráela, si quiere venir; **he seemed quite ~ to coming** parecía dispuesto a venir

agreed /ə'griːd/ *adj* **(a)** (in agreement) *(pred)* de acuerdo **(b)** (prearranged): **we met at ten, as ~** nos encontramos a las diez como habíamos quedado; *(before n)* ‹*price/terms*› acordado

agreement /ə'griːmənt/ *n* **1** **(a)** (shared opinion) acuerdo *m*; **to be in ~ (with sb)** estar* de acuerdo (con algn) **(b)** (written arrangement) acuerdo *m*; (Busn) contrato *m* **2** (consent) consentimiento *m*

agricultural /'ægrɪ'kʌltʃərəl/ *adj* agrícola

agriculture /'ægrɪkʌltʃər ‖ 'ægrɪkʌltʃə(r)/ *n* agricultura *f*

aground /ə'graʊnd/ *adv*: **to go** *o* **run ~ (ON sth)** encallar (EN algo)

ahead /ə'hed/ *adv* **1** **(a)** (indicating movement): **go straight ~** siga todo recto; **I'll go on ~** yo iré delante **(b)** (indicating position): **the post office is straight ~** la oficina de correos está siguiendo recto **(c)** (in race, competition): **our team was ~** nuestro equipo llevaba la delantera **(d)** (in time): **the months ~** los meses venideros, los próximos meses
2 **ahead of (a)** (in front of) delante de **(b)** (in race, competition) por delante de; **the Japanese are way ~ of us in this field** los japoneses nos llevan mucha ventaja en este campo **(c)** (before): **she got there an hour ~ of him** llegó una hora antes que él

aid¹ /eɪd/ *n* **(a)** (assistance, support) ayuda *f*; **to come/go to sb's ~** venir*/ir* en ayuda de algn **(b)** (monetary) ayuda *f*, asistencia *f*; **a concert in ~ of ...** un concierto a beneficio de ...

aid² *vt* ayudar; **to ~ and abet sb** (Law) instigar* *or* secundar a algn *(en la comisión de un delito)*

aide /eɪd/ *n* asesor, -sora *m,f*

AIDS /eɪdz/ *n* (= **acquired immune deficiency syndrome**) sida *m*, SIDA *m*

ailing /ˈeɪlɪŋ/ *adj* ⟨person⟩ enfermo; ⟨economy⟩ renqueante

ailment /ˈeɪlmənt/ *n* enfermedad *f*, dolencia *f* ⟨fml⟩

aim¹ /eɪm/ *vt*: he ~ed the gun at her le apuntó con la pistola; she ~ed a blow at his head intentó darle en la cabeza; the movie is ~ed at a young audience la película está dirigida a un público joven

■ ~ *vi* **(a)** ⟨point weapon⟩ apuntar; **to ~ AT sth/sb** apuntar(le) A algo/algn **(b)** ⟨intend⟩ **to ~ to +** INF querer* + INF

aim² *n* **(a)** ⟨goal, object⟩ objetivo *m* **(b)** ⟨with weapon⟩ puntería *f*; **to take ~** hacer* puntería, apuntar

aimless /ˈeɪmləs ‖ˈeɪmlɪs/ *adj* ⟨wandering⟩ sin rumbo ⟨fijo⟩; ⟨existence⟩ sin norte

ain't /eɪnt/ ⟨colloq & dial⟩ **(a)** = **am not (b)** = **is not (c)** = **are not (d)** = **has not (e)** = **have not**

air¹ /er ‖eə(r)/ *n* **1** aire *m*; **to go by ~** ir* en avión; **to be up in the ~** «plans» estar* en el aire; **to vanish into thin ~** esfumarse; ⟨before n⟩ ⟨route/attack⟩ aéreo; ⟨pollution⟩ de la atmósfera; **~ pressure** presión *f* atmosférica **2** ⟨Rad, TV⟩: **to be on the ~** estar* en el aire; **to come** o **go on the ~** salir* al aire **3** **(a)** ⟨manner, look, atmosphere⟩ aire *m* **(b) airs** *pl* ⟨affectations⟩ aires *mpl*

air² *vt* **1** **(a)** ⟨clothes/linen⟩ airear, orear; ⟨bed/room⟩ ventilar, airear **(b)** ⟨opinion/grievance⟩ manifestar*; ⟨knowledge⟩ hacer* alarde de **2** ⟨broadcast⟩ ⟨AmE⟩ ⟨program⟩ transmitir, emitir

air: **~ bag** *n* ⟨Auto⟩ bolsa *f* de aire; **~ base** *n* base *f* aérea; **~ bed** *n* ⟨BrE⟩ colchón *m* inflable; **~borne** *adj* ⟨seeds/dust⟩ transportado por el aire; ⟨troops/units⟩ aerotransportado **(b)** ⟨off the ground⟩: **the plane is now ~borne** el avión ha despegado; **~-conditioned** /ˈerkənˈdɪʃənd ‖ˈeəkəndɪʃənd/ *adj* con aire acondicionado, climatizado; **~ conditioning** *n* aire *m* acondicionado

aircraft /ˈerkræft ‖ˈeəkrɑːft/ *n* (*pl* ~) avión *m*

aircraft carrier *n* portaaviones *m*

air: **~fare** *n* precio *m* del pasaje *or* ⟨Esp tb⟩ del billete de avión; **~fares are set to rise** van a subir las tarifas aéreas; **~field** *n* aeródromo *m*; **~ force** *n* ⟨of nation⟩ fuerza *f* aérea; **~ freshener** /ˈfreʃnər ‖ˈfreʃnə(r)/ *n* ambientador *m*, desodorante *m* ambiental *or* de ambientes ⟨CS⟩; **~ gun** *n* ⟨revolver⟩ pistola *f* de aire comprimido; ⟨rifle⟩ escopeta *f* *or* rifle *m* de aire comprimido; **~ hostess** *n* azafata *f*, aeromoza *f* ⟨AmL⟩; **~ letter** *n* aerograma *m*; **~lift** *n* puente *m* aéreo; **~line** *n* línea *f* aérea, aerolínea *f*; **~mail** *n* correo *m* aéreo; **to send sth (by) ~mail** mandar algo por avión *or* por vía aérea; ⟨before n⟩ ⟨paper/envelope⟩ de avión; **~plane** *n* ⟨AmE⟩ avión *m*; **~port** *n* aeropuerto *m*; **~ raid** *n* ataque *m* aéreo; ⟨before n⟩ **~raid shelter** refugio *m* antiaéreo; **~ship** *n* dirigible *m*, zepelín *m*; **~sick** *adj*: **to be ~sick** estar* mareado (en un avión); **to get ~sick** marearse (al viajar en avión); **~sickness** *n* mareo *m* (al viajar en avión); **~ strike** *n* ataque *m* aéreo; **~strip** *n*

pista *f* de aterrizaje; **~tight** *adj* ⟨room/box⟩ hermético; ⟨alibi/argument⟩ a toda prueba; **~ traffic control** *n* control *m* del tráfico aéreo; **~ traffic controller** *n* controlador aéreo, controladora aérea *m,f*, **~worthy** *adj*: **to be ~worthy** estar* en condiciones de vuelo

airy /ˈeri ‖ˈeəri/ *adj* **airier, airiest (a)** ⟨room/house⟩ espacioso y aireado **(b)** ⟨manner/reply⟩ displicente

aisle /aɪl/ *n* ⟨gangway⟩ pasillo *m*; ⟨Archit⟩ nave *f* lateral

ajar /əˈdʒɑːr ‖əˈdʒɑː(r)/ *adj* ⟨pred⟩ entreabierto

AK = **Alaska**

akin /əˈkɪn/ *adj* ⟨pred⟩ **to be ~** ⟨TO sth⟩ ser* similar ⟨A algo⟩

AL = **Alabama**

Ala = **Alabama**

à la carte /ˈɑːləˈkɑːrt ‖ˌɑːlɑːˈkɑːt/ *adj/adv* a la carta

alarm¹ /əˈlɑːrm ‖əˈlɑːm/ *n* **1** (apprehension) gran preocupación *f* **2** (warning, device) alarma *f*

alarm² *vt* (worry) alarmar; (scare) asustar

alarm clock *n* ⟨reloj *m*⟩ despertador *m*

alarmed /əˈlɑːrmd ‖əˈlɑːmd/ *adj* (apprehensive): **don't be ~** no te asustes; **I began to be ~** empecé a alarmarme

alarming /əˈlɑːrmɪŋ ‖əˈlɑːmɪŋ/ *adj* alarmante

alas /əˈlæs/ *interj* (liter or frml) ¡ay! (liter)

Albania /ælˈbeɪniə/ *n* Albania *f*

Albanian¹ /ælˈbeɪniən/ *adj* albanés

Albanian² *n* **(a)** (person) albanés, -nesa *m,f* **(b)** (language) albanés *m*

albeit /ɔːlˈbiːɪt/ *conj* (frml) aunque

albino /ælˈbaɪnəʊ ‖ælˈbiːnəʊ/ *n* (*pl* **-nos**) albino, -na *m,f*; (before n) albino

album /ˈælbəm/ *n* **(a)** (book) álbum *m*; **photograph ~** álbum de fotos **(b)** (Audio) álbum *m*

alchemist /ˈælkəməst ‖ˈælkəmɪst/ *n* alquimista *mf*

alcohol /ˈælkəhɔːl ‖ˈælkəhɒl/ *n* alcohol *m*

alcoholic¹ /ˈælkəˈhɔːlɪk ‖ˌælkəˈhɒlɪk/ *adj* alcohólico

alcoholic² *n* alcohólico, -ca *m,f*

alcoholism /ˈælkəhɔːlɪzəm ‖ˈælkəhɒlɪzəm/ *n* alcoholismo *m*

alcove /ˈælkəʊv/ *n* (recess) hueco *m*; (niche) hornacina *f*

alderman /ˈɔːldərmən ‖ˈɔːldəmən/ *n* (*pl* **-men** /-mən/) **(a)** (in UK) regidor, -dora *m,f* **(b)** (in US) concejal *m*

alderwoman /ˈɔːldərˌwʊmən ‖ˈɔːldəˌwʊmən/ *n* (*pl* **-women**) (in US) concejala *f*

ale /eɪl/ *n* cerveza *f*

alert¹ /əˈlɜːrt ‖əˈlɜːt/ *adj* alerta *adj inv*; **to be ~** (vigilant) estar* alerta; (lively-minded) estar* despierto

alert² *n* alerta *f*; **to be on the ~** estar* alerta

alert³ *vt* **to ~ sb** ⟨TO sth⟩ alertar a algn ⟨DE algo⟩

A level *n* (in UK) *estudios de una asignatura a nivel de bachillerato superior*

alga /ˈælgə/ *n* (*pl* **algae** /ˈældʒiː, ˈælgiː/) alga *f*‡

algebra /ˈældʒəbrə ‖ˈældʒɪbrə/ *n* álgebra *f*‡

Algeria /ælˈdʒɪriə ‖ælˈdʒɪəriə/ *n* Argelia *f*

Algerian /æl'dʒɪəriən ‖æl'dʒɪəriən/ *adj* argelino

alias /'eɪliəs/ *adv* alias

alibi /'æləbaɪ ‖'ælɪbaɪ/ *n* coartada *f*

alien¹ /'eɪliən/ *n* (a) (foreigner) extranjero, -ra *m,f* (b) (in science fiction) extraterrestre *mf*

alien² *adj* (a) (strange, foreign) extraño; **to be ~ TO sb/sth** serle* ajeno A algn/algo (b) (in science fiction) extraterrestre

alienate /'eɪliəneɪt/ *vt* (Pol, Psych) alienar; (estrange): **he has ~d all his friends** ha hecho que todos sus amigos se alejen *or* se distancien de él

alight¹ /ə'laɪt/ *adj* (*pred*) **to be ~** estar* ardiendo; **to set sth ~** prender(le) fuego a algo

alight² *vi* (frml) «*passenger*» apearse (frml); (land) «*bird/insect*» posarse

align /ə'laɪn/ *vt* alinear

alignment /ə'laɪnmənt/ *n* (a) (Tech) alineación *f* (b) (Pol) alineamiento *m*

alike¹ /ə'laɪk/ *adj* (*pred*) parecido

alike² *adv* «*think/act*» igual; **popular with young and old ~** popular tanto entre los jóvenes como entre los mayores

alimony /'æləməʊni ‖'ælɪməni/ *n* pensión *f* alimenticia

alive /ə'laɪv/ *adj* (*pred*) vivo; **is he still ~?** ¿todavía vive?; **to stay ~** sobrevivir; **she's ~ and well** está sana y salva; **the place was ~ with insects** el lugar estaba plagado de insectos

alkaline /'ælkəlaɪn/ *adj* alcalino

all¹ /ɔːl/ *adj* (*before n*) todo, -da; (*pl*) todos, -das; **~ four of us went** fuimos los cuatro; **~ morning** toda la mañana; **of ~ the stupid things to do!** ¡qué estupidez!; *see also* ALL³ 3D

all² *pron* ① (everything) (+ *sing vb*) todo; **will that be ~, madam?** ¿algo más señora?; **when ~ is said and done** a fin de cuentas; **for ~ I care** por lo que a mí me importa
② all of: **~ of the children go to school** todos los niños van al colegio; **~ of the cheese** todo el queso
③ (*after n, pron*) todo, -da; (*pl*) todos, -das; **it was ~ gone** no quedaba nada
④ (*in phrases*) (a) **all in all** en general (b) **all told** en total (c) **and all** y todo; **he ate it, skin and ~** se lo comió con la cáscara y todo (d) **at all: they don't like him at ~** no les gusta nada; **thank you — not at ~** gracias — de nada *or* no hay de qué; **it's not at ~ bad** no está nada mal (e) **in all** en total

all³ *adv* ① (completely): **you've gone ~ red** te has puesto todo colorado/toda colorada; **she was ~ alone** estaba sola sola
② (each, apiece) (Sport): **the score was one ~** iban (empatados) uno a uno; **30 ~** 30 iguales
③ (*in phrases*) (a) **all along** desde el primer momento (b) **all but** casi; **the game had ~ but finished** ya casi había terminado el partido (c) **all that** (particularly) (*usu neg*): **I don't know her ~ that well** no la conozco tan bien; **I don't care ~ that much** no me importa demasiado (d) **all the**

(+ *comp*): **~ the more reason to fire them!** ¡más razón para echarlos!; **~ the more so because ...** tanto más cuanto que ...

Allah /'ælə/ *n* Alá

all: ~-American /'ɔːləˈmerəkən ‖ˌɔːləˈmerɪkən/ *adj* «*boy/girl*» típicamente americano; **~-around** /'ɔːləˈraʊnd/ *adj* (AmE) (*before n*) (a) (versatile) «*athlete/scholar*» completo (b) «*experience/visibility*» amplio

allay /ə'leɪ/ *vt* «*doubt/fear*» disipar

all-clear /'ɔːl'klɪr ‖'ɔːl'klɪə(r)/ *n*: **to give sb/sth the ~** dar* luz verde a algn/algo

allegation /'ælɪˈɡeɪʃən/ *n* acusación *f*

allege /ə'ledʒ/ *vt* afirmar; **she is ~d to have accepted bribes** se dice que aceptó sobornos

alleged /ə'ledʒd/ *adj* (*before n*) «*thief/violation*» presunto

allegedly /ə'ledʒədli ‖ə'ledʒɪdli/ *adv* (*indep*) supuestamente

allegiance /ə'liːdʒəns/ *n* lealtad *f*; (political) filiación *f*

allergic /ə'lɜːrdʒɪk ‖ə'lɜːdʒɪk/ *adj* alérgico; **to be ~ TO sth** ser alérgico A algo

allergy /'ælərdʒi ‖'ælədʒi/ *n* (*pl* **-gies**) alergia *f*

alleviate /ə'liːvieɪt/ *vt* «*pain*» aliviar; «*problem*» paliar

alley /'æli/ *n* (*pl* **alleys**) callejón *m*

alleyway /'æliweɪ/ *n* callejón *m*

alliance /ə'laɪəns/ *n* alianza *f*

allied /'ælaɪd/ *adj* (a) (combined) (*pred*) **~ WITH** *o* **TO** unido A algo (b) «*nations/groups*» aliado (c) (related) «*subjects/industries*» relacionado

alligator /'æləɡeɪtər ‖'ælɪɡeɪtə(r)/ *n* aligátor *m*

all: ~-important /'ɔːlɪmˈpɔːrtənt ‖ˌɔːlɪmˈpɔːtənt/ *adj* de suma importancia; **~-night** /'ɔːl'naɪt/ *adj* «*party/show*» que dura toda la noche; «*café/store*» que está abierto toda la noche

allocate /'æləkeɪt/ *vt* asignar; (distribute) repartir; **$3 million has been ~d for research** se han destinado tres millones de dólares a la investigación

allot /ə'lɑːt ‖ə'lɒt/ *vt* **-tt-** (distribute) repartir; (assign) asignar

all: ~out /'ɔːl'aʊt/ *adj* «*attack*» con todo; «*opposition*» acérrimo; «*strike*» general; «*war*» total; **~ over** *adv* «*search*» por todas partes; **people came from ~ over** vino gente de todas partes

allow /ə'laʊ/ *vt* ① (a) (permit) permitir; 🚫 **no dogs allowed** no se admiten perros (b) (give, grant) dar*; **they are ~ed an hour for lunch** les dan una hora para comer; **within the time ~ed** dentro del plazo concedido ② (plan for): **~ a good two hours to reach the coast** calculen que les va a llevar por lo menos dos horas llegar a la costa; **I normally ~ about £50 for spending money** normalmente calculo unas 50 libras para gastos ③ (Sport) «*referee*» «*goal*» dar* por bueno
■ **allow for** [*v* + *prep* + *o*] «*contingency*» tener* en cuenta

---

a

allowance /əˈlaʊəns/ n **1** (from employer) complemento m; (from state) prestación f; (private) asignación f; (from parents) mensualidad f, mesada f (AmL) **2** to make ~(s) for sb ser* indulgente con algn; **we've made ~(s) for delays** hemos tenido en cuenta posibles retrasos

alloy /ˈælɔɪ/ n aleación f

all-powerful /ˈɔːlˈpaʊərfəl ‖ ˌɔːlˈpaʊəfəl/ adj todopoderoso

all right¹ adj (pred): **are you ~ ~?** ¿estás bien?; **the hotel looks ~ ~** el hotel no parece estar mal; **do I look ~ ~ in this dress?** ¿estoy bien con este vestido?; **I'll pay you back tomorrow: is that ~ ~?** mañana te devuelvo el dinero ¿okey? or (Esp) ¿vale?; **I'm sorry — that's ~ ~** lo siento — no tiene importancia; **it's ~ ~: I'm not going to hurt you** tranquilo, que no te voy a hacer daño

all right² adv bien

all right³ interj (colloq): **I won't be home till late, ~ ~?** volveré tarde ¿okey? or (Esp) ¿vale? (fam); **can I come too? — all right** ¿puedo ir yo también? — bueno

all: ~-round /ˈɔːlˈraʊnd/ adj (esp BrE) ▶ ALL-AROUND; **A~ Saints' Day** n día m de Todos los Santos; **~-time** adj ⟨record⟩ sin precedentes; ⟨favorite⟩ de todos los tiempos

allude /əˈluːd/ vi to ~ TO sth/sb aludir A algo/algn

alluring /əˈlʊrɪŋ ‖ əˈlʊərɪŋ/ adj seductor

allusion /əˈluːʒən/ n alusión f

ally¹ /ˈælaɪ/ n (pl **allies**) aliado, -da m,f

ally² v refl **allies, allying, allied**: to ~ oneself WITH sb aliarse CON algn; see also ALLIED

almanac /ˈɔːlmənæk/ n (yearbook) anuario m; (calendar) almanaque m

almighty /ɔːlˈmaɪti/ adj todopoderoso

almond /ˈɑːmənd/ n almendra f

almost /ˈɔːlməʊst/ adv casi

■ Note Where almost is used with a verb in the past tense, it is translated by casi or por poco, and the verb is usually in the present tense: I almost fell casi me caigo; we almost missed the train casi or por poco perdemos el tren. In some Latin American countries the preterite tense is often used: we almost missed the train casi or por poco perdimos el tren.

alms /ɑːmz/ pl n limosnas fpl

aloft /əˈlɔːft ‖ əˈlɒft/ adv en el aire; **he held the cup ~** levantó la copa en alto

alone¹ /əˈləʊn/ adj **(a)** (without others) solo; **I want to be ~ with you** quiero estar a solas contigo; **leave me ~** ¡déjame en paz! **(b)** let alone: **I can't afford beer, let ~ champagne** no puedo comprar ni cerveza, para qué hablar de champán; **she can't sew a button on, let ~ make a dress** no sabe ni pegar un botón menos aún hacer un vestido

alone² adv solo

along¹ /əˈlɔːŋ ‖ əˈlɒŋ/ adv **(a)** (forward): **a bit further ~ on the right** un poco más adelante, a mano derecha; **I was walking ~** iba caminando; see also COME, GET, MOVE etc ALONG **(b)** (with one): **why don't you come ~?** ¿por qué no vienes conmigo/con nosotros?; **she brought her brother ~** trajo a su hermano; see also SING ALONG **(c)** **along with** (junto) con

along² prep: **we walked ~ the shore** caminamos por la playa; **a bit further ~ the road** un poco más adelante

alongside¹ /əˈlɔːŋsaɪd ‖ əˈlɒŋsaɪd/ prep al lado de

alongside² adv al costado

aloof /əˈluːf/ adj distante

aloud /əˈlaʊd/ adv en alto, en voz alta

alphabet /ˈælfəbet/ n alfabeto m

alphabetical /ˌælfəˈbetɪkəl/ adj alfabético; **in ~ order** en or por orden alfabético

alpine /ˈælpaɪn/ adj **(a)** (of high mountains) alpino **(b)** **Alpine** ⟨scenery/people⟩ de los Alpes, alpino

Alps /ælps/ pl n the ~ los Alpes

already /ɔːlˈredi/ adv ya; **I've ~ been there** ya he estado allí, ya estuve allí (AmL)

alright /ɔːlˈraɪt/ adj/adv/interj ▶ ALL RIGHT

Alsatian /ælˈseɪʃən/ n (esp BrE) ▶ GERMAN SHEPHERD (DOG)

also /ˈɔːlsəʊ/ adv **(a)** (as well) también **(b)** (moreover) (as linker) además

altar /ˈɔːltər ‖ ˈɔːltə(r)/ n altar m

alter /ˈɔːltər ‖ ˈɔːltə(r)/ vt ⟨text/situation⟩ cambiar; ⟨garment⟩ arreglar
■ ~ vi cambiar

alteration /ˌɔːltəˈreɪʃən/ n (to text) cambio m; (to building) reforma f, (to garment) arreglo m

alternate¹ /ˈɔːltərnət ‖ ɔːlˈtɜːnət/ adj (before n) **(a)** (every second): **she works ~ Tuesdays** trabaja un martes sí y otro no; **write on ~ lines** escriba dejando un renglón por medio **(b)** (happening by turns) alterno **(c)** (AmE) ▶ ALTERNATIVE¹ A

alternate² /ˈɔːltərneɪt ‖ ˈɔːltəneɪt/ vt/i alternar

alternately /ˈɔːltərnətli ‖ ɔːlˈtɜːnətli/ adv: **he and she take the class ~** se turnan para dar la clase

alternating /ˈɔːltərneɪtɪŋ ‖ ˈɔːltəneɪtɪŋ/ adj alterno

alternating current n corriente f alterna

alternative¹ /ɔːlˈtɜːrnətɪv ‖ ɔːlˈtɜːnətɪv/ adj (before n) **(a)** (other) ⟨plan/method⟩ diferente **(b)** (progressive) ⟨lifestyle/medicine⟩ alternativo

alternative² n alternativa f

alternatively /ɔːlˈtɜːrnətɪvli ‖ ɔːlˈtɜːnətɪvli/ adv (indep): **~, you could stay with us** si no, te podrías quedar con nosotros

although /ɔːlˈðəʊ/ conj aunque

altitude /ˈæltɪtuːd ‖ ˈæltɪtjuːd/ n altitud f

alto¹ /ˈæltəʊ/ n (pl **altos**) contralto f

alto² adj alto

altogether /ˌɔːltəˈɡeðər ‖ ˌɔːltəˈɡeðə(r)/ adv **(a)** (completely) totalmente; **the decision wasn't ~ wise** la decisión no fue del todo acertada **(b)** (in total) en total **(c)** (on the whole) (indep) en general

aluminum /əˈluːmɪnəm/, (BrE) **aluminium** /ˈæljəˈmɪniəm/ n aluminio m

always /ˈɔːlweɪz/ adv siempre

am¹ /æm, weak form əm/ 1st pers sing of BE

am² /ˈeɪem/ (before midday) a.m.; **at 7 ~** a las 7 de la mañana or 7 a.m.

amalgamate /əˈmælɡəmeɪt/ vt ⟨collections/indexes⟩ unir, amalgamar; ⟨companies/departments⟩ fusionar
■ ~ vi «companies» fusionarse

amass /ə'mæs/ vt ⟨fortune⟩ amasar; ⟨arms/ information/debts⟩ acumular

amateur¹ /'æmətər ‖'æmətə(r)/ n amateur mf

amateur² adj ⟨athlete/musician⟩ amateur; ⟨sport/competition⟩ para amateurs; **an ∼ photographer** un aficionado a la fotografía

amaze /ə'meɪz/ vt asombrar

amazed /ə'meɪzd/ adj ⟨expression⟩ de asombro; **to be ∼** estar* asombrado

amazement /ə'meɪzmənt/ n asombro m

amazing /ə'meɪzɪŋ/ adj increíble

Amazon /'æməzɑːn ‖'æməzən/ n **(a)** (Myth) amazona f **(b)** (Geog) **the ∼** el Amazonas; ⟨before n⟩ ⟨rain forest⟩ amazónico

ambassador /æm'bæsədər ‖æm'bæsədə(r)/ n embajador, -dora m,f

amber /'æmbər ‖'æmbə(r)/ n **(a)** (substance, color) ámbar m **(b)** (BrE Aut) amarillo

ambidextrous /'æmbɪ'dekstrəs/ adj ambidiestro, ambidextro

ambiguity /'æmbə'gjuːəti ‖'æmbɪ'gjuːəti/ n (pl **-ties**) ambigüedad f

ambiguous /æm'bɪgjuəs/ adj ambiguo

ambition /æm'bɪʃən/ n ambición f

ambitious /æm'bɪʃəs/ adj **(a)** ⟨person/plan⟩ ambicioso **(b)** (overadventurous) ⟨pred⟩: **aren't you being a bit ∼?** ¿no estás pretendiendo hacer demasiado?

ambivalent /æm'bɪvələnt/ adj ambivalente

amble /'æmbəl/ vi: **to ∼ along** ir* tranquilamente

ambulance /'æmbjələns ‖'æmbjʊləns/ n ambulancia f

ambulanceman /'æmbjələnsmən ‖'æmbjʊlənsmən/ n (pl **-men** /-mən/) (BrE) ambulanciero m

ambush¹ /'æmbʊʃ/ vt tenderle* una emboscada a

ambush² n emboscada f

ameba /ə'miːbə/ (AmE) ▶ AMOEBA

amen /'ɑː'men, 'eɪ'men/ interj amén

amenable /ə'miːnəbəl/ adj ⟨temperament⟩ dócil; **they proved quite ∼ to the idea** se mostraron bien dispuestos frente a la idea

amend /ə'mend/ vt **(a)** ⟨text⟩ corregir* **(b)** (Law) enmendar*

amendment /ə'mendmənt/ n **(a)** (alteration) corrección f **(b)** (Law) enmienda f

amends /ə'mendz/ pl n: **to make ∼ to sb** desagraviar a algn; **to make ∼** reparar el daño

amenity /ə'miːnəti/ n (pl **-ties**) servicio m

America /ə'merəkə ‖ə'merɪkə/ n (USA) Norteamérica f, Estados mpl Unidos, América f; (continent) América f

American¹ /ə'merəkən ‖ə'merɪkən/ adj (of USA) estadounidense, norteamericano, americano

American² n (from USA) estadounidense mf, norteamericano, -na m,f, americano, -na m,f

amethyst /'æməθəst ‖'æməθɪst/ n amatista f

amiable /'eɪmiəbəl/ adj afable

amicable /'æmɪkəbəl/ adj ⟨person⟩ amigable; ⟨relations⟩ cordial

amid /ə'mɪd/, **amidst** /ə'mɪdst/ prep en medio de, entre

amiss /ə'mɪs/ adj ⟨pred⟩: **there was nothing ∼** no había ningún problema; **there's something ∼** pasa algo

ammunition /'æmjə'nɪʃən ‖'æmjʊ'nɪʃən/ n munición f

amnesia /æm'niːʒə ‖æm'niːziə/ n amnesia f

amnesty /'æmnəsti/ n (pl **-ties**) amnistía f

amoeba, (AmE also) **ameba** /ə'miːbə/ n ameba f, amiba f

amok /ə'mʌk ‖ə'mɒk/ adv **to run ∼** ⟨person⟩ tener* un ataque de locura

among /ə'mʌŋ/, **amongst** /ə'mʌŋst/ prep entre

amount /ə'maʊnt/ n cantidad f
■ **amount to** [v + prep + o] **(a)** (add up to) ⟨debt/ assets⟩ ascender* a **(b)** (be equivalent to) equivaler* a; **it ∼s to the same thing** viene a ser lo mismo

amp /æmp/ n **(a)** (Elec) amperio m **(b)** (amplifier) (colloq) amplificador m

amphetamine /æm'fetəmiːn/ n anfetamina f

amphibian /æm'fɪbiən/ n (Zool) anfibio m

amphibious /æm'fɪbiəs/ adj anfibio

amphitheater, (BrE) **amphitheatre** /'æmfɪˌθiːətər ‖'æmfɪˌθiːətə(r)/ n anfiteatro m

ample /'æmpəl/ adj **(a)** ⟨space⟩ amplio; ⟨funds/ resources⟩ abundante; ⟨helping⟩ generoso **(b)** (plenty) ⟨pred⟩ más que suficiente

amplifier /'æmpləfaɪər ‖'æmplɪfaɪə(r)/ n amplificador m

amplify /'æmpləfaɪ ‖'æmplɪfaɪ/ vt **-fies, -fying, -fied** amplificar*

amputate /'æmpjəteɪt ‖'æmpjʊteɪt/ vt amputar

Amtrak /'æmtræk/ n (in US) Ferrocarriles mpl de los EEUU

amuse /ə'mjuːz/ vt **(a)** (entertain) entretener* **(b)** (make laugh) divertir*
■ v refl **to ∼ oneself** (entertain oneself) entretenerse*; (have fun) divertirse*

amused /ə'mjuːzd/ adj ⟨expression⟩ divertido; **she was ∼ at the look on his face** le hizo gracia la cara que puso

amusement /ə'mjuːzmənt/ n **(a)** (entertainment) distracción f, entretención f (AmL) **(b)** (mirth) diversión f, **much to our ∼** para nuestro gran regocijo; ⟨before n⟩ **∼ arcade** sala f de juegos recreativos; **∼ park** parque m de diversiones or (Esp) atracciones

amusing /ə'mjuːzɪŋ/ adj divertido

an /æn, weak form ən/ indef art before vowel ▶ A

anachronism /ə'nækrənɪzəm/ n anacronismo m

anaemia etc (BrE) ▶ ANEMIA etc

anaesthetic n (BrE) ▶ ANESTHETIC

anagram /'ænəgræm/ n anagrama m

analogy /ə'nælədʒi/ n (pl **-gies**) analogía f

analyse vt (BrE) ▶ ANALYZE

analysis /ə'næləsəs ‖ə'nælɪsɪs/ n (pl **-lyses** /-lɪsiːz/) **(a)** (examination) análisis m **(b)** (Psych) psicoanálisis m, análisis m

analyst /'ænləst ‖'ænəlɪst/ n **(a)** (of data) analista mf **(b)** (Psych) psicoanalista mf, analista mf

analytical /'ænə'lɪtɪkəl/ adj analítico

analyze, (BrE) **analyse** /'ænəlaɪz/ *vt* **(a)**
⟨*data*⟩ analizar* **(b)** (Psych) psicoanalizar*,
analizar*

anarchist /'ænərkəst ‖'ænəkɪst/ *n* anarquista
mf

anarchy /'ænərki ‖'ænəki/ *n* anarquía *f*

anatomy /ə'nætəmi/ *n* anatomía *f*

ancestor /'ænsestər ‖'ænsestə(r)/ *n*
antepasado, -da *m,f*

ancestry /'ænsestri/ *n* ascendencia *f*

anchor[1] /'æŋkər ‖'æŋkə(r)/ *n* (Naut) ancla *f*‡

anchor[2] *vt* ⟨*ship*⟩ anclar; ⟨*rope/tent*⟩ sujetar

anchor: ~**man** /'æŋkərmæn ‖'æŋkəmæn/ *n*
(*pl* **-men** /-men/) (TV) presentador *m*;
~**woman** *n* (TV) presentadora *f*

anchovy /'æntʃəʊvi ‖'æntʃəvi/ *n* (*pl* **-vies** or
-vy) anchoa *f*

ancient /'eɪnʃənt/ *adj* **(a)** ⟨*civilizations/ruin*⟩
antiguo; A~ Greek griego *m* clásico **(b)** (colloq)
(old) ⟨*car*⟩ del año de la pera (fam)

and /ænd, *weak form* ənd/ *conj*

■ **Note** The usual translation of *and*, *y*, becomes *e*
when it precedes a word beginning with *i*, *hi*, or *y*.

(a) y; bread ~ butter pan con mantequilla **(b)** (in
numbers): one ~ a half uno y medio; two hundred
~ twenty doscientos veinte **(c)** (showing continuation,
repetition): faster ~ faster cada vez más rápido **(d)**
(*with inf*): try ~ finish this today trata de
terminar esto hoy

Andalusia /ændə'lu:ʒə ‖,ændə'lu:siə/ *n*
Andalucía *f*

Andalusian[1] /,ændə'lu:ʒən ‖,ændə'lu:siən/
adj andaluz

Andalusian[2] *n* andaluz, -luza *m,f*

Andes /'ændi:z/ *pl n* the ~ los Andes

Andorra /æn'dɔːrə/ *n* Andorra *f*

anecdote /'ænɪkdəʊt/ *n* anécdota *f*

anemia, (BrE) **anaemia** /ə'ni:miə/ *n* anemia *f*

anemic, (BrE) **anaemic** /ə'ni:mɪk/ *adj*
anémico

anemone /ə'nemɪni/ *n* (Bot) anémona *f*

anesthetic, (BrE) **anaesthetic** /ænəs'θetɪk
‖,ænɪs'θetɪk/ *n* anestésico *m*; **to be under** ~
estar* bajo los efectos de la anestesia

anesthetize, (BrE) **anaesthetize**
/ə'nesθetaɪz ‖ə'ni:sθətaɪz/ *vt* anestesiar

anew /ə'nu: ‖ə'nju:/ *adv* (liter) de nuevo, otra
vez

angel /'eɪndʒəl/ *n* ángel *m*

angelic /æn'dʒelɪk/ *adj* angelical

anger /'æŋgər ‖'æŋgə(r)/ *n* ira *f*, enojo *m* (esp
AmL), enfado *m* (esp Esp)

angina /æn'dʒaɪnə/ *n* angina *f* (de pecho)

angle /'æŋgəl/ *n* [1] ángulo *m*; she wore her hat
at an ~ llevaba el sombrero ladeado [2] (point of
view) perspectiva *f*

angler /'æŋglər ‖'æŋglə(r)/ *n* pescador, -dora
m,f (de caña)

Anglican[1] /'æŋglɪkən/ *n* anglicano, -na *m,f*

Anglican[2] *adj* anglicano

angling /'æŋglɪŋ/ *n* pesca *f* (con caña)

Anglo-Saxon[1] /'æŋgləʊ'sæksən/ *adj*
anglosajón

Anglo-Saxon[2] *n* **(a)** (person) anglosajón, -jona
m,f **(b)** (language) anglosajón *m*

Angola /æŋ'gəʊlə/ *n* Angola *f*

Angolan /æŋ'gəʊlən/ *adj* angoleño

angrily /'æŋgrəli ‖'æŋgrɪli/ *adv* con ira

angry /'æŋgri/ *adj* **angrier, angriest**
⟨*person*⟩ enojado (esp AmL), enfadado (esp Esp); **to
get** ~ enojarse (esp AmL), enfadarse (esp Esp)

anguish /'æŋgwɪʃ/ *n* angustia *f*

angular /'æŋgjələr ‖'æŋgjʊlə(r)/ *adj* ⟨*shape*⟩
angular; ⟨*features*⟩ anguloso

animal /'ænəməl ‖'ænɪməl/ *n* animal *m*

animate /'ænəmeɪt ‖'ænɪmeɪt/ *vt* animar

animated /'ænəmeɪtəd ‖'ænɪmeɪtɪd/ *adj*
animado

animation /'ænə'meɪʃən ‖,ænɪ'meɪʃən/ *n*
animación *f*

animator /'ænəmeɪtər ‖'ænɪmeɪtə(r)/ *n*
animador, -dora *m,f*

animosity /'ænə'mɑːsəti ‖,ænɪ'mɒsəti/ *n* (*pl*
-ties) animosidad *f*

aniseed /'ænəsi:d ‖'ænɪsi:d/ *n* anís *m*

ankle /'æŋkəl/ *n* tobillo *m*; (*before n*) ~ boot
botín *m*; ~ sock calcetín *m* corto, soquete *m* (CS)

annex[1] /ə'neks/ *vt* ⟨*territory*⟩ anexar

annex[2], (BrE) **annexe** /'æneks/ *n* anexo *m*,
anejo *m*

annihilate /ə'naɪəleɪt/ *vt* ⟨*army/city*⟩ aniquilar

anniversary /'ænə'vɜːrsəri ‖,ænɪ'vɜːsəri/ *n*
(*pl* **-ries**) aniversario *m*; (wedding) ~
aniversario *m* de boda de casados

announce /ə'naʊns/ *vt* **(a)** ⟨*flight/guest/*
marriage⟩ anunciar **(b)** (declare) anunciar **(c)**
(AmE Rad, TV) ⟨*game/race*⟩ comentar

announcement /ə'naʊnsmənt/ *n* anuncio *m*

announcer /ə'naʊnsər ‖ə'naʊnsə(r)/ *n* (Rad,
TV) **(a)** (commentator) (AmE) comentarista *mf* **(b)**
(between programs) (BrE) locutor, -tora *m,f* de
continuidad

annoy /ə'nɔɪ/ *vt* molestar, irritar

annoyance /ə'nɔɪəns/ *n* **(a)** (irritation) irritación
f; (anger) enojo *m* (esp AmL), enfado *m* (esp Esp) **(b)**
(cause of irritation) molestia *f*

annoyed /ə'nɔɪd/ *adj* enojado (esp AmL),
enfadado (esp Esp)

annoying /ə'nɔɪɪŋ/ *adj* ⟨*person*⟩ pesado; ⟨*noise/*
habit⟩ molesto; how ~! ¡qué rabia!

annual[1] /'ænjuəl/ *adj* (*before n*) anual

annual[2] *n* [1] (plant) planta *f* anual
[2] (publication) anuario *m*

annually /'ænjuəli/ *adv* anualmente

annul /ə'nʌl/ *vt* **-ll-** anular

annulment /ə'nʌlmənt/ *n* anulación *f*

anoint /ə'nɔɪnt/ *vt* ungir*

anonymity /'ænə'nɪməti/ *n* anonimato *m*

anonymous /ə'nɑːnəməs ‖ə'nɒnɪməs/ *adj*
anónimo; to remain ~ permanecer* en el
anonimato; ~ letter anónimo *m*

anorak /'ænəræk/ *n* (BrE) anorak *m*

anorexia (nervosa) /'ænə'reksiə (nər'vəʊsə)
‖,ænə'reksiə (nɜː'vəʊsə)/ *n* anorexia *f* (nerviosa)

another[1] /ə'nʌðər ‖ə'nʌðə(r)/ *adj* otro, otra;
(*pl*) otros, otras

another[2] *pron* otro, otra

answer¹ /'ænsər ‖'ɑːnsə(r)/ n **1** (a) (reply) respuesta f, contestación f; **in ~ to your question** para contestar tu pregunta (b) (response): **her ~ to his rudeness was to ignore it** respondió a su grosería ignorándola; **Britain's ~ to Elvis Presley** el Elvis Presley británico **2** (a) (in exam, test, quiz) respuesta f (b) (solution) solución f; **~ TO sth** solución DE algo

answer² vt **1** (a) (reply to) ⟨person/letter⟩ contestar (b) ⟨telephone⟩ contestar, atender* (AmL), coger* (Esp); **will you ~ the door?** ¿vas tú (a abrir)? (c) ⟨critic/criticism⟩ responder a **2** (fit): **to ~ (to) a description** responder a una descripción
■ ~ vi contestar, responder
■ **answer back** **1** [v + adv] (rudely) contestar **2** [v + o + adv] **to ~ sb back** contestarle mal or de mala manera a algn
■ **answer for** [v + prep + o] (accept responsibility for) ⟨conduct/consequences⟩ responder de; **his parents have a lot to ~ for** sus padres tienen mucha culpa

answerable /'ænsərəbəl ‖'ɑːnsərəbəl/ adj: **she said she was not ~ for his behavior** dijo que ella no era responsable de lo que él hiciera; **I'm ~ to no one** no tengo que rendirle cuentas a nadie

answering machine /'ænsərɪŋ ‖'ɑːnsərɪŋ/ n contestador m (automático)

answerphone /'ænsərfəʊn ‖'ɑːnsəfəʊn/ n contestador m (automático)

ant /ænt/ n hormiga f

antagonize /æn'tægənaɪz/ vt suscitar el antagonismo de

Antarctic¹ /ænt'ɑːrktɪk ‖æn'tɑːktɪk/ adj antártico; **the ~ Ocean** el Océano Antártico; **the ~ Circle** el círculo polar antártico

Antarctic² n **the ~** la región antártica

Antarctica /ænt'ɑːrktɪkə ‖æn'tɑːktɪkə/ n la Antártida

anteater /'ænt,iːtər ‖'ænt,iːtə(r)/ n oso m hormiguero

antecedent /,æntə'siːdn̩t ‖,æntɪ'siːdənt/ n antecedente m

antelope /'æntələʊp ‖'æntɪləʊp/ n (pl **~s** or **~**) antílope m

antenatal /'ænti'neɪtl̩/ adj prenatal; **~ clinic** consulta médica para mujeres embarazadas

antenna /æn'tenə/ n (a) (pl **-nae** /-niː/) (Zool) antena f (b) (pl **-nas**) (Rad, TV) antena f

anthem /'ænθəm/ n himno m; **national ~** himno nacional

anthology /æn'θɑːlədʒi ‖æn'θɒlədʒi/ n (pl **-gies**) antología f

anthropologist /'ænθrə'pɑːlədʒəst ‖,ænθrə'pɒlədʒɪst/ n antropólogo, -ga m,f

anthropology /'ænθrə'pɑːlədʒi ‖,ænθrə'pɒlədʒi/ n antropología f

anti- /æntaɪ, 'ænti ‖'ænti/ pref anti-

antiaircraft /'æntaɪ'erkræft ‖,ænti'eəkrɑːft/ adj antiaéreo

antibiotic /'æntɪbaɪ'ɑːtɪk ‖,æntɪbaɪ'ɒtɪk/ n antibiótico m

antibody /'ænti,bɑːdi ‖'ænti,bɒdi/ n (pl **-dies**) anticuerpo m

anticipate /æn'tɪsəpeɪt ‖æn'tɪsɪpeɪt/ vt **1** (a) (expect) ⟨consequences⟩ prever*; **I don't ~ any problems** no creo que vaya a haber ningún problema (b) (look forward to) esperar **2** (a) (foresee and act accordingly) ⟨movements/objections/needs⟩ prever* (b) (pre-empt) anticiparse a

anticipation /æn'tɪsə'peɪʃən ‖æn,tɪsɪ'peɪʃən/ n (a) (foresight) previsión f; **thanking you in ~** agradeciéndole de antemano su atención (b) (expectation) expectativa f

anticlimax /'æntaɪ'klaɪmæks ‖,æntɪ'klaɪmæks/ n suceso caracterizado por un descenso de la tensión; (disappointment) decepción f

anticlockwise /'æntɪ'klɑːkwaɪz ‖,æntɪ'klɒkwaɪz/ adj/adv (BrE) en sentido contrario a las agujas del reloj

antics /'æntɪks/ pl n (clowning) payasadas fpl; (of naughty children) travesuras fpl

antidote /'æntɪdəʊt/ n ~ (TO sth) antídoto m (CONTRA algo)

antifreeze /'æntɪfriːz/ n anticongelante m

antihero /'ænti,hiːrəʊ ‖'ænti,hɪərəʊ/ n (pl **-roes**) antihéroe m

antipathy /æn'tɪpəθi/ n (pl **-thies**) antipatía f

antiperspirant /'æntɪ'pɜːrspərənt ‖,æntɪ'pɜːspɪrənt/ n antitranspirante m

antique¹ /æn'tiːk/ n antigüedad f; (before n) **~ shop** tienda f de antigüedades

antique² adj antiguo

antiquity /æn'tɪkwəti/ n (pl **-ties**) **1** (ancient times, age) antigüedad f **2** **antiquities** pl antigüedades fpl

anti-Semitic /'æntɪsə'mɪtɪk ‖,æntɪsɪ'mɪtɪk/ adj antisemita

anti-Semitism /,ænti'semətɪzəm ‖,ænti'semɪtɪzəm/ n antisemitismo m

antiseptic¹ /'æntɪ'septɪk/ n antiséptico m

antiseptic² adj (Pharm) antiséptico

antisocial /'æntɪ'səʊʃəl/ adj (a) (offensive to society) antisocial (b) (unsociable) poco sociable

antithesis /æn'tɪθəsɪs ‖æn'tɪθəsɪs/ n (pl **-eses** /-əsiːz/) antítesis f

antler /'æntlər ‖'æntlə(r)/ n cuerno m, asta f; **the animal's ~s** la cornamenta del animal

anus /'eɪnəs/ n ano m

anvil /'ænvəl ‖'ænvɪl/ n yunque m

anxiety /æŋ'zaɪəti/ n (pl **-ties**) (a) (distress, concern) preocupación f (b) (problem, worry) preocupación f (c) (Med, Psych) ansiedad f

anxious /'æŋkʃəs/ adj (a) (worried) preocupado (b) (worrying) ⟨time/moment⟩ (lleno) de preocupación (c) (eager) deseoso; **he's very ~ to please** tiene mucho afán de agradar

anxiously /'æŋkʃəsli/ adv (a) (worriedly) con preocupación (b) (eagerly) ansiosamente

any¹ /'eni/ adj

I **1** *(in questions)* **(a)** *(+ pl n)*: **are there ~ questions?** ¿alguien tiene alguna pregunta?; **does she have ~ children?** ¿tiene hijos? **(b)** *(+ uncount n)*: **do you need ~ help?** ¿necesitas ayuda?; **do you want ~ more coffee?** ¿quieres más café? **(c)** *(+ sing count n: as indef art)* algún, -guna; **is there ~ chance they'll come?** ¿existe alguna posibilidad de que vengan?

2 *(in 'if' clauses and suppositions)* **(a)** *(+ pl n)*: **call me if there are ~ changes** llámame si hay algún cambio; **if you see ~ flowers, buy some** si ves flores, compra algunas **(b)** *(+ uncount n)*: **let me know if you have ~ pain** avíseme si siente dolor; **take ~ money you need** toma el dinero que necesites **(c)** *(+ sing count n)*: **~ upset could kill him** cualquier disgusto podría matarlo; **~ act of disobedience will be punished** toda desobediencia será castigada

3 *(with neg and implied neg)* **(a)** *(+ pl n)*: **don't buy ~ more eggs** no compres más huevos; **aren't there ~ apples left?** ¿no queda ninguna manzana? **(b)** *(+ uncount n)*: **don't make ~ noise** no hagas ruido; **it doesn't make ~ sense** no tiene ningún sentido

II **1** **(a)** *(no matter which)*: **take ~ book you want** llévate cualquier libro; **~ day now** cualquier día de estos **(b)** *(every, all)*: **in ~ large school, you'll find that ...** en cualquier *or* todo colegio grande, verás que ...

2 *(countless, a lot)*: **~ number/amount of sth** cualquier cantidad de algo

any² *pron* **1** *(in questions)* **(a)** *(referring to pl n)* alguno, -na; **those chocolates were nice, are there ~ left?** ¡qué ricos esos bombones! ¿queda alguno? **(b)** *(referring to uncount n)*: **we need sugar; did you buy ~?** nos hace falta azúcar ¿compraste?; **is there ~ of that cake left?** ¿queda algo de ese pastel?

2 *(in 'if' clauses and suppositions)* **(a)** *(referring to pl n)*: **buy some red ones if you can find ~** compra algunas rojas si encuentras; **if ~ of my friends calls, take a message** si llama alguno de mis amigos, toma el recado **(b)** *(referring to uncount n)*: **help yourself to cake if you want ~** sírvete pastel si quieres

3 *(with neg and implied neg)* **(a)** *(referring to pl n)*: **some children were here — I didn't see ~** aquí había unos niños — yo no vi (a) ninguno *or* no los vi; **you'll have to go without cigarettes; I forgot to buy ~** te vas a tener que arreglar sin cigarrillos porque me olvidé de comprar **(b)** *(referring to uncount n)*: **she offered me some wine, but I didn't want ~** me ofreció vino, pero no quise; **I didn't understand ~ of that lecture** no entendí nada de esa conferencia

any³ *adv* **1** *(with comparative)*: **do you feel ~ better now?** ¿te sientes (algo) mejor ahora?; **they don't live here ~ more** ya no viven aquí **2** *(at all)* (AmE): **have you thought about it ~ since then?** ¿has pensado en ello desde entonces?; **it doesn't seem to have affected him ~** no parece haberlo afectado en absoluto

anybody /'eni.bɑːdi ‖ 'eni.bɒdi/ *pron* **1** **(a)** *(somebody)* *(in interrog, conditional sentences)* alguien; **will ~ be seeing Emma today?** ¿alguno de ustedes va a ver a Emma hoy? **(b)** *(with neg)* nadie; **don't tell ~!** ¡no se lo digas a nadie! **2** **(a)** *(whoever, everybody)*: **give it to ~ you like** dáselo a quien quieras; **~ who's been to Paris knows ...**

cualquier persona que haya estado en París sabe ...; **before ~ could stop her** antes de que nadie pudiera detenerla **(b)** *(no matter who)* cualquiera; **~ could do it** cualquiera podría hacerlo

anyhow /'enihaʊ/ *adv* **1** ▶ ANYWAY **2** *(haphazardly)* de cualquier manera

anyone /'eniwʌn/ *pron* ▶ ANYBODY

anyplace /'enipleɪs/ *adv* (AmE) ▶ ANYWHERE¹ 1

anything /'eniθɪŋ/ *pron* **1** **(a)** *(something)* *(in interrog, conditional sentences)* algo; **have you ever heard ~ so ridiculous?** ¡habráse oído semejante ridiculez! **(b)** *(a single thing)* *(with neg)* nada; **don't say ~!** ¡no digas nada! **2** **(a)** *(whatever)*: **~ you say!** ¡lo que tú digas!; **we'll do ~ we can to help** haremos todo lo que podamos para ayudar **(b)** *(no matter what)*: **~ is possible** todo es posible; **~ could happen** podría pasar cualquier cosa **3** *(used for emphasis)*: **was it interesting? — ~ but!** ¿fue interesante? — ¡qué va!; **the portrait doesn't look ~ like her** el retrato no se parece en nada a ella

anyway /'eniweɪ/ *adv* **1** *(in any case)* de todos modos **2** *(changing the subject, moving conversation on)* *(as linker)* bueno; **~, to cut a long story short, ...** bueno, en resumidas cuentas ...

anywhere¹ /'enihwer ‖ 'eniweə(r)/ *adv* **1** **(a)** *(no matter where)* en cualquier sitio *or* lugar; **you can sit ~ you like** te puedes sentar donde quieras **(b)** *(in, to any unspecified place)*: **have you seen my book ~?** ¿has visto mi libro por alguna parte *or* por algún lado?; **we never go ~ together** nunca vamos juntos a ningún lado **2** **anywhere near:** **is it ~ near Portland?** ¿queda cerca de Portland?; **we aren't ~ near ready yet** todavía no estamos listos ni mucho menos

anywhere² *pron*: **is there ~ that sells oysters?** ¿hay algún sitio donde vendan ostras?; **she hasn't ~ to stay** no tiene donde quedarse

apace /ə'peɪs/ *adv* (liter *or* journ) a paso *or* ritmo acelerado

apart /ə'pɑːrt ‖ ə'pɑːt/ *adv* **1** **(a)** *(separated)*: **they've lived ~ for some years** ya hace algunos años que viven separados; **keep them ~** manténgalos separados **(b)** *(into pieces)*: ▶ COME, FALL, PULL, TAKE *etc* APART **2** *(distant)*: **in places as far ~ as Tokyo and Paris** en lugares tan alejados el uno del otro como Tokio y París **3** *(excluded)* *(after n)*: **these faults ~ ...** aparte de estos defectos ...; **joking ~ ...** bromas aparte ... **4** **apart from** *(as prep)* **(a)** *(except for)* excepto, aparte de **(b)** *(separated from)*: **she always sits ~ from the rest of the group** siempre se sienta apartada del resto del grupo

apartheid /ə'pɑːrteɪt ‖ ə'pɑːteɪt/ *n* apartheid *m*

apartment /ə'pɑːrtmənt ‖ ə'pɑːtmənt/ *n* (set of rooms) apartamento *m*, departamento *m* (AmL), piso *m* (Esp); *(before n)*: **~ building** edificio *m* de apartamentos *or* (AmL tb) de departamentos

apathetic /ˌæpə'θetɪk/ *adj* apático

apathy /'æpəθi/ *n* apatía *f*

ape¹ /eɪp/ *n* simio *m*, mono *m*

ape² *vt* remedar, imitar

aperitif /ə'perəˌtiːf ‖ əˈperətif/ *n* aperitivo *m*

aperture /'æpərtʃər ‖'æpətʃə(r)/ n (a) (Opt, Phot) apertura f (b) (hole, opening) (frml) orificio m; (long and narrow) rendija f

apex /'eɪpeks/ n (pl **apexes** or **apices**) (a) (Math) vértice m (b) (pinnacle) cúspide f (c) (pointed end, tip) ápice m

APEX /'eɪpeks/ adj (= **advance purchase excursion**) (before n) ⟨ticket/booking⟩ Apex adj inv

aphid /'eɪfəd ‖'eɪfɪd/ n afídido m, áfido m

aphrodisiac /'æfrə'dɪziæk/ n afrodisíaco m

apices /'eɪpɪsiːz ‖'eɪpɪsiːz/ pl of APEX

apiece /ə'piːs/ adv cada uno

apocalypse /ə'pɑːkəlɪps ‖ə'pɒkəlɪps/ n apocalipsis m

apologetic /ə'pɑːlə'dʒetɪk ‖ə,pɒlə'dʒetɪk/ adj ⟨letter/look⟩ de disculpa; **she was very ~** se deshizo en disculpas

apologize /ə'pɑːlədʒaɪz ‖ə'pɒlədʒaɪz/ vi pedir* perdón, disculparse; **we ~ for the delay** rogamos disculpen el retraso; **you must ~ to her for being so rude** tienes que pedirle perdón por haber sido tan grosero

apology /ə'pɑːlədʒi ‖ə'pɒlədʒi/ n (pl **-gies**) (often pl) disculpa f; **please accept my apologies** le ruego me disculpe

apostle /ə'pɑːsəl ‖ə'pɒsəl/ n apóstol m

apostrophe /ə'pɑːstrəfi ‖ə'pɒstrəfi/ n apóstrofo m

appall, (BrE) **appal** /ə'pɔːl/ vt (BrE) **-ll-** horrorizar*

appalling /ə'pɔːlɪŋ/ adj ⟨conditions⟩ atroz; **the play is absolutely ~** la obra es pésima

apparatus /'æpə'rætəs ‖,æpə'reɪtəs/ n (pl ~) (a) (equipment) aparatos mpl; **a piece of ~** un aparato (b) (Pol) aparato m

apparel /ə'pærəl/ n (a) (finery) (liter) atavío m (liter) (b) (AmE Busn) ropa f

apparent /ə'pærənt/ adj (a) (evident): **for no ~ reason** sin motivo aparente; **it was ~ that ...** estaba claro que ..., era evidente que ... (b) (seeming) ⟨interest/concern⟩ aparente

apparently /ə'pærəntli/ adv (a) (indep) al parecer, por lo visto, según parece (b) (seemingly) ⟨intelligent/happy⟩ aparentemente

apparition /'æpə'rɪʃən/ n aparición f

appeal[1] /ə'piːl/ n **1** (call) llamamiento m, llamado m (AmL); (request) solicitud f, pedido m (AmL); (plea) ruego m **2** (Law) apelación f **3** (fund, organization) campaña para recaudar fondos **4** (attraction) atractivo m

appeal[2] vi **1** (call) **to ~ FOR sth** ⟨for funds⟩ pedir* algo; **the police ~ed to witnesses to come forward** la policía hizo un llamamiento or (AmL tb) un llamado para que se presentaran testigos del hecho **2** (Law) apelar **3** (be attractive) **to ~ TO sb** atraerle* A algn
 ■ ~ vt (AmE) ⟨decision/verdict⟩ apelar contra or de

appealing /ə'piːlɪŋ/ adj atractivo

appear /ə'pɪr ‖ə'pɪə(r)/ vi **1** (a) (come into view) aparecer* (b) (be published): **to ~ (in print)** publicarse* (c) (Law) comparecer* **2** (seem) parecer*; **so it ~s** eso parece; **to ~ to + INF** parecer* + INF; **we ~ to be lost** parece que nos hemos perdido

appearance /ə'pɪrəns ‖ə'pɪərəns/ n **1** (a) (coming into view) aparición f (b) (Law) comparecencia f (c) (of book) publicación f **2** (a) (look) aspecto m (b) **appearances** pl apariencias fpl; **to keep up ~s** guardar las apariencias

appease /ə'piːz/ vt ⟨person⟩ apaciguar*; ⟨anger⟩ aplacar*

appendices /ə'pendəsiːz ‖ə'pendɪsiːz/ pl of APPENDIX

appendicitis /ə'pendə'saɪtəs ‖ə,pendɪ'saɪtɪs/ n apendicitis f

appendix /ə'pendɪks/ n (pl **-dixes** or **-dices**) apéndice m

appetite /'æpətaɪt ‖'æpɪtaɪt/ n apetito m

appetizer /'æpətaɪzər ‖'æpɪtaɪzə(r)/ n (a) (drink) aperitivo m (b) (snack) aperitivo m, tapa f (Esp), botana f (Méx)

appetizing /'æpətaɪzɪŋ ‖'æpɪtaɪzɪŋ/ adj apetitoso

applaud /ə'plɔːd/ vt/i aplaudir

applause /ə'plɔːz/ n aplausos mpl

apple /'æpəl/ n manzana f; (before n) ~ **pie** pastel m de manzana, pay m de manzana (Méx); ~ **tree** manzano m

appliance /ə'plaɪəns/ n aparato m; **electrical ~s** electrodomésticos mpl

applicable /'æplɪkəbəl, ə'plɪkəbəl/ adj (frml): **these regulations are only ~ to foreigners** estas normas se refieren únicamente a los extranjeros; **delete as ~** tache lo que no corresponda

applicant /'æplɪkənt ‖'æplɪkənt/ n (for job) candidato, -ta m,f, postulante mf (CS), aplicante mf (Ven)

application /'æplə'keɪʃən ‖,æplɪ'keɪʃən/ n **1** (request) solicitud f; ~ **FOR sth** ⟨for loan/grant/visa⟩ solicitud DE algo; (before n) ~ **form** (impreso m de) solicitud f **2** (a) (of method, skills, theory) aplicación f (b) (of paint, ointment) aplicación f

applied /ə'plaɪd/ adj aplicado

apply /ə'plaɪ/ **applies, applying, applied** vt (a) (put on) aplicar* (b) ⟨method/theory/rules⟩ aplicar*; **to ~ the brakes** frenar; **she applied herself to her work** se puso a trabajar con diligencia
 ■ ~ vi (a) (make application): **please ~ in writing to ...** diríjase por escrito a ...; **to ~ FOR sth** ⟨for loan/permission⟩ solicitar algo; **to ~ for a job** solicitar un trabajo, aplicar* a un trabajo (Ven), postular para un trabajo (CS) (b) (be applicable) «regulation/criterion» aplicarse*

appoint /ə'pɔɪnt/ vt **1** (name, choose) nombrar **2** (frml) ⟨date⟩ designar (frml)

appointment /ə'pɔɪntmənt/ n **1** (arrangement to meet) cita f; (with doctor, hairdresser) hora f, cita f; **to make an ~** pedir* hora or una cita **2** (a) (act of appointing) nombramiento m (b) (post) (frml) puesto m

appraisal /ə'preɪzəl/ n (of situation, employee) evaluación f; (of work, novel) valoración f; (of property) tasación f

appraise /ə'preɪz/ vt ⟨situation/employee⟩ evaluar*; ⟨novel/painting⟩ valorar; ⟨property⟩ tasar, avaluar* (AmL)

appreciable /ə'priːʃəbəl/ adj ⟨change/difference⟩ apreciable; ⟨loss/sum⟩ importante

appreciate /ə'priːʃieɪt/ vt (a) (value) ⟨food/ novel⟩ apreciar (b) (be grateful for) agradecer* (c) (understand) ⟨danger/difficulties⟩ darse* cuenta de; I ~ that, but … lo comprendo, pero …
■ ~ vi «shares/property» (re)valorizarse*

appreciation /ə'priːʃi'eɪʃən/ n (a) (gratitude) agradecimiento m (b) (discriminating enjoyment): he showed a genuine ~ of music demostró saber apreciar la música

appreciative /ə'priːʃətɪv/ adj (a) (grateful) ⟨smile/gesture⟩ de agradecimiento (b) (of art, good food) apreciativo

apprehend /ˌæprɪ'hend/ vt (frml) apresar, detener*

apprehension /ˌæprɪ'hentʃən/ ‖ ˌæprɪ'henʃən/ n aprensión f

apprehensive /ˌæprɪ'hensɪv/ adj ⟨look⟩ aprensivo, de aprensión; I'm rather ~ about the consequences estoy algo inquieto por lo que pueda pasar

apprentice¹ /ə'prentəs ‖ ə'prentɪs/ n aprendiz, -diza m,f

apprentice² vt: to be ~d TO sb estar* de aprendiz CON algn

apprenticeship /ə'prentəsʃɪp ‖ ə'prentɪsʃɪp/ n aprendizaje m (de un oficio); to serve an ~ in sth hacer* el aprendizaje de algo

approach¹ /ə'prəʊtʃ/ vi acercarse*, aproximarse
■ ~ vt (a) (draw near to) aproximarse or acercarse* a (b) (talk to) have you ~ed her about it? ¿ya se lo ha planteado?, ¿ya ha hablado con ella del asunto?; he ~ed me for a loan se dirigió a mí para pedirme un préstamo (c) (tackle) ⟨problem/ question⟩ enfocar*

approach² n ① (method, outlook) enfoque m ② (overture — offering sth) propuesta f; (— requesting sth) solicitud f, petición f, pedido m (AmL) ③ (drawing near): at the ~ of winter al acercarse el invierno ④ (means of entering) acceso m

approachable /ə'prəʊtʃəbəl/ adj ⟨person/ place⟩ accesible

appropriate¹ /ə'prəʊpriət/ adj apropiado

appropriate² /ə'prəʊprieɪt/ vt ⟨possessions⟩ apropiarse de; ⟨money⟩ destinar

approval /ə'pruːvəl/ n aprobación f; on ~ a prueba

approve /ə'pruːv/ vi to ~ (OF sth/sb): they don't ~ of my smoking les parece mal que fume; mother seems to ~ of him a mamá parece gustarle; I don't ~ of his methods no estoy de acuerdo con sus métodos
■ ~ vt ⟨decision/plan⟩ aprobar*

approving /ə'pruːvɪŋ/ adj ⟨smile/look⟩ de aprobación

approximate /ə'prɒksəmət ‖ ə'prɒksɪmət/ adj aproximado

approximately /ə'prɒksəmətli ‖ ə'prɒksɪmətli/ adv aproximadamente

approximation /ə'prɒksə'meɪʃən ‖ əˌprɒksɪ'meɪʃən/ n aproximación f

apricot /'æprəkɒt ‖ 'eɪprɪkɒt/ n albaricoque m or (Méx) chabacano m or (AmS) damasco m

April /'eɪprəl ‖ 'eɪprɪl/ n abril m; (before n) ~ Fools' Day ≈ el día de los (Santos) Inocentes (en EEUU y GB se celebra el 1º de abril)

apron /'eɪprən/ n delantal m, mandil m (Esp)

apt /æpt/ adj (a) (fitting, suitable) acertado (b) (likely) to be ~ to + INF ser* propenso A + INF

aptitude /'æptɪtuːd ‖ 'æptɪtjuːd/ n ~ (FOR sth) aptitud f (PARA algo)

aquarium /ə'kweriəm ‖ ə'kweəriəm/ n (pl -riums or -ria /-riə/) acuario m

Aquarius /ə'kweriəs ‖ ə'kweəriəs/ n (a) (sign) (no art) Acuario (b) (person) Acuario or acuario mf, acuariano, -na m,f

aquatic /ə'kwætɪk, ə'kwɑːtɪk ‖ ə'kwætɪk/ adj acuático

AR = **Arkansas**

Arab¹ /'ærəb/ adj árabe

Arab² n árabe mf

Arabian /ə'reɪbiən/ adj árabe; the ~ Sea el Mar de Omán

Arabic¹ /'ærəbɪk/ adj árabe; a~ numerals números mpl arábigos

Arabic² n árabe m

arable /'ærəbəl/ adj arable; ~ land tierras fpl de cultivo

arbiter /'ɑːrbətər ‖ 'ɑːbɪtə(r)/ n árbitro, -tra m,f

arbitrary /'ɑːrbəˌtreri ‖ 'ɑːbɪtrəri/ adj arbitrario

arbitrate /'ɑːrbətreɪt ‖ 'ɑːbɪtreɪt/ vt ⟨dispute⟩ arbitrar (en)
■ ~ vi arbitrar

arbitration /ˌɑːrbə'treɪʃən ‖ ˌɑːbɪ'treɪʃən/ n arbitraje m

arc /ɑːrk ‖ ɑːk/ n arco m

arcade /ɑːr'keɪd ‖ ɑː'keɪd/ n (a) (Archit) arcada f; (around square, along street) soportales mpl, recova f (Arg) (b) (of shops) galería f comercial

arch¹ /ɑːrtʃ ‖ ɑːtʃ/ n arco m

arch² vt ⟨eyebrows/back⟩ arquear
■ ~ vi formar un arco

archaeologist etc (BrE) ▶ ARCHEOLOGIST etc

archaic /ɑːr'keɪɪk ‖ ɑː'keɪɪk/ adj arcaico

archangel /'ɑːrkˌeɪndʒəl ‖ 'ɑːkˌeɪndʒəl/ n arcángel m

archbishop /ˌɑːrtʃ'bɪʃəp ‖ ˌɑːtʃ'bɪʃəp/ n arzobispo m

archenemy /ˌɑːrtʃ'enəmi ‖ ˌɑːtʃ'enəmi/ n (pl -mies) archienemigo, -ga m,f

archeologist, (BrE) **archaeologist** /ˌɑːrki'ɑːlədʒəst ‖ ˌɑːki'ɒlədʒɪst/ n arqueólogo, -ga m,f

archeology, (BrE) **archaeology** /ˌɑːrki'ɑːlədʒi ‖ ˌɑːki'ɒlədʒi/ n arqueología f

archer /'ɑːrtʃər ‖ 'ɑːtʃə(r)/ n arquero, -ra m,f

archery /'ɑːrtʃəri ‖ 'ɑːtʃəri/ n tiro m con or al arco

architect /'ɑːrkətekt ‖ 'ɑːkɪtekt/ n arquitecto, -ta m,f

architecture /'ɑːrkətektʃər ‖ 'ɑːkɪtektʃə(r)/ n arquitectura f

archive /'ɑːrkaɪv ‖ 'ɑːkaɪv/ n (often pl) archivo m

Arctic¹ /'ɑːrktɪk ‖ 'ɑːktɪk/ adj ártico; the ~ Ocean el Océano (Glacial) Ártico, el Ártico; the ~ Circle el círculo polar ártico

Arctic² n the ~ la región ártica, el Ártico

ardent /'ɑːrdnt ‖ 'ɑːdnt/ adj ⟨supporter⟩ apasionado; ⟨plea/desire⟩ ferviente

ardor, (BrE) **ardour** /'ɑːrdər ‖'ɑːdə(r)/ n (liter) (zeal) fervor m, ardor m; (love) pasión f

arduous /'ɑːrdʒuəs ‖'ɑːdjuːəs/ adj ‹task› arduo; ‹training/conditions› duro; ‹march/climb› difícil

are /ɑːr ‖ɑː(r), weak form ər/ 2nd pers sing, 1st, 2nd & 3rd pers pl pres of BE

area /'eriə ‖'eəriə/ n [1] (geographical) zona f, área f‡; región f; (neighborhood) barrio m; (urban) zona f [2] (part of room, building) zona f; **play** ~ zona de recreo [3] (expanse, patch): **the shaded** ~ **represents ...** el área sombreada representa ...; **the wreckage was scattered over a wide** ~ los restos del siniestro quedaron esparcidos sobre una extensa zona [4] (Math) superficie f, área f‡; (of room, land) superficie f [5] (field, sphere) terreno m; (of knowledge) campo m

area code n (AmE) código m de la zona (AmL), prefijo m (local) (Esp)

arena /ə'riːnə/ n (a) (of stadium) arena f (b) (scene of activity) ruedo m; **the political** ~ el ruedo político

aren't /ɑːrnt ‖ɑːnt/ = **are not**

Argentina /'ɑːrdʒən'tiːnə ‖,ɑːdʒən'tiːnə/ n Argentina f

Argentine /'ɑːrdʒəntaɪn ‖'ɑːdʒəntaɪn/ adj argentino

Argentinian¹ /'ɑːrdʒən'tɪniən ‖,ɑːdʒən'tɪniən/ adj argentino

Argentinian² n argentino, -na m,f

arguably /'ɑːrgjuəbli ‖'ɑːgjuəbli/ adv (indep): **this is** ~ **his best novel** podría decirse que esta es su mejor novela

argue /'ɑːrgju ‖'ɑːgjuː/ vi [1] (quarrel) discutir; (more heatedly) pelear(se), reñir* (esp Esp); **don't** ~ **with me!** ¡no me discutas! [2] (reason): **she** ~s **convincingly** sabe expresar su punto de vista de manera muy convincente; **he** ~s **against changing the law** da razones en contra de que se cambie la ley

■ ~ vt (a) (put forward) (case) exponer* (b) (present as argument) argüir*, sostener*; **supporters of the bill** ~ **that ...** los partidarios del proyecto arguyen or sostienen que ...

argument /'ɑːrgjəmənt ‖'ɑːgjʊmənt/ n [1] (quarrel) discusión f, (more heated) pelea f, riña f (esp Esp); **to have an** ~ **with sb** tener* una discusión con algn; (more heatedly) pelearse or (esp Esp) reñir* con algn [2] (debate) polémica f [3] (a) (case) ~ (**FOR/AGAINST**) sth razones fpl or argumentos mpl (**A FAVOR/EN CONTRA DE**) algo (b) (line of reasoning) razonamiento m

argumentative /'ɑːrgjə'mentətɪv ‖,ɑːgjʊ'mentətɪv/ adj discutidor

arid /'ærəd ‖'ærɪd/ adj árido

Aries /'eriːz ‖'eəriːz/ n (a) (sign) (no art) Aries (b) (person) Aries or aries mf, ariano, -na m,f

arise /ə'raɪz/ vi (past **arose**; past p **arisen** /ə'rɪzən/) ‹‹difficulty/opportunity›› surgir*; **if the need** ~s si fuera necesario

aristocracy /'ærə'stɑːkrəsi ‖,ærɪ'stɒkrəsi/ n (pl -**cies**) aristocracia f

aristocrat /ə'rɪstəkræt ‖'ærɪstəkræt/ n aristócrata mf

aristocratic /ə'rɪstə'krætɪk ‖,ærɪstə'krætɪk/ adj aristocrático

arithmetic /ə'rɪθmətɪk/ n aritmética f

Ariz = **Arizona**

Ark¹ = **Arkansas**

Ark² /ɑːrk ‖ɑːk/ n arca f‡; **Noah's** ~ el arca de Noé

arm¹ /ɑːrm ‖ɑːm/ n [1] (Anat) brazo m; **they walked along** ~ **in** ~ iban del brazo [2] (a) (of chair, crane) brazo m (b) (of garment) manga f [3] **arms** pl (weapons) armas fpl

arm² vt armar; see also ARMED

armament /'ɑːrməmənt ‖'ɑːməmənt/ n armamento m

arm: ~**band** n (to denote rank, mourning etc) brazalete m; (for swimming) flotador m (que se coloca en el brazo), alita f (AmS); ~**chair** n sillón m, butaca f

armed /ɑːrmd ‖ɑːmd/ adj ‹resistance/struggle› armado; **the** ~ **forces** las fuerzas armadas; ~ **robbery** robo m a mano armada

Armenia /ɑːr'miːniə ‖ɑː'miːniə/ n Armenia f

Armenian /ɑːr'miːniən ‖ɑː'miːniən/ adj armenio

armistice /'ɑːrməstəs ‖'ɑːmɪstɪs/ n armisticio m

armor, (BrE) **armour** /'ɑːrmər ‖'ɑːmə(r)/ n armadura f; **suit of** ~ armadura f

armored, (BrE) **armoured** /'ɑːrmərd ‖'ɑːməd/ adj blindado

armor-plated, (BrE) **armour-plated** /'ɑːrmər'pleɪtəd ‖,ɑːmə'pleɪtɪd/ adj blindado

armory, (BrE) **armoury** /'ɑːrməri ‖'ɑːməri/ n (pl -**ries**) (a) (storehouse) arsenal m (b) (factory) (AmE) fábrica f de armas

arm: ~**pit** n axila f, sobaco m; ~**rest** n (of chair, sofa) brazo m; (of car, airplane seat) apoyabrazos m

arms race n carrera f armamentista

army /'ɑːrmi ‖'ɑːmi/ n (pl **armies**) ejército m

aroma /ə'raʊmə/ n aroma m

aromatic /'ærə'mætɪk/ adj aromático

arose /ə'raʊz/ past of ARISE

around¹ /ə'raʊnd/ adv [1] (a) (in a circle): ~ **and** ~ **they drove** estuvieron dando vueltas y vueltas con el coche (b) (so as to face in different direction): **she glanced** ~ echó un vistazo a su alrededor; see also TURN etc AROUND (c) (on all sides): **there's nothing for miles** ~ no hay nada en millas a la redonda; **everyone crowded** ~ todo el mundo se apiñó alrededor [2] (in the vicinity): **is John** ~? ¿anda or está John por ahí?; **there's no one** ~ aquí no hay nadie [3] (from one place to another): **he keeps following me** ~ me sigue a todas partes; **he knows his way** ~ conoce la ciudad (or la zona etc)

AmC	Central America	Arg	Argentina	Cu	Cuba	Per	Peru
AmL	Latin America	Bol	Bolivia	Ec	Ecuador	RPI	River Plate Area
AmS	South America	Chi	Chile	Esp	Spain	Ur	Uruguay
Andes	Andean Region	CS	Southern Cone	Méx	Mexico	Ven	Venezuela

4 (approximately) más o menos; **he must be ~ 35** debe (de) tener unos 35; **at ~ five thirty** alrededor de *or* a eso de las cinco y media, sobre las cinco y media (Esp); **~ 1660** alrededor de 1660

around² *prep* **1** (encircling) alrededor de; **he put his arm ~ her** la rodeó con el brazo; **they sailed ~ the world** dieron la vuelta al mundo en un velero **2 (a)** (in the vicinity of) alrededor de; **do you live ~ here?** ¿vives por aquí? **(b)** (within, through): **they traveled ~ Europe** viajaron por Europa; **she took them ~ the house** les mostró la casa

arouse /əˈraʊz/ *vt* ⟨interest/suspicion⟩ despertar*; (sexually) excitar

arrange /əˈreɪndʒ/ *vt* **1 (a)** (put in certain order, position) ⟨furniture/flowers⟩ arreglar **(b)** (put in order) arreglar **2** (fix up in advance) ⟨meeting/party⟩ organizar*; ⟨date/fee⟩ fijar; ⟨deal/appointment⟩ concertar*; ⟨loan⟩ tramitar; **she had ~d to meet them for lunch** había quedado en encontrarse con ellos para comer, había quedado con ellos para comer (Esp)

■ **~** *vi*: **could you ~ for the carpets to be cleaned?** ¿podría encargarse de que alguien venga a limpiar las alfombras?; **we've ~d for you to see the specialist** le hemos pedido hora *or* una cita con el especialista

arrangement /əˈreɪndʒmənt/ *n* **1** (of furniture) disposición *f*; **a flower ~** un arreglo floral **2** (agreement): **we made an ~ to meet the next day** quedamos en encontrarnos al día siguiente; **I have an ~ with the bank** tengo un acuerdo con el banco **3 arrangements** *pl* (plans) planes *mpl*; (for a funeral) preparativos *mpl*; **what are the sleeping ~s?** ¿cómo vamos (*or* van *etc*) a dormir? **4** (Mus) arreglo *m*

array /əˈreɪ/ *n* selección *f*

arrears /əˈrɪrz ‖əˈrɪəz/ *pl n* atrasos *mpl*; **to be in ~ with the rent** estar* atrasado en el pago del alquiler; **salaries are paid monthly in ~** los sueldos se pagan mensualmente, una vez cumplido cada mes de trabajo

arrest¹ /əˈrest/ *n* detención *f*, arresto *m*; **to be under ~** estar* detenido *or* arrestado

arrest² *vt* **1** (detain) detener*, arrestar **2** ⟨progress/growth⟩ (hinder) dificultar; (halt) detener*; ⟨decline⟩ atajar

arrival /əˈraɪvəl/ *n* llegada *f*, arribo *m* (esp AmL frml); **on ~** al llegar

arrive /əˈraɪv/ *vi* llegar*; **to ~ AT** llegar* A

arrogance /ˈærəgəns/ *n* arrogancia *f*

arrogant /ˈærəgənt/ *adj* arrogante

arrow /ˈærəʊ/ *n* flecha *f*

arse /ɑːrs ‖ɑːs/ *n* (BrE vulg) culo *m* (fam: en algunas regiones vulg)

arsenal /ˈɑːrsnəl ‖ˈɑːsənl/ *n* arsenal *m*

arson /ˈɑːrsn̩ ‖ˈɑːsn̩/ *n* incendiarismo *m*

arsonist /ˈɑːrsnəst ‖ˈɑːsənɪst/ *n* incendiario, -ria *m,f*, pirómano, -na *m,f*

art /ɑːrt ‖ɑːt/ *n* **1 (a)** arte *m*; **she's studying ~** estudia Bellas Artes; (*before n*) ⟨class⟩ de arte; (in school) de dibujo; **~ gallery** (museum) museo *m* de arte; (commercial) galería *f* de arte; **~ school** *o* **college** escuela *f* de Bellas Artes **(b)** (artwork) trabajos *mpl* artísticos; **~s and crafts** artesanía **2 arts** *pl* **(a) the ~s** la cultura y las artes **(b)** (BrE Educ) letras *fpl*

artefact /ˈɑːrtɪfækt ‖ˈɑːtɪfækt/ *n* (BrE) artefacto *m*

artery /ˈɑːrtəri ‖ˈɑːtəri/ *n* (*pl* **-ries**) arteria *f*

arthritis /ɑːrˈθraɪtəs ‖ɑːˈθraɪtɪs/ *n* artritis *f*

artichoke /ˈɑːrtətʃəʊk ‖ˈɑːtɪtʃəʊk/ *n* **(a)** (globe **~**) alcachofa *f*, alcaucil *m* (RPl) **(b)** (Jerusalem **~**) aguaturma *f*, pataca *f*

article /ˈɑːrtɪkəl ‖ˈɑːtɪkəl/ *n* **1** (thing, item) artículo *m*; **an ~ of clothing** una prenda (de vestir) **2** (in newspaper, encyclopedia) artículo *m* **3** (Ling) artículo *m*

articulate¹ /ɑːrˈtɪkjələɪt ‖ɑːˈtɪkjʊleɪt/ *vt* **(a)** ⟨idea/feeling⟩ expresar **(b)** ⟨word/sound⟩ articular

articulate² /ɑːrˈtɪkjələt ‖ɑːˈtɪkjʊlət/ *adj* ⟨utterance⟩ articulado; **he's very ~** se expresa muy bien

articulated lorry /ɑːrˈtɪkjʊleɪtəd ‖ɑːˈtɪkjəleɪtɪd/ *n* (BrE) camión *m* articulado

artifact /ˈɑːrtɪfækt/, (BrE) **artefact** *n* artefacto *m*

artificial /ˌɑːrtəˈfɪʃəl ‖ˌɑːtɪˈfɪʃəl/ *adj* artificial; ⟨leather⟩ sintético; ⟨arm/leg⟩ ortopédico; **~ respiration** respiración *f* artificial

artillery /ɑːrˈtɪləri ‖ɑːˈtɪləri/ *n* artillería *f*

artisan /ˈɑːrtəzən ‖ˌɑːtɪˈzæn/ *n* artesano, -na *m,f*

artist /ˈɑːrtəst ‖ˈɑːtɪst/ *n* **(a)** (writer, musician, painter, sculptor) artista *mf* **(b)** (performer) (Mus) intérprete *mf*; (Theat) actor, -triz *m,f*, artista *mf*

artistic /ɑːrˈtɪstɪk ‖ɑːˈtɪstɪk/ *adj* artístico

as¹ /æz, *weak form* əz/ *conj* **1 (a)** (when, while) cuando; **~ she was eating breakfast …** cuando *or* mientras tomaba el desayuno … **(b)** (indicating progression) a medida que; **~ the date drew closer, …** a medida que se acercaba la fecha, … **2** (because, since) como **3** (though): **try ~ he might, he could not open it** por más que trató, no pudo abrirlo; **strange ~ it may seem** por extraño que parezca **4** (in accordance with) como; **~ I was saying** como iba diciendo **5 (a)** (in the way that) como; **do ~ I say** haz lo que te digo; **I'm only interested in the changes ~ they affect them** solo me interesan los cambios en la medida en que me afectan a mí **(b)** (*in phrases*) **as it is: we've got too much work ~ it is** ya tenemos demasiado trabajo; **as it were** por así decirlo **6** (in comparisons of equal degree) **as … as** tan … como; **there weren't ~ many people ~ last time** no había tanta gente como la última vez **7 as if/as though** como si (+ *subj*)

as² *adv* **1** (equally): **it's not ~ cold today** hoy no hace tanto frío; **I can't run ~ quickly now** no puedo correr tan rápido ahora **2 as … as: ~ many ~ 400 people** hasta 400 personas; **~ long ago ~ 1960** ya en 1960

as³ *prep* **1** (in the condition, role of): **~ a child she adored dancing** de pequeña le encantaba bailar; **~ a teacher …** como maestro …; **he works ~ a clerk** trabaja de oficinista **2** (*in phrases*) **as for** en cuanto a; **as of** *o* (BrE) **as from** desde, a partir de

asbestos /æsˈbestəs/ *n* asbesto *m*, amianto *m*

ascend /əˈsend/ *vi* (frml) **(a)** ⟨person/rocket⟩ ascender* (frml) **(b) ascending** *pres p* ⟨slope/spiral/scale⟩ ascendente

⋯⋮

a

■ ~ vt (frml) ⟨steps⟩ subir; ⟨mountain⟩ escalar

ascension /əˈsentʃən ‖əˈsenʃən/ n the A~ (Relig) la Ascensión

ascent /əˈsent/ n (a) (of mountain) escalada f (b) (rise) ascenso m (c) (slope) subida f

ascertain /ˌæsərˈteɪn ‖ˌæsəˈteɪn/ vt establecer*

ASCII /ˈæski/ (no art) (= **American standard code for information interchange**) ASCII m

ascribe /əˈskraɪb/ vt to ~ sth TO sth/sb atribuirle* algo A algo/algn

aseptic /erˈseptɪk/ adj aséptico

ash /æʃ/ n **1** (a) (often pl) ceniza f (b) **ashes** pl (cremated remains) cenizas fpl **2** ~ (**tree**) fresno m

ashamed /əˈʃeɪmd/ adj (pred) avergonzado, apenado (AmL exc CS); **she was ~ of what she'd done** estaba avergonzada de or (AmL exc CS) apenada por lo que había hecho; **to be ~ OF sb** avergonzarse* DE algn; **he's ~ to ask** le da vergüenza or (AmL exc CS) pena preguntar

ashcan /ˈæʃkæn/ n (AmE) ▶ GARBAGE CAN

ashore /əˈʃɔːr/ adv en tierra; **to go ~** desembarcar*; **we swam ~** nadamos hasta la orilla

ash: ~**tray** n cenicero m; **A~ Wednesday** n miércoles m de Ceniza

Asia /ˈeɪʒə, ˈeɪʃə ‖ˈeɪʃə/ n Asia f‡

Asian[1] /ˈeɪʒən, ˈeɪʃən ‖ˈeɪʃən/ adj (a) (of Asia) asiático (b) (from the Indian subcontinent) (BrE) de India, Pakistán etc

Asian[2] n (a) (from Asia) asiático, -ca m,f (b) (from the Indian subcontinent) (BrE) persona proveniente de India, Pakistán etc

aside[1] /əˈsaɪd/ adv **1** a un lado; see also PUT ASIDE, SET ASIDE, STAND² 2A, STEP ASIDE, TAKE ASIDE **2** **aside from** (as prep) (esp AmE) (except for) aparte de (b) (as well as) aparte de, además de

aside[2] n aparte m

ask /æsk ‖ɑːsk/ vt **1** (inquire) preguntar; (inquire of) preguntarle a; **to ~ sb sth** preguntarle algo A algn; **have you ~ed him about his trip?** ¿le has preguntado por el viaje? **2** (request) ⟨approval/advice/favor⟩ pedir*; **to ~ sb FOR sth** pedirle* algo A algn; **to ~ sb to + INF** pedirle* A algn QUE (+ subj); **I ~ed to see the manager** pedí hablar con el director **3** (invite) invitar; **to ~ sb (TO sth)** invitar A algn (A algo); **to ~ sb out** invitar a algn a salir ■ ~ vi **1** (inquire) preguntar **2** (request): **there's no harm in ~ing** con preguntar no se pierde nada; **to ~ FOR sth** pedir* algo; **to ~ FOR sb** preguntar POR algn

■ **ask after** [v + prep + o] preguntar por

askance /əˈskæns/ adv: **to look ~ at sb** mirar a algn con recelo

askew /əˈskjuː/ adv torcido

asleep /əˈsliːp/ adj (pred): **to be ~** estar* dormido; **to fall ~** dormirse*

asparagus /əˈspærəgəs/ n espárrago m

ASPCA n = **American Society for the Prevention of Cruelty to Animals**

aspect /ˈæspekt/ n **1** (feature, facet) aspecto m **2** (frml) (orientation) orientación f

aspersions /əˈspɜːrʒənz ‖əˈspɜːʃənz/ pl n (sometimes sing): **to cast ~ on sth/sb** poner* algo/a algn en entredicho

asphalt /ˈæsfɔːlt ‖ˈæsfælt/ n asfalto m

asphyxiate /æsˈfɪksɪeɪt/ vt asfixiar

aspiration /ˌæspəˈreɪʃən ‖ˌæspɪˈreɪʃən/ n aspiración f

aspire /əˈspaɪr ‖əˈspaɪə(r)/ vi (a) to ~ TO sth aspirar A algo (b) **aspiring** pres p: **aspiring writers** personas que aspiran a ser escritores

aspirin /ˈæsprən ‖ˈæsprɪn/ n (pl ~ or -**rins**) aspirina f

ass /æs/ n **1** (a) (donkey) (liter) asno m, jumento m (liter) (b) (idiot) (colloq) imbécil mf **2** (part of body) (AmE vulg) culo m (fam: en algunas regiones vulg)

assailant /əˈseɪlənt/ n (frml) agresor, -sora m,f

assassin /əˈsæsn ‖əˈsæsɪn/ n asesino, -na m,f (de un personaje importante)

assassinate /əˈsæsɪnett ‖əˈsæsɪneɪt/ vt asesinar (a un personaje importante)

assassination /əˈsæsəˈneɪʃən ‖əˌsæsɪˈneɪʃən/ n asesinato m (de un personaje importante)

assault[1] /əˈsɔːlt/ n **1** (Law) (violence) agresión f; (molestation) agresión f sexual **2** (a) (Mil) asalto m (b) (onslaught) ~ (ON sth) ataque m (A algo)

assault[2] vt (use violence against) agredir*; (sexually) agredir* sexualmente

assemble /əˈsembl/ vt (a) (construct) montar; ⟨model⟩ armar (b) (get together) reunir* (c) (gather) ⟨facts⟩ recopilar; ⟨collection⟩ reunir* ■ ~ vi (gather) reunirse*

assembly /əˈsembli/ n (pl -**blies**) **1** (a) (coming together) reunión f (b) (group) concurrencia f (c) (Govt) asamblea f (d) (Educ) (no art) reunión de profesores y alumnos, al iniciarse la jornada escolar **2** (Tech)(process) montaje m; (before n) ~ **line** cadena f de montaje

assent[1] /əˈsent/ n asentimiento m; **to give one's ~ to sth** dar* su (or mi etc) conformidad a algo

assent[2] vi asentir*; **to ~ TO sth** acceder A algo

assert /əˈsɜːrt ‖əˈsɜːt/ vt (a) (declare) afirmar (b) (demonstrate, enforce) ⟨superiority⟩ reafirmar; ⟨rights/claims⟩ hacer* valer ■ v refl to ~ oneself hacerse* valer

assertion /əˈsɜːrʃən ‖əˈsɜːʃən/ n (a) (declaration) afirmación f (b) (demonstration) reafirmación f

assertive /əˈsɜːrtɪv ‖əˈsɜːtɪv/ adj ⟨tone⟩ autoritario; **to be ~** ser* firme y enérgico

assess /əˈses/ vt ⟨value/amount⟩ calcular; ⟨student/performance⟩ evaluar*; ⟨situation⟩ aquilatar

assessment /əˈsesmənt/ n (of performance, results) evaluación f; (of amount) cálculo m

asset /ˈæset/ n (a) (valuable quality): **her intelligence is her greatest ~** su inteligencia es su gran baza; **she's an ~ to the company** es una empleada muy valiosa para la compañía (b) **assets** pl (Fin) activo m

asset stripping /ˈstrɪpɪŋ/ n vaciamiento m

assiduous /əˈsɪdʒuəs ‖əˈsɪdjuəs/ adj (frml) ⟨student⟩ diligente

assign /əˈsaɪn/ vt (a) (appoint) to ~ sb TO sth nombrar a algn PARA algo (b) (allocate) asignar

assignment /ə'saɪnmənt/ n ① (a) (mission) misión f (b) (task) función f (c) (schoolwork) tarea f ② (a) (posting) nombramiento m (b) (allocation) asignación f

assimilate /ə'sɪməleɪt ‖ə'sɪmɪleɪt/ vt asimilar

assimilation /ə'sɪmə'leɪʃən ‖ə,sɪmɪ'leɪʃən/ n asimilación f

assist /ə'sɪst/ vt ayudar

assistance /ə'sɪstəns/ n ayuda f

assistant¹ /ə'sɪstənt/ n (a) (in shop) dependiente, -ta m,f, empleado, -da m,f (AmL) (b) (subordinate, helper) ayudante mf; **clerical ~** auxiliar administrativo, -va m,f (c) (language **~**) (BrE) (in university) ayudante mf or (Esp) lector, -tora m,f, (in school) auxiliar mf de lengua

assistant² adj (before n): **~ manager** subdirector, -tora m,f

associate¹ /ə'səʊʃieɪt, -sieɪt/ vt (a) (involve, connect) (usu pass) vincular (b) (link in mind) asociar
■ **~** vi **to ~ (WITH sb)** relacionarse (CON algn)

associate² /ə'səʊʃiət, -siət/ n (a) (in business, profession) colega mf (b) (member of professional body) colegiado, -da m,f

associate³ /ə'səʊʃiət, -siət/ adj (before n) ‹member› no numerario; ‹editor/professor› (AmE) adjunto

association /ə'səʊʃi'eɪʃən, -si'eɪʃən/ n asociación f; **in ~ with** (as prep) en asociación con

assorted /ə'sɔːtəd ‖ə'sɔːtɪd/ adj (before n) surtido

assortment /ə'sɔːtmənt ‖ə'sɔːtmənt/ n surtido m

assuage /ə'sweɪdʒ/ vt (liter) (a) (satisfy) ‹hunger/ desire› saciar (liter) (b) (ease) ‹pain/grief› aliviar (c) (calm) ‹anxiety› calmar; ‹fear› disipar

assume /ə'suːm ‖ə'sjuːm/ vt ① (suppose) suponer* ② (frml) ‹duties/command/responsibility› asumir; **~d name** nombre m ficticio

assumption /ə'sʌmpʃən/ n ① (supposition): **the ~ was that ...** se suponía que ...; **his reasoning is based on the ~ that ...** su razonamiento se basa en el supuesto de que ... ② (frml) (of duties, leadership, responsibility) asunción f

assurance /ə'ʃʊrəns ‖ə'ʃʊərəns, ə'ʃɔːrəns/ n ① (guarantee): **she gave me her ~ that ...** me aseguró que ... ② (self-confidence) seguridad f en sí mismo ③ (insurance) (BrE) seguro m

assure /ə'ʃʊr ‖ə'ʃʊə(r), ə'ʃɔː(r)/ vt ① (a) (guarantee) asegurar (b) (convince) convencer* ② (make certain) **to ~ sb (OF) sth: this work will ~ me (of) a regular income** este trabajo me asegurará una entrada fija ③ (insure) (BrE) ‹life› asegurar

asterisk /'æstərɪsk/ n asterisco m

asteroid /'æstərɔɪd/ n asteroide m

asthma /'æzmə ‖'æsmə/ n asma f‡

asthmatic /æz'mætɪk ‖æs'mætɪk/ adj asmático

astonish /ə'stɑːnɪʃ ‖ə'stɒnɪʃ/ vt asombrar; (more intensely) dejar pasmado

astonished /ə'stɑːnɪʃt ‖ə'stɒnɪʃt/ adj asombrado; **the ~ look on their faces** la cara de asombro que pusieron; **I'm ~ (that) he got so far** me asombra que haya llegado tan lejos

astonishing /ə'stɑːnɪʃɪŋ ‖ə'stɒnɪʃɪŋ/ adj asombroso; (more intensely) pasmoso

astonishment /ə'stɑːnɪʃmənt ‖ə'stɒnɪʃmənt/ n asombro m; (more intense) estupefacción f

astound /ə'staʊnd/ vt dejar estupefacto

astounded /ə'staʊndəd ‖ə'staʊndɪd/ adj atónito

astounding /ə'staʊndɪŋ/ adj increíble

astray /ə'streɪ/ adv: **to go ~** (get lost) extraviarse*; (do wrong) (euph or hum) descarriarse*; **to lead sb ~** (euph or hum) llevar a algn por mal camino

astride /ə'straɪd/ prep: **he sat ~ the fence/ horse** estaba sentado en la valla/montado en el caballo a horcajadas

astringent /ə'strɪndʒənt/ adj astringente

astrologer /ə'strɑːlədʒər ‖ə'strɒlədʒə(r)/ n astrólogo, -ga m,f

astrology /ə'strɑːlədʒi ‖ə'strɒlədʒi/ n astrología f

astronaut /'æstrənɔːt/ n astronauta mf

astronomer /ə'strɑːnəmər ‖ə'strɒnəmə(r)/ n astrónomo, -ma m,f

astronomical /'æstrə'nɑːmɪkəl ‖,æstrə'nɒmɪkəl/ adj astronómico

astronomy /ə'strɑːnəmi ‖ə'strɒnəmi/ n astronomía f

astute /ə'stuːt ‖ə'stjuːt/ adj ‹person› sagaz; ‹decision› inteligente

asylum /ə'saɪləm/ n (a) (refuge) asilo m (b) (lunatic **~**) manicomio m

at /æt, weak form ət/ prep ① (location) en; **she's ~ the office** está en la oficina; **he's ~ the bank** ha ido al banco ② (direction): **to point ~ sth/sb** señalar algo/a algn; **he smiled ~ me** me sonrió ③ (time): **~ 6 o'clock** a las seis; **~ Christmas** Navidad, por Navidades (Esp); **~ night** por la noche, de noche ④ (a) (indicating state): **~ a disadvantage** en desventaja; **~ war/peace** en guerra/paz (b) (occupied with): **people ~ work** gente trabajando; **children ~ play** niños jugando ⑤ (with measurements, numbers, rates etc): **they sell them ~ around $80** las venden a alrededor de $80 ⑥ (because of): **he was surprised ~ the decision** le sorprendió la decisión

ate /eɪt/ past of EAT

atheism /'eɪθiɪzəm/ n ateísmo m

atheist /'eɪθiəst ‖'eɪθiɪst/ n ateo, atea m,f

Athens /'æθənz/ n Atenas f

athlete /'æθliːt/ n atleta mf

athlete's foot n pie m de atleta

athletic /æθ'letɪk/ adj atlético

athletics /æθ'letɪks/ n (+ sing or pl vb) (a) (active sports) (AmE) deportes mpl (b) (track and field) (esp BrE) atletismo m

Atlantic¹ /ət'læntɪk/ adj atlántico

Atlantic² n **the ~ (Ocean)** el (océano) Atlántico

atlas /'ætləs/ n atlas m

ATM n (AmE) (= **automated** or **automatic teller machine**) cajero m automático or permanente

atmosphere /'ætməsfɪr ‖'ætməsfɪə(r)/ n **(a)** (of planet) atmósfera f **(b)** (feeling, mood) ambiente m

atmospheric /ˌætməs'ferɪk/ adj atmosférico

atom /'ætəm/ n átomo m

atomic /ə'tɑːmɪk ‖ə'tɒmɪk/ adj ‹warfare/ energy› atómico; ~ **bomb** bomba f atómica

atone /ə'təʊn/ vi (frml) to ~ **FOR** sth ‹for sins› expiar* algo; ‹for crime/harm› reparar algo

atrocious /ə'trəʊʃəs/ adj **(a)** (very bad) (colloq) ‹spelling/manners› espantoso (fam) **(b)** (horrifying) ‹injuries/conditions› atroz

atrocity /ə'trɑːsəti ‖ə'trɒsəti/ n (pl **-ties**) atrocidad f

attach /ə'tætʃ/ vt (fasten) sujetar; (tie) atar, amarrar (AmL exc RPI); (stick) pegar*; (to letter, document) adjuntar; **it is ~ed to the wall with screws** está sujeto a la pared con tornillos; **the ~ed form** el formulario adjunto; **to ~ importance to sth** dar(le) importancia a algo

attaché /ˌætæ'ʃeɪ ‖ə'tæʃeɪ/ n agregado, -da m,f

attaché case n maletín m

attached /ə'tætʃt/ adj (pred) (fond) **to be ~ TO sb/sth** tenerle* mucho cariño A algn/algo

attachment /ə'tætʃmənt/ n **1** **(a)** (part) accesorio m **(b)** (Comput) documento m adjunto **2** (fondness) ~ (**TO** sb/sth) cariño m (**POR** algn/algo)

attack¹ /ə'tæk/ n **(a)** (physical, verbal) ataque m; **terrorist ~s** atentados mpl terroristas **(b)** (Med) ataque m; **heart ~** infarto m

attack² vt **1** (physically, verbally) atacar* **2** ‹task› acometer; ‹problem› combatir ■ ~ vi (Mil, Sport) atacar*

attacker /ə'tækər ‖ə'tækə(r)/ n agresor, -sora m,f

attain /ə'teɪn/ vt (frml) ‹position/goal› alcanzar*, lograr; ‹ambition› realizar*

attempt¹ /ə'tempt/ vt **(a)** (try) to ~ to + **INF/-ING** tratar **DE** or intentar + **INF** **(b)** (have a try at) «student» ‹exam question› intentar responder a (frml) **(c)** **attempted** past p: ~ed **suicide/ murder** intento m de suicidio/tentativa f de asesinato

attempt² n intento m; **I made an ~ at conversation** traté de or intenté entablar conversación; **to make an ~ on sb's life** atentar contra la vida de algn

attend /ə'tend/ vt **1** (frml) **(a)** (be present at) asistir a (frml) **(b)** (go to regularly) ‹church/school/ classes› ir* a **2** ‹patient› atender* ■ ~ vi **1** (be present) asistir **2** (pay attention) **to ~** (**TO** sth) atender* (**A** algo), poner* atención (**A** algo) (AmL) ■ **attend to** [v + prep + o] ‹patient/customer› atender*; ‹correspondence/filing› ocuparse de

attendance /ə'tendəns/ n **(a)** (presence) asistencia f; **to be in ~** estar* presente **(b)** (people present): **what was the ~?** ¿cuántos asistentes hubo?; **to take ~** (AmE) pasar lista

attendant /ə'tendənt/ n (in museum, parking lot) guarda m; (in pool, toilets) encargado, -da m,f

attention /ə'tenʃən ‖ə'tenʃən/ n **1** **(a)** (concentration) atención f; **to pay ~ to sth/sb** prestarle atención a algo/algn **(b)** (notice) atención f; **to catch sb's ~** atraer* la atención de algn; **it has been brought to my ~** o **it has come to my ~ that ...** me han informado que ... **(c)** (care) atención f **2** (Mil): **to stand to ~** ponerse* en posición de firme(s)

attentive /ə'tentɪv/ adj atento

attenuate /ə'tenjueɪt/ vt atenuar*; **attenuating circumstances** circunstancias fpl atenuantes

attic /'ætɪk/ n desván m, ático m, altillo m (esp AmL)

attire /ə'taɪr ‖ə'taɪə(r)/ n (liter) atuendo m (frml), atavío m (liter)

attitude /'ætətuːd ‖'ætɪtjuːd/ n actitud f

attorney /ə'tɜːrni ‖ə'tɜːni/ n (pl **-neys**) (AmE) abogado, -da m,f; see also POWER OF ATTORNEY

Attorney General n (pl ~**s** or ~**s** ~) (in US — at national level) ≈Ministro, -tra m,f de Justicia; (— at state level) ≈Fiscal mf General

attract /ə'trækt/ vt atraer*

attraction /ə'trækʃən/ n **(a)** (Phys) atracción f **(b)** (interest): **I still feel a great ~ toward the place** todavía me atrae mucho el lugar; **what's the ~?** ¿qué atractivo tiene? **(c)** (attractive feature) atractivo m; **tourist ~** atracción f turística

attractive /ə'træktɪv/ adj atractivo

attribute¹ /ə'trɪbjət ‖ə'trɪbjuːt/ vt **to ~ sth TO sth/sb** atribuirle* algo A algo/algn

attribute² /'ætrəbjuːt ‖'ætrɪbjuːt/ n atributo m

attrition /ə'trɪʃən/ n **1** (destruction) desgaste m; **war of ~** guerra f de desgaste **2** (AmE Lab Rel) bajas fpl vegetativas

aubergine /'əʊbərʒiːn ‖'əʊbəʒiːn/ n (BrE) berenjena f

auburn /'ɔːbərn ‖'ɔːbən/ adj castaño rojizo adj inv

auction¹ /'ɔːkʃən/ n subasta f, remate m (AmL)

auction² vt subastar, rematar (AmL)

auctioneer /ˌɔːkʃə'nɪr ‖ˌɔːkʃə'nɪə(r)/ n subastador, -dora m,f, rematador, -dora m,f (AmL)

audacious /ɔː'deɪʃəs/ adj **(a)** (daring) ‹act/plan› audaz **(b)** (impudent) ‹behavior/person› atrevido

audacity /ɔː'dæsəti/ n (daring) audacia f; (impudence) atrevimiento m

audible /'ɔːdəbəl/ adj audible

audience /'ɔːdɪəns/ n **1** (at play, film) público m; (at concert, lecture) auditorio m; (TV) audiencia f **2** (interview) audiencia f

audio- /'ɔːdɪəʊ/ pref audio-

audio-: ~**book** n audiolibro m; ~**visual** adj audiovisual

audit¹ /'ɔːdət ‖'ɔːdɪt/ vt **(a)** (Busn, Fin) ‹accounts› auditar **(b)** (AmE Educ) ‹classes/course› asistir como oyente a

audit² n (Busn, Fin) **(a)** (inspection) auditoría f **(b)** (report) (AmE) informe m de auditoría

audition¹ /ɔː'dɪʃən/ vi: **to ~ (FOR sth)** dar* una audición (PARA algo)

audition² n audición f

auditor /'ɔːdətər ‖'ɔːdɪtə(r)/ n **(a)** (Busn, Fin) auditor, -tora m,f **(b)** (AmE Educ) oyente mf

auditorium /'ɔːdə'tɔːriəm ‖,ɔːdɪ'tɔːriəm/ n (pl **-riums** or **-ria** /-riə/) auditorio m

augment /ɔːg'ment/ vt (frml) aumentar, incrementar (frml)

augur /'ɔːgər ‖'ɔːgə(r)/ vi: **to ~ well/ill** ser* de buen/mal agüero

august /ɔː'gʌst/ adj augusto

August /'ɔːgəst/ n agosto m

aunt /ænt ‖ɑːnt/ n tía f

auntie, aunty /'ænti ‖'ɑːnti/ n (colloq) tía f, tiíta f (fam)

au pair /'əʊ'per ‖,əʊ'peə(r)/ n au pair mf

aura /'ɔːrə/ n halo m, aura m

aural /'ɔːrəl/ adj auditivo

auspices /'ɔːspəsəz ‖'ɔːspɪsɪz/ pl n (frml): **under the ~ of sb/sth** bajo los auspicios de algn/algo

auspicious /ɔː'spɪʃəs/ adj (frml) prometedor, auspicioso (CS)

austere /ɔː'stɪr ‖ɒ'stɪə(r), ɔː'stɪə(r)/ adj austero

austerity /ɔː'sterəti ‖ɒ'sterəti, ɔː'sterəti/ n austeridad f

Australasia /'ɔːstrə'leɪʒə, -'leɪʃə ‖,ɒstrə'leɪʒə, -'leɪʃə/ n Australasia f

Australia /ɔː'streɪliə ‖ɒ'streɪliə/ n Australia f

Australian¹ /ɔː'streɪliən ‖ɒ'streɪliən/ adj australiano

Australian² n australiano, -na m,f

Austria /'ɔːstriə ‖'ɒstriə/ n Austria f

Austrian¹ /'ɔːstriən ‖'ɒstriən/ adj austriaco, austríaco

Austrian² n austriaco, -ca m,f, austríaco, -ca m,f

authentic /ə'θentɪk ‖ɔː'θentɪk/ adj **(a)** (genuine) auténtico **(b)** (realistic) ⟨atmosphere⟩ realista

authenticate /ə'θentɪkeɪt ‖ɔː'θentɪkeɪt/ vt **(a)** (declare genuine) autenticar* **(b)** (prove, confirm) probar*

authenticity /'ɔːθen'tɪsəti/ n (of manuscript, painting) autenticidad f

author /'ɔːθər ‖'ɔːθə(r)/ n (writer) escritor, -ra m,f, (in relation to her/his works) autor, -tora m,f

authoritarian /ɔː'θɔːrə'teriən ‖ɔː,θɒrɪ'teəriən/ adj autoritario

authoritative /ə'θɔːrəteɪtɪv ‖ɔː'θɒrətətɪv/ adj **1** ⟨manner/tone⟩ de autoridad **2** (reliable, respected) ⟨source⟩ fidedigno; ⟨work/study⟩ autorizado

authority /ə'θɔːrəti ‖ɔː'θɒrəti/ n (pl **-ties**) **1** **(a)** (power) autoridad f **(b)** (authorization) **~ to + INF** autorización f PARA + INF **2** (person, body) autoridad f; **she was detained by the Belgian authorities** fue detenida por las autoridades belgas **3 (a)** (expert) **~ (ON sth)** autoridad f (EN algo) **(b)** (source) autoridad f; **to have sth on good ~** saber* algo de buena fuente

authorize /'ɔːθəraɪz/ vt **(a)** ⟨publication/

transaction⟩ autorizar*; ⟨funds⟩ aprobar* **(b)** (empower) **to ~ sb to + INF** autorizar* a algn PARA + INF

autistic /ɔː'tɪstɪk/ adj autista

autobiographical /'ɔːtə,baɪə'græfɪkəl/ adj autobiográfico

autobiography /'ɔːtəbaɪ'ɑːgrəfi ‖'ɔːtəbaɪɒgrəfi/ n (pl **-phies**) autobiografía f

autocratic /'ɔːtə'krætɪk/ adj autocrático

autograph¹ /'ɔːtəgræf ‖'ɔːtəgrɑːf/ n autógrafo m

autograph² vt autografiar*

automata /ɔː'tɑːmətə ‖ɔː'tɒmətə/ pl of AUTOMATON

automate /'ɔːtəmeɪt/ vt automatizar*

automatic¹ /'ɔːtə'mætɪk/ adj automático

automatic² n (car) coche m automático; (pistol) automática f

automatically /'ɔːtə'mætɪkli/ adv automáticamente

automation /'ɔːtə'meɪʃən/ n automatización f

automaton /ɔː'tɑːmətən ‖ɔː'tɒmətən/ n (pl **automata** or **-tons**) autómata m

automobile /'ɔːtəməbiːl/ n (esp AmE) coche m, carro m (AmL exc CS), auto m (esp CS), automóvil m (frml)

autonomous /ɔː'tɑːnəməs ‖ɔː'tɒnəməs/ adj autónomo

autonomy /ɔː'tɑːnəmi ‖ɔː'tɒnəmi/ n autonomía f

autopsy /'ɔːtɑːpsi ‖'ɔːtɒpsi/ n (pl **-sies**) autopsia f

autumn /'ɔːtəm/ n (esp BrE) otoño m; (before n) ⟨day/weather⟩ de otoño, otoñal

auxiliary¹ /ɔːg'zɪljəri/ adj auxiliar

auxiliary² n (pl **-ries**) auxiliar mf; **nursing ~** enfermero, -ra m,f auxiliar

avail¹ /ə'veɪl/ v refl (frml) **to ~ oneself OF sth** aprovechar algo

avail² n (liter): **to no ~** en vano

available /ə'veɪləbəl/ adj **(a)** (obtainable) (pred): **to be readily ~** ser* fácil de conseguir; **brochures are ~ on request** hay folletos a disposición de quien los solicite **(b)** (at sb's disposal) ⟨resources/manpower⟩ disponible; **to make sth ~ to sb** poner* algo a disposición de algn **(c)** (free, contactable) (pred) libre; (for work, job) disponible

avalanche /'ævəlæntʃ ‖'ævəlɑːnʃ/ n alud m, avalancha f

avant-garde /'ɑːvɑːn'gɑːrd ‖,ævɒn'gɑːd/ adj vanguardista, de vanguardia

avarice /'ævərəs ‖'ævərɪs/ n (liter) codicia f (liter)

avaricious /'ævə'rɪʃəs/ adj (liter) codicioso

Ave (= **Avenue**) Avda., Av.

avenge /ə'vendʒ/ vt vengar*

avenue /'ævənu ‖'ævənjuː/ n **1 (a)** (tree-lined walk) paseo m ⟨arbolado⟩ **(b)** (broad street) avenida f **2** (means, method) vía f

average¹ /'ævrɪdʒ , 'ævərɪdʒ/ n (Math) promedio m, media f

average² adj **(a)** (Math) ⟨time/age⟩ medio, promedio adj inv; **he is of ~ height** es de ⋯⋯⟩

estatura mediana **(b)** (typical): **the ~ family** la familia tipo **(c)** (ordinary): **how was the movie? —** *average* ¿qué tal la película? — normal

■ **average out** [v + adv]: **our speed ~d out at about 60mph** hicimos una media *or* un promedio de 60 millas por hora

averse /ə'vɜːrs ‖ə'vɜːs/ *adj* (*pred*) **to be ~ TO sth** ⟨*to an idea*⟩ ser* reacio A algo

aversion /ə'vɜːrʒən, -ʃən ‖ə'vɜːʃən/ *n* (*no pl*) aversión *f*

avert /ə'vɜːrt ‖ə'vɜːt/ *vt* **(a)** ⟨*eyes/gaze*⟩ apartar **(b)** ⟨*danger/suspicion*⟩ evitar; ⟨*accident/strike*⟩ impedir*

aviary /'eɪvieri ‖'eɪvɪəri/ *n* (*pl* **-ries**) pajarera *f*

aviation /ˌeɪvi'eɪʃən/ *n* aviación *f*

avid /'ævəd ‖'ævɪd/ *adj* ⟨*reader/interest*⟩ ávido; ⟨*fan/follower*⟩ ferviente

avocado /ˌævə'kɑːdəʊ/ *n* (*pl* **-dos**) ~ (**pear**) aguacate *m or* (Bol, CS, Per) palta *f*

avoid /ə'vɔɪd/ *vt* ⟨*obstacle/place/topic*⟩ evitar; ⟨*blow*⟩ esquivar; **why are you ~ing me?** ¿por qué me rehúyes?

avoidable /ə'vɔɪdəbəl/ *adj* evitable

avowed /ə'vaʊd/ *adj* (*before n*) declarado

await /ə'weɪt/ *vt* esperar

awake[1] /ə'weɪk/ *adj* (*pred*) **to be ~** estar* despierto

awake[2] (*past* **awoke**; *past p* **awoken**), **awaken** /ə'weɪkən/ *vt/i* despertar*

awakening /ə'weɪkənɪŋ/ *n* despertar *m*

award[1] /ə'wɔːrd ‖ə'wɔːd/ *vt* **(a)** ⟨*prize/medal/pay increase*⟩ conceder; ⟨*honor*⟩ conferir* **(b)** (Sport) ⟨*penalty/free kick*⟩ conceder

award[2] *n* **(a)** (prize) galardón *m*; (medal) condecoración *f* **(b)** (sum of money) asignación *f*

award-winning /ə'wɔːrd'wɪnɪŋ ‖ə'wɔːd,wɪnɪŋ/ *adj* (*before n*) galardonado

aware /ə'wer ‖ə'weə(r)/ *adj* (conscious) (*pred*) **to be ~ OF sth** ser* *or* (Chi, Méx) estar* consciente DE algo; **is your father ~ that you drink?** ¿sabe tu padre que bebes?

awareness /ə'wernəs ‖ə'weənɪs/ *n* conciencia *f*

awash /ə'wɔːʃ ‖ə'wɒʃ/ *adj* (*pred*) **to be ~** (WITH sth) estar* inundado (DE algo)

away /ə'weɪ/ *adv* **[1]** (from place, person): **I looked ~** aparté la vista; **he limped ~** se alejó cojeando **[2] (a)** (in the distance): **it isn't far ~** no queda lejos; **it's 20 miles ~** queda a 20 millas; **Easter is a long way ~** falta mucho para Pascua **(b)** (absent): **she's**

~ in Canada está en Canadá; **I'll be ~ all next week** toda la semana que viene no voy a estar **(c)** (esp BrE Sport): **to play ~** jugar* fuera (de casa) **[3]** (continuously): **he's been painting ~ all morning** se ha pasado toda la mañana pintando; **I could hear him singing ~** lo oía cantar

[4] away from (*as prep*) **(a)** (in opposite direction to): **she pulled him ~ from the cliff edge** lo apartó del borde del acantilado **(b)** (at a distance, separated from) lejos de; **to get ~ from it all** alejarse del mundanal ruido

awe /ɔː/ *n* sobrecogimiento *m*; **to be in ~ of sb** sentirse* intimidado por algn

awe-inspiring /'ɔːɪn'spaɪrɪŋ ‖'ɔːɪn,spaɪərɪŋ/ *adj* impresionante

awesome /'ɔːsəm/ *adj* imponente

awestruck /'ɔːstrʌk/ *adj* atemorizado

awful /'ɔːfəl/ *adj* (colloq) ⟨*journey/weather/day*⟩ horrible; ⟨*clothes*⟩ horroroso; ⟨*joke/movie*⟩ malísimo; **I felt ~** me sentía fatal

awkward /'ɔːkwərd ‖'ɔːkwəd/ *adj* **[1]** (clumsy) ⟨*movement/person*⟩ torpe; ⟨*phrase*⟩ poco elegante **[2] (a)** (difficult, inconvenient) ⟨*shape/angle*⟩ incómodo; **at a rather ~ moment** en mal momento; **she could make things very ~ for you** te podría hacer la vida imposible **(b)** (difficult to deal with) difícil **[3] (a)** (embarrassing) ⟨*decision/subject*⟩ delicado; **you've put me in a very ~ position** me has puesto en una situación muy violenta **(b)** (embarrassed) ⟨*silence*⟩ incómodo; **I felt very ~** me sentí muy incómodo

awning /'ɔːnɪŋ/ *n* toldo *m*

awoke /ə'wəʊk/ *past of* AWAKE[2]

awoken /ə'wəʊkən/ *past p of* AWAKE[2]

awry /ə'raɪ/ *adj* (*pred*) torcido; **to go ~** salir* mal

ax[1], (BrE) **axe** /æks/ *n* hacha *f*; **to have an ~ to grind** tener* un interés personal

ax[2], (BrE) **axe** *vt* ⟨*joum*⟩ ⟨*project/services/jobs*⟩ suprimir; ⟨*employee*⟩ despedir*

axis /'æksəs ‖'æksɪs/ *n* (*pl* **axes** /'æksiːz/) eje *m*

axle /'æksəl/ *n* eje *m*

AZ = **Arizona**

Azerbaijan /ˌæzərbaɪ'dʒɑːn ‖ˌæzəbaɪ'dʒɑːn/ *n* Azerbaiyán *m*, Azerbaiján *m*

Azerbaijani /ˌæzərbaɪ'dʒɑːni ‖ˌæzəbaɪ'dʒɑːni/ *adj* azerbaiyaní

Aztec[1] /'æztek/ *adj* azteca

Aztec[2] *n* azteca *mf*

azure /'æʒər ‖'æzjə(r), 'æzjʊə(r)/ *adj* (liter) azur (liter)

Bb

B, b /biː/ *n* (a) (letter) B, b *f* (b) (Mus) si *m*

b (= **born**) n.

BA *n* = **Bachelor of Arts**

babble /'bæbəl/ *vi* (talk foolishly) parlotear (fam); (talk unintelligibly) farfullar; «*baby*» balbucear; **a babbling brook** (liter) un arroyo rumoroso (liter)

baby /'beɪbi/ *n* (*pl* **babies**) **(a)** (infant) bebé *m*, niño, -ña *m,f*, bebe, -ba *m,f* (Per, RPl), guagua *f* (Andes); **to have a ~** tener* un hijo *or* un niño **(b)** (animal) cría *f* **(c)** (youngest member) benjamín, -mina *m,f*

baby: **~ buggy**, **~ carriage** *n* (AmE) cochecito *m* de bebé, carriola *f* (Méx); **~-sit** *vi* (*pres p* **-sitting**; *past & past p* **-sat**) cuidar niños, hacer* de canguro (Esp); **~-sitter** /'beɪbi,sɪtər ‖ 'beɪbi,sɪtə(r)/ *n* baby sitter *mf*, canguro *mf* (Esp)

bachelor /'bætʃələr ‖ 'bætʃələ(r)/ *n* **1** (single man) soltero *m* **2** (Educ) licenciado, -da *m,f*; **B~ of Arts/Science** (degree) licenciatura *f* en Filosofía y Letras/en Ciencias

back¹ /bæk/ *n* **1** (Anat) (of human) espalda *f*; (of animal) lomo *m*; **they laugh at him behind his ~** se ríen de él a sus espaldas; **to turn one's ~ on sb** volverle* la espalda a algn

2 **(a)** (of chair) respaldo *m*; (of dress, jacket) espalda *f*; (of electrical appliance, watch) tapa *f* **(b)** (reverse side — of envelope, photo) dorso *m*; (— of head) parte *f* posterior; (— of hand) dorso *m*; **your sweater is on ~ to front** te has puesto el suéter al revés; ▸ HAND¹ 2

3 (rear part): **the ~ of the house** la parte de atrás de la casa; **at the ~ of the drawer** en el fondo del cajón; **we sat at the ~** nos sentamos al fondo; **I'll sit in the ~** (of car) yo me siento detrás *or* (en el asiento de) atrás; **in the ~ of beyond** quién sabe dónde, donde el diablo perdió el poncho (AmS fam), en el quinto pino (Esp fam)

4 (Sport) defensa *mf*, zaguero, -ra *m,f*

back² *adj* (*before n, no comp*) **1** «*door*» trasero; «*garden*» de atrás **2** (*of an earlier date*): **~ number** *o* **issue** número *m* atrasado; **~ pay** atrasos *mpl*

back³ *adv* **1** (indicating return, repetition): **the journey ~** el viaje de vuelta; **he's ~ from Paris** ha vuelto de París; **long hair is ~** (in fashion) vuelve (a estar de moda) el pelo largo; **to run/fly ~** volver* corriendo/en avión; **he asked for the ring ~** pidió que le devolviera el anillo; *see also* GO, TAKE *etc* BACK

2 (in reply, reprisal): **he slapped her and she slapped him ~** él la abofeteó y ella le devolvió la bofetada

3 (backward): **take two steps ~** da dos pasos atrás

4 (in the past): **~ in 1972** (ya) en 1972

5 **back and forth** = **backward(s) and forward(s)**; ▸ BACKWARD² A

back⁴ *vt* **1** **(a)** «*person/decision*» respaldar **(b)** (bet money on) «*horse/winner*» apostar* por

2 (reverse): **he ~ed the car out of the garage** sacó el coche del garaje dando marcha atrás *or* (Col, Méx) en reversa

3 (Mus) acompañar

■ **~** *vi* «*vehicle/driver*» dar* marcha atrás, meter reversa (Col, Méx); **he ~ed into a lamppost** se dio contra una farola al dar marcha atrás *or* al meter reversa

■ **back away** [*v + adv*] echarse atrás

■ **back down** [*v + adv*] volverse* atrás

■ **back out** [*v + adv*] volverse* atrás; **they ~ed out of the deal** no cumplieron el trato

■ **back up** **1** [*v + o + adv, v + adv + o*] **(a)** (support) respaldar, apoyar **(b)** (Comput) «*file*» hacer* una copia de seguridad de

2 [*v + adv*] (reverse) dar* marcha atrás, meter reversa (Col, Méx)

back: **~ache** *n* dolor *m* de espalda; **~bencher** /'bæk'bentʃər ‖ ,bæk'bentʃə(r)/, **~ bench MP** *n* (in UK) diputado, -da *m,f* (*sin cargo específico en el gobierno o la oposición*); **~bone** *n* (Anat) columna *f* (vertebral); (main strength) columna *f* vertebral, eje *m*; **~date** /'bæk'deɪt/ *vt* «*wage increase*» pagar* con retroactividad; «*check*» ponerle* una fecha anterior a; **~drop** *n* telón *m* de fondo

backer /'bækər ‖ 'bækə(r)/ *n* patrocinador, -dora *m,f*

backfire /'bækfaɪr ‖ bæk'faɪə(r)/ *vi* **(a)** «*car*» producir* detonaciones en el escape **(b)** (fail) fracasar

background¹ /'bækɡraʊnd/ *n* **(a)** (of picture, scene) fondo *m*; **she prefers to stay in the ~** prefiere permanecer en un segundo plano **(b)** (of events) **~** (**TO sth**) antecedentes *mpl* (DE algo) **(c)** (of person — origin) origen *m*; (— education) formación *f*; (— previous activities) experiencia *f*

background² *adj* (*before n*) «*noise/music*» de fondo; **~ reading** lecturas *fpl* preparatorias (*acerca del momento histórico, antecedentes etc*)

backhand /'bækhænd/ *n* revés *m*

backing /'bækɪŋ/ *n* **(a)** (support) respaldo *m* **(b)** (Mus) acompañamiento *m*

backlash /'bæklæʃ/ *n* reacción *f* violenta; (Mech Eng) contragolpe *m*

backless /'bækləs ‖ 'bæklɪs/ *adj* sin espalda

back: **~log** *n* atraso *m*; **a ~log of work** trabajo atrasado; **~pack** *n* mochila *f*; **~ seat** *n* asiento *m* trasero *or* de atrás; **~side** /'bæk'saɪd/ *n* (colloq) trasero *m* (fam); **~stage** /'bæk'steɪdʒ/ *adj/adv* entre bastidores; **~street** *n* callejuela *f*; (*before n*) «*abortion*» clandestino; **~stroke** *n* estilo *m* espalda; **~track** *vi* **(a)** (retrace one's steps) retroceder **(b)** (reverse opinion, plan) dar* marcha atrás; **~up** *n* **(a)** (support) respaldo *m*, apoyo *m*; (*before n*) «*team/equipment*» de refuerzo **(b)** (Comput) copia *f* de seguridad; (*before n*) «*disk/file*» de reserva, de seguridad

backward¹ /'bækwərd ‖ 'bækwəd/ *adj* ⋯❖

1 (before n) ⟨movement⟩ hacia atrás; **a ∼ glance** una mirada atrás **2** ⟨child⟩ retrasado; ⟨nation⟩ atrasado

backward², (esp BrE) **backwards** /'bækwərd ‖'bækwədz/ adv **(a)** (toward rear) hacia atrás; **∼ and forward(s)** para atrás y para adelante; ▶ KNOW¹ vt 1A **(b)** (back to front, in reverse order) al revés

back yard n (paved) patio m trasero; (grassed) (AmE) jardín m trasero, fondo m (RPl)

bacon /'beɪkən/ n tocino m or (Esp) bacon m or (RPl) panceta f

bacteria /bæk'tɪriə ‖bæk'tɪəriə/ pl n bacterias mpl

bad¹ /bæd/ adj

■ **Note** The usual translation of bad, malo, becomes mal when it is used before a masculine singular noun.

(comp **worse;** superl **worst**) **1** (not good) malo; **to be ∼ AT** sth/-ING ser* malo PARA algo/+ INF; **to go from ∼ to worse** ir* de mal en peor; **too much food is ∼ for you** comer demasiado es malo; **she's got a ∼ knee** tiene problemas con la rodilla; **I feel ∼ about not having written to her** me da no sé qué no haberle escrito; **to be in a ∼ way** (colloq) estar* fatal (fam) **2** (serious) ⟨mistake/injury⟩ grave; ⟨headache⟩ fuerte **3** (rotten) ⟨egg/fruit⟩ podrido; **to go ∼** echarse a perder

bad² n: **all the ∼ that he's done** todo el mal que ha hecho; **there's good and ∼ in everybody** todos tenemos cosas buenas y malas

bad³ adv (esp AmE colloq): **to need sth real ∼** necesitar algo desesperadamente

bade /bæd, beɪd/ past of BID¹ vt 2

badge /bædʒ/ n (pin-on) chapa f, botón m (AmL); (sew-on) insignia f

badger¹ /'bædʒər ‖'bædʒə(r)/ n tejón m

badger² vt fastidiar

badly /'bædli/ adv (comp **worse;** superl **worst**) **1** (poorly) ⟨play/sing⟩ mal **2** (improperly) ⟨behave/treat⟩ mal **3** (as intensifier) ⟨fail⟩ miserablemente; **∼ injured** gravemente herido

badly off adj (comp **worse off;** superl **worst off**) (pred) mal de dinero

badminton /'bædmɪntn/ n bádminton m

bad-tempered /'bæd'tempərd ‖,bæd'tempəd/ adj ⟨reply/tone⟩ malhumorado; ⟨person⟩ (as permanent characteristic) de mal genio; (in a bad mood) de mal humor

baffle /'bæfəl/ vt **(a)** ⟨perplex⟩ desconcertar* **(b)** ⟨frustrate⟩ ⟨efforts⟩ frustrar

baffled /'bæfəld/ adj perplejo; ⟨expression⟩ de perplejidad

bag /bæg/ n **1 (a)** (container, bagful) bolsa f; **a paper ∼** una bolsa de papel; (hand∼) (esp BrE) cartera f or (Esp) bolso m or (Méx) bolsa f **(b)** (piece of luggage) maleta f, valija f (RPl), petaca f (Méx); **to pack one's ∼s** hacer* la maleta (or

valija etc) **2** (of skin) bolsa f; **to have ∼s under one's eyes** (of skin) tener* bolsas en los ojos; (dark rings) tener* ojeras

baggage /'bægɪdʒ/ n equipaje m; (before n) **∼ room** (AmE) consigna f

baggy /'bægi/ adj **-gier, -giest** ancho, guango (Méx)

bagpipes /'bægpaɪps/ pl n gaita f

Bahamas /bə'hɑːməz/ pl n **the ∼** las Bahamas

bail /beɪl/ n (Law) fianza f; **he was released on ∼** fue puesto en libertad bajo fianza

■ **bail out** **1** [v + o + adv, v + adv + o] **(a)** (Law): **to ∼ sb out** pagarle* la fianza a algn **(b)** (Naut) ⟨water⟩ achicar* **2** [v + o + adv, v + adv + o] (rescue) sacar* de apuros **3** [v + adv] (Aviat) tirarse en paracaídas

bailiff /'beɪləf ‖'beɪlɪf/ n (Law) **(a)** (in UK) alguacil mf **(b)** (in US) funcionario que custodia al acusado en el juzgado

bait¹ /beɪt/ n cebo m

bait² vt **1** ⟨hook/trap⟩ cebar **2** (persecute) acosar

bake /beɪk/ vt: **∼ in a hot oven** hornear en horno caliente; **she ∼s her own bread** hace el pan en casa; **∼d potato** papa f or (Esp) patata f asada

■ **∼** vi hacer* pasteles (or pan etc)

baked beans /beɪkt/ pl n **(a)** (in can) frijoles mpl or (Esp) judías fpl or (CS) porotos mpl en salsa de tomate **(b)** (dish) (AmE) el mismo plato preparado con cerdo

baker /'beɪkər ‖'beɪkə(r)/ n panadero, -ra m,f; **∼'s (shop)** panadería f

bakery /'beɪkəri/ n (pl **-ries**) panadería f

baking /'beɪkɪŋ/ n: **we do a lot of ∼** hacemos muchos pasteles (or pan etc); (before n) **∼ dish** fuente f para el horno; **∼ powder** polvo m de hornear, Royal® m, levadura f en polvo (Esp); **∼ tin** molde m; **∼ tray** bandeja f (de horno)

balance¹ /'bæləns/ n **1** (apparatus) balanza f **2** (equilibrium) equilibrio m; **to lose one's ∼** perder* el equilibrio **3 (a)** (in accounting) balance m **(b)** (bank ∼) saldo m **(c)** (difference, remainder) resto m; (of sum of money) saldo m

balance² vt **1** ⟨load⟩ equilibrar; ⟨object⟩ mantener* en equilibrio **2** (Fin) ⟨account⟩ hacer* el balance de

balanced /'bælənst/ adj equilibrado

balance of payments n balanza f de pagos

balcony /'bælkəni/ n (pl **-nies**) **(a)** (Archit) balcón m; (large) terraza f **(b)** (Theat) (in US) platea f alta; (in UK) galería f

bald /bɔːld/ adj **-er, -est (a)** ⟨man⟩ calvo, pelón (AmC, Méx), pelado (CS); **to go ∼** quedarse calvo (or pelón etc) **(b)** (worn) ⟨tire⟩ gastado

bale /beɪl/ n paca f

■ **bale out** (BrE) ▶ BAIL OUT

Balearic Islands /'bæli'ærɪk/ pl n **the ∼ ∼** las (Islas) Baleares

baleful /'beɪlfəl/ adj torvo

Balkan /'bɔːlkən/ *adj* balcánico

Balkans /'bɔːlkənz/ *pl n* **the ~** los países balcánicos

ball /bɔːl/ *n* **1** (in baseball, golf) pelota *f*, bola *f*; (in basketball, football) pelota *f* (esp AmL), balón *m* (esp Esp); (in billiards) bola *f*; **to be on the ~** (colloq) ser* muy espabilado **2** **(a) to play ~ (with sb)** (lit: play game) jugar* a la pelota (con algn); (cooperate) (colloq) cooperar (con algn) **(b)** (base~) (AmE) béisbol *m* **3** **(a)** (round mass) bola *f*; (of string, wool) ovillo *m* **(b)** (Anat): **the ~ of the foot** la parte anterior de la planta del pie **4** (dance) baile *m*

ballad /'bæləd/ *n* (narrative poem, song) romance *m*; (sentimental song) balada *f*

ballast /'bæləst/ *n* (Aviat, Naut) lastre *m*

ballerina /bælə'riːnə/ *n* bailarina *f* (de ballet)

ballet /'bæleɪ/ *n* ballet *m*; (*before n*) **~ dancer** bailarín, -rina *m,f* de ballet

ball game *n* juego *m* de pelota; (baseball game) (AmE) partido *m* de béisbol; (US football game) (AmE) partido *m* de fútbol *or* (AmC, Méx) futbol americano

ballistics /bə'lɪstɪks/ *n* (+ *sing vb*) balística *f*

balloon /bə'luːn/ *n* **(a)** (toy) globo *m*, bomba *f* (Col), chimbomba *f* (AmC) **(b)** (Aviat) globo *m*

ballot /'bælət/ *n* votación *f*; (*before n*) **~ box** urna *f*; **~ (paper)** papeleta *f*, boleta *f* electoral (Méx, RPl)

ball: **~park** *n* (AmE Sport) estadio *m or* (Méx) parque *m* de béisbol; (*before n*) **a ~park figure** una cifra aproximada; **~player** *n* (AmE) (in baseball) jugador, -dora *m,f* de béisbol, beisbolista *mf*; (in US football) jugador, -dora *m,f* de fútbol *or* (AmC, Méx) de futbol americano; (in basketball) jugador, -dora *m,f* de baloncesto, baloncestista *mf*, basquetbolista *mf* (AmL); **~point (pen)** *n* bolígrafo *m*, esfero(gráfico) *m* (Col), pluma *f* atómica (Méx), birome *f* (RPl), lápiz *m* de pasta (Chi); **~room** *n* sala *f or* salón *m* de baile; **~room dancing** *n* baile *m* de salón

balm /bɑːm/ *n* bálsamo *m*

Baltic /'bɔːltɪk/ *n* **the ~ (Sea)** el (mar) Báltico

bamboo /bæm'buː/ ‖bæm'buː/ *n* (*pl* **-boos**) bambú *m*

ban¹ /bæn/ *vt* **-nn-** ⟨book/smoking⟩ prohibir*; ⟨organization⟩ proscribir*; **he was ~ned from the club** le prohibieron la entrada al club

ban² *n* prohibición *f*

banal /bə'nɑːl, 'beɪnl/ ‖bə'nɑːl/ *adj* banal

banana /bə'nænə/ ‖bə'nɑːnə/ *n* plátano *m*, banana *f* (Per, RPl), banano *m* (AmC, Col), cambur *m* (Ven)

band /bænd/ *n* **1** **(a)** (group) grupo *m*; (of thieves, youths) pandilla *f* **(b)** (Mus) (jazz ~) grupo *m or* conjunto *m* de jazz; (rock ~) grupo *m* de rock **2** **(a)** (ribbon) cinta *f*; (strip — of cloth) banda *f*; (— for hat) cinta *f* **(b)** (stripe) franja *f*
∎ **band together** [*v + adv*] unirse

bandage¹ /'bændɪdʒ/ *n* venda *f*

bandage² *vt* vendar

Band-Aid® /'bændeɪd/ *n* (AmE) curita® *f*, tirita® *f* (Esp)

B & B /'biːən'biː/ *n* = **bed and breakfast**

bandit /'bændət/ ‖'bændɪt/ *n* bandido, -da *m,f*, bandolero, -ra *m,f*

band: **~stand** *n* quiosco *m* de música; **~wagon** *n*: *to jump on the ~wagon* subirse al carro

bandy¹ /'bændi/ *adj* **-dier, -diest** arqueado, torcido

bandy² **-dies, -dying, -died** *vt* ⟨remarks/ jokes⟩ intercambiar

bane /beɪn/ *n*: **to be the ~ of sb's life** ser* la cruz de algn

bang¹ /bæŋ/ *n* **1** (loud noise) estrépito *m*; (explosion) explosión *f* **2** (blow) golpe *m*, trancazo *m* **3** **bangs** *pl* (AmE) (fringe) flequillo *m*, cerquillo *m* (AmL), chasquilla *f* (Chi), capul *f* (Col), fleco *m* (Méx), pollina *f* (Ven)

bang² *vt* **(a)** (strike) golpear **(b)** (slam): **he ~ed the door** dio un portazo (fam)
∎ **~** *vi* **(a)** (strike) **to ~ on sth** golpear algo; **to ~ into sth** darse* contra algo **(b)** (slam) «*door*» cerrarse* de un golpe

bang³ *adv* **1** : **to go ~** «*gun*» dispararse **2** (*as intensifier*) (esp BrE colloq): **~ on time** a la hora justa

banger /'bæŋər ‖'bæŋə(r)/ *n* (BrE colloq) **(a)** (sausage) salchicha *f* **(b)** (firework) petardo *m* **(c)** (car) (old ~) cacharro *m* (fam)

Bangkok /'bæŋkɑːk ‖ˌbæŋ'kɒk/ *n* Bangkok *m*

Bangladesh /'bɑːŋglə'deʃ ‖ˌbæŋglə'deʃ/ *n* Bangladesh *m*

Bangladeshi /'bɑːŋglə'deʃi ‖ˌbæŋglə'deʃi/ *adj* bangladesí

bangle /'bæŋgl/ *n* pulsera *f*, brazalete *m*; (thin, of gold or silver) esclava *f*, aro *m*

banish /'bænɪʃ/ *vt* **(a)** (exile) desterrar*; ⟨fear/ doubts⟩ hacer* olvidar **(b)** (prohibit) prohibir*

banister /'bænəstər ‖'bænɪstə(r)/ *n* pasamanos *m*

bank¹ /bæŋk/ *n* **1** **(a)** (Fin) banco *m*; (*before n*) **~ balance** saldo *m* **(b)** (store, supply) banco *m*; **blood ~** banco de sangre **2** (edge of river) orilla *f*, ribera *f* **3** **~ of earth/snow** montículo *m* de tierra/nieve

bank² *vt* depositar *or* (esp Esp) ingresar (en el banco)
∎ **~** *vi* **1** (Fin): **I ~ with the National** tengo la cuenta en el National **2** (Aviat) ladearse
∎ **bank on** [*v + prep + o*] ⟨victory/help⟩ contar* con; **I wouldn't ~ on it** yo no me confiaría demasiado

bank: **~ account** *n* cuenta *f* bancaria; **~book** *n* libreta *f* de ahorros; **~card** *n* (AmE) tarjeta *f* de crédito (*expedida por un banco*); (BrE) tarjeta *f* bancaria

banker /'bæŋkər ‖'bæŋkə(r)/ *n* **(a)** (Fin) banquero, -ra *m,f* **(b)** (in gambling) banca *f*

bank holiday *n* (BrE) día *m* festivo, feriado *m* (esp AmL)

banking /'bæŋkɪŋ/ *n* banca *f*

bank: **~ note** *n* **(a)** (promissory note) (AmE) pagaré *m* **(b)** (paper money) (BrE) billete *m* de banco; **~ rate** *n* tasa *f or* (esp Esp) tipo *m* de interés

bankrupt¹ /'bæŋkrʌpt/ *adj* en quiebra, en bancarrota; **to be ~** estar* en quiebra *or* en bancarrota; **to go ~** quebrar*, ir* a la bancarrota

bankrupt² *n* fallido, -da *m,f*

bankrupt³ *vt* llevar a la quiebra *or* a la bancarrota

bankruptcy /'bæŋkrʌptsi/ *n* (*pl* **-cies**) quiebra *f*, bancarrota *f*

banner /'bænər ‖'bænə(r)/ *n* (flag) estandarte *m*; (in demonstration) pancarta *f*

bannister *n* ▶ BANISTER

banns /bænz/ *pl n* amonestaciones *fpl*

banquet /'bæŋkwət ‖'bæŋkwɪt/ *n* banquete *m*

banter /'bæntər ‖'bæntə(r)/ *n* bromas *fpl*

baptism /'bæptɪzəm/ *n* bautismo *m*

Baptist /'bæptəst ‖'bæptɪst/ *n* baptista *mf*, bautista *mf*

baptize /bæp'taɪz/ *vt* bautizar*

bar¹ /bɑːr ‖bɑː(r)/ *n* **1** (rod, rail) barra *f*; (— on cage, window) barrote *m* **2** (Sport) (cross~) (in soccer) larguero *m*; (in rugby) travesaño *m*; (in high jump) barra *f or* (Esp) listón *m*; (horizontal ~) barra *f* (fija) **3** (block) barra *f*; ~ **of chocolate** barra *f* de chocolate; **gold** ~ lingote *m* de oro; ~ **of soap** pastilla *f or* (CS) barra *f* de jabón **4** (establishment) bar *m*; (counter) barra *f*, mostrador *m* **5** (Law) **the Bar** (legal profession) (AmE) la abogacía; (barristers) (BrE) *el conjunto de* BARRISTERS **6** (Mus) compás *m*

bar² *vt* **-rr-** **1** (secure) ⟨*door/window*⟩ atrancar* **2** (block) ⟨*path/entrance*⟩ bloquear **3** (prohibit) ⟨*smoking/jeans*⟩ prohibir*; ⟨*person/group*⟩ excluir*

bar³ *prep* salvo, excepto, a *or* con excepción de

barb /bɑːrb ‖bɑːb/ *n* (of fishhook, arrow) lengüeta *f*

Barbados /bɑːr'beɪdəʊs ‖bɑː'beɪdɒs/ *n* Barbados *m*

barbarian /bɑːr'beriən ‖bɑː'beəriən/ *n* bárbaro, -ra *m,f*

barbaric /bɑːr'bærɪk ‖bɑː'bærɪk/ *adj* (primitive) primitivo; (brutal) brutal

barbarity /bɑːr'bærəti ‖bɑː'bærəti/ *n* (*pl* **-ties**) brutalidad *f*

barbecue /'bɑːrbɪkjuː ‖'bɑːbɪkjuː/ *n* **1** (grid and fireplace) barbacoa *f*, parrilla *f*, asador *m* (AmL) **2** (social occasion) barbacoa *f*, parrillada *f*, asado *m* (AmL)

barbed wire /bɑːrbd ‖bɑːbd/ *n* alambre *m* de púas *or* (Esp tb) de espino

barber /'bɑːrbər ‖'bɑːbə(r)/ *n* peluquero *m*, barbero *m* (ant); **the** ~**('s)** la peluquería

barbwire /'bɑːrb'waɪr ‖,bɑːb'waɪə(r)/ *n* (AmE) ▶ BARBED WIRE

bar code *n* código *m* de barras

bare¹ /ber ‖beə(r)/ *adj* **barer** /'berər ‖'beərə(r)/, **barest** /'berəst ‖'beərɪst/ (uncovered) ⟨*blade/flesh/walls*⟩ desnudo; ⟨*head*⟩ descubierto; ⟨*foot*⟩ descalzo; ⟨*floorboards*⟩ sin alfombrar; ⟨*tree*⟩ pelado; ⟨*wire*⟩ pelado *or* (Esp) desnudo; ⟨*room*⟩ con pocos muebles; **the** ~ **essentials** lo estrictamente esencial; **he gave me the** ~ **facts** se ciñó a los hechos; **to lay sth** ~ poner* *or* dejar algo al descubierto

bare² *vt*: **to** ~ **one's head** descubrirse* (la cabeza); **the dog** ~**d its teeth** el perro enseñó *or* mostró los dientes

bareback /'berbæk ‖'beəbæk/ *adv* ⟨*ride*⟩ a pelo

barefoot¹ /'berfʊt ‖'beəfʊt/ *adj* descalzo

barefoot² *adv*: **she ran** ~ corrió descalza

barely /'berli ‖'beəli/ *adv* (hardly) apenas

bargain¹ /'bɑːrgən ‖'bɑːgən/ *n* **1** (cheap purchase) ganga *f*; (before *n*) ⟨*price*⟩ de ganga *or* oferta **2** (deal, agreement) trato *m*, acuerdo *m*; **to strike a** ~ llegar a un acuerdo; **into** *o* (AmE also) **in the** ~ encima, por si fuera poco

bargain² *vi* **(a)** (haggle) regatear **(b)** (negotiate) negociar

■ **bargain for** [*v* + *prep* + *o*]: **we hadn't** ~**ed for such an eventuality** no habíamos tenido en cuenta esa posibilidad; **I got more than I had** ~**ed for** no me esperaba algo así

bargaining /'bɑːrgənɪŋ ‖'bɑːgənɪŋ/ *n* **(a)** (haggling) regateo *m* **(b)** (negotiating) negociaciones *fpl*; (before *n*) ⟨*strategy/position*⟩ negociador

barge¹ /bɑːrdʒ ‖bɑːdʒ/ *n* barcaza *f*

barge² *vi* (+ *adv compl*): **he** ~**d past (me)** me dio un empujón para pasar; **he always** ~**s in when we're trying to talk** siempre se entromete cuando queremos hablar

baritone /'bærətəʊn ‖'bærɪtəʊn/ *n* barítono *m*

bark¹ /bɑːrk ‖bɑːk/ *n* **1** (on tree) corteza *f* **2** (of dog) ladrido *m*

bark² *vi* ladrar;
■ ~ *vt* (shout) espetar; **to** ~ **(out) an order** gritar una orden

barkeep /'bɑːrkiːp ‖'bɑːkiːp/, **barkeeper** /-,kiːpər ‖-,kiːpə(r)/ *n* (AmE) (male) barman *m*, camarero *m* (Esp, Ven); (female) mesera *f or* (Esp, Ven) camarera *f or* (AmS) moza *f*

barley /'bɑːrli ‖'bɑːli/ *n* cebada *f*

bar: ~**maid** *n* mesera *f or* (Esp, Ven) camarera *f or* (AmS) moza *f*; ~**man** /'bɑːrmən ‖'bɑːmən/ *n* (*pl* **-men** /-mən/) (BrE) barman *m*, camarero *m* (Esp, Ven)

barn /bɑːrn ‖bɑːn/ *n* **(a)** (for crops) granero *m*; (for livestock) establo *m* **(b)** (for vehicles) (AmE) cochera *f*

barometer /bə'rɑːmətər ‖bə'rɒmɪtə(r)/ *n* barómetro *m*

baron /'bærən/ *n* **(a)** (nobleman) barón *m* **(b)** (magnate) magnate *m*

baroness /'bærə'nes, 'bærənəs/ *n* baronesa *f*

barracks /'bærəks/ *n* (*pl* ~) (+ *sing or pl vb*) cuartel *m*

barrage /bə'rɑːʒ ‖'bærɑːʒ/ *n* (Mil) (action) descarga *f*; (fire) cortina *f* de fuego

barrel /'bærəl/ *n* **1** (container) barril *m*, tonel *m* **2** (of handgun) cañón *m*; (of cannon) tubo *m*

barren /'bærən/ *adj* **-er, -est** ⟨*land/soil*⟩ estéril; ⟨*tree/plant/animal*⟩ (no *comp*) estéril; ⟨*woman*⟩ (dated or liter) infecunda

barrette /bə'ret ‖bə'ret/ *n* (AmE) pasador *m*, broche *m* (Méx, Ur), hebilla *f* (Arg)

barricade¹ /'bærəkeɪd ‖,bærɪ'keɪd/ *n* barricada *f*

barricade² *vt* cerrar* con barricadas; **they** ~**d themselves into the building** se atrincheraron en el edificio

barrier /'bæriər ‖'bæriə(r)/ *n* barrera *f*; **language** ~ barrera idiomática

Barrier Reef *n* **the Great** ~ ~ el Gran Arrecife Coralino, la Gran Barrera Coral

barrister /'bærəstər ‖'bærɪstə(r)/ *n* (BrE) abogado, -da *m,f* (*habilitado para alegar ante un tribunal superior*)

barrow /'bærəʊ/ n (wheel~) carretilla f

bar: ~**stool** n taburete m; ~**tender** n (esp AmE) (male) barman m, camarero m (Esp, Ven); (female) mesera f or (Esp, Ven) camarera f or (AmS) moza f

barter /'bɑːrtər ‖'bɑːtə(r)/ vt cambiar, trocar* ■ ~ vi hacer* trueques

base¹ /beɪs/ n **1** (of column, wall) base f; (of mountain, tree) pie m; (of spine, skull) base f; (of lamp) pie m **2** (foundation, basis) base f **3** (of patrol, for excursion) base f; (of organization) sede f **4** (in baseball) base f

base² vt **1** (found) to ~ sth ON sth ⟨opinion/ conclusion⟩ basar algo EN algo; **the movie is ~d on a real event** la película se basa en una historia real **2** (locate) basar; **the company is ~d in Madrid** la compañía tiene su base en Madrid

base³ adj baser, basest ⟨conduct/motive⟩ abyecto

baseball /'beɪsbɔːl/ n (a) (game) béisbol m; (before n) ~ **bat** bate m de béisbol (b) (ball) pelota f de béisbol

basement /'beɪsmənt/ n sótano m

base pay n (AmE) sueldo m base or básico

bases¹ /'beɪsiːz/ pl of BASIS

bases² /'beɪsəz ‖'beɪsɪz/ pl of BASE¹

bash¹ /bæʃ/ n (colloq) **1** (blow) golpe m, madrazo m (Méx fam) **2** (party) juerga f (fam)

bash² vt (colloq) pegarle* a

bashful /'bæʃfəl/ adj tímido, penoso (AmL exc CS)

basic /'beɪsɪk/ adj **1** (fundamental) fundamental **2** (simple, rudimentary) ⟨knowledge/need⟩ básico; ⟨hotel/food⟩ sencillo **3** (Econ) ⟨pay⟩ básico

basically /'beɪsɪkli/ adv fundamentalmente

basics /'beɪsɪks/ pl n lo básico

basil /'beɪzəl ‖'bæzəl/ n albahaca f

basin /'beɪsn̩/ n (a) (for liquid, food) cuenco m, bol m, tazón m (b) (hand ~) (BrE) lavamanos m, lavabo m, pileta f (RPl) (c) (Geog, Geol) cuenca f

basis /'beɪsəs ‖'beɪsɪs/ n (pl bases /'beɪsiːz/) **1** (foundation, grounds) base f **2** (system, level) (no pl): **employed on a daily** ~ contratado por día; **on a regional** ~ a nivel regional

bask /bæsk ‖bɑːsk/ vi: to ~ **in the sun** disfrutar (del calor) del sol; **she** ~**ed in their adulation** se deleitaba or se regodeaba con su adulación

basket /'bæskət ‖'bɑːskɪt/ n **1** (for shopping) canasta f (esp AmL), cesta f (esp Esp) **2** (in basketball) (a) (goal) canasta f, cesto m (b) (score) canasta f, enceste m

basketball /'bæskətbɔːl ‖'bɑːskɪtbɔːl/ n (a) (game) baloncesto m, básquetbol m (AmL) (b) (ball) pelota f de básquetbol or (Esp) balón m de baloncesto

Basque¹ /bæsk ‖bæsk, bɑːsk/ adj vasco; **the** ~ **Country** el País Vasco, Euskadi m

Basque² n (a) (person) vasco, -ca m,f (b) (language) euskera m, vasco m, vascuence m

bass¹ n /beɪs/ (pl ~es) (Mus) (a) (voice, singer) bajo m (b) (double bass or bass guitar) (contra)bajo m (c) (Audio) graves mpl

bass² adj ⟨voice⟩ de bajo

bass clef clave f de fa

bassoon /bə'suːn/ n fagot m

bastard /'bæstərd ‖'bɑːstəd/ n **1** (illegitimate child) bastardo, -da m,f **2** (colloq or vulg) cabrón m (fam o vulg), hijo m de puta (vulg)

baste /beɪst/ vt (a) (Culin) rociar con su jugo o con mantequilla etc durante la cocción (b) (sew loosely) hilvanar

bastion /'bæstʃən ‖'bæstɪən/ n (a) (Archit) bastión m (b) (stronghold) baluarte m, bastión m

bat¹ /bæt/ n **1** (in baseball, cricket) bate m; (in table tennis) (BrE) paleta f, raqueta f **2** (Zool) murciélago m

bat² vi -tt- (Sport) batear

batch /bætʃ/ n **1** (of cakes) hornada f; (of goods) (Busn) lote m; (of trainees, candidates) grupo m; (of mail, paperwork) pila f; (Comput) lote m

bated /'beɪtəd ‖'beɪtɪd/ adj: with ~ **breath** con ansiedad

bath¹ /bæθ ‖bɑːθ/ n (pl baths /bæðz ‖bɑːðz/) **1** (a) (wash) baño m; **to have** o (AmE also) **take a** ~ bañarse, darse* un baño (b) (tub) bañera f, tina f (AmL) **2** baths pl (swimming ~s) (BrE) piscina f, alberca f (Méx), pileta f (RPl)

bath² (BrE) vt bañar

bathe /beɪð/ vt (wash) ⟨wound/eyes⟩ lavar; ⟨baby/dog⟩ (AmE) bañar
■ ~ vi (a) (take bath) (AmE) bañarse (b) (go swimming) (BrE) bañarse

bathing suit, (BrE also) **bathing costume** /'beɪðɪŋ/ n traje m de baño, bañador m (Esp), malla f (de baño) (RPl), vestido m de baño (Col)

bath: ~**mat** n alfombrilla f or tapete m or (Chi) piso m de baño; ~**robe** n bata f de baño, albornoz m (Esp); ~**room** n (a) (room with bath) (cuarto m de) baño m (b) (toilet) (esp AmE) baño m, servicio m; ~**tub** n bañera f, tina f (AmL), bañadera f (Arg)

baton /bə'tɑːn ‖'bætən/ n (a) (Mus) batuta f (b) (truncheon) (BrE) bastón m (c) (in relay race) testigo m

battalion /bə'tæljən/ n batallón m

batter¹ /'bætər ‖'bætə(r)/ vt **1** (beat) ⟨victim/ opponent⟩ apalear; ⟨child/wife⟩ maltratar **2** (cover with batter) rebozar*

batter² n **1** (for fried fish, etc) rebozado m; (for pancakes) masa f; (for cake) (AmE) masa f **2** (in baseball) bateador, -dora m,f

battered /'bætərd ‖'bætəd/ adj ⟨car⟩ abollado; ⟨hat/suitcase⟩ estropeado; ⟨reputation/image⟩ maltrecho; ⟨baby/wife⟩ maltratado

battering ram /'bætərɪŋ/ n ariete m

battery /'bætəri/ n (pl -ries) **1** (in radio, lamp) pila f; (in car, motorcycle) batería f **2** (artillery) batería f **3** (Agr) batería f ⟨conjunto de jaulas instaladas para la explotación avícola intensiva⟩; (before n) ⟨eggs/hens⟩ de criadero, de batería; ~ **farming** cría f intensiva

battle¹ /'bætl/ n batalla f; **to fight a losing** ~ luchar por una causa perdida

battle² vi luchar

battle: ~**field** n campo m de batalla; ~**ground** n campo m de batalla

battlements /'bætlmənts/ pl n almenas fpl

battleship /'bætlʃɪp/ n acorazado m

baud /bɔːd/ n (Comput) baudio m

bawdy /'bɔːdi/ adj -dier, -diest subido de tono

b

bawl /bɔːl/ *vi* **(a)** (shout) vociferar **(b)** (cry noisily) berrear

bay¹ /beɪ/ *n* **1** (Geog) bahía *f* **2 (a)** (loading ∼) muelle *m or* plataforma *f* de carga **(b)** (area, recess) espacio *m* **3** : at ∼ acorralado; **to keep *o* hold sth/sb at ∼** mantener* algo/a algn a raya **4** ∼ **(tree)** laurel *m*

bay² *vi* «*hounds*» aullar*

bayleaf /'beɪliːf/ *n* (*pl* **-leaves**) hoja *f* de laurel

bayonet /'beɪənət/ *n* bayoneta *f*

bay window *n* ventana *f* en saliente

bazaar /bə'zɑːr ‖ bə'zɑː(r)/ *n* **(a)** (oriental market) bazar *m* **(b)** (charity sale) venta *f* benéfica

BBC *n* (= **British Broadcasting Corporation**) the ∼ la BBC

BC (= **before Christ**) antes de Cristo; (written form) aC, a. de C., a. de J.C.

be /biː, *weak form* bi/ (*pres* **am, are, is**; *past* **was, were**; *past p* **been**) *vi* [*See notes at* SER *and* ESTAR]

I **1** (*followed by an adjective*): **she's French** es francesa; **he's worried** está preocupado; **how are you?** ¿cómo estás?; **I'm much better** estoy *or* me encuentro mucho mejor; **she's pregnant/tired/ill** está embarazada/cansada/enferma; **I'm cold/hot/ hungry/thirsty** tengo frío/calor/hambre/sed; **he's dead** está muerto; **he's blind** es *or* (Esp tb) está ciego; **he's short** es bajo; **Tony is married/ divorced** Tony está *or* (esp AmL) es casado/ divorciado; **these shoes are new** estos zapatos son nuevos; **she was very rude to me** estuvo *or* fue muy grosera conmigo; **she's very rude** es muy grosera; ∼ **good** sé bueno

2 (*followed by a noun*) ser*; **if I were you, I'd stay** yo que tú me quedaría

3 (a) (talking about age) tener*; **how old are you?** ¿cuántos años tienes?; **I'm 31** tengo 31 años; **Paul was four last Monday** Paul cumplió cuatro años el lunes pasado; **our house is over 100 years old** nuestra casa tiene más de 100 años **(b)** (giving cost, measurement, weight): **they are $15 each** cuestan *or* valen 15 dólares cada una; **two plus two is four** dos más dos son cuatro; **how tall is he?** ¿cuánto mide?; **Jim's over six feet tall** Jim mide más de seis pies

II **1 (a)** (exist, live): **to let sth/sb** ∼ dejar tranquilo algo/a algn **(b)** (in expressions of time): **I'm drying my hair, I won't** ∼ **long** me estoy secando el pelo, enseguida estoy; **the party is tomorrow** la fiesta es mañana

2 (be situated, present) estar*; **where is the library?** ¿dónde está la biblioteca?

3 (*only in perfect tenses*) (visit) estar*; **I've never been to India** nunca he estado en la India

■ ∼ *v impers* **1 (a)** (talking about physical conditions, circumstances): **it's cold/hot** hace frío/calor; **it's so noisy in here!** ¡qué ruido hay aquí! **(b)** (in expressions of time) ser*; **it's three o'clock** son las tres; **it's Wednesday today** hoy es miércoles **(c)** (talking about distance) estar*; **it's 500 miles from here to Detroit** Detroit queda a 500 millas de aquí

2 (introducing person, object) ser*; **it's me/Daniel** soy yo/es Daniel

■ ∼ *v aux* **1 to** ∼ **-ING** estar* + GER; **I'm working** estoy trabajando; **how long have you been waiting?** ¿cuánto (tiempo) hace que esperas?; **when are you seeing her?** ¿cuándo la vas a ver?

2 (*in the passive voice*) ser* [*The passive voice, however, is less common in Spanish than it is in English*] **it was built in 1903** fue construido en 1903, se construyó en 1903, lo construyeron en 1903; **it is known that … ** se sabe que …

3 to ∼ **to** + INF **(a)** (with future reference): **the dessert is (still) to come** todavía falta el postre **(b)** (expressing possibility): **what are we to do?** ¿qué podemos hacer?; **it was nowhere to** ∼ **found** no se lo pudo encontrar por ninguna parte

4 (a) (*in tag questions*): **she's right, isn't she?** tiene razón, ¿no? *or* ¿verdad? **(b)** (*in elliptical uses*): **are you disappointed? — yes, I am/no, I'm not** ¿estás desilusionado? — sí (, lo estoy)/no (, no lo estoy); **she was told the news, and so was he/ but I wasn't** a ella le dieron la noticia, y también a él/pero a mí no

beach /biːtʃ/ *n* playa *f*

beacon /'biːkən/ *n* (light) faro *m*; (fire) almenara *f*

bead /biːd/ *n* cuenta *f*, abalorio *m*; (drop) gota *f*; ∼**s of sweat** gotas *fpl* de sudor

beady /'biːdi/ *adj*: ∼ **eyes** ojos redondos y brillantes

beak /biːk/ *n* pico *m*

beaker /'biːkər ‖ 'biːkə(r)/ *n* **(a)** (Chem) vaso *m* de precipitados **(b)** (cup) (BrE) taza *f* (*gen alta y sin asa*)

be-all and end-all /'biːɔːlən'endɔːl/ *n*: **it is the** ∼ ∼ ∼ **of his life** es su razón de ser; **work isn't the** ∼ ∼ ∼ el trabajo no lo es todo

beam¹ /biːm/ *n* **1** (in building) viga *f*; (in ship) bao *m* **2** (ray) rayo *m*; (broad) haz *m* de luz; **keep the headlights on high *o* (BrE) full *o* main** ∼ (Auto) deja las (luces) largas *or* (Chi) altas

beam² *vi* **(a)** (shine) brillar **(b)** (smile) sonreír* (*abiertamente*)

■ ∼ *vt* (broadcast) transmitir

bean /biːn/ *n* **(a)** (fresh, in pod) ▶ GREEN BEAN **(b)** (dried) frijol *m or* (Esp) alubia *f or* judía *f or* (CS) poroto *m or* (Ven) caraota *f*; **to be full of** ∼**s** (colloq) estar* lleno de vida

bean-: ∼ **curd** *n* tofu *m*, queso *m* de soya (AmL) *or* (Esp) soja; ∼**shoot,** ∼ **sprout** *n* frijol *m* germinado *or* (Esp) judía *f* germinada *or* (CS) poroto *m* germinado *or* (of soy bean) brote *m or* germinado *m* de soya (AmL) *or* (Esp) soja

bear¹ /ber ‖ beə(r)/ (*past* **bore**; *past p* **borne**) *vt* **1 (a)** (support) «*weight*» aguantar; «*cost*» correr con; «*responsibility*» cargar* con **(b)** (endure) «*pain/uncertainty*» soportar **(c)** (put up with, stand) (colloq) (*with can*) «*person*» aguantar (fam); «*noise*» aguantar **(d)** (stand up to): **her argument doesn't** ∼ **close scrutiny** su razonamiento no resiste un análisis cuidadoso; **it doesn't** ∼ **thinking about** da miedo solo de pensarlo

b

[2] **(a)** (carry) (liter) ‹*banner/coffin*› llevar, portar (liter) **(b)** (harbor): **she's not one to ~ a grudge** no es rencorosa; **to ~ sb malice** guardarle rencor a algn

[3] (have, show) ‹*title/signature*› llevar; ‹*scars*› tener*; ‹*resemblance*› tener*

[4] **(a)** (produce) ‹*fruit/crop*› dar*; ‹*interest*› devengar* **(b)** (give birth to) ‹*child*› dar* a luz; *see also* BORN¹

■ ~ *vi* (turn) torcer*; **~ left** tuerza a la izquierda

■ **bear out** [*v + o + adv, v + adv + o*] ‹*theory*› confirmar

■ **bear up** [*v + adv*]: **she bore up well under the strain** sobrellevó muy bien la situación

■ **bear with** [*v + prep + o*] ‹*person/mood*› tener* paciencia con; **if you'll just ~ with me for a moment, ...** (asking to wait) si tienen la bondad de esperar un momento, ...; (asking for patience) si puedo poner a prueba su paciencia, ...

bear² *n* oso, osa *m,f*

bearable /'berəbəl ‖'beərəbəl/ *adj* soportable

beard /bɪrd ‖bɪəd/ *n* barba *f*

bearded /'bɪrdəd ‖'bɪədɪd/ *adj* con *or* de barba

bearer /'berər ‖'beərə(r)/ *n* **(a)** (of news) portador, -dora *m,f* **(b)** (carrier, porter) portador, -dora *m,f*, porteador, -dora *m,f* **(c)** (holder — of check) portador, -dora *m,f*; (— of passport) titular *mf*

bearing /'berɪŋ ‖'beərɪŋ/ *n* [1] **(a)** (Aviat, Naut) demora *f*; **to get/lose one's ~s** orientarse/ desorientarse **(b)** (relevance): **that has no ~ on the subject** eso no tiene ninguna relación con el tema [2] (way of standing) porte *m*

beast /biːst/ *n* bestia *f*

beat¹ /biːt/ (*past* **beat**; *past p* **beaten** /'biːtn̩/) *vt* [1] **(a)** (hit) golpear; ‹*carpet*› sacudir; ‹*wings*› batir; ‹*child/wife*› maltratar **(b)** (hammer) ‹*metal*› batir **(c)** (Culin) batir

[2] ‹*opponent*› ganarle a; ‹*record*› batir; **our prices can't be ~en** nuestros precios son imbatibles

[3] (arrive before, anticipate): **I ~ him to the telephone** llegué antes que él al teléfono; **to ~ sb to it** adelantársele a algn

[3] (Mus) ‹*time*› marcar*

■ ~ *vi* (strike): **he could hear them ~ing on the door** los oía golpear la puerta; **the waves were ~ing against the cliff** las olas golpeaban contra el acantilado **(b)** (pulsate) «*heart*» latir, palpitar; «*drum*» redoblar; «*wings*» batir

■ **beat down** [1] [*v + o + adv, v + adv + o*] ‹*door*› tirar abajo; ‹*crop*› aplastar

[2] [*v + adv*] «*sun*» caer* de lleno; «*rain*» llover* con fuerza

■ **beat up** [*v + o + adv, v + adv + o*] (colloq) darle* una paliza a (fam)

■ **beat up on** [*v + adv + prep + o*] (AmE colloq) darle* una paliza a

beat² *n* [1] (of heart) latido *m*; (of drum) golpe *m* [2] (Mus) (rhythmic accent) tiempo *m*; (rhythm) ritmo *m* [3] (of policeman) ronda *f*

beat³ *adj* (colloq) (*pred*): **to be (dead) ~** estar* reventado (fam)

beaten /'biːtn̩/ *past p of* BEAT¹

beating /'biːtɪŋ/ *n* **(a)** (thrashing) paliza *f* **(b)** (defeat) paliza *f* (fam) **(c)** (surpassing): **her time will take some ~** va a ser difícil superar su marca

beautiful /'bjuːtəfəl ‖'bjuːtɪfəl/ *adj* **(a)** (in

appearance) precioso, hermoso, bello (liter) **(b)** (very good) (colloq) ‹*meal/weather*› estupendo **(c)** (kind) (esp AmE) ‹*person*› encantador

beautifully /'bjuːtəfli ‖'bjuːtɪfəli/ *adv* (excellently, very well) ‹*sing/dance*› maravillosamente (bien); **she was ~ dressed** iba elegantísima

beauty /'bjuːti/ *n* (*pl* **-ties**) [1] (quality) belleza *f*, hermosura *f*; (*before n*) ~ **contest** *o* (esp AmE) **pageant** concurso *m* de belleza; ~ **queen** reina *f* de la belleza [2] (woman) belleza *f*

beauty: ~ **salon** *n* salón *m* de belleza; ~ **shop** *n* (AmE) salón *m* de belleza; ~ **spot** *n* [1] (place) lugar *m* pintoresco; [2] (on face) lunar *m*

beaver /'biːvər ‖'biːvə(r)/ *n* castor *m*

became /bɪ'keɪm/ *past of* BECOME

because /bə'kɔːz, bɪ'kʌz/ *conj* [1] porque [2] **because of** (*as prep*) por, a *or* por causa de (frml)

beck /bek/ *n*: **to be at sb's ~ and call** estar* siempre a entera disposición de algn

beckon /'bekn/ *vt*: **to ~ sb over** hacerle* señas a algn para que se acerque

■ ~ *vi* hacer* una seña; **she ~ed to him to follow** le hizo señas para que la siguiera

become /bɪ'kʌm/ (*past* **became**; *past p* **become**) *vi*: **to ~ famous** hacerse* famoso; **to ~ accustomed to sth** acostumbrarse a algo; **she soon became bored** pronto se aburrió; **the heat became unbearable** el calor se hizo insoportable; **they became friends** se hicieron amigos

■ ~ *vt* **(a)** (befit) (frml) (*often neg*) ser* apropiado para **(b)** (suit) favorecer*

■ **become of** (*usu interrog*) ser* de; **what's to ~ of me?** ¿qué va a ser de mí?

becoming /bɪ'kʌmɪŋ/ *adj* **(a)** (fitting) (frml) apropiado **(b)** ‹*outfit/hat*› favorecedor, sentador (AmL)

bed /bed/ *n* [1] **(a)** (for sleeping) cama *f*; **to make the ~** hacer* *or* (AmL tb) tender* la cama; **to get into/ out of ~** acostarse*/levantarse; **to go to ~** acostarse*; **he's in ~ with measles** está en cama con sarampión; **we put the children to ~ early** acostamos a los niños temprano [2] (for plants) arriate *m*, cantero *m* (RPl) [3] (of river) lecho *m*, cauce *m*; (of sea) fondo *m* [4] (base, support) base *f*

bed: ~ **and breakfast** /'bednˈbrekfəst/ *n* **(a)** (service): **they do ~ and breakfast** dan alojamiento y desayuno **(b)** (establishment) ≈ pensión *f*; ~**clothes** *pl n* ropa *f* de cama

bedding /'bedɪŋ/ *n* **(a)** ▶ BEDCLOTHES **(b)** (for animals) cama *f*

bedlam /'bedləm/ *n* (colloq): **there was ~ when he announced the news** se armó la de San Quintín cuando anunció la noticia (fam)

bedpan /'bedpæn/ *n* (Med) cuña *f*

bedraggled /bɪ'drægəld/ *adj* desaliñado; ‹*hair*› despeinado

bed: ~**ridden** *adj* postrado en cama; ~**room** *n* dormitorio *m*, cuarto *m*, pieza *f* (esp AmL), recámara *f* (esp Méx); ~**side** *n*: **they sat at his ~side throughout the night** pasaron toda la noche junto a su cabecera; (*before n*) ~**side table** mesita *f* de noche, velador *m* (AmS), mesa *f* de luz (RPl); ~**sit**, ~**sitter** /'bed,sɪtər ‖,bed'sɪtə(r)/ *n* (BrE colloq) habitación *f* amueblada (*cuyo alquiler suele incluir el uso de baño y cocina comunes*); ~**sore** ⋯⋰

n escara *f*, úlcera *f* de decúbito (frml) (*llaga que se produce por estar mucho tiempo en cama*); **~spread** *n* cubrecama *m*, colcha *f*; **~time** *n* hora *f* de acostarse

bee /biː/ *n* ① (Zool) abeja *f* ② (social gathering) (esp AmE) círculo *m*

beech /biːtʃ/ *n* ~ (**tree**) haya *f*

beef /biːf/ *n* carne *f* de vaca *or* (AmC, Méx) de res, ternera *f* (Esp)

beefburger /'biːfˌbɜːrgər ‖'biːfˌbɜːgə(r)/ *n* (esp BrE) hamburguesa *f*

bee: ~hive *n* colmena *f*; **~line** *n*: **to make a ~line for sb/sth** (colloq) irse* derechito a algn/algo (fam)

been /bɪn ‖biːn/ (a) *past p of* BE (b) *past p of* GO¹ *vi* I 2

beep¹ /biːp/ *n* (colloq) pitido *m*

beep² *vt/i* (colloq) pitar

beer /bɪr ‖bɪə(r)/ *n* cerveza *f*

beer: ~ garden *n*: jardín o patio abierto de un bar; **~ mat** *n* posavasos *m* (*de cartón*)

beeswax /'biːzwæks/ *n* cera *f* de abeja

beet /biːt/ *n* (*pl* **~s**) (AmE) remolacha *f or* (Méx) betabel *m or* (Chi) betarraga *f*

beetle /'biːtl/ *n* escarabajo *m*

beetroot /'biːtruːt/ *n* (BrE) ▶ BEET

befall /bɪ'fɔːl/ *vt* (*past* **befell** /bɪ'fel/ *past p* **befallen** /bɪ'fɔːlən/) (liter) sucederle *or* ocurrirle a

before¹ /bɪ'fɔːr ‖bɪ'fɔː(r)/ *prep* ① (preceding in time) antes de; **~ long** dentro de poco; **~ going in** antes de entrar ② (a) (in front of) delante de, ante (frml) (b) (in rank, priority): **she puts her work ~ her family** antepone el trabajo a su familia

before² *conj* (a) (earlier than) antes de que (+ *subj*), antes de (+ *inf*) (b) (rather than) antes que

before³ *adv* (preceding) antes; **the day ~** el día anterior; **have you been to Canada ~?** ¿ya has estado en el Canadá?

beforehand /bɪ'fɔːrhænd ‖bɪ'fɔːhænd/ *adv* (earlier) antes; (in advance) de antemano

befriend /bɪ'frend/ *vt* hacerse* amigo de

beg /beg/ **-gg-** *vt* ① ⟨*money/food*⟩ pedir*, mendigar* ② (frml) (a) (entreat) ⟨*person*⟩ suplicarle* a, rogarle* a (b) (ask for) ⟨*forgiveness*⟩ suplicar*, rogar*
■ **~** *vi* «*beggar*» pedir*, mendigar*; **to ~ for mercy** pedir* *or* suplicar* clemencia

began /bɪ'gæn/ *past of* BEGIN

beget /bɪ'get/ *vt* (*pres p* **begetting**; *past* **begot** *or* (arch) **begat** /bɪ'gæt/; *past p* **begotten**) (liter) engendrar

beggar /'begər ‖'begə(r)/ *n* mendigo, -ga *m,f*

begin /bɪ'gɪn/ (*pres p* **beginning**; *past* **began**; *past p* **begun**) *vt* empezar*, comenzar*; **to ~ to** *+* **-ING/to** *+* **INF** empezar* *or* comenzar* A *+* INF
■ **~** *vi* empezar*, comenzar*; «*custom*» originarse; **to ~ with** para empezar

beginner /bɪ'gɪnər ‖bɪ'gɪnə(r)/ *n* principiante *mf*

beginning /bɪ'gɪnɪŋ/ *n* (a) (in time, place) principio *m*; **at the ~ of the year/of June** a principios del año/de junio; **I'll start again from the ~** volveré a empezar desde el principio; **from**

~ to end de principio a fin (b) (origin, early stage) (*often pl*) comienzo *m* (c) (start, debut) (*no pl*) comienzo *m*

begot /bɪ'gɑːt ‖bɪ'gɒt/ *past of* BEGET

begotten /bɪ'gɑːtn̩ ‖bɪ'gɒtn̩/ *past p of* BEGET

begrudge /bɪ'grʌdʒ/ *vt*: **I ~ paying so much** me da rabia pagar tanto; **I don't ~ you your success** no te envidio el éxito que tienes

beguile /bɪ'gaɪl/ *vt* (charm) cautivar, seducir*

beguiling /bɪ'gaɪlɪŋ/ *adj* cautivador, seductor

begun /bɪ'gʌn/ *past p of* BEGIN

behalf /bɪ'hæf ‖bɪ'hɑːf/ *n*: **on ~ of sb**, on (AmE also) **in ~ of sb**, on (AmE also) **in sb's ~** ① (as representative of): **I'd like to thank you on ~ of the team** quisiera darle las gracias en nombre de *or* de parte de todo el equipo; **he accepted the award on her ~** aceptó el premio en su nombre ② (in the interest of): **he argued on her ~ that ...** alegó en su defensa *or* en su favor que ...

behave /bɪ'heɪv/ *vi* (a) (act) comportarse; (esp of children) portarse (b) (be good) «*child/animal*» portarse bien, comportarse
■ *v refl* **to ~ oneself** portarse bien, comportarse

behavior, (BrE) **behaviour** /bɪ'heɪvjər ‖bɪ'heɪvjə(r)/ *n* conducta *f*, comportamiento *m*

behead /bɪ'hed/ *vt* decapitar

beheld /bɪ'held/ *past and past p of* BEHOLD

behind¹ /bɪ'haɪnd/ *prep* ① (a) (to the rear of) detrás de, atrás de (AmL); **we're ten years ~ the Japanese in microelectronics** en microelectrónica llevamos un retraso de diez años respecto a los japoneses (b) (on the other side of) detrás de, atrás de (AmL) ② (responsible for) detrás de; **the motives ~ his decision** los motivos que lo llevaron a esa decisión ③ (in time): **all that is ~ us now** todo eso ha quedado atrás; **I'm ~ schedule** voy retrasado (con el trabajo *or* los preparativos *etc*)

behind² *adv* (a) (to the rear, following): **he ran along ~** iba corriendo detrás *or* (AmL tb) atrás; **I was attacked from ~** me atacaron por la espalda; **keep an eye on the car ~** no pierdas de vista al coche de atrás (b) (in race, competition): **England were two goals ~** Inglaterra iba perdiendo por dos goles (c) (in arrears): **I'm ~ with my work/payments** estoy atrasada con el trabajo/en los pagos

behind³ *n* (colloq & euph) trasero *m* (fam)

behold /bɪ'həʊld/ (*past and past p* **beheld**) *vt* (liter) contemplar (liter)

beige /beɪʒ/ *adj* beige *adj inv*, beis *adj inv* (Esp)

Beijing /'beɪ'dʒɪŋ/ *n* Beijing *m*

being /'biːɪŋ/ *n* ser *m*

Belarus /'belə'ruːs/ *n* Bielorrusia *f*

belated /bɪ'leɪtəd ‖bɪ'leɪtɪd/ *adj* tardío

belch /beltʃ/ *vi* «*person*» eructar; **flames ~ed from the cannon** la boca del cañón escupía llamas

Belgian¹ /'beldʒən/ *adj* belga

Belgian² *n* belga *mf*

Belgium /'beldʒəm/ *n* Bélgica *f*

belie /bɪ'laɪ/ *vt* **belies, belying, belied** (a) (disguise) no dejar traslucir (b) (show to be false): **this ~s the notion that ...** esto demuestra que no es cierto que ...

belief /bəˈliːf ‖brˈliːf/ n (a) (conviction, opinion) creencia f (b) (confidence) ~ IN sb/sth confianza f or fe f EN algn/algo (c) (Relig) fe f

believable /bəˈliːvəbəl ‖brˈliːvəbəl/ adj ⟨story/ account⟩ verosímil

believe /bəˈliːv ‖brˈliːv/ vt (a) ⟨statement/story⟩ creer*; ⟨person⟩ creerle* a; **I don't ~ it!** ¡no puedo creerlo!; **to make ~ (that)** hacer* de cuenta que (b) (think) creer*
■ ~ vi creer*; **to ~ IN sth/sb** creer* EN algo/algn

believer /bəˈliːvər ‖brˈliːvə(r)/ n creyente mf

belittle /brˈlɪtl/ vt ⟨achievements⟩ menospreciar; ⟨person⟩ denigrar

bell /bel/ n (of church, clock) campana f; (on cat, toy) cascabel m; (on door, bicycle) timbre m; (of telephone, timer) timbre m; **to ring a ~:** the name rings a ~ me suena el nombre; (before n) ~ **tower** campanario m

belligerent /bəˈlɪdʒərənt/ adj agresivo

bellow /ˈbeləʊ/ vi bramar; (shout) gritar

bellows /ˈbeləʊz/ n (pl ~) (for fire) fuelle m

bell pepper n (AmE) ▶ CAPSICUM

belly /ˈbeli/ n (pl **-lies**) (a) (of person) vientre m, barriga f (fam); (of animal) panza f, vientre m; (before n) ~ **button** (colloq) ombligo m; **to do a ~ flop** darse* un planchazo or (Andes) un guatazo (fam)

belong /brˈlɔːŋ ‖brˈlɒŋ/ vi [1] (a) (be property) **to ~ TO sb** ser* DE algn, pertenecerle* A algn (be member) **to ~ TO sth** ⟨to a club⟩ ser* socio DE algo; ⟨to a union/political party⟩ estar* afiliado A algo [2] (have as usual place) ir*; **put them back where they ~** vuélvelos a poner en su lugar

belongings /brˈlɔːŋɪŋz ‖brˈlɒŋɪŋz/ pl n pertenencias fpl

beloved /brˈlʌvəd ‖brˈlʌvɪd/ adj (before n) querido

below¹ /brˈləʊ/ prep [1] (under) debajo de, abajo de (AmL) [2] (inferior, junior to) por debajo de [3] (less than) por debajo de; **~ zero** bajo cero

below² adv [1] (underneath) abajo; **put it on the shelf ~** ponlo en el estante de abajo [2] (in text) más abajo [3] (of temperature): **20 (degrees) ~** 20 (grados) bajo cero

belt¹ /belt/ n [1] (Clothing) cinturón m [2] (Mech Eng) correa f

belt² vt (colloq) darle* una paliza a

beltway /ˈbeltweɪ/ n (AmE) carretera f de circunvalación

bemoan /brˈməʊn/ vt lamentarse de

bemused /brˈmjuːzd/ adj de desconcierto

bench /bentʃ/ n [1] (a) (seat) banco m (b) (work~) mesa f de trabajo [2] (Law) **the bench** or **the Bench** (judges collectively) la judicatura; (tribunal) el tribunal

bend¹ /bend/ n (a) (in road, river) curva f (b) **bends** pl **the ~s** la enfermedad del buzo

bend² (past and past p **bent**) vt ⟨wire/branch⟩ torcer*, curvar; ⟨back/leg⟩ doblar; ⑤ **do not bend** no doblar
■ ~ vi (a) «pipe/wire» torcerse* (b) «person» ▶ BEND DOWN (c) «road/river» hacer* una curva
■ **bend down** [v + adv] agacharse
■ **bend over** [v + adv] inclinarse

beneath¹ /brˈniːθ/ prep [1] (under) bajo [2] (a)

(inferior to): **she married ~ her** no se casó bien (b) (unworthy of): **it's ~ her** es indigno de ella; **you're ~ contempt** no mereces ni desprecio

beneath² adv: **the floor ~** el piso de abajo; **I wondered what lay ~** me preguntaba qué habría debajo or abajo

benefactor /ˈbenəfæktər ‖ˈbenɪfæktə(r)/ n benefactor, -tora m,f

beneficial /benəˈfɪʃəl ‖ˌbenɪˈfɪʃəl/ adj beneficioso

beneficiary /benəˈfɪʃieri ‖ˌbenɪˈfɪʃəri/ n (pl **-ries**) beneficiario, -ria m,f

benefit¹ /ˈbenəfɪt ‖ˈbenɪfɪt/ n [1] (good) beneficio m, bien m; (advantage) provecho m; **to give sb the ~ of the doubt** darle* a algn el beneficio de la duda [2] (Soc Adm) prestación f; see also UNEMPLOYMENT [3] (concert, performance) beneficio m; (before n) con fines benéficos

benefit² **-t-** or (AmE also) **-tt-** vt beneficiar
■ ~ vi beneficiarse; **to ~ FROM sth** beneficiarse CON algo

benevolent /bəˈnevələnt/ adj ⟨person/smile⟩ benévolo; ⟨gesture⟩ de benevolencia

benign /brˈnaɪn/ adj (a) ⟨person/attitude⟩ benévolo (b) (Med) benigno

bent¹ /bent/ past and past p of BEND²

bent² adj [1] ⟨pipe⟩ curvado, torcido [2] (determined) **to be ~ ON doing sth** estar* empeñado EN hacer algo

bequeath /brˈkwiːð, -ˈkwiːθ/ vt **to ~ sth TO sb** legarle* algo A algn

bequest /brˈkwest/ n legado m

berate /brˈreɪt/ vt (fml) **to ~ sb (FOR sth)** reprender a algn (POR algo)

bereaved /brˈriːvd/ adj desconsolado (por la muerte de un ser querido)

bereavement /brˈriːvmənt/ n dolor m (por la muerte de un ser querido)

beret /bəˈreɪ ‖ˈbereɪ/ n boina f

Berlin /bɜːˈlɪn ‖bɜːˈlɪn/ n Berlín m

Bermuda /bərˈmjuːdə ‖bəˈmjuːdə/ n las (islas) Bermudas

berry /ˈberi/ n (pl **-ries**) (Bot) baya f; (Culin) fresas, frambuesas, moras etc

berserk /bərˈsɜːrk ‖bəˈsɜːk/ adj: **to go ~** ponerse* como una fiera

berth¹ /bɜːrθ ‖bɜːθ/ n (a) (bunk) litera f, cucheta f (RPl); (cabin) camarote m (b) (mooring) atracadero m; **to give sb a wide ~** eludir a algn

berth² vt/i atracar*

beseech /brˈsiːtʃ/ vt (past & past p **beseeched** or **besought**) (liter) suplicar*, rogar*

beset /brˈset/ vt (pres p **besetting**; past & past p **beset**) «anxieties/fears» acuciar; **he was ~ by doubts** lo acosaban las dudas

beside¹ /brˈsaɪd/ prep (at the side of) al lado de; **to be ~ oneself:** he was ~ **himself** with rage estaba fuera de sí (de la rabia); **she's ~ herself with happiness** está que no cabe en sí de la alegría (b) (compared with) comparado con (c) (extraneous to): **that's ~ the point** eso no tiene nada que ver (d) ▶ BESIDES¹

beside² adv (a) (alongside) al lado (b) ▶ BESIDES²

besides¹ /bɪˈsaɪdz/ prep (a) (in addition to) además de (b) (apart from) excepto, aparte de

besides² adv además

besiege /bɪˈsiːdʒ/ vt sitiar, asediar; **the village was ∼d by reporters** el pueblo se vio asediado por periodistas

besotted /bɪˈsɑːtəd ‖bɪˈsɒtɪd/ adj (usu pred): **he's totally ∼ with her** está perdidamente enamorado de ella

besought /bɪˈsɔːt/ past & past p of BESEECH

bespectacled /bɪˈspektɪkəld/ adj de anteojos or lentes (AmL), con gafas (esp Esp)

best¹ /best/ adj (superl of GOOD¹) mejor; **for the ∼ part of an hour/a month** durante casi una hora/un mes; **she's not very tolerant at the ∼ of times** la tolerancia no es precisamente una de sus características

best² adv (superl of WELL¹,²) mejor; **I did it as ∼ I could** lo hice lo mejor que pude; **it's ∼ forgotten** más vale olvidarlo

best³ n **1** **the ∼ (a)** (+ sing vb) lo mejor; **to do one's ∼** hacer* todo lo posible; **we'll just have to make the ∼ of what we've got** tendremos que arreglarnos con lo que tenemos; **(b)** (+ pl vb): **they're (the) ∼ of friends** son de lo más amigos; **she can ski with the ∼ of them** (colloq) esquía tan bien como el mejor **2** **(a) at best: at ∼, we'll just manage to cover costs** como mucho, podremos cubrir los gastos **(b) at/past one's best: at his ∼, his singing rivals that of Caruso** en sus mejores momentos puede compararse a Caruso; **the roses were past their ∼** las rosas ya no estaban en su mejor momento **3 (a)** (in greetings): **all the ∼!** ¡buena suerte! **(b)** (Sport) récord m; **a personal ∼ for Flynn** un récord para Flynn

best man n: amigo que acompaña al novio el día de la boda, ≈padrino m, testigo m

bestow /bɪˈstəʊ/ vt (fml or liter) **to ∼ sth ON** o **UPON sb** ⟨title/award⟩ conferirle* algo A algn (fml)

best-seller /ˈbestselər ‖ˌbestˈselə(r)/ n (book) bestseller m; (product) superventas m; (author) autor, -tora m,f de bestsellers

bet¹ /bet/ n apuesta f; **I had a ∼ with Charlie that Brazil would win** le aposté a Charlie que ganaría Brasil; **your best ∼ is to stay here** lo mejor que puedes hacer es quedarte aquí

bet² (pres p **betting**; past & past p **bet**) vt apostar*
■ ∼ vi jugar*; **to ∼ ON sth/sb** apostarle* A algo/algn; **I wouldn't ∼ on it if I were you** yo no estaría tan seguro, yo no me fiaría

betray /bɪˈtreɪ/ vt ⟨ally⟩ traicionar; **he ∼ed us to the enemy** nos vendió al enemigo; **her voice ∼ed her nervousness** su voz revelaba el miedo que sentía

betrayal /bɪˈtreɪəl/ n traición f

betrothal /bɪˈtrəʊðəl/ n (fml) esponsales mpl (fml)

better¹ /ˈbetər ‖ˈbetə(r)/ adj **1** (comp of

GOOD¹) mejor; **to get ∼** mejorar; **if they can both come, so much the ∼** si pueden venir los dos, mucho or tanto mejor **2** (pred) (recovered from illness): **to be ∼** estar* mejor; **to get ∼** recuperarse

better² adv **1** (comp of WELL¹,²) mejor **2** had better (ought): **I'd ∼ leave before it gets dark** va a ser mejor que me vaya antes de que oscurezca; **well, I'd ∼ be off** bueno, me tengo que ir

better³ n **(a)** (superior of two): **the ∼ of the two** el mejor de los/las dos; **for the ∼** para bien; **to get the ∼ of sb/sth** ganarle la batalla a algn/algo **(b) betters** pl (superiors) superiores mpl; **his elders and ∼s** sus mayores

better⁴ vt mejorar; **to ∼ oneself** superarse

better-off /ˌbetərˈɔːf ‖ˌbetərˈɒf/ adj (pred **better off (a)** (financially) de mejor posición económica **(b)** (emotionally, physically) (pred) mejor

betting shop /ˈbetɪŋ/ n (BrE) agencia f de apuestas

between¹ /bɪˈtwiːn/ prep entre

between² adv: **the one ∼** el/la de en medio

beverage /ˈbevərɪdʒ/ n bebida f

beware /bɪˈwer ‖bɪˈweə(r)/ vi (only in inf and imperative): **∼!** ¡(ten) cuidado!; 🔊 **beware of the dog** cuidado con el perro

bewildered /bɪˈwɪldərd ‖bɪˈwɪldəd/ adj desconcertado; (overwhelmed) apabullado

bewildering /bɪˈwɪldərɪŋ/ adj desconcertante; (overwhelming) apabullante

bewitch /bɪˈwɪtʃ/ vt (cast spell on) embrujar; (entrance, delight) cautivar

beyond¹ /bɪˈɑːnd ‖bɪˈjɒnd/ prep **1** (on other side of): **I live just ∼ the station** vivo justo pasando la estación; **∼ this point** de aquí en adelante **2 (a)** (further than): **try to think ∼ the immediate future** trata de pensar más allá del futuro inmediato **(b)** (more than, apart from): **I can't tell you anything ∼ that** no te puedo decir nada más que eso **3** (past): **it's ∼ repair** ya no tiene arreglo; **circumstances ∼ our control** circunstancias ajenas a nuestra voluntad; **it's ∼ me what she sees in him** (colloq) no puedo entender qué es lo que ve en él; **to live ∼ one's means** vivir por encima de sus (or mis etc) posibilidades

beyond² adv **(a)** (in space) más allá **(b)** (in time): **we're planning for the year 2000 and ∼** estamos haciendo planes para el 2000 y más allá del 2000

bias /ˈbaɪəs/ n parcialidad f; **the course has a scientific ∼** el curso tiene un enfoque científico

biased, biassed /ˈbaɪəst/ adj ⟨report/criticism⟩ tendencioso; ⟨judge⟩ parcial; **to be ∼ AGAINST/TOWARD(S) sth/sb** estar* predispuesto EN CONTRA DE/A FAVOR DE algo/algn

bib /bɪb/ n **(a)** (for baby) babero m **(b)** (on dungarees) peto m

Bible /ˈbaɪbəl/ n Biblia f

biblical /ˈbɪblɪkəl/ adj bíblico

bibliography /ˌbɪbliˈɑːgrəfi ‖ˌbɪbliˈɒgrəfi/ n (pl **-phies**) bibliografía f

AmC	Central America	Arg	Argentina	Cu	Cuba	Per	Peru
AmL	Latin America	Bol	Bolivia	Ec	Ecuador	RPI	River Plate Area
AmS	South America	Chi	Chile	Esp	Spain	Ur	Uruguay
Andes	Andean Region	CS	Southern Cone	Méx	Mexico	Ven	Venezuela

bicarbonate of soda /baɪˈkɑːrbəneɪt ‖ baɪˈkɑːbəneɪt/ n bicarbonato m de sodio or de soda or (Esp) de sosa

biceps /ˈbaɪseps/ n (pl ~) bíceps m

bicker /ˈbɪkər ‖ ˈbɪkə(r)/ vi pelear, discutir

bicycle /ˈbaɪsɪkəl/ n bicicleta f

bid¹ /bɪd/ vt [1] (pres p **bidding**; past & past p **bid**) (at auction) ofrecer* [2] (pres p **bidding**; past **bade** or **bid**; past p **bidden** or **bid**) (liter) (a) (wish, say): **to ~ sb farewell** despedirse* de algn (b) (request) **to ~ sb (to)** + INF pedirle* a algn QUE + SUBJ

■ ~ vi (pres p **bidding**; past & past p **bid**) (at auction) hacer* ofertas, pujar; **to ~ FOR sth** pujar POR algo

bid² n [1] (at auction) oferta f, puja f [2] (attempt) intento m, tentativa f; (unsuccessful) intentona f, intento m; **~ to** + INF intento m DE + INF

bidden /ˈbɪdn/ past p of BID¹ vt 2

bidder /ˈbɪdər ‖ ˈbɪdə(r)/ n postor, -tora m,f

bidding /ˈbɪdɪŋ/ n [1] (at auction): **the ~ opened at $100** la subasta abrió con una oferta de $100 [2] (wishes): **they had servants to do their ~** tenían criados para lo que se les antojara; **at his father's ~** a petición de su padre

bide /baɪd/ vt: **to ~ one's time** esperar el momento oportuno

bidet /bɪˈdeɪ ‖ ˈbiːdeɪ/ n bidet m, bidé m

biennial /baɪˈeniəl/ adj bienal

bier /bɪr ‖ bɪə(r)/ n andas fpl

bifocals /ˈbaɪfəʊkəlz/ pl n anteojos mpl or (esp Esp) gafas fpl bifocales

big /bɪg/ adj

■ Note The usual translation of big, grande, becomes gran when it is used before a singular noun.

-gg- grande; **a ~ garden** un jardín grande, un gran jardín; **how ~ is the table?** ¿cómo es de grande la mesa?; **a ~ hug/kiss** un abrazote/ besote (fam); **a ~ decision** una gran decisión; **our ~gest customer** nuestro cliente más importante; **she's really ~ in Europe** es muy conocida en Europa; **my ~ brother** mi hermano mayor

bigamist /ˈbɪgəməst ‖ ˈbɪgəmɪst/ n bígamo, -ma m,f

bigamy /ˈbɪgəmi/ n bigamia f

big: ~ business n el gran capital; **to be ~ business** ser* un gran negocio; **~-headed** /ˈbɪgˈhedəd ‖ ˌbɪgˈhedɪd/ adj (colloq) creído (fam); **~ league** n (in US) (Sport) liga f mayor; (top rank) los grandes; **~mouth** n (colloq) (boaster) fanfarrón, -rrona m,f; (gossip) chismoso, -sa m,f, cotilla mf (Esp fam), hocicón, -cona m,f (Chi, Méx fam)

bigot /ˈbɪgət/ n intolerante mf

bigotry /ˈbɪgətri/ n intolerancia f

big: ~ shot n (colloq) pez m gordo (fam); **~ top** n carpa f de circo

bike /baɪk/ n (colloq) (bicycle) bici f (fam); (motorcycle) moto f

bikini /bɪˈkiːni/ n bikini m or (RPl) f

bilateral /ˈbaɪˈlætərəl/ adj bilateral

bilberry /ˈbɪlˌberi ‖ ˈbɪlbəri/ n (pl **-ries**) arándano m

bilingual /baɪˈlɪŋgwəl/ adj bilingüe

bilious /ˈbɪliəs/ adj: **to feel ~** sentirse* descompuesto; **~ attack** ataque m al or de hígado

bill¹ /bɪl/ n [1] (a) (invoice) factura f, cuenta f; **the telephone ~** la cuenta or (Esp tb) el recibo del teléfono (b) (in restaurant) (esp BrE) cuenta f, adición f (RPl) [2] (AmE Fin) (banknote) billete m [3] (Govt) proyecto m de ley [4] (program) programa m; **to top the ~** encabezar* el reparto [5] (certificate): **~ of sale** contrato m de venta; **a clean ~ of health** (favorable report) el visto bueno [6] (beak) pico m

bill² vt [1] (invoice, charge) pasarle la cuenta or la factura a [2] (advertise) ⟨play/performer⟩ anunciar

billboard /ˈbɪlbɔːrd ‖ ˈbɪlbɔːd/ n (esp AmE) cartelera f

billet /ˈbɪlət ‖ ˈbɪlɪt/ vt alojar

billfold /ˈbɪlfəʊld/ n (AmE) billetera f, cartera f

billiards /ˈbɪljərdz ‖ ˈbɪljədz/ n (+ sing vb) billar m

billion /ˈbɪljən/ n mil millones mpl, millar m de millones

billow /ˈbɪləʊ/ vi (a) **~ (out)** ⟨sail/parachute⟩ hincharse (b) ⟨smoke⟩: **smoke ~ed from the window** nubes de humo salían de or por la ventana

billy /ˈbɪli/ n (pl **-lies**) **~ (goat)** macho m cabrío

bin /bɪn/ n (for kitchen refuse etc) (BrE) cubo m or (CS) tacho m or (Méx) bote m or (Col) caneca f or (Ven) tobo m de la basura; (wastepaper basket) (BrE) papelera f, papelero m, caneca f (Col); (litter ~) papelera f, basurero m (Chi, Méx), caneca f (Col)

binary /ˈbaɪnəri/ adj binario

bind¹ /baɪnd/ vt (past & past p **bound**) [1] (tie, fasten) ⟨person⟩ atar, amarrar; ▶ BOUND⁴ 1A [2] (a) (wrap) envolver* (b) **~ (up)** ⟨wound⟩ vendar [3] (Law) obligar* [4] ⟨book⟩ encuadernar [5] (Culin) ligar*

bind² n (colloq) (difficult situation) aprieto m, apuro m; (nuisance) (BrE) lata f (fam), rollo m (Esp fam)

binder /ˈbaɪndər ‖ ˈbaɪndə(r)/ n (file, folder) carpeta f

binding¹ /ˈbaɪndɪŋ/ n (a) (book cover) tapa f, cubierta f (b) (tape) ribete m

binding² adj ⟨promise/commitment⟩ que hay que cumplir; (Law) vinculante

binge /bɪndʒ/ n (colloq): **to go on a ~** irse* de juerga (fam)

bingo /ˈbɪŋgəʊ/ n bingo m

binliner /ˈbɪnˌlaɪnər ‖ ˈbɪnˌlaɪnə(r)/ n (BrE) bolsa f de (la) basura

binoculars /bəˈnɑːkjələrz ‖ bɪˈnɒkjʊləz/ pl n gemelos mpl, prismáticos mpl, anteojos fpl de larga vista (esp AmL)

biochemistry /ˈbaɪəʊˈkeməstri ‖ ˌbaɪəʊˈkemɪstri/ n bioquímica f

biodegradable /ˈbaɪəʊdɪˈgreɪdəbəl/ adj biodegradable

biographer /baɪˈɑːgrəfər ‖ baɪˈɒgrəfə(r)/ n biógrafo, -fa m,f

biographical /ˈbaɪəˈgræfɪkəl/ adj biográfico

biography /baɪˈɑːgrəfi ‖ baɪˈɒgrəfi/ n (pl **-phies**) biografía f

biological /ˈbaɪəˈlɑːdʒɪkəl ‖ ˌbaɪəˈlɒdʒɪkəl/ adj biológico

biologist /baɪˈɑːlədʒəst ‖baɪˈɒlədʒɪst/ n
biólogo, -ga m,f

biology /baɪˈɑːlədʒi ‖baɪˈɒlədʒi/ n biología f

biopsy /ˈbaɪɑːpsi ‖ˈbaɪɒpsi/ n (pl **-sies**)
biopsia f

birch /bɜːrtʃ ‖bɜːtʃ/ n ~ (**tree**) abedul m

bird /bɜːrd ‖bɜːd/ n (small) pájaro m; (large) ave
f‡; **to kill two ~s with one stone** matar dos
pájaros de un tiro

bird: ~**cage** n jaula f de pájaros; (large)
pajarera f; ~ **of prey** n (pl ~**s of prey**) ave f‡
rapaz or de rapiña or de presa; ~**'s-eye view**
n vista f aérea; ~**watcher** /ˈbɜːrdˌwɑːtʃər
‖ˈbɜːdˌwɒtʃə(r)/ n observador, -dora m,f de aves;
~**watching** /ˈbɜːrdˌwɑːtʃɪŋ ‖ˈbɜːdˌwɒtʃɪŋ/ n
observación f de las aves (como hobby)

Biro®, **biro** /ˈbaɪrəʊ ‖ˈbaɪərəʊ/ n (pl **biros**)
(BrE) bolígrafo m, birome f (RPl), esfero m (Col),
lápiz m de pasta (Chi), boli m (Esp fam)

birth /bɜːrθ ‖bɜːθ/ n nacimiento m; (childbirth)
parto m; **at** ~ al nacer; **date of** ~ fecha f de
nacimiento; **to give** ~ dar* a luz, parir

birth: ~ **certificate** n partida f or certificado
m or (Méx) acta f de nacimiento; ~ **control** n
control m de la natalidad

birthday /ˈbɜːrθdeɪ ‖ˈbɜːθdeɪ/ n cumpleaños m;
(of institution) aniversario m; **it'll be his fifth** ~
cumple cinco años; **happy** ~! ¡feliz cumpleaños!;
(before n) ⟨cake/card/party⟩ de cumpleaños

birth: ~**mark** n mancha f or marca f de
nacimiento, antojo m; ~**place** n (of person) lugar
m de nacimiento; (of movement, fashion, idea) cuna f

biscuit /ˈbɪskɪt/ n (Culin) **(a)** (AmE) bollo m,
panecillo m, bísquet m (Méx) **(b)** (cookie, cracker)
(BrE) galleta f, galletita f (RPl)

bisect /baɪˈsekt/ vt bisecar*

bisexual /ˌbaɪˈsekʃuəl/ adj bisexual

bishop /ˈbɪʃəp/ **(a)** n (Relig) obispo m **(b)** (in
chess) alfil m

bison /ˈbaɪsn/ n (pl ~) bisonte m

bit¹ /bɪt/ past of BITE¹

bit² n [1] (fragment, scrap) pedazo m, trozo m; **to
smash sth to** ~**s** hacer* pedazos algo; ~**s and
pieces** (assorted items) cosas fpl; (belongings) cosas
fpl; (broken fragments) pedazos mpl
[2] (section, piece) parte f
[3] **a bit of** (+ uncount noun) un poco de; **they
have quite a** ~ **of work to do** tienen bastante
trabajo que hacer
[4] **a bit** (as adv) **(a)** (somewhat) un poco; **the
town's changed a** ~ la ciudad ha cambiado algo
or un poco; **she hasn't changed a** ~ no ha
cambiado (para) nada **(b)** (a while) un momento
or rato
[5] (in adv phrases) **(a)** bit by bit poco a poco, de
a poco (AmL) **(b)** every bit: **I'm every** ~ **as
disappointed as you** estoy absolutamente tan
decepcionado como tú
[6] (Comput) bit m
[7] (of bridle) freno m, bocado m

bitch /bɪtʃ/ n [1] (female dog) perra f [2] (spiteful
woman) (AmE vulg, BrE sl) bruja f (fam), arpía f
(fam), cabrona f (Esp, Méx vulg)

bite¹ /baɪt/ (past **bit**; past p **bitten**) vt
⟨person/dog⟩ morder*; ⟨bug⟩ picar*; **to** ~ **off**

more than one can chew tratar de abarcar más
de lo que se puede; **once bitten, twice shy** el gato
escaldado del agua fría huye
■ ~ vi [1] **(a)** ⟨person/dog⟩ morder*;
⟨mosquito⟩ picar*; ⟨wind/frost⟩ cortar; **to** ~
INTO sth darle* un mordisco A algo **(b)** (take bait)
⟨fish⟩ picar* [2] ⟨law/recession⟩ hacerse*
sentir

bite² n [1] (act) mordisco m; (fierce) tarascada f
[2] (wound — from insect) picadura f; (— from dog,
snake) mordedura f [3] (snack) (colloq) (no pl)
bocado m; **to have a** ~ (to eat) comer un bocado,
comer algo

biting /ˈbaɪtɪŋ/ adj ⟨wind⟩ cortante; ⟨sarcasm/
criticism⟩ mordaz

bit part n papel m pequeño

bitten /ˈbɪtn/ past p of BITE¹

bitter¹ /ˈbɪtər ‖ˈbɪtə(r)/ adj [1] **(a)** (in taste)
amargo **(b)** (very cold) ⟨weather⟩ glacial; ⟨wind/
frost⟩ cortante [2] **(a)** (painful, hard)
⟨disappointment⟩ amargo; **they fought on to the** ~
end lucharon valientemente hasta el final **(b)**
⟨person⟩ resentido, amargado **(c)** ⟨enemies/
hatred⟩ implacable; ⟨struggle⟩ enconado

bitter² n (BrE) tipo de cerveza ligeramente
amarga

bitterly /ˈbɪtərli ‖ˈbɪtəli/ adv [1] ⟨cold⟩: **it was**
~ **cold** hacía un frío glacial [2] **(a)**
⟨disappointed⟩ tremendamente; ⟨weep/complain/
say⟩ amargamente **(b)** (implacably)
implacablemente

bitterness /ˈbɪtərnəs ‖ˈbɪtənɪs/ n [1] (of taste)
amargor m [2] (of person, disappointment) amargura f

bittersweet /ˈbɪtərswiːt ‖ˌbɪtəˈswiːt/ adj
agridulce; ⟨chocolate⟩ (AmE) amargo

bizarre /bɪˈzɑːr ‖bɪˈzɑː(r)/ adj ⟨story/
coincidence⟩ extraño; ⟨appearance/behavior⟩
estrambótico

black¹ /blæk/ adj **-er, -est** [1] ⟨dress/hair/
ink⟩ negro; ⟨sky⟩ oscuro; ⟨coffee⟩ negro (AmL),
solo (Esp), tinto (Col), puro (Chi); ⟨tea⟩ solo, sin
leche, puro (Chi);~ **cloud** nubarrón m [2] also
Black ⟨person/community⟩ negro [3] (sad,
hopeless) negro

black² n [1] (color) negro m [2] also **Black**
(person) negro, -gra m,f [3] (freedom from debt): **to
be in the** ~ no estar* en números rojos
■ **black out** [1] [v + adv] (lose consciousness)
perder* el conocimiento [2] [v + o + adv, v + adv
+ o] (in wartime) ⟨windows⟩ tapar; ⟨lights⟩ apagar*;
(by accident) ⟨town/district⟩ dejar sin luz

black: ~ **and white** n (Cin, Phot, TV) blanco y
negro m; **she sees things in** ~ **and white** para
ella no hay términos medios; ~**-and-white**
/ˈblækənˌhwaɪt ‖ˈblækənˌwaɪt/ adj (pred ~ **and
white**) en blanco y negro; ~ **belt** n cinturón m
negro, cinta f negra (Méx); (person) cinturón mf
negro, cinta mf negra (Méx); ~**berry**
/ˈblækˌberi ‖ˈblækbəri/ n mora f; ~**bird** n
(European) mirlo m; (North American) totí m;
~**board** n pizarra f, pizarrón m (AmL), tablero
m (Col); ~ **box** n (Aviat) caja f negra; ~**currant**
/ˈblækˈkɜːrənt ‖ˌblækˈkʌrənt/ n grosella f negra

blacken /ˈblækən/ vt **(a)** (make black)
ennegrecer* **(b)** (defame) ⟨person⟩ deshonrar;
⟨reputation⟩ manchar

black: ~ **eye** n ojo m morado, ojo m a la

funerala (Esp fam), ojo *m* en compota (CS fam), ojo *m* en tinta (Chi fam); **~head** *n* espinilla *f*; **~ hole** *n* agujero *m* negro; **~ ice** *n* capa fina de hielo en las carreteras

blacklist¹ /'blæklɪst/ *n* lista *f* negra

blacklist² *vt* poner* en la lista negra

blackmail¹ /'blækmeɪl/ *n* chantaje *m*

blackmail² *vt* chantajear, hacerle* chantaje a

black: ~ mark *n* punto *m* en contra; **~ market** *n* mercado *m* negro; **~out** /'blækaʊt/ *n* [1] (loss of consciousness) desvanecimiento *m*, desmayo *m*; [2] (in wartime) oscurecimiento de la ciudad para que esta no sea visible desde los aviones enemigos; **B~ Sea** *n* the B~ Sea el Mar Negro; **~ sheep** *n* oveja *f* negra; **~smith** *n* herrero *m*

bladder /'blædər ‖'blædə(r)/ *n* (Anat) vejiga *f*

blade /bleɪd/ *n* [1] (of knife, razor) hoja *f* [2] (of propeller) pala *f*, paleta *f* [3] (Bot) (of grass) brizna *f*

blame¹ /bleɪm/ *vt* echarle la culpa a, culpar; **to ~ sb FOR sth** culpar a algn DE algo, echarle la culpa DE algo A algn; **to be to ~ for sth** tener* la culpa de algo; **to ~ sth ON sb/sth** echarle la culpa DE algo A algn/algo

blame² *n* culpa *f*; **it's always me that gets the ~** siempre me echan la culpa a mí

bland /blænd/ *adj* **-er, -est** (a) ‹colors/music› soso; ‹food/taste› insípido; ‹statement/reply› anodino; ‹smile/manner› insulso (b) (mild) ‹food› suave

blank¹ /blæŋk/ *adj* (a) (empty) ‹page/space› en blanco; ‹tape› virgen; **my mind went ~** me quedé en blanco; **a ~ expression** un rostro carente de expresión (b) (uncompromising) ‹refusal/rejection› rotundo (c) (Mil) ‹ammunition› de fogueo

blank² *n* (a) (empty space) espacio *m* en blanco; **to draw a ~** no obtener* ningún resultado (b) (Mil) cartucho *m* de fogueo

blank check, (BrE) **cheque** *n* cheque *m* en blanco

blanket¹ /'blæŋkət ‖'blæŋkɪt/ *n* manta *f*, cobija *f* (AmL), frazada *f* (AmL)

blanket² *adj* (before n, no comp) ‹measure› global

blare /bler ‖bleə(r)/*vi* atronar*

■ **blare out** [*v* + *adv* + *o*]: **the radio was blaring out music** el radio emitía música retumbante

blasphemous /'blæsfəməs/ *adj* blasfemo

blasphemy /'blæsfəmi/ *n* (*pl* **-mies**) blasfemia *f*

blast¹ /blæst ‖blɑːst/ *n* [1] (of air, wind) ráfaga *f*; (of water) chorro *m* [2] (explosion) (journ) explosión *f* [3] (of sound) toque *m*; **he had the TV on full ~** tenía la tele a todo lo que daba (fam)

blast² *vt* (a) (blow) ‹rock› volar*; **they used dynamite to ~ the safe open** usaron dinamita para volar la caja fuerte (b) (attack) (journ) atacar*

■ **blast off** [*v* + *adv*] despegar*

blast-off /'blæstɔːf ‖'blɑːstɒf/ *n* despegue *m*

blatant /'bleɪtn̩t/ *adj* ‹prejudice/disrespect› descarado; ‹lie› flagrante; ‹incompetence› patente

blatantly /'bleɪtn̩tli/ *adv* descaradamente; **it's ~ obvious that ...** está clarísimo que ...

blaze¹ /bleɪz/ *n* [1] (in grate) fuego *m*; (bonfire) fogata *f*; (flames) llamaradas *fpl*; (dangerous fire)

(journ) incendio *m* [2] (dazzling display) (no *pl*): **a ~ of color** un derroche de color; **in a ~ of glory** cubierto de gloria

blaze² *vi* «*fire*» arder; «*lights*» brillar; «*eyes*» centellear

blazer /'bleɪzər ‖'bleɪzə(r)/ *n* blazer *m*

bleach¹ /bliːtʃ/ *n* lejía *f*, blanqueador *m* (Col, Méx), lavandina *f* (Arg), agua *f*‡ Jane® (Ur), cloro *m* (AmC, Chi)

bleach² *vt* ‹cloth› (in the sun) blanquear; (with bleach) poner* en lejía (*or* blanquear *etc*)

bleachers /'bliːtʃərz ‖'bliːtʃəz/ *pl n* (AmE) tribuna *f* descubierta

bleak /bliːk/ *adj* **-er, -est** (a) ‹landscape› inhóspito; ‹room› lóbrego (b) ‹winter› crudo; ‹day› gris y deprimente (c) (miserable, cheerless) ‹prospects/news› sombrío

bleary-eyed /'blɪriˈaɪd ‖'blɪəriˈaɪd/ *adj* con cara de sueño

bleat /bliːt/ *vi* balar

bleed /bliːd/ (*past & past p* **bled** /bled/) *vi* sangrar; **he bled to death** murió desangrado

■ **~** *vt* (a) (Med) sangrar; **to ~ sb dry** chuparle la sangre a algn (fam) (b) ‹brakes/radiator› purgar*

bleeding /'bliːdɪŋ/ *n* hemorragia *f*

bleep¹ /bliːp/ *n* pitido *m*

bleep² *vi* (BrE) emitir un pitido

blemish /'blemɪʃ/ *n* (on skin) imperfección *f*; (on reputation) mancha *f*

blend¹ /blend/ *n* combinación *f*, mezcla *f*

blend² *vt* mezclar, combinar; (in blender) licuar*

■ **~** *vi* «*flavors/colors*» armonizar*

■ **blend in** [1] [*v* + *o* + *adv*, *v* + *adv* + *o*] ‹ingredients› añadir *y* mezclar [2] [*v* + *adv*] (merge, harmonize) armonizar*

blender /'blendər ‖'blendə(r)/ *n* licuadora *f*

bless /bles/ *vt* (*past* **blessed**; *past p* **blessed** *or* (arch) **blest**) (a) (Relig) bendecir* (b) (*in interj phrases*) **~ you!** (to sb who sneezes) ¡salud! *or* (Esp) ¡Jesús!; **~ my soul!** (colloq) ¡válgame Dios!

blessed /'blesəd ‖'blesɪd/ *adj* bienaventurado

blessing /'blesɪŋ/ *n* [1] (a) (Relig – benediction) bendición *f*; (– of bread, wine) consagración *f* (b) (approval) aprobación *f* [2] (fortunate thing) bendición *f* (del cielo); **to be a mixed ~** tener* sus pros y sus contras

blest /blest/ (arch) *past & past pt of* BLESS

blew /bluː/ *past of* BLOW²

blight¹ /blaɪt/ *n* (Agr, Hort) añublo *m*; (loosely) peste *f*; (curse) plaga *f*

blight² *vt* ‹crop/career/health› arruinar; ‹region› asolar*; ‹hopes› malograr

blind¹ /blaɪnd/ *adj* [1] (a) (Med) ciego; **to go ~** quedarse ciego; **to be ~ TO sth** no ver* algo (b) (Auto) ‹corner› de poca visibilidad [2] ‹faith/fury› ciego

blind² *vt* (a) (permanently) dejar ciego (b) «*ambition/passion*» cegar*, enceguecer* (AmL); «*light/wealth*» deslumbrar

blind³ *n* [1] (outside window) persiana *f*; (roller ~) persiana *f* (de enrollar), estor *m* (Esp); (venetian ~) persiana *f* veneciana [2] (blind people) (+ *pl vb*) **the ~** los ciegos

blind date *n* cita *f* con un desconocido/una desconocida

blinders /'blaɪndərz ‖'blaɪndəz/ *n pl* (AmE) (on horse) anteojeras *fpl*

blindfold¹ /'blaɪndfəʊld/ *vt* vendarle los ojos a

blindfold² *n* venda *f* (*para tapar los ojos*)

blindfold³ *adv* con los ojos vendados

blindly /'blaɪndli/ *adv* **(a)** (without seeing) ⟨grope⟩ a ciegas **(b)** (without reasoning) ⟨follow⟩ ciegamente

blindness /'blaɪndnəs ‖'blaɪndnɪs/ *n* ceguera *f*

blind spot *n* **(a)** (weak point) punto *m* flaco **(b)** (Auto) punto *m* ciego

blink¹ /blɪŋk/ *n* parpadeo *m*, pestañeo *m*; **to be on the ~** (colloq) no marchar, no andar* bien (AmL)

blink² *vi* «*eye/person*» pestañear, parpadear; «*light*» parpadear

blinker /'blɪŋkər ‖'blɪŋkə(r)/ *n* **1** **(a)** (Auto colloq) intermitente *m*, direccional *f* (Col, Méx), señalizador *m* (de viraje) (Chi) **(b)** (AmE Transp) señal *f* intermitente **2** **blinkers** *pl* (on horse) anteojeras *fpl*

blinkered /'blɪŋkərd ‖'blɪŋkəd/ *adj* ⟨attitude⟩ de miras estrechas; ⟨view/outlook⟩ estrecho

blip /blɪp/ *n* **(a)** (sound) bip *m*, pitidito *m* **(b)** (irregularity) accidente *m*; (problem) problema *m* pasajero

bliss /blɪs/ *n* dicha *f*

blissful /'blɪsfəl/ *adj* ⟨smile⟩ de gozo

blissfully /'blɪsfəli/ *adv* ⟨smile/sigh⟩ con gran felicidad

blister¹ /'blɪstər ‖'blɪstə(r)/ *n* **(a)** (Med) ampolla *f* **(b)** (on paintwork) ampolla *f*, burbuja *f*

blister² *vi* ampollarse

blithely /'blaɪðli/ *adv* alegremente

blitz /blɪts/ *n* **(a)** (Aviat, Mil) bombardeo *m* aéreo **(b)** (intense attack): **this weekend we're going to have a ~ on the garden** (colloq) este fin de semana vamos a atacar el jardín

blizzard /'blɪzərd ‖'blɪzəd/ *n* ventisca *f*

bloated /'bləʊtəd ‖'bləʊtɪd/ *adj* hinchado

blob /blɑːb ‖blɒb/ *n* **(a)** (drip) gota *f* **(b)** (indistinct shape) mancha *f*

bloc /blɑːk ‖blɒk/ *n* (Pol) bloque *m*

block¹ /blɑːk ‖blɒk/ *n* **1** (of stone, wood) bloque *m*; (starting ~) (Sport) taco *m* de salida; (of paper) bloc *m*
2 **(a)** (space enclosed by streets) manzana *f*; (distance between two streets): **it's eight ~s from here** (AmE) está a ocho cuadras *or* (Esp) calles de aquí **(b)** (building): **a ~ of flats** (BrE) un edificio de apartamentos *or* de departamentos (AmL), una casa de pisos (Esp); **an office ~** un edificio de oficinas
3 (section of text) sección *f*, bloque *m*
4 (Comput) bloque *m*
5 (blockage) obstrucción *f*, bloqueo *m*; **I have a mental ~ about physics** tengo un bloqueo mental con la física
6 (Sport) bloqueo *m*

block² *vt* **1** **(a)** (obstruct) ⟨road/entrance⟩ bloquear; **you're ~ing my way** me estás

impidiendo el paso; **that fat man is ~ing my view** ese gordo no me deja ver **(b)** ⟨drain/sink⟩ atascar*, tapar (AmL); **my nose is ~ed** tengo la nariz tapada
2 **(a)** (prevent) ⟨progress⟩ obstaculizar*; ⟨funds/sale⟩ congelar **(b)** (Sport) bloquear
■ **~** *vi* (Sport) bloquear

■ **block in** [*v + o + adv*, *v + adv + o*] cerrarle* el paso a

■ **block off** [*v + o + adv*, *v + adv + o*] ⟨street⟩ cortar

■ **block out** [*v + o + adv*, *v + adv + o*] **(a)** (shut out) ⟨thought⟩ ahuyentar **(b)** (obstruct) ⟨light⟩ tapar

■ **block up** [*v + o + adv*, *v + adv + o*] **(a)** (seal) ⟨entrance/window⟩ tapiar **(b)** (cause obstruction in) ⟨drain/sink⟩ atascar*, tapar (AmL); **my nose is ~ed up** tengo la nariz tapada

blockade¹ /blɑːˈkeɪd ‖blɒˈkeɪd/ *n* bloqueo *m*

blockade² *vt* bloquear

blockage /'blɑːkɪdʒ ‖'blɒkɪdʒ/ *n* (in pipe, road) obstrucción *f*, (Med) oclusión *f*

block capitals, block letters *pl n* (letras *fpl*) mayúsculas *fpl* de imprenta

bloke /bləʊk/ *n* (BrE colloq) tipo *m* (fam), tío *m* (Esp fam)

blond /blɑːnd ‖blɒnd/ *adj* (*f* **blonde**) rubio *or* (Méx) güero *or* (Col) mono *or* (Ven) catire

blood /blʌd/ *n* sangre *f*; **in cold ~** a sangre fría; *(before n)* **~ donor** donante *mf* de sangre; **~ group** grupo *m* sanguíneo; **~ test** análisis *m* de sangre; **~ transfusion** transfusión *f* de sangre

blood: ~ bath *n* masacre *f*; **~curdling** /'blʌd.kɜːrdlɪŋ ‖'blʌd.kɜːdlɪŋ/ *adj* espeluznante, aterrador

bloodless /'blʌdləs ‖'blʌdlɪs/ *adj* ⟨coup⟩ sin derramamiento de sangre

blood: ~ pressure *n* tensión *f or* presión *f* (arterial); **~shed** *n* derramamiento *m* de sangre; **~shot** *adj* rojo, inyectado de sangre; **~ sport** *n* deporte *m* sangriento; **~stain** *n* mancha *f* de sangre; **~stained** /'blʌdsteɪnd/ *adj* manchado de sangre; **~stream** *n* the **~stream** el torrente sanguíneo; **~thirsty** *adj* **(a)** (cruel) sanguinario **(b)** ⟨story/description⟩ sangriento; **~ vessel** *n* vaso *m* sanguíneo

bloody¹ /'blʌdi/ *adj* **-dier, -diest** **1** **(a)** ⟨hands/clothes⟩ ensangrentado; ⟨wound⟩ que sangra, sangrante **(b)** ⟨battle⟩ sangriento **2** (esp BrE vulg *or* colloq) (*no comp*) (expressing annoyance, surprise, shock etc): **where's that ~ dog?** ¿dónde está ese maldito *or* (Méx) pinche perro? (fam); **~ hell!** ¡coño! (vulg), ¡chingado! (Méx vulg), ¡hostias! (Esp vulg)

bloody² *adv* (BrE vulg *or* colloq) (*as intensifier*): **the weather was ~ awful!** ¡hizo un tiempo de mierda! (vulg)

bloom¹ /bluːm/ *n* **1** **(a)** (flower) flor *f* **(b)** to be in **~** estar* en flor; **to be in full ~** estar* en plena floración **2** (on fruits, leaves) vello *m*

bloom² *vi* «*plant/garden*» florecer*; «*flower*» abrirse*

blossom¹ /'blɑːsəm ‖'blɒsəm/ n (a) (mass of flowers) flores fpl (b) (by single bloom) flor f

blossom² vi (a) (flower) «tree» florecer* (b) (flourish) «arts» florecer*; «person/relationship» alcanzar* su plenitud

blot¹ /blɑːt ‖blɒt/ n (a) (of ink) borrón m (b) (blemish): **the factory is a ~ on the landscape** la fábrica afea el paisaje

blot² -tt- vt (a) (stain, smear) ⟨page/word⟩ emborronar (b) (dry) ⟨ink⟩ secar* (con papel secante)

■ **blot out** [v + o + adv, v + adv + o] ⟨word⟩ tachar; ⟨view⟩ tapar; ⟨memory⟩ borrar

blotchy /'blɑːtʃi ‖'blɒtʃi/ adj **blotchier, blotchiest** ⟨skin⟩ lleno de manchas

blotting paper /'blɑːtɪŋ ‖'blɒtɪŋ/ n papel m secante

blouse /blaʊs ‖blaʊz/ n blusa f

blow¹ /bləʊ/ n golpe m; **to come to ~s** llegar* a las manos; **his death came as a ~ to us** su muerte fue un duro golpe para nosotros

blow² (past **blew**; past p **blown**) vt
1 (propel): **stop ~ing smoke in my face!** ¡no me eches el humo a la cara!; **a gust of wind blew the door shut** una ráfaga de viento cerró la puerta de golpe; **the plane was ~n off course** el viento sacó el avión de su curso
2 (a) (make by blowing): **to ~ bubbles** hacer* pompas de jabón (b) (clear): **to ~ one's nose** sonarse* la nariz (c) (play) ⟨note⟩ tocar*; ⟨signal⟩ dar*; **the referee blew the whistle** el árbitro tocó el silbato or pito
3 (a) (smash) ⟨bridge/safe⟩ volar* (b) (burn out) ⟨fuse⟩ hacer* saltar, quemar (c) (burst) ⟨gasket⟩ reventar*
4 (colloq) (a) (squander) ⟨money⟩ despilfarrar (b) (spoil): **I blew it** la pifié (fam); **I blew the oral test** la pifié en el oral (fam), la regué en el oral (Méx fam)
■ ~ vi **1** ⟨wind⟩ soplar (b) «person» soplar; **she came up the stairs, puffing and ~ing** subió las escaleras bufando y resoplando
2 (be driven by wind): **litter was ~ing everywhere** volaba basura por todas partes; **his hat blew off** se le voló el sombrero; **the door blew open** la puerta se abrió con el viento
3 (produce sound) «whistle» sonar*
4 (burn out) «fuse» saltar, quemarse
■ **blow down 1** [v + o + adv, v + adv + o] tirar (abajo)
2 [v + adv] caerse* (con el viento)
■ **blow out 1** [v + o + adv, v + adv + o] ⟨match/flame⟩ apagar* (soplando); **to ~ sb's brains out** (colloq) saltarle la tapa de los sesos a algn (fam)
2 [v + adv] «candle» apagarse*
■ **blow over** [v + adv] «trouble» caer* en el olvido; «storm» pasar
■ **blow up 1** [v + o + adv] (a) (explode) «bomb» estallar; «car» saltar por los aires (b) (begin) «wind/storm» levantarse; «conflict» estallar; **the affair blew up into a major scandal** el caso terminó en un gran escándalo
2 [v + o + adv, v + adv + o] (a) ⟨mine/car⟩ volar* (b) ⟨balloon⟩ inflar (c) (colloq) ⟨incident⟩ exagerar (d) ⟨photo⟩ ampliar*

blow: ~-**by**-~ /'bləʊbaɪ'bləʊ/ adj (before n) ⟨account⟩ con pelos y señales (fam); ~-**dry** vt

-**dries, -drying, -dries: to ~-dry one's hair** hacerse* un brushing (secarse el pelo con secador de mano y cepillo); ~**gun** n (AmE) cerbatana f

blown /bləʊn/ past p of BLOW²

blow: ~**out** n (a) (feast) (colloq) comilona f (fam) (b) (burst tire) reventón m; ~**pipe** n cerbatana f; ~**torch** n soplete m

blubber¹ /'blʌbər ‖'blʌbə(r)/ n grasa f de ballena

blubber² vi (colloq & pej) lloriquear

bludgeon /'blʌdʒən/ vt aporrear

blue¹ /bluː/ adj **bluer, bluest** **1** ⟨dress/sea/sky⟩ azul **2** (pornographic) (colloq) verde, porno adj inv, colorado (Méx) **3** (unhappy) (esp AmE) triste, deprimido

blue² n azul m; **out of the ~** ⟨call/arrive⟩ cuando menos lo (or me etc) lo esperaba

blue: ~**bell** n jacinto m silvestre; ~**berry** /'bluːˌberi ‖'bluːbəri/ n arándano m; ~-**blooded** /'bluːblʌdəd ‖ˌbluːˈblʌdɪd/ adj de sangre azul; ~**bottle** n mosca f azul; ~-**collar** /'bluːkɑːlər ‖ˌbluːˈkɒlə(r)/ adj ⟨union⟩ obrero; ⟨job⟩ manual; ~-**collar workers** los obreros; ~**print** n (of technical drawing) plano m; (plan of action) programa m

blues /bluːz/ pl n **1** (depression) (colloq): **the ~** la depre (fam) **2** (Mus) blues m

bluff¹ /blʌf/ vi hacer* un bluff or (Col, Méx) blof
■ ~ vt: **he managed to ~ his way out of it** logró salir del apuro embaucándolos

bluff² n (pretense) bluff m, blof m (Col, Méx); **to call sb's ~** poner* a algn en evidencia

blunder¹ /'blʌndər ‖'blʌndə(r)/ vi **1** (move clumsily, stumble): **he ~ed into the table** se topó con el jefe en el pasillo; **he ~ed around in the dark** andaba dando tumbos en la oscuridad **2** (make mistake) cometer un error garrafal

blunder² n (mistake) error m garrafal; (faux pas) metedura f or (AmL tb) metida f de pata (fam)

blunt¹ /blʌnt/ adj -**er**, -**est** (a) (not sharp) ⟨pencil⟩ desafilado, mocho (esp AmL); ⟨tip/edge⟩ romo; **a ~ instrument** un objeto contundente (b) (straightforward) ⟨person/manner⟩ directo, franco; ⟨refusal⟩ rotundo

blunt² vt (a) ⟨pencil⟩ despuntar; ⟨knife/scissors⟩ desafilar (b) (make dull) ⟨senses/intellect⟩ embotar

bluntly /'blʌntli/ adv ⟨say⟩ sin rodeos; ⟨refuse⟩ rotundamente

blur /blɜːr ‖blɜː(r)/ -**rr**- vt ⟨outline⟩ desdibujar; ⟨distinction⟩ hacer* menos claro; ⟨memory⟩ hacer* borroso
■ ~ vi «outline» desdibujarse

blurred /blɜːrd ‖blɜːd/ adj ⟨outline/vision⟩ borroso

blurt out /blɜːrt ‖blɜːt/ [v + o + adv, v + adv + o] espetar

blush /blʌʃ/ vi ruborizarse*, ponerse* colorado

blusher /'blʌʃər ‖'blʌʃə(r)/ n colorete m, rubor m (Méx, RPl)

bluster¹ /'blʌstər ‖'blʌstə(r)/ vi bravuconear

bluster² n bravatas fpl, bravuconería f

B-movie /'biːˌmuːvi/ n película f de serie B or de bajo presupuesto

boa /'bəʊə/ n (Zool) boa f; **a ~ constrictor** una boa constríctor

boar /bɔːr ‖bɔː(r)/ n (pl ~**s** or ~) **(a)** (male pig) cerdo m macho, verraco m **(b)** (wild ~) jabalí m

board¹ /bɔːrd ‖bɔːd/ n **1** (plank) tabla f, tablón m

2 (a) (diving ~) trampolín m **(b)** (for surfing, windsurfing) tabla f (de surf) **(c)** (Games) tablero m

3 (a) (notice~) tablero m or (Esp) tablón m de anuncios, cartelera f (AmL), diario m mural (Chi) **(b)** (sign) letrero m, cartel m **(c)** (score~) marcador m **(d)** (blackboard) pizarra f, pizarrón m (AmL), tablero m (Col)

4 (a) (committee) junta f, consejo m **(b)** (administrative body): **the Water/Gas B~** la compañía del agua/gas **(c)** ~ **(of directors)** (Busn) junta f directiva, consejo m de administración **(d)** (of examiners) tribunal m

5 (provision of meals): ~ **and lodging** comida y alojamiento; **full/half** ~ pensión f completa/media pensión f

6 (in phrases) across the board: **they have promised to reduce taxation across the** ~ han prometido una reducción general de impuestos; **on board** a bordo; **on** ~ **the ship/plane** a bordo del barco/avión

board² vt **1** (go aboard): **to** ~ **a ship** embarcar(se)*, abordar (Méx) **2** (accommodate) hospedar
■ ~ vi **1** (go aboard) embarcar(se)*, abordar (Col, Méx) **2** (be accommodated) **to** ~ **with sb** alojarse or hospedarse en casa de algn
■ **board up** [v + o + adv, v + adv + o] cerrar* con tablas

boarder /ˈbɔːrdər ‖ˈbɔːdə(r)/ n **(a)** (lodger) huésped mf **(b)** (at boarding school) (esp BrE) interno, -na m,f

board game n juego m de mesa

boarding /ˈbɔːrdɪŋ ‖ˈbɔːdɪŋ/: ~ **card** n ▶ ~ PASS; ~ **house** n pensión f; ~ **pass** n tarjeta f de embarque, pase m de abordar (Chi, Méx); ~ **school** n internado m

board: ~**room** n sala f or salón m de juntas; ~**walk** n (AmE) paseo marítimo entarimado

boast¹ /bəʊst/ vi presumir, fanfarronear (fam); **to** ~ **ABOUT** sth alardear or jactarse or vanagloriarse DE algo
■ ~ vt **(a)** (brag): **I won, he** ~**ed** —gané yo —dijo vanagloriándose **(b)** (possess) contar* con

boast² n alarde m

boastful /ˈbəʊstfəl/ adj jactancioso

boat /bəʊt/ n barco m or (small, open) bote m, barca f; **by** ~ en barco

boating /ˈbəʊtɪŋ/ n: **to go** ~ ir* a dar un paseo en bote or barca

boat: ~**man** n cobertizo m (para botes); ~**man** /ˈbəʊtmən/ n (pl -**men** /-mən/) barquero m; ~ **race** n regata f; ~**swain** /ˈbəʊsn̩/ n contramaestre m

bob¹ /baːb ‖bɒb/ n **1 (a)** (movement of head) inclinación f **(b)** (curtsy) reverencia f **2** (haircut) melena f

bob² vi -**bb**- (move abruptly): **the cork** ~**bed up and down on the water** el corcho cabeceaba en el agua

bobbin /ˈbaːbən ‖ˈbɒbɪn/ n bobina f

bobby /ˈbaːbi ‖ˈbɒbi/: ~ **pin** n (AmE) horquilla

f, pasador m (Méx), pinche m (Chi); ~ **socks,** (AmE also) ~ **sox** /saːks ‖sɒks/ pl n calcetines mpl cortos

bode /bəʊd/ vi (liter): **to** ~ **well/ill** ser* buena/ mala señal

bodice /ˈbaːdəs ‖ˈbɒdɪs/ n (of dress) canesú m; (undergarment) corpiño m

bodily¹ /ˈbaːdl̩i ‖ˈbɒdɪli/ adj (before n) corporal; ~ **functions** funciones fpl fisiológicas

bodily² adv: **they dragged him** ~ **into the car** lo agarraron y lo metieron en el coche a la fuerza

body /ˈbaːdi ‖ˈbɒdi/ n (pl **bodies**) **1 (a)** (of human, animal) cuerpo m; (before n) ~ **language** lenguaje m corporal **(b)** (trunk) cuerpo m **(c)** (dead) cadáver m; **over my dead** ~**!** ¡tendrán (or tendrá etc) que pasar por encima de mi cadáver! **2** (main part — of plane) fuselaje m; (— of ship) casco m; (Auto) carrocería f **3 (a)** (organization) organismo m **(b)** (unit) (no pl): **they walked out in a** ~ salieron en masa **(c)** (collection): **a** ~ **of evidence** un conjunto de pruebas; **a growing** ~ **of opinion** una creciente corriente de opinión **(d)** (of water) masa f **4** (object) cuerpo m; **heavenly** ~ (poet) cuerpo m celeste **5** (density — of wine) cuerpo m; (— of hair) volumen m, cuerpo m

body: ~ **builder** n fisiculturista mf; ~ **building** n fisiculturismo m; ~**guard** n guardaespaldas mf; (group) escolta f; ~ **stocking** n body m; ~**work** n carrocería f

bog /baːg, baːg ‖bɒg/ n ciénaga f; (peat ~) tremedal m
■ **bog down:** -**gg**- [v + o + adv] (usu pass): **to be** ~**ged down with work** estar* inundado de trabajo; **don't get** ~**ged down in too much detail** no te enredes con demasiados detalles

boggle /ˈbaːgəl ‖ˈbɒgəl/ vi: **the mind** ~**s** (hum) uno se queda helado, uno alucina (Esp, Méx fam)

bogus /ˈbəʊgəs/ adj ‹claim/name› falso; ‹argument› falaz

Bohemian /bəʊˈhiːmiən/ adj also **bohemian** (unconventional) bohemio

boil¹ /bɔɪl/ n **1** (Med) furúnculo m **2** (boiling point): **the vegetables are on the** ~ las verduras se están haciendo; **bring the water to the** ~ dejar que el agua rompa el hervor

boil² vi ‹water/vegetables› hervir*; **the rice has** ~**ed dry** el arroz se ha quedado sin agua
■ ~ vt **1** (bring to boiling point) hervir*; (keep at boiling point) hervir*, dejar hervir; (cook in boiling water) cocer*, hervir* **2** (boiled) past p ‹potatoes/rice› hervido; ‹ham› cocido; ‹egg› (soft) pasado por agua; (hard) duro
■ **boil down to** [v + adv + prep + o] reducirse* a
■ **boil over** [v + adv] ‹milk› irse* por el fuego; ‹pan› desbordarse; ‹person› perder* el control

boiler /ˈbɔɪlər ‖ˈbɔɪlə(r)/ n caldera f

boiler suit n (BrE) overol m (AmE), mono m (Esp, Méx)

boiling /ˈbɔɪlɪŋ/ adj (colloq): **this coffee is** ~ este café está hirviendo; **I'm** ~ estoy asado (fam); **it's** ~ **hot today/in here** (as adv) hace un calor espantoso hoy/aquí

boiling point n punto m de ebullición

boisterous /ˈbɔɪstərəs/ adj bullicioso

b

bold /bəʊld/ adj **-er, -est** [1] (daring) audaz [2] (impudent) ⟨smile/advances⟩ descarado [3] ⟨pattern⟩ llamativo; ⟨color⟩ fuerte

boldly /'bəʊldli/ adv [1] (daringly) con audacia, audazmente [2] (impudently) descaradamente

Bolivia /bə'lɪvɪə/ n Bolivia f

Bolivian¹ /bə'lɪvɪən/ adj boliviano

Bolivian² n boliviano, -na m,f

bollard /'bɑːlərd ‖'bɒlɑːd/ n **(a)** (on quay) noray m, bolardo m **(b)** (by road) (BrE) baliza f

bolster¹ /'bəʊlstər ‖'bəʊlstə(r)/ vt **to ~ (up)** ⟨popularity/economy⟩ reforzar*; ⟨argument⟩ reafirmar; ⟨morale⟩ levantar

bolster² n cabezal m (almohada de forma cilíndrica)

bolt¹ /bəʊlt/ n [1] (Tech) tornillo m, perno m [2] **(a)** (on door) pestillo m, pasador m, cerrojo m **(b)** (on firearm) cerrojo m

bolt² vt [1] (fasten with bolt) atornillar, sujetar con un tornillo or perno [2] ⟨door⟩ echarle el pestillo or el pasador or el cerrojo a [3] **~ (down)** ⟨food/meal⟩ engullir*
■ ~ vi «horse» desbocarse*; «person» salir* disparado

bolt³ adv: **~ upright** muy erguido; **he sat ~ upright in bed** se irguió en la cama

bomb¹ /bɑːm ‖bɒm/ n bomba f; **(before n) ~ disposal** desactivación f de explosivas; **~ scare** amenaza f de bomba; **~ squad** (colloq) brigada f antiexplosivos

bomb² vt (from air) bombardear; (plant bomb in) colocar* una bomba en

bombard /bɑːm'bɑːrd ‖bɒm'bɑːd/ vt (Mil) bombardear; **she was ~ed with questions** la acribillaron a preguntas

bomber /'bɑːmər ‖'bɒmə(r)/ n **(a)** (aircraft) bombardero m **(b)** (terrorist) terrorista mf (que perpetra atentados colocando bombas)

bomber jacket n chaqueta f or (Esp) cazadora f or (Méx) chamarra f or (RPl) campera f de aviador

bombing /'bɑːmɪŋ ‖'bɒmɪŋ/ n **(a)** (from aircraft) bombardeo m **(b)** (by terrorists) atentado m (terrorista)

bombshell /'bɑːmʃel ‖'bɒmʃel/ n (shocking news) bomba f

bona fide /'bəʊnəfaɪd ‖,bəʊnə'faɪdɪ/ adj genuino, auténtico

bonanza /bə'nænzə/ n **(a)** (piece of luck) filón m **(b)** (plentiful supply) superabundancia f

bond¹ /bɑːnd ‖bɒnd/ n [1] **(a)** (link) vínculo m **(b) bonds** pl (fetters) cadenas fpl [2] (adhesion) adherencia f

bond² vi **(a)** (stick) adherirse* **(b)** (form relationship) establecer* vínculos afectivos
■ ~ vt (stick) **to ~ sth TO sth** adherir* or pegar* algo A algo

bondage /'bɑːndɪdʒ ‖'bɒndɪdʒ/ n (enslavement) (liter) cautiverio m (liter)

bone¹ /bəʊn/ n **(a)** (Anat) hueso m; **to have a ~ to pick with sb** tener* que ajustar cuentas con algn **(b)** (of fish) espina f

bone² vt ⟨meat⟩ deshuesar; ⟨fish⟩ quitarle las espinas a

bone: ~ china n porcelana f fina; **~-dry** /'bəʊn'draɪ/ (pred ~ **dry**) adj completamente seco

bonfire /'bɑːnfaɪr ‖'bɒnfaɪə(r)/ n hoguera f

bonnet /'bɑːnət ‖'bɒnɪt/ n [1] (Clothing) sombrero m; (for baby) gorrito m [2] (BrE Auto) capó m, capote m (Méx)

bonus /'bəʊnəs/ n [1] (payment to employee) plus m, prima f [2] (added advantage): (added) ~ ventaja f

bony /'bəʊni/ adj **bonier, boniest (a)** ⟨knee⟩ huesudo **(b)** (made of bone) óseo

boo¹ /buː/ interj ¡bu!

boo² n ≈silba f

boo³, boos, booing, booed vt/i abuchear

booby /buːbi/: **~ prize** n premio m al peor; **~ trap** n (Mil) trampa f; (bomb) bomba f trampa; **~-trap** vt **-pp-** (Mil): **his car was ~-trapped** le pusieron una bomba en el coche

book¹ /bʊk/ n [1] (printed work) libro m; **to go by the ~** ceñirse* (estrictamente) a las normas or reglas; **to throw the ~ at sb** castigar* duramente a algn [2] **(a)** (exercise ~) cuaderno m **(b)** (note~) libreta f or cuaderno m (de apuntes) [3] (set — of samples) muestrario m; (— of matches, stamps) librito m [4] **books** pl (Busn, Fin): **the ~s** los libros

book² vt (esp BrE) [1] **(a)** ⟨room/seat/flight⟩ reservar; ⟨appointment⟩ concertar*; **the hotel/flight is fully ~ed** el hotel/vuelo está completo; **I'm ~ed (up) this week** tengo toda la semana ocupada **(b)** ⟨performer⟩ contratar [2] (record) ⟨order⟩ asentar* [3] **(a)** (record charge against) multar **(b)** (in soccer) (BrE) amonestar
■ ~ vi (esp BrE) hacer* una reserva
■ **book in** [v + o + adv, v + adv + o] (reserve room for): **she'd ~ed us in at the Hilton** nos había reservado habitación en el Hilton
■ **book up** [v + o + adv, v + adv + o] (reserve) (often pass): **the hotels are all ~ed up** los hoteles están todos completos; **tonight's performance is ~ed up** no quedan localidades para la función de esta noche

book: ~case n biblioteca f, librería f (Esp), librero m (Méx); **~end** n sujetalibros m

booking /'bʊkɪŋ/ n (esp BrE) **(a)** (reservation) reserva f, reservación f (AmL) **(b)** (engagement) compromiso m

booking office n (BrE Theat) taquilla f, boletería f (AmL)

bookkeeping /'bʊk,kiːpɪŋ/ n contabilidad f, teneduría f de libros

booklet /'bʊklət ‖'bʊklɪt/ n folleto m

bookmaker n /'bʊk,meɪkər‖'bʊk,meɪkə(r)/ corredor, -dora m,f de apuestas

bookmark¹ /'bʊkmɑːrk ‖'bʊkmɑːk/ n **(a)** (for book) señalador m, marcador m **(b)** (Comput) marcador m

bookmark² vt marcar

book: ~seller n librero m **~shelf** n **(a)** (shelf) estante m, balda f (Esp) (para libros) **(b) ~shelves** ▶ BOOKCASE; **~shop** n librería f, **~store** n (AmE) librería f; **~ token** n (BrE) cheque m regalo, vale m (canjeable por libros)

boom¹ /buːm/ n [1] (Econ, Fin) boom m [2] (sound of guns, explosion) estruendo m

boom² vi ⎡1⎤ «guns» tronar*; «voice/thunder» retumbar ⎡2⎤ (usu in -ing form) «market/industry» vivir un boom

boomerang /'bu:məræŋ/ n bumerang m

booming /'bu:mɪŋ/ adj (a) ‹sound› retumbante (b) ‹industry› en auge

boon /bu:n/ n gran ayuda f

boost¹ /bu:st/ n (uplift): to give a ~ to sth dar* empuje a algo; **it was a tremendous ~ to her confidence** le dio mucha más confianza en sí misma

boost² vt ‹economy/production› estimular; ‹sales› aumentar; ‹morale› levantar

booster /'bu:stər ‖'bu:stə(r)/ n (a) (Rad, Telec, TV) repetidor m (b) (Med) ~ (**shot**) (vacuna f de) refuerzo m

booster cable n (AmE) cable m de arranque

boot¹ /bu:t/ n ⎡1⎤ (Clothing) bota f; (short) botín m ⎡2⎤ (kick) (colloq) (no pl) patada f, puntapié m ⎡3⎤ (BrE Auto) maletero m, portamaletas m, cajuela f (Méx), baúl m (Col, CS, Ven), maleta f (Chi), maletera f (Per) ⎡4⎤ **to boot** (as linker) para rematarla

boot² vt (a) (kick) (colloq) darle* un puntapié a (b) (Comput) ~ (**up**) cargar*

booth /bu:θ ‖bu:ð, bu:θ/ n (a) (cabin) cabina f; **photo ~** fotomatón m (b) (polling ~) cabina f de votación (c) (telephone ~) cabina f (de teléfono) (d) (stall — at fair) barraca f, caseta f; (— at exhibition) stand m

bootleg /'bu:tleg/ adj (before n) ‹liquor› de contrabando; ‹tape› pirata adj inv

booty /'bu:ti/ n botín m

booze¹ /bu:z/ n (colloq) bebida f, trago m (esp AmL fam)

booze² vi (colloq) beber, tomar (esp AmL)

border¹ /'bɔ:rdər ‖'bɔ:də(r)/ n ⎡1⎤ (Pol) frontera f; (before n) ‹dispute/town› fronterizo ⎡2⎤ (a) (edge) borde m (b) (edging — on fabric, plate) cenefa f

border² vt (a) ‹country/state› limitar con; ‹fields/lands› lindar con (b) (edge — with ribbon, binding) ribetear

■ **border on** [v + prep + o] (a) ‹country› limitar con (b) (verge on) rayar en, lindar con

borderline /'bɔ:rdərlaɪn ‖'bɔ:dəlaɪn/ adj ‹case/score› dudoso; ‹candidate› en el límite entre el aprobado y el reprobado or (Esp) el suspenso

bore¹ /bɔ:r ‖bɔ:(r)/ past of BEAR¹

bore² vt ⎡1⎤ ‹shaft/tunnel› hacer*, abrir* ⎡2⎤ (weary) aburrir

bore³ n ⎡1⎤ (person) pesado, -da m,f (fam); (thing) aburrimiento m, lata f (fam) ⎡2⎤ (of cylinder, gun barrel) calibre m

bored /bɔ:rd ‖bɔ:d/ adj aburrido; **to be ~ WITH sth** estar* aburrido DE algo; **to get ~** aburrirse

boredom /'bɔ:rdəm ‖'bɔ:dəm/ n aburrimiento m

boring /'bɔ:rɪŋ/ adj aburrido, aburridor (AmL)

born¹ /bɔ:rn ‖bɔ:n/ (past p of BEAR¹): **to be ~** nacer*

born² adj (before n) ‹teacher/leader› nato; **he's a ~ loser** siempre ha sido y será un perdedor

born-again /'bɔ:rnə'gen ‖,bɔ:nə'gen/ adj (before n): ~ **Christian** cristiano convertido, especialmente a una secta evangélica

borne /bɔ:rn ‖bɔ:n/ past p of BEAR¹

borough /'bɜ:rəʊ ‖'bʌrə/ n (a) (in US) distrito m municipal (b) (in UK) municipio m

borrow /'bɑ:rəʊ ‖'bɒrəʊ/ vt ⎡1⎤ (a) (have on loan): **may I ~ your pencil?** ¿me prestas or (Esp tb) me dejas el lápiz?; **to ~ sth FROM sb** pedirle* prestado algo A algn; **I ~ed $5,000 from the bank** pedí un préstamo de 5.000 dólares al banco (b) (from library) sacar* ⎡2⎤ ‹idea› sacar*; ‹word› tomar

borrower /'bɑ:rəʊər ‖'bɒrəʊə(r)/ n (a) (Fin) prestatario, -ria m,f; (b) (from library) usuario, -ria m,f

borrowing /'bɑ:rəʊɪŋ ‖'bɒrəʊɪŋ/ n (Fin) préstamos mpl

Bosnia Herzegovina /'bɑ:zniə,hertsəgəʊ'vi:nə ‖,bɒzniə,hɜ:tsəgəʊ'vi:nə/ n Bosnia Herzegovina f

Bosnian /'bɑ:zniən ‖'bɒzniən/ adj bosnio

bosom /'bʊzəm/ n (a) (breast, chest) (liter) pecho m; (before n) ‹friend› del alma (b) (of woman — bust) pecho m, busto m; (— breast) pecho m, seno m (c) (heart, center) (liter) seno m

boss /bɑ:s ‖bɒs/ n (colloq) (a) (superior) jefe, -fa m,f; (employer, factory owner) patrón, -trona m,f (b) (leader) dirigente mf

■ **boss around**, (BrE also) **boss about** [v + o + adv] (colloq) mandonear (fam)

bossy /'bɑ:si ‖'bɒsi/ adj **bossier, bossiest** (colloq) mandón (fam)

bosun /'bəʊsn̩/ n ▶ BOATSWAIN

botanic /bə'tænɪk/, **-ical** /-ɪkəl/ adj botánico

botanist /'bɑ:tn̩əst ‖'bɒtənɪst/ n botánico, -ca m,f

botany /'bɑ:tn̩i ‖'bɒtəni/ n botánica f

botch /bɑ:tʃ ‖bɒtʃ/ vt (colloq) ~ (**up**) ‹repair› hacer* una chapuza de (fam); ‹plan› estropear

both¹ /bəʊθ/ adj ambos, -bas, los dos, las dos

both² pron ambos, -bas, los dos, las dos; **we ~ like chess** a los dos nos gusta el ajedrez; **the coats are ~ too big** los dos abrigos son demasiado grandes

both³ conj **both ... and ...**: ~ **Paul and John are in Italy** tanto Paul como John están en Italia, Paul y John están los dos en Italia; **she ~ wrote and played the music** compuso y tocó la música ella misma

bother¹ /'bɑ:ðər ‖'bɒðə(r)/ vt (a) (irritate, pester) molestar; **sorry to ~ you** perdone (que lo moleste) (b) (trouble) preocupar; **she's very quiet, but don't let it ~ you** es muy callada, no te inquietes por ello (c) (make effort) **not to ~ -ING**: **don't ~ writing a long letter** no hace falta que escribas una carta larga; **to ~ to + INF** tomarse la molestia DE + INF

· ·

■ ~ *vi* (a) (make effort) molestarse (b) (worry) **to ~ ABOUT sth/sb** preocuparse POR algo/algn

bother² *n* molestia *f*; (work) trabajo *m*; (problems) problemas *mpl*

bothered /'bɑːðərd ‖'bɒðəd/ *adj* (*pred*): **I can't be ~ to go** me da pereza ir; **she yelled at him, but he wasn't a bit ~** le pegó un berrido, pero él ni se inmutó

bottle¹ /'bɑːtl̩ ‖'bɒtl̩/ *n* (container, contents) botella *f*; (of perfume) frasco *m*; **baby's ~** biberón *m*, mamila *f* (Méx), mamadera *f* (CS, Per), tetero *m* (Col); (*before n*) **~ opener** abrebotellas *m*, destapador *m* (AmL)

bottle² *vt* (a) ⟨*wine/milk*⟩ embotellar; **~d milk** leche *f* en *or* de botella; **~d water** agua *f*, embotellada (b) (BrE) ⟨*fruit/vegetables*⟩ poner* en conserva

■ **bottle up** [*v + o + adv, v + adv + o*] (colloq) ⟨*emotion*⟩ reprimir

bottle: ~ bank *n* contenedor *m* de recogida de vidrio; **~feed** *vt* (*past & past p* **-fed**) alimentar con biberón *or* (Méx) con mamila *or* (CS, Per) con mamadera *or* (Col) con tetero; **~neck** *n* (narrow stretch of road) cuello *m* de botella; (hold-up) embotellamiento *m*

bottom¹ /'bɑːtəm ‖'bɒtəm/ *n* [1] (a) (of box, bottle, drawer) fondo *m*; (of hill, stairs) pie *m*; (of page) final *m*, pie *m*; (of pile) parte *f* de abajo; **to get to the ~ of sth** llegar* al fondo de algo (b) (underneath — of box) parte *f* de abajo; (— of ship) fondo *m* (c) (of bed) pies *mpl*; (of garden) fondo *m*; (of road) final *m* (d) (of sea, river, lake) fondo *m* [2] (of hierarchy): **he is at the ~ of the class** es el último de la clase; **she started out at the ~** empezó desde abajo [3] (a) (of person) trasero *m* (fam), traste *m* (CS fam) (b) (of pyjamas, tracksuit) (*often pl*) pantalón *m*, pantalones *mpl*; (of bikini) parte *f* de abajo

bottom² *adj* (*before n*) ⟨*shelf/layer*⟩ de más abajo; ⟨*grade*⟩ más bajo; ⟨*part/edge/lip*⟩ inferior

bottomless /'bɑːtəmləs ‖'bɒtəmlɪs/ *adj* ⟨*well/shaft*⟩ sin fondo

bough /baʊ/ *n* rama *f*

bought /bɔːt/ *past & past p of* BUY¹

boulder /'bəʊldər ‖'bəʊldə(r)/ *n* roca *f* (grande, alisada por la erosión)

boulevard /'bʊləvɑːrd ‖'buːləvɑːd/ *n* bulevar *m*

bounce¹ /baʊns/ *vi* (a) ⟨*ball/object*⟩ rebotar, picar* (AmL), botar (Esp, Méx); **the child was bouncing up and down on the sofa** el niño saltaba en el sofá (b) ⟨*check*⟩ (colloq) ser* devuelto, rebotar (fam)
■ ~ *vt* (a) ⟨*ball/object*⟩ hacer* rebotar, hacer* picar (AmL), (hacer*) botar (Esp, Méx) (b) ⟨*check*⟩ (colloq) devolver*
■ **bounce back** [*v + adv*] (colloq) levantarse

bounce² *n* (a) (action) rebote *m*, pique *m* (AmL) (b) (springiness, vitality): **this shampoo puts the ~ back into your hair** este champú les da nueva vida a sus cabellos; **she's full of ~** es una persona llena de vida

bouncer /'baʊnsər ‖'baʊnsə(r)/ *n* (colloq) gorila *m* (fam), sacabullas *m* (Méx fam)

bound¹ /baʊnd/ *n* [1] **bounds** *pl* (limits) límites *mpl*; **within the ~s of possibility** dentro de lo

posible; **the shop is out of ~s to schoolchildren** los niños tienen prohibido entrar en la tienda [2] (jump) salto *m*, brinco *m*

bound² *vi* saltar; **to ~ in/out** entrar/salir* dando saltos

bound³ *past & past p of* BIND¹

bound⁴ *adj* [1] (a) (tied up) atado, amarrado (AmL exc RPI) (b) (obliged): **they are ~ by law to supply the goods** están obligados por ley a suministrar los artículos; **I'm duty ~ to tell you the truth** es mi deber decirte la verdad [2] (*pred*) (certain): **it was ~ to happen sooner or later** tarde o temprano tenía que suceder; **it was ~ to go wrong** no cabía duda de que iba a salir mal [3] (headed) (*pred*): **the truck was ~ for Italy** el camión iba rumbo a Italia; **they are Moscow ~** van camino a Moscú

boundary /'baʊndri, -dəri/ *n* (*pl* **-ries**) límite *m*

bountiful /'baʊntɪfəl/ *adj* (liter) ⟨*king/nature*⟩ munificente (liter); ⟨*harvest/gifts*⟩ copioso

bounty /'baʊnti/ *n* (*pl* **-ties**) [1] (liter) (generosity) munificencia *f* (liter) [2] (reward) recompensa *f*; (*before n*) **~ hunter** cazador, -dora *m,f* de recompensas

bouquet /bəʊ'keɪ, buː'keɪ ‖bʊ'keɪ, bəʊ'keɪ/ *n* [1] (of flowers) ramo *m*; (small) ramillete *m* [2] (of wine) bouquet *m*

bourbon /'bɜːrbən ‖'bɜːbən/ *n* bourbon *m*

bourgeois /'bʊrʒwɑ ‖'bɔːʒwɑː, 'bʊəʒ-/ *adj* burgués

bout /baʊt/ *n* [1] (period, spell): **I had a ~ of flu** tuve una gripe *or* (Col, Méx) una gripa muy mala; **a drinking ~** una borrachera [2] (in boxing, wrestling) combate *m*, encuentro *m*

boutique /buː'tiːk/ *n* boutique *f*

bow¹ /baʊ/ *n* [1] (movement) reverencia *f* [2] (of ship) (*often pl*) proa *f*

bow² /baʊ/ *vi* hacer* una reverencia; **they ~ed to government pressure** cedieron ante la presión del gobierno
■ ~ *vt* ⟨*head*⟩ inclinar
■ **bow out** [*v + adv*] retirarse

bow³ /bəʊ/ *n* [1] (knot) lazo *m*, moño *m* (esp AmL) [2] (weapon) arco *m* [3] (Mus) arco *m*

bow⁴ /bəʊ/ *vi* «*branch/plank*» arquearse, pandearse (esp AmL)

bowel /'baʊəl/ *n* (Anat) intestino *m* grueso; **in the ~s of the earth** (liter) en las entrañas de la tierra

bowl¹ /bəʊl/ *n* [1] (a) (container) (Culin) bol *m*, tazón *m*, cuenco *m*; (for washing etc) palangana *f*, barreño *m*; **fruit ~** frutero *m*, frutera *f* (CS); **soup ~** sopero *m* (b) (contents) bol *m*, tazón *m* (c) (of toilet) taza *f* [2] (in game of bowls) bola *f*, bocha *f*; *see also* BOWLS

bowl² *vt/i* lanzar*
■ **bowl over** [*v + o + adv, v + adv + o*] derribar; **we were ~ed over by the beauty of the island** la belleza de la isla nos dejó pasmados

bowlegged /'bəʊlegd/ *adj* patizambo

bowler /'bəʊlər ‖'bəʊlə(r)/ *n* [1] (in cricket) lanzador, -dora *m,f*; (in bowling, bowls) jugador, -dora *m,f* [2] **~ (hat)** bombín *m*, sombrero *m* de hongo

bowling /'bəʊlɪŋ/ n (a) (in bowling alley) bolos mpl (b) (on grass) ▶ BOWLS

bowling: ∼ **alley** n bolera f, bowling m; ∼ **green** n: pista donde se juega a los BOWLS

bowls /bəʊlz/ n (+ sing vb) juego semejante a la petanca que se juega sobre césped

bow tie /bəʊ/ n corbata f de moño (AmL), pajarita f (Esp)

box¹ /bɑːks ‖bɒks/ n **1** (container, contents) caja f; (large) cajón m; (for watch, pen) estuche m **2** (on form) casilla f **3** (a) (in theater) palco m (b) (booth) cabina f

box² vi boxear
■ ∼ vt poner* en una caja, embalar
■ **box in** [v + o + adv, v + adv + o] (a) (restrict, surround) cerrarle* el paso a (b) (enclose) ⟨pipes⟩ esconder (tapando con una tabla etc)

boxer /'bɑːksər ‖'bɒksə(r)/ n (a) (person) boxeador, -dora m,f (b) (dog) bóxer mf

boxer shorts pl n calzoncillos mpl, calzones mpl (Méx), interiores mpl (Col, Ven)

boxing /'bɑːksɪŋ ‖'bɒksɪŋ/ n boxeo m; (before n) ∼ **ring** ring m, cuadrilátero m

Boxing Day /'bɑːksɪŋ ‖'bɒksɪŋ/ n: el 26 de diciembre, día festivo en Gran Bretaña

box: ∼ **number** n (at post office) apartado m (de correos), apartado m postal (Méx), casilla f postal or de correo (CS); ∼ **office** n taquilla f, boletería f (AmL)

boy /bɔɪ/ n (a) (baby, child) niño m, chico m (b) (son) hijo m, chico m (c) (young man) (colloq) muchacho m, chico m

boycott¹ /'bɔɪkɑːt ‖'bɔɪkɒt/ n boicot m

boycott² vt boicotear

boyfriend /'bɔɪfrend/ n novio m, pololo m (Chi fam)

boyish /'bɔɪʃ/ adj ⟨enthusiasm/smile⟩ de chico, de niño; (used of woman) de muchacho, de chico

boy scout n boy scout m, explorador m

bra /brɑː/ n sostén m, sujetador m (Esp), brasier m (Col, Méx), corpiño m (RPl), soutien m (Ur)

brace¹ /breɪs/ n **1** (support) abrazadera f **2** (Dent) ▶ 4B **3** (drill) berbiquí m **4** **braces** pl (a) (BrE Clothing) tirantes mpl, cargaderas fpl (Col), tiradores mpl (RPl), suspensores mpl (Chi) (b) (esp AmE Dent) aparato(s) m(pl), frenos mpl (Méx), fierros mpl (Méx, Per), frenillos mpl (Chi) **5** (pl ∼) (pair) (BrE) par m

brace² vt (support) apuntalar
■ v refl to ∼ oneself for sth prepararse para algo

bracelet /'breɪslət ‖'breɪslɪt/ n pulsera f, brazalete m

bracing /'breɪsɪŋ/ adj vigorizante

bracken /'brækən/ n helechos mpl

bracket¹ /'brækət ‖'brækɪt/ n **1** (a) (Print) (square bracket) corchete m (b) (parenthesis) (BrE) paréntesis m **2** (category): income ∼ nivel m de ingresos; the 25-30 age ∼ el grupo etario de entre 25 y 30 años **3** (support) soporte m; (for shelves) escuadra f

bracket² vt (a) ⟨word/phrase⟩ poner* entre corchetes; (in parentheses) (BrE) poner* entre paréntesis (b) (categorize) catalogar*

brag /bræg/ vi/t -gg- fanfarronear (fam)

braid¹ /breɪd/ n (a) (of hair) (esp AmE) trenza f (b) (Tex) galón m

braid² vt trenzar*

braille, Braille /breɪl/ n braille m, Braille m

brain /breɪn/ n cerebro m; (before n) ∼ **damage** lesión f cerebral; ∼ **tumor** tumor m cerebral

brain: ∼**child** n creación m; ∼**-dead** adj clínicamente muerto

brains /breɪnz/ n **1** (+ pl vb) (a) (substance) sesos mpl; (Culin) sesos mpl (b) (intelligence) inteligencia f **2** (+ sing vb) (mastermind) cerebro m, autor, -tora m,f intelectual (AmL); he's the ∼ of the family es la lumbrera de la familia

brain: ∼**wash** vt hacerle* un lavado de cerebro a; ∼**wave** n (colloq) idea f genial, lamparazo m (Col fam)

braise /breɪz/ vt estofar

brake¹ /breɪk/ n (on vehicle) freno m; (before n) ∼ **lights** luces fpl de freno

brake² vi/t frenar

bramble /'bræmbəl/ n zarza f

bran /bræn/ n salvado m, afrecho m

branch¹ /bræntʃ ‖brɑːntʃ/ n (of tree) rama f; (of river, road, railway) ramal m; (of family, field of study) rama f; (of company, bank) sucursal f

branch² vi «river/family» ramificarse*; «road» bifurcarse*; a path ∼es (off) to the right un sendero sale a la derecha
■ **branch out** [v + adv] (a) (take on new activity) diversificar* sus (or nuestras etc) actividades; the company has ∼ed out into publishing la compañía ha diversificado sus actividades lanzándose al campo editorial (b) (become independent): he has ∼ed out on his own «business partner» se ha establecido por su cuenta

brand¹ /brænd/ n **1** (a) (Busn) marca f (b) (type) tipo m; (style) estilo m **2** (identification mark) marca f (hecha a fuego)

brand² vt (a) (mark) ⟨cattle⟩ marcar* (con hierro candente) (b) (label) to ∼ sb AS sth tachar a algn DE algo

brandish /'brændɪʃ/ vt blandir

brand: ∼ **name** n marca f; ∼**-new** /'brænd'nuː ‖,brænd'njuː/ adj nuevo

brandy /'brændi/ n (pl -dies) coñac m, brandy m

brash /bræʃ/ adj -er, -est excesivamente desenvuelto

brass /bræs ‖brɑːs/ n (a) (Metall) latón m; (before n) ⟨button⟩ dorado (b) (Mus) (+ sing or pl vb) bronces mpl, metales mpl

brass band n banda f de música, tambora f (Méx)

brassiere /brə'zɪr ‖'bræziə(r)/ n ▶ BRA

brass knuckles pl n (AmE) nudilleras fpl de metal, manoplas fpl (AmL)

brat /bræt/ n (pej) mocoso, -sa m,f (pey)

bravado /brə'vɑːdəʊ/ n bravuconadas fpl

brave¹ /breɪv/ adj -ver, -vest valiente

brave² vt ⟨peril⟩ afrontar; to ∼ the weather hacerle frente al mal tiempo

brave³ n **1** (North American Indian) guerrero m piel roja **2** (liter) (+ pl vb) the ∼ los valientes

bravely /'breɪvli/ adv valientemente

bravery /'breɪvəri/ n valentía f, valor m

bravo /'brɑːvəʊ ‖brɑː'vəʊ/ interj ¡bravo!

brawl¹ /brɔːl/ n pelea f

brawl² *vi* pelearse

brawny /'brɔːni/ *adj* **-nier, -niest** musculoso

bray /breɪ/ *vi* «*donkey*» rebuznar; «*person*» cacarear

brazen /'breɪzn̩ ‖ 'breɪzən/ *adj* descarado

brazier /'breɪʒər, 'breɪzɪər ‖ 'breɪzɪə(r)/ *n* brasero *m*

Brazil /brə'zɪl/ *n* Brasil *m*

Brazilian /brə'zɪlɪən/ *adj* brasileño

brazil nut /brə'zɪl/ *n* coquito *m* del Brasil, castaña *f* de Pará (RPl)

breach¹ /briːtʃ/ *n* **1** (of law) infracción *f*; ~ **of contract** incumplimiento *m* de contrato; **she was arrested for** ~ **of the peace** la detuvieron por alterar el orden público **2** (gap, opening) (fml) brecha *f* **3** (break) (fml) ruptura *f*

breach² *vt* **(a)** «*rule*» infringir*, violar; «*security*» poner* en peligro **(b)** (fml) «*defenses*» abrir* una brecha en

bread /bred/ *n* pan *m*; ~ **and butter** pan con mantequilla *or* (RPl) manteca

bread: ~**bin** *n* (BrE) ▶ ~BOX; ~**board** *n* tabla *f* de cortar el pan; ~**box** *n* (AmE) panera *f* (*para guardar el pan*); ~**crumb** *n* miga *f* (de pan); ~**crumbs** (Culin) pan *m* rallado *or* (Méx) molido; ~**line** *n*: **they're on the** ~**line** (colloq) apenas tienen para vivir

breadth /bredθ/ *n* **(a)** (width) anchura *f*, ancho *m* **(b)** (extent) amplitud *f*; ~ **of vision** amplitud de miras

breadwinner /'bred,wɪnər ‖ 'bred,wɪnə(r)/ *n*: **she's the** ~ **of the family** es la que mantiene a la familia

break¹ /breɪk/ (*past* **broke**; *past p* **broken**) *vt* **1** «*window/plate*» romper*; «*stick*» partir, quebrar* (AmL); **he broke his wrist** se rompió la muñeca
2 (render useless) «*machine*» romper*, descomponer* (AmL)
3 (violate) «*rule*» infringir*; «*promise*» no cumplir; «*contract*» incumplir; «*strike*» romper*; ▶ LAW B
4 (end) «*strike*» poner* fin a; «*drug ring*» desarticular; «*impasse*» salir* de; «*habit*» dejar
5 **(a)** (ruin) «*person/company*» arruinar a **(b)** (crush) «*person*» destrozar*
6 (impart): **Sue broke the news to him** Sue le dio la noticia; **they broke it to her gently** se lo dijeron con mucho tacto
7 (exceed) «*record*» batir
8 (disrupt) «*pattern/monotony*» romper*
9 (decipher) «*code*» descifrar
■ ~ *vi* **1** «*window/plate*» romperse*; «*stick*» partirse, quebrarse* (AmL)
2 (give in) «*resistance*» desmoronarse; **she broke under constant interrogation** no resistió el constante interrogatorio
3 **(a)** (begin) «*storm*» estallar; «*day*» romper* **(b)** (change) «*weather*» cambiar; **his voice is** ~**ing** le está cambiando la voz; **his voice broke** (with emotion) se le entrecortó la voz
4 «*wave/surf*» romper*
■ **break away** [*v* + *adv*] **to** ~ **away** (FROM sth) «*piece*» desprenderse (DE algo); «*faction/region*» escindirse (DE algo)
■ **break down**
I [*v* + *adv*] **1** «*vehicle/machine*» estropearse,

averiarse*, descomponerse* (AmL), quedarse en pana (Chi), quedarse varado (Col); «*system*» fallar; «*talks*» fracasar
2 (lose composure) perder* el control
II [*v* + *o* + *adv*, *v* + *adv* + *o*] **1** «*door/barrier*» echar abajo
2 (divide up) «*expenditure*» desglosar; «*sentence*» descomponer*; **the process can be broken down into three steps** el proceso puede dividirse en tres pasos
■ **break in** **1** [*v* + *adv*] «*intruder*» entrar (*para robar etc*)
2 [*v* + *o* + *adv*, *v* + *adv* + *o*] «*horse*» domar
■ **break into** [*v* + *prep* + *o*] «*building*» entrar en (*para robar etc*)
■ **break off** **1** [*v* + *o* + *adv*, *v* + *adv* + *o*] **(a)** (detach) partir **(b)** «*engagement/diplomatic relations*» romper*
2 [*v* + *adv*] (snap off, come free) «*piece of ice*» desprenderse; **the handle broke off** se le rompió el asa
■ **break out** [*v* + *adv*] **1** (start) «*war/epidemic/rioting*» estallar
2 (escape) «*prisoner*» escaparse, fugarse*
■ **break through** **1** [*v* + *adv*] (penetrate) (Mil) penetrar en las defensas enemigas; «*sun*» salir*
2 [*v* + *prep* + *o*] «*barrier*» atravesar*, romper*; **they broke through our defenses** penetraron en nuestras defensas
■ **break up**
I [*v* + *o* + *adv*, *v* + *adv* + *o*] **1** (divide) «*land*» dividir; «*ship*» desaguazar*; «*sentence*» descomponer*
2 **(a)** «*demonstration*» disolver* **(b)** (wreck, ruin) «*home*» deshacer*
II [*v* + *adv*] **(a)** «*lovers/band*» separarse; **their marriage broke up** su matrimonio fracasó; **to** ~ **up WITH sb** romper* CON algn **(b)** «*meeting*» terminar; «*crowd*» dispersarse

break² *n* **1** **(a)** (Rad, TV) pausa *f* (comercial); (Theat) entreacto *m*, intermedio *m* **(b)** (rest period) descanso *m*; (at school) (BrE) recreo *m* **(c)** (short vacation) vacaciones *fpl* **(d)** (change, respite) cambio *m*; **I need a** ~ **from all this** necesito descansar de todo esto; **(a holiday)** necesito un cambio de aires
2 (gap) interrupción *f* **3** (fracture) fractura *f*, rotura *f*; **to make a clean** ~ cortar por lo sano

breakable /'breɪkəbəl/ *adj* frágil

breakage /'breɪkɪdʒ/ *n* **(a)** (action) rotura *f* **(b)** **breakages** *pl* (objects broken) roturas *fpl*

break: ~**away** *n* (separation) ruptura *f*, escisión *f*; (before *n*) «*faction*» disidente, escindido; ~**down** *n* **1** **(a)** (failure — of car, machine) avería *f*, descompostura *f* (Méx), varada *f* (Col), pana *f* (Chi); (— of service, communications) interrupción *f*; (— of negotiations) fracaso *m*; (before *n*) ~**down truck** grúa *f* **(b)** (nervous ~down) crisis *f* nerviosa; **2** (analysis): **a** ~**down of expenditure** un desglose de los gastos

breaker /'breɪkər ‖ 'breɪkə(r)/ *n* gran ola *f*

breakfast /'brekfəst/ *n* desayuno *m*; **to have** ~ desayunar, tomar el desayuno; (before *n*) ~ **television** televisión *f* matinal

break-in /'breɪkɪn/ *n* robo *m* (con escalamiento)

breaking /'breɪkɪŋ/**:** ~ **and entering** /'breɪkɪŋəndentərɪŋ/ *n* allanamiento *m* de morada; ~ **point** *n* límite *m*

break: ~**through** *n* gran avance *m*; ~**up** *n* ····⫶·

(of structure, family) desintegración *f*; (of empire, company) desmembramiento *m*; (of political party) disolución *f*; (of talks) fracaso *m*; **the ~up of their marriage** su separación; **~water** *n* rompeolas *m*

breast /brest/ *n* (a) (of woman) pecho *m*, seno *m*; (before *n*) ~ **cancer** cáncer *m* de mama *or* de pecho (b) (chest) (liter) pecho *m* (c) (Culin) (of chicken, turkey) pechuga *f*

breast: ~**feed** (*past & past p* **-fed**) *vt* darle* el pecho a, darle* de mamar a ■ ~ *vi* dar* el pecho, dar* de mamar; ~**stroke** *n* (estilo) pecho *m* (AmL), braza *f* (Esp)

breath /breθ/ *n* aliento *m*; **to have bad ~** tener* mal aliento; **to take a ~** aspirar, inspirar; **take a deep ~** respire hondo; **out of ~** sin aliento; **to hold one's ~** contener* la respiración; **to take sb's ~ away** dejar a algn sin habla

Breathalyzer®, Breathalyser® /'breθəlaɪzər ‖ 'breθəlaɪzə(r)/ *n* alcohómetro *m*, alcoholímetro *m*; (before *n*) ~ **test** prueba *f* del alcohol *or* de la alcoholemia

breathe /briːð/ *vi* respirar
■ ~ *vt* ⟨air/fumes⟩ aspirar, respirar
■ **breathe in** ① [*v + adv*] ② [*v + o + adv, v + adv + o*] ⟨air/fumes⟩ aspirar, respirar
■ **breathe out** ① [*v + adv*] espirar ② [*v + o + adv, v + adv + o*] ⟨smoke⟩ expeler; ⟨air⟩ exhalar

breathing /'briːðɪŋ/ *n* respiración *f*

breathing space *n* respiro *m*

breathless /'breθləs ‖ 'breθlɪs/ *adj*: **the blow left me ~** el golpe me dejó sin aliento; **he arrived ~** llegó jadeando

breathtaking /'breθ,teɪkɪŋ/ *adj* impresionante

bred /bred/ *past & past p of* BREED²

breeches /'brɪtʃəz ‖ 'brɪtʃɪz/ *pl n* (knee ~) (pantalones *mpl*) bombachos *mpl*; (riding ~) pantalones *mpl* de montar

breed¹ /briːd/ *n* (of animals) raza *f*; (of plants) variedad *f*

breed² (*past & past p* **bred**) *vt* ⟨animals⟩ criar*; ⟨violence⟩ engendrar
■ ~ *vi* reproducirse*

breeder /'briːdər ‖ 'briːdə(r)/ *n* (of animals) criador, -dora *m,f*; (of plants) cultivador, -dora *m,f*

breeding /'briːdɪŋ/ *n* (a) (reproduction) reproducción *f* (b) (raising — of animals) cría *f*; (— of plants) cultivo *m* (c) (upbringing): **politeness is a sign of good ~** la cortesía es señal de buena educación

breeze¹ /briːz/ *n* brisa *f*

breeze² *vi* (colloq): **to ~ in/out** entrar/salir* tan campante (fam)

breezy /'briːzi/ *adj* **-zier, -ziest** ① (windy) ⟨spot⟩ ventoso; **it's a bit ~ today** hace un poco de vientecito hoy ② (lively) (colloq) ⟨person⟩ dinámico

brethren /'breðrən/ *pl n* (arch *or* liter) hermanos *mpl*

brevity /'brevəti/ *n* brevedad *f*

brew /bruː/ *vt* (a) ⟨beer⟩ fabricar* (b) ⟨tea⟩ preparar (c) ⟨mischief⟩ tramar

■ ~ *vi* (a) (make beer) fabricar* cerveza (b) ⟨tea⟩: **the tea is ~ing** el té se está haciendo (c) ⟨storm⟩ avecinarse; ⟨trouble⟩ gestarse

brewer /'bruːər ‖ 'bruːə(r)/ *n* cervecero, -ra *m,f*

brewery /'bruːəri/ *n* (*pl* **-ries**) fábrica *f* de cerveza, cervecería *f*

bribe¹ /braɪb/ *n* soborno *m*

bribe² *vt* sobornar

bribery /'braɪbəri/ *n* soborno *m*

bric-a-brac /'brɪkəbræk/ *n* baratijas *fpl*

brick /brɪk/ *n* ladrillo *m*

bricklayer /'brɪk,leɪər ‖ 'brɪk,leɪə(r)/ *n* albañil *m*

bridal /'braɪdl̩/ *adj* ⟨procession⟩ nupcial; ⟨shop⟩ para novias

bride /braɪd/ *n* novia *f*; **the ~ and groom** los novios; (after ceremony) los recién casados

bride: ~**groom** *n* novio *m*; ~**smaid** *n* dama *f* de honor; (child) niña *que acompaña a la novia*

bridge¹ /brɪdʒ/ *n* ① (a) puente *m* (b) (on ship) puente *m* (de mando) (c) (of nose) caballete *m* ② (Dent) puente *m* ③ (card game) bridge *m*

bridge² *vt* ⟨river⟩ tender* un puente sobre; ⟨differences⟩ salvar

bridle /'braɪdl̩/ *n* brida *f*

brief¹ /briːf/ *adj* breve; **in ~** en resumen

brief² *n* (a) (Law) *expediente entregado por el abogado al* BARRISTER (b) (instructions) instrucciones *fpl* (c) (area of responsibility) competencia *f*

brief³ *vt* ⟨lawyer⟩ instruir*; ⟨pilot/spy⟩ darle* instrucciones a; ⟨committee⟩ informar

briefcase /'briːfkeɪs/ *n* maletín *m*, portafolio(s) *m* (esp AmL)

briefing /'briːfɪŋ/ *n* (a) (~ session) sesión *f* para dar instrucciones (b) (press ~) reunión *f* informativa (para la prensa)

briefly /'briːfli/ *adv* (a) ⟨visit/rule⟩ por poco tiempo (b) ⟨reply/speak⟩ brevemente (c) (indep) en resumen

briefs /briːfs/ *pl n* (man's) calzoncillos *mpl*, slip *m*; (woman's) calzones *mpl* (esp AmL), bragas *fpl* (Esp), bombachas *fpl* (RPl), pantaletas *fpl* (AmC, Ven)

brigade /brɪ'geɪd/ *n* brigada *f*

bright /braɪt/ *adj* **-er, -est** ① (a) ⟨star/light⟩ brillante; ⟨room⟩ con mucha luz (b) ⟨color⟩ fuerte ② (a) (cheerful) ⟨eyes⟩ lleno de vida (b) (hopeful) ⟨future⟩ prometedor; **to look on the ~ side of sth** mirar el lado bueno de algo ③ (intelligent) ⟨person⟩ inteligente; **whose ~ idea was it to …?** (iro) ¿quién tuvo la brillante idea de …? (iró)

brighten /'braɪtn̩/ *vi* (a) (become brighter) ⟨light⟩ hacerse* más brillante (b) ~ (up) (become cheerful, hopeful) ⟨person⟩ animarse; ⟨situation/prospects⟩ mejorar
■ ~ *vt* (a) (make brighter) iluminar (b) ~ (up) ⟨room⟩ alegrar; ⟨occasion/party⟩ animar

brightly /'braɪtli/ *adv* (a) ⟨shine⟩ intensamente (b) ⟨say/smile⟩ alegremente

brights /braɪts/ *pl n* (Auto) (AmE colloq) (luces *fpl*) largas *or* (Andes, Méx) altas *fpl*

brilliance /ˈbrɪljəns/ *n* **(a)** (brightness) resplandor *m* **(b)** (skill, intelligence) brillantez *f*

brilliant /ˈbrɪljənt/ *adj* ‹light› brillante; ‹sunshine› radiante; ‹red/green› brillante **(b)** ‹student/performance› brillante

brilliantly /ˈbrɪljəntli/ *adv* **(a)** ‹shine› intensamente **(b)** ‹write› con brillantez

brim¹ /brɪm/ *n* ⌷**1** (of hat) ala *f*‡ ⌷**2** (of vessel) borde *m*

brim² *vi* **-mm-**: her eyes were ~ming with tears tenía los ojos llenos de lágrimas; **to ~ with confidence** rebosar seguridad

brine /braɪn/ *n* **(a)** (saltwater) salmuera *f* **(b)** (seawater) agua *f*‡ salada *or* de mar

bring /brɪŋ/ (*past & past p* **brought**) *vt* traer*; **I couldn't ~ myself to do it** no pude hacerlo; **it brought tears to my eyes** hizo que se me llenaran los ojos de lágrimas; **to ~ sth to bear: to ~ pressure to bear on sb** ejercer* presión sobre algn
■ **bring about** [*v + o + adv, v + adv + o*] dar* lugar a
■ **bring along** [*v + o + adv, v + adv + o*] traer*
■ **bring back** [*v + o + adv, v + adv + o*] **(a)** (return): **I'll ~ your book back tomorrow** te devolveré *or* (AmL exc CS) te regresaré el libro mañana; **to ~ sb back to life** devolverle* la vida a algn **(b)** ‹gift/souvenir› traer* **(c)** (reintroduce) ‹custom› volver* a introducir **(d)** (recall) recordar*; **it brought back memories** me (*or* le *etc*) trajo recuerdos
■ **bring down** [*v + o + adv, v + adv + o*] **(a)** (lower) ‹price› reducir*; ‹temperature› hacer* bajar **(b)** (cause to fall) ‹tree/wall› tirar; ‹player/opponent/plane› derribar; ‹government› derrocar*
■ **bring forward** [*v + o + adv, v + adv + o*] **(a)** (present) ‹witness› hacer* comparecer; ‹evidence/idea› presentar **(b)** (to earlier time) ‹meeting/appointment› adelantar
■ **bring home** [*v + o + adv, v + adv + o*]: **her letter brought home to me the seriousness of the situation** su carta me hizo dar cuenta cabal de la gravedad de la situación
■ **bring off** [*v + o + adv, v + adv + o*] ‹feat/victory› conseguir*, lograr; ‹plan› llevar a cabo; ‹deal› conseguir*
■ **bring on** [*v + o + adv, v + adv + o*] ‹attack/breakdown› provocar*; **what brought this on?** ¿esto a qué se debe?
⌷**2** [*v + o + prep + o*] (cause to befall): **he brought it all on himself** él (mismo) se lo buscó
■ **bring out** [*v + o + adv, v + adv + o*] **(a)** ‹product/model› sacar* (al mercado); ‹edition/book› publicar* **(b)** (accentuate): **children ~ out the best in her** el trato con niños hace resaltar sus mejores cualidades
■ **bring together** [*v + o + adv, v + adv + o*]: **the conference will ~ together scientists from all over the world** el congreso reunirá a científicos de todo el mundo; **a tragedy like this can ~ a family together** una tragedia así puede unir a una familia
■ **bring up** [*v + o + adv, v + adv + o*] **(a)** (rear) ‹child› criar* **(b)** (mention) ‹subject› sacar* **(c)** (vomit) vomitar, devolver*

brink /brɪŋk/ *n* borde *m*; **to be on the ~ of** -ING estar* a punto de +INF

brisk /brɪsk/ *adj* **(a)** (lively, quick) ‹pace› rápido y enérgico; ‹walk› a paso ligero; **ice-cream sellers did a ~ trade** los vendedores de helados vendieron muchísimo **(b)** (efficient) ‹person/manner› enérgico *or* dinámico y eficiente

bristle¹ /ˈbrɪsəl/ *n* (on animal) cerda *f*; (on person): **his face was covered in ~(s)** tenía la barba crecida

bristle² *vi* **(a)** (stand up) «hair» erizarse*, ponerse* de punta **(b)** (show annoyance) erizarse*

Britain /ˈbrɪtn̩ ‖ˈbrɪtən/ *n* Gran Bretaña *f*

British¹ /ˈbrɪtɪʃ/ *adj* británico

British² *pl n* **the ~** los británicos

Britisher /ˈbrɪtɪʃər ‖ˈbrɪtɪʃə(r)/ *n* (AmE) británico, -ca *m,f*

British: ~ Isles *pl n* **the ~ Isles** las Islas Británicas; **~ Summer Time** *n* hora de verano en Gran Bretaña, adelantada en una hora con respecto a la hora de Greenwich

Briton /ˈbrɪtn̩ ‖ˈbrɪtən/ *n* ciudadano británico, ciudadana británica *m,f*; **the ancient ~s** los antiguos britanos

Brittany /ˈbrɪtni ‖ˈbrɪtəni/ *n* Bretaña *f*

brittle /ˈbrɪtl̩/ *adj* quebradizo

broach /brəʊtʃ/ *vt* ‹subject› mencionar

broad¹ /brɔːd/ *adj* ⌷**1** ‹avenue› ancho; ‹valley› grande; ‹forehead› despejado; ‹grin› de oreja a oreja ⌷**2** **(a)** (extensive) ‹syllabus› amplio; ‹interests› numeroso; **in its ~est sense** en su sentido más amplio **(b)** (general) ‹guidelines/conclusions› general ⌷**3** **(a)** **a ~ hint** una indirecta muy clara **(b)** ‹accent› cerrado

broad² *n* (woman) (AmE sl) tipa *f* (fam), vieja *f* (Col, Méx, Ven fam)

broad bean *n* haba *f*

broadcast¹ /ˈbrɔːdkæst ‖ˈbrɔːdkɑːst/ *vt/i* (*past & past p* **broadcast**) transmitir, emitir

broadcast² *n* programa *m*, emisión *f* (frml)

broadcaster /ˈbrɔːdkæstər ‖ˈbrɔːdkɑːstə(r)/ *n*: presentador, locutor *etc* de radio o televisión

broadcasting /ˈbrɔːdkæstɪŋ ‖ˈbrɔːdkɑːstɪŋ/ *n* (Rad) radiodifusión *f*; (TV) televisión *f*

broaden /ˈbrɔːdn̩/ *vt* ‹scope/horizons/interests› ampliar*

broadly /ˈbrɔːdli/ *adv*: **the two systems are ~ similar** en líneas generales, los dos sistemas son similares; **~ speaking** en líneas generales

broad: ~-minded /ˈbrɔːdˈmaɪndəd ‖ˌbrɔːdˈmaɪndɪd/ *adj* de criterio amplio; **~sheet** *n*: periódico de formato grande

brocade /brəʊˈkeɪd ‖brəˈkeɪd/ *n* brocado *m*

broccoli /ˈbrɑːkəli ‖ˈbrɒkəli/ *n* brócoli *m*, brécol *m*

brochure /brəʊˈʃʊr ‖ˈbrəʊʃə(r)/ *n* folleto *m*

brogue /brəʊg/ *n* ⌷**1** (shoe) zapato bajo de cuero ⌷**2** (Irish accent) (*no pl*) acento *m* irlandés

broil /brɔɪl/ *vt* (esp AmE) asar a la parrilla *or* al grill

broiler /ˈbrɔɪlər ‖ˈbrɔɪlə(r)/ *n* (AmE) parrilla *f*, grill *m*

broke¹ /brəʊk/ *past of* **BREAK¹**

broke² /adj (colloq) (pred): **to be ~** estar* pelado; **to be flat ~** estar* pelado or (Esp) sin un duro or (Col) en la olla

broken¹ /'brəʊkən/ past p of BREAK¹

broken² adj [1] (a) ⟨window/vase/chair/glass⟩ roto; ⟨bone⟩ roto, quebrado (AmL) (b) (not working) roto [2] ⟨voice⟩ quebrado; **to die of a ~ heart** morirse* de pena; **he's a ~ man** está destrozado [3] ⟨home/marriage⟩ deshecho [4] (imperfect): **in ~ English** en inglés chapurreado

broken-down /'brəʊkən'daʊn/ adj ⟨car/ machine⟩ averiado, descompuesto (AmL), en pana (Chi), varado (Col); ⟨shed/gate⟩ destartalado

broker /'brəʊkər ‖'brəʊkə(r)/ n (a) (agent) agente mf; **insurance ~** agente mf de seguros (b) (stock~) corredor, -dora mf de bolsa

bronchitis /brɒŋ'kaɪtəs ‖brɒŋ'kaɪtɪs/ n bronquitis f

bronze /brɑːnz ‖brɒnz/ n (Metall) bronce m

brooch /brəʊtʃ/ n prendedor m, broche m

brood¹ /bruːd/ n (of birds) nidada f; (of mammals) camada f; (of children) (hum) prole f (fam & hum)

brood² vi (reflect): **she sat ~ing on the unfairness of life** rumiaba lo injusta que era la vida; **stop ~ing over it** deja de darle vueltas al asunto

brook /brʊk/ n arroyo m

broom /bruːm/ n [1] (brush) escoba f [2] (plant) retama f, hiniesta f

broomstick /'bruːmstɪk/ n palo m de escoba; (of a witch) escoba f

broth /brɔːθ ‖brɒθ/ n caldo m

brothel /'brɑːθəl ‖'brɒθəl/ n burdel m

brother /'brʌðər ‖'brʌðə(r)/ n hermano m; **do you have any ~s and sisters?** ¿tienes hermanos?

brotherhood /'brʌðərhʊd ‖'brʌðəhʊd/ n (a) (fellowship) fraternidad f (b) (association) hermandad f; (Relig) cofradía f

brother-in-law /'brʌðərɪn,lɔː/ n (pl **brothers-in-law**) cuñado m

brotherly /'brʌðərli ‖'brʌðəli/ adj fraternal

brought /brɔːt/ past & past p of BRING

brow /braʊ/ n (a) (forehead) (liter) frente f (b) (eye~) ceja f (c) (of hill) cima f

browbeat /'braʊbiːt/ vt (past **browbeat**; past p **browbeaten** /'braʊ,biːtn̩/) intimidar

brown¹ /braʊn/ adj **-er, -est** ⟨shoe/dress/eyes⟩ marrón, café adj inv (AmC, Chi, Méx), carmelito (Col); ⟨hair⟩ castaño; ⟨skin/person⟩ (naturally) moreno; (suntanned) bronceado; **to get ~** broncearse

brown² n marrón m, café m (AmC, Chi, Méx), carmelito m (Col)

brown³ vt (a) (Culin) dorar (b) (tan) broncear

brown bread n pan m negro or (Esp) moreno

brownie /'braʊni/ n [1] (cake) bizcocho de chocolate y nueces [2] **Brownie**, (BrE) **Brownie (Guide)** alita f

brown: ~ **paper** n papel m de estraza; ~ **rice** n arroz m integral; ~ **sugar** n azúcar m moreno, azúcar f morena

browse /braʊz/ vi (look) mirar (en una tienda, catálogo etc); **she was browsing through a magazine** estaba hojeando una revista

browser /'braʊzər ‖'braʊzə(r)/ n (Comput) navegador m

bruise¹ /bruːz/ n moretón m, cardenal m, morado m (Esp, Ven)

bruise² vt ⟨body/arm⟩ contusionar (frml); ⟨fruit⟩ magullar, mallugar* (Méx, Ven)

brunch /brʌntʃ/ n (colloq) brunch m (combinación de desayuno y almuerzo)

brunette /bruː'net/ n morena f, morocha f (CS)

brunt /brʌnt/ n: **to bear** o **take the ~ of sth** sufrir algo

brush¹ /brʌʃ/ n [1] (for cleaning) cepillo m; (for hair) (paint~) pincel m; (large) brocha f [2] (of fox) cola f [3] (a) (act): **I gave my hair a ~** me cepillé el pelo (b) (faint touch) roce m (c) (encounter) ~ **WITH sth/sb** ⟨with the law/the police⟩ roce m CON algo/algn [4] (scrub) maleza f

brush² vt (a) (clean, groom) ⟨jacket/hair⟩ cepillar; **to ~ one's teeth** lavarse los dientes (b) (sweep): **he ~ed the crumbs off the table** quitó las migas de la mesa (c) (touch lightly) rozar*
■ ~ vi **to ~ AGAINST sth/sb** rozar* algo/a algn
■ **brush off** (a) [v + o + adv, v + adv + o] ⟨mud/ hair⟩ quitar (cepillando) (b) ⟨advances/ suggestions⟩ no hacer* caso de
■ **brush up** (a) [v + o + adv, v + adv + o] (colloq) darle* un repaso a (b) [v + adv] **to ~ up ON sth** darle* un repaso A algo

brusque /brʌsk ‖brʊsk/ adj brusco

Brussels /'brʌsəlz/ n Bruselas f

brussels sprout, Brussels Sprout n col f or (AmS) repollito m de Bruselas

brutal /'bruːtl̩/ adj brutal

brutality /bruː'tæləti/ n (pl **-ties**) brutalidad f

brutally /'bruːtl̩i/ adv (a) (cruelly) ⟨attack/treat⟩ brutalmente (b) (mercilessly) ⟨frank⟩ crudamente

brute¹ /bruːt/ n (colloq) (a) (person) animal mf (fam) (b) (animal) bestia f (fam)

brute² adj (before n) ~ **force** fuerza f bruta

BS n (AmE), **BSc** n (BrE) = **Bachelor of Science**

BST = **British Summer Time**

bubble¹ /'bʌbl̩/ n (of air, gas) burbuja f; (of soap) pompa f

bubble² vi [1] (form bubbles) «lava» bullir*; «champagne» burbujear [2] «person»: **she ~s with enthusiasm** rebosa (de) entusiasmo

bubble: ~ **bath** n baño m de burbujas or espuma; ~ **gum** n chicle m (de globos), chicle m de bomba (Col, Ven), chicle m globero (Ur); ~**-wrapped** adj envuelto en plástico con burbujas

bubbly /'bʌbli/ adj **-lier, -liest** (a) ⟨person⟩ lleno de vida; ⟨personality⟩ efervescente (b) (full of bubbles) burbujeante

Bucharest /'buːkərest ‖,buːkə'rest/ n Bucarest m

buck¹ /bʌk/ n [1] (male deer) ciervo m (macho); (male rabbit) conejo m (macho) [2] (dollar) (esp AmE colloq) dólar m, verde m (AmL fam) [3] (responsibility): **to pass the ~** (colloq) pasar la pelota (fam); **the ~ stops here** la responsabilidad es mía (or nuestra etc)

buck² vi «horse» corcovear
■ ~ vt ⟨trend⟩ resistirse a

■ **buck up** (colloq) **1** [v + adv] (become cheerful) levantar el ánimo **2** [v + o + adv, v + adv + o] (cheer up) ‹person› levantarle el ánimo a

bucket /'bʌkət ‖'bʌkɪt/ n balde m or (Esp) cubo m or (Méx) cubeta f or (Ven) tobo m; **to kick the ∼** (colloq & hum) estirar la pata (fam & hum)

buckle¹ /'bʌkəl/ n hebilla f

buckle² vt abrochar
■ **∼** vi (bend, crumple) «wheel/metal» torcerse*; **his knees ∼d beneath him** se le doblaron las rodillas

bud /bʌd/ n brote m, yema f; (of flower) capullo m

Budapest /'bu:dəpest ‖,bu:də'pest/ n Budapest m

Buddha /'bu:də ‖'bʊdə/ n Buda m

Buddhism /'bu:dɪzəm ‖'bʊdɪzəm/ n budismo m

Buddhist¹ /'bu:dəst ‖'bʊdɪst/ n budista mf

Buddhist² adj budista

budding /'bʌdɪŋ/ adj (before n) ‹artist/genius› en ciernes

buddy /'bʌdi/ n (pl **-dies**) (AmE colloq) amigo m, compinche m (fam), cuate m (Méx fam)

budge /bʌdʒ/ vi (usu with neg) (a) (move) moverse* (b) (change opinion) cambiar de opinión
■ **∼** vt (a) (move) correr (b) (persuade) convencer*

budgerigar /'bʌdʒərigɑ:r ‖'bʌdʒərigɑ:(r)/ n periquito m

budget¹ /'bʌdʒət ‖'bʌdʒɪt/ n presupuesto m

budget² vi administrarse; **to learn to ∼** aprender a administrar el dinero; **I hadn't ∼ed for staying in a hotel** no había contado con gastos de hotel

budgie /'bʌdʒi/ n (BrE colloq) periquito m

buff¹ /bʌf/ n (colloq) aficionado, -da m,f; **film ∼** cinéfilo, -la m,f

buff² vt ‹metal› pulir; ‹shoes› sacar* brillo a

buffalo /'bʌfələʊ/ n (pl **-loes** or **-los**) (a) (wild ox) búfalo m; (water ∼) búfalo m de agua, carabao m (b) (bison) (AmE) bisonte m

buffer /'bʌfər ‖'bʌfə(r)/ n **1** (a) (AmE Auto) parachoques m, paragolpes m (RPl) (b) (BrE Rail) (on train) tope m; (in station) parachoques m; (before n) **∼ state** estado m tapón **2** (Comput) memoria f intermedia

buffet¹ /bə'feɪ ‖'bʊfeɪ, 'bʌfeɪ/ n **1** (meal) buffet m **2** (BrE) (a) (in train) bar m; (before n) **∼ car** (also AmE) coche m restaurante, coche m comedor (b) (cafeteria) bar m (en una estación)

buffet² /'bʌfət ‖'bʌfɪt/ vt zarandear, sacudir

bug¹ /bʌg/ n **1** (a) (biting insect) chinche f or m; (any insect) (esp AmE) bicho m **2** (germ, disease) (colloq): **he picked up a stomach ∼** se agarró algo al estómago; **she got the travel ∼** le entró la fiebre de los viajes **3** (listening device) (colloq) micrófono m oculto

bug² vt **-gg-** (colloq) **1** ‹room/telephone› colocar* micrófonos ocultos en **2** (bother, irritate) fastidiar

bugger /'bʌgər ‖'bʌgə(r)/ n (BrE vulg) hijo, -ja m,f de puta (vulg)

buggy /'bʌgi/ n (pl **-gies**) **1** (horse-drawn vehicle) calesa f **2** (baby ∼) (baby carriage) (AmE) cochecito m; (pushchair) (BrE) sillita f de paseo (plegable)

bugle /'bju:gəl/ n clarín m

build¹ /bɪld/ (past & past p **built**) vt ‹house/ road/ship/wall› construir*; ‹fire/nest› hacer*
■ **build up** **1** [v + o + adv, v + adv + o] (a) (make

bigger, stronger) fortalecer* (b) (accumulate) ‹supplies/experience› acumular; ‹reserves› acrecentar* (c) (develop) ‹reputation› forjarse; **to ∼ up one's hopes** hacerse* ilusiones; **he built the firm up from nothing** levantó la empresa de la nada **2** [v + adv] (increase) ‹pressure/noise› ir* en aumento; **the tension ∼s up to a climax** la tensión va en aumento hasta llegar a un punto culminante

build² n complexión f

builder /'bɪldər ‖'bɪldə(r)/ n albañil mf; (contractor) contratista mf

building /'bɪldɪŋ/ n (a) (edifice) edificio m (b) (construction) construcción f; (before n) **∼ contractor** contratista mf (de obras); **∼ site** obra f

building society n (in UK) sociedad f de crédito hipotecario

buildup /'bɪldʌp/ n (a) (accumulation) acumulación f; (of tension, pressure) aumento m (b) (of troops) concentración f (c) (publicity) propaganda f

built /bɪlt/ past & past p of BUILD¹

built: **∼-in** /'bɪlt'ɪn/ adj (before n) ‹bookcase/ desk› empotrado; ‹equipment› fijo; ‹mechanism/ feature› incorporado; **∼-up** /'bɪlt'ʌp/ adj (before n) ‹area› urbanizado

bulb /bʌlb/ n **1** (Bot, Hort) (of flower) bulbo m, papa f (Chi); (of garlic) cabeza f **2** (light ∼) bombilla f or (Méx) foco m or (Col, Ven) bombillo m or (RPl) bombita f or lamparita f or (Chi) ampolleta f or (AmC) bujía f

bulbous /'bʌlbəs/ adj ‹growth› bulboso; ‹nose› protuberante

Bulgaria /bʌl'geriə ‖bʌl'geəriə/ n Bulgaria f

Bulgarian¹ /bʌl'geriən ‖bʌl'geəriən/ adj búlgaro

Bulgarian² n (a) (person) búlgaro, -ra m,f (b) (language) búlgaro m

bulge¹ /bʌldʒ/ n bulto m

bulge² vi (a) (protrude) sobresalir*; **the bag was bulging with books** la bolsa estaba repleta de libros (b) **bulging** pres p ‹pocket/bag› repleto; ‹eyes› saltón

bulimia (nervosa) /bju:'li:miə(nɜ:r'vəʊsə) ‖bju:'lɪmiə(nɜ:'vəʊsə)/ n bulimia f (nerviosa)

bulk /bʌlk/ n **1** (a) (Busn) (large quantity): **in ∼** en grandes cantidades (b) (large mass) mole f **2** (largest part): **the ∼ of sth** la mayor parte de algo

bulky /'bʌlki/ adj **-kier, -kiest** ‹package› voluminoso; ‹person› corpulento; ‹sweater› (AmE) grueso

bull /bʊl/ n toro m

bull: **∼dog** n bull(l)dog m; **∼doze** vt demoler*; **∼dozer** /'bʊldəʊzər ‖'bʊldəʊzə(r)/ n bulldozer m, topadora f (Arg)

bullet /'bʊlət ‖'bʊlɪt/ n bala f

bulletin /'bʊlətn ‖'bʊlətɪn/ n (notice) anuncio m; (newsletter) boletín m; (report) (Journ) boletín m (informativo)

bulletin board n (AmE) tablero m or (Esp) tablón m de anuncios, cartelera f (AmL), diario m mural (Chi)

bulletproof /'bʊlətpru:f ‖'bʊlɪtpru:f/ adj ‹vest› antibalas adj inv; ‹vehicle› blindado

bull: ~**fight** n corrida f de toros; ~**fighter** n torero, -ra m,f, ~**fighting** n (deporte m de) los toros; (art) tauromaquia f; ~**frog** n rana f toro

bullion /'bʊljən ‖'bʊljən/ n: **gold/silver** ~ oro/plata en lingotes

bullock /'bʊlək/ n (a) (castrated bull) buey m (b) (young bull) (esp AmE) novillo m

bull: ~**ring** n plaza f de toros; ~**seye** n diana f; ~**shit** /'bʊlʃɪt/ n (vulg) sandeces fpl (fam), pendejadas (AmL exc CS vulg), gilipolleces fpl (Esp arg), huevadas fpl (Andes, Ven vulg), boludeces fpl (Col, RPl vulg), mamadas fpl (Méx vulg)

bully¹ /'bʊli/ n (pl **-lies**) matón, -tona m,f

bully² vt **-lies, -lying, -lied** intimidar

bum /bʌm/ n (colloq) **1** (a) (worthless person) vago, -ga m,f (fam) (b) (vagrant) (AmE) vagabundo, -da m,f **2** (buttocks) (BrE) trasero m (fam), culo m (fam o vulg), traste m (CS fam), poto m (Chi, Per fam)

bumblebee /'bʌmbəl‚bi:/ n abejorro m

bumbling /'bʌmblɪŋ/ adj torpe

bump¹ /bʌmp/ n **1** (blow) golpe m; (jolt) sacudida f; (collision) topetazo m **2** (lump — in surface) bulto m; (— on head) chichón m; (— on road) bache m

bump² vt: I ~ed my elbow on o against the door me di en el codo con or contra la puerta; I ~ed the post as I was reversing choqué con or contra el poste al dar marcha atrás

■ ~ vi (hit, knock) to ~ (**AGAINST sth**) darse* or chocar* (**CONTRA** or **CON** algo)

■ **bump into** [v + prep + o] (a) (collide with) darse* or chocar* con (b) (meet by chance) (colloq) toparse or tropezarse* con

bumper¹ /'bʌmpər ‖'bʌmpə(r)/ n (Auto) parachoques m, paragolpes m (AmL)

bumper² adj (before n) ‹crop/year› récord adj inv; ‹edition› extra; ‹pack› gigante

bumper car n coche m de choque, autito m chocador (RPl), carro m loco (Andes), carrito m chocón (Méx, Ven)

bumpkin /'bʌmpkɪn/ n: (country) ~ pueblerino, -na m,f, paleto, -ta m,f (Esp fam), pajuerano, -na m,f (RPl fam)

bumpy /'bʌmpi/ adj **-pier, -piest** ‹surface› desigual; ‹road› lleno de baches; **we had a** ~ **flight** el avión se movió mucho

bun /bʌn/ n **1** (a) (sweetened) bollo m (b) (bread roll) panecillo m, pancito m (CS), bolillo m (Méx) **2** (hairstyle) moño m, rodete m (RPl), chongo m (Méx) **3** **buns** pl (AmE colloq) trasero m (fam), culo m (fam o vulg), traste m (CS fam), poto m (Chi, Per fam)

bunch /bʌntʃ/ n (a) (of flowers) ramo m, bonche m (Méx); (small) ramillete m; (of bananas) racimo m, penca f (Méx), cacho m (RPl); (of grapes) racimo m; (of keys) manojo m (b) (group) grupo m; **they're an odd** ~ son gente de lo más rara

bundle¹ /'bʌndl/ n (of clothes) lío m, fardo m, atado m (AmL); (of newspapers, letters) paquete m; (of money) fajo m; (of sticks) haz m, atado m (AmL)

bundle² vt (a) (make into a bundle) liar*, atar (b)

(push) (+ adv compl): **she** ~**d them off to school** los despachó al colegio; **they** ~**d him into the car** lo metieron a empujones en el coche

bung /bʌŋ/ n tapón m

bungalow /'bʌŋgələʊ/ n casa f de una planta

bungle /'bʌŋgl/ vt echar a perder; **a** ~**d attempt** un intento fallido

bungling /'bʌŋglɪŋ/ adj (before n, no comp) torpe

bunion /'bʌnjən/ n juanete m

bunk /bʌŋk/ n litera f

■ **bunk off** ▶ SKIVE OFF

bunk bed n litera f

bunny (pl **-nies**), **bunny rabbit** /'bʌni/ n (used to or by children) conejito m (fam)

bunting /'bʌntɪŋ/ n (esp AmE) tela usada para la confección de banderas

buoy /bɔɪ, 'bu:i ‖bɔɪ/ n boya f

■ **buoy up** [v + o + adv, v + adv + o] (a) ‹boat/person› mantener* a flote (b) (keep cheerful) animar

buoyant /'bɔɪənt/ adj (a) (able to float) flotante (b) ‹mood/spirits› optimista (c) (Fin) ‹currency› fuerte; ‹market› alcista

burble /'bɜːrbl ‖'bɜːbəl/ vi (a) «stream/spring» borbotar, borbotear (b) (talk meaninglessly) parlotear (fam), cotorrear (fam); (talk excitedly) hablar atropelladamente

burden¹ /'bɜːrdn ‖'bɜːdn/ n carga f

burden² vt cargar*; **I don't want to** ~ **you with my problems** no te quiero preocupar con mis problemas

bureau /'bjʊrəʊ ‖'bjʊərəʊ/ n (pl **bureaus** or **bureaux** /-z/) **1** (a) (agency) agencia f (b) (government department) (AmE) departamento m **2** (a) (chest of drawers) (AmE) cómoda f (b) (desk) (BrE) buró m, escritorio m

bureaucracy /bjʊ'rɑːkrəsi ‖bjʊə'rɒkrəsi/ n (pl **-cies**) burocracia f

bureaucrat /'bjʊrəkræt ‖'bjʊərəkræt/ n burócrata mf

bureaucratic /‚bjʊrə'krætɪk ‖‚bjʊərə'krætɪk/ adj burocrático

bureau de change /'bjʊrəʊdə'ʃɑːnʒ ‖'bjʊərəʊdə'ʃɑ̃ʒ/ n (pl **bureaux de change**) (casa f de) cambio m

burgeon /'bɜːrdʒən ‖'bɜːdʒən/ vi (liter) florecer*

burglar /'bɜːrglər ‖'bɜːglə(r)/ n ladrón, -drona m,f; (before n) ~ **alarm** alarma f antirrobo

burglarize /'bɜːrgləraɪz ‖'bɜːgləraɪz/ vt (AmE) robar

burglary /'bɜːrgləri ‖'bɜːgləri/ n (pl **-ries**) robo m (con allanamiento de morada o escalamiento)

burgle /'bɜːrgl ‖'bɜːgəl/ vt robar

burial /'beriəl/ n entierro m

Burkina Faso /bɜːr'kiːnəˈfæsəʊ ‖‚bɜːkiːnəˈfæsəʊ/ n Burkina Faso m

burlesque /bɜːr'lesk ‖bɜː'lesk/ n obra f burlesca

burly /'bɜːrli ‖'bɜːli/ adj **-lier, -liest** fornido

Burma /'bɜːrmə ‖'bɜːmə/ n Birmanía f

Burmese[1] /'bɜːr'miːz ‖bɜː'miːz/ adj birmano

Burmese[2] n (pl ∼) (a) (person) birmano, -na m,f (b) (language) birmano m

burn[1] /bɜːrn ‖bɜːn/ (past & past p **burned** or **burnt**) vi [1] (a) ⟨fire/building/wood/coal⟩ arder; ⟨food⟩ quemarse (b) (in sun) ⟨skin⟩ quemarse [2] (sting) ⟨eyes/wound⟩ escocer*, arder (esp AmL); **a ∼ing sensation** un escozor, un ardor (esp AmL)

■ ∼ vt (a) ⟨letter/rubbish/food⟩ quemar; ⟨building/town⟩ incendiar; **I ∼ed a hole in my sleeve** me quemé la manga (con un cigarrillo etc) (b) (injure) quemar

■ **burn down** [1] [v + o + adv, v + adv + o] incendiar [2] [v + adv] incendiarse

burn[2] n quemadura f

burner /'bɜːrnər ‖'bɜːnə(r)/ n quemador m

burning /'bɜːrnɪŋ ‖'bɜːnɪŋ/ adj (before n) (a) (hot) ⟨sand⟩ ardiente; ⟨sun⟩ abrasador (b) (intense) ⟨desire⟩ ardiente; ⟨hatred⟩ violento

burnt /bɜːrnt ‖bɜːnt/ past & past p of BURN[1]

burp v eructar

burrow[1] /'bɜːroʊ ‖'bʌrəʊ/ n madriguera f; (of rabbits) conejera f

burrow[2] vi cavar

bursar /'bɜːrsər ‖'bɜːsə(r)/ n administrador, -dora m,f

burst[1] /bɜːrst ‖bɜːst/ (past & past p **burst**) vi [1] «balloon/tire» reventarse*; «pipe» reventar*, romperse*; «dam» romperse*; **to ∼ open** abrirse* de golpe [2] (move suddenly) (+ adv compl): **he ∼ into the room** entró de sopetón en la habitación; **they ∼ through the police cordon** rompieron el cordón policial

■ ∼ vt ⟨balloon/bubble⟩ reventar*; **the river ∼ its banks** el río se desbordó

■ **burst into** [v + prep + o]: **to ∼ into tears** echarse a llorar; **to ∼ into song** ponerse* a cantar; **to ∼ into flames** estallar en llamas

burst[2] n [1] (of applause) salva f; (of activity) arrebato m; (of gunfire) ráfaga f [2] (of pipe) rotura f

bursting /'bɜːrstɪŋ ‖'bɜːstɪŋ/ adj (pred, no comp) **to be ∼** (WITH sth) estar* repleto (DE algo); **he was ∼ with energy** rebosaba (de) energía

bury /'beri/ **buries, burying, buried** vt (inter) enterrar*; **the village was buried by the avalanche** el pueblo fue sepultado por la avalancha; **he buried his head in his hands** ocultó la cabeza entre las manos

■ v refl **to ∼ oneself** IN sth ⟨in one's work/one's books⟩ enfrascarse* EN algo

bus /bʌs/ n (pl **buses** or (AmE also) **busses**) (Transp) (a) (local) autobús m, bus m (AmL), camión m (AmC, Méx), colectivo m (Arg), ómnibus m (Per, Ur), micro f (Chi), guagua f (Cu); (before n) ∼ **conductor** cobrador, -dora m,f, guarda mf (RPl) de autobuses; ∼ **driver** conductor, -tora m,f or chofer mf or (Esp) chófer mf de autobús, camionero, -ra m,f (AmC, Méx), colectivero, -ra m,f (Arg), microbusero, -ra m,f (Chi); ∼ **stop** parada f or (AmL exc RPl) paradero m de autobús (or bus etc) (b) (long-distance) autobús m, autocar m (Esp), pullman m (CS)

bush /bʊʃ/ n [1] (shrub) arbusto m; **to beat about the ∼** andarse* con rodeos [2] (wild country) **the ∼** el monte

bushy /'bʊʃi/ adj **bushier, bushiest** ⟨beard⟩ poblado; ⟨eyebrows⟩ tupido; ⟨undergrowth⟩ espeso

busily /'bɪzəli ‖'bɪzɪli/ adv ⟨work⟩ afanosamente

business /'bɪznəs ‖'bɪznɪs/ n [1] (Busn) (a) (world of commerce, finance) negocios mpl; (before n) ∼ **studies** (ciencias fpl) empresariales fpl (b) (commercial activity, trading) comercio m; **the firm has been in ∼ for 50 years** la empresa tiene 50 años de actividad comercial; **they went into ∼ together** montaron un negocio juntos; **she's away on ∼** está de viaje por negocios; **to go out of ∼** cerrar*; **to get down to ∼** ir* al grano; **to mean ∼** decir* algo muy en serio; (before n) ⟨appointment/lunch⟩ de trabajo, de negocios; ∼ **hours** horas fpl de oficina; ∼ **letter** carta f comercial; ∼ **trip** viaje m de negocios (c) (custom, clients): **to lose ∼** perder* clientes or clientela [2] (a) (firm) negocio m, empresa f (b) (branch of commerce): **I'm in the antiques ∼** trabajo en la compra y venta de antigüedades; **the music ∼** la industria de la música

[3] (rightful occupation, concern) asunto m; **mind your own ∼!** ¡no te metas en lo que no te importa!; **that's none of your ∼** eso no es asunto tuyo [4] (affair, situation, activity) (colloq) (no pl) asunto m; **what's all this ∼ about you leaving?** ¿qué es eso de que te vas?

business: ∼**like** adj ⟨person/manner⟩ (serious) formal; (efficient) eficiente; ⟨discussion⟩ serio; ∼**man** /'bɪznəsmæn ‖'bɪznɪsmən/ n (pl **-men** /-men ‖-mən/) empresario m, hombre m de negocios; ∼**woman** n empresaria f, mujer f de negocios

busker /'bʌskər ‖'bʌskə(r)/ n (BrE) músico m callejero

bust[1] /bʌst/ vt (a) (past & past p **busted** or (BrE also) **bust**) (break) (colloq) romper* (b) (past & past p **busted**) (raid) (sl) ⟨person⟩ agarrar (fam), trincar* (Esp fam); ⟨premises⟩ hacer* una redada en

bust[2] n (a) (sculpture) busto m (b) (bosom) busto m, pecho m

bust[3] adj (bankrupt) (colloq): **to go ∼** quebrar*, ir(se)* a la bancarrota, fundirse (Per, RPl fam)

bustle[1] /'bʌsl/ vi (a) (move busily): **to ∼ around** ir* de aquí para allá (b) (be crowded, lively) «street/store» **to ∼** (WITH sth) bullir* (DE algo)

bustle[2] n ajetreo m

bustling /'bʌslɪŋ/ adj ⟨street/shop⟩ animado

bust-up /'bʌstʌp/ n (a) (breakup) ruptura f (b) (quarrel) (BrE colloq) pelea f, bronca f (Esp)

busy[1] /'bɪzi/ adj **busier, busiest** [1] ⟨person⟩ ocupado; **the children keep me very ∼** los niños me tienen muy atareada [2] ⟨street/market⟩ concurrido; **I've had a ∼ day** he tenido un día de mucho trabajo; **a ∼ road** una carretera con mucho tráfico [3] (AmE Telec) ocupado (AmL), comunicando (Esp); **the ∼ signal** la señal de ocupado or (Esp) de comunicando

busy[2] v refl **busies, busying, busied**: **to ∼ oneself** WITH sth entretenerse* CON algo

busybody /'bɪzi,bɑːdi ‖'bɪzi,bɒdi/ n (pl **-dies**) (colloq) entrometido, -da m,f, metomentodo mf (fam)

b

but¹ /bʌt, *weak form* bət/ *conj* pero; **not ... ~ ...** no ... sino ...; **~ then you never were very ambitious, were you?** pero la verdad es que tú nunca fuiste muy ambicioso ¿no?; **not only did she hit him, ~ she also ...** no solo le pegó, sino que también ...

but² *prep*: **everyone ~ me** todos menos *or* excepto yo; **the last street ~ one** la penúltima calle; **~ for them, we'd have lost everything** de no haber sido por ellos, habríamos perdido todo

but³ *adv* (frml): **we can ~ try** con intentarlo no se pierde nada

butane /'bju:tem/ *n* butano *m*

butcher¹ /'bʊtʃər ||'bʊtʃə(r)/ *n* **(a)** (meat dealer) carnicero, -ra *m,f*; **~'s (shop)** carnicería *f* **(b)** (murderer) asesino, -na *m,f*

butcher² *vt* **(a)** ‹*cattle/pig*› matar, carnear (CS) **(b)** ‹*people*› masacrar

butler /'bʌtlər ||'bʌtlə(r)/ *n* mayordomo *m*

butt¹ /bʌt/ *n* **1** **(a)** (of rifle) culata *f* **(b) ~ (end)** (blunt end) extremo *m* **(c)** (of cigarette) colilla *f*, bacha *f* (Méx fam) **2** (target of jokes or criticism) blanco *m* **3** **(a)** (from goat) topetazo *m* **(b)** (head **~**) cabezazo *m* **4** (buttocks) (AmE colloq) trasero *m* (fam), culo *m* (fam *o* vulg), traste *m* (CS fam), poto *m* (Chi, Per fam)

butt² *vt* «*goat*» topetar

▪ **butt in** [*v* + *adv*] interrumpir

butter¹ /'bʌtər ||'bʌtə(r)/ *n* mantequilla *f*, manteca *f* (RPl)

butter² *vt* ‹*bread*› untar con mantequilla *or* (RPl) manteca

butter: ~ bean *n* **(a)** (dried bean) *tipo de frijol blanco*, poroto *m* de manteca (RPl) **(b)** (wax bean) (AmE) *tipo de frijol fresco con vaina amarilla*; **~cup** *n* ranúnculo *m*; **~fly** *n* **(a)** (Zool) mariposa *f*; **to have ~flies (in one's stomach)** ponerse*/estar* nervioso **(b)** (swimming stroke) estilo *m* mariposa

buttock /'bʌtək/ *n* nalga *f*

button¹ /'bʌtn̩/ *n* botón *m*

button² *vt* abotonar

▪ **~** *vi* abotonarse

▪ **button up** [*v* + *o* + *adv*, *v* + *adv* + *o*] abotonar

buttonhole /'bʌtn̩həʊl/ *n* **(a)** (Clothing) ojal *m* **(b)** (flower) (BrE) *flor que se lleva en el ojal*

buttress /'bʌtrəs ||'bʌtrɪs/ *n* (Archit) contrafuerte *m*; **flying ~** arbotante *m*

buxom /'bʌksəm/ *adj* con mucho busto *or* pecho

buy¹ /baɪ/ (*past & past p* **bought**) *vt* comprar; **to ~ sb sth** comprarle algo a algn; **to ~ sth FROM sb** comprarle algo A algn; **to ~ sth FOR sb** comprar algo PARA algn

▪ **~** *vi* comprar; **to ~ FROM sb** comprarle A algn

▪ **buy off** [*v* + *o* + *adv*, *v* + *adv* + *o*] sobornar

▪ **buy out** [*v* + *o* + *adv*, *v* + *adv* + *o*] ‹*partner/shareholder*› comprarle su parte a

▪ **buy up** [*v* + *adv* + *o*] comprarse todas las existencias de

buy² *n* compra *f*

buyer /'baɪər ||'baɪə(r)/ *n* **(a)** (customer) comprador, -dora *m,f* **(b)** (buying agent) encargado, -da *m,f* de compras

buzz¹ /bʌz/ *n* (of insect) zumbido *m*; (of voices) rumor *m*; (as signal) zumbido *m*

buzz² *vi* «*insect*» zumbar; «*telephone/alarm clock*» sonar*; **my ears were ~ing** me zumbaban los oídos

buzzard /'bʌzərd ||'bʌzəd/ *n* **(a)** (hawk) (esp BrE) águila *f*‡ ratonera **(b)** (vulture) (AmE) aura *f*‡, gallinazo *m*, zopilote *m* (AmC, Méx)

buzzer /'bʌzər ||'bʌzə(r)/ *n* timbre *m*

by¹ /baɪ/ *prep* **1** (indicating agent, cause) (*with passive verbs*) por [*The passive voice is, however, less common in Spanish than it is in English*] **she was brought up ~ her grandmother** la crio su abuela; **a play ~ Shakespeare** una obra de Shakespeare

2 **(a)** (indicating means, method): **made ~ hand** hecho a mano; **to travel ~ car/train/plane** viajar en coche/tren/avión; **to pay ~ credit card** pagar* con tarjeta de crédito; **I'll begin ~ introducing myself** empezaré por presentarme **(b)** (owing to, from): **~ chance** por casualidad; **they have lost public support ~ being too extreme** han perdido apoyo popular por ser demasiado extremistas

3 **(a)** (at the side of, near to) al lado de; **it's right ~ the door** está justo al lado de la puerta **(b)** (to hand) (AmE): **I always keep some money ~ me** siempre llevo algo de dinero encima

4 **(a)** (past): **I said hello, but he walked right ~ me** lo saludé pero él pasó de largo **(b)** (via, through) por; **~ land/sea/air** por tierra/mar/avión

5 **(a)** (indicating rate) por; **we are paid ~ the hour** nos pagan por hora(s) **(b)** (indicating extent of difference): **she broke the record ~ several seconds** batió el récord en *or* por varios segundos **(c)** (indicating gradual progression): **one ~ one** uno por uno

6 **(a)** (not later than): **he told her to be home ~ 11** le dijo que volviera antes de las 11; **they should be there ~ now** ya deberían estar allí; **~ the time he arrived, Ann had left** cuando llegó, Ann se había ido **(b)** (during, at) **~ day/night** de día/noche

7 (according to): **~ that clock it's almost half past** según ese reloj son casi y media; **that's fine ~ me** por mí no hay problema

8 (Math) por; **multiply two ~ three** multiplica dos por tres; **a room 20ft ~ 12ft** una habitación de 20 pies por 12

9 **by oneself** (alone, without assistance) solo

by² *adv* **(a)** (past): **she rushed ~ without seeing me** pasó corriendo y no me vio; **they watched the parade march ~** vieron pasar el desfile **(b)** (to sb's residence): **call *o* stop ~ on your way to work** pasa por casa de camino al trabajo **(c)** (*in phrases*) **by and by**: **~ and ~ they came to the clearing** al poco rato llegaron al claro; **by and large** por lo general, en general

bye, (AmE) **'bye** /baɪ/ *interj* (colloq) ¡adiós!, ¡chao *or* chau! (esp AmL fam)

bye-bye /'baɪ'baɪ/ *interj* (colloq) ¡adiós!, ¡chaucito! (AmL fam), ¡chaíto! (Chi fam)

by: ~gone *adj* (liter) (*before n*) ‹*age/days*› de antaño (liter); ***to let ~gones be ~gones*** olvidar el pasado; **~law** *n* (BrE) ordenanza *f* municipal

bypass¹ /'baɪpæs ||'baɪpɑ:s/ *n* **(a)** (road) (BrE) carretera *f* de circunvalación **(b)** (Med) bypass *m*

bypass² *vt* **(a)** (circumvent) ‹*person/difficulty*› eludir **(b)** (Transp) «*road*» circunvalar; «*driver*» evitar entrar en

by: ~-product *n* (in manufacture) subproducto *m*; (consequence) consecuencia *f*; **~road** *n* carretera *f* secundaria; **~stander** /'baɪˌstændər ‖'baɪˌstændə(r)/ *n*: **they opened fire, killing innocent ~standers** abrieron fuego y mataron a varias personas inocentes *or* a varios transeúntes

byte /baɪt/ *n* byte *m*, octeto *m*

by: **~way** *n* camino *m* (*apartado*); **~word** *n*: **to be a ~word FOR sth** ser* sinónimo DE algo; **~-your-leave** /'baɪjər'liːv ‖ˌbaɪjɔː'liːv/ *n*: **without so much as a ~-your-leave** sin (ni) siquiera pedir permiso

Cc

C, c /siː/ *n* **(a)** (letter) C, c *f* **(b)** (Mus) re *m*
c (a) (Corresp) = **copy to (b)** (in US) (= **cent(s)**) centavo(s) *m*(*pl*) **(c)** = **circa**
C (= **Celsius** *or* **centigrade**) C
ca = **circa**
CA, Ca = California
cab /kæb/ *n* **1** (taxi) taxi *m*; (*before n*) **~ driver** taxista *mf* **2** (driver's compartment) cabina *f*
cabaret /ˌkæbə'reɪ ‖'kæbəreɪ/ *n* cabaret *m*
cabbage /'kæbɪdʒ/ *n* repollo *m*, col *f*
cabin /'kæbən ‖'kæbɪn/ *n* **(a)** (hut) cabaña *f* **(b)** (Naut) camarote *m* **(c)** (Aerosp, Auto, Aviat) cabina *f*
cabinet /'kæbənət ‖'kæbɪnɪt/ *n* **1** (cupboard) armario *m*; (with glass front) vitrina *f* **2** *also* **Cabinet** (Govt) gabinete *m* (ministerial)
cable /'keɪbəl/ *n* **(a)** (Elec, Naut) cable *m* **(b)** (Telec) cable *m* **(c)** ▶ CABLE TELEVISION
cable: **~ car** *n* (suspended) teleférico *m*; (funicular) funicular *m*; (streetcar) (AmE) tranvía *m*; **~ television** *n* televisión *f* por cable, cablevisión *f* (esp AmL)
caboose /kə'buːs/ *n* (AmE Rail) furgón *m* de cola
cache /kæʃ/ *n* alijo *m*
cackle /'kækəl/ *vi* «*hen*» cacarear; «*person*» reírse* socarronamente
cactus /'kæktəs/ *n* (*pl* **-ti** /-taɪ/ *or* **-tuses**) cactus *m*
caddie, caddy (*pl* **-dies**) /'kædi/ *n* caddie *mf*
cadet /kə'det/ *n* cadete *mf*
cadge /kædʒ/ (colloq) *vt* **to ~ sth FROM** *o* **OFF sb** gorronearle *or* gorrearle *or* (RPl) garronearle *or* (Chi) bolsearle algo A algn (fam)
Caesarean (section) /sɪ'zæriən ‖sɪ'zeəriən/ *n* ▶ CESAREAN (SECTION)
café, cafe /kæ'feɪ ‖'kæfeɪ/ *n* (coffee bar) café *m*, cafetería *f*; (restaurant) *restaurante económico*
cafeteria /ˌkæfə'tɪriə ‖ˌkæfə'tɪəriə/ *n* (in hospital, college) cantina *f*, cafetería *f*; (restaurant) restaurante *m* autoservicio, self-service *m*
caffeine /'kæfiːn ‖'kæfiːn/ *n* cafeína *f*
cage¹ /keɪdʒ/ *n* jaula *f*; (in basketball) canasta *f*, cesta *f*; (in ice hockey) portería *f*, meta *f*, arco *m* (Col, CS)
cage² *vt* (*usu pass*) enjaular
Cairo /'kaɪrəʊ ‖'kaɪərəʊ/ *n* El Cairo
cajole /kə'dʒəʊl/ *vt* convencer* con zalamerías
cake¹ /keɪk/ *n*(Culin) (large) pastel *m*, tarta *f*

(Esp), torta *f* (esp CS); (small, individual) pastel *m*, masa *f* (RPl); **to be a piece of ~** (colloq) ser* pan comido (fam)
cake² *vt* (*usu pass*): **our shoes were ~d with mud** teníamos los zapatos cubiertos de barro endurecido
cake tin *n* (BrE) (for baking) molde *m* (para pastel); (for storage) lata *f* (*para guardar pasteles*)
Cal = California
calamity /kə'læməti/ *n* (*pl* **-ties**) calamidad *f*
calcium /'kælsiəm/ *n* calcio *m*
calculate /'kælkjʊleɪt ‖'kælkjʊleɪt/ *vt* calcular
calculating /'kælkjəleɪtɪŋ ‖'kælkjʊleɪtɪŋ/ *adj* calculador
calculation /ˌkælkjə'leɪʃən ‖ˌkælkjʊ'leɪʃən/ *n* cálculo *m*
calculator /'kælkjəleɪtər ‖'kælkjʊleɪtə(r)/ *n* calculadora *f*
calendar /'kæləndər ‖'kælɪndə(r)/ *n* calendario *m*, almanaque *m*; (*before n*) **~ month** mes *m* (del calendario)
calf /kæf ‖kɑːf/ *n* (*pl* **calves**) **1** (Zool) **(a)** (animal) ternero, -ra *m,f*, becerro, -rra *m,f* **(b)** (leather) (piel *f or* cuero *m* de) becerro *m* **2** (Anat) pantorrilla *f*
caliber, (BrE) **calibre** /'kæləbər ‖'kælɪbə(r)/ *n* calibre *m*
Calif = California
calipers, (BrE) **callipers** /'kæləpərz ‖'kælɪpəz/ *pl n* **(a)** (for measuring) calibrador *m* **(b)** (Med) aparato *m* ortopédico (*para la pierna*)
call¹ /kɔːl/ *n* **1** (by telephone) llamada *f*; **to give sb a ~** llamar a algn (por teléfono) **2 (a)** (of person — cry) llamada *f*, llamado *m* (AmL); (— shout) grito *m* **(b)** (of animal) grito *m*; (of bird) reclamo *m* **3** (summons): **to be on ~** estar* de guardia; **beyond the ~ of duty** más de lo que el deber exigía (*or* exige *etc*) (frml) **4** (demand) llamamiento *m*, llamado *m* (AmL); **there were ~s for his resignation** pidieron su dimisión **5** (*usu with neg*) **(a)** (reason) motivo *m* **(b)** (demand) demanda *f*; **there's not much ~ for this product** no hay mucha demanda para este producto **6** (visit) visita *f* **7** (Sport) decisión *f*, cobro *m* (Chi)
call² *vt* **(a)** (shout) llamar; **to ~ the roll** *o* **register** (Educ) pasar lista **(b)** ⟨*police/taxi/doctor*⟩ llamar; ⟨*strike*⟩ llamar a, convocar* **(c)** (by telephone) llamar **(d)** (name, describe as) llamar; **we ~ her** ⋯⟶

Betty la llamamos *or* (esp AmL) le decimos Betty;
what are you going to ~ the baby? ¿qué nombre
le van a poner al bebé? **what's this** ~**ed in**
Italian? ¿cómo se llama esto en italiano?
■ ~ *vi* (a) «*person*» llamar (b) (by telephone)
llamar; **who's** ~**ing, please?** ¿de parte de quién,
por favor? (c) (visit) pasar

■ **call around** [*v* + *adv*] (a) (Telec) llamar (*a*
varias personas) (b) (visit) pasar (por casa)

■ **call at** [*v* + *prep* + *o*]: «*train*» parar en; **I** ~**ed**
at your place yesterday ayer pasé por tu casa

■ **call back** ⒈ (Telec) [*v* + *o* + *adv*] llamar más
tarde
⒉ [*v* + *adv*] (Telec) volver* a llamar

■ **call for** [*v* + *prep* + *o*] (a) (require) requerir*,
exigir* (b) (demand) pedir* (c)
(collect) pasar a buscar *or* a recoger

■ **call in** ⒈ [*v* + *o* + *adv*, *v* + *adv* + *o*] (a) «*expert*/
doctor» llamar (b) «*coin*/*note*» retirar de
circulación
⒉ [*v* + *adv*] **to** ~ **in** (**on sb**) pasar a ver a algn

■ **call off** [*v* + *o* + *adv*, *v* + *adv* + *o*] (a) (cancel)
suspender (b) «*dog*» llamar

■ **call on** [*v* + *prep* + *o*] (a) (visit) pasar a ver a
(b) ▶ CALL UPON

■ **call out** [*v* + *o* + *adv*, *v* + *adv* + *o*] (a) «*fire*
brigade/*doctor*» llamar (b) (utter): **he** ~**ed out her**
name la llamó

■ **call round** [*v* + *adv*] (BrE) ▶ CALL AROUND

■ **call up** [*v* + *o* + *adv*, *v* + *adv* + *o*] (a) «*spirits*»
invocar* (b) (telephone) (esp AmE) llamar (c) (Mil)
(*often pass*) llamar (a filas)

■ **call upon** [*v* + *prep* + *o*] (a) (invite): **to** ~ (**on**)
sb to speak dar* la palabra a algn (b) (appeal to)
apelar a

call:~ **box** *n* (BrE) cabina *f* telefónica; ~
center, (BrE) ~ **centre** *n* (Telec) centro *m* de
llamadas

caller /'kɔːlər ‖ 'kɔːlə(r)/ *n*: **we didn't have many**
~**s** no vino mucha gente; (Telec) no tuvimos *or* no
hubo muchas llamadas; **the** ~ **didn't leave her**
name la persona que llamó no dejó su nombre

callipers *n* (BrE) ▶ CALIPERS

callous /'kæləs/ *adj* insensible, cruel

callus /'kæləs/ *n* (*pl* -**luses**) (Med) callo *m*

calm[1] /kɑːm/ *adj* -**er**, -**est** «*sea*» en calma,
calmo (esp AmL); «*person*/*voice*» tranquilo, calmo
(esp AmL)

calm[2] *vt* tranquilizar*, calmar
■ **calm down** (a) [*v* + *o* + *adv*, *v* + *adv* + *o*]
tranquilizar*, calmar (b) [*v* + *adv*]
tranquilizarse*; ~ **down!** ¡tranquilízate!,
¡tranquilo!

calm[3] *n* calma *f*

calmly /'kɑːmli/ *adv* con calma

Calor Gas® /'kælər ‖ 'kælə(r)/ *n* (BrE) (gas *m*)
butano *m*, supergás® *m* (RPl)

calorie /'kæləri/ *n* (Culin) (kilo)caloría *f*

calves /kævz ‖ kɑːvz/ *pl of* CALF

camcorder /'kæm,kɔːrdər ‖ 'kæm,kɔːdə(r)/ *n*
videocámara *f*, camcórder *m*

came /keɪm/ *past of* COME

camel /'kæməl/ *n* camello *m*

cameo /'kæmiəʊ/ *n* ⒈ (jewelry) camafeo *m*
⒉ (Cin, TV) actuación *f* especial

camera /'kæmərə/ *n* cámara *f* (fotográfica),
máquina *f* fotográfica *or* de fotos

camera: ~**man** /'kæmərəmæn/ *n* (*pl* -**men**
/-men/) camarógrafo, -fa *m,f*, cameraman *mf* (esp
AmL), cámara *mf* (Esp); ~**work** *n* fotografía *f*

Cameroon /'kæmə'ruːn/ *n* Camerún *m*

camomile /'kæməmaɪl/ *n* ▶ CHAMOMILE

camouflage[1] /'kæməflɑːʒ/ *n* camuflaje *m*

camouflage[2] *vt* camuflar, camuflajear (AmL)

camp[1] /kæmp/ *n* (collection of tents, huts)
campamento *m*; (**summer**) ~ (in US) campamento
m de verano, colonia *f* de vacaciones *or* verano

camp[2] *vi* acampar; **to go** ~**ing** ir* de camping

camp[3] *adj* (a) (effeminate) amanerado,
afeminado (b) «*performance*» afectado, exagerado

campaign[1] /kæm'peɪn/ *n* campaña *f*

campaign[2] *vi* (Pol, Sociol) **to** ~ **FOR**/**AGAINST**
sth hacer* una campaña A FAVOR DE/EN CONTRA
DE algo

campaigner /kæm'peɪnər ‖ kæm'peɪnə(r)/ *n*
(Pol, Sociol) defensor, -sora *m,f*

camper /'kæmpər ‖ 'kæmpə(r)/ *n* (a) (person)
campista *mf* (b) (Transp) cámper *f*

campground /'kæmpgraʊnd/ (AmE),
campsite /'kæmpsaɪt/ *n* camping *m*

camping /'kæmpɪŋ/ *n*: **I like** ~ me gusta ir de
camping

campus /'kæmpəs/ *n* (*pl* -**puses**) campus *m*

can[1] /kæn/ *n* (a) (container) lata *f*, bote *m* (Esp),
tarro *m* (Chi); (*before n*) ~ **opener** abrelatas *m* (b)
(for petrol, water) bidón *m*; (for garbage) (AmE) cubo
m or (CS) tacho *m or* (Col) caneca *f*, bote *m* (Méx),
tobo *m* de la basura (Ven)

can[2] *vt* -**nn**- (put in cans) enlatar; (bottle) (AmE)
«*fruit*» preparar conservas de

can[3] /kæn, *weak form* kən/ *v mod*

■ **Note** When *can* means *to be capable of* or *to be*
allowed to, it is translated by *poder*: **he can't eat** no
puede comer; **can you come out tonight?** ¿puedes
salir esta noche? When *can* means *to know how to*, it
is translated by *saber*: **can you swim?** ¿sabes nadar?;
she can already read and write ya sabe leer y
escribir.When *can* is used with a verb of perception
such as *see*, *hear*, or *feel*, it is often not translated:
can you see her from here? ¿la ves desde aquí?; **she**
couldn't feel anything no sentía nada.

(*past* **could**) ⒈ (indicating ability) poder*; (referring
to particular skills) saber*; **she couldn't answer the**
question no pudo contestar la pregunta; ~ **you**
swim? ¿sabes nadar?

⒉ (a) (with verbs of perception): **I** ~**'t see very well**
no veo muy bien; ~ **you hear me?** ¿me oyes? (b)
(with verbs of mental activity): **I** ~**'t understand it** no
lo entiendo; ~**'t you tell he's lying?** ¿no te das
cuenta de que está mintiendo?

⒊ (a) (indicating, asking etc permission) poder*; ~ **I**
come with you? ¿puedo ir contigo? (b) (in requests)

AmC	América Central	Arg	Argentina	Cu	Cuba	Per	Perú
AmL	América Latina	Bol	Bolivia	Ec	Ecuador	RPI	Río de la Plata
AmS	América del Sur	Chi	Chile	Esp	España	Ur	Uruguay
Andes	Región andina	CS	Cono Sur	Méx	México	Ven	Venezuela

poder*; ∼ **you turn that music down, please?**
¿puedes bajar esa música, por favor? **(c)** (in
offers): ∼ **I help you?** ¿me permite?; (in shop) ¿lo/la
atienden?, ¿qué desea?; ∼ **I carry that for you?**
¿quieres que (te) lleve eso? **(d)** (in suggestions,
advice): ∼'t **you give it another try?** ¿por qué no lo
vuelves a intentar?
4 (indicating possibility) poder*; **it** ∼'t **be true!** ¡no
puede ser!, ¡no es posible!

Canada /'kænədə/ n (el) Canadá m
Canadian¹ /kə'neɪdɪən/ adj canadiense
Canadian² n canadiense mf
canal /kə'næl/ n canal m
Canaries /kə'neriz ‖kə'neəriz/ pl n **the** ∼ (las)
Canarias
canary /kə'neri ‖kə'neəri/ n (pl **-ries**) canario
m
Canary Islands pl n **the** ∼ ∼ las Islas
Canarias
cancel /'kænsəl/, (BrE) **-ll-** vt cancelar; ‹check›
anular
■ **cancel out** [v + o + adv, v + adv + o] ‹deficit/
loss› compensar; ‹debt› cancelar
cancellation /ˌkænsə'leɪʃən/ n cancelación f;
(Theat) devolución f
cancer /'kænsər ‖'kænsə(r)/ n **1** (disease)
cáncer m **2** **Cancer** (Astrol) **(a)** (sign) (no art)
Cáncer **(b)** (person) Cáncer or cáncer mf,
canceriano, -na m,f
candid /'kændəd ‖'kændɪd/ adj franco
candidate /'kændədeɪt ‖'kændɪdət/ n
candidato, -ta m,f
candle /'kændl/ n (for domestic use) vela f; (for
altar) cirio m
candle: ∼**light** n: **by** ∼**light** a la luz de una
vela/de las velas; ∼**stick** n candelero m; (flat)
palmatoria f
candy /'kændi/ n (pl **-dies**) (AmE) **(a)**
(confectionery) golosinas fpl, dulces mpl (AmL exc
RPl) **(b)** (individual piece) caramelo m, dulce m (AmL
exc RPl)
cane¹ /keɪn/ n **1** (for wickerwork) mimbre m
2 (walking stick) bastón m; (for punishment) palmeta
f; (for supporting plants) rodrigón m
cane² vt castigar* con la palmeta
canine¹ /'keɪnaɪn/ n **1** (Zool) canino m, cánido
m **2** ∼ (**tooth**) (diente m) canino m, colmillo m
canine² adj canino
canister /'kænəstər ‖'kænɪstə(r)/ n **(a)** (for tea,
coffee) lata f, bote m (Esp) **(b)** (Mil) bote m (de
humo, metralla etc)
cannabis /'kænəbəs ‖'kænəbɪs/ n hachís m,
cannabis m
canned /kænd/ adj **(a)** ‹food› enlatado, en or
de lata, en conserva **(b)** (pre-recorded) (colloq)
‹music› enlatado (fam); ‹laughter› grabado
cannibal /'kænəbəl ‖'kænɪbəl/ n caníbal mf,
antropófago, -ga m,f
cannon /'kænən/ n (pl also ∼) cañón m
cannonball /'kænənbɔːl/ n (Mil) bala f de
cañón
cannot /'kænɑːt ‖'kænɒt/ = **can not**
canoe¹ /kə'nuː/ n canoa f, piragua f
canoe² vi **-noes, -noeing, -noed** ir* en
canoa or piragua

canoeing /kə'nuːɪŋ/ n piragüismo m, canotaje
m
canopy /'kænəpi/ n (pl **-pies**) (over bed, throne)
dosel m, baldaquín m, baldaquino m; (over person)
palio m, dosel m
can't /kænt ‖kɑːnt/ = **can not**
canteen /kæn'tiːn/ n **1** (dining hall) (BrE)
cantina f, comedor m, casino m (Chi) (en un lugar
de trabajo, colegio etc) **2** (water bottle) cantimplora
f
canter /'kæntər ‖'kæntə(r)/ vi ir* a medio
galope
canvas /'kænvəs/ n **1** (cloth) lona f **2** (Art) (for
painting) lienzo m, tela f
canvass /'kænvəs/ vt **1** (Pol): **to** ∼ **voters in
an area** hacer* campaña entre los votantes de
una zona **2** (scrutinize) (AmE): **to** ∼ **the votes**
hacer* el escrutinio de los votos
■ ∼ vi (Pol) **to** ∼ (**for sb**) hacer* campaña (A or
EN FAVOR DE algn)
canyon /'kænjən/ n cañón m
cap¹ /kæp/ n **1** (hat) gorra f; **swimming** ∼
gorro m or (esp AmL) gorra f de baño; **baseball**/
golf ∼ gorra de béisbol/golf **2** (of bottle) tapa f,
tapón m; (metal) chapa f, tapa f; (of pen) capuchón
m, tapa f **3** (upper limit) tope m
cap² vt **-pp-** **1** ‹bottle/tube› tapar **2** (crown): **to**
∼ **it all off** o (BrE) **to** ∼ **it all …** para colmo (de
desgracias or de males) …, para rematarla …
(fam) **3** ‹expenditure› poner* un tope a
4 (Dentistry): **to have a tooth** ∼**ped** ponerse* una
funda or una corona
CAP n (= **Common Agricultural Policy**)
PAC f
capability /ˌkeɪpə'bɪləti/ n (pl **-ties**) **(a)**
(ability) capacidad f **(b)** **capabilities** pl
aptitudes fpl
capable /'keɪpəbəl/ adj **(a)** (competent) capaz
(b) (pred) (able) **to be** ∼ **OF** -ING ser* capaz DE +
INF
capacity /kə'pæsəti/ n (pl **-ties**) **1** **(a)**
(maximum content) capacidad f; (before n) **a** ∼
crowd un lleno completo **(b)** (output) capacidad f
2 (ability) capacidad f; ∼ **FOR sth** capacidad DE
algo; ∼ **to** + INF capacidad PARA + INF; **the job
was beyond her** ∼ el trabajo estaba por encima
de su capacidad **3** (role) calidad f; **in his** ∼ **as
union delegate** en su calidad de delegado del
sindicato
cape /keɪp/ n **1** (Clothing) capa f **2** (Geog) cabo
m
caper¹ /'keɪpər ‖'keɪpə(r)/ n **1** (jump) salto m
2 (prank) travesura f **3** (Bot, Culin) alcaparra f
caper² vi correr y brincar*, dar* saltos or
brincos
capital¹ /'kæpət ‖'kæpɪtl/ n **(a)** (city) capital f
(b) (letter) mayúscula f **(c)** (Fin) capital m
capital² adj **(a)** (Law): ∼ **punishment** pena f
capital **(b)** (Geog, Pol): ∼ (**city**) capital f **(c)** (Print)
‹letter› mayúscula
capitalism /'kæpətlɪzəm ‖'kæpɪtəlɪzəm/ n
capitalismo m
capitalist¹ /'kæpətləst ‖'kæpɪtəlɪst/ n
capitalista mf
capitalist² adj capitalista

capitulate /kə'pɪtʃəleɪt ‖kə'pɪtjʊleɪt/ *vi* capitular

Capricorn /'kæprɪkɔːrn ‖'kæprɪkɔːn/ *n* **(a)** (sign) (*no art*) Capricornio **(b)** (person) Capricornio *or* capricornio *mf*, capricorniano, -na *m,f*

caps = **capital letters**

capsicum /'kæpsɪkəm/ *n* pimiento *m*, pimentón *m* (AmS exc RPl), ají *m* (RPl)

capsize /'kæpsaɪz ‖kæp'saɪz/ *vi* volcarse*

capsule /'kæpsəl ‖'kæpsjuːl/ *n* cápsula *f*

captain¹ /'kæptən ‖'kæptɪn/ *n* **(a)** (rank) capitán *m* **(b)** (person in command) capitán, -tana *m,f*; (of airline plane) comandante *mf*

captain² *vt* (Naut, Sport) capitanear

caption /'kæpʃən/ *n* (under picture) leyenda *f*, pie *m* de foto (*or* ilustración *etc*); (headline) título *m*

captivate /'kæptəveɪt ‖'kæptɪveɪt/ *vt* cautivar

captive¹ /'kæptɪv/ *n* (liter) cautivo, -va *m,f*

captive² *adj*: **to take/hold sb** ~ tomar prisionero/mantener* cautivo a algn; **to have a** ~ **audience** tener* un público que no tiene más remedio que escuchar

captivity /kæp'tɪvəti/ *n* cautiverio *m*, cautividad *f*

captor /'kæptər ‖'kæptə(r)/ *n* captor, -tora *m,f*

capture¹ /'kæptʃər ‖'kæptʃə(r)/ *vt* [1] ⟨person/animal⟩ capturar; ⟨city⟩ tomar [2] **(a)** ⟨attention/interest⟩ captar, atraer* **(b)** ⟨mood/atmosphere⟩ captar, reproducir*

capture² *n* (of person, animal) captura *f*; (of city) conquista *f*, toma *f*

car /kɑːr ‖kɑː(r)/ *n* **(a)** (Auto) coche *m*, automóvil *m* (frml), carro *m* (AmL exc CS), auto *m* (esp CS) **(b)** (Rail, Transp) vagón *m*, coche *m*

caramel /'kɑːrml ‖'kærəmel, -məl/ *n* caramelo *m*

carat /'kærət/ *n* **(a)** (for gold) (AmE also **karat**) quilate *m*; (before n) **18-**~ **gold** oro *m* de 18 quilates **(b)** (for precious stones) quilate *m*

caravan /'kærəvæn/ *n* **(a)** (group) caravana *f* **(b)** (vehicle) (BrE) caravana *f*, rulot *f* (Esp), casa *f* rodante (CS), tráiler *m* (Andes, Méx); (before n) ~ **park** o **site** camping *m* para caravanas

carbohydrate /ˌkɑːrbəʊ'haɪdreɪt ‖ˌkɑːbə'haɪdreɪt/ *n* hidrato *m* de carbono

car bomb *n* coche *m* bomba

carbon /'kɑːrbən ‖'kɑːbən/ *n* carbono *m*

carbon: ~ **copy** *n* copia *f* (hecha con papel carbón); ~ **dioxide** /daɪˈɑːksaɪd ‖daɪˈɒksaɪd/ *n* anhídrido *m* carbónico; ~ **monoxide** /məˈnɑːksaɪd ‖məˈnɒksaɪd/ *n* monóxido *m* de carbono

carburetor, (BrE) **carburettor** /ˌkɑːrbəˈreɪtər ‖ˌkɑːbəˈretə(r)/ *n* carburador *m*

carcass, (BrE also) **carcase** /'kɑːrkəs ‖'kɑːkəs/ *n* (dead animal) *cuerpo de animal muerto*; (for meat) res *f* (muerta)

card /kɑːrd ‖kɑːd/ *n* [1] **(a)** (for identification, access) tarjeta *f*; (business ~) tarjeta (de visita); (credit ~) tarjeta (de crédito) **(b)** (greeting ~) tarjeta *f* (de felicitación) **(c)** (index ~) ficha *f*; (before n) ~ **index** fichero *m* **(d)** (post~) (tarjeta *f*) postal *f* [2] (thin cardboard) cartulina *f* [3] (playing

card) carta *f*, naipe *m*, baraja *f* (AmC, Col, Méx, RPl); **to play** ~**s** jugar* a las cartas *or* (Col) jugar* cartas

cardamom /'kɑːrdəməm ‖'kɑːdəməm/ *n* cardamomo *m*

cardboard /'kɑːrdbɔːrd ‖'kɑːdbɔːd/ *n* (stiff) cartón *m*; (thin) cartulina *f*; (before n) ~ **box** caja *f* de cartón

cardiac /'kɑːrdiæk ‖'kɑːdiæk/ *adj* cardíaco; ~ **arrest** paro *m* cardíaco

cardigan /'kɑːrdɪgən ‖'kɑːdɪgən/ *n* cárdigan *m*, chaqueta *f* de punto, rebeca *f* (esp Esp), saco *m* (tejido) (RPl), chaleca *f* (Chi)

cardinal /'kɑːrdnəl ‖'kɑːdɪnl/ *n* [1] (Relig) cardenal *m* [2] ~ **(number)** número *m* cardinal

care¹ /ker ‖keə(r)/ *n* [1] (attention, carefulness) cuidado *m*, atención *f*; **to take** ~ tener* cuidado; **take** ~! (saying goodbye) ¡cuídate!; (as a warning) ¡ten cuidado!
[2] (of people): **medical** ~ asistencia *f* médica; (of animals, things) cuidado *m*; **in** ~ of (AmE), ~ of (BrE) (on letters) en casa de
[3] **to take** ~ **of sb/sth (a)** (look after) ⟨of patient⟩ atender* a algn, cuidar de algn; ⟨of children⟩ cuidar a *or* de algn, ocuparse de algn; ⟨of pet/plant/machine⟩ cuidar algo; **I can take** ~ **of myself** yo sé cuidarme **(b)** (deal with) ocuparse *or* encargarse* de algn/algo
[4] (worry) preocupación *f*

care² *vi* **to** ~ **to** ⟨ABOUT sth/sb⟩ preocuparse (POR algo/algn); **I don't** ~ no me importa
■ ~ *vt* **(a)** (feel concern) (*usu neg, interrog*): **I couldn't** ~ **less what he does** me tiene sin cuidado lo que haga **(b)** (wish) (frml) **to** ~ **to** + INF: **would you** ~ **to join us for dinner?** ¿le gustaría cenar con nosotros?
■ **care for** [*v* + *prep* + *o*] **(a)** (look after) ⟨patient⟩ cuidar (de), atender* **(b)** (be fond of) querer*, sentir* afecto *or* cariño por

career¹ /kəˈrɪr ‖kəˈrɪə(r)/ *n* carrera *f*

career² *vi* ir* a toda velocidad

carefree /'kerfriː ‖'keəfriː/ *adj* despreocupado

careful /'kerfəl ‖'keəfəl/ *adj* [1] (cautious) cuidadoso, prudente; **to be** ~ **OF/WITH sth** tener* cuidado CON algo [2] (painstaking) ⟨planning⟩ cuidadoso; ⟨work⟩ cuidado, esmerado; ⟨worker⟩ meticuloso

carefully /'kerfli ‖'keəfəli/ *adv* ⟨handle/drive⟩ con cuidado; ⟨plan/examine⟩ cuidadosamente; ⟨designed/chosen⟩ con esmero

careless /'kerləs ‖'keəlɪs/ *adj* ⟨person⟩ descuidado; ⟨work⟩ poco cuidado; ⟨driving⟩ negligente; **you made some** ~ **mistakes** cometiste errores por descuido

carelessly /'kerləsli ‖'keəlɪsli/ *adv* sin cuidado, sin la debida atención

carelessness /'kerləsnəs ‖'keəlɪsnɪs/ *n* falta *f* de atención *or* de cuidado

carer /'kerər ‖'keərə(r)/ *n*: *persona que tiene a su cuidado a un incapacitado sin recibir por ello remuneración*

caress¹ /kəˈres/ *n* caricia *f*

caress² *vt* acariciar

caretaker /'kerˌteɪkər ‖'keəˌteɪkə(r)/ *n* conserje *mf*

cargo /'kɑːrgəʊ ‖'kɑːgəʊ/ *n* (*pl* **-goes** *or* **-gos**) **(a)** (load) cargamento *m* **(b)** (goods) carga *f*

Caribbean¹ /ˌkærəˈbiːən, kəˈrɪbiən ‖ˌkærɪˈbiːən/ *adj* caribeño, del Caribe
Caribbean² *n* the ~ (Sea) el (mar) Caribe; the ~ (region) el Caribe, las Antillas
caricature /ˈkærɪkətʃər ‖ˈkærɪkətʃʊə(r)/ *n* caricatura *f*
caring /ˈkerɪŋ ‖ˈkeərɪŋ/ *adj* ⟨society/approach⟩ humanitario; ⟨person⟩ (kindly) bondadoso; (sympathetic) comprensivo
carnage /ˈkɑːrnɪdʒ ‖ˈkɑːnɪdʒ/ *n* carnicería *f*
carnation /kɑːrˈneɪʃən ‖kɑːˈneɪʃən/ *n* clavel *m*
carnival /ˈkɑːrnəvəl ‖ˈkɑːnɪvəl/ *n* carnaval *m*
carnivorous /kɑːrˈnɪvərəs ‖kɑːˈnɪvərəs/ *adj* carnívoro
carol /ˈkærəl/ *n* villancico *m*
carousel /ˌkærəˈsel/ *n* (a) ▶ MERRY-GO-ROUND (b) (for baggage) cinta *f or* correa *f* transportadora (c) (in shops) (AmE) expositor *m* giratorio
car park *n* (BrE) (open space) ▶ PARKING LOT; (building) ▶ PARKING GARAGE
carpenter /ˈkɑːrpəntər ‖ˈkɑːpəntə(r)/ *n* carpintero, -ra *m,f*
carpentry /ˈkɑːrpəntri ‖ˈkɑːpəntri/ *n* carpintería *f*
carpet /ˈkɑːrpət ‖ˈkɑːpɪt/ *n* (a) (rug) alfombra *f*, tapete *m* (Col, Méx, Ven); ▶ SWEEP² *vt* 1B (b) (wall-to-wall) alfombra *f*, moqueta *f* (Esp), moquette *f* (RPl) (c) (of flowers, leaves, moss) (liter) alfombra *f* (liter)
carphone /ˈkɑːrfəʊn ‖ˈkɑːfəʊn/ *n* teléfono *m* de automóvil
carriage /ˈkærɪdʒ/ *n* 1 (a) (horse-drawn) carruaje *m*, coche *m* (b) (BrE Rail) vagón *m* (c) (baby ~) (AmE) cochecito *m*, carriola *f* (Méx) 2 (transport) transporte *m* 3 (bearing) (frml) porte *m*
carrier /ˈkærɪər ‖ˈkærɪə(r)/ *n* 1 (company) compañía *f or* empresa *f* de transportes; (Aviat) línea *f* aérea 2 (of disease, gene) portador, -dora *m,f*
carrier bag *n* (BrE) bolsa *f* (de plástico *or* papel)
carrion /ˈkærɪən/ *n* carroña *f*
carrot /ˈkærət/ *n* zanahoria *f*
carry /ˈkæri/ -ries, -rying, -ried *vt* 1 (a) (bear, take) llevar; **I can't ~ this, it's too heavy** no puedo cargar con esto, pesa demasiado (b) (have with one) llevar encima (c) (be provided with) ⟨guarantee⟩ tener* (d) (be pregnant with) estar* embarazada *or* encinta de
2 (a) (convey) ⟨goods/passengers⟩ llevar, transportar; **she was carried along by the crowd** fue arrastrada por la multitud (b) (channel, transmit) ⟨oil/water/sewage⟩ llevar (c) ⟨disease⟩ ser*/portador de
3 (support) ⟨weight⟩ soportar
4 (involve, entail) ⟨responsibility⟩ conllevar
5 (gain support for) ⟨bill/motion⟩ aprobar*
6 (stock) ⟨model⟩ tener*, vender
■ ~ *vi*: **sound carries further in the mountains** en la montaña los sonidos llegan más lejos; **her voice carries well** su voz tiene mucha proyección
■ **carry away** [v + o + adv, v + adv + o] (usu pass): **I got carried away and painted the window**

as well me entusiasmé y pinté la ventana también; **there's no need to get carried away** no te pases
■ **carry off** [v + o + adv, v + adv + o] 1 (abduct) ⟨victim/hostage⟩ llevarse
2 (a) (win) ⟨trophy/cup⟩ llevarse (b) (succeed with): **she tried to appear disinterested but failed to ~ it off** intentó aparentar desinterés pero no lo logró
■ **carry on** 1 (a) [v + o + adv, v + adv + o] ⟨practice⟩ seguir* *or* continuar* con (b) [v + adv + o] ⟨conversation/correspondence⟩ mantener*
2 [v + adv] (a) (continue) seguir*, continuar* (b) (make a fuss) (colloq): **what a way to ~ on!** ¡qué manera de hacer escándalo, por favor!
■ **carry out** [v + o + adv, v + adv + o] ⟨work/repairs/investigation⟩ llevar a cabo; ⟨order⟩ cumplir; ⟨duty⟩ cumplir con
carry: ~**all** *n* (AmE) bolso *m* de viaje, bolsón *m* (RPl); ~**cot** *n* (BrE) cuna *f* portátil; ~**on** *adj* (AmE) (before n) ⟨bag/baggage⟩ de mano; ~**out** *n* (esp AmE) comida preparada o bebida que se vende para consumir fuera del lugar de venta
car: ~ **seat** *n* asiento *m* del coche; (for infant) asiento *m* de bebé (*para el coche*); ~**sick** *adj* mareado (*por viajar en coche*)
cart¹ /kɑːrt ‖kɑːt/ *n* (a) (waggon) carro *m*, carreta *f* (b) (in supermarket, airport) (AmE) carrito *m*
cart² *vt* (colloq): **I had to ~ the books around all day** tuve que cargar con los libros todo el día
cartel /kɑːrˈtel ‖kɑːˈtel/ *n* cártel *m*
carthorse /ˈkɑːrthɔːrs ‖ˈkɑːthɔːs/ *n* caballo *m* de tiro
cartilage /ˈkɑːrtlɪdʒ ‖ˈkɑːtɪlɪdʒ/ *n* cartílago *m*
carton /ˈkɑːrtn ‖ˈkɑːtn/ *n* (of cigarettes) cartón *m*; **a ~ of milk** una leche en cartón
cartoon /kɑːrˈtuːn ‖kɑːˈtuːn/ *n* (a) (humorous drawing) chiste *m* ⟨gráfico⟩, viñeta *f* (Esp), mono *m* (Chi) (b) (Cin) dibujos *mpl* animados
cartridge /ˈkɑːrtrɪdʒ ‖ˈkɑːtrɪdʒ/ *n* (for gun, pen) cartucho *m*
cartwheel /ˈkɑːrthwiːl ‖ˈkɑːtwiːl/ *n* voltereta *f* lateral, rueda *f*, rueda *f* de carro (Méx, RPl)
carve /kɑːrv ‖kɑːv/ *vt* 1 (Art) ⟨wood/stone⟩ tallar; ⟨figure/bust⟩ esculpir, tallar; ⟨initials⟩ grabar 2 (Culin) ⟨meat⟩ cortar, trinchar
■ **carve out** [v + o + adv, v + adv + o] ⟨reputation⟩ forjarse; ⟨name⟩ hacerse*
carving /ˈkɑːrvɪŋ ‖ˈkɑːvɪŋ/ *n* talla *f*, escultura *f*
carving knife *n* trinchante *m*, cuchillo *m* de trinchar
car wash *n* túnel *m or* tren *m* de lavado
cascade¹ /kæsˈkeɪd/ *n* cascada *f*
cascade² *vi* caer* en cascada
case /keɪs/ *n* 1 (matter) caso *m*; **to lose/win a ~** (Law) perder*/ganar un pleito *or* juicio
2 (a) (Med, Soc Adm) caso *m* (b) (eccentric) (colloq) caso *m* (fam)
3 (instance, situation) caso *m*; **if that's the ~** si es así; **in that ~, I'm not interested** en ese caso, no me interesa
4 (in phrases) **in any case** de todas maneras *or* formas; **in case** (as conj): **make a note in ~ you forget** apúntalo por si te olvidas; **just in case** por si acaso

5 (argument): **she has a good ~** sus argumentos son buenos; **there is a ~ for doing nothing** hay razones para no hacer nada
6 (a) (suit~) maleta f, valija f (RPI) **(b)** (attaché ~) maletín m **(c)** (crate) caja f, cajón m, jaba f (Chi, Per); (of wine, liquor) *caja de 12 botellas* **(d)** (hard container — for small objects) estuche f; (— for large objects) caja f; (soft container) funda f

case: ~ history n (Med) historial m clínico, historia f clínica (AmL); **~ study** n estudio m

cash¹ /kæʃ/ n **(a)** (notes and coins) dinero m (en) efectivo; **(in) ~** en efectivo; **~ on delivery** entrega f contra reembolso; (before n) ⟨payment⟩ en efectivo; ⟨refund⟩ al contado **(b)** (funds) (colloq) dinero m, lana f (AmL fam), plata f (AmS fam), tela f (Esp fam)

cash² vt ⟨check⟩ cobrar
■ **cash in** **1** [v + o + adv, v + adv + o] (exchange for money) canjear **2** [v + adv] (profit) **to ~ in** (ON sth) aprovecharse (DE algo)

cash: ~ and carry n: *tienda de venta al por mayor*; **~ crop** n cultivo m industrial or comercial; **~ desk** n (BrE) caja f; **~ dispenser** n (BrE) cajero m automático or permanente

cashew (nut) /ˈkæʃuː/ n anacardo m, castaña f de cajú (CS, Ven), nuez f de la India (Méx)

cash flow n flujo m de caja, cash-flow m

cashier /kæˈʃɪr ‖ kæˈʃɪə(r)/ n cajero, -ra m,f

cashier's check n (AmE) cheque m bancario or de caja or de gerencia

cashmere /ˈkæʒmɪr ‖ ˌkæʃˈmɪə(r)/ n cachemir m, cachemira f

cash: ~point n (BrE) cajero m automático or permanente; **~ register** n caja f registradora

casing /ˈkeɪsɪŋ/ n (cover) cubierta f; (case) caja f

casino /kəˈsiːnəʊ/ n (pl **-nos**) casino m

cask /kæsk ‖ kɑːsk/ n barril m, tonel m

casket /ˈkæskət ‖ ˈkɑːskɪt/ n **(a)** (for jewels) cofre m **(b)** (coffin) (AmE) ataúd m, féretro, cajón (AmL)

casserole /ˈkæsərəʊl/ n **(a)** (dish) cazuela f **(b)** (food) guiso m, guisado m (Méx)

cassette /kəˈset/ n (Audio) cassette f or m; (before n) **~ player** pasacintas m, cassette m (Esp), pasacassettes m (RPI), tocacassettes m (Chi)

cast¹ /kæst ‖ kɑːst/ n **1 (a)** (molded object) (Art) vaciado m; (Metall) pieza f fundida **(b)** (mold) molde m **2** (Cin, Theat) (+ sing or pl vb) reparto m, elenco m (esp AmL)

cast² (past & past p **cast**) vt **1 (a)** ⟨stone⟩ arrojar, lanzar*, tirar*; ⟨line⟩ lanzar*; ⟨net⟩ echar **(b)** ⟨shadow/light⟩ proyectar; **to ~ doubt on sth** poner* algo en duda **(c)** ⟨vote⟩ emitir **2** «snake» ⟨skin⟩ mudar de, mudar **3** (Cin, Theat) ⟨role⟩ asignar; **she was ~ as the princess** le dieron el papel de la princesa
■ **~** vi (in angling) lanzar*
■ **cast away** [v + o + adv]: **they were ~ away on a desert island** llegaron a una isla desierta tras naufragar

■ **cast off** [v + adv] **1 (a)** (in knitting) cerrar* **(b)** (Naut) soltar* amarras
2 [v + o + adv, v + adv + o] **(a)** (in knitting) ⟨stitch⟩ cerrar* **(b)** (abandon) ⟨friend/lover⟩ dejar
■ **cast on** **1** [v + adv] (in knitting) poner* or montar los puntos
2 [v + o + adv, v + adv + o] ⟨stitch⟩ montar, poner*
■ **cast out** [v + o + adv, v + adv + o] (liter) expulsar

castanets /ˌkæstəˈnets/ pl n castañuelas fpl

castaway /ˈkæstəweɪ ‖ ˈkɑːstəweɪ/ n náufrago, -ga m,f

caste /kæst ‖ kɑːst/ n casta f

caster /ˈkæstər ‖ ˈkɑːstə(r)/ n ruedecita f, ruedita f (esp AmL)

caster sugar n (BrE) azúcar blanca de granulado muy fino

Castile /kæsˈtiːl ‖ kæsˈtiːl/ n Castilla f

Castilian¹ /kæsˈtɪljən ‖ kəˈstɪliən/ adj castellano

Castilian² n **(a)** (person) castellano, -na m,f **(b)** (language) castellano m

cast: ~ iron n hierro m fundido or colado; **~-iron** adj (before n) ⟨guarantee⟩ sólido; ⟨alibi⟩ a toda prueba

castle /ˈkæsəl ‖ ˈkɑːsəl/ n **(a)** (Archit) castillo m **(b)** (in chess) torre f

castoff /ˈkæstɔːf ‖ ˈkɑːstɒf/ n: **she gave me her ~s** me dio la ropa que ya no quería

castrate /kæsˈtreɪt ‖ kæˈstreɪt/ vt castrar

casual /ˈkæʒuəl/ adj **1 (a)** (superficial) (before n) ⟨inspection⟩ superficial; **a ~ acquaintance** un conocido, una conocida; **~ sex** relaciones fpl sexuales promiscuas **(b)** (chance) (before n) ⟨visit/reader⟩ ocasional **(c)** (informal) ⟨chat⟩ informal; ⟨clothes⟩ de sport, informal **2** (unconcerned) ⟨attitude/tone⟩ despreocupado; ⟨remark⟩ hecho al pasar **3** (not regular) ⟨employment/labor⟩ eventual, ocasional

casually /ˈkæʒuəli/ adv **(a)** (informally) ⟨dressed⟩ de manera informal; ⟨chat⟩ informalmente **(b)** (with indifference) con indiferencia

casualty /ˈkæʒuəlti/ n (pl **-ties**) **1** (injured person) herido, -da m,f; (dead person) víctima f; (Mil) baja f **2** (hospital department) (BrE) (no art) urgencias fpl

cat /kæt/ n gato, -ta m,f; **to let the ~ out of the bag** descubrir* el pastel, levantar la liebre or (RPI) la perdiz; **to rain ~s and dogs** llover* a cántaros

Catalan¹ /ˈkætljæn ‖ ˈkætələn/ adj catalán

Catalan² n **(a)** (person) catalán, -lana m,f **(b)** (language) catalán m

catalog¹, catalogue /ˈkætlɔːg ‖ ˈkætəlɒg/ n catálogo m

catalog², catalogue vt catalogar*

Catalonia /ˌkætlˈəʊniə ‖ ˌkætəˈləʊniə/ n Cataluña f

catalyst /ˈkætləst ‖ ˈkætəlɪst/ n catalizador m

catalytic converter /ˌkætlˈɪtɪk kənˈvɜːrtər ‖ˌkætəˈlɪtɪk kənˈvɜːtə(r)/ n catalizador m

catapult¹ /ˈkætəpʊlt ‖ˈkætəpʌlt/ n (Aviat, Mil) catapulta f

catapult² vt catapultar

cataract /ˈkætərækt/ n [1] (over a precipice) catarata f; (in a river) rápido m [2] (Med) catarata f

catarrh /kəˈtɑːr ‖kəˈtɑː(r)/ n catarro m

catastrophe /kəˈtæstrəfi/ n catástrofe f

catch¹ /kætʃ/ (past & past p **caught**) vt [1] ⟨ball/object⟩ agarrar, coger* (esp Esp) [2] (capture) ⟨mouse/lion⟩ atrapar, coger* (esp Esp); ⟨fish⟩ pescar*, coger* (esp Esp); ⟨thief⟩ atrapar [3] (a) (take by surprise) agarrar, pillar (fam), pescar* (fam); **we got caught in the rain** nos sorprendió la lluvia (b) (intercept) ⟨person⟩ alcanzar*; ~ **you later** (colloq) nos vemos [4] (a) ⟨train/plane⟩ (take) tomar, coger* (esp Esp); (be in time for) alcanzar* (b) (manage to see, hear): **we'll just** ~ **the end of the game** todavía podemos pescar el final del partido (fam); **we could** ~ **a movie before dinner** (AmE) podríamos ir al cine antes de cenar [5] (entangle, trap): **I caught my skirt on a nail** se me enganchó or (Méx tb) se me atoró or (Chi) se me pescó la falda en un clavo; **I caught my finger in the drawer** me pillé or (AmL tb) me agarré el dedo en el cajón [6] (hear or understand clearly): **did you** ~ **what she said?** ¿oíste lo que dijo? [7] ⟨disease⟩ contagiarse de; **to** ~ **a cold** resfriarse*, agarrar or (esp Esp) coger* un resfriado [8] (hit): **he caught his head on the beam** se dio en la cabeza con la viga

■ ~ vi [1] (a) (grasp) agarrar, coger* (esp Esp), cachar (Méx) (b) (become hooked) engancharse [2] (ignite) ⟨fire⟩ prender, agarrar (AmL)

■ **catch on** [v + adv] (colloq) (a) (become popular) ⟨fashion/idea⟩ imponerse*; ⟨game/style⟩ ponerse* de moda (b) (understand) caer* (fam)

■ **catch out** [v + o + adv, v + adv + o] (a) **to** ~ **sb out** pillar or agarrar a algn desprevenido (b) (trick) pillar (fam), agarrar (CS fam)

■ **catch up** [1] [v + adv] (with work, studies) ponerse* al día; **to** ~ **up** WITH **sb/sth** (physically) alcanzar* a algn/algo; **she had to** ~ **up with the rest of the class** tuvo que ponerse al nivel del resto de la clase [2] [v + o + adv] (draw level with) (BrE) alcanzar* [3] (trap, involve) **to be/get caught up in sth** ⟨in barbed wire/thorns⟩ estar*/quedar enganchado or atrapado en algo; ⟨in scandal/dispute⟩ verse* envuelto en algo; ⟨in excitement/enthusiasm⟩ contagiarse de algo; **I got caught up in the traffic** me agarró or (esp Esp) me cogió el tráfico

catch² n [1] (a) (Sport) atrapada f, atajada f (CS) (b) (of fish) pesca f [2] (on door) pestillo m, pasador m (AmL); (on window, box, necklace) cierre m [3] (hidden drawback) trampa f; **I knew there'd be a** ~ **in it somewhere** ya sabía yo que tenía que haber gato encerrado; **it's a C**~-**22 situation** es una situación sin salida

catcher /ˈkætʃər ‖ˈkætʃə(r)/ n (in baseball) receptor, -tora m,f, catcher mf

catching /ˈkætʃɪŋ/ adj ⟨pred⟩ contagioso

catchment area /ˈkætʃmənt/ n zona f de captación (distrito que corresponde a un hospital, colegio etc)

catch: ~**phrase** n (of person) latiguillo m; (of political party) eslogan m; ~**word** n (a) (slogan) eslogan m (b) ▶ ~PHRASE

catchy /ˈkætʃi/ adj **catchier, catchiest** pegadizo, pegajoso (AmL exc RPl)

categorical /ˌkætəˈgɒrɪkəl ‖ˌkætəˈgɒrɪkəl/ adj categórico; ⟨refusal⟩ rotundo

categorize /ˈkætəgəraɪz/ vt ⟨things⟩ clasificar*; ⟨people⟩ catalogar*

category /ˈkætəgɔːri ‖ˈkætəgəri/ n (pl **-ries**) categoría f

cater /ˈkeɪtər ‖ˈkeɪtə(r)/ vt (AmE) encargarse* del buffet de

■ **cater to**, (BrE) **cater for** [v + prep + o]: **to** ~ **to** o **for people of all ages** ofrecer* servicios para gente de todas las edades; **we try to** ~ **to** o **for all needs** tratamos de satisfacer todas las necesidades

caterer /ˈkeɪtərər ‖ˈkeɪtərə(r)/ n: persona o firma que se encarga del servicio de comida y bebida para fiestas, cafeterías etc

catering /ˈkeɪtərɪŋ/ n (a) (provision of food): **to do the** ~ encargarse* del servicio de comida y bebida (or del buffet etc) (b) (trade, department) restauración f

caterpillar /ˈkætərpɪlər ‖ˈkætəpɪlə(r)/ n oruga f, azotador m (Méx), cuncuna f (Chi)

cathedral /kəˈθiːdrəl/ n catedral f

Catholic¹ /ˈkæθəlɪk/ n católico, -ca m,f

Catholic² adj [1] (Relig) católico; **the Roman** ~ **Church** la iglesia católica (apostólica romana) [2] **catholic** ⟨tastes/interests⟩ variado

Catholicism /kəˈθɒːləsɪzəm ‖kəˈθɒlɪsɪzəm/ n catolicismo m

cat: ~**nap** n siestecita f; **C**~**'s-eye**® n (Transp) catafaros m, ojo m de gato (CS), estoperol m (Col)

catsup /ˈkætsəp/ n (AmE) ▶ KETCHUP

cattle /ˈkætl/ n pl n ganado m, reses fpl; (before n) ~ **breeder** ganadero, -ra m,f

catwalk /ˈkætwɔːk/ n pasarela f

Caucasian /kɔːˈkeɪʒən/ n (Anthrop) caucásico, -ca m,f; **the suspect is a male** ~ el sospechoso es un hombre de raza blanca

caught /kɔːt/ past & past p of CATCH¹

cauliflower /ˈkɑːlɪflaʊər ‖ˈkɒlɪflaʊə(r)/ n coliflor f

cause¹ /kɔːz/ n [1] (a) (of accident, event, death) causa f (b) (reason, grounds) motivo m, razón f; **there's no** ~ **for concern** no hay por qué preocuparse [2] (ideal, movement) causa f

cause² vt causar; **to** ~ **sb problems** causarle problemas a algn; **to** ~ **sb/sth** TO + INF hacer* que algn/algo (+ subj)

causeway /ˈkɔːzweɪ/ n (path) paso m elevado; (road) carretera f elevada

caustic /ˈkɔːstɪk/ adj cáustico

caution¹ /ˈkɔːʃən/ n (a) (care, prudence) cautela f, prudencia f (b) (warning) advertencia f, aviso m; (Law, Sport) amonestación f

caution² vt (a) (warn) advertir* (b) (inform of rights) informar de sus derechos

cautious /ˈkɔːʃəs/ adj cauteloso, cauto

cautiously /ˈkɔːʃəsli/ adv cautelosamente

cavalry /'kævəlri/ n caballería f

cave /keɪv/ n cueva f; (before n) ~ **painting** pintura f rupestre
■ **cave in** [v + adv] derrumbarse

caveman /'keɪvmæn/ n (pl **-men** /-men/) hombre m de las cavernas

cavern /'kævən/ n caverna f

caviar, caviare /'kævɪɑːr ‖'kævɪɑː(r)/ n caviar m

cavity /'kævəti/ n (pl **-ties**) cavidad f; (Dent) caries f

caw /kɔː/ vi graznar

CBS n (in US) (no art) (= **Columbia Broadcasting System**) la CBS

cc (= **cubic centimeter** o (BrE) **centimetre**) c.c.

CCTV n = **closed-circuit television**

CD n (= **compact disc** or (AmE also) **disk**) CD m

CD-ROM n (= **compact disc read-only memory**) CD-ROM m

cease /siːs/ vt (a) to ~ to + INF/ to ~ -ING dejar DE + INF (b) ⟨production/publication⟩ interrumpir, suspender
■ ~ vi «noise» cesar; «production» interrumpirse; «work» detenerse*

cease-fire /'siːs'faɪr ‖'siːsfaɪə(r)/ n alto m el fuego, cese m del fuego (AmL)

ceaseless /'siːsləs ‖'siːslɪs/ adj incesante

cedar /'siːdər ‖'siːdə(r)/ n cedro m

cede /siːd/ vt to ~ sth (TO sb) ceder(le) algo (A algn)

ceiling /'siːlɪŋ/ n (Const) techo m, cielo m raso; (upper limit) límite m, tope m

celebrate /'seləbreɪt ‖'selɪbreɪt/ vt celebrar
■ ~ vi: we won: let's ~! ¡ganamos, vamos a celebrarlo!

celebration /,selə'breɪʃən ‖,selɪ'breɪʃən/ n (event) fiesta f; he attended the ~s asistió a los festejos

celebrity /sə'lebrəti ‖sɪ'lebrəti/ n (pl **-ties**) famoso, -sa m,f, celebridad mf

celery /'seləri/ n apio m, celeri m (Ven)

celibate /'seləbət ‖'selɪbət/ adj célibe

cell /sel/ n 1 (in prison) celda f 2 (Biol, Elec) célula f

cellar /'selər ‖'selə(r)/ n sótano m; (for coal) carbonera f; (for wine) bodega f

cello /'tʃeləʊ/ n (pl **-los**) violoncelo m, violonchelo m, chelo m

cellophane, (BrE) Cellophane® /'seləfeɪn/ n celofán m

cellphone /'selfəʊn/ n teléfono m celular

cellulite /'seljəlaɪt ‖'seljʊlaɪt/ n celulitis f

celluloid /'seljəlɔɪd ‖'seljʊlɔɪd/ n celuloide m

cellulose /'seljələʊs ‖'seljʊləʊs/ n celulosa f

Celsius /'selsiəs/ adj: 20 degrees ~ 20 grados centigrados or Celsio(s)

Celt /kelt/ n celta mf

Celtic /'keltɪk/ adj celta

cement¹ /sɪ'ment/ n cemento m

cement² vt (a) (Const) unir con cemento (b) ⟨friendship/alliance⟩ consolidar, fortalecer*

cement mixer n hormigonera f

cemetery /'semətəri ‖'semətri/ n (pl **-ries**) cementerio m

censor¹ /'sensər ‖'sensə(r)/ n censor, -sora m,f

censor² vt censurar

censorship /'sensərʃɪp ‖'sensəʃɪp/ n censura f

censure /'sentʃər ‖'sensjə(r)/ vt censurar

census /'sensəs/ n (pl **-suses**) censo m

cent /sent/ n (of dollar) centavo m; (of euro) céntimo m

centenary /sen'tenəri ‖sen'tiːnəri/ n (pl **-ries**) centenario m

centennial /sen'teniəl/ n (esp AmE) centenario m

center¹, (BrE) **centre** /'sentər ‖'sentə(r)/ n 1 (middle point, area) centro m 2 (site of activity) centro m 3 (Sport) (in US football, rugby) centro mf; (in basketball) pivot mf, pivote mf (AmL)

center², (BrE) **centre** vt centrar
■ ~ vi (a) (focus on) to ~ ON o UPON sth/sb centrarse EN algo/algn (b) (revolve around) to ~ ON o AROUND sth/sb girar ALREDEDOR DE algo/algn

center: ~ **forward** n delantero mf centro; ~ **half** (pl halfs or halves) n medio mf centro; ~**piece** n (decoration) centro m (de mesa); (main feature) eje m

centigrade /'sentɪgreɪd/ adj centígrado

centimeter, (BrE) **centimetre** /'sentə,miːtər ‖'sentɪ,miːtə(r)/ n centímetro m

centipede /'sentəpiːd ‖'sentɪpiːd/ n ciempiés m

central /'sentrəl/ adj (a) (main) central; ⟨problem⟩ fundamental (b) (in the center) ⟨area/street⟩ céntrico; in ~ Chicago en el centro de Chicago

central: **C~ America** n Centroamérica f, América f Central; **C~ American** adj centroamericano, de (la) América Central; **C~ Europe** n Europa f Central; ~ **heating** n calefacción f central

centralize /'sentrəlaɪz/ vt centralizar*

central reservation n (BrE) mediana f, bandejón m (central) (Chi), camellón m (Méx)

centre etc (BrE) ▶ CENTER etc

century /'sentʃəri/ n (pl **-ries**) siglo m; in the 19th ~ en el siglo XIX

ceramic /sə'ræmɪk ‖sɪ'ræmɪk/ adj ⟨pot⟩ de cerámica; ~ **tile** (for walls) azulejo m; (for floors) baldosa f (de cerámica)

ceramics /sə'ræmɪks ‖sɪ'ræmɪks/ n (+ pl vb) objetos mpl de cerámica, cerámicas fpl

cereal /'sɪriəl ‖'sɪəriəl/ n (a) (plant, grain) cereal m (b) (breakfast ~) cereales mpl

cerebral palsy /sə'riːbrəl 'pɔːlzi ‖'serɪbrəl 'pɔːlzi/ n parálisis f

ceremonial /,serə'məʊniəl ‖,serɪ'məʊniəl/ adj ⟨robes⟩ ceremonial; ⟨occasion⟩ solemne

ceremony /'serəməʊni ‖'serɪməni/ n (pl **-nies**) ceremonia f

certain /'sɜːrtn̩ ‖'sɜːtn̩/ adj 1 (a) (definite) seguro; to make ~ OF sth asegurarse or cerciorarse DE algo; for ~ con certeza (b) (convinced) ⟨pred⟩ to be ~ (OF sth) estar* seguro (DE algo); I checked the list to make ~ (that) ... revisé la lista para asegurarme de que ...

2 (particular) (before n) cierto; **he has a ~ something** tiene un no sé qué or (un) algo especial

certainly /'sɜːtn̩li ‖'sɜːtn̩li/ adv **(a)** (definitely): **we're almost ~ going to win** es casi seguro que vamos a ganar; **do you see what I mean? — certainly** ¿te das cuenta de lo que quiero decir? — desde luego **(b)** (emphatic): **I ~ won't be buying anything there again!** por cierto que no voy a volver a comprar nada allí; **may I use your phone? — certainly!** ¿puedo llamar por teléfono? — pues claro ¡(no) faltaría más!; **~ not!** ¡de ninguna manera!

certainty /'sɜːtn̩ti ‖'sɜːtn̩ti/ n (pl **-ties**) certeza f, seguridad f; **defeat is now a ~** la derrota es algo seguro

certificate /sər'tɪfɪkət ‖sə'tɪfɪkət/ n certificado m

certify /'sɜːrtəfaɪ ‖'sɜːtɪfaɪ/ vt **-fies, -fying, -fied (a)** ⟨facts/claim/death⟩ certificar*; **this is to ~ that ...** por la presente certifico que ... **(b)** (declare insane) (usu pass) declarar demente **(c)** (license) (AmE): **he isn't certified to teach in this state** no está habilitado para ejercer la docencia en este estado **(d) certified** past p (AmE) certificado; **certified public accountant** contador público, contadora pública m,f (AmL), censor jurado, censora jurada m,f de cuentas (Esp)

cervical /'sɜːrvɪkəl ‖sɜː'vaɪkəl/ adj del cuello del útero; **~ smear** (BrE) citología f, Papanicolau m (AmL)

cervix /'sɜːrvɪks ‖'sɜːvɪks/ n (pl **-vixes** or **-vices** /-vəsiːz/) cuello m del útero

Cesarean (section), Cesarian (section) /sɪ'zæriən ‖sɪ'zeəriən/ n (AmE) cesárea f

cesspit /'sespɪt/ n pozo m negro or séptico or ciego

cf (compare) cf.

CFC n = **chlorofluorocarbon**

ch n (pl **chs**) (= chapter) c.

chafe /tʃeɪf/ vt/i rozar*

chaff /tʃæf ‖tʃɑːf/ n barcia f

chagrin /ʃə'ɡrɪn ‖'ʃæɡrɪn/ n (liter) disgusto m; **to his ~** para su disgusto

chain¹ /tʃeɪn/ n cadena f; **a ~ of events** una cadena de acontecimientos

chain² vt **to ~ sth/sb TO sth** encadenar algo/a algn A algo

chain: ~ reaction n reacción f en cadena; **~smoke** vi fumar un cigarrillo tras otro; **~ store** n tienda f de una cadena

chair¹ /tʃer ‖tʃeə(r)/ n **1** (seat) silla f; (arm~) sillón m, butaca f (esp Esp) **2 (a)** (at university) cátedra f **(b)** (in meeting) presidencia f; **to take the ~** presidir

chair² vt ⟨meeting⟩ presidir

chair: ~lift n telesilla f or (Esp) telesquí m; **~man** /'tʃermən ‖'tʃeəmən/ n (pl **-men** /-mən/) presidente, -ta m,f; **~woman** n presidenta f

chalet /'ʃæleɪ/ n **(a)** (cabin) chalet m (de montaña) **(b)** (in motel) (BrE) bungalow m

chalk /tʃɔːk/ n **1** (Geol) creta f, caliza f **2** (for writing) tiza f, gis m (Méx)

challenge¹ /'tʃælənʤ ‖'tʃælɪnʤ/ vt **1 (a)** (summon) desafiar*, retar; **to ~ sb to + INF** desafiar* a algn A QUE (+ subj) **(b)** (question) ⟨authority/findings⟩ cuestionar **2** (stop) (Mil) darle* el alto a

challenge² n desafío m, reto m

challenger /'tʃælənʤər ‖'tʃælɪnʤə(r)/ n contendiente mf, rival mf

chamber /'tʃeɪmbər ‖'tʃeɪmbə(r)/ n **1** (room) (arch) cámara f (arc) **2** (of gun) recámara f

chamber: ~maid n camarera f (en un hotel); **~ music** n música f de cámara; **~ of commerce** n cámara f de comercio; **~ pot** n orinal m or (AmL exc RPl) bacinilla f or (CS) escupidera f

chameleon /kə'miːliən/ n camaleón m

chamois (leather) /'ʃæmi/ n gamuza f

chamomile /'kæməmaɪl/ n manzanilla f, camomila f; **~ tea** manzanilla f

champagne /ʃæm'peɪn/ n champán m, champaña f or m

champion¹ /'tʃæmpiən/ n **(a)** (Sport) campeón, -peona m,f **(b)** (of cause) defensor, -sora m,f

champion² vt abogar* por, defender*

championship /'tʃæmpiənʃɪp/ n (Sport) (often pl) campeonato m

chance¹ /tʃæns ‖tʃɑːns/ n **1** (fate) casualidad f, azar m; **by ~** por or de casualidad; (before n) ⟨meeting⟩ fortuito **2** (risk) riesgo m; **don't take any ~s** no te arriesgues **3** (opportunity) oportunidad f **4** (likelihood) posibilidad f, chance f or m (esp AmL); **(the) ~s are (that) ...** (colloq) lo más probable es que ...

chance² vt: **to ~ it** arriesgarse*

chancellor /'tʃænsələr ‖'tʃɑːnsələ(r)/ n **(a) Chancellor (of the Exchequer)** (in UK) ≈ministro, -tra m,f de Economía/Hacienda **(b)** (premier) canciller mf **(c)** (of university) rector, -tora m,f

chandelier /ˌʃændə'lɪr ‖ˌʃændə'lɪə(r)/ n araña f (de luces)

change¹ /tʃeɪnʤ/ n **1 (a)** cambio m; **a ~ in temperature** un cambio de temperatura; **for a ~** para variar **(b)** (of clothes) muda f **2 (a)** (coins) cambio m, monedas fpl, sencillo m (AmL), menudo m (Col), dinero m suelto, plata f suelta (AmS) **(b)** (money returned) cambio m, vuelto m (AmL), vuelta f (Esp), vueltas fpl (Col)

change² vt cambiar; **the witch ~d her into a stone** la bruja la convirtió en una piedra; **to ~ one's clothes** cambiarse de ropa; **to ~ color** cambiar de color; **let's ~ the subject** cambiemos de tema; **I wouldn't want to ~ places with her** no quisiera estar en su lugar; **to change train(s)** hacer* transbordo, cambiar (de tren); **to ~ dollars into pesos** cambiar dólares a or (Esp tb) en pesos

■ **~** vi **1 (a)** (become different) cambiar; **to ~ INTO sth** convertirse* EN algo **(b) changing** pres p ⟨needs/role/moods⟩ cambiante **2 (a)** (put on different clothes) cambiarse; **she ~d into a black dress** se cambió y se puso un vestido negro; **to get ~d** cambiarse **(b)** (Transp) cambiar, hacer* transbordo

■ **change over** [v + adv] cambiar

changeable /'tʃeɪnʤəbəl/ adj cambiante

change: ~over n (transition) **~over (FROM sth) (TO sth)** cambio m (DE algo) (A algo); **~ purse** n (AmE) monedero m, portamonedas m

changing room /'tʃeɪndʒɪŋ/ n (BrE) **(a)** (Sport) vestuario m, vestidor m (Chi, Méx) **(b)** (in shop) probador m

channel¹ /'tʃænl/ n **1** (strait) canal m; (course of river) cauce m; (navigable course) canal m; **the** (**English**) **C~** el Canal de la Mancha **2** (for irrigation) canal m, acequia f **3** (system, method) vía f; **you must go through the official ~s** tiene que hacer el trámite por los conductos oficiales **4** (Comput, TV) canal m

channel² vt, (BrE) **-ll-** ⟨water/proposals/ complaints⟩ canalizar*; ⟨efforts/energies⟩ encauzar*

channel: C~ Islands pl n the C~ Islands las Islas Anglonormandas, las islas del Canal de la Mancha; **C~ Tunnel** n the C~ Tunnel el Eurotúnel, el túnel del Canal de la Mancha

chant¹ /tʃænt ‖tʃɑːnt/ n (of demonstrators) consigna f; (of sports fans) alirón m, canción f

chant² vt/i (Mus, Relig) salmodiar; «crowd» gritar

chaos /'keɪɑːs ‖'keɪɒs/ n caos m

chaotic /ker'ɑːtɪk ‖ker'ɒtɪk/ adj caótico

chap /tʃæp/ n (colloq) tipo m (fam)

chap. n (pl **chaps**) (= **chapter**) c., cap.

chapel /'tʃæpəl/ n capilla f

chaperon, chaperone /'ʃæpərəʊn/ n (of young lady) acompañante f, chaperona f; (for young people) (AmE) acompañante mf

chaplain /'tʃæplən ‖'tʃæplɪn/ n capellán m

chapped /tʃæpt/ adj ⟨lips⟩ agrietado

chapter /'tʃæptər ‖'tʃæptə(r)/ n capítulo m

char /tʃɑː ‖tʃɑː(r)/ vt **-rr-** carbonizar*

character /'kærəktər ‖'kærəktə(r)/ n **1** (of person, thing) carácter m; **to be in/out of ~** ser*/no ser* típico; **her face is full of ~** tiene una cara con mucha personalidad **2** **(a)** (in novel, play, movie) personaje m **(b)** (person) tipo m (fam) **(c)** (eccentric person) caso m **3** (symbol) carácter m

characteristic¹ /'kærəktə'rɪstɪk/ n característica f

characteristic² adj característico

characterize /'kærəktəraɪz/ vt caracterizar*

charade /ʃə'reɪd ‖ʃə'rɑːd/ n farsa f; **~s** (+ sing vb) (game) charada f

charcoal /'tʃɑːrkəʊl ‖'tʃɑːkəʊl/ n carbón m (vegetal); (Art) carboncillo m, carbonilla f (RPl)

charge¹ /tʃɑːrdʒ ‖tʃɑːdʒ/ n **1** (Law) cargo m, acusación f; **to bring** o **press ~s against sb** formular cargos contra algn **2** (price) precio m; (fee) honorario m; **free of ~** gratuitamente, gratis **3** (responsibility): **the person in ~** la persona responsable; **to be in ~ of sth/sb** tener* algo/a algn a su (or mi etc) cargo; **to take ~ of** (of situation) hacerse* cargo de; (of class, guests) hacerse* cargo de, encargarse* de; (of task) encargarse* de, ocuparse de **4** (Elec, Phys) carga f **5** (of explosive) carga f **6** (attack) carga f

charge² vt **1** (accuse) **to ~ sb WITH sth/-ING** acusar a algn DE algo/+ INF **2** (ask payment) cobrar **3** (obtain on credit): **to ~ sth TO sb** cargar*

algo a la cuenta de algn **4** **(a)** (entrust) (frml) **to ~ sb WITH sth/-ING** encomendarle* A algn algo/QUE (+ subj) **(b)** (allege) (AmE) aducir* **5** (attack) (Mil) cargar* contra; «animal» embestir* or arremeter contra **6** (Elec) ⟨battery⟩ cargar*
■ **~** vi **to ~** (AT **sth/sb**) (Mil) cargar* (CONTRA algo/algn); «animal» arremeter or embestir* (CONTRA algo/algn)

charge: ~ account n cuenta f de crédito; **~ card** n tarjeta f de pago

charger /'tʃɑːrdʒər ‖'tʃɑːdʒə(r)/ n (battery ~) cargador m de pilas; (Auto) cargador m de baterías

chariot /'tʃæriət/ n carro m (de guerra)

charisma /kə'rɪzmə/ n carisma m

charismatic /'kærəz'mætɪk ‖,kærɪz'mætɪk/ adj carismático

charitable /'tʃærətəbəl ‖'tʃærɪtəbəl/ adj **(a)** (generous, giving) caritativo **(b)** (kind) ⟨person⟩ bueno; ⟨interpretation⟩ benévolo, generoso

charity /'tʃærəti/ n (pl **-ties**) **1** **(a)** (organization) organización f benéfica or de beneficencia **(b)** (relief) obras fpl de beneficencia; **to raise money for ~** recaudar dinero para un fin benéfico; ⟨before n⟩ ⟨work⟩ de beneficencia, benéfico **2** (generosity, kindness) caridad f

charm¹ /tʃɑːrm ‖tʃɑːm/ n **1** **(a)** (attractiveness) encanto m **(b)** (attractive quality, feature) encanto m **2** (spell) hechizo m **3** (amulet) amuleto m, fetiche m; (on bracelet) dije m

charm² vt cautivar

charming /'tʃɑːrmɪŋ ‖'tʃɑːmɪŋ/ adj ⟨person⟩ encantador; ⟨room/house⟩ precioso

chart¹ /tʃɑːrt ‖tʃɑːt/ n **1** (Aviat, Naut) carta f de navegación; (diagram, graph) gráfico m; (table) tabla f **2** **charts** pl (best-selling records) **the ~s** la lista de éxitos

chart² vt ⟨course⟩ trazar*; ⟨progress/changes⟩ (follow closely) seguir* atentamente; (record) registrar gráficamente

charter¹ /'tʃɑːrtər ‖'tʃɑːtə(r)/ n **1** **(a)** (constitution) carta f **(b)** (guarantee of rights) fuero m, privilegio m **2** (Transp) ⟨before n⟩ ⟨flight/plane⟩ chárter adj inv

charter² vt **1** ⟨plane/ship/bus⟩ fletar, alquilar **2** (BrE) **chartered** past p ⟨engineer/surveyor⟩ colegiado; **~ed accountant** contador público, contadora pública m,f (AmL), censor jurado, censora jurada m,f de cuentas (Esp)

chase¹ /tʃeɪs/ n persecución f

chase² vt perseguir*
■ **~** vi: **we ~d after the thief** fuimos tras el ladrón; **to ~ after girls** ir* detrás de las chicas
■ **chase up** [v + o + adv, v + adv + o] (colloq): **~ up this order for me, please** averíguame qué pasó con este pedido, por favor; **I'll have to ~ him up about the report** voy a tener que recordarle lo del informe

chasm /'kæzəm/ n sima f, abismo m

chassis /'tʃæsi ‖'ʃæsi/ n (pl **chassis** /'tʃæsiz ‖'ʃæ-/) (Auto) chasis m, bastidor m (Esp)

---

chastise /tʃæs'taɪz/ vt (fml) (verbally) reprender; (physically) castigar*

chastity /'tʃæstəti/ n castidad f

chat¹ /tʃæt/ n charla f, conversación f (esp AmL), plática f (AmC, Méx)

chat² vi **-tt-** to ∼ (**to** o **with** sb) charlar or (esp AmL) conversar or (AmC, Méx) platicar* (**con** algn)

chat: ∼ **line** n chat m; ∼ **show** n (BrE) programa m de entrevistas

chatter /'tʃætər ‖ 'tʃætə(r)/ vi «person» charlar; «monkeys» parlotear; «birds» cotorrear; **his teeth are** ∼**ing** le castañetean los dientes

chatterbox /'tʃætərbɑːks ‖ 'tʃætəbɒks/ n charlatán, -tana m,f

chatty /'tʃæti/ adj **-tier, -tiest** ⟨person⟩ conversador; ⟨letter⟩ simpático y lleno de noticias

chauffeur /'ʃəʊfər ‖ 'ʃəʊfə(r)/ n chofer mf or (Esp) chófer mf

chauvinism /'ʃəʊvənɪzəm ‖ 'ʃəʊvɪnɪzəm/ n chovinismo m; **male** ∼ machismo m

chauvinist /'ʃəʊvənəst ‖ 'ʃəʊvɪnɪst/ n chovinista mf; (**male**) ∼ machista m

cheap /tʃiːp/ adj **-er, -est** [1] (a) (inexpensive) barato; ⟨restaurant/hotel⟩ económico (b) (shoddy) ⟨merchandise/jewelry⟩ ordinario, de baratillo; ⟨mechanic/electrician⟩ (AmE) chapucero [2] (a) (vulgar, contemptible) ⟨joke/gimmick⟩ de mal gusto; ⟨trick/tactics⟩ bajo; ⟨liar/crook⟩ vil (b) (worthless) ⟨flattery/promises⟩ fácil

cheapen /'tʃiːpən/ vt quitarle valor a, degradar

cheaply /'tʃiːpli/ adv ⟨buy/sell/get⟩ barato; ⟨dress/eat/live⟩ con poco dinero

cheat¹ /tʃiːt/ vt estafar, engañar
■ ∼ vi (a) (act deceitfully) hacer* trampas (b) (be unfaithful) **to** ∼ **on** sb engañar a algn

cheat² n (swindler) estafador, -dora m,f; (at cards, in exam) tramposo, -sa m,f

check¹ /tʃek/ n [1] (stop, restraint) control m [2] (inspection — of passport, documents) control m; (— of work) examen m, revisión f; (— of machine, product) inspección f; **to keep a** ∼ **on** sth controlar algo [3] (before n) ⟨jacket/shirt⟩ a or de cuadros [4] (in chess) jaque m [5] (Fin), (BrE) **cheque** cheque m, talón m (Esp); **to pay by** ∼ pagar* con cheque or (Esp) con talón [6] (restaurant bill) (AmE) cuenta f, adición f (RPl) [7] (tick) (AmE) signo m, tic m, visto m (Esp), palomita f (Méx fam)

check² vt [1] (restrain) ⟨anger/impulse⟩ contener* [2] (a) (inspect) ⟨passport/ticket⟩ revisar, checar* (Méx); ⟨machine/product⟩ inspeccionar; ⟨quality⟩ controlar; ⟨temperature/pressure/volume⟩ comprobar*, checar* (Méx) (b) (verify) ⟨facts/information⟩ comprobar*, verificar*, checar* (Méx); ⟨accounts/bill⟩ revisar [3] (AmE) (a) (in cloakroom) dejar en el guardarropa; (in baggage office) dejar or (frml) depositar en consigna (b) (Aviat) ⟨baggage⟩ facturar, chequear (AmL) [4] (tick) (AmE) marcar*, hacer* un tic or (Méx fam) una palomita en, poner* un visto en (Esp)
■ ∼ vi comprobar*, verificar*, checar* (Méx)
■ **check in** [1] [v + adv] (at airport) facturar or (AmL tb) chequear el equipaje; (at hotel) registrarse [2] [v + o + adv, v + adv + o] (Aviat) ⟨luggage⟩ facturar, chequear (AmL)

■ **check out** [1] [v + adv] dejar el hotel (or pensión etc) (habiendo pagado la factura etc) [2] [v + adv] (tally) (AmE) «story» cuadrar [3] [v + o + adv, v + adv + o] (a) ⟨facts/story⟩ verificar*, comprobar*, checar* (Méx) (b) (esp AmE) ⟨shopping⟩ «customer» pagar*; «cashier» cobrar

■ **check up** [v + adv]: we ∼ed up and found out he was lying hicimos averiguaciones y comprobamos que mentía; **can you** ∼ **up on that?** ¿puedes comprobarlo?

checkbook, (BrE) **chequebook** /'tʃekbʊk/ n chequera f, talonario m de cheques (esp Esp)

checked /tʃekt/ adj (no comp) a or de cuadros

checker /'tʃekər ‖ 'tʃekə(r)/ n (AmE) (cashier) cajero, -ra m,f

checkered, (BrE) **chequered** /'tʃekərd ‖ 'tʃekəd/ adj ⟨career/history⟩ accidentado

checkers /'tʃekərz ‖ 'tʃekəz/ n (AmE) (+ sing vb) damas fpl

check-in /'tʃekɪn/ n facturación f de equipajes

checking account /'tʃekɪŋ/ n (AmE) cuenta f corriente

check: ∼**list** n lista f de control; ∼**mate** n (jaque m) mate m; ∼**out** n caja f; ∼**point** n control m; ∼**room** n (AmE) guardarropa m; ∼**up** n (Med) chequeo m, revisión f

cheek /tʃiːk/ n [1] (of the face) mejilla f, cachete m (AmL fam) [2] (colloq) (impudence) descaro m, cara f (fam)

cheekbone /'tʃiːkbəʊn/ n pómulo m

cheeky /'tʃiːki/ adj **-kier, -kiest** (esp BrE) ⟨boy/girl⟩ fresco, descarado; ⟨grin⟩ pícaro

cheep /tʃiːp/ vi piar*

cheer¹ /tʃɪr ‖ tʃɪə(r)/ n [1] (of encouragement, approval) ovación f, aclamación f; **three** ∼**s for** Fred! ¡viva Fred! [2] **cheers** pl (as interj) (drinking toast) ¡salud!

cheer² vt (a) (shout in approval) aclamar, vitorear (b) ∼ (**on**) (shout encouragement at) animar
■ ∼ vi aplaudir
■ **cheer up** [1] [v + adv] animarse [2] [v + o + adv, v + adv + o] ⟨person⟩ animar

cheerful /'tʃɪrfəl ‖ 'tʃɪəfəl/ adj alegre; ⟨news/prospect⟩ alentador

cheerleader /'tʃɪrˌliːdər ‖ 'tʃɪəˌliːdə(r)/ n animador, -dora m,f (en encuentros deportivos, mítines políticos), porrista mf (Col, Méx)

cheese /tʃiːz/ n queso m

cheese: ∼**board** n tabla f de quesos; ∼**cake** n tarta f de queso; ∼**burger** n hamburguesa f con queso; ∼**cloth** n estopilla f, bambula f

cheetah /'tʃiːtə/ n guepardo m, chita f

chef /ʃef/ n chef m, jefe -fa m,f de cocina

chemical¹ /'kemɪkəl/ n sustancia f química, producto m químico

chemical² adj químico

chemist /'keməst ‖ 'kemɪst/ n (a) (scientist) químico, -ca m,f (b) (pharmacist) (BrE) farmacéutico, -ca m,f; **the** ∼**'s** la farmacia

chemistry /'keməstri ‖ 'kemɪstri/ n química f

chemotherapy /ˌkiːməʊ'θerəpi/ n quimioterapia f

cheque /tʃek/ n (BrE) ▶ CHECK¹ 5

chequebook /'tʃekbʊk/ n (BrE) ▶ CHECKBOOK

chequered /'tʃekərd ‖'tʃekəd/ adj (BrE) ▶
CHECKERED

cherish /'tʃerɪʃ/ vt **(a)** (care for, value) apreciar
(b) (cling to) ⟨memory/hope⟩ conservar

cherry /'tʃeri/ n (pl **-ries**) cereza f; (before n)
~ **tree** cerezo m

chess /tʃes/ n ajedrez m

chessboard /'tʃesbɔːrd ‖'tʃesbɔːd/ n tablero
m de ajedrez

chest /tʃest/ n **1** (Anat) pecho m; **to get sth off
one's** ~ desahogarse* contando/confesando algo
2 (box) arcón m **3** (AmE) (treasury) tesorería f;
(funds) fondos mpl

chestnut¹ /'tʃesnʌt/ n castaña f; (before n) ~
tree castaño m

chestnut² adj castaño

chest of drawers n (pl ~**s** ~ ~) cómoda
f

chew /tʃuː/ vt ⟨food⟩ mascar*, masticar*; ⟨gum⟩
mascar*

chewing gum /'tʃuːɪŋ/ n chicle m

chick /tʃɪk/ n (young bird) polluelo, -la m,f; (young
chicken) pollito, -ta m,f

chicken /'tʃɪkən ‖'tʃɪkɪn/ n **(a)** (hen) gallina f;
(as generic term) pollo m **(b)** (Culin) pollo m
■ **chicken out** [v + adv] (colloq) acobardarse,
achicarse* (fam), rajarse (fam)

chickenpox /'tʃɪkənpɑːks ‖'tʃɪkɪnpɒks/ n
varicela f, peste f cristal (Chi)

chickpea /'tʃɪkpiː/ n garbanzo m

chicory /'tʃɪkəri/ n (Bot) endivia f; (in coffee)
achicoria f

chief¹ /tʃiːf/ n jefe, -fa m,f, líder mf; ~ **of police**
jefe de policía

chief² adj (before n, no comp) principal

chief: ~ **constable** n jefe, -fa m,f de policía;
~ **justice** (in US) presidente, -ta m,f del
tribunal

chilblain /'tʃɪlbleɪn/ n sabañón m

child /tʃaɪld/ n (pl **children** /'tʃɪldrən/) **(a)**
(boy) niño m; (girl) niña f **(b)** (son) hijo m;
(daughter) hija f

childbirth /'tʃaɪldbɜːrθ ‖'tʃaɪldbɜːθ/ n parto m

childhood /'tʃaɪldhʊd/ n niñez f, infancia f

childish /'tʃaɪldɪʃ/ adj infantil

childlike /'tʃaɪldlaɪk/ adj ingenuo, de niño

children /'tʃɪldrən/ pl of CHILD

Chile /'tʃɪli/ n Chile m

Chilean¹ /'tʃɪliən/ adj chileno

Chilean² n chileno, -na m,f

chili, chilli /'tʃɪli/ n (pl **-lies**) ají m, chile m

chill¹ /tʃɪl/ n **(a)** (coldness — of weather) frío m,
fresco m **(b)** (Med) enfriamiento m, resfriado m

chill² vt enfriar*; ⟨wine/food⟩ poner* a enfriar

chilli n (pl **-lies**) ▶ CHILI

chilly /'tʃɪli/ adj **-lier, -liest** frío

chime¹ /tʃaɪm/ n (of bells, clock) campanada f; (of
doorbell) campanilla f

chime² vi «bell» sonar*; «clock» dar* la hora

chimney /'tʃɪmni/ n chimenea f

chimney sweep n deshollinador, -dora m,f

chimpanzee /'tʃɪmpænˈziː ‖ˌtʃɪmpənˈziː/ n
chimpancé m

chin /tʃɪn/ n barbilla f, mentón m

china /'tʃaɪnə/ n loza f; (fine) porcelana f

China /'tʃaɪnə/ n China f

Chinese¹ /tʃaɪˈniːz/ adj chino

Chinese² n (pl ~) **(a)** (person) chino, -na m,f
(b) (language) chino m

chink /tʃɪŋk/ n grieta f, abertura f

chip¹ /tʃɪp/ n **1** **(a)** (of wood) astilla f; (of stone)
esquirla f; **to have a** ~ **on one's shoulder** ser* un
resentido **(b)** (in cup) desportilladura f **2** (Culin)
(a) (in packet) (AmE) papa f or (Esp) patata f frita,
papa f chip (Ur) **(b)** (French fry) (BrE) papa f or
(Esp) patata f frita **3** (Games) ficha f **4** (Comput,
Electron) chip m

chip² **-pp-** vt ⟨crockery⟩ desportillar, cascar*
(RPl), saltar (Chi); ⟨tooth⟩ romper* un trocito de
■ ~ vi «china/cup» desportillarse, cascarse*
(RPl), saltarse (Chi); «paint/varnish» saltarse,
desconcharse

chipboard /'tʃɪpbɔːrd ‖'tʃɪpbɔːd/ n **(a)** (of
wood) madera f prensada or aglomerada,
aglomerado m **(b)** (of paper) (AmE) cartón m
prensado

chipmunk /'tʃɪpmʌŋk/ n ardilla f listada

chiropodist /kəˈrɑːpədəst ‖kɪˈrɒpədɪst/ n
pedicuro, -ra m,f, podólogo, -ga m,f, callista mf

chirp /tʃɜːrp ‖tʃɜːp/ vi piar*

chisel¹ /'tʃɪzəl/ n (for stone) cincel m; (for wood)
formón m, escoplo m

chisel² vt, (BrE) **-ll-** ⟨stone⟩ cincelar; ⟨wood⟩
labrar

chivalry /'ʃɪvəlri/ n caballerosidad f, cortesía f

chives /tʃaɪvz/ pl n cebollinos mpl, cebolletas
fpl

chlorine /'klɔːriːn/ n cloro m

chlorofluorocarbon
/ˈklɔːrəʊˈflʊərəʊˈkɑːrbən ‖ˌklɔːrəʊˌflʊərəʊˈkɑːbən,
-flɔːrə-/ n clorofluorocarbono m

chloroform /'klɔːrəfɔːrm ‖'klɒrəfɔːm/ n
cloroformo m

chocolate /'tʃɑːklət ‖'tʃɒklət/ n **(a)**
chocolate m; (candy, sweet) bombón m **(b)** (drinking
~) chocolate m en polvo; **a cup of hot** ~ una
taza de chocolate

choice¹ /tʃɔɪs/ n **(a)** (act, option) elección f; **I
don't work here out of** ~ no es por (mi) gusto que
trabajo aquí **(b)** (person, thing chosen): **she's a
possible** ~ **for the job** es una de las candidatas
posibles para el puesto; **it was an unfortunate** ~
of words no fue la mejor manera de decirlo **(c)**
(variety) (no pl) surtido m, selección f

choice² adj **choicer, choicest** ⟨fruit/wine⟩
selecto; ⟨beef/veal⟩ (in US) de primera

choir /kwaɪr ‖ˈkwaɪə(r)/ n coro m

choke¹ /tʃəʊk/ vt estrangular, ahogar*, asfixiar
■ ~ vi ahogarse*, asfixiarse; **to** ~ **ON sth**
atragantarse or (AmL tb) atorarse CON algo

choke² n (Auto) choke m, estárter m, cebador m
(RPl), ahogador m (Chi, Méx)

cholera /'kɑːlərə ‖'kɒlərə/ n cólera m

cholesterol /kəˈlestərəʊl ‖kəˈlestərɒl/ n
colesterol m

choose /tʃuːz/ (past **chose**; past p **chosen**)
vt **(a)** (select) elegir*, escoger*; ⟨candidate⟩ elegir*
(b) (decide) **to** ~ **to** + INF decidir + INF, optar POR
+ INF
■ ~ vi elegir*, escoger*

choosy /'tʃuːzi/ adj **-sier, -siest** (colloq)
exigente

chop¹ /tʃɑːp ‖tʃɒp/ n ⊡ (with ax, cleaver)
hachazo m; (with hand) manotazo m; (in karate)
golpe m ⊡ (Culin) chuleta f, costilla f (AmS)

chop² **-pp-** vt **(a)** (cut) ⟨wood⟩ cortar; ⟨meat/
apple⟩ cortar ⟨en trozos pequeños⟩; ⟨parsley/onion⟩
picar* **(b) chopped** past p ⟨onions/herbs⟩
picado; ⟨meat⟩ (AmE) molido or (Esp, RPl) picado
■ **chop down** [v + o + adv, v + adv + o] cortar
■ **chop off** [v + o + adv, v + adv + o] ⟨branch⟩
cortar
■ **chop up** [v + o + adv, v + adv + o] ▶ CHOP² A

chopper /'tʃɑːpər ‖tʃɒpə(r)/ n **(a)** (hatchet)
hacha f; pequeña **(b)** (helicopter) (colloq)
helicóptero m

chopping board /'tʃɑːpɪŋ ‖'tʃɒpɪŋ/ n tabla f
de picar

choppy /'tʃɑːpi ‖'tʃɒpi/ adj **-pier, -piest**
⟨sea⟩ picado

chopstick /'tʃɑːpstɪk ‖'tʃɒpstɪk/ n palillo m
(para comer comida oriental)

chord /kɔːrd ‖kɔːd/ n (Mus) acorde m

chore /tʃɔːr ‖tʃɔː(r)/ n (routine task) tarea f;
(tedious task) lata f (fam)

choreographer /ˌkɔːri'ɑːgrəfər
‖ˌkɒri'ɒɡrəf(r)/ n coreógrafo, -fa m,f

choreography /ˌkɔːri'ɑːɡrəfi ‖ˌkɒri'ɒɡrəfi/ n
coreografía f

chortle /'tʃɔːrtl ‖'tʃɔːtl/ vi reírse* (con
satisfacción)

chorus /'kɔːrəs/ n ⊡ (+ sing o pl vb) (in musical,
opera) coro m ⊡ (refrain) estribillo m; (choral piece)
coral m

chose /tʃəʊz/ past of CHOOSE

chosen /'tʃəʊzən/ past p of CHOOSE

Christ /kraɪst/ n **(a)** (Relig) Cristo **(b)** (as interj)
(colloq) ¡Jesús! (fam); **for** ~**'s sake!** ¡por amor de
Dios!

christen /'krɪsn/ vt bautizar*

christening /'krɪsnɪŋ/ n bautismo m, bautizo
m

Christian¹ /'krɪstʃən/ n cristiano, -na m,f
Christian² adj cristiano

Christianity /ˌkrɪsti'ænəti, ˌkrɪstʃi-
‖ˌkrɪsti'ænəti/ n (faith) cristianismo m; (believers)
los cristianos

Christian name n nombre m de pila

Christmas /'krɪsməs/ n Navidad f, Pascua f
(Chi, Per); ⟨~time⟩ las Navidades, la Navidad, la
Pascua (Chi, Per); **merry** o (BrE also) **happy** ~**!**
¡Feliz Navidad!, ¡Felices Pascuas!; (before n) ~
cake pastel m de Navidad (pastel de frutas
cubierto de mazapán y azúcar glaseado); ~ **card**
tarjeta f de Navidad, tarjeta f de Pascua (Chi, Per),
crismas m (Esp); ~ **Day** día m de Navidad or (Chi,
Per tb) de Pascua; ~ **Eve** (day) la víspera de
Navidad; (evening) Nochebuena f; ~ **tree** árbol m
de Navidad or (Chi, Per tb) de Pascua

chrome /krəʊm/ n cromo m

chromium /'krəʊmiəm/ n cromo m

chromosome /'krəʊməsəʊm/ n cromosoma m

chronic /'krɑːnɪk ‖'krɒnɪk/ adj (Med) crónico;
⟨unemployment/shortages⟩ crónico; ⟨smoker/liar⟩
empedernido

chronicle /'krɑːnɪkəl ‖'krɒnɪkəl/ n crónica f

chronological /ˌkrɑːnə'lɑːdʒɪkəl
‖ˌkrɒnə'lɒdʒɪkəl/ adj cronológico

chrysalis /'krɪsələs ‖'krɪsəlɪs/ n crisálida f

chubby /'tʃʌbi/ adj **-bier, -biest** (colloq) ⟨legs/
cheeks/face⟩ regordete (fam); ⟨person⟩ gordinflón
(fam)

chuck /tʃʌk/ vt (colloq) **(a)** (throw) tirar, aventar*
(Méx) **(b)** (throw away) tirar, botar (AmL exc RPl)
(c) (give up) (colloq) ⟨job⟩ dejar, plantar (fam);
⟨boyfriend/girlfriend⟩ plantar (fam), botar (AmC,
Chi fam), largar* (RPl fam)

chuckle /'tʃʌkəl/ vi reírse*

chum /tʃʌm/ n (colloq) amigo, -ga m,f,
compinche mf (fam), cuate m (Méx fam), pata m
(Per fam), pana mf (Ven fam)

chunk /tʃʌŋk/ n pedazo m, trozo m

chunky /'tʃʌŋki/ adj **-kier, -kiest** ⟨person⟩
fornido; ⟨sweater⟩ grueso

church /tʃɜːrtʃ ‖tʃɜːtʃ/ n iglesia f

churchgoer /'tʃɜːrtʃˌɡəʊər ‖'tʃɜːtʃˌɡəʊə(r)/ n
practicante mf

churn¹ /tʃɜːrn ‖tʃɜːn/ n mantequera f

churn² vt ⟨milk⟩ batir; ⟨butter⟩ hacer*
■ **churn out** [v + o + adv, v + adv + o] (colloq)
producir* como salchichas (fam)
■ **churn up** [v + o + adv, v + adv + o] revolver*

chute /ʃuːt/ n tolva f, vertedor m; (in swimming
pool, amusement park) tobogán m, rodadero m (Col)

CIA n (= **Central Intelligence Agency**)
CIA f

cider /'saɪdər ‖'saɪdə(r)/ n **(a)** (alcoholic) sidra f;
hard ~ (AmE) sidra f fermentada **(b)** (non-alcoholic)
(AmE): ⟨sweet⟩ ~ jugo m or (Esp) zumo m de
manzana

cigar /sɪˈɡɑːr ‖sɪˈɡɑː(r)/ n cigarro m, puro m,
tabaco m (Col)

cigarette /ˌsɪɡə'ret/ n cigarrillo m; (before n)
~ **end** colilla f; ~ **holder** boquilla f; ~ **lighter**
encendedor m, mechero m (Esp)

cinch /sɪntʃ/ n (colloq) (no pl) (easy task): **it's a** ~
es pan comido (fam), es tirado (Esp fam), es una
papa or un bollo (RPl fam), es botado (Chi fam)

cinder /'sɪndər ‖'sɪndə(r)/ n **(a)** (ember)
carbonilla f, carboncillo m; **the dinner was burnt
to a** ~ la cena estaba carbonizada **(b) cinders**
pl (ashes) ceniza f, rescoldo m

cinecamera /'sɪniˌkæmərə/ n (BrE) filmadora
f (AmL), tomavistas m (Esp); (large, professional)
cámara f cinematográfica

cinema /'sɪnəmə ‖'sɪnəmɑː/ n cine m

cinnamon /'sɪnəmən/ n canela f

cipher /'saɪfər ‖'saɪfə(r)/ n clave f, cifra f

circa /'sɜːrkə ‖'sɜːkə/ prep alrededor de, hacia

circle¹ /'sɜːrkəl ‖'sɜːkəl/ n círculo m; **their** ~
of friends su círculo de amigos; **to come/go full**
~ volver* al punto de partida

circle² vt ⊡ (move around) dar* vueltas
alrededor de; (be around) rodear, cercar* ⊡ (draw
circle around) trazar* un círculo alrededor de
■ ~ vi dar* vueltas; ⟨aircraft/bird⟩ volar* en
círculos

circuit /'sɜːrkət ‖'sɜːkɪt/ n ⊡ (passage around)
recorrido m, vuelta f ⊡ (Elec) circuito m

circular¹ /'sɜːrkjələr ‖'sɜːkjʊlə(r)/ adj circular

circular² n circular f

circulate /'sɜːrkjəleɪt ‖ 'sɜːrkjʊleɪt/ vi circular ■ ~ vt ⟨report/news⟩ hacer* circular, divulgar*

circulation /sɜːrkjə'leɪʃən ‖ sɜːrkjʊ'leɪʃən/ n circulación f

circumcise /'sɜːrkəmsaɪz ‖ 'sɜːrkəmsaɪz/ vt circuncidar

circumference /sər'kʌmfərəns ‖ sə'kʌmfərəns/ n circunferencia f

circumflex (accent) /'sɜːrkəmfleks ‖ 'sɜːrkəmfleks/ n ⟨acento m⟩ circunflejo m

circumstance /'sɜːrkəmstæns ‖ 'sɜːrkəmstəns/ n **1** (condition, fact) circunstancia f; **in** o **under the ~s** dadas las circunstancias; **under no ~s** bajo ningún concepto, bajo ninguna circunstancia **2 circumstances** pl (financial position): **a person in my ~s** una persona en mi situación económica

circumstantial /'sɜːrkəm'stænʃəl ‖ sɜːkəm'stænʃəl/ adj ⟨evidence⟩ circunstancial

circus /'sɜːrkəs ‖ 'sɜːkəs/ n circo m

cirrhosis /sə'rəʊsəs ‖ sɪ'rəʊsɪs/ n cirrosis f

CIS n (= **Commonwealth of Independent States**) CEI f

cistern /'sɪstərn ‖ 'sɪstən/ n cisterna f

cite /saɪt/ vt citar

citizen /'sɪtəzən ‖ 'sɪtɪzən/ n ciudadano, -na m,f

citizenship /'sɪtəzənʃɪp ‖ 'sɪtɪzənʃɪp/ n ciudadanía f

citrus /'sɪtrəs/ adj (before n) cítrico

city /'sɪti/ n (pl **cities**) ciudad f; (before n) ~ **center** centro m de la ciudad

city: ~ **hall** n (AmE) ayuntamiento m, municipio m; ~ **planner** n (AmE) urbanista mf; ~ **planning** n (AmE) urbanismo m

civic /'sɪvɪk/ adj ⟨authorities⟩ civil; ⟨leader⟩ de la ciudad; ⟨duty/virtues⟩ cívico; ~ **center** edificios mpl municipales

civil /'sɪvəl ‖ 'sɪvl/ adj **(a)** (of society, citizens) civil **(b)** (polite) cortés

civilian /sə'vɪljən ‖ sɪ'vɪljən/ n civil mf

civilization /sɪvələ'zeɪʃən ‖ sɪvəlaɪ'zeɪʃən/ n civilización f

civilized /'sɪvəlaɪzd/ adj ⟨society⟩ civilizado; ⟨person⟩ educado

civil: ~ **liberties** pl n derechos mpl civiles; ~ **rights** pl n derechos mpl civiles; ~ **servant** n funcionario, -ria m,f (del Estado); ~ **service** n the ~ **service** la administración pública; (employees) el funcionariado (del Estado); ~ **war** n guerra f civil; **the C~ War** (in US) la guerra de Secesión

claim¹ /kleɪm/ n **1** (demand): **wage** o **pay** ~ reivindicación f salarial; **insurance** ~ reclamación f al seguro; **a** ~ **for expenses** una solicitud de reembolso de gastos **2** (to right, title) ~ **(TO** sth) derecho m (A algo) **3** (allegation) afirmación f

claim² vt **1 (a)** ⟨throne/inheritance/land⟩ reclamar; ⟨right⟩ reivindicar*; ⟨diplomatic

immunity⟩ alegar* **(b)** ⟨lost property⟩ reclamar **(c)** ⟨social security/benefits⟩ (apply for) solicitar; (receive) cobrar; **you can** ~ **your expenses back** puedes pedir que te reembolsen los gastos **2** (allege, profess): **no one has ~ed responsibility for the attack** nadie ha reivindicado el atentado; **he ~ed (that) he knew nothing about it** aseguraba or afirmaba no saber nada de ello

claimant /'kleɪmənt/ n **(a)** (Soc Adm) solicitante mf **(b)** (to throne) pretendiente, -ta m,f

clairvoyant /kler'vɔɪənt ‖ kleə'vɔɪənt/ n clarividente mf

clam /klæm/ n almeja f ■ **clam up:** -**mm**- [v + adv] (colloq) ponerse* muy poco comunicativo

clamber /'klæmbər ‖ 'klæmbə(r)/ vi trepar; **they ~ed over the wall** treparon al muro y saltaron

clammy /'klæmi/ adj -**mier, -miest** ⟨handshake⟩ húmedo; ⟨weather⟩ bochornoso

clamor, (BrE) **clamour** /'klæmər ‖ 'klæmə(r)/ vi gritar; **to** ~ **FOR** sth ⟨for war/resignation⟩ pedir* algo a gritos

clamp¹ /klæmp/ n **(a)** (Const) abrazadera f; (in carpentry) tornillo m de banco **(b)** (wheel ~) (BrE) cepo m

clamp² vt **(a)** (join, fasten) sujetar con abrazaderas **(b)** (BrE Auto) (colloq) ⟨car⟩ ponerle* el cepo a ■ **clamp down** [v + adv] **to** ~ **down ON** sth/sb tomar medidas drásticas CONTRA algo/algn

clampdown /'klæmpdaʊn/ n (colloq): **a** ~ **on illegal immigrants** medidas fpl drásticas contra los inmigrantes ilegales; **there's been a** ~ **on loans** se ha restringido severamente la concesión de créditos

clan /klæn/ n clan m

clandestine /klæn'destən ‖ klæn'destɪn/ adj clandestino

clang /klæŋ/ vi «bells» sonar*

clank /klæŋk/ vi hacer* ruido

clap¹ /klæp/ n **(a)** (applause): **to give sb a** ~ aplaudir a algn **(b)** **a** ~ **of thunder** un trueno

clap² -**pp**- vt (applaud) aplaudir; **to** ~ **one's hands to the music** dar* palmadas al compás de la música ■ ~ vi (applaud) aplaudir; (to music etc) dar* una palmada

clapping /'klæpɪŋ/ n aplausos mpl

clarify /'klærəfaɪ ‖ 'klærɪfaɪ/ -**fies, -fying, -fied** vt **(a)** (explain, make clear) aclarar **(b)** (purify) ⟨butter/wine⟩ clarificar*

clarinet /'klærə'net/ n clarinete m

clarity /'klærəti/ n claridad f

clash¹ /klæʃ/ n **1** (of interests) conflicto m; (of cultures, personalities) choque m; (of opinions, views) disparidad f **2** (between armies, factions) enfrentamiento m, choque m **3** (noise): **the** ~ **the cymbals** el sonido de los platillos

clash² vi **(a)** «personalities» chocar*; «colors/

AmC	Central America	Arg	Argentina	Cu Cuba
AmL	Latin America	Bol	Bolivia	Ec Ecuador
AmS	South America	Chi	Chile	Esp Spain
Andes	Andean Region	CS	Southern Cone	Méx Mexico

Per	Peru
RPI	River Plate Area
Ur	Uruguay
Ven	Venezuela

patterns» desentonar **(b)** «armies/factions/
leaders» chocar* **(c)** «dates» coincidir **(d)**
«cymbals/swords» sonar* (al entrechocarse)

clasp¹ /klæsp ‖klɑːsp/ n broche m, cierre m

clasp² vt: she ~ed her bag firmly sujetó
firmemente el bolso; he ~ed her in his arms la
estrechó entre sus brazos

class¹ /klæs ‖klɑːs/ n **1** (social stratum) clase f
2 (group of students) clase f; (lesson) clase f; the ~
of '86 la promoción del 86 **3** (group, type) clase f
4 **(a)** (Transp) clase f **(b)** (in UK) (Post): **send the
letter first/second** ~ manda la carta por correo
preferente/normal **5** (style) (colloq) clase f

class² vt catalogar*

classic¹ /'klæsɪk/ adj clásico; ‹scene/line›
memorable

classic² n clásico m; see also CLASSICS

classical /'klæsɪkəl/ adj (of Greece, Rome)
clásico; ~ **music** música f clásica

classics /'klæsɪks/ n (+ sing vb) clásicas fpl

classification /ˌklæsəfə'keɪʃən
‖ˌklæsɪfɪ'keɪʃən/ n clasificación f

classified /'klæsɪfaɪd ‖'klæsɪfaɪd/ adj **(a)**
(categorized) clasificado; ~ **advertising** anuncios
mpl por palabras, avisos mpl clasificados (AmL)
(b) (secret) ‹information› secreto

classify /'klæsəfaɪ ‖'klæsɪfaɪ/ vt **-fies,
-fying, -fied** ‹books/data› clasificar*

class: ~**mate** n compañero, -ra m,f de clase;
~**room** n aula fȝ, clase f

clatter¹ /'klætər ‖'klætə(r)/ vi «pans» hacer*
ruido; «typewriter» repiquetear

clatter² n (of trains) traqueteo m; (of typewriters)
repiqueteo m; (of hooves) chacoloteo m

clause /klɔːz/ n **(a)** (in contract) cláusula f **(b)**
(Ling) oración f, cláusula f

claustrophobia /ˌklɔːstrə'fəʊbiə
‖ˌklɒstrə'fəʊbiə/ n claustrofobia f

claustrophobic /ˌklɔːstrə'fəʊbɪk
‖ˌklɒstrə'fəʊbɪk/ adj claustrofóbico

claw /klɔː/ n (of tiger, lion) zarpa f, garra f; (of
eagle) garra f; (of crab, lobster) pinza f

clay /kleɪ/ n arcilla f; (for children) (AmE)
plastilina® f, plasticina® f (CS)

clean¹ /kliːn/ adj **-er, -est** limpio; ‹joke›
inocente; ‹game/player› limpio; ‹driver's license›
donde no constan infracciones; ‹stroke/features›
bien definido, nítido; **she made a** ~ **break with
the past** cortó radicalmente con el pasado

clean² adv (colloq) **(a)** (completely): **I** ~ **forgot
about it** se me olvidó por completo **(b)** (fairly)
‹fight/play› limpio, limpiamente

clean³ vt **(a)** limpiar; ‹blackboard› borrar; **to**
~ **one's teeth** lavarse los dientes; **you can** ~ **it
off with a sponge** lo puedes quitar con una
esponja **(b)** (dry-clean) limpiar en seco

■ **clean out** [v + o + adv, v + adv + o] (clean
thoroughly) vaciar* y limpiar (a fondo)

■ **clean up** **1** [v + o + adv, v + adv + o]
(physically, morally) limpiar **2** [v + adv] (do cleaning)
limpiar

clean-cut /'kliːn'kʌt/ adj ‹outline› bien
definido; ‹appearance› muy cuidado

cleaner /'kliːnər ‖'kliːnə(r)/ n **(a)** (person)
limpiador, -dora m,f **(b)** (substance) producto m de
limpieza

cleaning /'kliːnɪŋ/ n limpieza f; (before n) ~
fluid líquido m limpiador; **the** ~ **lady** la señora
de la limpieza

cleanliness /'klenlɪnəs ‖'klenlɪnɪs/ n
limpieza f; **personal** ~ el aseo personal

cleanse /klenz/ vt limpiar

cleanser /'klenzər ‖'klenzə(r)/ n (for household
use) producto m de limpieza; (for skin) leche f (or
crema f etc) limpiadora or de limpieza

clean-shaven /'kliːn'ʃeɪvən/ adj ‹face› bien
afeitado or (esp Méx) rasurado

cleansing /'klenzɪŋ/ adj limpiador; ~ **lotion**
loción f limpiadora or de limpieza

clear¹ /klɪr ‖klɪə(r)/ adj **-er, -est** **1** ‹sky›
despejado; **she has very** ~ **skin** tiene muy buen
cutis; **to keep a** ~ **head** mantener* la mente
despejada **2** (distinct) ‹outline/picture› nítido,
claro; ‹voice› claro **3** **(a)** (plain, evident): **it's a** ~
case of suicide es un caso evidente de suicidio; **it
became** ~ **that ...** se hizo evidente que ... **(b)**
‹explanation/instructions› claro **4** (free,
unobstructed) ‹space/road› despejado

clear² adv: **stand** ~ **of the doors** manténganse
alejados de las puertas; **the curtains should hang**
~ **of the radiators** las cortinas no deben tocar los
radiadores; **to keep/stay** ~ **(of sth)** mantenerse*
alejado (de algo), no acercarse* (a algo)

clear³ vt **1** (make free, unobstructed) ‹room›
vaciar*; ‹surface› despejar; ‹drain/pipe›
desatascar*, destapar (AmL); ‹building› desalojar;
‹land› despoblar de árboles, desmontar; **to** ~ **the
table** levantar or (Esp tb) quitar la mesa; **to** ~
one's throat carraspear
2 ‹fence/ditch› salvar; **to** ~ **customs** pasar por
la aduana
3 (free from suspicion) ‹name› limpiar; **he was** ~**ed
of all charges** lo absolvieron de todos los cargos
4 (authorize) autorizar*
5 ‹debt/account› liquidar, saldar

■ ~ vi **1** ‹sky/weather/traffic› despejarse;
«water» aclararse; «fog/smoke» levantarse
2 (Fin) «check» ser* compensado

■ **clear off** [v + adv] (colloq) largarse* (fam)

■ **clear out** [v + o + adv, v + adv + o] ‹cupboard/
drawer› vaciar* y ordenar

■ **clear up** **1** [v + o + adv, v + adv + o] **(a)**
‹crime› esclarecer*; ‹misunderstanding/doubts›
aclarar **(b)** ‹rubbish/toys› recoger*
2 [v + adv] **(a)** (tidy) ordenar **(b)** «weather»
despejar **(c)** (get better) ‹cough/cold› mejorarse;
the rash has ~**ed up** se le (or me etc) ha ido el
sarpullido

clearance /'klɪrəns ‖'klɪərəns/ n
1 (authorization) autorización f; (from customs)
despacho m de aduana **2** (of building land)
desmonte m, despeje m **3** (of stock) liquidación f

clear-cut /'klɪr'kʌt ‖ˌklɪə'kʌt/ adj claro, bien
definido

clearing /'klɪrɪŋ ‖'klɪərɪŋ/ n (in forest) claro m

clearly /'klɪrli ‖'klɪəli/ adv ‹visible/marked›
claramente; ‹speak/write/think› con claridad,
claramente; **it's** ~ **impossible** es a todas luces
imposible, está claro que es imposible

cleavage /'kliːvɪdʒ/ n escote m

cleaver /'kliːvər ‖'kliːvə(r)/ n cuchilla f de
carnicero

clef /klef/ n clave f

cleft[1] /kleft/ adj ‹chin› partido; ~ **palate** paladar *m* hendido, fisura *f* del paladar

cleft[2] *n* hendidura *f*, grieta *f*

clench /klentʃ/ *vt* (a) ‹fist/jaw› apretar* (b) (grip) apretar*, agarrar

clergy /'klɜ:rdʒi ‖'klɜːdʒi/ *n* (+ *sing or pl vb*) clero *m*

clerical /'klerɪkəl/ *adj* [1] (Relig) clerical [2] ‹job/work› de oficina; ~ **assistant** oficinista *mf*

clerk /klɜ:rk ‖klɑːk/ *n* (in office) empleado (administrativo), empleada (administrativa) *m,f*, oficinista *mf*; (in bank) empleado, -da *m,f*, bancario, -ria *m,f* (CS); (sales ~) (AmE) vendedor, -dora *m,f*, dependiente, -ta *m,f*; (desk ~) (AmE) recepcionista *mf*

clever /'klevər ‖'klevə(r)/ *adj* **-verer, -verest** (a) (intelligent) inteligente, listo (b) (artful) (pej) listo (c) (skillful, adept) ‹player/politician› hábil; ‹invention/solution› ingenioso

cliché /kli:'ʃeɪ ‖'kli:ʃeɪ/ *n* lugar *m* común, cliché *m*

click[1] /klɪk/ *vt* ‹fingers› chasquear, tronar* (Méx); ‹tongue› chasquear
■ ~ *vi* hacer* un ruidito seco

click[2] *n* (of fingers, tongue) chasquido *m*; (of camera, switch) clic *m*

client /'klaɪənt/ *n* cliente, -ta *m,f*

clientele /ˌklaɪən'tel ‖ˌkli:ɒn'tel, ˌkli:ən'tel/ *n* (+ *sing or pl vb*) clientela *f*

cliff /klɪf/ *n* acantilado *m*; (not by sea) precipicio *m*

cliffhanger /'klɪf,hæŋər ‖'klɪf,hæŋə(r)/ *n* situación *f* de suspenso *or* (Esp) de suspense

climate /'klaɪmət ‖'klaɪmɪt/ *n* clima *m*

climax /'klaɪmæks/ *n* (pl **-maxes**) clímax *m*; (orgasm) orgasmo *m*

climb[1] /klaɪm/ *vt* ‹mountain› escalar, subir a; ‹tree› trepar a, subirse a, treparse a (esp AmL); ‹stairs› subir
■ ~ *vi* (a) (clamber) trepar, treparse; **she ~ed onto the table** se subió a la mesa, trepó *or* se trepó a la mesa (b) (rise) subir
■ **climb down** [1] [v + prep + o] ‹rope› bajarse por; ‹tree› bajarse de [2] [v + adv] (concede) (colloq) ceder

climb[2] *n* (a) (ascent) subida *f* (b) (Aviat) ascenso *m*

climber /'klaɪmər ‖'klaɪmə(r)/ *n* (a) (rock ~) escalador, -dora *m,f*; (mountaineer) alpinista *mf*, andinista *mf* (AmL) (b) (Hort) enredadera *f*, trepadora *f*

climbing /'klaɪmɪŋ/ *n* (Sport) alpinismo *m*, andinismo *m* (AmL)

clinch /klɪntʃ/ *vt* ‹deal› cerrar*; ‹title› ganar; ‹argument› resolver* de forma contundente

cling /klɪŋ/ *vi* (past & past p **clung**) [1] (a) (hold fast) **to ~ to sth/sb** estar* aferrado A algo/ algn (b) (be dependent) (pej) **to ~ (to sb)** pegársele* A algn [2] (stick) **to ~ (to sth)** pegarse* (A algo)

clingfilm /'klɪŋfɪlm/ *n* (BrE) film *m* transparente (*para envolver alimentos*)

clinic /'klɪnɪk/ *n* (treatment center) centro *m* médico; (in state hospital) consultorio *m*; (private hospital) clínica *f*

clinical /'klɪnɪkəl/ *adj* (a) (Med) (before n) clínico (b) (unemotional) ‹manner/detachment› frío

clink /klɪŋk/ *vt* hacer* tintinear
■ ~ *vi* tintinear

clip[1] /klɪp/ *n* [1] (device) clip *m*, gancho *m* [2] (from film) fragmento *m*, clip *m*

clip[2] *vt* **-pp-** [1] (a) (cut) ‹hair/nails/grass/ hedge› cortar; ‹sheep› trasquilar; ‹dog› recortarle el pelo a (b) (punch) ‹ticket› picar*, perforar [2] (cut out) (AmE) recortar [3] (attach) sujetar (*con un clip*)

clip-on /'klɪpɑːn ‖'klɪpɒn/ *adj* (before n) ‹sunglasses› que se engancha; ‹earrings› de clip

clippers /'klɪpərz ‖'klɪpəz/ *pl n* (for nails) cortaúñas *m*; (for hair) maquinilla *f* (*para cortar el pelo*); (for hedge, lawn) podadera *f*, tijeras *fpl* de podar

clipping /'klɪpɪŋ/ *n* (from newspaper) recorte *m*

clique /kli:k/ *n* camarilla *f*

cloak[1] /kləʊk/ *n* capa *f*; (disguise) tapadera *f*

cloak[2] *vt* ‹purpose/activities› encubrir*; ~**ed in secrecy** rodeado de un velo de misterio

cloakroom /'kləʊkru:m, -rʊm/ *n* guardarropa *m*

clock /klɑːk ‖klɒk/ (a) *n* (timepiece) reloj *m*; **to work around** *o* **round the ~** trabajar las veinticuatro horas del día (b) (Auto) (mileometer) cuentakilómetros *m*; (speedometer) velocímetro *m*
■ **clock in,** (BrE) **clock on** [v + adv] fichar, marcar* *or* (Méx) checar* tarjeta (*al entrar al trabajo*)
■ **clock out,** (BrE) **clock off** [v + adv] fichar, marcar* *or* (Méx) checar* tarjeta (*al salir del trabajo*)

clockwise[1] /'klɑːkwaɪz ‖'klɒkwaɪz/ *adj* ‹direction› de las agujas del reloj

clockwise[2] *adv* en el sentido de las agujas del reloj

clockwork /'klɑːkwɜ:rk ‖'klɒkwɜːk/ *n* mecanismo *m* de relojería; **like/regular as ~** como un reloj; (before n) ~ **toy** (esp BrE) juguete *m* de cuerda

clog[1] /klɑːg ‖klɒg/ *n* zueco *m*

clog[2] **-gg-** ~ **(up)** *vt* ‹pipe/filter› obstruir*, atascar*
■ ~ *vi* «pipe/filter» obstruirse*, atascarse*

cloister /'klɔɪstər ‖'klɔɪstə(r)/ *n* claustro *m*

clone /kləʊn/ *vt* clonar

close[1] /kləʊs/ *adj* **closer, closest** [1] (a) (near) próximo, cercano (b) ‹shave› al ras, apurado; **that was a ~ shave** (colloq) se salvó (*or* me salvé *etc*) por un pelo *or* por los pelos (fam) [2] ‹link/connection› estrecho; ‹contact› directo; ‹relative› cercano; **they are ~ friends** son muy amigos [3] (in similarity): **he bears a ~ resemblance to his brother** tiene un gran parecido a *or* con su hermano [4] ‹fit› ajustado [5] (careful) ‹examination› detenido; **to keep a ~ watch on sth/sb** vigilar algo/a algn de cerca [6] ‹contest/ finish› reñido [7] ‹weather/atmosphere› pesado, bochornoso

close[2] /kləʊs/ *adv* **closer, closest** [1] (in position) cerca; **to draw/get/come ~** acercarse*; ~ **to sth/sb** cerca DE algo/algn [2] (in intimacy): **the tragedy brought them ~r together** la tragedia los acercó más [3] (in approximation): **the temperature is ~ to ...** la temperatura es casi ...; **he was ~ to**

tears estaba a punto de llorar **4** (*in phrases*)
close by cerca; **close together** (physically) juntos;
close up de cerca

close³ /kləʊz/ *n* fin *m*; **to come/draw to a ~**
llegar*/acercarse* a su fin

close⁴ /kləʊz/ *vt* cerrar*

■ ~ *vi* **1** «*door/window*» cerrar(se)*; «*gap/
wound*» cerrarse*
2 «*shop/library/museum*» cerrar*
3 (a) (finish, end) «*lecture/book*» terminar,
concluir* (b) **closing** *pres p* «*minutes*» último;
«*speech*» de clausura

■ **close down 1** [*v + o + adv, v + adv + o*]
«*shop/factory*» cerrar*
2 [*v + adv*] «*shop/factory*» cerrar*

■ **close in** [*v + adv*] (a) «*pursuers/enemy*»
acercarse*; **to ~ in ON sth/sb** cercar* algo/a algn
(b) «*winter*» acercarse* (c) (get shorter) «*day*»
acortarse

■ **close off** [*v + o + adv, v + adv + o*] clausurar

■ **close out** [*v + o + adv, v + adv + o*] (AmE)
liquidar

■ **close up 1** [*v + adv*] «*shop/museum*»
cerrar*; «*wound/gash*» cerrarse*
2 [*v + o + adv, v + adv + o*] «*shop/museum*»
cerrar*

closed /kləʊzd/ *adj* cerrado

closed circuit *n* circuito *m* cerrado; (*before
n*) **closed-circuit television** televisión *f* en circuito
cerrado

close /kləʊs/**: ~-fitting** *adj* ajustado, ceñido;
~-knit *adj* unido

closely /'kləʊsli/ *adv* **1** «*connected/associated*»
estrechamente; **they worked ~ with the French**
trabajaron en estrecha colaboración con los
franceses **2** (a) (at a short distance) «*follow/mark*»
de cerca (b) (carefully) «*study/examine*»
detenidamente; «*watch*» de cerca; «*question*» a
fondo; **a ~ guarded secret** un secreto muy bien
guardado **3** (in approximation): **somebody who
resembled her ~** alguien que se le parecía mucho

closet /'klɑːzət ‖'klɒzɪt/ *n* (AmE) (cupboard)
armario *m*, placard *m* (RPl); (for clothes) armario
m, closet *m* (AmL exc RPl), placard *m* (RPl)

close-up /'kləʊsʌp/ *n* primer plano *m*

closing /'kləʊzɪŋ/**: ~ date** *n* fecha *f* límite,
fecha *f* tope; **~ time** *n* hora *f* de cierre

closure /'kləʊʒər ‖'kləʊʒə(r)/ *n* cierre *m*

clot¹ /klɑːt ‖klɒt/ *n* (blood ~) coágulo *m*

clot² *vi* **-tt-** «*blood*» coagularse

cloth /klɔːθ ‖klɒθ/ *n* (a) (fabric) tela *f*, género *m*;
(thick, woolen) paño *m* (b) (for cleaning) trapo *m*

clothe /kləʊð/ *vt* vestir*

clothes /kləʊðz/ *pl n* ropa *f*; **he had no ~ on**
estaba desnudo; (*before n*) **~ brush** cepillo *m*
para *or* de la ropa, escobilla *f* de ropa (Chi); **~
horse** tendedero *m* (*plegable*); **~ line** cuerda *f* de
tender; **~ shop** tienda *f* *or* casa *f* de modas

clothespin /'kləʊðzpɪn/ (AmE), **clothes-peg**
/'kləʊðzpeg/ (BrE) *n* pinza *f* *or* (Arg) broche *m* *or*
(Chi) perrito *m* *or* (Ur) palillo *m* (de tender la
ropa)

clothing /'kləʊðɪŋ/ *n* ropa *f*

cloud¹ /klaʊd/ *n* (a) (Meteo) (single) nube *f*;
(mass) nubes *fpl*, nubosidad *f* (b) (of smoke, dust)
nube *f*; (of suspicion) halo *m*, nube *f*

cloud² *vt* «*view/vision*» nublar

cloud over [*v + adv*] nublarse

cloudiness /'klaʊdinəs ‖'klaʊdɪnɪs/ *n* (of sky)
lo nublado; (of liquid) lo turbio

cloudless /'klaʊdləs ‖'klaʊdlɪs/ *adj*
totalmente despejado, sin una nube

cloudy /'klaʊdi/ *adj* **-dier, -diest** «*day/sky*»
nublado; «*liquid*» turbio; **it's ~** está nublado

clout¹ /klaʊt/ *n* (colloq) **1** (blow) tortazo *m* (fam)
2 (power, influence) peso *m*, influencia *f*

clout² *vt* (colloq) darle* un tortazo a (fam)

clove /kləʊv/ *n* (a) (spice) clavo *m* (de olor) (b)
(of garlic) diente *m*

clover /'kləʊvər ‖'kləʊvə(r)/ *n* trébol *m*

clown¹ /klaʊn/ *n* payaso, -sa *m,f*

clown² *vi* **~ (around *o* about)** hacer*
payasadas, payasear (AmL fam), hacer* el payaso
(Esp)

cloying /'klɔɪɪŋ/ *adj* empalagoso

club¹ /klʌb/ *n* **1** (a) (cudgel) garrote *m*,
cachiporra *f* (b) (golf ~) palo *m* de golf **2** (society,
association) club *m* **3** (Games) **clubs** *pl* (suit) (+
sing or pl vb) tréboles *mpl*; (in Spanish pack) bastos
mpl

club² **-bb-** *vt* aporrear

■ ~ *vi* (visit nightclubs): **to go ~bing** ir* de
nightclubs

cluck /klʌk/ *vi* «*hen*» cloquear

clue /kluː/ *n* pista *f*; (in crosswords) clave *f*; **not to
have a ~** (colloq) no tener* ni (la más mínima *or*
la menor) idea (fam)

clump /klʌmp/ *n* (a) (of trees) grupo *m*; (of
flowers) macizo *m* (b) (of earth) terrón *m*

clumsily /'klʌmzəli ‖'klʌmzɪli/ *adv* «*handle/
apologize*» torpemente

clumsy /'klʌmzi/ *adj* **-sier, -siest** «*person/
movement*» torpe; «*tool/shape*» tosco; «*translation*»
burdo

clung /klʌŋ/ *past & past p of* CLING

cluster¹ /'klʌstər ‖'klʌstə(r)/ *n* (of people,
buildings, stars) grupo *m*; (of berries, bananas) racimo
m

cluster² *vi* apiñarse, agruparse

clutch¹ /klʌtʃ/ *n* **1** **clutches** *pl* garras *fpl*;
to be in/fall into sb's ~es estar*/caer* en las
garras de algn **2** (Auto) embrague *m*, clutch *m*
(AmC, Col, Méx) **3** (of eggs) nidada *f*

clutch² *vt* tener* firmemente agarrado

■ ~ *vi* **to ~ AT sth** tratar de agarrarse DE algo

clutter /'klʌtər ‖'klʌtə(r)/ *vt* **~ (up)** abarrotar

cluttered /'klʌtərd ‖'klʌtəd/ *adj* abarrotado
de cosas

cm (= **centimeter(s)** *or* (BrE)
centimetre(s)) cm.

c/o (= **in care of** *or* (BrE) **care of**): **John
Smith, c/o Ana Mas** John Smith, en casa de Ana
Mas

Co (a) /kəʊ/ (= **company**) Cía. (b) (Geog)
= **County**

CO **1** (Geog) = **Colorado** **2** (Mil)
= **Commanding Officer**

coach¹ /kəʊtʃ/ *n* **1** (a) (horse-drawn carriage)
coche *m* (de caballos), carruaje *m* (b) (long-distance
bus) (BrE) autobús *m*, autocar *m* (Esp), pullman *m*
(CS) **2** (Rail) (a) (AmE) vagón *m* de tercera (clase)
(b) (BrE) vagón *m* **3** (a) (tutor) profesor, -sora ····❖

m,f particular **(b)** (team manager) entrenador, -dora *m,f*, director técnico, directora técnica *mf* (AmL)

coach² *vt* ‹team/player› entrenar; ‹pupil/ student/singer› preparar

coal /kəʊl/ *n* carbón *m*; (before *n*) ~ **fire** fuego *m* de or a carbón

coalition /ˌkəʊəˈlɪʃən/ *n* coalición *f*

coal: ~**man** /ˈkəʊlmæn/ *n* (pl -**men** /-men/) carbonero *m*; ~**mine** *n* mina *f* de carbón; ~**miner** *n* minero, -ra *m,f* de carbón

coarse /kɔːrs ‖kɔːs/ *adj* **coarser, coarsest (a)** ‹sand/filter› grueso; ‹cloth› basto, ordinario, burdo; ‹features› tosco **(b)** ‹person/manners/ language› ordinario, basto

coast¹ /kəʊst/ *n* **(a)** (shoreline) costa *f*; **the ~ is clear** no hay moros en la costa **(b)** (region) costa *f*, litoral *m*

coast² *vi* «car» deslizarse* (sin llevar el motor en marcha)

coastal /ˈkəʊstl/ *adj* (before *n*) costero

coaster /ˈkəʊstər ‖ˈkəʊstə(r)/ *n* **(a)** (ship) barco *m* de cabotaje **(b)** (drink mat) posavasos *m*

coast: ~**guard** *n* guardacostas *mf*; ~**line** *n* costa *f*, litoral *m*; ~ **to** ~ *adv* (AmE) a lo largo y ancho del país; ~**to-**~ /ˈkəʊsttəˈkəʊst/ *adj* (AmE) de costa a costa

coat¹ /kəʊt/ *n* **1** (Clothing) (over~) (for men) abrigo *m* or (RPl) sobretodo *m*; (for women) abrigo *m* or (RPl) tapado *m*; (jacket) chaqueta *f*; chaquetón *m*; (before *n*) ~ **hanger** percha *f*; ~ **stand** perchero *m* **2** (of animals) pelaje *m* **3** (layer) capa *f*; (of paint) capa *f*, mano *f*

coat² *vt* cubrir*

coating /ˈkəʊtɪŋ/ *n* capa *f*

coat of arms *n* (pl ~**s** or ~) escudo *m* de armas

coax /kəʊks/ *vt*: **I** ~**ed the animal into the cage** con paciencia logré que el animal se metiera en la jaula; **I managed to** ~ **the information out of her** logré sonsacarle la información

cobbled /ˈkɑːbəld ‖ˈkɒbəld/ *adj* adoquinado

cobbler /ˈkɑːblər ‖ˈkɒblə(r)/ *n* zapatero *m* (remendón)

cobblestone /ˈkɑːbəlstəʊn ‖ˈkɒbəlstəʊn/ *n* adoquín *m*

cobra /ˈkəʊbrə/ *n* cobra *f*

cobweb /ˈkɑːbweb ‖ˈkɒbweb/ *n* telaraña *f*

cocaine /kəʊˈkeɪn/ *n* cocaína *f*

cock¹ /kɑːk ‖kɒk/ *n* (male fowl) gallo *m*; (male bird) macho *m*

cock² *vt* **1** ‹gun› montar **2** ‹head› ladear; ‹ears› levantar, parar (AmL)

cockerel /ˈkɑːkrəl ‖ˈkɒkərəl/ *n* gallito *m*

cockeyed /ˈkɑːkaɪd ‖ˈkɒkaɪd/ *adj* **(a)** (ridiculous) disparatado **(b)** (askew) torcido, chueco (AmL)

cockle /ˈkɑːkəl ‖ˈkɒkəl/ *n* berberecho *m*

Cockney, cockney /ˈkɑːkni ‖ˈkɒkni/ *n* (pl -**neys**) cockney *mf* (persona nacida en el East End de Londres, tradicionalmente de clase obrera)

cockpit /ˈkɑːkpɪt ‖ˈkɒkpɪt/ *n* (Aviat) cabina *f* de mando

cockroach /ˈkɑːkrəʊtʃ ‖ˈkɒkrəʊtʃ/ *n* cucaracha *f*

cocktail /ˈkɑːkteɪl ‖ˈkɒkteɪl/ *n* **(a)** (drink) cóctel *m*, coctel *m*, combinado *m*; (before *n*) ~ **bar** bar *m*, coctelería *f*; ~ **cabinet** mueble-bar *m*; ~ **party** cóctel *m*, coctel *m*; ~ **stick** palillo *m*, mondadientes *m* **(b)** (food): shrimp o (BrE) prawn ~ cóctel *m* de camarones or (Esp) de gambas or (CS) de langostinos, langostinos *mpl* con salsa golf (RPl)

cocky /ˈkɑːki ‖ˈkɒki/ *adj* **cockier, cockiest** (colloq) gallito (fam), chulo (Esp fam)

cocoa /ˈkəʊkəʊ/ *n* (powder) cacao *m*, cocoa *f* (AmL); (drink) chocolate *m*, cocoa *f* (AmL)

coconut /ˈkəʊkənʌt/ *n* coco *m*

cocoon /kəˈkuːn/ *n* capullo *m*

cod /kɑːd ‖kɒd/ *n* (pl ~ or ~**s**) bacalao *m*

COD *adv* (= **cash** or (AmE also) **collect on delivery**) contra reembolso

code¹ /kəʊd/ *n* **1** **(a)** (cipher) clave *f*, código *m*; **in** ~ en clave, cifrado **(b)** (for identification) código *m* **(c)** (Comput) código *m* **(d)** (Telec) código *m*, prefijo *m* **2** (social, moral) código *m*

code² *vt* **(a)** (encipher) cifrar, poner* en clave **(b)** (give identifying number, mark) codificar*

coerce /kəʊˈɜːrs ‖kəʊˈɜːs/ *vt* **to** ~ **sb** (**INTO** -**ING**) coaccionar a algn (**PARA QUE** (+ *subj*))

coexist /ˌkəʊɪgˈzɪst/ *vi* **to** ~ (**WITH sb/sth**) coexistir (**CON** algn/algo)

coffee /ˈkɔːfi ‖ˈkɒfi/ *n* (beans, granules, drink) café *m*; **black** ~ café negro or (Esp) solo or (Chi) puro or (Col) tinto; **white** ~ (BrE) café con leche; (before *n*) ~ **bean** grano *m* de café; ~ **break** pausa *f* del café; ~ **maker** cafetera *f*; ~ **mill** o **grinder** molinillo *m* de café

coffee: ~ **klatsch** /klætʃ, klɑːtʃ / *n* (AmE) tertulia *f*; ~**pot** *n* cafetera *f*; ~ **table** *n* mesa *f* de centro, mesa *f* ratona (RPl)

coffin /ˈkɔːfən ‖ˈkɒfɪn/ *n* ataúd *m*, féretro *m*, cajón *m* (AmL)

cog /kɑːg ‖kɒg/ *n* **(a)** (tooth) diente *m* **(b)** (wheel) piñón *m*, rueda *f* dentada

cognac /ˈkɑːnjæk ‖ˈkɒnjæk/ *n* coñac *m*, coñá *m*

cohabit /kəʊˈhæbət ‖kəʊˈhæbɪt/ *vi* (fml) cohabitar (fml)

coherent /kəʊˈhɪrənt ‖kəʊˈhɪərənt/ *adj* coherente

coil¹ /kɔɪl/ *n* **1** **(a)** (series of loops — of rope, wire) rollo *m*; (— of smoke) espiral *f*, volutas *fpl* **(b)** (single loop) lazada *f*, vuelta *f* **2** (contraceptive) (BrE) espiral *f*

coil² *vt* enrollar

coin¹ /kɔɪn/ *n* moneda *f*

coin² *vt* ‹*word/expression*› acuñar; **to ~ a phrase** (set phrase) como se suele decir

coin box *n* depósito *m* de monedas

coincide /ˈkəʊənˈsaɪd ‖ˌkəʊɪnˈsaɪd/ *vi* **to ~ (WITH sth)** coincidir (CON algo)

coincidence /kəʊˈɪnsədəns ‖kəʊˈɪnsɪdəns/ *n* casualidad *f*, coincidencia *f*

coincidental /kəʊˈɪnsəˈdentl̩ ‖kəʊˈɪnsɪdentl̩/ *adj* casual, fortuito

coin-operated /ˈkɔɪnˈɑːpəreɪtəd ‖ˈkɔɪnˌɒpəreɪtɪd/ *adj* que funciona con monedas

coke /kəʊk/ *n* **1** (fuel) (carbón *m* de) coque *m* **2** (cocaine) (colloq) coca *f* (fam) **3** **Coke®** (colloq) Coca-Cola® *f*

colander /ˈkʌləndər ‖ˈkʌləndə(r)/ *n* colador *m*, escurridor *m* (*de pasta, verduras*)

cold¹ /kəʊld/ *adj* frío; **I'm ~** tengo frío; **my feet are ~** tengo los pies fríos, tengo frío en los pies; **it's ~ today** hoy hace frío; **your dinner's getting ~** se te está enfriando la comida; **I got a very ~ reception** me recibieron con mucha frialdad; **I came to the job ~** empecé el trabajo sin ninguna preparación

cold² *n* **1** (low temperature) frío *m*; **come in out of the ~** entra, que hace frío; **to feel the ~** ser* friolento *or* (Esp) friolero, sentir* el frío **2** (Med) resfriado *m*, constipado *m* (Esp), resfrío *m* (CS); **to have a ~** estar* resfriado

cold: ~-blooded /ˈkəʊldˈblʌdəd ‖ˌkəʊldˈblʌdɪd/ *adj* **(a)** ‹*murder*› a sangre fría; ‹*killer*› despiadado, cruel **(b)** (Zool) de sangre fría; **~ cream** *n* crema *f* limpiadora *or* de limpieza, cold cream *f*; **~ cuts** *pl n* (AmE) fiambres *mpl*; **~-hearted** /ˈkəʊldˈhɑːrtəd ‖ˌkəʊldˈhɑːtɪd/ *adj* frío, insensible

coldly /ˈkəʊldli/ *adv* con frialdad, fríamente

cold: ~ sore *n* herpes *m* (labial), fuego *m* (AmL), pupa *f* (Esp fam); **~ storage** *n* almacenamiento *m* en cámaras frigoríficas; **~ war** *n* guerra *f* fría

coleslaw /ˈkəʊlslɔː/ *n* ensalada de repollo, zanahoria y cebolla con mayonesa

collaborate /kəˈlæbəreɪt/ *vi* colaborar

collaboration /kəˈlæbəˈreɪʃən/ *n* (cooperation) colaboración *f*; (with enemy) colaboracionismo *m*

collaborator /kəˈlæbəreɪtər ‖kəˈlæbəreɪtə(r)/ *n* (partner) colaborador, -dora *m,f*; (with enemy) colaboracionista *mf*

collapse¹ /kəˈlæps/ *vi* **1** «*building*» derrumbarse, desmoronarse **2** «*person*» desplomarse; (Med) sufrir un colapso **3** (fail) fracasar **4** (fold up) «*table/chair*» plegarse*

collapse² *n* **(a)** (of building) derrumbe *m*, desmoronamiento *m* **(b)** (Med) colapso *m* **(c)** (of company) quiebra *f*

collapsible /kəˈlæpsəbəl/ *adj* plegable

collar /ˈkɑːlər ‖ˈkɒlə(r)/ *n* **(a)** (Clothing) cuello *m* **(b)** (for animal) collar *m*

collarbone /ˈkɑːlərbəʊn ‖ˈkɒləbəʊn/ *n* clavícula *f*

colleague /ˈkɑːliːg ‖ˈkɒliːg/ *n* colega *mf*

collect¹ /kəˈlekt/ *vt* **1** ‹*information/evidence/data*› reunir*; ‹*dust*› acumular **2** (as hobby) coleccionar, juntar (esp AmL) **3** (fetch, pick up)

recoger* **4** (obtain payment) ‹*rent*› cobrar; ‹*taxes*› recaudar **5** (put in order): **give me some time to ~ my thoughts** déjame pensar un momento

■ **~** *vi* **1** **(a)** (gather, assemble) «*people*» reunirse* **(b)** (accumulate) «*dust/water*» acumularse **2** (for charity etc) recaudar dinero

collect² *adj* (AmE) ‹*call*› a cobro revertido, por cobrar (Chi, Méx)

collect³ *adv* (AmE) ‹*call*› a cobro revertido, por cobrar (Chi, Méx)

collection /kəˈlekʃən/ *n* **1** **(a)** (of evidence) recopilación *f*; (of rent, debts) cobro *m*; (of taxes) recaudación *f* **(b)** (act of fetching): **the goods are ready for ~** puede recoger *or* pasar a buscar las mercancías **(c)** (of mail, refuse) recogida *f* **2** (of money) colecta *f* **3** (group of objects) colección *f*

collective /kəˈlektɪv/ *adj* (*usu before n*) colectivo

collector /kəˈlektər ‖kəˈlektə(r)/ *n* **(a)** coleccionista *mf*; **a ~'s item** una pieza de colección *f* **(b)** (official) cobrador, -dora *m,f*

college /ˈkɑːlɪdʒ ‖ˈkɒlɪdʒ/ *n* **(a)** (university) (esp AmE) universidad *f* **(b)** (for vocational training) escuela *f*, instituto *m*; *see also* TEACHERS COLLEGE **(c)** (department of university) facultad *f*, departamento *m*; (in Britain) colegio *m* universitario

collegiate /kəˈliːdʒət, -dʒiət/ *adj* (esp AmE) universitario

collide /kəˈlaɪd/ *vi* ‹*vehicle*› chocar*, colisionar (frml); **to ~ WITH sth/sb** chocar* CON algo/algn; **we ~ed in the corridor** nos chocamos en el pasillo

collie /ˈkɑːli ‖ˈkɒli/ *n* collie *mf*, pastor escocés, pastora escocesa *m,f*

collision /kəˈlɪʒən/ *n* (of cars, trains) choque *m*, colisión *f* (frml); (of boats) abordaje *m*, colisión *f* (frml)

colloquial /kəˈləʊkwiəl/ *adj* coloquial

collusion /kəˈluːʒən/ *n* colusión *f*

Colo = Colorado

cologne /kəˈləʊn/ *n* (eau de ~) colonia *f*

Colombia /kəˈlʌmbiə/ *n* Colombia *f*

Colombian /kəˈlʌmbiən/ *adj* colombiano

colon /ˈkəʊlən/ *n* **(a)** (Anat) colon *m* **(b)** (in punctuation) dos puntos *mpl*

colonel /ˈkɜːrnl̩ ‖ˈkɜːnl̩/ *n* coronel, -nela *m,f*

colonial /kəˈləʊniəl/ *adj* colonial

colonize /ˈkɑːlənaɪz ‖ˈkɒlənaɪz/ *vt* colonizar*

colony /ˈkɑːləni ‖ˈkɒləni/ *n* (*pl* **-nies**) colonia *f*

color¹, (BrE) **colour** /ˈkʌlər ‖ˈkʌlə(r)/ *n* **1** color *m*; **what ~ is the ball?** ¿de qué color es la pelota?; (*before n*) ‹*photograph*› en colores *or* (Esp) en color; ‹*television*› a color(es) *or* en colores *or* (Esp) en color **2** **colors** *pl* **(a)** (flag) bandera *f*; **with flying ~s: he passed his exams with flying ~s** le fue estupendamente en los exámenes **(b)** (BrE Sport): **the team ~s** los colores del equipo

color², (BrE) **colour** *vt* **(a)** (Art) pintar, colorear; **to ~ sth blue** colorear algo de azul **(b)** (dye) teñir* **(c)** (influence, bias) ‹*atmosphere*› empañar; **you shouldn't let that ~ your judgment** no deberías dejar que eso influya en tu opinión ⋯

c

■ ~ *vi* (flush) ruborizarse*, sonrojarse, ponerse* colorado

color: ~**-blind** *adj* daltónico, daltoniano; ~**-coded** /'kʌlər'kəʊdəd ‖,kʌlə'kəʊdɪd/ *adj* codificado con colores

colored, (BrE) **coloured** /'kʌlərd ‖'kʌləd/ *adj* ⟨walls/blouse⟩ de color

-colored, (BrE) **-coloured** /,kʌlərd ‖'kʌləd/ *suff*: slate~/coral~ de color pizarra/coral

colorful, (BrE) **colourful** /'kʌlərfəl ‖'kʌləfəl/ *adj* ⟨clothes/plumage⟩ de colores muy vivos; ⟨parade/description⟩ lleno de color

coloring, (BrE) **colouring** /'kʌlərɪŋ/ *n* [1] (of skin) color *m*, tono *m*; (of fur, plumage) colorido *m* [2] (food ~) colorante *m*

colorless, (BrE) **colourless** /'kʌlərləs ‖'kʌləlɪs/ *adj* incoloro, sin color; ⟨person/life⟩ anodino, gris

color: ~ **scheme** *n* (combinación *f* de) colores *mpl*; ~ **supplement** *n* suplemento *m* a todo color *or* en color

colossal /kə'lɒsəl ‖'lɒsəl/ *adj* (colloq) colosal

colour *etc* (BrE) ▶ COLOR *etc*

colt /kəʊlt/ *n* potro *m*

column /'kɑːləm ‖'kɒləm/ *n* columna *f*

columnist /'kɑːləmnəst, 'kɑːləməst ‖'kɒləmnɪst, 'kɒləmɪst/ *n* columnista *mf*

coma /'kəʊmə/ *n* (*pl* ~s) (Med) coma *m*

comb¹ /kəʊm/ *n* (for hair) peine *m*, peinilla *f* (AmL), peineta *f* (Chi)

comb² *vt* (a) (pass a comb through): to ~ one's hair peinarse (b) (search) ⟨area/field⟩ peinar

combat¹ /kəm'bæt ‖'kɒmbæt/ *vt*, (BrE) **-tt-** combatir

combat² /'kɑːmbæt ‖'kɒmbæt/ *n* combate *m*

combination /'kɑːmbə'neɪʃən ‖,kɒmbɪ'neɪʃən/ *n* combinación *f*

combine /kəm'baɪn/ *vt* ⟨elements⟩ combinar; ⟨ingredients⟩ (Culin) mezclar; ⟨efforts⟩ aunar* ■ ~ *vi* ⟨elements⟩ combinarse; ⟨ingredients⟩ mezclarse; ⟨teams/forces⟩ unirse

combined /kəm'baɪnd/ *adj* conjunto; our ~ efforts led to success la suma de nuestros esfuerzos nos condujo al éxito

combine harvester /'kɑːmbaɪn 'hɑːrvəstər ‖'kɒmbaɪn 'hɑːvɪstə(r)/ *n* cosechadora *f*

combustion /kəm'bʌstʃən/ *n* combustión *f*; (before *n*) ~ **engine** motor *m* de combustión

come /kʌm/ (*past* came; *past p* come) *vi* [1] (a) (advance, approach, travel) venir*; ~ here ven (aquí); we've ~ a long way since ... (made much progress) hemos avanzado mucho desde que ...; can I ~ with you? ¿puedo ir contigo?, ¿te puedo acompañar?; after a while, you'll ~ to a crossroads al cabo de un rato, llegarás a un cruce; I'm coming, I won't be a moment enseguida voy (b) (originate): where do you ~ from? ¿de dónde eres?; it ~s from Italy viene de Italia (c) to come and go ir* y venir*; three o'clock came and went and he still hadn't arrived pasaron las tres y no llegaba [2] (a) (occur in time, context): Christmas is coming ya llega la Navidad; it came as a complete surprise fue una sorpresa total; to take life as it ~s aceptar la vida tal (y) como se presenta; ~ what may pase lo que pase (b) (as prep) para; I'll

be tired out ~ Friday estaré agotado para el viernes (c) **coming** *pres p*: this coming Friday este viernes que viene (d) to come (in the future) (*as adv*): in years to ~ en años venideros; a taste of things to ~ una muestra de lo que nos espera [3] (reach) (+ *adv compl*) llegar*; the water came up to our knees el agua nos llegaba a las rodillas [4] (be gained): it'll ~, just keep practicing ya te va a salir; sigue practicando; driving didn't ~ easily to me aprender a manejar *or* (Esp) conducir no me fue fácil [5] (be available, obtainable) (+ *adv compl*) venir*; sugar ~s in half-pound bags el azúcar viene en paquetes de media libra; the car ~s with the job el coche te lo dan con el trabajo [6] (+ *adv compl*) (a) (in sequence, list, structure): Cancer ~s between Gemini and Leo Cáncer está entre Géminis y Leo (b) (in race, competition) llegar*; to ~ first (in a race) llegar* el primero; (in an exam) quedar *or* salir* el primero (c) (be ranked) estar*; my children ~ first primero están mis hijos [7] (a) (become) (+ *adj compl*): my dream has ~ true mi sueño se ha hecho realidad (b) (reach certain state) to ~ to + INF llegar* a + INF; ~ to think of it ... ahora que lo pienso ... [8] (*in phrases*): come, come! ¡vamos, vamos!, ¡dale! (CS fam); how come? (colloq) ¿cómo?

■ **come across** [1] [*v* + *prep* + *o*] (find) encontrar(se)*; (meet) ⟨person⟩ encontrarse* con [2] [*v* + *adv*] (communicate, be communicated) ⟨meaning⟩ ser* comprendido; ⟨feelings⟩ transmitirse; he came across very well in the interview hizo muy buena impresión en la entrevista

■ **come along** [*v* + *adv*] [1] (*in imperative*) (a) (hurry up): ~ along, children ¡vamos, niños!, ¡apúrense, niños! (AmL), ¡órale, niños! (Méx fam) (b) (as encouragement, rebuke) ~ along! ¡vamos! [2] (accompany): can I ~ along? ¿puedo ir (yo) también?; ~ along with me ven conmigo, acompáñame [3] (progress) ir*, marchar

■ **come apart** [*v* + *adv*] (a) (fall apart) deshacerse* (b) (have detachable parts) desmontarse

■ **come around**, (BrE also) **come round** [1] [*v* + *prep* + *o*] (turn) ⟨bend⟩ ⟨corner⟩ doblar [2] [*v* + *adv*] (a) (visit) (esp BrE) venir* (a casa) (b) (recover consciousness) volver* en sí (c) (change mind): he'll ~ around eventually ya se va a convencer

■ **come away** [*v* + *adv*] [1] (leave, depart) to ~ away (FROM sth) ⟨from meeting/stadium⟩ salir* (DE algo) [2] (become detached) ⟨handle⟩ salirse*

■ **come back** [*v* + *adv*] (a) (return) volver* (b) (be remembered): it's all coming back (to me) estoy volviendo a recordarlo todo

■ **come down** [*v* + *adv*] [1] (a) (descend) bajar (b) (reach) llegar* (c) (collapse) ⟨ceiling/wall⟩ caerse* (d) ⟨plane⟩ aterrizar*; (in accident) caer* [2] (decrease) ⟨price⟩ bajar

■ **come down to** [*v* + *adv* + *prep* + *o*] (*impers*) ser* cuestión de

■ **come forward** [*v* + *adv*] ⟨witness⟩ presentarse; ⟨volunteer⟩ ofrecerse*; ⟨culprit⟩ darse* a conocer

■ **come in** [*v* + *adv*] [1] (enter) entrar; ~ in! ¡adelante!

2 (a) «*boat*» llegar* (b) «*tide*» subir
3 (be received) «*applications/reports/donations*» llegar*
4 (play useful role): **where do I ~ in?** ¿cuál es mi papel?; **that's where these boxes ~ in** para eso están las cajas

■ **come in for** [*v* + *adv* + *prep* + *o*] «*criticism*» ser* objeto de

■ **come into** [*v* + *prep* + *o*] (a) (enter into) entrar en, entrar a (AmL) (b) (inherit) heredar (c) (be, become relevant): **principles don't ~ into it** no es cuestión de principios

■ **come off** **1** (a) [*v* + *adv*] (detach itself) «*handle*» soltarse*; «*button*» desprenderse; «*wallpaper*» despegarse*; «*dirt/grease*» quitarse (b) [*v* + *prep* + *o*] (fall off) «*horse/motorcycle*» caerse* de
2 [*v* + *adv*] (fare, acquit oneself): **he always ~s off worst** siempre sale perdiendo
3 [*v* + *prep* + *o*] (a) (stop taking) «*drug*» dejar de tomar (b) (be serious): **~ off it!** (colloq) ¡anda! ¡no digas tonterías! (fam)

■ **come on** [*v* + *adv*] **1** (urging sb) (*only in imperative*): **~ on!** ¡vamos! ¡date prisa! *or* (AmL tb) ¡apúrate!, ¡órale! (Méx fam)
2 (a) (begin) «*night/winter*» entrar (b) (begin to operate) «*heating/appliance*» encenderse*, ponerse* en funcionamiento; «*light*» encenderse*

■ **come out**
I [*v* + *adv* (+ *prep* + *o*)] **1** (from inside) salir*
2 «*tooth/hair*» caerse*; «*stain*» salir*
II [*v* + *adv*] **1** (appear) «*sun/stars*» salir*; «*flowers*» florecer*, salir*
2 (be said, spoken) salir*; (be revealed, emphasized) «*secret/truth*» revelarse, salir* a la luz
3 (a) (declare oneself) declararse; **to ~ out on strike** declararse en huelga (b) (as being gay) destaparse (fam), declararse abiertamente homosexual
4 «*newspaper/record/product*» salir*

■ **come over** **1** [*v* + *adv*] (to sb's home) venir* (a casa)
2 [*v* + *prep* + *o*] (affect, afflict): **I don't know what came over me** no sé qué me pasó

■ **come round** (BrE) ▶ COME AROUND

■ **come through** **1** «*message/news/supplies*» llegar*; **you're coming through loud and clear** te recibimos muy bien
2 [*v* + *prep* + *o*] «*ordeal/illness*» salir* de; «*war*» sobrevivir a

■ **come to**
I [*v* + *prep* + *o*] **1** (a) (reach) llegar* a; **what's the world coming to!** ¡hasta dónde vamos a llegar! (b) (occur) «*idea/answer/name*» ocurrírse; **it came to me in a flash** se me ocurrió de repente (c) (be a question of): **when it ~s to ...** cuando se trata de ...
2 (amount to) «*total*» ascender* a (frml); **it ~s to $15 exactly** son 15 dólares justos; **the plan never came to anything** el plan nunca llegó a nada
II [*v* + *adv*] (recover consciousness) volver* en sí

■ **come up** [*v* + *adv*] **1** (a) (ascend, rise) «*person*» subir*; «*sun/moon*» salir* (b) (approach) acercarse*; **to ~ up TO sb** acercársele* A algn
2 (a) (occur, arise) «*problem*» surgir*; **something important has just ~ up** acaba de surgir algo importante (b) (be raised, mentioned) «*subject/point*» surgir*; «*name*» ser* mencionado

■ **come up against** [*v* + *adv* + *prep* + *o*] ⟨*opposition/prejudice*⟩ enfrentarse a

■ **come up for** [*v* + *adv* + *prep* + *o*]: **the car is coming up for its annual service** dentro de poco hay que hacerle la revisión anual al coche; **I should ~ up for promotion next year** me deberían considerar para un ascenso el año que viene

■ **come up to** [*v* + *adv* + *prep* + *o*] (a) (reach as far as) llegar* a *or* hasta (b) (attain) ⟨*standard*⟩ alcanzar*, llegar* a

■ **come up with** [*v* + *adv* + *prep* + *o*] ⟨*plan/scheme*⟩ idear; ⟨*proposal*⟩ presentar; ⟨*money*⟩ conseguir*; **if you can ~ up with a better idea** si a ti se te ocurre algo mejor

comeback /'kʌmbæk/ *n* **1** (return, revival) vuelta *f*, retorno *m*; **to make a ~** volver* a la escena (*or* a la política *etc*) **2** (redress) (*no pl*): **the trouble is that you have no ~ at all** el problema es que no puedes hacer ninguna reclamación

comedian /kə'mi:diən/ *n* humorista *mf*, cómico, -ca *m,f*

comedy /'kɒmədi ǁ'kɒmədi/ *n* (*pl* **-dies**) (a) (play, film) comedia *f* (b) (comic entertainment) humorismo *m*; (*before n*) ⟨*show/program*⟩ humorístico

comet /'kɒmət ǁ'kɒmɪt/ *n* cometa *m*

comfort¹ /'kʌmfərt ǁ'kʌmfət/ *n* **1** (a) (physical, material) comodidad *f*, confort *m* (b) (sth pleasant, luxury) comodidad *f* **2** (mental) consuelo *m*; **to take ~ from sth** consolarse* con algo

comfort² *vt* ⟨*child/bereaved person*⟩ consolar*

comfortable /'kʌmftərbəl ǁ'kʌmftəbəl/ *adj* **1** ⟨*chair/clothes*⟩ cómodo; ⟨*house/room*⟩ confortable; **a ~ lifestyle** una vida desahogada **2** ⟨*margin/majority*⟩ amplio, holgado

comfortably /'kʌmftərbli ǁ'kʌmftəbli/ *adv* ⟨*lie/sit*⟩ cómodamente; ⟨*live/win*⟩ holgadamente

comforter /'kʌmfərtər ǁ'kʌmfətə(r)/ *n* (a) (bedcover) (AmE) edredón *m* (b) (for baby) (BrE) ▶ PACIFIER

comforting /'kʌmfərtɪŋ ǁ'kʌmfətɪŋ/ *adj* ⟨*words*⟩ de consuelo; **it's a ~ thought** es reconfortante pensarlo

comic¹ /'kɒmɪk ǁ'kɒmɪk/ *adj* ⟨*actor/scene*⟩ cómico; ⟨*writer*⟩ humorístico

comic² *n* **1** (comedian) cómico, -ca *m,f*, humorista *mf* **2** (a) (BrE) (book) comic *m*, libro *m* de historietas; (magazine) ▶ COMIC BOOK (b) **comics** *pl* (comic strips) (AmE) tiras *fpl* cómicas, historietas *fpl*, monitos *mpl* (Andes, Méx)

comical /'kɒmɪkəl ǁ'kɒmɪkəl/ *adj* cómico

comic: ~ book *n* (AmE) revista *f* de historietas, tebeo *m* (Esp), revista *f* de chistes (RPl); (for adults) comic *m*; **~ strip** *n* tira *f* cómica, historieta *f*

coming /'kʌmɪŋ/ *adj* (*before n*) ⟨*week/year*⟩ próximo; **this ~ Monday** este lunes, el lunes que viene

comma /'kɒmə ǁ'kɒmə/ *n* coma *f*

command¹ /kə'mænd ǁkə'mɑːnd/ *vt* **1** (a) (order) **to ~ sb to + INF** ordenarle A algn QUE (+ *subj*) (b) ⟨*army/ship*⟩ estar* al mando de **2** ⟨*wealth/resources*⟩ contar* con **3** ⟨*respect*⟩ imponer*; ⟨*fee*⟩ exigir*; ⟨*price*⟩ alcanzar*

command² *n* **1** (a) (order) orden *f* (b)   ····⟶

(authority) mando m; **under sb's ~** bajo las órdenes or el mando de algn **2** (mastery) dominio m **3** (Comput) orden f, comando m

commandant /ˈkɑːməndænt ‖ˈkɒməndænt/ n comandante mf

commandeer /ˌkɑːmənˈdɪr ‖ˌkɒmənˈdɪə(r)/ vt (Mil) requisar

commander /kəˈmændər ‖kəˈmɑːndə(r)/ n **(a)** (officer in command) comandante mf **(b)** (navy rank) ≈ capitán m de fragata

commanding /kəˈmændɪŋ ‖kəˈmɑːndɪŋ/ adj **(a)** ⟨position⟩ de superioridad; ⟨lead⟩ considerable **(b)** ⟨presence⟩ que impone; ⟨tone⟩ autoritario

commanding officer n oficial mf al mando

commandment /kəˈmændmənt ‖kəˈmɑːndmənt/ n precepto m; **the Ten C~s** los diez mandamientos

commando /kəˈmændəʊ ‖kəˈmɑːndəʊ/ n (pl **-dos** or **-does**) comando m

commemorate /kəˈmeməreɪt/ vt conmemorar

commence /kəˈmens/ vi (frml) «session/ celebration» dar* comienzo (frml); «person» comenzar*
■ ~ vt (frml) ⟨work/discussion⟩ dar* comienzo a (frml)

commend /kəˈmend/ vt **1 (a)** (praise) elogiar **(b)** (recommend) recomendar* **2** (frml) (entrust) **to ~ sb/sth to sb** encomendar(le)* algn/algo a algn

commendable /kəˈmendəbəl/ adj loable, encomiable

commendation /ˌkɑːmənˈdeɪʃən ‖ˌkɒmenˈdeɪʃən/ n **(a)** (praise) (frml) encomio m (frml), elogios mpl **(b)** (award) mención f de honor, accésit m

comment¹ /ˈkɑːment ‖ˈkɒment/ n **(a)** (remark) comentario m **(b)** (reaction) comentarios mpl; **no ~** sin comentarios

comment² vi **to ~ (on sth)** hacer* comentarios (sobre algo)
■ ~ vt comentar

commentary /ˈkɑːmənteri ‖ˈkɒməntəri, -tri/ n (pl **-ries**) (Rad, Sport, TV) comentarios mpl, crónica f; (analysis) comentario m

commentator /ˈkɑːmənteɪtər ‖ˈkɒmənt(eɪtə(r)/ n comentarista mf

commerce /ˈkɑːmərs ‖ˈkɒmɜːs/ n comercio m

commercial¹ /kəˈmɜːrʃəl ‖kəˈmɜːʃəl/ adj comercial

commercial² n spot m publicitario, anuncio m, aviso m (AmL), comercial m (AmL)

commercialize /kəˈmɜːrʃəlaɪz ‖kəˈmɜːʃəlaɪz/ vt comercializar*

commiserate /kəˈmɪzəreɪt/ vi: **I ~d with him about losing his job** le dije cuánto sentía que se hubiera quedado sin trabajo

commiseration /kəˌmɪzəˈreɪʃən/ n (often pl) conmiseración f

commission¹ /kəˈmɪʃən/ n **1** (group)

comisión f **2** (for sales) comisión f **3 (a)** (for music, painting, building) encargo m, comisión f (esp AmL) **(b)** (office) (Govt) cargo m

commission² vt **1 (a) to ~ sb to +** inf ⟨artist/writer/researcher⟩ encargarle* a algn que (+ subj) **(b)** ⟨painting/novel/study⟩ encargar*, comisionar (esp AmL) **2 (a)** (Mil) nombrar oficial; **~ed officer** oficial mf (del ejército) (con grado de teniente o superior a teniente) **(b)** (Naut) ⟨ship⟩ poner* en servicio

commissioner /kəˈmɪʃənər ‖kəˈmɪʃənə(r)/ n **(a)** (commission member) comisionado, -da m,f, miembro mf de la comisión **(b)** (of police) (BrE) inspector, -tora m,f jefe

commit /kəˈmɪt/ **-tt-** vt **1** (perpetrate) ⟨crime/ error/sin⟩ cometer **2** (assign) ⟨funds/time/ resources⟩ asignar **3** (send): **to ~ sb to an asylum** internar a algn en un manicomio
■ v refl **to ~ (oneself) TO -ING/+** inf comprometerse (A + inf)

commitment /kəˈmɪtmənt/ n **1 (a)** (responsibility) responsabilidad f; (obligation) obligación f **(b)** (engagement) compromiso m **2** (dedication) dedicación f

committed /kəˈmɪtəd ‖kəˈmɪtɪd/ adj ⟨Christian/feminist⟩ comprometido; ⟨teacher/ worker⟩ entregado a su trabajo

committee /kəˈmɪti/ n (of club, society) comité m, comisión f; (of parliament) comisión f

commodity /kəˈmɑːdəti ‖kəˈmɒdəti/ n (pl **-ties**) **(a)** (product) artículo m, producto m, mercadería f (AmS) **(b)** (Fin) materia f prima

common¹ /ˈkɑːmən ‖ˈkɒmən/ adj **1 (a)** (widespread, prevalent) común; **the ~ cold** el resfriado común **(b)** (average, normal) ⟨soldier⟩ raso; **the ~ people** la gente común y corriente **(c)** (low-class, vulgar) ordinario **2 (a)** (shared, mutual) común **(b)** (public): **it's ~ knowledge** todo el mundo lo sabe

common² n **1** (in phrases) **in common** en común; **to have sth in ~ (with sb)** tener* algo en común (con algn); see also **COMMONS 2** (in UK) terreno perteneciente al municipio

common-: ~ law n derecho m consuetudinario; (before n) **common-law wife** concubina f, conviviente f (Chi); **C~ Market** n **the C~ Market** el Mercado Común; **~-or-garden** /ˈkɑːmənɔːrˈɡɑːrdn ‖ˈkɒmənɔːˈɡɑːdn/ adj (BrE colloq) vulgar or común y corriente

commonplace /ˈkɑːmənpleɪs ‖ˈkɒmənpleɪs/ adj (ordinary) común; (trite) banal

Commons /ˈkɑːmənz ‖ˈkɒmənz/ n (in UK) (+ sing or pl vb) **the ~** la Cámara de los Comunes

common sense n sentido m común

Commonwealth /ˈkɑːmənwelθ ‖ˈkɒmənwelθ/ n **the ~** la or el Commonwealth

commotion /kəˈməʊʃən/ n (no pl) **(a)** (outrage) conmoción f; **to cause (a) ~** producir* una conmoción **(b)** (noise) alboroto m

communal /kəˈmjuːnl ‖ˈkɒmjʊnl, kəˈmjuːnl/

AmC	Central America	Arg	Argentina	Cu	Cuba	Per	Peru
AmL	Latin America	Bol	Bolivia	Ec	Ecuador	RPI	River Plate Area
AmS	South America	Chi	Chile	Esp	Spain	Ur	Uruguay
Andes	Andean Region	CS	Southern Cone	Méx	Mexico	Ven	Venezuela

adj **(a)** ‹*land/ownership*› comunal; ‹*kitchen/ bathroom*› común; ‹*life*› comunitario **(b)** (between groups) ‹*violence*› interno

commune /'kɑ:mju:n ‖'kɒmju:n/ *n* comuna *f*

communicate /kə'mju:nɪkeɪt/ *vi* comunicarse*
■ ~ *vt* comunicar*

communication /kə,mju:nə'keɪʃən ‖kə,mju:nɪ'keɪʃən/ *n* **1** (act) comunicación *f* **2 communications** *pl* comunicaciones *fpl*

communicative /kə'mju:nəkeɪtɪv ‖kə'mju:nɪkətɪv/ *adj* comunicativo

communion /kə'mju:njən/ *n* **1** (Holy C~) la Santa *or* Sagrada Comunión **2** (exchange of ideas, fellowship) (frml) comunión *f*

communism, Communism /'kɑ:mjənɪzəm ‖'kɒmjʊnɪzəm/ *n* comunismo *m*

communist[1], Communist /'kɑ:mjənəst ‖'kɒmjʊnɪst/ *adj* comunista

communist[2], Communist *n* comunista *mf*

community /kə'mju:nəti/ *n* (*pl* **-ties**) comunidad *f*; **the city's black ~** la población *or* comunidad negra de la ciudad

community: ~ center, (BrE) **~ centre** *n* centro *m* social; **~ chest** *n* (in US) *fondos reunidos voluntariamente por la comunidad, destinados a beneficencia y bienestar social;* **~ service** trabajo *m* comunitario (*prestado en lugar de cumplir una pena de prisión*)

commute /kə'mju:t/ *vi* viajar todos los días (*entre el lugar de residencia y el de trabajo*)
■ ~ *vt* ‹*sentence/punishment*› conmutar

commuter /kə'mju:tər ‖kə'mju:tə(r)/ *n: persona que viaja diariamente una distancia considerable entre su lugar de residencia y el de trabajo*

compact[1] /kəm'pækt/ *adj* compacto

compact[2] /'kɑ:mpækt ‖'kɒmpækt/ *n* **1** (**powder**) ~ polvera *f* **2** (agreement) (frml) pacto *m*

compact disc, compact disk /'kɑ:mpækt ‖'kɒmpækt/ *n* disco *m* compacto, compact-disc *m*; (*before n*) **~ ~ player** (reproductor *m* de) compact-disc *m*

companion /kəm'pænjən/ *n* compañero, -ra *m,f*

companionship /kəm'pænjənʃɪp/ *n* compañía *f*

company /'kʌmpəni/ (*pl* **-nies**) *n* **1** (companionship, companions) compañía *f*; **to keep sb ~** hacerle* compañía a algn; **to part ~** separarse; **she's excellent ~** es muy agradable (*or* divertido *etc*) estar con ella; **we've got ~** tenemos visita **2** (Busn) compañía *f*, empresa *f*; (*before n*) ‹*car*› de la compañía *or* empresa **3** **(a)** (Theat) compañía *f* **(b)** (Mil) compañía *f* **(c)** (Naut): **ship's ~** tripulación *f*, dotación *f*

comparable /'kɑ:mpərəbəl ‖'kɒmpərəbəl/ *adj* comparable

comparative[1] /kəm'pærətɪv/ *adj* relativo; ‹*literature/linguistics*› comparado; ‹*analysis/ study*› comparativo

comparative[2] *n* (Ling) comparativo *m*

compare /kəm'per ‖kəm'peə(r)/ *vt* **(a)** (make comparison between) comparar; **to ~ sth/sb TO o** WITH sth/sb comparar algo/a algn CON algo/algn **(b)** (liken) **to ~ sth/sb TO sth/sb** comparar algo/a algn CON *or* A algo/algn
■ ~ *vi*: **how do the two models ~ for speed?** en cuanto a velocidad ¿qué diferencia hay entre los dos modelos?; **this novel ~s favorably with the previous one** esta novela no desmerece de la anterior

comparison /kəm'pærəsən ‖kəm'pærɪsən/ *n* comparación *f*

compartment /kəm'pɑ:rtmənt ‖kəm'pɑ:tmənt/ *n* **(a)** (of bag, desk, refrigerator) compartimento *m*, compartimiento *m* **(b)** (in train) (BrE Rail) compartimento *m*, compartimiento *m*

compass /'kʌmpəs/ *n* **(a)** (magnetic ~) brújula *f* **(b)** (Math) (*often pl*) compás *m*

compassion /kəm'pæʃən/ *n* compasión *f*

compassionate /kəm'pæʃənət/ *adj* compasivo

compatible /kəm'pætəbəl/ *adj* **(a)** ‹*people/ ideas/principles*› compatible **(b)** (Comput) compatible; **an IBM ~ computer** una computadora *or* (Esp tb) un ordenador compatible con IBM

compel /kəm'pel/ *vt* **-ll-** **to ~ sb to +** INF obligar* a algn A + INF

compelling /kəm'pelɪŋ/ *adj* ‹*argument*› convincente; ‹*book*› absorbente

compendium /kəm'pendiəm/ *n* (*pl* **-diums** *or* **-dia** /-dɪə/) (BrE) **(a)** (book) compendio *m* **(b)** (of games) juegos *mpl* reunidos

compensate /'kɑ:mpənseɪt ‖'kɒmpenseɪt/ *vt* indemnizar*, compensar; **to ~ sb FOR sth** indemnizar* *or* compensar a algn POR algo
■ ~ *vi* **to ~ FOR sth** compensar algo

compensation /'kɑ:mpən'seɪʃən ‖,kɒmpen'seɪʃən/ *n* **(a)** (recompense) indemnización *f*, compensación *f*; **I received $20,000 as o in ~ for the damage** me dieron 20.000 dólares de indemnización *or* en compensación por los daños **(b)** (remuneration) (AmE) remuneración *f*

compete /kəm'pi:t/ *vi* competir*; **to ~ FOR sth** competir* POR algo

competence /'kɑ:mpətəns ‖'kɒmpɪtəns/ *n* competencia *f*

competent /'kɑ:mpətənt ‖'kɒmpɪtənt/ *adj* competente

competition /'kɑ:mpə'tɪʃən ‖,kɒmpə'tɪʃən/ *n* **1** **(a)** (competing) competencia *f*; **to be in ~ with sb/sth** competir* con algn/algo **(b)** (opposition) competencia *f* **2** (contest) concurso *m*; (Sport) competencia *f* (AmL), competición *f* (Esp)

competitive /kəm'petətɪv ‖kəm'petɪtɪv/ *adj* competitivo

competitiveness /kəm'petətɪvnəs ‖kəm'petɪtɪvnɪs/ *n* **(a)** (of business, economy) competitividad *f* **(b)** (of person) espíritu *m* competitivo

competitor /kəm'petətər ‖kəm'petɪtə(r)/ *n* **(a)** (contestant) participante *mf*, concursante *mf* **(b)** (rival) (Busn) competidor, -dora *m,f*, rival *mf*; (Sport) contrincante *mf*

compile /kəm'paɪl/ *vt* **(a)** ‹*dictionary/index*› compilar **(b)** ‹*information*› recopilar, reunir*

complacent /kəm'pleɪsn̩t/ *adj* ‹*person*› satisfecho de sí mismo; ‹*attitude*› displicente

complain /kəm'pleɪn/ vi/t quejarse

complaint /kəm'pleɪnt/ n (a) (grievance) queja f, reclamo m (AmL); **to make a ~** quejarse (b) (ailment) dolencia f (frml)

complement¹ /'kɑːmpləmənt ‖'kɒmplɪmənt/ n **1** ~ (**to** sth) complemento m (DE algo) **2** (full number): **the orchestra had the full ~ of strings** la orquesta contaba con una sección de cuerdas completa

complement² vt complementar

complementary /'kɑːmplə'mentri ‖ˌkɒmplɪ'mentri/ adj complementario

complete¹ /kəm'pliːt/ adj **1** (a) (entire) completo (b) (finished) terminado, concluido **2** (thorough, absolute) (as intensifier) total, completo; **it came as a ~ surprise** fue una auténtica sorpresa

complete² vt (a) (finish) ⟨building/education⟩ acabar, terminar; ⟨sentence⟩ cumplir; ⟨investigations⟩ completar, concluir* (b) (make whole) ⟨set/collection⟩ completar (c) (fill in) (frml) ⟨form⟩ llenar, rellenar

completely /kəm'pliːtli/ adv completamente, totalmente

completion /kəm'pliːʃən/ n finalización f, terminación f

complex¹ /'kɑːmpleks ‖'kɒmpleks/ adj complejo

complex² n **1** (buildings) complejo m **2** (Psych) complejo m

complexion /kəm'plekʃən/ n cutis m; (in terms of color) tez f

complexity /kəm'pleksəti/ n (pl **-ties**) complejidad f

complicate /'kɑːmpləkeɪt ‖'kɒmplɪkeɪt/ vt complicar*

complicated /'kɑːmpləkeɪtəd ‖'kɒmplɪkeɪtɪd/ adj complicado

complication /'kɑːmplə'keɪʃən ‖ˌkɒmplɪ'keɪʃən/ n complicación f; **~s set in** (Med) surgieron complicaciones

compliment¹ /'kɑːmpləmənt ‖'kɒmplɪmənt/ n (a) (expression of praise) cumplido m, halago m; **to pay sb a ~** hacerle* un cumplido a algn, halagar* a algn (b) **compliments** pl (best wishes) saludos mpl; **with the ~s of the management** gentileza de la casa

compliment² vt **to ~ sb** (**on** sth) felicitar a algn (POR algo)

complimentary /'kɑːmplə'mentəri ‖ˌkɒmplɪ'mentri/ adj (a) (flattering) elogioso, halagüeño (b) (free) ⟨copy⟩ de obsequio or regalo; **~ ticket** invitación f

comply /kəm'plaɪ/ vi **-plies, -plying, -plied**: **to ~ with a request/an order** acceder a una solicitud/cumplir una orden

component¹ /kəm'pəʊnənt/ n componente m; (Auto) pieza f; (Electron) componente m

component² adj componente; ⟨element⟩ constituyente; **~ part** componente m

compose /kəm'pəʊz/ vt **1** (constitute) (usu pass) **to be ~d** OF sth estar* compuesto DE algo **2** ⟨music⟩ componer*; ⟨letter⟩ redactar **3** (calm, control) (liter): **to ~ oneself** serenarse, recobrar la compostura

composed /kəm'pəʊzd/ adj sereno

composer /kəm'pəʊzər ‖kəm'pəʊzə(r)/ n compositor, -tora m,f

composition /'kɑːmpə'zɪʃən ‖ˌkɒmpə'zɪʃən/ n composición f

compost /'kɑːmpəʊst ‖'kɒmpɒst/ n abono m orgánico

composure /kəm'pəʊʒər ‖kəm'pəʊʒə(r)/ n compostura f

compound¹ /'kɑːmpaʊnd ‖'kɒmpaʊnd/ adj ⟨number/interest⟩ compuesto

compound² /'kɑːmpaʊnd ‖'kɒmpaʊnd/ n **1** (a) (Chem) compuesto m (b) (word) palabra f compuesta **2** (residence) complejo m habitacional; (for prisoners etc) barracones mpl

compound³ /kəm'paʊnd ‖kəm'paʊnd/ vt ⟨problem⟩ agravar; ⟨risk/difficulties⟩ acrecentar*

comprehend /'kɑːmprɪ'hend ‖ˌkɒmprɪ'hend/ vt comprender

comprehension /'kɑːmprɪ'hentʃən ‖ˌkɒmprɪ'henʃən/ n (a) (understanding) comprensión f (b) (school exercise) (BrE) ejercicio m de comprensión

comprehensive /'kɑːmprɪ'hensɪv ‖ˌkɒmprɪ'hensɪv/ adj (a) ⟨survey/report⟩ exhaustivo, global; ⟨view⟩ integral, de conjunto; ⟨list/range⟩ completo; ⟨insurance/cover⟩ contra todo riesgo (b) (Educ) (in UK) relativo al sistema educativo en el cual no se separa a los alumnos según su nivel de aptitud

comprehensive (school) n (in UK) instituto de segunda enseñanza para alumnos de cualquier nivel de aptitud

compress¹ /kəm'pres/ vt comprimir

compress² /'kɑːmpres ‖'kɒmpres/ n compresa f

comprise /kəm'praɪz/ vt (a) (consist of) comprender (b) (constitute, make up) componer*

compromise¹ /'kɑːmprəmaɪz ‖'kɒmprəmaɪz/ n acuerdo m mutuo, arreglo m, compromiso m

compromise² vi transigir*, transar (AmL) ■ **~** vt (a) (discredit) comprometer; **to ~ oneself** ponerse* en una situación comprometida (b) (endanger) comprometer

compromising /'kɑːmprəmaɪzɪŋ ‖'kɒmprəmaɪzɪŋ/ adj ⟨evidence⟩ comprometedor; ⟨situation⟩ comprometido

compulsion /kəm'pʌlʃən/ n (a) (force, duress) coacción f (b) (obsession) compulsión f

compulsive /kəm'pʌlsɪv/ adj (a) (compelling): **the book is ~ reading** es uno de esos libros que se empiezan y no se pueden dejar (b) (obsessive) ⟨behavior⟩ compulsivo; **he's a ~ eater/liar** come/miente por compulsión

compulsory /kəm'pʌlsəri/ adj ⟨attendance⟩ obligatorio; ⟨retirement⟩ forzoso; **~ education** enseñanza f obligatoria

computer /kəm'pjuːtər ‖kəm'pjuːtə(r)/ n computadora f (esp AmL), computador m (esp AmL), ordenador m (Esp); ⟨before n⟩ ⟨society/age/revolution⟩ de la informática; ⟨program/game⟩ de computadora (or ordenador etc)

computer: ~ crime n delito m informático; **~ dating** n citas fpl por computadora or (Esp tb) ordenador

computerize /kəm'pju:təraɪz/ *vt* computarizar*, computerizar*; ⟨company/ department⟩ informatizar*

computer: ∼-literate *adj* capacitado para operar un ordenador; ∼ **programmer** *n* programador, -dora *m,f*; ∼ **programming** *n* programación *f*; ∼ **science** *n* informática *f*; ∼ **studies** *n* informática *f*, computación *f*

computing /kəm'pju:tɪŋ/ *n* informática *f*, computación *f*

comrade /'kɑ:mræd ‖'kɒmreɪd/ *n* compañero, -ra *m,f*, camarada *mf*

con¹ /kɑ:n ‖kɒn/ *n* **1** (fraud) (colloq) timo *m* (fam), estafa *f* **2** (convict) (sl) preso, -sa *m,f* **3** (colloq) (objection) contra *m*; *see also* PRO 2

con² *vt* **-nn-** (colloq) timar (fam), estafar

concave /'kɑ:nkeɪv ‖'kɒŋkeɪv/ *adj* cóncavo

conceal /kən'si:l/ *vt* ⟨object/facts⟩ ocultar; ⟨emotions⟩ disimular; **to ∼ sth FROM sb** ocultar(le) algo A algn

concede /kən'si:d/ *vt* **(a)** (admit) reconocer* **(b)** (allow) ⟨right/privilege⟩ conceder **(c)** (give away) ⟨game/penalty⟩ conceder

conceit /kən'si:t/ *n* engreimiento *m*, presunción *f*

conceited /kən'si:təd ‖kən'si:tɪd/ *adj* engreído, presuntuoso

conceivable /kən'si:vəbəl/ *adj* imaginable

conceive /kən'si:v/ *vt* **1 (a)** (devise) ⟨plan⟩ concebir* **(b)** (imagine) imaginar; (consider) considerar **2** ⟨child⟩ concebir* ■ ∼ *vi* concebir*

concentrate¹ /'kɑ:nsəntreɪt ‖'kɒnsəntreɪt/ *vt* **to ∼ sth** (ON sth) concentrar algo (EN algo) ■ ∼ *vi* «person» concentrarse; «talks» centrarse; **∼ on getting this finished** concéntrate en terminar esto

concentrate² *n* concentrado *m*

concentrated /'kɑ:nsəntreɪtɪd ‖'kɒnsəntreɪtɪd/ *adj* **(a)** ⟨effort⟩ intenso y continuado **(b)** ⟨solution/juice⟩ concentrado

concentration /'kɑ:nsən'treɪʃən ‖,kɒnsən'treɪʃən/ *n* concentración *f*

concentration camp *n* campo *m* de concentración

concept /'kɑ:nsept ‖'kɒnsept/ *n* concepto *m*

conception /kən'sepʃən/ *n* **1** (idea) noción *f* **2** (of baby, plan) concepción *f*

concern¹ /kən'sɜ:rn ‖kən'sɜ:n/ *n* **1** (business, affair) asunto *m*; **that's no ∼ of yours** eso no es asunto tuyo **2 (a)** (anxiety) preocupación *f*, inquietud *f* **(b)** (interest) ∼ **FOR** sb/sth interés *m* POR algn/algo; **to be of ∼ to sb** importarle a algn **3** (firm) empresa *f*; ▸ GOING²

concern² *vt* **1** (affect, involve) concernir*, incumbir; **to be ∼ed WITH sth** ocuparse DE algo; **as far as I'm ∼ed** en lo que a mí respecta, por mi parte; **to whom it may ∼** (fml) a quien corresponda (fml) **2 (a)** (interest) interesar **(b)** (worry, bother) preocupar, inquietar **3** (relate to): **item one ∼s the new office** el primer punto trata de la nueva oficina

concerned /kən'sɜ:rnd ‖kən'sɜ:nd/ *adj* ⟨person⟩ preocupado; ⟨look⟩ de preocupación; **to be ∼ ABOUT/FOR sb/sth** estar* preocupado POR algn/algo

concerning /kən'sɜ:rnɪŋ ‖kən'sɜ:nɪŋ/ *prep* sobre, acerca de, con respecto a

concert¹ /'kɑ:nsərt ‖'kɒnsət/ *n* concierto *m*; **in** ∼ en vivo, en concierto; (before *n*) ∼ **hall** sala *f* de conciertos, auditorio *m*

concert² /kən'sɜ:rt ‖kən'sɜ:t/ *vt* (fml) concertar*, coordinar; **we made a ∼ed effort to ...** coordinamos or concertamos nuestros esfuerzos para ...

concerto /kən'tʃertəʊ ‖kən'tʃɜ:təʊ, kən'tʃeətəʊ/ *n* (*pl* **-tos** or **-ti** /-ti/) concierto *m*

concession /kən'seʃən/ *n* concesión *f*

conciliation /kən'sɪli'eɪʃən/ *n* conciliación *f*

conciliatory /kən'sɪliətɔ:ri ‖kən'sɪliətəri/ *adj* conciliador, conciliatorio

concise /kən'saɪs/ *adj* conciso

conclude /kən'klu:d/ *vt* **1 (a)** (end) concluir* (fml), finalizar* **(b)** (settle) ⟨deal⟩ cerrar*; ⟨agreement⟩ llegar* a; ⟨treaty⟩ firmar; ⟨alliance⟩ pactar **2** (infer) concluir* (fml) ■ ∼ *vi* concluir* (fml), terminar

conclusion /kən'klu:ʒən/ *n* **1** (end) conclusión *f*; **in** ∼ (as linker) para concluir **2** (decision, judgment) conclusión *f*; **to come to** *o* **reach a** ∼ llegar* a una conclusión; **to jump to** ∼s precipitarse (a sacar conclusiones)

conclusive /kən'klu:sɪv/ *adj* ⟨evidence/ argument⟩ concluyente; ⟨victory⟩ decisivo

concoct /kən'kɑ:kt ‖kən'kɒkt/ *vt* ⟨meal/drink⟩ preparar; ⟨excuse/story⟩ inventarse; ⟨plan⟩ tramar

concrete¹ /kɑ:n'kri:t, 'kɑ:nkri:t ‖'kɒnkri:t/ *adj* concreto

concrete² /'kɑ:nkri:t ‖'kɒnkri:t/ *n* hormigón *m*, concreto *m* (AmL)

concur /kən'kɜ:r ‖kən'kɜ:(r)/ *vi* **-rr-** (fml) **to ∼** (WITH sb/sth) coincidir (CON algn/algo)

concuss /kən'kʌs/ *vt* (*usu pass*): **to be ∼ed** sufrir una conmoción (cerebral) *or* una concusión

concussion /kən'kʌʃən/ *n* conmoción *f* cerebral, concusión *f*

condemn /kən'dem/ *vt* **1 (a)** (sentence) condenar **(b)** (censure) condenar **2 (a)** (declare unusable) ⟨building⟩ declarar ruinoso **(b)** (in US: convert to public use) ⟨building⟩ expropiar (*por causa de utilidad pública*)

condemnation /'kɑ:ndem'neɪʃən ‖,kɒndem'neɪʃən/ *n* condena *f*

condensation /'kɑ:nden'seɪʃən ‖,kɒnden'seɪʃən/ *n* **(a)** (process) condensación *f* **(b)** (on windows etc) vapor *m*, vaho *m*

condense /kən'dens/ *vt* **1** (abridge) ⟨book/ article⟩ condensar **2** (Chem) condensar

condensed /kən'densd/ *adj* condensado; ∼ **milk** leche *f* condensada

condescend /'kɑ:ndɪ'send ‖,kɒndɪ'send/ *vi* **to ∼ to + INF** dignarse *or* condescender* A + INF

condescending /'kɑ:ndɪ'sendɪŋ ‖,kɒndɪ'sendɪŋ/ *adj* ⟨tone/smile⟩ condescendiente

condiment /'kɑ:ndəmənt ‖'kɒndɪmənt/ *n* (seasoning) condimento *m*, aliño *m*; (relish) salsa *f* (*para condimentar*)

condition¹ /kən'dɪʃən/ *n* **1** (stipulation, requirement) condición *f*; **on ∼ that** con la condición de que **2 (a)** (state) (*no pl*) estado *m*, ⋯⟩

condiciones fpl; **in good** ∼ **en buen estado (b)** (state of fitness): **to be in/out of** ∼ estar*/no estar* en forma **(c)** (Med) afección f (frml), enfermedad f **3** **conditions** pl **(a)** (circumstances) condiciones fpl; **working/housing** ∼s condiciones de trabajo/ vivienda **(b)** (Meteo): **weather** ∼s **are good** el estado del tiempo es bueno

condition² vt **(a)** (influence, determine) condicionar **(b)** ⟨hair⟩ acondicionar

conditional /kən'dɪʃnəl ‖kən'dɪʃənl/ adj **(a)** (provisional) condicional **(b)** (Ling) condicional

conditioner /kən'dɪʃnər ‖kən'dɪʃnə(r)/ n (hair ∼) acondicionador m, enjuague m (AmL), suavizante m (Esp), bálsamo m (Chi); (fabric ∼) suavizante m

conditioning /kən'dɪʃnɪŋ/ n (Psych) condicionamiento m

condo /'kɑːndəʊ ‖'kɒndəʊ/ n (AmE colloq) ▶ CONDOMINIUM

condolences /kən'dəʊlənsɪz/ pl n (frml) condolencias fpl (frml)

condom /'kɑːndəm ‖'kɒndɒm/ n preservativo m, condón m

condominium /ˌkɑːndə'mɪniəm ‖ˌkɒndə'mɪniəm/ n (pl ∼s) (AmE) apartamento m, piso m (Esp) (en régimen de propiedad horizontal)

condone /kən'dəʊn/ vt aprobar*

conduct¹ /'kɑːndʌkt ‖'kɒndʌkt/ n conducta f

conduct² /kən'dʌkt/ vt **(a)** ⟨inquiry/ experiment/business⟩ llevar a cabo, realizar*; ⟨conversation⟩ mantener* **(b)** (Mus) dirigir* **(c)** ⟨visitor/tour/party⟩ guiar* **(d)** ⟨heat/electricity⟩ conducir*

conductor /kən'dʌktər ‖kən'dʌktə(r)/ n **1** (Mus) director, -tora m,f (de orquesta) **2** (on bus) cobrador, -dora m,f, guarda mf (RPl); (on train) (AmE) cobrador, -dora m,f **3** (Elec, Phys) conductor m

cone /kəʊn/ n **(a)** (Auto, Math) cono m **(b)** (ice-cream ∼) cucurucho m or barquillo m or (Ven) barquilla f or (Col) cono m

confectionery /kən'fekʃəneri ‖kən'fekʃənəri/ n productos mpl de confitería

confer /kən'fɜːr ‖kən'fɜː(r)/ **-rr-** vt (bestow) conceder, conferir* (frml); **to** ∼ **sth** ON o UPON sb/ sth concederle or (frml) conferirle* algo A algn/ algo
■ ∼ vi (discuss) consultar

conference /'kɑːnfrəns ‖'kɒnfərəns/ n **(a)** (large assembly, convention) congreso m, conferencia f; (before n) ∼ **center** o (BrE) **centre** centro m de conferencias **(b)** (meeting, discussion) conferencia f; (before n) ∼ **room** sala f de juntas

confess /kən'fes/ vt confesar*
■ ∼ vi **(a)** (admit) confesar* **(b)** (Relig) confesarse*

confession /kən'feʃən/ n **(a)** (statement) confesión f **(b)** (Relig) confesión f

confetti /kən'feti/ n confeti m or (Chi) chaya f or (RPl) papel m picado or (Ven) papelillos mpl

confide /kən'faɪd/ vi (tell secrets) **to** ∼ **IN** sb confiarse* A algn
■ ∼ vt **to** ∼ **sth TO** sb confiarle* algo A algn

confidence /'kɑːnfədəns ‖'kɒnfɪdəns/ n **1** **(a)** (trust, faith) confianza f **(b)** (self-confidence) confianza f en sí mismo **2** (confidentiality): **he took her into his** ∼ se confió a ella; **in** ∼ en confianza

confidence game n (AmE), **confidence trick** n estafa f, timo m (fam)

confident /'kɑːnfədənt ‖'kɒnfɪdənt/ adj **(a)** (sure) ⟨statement/forecast⟩ hecho con confianza; **to be** ∼ **OF** sth confiar* EN algo **(b)** (self-confident) ⟨person⟩ seguro de sí mismo

confidential /ˌkɑːnfə'dentʃəl ‖ˌkɒnfɪ'denʃəl/ adj confidencial

confidentiality /ˌkɑːnfə'dentʃi'æləti ‖ˌkɒnfɪdenʃɪ'æləti/ n confidencialidad f

confine /kən'faɪn/ vt **(a)** (limit, restrict) **to** ∼ **sth TO** sth limitar algo A algo **(b)** (shut in, imprison) ⟨person⟩ confinar, recluir*; ⟨animal⟩ encerrar*

confined /kən'faɪnd/ adj ⟨space⟩ limitado

confinement /kən'faɪnmənt/ n **(a)** (act, state) reclusión f, confinamiento m **(b)** (in childbirth) parto m

confines /'kɑːnfaɪnz ‖'kɒnfaɪnz/ pl n confines mpl

confirm /kən'fɜːrm ‖kən'fɜːm/ vt **1** **(a)** (substantiate) ⟨report/reservation⟩ confirmar **(b)** **confirmed** past p ⟨bachelor/liar⟩ empedernido **2** (Relig) confirmar

confirmation /ˌkɑːnfər'meɪʃən ‖ˌkɒnfə'meɪʃən/ n **1** **(a)** (substantiation) confirmación f **(b)** (ratification) (frml) ratificación f **2** (Relig) confirmación f

confiscate /'kɑːnfəskeɪt ‖'kɒnfɪskeɪt/ vt confiscar*

conflict¹ /'kɑːnflɪkt ‖'kɒnflɪkt/ n conflicto m

conflict² /kən'flɪkt/ vi discrepar

conflicting /kən'flɪktɪŋ/ adj ⟨interests⟩ opuesto; ⟨views/accounts/emotions⟩ contradictorio

conform /kən'fɔːrm ‖kən'fɔːm/ vi **(a)** (be in accordance) **to** ∼ **TO** o **WITH** sth ajustarse A or cumplir CON algo **(b)** (act in a conformist way) ser* conformista; **he usually** ∼s **to their wishes** por lo general se aviene a sus deseos

confound /kən'faʊnd/ vt **(a)** (perplex) ⟨person⟩ confundir **(b)** (thwart) ⟨attempt⟩ frustrar

confront /kən'frʌnt/ vt **(a)** (come face to face with) ⟨danger/problem⟩ afrontar, enfrentar; **police were** ∼ed **by a group of demonstrators** la policía se vio enfrentada a un grupo de manifestantes **(b)** (face up to) ⟨enemy/fear/crisis⟩ hacer* frente a

confrontation /ˌkɑːnfrʌn'teɪʃən ‖ˌkɒnfrʌn'teɪʃən/ n **(a)** (conflict) enfrentamiento m, confrontación f **(b)** (encounter) confrontación f

confuse /kən'fjuːz/ vt **1** **(a)** (bewilder) confundir **(b)** (blur) ⟨situation⟩ complicar* **2** (mix up, be unable to distinguish) ⟨ideas/sounds⟩ confundir

confused /kən'fjuːzd/ adj **(a)** (perplexed) confundido; **to get** ∼ confundirse **(b)** (unclear) ⟨argument⟩ confuso

confusing /kən'fjuːzɪŋ/ *adj* confuso

confusion /kən'fjuːʒən/ *n* **(a)** (turmoil) confusión *f* **(b)** (disorder) desorden *m*

congeal /kən'dʒiːl/ *vi* «*fat*» solidificarse*; ~ed blood sangre *f* coagulada

congested /kən'dʒestəd ‖kən'dʒestɪd/ *adj* **(a)** (with traffic) congestionado; (with people) abarrotado de gente **(b)** (Med) congestionado

congestion /kən'dʒestʃən/ *n* **(a)** (with traffic) congestión *f*; (with people) abarrotamiento *m* **(b)** (Med) congestión *f*

Congo /'kɑːŋgəʊ ‖'kɒŋgəʊ/ *n* el Congo

congratulate /kən'grætʃəleɪt ‖kən'grætjʊleɪt/ *vt* felicitar; **to ~ sb ON sth/-ING** felicitar *or* darle* la enhorabuena a algn POR algo/+ INF

congratulation /kən'grætʃə'leɪʃən ‖kən,grætjʊ'leɪʃən/ *n* **(a)** (praise) felicitación *f* **(b) congratulations** *pl* enhorabuena *f*, felicitaciones *fpl*; (*as interj*) **~s!** ¡enhorabuena!, ¡felicitaciones! (AmL)

congregate /'kɑːŋgrɪgeɪt ‖'kɒŋgrɪgeɪt/ *vi* congregarse*

congregation /'kɑːŋgrɪ'geɪʃən ‖,kɒŋgrɪ'geɪʃən/ *n* (Relig) (attending service) fieles *mpl*; (parishioners) feligreses *mpl*

congress /'kɑːŋgrəs ‖'kɒŋgres/ *n* **(a)** (conference) congreso *m* **(b) Congress** (in US) el Congreso (de los Estados Unidos)

congress: ~man /'kɑːŋgrəsmən ‖'kɒŋgresmən/ *n* (*pl* **-men** /-mən/) (in US) miembro *m* del Congreso; **~woman** *n* (in US) miembro *f* del Congreso

conifer /'kɑːnəfər ‖'kɒnɪfə(r)/ *n* conífera *f*

conjecture¹ /kən'dʒektʃər ‖kən'dʒektʃə(r)/ *n*: it's pure ~ no son más que conjeturas

conjecture² *vt/i* (fml) conjeturar

conjugal /'kɑːndʒəgəl ‖'kɒndʒʊgəl/ *adj* (fml) conyugal

conjunctivitis /kən'dʒʌŋktɪ'vaɪtəs ‖kən,dʒʌŋktɪ'vaɪtɪs/ *n* conjuntivitis *f*

conjurer /'kɑːndʒərər ‖'kʌndʒərə(r)/ *n* prestidigitador, -dora *m,f*, mago, -ga *m,f*

conjure up /'kɑːndʒər ‖'kʌndʒə(r)/ [*v* + *o* + *adv*, *v* + *adv* + *o*] (evoke) evocar*; it ~s ~ images of ... hace pensar en ...

conjuror *n* ▶ CONJURER

con man *n* estafador *m*, timador *m*

Conn = Connecticut

connect /kə'nekt/ *vt* **1 (a)** (attach) **to ~ sth (TO sth)** conectar algo (A algo) **(b)** (link together) «*rooms/buildings*» comunicar*; «*towns*» conectar **(c)** (Telec): I'm trying to ~ you un momento que lo comunico *or* (Esp) le pongo con el número **(d)** «*phone/gas*» conectar

2 (associate) «*people/ideas/events*» relacionar

■ ~ *vi* **1 (a)** (be joined together) «*rooms*» comunicarse*; «*pipes*» empalmar **(b)** (be fitted) to ~ (TO sth) estar* conectado (a algo)

2 (Transp) **to ~ WITH sth** «*train/flight*» enlazar* CON algo, conectar CON algo (AmL)

■ **connect up 1** [*v* + *o* + *adv*, *v* + *adv* + *o*] «*wires/apparatus*» conectar

2 [*v* + *adv*] «*wires*» conectarse*; it all ~s up todo está relacionado

connected /kə'nektəd ‖kə'nektɪd/ *adj* «*ideas/ events*» relacionado; **to be ~ed WITH sth** estar* relacionado CON algo

connection /kə'nekʃən/ *n* **1 (a)** (link) ~ (**WITH sth**) enlace *m* or conexión *f* (CON algo) **(b)** (Elec) conexión *f* **2** (Transp) ~ (**WITH sth**) conexión *f* or enlace *m* (CON algo) **3** (relation) relación *f* or conexión *f* **4 connections** *pl* (links, ties) lazos *mpl*; (influential people) contactos *mpl*, conexiones *fpl* (AmL)

connive /kə'naɪv/ *vi* **(a)** (plot) **to ~ (WITH sb)** actuar* en complicidad (CON algn) **(b)** (cooperate) **to ~ AT sth** ser* cómplice EN algo

connoisseur /'kɑːnə'sɜːr ‖,kɒnə'sɜː(r)/ *n* entendido, -da *m,f*

connotation /'kɑːnə'teɪʃən ‖,kɒnə'teɪʃən/ *n* connotación *f*

conquer /'kɑːŋkər ‖'kɒŋkə(r)/ *vt* «*country/ mountain*» conquistar; «*enemy/fear*» vencer

conqueror /'kɑːŋkərər ‖'kɒŋkərə(r)/ *n* conquistador, -dora *m,f*

conquest /'kɑːŋkwest ‖'kɒŋkwest/ *n* conquista *f*

conscience /'kɑːnʃəns ‖'kɒnʃəns/ *n* conciencia *f*; **to have a clear ~** tener* la conciencia tranquila

conscientious /'kɑːnʃi'enʃəs ‖,kɒnʃi'enʃəs/ *adj* «*work*» concienzudo; «*student*» aplicado

conscientious objector *n* /əb'dʒektər ‖əb'dʒektə(r)/ objetor, -tora *m,f* de conciencia

conscious /'kɑːnʃəs ‖'kɒnʃəs/ *adj* **1 (a)** (awake, alert) (*no comp*) consciente **(b)** (aware) (*pred*) **to be ~ OF sth** ser* or (Chi, Méx tb) estar* consciente DE algo **2** (deliberate) «*decision*» deliberado; **she made a ~ effort to be nice** se esforzó por ser amable

consciousness /'kɑːnʃəsnəs ‖'kɒnʃəsnɪs/ *n* **(a)** (state of being awake, alert) conocimiento *m* **(b)** (awareness) conciencia *f*

conscript¹ /'kɑːnskrɪpt ‖'kɒnskrɪpt/ *n* recluta *mf*, conscripto, -ta *m,f* (AmL)

conscript² /kən'skrɪpt/ *vt* reclutar

conscription /kən'skrɪpʃən/ *n* conscripción *f* (esp AmL), reclutamiento *m* (para el servicio militar obligatorio en casos de guerra)

consecrate /'kɑːnsəkreɪt ‖'kɒnsɪkreɪt/ *vt* consagrar

consecutive /kən'sekjətɪv ‖kən'sekjʊtɪv/ *adj* «*numbers*» consecutivo; **he was absent on three ~ days** faltó tres días seguidos

consensus /kən'sensəs/ *n* consenso *m*

consent¹ /kən'sent/ *vi* acceder; **to ~ TO sth** acceder A *or* consentir* EN algo

consent² *n* consentimiento *m* de común acuerdo; **age of ~** (Law) edad a partir de la cual es válido el consentimiento que se da para tener relaciones sexuales

consequence /'kɑːnsəkwens ‖'kɒnsɪkwəns/ *n* **1** (result) consecuencia *f* **2** (importance) trascendencia *f*

consequently /'kɑːnsəkwentli ‖'kɒnsɪkwəntli/ *adv* consiguientemente, por consiguiente

conservation /ˌkɑːnsərˈveɪʃən ‖ˌkɒnsəˈveɪʃən/ n protección f or conservación f del medio ambiente

conservationist /ˌkɑːnsərˈveɪʃənəst ‖ˌkɒnsəˈveɪʃənɪst/ n conservacionista mf

conservative /kənˈsɜːrvətɪv ‖kənˈsɜːvətɪv/ adj (a) (traditional) conservador (b)
Conservative (in UK) (before n) conservador (c) (cautious) cauteloso; **a ~ estimate** un cálculo por lo bajo
Conservative n (in UK) conservador, -dora m,f

conservatory /kənˈsɜːrvətɔːri ‖kənˈsɜːvətri/ n (pl **-ries**) (a) (greenhouse) jardín m de invierno (b) (school of music) conservatorio m

conserve /kənˈsɜːrv ‖kənˈsɜːv/ vt (a) (preserve) ⟨wildlife/rivers⟩ proteger*, conservar (b) (save) ⟨energy/resources⟩ conservar

consider /kənˈsɪdər ‖kənˈsɪdə(r)/ vt (a) (think about, of) considerar; **we're ~ing moving house** estamos pensando en mudarnos; **~ yourself lucky** puedes darle por afortunado (b) (take into account) tener* en cuenta, considerar; **all things ~ed, I think that …** bien considerado, creo que …

considerable /kənˈsɪdərəbəl/ adj ⟨achievement/risk⟩ considerable; ⟨sum⟩ importante; **with ~ difficulty** con bastante dificultad

considerably /kənˈsɪdərəbli/ adv bastante, considerablemente

considerate /kənˈsɪdərət/ adj atento, considerado

consideration /kənˌsɪdəˈreɪʃən/ n **1** (a) (attention, thought): **their case has been given careful ~** su caso ha sido estudiado or considerado detenidamente; **to take sth into ~** tener* algo en cuenta (b) (factor): **a major ~ is the cost** un factor muy a tener en cuenta es el costo
2 (thoughtfulness) consideración f **3** (importance): **of little/no ~** de poca/ninguna importancia

considering[1] /kənˈsɪdərɪŋ/ prep teniendo en cuenta

considering[2] conj: **~ (that) she's only two years old** teniendo en cuenta que tiene solo dos años

consignment /kənˈsaɪnmənt/ n (a) (goods sent) envío m, remesa f (b) (sending) envío m

consist /kənˈsɪst/ vi **to ~ OF sth** constar DE algo

consistency /kənˈsɪstənsi/ n (pl **-cies**) (a) (regularity) regularidad f (b) (of mixture) consistencia f

consistent /kənˈsɪstənt/ adj (a) (compatible) **to be ~ (WITH sth)** ⟨statements/beliefs⟩ concordar* (CON algo) (b) (constant) ⟨excellence/failure⟩ constante; ⟨denial⟩ sistemático

consistently /kənˈsɪstəntli/ adv (a) (without change) ⟨argue⟩ coherentemente; ⟨behave⟩ consecuentemente (b) (constantly) ⟨claim/refuse⟩ sistemáticamente

consolation /ˌkɑːnsəˈleɪʃən ‖ˌkɒnsəˈleɪʃən/ n consuelo m; (before n) **~ prize** premio m de consolación, premio m (de) consuelo (CS)

console[1] /ˈkɑːnsəʊl ‖ˈkɒnsəʊl/ n consola f

console[2] /kənˈsəʊl/ vt consolar*

consolidate /kənˈsɑːlədeɪt ‖kənˈsɒlɪdeɪt/ vt (a) (reinforce) ⟨support/position⟩ consolidar (b) (combine) ⟨companies⟩ fusionar; ⟨debts⟩ consolidar

consonant /ˈkɑːnsənənt ‖ˈkɒnsənənt/ n consonante f

consort /ˈkɑːnsɔːrt ‖ˈkɒnsɔːt/ n (fml) consorte mf (fml)

consortium /kənˈsɔːrʃəm ‖kənˈsɔːtiəm/ n (pl **-tia** /-tiə/ or **-tiums**) consorcio m

conspicuous /kənˈspɪkjuəs/ adj ⟨hat/badge⟩ llamativo; ⟨differences/omissions⟩ manifiesto, evidente; **to make oneself ~** llamar la atención; **to be ~ by one's absence** brillar por su (or mi etc) ausencia

conspiracy /kənˈspɪrəsi/ n (pl **-cies**) conspiración f

conspirator /kənˈspɪrətər ‖kənˈspɪrətə(r)/ n conspirador, -dora m,f

conspire /kənˈspaɪr ‖kənˈspaɪə(r)/ vi conspirar; **to ~ to + INF** conspirar PARA + INF

constable /ˈkɑːnstəbəl ‖ˈkʌnstəbəl/ n (BrE) agente mf de policía

constant /ˈkɑːnstənt ‖ˈkɒnstənt/ adj (a) (continual) ⟨pain/complaints⟩ constante (b) (unchanging) ⟨temperature/speed⟩ constante (c) (loyal) (liter) fiel, leal

constantly /ˈkɑːnstəntli ‖ˈkɒnstəntli/ adv constantemente

constellation /ˌkɑːnstəˈleɪʃən ‖ˌkɒnstəˈleɪʃən/ n constelación f

constipated /ˈkɑːnstəpeɪtəd ‖ˈkɒnstɪpeɪtɪd/ adj estreñido

constipation /ˌkɑːnstəˈpeɪʃən ‖ˌkɒnstɪˈpeɪʃən/ n estreñimiento m

constituency /kənˈstɪtʃuənsi ‖kənˈstɪtjʊənsi/ n (pl **-cies**) (area) circunscripción f or distrito m electoral; (supporters) electores mpl potenciales (de una circunscripción electoral)

constituent[1] /kənˈstɪtʃuənt ‖kənˈstɪtjʊənt/ n **1** (Pol) elector, -tora m,f **2** (component) (fml) componente m, elemento m constitutivo or constituyente

constituent[2] adj (before n) ⟨part/element⟩ constituyente, constitutivo

constitute /ˈkɑːnstətuːt ‖ˈkɒnstɪtjuːt/ vt (fml) constituir* (fml)

constitution /ˌkɑːnstəˈtuːʃən ‖ˌkɒnstɪˈtjuːʃən/ n **1** (of country) constitución f; (of association, party) estatutos mpl **2** (of person) constitución f

constitutional /ˌkɑːnstəˈtuːʃnəl ‖ˌkɒnstɪˈtjuːʃənl/ adj constitucional

constrain /kənˈstreɪn/ vt (often pass) obligar*

constraint /kənˈstreɪnt/ n (a) (compulsion) coacción f (b) (restriction) (often pl) restricción f, limitación f

constrict /kənˈstrɪkt/ vt ⟨opening/channel⟩ estrechar; ⟨flow/breathing⟩ dificultar; ⟨freedom⟩ coartar

construct /kənˈstrʌkt/ vt (a) (build) (fml) construir* (b) (put together) ⟨model⟩ armar, montar

construction /kənˈstrʌkʃən/ n **1** (a) (of building) construcción f; (before n) ⟨industry/worker⟩ de la construcción (b) (Ling, Math) construcción f **2** (structure) estructura f

constructive /kən'strʌktɪv/ *adj* constructivo

consul /'kɑːnsəl ‖'kɒnsəl/ *n* cónsul *mf*

consulate /'kɑːnsələt ‖'kɒnsjʊlət/ *n* consulado *m*

consult /kən'sʌlt/ *vt* consultar
- ∎ ∼ *vi*: I ought to ∼ with my wife first primero debería consultárselo a mi mujer

consultancy /kən'sʌltənsi/ *n* (*pl* **-cies**) (Busn) asesoría *f*, consultoría *f*

consultant /kən'sʌltənt/ *n* (adviser) asesor, -sora *m,f*, consultor, -tora *m,f*; (BrE Med) especialista *mf*

consultation /'kɑːnsəl'teɪʃən ‖,kɒnsəl'teɪʃən/ *n* (a) (with doctor, lawyer) consulta *f* (b) (of dictionary, notes) consulta *f* (c) (discussion): there was no ∼ with the tenants no se consultó a los inquilinos; in ∼ with sb en conferencia con algn

consulting /kən'sʌltɪŋ/ *adj* (before n) (Med): ∼ room consultorio *m*, consulta *f*

consume /kən'suːm ‖kən'sjuːm/ *vt* consumir; he was ∼d by *o* with jealousy lo consumían los celos

consumer /kən'suːmər ‖kən'sjuːmə(r)/ *n* consumidor, -dora *m,f*; (before n) ∼ goods artículos *mpl* or bienes *mpl* de consumo; the ∼ society la sociedad de consumo

consummate¹ /'kɑːnˌsəmət ‖'kɒnsəmət/ *adj* (fml) (before n) ⟨actor/liar⟩ consumado

consummate² /'kɑːnsəmeɪt ‖'kɒnsəmeɪt/ *vt* consumar

consumption /kən'sʌmpʃən/ *n* consumo *m*

contact¹ /'kɑːntækt ‖'kɒntækt/ *n* (a) (physical) contacto *m*; to come into ∼ with sth hacer* contacto con algo (b) (communication) contacto *m*; to come in/into ∼ with sb tratar a algn; to be/get in ∼ with sb estar*/ponerse* en contacto con algn

contact² *vt* ponerse* en contacto con

contact lens *n* lente *f or* (AmL) lente *m* de contacto, lentilla *f* (Esp)

contagious /kən'teɪdʒəs/ *adj* contagioso

contain /kən'teɪn/ *vt* [1] (hold) contener* [2] ⟨enemy/fire/epidemic⟩ contener*; ⟨anger/laughter⟩ contener*; to ∼ oneself contenerse*

container /kən'teɪnər ‖kən'teɪnə(r)/ *n* (receptacle) recipiente *m*; (as packaging) envase *m*; (Transp) contenedor *m*, contáiner *m*; (before n) ∼ ship buque *m* portacontenedores

contaminate /kən'tæmɪneɪt ‖kən'tæmɪneɪt/ *vt* contaminar

contamination /kən'tæmə'neɪʃən ‖kən,tæmɪ'neɪʃən/ *n* contaminación *f*

contd (= **continued**) sigue

contemplate /'kɑːntəmpleɪt ‖'kɒntəmpleɪt/ *vt* contemplar; I ∼d phoning her pensé (en) llamarla

contemporary¹ /kən'tempəreri ‖kən'tempərəri/ *adj* (a) (of the same period) ⟨person⟩ contemporáneo, coetáneo; ⟨object⟩ de la época (b) (present-day) contemporáneo, actual

contemporary² *n* (*pl* **-ries**) (a) (sb living at same time) contemporáneo, -nea *m,f*, coetáneo, -na *m,f* (b) (sb of same age): he looks older than his contemporaries parece mayor que la gente de su edad

contempt /kən'tempt/ *n* desprecio *m*; to be beneath ∼ ser* despreciable; ∼ (of court) (Law) desacato *m* al tribunal

contemptible /kən'temptəbəl/ *adj* despreciable

contemptuous /kən'temptʃuəs ‖kən'temptjuəs/ *adj* despectivo

contend /kən'tend/ *vi* (a) (compete) to ∼ (with sb) (for sth) competir* (con algn) (por algo) (b) (face) to ∼ with sth lidiar con algo
- ∎ ∼ *vt* argüir*

contender /kən'tendər ‖kən'tendə(r)/ *n* ∼ (for sth) aspirante *mf* (a algo)

content¹ /'kɑːntent ‖'kɒntent/ *n*
[1] **contents** *pl* (of box, bottle) contenido *m*; ∼s (of book) índice *m* de materias; (in magazine) sumario *m* [2] (amount contained) contenido *m*

content² /kən'tent/ *adj* (pred) contento

content³ /kən'tent/ *v refl* to ∼ oneself with sth/-ING contentarse con algo/+ INF

contented /kən'tentəd ‖kən'tentɪd/ *adj* ⟨sigh/purr⟩ de satisfacción; ⟨person/workforce⟩ satisfecho; to be ∼ with sth contentarse con algo

contention /kən'tentʃən ‖kən'tenʃən/ *n*
[1] (dispute): there is considerable ∼ over ... existe un gran desacuerdo sobre ... [2] (assertion) opinión *f*; it is her ∼ that ... ella sostiene que ...

contentious /kən'tentʃəs ‖kən'tenʃəs/ *adj* ⟨issue⟩ polémico

contentment /kən'tentmənt/ *n* satisfacción *f*

contest¹ /'kɑːntest ‖'kɒntest/ *n* (a) (competition) (Games) concurso *m*; (Sport) competencia *f* (AmL), competición *f* (Esp); (in boxing) combate *m* (b) (struggle) lucha *f*

contest² /kən'test/ *vt* (a) ⟨allegation⟩ refutar; ⟨will⟩ impugnar; ⟨decision⟩ protestar contra (b) ⟨election⟩ presentarse como candidato a

contestant /kən'testənt/ *n* concursante *mf*

context /'kɑːntekst ‖'kɒntekst/ *n* contexto *m*

continent /'kɑːntɪnənt ‖'kɒntɪnənt/ *n* continente *m*; the C∼ Europa *f* (continental)

continental /'kɑːntɪn'entl ‖,kɒntɪ'nentl/ *adj* continental; C∼ (European) de Europa (continental)

continental: ∼ breakfast *n* desayuno *m* continental (desayuno de café o té y bollos con mantequilla y mermelada); **∼ quilt** *n* (BrE) ▶ DUVET

contingency /kən'tɪndʒənsi/ *n* (*pl* **-cies**) (eventuality) contingencia *f*; (before n) ⟨fund⟩ (para casos) de emergencia; a ∼ plan un plan para prever

continual /kən'tɪnjuəl/ *adj* continuo, constante

continually /kən'tɪnjuəli/ *adv* continuamente, constantemente

continuation /kən'tɪnjuˈeɪʃən/ *n* continuación *f*

continue /kən'tɪnjuː/ *vi* continuar*, seguir*; we ∼d on our way reanudamos el camino
- ∎ ∼ *vt* (a) (keep on) continuar*, seguir* con; to ∼ -ING/to + INF continuar* or seguir* + GER (b) (resume) continuar*, seguir* con, proseguir* (fml); to be ∼d continuará (c) (extend, prolong) prolongar*

continuity /ˌkɑːntn̩'uːəti ‖ˌkɒntrɪ'njuːɪti/ n
continuidad f

continuous /kən'tɪnjuəs/ adj continuo; ∼
assessment (Educ) evaluación f continua

continuously /kən'tɪnjuəsli/ adv
continuamente, sin interrupción

contort /kən'tɔːrt ‖kən'tɔːt/ vt ‹face› contraer*;
to ∼ **oneself** contorsionarse
■ ∼ vi crisparse

contortion /kən'tɔːrʃən ‖kən'tɔːʃən/ n
contorsión f

contour /'kɑːntʊr ‖'kɒntʊə(r)/ n contorno m;
(before n) ∼ **line** curva f de nivel, cota f

contraband /'kɑːntrəbænd ‖'kɒntrəbænd/ n
contrabando m

contraception /ˌkɑːntrə'sepʃən
‖ˌkɒntrə'sepʃən/ n anticoncepción f,
contracepción f

contraceptive /ˌkɑːntrə'septɪv
‖ˌkɒntrə'septɪv/ n anticonceptivo m,
contraconceptivo m

contract¹ /'kɑːntrækt ‖'kɒntrækt/ n
(agreement, document) contrato m; (for public works)
contrata f; ∼ **killer** asesino, -na m,f a sueldo,
sicario, -ria m,f

contract² /kən'trækt/ vt also /'kɑːntrækt/ (a)
(place under contract) ‹person› contratar (b) ‹debt/
disease› contraer* (frml) (c) ‹muscle› contraer*
■ ∼ vi (become smaller/tighter) contraerse*
■ **contract out** /'kɑːntrækt ‖'kɒntrækt/ [v + o
+ adv, v + adv + o] ‹job/work› subcontratar

contraction /kən'trækʃən/ n contracción f

contractor /kən'træktər ‖kən'træktə(r)/ n
contratista mf

contradict /ˌkɑːntrə'dɪkt ‖ˌkɒntrə'dɪkt/ vt
contradecir*

contradiction /ˌkɑːntrə'dɪkʃən
‖ˌkɒntrə'dɪkʃən/ n contradicción f; **a** ∼ **in terms**
un contrasentido

contradictory /ˌkɑːntrə'dɪktəri
‖ˌkɒntrə'dɪktəri/ adj contradictorio

contralto /kən'træltəʊ/ n (pl ∼s) contralto f

contraption /kən'træpʃən/ n (colloq) artilugio
m

contrary¹ adj ① /'kɑːntreri ‖'kɒntrəri/ (a)
(opposed, opposite) contrario (b) ∼ **to** (as prep)
contrariamente a, al contrario de ② /'kɑːntreri,
kən'treri ‖kən'treəri/ (obstinate): **he's so** ∼
siempre tiene que llevar la contraria

contrary² /'kɑːntreri ‖'kɒntrəri/ n (pl -ries):
the ∼ lo contrario; **on the** ∼ (as linker) al
contrario

contrast¹ /'kɑːntræst ‖'kɒntrɑːst/ n contraste
m; **by** ∼ (as linker) por contraste; **in** ∼ **to** o **with**
(as prep) en contraste con

contrast² /kən'træst ‖kən'trɑːst/ vt contrastar
■ ∼ vi (a) (differ) contrastar (b) **contrasting**
pres p ‹opinions/approaches› contrastante

contribute /kən'trɪbət, -bjuːt/ vt (a) ‹money/
time› contribuir* con, aportar, hacer* una

aportación or (esp AmL) un aporte de;
‹suggestions/ideas› aportar (b) ‹article/poem/
paper› escribir*
■ ∼ vi (a) (play significant part) **to** ∼ (**TO sth**)
contribuir* (A algo) (b) (give money) contribuir*
(c) (participate) **to** ∼ **TO sth** participar EN algo (d)
(Journ) **to** ∼ **TO sth** escribir* PARA algo

contribution /ˌkɑːntrə'bjuːʃən
‖ˌkɒntrɪ'bjuːʃən/ n (a) (participation, part played)
contribución f (b) (payment, donation) contribución
f; (to a fund) aportación f, aporte m (esp AmL)

contributor /kən'trɪbjətər ‖kən'trɪbjʊtə(r)/ n
(a) (writer) colaborador, -dora m,f (b) (donor)
donante mf

contrive /kən'traɪv/ vt (a) (manage) **to** ∼ **to** +
INF lograr + INF/QUE (+ subj), ingeniárselas or
arreglárselas PARA + INF/PARA QUE (+ subj) (b)
(create) ‹method/device› idear

contrived /kən'traɪvd/ adj artificioso

control¹ /kən'trəʊl/ vt **-ll-** controlar; ‹traffic›
dirigir*; **to** ∼ **oneself** controlarse

control² n ① control m; **to be in** ∼ **of sth**
dominar algo; **to gain** ∼ **of sth** hacerse* con;
circumstances beyond our ∼ circunstancias
ajenas a nuestra voluntad; **to be out of** ∼ estar*
fuera de control; **to get out of** ∼ descontrolarse
② price ∼(s) control m de precios ③ **controls**
pl (of vehicle) mandos mpl ④ (mastery) dominio m

controlled /kən'trəʊld/ adj ‹voice/emotion›
contenido; ‹response› mesurado; ‹conditions/
experiment› controlado

controller /kən'trəʊlər ‖kən'trəʊlə(r)/ n
director, -tora m,f

control: ∼ **room** n (Mil, Naut) centro m de
operaciones; (Audio, Rad, TV) sala f de control; ∼
tower n torre f de control

controversial /ˌkɑːntrə'vɜːrʃəl
‖ˌkɒntrə'vɜːʃəl/ adj controvertido

controversy /'kɑːntrəvɜːrsi ‖'kɒntrəvɜːsi,
kən'trɒvəsi/ n (pl **-sies**) controversia f

conundrum /kə'nʌndrəm/ n adivinanza f

conurbation /ˌkɑːnɜːr'beɪʃən ‖ˌkɒnɜː'beɪʃən/
n conurbación f

convalesce /ˌkɑːnvə'les ‖ˌkɒnvə'les/ vi
recuperarse, convalecer*

convene /kən'viːn/ vi reunirse*

convenience /kən'viːniəns/ n (a) (comfort,
practicality) conveniencia f; **at your** ∼ cuando le
resulte conveniente (b) (amenity, appliance): **with
every modern** ∼ con todas las comodidades
modernas

convenience food n comida f de
preparación rápida

convenient /kən'viːniənt/ adj (a) (opportune,
suitable) conveniente (b) (practical) práctico; **a very**
∼ **way of storing things** una manera muy
práctica de guardar las cosas (c) (handy, close): **it's
very** ∼ **having the school so near** resulta tan
práctico tener la escuela tan cerca

conveniently /kən'viːniəntli/ adv (a) (handily)
convenientemente (b) (expediently): **the**

AmC	Central America	Arg	Argentina	Cu	Cuba	Per	Peru
AmL	Latin America	Bol	Bolivia	Ec	Ecuador	RPI	River Plate Area
AmS	South America	Chi	Chile	Esp	Spain	Ur	Uruguay
Andes	Andean Region	CS	Southern Cone	Méx	Mexico	Ven	Venezuela

government ~ forgets its election promises le resulta muy cómodo al gobierno olvidarse de sus promesas electorales

convent /'kɑ:nvənt ‖'kɒnvənt/ n convento m

convention /kən'ventʃən ‖kən'venʃən/ n [1] (a) (social code) convenciónes fpl, convencionalismos mpl (b) (established practice) convención f [2] (agreement) convención f [3] (conference) convención f, congreso m

conventional /kən'ventʃnəl ‖kən'venʃn̩l/ adj convencional

converge /kən'vɜ:rdʒ ‖kən'vɜ:dʒ/ vi «lines/roads» converger*, convergir*; «crowd/armies» reunirse*

conversation /'kɑ:nvər'seɪʃən ‖,kɒnvə'seɪʃən/ n conversación f

conversational /'kɑ:nvər'seɪʃnəl ‖,kɒnvə'seɪʃn̩l/ adj familiar, coloquial

converse /kən'vɜ:rs ‖kən'vɜ:s/ vi conversar

conversion /kən'vɜ:rʒən ‖kən'vɜ:ʃən/ n [1] (a) (change) conversión f (b) (of house): to do a ~ transformar una casa (c) (Relig) conversión f [2] (in rugby) conversión f, transformación f

convert¹ /'kɑ:nvɜ:rt ‖'kɒnvɜ:t/ n converso, -sa m,f

convert² /kən'vɜ:rt ‖kən'vɜ:t/ vt [1] «building» remodelar; «vehicle» transformar; to ~ sth INTO sth convertir* algo EN algo [2] (cause to change view, religion) convertir* [3] (in rugby) transformar, convertir*
■ ~ vi (Pol, Relig) convertirse*

convertible¹ /kən'vɜ:rtəbəl ‖kən'vɜ:təbəl/ adj convertible

convertible² n (Auto) descapotable m, convertible m (AmL)

convex /'kɑ:nveks ‖'kɒnveks/ adj convexo

convey /kən'veɪ/ vt «goods/people» transportar; «feeling» expresar; «thanks» hacer* llegar

conveyor (belt) /kən'veɪər ‖kən'veɪə(r)/ n cinta f or correa f transportadora, banda f transportadora (Méx)

convict¹ /'kɑ:nvɪkt ‖'kɒnvɪkt/ n recluso, -sa m,f, presidiario, -ria m,f

convict² /kən'vɪkt/ vt (often pass) declarar culpable, condenar; to be ~ed OF sth ser* condenado POR algo

conviction /kən'vɪkʃən/ n [1] (Law) condena f [2] (certainty) convicción f

convince /kən'vɪns/ vt convencer*; to ~ sb THAT convencer* a algn DE QUE

convinced /kən'vɪnst/ adj (persuaded) (pred): to be ~ OF sth/THAT estar* convencido DE algo/DE QUE

convincing /kən'vɪnsɪŋ/ adj convincente

convivial /kən'vɪviəl/ adj «atmosphere» cordial; «person» simpático

convoy /'kɑ:nvɔɪ ‖'kɒnvɔɪ/ n convoy m

convulsion /kən'vʌlʃən/ n convulsión f

coo /ku:/ vi «dove/pigeon» arrullar

cook¹ /kʊk/ n cocinero, -ra m,f; he's a good ~ cocina muy bien, es muy buen cocinero

cook² vt «food/meal» hacer*, preparar
■ ~ vi (a) (prepare food) cocinar, guisar (b) (become ready) «food» hacerse*

cookbook /'kʊkbʊk/ n libro m de cocina or de recetas

cooker /'kʊkər ‖'kʊkə(r)/ n (BrE) (stove) cocina f or (Col, Méx) estufa f

cookery /'kʊkəri/ n cocina f; (before n) ~ book (BrE) ▶ COOKBOOK

cookie /'kʊki/ n (AmE Culin) galleta f, galletita f (RPl)

cooking /'kʊkɪŋ/ n: to do the ~ cocinar; it is used in ~ se usa para cocinar; home ~ la comida casera; Spanish ~ la cocina española

cooky n ▶ COOKIE

cool¹ /ku:l/ adj -er, -est [1] (cold) fresco; it's ~ today hace or está fresco hoy [2] (reserved, hostile) «reception/behavior» frío [3] (calm) sereno, tranquilo; keep ~! ¡tranquilo!, no te pongas nervioso; he's a very ~ customer tiene una sangre fría impresionante [4] (sl) (trendy, laid-back): he's really ~ es muy en la onda (fam)

cool² n [1] (low temperature): let's stay here in the ~ quedémonos aquí al fresco [2] (composure) calma f; to keep/lose one's ~ mantener*/perder* la calma

cool³ vt «air/room» refrigerar; «engine/food/enthusiasm» enfriar*
■ ~ vi «air/room» refrigerarse; «engine/food/enthusiasm» enfriarse*
■ **cool down** [v + adv] (a) (become cooler) «food/iron» enfriarse*; «person» refrescarse* (b) (become calmer) calmarse
■ **cool off** [v + adv] (a) (become cooler) «person» refrescarse* (b) (become calmer) calmarse

coolly /'ku:lli/ adv (a) (calmly) con serenidad or calma (b) (boldly) descaradamente, con la mayor frescura (c) (with reserve, hostility) fríamente, con frialdad

coop /ku:p/ n: chicken/hen ~ gallinero m
■ **coop up** [v + o + adv, v + adv + o] (usu passive) encerrar*

co-op /'kəʊɑ:p ‖'kəʊɒp/ n cooperativa f

cooperate /kəʊ'ɑ:pəreɪt ‖kəʊ'ɒpəreɪt/ vi cooperar, colaborar

cooperation /kəʊ'ɑ:pə'reɪʃən ‖kəʊ,ɒpə'reɪʃən/ n cooperación f, colaboración f

cooperative¹ /kəʊ'ɑ:pərətɪv ‖kəʊ'ɒpərətɪv/ adj (a) «attitude» de colaboración, cooperativo (b) «effort/venture» conjunto

cooperative² n cooperativa f

co-opt /kəʊ'ɑ:pt ‖kəʊ'ɒpt/ vt: to ~ sb onto a committee invitar a algn a formar parte de una comisión

coordinate¹ /kəʊ'ɔ:rdneɪt ‖,kəʊ'ɔ:dɪneɪt/ vt coordinar

coordinate² /kəʊ'ɔ:rdnət ‖kəʊ'ɔ:dɪnət/ n [1] (Math) coordenada f [2] **coordinates** pl prendas fpl para combinar, coordinados mpl

coordination /kəʊ'ɔ:rdn'eɪʃən ‖kəʊ,ɔ:dɪ'neɪʃən/ n coordinación f

coordinator /kəʊ'ɔ:rdneɪtər ‖kəʊ'ɔ:dɪmeɪtə(r)/ n coordinador, -dora m,f

coowner /'kəʊ'əʊnər ‖kəʊ'əʊnə(r)/ n copropietario, -ria m,f

cop /kɑ:p ‖kɒp/ n (colloq) poli mf (fam), tira mf (Méx fam), cana mf (RPl arg), cachaco, -ca m,f (Per fam), paco, -ca m,f (Chi fam)

cope /kəʊp/ vi: I can't ~ with all this work no doy abasto or no puedo con tanto trabajo; how do you ~ without a washing machine? ¿cómo te las ⋯⟶

arreglas sin lavadora?; **how is he coping on his own?** ¿qué tal se las arregla solo?; **these are some of the problems they have to ~ with** estos son algunos de los problemas a los que tienen que enfrentarse

Copenhagen /ˈkəʊpənˈheɪgən/ n Copenhague m

copious /ˈkəʊpiəs/ adj copioso

copper /ˈkɑːpər ‖ˈkɒpə(r)/ n **1** **(a)** (metal) cobre m **(b)** **coppers** pl (coins) (colloq) peniques mpl, perras fpl (Esp fam), quintos mpl (Méx fam), chauchas fpl (Chi fam), vintenes mpl (Ur fam) **(c)** (color) color m cobre; (before n) cobrizo **2** (police officer) (colloq) ▶ COP

co-production /ˈkəʊprəˌdʌkʃən/ n coproducción f

copy¹ /ˈkɑːpi ‖ˈkɒpi/ n (pl **copies**) **1** (of painting, document) copia f **2** (of newspaper, book) ejemplar m **3** (text): **he/she must be able to produce clear ~** debe saber redactar con claridad

copy² **copies, copying, copied** vt **1** **(a)** (reproduce, transcribe) copiar **(b)** (photocopy) fotocopiar **2** (imitate) ⟨painter/singer⟩ copiarle a; ⟨style/behavior⟩ copiar

copy: **~cat** n (colloq) copión, -piona m,f (fam), imitamonos mf (Méx fam); **~right** n copyright m, derechos mpl de reproducción

coral /ˈkɔːrəl ‖ˈkɒrəl/ n coral m

cord /kɔːrd ‖kɔːd/ n **1** **(a)** (string, rope) cuerda f; (of pajamas, curtains) cordón m **(b)** (AmE Elec) cordón m, cable m **(c)** (Anat) ▶ SPINAL CORD, UMBILICAL CORD, VOCAL CORDS **2** (Tex) pana f, corderoy m (AmS), cotelé m (Chi)

cordial¹ /ˈkɔːrdʒəl ‖ˈkɔːdiəl/ adj cordial

cordial² n refresco m (concentrado)

cordless /ˈkɔːrdləs ‖ˈkɔːdlɪs/ adj inalámbrico

cordon /ˈkɔːrdn̩ ‖ˈkɔːdn̩/ n cordón m
■ **cordon off** [v + o + adv, v + adv + o] acordonar

corduroy /ˈkɔːrdərɔɪ ‖ˈkɔːdərɔɪ/ n pana f, corderoy m (AmS), cotelé m (Chi)

core¹ /kɔːr ‖kɔː(r)/ n (of apple, pear) corazón m; (of Earth) centro m; (of nuclear reactor) núcleo m; (of problem) meollo m

core² vt ⟨apple⟩ quitarle el corazón a

coriander /ˈkɔːriændər ‖ˌkɒriˈændə(r)/ n cilantro m, culantro m

cork /kɔːrk ‖kɔːk/ n corcho m

corkscrew /ˈkɔːrkskruː ‖ˈkɔːkskruː/ n sacacorchos m, tirabuzón m

corn /kɔːrn ‖kɔːn/ n **1** **(a)** (cereal crop — in general) grano m; (maize) (AmE) maíz m; (wheat) (BrE) trigo m; (oats) (BrE) avena f **(b)** (foodstuff) maíz m, choclo m (AmS); **~ on the cob** mazorca f de maíz or (AmS) de choclo, elote f (Méx) **2** (on toe) callo m

corner¹ /ˈkɔːrnər ‖ˈkɔːnə(r)/ n **1** **(a)** (inside angle — of room, cupboard) rincón m; (— of field) esquina f; (— of mouth) comisura f; (— of page) ángulo m **(b)** (outside angle — of street, page) esquina f; (— of table) punta f, punta f; (bend in road) curva f; **I'll meet you on** o **at the ~** te veo en la esquina; **to cut ~s** (financially) hacer* economías; (in a process) simplificar*; (before n) **~ shop** (BrE) tienda f de la esquina; (local shop) tienda f de barrio

2 (in soccer) (~ kick) córner m, tiro m or saque m de esquina
3 (in boxing) esquina f

corner² vt **1** (trap) acorralar **2** (monopolize) acaparar
■ **~** vi tomar una curva; **this car ~s well** este coche tiene buen agarre en las curvas

cornerstone /ˈkɔːrnərstəʊn ‖ˈkɔːnəstəʊn/ n piedra f angular

corn: **~flakes** pl n copos mpl or hojuelas fpl de maíz; **~flour** n (BrE) maizena® f

Cornish /ˈkɔːrnɪʃ ‖ˈkɔːnɪʃ/ adj de Cornualles

cornstarch /ˈkɔːrnstɑːrtʃ ‖ˈkɔːnstɑːtʃ/ n (AmE) maizena® f

Cornwall /ˈkɔːrnwɔːl ‖ˈkɔːnwɔːl/ n Cornualles m

corny /ˈkɔːrni ‖ˈkɔːni/ adj **-nier, -niest** (colloq) **(a)** ⟨song/movie⟩ cursi, sensiblero **(b)** (BrE) ⟨joke⟩ malo

coronary¹ /ˈkɔːrəneri ‖ˈkɒrənri/ adj coronario

coronary² n (pl **-ries**) infarto m (de miocardio)

coronation /ˌkɔːrəˈneɪʃən ‖ˌkɒrəˈneɪʃən/ n coronación f

coroner /ˈkɔːrənər ‖ˈkɒrənə(r)/ n: funcionario encargado de investigar las causas de muertes violentas, repentinas o sospechosas, ≈ juez mf de instrucción

corporal /ˈkɔːrprəl ‖ˈkɔːpərəl/ n cabo m

corporal punishment n castigos mpl corporales

corporate /ˈkɔːrpərət ‖ˈkɔːpərət/ adj **1** **(a)** (of a company) ⟨headquarters/lawyer⟩ de la empresa or compañía **(b)** ⟨mentality/jargon⟩ empresarial **2** (joint, collective) ⟨action/decision⟩ colectivo

corporation /ˈkɔːrpəˈreɪʃən ‖ˌkɔːpəˈreɪʃən/ n (company — in US) sociedad f anónima; (— in UK) compañía f, empresa f, corporación f

corpse /kɔːrps ‖kɔːps/ n cadáver m

corpuscle /ˈkɔːrpʌsəl ‖ˈkɔːpʌsəl/ n corpúsculo m

corral /kəˈræl ‖kəˈrɑːl/ n corral m

correct¹ /kəˈrekt/ vt corregir*

correct² adj correcto

correction /kəˈrekʃən/ n corrección f

correctly /kəˈrektli/ adv correctamente

correlate /ˈkɔːrəleɪt ‖ˈkɒr-/ vi **to ~ (with sth)** estar* correlacionado (con algo)

correlation /ˌkɔːrəˈleɪʃən ‖ˌkɒrəˈleɪʃən/ n correlación f (frml)

correspond /ˈkɔːrəˈspɑːnd ‖ˌkɒrəˈspɒnd/ vi **1** **(a)** (tally) **to ~ (with sth)** corresponderse or concordar* (con algo) **(b)** (be equivalent) **to ~ (to sth)** equivaler* or corresponder (a algo) **2** (communicate by letter) **to ~ (with sb)** mantener* correspondencia (con algn)

correspondence /ˈkɔːrəˈspɑːndəns ‖ˌkɒrəˈspɒndəns/ n **1** (agreement) correspondencia f **2** (letters, letter writing) correspondencia f

correspondence course n curso m por correspondencia

correspondent /ˌkɔːrəˈspɑːndənt ‖ˌkɒrəˈspɒndənt/ n (a) (letter writer) corresponsal mf (b) (Journ) corresponsal mf

corridor /ˈkɔːrədər ‖ˈkɒrɪdɔː(r)/ n pasillo m, corredor m

corroborate /kəˈrɑːbəreɪt ‖kəˈrɒbəreɪt/ vt corroborar

corrode /kəˈrəʊd/ vt corroer*
■ ~ vi corroerse*

corrosion /kəˈrəʊʒən/ n (a) (action) corrosión f (b) (substance) herrumbre f, orín m

corrosive /kəˈrəʊsɪv/ adj corrosivo

corrugated /ˈkɔːrəgeɪtəd ‖ˈkɒrəgeɪtɪd/ adj ondulado; ~ **cardboard** cartón m corrugado; ~ **iron** chapa f de zinc, calamina f (Chi, Per)

corrupt¹ /kəˈrʌpt/ vt (deprave) corromper; (bribe) sobornar; (Comput) corromper

corrupt² adj ⟨person/government⟩ corrompido, corrupto

corruption /kəˈrʌpʃən/ n corrupción f

corset /ˈkɔːrsət ‖ˈkɔːsɪt/ n (often pl) corsé m

cosmetic /kɑːzˈmetɪk ‖kɒzˈmetɪk/ adj (a) (beautifying) ⟨powder/cream⟩ cosmético; ~ **surgery** cirugía f estética (b) (superficial) ⟨reforms/changes⟩ superficial

cosmetics /kɑːzˈmetɪks ‖kɒzˈmetɪks/ pl n cosméticos mpl

cosmic /ˈkɑːzmɪk ‖ˈkɒzmɪk/ adj cósmico

cosmonaut /ˈkɑːzmənɔːt ‖ˈkɒzmənɔːt/ n cosmonauta mf

cosmopolitan /ˌkɑːzməˈpɑːlətn̩ ‖ˌkɒzməˈpɒlɪtn̩/ adj cosmopolita

cosmos /ˈkɑːzməʊs ‖ˈkɒzmɒs/ n the ~ el cosmos

cost¹ /kɔːst ‖kɒst/ n **1** (a) (expense) (often pl) costo m (esp AmL), coste m (Esp); to cut ~s reducir* los gastos (b) **costs** pl (Law) costas fpl **2** (loss, sacrifice): she helped me out, at great ~ to herself sacrificó mucho al ayudarme; at all ~s a toda costa

cost² vt **1** (past & past p cost) (a) «article/service» costar* (b) (cause to lose) costar*; one slip ~ him the title un error le costó el título **2** (past & past p costed) (calculate cost of) calcular el costo or (Esp) coste de

co-star /ˈkəʊstɑːr ‖ˈkəʊstɑː(r)/ n coprotagonista mf

Costa Rica /ˈkɑːstəˈriːkə ‖ˈkɒstəˈriːkə/ n Costa Rica f

Costa Rican¹ /ˈkɑːstəˈriːkən ‖ˈkɒstəˈriːkən/ adj costarricense

Costa Rican² n costarricense mf

cost-effective /ˌkɔːstɪˈfektɪv ‖ˌkɒstɪˈfektɪv/ adj rentable

costly /ˈkɔːstli ‖ˈkɒstli/ adj **-lier, -liest** costoso

cost: of living n costo m or (Esp) coste m de (la) vida; ~ **price** n precio m de costo or (Esp) de coste

costume /ˈkɑːstuːm ‖ˈkɒstjuːm/ n (a) (style of dress) traje m; (for parties, disguise) disfraz m (b) (wardrobe) (Theat) vestuario m; (individual outfit) traje m (c) (swimming ~) traje m de baño

costume jewelry, (BrE) **costume jewellery** n bisutería f, alhajas fpl de fantasía

cosy¹ /ˈkəʊzi/ adj **cosier, cosiest** (BrE) ▶ cozy¹

cosy² n (pl **cosies**) (BrE) ▶ cozy²

cot /kɑːt ‖kɒt/ n (a) (campbed) (AmE) catre m (b) (for child) (BrE) cuna f, cama f (con barandas)

cottage /ˈkɑːtɪdʒ ‖ˈkɒtɪdʒ/ n casita f

cottage cheese n requesón m

cotton /ˈkɑːtn̩ ‖ˈkɒtn̩/ n (a) (cloth) algodón m; (before n) ⟨dress/sheet/print⟩ de algodón (b) (thread) (BrE) hilo m (de coser) (c) (absorbent ~) (AmE) algodón m (hidrófilo)

cotton wool n (BrE) algodón m (hidrófilo)

couch /kaʊtʃ/ n (sofa) sofá m; (doctor's, psychoanalyst's) diván m

couch potato /kaʊtʃ/ n (colloq) teleadicto, -ta m,f (fam)

cough¹ /kɔːf ‖kɒf/ n tos f; (before n) ~ **mixture** jarabe m para la tos

cough² vi toser
■ ~ vt ~ (up) expectorar
■ **cough up** **1** [v + adv + o] (pay) (colloq) ⟨money⟩ soltar* (fam), aflojar (fam) **2** [v + adv] (pay) soltar* la plata or (Esp) la pasta or (AmL tb) la lana (fam)

could /kʊd/ v mod **1** past of CAN³ **2** (indicating possibility) poder*; **I would help you if I ~** te ayudaría si pudiera; **you ~ have killed us all!** ¡podrías or podías habernos matado a todos!; **you ~ be right** puede (ser) que tengas razón **3** (a) (asking permission): ~ **I use your bathroom?** ¿podría or me permitiría pasar al baño? (b) (in requests): ~ **you sign here please?** ¿quiere firmar aquí, por favor? **4** (a) (in suggestions) poder*; **you ~ try doing it this way** podrías tratar de hacerlo de esta manera (b) (indicating strong desire) poder*; **I ~ have killed her** la hubiera matado, la podría or podía haber matado

couldn't /ˈkʊdn̩t/ = **could not**

council /ˈkaʊnsl̩/ n (a) (advisory group) consejo m (b) (Govt) ayuntamiento m, municipio m; ~ **housing** (BrE) viviendas de alquiler subvencionadas por el ayuntamiento

councillor n (BrE) ▶ COUNCILOR

Council of Europe n the ~ ~ ~ el Consejo de Europa

councilor, (BrE) **councillor** /ˈkaʊnsələr ‖ˈkaʊnsələ(r)/ n concejal, -jala m,f

council tax n (in UK) ≈ contribución f (municipal or inmobiliaria)

counsel¹ /ˈkaʊnsl̩/ n (pl ~) (no art) (Law) abogado, -da m,f; ~ **for the defense** abogado defensor, abogada defensora m,f; ~ **for the prosecution** fiscal mf

counsel² vt, (BrE) **-ll-** (frml) aconsejar

counseling, (BrE) **counselling** /ˈkaʊnsəlɪŋ/ n (Educ, Psych) orientación f psicopedagógica

counselor, (BrE) **counsellor** /ˈkaʊnsələr ‖ˈkaʊnsələ(r)/ n (a) (Educ, Psych) consejero, -ra m,f, orientador, -dora m,f (b) (AmE Law) abogado, -da m,f

count¹ /kaʊnt/ n **1** (a) (act of counting) recuento m, cómputo m; (of votes) escrutinio m, recuento m, cómputo m, conteo m (Andes, Ven); to keep/lose ~ of sth llevar/perder* la cuenta de algo (b) (total) total m; the final ~ (of votes) el recuento or ⋯⋗

cómputo final **2** (point): **it has been criticized on several ~s** ha sido criticado por varios motivos **3** (rank) conde *m*

count² *vt* **1** (enumerate, add up) contar* **2** (include) contar*; **not ~ing the driver** sin contar al conductor **3** (consider) considerar; **to ~ oneself lucky** darse* por afortunado
■ **~** *vi* **1** (enumerate) contar* **2** (be valid, matter) contar*; **that doesn't ~** eso no cuenta *or* no vale; **every minute ~s** cada minuto cuenta
■ **count for** [*v + prep + o*] contar*; **your opinion ~s for a great deal/won't ~ for much** tu opinión importa mucho/no va a contar mucho
■ **count on** [*v + prep + o*] **(a)** (rely on) ⟨*friend/help*⟩ contar* con **(b)** (expect) esperar; **we hadn't ~ed on that happening** no esperábamos que fuera a pasar eso
■ **count out 1** [*v + o + adv*]: **you can ~ me out** a mí no me incluyan, no cuenten conmigo **2** [*v + o + adv, v + adv + o*] ⟨*money/objects*⟩ contar* (*uno por uno*)

countdown /ˈkaʊntdaʊn/ *n* cuenta *f* atrás *or* regresiva, conteo *m* regresivo (Andes, Ven)

counter¹ /ˈkaʊntər ‖ ˈkaʊntə(r)/ *n* **1** (in shop) mostrador *m*; (in café) barra *f*; (in bank, post office) ventanilla *f*; (in kitchen) (AmE) encimera *f* **2** (Games) ficha *f*

counter² *vt* **(a)** (oppose) ⟨*deficiency/trend*⟩ contrarrestar **(b)** (in debate) ⟨*idea/statement*⟩ rebatir, refutar; **to ~ THAT** responder *or* replicar* QUE

counter³ *adv*: **to run** *o* **go ~ to sth** ser* contrario a *or* oponerse* a algo

counteract /kaʊntərˈækt/ *vt* contrarrestar

counterattack¹ /ˈkaʊntərəˈtæk/ *n* contraataque *m*

counterattack² *vi* contraatacar*

counterbalance /ˈkaʊntərˈbæləns ‖ ˈkaʊntəˌbæləns/ *n* contrapeso *m*

counterclockwise /ˈkaʊntərˈklɑːkwaɪz ‖ ˌkaʊntəˈklɒkwaɪz/ *adj/adv* (AmE) en sentido contrario a las agujas del reloj

counterfeit¹ /ˈkaʊntərfɪt ‖ ˈkaʊntəfɪt/ *n* falsificación *f*

counterfeit² *adj* ⟨*money*⟩ falso

counter-: ~foil *n* talón *m* (AmL), matriz *f* (Esp); **~part** *n* (person) homólogo, -ga *m,f*; (thing) equivalente *m*; **~point** *n* (Mus) contrapunto *m*; **~productive** /ˈkaʊntərprəˈdʌktɪv ‖ ˌkaʊntəprəˈdʌktɪv/ *adj* contraproducente

countess /ˈkaʊntəs ‖ ˈkaʊntes/ *n* condesa *f*

countless /ˈkaʊntləs ‖ ˈkaʊntlɪs/ *adj* ⟨*stars/hours*⟩ incontables, innumerables

country /ˈkʌntri/ *n* (*pl* **-tries**) **1** (nation) país *m*; (people) pueblo *m*; (native land) patria *f* **2** (rural area) **the ~** el campo; (*before n*) ⟨*people*⟩ del campo; ⟨*cottage*⟩ de campo **3** (region) terreno *m* **4** (Mus) (música *f*) country *m*

country: ~-and-western /ˈkʌntriənˈwestərn

‖ ˌkʌntriənˈwestən/ *n* (música *f*) country *m*; **~ dancing** *n* (esp BrE) danzas *fpl* folklóricas; **~ house** *n* casa *f* solariega, quinta *f*; **~man** /ˈkʌntrimən/ *n* (*pl* **-men** /-mən/) (fellow ~man) (liter) compatriota *m*; **~side** *n* campiña *f*, campo *m*; **~wide** /ˈkʌntriwaɪd/ *adj/adv* a escala nacional

county /ˈkaʊnti/ *n* (*pl* **-ties**) condado *m*

county: ~ council *n* (in UK) corporación *f* de gobierno a nivel de condado; **~ court** *n* (in US) juzgado *m* comarcal; (in UK) juzgado *m* comarcal (*que conoce de causas de derecho civil*)

coup /kuː/ *n* (*pl* **~s** /kuːz/) **1** (successful action) golpe *m* maestro **2** **~ (d'état)** /deɪˈtɑː/ (Pol) golpe *m* (de estado)

couple¹ /ˈkʌpəl/ *n* **1** (two people) (+ *sing o pl vb*) pareja *f*; **a married ~** un matrimonio **2** (two or small number): **a ~ (of sth)** (+ *pl vb*) un par (de algo)

couple² *vt* **(a)** (connect) (Rail) enganchar; ⟨*theories/events*⟩ asociar; **to ~ sth/sb WITH sth/sb** asociar algo/a algn CON algo/algn **(b)** (combine) (*often pass*): **the fall in demand, ~d with competition from abroad** el descenso de la demanda, unido a la competencia extranjera

coupon /ˈkuːpɑːn ‖ ˈkuːpɒn/ *n* **(a)** (voucher — for discount) vale *m*; (— in rationing) cupón *m* de racionamiento **(b)** (form — in advertisement) cupón *m*; (— for competition) boleto *m*

courage /ˈkərɪdʒ ‖ ˈkʌrɪdʒ/ *n* valor *m*, coraje *m*

courageous /kəˈreɪdʒəs/ *adj* ⟨*person*⟩ valiente, corajudo; ⟨*words*⟩ valiente; ⟨*act*⟩ valeroso

courgette /kʊrˈʒet ‖ kɔːˈʒet/ *n* (BrE) ▶ ZUCCHINI

courier /ˈkʊriər ‖ ˈkʊriə(r)/ *n* **(a)** (guide) guía *mf* **(b)** (messenger) (BrE) mensajero, -ra *m,f*, correo *mf*, rutero, -ra *m,f*

course /kɔːrs ‖ kɔːs/ *n* **1** **(a)** (of river) curso *m*; (of road) recorrido *m* **(b)** (way of proceeding): **the best ~ of action** las mejores medidas que se pueden tomar **(c)** (progress, direction) (*no pl*): **in the normal ~ of events** normalmente; **in due ~** a su debido tiempo; **it changed the ~ of history** cambió el curso de la historia **2** **of course** claro, desde luego, por supuesto; **of ~ not** claro *or* por supuesto que no **3** (Aviat, Naut) rumbo *m*; **to go off ~** desviarse* de rumbo; **to change ~** cambiar de rumbo **4** **(a)** (Educ) curso *m*; **to take a ~ IN/ON sth** curso DE/SOBRE algo; **to take a ~** hacer* un curso **(b)** (Med): **a ~ of treatment** un tratamiento **5** (part of a meal) plato *m*; **main ~** plato principal *or* fuerte; **a three-~ meal** una comida de dos platos y postre **6** (Sport) (race~) hipódromo *m*, pista *f* (de carreras); (golf ~) campo *m or* (CS *tb*) cancha *f* (de golf)

court¹ /kɔːrt ‖ kɔːt/ *n* **1** (Law) **(a)** (tribunal) tribunal *m*; **to take sb to ~** demandar a algn, llevar a algn a juicio; (*before n*) **~ case** causa *f*, juicio *m* **(b)** (building) juzgado *m* **2** (of sovereign) corte *f* **3** (Sport) cancha *f* (AmL), pista *f* (Esp) **4** (courtyard) patio *m*

court² *vt* **(a)** ⟨girl⟩ (dated) cortejar (ant), hacerle* la corte a (ant) **(b)** (seek) ⟨danger/favor⟩ buscar*; ⟨danger⟩ exponerse* a

courteous /'kɜːrtiəs ‖'kɜːtiəs/ *adj* cortés

courtesy /'kɜːrtəsi ‖'kɜːtəsi/ *n* cortesía *f*; ~ **of** por atención de

courthouse /'kɔːrthaʊs ‖'kɔːthaʊs/ *n* juzgado *m*

courtier /'kɔːrtiər ‖'kɔːtiə(r)/ *n* cortesano, -na *m,f*

court-martial¹ /'kɔːrt'mɑːrʃəl ‖,kɔːt'mɑːʃəl/ *n* (*pl* **courts-martial** /'kɔːrts-/) consejo *m* de guerra

court-martial² *vt*, (BrE) **-ll-** formarle consejo de guerra a

court: ~room *n* sala *f* (de un tribunal); **~ shoe** *n* (BrE) zapato *m* (de) salón; **~yard** *n* patio *m*

cousin /'kʌzn̩/ *n* primo, -ma *m,f*; **first ~** primo hermano *or* carnal, prima hermana *or* carnal; **second ~** primo segundo, prima segunda

cove /kəʊv/ *n* cala *f*, caleta *f*

covenant /'kʌvənənt/ *n* pacto *m*

cover¹ /'kʌvər ‖'kʌvə(r)/ *n* **1 (a)** (lid, casing) tapa *f*, cubierta *f*; (for cushion, sofa, typewriter) funda *f*; (for book) forro *m* **(b) covers** *pl* (bedclothes) **the ~s** las mantas, las cobijas (AmL), las frazadas (AmL)

2 (of book) tapa *f*, cubierta *f*; (of magazine) portada *f*, carátula *f* (Andes); (front ~) portada *f*; **to read sth from ~ to ~** leer* algo de cabo a rabo **3 (a)** (shelter, protection): **to take ~** guarecerse*, ponerse* a cubierto; **to run for ~** correr a guarecerse *or* a ponerse a cubierto; **under ~ of darkness** al abrigo de la oscuridad **(b)** (front, pretense) tapadera *f*, pantalla *f*; **to blow sb's ~** desenmascarar a algn

4 (insurance) (BrE) cobertura *f*

cover² *vt* **1 (a)** (overlay) cubrir*; **to be ~ed IN sth** estar* cubierto DE algo **(b)** ⟨hole/saucepan⟩ tapar **(c)** ⟨cushion⟩ ponerle* una funda a; ⟨book⟩ forrar; ⟨sofa⟩ tapizar*, recubrir* **(d)** ⟨passage/terrace⟩ techar, cubrir*

2 (a) (extend over) ⟨area/floor⟩ cubrir*; ⟨page⟩ llenar **(b)** (travel) ⟨distance⟩ recorrer **3 (a)** (deal with) ⟨syllabus⟩ cubrir*; ⟨topic⟩ tratar **(b)** (report on) (Journ) cubrir*

4 (a) (hide) tapar; **to ~ one's head** cubrirse* (la cabeza) **(b)** (mask) ⟨surprise/ignorance⟩ disimular; ⟨mistake⟩ ocultar

5 (a) (guard, protect) cubrir* **(b)** (point gun at) apuntarle a **(c)** (Sport) ⟨opponent⟩ marcar*; ⟨shot/base⟩ cubrir*

6 (Fin) **(a)** ⟨costs/expenses⟩ cubrir*; ⟨liabilities⟩ hacer* frente a; **will $100 ~ it?** ¿alcanzará con 100 dólares? **(b)** (insurance) cubrir*

■ ~ *vi* **(a)** (deputize) **to ~ FOR sb** sustituir* a algn **(b)** (conceal truth) **to ~ FOR sb** encubrir* a algn

■ **cover up** **1** [v + o + adv, v + adv + o] **(a)** (cover completely) cubrir*, tapar **(b)** (conceal) ⟨facts/truth⟩ ocultar; ⟨mistake⟩ disimular

2 [v + adv] (conceal error) disimular; (conceal truth) **to ~ up FOR sb** encubrir* a algn

coverage /'kʌvərɪdʒ/ *n* (Journ) cobertura *f*

cover-alls /'kʌvərɔːlz/ *pl n* (AmE) overol *m* (AmL), mono *m* (Esp, Méx)

covering letter /'kʌvərɪŋ/ *n* carta *f* adjunta

covert /'kəʊvərt ‖'kʌvət, 'kəʊ-/ *adj* encubierto

cover-up /'kʌvərʌp/ *n* (of crime) encubrimiento *m*

covet /'kʌvət/ *vt* codiciar

cow /kaʊ/ *n* **(a)** (Agr) vaca *f* **(b)** (female whale, elephant, seal) hembra *f*

coward /'kaʊərd ‖'kaʊəd/ *n* cobarde *mf*

cowardice /'kaʊərdəs ‖'kaʊədɪs/ *n* cobardía *f*

cowardly /'kaʊərdli ‖'kaʊədli/ *adj* cobarde

cowboy /'kaʊbɔɪ/ *n* (in Western US) vaquero *m*; (in Wild West) vaquero *m*, cowboy *m*

cower /'kaʊər ‖'kaʊə(r)/ *vi* encogerse* (de miedo)

coworker /'kəʊ'wɜːrkər ‖'kəʊ'wɜːkə(r)/ *n* (esp AmE) (workmate) colega *mf*, compañero, -ra *m,f* de trabajo; (collaborator) colaborador, -dora *m,f*

coy /kɔɪ/ *adj* **coyer, coyest** (shy) tímido; (evasive) evasivo

coyote /kaɪ'əʊti ‖kɔɪ'əʊti/ *n* (*pl* **-otes** or **-ote**) coyote *m*

cozy¹, (BrE) **cosy** /'kəʊzi/ *adj* **cozier, coziest (a)** ⟨room⟩ acogedor **(b)** ⟨chat⟩ íntimo y agradable

cozy², (BrE) **cosy** *n* (*pl* **-ies**) (tea ~) cubreteteras *m*

CPA *n* (in US) = **Certified Public Accountant**

crab /kræb/ *n*(animal, meat) cangrejo *m*, jaiba *f* (AmL)

crack¹ /kræk/ *n* **1 (a)** (in ice, wall, pavement) grieta *f*; (in glass, china) rajadura *f* **(b)** (chink, slit) rendija *f* **2** (sound — of whip, twig) chasquido *m*; (— of rifle shot) estallido *m*; (— of thunder) estruendo *m* **3** (blow) golpe *m* **4** (instant): **at the ~ of dawn** al amanecer **5** (attempt) (colloq) intento *m*; **to have a ~ at sth** intentar algo **6** (colloq) (wisecrack) comentario *m* socarrón **7** (drug) crack *m*

crack² *adj* (before n) ⟨shot/troops⟩ de primera

crack³ *vt* **1 (a)** ⟨cup/glass⟩ rajar; ⟨ground/earth/skin⟩ agrietar; **he ~ed a rib** se fracturó una costilla

2 (a) (break open) ⟨egg/nut⟩ cascar*; ⟨safe⟩ forzar*; ⟨drugs ring/spy ring⟩ desmantelar **(b)** (decipher, solve) ⟨code⟩ descifrar; ⟨problem⟩ resolver*

3 (make cracking sound with) ⟨whip⟩ (hacer*) chasquear; ⟨finger/knuckle⟩ hacer* crujir

4 (hit sharply) pegar*

5 ⟨joke⟩ (colloq) contar*

■ ~ *vi* **1 (a)** «cup/glass» rajarse; «rock/paint/skin» agrietarse **(b)** (make cracking sound) «whip» chasquear; «bones/twigs» crujir **(c)** «voice» quebrarse* **(d)** (break down): **she ~ed under the strain** sufrió una crisis nerviosa a causa de la tensión

2 (be active, busy): **to get ~ing** (colloq) poner(se)* manos a la obra

■ **crack down** [v + adv] **to ~ down ON sb/sth** tomar medidas enérgicas CONTRA algn/algo

■ **crack up** [v + adv] **(a)** (break down) (colloq) «person» sufrir un ataque de nervios, sucumbir a la presión **(b)** (burst out laughing) (colloq) soltar* una carcajada

cracked /krækt/ *adj* **(a)** ⟨cup/glass⟩ rajado; ⟨rib⟩ fracturado; ⟨wall/ceiling⟩ con grietas; ⟨lips⟩ partido; ⟨skin⟩ agrietado **(b)** (crazy) (colloq) ⟨person⟩ loco, chiflado (fam) **(c)** ⟨voice⟩ cascado

cracker /'krækər ‖ 'krækə(r)/ n **1** (biscuit) cracker f, galleta f (salada) **2** (a) (fire~) petardo m (b) (BrE) sorpresa f (que estalla al abrirla) **3** (Comput colloq) intruso, -sa m,f

crackle¹ /'krækəl/ vi «fire» crepitar; «twigs/paper» crujir

crackle² n (of twigs, paper) crujido m; (of fire) chisporroteo m

cradle¹ /'kreɪdl/ n cuna f

cradle² vt ‹baby› acunar, mecer*

craft /kræft ‖ krɑːft/ n **1** (a) (trade) oficio m; (skill) arte m (b) **crafts** pl artesanía f; see also ART 1B **2** (guile, deceit) (liter) artimañas fpl **3** (pl ~) (Naut) embarcación f; (Aerosp, Aviat) nave f

craftsman /'kræftsmən ‖ 'krɑːftsmən/ n (pl -men /mən/) artesano m, artífice m

crafty /'kræfti ‖ 'krɑːfti/ adj -tier, -tiest ‹person› astuto; ‹methods/tactics› hábil

craggy /'krægi/ adj -gier, -giest escarpado; he had a ~, weather-beaten face tenía un rostro curtido y de facciones bien marcadas

cram /kræm/ -mm- vt (stuff) meter; the room was ~med with books la habitación estaba abarrotada de libros; I ~med three meetings into one morning logré asistir a tres reuniones en una mañana
■ ~ vi (for exam) empollar (Esp fam), zambutir (Méx), tragar* (RPl fam), matearse (Chi fam), empacarse* (Col fam)

cramp¹ /kræmp/ n (in leg) calambre m, rampa f (Esp); **stomach ~s** retorcijones mpl or (Esp) retortijones mpl en el estómago

cramp² vt (limit) ‹work/progress› entorpecer*; to ~ sb's style cortarle los vuelos a algn

cramped /kræmpt/ adj ‹handwriting› apretado; they work in ~ conditions están muy estrechos en el trabajo; they live in ~ conditions viven hacinados

cranberry /'kræn,beri ‖ 'krænbəri/ n (pl -ries) arándano m (rojo y agrio)

crane¹ /kreɪn/ n **1** (for lifting) grúa f **2** (Zool) grulla f

crane² vt: to ~ one's neck estirar el cuello

crank /kræŋk/ n **1** (a) (Mech Eng) cigüeñal m (b) ~ (handle) (Auto) manivela f (de arranque) **2** (colloq) (a) (eccentric) maniático, -ca m,f (b) (bad-tempered person) (AmE) cascarrabias mf

cranny /'kræni/ n (pl -nies) ranura f; ▶ NOOK

crap /kræp/ n (a) (excrement) (vulg) mierda f (vulg) (b) (nonsense) (sl) estupideces fpl, gilipolleces fpl (Esp fam o vulg), pendejadas fpl (AmL exc CS fam), huevadas fpl (Andes, Ven vulg), boludeces fpl (Col, RPl vulg)

crash¹ /kræʃ/ n (a) (loud noise) estrépito m (b) (collision, accident) accidente m, choque m (c) (financial failure) crac m, crack m

crash² vt **1** (smash): he ~ed the car tuvo un accidente con el coche, chocó **2** (colloq) to ~ a party colarse* en una fiesta (fam)
■ ~ vi (a) (collide) to ~ (INTO sth) estrellarse or chocar* (CONTRA algo) (b) (make loud noise) «thunder» retumbar; the dishes ~ed to the floor los platos se cayeron al suelo estrepitosamente (c) (Fin) «shares» caer* a pique

crash³ adj (before n) ‹program/course› intensivo; ~ diet régimen m muy estricto

crash: ~ **barrier** n barrera f de protección; ~ **helmet** n casco m (protector); ~**landing** /'kræʃlændɪŋ/ n aterrizaje m forzoso

crate /kreɪt/ n cajón m (de embalaje), jaba f (Chi)

crater /'kreɪtər ‖ 'kreɪtə(r)/ n cráter m

cravat /krə'væt/ n pañuelo m de cuello (de caballero)

crave /kreɪv/ vt ‹admiration› ansiar*; ‹affection› tener* ansias de; ‹food/drink› morirse* por (fam)

craving /'kreɪvɪŋ/ n (a) (strong desire) ansias fpl (b) (in pregnancy) antojo m

crawfish /'krɔːfɪʃ/ n (pl -fish or -fishes) ▶ CRAYFISH

crawl¹ /krɔːl/ vi **1** (a) (creep) arrastrarse; «baby» gatear, ir* a gatas; «insect» andar* (b) (go slowly) «traffic/train» avanzar* muy lentamente **2** (teem): the beach was ~ing with tourists la playa estaba plagada de turistas **3** (demean oneself) (colloq) arrastrarse

crawl² n **1** (slow pace) (no pl): to go at a ~ avanzar* muy lentamente **2** (swimming stroke) crol m

crayfish /'kreɪfɪʃ/ n (pl -fish or -fishes) (freshwater) ástaco m, cangrejo m de río; (marine) langosta f (pequeña), cigala f

crayon /'kreɪɑːn ‖ 'kreɪən/ n (pencil) lápiz m de color; (wax ~) crayola® f, crayón m (Méx, RPl), lápiz m de cera (Chi)

craze /kreɪz/ n (fashion) moda f; (fad) manía f

crazy /'kreɪzi/ adj -zier, -ziest loco; to go ~ volverse* loco; to be ~ ABOUT o (AmE) FOR o (AmE) OVER sb estar* loco POR algn (fam)

creak /kriːk/ vi «door» chirriar*; «bedsprings/floorboards/joints» crujir

cream¹ /kriːm/ n **1** (Culin) crema f (de leche) (esp AmL), nata f (Esp) **2** (lotion) crema f **3** (elite) the ~ of society la flor y nata de la sociedad **4** (color) color m crema

cream² adj color crema adj inv

cream³ vt ‹butter/sugar› batir (hasta obtener una consistencia cremosa); ~ed potatoes puré m de papas or (Esp) patatas

cream cheese n queso m crema (AmL), queso m para untar (Esp)

creamer /'kriːmər ‖ 'kriːmə(r)/ n **1** (jug) (AmE) jarrita f para crema **2** (powder) leche f en polvo

creamy /'kriːmi/ adj -mier, -miest (containing cream) con crema; (smooth) cremoso

crease¹ /kriːs/ n (in paper, clothes) arruga f; (in trousers) raya f, pliegue m (Méx, Ven)

crease² vi arrugarse*
■ ~ vt ‹clothes› arrugar*; ‹paper› doblar, plegar*

create /kri'eɪt/ vt crear; ‹impression› producir*

creation /kri'eɪʃən/ n creación f

creative /kri'eɪtɪv/ adj creativo

creativity /ˌkriːeɪ'tɪvəti/ n creatividad f

creator /kri'eɪtər ‖ kri'eɪtə(r)/ n creador, -dora m,f

creature /'kriːtʃər ‖ 'kriːtʃə(r)/ n (a) (animate being) criatura f; sea ~ animal m marino (b) (person) ser m, criatura f

creche, crèche /kreʃ/ n (a) (hospital for foundlings) (AmE) orfanato m, orfelinato m, orfanatorio *m* **(b)** (day nursery) (BrE) guardería *f* (infantil) (*puede ser en el lugar de trabajo para los empleados etc.*)

credentials /krɪ'dentʃəlz ‖krɪ'denʃəlz/ *pl n* (of ambassador) cartas *fpl* credenciales; (references) referencias *fpl*; (identifying papers) documentos *mpl* (de identidad)

credibility /'kredə'bɪləti/ *n* credibilidad *f*

credible /'kredəbəl/ *adj* creíble

credit¹ /'kredət ‖'kredɪt/ *n* **1** (Fin) **(a)** (in store) crédito *m*; **on ~** a crédito **(b)** (in banking): **to keep one's account in ~** mantener* un saldo positivo; (*before n*) **~ balance** saldo *m* positivo; **~ limit** límite *m* de crédito **(c)** (on balance sheet) saldo *m* acreedor *or* a favor
2 (honor, recognition) mérito *m*; **Jim must take the ~ for the excellent organization** la excelente organización es obra de Jim; **your children are a ~ to you** puedes estar orgulloso de tus hijos
3 (Educ) **(a)** (for study) crédito *m* (*unidad de valor de una asignatura dentro de un programa de estudios*) **(b)** (grade) ≈ notable *m*
4 credits *pl* (Cin, TV, Video) créditos *mpl*

credit² *vt* **1** to **~ money to an account** abonar *or* ingresar dinero en una cuenta **2 (a)** (ascribe to) **please, ~ me with some intelligence** reconóceme algo de inteligencia, por favor; **they are ~ed with having invented the game** se les atribuye la invención del juego **(b)** (believe) creer*

credit card *n* tarjeta *f* de crédito

creditor /'kredətər ‖'kredɪtə(r)/ *n* acreedor, -dora *m,f*

creed /kriːd/ *n* credo *m*

creek /kriːk/ *n* **(a)** (stream) (AmE) arroyo *m*, riachuelo *m* **(b)** (inlet) (BrE) cala *f*

creep¹ /kriːp/ (*past & past p* **crept**) *vi* (+ *adv compl*) **(a)** (crawl) arrastrarse **(b)** (move stealthily): **to ~ into a room** entrar en un cuarto sigilosamente; **a note of suspicion crept into his voice** se empezó a notar un elemento de sospecha en su voz

creep² *n* (colloq) **(a)** (unpleasant person) asqueroso, -sa *m,f* **(b)** (favor-seeking person) adulador, -dora *m,f*, pelota *mf* (Esp fam), chupamedias *mf* (CS, Ven fam), lambiscón, -cona *m,f* (Méx fam), lambón, -bona *m,f* (Col fam)

creeper /'kriːpər ‖'kriːpə(r)/ *n* planta *f* trepadora

cremate /'kriːmeɪt ‖krɪ'meɪt/ *vt* incinerar, cremar

cremation /krɪ'meɪʃən/ *n* incineración *f*, cremación *f*

crematorium /'kriːmə'tɔːriəm ‖,kremə'tɔːriəm/ *n* (*pl* **-riums** *or* **-ria** /-riə/) crematorio *m*

crepe, crêpe /kreɪp/ *n* **1** (fabric) crep *m*, crepé *m* **2** (pancake) (Culin) crep *m*, crêpe *f*, panqueque *m* (AmC, CS), crepa *f* (Méx)

crepe paper *n* papel *m* crepé *or* crep¹

crept /krept/ *past & past p of* CREEP¹

crescendo /krə'ʃendəʊ ‖krɪ'ʃendəʊ/ *n* (*pl* **-dos**) (Mus) crescendo *m*; (climax) punto *m* culminante

crescent /'kresn̩t/ *n* **1** (moon) creciente *m* **2 (a)** (shape) media luna *f* **(b)** (street) *calle en forma de media luna*

cress /kres/ *n* mastuerzo *m*

crest /krest/ *n* **1** (Zool) (of skin) cresta *f*; (of feathers) penacho *m* **2** (in heraldry) emblema *m*, divisa *f* **3** (of wave) cresta *f*; (of mountain) cima *f*

crestfallen /'krest,fɔːlən/ *adj* alicaído

crevice /'krevəs ‖'krevɪs/ *n* grieta *f*

crew /kruː/ *n* **(a)** (Aviat, Naut) tripulación *f* **(b)** (team) equipo *m*; **film ~** (Cin) equipo *m* de rodaje **(c)** (gang, band) banda *f*, pandilla *f*

crew: **~ cut** *n* pelo *m* cortado al rape; **~ neck** *n* cuello *m* redondo

crib /krɪb/ *n* **1 (a)** (child's bed) (AmE) cuna *f* **(b)** (Nativity scene) nacimiento *m*, pesebre *m*, belén *m* (Esp) **2** (Agr) **(a)** (manger) pesebre *m* **(b)** (for storing grain) (AmE) granero *m*

crick /krɪk/ *vt*: **to ~ one's neck** hacer* un mal movimiento con el cuello

cricket /'krɪkət ‖'krɪkɪt/ *n* **1** (Zool) grillo *m* **2** (Sport) críquet *m*

cricketer /'krɪkətər ‖'krɪkɪtə(r)/ *n* jugador, -dora *m,f* de críquet

crime /kraɪm/ *n* **(a)** (wrongful act) delito *m*; (murder) crimen *m* **(b)** (criminal activity) delincuencia *f*; **~ wave** ola *f* delictiva

criminal¹ /'krɪmənl̩ ‖'krɪmɪnl̩/ *n* delincuente *mf*; (serious offender) criminal *mf*

criminal² *adj* ⟨act⟩ delictivo; ⟨organization/mind⟩ criminal; **~ court** juzgado *m* en lo penal; **~ law** derecho *m* penal; **~ offense** delito *m*

criminal record *n* antecedentes *mpl* penales, prontuario *m* (CS)

crimson¹ /'krɪmzən/ *n* carmesí *m*

crimson² *adj* carmesí *adj inv*

cringe /krɪndʒ/ *vi* **(a)** (shrink, cower) encogerse* **(b)** (grovel) arrastrarse

crinkle /'krɪŋkəl/ **~ (up)** *vt* arrugar*
■ **~** *vi* arrugarse*

cripple¹ /'krɪpəl/ *n* lisiado, -da *m,f*

cripple² *vt* **(a)** (lame, disable): **he was ~d for life** quedó lisiado de por vida; **he's ~d with arthritis** la artritis lo tiene casi inmovilizado **(b)** (make inactive, ineffective) ⟨ship/plane⟩ inutilizar*; ⟨industry⟩ paralizar*

crippling /'krɪplɪŋ/ *adj* ⟨costs/debts⟩ agobiante; ⟨losses/strike⟩ de consecuencias catastróficas; ⟨pain⟩ atroz

crisis /'kraɪsəs ‖'kraɪsɪs/ *n* (*pl* **-ses** /-siːz/) crisis *f*; (*before n*) **to reach ~ point** hacer* crisis

crisp¹ /krɪsp/ *adj* **-er**, **-est** **1 (a)** (crunchy) ⟨toast/bacon⟩ crujiente, crocante (RPl); ⟨lettuce⟩ fresco; ⟨apple/snow⟩ crujiente **(b)** ⟨sheets⟩ limpio y almidonado **(c)** (cold) ⟨air⟩ frío y vigorizante **2** (brisk, concise) ⟨manner⟩ seco; ⟨style⟩ escueto

crisp² *n* (potato **~**) (BrE) papa *f or* (Esp) patata *f* frita (*de bolsa*), papa *f* chip (Ur)

crisscross¹ /'krɪskrɔːs ‖'krɪskrɒs/ *adj* entrecruzado

crisscross² *vt* entrecruzar*

criterion /kraɪ'trɪən ‖kraɪ'tɪəriən/ *n* (*pl* **-ria** /-riə/) criterio *m*

critic /'krɪtɪk/ *n* (Art, Theat, Lit) crítico, -ca *m,f*; (detractor) detractor, -tora *m,f*

critical /'krɪtɪkəl/ *adj* **1** ⟨remark/report⟩ crítico **2 (a)** (very serious) ⟨condition/shortage⟩ crítico **(b)** (crucial) ⟨period⟩ crítico

critically /'krɪtɪkli/ adv **1** ⟨ill⟩ gravemente **2** (a) (as a critic): she looked ~ at her reflection miró con ojo crítico la imagen que le devolvía el espejo (b) (censoriously): she spoke rather ~ of him habló de él en tono de crítica

criticism /'krɪtəsɪzəm ‖'krɪtɪsɪzəm/ n crítica f

criticize /'krɪtɪsaɪz ‖'krɪtɪsaɪz/ vt criticar*

croak¹ /krəʊk/ n (of frog) croar m; (of raven) graznido m; (of person) voz f ronca

croak² vi «frog» croar; «raven» graznar; «person» hablar con voz ronca
■ ~ vt decir* con voz ronca

Croat /'krəʊæt/ n croata mf

Croatia /krəʊ'eɪʃə/ n Croacia f

Croatian /krəʊ'eɪʃən/ adj croata

crochet¹ /'krəʊʃeɪ ‖'krəʊʃeɪ/ vt tejer a crochet or a ganchillo; (before n) ~ hook aguja f de crochet, ganchillo m, crochet m (Chi)

crochet² n crochet m, ganchillo m

crockery /'krɑːkəri ‖'krɒkəri/ n vajilla f, loza f

crocodile /'krɑːkədaɪl ‖'krɒkədaɪl/ n cocodrilo m

crocus /'krəʊkəs/ n (pl **-cuses**) azafrán m de primavera

crook /krʊk/ n sinvergüenza mf

crooked /'krʊkəd ‖'krʊkɪd/ adj (a) ⟨line/legs⟩ torcido, chueco (AmL); ⟨back⟩ encorvado; ⟨path⟩ sinuoso (b) (dishonest) (colloq) ⟨person/deal⟩ deshonesto, chueco (Chi, Méx fam)

crop¹ /krɑːp ‖krɒp/ n **1** (a) (quantity of produce) cosecha f (b) (type of produce) cultivo m **2** (haircut) corte m de pelo muy corto **3** (riding ~) fusta f, fuete m (AmL exc CS)

crop² -pp- vt ⟨hair⟩ cortar muy corto
■ **crop up** [v + o + adv, v + adv + o] (colloq) surgir*

croquet /krəʊ'keɪ ‖'krəʊkeɪ/ n croquet m

croquette /krəʊ'ket/ n (potato ~) rollito de puré de papa envuelto en pan rallado y frito

cross¹ /krɔːs ‖krɒs/ n **1** (a) (Relig) cruz f (b) (mark, sign) cruz f **2** (hybrid) cruce m, cruza f (AmL) **3** (Sport) (a) (in soccer) pase m cruzado (b) (in boxing) cruzado m, cross m

cross² vt **1** (go across) ⟨road/river/desert⟩ cruzar*; it ~ed my mind that ... se me ocurrió que ... **2** ⟨arms/legs⟩ cruzar* **3** ⟨plants/breeds⟩ cruzar* **4** (go against) ⟨person⟩ contrariar*; ⟨plans⟩ frustrar
■ ~ vi (a) (walk across road) cruzar* (b) «paths/letters» cruzarse*
■ v refl to ~ oneself persignarse, santiguarse*
■ **cross out** [v + o + adv, v + adv + o] tachar

cross³ adj -er, -est (esp BrE) enojado (esp AmL), enfadado (esp Esp); to get ~ enojarse (esp AmL), enfadarse (esp Esp)

cross: ~**bar** n (on bicycle) barra f; (of goal) larguero m; ~**bow** /'krɔːsbəʊ ‖'krɒsbəʊ/ n ballesta f; ~**breed** vt (past & past p -**bred**) cruzar*; ~**Channel** /'krɔːs'tʃænl ‖,krɒs'tʃænl/ adj (before n) ⟨ferry/traffic⟩ que cruza el Canal de la Mancha; ~**check** /'krɔːs'tʃek ‖,krɒs'tʃek/ vt

⟨facts/references⟩ verificar* (consultando otras fuentes); to ~check sth AGAINST sth cotejar algo CON algo; ~**country** /'krɔːs'kʌntri ‖krɒs'kʌntri/ adj ⟨route/drive⟩ campo a través; ~**examination** /'krɔːsɪg,zæmə'neɪʃən ‖,krɒsɪg,zæmɪ'neɪʃən/ n repreguntas fpl, contrainterrogación f (Chi); ~**examine** /'krɔːsɪg'zæmən ‖'krɒsɪg'zæmɪn/ vt ⟨witness⟩ repreguntar; ~**eyed** /'krɔːs'aɪd ‖'krɒsaɪd/ adj bizco; ~**fire** n fuego m cruzado

crossing /'krɔːsɪŋ ‖'krɒsɪŋ/ n **1** (across sea) travesía f, cruce m (AmS) **2** (for pedestrians) cruce m peatonal or de peatones

cross: ~**legged** /'krɔːs'legd ‖,krɒs'legd/ adv con las piernas cruzadas (en el suelo); ~**purposes** /'krɔːs'pɜːrpəsəz ‖,krɒs'pɜːpəsɪz/ pl n: we're (talking) at ~purposes estamos hablando de cosas distintas; ~**question** /'krɔːs'kwestʃən ‖,krɒs'kwestʃən/ vt interrogar*; ~**reference** /'krɔːs'refrəns ‖,krɒs'refrəns/ n remisión f; ~**roads** n (pl ~**roads**) cruce m, encrucijada f (liter); ~ **section,** (BrE) ~**section** /'krɔːs'sekʃən ‖,krɒs'sekʃən/ n (Biol, Eng) sección f, corte m transversal; ~**walk** n (AmE) cruce m peatonal or de peatones; ~**word** (**puzzle**) n crucigrama f, palabras fpl cruzadas (CS)

crotch /krɑːtʃ ‖krɒtʃ/ n entrepierna f

crotchet /'krɑːtʃət ‖'krɒtʃɪt/ n (BrE Mus) negra f

crouch /kraʊtʃ/ vi agacharse, ponerse* en cuclillas

croupier /'kruːpiər ‖'kruːpiə(r)/ n crupier mf, croupier mf

crow¹ /krəʊ/ n cuervo m; as the ~ flies en línea recta

crow² vi (a) «cock» cacarear (b) (exult) alardear

crowbar /'krəʊbɑːr ‖'krəʊbɑː(r)/ n palanca f

crowd¹ /kraʊd/ n (a) (gathering of people) muchedumbre f, multitud f; the game attracted a good ~ el partido atrajo mucho público (b) (masses, average folk) (pej): to follow the ~ seguir* (a) la manada; to stand out from the ~ destacar(se)* (c) (group, set) (colloq): they are a nice ~ son gente simpática

crowd² vi aglomerarse
■ ~ vt ⟨hall/entrance⟩ llenar, abarrotar

crowded /'kraʊdəd ‖'kraʊdɪd/ adj ⟨street/room/bus⟩ abarrotado, atestado; the beach gets very ~ la playa se llena de gente

crown¹ /kraʊn/ n **1** (of monarch) corona f **2** (top — of hill) cima f; (— of tree) copa f; (— of tooth) corona f; (— of head) coronilla f; (— of hat) copa f **3** (Fin) corona f

crown² vt **1** (make monarch) coronar **2** (be culmination of) coronar; to ~ it all, I lost my wallet y para rematarla, perdí la billetera

crown court n (in UK) juzgado m (que conoce de causas de derecho penal)

crowning /'kraʊnɪŋ/ adj (before n) ⟨success/achievement⟩ supremo, mayor

crown: ~ **jewels** pl n joyas fpl de la corona; ~ **prince** n príncipe m heredero

crow's feet pl n patas fpl de gallo

crucial /'kru:ʃəl/ adj crucial, decisivo

crucifixion /'kru:sə'fɪkʃən ‖,kru:sɪ'fɪkʃən/ n crucifixión f

crucify /'kru:səfaɪ ‖'kru:sɪfaɪ/ vt (past & past p **-fied**) crucificar*

crude /kru:d/ adj **-der, -dest (a)** (vulgar) ordinario, grosero **(b)** (unsophisticated) rudimentario, burdo **(c)** (containing impurities) (before n) ‹oil› crudo

cruel /'kru:əl/ adj **crueller, cruellest** cruel

cruelty /'kru:əlti/ n (pl **-ties**) crueldad f

cruet /'kru:ət ‖'kru:ɪt/ n (Culin) vinagrera f, aceitera f, alcuza f (Chi)

cruise[1] /kru:z/ vi [1] **(a)** (Naut) hacer* un crucero **(b)** ‹police car› patrullar [2] (travel at steady speed) ‹plane› volar*; ‹car› ir* (a una velocidad constante)

cruise[2] n crucero m

cruiser /'kru:zər ‖'kru:zə(r)/ n (warship) crucero m; (cabin ~) lancha f

crumb /krʌm/ n miga f

crumble /'krʌmbəl/ vi ‹cake/soil› desmenuzarse*; ‹wall› desmoronarse; ‹democracy/resolve› desmoronarse
■ ~ vt ‹earth/cake› desmenuzar*; ‹bread› desmigajar

crummy /'krʌmi/ adj **-mier, -miest** (colloq) malo, horrible

crumpet /'krʌmpət ‖'krʌmpɪt/ n (Culin) panecillo de levadura que se come tostado

crumple /'krʌmpəl/ vt ‹paper/clothes› arrugar*; ‹metal› abollar; **she ~d the sheet of paper into a ball** hizo una bola estrujando la hoja de papel

crunch[1] /krʌntʃ/ vt **(a)** (eat noisily) mascar*, ronchar **(b)** (crush) aplastar (haciendo crujir)

crunch[2] n [1] (noise) crujido m [2] (crisis): **when it comes to the ~** a la hora de la verdad

crunchy /'krʌntʃi/ adj **-chier, -chiest** crujiente

crusade /kru:'seɪd/ n (a) (Hist) also **Crusade** cruzada f **(b)** (campaign) cruzada f

crush[1] /krʌʃ/ vt [1] (squash) ‹box/car/person/fingers› aplastar; ‹grapes› prensar; ‹dress/suit› arrugar* [2] (subdue) ‹resistance/enemy› aplastar

crush[2] n [1] (crowd) (no pl) aglomeración f [2] (infatuation) (colloq) enamoramiento m; **to have a ~ on sb** estar* chiflado por algn (fam)

crush barrier n valla f de protección

crushing /'krʌʃɪŋ/ adj ‹defeat› aplastante; ‹reply/contempt› apabullante

crust /krʌst/ n **(a)** (on bread) corteza f **(b)** (thin outer layer) costra f, corteza f; **the earth's ~** la corteza terrestre

crustacean /krʌ'steɪʃən/ n crustáceo m

crusty /'krʌsti/ adj **-tier, -tiest (a)** (crispy) ‹bread› crujiente **(b)** (irascible) malhumorado

crutch /krʌtʃ/ n [1] (walking aid) muleta f [2] (BrE) ▶ CROTCH

crux /krʌks/ n (no pl) **the ~** (of the matter) el quid (de la cuestión)

cry[1] /kraɪ/ n (pl **cries**) [1] **(a)** (exclamation) grito m; **to be a far ~ from sth** ser* muy distinto

de or a algo **(b)** (of street vendor) pregón m **(c)** (no pl) (call of seagull) chillido m [2] (weep) (colloq) (no pl) llanto m; **to have a ~** llorar

cry[2] **cries, crying, cried** vi [1] (weep) llorar [2] (call) ‹bird› chillar; ‹person› gritar
■ **cry out** [v + adv] **(a)** (call out) gritar **(b)** (need) **to ~ out FOR sth** pedir* algo a gritos

crypt /krɪpt/ n cripta f

cryptic /'krɪptɪk/ adj enigmático

crystal /'krɪstl/ n **(a)** (Chem) cristal m **(b)** ~ (glass) cristal m

crystal: ~ **ball** n bola f de cristal; ~**clear** /'krɪstl'klɪr ‖,krɪstl'klɪə(r)/ adj ‹water› (liter) cristalino; ‹sound/image› nítido, claro

crystallize /'krɪstəlaɪz/ vt **(a)** (Chem, Geol) cristalizar*; ‹idea/plan› materializar* **(b)** (Culin) ‹fruit› confitar, escarchar, abrillantar (RPl), cristalizar* (Méx)

CS gas /'si:'es/ n gas m lacrimógeno

CST (in US) = **Central Standard Time**

CT = **Connecticut**

cub /kʌb/ n **(a)** (young animal) cachorro m **(b)** **Cub** (Scout) lobato m

Cuba /'kju:bə/ n Cuba f

Cuban[1] /'kju:bən/ adj cubano

Cuban[2] n cubano, -na m,f

cubbyhole /'kʌbihəʊl/ n cuchitril m

cube[1] /kju:b/ n (solid, shape) cubo m; (of meat, cheese) dado m, cubito m; (of sugar) terrón m

cube[2] vt (Math) elevar al cubo, cubicar*

cubic /'kju:bɪk/ adj (of measure, shape) cúbico; ~ **capacity** volumen m; (of engine) cilindrada f, cubicaje m

cubicle /'kju:bɪkəl/ n (in dormitory, toilets) cubículo m; (booth) cabina f; (in store) probador m

cuckoo /'kʊku: ‖'kʊku:/ n (pl **cuckoos**) cuco m, cucú m, cuclillo m

cuckoo clock n reloj m de cuco or cucú

cucumber /'kju:kʌmbər ‖'kju:kʌmbə(r)/ n pepino m

cud /kʌd/ n: **to chew the ~** (lit) ‹cow› rumiar; ‹person› rumiar el asunto

cuddle[1] /'kʌdl/ vt abrazar*

cuddle[2] n abrazo m

cuddly /'kʌdli/ adj **-dlier, -dliest** adorable; ~ **toy** muñeco m de peluche

cudgel /'kʌdʒəl/ n garrote m, porra f

cue /kju:/ n [1] (Mus) entrada f; (Theat) pie m; **right on ~** en el momento justo [2] (in snooker) taco m

cuff[1] /kʌf/ n [1] **(a)** (of sleeve) puño m; (of pants) (AmE) vuelta f or (Chi) bastilla f or (Méx) valenciana f or (RPl) botamanga f **(b)** (in phrases) **off the cuff** (as adv): **he spoke off the ~** habló improvisando; (as adj): **an off-the-~ speech** un discurso improvisado [2] (blow — on side of head) cachete m, bofetón m, cachetada f (AmL); (— on head) coscorrón m

cuff[2] vt darle* un cachete (or coscorrón etc) a

cuff link n gemelo m or (Col) mancorna f or (Chi) collera f or (Méx) mancuernilla or mancuerna f

cuisine /kwɪ'zi:n/ n cocina f

cul-de-sac /'kʌldəsæk/ n calle f sin salida or (Col) ciega or (RPl) cortada f

cull /kʌl/ vt sacrificar de forma selectiva

culminate /'kʌlmənert ‖'kʌlmɪnert/ vi (reach peak) to ~ **IN** sth culminar **EN** algo

culprit /'kʌlprət ‖'kʌlprɪt/ n culpable mf

cult /kʌlt/ n (belief, worship) culto m; (sect) secta f; (before n) ▶ **figure** idolo m

cultivate /'kʌltəvert ‖'kʌltɪvert/ vt cultivar

cultural /'kʌltʃərəl/ adj cultural

culture¹ /'kʌltʃər ‖'kʌltʃə(r)/ n **1** (civilization) cultura f; (before n) ~ **shock** choque m cultural or de culturas **2** (Agr, Biol) cultivo m

culture² vt cultivar

cultured /'kʌltʃərd ‖'kʌltʃəd/ adj ⟨person/ mind⟩ culto; ⟨tastes⟩ refinado

cumbersome /'kʌmbərsəm ‖'kʌmbəsəm/ adj ⟨movements/gait⟩ pesado y torpe

cumin /'kʌmən ‖'kʌmɪn/ n comino m

cumulative /'kju:mjələtɪv ‖'kju:mjʊlətɪv/ adj acumulativo

cunning /'kʌnɪŋ/ adj (a) (clever, sly) astuto; ⟨smile⟩ malicioso (b) (ingenious) ⟨device⟩ ingenioso

cup¹ /kʌp/ n **1** (a) (container, contents, cupful) taza f; **paper** ~ vaso m de papel (b) (goblet) copa f **2** (trophy) copa f

cup² vt -**pp**-: to ~ **one's hands** (to drink) ahuecar* las manos; (to shout) hacer* bocina (con las manos)

cupboard /'kʌbərd ‖'kʌbəd/ n (a) (cabinet) armario m; (in dining-room) aparador m (b) (full-length, built-in) (BrE) armario m or (AmL exc RPl) clóset m or (RPl) placard m

curable /'kjʊrəbəl ‖'kjʊərəbəl/ adj curable

curate /'kjʊrət ‖'kjʊərət/ n coadjutor m

curator /kjʊ'rertər ‖kjʊə'rertə(r)/ n (of museum, art gallery) conservador, -dora m,f; (of exhibition) comisario, -ria m,f

curb¹ /kɜːrb ‖kɜːb/ n **1** (restraint) freno m **2** **curb**, (BrE) **kerb** /kɜːb/ n (in street) bordillo m (de la acera), borde m de la banqueta (Méx), cuneta f (Chi), sardinel m (Col), cordón m de la vereda (RPl)

curb² vt (control) ⟨anger⟩ dominar, refrenar; ⟨spending/prices⟩ poner* freno a, frenar

curd /kɜːrd ‖kɜːd/ n (often pl) cuajada f

curdle /'kɜːrdḷ ‖'kɜːdl̩/ vi (a) (go bad, separate) «milk/sauce» cortarse (b) (form curds) «milk» cuajarse

cure¹ /kjʊr ‖kjʊə(r)/ vt **1** (Med) curar **2** ⟨meat⟩ curar

cure² n cura f

curfew /'kɜːrfju: ‖'kɜːfju:/ n toque m de queda

curiosity /ˌkjʊri'ɑːsəti ‖ˌkjʊəri'ɒsəti/ n (pl -**ties**) curiosidad f

curious /'kjʊriəs ‖'kjʊəriəs/ adj (a) (inquisitive) curioso (b) (strange) curioso, extraño

curiously /'kjʊriəsli ‖'kjʊəriəsli/ adv (with curiosity) con curiosidad; (strangely) curiosamente; ~ **enough**, ... (indep) curiosamente, ...

curl¹ /kɜːrl ‖kɜːl/ n rizo m, rulo m (CS), chino m (Méx); (ringlet) bucle m, tirabuzón m

curl² vt ⟨hair⟩ rizar*, encrespar (CS), enchinar (Méx), enrular (RPl)
■ ~ vi «hair» rizarse*, encresparse (CS), enchinarse (Méx), enrularse (RPl); «paper/leaf/ edge» ondularse

■ ~ **up** [v + adv] (twist) «leaf/pages» ondularse; «cat» hacerse* un ovillo; to ~ **up in a chair** acurrucarse* en un sillón

curler /'kɜːrlər ‖'kɜːlə(r)/ n (for hair) rulo m, rulero m (RPl), marrón m (Col), tubo m (Chi, Méx)

curling irons, curling tongs /'kɜːrlɪŋ ‖'kɜːlɪŋ/ pl n tenacillas fpl (para rizar el pelo)

curly /'kɜːrli ‖'kɜːli/ adj -**lier**, -**liest** ⟨hair⟩ rizado, crespo (CS), chino (Méx); ⟨tail⟩ enroscado

currant /'kɜːrənt ‖'kʌrənt/ n pasa f de Corinto

currency /'kɜːrənsi ‖'kʌrənsi/ n (pl -**cies**) moneda f; **foreign** ~ moneda f extranjera, divisas fpl

current¹ /'kɜːrənt ‖'kʌrənt/ adj **1** (before n) (a) (existing) ⟨situation/prices⟩ actual; ⟨year⟩ en curso (b) (most recent) ⟨issue⟩ último **2** (a) (valid) ⟨license/membership⟩ vigente (b) (prevailing) ⟨opinion/practice⟩ corriente

current² n (Elec) corriente f

current: ~ **account** n (BrE) cuenta f corriente; ~ **affairs** pl n sucesos mpl de actualidad

currently /'kɜːrəntli ‖'kʌrəntli/ adv (a) (at present) actualmente (b) (commonly) comúnmente

curriculum /kə'rɪkjələm ‖kə'rɪkjʊləm/ n (pl -**lums** or -**la** /-lə/) (a) (range of courses) plan m de estudios (b) (for single course) programa m (de estudio), currículo m, currículum m (AmL)

curriculum vitae /'viːtaɪ/ n (pl **curricula vitae**) (BrE) currículum m (vitae), historial m personal

curry¹ /'kɜːri ‖'kʌri/ n (pl **curries**) curry m

curry² vt -**ries**, -**rying**, -**ried** **1** (Culin) preparar al curry; **curried chicken** pollo m al curry **2** ▶ **FAVOR¹** 1A

curse¹ /kɜːrs ‖kɜːs/ n (a) (evil spell) maldición f (b) (oath) maldición f, palabrota f

curse² vt/i maldecir*

cursor /'kɜːrsər ‖'kɜːsə(r)/ n cursor m

cursory /'kɜːrsəri ‖'kɜːsəri/ adj ⟨glance⟩ rápido; ⟨description⟩ somero; ⟨interest⟩ superficial

curt /kɜːrt ‖kɜːt/ adj cortante, seco

curtail /kɜːr'teɪl ‖kɜː'teɪl/ vt (cut short) abreviar; (restrict) restringir*; (reduce) reducir*

curtain /'kɜːrtn̩ ‖'kɜːtn̩/ n (at window) cortina f; (Theat) telón m

curtain call n salida f a escena (para saludar), telón m (Méx)

curtsey¹ n (pl -**seys**) (esp BrE) ▶ **CURTSY¹**

curtsey² vi -**seys**, -**seying**, -**seyed** (BrE) ▶ **CURTSY²**

curtsy¹ /'kɜːrtsi ‖'kɜːtsi/ n (pl -**sies**) reverencia f (que hacen las mujeres agachándose)

curtsy² vi -**sies**, -**sying**, -**sied** hacer* una reverencia

curve¹ /kɜːrv ‖kɜːv/ n curva f

curve² vi «surface» estar* curvado; «river/ ball» describir* una curva

curved /kɜːrvd ‖kɜːvd/ adj curvo

cushion¹ /'kʊʃən/ n almohadón m; (before n) ~ **cover** funda f de almohadón

cushion² vt ⟨blow⟩ amortiguar*; (protect) to ~ **sb AGAINST sth** proteger* a algn **CONTRA** algo

cuss /kʌs/ (esp AmE colloq) vi (a) (complain) despotricar* (b) (swear) maldecir*

custard /'kʌstərd ‖'kʌstəd/ n (a) (sauce) (BrE) crema f; (cold, set) ≈natillas fpl (b) (egg ~) especie de flan

custodian /kʌ'stəʊdiən/ n (a) (of morals, tradition) guardián, -diana m,f, custodio, -dia m,f (b) (of museum, library) conservador, -dora m,f

custody /'kʌstədi/ n **1** (detention): **to be in** (police) ~ estar* detenido **2** (of child) custodia f

custom /'kʌstəm/ n **1** (convention, tradition, habit) costumbre f **2** (patronage) (esp BrE): **I'll take my ~ elsewhere** dejaré de ser su cliente **3 customs** pl aduana f

customary /'kʌstəməri/ adj (a) (traditional) tradicional; **it is ~ to + INF** es la costumbre + INF (b) (habitual) habitual, acostumbrado

custom-built /'kʌstəm'bɪlt/ adj ⟨car⟩ hecho de encargo; ⟨house⟩ construido según las especificaciones del cliente

customer /'kʌstəmər ‖'kʌstəmə(r)/ n cliente, -ta m,f, (before n) Ⓢ **customer services** información y reclamaciones

customize /'kʌstəmaɪz/ vt ⟨car/program⟩ hacer* (or adaptar etc) según los requisitos del cliente

custom-made /'kʌstəm'meɪd/ adj hecho de encargo; ⟨suit/shoes⟩ a la medida

cut¹ /kʌt/ n **1** (a) (wound) tajo m, corte m (b) (incision) corte m **2** (a) (reduction): **to make ~s in essential services** hacer* recortes en los servicios esenciales (b) (in text, film) corte m (c) (power ~) apagón m **3** (hair~) corte m de pelo (b) (of suit) corte m **4** (of meat — type) corte m; (— piece) trozo m **5** (share) (colloq) tajada f (fam), parte f **6** (blow — with knife) cuchillada f

cut² /kʌt/ (pres p **cutting**; past & past p **cut**) vt **1** ⟨wood/paper/wire/rope⟩ cortar; **to ~ sth in half** cortar algo por la mitad; **I ~ my finger** me corté el dedo; **to cut sb's throat** degollar* a algn; see also SHORT² 1

2 (a) (trim) ⟨hair/nails⟩ cortar; ⟨grass/corn⟩ cortar, segar*; **to get one's hair ~** cortarse el pelo (b) (shape) ⟨glass/stone⟩ tallar; ⟨key⟩ hacer* **3** (reduce) ⟨level/number⟩ reducir*; ⟨budget⟩ recortar; ⟨price/rate⟩ rebajar; ⟨service/workforce⟩ hacer* recortes en

4 (a) (shorten) ⟨text⟩ acortar (b) (remove) ⟨scene⟩ cortar (c) ⟨film⟩ (edit) editar; «censors» hacer* cortes en

5 (in cards) ⟨deck⟩ cortar

6 (colloq) (cease): **~ the jokes!** ¡basta ya de bromas!

■ ~ vi **1** «knife/scissors» cortar; **the rope ~ into her wrists** la cuerda le estaba cortando las muñecas

2 (Cin, Rad): **~!** ¡corte(n)!

3 (in cards) cortar

■ **cut across** [v + prep + o] (a) (take shortcut across) cortar por (b) (cross boundaries of) trascender*

■ **cut back 1** [v + o + adv, v + adv + o] (a) (prune) ⟨hedge⟩ podar (b) (reduce) ⟨spending⟩ recortar

2 [v + adv] (make reductions) hacer* economías; **to ~ back ON sth** reducir* algo

■ **cut down 1** [v + o + adv, v + adv + o] (a) (fell) ⟨tree⟩ cortar, talar (b) (kill) matar

2 [v + adv] (make reductions): **cigarette? — no, thanks, I'm trying to ~ down** ¿un cigarrillo? —

no, gracias, estoy tratando de fumar menos; **you should ~ down on carbohydrates** debería reducir el consumo de hidratos de carbono

■ **cut in** [v + adv] (a) (interrupt) interrumpir (b) (Auto) atravesarse*

■ **cut off 1** [v + o + adv, v + adv + o] (sever) ⟨branch/limb⟩ cortar

2 [v + o + adv, v + adv + o] (interrupt, block) ⟨supply/route⟩ cortar

3 [v + o + adv] (a) (isolate) aislar*; **to feel ~ off** sentirse* aislado; **the town was ~ off** la ciudad quedó sin comunicaciones (b) (on telephone): **we were ~ off** se cortó la comunicación

■ **cut out 1** [v + o + adv, v + adv + o] ⟨article/ photograph⟩ recortar

2 [v + o + adv, v + adv + o] (a) ⟨dress/cookies⟩ cortar (b) (exclude) ⟨noise/carbohydrates⟩ eliminar; **he ~ me out of his will** me excluyó de su testamento; **~ it out!** (colloq) ¡basta ya!

3 (suit): **to be ~ out FOR sth** estar* hecho para algo

4 [v + adv] «engine» pararse

■ **cut up** [v + o + adv, v + adv + o] ⟨vegetables/ wood⟩ cortar en pedazos

cut³ adj (before n) ⟨flowers⟩ cortado; ⟨glass⟩ tallado

cutback /'kʌtbæk/ n recorte m

cute /kjuːt/ adj **cuter, cutest** (a) (sweet) ⟨baby/face⟩ mono (fam), cuco (fam), rico (CS fam) (b) (attractive) (AmE) guapo

cut-glass /'kʌt'glæs ‖'kʌt'glɑːs/ adj de cristal tallado

cuticle /'kjuːtɪkəl/ n cutícula f

cutlery /'kʌtləri/ n cubiertos mpl, cubertería f, cuchillería f (Chi)

cutlet /'kʌtlət ‖'kʌtlɪt/ n chuleta f (pequeña)

cut: **~off** (point) n límite m; **~-price** /'kʌt'praɪs/ adj (BrE) ▶ **~-RATE**; **~-rate** /'kʌt'reɪt/ adj (AmE) a precio rebajado; **~-throat** adj ⟨competition⟩ feroz, salvaje

cutting¹ /'kʌtɪŋ/ n **1** (a) (from newspaper) (BrE) recorte m (b) (from plant) esqueje m **2** (for road, railway) (BrE) zanja f

cutting² adj (a) (before n) ⟨tool/blade⟩ cortante (b) (cold) ⟨wind⟩ cortante (c) (hurtful) ⟨remark⟩ hiriente

CV n = **curriculum vitae**

cwt n = **hundredweight**

cyanide /'saɪənaɪd/ n cianuro m

cybercafé /'saɪbərˌkæfeɪ ‖'saɪbəˌkæfeɪ/ n cibercafé m

cyberspace /'saɪbərspeɪs ‖'saɪbəspeɪs/ n ciberespacio m

cycle¹ /'saɪkəl/ n **1** (process) ciclo m **2** (Elec, Comput) ciclo m **3** (bicycle) bicicleta f

cycle² vi ir* en bicicleta

cycling /'saɪklɪŋ/ n ciclismo m

cyclist /'saɪklɪst ‖'saɪklɪst/ n ciclista m/f

cyclone /'saɪkləʊn/ n ciclón m

cylinder /'sɪləndər ‖'sɪlɪndə(r)/ n **1** (Math) cilindro m **2** (a) (of engine) cilindro m (b) (container — for liquid gas) tanque m or (Esp) bombona f or (RPl) garrafa f or (Chi) balón m

cymbal /'sɪmbəl/ n platillo m, címbalo m

cynic /'sɪnɪk/ n cínico, -ca m,f

cynical /'sɪnɪkəl/ adj cínico

cynicism /'sɪnəsɪzəm/ n cinismo m
cypher n (esp BrE) ▶ CIPHER
cypress /'saɪprəs/ n ciprés m
Cyprus /'saɪprəs/ n Chipre f
cyst /sɪst/ n quiste m
cystic fibrosis /ˌsɪstɪkfaɪ'brəʊsəs ‖ˌsɪstɪkfaɪ'brəʊsɪs/ n fibrosis f cística or pancreática
cystitis /sɪ'staɪtəs ‖sɪ'staɪtɪs/ n cistitis f
czar /zɑːr ‖zɑː(r)/ n (esp AmE) ▶ TSAR

Czech¹ /tʃek/ adj checo
Czech² n (a) (person) checo, -ca m,f (b) (language) checo m
Czechoslovakia /ˌtʃekəslə'vɑːkiə ‖ˌtʃekəslə'vækiə/ n (Hist) Checoslovaquia f
Czechoslovakian /ˌtʃekəslə'vɑːkiən ‖ˌtʃekəslə'vækiən/ adj (Hist) checoslovaco
Czech Republic n the ~ ~ la República Checa

Dd

D, d /diː/ n (a) (letter) D, d f (b) (Mus) re m
d' = **do**; d'you go there often? ¿vas ahí a menudo?
'd /d/ (a) = **had** (b) = **would** (c) = **did**
DA n (in US) = **district attorney**
dab /dæb/ vt: ~ the stain with a damp cloth frote suavemente la mancha con un trapo húmedo; ~ antiseptic on the cut dese unos toques de antiséptico en la herida
dabble /'dæbəl/ vi: to ~ in politics/journalism tener* escarceos con la política/el periodismo
dad /dæd/ n (colloq) papá m (fam)
daddy /'dædi/ n papi m (fam)
daddy longlegs /'lɔːŋlegz ‖'lɒŋlegz/ n (pl ~ ~) (colloq) (a) (harvestman) (AmE) segador m, falangio m (b) (cranefly) (BrE) típula f
daffodil /'dæfədɪl/ n narciso m
daft /dæft ‖dɑːft/ adj -er, -est (esp BrE colloq) tonto, bobo (fam)
dagger /'dægər ‖'dægə(r)/ n daga f, puñal m
dahlia /'dæljə ‖'deɪliə/ n dalia f
daily¹ /'deɪli/ adj (before n) ⟨newspaper/prayers⟩ diario; ⟨walk/visit⟩ diario, cotidiano
daily² adv a diario, diariamente
daily³ n (pl -lies) diario m, periódico m
dainty /'deɪnti/ adj -tier, -tiest ⟨flowers/vase⟩ delicado; ⟨appearance⟩ delicado, refinado
dairy /'deri ‖'deəri/ n (pl -ries) (a) (on farm) lechería f, (before n) ⟨produce⟩ lácteo; ⟨butter/cream⟩ de granja; ⟨cow/industry⟩ lechero (b) (shop) lechería f; (company) central f lechera
daisy /'deɪzi/ n (pl -sies) (cultivated) margarita f; (wild) margarita f de los prados, maya f
dally /'dæli/ vi -lies, -lying, -lied perder* el tiempo
dam¹ /dæm/ n dique m, presa f, represa f (AmS)
dam² vt -mm- construir* una presa or (AmS) una represa en

damage¹ /'dæmɪdʒ/ n **1** (to object) daño m; (to reputation, cause) daño m, perjuicio m
  2 damages pl (Law) daños y perjuicios mpl
damage² vt ⟨building/vehicle⟩ dañar; ⟨health⟩ perjudicar*, ser* perjudicial para; ⟨reputation/cause⟩ perjudicar*, dañar
damaging /'dæmɪdʒɪŋ/ adj perjudicial
dame /deɪm/ n **1 Dame** (title in UK) Dame (título honorífico) **2** (woman) (AmE sl) tipa f (fam), tía f (Esp fam)
damn¹ /dæm/ vt (a) (Relig) condenar (b) (condemn) condenar
damn² n (colloq) (no pl): not to give a ~: I don't give a ~ what they think me importa un bledo lo que piensen (fam), me vale madres lo que piensen (Méx vulg)
damn³ interj (colloq) ¡caray! (fam & euf)
damn⁴ adj (colloq) (before n) (as intensifier) condenado (fam), maldito (fam), pinche (Méx fam)
damnation /dæm'neɪʃən/ n condenación f
damned /dæmd/ ▶ DAMN⁴
damning /'dæmɪŋ/ adj (a) (condemnatory) ⟨evidence⟩ condenatorio (b) (critical) ⟨appraisal⟩ crítico
damp¹ /dæmp/ adj -er, -est húmedo; to smell ~ oler* a humedad
damp² n humedad f
damp³ vt ~ (down) ⟨fire⟩ sofocar*; ⟨enthusiasm/excitement⟩ apagar*, enfriar*
damp course n membrana f aislante
dampen /'dæmpən/ vt **1** (moisten) humedecer*, mojar **2** (discourage) ⟨hopes⟩ hacer* perder; ⟨enthusiasm⟩ hacer* perder, apagar*
damper /'dæmpər ‖'dæmpə(r)/ n (of piano) sordina f; to put a ~ on sth (colloq): the bad news put a ~ on the celebrations la mala noticia estropeó las fiestas
damp-: ~**proof** vt proteger* contra la humedad; ~**proof course** n ▶ DAMP COURSE
damson /'dæmzən/ n ciruela f damascena

dance¹ /dæns ‖ dɑːns/ n **(a)** (act, occasion) baile m; (before n) ⟨music⟩ de baile, bailable **(b)** (set of steps) baile m, danza f **(c)** (art form) danza f, baile m

dance² vi **1** **(a)** (to music) bailar **(b)** (skip) dar~ saltos **2** «eyes/flames» (liter) bailar, danzar* (liter);
■ ~ vt ⟨waltz/tango⟩ bailar

dancer /'dænsər ‖ 'dɑːnsə(r)/ n bailarín, -rina m,f

dancing /'dænsɪŋ ‖ 'dɑːnsɪŋ/ n baile m; (before n) ⟨lesson/shoes⟩ de baile

dandelion /'dændəlaɪən ‖ 'dændɪlaɪən/ n diente m de león

dandruff /'dændrʌf/ n caspa f; (before n) ~ shampoo champú m anti-caspa

Dane /deɪn/ n danés, -nesa m,f, dinamarqués, -quesa m,f

danger /'deɪndʒər ‖ 'deɪndʒə(r)/ n peligro m; in ~ en peligro or en riesgo; to be in ~ of -ING correr peligro or riesgo de + INF; (before n) to be on the ~ list encontrarse* en estado grave; ~ signal señal f

dangerous /'deɪndʒərəs/ adj peligroso

dangerously /'deɪndʒərəsli/ adv peligrosamente

dangle /'dæŋɡəl/ vi colgar*, pender
■ ~ vt hacer* oscilar

Danish¹ /'deɪnɪʃ/ adj danés, dinamarqués

Danish² n danés m

Danish (**pastry**) n: bollo cubierto de azúcar glaseado

dank /dæŋk/ adj frío y húmedo

dapper /'dæpər ‖ 'dæpə(r)/ adj atildado, pulcro

dare¹ /der ‖ deə(r)/ n reto m, desafío m

dare² v mod atreverse a, osar (liter); how ~ you! ¡cómo te atreves!; I ~ say you've had enough estarás harto(, me imagino)
■ ~ vt **1** (be so bold) to ~ to + INF atreverse a + INF, osar + INF (liter) **2** (challenge) to ~ sb to + INF retar or desafiar* a algn a + INF or A QUE (+ subj)

daredevil /'der‚devl ‖ 'deə‚devl/ n corajudo, -da m,f (fam); (before n) ⟨feat/exploit⟩ temerario

daring¹ /'derɪŋ ‖ 'deərɪŋ/ adj **(a)** ⟨explorer/pilot⟩ osado; ⟨plan⟩ audaz **(b)** ⟨dress/film⟩ atrevido

daring² n **(a)** (courage) arrojo m, coraje m **(b)** (audacity) audacia f

dark¹ /dɑːrk ‖ dɑːk/ adj **-er, -est** **1** (unlit) ⟨room/night⟩ oscuro; it's getting ~ está oscureciendo, se está haciendo de noche **2** **(a)** (in color) oscuro; ~ chocolate chocolate m sin leche; ~ glasses anteojos mpl oscuros (esp AmL), gafas fpl negras (Esp) **(b)** (in complexion) moreno

dark² n (absence of light) the ~ la oscuridad; to wait until ~ esperar hasta que anochezca; to keep sb in the ~ about sth ocultarle algo a algn

Dark Ages pl n the ~ ~ la Alta Edad Media, la Edad de las tinieblas

darken /'dɑːrkən ‖ 'dɑːkən/ vt **(a)** (make dark) oscurecer* **(b)** (make somber) ensombrecer*
■ ~ vi **(a)** (grow dark) ⟨room/color/sky⟩ oscurecerse* **(b)** (grow somber) ensombrecerse*

darkness /'dɑːrknəs ‖ 'dɑːknɪs/ n oscuridad f

darkroom /'dɑːrkruːm, -rʊm ‖ 'dɑːkruːm, -rʊm/ n cuarto m oscuro

darling¹ /'dɑːrlɪŋ ‖ 'dɑːlɪŋ/ n (as form of address) cariño

darling² adj (before n) querido

darn¹ /dɑːrn ‖ dɑːn/ vt zurcir*

dart¹ /dɑːrt ‖ dɑːt/ n **(a)** (weapon) dardo m **(b)** (Games) dardo m **(c)** (Clothing) pinza f

dart² vi: to ~ into/out of a room entrar como una flecha en/salir* como una flecha de una habitación
■ ~ vt ⟨look⟩ lanzar*

dartboard /'dɑːrtbɔːrd ‖ 'dɑːtbɔːd/ n diana f

darts /dɑːrts ‖ dɑːts/ n (+ sing vb) dardos mpl

dash¹ /dæʃ/ n **1** (small amount) poquito m; a ~ of milk un chorrito de leche **2** (punctuation mark) guion m

dash² vt **1** (hurl) tirar; she ~ed the plate to pieces hizo añicos or trizas el plato; the ship was ~ed against the rocks el barco se estrelló contra las rocas **2** (disappoint) ⟨hopes⟩ (usu pass) defraudar
■ ~ vi: I ~ed to the rescue me lancé al rescate; she ~ed out salió disparada
■ **dash off** **1** [v + o + adv, v + adv + o] (write hurriedly) escribir* corriendo **2** [v + adv] (leave hastily) irse* corriendo

dashboard /'dæʃbɔːrd ‖ 'dæʃbɔːd/ n tablero m de mandos, salpicadero m (Esp)

data /'deɪtə/ n **1** (facts, information) (+ pl vb) datos mpl, información f **2** (Comput) (+ sing vb) datos mpl

data: ~**base** n base f de datos; ~ **highway** n (Comput) autopista f de datos

date¹ /deɪt/ n **1** (of appointment, battle) fecha f; what's the ~ today? ¿a qué fecha estamos?; to ~ hasta la fecha, hasta el momento **2** (colloq) (appointment) cita f; Greg has a ~ with Ana on Sunday Greg sale con Ana el domingo **3** (fruit) dátil m

date² vt **1** **(a)** (mark with date) fechar **(b)** (give date to) ⟨remains/pottery/fossil⟩ datar, determinar la antigüedad de **2** (betray age) (colloq): that really ~s you eso delata tu edad, eso demuestra lo viejo que eres
■ ~ vi **1** (originate in) datar; it ~s from the 14th century data del siglo XIV; his title ~s back to the 14th century los orígenes de su título se remontan al siglo XIV **2** (become old-fashioned) pasar de moda

dated /'deɪtəd ‖ 'deɪtɪd/ adj ⟨fashion/word⟩ anticuado; his plays are ~ sus obras han perdido actualidad

date: ~ **rape** n violación f (cometida durante una cita); ~ **stamp** n (instrument) fechador m; (date) fecha f; ~**-stamp** vt fechar

daub /dɔːb/ vt (smear) to ~ sth WITH sth embadurnar algo DE algo

daughter /'dɔːtər ‖ 'dɔːtə(r)/ n hija f

daughter-in-law /'dɔːtərɪnlɔː/ n (pl **daughters-in-law**) nuera f

daunt /dɔːnt/ vt (usu pass) amilanar, intimidar

daunting /'dɔːntɪŋ/ adj ⟨prospect⟩ desalentador, sobrecogedor; ⟨task⟩ de enormes proporciones

dawdle /'dɔːdl̩/ vi entretenerse*

dawn¹ /dɔːn/ n amanecer m; at ~ al amanecer, al alba (liter)

d

dawn² *vi* (liter) «*day*» amanecer*, clarear, alborear (liter); «*new age*» alborear (liter), nacer*
■ **dawn on** [*v* + *prep* + *o*]: **it gradually ~ed on me that …** fui cayendo en la cuenta de que …
dawn chorus *n* **the ~ ~** el trino de los pájaros al amanecer
day /deɪ/ *n* **1** (día *m*; (working day) jornada *f*, día *m*; **twice a ~** dos veces al día; **all ~** todo el día; **every ~** todos los días; **one of these ~s** un día de estos; **~ by ~** día a día, de día en día; **it's not my/his ~** no es mi/su día; **to take a ~ off (from work)** tomarse un día libre; **in this ~ and age** hoy (en) día, el día de hoy; **these ~s** hoy (en) día; **that'll be the ~** (colloq & iro) cuando las ranas críen cola; **have a good** *o* **nice ~!** (AmE) ¡que le vaya bien!; **to call it a ~** (temporarily) dejarlo para otro día; (permanently) dejar de trabajar (*or* estudiar *etc*); **to make someone's ~** (colloq) alegrarle la vida a algn
2 days (*as adv*): **to work ~s** trabajar durante el día
day: **~break** *n* alba *f‡* (liter), amanecer *m*; **~-care center** *n* (AmE) guardería *f* infantil
daydream¹ /'deɪdriːm/ *n* ensueño *m*, ensoñación *f*
daydream² *vi* soñar* despierto, fantasear
day: **~light** *n* luz *f* (del día); **~light (saving) time** *n* (AmE) hora *f* de verano; **~ release** *n* (in UK) sistema que permite a un empleado ausentarse regularmente de su trabajo para seguir estudios relacionados con el mismo; **~room** *n*: sala de estar comunal en hospitales, prisiones *etc*; **~time** *n*: **in** *o* **during the ~time** de día *or* durante el día; **~-to-~** /'deɪtə'deɪ/ *adj* (*before n*) (occurrence) cotidiano, diario; (chores/difficulties) de cada día; (existence) diario; **~ trip** *n* excursión *f* de un día; **~-tripper** /,trɪpər ‖,trɪpə(r)/ *n* excursionista *mf*
daze /deɪz/ *n* (*no pl*) aturdimiento *m*; **to go about in a ~** estar* en las nubes
dazed /deɪzd/ *adj* aturdido
dazzle /'dæzəl/ *vt* «*light*» deslumbrar, encandilar; «*beauty/wit*» deslumbrar
dazzling /'dæzlɪŋ/ *adj* (bright) (light/glare) deslumbrante, resplandeciente, que encandila; (impressive) (wit/looks) deslumbrante, deslumbrador
DC (a) (= **direct current**) CC (b) = **District of Columbia**
D-day /'diːdeɪ/ *n* (a) (in World War II) día *m* D (*día del desembarco aliado en Normandía*) (b) (important day) el día señalado
DE = **Delaware**
DEA *n* (= **Drug Enforcement Administration**) DEA *f*
deacon /'diːkən/ *n* diácono *m*
deaconess /'diːkənəs ‖,diːkə'nes, 'diːkənɪs/ *n* diaconisa *f*
dead¹ /ded/ *adj* **1** (no longer alive) muerto; **he's ~** está muerto; **to drop ~** caerse* muerto; **I wouldn't be seen ~ in that dress** (colloq) yo no me pondría ese vestido ni muerta *or* ni loca; ▶ BODY 1c **2** (numb) (*usu pred*) dormido; **to go ~** «*limb*» dormirse* **3** (very tired, ill) (colloq) muerto (fam) **4** (obsolete) (*language*) muerto; (*custom*) en desuso **5** (a) (not functioning) (wire/circuit)

desconectado; (*telephone*) desconectado, cortado; (*battery*) descargado **(b)** (not alight) (fire/match) apagado **(c)** (not busy) (town/hotel/party) muerto
dead² *adv* **1** (a) (exactly) justo **(b)** (directly) justo, directamente; **~ ahead** justo delante **(c)** (suddenly): **to stop ~** parar en seco **2** (colloq) (straight/level) completamente; **~ slow** lentísimo; **to be ~ certain** estar* totalmente seguro; **it was ~ easy** estuvo regalado *or* tirado (fam)
dead³ *pl n*: **the ~** los muertos
deaden /'dedn/ *vt* (impact) amortiguar; (noise/vibration) reducir*; (pain) atenuar*, aliviar; (nerve) insensibilizar*; (faculties) entorpecer*
dead: **~ end** *n* callejón *m* sin salida; **~-end** /'ded'end/ *adj* (street) sin salida, ciego (Andes, Ven); **a ~-end job** (colloq) un trabajo sin porvenir *or* futuro; **~line** *n* fecha *f* tope *or* límite, plazo *m* de entrega; **~lock** *n* (*no pl*) punto *m* muerto
deadly¹ /'dedli/ *adj* **-lier, -liest** **1** (fatal) (disease/poison) mortal; (weapon) mortífero **2** (dull) (colloq) aburridísimo, terriblemente aburridor (AmL)
deadly² *adv* (*as intensifier*) (dull) terriblemente
dead: **~pan** *adj* (expression) de póquer *or* (fam) de palo; (voice/delivery) deliberadamente inexpresivo; **D~ Sea** *n* **the D~ Sea** el Mar Muerto; **~ weight** *n* peso *m* muerto
deaf /def/ *adj* sordo; **to go ~** quedarse sordo; **~ and dumb** sordomudo
deaf-aid /'defeɪd/ *n* (BrE) audífono *m*
deafen /'defən/ *vt* ensordecer*
deafening /'defənɪŋ/ *adj* ensordecedor
deaf-mute /'def'mjuːt/ *n* sordomudo, -da *m,f*
deafness /'defnəs ‖'defnɪs/ *n* sordera *f*
deal¹ /diːl/ *n* **1** (indicating amount): **it makes a great/good ~ of difference** cambia mucho/ bastante las cosas; **we've seen a great ~ of her lately** la hemos visto mucho *o* muy a menudo últimamente
2 (a) (agreement) trato *m*, acuerdo *m*; **to do a ~ with sb** llegar* a un acuerdo con algn, hacer* un trato *or* un pacto con algn; **it's no big ~** no es nada del otro mundo **(b)** (financial arrangement) acuerdo *m* **(c)** (bargain): **you'll get a better ~ if you shop around** lo conseguirás más barato si vas a otras tiendas
3 (treatment) trato *m*; **she's had a raw ~ in life** la vida la ha tratado muy mal
deal² (*past & past p* **dealt**) *vt/i* (Games) dar*, repartir
■ **deal in** [*v* + *prep* + *o*] (Busn) dedicarse* a la compra y venta de, comerciar en
■ **deal out** [*v* + *o* + *adv, v* + *adv* + *o*] (gifts/ money) repartir, distribuir*
■ **deal with** [*v* + *prep* + *o*] **1** (do business with) (company) tener* relaciones comerciales con; **I prefer to ~ with her** yo prefiero tratar con ella **2** (a) (tackle, handle) (complaint) ocuparse de, atender*; (situation) manejar **(b)** (be responsible for) ocuparse *or* encargarse* de **3** (issue) (discuss, treat) tratar; (have as subject) tratar de
dealer /'diːlər ‖'diːlə(r)/ *n* **1** (a) (trader): **she's a car ~** se dedica a la compra-venta de coches; **visit your local Hoover ~** visite a su representante Hoover más próximo; **drug ~**

traficante *mf* de drogas **(b)** (Fin) corredor, -dora
m,*f* de bolsa *or* de valores **2** (Games): **the** ~ el
que da *or* reparte las cartas

dealing /'diːlɪŋ/ *n* **1** **(a)** (business methods): **the
company has a reputation for honest/shady** ~ la
empresa tiene fama de honradez en los negocios/
de hacer negocios turbios **(b)** **dealings** *pl*
(contacts, relations) relaciones *fpl*, trato *m*
2 (trafficking) tráfico *m*

dealt /delt/ *past & past p of* DEAL²

dean /diːn/ *n* **1** (Relig) deán *m* **2** **(a)** (in
university) decano, -na *m*,*f*; **(b)** (in college, secondary
school) (AmE) *docente a cargo del asesoramiento y
de la disciplina de los estudiantes*

dear¹ /dɪr ‖dɪə(r)/ *adj* **dearer, dearest**
1 (loved) querido **2** (in direct address) (a) (in
speech): **my** ~ **Mrs Harper, I can assure you that …**
mi buena señora (Harper), le aseguro que … **(b)**
(in letter writing): **D~ Mr Jones** Estimado Sr. Jones;
D~ Sir or Madam Estimado/a Señor(a), Muy
señor mío/señora mía; **D~ Jimmy** Querido
Jimmy **3** (lovable) adorable **4** (expensive) caro

dear² *interj*: **oh** ~! ¡ay!, ¡qué cosa!

dear³ *n* (*as form of address*) querido, -da,
cariño; **(you) poor** ~! ¡pobre ángel!, ¡pobrecito!

dearly /'dɪrli ‖'dɪəli/ *adv* **1** (*as intensifier*): **I
love him** ~ lo quiero mucho *or* de verdad; ~
beloved (frml) (Relig) (amados) hermanos **2** (at
great cost) caro *adj*

death /deθ/ *n* muerte *f*, fallecimiento *m* (frml); **to
put sb to** ~ ejecutar a algn; **to be worried to** ~
(colloq) estar* preocupadísimo

death: ~**bed** *n* lecho *m* de muerte; ~
certificate *n* certificado *m* de defunción; ~
penalty *n* **the** ~ **penalty** la pena de muerte; ~
row /rəʊ/ *n* (*no art*) pabellón *m* de los
condenados a muerte, corredor *m* de la muerte;
~ **sentence** *n*: **the** ~ **sentence** la pena de
muerte; ~ **squad** *n* escuadrón *m* de la muerte;
~ **toll** *n* número *m* de víctimas (mortales) *or* de
muertos; ~ **trap** *n*: *edificio, vehículo etc muy
poco seguro*; ~ **warrant** *n* sentencia *f* de
muerte; ~ **wish** *n* (*no pl*) (Psych) pulsión *f* de
muerte

debar /dɪ'bɑːr ‖dɪ'bɑː(r)/ *vt* **-rr-** (frml) **the fact
that she didn't have a degree** ~**red her from
promotion** el hecho de no tener un título
universitario le impedía ascender; **he was** ~**red
from taking his final exam** se le prohibió rendir el
examen final

debase /dɪ'beɪs/ *vt* **(a)** (devalue) 〈*ideal/principle*〉
degradar, envilecer*; 〈*language*〉 corromper,
viciar **(b)** (demean) 〈*person*〉 degradar, rebajar

debate¹ /dɪ'beɪt/ *n* **(a)** (public, parliamentary)
debate *m* **(b)** (discussion) debate *m*, discusión *f*

debate² *vt* **(a)** 〈*question/topic/motion*〉 debatir,
discutir **(b)** (weigh up) 〈*idea/possibility*〉 darle*
vueltas a, considerar

debauchery /dɪ'bɔːtʃəri/ *n* disipación *f*,
libertinaje *m*

debenture /dɪ'bentʃər ‖dɪ'bentʃə(r)/ *n* ~
(bond) (Fin) obligación *f*, bono *m*

debilitating /dɪ'bɪlɪteɪtɪŋ ‖dɪ'bɪlɪteɪtɪŋ/ *adj*
〈*disease*〉 debilitante; 〈*climate*〉 extenuante

debit¹ /'debət ‖'debɪt/ *n* débito *m*, cargo *m*;
(*before n*) ~ **card** tarjeta *f* de cobro automático

debit² *vt* (Fin) debitar, cargar*

debonair /ˌdebə'ner ‖ˌdebə'neə(r)/ *adj* (suave)
elegante y desenvuelto; (courteous) cortés, afable

debriefing /'diː'briːfɪŋ/ *n*: **they were sent for** ~
los llamaron para que rindiesen informe *or*
diesen parte de su misión

debris /də'briː ‖'debriː, 'deɪbriː/ *n* **(a)** (rubble)
escombros *mpl*; (of plane, ship) restos *mpl*; (rubbish)
desechos *mpl* **(b)** (Geol) detritos *mpl*

debt /det/ *n* **(a)** (indebtedness) endeudamiento *m*;
I'm $200 in ~ debo 200 dólares, tengo deudas por
200 dólares; **to be in** ~ **to sb** (frml) estarle* en
deuda a algn, estar* en deuda con algn; **to get
into** ~ endeudarse, llenarse *or* cargarse* de
deudas **(b)** (money owing) deuda *f*; **bad** ~**s** deudas
incobrables

debtor /'detər ‖'detə(r)/ *n* deudor, -dora *m*,*f*

debunk /'diː'bʌŋk/ *vt* (colloq) desacreditar

debut, début /'deɪbjuː, 'de-/ (*pl* **-buts** /-bjuːz/)
n debut *m*

decade /'dekeɪd/ *n* década *f*

decadence /'dekədəns/ *n* decadencia *f*

decadent /'dekədənt/ *adj* decadente

decaffeinated /'diː'kæfəneɪtəd
‖ˌdiː'kæfɪneɪtɪd/ *adj* descafeinado

decanter /dɪ'kæntər ‖dɪ'kæntə(r)/ *n* licorera *f*

decapitate /dɪ'kæpɪteɪt/ *vt* decapitar

decathlon /dɪ'kæθlən/ *n* decatlón *m*

decay¹ /dɪ'keɪ/ *vi* 〈*foodstuffs/corpse*〉
descomponerse, pudrirse*; 〈*wood*〉 pudrirse*;
〈*tooth*〉 cariarse, picarse*; 〈*building/machine*〉
deteriorarse; 〈*empire/culture/civilization*〉
decaer*, declinar

decay² *n* (of organic matter) descomposición *f*;
(tooth ~) caries *f*; (of building) deterioro *m*; (of
culture) decadencia *f*

deceased¹ /dɪ'siːst/ *n* (*pl* ~) (frml) **the** ~ el
difunto, la difunta; (*pl*) los difuntos, las difuntas
(frml)

deceased² *adj* (frml) difunto

deceit /dɪ'siːt/ *n* engaño *m*

deceitful /dɪ'siːtfəl/ *adj* 〈*person*〉 falso,
embustero; 〈*action*〉 engañoso

deceive /dɪ'siːv/ *vt* engañar

deceiver /dɪ'siːvər ‖dɪ'siːvə(r)/ *n* impostor,
-tora *m*,*f*

decelerate /'diː'seləreɪt/ *vi* (frml) 〈*vehicle/
driver*〉 reducir* *or* aminorar la velocidad

December /dɪ'sembər ‖dɪ'sembə(r)/ *n*
diciembre *m*

decency /'diːsn̩si/ *n* **(a)** (of dress, conduct)
decencia *f*, decoro *m* **(b)** (propriety) buena
educación *f*, consideración *f*; **she didn't even
have the** ~ **to ask me** ni siquiera tuvo la
consideración de preguntarme

decent /'diːsn̩t/ *adj* **1** (appropriate, respectable)
decente, decoroso **2** (acceptable) 〈*person*〉 pasable,
aceptable; 〈*meal/housing*〉 decente, como es
debido

decently /'diːsn̩tli/ *adv* **1** (respectably) 〈*dress/
behave*〉 decentemente, con decencia
2 (acceptably) 〈*perform/cook*〉 bastante bien

decentralize /diː'sentrəlaɪz/ *vt*
descentralizar*

deception /dɪ'sepʃən/ *n* engaño *m*

decibel /'desəbəl ‖'desɪbel/ n decibelio m, decibel m

decide /dɪ'saɪd/ vt **1** (make up one's mind) decidir; **to ~ to + INF** decidir or resolver + INF **2** (settle) ⟨question/issue⟩ decidir; ⟨outcome⟩ determinar

■ ~ vi decidirse

decided /dɪ'saɪdəd ‖dɪ'saɪdɪd/ adj **(a)** (definite) (before n) ⟨improvement/advantage⟩ claro, marcado **(b)** (determined) ⟨character/tone⟩ decidido

deciduous /dɪ'sɪdʒuəs ‖dɪ'sɪdjʊəs/ adj de hoja caduca, caducifolio (téc)

decimal[1] /'desəməl ‖'desɪməl/ adj decimal

decimal[2] n decimal m

decimalization /desəmələ'zeɪʃən ‖,desɪmələr'zeɪʃən/ n decimalización f, conversión f al sistema decimal

decimal point n ≈ coma f (decimal o de los decimales), punto m decimal

decimate /'desəmeɪt ‖'desɪmeɪt/ vt diezmar

decipher /dɪ'saɪfər ‖dɪ'saɪfə(r)/ vt descifrar

decision /dɪ'sɪʒən/ n decisión f; **to make** o (BrE also) **take a ~** tomar una decisión

decision-making /dɪ'sɪʒən,meɪkɪŋ/ n toma f de decisiones; (before n) ⟨body/process⟩ decisorio

decisive /dɪ'saɪsɪv/ adj **1** (conclusive) ⟨battle/factor⟩ decisivo; ⟨victory⟩ contundente **2** (purposeful) ⟨person⟩ decidido, resuelto; ⟨leadership/answer⟩ firme

deck[1] /dek/ n **1** (a) (Naut) cubierta f **(b)** (of stadium) (AmE) nivel m **(c)** (sun ~) terraza f **(d)** (of bus) (BrE) piso m **2** (Audio) deck m (AmL), pletina f (Esp) **3** (AmE Games) ~ **(of cards)** baraja f, mazo m (de naipes or cartas) (esp AmL)

deck[2] vt **1** (adorn) **to ~ sth (out) WITH sth** engalanar or adornar algo CON algo; **he was all ~ed out in his Sunday best** iba muy endomingado **2** (knock down) (AmE colloq) tumbar (fam)

deckchair /'dektʃer ‖'dektʃeə(r)/ n silla f de playa, perezosa f (Col, Méx), reposera f (RPl)

declaim /dɪ'kleɪm/ vt/i declamar

declaration /'deklə'reɪʃən/ n **1** (statement) declaración f **2** (Law) (finding) pronunciamiento m (oficial); (statement) declaración f

declare /dɪ'kler ‖dɪ'kleə(r)/ vt **(a)** (state, announce) ⟨intention⟩ declarar; ⟨opinion⟩ manifestar*; **to ~ war** declarar la guerra; **to ~ war on sb/sth** declararle la guerra a algn/algo **(b)** (Tax) ⟨goods/income⟩ declarar

decline[1] /dɪ'klaɪn/ n (no pl) **(a)** (decrease) descenso m, disminución f **(b)** (downward trend) declive m, decadencia f, deterioro m; **to be in ~** estar* en declive or en decadencia

decline[2] vi **1** (a) (decrease) ⟨⟨production/strength⟩⟩ disminuir*, decrecer*; ⟨⟨interest⟩⟩ disminuir*, decaer* **(b)** (deteriorate) ⟨⟨health⟩⟩ deteriorarse*; ⟨⟨industry/region/standards⟩⟩ decaer* **(c) declining** pres p ⟨industry/region/

standards⟩ en declive, en decadencia **2** (refuse): **I invited him, but he ~d** lo invité, pero rehusó or declinó mi invitación

■ ~ vt ⟨offer/invitation⟩ rehusar, declinar

decode /'di:'kəʊd/ vt ⟨signal⟩ descodificar*; ⟨message⟩ descifrar

decompose /'di:kəm'pəʊz/ vi descomponerse*, pudrirse*

decor, décor /deɪ'kɔːr ‖'deɪkɔː(r)/ n (furnishings) decoración f

decorate /'dekəreɪt/ vt **(a)** ⟨room/house⟩ (with paint) pintar; (with wallpaper) empapelar **(b)** ⟨Christmas tree⟩ adornar, decorar (AmL); ⟨cake⟩ decorar

decoration /'dekə'reɪʃən/ n **1** (a) (act) decoración f **(b)** (ornamentation) decoración f **(c)** (ornament) adorno m **2** (Mil) condecoración f

decorative /'dekərətɪv/ adj ⟨object⟩ ornamental, de adorno

decorator /'dekəreɪtər ‖'dekəreɪtə(r)/ n **(a)** (painter) pintor, -tora m,f, (paperhanger) empapelador, -dora m,f **(b)** (designer) decorador, -dora m,f, interiorista mf

decorous /'dekərəs/ adj (frml) decoroso

decorum /dɪ'kɔːrəm/ n decoro m

decoy /'di:kɔɪ/ n (lure) señuelo m; (in hunting) señuelo m, reclamo m

decrease[1] /dɪ'kri:s, 'di:kri:s/ vi **(a)** (in quantity) «amount/numbers» disminuir*, decrecer*; «prices» bajar; «speed» disminuir* **(b)** (in intensity) «quality» disminuir*, bajar; «power/effectiveness» disminuir*, decrecer*; «interest» disminuir*, decaer*

■ ~ vt disminuir*, reducir*

decrease[2] /'di:kri:s, dɪ'kri:s/ n disminución f, descenso m

decree[1] /dɪ'kri:/ n decreto m

decree[2] vt decretar

decrepit /dɪ'krepət ‖dɪ'krepɪt/ adj **(a)** (dilapidated) ⟨bus/furniture⟩ destartalado; ⟨house⟩ deteriorado, viejo y en mal estado **(b)** (infirm) ⟨person/animal⟩ decrépito

decriminalize /di:'krɪmmələɪz/ vt despenalizar*

dedicate /'dedɪkeɪt/ vt **(a)** (devote) **to ~ sth TO sth/-ING** dedicar* algo A algo/+ INF **(b)** ⟨poem/book⟩ dedicar*

dedicated /'dedɪkeɪtəd ‖'dedɪkeɪtɪd/ adj **1** ⟨musician/nurse/teacher⟩ de gran dedicación, dedicado or entregado a su (or mi etc) trabajo; **to be ~ TO sth** estar* dedicado or entregado A algo **2** (Comput) (before n) dedicado

dedication /'dedɪ'keɪʃən/ n **1** (devotion) dedicación f, entrega f **2** (written message) dedicatoria f

deduce /dɪ'du:s ‖dɪ'dju:s/ vt deducir*, inferir*

deduct /dɪ'dʌkt/ vt deducir*, descontar*

deduction /dɪ'dʌkʃən/ n **1** (subtraction) deducción f, descuento m **2** (reasoning, conclusion) deducción f

· ·

AmC Central America	Arg Argentina	Cu Cuba	Per Peru
AmL Latin America	Bol Bolivia	Ec Ecuador	RPl River Plate Area
AmS South America	Chi Chile	Esp Spain	Ur Uruguay
Andes Andean Region	CS Southern Cone	Méx Mexico	Ven Venezuela

deed /diːd/ n [1] (action) hecho m [2] (Law) escritura f

deed poll n (BrE): **to change one's name by ~** ~ ≈ cambiarse el apellido oficialmente

deem /diːm/ vt (fml) considerar, juzgar*

deep¹ /diːp/ adj -er, -est [1] (a) ⟨water⟩ profundo; ⟨hole/pit⟩ profundo, hondo; ⟨gash⟩ profundo; ⟨dish⟩ hondo; ⟨pan⟩ alto; **the ditch is 6 ft ~** la zanja tiene 6 pies de profundidad (b) (horizontally) ⟨shelf⟩ profundo; **the soldiers were standing 12 ~** los soldados formaban columnas de 12 en fondo [2] ⟨sigh/groan⟩ profundo, hondo; **take a ~ breath** respire hondo [3] (a) ⟨voice⟩ profundo, grave; ⟨note⟩ grave (b) ⟨color⟩ intenso, subido [4] (a) (intense) ⟨sleep/love/impression⟩ profundo; **it is with ~ regret that ...** es con gran or profundo pesar que ... (b) ⟨thoughts⟩ profundo (c) ⟨mystery/secret⟩ profundo

deep² adv -er, -est [1] (of penetration): **to dig ~** cavar hondo; **feelings run very ~ among the population** hay un sentir muy fuerte entre la población; **he looked ~ into her eyes** la miró fijamente a los ojos; **to go ~er (into sth)** ahondar or profundizar* más (en algo) [2] (situated far from edge): **~ in the forest** en lo profundo del bosque; **~ down you know I'm right** en el fondo sabes que tengo razón

deepen /diːpən/ vt [1] ⟨canal/well⟩ hacer* más profundo or hondo [2] ⟨knowledge⟩ profundizar* or ahondar en; ⟨concern⟩ aumentar; ⟨friendship⟩ estrechar
■ ~ vi [1] ⟨gorge/river⟩ hacerse* or volverse* más hondo or profundo [2] «concern/love» hacerse* más profundo; «friendship» estrecharse; «mystery» crecer*, aumentar; «crisis» acentuarse*

deep: **~ end** n **the ~ end** (of swimming pool) la parte honda, lo hondo (fam); **to throw sb in (at) the ~ end** meter a algn de lleno en lo más difícil; **~ freeze** n congelador m, freezer f (AmL); **~-fry** /diːpfraɪ/ vt -fries, -frying, -fried freír* (en abundante aceite)

deeply /diːpli/ adv [1] ⟨sigh⟩ profundamente; **to breathe ~** respirar hondo [2] ⟨think⟩ a fondo; ⟨concerned⟩ profundamente; ⟨interested⟩ sumamente

deep: **~-sea** /diːpsiː/ adj (before n) **~-sea diving** buceo m de altura or en alta mar; **~-sea fishing** pesca f de altura; **~-seated** /diːpsiːtəd ‖diːpsiːtɪd/ adj ⟨prejudice/conviction⟩ profundamente arraigado; ⟨problem⟩ de raíces profundas; **~-set** /diːpset/ adj ⟨eyes⟩ hundido

deer /dɪr ‖dɪə(r)/ n (pl ~) ciervo m, venado m

deface /dɪfeɪs/ vt ⟨wall/notice⟩ pintarrajear

defamation /defəˈmeɪʃən/ n (fml) difamación f

default¹ /dɪˈfɔːlt/ n [1] (omission) omisión f; (on payments) mora f; (failure to appear) incomparecencia f; (Law) rebeldía f [2] (lack) falta f; **he was elected by ~** fue elegido por ausencia de otros candidatos; (before n) **~ option** (Comput) opción f por defecto

default² vi (a) (Fin) **to ~ (on sth)** no pagar* (algo) (b) (Law) estar* en rebeldía (c) (Sport) no presentarse

defeat¹ /dɪˈfiːt/ n [1] (by opponent) derrota f [2] (of motion, bill) (Adm, Govt) rechazo m

defeat² vt [1] ⟨opponent⟩ derrotar, vencer* [2] ⟨hopes/plans⟩ frustrar; **that would ~ the object of the exercise** eso iría en contra de lo que se pretende lograr [3] (Adm, Govt) ⟨opposition⟩ derrotar; ⟨bill/motion⟩ rechazar* [4] (baffle) (colloq): **it ~s me** no alcanzo a comprenderlo

defeatist /dɪˈfiːtəst ‖dɪˈfiːtɪst/ adj derrotista

defect¹ /ˈdiːfekt/ n defecto m; **a speech ~** un defecto en el habla

defect² /dɪˈfekt/ vi (Pol) desertar*, defeccionar (period)

defective /dɪˈfektɪv/ adj defectuoso

defector /dɪˈfektər ‖dɪˈfektə(r)/ n desertor, -tora m,f

defence etc (BrE) ▶ **DEFENSE** etc

defend /dɪˈfend/ vt defender*
■ ~ vi [1] (Law) actuar* por la defensa [2] (Sport): **he's better at ~ing** juega mejor como defensa

defendant /dɪˈfendənt/ n (Law) (in civil case) demandado, -da m,f; (in criminal case) acusado, -da m,f

defender /dɪˈfendər ‖dɪˈfendə(r)/ n (a) (of cause, course of action, opinion) defensor, -sora m,f (b) (Sport) defensa mf

defending /dɪˈfendɪŋ/ adj: **the ~ champion** el actual campeón (que defiende su título)

defense, (BrE) **defence** /dɪˈfens, ˈdiːfens ‖dɪˈfens/ n [1] (a) (Mil) defensa f (b) (on personal level) defensa f [2] (a) (protection) defensa f, protección f (b) (apologia) defensa f [3] **defenses** pl (Mil, Med, Psych) defensas fpl [4] (Law) defensa f [5] (a) (Sport) defensa f (b) (in chess) defensa f

defenseless, (BrE) **defenceless** /dɪˈfensləs ‖dɪˈfenslɪs/ adj indefenso

defensive /dɪˈfensɪv/ adj defensivo

defer /dɪˈfɜːr ‖dɪˈfɜː(r)/ -rr- vt (fml) diferir* (fml), aplazar*, postergar* (esp AmL)
■ **defer to** [v + prep + o] (fml) deferir* a (fml)

deference /ˈdefərəns/ n (fml) deferencia f

deferential /defəˈrenʃəl ‖defəˈrenʃəl/ adj deferente

deferment /dɪˈfɜːrmənt ‖dɪˈfɜːmənt/ n (fml) aplazamiento m

defiance /dɪˈfaɪəns/ n **an act of ~** un desafío, un acto de rebeldía; **in ~ of her orders** haciendo caso omiso de sus órdenes

defiant /dɪˈfaɪənt/ adj ⟨attitude/tone⟩ desafiante; ⟨person⟩ rebelde

deficiency /dɪˈfɪʃənsi/ n (pl -cies) deficiencia f

deficient /dɪˈfɪʃənt/ adj (fml) deficiente, insuficiente

deficit /ˈdefəsɪt ‖ˈdefɪsɪt/ n déficit m

define /dɪˈfaɪn/ vt (a) (state meaning of, describe) ⟨word/position⟩ definir (b) ⟨powers/duties⟩ delimitar (c) (characterize) distinguir*

definite /ˈdefənət, ˈdefnət ‖ˈdefɪnət/ adj [1] (a) (final) ⟨date/price/offer⟩ definitivo, en firme (b) (certain) seguro, confirmado (c) (firm, categorical) ⟨tone⟩ firme, terminante (d) (distinct): **it's a ~ advantage/possibility** es, sin duda, una ventaja/ posibilidad [2] (Ling): **~ article** artículo m determinado or definido

definitely /ˈdefənətli, ˈdefnətli ‖ˈdefɪnɪtli/ adv (a) (without doubt): **it's ~ true** es indudablemente ···⦂

cierto; **he ~ said we should meet here** seguro que dijo que nos encontráramos aquí **(b)** (definitively) ⟨*arrange/agree*⟩ definitivamente

definition /ˌdefəˈnɪʃən ‖ ˌdefrˈnɪʃən/ *n* **1** **(a)** (statement of meaning) definición *f*; **by ~** por definición **(b)** (categorization) definición *f*, delimitación *f*

definitive /dɪˈfɪnətɪv/ *adj* (*no comp*) **(a)** (final) ⟨*verdict/victory*⟩ definitivo **(b)** (authoritative) ⟨*biography/study*⟩ de mayor autoridad

deflate /dɪˈfleɪt/ *vt* **(a)** ⟨*balloon/tire*⟩ desinflar **(b)** (humble): **to ~ sb** bajarle los humos a algn **(c)** (depress) deprimir; **I felt ~d** me sentí por los suelos

deflation /dɪˈfleɪʃən/ *n* deflación *f*

deflect /dɪˈflekt/ *vt* **to ~ sth** (**FROM sth**) desviar* algo (DE algo)
■ **~** *vi* desviarse*

defogger /ˈdiːfɔːɡər ‖ ˌdiːˈfɒɡə(r)/ *n* (AmE) desempañador *m*

deforestation /diːˌfɔːrəˈsteɪʃən ‖ ˌdiːˌfɒrɪˈsteɪʃən/ *n* deforestación *f*, despoblación *f* forestal (Esp)

deformed /dɪˈfɔːrmd ‖ dɪˈfɔːmd/ *adj* deforme

deformity /dɪˈfɔːrməti ‖ dɪˈfɔːməti/ *n* (*pl* **-ties**) deformidad *f*

defraud /dɪˈfrɔːd/ *vt* ⟨*person*⟩ estafar

defray /dɪˈfreɪ/ *vt* (frml) ⟨*cost*⟩ sufragar* (frml)

defrost /diːˈfrɔːst ‖ ˌdiːˈfrɒst/ *vt* ⟨*food*⟩ descongelar; ⟨*refrigerator*⟩ deshelar*, descongelar
■ **~** *vi* «*meat*» descongelarse; «*refrigerator*» deshelarse*, descongelarse

deft /deft/ *adj* **-er, -est** ⟨*movement*⟩ hábil, diestro

deftly /ˈdeftli/ *adv* hábilmente, con destreza

defunct /dɪˈfʌŋkt/ *adj* ⟨*idea/theory*⟩ caduco; ⟨*institution*⟩ desaparecido, extinto, fenecido (frml)

defuse /diːˈfjuːz/ *vt* ⟨*bomb*⟩ desactivar; ⟨*situation*⟩ distender*; ⟨*crisis*⟩ calmar

defy /dɪˈfaɪ/ *vt* **defies, defying, defied** **(a)** (disobey) ⟨*order/authority*⟩ desacatar, desobedecer* **(b)** (resist): **to ~ understanding/description** ser* incomprensible/indescriptible **(c)** (ignore) ⟨*danger/death*⟩ desafiar*

degenerate¹ /dɪˈdʒenəreɪt/ *vi* degenerar; «*health*» deteriorarse

degenerate² /dɪˈdʒenərət/ *adj* degenerado

degeneration /dɪˌdʒenəˈreɪʃən/ *n* **(a)** (deterioration) degeneración *f*, deterioro *m* **(b)** (Med) (of tissue, organs) degeneración *f*

degrade /dɪˈɡreɪd/ *vt* degradar

degrading /dɪˈɡreɪdɪŋ/ *adj* degradante

degree /dɪˈɡriː/ *n* **1** (level, amount) grado *m*, nivel *m*; **there's a ~ of truth in what she says** hay cierta verdad en lo que dice; **to a ~** (extremely) en grado sumo; (to some extent) hasta cierto punto **2** (grade, step) grado *m*; **first/third ~ burns** quemaduras *fpl* de primer/tercer grado; **first/second ~ murder** (in US) homicidio *m* en primer/segundo grado; **by ~s** gradualmente, paulatinamente
3 (Math, Geog, Meteo, Phys) grado *m*; **12 ~s below zero** 12 grados bajo cero; **this wine is 12 ~s proof** este vino es de *or* tiene 12 grados

4 (Educ) título *m*; **first ~** licenciatura *f*; **he has o** (frml) **holds a ~ in chemistry** es licenciado en química

dehydrated /ˈdiːhaɪdreɪtəd ‖ ˌdiːhaɪˈdreɪtɪd/ *adj* deshidratado; **to become ~** deshidratarse

dehydration /ˌdiːhaɪˈdreɪʃən/ *n* deshidratación *f*

deign /deɪn/ *vi* **to ~ to +** INF dignarse (A) + INF

deity /ˈdiːəti/ *n* (*pl* **-ties**) deidad *f*

dejected /dɪˈdʒektəd ‖ dɪˈdʒektɪd/ *adj* abatido, desalentado

Del = **Delaware**

delay¹ /dɪˈleɪ/ *vt* **1** (make late, hold up) retrasar, demorar (esp AmL) **2** (defer) ⟨*decision/payment*⟩ retrasar, demorar (esp AmL)
■ **~** *vi* tardar, demorar (esp AmL)

delay² *n* **(a)** (waiting) tardanza *f*, dilación *f*, demora *f* (esp AmL) **(b)** (holdup) retraso *m*, demora *f* (esp AmL); **~s can be expected on major roads** se puede esperar embotellamientos en las principales carreteras

delayed action /dɪˈleɪd/ *n* acción *f* retardada

delectable /dɪˈlektəbəl/ *adj* **(a)** (delicious) delicioso, exquisito **(b)** (delightful) delicioso, encantador

delegate¹ /ˈdelɪɡeɪt/ *vt/i* delegar*

delegate² /ˈdelɪɡət/ *n* delegado, -da *m,f*

delegation /ˌdelɪˈɡeɪʃən/ *n* delegación *f*

delete /dɪˈliːt/ *vt* suprimir, eliminar; (by crossing out) tachar; (Comput) borrar, suprimir

delete key *n* (Comput) tecla *f* de borrar, tecla *f* de borrado

deliberate¹ /dɪˈlɪbərət, -brət/ *adj* **1** (intentional) ⟨*act/attempt*⟩ deliberado, intencionado **2** **(a)** (considered) reflexivo **(b)** (unhurried) pausado, lento

deliberate² /dɪˈlɪbəreɪt/ *vi* (frml) **to ~** (**ABOUT/ON sth**) deliberar (SOBRE algo)
■ **~** *vt* (frml) deliberar sobre

deliberately /dɪˈlɪbərətli, -brətli/ *adv* **1** (intentionally) adrede, a propósito **2** (unhurriedly) pausadamente, con parsimonia

deliberation /dɪˌlɪbəˈreɪʃən/ *n* (frml) **(a)** (consideration) deliberación *f* **(b)** **deliberations** *pl* (decision-making) deliberaciones *fpl*

delicacy /ˈdelɪkəsi/ *n* (*pl* **-cies**) **1** **(a)** (fineness, intricacy) delicadeza *f*, lo delicado; (fragility) fragilidad *f*, lo delicado **(b)** (tact) delicadeza *f* **(c)** (subtleness) lo delicado **2** (choice food) manjar *m*, exquisitez *f*

delicate /ˈdelɪkət/ *adj* **1** **(a)** (fine, intricate) ⟨*lace/features*⟩ delicado; ⟨*workmanship*⟩ fino, esmerado **(b)** (fragile, needing care) delicado **2** **(a)** (needing skill, tact) delicado **(b)** (tactful) delicado, discreto **3** (subtle) ⟨*shade/taste*⟩ delicado

delicately /ˈdelɪkətli/ *adv* **1** ⟨*carve/paint*⟩ con delicadeza, delicadamente **2** ⟨*treat*⟩ con delicadeza **3** ⟨*patterned/perfumed*⟩ delicadamente

delicatessen /ˌdelɪkəˈtesən/ *n* charcutería *f*, rotisería *f* (CS), salsamentaria *f* (Col), salchichonería *f* (Méx)

delicious /dɪˈlɪʃəs/ *adj* delicioso

delight¹ /dɪˈlaɪt/ *n* **(a)** (joy) placer *m*, deleite *m*; **to take ~ in sth** disfrutar *or* gozar* con algo **(b)** (source of joy) placer *m*

delight² *vt* **(a)** (make very happy) llenar de

alegría; **his success ∼ed them** su éxito los llenó
de alegría **(b)** (give pleasure to) deleitar; **the clown
∼ed the children** el payaso hizo las delicias de *or*
deleitó a los niños
■ ∼ *vi* **to ∼ IN** -ING deleitarse + GER

delighted /dɪˈlaɪtɪd ‖dɪˈlaɪtɪd/ *adj* ⟨grin/look⟩
de alegría; **I'm ∼ (that) you can come** me alegra
mucho que puedas venir; **to be ∼ WITH sth/sb**
estar* encantado CON algo/algn

delightful /dɪˈlaɪtfəl/ *adj* ⟨weather/evening⟩
muy agradable, delicioso; ⟨person⟩ encantador;
⟨dress⟩ precioso

delineate /dɪˈlɪnieɪt/ *vt* (fml) **(a)** (draw) trazar*,
delinear **(b)** (describe) ⟨problem⟩ definir

delinquency /dɪˈlɪŋkwənsi/ *n* (Law, Sociol)
delincuencia *f*

delinquent /dɪˈlɪŋkwənt/ *n* delincuente *mf*

delirious /dɪˈlɪriəs/ *adj* **(a)** (Med) delirante; **to
be ∼** delirar, desvariar* **(b)** (wildly excited, happy)
(colloq) loco de alegría (fam)

deliver /dɪˈlɪvər ‖dɪˈlɪvə(r)/ *vt* **1 (a)** (hand over)
entregar* **(b)** (distribute) repartir (*a domicilio*)
2 (a) (administer) ⟨blow/punch⟩ propinar, asestar
(b) (issue) ⟨ultimatum/lecture/sermon⟩ dar*;
⟨warning⟩ hacer*; ⟨speech⟩ pronunciar;
⟨judgment⟩ dictar, pronunciar, emitir **(c)**
(produce, provide): **he promised much, but ∼ed little**
cumplió muy poco de lo mucho que había
prometido **(d)** (Sport) ⟨ball⟩ lanzar* **(e)** (in
elections) (AmE) ⟨state⟩ ganar **3** (Med): **her
husband ∼ed the baby** su marido la asistió en el
parto
■ ∼ *vi* **1** (Busn): **we ∼ free of charge** hacemos
reparto(s) a domicilio gratuitamente **2** (produce
the necessary) (colloq) cumplir

delivery /dɪˈlɪvəri/ *n* (*pl* **-ries**) **1 (a)** (act)
entrega *f*; (before *n*) **∼ charges** gastos *mpl* de
envío *or* transporte; **∼ man** repartidor *m*; **∼
truck** *o* (BrE) **van** camioneta *f or* furgoneta *f* de los
repartos **(b)** (occasion) reparto *m*; **is there a ∼ on
Saturdays?** ¿hay reparto los sábados? **(c)**
(consignment) partida *f*, remesa *f* **2** (of baby) parto
m, alumbramiento *m* (fml) **3** (manner of speaking)
expresión *f* oral

delta /ˈdeltə/ *n* delta *m*

delude /dɪˈluːd/ *vt* engañar

deluge /ˈdeljuːdʒ/ *n* **1 (a)** (flood) inundación *f*
(b) (downpour) diluvio *m* **2** (of protests, questions,
letters) aluvión *m*, avalancha *f*

delusion /dɪˈluːʒən/ *n* (mistaken idea) error *m*;
(vain hope) falsa ilusión *f*

deluxe /dəˈlʊks/ *adj* de lujo

delve /delv/ *vi* (liter) **to ∼ INTO sth** ahondar EN
algo; **to ∼ into the past** hurgar* en el pasado

demand¹ /dɪˈmænd ‖dɪˈmɑːnd/ *vt*
1 «*person*» (call for, insist on) exigir*; **the unions
are ∼ing better conditions** los sindicatos
reclaman mejores condiciones **2** (require)
⟨determination/perseverance⟩ exigir*, requerir*

demand² *n* **1** (claim) exigencia *f*; (Lab Rel, Pol)
reivindicación *f*, reclamo *m*; (request) petición *f*,
pedido *m* (AmL); **the ∼s of the job** las exigencias
del trabajo; **abortion on ∼** aborto *m* libre aborto *m*
2 (requirement) demanda *f*; **he's in great ∼** está
muy solicitado, es popular

demanding /dɪˈmændɪŋ ‖dɪˈmɑːndɪŋ/ *adj*
⟨job⟩ que exige mucho; ⟨book/music⟩ difícil;
⟨teacher⟩ exigente

demarcation /ˈdiːmɑːrˈkeɪʃən
‖ˌdiːmɑːˈkeɪʃən/ *n* demarcación *f*; (before *n*) **∼
line** línea *f* de demarcación

demean /dɪˈmiːn/ *vt* (fml) degradar

demeaning /dɪˈmiːnɪŋ/ *adj* degradante

demeanor, (BrE) **demeanour** /dɪˈmiːnər
‖dɪˈmiːnə(r)/ *n* (fml) **(a)** (behavior)
comportamiento *m*, conducta *f* **(b)** (bearing) porte
m

demented /dɪˈmentəd ‖dɪˈmentɪd/ *adj*
⟨person⟩ demente; ⟨screams/mutterings⟩
enloquecido

dementia /dɪˈmentʃə ‖dɪˈmenʃə/ *n* demencia *f*

demerara (**sugar**) /ˈdeməˈrɑːrə
‖ˌdeməˈreərə/ *n* (BrE) azúcar *f* morena, azúcar *m*
moreno

demerit /diːˈmerət ‖diːˈmerɪt/ *n* (fml) demérito
m (fml)

demise /dɪˈmaɪz/ *n* (*no pl*) (fml) **(a)** (death)
fallecimiento *m* (fml), deceso *m* (AmL frml) **(b)**
(end) desaparición *f*

demister /ˈdiːˈmɪstər ‖ˌdiːˈmɪstə(r)/ *n* (BrE)
desempañador *m*

demo /ˈdeməʊ/ *n* (*pl* **demos**) **1** (Mus)
demostración *f*; (before *n*) **∼ tape** cinta *f* de
demostración **2** (protest) (BrE colloq)
manifestación *f*

demobilize /ˈdɪˈməʊbəlaɪz ‖diːˈməʊbɪlaɪz/ *vt*
desmovilizar*

democracy /dɪˈmɑːkrəsi ‖dɪˈmɒkrəsi/ *n* (*pl*
-cies) democracia *f*

democrat /ˈdeməkræt/ *n* **(a)** (believer in
democracy) demócrata *mf* **(b)** **Democrat** (in US)
demócrata *mf*

democratic /ˈdeməˈkrætɪk/ *adj* **(a)** ⟨country/
election⟩ democrático **(b)** **Democratic** (in US)
demócrata

demographic /ˈdeməˈgræfɪk/ *adj* demográfico

demography /dɪˈmɑːgrəfi ‖dɪˈmɒgrəfi/ *n*
demografía *f*

demolish /dɪˈmɑːlɪʃ ‖dɪˈmɒlɪʃ/ *vt* ⟨structure/
building⟩ demoler*, derribar, echar abajo;
⟨argument/theory⟩ demoler*, echar por tierra

demolition /ˈdeməˈlɪʃən/ *n* (of building)
demolición *f*, derribo *m*; (of theory) demolición *f*,
destrucción *f*

demon /ˈdiːmən/ *n* demonio *m*

demonstrate /ˈdemənstreɪt/ *vt* **(a)** (show)
⟨need/ability⟩ demostrar* **(b)** (Marketing) hacer*
una demostración de
■ ∼ *vi* (Pol) manifestarse*

demonstration /ˈdemənˈstreɪʃən/ *n* **1 (a)**
(expression) muestra *f*, demostración *f* **(b)** (display)
demostración *f* **2** (Pol) manifestación *f*

demonstrative /dɪˈmɑːnstrətɪv
‖dɪˈmɒnstrətɪv/ *adj* efusivo, expresivo,
demostrativo (AmL)

demonstrator /ˈdemənstreɪtər
‖ˈdemənstreɪtə(r)/ *n* manifestante *mf*

demoralize /dɪˈmɔːrəlaɪz ‖dɪˈmɒrəlaɪz/ *vt*
desmoralizar*

demoralizing /dɪˈmɔːrəlaɪzɪŋ ‖dɪˈmɒrəlaɪzɪŋ/
adj desalentador, desmoralizante

d

demote /dɪˈməʊt, ˈdiː-/ vt (in organization) bajar de categoría; (Mil) degradar

demotion /dɪˈməʊʃən, diː-/ n (in organization) descenso m de categoría; (Mil) degradación f

demur /dɪˈmɜːr ‖dɪˈmɜː(r)/ vi -rr- (fml) objetar

demure /dɪˈmjʊr ‖dɪˈmjʊə(r)/ adj recatado

den /den/ n **1** (of animals, thieves) guarida f **2** (room) (colloq) cuarto m de estar; (for study, work) estudio m

denial /dɪˈnaɪəl/ n **1** (of accusation, fact): to issue a ∼ of sth desmentir* algo **2** (of request, rights) denegación f **3** (repudiation) negación f, rechazo m **4** (abstinence) renuncia f

denier /ˈdenjər ‖ˈdenɪə(r)/ n denier m

denigrate /ˈdenɪɡreɪt/ vt (fml) ⟨character/person⟩ denigrar; ⟨effort⟩ menospreciar

denim /ˈdenəm ‖ˈdenɪm/ n(Tex) tela f vaquera or jeans, mezclilla f (Chi, Méx); (before n) ⟨jacket/skirt⟩ vaquero, tejano (Esp), de mezclilla (Chi, Méx)

Denmark /ˈdenmɑːrk ‖ˈdenmɑːk/ n Dinamarca f

denomination /dɪˌnɑːməˈneɪʃən ‖dɪˌnɒmɪˈneɪʃən/ n **1** (Relig) confesión f **2** (of currency) valor m, denominación f (AmL)

denominator /dɪˈnɑːməneɪtər ‖dɪˈnɒmɪneɪtə(r)/ n (Math) denominador m

denote /dɪˈnəʊt/ vt denotar

denouement /ˌdeɪnuːˈmɑːn ‖deɪˈnuːmɔːn/ n desenlace m

denounce /dɪˈnaʊns/ vt denunciar

dense /dens/ adj denser, densest **1** (a) (closely spaced) ⟨forest/jungle⟩ espeso; ⟨population/traffic⟩ denso; ⟨crowd⟩ compacto, apretado (b) (thick) ⟨fog/mist/smoke⟩ denso, espeso (c) (Phys) denso (d) (complicated) ⟨prose/article⟩ denso **2** (stupid) (colloq) burro (fam), duro de entendederas (fam)

densely /ˈdensli/ adv ⟨populated/forested⟩ densamente; ⟨packed⟩ apretadamente

density /ˈdensəti/ n (pl -ties) densidad f; (of fog) lo espeso, densidad f

dent¹ /dent/ n (in metal) abolladura f, abollón m; (in wood) marca f

dent² vt ⟨metal⟩ abollar; ⟨wood⟩ hacer* una marca en; ⟨popularity⟩ afectar; ⟨pride⟩ hacer* mella en

dental /ˈdentl/ adj dental; ⟨school⟩ de odontología

dental floss /flɑːs ‖flɒs/ n hilo m or seda f dental

dentist /ˈdentəst ‖ˈdentɪst/ n dentista mf, odontólogo, -ga m,f (fml)

dentistry /ˈdentəstri ‖ˈdentɪstri/ n odontología f

dentures /ˈdentʃərz ‖ˈdentʃəz/ pl n dentadura f postiza

deny /dɪˈnaɪ/ vt denies, denying, denied **1** ⟨accusation/fact⟩ negar*; ⟨rumors⟩ desmentir* **2** (refuse) ⟨request⟩ denegar*

deodorant /diːˈəʊdərənt/ n desodorante m

depart /dɪˈpɑːrt ‖dɪˈpɑːt/ vi (Transp) salir*, partir (fml); «person» (fml) partir (fml), salir*

department /dɪˈpɑːrtmənt ‖dɪˈpɑːtmənt/ n **1** (of store) sección f; (of company) departamento m, sección f **2** (a) (Govt) ministerio m, secretaría f (Méx) (b) (AmE Adm): the police/fire ∼ el cuerpo de policía/bomberos **3** (Educ) departamento m

department store n (grandes) almacenes mpl, tienda f de departamentos (Méx)

departure /dɪˈpɑːrtʃər ‖dɪˈpɑːtʃə(r)/ n(Transp) salida f, partida f (fml); (of person) (fml) partida f (fml), ida f; **point of** ∼ punto m de partida; **a** ∼ **from the norm** una desviación de la norma; (before n) ∼ **lounge** sala f de embarque

depend /dɪˈpend/ vi to ∼ **on** sb/sth depender DE algn/algo

dependable /dɪˈpendəbəl/ adj ⟨person⟩ formal, digno de confianza; ⟨ally/workman⟩ digno de confianza

dependant, (AmE also) **dependent** /dɪˈpendənt/ n carga f familiar, familiar mf a su (or mi etc) cargo

dependence /dɪˈpendəns/ n dependencia f

dependent¹ /dɪˈpendənt/ adj (a) (reliant) (pred) to be ∼ **on** sth depender DE algo/algn (b) (conditional) (pred) to be ∼ **on** sth depender DE algo

dependent² n (AmE) ▶ DEPENDANT

depict /dɪˈpɪkt/ vt (fml) (a) (portray) representar (b) (describe) describir*, pintar

depiction /dɪˈpɪkʃən/ n (fml) (a) (representation) representación f (b) (description) descripción f

depilatory /dɪˈpɪlətɔːri ‖dɪˈpɪlətri/ n (pl -ries) depilatorio m

deplete /dɪˈpliːt/ vt (reduce) ⟨supply/stock⟩ reducir*; (exhaust) ⟨energy source⟩ agotar

deplorable /dɪˈplɔːrəbəl/ adj (a) (disgraceful) deplorable, vergonzoso (b) (regrettable) lamentable

deplore /dɪˈplɔːr ‖dɪˈplɔː(r)/ vt (fml) (a) (condemn) deplorar, condenar (b) (regret) deplorar, lamentar

deploy /dɪˈplɔɪ/ vt **1** (position) (Mil) desplegar* **2** (distribute, use) (fml) utilizar*, hacer* uso de

deport /dɪˈpɔːrt ‖dɪˈpɔːt/ vt deportar

deportation /ˌdiːpɔːrˈteɪʃən ‖ˌdiːpɔːˈteɪʃən/ n deportación f

deportment /dɪˈpɔːrtmənt ‖dɪˈpɔːtmənt/ n (fml) (a) (carriage) porte m (b) (conduct) conducta f

depose /dɪˈpəʊz/ vt ⟨dictator/ruler⟩ deponer*, derrocar*; ⟨champion/king⟩ destronar

deposit¹ /dɪˈpɑːzət ‖dɪˈpɒzɪt/ vt **1** (a) (set down) depositar, poner* (b) (Geol) ⟨silt⟩ depositar **2** (a) (leave) depositar (b) ⟨money⟩ depositar, ingresar f (Esp)

deposit² n **1** (a) (payment into account) depósito m, ingreso m (Esp); (before n) ∼ **account** cuenta f de ahorros (b) (down payment — on large amounts) depósito m, entrega f inicial; (— on small amounts) depósito m, señal f, seña f (RPl) (c) (security)

depósito *m*, fianza *f* **2** (accumulation — of silt, mud)
depósito *m*; (— of dust) capa *f* **3** (Min) (of gas)
depósito *m*; (of gold, copper) yacimiento *m*

depot /'di:pəʊ ‖'depəʊ/ *n* **1** **(a)** (storehouse)
depósito *m*, almacén *m* **(b)** (Mil) depósito *m*
2 (esp AmE) (bus station) terminal *f or* (Chi) *m*,
estación *f* de autobuses; (train station) estación *f*
3 (esp BrE) (storage area) **(a)** (for buses) garage *m*
(esp AmL), cochera *f* (Esp), depósito *m* (Chi) **(b)** (for
trains) depósito *m* de locomotoras

depraved /dɪ'preɪvd/ *adj* depravado

depravity /dɪ'prævəti/ *n* depravación *f*

deprecating /'deprɪkeɪtɪŋ/ *adj* (fml) **(a)**
(disapproving) ⟨remark⟩ de desaprobación,
reprobatorio **(b)** (belittling) ⟨smile/laugh⟩ de
desprecio

depreciate /dɪ'pri:ʃieɪt/ *vt* (Fin) depreciar
■ ~ *vi* (Fin) depreciarse

depress /dɪ'pres/ *vt* **1** (sadden) deprimir,
abatir **2** (press down) (fml) ⟨lever⟩ bajar; ⟨button⟩
pulsar (fml) **3** (Econ) ⟨market⟩ deprimir; ⟨prices/
wages⟩ reducir*, hacer* bajar

depressed /dɪ'prest/ *adj* **1** (dejected)
deprimido, abatido; **to get ~** deprimirse, dejarse
abatir **2** (Econ) ⟨economy/market/area⟩
deprimido

depressing /dɪ'presɪŋ/ *adj* deprimente

depression /dɪ'preʃən/ *n* **1** (despondency)
depresión *f*, abatimiento *m* **2** (in flat surface)
depresión *f* **3** (Econ) depresión *f*, crisis *f*

deprivation /ˌdeprə'veɪʃən ‖ˌdeprɪ'veɪʃən/ *n*
(lack, loss) privación *f*, (hardship) privaciones *fpl*,
penurias *fpl*

deprive /dɪ'praɪv/ *vt*: **to ~ sb OF sth** privar a
algn DE algo

deprived /dɪ'praɪvd/ *adj* ⟨child⟩ carenciado,
desventajado; ⟨region⟩ carenciado

dept (= **department**) Dpto.

depth /depθ/ *n* **1** **(a)** (of hole, water)
profundidad *f*; **out of one's ~**: **when it comes to
computers I'm out of my ~** estoy muy flojo en
informática; **don't go out of your ~** (in water) no
vayas donde no haces pie *or* no tocas fondo **(b)**
(of shelf, cupboard) profundidad *f*, fondo *m*; (of hem)
ancho *m*
2 (of emotion, knowledge) profundidad *f*; **to study
sth in ~** estudiar algo a fondo *or* en profundidad
3 (of voice) profundidad *f*; (of sound) intensidad *f*
4 **depths** *pl n*: **in the ~s of the ocean** en las
profundidades del océano; **in the ~s of despair** en
lo más hondo de la desesperación

deputation /ˌdepjə'teɪʃən ‖ˌdepjʊ'teɪʃən/ *n*
delegación *f*

deputy /'depjəti/ *n* (*pl* **-ties**) **1** **(a)**
(second-in-command) segundo, -da *m,f*; (substitute)
suplente *m,f*, reemplazo *m,f* **(b)** ~ **(sheriff)** (AmE
Law) ayudante *m,f* del sheriff **2** (Govt) diputado,
-da *m,f*

derail /dɪ'reɪl/ *vt* **(a)** ⟨train⟩ hacer* descarrilar
(b) (upset) ⟨plan⟩ desbaratar

deranged /dɪ'reɪndʒd/ *adj* trastornado

derby /'dɜːrbi ‖'dɑːbi/ *n* (*pl* **derbies**)
1 (Sport): **the D~** (in UK) el Derby, el clásico de
Epsom; **the Kentucky D~** el Derby de Kentucky
2 (hat) (AmE) bombín *m*, sombrero *m* de hongo

deregulate /di:'regjəleɪt ‖di:'regjʊleɪt/ *vt*
desregular, liberalizar*

deregulation /ˌdi:regjə'leɪʃən
‖di:ˌregjʊ'leɪʃən/ *n* desregulación *f*,
liberalización *f*

derelict /'derəlɪkt/ *adj* abandonado y en ruinas

deride /dɪ'raɪd/ *vt* ridiculizar*, burlarse de

derision /dɪ'rɪʒən/ *n* escarnio *m* (fml), irrisión
f (fml)

derisive /dɪ'raɪsɪv/ *adj* ⟨smile/laughter⟩ burlón,
⟨attitude/remark⟩ desdeñoso y burlón

derisory /dɪ'raɪzəri/ *adj* ⟨sum/offer⟩ irrisorio

derivative[1] /dɪ'rɪvətɪv/ *adj* (unoriginal) ⟨novel⟩
carente de originalidad; ⟨plot/theme⟩ manido,
trillado; ⟨artist/writer⟩ adocenado

derivative[2] *n* (in industry) derivado *m*

derive /dɪ'raɪv/ *vt* **children can ~ great
enjoyment from the simplest things** las cosas más
simples pueden dar enorme placer a un niño; **the
name is ~d from the Greek** el nombre viene *or*
deriva del griego
■ ~ *vi* **to ~ FROM sth** «⟨attitude/problem⟩»
provenir* DE algo; «⟨idea⟩» tener* su origen EN
algo; (Ling) derivar(se) DE algo

dermatitis /ˌdɜːrmə'taɪtəs ‖ˌdɜːmə'taɪtɪs/ *n*
dermatitis *f*

derogatory /dɪ'rɑːgətɔːri ‖dɪ'rɒgətri/ *adj*
despectivo, peyorativo

descant /'deskænt/ *n* contrapunto *m*

descend /dɪ'send/ *vi* (move downwards)
descender* (fml), bajar; **in ~ing order of
importance** en orden decreciente *or* descendente
de importancia; **don't ~ to his level** no te pongas
a su nivel
■ ~ *vt* descender* (fml), bajar

descendant /dɪ'sendənt/ *n* descendiente *mf*

descended /dɪ'sendəd ‖dɪ'sendɪd/ *adj* (pred)
to be ~ FROM sb ser* descendiente DE algn,
descender* DE algn

descendent *n* (AmE) ▶ DESCENDANT

descent /dɪ'sent/ *n* **1** **(a)** (by climbers, plane)
descenso *m*, bajada *f* **(b)** (in terrain) pendiente *f*,
bajada *f* **2** (decline) caída *f* **3** (lineage)
ascendencia *f*

describe /dɪ'skraɪb/ *vt* describir*; **he ~s
himself as a socialist** se define como socialista

description /dɪ'skrɪpʃən/ *n* descripción *f*; **of
every ~** de todo tipo, de toda clase

descriptive /dɪ'skrɪptɪv/ *adj* descriptivo

desecrate /'desɪkreɪt/ *vt* profanar

desert[1] /'dezərt ‖'dezət/ *n* (Geog) desierto *m*;
(before n) ⟨region/climate⟩ desértico; ⟨tribe/sand⟩
del desierto

desert[2] /dɪ'zɜːrt ‖dɪ'zɜːt/ *vt* **(a)** (fml) ⟨place⟩
abandonar, huir* de **(b)** ⟨family⟩ abandonar;
⟨cause⟩ desertar de
■ ~ *vi* (Mil) desertar

deserted /dɪ'zɜːrtəd ‖dɪ'zɜːtɪd/ *adj* **(a)** ⟨streets/
village⟩ desierto **(b)** ⟨husband/wife⟩ abandonado

deserter /dɪ'zɜːrtər ‖dɪ'zɜːtə(r)/ *n* desertor,
-tora *m,f*

desertion /dɪ'zɜːrʃən ‖dɪ'zɜːʃən/ *n* **(a)** (Mil)
deserción *f* **(b)** (of family, place) abandono *m*

desert island /'dezərt ‖'dezət/ *n* isla *f*
desierta

deserts /dɪ'zɜːrts ‖dɪ'zɜːts/ *pl n*: **to get one's
just ~** recibir su (*or* tu *etc*) merecido

deserve /dɪˈzɜːrv ‖dɪˈzɜːv/ vt merecer(se)*; they got what they ∼d se llevaron su merecido

deserving /dɪˈzɜːrvɪŋ ‖dɪˈzɜːvɪŋ/ adj ⟨cause/case⟩ meritorio; the ∼ poor los pobres dignos de ayuda

desiccated /ˈdesɪkeɪtəd ‖ˈdesɪkeɪtɪd/ adj seco; ∼ coconut coco m rallado

design¹ /dɪˈzaɪn/ n [1] (a) (of product, car, machine) diseño m; (drawing) diseño m, boceto m (b) (pattern, decoration) diseño m, motivo m, dibujo m (c) (product, model) modelo m [2] (a) (Art) diseño m (b) (style) estilo m, líneas fpl [3] (a) (plan) (liter) plan m; by ∼ deliberadamente (b) **designs** pl n (intentions) propósitos mpl, designios mpl (liter)

design² vt ⟨house/garden⟩ diseñar, proyectar; ⟨dress/product⟩ diseñar; ⟨course/program⟩ planear, estructurar; a statement ∼ed to reassure the public una declaración destinada a tranquilizar al público

designate¹ /ˈdezɪgneɪt/ vt [1] (name officially) nombrar, designar [2] (call) (frml) designar

designate² /ˈdezɪgneɪt, -nət ‖ˈdezɪgnət/ adj (after n): the governor ∼ quien ha sido nombrado gobernador

designer /dɪˈzaɪnər ‖dɪˈzaɪnə(r)/ n diseñador, -dora m,f; (before n) ⟨clothes/jeans⟩ de diseño exclusivo; ⟨furniture/pen⟩ de diseño

desirable /dɪˈzaɪrəbəl ‖dɪˈzaɪərəbəl/ adj (a) ⟨property/location⟩ atractivo (b) (sexually) ⟨man/woman⟩ atractivo, deseable, apetecible (c) ⟨outcome⟩ deseable, conveniente; ⟨option⟩ conveniente, aconsejable

desire¹ /dɪˈzaɪr ‖dɪˈzaɪə(r)/ n [1] (wish) deseo m, anhelo m (liter) [2] (lust) deseo m

desire² vt (a) (want) ⟨happiness/success⟩ desear; to leave a lot to be ∼d dejar bastante que desear (b) (lust after) ⟨person⟩ desear

desirous /dɪˈzaɪrəs ‖dɪˈzaɪərəs/ adj (frml) (pred): we are ∼ of your success le deseamos éxito

desist /dɪˈzɪst/ vi (frml) to ∼ (FROM sth/-ING) (cease) desistir (DE algo/+ INF); (abstain) abstenerse* (DE algo/+ INF)

desk /desk/ n (a) (table) escritorio m, mesa f de trabajo; (in school) pupitre m; (before n) ⟨lamp⟩ de escritorio, de (sobre)mesa; a ∼ job un trabajo de oficina (b) (service counter) mostrador m (c) (Journ) sección f

desktop /ˈdesktɑːp ‖ˈdesktɒp/ adj (before n) ⟨calculator/computer⟩ de escritorio, de (sobre)mesa; ∼ publishing autoedición f, edición f electrónica

desolate /ˈdesələt/ adj [1] (deserted) ⟨place/landscape⟩ desierto, desolado [2] ⟨person⟩ desconsolado, desolado; ⟨outlook/existence⟩ sombrío, lúgubre

despair¹ /dɪˈsper ‖dɪˈspeə(r)/ n desesperación f; to be in ∼ estar* desesperado

despair² vi perder* las esperanzas, desesperar(se); honestly, I ∼ of you! ¡francamente, eres un caso perdido!

despairing /dɪˈsperɪŋ ‖dɪˈspeərɪŋ/ adj ⟨look/cry⟩ de desesperación

despatch /dɪˈspætʃ/ vt/n ▶ DISPATCH¹,²

desperate /ˈdespərət/ adj [1] (frantic) ⟨person/attempt⟩ desesperado; to be ∼ estar* desesperado [2] (critical) ⟨state/situation⟩ grave, desesperado; ⟨need⟩ apremiante

desperately /ˈdespərətli/ adv ⟨struggle⟩ desesperadamente; ⟨need⟩ urgentemente, con urgencia

desperation /despəˈreɪʃən/ n desesperación f

despicable /dɪˈspɪkəbəl/ adj vil, despreciable

despise /dɪˈspaɪz/ vt despreciar (profundamente)

despite /dɪˈspaɪt/ prep a pesar de

despondent /dɪˈspɑːndənt ‖dɪˈspɒndənt/ adj abatido, descorazonado

despot /ˈdespɑːt ‖ˈdespɒt/ n déspota mf

dessert /dɪˈzɜːrt ‖dɪˈzɜːt/ n postre m

dessertspoon /dɪˈzɜːrtspuːn ‖dɪˈzɜːtspuːn/ n cuchara f de postre

destabilize /ˈdiːˈsteɪbəlaɪz/ vt desestabilizar*

destination /destəˈneɪʃən ‖destɪˈneɪʃən/ n (a) (end of journey) destino m (b) (purpose) meta f

destined /ˈdestənd ‖ˈdestɪnd/ adj (pred) [1] (fated) to be ∼ to + INF estar* (pre)destinado A + INF [2] (a) (intended) ∼ FOR sth destinado A algo (b) (bound, on way): ∼ for the West Indies con destino al Caribe

destiny /ˈdestəni ‖ˈdestɪni/ n (pl -nies) destino m, sino m (liter)

destitute /ˈdestətuːt ‖ˈdestɪtjuːt/ adj indigente

destroy /dɪˈstrɔɪ/ vt (a) (ruin, wreck) ⟨building/forest⟩ destruir*; ⟨reputation/confidence⟩ acabar con; ⟨life⟩ arruinar (b) ⟨animal⟩ sacrificar* (euf)

destroyer /dɪˈstrɔɪər ‖dɪˈstrɔɪə(r)/ n destructor m

destruction /dɪˈstrʌkʃən/ n [1] (of city, books, forest) destrucción f; (of reputation, civilization) ruina f, destrucción f; (slaughter) exterminación f [2] (cause of downfall) (frml) ruina f, perdición f [3] (damage) destrucción f, estragos mpl, destrozos mpl

destructive /dɪˈstrʌktɪv/ adj ⟨storm/weapon⟩ destructor; ⟨tendency⟩ destructivo; ⟨child⟩ destrozón; ⟨criticism⟩ destructivo, negativo

desultory /ˈdesəltɔːri ‖ˈdezəltəri/ adj ⟨effort/attempt⟩ desganado

detach /dɪˈtætʃ/ vt (separate) separar, quitar; (unstick) despegar*; the headrest can be ∼ed el apoyacabezas se puede desmontar or quitar

detachable /dɪˈtætʃəbəl/ adj ⟨cover⟩ de quita y pon, de quitar y poner; ⟨lining⟩ desmontable

detached /dɪˈtætʃt/ adj [1] ⟨person/manner⟩ (aloof) distante, indiferente; (objective) objetivo, imparcial [2] (BrE) ⟨house⟩ no adosado

detachment /dɪˈtætʃmənt/ n [1] (aloofness) distancia f, indiferencia f; (objectivity) objetividad f, imparcialidad f [2] (act of detaching) (frml) desprendimiento m [3] (Mil) destacamento m

detail¹ /ˈditeɪl, ˈdiːteɪl ‖ˈdiːteɪl/ n [1] (a) (particular) detalle m, pormenor m; he asked for further ∼s pidió más información or información más detallada (b) (embellishment) detalle m (c) (insignificant matter) minucia f, detalle m (sin importancia) [2] (minutiae) detalles mpl; to go into ∼ entrar en detalles or pormenores; to explain sth in ∼ explicar* algo detalladamente or minuciosamente

detail² vt [1] (describe) exponer* en detalle, detallar [2] (Mil) destacar*

detailed /'di:teɪld/ *adj* ⟨*description*⟩ detallado, minucioso, pormenorizado; ⟨*examination*⟩ minucioso, detenido

detain /dɪ'teɪn/ *vt* (a) (delay) (fml): don't let me ∼ you no quiero entretenerlo *or* demorarlo (b) (in custody) detener*

detect /dɪ'tekt/ *vt* ⟨*object/substance*⟩ detectar

detection /dɪ'tekʃən/ *n* [1] (of error) descubrimiento *m*; (of act, crime, criminal): to escape ∼ pasar desapercibido *or* inadvertido [2] (of substance) detección *f*

detective /dɪ'tektɪv/ *n* (private) detective *mf*; (in police force) agente *mf*, oficial *mf*; (before *n*) ∼ story novela *f* policíaca *or* policial

detector /dɪ'tektər ‖dɪ'tektə(r)/ *n* detector *m*

detente /deɪ'tɑ:nt/ *n* (Pol) distensión *f*

detention /dɪ'tenʃən ‖dɪ'tenʃən/ *n* [1] (in custody) detención *f* [2] (Educ): to be in ∼ estar* castigado

deter /dɪ'tɜːr ‖dɪ'tɜː(r)/ *vt* -rr- ⟨*person*⟩ disuadir, hacer* desistir; ⟨*crime/war*⟩ impedir*; to ∼ sb FROM sth/-ING disuadir a algn DE algo/ + INF

detergent /dɪ'tɜːrdʒənt ‖dɪ'tɜːdʒənt/ *n* (Chem) detergente *m*; (for clothes) detergente *m*; (for dishes) lavavajillas *m*

deteriorate /dɪ'tɪriəreɪt ‖dɪ'tɪəriəreɪt/ *vi* «*health/relationship/material*» deteriorarse; «*weather/work*» empeorar

deterioration /dɪ,tɪriə'reɪʃən ‖dɪ,tɪəriə'reɪʃən/ *n* deterioro *m*

determination /dɪ,tɜːrmɪ'neɪʃən ‖dɪ,tɜːmɪ'neɪʃən/ *n* determinación *f*, resolución *f*

determine /dɪ'tɜːrmən ‖dɪ'tɜːmɪn/ *vt* [1] (ascertain) establecer*, determinar [2] (a) (influence) determinar, condicionar (b) (mark) ⟨*boundary/limit*⟩ definir, demarcar* [3] (liter) (resolve) decidir; to ∼ to + INF decidir + INF, tomar la determinación DE + INF

determined /dɪ'tɜːrmənd ‖dɪ'tɜːmɪnd/ *adj* ⟨*mood/person*⟩ decidido, resuelto; to be ∼ to + INF estar* decidido A + INF, estar* empeñado EN + INF; to be ∼ THAT estar* resuelto *or* decidido A QUE (+ *subj*)

deterrent /dɪ'terənt/ *n*: it may act as a ∼ to thieves puede servir para disuadir a los ladrones; the nuclear ∼ las armas nucleares como fuerza disuasoria

detest /dɪ'test/ *vt* detestar, odiar

dethrone /dɪ'θrəʊn/ *vt* destronar

detonate /'detəneɪt/ *vt* hacer* detonar

detour¹ /'di:tʊr ‖'di:tʊə(r)/ *n* (a) (deviation) rodeo *m*, vuelta *f*; to make a ∼ dar* un rodeo, desviarse* (b) (AmE Transp) desvío *m*, desviación *f*

detour² *vt* (AmE) ⟨*traffic*⟩ desviar*

detract /dɪ'trækt/ *vi*: I didn't wish to ∼ from her achievement no quise quitarle méritos *or* restarle valor a su logro; it ∼s from the beauty of the painting desmerece la belleza del cuadro

detractor /dɪ'træktər ‖dɪ'træktə(r)/ *n* detractor, -tora *m,f*

detriment /'detrəmənt ‖'detrɪmənt/ *n* (fml) detrimento *m*, perjuicio *m*; to the ∼ of sb/sth en detrimento *or* perjuicio de algn/algo

devalue /'di:'vælju:/ *vt* (Fin) devaluar*

devastate /'devəsteɪt/ *vt* (a) (lay waste) devastar, asolar* (b) (overwhelm) ⟨*opposition/*

argument⟩ aplastar, demoler*; I was ∼d when I heard quedé deshecho *or* anonadado cuando me enteré

devastating /'devəsteɪtɪŋ/ *adj* (a) ⟨*punch/shock*⟩ devastador (b) ⟨*accuracy/logic*⟩ abrumador, apabullante; ⟨*reply/defeat*⟩ demoledor, aplastante; ⟨*beauty*⟩ irresistible

devastation /'devə'steɪʃən/ *n* devastación *f*

develop /dɪ'veləp/ *vt* [1] (a) (elaborate, devise) desarrollar (b) (improve) ⟨*skill/ability/quality*⟩ desarrollar (c) (exploit) ⟨*land/area*⟩ urbanizar* (d) (expand) ⟨*business/range*⟩ ampliar* (e) (create) ⟨*drug/engine*⟩ crear [2] (acquire) ⟨*immunity/resistance*⟩ desarrollar; ⟨*disease*⟩ contraer* (fml); the machine ∼ed a fault la máquina empezó a funcionar mal [3] (Phot) revelar
■ ∼ *vi* [1] (a) (grow) «*person/industry*» desarrollarse; «*interest*» crecer*, aumentar (b) (evolve) to ∼ INTO sth convertirse *or* transformarse EN algo [2] (appear) «*problem/complication*» surgir*, aparecer*; «*crisis*» producirse*

developer /dɪ'veləpər ‖dɪ'veləpə(r)/ *n* [1] (of land, property) promotor inmobiliario, promotora inmobiliaria *m,f* [2] (Phot) revelador *m*

developing /dɪ'veləpɪŋ/ *adj* ⟨*country*⟩ en vías de desarrollo

development /dɪ'veləpmənt/ *n* [1] (of person, idea, situation) desarrollo *m* [2] (of drug, engine) creación *f* [3] (of land, area) urbanización *f* [4] (housing ∼) complejo *m* habitacional, fraccionamiento *m* (Méx), urbanización *f* (Esp) [5] (Econ) desarrollo *m* [6] (happening, event) acontecimiento *m*, suceso *m*

deviant /'di:viənt/ *adj* ⟨*practices/conduct*⟩ desviado, que se aparta de la norma; ⟨*person/personality*⟩ anormal

deviate /'di:vieɪt/ *vi* to ∼ FROM sth ⟨*from course*⟩ desviarse* DE algo; ⟨*from truth/norm*⟩ apartarse DE algo

deviation /'di:vi'eɪʃən/ *n* desviación *f*

device /dɪ'vaɪs/ *n* [1] (gadget, tool) artefacto *m*, dispositivo *m*, aparato *m*; (mechanism) dispositivo *m*, mecanismo *m* [2] (stratagem) recurso *m*, estratagema *f*; to leave sb to her/his own ∼s dejar que algn se las arregle solo

devil /'devl/ *n* [1] (a) (Relig) diablo *m*, demonio *m* (b) (evil spirit) demonio *m* [2] (colloq) (person): he's a little ∼! ¡es un diablillo!; poor ∼! ¡pobre diablo!

devious /'di:viəs/ *adj* (a) (underhand) ⟨*person*⟩ taimado, artero (b) (roundabout) ⟨*route/path*⟩ tortuoso, sinuoso

devise /dɪ'vaɪz/ *vt* ⟨*plan/system*⟩ idear, crear, concebir*; ⟨*machine/tool*⟩ inventar

devoid /dɪ'vɔɪd/ *adj* (pred) (fml) to be ∼ OF sth carecer* DE algo

devolution /'devə'lu:ʃən ‖,di:və'lu:ʃən/ *n* (a) (delegation) delegación *f*, transferencia *f* (b) (BrE Govt) transferencia de competencias del gobierno central a un gobierno regional

devolve /dɪ'vɑːlv ‖dɪ'vɒlv/ *vt* (fml) ⟨*power*⟩ delegar*, transferir*; ⟨*privilege/right*⟩ conceder

devote /dɪ'vəʊt/ *vt* to ∼ sth TO sth/-ING dedicar* algo A algo/ + INF
■ *v refl* to ∼ oneself TO sth/-ING dedicarse* A algo/ + INF

devoted /dɪ'vəʊtəd ‖dɪ'vəʊtɪd/ adj (a) (loving) ⟨couple/family⟩ unido; **to be ~ TO sb** sentir* devoción POR algn (b) (dedicated) ⟨before n⟩ ⟨follower/admirer⟩ ferviente, devoto; ⟨service/friendship⟩ leal

devotion /dɪ'vəʊʃən/ n(love) devoción f; (loyalty) lealtad f

devour /dɪ'vaʊr ‖dɪ'vaʊə(r)/ vt devorar

devout /dɪ'vaʊt/ adj (a) (Relig) devoto, piadoso (b) (earnest) (frml) ⟨before n⟩ ⟨supporter⟩ ferviente

dew /du: ‖dju:/ n rocío m

dexterity /dek'sterəti/ n (manual) destreza f, habilidad f; (skill) habilidad f

diabetes /daɪə'bi:ti:z/ n diabetes f

diabetic¹ /daɪə'betɪk/ adj diabético; ⟨jam/chocolate⟩ para diabéticos

diabetic² n diabético, -ca m,f

diabolical /daɪə'bɑ:lɪkəl ‖,daɪə'bɒlɪkəl/ adj ⟨machinations⟩ diabólico, satánico; ⟨cruelty⟩ perverso, satánico

diagnose /'daɪəgnəʊs, -əʊz ‖'daɪəgnəʊz/ vt ⟨illness⟩ diagnosticar*; ⟨cause/fault⟩ determinar

diagnosis /,daɪəg'nəʊsəs ‖,daɪəg'nəʊsɪs/ n (pl **-ses** /-si:z/) diagnóstico m

diagonal /daɪ'ægənl/ adj ⟨line⟩ diagonal; ⟨path⟩ en diagonal

diagram /'daɪəgræm/ n diagrama m, esquema m, gráfico m

dial¹ /'daɪl ‖'daɪəl/ n (on clock, watch) esfera f, (on measuring instrument) cuadrante m; (of telephone) disco m; (on radio) dial m

dial², (BrE) **-ll-** vt/i (Telec) marcar*, discar* (AmL)

dialect /'daɪəlekt/ n dialecto m

dialling tone /'daɪlɪŋ ‖'daɪəlɪŋ/ n (BrE) ▶ DIAL TONE

dialogue, (AmE also) **dialog** /'daɪəlɔ:g ‖'daɪəlɒg/ n diálogo m

dial tone n tono m de marcar or (AmL) de discado

diameter /daɪ'æmətər ‖daɪ'æmɪtə(r)/ n diámetro m

diamond /'daɪəmənd/ n [1] (Min) diamante m; (cut) brillante m, diamante m [2] (shape) rombo m [3] (Games) **diamonds** (suit) (+ sing or pl vb) diamantes mpl

diaper /'daɪpər ‖'daɪəpə(r)/ n (AmE) pañal m

diaphragm /'daɪəfræm/ n [1] (Anat) diafragma m [2] (contraceptive) diafragma m

diarrhea, (BrE) **diarrhoea** /'daɪə'ri:ə ‖,daɪə'rɪə/ n diarrea f

diary /'daɪəri/ n (pl **-ries**) [1] (personal record) diario m [2] (book for appointments) agenda f

dice¹ /daɪs/ n (pl ~) dado m

dice² pl of DIE² and of DICE¹

dice³ vt (Culin) cortar en dados or cubitos

dictate /'dɪkteɪt ‖dɪk'teɪt/ vt [1] (read out) dictar [2] (prescribe, lay down) ⟨law⟩ establecer*, dictar; ⟨common sense⟩ dictar

dictation /dɪk'teɪʃən/ n (Corresp, Educ) dictado m

dictator /'dɪkteɪtər ‖dɪk'teɪtə(r)/ n dictador, -dora m,f

dictatorial /,dɪktə'tɔ:riəl/ adj dictatorial

dictatorship /dɪk'teɪtərʃɪp ‖dɪk'teɪtəʃɪp/ n dictadura f

diction /'dɪkʃən/ n dicción f

dictionary /'dɪkʃəneri ‖'dɪkʃənri, 'dɪkʃənəri/ n (pl **-ries**) diccionario m

did /dɪd/ past of DO¹

didactic /daɪ'dæktɪk/ adj didáctico

diddle /'dɪdl/ vt (colloq) estafar, timar (fam)

didn't /'dɪdnt/ = **did not**

die¹ /daɪ/ **dies, dying, died** vi (a) (stop living) morir*; (violently) matarse, morir*; **to be dying FOR sth** (colloq) morirse* POR algo; **to be dying to + INF** (colloq) morirse* POR + INF, morirse* de ganas de + INF (b) (stop functioning) ⟨engine/motor⟩ apagarse*, dejar de funcionar

■ **~** vt: **to ~ a natural death** morir* de muerte natural; **to ~ a violent death** tener* or sufrir una muerte violenta

■ **die away** [v + adv] ⟨storm/wind⟩ amainar; ⟨anger⟩ pasar

■ **die down** [v + adv] ⟨fire/noise⟩ irse* apagando; ⟨storm/wind⟩ amainar; ⟨anger/excitement⟩ calmarse

■ **die out** [v + adv] ⟨race/species⟩ extinguirse*; ⟨custom⟩ morir*, caer* en desuso

die² n (pl **dice**) (Games) dado m

diehard /'daɪhɑ:rd ‖'daɪhɑ:d/ n intransigente mf; (before n) intransigente, acérrimo

diesel¹ /'di:zəl/ n (a) (vehicle) coche m (or camión m etc) diesel, diesel m (b) (fuel) diesel m, gasóleo m, gas-oil m

diesel² adj (before n) diesel adj inv

diet¹ /'daɪət/ n (a) (special food) régimen m, dieta f; **to be/go on a ~** estar*/ponerse* a régimen or a dieta; (before n) ⟨cola⟩ light adj inv (b) (nourishment) alimentación f, dieta f (alimenticia); **they live on a ~ of rice and fish** se alimentan de arroz y pescado

diet² vi hacer* régimen or dieta

differ /'dɪfər ‖'dɪfə(r)/ vi [1] (a) (be at variance) diferir*; **how do they ~?** ¿en qué difieren? (b) (be unlike) ser* distinto or diferente; **to ~ FROM sb/sth** diferenciarse or diferir* DE algn/algo [2] (disagree) discrepar, diferir* (frml)

difference /'dɪfrəns/ n diferencia f; **to tell the ~** notar or ver* la diferencia; **it could make a ~ in** o (BrE) **to the outcome** podría influir en el resultado; **it will make no ~ to you** a ti no te va a afectar

different /'dɪfrənt/ adj (a) (not the same) distinto, diferente; **~ FROM** o **TO** o (AmE also) **THAN sth/sb** distinto or diferente DE or A algo/algn (b) (unusual) diferente, original

differential /'dɪfə'rentʃəl ‖,dɪfə'renʃəl/ n diferencial m

differentiate /'dɪfə'rentʃieɪt ‖,dɪfə'renʃieɪt/ vi distinguir*

AmC	Central America	Arg	Argentina	Cu	Cuba
AmL	Latin America	Bol	Bolivia	Ec	Ecuador
AmS	South America	Chi	Chile	Esp	Spain
Andes	Andean Region	CS	Southern Cone	Méx	Mexico

Per	Peru
RPI	River Plate Area
Ur	Uruguay
Ven	Venezuela

■ ~ *vt* (frml): **to ~ sth (FROM sth)** diferenciar *or* distinguir* algo (DE algo)

differently /'dɪfrəntli/ *adv*: **they think ~ no** piensan igual *or* del mismo modo; **I view things ~** yo veo las cosas de otra forma *or* otro modo

difficult /'dɪfɪkəlt/ *adj* difícil; **the ~ part is ...** lo difícil es ..., la dificultad está en ...; **he's finding it ~ to give up smoking** le está resultando difícil dejar de fumar, le está costando dejar de fumar

difficulty /'dɪfɪkəlti/ *n* (*pl* **-ties**) **(a)** (of situation, task) dificultad *f*; **she had great ~ walking** caminaba con mucha dificultad **(b)** (problem) dificultad *f*, problema *m*; **to get into difficulties** meterse en líos

diffident /'dɪfədənt/ /'dɪfɪdənt/ *adj* ⟨person⟩ poco seguro de sí mismo; ⟨smile⟩ tímido

diffuse¹ /dɪ'fjuːz/ *vt* ⟨heat⟩ difundir, esparcir*; ⟨light⟩ tamizar*, difuminar; ⟨knowledge⟩ (frml) difundir

diffuse² /dɪ'fjuːs/ *adj* difuso

dig¹ /dɪg/ (*pres p* **digging**; *past & past p* **dug**) *vt* **1** ⟨ground⟩ cavar; ⟨hole/trench⟩ (by hand) cavar; (by machine) excavar **2** (jab, thrust) **to ~ sth INTO sth** clavar algo en algo
■ ~ *vi* **1** (excavate — by hand) cavar; (— by machine) excavar; «*dog*» escarbar; **to ~ for oil** hacer* prospecciones petrolíferas **2** (search) buscar*; **she dug in her pockets for the key** buscó la llave en los bolsillos
■ **dig up** [*v + o + adv, v + adv + o*] **(a)** ⟨lawn⟩ levantar; ⟨weeds/tree⟩ arrancar* **(b)** ⟨body/treasure⟩ desenterrar* **(c)** ⟨facts⟩ (colloq) sacar* a la luz

dig² *n* **1** (Archeol) excavación *f* **2** (jab — with elbow) codazo *m*; (— with pin) pinchazo *m* **3** (critical remark) (colloq) pulla *f*; (hint) indirecta *f*; **to have a ~ at sb/sth** meterse con algn/algo

digest¹ /daɪ'dʒest, də-/ /daɪ'dʒest, dɪ-/ *vt* ⟨food⟩ digerir*; (assimilate mentally) asimilar, digerir* (fam)

digest² /'daɪdʒest/ *n* (summary) compendio *m*; (journal) boletín *m*, revista *f*

digestible /daɪ'dʒestəbəl, də-/ /daɪ'dʒestəbəl, dɪ-/ *adj* (Physiol) digerible; (comprehensible) fácil de asimilar *or* (fam) digerir

digestion /daɪ'dʒestʃən, də-/ /daɪ'dʒestʃən, dɪ-/ *n* digestión *f*

digestive /daɪ'dʒestɪv, də-/ /daɪ'dʒestɪv, dɪ-/ *adj* digestivo

digger /'dɪgər/ /'dɪgə(r)/ *n* (machine) excavadora *f*; (person) excavador, -dora *m,f*

digit /'dɪdʒət/ /'dɪdʒɪt/ *n* **1** (Math) dígito *m* (frml) **2** (Anat) dedo *m*

digital /'dɪdʒətəl/ /'dɪdʒɪtl/ *adj* digital

digital: **~ camera** *n* cámara *f* (fotográfica) digital; **~ video disc** *n* videodisco *m* digital

dignified /'dɪgnəfaɪd/ /'dɪgnɪfaɪd/ *adj* **(a)** ⟨person/reply⟩ digno, circunspecto; ⟨silence/attitude⟩ digno **(b)** (stately) majestuoso

dignity /'dɪgnəti/ /-ɪ/ *n* (of person) dignidad *f*; (of occasion) solemnidad *f*

digress /daɪ'gres/ *vi*: **but I ~** pero estoy divagando; **to ~ FROM sth** apartarse DE algo

digression /daɪ'greʃən/ *n* digresión *f*

dike /daɪk/ *n* **1 (a)** (to keep out water) dique *m* **(b)** (causeway) terraplén *m* **(c)** (ditch) acequia *f* **2** ▶ DYKE 2

dilapidated /də'læpədeɪtəd/ /dɪ'læpɪdeɪtɪd/ *adj* ⟨building⟩ ruinoso; ⟨car⟩ destartalado

dilate /daɪ'leɪt/ *vi* dilatarse

dilemma /də'lemə, daɪ-/ /dɪ'lemə, daɪ-/ *n* dilema *m*

diligence /'dɪlədʒəns/ /'dɪlɪdʒəns/ *n* diligencia *f*

diligent /'dɪlədʒənt/ /'dɪlɪdʒənt/ *adj* ⟨worker⟩ diligente, cumplidor; ⟨student⟩ aplicado, diligente; ⟨work/study⟩ esmerado, concienzudo

dilute /daɪ'luːt/ /daɪ'ljuːt/ *vt* diluir*

dim¹ /dɪm/ *adj* **-mm-** **1 (a)** (dark) ⟨room⟩ oscuro, poco iluminado; ⟨light⟩ débil, tenue **(b)** (indistinct) ⟨memory/shape⟩ borroso; ⟨idea⟩ vago **(c)** (gloomy) ⟨prospects⟩ nada halagüeño, nada prometedor **2** (stupid) (colloq) corto (de luces) (fam), tonto (fam)

dim² *vt* **-mm-** ⟨lights⟩ atenuar*; **to ~ one's headlights** (AmE) poner* las (luces) cortas *or* de cruce *or* (AmL tb) las (luces) bajas

dime /daɪm/ *n* (AmE colloq) moneda de diez centavos

dimension /de'mentʃən, daɪ-/ /dɪ'menʃən, daɪ-/ *n* dimensión *f*

dime store *n* (AmE) tienda que vende artículos de bajo precio, ≈ baratillo *m*

diminish /də'mɪnɪʃ/ /dɪ'mɪnɪʃ/ *vi* «cost/number» disminuir*, reducirse*; «enthusiasm» disminuir*, apagarse*
■ ~ *vt* ⟨size/cost⟩ reducir*, disminuir*; ⟨enthusiasm⟩ disminuir*

diminutive /də'mɪnjətɪv/ /dɪ'mɪnjʊtɪv/ *adj* diminuto, minúsculo

dimly /'dɪmli/ *adv* ⟨shine⟩ débilmente; **a ~ lit room** una habitación poco iluminada *or* iluminada por una luz tenue

dimmer /'dɪmər/ /'dɪmə(r)/ *n* potenciómetro *m*, dimmer *m*

dimple /'dɪmpəl/ *n* (in cheeks, chin) hoyuelo *m*

dimwit /'dɪmwɪt/ *n* (colloq) tarado, -da (mental) *m,f* (fam)

din /dɪn/ *n* (colloq) (*no pl*) (of conversation, voices) barullo *m* (fam), bulla *f* (fam); (of drill, traffic) estruendo *m*, ruido *m*

dine /daɪn/ *vi* (frml) cenar

diner /'daɪnər/ /'daɪnə(r)/ *n* **1** (person) comensal *mf* **2 (a)** (restaurant) (AmE) cafetería *f* **(b)** ▶ DINING CAR

dinghy /'dɪŋi, 'dɪŋi/ *n* (*pl* **-ghies**) (sailing boat) bote *m*; (inflatable *o* rubber ~) bote *m* neumático

dingy /'dɪndʒi/ *adj* **-gier, -giest** ⟨building/room⟩ lúgubre, ⟨furnishings⟩ deslucido; (dirty) sucio

dining /'daɪnɪŋ/**:** **~ car** *n* coche *m* restaurante, coche *m* comedor; **~ room** *n* comedor *m*; **~ table** *n* mesa *f* (de comedor)

dinner /'dɪnər/ /'dɪnə(r)/ *n* **(a)** (in evening) cena *f*, comida *f* (AmL); **to eat** *o* **have ~** cenar, comer (AmL) **(b)** (formal) cena *f* (de gala) **(c)** (at midday) almuerzo *m*, comida *f* (esp Esp, Méx); **to eat** *o* **(BrE) have ~** almorzar*, comer (esp Esp, Méx)

dinner: **~ dance** *n* cena *f* con baile, comida *f* bailable (esp AmL), cena baile *f* (Méx); **~ jacket** *n* (esp BrE) esmoquin *m*, smoking *m*; **~ party** *n* cena *f*, comida *f* (AmL); **~ plate** *n* plato *m* llano *or* (Méx) plano *or* (RPl tb) playo *or* (Chi) bajo; **~** ⋯⋗

service n vajilla f; ~ **table** n mesa f; ~**time**
n (in evening) hora f de cenar or (esp AmL) de
comer; (at midday) hora f de almorzar or (esp Esp,
Méx) de comer

dinosaur /'daɪnəsɔːr ‖ 'daɪnəsɔː(r)/ n
dinosaurio m

dint /dɪnt/ n: **by** ~ **of sth** a fuerza de algo

diocese /'daɪəsəs ‖ 'daɪəsɪs/ n diócesis f

dip¹ /dɪp/ -**pp**- vt [1] **to** ~ **sth IN(TO) sth** meter
algo EN algo; (into liquid) mojar algo EN algo
[2] (Agr) ‹sheep› desinfectar (haciendo pasar por
un baño) [3] (a) (lower) ‹head› agachar, bajar (b)
(BrE Auto): **to** ~ **one's headlights** poner* las
(luces) cortas or de cruce or (AmL tb) las (luces)
bajas

■ ~ vi (a) (decrease) «sales/prices» bajar (b) (move
downward) «aircraft/bird» bajar en picada or (Esp)
en picado

dip² n [1] (swim) (colloq) (no pl) chapuzón m (fam)
[2] (Agr) baño m desinfectante [3] (depression,
hollow) hondonada f [4] (in sales, production) caída f,
descenso m [5] (Culin) salsa en la que se mojan
diferentes bocaditos (en una fiesta etc)

diphthong /'dɪfθɔːŋ ‖ 'dɪfθɒŋ/ n diptongo m

diploma /də'pləʊmə ‖ dɪ'pləʊmə/ n diploma m

diplomacy /də'pləʊməsi ‖ dɪ'pləʊməsi/ n
diplomacia f

diplomat /'dɪpləmæt/ n diplomático, -ca m,f

diplomatic /dɪplə'mætɪk/ adj (a) (Govt)
(before n) diplomático; ~ **immunity** inmunidad f
diplomática (b) (tactful) diplomático

dipstick /'dɪpstɪk/ n varilla f (medidora) del
aceite

dire /daɪr ‖ 'daɪə(r)/ adj **direr, direst** [1] (a)
‹news/consequences› funesto, nefasto; **to be in** ~
straits estar* en una situación desesperada (b)
(very bad) (BrE colloq) espantoso (fam), atroz
[2] (ominous) ‹warning› serio, grave [3] (desperate)
‹need/misery› extremo

direct¹ /də'rekt, daɪ- ‖ daɪ'rekt, dɪ-/ adj [1] (a)
‹route/flight› directo; ‹contact› directo; ‹cause/
consequence› directo (b) (Ling) (before n)
‹question/command› en estilo directo; ~
discourse o (BrE) **speech** estilo m directo [2] (frank,
straightforward) ‹person/manner› franco, directo;
‹question› directo

direct² adv [1] ‹write/phone› directamente; ‹go/
travel› (BrE) directo, directamente [2] (straight)
directamente; ~ **from Paris** (Rad, TV) en directo
desde París

direct³ vt [1] (a) (give directions to) indicarle* el
camino a (b) (address) ‹letter/parcel› mandar,
dirigir* [2] (aim) dirigir*; **it was** ~**ed at us** iba
dirigido a nosotros [3] ‹play/orchestra/traffic›
dirigir* [4] (order) (fml) ordenar; **to** ~ **sb to** + INF
ordenarle A algn QUE (+ subj)

■ ~ vi (Cin, Theat) dirigir*

direct: ~ **billing** /'bɪlɪŋ/ n (AmE) débito m
bancario or (Esp) domiciliación f de pagos; ~
current n corriente f continua; ~ **debit** n ► ~
BILLING; ~ **dialing**, (BrE) ~ **dialling** n discado
m directo or automático

direction /də'rekʃən, daɪ- ‖ daɪ'rekʃən, dɪ-/ n
[1] (course, compass point) dirección f; **sense of** ~
sentido m de (la) orientación; **in the** ~ **of** en
dirección a [2] (purpose): **he lacks** ~ no tiene un

norte [3] (supervision) dirección f [4] **directions**
pl (for route) indicaciones fpl; (for task, use, assembly)
instrucciones fpl, indicaciones fpl

directive /də'rektɪv, daɪ- ‖ daɪ'rektɪv, dɪ-/ n
directriz f, directiva f (esp AmL)

directly /də'rektli, daɪ- ‖ daɪ'rektli, dɪ-/ adv
[1] (a) (without stopping) ‹go/drive/fly›
directamente, directo (b) (without intermediaries)
‹report/deal› directamente; **he's** ~ **responsible** es
el responsable directo (c) (exactly) ‹opposite/
above› justo (d) (in genealogy) ‹related/descended›
por línea directa [2] (frankly, straightforwardly) ‹ask›
directamente; ‹speak› con franqueza [3] (now, at
once) inmediatamente, ahora mismo

director /də'rektər, daɪ- ‖ daɪ'rektə(r), dɪ-/ n
[1] (of company) directivo, -tiva m,f; (of department,
project) director, -tora m,f; see also MANAGING
DIRECTOR [2] (Cin, Theat) director, -tora m,f; (esp
AmE Mus) director, -tora m,f

directory /də'rektəri, daɪ- ‖ daɪ'rektəri, dɪ-/ n
(pl -**ries**) (a) (telephone ~) guía f telefónica or de
teléfonos, directorio m telefónico (Col, Méx) (b)
(index, yearbook) directorio m, guía f

dirt /dɜːrt ‖ dɜːt/ n suciedad f, mugre f

dirty¹ /'dɜːrti ‖ 'dɜːti/ adj -**tier, -tiest**
[1] (soiled) sucio; **to get** ~ ensuciarse [2] (a)
(obscene) ‹story/book› cochino (fam), guarro (Esp
fam); ‹leer/grin› lascivo; ‹joke› verde or (Méx)
colorado; ‹magazine› porno adj inv (b) (shameful)
‹job/work› sucio; **to do sb's** ~ **work** hacerle* el
trabajo sucio a algn

dirty² vt **dirties, dirtying, dirtied** ensuciar

dirty old man n (colloq) viejo m verde (fam)

disability /dɪsə'bɪləti/ n (pl -**ties**) (a) (state)
invalidez f, discapacidad f; (before n) ‹pension/
allowance› por invalidez (b) (particular handicap)
problema m

disable /dɪs'eɪbəl/ vt (a) «illness/accident/
injury» dejar inválido (or lisiado or ciego etc) (b)
‹machine/weapon› (Mil) inutilizar*

disabled /dɪs'eɪbəld/ adj discapacitado,
minusválido

disabuse /'dɪsə'bjuːz/ vt (fml) desengañar; **I
tried to** ~ **him of the notion that ...** intenté
sacarlo del error de que ...

disadvantage /'dɪsəd'væntɪdʒ
‖ ,dɪsəd'vɑːntɪdʒ/ n desventaja f, inconveniente
m; **to be at a** ~ estar* en desventaja

disadvantageous /dɪs'ædvæn'teɪdʒəs
‖ dɪs,ædvən'teɪdʒəs/ adj desventajoso,
desfavorable

disaffected /'dɪsə'fektəd ‖ ,dɪsə'fektɪd/ adj
desafecto

disagree /'dɪsə'griː/ vi [1] (a) (differ in opinion) **to**
~ (WITH sb/sth) no estar* de acuerdo (CON algn/
algo), discrepar (DE algn/algo) (fml) (b) (conflict)
«figures/accounts» no coincidir, discrepar
[2] (cause discomfort) ‹food› **to** ~ **WITH sb**
sentarle* or caerle* mal a algn

disagreeable /'dɪsə'griːəbəl/ adj ‹smell/
experience/person› desagradable; ‹task/job›
ingrato, desagradable

disagreement /'dɪsə'griːmənt/ n (a) (difference
of opinion) desacuerdo m, disconformidad f (b)
(quarrel) discusión f (c) (disparity) discrepancia f

disallow /'dɪsə'laʊ/ vt (fml) ‹claim/evidence›
(Law) rechazar*, desestimar; ‹goal› anular

disappear /ˌdɪsəˈpɪr ‖ˌdɪsəˈpɪə(r)/ vi **(a)** (become invisible) desaparecer* **(b)** (go away) «pain/problems» desaparecer*, irse*; «worries/fears» desvanecerse*

disappearance /ˌdɪsəˈpɪrəns ‖ˌdɪsəˈpɪərəns/ n desaparición f

disappoint /ˌdɪsəˈpɔɪnt/ vt ⟨person⟩ decepcionar; ⟨hopes/desires⟩ defraudar

disappointed /ˌdɪsəˈpɔɪntəd ‖ˌdɪsəˈpɔɪntɪd/ adj (pred) to be ~ estar* desilusionado or decepcionado; I'm ~ with the results los resultados me han decepcionado

disappointing /ˌdɪsəˈpɔɪntɪŋ/ adj decepcionante

disappointment /ˌdɪsəˈpɔɪntmənt/ n **(a)** (emotion) desilusión f, decepción f **(b)** (letdown) decepción f, chasco m

disapproval /ˌdɪsəˈpruːvəl/ n desaprobación f

disapprove /ˌdɪsəˈpruːv/ vi: he ~s of smoking está en contra del tabaco or del cigarrillo; she ~s of her son's fiancée no tiene buen concepto de la novia de su hijo

disapproving /ˌdɪsəˈpruːvɪŋ/ adj ⟨tone/look⟩ de reproche

disarm /dɪsˈɑːrm ‖dɪsˈɑːm/ vt ⏍**1** ⟨troops/opposition⟩ desarmar; ⟨bomb/mine⟩ desactivar; ⟨criticism⟩ desbaratar ⏍**2** (win confidence of) desarmar

■ ~ vi desarmarse

disarmament /dɪsˈɑːrməmənt ‖dɪsˈɑːməmənt/ n desarme m

disarming /dɪsˈɑːrmɪŋ ‖dɪsˈɑːmɪŋ/ adj que desarma

disarray /ˌdɪsəˈreɪ/ n (of political party) desorganización f; (of appearance) desaliño m; her papers were in total ~ sus papeles estaban completamente desordenados

disassociate /ˌdɪsəˈsəʊʃieɪt, -sieɪt/ vt ▶ DISSOCIATE

disaster /dɪˈzæstər ‖dɪˈzɑːstə(r)/ n ⏍**1** (flood, earthquake) catástrofe f, desastre m; (crash, sinking) siniestro m, desastre m; (before n) ~ fund fondo m para los damnificados ⏍**2** **(a)** (fiasco) desastre m **(b)** (hopeless person) (colloq) desastre m (fam) ⏍**3** (misfortune): ~ struck ocurrió or se produjo una catástrofe

disaster area n zona f siniestrada, zona f de desastre; my room is a real ~ ~ (colloq & hum) mi habitación está hecha un desastre (fam)

disastrous /dɪˈzæstrəs ‖dɪˈzɑːstrəs/ adj desastroso, catastrófico

disband /dɪsˈbænd/ vt ⟨organization⟩ disolver*; ⟨army⟩ licenciar

■ ~ vi «organization» disolverse*; «group» desbandarse

disbelief /ˌdɪsbəˈliːf/ n incredulidad f

disbelieve /ˌdɪsbəˈliːv/ vt (fml) ⟨statement⟩ no creer*; ⟨person⟩ no creerle* a

disc /dɪsk/ n (esp BrE) ▶ DISK

discard /dɪsˈkɑːrd ‖dɪsˈkɑːd/ vt **(a)** (dispose of) desechar, deshacerse* de **(b)** ⟨idea/belief⟩ desechar **(c)** (shed) ⟨skin/leaves⟩ mudar **(d)** (take off) ⟨clothing⟩ desembarazarse* de

discern /dɪˈsɜːrn ‖dɪˈsɜːn/ vt (fml) distinguir*, percibir

discerning /dɪˈsɜːrnɪŋ ‖dɪˈsɜːnɪŋ/ adj ⟨reader/customer⟩ exigente, con criterio; ⟨palate/taste⟩ exigente, fino; ⟨ear/eye⟩ educado

discharge¹ /dɪsˈtʃɑːrdʒ ‖dɪsˈtʃɑːdʒ/ vt ⏍**1** **(a)** (release) ⟨prisoner⟩ liberar, poner* en libertad; ⟨patient⟩ dar* de alta; ⟨juror⟩ dispensar; ⟨bankrupt⟩ rehabilitar **(b)** (dismiss) (fml) despedir* ⏍**2** **(a)** (send out) ⟨fumes⟩ despedir*; ⟨electricity⟩ descargar*; ⟨sewage/waste⟩ verter* **(b)** (unload) ⟨cargo⟩ descargar* **(c)** (shoot) ⟨volley/broadside⟩ descargar* ⏍**3** **(a)** ⟨duty⟩ cumplir con **(b)** ⟨debt⟩ saldar, liquidar

discharge² /ˈdɪstʃɑːrdʒ ‖ˈdɪstʃɑːdʒ/ n ⏍**1** (release — from army) baja f; (— from hospital) alta f; (— from prison) puesta f en libertad ⏍**2** **(a)** (Med) secreción f; (vaginal ~) flujo m (vaginal) **(b)** (of toxic fumes, gases) emisión f; (of sewage, waste) vertido m **(c)** (Elec) descarga f ⏍**3** (of debt, liabilities) liquidación f, pago m; (of duty) (frml) cumplimiento m

disciple /dɪˈsaɪpəl/ n (Relig) discípulo, -la m,f; (adherent) seguidor, -dora m,f

disciplinary /ˈdɪsəplənəri ‖ˌdɪsɪˈplɪnəri/ adj disciplinario

discipline¹ /ˈdɪsəplən ‖ˈdɪsɪplɪn/ n disciplina f

discipline² vt **(a)** (control) ⟨child/pupils⟩ disciplinar; ⟨emotions⟩ controlar **(b)** (punish) ⟨employee⟩ sancionar **(c)** (train) ⟨body/mind⟩ disciplinar

disc jockey n disc(-)jockey mf, pinchadiscos mf (Esp fam)

disclaim /dɪsˈkleɪm/ vt (deny): she ~ed all knowledge of his whereabouts negó conocer su paradero; he ~ed any connection with him negó tener ninguna relación con él

disclaimer /dɪsˈkleɪmər ‖dɪsˈkleɪmə(r)/ n (Law) descargo m de responsabilidad

disclose /dɪsˈkləʊz/ vt revelar

disclosure /dɪsˈkləʊʒər ‖dɪsˈkləʊʒə(r)/ n revelación f

disco /ˈdɪskəʊ/ n (pl **-cos**) discoteca f, disco f (fam)

discolor, (BrE) **discolour** /dɪsˈkʌlər ‖dɪsˈkʌlə(r)/ vt (fade) decolorar; (stain) dejar amarillento, manchar

discomfort /dɪsˈkʌmfərt ‖dɪsˈkʌmfət/ n **(a)** (lack of comfort) incomodidad f; (pain) molestia(s) f(pl), malestar m **(b)** (emotional, mental) inquietud f, desasosiego m

disconcert /ˌdɪskənˈsɜːrt ‖ˌdɪskənˈsɜːt/ vt desconcertar*

disconcerting /ˌdɪskənˈsɜːrtɪŋ ‖ˌdɪskənˈsɜːtɪŋ/ adj desconcertante

disconnect /ˌdɪskəˈnekt/ vt desconectar; I didn't pay my bills, so I was ~ed me cortaron el teléfono (or el gas etc) por no pagar

discontent /ˌdɪskənˈtent/ n descontento m

discontented /ˌdɪskənˈtentəd ‖ˌdɪskənˈtentɪd/ adj descontento

discontinue /ˌdɪskənˈtɪnjuː/ vt ⟨production⟩ suspender; ⟨model⟩ discontinuar*, descontinuar*; ⟨action/suit⟩ (Law) desistir de

discord /ˈdɪskɔːrd ‖ˈdɪskɔːd/ n ⏍**1** (conflict) ⋯⊱

discordia f ② (Mus) **(a)** (lack of harmony) discordancia f, disonancia f **(b)** (chord) acorde m disonante

discotheque /'dɪskətek/ n ▶ DISCO

discount¹ /'dɪskaʊnt/ n descuento m; **at a ~** ⟨sell⟩ con descuento, a precio reducido; (before n) ⟨store⟩ de saldos; ⟨goods⟩ de saldo

discount² /'dɪskaʊnt, dɪs'kaʊnt ‖dɪs'kaʊnt/ vt ① (Busn) **(a)** ⟨amount⟩ descontar* **(b)** ⟨goods⟩ rebajar **(c)** ⟨price⟩ reducir* ② (disregard) ⟨possibility⟩ descartar; ⟨claim/criticism⟩ pasar por alto

discourage /dɪs'kʌrɪdʒ ‖dɪs'kʌrɪdʒ/ vt **(a)** (depress) desalentar*, desanimar **(b)** (deter) ⟨crime/speculation⟩ poner* freno a; ⟨burglar⟩ ahuyentar, disuadir **(c)** (dissuade) **to ~ sb FROM -ING: she ~d me from taking the exam** trató de convencerme de que no me presentara al examen

discouraging /dɪs'kʌrɪdʒɪŋ ‖dɪs'kʌrɪdʒɪŋ/ adj ⟨news/result⟩ desalentador, descorazonador

discourse /'dɪskɔːrs ‖'dɪskɔːs/ n (fml) **(a)** (dissertation) disertación f **(b)** (talk) conversación f

discourteous /dɪs'kɜːrtiəs/ adj descortés

discover /dɪs'kʌvər ‖dɪs'kʌvə(r)/ vt descubrir*

discoverer /dɪs'kʌvərər ‖dɪs'kʌvərə(r)/ n descubridor, -dora m,f

discovery /dɪs'kʌvəri/ n (pl **-ries**) descubrimiento m

discredit¹ /dɪs'kredət ‖dɪs'kredɪt/ vt desacreditar

discredit² n descrédito m

discreet /dɪs'kriːt/ adj **(a)** (tactful) ⟨person/inquiries⟩ discreto **(b)** (restrained) ⟨elegance/colors⟩ discreto, sobrio

discreetly /dɪs'kriːtli/ adv discretamente, con discreción

discrepancy /dɪs'krepənsi/ n (pl **-cies**) discrepancia f

discretion /dɪs'kreʃən/ n ① (tact) discreción f ② (judgment) criterio m; **at the committee's ~** a criterio or a discreción de la comisión

discretionary /dɪs'kreʃəneri ‖dɪs'kreʃənəri, -ənri/ adj discrecional

discriminate /dɪs'krɪməneɪt ‖dɪ'skrɪmɪneɪt/ vi ① (act with prejudice) hacer* discriminaciones, discriminar; **to ~ AGAINST sb** discriminar a algn ② **(a)** (distinguish) distinguir*, discriminar **(b)** (be discerning) discernir*, utilizar* el sentido crítico

discriminating /dɪs'krɪməneɪtɪŋ ‖dɪ'skrɪmɪneɪtɪŋ/ adj (discerning) ⟨critic/customer⟩ exigente; ⟨judgment⟩ sagaz; ⟨taste⟩ refinado, educado

discrimination /dɪs'krɪmə'neɪʃən ‖dɪˌskrɪmɪ'neɪʃən/ n ① (unfair treatment) discriminación f ② (discernment) criterio m, discernimiento m

discus /'dɪskəs/ n (pl **-cuses**) disco m

discuss /dɪs'kʌs/ vt (talk about) ⟨person⟩ hablar de; ⟨topic⟩ hablar de, tratar; ⟨debate⟩ debatir; ⟨plan/problem⟩ discutir

discussion /dɪs'kʌʃən/ n discusión f, debate m

disdain /dɪs'deɪn/ n desdén m

disdainful /dɪs'deɪnfəl/ adj ⟨manner/tone⟩ despectivo, desdeñoso

disease /dɪ'ziːz/ n enfermedad f, dolencia f (fml)

diseased /dɪ'ziːzd/ adj ⟨organ/tissue⟩ afectado; ⟨plant/animal⟩ enfermo

disembark /'dɪsəm'bɑːrk ‖ˌdɪsɪm'bɑːk/ vi desembarcar*

disembodied /'dɪsəm'bɑːdid ‖ˌdɪsɪm'bɒdid/ adj incorpóreo

disembowel /'dɪsəm'baʊəl ‖ˌdɪsɪm'baʊəl/ vt, (BrE) **-ll-** destripar

disenchanted /'dɪsɪn'tʃæntəd ‖ˌdɪsɪn'tʃɑːntɪd/ adj **to be ~ WITH sb/sth** estar* desilusionado CON or DE algn/DE algo

disenfranchise /'dɪsɪn'fræntʃaɪz ‖ˌdɪsɪn'fræntʃaɪz/ vt ⟨person⟩ privar del derecho al voto; ⟨place⟩ privar del derecho de representación

disengage /'dɪsɪn'geɪdʒ ‖ˌdɪsɪn'geɪdʒ/ vt ① **(a)** (extricate) soltar* **(b)** (Mil) ⟨troops/forces⟩ retirar ② (Tech) ⟨gears/mechanism⟩ desconectar

disentangle /'dɪsɪn'tæŋgəl ‖ˌdɪsɪn'tæŋgəl/ vt ⟨rope/hair/wool⟩ desenredar, desenmarañar; ⟨mystery⟩ esclarecer*, desentrañar

disfavor, (BrE) **disfavour** /dɪs'feɪvər ‖dɪs'feɪvə(r)/ n (fml) desaprobación f

disfigure /dɪs'fɪgjər ‖dɪs'fɪgə(r)/ vt ⟨face/person⟩ desfigurar; ⟨landscape/building⟩ afear, estropear

disgrace¹ /dɪs'greɪs/ n vergüenza f, **she was sent upstairs in ~** la mandaron arriba castigada

disgrace² vt **(a)** (bring shame on) ⟨person/family/school⟩ deshonrar **(b)** (destroy reputation of) ⟨enemy/politician⟩ desacreditar

disgraceful /dɪs'greɪsfəl/ adj vergonzoso

disgruntled /dɪs'grʌntld/ adj ⟨child/look⟩ contrariado; ⟨employee⟩ descontento

disguise¹ /dɪs'gaɪz/ vt **(a)** ⟨person⟩ disfrazar*; ⟨voice⟩ cambiar **(b)** (conceal) ⟨mistake⟩ ocultar; ⟨disapproval/contempt⟩ disimular

disguise² n disfraz m; **in ~** disfrazado

disgust¹ /dɪs'gʌst/ vt darle* asco a

disgust² n (revulsion) indignación f; (physical, stronger) asco m, repugnancia f; **she stormed out of the meeting in ~** salió indignada or furiosa de la reunión

disgusted /dɪs'gʌstəd ‖dɪs'gʌstɪd/ adj indignado; (stronger) asqueado

disgusting /dɪs'gʌstɪŋ/ adj **(a)** ⟨smell/taste/food⟩ asqueroso, repugnante **(b)** ⟨conduct/attitude⟩ vergonzoso

dish /dɪʃ/ n ① **(a)** (plate) plato m; (serving ~) fuente f; **to wash the ~es** lavar los platos **(b)** (amount) plato m ② (Culin) plato m ③ (Telec, TV) antena f parabólica

■ **dish up** [*v* + *o* + *adv, v* + *adv* + *o*] [*v* + *adv*] (Culin) servir*

dishcloth /'dɪʃklɔ:θ ‖'dɪʃklʊθ/ *n* **(a)** (for drying) paño *m* de cocina, repasador *m* (RPl); limpión *m* (Col) **(b)** (BrE) ▶ DISHRAG

disheartening /dɪs'hɑ:rtn̩ɪŋ ‖dɪs'hɑ:tn̩ɪŋ/ *adj* descorazonador, desalentador

disheveled, (BrE) **dishevelled** /dɪ'ʃevəld/ *adj* despeinado

dishonest /dɪs'ɑ:nəst ‖dɪs'ɒnɪst/ *adj* ⟨person/ answer⟩ deshonesto; ⟨dealings/means⟩ fraudulento, deshonesto

dishonesty /dɪs'ɑ:nəsti ‖dɪs'ɒnɪsti/ *n* deshonestidad *f*, falta *f* de honradez; (of statement) falsedad *f*; (of dealings) fraudulencia *f*

dishonor, (BrE) **dishonour** /dɪs'ɑ:nər ‖dɪs'ɒnə(r)/ *n* deshonra *f*, deshonor *m*

dishonorable, (BrE) **dishonourable** /dɪs'ɑ:nərəbəl ‖dɪs'ɒnərəbəl/ *adj* deshonroso

dish: ~**rag** *n* (AmE) trapo *m*, bayeta *f*, fregón *m* (RPl); ~ **soap** *n* (AmE) lavavajillas *m*, detergente *m*; ~**towel** *n* ▶ DISHCLOTH A; ~**washer** /'dɪʃ'wɔ:ʃər ‖'dɪʃ,wɒʃə(r)/ *n* (machine) lavaplatos *m*, lavavajillas *m*; ~**washing liquid** /'dɪʃ,wɔ:ʃɪŋ ‖'dɪʃ,wɒʃɪŋ/ *n* (AmE) ▶ ~ SOAP; ~**water** *n* agua *f*; de fregar *or* de lavar los platos

disillusion /'dɪsə'lu:ʒən ‖,dɪsɪ'lu:ʒən/ *vt* desilusionar

disillusionment /'dɪsə'lu:ʒənmənt ‖,dɪsɪ'lu:ʒənmənt/ *n* desilusión *f*

disinfect /'dɪsɪn'fekt ‖,dɪsɪm'fekt/ *vt* desinfectar

disinfectant /'dɪsɪn'fektənt ‖,dɪsɪm'fektənt/ *n* desinfectante *m*

disinformation /,dɪsɪnfər'meɪʃən ‖,dɪsɪnfə'meɪʃən/ *n* desinformación *f*

disinherit /'dɪsɪn'herət ‖,dɪsɪm'herɪt/ *vt* desheredar

disintegrate /dɪs'ɪntəgreɪt ‖dɪs'ɪntɪgreɪt/ *vi* desintegrarse

disintegration /dɪs'ɪntə'greɪʃən ‖dɪs,ɪntɪ'greɪʃən/ *n* desintegración *f*

disinterested /dɪs'ɪntrəstəd ‖dɪs'ɪntrəstɪd/ *adj* ⟨decision/advice⟩ imparcial; ⟨action⟩ desinteresado

disjointed /dɪs'dʒɔɪntəd ‖dɪs'dʒɔɪntɪd/ *adj* inconexo, deshilvanado

disk /dɪsk/ *n* **(a)** (flat, circular object) disco *m* **(b)** (Comput, Audio, Anat) disco *m*

disk drive *n* unidad *f* de disco

diskette /dɪs'ket/ *n* disquete *m*

dislike[1] /dɪs'laɪk/ *vt*: I ~ dogs no me gustan los perros; **he** ~**s wearing a tie** le desagrada *or* no le gusta llevar corbata

dislike[2] *n* **(a)** (emotion): **I have a strong** ~ **of dogs** no me gustan nada los perros, (les) tengo aversión a los perros; **to take a** ~ **to sb** tomarle antipatía a algn **(b)** (sth disliked): **you'll have to tell us all your likes and** ~**s** tendrás que decirnos lo que te gusta y lo que no te gusta

dislocate /'dɪsləkərt/ *vt* (Med) dislocarse*

dislodge /dɪs'lɑ:dʒ ‖dɪs'lɒdʒ/ *vt* (shift, remove) sacar*; **the wind** ~**d some tiles** el viento causó que se soltaran varias tejas

disloyal /dɪs'lɔɪəl/ *adj* desleal

dismal /'dɪzməl/ *adj* **(a)** (gloomy) ⟨place/tone⟩

sombrío, deprimente, lúgubre **(b)** (very bad) ⟨news/prophecy⟩ funesto; ⟨future⟩ muy negro; ⟨weather⟩ malísimo; ⟨results/performance⟩ pésimo

dismantle /dɪs'mæntl/ *vt* ⟨machinery/ furniture⟩ desmontar; ⟨organization⟩ desmantelar

dismay[1] /dɪs'meɪ/ *n* consternación *f*; **they looked at him in** *o* **with** ~ **lo** miraron consternados; **much to my/his** ~ para mi/su desgracia

dismay[2] *vt* consternar

dismember /dɪs'membər ‖dɪs'membə(r)/ *vt* ⟨animal⟩ descuartizar*; ⟨corpse⟩ desmembrar*

dismiss /dɪs'mɪs/ *vt* [1] **(a)** ⟨employee⟩ despedir*; ⟨executive, minister⟩ destituir* **(b)** (send away) ⟨class⟩ dejar salir [2] ⟨possibility/ suggestion⟩ descartar, desechar; ⟨request/petition/ claim⟩ desestimar, rechazar* [3] (Law) ⟨charge/ appeal⟩ desestimar; **to** ~ **a case** sobreseer* una causa

dismissal /dɪs'mɪsəl/ *n* **(a)** (of employee) despido *m*; (of executive, minister) destitución *f* **(b)** (sending away) autorización *f* para retirarse **(c)** (of theory, request) rechazo *m* **(d)** (Law) desestimación *f*

dismount /dɪs'maʊnt/ *vi* desmontar

disobedience /'dɪsə'bi:diəns/ *n* desobediencia *f*

disobedient /'dɪsə'bi:diənt/ *adj* desobediente

disobey /'dɪsə'beɪ/ *vt* [1] desobedecer*

disorder /dɪs'ɔ:rdər ‖dɪs'ɔ:də(r)/ *n* [1] **(a)** (confusion) desorden *m* **(b)** (unrest) desórdenes *mpl*, disturbios *mpl* [2] (Med) afección *f* (frml), problema *m*

disorderly /dɪs'ɔ:rdərli ‖dɪs'ɔ:dəli/ *adj* **(a)** (untidy) desordenado **(b)** (unruly) ⟨crowd⟩ alborotado; ⟨person⟩ revoltoso; ~ **conduct** alteración *f* del orden público

disorganized /dɪs'ɔ:rgənaɪzd ‖dɪs'ɔ:gənaɪzd/ *adj* desorganizado

disorient /dɪs'ɔ:rient/, **disorientate** /dɪs'ɔ:riəntert/ *vt* desorientar

disown /dɪs'əʊn/ *vt* **(a)** (repudiate) renegar* de, repudiar **(b)** (deny responsibility for) no reconocer* como propio

disparaging /dɪs'pærədʒɪŋ/ *adj* desdeñoso, despreciativo

disparity /dɪs'pærəti/ *n* (inequality) disparidad *f*; (difference) discrepancia *f*

dispassionate /dɪs'pæʃənət/ *adj* ⟨account⟩ desapasionado, objetivo; ⟨adjudication/onlooker⟩ imparcial

dispatch[1] /dɪ'spætʃ/ *vt* [1] (send) despachar, enviar* [2] **(a)** (carry out) (frml) ⟨task/duty⟩ despachar **(b)** (kill) (euph) ⟨person/animal⟩ despachar (euf) **(c)** (consume) (hum) ⟨food/drink⟩ despacharse (hum)

dispatch[2] *n* [1] (message) despacho *m*; (Mil) parte *m* [2] (sending) despacho *m*, envío *m*, expedición *f*

dispel /dɪ'spel/ *vt* **-ll-** **(a)** ⟨doubts/fear⟩ disipar, hacer* desvanecer **(b)** ⟨fog⟩ disipar

dispensary /dɪ'spensəri/ *n* (*pl* **-ries**) (in hospital) dispensario *m*, farmacia *f*; (in school) enfermería *f*

dispensation /'dɪspən'seɪʃən/ *n* [1] **(a)** (exemption) exención *f* **(b)** (Relig) dispensa *f* [2] (of justice) administración *f*

d

dispense /dɪ'spens/ vt **1** (a) ⟨grants/alms⟩ dar*; ⟨advice⟩ ofrecer*, dar*; ⟨favors⟩ conceder* (b) «machine» ⟨coffee/soap⟩ expender **2** ⟨drugs/ prescription⟩ despachar, preparar **3** (administer) ⟨justice⟩ administrar
■ **dispense with** [v + prep + o] prescindir de

dispenser /dɪ'spensə(r)/ n (device): **a cash** ~ un cajero automático; **a soap** ~ un dispositivo que suministra jabón

disperse /dɪ'spɜːrs ‖dɪ'spɜːs/ vt dispersar
■ ~ vi dispersarse

dispirited /dɪ'spɪrətəd ‖dɪ'spɪrɪtɪd/ adj ⟨person⟩ desanimado, abatido

displace /dɪs'pleɪs/ vt (a) (Phys) ⟨liquid/ volume⟩ desplazar* (b) (replace) reemplazar* (c) (force from home) ⟨refugees/workers⟩ desplazar*

display¹ /dɪ'spleɪ/ vt (a) (put on show) ⟨exhibit⟩ exponer*; ⟨data/figures⟩ (Comput) visualizar* (b) (flaunt) ⟨finery/erudition⟩ hacer* despliegue or gala de; ⟨muscles⟩ lucir*, hacer* alarde de (c) (reveal) ⟨anger/interest⟩ demostrar*, manifestar*; ⟨feelings⟩ exteriorizar*, demostrar*; ⟨tendencies/ symptoms⟩ presentar; ⟨skill/courage⟩ demostrar*

display² n **1** (a) (exhibition) exposición f, muestra f; (show) show m; **to be on** ~ ⟨«painting/ wares»⟩ estar* expuesto; (before n) ~ **cabinet** vitrina f (b) (of feeling) exteriorización f, demostración f; (of courage, strength, knowledge) despliegue m; (of ignorance) demostración f **2** (Comput, Electron) display m, visualizador m **3** (Journ, Print) (before n) ~ **advertising** anuncios mpl destacados

displease /dɪs'pliːz/ vt desagradar, contrariar*

displeasure /dɪs'pleʒər ‖dɪs'pleʒə(r)/ n desagrado m

disposable /dɪ'spəʊzəbəl/ adj **1** ⟨cup/razor/ pen⟩ desechable, de usar y tirar **2** ⟨income⟩ disponible

disposal /dɪ'spəʊzəl/ n **1** (removal, riddance): **the problem of the** ~ **of waste** el problema de cómo deshacerse de residuos; **arrangements were made for the** ~ **of the body** se hicieron arreglos para que el cadáver fuera inhumado (or trasladado al crematorio etc) **2** (power to use) disposición f; **to have sth at one's** ~ disponer* de algo, tener* algo a su (or mi etc) disposición

disposed /dɪ'spəʊzd/ adj (pred) (a) (inclined) **to be** ~ **to + INF** estar* dispuesto A + INF (b) (liable) (frml) **to be** ~ **TO sth** ser* propenso A algo, tener* propensión A algo

dispose of /dɪ'spəʊz/ [v + prep + o] **1** (a) (get rid of) ⟨refuse/evidence⟩ deshacerse* de; ⟨rival/ opponent⟩ deshacerse* de, liquidar (fam) (b) (sell) ⟨house/car/land⟩ vender, enajenar (frml) (c) (deal with) ⟨problem/question/objection⟩ despachar **2** (have use of) (frml) ⟨funds/resources⟩ disponer* de

disposition /dɪspə'zɪʃən/ n **1** (a) (personality) manera f or modo m de ser, temperamento m (b) (inclination) (no pl) (frml) ~ **TO sth** predisposición f A algo **2** (arrangement) disposición f

dispossess /dɪspə'zes/ vt (frml) **to** ~ **sb OF sth** desposeer* or despojar a algn DE algo (frml)

disproportionate /dɪsprə'pɔːrʃnət ‖dɪsprə'pɔːʃənət/ adj ⟨number/size⟩ desproporcionado

disprove /dɪs'pruːv/ vt ⟨claim/assertion/charge⟩ desmentir*; ⟨doctrine/theory⟩ rebatir, refutar

dispute¹ /dɪ'spjuːt/ n (a) (controversy, clash) polémica f, controversia f (b) (debate) discusión f; (quarrel) disputa f (c) (Lab Rel) conflicto m (laboral)

dispute² vt **1** (a) (contest) discutir, cuestionar (b) ⟨will/decision⟩ impugnar (c) (argue) ⟨point/ question⟩ debatir, discutir (d) **disputed** past p ⟨decision⟩ discutido, polémico; ⟨territory⟩ en litigio **2** (fight for) ⟨possession/victory/territory⟩ disputarse

disqualify /dɪs'kwɑːləfaɪ ‖dɪs'kwɒlɪfaɪ/ vt **-fies, -fying, -fied** (a) (make ineligible): **as a professional she was disqualified from entering the Olympics** el hecho de ser profesional le impedía participar en las Olimpíadas; **a criminal record disqualifies you from jury service** tener antecedentes penales inhabilita para ser miembro de un jurado (b) (debar) (Sport) descalificar*

disquiet /dɪs'kwaɪət/ n (frml) inquietud f, intranquilidad f, desasosiego m

disregard¹ /dɪsrɪ'gɑːrd ‖dɪsrɪ'gɑːd/ vt ⟨danger/difficulty⟩ ignorar, despreciar; ⟨advice⟩ hacer* caso omiso de, no prestar atención a; ⟨feelings/wishes⟩ no tener* en cuenta

disregard² n ~ **FOR sth/sb** indiferencia f HACIA algo/algn

disrepair /dɪsrɪ'per ‖dɪsrɪ'peə(r)/ n mal estado m; **to be in (a state of)** ~ estar* en mal estado

disreputable /dɪs'repjətəbəl ‖dɪs'repjʊtəbəl/ adj ⟨person/firm⟩ de dudosa reputación, de mala fama; ⟨nightclub/district⟩ de mala fama; ⟨conduct/ action⟩ vergonzoso

disrepute /dɪsrɪ'pjuːt/ n (frml): **to fall into** ~ caer* en descrédito; **to bring sth into** ~ desacreditar algo

disrespect /dɪsrɪ'spekt/ n ~ (**FOR sth**) falta f de respeto (HACIA algo); **I meant no** ~ no fue mi intención ofenderlo, no quise faltarle al or (CS) el respeto

disrespectful /dɪsrɪ'spektfəl/ adj ⟨person⟩ irrespetuoso; ⟨attitude⟩ irreverente

disrupt /dɪs'rʌpt/ vt ⟨meeting/class⟩ perturbar el desarrollo de; ⟨traffic/communications⟩ crear problemas de, afectar a; ⟨plans⟩ desbaratar, trastocar*

disruption /dɪs'rʌpʃən/ n trastorno m

disruptive /dɪs'rʌptɪv/ adj ⟨influence⟩ perjudicial, negativo; **a** ~ **pupil** un alumno problema

dissatisfaction /dɪssætəs'fækʃən ‖dɪssætɪs'fækʃən/ n descontento m, insatisfacción f

dissatisfied /dɪs'sætəsfaɪd ‖dɪs'sætɪsfaɪd/ adj descontento, insatisfecho

dissect /dɪ'sekt, daɪ-/ vt ⟨animal/body⟩ diseccionar, hacer* la disección de

disseminate /dɪ'seməneɪt ‖dɪ'semɪneɪt/ vt (frml) diseminar

dissent /dɪ'sent/ n (frml) desacuerdo m

dissertation /dɪsər'teɪʃən ‖dɪsə'teɪʃən/ n (in US: for PhD) tesis f (doctoral); (in UK: for lower degree) tesis f, tesina f

disservice /ˈdɪsˈsɜːrvəs ‖dɪsˈsɜːvɪs/ *n* (fml): this report does him a ~ este informe no le hace justicia

dissident /ˈdɪsədənt ‖ˈdɪsɪdənt/ *n* disidente *mf*

dissimilar /dɪˈsɪmələr ‖dɪˈsɪmɪlə(r)/ *adj* distinto, diferente

dissipate /ˈdɪsəpeɪt ‖ˈdɪsɪpeɪt/ *vt* (fml) **(a)** (squander) ⟨inheritance⟩ disipar, dilapidar; ⟨energy/talents⟩ desperdiciar **(b)** (dispel) ⟨anxiety⟩ disipar, hacer* desvanecer
■ ~ *vi* (fml) «anger/doubts» disiparse, desvanecerse*

dissociate /dɪˈsəʊʃieɪt, -sieɪt/ *vt* **(a)** (separate) disociar **(b)** (distance) **to** ~ **oneself FROM sb/sth** desvincularse DE algn/algo

dissolute /ˈdɪsəluːt/ *adj* disoluto

dissolve /dɪˈzɑːlv ‖dɪˈzɒlv/ *vt* disolver*
■ ~ *vi* disolverse*

dissuade /dɪˈsweɪd/ *vt* **to** ~ **sb** (FROM sth) disuadir a algn (DE algo); **I managed to** ~ **her from leaving** logré convencerla de que no se fuera

distance¹ /ˈdɪstəns/ *n* distancia *f*; **in the (far)** ~ en la distancia *or* lejanía, a lo lejos; **to keep one's** ~ (remain aloof) guardar las distancias; (lit: keep away) no acercarse*

distance² *v refl* **to** ~ **oneself** (FROM sb/sth) (emotionally) distanciarse (DE algn/algo); (deny involvement) desvincularse (DE algn/algo)

distance learning *n* enseñanza *f* a distancia

distant /ˈdɪstənt/ *adj* ⟨spot/country⟩ distante, lejano; ⟨relative⟩ lejano; **in the** ~ **past** en el pasado remoto

distantly /ˈdɪstəntli/ *adv* ⟨hear/see⟩ en la lejanía; **we are** ~ **related** somos parientes lejanos

distaste /dɪsˈteɪst/ *n* desagrado *m*

distasteful /dɪsˈteɪstfəl/ *adj* **(a)** (unpleasant) ⟨task/chore⟩ desagradable **(b)** (offensive) ⟨remark/picture⟩ de mal gusto

distend /dɪˈstend/ *vt* dilatar, hinchar
■ ~ *vi* dilatarse, hincharse

distill, (BrE) **distil** *vt* **-ll-** /dɪˈstɪl/ destilar

distillery /dɪˈstɪləri/ *n* (*pl* **-ries**) destilería *f*

distinct /dɪˈstɪŋkt/ *adj* **1** ⟨shape/outline⟩ definido, claro, nítido; ⟨likeness⟩ obvio, marcado; ⟨improvement⟩ decidido, marcado; ⟨possibility⟩ nada desdeñable **2** (different, separate) distinto, bien diferenciado; **we are talking about English people as** ~ **from British people** nos referimos a los ingleses en particular y no a los británicos

distinction /dɪˈstɪŋkʃən/ *n* **1 (a)** (difference) distinción *f*; **we must make** *o* **draw a** ~ **between ... debemos distinguir entre ... (b)** (act of differentiating) distinción *f*; **without** ~ **of race or creed** sin distinción de raza o credo **2 (a)** (merit, excellence): **a writer of** ~ un distinguido *or* destacado escritor; **a car of** ~ un coche de categoría **(b)** (distinguished appearance) distinción *f* **(c)** (mark of recognition) honor *m*, distinción *f* **(d)** (BrE Educ) mención *f* especial

distinctive /dɪˈstɪŋktɪv/ *adj* ⟨marking/plumage⟩ distintivo, característico; ⟨gesture/laugh⟩ personal, inconfundible; ⟨decor/dress⟩ particular

distinctly /dɪˈstɪŋktli/ *adv* **(a)** ⟨speak/

enunciate⟩ con claridad **(b)** ⟨hear⟩ perfectamente, claramente; **I** ~ **remember telling you** me acuerdo perfectamente *or* muy bien de que te lo dije

distinguish /dɪˈstɪŋgwɪʃ/ *vt* **1 (a)** (differentiate) distinguir*, diferenciar **(b) distinguishing** *pres p* ⟨feature/mark⟩ distintivo, característico **2** (make out) distinguir*
■ ~ *vi* distinguir*

distinguished /dɪˈstɪŋgwɪʃt/ *adj* distinguido

distort /dɪˈstɔːrt ‖dɪˈstɔːt/ *vt* **(a)** (deform) ⟨metal/object⟩ deformar **(b)** (Opt) ⟨image/reflection⟩ deformar, distorsionar **(c)** (Electron) ⟨signal/sound⟩ distorsionar **(d)** (misrepresent) ⟨facts/statement⟩ tergiversar, distorsionar

distortion /dɪˈstɔːrʃən ‖dɪˈstɔːʃən/ *n* **(a)** (of metal, object) deformación *f*; (of features) distorsión *f* **(b)** (Opt) deformación *f*, distorsión *f* **(c)** (of facts, news) tergiversación *f*, distorsión *f*

distract /dɪˈstrækt/ *vt* **(a)** (divert) ⟨person⟩ distraer* **(b)** (amuse) entretener*, distraer*

distraction /dɪˈstrækʃən/ *n* **1 (a)** (interruption) distracción *f* **(b)** (entertainment) (fml) entretenimiento *m*, distracción *f* **2** (madness): **to drive sb to** ~ sacar* a algn de quicio

distraught /dɪˈstrɔːt/ *adj* ⟨voice/person⟩ consternado, angustiado

distress¹ /dɪˈstres/ *n* angustia *f*, aflicción *f*; **he was in great** ~ sufría mucho

distress² *vt* (upset) afligir*; (grieve) consternar

distressed /dɪˈstrest/ *adj* afligido

distressing /dɪˈstresɪŋ/ *adj* ⟨news/circumstance⟩ penoso, angustiante

distribute /dɪˈstrɪbjət, -bjuːt ‖dɪˈstrɪbjuːt/ *vt* distribuir*; ⟨profits⟩ repartir

distribution /ˈdɪstrɪˈbjuːʃən/ *n* distribución *f*, reparto *m*; (of dividends) reparto *m*

distributor /dɪˈstrɪbjətər ‖dɪˈstrɪbjʊtə(r)/ *n* **1** (Busn) distribuidor *m*; (Cin) distribuidora *f* **2** (Auto, Elec) distribuidor *m* (del encendido)

district /ˈdɪstrɪkt/ *n* **1 (a)** (region) zona *f*, región *f* **(b)** (locality) barrio *m* **2** (Govt) (in US: of state, city) distrito *m*

district: ~ **attorney** *n* (in US) fiscal *mf* del distrito; ~ **court** *n* (in US) tribunal *m* de distrito; ~ **nurse** *n* (in UK) enfermero que tiene a su cuidado a los pacientes de un distrito

distrust¹ /dɪsˈtrʌst/ *vt* desconfiar* de, no fiarse* de

distrust² *n* desconfianza *f*, recelo *m*

distrustful /dɪsˈtrʌstfəl/ *adj* desconfiado, receloso

disturb /dɪˈstɜːrb ‖dɪˈstɜːb/ *vt* **1 (a)** (interrupt): **the noise ~ed my concentration** el ruido me hizo perder la concentración; **the calm was ~ed by the arrival of the tourists** la llegada de los turistas vino a perturbar la calma **(b)** (inconvenience) molestar **(c)** (burst in upon) ⟨thief⟩ sorprender **2** (disarrange): **she found that her papers had been ~ed** notó que alguien había tocado sus papeles **3** (trouble) perturbar, inquietar, llenar de inquietud

disturbance /dɪˈstɜːrbəns ‖dɪˈstɜːbəns/ *n* **1 (a)** (noisy disruption): **to cause/create a** ~ provocar*/armar un alboroto **(b)** (interruption) interrupción *f* **2** (of routine) alteración *f* **3** (riot) disturbio *m*

disturbed /dɪ'stɜːrbd ‖dɪ'stɜːbd/ *adj* **1** **(a)**
(Psych) ‹person/mind› trastornado **(b)** (perturbed)
(*pred*): **I was greatly ~ to hear of his misfortune**
la noticia de su desgracia me impresionó *or*
afectó muchísimo **2** (restless) ‹sleep› agitado,
inquieto

disturbing /dɪ'stɜːrbɪŋ ‖dɪ'stɜːbɪŋ/ *adj*
(worrying, upsetting) inquietante, perturbador;
(alarming) alarmante

disuse /dɪʃ'uːs ‖dɪs'juːs/ *n* desuso *m*

disused /dɪʃ'uːzd ‖dɪs'juːzd/ *adj* ‹factory/
quarry› abandonado; ‹machinery› en desuso

ditch¹ /dɪtʃ/ *n* zanja *f*, (at roadside) cuneta *f*; (for
irrigation) acequia *f*

ditch² *vt* **1** (abandon) colloq ‹girlfriend/
boyfriend› plantar (fam), botar (AmC, Chi fam);
‹object› deshacerse* de, botar (AmL exc RPI), tirar
(Esp, RPI); ‹plan› abandonar, desechar **2** (Aviat):
to ~ a plane hacer* un amaraje *or* amarizaje
(forzoso)

dither /'dɪðər ‖'dɪðə(r)/ *vi* (colloq) **(a)** (become
agitated) (AmE) ponerse* muy nervioso **(b)** (be
indecisive) titubear, vacilar

ditto /'dɪtəʊ/ *adv* (colloq): **I'm fed up — ditto!**
estoy harto — ¡y yo ídem de ídem! (fam)

divan /dɪ'væn/ *n* **(a)** (sofa) diván *m*, canapé *m*
(b) **~ (bed)** cama *f* turca

dive¹ /daɪv/ *vi* (*past* **dived** *or* (AmE also) **dove**;
past p **dived**) **(a)** (from height) zambullirse*,
tirarse (al agua), tirarse *or* echarse un clavado
(AmL) **(b)** (from surface) «person/whale»
sumergirse*, zambullirse*; «submarine»
sumergirse* **(c)** (swoop) «plane/bird» bajar en
picada *or* (Esp) en picado

dive² *n* **1** **(a)** (into water) zambullida *f*, clavado
m (AmL); (Sport) salto *m* (de trampolín), clavado *m*
(AmL) **(b)** (of submarine, whale) inmersión *f* **(c)**
(swoop) descenso *m* en picada *or* (Esp) en picado
2 (lunge, sudden movement) (colloq): **he made a ~**
for the gun se abalanzó sobre la pistola
3 (disreputable club, bar) (colloq) antro *m*

dive-bomb /'daɪvbɑːm ‖'daɪvbɒm/ *vt*
bombardear en picada *or* (Esp) en picado

diver /'daɪvər ‖'daɪvə(r)/ *n* **(a)** (from diving board
etc) saltador, -dora *m,f*, clavadista *mf* **(b)**
(deep-sea) buzo *mf*, submarinista *mf*

diverge /də'vɜːrdʒ ‖daɪ'vɜːdʒ/ *vi* **(a)** «lines/
paths» separarse **(b)** «opinions/explanations»
divergir*

diverse /daɪ'vɜːrs ‖daɪ'vɜːs/ *adj* **(a)** (varied)
‹interests/tastes› diversos, variados; **plant life in**
the area is extremely ~ la vegetación en la zona
es muy variada **(b)** (unlike) diferentes, distintos

diversion /də'vɜːrʒən ‖daɪ'vɜːʃən/ *n* **1** **(a)** (of
river) desviación *f* **(b)** (of funds) malversación *f* **(c)**
(BrE Transp) desvío *m*, desviación *f* **2** (distraction)
(Mil) diversión *f*, divertimiento *m* estratégico
3 (amusement) (fml) diversión *f*, entretenimiento
m

diversity /də'vɜːrsəti ‖daɪ'vɜːsəti/ *n* diversidad
f

divert /də'vɜːrt ‖daɪ'vɜːt/ *vt* **1** **(a)** (redirect)
‹stream/flow› desviar*; ‹traffic› (BrE) desviar* **(b)**
(ward off) ‹blow/attack› eludir, esquivar
2 (distract) ‹attention/thoughts› distraer*
3 (amuse) (fml) divertir*, entretener*

divest /daɪ'vest/ *vt* (fml) **to ~ sb of sth**
despojar a algn DE algo (fml)

divide /də'vaɪd ‖dɪ'vaɪd/ *vt* **1** **(a)** (split up)
dividir; **to ~ sth INTO sth** dividir algo EN algo **(b)**
(separate) **to ~ sth FROM sth** separar algo DE algo
(c) (share) ‹cake/money/work› repartir **2** (cause to
disagree) dividir **3** (Math) dividir; ▸ **FOUR¹**
■ **~** *vi* **1** **(a)** (fork) ‹road/river› dividirse **(b)**
(split) «group/particles/cells» dividirse **2** (Math)
dividir
■ **divide up** **1** [*v + o + adv, v + adv + o*] dividir
2 [*v + adv*] dividirse

divided /də'vaɪdəd ‖dɪ'vaɪdɪd/ *adj* ‹opinion›
dividido

divided highway *n* (AmE) autovía *f*,
carretera *f* de doble pista

dividend /'dɪvədend ‖'dɪvɪdend/ *n* dividendo
m; **to pay ~s** dar* dividendos, reportar
beneficios

divider /də'vaɪdər ‖dɪ'vaɪdə(r)/ *n* **(a)** (screen)
mampara *f*; (in filing system) separador *m* **(b)**
dividers *pl* (Math) compás *m* de puntas fijas

dividing line /də'vaɪdɪŋ ‖dɪ'vaɪdɪŋ/ *n* línea *f*
divisoria

divine¹ /də'vaɪn ‖dɪ'vaɪn/ *adj* **1** (*before n*)
‹intervention/inspiration› divino **2** (wonderful)
divino, precioso

divine² *vt* **(a)** (discover, guess) (liter) adivinar **(b)**
‹water/minerals› descubrir* (con una varita de
zahorí)

diving /'daɪvɪŋ/ *n* **(a)** (from height) saltos *mpl* de
trampolín, clavados *mpl* (AmL) **(b)** (under water)
submarinismo *m*, buceo *m*

diving: ~ board *n* trampolín *m*; **~ suit** *n*
escafandra *f*, traje *m* de buzo

divinity /də'vɪnəti ‖dɪ'vɪnəti/ *n* (*pl* **-ties**) (fml)
(a) (divine nature, being) divinidad *f* **(b)** (theology)
teología *f*

division /də'vɪʒən ‖dɪ'vɪʒən/ *n* **1** **(a)**
(distribution) reparto *m*, división *f* **(b)** (boundary)
división *f*; **class ~s** divisiones de clase **(c)** (part)
división *f* **2** (disagreement) desacuerdo *m*
3 (department) división *f*, sección *f* **4** (Mil)
división *f* **5** (Sport) **(a)** (in boxing) categoría *f* **(b)**
(in US: area) zona *f* **(c)** (in UK: by standard) división *f*
6 (Math) división *f*

divisive /də'vaɪsɪv ‖dɪ'vaɪsɪv/ *adj* divisivo

divorce¹ /də'vɔːrs ‖dɪ'vɔːs/ *n* divorcio *m*

divorce² *vt* (Law) divorciarse de; **to get ~d**
divorciarse
■ **~** *vi* divorciarse

divorcee /də'vɔːr'seɪ ‖dɪ,vɔː'siː/ *n* divorciado,
-da *m,f*

divulge /daɪ'vʌldʒ/ *vt* divulgar*; **to ~ sth TO sb**
revelarle algo A algn

DIY *n* (BrE) (= **do-it-yourself**) bricolaje *m*

dizzy /'dɪzi/ *adj* **-zier, -ziest** (a) (giddy)
⟨*sensation*⟩ de mareo; **to feel** ~ estar* mareado
(b) (causing dizziness) ⟨*speed*⟩ vertiginoso; ⟨*height*⟩
de vértigo

DJ *n* = **disc jockey**

DNA *n* (= **deoxyribonucleic acid**) ADN *m*

do¹ /duː, *weak form* dʊ, də/ (*3rd pers sing pres*
does; *pres* **doing**; *past* **did**; *past p* **done**) *vt*
[1] hacer*; **to have something/nothing to** ~ tener*
algo/no tener* nada que hacer; **it was a silly thing
to** ~ fue una estupidez; **can I** ~ **anything to help?**
¿puedo ayudar en algo?

[2] (carry out) ⟨*job/task*⟩ hacer*; **to** ~ **the cooking**
cocinar; **well done!** ¡muy bien!

[3] (achieve, bring about): **she's done it: it's a new
world record** lo ha logrado: es una nueva marca
mundial; **it was climbing those stairs that did it**
fue por subir esa escalera; **that mustache really
does something for him** la verdad es que le queda
muy bien el bigote

[4] (a) (fix, arrange, repair): **I have to** ~ **my nails** me
tengo que arreglar las uñas; **she had her hair
done** se hizo peinar (b) (clean) ⟨*dishes*⟩ lavar;
⟨*brass/windows*⟩ limpiar

[5] (make, produce) ⟨*meal*⟩ preparar, hacer*;
⟨*drawing/translation*⟩ hacer*

[6] (travel): **he was** ~**ing 100 mph** iba a 100 millas
por hora; **the car has only done 4,000 miles** el
coche solo tiene 4.000 millas

■ ~ *vi* [1] (act, behave) hacer*; ~ **as you're told!**
¡haz lo que se te dice!; **his concern to** ~ **well by
his son** su preocupación por hacer todo lo
posible por su hijo

[2] (get along, manage): **how are you** ~**ing?** (colloq)
¿qué tal estás *or* andas *or* te va?; **how do you** ~**?**
(as greeting) mucho gusto, encantado; **how are we
** ~**ing for time?** ¿cómo *or* qué tal vamos *or*
andamos de tiempo?; **she did well in her exams** le
fue bien en los exámenes; **he's done well for
himself** ha sabido abrirse camino

[3] (go on, happen) (colloq) (*in* -*ing form*): **there's
nothing** ~**ing in town** no pasa nada en el pueblo;
nothing ~**ing!** ¡ni hablar!, ¡ni lo sueñes!

[4] (be suitable, acceptable): **look, this won't** ~!
¡mira, esto no puede ser!; **it's not ideal, but it'll** ~
no es lo ideal, pero sirve; **this box will** ~ **for** *o* **as
a table** esta caja nos servirá de mesa

[5] (be enough) ser* suficiente, alcanzar*, bastar*;
that'll ~! **shut up!** ¡basta! ¡cállate la boca!

■ ~ *v aux* [*El verbo auxiliar* DO *se usa para
formar el negativo* (I 1) *y el interrogativo* (I 2),
para agregar énfasis (I 3) *o para sustituir a un
verbo usado anteriormente* (II)]

I [1] (*used to form negative, interrogative,
exclamations*): **I** ~ **not** *o* **don't know** no sé; **not
only does it cost more, it also** ... no solo cuesta
más, sino que también ...; **did I frighten you?** ¿te
asusté?; **doesn't it make you sick!** ¡dime si no es
asqueante!

[2] (emphasizing): **you** ~ **exaggerate!** ¡cómo
exageras!; **you must admit, she did look ill** tienes
que reconocer que tenía mala cara

II [1] (*in elliptical uses*): ~ **you live here?** — **yes,
I** ~/**no, I don't** ¿vives aquí? — sí/no; **she says she
understands, but she doesn't** dice que
comprende, pero no es así

[2] (*in tag questions*): **you know Bob, don't you?**
conoces a Bob, ¿no? *or* ¿verdad? *or* ¿no es cierto?;
I told you, didn't I? te lo dije ¿no? *or* ¿no es
cierto?

■ **do away with** [*v* + *adv* + *prep* + *o*] (a) (abolish)
⟨*privilege/tax*⟩ abolir*, suprimir; ⟨*need*⟩ eliminar,
acabar con (b) (kill) (colloq) eliminar, liquidar
(fam)

■ **do up** [*v* + *o* + *adv, v* + *adv* + *o*] (a) (fasten) ⟨*coat/
necklace/button*⟩ abrochar; ⟨*zipper*⟩ subir; **to** ~ **up
one's shoes** atarse los cordones *or* (Méx) las
agujetas *or* (Per) los pasadores (de los zapatos) (b)
(wrap up) ⟨*parcel*⟩ envolver* (c) (dress up) (colloq):
she was all done up estaba muy elegante (d) (colloq)
⟨*house*⟩ arreglar (*pintando, empapelando etc*)

■ **do with** [*v* + *prep* + *o*] [1] (benefit from) (*with
can, could*): **that door could** ~ **with a coat of paint**
no le vendría mal una mano de pintura a esa
puerta; **you could** ~ **with a change** te hace falta
or te vendría bien un cambio

[2] (expressing connection) **I don't want to have
anything to** ~ **with him/this business** yo no
quiero tener nada que ver con él/este asunto; **it's
nothing to** ~ **with you!** no es nada que te
concierna *or* que te importe a ti

■ **do without** [1] [*v* + *prep* + *o*]: **to** ~ **without sth/
sb** prescindir de *or* arreglárselas sin algo/algn
[2] [*v* + *adv*] arreglárselas

do² /duː/ *n* (*pl* **dos**) [1] (party, gathering) (colloq)
fiesta *f*, reunión *f* [2] **do's and don'ts** (rules)
normas *fpl*

do³ /dəʊ/ *n* (*pl* **dos**) (Mus) do *m*

docile /'dɑːsəl ‖ 'dəʊsaɪl/ *adj* dócil, sumiso

dock¹ /dɑːk ‖ dɒk/ *n* [1] (Naut) (a) (wharf, quay)
muelle *m*; (for cargo ships) dársena *f*; (*before n*)
⟨*worker/strike*⟩ portuario (b) **docks** *pl* puerto *m*
[2] (Law) (*no pl*) **the** ~ el banquillo de los
acusados [3] (Bot) acedera *f*

dock² *vt* [1] (a) ⟨*tail*⟩ cortar (b) ⟨*wages*⟩
descontar* dinero de [2] ⟨*vessel/ship*⟩ fondear,
atracar*

■ ~ *vi* (a) (Naut) «*ship/vessel*» atracar*, fondear
(b) (Aerosp) acoplarse

docker /'dɑːkər ‖ 'dɒkə(r)/ *n* (BrE) estibador,
-dora *m,f*

dockyard /'dɑːkjɑːrd ‖ 'dɒkjɑːd/ *n* (*often pl*)
astillero *m*

doctor¹ /'dɑːktər ‖ 'dɒktə(r)/ *n* [1] (Med)
médico, -ca *m,f*, doctor, -tora *m,f*, facultativo, -va
m,f (frml); **D**~ **Jones** el doctor Jones [2] (Educ)
doctor, -tora *m,f*

doctor² *vt* (pej) (a) ⟨*food/drink*⟩ adulterar (b)
⟨*text*⟩ arreglar (c) ⟨*results/evidence*⟩ falsificar*

doctoral /'dɑːktərəl ‖ 'dɒktərəl/ *adj* ⟨*thesis/
dissertation*⟩ doctoral

doctorate /'dɑːktərət ‖ 'dɒktərət/ *n* doctorado
m

doctrine /'dɑːktrən ‖ 'dɒktrɪn/ *n* doctrina *f*

document¹ /'dɑːkjəmənt ‖ 'dɒkjʊmənt/ *n*
documento *m*

document² *vt* /'dɑːkjəment ‖ 'dɒkjʊment/
documentar

documentary¹ /'dɑːkjə'mentəri
‖ ˌdɒkjʊ'mentri/ *adj* documental

documentary² *n* (*pl* **-ries**) documental *m*

documentation /'dɑːkjəmen'teɪʃən
‖ ˌdɒkjʊmen'teɪʃən/ *n* documentación *f*

dodge /'dɑːdʒ ‖ dɒdʒ/ *vt* (a) ⟨*blow*⟩ esquivar;
⟨*pursuer*⟩ eludir (b) ⟨*question*⟩ esquivar,
soslayar; ⟨*problem/issue*⟩ soslayar; ⟨*work/
responsibility*⟩ eludir; ⟨*tax*⟩ evadir

⋯⟶

d

■ ~ *vi* echarse a un lado, apartarse; **she ~d behind the car** se escondío rápidamente detrás del coche

dodgem (car) /'dɑːdʒəm ‖'dɒdʒəm/ *n* ▶ BUMPER CAR

dodger /'dɑːdʒər ‖'dɒdʒə(r)/ *n*: **tax ~** evasor, -sora *m,f* de impuestos; **fare ~** *persona que intenta viajar sin pagar en un medio de transporte público*

doe /dəʊ/ *n* (of deer) hembra *f* de gamo, gama *f*; (of rabbit) coneja *f*

does /dʌz, *weak form* dəz/ *3rd pers sing pres of* DO¹

doesn't /'dʌznt/ = **does not**

dog¹ /dɔːg ‖dɒg/ *n* (Zool) perro, -rra *m,f*; (male canine) macho *m*; **it's ~ eat ~** hay una competencia brutal; **to go to the ~s** venirse* abajo; **let sleeping ~s lie** mejor no revolver el asunto; (*before n*) **~ show** exposición *f* canina

dog² *vt* **-gg-** (*often pass*) perseguir*

dog-eared /'dɔːgɪrd ‖'dɒgɪəd/ *adj* sobado y con las esquinas dobladas

dogged /'dɔːgəd ‖'dɒgɪd/ *adj* obstinado

doggedly /'dɔːgədli ‖'dɒgɪdli/ *adv* obstinadamente

doggerel /'dɔːgərəl ‖'dɒgərəl/ *n* ripios *mpl*

doghouse /'dɔːghaʊs ‖'dɒghaʊs/ *n* (AmE) casa *f* or casilla *f* or (Esp) caseta *f* or (Chi) casucha *f* del perro, perrera *f* (Col); **to be in the ~** (also BrE colloq) haber* caído en desgracia

dogma /'dɔːgmə ‖'dɒgmə/ *n* dogma *m*

dogmatic /dɔːg'mætɪk ‖dɒg'mætɪk/ *adj* dogmático

do-gooder /'duːguːdər ‖duː'guːdə(r)/ *n* (pej) hacedor, -dora *m,f* de buenas obras (hum)

dog: ~ paddle *n* estilo *m* perro *or* perrito; **~sbody** *n* (esp BrE colloq): **I'm just the general ~sbody around here** yo aquí no soy más que el botones

doh /dəʊ/ *n* (Mus) do *m*

doily /'dɔɪli/ *n* (*pl* **-lies**) **(a)** (on plate) blonda *f* **(b)** (under plate, ornament) tapete *m*, pañito *m*, carpeta *f* (Col, CS)

doing /'duːɪŋ/ *n* **1** (action): **that takes some ~** eso no es nada fácil; **it was none of our ~** nosotros no tuvimos nada que ver **2 doings** *pl* (activities, events) actividades *fpl*

do-it-yourself /'duːətʃər'self ‖,duːɪtjɔː'self/ *n* bricolaje *m*

doldrums /'dəʊldrəmz, 'dɑːl- ‖'dɒldrəmz/ *pl n*: **to be in the ~** estar* de capa caída

dole /dəʊl/ *n* (BrE): **to be on the ~** estar* cobrando subsidio de desempleo *or* (Chi tb) de cesantía, estar* en el paro (Esp)

■ **dole out** [*v + o + adv*, *v + adv + o*] *〈food/ money〉* dar*, repartir

doleful /'dəʊlfəl/ *adj* *〈face/look〉* compungido, triste; *〈sound/voice〉* plañidero, lúgubre

doll /dɑːl ‖dɒl/ *n* muñeca *f*

■ **doll up** [*v + o + adv*] (colloq): **to get (all) ~ed up** emperifollarse (fam)

dollar /'dɑːlər ‖'dɒlə(r)/ *n* dólar *m*; **you can bet your bottom ~** (colloq) puedes estar seguro, te lo doy firmado (fam); (*before n*) **~ bill** billete *m* de un dólar; **~ sign** signo *m* or símbolo *m* del dólar

dollhouse /'dɑːlhaʊs ‖'dɒlhaʊs/ (AmE) *n* casa *f* de muñecas

dollop /'dɑːləp ‖'dɒləp/ *n* (colloq) (served with a spoon) cucharada *f*; (serving, measure) porción *f*

doll's house *n* (BrE) casa *f* de muñecas

dolly /'dɑːli ‖'dɒli/ *n* (*pl* **-lies**) (used to or by children) muñequita *f*

dolphin /'dɑːlfən ‖'dɒlfɪn/ *n* (*pl* **~s** *or* **~**) delfín *m*

domain /də'meɪn, dəʊ-/ *n* **(a)** (sphere of influence, activity) campo *m*, esfera *f*; **in the public ~** de(l) dominio público **(b)** (Comput) dominio *m*

dome /dəʊm/ *n* (Archit) cúpula *f*

domestic /də'mestɪk/ *adj* **1** **(a)** (of the home) *〈life/problems〉* doméstico; *〈violence〉* violencia *f* en el hogar **(b)** (home-loving) casero, hogareño **2** *〈animal〉* doméstico **3** (Econ, Pol) *〈affairs/ policy/market〉* interno; *〈produce/flight〉* nacional

domesticated /də'mestɪkeɪtəd ‖də'mestɪkeɪtɪd/ *adj* *〈animal/species〉* domesticado

domesticity /'dəʊmes'tɪsəti ‖,dɒmes'tɪsəti, dəʊ-/ *n* (frml or hum) domesticidad *f*

domestic science *n* economía *f* doméstica, hogar *m* (Esp)

domicile /'dɑːməsaɪl ‖'dɒmɪsaɪl/ *n* (frml) domicilio *m* (frml)

dominance /'dɑːmənəns ‖'dɒmɪnəns/ *n* **(a)** (supremacy) dominio *m*, dominación *f* **(b)** (predominance) predominio *m*, preponderancia *f*

dominant /'dɑːmənənt ‖'dɒmɪnənt/ *adj* **(a)** (more powerful) *〈nation/influence〉* dominante **(b)** (predominant) *〈crop/industry〉* predominante, preponderante **(c)** (Biol, Ecol) dominante

dominate /'dɑːməneɪt ‖'dɒmɪneɪt/ *vt* dominar

domination /'dɑːmə'neɪʃən ‖,dɒmɪ'neɪʃən/ *n* dominación *f*

domineering /'dɑːmə'nɪrɪŋ ‖,dɒmɪ'nɪərɪŋ/ *adj* dominante

Dominican Republic /də'mɪnɪkən/ *n* **the ~ ~** la República Dominicana

dominion /də'mɪnjən/ *n* (liter) dominio *m*

domino /'dɑːmənəʊ ‖'dɒmɪnəʊ/ *n* (*pl* **-noes**) **(a)** (counter) ficha *f* de dominó **(b) dominoes** (+ *sing vb*) dominó *m*

don /dɑːn ‖dɒn/ *vt* **-nn-** (put on) (liter) ponerse*

donate /'dəʊneɪt, dəʊ'neɪt/ *vt* donar

donation /dəʊ'neɪʃən/ *n* **(a)** (gift) donativo *m*, donación *f* **(b)** (act) donación *f*

done¹ /dʌn/ *past p of* DO¹

done² *adj* (*no comp*) **1** (*pred*) **(a)** (finished) hecho **(b)** (cooked) cocido **(c)** (accepted): **it's not ~** *o* **not the ~ thing** no está bien visto

donkey /'dɑːŋki ‖'dɒŋki/ *n* (*pl* **-keys**) burro *m*, asno *m*

donor /'dəʊnər ‖'dəʊnə(r)/ *n* donante *mf*

don't /dəʊnt/ = **do not**

doodle /'duːdl/ *vi/t* garabatear, garrapatear

doom¹ /duːm/ *vt* (*usu pass*) condenar

doom² *n* **(a)** (fate) sino *m* (liter); (death) muerte *f* **(b)** (ruin) fatalidad *f*

doomsday /'duːmzdeɪ/ *n* (arch) día *m* del Juicio Final

door /dɔːr ‖dɔː(r)/ *n* puerta *f*; **double ~s** puerta de dos hojas; **there's someone at the ~** llaman a la puerta; **tickets are available at the** ～ se pueden comprar las localidades en la puerta *or* a la entrada; **he's not allowed out of** ～s no le permiten salir; *to show sb the* ～ mostrarle* *or* enseñarle la puerta a algn, echar a algn

door: ～**bell** *n* timbre *m*; ～ **knob** *n* pomo *m* (de la puerta); ～**man** /'dɔːrmən ‖'dɔːmən/ *n* (*pl* **-men** /-mən/) portero *m*; ～**mat** *n* felpudo *m*; ～**step** *n* umbral *m*; ～**stop** *n* cuña *f* (*para mantener la puerta abierta*); ～**-to-**～ /'dɔːrtə'dɔːr ‖,dɔːtə'dɔː(r)/ *adj* 〈*delivery/service*〉 de puerta a puerta; **a** ～**-to-**～ **salesman** un vendedor ambulante (*que va de puerta a puerta*); ～**way** *n* entrada *f*

dope¹ /dəʊp/ *n* **1** **(a)** (drugs) (sl) droga *f*, pichicata *f* (CS, Per fam); (cannabis) hachís *m*, chocolate *m* (Esp arg) **(b)** (Sport) estimulante *m*, droga *f*, doping *m*; (*before n*) 〈*test*〉 antidoping *adj inv* **2** (information) (sl) información *f* **3** (stupid person) (colloq) imbécil *mf*, tarugo *mf* (fam)

dope² *vt* (colloq) 〈*person/racehorse*〉 dopar (fam), drogar*; 〈*food/drink*〉 poner* droga en

dopey, dopy /'dəʊpi/ *adj* **dopier, dopiest** (colloq) **(a)** (stupid) lelo (fam), bobo (fam) **(b)** (befuddled) atontado, grogui (fam)

dormant /'dɔːrmənt ‖'dɔːmənt/ *adj* **1** **(a)** 〈*animal/plant*〉 aletargado **(b)** 〈*volcano*〉 inactivo **2** (frml) 〈*idea/emotion*〉 latente

dormice /'dɔːrmaɪs ‖'dɔːmaɪs/ *pl of* DORMOUSE

dormitory /'dɔːrmətɔːri ‖'dɔːmɪtri/ *n* (*pl* **-ries**) **(a)** (in school, hostel) dormitorio *m*; (*before n*) ～ **town** (BrE) ciudad *f* dormitorio **(b)** (students' residence) (AmE) residencia *f* de estudiantes

dormouse /'dɔːrmaʊs ‖'dɔːmaʊs/ *n* (*pl* **-mice** /-maɪs/) lirón *m*

dorsal /'dɔːrsəl ‖'dɔːsəl/ *adj* dorsal

DOS /dɑːs ‖dɒs/ *n* (= **disk-operating system**) DOS *m*

dosage /'dəʊsɪdʒ/ *n* dosis *f*

dose¹ /dəʊs/ *n* (of medication) dosis *f*; **a bad** ～ **of flu** (colloq) una gripe *or* (Col, Méx) una gripa muy mala

dose² *vt*: **I'm all** ～**d up with painkillers** me he tomado no sé cuántos analgésicos

dossier /'dɔːsieɪ ‖'dɒsiə(r), -ieɪ/ *n* dossier *m*, expediente *m*

dot¹ /dɑːt ‖dɒt/ *n* punto *m*; ～ ～ ～ puntos suspensivos; **on the** ～ en punto

dot² *vt* **-tt-** **1** (add dot) puntuar*; **to sign on the** ～**ted line** firmar la línea punteada *or* de puntos **2** (scatter) (*usu pass*) salpicar*; **her family is** ～**ted about all over Europe** su familia está desperdigada por toda Europa

dot.com /kɑːm ‖kɒm/ *n* (Comput) punto' *m* com; (*before n*) 〈*company*〉 punto com

dote /dəʊt/ *vi* **to** ～ **ON** sb adorar a algn

doting /'dəʊtɪŋ/ *adj*: **his** ～ **mother** su madre, que lo adora

dotty /'dɑːti ‖'dɒti/ *adj* **-tier, -tiest** (colloq) 〈*person*〉 chiflado (fam); 〈*idea*〉 descabellada

double¹ /'dʌbəl/ *adj* doble; 〈*bed*〉 de matrimonio, de dos plazas (AmL); **it's** ～ **that** es el doble de eso; **my number is** ～ **three seven** ～ **four eight** (esp BrE) mi número es tres tres siete, cuatro cuatro ocho; **it's spelled with a** ～ **'t'** se

escribe con dos tes; ～ **bend** curva *f* en S (*read as:* curva *en ese*); **inflation reached** ～ **figures** la inflación alcanzó/rebasó el 10%

double² *adv* 〈*pay/earn/cost*〉 el doble; **she spends** ～ **what she earns** gasta el doble de lo que gana; **to see** ～ ver* doble

double³ *n* **1** **(a)** (hotel room) doble *f* **(b)** (of spirits): **I'll have a** ～ (deme) uno doble **2** (lookalike) doble *mf* **3** (Sport) (double win) doblete *m* **4** (pace): **at** *o* **on the** ～ (Mil) a paso ligero

double⁴ *vt* **(a)** (increase twofold) 〈*earnings/profits*〉 doblar, duplicar*; 〈*efforts*〉 redoblar **(b)** (Games) 〈*stake/call/bid*〉 doblar

■ ～ *vi* **1** (increase twofold) 《*price/amount*》 duplicarse*, doblarse

2 (have dual role): **the table** ～**s as a desk** la mesa también se usa como escritorio; **somebody** ～**d for him in the dangerous scenes** alguien lo doblaba en las escenas peligrosas

■ **double back** [*v* + *adv*] 〈*person/animal*〉 volver* sobre sus pasos; **the path** ～**d back on itself** el camino doblaba sobre sí mismo

■ **double up** [*v* + *adv* (+ *o*)] **(a)** (bend): **to** ～ **up with laughter** morirse* *or* desternillarse de risa; **he was** ～**d up with pain** se retorcía de dolor **(b)** (redouble) (AmE) doblar

double: ～ **act** *n*: **they are a** ～ **act** actúan en pareja; ～**-barreled,** (BrE) ～**-barrelled** /'dʌbəl'bærəld/ *adj* **(a)** 〈*shotgun*〉 de dos cañones **(b)** (BrE) 〈*surname*〉 compuesto; ～ **bass** *n* contrabajo *m*; ～**-book** /'dʌbəl'bʊk/ *vt* (BrE): **the room had been** ～**-booked** la habitación había sido reservada para dos personas distintas; ～**-breasted** /'dʌbəl'brestəd ‖,dʌbəl'brestɪd/ *adj* cruzado; ～**-check** /'dʌbəl'tʃek/ *vi* volver* a mirar, verificar* dos veces ■ ～ *vt* 〈*facts/ information*〉 volver* a revisar; ～ **chin** *n* papada *f*; ～**-click** /'dʌbəl'klɪk/ *vi* (Comput) hacer* doble click; ～ **cream** *n* (BrE) crema *f* doble, nata *f* para montar (Esp), doble crema *f* (Méx); ～**-cross** /'dʌbəl'krɔːs ‖,dʌbəl'krɒs/ *vt* traicionar; ～**-decker** /'dʌbəl'dekər ‖,dʌbəl'dekə(r)/ *n* ～**-decker** (bus) (esp BrE) autobús *m* de dos pisos; ～ **Dutch** *n* (colloq) chino *m* (fam); ～**-edged** /'dʌbəl'edʒd/ *adj* 〈*knife/blade/scheme*〉 de doble filo; 〈*remark/comment*〉 de doble sentido; ～ **glazing** /'ɡleɪzɪŋ/ *n* (BrE) doble ventana *f*; ～**-jointed** /'dʌbəl'dʒɔɪntəd ‖,dʌbəl'dʒɔɪntɪd/ *adj*: **he's** ～**-jointed** tiene articulaciones dobles

doubles /'dʌbəlz/ *pl n* dobles *mpl*

double standard *n*: **to have a** ～**s** aplicar* una ley para unos y otra para otros

doubly /'dʌbli/ *adv* 〈*difficult/dangerous/ interesting*〉 doblemente

doubt¹ /daʊt/ *n* (uncertainty) duda *f*; **no** ～ **she will phone** con seguridad que llama, seguro que llama; **if in** ～, **don't go** si estás en (la) duda, no vayas; **I have my** ～**s** tengo mis dudas

doubt² *vt* **(a)** 〈*fact/truth*〉 dudar de **(b)** (consider unlikely) dudar; **to** ～ (THAT) *o* **if** *o* **whether** dudar QUE (+ *subj*)

doubtful /'daʊtfəl/ *adj* **(a)** (full of doubt) 〈*expression/tone*〉 de indecisión *or* duda, dubitativo; **I am** ～ **as to its value** tengo mis dudas acerca de su valor **(b)** (in doubt) dudoso; **the outcome remains** ～ el resultado sigue siendo dudoso *or* incierto

doubtfully /'daʊtfəli/ adv ⟨say⟩ sin convicción; ⟨agree⟩ con reserva

doubtless /'daʊtləs ‖'daʊtlɪs/ adv sin duda, indudablemente

dough /dəʊ/ n 1 (Culin) masa f 2 (money) (sl) guita f (arg), lana f (AmL fam), plata f (AmS fam), pasta f (Esp fam)

doughnut /'dəʊnʌt/ n donut m, rosquilla f

dour /daʊr, dʊr ‖dʊə(r)/ adj adusto

douse /daʊs/ vt ⟨flames⟩ sofocar*

dove¹ /dʌv/ n paloma f

dove² /dəʊv/ (AmE) past of DIVE¹

dovetail /'dʌvteɪl/ vi encajar

dowager /'daʊədʒər ‖'daʊədʒə(r)/ n: viuda de un noble

dowdy /'daʊdi/ adj -dier, -diest ⟨woman⟩ sin gracia, sin estilo

down¹ /daʊn/ adv 1 (a) (in downward direction): to go ~ bajar; to look ~ mirar (hacia or para) abajo; from the waist ~ desde la cintura para abajo; ~ with tyranny! ¡abajo la tiranía! (b) (downstairs): can you come ~? ¿puedes bajar? 2 (a) (of position) abajo; two floors ~ dos pisos más abajo; ~ here/there aquí/allí (abajo) (b) (downstairs): I'm ~ in the cellar estoy aquí abajo, en el sótano (c) (lowered, pointing downward) bajado; face ~ boca abajo (d) (prostrate): I was ~ with flu all last week estuve con gripe toda la semana pasada 3 (of numbers, intensity): my temperature is ~ to 38° C la temperatura me ha bajado a 38° C; they were two goals ~ iban perdiendo por dos goles 4 (a) (in, toward the south): to go/come ~ south ir*/venir* al sur (b) (at, to another place) (esp BrE): ~ on the farm en la granja; I'm going ~ to the library voy a la biblioteca 5 (a) (dismantled, removed): the room looks bare with the pictures ~ la habitación queda desnuda sin los cuadros; once this wall is ~ una vez que hayan derribado esta pared (b) (out of action): the telephone lines are ~ las líneas de teléfono están cortadas; the system is ~ (Comput) el sistema no funciona 6 down to (a) (as far as) hasta: ~ to the present day hasta nuestros días (b) (reduced to): we're ~ to our last can of tomatoes nos queda solo una lata de tomates

down² prep 1 (in downward direction): we ran ~ the slope corrimos cuesta abajo; it fell ~ a hole se cayó por un agujero; halfway ~ the page hacia la mitad de la página 2 (along): we drove on ~ the coast seguimos por la costa; the library is just ~ the street la biblioteca está un poco más allá

down³ adj 1 (before n) (going downward): the ~ escalator la escalera mecánica de bajada or para bajar 2 (depressed) (colloq) ⟨pred⟩ deprimido

down⁴ n (a) (on bird) plumón m (b) (on face, body) vello m, pelusilla f (c) (on plant, fruit) pelusa f

down⁵ vt (a) (drink) beberse or tomarse rápidamente (b) (knock down) ⟨person⟩ tumbar, derribar

down: ~ **and out** adj (colloq) ⟨pred⟩: to be ~

and out estar* en la miseria; ~**cast** adj (a) (dejected) alicaído, abatido (b) (directed downward): with ~cast eyes con la mirada baja; ~**fall** n (of person) perdición f, ruina f; (of king, dictator) caída f; ~**grade** ⟨employee/hotel⟩ bajar de categoría; ~**hearted** /'daʊn'hɑːrtəd ‖,daʊn'hɑːtɪd/ adj desanimado, desmoralizado; ~**hill** /'daʊn'hɪl/ adv ⟨walk/run⟩ cuesta abajo; to go ~hill ir* cuesta abajo, ir* de mal en peor

Downing Street /'daʊnɪŋ/ n Downing Street (calle de Londres donde se encuentra la residencia oficial del primer ministro británico)

download /'daʊn'ləʊd/ vt (Comput) trasvasar

downmarket¹ /'daʊn'mɑːrkət ‖,daʊn'mɑːkɪt/ adv: the paper has gone ~ el diario ha perdido categoría; (deliberately) el diario se dirige ahora a un sector más popular del público

downmarket² adj ⟨newspaper⟩ popular; ⟨store⟩ barato

down: ~ **payment** n cuota f or entrega f inicial, entrada f (Esp), pie m (Chi); ~**pour** n aguacero m, chaparrón m

downright¹ /'daʊnraɪt/ adj ⟨lie/insolence⟩ descarado; ⟨crook/liar/rogue⟩ redomado, de tomo y lomo (fam); ⟨madness⟩ total y absoluto

downright² adv: it was ~ dangerous! ¡fue peligrosísimo!; he was ~ rude! ¡estuvo de lo más grosero!

downriver /'daʊn'rɪvər ‖,daʊn'rɪvə(r)/ adv río abajo

Down's syndrome /daʊnz/ n síndrome m de Down; (before n) ⟨child⟩ afectado por el síndrome de Down

downstairs¹ /'daʊn'sterz ‖,daʊn'steəz/ adv abajo; he went ~ to open the door bajó a abrir la puerta

downstairs² n planta f baja; (before n) ⟨neighbor/toilet⟩ (del piso) de abajo

down: ~**stream** /'daʊn'striːm/ adv río abajo; ~**-to-earth** /'daʊntʊ'ɜːrθ ‖,daʊntə'ɜː θ/ adj ⟨pred⟩ ~ to earth realista, práctico

downtown¹ /'daʊn'taʊn/ n (AmE) centro m (de la ciudad); (before n) ~ New York el centro de Nueva York

downtown² adv (AmE): to go/live ~ ir* al/ vivir en el centro

downtrodden /'daʊn'trɑːdn ‖'daʊn,trɒdn/ adj oprimido

downward¹ /'daʊnwərd ‖'daʊnwəd/ adj ⟨direction/pressure⟩ hacia abajo; ⟨movement/ spiral⟩ descendente; ⟨tendency⟩ (Fin) a la baja

downward² /'daʊnwərd ‖'daʊnwəd/, (esp BrE) **downwards** /-z/ adv hacia abajo

downwind /'daʊn'wɪnd/ adv en la dirección del viento

dowry /'daʊəri/ n (pl -ries) dote f

doze /dəʊz/ vi dormitar
■ **doze off** [v + adv] quedarse dormido, dormirse*

AmC	América Central	Arg	Argentina	Cu	Cuba	Per	Perú
AmL	América Latina	Bol	Bolivia	Ec	Ecuador	RPI	Río de la Plata
AmS	América del Sur	Chi	Chile	Esp	España	Ur	Uruguay
Andes	Región andina	CS	Cono Sur	Méx	México	Ven	Venezuela

dozen¹ /'dʌzn/ n (pl ∼ or ∼s) docena f; **four dollars a** o **per ∼** cuatro dólares la docena; **I got ∼s of cards** recibí montones de tarjetas (fam)

dozen² adj docena f de; **a ∼/two ∼ eggs** una docena/dos docenas de huevos

dozy /'dəʊzi/ adj **dozier, doziest** amodorrado, adormilado

Dr /'dɑːktər ‖'dɒktə(r)/ (title) (= **Doctor**) Dr., Dra.

drab /dræb/ adj ‹clothing/decor/appearance› soso, sin gracia; ‹life/occupation› gris, monótono

draft¹ /dræft ‖drɑːft/ n ① (BrE) **draught** (cold air) corriente f de aire ② (formulation) versión f ③ (Fin) cheque m or efecto m bancario ④ (AmE) **the ∼** (Mil) el llamamiento or (AmL tb) llamado a filas

draft² vt ① (formulate) ‹document/contract/letter› redactar el borrador de; ‹speech› preparar ② (conscript) (AmE) reclutar, llamar a filas

draftproof /'dræftpruːf ‖'drɑːftpruːf/ adj hermético

draftsman, (BrE) **draughtsman** /'dræftsmən ‖'drɑːftsmən/ n (pl **-men** /-mən/) dibujante mf

drafty, (BrE) **draughty** /'dræfti ‖'drɑːfti/ adj **-tier, -tiest** con corrientes de aire

drag¹ /dræg/ **-gg-** vt ① (haul) arrastrar, llevar a rastras; **I couldn't ∼ myself away** (colloq) no tenía fuerzas para irme ② (allow to trail) ‹tail/garment/anchor› arrastrar; **to ∼ one's feet** o **heels** dar(le)* largas al asunto ③ (Comput) **∼ (and drop)** arrastrar (y soltar)
■ ∼ vi ① (a) (trail) «anchor» garrar; «coat» arrastrar (b) (lag) rezagarse* ② (go on slowly) «work/conversation» hacerse* pesado; «film/play» hacerse* largo
■ **drag on** [v + adv] alargarse* (interminablemente)

drag² n (no pl) ① (tiresome thing): **what a ∼!** ¡qué lata! (fam) ② (resistant force) resistencia f al avance ③ (women's clothes): **in ∼** vestido de mujer

dragon /'drægən/ n dragón m

dragonfly /'drægənflaɪ/ n (pl **-flies**) libélula f, caballito m del diablo, matapiojos m (Andes)

drain¹ /dreɪn/ n ① (a) (pipe) sumidero m, resumidero m (AmL); **the ∼s** (of town) el alcantarillado; (of building) las tuberías de desagüe (b) (grid) (BrE) sumidero m, resumidero m (AmL) ② (plughole) desagüe m ③ (no pl) (cause of depletion) **a ∼ on the country's resources** una sangría para el país; **the extra work is an enormous ∼ on my energy** el trabajo extra me está agotando

drain² vt ① (a) ‹container/tank› vaciar*; ‹land/swamp› drenar, avenar; ‹blood› drenar; ‹sap/water› extraer* (b) (Culin) ‹vegetables/pasta› escurrir, colar* (c) (Med) drenar ② (drink up) ‹glass/cup› vaciar*, apurar ③ (consume, exhaust) ‹resources/strength› agotar, consumir
■ ∼ vi (a) (dry) ‹dishes› escurrir(se) (b) (disappear): **all the strength seemed to ∼ from my limbs** los brazos y las piernas se me quedaron como sin fuerzas (c) (discharge) «pipes/river» desaguar*

drainage /'dreɪnɪdʒ/ n (a) (of household waste) desagüe m (de aguas residuales); (of rainwater)

canalización f (de agua de lluvia); (before n) **∼ system** (red f de) alcantarillado m (b) (of fields, marshes) drenaje m, avenamiento m

drainboard /'dreɪnbɔːrd ‖'dreɪnbɔːd/ n (AmE) escurridero m

draining board /'dreɪnɪŋ/ n (BrE) escurridero m

drainpipe /'dreɪnpaɪp/ n tubo m or caño m del desagüe, bajante f

drake /dreɪk/ n pato m (macho)

drama /'drɑːmə/ n (pl **-mas**) ① (Theat) (a) (play) obra f dramática, drama m (b) (plays collectively) teatro m, drama m; (dramatic art) arte m dramático ② (excitement) dramatismo m

dramatic /drə'mætɪk/ adj ① (Theat) (before n) dramático, teatral ② (a) (striking) ‹change/improvement› espectacular, drástico; ‹increase› espectacular (b) (momentous) ‹events/development› dramático

dramatically /drə'mætɪkli/ adv (a) (exaggeratedly) ‹pause/announce› dramáticamente, de manera teatral or histriónica (b) (strikingly) ‹change/improve/increase› de manera espectacular

dramatics /drə'mætɪks/ n (Theat) (+ sing vb): **amateur ∼** teatro m amateur or de aficionados

dramatist /'dræmətɪst/ n dramaturgo, -ga m,f

dramatize /'dræmətaɪz/ vt ① ‹story/novel› (Theat) dramatizar*, hacer* una adaptación teatral de; (Cin) llevar al cine ② (exaggerate) ‹situation/event› dramatizar*, exagerar

drank /dræŋk/ past of DRINK²

drape /dreɪp/ vt (a) (arrange): **they ∼d a flag over the tomb** colocaron una bandera formando pliegues sobre la tumba; **she ∼d herself over the sofa** se tendió sobre el sofá (b) (cover) cubrir*

drapes /dreɪps/ pl n (AmE) cortinas fpl

drastic /'dræstɪk/ adj drástico, radical

drastically /'dræstɪkli/ adv drásticamente

draught /dræft ‖drɑːft/ n ① (storage under pressure): **beer on ∼** cerveza f de barril; (before n) ‹beer/cider› de barril ② (liter) (of water, beer) trago m ③ (BrE) ▶ DRAFT¹ 1

draughtproof /'dræftpruːf ‖'drɑːftpruːf/ adj (BrE) ▶ DRAFTPROOF

draughts /drɑːfts ‖drɑːfts/ n (BrE) (+ sing vb) damas fpl

draughtsman /'dræftsmən ‖'drɑːftsmən/ n (BrE) ▶ DRAFTSMAN

draughty /'dræfti ‖'drɑːfti/ adj (BrE) ▶ DRAFTY

draw¹ /drɔː/ (past **drew**; past p **drawn**) vt ① (a) (move by pulling) ‹curtains/bolt› (open) descorrer; (shut) correr; **he drew her to one side** la llevó a un lado, la llevó aparte (b) (pull along) ‹cart/sled› tirar de, arrastrar ② (a) (pull out) ‹tooth/cork› sacar*, extraer* (fml); ‹gun› desenfundar, sacar*; ‹sword› desenvainar, sacar* (b) (cause to flow) sacar*; **to ∼ blood** sacar* sangre, hacer* sangrar; **to ∼ breath** respirar ③ (a) (Fin) ‹salary/pension› cobrar, percibir (fml); ‹check› girar, librar (b) (derive) ‹strength/lesson› sacar* ④ (establish) ‹distinction/parallel› establecer* ⑤ (a) (attract) ‹customers/crowd› atraer*; **to be** ····▷

~n to sb/sth sentirse* atraído por algn/algo **(b)**
(elicit) ⟨*praise*⟩ conseguir*; ⟨*criticism/protest*⟩
provocar*, suscitar
6 (sketch) ⟨*flower/picture*⟩ dibujar; ⟨*line*⟩ trazar*
7 (BrE Games, Sport) empatar

■ ~ *vi* **1** (move): to ~ close to sth/sb acercarse* a
algo/algn; to ~ to a close terminar, finalizar*
(frml); the train drew out of/into the station el tren
salió de/entró en la estación; to ~ ahead of sb/
sth adelantarse a algn/algo
2 (Art) dibujar
3 (BrE Games, Sport) empatar; (in chess game)
hacer* tablas

■ **draw back** [*v* + *adv*] **(a)** (retreat) retirarse **(b)**
(recoil) retroceder

■ **draw in** **1** [*v* + *o* + *adv*, *v* + *adv* + *o*] **(a)**
(retract) ⟨*claws*⟩ esconder, retraer* **(b)** (into quarrel,
war) involucrar; (into conversation) darle*
participación a
2 [*v* + *adv*] **(a)** (arrive) «*train*» llegar* **(b)**
⟨*days/nights*⟩ hacerse* más corto

■ **draw on** [*v* + *prep* + *o*] (make use of) ⟨*resources/
reserves*⟩ recurrir a, hacer* uso de; she drew on
her own experiences se inspiró en sus propias
experiencias

■ **draw out** **1** [*v* + *adv*] **(a)** (depart) «*train*»
salir* **(b)** (become longer) hacerse* más largo
2 [*v* + *o* + *adv*, *v* + *adv* + *o*] **(a)** (prolong)
alargar*, estirar **(b)** (extract, remove) ⟨*tooth/thorn*⟩
sacar*, extraer* (frml); ⟨*wallet/handkerchief*⟩
sacar*; ⟨*information*⟩ sacar*, sonsacar*;
⟨*confession*⟩ arrancar* **(c)** (withdraw) ⟨*money*⟩
sacar*

■ **draw up** **1** [*v* + *adv*] «*car*» detenerse*, parar
2 [*v* + *o* + *adv*, *v* + *adv* + *o*] **(a)** (prepare, draft)
⟨*contract/treaty*⟩ redactar, preparar; ⟨*list/plan*⟩
hacer* **(b)** (arrange in formation) ⟨*troops/competitors*⟩
alinear, formar **(c)** (bring near) ⟨*chair*⟩ acercar*,
arrimar

draw² *n* **1** (raffle) sorteo *m* **2** (tie) (Games, Sport)
empate *m*

draw: ~**back** *n* inconveniente *m*, desventaja *f*;
~**bridge** *n* puente *m* levadizo

drawer *n* /drɔːr ‖ˈdrɔː(r)/ **1** (in furniture) cajón
m, gaveta *f* (esp AmC, Méx) **2** **drawers** *pl*
(Clothing) calzones *mpl*

drawing /ˈdrɔːɪŋ/ *n* dibujo *m*

drawing: ~ **pin** *n* (BrE) ▶ THUMBTACK; ~
room *n* sala *f*, salón *m*

drawl /drɔːl/ *n*: acento caracterizado por la
longitud de las vocales

drawn¹ /drɔːn/ *past p of* DRAW¹

drawn² *adj* ⟨*features/face*⟩ demacrado

drawstring /ˈdrɔːstrɪŋ/ *n* cordón *m* (*del que se
tira para cerrar algo*); (*before n*) ⟨*bag/waist*⟩
fruncido con un cordón o una cinta

dread¹ /dred/ *vt* tenerle* terror *or* pavor a

dread² *n* terror *m*

dreadful /ˈdredfəl/ *adj* ⟨*news/experience/
weather*⟩ espantoso, terrible; I feel ~ me siento
pésimo

dreadfully /ˈdredfəli/ *adv* (as intensifier)
⟨*upset/late*⟩ terriblemente, enormemente

dream¹ /driːm/ *n* sueño *m*; a ~ come true un
sueño hecho realidad; (*before n*) he lives in a ~
world vive de ilusiones, vive en las nubes

dream² (*past & past p* dreamed *or* (BrE also)

dreamt /dremt/) *vi* soñar*; to ~ ABOUT sth/sb
soñar* CON algo/algn; would you do that? — I
wouldn't ~ of it! ¿harías eso? — ¡ni pensarlo!

■ ~ *vt* soñar*; I never ~ed he'd be so rude nunca
(me) imaginé que iba a ser tan grosero

■ **dream up** [*v* + *o* + *adv*, *v* + *adv* + *o*] ⟨*plan*⟩
idear

dreamer /ˈdriːmər ‖ˈdriːmə(r)/ *n* soñador,
-dora *m,f*

dreamt /dremt/ (BrE) *past & past p of* DREAM²

dreamy /ˈdriːmi/ *adj* **-mier, -miest** **(a)**
(abstracted) ⟨*person*⟩ soñador, fantasioso; ⟨*gaze*⟩
distraído **(b)** ⟨*music*⟩ etéreo, sutil

dreary /ˈdrɪri ‖ˈdrɪəri/ *adj* **-rier, -riest** **(a)**
⟨*room/landscape*⟩ deprimente, lóbrego, sombrío;
⟨*weather*⟩ gris, deprimente **(b)** ⟨*work/routine*⟩
monótono, aburrido (AmL)

dredge /dredʒ/ *vt* dragar*

■ **dredge up** [*v* + *o* + *adv*, *v* + *adv* + *o*] ⟨*mud/
sand*⟩ dragar*; ⟨*story/scandal*⟩ desenterrar*

dredger /ˈdredʒər ‖ˈdredʒə(r)/ *n* (machine)
draga *f*, (vessel) dragador *m*, draga *f*

dregs /dregz/ *pl n* posos *mpl*, cunchos *mpl* (Col),
conchos *mpl* (Chi); the ~ of society la escoria de
la sociedad

drench /drentʃ/ *vt* (usu pass) empapar

dress¹ /dres/ *n* **1** (for woman, girl) vestido *m*
2 (style of dressing): they adopted Western ~
adoptaron el modo de vestir *or* la vestimenta
occidental; (*before n*) she has no ~ sense tiene
mal gusto para vestirse

dress² *vt* **1** (put clothes on) vestir*; to get ~ed
vestirse*; he was ~ed in white iba (vestido) de
blanco **2** (Culin) **(a)** (prepare) ⟨*chicken/fish*⟩
preparar **(b)** (season) ⟨*salad*⟩ aliñar **3** (Med)
⟨*wound*⟩ vendar

■ ~ *vi* vestirse*

■ **dress up** [*v* + *adv*] **(a)** (dress smartly) ponerse*
elegante **(b)** (in fancy dress) disfrazarse*; to ~ up
AS sth disfrazarse* DE algo

dresser /ˈdresər ‖ˈdresə(r)/ *n* **1** (person): he's
a stylish ~ (se) viste con mucho estilo **2** **(a)** (in
bedroom) (AmE) tocador *m* **(b)** (in kitchen) (BrE)
aparador *m*

dressing /ˈdresɪŋ/ *n* **1** (Med) apósito *m*, gasa *f*;
(bandage) vendaje *m* **2** (Culin) (for salad) aliño *m*,
aderezo *m*; (stuffing) (AmE) relleno *m*

dressing: ~ **gown** *n* bata *f*, salto *m* de cama
(CS); ~ **room** *n* (Theat) camerino *m*; (in house)
vestidor *m*; ~ **table** *n* tocador *m*

dress: ~**maker** *n* modista *mf*; (designer)
modisto, -ta *m,f*; ~ **rehearsal** *n* ensayo *m*
general; ~ **suit** *n* traje *m* de etiqueta

dressy /ˈdresi/ *adj* **-sier, -siest** elegante

drew /druː/ *past of* DRAW¹

dribble /ˈdrɪbəl/ *vi* **1** (drool) babear **2** (Sport)
driblar, driblear

dribs and drabs /ˌdrɪbzənˈdræbz/ *pl n*: in ~
~ ~ poquito a poco

dried /draɪd/ *adj* ⟨*figs/flowers*⟩ seco; ⟨*fish*⟩
salado, seco; ⟨*milk/eggs*⟩ en polvo

drier /ˈdraɪər ‖ˈdraɪə(r)/ *n* ▶ DRYER

drift¹ /drɪft/ *vi* **1** **(a)** (on water) *moverse
empujado por la corriente* (be adrift) «*boat/
person*» ir* a la deriva **(c)** (in air) «*balloon*»
moverse empujado por el viento **2** (proceed

aimlessly): **the crowd began to ~ away** la muchedumbre comenzó a dispersarse; **to ~ apart** «*couple/friends*» distanciarse ③ (pile up) «*sand/ snow*» amontonarse

drift² n ① (of sand) montón m; (of snow) ventisquero m ② (meaning) (no pl) sentido m; **I didn't quite catch your ~** no entendí or capté muy bien lo que querías decir ③ (movement): **the ~ from the land** el éxodo rural

driftwood /'drɪftwʊd/ n madera, tablas etc que flotan en el mar a la deriva o que arrastra el mar hasta la playa

drill¹ /drɪl/ n ① (electric o power ~) taladradora f, taladro m; (hand ~) taladro m (manual); (Dent) torno m, fresa f; (Eng, Min) perforadora f, barreno m; (drill head) broca f ② (a) (Mil) instrucción f (b) (Educ) ejercicio m

drill² vt ① «*hole*» hacer*, perforar; «*wood/metal*» taladrar, perforar, barrenar; «*tooth*» trabajar or limpiar con la fresa ② (Mil) «*soldiers*» instruir*
■ ~ vi perforar, hacer* perforaciones; **to ~ for oil** perforar en busca de petróleo

drily /'draɪli/ adv secamente, con sequedad

drink¹ /drɪŋk/ n ① (a) (any liquid) bebida f (b) (alcohol) bebida f ② (a) (amount drunk, served, sold): **have a ~ of water/milk** bebe or (esp AmL) toma un poco de agua/leche (b) (alcoholic) copa f, trago m (fam); **to have a ~** tomar una copa

drink² (past **drank**; past p **drunk**) vt/i beber, tomar (esp AmL)
■ **drink up** ① [v + adv] bebérselo or (esp AmL) tomárselo todo, terminar su (or mi etc) copa (or leche etc) ② [v + o + adv, v + adv + o] beberse, tomarse (esp AmL)

drinkable /'drɪŋkəbəl/ adj «*water*» potable

drink-driving /ˌdrɪŋk'draɪvɪŋ/ n BrE ▶ DRUNK DRIVING

drinker /'drɪŋkər ‖ 'drɪŋkə(r)/ n: **he's a heavy ~** es un gran bebedor or un bebedor empedernido; **I'm a beer ~ myself** yo prefiero la cerveza

drinking /'drɪŋkɪŋ/ n (a) (of liquid) beber (b) (of alcohol): **his ~ is causing concern** lo mucho que bebe está causando preocupación

drinking: ~ chocolate n chocolate m en polvo; **~ water** n agua f‡ potable

drip¹ /drɪp/ vi **-pp-** «*washing/hair*» chorrear, gotear; «*faucet/tap*» gotear; **water was ~ping from the ceiling** el techo goteaba, caían gotas del techo

drip² n ① (of rainwater, tap) (no pl) goteo m ② (Med) suero m, gota a gota m ③ (ineffectual person) (colloq) soso, -sa m,f (fam)

drip-dry /'drɪp'draɪ/ adj «*fabric/garment*» de lava y pon, de lavar y poner

dripping /'drɪpɪŋ/ adj (colloq) empapado; (as intensifier) **to be ~ wet** estar* chorreando or empapado

drive¹ /draɪv/ (past **drove**; past p **driven**) vt ① (Transp) (a) «*car/bus/train*» manejar or (Esp) conducir* (b) (convey in vehicle) llevar en coche ② (a) (cause to move) (+ adv compl): **the Indians were ~n off their land** los indios fueron expulsados de sus tierras; **we drove them away with sticks** los ahuyentamos con palos (b) (Sport) «*ball*» mandar, lanzar* (c) (provide power for, operate) hacer* funcionar, mover*

③ (make penetrate) «*nail*» clavar; «*stake*» hincar* ④ (a) (cause to become) volver*; **to ~ sb mad** volver* loco a algn; **he ~s me crazy with his incessant chatter** me saca de quicio con su constante cháchara (b) (compel to act) **to ~ sb to +** INF llevar or empujar a algn A + INF; **she is ~n by ambition** la impulsa or motiva la ambición (c) (overwork): **he drove them mercilessly** los hizo trabajar como esclavos; **she ~s herself too hard** se exige demasiado a sí misma
■ ~ vi manejar or (Esp) conducir*; **she ~s to work** va a trabajar en coche
■ **drive out** [v + o + adv, v + adv + o] expulsar

drive² n ① (in vehicle): **to go for a ~** ir* a dar un paseo or una vuelta en coche; **it's a three-hour ~** es un viaje de tres horas en coche ② (a) (leading to house) camino m, avenida f (que lleva hasta una casa) (b) (in front of house) entrada f (para coches) ③ (in golf, tennis) golpe m fuerte ④ (a) (energy) empuje m, dinamismo m (b) (compulsion) (Psych) impulso m, instinto m; **the sex ~** el apetito sexual ⑤ (a) (organized effort) campaña f (b) (attacking move) (Mil) ofensiva f, avanzada f (c) (in US football) ataque m ⑥ (a) (propulsion system) transmisión f, propulsión f (b) (Auto): **front-wheel/rear-wheel ~** tracción f delantera/trasera

drive-in /'draɪvɪn/ n (AmE) (cinema) autocine m; (restaurant) drive in m (restaurante que sirve a los clientes en el propio automóvil)

drivel /'drɪvəl/ n tonterías fpl, estupideces fpl

driven /'drɪvən/ past p of DRIVE¹

driver /'draɪvər ‖ 'draɪvə(r)/ n (of car, truck, bus) conductor, -ra m,f, chofer m or (Esp) chófer mf; (of racing car) piloto mf; **she's a good ~** maneja or (Esp) conduce bien

driver's license n (AmE) licencia f or (Esp) permiso m de conducción; (less formally) carné m or permiso m (de conducir) (Esp), carné m (Chi) or (Ur) libreta f or (AmC, Méx, Ven) licencia f or (Col) pase m (de manejar), registro m (Arg), brevete m (Per)

driving¹ /'draɪvɪŋ/ n (Auto) conducción f (frml)

driving² adj (a) «*rain*» torrencial; «*wind*» azotador (b) (dynamic): **she's the ~ force behind the project** es el alma-máter or la impulsora del proyecto

driving: ~ instructor n instructor, -tora m,f de autoescuela; **~ licence** n (BrE) ▶ DRIVER'S LICENSE; **~ test** n examen m de conducir or (AmL tb) de manejar

drizzle¹ /'drɪzəl/ n llovizna f, garúa f (AmL)

drizzle² v impers lloviznar, garuar* (AmL)

droll /drəʊl/ adj (a) (comic) gracioso, con chispa (b) (quaint, curious) curioso

drone¹ /drəʊn/ n ① (bee) zángano m ② (sound — of bees, traffic, aircraft) zumbido m; (— of voice) cantinela f (fam), sonsonete m

drone² vi «*bee/engine/plane*» zumbar; **she ~d (on) for hours** estuvo horas con la misma perorata (fam)

drool /druːl/ vi «*dog/baby*» babear; **we ~ed at the sight of the cakes** se nos hizo la boca agua or agua la boca al ver los pasteles

droop /druːp/ vi (a) (sag) «*flowers*» ponerse* ····≻

mustio; **his shoulders ~ed** se encorvó (b) (flag)
«*spirits*» flaquear, decaer*; «*person*»
desfallecer*, decaer* **(c) drooping** *pres p* ⟨*head*⟩
gacho; ⟨*flowers*⟩ mustio

drop¹ /drɑːp ‖drɒp/ *n* **1** **(a)** (of liquid) gota *f*;
she's had a ~ too much ha bebido más de la
cuenta **(b) drops** *pl* (Med) gotas *fpl*; **nose ~s**
gotas para la nariz **(d)** (candy): **acid ~s** caramelos
mpl ácidos; **chocolate ~s** pastillas *fpl* de
chocolate **2** (fall) (*no pl*) (in temperature) descenso
m; (in prices) caída *f*, baja *f*; **a sheer ~** una caída a
plomo; **at the ~ of a hat** en cualquier momento

drop² **-pp-** *vt* **1** **(a)** (accidentally): **I/he ~ped the
cup** se me/le cayó la taza; **don't ~ it!** ¡que no se
te caiga! **(b)** (deliberately) ⟨*cup/vase*⟩ dejar caer,
tirar*; ⟨*bomb/supplies*⟩ lanzar*; **~ that gun!** ¡suelta
ese revólver!
2 (lower) ⟨*hem*⟩ alargar*, bajar; ⟨*eyes/voice*⟩ bajar
3 **(a)** (set down) ⟨*passenger/cargo*⟩ dejar **(b)**
(deliver) pasar a dejar
4 (send) (colloq) ⟨*card/letter*⟩ mandar; **~ me a line**
a ver si me mandas *or* me escribes unas líneas
5 (utter) ⟨*hint/remark*⟩ soltar*, dejar caer; **to let it
~ that …** (inadvertently) dejar escapar que …;
(deliberately) dejar caer que …
6 **(a)** (omit) ⟨*letter/syllable/word*⟩ omitir; **to ~ sb
from a team** sacar* a algn de un equipo **(b)** (give
up, abandon) ⟨*case*⟩ abandonar; ⟨*charges*⟩ retirar*;
⟨*plan/idea*⟩ abandonar, renunciar a; ⟨*friend/
associate*⟩ dejar de ver a; **to ~ the subject** dejar
el tema
■ **~** *vi* **1** **(a)** (fall) «*object*» caer(se)*; «*plane*»
bajar, descender*; **he ~ped to the ground**
(deliberately) se tiró al suelo; (fell) cayó de un golpe
(b) (collapse) desplomarse
2 **(a)** (decrease) «*wind*» amainar;
«*temperature*» bajar, descender*; «*prices*»
bajar, experimentar un descenso (frml); «*voice*»
bajar **(b)** (in height) «*terrain*» caer*
■ **drop in** [*v* + *adv*] (colloq) pasar; **to ~ in on sb**
pasar a ver a algn, caerle* a algn (fam)
■ **drop off** **1** [*v* + *adv*] **(a)** (fall off) caerse* **(b)**
(fall asleep) dormirse*, quedarse dormido **(c)**
(decrease) «*sales/numbers*» disminuir*
2 [*v* + *o* + *adv*] ⟨*person/goods*⟩ dejar
■ **drop out** [*v* + *adv*] **to ~ out of school**
abandonar los estudios; **to ~ out (of a
competition/race)** (before event) no presentarse (a
un concurso/una carrera); (during event)
abandonar (un curso/una carrera); **to ~ out (of
society)** marginarse, convertirse* en un
marginado

drop-dead /ˈdrɑːpˈded ‖ˈdrɒpded/ *adv*: **~
gorgeous** que te caes de espaldas de guapo

droplet /ˈdrɑːplət ‖ˈdrɒplɪt/ *n* gotita *f*

dropper /ˈdrɑːpər ‖ˈdrɒpə(r)/ *n* cuentagotas *m*,
gotero *m*

droppings /ˈdrɑːpɪŋz ‖ˈdrɒpɪŋz/ *pl n* (of bird,
flies) excremento *m* (frml), cagadas *fpl* (fam); (of
rabbit, sheep) cagarrutas *fpl*

dross /drɑːs ‖drɒs/ *n* **(a)** (waste) basura *f* **(b)**
(Metall) escoria *f*

drought /draʊt/ *n* sequía *f*

drove¹ /drəʊv/ *past of* DRIVE¹

drove² *n* **(a)** (of animals) manada *f* **(b) droves**
pl (of people) hordas *fpl*, manadas *fpl*

drown /draʊn/ *vt* **1** ⟨*person/animal*⟩ ahogar*
2 **~ (out)** (make inaudible) ⟨*noise/cries/screams*⟩
ahogar*
■ **~** *vi* ahogarse*, morir* ahogado

drowsy /ˈdraʊzi/ *adj* **-sier, -siest**
somnoliento, adormilado

drudge /drʌdʒ/ *n* esclavo, -va *m,f*

drudgery /ˈdrʌdʒəri/ *n*: **this job is sheer ~** este
trabajo es una pesadez

drug¹ /drʌg/ *n* **(a)** (narcotic) droga *f*,
estupefaciente *m* (frml); **to be on ~s** drogarse* **(b)**
(medication) medicamento *m*, medicina *f*, fármaco
m (frml)

drug² *vt* **-gg-** drogar*

drug addict *n* drogadicto, -ta *m,f*

druggist /ˈdrʌgɪst/ *n* (AmE) farmacéutico, -ca
m,f

drug: ~store *n* (AmE) establecimiento que vende
medicamentos, cosméticos, periódicos y una gran
variedad de artículos; **~taker** /ˌteɪkər
‖ˌteɪkə(r)/ *n* consumidor, -dora *m,f* de drogas;
~taking *n* consumo *m* de drogas

drum¹ /drʌm/ *n* **1** (Mus) **(a)** tambor *m* **(b)**
drums *pl* (in band) batería *f* **2** **(a)** (container)
bidón *m* **(b)** (machine part) tambor *m* **(c)** (spool)
tambor *m*

drum² **-mm-** *vt* ⟨*table/floor*⟩ golpetear; **to ~
one's fingers** tamborilear con los dedos
■ **~** *vi* **(a)** (Mus) tocar* el tambor **(b)** (beat, tap)
«*person*» dar* golpecitos, tamborilear; «*rain/
hail/hooves*» repiquetear
■ **drum up** [*v* + *adv* + *o*] ⟨*support*⟩ conseguir*,
obtener*

drum: ~beat *n* son *m* del tambor; **~kit** *n*
batería *f*

drummer /ˈdrʌmər ‖ˈdrʌmə(r)/ *n* (pop, jazz)
batería *mf*, baterista *mf* (AmL); (military) tambor *m*

drumstick /ˈdrʌmstɪk/ *n* **1** palillo *m* (de
tambor), baqueta *f* **2** (Culin) muslo *m*, pata *f*

drunk¹ /drʌŋk/ *past p of* DRINK²

drunk² *adj* (*pred*) borracho; **to get ~**
emborracharse; **~ and disorderly** (Law) en estado
de embriaguez y alterando el orden público (frml)

drunk³ *n* borracho, -cha *m,f*

drunkard /ˈdrʌŋkərd ‖ˈdrʌŋkəd/ *n* (frml & pej)
borracho, -cha *m,f*, beodo, -da *m,f* (frml)

drunk driving *n* (AmE) conducción *f* de un
vehículo bajo los efectos del alcohol

drunken /ˈdrʌŋkən/ *adj* (*before n*) ⟨*person/mob*⟩
borracho; ⟨*orgy/brawl*⟩ de borrachos

drunkenness /ˈdrʌŋkənnəs ‖ˈdrʌŋkənnɪs/ *n*
borrachera *f*, embriaguez *f* (frml)

dry¹ /draɪ/ *adj* **drier, driest** **1** **(a)** (not wet)
⟨*ground/washing*⟩ seco **(b)** (lacking natural moisture)
⟨*leaves/skin/hair*⟩ seco; ⟨*cough*⟩ seco **(c)** (dried-up)
⟨*well/river*⟩ seco; **to run ~** ⟨*river/well*⟩ secarse*
(d) (not rainy, not humid) ⟨*climate/weather/heat*⟩
seco; **tomorrow will be ~** mañana no lloverá

AmC	Central America	Arg	Argentina	Cu	Cuba	Per	Peru
AmL	Latin America	Bol	Bolivia	Ec	Ecuador	RPI	River Plate Area
AmS	South America	Chí	Chile	Esp	Spain	Ur	Uruguay
Andes	Andean Region	CS	Southern Cone	Méx	Mexico	Ven	Venezuela

2 (not sweet) ⟨wine/sherry⟩ seco **3** (ironic) ⟨humor/wit⟩ mordaz **4** (dull, boring) ⟨lecture/book⟩ árido

dry² dries, drying, dried vt secar*; to ~ one's eyes secarse* or (liter) enjugarse* las lágrimas
■ ~ vi secarse*
■ **dry up** [v + adv] (a) «stream/pond» secarse* (completamente) (b) «funds/resources/ inspiration» agotarse

dry: ~ clean vt limpiar en seco; ~ cleaner('s) n tintorería f; ~ dock n dique m seco

dryer /'draɪər ‖ 'draɪə(r)/ n (a) (for clothes — machine) secadora f; (— rack) tendedor m, tendedero m; (spin ~) secadora f (centrífuga); (tumble ~) secadora f (de aire caliente) (b) ▶ HAIRDRIER

dry: ~ goods pl n (a) (clothing) (AmE) artículos mpl or prendas fpl de confección; (before n) ~ goods store tienda f de confecciones (b) (groceries) (BrE) comestibles mpl no perecederos; ~ ice n hielo m seco

dryly adv ▶ DRILY

dryness /'draɪnəs ‖ 'draɪnɪs/ n **1** (of ground, hair, skin, climate) sequedad f **2** (of wine, sherry) lo seco **3** (of humor, wit) lo mordaz

dry: ~ rot n putrefacción de la madera producida por un hongo; ~ wall, (BrE) ~-stone wall n muro m de mampostería sin mortero

dual /'duːəl ‖ 'djuːəl/ adj (before n) ⟨role/ function⟩ doble; ⟨nationality⟩ doble

dual: ~ carriageway /'kærɪdʒweɪ/ n (BrE) autovía f, carretera f de doble pista; ~-control /'duːəlkəntrəʊl ‖ ,djuːəlkən'trəʊl/ adj ⟨car/ brakes⟩ de doble mando or control; ~-purpose /'duːəl'pɜːrpəs ‖ ,djuːəl'pɜːpəs/ adj ⟨utensil⟩ de doble uso; ⟨cleaner⟩ de doble acción; ⟨furniture⟩ de doble función or uso

dub /dʌb/ vt -bb- **1** (nickname) apodar **2** (a) (Cin) ⟨film⟩ doblar (b) (Audio) mezclar

dubious /'duːbiəs ‖ 'djuːbiəs/ adj (a) (questionable) ⟨honor/achievement⟩ dudoso, discutible; ⟨past⟩ turbio; ⟨motives/person⟩ sospechoso (b) (doubtful) to be ~ (ABOUT sth/sb) tener* reservas or dudas (SOBRE or ACERCA DE algo/algn)

duchess /'dʌtʃəs ‖ 'dʌtʃɪs/ n duquesa f

duchy /'dʌtʃi/ n (pl duchies) ducado m

duck¹ /dʌk/ n pato, -ta m,f

duck² vi (bow down) agacharse; (hide): I ~ed behind a pillar me escondí rápidamente detrás de una columna
■ ~ vt **1** (lower) ⟨head⟩ agachar, bajar **2** (submerge) hundir **3** (dodge) ⟨question⟩ eludir, esquivar; ⟨responsibility⟩ evadir, eludir

duckling /'dʌklɪŋ/ n patito m, anadón m

duct /dʌkt/ n (Tech, Anat) conducto m

dud¹ /dʌd/ n (colloq) (a) (useless thing) birria f (fam), porquería f (fam) (b) (useless person) calamidad f, inútil mf

dud² adj (colloq) (a) (useless, valueless) ⟨note/coin⟩ falso; ⟨check⟩ sin fondos (b) (Mil) ⟨shell/bomb⟩ que no estalla

dude /duːd ‖ djuːd/ n (AmE sl) tipo m (fam), tío m (Esp fam)

dudgeon /'dʌdʒən/ n: in high ~ indignadísimo, lleno de indignación

due¹ /duː ‖ djuː/ adj **1** (pred): the rent is ~ hay que pagar el alquiler; the respect ~ to one's elders el respeto que se les debe a los mayores; it's all ~ to you todo gracias a ti, te lo debemos todo a ti; when is the next train ~? ¿cuándo llega el próximo tren?; she's ~ back tomorrow vuelve mañana, su regreso está previsto para mañana **2** (before n) ⟨consideration/regard⟩ debido; with all ~ respect con el debido respeto **3** due to (as prep) (crit) debido a

due² adv: the fort is ~ west of the town el fuerte está justo or exactamente al oeste del pueblo; we headed ~ north nos dirigimos derecho hacia el norte

due³ n **1** to give him his ~, he is efficient tienes que reconocer que es eficiente **2** dues pl n (subscription) cuota f

duel /'duːəl/ n duelo m

duet /duː'et ‖ djuː'et/ n dúo m

duffel bag, (BrE) duffle bag /'dʌfəl/ n talego m, tula f (Col), bolso m marinero (RPl)

duffel coat, (BrE) duffle coat /'dʌfəl/ n trenca f, montgomery m (CS)

dug /dʌg/ past & past p of DIG¹

dugout /'dʌgaʊt/ n **1** (Mil) refugio m subterráneo **2** ~ (canoe) piragua f **3** (in baseball) dogaut m, caseta f

duke /duːk ‖ djuːk/ n duque m

dull¹ /dʌl/ adj **1** (a) (not bright) ⟨color⟩ apagado; ⟨light/glow⟩ pálido; ⟨eyes/complexion⟩ sin brillo (b) (not shiny) ⟨finish⟩ mate; ⟨hair⟩ sin brillo (c) (overcast) ⟨day/morning⟩ gris, feo **2** (boring) ⟨speech/person⟩ aburrido **3** (a) ⟨faculties⟩ torpe, lerdo; ⟨pain/ache⟩ sordo; ⟨sound⟩ sordo, amortiguado (b) ⟨edge/blade⟩ romo, embotado

dull² vt (a) (make less bright) ⟨color/surface⟩ quitar el brillo a, opacar* (b) (make less sharp) ⟨pain⟩ aliviar, calmar; ⟨senses⟩ entorpecer*, embotar

dully /'dʌlli/ adv (a) (dimly) ⟨glow/shine⟩ débilmente, pálidamente (b) (boringly) ⟨talk/write⟩ de manera aburrida

duly /'duːli ‖ 'djuːli/ adv debidamente; permission was ~ granted el permiso fue concedido, como era de esperar

dumb /dʌm/ adj **1** (unable to speak) mudo; to be struck ~ quedarse mudo or sin habla **2** (stupid) (colloq) bobo (fam)
■ **dumb down** [v + adv + o, v + o + adv] bajar el nivel intelectual de

dumb: ~bell n pesa f, mancuerna f; ~found /'dʌm'faʊnd/ vt (usu pass) anonadar; ~struck adj estupefacto; ~waiter /'dʌm'weɪtər ‖ ,dʌm'weɪtə(r)/ n (elevator) montaplatos m; (table) mesita f rodante

dummy¹ /'dʌmi/ n **1** (a) (in window display, for dressmaker) maniquí m (b) (in tests, stunts) muñeco m (c) (in US football) domi m **2** (for baby) (BrE) ▶ PACIFIER **3** (fool) (colloq) bobo, -ba m,f (fam)

dummy² adj ⟨gun/telephone⟩ de juguete

dump¹ /dʌmp/ n **1** (place for waste) vertedero m (de basura), basural m (AmL), tiradero m (Méx) **2** (temporary store) (Mil) depósito m **3** (unpleasant place) (colloq) lugar m de mala muerte **4** to be (down) in the ~s (colloq) estar* or andar* con la depre (fam)

dump² *vt* **1** (get rid of) ‹*waste/refuse*› tirar, botar (AmL exc RPI); ‹*boyfriend/girlfriend*› (colloq) plantar (fam), botar (AmS exc RPI fam), largar* (RPI fam) **2** **(a)** (set on ground) ‹*load/sand*› descargar*, verter*; **where can I ~ my things?** (colloq) ¿dónde puedo dejar *or* poner mis cosas? **(b)** (Comput) ‹*data/disks*› volcar*

dumper (**truck**) /'dʌmpər ‖'dʌmpə(r)/ *n* ▸ DUMP TRUCK

dumpling /'dʌmplɪŋ/ *n: bola de masa que se come en sopas o guisos*

Dumpster® /'dʌmpstər ‖'dʌmpstə(r)/ *n* (AmE) contenedor *m* (*para escombros*)

dump truck *n* volquete *m*, camión *m* volteador (RPI) *or* (Méx) de volteo, volqueta *f* (Col)

dumpy /'dʌmpi/ *adj* **-pier, -piest** regordete

dunce /dʌns/ *n* (pej) burro, -rra *m,f*

dune /duːn ‖djuːn/ *n* duna *f*

dung /dʌŋ/ *n* **(a)** (feces) boñiga *f*, bosta *f* **(b)** (manure) (esp BrE) estiércol *m*

dungarees /'dʌŋgə'riːz/ *pl n* (workman's) overol *m*; (fashion) pantalón *m* de peto *m*

dungeon /'dʌndʒən/ *n* mazmorra *f*, calabozo *m*

duo /'duːəʊ ‖'djuːəʊ/ *n* (*pl* **-os**) dúo *m*

dupe¹ /duːp ‖djuːp/ *vt* engañar, embaucar*

dupe² *n* inocentón, -tona *m,f*, primo, -ma *m,f* (Esp fam)

duplex /'duːpleks ‖'djuːpleks/ *n* (AmE) ~ (**apartment**) dúplex *m*; ~ (**house**) casa de dos viviendas adosadas

duplicate¹ /'duːplɪkət ‖'djuːplɪkət/ *adj* (before *n*): **a ~ copy** un duplicado; **a ~ key** un duplicado *or* una copia de una llave

duplicate² /'duːplɪkət ‖'djuːplɪkət/ *n* duplicado *m*, copia *f*

duplicate³ /'duːplɪkeɪt ‖'djuːplɪkeɪt/ *vt* **(a)** (copy) ‹*letter/document*› hacer* copias de **(b)** (repeat) ‹*work/efforts*› repetir* (*en forma innecesaria*)

durable /'dʊrəbəl ‖'djʊərəbəl/ *adj* durable

duration /dʊ'reɪʃən ‖'djʊə'reɪʃən/ *n* duración *f*

duress /dʊ'res ‖djʊə'res/ *n*: **under ~** bajo coacción

during /'dʊrɪŋ ‖'djʊərɪŋ/ *prep* durante

dusk /dʌsk/ *n* anochecer *m*

dust¹ /dʌst/ *n* polvo *m*; **to bite the ~** ‹‹person›› morder* el polvo

dust² *vt* **1** (remove dust from): **to ~ the furniture** quitarles el polvo a los muebles, sacudir los muebles (CS, Méx) **2** (sprinkle) **to ~ sth WITH sth** espolvorear algo CON algo

dust: ~ **bin** /'dʌstbɪn, 'dʌsbɪn/ *n* (BrE) cubo *m or* (CS, Per) tacho *m or* (Méx) tambo *m or* (Col) caneca *f or* (Ven) tobo *m* de la basura; ~**cart** /'dʌstkɑːrt, 'dʌskɑːrt ‖'dʌstkɑːt, dʌskɑːt/ *n* (BrE) camión *m* de la basura; ~ **cloth** *n* (AmE) trapo *m* del polvo, trapo *m* de sacudir (CS, Méx), sacudidor *m* (Méx)

duster /'dʌstər ‖'dʌstə(r)/ *n* **1** (Clothing) (housecoat) (AmE) guardapolvo *m* **2** (BrE) **(a)** (for blackboard) borrador *m* **(b)** ▸ DUST CLOTH

dust: ~ **jacket** *n* sobrecubierta *f*; ~**man** /'dʌstmən, 'dʌsmən/ *n* (*pl* **-men** /-mən/) (BrE) basurero *m*; ~**pan** /'dʌstpæn, 'dʌspæn/ *n* pala *f*, recogedor *m*

dusty /'dʌsti/ *adj* **-tier, -tiest** ‹*furniture*› cubierto de polvo; ‹*road/plain*› polvoriento

Dutch¹ /dʌtʃ/ *adj* holandés; **to go ~** pagar* a escote (fam), pagar* *or* ir* a la americana (AmL), pagar* *or* ir* a la inglesa (Chi fam)

Dutch² *n* **(a)** (language) holandés *m* **(b)** (people) (+ *pl vb*) **the ~** los holandeses

Dutch: ~**man** /'dʌtʃmən/ *n* (*pl* **-men** /-mən/) holandés *m*; ~**woman** *n* holandesa *f*

dutiful /'duːtɪfəl ‖'djuːtɪfəl/ *adj* consciente de sus deberes

duty /'duːti ‖'djuːti/ *n* (*pl* **duties**) **1** (obligation) deber *m*, obligación *f* **2** **(a)** (service) servicio *m*; **to do ~ as sth** hacer* las veces de algo, servir* de algo **(b)** (in phrases) **to be on/off ~** ‹‹nurse/doctor›› estar*/no estar* de turno *or* guardia; ‹‹policeman/fireman›› estar*/no estar* de servicio **(c)** **duties** *pl n* (responsibilities) (frml) funciones *fpl*, responsabilidades *fpl* **3** (Tax) (*often pl*) impuesto *m*

duty: ~**-free** /'duːti'friː ‖,djuːti'friː/ *adj* libre de impuestos; ~**-free shop** *n* duty free *m*, tienda *f* libre de impuestos

duvet /'duːveɪ/ *n* (BrE) edredón *m* (nórdico)

DVD *n* = **digital video disc**

dwarf¹ /dwɔːrf ‖dwɔːf/ *n* (*pl* ~**s** *or* **dwarves** /dwɔːrvz/) enano, -na *m,f*; (before *n*) ‹*tree/species*› enano

dwarf² *vt* ‹*building*› hacer* parecer pequeño

dwell /dwel/ (*past & past p* **dwelt** *or* **dwelled**) *vi* (liter) morar, (liter) vivir
■ **dwell on** [*v + prep + o*]: **try not to ~ on the past** trata de no pensar demasiado en el pasado; **the documentary ~s excessively on ...** el documental se detiene demasiado *or* hace demasiado hincapié en ...

dwelling /'dwelɪŋ/ *n* **(a)** (habitation) (liter) morada *f* (liter) **(b)** (house) (frml) vivienda *f*

dwelt /dwelt/ *past & past p of* DWELL

dwindle /'dwɪndl/ *vi* **(a)** ‹*numbers/population*› disminuir*, menguar*, reducirse* **(b)** **dwindling** *pres p*: **dwindling resources** recursos *mpl* cada vez más limitados

dye¹ /daɪ/ *n* tintura *f*, tinte *m*

dye² **dyes, dyeing, dyed** *vt* teñir*

dying /'daɪɪŋ/ *adj* (before *n*) **(a)** (near death, extinction) ‹*person/animal*› moribundo, agonizante; ‹*race/art*› en vías de extinción **(b)** (related to time of death) ‹*wish/words/breath*› último, postrero (liter)

dyke /daɪk/ *n* **1** ▸ DIKE 1 **2** (lesbian) (sl & often pej) tortillera *f* (arg)

dynamic /daɪ'næmɪk/ *adj* dinámico

dynamism /'daɪnəmɪzəm/ *n* dinamismo *m*

dynamite /'daɪnəmaɪt/ *n* dinamita *f*

dynamo /'daɪnəməʊ/ *n* (*pl* **-mos**) dínamo *m or* dinamo *m* (AmL), dínamo *f or* dinamo *f* (Esp)

dynasty /'daɪnəsti ‖'dɪnəsti/ *n* (*pl* **-ties**) dinastía *f*

dysentery /'dɪsntəri ‖'dɪsəntri/ *n* disentería *f*

dysfunction /dɪs'fʌŋkʃən/ *n* disfunción *f*

dysfunctional /dɪs'fʌŋkʃnəl ‖dɪs'fʌŋkʃənl/ *adj* disfuncional

dyslexia /dɪs'leksiə/ *n* dislexia *f*

dyslexic /dɪs'leksɪk/ *adj* disléxico

Ee

E, e /iː/ n (a) (letter) E, e f (b) (Mus) mi m

E (= east) E

each¹ /iːtʃ/ adj cada adj inv

each² pron [1] cada uno, cada una; **he questioned ∼ of them in turn** les preguntó uno por uno [2] **each other: they are always criticizing ∼ other** siempre se están criticando el uno al otro; (if more than two people) siempre se están criticando unos a otros; **their respect for ∼ other** su mutuo respeto

each³ adv: **we were paid $10 ∼** nos pagaron 10 dólares a cada uno; **the apples are 20 cents ∼** las manzanas valen 20 centavos por pieza or cada una

eager /ˈiːgər ‖ ˈiːgə(r)/ adj (excited, impatient) impaciente, ansioso; (keen) entusiasta; **he's ∼ to please** está deseoso de complacer; **she is ∼ for change** tiene muchos deseos de cambio

eagerly /ˈiːgərli ‖ ˈiːgəli/ adv ⟨accept/agree⟩ con entusiasmo; ⟨await⟩ ansiosamente, con ansiedad e impaciencia; ⟨listen/read⟩ con avidez

eagle /ˈiːgəl/ n águila f‡

ear /ɪr ‖ ɪə(r)/ n [1] **(a)** (Anat) oreja f; (organ) oído m **(b)** (sense of hearing) (no pl) oído m; **to play sth by ∼** tocar* algo de oído [2] (of corn) espiga f

ear: ∼ache n dolor m de oído; **∼drum** n tímpano m

earl /ɜːrl ‖ ɜːl/ n conde m

early¹ /ˈɜːrli ‖ ˈɜːli/ adj **-lier, -liest** [1] (before expected time) ⟨arrival/elections⟩ anticipado; **to be ∼** «person» llegar* temprano; **the bus was ∼** el autobús pasó (or salió etc) antes de la hora [2] (before normal time): **to have an ∼ night** acostarse* temprano; **∼ retirement** jubilación f anticipada **(b)** ⟨crop/variety⟩ temprano, tempranero [3] (far back in time): **∼ man** el hombre primitivo; **his earliest memories** sus primeros recuerdos [4] (toward beginning of period): **it's too ∼ to tell** es demasiado pronto para saber; **in ∼ June** a principios de junio; **he was in his ∼ twenties** tenía poco más de veinte años

early² adv **-lier, -liest** [1] (before expected time) temprano [2] (before usual time) temprano, pronto (Esp) [3] (toward beginning of period): **∼ in the morning** por la mañana temprano; **∼ in the year** a principios de año; **∼ (on) in her career** en los comienzos de su carrera [4] (soon) pronto; **they won't be here till nine at the earliest** por temprano que lleguen no estarán aquí antes de las nueve

ear: ∼mark vt ⟨money/funds⟩ destinar; **∼muffs** pl n orejeras fpl

earn /ɜːrn ‖ ɜːn/ vt [1] ⟨money/wages⟩ ganar; ⟨interest⟩ dar* [2] ⟨respect/gratitude⟩ ganarse; ⟨promotion⟩ ganar

earnest¹ /ˈɜːrnəst ‖ ˈɜːnɪst/ adj **(a)** (sincere) (frml) ⟨effort/attempt⟩ serio; ⟨wish⟩ ferviente **(b)** (serious) serio

earnest² n **in ∼** en serio

earnings /ˈɜːrnɪŋz ‖ ˈɜːnɪŋz/ pl n ingresos mpl

ear: ∼plug n tapón m para el oído; **∼ring** n arete m (AmL), aro m (CS), pendiente m (Esp), caravana f (Ur); **∼shot** n: **to be within/out of ∼shot** estar*/no estar* lo suficientemente cerca como para oír

earth /ɜːrθ ‖ ɜːθ/ n [1] **(a)** (Astron, Relig) tierra f; **the ∼** o **E∼** la Tierra **(b)** (as intensifier): **why on ∼ didn't you warn me?** ¿por qué diablos no me avisaste? [2] (land, soil) tierra f [3] (BrE Elec) tierra f

earthenware /ˈɜːrθənwər ‖ ˈɜːθənweə(r)/ n (material) barro m (cocido); (dishes) vajilla f de barro (cocido)

earth: ∼quake n terremoto m; **∼worm** n lombriz f (de tierra)

earwig /ˈɪrwɪg ‖ ˈɪəwɪg/ n tijereta f, cortapicos m

ease¹ /iːz/ n [1] (facility) facilidad f; **∼ of operation** facilidad de manejo; **for ∼ of access** para facilitar el acceso; **with ∼** fácilmente [2] **(a)** (freedom from constraint): **at ∼** a gusto; **to put sb at his/her ∼** hacer* que algn se sienta a gusto **(b)** (Mil): **(stand) at ∼!** ¡descansen!

ease² vt [1] **(a)** (relieve) ⟨pain⟩ calmar, aliviar; ⟨tension⟩ hacer* disminuir, aliviar; ⟨burden⟩ aligerar; **to ∼ sb's mind** tranquilizar* a algn **(b)** (make easier) ⟨situation/transition⟩ facilitar; **to ∼ the way for sth** preparar el terreno para algo [2] **(a)** ⟨rules/restrictions⟩ relajar **(b)** ⟨belt/rope⟩ aflojar [3] (move with care) (+ adv compl): **they ∼d him into the wheelchair** lo sentaron con cuidado en la silla de ruedas; **he ∼d the key into the lock** introdujo la llave en la cerradura con cuidado
■ **∼** vi ⟨pain⟩ aliviarse, calmarse; ⟨tension⟩ disminuir*
■ **ease off** [v + adv] «rain» amainar; «pain» aliviarse, calmarse; «pressure/traffic» disminuir*
■ **ease up** [v + adv] (slacken pace — of life) tomarse las cosas con más calma; (— of work, activity) bajar el ritmo

easel /ˈiːzəl/ n caballete m

easily /ˈiːzəli ‖ ˈiːzɪli/ adv [1] (without difficulty) fácilmente, con facilidad **(b)** (readily) ⟨break/stain/cry⟩ con facilidad [2] (by far) con mucho, (de) lejos (AmL fam); **there's ∼ enough for everybody** hay de sobra para todos

east¹ /iːst/ n [1] (point of the compass, direction) este m; **the ∼, the E∼** (region) el este [2] **the East** (the Orient) (el) Oriente

east² adj (before n) este adj inv, oriental; ⟨wind⟩ del este

east³ adv al este

east: ∼bound adj que va (or iba etc) en dirección este or hacia el este; **E∼ End** n (in UK) **the E∼ End of** (London) barrio del este de Londres de tradición obrera

Easter /'i:stər ‖'i:stə(r)/ n Pascua f (de Resurrección); (before n) ~ **Day** o **Sunday** (el) Domingo de Pascua or Resurrección; ~ **egg** huevo m de Pascua

easterly /'i:stərli ‖'i:stəli/ adj ⟨wind⟩ del este; **in an** ~ **direction** hacia el este, en dirección este

eastern /'i:stərn ‖'i:stən/ adj **(a)** (Geog) (before n) oriental, este adj inv; **heavy rain over** ~ **England** fuertes lluvias en or sobre el este de Inglaterra; **the** ~ **states** los estados del este; **E**~ **Europe** Europa Oriental or del Este **(b)** (oriental) ⟨appearance/custom⟩ oriental

eastward¹ /'i:stwərd ‖'i:stwəd/ adj (before n): **in an** ~ **direction** en dirección este, hacia el este

eastward², (BrE) **eastwards** /-z/ adv hacia el este

easy¹ /'i:zi/ adj **easier, easiest** [1] (not difficult) fácil; **it's** ~ **to see that ...** es fácil ver que ...; **she was an** ~ **winner** ganó sin problemas [2] (undemanding) ⟨life⟩ fácil; **to be** ~ **on the eye** ser* agradable a la vista

easy² adv [1] (without difficulty): **money doesn't come** ~ el dinero no es fácil de conseguir; ~ **come,** ~ **go** así como viene se va [2] (slowly, calmly) despacio, con calma; ~ **does it** despacio; **to take it** ~ tomárselo con calma

easy: ~ **chair** n sillón m, poltrona f, butaca f; ~**going** /'i:zi'gəʊɪŋ/ adj: **she's very** ~**going** es una persona de trato fácil or sin complicaciones

eat /i:t/ (past **ate**; past p **eaten**) vt/i comer
■ **eat away** [v + o + adv, v + adv + o] ⟨rats/mice⟩ roer*; ⟨moths⟩ picar*, comerse; ⟨acid⟩ corroer*
■ **eat into** [v + prep + o] ⟨acid/rust⟩ corroer*; ⟨profits/savings⟩ comerse
■ **eat up** [1] [v + o + adv, v + adv + o] (finish) ⟨meal/food⟩ comerse [2] [v + adv + o] (finish meal) terminar (de comer) [3] [v + adv + o] (consume) ⟨fuel/electricity⟩ consumir, gastar [4] [v + o + adv] ⟨curiosity/ambition⟩ consumir

eaten /'i:tn/ past p of EAT

eater /'i:tər ‖'i:tə(r)/ n: **he's a big** ~ come mucho, es muy comelón or (CS, Esp) comilón (fam); **we're big meat** ~**s** comemos mucha carne

eaves /i:vz/ pl n alero m

eavesdrop /'i:vzdrɑːp ‖'i:vzdrɒp/ vi **-pp-** to ~ (**on sth/sb**) escuchar (algo/a algn) a escondidas

ebb¹ /eb/ n **(a)** ⟨tide⟩ reflujo m; **the** ~ **and flow of the tide** el flujo y reflujo de la marea; **to be at a low** ~ ⟨person⟩ estar* decaído; ⟨diplomatic relations⟩ estar* en un punto bajo

ebb² vi **(a)** ⟨tide⟩ bajar, retroceder; **to** ~ **and flow** fluir* y refluir* **(b)** (dwindle) decaer*
■ **ebb away** [v + adv]: **his life was** ~**ing away** se consumía poco a poco; **I felt my strength** ~**ing away** sentí que me abandonaban las fuerzas

ebb tide n reflujo m

ebony /'ebəni/ n **(a)** (wood) ébano m **(b)** (color) color m (de) ébano; (before n) ⟨hair/skin⟩ negro como el ébano

EC n (= **European Community**) CE f

eccentric¹ /ɪk'sentrɪk, ek-/ adj excéntrico

eccentric² n excéntrico, -ca m,f

eccentricity /'eksen'trɪsəti/ n (pl **-ties**) excentricidad f

ecclesiastical /ɪ'kli:zi'æstɪkəl/ adj eclesiástico

echo¹ /'ekəʊ/ n (pl **-oes**) eco m

echo² vi ⟨footsteps/voices⟩ hacer* eco

eclair /eɪ'kleə(r), ɪ'kleə(r)/ n: pastel individual relleno de crema

eclipse¹ /ɪ'klɪps/ n eclipse m

eclipse² vt eclipsar

eco-friendly /'i:kəʊ,frendli/ adj ecológico, que no daña el medio ambiente

ecological /'i:kə'lɑːdʒəkəl ‖,i:kə'lɒdʒɪkəl/ adj ecológico

ecologist /ɪ'kɑːlədʒəst ‖i:'kɒlədʒɪst/ n (student of ecology) ecólogo, -ga m,f; (conservationist) ecologista mf

ecology /ɪ'kɑːlədʒi ‖i:'kɒlədʒi/ n ecología f

e-commerce /i:'kɑːmərs ‖i:'kɒmɜ:s/ n. comercio m electrónico, e-comercio m

economic /'ekə'nɑːmɪk, 'i:k- ‖,i:kə'nɒmɪk, ,ek-/ adj económico

economical /'ekə'nɑːmɪkəl, 'i:k- ‖,i:kə'nɒmɪkəl, ,ek-/ adj económico

economics /'ekə'nɑːmɪks, 'i:k- ‖,i:kə'nɒmɪks, ,ek-/ n **(a)** (+ sing vb) economía f **(b)** (financial aspect) (+ pl vb) aspecto m económico

economist /ɪ'kɑːnəməst ‖i:'kɒnəmɪst/ n economista mf

economize /ɪ'kɑːnəmaɪz ‖i:'kɒnəmaɪz/ vi economizar*; **to** ~ **on sth** economizar* algo

economy /ɪ'kɑːnəmi, i:- ‖i:'kɒnəmi/ n (pl **-mies**) [1] (economic state or system of country) economía f [2] **(a)** (saving): **to make economies** economizar*, hacer* economía(s) **(b)** (thrift) economía f; (before n) ⟨pack/size⟩ familiar; ~ **class** clase f turista

ecosystem /'i:kəʊ,sɪstəm/ n ecosistema m

ecstasy /'ekstəsi/ n (pl **-sies**) **(a)** (state) éxtasis m **(b)** (drug) éxtasis m

ecstatic /ɪk'stætɪk/ adj ⟨look/expression⟩ extasiado, extático; ⟨applause⟩ clamoroso

ECU /'i:kju:, eɪ'ku:/ n (pl **ECUs**) ecu m

Ecuador /'ekwədɔ:r ‖'ekwədɔ:(r)/ n Ecuador m

Ecuadorean¹ /'ekwə'dɔ:riən/ adj ecuatoriano

Ecuadorean² n ecuatoriano, -na m,f

eczema /ɪg'zi:mə, 'egzəmə ‖'eksɪmə/ n eczema m

eddy¹ /'edi/ n (pl **eddies**) remolino m, torbellino m

eddy² vi **eddies, eddying, eddied** ⟨water⟩ formar remolinos; ⟨smoke/dust⟩ arremolinarse

Eden /'i:dn/ n Edén m

edge /edʒ/ n [1] **(a)** (no pl) (border, brink — of town) afueras fpl; (— of forest) lindero m, borde m; (— of river, lake) orilla f, margen m; (— of cliff) borde m **(b)** (of plate, table, chair) borde m; (of coin)

· ·

AmC	América Central	Arg	Argentina	Cu	Cuba	Per	Perú
AmL	América Latina	Bol	Bolivia	Ec	Ecuador	RPI	Río de la Plata
AmS	América del Sur	Chi	Chile	Esp	España	Ur	Uruguay
Andes	Región andina	CS	Cono Sur	Méx	México	Ven	Venezuela

canto m; (of page) margen m **2** (cutting part) filo m; *to be on* ~ estar* nervioso, tener* los nervios de punta (fam)

edge² vt: the collar was ~d with fur el cuello estaba ribeteado de piel; the paper was ~d in black el papel tenía un borde negro

■ ~ vi (+ adv compl): to ~ forward/closer/away ir* avanzando/acercándose/alejándose (poco a poco)

edging /'edʒɪŋ/ n borde m

edgy /'edʒi/ adj tenso, con los nervios de punta

edible /'edəbəl/ adj (safe to eat) comestible; (eatable) pasable, comible

edifying /'edəfaɪŋ ǁ'edɪfaɪɪŋ/ adj edificante

Edinburgh /'edn̩ˌbɜːrə, -rəʊ ǁ'edɪnbrə/ n Edimburgo m

edit /'edət ǁ'edɪt/ vt **1** ⟨manuscript⟩ (correct) corregir*, editar; (cut) recortar, editar **2** ⟨movie/tape⟩ editar **3** (manage) ⟨newspaper/magazine⟩ dirigir*

edition /ɪ'dɪʃən/ n edición f

editor /'edətər ǁ'edɪtə(r)/ n **1** (of text) redactor, -tora m,f, editor, -tora m,f; (of collected works, series) editor, -tora m,f **2** (of newspaper, magazine) director, -tora m,f, redactor, -tora m,f responsable **3** (of movie, radio show) editor, -tora m,f

editorial¹ /ˌedə'tɔːriəl ǁˌedɪ'tɔːriəl/ adj **(a)** (Publ) ⟨assistant/director⟩ de redacción **(b)** (Journ) ⟨comment/decision/freedom⟩ editorial

editorial² n editorial m

EDT (in US) = **Eastern Daylight Time**

educate /'edʒəkeɪt ǁ'edjʊkeɪt/ vt **(a)** (teach, school) educar* **(b)** (make aware) concientizar* or (Esp) concienciar

educated /'edʒəkeɪtəd ǁ'edjʊkeɪtɪd/ adj ⟨person⟩ culto; to make an ~ guess hacer* una conjetura hecha con cierta base

education /ˌedʒə'keɪʃən ǁˌedjʊ'keɪʃən/ n educación f; (before n) ⟨system/policy⟩ educativo

educational /ˌedʒə'keɪʃn̩əl ǁˌedjʊ'keɪʃənl̩/ adj **(a)** ⟨establishment⟩ docente, de enseñanza; ⟨toy⟩ educativo **(b)** (instructive) instructivo

Edwardian /ed'wɔːrdiən ǁed'wɔːdiən/ adj eduardiano

EEC n (= **European Economic Community**) CEE f

eel /iːl/ n anguila f

e'er /er ǁeə(r)/ adv (poet & arch) ▶ EVER

eerie /'ɪri ǁ'ɪəri/ adj eerier, eeriest ⟨atmosphere/silence/cry⟩ inquietante, espeluznante; ⟨glow/place⟩ fantasmagórico

efface /ɪ'feɪs/ vt (fml) borrar

effect¹ /ɪ'fekt/ n **1** **(a)** (consequence) efecto m; to take ~ surtir efecto **(b)** in effect de hecho, realmente **(c)** (phenomenon) efecto m **2** (impression) impresión f; he only did it for ~ lo hizo sólo para llamar la atención **3** (applicability, operation): to come into ~, to take ~ entrar en vigor or en vigencia **4** (meaning): a statement was issued to the ~ that … (fml) se hizo público un comunicado anunciando que …; he said it wasn't true, or words to that ~ dijo que no era verdad o algo de ese tenor

5 **effects** pl **(a)** (special ~s) (Cin, TV) efectos mpl especiales **(b)** (belongings) (fml) efectos mpl (fml)

effect² vt (fml) ⟨reconciliation/cure⟩ lograr; ⟨escape⟩ llevar a cabo; ⟨repairs/payment⟩ efectuar* (fml)

effective /ɪ'fektɪv/ adj **(a)** (producing the desired result) ⟨method/treatment⟩ eficaz, efectivo **(b)** (striking) ⟨design/contrast⟩ de mucho efecto **(c)** (real) (before n) ⟨control/leader⟩ efectivo

effectively /ɪ'fektɪvli/ adv **(a)** ⟨manage/spend⟩ con eficacia, eficazmente **(b)** ⟨contrast/decorate⟩ con mucho gran efecto; ⟨speak⟩ convincentemente **(c)** (in effect) (indep) de hecho

effeminate /ə'femənət ǁɪ'femɪnət/ adj afeminado

effervescent /ˌefər'vesənt ǁˌefə'vesənt/ adj ⟨liquid/personality⟩ efervescente

efficiency /ɪ'fɪʃənsi/ n (pl -cies) (of person, system) eficiencia f; (Mech Eng, Phys) rendimiento m

efficient /ɪ'fɪʃənt/ adj ⟨person/system⟩ eficiente; ⟨machine/engine⟩ de buen rendimiento

efficiently /ɪ'fɪʃəntli/ adv eficientemente

effigy /'efədʒi ǁ'efɪdʒi/ n (pl -gies) efigie f

effluent /'efluənt/ n (liquid waste) vertidos mpl; (sewage) aguas fpl residuales

effort /'efərt ǁ'efət/ n esfuerzo m; to make an ~ hacer* un esfuerzo, esforzarse*; it's not worth the ~ no merece or vale la pena

effortless /'efərtləs ǁ'efətlɪs/ adj ⟨grace⟩ natural; ⟨prose/style⟩ fluido

e.g. (for example) p. ej. or vg. or e.g.; (in speech) por ejemplo

egalitarian /ɪˌgælə'teriən ǁɪˌgælɪ'teəriən/ adj igualitario

egg /eg/ n huevo m

■ **egg on** [v + o + adv, v + adv + o] incitar

egg: ~**cup** n huevera f; ~**plant** n (AmE) berenjena f; ~**shell** n cáscara f de huevo; ~ **timer** n (with sand) reloj m de arena (de tres minutos); (clockwork) avisador m; ~ **white** n clara f de huevo; ~ **yolk** n yema f de huevo

ego /'iːgəʊ, 'egəʊ/ n (pl **egos**) **(a)** (Psych) the ~ el yo, el ego **(b)** (self-regard) amor m propio, ego m

ego trip n (colloq): his autobiography is simply an ~ ~ su autobiografía es un regodeo ególatra

Egypt /'iːdʒəpt ǁ'iːdʒɪpt/ n Egipto m

Egyptian¹ /ɪ'dʒɪpʃən/ adj egipcio

Egyptian² n egipcio, -cia m,f

eiderdown /'aɪdərdaʊn ǁ'aɪdədaʊn/ n edredón m

eight /eɪt/ adj/n ocho adj inv/m; see also FOUR¹

eighteen /'eɪtiːn/ adj/n dieciocho adj inv/m; see also FOUR

eighteenth¹ /'eɪtiːnθ/ adj decimoctavo

eighteenth² adv en decimoctavo lugar

eighteenth³ n **(a)** (Math) dieciochoavo m; (part) dieciochoava parte f **(b)** (birthday): it's her ~ today hoy cumple dieciocho años

eighth¹ /eɪtθ/ adj octavo

eighth² adv en octavo lugar

eighth³ n (Math) octavo m; (part) octava parte f

eighth note n (AmE) corchea f

eightieth¹ /'eɪtiəθ/ adj octogésimo

eightieth² *adv* en octogésimo lugar

eightieth³ *n* (Math) ochentavo *m*; (part) ochentava *or* octogésima parte *f*

eighty /'eɪti/ *adj/n* ochenta *adj inv/m*; *see also* FOUR¹

Eire /'erə ‖'eərə/ *n* Eire *m*, Irlanda *f*

either¹ /'iːðər, 'aɪðər ‖'iːðə(r), 'aɪðə(r)/ *conj* either ... or ... o ... o ...

■ Note In the usual translation of *either ... or*, o ... o, o becomes *u* when it precedes a word beginning with o or ho.

either² *adj*: you can take ~ route puedes tomar cualquiera de las dos rutas; on ~ side of the path a ambos lados del camino

either³ *pron* (*esp* BrE) cualquiera; (*with neg*) ninguno, -na; (*in questions*) alguno, -na

either⁴ *adv* (*with neg*) tampoco; she can't cook and he can't ~ ella no sabe cocinar y él tampoco

ejaculate /ɪ'dʒækjəleɪt ‖ɪ'dʒækjʊleɪt/ *vi* (Physiol) eyacular

eject /ɪ'dʒekt/ *vt* ⟨troublemaker/cassette⟩ expulsar

■ ~ *vi* (Aviat) eyectarse

eke out /iːk/ [*v* + *adv* + *o*, *v* + *o* + *adv*] (a) (make last) ⟨resources/funds⟩ estirar, hacer* alcanzar (b) (barely obtain): to ~ out a living ganarse la vida a duras penas

elaborate¹ /ɪ'læbərət/ *adj* ⟨decoration/design/hairstyle⟩ complicado; ⟨meal⟩ de mucho trabajo; ⟨plan⟩ minucioso

elaborate² /ɪ'læbəreɪt/ *vt* elaborar

■ ~ *vi* dar* (más) detalles

elapse /ɪ'læps/ *vi* transcurrir

elastic¹ /ɪ'læstɪk/ *n* (a) (Tex) elástico *m* (b) (garter) (AmE) liga *f* (c) (AmE) ▶ ELASTIC BAND

elastic² *adj* ⟨waistband/garter⟩ de elástico; ⟨stocking⟩ elastizado; ⟨fiber/properties⟩ elástico

elastic band *n* (*esp* BrE) goma *f* (elástica), gomita *f*, liga *f* (Méx), caucho *m* (Col), elástico *m* (Chi), banda *f* elástica (Ven)

elated /ɪ'leɪtəd ‖ɪ'leɪtɪd/ *adj* eufórico

elbow¹ /'elbəʊ/ *n* codo *m*

elbow² *vt* darle* un codazo a; they ~ed us out of the way nos apartaron a empujones

elbow: ~ **grease** *n* (colloq): put some ~ grease into it! ¡dale con más fuerza! (fam); ~ **room** *n* espacio *m*

elder¹ /'eldər ‖'eldə(r)/ *adj* mayor

elder² *n* [1] (a) (older person): she's my ~ by two years me lleva dos años, es dos años mayor que yo (b) (senior person): the village/tribal ~s los ancianos del pueblo/de la tribu (c) (Relig) miembro *m* del consejo [2] (Bot) saúco *m*

elderberry /'eldər,beri ‖'eldəberi/ *n* (*pl* -ries) baya *f* del saúco

elderly¹ /'eldərli ‖'eldəli/ *adj* mayor, de edad

elderly² *pl n* the ~ los ancianos

eldest /'eldəst ‖'eldɪst/ *adj* (*before n*) ⟨brother/sister/child⟩ mayor; the ~ (*as pron*) el/la mayor, el/la de más edad

elect¹ /ɪ'lekt/ *vt* [1] (Adm, Govt) elegir* [2] (choose) (frml) to ~ to + INF optar POR + INF

elect² *adj* (*after n*): the president ~ el presidente electo, la presidenta electa

election /ɪ'lekʃən/ *n* (a) (event) elecciones *fpl*; to call/hold an ~ convocar*/celebrar elecciones; (*before n*) ⟨campaign/speech⟩ electoral; ⟨day/results⟩ de las elecciones (b) (act) elección *f*

elector /ɪ'lektər ‖ɪ'lektə(r)/ *n* elector, -tora *m,f*

electoral /ɪ'lektərəl/ *adj* (*usu before n*) ⟨system/reform⟩ electoral; ~ **register** *o* **roll** padrón *m* (AmL) *or* (Esp) censo *m or* (Chi, Ven) registro *m or* (Col) planilla *f* electoral

electorate /ɪ'lektərət/ *n* (+ *sing or pl vb*) electorado *m*

electric /ɪ'lektrɪk/ *adj* eléctrico; ⟨fence⟩ electrificado; ⟨performance/atmosphere⟩ electrizante

electrical /ɪ'lektrɪkəl/ *adj* eléctrico

electric: ~ **blanket** *n* manta *f or* (AmL exc CS) cobija *f or* (CS) frazada *f* eléctrica; ~ **chair** *n* silla *f* eléctrica

electrician /ɪ,lek'trɪʃən/ *n* electricista *mf*

electricity /ɪ,lek'trɪsəti/ *n* electricidad *f*

electric shock *n* descarga *f* eléctrica

electrify /ɪ'lektrəfaɪ ‖ɪ'lektrɪfaɪ/ *vt* -fies, -fying, -fied electrificar*; (excite, thrill) electrizar*

electrocute /ɪ'lektrəkjuːt/ *vt* electrocutar

electrode /ɪ'lektrəʊd/ *n* electrodo *m*

electrolysis /ɪ'lek'trɒləsɪs ‖,ɪlek'trɒləsɪs/ *n* electrólisis *f*

electron /ɪ'lektrɒːn ‖ɪ'lektrɒn/ *n* electrón *m*

electronic /ɪ'lek'trɒːnɪk ‖,ɪlek'trɒnɪk/ *adj* electrónico

electronic mail *n* correo *m* electrónico

electronics /ɪ'lek'trɒːnɪks ‖,ɪlek'trɒnɪks/ *n* (a) (subject) (+ *sing vb*) electrónica *f*; (*before n*) ⟨industry⟩ electrónico (b) (circuitry) (+ *sing or pl vb*) sistema *m* electrónico

elegance /'eligəns/ *n* elegancia *f*

elegant /'eligənt/ *adj* elegante

element /'eləmənt ‖'elɪmənt/ *n* [1] (a) (part, group) elemento *m*; an ~ of doubt elemento de duda; extremist ~s in society elementos extremistas de la sociedad (b) **elements** *pl* (rudiments): the basic ~s of self-defense los principios elementales de la defensa personal [2] (Chem) elemento *m* [3] **elements** *pl* (weather) (liter) the ~s los elementos [4] (preferred environment) elemento *m*; to be in one's ~ estar* en su (*or* mi *etc*) elemento [5] (of kettle, heater) resistencia *f*, elemento *m* (CS)

elementary /'elə'mentəri ‖,elɪ'mentri/ *adj* elemental

elementary: ~ **school** *n* (in US) escuela *f* (de enseñanza) primaria; ~ **teacher** *n* (in US) maestro, -tra *m,f* de enseñanza primaria

elephant /'eləfənt ‖'elɪfənt/ *n* elefante, -ta *m,f*

elevate /'eləveɪt ‖'elɪveɪt/ *vt* (a) (promote): to ~ sb to the peerage concederle a algn el título de lord/lady; he's been ~d to the position of manager (hum) lo han ascendido a director (b) (frml) ⟨spirit⟩ elevar (c) ⟨load/platform⟩ elevar (frml), subir

elevated railroad /'eləveɪtəd ‖'elɪvˈeɪtɪd/ *n* (AmE) ferrocarril *m* elevado

elevation /'elə'veɪʃən ‖,elɪ'veɪʃən/ *n* [1] (promotion) elevación *f* [2] (angle) elevación *f* [3] (altitude) altura *f*

elevator /'eləveɪtər ‖'elɪveɪtə(r)/ *n* (a) (for passengers) (AmE) ascensor *m*, elevador *m* (Méx) (b) (for goods) elevador *m*, montacargas *m*

eleven¹ /ɪ'levən/ *n* (a) (number) once *m; see also* FOUR¹ (b) (in soccer, field hockey) equipo *m*, once *m* (period)

eleven² *adj* once *adj inv*

eleventh¹ /ɪ'levənθ/ *adj* undécimo

eleventh² *adv* en undécimo lugar

eleventh³ *n* (Math) onceavo *m*; (part) onceava parte *f*

elf /elf/ *n* (*pl* **elves**) geniecillo *m*, elfo *m*

elicit /ɪ'lɪsət ‖ɪ'lɪsɪt/ *vt* ‹laughter/smile› provocar*; **to ~ sth** (FROM sb) ‹explanation/reply› obtener* algo (DE algn)

eligible /'elədʒəbəl ‖'elɪdʒəbəl/ *adj* (a) (qualified, suitable) ‹applicant/candidate› que reúne los requisitos necesarios; **he's ~ for a grant** tiene derecho a solicitar una beca; **he is not ~ to compete** no reúne los requisitos necesarios para competir (b) (marriageable): **an ~ bachelor** un buen partido

eliminate /ɪ'lɪməneɪt ‖ɪ'lɪmɪmeɪt/ *vt* eliminar; ‹possibility/suspect› descartar

elimination /ɪ'lɪmə'neɪʃən ‖ɪ,lɪmɪ'neɪʃən/ *n* (getting rid of) eliminación *f*; (ruling out) descarte *m*; **by a process of ~** por (un proceso de) eliminación *or* descarte

elite¹ /er'li:t, i-/ *n* (+ *sing or pl vb*) elite *f*, élite *f*

elite² *adj* (before n) selecto, de elite *or* élite

elitism /er'li:tɪzəm, i-/ *n* elitismo *m*

elitist /er'li:tɪst, i-/ *adj* elitista

elixir /ɪ'lɪksər ‖ɪ'lɪksə(r)/ *n* elixir *m*

Elizabethan /ɪ'lɪzə'bi:θən/ *adj* isabelino

elk /elk/ *n* (*pl* **~s** *or* **~**) (European animal) alce *m*; (American animal) uapití *m*

elm /elm/ *n* **~** (**tree**) olmo *m*

elocution /'elə'kju:ʃən/ *n* dicción *f*, elocución *f*

elongated /ɪ'lɔ:ŋgeɪtəd ‖'i:lɒŋgeɪtɪd/ *adj* alargado

elope /ɪ'ləup/ *vi* fugarse* (con un amante, novio para casarse)

eloquent /'eləkwənt/ *adj* elocuente

El Salvador /el'sælvədɔ:r ‖,el'sælvədɔ:(r)/ *n* El Salvador

else /els/ *adv* 1 (after pron): **somebody** *o* **someone ~** otra persona; **everybody** *o* **everyone ~** todos los demás; **everything ~** todo lo demás; **there's not much ~ we can do** no podemos hacer mucho más; **nobody ~** nadie más; **they have nowhere ~ to go** no tienen ningún otro sitio *or* lugar adonde ir; **anything ~?** ¿algo más? 2 (with interrog): **what/who ~?** ¿qué/quién más?; **what ~ can you expect from her?** ¿qué otra cosa se puede esperar de ella? 3 **or else** (as conj) si no

elsewhere /'elshwer ‖,els'weə(r)/ *adv*: **to go ~** ir* a otro sitio *or* lugar; **~ in Europe** en otras partes *or* otros lugares de Europa

elude /i:'lu:d ‖ɪ'lu:d/ *vt* (avoid) eludir; (escape from) escaparse de

elusive /i:'lu:sɪv ‖i'lu:sɪv/ *adj* ‹enemy/prey› escurridizo, difícil de aprehender; ‹goal/ agreement› difícil de alcanzar

elves /elvz/ *pl of* ELF

emaciated /ɪ'meɪʃieɪtəd ‖ɪ'meɪsieɪtɪd/ *adj* ‹person/animal› escuálido; ‹body/face› consumido

E-mail, e-mail /'i:meɪl/ *n* correo *m* electrónico

emanate /'eməneɪt/ *vi* **to ~ FROM sth** «gas/ light/sound» emanar DE algo; «ideas/ suggestions» provenir* DE algo

emancipate /ɪ'mænsəpeɪt ‖ɪ'mænsɪpeɪt/ *vt* (frml) emancipar

emancipated /ɪ'mænsəpeɪtəd ‖ɪ'mænsɪpeɪtɪd/ *adj* emancipado; ‹viewpoint/ lifestyle› independiente y progresista

emancipation /ɪ,mænsə'peɪʃən ‖ɪ,mænsɪ'peɪʃən/ *n* (frml) emancipación *f*

embankment /ɪm'bæŋkmənt/ *n* (for road, railroad) terraplén *m*; (as protection) muro *m* de contención

embargo /ɪm'bɑ:rgəu ‖ɪm'bɑ:gəu/ *n* (*pl* **-goes**) embargo *m*, prohibición *f*; **to put an ~ on sth** imponer* un embargo sobre algo

embark /ɪm'bɑ:rk ‖ɪm'bɑ:k/ *vi* (a) (on ship, plane) embarcar(se)* (b) (start) **to ~ ON** *o* **UPON sth** ‹on career/new life› emprender algo; ‹on adventure/undertaking› embarcarse* EN algo

embarrass /ɪm'bærəs/ *vt* hacerle* pasar vergüenza a, avergonzar*

embarrassed /ɪm'bærəst/ *adj*: **an ~ silence** un silencio violento; **I'm ~** me da vergüenza, me da pena (AmL exc CS)

embarrassing /ɪm'bærəsɪŋ/ *adj* ‹situation/ question› embarazoso; **how ~!** ¡qué vergüenza *or* (AmL exc CS) pena!

embarrassment /ɪm'bærəsmənt/ *n* (a) (shame) bochorno *m*, vergüenza *f*, pena *f* (AmL exc CS) (b) (cause of shame): **he's an ~ to his friends** les hace pasar vergüenza a sus amigos

embassy /'embəsi/ *n* (*pl* **-sies**) embajada *f*

embed /ɪm'bed/ *vt* **-dd-** (in rock, wood) enterrar*; **the bullet was ~ded in his arm** la bala quedó alojada en el brazo

ember /'embər ‖'embə(r)/ *n* brasa *f*, ascua *f*

embezzle /ɪm'bezəl/ *vt* desfalcar*, malversar

embittered /ɪm'bɪtərd ‖ɪm'bɪtəd/ *adj* ‹person› amargado; ‹fighting/rivalry› enconado

emblem /'embləm/ *n* emblema *m*

embody /ɪm'bɑ:di ‖ɪm'bɒdi/ *vt* **-dies, -dying, -died** (a) (personify) encarnar, personificar* (b) (express) ‹thought/idea› plasmar, expresar

emboss /ɪm'bɑ:s, 'embɔ:s ‖ɪm'bɒs/ *vt* (a) ‹leather/metal› repujar (b) **embossed** *past p* ‹stationery› con membrete en relieve; ‹wallpaper› estampado en relieve

embrace¹ /ɪm'breɪs/ *vt* (a) (hug) abrazar* (b) ‹idea/principle› abrazar*; ‹lifestyle/religion› *past p* adoptar
■ **~** *vi* abrazarse*

embrace² *n* abrazo *m*

embrocation /'embrə'keɪʃən/ *n* linimento *m*, embrocación *f* (ant)

embroider /ɪm'brɔɪdər ‖ɪm'brɔɪdə(r)/ *vt* ‹cloth/design› bordar; ‹story› adornar

embroidery /ɪm'brɔɪdəri/ *n* (*pl* **-ries**) bordado *m*

embroil /ɪm'brɔɪl/ *vt*: **to be/become ~ed in sth** estar*/verse* envuelto en algo

embryo /'embriəu/ *n* (*pl* **-os**) embrión *m*

emend /i:'mend ‖ɪ'mend/ *vt* (frml) enmendar*

emerald /'emərəld/ n (a) (gem) esmeralda f;
(b) (color) verde m esmeralda

emerge /ɪ'mɜːrdʒ ‖ɪ'mɜːdʒ/ vi (a) (come out)
salir*, aparecer* (b) (become evident, known)
«problem» surgir*; «pattern» dibujarse;
«truth» revelarse; «facts» salir* a la luz

emergency /ɪ'mɜːrdʒənsi ‖ɪ'mɜːdʒənsi/ n (pl
-cies) (a) (serious situation) emergencia f; in an ~
o in case of ~ en una emergencia or en caso de
emergencia (Med) urgencia f; (before n) «case/
operation» de urgencia (c) (Govt): «a state of ~
was declared» se declaró el estado de excepción

emergency: ~ **exit** n salida f de
emergencia; ~ **landing** n aterrizaje m forzoso;
~ **stop** n parada f de emergencia

emery /'eməri/: ~ **board** n lima f de esmeril;
~ **paper** n papel m de lija

emigrant /'emɪgrənt ‖'emɪgrənt/ n emigrante
mf

emigrate /'emɪgreɪt ‖'emɪgreɪt/ vi emigrar

emigration /emə'greɪʃən ‖emɪ'greɪʃən/ n
emigración f

eminent /'emənənt ‖'emɪnənt/ adj eminente,
ilustre

emission /i'mɪʃən ‖ɪ'mɪʃən/ n emisión f

emit /i'mɪt ‖i'mɪt/ vt -tt- «gas/smell/vapor»
despedir*; «heat/light/radiation/sound» emitir

emotion /ɪ'məʊʃən/ n (a) (feeling) sentimiento
m (b) (strength of feeling) emoción f

emotional /ɪ'məʊʃnəl ‖ɪ'məʊʃənl/ adj (a)
«disorder» emocional (b) (sensitive) «person/nature»
emotivo (c) (upset) emocionado; to get ~
emocionarse (d) (moving) «speech/experience/scene»
emotivo

empathize /'empəθaɪz/ vi to ~ WITH sb
establecer* lazos de empatía CON algn,
identificarse* CON algn

empathy /'empəθi/ n empatía f

emperor /'empərər ‖'empərə(r)/ n emperador
m

emphasis /'emfəsəs ‖'emfəsɪs/ n (pl -ses
/-siːz/) énfasis m; to lay o put ~ on sth hacer*
hincapié or poner* énfasis en la importancia de
algo

emphasize /'emfəsaɪz/ vt «phrase/word»
enfatizar*; «fact/point/warning» recalcar*, hacer*
hincapié en; «fault/value» poner* de relieve;
«shape/feature» resaltar, hacer* resaltar

emphatic /ɪm'fætɪk/ adj «gesture/tone»
enérgico, enfático; «assertion/refusal» categórico

empire /'empaɪr ‖'empaɪə(r)/ n imperio m

employ /ɪm'plɔɪ/ vt (a) «person» (take on)
contratar, emplear; (have working) emplear, dar*
empleo a (b) «method/tactics/tool» emplear

employee /ɪm'plɔɪiː/ n empleado, -da m,f

employer /ɪm'plɔɪər ‖ɪm'plɔɪə(r)/ n
empleador, -dora m,f; (of domestic worker etc)
patrón, -trona m,f

employment /ɪm'plɔɪmənt/ n (a) (work)
trabajo m; to be in ~ tener* trabajo; (before n) ~
agency agencia f de trabajo (b) (availability of work)
empleo m; full ~ pleno empleo m

empress /'emprəs ‖'emprɪs/ n emperatriz f

empty[1] /'empti/ adj -tier, -tiest «container/
table» vacío; «words/gesture/life» vacío; «threat/
promise» vano

empty[2] -ties, -tying, -tied vt «container/
warehouse» vaciar*; she emptied the contents all
over the floor vació la caja (or el bolso etc) en el
suelo
  ■ ~ vi «room/street» vaciarse*; «river/stream»
  to ~ INTO sth desaguar* EN algo
  ■ **empty out** [v + o + adv, v + adv + o] «bag/
  drawer/pockets» vaciar*; «garbage» tirar, botar
  (AmL exc RPl)

empty[3] n (pl -ties) (colloq) (bottle) envase m
(vacío), casco m (Esp, Méx)

empty-handed /'empti'hændəd
‖empti'hændɪd/ adv con las manos vacías

emu /'iːmjuː/ n emú m

emulate /'emjəleɪt ‖'emjʊleɪt/ vt emular

emulsion /ɪ'mʌlʃən/ n ~ (**paint**) pintura f al
agua

enable /ɪn'eɪbəl/ vt (a) (provide means for) to ~
sb to + INF permitir(le) a algn + INF (b) (make
possible) posibilitar, permitir

enact /ɪn'ækt/ vt [1] (Govt, Law) «law»
promulgar* [2] «play/role» representar

enamel /ɪ'næməl/ n esmalte m

enamored, (BrE) **enamoured** /ɪ'næmərd
‖ɪ'næməd/ adj (frml) to be ~ OF sb estar*
enamorado or prendado DE algn; I'm not very ~
of the idea no estoy muy entusiasmado con la
idea

enc (= **enclosed**) anexo

encampment /ɪn'kæmpmənt/ n campamento
m

encase /ɪn'keɪs/ vt revestir*, recubrir*; ~d IN
sth revestido or recubierto DE algo

enchant /ɪn'tʃænt ‖ɪn'tʃɑːnt/ vt (delight, charm)
cautivar; (Occult) hechizar*

enchanting /ɪn'tʃæntɪŋ ‖ɪn'tʃɑːntɪŋ/ adj
encantador

encircle /ɪn'sɜːrkəl ‖ɪn'sɜːkəl/ vt «camp/house»
rodear; «waist/wrist» ceñir*

enclave /'enkleɪv/ n enclave m

enclose /ɪn'kləʊz/ vt [1] (a) (surround)
encerrar*; (fence in) cercar* (b) **enclosed** past p
«area/space» cerrado [2] (in letter) adjuntar,
acompañar

enclosure /ɪn'kləʊʒər ‖ɪn'kləʊʒə(r)/ n recinto
m; a fenced ~ un cercado

encode /ɪn'kəʊd, en-/ vt codificar*, cifrar

encompass /ɪn'kʌmpəs/ vt (frml) abarcar*

encore /'ɑːnkɔːr ‖'ɒŋkɔː(r)/ n bis m; (as interj)
¡otra!

encounter[1] /ɪn'kaʊntər ‖ɪn'kaʊntə(r)/ vt (a)

(be faced with) ⟨*danger/difficulty/opposition*⟩ encontrar*, encontrarse* con **(b)** (come across) tropezar* *or* toparse con

encounter² *n* encuentro *m*

encourage /ɪnˈkʌrɪdʒ ‖ɪnˈkɜːrɪdʒ/ *vt* **(a)** (give hope, courage to) animar, alentar*; **she/it** ∼**d me to carry on** me animó a seguir adelante **(b)** ⟨*industry/competition/growth*⟩ fomentar

encouragement /ɪnˈkʌrɪdʒmənt ‖ɪnˈkɜːrɪdʒmənt/ *n* ánimo *m*

encouraging /ɪnˈkʌrɪdʒɪŋ ‖ɪnˈkɜːrɪdʒɪŋ/ *adj* alentador

encroach /ɪnˈkrəʊtʃ/ *vi* to ∼ ON *o* UPON sth ⟨*on land*⟩ invadir algo; ⟨*on rights*⟩ cercenar algo

encrypt /enˈkrɪpt/ *vt* (Comput) cifrar

encumber /ɪnˈkʌmbər ‖ɪnˈkʌmbə(r)/ *vt* cargar*

encyclopedia, (BrE also) **encyclopaedia** /ɪnˌsaɪkləˈpiːdiə/ *n* enciclopedia *f*

end¹ /end/ *n* **1 (a)** (extremity — of rope, stick) extremo *m*, punta *f*; (— of nose) punta *f*; (— of street) final *m*; **for weeks on** ∼ durante semanas y semanas, durante semanas enteras; **it measures five feet (from)** ∼ **to** ∼ mide cinco pies de un lado al otro *or* de punta a punta; *to make* ∼**s meet** llegar* a fin de mes **(b)** (remaining part) final *m*, resto *m*
2 (a) (finish, close) fin *m*, final *m*; **at the** ∼ **of January** a fines *or* a finales de enero; **in the** ∼ al final; **to put an** ∼ **to sth** poner* fin *or* poner* punto final a algo **(b)** (death, destruction) final *m*, fin *m* **(c)** (outcome) final *m*
3 (purpose) fin *m*; **to this** ∼ (frml) con este fin (frml)

end² *vt* **(a)** (stop) ⟨*argument/discussion/fight*⟩ terminar; ⟨*gossip/speculation*⟩ acabar *or* terminar con **(b)** (conclude) terminar
■ ∼ *vi* acabar, terminar
■ **end up** [*v + adv*] terminar, acabar

endanger /ɪnˈdeɪndʒər ‖ɪnˈdeɪndʒə(r)/ *vt* ⟨*life*⟩ poner* en peligro; ⟨*chances/reputation*⟩ hacer* peligrar **(b) endangered** *past p* ⟨*species*⟩ en peligro

endear /ɪnˈdɪr ‖ɪnˈdɪə(r)/ *vt* to ∼ **oneself** TO sb granjearse el cariño de algn

endearing /ɪnˈdɪrɪŋ ‖ɪnˈdɪərɪŋ/ *adj* atractivo

endearment /ɪnˈdɪrmənt ‖ɪnˈdɪəmənt/ *n* expresión *f* de cariño

endeavor¹, (BrE) **endeavour** /ɪnˈdevər ‖ɪnˈdevə(r)/ *n* (frml) esfuerzo *m*, intento *m*

endeavor², (BrE) **endeavour** *vt* (frml) to ∼ to + INF intentar por todos los medios + INF, esforzarse* POR + INF

ending /ˈendɪŋ/ *n* **(a)** (conclusion) final *m*, desenlace *m* **(b)** (Ling) desinencia *f*, terminación *f*

endless /ˈendləs ‖ˈendlɪs/ *adj* **(a)** ⟨*journey/ meeting*⟩ interminable; ⟨*plain/patience*⟩ sin límites; ⟨*chatter/complaining*⟩ continuo **(b)** (innumerable) innumerable; **the possibilities are** ∼ las posibilidades son infinitas

endorse /ɪnˈdɔːrs ‖ɪnˈdɔːs/ *vt* **1** (approve) ⟨*statement/decision*⟩ aprobar* **2** (sign) ⟨*check/bill*⟩ endosar

endorsement /ɪnˈdɔːrsmənt ‖ɪnˈdɔːsmənt/ *n* **1 (a)** (approval) aval *m*, aprobación *f* **(b)** (Pol) refrendo *m* **2** (on driving licence) (BrE) anotación *f* (*de una infracción de tráfico*)

endow /ɪnˈdaʊ/ *vt* **(a)** (provide) (*usu pass*) ∼**ed** WITH sth dotado DE algo **(b)** (provide income for) ⟨*college/school/hospital*⟩ dotar (de fondos) a

endowment /ɪnˈdaʊmənt/ *n* (Fin) donación *f*

end product *n* producto *m* final

endurance /ɪnˈdʊrəns ‖ɪnˈdjʊərəns/ *n* (physical) resistencia *f*; (mental) entereza *f*; (*before n*) ∼ **test** prueba *f* de resistencia

endure /ɪnˈdʊr ‖ɪnˈdjʊə(r)/ *vt* soportar
■ ∼ *vi* ⟨*fame/friendship/memories*⟩ perdurar

enemy /ˈenəmi/ *n* (*pl* **-mies**) enemigo, -ga *m,f*

energetic /ˌenərˈdʒetɪk ‖ˌenəˈdʒetɪk/ *adj* ⟨*person*⟩ lleno de energía; ⟨*exercise*⟩ enérgico

energy /ˈenərdʒi ‖ˈenədʒi/ *n* energía *f*; (power, effort) energías *fpl*

enforce /ɪnˈfɔːrs ‖ɪnˈfɔːs/ *vt* ⟨*law/regulation*⟩ hacer* respetar *or* cumplir; ⟨*claim/right*⟩ hacer* valer

engage /ɪnˈɡeɪdʒ/ *vt* **1** ⟨*attention/interest*⟩ captar **2** ⟨*cog/wheel*⟩ engranar con; ⟨*gear*⟩ engranar **3** (hire) ⟨*staff/performer*⟩ contratar
■ ∼ *vi* (take part) to ∼ IN sth ⟨*in politics/voluntary work/study*⟩ dedicarse* a algo; **they** ∼**d in a variety of activities** participaron en una variedad de actividades

engaged /ɪnˈɡeɪdʒd/ *adj* **1** (betrothed) prometido, comprometido (AmL); **to be** ∼ **TO sb** estar* prometido A algn, estar* comprometido CON algn (AmL); **to get** ∼ prometerse, comprometerse (AmL) **2** (pred) **(a)** (occupied) (frml) ocupado; **I'm otherwise** ∼ tengo otro compromiso; **they are** ∼ **in a new business venture** tienen un nuevo negocio entre manos **(b)** (BrE) ⟨*toilet*⟩ ocupado **(c)** (BrE Telec) ocupado, comunicando (Esp); **the** ∼ **tone** *o* **signal** la señal de ocupado *or* (Esp) de comunicando

engagement /ɪnˈɡeɪdʒmənt/ *n* **1** (pledge to marry) compromiso *m*; (period) noviazgo *m*; (*before n*) ∼ **ring** anillo *m* de compromiso **2** (appointment) compromiso *m*

engine /ˈendʒən ‖ˈendʒɪn/ *n* **(a)** (motor) motor *m* **(b)** (locomotive) locomotora *f*, máquina *f*

engine driver *n* (BrE) maquinista *mf*

engineer¹ /ˈendʒəˈnɪr ‖ˌendʒɪˈnɪə(r)/ *n* **1 (a)** (graduate) ingeniero, -ra *m,f* **(b)** (for maintenance) (BrE) técnico *mf*, ingeniero, -ra *m,f* (Méx) **2** (AmE Rail) maquinista *mf*

engineer² *vt* ⟨*plan*⟩ urdir, tramar; ⟨*defeat/ downfall*⟩ fraguar*

engineering /ˈendʒəˈnɪrɪŋ ‖ˌendʒɪˈnɪərɪŋ/ *n* ingeniería *f*

England /ˈɪŋɡlənd/ *n* Inglaterra *f*

English¹ /ˈɪŋɡlɪʃ/ *adj* inglés

English² *n* **(a)** (language) inglés *m*; (*before n*) ⟨*lesson/teacher*⟩ de inglés **(b)** (people) (+ *pl vb*) **the** ∼ los ingleses

English: ∼**man** /ˈɪŋɡlɪʃmən/ *n* (*pl* **-men** /-mən/) inglés *m*; ∼**woman** *n* inglesa *f*

engrave /ɪnˈɡreɪv/ *vt* grabar

engraving /ɪnˈɡreɪvɪŋ/ *n* grabado *m*

engross /ɪnˈɡrəʊs/ *vt* absorber*; **to be** ∼**ed IN sth** estar* absorto EN algo

engulf /ɪnˈɡʌlf/ *vt* ⟨*flames/fire/waves*⟩ envolver*; ⟨*lava*⟩ sepultar; ⟨*feeling*⟩ asaltar

enhance /ɪn'hæns ‖m'hɑːns/ vt ⟨beauty/taste⟩ realzar*; ⟨value⟩ aumentar; ⟨reputation/performance⟩ mejorar

enigma /ɪ'nɪɡmə/ n (pl **-mas**) enigma m

enigmatic /'enɪɡ'mætɪk/ adj enigmático

enjoy /ɪn'dʒɔɪ/ vt **1** (like): **I ~ traveling/music** me gusta viajar/la música; **I ~ed the party** lo pasé bien en la fiesta **2** (have, experience) ⟨good health⟩ disfrutar de, gozar* de
- **v refl** to **~ oneself** divertirse*, pasarlo or pasarla bien

enjoyable /ɪn'dʒɔɪəbəl/ adj agradable

enjoyment /ɪn'dʒɔɪmənt/ n placer m

enlarge /ɪn'lɑːdʒ ‖ɪn'lɑːdʒ/ vt ⟨hole/area⟩ agrandar; ⟨gland/heart⟩ dilatar; ⟨room/office⟩ ampliar; ⟨print/photograph⟩ ampliar*

enlighten /ɪn'laɪtn/ vt ⟨people/population⟩ ilustrar (frml); **would you care to ~ me?** ¿te importaría explicarme?

enlightened /ɪn'laɪtnd/ adj ⟨person/view⟩ progresista; ⟨decision⟩ inteligente

Enlightenment /ɪn'laɪtnmənt/ n (Hist) **the (Age of) ~** la Ilustración, el Siglo de las Luces

enlist /ɪn'lɪst/ vi alistarse
- **~ vt** ⟨soldiers/helpers/members⟩ reclutar, alistar; ⟨sailors⟩ enrolar; ⟨support/aid⟩ conseguir*

enlisted man /ɪn'lɪstəd ‖ɪn'lɪstɪd/ n (AmE) soldado m raso

en masse /ɑːn'mæs ‖ɒn'mæs/ adv en masa

enmity /'enmɪti/ n (pl **-ties**) (frml) enemistad f

enormous /ɪ'nɔːrməs ‖ɪ'nɔːməs/ adj enorme, inmenso

enormously /ɪ'nɔːrməsli ‖ɪ'nɔːməsli/ adv ⟨enjoy/benefit⟩ enormemente; **he's ~ fat** es gordísimo

enough¹ /ɪ'nʌf/ adj bastante, suficiente; (pl) bastantes, suficientes; **they had more than ~ time** tuvieron tiempo de sobra

enough² pron: **they don't pay us ~** no nos pagan bastante or lo suficiente; **I've had ~!** ¡ya estoy harto!

enough³ adv **you don't go out ~** no sales lo suficiente; **make sure it's big ~** asegúrate de que sea lo suficientemente grande; **curiously ~** curiosamente

- **Note** Where the meaning … enough to … is being translated, the translation uses the structure lo bastante or lo suficiente … como para …: you aren't eating enough (to stay healthy) no estás comiendo lo suficiente or lo bastante (como para mantenerte saludable).

enquire etc (BrE) /ɪn'kwaɪr ‖ɪn'kwaɪə(r)/ ▶ INQUIRE etc

enrage /ɪn'reɪdʒ/ vt enfurecer*

enrich /ɪn'rɪtʃ/ vt enriquecer*

enroll, (BrE) **enrol** /ɪn'rəʊl/ vi**-ll-** matricularse, inscribirse*
- **~ vt** matricular, inscribir*

enrollment, (BrE) **enrolment** /ɪn'rəʊlmənt/ n inscripción f, matrícula f

en route /ɑːn'ruːt ‖ɒn'ruːt/ adv por el camino, de camino

ensemble /ɑːn'sɑːmbəl ‖ɒn'sɒmbəl/ n **1** (group of performers) conjunto m **2** (Clothing) conjunto m

enslave /ɪn'sleɪv/ vt esclavizar*

ensue /ɪn'suː ‖ɪn'sjuː/ vi seguir*; **in the ensuing fight** en la pelea que tuvo lugar a continuación

en suite /ˌɑːn'swiːt ‖ˌɒn'swiːt/ adj adjunto, en suite

ensure /ɪn'ʃʊr ‖ɪn'ʃʊə(r), ɪn'ʃɔː(r)/ vt asegurar

entail /ɪn'teɪl/ vt ⟨risk⟩ implicar*, suponer*; ⟨expense⟩ acarrear, suponer*; ⟨responsibility⟩ conllevar

entangle /ɪn'tæŋɡəl/ vt enredar

enter /'entər ‖'entə(r)/ vt **1** (a) ⟨room/house/country⟩ entrar en, entrar a (esp AmL) (b) (penetrate) entrar en **2** (begin) ⟨period/phase⟩ entrar en **3** (a) (join) ⟨army⟩ alistarse en, entrar en; ⟨firm/organization⟩ entrar en, incorporarse a (b) (begin to take part in) ⟨war/negotiations⟩ entrar en; ⟨debate/dispute⟩ sumarse a (c) ⟨student/candidate⟩ presentar (d) ⟨race⟩ inscribirse* (para tomar parte) en; **to ~ a competition** presentarse a un concurso **4** (a) (record — en register) inscribir*; (— in ledger, book) anotar (b) (Comput) dar* entrada a
- **~ vi 1** entrar **2 to ~ (FOR sth)** ⟨for competition/race⟩ inscribirse* (EN algo); ⟨for examination⟩ presentarse (A algo)

enterprise /'entərpraɪz ‖'entəpraɪz/ n **1** (a) (project) empresa f (b) (initiative, daring) empuje m **2** (a) (company) empresa f (b) (business activity): **free ~** la libre empresa; **private ~** la iniciativa privada; (sector) el sector privado

entertain /'entər'teɪn ‖,entə'teɪn/ vt **1** (amuse) ⟨audience⟩ entretener* **2** (frml) ⟨idea/suggestion⟩ contemplar; ⟨doubt/suspicions⟩ abrigar* (frml)
- **~ vi 1** (provide entertainment) entretener* **2** (have guests) recibir

entertainer /'entər'teɪnər ‖,entə'teɪnə(r)/ n artista mf (del mundo del espectáculo); (presenter of program) (Rad, TV) animador, -dora m,f

entertaining /'entər'teɪnɪŋ ‖,entə'teɪnɪŋ/ adj ⟨book/movie/anecdote⟩ entretenido; ⟨person⟩ divertido

entertainment /'entər'teɪnmənt ‖,entə'teɪnmənt/ n (a) (amusement) entretenimiento m (b) (show) espectáculo m

enthrall, (BrE) **enthral** /ɪn'θrɔːl/ vt **-ll-** cautivar

enthusiasm /ɪn'θuːziæzəm ‖ɪn'θjuːziæzəm/ n entusiasmo m

enthusiast /ɪn'θuːziæst ‖ɪn'θjuːziæst/ n entusiasta mf

enthusiastic /ɪn'θuːzi'æstɪk ‖ɪn,θjuːzi'æstɪk/ adj entusiasta

entice /ɪn'taɪs/ vt atraer*

entire /ɪn'taɪr ‖ɪn'taɪə(r)/ adj (a) (whole) (before n) entero (b) (intact) (pred) intacto

entirely /ɪn'taɪrli ‖ɪn'taɪəli/ adv totalmente, completamente

entirety /ɪn'taɪrəti ‖ɪn'taɪərəti/ n: **in its ~** íntegramente, en su totalidad

entitle /ɪn'taɪtl/ vt **1** (give right) to **~ sb TO sth** darle* a algn derecho A algo; **to be ~d TO sth** tener* derecho A algo **2** (name) (frml) ⟨often pass⟩ titular

entity /'entəti/ n (pl **-ties**) entidad f

entourage /'ɑːntʊˈrɑːʒ ‖'ɒntʊˈrɑːʒ/ n séquito m

entrails /'entreɪlz/ *pl n* (of person) entrañas *fpl*; (of animal) vísceras *fpl*

entrance¹ /'entrəns/ *n* **1 (a)** (way in) entrada *f* **(b)** (foyer) hall *m*; (*before n*) ~ **hall** hall *m*, vestíbulo *m* **(c)** (access) (frml) entrada *f* **2** (admission — to club, museum) entrada *f*; (— to school, university) ingreso *m*; (*before n*) ~ **fee** (for entry) (precio *m* de) entrada *f*; (to join club) cuota *f* de ingreso *or* inscripción; (for exam, competition) cuota *f or* tasa *f* de inscripción **3** (act of entering) entrada *f*; (Theat) entrada *f* en escena

entrance² /ɪn'træns ‖ɪn'trɑːns/ *vt* embelesar, extasiar*

entrant /'entrənt/ *n* (in competition) participante *mf*; (for exam) candidato, -ta *m,f*

entreat /ɪn'triːt/ *vt* (liter) suplicar*, rogar*

entreaty /ɪn'triːti/ *n* (*pl* **-ties**) (liter) súplica *f*, ruego *m*

entrepreneur /ˌɑːntrəprə'nɜːr ‖ˌɒntrəprə'nɜː(r)/ *n* empresario, -ria *m,f*

entrust /ɪn'trʌst/ *vt* **to** ~ **sth** TO **sb** encomendarle* *or* confiarle* algo A algn

entry /'entri/ *n* (*pl* **entries**) **1** (coming, going in) entrada *f* **2** (access) entrada *f*, acceso *m*; **ⓢ no entry** (on door) prohibida la entrada; (on road sign) prohibido el paso **3 (a)** (in accounts) entrada *f*, asiento *m* **(b)** (in diary) anotación *f*, entrada *f* **(c)** (in dictionary — headword) entrada *f*; (in encyclopedia — article) artículo *m* **4** (in contest): **the winning** ~ **in the painting competition** el ejemplar ganador del concurso de pintura; **there were 20 entries** hubo 20 inscripciones **5** (door, gate) (AmE) entrada *f*

entryphone /'entrɪfəʊn/ *n* (BrE) portero *m* eléctrico *or* (Esp) automático, interfón *m* (Méx), intercomunicador *m* (Ven)

entwine /ɪn'twaɪn/ *vt* (liter) entrelazar*

envelop /ɪn'veləp/ *vt* envolver*

envelope /'enveləʊp/ *n* sobre *m*

enviable /'enviəbəl/ *adj* envidiable

envious /'enviəs/ *adj* envidioso; (*expression*) (lleno) de envidia

environment /ɪn'vaɪrənmənt ‖ɪn'vaɪərənmənt/ *n* **(a)** (Ecol) **the** ~ el medio ambiente **(b)** (surroundings): **she's studying gorillas in their natural** ~ estudia a las gorilas en su entorno *or* hábitat natural; **the home** ~ el ambiente del hogar

environmental /ɪn'vaɪrən'ment ‖ɪn,vaɪərən'mentl/ *adj* **(a)** (Ecol) (*factor*) ambiental; (*damage*) al medio ambiente, medioambiental; ~ **groups** grupos *mpl* ecologistas **(b)** (of surroundings) (*factor*) ambiental; (*influence*) del ambiente *or* entorno

environment-friendly /ɪn'vaɪrənmənt,frendli ‖ɪn'vaɪərənmənt,frendli/ *adj*: ~ **products** productos *mpl* ecológicos, productos *mpl* que no dañan al medio ambiente

environs /ɪn'vaɪrənz ‖ɪn'vaɪərənz/ *pl n* alrededores *mpl*, entorno *m*

envisage /ɪn'vɪzɪdʒ/ *vt* **(a)** (foresee) prever* **(b)** (visualize) imaginarse

envision /ɪn'vɪʒən/ *vt* (AmE) prever*

envoy /'envɔɪ/ *n* enviado, -da *m,f*

envy¹ /'envi/ *n* envidia *f*

envy² *vt* **envies, envying, envied** envidiar

enzyme /'enzaɪm/ *n* enzima *f*

epic¹ /'epɪk/ *adj* (*usu before n*) *(poem/poetry/ film)* épico; *(achievement/struggle)* colosal, de epopeya

epic² *n* (poem) poema *m* épico; (film) superproducción *f*; (novel) epopeya *f*

epidemic /'epə'demɪk ‖,epɪ'demɪk/ *n* epidemia *f*

epigram /'epəgræm ‖'epɪgræm/ *n* epigrama *m*

epilepsy /'epəlepsi ‖'epɪlepsi/ *n* epilepsia *f*

epileptic /'epə'leptɪk ‖,epɪ'leptɪk/ *adj* *(fit/ attack)* epiléptico, de epilepsia; **she's** ~ es epiléptica

epilogue, (AmE also) **epilog** /'epəlɔːg ‖'epɪlɒg/ *n* epílogo *m*

Epiphany /ɪ'pɪfəni/ *n* **the** ~ la Epifanía (del Señor)

episode /'epəsəʊd ‖'epɪsəʊd/ *n* episodio *m*

epistle /ɪ'pɪsəl/ *n* epístola *f*

epitaph /'epətæf ‖'epɪtɑːf/ *n* epitafio *m*

epitome /ɪ'pɪtəmi/ *n* (embodiment) personificación *f*; (typical example) arquetipo *m*

epitomize /ɪ'pɪtəmaɪz/ *vt* tipificar*; «*person*» ser* la personificación de

epoch /'epək ‖'iːpɒk/ *n* era *f*, época *f*

equal¹ /'iːkwəl/ *adj* igual; ~ **opportunities** igualdad *f* de oportunidades; **he doesn't feel** ~ **to the task** no se siente capaz de hacerlo

equal² *n* igual *mf*

equal³ *vt*, (BrE) **-ll- 1** (Math) ser* igual a; **three times three** ~**s nine** tres por tres son nueve *or* es igual a nueve **2** *(record/time)* igualar

equality /ɪ'kwɑːləti ‖ɪ'kwɒləti/ *n* igualdad *f*

equalize /'iːkwəlaɪz/ *vt* *(pressure/weight)* igualar; *(incomes)* equiparar ■ ~ *vi* (Sport) empatar

equalizer /'iːkwəlaɪzər ‖'iːkwəlaɪzə(r)/ *n* (Sport) gol *m* de la igualada *or* del empate

equally /'iːkwəli/ *adv* **1 (a)** (in equal amounts) *(divide/share)* por igual **(b)** (without bias) *(treat)* de la misma manera, (por) igual **2** (to an equal degree) igualmente; ~ **easily** con igual *or* con la misma facilidad **3** (*indep*) **(a)** (just as possibly) ~ (**well**) de igual modo **(b)** (at the same time) (*as linker*) al mismo tiempo

equate /ɪ'kweɪt/ *vt* (compare) equiparar; (identify) identificar*

equation /ɪ'kweɪʒən/ *n* ecuación *f*

equator /ɪ'kweɪtər ‖ɪ'kweɪtə(r)/ *n* **the** ~ **o E**~ el ecuador

equilibrium /'iːkwə'lɪbriəm ‖,iːkwɪ'lɪbriəm/ *n* (*pl* **-riums** *or* **-ria** /-riə/) equilibrio *m*

equinox /'iːkwənɒks, 'ek- ‖'iːkwɪnɒks, 'ek-/ *n* equinoccio *m*

equip /ɪ'kwɪp/ *vt* **-pp- (a)** (furnish, supply) *(troops/ laboratory)* equipar; **to** ~ **sth/sb** WITH **sth** proveer* algo/a algn DE algo **(b)** (prepare, make capable) preparar

equipment /ɪ'kwɪpmənt/ *n* equipo *m*; **office** ~ mobiliario, máquinas y material de oficina; **sports** ~ artículos *mpl* deportivos

equity /'ekwəti/ *n* **1** (fairness) (frml) equidad *f* (frml) **2** (Busn, Fin) **(a)** (shareholders' interest in company) patrimonio *m* neto **(b) equities** *pl n* (shares) valores *mpl* de renta variable

equivalent¹ /ɪ'kwɪvələnt/ *adj* **(a)** (equal) *(size/* ····⫶

value⟩ equivalente; **to be ~ TO sth/-ING**
equivaler* A algo/+ INF **(b)** (corresponding)
⟨*position/term*⟩ equivalente

equivalent² *n* equivalente *m*

era /'ɪrə, 'erə ‖'ɪərə/ *n* era *f*, época *f*

eradicate /ɪ'rædəkeɪt ‖ɪ'rædɪkeɪt/ *vt*
erradicar*

erase /ɪ'reɪs ‖ɪ'reɪz/ *vt* borrar

eraser /ɪ'reɪsər ‖ɪ'reɪzə(r)/ *n* goma *f* (de borrar)

erect¹ /ɪ'rekt/ *adj* **1** ⟨*bearing/posture*⟩ erguido
2 (Physiol) erecto

erect² *vt* ⟨*altar/monument*⟩ erigir* (frml),
levantar; ⟨*barricade/wall*⟩ levantar; ⟨*tent*⟩ armar

erection /ɪ'rekʃən/ *n* **1** (frml) **(a)** (of building,
monument) construcción *f*; (of barricade)
levantamiento *m* **(b)** (building) construcción *f*
2 (Physiol) erección *f*

erode /ɪ'rəʊd/ *vt* «*water/wind/waves*»
erosionar; «*acid*» corroer*; ⟨*confidence/faith*⟩
minar

erosion /ɪ'rəʊʒən/ *n* (by water, wind, waves)
erosión *f*; (by acid) corrosión *f*; (of confidence, power,
rights) menoscabo *m*

erotic /ɪ'rɑːtɪk ‖ɪ'rɒtɪk/ *adj* erótico

err /er ‖ɜː(r)/ *vi* (frml): **to ~ IN sth** equivocarse*
EN algo; to ~ on the side of caution pecar* de
cauteloso

errand /'erənd/ *n* mandado *m* (esp AmL), recado
m (Esp); **to run an ~ for sb** hacerle* un mandado
or (Esp) recado a algn

erratic /ɪ'rætɪk/ *adj* ⟨*performance/work*⟩
desigual; ⟨*person/moods*⟩ imprevisible; ⟨*course*⟩
errático

erroneous /ɪ'rəʊniəs/ *adj* erróneo

error /'erər ‖'erə(r)/ *n* error *m*

error message *n* (Comput) mensaje *m* de
error

erstwhile /'ɜːrsthwaɪl ‖'ɜːstwaɪl/ *adj* (liter)
antiguo

erudite /'erjədaɪt ‖'eruːdaɪt/ *adj* (frml) erudito

erupt /ɪ'rʌpt/ *vi* **(a)** «*volcano/geyser*» entrar en
erupción **(b)** (break out) «*violence/fighting*»
estallar

eruption /ɪ'rʌpʃən/ *n* **(a)** (of volcano) erupción *f*
(b) (of violence) brote *m*; (of anger) estallido *m*

escalate /'eskəleɪt/ *vi* **(a)** «*fighting/violence/
dispute*» intensificarse*; «*prices/claims*»
aumentar **(b) escalating** *pres p* ⟨*dispute/
tension*⟩ creciente

escalator /'eskəleɪtər ‖'eskəleɪtə(r)/ *n*
escalera *f* mecánica

escapade /'eskəpeɪd/ *n* aventura *f*

escape¹ /ɪ'skeɪp/ *vi* **1 (a)** (flee) escaparse;
«*prisoner*» fugarse*; **to ~ FROM sth** ⟨*from
prison*⟩ fugarse* DE algo; ⟨*from cage/zoo*⟩
escaparse DE algo; ⟨*from danger/routine*⟩ escapar
DE algo **(b)** «*air/gas/water*» escaparse *f* **2** (from
accident, danger) salvarse
■ **~** *vt* ⟨*pursuer/police*⟩ escaparse de; ⟨*capture*⟩

salvarse de; ⟨*responsibilities/consequences*⟩
librarse de; **that detail had ~d my notice** se me
había escapado ese detalle

escape² *n* **(a)** (from prison) fuga *f*, huida *f*; **to
make one's ~** escaparse **(b)** (from accident, danger):
to have a miraculous ~ salvarse milagrosamente;
there's no ~ no hay escapatoria posible **(c)** (of
gas, air, water) escape *m* **(d)** (from reality) evasión *f*
(e) (Comput): **press ~** pulse la tecla de escape;
(before in) **~ key** tecla *f* de escape

escapist /ɪ'skeɪpəst ‖ɪ'skeɪpɪst/ *adj* escapista

escort¹ /'eskɔːrt ‖'eskɔːt/ *n* **1** (guard) escolta *f*;
under police ~ escoltado por la policía
2 (companion) acompañante *mf*; (male companion)
(frml) acompañante *m*

escort² /ɪ'skɔːrt ‖ɪ'skɔːt/ *vt* **(a)** (accompany)
acompañar; ⟨*prisoner/intruder*⟩ llevar **(b)** (for
protection) ⟨*politician/procession/ship*⟩ escoltar

Eskimo *n* (*pl* **-mos**) esquimal *mf*

esoteric /'esə'terɪk ‖,iːsəʊ'terɪk, ,esəʊ-/ *adj*
esotérico

espadrille /,espə'drɪl/ *n* alpargata *f*

especially /ɪ'speʃli/ *adv* especialmente;
everyone was bored, ~ me estaba todo el mundo
aburrido, sobre todo *or* especialmente yo

espionage /'espiənɑːʒ/ *n* espionaje *m*

Esquire /ɪ'skwaɪr ‖ɪ'skwaɪə(r)/ *n* (as title):
Frederick Saunders, ~ Sr. Frederick Saunders,
Sr Don Frederick Saunders (esp Esp)

essay /'eseɪ/ *n* (literary composition) ensayo *m*;
(academic composition) trabajo *m*, ensayo *m*;
(language exercise) composición *f*, redacción *f*

essence /'esns/ *n* **1 (a)** (central feature, quality)
esencia *f*; **in ~** en esencia **(b)** (personification)
personificación *f* **2** (Culin): **vanilla ~** esencia *f* de
vainilla

essential¹ /ɪ'sentʃəl ‖ɪ'senʃəl/ *adj* esencial

essential² *n* **(a)** (sth indispensable) imperativo
m, elemento *m* esencial **(b) essentials** *pl n*
(fundamental features) puntos *mpl* esenciales

essentially /ɪ'sentʃəli ‖ɪ'senʃəli/ *adv*
esenciálmente; (indep) en lo esencial

EST (in US) = **Eastern Standard Time**

establish /ɪ'stæblɪʃ/ *vt* **(a)** ⟨*colony/company*⟩
establecer*, fundar; ⟨*committee/fund*⟩ instituir*,
crear **(b)** ⟨*procedure/diplomatic relations*⟩
establecer* **(c)** (prove) ⟨*guilt/innocence*⟩
establecer*; (ascertain) ⟨*motive/fact/identity*⟩
establecer*

established /ɪ'stæblɪʃt/ *adj* **1** ⟨*expert/
company*⟩ de reconocido prestigio; ⟨*star*⟩ de
renombre; ⟨*reputation*⟩ sólido; ⟨*practice*⟩
establecido; ⟨*fact*⟩ comprobado **2** ⟨*church/
religion*⟩ oficial

establishment /ɪ'stæblɪʃmənt/ *n* **1 (a)** (of
colony, business) fundación *f*; (of committee) creación
f **(b)** (of criteria, relations) establecimiento *m*
2 (club, hotel, shop) establecimiento *m* **3 the
Establishment** la clase dirigente, el establishment

estate /ɪ'steɪt/ *n* **1 (a)** (land, property) finca *f*,
propiedad *f* **(b)** (group of buildings): **a private ~** un

complejo habitacional, una urbanización (Esp),
un fraccionamiento (Méx) **2** (Law) patrimonio *m*;
(of deceased person) sucesión *f* **3** ~ **(car)** (BrE) ▶
STATION WAGON

estate agent *n* (BrE) agente *mf* de la
propiedad inmobiliaria

esteem /ɪ'stiːm/ *n* estima *f*; **I hold him in high**
~ lo aprecio mucho

esthetic /es'θetɪk ‖ i:s'θetɪk/ *adj* estético

estimate¹ /'estəmeɪt ‖ 'estɪmeɪt/ *vt* **(a)**
(calculate approximately) ‹price/number/age› calcular
(b) estimated *past p* ‹cost/speed› aproximado;
~d **time of arrival** hora *f* de llegada previsto **(c)**
(form judgment of) ‹outcome/ability› juzgar*,
valorar

estimate² /'estəmət ‖ 'estɪmət/ *n* **(a)** (rough
calculation) cálculo *m* aproximado **(b)** (of costs)
(Busn) presupuesto *m*

estimation /ˌestə'meɪʃən ‖ ˌestɪ'meɪʃən/ *n* **(a)**
(judgment, opinion) juicio *m*, valoración *f* **(b)**
(esteem): **to go up/down in sb's** ~ ganarse/
perder* la estima de algn

Estonia /es'təʊniə/ *n* Estonia *f*

Estonian /es'təʊniən/ *adj* estonio

estrange /ɪ'streɪndʒ/ *vt*: **his** ~**d wife** su mujer,
de quien está separado

estuary /'estʃueri ‖ 'estjʊəri/ *n* (*pl* **-ries**)
estuario *m*

etc (= **et cetera**) etc.

et cetera /ɪt'setrə/ *adv* etcétera

etch /etʃ/ *vt* (Art, Print) grabar

etching /'etʃɪŋ/ *n* grabado *m*

eternal /ɪ'tɜːnl̩ ‖ ɪ'tɜːnl̩/ *adj* eterno; (colloq)
‹noise/complaints› constante

eternity /ɪ'tɜːnəti ‖ ɪ'tɜːnəti/ *n* (*pl* **-ties**)
eternidad *f*

ethereal /ɪ'θɪriəl ‖ ɪ'θɪəriəl/ *adj* (liter) etéreo
(liter)

ethical /'eθɪkəl/ *adj* ‹dilemma› ético; ‹code› de
conducta

ethics /'eθɪks/ *n* **1** (Phil) (+ *sing vb*) ética *f*
2 (+ *pl vb*) (morality) ética *f*

Ethiopia /ˌiːθi'əʊpiə/ *n* Etiopía *f*

Ethiopian /ˌiːθi'əʊpiən/ *adj* etíope

ethnic /'eθnɪk/ *adj* ‹origin/group› étnico;
‹culture/art/vote› de las minorías étnicas; **an** ~
minority una minoría étnica; ~ **cleansing**
limpieza *f* étnica

etiquette /'etɪket/ *n* etiqueta *f*

etymology /ˌetə'mɒlədʒi ‖ ˌetɪ'mɒlədʒi/ *n* (*pl*
-gies) etimología *f*

EU *n* = **European Union**

eucalyptus /ˌjuːkə'lɪptəs/ *n* (*pl* **-tuses**)
eucalipto *m*

Eucharist /'juːkərəst ‖ 'juːkərɪst/ *n* Eucaristía
f

eulogy /'juːlədʒi/ *n* (*pl* **-gies**) (liter) elogio *m*,
loa *f* (liter)

eunuch /'juːnək/ *n* eunuco *m*

euphemism /'juːfəmɪzəm/ *n* eufemismo *m*

euphemistic /ˌjuːfə'mɪstɪk/ *adj* eufemístico

euphoria /juː'fɔːriə/ *n* euforia *f*

euphoric /juː'fɔːrɪk ‖ juː'fɒrɪk/ *adj* eufórico

euro /'jʊərəʊ ‖ 'jʊərəʊ/ *n* (*pl* **euros**) euro *m*

eurocheque /'jʊərəʊtʃek ‖ 'jʊərəʊtʃek/ *n* (BrE)
eurocheque *m*

Europe /'jʊərəp ‖ 'jʊərəp/ *n* **(a)** (Geog) Europa *f*
(b) (the EC) (BrE) Europa *f*

European¹ /ˌjʊərə'piːən ‖ ˌjʊərə'piən/ *adj*
europeo

European² *n* europeo, -pea *m,f*

European: ~ **Commission** *n* Comisión *f*
Europea, Comisión *f* de las Comunidades
Europeas; ~ **Currency Unit** *n* unidad *f*
monetaria europea; ~ **(Economic)**
Community *n* Comunidad *f* (Económica)
Europea; ~ **Union** *n* Unión *f* Europea

euthanasia /ˌjuːθə'neɪʒə ‖ ˌjuːθə'neɪziə/ *n*
eutanasia *f*

evacuate /ɪ'vækjueɪt/ *vt* evacuar*

evacuation /ɪˌvækju'eɪʃən/ *n* evacuación *f*

evade /ɪ'veɪd/ *vt* ‹arrest/enemy/responsibility›
eludir, evadir; ‹question/issue› eludir;
‹regulations/military service› eludir; ‹taxes›
evadir

evaluate /ɪ'væljueɪt/ *vt* **(a)** ‹ability/data›
evaluar* **(b)** (value) (AmE) valorar, tasar, avaluar*
(AmL)

evangelical /ˌiːvæn'dʒelɪkəl/ *adj* evangélico

evaporate /ɪ'væpəreɪt/ *vi* «liquid/support/
opposition» evaporarse; «hope/fear»
desvanecerse*; «confidence» esfumarse

evaporated milk /ɪ'væpəreɪtəd
‖ ɪ'væpəreɪtɪd/ *n* leche *f* evaporada, leche *f*
condensada (*sin azúcar*)

evasion /ɪ'veɪʒən/ *n* evasión *f*

evasive /ɪ'veɪsɪv/ *adj* ‹reply› evasivo

eve /iːv/ *n* (day, night before) (liter or journ) víspera *f*

even¹ /'iːvən/ *adv* **1** **(a)** hasta, incluso **(b)**
(*with neg*): **he can't** ~ **sew a button** no sabe ni
pegar un botón; **you're not** ~ **trying** ni siquiera lo
estás intentando **(c)** (*with comparative*) aún,
todavía **2** (*in phrases*) **even if** aunque (+ *subj*);
even so aun así; **even though** aun cuando, a
pesar de que

even² *adj* **1** **(a)** (flat, smooth) ‹ground/surface›
plano; ‹coat of paint› uniforme **(b)** (regular, uniform)
‹color/lighting› uniforme, parejo (AmL);
‹breathing› acompasado; ‹temperature› constante
2 (equal) ‹distribution› equitativo; **to break** ~
recuperar los gastos; **to get** ~ desquitarse; **I'll get**
~ **with her** me las pagará **3** (divisible by two)
‹number› par

even³ *vt* **1** (level) ‹surface› allanar, nivelar
2 (make equal) ‹score› igualar; ‹contest/situation›
equilibrar

■ **even out 1** [*v + o + adv, v + adv + o*]
compensar, nivelar **2** [*v + adv*] compensarse,
nivelarse

■ **even up** [*v + o + adv, v + adv + o*] ‹numbers/
amounts› equilibrar

evening /'iːvnɪŋ/ *n* **1** **(a)** (after dark) noche *f*;
(before dark) tarde *f*; **good** ~ (early on) buenas
tardes; (later) buenas noches; (*before n*) ~ **meal**
cena *f* **(b)** (period of entertainment) velada *f* (frml),
noche *f* **2** **evenings** (*as adv*) (before dark) por la
tarde, en la tarde (AmL), a la tarde *or* de tarde
(RPl); (after dark) por la noche, de noche, en la
noche (AmL)

evening: ~ **class** n clase f nocturna; ~ **dress** n (a) (for woman) traje m de noche (b) (formal wear) traje m de etiqueta

evenly /'iːvənli/ adv **1** (equally) ‹distribute/divide› equitativamente; ‹spread› uniformemente **2** (a) (calmly) ‹say/speak› sin alterar la voz (b) (steadily) ‹breathe› con regularidad

event /ɪ'vent/ n **1** (a) (happening, incident) acontecimiento m (b) (Sport) prueba f **2** (in phrases) **in the event:** **in the ~ of the reactor becoming overheated** en caso de que el reactor se recalentara; **in any event** en todo caso; **at all events** de cualquier modo

eventful /ɪ'ventfəl/ adj ‹week› lleno de incidentes; ‹life› rico en experiencias

eventuality /ɪ'ventʃu'æləti/ n (pl **-ties**) eventualidad f

eventually /ɪ'ventʃuəli/ adv finalmente, al final

ever /'evər ‖ 'evə(r)/ adv **1** (at any time): **have you ~ visited London?** ¿has estado en Londres (alguna vez)?; **nobody ~ comes to see me** nunca viene nadie a verme; **hardly ~** casi nunca **2** (after comp or superl): **these are our worst ~ results** estos son los peores resultados que hemos tenido hasta ahora; **the situation is worse than ~** la situación está peor que nunca **3** (always, constantly) **as ever** como siempre; **ever since:** **~ since we first saw her** desde que la vimos por primera vez; **we've been friends ~ since** somos amigos desde entonces; **for ever** para siempre **4** (as intensifier): **when will you ~ learn?** ¿cuándo vas a aprender?; **thanks ~ so much** (esp BrE colloq) muchísimas gracias

ever: ~**green** adj ‹tree/shrub› de hoja perenne; ~**lasting** /'evər'læstɪŋ ‖ ,evə'lɑːstɪŋ/ adj eterno

every /'evri/ adj **1** (each): ~ **room was searched** se registraron todas las habitaciones; ~ **minute is precious** cada minuto es precioso; **she comes ~ month** viene todos los meses **2** (indicating recurrence) cada; ~ **three days,** ~ **third day** cada tres días; ~ **other day** un día sí, otro no, día por medio (CS, Per); ~ **so often** cada tanto, de vez en cuando **3** (very great, all possible): **they have ~ confidence in us** confían plenamente en nosotros; **she made ~ effort to satisfy him** hizo lo indecible por satisfacerlo

everybody /'evrɪ,bɑːdi ‖ 'evrɪ,bɒdi/ pron todos; **is that ~?** ¿están todos?, ¿está todo el mundo?

everyday /'evri'deɪ/ adj (before n) ‹occurrence/problems/activities› de todos los días, cotidiano; ‹suit/clothes› de diario; ‹expression› corriente, de todos los días; ‹life› diario , cotidiano

everyone /'evriwʌn/ pron ▶ EVERYBODY

everything /'evriθɪŋ/ pron todo

everywhere /'evrihwer ‖ 'evriweə(r)/ adv ‹be› en todas partes; **I've looked ~ for it** lo he buscado por todas partes o por todos lados; **they go ~ by car** van a todos lados o a todas partes en coche

evict /ɪ'vɪkt/ vt ‹tenant/squatter› desahuciar, desalojar; ‹demonstrators› desalojar

eviction /ɪ'vɪkʃən/ n (of tenant, squatter) desalojo m, desahucio m

evidence /'evədəns ‖ 'evɪdəns/ n **1** (Law) (a) (proof) pruebas fpl (b) (testimony) testimonio m; **to give ~** declarar declaración **2** (sign, indication) indicio m, señal f

evident /'evədənt ‖ 'evɪdənt/ adj evidente

evidently /'evədəntli ‖ 'evɪdəntli/ adv (a) ‹embarrassed/unsuitable› claramente, obviamente (b) (indep) aparentemente, según parece

evil¹ /'iːvəl/ adj ‹demon/wizard› malvado; ‹deeds/thoughts/character› de gran maldad; ‹influence› maléfico; ‹plan/suggestion› diabólico; ‹spirit› maligno

evil² n mal m

evildoer /'iːvəl'duːər ‖ 'iːvəl,duːə(r)/ n malhechor, -chora m,f

evocative /ɪ'vɑːkətɪv ‖ ɪ'vɒkətɪv/ adj evocador

evoke /ɪ'vəʊk/ vt ‹response/admiration/sympathy› provocar*; ‹memories/associations› evocar*

evolution /'evə'luːʃən ‖ ,iːvə'luːʃən/ n evolución f

evolve /ɪ'vɑːlv ‖ ɪ'vɒlv/ vi evolucionar

ewe /juː/ n oveja f (hembra)

ex- /'eks/ pref ex(-); ~**wife** ex(-)esposa

exact¹ /ɪg'zækt/ adj (a) (precise) ‹number/size/time/date› exacto (b) (accurate) ‹description/definition› preciso

exact² vt ‹promise› arrancar*; **he ~ed his revenge** se vengó

exacting /ɪg'zæktɪŋ/ adj ‹work/job› que exige mucho; ‹supervisor/employer› exigente; ‹standards/conditions› riguroso

exactly /ɪg'zæktli/ adv ‹measure/calculate› exactamente; **at ~ six-thirty** a las seis y media en punto

exaggerate /ɪg'zædʒəreɪt/ vi/t exagerar

exaggeration /ɪg'zædʒə'reɪʃən/ n exageración f

exalt /ɪg'zɔːlt/ vt (frml) (a) (elevate) exaltar (frml), elevar (b) (praise) ensalzar*, exaltar (frml)

exam /ɪg'zæm/ n ▶ EXAMINATION 1

examination /ɪg'zæmə'neɪʃən ‖ ɪg,zæmɪ'neɪʃən/ n **1** (Educ) (frml) examen m **2** (a) (inspection — of accounts) revisión f, inspección f; (— of passports) control m; (— by doctor) reconocimiento m, examen m, revisación f (RPl) (b) (study, investigation) examen m; **on closer ~** al examinarlo más de cerca

examine /ɪg'zæmən ‖ ɪg'zæmɪn/ vt **1** (a) (inspect) examinar; ‹accounts› inspeccionar, revisar; ‹baggage› registrar, revisar (AmL) (b) (Med, Dent) examinar, revisar (AmL) (c) (study, investigate) examinar, estudiar **2** (a) (Educ) examinar (b) (Law) ‹witness/accused› interrogar*

examiner /ɪg'zæmənər ‖ ɪg'zæmɪnə(r)/ n examinador, -dora m,f

example /ɪg'zæmpəl ‖ ɪg'zɑːmpəl/ n **1** (specimen, sample) ejemplo m; **for ~** por ejemplo **2** (a) (model) ejemplo m (b) (warning): **to make an ~ of sb** darle* un castigo ejemplar a algn

exasperated /ɪg'zæspəreɪtəd ‖ ɪg'zæspəreɪtɪd/ adj exasperado

exasperating /ɪg'zæspəreɪtɪŋ/ adj exasperante

exasperation /ɪg'zæspə'reɪʃən/ n exasperación f

excavate /'ekskəveɪt/ *vt/i* excavar

excavation /'ekskə'veɪʃən/ *n* excavación *f*

exceed /ɪk'siːd/ *vt* **(a)** (be greater than) exceder de **(b)** (go beyond) ⟨*limit/minimum*⟩ rebasar; ⟨*expectations/hopes*⟩ superar; ⟨*powers*⟩ (frml) excederse en

excel /ɪk'sel/ *-ll-* *vi* **to** ~ **AT/IN** sth destacar* EN algo
■ *v refl* **to** ~ **oneself** lucirse*

excellence /'eksələns/ *n* excelencia *f*

excellent /'eksələnt/ *adj* excelente; (Educ) sobresaliente

except /ɪk'sept/ *prep* **(a)** (apart from): ~ **(for)** menos, excepto, salvo **(b)** ~ **for** (if it weren't for) si no fuera por

exception /ɪk'sepʃən/ *n* [1] excepción *f* [2] (offense): **to take** ~ **to** sth ofenderse por algo

exceptional /ɪk'sepʃnəl ‖ɪk'sepʃənl/ *adj* excepcional

excerpt /'eksɜːrpt ‖'eksɜːpt/ *n* pasaje *m*

excess¹ /ɪk'ses/ *n* [1] (*no pl*) exceso *m* [2] (surplus) excedente *m*; **in** ~ **of** superior a

excess² /ɪk'ses ‖'ekses/ *adj*: ~ **baggage/ weight** exceso *m* de equipaje/de peso

excessive /ɪk'sesɪv/ *adj* ⟨*price/charges*⟩ excesivo; ⟨*demands/pressure/interest*⟩ exagerado

exchange¹ /ɪks'tʃeɪndʒ/ *n* [1] **(a)** (of information, greetings, insults) intercambio *m*; (of prisoners, hostages) canje *m*; **in** ~ **for** sth a cambio de algo **(b)** (of students) intercambio *m* **(c)** (dialogue) intercambio *m* de palabras **(d)** (of currency) cambio *m* [2] (Telec) (telephone ~) central *f* telefónica

exchange² *vt* **(a)** (give in place of) **to** ~ sth **FOR** sth cambiar algo **POR** algo **(b)** ⟨*information/ addresses*⟩ intercambiar(se); ⟨*blows*⟩ darse*; ⟨*insults*⟩ intercambiar; ⟨*prisoners/hostages*⟩ canjear

exchange rate *n* tasa *f* or (esp Esp) tipo *m* de cambio

Exchequer /ɪks'tʃekər ‖ɪks'tʃekə(r)/ *n* (in UK) **the** ~ el tesoro público, el erario público; *see also* CHANCELLOR A

excise /'eksaɪz/ *n* impuestos *mpl* internos

excitable /ɪk'saɪtəbəl/ *adj* excitable

excite /ɪk'saɪt/ *vt* [1] **(a)** (make happy, enthusiastic) entusiasmar; (make impatient, boisterous) ⟨*children*⟩ alborotar **(b)** (sexually) excitar [2] ⟨*interest/ admiration*⟩ despertar*; ⟨*envy/curiosity*⟩ provocar*

excited /ɪk'saɪtəd ‖ɪk'saɪtɪd/ *adj* **(a)** (happy, enthusiastic) ⟨*person*⟩ entusiasmado, excitado; ⟨*shouts*⟩ de excitación *or* entusiasmo; **to get** ~ entusiasmarse **(b)** (nervous, worried) ⟨*person*⟩ excitado, agitado; ⟨*voice/gesture*⟩ vehemente, ansioso **(c)** (impatient, boisterous) ⟨*children*⟩ excitado, alborotado **(d)** (sexually) excitado

excitement /ɪk'saɪtmənt/ *n* (enthusiasm, happiness) excitación *f*, entusiasmo *m*; (agitation) agitación *f*, alboroto *m*

exciting /ɪk'saɪtɪŋ/ *adj* ⟨*events/experience*⟩ emocionante; ⟨*film/story*⟩ apasionante

exclaim /ɪk'skleɪm/ *vi/t* exclamar

exclamation /'eksklə'meɪʃən/ *n* exclamación *f*

exclamation point, (BrE) **exclamation mark** *n* signo *m* de admiración

exclude /ɪk'skluːd/ *vt* excluir*

excluding /ɪk'skluːdɪŋ/ *prep* sin incluir, excluyendo

exclusion /ɪk'skluːʒən/ *n* exclusión *f*

exclusive /ɪk'skluːsɪv/ *adj* [1] ⟨*rights/ ownership/privileges*⟩ exclusivo; ⟨*story/interview*⟩ en exclusiva [2] ⟨*club/gathering*⟩ selecto, exclusivo

excommunicate /'ekskə'mjuːnəkeɪt ‖,ekskə'mjuːnɪkeɪt/ *vt* excomulgar*

excrement /'ekskrəmənt ‖'ekskrɪmənt/ *n* (frml) excremento *m* (frml)

excruciating /ɪk'skruːʃieɪtɪŋ/ *adj* ⟨*pain*⟩ atroz; ⟨*boredom/embarrassment*⟩ espantoso

excursion /ɪk'skɜːrʒən ‖ɪk'skɜːʃən/ *n* excursión *f*

excuse¹ /ɪk'skjuːz/ *vt* [1] **(a)** (forgive) ⟨*mistake/ misconduct*⟩ disculpar, perdonar; ~ **me!** ¡perdón!; ~ **me, please** (con) permiso **(b)** (justify) ⟨*conduct/ rudeness*⟩ excusar, justificar* [2] (release from obligation) disculpar; **to** ~ sb **(FROM)** sth dispensar a algn DE algo

excuse² /ɪk'skjuːs/ *n* excusa *f*; **to make** ~s poner* excusas

ex-directory /'eksdaɪ'rektəri, -də- ‖,eksdaɪ'rektəri, -dɪ-/ *adj* (BrE Telec) (que no figura en la guía telefónica, privado (Méx)

execute /'eksɪkjuːt/ *vt* [1] (carry out, perform) ejecutar; ⟨*duties*⟩ desempeñar [2] (put to death) ejecutar

execution /'eksɪ'kjuːʃən/ *n* [1] (of order, plan) ejecución *f*; (of duties) desempeño *m* [2] (putting to death) ejecución *f*

executioner /'eksɪ'kjuːʃnər ‖,eksɪ'kjuːʃənə(r)/ *n* verdugo *m*

executive¹ /ɪg'zekjətɪv ‖ɪg'zekjʊtɪv/ *adj* [1] (Adm, Busn) (managerial) ejecutivo; ⟨*washroom/ suite/jet*⟩ para ejecutivos; ⟨*car/briefcase*⟩ de ejecutivo [2] (Govt) ⟨*powers/branch*⟩ ejecutivo

executive² *n* [1] (manager) ejecutivo, -va *m,f* [2] (branch of government) **the** ~ el (poder) ejecutivo **(b)** (~ committee) (esp BrE) comisión *f* directiva

executor /ɪg'zekjətər ‖ɪg'zekjʊtə(r)/ *n* albacea *mf*, testamentario, -ria *m,f*

exemplify /ɪg'zempləfaɪ ‖ɪg'zemplɪfaɪ/ *vt* **-fies, -fying, -fied (a)** (give example of) ejemplificar* **(b)** (be example of) demostrar*

exempt /ɪg'zempt/ *adj*: **to be** ~ **FROM** sth estar* exento DE algo

exemption /ɪg'zempʃən/ *n* ~ **FROM** sth exención *f* or exoneración *f* DE algo

exercise¹ /'eksərsaɪz ‖'eksəsaɪz/ *n* [1] (physical) ejercicio *m*; **to take** ~ hacer* ejercicio [2] (Sport, Educ) ejercicio *m*; (Mil) ejercicios *mpl*, maniobras *fpl* [3] (undertaking): **a public relations** ~ una operación de relaciones públicas [4] (use — of rights, power) (frml) ejercicio *m*; (— of caution, patience) uso *m*

exercise² *vt* [1] ⟨*body*⟩ ejercitar; ⟨*dog*⟩ pasear; ⟨*horse*⟩ ejercitar [2] ⟨*power/control/right*⟩ ejercer*; ⟨*patience/tact*⟩ hacer* uso de
■ ~ *vi* hacer* ejercicio

exercise book *n* cuaderno *m*

exert /ɪgˈzɜːrt ‖ɪgˈzɜːt/ *vt* ejercer*; ⟨force⟩ emplear
■ *v refl* **to ~ oneself** hacer* un (gran) esfuerzo

exertion /ɪgˈzɜːrʃən ‖ɪgˈzɜːʃən/ *n* (*often pl*) esfuerzo *m*

exhale /eksˈheɪl/ *vi* espirar

exhaust¹ /ɪgˈzɔːst/ *n* **(a)** (~ pipe) tubo *m or* (RPI) caño *m* de escape, mofle *m* (AmC, Méx), exhosto *m* (Col) **(b)** (system) escape *m*, exhosto *m* (Col) **(c)** (fumes) gases *mpl* del tubo de escape

exhaust² *vt* agotar

exhausted /ɪgˈzɔːstəd ‖ɪgˈzɔːstɪd/ *adj* agotado

exhausting /ɪgˈzɔːstɪŋ/ *adj* agotador

exhaustion /ɪgˈzɔːstʃən/ *n* agotamiento *m*

exhaustive /ɪgˈzɔːstɪv/ *adj* (fml) exhaustivo

exhibit¹ /ɪgˈzɪbət ‖ɪgˈzɪbɪt/ *vt* **1** ⟨goods/ paintings⟩ exponer* **2** (fml) ⟨skill/dexterity⟩ demostrar*; ⟨fear/courage⟩ mostrar*; ⟨symptoms⟩ presentar

exhibit² *n* **(a)** (in gallery, museum) *objeto en exposición* **(b)** (Law) *documento u objeto que se exhibe en un juicio como prueba* **(c)** (exhibition) (AmE) exposición *f*

exhibition /ˈeksəˈbɪʃən ‖ˌeksɪˈbɪʃən/ *n* (of paintings, goods) exposición *f*; **to make an ~ of oneself** dar* un espectáculo

exhilarate /ɪgˈzɪləreɪt/ *vt* **(a)** (make happy) llenar de júbilo **(b)** (stimulate) tonificar*

exhilarating /ɪgˈzɪləreɪtɪŋ/ *adj* ⟨experience⟩ excitante; ⟨climate⟩ tonificante

exile¹ /ˈeksaɪl/ *n* **(a)** (person — voluntary) exiliado, -da *m,f*, exilado, -da *m,f*; (— expelled) desterrado, -da *m,f*, exiliado, -da *m,f*, exilado, -da *m,f* **(b)** (state) exilio *m*, destierro *m*

exile² *vt* desterrar*, exiliar, exilar

exist /ɪgˈzɪst/ *vi* **1** (be real) existir **2** (survive) subsistir

existence /ɪgˈzɪstəns/ *n* **1** (being) existencia *f*; **this is the only copy in ~** este es el único ejemplar existente **2** (life) vida *f*, existencia *f*

existing /ɪgˈzɪstɪŋ/ *adj* existente

exit /ˈegzət ‖ˈeksɪt/ *n* salida *f*

exodus /ˈeksədəs/ *n* (*no pl*) éxodo *m*

exorbitant /ɪgˈzɔːrbətənt ‖ɪgˈzɔːbɪtənt/ *adj* (fml) ⟨price/rent⟩ exorbitante

exorcize /ˈeksɔːrsaɪz ‖ˈeksɔːsaɪz/ *vt* exorcizar*

exotic /ɪgˈzɑːtɪk ‖ɪgˈzɒtɪk/ *adj* exótico

expand /ɪkˈspænd/ *vt* **1** (enlarge) expandir; ⟨lungs⟩ ensanchar; ⟨chest⟩ desarrollar; ⟨horizons⟩ ampliar*; ⟨influence/role⟩ extender* **2** ⟨story/ summary⟩ ampliar*
■ ~ *vi* **(a)** «metal/gas» expandirse; «elastic/ rubber band» estirarse **(b)** **expanding** *pres p* ⟨industry/market⟩ en expansión

expanse /ɪkˈspæns/ *n* extensión *f*

expansion /ɪkˈspæntʃən ‖ɪkˈspænʃən/ *n* expansión *f*

expatriate /eksˈpeɪtrɪət ‖eksˈpætrɪət/ *n* expatriado, -da *m,f*

expect /ɪkˈspekt/ *vt* **1** (anticipate) esperar; **is he**

coming tonight? — I ~ so ¿va a venir esta noche? — supongo que sí; **we're not ~ing any trouble** no creemos que vaya a haber problemas; **to ~ to + INF: she ~s to win the match** espera ganar el partido
2 (imagine) suponer*, imaginarse
3 (await) esperar; **I'll ~ you at eight** te espero a las ocho; **to be ~ing a baby** esperar un bebé
4 (require): **he ~ed me to pay** esperaba que yo pagara; **that's the least you'd ~** es lo menos que se puede esperar
■ ~ *vi* (colloq): **she's ~ing** está esperando (familia)

expectancy /ɪkˈspektənsi/ *n* expectación *f*; **life ~** esperanza *f* or expectativas *fpl* de vida

expectant /ɪkˈspektənt/ *adj* expectante

expectation /ˈekspekˈteɪʃən/ *n* **1** (anticipation): **in ~ of victory** previendo la victoria; **an atmosphere of great ~** un ambiente de gran expectación **2** **expectations** *pl* (of inheritance, promotion) expectativas *fpl*

expedient¹ /ɪkˈspiːdɪənt/ *adj* (fml) (*usu pred*) conveniente

expedient² *n* (fml) recurso *m*, expediente *m* (fml)

expedition /ˈekspəˈdɪʃən ‖ˌekspɪˈdɪʃən/ *n* expedición *f*

expel /ɪkˈspel/ *vt* **-ll-** expulsar

expendable /ɪkˈspendəbəl/ *adj* prescindible

expenditure /ɪkˈspendɪtʃər ‖ɪkˈspendɪtʃə(r)/ *n* (amount) gastos *mpl*; (spending) gasto *m*

expense /ɪkˈspens/ *n* **1** (cost, outlay) gasto *m*; **they had a good laugh at my ~** se partieron de risa a costa mía; **at the ~ of sth/sb** (with the loss of) a expensas de algo/algn **2** **expenses** *pl* (Busn) (incidental costs) gastos *mpl*

expense account *n* cuenta *f* de gastos de representación

expensive /ɪkˈspensɪv/ *adj* caro

experience¹ /ɪkˈspɪriəns ‖ɪkˈspɪərɪəns/ *n* experiencia *f*

experience² *vt* ⟨loss/setback/delays⟩ sufrir; ⟨difficulty⟩ tener*; ⟨change/improvement/pleasure/ pain⟩ experimentar

experienced /ɪkˈspɪriənst ‖ɪkˈspɪərɪənst/ *adj* ⟨secretary/chef⟩ con experiencia; ⟨driver⟩ experimentado

experiment¹ /ɪkˈsperəmənt ‖ɪkˈsperɪmənt/ *n* experimento *m*

experiment² *vi* **to ~ on sth/sb** experimentar con algo/algn; **to ~ with sth** experimentar con algo

experimental /ɪkˈsperəˈmentl ‖ɪkˌsperɪˈmentl/ *adj* experimental

expert¹ /ˈekspɜːrt ‖ˈekspɜːt/ *n* experto, -ta *m,f*

expert² *adj* experto; **~ witness** perito, -ta *m,f*

expertise /ˈekspɜːrˈtiːz ‖ˌekspɜːˈtiːz/ *n* pericia *f*

expire /ɪkˈspaɪr ‖ɪkˈspaɪə(r)/ *vi* (run out) «visa/ passport/ticket» caducar*; «lease/contract» vencer*

---

expiry /ɪkˈspaɪri ‖ɪkˈspaɪəri/ n vencimiento m, caducidad f

explain /ɪkˈspleɪn/ vt explicar*
■ v refl to ~ oneself explicarse*
■ **explain away** [v + o + adv, v + adv + o] ⟨fact/result⟩ encontrar* una explicación convincente para

explanation /ˌekspləˈneɪʃən/ n explicación f

explanatory /ɪkˈsplænətɔ:ri ‖ɪkˈsplænətri/ adj explicativo

explicit /ɪkˈsplɪsət ‖ɪkˈsplɪsɪt/ adj explícito; ⟨denial/refutation⟩ categórico

explode /ɪkˈspləʊd/ vi (a) «gunpowder/bomb» estallar, hacer* explosión, explotar; «vehicle» hacer* explosión; (with emotion) explotar, estallar (b) «population/costs» dispararse
■ ~ vt ⟨1⟩ ⟨bomb/dynamite⟩ explosionar, hacer* explotar or estallar ⟨2⟩ (discredit) ⟨theory⟩ rebatir; ⟨myth⟩ destruir*

exploit¹ /ɪkˈsplɔɪt/ vt explotar; ⟨situation/relationship⟩ aprovecharse de

exploit² /ˈeksplɔɪt/ n hazaña f

exploitation /ˌeksplɔɪˈteɪʃən/ n explotación f

exploration /ˌekspləˈreɪʃən/ n exploración f

exploratory /ɪkˈsplɔ:rətɔ:ri ‖ɪkˈsplɒrətəri/ adj ⟨talks⟩ preliminar; ⟨surgery⟩ exploratorio

explore /ɪkˈsplɔ:r ‖ɪkˈsplɔ:(r)/ vt ⟨territory/town⟩ explorar; ⟨topic/possibility⟩ investigar*

explorer /ɪkˈsplɔ:rər ‖ɪkˈsplɔ:rə(r)/ n (a) (traveler) explorador, -dora m,f (b) **Explorer** (in US) boy scout m (mayor de 14 años)

explosion /ɪkˈspləʊʒən/ n (of bomb, gas) explosión f, estallido m; (of anger) estallido m, explosión f

explosive¹ /ɪkˈspləʊsɪv/ adj explosivo

explosive² n explosivo m

exponent /ɪkˈspəʊnənt/ n (of idea, theory) defensor, -sora m,f; (of art style) exponente mf

export¹ /ekˈspɔ:rt ‖ɪkˈspɔ:t/ vt exportar

export² /ˈekspɔ:rt ‖ˈekspɔ:t/ n (a) (item exported) artículo m or producto m de exportación (b) (act of exporting) exportación f

exporter /ekˈspɔ:rtər ‖ɪkˈspɔ:tə(r)/ n exportador, -dora m,f

expose /ɪkˈspəʊz/ vt ⟨1⟩ (lay bare) ⟨nerve/wire/wound⟩ exponer*; **to ~ oneself to criticism** exponerse* a las críticas ⟨2⟩ (uncover) ⟨secret/scandal⟩ poner* al descubierto, sacar* a la luz; ⟨inefficiency/weaknesses⟩ poner* en evidencia; ⟨criminal⟩ desenmascarar ⟨3⟩ (Phot) exponer*

exposition /ˌekspəˈzɪʃən/ n exposición f

exposure /ɪkˈspəʊʒər ‖ɪkˈspəʊʒə(r)/ n ⟨1⟩ (a) (contact) ~ TO sth exposición f a algo (b) (Med) congelación f; **to die from ~** morir* de frío ⟨2⟩ (a) (unmasking): **she was threatened with public ~** amenazaron con ponerla al descubierto (b) (publicity) publicidad f ⟨3⟩ (Phot) exposición f

expound /ɪkˈspaʊnd/ vt (fml) exponer*

express¹ /ɪkˈspres/ vt expresar

express² n (train) expreso m, rápido m; (bus) directo m

express³ adj ⟨1⟩ (fast) ⟨train⟩ expreso, rápido; ⟨bus⟩ directo; ⟨delivery/letter⟩ exprés adj inv ⟨2⟩ (specific) (fml) ⟨intention/wish⟩ expreso

expression /ɪkˈspreʃən/ n expresión f

expressive /ɪkˈspresɪv/ adj expresivo

expressly /ɪkˈspresli/ adv (fml) expresamente

expressway /ɪkˈspreswei/ n (AmE) autopista f; (urban) vía f rápida

expropriate /eksˈprəʊprieɪt/ vt expropiar

expulsion /ɪkˈspʌlʃən/ n expulsión f

exquisite /ekˈskwɪzət ‖ɪˈekskwɪzɪt/ adj (a) ⟨dress/meal/taste⟩ exquisito; ⟨carving/brooch⟩ de exquisita factura; ⟨work/workmanship⟩ intrincado (b) ⟨pleasure⟩ infinito

ex-serviceman /ˈeks·sɜ:rvəsmən ‖·sɜ:vɪsmən/ n (pl **-men** /·mən/) soldado (or marinero etc) m retirado

extend /ɪkˈstend/ vt ⟨1⟩ (a) (stretch out) ⟨limbs/wings/telescope⟩ extender*; ⟨rope/wire⟩ tender* (b) (lengthen) ⟨road/line/visit⟩ prolongar*; ⟨lease/contract/deadline⟩ prorrogar* (c) (enlarge) ⟨house/room⟩ ampliar*; ⟨range/scope/influence⟩ extender* ⟨2⟩ (offer) (fml): **to ~ an invitation to sb** invitar a algn; (of written invitations) cursarle invitación a algn (fml)
■ ~ vi (a) (stretch) «fence/property/influence» extenderse* (b) (in time) «talks» prolongarse* (c) (become extended) «ladder/antenna» extenderse*

extension /ɪkˈstentʃən ‖ɪkˈstenʃən/ n ⟨1⟩ (a) (of power, meaning) extensión f (b) (lengthening) prolongación f; (of deadline) prórroga f, extensión f ⟨2⟩ (to building) ampliación f ⟨3⟩ (Telec) (a) (line) extensión f, interno m (RPl), anexo m (Chi) (b) (telephone) supletorio m

extension cord, (BrE) **extension lead** n extensión f, alargador m, cable m (RPl)

extensive /ɪkˈstensɪv/ adj ⟨area/field⟩ extenso; ⟨knowledge⟩ vasto; ⟨experience/coverage⟩ amplio; ⟨search/inquiries⟩ exhaustivo; ⟨damage/repairs⟩ de consideración

extensively /ɪkˈstensɪvli/ adv (a) (widely): **he's traveled ~** ha viajado por todas partes; **this technique is used ~** esta técnica es de uso extendido (b) (thoroughly, at length) ⟨research/investigate⟩ exhaustivamente

extent /ɪkˈstent/ n ⟨1⟩ (size, area) extensión f ⟨2⟩ (range, degree — of knowledge) amplitud f; (— of problem) alcance m; **to some ~** hasta cierto punto; **to a large ~** en gran parte

extenuate /ɪkˈstenjueɪt/ vt (fml) atenuar*; **extenuating circumstances** circunstancias fpl atenuantes, atentuantes mpl or fpl

exterior¹ /ekˈstɪriər ‖ɪkˈstɪəriə(r)/ adj ⟨wall/surface⟩ exterior

exterior² n exterior m

exterminate /ɪkˈstɜ:rmɪneɪt ‖ɪkˈstɜ:mɪneɪt/ vt exterminar

external /ekˈstɜ:rnl ‖ɪkˈstɜ:nl/ adj (a) (exterior) ⟨appearance/sign⟩ externo, exterior; ⟨wall⟩ exterior; ⟨wound/treatment⟩ externo (b) ⟨aid/influence⟩ del exterior; ⟨pressure/evidence⟩ externo (c) (foreign) ⟨affairs/trade/policy⟩ exterior

extinct /ɪkˈstɪŋkt/ adj ⟨animal/species⟩ extinto, desaparecido; ⟨volcano⟩ extinto, apagado

extinction /ɪkˈstɪŋkʃən/ n extinción f

extinguish /ɪkˈstɪŋgwɪʃ/ vt (a) ⟨fire⟩ extinguir*; ⟨candle/cigar⟩ apagar* (b) (liter) ⟨hope/memory⟩ apagar* (liter); ⟨passion/life⟩ extinguir* (liter)

extinguisher /ɪkˈstɪŋgwɪʃər ‖ɪkˈstɪŋgwɪʃə(r)/ n (fire ~) extinguidor m (AmL), extintor m (Esp)

extortion /ɪk'stɔːrʃən ‖ɪk'stɔːʃən/ n extorsión f

extortionate /ɪk'stɔːrʃənət ‖ɪk'stɔːʃənət/ adj ⟨fee/price⟩ abusivo; ⟨demand⟩ excesivo

extra¹ /'ekstrə/ adj (a) (additional) ⟨before n⟩ de más; **we need ~ staff** necesitamos más personal; **at no ~ charge** sin cargo adicional; **they organized three ~ flights** organizaron tres vuelos adicionales; **~ time** (in soccer) prórroga f (b) (especial) ⟨before n⟩ ⟨care/caution⟩ especial

extra² adv (a) (as intensifier): **~ long** extralargo; **I worked ~ hard** trabajé más que nunca (b) (more): **to charge ~ for sth** cobrar algo aparte

extra³ n [1] (additional payment or expense) extra m; **optional ~s** (Auto) equipamiento m opcional, extras mpl [2] (Cin) extra mf

extract¹ /ɪk'strækt/ vt extraer*

extract² /'ekstrækt/ n [1] (excerpt) fragmento m [2] (concentrate) extracto m

extraction /ɪk'strækʃən/ n [1] (a) (Dent) extracción f (b) (of mineral, juice) extracción f [2] (ancestry) extracción f; **of Polish ~** de extracción polaca

extradite /'ekstrədaɪt/ vt extraditar

extradition /ekstrə'dɪʃən/ n extradición f; ⟨before n⟩ ⟨order/treaty⟩ de extradición

extraordinary /ɪk'strɔːrdṇeri ‖ɪk'strɔːdṇri/ adj [1] (exceptional) extraordinario; (very odd) ⟨sight/appearance⟩ insólito; (incredible) increíble [2] (frml) (Adm, Govt) ⟨powers/meeting⟩ extraordinario

extrapolate /ɪk'stræpəleɪt/ vt (frml) extrapolar

extrasensory /'ekstrə'sensəri/ adj extrasensorial; **~ perception** percepción f extrasensorial

extravagance /ɪk'strævəgəns/ n [1] (a) (lavishness, wastefulness) despilfarro m, derroche m (b) (luxury) lujo m [2] (of gestures, dress) extravagancia f; (of claim, story) lo insólito

extravagant /ɪk'strævəgənt/ adj (a) (lavish, wasteful) ⟨person⟩ derrochador, despilfarrador; ⟨lifestyle⟩ de lujo (b) ⟨claim/notions⟩ insólito; ⟨praise/compliments⟩ exagerado; ⟨behavior/dress/gesture⟩ extravagante

extravaganza /ɪk'strævə'gænzə/ n gran espectáculo m (realizado con alarde de color, fantasía y dinero)

extreme¹ /ɪk'striːm/ adj (a) (very great) ⟨poverty/caution/urgency⟩ extremo; ⟨annoyance/relief⟩ enorme; ⟨heat⟩ extremado (b) (not moderate) ⟨action/measure⟩ extremo; ⟨opinion⟩ extremista (c) (outermost) ⟨before n⟩: **in the ~ north/south** en la zona más septentrional/meridional

extreme² n extremo m; **~s of temperature** temperaturas fpl extremas

extremely /ɪk'striːmli/ adv (as intensifier) sumamente; **it's ~ difficult** es dificilísimo

extremist /ɪk'striːməst ‖ɪk'striːmɪst/ n extremista mf

extremity /ɪk'streməti/ n (pl **-ties**) [1] (a) (farthest point) extremo m (b) **extremities** pl (Anat) extremidades fpl [2] (critical degree, situation) (frml) extremo m

extricate /'ekstrəkeɪt ‖'ekstrɪkeɪt/ vt sacar* (con dificultad)

extrovert¹ /'ekstrəvɜːrt ‖'ekstrəvɜːt/ adj extrovertido

extrovert² /'ekstrəvɜːrt ‖'ekstrəvɜːt/ n extrovertido, -da m,f

exude /ɪg'zuːd ‖ɪg'zjuːd/ vt ⟨resin/fluid⟩ exudar; ⟨charm/confidence⟩ emanar

exult /ɪg'zʌlt/ vi (frml) exultar (frml)

exultation /'egzʌl'teɪʃən/ n (frml) exultación f (frml)

eye¹ /aɪ/ n [1] (a) (Anat) ojo m; **as far as the ~ can/could see** hasta donde alcanza/alcanzaba la vista; **I can't believe my ~s** si no lo veo, no lo creo; **to see ~ to ~ with sb** (usu with neg) estar* de acuerdo con algn; **to be up to one's ~s in sth** estar* hasta aquí de algo (fam) (b) (look, gaze) mirada f; **before my very ~s** ante mis propios ojos; **nothing caught my ~ in the store** no vi nada que me llamara la atención en la tienda; **to keep an ~ on sth/sb** vigilar or cuidar algo/a algn (c) (attention): **the company has been in the public ~ a lot recently** últimamente se ha hablado mucho de la compañía; **to have one's ~ on sth** echarle el ojo a algo (fam) (d) (ability to judge) ojo m; **to have an ~ for design** tener* ojo para el diseño [2] (a) (of needle) ojo m (b) (of hurricane, storm) ojo m (c) (in potato) ojo m

eye² vt (pres p **eying** or (BrE) **eyeing**) mirar

eye: ~ball /'aɪbɔːl/ n globo m ocular; **~brow** n ceja f; **to raise one's ~brows** arquear las cejas; **to raise one's ~brows at sth** asombrarse ante algo; **~catching** adj llamativo; **~drops** pl n colirio m

eyeful /'aɪfʊl/ n: **I got an ~ of dust** se me llenó el ojo de polvo

eye: ~glasses pl n (AmE) gafas fpl, anteojos mpl (esp AmL), lentes mpl (esp AmL); **~lash** n pestaña f

eyelet /'aɪlət ‖'aɪlɪt/ n ojete m

eye: ~lid n párpado m; **~liner** n delineador m (de ojos); **~-opener** n (colloq) (no pl) revelación f; **~ shadow** n sombra f de ojos; **~sight** n vista f; **~sore** n monstruosidad f, adefesio m; **~strain** n fatiga f visual; **~wash** n colirio m; **it's a lot of ~wash** (colloq) es un cuento chino (fam); **~witness** /'aɪ'wɪtnəs ‖'aɪwɪtnɪs/ n testigo mf ocular

Ff

F, f /ef/ *n* **(a)** (letter) F, f *f* **(b)** (Mus) fa *m*

F (= **Fahrenheit**) F

fa /fɑː/ *n* (Mus) fa *m*

FA *n* (in UK) = **Football Association**

fable /'feɪbəl/ *n* fábula *f*

fabric /'fæbrɪk/ *n* **(a)** (Tex) tela *f* **(b)** (of building, society) estructura *f*

fabricate /'fæbrɪkeɪt/ *vt* **(a)** (invent) inventar(se) **(b)** (manufacture) fabricar*

fabulous /'fæbjələs ‖ 'fæbjʊləs/ *adj* **(a)** (wonderful) (colloq) magnífico **(b)** (imaginary) fabuloso

facade, façade /fə'sɑːd/ *n* fachada *f*

face¹ /feɪs/ *n* **1** (of person, animal) cara *f*, rostro *m*; **a new ∼** una cara nueva; **in the ∼ of stiff opposition** en medio de una fuerte oposición; **to fall flat on one's ∼** caerse* de bruces; **to keep a straight ∼**: **I could hardly keep a straight ∼** casi no podía aguantarme (de) la risa; **to make** o (BrE also) **pull a ∼** poner* mala cara; **to put a brave ∼ on it** poner(le)* al mal tiempo buena cara; **to sb's ∼** a *or* en la cara
2 **(a)** (appearance, nature) (*no pl*) fisonomía *f*; **on the ∼ of it** aparentemente **(b)** (dignity): **to lose ∼** desprestigiarse; **to save ∼** guardar las apariencias
3 (of coin, medal, solid) cara *f*; (of clock, watch) esfera *f*, carátula *f* (Méx)
4 (of cliff) pared *f*; **to disappear off the ∼ of the earth** desaparecer* de la faz de la tierra

face² *vt* **1** (be opposite): **she turned to ∼ him** se volvió hacia él; **the hotel ∼s the sea** el hotel está frente al mar
2 (confront) enfrentarse a; **to be ∼d with sth** estar* *or* verse* frente a algo
3 **(a)** (be presented with) (*problem/increase*) enfrentarse a **(b)** (bear): **I can't ∼ going through all that again** no podría volver a pasar por todo eso; **I can't ∼ food first thing in the morning** no puedo ni oler la comida temprano por la mañana
■ **∼** *vi*: **the house ∼s north** la casa está orientada al norte; **I was facing the other way** miraba para el otro lado
■ **face up to** [*v + adv + prep + o*] afrontar

face: **∼cloth**, (BrE also) **∼ flannel** *n* toallita *f* (*para lavarse*); **∼ lift** *n* lifting *m*, estiramiento *m* (facial); **the building was given a ∼ lift** remozaron el edificio; **∼ pack** *n* mascarilla *f* (*de belleza*)

facet /'fæsət ‖ 'fæsɪt/ *n* faceta *f*

facetious /fə'siːʃəs/ *adj* burlón

face: **∼ to ∼** *adv* cara a cara; **∼ value** *n* valor *m* nominal; **to take sb/sth at ∼ value**: **I took her/what she said at ∼ value** me fie de ella/yo me creí lo que dijo

facial /'feɪʃəl/ *adj* facial

facile /'fæsəl ‖ 'fæsaɪl/ *adj* superficial, simplista

facilitate /fə'sɪləteɪt ‖ fə'sɪlɪteɪt/ *vt* (frml) facilitar

facility /fə'sɪləti/ *n* (*pl* **-ties**) **1** **facilities** *pl*:

facilities for the disabled instalaciones *fpl* para minusválidos; **the hotel has conference facilities** el hotel dispone de sala(s) de conferencia
2 (building) (AmE) complejo *m*, centro *m*

-facing /'feɪsɪŋ/ *suff*: **north/south∼** que da al norte/sur

facsimile /fæk'sɪməli/ *n* facsímil(e) *m*

fact /fækt/ *n* **1** (sth true) hecho *m*; **hard ∼s** datos *mpl* concretos; **to face (the) ∼s** aceptar la realidad **2** (reality): **this novel is based on ∼** esta novela está basada en hechos reales; **in ∼** de hecho, en realidad; **the ∼ of the matter is (that) ...** el hecho es que ...

fact: **∼-finding** /'fækt,faɪndɪŋ/ *adj* (*before n*) de investigación, investigador; **∼ sheet** *n* resumen *m* de datos esenciales

faction /'fækʃən/ *n* facción *f*

factor /'fæktər ‖ 'fæktə(r)/ *n* factor *m*

factory /'fæktri, -təri/ *n* (*pl* **-ries**) fábrica *f*

factory: **∼ farming** *n* (BrE) cría *f* intensiva; **∼ ship** *n* buque *m* factoría

factual /'fæktʃuəl/ *adj* (*account*) que se atiene a los hechos

faculty /'fækəlti/ *n* (*pl* **-ties**) **1** (sense) facultad *f* **2** (Educ) **(a)** (of university, college) facultad *f* **(b)** (academic personnel) (AmE) cuerpo *m* docente

fad /fæd/ *n* moda *f* pasajera

fade /feɪd/ *vi* **1** (*color*) apagarse*; (*fabric*) perder* color, desteñirse* **2** **(a)** (disappear) (*hope/memories*) desvanecerse*; (*beauty*) marchitarse; (*interest*) decaer*; (*sound*) debilitarse **(b)** (*flower/plant*) ajarse
■ **∼** *vt* (*fabric*) desteñir*, hacer* perder el color a
■ **fade away** [*v + adv*] irse* apagando

faded /'feɪdəd ‖ 'feɪdɪd/ *adj* (*color*) apagado; (*fabric*) desteñido

faeces /'fiːsiːz/ *pl n* (BrE frml) ▶ FECES

fag /fæg/ *n* **1** (male homosexual) (AmE sl & pej) maricón *m* (fam & pey) **2** (cigarette) (BrE colloq) cigarrillo *m*, pitillo *m* (fam)

fah /fɑː/ *n* (BrE Mus) fa *m*

Fahrenheit /'færənhaɪt/ *adj* Fahrenheit *adj inv*

fail¹ /feɪl/ *vi* **1** (not succeed) (*marriage/business/plan*) fracasar; **if all else ∼s** como último recurso; **he ∼ed to live up to our expectations** no dio todo lo que se esperaba de él
2 **(a)** (*brakes/lights*) fallar **(b)** (*crop*) perderse*, malograrse **(c)** (failing *pres p*): **he could no longer read because of his ∼ing eyesight** la vista se le había deteriorado tanto que ya no podía leer; **he retired because of ∼ing health** se retiró porque su salud se había deteriorado mucho
3 (in exam) ser* reprobado (AmL), suspender (Esp)
■ **∼** *vt* **1** **(a)** (*exam*) no pasar, ser* reprobado en ┈┈⟶

(AmL), suspender (Esp), reprobar* (Méx), perder* (Col, Ur), salir* mal en (Chi) **(b)** ⟨*student*⟩ reprobar* *or* (Esp) suspender **2** (let down): **his courage ~ed him** le faltó valor; **words ~ me!** ¡es el colmo!

fail² *n* **1** (in exam, test) (BrE) reprobado *m or* (Esp) suspenso *m or* (RPl) aplazo *m* **2** **without ~** sin falta

failing¹ /'feɪlɪŋ/ *n* defecto *m*

failing² *prep*: **~ that, try bleach** si eso no resulta, prueba con lejía

fail-safe /'feɪlseɪf/ *adj* ⟨*mechanism*⟩ de seguridad

failure /'feɪljər ‖ 'feɪljə(r)/ *n* (unsuccessful thing, act, person) fracaso *m*; **engine ~** falla *f* mecánica *or* (Esp) fallo *m* mecánico; **power ~** apagón *m*; **heart ~** insuficiencia *f* cardíaca; **~ to carry out orders** el incumplimiento de las órdenes

faint¹ /feɪnt/ *adj* **-er, -est** ⟨*line*⟩ apenas visible; ⟨*light*⟩ débil; ⟨*noise*⟩ apenas perceptible; ⟨*hope/smile*⟩ ligero; **I feel ~** estoy mareado; **I haven't the ~est** ⟨*idea*⟩ (colloq) no tengo la más mínima idea

faint² *vi* desmayarse

faint³ *n* desmayo *m*

faintly /'feɪntli/ *adv* **(a)** (barely perceptibly) ⟨*see/hear*⟩ apenas; ⟨*shine*⟩ débilmente **(b)** (slightly) ⟨*amused*⟩ ligeramente; ⟨*amusing/ridiculous*⟩ algo

fair¹ /fer ‖ feə(r)/ *adj* **-er, -est** **1** (just) ⟨*person/decision*⟩ justo; ⟨*contest/election*⟩ limpio; **~ enough** bueno, está bien; **I've had my ~ share of problems recently** ya he tenido bastantes problemas últimamente; **~ and square**: **he won ~ and square** ganó en buena ley **2** ⟨*hair*⟩ rubio, güero (Méx), mono (Col), catire (Ven); ⟨*skin*⟩ blanco **3** (beautiful) (liter) hermoso, bello **4** **(a)** (quite good) ⟨*work*⟩ pasable; **we have a ~ chance of winning** tenemos bastantes posibilidades de ganar **(b)** (considerable) ⟨*before n*⟩ ⟨*number/amount*⟩ bueno **5** (Meteo): **the weather tomorrow will be ~** mañana va a hacer buen tiempo

fair² *adv* (impartially) ⟨*play*⟩ limpio, limpiamente

fair³ *n* **1** (market) feria *f*; (trade **~**) feria *f* industrial/comercial **2** (funfair) (BrE) feria *f*

fair: **~ground** *n* (funfair) (BrE) feria *f*; (permanent) parque *m* de diversiones *or* (Esp) atracciones; **~-haired** /'fer'herd ‖ ˌfeə'heəd/ *adj* (BrE) rubio, güero (Méx), mono (Col), catire (Ven)

fairly /'ferli ‖ 'feəli/ *adv* **1** (justly) ⟨*play*⟩ limpio; ⟨*judge*⟩ con imparcialidad; ⟨*divide*⟩ equitativamente **2** (moderately) bastante; **I'm ~ sure** estoy casi segura

fairness /'fernəs ‖ 'feənɪs/ *n* imparcialidad *f*; **in all ~** sinceramente

fair: **~ play** *n* juego *m* limpio; **~-sized** /'fer'saɪzd ‖ ˌfeə'saɪzd/ *adj* ⟨*before n*⟩ bastante grande

fairy /'feri ‖ 'feəri/ *n* (*pl* **-ries**) hada *f*‡

fairy: **~ godmother** *n* hada *f*‡ madrina; **~land** *n* el país de las hadas; **~ story, ~ tale** *n* cuento *m* de hadas

faith /feɪθ/ *n* **1** (trust) confianza *f*; **to have ~ IN sb/sth** tener* confianza *or* fe EN algn/algo **2** (Relig) fe *f*

faithful /'feɪθfəl/ *adj* fiel

faithfully /'feɪθfəli/ *adv* **(a)** (in letters): **yours ~** (esp BrE) (le saluda) atentamente **(b)** ⟨*serve/record*⟩ fielmente

faith healer /'hi:lər ‖ 'hi:lə(r)/ *n* curandero, -ra *m,f*

fake¹ /feɪk/ *n* (object) falsificación *f*; (person) farsante *mf*

fake² *adj* ⟨*jewel/document*⟩ falso; ⟨*fur*⟩ sintético

fake³ *vt* ⟨*document/signature*⟩ falsificar*; ⟨*results/evidence*⟩ falsear ■ **~** *vi* fingir*

falcon /'fælkən ‖ 'fɔːlkən/ *n* halcón *m*

Falkland Islands /'fɔːlklənd/, **Falklands** /'fɔːlkləndz/ *pl n* **the ~ ~, the ~** las (Islas) Malvinas

fall¹ /fɔːl/ *n* **1** (tumble, collapse) caída *f* **2** (autumn) (AmE) otoño *m* **3** (decrease): **a ~ in temperature** un descenso de (las) temperaturas; **a ~ in prices** una bajada de precios **4** (of snow) nevada *f*; (of rocks) desprendimiento *m* **5** **falls** *pl* (waterfall) cascada *f*; (higher) catarata *f*

fall² (*past* **fell**; *past p* **fallen**) *vi* **1** **(a)** (tumble) caerse*; **I fell over a piece of wood** tropecé con un trozo de madera; **I fell down the stairs** me caí por la escalera **(b)** (descend) ⟨*night/rain*⟩ caer* **2** ⟨*temperature/price*⟩ bajar; **his face fell** puso cara larga **3** (be captured, defeated) **to ~** ⟨(TO sb) ⟨*city/country*⟩ caer* (en manos de algn) **4** (pass into specified state): **to ~ ill** *o* (esp AmE) **sick** caer* *or* (Esp tb) ponerse* enfermo, enfermarse (AmL); **to ~ silent** callarse **5** (land): **Christmas ~s on a Thursday this year** este año Navidad cae en (un) jueves; **the burden will ~ on the poor** los pobres serán los que sufrirán la carga

■ **fall apart** [*v + adv*] ⟨*clothing*⟩ deshacerse*; ⟨*system*⟩ venirse* abajo; ⟨*relationship*⟩ irse* a pique

■ **fall back** [*v + adv*] ⟨*troops*⟩ replegarse*

■ **fall back on** [*v + adv + prep + o*] ⟨*one's parents*⟩ recurrir a; ⟨*resources*⟩ echar mano de

■ **fall behind** [*v + adv*] [*v + adv + prep + o*] (in class, race) rezagarse*, quedarse atrás; **to ~ behind WITH sth** ⟨*with payments*⟩ atrasarse EN algo

■ **fall down** [*v + adv*] ⟨*person/tree*⟩ caerse*; ⟨*house/wall*⟩ venirse* abajo

■ **fall for** [*v + prep + o*] **(a)** (be attracted to) ⟨*man/woman*⟩ enamorarse de **(b)** (be deceived by) ⟨*trick/story*⟩ tragarse* (fam)

■ **fall in** [*v + adv*] **(a)** (tumble in) caerse* (a un pozo, al agua etc) **(b)** (collapse) ⟨*roof*⟩ venirse* abajo **(c)** (form ranks) (Mil) formar filas

■ **fall off** [*v + adv*] **(a)** (tumble down) caerse* (de una bicicleta, un caballo etc) **(b)** (break off) ⟨*button/handle*⟩ caerse* **(c)** (decline) ⟨*production/attendance*⟩ decaer*

■ **fall out** [*v* + *adv*] **(a)** (drop out) caerse* **(b)** (break ranks) (Mil) romper* filas **(c)** (quarrel) «*friends*» pelearse

■ **fall over** [*v* + *adv*] «*person/object*» caerse*

■ **fall through** [*v* + *adv*] (fail) no salir* adelante

fallacy /'fæləsi/ *n* (*pl* **-cies**) falacia *f*

fallen /'fɔːlən/ *past of* FALL²

fallible /'fæləbəl/ *adj* falible

falling /'fɔːlɪŋ/: ~**-off** /'fɔːlɪŋ'ɔːf ‖ ˌfɔːlɪŋ'ɒf/ *n* ▸ FALLOFF; ~**-out** /'fɔːlɪŋ'aʊt/ *n* (AmE) pelea *f*

falloff /'fɔːlɔːf ‖ 'fɔːlɒf/ *n* (*no pl*) (in speed) disminución *f*

Fallopian tube /fə'ləʊpiən/ *n* trompa *f* de Falopio

fallout /'fɔːlaʊt/ *n* lluvia *f* radiactiva; (*before n*) ~ **shelter** refugio *m* antinuclear

fallow /'fæləʊ/ *adj* ‹*land*› en barbecho

false /fɔːls/ *adj* ‹*statement/pride/name*› falso; ‹*belief*› erróneo; ‹*eyelashes/fingernails*› postizo; **true or** ~**?** ¿verdadero o falso?

false alarm *n* falsa alarma *f*

falsehood /'fɔːlshʊd/ *n* (frml) falsedad *f*

falsely /'fɔːlsli/ *adv* ‹*accuse*› falsamente

false: ~ **start** *n* (Sport) salida *f* en falso; (to career, speech) intento *m* fallido; ~ **teeth** *pl n* dentadura *f* postiza

falsify /'fɔːlsəfaɪ ‖ 'fɔːlsɪfaɪ/ *vt* **-fies, -fying, -fied** ‹*accounts/evidence*› falsificar*; ‹*truth*› falsear

falter /'fɔːltər ‖ 'fɔːltə(r)/ *vi* **(a)** (speak hesitantly) titubear, balbucear **(b)** «*enthusiasm/interest*» decaer*; «*courage/resolve*» flaquear

fame /feɪm/ *n* fama *f*

familiar /fə'mɪljər ‖ fə'mɪlɪə(r)/ *adj* **(a)** (well-known) ‹*sound/face*› familiar, conocido; **the name sounds** ~ el nombre me suena **(b)** (having knowledge of) **to be** ~ **WITH sth/sb** estar* familiarizado CON algo/algn

familiarity /fə'mɪli'ærəti/ *n* (*pl* **-ties**) **(a)** (knowledge): **she claimed extensive** ~ **with the method** dijo estar muy familiarizada con el método; **some** ~ **with computers would be an asset** se valorará la experiencia previa con computadoras **(b)** (of person, book, landscape) familiaridad *f*; ~ **breeds contempt** lo que se tiene no se aprecia

familiarize /fə'mɪljəraɪz ‖ fə'mɪlɪəraɪz/ *vt* **to** ~ **oneself WITH sth** familiarizarse* CON algo

family /'fæmli, 'fæməli ‖ 'fæmɪli, 'fæmli/ *n* (*pl* **-lies**) (relatives) familia *f*; (*before n*) ‹*business*› familiar; ‹*fortune*› de la familia

family: ~ **planning** *n* planificación *f* familiar; ~ **tree** *n* árbol *m* genealógico

famine /'fæmən ‖ 'fæmɪn/ *n* hambruna *f*

famished /'fæmɪʃt/ *adj* famélico; **I'm** ~**!** (colloq) ¡estoy muerto de hambre! (fam)

famous /'feɪməs/ *adj* famoso

fan¹ /fæn/ *n* **1** (hand-held) abanico *m*; (mechanical) ventilador *m* **2** (of group, actor) fan *m/f*; (of football team) hincha *m/f*

fan² **-nn-** *vt* ‹*person*› abanicar*; ‹*interest/curiosity*› avivar

■ **fan out** [*v* + *adv*] «*searchers*» abrirse* en abanico

fanatic /fə'nætɪk/ *n* fanático, -ca *m,f*

fanatical /fə'nætɪkəl/ *adj* ‹*believer*› fanático; ‹*belief*› ciego

fan belt *n* correa *f* or (Méx) banda *f* del ventilador

fanciful /'fænsɪfəl/ *adj* **(a)** (impractical) ‹*idea*› extravagante **(b)** (elaborate) ‹*design*› imaginativo

fan club *n* club *m* de fans

fancy¹ /'fænsi/ *vt* **fancies, fancying, fancied** (esp BrE) **1** (expressing surprise) (*in interj*): **(just)** ~ **that!** ¡pues mira tú!; ~ **meeting them here!** ¡qué casualidad encontrarnos con ellos aquí! **2** (feel desire for) (colloq): **I really** ~ **an ice-cream** ¡qué ganas de tomarme un helado!; **do you** ~ **going to see a movie?** ¿tienes ganas de ir al cine? **3** (be physically attracted to) (colloq): **I** ~ **her/him** me gusta mucho **4** (imagine) (frml) **to** ~ (THAT): **she fancied she saw his face in the crowd** creyó ver su cara entre la multitud

fancy² *adj* **-cier, -ciest (a)** (elaborate) elaborado **(b)** (superior) (pej) ‹*hotel*› de campanillas; ‹*car*› lujoso; ‹*ideas*› extravagante

fancy³ *n* (*pl* **-cies**) **1** (liking) (*no pl*): **to take a** ~ **to sb: she seems to have taken a** ~ **to you** parece que le has caído en gracia; **to tickle sb's** ~: **the idea rather tickled my** ~ la idea me resultó atractiva **2** (imagination) imaginación *f*

fancy: ~ **dress** *n* (BrE) disfraz *m*; (*before n*) ~**-dress party** fiesta *f* de disfraces; ~**-free** /'fænsi'friː/ *adj* ▸ FOOTLOOSE; ~ **goods** *pl n* (Busn) artículos *mpl* para regalo

fanfare /'fænfer ‖ 'fænfeə(r)/ *n* fanfarria *f*

fang /fæŋ/ *n* (of dog) colmillo *m*; (of snake) diente *m*

fan heater *n* electroconvector *m*

fanny /'fæni/ *n* (*pl* **-nies**) (buttocks) (AmE sl) culo *m* (fam: en algunas regiones vulg), traste *m* (CS fam), poto *m* (Chi, Per fam)

fantasize /'fæntəsaɪz/ *vi* fantasear

fantastic /fæn'tæstɪk/ *adj* **(a)** (wonderful) (colloq) fantástico **(b)** (incredible) ‹*story*› absurdo

fantasy /'fæntəsi/ *n* (*pl* **-sies**) **(a)** (unreality) fantasía *f* **(b)** (daydream) sueño *m*

FAQ *pl n* (Comput) = **frequently asked questions**

far¹ /fɑːr ‖ fɑː(r)/ *adv* **1** (*comp* **further** or **farther**; *superl* **furthest** or **farthest**) **(a)** (in distance) lejos; **how** ~ **is it?** ¿a qué distancia está?; ~ **away in the distance** a lo lejos **(b)** (in progress): **the plans are now quite** ~ **advanced** los planes están ya muy avanzados; **that girl will go** ~ esa chica va a llegar lejos **(c)** (in time): **Christmas isn't** ~ **away** *o* **off now** ya falta poco para Navidad; **I can't remember that** ~ **back** no recuerdo cosas tan lejanas **(d)** (in extent, degree): **the new legislation doesn't go** ~ **enough** la nueva legislación no tiene el alcance necesario; **his jokes went a bit too** ~ se pasó un poco con esos chistes

2 (very much): ~ **better** mucho mejor

3 (*in phrases*) **as** *o* **so far as: as** *o* **so** ~ **as I know** que yo sepa; **by far: their team was by** ~ **the worst** su equipo fue con mucho el peor; **so far: so** ~**, everything has gone according to plan** hasta ahora todo ha salido de acuerdo a lo planeado

far² *adj* (*comp* **farther**; *superl* **farthest**) **(a)** (distant) lejano **(b)** (most distant, extreme) (*before n*, ⋯⟩

no comp): **at the ~ end of the room** en el otro extremo de la habitación; **the ~ left/right** (Pol) la extrema izquierda/derecha

faraway /'fɑːrəˈweɪ/ *adj* (*before n*) ⟨*lands*⟩ lejano; ⟨*look*⟩ ausente

farce /fɑːrs ‖ fɑːs/ *n* farsa *f*

farcical /'fɑːrsɪkəl ‖ 'fɑːsɪkəl/ *adj* ridículo

fare /fer ‖ feə(r)/ *n* [1] (cost of travel — by air) pasaje *m or* (Esp) billete *m*; (— by bus, train) boleto *m or* (esp Esp) billete *m*; **~s will rise again next year** las tarifas subirán de nuevo en el próximo año [2] (food and drink) comida *f*

Far East *n* **the ~ ~** el Lejano *or* Extremo Oriente

farewell¹ /'fer'wel ‖ feə'wel/ *n* despedida *f*

farewell² *interj* (liter) adiós

far-fetched /'fɑːr'fetʃt ‖ fɑːˈfetʃt/ *adj* exagerado

farm¹ /fɑːrm ‖ fɑːm/ *n* (small) granja *f*, chacra *f* (CS, Per); (large) hacienda *f*, cortijo *m* (Esp), rancho *m* (Méx), estancia *f* (RPl), fundo *m* (Chi); (*before n*) ⟨*machinery/worker*⟩ agrícola

farm² *vt* ⟨*land*⟩ cultivar

■ **farm out** [*v + o + adv, v + adv + o*] ⟨*work*⟩ encargar* (*a terceros*)

farmer /'fɑːrmər ‖ 'fɑːmə(r)/ *n* agricultor, -tora *m,f*, granjero, -ra *m,f*, chacarero, -ra *m,f* (CS, Per); (owner of large farm) hacendado, -da *m,f*, ranchero, -ra *m,f* (Méx), estanciero, -ra *m,f* (RPl), dueño, -ña *m,f* de fundo (Chi)

farm: ~hand *n* peón *m or* (Esp) mozo *m* de labranza; **~house** *n* casa *f* de labranza, alquería *f* (*en Esp*), ≈ casco *m* de la estancia (*en RPl*)

farming /'fɑːrmɪŋ ‖ 'fɑːmɪŋ/ *n* (of land) labranza *f*; (of animals) crianza *f*; (*before n*) ⟨*community*⟩ agrícola; ⟨*methods*⟩ de labranza

farm: ~land *n* tierras *fpl* de labranza; **~yard** *n* corral *m*

far: ~-off /'fɑːr'ɔːf ‖ 'fɑːrɒf/ *adj* (*pred ~ off*) (in space) remoto; (in time) distante; **~-reaching** /'fɑːˈriːtʃɪŋ ‖ fɑːˈriːtʃɪŋ/ *adj* de gran alcance; **~-sighted** /'fɑːr'saɪtəd ‖ fɑːˈsaɪtɪd/ *adj* (a) (showing foresight) con visión de futuro (b) (AmE Med) hipermétrope

fart¹ /fɑːrt ‖ fɑːt/ *n* (vulg) pedo *m* (fam)

fart² *vi* (vulg) tirarse *or* echarse un pedo (fam)

farther¹ /'fɑːrðər ‖ 'fɑːðə(r)/ *adv comp of* FAR¹ 1

farther² *adj comp of* FAR²

farthest¹ /'fɑːrðəst ‖ 'fɑːðɪst/ *adv superl of* FAR¹ 1

farthest² *adj superl of* FAR²

fascinate /'fæsɪneɪt ‖ 'fæsɪneɪt/ *vt* fascinar

fascinated /'fæsɪneɪtəd ‖ 'fæsɪneɪtɪd/ *adj* fascinado

fascinating /'fæsɪneɪtɪŋ ‖ 'fæsɪneɪtɪŋ/ *adj* fascinante

fascination /ˌfæsɪˈneɪʃən ‖ ˌfæsɪˈneɪʃən/ *n* fascinación *f*

fascism /'fæʃɪzəm/ *n* fascismo *m*

fascist¹ /'fæʃəst ‖ 'fæʃɪst/ *n* fascista *mf*

fascist² *adj* fascista

fashion¹ /'fæʃən/ *n* [1] (vogue) moda *f*; **to be in/out of ~** estar* de moda/estar* pasado de moda; (*before n*) **~ designer** diseñador, -dora *m,f* de

modas [2] (custom) costumbre *f* [3] (manner) manera *f*; **after a ~: can you swim? — well, after a ~** ¿sabes nadar? — bueno, a mi manera

fashion² *vt* crear

fashionable /'fæʃnəbəl/ *adj* ⟨*clothes/designs*⟩ a la moda; ⟨*restaurant/people/idea*⟩ de moda

fashionably /'fæʃnəbli/ *adv* a la moda

fashion show *n* desfile *m* de modas

fast¹ /fæst ‖ fɑːst/ *adj* **-er, -est** [1] (a) (speedy) rápido (b) (of clock, watch) (*pred*): **my watch is five minutes ~** mi reloj (se) adelanta cinco minutos [2] (color) inalterable

fast² *adv* [1] (quickly) rápidamente, rápido [2] (firmly): **the car was stuck ~ in the mud** el coche estaba atascado en el barro completamente; **to be ~ asleep** estar* profundamente dormido

fast³ *vi* ayunar

fast⁴ *n* ayuno *m*

fasten /'fæsn ‖ 'fɑːsn/ *vt* (a) (attach) sujetar; (tie) atar (b) (do up, close) ⟨*case*⟩ cerrar*; ⟨*coat/seat belt*⟩ abrochar

■ **~** *vi* «*suitcase*» cerrar*; «*skirt/necklace*» abrocharse

fastener /'fæsnər ‖ 'fɑːsnə(r)/ *n* cierre *m*

fast: ~ food *n* comida *f* rápida; **~-forward** /'fæst'fɔːrwərd ‖ fɑːst'fɔːwəd/ *vt/i* avanzar*

fastidious /fæs'tɪdiəs/ *adj* (a) (demanding) muy exigente (b) (fussy) maniático, mañoso (AmL)

fast track *n* vía *f* rápida

fat¹ /fæt/ *adj* **-tt-** ⟨*person/animal*⟩ gordo ⟨*book/cigar*⟩ grueso; **to get ~** engordar; **a ~ lot of good that'll do!** (iro) ¡para lo que va a servir!

fat² *n* grasa *f*

fatal /'feɪtl/ *adj* (a) (causing death) mortal (b) (disastrous) ⟨*decision/mistake*⟩ fatídico

fatalistic /'feɪtl'ɪstɪk ‖ feɪtə'lɪstɪk/ *adj* fatalista

fatality /fer'tælətɪ ‖ fə'tæləti/ *n* (*pl* **-ties**) muerto *m*

fatally /'feɪtli ‖ 'feɪtəli/ *adv* mortalmente

fate /feɪt/ *n* (a) (destiny) destino *m* (b) (*no pl*) (one's lot, end) suerte *f*

fated /'feɪtəd ‖ 'feɪtɪd/ *adj* (destined) **to be ~ to +** INF (liter) estar* predestinado A + INF

fateful /'feɪtfəl/ *adj* (a) (momentous) ⟨*day/decision*⟩ fatídico (b) (prophetic) ⟨*words*⟩ profético

father¹ /'fɑːðər ‖ 'fɑːðə(r)/ *n* padre *m*

father² *vt* ⟨*child*⟩ engendrar, tener*

Father Christmas *n* (BrE) Papá *m* Noel, viejo *m* Pascuero (Chi)

fatherhood /'fɑːðərhʊd ‖ 'fɑːðəhʊd/ *n* paternidad *f*

father: ~-in-law *n* (*pl* **~s-in-law**) suegro *m*; **~land** *n* patria *f*

fatherly /'fɑːðərli ‖ 'fɑːðəli/ *adj* paternal

fathom¹ /'fæðəm/ *n* braza *f*

fathom² *vt* **~ (out)** entender*

fatigue /fə'tiːg/ *n* fatiga *f*

fatten /'fætn/ *vt* **~ (up)** ⟨*animal*⟩ cebar

fattening /'fætnɪŋ/ *adj*: **cakes are extremely ~** los pasteles engordan muchísimo

fatty /'fæti/ *adj* **-tier, -tiest** ⟨*food/substance*⟩ graso, grasoso (AmL)

faucet /'fɔːsət/ n (AmE) llave f or (Esp) grifo m or (RPl) canilla f or (Per) caño m or (AmC) paja f, chorro m (AmC, Ven)

fault¹ /fɔːlt/ n **1** (responsibility, blame) culpa f; they're always finding ~ with me todo lo que hago les parece mal **2** (a) (failing) defecto m; she is generous to a ~ es generosa en extremo (b) (in machine) avería f; (in goods) defecto m **3** (Geol) falla f **4** (in tennis, show jumping) falta f

fault² vt encontrarle* defectos a

faultless /'fɔːltləs ‖'fɔːltlɪs/ adj impecable

faulty /'fɔːlti/ adj **-tier, -tiest** ⟨goods/design⟩ defectuoso; ⟨workmanship⟩ imperfecto

faux pas /fəʊ'pɑː/ n (pl ~ ~ /-z/) metedura f or (AmL tb) metida f de pata (fam)

favor¹, (BrE) **favour** /'feɪvər ‖'feɪvə(r)/ n **1** (approval): to find ~ with sb (fml) merecer* or tener* buena acogida por parte de algn (fml); to curry ~ with sb tratar de congraciarse con algn **2** in ~ a favor; to be in ~ of sth estar* a favor de algo **3** (act of kindness) favor m; to do/ask sb a ~ hacerle*/pedirle* un favor a algn

favor², (BrE) **favour** vt (a) (be in favor of) estar* a favor de (b) (benefit) favorecer* (c) (treat preferentially) favorecer*

favorable, (BrE) **favourable** /'feɪvrəbəl/ adj favorable; to be ~ TO sth favorecer* algo

favorite¹, (BrE) **favourite** /'feɪvrət ‖'feɪvərɪt/ adj preferido

favorite², (BrE) **favourite** n (a) (person, thing) preferido, -da m,f, (Sport) favorito, -ta m,f (b) (of teacher, ruler) favorito, -ta m,f

favoritism, (BrE) **favouritism** /'feɪvrətɪzəm ‖'feɪvərɪtɪzəm/ n favoritismo m

fawn¹ /fɔːn/ n **1** (young deer) cervato m **2** (color) beige m, beis m (Esp); (before n) ⟨sweater/coat⟩ beige adj inv, beis adj inv (Esp)

fawn² vi (flatter) to ~ ON sb «person» (pej) adular a algn

fax¹ /fæks/ n fax m; (before n) ~ machine fax m

fax² vt faxear

faze /feɪz/ vt (colloq) perturbar

FBI n (in US) (= Federal Bureau of Investigation) FBI m

FDA n (in US) = Food and Drug Administration

fear¹ /fɪr ‖fɪə(r)/ n miedo m, temor m; ~ of heights miedo a las alturas; no ~! (as interj) (colloq) ¡ni loco! or ¡ni muerto!

fear² vt (a) (dread) temer (b) (suspect) to ~ (THAT) temerse QUE
■ ~ vi temer; to ~ FOR sb/sth temer POR algn/algo

fearful /'fɪrfəl ‖'fɪəfəl/ adj **1** (frightening) aterrador **2** (timid) miedoso

fearless /'fɪrləs ‖'fɪəlɪs/ adj intrépido

fearsome /'fɪrsəm ‖'fɪəsəm/ adj ⟨enemy⟩ aterrador; ⟨task⟩ tremendo

feasibility /ˌfiːzə'bɪləti/ n viabilidad f; (before n) ~ study estudio m de viabilidad

feasible /'fiːzəbəl/ adj (practicable) viable; (possible) posible

feast¹ /fiːst/ n **1** (banquet) banquete m **2** (Relig) fiesta f; (before n) ~ day día m festivo

feast² vi festejar
■ ~ vt to ~ one's eyes ON sth regalarse los ojos CON algo

feat /fiːt/ n hazaña f

feather /'feðər ‖'feðə(r)/ n pluma f; as light as a ~ ligero or (esp AmL) liviano como una pluma; (before n) ~ bed colchón m de plumas; ~ duster plumero m

feature¹ /'fiːtʃər ‖'fiːtʃə(r)/ n **1** (a) (of face) rasgo m (b) (of character, landscape, machine, style) característica f **2** (a) ~ (film) película f (b) (Journ) artículo m (c) (Rad, TV) documental m

feature² vt **1** (Journ, Cin): he was ~d in 'The Globe' recently 'The Globe' publicó un artículo sobre él hace poco; featuring John Ball con la actuación de John Ball **2** (a) (have as feature) ⟨hotel/house⟩ ofrecer* (b) (depict) mostrar*
■ ~ vi figurar; rice ~s prominently in their diet el arroz ocupa un lugar importante en su alimentación

February /'februeri ‖'februəri/ n febrero m

feces, (BrE) **faeces** /'fiːsiːz/ pl n (fml) heces fpl (fml)

fed /fed/ past & past p of FEED¹

federal /'fedərəl/ adj federal

federal: F~ Republic of Germany n the F~ Republic of Germany la República Federal de Alemania; **F~ Reserve Board** n (in US) la Junta de Gobernadores de la Reserva Federal

federation /ˌfedə'reɪʃən/ n federación f

fed up adj (colloq) (usu pred) to be ~ ~ (WITH sb/sth/algo/+ ING) estar* harto (DE algn/algo/+ INF)

fee /fiː/ n (a) (payment: to doctor, lawyer) honorarios mpl; (— to actor, singer) caché m (b) (charge) (often pl): on payment of a small ~ por una módica suma; membership ~(s) cuota f (de socio)

feeble /'fiːbəl/ adj **-bler** /-blər ‖-blə(r)/, **-blest** /-bləst ‖-blɪst/ (a) (weak) débil (b) (poor) ⟨joke⟩ flojo; ⟨excuse⟩ pobre

feed¹ /fiːd/ (past & past p **fed**) vt **1** (a) (give food to) dar* de comer a; ⟨baby⟩ (breastfeed) darle* el pecho a; (with a bottle) darle* el biberón or (CS, Per) la mamadera or (Col, Ven) el tetero a (b) (provide food for) alimentar (give as food) to ~ sth TO sb dar* algo (de comer) A algn **2** (insert) to ~ sth INTO sth ⟨into a machine⟩ introducir* algo EN algo **3** (sustain) ⟨imagination/rumor⟩ avivar; ⟨hope/fire⟩ alimentar
■ ~ vi comer; to ~ ON sth alimentarse DE algo

feed² n (a) (act of feeding): it's time for the baby's ~ es hora de darle de comer al niño (b) (food) alimento m; (for cattle) pienso m

feedback /'fiːdbæk/ n (reaction) reacción f; (Audio, Electron) retroalimentación f

feeding bottle /'fiːdɪŋ/ n (BrE) biberón m, mamila f (Méx), mamadera f (CS, Per), tetero m (Col)

feel¹ /fiːl/ (past & past p **felt**) vi **1** (physically, emotionally) sentirse*; to ~ hot/cold/hungry/thirsty tener* calor/frío/hambre/sed **2** (have opinion): it's something I ~ strongly about es algo que me parece muy importante; how do you ~ about these changes? ¿qué opinas de estos cambios? **3** to ~ like -ING (be in the mood for) tener* ganas DE + INF **4** (seem): your hands ~ cold tienes las manos frías; how does that ~? — it's still too tight ¿cómo lo sientes? — todavía me queda apretado ···⟩

5 (grope) to ~ FOR sth buscar* algo a tientas
■ ~ vt **1** (touch) tocar*; to ~ one's way ir* a tientas
2 ⟨sensation/movement/shame⟩ sentir*; I couldn't ~ my fingers no sentía los dedos
3 (consider) considerar; I ~ that ... me parece que ...

feel² n (no pl) **1** (a) (sensation) sensación f **(b)** (sense of touch) tacto m **2** (a) (atmosphere — of house, room) ambiente m **(b)** (instinct): to have a ~ for sth tener* sensibilidad para algo; to get the ~ of sth acostumbrarse a algo

feeler /'fiːlər ‖'fiːlə(r)/ n **(a)** (Zool) (antenna) antena f; (tentacle) tentáculo m **(b)** (tentative approach): to put out ~s tantear el terreno

feeling /'fiːlɪŋ/ n **1** (a) (physical sensitivity) sensibilidad f **(b)** (physical, emotional sensation) sensación f **2** (a) (sincere emotion) sentimiento m **(b) feelings** pl (sensitivity) sentimientos mpl **3** (opinion) opinión f **4** (no pl) (impression) impresión f; I've a ~ that he knows already tengo or me da la sensación de que ya lo sabe

feet /fiːt/ n pl of FOOT¹

feign /feɪn/ vt fingir*

feline /'fiːlaɪn/ adj felino

fell¹ /fel/ past of FALL²

fell² vt ⟨tree⟩ talar; ⟨person⟩ derribar

fellow¹ /'feləʊ/ n **1** (man) tipo m (fam), hombre m **2** (member — of college) miembro del cuerpo docente y de la junta rectora de una universidad; (— of learned society) miembro mf de número

fellow² adj (before n): ~ worker/traveler compañero, -ra m,f, de trabajo/viaje; ~ citizen conciudadano, -na m,f; he has no love for his ~ men no le tiene amor al prójimo

fellow feeling n camaradería f

fellowship /'feləʊʃɪp/ n **1** (Educ) **(a)** (at university) título m de FELLOW¹ 2 **(b)** (endowment) beca f de investigación **2** (a) (companionship) (liter) hermandad f (liter) **(b)** (fraternity) fraternidad f

felon /'felən/ n (in US law) delincuente mf (que ha cometido un delito grave)

felony /'feləni/ n (pl **-nies**) (in US Law) delito m grave

felt¹ /felt/ n fieltro m

felt² past & past p of FEEL¹

felt pen, felt-tip (pen) /'felttɪp/ n rotulador m, marcador m (AmL)

female¹ /'fiːmeɪl/ adj ⟨sex⟩ femenino; ⟨animal/plant⟩ hembra; the victim was ~ la víctima era una mujer

female² n hembra f; (woman, girl) mujer f

feminine /'femənən ‖'femɪnɪn/ adj femenino

femininity /ˌfemə'nɪməti ‖ˌfemɪ'nɪnəti/ n feminidad f, femineidad f

feminism /'femənəzəm ‖'femɪnɪzəm/ n feminismo m

feminist¹ /'femənəst ‖'femɪnɪst/ n feminista mf

feminist² adj feminista

fence¹ /fens/ n **1** (a) (barrier) cerca f, cerco m (AmL); to sit on the ~ nadar entre dos aguas **(b)** (in showjumping) valla f **2** (receiver of stolen goods) (colloq) persona que comercia con objetos robados, reducidor, -dora m,f (AmS)

fence² vt cercar*
■ ~ vi (Sport) practicar* la esgrima
■ **fence in** [v + adv + o, v + o + adv] cercar*
■ **fence off** [v + adv + o, v + o + adv] separar con una cerca

fencer /'fensər ‖'fensə(r)/ n esgrimista mf

fencing /'fensɪŋ/ n **1** (Sport) esgrima f **2** (a) (material) materiales para cercos o vallas **(b)** (fence) cerca f

fend /fend/ vi: to ~ for oneself valerse* por sí mismo
■ **fend off** [v + o + adv, v + adv + o] ⟨attack/enemy⟩ rechazar*; ⟨blow⟩ esquivar; ⟨questions⟩ eludir

fender /'fendər ‖'fendə(r)/ n **1** (around fireplace) rejilla f **2** (on car) (AmE) guardabarros m or (Méx) salpicadera f or (Chi, Per) tapabarro(s) m; (on boat) defensa f

fennel /'fenl/ n hinojo m

ferment /fər'ment ‖fə'ment/ vi fermentar

fern /fɜːrn ‖fɜːn/ n helecho m

ferocious /fə'rəʊʃəs/ adj feroz

ferocity /fə'rɑːsəti ‖fə'rɒsəti/ n ferocidad f

ferret /'ferət ‖'ferɪt/ n hurón m
■ **ferret around, ferret about** [v + adv] husmear
■ **ferret out** [v + o + adv, v + adv + o] (colloq) descubrir*

ferry¹ /'feri/ n (pl **-ries**) (boat) transbordador m, ferry m; (smaller) balsa f

ferry² vt **-ries, -rying, -ried** llevar; we ~ the children to and from school in the car llevamos a los niños al colegio y los vamos a buscar en coche

fertile /'fɜːrtl ‖'fɜːtaɪl/ adj ⟨woman/animal/plant/soil⟩ fértil; ⟨seed/egg⟩ fecundado; ⟨imagination⟩ fértil

fertility /fər'tɪləti ‖fə'tɪləti/ n fertilidad f

fertilize /'fɜːrtlaɪz ‖'fɜːtaɪz/ vt ⟨egg/plant/cell⟩ fecundar; ⟨soil/crop⟩ abonar

fertilizer /'fɜːrtlaɪzər ‖'fɜːtaɪzə(r)/ n fertilizante m

fervent /'fɜːrvənt ‖'fɜːvənt/ adj ferviente

fervor, (BrE) **fervour** /'fɜːrvər ‖'fɜːvə(r)/ n fervor m

fester /'festər ‖'festə(r)/ vi enconarse

festival /'festəvəl ‖'festɪvəl/ n **(a)** (Relig) fiesta f **(b)** (Cin, Mus, Theat) festival m **(c)** (celebration) fiesta f

festive /'festɪv/ adj festivo; the ~ season (set phrase) las Navidades

festivity /fes'tɪvəti/ n (usu pl) celebración f

festoon /fe'stuːn/ vt to ~ sth/sb (WITH sth) adornar algo/a algn (CON algo)

---

fetch /fetʃ/ *vt* **1** (bring) traer*, ir* a por (Esp) **2** (sell for) (colloq): **the car ~ed $4,000** el coche se vendió en 4.000 dólares

■ ~ *vi*: **to ~ and carry** ser* el recadero/la recadera

fetching /'fetʃɪŋ/ *adj* ‹smile› atractivo; ‹dress/ hat› sentador, que sienta bien (Esp)

fete, fête /feɪt/ *n* **(a)** (fund-raising event) (BrE) feria *f* ‹benéfica›, kermesse *f* (CS, Méx), bazar *m* (Col) **(b)** (party) (AmE) fiesta *f* ‹en un jardín›

fetish /'fetɪʃ/ *n* fetiche *m*

fetter /'fetər ‖ 'fetə(r)/ *vt* (liter) encadenar; **he felt ~ed by convention** se sentía prisionero de los convencionalismos

fetters /'fetərz ‖ 'fetəz/ *pl n* (liter) grillos *mpl*

fettle /'fetl/ *n*: **to be in fine ~** estar* en (buena) forma

fetus, (BrE) **foetus** /'fi:təs/ *n* feto *m*

feud¹ /fju:d/ *n* contienda *f* (frml)

feud² *vi* contender* (frml)

feudal /'fju:dl/ *adj* feudal

fever /'fi:vər ‖ 'fi:və(r)/ *n* fiebre *f*

feverish /'fi:vərɪʃ/ *adj* (Med) con fiebre; (frantic) febril

fever pitch *n*: **to reach ~ ~** llegar* al paroxismo

few¹ /fju:/ *adj* **-er, -est** pocos, -cas; **the last ~ days have been difficult** estos últimos días han sido difíciles; **there were ~er people than usual** había menos gente que de costumbre; **I've been there a ~ times** he estado allí unas cuantas veces

few² *pron* **-er, -est** pocos, -cas; **the privileged ~** la minoría privilegiada; **a ~ of us complained** algunos (de nosotros) nos quejamos

fiancé /fi:'ɑ:nseɪ, fi:'ɑ:nseɪ ‖ fi:'ɒnseɪ/ *n* prometido *m*

fiancée /fi:'ɑ:nseɪ, fi:'ɑ:nseɪ ‖ fi:'ɒnseɪ/ *n* prometida *f*

fiasco /fi'æskəʊ/ *n* (*pl* **-cos** *or* **-coes**) fracaso *m*

fib¹ /fɪb/ *n* (colloq) mentirilla *f*, bola *f* (fam)

fib² *vi* **-bb-** (colloq) mentir*, decir* mentirillas *or* (fam) bolas

fiber, (BrE) **fibre** /'faɪbər ‖ 'faɪbə(r)/ *n* fibra *f*; (dietary) ~ fibra *f*

fiberglass /'faɪbərglæs ‖ 'faɪbəglɑ:s/ *n* fibra *f* de vidrio

fickle /'fɪkəl/ *adj* veleidoso

fiction /'fɪkʃən/ *n* ficción *f*

fictional /'fɪkʃnəl ‖ 'fɪkʃənl/ *adj* ficticio

fictitious /fɪk'tɪʃəs/ *adj* **(a)** (false) ‹name› ficticio **(b)** (imaginary) imaginario

fiddle¹ /'fɪdl/ *n* **1** (violin) violín *m*; **as fit as a ~** rebosante de salud **2** (cheat) (BrE colloq) chanchullo *m* (fam)

fiddle² *vt* (BrE colloq) ‹accounts› hacer* chanchullos con (fam); ‹results› amañar

■ ~ *vi* (fidget) **to ~ with sth** juguetear con algo

fiddler /'fɪdlər ‖ 'fɪdlə(r)/ *n* violinista *mf*

fidelity /fə'deləti ‖ fɪ'deləti/ *n* fidelidad *f*

fidget /'fɪdʒət ‖ 'fɪdʒɪt/ *vi*: **stop ~ing** ¡estate quieto!

field¹ /fi:ld/ *n* **1** (Agr) campo *m* **2** (Sport) **(a)** (area of play) campo *m*, cancha *f* (AmL) **(b)** (competitors) (+ *sing o pl vb*): **to lead the ~** llevar la delantera; **our products lead the ~** nuestros

productos son los líderes del mercado **3** (of study, work) campo *m*; (of activities) esfera *f* **4** (Opt, Phot, Phys) campo *m*; **~ of vision** campo visual

field² *vt* (Sport) fildear

field: **~ day** *n*: **to have a ~ day** hacer* su agosto; **~ glasses** *pl n* gemelos *mpl*, prismáticos *mpl*; **~ hockey** *n* (AmE) hockey *m* (sobre hierba); **~ marshal** *n* mariscal *m* de campo; **~ trip** *n* viaje *m* de estudio; **~work** *n* trabajo *m* de campo

fiend /fi:nd/ *n* **(a)** (demon) demonio *m* **(b)** (cruel person) (journ *or* hum) desalmado, -da *m,f*

fiendish /'fi:ndɪʃ/ *adj* **(a)** (wicked) diabólico **(b)** (very difficult) (colloq) endemoniado (fam)

fierce /fɪrs ‖ fɪəs/ *adj* **fiercer, fiercest (a)** ‹dog/lion› fiero; ‹temper› feroz; ‹hatred/love› intenso; ‹fighting› encarnizado; ‹criticism/ opposition› violento **(c)** ‹storm› violento; ‹wind› fortísimo; **the ~ tropical sun** el implacable sol del trópico

fiercely /'fɪrsli ‖ 'fɪəsli/ *adv* **(a)** ‹growl› con ferocidad **(b)** ‹fight› con fiereza; ‹criticize/ competitive/independent› extremadamente

fiery /'faɪri ‖ 'faɪəri/ *adj* **-rier, -riest** ‹glow› ardiente; ‹red› encendido; ‹heat/sun› abrasador; ‹liquor› muy fuerte; ‹temper› exaltado; ‹speech› fogoso

FIFA /'fi:fə/ *n* (*no art*) la FIFA

fifteen /fɪf'ti:n/ *adj/n* quince *adj inv/m*; *see also* FOUR¹

fifteenth¹ /fɪf'ti:nθ/ *adj* decimoquinto

fifteenth² *adv* en decimoquinto lugar

fifteenth³ *n* (Math) quinceavo *m*; (part) quinceava parte *f*

fifth¹ /fɪfθ/ *adj* quinto

fifth² *adv* en quinto lugar

fifth³ *n* **1** (a) (Math) quinto *m*; (part) quinta parte *f*, quinto *m* **(b)** (Mus) quinta *f* **(c)** (in competition): **he finished a disappointing ~** llegó en un deslucido quinto lugar **2** ~ (gear) (*no art*) quinta *f*

fiftieth¹ /'fɪftiəθ/ *adj* quincuagésimo

fiftieth² *adv* en quincuagésimo lugar

fiftieth³ *n* (Math) cincuentavo *m*; (part) cincuentava *or* quincuagésima parte *f*

fifty /'fɪfti/ *adj/n* cincuenta *adj inv/m*; *see also* FOUR¹

fifty-fifty¹ /'fɪfti'fɪfti/ *adv* (colloq) a medias

fifty-fifty² *adj* (colloq): **a ~ chance** un 50% de posibilidades; **on a ~ basis** a medias

fig /fɪg/ *n* higo *m*; (*before n*) ~ **tree** higuera *f*

fight¹ /faɪt/ (*past & past p* **fought**) *vi* «army/ country/animal» luchar; «person» pelear; **to ~** FOR/AGAINST sb/sth luchar POR/CONTRA algn/algo; **to ~ OVER sth** pelearse POR algo

■ ~ *vt* **1 (a)** ‹army/country› luchar contra **(b)** ‹fire/disease/measure› combatir **2 (a)** (conduct): **they fought a long war against the rebels** lucharon contra los rebeldes durante largo tiempo **(b)** (contest) ‹election› presentarse a; **we intend to ~ the case** (Law) pensamos llevar el caso a los tribunales (*or* defendernos *or*)

■ **fight back 1** [*v* + *adv*] defenderse*; **to ~ back** AGAINST sb/sth luchar CONTRA algn/algo ···⟩

2 [v + o + adv, v + adv + o] ⟨tears⟩ contener*; ⟨anger⟩ reprimir

■ **fight off** [v + o + adv, v + adv + o] ⟨attack/ enemy⟩ rechazar*; ⟨cold⟩ combatir

■ **fight out** [v + o + adv]: **you'll have to ~ it out among yourselves** tendrán que resolverlo entre ustedes

fight² n **1** (a) (between persons) pelea f; (between armies, companies) lucha f (b) (boxing match) pelea f **2** (a) (struggle) lucha f (b) (quarrel) pelea f

fighter /ˈfaɪtər ‖ˈfaɪtə(r)/ n **1** (a) (person) luchador, -dora m,f (b) (boxer) boxeador, -dora m,f **2** (plane) caza m; (before n) ~ **pilot** piloto m de caza

fighting /ˈfaɪtɪŋ/ n (Mil) enfrentamientos mpl; (brawling, arguing) peleas fpl

figment /ˈfɪgmənt/ n: **a ~ of the imagination** (un) producto de la imaginación

figurative /ˈfɪgjərətɪv ‖ˈfɪgərətɪv/ adj figurado

figure¹ /ˈfɪgjər ‖ˈfɪgə(r)/ n **1** (digit) cifra f; **recent ~s show that ...** estadísticas recientes muestran que ... **2** (a) (person) figura f; **a public ~** un personaje público (b) (body shape) figura f **3** (Art, Math, Mus) figura f

figure² vi **1** (feature) figurar; **to ~ prominently** destacarse* **2** (make sense) (colloq): **it just doesn't ~** no me lo explico

■ ~ vt (reckon) (AmE colloq) calcular

■ **figure on** [v + prep + o] (AmE colloq) contar* con

■ **figure out** [v + o + adv, v + adv + o] (a) (understand) entender* (b) (calculate) ⟨sum/result⟩ calcular; ⟨problem⟩ resolver*

figure: ~**head** n (Naut) mascarón m de proa; **he's merely a ~head** no es más que una figura decorativa; ~ **of speech** n figura f retórica; ~ **skating** n patinaje m artístico

Fiji /ˈfiːdʒiː/ n Fiji

filament /ˈfɪləmənt/ n filamento m

filch /fɪltʃ/ vt (colloq) birlar (fam)

file¹ /faɪl/ n **1** (tool) lima f **2** (a) (folder) carpeta f; (box ~) clasificador m; (for card index) fichero m (b) (collection of documents) archivo m; (of a particular case) expediente m (c) (Comput) archivo m

file² vt **1** (sort) ⟨papers⟩ archivar **2** ⟨application/suit⟩ presentar **3** ⟨metal⟩ limar; **to ~ one's nails** limarse las uñas

■ ~ vi **1** (walk in line) (+ adv compl): **they ~d into the room** entraron en la habitación en fila; **the crowd ~d past the tomb** la multitud desfiló ante la tumba **2** (Law): **to ~ for divorce** presentar una demanda de divorcio

file: ~ **card** n (AmE) ficha f; ~ **clerk** n (AmE) administrativo, -va m,f (encargado de archivar)

filing /ˈfaɪlɪŋ/ n: **there's a lot of ~ to do** hay mucho que archivar

filing: ~ **cabinet** n archivador m; ~ **clerk** n (BrE) ▶ FILE CLERK

Filipino /fɪləˈpiːnəʊ ‖ˌfɪlɪˈpiːnəʊ/ adj filipino

fill¹ /fɪl/ vt **1** (a) (make full) **to ~ sth** (WITH sth) llenar algo (DE algo) (b) ⟨cake/sandwich⟩ rellenar algo (DE algo) (b) (plug) ⟨hole/crack⟩ rellenar; ⟨tooth⟩ empastar, tapar (Andes), emplomar (RPl), calzar* (Col)

2 ⟨vacancy⟩ cubrir*

■ ~ vi «bath/auditorium»: **to ~** (WITH sth) llenarse (DE algo)

fill in 1 [v + o + adv, v + adv + o] (a) ⟨hole/ outline⟩ rellenar (b) ⟨form⟩ rellenar

2 [v + o + adv] (inform) (colloq) **to ~ sb in** (ON sth) poner* a algn al corriente (DE algo)

3 [v + adv] (deputize) **to ~ in FOR sb** sustituir* a algn

■ **fill out** [v + o + adv, v + adv + o] ⟨form⟩ rellenar

■ **fill up 1** [v + o + adv, v + adv + o] (a) (make full) llenar (b) (Auto): ~ **her up!** ¡llénelo! **2** [v + adv] (a) (become full) llenarse (b) (buy fuel) echar gasolina

fill² n: **to eat one's ~ of sth** (liter) comer algo hasta saciarse; **to have had one's ~ of sth** estar* harto de algo

filler /ˈfɪlər ‖ˈfɪlə(r)/ n (for cracks) masilla f

fillet¹ /ˈfɪlət ‖ˈfɪlɪt/ n (of beef) filete m, solomillo m (Esp), lomo m (AmS); (of pork) lomo m; (of fish) filete m; (before n) **a ~ steak** un filete, un solomillo de ternera (Esp), un bife de lomo (RPl)

fillet² vt ⟨meat⟩ cortar en filetes; ⟨fish⟩ quitarle la espina a

filling¹ /ˈfɪlɪŋ/ n **1** (Dent) empaste m, tapadura f (Chi, Méx), emplomadura f (RPl), calza f (Col) **2** (Culin) relleno m

filling² adj: **pasta's very ~** la pasta llena mucho

filling station n ▶ GAS STATION

filly /ˈfɪli/ n (pl **-lies**) n potra f

film¹ /fɪlm/ n **1** (a) (Phot) película f (fotográfica) (b) (movie) película f, film(e) m (period); (before n) ~ **star** estrella f de cine **2** (a) (thin covering) película f (b) (wrap) film m transparente

film² vt ⟨scene⟩ filmar; ⟨novel/play⟩ llevar al cine

■ ~ vi rodar*; ~**ing starts tomorrow** el rodaje empieza mañana

filmstrip /ˈfɪlmstrɪp/ n: película o serie de filminas para proyección fija

Filofax® /ˈfaɪləfæks/ n filofax® m

filter¹ /ˈfɪltər ‖ˈfɪltə(r)/ n **1** (device) filtro m; (before n) ~ **coffee** café m americano **2** (BrE Transp) flecha f (que autoriza el giro a derecha o izquierda en algunos semáforos); (before n) ~ **lane** carril m de giro

filter² vt filtrar

■ ~ vi ⟨gas/light/sound⟩ filtrarse

filter-tipped /ˈfɪltərtɪpt ‖ˌfɪltəˈtɪpt/ adj con filtro

filth /fɪlθ/ n mugre f

filthy /ˈfɪlθi/ adj **-thier, -thiest** (a) (dirty) mugriento (b) (obscene) ⟨language⟩ obsceno (c) (unpleasant) (BrE colloq) ⟨weather/habit⟩ asqueroso (fam)

fin /fɪn/ n aleta f

final¹ /ˈfaɪnl/ adj **1** (last) (before n) último; **a ~ demand** (for payment) (Busn) un último aviso de pago **2** (definitive) final; **the judges' decision is ~** (frml) la decisión del jurado es inapelable

final² n **1** (Games, Sport) (often pl) final f **2** **finals** pl (Educ) exámenes mpl finales

finale /fəˈnæli ‖fɪˈnɑːli/ n (a) (Mus) final m (b) (Theat) apoteosis f

finalist /ˈfaɪnəlɪst ‖ˈfaɪnəlɪst/ n finalista mf

finalize /ˈfaɪnəlaɪz ‖ˈfaɪnəlaɪz/ vt ultimar

finally /ˈfaɪnli ‖ˈfaɪnəli/ adv (a) (lastly) (indep) por último (b) (at last) por fin

finance¹ /fəˈnæns, faɪ- ‖ˈfaɪmæns, faɪˈnæns/ *n*
(a) (banking, business) finanzas *fpl* (b) **finances**
pl recursos *mpl* financieros (c) (funding)
financiación *f*, financiamiento *m* (esp AmL)

finance² *vt* financiar

financial /fəˈnæntʃəl ‖faɪˈnænʃəl/ *adj* ⟨system/
risk⟩ financiero; ⟨difficulties/independence⟩
económico; ⟨news⟩ de economía, de negocios; ~
advice asesoría *f* económica; ~ **management**
gestión *f* financiera

financial year *n* (BrE) (of company) ejercicio
m; (of government) año *m* fiscal

financier /ˈfɪnənsɪr ‖faɪˈnænsɪə(r)/ *n*
financiero, -ra *m,f*

find¹ /faɪnd/ (*past & past p* **found**) *vt*
encontrar*; I can't ~ it no lo encuentro; I found
(that) it was easier to do it this way descubrí que
era más fácil hacerlo así; I ~ **that hard to believe!**
¡me cuesta creerlo!; **to ~ sb guilty/not guilty** (Law)
declarar a algn culpable/inocente
■ *v refl* **to ~ oneself** encontrarse* a sí (*or* mí *etc*)
mismo
■ **find out** **1** [*v + o + adv, v + adv + o*] (discover)
⟨truth⟩ descubrir*; ⟨information⟩ (by making
enquiries) averiguar*
2 [*v + adv*] (a) (learn) enterarse; **to ~ out ABOUT**
sth enterarse DE algo (b) (make inquiries)
averiguar*

find² *n* hallazgo *m*

findings /ˈfaɪndɪŋz/ *pl n* conclusiones *fpl*

fine¹ /faɪn/ *adj* **finer, finest** **1** (*usu before n*)
(a) (excellent) ⟨house/speech/example⟩ magnífico;
⟨wine/ingredients⟩ de primera calidad (b) (fair)
⟨weather⟩ bueno **2** (colloq) (*pred*) (a) (in good
health) muy bien (b) (OK) bien; (perfect) perfecto
3 (thin, delicate) ⟨hair/china/point⟩ fino **4** (subtle)
⟨distinction/nuance⟩ sutil; ⟨balance⟩ delicado;
⟨adjustment⟩ preciso

fine² *adv* (adequately) bien; (very well) muy bien

fine³ *n* multa *f*

fine⁴ *vt* multar

fine art *n* arte *m*; **the ~ ~s** las bellas artes; **to**
have (got) sth down to a ~ ~ hacer* algo a la
perfección

finely /ˈfaɪnli/ *adv* (a) (in small pieces): **to chop**
sth ~ picar* algo muy fino (b) (subtly) ⟨adjust⟩
con precisión

fine print *n* (AmE) **the ~ ~** la letra pequeña *or*
menuda, la letra chica (AmL)

finery /ˈfaɪnəri/ *n*: **in all their ~** con sus mejores
galas

finesse /fəˈnes ‖fɪˈnes/ *n* (a) (refinement) finura *f*
(b) (tact) diplomacia *f*

fine-tooth(ed) comb /ˈfaɪnˈtuːθ(t)/ *n*: **to go**
over sth with a ~-tooth(ed) comb mirar algo con
lupa

finger¹ /ˈfɪŋgər ‖ˈfɪŋgə(r)/ *n* (of hand, glove) dedo
m; **index ~** (dedo) índice *m*; **middle ~** (dedo)
corazón *m or* medio *m*; **ring ~** (dedo) anular *m*;
little ~ (dedo) meñique *m*; **to cross one's ~s**: **I'll**
keep my ~s crossed for you ojalá (que) tengas
suerte; **to snap one's ~s** chasquear *or* (Méx)
tronar* los dedos

finger² *vt* toquetear, tentalear (Méx)

finger: **~nail** *n* uña *f*; **~print** *n* huella *f*
digital; **~tip** *n* yema *f* del dedo

finish¹ /ˈfɪnɪʃ/ *vt* **1** (a) (complete) terminar,
acabar; **we ~ work at four o'clock today** hoy
salimos a las cuatro; **to ~ -ING** terminar *or*
acabar DE + INF (b) (consume) ⟨drink/rations⟩
terminar, acabar
2 ⟨cloth/porcelain⟩ terminar; ⟨wood⟩ pulir
3 (destroy) (colloq) acabar con
■ ~ *vi* terminar, acabar
■ **finish off** **1** [*v + o + adv, v + adv + o*] (a)
(complete) terminar, acabar (b) (exhaust) dejar
agotado (c) (consume) terminar (d) (kill) matar
2 [*v + adv*] (conclude) terminar, acabar
■ **finish up** **1** [*v + o + adv, v + adv + o*] ⟨food/
paint⟩ terminar
2 [*v + adv*] (end up) acabar

finish² *n* **1** (*no pl*) (end) fin *m*, final *m*; (of race)
llegada *f* **2** (surface texture) acabado *m*

finished /ˈfɪnɪʃt/ *adj* (*pred*) (a) (complete,
achieved): **to get sth ~** terminar *or* acabar algo;
I'm ~ with the scissors no necesito más la tijera
(b) (ruined) acabado

finishing /ˈfɪnɪʃɪŋ/: **~ line** *n* (BrE) ▶ FINISH
LINE; **~ school** *n*: colegio privado para
señoritas donde se aprende a comportarse en
sociedad; **~ touch** *n*: **to put the ~ touch(es) to**
sth darle* los últimos toques a algo

finish line, (BrE) **finishing line** *n* meta *f*,
línea *f* de llegada

finite /ˈfaɪnaɪt/ *adj* finito

Finland /ˈfɪnlənd/ *n* Finlandia *f*

Finn /fɪn/ *n* finlandés, -desa *m,f*, finés, -nesa *m,f*

Finnish¹ /ˈfɪnɪʃ/ *adj* finlandés, finés

Finnish² *n* finlandés *m*

fiord /fiˈɔːrd ‖fiˈɔːd/ *n* fiordo *m*

fir /fɜːr ‖fɜː(r)/ *n* abeto *m*

fire¹ /faɪr ‖ˈfaɪə(r)/ *n* **1** (a) (flames) fuego *m*; **to**
be on ~ estar* en llamas; **to set sth on ~** *o* **to set**
~ to sth prenderle fuego a algo; **to catch ~**
prender fuego (b) (outdoors) hoguera *f*; (in hearth)
fuego *m* **2** (blaze which destroys a building) incendio
m; (*as interj*) ~! ¡fuego!; (*before n*) ~ **curtain**
telón *m* contra incendios; **this is a ~ hazard** esto
podría causar un incendio **3** (heater) (BrE) estufa
f **4** (of guns) fuego *m*; **to open ~ on sb/sth** abrir*
fuego sobre algn/algo

fire² *vt* **1** ⟨gun/shot⟩ disparar; ⟨rocket⟩ lanzar*;
to ~ questions at sb hacerle* preguntas a algn
2 (dismiss) (colloq) echar, despedir*
3 ⟨imagination⟩ avivar
■ ~ *vi* (shoot) disparar; **to ~ AT sb/sth** disparar
CONTRA algn/algo; **ready, aim, ~!** apunten ¡fuego!

fire: **~ alarm** *n* (apparatus) alarma *f* contra
incendios; (signal) alarma *f*; **~arm** *n* arma *f*; de
fuego; **~ department,** (BrE) **~ brigade** *n*
cuerpo *m* de bomberos; **~ door** *n* puerta *f*
contra incendios; **~ drill** *n* simulacro *m* de
incendio; **~ engine** *n* (BrE) ▶ ~ TRUCK; **~**
escape *n* escalera *f* de incendios; **~**
extinguisher *n* extinguidor *m* (de incendios)
(AmL), extintor *m* (Esp); **~fighter** *n* bombero *mf*;
~ guard *n* rejilla *f* de chimenea; **~lighter** *n*:
líquido o pastilla utilizados para facilitar el
encendido del fuego de leña o carbón; **~man**
/ˈfaɪrmən ‖ˈfaɪəmən/ (*pl* **-men** /-mən/) *n*
bombero *m*; **~place** *n* chimenea *f*, **~proof** *adj*
ignífugo; **~side** *n* hogar *m*; **~ station** *n*
estación *f or* (Esp) parque *m or* (RPl) cuartel *m* de ⋯▸

bomberos, bomba f (Chi); **~ truck** n (AmE) carro m or (Esp) coche m de bomberos, autobomba m (RPl), bomba f (Chi); **~wood** n leña f; **~works** pl n fuegos mpl artificiales

firing /'faɪrɪŋ || faɪrɪŋ/ **: ~ line** n: **to be on** o (BrE) **in the ~ line** (exposed to criticism) estar* expuesto a las críticas; (Mil) estar* en la línea de combate; **~ squad** n pelotón m de fusilamiento

firm¹ /fɜːm ||fɜːm/ adj **1** (a) (secure) ‹grasp› firme (b) (not yielding) ‹surface/muscles› firme; ‹mattress› duro; ‹foundation› sólido **2** (a) (steadfast) ‹friendship› sólido; ‹support› firme (b) (strict) estricto **3** (definite) ‹offer/date› en firme

firm² n empresa f, firma f

firmly /'fɜːmli ||'fɜːmli/ adv ‹grasp/believe› con firmeza; ‹fixed/supported› firmemente

first¹ /fɜːst ||fɜːst/ adj

■ **Note** The usual translation of first, primero, becomes primer when it precedes a masculine singular noun.

1 (initial) primero; **the ~ president of the USA** el primer presidente de los EE UU; **who's going to be ~?** ¿quién va a ser el primero?; **~ things first** primero lo más importante **2** (elliptical use): **he'll be arriving on the ~ (of the month)** llegará el primero or (Esp tb) el uno (del mes); **she was the ~ to arrive** fue la primera en llegar **3** (in phrases) **at first** al principio; **from first to last** de(l) principio a(l) fin

first² adv **1** (a) (ahead of others) primero; **he came ~ in the exam** sacó la mejor nota en el examen; **I always put my children ~** para mí antes que nada están mis hijos; **ladies ~** primero las damas (b) (before other actions, events) primero (c) (beforehand) antes (d) (for the first time) por primera vez **2** (in phrases) **first and foremost** ante todo; **first and last** por encima de todo; **first of all** en primer lugar

first³ (a) **~ (gear)** (Auto) (no art) primera f (b) (original idea, accomplishment) primicia f

first: **~ aid** n primeros auxilios mpl; (before n) **~-aid kit** botiquín m (de primeros auxilios); **~-aid station** o (BrE) **post** puesto m de primeros auxilios; **~ class** adv ‹travel› en primera (clase); **~-class** /'fɜːst'klæs ||,fɜːst'klɑːs/ adj (pred **~ class**) (a) (of highest grade) ‹hotel/ticket› de primera clase; ‹travel› en primera (clase) (b) (excellent) de primera (c) (BrE Corresp) **~-class mail** correspondencia enviada a una tarifa superior, que garantiza una rápida entrega; **~-hand** /'fɜːst'hænd ||,fɜːst'hænd/ adj ‹news› de primera mano; **~ lady** n primera dama f

firstly /'fɜːstli ||'fɜːstli/ adv (as linker) en primer lugar

first: **~ name** n nombre m de pila; **~-rate** /'fɜːst'reɪt ||,fɜːst'reɪt/ adj de primera; **~-time buyer** n: persona que compra algo, gen una vivienda, por primera vez

fiscal /'fɪskəl/ adj fiscal

fiscal year n (AmE) año m fiscal

fish¹ /fɪʃ/ n (pl **fish** or **fishes**) (a) (Zool) pez m; (before n) **~ pond** estanque m; **~ tank** pecera f (b) (Culin) pescado m; **~ and chips** (esp BrE) pescado m frito con papas or (Esp) patatas fritas

fish² vi pescar*; **to go ~ing** ir* de pesca; **to ~ FOR sth** ‹for trout› pescar* algo; ‹for compliments› andar* a la caza de algo; **to ~ (around) in one's pockets/bag** rebuscar* en los bolsillos/la bolsa
■ **fish out** [v + o + adv, v + adv + o] sacar*

fish: **~bone** n espina f (de pez); **~cake** n ≈ croqueta f (de pescado y papas)

fisherman /'fɪʃərmən ||'fɪʃəmən/ n (pl **-men** /-mən/) pescador m

fishery /'fɪʃəri/ n (pl **-eries**) **1** ▶ FISH FARM **2** **fisheries** pl (industry) industria f pesquera, pesca f

fish: **~ farm** n piscifactoría f; **~ finger** n (BrE) ▶ FISH STICK; **~hook** n anzuelo m

fishing /'fɪʃɪŋ/ n pesca f; (before n) ‹industry/port/vessel/fleet› pesquero

fishing: **~ net** n red f de pesca; **~ pole** (AmE), **~ rod** n caña f de pescar

fish: **~monger** /'fɪʃ,mɑːŋər ||'fɪʃ,mʌŋɡə(r)/ n (BrE) pesficadero, -ra m,f; **at the ~monger('s)** en la pescadería; **~net** n (a) (AmE) ▶ FISHING NET (b) (Tex) red f; (before n) ‹stockings› de malla gruesa or de red; **~ slice** n (BrE) espumadera f; **~ stick** n (AmE) palito m de bacalao (or merluza etc) (trozo de pescado rebozado y frito)

fishy /'fɪʃi/ adj **fishier, fishiest 1** ‹smell/taste› a pescado **2** (suspicious) (colloq) sospechoso

fission /'fɪʃən/ n fisión f

fist /fɪst/ n puño m

fistfight /'fɪstfaɪt/ n pelea f (a puñetazos)

fit¹ /fɪt/ adj **-tt- 1** (healthy) en forma; **to keep ~** mantenerse* en forma; **to be ~ to + INF** ‹to play/travel› estar* en condiciones DE + INF **2** (suitable) ‹person/conduct› adecuado; **this isn't ~ to eat** (harmful) esto no está en buenas condiciones; (unappetizing) esto está incomible; **he's not ~ to be a father** no es digno de ser padre; **he did not see ~ to reply to our letter** ni se dignó contestar a nuestra carta

fit² **-tt-** vt **1** (a) (Clothing): **the dress ~s you perfectly** el vestido te queda perfecto; **the jacket doesn't ~ me** la chaqueta no me queda bien (b) (be right size, shape for) ‹socket› encajar en (c) (correspond to) ‹theory› concordar* con; **to ~ a description** responder a una descripción **2** (install) (esp BrE) ‹carpet/lock› poner*; ‹double glazing› instalar **3** (accommodate) **to ~ sth INTO sth** meter algo EN algo
■ **~** vi (a) (Clothing): **these shoes don't ~** estos zapatos no me quedan bien; **to make sth ~** ajustar algo (b) (be right size, shape) «lid» ajustar; «key/peg» encajar (c) (correspond) «facts/description» encajar
■ **fit in** **1** [v + adv] (a) (have enough room) caber* (b) (accord) «detail/event» **to ~ in (WITH sth)** concordar* (CON algo) (c) (belong): **she doesn't ~**

in here esto no es para ella **(d)** (conform to): **he'll have to ~ in with our plans** tendrá que amoldarse a nuestros planes

2 [v + o + adv, v + adv + o] **(a)** (find space for) acomodar **(b)** (find time for): **I can ~ you in at ten o'clock** puedo atenderla a las diez; **she hoped to ~ in some sightseeing** esperaba tener un poco de tiempo para salir a conocer el lugar

■ **fit out** [v + o + adv, v + adv + o] equipar; **to ~ sb out WITH sth** ⟨with boots/equipment⟩ equipar a algn CON algo; ⟨with uniform⟩ proveer* a algn DE algo

fit³ n **1** **(a)** (attack) ataque m; **epileptic ~** ataque epiléptico; **to have a ~** (colloq): **I nearly had a ~** casi me da un ataque (fam) **(b)** (short burst): **a ~ of coughing** un acceso de tos; **in ~s and starts** a los tropezones **2** (of clothes) (no pl): **my new jacket is a good ~** la chaqueta nueva me queda bien; **it's a tight ~** es muy entallado

fitful /'fɪtfʊl/ adj ⟨progress/sunshine⟩ intermitente; ⟨sleep⟩ irregular

fitfully /'fɪtfəli/ adv de manera irregular

fitness /'fɪtnəs ‖'fɪtnɪs/ n **1** (healthiness) salud f; **(physical) ~** (buena) forma f física **2** (suitability) aptitud f

fitted /'fɪtəd ‖'fɪtɪd/ adj **(a)** ⟨cupboard⟩ empotrado; ⟨shelves⟩ hecho a medida; ⟨sheet⟩ ajustable, de cajón (Méx); **~ carpet** (esp BrE) alfombra f de pared a pared, moqueta f (Esp) **(b)** ⟨kitchen⟩ integral

fitter /'fɪtər ‖'fɪtə(r)/ n **1** (Clothing) probador, -dora m,f **2** (mechanic – in garage) mecánico, -ca m,f; (– in car industry, shipbuilding) operario, -ria m,f

fitting¹ /'fɪtɪŋ/ adj ⟨conclusion⟩ adecuado; ⟨tribute⟩ digno

fitting² n **1** (Clothing) **(a)** (trying on) prueba f **(b)** (BrE) (size – of clothes) medida f; (– of shoe) horma f **2** **(a)** (accessory) accesorio m **(b)** **fittings** pl (esp BrE Const) accesorios mpl; **electrical ~s** instalaciones fpl eléctricas; **bathroom ~s** grifería f y accesorios mpl de baño

fitting room n probador m

five /faɪv/ adj/n cinco adj inv/m; see also FOUR¹

fiver /'faɪvər ‖'faɪvə(r)/ n **(a)** ($5) (AmE sl) cinco dólares mpl **(b)** (£5) (BrE colloq) cinco libras fpl

fix¹ /fɪks/ vt

I **1** ⟨plank/shelf⟩ sujetar; **to ~ a notice on a door** poner* un anuncio en una puerta; **to ~ sth in one's memory** grabar algo en la memoria **2** (direct steadily): **his eyes were ~ed on the road ahead** tenía la mirada fija en la carretera; **he ~ed her with a stony gaze** clavó en ella una mirada glacial

II **1** ⟨date/time/price⟩ fijar **2** (repair) (colloq) arreglar **3** (prepare) (esp AmE colloq) preparar **4** (colloq) ⟨election/contest⟩ amañar (fam)

■ ~ vi (make plans) (AmE): **we're ~ing to go fishing on Sunday** estamos planeando ir de pesca el domingo

■ **fix up** [v + o + adv, v + adv + o] **(a)** (provide for): **I need somewhere to stay: can you ~ me up?** necesito alojamiento ¿me lo puedes arreglar?; **she ~ed me up with a job** me encontró un trabajo **(b)** (repair) ⟨house/room⟩ (AmE) arreglar

fix² n (predicament) (colloq) aprieto m, apuro m

fixation /fɪk'seɪʃən/ n obsesión f

fixed /fɪkst/ adj **1** ⟨price/rate/ideas⟩ fijo; ⟨principles/position⟩ rígido; **a ~-term contract** un contrato a plazo fijo **2** ⟨gaze⟩ fijo; ⟨smile⟩ petrificado

fixed: **~ assets** pl n activo m fijo; **~-rate** /'fɪkst'reɪt/ adj a una tasa de interés fija or (esp Esp) a tipo de interés fijo

fixture /'fɪkstʃər ‖'fɪkstʃə(r)/ n **1** **(a)** (in building) elemento m de la instalación, como los artefactos del baño, cocina etc **(b)** (permanent feature) parte f integrante **2** (BrE Sport) encuentro m

fizz /fɪz/ vi ⟨champagne/cola⟩ burbujear

fizzle out /'fɪzəl/ [v + adv] ⟨fire/firework⟩ apagarse*; ⟨excitement⟩ esfumarse

fizzy /'fɪzi/ adj **-zier, -ziest** gaseoso, efervescente; **~ water** (colloq) agua f‡ mineral con gas

fjord /fi'ɔːrd ‖fi'ɔːd/ n fiordo m

FL, Fla = **Florida**

flabbergasted /'flæbər,gæstəd ‖'flæbə,gɑːstɪd/ adj estupefacto

flabby /'flæbi/ adj **-bier, -biest** ⟨stomach⟩ fofo; ⟨muscle⟩ flojo

flag¹ /flæg/ n bandera f

flag² **-gg-** vi ⟨person/animal⟩ desfallecer*; ⟨interest/conversation/spirits⟩ decaer*; ⟨attendance⟩ disminuir*

■ ~ vt **(a)** (mark with flags) marcar* con banderas **(b)** (mark for special attention) marcar*

■ **flag down** [v + o + adv, v + adv + o] parar ⟨haciendo señas⟩

flagpole /'flægpəʊl/ n asta f‡ de (la) bandera

flagrant /'fleɪgrənt/ adj flagrante

flag: **~ship** n (Naut) buque m insignia; (showpiece) producto m (or programa m etc) bandera; **~stone** n losa f

flair /fler ‖fleə(r)/ n **(a)** (natural aptitude) (no pl): **a ~ for languages/business** facilidad f para los idiomas/olfato m para los negocios **(b)** (stylishness) estilo m

flak /flæk/ n **(a)** (Aviat, Mil) fuego m antiaéreo **(b)** (criticism) críticas fpl

flake¹ /fleɪk/ n (of snow, cereals) copo m; (of paint, rust, skin) escama f

flake² vi ⟨paint/plaster⟩ descascararse

flaky, flakey /'fleɪki/ adj **-kier, -kiest** ⟨piecrust⟩ hojaldrado; ⟨paint/plaster⟩ que se desconcha; **~ pastry** masa tipo hojaldre

flamboyant /flæm'bɔɪənt/ adj **(a)** (dashing) ⟨style/person⟩ exuberante; ⟨gesture⟩ ampuloso **(b)** (brilliant) ⟨color⟩ vistoso; ⟨hat/dress⟩ llamativo

flame /fleɪm/ n **(a)** (llama f; **to be in ~s** estar* (envuelto) en llamas; **to go up in ~s** incendiarse **(b)** (lover): **he's an old ~ of mine** es un antiguo enamorado mío

flame: **~proof** adj ⟨fabric⟩ ininflamable; ⟨dish⟩ resistente al fuego; **~thrower** /'fleɪm'θrəʊər ‖'fleɪm,θrəʊə(r)/n lanzallamas m

flamingo /flə'mɪŋgəʊ/ n (pl **-gos** or **-goes**) flamenco m

flammable /'flæməbəl/ adj inflamable, flamable (Méx)

flan /flæn/ n (sweet) tarta f, kuchen m (Chi); (individual) tartaleta f, tarteleta f (RPl)

flank¹ /flæŋk/ n **(a)** (of animal) ijada f, ijar m; (of person) costado m **(b)** (Mil, Sport) flanco m

flank² vt (often pass) flanquear

flannel /'flænl/ n **1** **(a)** (fabric) franela f; (before n) ⟨shirt/nightgown⟩ de franela **(b)** **flannels** pl (trousers) pantalón m de franela **2** (face ∼) (BrE) toallita f (para lavarse)

flap¹ /flæp/ n **1** **(a)** (cover) tapa f; (of pocket, envelope) solapa f; (of table) hoja f; (of jacket, coat) faldón m; (of tent) portezuela f; (ear ∼) orejera f; **a cat ∼** una gatera **(b)** (Aviat) alerón m **2** (motion) aletazo m **3** (commotion, agitation) (colloq): **to be in/get into a ∼** estar*/ponerse* como loco (fam)

flap² **-pp-** vi ⟨sail/curtain⟩ agitarse; ⟨flag⟩ ondear
■ ∼ vt ⟨wings⟩ batir; ⟨arms⟩ agitar

flapjack /'flæpdʒæk/ n **1** (pancake) (esp AmE) crepe o panqueque pequeño y grueso **2** (cookie) (BrE) tipo de galleta dulce de avena

flare /fler ‖flea(r)/ n **1** **(a)** (marker light) bengala f; (on runway, road) baliza f **(b)** (sudden light) destello m; (flame) llamarada f **2** (Clothing) **(a)** (on jacket) vuelo m **(b)** **flares** (BrE) pantalones mpl acampanados
■ **flare up** [v + adv] **(a)** ⟨fire⟩ llamear; ⟨fighting⟩ estallar **(b)** ⟨infection/disease⟩ recrudecer* **(c)** (lose temper) explotar

flared /flerd ‖flead/ adj ⟨skirt⟩ con mucho vuelo, evasé (RPl); ⟨trousers⟩ acampanado

flare-up /'flerʌp ‖'fleaʌp/ n (of violence) brote m

flash¹ /flæʃ/ n **1** **(a)** (of light) destello m; (from explosion) fogonazo m; **a ∼ of inspiration** un ramalazo de inspiración; (as) **quick as a ∼** como un rayo; **in a ∼**: **it came to me in a ∼** de repente lo vi claro **(b)** (Phot) flash m **2** (news ∼) avance m informativo

flash² vt **1** (direct): **they ∼ed a light in my face** me enfocaron la cara con una luz; **to ∼ one's headlights at sb** hacerle* una señal con los faros a algn
2 (show) ⟨card⟩ mostrar*, enseñar (esp Esp); **she loves ∼ing her money around** le encanta ir por ahí haciendo ostentación de su dinero
■ ∼ vi **1** **(a)** (emit sudden light) destellar **(b)** (Auto) hacer* una señal con los faros **(c)** **flashing** pres p ⟨sign/light⟩ intermitente; ⟨eyes/smile⟩ brillante **2** (move fast) (+ adv compl): **a message ∼ed across the screen** un mensaje apareció fugazmente en la pantalla; **to ∼ by** o **past** «⟨train/car/person⟩» pasar como una bala

flash: ∼**back** n (Cin, Lit) flashback m; ∼**bulb** n (Phot) lámpara f de flash; ∼**cube** n (Phot) cubo m (de) flash; ∼**gun** n flash m electrónico; ∼**light** n (AmE) linterna f

flashy /'flæʃi/ adj **-shier, -shiest** llamativo

flask /flæsk ‖flɑːsk/ n (bottle) frasco m; (in laboratory) matraz m; (hip ∼) petaca f, nalguera f (Méx); (vacuum ∼) (BrE) termo m

flat¹ /flæt/ adj **-tt-** **1** **(a)** ⟨surface⟩ plano; ⟨countryside⟩ llano; ∼ **feet** pies mpl planos; **I was ∼ on my back for two months** estuve en cama durante dos semanas; ⟨dish⟩ llano, bajo (Chi), playo (RPl); ∼ **shoes** zapatos mpl bajos, zapatillas fpl de piso (Méx) **(c)** (deflated) ⟨ball⟩ desinflado,

ponchado (Méx); **you have a ∼ tire** o (BrE) **tyre** tienes un neumático desinflado or (Méx) una llanta ponchada
2 **(a)** ⟨lemonade/beer⟩ sin efervescencia **(b)** ⟨battery⟩ descargado
3 (dull, uninteresting) ⟨conversation/party⟩ soso (fam); ⟨joke⟩ sin gracia; ⟨voice⟩ monótono; **to fall ∼** «⟨play/project⟩» fracasar*; **the joke fell very ∼** el chiste no hizo ni pizca de gracia
4 (total, firm) ⟨denial/refusal⟩ rotundo
5 (Mus) (referring to key) bemol; **A ∼** la m bemol
6 (fixed) (before n) ⟨rate⟩ fijo

flat² adv **1** **(a)** ⟨refuse/turn down⟩ de plano **(b)** (exactly): **it took him two hours ∼** tardó dos horas justas **2** (Mus) demasiado bajo

flat³ n **1** (apartment) (BrE) apartamento m, departamento m (AmL), piso m (Esp) **2** **(a)** (surface — of sword) cara f de la hoja; (— of hand) palma f **(b)** (level ground) llano m **3** (Mus) bemol m

flatly /'flætli/ adv de plano

flatmate /'flætmeɪt/ n (BrE) compañero, -ra m,f de apartamento or (Esp) de piso

flat out¹ adj (colloq) (pred) (prostrate) tirado

flat out² adv (at full speed) (colloq) a toda máquina

flat-rate /'flætreɪt/ adj (BrE) a una tasa de interés fija or (esp Esp) a un tipo de interés fijo

flatten /'flætn/ vt ⟨surface⟩ aplanar; ⟨path/lawn⟩ allanar; ⟨city⟩ arrasar

flatter /'flætər ‖'flætə(r)/ vt **(a)** (gratify) halagar* **(b)** (show to advantage) favorecer*

flattering /'flætərɪŋ/ adj **(a)** ⟨words/speech⟩ halagador **(b)** ⟨clothes/hairstyle⟩ favorecedor

flattery /'flætəri/ n halagos mpl

flaunt /flɔːnt/ vt ⟨possessions⟩ hacer* ostentación de; ⟨knowledge⟩ alardear de

flavor¹, (BrE) **flavour** /'fleɪvər ‖'fleɪvə(r)/ n sabor m, gusto m

flavor², (BrE) **flavour** vt sazonar; **chocolate-∼ed** con sabor or gusto a chocolate

flavoring, (BrE) **flavouring** /'fleɪvərɪŋ/ n condimento m

flaw /flɔː/ n (in material, character) defecto m; (in argument) error m

flawless /'flɔːləs ‖'flɔːlɪs/ adj ⟨performance/logic⟩ impecable; ⟨conduct⟩ intachable; ⟨complexion/gem⟩ perfecto

flax /flæks/ n lino m

flay /fleɪ/ vt desollar*

flea /fliː/ n pulga f; (before n) ⟨collar/powder⟩ antipulgas adj inv

flea market n mercado m de las pulgas or (CS) de pulgas, rastro m (Esp)

fleck¹ /flek/ n (of dust) mota f; (of paint, mud) salpicadura f

fleck² vt (with mud) salpicar*; **beige ∼ed with brown** beige moteado de marrón

fled /fled/ past & past p of FLEE

fledgling, fledgeling /'fledʒlɪŋ/ n polluelo m; (before n) **a ∼ democracy** una democracia en ciernes

flee /fliː/ (past & past p **fled**) vi huir*
■ ∼ vt huir* de

fleece¹ /fliːs/ n (on sheep) lana f; (from sheep) vellón m

fleece² *vt* (colloq) desplumar (fam)

fleet /fliːt/ *n* **(a)** (naval unit, body of shipping) flota *f* **(b)** (navy) armada *f* **(c)** (of cars) parque *m* móvil, flota *f*

fleeting /'fliːtɪŋ/ *adj* (*usu before n*) fugaz

Flemish¹ /'flemɪʃ/ *adj* flamenco

Flemish² *n* flamenco *m*

flesh /fleʃ/ *n* carne *f*; **in the ~** en persona; **~ and blood**: **after all, I'm only ~ and blood** después de todo, soy de carne y hueso

fleshy /'fleʃi/ *adj* **-shier, -shiest** *adj* ⟨*arms/ person*⟩ rollizo; ⟨*plant/leaf*⟩ carnoso

flew /fluː/ *past of* FLY²

flex¹ /fleks/ *vt* ⟨*arm/knees/body*⟩ doblar; **to ~ one's muscles** (to warm up) hacer* ejercicios de calentamiento; (in body building) mostrar* los músculos; «*regime*» mostrar* su poderío

flex² *n* (BrE) cable *m* (eléctrico)

flexible /'fleksəbəl/ *adj* flexible

flextime /'flekstaɪm/, (BrE) **flexitime** /'fleksɪtaɪm/ *n* horario *m* flexible

flick¹ /flɪk/ *vt* **(a)** (strike lightly): **she ~ed a piece of bread at me** me tiró un pedazo de pan **(b)** (remove): **he ~ed the ash off his lapel** se sacudió la ceniza de la solapa
■ **flick through** [*v* + *prep* + *o*] ⟨*book*⟩ hojear; ⟨*pages*⟩ pasar

flick² *n* (of tail) coletazo *m*; (of wrist) giro *m*

flicker¹ /'flɪkər ‖ 'flɪkə(r)/ *vi* parpadear

flicker² *n* parpadeo *m*

flier /'flaɪər ‖ 'flaɪə(r)/ *n* **1** **(a)** (pilot) aviador, -dora *m,f* **(b)** (passenger) usuario -ria *m,f* (regular) del avion **2** (handbill) (AmE) folleto *m* (publicitario); volante *m* (AmL)

flight /flaɪt/ *n* **1** **(a)** (of bird, aircraft) vuelo *m*; (of ball, projectile) trayectoria *f*; **in ~** en vuelo **(b)** (air journey) vuelo *m*; (before *n*) **~ path** ruta *f*; **~ recorder** caja *f* negra **2** (group of birds) bandada *f* **3** (of stairs) tramo *m* **4** (act of fleeing) huida *f*; **to take ~** darse* a la fuga

flight: **~ attendant** *n* auxiliar *mf* de vuelo; **~ deck** *n* (on plane) cabina *f* de mando; (on aircraft carrier) cubierta *f* de vuelo

flimsy /'flɪmzi/ *adj* **-sier, -siest (a)** ⟨*material/ garment*⟩ ligerísimo **(b)** ⟨*construction/object*⟩ endeble **(c)** ⟨*excuse*⟩ pobre; ⟨*argument/evidence*⟩ poco sólido

flinch /flɪntʃ/ *vi* estremecerse*

fling¹ /flɪŋ/ *vt* (*past & past p* **flung**) lanzar*, aventar* (Col, Méx, Per)

fling² *n* (colloq) **(a)** (love affair) aventura *f*; **to have a ~** tener* una aventurilla **(b)** (wild time) juerga *f* (fam); **to have a ~** irse* de juerga

flint /flɪnt/ *n* **(a)** (Geol) sílex *m*, pedernal *m*; (piece of stone) pedernal *m* **(b)** (for cigarette lighter) piedra *f*

flip /flɪp/ *vt* **-pp-** *vt* tirar, aventar* (Méx); **we'll ~ a coin to decide** vamos a echarlo a cara o cruz *or* (Andes, Ven) a cara o sello *or* (Arg) a cara o ceca, vamos a echar un volado (Méx)
■ **~** *vi* (sl) (lose self-control) perder* la chaveta (fam)

flip-flop /'flɪpflɑːp ‖ 'flɪpflɒp/ *n* (BrE) ▶ THONG B

flippant /'flɪpənt/ *adj* ⟨*remark*⟩ frívolo; ⟨*attitude*⟩ displicente

flipper /'flɪpər ‖ 'flɪpə(r)/ *n* aleta *f*

flip side *n* **the ~ ~** (Audio) la cara B; (of a situation) (colloq) la otra cara de la moneda (fam)

flirt¹ /flɜːrt ‖ flɜːt/ *vi* flirtear

flirt² *n*: **he is a terrible ~** le encanta flirtear

flirtation /flɜːr'teɪʃən ‖ ˌflɜː'teɪʃən/ *n* **(a)** (relationship) flirt *m* **(b)** (coquetry) flirteo *m*

flit /flɪt/ *vi* **-tt-** «*bird/butterfly/bat*» revolotear

float¹ /fləʊt/ *vi* **(a)** (on water) flotar; **to ~ (up) to the surface** salir* a flote **(b)** «*cloud/smoke*» flotar en el aire
■ **~** *vt* **1** ⟨*ship/boat*⟩ poner* a flote; ⟨*raft/logs*⟩ llevar **2** (Fin) **(a)** (establish): **to ~ a company** introducir* una compañía en Bolsa **(b)** ⟨*shares/ stock*⟩ emitir **(c)** ⟨*currency*⟩ dejar flotar **3** (circulate) ⟨*idea*⟩ presentar

float² *n* **1** **(a)** (for fishing, for buoyancy) flotador *m* **(b)** (in cistern, carburetor) flotador *m* **(c)** (raft, platform) plataforma *f* (flotante) **2** **(a)** (in parade) carroza *f*, carro *m* alegórico (CS, Méx) **(b)** (milk **~**) (BrE) furgoneta *f* (*del reparto de leche*) **3** (ready cash) caja *f* chica; (Busn, Fin) fondo *m* fijo

floating /'fləʊtɪŋ/ *adj* (before *n*) **1** ⟨*harbor/ restaurant*⟩ flotante **2** (Fin) ⟨*currency*⟩ flotante; ⟨*assets*⟩ circulante **3** ⟨*population*⟩ flotante; ⟨*voter*⟩ (BrE) indeciso

flock¹ /flɑːk ‖ flɒk/ *n* (+ *sing* or *pl vb*) (of sheep) rebaño *m*; (of birds) bandada *f*; (of people) (*often pl*) tropel *m*, multitud *f*

flock² *vi* acudir (en gran número, en masa)

floe /fləʊ/ *n* témpano *m* de hielo

flog /flɑːg ‖ flɒg/ *vt* **-gg-** **1** (beat) azotar **2** (sell) (BrE sl) vender

flood¹ /flʌd/ *n* (of water) inundación *f*; (of complaints, calls) avalancha *f*; **she was in ~s of tears** estaba hecha un mar de lágrimas

flood² *vt* inundar; ⟨*engine*⟩ ahogar*; **to ~ the market with imports** (Busn) inundar el mercado de productos importados
■ **~** *vi* «*river/sewers*» desbordarse; «*mine/ basement*» inundarse; (Auto) ahogarse*; **to ~ in** «*sunshine*» entrar a raudales; **donations came ~ing in** llovieron los donativos

flooding /'flʌdɪŋ/ *n* inundación *f*

floodlight¹ /'flʌdlaɪt/ *n* reflector *m*, foco *m*

floodlight² *vt* (*past & past p* **floodlit** /'flʌd-lɪt/) **(a)** iluminar (*con reflectores o focos*) **(b)** **floodlit** *past p* ⟨*arena/building*⟩ iluminado; ⟨*game*⟩ que se juega con luz artificial

flood: **~ tide** *n* pleamar *f*; **~water** *n* (*often pl*) crecida *f*

floor¹ /flɔːr ‖ flɔː(r)/ *n* **1** **(a)** (of room, vehicle) suelo *m*, piso *m* (AmL) **(b)** (for dancing) pista *f* (de baile) **(c)** (of ocean, valley, forest) fondo *m* **2** (storey) piso *m*; **we live on the first/second ~** (AmE) vivimos en la planta baja/el primer piso *or* (Chi) en el primer/segundo piso; (BrE) vivimos en el primer/segundo piso *or* (Chi) en el segundo/tercer piso

floor² *vt* **(a)** (knock down) derribar **(b)** (nonplus) (colloq) dejar helado (fam)

floorboard /'flɔːrbɔːrd ‖ 'flɔːbɔːd/ *n* tabla *f* del suelo, duela *f* (Méx)

flooring /'flɔːrɪŋ/ *n* revestimiento *m* para suelos

floor show *n* espectáculo *m* (*de cabaret*)

flop¹ /flɑːp ‖ flɒp/ *vi* **-pp-** **1** (fall, move slackly) (+ ⋯⋗

adv compl): she ~ped down into a chair se dejó caer en un sillón; he ~ped down exhausted onto the bed se desplomó en la cama muerto de cansancio **2** (fail) (colloq) fracasar estrepitosamente

flop² *n* (colloq) fracaso *m*

floppy¹ /'flɑːpi ‖'flɒpi/ *adj* ‹hat/bag› flexible; ‹ears/tail› caído

floppy² *n* (*pl* -**pies**) (colloq) ▶ FLOPPY DISK

floppy disk *n* disquete *m*, floppy (disk) *m*

floral /'flɔːrəl/ *adj* ‹fabric/dress› floreado; **a ~ print** un estampado de flores

florid /'flɔːrəd ‖'flɒrɪd/ *adj* **(a)** (red) ‹complexion› rubicundo **(b)** (ornate) ‹decoration/style› recargado; ‹language› florido

florist /'flɔːrəst ‖'flɒrɪst/ *n* (person) florista *mf*; **is there a ~'s near here?** ¿hay una floristería *or* (AmL tb) florería cerca de aquí?

flotation /fləʊ'teɪʃən/ *n* (of company) salida *f* a Bolsa; (of shares) emisión *f*

flotsam /'flɑːtsəm ‖'flɒtsəm/ *n* restos *mpl* flotantes ‹de un naufragio›; **~ and jetsam** desechos *mpl*

flounce¹ /flaʊns/ *vi* (+ *adv compl*): **to ~ in/out** entrar/salir* airada (*or* airado *etc*)

flounce² *n* (ruffle) volante *m*, elán *m* (Méx), volado *m* (RPl), vuelo *m* (Chi)

flounder /'flaʊndər ‖'flaʊndə(r)/ *vi* **(a)** (in water) luchar para mantenerse a flote **(b)** «*speaker*» quedarse sin saber qué decir

flour /flaʊər ‖'flaʊə(r)/ *n* harina *f*

flourish¹ /'flɜːrɪʃ ‖'flʌrɪʃ/ *vi* «*arts/trade*» florecer*; «*business*» prosperar; «*plant*» darse* *or* crecer* bien
■ ~ *vt* ‹stick/letter› blandir

flourish² *n* **(a)** (showy gesture) floreo *m* **(b)** (embellishment) floritura *f*, firulete *m* (AmL); (in signature) rúbrica *f*

flourishing /'flɜːrɪʃɪŋ ‖'flʌrɪʃɪŋ/ *adj* ‹business› próspero

flout /flaʊt/ *vt* desobedecer* abiertamente

flow¹ /fləʊ/ *vi* **(a)** «*liquid/electric current*» fluir*; «*tide*» subir; «*blood*» correr; (from wound) manar **(b)** (run smoothly, continuously) «*traffic*» circular con fluidez; «*music/words*» fluir*

flow² *n* **1** **(a)** (of liquid, current) flujo *m* **(b)** (of traffic, information) circulación *f*; (of capital, money) movimiento *m* **2** (stream — of water, lava) corriente *f*

flow chart, flow diagram *n* organigrama *m*

flower¹ /flaʊər ‖'flaʊə(r)/ *n* flor *f*

flower² *vi* florecer*, florear (Chi, Méx)

flower: ~bed *n* arriate *m* (Esp, Méx), parterre *m* (Esp), cantero *m* (Cu, RPl), tiesto *m* (Esp); **~pot** *n* maceta *f*, tiesto *m* (Esp), macetero *m* (AmS)

flowery /'flaʊri ‖'flaʊəri/ *adj* ‹pattern› floreado; ‹meadow› florido; ‹style/prose› florido

flowing /'fləʊɪŋ/ *adj* **(a)** ‹beard/robe› largo y suelto **(b)** ‹handwriting/movement› fluido

flown /fləʊn/ *past p of* FLY²

flu /fluː/ *n* gripe *f*, gripa *f* (Col, Méx)

fluctuate /'flʌktʃʊeɪt ‖'flʌktjʊeɪt/ *vi* fluctuar*

fluctuation /ˌflʌktʃʊ'eɪʃən ‖ˌflʌktjʊ'eɪʃən/ *n* fluctuación *f*

flue /fluː/ *n* tiro *m*

fluency /'fluːənsi/ *n* fluidez *f*

fluent /'fluːənt/ *adj*: **to speak ~ Italian** hablar italiano con fluidez

fluently /'fluːəntli/ *adv* con fluidez

fluff /flʌf/ *n* pelusa *f*

fluffy /'flʌfi/ *adj* -**fier**, -**fiest** ‹fabric/garment› suave y esponjoso; ‹fur/hair› suave y sedoso

fluid¹ /'fluːəd ‖'fluːɪd/ *n* fluido *m*

fluid² *adj* fluido

fluke /fluːk/ *n* (colloq) chiripa *f* (fam)

flummox /'flʌməks/ *vt* (colloq) desconcertar*

flung /flʌŋ/ *past & past p of* FLING¹

fluorescent /flʊ'resənt ‖fluə'resənt, flɔː-/ *adj* fluorescente; **~ light** tubo *m* fluorescente, tubolux® *m* (RPl)

fluoride /'flʊəraɪd ‖'flɔːraɪd/ *n* (Chem) fluoruro *m*; (Dent) flúor *m*; (before *n*) **~ toothpaste** dentífrico *m* con flúor

flurry /'flɜːri ‖'flʌri/ *n* (*pl* -**ries**) **1** (of snow, wind) ráfaga *f*, (of rain) chaparrón *m* **2** (sudden burst): **a ~ of excitement/activity** una oleada de emoción/un frenesí de actividad

flush¹ /flʌʃ/ *n* **1** **(a)** (blush) rubor *m* **(b)** (of anger, passion) arrebato *m*; **in the first ~ of success** con la euforia del triunfo **2** (in cards) flor *f*

flush² *vt* **1** ‹toilet›: **to ~ the toilet** tirar de la cadena, jalarle (a la cadena) (AmL exc CS) **2** (drive out) ~ (out) ‹person/criminal› hacer* salir
■ ~ *vi* **1** «*toilet*» funcionar **2** (blush) «*person/face*» (with anger) enrojecer*; (with embarrassment) ruborizarse*

flush³ *adj* alineado

flushed /flʌʃt/ *adj* ‹cheeks› colorado; **~ with success** exaltado por el éxito

fluster /'flʌstər ‖'flʌstə(r)/ *vt* poner* nervioso; **to get ~ed** ponerse* nervioso

flute /fluːt/ *n* flauta *f*

flutter¹ /'flʌtər ‖'flʌtə(r)/ *vi* «*bird/butterfly*» revolotear; «*flag*» ondear, agitarse; «*heart*» latir con fuerza
■ ~ *vt* ‹wings› batir, sacudir

flutter² *n* ~ (of wings) (no *pl*) aleteo *m*

flux /flʌks/ *n*: **to be in (a state of) ~** estar* en un estado de cambio

fly¹ /flaɪ/ *n* (*pl* **flies**) **1** (insect) mosca *f* **2** (on trousers) (often *pl in BrE*) bragueta *f*, marrueco *m* (Chi)

fly² (*3rd pers sing pres* **flies**; *pres p* **flying**; *past* **flew**; *past p* **flown**) *vi* **1** volar*; «*passenger*» ir* en avión; **to ~ away** irse* volando; **to ~ in/out** «*bird/bee*» entrar/salir* volando; «*plane/pilot*» llegar*/salir* (*en avión*) **(b)** «*flag*» ondear **2** **(a)** (rush) «*person*» correr, ir* (*or* salir* *etc*) volando; **to ~ AT sb** lanzarse* SOBRE algn; **to ~ into a rage** ponerse* hecho una furia **(b)** (move, be thrown) volar*; **I tripped and went ~ing** tropecé y salí volando **(c)** (pass quickly) «*time*» pasar volando

■ **~** *vt* **1 (a)** (control) ⟨*plane/glider/balloon*⟩ pilotar; ⟨*kite*⟩ hacer* volar *or* encumbrar (Andes), remontar (RPl) **(b)** (carry) ⟨*cargo*⟩ transportar (*en avión*); ⟨*person*⟩ llevar (*en avión*) **(c)** (travel over) ⟨*distance*⟩ recorrer (*en avión*) **2** ⟨*flag*⟩ izar*, enarbolar

flyer /'flaɪər ‖'flaɪə(r)/ *n* ▶ FLIER

flying¹ /'flaɪɪŋ/ *adj* (*before n*) **(a)** (hurried): **a ~ visit** una visita relámpago **(b)** ⟨*glass/debris*⟩ que vuela (por los aires)

flying² *n* **(a)** (as pilot) pilotaje *m*; (*before n*) ⟨*time/lesson*⟩ de vuelo; ⟨*helmet/jacket*⟩ de piloto **(b)** (as passenger): **I hate ~** odio viajar en avión

flying: ~ saucer *n* platillo *m* volador *or* (Esp) volante; **~ start** *n* salida *f* lanzada; **to get off to a ~ start** «*person/business*» empezar* con muy buen pie

fly: ~leaf *n* guarda *f*; **~-on-the-wall** *adj* ⟨*documentary*⟩ en el que las cámaras son meras espectadoras de la acción; **~over** *n* (BrE Transp) paso *m* elevado, paso *m* a desnivel (Méx); **~ spray** *n* insecticida *m* (*en aerosol*); **~swatter** /'flaɪˌswɑːtər ‖'flaɪˌswɒtə(r)/ *n* matamoscas *m*; **~wheel** *n* volante *m*

FM *n* (= **frequency modulation**) FM *f*

foal /fəʊl/ *n* (male) potro *m*, potrillo *m*; (female) potranca *f*, potra *f*

foam¹ /fəʊm/ *n* espuma *f*

foam² *vi* «*sea/waves*» hacer* espuma; **to ~ at the mouth** echar espuma por la boca

foam rubber *n* goma espuma *f*, hule *m* espuma (Méx)

fob /fɑːb ‖fɒb/ *n* (watchchain) leontina *f*; (*before n*) **~ watch** reloj *m* de bolsillo
■ **fob off: -bb-** [*v + o + adv*] (placate) **to ~ sb off** (WITH sth) engatusar a algn (CON algo)

focal /'fəʊkəl/ *adj* (*before n*) **(a)** (Opt) focal **(b)** ⟨*issue*⟩ central

focal point *n* **(a)** (Opt) foco *m* **(b)** (of attention, activity) centro *m*

focus¹ /'fəʊkəs/ *n* (*pl* **-cuses** *or* **foci** /'fəʊsaɪ/) **1** (Opt, Phot) foco *m*; **to be in/out of ~** estar* enfocado/desenfocado **2** (central point) centro *m*

focus² **-s-** *or* **-ss-** *vt* **(a)** (Opt, Phot) enfocar* **(b)** (concentrate) **to ~ sth** (ON sth) ⟨*attention*⟩ centrar algo (EN algo)
■ **~** *vi* **(a)** «*camera/eyes*» enfocar* **(b)** «*lecturer/ chapter/attention*» **to ~ ON sth/sb** centrarse EN algo/algn

focus group *n* grupo *m* analizado

fodder /'fɑːdər ‖'fɒdə(r)/ *n* forraje *m*

foe /fəʊ/ *n* (liter) enemigo, -ga *m,f*

foetus /'fiːtəs/ *n* (BrE) ▶ FETUS

fog /fɔːg ‖fɒg/ *n* (Meteo) niebla *f*

fogbound /'fɔːgbaʊnd ‖'fɒgbaʊnd/ *adj* ⟨*airport/road*⟩ afectado por la niebla; ⟨*plane/ ferry*⟩ retenido a causa de la niebla

foggy /'fɔːgi ‖'fɒgi/ *adj* **-gier, -giest (a)** ⟨*day*⟩ de niebla; ⟨*weather*⟩ nebuloso; **it's ~** hay niebla **(b)** (confused) confuso

fog: ~horn *n* sirena *f* (*de niebla*); **~ light, ~ lamp** *n* faro *m* antiniebla

foible /'fɔɪbəl/ *n* debilidad *f*

foil¹ /fɔɪl/ *n* **(a)** (metal sheet) lámina *f* de metal **(b)** (Culin) (kitchen **~**) papel *m* de aluminio *or* de plata

foil² *vt* ⟨*plan/attempt*⟩ frustrar

foist /fɔɪst/ *vt* **to ~ sth** (OFF) ON *o* ONTO **sb** endilgarle* algo a algn

fold¹ /fəʊld/ *vt* **1 (a)** (bend, bring together) ⟨*paper/ sheet*⟩ doblar; **to ~ one's arms** cruzar* los brazos **2** (Culin) **to ~ sth** INTO sth incorporar algo A algo
■ **~** *vi* **1 (a)** «*chair/table*» plegarse*; «*map/ poster*» doblarse **(b) folding** *pres p* ⟨*chair/table*⟩ plegable **2** (fail) «*project*» venirse* abajo; «*play*» bajar de cartel; «*business*» cerrar* (sus puertas)
■ **fold up** [*v + o + adv*, *v + adv + o*] ⟨*sheet/ newspaper*⟩ doblar; ⟨*chair/table*⟩ plegar*

fold² *n* **1** (crease) doblez *m* **2** (sheep pen) redil *m*

-fold /fəʊld/ *suff*: **his income increased five~** sus ingresos se multiplicaron por cinco *or* se quintuplicaron; **the problem is three~** el problema tiene tres aspectos

folder /'fəʊldər ‖'fəʊldə(r)/ *n* **(a)** (for papers) carpeta *f* **(b)** (Comput) carpeta *f*

foliage /'fəʊliɪdʒ/ *n* follaje *m*

folio /'fəʊliəʊ/ *n* (*pl* **folios**) (sheet) pliego *m*; (numbered leaf) folio *m*

folk /fəʊk/ *n* **1 (a)** *also* **folks** *pl* (people) (colloq) gente *f* **(b) folks** *pl* (esp AmE colloq) (relatives) familia *f*; (parents) padres *mpl*, viejos *mpl* (fam) **2** (+ *pl vb*) (Anthrop) pueblo *m*; (*before n*) ⟨*art/ medicine*⟩ popular; ⟨*dancing*⟩ folklórico

folk: ~lore *n* folklore *m*; **~ music** *n* (traditional) música *f* folklórica; (modern) música *f* folk; **~ song** *n* (traditional) canción *f* popular; (modern) canción *f* folk

follow /'fɑːləʊ ‖'fɒləʊ/ *vt* **1** (go, come after) seguir*; **the lecture was ~ed by a discussion** después de la conferencia hubo un debate **2** (keep to, conform to) ⟨*road*⟩ seguir* (por); ⟨*trail*⟩ seguir*; ⟨*instructions*⟩ seguir*; ⟨*order*⟩ cumplir; ⟨*fashion/example*⟩ seguir* **3** (pay close attention to) ⟨*movement/progress*⟩ seguir* de cerca; ⟨*news*⟩ mantenerse* al tanto de; ⟨*TV serial*⟩ seguir* **4** ⟨*argument/reasoning*⟩ entender*
■ **~** *vi* **1** (come after): **you go first, and I'll ~** tú ve delante que yo te sigo; **the winners were as ~s ...** los ganadores fueron ... **2** (be logical consequence) deducirse*; **that doesn't necessarily ~** una cosa no implica la otra **3** (understand) entender*
■ **follow up** [*v + o + adv*, *v + adv + o*] seguir*

follower /'fɑːləʊər ‖'fɒləʊə(r)/ *n* seguidor, -dora *m,f*

following¹ /'fɑːləʊɪŋ ‖'fɒləʊɪŋ/ *adj* (*before n*) (next) siguiente; **(on) the ~ day** al día siguiente

following² *n* **1** (followers) seguidores *mpl*; (admirers) admiradores *mpl* **2** (what, who comes next) **the ~: the ~ are to play in tomorrow's game** ... los siguientes jugarán en el partido de mañana ...; **the letter said the ~ ...** la carta decía lo siguiente ...

follow-up /'fɑːləʊʌp ‖'fɒləʊʌp/ n (sequel) continuación f; (before n): **she sent a ~ letter** mandó una segunda (or tercera etc) carta

folly /'fɑːli ‖'fɒli/ n (pl **-lies**) locura f

fond /fɑːnd ‖fɒnd/ adj **-er, -est** [1] (pred): **she's very ~ of Sue** le tiene mucho cariño a Sue; **he was ~ of chocolate** le gustaba el chocolate [2] (before n) (loving) ‹gesture/look› cariñoso

fondle /'fɑːndl ‖'fɒndl/ vt acariciar

fondly /'fɑːndli ‖'fɒndli/ adv **(a)** (lovingly) cariñosamente; ‹remember› con cariño **(b)** (foolishly) ingenuamente

fondness /'fɑːndnəs ‖'fɒndnɪs/ n (love) cariño m; (liking) afición f

font /fɑːnt ‖fɒnt/ n [1] (baptismal) pila f bautismal [2] **(a)** (Print) fuente f **(b)** (Comput) font m, fuente f, juego m de caracteres

food /fuːd/ n **(a)** (in general) comida f; (before n) ‹shortage/exports› de alimentos **(b)** (specific kind) alimento m

food: ~ **poisoning** n intoxicación f (por alimentos); ~ **processor** /'prɑːsesər, 'prəʊ- ‖'prəʊsesə(r)/ n robot m de cocina; ~**stuffs** pl n productos mpl alimenticios

fool[1] /fuːl/ n idiota mf; **to make a ~ of oneself** hacer* el ridículo

fool[2] vt engañar
■ **fool around,** (BrE also) **fool about** [v + adv] hacer* payasadas, hacer* el tonto (Esp)

foolhardy /'fuːlhɑːrdi ‖'fuːlhɑːdi/ adj imprudente

foolish /'fuːlɪʃ/ adj ‹person/prank› tonto; ‹look/ grin› de tonto; ‹decision/plan› insensato

fool: ~**proof** adj ‹idea/plan› infalible; ‹machine› sencillo de manejar; ~**scap** /'fuːlskæp/ n pliego de aprox 33 x 22 cm

foot[1] /fʊt/ n (pl **feet**) [1] (of person) pie m; (of animal) pata f; (on sewing machine) pie m; **to be on one's feet** estar* de pie, estar* parado (AmL); **to go/come on ~** ir*/venir* a pie; **to find one's feet**: **it didn't take him long to find his feet in his new school** no tardó en habituarse a la nueva escuela; **to put one's ~ down** (be firm) imponerse*; (accelerate vehicle) (colloq) apretar* el acelerador, meterle (AmL fam); **to put one's ~ in it** (colloq) meter la pata (fam); **under sb's feet**: **the cat keeps getting under my feet** el gato siempre me anda alrededor [2] (lower end) (no pl) pie m; **the ~ of the bed** los pies de la cama [3] (measure) (pl **foot** or **feet**) pie m

foot[2] vt: **to ~ the bill** pagar*

footage /'fʊtɪdʒ/ n (Cin) secuencias fpl (filmadas)

foot-and-mouth (**disease**) /'fʊtņ'maʊθ/ n fiebre f aftosa, glosopeda f

football /'fʊtbɔːl/ n [1] **(a)** (American ~) fútbol m or (AmC, Méx) futbol m americano **(b)** (soccer) fútbol m or (AmC, Méx) futbol m; (before n) ~ **match** partido m de fútbol or (AmC, Méx) futbol; ~ **player** ▶ FOOTBALLER [2] (ball) balón m or (esp AmL) pelota f de fútbol or (AmC, Méx) futbol

footballer /'fʊtbɔːlər ‖'fʊtbɔːlə(r)/ n (BrE) futbolista mf, jugador, -dora m,f de fútbol or (AmC, Méx) futbol

football: ~ **pool** n (AmE) apuesta f colectiva, polla f (AmL); ~ **pools** pl n (BrE) **the ~ pools**

juego de apuestas en que se trata de acertar los resultados de los partidos de la liga de fútbol, ≈el pronóstico deportivo (en Méx), ≈las quinielas (en Esp), ≈el prode (en Arg), ≈el totogol (en Col), ≈la polla-gol (en Chi), ≈la polla (en Per)

-footed /'fʊtəd ‖'fʊtɪd/ suff: **four~** de cuatro patas; **light~** ligero de pies

foot: ~**hills** pl n estribaciones fpl; ~**hold** n punto m de apoyo (para el pie); **to gain a ~hold** «ideology» prender*

footing /'fʊtɪŋ/ n (no pl) [1] (balance) equilibrio m; **to miss one's ~** resbalar [2] (basis): **on an equal ~** en igualdad de condiciones

foot: ~**lights** pl n candilejas fpl; ~**loose** adj libre y sin compromiso; ~**loose and fancy-free** libre como el viento; ~**man** /'fʊtmən/ n (pl **-men** /-mən/) lacayo m; ~**note** n nota f a pie de página; ~**path** n (path) sendero m; (pavement) (BrE) acera f, banqueta f (Méx), vereda f (CS, Per); ~**print** n huella f; ~**step** n paso m; ~**wear** n calzado m

for[1] /fɔːr ‖fɔː(r), weak form fər ‖fə(r)/ prep

I [1] (intended for) para; **is there a letter ~ me?** ¿hay carta para mí?; **my love ~ her** mi amor por ella

[2] **(a)** (on behalf of, representing): **I did it ~ you** lo hice por ti; **he plays ~ England** forma parte de or juega en la selección inglesa; **D ~ David** D de David **(b)** (as): **we're having chicken ~ dinner** vamos a cenar pollo; **I can see him now ~ what he is** ahora me doy cuenta de cómo es en realidad **(c)** (in favor of) a favor de

[3] (indicating purpose): **what's that ~?** ¿para qué es eso?; **it's ~ decoration** es de adorno; **it's ~ your own good!** ¡es por tu (propio) bien!

[4] (giving reason) por; ~ **that reason** por esa razón; **if it weren't ~ Joe ...** si no fuera por Joe ...

[5] (in exchange for) por; **I bought the book ~ $10** compré el libro por 10 dólares; **she left him ~ somebody else** lo dejó por otro

[6] (as concerns) para; **it's too cold ~ me here** aquí hace demasiado frío para mí

[7] **(a)** (in spite of): ~ **all her faults, she's been very kind to us** tendrá sus defectos, pero con nosotros ha sido muy buena **(b)** (with infinitive clause): **it's unusual ~ me to forget a name** es raro que se me olvide un nombre; **it's not ~ me to decide** no me corresponde a mí decidir

II [1] (in the direction of) para; **the plane ~ New York** el avión para or de Nueva York

[2] **(a)** (indicating duration): **he spoke ~ half an hour** habló (durante) media hora; **I've only been here ~ a day** solo llevo un día aquí; **how long are you going ~?** ¿por cuánto tiempo vas? **(b)** (on the occasion of) para; **he gave it to me ~ my birthday** me lo regaló para mi cumpleaños **(c)** (by, before) para; **we have to be there ~ six o'clock** tenemos que estar allí a las seis

[3] (indicating distance): **we drove ~ 20 miles** hicimos 20 millas; **we could see ~ miles** se podía ver hasta muy lejos

for[2] conj (liter) pues (liter), puesto que (fml)

forage /'fɔːrɪdʒ ‖'fɒrɪdʒ/ vi **(a)** «animal» forrajear **(b)** (for supplies) **to ~ FOR sth** buscar* algo

foray /'fɔːreɪ ‖'fɒreɪ/ n (Mil) incursión f

forbid /fər'bɪd ‖fə'bɪd/ vt (past **forbad(e)** /fər'bæd, -'beɪd ‖fə'bæd, -'beɪd/; past p

forbidden /fərˈbɪdn̩ ‖fəˈbɪdn̩/) (not allow) prohibir*; **to ~ sb to + INF** prohibirle* A algn + INF, prohibirle* A algn QUE (+ subj)

force¹ /fɔːrs ‖fɔːs/ n fuerza f; **the** (armed) ~**s** las fuerzas armadas; **a ~ eight gale** vientos de fuerza ocho; **to join ~s with sb** unirse a algn; **to come into ~** entrar en vigor or vigencia; **to be in ~** estar* en vigor or vigencia

force² vt ⓵ (compel) **to ~ sb to + INF** obligar* a algn A + INF ⓶ (push, drive) ⟨door/link⟩ forzar*; **they ~d their way in** entraron por la fuerza
■ **force down** [v + o + adv, v + adv + o] **(a)** ⟨aircraft/pilot⟩ obligar* a aterrizar **(b)** ⟨food⟩ tragar* (a duras penas)

forced /fɔːrst ‖fɔːst/ adj (before n) ⟨labor/smile⟩ forzado; ⟨landing/stopover⟩ forzoso

force-feed /ˈfɔːrsˈfiːd ‖ˈfɔːsfiːd/ vt ⟨past & past p **-fed**⟩ alimentar por la fuerza

forceful /ˈfɔːrsfəl ‖ˈfɔːsfəl/ adj **(a)** (vigorous) ⟨person⟩ con carácter; ⟨personality⟩ fuerte **(b)** (persuasive) ⟨words/argument⟩ convincente

forceps /ˈfɔːrsəps ‖ˈfɔːseps/ pl n fórceps m

forcible /ˈfɔːrsəbəl ‖ˈfɔːsəbəl/ adj forzoso

ford /fɔːrd ‖fɔːd/ n vado m

fore /fɔːr ‖fɔː(r)/ n: **to come to the ~** «issue» saltar a primera plana

forearm /ˈfɔːrɑːrm ‖ˈfɔːrɑːm/ n antebrazo m

foreboding /fɔːrˈbəʊdɪŋ ‖fɔːˈbəʊdɪŋ/ n **(a)** (apprehension) aprensión f **(b)** (presentiment) premonición f

forecast¹ /ˈfɔːrkæst ‖ˈfɔːkɑːst/ n (weather ~) pronóstico m del tiempo; (prediction) previsión f

forecast² vt ⟨past & past p **forecast** or **forecasted**⟩ ⟨weather⟩ pronosticar*; ⟨result/trend⟩ prever*

forecourt /ˈfɔːrkɔːrt ‖ˈfɔːkɔːt/ n patio m delantero

forefathers /ˈfɔːrˌfɑːðərz ‖ˈfɔːfɑːðəz/ pl n (liter) antepasados mpl

forefinger /ˈfɔːrˌfɪŋɡər ‖ˈfɔːfɪŋɡə(r)/ n índice m

forefront /ˈfɔːrfrʌnt ‖ˈfɔːfrʌnt/ n: **in** o **at the ~ of sth** al frente de algo; (in the vanguard) a la vanguardia de algo

forego /fɔːrˈɡəʊ ‖fɔːˈɡəʊ/ vt ⟨3rd pers sing pres **-goes**; pres p **-going**; past **-went**; past p **-gone**⟩ ▶ FORGO

foregone /ˈfɔːrɡɑːn ‖ˈfɔːɡɒn/ adj: **the result was a ~ conclusion** el resultado era de prever

foreground /ˈfɔːrɡraʊnd ‖ˈfɔːɡraʊnd/ n: **in the ~** en primer plano

forehand /ˈfɔːrhænd ‖ˈfɔːhænd/ n golpe m de derecho

forehead /ˈfɑːrəd, ˈfɔːrhed ‖ˈfɒrɪd, ˈfɔːhed/ n frente f

foreign /ˈfɔːrən, ˈfɑː- ‖ˈfɒrən/ adj ⓵ **(a)** ⟨custom/country/language⟩ extranjero **(b)** ⟨policy/trade/relations⟩ exterior; **~ debt** deuda f externa ⓶ (Med) extraño; **a ~ body** un cuerpo extraño

foreigner /ˈfɔːrənər, ˈfɑː- ‖ˈfɒrənə(r)/ n extranjero, -ra m,f

foreign: ~ exchange n divisas fpl; **F~ minister** n ministro, -tra or (Méx) secretario, -ria m,f de relaciones or (Esp) asuntos exteriores, canciller mf (AmS); **F~ Office** n (in UK) **the F~ Office** el Foreign Office, el ministerio de relaciones exteriores de Gran Bretaña; **F~ Secretary** n (in UK) ▶ F~ MINISTER

foreleg /ˈfɔːrleɡ ‖ˈfɔːleɡ/ n pata f delantera

foreman /ˈfɔːrmən ‖ˈfɔːmən/ n (pl **-men** /-mən/) **(a)** (supervisor) capataz m **(b)** (of jury) presidente m

foremost¹ /ˈfɔːrməʊst ‖ˈfɔːməʊst/ adj más importante

foremost² adv en primer lugar

forename /ˈfɔːrneɪm ‖ˈfɔːneɪm/ n nombre m (de pila)

forensic /fəˈrensɪk/ adj (before n) forense

forerunner /ˈfɔːrˌrʌnər ‖ˈfɔːˌrʌnə(r)/ n precursor, -sora m,f

foresee /fɔːrˈsiː ‖fɔːˈsiː/ vt ⟨past **foresaw**; past p **foreseen**⟩ prever*

foreshore /ˈfɔːrʃɔːr ‖ˈfɔːʃɔː(r)/ n: parte de la playa entre la pleamar y la bajamar

foresight /ˈfɔːrsaɪt ‖ˈfɔːsaɪt/ n previsión f

foreskin /ˈfɔːrskɪn ‖ˈfɔːskɪn/ n prepucio m

forest /ˈfɔːrəst ‖ˈfɒrɪst/ n (wood) bosque m; (tropical) selva f; (before n) forestal

forestall /fɔːrˈstɔːl ‖fɔːˈstɔːl/ vt **(a)** (prevent) prevenir* **(b)** (preempt) adelantarse a

forestry /ˈfɔːrəstri ‖ˈfɒrɪstri/ n silvicultura f

foretaste /ˈfɔːrteɪst ‖ˈfɔːteɪst/ n anticipo m

foretell /fɔːrˈtel ‖fɔːˈtel/ vt ⟨past & past p **foretold**⟩ predecir*

forever /fəˈrevər ‖fəˈrevə(r)/ adv: **those days are gone ~** esos días no volverán; **nothing lasts ~** nada dura eternamente

forewarn /fɔːrˈwɔːrn ‖fɔːˈwɔːn/ vt **to ~ sb OF sth** advertir* A algn DE algo

forewent /fɔːrˈwent ‖fɔːˈwent/ past of FOREGO

foreword /ˈfɔːrwɜːrd ‖ˈfɔːwɜːd/ n prólogo m

forfeit¹ /ˈfɔːrfət ‖ˈfɔːfɪt/ vt ⟨property⟩ perder* el derecho a; ⟨rights/respect/game⟩ perder*

forfeit² n **(a)** (penalty) multa f **(b)** (Games) prenda f

forgave /fərˈɡeɪv ‖fəˈɡeɪv/ past of FORGIVE

forge¹ /fɔːrdʒ ‖fɔːdʒ/ vt ⓵ ⟨metal/bond⟩ forjar ⓶ (counterfeit) falsificar*

forge² n **(a)** (smithy) forja f **(b)** (furnace) fragua f

forger /ˈfɔːrdʒər ‖ˈfɔːdʒə(r)/ n falsificador, -dora m,f

forgery /ˈfɔːrdʒəri ‖ˈfɔːdʒəri/ n (pl **-ries**) falsificación f

forget /fərˈɡet ‖fəˈɡet/ ⟨pres p **forgetting**; past **forgot**; past p **forgotten**⟩ vt olvidarse de, olvidar
■ **~** vi: **to ~** (ABOUT sth) olvidarse (DE algo)

forgetful /fərˈɡetfəl ‖fəˈɡetfəl/ adj olvidadizo

forget-me-not /fərˈɡetmiˈnɑːt ‖fəˈɡetmɪnɒt/ n nomeolvides m

forgive /fərˈɡɪv ‖fəˈɡɪv/ vt ⟨past **forgave**; past p **forgiven**⟩ perdonar; **to ~ sb FOR sth** perdonarle algo a algn

forgiveness /fərˈɡɪvnəs ‖fəˈɡɪvnɪs/ n (quality) clemencia f; **to ask sb's ~ for sth** pedirle* perdón a algn por algo

forgo /fɔːrˈɡəʊ ‖fɔːˈɡəʊ/ vt ⟨3rd pers sing pres **-goes**; pres p **-going**; past **-went**; past p **-gone**⟩ (frml) privarse de

forgot /fərˈɡɑːt ‖fəˈɡɒt/ past of FORGET

forgotten /fəˈɡɑːtn̩ ‖fəˈɡɒtn̩/ *past p of* FORGET

fork¹ /fɔːrk ‖fɔːk/ *n* (Culin) tenedor *m*; (for gardening) horca *f*

fork² *vi* (a) (split) «*branch/road/river*» bifurcarse* (b) (turn): **to ~ (to the) right** desviarse* a la derecha

forklift (truck) /ˈfɔːrkˌlɪft ‖ˈfɔːklɪft/ *n* carretilla *f* elevadora (*de horquilla*)

forlorn /fərˈlɔːrn ‖fəˈlɔːn/ *adj* (a) «*glance/smile*» triste; «*appearance*» de tristeza y desamparo (b) «*attempt*» desesperado

form¹ /fɔːrm ‖fɔːm/ *n* [1] (shape, manner) forma *f* [2] (type, kind) tipo; **other ~s of life** otras formas de vida [3] (fitness, ability) forma *f*; **to be on ~** estar* en forma [4] (document) formulario *m*, forma *f* (Méx) [5] (BrE Educ) (class) clase *f*; (year) curso *m*

form² *vt* «*character/shape/company/basis*» formar; «*opinion*» formarse; «*habit*» adquirir* ■ ~ *vi* «*idea/plan*» tomar forma; «*ice/fog*» formarse

formal /ˈfɔːrməl ‖ˈfɔːməl/ *adj* «*reception/dinner/language*» formal; «*manner/person*» ceremonioso; **~ dress** traje *m* de etiqueta

formality /fɔːrˈmæləti ‖fɔːˈmæləti/ *n* (*pl* **-ties**) [1] (formal quality) ceremonia *f* [2] (convention) formalidad *f*

formalize /ˈfɔːrməlaɪz ‖ˈfɔːməlaɪz/ *vt* formalizar*

formally /ˈfɔːrməli ‖ˈfɔːməli/ *adv* «*invite/reprimand*» formalmente

format¹ /ˈfɔːrmæt ‖ˈfɔːmæt/ *n* formato *m*

format² *vt* **-tt-** formatear

formation /fɔːrˈmeɪʃən ‖fɔːˈmeɪʃən/ *n* formación *f*

former¹ /ˈfɔːrmər ‖ˈfɔːmə(r)/ *adj* [1] (previous) antiguo [2] (first-mentioned) primero

former² *n* **the ~** el primero, la primera; (*pl*) los primeros, las primeras

formerly /ˈfɔːrmərli ‖ˈfɔːməli/ *adv* antes

formidable /ˈfɔːrmədəbəl ‖ˈfɔːmɪdəbəl, fɔːˈmɪdəbəl/ *adj* «*task*» imponente; «*problem/obstacle*» tremendo; «*opponent*» temible

formula /ˈfɔːrmjələ ‖ˈfɔːmjʊlə/ *n* (*pl* **-las** o (fml) **-lae** /-liː/) fórmula *f*; **~ one** (motor racing) fórmula uno

formulate /ˈfɔːrmjələrt ‖ˈfɔːmjʊleɪt/ *vt* formular

fornication /ˌfɔːrnəˈkeɪʃən ‖ˌfɔːnɪˈkeɪʃən/ *n* (fml) fornicación *f* (fml)

for-profit /fərˈprɑːfət ‖fəˈprɒfɪt/ *adj* comercial, con fines de lucro

forsake /fərˈseɪk ‖fəˈseɪk/ *vt* (*past* **forsook** /fərˈsʊk ‖fəˈsʊk/; *past p* **forsaken** /fərˈseɪkən ‖fəˈseɪkən/) (liter) (a) (abandon) abandonar (b) (relinquish) «*pleasure/habits*» renunciar a

fort /fɔːrt ‖fɔːt/ *n* fuerte *m*; (small) fortín *m*

forte /ˈfɔːrteɪ ‖ˈfɔːteɪ/ *n* fuerte *m*

forth /fɔːrθ ‖fɔːθ/ *adv* (liter) (a) (out): **~ he went**

to battle with his enemy marchó a luchar con su enemigo (b) (in time): **from this day ~** de hoy en adelante

forthcoming /ˌfɔːrθˈkʌmɪŋ ‖ˌfɔːθˈkʌmɪŋ/ *adj* [1] (a) (approaching) (*usu before n*) «*event*» próximo (b) (about to appear) «*article/record*» de próxima aparición; «*film*» a estrenarse próximamente [2] (available) (*pred*): **no explanation was ~** no dieron (*or* dio *etc*) ninguna explicación [3] (open, helpful): **he was not very ~** no estuvo muy comunicativo

forthright /ˈfɔːrθraɪt ‖ˈfɔːθraɪt/ *adj* directo

forthwith /ˌfɔːrθˈwɪð ‖ˌfɔːθˈwɪθ/ *adv* (frml or liter) inmediatamente

fortieth¹ /ˈfɔːrtiəθ ‖ˈfɔːtiəθ/ *adj* cuadragésimo

fortieth² *adv* en cuadragésimo lugar

fortieth³ *n* (Math) cuarentavo *m*; (part) cuarentava *or* cuadragésima parte *f*

fortification /ˌfɔːrtəfəˈkeɪʃən ‖ˌfɔːtɪfɪˈkeɪʃən/ *n* (Mil) fortificación *f*

fortify /ˈfɔːrtəfaɪ ‖ˈfɔːtɪfaɪ/ *vt* **-fies, -fying, -fied** «*town/building*» fortificar*; «*person/determination*» fortalecer*; «*argument*» reforzar*; **fortified wine** vino *m* fortificado

fortnight /ˈfɔːrtnaɪt ‖ˈfɔːtnaɪt/ *n* (esp BrE) quince días, dos semanas

fortnightly¹ /ˈfɔːrtnaɪtli ‖ˈfɔːtnaɪtli/ *adv* (esp BrE) cada dos semanas

fortnightly² *adj* (esp BrE) quincenal

fortress /ˈfɔːrtrəs ‖ˈfɔːtrɪs/ *n* fortaleza *f*

fortuitous /fɔːrˈtuːɪtəs ‖fɔːˈtjuːɪtəs/ *adj* fortuito

fortunate /ˈfɔːrtʃnət ‖ˈfɔːtʃənət/ *adj* afortunado; **it was ~ that he came** fue una suerte que viniera

fortunately /ˈfɔːrtʃnətli ‖ˈfɔːtʃənətli/ *adv* (*indep*) afortunadamente

fortune /ˈfɔːrtʃən ‖ˈfɔːtʃən, ˈfɔːtʃuːn/ *n* [1] (money, prosperity) fortuna *f*; (a lot of money) (colloq) (*no pl*) dineral *m*, platal *m* (AmL fam), pastón *m* (Esp fam) [2] (destiny) destino *m*; **to tell sb's ~** decirle* la buenaventura a algn [3] (luck) **good ~** suerte *f*

fortune-teller /ˈfɔːrtʃənˌtelər ‖ˈfɔːtʃənˌtelə(r), ˈfɔːtʃuːn-/ *n* adivino, -na *m,f*

forty /ˈfɔːrti ‖ˈfɔːti/ *adj/n* cuarenta *adj inv/m*; *see also* FOUR¹

forum /ˈfɔːrəm ‖ˈfɔːrəm/ *n* foro *m*

forward¹ /ˈfɔːrwərd ‖ˈfɔːwəd/, (esp BrE) **forwards** /ˈfɔːrwərdz ‖ˈfɔːwədz/ *adv* (a) «*bend/slope/lean*» hacia adelante (b) (in time) (frml) en adelante; **from this day ~** desde hoy en adelante

forward² *adj* [1] (*before n*) «*movement*» hacia adelante [2] (advance): **~ planning** planificación *f* [3] (assertive) atrevido

forward³ *vt* (send) (Busn) enviar*; **☉ please forward** hacer* seguir

forward⁴ *n* (Sport) delantero *mf*

forwent /fɔːrˈwent ‖fɔːˈwent/ *past of* FORGO

fossil /ˈfɑːsəl ‖ˈfɒsəl/ *n* fósil *m*

fossil fuel n combustible m fósil

foster[1] /ˈfɒstər ‖ˈfɒstə(r)/ vt ① ‹child› (BrE) acoger en el hogar sin adoptarlo legalmente ② ‹suspicion/talent› fomentar; ‹reconciliation› promover*

foster[2] adj ‹child› ≈adoptivo; ~ **home** casa f de acogida de menores

fought /fɔːt/ past & past p of FIGHT[1]

foul[1] /faʊl/ adj **-er, -est** ① (offensive) ‹smell› nauseabundo; ‹taste› repugnante ② (horrible) (colloq) ‹person› asqueroso (fam); ‹weather› pésimo ③ (obscene) ‹language/gesture› ordinario

foul[2] n falta f, faul m or foul m (AmL)

foul[3] vt ① (pollute) contaminar ② (a) (block) ‹drain/chimney› obstruir* (b) (entangle) ‹rope/chain› enredar ③ (Sport) cometer una falta or (AmL tb) un foul or faul contra, faulear (AmL)

foul: ~**-mouthed** /ˈfaʊlˈmaʊðd/ adj malhablado; ~ **play** n (a) (Law): **they suspect ~ play** sospechan que se trata de un crimen (b) (Sport) juego m sucio

found[1] /faʊnd/ past & past p of FIND[1]

found[2] vt ① (a) (establish) fundar (b) **founding** pres p fundador ② (base) **to ~ sth on sth** fundar algo EN algo

foundation /faʊnˈdeɪʃən/ n ① (a) (establishing) fundación f (b) (institution) fundación f ② (often pl) (a) (Const) cimientos mpl (b) (groundwork, basis) fundamentos mpl; ‹before n› ~ **course** curso m preparatorio ③ (grounds) fundamento m ④ (cosmetic) base f de maquillaje

founder[1] /ˈfaʊndər ‖ˈfaʊndə(r)/ n fundador, -dora m,f

founder[2] vi «ship» hundirse; «plan/project» irse* a pique

foundry /ˈfaʊndri/ n (pl **-ries**) fundición f

fountain /ˈfaʊntn̩ ‖ˈfaʊntɪn/ n (a) (ornamental) fuente f (b) (drinking ~) fuente f, bebedero m (CS, Méx)

fountain pen n pluma f (estilográfica), pluma f fuente (AmL), estilográfica f, lapicera f fuente (CS)

four[1] /fɔːr ‖fɔː(r)/ n cuatro m; **4 + 1 = 5** (léase: four plus one equals o is five) 4 + 1 = 5 (read as: cuatro más uno es igual a cinco); **4 - 1 = 3** (léase: four minus one equals o is three) 4 - 1 = 3 (read as: cuatro menos uno es igual a tres); **3 x 4 = 12** (léase: three times four equals o is twelve, o three fours are twelve) 3 x 4 = 12 (read as: tres fours are twelve) 3 x 4 = 12 (read as: tres (multiplicado) por cuatro (son) doce); **4 ÷ 2 = 2** (léase: four divided by two equals o is two) 4 ÷ 2 = 2 (read as: cuatro dividido por dos es (igual a) dos); **on all ~s** en or a cuatro patas, a gatas

four[2] adj cuatro adj inv

four: ~**-by-**~ n todoterreno m; ~**-poster (bed)** /ˈfɔːrˈpəʊstər ‖ˌfɔːˈpəʊstə(r)/ n: cama con cuatro columnas, gen con dosel; ~**-seater** /ˈfɔːrˈsiːtər ‖ˈfɔːˌsiːtə(r)/ n coche m/avión m de cuatro plazas

foursome /ˈfɔːrsəm ‖ˈfɔːsəm/ n: grupo de cuatro personas

fourteen /ˈfɔːrtiːn ‖ˌfɔːˈtiːn/ adj/n catorce adj inv/m; see also FOUR[1]

fourteenth[1] /ˈfɔːrtiːnθ ‖ˌfɔːˈtiːnθ/ adj decimocuarto

fourteenth[2] adv en decimocuarto lugar

fourteenth[3] n (Math) catorceavo m; (part) catorceava parte f

fourth[1] /fɔːrθ ‖fɔːθ/ adj cuarto

fourth[2] adv (a) (in position, time, order) en cuarto lugar (b) (fourthly) en cuarto lugar

fourth[3] n ① (part) cuarto m ② ~ **(gear)** (Auto) (no art) cuarta f

fourthly /ˈfɔːrθli ‖ˈfɔːθli/ adv (indep) en cuarto lugar

four-wheel drive /ˈfɔːrhwiːl ‖ˈfɔːwiːl/ n tracción f integral

fowl /faʊl/ n (pl ~**s** or ~) ave f꞉ (de corral)

fox[1] /fɑːks ‖fɒks/ n zorro m

fox[2] vt (colloq) confundir

fox: ~**glove** n dedalera f, digital f; ~**-hunting** n caza f del zorro

foyer /ˈfɔɪeɪ/ n (of theatre) foyer m; (of hotel) vestíbulo m

fracas /ˈfreɪkəs, ˈfrækəs ‖ˈfrækɑː/ n (pl **fracases** or (BrE) **fracas** /-z/) (liter) altercado m

fraction /ˈfrækʃən/ n fracción f

fracture[1] /ˈfræktʃər ‖ˈfræktʃə(r)/ n fractura f

fracture[2] vt fracturar

fragile /ˈfrædʒəl ‖ˈfrædʒaɪl/ adj (a) ‹object/china/glass› frágil; ‹relationship/link/agreement› precario (b) ‹person› débil; ‹health› delicado

fragment /ˈfrægmənt/ n fragmento m

fragrance /ˈfreɪgrəns/ n (smell) fragancia f; (perfume) perfume m

fragrant /ˈfreɪgrənt/ adj fragante

frail /freɪl/ adj **-er, -est** (a) (physically delicate) ‹person› débil; ‹health› delicado (b) (morally weak) débil (c) (fragile) precario

frame[1] /freɪm/ n (a) (structure — of building, ship, plane) armazón m or f; (— of car, motorcycle, bed, door) bastidor m; (— of bicycle) cuadro m, marco m (Chi, Col) (b) (edge — of picture, window, door) marco m (c) **frames** pl (for spectacles) montura f

frame[2] vt ① ‹picture/photograph› enmarcar*; ‹plan/policy/question› formular, elaborar ② (incriminate unjustly) (colloq): **I was ~d** me tendieron una trampa para incriminarme

frame: ~ **of mind** n (pl ~**s of mind**) estado m de ánimo; ~**work** n (basis) marco m; (plan) esquema m; (Eng) armazón m or f

franc /fræŋk/ n franco m

France /fræns ‖frɑːns/ n Francia f

franchise /ˈfræntʃaɪz/ n ① (Busn) (a) (right — to operate retail outlet) franquicia f; (— to market product, service) concesión f (b) (retail outlet) franquicia f ② (Pol frml) **the** ~ el derecho de or al voto

frank[1] /fræŋk/ adj **-er, -est** (a) (candid) sincero (b) (outspoken) franco

frank[2] vt (a) ‹letter/parcel/envelope› franquear (b) (postmark) ‹stamp/letter› matasellar

frankfurter /ˈfræŋkfɜːrtər ‖ˈfræŋkfɜːtə(r)/ n salchicha f de Frankfurt or (Arg, Col) de Viena, frankfurter m (Ur), vienesa f (Chi), salchicha f alemana (Ven)

frankincense /ˈfræŋkənsens ‖ˈfræŋkɪnsens/ n incienso m

frankly /ˈfræŋkli/ adv francamente

frantic /'fræntɪk/ adj (a) (very worried) desesperado (b) (frenzied) ⟨activity⟩ frenético

fraternal /frə'tɜːrn̩l ‖ frə'tɜːnl/ adj ⟨love⟩ fraternal, fraterno; ⟨jealousy⟩ entre hermanos

fraternity /frə'tɜːrnəti ‖ frə'tɜːnəti/ n (pl **-ties**) [1] (virtue of brotherhood) fraternidad f [2] (a) (Relig) hermandad f (b) (university club) asociación f estudiantil

fraternize /'frætərnaɪz ‖ 'frætənaɪz/ vi confraternizar*

fraud /frɔːd/ n [1] (deception) fraude m [2] (person) farsante mf

fraudulent /'frɔːdʒələnt ‖ 'frɔːdjʊlənt/ adj fraudulento

fraught /frɔːt/ adj (a) (pred) **to be ~ WITH** sth ⟨with danger/problems⟩ estar* lleno DE algo (b) (tense) ⟨atmosphere/relationship⟩ tirante

fray¹ /freɪ/ vi «cloth/collar/rope» deshilacharse; «wire» pelarse

fray² n refriega f

frayed /freɪd/ adj (a) ⟨collar/cloth⟩ deshilachado; ⟨rope/wire⟩ desgastado (b) ⟨nerves⟩ crispado; **tempers were getting ~** se estaban exaltando los ánimos

freak¹ /friːk/ n (a) (abnormal specimen) fenómeno m; (monster) monstruo m (b) (unnatural event) fenómeno m

freak² adj (before n) ⟨weather⟩ inusitado; ⟨happening⟩ inesperado
■ **freak out** (sl) [1] [v + adv] flipar (arg), friquear(se) (Méx arg) [2] [v + o + adv] alucinar (fam), friquear (Méx arg)

freckle /'frekəl/ n peca f

free¹ /friː/ adj freer /'friːər ‖ 'friːə(r)/, freest /'friːəst ‖ 'friːɪst/ [1] (a) (at liberty) (usu pred) libre; **to set sb ~** dejar or poner* a algn en libertad (b) ⟨country/people/press⟩ libre; **the right of ~ speech** la libertad de expresión (c) (loose) ⟨sth stuck or caught⟩ suelto; **to work ~** soltarse* [2] (pred) (without, rid of) **~ FROM** o **OF** sth libre DE algo; **~ of** o **from** additives sin aditivos; **~ of charge** gratis [3] (costing nothing) ⟨ticket/sample⟩ gratis adj inv; ⟨schooling/health care⟩ gratuito [4] (not occupied) ⟨table/time⟩ libre

free² adv (a) (without payment) gratuitamente; **I got in for ~** (colloq) entré gratis (b) (without restriction) ⟨roam/run⟩ a su (or mi etc) antojo

free³ vt [1] (liberate) ⟨prisoner/hostage⟩ poner* or dejar en libertad; ⟨animal⟩ soltar*; ⟨nation/slave⟩ liberar [2] (a) (release) ⟨bound person⟩ soltar*; ⟨trapped person⟩ rescatar (b) (loose, clear) ⟨sth stuck or caught⟩ desenganchar

-free /friː/ suff: **trouble~** sin problemas; **nuclear~ zone** zona f desnuclearizada

freedom /'friːdəm/ n libertad f

freedom fighter n guerrillero, -ra m,f

free: ~-for-all /'friːfər'ɔːl/ n gresca f; **~hold** adj (esp BrE): **~hold property** bien m raíz (que se compra o vende en plena propiedad junto con el suelo sobre el que está edificado); **~ kick** n (in soccer) tiro m libre; (in rugby) patada f libre

freelance¹ /'friːlæns ‖ 'friːlɑːns/ adj por cuenta propia, por libre (Esp)

freelance² adv por cuenta propia, por libre (Esp)

freely /'friːli/ adv [1] (a) (without restriction) libremente (b) (openly) ⟨speak/write⟩ con libertad (c) (willingly) ⟨offer⟩ de buen grado [2] (a) (generously) ⟨spend/give⟩ a manos llenas (b) (copiously) ⟨flow/pour⟩ profusamente

free: F~mason /'friːmeɪsən ‖ 'friːmeɪsn/ n masón, -sona m,f, francmasón, -sona m,f; **~-range** /'friːˈreɪndʒ/ adj ⟨chicken/eggs⟩ de granja; **~style** n estilo m libre; **~ trade** n libre comercio m; **~ware** n (Comput) programas mpl de libre distribución; **~way** n (AmE) autopista f (sin peaje); **~wheel** /'friːˈhwiːl ‖ ˌfriːˈwiːl/ vi: **he ~wheeled down the hill** (on bike) bajó la cuesta sin pedalear; (in car) bajó la cuesta en punto muerto; **~ will** n: **of one's own ~ will** por su (or mi etc) propia voluntad

freeze¹ /friːz/ (past **froze**; past p **frozen**) vi [1] ⟨pipe/lock/ground/person⟩ helarse*; **I'm freezing!** ¡estoy helado! [2] (stand still) quedarse inmóvil
■ ~ vt ⟨water/stream/pipe⟩ helar*; ⟨food⟩ congelar [2] (Fin) ⟨assets/account/prices⟩ congelar
■ ~ v impers helar*
■ **freeze over** [v + adv] helarse*
■ **freeze up** [v + adv] helarse*

freeze² n congelación f; **a wage/price ~** una congelación salarial/de precios

freezer /'friːzər ‖ 'friːzə(r)/ n (deep freeze) freezer m; (freezing compartment) congelador m

freezing¹ /'friːzɪŋ/ adj ⟨temperatures⟩ bajo cero; ⟨weather⟩ con temperaturas bajo cero; ⟨hands/feet⟩ helado; **it's ~** (cold) **in here** aquí hace un frío que pela (fam)

freezing² n [1] **~ (point)** punto m de congelación; **three degrees below ~** tres grados sobre/bajo cero [2] (process) congelación f

freight /freɪt/ n (a) (goods transported) carga f (b) (transportation) transporte m, flete m (AmL)

freighter /'freɪtər ‖ 'freɪtə(r)/ n buque m de carga

freight train n tren m de carga

French¹ /frentʃ/ adj francés

French² n (a) (language) francés m (b) (people) + pl vb the **~** los franceses

French: ~ bean pl n (BrE) ▶ GREEN BEAN; **~ doors** pl n (AmE) ▶ **~ WINDOWS**; **~ dressing** n aliño para ensaladas a base de aceite, vinagre y mostaza; (AmE) aderezo (para ensaladas) a base de aceite, vinagre y tomate; **~ fries** pl n papas fpl or (Esp) patatas fpl fritas, papas fpl a la francesa (Col, Méx); **~man** /'frentʃmən/ n (pl **-men** /-mən/) francés m; **~ windows** pl n puerta f ventana, cristalera f (Esp); **~woman** n francesa f

frenetic /frə'netɪk/ adj ⟨activity⟩ frenético; ⟨attempt⟩ desesperado

frenzy /'frenzi/ n (no pl) frenesí m

frequency /'friːkwənsi/ n (pl **-cies**) frecuencia f

frequent¹ /'friːkwənt/ adj ⟨attempts/journeys⟩ frecuente; ⟨visitor⟩ asiduo

frequent² /frɪ'kwent/ vt frecuentar

frequently /'friːkwəntli/ adv con frecuencia, a menudo

fresh /freʃ/ adj **-er, -est** [1] (a) (not stale, frozen or canned) ⟨food⟩ fresco; **to get some ~ air** tomar el fresco (b) (not tired) ⟨complexion/appearance⟩

freshen ···❯ frontbencher ···

fresco **2** (not salty): ~ **water** agua *f*; dulce **3** (a) (new, clean) ‹*clothes/linen*› limpio (b) (new, additional) ‹*supplies/initiative*› nuevo

freshen /'freʃən/ *vt* refrescar*
■ **freshen up** [*v* + *adv*] lavarse

fresher /'freʃər ‖'freʃə(r)/ *n* (BrE colloq) ▶ FRESHMAN

freshly /'freʃli/ *adv* recién

freshman /'freʃmən/ *n* (*pl* **-men** /-mən/) (Educ) estudiante *mf* de primer año, mechón, -chona *m,f* (Chi fam)

freshness /'freʃnəs ‖'freʃnɪs/ *n* frescura *f*

freshwater /'freʃ'wɔːtər ‖'freʃ,wɔːtə(r)/ *adj* (*before n*) de agua dulce

fret /fret/ *vi* **-tt-** preocuparse

fretful /'fretfəl/ *adj* (a) (querulous) quejoso (b) (anxious) inquieto

friar /'fraɪər ‖'fraɪə(r)/ *n* fraile *m*

friction /'frɪkʃən/ *n* **1** (Phys, Tech) rozamiento *m*, fricción *f* **2** (discord) tirantez *f*

Friday /'fraɪdeɪ, -di/ *n* viernes *m*; *see also* MONDAY

fridge /frɪdʒ/ *n* (colloq) nevera *f*, refrigerador *m*, frigorífico *m* (Esp), heladera *f* (RPl), refrigeradora *f* (Col, Per)

fried /fraɪd/ *adj* frito; **a ~ egg** un huevo frito *or* (Méx) estrellado

friend /frend/ *n* amigo, -ga *m,f*; **he soon made ~s with her** en poco tiempo se hizo amigo suyo

friendliness /'frendlɪnəs ‖'frendlɪnɪs/ *n* simpatía *f*

friendly /'frendli/ *adj* **-lier, -liest** (a) ‹*person/ pet*› simpático; ‹*place/atmosphere*› agradable; ‹*welcome*› cordial; **to be ~ WITH sb** ser* amigo, -ga DE algn (b) (good-natured) ‹*rivalry/match*› amistoso

friendship /'frendʃɪp/ *n* amistad *f*

frieze /friːz/ *n* (on building, wall) friso *m*; (on wallpaper) greca *f*

frigate /'frɪgət ‖'frɪgɪt/ *n* fragata *f*

fright /fraɪt/ *n* (a) (fear) miedo *m*; **to take ~ at sth** asustarse por algo (b) (shock) susto *m*

frighten /'fraɪtn̩/ *vt* asustar
■ **frighten away, frighten off** [*v* + *o* + *adv*, *v* + *adv* + *o*] espantar

frightened /'fraɪtn̩d/ *adj* ‹*person/animal*› asustado; **to be ~ OF sb/sth** tenerle* miedo A algn/algo

frightening /'fraɪtn̩ɪŋ/ *adj* ‹*experience*› espantoso; (stronger) aterrador

frightful /'fraɪtfəl/ *adj* **1** (horrific) aterrador **2** (BrE colloq) (very unpleasant) horroroso

frigid /'frɪdʒəd ‖'frɪdʒɪd/ *adj* frígido

frill /frɪl/ *n* volante *m or* (RPl) volado *m or* (Méx) olán *m or* (Chi) vuelo *m*; **a ceremony with no ~s** una ceremonia sencilla

frilly /'frɪli/ *adj* **-lier, -liest** ‹*dress/petticoat*› de volantes *or* (RPl) de volados *or* (Méx) de olanes *or* (Chi) de vuelos

fringe /frɪndʒ/ *n* **1** (on shawl, carpet, tablecloth) fleco *m* **2** (of hair) (BrE) flequillo *m*, cerquillo *m* (AmL), fleco *m* (Méx), chasquilla *f* (Chi), capul *m* (Col), pollina *f* (Ven) **3** (periphery) (*often pl*): **to live on the ~(s) of society** vivir al margen de la sociedad; (*before n*) ‹*area/group*› marginal; ‹*music/medicine*› alternativo

fringe benefit *n* (a) (Lab Rel) incentivo *m* (b) (incidental advantage) ventaja *f* adicional

frisk /frɪsk/ *vt* cachear, catear (Méx)

frisky /'frɪski/ *adj* **-kier, -kiest** retozón

fritter /'frɪtər ‖'frɪtə(r)/ *n* buñuelo *m*, fruta *f* de sartén (Esp)
■ **fritter away** [*v* + *o* + *adv*, *v* + *adv* + *o*] ‹*money*› malgastar; ‹*fortune*› dilapidar; ‹*time*› desperdiciar

frivolous /'frɪvələs/ *adj* frívolo

frizzy /'frɪzi/ *adj* **-zier, -ziest** crespo, chino (Méx), como mota (CS)

frock /frɑːk ‖frɒk/ *n* vestido *m*

frog /frɔːg ‖frɒg/ *n* rana *f*; **to have a ~ in the** *o* **one's throat** tener* carraspera

frog: ~man /'frɔːgmæn ‖'frɒgmən/ *n* (*pl* **-men** /-mən/) hombre *m* rana; **~spawn** *n* (BrE) huevos *mpl* de rana

frolic /'frɑːlɪk ‖'frɒlɪk/ *vi* **-ck-** retozar*

from /frɑːm ‖frɒm, *weak form* frəm/ *prep* **1** (indicating starting point) desde; **~ the beginning** desde el principio **2** (indicating distance): **2cm ~ the edge** a 2cm del borde; **we're still three hours ~ Tulsa** todavía faltan tres horas para llegar a Tulsa **3** (after): **~ today** a partir de hoy; **50 years ~ now** dentro de 50 años **4** (indicating origin) de; **I'm ~ Texas** soy de Texas; **the flight ~ Madrid** el vuelo procedente de Madrid; **a letter ~ my lawyer** una carta de mi abogado **5** **from ... to ...:** **they flew ~ New York to Lima** volaron de Nueva York a Lima; **they stretch ~ Derbyshire to the borders of Scotland** se extienden desde el condado de Derbyshire hasta el sur de Escocia; **we work ~ nine to five** trabajamos de nueve a cinco; **~ $50 to $100** entre 50 y 100 dólares **6** (as a result of) de; **his eyes were red ~ crying** tenía los ojos rojos de tanto llorar; **~ experience I would say that ...** según mi experiencia diría que ... **7** (out of, off) de; **~ the cupboard/shelf** del armario/estante; **if you take 5 ~ 10** si le restas 5 a 10 **8** (with preps & advs): **~ above/below** desde arriba/abajo; **he crawled out ~ under the table** salió gateando de debajo de la mesa

frond /frɑːnd ‖frɒnd/ *n* (of fern) fronda *f*; (of palm) hoja *f*

front¹ /frʌnt/ *n* **1** (forward part) frente *m*; (of building) frente *m*, fachada *f*; (of dress) delantera *f*; **you sit in the ~** siéntate delante *or* (esp AmL) adelante **2** (*in phrases*) **in front** (*as adv*) delante, adelante (esp AmL); **in front of sb/sth** delante *or* (esp AmL) adelante de algn/algo; (facing) enfrente de algn/algo **3** (Meteo, Mil, Pol) frente *m* **4** (outward show) fachada *f*; (— for illegal activity) pantalla *f* **5** (overlooking sea) paseo *m* marítimo, malecón *m* (AmL), rambla *f* (RPl)

front² *adj* (at front) ‹*seat/wheel/leg*› delantero, de delante *or* (esp AmL) de adelante; **the ~ door** la puerta de (la) calle; **the ~ yard** *o* (BrE) **garden** el jardín del frente; **a ~-row seat** un asiento en primera fila

frontbencher /'frʌnt'bentʃər ···❯

‖ ˌfrʌntˈbentʃə(r)/ n (BrE) *diputado con cargo ministerial en el gobierno o en el gabinete fantasma*

frontier /frʌnˈtɪr ‖ ˈfrʌntɪə(r)/ n frontera f; (*before n*) ⟨guard/zone⟩ fronterizo

frontispiece /ˈfrʌntɪspiːs/ n frontispicio m

front room n salón m, living m (esp AmL)

frost¹ /frɔːst ‖ frɒst/ n **(a)** (sub-zero temperature) helada f **(b)** (frozen dew) escarcha f

frost² vt **1** (Meteo) helar*; ⟨plant⟩ quemar **2** (AmE Culin) bañar

frostbite /ˈfrɔːstbaɪt ‖ ˈfrɒstbaɪt/ n congelación f

frosting /ˈfrɔːstɪŋ ‖ ˈfrɒstɪŋ/ n (AmE Culin) baño m

frosty /ˈfrɔːsti ‖ ˈfrɒsti/ adj **-tier, -tiest** ⟨weather/air⟩ helado; ⟨night⟩ de helada; ⟨manner/reception⟩ glacial

froth /frɔːθ ‖ frɒθ/ n espuma f

frothy /ˈfrɔːθi ‖ ˈfrɒθi/ adj **frothier, frothiest** espumoso

frown¹ /fraʊn/ vi fruncir* el ceño; **to ~ AT sb** mirar a algn con el ceño fruncido
■ **frown on, frown upon** [v + prep + o]: **that sort of thing is ~ed upon** eso está muy mal visto

frown² n ceño m fruncido

froze /frəʊz/ past of FREEZE¹

frozen¹ /ˈfrəʊzn/ past p of FREEZE¹

frozen² adj **1 (a)** ⟨water/lock/pipe/food⟩ congelado; (region) helado; **my feet are ~** (colloq) tengo los pies helados **(b)** (Fin) ⟨prices/incomes⟩ congelado **2** (motionless): **I stood there ~ (to the spot)** me quedé allí clavado, paralizado por el terror

frugal /ˈfruːɡəl/ adj frugal

fruit /fruːt/ n **1 (a)** (collectively) fruta f; **dried ~** (BrE) fruta f seca; ⟨before noun⟩ ~ **juice** jugo m or (Esp) zumo m de frutas; ~ **tree** árbol m frutal **(b)** (type — as food) fruta f; (Bot) fruto m **2** (product) fruto m; **to bear ~** dar* (su) fruto

fruit: ~**cake** n plum-cake m, ponqué m de frutas (Col), fruit cake m (Méx), budín m inglés (RPl); ~ **cocktail** n (dish) ensalada f or macedonia f or cóctel m de frutas; ~ **cup** n (AmE) ▶ COCKTAIL

fruitful /ˈfruːtfəl/ adj provechoso, fructífero

fruition /fruːˈɪʃn/ n (frml): **their plan never came to ~** su plan nunca cristalizó

fruitless /ˈfruːtləs ‖ ˈfruːtlɪs/ adj infructuoso

fruit: ~ **machine** n (BrE) máquina f tragamonedas or (Esp tb) tragaperras; ~ **salad** n **(a)** (AmE) ensalada de frutas, gen en gelatina **(b)** (BrE) ▶ FRUIT COCKTAIL

frustrate /ˈfrʌstreɪt ‖ frʌsˈtreɪt/ vt frustrar

frustrated /ˈfrʌstreɪtəd ‖ frʌsˈtreɪtɪd/ adj **(a)** (thwarted) frustrado **(b)** (dissatisfied) descontento; (sexually) ~ sexualmente frustrado

frustrating /ˈfrʌstreɪtɪŋ ‖ frʌsˈtreɪtɪŋ/ adj frustrante

frustration /frʌsˈtreɪʃn/ n frustración f

fry¹ /fraɪ/ **fries, frying, fried** vt freír*
■ ~ vi freírse*

fry² n (pl **fries**) **1 fries** pl (French fries) papas or (Esp) patatas fritas, papas fpl a la francesa (Col, Méx) **2 (a)** (+ pl vb) (Zool) alevines mpl, majuga f (Ur) **(b)** (people): **small ~** gente f de poca monta

frying pan /ˈfraɪŋ/, (AmE also) **fry pan** n sartén f, sartén m or f (AmL)

ft = **foot/feet**

FTP n (Comput) (= **file transfer protocol**) FTP m

fuchsia /ˈfjuːʃə/ n (Bot) fucsia f, aljaba f (RPl)

fuck /fʌk/ vt (vulg) (copulate with) joder (vulg), tirarse (vulg), follarse (Esp vulg), coger* (Méx, RPl, Ven vulg)
■ ~ vi (vulg) joder (vulg), tirar (vulg), coger* (Méx, RPl, Ven vulg), follar (Esp vulg), cachar (Chi, Per vulg)
■ **fuck off** [v + adv] (vulg): ~ **off!** ¡vete a la mierda! (vulg), ¡vete a tomar por (el) culo! (Esp vulg), ¡vete a la chingada! (Méx vulg), ¡andá a cagar! (RPl vulg)

fucking /ˈfʌkɪŋ/ adj (vulg) (before n): ~ **hell!** ¡puta madre! (vulg)

fudge¹ /fʌdʒ/ n (Culin) *especie de caramelo de dulce de leche*

fudge² vt (colloq) **(a)** (falsify) ⟨figures⟩ amañar **(b)** (evade) ⟨issue⟩ esquivar

fuel¹ /ˈfjuːəl/ n combustible m

fuel² vt (BrE) **-ll-** **1** ⟨ship/plane⟩ abastecer* de combustible; ⟨stove/furnace⟩ alimentar **2** ⟨hope/passion⟩ alimentar; ⟨debate⟩ avivar; ⟨fear⟩ exacerbar

fuel oil n fuel-oil m

fugitive /ˈfjuːdʒətɪv/ n fugitivo, -va m,f

fulfill, (BrE) **fulfil** /fʊlˈfɪl/ **-ll-** vt **1 (a)** (carry out) ⟨duty⟩ cumplir con; ⟨task⟩ llevar a cabo **(b)** (obey, keep) ⟨order/promise/contract⟩ cumplir **(c)** (serve) ⟨need⟩ satisfacer* **(d)** (meet) ⟨requirements⟩ satisfacer* **2** (realize) ⟨ambition⟩ hacer* realidad; ⟨potential⟩ alcanzar* **3** (make content) ⟨person⟩ satisfacer*
■ v refl **to ~ oneself** realizarse*

fulfilled /fʊlˈfɪld/ adj (usu pred) realizado

fulfillment, (BrE) **fulfilment** /fʊlˈfɪlmənt/ n **(a)** (of duty, promise) cumplimiento m **(b)** (satisfaction): **her family gave her a sense of ~** su familia la hacía sentirse realizada

full¹ /fʊl/ adj **-er, -est** **1** (filled) lleno; **I'm ~ (up)** estoy lleno; ~ **OF sth** lleno DE algo **2 (a)** (complete) ⟨report/description⟩ detallado; ⟨name/answer⟩ completo; **you have my ~ support** tienes todo mi apoyo; **to lead a very ~ life** llevar una vida muy activa **(b)** (maximum): **at ~ speed** a toda velocidad; ~ **employment** (Econ) pleno empleo m **3** ⟨figure⟩ regordete

full² adv **1** (as intensifier) ~ **well** muy bien **2** (directly): **the sun was shining ~ in my face** el sol me daba de lleno en la cara **3** in full: **write your name in ~** escriba su nombre completo; **it will be paid in ~** será pagado en su totalidad

full: ~**-blown** /ˈfʊlˈbləʊn/ adj (before n)

AmC	Central America	Arg	Argentina	Cu	Cuba	Per	Peru
AmL	Latin America	Bol	Bolivia	Ec	Ecuador	RPl	River Plate Area
AmS	South America	Chi	Chile	Esp	Spain	Ur	Uruguay
Andes	Andean Region	CS	Southern Cone	Méx	Mexico	Ven	Venezuela

verdadero; **~-fledged** /'fʊl'fledʒd/ adj (AmE) [1] ⟨chick⟩ capaz de volar; [2] ⟨lawyer/nurse⟩ hecho y derecho; **~-grown** /'fʊl'grəʊn/ adj ⟨before n⟩ totalmente desarrollado; **~ house** n (Cin, Theat) lleno m; **~-length** /'fʊl'leŋθ/ adj ⟨portrait/mirror⟩ de cuerpo entero; ⟨dress/skirt⟩ largo

fullness /'fʊlnəs ‖ 'fʊlnɪs/ n plenitud f; **in the ~ of time** con el tiempo

full: **~-scale** /'fʊl'skeɪl/ adj [1] (actual size) a escala natural; [2] (major) ⟨work⟩ de envergadura; ⟨investigation⟩ a fondo; ⟨test⟩ a escala real; ⟨war⟩ declarado; **~-size** /'fʊl'saɪz/, **~-sized** /-d/ adj (a) (life-size) de tamaño natural (b) (of adult size) ⟨bicycle/bed⟩ de adulto; **~ stop** n (BrE) punto m

full-time¹ /'fʊltaɪm/ adj ⟨student/soldier⟩ de tiempo completo; ⟨employment/post⟩ de jornada completa

full-time² /fʊl'taɪm/ adv a tiempo completo

fully /'fʊli/ adv [1] (a) (completely): **I ~ understand** comprendo muy bien; **she's a ~ trained nurse** es una enfermera diplomada (b) (in full) enteramente [2] (at least) por lo menos, como poco

fully-fledged /'fʊli'fledʒd/ adj (BrE) ▶ FULL-FLEDGED

fulsome /'fʊlsəm/ adj ⟨praise⟩ empalagoso; ⟨manner⟩ excesivamente efusivo

fumble /'fʌmbəl/ vi: **she ~d in her pockets** revolvió en sus bolsillos; **he ~d for the right words** tartamudeó, tratando de encontrar las palabras adecuadas; **she ~d with her buttons** intentó torpemente abrocharse/desabrocharse

fume /fjuːm/ vi [1] (smoke) (Chem) despedir* gases [2] (be angry) (colloq): **she was absolutely fuming** estaba que echaba humo

fumes /fjuːmz/ pl n gases mpl

fumigate /'fjuːməgeɪt ‖ 'fjuːmɪgeɪt/ vt fumigar*

fun /fʌn/ n diversión f; **to have ~** divertirse*; **he's good ~** es muy divertido; **to do sth for ~** hacer* algo por gusto; **to make ~ of sb/sth** reírse* de algn/algo

function¹ /'fʌŋkʃən/ n [1] (of tool, organ, person) función f; **to carry out/perform a ~** cumplir/ desempeñar una función [2] (reception, party) recepción f [3] (Comput, Math) función f; ⟨before n⟩ **~ key** tecla f de función

function² vi (a) (operate) «machine/organ» funcionar (b) (serve) **to ~ AS sth** «object/ building» hacer* (las veces) DE algo

functional /'fʌŋkʃnəl ‖ 'fʌŋkʃənl/ adj (a) (functioning) ⟨machine/part⟩ en buen estado (de funcionamiento) (b) (practical) ⟨furniture/design⟩ funcional

fund¹ /fʌnd/ n (a) (money reserve) fondo m (b) **funds** pl (resources, money) fondos mpl

fund² vt (a) (finance) ⟨research/organization⟩ financiar (b) (Fin) ⟨debt⟩ consolidar

fundamental /ˌfʌndə'mentl/ adj (a) (basic) ⟨principle/error/concept⟩ fundamental (b) (essential) ⟨skill/constituent⟩ esencial (c) (intrinsic, innate) ⟨absurdity/truth⟩ intrínseco

fundamentalism /ˌfʌndə'mentəlɪzəm/ n integrismo m, fundamentalismo m

fundamentalist /ˌfʌndə'mentləst ‖ fʌndə'mentəlɪst/ n integrista mf, fundamentalista mf

fundamentally /ˌfʌndə'mentli ‖ ˌfʌndə'mentəli/ adv (a) (radically) ⟨different/ mistaken⟩ fundamentalmente (b) (in essence) ⟨correct/justified⟩ esencialmente

fundamentals /ˌfʌndə'mentlz/ pl n fundamentos mpl

funding /'fʌndɪŋ/ n (act) financiación f; (resources) fondos mpl

fund-raising /'fʌndˌreɪzɪŋ ‖ 'fʌndˌreɪzɪŋ/ n recaudación f de fondos

funeral /'fjuːnərəl/ n funerales mpl

funeral: **~ director** n (frml) director, -tora m,f de una funeraria; **~ home** (AmE), **~ parlour** (BrE) n funeraria f

funfair /'fʌnfer ‖ 'fʌnfeə(r)/ n (BrE) (traveling) feria f; (permanent) parque m de diversiones or (Esp) de atracciones

fungus /'fʌŋgəs/ n (pl **fungi** /'fʌŋgaɪ/) hongo m

funnel /'fʌnl/ n (a) (for pouring) embudo m (b) (on steamship, steam engine) (BrE) chimenea f

funnily /'fʌnli ‖ 'fʌnɪli/ adv (a) (strangely) (esp BrE) de modo extraño (b) **~ enough** (indep) casualmente

funny /'fʌni/ adj **-nier, -niest** [1] (amusing) ⟨joke⟩ gracioso; ⟨person⟩ divertido [2] (strange) raro; **(it's) ~ (that) you should mention it** es curioso que lo menciones; **to taste/smell ~** saber*/oler* raro [3] (colloq) (unwell): **I feel a bit ~** me siento medio mal

fur /fɜːr ‖ fɜː(r)/ n (a) (of animal) (Zool) pelo m, pelaje m; (Clothing) piel f; ⟨before n⟩ **~ coat** abrigo m de piel or (Esp tb) de pieles (b) (pelt) piel f

furious /'fjʊriəs ‖ 'fjʊəriəs/ adj (a) (angry) furioso (b) (violent, intense) ⟨struggle⟩ feroz; ⟨speed⟩ vertiginoso; ⟨storm⟩ violento; ⟨activity⟩ febril

furiously /'fjʊriəsli ‖ 'fjʊəriəsli/ adv (a) (angrily) con furia (b) (violently, intensely) frenéticamente

furlough /'fɜːrləʊ ‖ 'fɜːləʊ/ n (AmE) permiso m, licencia f; **on ~** de permiso, con licencia

furnace /'fɜːrnəs ‖ 'fɜːnɪs/ n (in industry) horno m; (for heating) caldera f

furnish /'fɜːrnɪʃ ‖ 'fɜːnɪʃ/ vt (a) ⟨house/ room⟩ amueblar, amoblar* (AmL) (b) **furnished** past p ⟨room/apartment⟩ amueblado, amoblado (AmL) [2] (supply) (frml) proporcionar; **to ~ sb WITH sth** ⟨with information⟩ proporcionarle algo a algn

furnishings /'fɜːrnɪʃɪŋz ‖ 'fɜːnɪʃɪŋz/ pl n: mobiliario, cortinas, alfombras

furniture /'fɜːrnɪtʃər ‖ 'fɜːnɪtʃə(r)/ n (in home, office) muebles mpl, mobiliario m; **a piece of ~** un mueble; ⟨before n⟩ **~ mover** o (BrE) **remover** empresa f de mudanzas; **~ polish** cera f para muebles

furor /'fjʊrɔːr ‖ 'fjʊərɔː(r)/, (BrE) **furore** /fjʊə'rɔːri ‖ fjʊəˈrɔːri/ n escándalo m

furrow /'fɜːrəʊ ‖ 'fʌrəʊ/ n surco m

furry /'fɜːri/ adj **-rier, -riest** ⟨animal⟩ peludo; ⟨toy⟩ de peluche; ⟨covering/lining⟩ afelpado

further¹ /'fɜːrðər ‖ 'fɜːðə(r)/ adj [1] comp of FAR¹ 1 (a) (in distance): **they live even ~ away** ellos viven aún más lejos; **how much ~ is it?** ¿cuánto camino nos queda por hacer?; **~ on, there's another set of traffic lights** más adelante, hay otro semáforo (b) (in progress): **the legislation should have gone ~** la legislación debería haber ido ⋯⊹

más lejos; **have you got any ~ with that essay?** ¿has adelantado ese trabajo? **(c)** (in time): **we must look back even ~** tenemos que retroceder aún más en el tiempo; **this vase dates back even ~** este jarrón es aún más antiguo **(d)** (in extent, degree): **I'll look ~ into that possibility** voy a estudiar esa posibilidad más a fondo; **the situation is ~ complicated by her absence** el hecho de que ella no esté complica aún más la situación

2 further to (Corresp) (as prep): **~ to your letter of June 6, ...** con relación a su carta del 6 de junio, ...

3 (furthermore) (as linker) además

further² adj más; **have you any ~ questions?** ¿tienen más preguntas?; **until ~ notice** hasta nuevo aviso

further³ vt ⟨cause/aims⟩ promover*; ⟨career/interests⟩ favorecer*

further education n (BrE) programa de cursos de extensión cultural para adultos

furthermore /ˈfɜːrðərmɔːr ‖ ˌfɜːðəˈmɔː(r)/ adv además

furthest /ˈfɜːrðəst ‖ ˈfɜːðɪst/ adv superl of FAR¹ 1

furtive /ˈfɜːrtɪv ‖ ˈfɜːtɪv/ adj **(a)** (stealthy) ⟨movement/look⟩ furtivo; ⟨person⟩ solapado **(b)** (suspicious, shifty) ⟨appearance⟩ sospechoso; ⟨manner⟩ solapado

furtively /ˈfɜːrtɪvli ‖ ˈfɜːtɪvli/ adv ⟨creep⟩ sigilosamente; ⟨peep/listen⟩ a hurtadillas

fury /ˈfjʊri ‖ ˈfjʊəri/ n (pl **furies**) ira f

fuse¹ /fjuːz/ n **1** (Elec) fusible m, plomo m (Esp), tapón m (CS) **2** (for explosives) mecha f

fuse² vt **1** (Elec) **(a)** (short-circuit) (BrE): **to ~ the**

lights hacer* saltar los fusibles or (CS tb) los tapones, fundir los plomos (Esp) **(b)** **fused** past p con fusible **2** **(a)** (melt together) alear **(b)** (merge) fusionar

fuse box n caja f de fusibles or (Esp tb) de plomos or (CS tb) de tapones

fuselage /ˈfjuːzəlɑːʒ/ n fuselaje m

fusion /ˈfjuːʒən/ n fusión f

fuss¹ /fʌs/ n alboroto m; **to kick up a ~** armar un lío, montar un número (Esp fam); **to make** o (AmE also) **raise a ~** hacer* un escándalo

fuss² vi preocuparse

fussbudget /ˈfʌsˌbʌdʒɪt/, (BrE also) **fusspot** /ˈfʌspɑːt ‖ ˈfʌspɒt/ n maniático, -ca m,f, mañoso, -sa m,f (AmL)

fussy /ˈfʌsi/ adj **-sier, -siest** exigente; **I'm a ~ eater** soy muy maniático or (AmL tb) mañoso para comer

futile /ˈfjuːtl ‖ ˈfjuːtaɪl/ adj ⟨attempt⟩ inútil; ⟨suggestion/question⟩ trivial

futility /fjuˈtɪləti/ n inutilidad f

future¹ /ˈfjuːtʃər ‖ ˈfjuːtʃə(r)/ n **1** (time ahead) **the ~** el futuro; **in ~** de ahora en adelante **2** (prospects) futuro m; **a job with a ~** un trabajo con futuro **3** (Ling) futuro m **4** **futures** pl (Fin) futuros mpl

future² adj (before n) **(a)** ⟨husband/home⟩ futuro **(b)** (Ling): **the ~ tense** el futuro

futuristic /ˈfjuːtʃəˈrɪstɪk/ adj futurista

fuze /fjuːz/ n (AmE) ▶ FUSE¹ 2

fuzzy /ˈfʌzi/ adj **-zier, -ziest** **1** ⟨hair⟩ muy rizado; ⟨beard⟩ enmarañado **2** (blurred) ⟨sound⟩ confuso; ⟨picture/outline⟩ borroso

Gg

G, g /dʒiː/ n **(a)** (letter) G, g f **(b)** (Mus) sol m

g (= **gram(s)**) g., gr.

G (in US) (Cin) (= **general**) apta para todo público

GA, Ga = Georgia

gab /gæb/ vi **-bb-** (colloq) charlar (fam)

gabble /ˈgæbəl/ vi (speak incoherently) hablar atropelladamente, farfullar; (speak quickly) parlotear (fam)

gable /ˈgeɪbəl/ n gablete m; **~ (end)** hastial m

gadget /ˈgædʒət ‖ ˈgædʒɪt/ n (colloq) aparato m, chisme m (Esp fam)

Gaelic /ˈgeɪlɪk/ n gaélico m

gaffe /gæf/ n metedura f or (AmL tb) metida f de pata (fam)

gag¹ /gæg/ n **1** (for mouth) mordaza f **2** (joke) (colloq) chiste m (fam)

gag² **-gg-** vt amordazar*
■ **~** vi hacer* arcadas

gage /geɪdʒ/ vt/n (AmE) ▶ GAUGE¹,²

gaggle /ˈgægəl/ n (of geese) bandada f

gain¹ /geɪn/ vt **1** (acquire) ⟨control⟩ conseguir*; ⟨experience⟩ adquirir*; ⟨recognition⟩ obtener* **2** (increase) ⟨strength/speed⟩ ganar **3** ⟨time⟩ ganar; **my watch is ~ing ten minutes a day** mi reloj (se) adelanta diez minutos por día
■ **~** vi **1 (a)** (improve) **to ~ in value** subir or aumentar de valor; **she's gradually ~ing in confidence** poco a poco va adquiriendo confianza en sí misma **(b)** (benefit) beneficiarse **2 (a)** (go fast) «clock/watch» adelantar(se) **(b)** (move nearer) **to ~ on sb** acortar (las) distancias con respecto a algn

gain² n **1** (profit) ganancia f **2** (increase) aumento m

gainful /ˈgeɪnfəl/ adj retribuido

gait /geɪt/ n (no pl) modo m de andar

gala /ˈgælə, ˈgeɪlə ‖ ˈgɑːlə/ n fiesta f

Galapagos Islands /gəˈlɑːpəgəs ‖ gəˈlæpəgəs/ pl n **the ~ ~** las Islas Galápagos

galaxy /ˈgæləksi/ n (pl **-xies**) galaxia f

gale /geɪl/ n vendaval f; (before n) **~-force winds** vientos mpl (huracanados)

Galicia /gə'lɪʃiə, gə'lɪsiə/ n Galicia f

Galician¹ /gə'lɪʃiən, gə'lɪsiən/ n **(a)** (person) gallego, -ga m,f **(b)** (language) gallego m

Galician² adj gallego

gallant adj **(a)** /'gælənt/ (brave) (liter) aguerrido (liter) **(b)** /gə'lænt/ (chivalrous) galante

gall bladder /gɔːl/ n vesícula f (biliar)

galleon /'gælɪən/ n galeón m

gallery /'gælərɪ/ n (pl **-ries**) **1** (Art) museo m (de Bellas Artes); (commercial) galería f (de arte) **2** (Archit) galería f; (for press, spectators) tribuna f

galley /'gælɪ/ n **1** (ship) galera f **2** (kitchen on boat, plane) cocina f

gallon /'gælən/ n galón m (*EEUU: 3,78 litros, RU: 4,55 litros*)

gallop¹ /'gæləp/ n galope m

gallop² vi galopar

gallows /'gæləʊz/ n (pl ∼) (+ sing o pl vb) horca f

gallstone /'gɔːlstəʊn/ n cálculo m biliar

galore /gə'lɔːr ‖gə'lɔː(r)/ adj (after n) en abundancia

galvanize /'gælvənaɪz/ vt **1** (rouse) to ∼ sb (INTO sth/-ING) impulsar a algn (A algo /+ INF) **2 galvanized** past p ⟨iron/steel⟩ galvanizado

Gambia /'gæmbiə/ n Gambia f

gambit /'gæmbət 'gæmbɪt/ n (stratagem) táctica f; (in chess) gambito m

gamble¹ /'gæmbəl/ vi jugar*; to ∼ on a horse apostar* a un caballo
■ ∼ vt jugarse*

gamble² n (no pl) **(a)** (bet) apuesta f **(b)** (risk): to take a ∼ arriesgarse*

gambler /'gæmblər ‖'gæmblə(r)/ n jugador, -dora m,f

gambling /'gæmblɪŋ/ n juego m

gambol /'gæmbəl/ vi, (BrE) **-ll-** retozar*

game¹ /geɪm/ n **1** **(a)** (amusement) juego m **(b)** (type of sport) deporte m **2** **(a)** (complete match) (Sport) partido m; (in board games, cards) partida f **(b)** (part of tennis, squash match) juego m **3** (underhand scheme, ploy) juego m **4** (in hunting) caza f; **big** ∼ caza mayor **5** (Culin) caza f

game² adj we're going swimming, are you ∼? vamos a nadar ¿te apuntas?; **she's** ∼ **for anything** se apunta a todo

game: ∼**keeper** n guardabosque(s) mf; ∼ **reserve** n coto m de caza; ∼ **show** n programa m concurso

gammon /'gæmən/ n (esp BrE) jamón m fresco

gamut /'gæmət/ n gama f; **to run the (whole)** ∼ **of sth** cubrir* toda la gama de algo

gander /'gændər ‖'gændə(r)/ n (Zool) ganso m (macho)

gang /gæŋ/ n (of criminals) banda f; (of youths, children) pandilla f
■ **gang up** [v + adv] (colloq) to ∼ up AGAINST o ON sb ponerse*/estar* en contra de algn

gang: ∼**land** n (journ) hampa f‡, mundo m del crimen organizado; ∼**plank** n plancha f

gangrene /'gæŋgriːn/ n gangrena f

gangster /'gæŋstər ‖'gæŋstə(r)/ n gángster mf

gangway /'gæŋweɪ/ n **1** (walkway) pasarela f **2** (between rows of seats) (BrE) pasillo m

gantlet /'gɔːntlət/ n (AmE) ▶ GAUNTLET

gaol /dʒeɪl/ n/vt (esp BrE) ▶ JAIL¹, ²

gap /gæp/ n **1** (space) espacio m; (in fence, hedge) hueco m **2** **(a)** (in knowledge) laguna f **(b)** (in time) intervalo m, interrupción f **(c)** (disparity) distancia f, brecha f **(d)** (void) vacío m

gape /geɪp/ vi **1** (stare) mirar boquiabierto **2** (be open) estar* abierto

gaping /'geɪpɪŋ/ adj ⟨wound⟩ abierto; ⟨hole⟩ enorme

garage /gə'rɑːʒ ‖'gærɑːdʒ, -ɪdʒ/ n **1** (for parking) garaje m, garage m (esp AmL) **2** **(a)** (for repairs) taller m (mecánico), garaje m, garage m (esp AmL) **(b)** (for fuel) (BrE) ▶ GAS STATION

garb /gɑːrb ‖gɑːb/ n (liter o hum) atuendo m (liter o hum)

garbage /'gɑːrbɪdʒ ‖'gɑːbɪdʒ/ n **(a)** (AmE) (refuse) basura f; (before n) ∼ **dump** vertedero m (de basuras), basurero m, basural m (AmL) **(b)** (junk) (colloq) trastos mpl, cachivaches mpl (fam), porquerías fpl (fam); **this book is absolute** ∼ este libro es una auténtica porquería

garbage: ∼ **bag** n (AmE) bolsa f de la basura; ∼ **can** n (AmE) cubo m or (CS) tacho m or (Col) caneca f or (Méx) bote m or (Ven) tobo m de la basura; ∼**man** /'gɑːrbɪdʒmæn/ n (pl **-men** /-men/) (AmE) basurero m; ∼ **truck** n (AmE) camión m de la basura

garbled /'gɑːrbəld ‖'gɑːbəld/ adj ⟨account⟩ confuso; ⟨message⟩ incomprensible

garden¹ /'gɑːrdn ‖'gɑːdn/ n **(a)** (for ornamental plants) jardín m; (for vegetables) huerta f, huerto m **(b)** **gardens** pl (public, on private estate) jardines mpl, parque m

garden² vi trabajar en el jardín

garden center, (BrE) **garden centre** n vivero m, centro m de jardinería

gardener /'gɑːrdnər ‖'gɑːdnə(r)/ n jardinero, -ra m,f

gardening /'gɑːrdnɪŋ ‖'gɑːdnɪŋ/ n jardinería f; (vegetable growing) horticultura f; **he does the** ∼ él se encarga del jardín

garden: ∼ **party** n recepción f al aire libre; ∼**-variety** adj (AmE colloq) (before n) vulgar or común y corriente

gargle /'gɑːrgəl ‖'gɑːgəl/ vi hacer* gárgaras

gargoyle /'gɑːrgɔɪl ‖'gɑːgɔɪl/ n gárgola f

garish /'gerɪʃ ‖'geərɪʃ/ adj ⟨color⟩ chillón, charro (AmL fam); ⟨garment⟩ estridente, charro (AmL fam)

garland /'gɑːrlənd ‖'gɑːlənd/ n guirnalda f

garlic /'gɑːrlɪk ‖'gɑːlɪk/ n ajo m

garment /'gɑːrmənt ‖'gɑːmənt/ n prenda f (de ropa)

garnet /'gɑːrnət ‖'gɑːnɪt/ n granate m

garnish¹ /'gɑːrnɪʃ ‖'gɑːnɪʃ/ vt adornar

garnish² n adorno m, aderezo m; (more substantial) guarnición f

garret /'gærət/ n buhardilla f

garrison /'gærəsən ‖'gærɪsən/ n **(a)** (place) plaza f fuerte or de armas **(b)** (troops) guarnición f

garrulous /'gærələs/ adj charlatán

garter /'gɑːrtər ‖'gɑːtə(r)/ n liga f

gas¹ /gæs/ n (pl **gases** or **gasses**) **1** (Phys) ···⟫

gas m [2] (a) (fuel) gas m; (before n) ⟨ring/heater⟩ de or a gas (b) (anesthetic) gas m [3] (gasoline) (AmE) ▶ GASOLINE [4] (flatulence) gases mpl

gas² vt **-ss-** (Mil) gasear; (kill) asfixiar con gas; (in gas chamber) ejecutar en la cámara de gas

gas chamber n cámara f de gas

gaseous /'gæsiəs/ adj gaseoso

gash¹ /gæʃ/ n tajo m, corte m profundo

gash² vt hacer* un tajo en, cortar (profundamente)

gasket /'gæskət ‖'gæskɪt/ n junta f

gas: ∼**light** n (illumination) luz f de gas; ∼ **mask** n máscara f antigás

gasoline /'gæsəliːn/ n (AmE) gasolina f, nafta f (RPl), bencina f (Andes)

gasp¹ /gæsp ‖gɑːsp/ vi (a) (inhale sharply) dar* un grito ahogado (b) (pant) respirar entrecortadamente, jadear
■ ∼ vt decir* jadeando

gasp² n exclamación f, grito m (entrecortado o ahogado)

gas: ∼ **pedal** n (esp AmE) acelerador m; ∼ **pump** n (AmE) (in service station) surtidor m, bomba f bencinera (Andes); ∼ **station** n (AmE) estación f de servicio or (RPl tb) de nafta, gasolinera f, bomba f (Andes, Ven), grifo m (Per); ∼ **tank** n (AmE) depósito m or tanque m de gasolina or (RPl) de nafta or (Andes) de bencina

gastric /'gæstrɪk/ adj gástrico

gastroenteritis /'gæstrəʊˌentə'raɪtəs ‖ˌgæstrəʊˌentə'raɪtɪs/ n gastroenteritis f

gasworks /'gæswɜːrks ‖'gæswɜːks/ n (pl ∼) (+ sing o pl vb) fábrica f de gas

gate /geɪt/ n (a) (to garden — wooden) puerta f (del jardín); (— wrought-iron) verja f, cancela f (Esp); (to field) tranquera f (AmL), portillo m (Esp) (b) (to castle, city) (usu pl) puerta f (c) (controlling admission) entrada f (d) (at airport) puerta f (de embarque)

gate: ∼**crash** vi colarse*; ∼**way** n verja f, portalón m

gather¹ /'gæðər ‖'gæðə(r)/ vi congregarse*, reunirse*
■ ∼ vt [1] (a) (collect) ⟨wood/berries⟩ recoger*, coger* (esp Esp); ⟨information⟩ reunir*, juntar; ⟨people⟩ reunir*; to ∼ **dust** juntar or acumular polvo (b) ⟨thoughts⟩ poner* en orden; ⟨strength⟩ juntar, hacer* acopio de (c) ⟨speed⟩ ir* adquiriendo [2] (conclude) deducir*; I ∼ you're **moving** tengo entendido que te mudas (de casa) [3] (by sewing) fruncir*
■ **gather in** [v + o + adv, v + adv + o] recoger*

gather² n fruncido m, frunce m

gathering¹ /'gæðərɪŋ/ n (meeting) reunión f; (group of people) concurrencia f

gathering² adj (before n) creciente; **the** ∼ **storm** la tormenta que se avecinaba

gaudy /'gɔːdi/ adj chillón, charro (AmL fam)

gauge¹, (AmE also) **gage** /geɪdʒ/ vt (a) (estimate) ⟨size⟩ calcular (b) (judge) ⟨effects⟩ evaluar* (c) (measure) medir*

gauge², (AmE also) **gage** n [1] (instrument) indicador m [2] (measure, indication) indicio m [3] (Rail): **narrow** ∼ vía f estrecha, trocha f angosta (CS)

gaunt /gɔːnt/ adj ⟨person⟩ descarnado, delgado y adusto; (from illness, tiredness) demacrado

gauntlet /'gɔːntlət ‖'gɔːntlɪt/ n guante m (con el puño largo); (of suit of armor) guantelete m, manopla f

gauze /gɔːz/ n (Tex, Med) gasa f; (fine mesh) malla f

gave /geɪv/ past of GIVE¹

gavel /'gævəl/ n mazo m or martillo m (usado por jueces, subastadores etc)

gay /geɪ/ adj [1] (homosexual) gay adj inv [2] (dated) (merry) alegre

gaze¹ /geɪz/ vi mirar (larga y fijamente); **to** ∼ **AT sth/sb** mirar algo/a algn

gaze² n mirada f (larga y fija)

gazelle /gə'zel/ n (pl ∼**s** or ∼) gacela f

gazette /gə'zet/ n gaceta f

gazetteer /ˌgæzə'tɪr ‖ˌgæzə'tɪə(r)/ n índice m geográfico

GB = **Great Britain**

GCSE n (in UK) = **General Certificate of Secondary Education** ≈ bachillerato m elemental (exámenes que se toman en diferentes asignaturas alrededor de los 16 años)

gear¹ /gɪr ‖'gɪə(r)/ n [1] (Mech Eng) engranaje m; (Auto) marcha f, velocidad f, cambio m; **to shift** o (BrE) **change** ∼ cambiar de marcha, cambiar de velocidad, hacer* un cambio [2] (a) (equipment) equipo m; (tools) herramientas fpl; (fishing ∼) aparejo(s) m(pl) de pesca (b) (miscellaneous items) (colloq) cosas fpl

gear² vt orientar; (to be) ∼ed **TO/TOWARD sth/sb** (estar*) dirigido A algo/algn
■ **gear up** [1] [v + adv] (prepare) prepararse [2] [v + o + adv, v + adv + o] preparar

gearbox /'gɪrbɑːks ‖'gɪəbɒks/ n (Auto) caja f de cambios or velocidades

gee /dʒiː/ interj (AmE colloq): ∼, **I'm sorry to hear that** oye, lo siento; ∼, **thanks!** ¡pero … gracias!

geese /giːs/ pl of GOOSE

gel¹ /dʒel/ n gel m

gel² vi **-ll-** (a) ⟨liquid⟩ gelificarse* (b) (BrE) ⟨plans/ideas⟩ cuajar

gelatin /'dʒelətn ‖'dʒelətɪn/, **gelatine** /'dʒeləˌtiːn/ n gelatina f

gem /dʒem/ n (a) (stone) gema f, piedra f preciosa/semipreciosa; (jewel) joya f, alhaja f (b) (wonderful example) joya f

Gemini /'dʒemənaɪ, -niː ‖'dʒemɪnaɪ, -niː/ n (a) (sign) (no art) Géminis (b) (person) Géminis or géminis mf, geminiano, -na m,f

gender /'dʒendər ‖'dʒendə(r)/ n (a) (Ling) género m (b) (sex) sexo m

gene /dʒiːn/ n gen m, gene m

genealogy /ˌdʒiːni'ælədʒi/ n genealogía f

general¹ /'dʒenrəl/ adj [1] (not detailed or specific)

AmC	América Central		Arg	Argentina
AmL	América Latina		Bol	Bolivia
AmS	América del Sur		Chi	Chile
Andes	Región andina		CS	Cono Sur

Cu	Cuba		Per	Perú
Ec	Ecuador		RPl	Río de la Plata
Esp	España		Ur	Uruguay
Méx	México		Ven	Venezuela

general; **in ~** en general **2** (widespread) ⟨*tendency*⟩ generalizado **3** (usual) general; **as a ~ rule** por lo general, por regla general **4** (chief) ⟨*manager*⟩ general **5** (Med) ⟨*anesthetic*⟩ general

general² n (Mil) general *mf*

general: ~ delivery n (AmE) lista f de correos, poste f restante (AmL); **~ election** n elecciones *fpl* generales

generalization /'dʒenrələ'zeɪʃən ‖,dʒenrələ'zeɪʃən/ n generalización f

generalize /'dʒenrəlaɪz/ *vi/t* generalizar*

general knowledge n cultura f general

generally /'dʒenrəli/ adv **(a)** (usually, as a rule) generalmente, por lo general **(b)** (broadly) ⟨*indep*⟩ **~ (speaking)** por lo general, en general **(c)** (as a whole) en general

general: ~ practitioner n médico, -ca *m,f* de medicina general; **~ public** n the **~ public** el público en general, el gran público; **~-purpose** adj ⟨*tool*⟩ para todo uso; ⟨*dictionary*⟩ de uso general; **~ store** n (AmE) tienda f (*que vende todo tipo de artículos en una comunidad pequeña*), almacén m (CS); **~ strike** n huelga f general, paro m general (AmL)

generate /'dʒenəreɪt/ *vt* generar

generation /'dʒenə'reɪʃən/ n **1** generación f; **the older ~** la gente de más edad; **first-~ computers** computadoras *fpl* or (Esp tb) ordenadores *mpl* de primera generación **2** (act of generating) generación f

generation gap n brecha f generacional

generator /'dʒenəreɪtə(r)/ n generador m, grupo m electrógeno

generic /dʒə'nerɪk/ adj ⟨*term*⟩ genérico

generosity /'dʒenə'rɑːsəti ‖,dʒenə'rɒsəti/ n generosidad f

generous /'dʒenrəs ‖'dʒenərəs/ adj **(a)** (open-handed) generoso **(b)** (ample, large) abundante, generoso

genetic /dʒə'netɪk ‖dʒɪ'netɪk/ adj genético

genetically /dʒə'netɪkli/ adv genéticamente; **~ modified** transgénico, genéticamente modificado

genetics /dʒə'netɪks ‖dʒɪ'netɪks/ n (+ *sing vb*) genética f

genial /'dʒiːnjəl ‖'dʒiːniəl/ adj ⟨*person*⟩ simpático; ⟨*welcome/smile*⟩ cordial

genie /'dʒiːni/ n genio m

genitals /'dʒenətlz ‖'dʒenɪtlz/ *pl* n genitales *mpl*

genius /'dʒiːniəs/ n **1** (clever person) genio m **2** (brilliance) genialidad f

genre /'ʒɑːnrə ‖ʒɒnrə/ n género m

gent /dʒent/ n (BrE colloq) caballero m; **Ⓢ Gents** Caballeros

gentle /'dʒentl/ adj **gentler** /'dʒentlər ‖'dʒentlə(r)/, **gentlest** /'dʒentləst ‖'dʒentlɪst/ **1 (a)** ⟨*person*⟩ dulce; ⟨*character*⟩ suave **(b)** (of voice): **in a ~ voice** en un tono suave or dulce **2** ⟨*murmur/breeze*⟩ suave; ⟨*exercise*⟩ moderado; ⟨*slope*⟩ poco empinado; ⟨*reminder*⟩ discreto

gentleman /'dʒentlmən/ n (pl **-men** /-mən/) **(a)** (man) caballero m, señor m **(b)** (well-bred man) caballero m

gently /'dʒentli/ adv **(a)** (not roughly or violently)

⟨*handle*⟩ con cuidado; ⟨*tap*⟩ ligeramente; ⟨*hint*⟩ con tacto **(b)** (tenderly) dulcemente; (tactfully) con delicadeza

gentry /'dʒentri/ n (+ *sing o pl vb*) alta burguesía f, pequeña nobleza f

genuine /'dʒenjuən ‖'dʒenjɔɪn/ adj **(a)** ⟨*interest/person*⟩ genuino, sincero; ⟨*inquiry/buyer/mistake*⟩ serio; **it was a ~ mistake** fue realmente un error **(b)** ⟨*antique*⟩ auténtico; ⟨*leather*⟩ legítimo

genuinely /'dʒenjuənli ‖'dʒenjuɪmli/ adv **(a)** (sincerely) sinceramente **(b)** (really) realmente

geographical /'dʒiːə'græfɪkəl ‖,dʒiə'græfɪkəl/ adj geográfico

geography /dʒi'ɑːgrəfi ‖dʒɪ'ɒgrəfi/ n geografía f

geological /'dʒiːə'lɑːdʒɪkəl ‖,dʒiə'lɒdʒɪkəl/ adj geológico

geologist /dʒi'ɑːlədʒəst ‖dʒi'ɒlədʒɪst/ n geólogo, -ga *m,f*

geology /dʒi'ɑːlədʒi ‖dʒi'ɒlədʒi/ n geología f

geometrical /'dʒiːə'metrɪkəl ‖,dʒiə'metrɪkəl/ adj geométrico

geometry /dʒi'ɑːmətri ‖dʒi'ɒmətri/ n geometría f

Georgia /'dʒɔːrdʒə ‖'dʒɔːdʒə/ n **(a)** (republic in the Caucasus) Georgia f **(b)** (US state) Georgia f

Georgian¹ /'dʒɔːrdʒən ‖'dʒɔːdʒən/ adj **(a)** (of Georgia in the Caucasus) georgiano **(b)** (of Georgia in USA) georgiano **(c)** (in architecture, UK history) georgiano

Georgian² n **(a)** (from the Caucasus) georgiano, -na *m,f* **(b)** (language) georgiano m **(c)** (from USA) georgiano, -na *m,f*

geriatric /'dʒeri'ætrɪk/ adj (Med) ⟨*patient*⟩ anciano; ⟨*ward*⟩ de geriatría

geriatrician /,dʒeriə'trɪʃən/ n geriatra *mf*

germ /dʒɜːrm ‖dʒɜːm/ n **1** (Med) microbio m, germen m **2** (Biol, Bot) germen m

German¹ /'dʒɜːrmən ‖'dʒɜːmən/ adj alemán

German² n **(a)** (language) alemán m **(b)** (person) alemán, -mana *m,f*

German: ~ measles n (+ *sing vb*) rubéola f, rubeola f; **~ shepherd (dog)** n pastor m or (CS) ovejero m alemán

Germany /'dʒɜːrməni ‖'dʒɜːməni/ n Alemania f

germinate /'dʒɜːrməneɪt ‖'dʒɜːmɪneɪt/ *vi* germinar

gerund /'dʒerənd/ n gerundio m

gestation /dʒe'steɪʃən/ n gestación f

gesticulate /dʒe'stɪkjəleɪt ‖dʒe'stɪkjʊleɪt/ *vi* gesticular

gesture¹ /'dʒestʃər ‖'dʒestʃə(r)/ n **(a)** (of body) gesto m, ademán m **(b)** (token, expression) gesto m; **a ~ of good will** un gesto de buena voluntad; **it was a nice ~** fue todo un detalle

gesture² *vi* hacer* gestos

get /get/ (*pres p* **getting**; *past* **got**; *past p* **got** or (AmE also) **gotten**) *vt*

I ▪ 1 (a) (obtain) conseguir*, obtener*; ⟨*job/staff*⟩ conseguir*; ⟨*idea*⟩ sacar*; **where did you ~ that beautiful rug?** ¿dónde conseguiste esa alfombra tan preciosa? **(b)** (buy) comprar; **I got it from Harrods** lo compré en Harrods **(c)** (achieve, win) ⟨*prize/grade*⟩ sacar*, obtener* (fml) **(d)** (on the ⋯▷

telephone) ⟨person⟩ lograr comunicarse con; **you've got the wrong number** se ha equivocado de número

2 (a) (receive) ⟨letter/reward/reprimand⟩ recibir; **I got a stereo for my birthday** me regalaron un estéreo para mi cumpleaños **(b)** (be paid) ⟨salary/pay⟩ ganar; **I got £200 for the piano** me dieron 200 libras por el piano **(c)** (experience) ⟨shock/surprise⟩ llevarse; **I ~ the feeling that …** tengo la sensación de que … **(d)** (suffer): **how did you ~ that bump on your head?** ¿cómo te hiciste ese chichón en la cabeza?

3 (fetch) ⟨hammer/scissors⟩ traer*, ir* a buscar; ⟨doctor/plumber⟩ llamar; **~ your coat** anda *or* vete a buscar tu abrigo

4 (take hold of) agarrar, coger* (esp Esp) **(b)** (catch, trap) pillar (fam), agarrar (AmL), coger* (esp Esp)

5 (contract) ⟨cold/flu⟩ agarrar, pescar* (fam), pillar (fam), coger* (esp Esp)

6 (catch) ⟨bus/train⟩ tomar, coger* (Esp)

7 (colloq) **(a)** (irritate) fastidiar **(b)** (puzzle): **what ~s me is how …** lo que no entiendo es cómo …

8 (a) (understand) (colloq) entender*; **don't ~ me wrong** no me malentiendas **(b)** (take note of): **did you ~ the number?** ¿tomaste nota del número?

9 (possess) **to have got** ▶ HAVE *vt*

II 1 (bring, move, put) (+ *adv compl*): **we'll ~ it there by two o'clock** lo tendremos allí antes de las dos; **they couldn't ~ it up the stairs** no lo pudieron subir por las escaleras

2 (cause to be) (+ *adj compl*): **he got the children ready** preparó a los niños; **I can't ~ the window open** no puedo abrir la ventana; **they got their feet wet** se mojaron los pies

3 to ~ sb/sth + *pp* (a) (with action carried out by subject): **we must ~ some work done** tenemos que trabajar un poco; **to ~ oneself organized** organizarse* **(b)** (with action carried out by somebody else): **he got the house painted** hizo pintar la casa; **I must ~ this watch fixed** tengo que llevar a *or* (AmL tb) mandar a arreglar este reloj

4 (arrange, persuade, force) **to ~ sb/sth to + INF**: **I'll ~ him to help you** (order) le diré que te ayude; (ask) le pediré que te ayude; (persuade) lo convenceré de que te ayude; **I can't ~ it to work** no puedo hacerlo funcionar

■ **~ vi 1** (reach) (+ *adv compl*) llegar*; **can you ~ there by train?** ¿se puede ir en tren?

2 (become): **to ~ tired** cansarse; **to ~ dressed** vestirse*; **he got very angry** se puso furioso; ▶ MARRIED, COLD *etc*

3 to ~ to + INF (a) (come to) llegar* a + INF; **I never really got to know him** nunca llegué a conocerlo de verdad **(b)** (have opportunity to): **in this job you ~ to meet many interesting people** en este trabajo uno tiene la oportunidad de conocer a mucha gente interesante; **when do we ~ to open the presents?** ¿cuándo podemos abrir los regalos?

4 (start) **to ~ -ING** empezar* a + INF, ponerse* a + INF

■ **get about** [*v + adv*] [*v + prep + o*] (BrE) ▶ GET AROUND I 1

■ **get above** [*v + prep + o*]: **to ~ above oneself** llenarse de ínfulas

■ **get across 1** [*v + prep + o*] [*v + adv*] (cross) ⟨river⟩ atravesar*, cruzar*; ⟨road⟩ cruzar*

2 [*v + o + adv, v + adv + o*] ⟨meaning/concept⟩ hacer* entender

3 [*v + adv*] (be understood) «teacher/speaker» hacerse* entender

■ **get ahead** [*v + adv*] **(a)** (get in front) «student/worker» adelantar **(b)** (progress, succeed) progresar

■ **get along** [*v + adv*] **1** (manage, cope) arreglárselas

2 (progress) «work/patient» marchar, andar*; **he's ~ting along just fine at school** le va muy bien en el colegio

3 (be on good terms) **to ~ along (WITH sb)** llevarse bien (CON algn)

■ **get around**

I 1 [*v + adv*] **(a)** (walk, move about) caminar, andar*; (using transport, car) desplazarse* **(b)** (travel) viajar **(c)** (circulate): **it *o* word got around that …** pronto corrió el rumor de que …

2 [*v + prep + o*] (gather in circle): **we can't all ~ around this table** no cabemos todos alrededor de esta mesa

II [*v + prep + o*] **(a)** (avoid, circumvent) ⟨difficulty/obstacle⟩ sortear, evitar; ⟨rule/law⟩ eludir el cumplimiento de **(b)** (persuade) ⟨person⟩ engatusar

III [*v + adv*] (go) ir*; (come) venir*

■ **get around to** [*v + adv + prep + o*]: **I meant to write to you, I just never got around to it** tenía intenciones de escribirte pero nunca llegué a hacerlo; **I must ~ around to writing those letters** debo ponerme a escribir esas cartas

■ **get at** [*v + prep + o*] **1 (a)** (reach) ⟨pipe/wire⟩ llegar* a **(b)** (ascertain) ⟨facts/truth⟩ establecer*

2 (nag, criticize) (colloq) criticar*, meterse con (fam)

3 (hint at, mean) (colloq): **what are you ~ting at?** ¿qué quieres decir?

■ **get away** [*v + adv*] **1** (escape) escaparse

2 (leave) salir* **(b)** (go on vacation) irse* de vacaciones; **to ~ away from it all** alejarse del mundanal ruido

■ **get away with** [*v + adv + prep + o*] **1** (make off with) llevarse, escaparse con

2 (a) (go unpunished for): **you won't ~ away with this** esto no va a quedar así; **don't let them ~ away with it** no dejes que se salgan con la suya **(b)** (be let off with) ⟨fine/warning⟩ escaparse *or* librarse con

■ **get back 1** [*v + adv*] **(a)** (return) volver*, regresar; (arrive home) llegar* (a casa) **(b)** (retreat): **~ back!** ¡atrás!

2 [*v + o + adv, v + adv + o*] (regain possession of) ⟨property⟩ recuperar; ⟨health⟩ recobrar; **we never got our money back** nos devolvieron el dinero

■ **get behind 1** [*v + adv*] (fall behind) **to ~ behind (WITH sth)** atrasarse (CON algo)

2 [*v + prep + o*] (move to rear of) ponerse* detrás de; (fall behind) rezagarse*, quedarse atrás

■ **get by** [*v + adv*] (manage) arreglárselas; **I speak enough French to ~ by** me defiendo en francés; **to ~ by ON sth** arreglárselas CON algo

■ **get down 1** [*v + adv*] **(a)** (descend) bajar **(b)** (crouch) agacharse

2 [*v + o + adv, v + adv + o*] **(a)** (take, lift, bring down) bajar **(b)** (write down) anotar, tomar nota de

3 [*v + o + adv*] **(a)** (reduce) ⟨costs/inflation⟩ reducir*; ⟨blood pressure⟩ bajar **(b)** (depress) deprimir

4 [v + prep + o] (descend) ‹stairs› bajar; ‹ladder› bajarse de; ‹rope› bajar por

■ **get down to** [v + adv + prep + o] (start work on) ponerse* a

■ **get in** **1** (a) [v + adv] (enter) entrar (b) [v + prep + o] ▶ GET INTO 1A

2 [v + adv] (a) (arrive) «person/train» llegar* (b) (gain admission to, be selected for) entrar, ser* admitido (c) (be elected) (Pol) ganar, resultar elegido

3 [v + o + adv, v + adv + o] (a) (bring in, collect up) ‹washing/chairs› entrar; ‹harvest› recoger* (b) (buy, obtain) (BrE) ‹wood/coal/food› aprovisionarse de (c) (call out) ‹doctor/plumber› llamar (d) (interpose) ‹blow/kick› dar*; ‹remark› hacer*

■ **get into** **1** [v + prep + o] (a) (enter) ‹house› entrar en or (AmL tb) a; ‹car› subir a; ‹hole› meterse en (b) (arrive at) ‹station/office› llegar* a (c) (be selected for, elected to) ‹college/club/Congress› entrar en or (AmL tb) a (d) (put on) ‹coat/robe› ponerse*; (fit into) I can't ~ into this dress any more este vestido ya no me entra (e) (into a given state): to ~ into a rage/a mess ponerse* furioso/meterse en un lío; (f) (affect): I don't know what's got into him lately no sé qué le pasa últimamente

2 [v + o + prep + o] (a) (bring, take, put in) meter (b) (involve): you got me into this tú me metiste en esto

■ **get off** **1** [v + adv] [v + prep + o] (a) (alight, dismount) bajarse; to ~ off a train/horse/bicycle bajarse de un tren/de un caballo/de una bicicleta (b) (remove oneself from) ‹flowerbed/lawn› salir* de (c) (finish) ‹work/school› salir* de

2 [v + adv] (a) (leave) «person/letter» salir* (b) (escape unpunished) «person accused» salir* libre; he got off lightly o (AmE also) easy no recibió el castigo que se merecía; he got off with a fine se escapó con solo una multa

3 [v + prep + o] (a) (get up from) ‹floor› levantarse de (b) (deviate from) ‹track/tourist routes› salir* or alejarse de; ‹point› desviarse* or irse* de; I tried to ~ him off the subject intenté hacerlo cambiar de tema (c) (evade) ‹duty› librarse or salvarse de

4 [v + o + adv] (remove) ‹lid/top/stain› quitar

5 [v + o + adv] (send, see off): we got the children off to school mandamos a los niños a la escuela

6 (save from punishment) salvar

■ **get on**

I [v + adv] **1** (move on) seguir* adelante; to ~ on TO sth pasar A algo; ~ on with what you're doing sigue con lo que estás haciendo

2 (a) (fare): how's Joe ~ting on nowadays? ¿qué tal anda Joe?; how did he ~ on at the interview? ¿cómo le fue en la entrevista? (b) (succeed) tener* éxito; to ~ on in life tener éxito en la vida

3 (be friends, agree) to ~ on (WITH sb) llevarse bien (CON algn)

4 (in -ing form) (a) (in time) it's ~ting on se está haciendo tarde (b) (in age): she's ~ting on (in years) está vieja, ya no es joven

II [v + adv] (climb on, board) subirse; to ~ on the bus/a horse subirse al autobús/subirse a un caballo

III [v + o + adv] [v + o + prep + o] (place, fix on) poner; I can't ~ the top on (it) no puedo ponerle la tapa

IV [v + o + adv] (put on) ‹clothes› ponerse*

■ **get on for** [v + adv + prep + o] (approach) (BrE) (usu in -ing form): it's ~ting on for six o'clock van a ser las seis; he must be ~ting on for 40 debe (de) andar rondando los 40

■ **get onto** [v + prep + o] **1** (a) (contact) ‹person/department› ponerse* en contacto con (b) (begin discussing) ‹subject› empezar* a hablar de

2 (mount, board) ‹table/bus/train› subirse a; ‹horse/bicycle› montarse en

■ **get out**

I [v + adv] **1** (a) (of car, bus, train) bajar(se); (of hole) salir*; (of bath) salir*; to ~ out of bed levantarse (de la cama) (b) (of room, country) salir*; ~ out! ¡fuera (de aquí)!

2 (a) (escape) ‹animal/prisoner› escaparse (b) (become known) «news/truth» saberse*

II [v + o + adv, v + adv + o] (a) (remove, extract) ‹stopper/nail› sacar*; ‹stain› quitar, sacar* (esp AmL) (b) (take out) ‹knife/map› sacar* (c) (withdraw) ‹money› sacar* (d) (borrow) ‹library book› sacar*

III [v + o + adv] **1** (remove) ‹tenant› echar; ~ that dog out of here! ¡saquen (a) ese perro de aquí!; I can't ~ you out of this mess no te puedo sacar de este lío

2 (send for) ‹doctor/repairman› llamar

■ **get out of** **1** [v + adv + prep + o] (a) (avoid) ‹obligation› librarse or salvarse de; to ~ out of -ING librarse or salvarse de + INF (b) (give up): you must ~ out of that bad habit tienes que sacarte esa mala costumbre; I'd got out of the habit of setting my alarm clock había perdido la costumbre de poner el despertador

2 [v + o + adv + prep + o] (a) (extract) ‹information/truth› sonsacar*, sacar* (b) (derive, gain) ‹money/profit› sacar*

■ **get over** **1** [v + prep + o] ‹river/chasm› cruzar*; ‹wall/fence› pasar por encima de; ‹hill/ridge› atravesar*; ‹obstacle› superar

2 [v + prep + o] ‹loss/tragedy/difficulty› superar; ‹illness/shock› reponerse* de; he's very disappointed — he'll ~ over it ha quedado muy decepcionado — ya se le pasará

3 [v + o + adv] (cause to come, take): ~ those documents over to Wall Street right away manda esos documentos a Wall Street enseguida; to ~ sth over with: I'd like to ~ it over with as quickly as possible quisiera salir de eso or quitarme eso de encima lo más pronto posible

4 [v + o + adv] (communicate) ‹emotion› comunicar*

■ **get past** **1** [v + adv] (move past) pasar

2 [v + prep + o] (a) (move past) ‹vehicle› pasar, adelantarse a; ‹opponent/attacker› eludir (b) (get beyond) ‹obstacle› superar; ‹semifinals› pasar

■ **get round** (esp BrE) ▶ GET AROUND

■ **get through**

I [v + prep + o] [v + adv] (a) (pass through) ‹gap/hole› pasar por (b) (ordeal) superar; ‹winter/difficult time› pasar (c) (Sport) ‹heat› pasar

II [v + adv] **1** (a) (reach destination) «supplies/messenger» llegar* a destino; «news/report» llegar* (b) (on the telephone) to ~ through (TO sb/sth) comunicarse* (CON algn/algo) (c) (make understand): am I ~ting through to you? ¿me entiendes?; I can't ~ through to him no logro hacerme entender con él

2 (finish) (AmE) terminar, acabar

III [v + prep + o] **(a)** (use up) (BrE) ⟨money⟩ gastarse; ⟨materials⟩ usar; ⟨shoes⟩ destrozar* **(b)** (deal with): **I've only got ten more pages to ∼ through** me quedan solo diez páginas por leer (or estudiar etc)
IV [v + o + adv] [v + o + prep + o] (bring through) pasar; **to ∼ sth through customs** pasar algo por la aduana
V [v + o + adv] **(a)** (send) ⟨supplies/message⟩ hacer* llegar **(b)** (make understood) hacer* entender

■ **get together** **1** [v + adv] **(a)** (meet up) reunirse*, quedar (Esp); (have a family reunion) juntarse, reunirse* **(b)** (join forces) «nations/unions» unirse **(c)** (become couple, team) (colloq) juntarse
2 [v + o + adv, v + adv + o] (assemble) ⟨people/money⟩ reunir*; **∼ your things together** junta or recoge tus cosas

■ **get up** **1** [v + prep + o] [v + adv] (climb up) subir; **to ∼ up ON sth** subir(se) A algo
2 [v + adv] **(a)** (out of bed) levantarse **(b)** (stand up) levantarse
3 [v + o + adv] (raise, lift) ⟨person⟩ levantar
4 [v + o + adv, v + adv + o] (develop, arouse) ⟨appetite/enthusiasm⟩ despertar*; ⟨speed⟩ agarrar, coger* (esp Esp); **she didn't want to ∼ their hopes up** no quería despertarles or darles esperanzas

■ **get up to** [v + adv + prep + o] **1** (reach): **when he got up to them ...** cuando los alcanzó ...; **we got up to page 161** llegamos hasta la página 161
2 (be involved in) (colloq) hacer*; **to ∼ up to mischief** hacer* travesuras or de las suyas

get: **∼away** n huida f, fuga f; **to make one's ∼away** escaparse, huir*; **∼together** n (colloq) reunión f

geyser /'gaɪzər ‖'giːzə(r)/ n (Geog) géiser m

Ghana /'gɑːnə/ n Ghana f

Ghanaian /gɑː'neɪən/ adj ghanés

ghastly /'gæstli ‖'gɑːstli/ adj **(a)** (very bad, awful) (colloq) espantoso, horrendo (fam) **(b)** (horrible, hideous) horrible, espantoso

gherkin /'gɜːrkən ‖'gɜːkɪn/ n pepinillo m

ghetto /'getəʊ/ n (pl -tos or -toes) gueto m

ghost /gəʊst/ n fantasma m, espíritu m

ghostly /'gəʊstli/ adj -lier, -liest fantasmal, fantasmagórico

ghoul /guːl/ n **(a)** (person) morboso, -sa m,f **(b)** (evil spirit) demonio m necrófago

GI n (colloq) soldado m estadounidense

giant¹ /'dʒaɪənt/ n gigante, -ta m,f

giant² adj (before n) ⟨organization⟩ gigantesco; ⟨insect⟩ gigante; ⟨stride⟩ gigantesco

gibber /'dʒɪbər ‖'dʒɪbə(r)/ vi farfullar

gibberish /'dʒɪbərɪʃ/ n galimatías m; **to talk ∼** decir* sandeces (fam)

gibe /dʒaɪb/ n pulla f

giblets /'dʒɪbləts ‖'dʒɪblɪts/ pl n menudillos mpl, menudos mpl

Gibraltar /dʒə'brɔːltər ‖dʒɪ'brɔːltə(r)/ n Gibraltar

giddy /'gɪdi/ adj **-dier, -diest** ⟨sensation⟩ de mareo or aturdimiento; **to feel ∼** sentirse* mareado

gift /gɪft/ n **1** (present) regalo m; **it was a ∼** me lo regalaron, es un regalo **2** (talent) don m; **she has a ∼ for poetry** tiene talento para la poesía

gift certificate n (AmE) vale m (canjeable por artículos en una tienda), cheque regalo m

gifted /'gɪftəd ‖'gɪftɪd/ adj ⟨person⟩ de talento, talentoso

gift: **∼ token**, **∼ voucher** n (BrE) ▶ GIFT CERTIFICATE; **∼-wrap** vt **-pp-** envolver* para regalo or (frml) obsequio

gig /gɪg/ n (sl) actuación f

gigabyte /'gɪgəbaɪt/ n gigabyte m

gigantic /dʒaɪ'gæntɪk/ adj gigantesco; ⟨success/appetite⟩ enorme; ⟨effort⟩ titánico

giggle¹ /'gɪgəl/ vi reírse* tontamente

giggle² n risita f

gild /gɪld/ vt dorar

gill n **1** /dʒɪl/ medida para líquidos equivalente a la cuarta parte de una pinta o 0,142 l **2** /gɪl/ (Zool) agalla f, branquia f

gilt /gɪlt/ n dorado m

gimmick /'gɪmɪk/ n **(a)** (ingenious idea, device) truco m **(b)** (catch, snag) (AmE) trampa f

gin /dʒɪn/ n ginebra f, gin m

ginger¹ /'dʒɪndʒər ‖'dʒɪndʒə(r)/ n jengibre m

ginger² adj ⟨hair⟩ color zanahoria; ⟨cat⟩ rojizo

ginger: **∼ ale** n ginger ale m, refresco m de jengibre; **∼ beer** n cerveza f de jengibre; **∼bread** n (cake) pan m de jengibre; (cookie) galleta f de jengibre

gipsy, Gipsy /'dʒɪpsi/ n ▶ GYPSY

giraffe /dʒə'ræf ‖dʒɪ'rɑːf/ n jirafa f

girder /'gɜːrdər ‖'gɜːdə(r)/ n viga f (de metal)

girdle /'gɜːrdl̩ ‖'gɜːdl̩/ n faja f

girl /gɜːrl ‖gɜːl/ n **1** **(a)** (baby, child) niña f, nena f (esp RPI) **(b)** (young woman) chica f, muchacha f **2** (daughter) hija f, niña f

girl: **∼friend** n **(a)** (of man) novia f **(b)** (of woman) (esp AmE) amiga f; (in lesbian couple) compañera f; **∼ guide** (BrE) ▶ GIRL SCOUT

girlish /'gɜːrlɪʃ ‖'gɜːlɪʃ/ adj de niña

girl scout n (AmE) guía f (de los scouts), exploradora f

giro /'dʒaɪrəʊ/ n (pl -ros) (in UK) (system) transferencia f, giro m

girth /gɜːrθ ‖gɜːθ/ n **1** (of person, object) circunferencia f **2** (Equ) cincha f

gist /dʒɪst/ n lo esencial; **to get the ∼ of sth** captar lo esencial de algo

give¹ /gɪv/ (past **gave**; past p **given**) vt
I **1** **(a)** (hand, pass) dar*; **∼ her/me/them a glass of water** dale/dame/dales un vaso de agua **(b)** (as gift) regalar; **to ∼ sb a present** hacerle* un regalo a algn, regalarle algo a algn **(c)** (donate) dar*, donar **(d)** (dedicate, devote) ⟨love/affection⟩ dar*;

⟨attention⟩ prestar; **I'll ~ it some thought** lo pensaré **(e)** (sacrifice) ⟨life⟩ dar*, entregar* **(f)** ⟨injection/sedative⟩ dar*, administrar (frml)

2 **(a)** (supply, grant) ⟨help⟩ dar*, brindar; ⟨idea⟩ dar* **(b)** (allow, concede) ⟨opportunity/permission⟩ dar*, conceder (frml)

3 **(a)** (cause) ⟨pleasure/shock⟩ dar*; ⟨cough⟩ dar* **(b)** (yield) ⟨results/fruit⟩ dar*

4 **(a)** (award, allot) ⟨title/authority/right⟩ dar*, otorgar* (frml); ⟨contract⟩ dar*, adjudicar*; ⟨mark⟩ dar*, poner* **(b)** (entrust) ⟨task/responsibility⟩ dar*, confiar*

5 (pay, exchange) dar*; **I'd ~ anything for a cigarette** no sé qué daría por un cigarrillo

6 (care) (colloq): **I don't ~ a damn** me importa un bledo (fam)

II **1** (convey, state) ⟨apologies/information⟩ dar*; **she gave a detailed description of the place** describió el lugar detalladamente

2 (make sound, movement) ⟨cry/jump⟩ dar*; ⟨laugh⟩ soltar*

3 (indicate) ⟨speed/temperature⟩ señalar

4 (hold) ⟨party/dinner⟩ dar*, ofrecer* (frml); ⟨concert⟩ dar*; ⟨speech⟩ decir*

■ ~ *vi* **1** **(a)** (yield under pressure) ceder, dar* de sí **(b)** (break, give way) «planks/branch» romperse* **2** (make gift) dar*; **to ~ to charity** dar* dinero a organizaciones de caridad

■ **give away** [*v + o + adv, v + adv + o*] **1** **(a)** (free of charge) regalar **(b)** ⟨prizes⟩ hacer* entrega de

2 **(a)** (disclose) revelar; **he didn't ~ anything away** no dejó entrever nada **(b)** (betray) delatar **3** ⟨bride⟩ entregar* en matrimonio

■ **give back** [*v + o + adv, v + adv + o*] devolver*

■ **give in** [*v + adv*] (surrender, succumb) ceder; (in guessing games) rendirse*; **we will not ~ in to terrorists** no vamos a ceder frente a los terroristas

■ **give off** [*v + adv + o*] ⟨smell/fumes⟩ despedir*, largar* (RPl fam); ⟨heat⟩ dar*; ⟨radiation⟩ emitir

■ **give out** **1** [*v + o + adv, v + adv + o*] ⟨leaflets⟩ repartir, distribuir*

2 [*v + adv + o*] **(a)** (let out) ⟨cry/yell⟩ dar* **(b)** (emit) ⟨heat⟩ dar*; ⟨signal⟩ emitir

■ **give up**

I [*v + o + adv, v + adv + o*] **1** **(a)** (renounce, cease from) ⟨alcohol⟩ dejar; ⟨fight⟩ abandonar; **to ~ up hope** perder* las esperanzas; **to ~ up -ING** dejar DE + INF **(b)** (relinquish, hand over) ⟨territory/position⟩ ceder; **to ~ up one's seat for sb** cederle el asiento a algn

2 (surrender): **to ~ oneself up** entregarse*

II [*v + adv*] **(a)** (cease fighting, trying) rendirse*; **I've ~n up on them** yo con ellos no insisto más, no pierdo más tiempo **(b)** (stop doing sth) dejar

III [*v + o + adv*] (abandon hope for): **to ~ sb up for lost** dar* a algn por desaparecido

give² *n* elasticidad *f*

give: **~-and-take** */*gɪvən'teɪk/ *n* concesiones *fpl* mutuas, toma y daca *m*; **~away** *n*
1 (evidence): **her accent is a real ~away** el acento la delata *or* (fam) la vende; **2** **(a)** (free gift) regalo *m*; (before *n*) **at ~away prices** a precio de regalo **(b)** (sth easily done, obtained): **the last question was a ~away** la última pregunta estaba regalada *or* tirada (fam)

given¹ */*gɪvən/ *past p of* GIVE¹

given² *adj* ⟨amount/time⟩ determinado, dado

given³ *prep* **1** (in view of) dado **2** (as conj) ~ (THAT) dado que

given name *n* (AmE) nombre *m* de pila

glacé */*glæ'seɪ ‖'glæseɪ/ *adj* (before *n*) glaseado

glacier */*'gleɪʃər ‖'glæsɪə(r), 'gleɪsɪə(r)/ *n* glaciar *m*

glad */*glæd/ *adj* **-dd-** (pred) **to be ~** (ABOUT sth) alegrarse DE algo; **to be ~** (THAT) alegrarse DE QUE (+ subj); **I'm only too ~ to help** es un placer poder ser útil

gladden */*'glædn/ *vt* (liter) llenar de alegría *or* (liter) de gozo

gladly */*'glædli/ *adv* con mucho gusto

glamor */*'glæmər ‖'glæmə(r)/ *n* (AmE) ▶ GLAMOUR

glamorous */*'glæmərəs/ *adj* ⟨person/dress⟩ glamoroso; ⟨lifestyle⟩ sofisticado; ⟨job⟩ rodeado de glamour

glamour, (AmE also) **glamor** */*'glæmər ‖'glæmə(r)/ *n* glamour *m*

glance¹ */*glæns ‖glɑːns/ *n* mirada *f*; **to take a ~ at sth** echarle un vistazo *or* una ojeada a algo; **at first ~** a primera vista

glance² *vi* mirar; **to ~ AT sth** echarle una ojeada *or* un vistazo A algo; **to ~ AT sb** echarle una mirada A algn

glancing */*'glænsɪŋ ‖'glɑːnsɪŋ/ *adj* (before *n*): **to strike sb a ~ blow** pegarle* a algn de refilón

gland */*glænd/ *n* **(a)** (organ) glándula *f* **(b)** (lymph node) ganglio *m*

glandular fever */*'glændjələr ‖'glændjʊlə(r)/ *n* mononucleosis *f* (infecciosa)

glare¹ */*gler ‖gleə(r)/ *n* **1** (stare) mirada *f* (hostil, feroz, de odio etc) **2** (light) resplandor *m*

glare² *vi* **1** (stare) **to ~ AT sb** fulminar a algn con la mirada **2** (shine) brillar

glaring */*'glerɪŋ ‖'gleərɪŋ/ *adj* **(a)** ⟨light⟩ deslumbrante **(b)** (flagrant) (before *n*) ⟨error⟩ mayúsculo

glass */*glæs ‖glɑːs/ *n* **1** (material) vidrio *m*, cristal *m* (Esp) **2** (vessel) vaso *m*; (with stem) copa *f*; **a ~ of wine** una copa de vino **3** **glasses** *pl* (spectacles) gafas *fpl*, lentes *mpl* (esp AmL), anteojos *mpl* (esp AmL) **4** (magnifying ~) lupa *f*, lente *f* de aumento

glassblowing */*'glæs,bləʊɪŋ ‖'glɑːs,bləʊɪŋ/ *n* soplado *m* del vidrio

glassy */*'glæsi ‖'glɑːsi/ *adj* **(a)** (like glass) vítreo **(b)** (dull, lifeless) ⟨stare⟩ vidrioso

glaze¹ */*gleɪz/ *n* **(a)** (on pottery) vidriado *m* **(b)** (Culin) glaseado *m*

glaze² *vt* **1** (fit with glass) ⟨window/door⟩ acristalar; **to ~ a window** ponerle* vidrio(s) *or* (Esp) cristal(es) a **2** (make shiny, glossy) **(a)** ⟨pottery⟩ vidriar **(b)** (Culin) glasear

■ ~ *vi* ~ (over) «eyes» vidriarse

glazed */*gleɪzd/ *adj* **1** (fitted with glass) ⟨window/door⟩ con vidrio *or* (Esp) cristal **2** **(a)** (Culin) glaseado **(b)** ⟨expression⟩ vidrioso

glazier */*'gleɪʒər ‖'gleɪzɪə(r)/ *n* vidriero, -ra *m,f*, cristalero, -ra *m,f*(Esp)

gleam¹ */*gliːm/ *vi* «metal» relucir*

gleam² *n* (on metal, water) reflejo *m*; **he had a wicked ~ in his eyes** sus ojos despedían un destello maléficoso

gleaming */*'gliːmɪŋ/ *adj* reluciente

glean /gliːn/ *vt* ⟨*information*⟩ recoger*

glee /gliː/ *n* regocijo *m*

gleeful /ˈgliːfəl/ *adj* lleno de alegría

glen /glen/ *n* cañada *f*

glib /glɪb/ *adj* -**bb**- ⟨*remark/answer*⟩ simplista; ⟨*salesman/politician*⟩ con mucha labia

glide /glaɪd/ *vi* [1] (move smoothly over a surface) deslizarse* [2] ⟨*bird/plane*⟩ planear

glider /ˈglaɪdər ‖ˈglaɪdə(r)/ *n* planeador *m*

glimmer¹ /ˈglɪmər ‖ˈglɪmə(r)/ *vi* brillar con luz trémula

glimmer² *n* luz *f* débil; **a ~ of hope** un rayo de esperanza

glimpse¹ /glɪmps/ *n*: **I caught a ~ of the room** pude ver brevemente la habitación; **a ~ of life in rural England** una visión de la vida en la Inglaterra rural

glimpse² *vt* alcanzar* a ver

glint¹ /glɪnt/ *vi* destellar

glint² *n* (of metal, light) destello *m*; (in eye) ⟨*no pl*⟩ chispa *f*, brillo *m*

glisten /ˈglɪsən/ *vi* brillar

glitter¹ /ˈglɪtər ‖ˈglɪtə(r)/ *vi* relumbrar

glitter² *n* **(a)** (sparkle) ⟨*no pl*⟩ destello *m* **(b)** (superficial attractiveness) oropel *m* **(c)** (decoration) purpurina *f*, brillantes *mpl* (Arg), brillantina *f* (Ur, Ven), brillo *m* (Chi)

gloat /gləʊt/ *vi* **to ~** ⟨OVER *sth*⟩ regodearse ⟨CON algo⟩

global /ˈgləʊbəl/ *adj* **(a)** (worldwide) a escala mundial, global; **~ warming** calentamiento *m* global **(b)** (overall, comprehensive) global

globe /gləʊb/ *n* **(a)** (world) **the ~** el globo **(b)** (model) globo *m* terráqueo

globe: ~ artichoke *n* alcachofa *f*, alcaucil *m* (RPl); **~trotter** /ˈgləʊb,trɒtər ‖ˈgləʊb,trɒtə(r)/ *n* trotamundos *mf*

globule /ˈglɒbjuːl ‖ˈglɒbjuːl/ *n* glóbulo *m*

gloom /gluːm/ *n* **(a)** (darkness) penumbra *f*, oscuridad *f* **(b)** (melancholy) melancolía *f*

gloomily /ˈgluːməli ‖ˈgluːmɪli/ *adv* ⟨*sigh/stare*⟩ tristemente; ⟨*predict*⟩ con pesimismo

gloomy /ˈgluːmi/ *adj* -**mier**, -**miest** **(a)** (dark) ⟨*day/place*⟩ sombrío **(b)** (dismal) ⟨*person*⟩ lúgubre, fúnebre; ⟨*prospect*⟩ nada halagüeño; ⟨*prediction*⟩ pesimista

glorify /ˈglɔːrəfaɪ ‖ˈglɔːrɪfaɪ/ *vt* -**fies**, -**fying**, -**fied** ⟨*person*⟩ ensalzar*; ⟨*violence/war*⟩ exaltar

glorious /ˈglɔːriəs/ *adj* **(a)** (deserving glory) glorioso **(b)** (wonderful) ⟨*view/weather*⟩ maravilloso

glory¹ /ˈglɔːri/ *n* ⟨*pl* -**ries**⟩ **(a)** (fame) gloria *f* **(b)** (beauty, magnificence) esplendor *m*

glory² *vi* -**ries**, -**rying**, -**ried**: **to ~ IN sth** (take pleasure) disfrutar ⟨DE algo⟩; (in unpleasant way) regodearse ⟨CON algo⟩

gloss /glɑːs ‖glɒs/ *n* **(a)** (shine) brillo *m*; ⟨*before n*⟩ **~ finish** acabado *m* brillante **(b)** **~ (paint)** (pintura *f* al or de) esmalte *m*

■ **gloss over** [*v* + *adv* + *o*] (make light of) quitarle importancia a; (ignore) pasar por alto

glossary /ˈglɑːsəri ‖ˈglɒsəri/ *n* ⟨*pl* -**ries**⟩ glosario *m*

glossy /ˈglɑːsi ‖ˈglɒsi/ *adj* -**sier**, -**siest** ⟨*coat of animal*⟩ brillante, lustroso; ⟨*hair*⟩ brillante,

brilloso (AmL); ⟨*photograph*⟩ brillante; **~ magazine** revista *f* ilustrada (*impresa en papel satinado*)

glove /glʌv/ *n* guante *m*

glove compartment *n* guantera *f*

glow¹ /gləʊ/ *vi* ⟨*fire*⟩ brillar; ⟨*metal*⟩ estar* al rojo vivo; **to ~ with health** rebosar (de) salud; **to be ~ing with happiness** estar* radiante de felicidad

glow² *n* ⟨*no pl*⟩ brillo *m*; **he felt a ~ of pride** sintió una oleada de orgullo

glower /ˈglaʊər ‖ˈglaʊə(r)/ *vi* tener* el ceño fruncido; **to ~ AT sb** lanzarle* miradas fulminantes/una mirada fulminante A algn

glowing /ˈgləʊɪŋ/ *adj* **(a)** (shining) ⟨*before n*⟩ ⟨*cheeks*⟩ encendido; **the ~ embers** las brasas **(b)** (expressing praise) ⟨*report*⟩ elogioso

glucose /ˈgluːkəʊs, -kəʊz/ *n* glucosa *f*

glue¹ /gluː/ *n* goma *f* de pegar, pegamento *m*

glue² *vt* **glues**, **glueing**, **glued** **(a)** (stick) pegar* **(b)** (fix): **he was ~d to the television** estaba pegado a la televisión

glum /glʌm/ *adj* -**mm**- apesadumbrado

glut /glʌt/ *n* superabundancia *f*

glutton /ˈglʌtn̩/ *n* glotón, -tona *m,f*

gluttony /ˈglʌtn̩i ‖ˈglʌtəni/ *n* glotonería *f*

glycerin /ˈglɪsərən ‖ˈglɪsərɪn/, **glycerine** /ˈglɪsərən ‖ˈglɪsəriːn/ *n* glicerina *f*

GM *adj* = **genetically modified**

GMO *n* (= **genetically modified organism**) OGM *m*

GMT (= **Greenwich Mean Time**) GMT

gnarled /nɑːrld ‖nɑːld/ *adj* ⟨*wood/fingers*⟩ nudoso; ⟨*tree*⟩ retorcido

gnash /næʃ/ *vt*: **to ~ one's teeth** hacer* rechinar los dientes

gnat /næt/ *n* jején *m*; (general usage) mosquito *m*

gnaw /nɔː/ *vt* roer*

■ **~** *vi* **to ~ AT sth** roer* algo

gnome /nəʊm/ *n* gnomo *m*

go¹ /gəʊ/ ⟨*3rd pers sing pres* **goes**; *past* **went**; *past p* **gone**⟩ *vi*

I [1] **(a)** (move, travel) ir*; **where do we ~ from here?** ¿y ahora qué hacemos? **(b)** (start moving, acting): **ready, (get) set, ~!** preparados *or* en sus marcas, listos ¡ya!; **let's ~!** ¡vamos!; **here ~es!** ¡allá vamos (*or* voy *etc*)!

[2] (*past p* **gone/been**) **(a)** (travel to) ir*; **she's gone to France** se ha ido a Francia; **I have never been abroad** no he estado nunca en el extranjero; **to ~ by car/bus** ir* en coche/autobús; **to ~ on foot** ir* a pie; **to ~ for a walk** ir* a dar un paseo; **~ and see what she wants** anda *or* vete a ver qué quiere **(b)** (attend) ir*; **to ~ on a course** hacer* un curso; **to ~ -ING** ir* A + INF; **to ~ swimming** ir* a nadar

[3] (attempt, make as if to) **to ~ to + INF** ir* A + INF

II [1] (leave, depart) ⟨*visitor*⟩ irse*, marcharse (esp Esp); ⟨*bus/train*⟩ salir*; ▸ LET² 1C

[2] **(a)** (pass) ⟨*time*⟩ pasar; **the time ~es quickly** el tiempo pasa volando **(b)** (disappear) ⟨*headache/pain/fear*⟩ pasarse *or* irse* (+ *me/te/le etc*) **(c)** ⟨*money*⟩ (be spent) irse*; (be used up) acabarse

[3] **(a)** (be disposed of): **that sofa will have to ~**

nos vamos (*or* se van *etc*) a tener que deshacer de ese sofá **(b)** (be sold) venderse; **the painting went for £1,000** el cuadro se vendió en 1.000 libras
4 **(a)** (cease to function, wear out) «*bulb/fuse*» fundirse; «*thermostat/fan/exhaust*» estropearse; **her memory/eyesight is ∼ing** está fallándole la memoria/la vista; **my legs went (from under me)** me fallaron las piernas **(b)** (die) (colloq) morir*
5 **to go (a)** (remaining): **only two weeks to ∼ till he comes** solo faltan dos semanas para que llegue; **I still have 50 pages to ∼** todavía me faltan *or* me quedan 50 páginas **(b)** (take away) (AmE): **two burgers to ∼** dos hamburguesas para llevar
III 1 (a) (lead) «*path/road*» ir*, llevar **(b)** (extend, range) «*road/railway line*» ir*; **it only ∼es as far as Croydon** solo va hasta Croydon
2 (have place) ir*; (fit) caber*; *see also* GO IN, GO INTO
IV 1 (a) (become): **to ∼ blind** quedarse ciego; **to ∼ crazy** volverse* loco; **her face went red** se puso colorada **(b)** (be, remain): **to ∼ barefoot** ir* *or* andar* descalzo; **to ∼ hungry** pasar hambre
2 (turn out, proceed, progress) ir*; **how are things ∼ing?** ¿cómo van *or* andan las cosas?
3 (a) (be available) (*only in -ing form*): **I'll take any job that's ∼ing** estoy dispuesto a aceptar el trabajo que sea **(b)** (in general): **it's not expensive as dishwashers ∼** no es caro, para lo que cuestan los lavavajillas
V 1 (a) (function, work) «*heater/engine/clock*» funcionar **(b) to get going: the car's OK once it gets ∼ing** el coche marcha bien una vez que arranca; **we'd better get ∼ing** más vale que nos vayamos; **we tried to get a fire ∼ing** tratamos de hacer fuego **(c) to keep going** (continue to function) aguantar; (not stop) seguir*; **to keep a project ∼ing** mantener* a flote un proyecto
2 (continue, last out) seguir*; **the club's been ∼ing for 12 years now** el club lleva 12 años funcionando
3 (a) (sound) «*bell/siren*» sonar* **(b)** (make sound, movement) hacer*
4 (a) (contribute): **everything that ∼es to make a good school** todo lo que contribuye a que una escuela sea buena; **it just ∼es to show: we can't leave them on their own** está visto que no los podemos dejar solos **(b)** (be used) **all their savings are ∼ing toward the trip** van a gastar todos sus ahorros en el viaje; **the money will ∼ to pay the workmen** el dinero se usará para pagar a los obreros
5 (run, be worded) decir*; **how does the song ∼?** ¿cómo es (la letra/música de la) canción?
6 (a) (be permitted): **anything ∼es** todo vale **(b)** (be necessarily obeyed, believed): **what the boss says ∼es** lo que dice el jefe, va a misa **(c)** (match, suit) pegar*, ir*
■ **∼** *v aux* (*only in -ing form*) **to be ∼ing to +** INF (expressing intention, prediction) ir* A + INF
■ **go about** [*v + prep + o*] **(a)** (tackle) «*task*» acometer; **how would you ∼ about solving this equation?** ¿cómo harías para resolver esta ecuación? **(b)** (occupy oneself with): **to ∼ about one's business** ocuparse de sus (*or* mis *etc*) cosas
■ **go after** [*v + prep + o*] (pursue, chase) perseguir*, dar* caza a
■ **go against** [*v + prep + o*] **(a)** (oppose, resist)

«*instructions/policy/person*» oponerse* a, ir* en contra de **(b)** (be unfavorable to): **the decision went against them** la decisión les fue desfavorable
■ **go ahead** [*v + adv*] **(a)** (proceed, begin) **to ∼ ahead (WITH sth)** seguir* adelante (CON algo); **may I ask you a question? — ∼ ahead!** ¿le puedo hacer una pregunta? — por supuesto *or* (AmL tb) pregunte nomás
■ **go along** [*v + adv*] **(a)** (accompany, be present) ir* **(b)** (proceed, progress) ir*; **I usually make corrections as I ∼ along** normalmente hago correcciones sobre la marcha **(c)** (acquiesce): **to ∼ along with a proposal** secundar una propuesta
■ **go around**, (BrE also) **go round**
I [*v + prep + o*] **(a)** (turn) «*corner*» doblar, dar* la vuelta a, dar* vuelta (CS); «*bend*» tomar **(b)** (make detour) «*obstacle*» rodear
2 (visit, move through) «*country/city*» recorrer; «*museum/castle*» visitar; **to ∼ around the world** dar* la vuelta al mundo
II [*v + adv*] **1 (a)** (move, travel, be outdoors) andar*; **to ∼ around -**ING ir* por ahí + GER **(b)** (circulate) «*joke/rumor*» correr **(c)** (be sufficient for everybody): **there aren't enough to ∼ around** no alcanzan
2 (revolve) «*wheel/world*» dar* vueltas
3 (visit) ir*; **I'll ∼ around and see him** iré a verlo
■ **go away** [*v + adv*] **(a)** (depart, leave) irse* **(b)** (from home): **I'm ∼ing away this weekend** voy a salir este fin de semana; **to ∼ away on vacation** irse* de vacaciones **(c)** (disappear, fade away) «*smell*» irse*; «*pain*» pasarse *or* irse* (+ *me/te/le etc*)
■ **go back** [*v + adv*] **1** (return) volver*; **∼ back!** ¡vuelve atrás!, ¡retrocede!
2 (a) (date, originate) «*tradition/dynasty*» remontarse; **we ∼ back a long way** (colloq) nos conocemos desde hace mucho **(b)** «*clocks*» atrasarse
■ **go back on** [*v + adv + prep + o*] «*one's promise*» dejar de cumplir; «*one's word*» faltar a
■ **go before** [*v + prep + o*] «*court/committee*» presentarse ante
■ **go by 1** [*v + adv*] **(a)** (move past) pasar; **to let an opportunity ∼ by** dejar pasar una oportunidad **(b)** (elapse) «*days/years*» pasar; **as time goes by** con el tiempo
2 [*v + prep + o*] **(a)** (be guided by) «*instinct*» dejarse llevar por; «*rules*» seguir* **(b)** (base judgment on) «*appearances*» guiarse* *or* dejarse llevar por; **if previous experience is anything to ∼ by** a juzgar por lo que ha sucedido en otras ocasiones
■ **go down** [*v + adv*] **1 (a)** (descend) «*person*» bajar; «*sun*» ponerse*; «*curtain*» (Theat) caer* **(b)** (fall) «*boxer/horse*» caerse*; «*plane*» caer*, estrellarse **(c)** (sink) «*ship*» hundirse **(d)** «*computer*» dejar de funcionar, descomponerse* (AmL) **(e)** (be defeated) (Sport) perder*; **to ∼ down fighting** caer* luchando
2 (a) (decrease) «*temperature/exchange rate*» bajar; «*population/unemployment*» disminuir*; **to ∼ down in value** perder* valor **(b)** (decline) «*standard/quality*» empeorar **(c)** (abate) «*wind/storm*» amainar; «*floods/swelling*» bajar; **his temperature's gone down** le ha bajado la fiebre **(d)** (deflate) «*tire*» perder* aire
3 (extend): **this road ∼es down to the beach** ⋯⟶

este camino baja a or hasta la playa; **the skirt ~es down to her ankles** la falda le llega a los tobillos
4 (a) (be swallowed): **it just won't ~ down** no lo puedo tragar; **it went down the wrong way** se me fue por el otro camino **(b)** «*present/proposal/ remarks*»: **how did the announcement ~ down?** ¿qué tipo de acogida tuvo el anuncio?; **that won't ~ down too well with your father** eso no le va a caer muy bien a tu padre
5 (be recorded, written): **all these absences will ~ down on your record** va a quedar constancia de estas faltas en tu ficha; **to ~ down in history as sth** pasar a la historia como algo

■ **go down with** [*v + adv + prep + o*] (BrE): **to ~ down with flu/hepatitis** caer* en cama con gripe/ hepatitis

■ **go for** [*v + prep + o*] **1 (a)** (head toward, reach for): **he went for his gun** fue a echar mano de la pistola **(b)** (attack): **he went for Bill** se le echó encima a Bill
2 (choose) decidirse por
3 (aim at): **~ for it!** ¡haz la tentativa!, ¡a por ello! (Esp)

■ **go in** [*v + adv*] **1 (a)** (enter) entrar **(b)** «*screw/ key*» entrar; **the big case won't ~ in** la maleta grande no cabe **(c)** (to work) ir* a trabajar
2 (be obscured) «*sun/moon*» ocultarse

■ **go in for** [*v + adv + prep + o*] **(a)** (enter) ‹*competition*› participar en; ‹*exam/test*› presentarse a **(b)** (take up, practice): **he'd thought of ~ing in for teaching** había pensado dedicarse a la enseñanza

■ **go into** [*v + prep + o*] **1 (a)** (enter) ‹*room/ building*› entrar a, entrar a (AmL) **(b)** (crash into) ‹*car/wall*› chocar* contra **(c)** (fit into) entrar en
2 (a) (start, embark on) ‹*phase/era*› entrar en **(b)** (enter certain state) ‹*coma/trance*› entrar en **(c)** (enter profession) ‹*television/Parliament*› entrar en
3 (a) (discuss, explain) entrar en; **I don't want to ~ into that** no quiero entrar en ese tema **(b)** (investigate, analyze) ‹*problem/motives*› analizar*
4 (be devoted to): **after all the money/work that has gone into this!** ¡después de todo el dinero/ trabajo que se ha metido en esto!

■ **go off**
I [*v + adv*] **1** (depart) irse*, marcharse (esp Esp); **to ~ off with sth** llevarse algo
2 «*milk/meat/fish*» echarse a perder
3 (a) «*bomb/firework*» estallar; «*gun*» dispararse **(b)** «*alarm*» sonar
4 (stop operating) «*heating/lights*» apagarse*
II [*v + prep + o*] (lose liking for) (BrE): **to ~ off one's food** perder* el apetito; **I've gone off the idea** ya no me atrae la idea

■ **go on** [*v + adv*] **1 (a)** (go further) seguir*; **I can't ~ on** no puedo más **(b)** (go ahead): **you ~ on, we'll follow** tú vete que nosotros ya iremos; **he went on ahead to look for a hotel** él fue antes para buscar hotel
2 (continue) «*fight/struggle*» continuar*; **we can't ~ on like this** no podemos seguir así; **the**

discussion went on for hours la discusión duró horas; **to ~ on -ING** seguir* + GER; **he went on to become President** llegó a ser presidente; **to ~ on with sth** seguir* con algo; **~ on!** (encouraging, urging) ¡dale!, ¡vamos!, ¡ándale! (Méx), ¡ándele! (Col), ¡venga! (Esp)
3 (a) (continue speaking) seguir*, continuar* **(b)** (talk irritatingly) (pej): **he went on and on** siguió dale que dale; **to ~ on ABOUT sth** hablar insistentemente DE algo
4 (happen): **what's ~ing on?** ¿qué pasa?; **is there anything ~ing on between them?** ¿hay algo entre ellos?; **how long has this been ~ing on?** ¿desde cuándo viene sucediendo esto?
5 (a) (onto stage) salir* a escena; (onto field of play) salir* al campo **(b)** (fit, be placed): **the lid won't ~ on** no lo puedo (or podemos etc) poner la tapa

■ **go out** [*v + adv*] **1 (a)** (leave, exit) salir*; **to ~ out hunting/shopping** salir* de caza/de compras **(b)** (socially, for entertainment) salir*; **to ~ out for a meal** salir* a comer fuera **(c)** (as boyfriend, girlfriend) **to ~ out (WITH sb)** salir* (CON algn)
2 (a) (be broadcast) «*TV, radio program*» emitirse **(b)** (be issued, distributed): **a warrant has gone out for her arrest** se ha ordenado su detención; **the invitations have already gone out** ya se han mandado las invitaciones
3 (be extinguished) «*fire/cigarette/light*» apagarse*
4 «*tide*» bajar
5 (become outmoded) «*clothes/style*» pasar de moda

■ **go over**
I [*v + prep + o*] **1** (check) ‹*text/figures/work*› revisar; ‹*car*› revisar; ‹*house/premises*› inspeccionar
2 (revise, review) ‹*notes/chapter*› repasar
II [*v + adv*] **1** (make one's way, travel) ir*; **she went over to Jack and took his hand** se acercó a Jack y le tomó la mano
2 (change sides) pasarse

■ **go past** [*v + adv*] [*v + prep + o*] pasar
■ **go round** (BrE) ► GO AROUND
■ **go through**
I [*v + prep + o*] **1 (a)** (pass through) ‹*process/ stage*› pasar por **(b)** (perform): **let's ~ through the procedure once more** repitamos otra vez todos los pasos del procedimiento **(c)** (endure) ‹*ordeal/ hard times*› pasar por
2 (a) (search) ‹*attic/suitcase*› registrar, revisar (AmL); ‹*drawers/desk*› hurgar* en; **to ~ through sb's mail** abrirle* las cartas a algn **(b)** ► GO OVER I 2
3 (consume, use up) ‹*money/fortune*› gastarse; **he ~es through ten shirts a week** ensucia diez camisas por semana
II [*v + adv*] **(a)** (be carried out) «*changes/ legislation*» ser* aprobado; «*business deal*» llevarse a cabo; **when his divorce ~es through** cuando obtenga el divorcio **(b)** (Sport): **to ~ through to the next round** pasar a la siguiente etapa

■ **go through with** [*v + adv + prep + o*] ‹*threat/ plans*› llevar a cabo
■ **go together** [*v + adv*] «*colors/patterns*» combinar; **lamb and mint sauce ~ well together** el cordero queda muy bien con salsa de menta

■ **go under** [v + adv] **(a)** (sink) «*ship*» hundirse; «*submarine/diver*» sumergirse* **(b)** (fail, go bankrupt) hundirse

■ **go up** [v + adv] **1 (a)** (ascend) «*person*» subir; «*balloon/plane*» subir; «*curtain*» (Theat) levantarse **(b)** (approach) **to ~ up TO sb/sth** acercarse* A algn/algo **2 (a)** (increase) «*temperature/price/cost*» subir, aumentar; «*population/unemployment*» aumentar; **to ~ up in price** subir or aumentar de precio **(b)** (improve) «*standard*» mejorar **3** (burst into flames) prenderse fuego; (explode) estallar; **to ~ up in flames** incendiarse

■ **go with** [v + prep + o] **(a)** (be compatible with): **this sauce ~es well with hamburgers** esta salsa queda muy bien con hamburguesas; **choose a tie to ~ with your shirt** elija una corbata que quede bien con su camisa **(b)** (accompany, be associated with): **the house ~es with the job** la casa va con el puesto

■ **go without (a)** [v + prep + o] (do without) pasar sin; **she often went without food** a menudo pasaba sin comer; **they went without food/sleep for days** (not by choice) no comieron nada/no durmieron durante días **(b)** [v + adv]: **in order to feed her children she herself often went without** para darles de comer a los niños a menudo pasaba privaciones; **there's no coffee left, you'll just have to ~ without** no queda café, así que tendrás que pasar sin él

go² n (pl **goes**) **1 (a)** (attempt): **at one ~** (AmE), **in one ~** (BrE) «*empty/eat*» de un tirón (fam); «*drink*» de un trago; **she succeeded in lifting it at the third ~** consiguió levantarlo al tercer intento; **I want to have a ~ at learning Arabic** quiero intentar aprender árabe; **have a ~** prueba a ver, inténtalo; **to have a ~ at sb** (colloq): **she had a ~ at me for not having told her** se la agarró conmigo por no habérselo dicho (fam) **(b)** (turn): **whose ~ is it?** ¿a quién le toca?; **it's my ~** me toca a mí **2** (energy, drive) empuje m; **(to be) on the ~**: **I've been on the ~ all morning** no he parado en toda la mañana

goad /ɡəʊd/ vt «*person*» acosar; «*animal*» aguijonear

go-ahead /ˈɡəʊəhed/ n: **to give sb/sth the ~** darle* luz verde a algn/algo

goal /ɡəʊl/ n **1** (Sport) **(a)** (structure) portería f, arco m (AmL) **(b)** (point) gol m **2** (aim) meta f

goal: **~keeper** n portero, -ra m,f, guardameta m/f, arquero, -ra m,f (AmL); **~post** n poste m de la portería or (AmL tb) del arco; **~tender** n (AmE) ▶ **~KEEPER**

goat /ɡəʊt/ n (Zool) cabra f

gobble /ˈɡɑːbəl ‖ˈɡɒbəl/ vt engullirse*

■ **gobble up** [v + o + adv, v + adv + o] tragarse*

gobbledygook /ˈɡɑːbəldiˈɡuːk ‖ˈɡɒbəldiˌɡuːk/ n (colloq & pej) jerigonza f

go-between /ˈɡəʊbɪtwiːn/ n (intermediary) intermediario, -ria m,f; (messenger) mensajero, -ra m,f

goblet /ˈɡɑːblət ‖ˈɡɒblɪt/ n copa f

goblin /ˈɡɑːblən ‖ˈɡɒblɪn/ n duende m travieso, trasgo m

god /ɡɑːd ‖ɡɒd/ n **1 God** Dios m; **G~ bless (you)** que Dios te bendiga; **G~!** ¡Dios (santo)! **2** (deity, idol) dios m

god: **~child** n ahijado, -da m,f; **~dam, ~damn** adj (AmE sl) (before n) condenado (fam); **~daughter** /ˈɡɑːdˈdɔːtər ‖ˈɡɒdˌdɔːtə(r)/ n ahijada f

goddess /ˈɡɑːdəs ‖ˈɡɒdɪs/ n diosa f

god: **~father** /ˈɡɑːdˈfɑːðər ‖ˈɡɒdˌfɑːðə(r)/ n padrino m; **~mother** /ˈɡɑːdˈmʌðər ‖ˈɡɒdˌmʌðə(r)/ n madrina f; **~parent** /ˈɡɑːdˈperənt ‖ˈɡɒdˌpeərənt/ n (man) padrino m; (woman) madrina f; **my ~parents** mis padrinos; **~send** n bendición f (del cielo); **~son** n ahijado m

goggle /ˈɡɑːɡəl ‖ˈɡɒɡəl/ vi (pej) **to ~ AT sth/sb** mirar algo/a algn con los ojos desorbitados

goggles /ˈɡɑːɡəlz ‖ˈɡɒɡəlz/ pl n (Sport) gafas fpl or anteojos mpl (esp AmL) de esquí (or natación etc); (for welders) gafas fpl protectoras, anteojos mpl protectores (esp AmL)

going¹ /ˈɡəʊɪŋ/ n (no pl) **1** (progress): **once at the top, the ~ was easier** una vez en la cima, la marcha fue más fácil; **I found that lecture hard ~** me resultó difícil seguir la conferencia; **the novel was heavy ~** la novela era pesada **2** (departure) partida f **3** (situation) situación f; **if I were you, I'd buy it while the ~ is good** yo que tú lo compraría ahora, aprovechando el buen momento; **when the ~ got tough** cuando las cosas se pusieron difíciles

going² adj (before n) **(a)** (in operation) en marcha; **a ~ concern** (Busn) un negocio or una empresa en marcha **(b)** (present, current): **that's the ~ rate** es lo que se suele cobrar/pagar

gold /ɡəʊld/ n **1** (metal) oro m; (money) (monedas fpl de) oro m; (before n) «*ring/medal*» de oro **2** (color) dorado m, color m (de) oro

gold dust n oro m en polvo

golden /ˈɡəʊldən/ adj **1 (a)** (made of gold) de oro **(b)** (in color) dorado **2 (a)** (happy, prosperous) «*years*» dorado **(b)** (excellent): **a ~ opportunity** una excelente oportunidad

golden: **~ age** n época f dorada, edad f de oro; **~ wedding (anniversary)** n bodas fpl de oro

gold: **~fish** n (pl **-fish** or **-fishes**) pececito m (rojo); (plural) peces mpl de colores; **~ leaf** n oro m batido, pan m de oro; **~ mine** n mina f de oro; **~-plated** /ˈɡəʊldˈpleɪtəd ‖ˌɡəʊldˈpleɪtɪd/ adj chapado en oro; **~ rush** n fiebre f del oro; **~smith** n orfebre m/f

golf /ɡɑːlf ‖ɡɒlf/ n golf m

golf: **~ ball** n (Sport) pelota f de golf; **~ club** n **(a)** (stick) palo m de golf **(b)** (place) club m de golf; **~ course** n campo m or (AmL tb) cancha f de golf

golfer /ˈɡɑːlfər ‖ˈɡɒlfə(r)/ n golfista m/f

gone¹ /ɡɔːn ‖ɡɒn/ past p of GO¹

gone² adj (pred) **(a)** (not here): **my briefcase is ~!** ¡se me ha desaparecido la cartera!; **how long has she been ~?** ¿cuánto hace que se fue? **(b)** (past): **those days are (long) ~** de eso hace ya mucho, ha llovido mucho desde entonces **(c)** (used up): **the money is all ~** se ha acabado el dinero, no queda nada de dinero

gone³ prep (BrE): **it's just ~ five** acaban de dar las cinco

gong /ɡɑːŋ ‖ɡɒŋ/ n gong m

gonna /ˈɡənə ‖ˈɡɒnə/ (colloq) (= **going to**) ▶ GO¹ v aux

gonorrhea, (BrE) **gonorrhoea** /ˌgɑːnəˈriːə ‖ˌgɒnəˈriə/ n gonorrea f

goo /guː/ n (colloq) mugre f

good¹ /gʊd/ adj

■ Note The usual translation of *good*, *bueno*, becomes *buen* when it precedes a masculine singular noun.

(*comp* **better;** *superl* **best**) **1** ⟨*food/quality/book/work/reputation*⟩ bueno; **it smells ~** huele bien; **her French is very ~** habla muy bien (el) francés; **is this a ~ time to phone?** ¿es buena hora para llamar?; **it's ~ to be back home** ¡qué alegría estar otra vez en casa!; **I had a ~ night's sleep** dormí bien

2 (advantageous, useful) ⟨*deal/offer/advice*⟩ bueno; **burn it; that's all it's ~ for** quémalo, no sirve para otra cosa; **~ idea!, ~ thinking!** ¡buena idea!

3 (healthy) ⟨*diet/habit/exercise*⟩ bueno; **I'm not feeling too ~** (colloq) no me siento bien; **spinach is ~ for you** las espinacas son buenas para la salud

4 (attractive): **it looks ~** tiene buen aspecto; **that dress looks really ~ on her** ese vestido le queda *or* le sienta muy bien

5 (a) (in interj phrases): **~! now to the next question** bien, pasemos ahora a la siguiente pregunta; **~ for you!** ¡bien hecho! (b) (for emphasis) (colloq): **I'll do it when I'm ~ and ready** lo haré cuando me parezca; **the water's ~ and hot** el agua está bien caliente (c) **as good as: it's as ~ as new** está como nuevo; **he as ~ as admitted it** prácticamente lo admitió

6 (skilled, competent) bueno; **he's no ~ in emergencies** en situaciones de emergencia no sabe qué hacer; **to be ~ at languages** tener* facilidad para las idiomas; **he is ~ with children** tiene buena mano con los niños; **she is ~ with her hands** es muy habilidosa

7 (well-behaved, virtuous) bueno; **~ boy!** ¡muy bien!

8 (kind) bueno; **she was very ~ to me** fue muy amable conmigo

9 (valid) ⟨*argument/excuse*⟩ bueno; **this ticket is ~ for another week** este billete vale para una semana más; **it's simply not ~ enough!** ¡esto no puede ser!

10 (substantial, considerable) ⟨*meal/salary/distance*⟩ bueno; **there were a ~ many people there** había bastante gente allí

11 (not less than): **it'll take a ~ hour** va a llevar su buena hora *or* una hora larga; **a ~ half of all the people interviewed** más de la mitad de los entrevistados

good² n **1** (moral right) bien m; **to do ~** hacer* el bien; **there is some ~ in everyone** todos tenemos algo bueno; **to be up to no ~** (colloq) estar* tramando algo, traerse* algo entre manos **2** (a) (benefit) bien m; **no ~ will come of it** nada bueno saldrá de ello; **to do sb ~** hacerle* bien a algn (b) (use): **this knife is no ~ (at all)** este cuchillo no sirve (para nada); **this book is no ~** este libro no vale nada (c) **for good** para siempre **3 goods** pl (a) (merchandise) artículos mpl, mercancías fpl, mercaderías fpl (AmS); **manufactured ~s** productos mpl manufacturados, manufacturas fpl (b) (property) (frml) bienes mpl

goodbye¹ /gʊdˈbaɪ/ interj ¡adiós!, ¡chao! *or* ¡chau! (esp AmL)

goodbye² n: **to say ~ to sb** decirle* adiós a algn

good: G~ Friday n Viernes m Santo; **~-humored,** (BrE) **~-humoured** /ˈgʊdˈhjuːmərd ‖ˌgʊdˈhjuːməd/ adj ⟨*person*⟩ (permanent characteristic) alegre, jovial; (in good mood) de buen humor; ⟨*joke*⟩ sin mala intención; **~-looking** /ˈgʊdˈlʊkɪŋ/ adj ⟨*man*⟩ buen mozo (esp AmL), guapo (esp Esp); **a ~-looking woman** una mujer bonita *or* (esp Esp) guapa; **~-natured** /ˈgʊdˈneɪtʃərd ‖ˌgʊdˈneɪtʃəd/ adj (as permanent characteristic) bueno, de natural bondadoso

goodness /ˈgʊdnəs ‖ˈgʊdnɪs/ n **1** (a) (moral worth) bondad f (b) (of food) valor m nutritivo **2** (in interj phrases, as intensifier): **(my) ~!** ¡Dios (mío)!; **~ me!** ¡Dios mío!, ¡válgame Dios!

goodwill /ˈgʊdˈwɪl/ n (a) (benevolence) buena voluntad f (b) (Busn, Fin) fondo m de comercio, llave f (CS)

goofy /ˈguːfi/ adj **-fier, -fiest** (AmE sl) ⟨*person*⟩ memo (fam); ⟨*smile*⟩ bobalicón (fam)

goose /guːs/ n (pl **geese**) (a) (Zool) oca f, ganso m (b) (Culin) ganso m

goose: ~berry /ˈguːsˌberi ‖ˈgʊzbəri/ n **1** (Bot) grosella f espinosa, uva f espina; **2** (unwanted third person) (BrE colloq) carabina f (fam), chaperón, -rona m,f, violinista mf (Chi fam); **to play ~berry** hacer* de carabina (Esp fam), tocar* el violín (Chi fam); **~ bumps** pl n (AmE colloq), **~flesh** n, **~ pimples** pl n carne f de gallina

gore /gɔːr ‖gɔː(r)/ vt cornear

gorge¹ /gɔːrdʒ ‖gɔːdʒ/ n (Geog) desfiladero m, cañón m

gorge² v refl **to ~ oneself** atiborrarse de comida

gorgeous /ˈgɔːrdʒəs ‖ˈgɔːdʒəs/ adj (a) (lovely) (colloq) ⟨*girl*⟩ precioso, guapísimo; ⟨*dress*⟩ precioso, divino; ⟨*day*⟩ maravilloso, espléndido (b) (splendid) ⟨*color*⟩ magnífico

gorilla /gəˈrɪlə/ n gorila m

gorse /gɔːrs ‖gɔːs/ n aulaga f, tojo m

gory /ˈgɔːri/ adj **gorier, goriest** (colloq) sangriento

gosh /gɑːʃ ‖gɒʃ/ interj (colloq) ¡(mi) Dios!, ¡Dios mío!

gospel /ˈgɑːspəl ‖ˈgɒspəl/ n (a) **Gospel** (in New Testament) evangelio m (b) (Christian teaching) (no pl) Evangelio m; (before n) **it's ~ (truth)** es la pura verdad f (c) **~ (music)** (Mus) gospel m

gossamer /ˈgɑːsəmər ‖ˈgɒsəmə(r)/ n (liter) telaraña f; (before n) ⟨*threads*⟩ tenue

gossip¹ /ˈgɑːsəp ‖ˈgɒsɪp/ n (a) (speculation, scandal) chismorreo m (fam), cotilleo m (Esp fam); **an interesting piece of ~** un chisme interesante; (before n) **~ column** crónica f de sociedad (b) (chat): **to have a ~ with sb** chismorrear (fam) *or* (Esp tb) cotillear con algn (c) (person) chismoso, -sa m,f (fam), cotilla mf (Esp fam)

gossip² vi (a) (chatter) chismorrear (fam), cotillear (Esp fam) (b) (spread tales) contar* chismes

got /gɑːt ‖gɒt/ **1** past & past p of GET **2** (crit) pres of HAVE

Gothic /ˈgɑːθɪk ‖ˈgɒθɪk/ adj (Archit, Lit) gótico

gotta /ˈgɑːtə ‖ˈgɒtə/ (sl) = **have got to**

gotten /ˈgɑːtn̩ ‖ˈgɒtn̩/ (AmE) past p of GET

gouge /gaʊdʒ/ vt ⟨hole⟩ abrir*
■ **gouge out** [v + o + adv, v + adv + o] sacar*
gourd /gʊrd, gɔːrd ‖gʊəd/ n (Bot) calabaza f, jícaro m (AmC, Col, Méx)
gourmet /'gʊrmeɪ ‖'gʊəmeɪ/ n gourmet mf, gastrónomo, -ma m,f
gout /gaʊt/ n gota f
govern /'gʌvərn ‖'gʌvən/ vt (a) (rule) gobernar* (b) (determine) determinar (c) **governing** pres p ⟨party⟩ de gobierno; ⟨principle⟩ rector; **~ing body** organismo m rector
■ ~ vi gobernar*
governess /'gʌvərnəs ‖'gʌvənɪs/ n institutriz f
government /'gʌvərnmənt ‖'gʌvənmənt/ n gobierno m; (before n) ~ **policy** política f gubernamental
governor /'gʌvənər ‖'gʌvənə(r)/ n [1] (of state, province, colony) gobernador, -dora m,f [2] (of institution): prison ~ (BrE) director, -tora m,f de una cárcel; school ~ (BrE) miembro de un consejo escolar
gown /gaʊn/ n [1] (a) (dress) vestido m; **evening ~** traje m de fiesta (b) (night~) (AmE) camisón m [2] (a) (Educ, Law) toga f (b) (Med) bata f
GP n (= **general practitioner**) médico, -ca m,f de medicina general; **my ~** mi médico de cabecera
gr (= **gram(s)**) gr., g.
grab /græb/ **-bb-** vt (a) (seize) ⟨rope/hand⟩ agarrar; ⟨chance⟩ aprovechar (b) (appropriate) ⟨land⟩ apropiarse de; ⟨money⟩ llevarse (c) (appeal to) (colloq) «idea» atraer*; **how does that ~ you?** ¿qué te parece?
■ ~ vi: to ~ **AT** sth: she ~bed at the rope trató de agarrar la cuerda
grace /greɪs/ n [1] (elegance — of movement) gracia f, garbo m; (— of expression, form) elegancia f
[2] (a) (courtesy) cortesía f, gentileza f (b) (good nature): **to do sth with good/bad ~** hacer* algo de buen talante/a regañadientes (c) (good quality): **her saving ~ is her sense of humor** lo que la salva es que tiene sentido del humor; **social ~s** modales mpl
[3] (Relig) (a) (mercy) gracia f; **by the ~ of God ...** gracias a Dios ... (b) (prayer): **to say ~** (before a meal) bendecir* la mesa
[4] (respite) gracia f; **16 days' ~** (BrE Law) 16 días de gracia
graceful /'greɪsfəl/ adj ⟨dancer/movement⟩ lleno de gracia, grácil (liter); ⟨style⟩ elegante
gracefully /'greɪsfəli/ adv con gracia or garbo
gracious¹ /'greɪʃəs/ adj (a) ⟨smile/act⟩ gentil, cortés (b) (merciful) misericordioso
gracious² interj: (good o goodness) ~! (expressing surprise) ¡Dios Santo!; (expressing exasperation) ¡por favor!
graciously /'greɪʃəsli/ adv ⟨smile/apologize⟩ gentilmente
grade¹ /greɪd/ n [1] (a) (quality) calidad f; **~ A tomatoes** tomates mpl de la mejor calidad (b) (degree, level): **it divides hotels into four ~s** divide a los hoteles en cuatro categorías (c) (in seniority) grado m (del escalafón); (Mil) rango m [2] (Educ) (a) (class) (AmE) grado m, año m, curso m (b) (in exam) nota f

grade² vt [1] (a) (classify) clasificar* (b) (order in ascending scale) ⟨exercise/questions⟩ ordenar por grado de dificultad (c) (mark) (AmE) ⟨test/exercise⟩ corregir* y calificar* (d) **graded** past p ⟨produce⟩ clasificado [2] (make more level) ⟨surface/soil⟩ (AmE) nivelar
grade: ~ **crossing** n (AmE) paso m a nivel, crucero m (Méx); ~ **school** n (AmE) escuela f primaria
gradient /'greɪdiənt/ n (slope) pendiente f, gradiente f (AmL)
gradual /'grædʒuəl/ adj ⟨improvement⟩ gradual; ⟨slope⟩ no muy empinado
gradually /'grædʒuəli/ adv ⟨improve⟩ gradualmente, poco a poco; ⟨rise/slope⟩ suavemente
graduate¹ /'grædʒueɪt/ vi [1] (Educ) (a) (from a college, university) terminar la carrera, recibirse (AmL), graduarse*; (obtain bachelor's degree) licenciarse (b) (from high school) (AmE) terminar el bachillerato, recibirse de bachiller [2] (progress) **to ~** (**FROM sth**) **TO sth** pasar (DE algo) A algo
graduate² /'grædʒuət/ n (a) (from higher education) persona con título universitario; (with a bachelor's degree) licenciado, -da m,f; (before n) ⟨course/student⟩ de posgrado or postgrado; **he went to ~ school** (AmE) hizo un curso de posgrado (b) (from high school) (AmE) bachiller mf
graduated /'grædʒueɪtəd ‖'grædʒueɪtɪd/ adj (a) (progressive) ⟨scale⟩ graduado; ⟨payments⟩ escalonado (b) (calibrated) ⟨flask/test tube⟩ graduado
graduation /ˌgrædʒu'eɪʃən/ n (Educ) graduación f
graffiti /grə'fiːti/ n (+ sing o pl vb) graffiti mpl
graft¹ /grɑːft ‖grɑːft/ vt (Hort) injertar
graft² n [1] (Hort, Med) injerto m [2] (bribery, corruption) (AmE colloq) chanchullos mpl (fam)
grain /greɪn/ n [1] (of cereal, salt, sugar, sand) grano m [2] (Agr) grano m, cereal m [3] (of wood — pattern) veta f, veteado m; (— texture) grano m; **to go against the ~: it goes against the ~ for me to support them** apoyarlos va en contra de mis principios
gram, (BrE also) **gramme** /græm/ n gramo m
grammar /'græmər ‖'græmə(r)/ n gramática f
grammar school n (a) (in US) ▶ ELEMENTARY SCHOOL (b) (in UK) colegio de enseñanza secundaria para ingresar al cual hay que aprobar un examen de aptitud
grammatical /grə'mætɪkəl/ adj (a) (of grammar) gramatical (b) (correct) gramaticalmente correcto
gramme /græm/ n (BrE) ▶ GRAM
granary /'greɪnəri, 'grænəri ‖'grænəri/ n (pl **-ries**) granero m
grand /grænd/ adj **-er, -est** [1] (a) (impressive) magnífico (b) (ostentatious) ⟨gesture⟩ grandilocuente; ⟨entrance⟩ triunfal (c) (ambitious, lofty) ⟨vision⟩ grandioso; ⟨ideal⟩ elevado (d) (overall) (before n, no comp) global; **the ~ total** el total f [2] (formal, ceremonial) ⟨opening/occasion⟩ solemne [3] (very good) (colloq) ⟨day/weather⟩ espléndido
grandad /'grændæd/ n abuelo m

grand: G~ Canyon n the G~ Canyon el Cañón del Colorado; **~child** /'græntʃaɪld/ n nieto, -ta m,f; **~dad** /'grændæd/ n abuelo m; **~daughter** /'græn,dɔːtər ‖'græn,dɔːtə(r)/ n nieta f

grandeur /'grændʒər ‖'grændʒə(r)/ n grandiosidad f

grandfather /'græn,fɑːðər ‖'græn,fɑːðə(r)/ n abuelo m; (before n) **~ clock** reloj m de pie

grandiose /'grændiəʊs/ adj ⟨claim/scheme/ notion⟩ fatuo; ⟨speech⟩ altisonante

grand: ~ jury n (in US) jurado m de acusación (jurado que decide si hay suficientes pruebas para procesar); **~ma** /'grænmɑː/ n (colloq) abuela f; **~mother** /'græn,mʌðər ‖'græn,mʌðə(r)/ n abuela f; **~pa** /'grænpɑː/ n abuelo m; **~parent** /'græn,peərənt ‖'græn,peərənt/ n abuelo, -la m,f; my **~parents** mis abuelos; **~ piano** n piano m de cola; **~son** /'grænsʌn/ n nieto m; **~stand** n tribuna f, (before n) ⟨ticket/seat⟩ de tribuna

granite /'grænət ‖'grænɪt/ n granito m

granny, grannie /'græni/ n (pl **-nies**) abuelita f (fam)

grant¹ /grænt ‖grɑːnt/ vt **1** (a) ⟨desire/ request⟩ conceder (b) ⟨interview/audience⟩ conceder (c) ⟨land/pension⟩ otorgar* **2** (admit) reconocer* **3 granted** past p (admittedly): **~ed,** it's very expensive, but ... de acuerdo, es muy caro, pero ...; to take sth for **~ed** dar* algo por sentado

grant² n (subsidy — to body, individual) subvención f, subsidio m (AmL); (— to student) (esp BrE) beca f

granulated /'grænjəleɪtəd ‖'grænjʊleɪtɪd/ adj: **~ sugar** azúcar f granulada, azúcar m granulado

granule /'grænjuːl/ n gránulo m

grape /greɪp/ n (fruit) uva f; it's sour **~s** (set phrase) las uvas están verdes (fr hecha)

grape: ~fruit n (pl **-fruit** or **-fruits**) toronja f (AmL exc CS), pomelo m (CS, Esp); **~vine** n (a) (Agr, Bot) parra f (b) (source of information) (colloq): I heard it on o through the **~vine** me lo dijo un pajarito (fam), lo he escuchado en radio macuto (Esp fam)

graph /græf ‖grɑːf/ n gráfico m, gráfica f

graphic /'græfɪk/ adj **1** (vivid) ⟨account/ description⟩ muy gráfico; in **~ detail** con todo lujo de detalles **2** (Art) gráfico; **~ design** diseño m gráfico

graphics /'græfɪks/ pl n **1** (graphic design) diseño m gráfico **2** (Comput) gráficos mpl

graph paper n papel m milimetrado or (Méx) cuadriculado

grapple /'græpl/ vi to **~** (WITH sb/sth) forcejear (CON algn/algo); to **~ with one's conscience** tener* escrúpulos de conciencia

grasp¹ /græsp ‖grɑːsp/ vt **1** (a) (seize) ⟨object/ person⟩ agarrar; ⟨opportunity/offer⟩ aprovechar (b) (hold tightly) tener* agarrado **2** (understand) ⟨concept⟩ captar
■ **~** vi to **~ AT sth** tratar de agarrar algo; ⟨opportunity⟩ aprovechar

grasp² n (no pl) **1** (a) (grip): he tightened his **~** on my arm me apretó más el brazo (b) (reach) alcance m **2** (understanding) comprensión f; (knowledge) conocimientos mpl

grasping /'græspɪŋ ‖'grɑːspɪŋ/ adj avaricioso

grass /græs ‖grɑːs/ n **1** (a) (as pasture) pasto m, zacate m (Méx); (lawn) césped m, hierba f, pasto m (AmL), grama (AmC, Ven); the **~** is always greener on the other side nadie está contento con su suerte (b) (Bot) hierba f **2** (marijuana) (sl) maría f (arg), hierba f (arg), monte m (AmC, Col, Ven arg), mota f (Méx arg)

grass: ~hopper /'græs,hɑːpər ‖'grɑːs,hɒpə(r)/ n saltamontes m; **~ roots** pl n (ordinary members) (before n) ⟨support/opinion⟩ de las bases

grassy /'græsi ‖'grɑːsi/ adj **-sier, -siest** cubierto de hierba

grate¹ /greɪt/ vt (Culin) rallar; **~d cheese** queso m rallado
■ **~** vi (a) (irritate) ser* crispante (b) (make harsh noise) chirriar*

grate² n (metal frame in fireplace) rejilla f, (fireplace) chimenea f

grateful /'greɪtfəl/ adj agradecido; I'm very **~** to you for your advice le agradezco mucho sus consejos

grater /'greɪtər ‖'greɪtə(r)/ n rallador m

gratify /'grætəfaɪ ‖'grætɪfaɪ/ vt **-fies, -fying, -fied** (a) (fulfill) satisfacer* (b) (give satisfaction) complacer*

grating¹ /'greɪtɪŋ/ adj (a) (harsh) ⟨noise/sound⟩ chirriante (b) (irritating) crispante

grating² n rejilla f

gratitude /'grætətuːd ‖'grætɪtjuːd/ n gratitud f

gratuitous /grə'tuːətəs ‖grə'tjuːɪtəs/ adj (pej) gratuito

grave¹ /greɪv/ adj **graver, gravest** **1** ⟨error/danger/voice⟩ grave **2** /grɑːv/ (Ling) ⟨accent⟩ grave

grave² n tumba f, sepultura f

gravedigger /'greɪv,dɪgər ‖'greɪv,dɪgə(r)/ n sepulturero, -ra m,f

gravel /'grævəl/ n grava f, (finer) gravilla f

gravely /'greɪvli/ adv (a) (seriously) gravemente (b) (solemnly) con gravedad

grave: ~stone n lápida f; **~yard** n cementerio m, panteón m (Méx)

gravitate /'grævəteɪt ‖'grævɪteɪt/ vi: people of similar interests naturally **~** toward each other uno tiende a acercarse a gente con intereses afines; young people tend to **~** toward the big cities las grandes ciudades son un polo de atracción para los jóvenes

gravity /'grævəti/ n **1** (Phys) gravedad f **2** (seriousness) gravedad f

gravy /'greɪvi/ n (Culin) salsa hecha con el jugo de la carne asada

gray¹, (BrE) **grey** /greɪ/ adj **-er, -est** gris; ⟨outlook/future⟩ poco prometedor; a **~** hair una cana; she has **~** hair es canosa

AmC	Central America	Arg	Argentina	Cu	Cuba	Per	Peru
AmL	Latin America	Bol	Bolivia	Ec	Ecuador	RPI	River Plate Area
AmS	South America	Chi	Chile	Esp	Spain	Ur	Uruguay
Andes	Andean Region	CS	Southern Cone	Méx	Mexico	Ven	Venezuela

gray², (BrE) **grey** n gris m

graze¹ /greɪz/ vt **(a)** (cut, injure) rasguñarse **(b)** (touch, brush) rozar*

■ ~ vi (Agr) pastar

graze² n rasguño m

grease¹ /griːs/ n grasa f

grease² vt **(a)** (lubricate) ⟨machinery/hinge⟩ engrasar **(b)** (Culin): **to ~ (with butter)** enmantequillar, enmantecar* (RPl); **to ~ (with oil)** aceitar

grease: ~**paint** n maquillaje m teatral; ~**proof paper** n (BrE) papel m encerado or (Esp) parafinado, papel m manteca (RPl), papel m mantequilla (Chi)

greasy /griːsi/ adj **-sier, -siest (a)** (soiled) ⟨hands⟩ grasiento; ⟨overalls⟩ cubierto de grasa **(b)** (containing grease) ⟨food⟩ graso; (pej) grasiento **(c)** ⟨hair/skin⟩ graso, grasoso (esp AmL)

great¹ /greɪt/ adj **1** (before n) (large in size, number, quantity) (sing) gran (delante del n); (pl) grandes (delante del n); **a ~ many people** muchísima gente **2** (before n) **(a)** (important) ⟨landowner/occasion⟩ (sing) gran (delante del n); (pl) grandes (delante del n); **Catherine the G~** Catalina la Grande **(b)** (genuine, real) ⟨friend/rival⟩ (sing) gran (delante del n); (pl) grandes (delante del n) **3** (excellent) (colloq) ⟨goal/movie/meal⟩ sensacional; **he's a really ~ guy** es un tipo or (Esp tb) tío sensacional (fam); (as interj) **(that's) ~!** ¡fenomenal!, ¡estupendo! (fam)

great² adv (esp AmE colloq) fenomenal (fam)

great: ~**aunt** /ˈɡreɪtˈænt ‖ˌɡreɪtˈɑːnt/ n tía f abuela; **G~ Britain** n Gran Bretaña f; **G~ Dane** n gran danés m; ~**granddaughter** /ˈɡreɪtˈɡrænˌdɔːtər ‖ˌɡreɪtˈɡrænˌdɔːtə(r)/ n bisnieta f, biznieta f; ~**grandfather** /ˈɡreɪtˈɡrænˌfɑːðer ‖ˌɡreɪtˈɡrænˌfɑːðə(r)/ n bisabuelo m; ~**grandmother** /ˈɡreɪtˈɡrænˌmʌðər ‖ˌɡreɪtˈɡrænˌmʌðə(r)/ n bisabuela f; ~**grandson** /ˈɡreɪtˈɡrænsʌn/ n bisnieto m, biznieto m

greatly /ˈɡreɪtli/ adv (as intensifier) ⟨admire/improve⟩ enormemente

great-uncle /ˈɡreɪtˈʌŋkəl/ n tío m abuelo

Greece /griːs/ n Grecia f

greed /griːd/ n **(a)** (for food) gula f, angurria f (CS) **(b)** (for power, money) codicia f

greedy /ˈɡriːdi/ adj **-dier, -diest (a)** (for food, drink) glotón, angurriento (CS) **(b)** (for power, wealth) **to be ~ FOR sth** tener* ansias DE algo

Greek¹ /griːk/ adj griego

Greek² n **(a)** (language) griego m **(b)** (person) griego, -ga m,f

green¹ /griːn/ adj **-er, -est 1** (in color) verde; **he was ~ with envy** se moría de envidia; **to have a ~ thumb** o (BrE) ~ **fingers** tener* mano para las plantas **2 (a)** (unripe) verde **(b)** (colloq) (pred) (inexperienced) verde (fam) **3** (Pol) verde, ecologista

green² n **1** (color) verde m **2** (in village, town) ≈ plaza f (con césped) **3 greens** pl (vegetables) verdura f (de hoja verde)

green: ~**back** n (AmE colloq) dólar m, verde m (esp AmL fam); ~ **bean** n habichuela f or (Esp) judía f verde or (Méx) ejote m or (RPl) chaucha f or (Chi) poroto m verde or (Ven) vainita f; ~ **belt** n (esp BrE) zona f verde; ~ **card** n (in US)

permiso m de residencia y trabajo; ~**field site** n: terreno en zona rural; ~**fly** n (pl **-flies** or **-fly**) (BrE) pulgón m; ~**grocer** n (BrE) verdulero, -ra m,f; **the ~grocer('s)** la verdulería; ~**house** n invernadero m; (before n) **the ~house effect** (Ecol) el efecto invernadero; **G~land** /ˈɡriːnlənd/ n Groenlandia f; ~ **onion** n (AmE) cebolleta f, cebollino m; ~ **pepper** n ▶ PEPPER¹ 2

Greenwich Mean Time /ˈɡrenɪdʒ, ˈɡrenɪtʃ/ n hora f de Greenwich

greet /griːt/ vt **1 (a)** (welcome, receive) ⟨guest/client⟩ recibir **(b)** (say hello to) saludar **2** (reactto) acoger* **3** (meet): **a strange sight ~ed our eyes** un extraño espectáculo se ofreció a nuestra vista

greeting /ˈɡriːtɪŋ/ n **(a)** (spoken) saludo m; (as interj) ~**s!** (arch or hum) ¡buenas! (fam) **(b)** (message) (usu pl): ⊛ **birthday/Christmas greetings** feliz cumpleaños/Navidad; (before n) **a ~ card** (BrE also) ~**s card** una tarjeta de felicitación

gregarious /ɡrɪˈɡeriəs ‖ɡrɪˈɡeəriəs/ adj ⟨person⟩ sociable; (Zool) gregario

Grenada /ɡrəˈneɪdə/ n Granada f

grenade /ɡrəˈneɪd/ n granada f

grew /ɡruː/ past of GROW

grey adj/n (BrE) ▶ GRAY¹,²

greyhound /ˈɡreɪhaʊnd/ n galgo m

grid /ɡrɪd/ n **1** (grating over opening) rejilla f **2** (on map) (Geog) cuadriculado m; (before n) ~ **reference** coordenadas fpl cartográficas

griddle /ˈɡrɪdl/ n plancha f

grid: ~**iron** /ˈɡrɪdˌaɪərn ‖ˈɡrɪdaɪən/ n **1** (Culin) parrilla f; **2** (in US football) campo m, cancha f (AmL), emparrillado m (Méx); ~**lock** n (esp AmE) paralización f total del tráfico; ~**locked** /ˈɡrɪdlɑːkt ‖ˈɡrɪdlɒkt/ adj colapsado, paralizado

grief /griːf/ n dolor m, profunda pena f; **to come to ~** «plans» fracasar, irse* al traste (fam); **he'll come to ~ one day** va a acabar mal

grievance /ˈɡriːvəns/ n **(a)** (ground for complaint) motivo m de queja; **to air one's ~s** quejarse **(b)** (Lab Rel) queja f formal; (before n) ~ **procedure** procedimiento m conciliatorio

grieve /ɡriːv/ vi sufrir; **to ~ FOR sb** llorar a algn

■ ~ vt apenar

grievous /ˈɡriːvəs/ adj (liter) ⟨loss⟩ doloroso; ⟨wound/injury⟩ de extrema gravedad; ~ **bodily harm** (Law) lesiones fpl (corporales) graves

grill¹ /ɡrɪl/ vt **1** (BrE Culin) (in electric, gas grill) hacer* al grill; (over hot fire) hacer* a la parrilla **2** (interrogate) (colloq) interrogar*

grill² n **(a)** (on stove) (esp BrE) grill m, gratinador m **(b)** (on barbecue) parrilla f

grille /ɡrɪl/ n **(a)** (partition) reja f **(b)** (protective covering) (Tech) rejilla f; (Auto) calandra f

grim /ɡrɪm/ adj **-mm-** ⟨person/expression⟩ adusto; (gloomy) ⟨outlook/situation⟩ nefasto; **she carried on with ~ determination** siguió adelante, resuelta a no dejarse vencer

grimace¹ /ˈɡrɪməs, ɡrɪˈmeɪs/ n mueca f

grimace² vi hacer* una mueca

grime /ɡraɪm/ n mugre f

grimy /ˈɡraɪmi/ adj **-mier, -miest** mugriento

grin¹ /ɡrɪn/ vi **-nn-** sonreír* (abiertamente o burlonamente); **to ~ and bear it** aguantarse

grin² n sonrisa f

grind¹ /graɪnd/ (past & past p ground) vt ⟨coffee/wheat⟩ moler*; (in mortar) machacar*; ⟨meat⟩ (AmE) moler* or (Esp, RPl) picar*; ⟨crystals/ore⟩ triturar; **he ~s his teeth in his sleep** le rechinan los dientes cuando duerme
■ ~ vi (move with friction) rechinar, chirriar*; **to ~ to a halt** o **standstill** ⟨vehicle⟩ pararse or detenerse* con un chirrido; ⟨negotiations⟩ llegar* a un punto muerto

grind² n (a) (drudgery, colloq) (no pl): **the daily ~** el monótono trajín diario (b) (over-conscientious worker) (AmE colloq): **she's the office ~** es la niña aplicada de la oficina (iró)

grinder /ˈgraɪndər ‖ˈgraɪndə(r)/ n (machine) molinillo m; **a coffee ~** un molinillo de café

grindstone /ˈgraɪnstəʊn, ˈgraɪndstəʊn ‖ˈgraɪndstəʊn/ n muela f, piedra f de afilar; **back to the ~!** ¡de vuelta al yugo!

grip¹ /grɪp/ n ⟨1⟩ (a) (hold): **she held his arm in a strong ~** lo tenía agarrado or asido fuertemente del brazo; **he kept a firm ~ on expenses** llevaba un rígido control de los gastos; **get a ~ on yourself!** ¡contrólate!; **the region is in the ~ of an epidemic** una epidemia asola la región; **to come to ~s with sth** ⟨idea/situation⟩ aceptar or asumir algo; **to get to ~s with sth** ⟨subject⟩ entender* algo; ⟨new system⟩ aprender algo (b) (of tires) adherencia f
⟨2⟩ (on handle) empuñadura f
⟨3⟩ (hair ~) (BrE) horquilla f, pinche m (Chi), pasador m (Méx)

grip² vt **-pp-** ⟨1⟩ (take hold of) agarrar; (have hold of) tener* agarrado ⟨2⟩ (of feelings, attention): **the audience was ~ped by the play** la obra captó la atención del público

gripping /ˈgrɪpɪŋ/ adj apasionante

grisly /ˈgrɪzli/ adj **-lier, -liest** truculento

gristle /ˈgrɪsəl/ n cartílago m

grit¹ /grɪt/ n ⟨1⟩ (a) (dirt) polvo m (b) (gravel) arenilla f ⟨2⟩ (courage) (colloq) agallas fpl (fam) ⟨3⟩ **grits** pl (hominy ~s) (AmE Culin) sémola f de maíz

grit² vt **-tt-** (a) (BrE) ⟨road⟩ echar arenilla en (b)
▶ TOOTH A

grizzly /ˈgrɪzli/ n (pl **-lies**), **grizzly bear** oso m pardo

groan¹ /grəʊn/ vi ⟨1⟩ (a) (with pain, suffering) gemir* (b) (with dismay) gruñir* (c) (creak) ⟨door/timber⟩ crujir ⟨2⟩ (grumble) (colloq) refunfuñar (fam)

groan² n (a) (of pain, suffering) quejido m (b) (of dismay) gruñido m (c) (creak) crujido m

grocer /ˈgrəʊsər ‖ˈgrəʊsə(r)/ n tendero, -ra m,f, almacenero, -ra m,f (esp CS); **the ~'s** (BrE) la tienda de comestibles or de ultramarinos, la bodega (Cu, Per, Ven), la tienda de abarrotes (AmC, Andes, Méx), el almacén (esp CS)

grocery /ˈgrəʊsəri/ n (pl **-ries**) (a) (shop) tienda f de comestibles or de ultramarinos, bodega f (Cu, Per, Ven), tienda f de abarrotes (AmC, Andes, Méx), almacén m (esp CS) (b) **groceries** pl (provisions) comestibles mpl, provisiones fpl

groggy /ˈgrɑːgi ‖ˈgrɒgi/ adj **-gier, -giest** (colloq) grogui (fam)

groin /grɔɪn/ n (Anat) ingle f

groom¹ /gruːm/ vt (a) ⟨dog⟩ cepillar; ⟨horse⟩

cepillar, almohazar* (b) (make neat, attractive) (usu pass): **well ~ed** bien arreglado (c) (prepare) preparar; **to ~ sb for sth** preparar a algn para algo

groom² n ⟨1⟩ (Equ) mozo m de cuadra
⟨2⟩ (bride~) novio m

groove /gruːv/ n ranura f; (Audio) surco m

grope /grəʊp/ vi andar* a tientas; **to ~ FOR sth** buscar* algo a tientas
■ ~ vt ⟨person⟩ (colloq) manosear, meterle mano a (fam)

gross¹ /grəʊs/ adj ⟨1⟩ (extreme, flagrant) (before n) ⟨disregard/injustice⟩ flagrante; ⟨exaggeration⟩ burdo ⟨2⟩ (total) ⟨weight/profit/income⟩ bruto; **~ national product** (Econ) producto m nacional bruto ⟨3⟩ (a) (fat) obeso (b) (disgusting) ⟨person⟩ asqueroso; ⟨language/joke⟩ soez

gross² vt ⟨worker/earner⟩ tener* una entrada bruta de; **their profits ~ed 2 million** tuvieron beneficios brutos de 2 millones

gross³ n ⟨1⟩ (pl **~**) (144) gruesa f ⟨2⟩ (pl **grosses**) (gross profit) (AmE) ingresos mpl brutos

grossly /ˈgrəʊsli/ adv ⟨exaggerated/unfair⟩ terriblemente

grotesque /grəʊˈtesk/ adj grotesco

grotto /ˈgrɑːtəʊ ‖ˈgrɒtəʊ/ n (pl **-toes** or **-tos**) gruta f

ground¹ /graʊnd/ n ⟨1⟩ (land, terrain) terreno m; **to gain/lose ~** ganar/perder* terreno; **to stand one's ~** (in argument) mantenerse* firme; (in battle) no ceder terreno
⟨2⟩ **grounds** pl (premises) terreno m; (gardens) jardines mpl
⟨3⟩ (surface of the earth) suelo m; (soil) tierra f; **to break new ~** abrir* nuevos caminos; **to get off the ~** ⟨plan/project⟩ llegar* a concretarse; ⟨talks⟩ empezar* a encaminarse; **to get sth off the ~** ⟨project⟩ poner* algo en marcha; **to suit sb down to the ~** (colloq) ⟨arrangement⟩ venirle* de perlas a algn (fam); ⟨hat⟩ quedarle que ni pintado a algn (fam)
⟨4⟩ (matter, subject): **we covered a lot of ~ in our discussions** tratamos muchos puntos en nuestras conversaciones
⟨5⟩ (outdoor site): **football ~** (BrE) campo m de fútbol, cancha f de fútbol (AmL); **recreation ~** parque m ⟨donde se practican deportes⟩
⟨6⟩ (AmE Elec) tierra f
⟨7⟩ (justification) (usu pl) motivo m; **~s for divorce** causal f de divorcio; **on ~s of ill health** por motivos de salud; **they refused, on the ~s that ...** se negaron, alegando que ...
⟨8⟩ **grounds** pl (dregs): **coffee ~s** posos mpl de café

ground² vt ⟨1⟩ (usu pass) (a) (base) ⟨argument/theory⟩ fundar (b) (instruct): **we were well ~ed in German** se nos dio una sólida base en alemán
⟨2⟩ (a) ⟨plane⟩ retirar del servicio (b) ⟨child/teenager⟩ (esp AmE colloq): **I can't go out tonight; I'm ~ed** no puedo salir esta noche, estoy castigado or no me dejan ⟨3⟩ (Naut) ⟨ship⟩ hacer* encallar

ground³ past & past p of GRIND¹

ground⁴ adj ⟨coffee/pepper⟩ molido; **~ beef** (AmE) carne f molida or (Esp, RPl) picada

ground: ~cloth, (BrE) **~sheet** n suelo m

impermeable (*de una tienda de campaña*); ~ **control** *n* control *m* de tierra; ~ **floor** *n* (BrE) the ~ **floor** la planta baja, el primer piso (Chi)

grounding /'graʊndɪŋ/ *n* (*no pl*) base *f*

groundless /'graʊndləs ǁ'graʊndlɪs/ *adj* infundado

ground: ~ **level** *n*: at ~ **level** a ras del suelo; above ~ **level** sobre el nivel del suelo; below ~ **level** bajo tierra; ~ **rule** *n* **1** (guiding principle) directriz *f*, **2** (AmE Sport) regla *f* de terreno *or* de campo, regla local (Ven); ~**sheet** *n* (BrE) ▶ GROUNDCLOTH; ~**work** *n* trabajo *m* preliminar *or* de base

group¹ /gruːp/ *n* **1** (+ *sing o pl vb*) **(a)** (of people) grupo *m*; **a women's/gay** ~ una agrupación de mujeres/gay; (*before n*) ⟨*discussion/visit*⟩ en grupo; ⟨*portrait*⟩ de conjunto **(b)** (Mus) grupo *m*, conjunto *m* **2** (Busn, Chem, Math) grupo *m*

group² *vt* agrupar

■ ~ *vi*: **to** ~ **together** agruparse

grouse¹ /graʊs/ *n* (*pl* ~) (bird) urogallo *m*

grouse² *vi* (colloq) gruñir* (fam); **to** ~ **ABOUT sb/sth** quejarse DE algn/algo

grout /graʊt/ *vt* ⟨*tiles*⟩ enlechar

grove /grəʊv/ *n* (of trees) bosquecillo *m*; **an orange** ~ un naranjal

grovel /'grɑːvəl ǁ'grɒvəl/ *vi*, (BrE) **-ll-** (physically) postrarse; (abase oneself) arrastrarse

grow /grəʊ/ (*past* **grew**; *past p* **grown**) *vi* **1** (get bigger) crecer*; (develop emotionally) madurar; (expand, increase) «*city/company/influence*» crecer*; «*quantity/population/membership*» aumentar; **his hair has** ~**n** le creció el pelo; **the economy is** ~**ing** **again** la economía vuelve a experimentar un período de crecimiento *or* expansión

2 (a) (become): **to** ~ **careless** volverse* descuidado; **to** ~ **old** envejecer* (fam); **(b)** (get) **to** ~ **to** **+ INF**: **she grew to love him** llegó a quererlo

■ ~ *vt* ⟨*flowers/plants/crops*⟩ cultivar; **to** ~ **a beard** dejarse (crecer) la barba; **to** ~ **one's hair** **(long)** dejarse crecer el pelo

■ **grow into** [*v + prep + o*] **(a)** (become) convertirse* en **(b)** (grow to fit): **she will soon** ~ **into these dresses** pronto podrá usar estos vestidos

■ **grow on** [*v + prep + o*] (colloq): **it** ~**s on you** «*music/place*» llega a gustar con el tiempo

■ **grow out of** [*v + adv + prep + o*] **(a)** ⟨*habit*⟩ perder*, quitarse (*con el tiempo o la edad*); **it's just a phase, she'll** ~ **out of it** son cosas de la edad, ya se le pasará **(b)** ⟨*clothes*⟩: **she's** ~**n out of those shoes already** esos zapatos ya le quedan chicos *or* (Esp) le están pequeños

■ **grow up** [*v + adv*] **(a)** (spend childhood) criarse*, crecer* **(b)** (become adult) hacerse* mayor; **when I** ~ **up** cuando sea grande; ~ **up!** ¡no seas infantil! **(c)** (arise) «*friendship/custom/feeling*» surgir*; «*settlement/town*» desarrollarse

grower /'grəʊər ǁ'grəʊə(r)/ *n* cultivador, -dora *m,f*

growing /'grəʊɪŋ/ *adj* (*before n*) **(a)** ⟨*quantity/ reputation*⟩ cada vez mayor; ⟨*influence*⟩ creciente **(b)** ⟨*child*⟩: **you need a lot to eat; you're a** ~ **boy** tienes que comer mucho, estás creciendo **(c)** ⟨*plant/stem/vegetable*⟩ que está creciendo

growl¹ /graʊl/ *vi* gruñir*

growl² *n* gruñido *m*

grown¹ /grəʊn/ *past p of* GROW

grown² *adj*: **he's a** ~ **man** es un hombre hecho y derecho; **when the young are fully** ~ (Zool) cuando las crías han alcanzado su pleno desarrollo

grown-up¹ /'grəʊnʌp/ *n* persona *f* mayor

grown-up² *adj* **(a)** (adult) mayor **(b)** (mature) (colloq) maduro, adulto

growth /grəʊθ/ *n* **1** (of animals, plants, humans) crecimiento *m* **2** (of population, city, business) crecimiento *m*; (of quantity, profits) aumento *m*; (in popularity) aumento *m* **3 (a)** (what grows): **new** ~ brotes *mpl* nuevos; **several days' ** ~ **of beard** una barba de varios días **(b)** (Med) bulto *m*, tumor *m*

growth industry *n* industria *f* en crecimiento *or* en expansión

grub /grʌb/ *n* **1** (Zool) larva *f* **2** (food) (colloq) comida *f*, papeo *m* (Esp arg), morfe *m* (CS arg)

grubby /'grʌbi/ *adj* **-bier, -biest** mugriento

grudge¹ /grʌdʒ/ *n* rencilla *f*; **to bear sb a** ~ tenerle* *or* guardarle rencor a algn

grudge² *vt* ▶ BEGRUDGE

grueling, (BrE) **gruelling** /'gruːəlɪŋ/ *adj* ⟨*journey*⟩ extenuante; ⟨*experience/ordeal*⟩ penoso

gruesome /'gruːsəm/ *adj* truculento

gruff /grʌf/ *adj* **-er, -est** ⟨*voice*⟩ áspero; ⟨*manner/reply*⟩ brusco

grumble /'grʌmbəl/ *vi* refunfuñar (fam), rezongar (fam); **to** ~ **ABOUT sth/sb** quejarse DE algo/ algn

grumpy /'grʌmpi/ *adj* **-pier, -piest** ⟨*person*⟩ gruñón; ⟨*remark/voice*⟩ malhumorado

grunt¹ /grʌnt/ *vi* gruñir*

grunt² *n* gruñido *m*

guarantee¹ /'gærən'tiː/ *n* garantía *f*

guarantee² *vt* garantizar*

guarantor /'gærən'tɔːr ǁ,gærən'tɔː(r)/ *n* garante *mf*

guard¹ /gɑːrd ǁgɑːd/ *vt* **(a)** ⟨*building/prisoner*⟩ vigilar; ⟨*person/reputation*⟩ proteger*; ⟨*secret*⟩ guardar **(b)** (AmE Sport) marcar*

■ **guard against** [*v + prep + o*] ⟨*injury/ temptation*⟩ evitar; ⟨*risk*⟩ protegerse* contra

guard² *n* **1 (a)** (sentry, soldier) guardia *mf*; **security** ~ guarda *mf* de seguridad; **prison** ~ (AmE) carcelero, -ra *m,f*, oficial *mf* de prisiones **(b)** (squad) (*no pl*) guardia *f* **(c)** (Sport) (in US football) defensa *mf*; (in basketball) escolta *mf* **2** (surveillance) guardia *f*; **to be on** ~ estar* de guardia; (*before n*) ~ **duty** guardia *f*, posta *f* (AmC) **3** (in boxing, fencing) guardia *f*; **to be on/off (one's)** ~ estar* alerta/desprevenido **4 (a)** (fire ~) guardallama(s) *m* **(b)** (on machinery) cubierta *f* (*or* dispositivo *m* *etc*) de seguridad **5** (BrE Rail) jefe, -fa *m,f* de tren

guard dog *n* perro *m* guardián

guarded /'gɑːrdəd ǁ'gɑːdɪd/ *adj* ⟨*reply/ admission*⟩ cauteloso; ⟨*optimism*⟩ cauto

guardian /'gɑːrdiən ǁ'gɑːdiən/ *n* **(a)** (of child) tutor, -tora *m,f* **(b)** (protector) defensor, -sora *m,f*, custodio, -dia *m,f*

guardian angel n ángel m de la guarda, ángel m custodio

guard: ~**rail** n (in staircase) barandilla f; (in roads etc) barrera f de seguridad; ~**'s van** n (BrE Rail) furgón m de cola

Guatemala /ˌgwɑːtəˈmɑːlə/ n Guatemala f

Guatemalan[1] /ˌgwɑːtəˈmɑːlən/ adj guatemalteco

Guatemalan[2] n guatemalteco, -ca m,f

Guernsey /ˈgɜːnzi ‖ ˈgɜːnzi/ n Guernesey

guerrilla /gəˈrɪlə/ n guerrillero, -ra m,f; (before n) ⟨tactics/leader⟩ guerrillero; ~ **warfare** guerrilla f

guess[1] /ges/ n: **have a** ~! ¡a ver si adivinas!; **your** ~ **is as good as mine** quién sabe, vete tú a saber

guess[2] vt (a) (conjecture, estimate) adivinar; ~ **what!** ¿sabes qué?; **you'll never** ~ **what he said** no te puedes imaginar lo que dijo (b) (suppose) (esp AmE colloq) suponer*; **I** ~ **so** supongo (que sí)
■ ~ vi: **how did you** ~? ¿cómo adivinaste? or (Esp) ¿cómo lo has adivinado?; **to** ~ **right** acertar*, adivinar, atinar(le) (Méx)

guesswork /ˈgeswɜːrk ‖ ˈgeswɜːk/ n conjeturas fpl

guest /gest/ n (visitor) invitado, -da m,f; (in hotel) huésped mf, cliente, -ta m,f; (before n) ~ **list** lista f de invitados; ~ **speaker** conferenciante invitado, -da m,f; ~ **star** estrella f invitada

guest: ~**house** n (a) (in US, attached to mansion) pabellón m de huéspedes (b) (Tourism) (in UK) casa f de huéspedes, pensión f; ~**room** n cuarto m de huéspedes or (Chi) de alojados

guffaw[1] /gʌˈfɔː/ n risotada f

guffaw[2] vi reírse* a carcajadas

guidance /ˈgaɪdəns/ n orientación f; **he needs** ~ necesita que lo orienten; (before n) ~ **counselor** (AmE) orientador, -dora m,f vocacional

guide[1] /gaɪd/ n ① (a) (Tourism) (person) guía mf; (publication) guía f (b) (adviser) consejero, -ra m,f ② **Guide** (BrE) exploradora f, guía f ③ (indicator) guía f; **to use** o **take sth as a** ~ guiarse* por algo

guide[2] vt (a) ⟨tourist/stranger⟩ guiar*; **a priest** ~**d them round the cathedral** un sacerdote les hizo de guía en la catedral (b) (help, advise) guiar*, aconsejar (c) (steer, manipulate) (+ adv compl): **the captain** ~**d the ship between the rocks** el capitán condujo or guio el barco por entre las rocas

guide: ~**book** n guía f; ~ **dog** n perro m guía, perro m lazarillo

guided tour /ˈgaɪdəd ‖ ˈgaɪdɪd/ n visita f guiada

guideline /ˈgaɪdlaɪn/ n pauta f

guild /gɪld/ n (a) (of workers) gremio m (b) (club, society) asociación f

guile /gaɪl/ n astucia f

guillotine /ˈgɪlətiːn/ n guillotina f

guilt /gɪlt/ n (a) (blame) culpa f; (Law) culpabilidad f (b) (Psych) culpa f

guilty /ˈgɪlti/ adj **-tier, -tiest** (a) (Law) (no comp) culpable; **to be** ~ **of** sth ser* culpable DE algo (b) (ashamed, remorseful) culpable (c) (shameful) (before n) ⟨secret⟩ vergonzoso

guinea /ˈgɪni/ n guinea f

guinea pig n (a) (Zool) cobayo m, cobaya f, conejillo m de Indias, cuy m (AmS) (b) (person) conejillo m de Indias

guise /gaɪz/ n: **under the** ~ **of friendship** bajo una apariencia de amistad; **in many different** ~**s** de muchas formas distintas

guitar /gəˈtɑːr ‖ gɪˈtɑː(r)/ n guitarra f

guitarist /gəˈtɑːrəst ‖ gɪˈtɑːrɪst/ n guitarrista mf

gulf /gʌlf/ n (a) (Geog) golfo m (b) (gap) abismo m

gull /gʌl/ n (Zool) gaviota f

gullet /ˈgʌlət ‖ ˈgʌlɪt/ n garganta f

gulley /ˈgʌli/ n (pl **-leys**) ▶ GULLY

gullible /ˈgʌləbəl/ adj crédulo

gully /ˈgʌli/ n (pl **-lies**) (a) (small valley) barranco m (b) (channel) surco m, cauce m

gulp[1] /gʌlp/ vi tragar* saliva
■ ~ vt **~** (down) ⟨food⟩ engullir*; ⟨drink/medicine⟩ beberse de un trago

gulp[2] n (of liquid) trago m; (of air) bocanada f; **in one** ~ de un trago

gum /gʌm/ n ① (Anat) encía f ② (chewing ~) chicle m, goma f de mascar ③ (a) (glue) (BrE) goma f de pegar (b) (from plant) resina f

gun /gʌn/ n (pistol) pistola f, revólver m; (shotgun, rifle) escopeta f, fusil m, rifle m; (artillery piece) cañón m
■ **gun down** [v + o + adv, v + adv + o] abatir a tiros

gun: ~**dog** n perro m de caza; ~**fight** n tiroteo m, balacera f (AmL); ~**fire** n disparos mpl; (from heavy artillery) cañoneo m, cañonazos mpl; ~**man** /ˈgʌnmən/ n (pl **-men** /-mən/) pistolero m, gatillero m (Méx); ~**point** n: **at** ~**point** a punta de pistola; ~**powder** n pólvora f; ~**running** n tráfico m de armas; ~**shot** n disparo m; (before n) ~**shot wound** herida f de bala; ~**smith** n armero, -ra m,f

gurgle[1] /ˈgɜːrgəl ‖ ˈgɜːgəl/ vi «water/brook» borbotar; «baby» gorjear

gurgle[2] n (of water, liquid) borboteo m; (of delight) gorjeo m

gush /gʌʃ/ vi «liquid» salir* a borbotones

gushing /ˈgʌʃɪŋ/ adj (pej) demasiado efusivo

gusset /ˈgʌsət ‖ ˈgʌsɪt/ n entretela f

gust /gʌst/ n ráfaga f

gusto /ˈgʌstəʊ/ n entusiasmo m; **with** ~ ⟨eat⟩ con ganas; ⟨sing/play⟩ con brío

gusty /ˈgʌsti/ adj **-tier, -tiest** ⟨wind⟩ racheado; ⟨weather/day⟩ ventoso

gut /gʌt/ n (a) (intestine) intestino m (b) (belly) (colloq) barriga f (fam); (before n) ⟨reaction⟩ instintivo

AmC	América Central	Arg	Argentina	Cu	Cuba	Per	Perú
AmL	América Latina	Bol	Bolivia	Ec	Ecuador	RPI	Río de la Plata
AmS	América del Sur	Chi	Chile	Esp	España	Ur	Uruguay
Andes	Región andina	CS	Cono Sur	Méx	México	Ven	Venezuela

gut² *vt* **-tt-** (a) ⟨*fish/chicken/rabbit*⟩ limpiar (b) ⟨*building*⟩ destruir* el interior de

guts /gʌts/ *n* [1] (+ *pl vb*) (colloq) (bowels) tripas *fpl* (fam) [2] (+ *sing o pl vb*) (courage) (colloq) agallas *fpl* (fam)

gutter /'gʌtər ‖ 'gʌtə(r)/ *n* (a) (on roof) canaleta *f*, canalón *m* (Esp) (b) (in street) alcantarilla *f* (c) (lowest section of society) **the ~** el arroyo; ⟨*before n*⟩ **the ~ press** la prensa sensacionalista

guttural /'gʌtərəl/ *adj* gutural

guy /gaɪ/ *n* (colloq) (a) (man) tipo *m* (fam), tío *m* (Esp fam), chavo *m* (Méx fam) (b) **guys** *pl* (people) (AmE) gente *f*

Guyana /gaɪ'ænə/ *n* Guyana *f*, Guayana *f*

Guyanese /ˌgaɪə'niːz/ *adj* guyanés, guayanés

guzzle /'gʌzəl/ *vt* (a) (drink greedily) chupar (fam) (b) (eat greedily) (BrE) engullirse*, tragarse*

gym /dʒɪm/ *n* (a) (gymnasium) gimnasio *m* (b) (gymnastics) gimnasia *f*

gymnasium /dʒɪm'neɪziəm/ *n* (*pl* **-siums** *or* **-sia** /-ziə/) gimnasio *m*

gymnast /'dʒɪmnæst/ *n* gimnasta *mf*

gymnastics /dʒɪm'næstɪks/ *n* (a) (activity) (+ *sing vb*) gimnasia *f* (b) (exercises) (+ *pl vb*) gimnasia *f*

gynecologist, (BrE) **gynaecologist** /'gaɪnə'kɑːlədʒəst ‖ ˌgaɪnə'kɒlədʒɪst/ *n* ginecólogo, -ga *m,f*

gynecology, (BrE) **gynaecology** /'gaɪnə'kɑːlədʒi ‖ ˌgaɪnə'kɒlədʒi/ *n* ginecología *f*

gypsy, Gypsy /'dʒɪpsi/ *n* (*pl* **-sies**) gitano, -na *m,f*

gyrate /'dʒaɪreɪt ‖ dʒaɪ'reɪt/ *vi* girar

Hh

H, h /eɪtʃ/ *n* H, h *f*

haberdashery /'hæbər,dæʃəri ‖ 'hæbə,dæʃəri/ *n* (a) (clothes) (AmE) ropa *f* y accesorios *mpl* (b) (sewing materials) (BrE) (artículos *mpl* de) mercería *f*

habit /'hæbət ‖ 'hæbɪt/ *n* [1] (a) (usual piece of behavior) costumbre *f*, hábito *m*; (bad) vicio *m*, mala costumbre *f*, mal hábito *m*; **to get out of/ into the ~ of doing sth** perder*/tomar la costumbre de hacer algo (b) (customary behavior) costumbre *f*; **by** *or* **out of** *or* **from force of ~** por fuerza de la costumbre [2] (Clothing) hábito *m*

habitat /'hæbətæt ‖ 'hæbɪtæt/ *n* hábitat *m*

habitation /'hæbə'teɪʃən ‖ ˌhæbɪ'teɪʃən/ *n* (frml): **unfit for human ~** inhabitable

habitual /hə'bɪtʃuəl/ *adj* (a) (usual) habitual, acostumbrado (b) (compulsive) ⟨*liar/gambler*⟩ empedernido

hack¹ /hæk/ *vt* cortar a tajos, tajear (Andes)
■ ~ *vi* [1] (to cut): **to ~ at sth** darle* (golpes) a algo; **we ~ed through the undergrowth** nos abrimos paso a machetazos (*or* hachazos *etc*) a través de la espesura [2] (Comput colloq) **to ~ into** ⟨*system*⟩ piratear

hack² *n* [1] (pej *or* hum) (writer) escritorzuelo, -la *m,f* (pey); (journalist) gacetillero, -ra *m,f* (pey) [2] (horse — for hire) caballo *m* de alquiler; (— worn-out) jaco *m*, jamelgo *m* [3] (AmE colloq) (a) (taxi driver) taxista *mf*, tachero, -ra *m,f* (RPl fam), ruletero, -ra *m,f* (Méx fam) (b) (taxi) taxi *m*, tacho *m* (RPl fam)

hacker /'hækər ‖ 'hækə(r)/ *n* (Comput colloq) pirata informático, -ca *m,f*

hacking /'hækɪŋ/ *adj* ⟨*cough*⟩ áspero

hackles /'hækəlz/ *pl n* **to make sb's ~ rise** poner* furioso a algn; **his ~ rose** se enfureció

hackneyed /'hæknid/ *adj* manido, trillado

hacksaw /'hæksɔː/ *n* sierra *f* de arco (*para metales*)

had /hæd/, *weak form* həd, əd/ *past & past p of* HAVE

haddock /'hædək/ *n* (*pl* **~**) (a) (Zool) eglefino *m* (b) (Culin) abadejo *m*

hadn't /'hædn̩t/ = **had not**

haem- *etc* (BrE) ▶ HEM- *etc*

hag /hæg/ *n* bruja *f*, arpía *f*

haggard /'hægərd ‖ 'hægəd/ *adj* demacrado

haggis /'hægəs ‖ 'hægɪs/ *n* (*pl* **-gis** *or* **-gises**) plato escocés hecho con vísceras de cordero y avena

haggle /'hægəl/ *vi* regatear

Hague /heɪg/ *n* **The ~** La Haya

hail¹ /heɪl/ *n* (a) (Meteo) granizo *m*, pedrisco *m* (b) (of bullets, insults) (*no pl*) lluvia *f*

hail² *v impers* (Meteo) granizar*
■ ~ *vt* [1] (call to) ⟨*person*⟩ llamar; ⟨*ship*⟩ saludar; ⟨*taxi*⟩ hacerle* señas a [2] (acclaim, welcome) ⟨*king/ leader*⟩ aclamar; **it was ~ed as a major breakthrough** fue acogido como un importantísimo avance
■ ~ *vi* **to ~ FROM** «*person*» ser* DE

hail: H~ Mary /'meri ‖ 'meəri/ *n* Avemaría *m*; **~stone** *n* granizo *m*, piedra *f* (de granizo)

hair /her ‖ heə(r)/ *n* (a) (on human head) pelo *m*, cabello *m* (frml o liter); **to have one's ~ done** peinarse (*en la peluquería*); ⟨*before n*⟩ ⟨*gel/ lacquer/oil*⟩ para el pelo; ⟨*transplant*⟩ capilar (b) (on human body) vello *m*; (on animal, plant) pelo *m* (c) (single strand) pelo *m*

hair: ~band *n* (elastic) cinta *f*, huincha *f* (Bol, Chi, Per), balaca *f* (Col), banda *f* (Méx), vincha *f* (RPl, Ven); (rigid) diadema *f*, cintillo *m*, vincha *f* (RPl, Ven); **~brush** *n* cepillo *m* (del pelo); **~clip** *n* (BrE) horquilla *f*, pinche *m* (Chi), pasador *m* (Méx); **~cut** *n* corte *m* de pelo; **~do** *n* (colloq) peinado *m*; **~dresser** *n* peluquero, -ra *m,f*; **the ~dresser's** la peluquería; **~drier, ~dryer** *n* secador *m* or (Méx) secadora *f*; **~grip** *n* (BrE) horquilla *f*, pinche *m* (Chi), pasador *m* (Méx); ····⦂

∼line n (a) (where hair begins) nacimiento m del pelo (b) (fine line) línea f delgada; (before n) a **∼line fracture** una pequeña fisura; **∼net** n redecilla f; **∼piece** n postizo m; **∼pin** n horquilla f (de moño); (before n) **∼pin turn** o (BrE) bend curva f muy cerrada; **∼raising** /'her,reɪzɪŋ ‖heə,reɪzɪŋ/ adj espeluznante; **∼'s breadth, ∼sbreadth** n (no pl): by a **∼'s breadth** por un pelo (fam); (before n) **∼** BARRETTE; **∼spray** n laca f, fijador m (para el pelo); **∼style** n peinado m, corte m de pelo

hairy /'heri ‖'heəri/ adj **-rier, -riest** ⟨legs/ chest⟩ peludo, velludo

Haiti /'heɪti/ n Haití m

Haitian /'heɪʃən/ adj haitiano

hake /heɪk/ n (pl **∼**) merluza f

halal /hɑːˈlɑːl/ adj (Culin) ⟨meat⟩ de animales faenados or (Esp) sacrificados según la ley musulmana

hale /heɪl/ adj (liter): **∼ and hearty** (fuerte) como un roble

half¹ /hæf ‖hɑːf/ n (pl **halves**) **1** (a) (part) mitad f; **to break sth in ∼** romper* algo por la mitad or en dos; **to go halves** (colloq) pagar* a medias (b) (Math) medio m (c) (elliptical use): **an hour and a ∼** una hora y media; **it's ∼ past ten** son las diez y media **2** (Sport) (a) (period) tiempo m (b) (of pitch) campo m (c) (interval) (AmE) descanso m, medio tiempo m (AmL)

half² pron la mitad

half³ adj medio, -dia; **∼ a pint of milk** media pinta de leche; **one and a ∼ hours** una hora y media

half⁴ adv medio; **she was ∼ asleep** estaba medio dormida or semidormida; **the work is only ∼ done** el trabajo está a medio hacer; **she is ∼ Italian, ∼ Greek** es hija de italianos y griegos; **they are paid ∼ as much as we are** les pagan la mitad que a nosotros

half- /'hæf ‖hɑːf/ pref: **∼closed/∼open** entreabierto; **∼starved** medio muerto de hambre

half: **∼ a dozen** n (no pl) media docena f, **∼ a dozen eggs** media docena de huevos; **∼ an hour** n media hora f; **∼ brother** n hermanastro m, medio hermano m; **∼hearted** /'hæfhɑːrtəd ‖hɑːfˈhɑːtɪd/ adj poco entusiasta; **∼hour** /'hæfaʊr ‖hɑːfaʊə(r)/ n media hora f; **∼light** n penumbra f; **∼mast** /'hæfmæst ‖hɑːfmɑːst/ n: **at ∼mast** a media asta; **∼ measures** pl n medias tintas fpl; **∼moon** /'hæfmuːn ‖hɑːfmuːn/ n media luna f; **∼ note** n (AmE) blanca f; **∼penny** /'heɪpni/ n (Hist) (a) (pl **-pennies**) (coin) medio penique m (b) (pl **-pence** /'heɪpəns/) (value) medio penique m; **∼ price** n mitad f de precio; **it's ∼ price** está a mitad de precio; **∼ sister** n hermanastra f, media hermana f; **∼staff** n (AmE) ▸ **∼MAST**; **∼ term** n (in UK) vacaciones fpl de mitad de trimestre; **∼time** n (a) (Sport) descanso m, medio tiempo m (AmL); (b) (Busn, Lab Rel) media jornada f

half-way¹ /'hæfweɪ ‖hɑːfˈweɪ/ adv (at, to mid point) a mitad de camino; **I'm about ∼ through** voy por la mitad; **to meet sb ∼** (compromise) llegar* a una solución intermedia con algn; (lit: on journey) encontrarse* con algn a mitad de camino

half-way² adj (before n) ⟨point⟩ medio; ⟨stage⟩ intermedio; **the ∼ mark** el punto medio, la mitad

half-yearly /'hæfjɪrli ‖hɑːfˈjɪəli/ adj semestral

hall /hɔːl/ n **1** (a) (vestibule) vestíbulo m, entrada f (b) (corridor) (AmE) pasillo m, corredor m **2** (a) (for gatherings) salón m (b) (in castle, mansion) sala f **3** (student residence) (BrE) residencia f universitaria or de estudiantes, colegio m mayor (Esp) **4** (large country house) (BrE) casa f solariega

halleluja /ˌhæleˈluːjə ‖ˌhælɪˈluːjə/ interj ¡aleluya!

hallmark /'hɔːlmɑːrk ‖'hɔːlmɑːk/ n (a) (on gold, silver) contraste m, sello m (de contraste) (b) (distinguishing characteristic) distintivo m, sello m

hallo /həˈləʊ/ interj ▸ HELLO

hall of residence n (pl **∼s of residence**) (BrE) ▸ HALL 3

Halloween, Hallowe'en /ˌhæləʊˈiːn/ n víspera f del día de Todos los Santos

hallucination /həˌluːsɪˈneɪʃən ‖həˌluːsɪˈneɪʃən/ n alucinación f

hallway /'hɔːlweɪ/ n ▸ HALL 1

halo /'heɪləʊ/ n (pl **-los** or **-loes**) (a) (Art, Relig) aureola f, halo m (b) (Astron, Opt) halo m

halt¹ /hɔːlt ‖hɒlt, hɔːlt/ n: **to come to a ∼** pararse

halt² vi detenerse* (frml); **∼!** (Mil) ¡alto!
∎ **∼** vt ⟨vehicle/troops⟩ detener* (frml); ⟨process⟩ atajar, detener* (frml); ⟨work/production⟩ interrumpir

halter /'hɔːltər ‖'hɒltə(r), 'hɔː-/ n cabestro m, ronzal m

halve /hæv ‖hɑːv/ vt (a) (reduce by half) ⟨expense/time/length⟩ reducir* a la mitad or en un 50%; ⟨number⟩ dividir por dos (b) (divide into halves) partir por la mitad
∎ **∼** vi reducirse* a la mitad or en un 50%

halves /hævz ‖hɑːvz/ pl of HALF¹

ham /hæm/ n **1** (Culin) (cured) jamón m (crudo), jamón m serrano (Esp); (cooked) jamón m (cocido), jamón m (de) York (Esp) **2** (Theat) actor extravagantemente histriónico

hamburger /'hæmbɜːrgər ‖'hæmbɜːgə(r)/ n hamburguesa f

hamlet /'hæmlət ‖'hæmlɪt/ n aldea f, caserío m

hammer¹ /'hæmər ‖'hæmə(r)/ n martillo m

hammer² vt ⟨nail⟩ clavar (con un martillo); ⟨metal⟩ martillar, batir
∎ **∼** vi (strike) dar* golpes; (with hammer) dar* martillazos; **to ∼ at or on the door** golpear la puerta
∎ **hammer home** [v + o + adv, v + adv + o] ⟨nail⟩ remachar; ⟨point⟩ recalcar*, machacar*
∎ **hammer out** [v + o + adv, v + adv + o] ⟨metal/ dent⟩ alisar a martillazos; ⟨compromise/deal⟩ negociar ⟨con mucho toma y daca⟩

hammock /'hæmək/ n hamaca f, hamaca f paraguaya (RPl); (Naut) coy m

hamper¹ /'hæmpər ‖'hæmpə(r)/ vt dificultar

hamper² n cesta f, canasta f

hamster /'hæmstər ‖'hæmstə(r)/ n hámster m

hamstring /'hæmstrɪŋ/ n (of person) ligamento m de la corva; (of horse) tendón m del corvejón or jarrete

hand¹ /hænd/ n **1** (Anat) mano f; ~s off! ¡quita las manos de ahí!; ~s up all those in favor que levanten la mano los que estén a favor; ~s up! ¡manos arriba!

2 (in phrases) **at hand: help was at ~** la ayuda estaba en camino; **by hand** ⟨make/write/wash⟩ a mano; ⟨deliver⟩ en mano; **hand in hand** (tomados or agarrados or (esp Esp) cogidos) de la mano; **poverty and disease go ~ in ~** la pobreza y la enfermedad van de la mano; **on hand: the police were on ~** la policía estaba cerca; **to have sth on ~** tener* algo a mano; **out of hand: the situation is getting out of ~** la situación se nos (or les etc) va de las manos; **to reject sth out of ~** rechazar* algo de plano; **to hand** (BrE) (within reach) al alcance de la mano, a (la) mano; (available) disponible; **to beat sb/win ~s down** ganarle a algn/ganar sin problemas; **to get one's ~s on sb/ sth: just wait till I get my ~s on him!** ¡vas a ver cuando lo agarre!; **she can't wait to get her ~s on the new computer** se muere por usar la computadora nueva; **to give sb/have a free ~** darle* a algn/tener* carta blanca; **to know a place like the back of one's ~** conocer* un sitio al dedillo; **to try one's ~ (at sth)** probar* (a hacer algo)

3 (a) (agency) mano f; **to have a ~ in sth** tener* parte en algo; **the town had suffered at the ~s of invaders** la ciudad había sufrido a manos de los invasores (b) (assistance) (colloq): **to give sb a ~** echarle or darle* una mano a algn; **if you need a ~** si necesitas ayuda (c) **hands** pl (possession, control, care): **to change ~s** cambiar de dueño; **in good/capable ~s** en buenas manos; **my life is in your ~s** mi vida depende de ti; **we've got a problem on our ~s** tenemos un problema; **the matter is out of my ~s** el asunto no está en mis manos

4 (side): **on sb's right/left ~** a la derecha/ izquierda de algn; **on the one ~ ... on the other (~)** ... por un lado ... por otro (lado) ...

5 (Games) (a) (set of cards) mano f, cartas fpl (b) (round of card game) mano f

6 (a) (worker) obrero, -ra m,f; (farm ~) peón m (b) (Naut) marinero m (c) (experienced person): **an old ~** un veterano, una veterana

7 (applause) (colloq) (no pl): **a big ~ for ...** un gran aplauso para ...

8 (handwriting) (liter) letra f

9 (on clock) manecilla f, aguja f, puntero m (Andes)

hand² vt **to ~ sb sth, to ~ sth TO sb** pasarle algo A algn

■ **hand around,** (BrE also) **hand round** [v + o + adv, v + adv + o] (distribute) repartir, distribuir*; (offer round) ⟨cakes⟩ ofrecer*

■ **hand down** [v + o + adv, v + adv + o] (pass down) ⟨custom/heirloom/story⟩ transmitir; ⟨clothes⟩ pasar

■ **hand in** [v + o + adv, v + adv + o] ⟨homework/ form/ticket⟩ entregar*; ⟨resignation⟩ presentar

■ **hand on** [v + o + adv, v + adv + o] ⟨skills/ knowledge⟩ transmitir, pasar; ⟨object/photograph⟩ pasar

■ **hand out** [v + o + adv, v + adv + o] repartir, distribuir*; ⟨advice⟩ dar*

■ **hand over** [v + o + adv, v + adv + o] (a) (relinquish) entregar* (b) (transfer) transferir*

■ **hand round** (BrE) ▶ HAND AROUND

hand: ~**bag** n (used by women) cartera f or (Esp) bolso m or (Méx) bolsa f; (small suitcase) (AmE) maletín m; ~ **baggage,** (BrE) ~ **luggage** n equipaje m de mano; ~**ball** n (a) (game — in US) frontón m, pelota f; (— in Europe) balonmano m, handball m (AmL) (b) (in soccer) mano f; ~**book** n manual m; ~**brake** n (on bicycle) (AmE) freno m (de pastilla); (BrE Auto) freno m de mano; ~**craft** n ▶ HANDICRAFT; ~ **cream** n crema f de manos or para las manos; ~**cuff** vt esposar, ponerle* esposas a; ~**cuffs** npl n esposas fpl

handful /'hændful/ n (a) (amount) puñado m (b) (small number) (+ sing o pl vb) puñado m; **a ~ of people** unas cuantas personas (c) (troublesome person or people) (no pl): **that child is a real ~** ese niño da mucho trabajo

hand grenade n granada f (de mano)

handicap¹ /'hændɪkæp/ n **1** (a) (disability): **physical ~** impedimento m físico; **mental ~** retraso m mental (b) (disadvantage) desventaja f **2** (Sport) (in golf, polo) hándicap m; (penalty) desventaja f

handicap² vt -pp- ⟨person/chances⟩ perjudicar*

handicapped /'hændɪkæpt/ adj disminuido, discapacitado, minusválido; **mentally/physically ~** disminuido or discapacitado or minusválido psíquico/físico

handicraft /'hændɪkræft ‖ 'hændɪkrɑːft/, **handcraft** n (a) (skill) artesanía f, trabajo m artesanal (b) (product) producto m de artesanía

handiwork /'hændiwɜːrk ‖ 'hændiwɜːk/ n (a) (craftsmanship) trabajo m (b) (product) artesanías fpl, objetos mpl artesanales (c) (doing) (pej) obra f; **it looks like Laura's ~ to me** a mí me parece obra de Laura

handkerchief /'hæŋkərtʃəf, -tʃiːf ‖ 'hæŋkətʃɪf, -tʃiːf/ n (pl **-chieves** /-tʃiːvz/ or **-chiefs**) pañuelo m

handle¹ /'hændl/ n (of cup, jug, bag) asa f‡; (of door) picaporte m; (knob) pomo m; (of drawer) tirador m, manija f; (of broom, knife, spade) mango m; (of wheelbarrow) brazo m; (of pump) manivela f

handle² vt **1** (a) (touch) tocar*; **ⓢ handle with care** frágil (b) (manipulate, manage) ⟨vehicle/ weapon⟩ manejar; ⟨chemicals⟩ manipular **2** (deal with) ⟨people⟩ tratar; ⟨situation/affair⟩ manejar; **he can't ~ the job** (colloq) no puede con el trabajo **3** (a) (be responsible for) ⟨business/financial matters⟩ encargarse* or ocuparse de, llevar (b) (do business in) ⟨goods/commodities⟩ comerciar con (c) ⟨computer⟩ ⟨data⟩ procesar

handlebar /'hændlbɑːr ‖ 'hændlbɑː(r)/ n (often pl) ~(s) manillar m, manubrio m (AmL)

handling /'hændlɪŋ/ n **1** (treatment — of situation) manejo m; (— of subject) tratamiento m **2** (a) (Busn) porte m (b) (Aviat) handling m (c) (Auto) manejo m

handling charge n cargo m por tramitación

hand: ~ **luggage** n (BrE) equipaje m de mano; ~**made** /'hændmeɪd/ adj hecho a mano; ~**-me-down** n: prenda usada o heredada; ~**out** n (a) (of money, food) dádiva f (b) (advertising ⋯⟩

leaflet) folleto *m* **(c)** (at lecture, in class) notas *fpl* (*que se distribuyen a los asistentes*); **~-picked** /ˈhænd'pɪkt/ *adj* cuidadosamente seleccionado; **~rail** *n* (on stairs, slope) pasamanos *m*; (on bridge, ship) baranda *f*, barandilla *f*; **~set** *n* auricular *m*, tubo *m* (RPI); **~shake** *n* apretón *m* de manos; **~ signal** *n* (Auto) seña *f* (*hecha con la mano*); (by referee, coach) (AmE) señal *f*

handsome /ˈhænsəm/ **handsomer, handsomest** *adj* **(a)** (attractive) ⟨man⟩ apuesto, buen mozo (AmL), guapo (esp Esp, Méx) **(b)** ⟨gift/ offer⟩ generoso

hand: ~s-on /ˈhændz'ɑːn ‖ˈhændz'ɒn/ *adj* (*before n*) **(a)** ⟨instruction/experience⟩ práctico **(b)** (Comput) manual; **~stand** *n*: to do a **~stand** hacer* la vertical *or* (Esp) el pino, pararse de manos (AmL); **~-to-mouth** /ˈhændtə'maʊθ/ *adj* pobre, precario; **~-wash** /ˈhænd'wɔːʃ ‖ˈhænd,wɒʃ/ *vt* lavar a mano; **~writing** *n* letra *f*; **~written** /ˈhænd'rɪtn̩/ *adj* manuscrito, escrito a mano

handy /ˈhændi/ *adj* **-dier, -diest** (colloq) ⟨1⟩ ⟨*pred*⟩ **(a)** (readily accessible) a mano **(b)** (conveniently situated) cerca, a mano ⟨2⟩ (useful) práctico; **to come in ~** venir* bien, resultar útil ⟨3⟩ ⟨person⟩ hábil, habilidoso

handyman /ˈhændimæn/ *n* (*pl* **-men** /-men/) *hombre habilidoso para trabajos de carpintería, albañilería etc*

hang¹ /hæŋ/ *vt* ⟨1⟩ (*past & past p* **hung**) **(a)** (suspend) ⟨coat/picture⟩ colgar* **(b)** (put in position) ⟨door/gate⟩ colocar* **(c)** to **~** one's head bajar la cabeza
⟨2⟩ (*past & past p* **hanged** *or* **hung**) (execute) ahorcar*

■ **~** *vi* ⟨1⟩ (*past p* **hung**) **(a)** (be suspended) colgar*, estar* colgado; **to ~ BY/FROM/ON sth** colgar* DE algo; **it's ~ing on the wall** está colgado en la pared **(b)** (hover) «*fog/smoke*» flotar; «*bird*» planear, cernerse*; **he still has the court case ~ing over him** todavía tiene el juicio pendiente **(c)** «*clothing/fabric*» caer*
⟨2⟩ (*past & past p* **hanged** *or* **hung**) (be executed): **he should ~ for his crime** debería ir a la horca por este crimen

■ **hang about** [*v + adv*] ▸ **HANG AROUND**

■ **hang around** (colloq) [*v + adv*] **(a)** (wait) esperar **(b)** (stay) quedarse **(c)** (spend time idly): **they just ~ around on street corners** pasan el tiempo en la calle, holgazaneando; **to ~ around WITH sb** andar* *or* juntarse CON algn

■ **hang on** ⟨1⟩ [*v + adv*] **(a)** (wait) esperar **(b)** (keep hold) **to ~ on TO sth: you ~ on to this end of the rope** tú sostén esta punta de la cuerda **(c)** (keep) (colloq) **to ~ on TO sth** conservar *or* guardar algo **(d)** (in a crisis) aguantar, resistir
⟨2⟩ [*v + prep + o*] (depend on) «*outcome/decision*» depender de

■ **hang out** ⟨1⟩ [*v + o + adv, v + adv + o*] ⟨washing⟩ tender*, colgar*; ⟨flag⟩ poner*
⟨2⟩ [*v + adv*] (dangle) «*wires*» estar* suelto; **with his shirt/tongue ~ing out** con la camisa/la lengua afuera

■ **hang up** ⟨1⟩ [*v + adv*] (put down receiver) colgar*, cortar (CS)
⟨2⟩ [*v + o + adv, v + adv + o*] ⟨coat⟩ colgar*

hang² *n* (*no pl*) **to get the ~ of sth** (colloq) agarrarle la onda a algo (AmL fam), cogerle* el tranquillo a algo (Esp fam), agarrarle la mano a algo (CS fam)

hangar /ˈhæŋər ‖ˈhæŋə(r)/ *n* hangar *m*

hanger /ˈhæŋər ‖ˈhæŋə(r)/ *n* (clothes or coat **~**) percha *f*, gancho *m* (para la ropa) (AmL)

hang: ~ glider *n* ala *f‡* delta, deslizador *m* (Méx); **~ gliding** /ˈglaɪdɪŋ/ *n* vuelo *m* con ala delta *or* (Méx) en deslizador

hanging /ˈhæŋɪŋ/ *n* ⟨1⟩ (execution) ejecución *f* (*en la horca*) ⟨2⟩ (wall **~**) tapiz *m*

hanging basket *n*: *cesto colgante para plantas*

hang: ~man *n* (*pl* **-men** /-mən/) verdugo *m*; **~over** *n* **(a)** (from drinking) resaca *f*, cruda *f* (AmC, Méx fam), guayabo *m* (Col fam), ratón *m* (Ven fam) **(b)** (something surviving) vestigio *m*, reliquia *f*; **~-up** *n* (colloq) complejo *m*, trauma *m*

hanker /ˈhæŋkər ‖ˈhæŋkə(r)/ *vi* **to ~ AFTER** *o* **FOR sth** anhelar *or* ansiar* algo

hanky, hankie /ˈhæŋki/ *n* (*pl* **-kies**) (colloq) pañuelo *m*

Hanukkah, Hanukah /ˈhɑːnəkə/ *n* Januká *m*, Hanukkah *m* (*fiesta judía de la dedicación del Templo*)

haphazard /ˈhæp'hæzərd ‖ˌhæp'hæzəd/ *adj* **(a)** (random): **they promote people in a very ~ way** ascienden a la gente caprichosamente *or* al azar **(b)** (without order): **his approach is very ~** no es coherente en su enfoque

hapless /ˈhæpləs ‖ˈhæplɪs/ *adj* (*before n*) (liter or jour) desafortunado, desventurado (liter)

happen /ˈhæpən/ *vi* ⟨1⟩ **(a)** (occur) pasar, suceder, ocurrir **(b)** (befall, become of) **to ~ TO sb** pasarle a algn ⟨2⟩ **to ~ to + INF: she ~ed to be there** dio la casualidad de que estaba ahí; **if you ~ to see her ...** si por casualidad la ves ...

■ **~** *v impers*: **it (just) so ~s that ...** da la casualidad de que ...

happening /ˈhæpənɪŋ/ *n* suceso *m*

happily /ˈhæpəli ‖ˈhæpɪli/ *adv* ⟨1⟩ **(a)** ⟨smile/ laugh⟩ alegremente; **to be ~ married** ser* feliz en el matrimonio **(b)** (gladly) (*usu before vb*) ⟨help⟩ con mucho gusto ⟨2⟩ (fortunately) (*indep*) por suerte, afortunadamente

happiness /ˈhæpinəs ‖ˈhæpinɪs/ *n* felicidad *f*

happy /ˈhæpi/ *adj* **-pier, -piest** ⟨1⟩ **(a)** ⟨joyful, content⟩ ⟨person/home⟩ feliz; ⟨smile⟩ de felicidad, alegre **(b)** (pleased) (*pred*) **to be ~** alegrarse **(c)** (satisfied) (*pred*) **to be ~ (WITH sth)** estar* contento (CON algo) ⟨2⟩ ⟨days/occasion⟩ feliz; **~ birthday** feliz cumpleaños

happy-go-lucky /ˈhæpigəʊ'lʌki/ *adj* despreocupado

harangue /hə'ræŋ/ *vt* arengar*

harass /ˈhærəs, hə'ræs/ *vt* **(a)** (persistently annoy) acosar **(b)** (Mil) hostigar*

AmC	Central America	Arg	Argentina	Cu	Cuba	Per	Peru
AmL	Latin America	Bol	Bolivia	Ec	Ecuador	RPI	River Plate Area
AmS	South America	Chi	Chile	Esp	Spain	Ur	Uruguay
Andes	Andean Region	CS	Southern Cone	Méx	Mexico	Ven	Venezuela

harassment /'hærəsmənt, hə'ræs-/ n acoso m; **racial** ~ hostilidad f racial; **sexual** ~ acoso m sexual

harbor¹, (BrE) **harbour** /'hɑːrbər ‖ 'hɑːbə(r)/ n puerto m

harbor², (BrE) **harbour** vt (a) (shelter) ⟨fugitive⟩ albergar, dar* refugio a (b) ⟨desire/suspicion⟩ albergar* (liter); **to** ~ **a grudge** guardar rencor

hard¹ /hɑːrd ‖ hɑːd/ adj **-er, -est** ⓵ (a) (firm, solid) ⟨object/surface⟩ duro (b) (forceful) ⟨push/knock⟩ fuerte
⓶ (a) (difficult) ⟨question/subject⟩ difícil; ⟨task⟩ arduo; **I find that** ~ **to believe** me cuesta creerlo; **to learn sth the** ~ **way** aprender algo a base de cometer errores (b) (severe) ⟨winter/climate/master⟩ duro, severo; **to give sb a** ~ **time** hacérselas* pasar mal a algn; **don't be too** ~ **on him** no seas demasiado duro con él; ~ **luck** mala suerte (c) (tough, cynical) ⟨person/attitude⟩ duro
⓷ (concentrated, strenuous) ⟨work⟩ duro; **children are very** ~ **work** los niños dan mucho trabajo; **he's a** ~ **worker** es muy trabajador
⓸ (definite) ⟨evidence⟩ concluyente
⓹ (sharp, harsh) ⟨light/voice⟩ fuerte
⓺ (a) (in strongest form): ~ **drugs** drogas fpl duras; ~ **liquor** bebidas fpl (alcohólicas) fuertes; ~ **porn** porno m duro (b) ⟨water⟩ duro

hard² adv **-er, -est** ⓵ (a) (with force) ⟨pull/push⟩ con fuerza; ⟨hit⟩ fuerte (b) (strenuously) ⟨work⟩ mucho, duro (c) (intently) ⟨listen⟩ atentamente ⓶ (heavily) ⟨rain/snow⟩ fuerte, mucho; ⟨pant/breathe⟩ pesadamente ⓷ (severely): **to be** ~ **hit** ser* muy afectado; **to feel** ~ **done by**: **she feels** ~ **done by** piensa que la han tratado injustamente

hard: ~-**and-fast** /'hɑːrdn̩'fæst ‖ 'hɑːdən'fɑːst/ adj (no comp, usu before n) absoluto; ~**back** n (book) libro m de tapa dura or en cartoné; ~**ball** n (AmE) béisbol m; ~**board** n cartón m madera; ~-**boiled** /'hɑːrd'bɔɪld ‖ ,hɑːd'bɔɪld/ adj (a) ⟨egg⟩ duro (b) (unsentimental) endurecido; ~ **disk** n disco m duro; ~-**earned** /'hɑːrd'ɜːrnd ‖ 'hɑːd,ɜːnd/ adj (usu before n) ⟨cash⟩ ganado con el sudor de la frente

harden /'hɑːrdn̩ ‖ 'hɑːdn̩/ vt (a) (make hard) ⟨clay/cement/skin⟩ endurecer*; ⟨steel/glass⟩ templar (b) (make tough, unfeeling) ⟨person⟩ endurecer*; **you must** ~ **your heart and tell him to go** tienes que hacerte fuerte y decirle que se vaya
■ ~ vi (a) (become hard, rigid) endurecerse* (b) (become inflexible) ⟨attitude⟩ volverse* inflexible

hardened /'hɑːrdn̩d ‖ 'hɑːdn̩d/ adj (before n) ⟨sinner/drinker⟩ empedernido; ⟨criminal⟩ habitual

hard: ~ **hat** n (Clothing, Const) casco m; ~-**headed** /'hɑːrd'hedəd ‖ ,hɑːd'hedɪd/ adj (a) (practical, realistic) práctico, realista (b) (stubborn) (AmE) testarudo, cabezota (fam); ~-**hearted** /'hɑːrd'hɑːrtəd ‖ ,hɑːd'hɑːtɪd/ adj duro de corazón; ~-**hitting** /'hɑːrd'hɪtɪŋ ‖ ,hɑːd'hɪtɪŋ/ adj implacable, feroz; ~ **labor,** (BrE) ~ **labour** n trabajos mpl forzados; ~-**liner** /'hɑːrd'laɪnər ‖ ,hɑːd'laɪnə(r)/ n partidario, -ria m,f de la línea dura

hardly /'hɑːrdli ‖ 'hɑːdli/ adv (a) (scarcely): ~ **anyone/anything** casi nadie/nada; ~ **ever** casi

nunca; **he** ~ **knew her** apenas la conocía (b) (surely not): **it's** ~ **what you'd call a masterpiece** no es precisamente una obra maestra

hardness /'hɑːrdnəs ‖ 'hɑːdnɪs/ n dureza f

hard: ~ **of hearing** adj duro de oído; ~-**pressed** /'hɑːrd'prest ‖ ,hɑːd'prest/ adj ⟨pred ~ **pressed**⟩ ⟨industry/nation/staff⟩ en apuros; ~ **sell** n (no pl) venta f agresiva

hardship /'hɑːrdʃɪp ‖ 'hɑːdʃɪp/ n: **to experience** o **suffer great** ~ pasar muchos apuros; **the** ~**s of the journey** las penurias del viaje

hard: ~ **shoulder** n (BrE) arcén m, berma f (Andes), acotamiento m (Méx), banquina f (RPl), hombrillo m (Ven); ~ **up** adj (colloq) ⟨pred⟩ **to be** ~ **up** estar* mal de dinero; ~**ware** /'hɑːrdwer ‖ 'hɑːdweə(r)/ n (a) (ironmongery) ferretería f; ⟨before n⟩ ~**ware store** ferretería f (b) (Mil): **military** ~**ware** armamento m (c) (Comput) hardware m, soporte m físico, equipo m; ~-**wearing** /'hɑːrd'werɪŋ ‖ ,hɑːd'weərɪŋ/ adj (BrE) resistente; ~-**working** /'hɑːrd'wɜːrkɪŋ ‖ ,hɑːd'wɜːkɪŋ/ adj trabajador

hardy /'hɑːrdi ‖ 'hɑːdi/ adj **-dier, -diest** ⟨person/animal⟩ fuerte; ⟨plant⟩ resistente (a las heladas etc)

hare /her ‖ heə(r)/ n liebre f

haricot (**bean**) /'hærɪkəʊ/ n frijol m or (Esp) alubia f or judía f or (CS) poroto m (de color blanco)

hark back /hɑːrk ‖ hɑːk/ vi **to** ~ ~ **TO sth** «person» rememorar algo; «book» evocar* algo

harm¹ /hɑːrm ‖ hɑːm/ n daño m; **to do** ~ **to sb/sth** hacerle* daño a algn/algo; **there's no** ~ **in asking** con preguntar no se pierde nada; **he won't come to any** ~ no le va a pasar nada; **to be out of** ~'**s way** estar* a salvo

harm² vt ⟨person/object⟩ hacerle* daño a; ⟨reputation/career⟩ perjudicar*

harmful /'hɑːrmfəl ‖ 'hɑːmfəl/ adj ⟨substance⟩ nocivo; ⟨influence⟩ pernicioso, dañino; ⟨effect⟩ perjudicial

harmless /'hɑːrmləs ‖ 'hɑːmlɪs/ adj ⟨animal/person⟩ inofensivo; ⟨substance⟩ inocuo; ⟨joke/suggestion/fun⟩ inocente

harmonica /hɑːr'mɑːnɪkə ‖ hɑː'mɒnɪkə/ n armónica f

harmonious /hɑːr'məʊniəs ‖ hɑː'məʊniəs/ adj armonioso

harmonize /'hɑːrmənaɪz ‖ 'hɑːmənaɪz/ vi (Mus) cantar en armonía; (be in accord) «colors/ideas» armonizar*
■ ~ vt ⟨policies/plans⟩ armonizar

harmony /'hɑːrməni ‖ 'hɑːməni/ n (pl **-nies**) (Mus) armonía f; **in** ~ en armonía

harness¹ /'hɑːrnəs ‖ 'hɑːnɪs/ n (a) (for horse) arnés m, arreos mpl (b) (for baby, on parachute) arnés m (c) (safety ~) arnés m de seguridad

harness² vt (a) (put harness on) ⟨horse⟩ enjaezar*, ponerle* los arreos or el arnés a (b) (utilize) ⟨energy/resources⟩ aprovechar, utilizar*

harp /hɑːrp ‖ hɑːp/ n arpa f‡
■ **harp on** [v + adv] (colloq) **to** ~ ~ **on ABOUT sth** insistir SOBRE algo

harpoon¹ /hɑːr'puːn ‖ hɑː'puːn/ n arpón m

harpoon² vt arponear

harrowing /'hærəʊɪŋ/ adj ‹experience›
angustioso, terrible; ‹tale› desgarrador

harry /'hæri/ vt **-ries, -rying, -ried (a)** (raid)
‹enemy› hostilizar* **(b)** (pester) hostigar*, acosar

harsh /hɑːrʃ ‖ hɑːʃ/ adj ‹punishment› duro,
severo; ‹words/conditions› duro; ‹light› fuerte;
‹climate› riguroso; ‹contrast› violento; ‹color›
chillón; ‹sound› discordante; ‹tone/texture›
áspero

harshly /'hɑːrʃli ‖ 'hɑːʃli/ adv ‹judge/punish/
speak› severamente, con severidad

harvest¹ /'hɑːrvəst ‖ 'hɑːvɪst/ n **(a)** (of grain)
cosecha f, siega f; (of fruit, vegetables) cosecha f,
recolección f; (of grapes) vendimia f **(b)** (yield)
cosecha f

harvest² vt ‹crop/wheat› cosechar; ‹grapes›
vendimiar; ‹field› realizar* la cosecha en

harvester /'hɑːrvəstər ‖ 'hɑːvɪstə(r)/ n **(a)**
(machine) cosechadora f **(b)** (person) segador, -dora
m,f

has /hæz, weak form həz, əz/ 3rd pers sing pres
of HAVE

has-been /'hæzbɪn ‖ 'hæzbiːn/ n (colloq & pej)
nombre m del pasado

hash /hæʃ/ n **(a)** (Culin) plato de carne y
verduras picadas y doradas **(b)** (muddle): **to make
a ∼ of sth** (colloq) hacer* algo muy mal

hash browns pl n (AmE colloq) papas y cebolla
doradas en la sartén

hashish /'hæʃiːʃ/ n hachís m

hasn't /'hæznt/ = **has not**

hassle¹ /'hæsəl/ n (colloq) lío m (fam), rollo m
(fam)

hassle² vt (colloq) fastidiar, jorobar (fam)

haste /heɪst/ n prisa f, apuro m (AmL)

hasten /'heɪsn/ vt ‹process› acelerar; ‹defeat/
death› adelantar
∎ ∼ vi apresurarse, apurarse (AmL)

hastily /'heɪstəli ‖ 'heɪstɪli/ adv **(a)** (quickly)
‹built/thought up› a toda prisa, apresuradamente
(b) (rashly) ‹speak/act› con precipitación,
precipitadamente

hasty /'heɪsti/ adj **-tier, -tiest (a)** (quick)
‹glance/meal› rápido **(b)** (rash) ‹move/decision/
judgment› precipitado; **I think you're being rather
∼** creo que te precipitas

hat /hæt/ n sombrero m

hatch¹ /hætʃ/ vt **(a)** ‹egg› incubar **(b) ∼ (out)**
‹chick› empollar **(c)** (devise) (pej) ‹plot/scheme›
tramar, urdir
∎ ∼ vi **(a)** «egg» romperse* **(b) ∼ (out)** «chick»
salir* del cascarón, nacer*

hatch² n **(a)** (opening, cover) trampilla f; (Aviat,
Naut) escotilla f **(b)** (serving ∼) ventanilla f (que
comunica cocina y comedor)

hatchback /'hætʃbæk/ n (car) coche m con
tres/cinco puertas; (door) puerta f trasera

hatchet /'hætʃət ‖ 'hætʃɪt/ n hacha f‡,
hachuela f; **to bury the ∼** enterrar* el hacha de
guerra

hate¹ /heɪt/ vt odiar, detestar

hate² n **(a)** (hatred) odio m **(b)** (object of hatred) ▶
PET² B

hatred /'heɪtrəd ‖ 'heɪtrɪd/ n odio m

hat trick n: **to score a ∼ ∼** marcar* tres goles
(or tantos etc) en un partido

haughty /'hɔːti/ adj **-tier, -tiest** altivo,
altanero

haul¹ /hɔːl/ vt **(a)** (drag) ‹logs/load› llevar
arrastrando; **the fishermen ∼ed in their nets** los
pescadores cobraron las redes **(b)** (Transp)
transportar

haul² n **1** (catch — of fish) redada f; (— of stolen
goods) botín m **2** (distance) (Transp) recorrido m,
trayecto m

haulage /'hɔːlɪdʒ/ n **(a)** (activity) transporte m;
(before n) **∼ contractor** transportista mf **(b)**
(charge) (gastos mpl de) transporte m

hauler /'hɔːlər ‖ 'hɔːlə(r)/, (BrE) **haulier**
/'hɔːljə(r)/ n (person) transportista mf; (business)
empresa f de transportes

haunch /hɔːntʃ/ n (usu pl) (of animal) anca f‡; (of
horse) grupa f, anca f‡; (of person) cadera f

haunt¹ /hɔːnt/ vt «ghost» rondar; «memory/
idea» perseguir*

haunt² n: **we went to all her old ∼s** fuimos a
todos los sitios a los que solía ir

haunted /'hɔːntəd ‖ 'hɔːntɪd/ adj ‹house›
embrujado; ‹look› angustiado

haunting /'hɔːntɪŋ/ adj evocador e inquietante

Havana /hə'vænə/ n La Habana

have /hæv, weak forms həv, əv/ (3rd pers sing
pres **has**; past & past p **had**) vt
I 1 (possess) tener*; **I ∼ o** (esp BrE) **I've got two
cats** tengo dos gatos
2 (hold, have at one's disposal) tener*; **can I ∼ a
sheet of paper?** ¿me das una hoja de papel?; **I've
(got) a lot to do** tengo mucho que hacer
3 (a) (receive) ‹letter/news› tener*, recibir; **to ∼
had it** (colloq): **I've had it** (I'm in trouble) estoy frito
(AmL), me la he cargado (Esp fam); (I've lost my
chance) la he fastidiado (fam); **to ∼ it in for sb**
(colloq) tenerle* manía or tirria a algn (fam) **(b)**
(obtain) conseguir*; **they were the only seats to be
had** eran los únicos asientos que había
4 (consume) ‹steak/spaghetti› comer, tomar (Esp);
‹champagne/beer› tomar; ‹cigarette› fumar(se); **to
∼ something to eat/drink** comer/beber algo; **to ∼
breakfast** desayunar; **to ∼ lunch** almorzar* or
(esp Esp, Méx) comer; **to ∼ dinner** cenar, comer
(AmL)
5 (a) (experience, undergo) ‹accident› tener*; **∼ a
nice day!** ¡adiós! ¡que le (or te etc) vaya bien!; **we
had a very pleasant evening** pasamos una noche
muy agradable; **she had a heart attack** le dio un
ataque al corazón **(b)** (organize) ‹party› hacer*,
dar*; ‹meeting› tener* **(c)** (suffer from) ‹cancer/
diabetes/flu› tener*; **to ∼ a cold** estar* resfriado
6 (give birth to) ‹baby› tener*
7 (colloq) (swindle, dupe): **you've been had!** ¡te han
timado or engañado!
II 1 (causative use): **we'll ∼ it clean in no time**
enseguida lo limpiamos or lo dejamos limpio; **he
had them all in tears** hizo llorar a todos; **you
had me worried** me tenías preocupado; **to ∼ sth +
PAST P: we had it repaired** lo hicimos arreglar, lo
mandamos (a) arreglar (AmL); **to ∼ one's hair cut**
cortarse el pelo
2 (indicating what happens to sb): **to have sth + PAST
P: he had his bicycle stolen** le robaron la
bicicleta
3 (a) (allow) (with neg) tolerar, consentir*; **I**

won't ∼ it! ¡no lo consentiré *or* toleraré! **(b)**
(accept, believe) aceptar, creer*; **she wouldn't ∼ it**
no lo quiso aceptar *or* creer
4 (indicating state, position) tener*; **I had the radio
on** tenía la radio puesta
■ ∼ *v aux*
I 1 (*used to form perfect tenses*) haber*; **I ∼/had
seen her** la he/había visto; **∼ you been waiting
long?** ¿hace mucho que esperas?; **if I'd known that
…** si hubiera sabido que …; **when he had
finished, she …** cuando terminó *or* (liter) cuando
hubo terminado, ella …
2 **(a)** (in tags): **you've met Joe, ∼n't you?**
conoces a Joe ¿no? *or* ¿no es cierto? *or* ¿no es
verdad?; **∼n't lost the key, ∼ you?** ¡no
habrás perdido la llave …! **(b)** (elliptical use): **you
may ∼ forgiven him, but I ∼n't** puede que tú lo
hayas perdonado, pero yo no; **the clock has
stopped — so it has!** el reloj se ha parado — ¡es
verdad! *or* ¡es cierto!; **you've forgotten something
— ∼ I?** te has olvidado de algo — ¿sí?
II (expressing obligation): **to ∼ to + INF** tener* QUE +
INF; **you don't ∼ to be an expert to realize that** no
hay que *or* no se necesita ser un experto para
darse cuenta de eso
■ **have back** 1 [*v + o + adv, v + adv + o*]
(receive back): **can I ∼ the ring back?** ¿me
devuelves el anillo?
2 [*v + o + adv*] ⟨guests⟩ **to ∼ sb back** (invite again)
volver* a invitar a algn; (reciprocate invitation)
devolverle* a algn una invitación
■ **have on** [*v + o + adv*] (tease) (colloq) **to ∼ sb on**
tomarle el pelo a algn (fam)
■ **have out** [*v + o + adv*] **(a)** (have removed): **to ∼
a tooth out** sacarse* una muela; **she had her
tonsils out** la operaron de las amígdalas **(b)**
(discuss forcefully) **to ∼ it out WITH sb** ponerle* las
cosas claras A algn

haven /'heɪvən/ *n* **(a)** (refuge) refugio *m* **(b)**
(port) (liter) puerto *m*

haven't /'hævənt/ = **have not**

haversack /'hævərsæk ‖'hævəsæk/ *n*
mochila *f*, morral *m*

haves /hævz/ *pl n* **the ∼ and the have-nots** los
ricos y los pobres *or* los desposeídos

havoc /'hævək/ *n*: **the accident caused ∼** el
accidente creó gran confusión; **the children
created ∼** los niños armaron un lío tremendo
(fam); **to play ∼ with sth** trastocar* *or* desbaratar
algo

Hawaii /hə'waɪiː/ *n* Hawai *m*

Hawaiian /hə'waɪən/ *adj* hawaiano

hawk[1] /hɔːk/ *n* halcón *m*

hawk[2] *vt* ⟨goods/wares⟩ vocear, pregonar

hawthorn /'hɔːθɔːrn ‖'hɔːθɔːn/ *n* espino *m*

hay /heɪ/ *n* heno *m*

hay: ∼ **fever** *n* fiebre *f* del heno; ∼**rick**
/'heɪrɪk/ *n* almiar *m*; ∼**seed** *n* (AmE sl) ▶ YOKEL;
∼**stack** *n* almiar *m*; ∼**wire** *adj* (colloq) (pred):
to go ∼**wire** ⟨person⟩ perder* la chaveta (fam);
⟨machine⟩ estropearse, descomponerse* (AmL)

hazard[1] /'hæzərd ‖'hæzəd/ *n* peligro *m*, riesgo
m

hazard[2] *vt* (fml) ⟨remark/question⟩ aventurar;
to ∼ a guess aventurar una respuesta

hazard lights, (BrE also) **hazard warning
lights** *pl n* (Auto) luces *fpl* de emergencia

hazardous /'hæzərdəs ‖'hæzədəs/ *adj*
peligroso, arriesgado

haze /heɪz/ *n* (*no pl*) (due to humidity) neblina *f*,
bruma *f*; (due to heat) calima *f*

hazel /'heɪzl/ *n* **(a)** (plant) avellano *m* **(b)** (wood)
(madera *f* de) avellano *m* **(c)** (color) color *m*
avellana; ⟨before n⟩ ⟨eyes⟩ color avellana *adj inv*

hazelnut /'heɪzəlnʌt/ *n* avellana *f*

hazy /'heɪzi/ *adj* **hazier, haziest** **(a)** ⟨day⟩
(due to humidity) neblinoso, brumoso; (due to heat)
de calima **(b)** ⟨memory/idea/distinction⟩ vago,
confuso

he /hiː, *weak form* i/ *pron* él

■ **Note** Although *él* is given as the main translation of
he, it is in practice used only for emphasis, or to avoid
ambiguity: *he went to the theater* fue al teatro; *she
went to the theater, he went to the cinema* ella fue al
teatro y él fue al cine; *he did it* él lo hizo.

head[1] /hed/ *n* 1 (Anat) cabeza *f*; **a fine ∼ of hair**
una buena cabellera; **from ∼ to foot** *o* **toe** de pies
a cabeza, de arriba (a) abajo; **∼ over heels**: **she
tripped and went ∼ over heels down the steps**
tropezó y cayó rodando escaleras abajo; **to be ∼
over heels in love** estar* locamente enamorado;
to go to sb's ∼ subírsele a la cabeza a algn; **to
make ∼ or tail** *o* (AmE also) ∼**s or tails of sth**
entender* algo
2 (mind, brain) cabeza *f*; **I said the first thing that
came into my ∼** dije lo primero que se me
ocurrió; **she added it up in her ∼** hizo la suma
mentalmente; **she has a good ∼ for business**
tiene cabeza para los negocios; **I've no ∼ for
heights** sufro de vértigo; **it never entered my ∼
that …** ni se me pasó por la cabeza que …; **to
keep/lose one's ∼** mantener/perder* la calma
3 **(a)** (of nail, tack, pin) cabeza *f*; (of spear, arrow)
punta *f*; (of hammer) cabeza *f*; (on beer) espuma *f*
(b) (top end — of bed, table) cabecera *f*; (— of page,
letter) encabezamiento *m*; (— of procession, line)
cabeza *f*
4 **(a)** (chief) director, -tora *m,f*; **∼ of state** jefe,
-fa *m,f* de Estado; **the ∼ of the household** el/la
cabeza de familia; ⟨before n⟩ **∼ waiter** maître *m*,
capitán *m* de meseros (Méx) **(b)** (∼ teacher) (esp
BrE) director, -tora *m,f* (de colegio)
5 (person): **\$15 per ∼** 15 dólares por cabeza *or*
persona
6 (crisis): **to come to a ∼** hacer* crisis
7 **(a)** (magnetic device) (Audio, Comput) cabeza *f*,
cabezal *m* **(b)** (of drill) cabezal *m*
8 (Geog) cabo *m*

head[2] *vt* 1 **(a)** ⟨march/procession⟩ encabezar*,
ir* a la cabeza de **(b)** ⟨revolt⟩ acaudillar; ⟨team⟩
capitanear; ⟨expedition/department⟩ dirigir*
2 (direct) (+ adv compl) ⟨vehicle/ship⟩ dirigir*
3 (in soccer) ⟨ball⟩ cabecear
4 ⟨page/chapter⟩ encabezar*
■ ∼ *vi*: **to ∼ west/north** ir* en dirección oeste/
norte
■ **head for** [*v + prep + o*] **(a)** (go toward) ⟨ship⟩
ir* con rumbo a; **to ∼ for home** ponerse* en
camino a casa; **the car was ∼ing straight for me**
el coche venía derecho hacia mí **(b)** (be in danger
of): **to be ∼ed** *o* ∼**ing for sth** ir* camino de algo
■ **head off** 1 [*v + adv*] (set out) salir*
2 [*v + o + adv, v + adv + o*] **(a)** (get in front of)
atajar, cortarle el paso a algn **(b)** (prevent, forestall)
⟨criticism/threat⟩ prevenir*

head: ~**ache** n dolor m de cabeza; **I've got a** ~**ache** tengo dolor de cabeza, me duele la cabeza; ~**band** n cinta f del pelo, vincha f (AmS), huincha f (Bol, Chi, Per); ~**board** n cabecera f; ~**dress** n tocado m

headed /'hedəd ‖'hedɪd/ adj ⟨notepaper⟩ con membrete, membretado, membreteado (Andes)

header /'hedər ‖'hedə(r)/ n (in soccer) cabezazo m

head: ~**first** /'hed'fɜːrst ‖'hed'fɜːst/ adv (a) (with head foremost) de cabeza (b) (over-hastily) precipitadamente; ~**hunt** vt ofrecerle* un puesto a; ~**hunter** n (Busn) cazatalentos m

heading /'hedɪŋ/ n (title) encabezamiento m, título m, acápite m (AmL); (letterhead) membrete m

head: ~**lamp** n faro m; ~**land** /'hedlənd/ n cabo m; ~**light** n faro m; ~**line** n titular m; **the news** ~**lines** el resumen informativo or de noticias; ~**long** adv (a) (hastily) precipitadamente (b) (with head foremost) de cabeza; ~**master** /'hed'mæstər ‖,hed'mɑːstə(r)/ n director m (de colegio); ~**mistress** /'hed'mɪstrəs ‖,hed'mɪstrɪs/ n directora f (de colegio); ~ **office** n (oficina f) central f; ~**on** /'hed'ɑːn ‖,hed'ɒn/ adj ⟨crash/collision⟩ frontal, de frente; ~**phones** pl n auriculares mpl, cascos mpl; ~**quarters** /'hed'kwɔːrtərz ‖,hed'kwɔːtəz/ n (pl ~**quarters**) (+ sing or pl vb) oficina f central; (Mil) cuartel m general; ~**rest** n reposacabezas m, apoyacabezas m; ~**room** n altura f

heads /hedz/ adv (on coin) cara f, águila f⃗ (Méx); ~ **or tails?** ¿cara o cruz, ¿águila o sol? (Méx), ¿cara o sello? (Andes, Ven), ¿cara o ceca? (Arg)

head: ~**scarf** n pañuelo m (de cabeza); ~**set** n auriculares mpl, cascos mpl; ~**stand** n: **to do a** ~**stand** pararse de cabeza (AmL), hacer* el pino (Esp); ~ **start** n ventaja f; ~**stone** n lápida f; ~**strong** adj testarudo, obstinado; ~**teacher** /'hed'tiːtʃər ‖,hed'tiːtʃə(r)/ n (BrE) director, -tora m, f (de colegio); ~**way** n: **to make** ~**way** hacer* progresos, avanzar*

heady /'hedi/ adj -**dier**, -**diest** ⟨scent⟩ embriagador; ⟨wine⟩ que se sube a la cabeza

heal /hiːl/ vt curar
■ ~ vi cicatrizar*, cerrarse*

health /helθ/ n salud f; **to be in good/poor** ~ estar* bien/mal de salud; **your (good)** ~! (proposing a toast) ¡salud!; (before n) ⟨policy/services⟩ sanitario, de salud pública; ⟨inspector/regulations⟩ de sanidad; ~ **hazard** riesgo m or peligro m para la salud

health: ~ **care** n asistencia f sanitaria or médica; ~ **centre** n (BrE) centro m médico or de salud; ~ **food** n alimentos mpl naturales; ~ **insurance** n seguro m de enfermedad; ~ **service** n (in UK) ▶ NATIONAL HEALTH (SERVICE)

healthy /'helθi/ adj -**thier**, -**thiest** [1] (a) (in good health) ⟨person/animal/complexion⟩ sano; **she has a** ~ **appetite** tiene buen apetito (b) (promoting good health) ⟨diet/living/environment⟩ sano, saludable (c) (sound) ⟨respect⟩ sano [2] ⟨economy/finances⟩ próspero

heap¹ /hiːp/ n (a) (pile) montón m, pila f (b) (car) (colloq) cacharro m (fam)

heap² vt (a) (make pile) amontonar, apilar (b) (supply liberally): **she** ~**ed his plate with food** le llenó el plato de comida; **a** ~**ing spoonful** (AmE) o (BrE) ~**ed spoonful** (Culin) una cucharada colmada

hear /hɪr ‖hɪə(r)/ (past & past p **heard** /hɜːrd ‖hɜːd/) vt [1] ⟨sound⟩ oír* [2] (get to know) oír*; **I've** ~**d so much about you** me han hablado tanto de ti, he oído hablar tanto de ti; **he's very ill, I** ~ me han dicho que está muy enfermo [3] (listen to) (a) ⟨lecture/broadcast/views⟩ escuchar, oír* (b) (Law) ⟨case⟩ ver*; ⟨charge⟩ oír*
■ ~ vi [1] (perceive) oír*; ~, ~! ¡eso, eso!, ¡bien dicho! [2] (get news): **have you** ~**d?** ¿te has enterado?; **to** ~ **ABOUT sth** enterarse DE algo; **I haven't** ~**d from them for months** hace meses que no sé nada de ellos or que no tengo noticias suyas
■ **hear of** [v + prep + o] (a) (encounter, come to know of): **I've** ~**d of him** he oído hablar de él; **if you** ~ **of anything interesting, let me know** si te enteras de algo interesante, me lo dices (b) (have news of) tener* noticias or saber* de (c) (allow): **I won't** ~ **of it!** ¡ni hablar!
■ **hear out** [v + o + adv, v + adv + o] escuchar ⟨hasta el final⟩

hearing /'hɪrɪŋ ‖'hɪərɪŋ/ n [1] (sense) oído m [2] (a) (consideration) **to give sb a** ~ escuchar a algn (b) (trial) vista f

hearing aid n audífono m

hearsay /'hɪrseɪ ‖'hɪəseɪ/ n habladurías fpl

hearse /hɜːrs ‖hɜːs/ n coche m fúnebre

heart /hɑːrt ‖hɑːt/ n [1] (Anat) corazón m; (before n) ⟨disease⟩ del corazón, cardíaco; ⟨operation⟩ de(l) corazón [2] (seat of emotions): **to have a kind** ~ tener* buen corazón, ser* de buen corazón; **to have sb's interests at** ~ preocuparse por algn; **to learn/know sth by** ~ aprender/saber* algo de memoria; **my/her/his** ~ **wasn't in it** lo hacía sin ganas; **to take sth to** ~ tomarse algo a pecho [3] (courage, morale) ánimos mpl; **to lose** ~ descorazonarse, desanimarse; **to take** ~ animarse; **not to have the** ~ **to do sth**: **I didn't have the** ~ **to tell him** no tuve el valor para decírselo [4] (a) (central part): **the** ~ **of the city/country** el corazón or centro de la ciudad/del país; **the** ~ **of the matter** el meollo del asunto (b) (of cabbage, lettuce) cogollo m [5] (Games) **hearts** (suit) (+ sing or pl vb) corazones mpl

heart: ~**ache** n pena f, dolor m; ~ **attack** n ataque m al corazón, infarto m; ~**beat** n latido m (del corazón); ~**break** n (a) (grief) congoja f, sufrimiento m (b) (cause of grief) desengaño m; ~**breaking** adj desgarrador; ~**broken** adj

---

AmC	América Central	Arg	Argentina	Cu	Cuba	Per	Perú
AmL	América Latina	Bol	Bolivia	Ec	Ecuador	RPI	Río de la Plata
AmS	América del Sur	Chi	Chile	Esp	España	Ur	Uruguay
Andes	Región andina	CS	Cono Sur	Méx	México	Ven	Venezuela

⟨*look/sobs*⟩ desconsolado; **she was ∼broken when he died** su muerte la dejó destrozada; **∼burn** *n* ardor *m* de estómago; **∼felt** *adj* sincero

hearth /hɑːrθ ‖hɑːθ/ *n* chimenea *f*, hogar *m*

heartily /'hɑːrtli ‖'hɑːtɪli/ *adv* **(a)** (warmly) ⟨*congratulate/greet*⟩ efusivamente **(b)** (with enthusiasm) ⟨*laugh/eat*⟩ con ganas

heartless /'hɑːrtləs ‖'hɑːtlɪs/ *adj* ⟨*person*⟩ sin corazón; ⟨*refusal*⟩ cruel

heart: **∼-shaped** *adj* ⟨*card/cake*⟩ con forma de corazón; ⟨*face*⟩ en forma de corazón; **∼-to-∼** *n* (colloq) charla *f* íntima

hearty /'hɑːrti ‖'hɑːti/ *adj* **-tier, -tiest** ⟨*person*⟩ campechano; ⟨*welcome*⟩ caluroso; ⟨*appetite*⟩ bueno

heat¹ /hiːt/ *n* **1** **(a)** (warmth) calor *m* **(b)** (for cooking) fuego *m* **2** **in the ∼ of the moment** en un momento de enojo (*or* exaltación *etc*) **3** (estrus) celo *m*; **to be in** *o* (BrE) **on ∼** estar* en celo **4** (Sport) (prueba) eliminatoria *f*

heat² *vt* calentar*; ⟨*house*⟩ calentar*, calefaccionar (CS)
▪ **heat up** **1** [*v + adv*] calentarse* **2** [*v + o + adv, v + adv + o*] calentar*

heated /'hiːtəd ‖'hiːtɪd/ *adj* **(a)** (warmed) ⟨*pool*⟩ climatizado; ⟨*seat/rear window*⟩ térmico **(b)** (impassioned) ⟨*argument*⟩ acalorado; **to get ∼** acalorarse

heater /'hiːtər ‖'hiːtə(r)/ *n* calentador *m*, estufa *f*; (water ∼) calentador *m* (de agua)

heath /hiːθ/ *n* brezal *m*, monte *m*

heathen /'hiːðən/ *n* pagano, -na *m,f*

heather /'heðər ‖'heðə(r)/ *n* brezo *m*

heating /'hiːtɪŋ/ *n* calefacción *f*

heat wave *n* ola *f* de calor

heave¹ /hiːv/ *vt* **1** **(a)** (move with effort): **we ∼d the box onto the shelf** con esfuerzo logramos subir la caja al estante; **they ∼d it into place** lo colocaron empujando/levantándolo **(b)** (throw) (colloq) tirar **2** (utter): **to ∼ a sigh** suspirar
▪ **∼** *vi* **1** (pull) tirar, jalar (AmL exc CS) **2** (rise and fall): **his chest ∼d** respiraba agitadamente

heave² *n* (pull) tirón *m*, jalón *m* (AmL exc CS); (push) empujón *m*

heaven /'hevən/ *n* cielo *m*; (good) **∼s!** ¡Dios mío!; **thank ∼** gracias a Dios

heavenly /'hevənli/ *adj* **(a)** (Relig) celestial **(b)** (Astron) celeste **(c)** (superb) (colloq) divino (fam)

heavily /'hevəli ‖'hevɪli/ *adv* **1** **(a)** ⟨*tread/fall*⟩ pesadamente; **to be ∼ built** ser* corpulento; **to breathe ∼** jadear **(b)** (thickly) ⟨*underlined*⟩ con trazo grueso; **she was ∼ made-up** iba muy maquillada **2** **(a)** (copiously) ⟨*rain/snow*⟩ mucho **(b)** (immoderately) ⟨*drink/smoke*⟩ en exceso **(c)** (greatly): **to borrow ∼** contraer* considerables deudas; **∼ pregnant** en avanzado estado de gravidez (frml) *or* (period) de gestación

heavy¹ /'hevi/ *adj* **-vier, -viest** **1** **(a)** (weighty) ⟨*load/suitcase/weight*⟩ pesado; ⟨*fabric/garment*⟩ grueso, pesado; ⟨*saucepan*⟩ de fondo grueso; ⟨*boots*⟩ fuerte; ⟨*work*⟩ pesado; **it's very ∼** es muy pesado, pesa mucho **(b)** (large-scale) (*before n*) ⟨*artillery/machinery*⟩ pesado **2** **(a)** (ponderous) ⟨*tread/footstep/fall*⟩ pesado; ⟨*thud*⟩ sordo **(b)** (features) tosco; ⟨*irony*⟩ poco sutil **3** **(a)** (oppressive) ⟨*clouds/sky*⟩ pesado **(b)** (loud) ⟨*sigh*⟩ profundo **4** **(a)** (bigger than usual)

⟨*expenditure*⟩ cuantioso **(b)** (intense) ⟨*book*⟩ pesado, denso; ⟨*rain*⟩ fuerte; ⟨*traffic*⟩ denso; ⟨*schedule*⟩ apretado; **to be a ∼ drinker/smoker** beber/fumar mucho **(c)** (severe) ⟨*sentence*⟩ severo; ⟨*casualties*⟩ numeroso; ⟨*blow*⟩ duro, fuerte

heavy² *n* (*pl* **-vies**) (colloq) matón *m* (fam)

heavy: **∼ cream** *n* (AmE) crema *f* doble, nata *f* para montar (Esp), doble crema *f* (Méx); **∼-duty** /'hevi'duːti ‖,hevi'djuːti/ *adj* ⟨*material/sacks*⟩ muy resistente; ⟨*machine*⟩ para uso industrial; ⟨*clothing/overalls*⟩ de trabajo; **∼-handed** /'hevi'hændəd ‖,hevi'hændɪd/ *adj* torpe; **∼ metal** *n* (Mus) heavy *m* (metal), rock *m* duro

heavyweight¹ /'heviweɪt/ *n* (Sport) peso *m* pesado; **a political ∼** un peso pesado de la política

heavyweight² *adj* **(a)** (Sport) (*before n*) ⟨*boxer/wrestler*⟩ de la categoría de los pesos pesados; ⟨*title*⟩ de los pesos pesados **(b)** (Tex) ⟨*cotton/denim*⟩ grueso *y* resistente

Hebrew¹ /'hiːbruː/ *adj* hebreo

Hebrew² *n* hebreo *m*

Hebrides /'hebrədiːz ‖'hebrɪdiːz/ *pl* **in the ∼** las (islas) Hébridas

heck /hek/ *n* (colloq & euph): **∼!** ¡caray! (fam & euf); **what the ∼!** ¡qué diablos! (fam)

heckle /'hekl/ *vt* interrumpir (con preguntas *o* comentarios molestos)

heckler /'heklər ‖'heklə(r)/ *n*: persona que interrumpe a un orador para molestar

hectare /'hekter ‖'hekteə(r)/ *n* hectárea *f*

hectic /'hektɪk/ *adj* ⟨*day/week*⟩ ajetreado, agitado; ⟨*journey/pace*⟩ agotador; ⟨*activity*⟩ frenético, febril

he'd /hiːd/ **(a)** = **he had (b)** = **he would**

hedge¹ /hedʒ/ *n* seto *m* (verde *or* vivo)

hedge² *vt* ⟨*field/garden*⟩ cercar* (con seto)
▪ **∼** *vi* (evade the issue) dar* rodeos

hedgehog /'hedʒhɔːɡ ‖'hedʒhɒɡ/ *n* erizo *m*

hedgerow /'hedʒrəʊ/ *n* (*usu pl*) seto *m* (verde *or* vivo)

hedonism /'hiːdn̩ɪzəm ‖'hiːdənɪzəm/ *n* hedonismo *m*

hedonist /'hiːdn̩ɪst ‖'hiːdənɪst/ *n* hedonista *mf*

heed¹ /hiːd/ *n*: **to take ∼** tener* cuidado

heed² *vt* prestar atención a, hacer* caso de

heedless /'hiːdləs ‖'hiːdlɪs/ *adj* (frml) **∼ of** sth: **∼ of the danger** ... haciendo caso omiso del peligro ...

heel¹ /hiːl/ *n* **(a)** (Anat) talón *m* **(b)** (of shoe) tacón *m*, taco *m* (CS)

heel² *vt* ⟨*shoes*⟩ ponerles* tacones *or* (CS) tacos nuevos a; ⟨*high-heeled shoes*⟩ ponerles* tapas *or* (Chi) tapillas a

hefty /'hefti/ *adj* **-tier, -tiest** (colloq) **(a)** (large and heavy) ⟨*person*⟩ robusto, fornido, corpulento; ⟨*load/case*⟩ pesado **(b)** (strong) fuerte **(c)** (substantial) ⟨*price/salary*⟩ alto; ⟨*fine*⟩ considerable

heifer /'hefər ‖'hefə(r)/ *n* vaquilla *f*, novilla *f*

height /haɪt/ *n* **1** **(a)** (tallness — of object) altura *f*; (— of person) estatura *f*, talla *f*; **what ∼ are you?** ¿cuánto mides? **(b)** (Aviat) altura *f*; **to gain/lose ∼** ganar/perder* altura **2** (peak) (*no pl*): **to be at the ∼ of one's power** estar* en la cima *or* en la cumbre *or* en la ⋯>

cúspide de su (*or* mi *etc*) poder; **at the ∼ of the season** en plena temporada; **it's the ∼ of stupidity** es el colmo de la estupidez

3 **heights** *pl* **(a)** (high ground) cerros *mpl*, cumbres *fpl* **(b)** **to be afraid of ∼s** sufrir de vértigo

heighten /'haɪtn̩/ *vt* ‹effect/impression› destacar*, realzar*; ‹suspense/admiration/respect› aumentar

heinous /'heɪnəs/ *adj* (frml) atroz, abyecto

heir /er ‖eə(r)/ *n* heredero, -ra *m,f*; **∼ to sth** (to fortune, title) heredero DE algo; (to throne) heredero A algo

heiress /'erəs ‖'eəres/ *n* heredera *f*

heirloom /'erlu:m ‖'eəlu:m/ *n* reliquia *f*

heist /haɪst/ *n* (AmE colloq) golpe *m* (fam), atraco *m*

held /held/ *past & past p of* HOLD¹

helicopter /'heləkɑ:ptər ‖'helɪkɒptə(r)/ *n* helicóptero *m*

heliport /'heləpɔ:rt ‖'helɪpɔ:t/ *n* helipuerto *m*

helium /'hi:liəm/ *n* helio *m*

hell /hel/ *n* **1** (Relig) infierno *m*; **three months of sheer ∼** tres meses infernales; **to make sb's life ∼** (colloq) hacerle* la vida imposible a algn **2** (colloq) (*as intensifier*): **how/why the ∼ ...?** ¿cómo/por qué demonios *or* diablos ...? (fam); **he's a ∅ one ∼ of a guy** es un tipo sensacional (fam); **to run like ∼** correr como un loco (fam); **oh, well, what the ∼!** bueno ¿qué importa? (fam)

he'll /hi:l/ **(a)** = **he will** **(b)** = **he shall**

hello /hə'ləʊ/ *interj* **(a)** (greeting) ¡hola! **(b)** (answering the telephone) sí, aló (AmS), diga *or* dígame (Esp), bueno (Méx), olá (RPl)

helm /helm/ *n* (Naut) timón *m*

helmet /'helmət ‖'helmɪt/ *n* (headgear) casco *m*; (armor) yelmo *m*

help¹ /help/ *vt* **1** (assist) ayudar; **to ∼ sb (to) +** INF ayudar a algn A + INF **2** (avoid, prevent) (*usu neg or interrog*): **I can't ∼ it** no lo puedo remediar; **they can't ∼ being poor** no tienen la culpa de ser pobres
■ **∼** *vi* ‹person/remark› ayudar; ‹tool› servir*
■ *v refl* **to ∼ oneself** **1** (assist) ayudarse (a sí mismo) **2** (resist impulse) (*usu neg*) controlarse; **I can't ∼ myself** no me puedo controlar **3** (take) **to ∼ oneself** (TO sth) ‹to food/a drink› servirse* (algo)
■ **help out** **1** [*v + o + adv, v + adv + o*] ayudar **2** [*v + adv*] ayudar

help² *n* **(a)** (rescue) ayuda *f*; (*as interj*) **∼!** ¡socorro!, ¡auxilio! **(b)** (assistance) ayuda *f*; **can I be of (any) ∼ to you?** ¿la/lo puedo ayudar (en algo)?

help desk *n* servicio *m* de asistencia, ayuda *f* al usuario

helper /'helpər ‖'helpə(r)/ *n* ayudante, -ta *m,f*

helpful /'helpfəl/ *adj* **(a)** (obliging) ‹person/attitude› servicial, amable **(b)** (useful) ‹advice› útil

helping /'helpɪŋ/ *n* porción *f* (esp AmL), ración *f* (esp Esp)

helpless /'helpləs ‖'helplɪs/ *adj* **(a)** (defenseless) ‹prey/victim› indefenso **(b)** (powerless) ‹look/expression› de impotencia; **to be ∼ to +** INF ser* incapaz DE + INF **(c)** (incapacitated): **to leave sb ∼** dejar a algn sin recursos

helplessly /'helpləsli ‖'helplɪsli/ *adv* ‹look on/stand by› sin poder hacer nada; ‹struggle/try› en vano, inútilmente

helpline /'helplaɪn/ *n* servicio *m* telefónico de asistencia, línea *f* directa

helter-skelter /'heltər'skeltər ‖,heltə'skeltə(r)/ *adv* atropelladamente, a la desbanda

hem /hem/ *n* dobladillo *m*, basta *f* (Chi)
■ **hem in**: **-mm-** [*v + o + adv, v + adv + o*] encerrar*

hemisphere /'heməsfɪr ‖'hemɪsfɪə(r)/ *n* (Geog) hemisferio *m*

hemline /'hemlaɪn/ *n* bajo *m*, ruedo *m*

hemoglobin, (BrE) **haemoglobin** /'hi:məgləʊbən ‖,hi:mə'gləʊbɪn/ *n* hemoglobina *f*

hemophilia, (BrE) **haemophilia** /'hi:mə'fɪliə/ *n* hemofilia *f*

hemophiliac, (BrE) **haemophiliac** /,hi:mə'fɪliæk/ *n* hemofílico, -ca *m,f*

hemorrhage¹, (BrE) **haemorrhage** /'hemərɪdʒ/ *n* (Med) hemorragia *f*

hemorrhage², (BrE) **haemorrhage** *vi* «patient» tener* *or* (frml) sufrir una hemorragia; «wound/blood vessel» sangrar mucho

hemorrhoids, (BrE) **haemorrhoids** /'hemərɔɪdz/ *pl n* hemorroides *fpl*, almorranas *fpl*

hemp /hemp/ *n* (fiber) cáñamo *m*; (drug) marihuana *f*, cannabis *m*; (plant) cannabis *m*, cáñamo *m* índico *or* de la India

hen /hen/ *n* (chicken) gallina *f*; (female bird) hembra *f*

hence /hens/ *adv* **1** **(a)** (that is the reason for) de ahí **(b)** (therefore) por lo tanto, por consiguiente **2** (from now) (frml): **a few years ∼** dentro de algunos años

henceforth /'hens'fɔ:rθ ‖,hens'fɔ:θ/ *adv* (liter) a partir de ahora, de ahora en adelante

henchman /'hentʃmən/ *n* (*pl* **-men** /-mən/) secuaz *m*

henna /'henə/ *n* henna *f*

hen: **∼ night, hen party** *n* **(a)** (all-female celebration) fiesta *f* de mujeres **(b)** (before wedding) despedida *f* de soltera; **∼pecked** /'henpekt/ *adj* (colloq): **a ∼pecked husband** un marido dominado por su mujer, un mandilón (Méx fam), un calzonazos (Esp fam)

hepatitis /'hepə'taɪtəs ‖,hepə'taɪtɪs/ *n* hepatitis *f*

her¹ /hɜ:r ‖hɜ:(r), *weak form* ər ‖ə(r)/ *pron* **1** **(a)** (as direct object) la; **I can't stand ∼** no la soporto; **call ∼** llámala **(b)** (as indirect object) le; (with direct object pronoun present) se; **I wrote ∼ a letter** le escribí una carta **(c)** (after preposition) ella **2** (emphatic use) ella; **it's ∼** es ella

her² *adj*

─────────────────────────────

■ **Note** The translation *su* agrees in number with the noun which it modifies: *her* is translated by *su, sus*, according to what follows: *her father/mother* su padre/madre; *her books/magazines* sus libros/revistas.

─────────────────────────────

(*sing*) su; (*pl*) sus; **she took ∼ hat off** se quitó el sombrero; **she broke ∼ arm** se rompió el brazo

herald¹ /'herəld/ n (Hist) heraldo m

herald² vt anunciar

heraldry /'herəldri/ n heráldica f

herb /ɜːrb, hɜːrb ‖hɜːb/ n hierba f, yuyo m (Per, RPI)

herbal /'ɜːrbəl, 'hɜːrbəl‖'hɜːbəl/ adj ⟨shampoo⟩ de hierbas; ~ **tea** (esp BrE) ▶ HERB TEA

herb tea n infusión f, agua f‡ (AmC, Andes), té m de yuyos (Per, RPI)

herd¹ /hɜːrd ‖hɜːd/ n (a) (of cattle) manada f, vacada f; (of goats) rebaño m; (of pigs) piara f, manada f; (of wild animals) manada f (b) (of people) (pej) tropel m

herd² vt ⟨animals⟩ arrear, arriar (RPI); **the refugees were ~ed into trucks** metieron a los refugiados en camiones como si fueran ganado

here /hɪr ‖hɪə(r)/ adv **1** (a) (at, to this place) aquí, acá (esp AmL); (less precise) acá **(b)** (in phrases) **here and there** aquí y allá; **here, there and everywhere** por todas partes **2** (calling attention to sth, sb): ~'s **£20** toma 20 libras; ~ **he is** aquí está **3** (a) (present): **he isn't ~ today** hoy no está **(b)** (arrived): **they're ~!** ¡ya llegaron!, ¡ya están aquí! **4** (as interj): ~, **let me do it** trae, deja que lo haga yo

hereabouts /ˌhɪrə'baʊts ‖ˌhɪərə'baʊts/ adv por aquí, por acá

hereafter /ˌhɪr'æftər ‖ˌhɪər'ɑːftə(r)/ adv (frml: used esp in legal texts) (from now on) de aquí en adelante; (in the future) en el futuro, en lo sucesivo

hereditary /hə'redətəri ‖hɪ'redɪtri/ adj hereditario

heredity /hə'redəti ‖hɪ'redəti/ n herencia f

heresy /'herəsi/ n (pl **-sies**) herejía f

heretic /'herətɪk/ n hereje mf

heritage /'herətɪdʒ ‖'herɪtɪdʒ/ n (no pl) patrimonio m

hermetically /hɜːr'metɪkli ‖hɜː'metɪkli/ adv: ~ **sealed** herméticamente cerrado

hermit /'hɜːrmət ‖'hɜːmɪt/ n ermitaño, -ña m,f, eremita mf

hernia /'hɜːrniə ‖'hɜːniə/ n hernia f

hero /'hiːrəʊ ‖'hɪərəʊ/ n (pl **heroes**) héroe m; (of novel, film) protagonista mf

heroic /hɪ'rəʊɪk/ adj heroico

heroin /'herəʊɪn/ n heroína f; (before n) ~ **addict** heroinómano, -na m,f

heroine /'herəʊɪn/ n (brave, admirable woman) heroína f; (of novel, film) protagonista f

heroism /'herəʊɪzəm/ n heroísmo m

heron /'herən/ n garza f (real)

hero worship n adoración f (de alguien a quien se tiene como ídolo)

herpes /'hɜːrpiːz ‖'hɜːpiːz/ n herpes m, herpe f

herring /'herɪŋ/ n (pl **herrings** or **herring**) arenque m

hers /hɜːrz ‖hɜːz/ pron

■ **Note** The translation suyo reflects the gender and number of the noun it is standing for; hers is translated by el suyo, la suya, los suyos, las suyas, depending on what is being referred to.

(sing) suyo, -ya; (pl) suyos, -yas, de ella; **they're** ~ son suyos/suyas, son de ella; ~ **is blue** el suyo/la suya es azul, el/la de ella es azul; **a friend of** ~ un amigo suyo or de ella

herself /hər'self ‖hə'self/ pron **(a)** (reflexive): **she cut** ~ se cortó; **she bought** ~ **a hat** se compró un sombrero; **she only thinks of** ~ solo piensa en sí misma; **by** ~ sola; **she was talking to** ~ estaba hablando sola **(b)** (emphatic use) ella misma; **she told me so** ~ me lo dijo ella misma **(c)** (normal self): **she's not** ~ no es la de siempre

he's /hiːz/ **(a)** = **he is (b)** = **he has**

hesitant /'hezətənt ‖'hezɪtənt/ adj ⟨voice⟩ vacilante; ⟨manner⟩ inseguro; ⟨steps⟩ vacilante; **he seemed a little** ~ parecía un poco indeciso

hesitate /'hezəteɪt ‖'hezɪteɪt/ vi vacilar, titubear

hesitation /ˌhezə'teɪʃən ‖ˌhezɪ'teɪʃən/ n vacilación f

heterosexual¹ /ˌhetərəʊ'sekʃʊəl/ adj heterosexual

heterosexual² n heterosexual mf

heterosexuality /ˌhetərəʊsekʃʊ'æləti/ n heterosexualidad f

hew /hjuː/ vt (past **hewed**; past p **hewed** or **hewn** /hjuːn/) (extract) extraer*; (fashion) ⟨stone⟩ labrar

hexagon /'heksəgɑːn ‖'heksəgən/ n hexágono m

hey /heɪ/ interj **(a)** (calling attention) ¡eh! **(b)** (expressing dismay, protest, indignation) ¡oye!, ¡oiga(n)!

heyday /'heɪdeɪ/ n apogeo m, auge m; **in his** ~ en sus buenos tiempos

HGV n (BrE) (= **heavy goods vehicle**) vehículo m pesado

hi /haɪ/ interj (colloq) ¡hola! (fam)

HI = **Hawaii**

hiatus /haɪ'eɪtəs/ n (pl **-tuses**) (frml) paréntesis m (frml)

hibernate /'haɪbərneɪt ‖'haɪbəneɪt/ vi hibernar

hibernation /ˌhaɪbər'neɪʃən ‖ˌhaɪbə'neɪʃən/ n hibernación f; **to go into** ~ entrar en estado de hibernación

hiccough /'hɪkʌp/ n/vi ▶ HICCUP¹,²

hiccup¹ /'hɪkʌp/ n **(a)** hipo m; **to have (the)** ~**s** tener* hipo **(b)** (brief interruption) dificultad f

hiccup² vi, (BrE also) **-pp-** hipar

hick /hɪk/ n (AmE colloq & pej) pueblerino, -na m,f, paleto, -ta m,f (Esp fam & pey), pajuerano, -na m,f (RPI fam & pey)

hid /hɪd/ **(a)** past of HIDE¹ **(b)** (arch) past p of HIDE¹

hidden¹ /'hɪdn̩/ adj ⟨entrance/camera/reserves⟩ oculto; ⟨cost⟩ no aparente

hidden² past p of HIDE¹

hide¹ /haɪd/ (past **hid** /hɪd/; past p **hidden** or (arch) **hid**) vt **(a)** (conceal) esconder; **she hid the money from the police** escondió el dinero para que no lo encontrara la policía; **to** ~ **oneself** esconderse **(b)** (keep secret) ⟨feelings/thoughts⟩ ocultar; **to** ~ **sth FROM sb** ocultarle algo A algn **(c)** (mask, screen) tapar
■ ~ vi esconderse

■ **hide away 1** [v + adv] esconderse **2** [v + o + adv, v + adv + o] esconder

hide² n (raw) piel f; (tanned) cuero m

hide: hide-and-seek~**-and-seek** /'haɪdn̩'siːk/, (AmE & Scot also) ~**-and-go-seek** /'haɪdn̩gəʊ'siːk/ n: **to play** ~**-and-seek** jugar* al ⋯⟶

escondite, jugar* a las escondidas (AmL); **~away** n (a) (hiding place) (AmE) escondite m (b) (secluded spot) rincón m

hideous /'hɪdiəs/ adj ⟨monster/sight⟩ horroroso, horrible; ⟨crime/fate⟩ espantoso; ⟨color/furniture⟩ (colloq) horrendo, espantoso

hideout /'haɪdaʊt/ n guarida f

hiding /'haɪdɪŋ/ n ① (concealment): **to be in ~/go into ~** estar* escondido/esconderse; (before n) **~ place** escondite m, escondrijo m ② (beating) (colloq) paliza f, tunda f

hierarchy /'haɪərɑːrki ‖ 'haɪərɑːki/ n (pl **-chies**) jerarquía f

hieroglyphics /haɪərə'glɪfɪks/ pl n jeroglíficos mpl

hi-fi /'haɪfaɪ/ n (a) (equipment) alta fidelidad f (b) (set) equipo m de alta fidelidad, hi-fi m

higgledy-piggledy /'hɪgəldi'pɪgəldi/ adv (colloq) sin orden ni concierto, de cualquier manera

high¹ /haɪ/ adj **-er, -est** ① (a) (tall) ⟨wall/mountain⟩ alto; **how ~ is it?** ¿qué altura tiene?; **the tower is 40 m ~** la torre tiene 40 m de alto or de altura (b) (high up) ⟨window/balcony⟩ alto; ⟨plateau⟩ elevado; **at a ~ altitude** a gran altitud; **~ cheekbones** pómulos mpl salientes (c) (in status) ⟨office/rank⟩ alto; **he has friends in ~ places** tiene amigos muy bien situados; **~ society** la alta sociedad (d) (morally, ethically) ⟨ideals/principles⟩ elevado (e) (in pitch) ⟨voice⟩ agudo; ⟨note⟩ alto ② (greater than usual) ⟨temperature/speed/pressure⟩ alto; ⟨wind⟩ fuerte; **unemployment is very ~** hay mucho desempleo; **to be ~ in vitamins** ser* rico en vitaminas ③ (climactic) culminante; **the ~ point** el punto culminante ④ (a) (happy, excited): **she was in ~ spirits** estaba muy animada (b) (intoxicated) (colloq) drogado, colocado (Esp fam) ⑤ (of time): **~ noon** mediodía m; **in ~ summer** en pleno verano ⑥ ⟨meat⟩ pasado; ⟨game⟩ que tiene un olor fuerte

high² adv **-er, -est** ① ⟨fly⟩ alto; **~ up** arriba, en lo alto; **to search ~ and low (for sth)** remover* cielo y tierra (para encontrar algo) ② (in pitch) ⟨sing⟩ alto

high³ n ① (level) récord m ② (Meteo) (anticyclone) zona f de altas presiones; (high temperature) máxima f ③ (top gear) (AmE Auto) (no art) directa f

high- /haɪ/ pref: **~quality** de alta calidad, de gran calidad; **~speed** ⟨train⟩ de alta velocidad

high: **~brow** adj (colloq) ⟨tastes⟩ de intelectual; ⟨art/music⟩ para intelectuales; **~chair** n silla f alta (para niño); **~class** /'haɪ'klæs ‖ ,haɪ'klɑːs/ adj ⟨restaurant/hotel⟩ de lujo; ⟨merchandise⟩ de primera calidad; **H~ Court** n (in England and Wales) una de las dos ramas del Tribunal Supremo, con competencia para conocer de causas civiles cuyo coste excede cierta cuantía

higher /'haɪər ‖ 'haɪə(r)/ adj (a) comp of HIGH¹ (b) (before n) ⟨mammals/organs⟩ superior

higher education n enseñanza f superior

high: **~ finance** n altas finanzas fpl; **~flier, ~flyer** /'haɪ'flaɪər ‖ ,haɪ'flaɪə(r)/ n persona f muy prometedora; **~flown** adj altisonante; **~-frequency** /'haɪ'friːkwənsi/ adj de alta frecuencia; **~grade** adj de calidad superior; **~-handed** /'haɪ'hændəd ‖ ,haɪ'hændɪd/ adj arbitrario; **~-heeled** /'haɪ'hiːld/ adj de tacón or (CS) de taco alto; **~ jump** n salto m de altura, salto m alto (AmL); **~lands** /'haɪləndz/ pl n (a) (uplands) tierras fpl altas, altiplanicie f (b) (in Scotland) **the H~lands** las or los Highlands, las tierras altas; **~-level** /'haɪ'levəl/ adj ⟨talks/delegation⟩ de alto nivel (b) ⟨bridge/road⟩ elevado (c) (Comput) de alto nivel

highlight¹ /'haɪlaɪt/ vt (past & past p **-lighted**) ① (call attention to) ⟨problem/question⟩ destacar*, poner* de relieve ② (Art, Phot) realzar*, dar* realce a

highlight² n ① (most memorable part) lo más destacado; **her performance was the ~ of the evening** su actuación fue el plato fuerte de la velada ② (a) (Art, Phot) toque m de luz (b) **highlights** pl (in hair) reflejos mpl, claritos mpl (RPl), visos mpl (Chi), luces fpl (Méx), mechones mpl (Col)

highlighter /'haɪlaɪtər ‖ 'haɪlaɪtə(r)/ n (a) (makeup) sombra f clara de ojos (b) (pen) rotulador m, marcador m (AmL)

highly /'haɪli/ adv (a) (to a high degree): **~ unlikely** muy poco probable; **~ intelligent** inteligentísimo; **~ trained** altamente capacitado (b) (favorably): **his boss speaks/thinks very ~ of him** su jefe habla muy bien/tiene muy buena opinión de él (c) (at a high rate): **a ~ paid job** un trabajo muy bien pagado

highly-strung /'haɪli'strʌŋ/ adj (BrE) ▶ HIGH-STRUNG

Highness /'haɪnəs ‖ 'haɪnɪs/ n: **Her/His/Your (Royal) ~** Su Alteza (Real)

high: **~-pitched** /'haɪ'pɪtʃt/ adj ⟨voice/sound⟩ agudo; ⟨instrument⟩ de tono agudo or alto; **~-powered** /'haɪ'paʊərd ‖ ,haɪ'paʊəd/ adj ⟨car/machine⟩ muy potente, de gran potencia; ⟨executive/campaign⟩ dinámico, enérgico; ⟨job⟩ de alto(s) vuelo(s); **~-profile** /'haɪ'prəʊfaɪl/ adj prominente; **~-ranking** /'haɪ'ræŋkɪŋ/ adj ⟨officer⟩ de alto rango; ⟨official⟩ alto, de alta jerarquía; **~ rise** n (esp AmE) torre f de apartamentos or (Esp) pisos); **~-rise** /'haɪ'raɪz/ adj (before n) ⟨building/block⟩ alto, de muchas plantas; ⟨apartment⟩ de una torre, de un edificio alto; **~-risk** /'haɪ'rɪsk/ adj de alto riesgo; **~road** n carretera f; **~ school** n colegio m secundario, ≈ instituto m (en Esp), ≈ liceo m (en CS, Ven); **~ season** n temporada f alta; **~-spirited** /'haɪ'spɪrətəd ‖ ,haɪ'spɪrɪtɪd/ adj lleno de vida, brioso; **~ street** n (BrE) calle f principal, calle f mayor (Esp); **~-strung** /'haɪ'strʌŋ/, (BrE) **highly-strung** adj ⟨person⟩

nervioso; ⟨*dog*/*horse*⟩ muy excitable; **~-tech**
/'haɪ'tek/ *adj* de alta tecnología; ⟨*era*⟩ high tech
adj inv; **~-up** *n* (esp AmE colloq) gerifalte *mf*,
capo, -pa *m,f* (fam); **~way** *n* (main road) carretera
f; (public way) vía *f* pública; (*before n*) ⟨*patrol*/
patrolman⟩ (AmE) de carretera; **H~way Code**
n (in UK) Código *m* de la Circulación;
~wayman /'haɪweɪmən/ *n* (*pl* **-men** /-mən/)
salteador *m* de caminos, bandolero *m*; **~ wire** *n*
cuerda *f* floja

hijack¹ /'haɪdʒæk/ *vt* secuestrar

hijack² *n* secuestro *m*

hijacker /'haɪdʒækər ‖ 'haɪdʒækə(r)/ *n*
secuestrador, -dora *m,f*; (of planes) pirata aéreo,
-rea *m,f*

hike¹ /haɪk/ *n* **1** (long walk) caminata *f*,
excursión *f* **2** (increase) subida *f*

hike² *vi* (walk) ir* de caminata *or* de excursión;
to go hiking hacer* excursionismo

hiker /'haɪkər ‖ 'haɪkə(r)/ *n* excursionista *mf*

hilarious /hɪ'leriəs ‖ hɪ'leəriəs/ *adj*
divertidísimo, comiquísimo

hill /hɪl/ *n* (low) colina *f*, cerro *m*, collado *m*;
(higher) montaña *f*; (slope, incline) cuesta *f*

hill: **~billy** *n* (AmE colloq) rústico, -ca *m,f*,
paleto, -ta *m,f* (Esp fam & pey), pajuerano, -na *m,f*
(RPl fam & pey); **~side** *n* ladera *f*; **~top** *n* cima
f, cumbre *f*

hilly /'hɪli/ *adj* **-lier, -liest** accidentado

hilt /hɪlt/ *n* empuñadura *f*, puño *m*

him /hɪm, *weak form* ɪm/ *pron* **1** (a) (as direct
object) lo, le (Esp); **I saw ~** lo *or* (Esp tb) le vi; **call
~** llámalo, llámale (Esp) **(b)** (as indirect object) le;
(with direct object pronoun present) se; **I sent ~ a card**
le mandé una tarjeta **(c)** (after preposition) él
2 (emphatic use) él; **it's ~** es él

Himalayas /'hɪmə'leɪəz/ *pl n* the **~** el
Himalaya

himself /hɪm'self/ *pron* **(a)** (reflexive): **he cut**/
hurt ~ se cortó/lastimó; **he bought ~ a hat** se
compró un sombrero; **he only thinks of ~** solo
piensa en sí mismo; **by ~** solo; **he was talking to
~** estaba hablando solo **(b)** (emphatic use) él
mismo; **he told me so ~** me lo dijo él mismo **(c)**
(normal self): **he's not ~** no es el de siempre

hind /haɪnd/ *adj* (before n, no comp) ⟨*legs*⟩
trasero

hinder /'hɪndər ‖ 'hɪndə(r)/ *vt* dificultar

Hindi /'hɪndi/ *n* indi *m*, hindi *m*

hindrance /'hɪndrəns/ *n* estorbo *m*

hindsight /'haɪndsaɪt/ *n*: **with (the benefit of)
~** a posteriori, en retrospectiva

Hindu¹ /'hɪnduː/ *n* hindú *mf*

Hindu² *adj* hindú

Hinduism /'hɪnduːɪzəm/ *n* hinduismo *m*

hinge¹ /hɪndʒ/ *n* (of door, window, gate) bisagra *f*,
gozne *m*; (of box, lid) bisagra *f*

hinge² hinges, hinging, hinged *vi* **to ~ on**
sth (turn) girar SOBRE algo; (be fixed) ir* asegurado
con bisagras A algo; (depend) depender DE algo

hint¹ /hɪnt/ *n* **1** (a) (oblique reference)
insinuación *f*, indirecta *f*; (clue) pista *f*; **to drop a
~ to** sb lanzarle* una indirecta a algn; **to take
the ~** captar *or* (Esp tb) coger* la indirecta **(b)**

(trace – of bitterness, sadness) dejo *m*; (– of color)
toque *m*, matiz *m*; (– of garlic, lemon) dejo *m*, gusto
m **2** (tip) consejo *m*

hint² *vt* insinuar*, dar* a entender
■ **~** *vi* lanzar* indirectas; **to ~** AT sth insinuar*
or dar* a entender algo

hip¹ /hɪp/ *n* cadera *f*

hip² *interj*: **~, ~,** hooray *o* hurrah! ¡hurra!, ¡viva!

hippie /'hɪpi/ *n* ▶ HIPPY

hippo /'hɪpəʊ/ *n* (*pl* **-pos**) (colloq) hipopótamo *m*

hippopotamus /'hɪpə'pɑːtəməs
‖ ˌhɪpə'pɒtəməs/ *n* (*pl* **-muses** *or* **-mi** /-maɪ/)
hipopótamo *m*

hippy, hippie /'hɪpi/ *n* (*pl* **-pies**) hippy *mf*

hire¹ /haɪr ‖ 'haɪə(r)/ *vt* **1** (a) ⟨*hall*/*boat*/*suit*⟩
alquilar, arrendar* **(b)** (Busn, Lab Rel) ⟨*staff*/
person⟩ contratar **(c)** **hired** *past p* ⟨*car*⟩
alquilado **2** ▶ HIRE OUT
■ **hire out** [*v + o + adv, v + adv + o*] (BrE)
alquilar, arrendar*

hire² *n* **1** (of hall/car/suit) alquiler *m*, arriendo *m*;
☉ for hire se alquila *or* se arrienda; (on taxis)
libre **2** (payment) alquiler *m*, arriendo *m*

hire purchase *n* (BrE) compra *f* a plazos; **to
buy sth on ~ ~** comprar algo a plazos, comprar
algo en cuotas (esp AmL)

his¹ /hɪz, *weak form* ɪz/ *adj*

■ **Note** The translation *su* agrees in number with the
noun which it modifies; *his* is translated by *su, sus,*
according to what follows: *his father*/*mother* su padre/
madre; *his books*/*magazines* sus libros/revistas.

(*sing*) su; (*pl*) sus; **he injured ~ knee** se lesionó
la rodilla

his² *pron*

■ **Note** The translation *suyo* reflects the gender and
number of the noun it is standing for; *his* is translated
by *el suyo, la suya, los suyos, las suyas,* depending
on what is being referred to.

(*sing*) suyo, -ya; (*pl*) suyos, -yas, de él; **they're ~**
son suyos/suyas, son de él; **~ is blue** el suyo/la
suya es azul, el/la de él es azul; **a friend of ~** un
amigo suyo *or* de él

Hispanic¹ /hɪ'spænɪk/ *adj* hispánico, hispano;
⟨*community*/*voter*⟩ (in US) hispano

Hispanic² *n* (esp AmE) hispano, -na *m,f*

hiss¹ /hɪs/ *vi* silbar; «*cat*» bufar
■ **~** *vt* decir* entre dientes

hiss² *n* (of snake, audience) silbido *m*; (of cat)
bufido *m*

historian /hɪ'stɔːriən/ *n* historiador, -dora *m,f*

historic /hɪ'stɔːrɪk ‖ hɪ'stɒrɪk/ *adj* **(a)**
(momentous) ⟨*event*/*moment*⟩ memorable **(b)** (old)
⟨*house*/*building*⟩ histórico

historical /hɪ'stɔːrɪkəl ‖ hɪ'stɒrɪkəl/ *adj* **(a)**
(relating to history) histórico **(b)** (crit) ▶ HISTORIC

history /'hɪstəri/ *n* (*pl* **-ries**) **1** historia *f*; **the
worst earthquake in ~** el peor terremoto de la
historia **2** (record, background) historial *m*

hit¹ /hɪt/ (*pres p* **hitting**; *past & past p* **hit**) *vt*
1 (a) (deal blow to) ⟨*door*/*table*⟩ dar* un golpe en,
golpear; ⟨*person*⟩ pegarle* a **(b)** (strike) golpear;
the truck ~ a tree el camión chocó con *or* contra
un árbol; **the house was ~ by a bomb** una bomba
cayó sobre la casa; **the bullet ~ him in the leg** la ⋯✧

bala le dio *or* lo alcanzó en la pierna; **to ~ one's
head on sth** darse* un golpe en la cabeza contra
algo; **to ~ it off with sb** congeniar con algn
2 (a) (strike accurately) ⟨*target*⟩ dar* en **(b)** (attack)
⟨*opponent/enemy*⟩ atacar* **(c)** (score) (Sport)
anotarse, marcar*
3 (affect adversely) afectar (a)
4 (a) (meet with, run into) ⟨*difficulty/problem*⟩
toparse con **(b)** (reach) ⟨*goal*⟩ llegar* a, alcanzar*
5 (occur to): **suddenly it ~ me: why had he … ?**
de repente se me ocurrió: ¿por qué había … ?
■ **hit back (a)** [*v + adv*] (strike in return) devolver*
el golpe; **she ~ back at her critics** arremetió
contra sus detractores **(b)** [*v + o + adv*]
devolverle* el golpe a
■ **hit on** [*v + prep + o*] ⟨*solution*⟩ dar* con
■ **hit out** [*v + adv*] **(a)** (strike) **to ~ out (AT sb)**
(once) lanzar*(le) un golpe (A algn); (repeatedly)
tirar(le) golpes (A algn) **(b)** (attack verbally) **to ~
out AT *o* AGAINST sth/sb** atacar* algo/a algn
■ **hit upon** ▶ HIT ON

hit² *n* **1 (a)** (blow, stroke) (Sport) golpe *m* **(b)** (in
shooting) blanco *m* **2** (success) (colloq) éxito *m*
3 (Comput) impacto *m*

hit-: ~-and-miss /'hɪtən'mɪs/ *adj* (*pred* **~ and
miss**) ▶ HIT-OR-MISS; **~-and-run** /'hɪtən'rʌn/
adj (*before n*) ⟨*driver*⟩ que se da a la fuga tras
atropellar a algn

hitch¹ /hɪtʃ/ *n* **1** (difficulty) complicación *f*,
problema *m*, pega *f* (Esp fam); **a technical ~** un
problema técnico **2** (limp) (AmE) cojera *f*,
renguera *f* (AmL)

hitch² *vt* **1** (attach) **to ~ sth TO sth** enganchar
algo A algo **2** (thumb) (colloq): **to ~ a ride** *o* (BrE
also) **a lift** hacer* dedo (fam), hacer* autostop, ir*
de aventón (Col, Méx fam), pedir* cola (Ven fam)
■ **~** *vi* ▶ HITCHHIKE

hitch-: ~hike *vi* hacer* autostop, hacer* dedo
(fam), ir* de aventón (Col, Méx fam), pedir* cola
(Ven fam); **~hiker** *n* autoestopista *mf*

hi-tech /'haɪ'tek/ *adj* ▶ HIGH-TECH

hitherto /'hɪðər'tu: ‖,hɪðə'tu:/ *adv* (frml) hasta
ahora, hasta la fecha

hit-: ~ list *n* (colloq) (murder list) lista *f* de
sentenciados; (blacklist) lista *f* negra; **~ man** *n*
(colloq) (assassin) asesino *m* a sueldo, sicario *m*;
~-or-miss /'hɪtər'mɪs ‖,hɪtɔ:'mɪs/ *adj* (*pred* **~
or miss**) ⟨*method/approach*⟩ poco científico

hitter /'hɪtər ‖'hɪtə(r)/ *n* (in baseball) bateador,
-dora *m,f*; (in US football) liniero, -ra *m,f*

HIV *n* (= **Human Immunodeficiency
Virus**) VIH *m*, virus *m* del sida; **he's ~ positive**
es seropositivo

hive /haɪv/ *n* (home of bees) colmena *f*; (bee colony)
enjambre *m*

hives /haɪvz/ *n* (Med) urticaria *f*

HM (= **Her/His Majesty**) S.M.

HMS (in UK) = **Her/His Majesty's Ship**

hoard¹ /hɔːrd ‖hɔːd/ *n* (of food) reserva *f*, **a ~
of treasure** un tesoro escondido

hoard² *vt* acumular, juntar; (anticipating a
shortage) acaparar

hoarding /'hɔːrdɪŋ ‖'hɔːdɪŋ/ *n* **1** (anticipating a
shortage) acaparamiento *m* **2** (billboard) (BrE) valla
f publicitaria, barda *f* de anuncios (Méx)

hoarse /hɔːrs ‖hɔːs/ *adj* **hoarser, hoarsest**
ronco

hoax /həʊks/ *n* (deception) engaño *m*; (joke)
broma *f*; (tall story) patraña *f*

hob /hɑːb ‖hɒb/ *n* **(a)** (beside open fire) placa *f* **(b)**
(of cooker) (BrE) hornillas *fpl* (AmL exc CS),
hornillos *mpl* (Esp), hornallas *fpl* (RPl), platos
mpl (Chi)

hobble /'hɑːbəl ‖'hɒbəl/ *vi* cojear, renguear
(AmL)

hobby /'hɑːbi ‖'hɒbi/ *n* (*pl* **-bies**) hobby *m*,
pasatiempo *m*, afición *f*

hobnailed /'hɑːbneɪld ‖'hɒbneɪld/ *adj* con
tachuelas

hobo /'həʊbəʊ/ *n* (*pl* **-boes** *or* **-bos**) (AmE
colloq) vagabundo, -da *m,f*, linyera *mf* (CS fam)

hockey /'hɑːki ‖'hɒki/ *n* **(a)** (ice ~) (AmE)
hockey *m* sobre hielo **(b)** (played on grass) (BrE)
hockey *m* (sobre hierba)

hod /hɑːd ‖hɒd/ *n* (for bricks) capacho *m* (*para
acarrear ladrillos*)

hoe¹ /həʊ/ *n* azada *f*, azadón *m*

hoe² *vt* azadonar, pasar la azada por

hog¹ /hɔːg ‖hɒg/ *n* **1** (AmE Agr, Zool) cerdo, -da
m,f, puerco, -ca *m,f*, chancho, -cha *m,f* (AmL)
2 (person) (colloq) tragón, -gona *m,f* (fam),
angurriento, -ta *m,f* (CS fam)

hog² *vt* **-gg-** (colloq) ⟨*food/bathroom/limelight*⟩
acaparar; ⟨*discussion*⟩ monopolizar*

Hogmanay /'hɑːgməneɪ ‖'hɒgməneɪ/ *n* (Scot)
Nochevieja *f*, noche *f* de fin de año

hoist¹ /hɔɪst/ *vt* (lift) levantar, alzar*; ⟨*sail/flag*⟩
izar*

hoist² *n* (elevator) montacargas *m*; (crane, derrick)
grúa *f*

hokum /'həʊkəm/ *n* (colloq) **(a)** (nonsense)
paparruchas *fpl* (fam) **(b)** (corny material) (AmE)
recursos efectistas de tipo melodramático o cómico

hold¹ /həʊld/ (*past & past p* **held**) *vt* **1 (a)**
(have in one's hand(s)) tener* (en la mano); **will you
~ this for me?** ¿me puedes tener *or* (esp AmL)
agarrar esto por favor? **(b)** (clasp): **~ it with both
hands** sujétala *or* (esp AmL) agárralo con las dos
manos; **he was ~ing her hand** la tenía agarrada
or (esp Esp) cogida de la mano **(c)** (grip) (Auto)
agarrar, adherirse*
2 (have room for) ⟨*cup/jug*⟩ tener* una capacidad
de; ⟨*stadium*⟩ tener* capacidad *or* cabida para;
this report ~s all the answers to … este informe
contiene todas las respuestas a …; **who knows what
the future ~s** quién sabe qué nos deparará el futuro
3 (a) (keep in position) ⟨*ladder*⟩ sujetar, sostener*
(b) (maintain) ⟨*attention/interest*⟩ mantener*; **she
held the lead throughout the race** se mantuvo a la
cabeza durante toda la carrera
4 (a) (keep) ⟨*tickets/room*⟩ reservar, guardar **(b)**
(detain, imprison): **she is being held at the police
station for questioning** está detenida en la
comisaría para ser interrogada **(c)** (restrain)
detener* **(d)** (control) ⟨*troops/rebels*⟩ ocupar
5 (a) (have) ⟨*passport/permit*⟩ tener*, estar* en
posesión de (frml); ⟨*degree/shares*⟩ tener*; ⟨*record*⟩
ostentar, tener*; ⟨*post/position*⟩ tener*, ocupar;
he ~s the view that … sostiene *or* mantiene que
… **(b)** (consider) considerar; (assert) sostener*,
mantener*; **to ~ sb responsible for sth**
responsabilizar* a algn de algo **(c)** (conduct)
⟨*meeting/elections*⟩ celebrar; ⟨*demonstration*⟩
hacer*; ⟨*party*⟩ dar*; ⟨*conversation*⟩ mantener*

6 (stop): ~ it! ¡espera!

■ ~ *vi* 1 (clasp, grip): ~ **tight!** ¡agárrate fuerte!
2 **(a)** (stay firm) «*rope/door*» aguantar, resistir
(b) (continue) «*weather*» seguir* *or* continuar*
bueno; **if our luck ~s** si nos sigue acompañando
la suerte

■ **hold against** [*v + o + prep + o*]: **I won't ~ that
against him** no se lo voy a tomar en cuenta

■ **hold back** 1 [*v + o + adv, v + adv + o*] **(a)**
(restrain) ‹*crowds/water/tears*› contener* **(b)**
(withhold, delay) ‹*information*› no revelar;
‹*payment*› retrasar
2 [*v + adv*] (restrain oneself) contenerse*, frenarse

■ **hold down** [*v + o + adv, v + adv + o*] **(a)** (force,
press down) ‹*lid/papers*› sujetar; ‹*person*›
inmovilizar **(b)** ‹*job*›: **he can't ~ down a job** es
incapaz de tener un trabajo y cumplir con él **(c)**
(limit) ‹*price/increase*› moderar, contener*

■ **hold in** [*v + o + adv, v + adv + o*] ‹*stomach*›
meter; ‹*feelings/laughter*› contener*

■ **hold off** 1 [*v + o + adv, v + adv + o*] **(a)** (resist)
‹*attack/enemy*› resistir **(b)** (defeat) ‹*challenger/
rival*› derrotar
2 [*v + adv*] (be delayed): **if the rain ~s off** si no
empieza a llover

■ **hold on** [*v + adv*] **(a)** (wait) esperar **(b)** (survive)
resistir, aguantar **(c)** (clasp, grip) agarrarse; **to ~
on TO sth/sb** agarrarse A *or* DE algo/algn **(d)**
(keep) **to ~ on TO sth** ‹*receipt/photo*› conservar *or*
guardar algo

■ **hold out** 1 [*v + o + adv, v + adv + o*] (extend)
‹*hands/arms*› tender*, alargar*
2 [*v + adv + o*] **(a)** (offer) ‹*possibility*› ofrecer*;
‹*hope*› dar* **(b)** (have, retain) ‹*hope*› tener*; **I don't
~ out much hope of getting the job** no tengo
muchas esperanzas de que me den el trabajo
3 [*v + adv*] **(a)** (survive, last) «*person*» aguantar
(b) (resist, make a stand) «*army/town*» resistir

■ **hold over** [*v + o + adv, v + adv + o*] (postpone)
‹*meeting/decision*› aplazar*, postergar* (esp AmL)

■ **hold together** 1 [*v + adv*] «*arguments*»
tener* lógica *or* solidez; «*people*» mantenerse*
unidos
2 [*v + o + adv*] (keep united) ‹*family/group*›
mantener* unido

■ **hold up** 1 [*v + o + adv, v + adv + o*] **(a)** (raise)
‹*hand/banner*› levantar; ‹*head*› mantener*
erguido **(b)** (support) ‹*roof/walls*› sostener* **(c)**
(delay) ‹*person/arrival*› retrasar; ‹*progress*›
entorpecer* **(d)** (rob) atracar*, asaltar
2 [*v + adv*] «*theory/argument*» resultar válido

■ **hold with** [*v + prep + o*] (*usu neg*) estar* de
acuerdo con

hold² *n* 1 **(a)** (grip, grasp): **to catch** *o* **grab** *o*
take ~ of sth agarrar *or* (esp Esp) coger* algo; (so
as not to fall etc) agarrarse *or* asirse de *or* a algo; **to
get ~ of sb** (find) localizar* *or* (AmL tb) ubicar* a
algn; **to get ~ of sth** (manage to get) conseguir*
algo **(b)** (control): **the ~ they have over the
members of the sect** el dominio que ejercen sobre
los miembros de la secta
2 **(a)** (in wrestling, judo) llave *f*; **with no ~s barred**
sin ningún tipo de restricciones **(b)** (in
mountaineering) asidero *m*
3 (delay, pause) demora *f*; **I've got Mr Brown on ~**
(Telec) el Sr Brown está esperando para hablar
con usted; **to put sth on ~** ‹*project*› dejar algo
aparcado

4 (of ship, aircraft) bodega *f*

holdall /ˈhəʊldɔːl/ *n* (BrE) bolso *m* de viaje,
bolsón *m* (RPl)

holder /ˈhəʊldər ‖ˈhəʊldə(r)/ *n* 1 (of permit,
passport, job) titular *mf*; (of ticket) poseedor, -dora
m,f; (of bonds etc) titular *mf*, tenedor, -dora *m,f*;
(of title, cup) poseedor, -dora *m,f* 2 (wallet) funda *f*

holdup /ˈhəʊldʌp/ *n* **(a)** (delay) demora *f*, retraso
m; (in traffic) atasco *m*, embotellamiento *m* **(b)**
(armed robbery) atraco *m*

hole /həʊl/ *n* 1 **(a)** (in belt, material, clothing)
agujero *m*; (in ground) hoyo *m*, agujero *m*; (in road)
bache *m*; (in wall) boquete *m*; **to make a ~ in sth**
hacer* un agujero en algo, agujerear algo **(b)** (in
argument, proposal) punto *m* débil; **to pick ~s in sth**
encontrarle* defectos *or* faltas a algo **(c)** (of
animal) madriguera *f* 2 (in golf) hoyo *m*
3 (unpleasant place) (colloq): **this town is a real ~!**
¡qué pueblo de mala muerte! (fam)

holiday /ˈhɒlədeɪ ‖ˈhɒlədeɪ/ *n* **(a)** (day) fiesta *f*,
día *m* festivo, (día *m*) feriado *m* (AmL) **(b)** (period
away from work) (esp BrE) (*often pl*) vacaciones *fpl*,
licencia *f* (Col, Méx, RPl); **to go/be on ~** irse*/
estar* de vacaciones; (*before n*) ‹*mood/spirit*›
festivo; ‹*cottage*› de vacaciones **(c)** (BrE Educ)
(*often pl*) vacaciones *fpl*

holiday: ~ **camp** *n* (BrE) colonia *f* de
vacaciones; ~**maker** *n* (BrE) turista *mf*; (on
summer holidays) veraneante *mf*; ~ **resort** *n*
centro *m* turístico

Holland /ˈhɒlənd ‖ˈhɒlənd/ *n* Holanda *f*

holler /ˈhɒlər ‖ˈhɒlə(r)/ *vt/i* (AmE colloq) gritar

hollow¹ /ˈhɒləʊ ‖ˈhɒləʊ/ *adj* 1 ‹*tree/tooth/
wall*› hueco; ‹*sound*› hueco; ‹*voice*› apagado;
‹*cheeks/eyes*› hundido 2 ‹*success/triumph*› vacío;
‹*person*› vacío, vacuo; ‹*promises/threats*› vano,
falso; ‹*words*› hueco, vacío

hollow² *n* **(a)** (empty space) hueco *m*; (depression)
hoyo *m*, depresión *f* **(b)** (dell, valley) hondonada *f*

■ **hollow out** [*v + o + adv, v + adv + o*] vaciar*,
ahuecar*

holly /ˈhɒli ‖ˈhɒli/ *n* acebo *m*

holocaust /ˈhɒləkɔːst, ˈhɑː- ‖ˈhɒləkɔːst/ *n*
hecatombe *f*, desastre *m*; **nuclear ~** holocausto *m*
nuclear; **the H~** el Holocausto

hologram /ˈhɒləgræm, ˈhɑː- ‖ˈhɒləgræm/ *n*
holograma *m*

holster /ˈhəʊlstər ‖ˈhəʊlstə(r)/ *n* pistolera *f*,
funda *f* de pistola (*or* revólver *etc*)

holy /ˈhəʊli/ *adj* **-lier, -liest** ‹*ground/place*›
sagrado, santo; ‹*day*› de precepto, de guardar;
‹*water*› bendito; ‹*person/life/virtue*› santo; **the H~
Bible** la Sagrada *or* Santa Biblia; **H~ Week**
Semana Santa

holy: **H~ Ghost** *n* **the H~ Ghost** el Espíritu
Santo; **H~ Spirit** *n* **the H~ Spirit** el Espíritu
Santo

homage /ˈhɒmɪdʒ ‖ˈhɒmɪdʒ/ *n* (frml) homenaje
m; **to pay ~ to sb/sth** rendir* homenaje a algn/
algo

home¹ /həʊm/ *n* 1 (of person) **(a)** (dwelling) casa
f (& in wider sense): **New York is my ~ now**
Nueva York es donde vivo ahora; ~ **sweet ~**
hogar dulce hogar; **to leave ~** irse* de casa **(c)**
(family environment) hogar *m*
2 (of animal, plant) (Bot, Zool) hábitat *m*
3 **at home (a)** (in house) en casa **(b)** (at ease): ⋯▸

make yourself at ∼ ponte cómodo, estás en tu casa **(c)** (not abroad): at ∼ **and abroad** dentro y fuera del país **(d)** (Sport) en casa
4 (institution) (for children) asilo *m* (AmL), orfanatorio *m* (Méx), centro *m* de acogida de menores (Esp); (for old people) residencia *f* de ancianos; **dogs'** ∼ (BrE) perrera *f*
■ **home in** [*v* + *adv*] **to** ∼ **in on** sth localizar* y dirigirse* HACIA algo

home² *adv* **1** (where one lives) ⟨*come/arrive*⟩ a casa; **I'll be** ∼ **at five** estaré en casa a las cinco **2** (to desired place): **to hit** ∼ dar* en el blanco; **to drive** sth ∼ **(to sb)** hacer(le)* entender algo (a algn)

home³ *adj* (*before n*) **(a)** ⟨*address/telephone number*⟩ particular; ⟨*background/environment*⟩ familiar; ⟨*cooking/perm*⟩ casero; ∼ **delivery** (of purchases) entrega *f* a domicilio; ∼ **visit** (by doctor) (BrE) visita *f* a domicilio **(b)** (of origin): ∼ **state** (in US) estado *m* natal *or* de procedencia **(c)** (not foreign) ⟨*affairs/market*⟩ nacional **(d)** (Sport) ⟨*team*⟩ de casa, local; ⟨*game*⟩ en casa

home: ∼ **base** *n* (AmE) (Busn, Mil) base *f* de operaciones (in baseball) ▶ HOME PLATE; ∼**boy** *n* (AmE sl) compinche *m* (fam), cuate *m* (Méx fam); ∼ **brew** *n* cerveza hecha en casa; ∼**coming** *n* **(a)** (return home) regreso *m*, vuelta *f* (a casa, a la patria etc) **(b)** (at school, college) (AmE) *fiesta estudiantil al comienzo del año académico con asistencia de ex-alumnos*; **H**∼ **Counties** *pl n* (in UK) **the H**∼ **Counties** *los condados de los alrededores de Londres*; ∼**grown** /'həʊm'grəʊn/ *adj* (from one's own garden) de la huerta propia; (not foreign) del país, local, nacional; ∼ **help** *n* (BrE) auxiliar *mf*; ∼**land** *n* patria *f*, tierra *f* natal

homeless /'həʊmləs ‖'həʊmlɪs/ *adj* sin hogar, sin techo

homely /'həʊmli/ *adj* **-lier, -liest (a)** (characteristic of home) ⟨*meal/food*⟩ casero; ⟨*atmosphere/room*⟩ acogedor, hogareño **(b)** (plain) (AmE) feo

home: ∼**made** /'həʊm'meɪd/ *adj* ⟨*clothes*⟩ hecho en casa; ⟨*food*⟩ casero; ∼**maker** *n* ama *f* de casa; ∼ **movie** *n* película *f* casera; ∼ **office** *n* (AmE) oficina *f* central; **H**∼ **Office** *n* (in UK) **the H**∼ **Office** *el Home Office, el Ministerio del Interior británico*

homeopathic, (BrE) **homoeopathic** /'həʊmiə'pæθɪk/ *adj* homeopático

home: ∼ **owner** *n* propietario, -ria *m,f* (*de una vivienda*); ∼ **page** *n* (Comput) página *f* frontal, página *f* inicial; ∼ **plate** *n* home *m*, pentágono *m* (Méx)

homer /'həʊmər ‖'həʊmə(r)/ *n* (AmE colloq) ▶ HOME RUN

home: ∼**room** *n* (AmE Educ) clase *f* or aula *f*‡ del curso; ∼ **rule** *n* autogobierno *m*; ∼ **run** *n* cuadrangular *m*, jonrón *m* (AmL); **H**∼ **Secretary** *n* (in UK) ministro, -tra *m,f* del Interior; ∼**sick** *adj*: **I am o feel** ∼**sick** echo de menos *or* (AmL tb) extraño a mi familia (*or* mi país *etc*)

homestead /'həʊmsted/ *n* (AmE) casa *f* (*en una granja, hacienda etc*)

home: ∼ **straight,** ∼ **stretch** *n* (Sport) recta *f* final *or* de llegada; ∼**town** /'həʊm'taʊn/ *n* ciudad *f*/pueblo *m* natal; ∼ **truth** *n* (*usu pl*) verdad *f* (*desagradable*)

homeward¹ /'həʊmwərd ‖'həʊmwəd/ **(a)** (BrE also) **homewards** /-z/ *adv* ⟨*travel/journey/sail*⟩ de vuelta a casa **(b) to be** ∼ **bound** ir* de camino *or* de vuelta a casa

homeward² *adj* (*before n*) ⟨*journey*⟩ de vuelta *or* de regreso

homework /'həʊmwɜːrk ‖'həʊmwɜːk/ *n* deberes *mpl*, tarea *f*

homey /'həʊmi/ *adj* **homier, homiest** (AmE colloq) ⟨*atmosphere/place*⟩ hogareño, acogedor; ⟨*manner*⟩ campechano

homicidal /'hɑːmə'saɪdl ‖,hɒmɪ'saɪdl/ *adj* ⟨*tendency*⟩ homicida; ⟨*rage*⟩ asesino

homicide /'hɑːməsaɪd ‖'hɒmɪsaɪd/ *n* **(a)** (crime, act) homicidio *m* **(b)** (murderer) (frml) homicida *mf*

homing /'həʊmɪŋ/ *adj* (*before n*) ⟨*instinct*⟩ de volver al hogar; ⟨*device/missile*⟩ buscador; ∼ **pigeon** paloma *f* mensajera

homeopathic /'həʊmiə'pæθɪk/ *adj* (BrE) ▶ HOMEOPATHIC

homogeneous /'həʊmə'dʒiːniəs ‖,hɒmə'dʒiːniəs/ *adj* homogéneo

homosexual¹ /'həʊmə'sekʃuəl ‖,həʊmə'sekʃuəl, ,hɒmə-/ *adj* homosexual

homosexual² *n* homosexual *mf*

homosexuality /'həʊmə'sekʃu'æləti ‖,həʊməsekʃʊ'æləti, ,hɒmə-/ *n* homosexualidad *f*

Hon /ɑːn ‖ɒn/ (in UK) = **Honourable**

Honduran¹ /hɑːn'dʊrən ‖hɒn'djʊərən/ *adj* hondureño

Honduran² *n* hondureño, -ña *m,f*

Honduras /hɑːn'dʊrəs ‖hɒn'djʊərəs/ *n* Honduras *f*

hone /həʊn/ *vt* ⟨*blade/edge*⟩ afilar; ⟨*style/skill*⟩ afinar

honest /'ɑːnəst ‖'ɒnɪst/ *adj* **(a)** (trustworthy, upright) ⟨*person/action*⟩ honrado, honesto; ⟨*face*⟩ de persona honrada *or* honesta **(b)** (sincere) ⟨*appraisal/opinion*⟩ sincero; **to be** ∼ **with you** ... si quieres que te diga la verdad ...

honestly /'ɑːnəstli ‖'ɒnɪstli/ *adv* **(a)** (sincerely) ⟨*answer/say/think*⟩ sinceramente, francamente **(b)** (indep) en serio, de verdad **(c)** (as interj) (expressing exasperation) ¡por favor! **(d)** (legitimately) ⟨*act/earn*⟩ con honradez, honradamente

honesty /'ɑːnəsti ‖'ɒnɪsti/ *n* **(a)** (probity) honradez *f*, honestidad *f*, rectitud *f* **(b)** (truthfulness) franqueza *f*, sinceridad *f*; **in all** ∼ ... para ser sincero ...

honey /'hʌni/ *n* (*pl* **honeys**) **1** miel *f* **2** (*as form of address*) (colloq) cariño (fam)

honey: ∼ **bee** *n* abeja *f*; ∼**comb** *n* panal *m*; ∼**moon** *n* luna *f* de miel; ∼**suckle** *n* madreselva *f*

AmC	América Central	Arg Argentina	Cu Cuba	Per Perú
AmL	América Latina	Bol Bolivia	Ec Ecuador	RPI Río de la Plata
AmS	América del Sur	Chi Chile	Esp España	Ur Uruguay
Andes	Región andina	CS Cono Sur	Méx México	Ven Venezuela

Hong Kong /ˈhɑːŋˈkɑːŋ ‖ ˌhɒŋˈkɒŋ/ n
Hong-Kong m

honk vi (hoot) «goose» graznar; «driver» tocar* el claxon, pitar

honor¹, (BrE) **honour** /ˈɑːnər ‖ ˈɒnə(r)/ n
[1] (good name) honor m [2] (privilege, mark of distinction) honor m; **to have the ~ to + INF o of -ING** (frml) tener* el honor DE + INF (frml); **a reception in ~ of the delegates** una recepción en honor de los delegados [3] **Honor** (as title) **Your/His H~** Su Señoría [4] **honors** pl (a) (special mention) (before n) **~s list** (AmE) cuadro m de honor (b) (Educ): **to graduate with ~s** licenciarse con matrícula (de honor) or con honores; (before n) **an honours degree** (BrE) ≈ una licenciatura

honor², (BrE) **honour** vt [1] (show respect) honrar [2] (a) (keep to) ‹agreement/obligation› cumplir (con) (b) (Fin) ‹bill/debt› satisfacer* (frml), pagar*; ‹check/draft› pagar*, aceptar

honorable, (BrE) **honourable** /ˈɑːnərəbəl ‖ ˈɒnərəbəl/ adj [1] (a) (honest, respectable) ‹person/action› honorable (b) (creditable) ‹peace/settlement› honroso [2] **Honourable** (in UK) tratamiento dado a representantes parlamentarios y a hijos de vizcondes, barones y condes

honorary /ˈɑːnəreri ‖ ˈɒnərəri/ adj honorario; ‹doctorate› honoris causa

honour etc (BrE) ▶ HONOR etc

hood /hʊd/ n [1] (a) (on coat, jacket) capucha f; (pointed) capirote m; (of monk) capucha f, capuchón m (b) (on chimney, cooker) campana f; (on machine) cubierta f (b) (AmE Auto) capó m (c) (folding cover) (BrE) capota f

hoodlum /ˈhuːdləm/ n (a) (thug) (AmE) matón, -tona m,f (fam), (for fishing) anzuelo m; vándalo, -la m,f, gamberro, -rra m,f (Esp)

hoodwink /ˈhʊdwɪŋk/ vt engañar; **to ~ sb INTO -ING** engañar a algn PARA QUE (+ subj)

hoof /hʊf ‖ huːf/ n (pl **hoofs** or **hooves**) (of horse) casco m, vaso m (RPl), pezuña f (Méx); (of cow) pezuña f

hoof-and-mouth disease /ˈhʊfənˈmaʊθ ‖ ˌhuːfənˈmaʊθ/ n (AmE) fiebre f aftosa, glosopeda f (téc)

hook¹ /hʊk/ n [1] (a) (for hanging clothes) percha f, gancho m; (for hanging clothes) percha f, gancho m; (for fishing) anzuelo m; **to take the phone off the ~** descolgar* el teléfono; **to let sb off the ~** dejar salir a algn del atolladero (b) (Clothing) corchete m, ganchito m; **~s and eyes** corchetes (macho y hembra) [2] (in boxing) gancho m

hook² vt (grasp, secure) enganchar
■ **hook up** [1] [v + o + adv, v + adv + o] (a) (fasten) ‹dress/bra› abrochar (b) (connect, link) enganchar [2] [v + adv] (a) (Rad, TV) conectarse, transmitir en cadena (b) (fasten) «dress» abrocharse

hooked /hʊkt/ adj [1] (hook-shaped) ‹tool› en forma de gancho; ‹beak› aguileño [2] (addicted) (colloq) **to be/get ~ ON sth** estar* enviciado/enviciarse CON algo, estar* enganchado/engancharse A algo (Esp)

hooker /ˈhʊkər ‖ ˈhʊkə(r)/ n (esp AmE colloq) prostituta f, puta f (vulg)

hooky, hookey /ˈhʊki/ n: **to play ~** (esp AmE colloq) faltar a clase, hacer* novillos or (Méx) irse*

de pinta or (RPl) hacerse* la rata or la rabona or (Per) la vaca or (Chi) hacer* la cimarra or (Col) capar clase or (Ven) jubilarse (fam)

hooligan /ˈhuːlɪgən/ n vándalo, -la m,f, gamberro, -rra m,f (Esp)

hoop /huːp/ n aro m

hooray /hʊˈreɪ/ interj ¡hurra!

hoot¹ /huːt/ n (of owl) grito m, ululato m; **~s of laughter** risotadas fpl, carcajadas fpl

hoot² vi «owl» ulular; «car/driver» tocar* el claxon, pitar

hooter /ˈhuːtər ‖ ˈhuːtə(r)/ n (BrE) (a) (siren) sirena f (b) (horn) claxon m, bocina f

hoover /ˈhuːvər ‖ ˈhuːvə(r)/ (BrE) vt pasar la aspiradora or el aspirador por, aspirar (AmL)

Hoover®, hoover /ˈhuːvər ‖ ˈhuːvə(r)/ n (BrE) aspiradora f, aspirador m

hooves /hʊvz ‖ huːvz/ pl of HOOF

hop¹ /hɑːp ‖ hɒp/ n [1] (jump — of person) salto m a la pata coja, brinco m de cojito (Méx); (— of rabbit) salto m, brinco m; (— of bird) saltito m [2] (Bot, Culin) (usu pl) lúpulo m

hop² -**pp**- vi (a) «frog/rabbit» brincar*, saltar; «bird» dar* saltitos (b) «person/child» saltar a la pata coja, brincar* de cojito (Méx) (c) (move quickly) (colloq): **~ in**, I'll take you to the station súbete, que te llevo a la estación; **to ~ on a bus** tomarse un autobús
■ **~** vt (AmE colloq) ‹flight/train› tomar, pillar (fam)

hope¹ /həʊp/ n esperanza f; **she did it in the ~ of a reward** lo hizo con la esperanza de obtener una recompensa

hope² vi esperar; **I ~ so/not** espero que sí/que no; **we're hoping for good weather** esperamos tener buen tiempo
■ **~** vt **to ~** (THAT) esperar QUE (+ subj); **to ~ to + INF** esperar + INF

hope chest n (AmE) baúl m or arcón m del ajuar

hopeful¹ /ˈhəʊpfəl/ adj (a) ‹person› esperanzado, optimista (b) (promising) esperanzador, prometedor

hopeful² n aspirante mf, candidato, -ta m,f

hopefully /ˈhəʊpfəli/ adv (a) (in hopeful way): **can you pay me in dollars? she asked ~** — ¿puedes pagarme en dólares? — preguntó esperanzada (b) (crit) (indep): **when do you leave? — ~, on Friday** ¿cuándo te vas? — el viernes, espero

hopeless /ˈhəʊpləs ‖ ˈhəʊplɪs/ adj [1] (allowing no hope) ‹situation› desesperado; ‹task› imposible; **he's a ~ case** «patient» está desahuciado; (colloq) «pupil» no tiene remedio [2] (incompetent, inadequate) (colloq): **you're ~!** ¡eres un inútil!; **the train service on this line is ~** el servicio de trenes en esta línea es desastroso or es un desastre; **to be ~ AT sth** ser* negado PARA algo

hopelessly /ˈhəʊpləsli ‖ ˈhəʊplɪsli/ adv (a) (irredeemably) (as intensifier): **to be ~ lost/in love** estar* completamente perdido/perdidamente enamorado (b) (without hope) sin esperanzas

hopelessness /ˈhəʊpləsnəs ‖ ˈhəʊplɪsnɪs/ n (a) (of situation) lo desesperado (b) (despair) desesperanza f

hopping /ˈhɑːpɪŋ ‖ ˈhɒpɪŋ/ adj: **to be ~ mad** (colloq) estar* furioso

h

hopscotch /'hɑːpskɑːtʃ ‖'hɒpskɒtʃ/ n: to play ~ jugar* al tejo or (Méx) al avión or (RPl) a la rayuela or (Col) a la golosa or (Chi) al luche

horde /hɔːrd ‖hɔːd/ n (colloq) multitud f, horda f

horizon /həˈraɪzən/ n (Geog) the ~ el horizonte

horizontal /ˈhɔːrəˈzɑːntl̩ ‖ˌhɒrɪˈzɒntl̩/ adj horizontal

hormone /'hɔːrməʊn ‖'hɔːməʊn/ n hormona f; (before n) ~ **replacement therapy** terapia f hormonal sustitiva

horn /hɔːrn ‖hɔːn/ n **1** (a) (Zool) (of animal) cuerno m, asta f, cacho m (AmS), guampa f (CS) **2** (Mus) (a) (wind instrument) cuerno m (b) (French ~) trompa f **3** (Auto) claxon m, bocina f, (Naut) sirena f

hornet /'hɔːrnət ‖'hɔːnɪt/ n avispón m

horoscope /'hɔːrəskəʊp ‖'hɒrəskəʊp/ n horóscopo m

horrendous /hɔːˈrendəs ‖hɒˈrendəs/ adj (a) (horrifying) ⟨crime/account⟩ horrendo, horroroso (b) (dreadful) (colloq) ⟨price/mistake⟩ terrible

horrible /'hɔːrəbəl ‖'hɒrɪbəl/ adj horrible, horroroso

horrid /'hɔːrəd ‖'hɒrɪd/ adj (esp BrE colloq) ⟨weather/taste⟩ horroroso

horrific /hɔːˈrɪfɪk ‖hɒˈrɪfɪk, hə-/ adj horroroso, espantoso

horrify /'hɔːrəfaɪ ‖'hɒrɪfaɪ/ vt **-fies, -fying, -fied** horrorizar*

horrifying /'hɔːrəfaɪɪŋ ‖'hɒrɪfaɪɪŋ/ adj horroroso, horrendo, horripilante

horror /'hɔːrər ‖'hɒrə(r)/ n horror m; (before n) ⟨movie/story⟩ de terror

horror-struck /'hɔːrərstrʌk ‖'hɒrəstrʌk/ adj horrorizado

hors d'oeuvre /ɔːrˈdɜːrv ‖ɔːˈdɜːvrə/ n (pl **hors d'oeuvres** /-ˈdɜːrv ‖-ˈdɜːvrə/) entremés m, botana f (Méx)

horse /hɔːrs ‖hɔːs/ n **1** (Zool) caballo m; **I could eat a ~** tengo un hambre canina; (before n) ~ **riding** (BrE) equitación f **2** (vaulting ~) potro m, caballo m (Méx)

horse: ~**back** n: on ~back a caballo; (before n) ~back riding (AmE) equitación f; ~**box** n (BrE) ▶ ~CAR; ~**car** n (AmE) (for transporting horses) remolque m or trailer m (para transportar caballos); ~ **chestnut** n (a) (tree) castaño m de Indias (b) (fruit) castaña f de Indias; ~**drawn** adj tirado por caballos; ~**fly** n tábano m; ~**man** /'hɔːrsmən ‖'hɔːsmən/ n (pl -**men** /-mən/) jinete m; ~**power** n caballo m (de fuerza); ~ **racing** n carreras fpl de caballos, hípica f; ~**radish** /'hɔːrsˈrædɪʃ ‖'hɔːsrædɪʃ/ n rábano m picante; ~**shoe** n herradura f, ~ **show** n concurso m hípico

horticulture /'hɔːrtəˌkʌltʃər ‖'hɔːtɪˌkʌltʃə(r)/ n horticultura f

hose /həʊz/ n **1** (~pipe) manguera f, manga f, (Auto) manguito m **2** (Clothing) (+ pl vb) (a) (tights) (Hist, Theat) calzas fpl, malla f (b) (AmE) ▶ PANTYHOSE

■ **hose down** [v + o + adv, v + adv + o] lavar (con manguera)

hosepipe /'həʊzpaɪp/ n (esp BrE) ▶ HOSE 1

hosiery /'həʊʒəri ‖'həʊzɪəri/ n (fml) calcetería f

hospice /'hɑːspəs ‖'hɒspɪs/ n: residencia para enfermos desahuciados

hospitable /hɑːˈspɪtəbəl ‖hɒˈspɪtəbəl/ adj hospitalario

hospital /'hɑːspɪtl̩ ‖'hɒspɪtl̩/ n hospital m

hospitality /ˌhɑːspəˈtæləti ‖ˌhɒspɪˈtæləti/ n hospitalidad f

hospitalize /'hɑːspɪtl̩aɪz ‖'hɒspɪtl̩aɪz/ vt hospitalizar*, internar (CS, Méx)

host¹ /həʊst/ n **1** (a) (person dispensing hospitality) anfitrión, -triona m,f; (before n) ⟨country/government⟩ anfitrión (b) (Rad, TV) presentador, -dora m,f **2** (of parasite) huésped m **3** (multitude) gran cantidad f **4** **the Host** (Relig) la Sagrada Hostia

host² vt (a) (be the venue for) ⟨conference/event⟩ ser* la sede de (b) (Rad, TV) ⟨program⟩ presentar

hostage /'hɑːstɪdʒ ‖'hɒstɪdʒ/ n rehén m

hostel /'hɑːstl̩ ‖'hɒstl̩/ n (a) (youth ~) albergue m juvenil or de juventud (b) (for students) (BrE) residencia f; (for homeless people, battered wives etc) hogar m

hostess /'həʊstəs ‖'həʊstes/ n (a) (in private capacity) anfitriona f (b) (air ~) (esp BrE) ▶ STEWARDESS B (c) (on TV show) (presenter) presentadora f; (assistant) azafata f

hostile /'hɑːstl̩ ‖'hɒstaɪl/ adj hostil

hostility /hɑːˈstɪləti ‖hɒˈstɪləti/ n hostilidad f

hot /hɑːt ‖hɒt/ adj **-tt-** **1** (a) ⟨food/water⟩ caliente; ⟨weather/day/country⟩ caluroso; ⟨climate⟩ cálido; **it's** ~ **today** hoy hace calor; **I'm** ~ tengo calor; **to be** ~ «object» estar* caliente; **to get** ~ «oven/iron/radiator» calentarse* (b) (spicy) picante, picoso (Méx) **2** (a) (fresh) ⟨news/scent⟩ reciente, fresco (b) (current) ⟨story/issue⟩ de plena actualidad (c) (popular, in demand) ⟨product⟩ de gran aceptación; ⟨play/movie⟩ taquillero **3** (colloq) (knowledgeable, keen): **he's very** ~ **on current affairs** está muy al tanto en temas de actualidad; **she's** ~ **on punctuality** le da mucha importancia a la puntualidad

hot: ~ **air** n palabrería f, ~**air balloon** /'hɑːt'er ‖ˌhɒt'eə/ n globo m de aire caliente; ~**bed** n (of crime, unrest) semillero m; ~**blooded** /'hɑːt'blʌdəd ‖ˌhɒt'blʌdɪd/ adj apasionado; ~ **dog** n perro m or perrito m caliente, pancho m (RPl)

hotel /həʊˈtel/ n hotel m

hotelier /həʊˈteljər ‖həʊˈteliə(r)/ n hotelero, -ra m,f

hot: ~ **flush,** (AmE) ~ **flash** n sofoco m, bochorno m, calor m (RPl fam); ~**headed** /'hɑːt'hedəd ‖ˌhɒt'hedɪd/ adj exaltado; ~**house** n invernadero m; (before n) ⟨plant/flowers⟩ de invernadero; ~ **line** n (Pol) teléfono m rojo; (for public) línea f directa

hotly /'hɑːtli ‖'hɒtli/ adv ⟨dispute/deny⟩ con vehemencia; ⟨debated⟩ acaloradamente

hot: ~ **pepper** n (AmE) pimiento m picante, ají m picante (AmS), chile m (Méx); ~**plate** n (for cooking) placa f, hornilla f (AmL exc CS), hornalla f (RPl), plato m (Chi); (for keeping food warm) calientaplatos m; ~ **seat** n (colloq): **to be in the** ~ **seat** estar* en la línea de fuego; ~**shot** n personaje m; ~ **spot** n (colloq) (a) (Pol) punto m conflictivo (b) (night club) club m nocturno; ~ **spring** n fuente f termal; ~**tempered**

/ˈhɑːtˈtempərd ‖ˌhɒtˈtempəd/ *adj* irascible;
~-water bottle /ˈhɑːtˈwɔːtər ‖ˌhɒtˈwɔːtə/ *n* bolsa *f* de agua caliente

hound¹ /haʊnd/ *n* perro *m* de caza, sabueso *m*

hound² *vt* acosar

hour /aʊr ‖aʊə(r)/ *n* **(a)** (60 minutes) hora *f* **(b)** (time of day) hora *f*; **on the ~** a la hora en punto; **at 1600 ~s** a las 16:00 horas **(c)** (particular moment) momento *m*; **her finest ~** su mejor momento

hourly¹ /ˈaʊrli ‖ˈaʊəli/ *adj* ‹rate/wage› por hora

hourly² *adv* **(a)** (every hour) ‹run/broadcast› cada hora **(b)** (by the hour) ‹pay/charge› por hora(s)

house¹ /haʊs/ *n* (*pl* **houses** /ˈhaʊzəz ‖ˈhaʊzɪz/) **1** (dwelling, household) casa *f*; **to put one's (own) ~ in order** poner* sus (*or* mis *etc*) asuntos en orden; **to set up ~** poner* casa **2** (Govt) Cámara *f*; **the H~ of Representatives** (in US) la Cámara de Representantes *or* de Diputados; **the H~ of Commons/of Lords** (in UK) la Cámara de los Comunes/de los Lores; **the H~s of Parliament** (in UK) el Parlamento **3** (Busn) casa *f*, empresa *f*; **publishing ~** editorial *f*; **drinks are on the ~** invita la casa; (*before n*) **~ wine** vino *m* de la casa **4** (Theat) **(a)** (auditorium) sala *f* **(b)** (audience) público *m*

house² /haʊz/ *vt* **(a)** (accommodate) ‹person/ family› alojar **(b)** (contain) ‹office/museum› albergar*

house /haʊs/: **~ arrest** *n* arresto *m* domiciliario; **~boat** *n* casa *f* flotante; **~bound** *adj*: **she's 85 and completely ~bound** tiene 85 años y está completamente confinada a su casa; **~broken** *adj* (AmE) ‹pet› enseñado; **~fly** *n* mosca *f* común *or* doméstica

household /ˈhaʊshəʊld/ *n* casa *f*; **~s with more than one wage earner** las familias *or* (frml) los hogares donde trabajan dos o más personas; (*before n*) **a ~ name** un nombre muy conocido

householder /ˈhaʊshəʊldər ‖ˈhaʊshəʊldə(r)/ *n* dueño, -ña *m,f* de casa

house /haʊs/: **~-hunt** *vi* (usu in -ing form) buscar* casa (*para comprar o alquilar*); **~husband** *n* (hum) hombre que se ocupa de la casa mientras su mujer sale a trabajar, amo *m* de casa (hum); **~keeper** *n* (woman) ama *f*‡ de llaves; (in hotel) gobernanta *f*; (man) encargado *m* de la casa; **~keeping** *n* **(a)** (running of home) gobierno *m* de la casa **(b)** **~keeping (money)** dinero *m* (para los gastos) de la casa; **~maid** *n* criada *f*, mucama *f* (AmL); **~plant** *n* planta *f* de interior; **~-proud** *adj* (esp BrE) muy meticuloso (*en la limpieza y el arreglo de la casa*); **~-to-~** /ˈhaʊstəˈhaʊs/ *adj* ‹inquiries/search› puerta a puerta; **~-trained** *adj* (BrE) ‹pet› enseñado; **~warming (party)** /ˈhaʊsˌwɔːrmɪŋ ‖ˈhaʊsˌwɔːmɪŋ/ *n*: fiesta de inauguración de una casa; **~wife** *n* ama *f*‡ de casa; **~work** *n* tareas *fpl* domésticas, trabajo *m* de la casa

housing /ˈhaʊzɪŋ/ *n* **(a)** (dwellings) viviendas *fpl* **(b)** (provision of houses): **the government's policy on ~** la política del gobierno en cuanto al problema de la vivienda

housing: ~ association *n* (in UK) asociación que construye o renueva viviendas para alquilarlas a precios módicos; **~ development**

n (AmE) complejo *m* habitacional, urbanización *f* (Esp), fraccionamiento *m* (Méx); **~ estate** *n* (BrE) **(a)** (council estate) urbanización de viviendas de alquiler subvencionadas por el ayuntamiento **(b)** (privately owned) ▶ **~ DEVELOPMENT**; **~ project** *n* (in US) complejo *m* de viviendas subvencionadas

hovel /ˈhʌvəl ‖ˈhɒvəl/ *n* casucha *f*, rancho *m* (RPl)

hover /ˈhʌvər ‖ˈhɒvə(r)/ *vi* «helicopter» sostenerse* en el aire (*sin avanzar*); «bird» cernerse*; **the temperature ~ed around 20°** la temperatura rondaba los 20°; **the waiter ~ed around, waiting for a tip** el mesero estuvo rodando la mesa, esperando una propina

hovercraft /ˈhʌvərkræft ‖ˈhɒvəkrɑːft/ *n* (*pl* **-craft** *or* **-crafts**) aerodeslizador *m*

how /haʊ/ *adv* **1** (in questions) cómo; **~ are you?** ¿cómo estás? **2** (with adjs, advs) **(a)** (in questions): **~ wide is it?** ¿cuánto mide *or* tiene de ancho?, ¿qué tan ancho es? (AmL exc CS); **~ heavy is it?** ¿cuánto pesa?; **~ often do you meet?** ¿con qué frecuencia se reúnen?; **~ old are you?** ¿cuántos años tienes? **(b)** (in exclamations) qué; **~ strange/rude!** ¡qué raro/grosero! **3** (in phrases) **how about** *o* (colloq) **how's about sth: Thursday's no good; ~ about Friday?** el jueves no puede ser ¿qué te parece el viernes?; **I'd love to go; ~ about you?** me encantaría ir ¿y a ti?; **how come** (colloq): **~ come the door's locked?** ¿cómo es que la puerta está cerrada con llave?

however /haʊˈevər ‖haʊˈevə(r)/ *adv* **1** (as linker) sin embargo, no obstante (frml) **2** (used before adj or adv) (no matter how): **~ hard she tried ... por más que trataba ...** **3** (interrog) cómo

howl¹ /haʊl/ *vi* **(a)** «dog/wolf» aullar*; «person» dar* alaridos; «wind/gale» aullar*, bramar **(b)** (weep noisily) (colloq) berrear (fam)

howl² *n* (of dog, wolf) aullido *m*; (of person) alarido *m*, aullido *m*

hp (= **horsepower**) CV, HP

HP *n* (BrE) = **hire purchase**

HQ *n* = **headquarters**

hr (= **hour**) h.

HRH (in UK) (= **Her/His Royal Highness**) S.A.R.

HRT *n* = **hormone replacement therapy**

HTML *n* (Comput) (= **hypertext markup language**) HTML *m*

hub /hʌb/ *n* **(a)** (of wheel) cubo *m* **(b)** (focal point) centro *m*

hub cap *n* tapacubos *m*, taza *f* (RPl)

huddle¹ /ˈhʌdl/ *vi* **(a)** **~ (together)** (crowd together) apiñarse **(b)** **~ (up)** (curl up) acurrucarse*

huddle² *n* (tight group) grupo *m*, corrillo *m*; (in US football) timbac *m*, jol *m*

hue /hjuː/ *n* (liter) (color) color *m*; (shade) tono *m*

hue and cry *n* (no pl) revuelo *m*

huff /hʌf/ *n* (no pl): **to be in a ~** estar* enfurruñado, estar* con mufa (RPl fam)

hug¹ /hʌg/ *vt* **-gg-** **(a)** (embrace) abrazar* **(b)** (keep close to) ir* pegado a

hug² *n* abrazo *m*

huge /ˈhjuːdʒ/ *adj* enorme

hull /hʌl/ *n* (of ship, plane, tank) casco *m*

hullo /hə'ləʊ ‖hʌ'ləʊ/ (esp BrE) ▶ HELLO

hum¹ /hʌm/ **-mm-** vi «machinery/bee/wire»
zumbar; «person» tararear (con la boca cerrada)
■ ~ vt «tune» tararear (con la boca cerrada)

hum² n (no pl) (of bees, machinery) zumbido m; (of
voices, traffic) murmullo m

human¹ /'hju:mən/ adj humano

human² n ser* m humano

human being n ser m humano

humane /hju:'meɪn/ adj humanitario, humano

humanism /'hju:mənɪzəm/ n humanismo m

humanist /'hju:mənəst ‖'hju:mənɪst/ n
humanista mf

humanitarian /hju:ˌmænə'teriən
‖hju:ˌmænɪ'teəriən/ adj humanitario

humanities /hju:'mænətɪz/ n (a) (+ pl vb) the
~ las humanidades, las artes y las letras (b)
(discipline) (+ sing vb) humanidades fpl

humanity /hju:'mænəti/ n humanidad f

human: ~ **nature** n naturaleza f humana; ~
rights pl n derechos mpl humanos

humble /'hʌmbəl/ adj humilde

humbly /'hʌmbli/ adv humildemente

humdrum /'hʌmdrʌm/ adj monótono,
rutinario

humid /'hju:məd ‖'hju:mɪd/ adj húmedo

humidity /hju:'mɪdəti/ n humedad f

humiliate /hju:'mɪlieɪt/ vt humillar

humiliating /hju:'mɪlieɪtɪŋ/ adj humillante

humiliation /hju:ˌmɪli'eɪʃən/ n humillación f

humility /hju:'mɪləti/ n humildad f

humor¹, (BrE) **humour** /'hju:mər ‖'hju:mə(r)/
n humor m

humor², (BrE) **humour** vt seguirle* la
corriente a

humorless, (BrE) **humourless** /'hju:mərləs
‖'hju:məlɪs/ adj «person» sin sentido del humor

humorous /'hju:mərəs/ adj «novel/play/speech»
humorístico; «situation» cómico, gracioso

humour n/vt (BrE) ▶ HUMOR¹,²

hump /hʌmp/ n (a) (of camel) joroba f, giba f; (of
person) joroba f (b) (in ground) montículo m

hunch¹ /hʌntʃ/ vt «back/shoulders» encorvar

hunch² n (intuitive feeling) (colloq) presentimiento
m, pálpito m, corazonada f

hunch: ~**back** n (person) jorobado, -da m,f;
(hump) joroba f; ~**backed** /'hʌntʃbækt/ adj
jorobado

hundred /'hʌndrəd/ n cien m; a/one ~ cien; a/
one ~ **and one** ciento uno; **two** ~ doscientos; **five**
~ quinientos; **five** ~ **pages** quinientas páginas;
in (the year) fifteen ~ en el (año) mil quinientos;
she lived in the seventeen ~**s** vivió en el siglo
XVIII; **ten** ~**s are a thousand** diez centenas son
un millar; **they are sold by the** ~ o in ~**s** se
venden de a cien or (Esp) de cien en cien; a/one
~ **thousand/million** cien mil/millones; ~**s of
times** cientos de veces

hundredfold /'hʌndrədfəʊld/ adj/adv ▶ -FOLD

hundredth¹ /'hʌndrədθ/ adj centésimo

hundredth² adv en centésimo lugar

hundredth³ n (Math) centésimo m; (part)
centésima parte f

hundredweight /'hʌndrədweɪt/ n (pl ~)
unidad de peso equivalente a 45,36kg. en EEUU y a
50,80kg. en RU

hung /hʌŋ/ past & past p of HANG¹

Hungarian¹ /hʌŋ'geriən ‖hʌŋ'geəriən/ adj
húngaro

Hungarian² n (a) (language) húngaro m (b)
(person) húngaro, -ra m,f

Hungary /'hʌŋgəri/ n Hungría f

hunger /'hʌŋgər ‖'hʌŋgə(r)/ n (a) (physical)
hambre f⚥ (b) (strong desire) (no pl): **a** ~ **for
adventure** un ansia f⚥or (liter) hambre de aventura

hunger strike n huelga f de hambre

hung: ~ **jury** n: jurado que se disuelve al no
ponerse de acuerdo sus miembros; ~**over**
/hʌŋ'əʊvər‖hʌŋ'əʊvə(r)/ adj **to be** ~**over** tener*
resaca or (Col fam) guayabo or (AmL, Méx fam)
cruda or (Ven fam) ratón

hungrily /'hʌŋgrəli ‖'hʌŋgrɪli/ adv ávidamente

hungry /'hʌŋgri/ adj **-grier, -griest**
hambriento; **to be** ~ tener* hambre; **to be** ~ **FOR
sth** estar* ávido DE algo

hunk /hʌŋk/ n (a) (chunk) trozo m, pedazo m (b)
(man) (colloq): **he's a real** ~ está buenísimo (fam)

hunt¹ /hʌnt/ vt ① «game/fox» cazar* ② (search
for) buscar*
■ ~ vi (a) (pursue game) cazar*; **to go** ~**ing** ir* de
caza or de cacería (b) (search) **to** ~ (**FOR sth**)
buscar* (algo)
■ **hunt down** [v + o + adv, v + adv + o] «animal/
fugitive» darle* caza a

hunt² n ① (a) (chase) caza f, cacería f (b)
(hunters) partida f de caza, cacería f ② (search)
búsqueda f

hunter /'hʌntər ‖'hʌntə(r)/ n (person) cazador,
-dora m,f; (horse) caballo m de caza

hunting /'hʌntɪŋ/ n (Sport) caza f, cacería f

hurdle /'hɜ:rdl ‖'hɜ:dl/ n (a) (Sport) (obstacle)
obstáculo m, valla f; see also HURDLES (b)
(problem) obstáculo m

hurdles /'hɜ:rdlz ‖'hɜ:dlz/ n (+ sing vb) vallas
fpl

hurl /hɜ:rl ‖hɜ:l/ vt tirar, arrojar, lanzar*

hurrah /hʊ'rɑ:/, **hurray** /hʊ'reɪ/ interj ▶
HOORAY

hurricane /'hɜ:rəkem ‖'hʌrɪkən, -keɪn/ n
huracán m

hurry¹ /'hɜ:ri ‖'hʌri/ n (no pl) prisa f, apuro m
(AmL); **I'm in a** ~ tengo prisa, estoy apurado
(AmL); **he wrote it in a** ~ lo escribió deprisa (fam)

hurry² **-ries, -rying, -ried** vi (a) (make haste)
darse* prisa, apurarse (AmL) (b) (move hastily) (+
adv compl): **she hurried after him** corrió tras él;
he hurried back/in/out volvió/entró/salió
corriendo

AmC	Central America	Arg	Argentina	Cu	Cuba	Per	Peru
AmL	Latin America	Bol	Bolivia	Ec	Ecuador	RPI	River Plate Area
AmS	South America	Chi	Chile	Esp	Spain	Ur	Uruguay
Andes	Andean Region	CS	Southern Cone	Méx	Mexico	Ven	Venezuela

■ ~ *vt* **(a)** ⟨*person*⟩ meterle prisa a, apurar (AmL) **(b)** ⟨*work*⟩ hacer* apresuradamente

■ **hurry away, hurry off** [*v* + *adv*] alejarse rápidamente

■ **hurry up** ⓵ [*v* + *adv*] darse* prisa, apurarse (AmL) ⓶ [*v* + *o* + *adv*, *v* + *adv* + *o*] ⟨*person*⟩ meterle prisa a, apurar (AmL); ⟨*work*⟩ acelerar, apurar (AmL)

hurt¹ /hɜːrt ‖hɜːt/ (*past & past p* **hurt**) *vt* ⓵ **(a)** (cause pain): **you're ~ing her/me!** ¡le/me estás haciendo daño!, ¡la/me estás lastimando! (esp AmL) **(b)** (injure): **I ~ my ankle** me hice daño en el tobillo, me lastimé el tobillo (esp AmL); **to ~ oneself, to get ~** hacerse* daño, lastimarse (esp AmL)

⓶ (distress emotionally): **I've been ~ too often** me han hecho sufrir demasiadas veces; **to ~ sb's feelings** herir* los sentimientos de algn

■ ~ *vi* ⓵ (be source of pain) doler*; **my leg ~s** me duele la pierna

⓶ (have adverse effects): **it won't ~ to postpone it for a while** no pasa nada si lo dejamos por el momento

⓷ (suffer adverse effects) (AmE colloq): **to be ~ing** estar* pasándola *or* pasándolo mal (fam)

hurt² *n* (emotional) dolor *m*, pena *f*

hurt³ *adj* **(a)** (physically) ⟨*finger/foot*⟩ lastimado; **she was badly ~** estaba gravemente herida **(b)** (emotionally) ⟨*feelings/pride*⟩ herido; ⟨*tone/ expression*⟩ dolido; **to feel/be ~** sentirse*/estar* dolido

hurtful /'hɜːrtfəl ‖'hɜːtfəl/ *adj* hiriente

hurtle /'hɜːrtl ‖'hɜːtl/ *vi* (+ *adv compl*): **to ~ along/past** ir*/pasar volando *or* a toda velocidad

husband /'hʌzbənd/ *n* marido *m*, esposo *m*

hush¹ /hʌʃ/ *n* (*no pl*) silencio *m*

hush² *vt* (quieten) hacer* callar; (calm down) calmar

■ **hush up** ⓵ [*v* + *o* + *adv*, *v* + *adv* + *o*] ⟨*scandal/ story*⟩ acallar ⓶ [*v* + *adv*] (be quiet) (AmE colloq) callarse

hush³ *interj*: **~!** ¡shh!, ¡chitón!

hushed /hʌʃt/ *adj* (before *n*) silencioso; **in ~ tones** en voz muy baja, en murmullos

hush-hush *adj* (colloq) super secreto (fam)

husk /hʌsk/ *n* (of wheat, rice) cáscara *f*, cascarilla *f*; (of maize) chala *f or* (Esp) farfolla *f*

husky¹ /'hʌski/ *adj* **-kier, -kiest** ronco

husky² *n* (*pl* **-kies**) husky *mf*, perro, -rra *m,f* esquimal

hustings /'hʌstɪŋz/ *pl n* **the ~** la campaña electoral

hustle¹ /'hʌsəl/ *vt* ⓵ **(a)** (move hurriedly) (+ *adv compl*): **she was ~d into the car** la metieron en el coche a empujones; **he was ~d away by his bodyguards** sus guardaespaldas se lo llevaron precipitadamente **(b)** (pressure) apremiar, meterle prisa a, apurar (AmL) ⓶ (AmE colloq) (a) (obtain aggressively) hacerse* con (b) (hawk, sell) vender

hustle² *n* ⓵ (hurry) ajetreo *m*; **the ~ and bustle of the big city** el ajetreo y bullicio de la gran ciudad ⓶ (trick, swindle) (AmE colloq) chanchullo *m* (fam)

hustler /'hʌslər ‖'hʌslə(r)/ *n* (AmE) **(a)** (hard worker) (colloq) persona *f* trabajadora **(b)** (swindler) (sl) estafador, -dora *m,f* **(c)** (prostitute) (sl) puto, -ta *m,f* (vulg)

hut /hʌt/ *n* **(a)** (cabin) cabaña *f*; (of mud, straw) choza *f* **(b)** (hovel) casucha *f*

hutch /hʌtʃ/ *n* (rabbit **~**) conejera *f*

hyaena /haɪˈiːnə/ *n* ▶ HYENA

hybrid /'haɪbrəd ‖'haɪbrɪd/ *n* híbrido *m*

hydrant /'haɪdrənt/ *n* boca *f* de riego, toma *f* de agua, hidrante *m* (AmC, Col); (fire **~**) boca *f* de incendios *or* (Esp) de riego, toma *f* de agua, hidrante *m* de incendios (AmC, Col), grifo *m* (Chi)

hydraulic /haɪˈdrɔːlɪk ‖haɪˈdrɔːlɪk, haɪˈdrɒlɪk/ *adj* hidráulico

hydrocarbon /ˌhaɪdrəʊˈkɑːrbən ‖ˌhaɪdrəˈkɑːbən/ *n* hidrocarburo *m*

hydroelectric /'haɪdrəʊrˈlektrɪk/ *adj* hidroeléctrico

hydrofoil /'haɪdrəfɔɪl/ *n* (vessel) hidrodeslizador *m*, aliscafo *m*

hydrogen /'haɪdrədʒən/ *n* hidrógeno *m*

hyena /haɪˈiːnə/ *n* hiena *f*

hygiene /'haɪdʒiːn/ *n* higiene *f*

hygienic /haɪˈdʒiːnɪk/ *adj* higiénico

hymn /hɪm/ *n* (Relig) cántico *m*, himno *m*

hype¹ /haɪp/ *n* (colloq) despliegue *m or* bombo *m* publicitario

hype² *vt* (colloq) promocionar con bombos y platillos *or* (Esp) a bombo y platillo

■ **hype up** [*v* + *adv* + *o*, *v* + *o* + *adv*] (colloq) ⟨*movie*⟩ promocionar con bombos y platillos *or* (Esp) a bombo y platillo; ⟨*person*⟩ poner* nervioso

hyperactive /'haɪpərˈæktɪv/ *adj* hiperactivo

hypermarket /'haɪpərˌmɑːrkət ‖'haɪpəmɑːkɪt/ *n* (BrE) hipermercado *m*

hypertension /'haɪpərˈtentʃən ‖,haɪpəˈtenʃən/ *n* hipertensión *f*

hypertext markup language /'haɪpərtekst ‖'haɪpətekst/ *n* (Comput) lenguaje *m* de marcado de hipertexto

hyperventilate /'haɪpərˈventleɪt ‖,haɪpəˈventleɪt/ *vi* hiperventilarse

hyphen /'haɪfən/ *n* guion *m*

hypnosis /hɪpˈnəʊsəs ‖hɪpˈnəʊsɪs/ *n* hipnosis *f*

hypnotic /hɪpˈnɑːtɪk ‖hɪpˈnɒtɪk/ *adj* ⟨*suggestion/state*⟩ hipnótico; ⟨*voice/eyes/rhythm*⟩ hipnotizador, hipnotizante

hypnotism /'hɪpnətɪzəm/ *n* hipnotismo *m*

hypnotist /'hɪpnətəst ‖'hɪpnətɪst/ *n* hipnotizador, -dora *m,f*

hypnotize /'hɪpnətaɪz/ *vt* hipnotizar*

hypoallergenic /'haɪpəʊˌæler'dʒenɪk ‖,haɪpəʊˌælə'dʒenɪk/ *adj* hipoalérgeno

hypochondriac /'haɪpə'kɑːndriæk ‖,haɪpə'kɒndriæk/ *n* hipocondríaco, -ca *m,f*

hypocrisy /hɪˈpɑːkrəsi ‖hɪˈpɒkrɪsi/ *n* (*pl* **-sies**) hipocresía *f*

hypocrite /'hɪpəkrɪt/ *n* hipócrita *mf*

hypocritical /'hɪpə'krɪtɪkəl/ *adj* hipócrita

hypodermic¹ /'haɪpə'dɜːrmɪk ‖,haɪpə'dɜːmɪk/ *adj* hipodérmico

hypodermic² *n* (aguja *f*) hipodérmica *f*

hypothermia /'haɪpə'θɜːrmiə ‖,haɪpə'θɜːmiə/ *n* hipotermia *f*

hypothesis /haɪˈpɑːθəsəs ‖haɪˈpɒθəsɪs/ *n* (*pl* **-ses** /-siːz/) hipótesis *f*

hypothetical /'haɪpə'θetɪkəl/ *adj* hipotético

hysterectomy /ˌhɪstəˈrektəmi/ n (pl **-mies**) histerectomía f

hysteria /hɪˈstɪriə ‖ hɪˈstɪəriə/ n histerismo m, histeria f

hysterical /hɪˈsterɪkəl/ adj (a) (Psych) histérico (b) (very funny) (colloq) para morirse de (la) risa

hysterics /hɪˈsterɪks/ pl n (a) (nervous agitation) histeria f, histerismo m; **to go into** or **have** ∼ ponerse* histérico (b) (laughter) (colloq) **to be in** ∼ estar* como loco

I i

I, i /aɪ/ n I, i f

I /aɪ/ pron yo

■ **Note** Although yo is given as the main translation of *I*, it is in practice used only for emphasis, or to avoid ambiguity: *I went to the theater* fui al teatro; *I was singing, he was playing the piano* yo cantaba y él tocaba el piano; *I did it* yo lo hice.

IA = **Iowa**

IBA n (in UK) = **Independent Broadcasting Authority**

Iberian /aɪˈbɪriən ‖ aɪˈbɪəriən/ adj ibérico

ice¹ /aɪs/ n [1] (frozen water) hielo m; **to break the** ∼ (overcome reserve) romper* el hielo; (make a start) (AmE) dar* los primeros pasos [2] (sherbet) (AmE) sorbete m, helado m de agua (AmL), nieve f (Méx)

ice² vt ⟨cake⟩ bañar ⟨con fondant⟩

Ice Age n: **the** ∼ la edad de hielo

iceberg /ˈaɪsbɜːrg ‖ ˈaɪsbɜːg/ n iceberg m

ice: ∼**box** n (a) (refrigerator) (AmE colloq & dated) refrigerador m, nevera f, heladera f (RPl) (b) (freezing compartment) (BrE) congelador m; ∼ **cream** n helado m; ∼ **cube** n cubito m de hielo

iced /aɪst/ adj [1] (chilled) helado [2] (Culin) glaseado

ice hockey n hockey m sobre hielo

Iceland /ˈaɪslənd/ n Islandia f

Icelandic¹ /aɪsˈlændɪk/ adj islandés

Icelandic² n islandés m

ice: ∼ **lolly** n (BrE) paleta f helada or (Esp) polo m or (RPl) palito m helado or (CS) chupete m helado; ∼ **rink** n (BrE) pista f de (patinaje sobre) hielo; ∼ **skating** n patinaje m sobre hielo

icicle /ˈaɪsɪkəl/ n carámbano m (de hielo)

icing /ˈaɪsɪŋ/ n (Culin) glaseado m

icing sugar n (BrE) azúcar m or f glas(é) or (RPl) impalpable or (Chi) flor or (Col) en polvo

icon /ˈaɪkɒn ‖ ˈaɪkɒn/ n icono m, ícono m

icy /ˈaɪsi/ adj **icier, iciest** (a) ⟨wind/rain⟩ helado, glacial; ⟨feet/hands⟩ helado; ⟨as adv⟩ ∼ **cold** helado (b) ⟨stare/reception⟩ glacial (c) ⟨roads/ground⟩ cubierto de hielo

ID (a) = **identification** (b) = **Idaho**

idea /aɪˈdiːə ‖ aɪˈdɪə/ n idea f; **I had an** ∼ se me ocurrió una idea; **that's the general** ∼ de eso se trata; **that's not my** ∼ **of fun** eso no es lo que yo entiendo por diversión; **where is he? — (I've) no** ∼! ¿dónde está? — (no tengo) ni idea

ideal¹ /aɪˈdiːəl/ adj ideal

ideal² n ideal m

idealism /aɪˈdiːəlɪzəm/ n idealismo m

idealist /aɪˈdiːəlɪst ‖ aɪˈdiːəlɪst/ n idealista mf

idealistic /aɪˌdiːəˈlɪstɪk ‖ ˌaɪdɪəˈlɪstɪk/ adj idealista

idealize /aɪˈdiːəlaɪz ‖ aɪˈdɪəlaɪz/ vt idealizar*

ideally /aɪˈdiːəli ‖ aɪˈdɪəli/ adv ⟨located/placed/equipped⟩ inmejorablemente; **they are** ∼ **suited** están hechos el uno para el otro; ∼, **no one would have to do it** (indep) lo ideal sería que nadie tuviera que hacerlo

identical /aɪˈdentɪkəl/ adj idéntico; ∼ **twins** gemelos mpl univitelinos (téc), gemelos mpl (AmL), gemelos mpl idénticos (Esp); **to be** ∼ **TO** o **WITH sth** ser* idéntico A algo

identification /aɪˌdentəfəˈkeɪʃən ‖ aɪˌdentɪfɪˈkeɪʃən/ n (a) (act of identifying) identificación f (b) (evidence of identity): **have you got any** ∼? ¿tiene algún documento que acredite su identidad?

identification parade n (BrE) rueda f de identificación or de sospechosos

identify /aɪˈdentəfaɪ ‖ aɪˈdentɪfaɪ/ **-fies, -fying, -fied** vt identificar*
■ v refl (reveal identity) **to** ∼ **oneself** identificarse*
■ ∼ vi **to** ∼ **WITH sb/sth** identificarse* CON algn/algo

Identikit® /aɪˈdentəkɪt ‖ aɪˈdentɪkɪt/ n: ∼ **picture** Identikit® m, retrato m hablado (AmS) or (Méx) reconstruido or (Esp) robot

identity /aɪˈdentəti/ n (pl **-ties**) identidad f; ⟨before n⟩ ∼ **card** carné m or (AmL tb) cédula f de identidad

ideological /ˌaɪdiəˈlɒdʒɪkəl ‖ ˌaɪdɪəˈlɒdʒɪkəl/ adj ideológico

ideology /ˌaɪdiˈɒlədʒi ‖ ˌaɪdɪˈɒlədʒi/ n (pl **-gies**) ideología f

idiom /ˈɪdiəm/ n modismo m

idiomatic /ˌɪdiəˈmætɪk/ adj idiomático

idiosyncrasy /ˌɪdiəˈsɪŋkrəsi/ n (pl **-sies**) idiosincrasia f

idiosyncratic /ˌɪdiəsɪnˈkrætɪk ‖ ˌɪdiəsɪŋˈkrætɪk/ adj idiosincrásico

idiot /ˈɪdiət/ n idiota mf

idiotic /ˌɪdiˈɒtɪk ‖ ˌɪdiˈɒtɪk/ adj idiota

idle¹ /ˈaɪdl/ adj **idler** /ˈaɪdlər ‖ ˈaɪdlə(r)/, **idlest** /ˈaɪdləst ‖ ˈaɪdlɪst/ [1] (a) (not in use or employment): **to be** ∼ ⟨worker⟩ no tener* trabajo; ⟨machine/

factory» estar* parado **(b)** (unoccupied) ⟨*hours/ moment*⟩ de ocio **2** (lazy) holgazán **3** (frivolous): **it was ~ curiosity** era pura curiosidad; **~ speculation** conjeturas *fpl* inútiles

idle² *vi* **(a)** (be lazy) holgazanear **(b)** (Auto) «*engine*» andar* al ralentí

idleness /'aɪdlnəs ‖'aɪdlnɪs/ *n* **(a)** (involuntary inactivity) inactividad *f* **(b)** (laziness) holgazanería *f*

idol /'aɪdl/ *n* ídolo *m*

idolize /'aɪdlaɪz/ *vt* idolatrar

idyll /'aɪdl ‖'ɪdɪl/ *n* idilio *m*

idyllic /aɪ'dɪlɪk ‖ɪ'dɪlɪk/ *adj* idílico

i.e. /'aɪ'i:/ (that is) (in writing) i.e.; (in speech) esto es

if /ɪf/ *conj* **1** (on condition that) si; **~ I were you, I wouldn't do it** yo en tu lugar *or* yo que tú, no lo haría; **she was very offhand, ~ not downright rude** estuvo muy brusca, por no decir verdaderamente grosera; **~ nothing else** aunque no sea más que eso; **~ so** (as linker) si es así **2** (whether) si **3** (though) aunque, si bien

igloo /'ɪglu:/ *n* iglú *m*

ignite /ɪg'naɪt/ *vt* prenderle fuego a ∎ **~** *vi* «*fuel/paper*» prenderse fuego

ignition /ɪg'nɪʃən/ *n* **(a)** (act) encendido *m* **(b)** (mechanism) (Auto) encendido *m*; (before *n*) **~ key** llave *f* de contacto *or* (AmL tb) del arranque

ignorance /'ɪgnərəns/ *n* ignorancia *f*

ignorant /'ɪgnərənt/ *adj* (lacking knowledge) ignorante; **to be ~ of sth** ignorar algo

ignore /ɪg'nɔːr ‖ɪg'nɔː(r)/ *vt* ⟨*person/remark*⟩ ignorar; ⟨*warning*⟩ hacer* caso omiso de; **we can't ~ the fact that …** no podemos dejar de tener en cuenta el hecho de que …

IL = **Illinois**

ilk /ɪlk/ *n* tipo *m*

ill¹ /ɪl/ *adj* **1** **-er, -est** (unwell) enfermo; **to feel ~** sentirse* mal **2** (bad) (before *n*): **~ effects** efectos *mpl* negativos; **his ~ health** su mala salud

ill² *adv* (no comp) **(a)** (hardly): **I can ~ afford to buy a new car** mal puedo yo permitirme comprar un coche nuevo **(b)** (badly) (frml) mal; **to speak ~ of sb** hablar mal de algn

ill³ *n* mal *m*

Ill = **Illinois**

I'll /aɪl/ = **I will, I shall**

ill: ~-advised /'ɪləd'vaɪzd/ *adj* ⟨*action*⟩ desacertado; **you would be ~-advised to go no** sería aconsejable que fueras; **~ at ease** *adj* (pred) (uncomfortable) incómodo; (anxious) inquieto; **~-bred** /'ɪl'bred/ *adj* sin educación

illegal /ɪ'li:gəl/ *adj* **(a)** (unlawful) ilegal **(b)** (AmE Sport) antirreglamentario

illegible /ɪ'ledʒəbəl/ *adj* ilegible

illegitimate /'ɪlɪ'dʒɪtəmət ‖ ‚ɪlɪ'dʒɪtɪmət/ *adj* ilegítimo

ill: ~-fated /'ɪl'feɪtəd ‖‚ɪl'feɪtɪd/ *adj* infortunado; **~ feeling** *n* resentimiento *m*, rencor *m*; **~-gotten** /'ɪl'gɑːtn ‖‚ɪl'gɒtn/*adj*: **~-gotten gains** dinero *m* mal habido

illicit /ɪ'lɪsət ‖ɪ'lɪsɪt/ *adj* ilícito

ill-informed /'ɪlɪn'fɔːrmd ‖‚ɪlɪn'fɔːmd/ *adj* mal informado

illiteracy /ɪ'lɪtərəsi/ *n* analfabetismo *m*

illiterate /ɪ'lɪtərət/ *adj* analfabeto

illness /'ɪlnəs ‖'ɪlnɪs/ *n* enfermedad *f*

illogical /ɪ'lɑ:dʒɪkəl ‖ɪ'lɒdʒɪkəl/ *adj* ilógico

ill: ~-treat /'ɪl'tri:t/ *vt* maltratar; **~-treatment** /'ɪl'tri:tmənt/ *n* malos tratos *mpl*

illuminate /ɪ'lu:məneɪt ‖ɪ'lu:mɪneɪt/ *vt* iluminar

illumination /ɪ'lu:mə'neɪʃən ‖ɪ‚lu:mɪ'neɪʃən/ *n* iluminación *f*

illusion /ɪ'lu:ʒən/ *n* **(a)** (false appearance): **to give** *o* **create an ~ of sth** dar* la impresión de algo; (Art) crear la ilusión de algo; **an optical ~** una ilusión óptica **(b)** (false idea) ilusión *f*

illustrate /'ɪləstreɪt/ *vt* **1** ⟨*book/magazine*⟩ ilustrar **2** **(a)** (explain by examples) ilustrar **(b)** (show) poner* de manifiesto

illustration /'ɪlə'streɪʃən/ *n* **1** (picture, technique) ilustración *f* **2** (example) ejemplo *m*

illustrator /'ɪləstreɪtər ‖'ɪləstreɪtə(r)/ *n* ilustrador, -dora *m,f*

illustrious /ɪ'lʌstriəs/ *adj* (liter) ilustre

ill will *n* **(a)** (hostility) animadversión *f* **(b)** (spite) rencor *m*

I'm /aɪm/ = **I am**

image /'ɪmɪdʒ/ *n* imagen *f*; **to be the (spitting) ~** *o* **spit and ~ of sb** ser* la viva imagen de algn

imagery /'ɪmɪdʒəri/ *n* imaginería *f*, imágenes *fpl*

imaginable /ɪ'mædʒənəbəl ‖ɪ'mædʒɪnəbəl/ *adj* imaginable

imaginary /ɪ'mædʒəneri ‖ɪ'mædʒɪnəri/ *adj* imaginario

imagination /ɪ'mædʒə'neɪʃən ‖ɪ‚mædʒɪ'neɪʃən/ *n* imaginación *f*

imaginative /ɪ'mædʒənətɪv ‖ɪ'mædʒɪnətɪv/ *adj* imaginativo

imagine /ɪ'mædʒən ‖ɪ'mædʒɪn/ *vt* **(a)** (picture to oneself) imaginarse; **I can just ~ her saying that** ya me la imagino diciendo eso **(b)** (fancy mistakenly): **you're imagining things** son imaginaciones *or* figuraciones tuyas **(c)** (assume) imaginarse; **I ~ she's very tired** me imagino que estará muy cansada

imbalance /ɪm'bæləns/ *n* desequilibrio *m*

imbecile /'ɪmbəsəl ‖'ɪmbəsi:l/ *n* imbécil *mf*

imbed /ɪm'bed/ *vt* **-dd-** (AmE) ▶ **EMBED**

IMF *n* (= **International Monetary Fund**) FMI *m*

imitate /'ɪməteɪt ‖'ɪmɪteɪt/ *vt* imitar

imitation¹ /'ɪmə'teɪʃən ‖‚ɪmɪ'teɪʃən/ *n* imitación *f*

imitation² *adj* ⟨*gold/pearls*⟩ de imitación

immaculate /ɪ'mækjələt ‖ɪ'mækjʊlət/ *adj* impecable

immaterial /'ɪmə'tɪriəl ‖‚ɪmə'tɪəriəl/ *adj* irrelevante

immature /'ɪmə'tʊr ‖‚ɪmə'tjʊə(r)/ *adj* **(a)** ⟨*tree/ animal*⟩ joven; ⟨*fruit*⟩ verde, inmaduro **(b)** (childish) ⟨*person/attitude*⟩ inmaduro

immaturity /'ɪmə'tʊrəti ‖‚ɪmə'tjʊərəti/ *n* inmadurez *f*

immediate /ɪ'mi:diət/ *adj* **1** **(a)** (instant, prompt) inmediato **(b)** ⟨*problem/need*⟩ urgente, apremiante **2** (before *n*) (close): **in the ~ future** en el futuro inmediato; **in the ~ vicinity** en las inmediaciones

immediately /ɪˈmiːdiətli/ adv **1** (at once)
inmediatamente **2** ⟨before/after/above/below⟩
justo

immemorial /ˈɪməˈmɔːriəl/ adj (liter)
inmemorial (liter)

immense /ɪˈmens/ adj inmenso, enorme

immensely /ɪˈmensli/ adv ⟨enjoy/like⟩
enormemente; ⟨popular/powerful⟩ inmensamente

immerse /ɪˈmɜːrs ‖ɪˈmɜːs/ vt (a) (submerge) to
~ sth/sb (IN sth) sumergir* algo/a algn (EN algo)
(b) (absorb, involve) to be ~d IN sth estar* absorto
EN algo

immersion heater /ɪˈmɜːrʒən ‖ɪˈmɜːʃən/ n
calentador m eléctrico (de agua), termo m (Chi),
termofón m (RPl)

immigrant /ˈɪməɡrənt ‖ˈɪmɪɡrənt/ n
inmigrante mf; ⟨before n⟩ ⟨worker/population⟩
inmigrante

immigration /ˈɪməˈɡreɪʃən ‖ˌɪmɪˈɡreɪʃən/ n
inmigración f

imminent /ˈɪmənənt ‖ˈɪmɪnənt/ adj inminente

immobile /ɪˈməʊbəl ‖ɪˈməʊbaɪl/ adj inmóvil

immobilize /ɪˈməʊbəlaɪz ‖ɪˈməʊbɪlaɪz/ vt
inmovilizar*

immoderate /ɪˈmɑːdərət ‖ɪˈmɒdərət/ adj
⟨demands/appetite⟩ desmedido

immodest /ɪˈmɑːdəst ‖ɪˈmɒdɪst/ adj (a)
(conceited) presuntuoso, inmodesto (b) (indecent)
⟨behavior/suggestion⟩ impúdico, inmodesto

immoral /ɪˈmɔːrəl ‖ɪˈmɒrəl/ adj inmoral

immorality /ˈɪmɔːˈræləti ‖ˌɪməˈræləti/ n
inmoralidad f

immortal /ɪˈmɔːrtl̩ ‖ɪˈmɔːtl̩/ adj inmortal

immortality /ˈɪmɔːrˈtæləti ‖ˌɪmɔːˈtæləti/ n
inmortalidad f

immortalize /ɪˈmɔːrtl̩aɪz ‖ɪˈmɔːtl̩aɪz/ vt
inmortalizar*

immune /ɪˈmjuːn/ adj (a) (not susceptible) to be
~ TO sth inmune A algo (b) ⟨before n⟩
⟨system/response⟩ inmunológico

immunity /ɪˈmjuːnəti/ n inmunidad f

immunization /ˈɪmjənəˈzeɪʃən ‖ˌɪmjʊnaɪˈzeɪʃən/ n inmunización f

immunize /ˈɪmjənaɪz ‖ˈɪmjʊnaɪz/ vt
inmunizar*

imp /ɪmp/ n diablillo m (fam)

impact /ˈɪmpækt/ n impacto m

impair /ɪmˈper ‖ɪmˈpeə(r)/ vt afectar; ~ed
vision/hearing problemas mpl de vista/audición

impale /ɪmˈpeɪl/ vt to ~ sth/sb ON sth
atravesar* algo/a algn CON algo

impart /ɪmˈpɑːrt ‖ɪmˈpɑːt/ vt (frml) ⟨news⟩
comunicar*; ⟨knowledge⟩ impartir; ⟨feeling/
quality⟩ conferir* (frml)

impartial /ɪmˈpɑːrʃəl ‖ɪmˈpɑːʃəl/ adj imparcial

impassable /ɪmˈpæsəbəl ‖ɪmˈpɑːsəbəl/ adj
⟨river/barrier⟩ infranqueable; ⟨road⟩
intransitable

impasse /ˈɪmpæs ‖ˈæmpæs/ n impasse m

impassioned /ɪmˈpæʃənd/ adj apasionado

impassive /ɪmˈpæsɪv/ adj impasible

impatience /ɪmˈpeɪʃəns/ n impaciencia f

impatient /ɪmˈpeɪʃənt/ adj ⟨person⟩
impaciente; ⟨gesture/voice⟩ de impaciencia

impatiently /ɪmˈpeɪʃəntli/ adv con
impaciencia

impeach /ɪmˈpiːtʃ/ vt (Law) acusar a un alto
cargo de delitos cometidos en el desempeño de sus
funciones

impeccable /ɪmˈpekəbəl/ adj impecable

impecunious /ˈɪmpɪˈkjuːniəs/ adj (liter or hum)
sin peculio (liter o hum)

impede /ɪmˈpiːd/ vt dificultar

impediment /ɪmˈpedəmənt ‖ɪmˈpedɪmənt/ n
(a) (hindrance) impedimento m (b) (physical defect)
defecto m; **a speech** ~ un defecto del habla

impel /ɪmˈpel/ vt **-ll-** impeler

impending /ɪmˈpendɪŋ/ adj ⟨before n⟩
inminente

impenetrable /ɪmˈpenətrəbəl/ adj
impenetrable

imperative¹ /ɪmˈperətɪv/ adj **1** (a) (essential)
imprescindible, fundamental (b) ⟨need⟩
imperioso, imperativo **2** (Ling) ⟨mood⟩
imperativo; ⟨sentence⟩ en imperativo

imperative² n imperativo m

imperceptible /ˈɪmpərˈseptəbəl ‖ˌɪmpəˈseptəbəl/ adj imperceptible

imperfect¹ /ɪmˈpɜːrfɪkt ‖ɪmˈpɜːfɪkt/ adj
imperfecto

imperfect² n imperfecto m

imperfection /ˈɪmpərˈfekʃən ‖ˌɪmpəˈfekʃən/
n imperfección f

imperial /ɪmˈpɪriəl ‖ɪmˈpɪəriəl/ adj (of empire)
⟨before n⟩ imperial, del imperio

imperialism /ɪmˈpɪriəlɪzəm ‖ɪmˈpɪəriəlɪzəm/
n imperialismo m

imperialist /ɪmˈpɪriələst ‖ɪmˈpɪəriəlɪst/ n
imperialista mf

imperil /ɪmˈperəl ‖ɪmˈperɪl, ɪmˈperəl/ vt, (BrE)
-ll- poner* en peligro

imperious /ɪmˈpɪriəs ‖ɪmˈpɪəriəs/ adj
imperioso

impermeable /ɪmˈpɜːrmiəbəl ‖ɪmˈpɜːmiəbəl/
adj impermeable

impersonal /ɪmˈpɜːrsnəl ‖ɪmˈpɜːsənl̩/ adj
impersonal

impersonate /ɪmˈpɜːrsəneɪt ‖ɪmˈpɜːsəneɪt/ vt
(a) (pretend to be) hacerse* pasar por (b) (mimic)
imitar, impersonar (Méx)

impersonator /ɪmˈpɜːrsəneɪtər
‖ɪmˈpɜːsəneɪtə(r)/ n imitador, -dora m,f,
impersonador, -dora m,f (Méx)

impertinent /ɪmˈpɜːrtnənt ‖ɪmˈpɜːtɪnənt/ adj
impertinente

impervious /ɪmˈpɜːrviəs ‖ɪmˈpɜːviəs/ adj (a)
⟨rock/material⟩ impermeable (b) (unaffected) to be
~ TO sth ⟨to criticism/doubt⟩ ser* impermeable A
algo

impetuous /ɪm'petʃuəs/ *adj* ‹person›
impetuoso; ‹action/decision› impulsivo

impetus /'ɪmpətəs/ ‖ /'ɪmpɪtəs/ *n* ímpetu *m*

impinge /ɪm'pɪndʒ/ *vi* **to ~ on** *o* **upon sth**
‹privacy/freedom› vulnerar algo

implacable /ɪm'plækəbəl/ *adj* implacable

implant /ɪm'plænt/ ‖ /ɪm'plɑːnt/ *vt* (a) ‹idea/
ideal› inculcar* (b) ‹embryo/hair› implantar

implausible /ɪm'plɔːzəbəl/ *adj* inverosímil

implement¹ /'ɪmpləmənt/ ‖ /'ɪmplɪmənt/ *vt*
implementar

implement² /'ɪmpləmənt/ ‖ /'ɪmplɪmənt/ *n*
instrumento *m*, implemento *m* (AmL)

implicate /'ɪmpləkeɪt/ ‖ /'ɪmplɪkeɪt/ *vt* implicar*

implication /ɪmplə'keɪʃən/ ‖ /ɪmplɪ'keɪʃən/ *n*
[1] ‹consequence, significance› repercusión *f*,
implicación *f* [2] ‹involvement› implicación *f*

implicit /ɪm'plɪsɪt/ ‖ /ɪm'plɪsɪt/ *adj* (a) ‹threat›
implícito (b) ‹confidence/trust› incondicional,
total

implode /ɪm'pləʊd/ *vi* implosionar

implore /ɪm'plɔːr/ ‖ /ɪm'plɔː(r)/ *vt* implorar

imply /ɪm'plaɪ/ *vt* **implies, implying,
implied** [1] ‹suggest, hint› dar* a entender,
insinuar* [2] ‹involve› implicar*, suponer*

impolite /ɪmpə'laɪt/ *adj* maleducado, descortés

import¹ /'ɪmpɔːrt/ ‖ /'ɪmpɔːt/ *n* [1] (Busn) (a) (act)
importación *f* (b) (article): **a foreign ~** un artículo
de importación [2] (significance) (frml) importancia *f*

import² /ɪm'pɔːrt/ ‖ /ɪm'pɔːt/ *vt* importar

importance /ɪm'pɔːrtns/ ‖ /ɪm'pɔːtns/ *n*
importancia *f*

important /ɪm'pɔːrtnt/ ‖ /ɪm'pɔːtnt/ *adj*
importante

importer /ɪm'pɔːrtər/ ‖ /ɪm'pɔːtə(r)/ *n*
importador, -dora *m,f*

impose /ɪm'pəʊz/ *vt* imponer*
■ **~** *vi* molestar; **to ~ on sb's goodwill** abusar de
la buena voluntad de algn

imposing /ɪm'pəʊzɪŋ/ *adj* imponente

imposition /ɪmpə'zɪʃən/ *n* (a) (enforcement)
imposición *f* (b) (taking unfair advantage) abuso *m*

impossibility /ɪmpɑːsə'bɪləti/ ‖ /ɪmpɒsə'bɪləti/
n imposibilidad *f*

impossible¹ /ɪm'pɑːsəbəl/ ‖ /ɪm'pɒsəbəl/ *adj*
(a) ‹job/request› imposible; **it's ~ for me to arrive
by twelve** me es imposible llegar para las doce
(b) (intolerable) intolerable

impossible² *n* **to ask/attempt the ~** pedir*/
intentar lo imposible

impostor /ɪm'pɑːstər/ ‖ /ɪm'pɒstə(r)/ *n* impostor,
-tora *m,f*

impotence /'ɪmpətəns/ *n* impotencia *f*

impotent /'ɪmpətənt/ *adj* impotente

impound /ɪm'paʊnd/ *vt* (a) ‹possessions/assets›
incautar(se de) (b) ‹vehicle› llevar al depósito
municipal

impoverished /ɪm'pɑːvərɪʃt/ ‖ /ɪm'pɒvərɪʃt/
adj (financially, spiritually) empobrecido; ‹soil/diet›
pobre

impractical /ɪm'præktɪkəl/ *adj* poco práctico

impregnable /ɪm'pregnəbəl/ *adj* ‹fortress›
inexpugnable; ‹organization› impenetrable

impregnate /ɪm'pregneɪt/ ‖ /'ɪmpregneɪt/ *vt*
[1] (saturate) **to ~ sth with sth** impregnar algo
con *or* de algo [2] (make pregnant) (frml) fecundar

impresario /ɪmprə'sɑːriəʊ/ ‖ /ɪmprɪ'sɑːriəʊ/
(*pl* **-os**) *n* empresario, -ria *m,f* teatral

impress /ɪm'pres/ *vt* [1] (make impression on): **we
were ~ed by your work** tu trabajo nos causó muy
buena impresión; **he only did it to ~ her** lo hizo
sólo para impactarla [2] (emphasize) **to ~ sth on** *o*
upon sb recalcarle* algo a algn
■ **~** *vi* impresionar

impression /ɪm'preʃən/ *n* [1] (a) (idea, image)
impresión *f*; **to be under the ~ (that)** ... creer* *or*
pensar* que ... (b) (effect) impresión *f*; **to make** *o*
create a good/bad ~ on sb causarle a algn una
buena/mala impresión [2] (imprint) impresión *f*,
huella *f* [3] (impersonation) imitación *f*

impressionable /ɪm'preʃnəbəl/ *adj* (a)
(easily influenced) influenciable (b) (easily frightened,
upset) impresionable

impressionism /ɪm'preʃənɪzəm/ *n*
impresionismo *m*

impressionist /ɪm'preʃənəst/ ‖ /ɪm'preʃənɪst/
n (a) (Art) impresionista *mf* (b) (impersonator)
imitador, -dora *m,f*

impressive /ɪm'presɪv/ *adj* ‹record/work›
admirable; ‹building/ceremony› imponente

imprint¹ /'ɪmprɪnt/ *n* marca *f*, huella *f*

imprint² /ɪm'prɪnt/ *vt* (physically) imprimir*; (on
mind) grabar

imprison /ɪm'prɪzən/ *vt* (Law) encarcelar

imprisonment /ɪm'prɪzənmənt/ *n* (act)
encarcelamiento *m*; (state) prisión *f*; **life ~** cadena
f perpetua

improbable /ɪm'prɑːbəbəl/ ‖ /ɪm'prɒbəbəl/ *adj*
(a) (unlikely) improbable (b) (implausible)
inverosímil

impromptu /ɪm'prɑːmptu/ ‖ /ɪm'prɒmptjuː/ *adj*
improvisado

improper /ɪm'prɑːpər/ ‖ /ɪm'prɒpə(r)/ *adj*
[1] ‹behavior/language› indecoroso; ‹suggestion›
deshonesto [2] (incorrect) (frml) ‹use› indebido;
‹term› incorrecto

improve /ɪm'pruːv/ *vt* (a) ‹design/results›
mejorar; ‹chances› aumentar; **to ~ one's mind**
cultivarse (b) ‹property› hacer* mejoras en
■ **~** *vi* ‹‹situation/weather/health›› mejorar;
‹‹chances›› aumentar

improvement /ɪm'pruːvmənt/ *n* (in design,
situation) mejora *f*; (in health) mejoría *f*

improvise /'ɪmprəvaɪz/ *vi/t* improvisar

imprudent /ɪm'pruːdnt/ *adj* (frml) imprudente

impudence /'ɪmpjədəns/ ‖ /'ɪmpjʊdəns/ *n*
insolencia *f*

impudent /'ɪmpjədənt/ ‖ /'ɪmpjʊdənt/ *adj*
insolente

impulse /'ɪmpʌls/ *n* impulso *m*; **I did it on ~** lo
hice sin pensarlo

impulsive /ɪm'pʌlsɪv/ *adj* impulsivo

impunity /ɪm'pjuːnəti/ *n* (frml) impunidad *f*

impure /ɪm'pjʊr/ ‖ /ɪm'pjʊə(r)/ *adj* impuro

impurity /ɪm'pjʊrəti/ ‖ /ɪm'pjʊərəti/ *n* (*pl* **-ties**)
impureza *f*

in¹ /ɪn/ *prep* [1] (a) (indicating place, location) en; **~
Japan** en (el) Japón; **he went ~ the shop** entró en
la tienda; **who's that ~ the photo?** ¿quién es ese ···⟩

de la foto?; ~ **here/there** aquí/allí dentro or (esp AmL) adentro; ~ **the rain** bajo la lluvia **(b)** (with superl) de; **the highest mountain** ~ **Italy** la montaña más alta de Italia; **the worst storm** ~ **living memory** la peor tormenta que se recuerda **2** (indicating time) en; ~ **spring/January/1924** en primavera/enero/1924; **at four o'clock** ~ **the morning** a las cuatro de la mañana; **she did it** ~ **three hours** lo hizo en tres horas; ~ **two months' time** dentro de dos meses **3 (a)** (indicating manner) en; ~ **dollars** en dólares; ~ **French** en francés; ~ **twos** de dos en dos, de a dos (AmL); **cut it** ~ **half** córtalo por la mitad; **they came** ~ **their thousands** vinieron miles y miles **(b)** (wearing): **he turned up** ~ **a suit** apareció de traje; **are you going** ~ **that dress?** ¿vas a ir con ese vestido? **4** (indicating circumstances, state): **the company is** ~ **difficulties** la empresa está pasando dificultades; **to be** ~ **a good mood** estar* de buen humor; **he's** ~ **pain** está dolorido; **low** ~ **calories** bajo en calorías **5** (indicating ratio): **one** ~ **four** uno de cada cuatro; **she's one** ~ **a million** es única **6 (a)** (+ gerund): ~ **so doing, they set a precedent** al hacerlo, sentaron precedente **(b)** in that (as conj): **the case is unusual** ~ **that ...** el caso es poco común en el sentido de que ...

in² adv **1 (a)** (inside): **is the cat** ~? ¿el gato está dentro or (esp AmL) adentro?; ~ **you go!** ¡entra! **(b)** (at home, work): **is Lisa** ~? ¿está Lisa?; **there was nobody** ~ no había nadie **2 (a)** (in position): **she had her curlers** ~ llevaba or tenía los rulos puestos **(b)** (at destination): **the train isn't** ~ **yet** el tren no ha llegado todavía; **application forms must be** ~ **by October 5** las solicitudes deben entregarse antes del 5 de octubre **3** (involved): **we were** ~ **on the planning stage** participamos en la planificación; **to be** ~ **for sth**: **it looks like we're** ~ **for some rain** parece que va a llover; **you're** ~ **for a big surprise** te vas a llevar una buena sorpresa

in³ adj **1 (a)** (fashionable) (colloq) (no comp): **black is** ~ **this season** el negro está de moda esta temporada; **the** ~ **place** el lugar in (fam) **(b)** (exclusive, private) (before n): **an** ~ **joke** un chiste para iniciados **2** (pred) (in tennis, badminton, etc): **the ball was** ~ la pelota fue buena or cayó dentro or (esp AmL) adentro

in⁴ n: **the** ~**s and outs (of sth)** los pormenores (de algo)

in⁵ (pl **in** or **ins**) = **inch(es)**

IN = **Indiana**

inability /ˌɪnəˈbɪləti/ n incapacidad f; ~ **to** + **INF** incapacidad PARA + INF

inaccessible /ˌɪnəkˈsesəbəl ‖ ˌɪnækˈsesəbəl/ adj inaccesible

inaccurate /ɪnˈækjərət/ adj **(a)** ⟨translation/ estimate⟩ inexacto **(b)** ⟨aim/shot⟩ impreciso

inactive /ɪnˈæktɪv/ adj inactivo

inactivity /ˌɪnækˈtɪvəti/ n inactividad f

inadequate /ɪnˈædɪkwət/ adj **(a)** ⟨resources/ measures⟩ insuficiente **(b)** ⟨person⟩ inepto

inadvertently /ˌɪnədˈvɜːtntli ‖ ˌɪnədˈvɜːrtntli/ adv sin querer

inadvisable /ˌɪnədˈvaɪzəbəl/ adj desaconsejable

inane /ɪˈneɪn/ adj estúpido, idiota

inanimate /ɪnˈænəmət ‖ ɪnˈænɪmət/ adj inanimado

inapplicable /ɪnˈæplɪkəbəl, ˌɪnəˈplɪkəbəl/ adj inaplicable, no aplicable

inappropriate /ˌɪnəˈprəʊpriət/ adj ⟨measure/ dress⟩ inadecuado; ⟨moment⟩ inoportuno

inarticulate /ˌɪnɑːˈtɪkjələt ‖ ˌɪnɑːˈtɪkjʊlət/ adj ⟨babbling/grunt⟩ inarticulado; ⟨person⟩ con dificultad para expresarse

inasmuch as /ˌɪnəzˈmʌtʃ/ conj (frml) **(a)** (since, seeing that) ya que, puesto que **(b)** ▶ INSOFAR AS

inattentive /ˌɪnəˈtentɪv/ adj ⟨pupil/listener⟩ distraído, poco atento

inaudible /ɪnˈɔːdəbəl/ adj inaudible

inaugural /ɪˈnɔːɡjərəl ‖ ɪˈnɔːɡjʊrəl/ adj **(a)** ⟨speech/lecture⟩ inaugural **(b)** (of official) ⟨speech⟩ de toma de posesión; ⟨ceremony⟩ de investidura

inaugurate /ɪˈnɔːɡjəreɪt ‖ ɪˈnɔːɡjʊreɪt/ vt **(a)** (begin, open) inaugurar **(b)** (frml) ⟨president⟩ investir*

inauguration /ɪˌnɔːɡjəˈreɪʃən ‖ ɪˌnɔːɡjʊˈreɪʃən/ n **(a)** (investiture) investidura f; (before n) **I~ Day** (in US) día de la toma de posesión del presidente de los EEUU **(b)** (opening) inauguración f

inbreeding /ˈɪnˌbriːdɪŋ/ n endogamia f

Inc /ɪŋk/ (AmE) = **Incorporated**

Inca¹ /ˈɪŋkə/ adj incaico, inca

Inca² n inca mf

incapable /ɪnˈkeɪpəbəl/ adj (pred) **(a)** (not able) **to be** ~ OF **-ING** ser* incapaz DE + INF **(b)** (helpless) inútil, incapaz

incapacitate /ˌɪnkəˈpæsəteɪt ‖ ˌɪnkəˈpæsɪteɪt/ vt **(a)** (disable) incapacitar **(b)** (Law) inhabilitar

incarcerate /ɪnˈkɑːrsəreɪt ‖ ɪnˈkɑːsəreɪt/ vt encarcelar

incarnate /ɪnˈkɑːrnət ‖ ɪnˈkɑːnət/ adj (liter) (usu pred) encarnado

incarnation /ˌɪnkɑːrˈneɪʃən ‖ ˌɪnkɑːˈneɪʃən/ n encarnación f

incendiary /ɪnˈsendieri ‖ ɪnˈsendiəri/ adj incendiario

incense¹ /ˈɪnsens/ n incienso m

incense² /ɪnˈsens/ vt indignar

incentive /ɪnˈsentɪv/ n incentivo m

inception /ɪnˈsepʃən/ n (frml) inicio m

incessant /ɪnˈsesnt/ adj incesante

incessantly /ɪnˈsesntli/ adv sin cesar

incest /ˈɪnsest/ n incesto m

incestuous /ɪnˈsestʃuəs ‖ ɪnˈsestjuəs/ adj incestuoso

inch¹ /ɪntʃ/ n pulgada f (2,54 centímetros); **I've searched every** ~ **of the house** he buscado hasta en el último rincón de la casa; **she wouldn't budge** o **give an** ~ no cedió ni un ápice

inch² vi: **to** ~ **forward** avanzar* lentamente

incidence /ˈɪnsədəns ‖ ˈɪnsɪdəns/ n **1** (frequency) índice m **2** (Opt, Phys) incidencia f

incident /ˈɪnsədənt ‖ ˈɪnsɪdənt/ n incidente m

incidental /ˌɪnsəˈdentl ‖ ˌɪnsɪˈdentl/ adj **(a)** (accompanying) ⟨effect⟩ secundario; ⟨advantage/ benefit⟩ adicional; ⟨expenses⟩ imprevisto **(b)** (minor) incidental

incidentally /ˌɪnsəˈdentli ‖ ˌɪnsɪˈdentli/ adv (indep) a propósito

incinerate /ɪnˈsɪnəreɪt/ vt incinerar
incinerator /ɪnˈsɪnəreɪtər ‖ɪnˈsɪnəreɪtə(r)/ n
incinerador m
incision /ɪnˈsɪʒən/ n incisión f
incisor /ɪnˈsaɪzər ‖ɪnˈsaɪzə(r)/ n incisivo m
incite /ɪnˈsaɪt/ vt ⟨hatred/violence⟩ instigar* a,
incitar a; ⟨person⟩ to ∼ sb TO sth/+ INF instigar*
or incitar a algn A algo/+ INF
inclination /ˌɪnkləˈneɪʃən ‖ˌɪnklɪˈneɪʃən/ n (a)
(leaning) tendencia f (b) (desire) to have an/no ∼ to
+ INF tener*/no tener* deseos de + INF
incline¹ /ɪnˈklaɪn/ vt (frml) ⟨head⟩ inclinar
■ ∼ vi (frml) to ∼ TO sth: she ∼s to the opposite
view se inclina a pensar lo contrario
incline² /ˈɪnklaɪn/ n (frml) pendiente f
inclined /ɪnˈklaɪnd/ adj (disposed) ∼ to + INF:
I'm ∼ to agree yo me inclino a pensar lo mismo;
she's ∼ to be irritable in the morning tiende a
estar de mal humor por la mañana
include /ɪnˈkluːd/ vt incluir*; (with letter)
adjuntar; **service isn't** ∼d el servicio no está
incluido
including /ɪnˈkluːdɪŋ/ prep: up to and ∼ page
25 hasta la página 25 inclusive; **not** ∼ **insurance**
sin incluir el seguro
inclusion /ɪnˈkluːʒən/ n inclusión f
inclusive /ɪnˈkluːsɪv/ adj ⟨price/charge⟩ global;
to be ∼ OF sth incluir* algo
incognito /ˌɪnkɑːgˈniːtəʊ ‖ˌɪnkɒgˈniːtəʊ/ adv
de incógnito
incoherent /ˌɪnkəʊˈhɪrənt ‖ˌɪnkəʊˈhɪərənt/
adj incoherente
income /ˈɪnkʌm/ n ingresos mpl
income: ∼ **support** n (in UK) subsidio
otorgado a personas de bajos ingresos; ∼ **tax** n
impuesto m sobre or a la renta, impuesto m a los
réditos (Arg)
incoming /ˈɪnkʌmɪŋ/ adj (before n) (a)
(inbound): **the area has been closed to** ∼ **traffic** no
se permite la entrada de vehículos a la zona; **the
secretary takes all** ∼ **calls** la secretaria atiende
todas las llamadas (b) (about to take office)
⟨president⟩ entrante
incommunicado /ˈɪnkəˌmjuːnəˈkɑːdəʊ
‖ˌɪnkəˌmjuːnɪˈkɑːdəʊ/ adj (pred) to be ∼ estar*
incomunicado
incomparable /ɪnˈkɑːmpərəbəl
‖ɪnˈkɒmpərəbəl/ adj (liter) incomparable
incompatibility /ˌɪnkəmpætəˈbɪləti/ n
incompatibilidad f
incompatible /ˈɪnkəmˈpætəbəl/ adj
incompatible
incompetence /ɪnˈkɑːmpətəns
‖ɪnˈkɒmpɪtəns/ n incompetencia f
incompetent /ɪnˈkɑːmpətənt ‖ɪnˈkɒmpɪtənt/
adj ⟨person⟩ incompetente; ⟨work⟩ deficiente
incomplete /ˈɪnkəmˈpliːt/ adj (a) (with sth or sb
missing) incompleto (b) (unfinished) inacabado
incomprehensible /ɪnˈkɑːmprəˈhensəbəl
‖ɪnˌkɒmprɪˈhensəbəl/ adj incomprensible
incomprehension /ɪnˈkɑːmprɪˈhentʃən
‖ɪnˌkɒmprɪˈhenʃən/ n incomprensión f
inconceivable /ˈɪnkənˈsiːvəbəl/ adj
inconcebible
inconclusive /ˈɪnkənˈkluːsɪv/ adj ⟨evidence/
findings⟩ no concluyente

incongruous /ɪnˈkɑːŋgruəs ‖ɪnˈkɒŋgruəs/ adj
⟨behavior/remark⟩ fuera de lugar, inapropiado;
⟨appearance⟩ extraño, raro
inconsequential /ɪnˈkɑːnsəˈkwentʃəl
‖ɪnˌkɒnsɪˈkwenʃəl/ adj intrascendente
inconsiderate /ˈɪnkənˈsɪdərət/ adj
desconsiderado
inconsistent /ˈɪnkənˈsɪstənt/ adj (a)
(contradictory) contradictorio; to be ∼ WITH sth no
concordar* CON algo; ⟨with principles/ideas⟩ no
compadecerse* CON algo (b) (changeable) ⟨person/
attitude⟩ inconsecuente
inconspicuous /ˈɪnkənˈspɪkjuəs/ adj que no
llama la atención
incontinent /ɪnˈkɑːntɪnənt ‖ɪnˈkɒntɪnənt/ adj
(Med) incontinente
inconvenience¹ /ˈɪnkənˈviːniəns/ n (a)
(unsuitability, troublesomeness) inconveniencia f (b)
(trouble) molestias fpl (c) (drawback, nuisance)
inconveniente m
inconvenience² vt causarle molestias a
inconvenient /ˈɪnkənˈviːniənt/ adj ⟨moment⟩
poco conveniente; ⟨position⟩ poco práctico
incorporate /ɪnˈkɔːrpəreɪt ‖ɪnˈkɔːpəreɪt/ vt
⌐1⌐ (a) (take in) ⟨idea/plan⟩ incorporar; to ∼ sth
INTO sth incorporar algo A algo (b) (include,
contain) incluir* ⌐2⌐ (Busn, Law) ⟨business/
enterprise⟩ constituir* (en sociedad)
incorrect /ˈɪnkəˈrekt/ adj ⟨answer/spelling⟩
incorrecto; ⟨statement/belief⟩ equivocado
incorrigible /ɪnˈkɔːrədʒəbəl ‖ɪnˈkɒrɪdʒəbəl/
adj incorregible
increase¹ /ɪnˈkriːs/ vi «number/size/prices/
output» aumentar; «influence/popularity»
crecer*; to ∼ in size aumentar de tamaño; to ∼
in number crecer* en número; to ∼ in value
aumentar de valor
■ ∼ vt aumentar
increase² /ˈɪnkriːs/ n aumento m; to be on the
∼ estar* or ir* en aumento
increasing /ɪnˈkriːsɪŋ/ adj (before n) creciente
increasingly /ɪnˈkriːsɪŋli/ adv: ∼ difficult
cada vez más difícil; it is becoming ∼ clear that
... resulta cada vez más claro que ...
incredible /ɪnˈkredəbəl/ adj increíble
incredibly /ɪnˈkredəbli/ adv (colloq) (as
intensifier) increíblemente
incredulous /ɪnˈkredʒələs ‖ɪnˈkredjʊləs/ adj
de incredulidad
increment /ˈɪŋkrəmənt/ n (in salary)
incremento m (salarial) (frml)
incriminate /ɪnˈkrɪməneɪt ‖ɪnˈkrɪmɪneɪt/ vt
incriminar (frml)
incriminating /ɪnˈkrɪməneɪtɪŋ
‖ɪnˈkrɪmɪneɪtɪŋ/ adj ⟨evidence/document⟩
comprometedor
incubate /ˈɪŋkjəbeɪt ‖ˈɪŋkjubeɪt/ vt incubar
■ ∼ vi «bird» empollar; «egg/bacteria»
incubarse
incubation /ˈɪŋkjəˈbeɪʃən ‖ˌɪŋkjʊˈbeɪʃən/ n
incubación f
incubator /ˈɪŋkjəbeɪtər ‖ˈɪŋkjubeɪtə(r)/ n
incubadora f
inculcate /ˈɪŋkʌlkeɪt/ vt (frml) to ∼ sth IN(TO)
sb, to ∼ sb WITH sth inculcarle* algo A algn,
inculcar* algo EN algn

incumbent¹ /ɪnˈkʌmbənt/ adj (frml) to be ~ ON o UPON sb incumbirle A algn

incumbent² n titular mf del cargo

incur /ɪnˈkɜːr ‖ ɪnˈkɜː(r)/ vt -rr- (frml) ⟨anger⟩ provocar*, incurrir en (frml); ⟨penalty⟩ acarrear; ⟨damage/loss⟩ sufrir; ⟨debt/liability⟩ contraer*; ⟨expense⟩ incurrir en (frml)

incurable /ɪnˈkjʊrəbəl ‖ ɪnˈkjʊərəbəl/ adj ⟨illness⟩ incurable; ⟨optimist/romantic⟩ empedernido

incursion /ɪnˈkɜːrʒən ‖ ɪnˈkɜːʃən/ n incursión f

Ind = **Indiana**

indebted /ɪnˈdetəd ‖ ɪnˈdetɪd/ adj to be ~ TO sb (FOR sth) estar* en deuda CON algn (POR algo)

indecency /ɪnˈdiːsnsi/ n indecencia f

indecent /ɪnˈdiːsnt/ adj indecente

indecent assault n abusos mpl deshonestos

indecipherable /ˈɪndɪˈsaɪfərəbəl/ adj indescifrable

indecision /ˈɪndɪˈsɪʒən/ n indecisión f

indecisive /ˈɪndɪˈsaɪsɪv/ adj (a) (hesitant) indeciso (b) (inconclusive) no decisivo

indeed /ɪnˈdiːd/ adv **1** (as intensifier): thank you very much ~ muchísimas gracias; this is ~ a great privilege este es un auténtico o verdadero privilegio **2** (in fact): the wheel was ~ loose en efecto, la rueda estaba suelta; if ~ he is right sí es que tiene razón

indefensible /ˈɪndɪˈfensəbəl/ adj inexcusable

indefinite /ɪnˈdefənət ‖ ɪnˈdefmət/ adj **1** ⟨number/period/outline⟩ indefinido **2** (Ling): ~ article artículo m indefinido

indelible /ɪnˈdeləbəl/ adj indeleble

indelicate /ɪnˈdeləkət ‖ ɪnˈdelɪkət/ adj (a) (vulgar) indelicado (b) (tactless) indiscreto

indemnify /ɪnˈdemnəfaɪ ‖ ɪnˈdemnɪfaɪ/ vt -fies, -fying, -fied (a) (insure) asegurar (b) (compensate) indemnizar*

indemnity /ɪnˈdemnəti/ n (pl -ties) (a) (insurance) indemnidad f (b) (compensation) indemnización f

indent /ɪnˈdent/ vt (a) ⟨line/paragraph⟩ sangrar (b) ⟨surface/edge⟩ marcar*

independence /ˈɪndɪˈpendəns/ n independencia f

Independence Day n día m de la Independencia

independent /ˈɪndɪˈpendənt/ adj independiente

in-depth /ˈɪnˈdepθ/ adj (before n) a fondo

indescribable /ˈɪndɪˈskraɪbəbəl/ adj indescriptible

indestructible /ˈɪndɪˈstrʌktəbəl/ adj indestructible

indeterminate /ˈɪndɪˈtɜːrmənət ‖ ˈɪndɪˈtɜːmɪnət/ adj indeterminado

index¹ /ˈɪndeks/ n **1** (pl **indexes**) (a) (in book, journal) índice m (b) (list) lista f; (before n) ~ **card** ficha f **2** (pl **indexes** o **indices**) (Econ, Fin) índice m **3** (pl **indices**) (Math) índice m

index² vt **1** (Publ) (a) (provide with index) ponerle* un índice a (b) (enter in index) incluir* en un índice **2** (Econ, Fin) ⟨prices/wages⟩ indexar

index: ~ **finger** n (dedo m) índice m; ~-**linked** /ˈɪndeksˈlɪŋkt/ adj (esp BrE) indexado

India /ˈɪndiə/ n la India

Indian¹ /ˈɪndiən/ adj **1** (of India) indio **2** (of America) indígena, indio

Indian² n **1** (person from India) indio, -dia m,f **2** (American ~) indígena mf, indio, -dia m,f

Indian: ~ **Ocean** n the ~ Ocean el (Océano) Índico; ~ **summer** n (in northern hemisphere) ≈ veranillo m de San Martín or de San Miguel; (in southern hemisphere) ≈ veranillo m de San Juan

indicate /ˈɪndɪkeɪt ‖ ˈɪndɪkeɪt/ vt **1** (a) (point out) señalar (b) (Auto) indicar* **2** (a) (show) ⟨change/condition⟩ ser* indicio de (b) (state) señalar
■ ~ vi (BrE Auto) indicar*, señalizar*, poner* el intermitente or (Col, Méx) las direccionales or (Chi) el señalizador

indication /ˈɪndəˈkeɪʃən ‖ ˈɪndɪˈkeɪʃən/ n (a) (sign, hint) indicio m (b) (Med) indicación f

indicative¹ /ɪnˈdɪkətɪv/ adj **1** (revealing) (frml) to be ~ OF sth ser* indicio DE algo **2** (Ling) ⟨mood/form⟩ indicativo

indicative² n (Ling) indicativo m

indicator /ˈɪndəkeɪtər ‖ ˈɪndɪkeɪtə(r)/ n **1** (a) (pointer) indicador m (b) (instrument) indicador m **2** (Auto) intermitente m, direccional f (Col, Méx), señalizador m (de viraje) (Chi) **3** (sign) indicador m

indices /ˈɪndəsiːz ‖ ˈɪndɪsiːz/ pl of INDEX¹ 2,3

indict /ɪnˈdaɪt/ vt (Law) acusar

indictment /ɪnˈdaɪtmənt/ n **1** (Law) acusación f **2** (criticism): the report was an ~ of his management el informe censuraba su gestión

indifference /ɪnˈdɪfrəns/ n indiferencia f

indifferent /ɪnˈdɪfrənt/ adj **1** (uninterested) indiferente **2** (mediocre) mediocre

indigenous /ɪnˈdɪdʒənəs/ adj ⟨population/language⟩ indígena, autóctono; ⟨species⟩ autóctono

indigestible /ˈɪndaɪˈdʒestəbəl, -də- ‖ ˈɪndɪˈdʒestəbəl/ adj (impossible to digest) no digerible; (hard to digest) indigesto

indigestion /ˈɪndaɪˈdʒestʃən, -də- ‖ ˈɪndɪˈdʒestʃən/ n indigestión f

indignant /ɪnˈdɪɡnənt/ adj indignado

indignation /ˈɪndɪɡˈneɪʃən/ n indignación f

indignity /ɪnˈdɪɡnəti/ n (pl -ties) humillación f

indigo /ˈɪndɪɡəʊ/ n índigo m, añil m; (before n) ⟨ink/sea⟩ color añil adj inv

indirect /ˈɪndəˈrekt, -daɪ- ‖ ˈɪndɪˈrekt, -daɪ-/ adj **1** (a) ⟨route/method⟩ indirecto; ⟨result/benefit⟩ indirecto (b) (Ling) ⟨statement/question⟩ indirecto; ~ **discourse** o (BrE) **speech** estilo m indirecto **2** (Fin) ⟨costs/taxes⟩ indirecto

AmC	Central America	Arg	Argentina	Cu	Cuba	Per	Peru
AmL	Latin America	Bol	Bolivia	Ec	Ecuador	RPl	River Plate Area
AmS	South America	Chi	Chile	Esp	Spain	Ur	Uruguay
Andes	Andean Region	CS	Southern Cone	Méx	Mexico	Ven	Venezuela

indirectly /ˌɪndəˈrektli, -daɪ- ‖ˌɪndɪˈrektli, -daɪ-/ *adv* indirectamente

indiscreet /ˌɪndɪsˈkriːt/ *adj* indiscreto

indiscretion /ˌɪndɪsˈkreʃən/ *n* indiscreción *f*

indiscriminate /ˌɪndɪsˈkrɪmənət ‖ˌɪndɪsˈkrɪmmət/ *adj* indiscriminado

indispensable /ˌɪndɪsˈpensəbəl/ *adj* indispensable

indisposed /ˌɪndɪsˈpəʊzd/ *adj* (fml) (*pred*) (ill) **to be ∼** estar* indispuesto (fml)

indisputable /ˌɪndɪˈspjuːtəbəl/ *adj* ⟨evidence/proof⟩ irrefutable; ⟨leader/winner⟩ indiscutible

indistinct /ˌɪndɪˈstɪŋkt/ *adj* ⟨sound/shape⟩ poco definido; ⟨speech⟩ poco claro

indistinguishable /ˌɪndɪˈstɪŋgwɪʃəbəl/ *adj* **∼ (FROM sth)** indistinguible (DE algo)

individual¹ /ˌɪndəˈvɪdʒuəl ‖ˌɪndɪˈvɪdjuəl/ *adj* ⌐1⌐ (*before n*) (*no comp*) (a) (for one person) ⟨portion⟩ individual; ⟨tuition⟩ personal (b) (single, separate): **you can purchase the whole set or ∼** se puede comprar el juego o cada pieza por separado (c) (particular, personal) ⟨style⟩ personal ⌐2⌐ (distinctive) personal

individual² *n* (a) (single person, animal) individuo *m* (b) (person) (colloq) individuo, -dua *m,f*

indivisible /ˌɪndəˈvɪzəbəl ‖ˌɪndɪˈvɪzəbəl/ *adj* indivisible

indoctrinate /ɪnˈdɑːktrəneɪt ‖ɪnˈdɒktrɪneɪt/ *vt* adoctrinar

indolent /ˈɪndələnt/ *adj* (fml) indolente

Indonesia /ˌɪndəˈniːʒə ‖ˌɪndəˈniːziə/ *n* Indonesia *f*

Indonesian¹ /ˌɪndəˈniːʒən ‖ˌɪndəˈniːziən/ *adj* indonesio

Indonesian² *n* (a) (person) indonesio, -sia *m,f* (b) (language) indonesio *m*

indoor /ˈɪndɔːr ‖ˈɪndɔː(r)/ *adj* (*before n*) ⟨clothes/shoes⟩ para estar en casa; ⟨plants⟩ de interior(es); ⟨swimming pool⟩ cubierto, techado

indoors /ˈɪnˈdɔːrz ‖ˌɪnˈdɔːz/ *adv* dentro, adentro (esp AmL)

induce /ɪnˈduːs ‖ɪnˈdjuːs/ *vt* ⌐1⌐ (persuade) **to ∼ sb to + INF** inducir* a algn A + INF ⌐2⌐ (Med) ⟨sleep/labor⟩ inducir*

inducement /ɪnˈduːsmənt ‖ɪnˈdjuːsmənt/ *n* incentivo *m*

induction /ɪnˈdʌkʃən/ *n* ⌐1⌐ (introduction) **∼ (INTO sth)** iniciación *f* (EN algo); (*before n*) ⟨course/period⟩ introductorio ⌐2⌐ (Med) (of labor) inducción *f*

indulge /ɪnˈdʌldʒ/ *vt* ⟨child⟩ consentir*, mimar; ⟨desire⟩ satisfacer*; **it doesn't hurt to ∼ oneself every now and again** es bueno darse algún gusto de vez en cuando
■ **∼** *vi* **to ∼ IN sth** permitirse algo

indulgence /ɪnˈdʌldʒəns/ *n* (a) (extravagance): **an occasional cigar is my only ∼** un puro de vez en cuando es el único lujo que me permito (b) (partaking): **too much ∼ in anything is bad** es malo abusar de cualquier placer

indulgent /ɪnˈdʌldʒənt/ *adj* indulgente

industrial /ɪnˈdʌstriəl/ *adj* ⟨town/production/engineering⟩ industrial; **∼ dispute** conflicto *m* laboral

industrial estate *n* (BrE) zona *f* industrial, polígono *m* industrial (Esp)

industrialist /ɪnˈdʌstriələst ‖ɪnˈdʌstriəlɪst/ *n* industrial *mf*

industrialize /ɪnˈdʌstriəlaɪz/ *vt* industrializar*

industrial: ∼ park *n* (AmE) zona *f* industrial, polígono *m* industrial (Esp); **I∼ Revolution** *n* **the I∼ Revolution** la Revolución Industrial

industrious /ɪnˈdʌstriəs/ *adj* ⟨worker⟩ trabajador; ⟨student⟩ aplicado

industry /ˈɪndəstri/ *n* (*pl* **-tries**) industria *f*; **the steel ∼** la industria siderúrgica; **the tourist ∼** el turismo

inebriated /ɪnˈiːbrieɪtəd ‖ɪnˈiːbrieɪtɪd/ *adj* (fml) ⟨person⟩ beodo (fml), ebrio (fml); ⟨state⟩ de embriaguez (fml)

inedible /ɪnˈedəbəl/ *adj* (impossible to eat) no comestible; (unpalatable) incomible

ineffective /ˈɪnəˈfektɪv ‖ˌɪnɪˈfektɪv/ *adj* ⟨measure⟩ ineficaz; ⟨attempt⟩ infructuoso; ⟨person⟩ incompetente

inefficiency /ˈɪnəˈfɪʃənsi ‖ˌɪnɪˈfɪʃənsi/ *n* (of machinery) falta *f* de eficiencia; (of persons, method) ineficiencia *f*

inefficient /ˈɪnəˈfɪʃənt ‖ˌɪnɪˈfɪʃənt/ *adj* ineficiente

ineligible /ɪnˈelədʒəbəl ‖ɪnˈelɪdʒəbəl/ *adj* (usu pred) ⟨candidate⟩ inelegible; **she was ∼ to vote** no tenía derecho a votar

inept /ɪˈnept/ *adj* ⟨person⟩ inepto; ⟨conduct⟩ torpe

inequality /ˌɪnɪˈkwɑːləti ‖ˌɪnɪˈkwɒləti/ *n* (*pl* **-ties**) desigualdad *f*

inert /ɪˈnɜːrt ‖ɪˈnɜːt/ *adj* inerte

inertia /ɪˈnɜːrʃə ‖ɪˈnɜːʃə/ *n* inercia *f*

inevitable¹ /ɪnˈevətəbəl ‖ɪnˈevɪtəbəl/ *adj* inevitable

inevitable² *n* **the ∼** lo inevitable

inevitably /ɪnˈevətəbli ‖ɪnˈevɪtəbli/ *adv* inevitablemente

inexact /ˌɪnɪgˈzækt/ *adj* inexacto

inexcusable /ˌɪnɪkˈskjuːzəbəl/ *adj* imperdonable

inexpensive /ˌɪnɪkˈspensɪv/ *adj* económico

inexperience /ˈɪnɪkˈspɪriəns ‖ˌɪnɪkˈspɪəriəns/ *n* inexperiencia *f*, falta *f* de experiencia

inexperienced /ˈɪnɪkˈspɪriənst ‖ˌɪnɪkˈspɪəriənst/ *adj* ⟨nurse/pilot⟩ sin experiencia; ⟨swimmer/driver⟩ inexperto, novato

inexpert /ɪnˈekspɜːrt ‖ɪnˈekspɜːt/ *adj* inexperto

inexplicable /ˌɪnɪkˈsplɪkəbəl/ *adj* inexplicable

inextricably /ˌɪnɪkˈstrɪkəbli/ *adv* inextricablemente

infallibility /ˌɪnˌfæləˈbɪləti/ *n* infalibilidad *f*

infallible /ɪnˈfæləbəl/ *adj* infalible

infamous /ˈɪnfəməs/ *adj* (a) (notorious) de triste fama (b) (shameful) infame

infancy /ˈɪnfənsi/ *n* primera infancia *f*

infant /ˈɪnfənt/ *n* (a) (baby) bebé *m*, niño, -ña *m,f*; (*before n*) **∼ mortality** mortalidad *f* infantil (b) (BrE Educ) niño, -ña *m,f* (entre cinco y siete años de edad); (*before n*) **∼ school** (in UK) escuela para niños de entre cinco y siete años de edad

infantile /ˈɪnfəntaɪl/ *adj* pueril, infantil

infantry /'ɪnfəntri/ n (+ sing or pl vb) infantería f

infatuated /ɪn'fætʃʊeɪtəd ‖ɪn'fætʃʊeɪtɪd/ adj to be ~ WITH sb estar* encaprichado CON or (Esp tb) DE algn

infatuation /ɪnˌfætʃu'eɪʃən ‖ɪnˌfætʃʊ'eɪʃən/ n encaprichamiento m

infect /ɪn'fekt/ vt ⟨wound/cut⟩ infectar; ⟨person/animal⟩ contagiar; the wound became ~ed la herida se infectó

infection /ɪn'fekʃən/ n (a) (disease) infección f (b) (of wound) infección f; (of person) contagio m

infectious /ɪn'fekʃəs/ adj ⟨disease⟩ infeccioso, contagioso; ⟨laughter/enthusiasm⟩ contagioso

infer /ɪn'fɜːr ‖ɪn'fɜː(r)/ vt -rr- (deduce) to ~ sth (FROM sth) inferir* or deducir* algo (DE algo)

inferior¹ /ɪn'fɪriər ‖ɪn'fɪəriə(r)/ adj (no comp) ⟨product⟩ (de calidad) inferior; ⟨workmanship/rank⟩ inferior

inferior² n inferior mf

inferiority /ɪnˌfɪri'ɔːrəti ‖ɪnˌfɪəri'ɒrəti/ n inferioridad f; (before n) ~ complex complejo m de inferioridad

inferno /ɪn'fɜːrnəʊ ‖ɪn'fɜːnəʊ/ n (pl -noes) (journ): the building was a blazing ~ el edificio estaba totalmente envuelto en llamas

infertile /ɪn'fɜːrtl̩ ‖ɪn'fɜːtaɪl/ adj ⟨land⟩ estéril, infecundo; ⟨woman/man/animal⟩ estéril

infertility /ɪnfər'tɪləti ‖ɪnfə'tɪləti/ n (Agr) infecundidad f; (Biol) esterilidad f

infest /ɪn'fest/ vt infestar

infidelity /ɪnfə'deləti ‖ɪnfɪ'deləti/ n (pl -ties) infidelidad f

infighting /'ɪnˌfaɪtɪŋ/ n luchas fpl internas

infiltrate /ɪn'fɪltreɪt ‖'ɪnfɪltreɪt/ vt infiltrarse en

infiltrator /ɪn'fɪltreɪtər ‖'ɪnfɪltreɪtə(r)/ n infiltrado, -da m,f

infinite /'ɪnfənət ‖'ɪnfɪnət/ adj infinito

infinitesimal /'ɪnfɪnə'tesɪml̩ ‖ˌɪnfɪnɪ'tesɪml̩/ adj infinitesimal

infinitive /ɪn'fɪnətɪv/ n infinitivo m

infinity /ɪn'fɪnəti/ n (a) (Math) infinito m (b) (endless space) infinito m (c) (vast number, quantity) (liter) (no pl) infinidad f

infirm /ɪn'fɜːrm ‖ɪn'fɜːm/ adj (weak) endeble; (ill) enfermo

infirmary /ɪn'fɜːrməri ‖ɪn'fɜːməri/ n (pl -ries) (used in titles) hospital m

infirmity /ɪn'fɜːrməti ‖ɪn'fɜːməti/ n (pl -ties) dolencia f (frml), padecimiento m

inflame /ɪn'fleɪm/ vt ⟨person/passion⟩ encender*; ⟨situation⟩ exacerbar

inflamed /ɪn'fleɪmd/ adj inflamado; to become ~ inflamarse

inflammable /ɪn'flæməbəl/ adj inflamable, flamable (Méx)

inflammation /'ɪnflə'meɪʃən/ n inflamación f

inflate /ɪn'fleɪt/ vt (with air, gas) inflar, hinchar (Esp)

inflation /ɪn'fleɪʃən/ n inflación f

inflexible /ɪn'fleksəbəl/ adj ⟨personality/regulations⟩ inflexible; ⟨material⟩ rígido

inflict /ɪn'flɪkt/ vt ⟨pain/damage⟩ causar; ⟨punishment⟩ imponer*; to ~ sth ON sb: the suffering which he ~ed on his family el sufrimiento que le causó a su familia

influence¹ /'ɪnfluəns/ n influencia f; to be under the ~ of sb/sth estar* bajo la influencia de algn/algo; she's a good/bad ~ on him ejerce buena/mala influencia sobre él

influence² vt influir* en, influenciar

influential /'ɪnflu'entʃəl ‖ɪnflʊ'enʃəl/ adj influyente

influenza /'ɪnflu'enzə/ n (Med) gripe f or (Chi tb) influenza f or (Col, Méx) gripa f

influx /'ɪnflʌks/ n (of people) afluencia f; (of goods) entrada f; (of ideas) llegada f

inform /ɪn'fɔːrm ‖ɪn'fɔːm/ vt informar; to keep sb ~ed mantener* a algn informado or al corriente

■ ~ vi to ~ ON sb delatar or denunciar a algn

informal /ɪn'fɔːrməl ‖ɪn'fɔːməl/ adj informal

informality /'ɪnfɔːr'mæləti ‖ɪnfɔː'mæləti/ n falta f de ceremonia, informalidad f

informally /ɪn'fɔːrməli ‖ɪn'fɔːməli/ adv (a) (casually) ⟨talk/dress⟩ de manera informal (b) (unofficially) ⟨meet/discuss⟩ informalmente

informant /ɪn'fɔːrmənt ‖ɪn'fɔːmənt/ n informante mf

information /'ɪnfər'meɪʃən ‖ˌɪnfə'meɪʃən/ n información f; a piece of ~ un dato; (before n) ~ desk información f

information: ~ **highway** n (Comput) autopista f de información, infovía f; ~ **technology** n informática f

informative /ɪn'fɔːrmətɪv ‖ɪn'fɔːmətɪv/ adj ⟨article/lecture⟩ instructivo, informativo; ⟨guidebook⟩ lleno de información, informativo

informed /ɪn'fɔːrmd ‖ɪn'fɔːmd/ adj ⟨source⟩ bien informado; ⟨criticism/approach⟩ bien fundado

informer /ɪn'fɔːrmər ‖ɪn'fɔːmə(r)/ n informante mf

infrared /'ɪnfrə'red/ adj infrarrojo

infrastructure /'ɪnfrəˌstrʌktʃər ‖'ɪnfrəˌstrʌktʃə(r)/ n infraestructura f

infrequent /ɪn'friːkwənt/ adj poco frecuente

infringe /ɪn'frɪndʒ/ vt ⟨contract⟩ no cumplir (con); ⟨treaty/rule⟩ infringir*

■ ~ vi to ~ ON o UPON sth violar algo

infringement /ɪn'frɪndʒmənt/ n (of law) contravención f, violación f; (of contract) incumplimiento m; (Sport) falta f; (of rights) violación f

infuriate /ɪn'fjʊrieɪt ‖ɪn'fjʊərieɪt/ vt enfurecer*

infuriating /ɪn'fjʊrieɪtɪŋ ‖ɪn'fjʊərieɪtɪŋ/ adj exasperante

infuse /ɪn'fjuːz/ vt ⟨tea/herb⟩ hacer* una infusión de

infusion /ɪn'fjuːʒən/ n infusión f

ingenious /ɪn'dʒiːnjəs ‖ɪn'dʒiːniəs/ adj ingenioso

ingenuity /ˌɪndʒə'nuːəti ‖ˌɪndʒə'njuːəti/ n (of person) ingenio m; (of gadget, idea) lo ingenioso

ingenuous /ɪn'dʒenjuəs/ adj ingenuo

ingot /'ɪŋgət/ n lingote m

ingrained /ɪnˈɡreɪnd/ *adj* **(a)** ‹belief/habit› arraigado **(b)** ‹dirt› incrustado

ingratiate /ɪnˈɡreɪʃieɪt/ *v refl* **to ~ oneself (WITH sb)** congraciarse (CON algn)

ingratitude /ɪnˈɡrætətuːd ‖ ɪnˈɡrætɪtjuːd/ *n* ingratitud *f*

ingredient /ɪnˈɡriːdiənt/ *n* **(a)** (Culin) ingrediente *m* **(b)** (Pharm) componente *m* **(c)** (element) elemento *m*

ingrowing /ˈɪnˌɡrəʊɪŋ/ *adj* (BrE) ‹toenail› encarnado

ingrown /ˈɪnɡrəʊn/ *adj* ‹toenail› encarnado

inhabit /ɪnˈhæbət ‖ ɪnˈhæbɪt/ *vt* habitar (frml), vivir en

inhabitant /ɪnˈhæbətənt ‖ ɪnˈhæbɪtənt/ *n* habitante *mf*

inhale /ɪnˈheɪl/ *vi* aspirar

inhaler /ɪnˈheɪlər ‖ ɪnˈheɪlə(r)/ *n* inhalador *m*

inherent /ɪnˈhɪrənt, -ˈher- ‖ ɪnˈhɪərənt, -ˈher-/ *adj* inherente; **to be ~ IN sth** ser* inherente A algo

inherit /ɪnˈherət ‖ ɪnˈherɪt/ *vt* heredar

inheritance /ɪnˈherətəns ‖ ɪnˈherɪtəns/ *n* **(a)** (sth inherited) herencia *f* **(b)** (act) sucesión *f*

inhibit /ɪnˈhɪbət ‖ ɪnˈhɪbɪt/ *vt* (frml) inhibir

inhibited /ɪnˈhɪbətəd ‖ ɪnˈhɪbɪtɪd/ *adj* inhibido

inhibition /ˌɪnəˈbɪʃən ‖ ˌɪnhɪˈbɪʃən/ *n* inhibición *f*

inhospitable /ˌɪnhɑːˈspɪtəbəl ‖ ˌɪnhɒˈspɪtəbəl/ *adj* ‹person› poco hospitalario; ‹climate/region› inhóspito

in-house /ˈɪnhaʊs/ *adj* ‹training› en la empresa (*or* organización *etc*); ‹staff› interno

inhuman /ɪnˈhjuːmən/ *adj* inhumano

inhumane /ˌɪnhjuːˈmeɪn/ *adj* ‹treatment› inhumano; ‹person› cruel

inhumanity /ˌɪnhjuːˈmænəti/ *n* (*pl* -ties) **(a)** (cruelty) crueldad *f* **(b)** (cruel act) atrocidad *f*

inimitable /ɪnˈɪmətəbəl ‖ ɪˈnɪmɪtəbəl/ *adj* inimitable

initial¹ /ɪˈnɪʃəl/ *adj* inicial

initial² *n* inicial *f*

initial³ *vt*, (BrE) **-ll-** inicialar

initially /ɪˈnɪʃəli/ *adv* inicialmente

initiate /ɪˈnɪʃieɪt/ *vt* **1** (start) (frml) ‹talks› iniciar (frml); ‹reform/plan› poner* en marcha **2** (admit, introduce) **to ~ sb (INTO sth)** iniciar a algn (EN algo)

initiation /ɪˌnɪʃiˈeɪʃən/ *n* **1** (admission) iniciación *f*; (before n) **~ ceremony** ceremonia *f* iniciática **2** (of plan, talks) inicio *m* (frml)

initiative /ɪˈnɪʃətɪv/ *n* iniciativa *f*; **on one's own ~** por iniciativa propia; **to take the ~** tomar la iniciativa

inject /ɪnˈdʒekt/ *vt* ‹drug› inyectar; **to ~ sth (INTO sth)** ‹capital/resources› inyectarle algo (A algo)

injection /ɪnˈdʒekʃən/ *n* inyección *f*

injunction /ɪnˈdʒʌŋkʃən/ *n* (Law) mandamiento *m* judicial

injure /ˈɪndʒər ‖ ˈɪndʒə(r)/ *vt* **(a)** ‹person/feelings› herir* **(b) injured** *past p*: **she gave me an ~d look** me miró con expresión ofendida; **I am the ~d party** soy yo quien sufrió el agravio

injurious /ɪnˈdʒʊriəs ‖ ɪnˈdʒʊəriəs/ *adj* (frml) perjudicial

injury /ˈɪndʒəri/ *n* (*pl* **-ries**) herida *f*; (before n) **~ time** (BrE Sport) tiempo *m* de descuento

injustice /ɪnˈdʒʌstəs ‖ ɪnˈdʒʌstɪs/ *n* injusticia *f*; **to do sb an ~** cometer una injusticia con algn

ink /ɪŋk/ *n* tinta *f*

inkling /ˈɪŋklɪŋ/ *n*: **I had an ~ something had gone wrong** tuve el presentimiento *or* (CS, Per tb) el pálpito de que algo había salido mal

inkwell /ˈɪŋkwel/ *n* tintero *m* (empotrado en un escritorio)

inlaid¹ /ˈɪnleɪd/ *past & past p of* INLAY²

inlaid² *adj* ‹design› de marquetería; ‹box/lid› con incrustaciones

inland¹ /ˈɪnlənd/ *adj* (before n) ‹town› del interior; ‹sea› interior

inland² /ˈɪnlænd/ *adv* tierra adentro

Inland Revenue /ˈɪnlənd/ *n* (in UK) **the ~ ~** ≈ Hacienda, ≈ la Dirección General Impositiva (*en RPl*), ≈ Impuestos Internos (*en Chi*)

in-laws /ˈɪnlɔːz/ *pl n* (colloq) (spouse's parents) suegros *mpl*; (spouse's family) parientes *mpl* políticos

inlay¹ /ˈɪnleɪ/ *n* (of wood, metal, ivory) incrustación *f*

inlay² /ɪnˈleɪ/ *vt* (*past & past p* **inlaid**) **to ~ sth WITH sth** hacer* incrustaciones de algo EN algo

inlet /ˈɪnlet/ *n* (in coastline) ensenada *f*, entrada *f*; (of river, sea) brazo *m*

inmate /ˈɪnmeɪt/ *n* (of asylum) interno, -na *m,f*; (of prison) preso, -sa *m,f*; (of hospital) paciente hospitalizado, -da *m,f*

inmost /ˈɪnməʊst/ *adj* ▶ INNERMOST

inn /ɪn/ *n* (tavern) taberna *f*; (hotel) hostal *m*

innards /ˈɪnərdz ‖ ˈɪnədz/ *pl n* tripas *fpl* (fam)

innate /ɪˈneɪt/ *adj* innato

inner /ˈɪnər ‖ ˈɪnə(r)/ *adj* (before n, no comp) **(a)** ‹room/part› interior; **the ~ city** la zona del centro urbano habitada por familias de escasos ingresos, caracterizada por problemas sociales *etc* **(b)** (of person) ‹life› interior; ‹thoughts› íntimo

innermost /ˈɪnərməʊst ‖ ˈɪnəməʊst/ *adj* ‹part/chamber› más recóndito; ‹thoughts› más íntimo

inner tube *n* cámara *f*

inning /ˈɪnɪŋ/ *n* (in baseball) entrada *f*, manga *f*

innings /ˈɪnɪŋz/ *n* (*pl* **~**) (in cricket) entrada *f*

innkeeper /ˈɪnˌkiːpər ‖ ˈɪnˌkiːpə(r)/ *n* posadero, -ra *m,f*

innocence /ˈɪnəsəns/ *n* inocencia *f*

innocent /ˈɪnəsənt/ *adj* inocente

innocuous /ɪˈnɑːkjuəs ‖ ɪˈnɒkjuəs/ *adj* ‹drug› inocuo; ‹person/comment› inofensivo

innovation /ˌɪnəˈveɪʃən/ *n* innovación *f*

innovative /ˈɪnəveɪtɪv ‖ ˈɪnəvətɪv/ *adj* innovador

innuendo /ˌɪnjuˈendəʊ/ *n* (*pl* **-dos** *or* **-does**) indirecta *f*, insinuación *f*

innumerable /ɪˈnuːmərəbəl ‖ ɪˈnjuːmərəbəl/ *adj* innumerable

inoculate /ɪˈnɑːkjəleɪt ‖ ɪˈnɒkjʊleɪt/ *vt* inocular

inoculation /ɪˌnɑːkjəˈleɪʃən ‖ ɪˌnɒkjʊˈleɪʃən/ *n* inoculación *f*

inoffensive /ˌɪnəˈfensɪv/ adj inofensivo

inordinate /ɪˈnɔːrdnət ‖ɪnˈɔːdɪnət/ adj: **an ~ amount of money** una cantidad exorbitante de dinero; **they are making ~ demands** lo que piden es excesivo

inpatient /ˈɪnˌpeɪʃənt/ n paciente hospitalizado, -da m,f

input¹ /ˈɪnpʊt/ n **1** **(a)** (of resources) aportación f, aporte m (esp AmL) **(b)** (contribution) aportación f, aporte m (esp AmL) **2** (Comput) entrada f

input² vt (pres p **inputting**; past & past p **input** or **inputted**) ‹data› entrar

inquest /ˈɪnkwest/ n investigación f

inquire, (BrE) **enquire** /ɪnˈkwaɪr ‖ɪnˈkwaɪə(r)/ vt preguntar
■ **~** vi preguntar; **to ~ ABOUT sth** informarse ACERCA DE algo

inquiring, (BrE) **enquiring** /ɪnˈkwaɪrɪŋ ‖ɪnˈkwaɪərɪŋ/ adj (before n) ‹mind› curioso; ‹look› inquisitivo

inquiry, (BrE) **enquiry** /ɪnˈkwaɪri, ˈɪnkwəri ‖ɪnˈkwaɪəri/ n (pl **-ries**) **(a)** (question): **we made inquiries about** o **into his past** hicimos averiguaciones sobre su pasado; **all inquiries to ...** para cualquier información dirigirse a ...; **ⓢ inquiries** información f **(b)** (investigation) investigación f

inquisition /ˌɪnkwəˈzɪʃən ‖ˌɪnkwɪˈzɪʃən/ n **(a)** (severe questioning) interrogatorio m **(b)** the **Spanish I~** la (Santa) Inquisición, el Santo Oficio

inquisitive /ɪnˈkwɪzətɪv/ adj ‹mind› inquisitivo; ‹person/animal› muy curioso

inroads /ˈɪnrəʊdz/ pl n: **we are making ~ into the Japanese market** estamos haciendo avances en el mercado japonés; **this made substantial ~ into her savings** esto le comió buena parte de los ahorros

INS n (in US) = **Immigration and Naturalization Service**

insane /ɪnˈseɪn/ adj (mad) demente; (foolish) insensato

insanitary /ɪnˈsænətəri ‖ɪnˈsænɪtəri/ adj malsano, insanitario

insanity /ɪnˈsænəti/ n demencia f

insatiable /ɪnˈseɪʃəbəl/ adj insaciable

inscribe /ɪnˈskraɪb/ vt **to ~ sth** (ON sth) ‹letters› inscribir* algo (EN algo); ‹design› grabar algo (EN algo)

inscription /ɪnˈskrɪpʃən/ n inscripción f

insect /ˈɪnsekt/ n insecto m

insecticide /ɪnˈsektəsaɪd ‖ɪnˈsektɪsaɪd/ n insecticida m

insecure /ˌɪnsɪˈkjʊr ‖ˌɪnsɪˈkjʊə(r)/ adj **(a)** (unsafe, exposed) inseguro **(b)** (not firmly fixed) poco seguro **(c)** (not confident) inseguro

insecurity /ˌɪnsɪˈkjʊrəti ‖ˌɪnsɪˈkjʊərəti/ n (pl **-ties**) inseguridad f

insemination /ɪnˌseməˈneɪʃən ‖ɪnˌsemɪˈneɪʃən/ n inseminación f

insensible /ɪnˈsensəbəl/ adj (frml) **(a)** (unconscious) inconsciente **(b)** (without sensation) insensible

insensitive /ɪnˈsensətɪv/ adj ‹person› insensible; ‹behavior› falto de sensibilidad

insensitivity /ɪnˌsensəˈtɪvəti/ n falta f de sensibilidad

inseparable /ɪnˈseprəbəl/ adj inseparable

insert /ɪnˈsɜːrt ‖ɪnˈsɜːt/ vt ‹coin/token› introducir*; ‹zipper› poner*; ‹word/paragraph› insertar

insertion /ɪnˈsɜːrʃən ‖ɪnˈsɜːʃən/ n introducción f

inshore¹ /ˈɪnˈʃɔːr ‖ˌɪnˈʃɔː(r)/ adj costero

inshore² adv hacia la costa

inside¹ /ˈɪnˈsaɪd/ n **1** (interior part) interior m; (inner side, surface) parte f de dentro or (esp AmL) de adentro **2** **insides** pl (internal organs) (colloq) tripas fpl (fam); **~ out** adv: **turn it ~ out** ponlo de adentro para fuera; **you've got your socks on ~ out** llevas los calcetines del or al revés

inside² prep **(a)** (within) dentro de; **we did the journey ~ 3 hours** (colloq) hicimos el viaje en menos de 3 horas **(b)** (into): **he followed her ~ the bar** la siguió al interior del bar

inside³ adv **(a)** (within, indoors) dentro, adentro (esp AmL); **come ~** entra, pasa **(b)** (in prison) (colloq) entre rejas (fam), a la sombra (fam)

inside⁴ adj (before n) **(a)** ‹pages› interior; ‹pocket› interior, de adentro (esp AmL) **(b)** the **~ lane** (Auto) el carril de la derecha; (in UK etc) el carril de la izquierda; (Sport) el carril (AmL) or (Esp) la calle número uno **(c)** (from within group) ‹information› de dentro, de adentro (esp AmL)

insider /ɪnˈsaɪdər ‖ɪnˈsaɪdə(r)/ n: persona que pertenece a una organización determinada o que tiene acceso a información confidencial

insidious /ɪnˈsɪdiəs/ adj insidioso

insight /ˈɪnsaɪt/ n **(a)** (perceptiveness) perspicacia f **(b)** (comprehension): **to gain an ~ into sth** llegar* a comprender bien algo

insignia /ɪnˈsɪɡniə/ n (pl **~** or **~s**) insignia f

insignificant /ˌɪnsɪɡˈnɪfɪkənt/ adj ‹person/ amount› insignificante; ‹detail› nimio

insincere /ˌɪnsɪnˈsɪr ‖ˌɪnsɪnˈsɪə(r)/ adj ‹offer› poco sincero; ‹person/smile› falso

insincerity /ˌɪnsɪnˈserəti/ n falta f de sinceridad

insinuate /ɪnˈsɪnjueɪt/ vt insinuar*

insinuation /ɪnˌsɪnjuˈeɪʃən/ n insinuación f

insipid /ɪnˈsɪpəd ‖ɪnˈsɪpɪd/ adj ‹food/drink› insípido; ‹person/novel› insulso

insist /ɪnˈsɪst/ vt **(a)** (demand) **to ~ (THAT)** insistir EN QUE (+ subj) **(b)** (maintain) **to ~ (THAT)** insistir EN QUE
■ **~** vi insistir
■ **insist on** [v + prep + o] **to ~ on -ING** insistir EN + INF/EN QUE (+ subj)

insistence /ɪnˈsɪstəns/ n insistencia f

insistent /ɪnˈsɪstənt/ adj (a) (persistent) insistente; **to be ~ THAT** insistir EN QUE (b) (pressing) ⟨need⟩ apremiante

insofar as /ˌɪnsəˈfɑːr ‖ ˌɪnsəˈfɑː(r)/ conj (frml) en la medida en que

insole /ˈɪnsəʊl/ n plantilla f

insolence /ˈɪnsələns/ n insolencia f

insolent /ˈɪnsələnt/ adj insolente

insolvent /ɪnˈsɑːlvənt ‖ ɪnˈsɒlvənt/ adj insolvente

insomnia /ɪnˈsɑːmniə ‖ ɪnˈsɒmniə/ n insomnio m

insomniac /ɪnˈsɑːmniæk ‖ ɪnˈsɒmniæk/ n insomne mf

inspect /ɪnˈspekt/ vt (a) (look closely at) ⟨car/camera⟩ revisar, examinar; (examine officially) ⟨school/restaurant/equipment⟩ inspeccionar (b) ⟨troops⟩ pasar revista a

inspection /ɪnˈspekʃən/ n (a) (official examination) inspección f (b) (of troops) revista f (c) (scrutiny) examen m, revisión f

inspector /ɪnˈspektər ‖ ɪnˈspektə(r)/ n (a) (official) inspector, -tora m,f (b) (police officer) inspector, -tora m,f (de policía)

inspiration /ˈɪnspəˈreɪʃən/ n inspiración f

inspire /ɪnˈspaɪr ‖ ɪnˈspaɪə(r)/ vt inspirar; ⟨hope/courage⟩ infundir; **what ~d you to do that?** ¿qué te movió or te llevó a hacer eso?

inspired /ɪnˈspaɪrd ‖ ɪnˈspaɪəd/ adj inspirado

inspiring /ɪnˈspaɪrɪŋ ‖ ɪnˈspaɪərɪŋ/ adj inspirador

instability /ˈɪnstəˈbɪləti/ n inestabilidad f

install, instal /ɪnˈstɔːl/ vt -ll- instalar

installation /ˈɪnstəˈleɪʃən/ n instalación f

installment, (BrE) instalment /ɪnˈstɔːlmənt/ n [1] (payment) plazo m, cuota f (esp AmL); **to pay in** o **by ~s** pagar* a plazos, pagar* en cuotas (esp AmL) [2] (of publication) entrega f; (of TV, radio serial) episodio m

installment plan n (AmE) plan m de financiación; **to buy sth on an ~** comprar algo a plazos, comprar algo en cuotas (esp AmL)

instance /ˈɪnstəns/ n (a) (example) ejemplo m; **for ~** por ejemplo (b) (case) caso m; **in this ~** en este caso

instant¹ /ˈɪnstənt/ adj instantáneo

instant² n (a) (precise moment) instante m (b) (short time) momento m

instantaneous /ˈɪnstənˈteɪniəs/ adj instantáneo

instantly /ˈɪnstəntli/ adv al instante

instant replay n repetición f (de la jugada)

instead /ɪnˈsted/ adv: **I couldn't go, so she went ~** no pude ir, así que fue ella (en vez de mí); **~ of** (as prep) en vez de, en lugar de

instep /ˈɪnstep/ n (of foot — arch) arco m (del pie); (— upper surface) empeine m

instigate /ˈɪnstəgeɪt ‖ ˈɪnstɪgeɪt/ vt ⟨rebellion/mutiny⟩ instigar* a

instigation /ˈɪnstəˈgeɪʃən ‖ ˌɪnstɪˈgeɪʃən/ n instigación f; **it was carried out at the director's ~** se llevó a cabo a instancias del director

instill, instil /ɪnˈstɪl/ vt -ll-: **to ~ sth IN/INTO sb** ⟨habit/attitude⟩ inculcarle* algo A algn; ⟨courage/fear⟩ infundirle algo A algn

instinct /ˈɪnstɪŋkt/ n instinto m

instinctive /ɪnˈstɪŋktɪv/ adj instintivo

institute¹ /ˈɪnstətuːt ‖ ˈɪnstɪtjuːt/ vt (frml) ⟨search/inquiry⟩ iniciar; ⟨proceedings⟩ entablar

institute² n instituto m

institution /ˈɪnstəˈtuːʃən ‖ ˌɪnstɪˈtjuːʃən/ n [1] (established practice) institución f [2] (a) (organization) organismo m; (building) institución f (b) (hospital, asylum, home) establecimiento sanitario, penitenciario o de asistencia social

institutional /ˈɪnstəˈtuːʃnəl ‖ ˌɪnstɪˈtjuːʃn̩l/ adj institucional

instruct /ɪnˈstrʌkt/ vt [1] (command) **to ~ sb to + INF** ordenar a algn QUE (+ subj) [2] (frml) (teach) **to ~ sb IN sth** enseñarle algo a algn

instruction /ɪnˈstrʌkʃən/ n instrucción f; **ⓢ instructions (for use)** instrucciones; **they were acting on the ~s of the chief of police** cumplían órdenes del jefe de policía

instructive /ɪnˈstrʌktɪv/ adj instructivo

instructor /ɪnˈstrʌktər ‖ ɪnˈstrʌktə(r)/ n (a) (teacher) (Mil) instructor, -tora m,f (b) (in US colleges) profesor, -sora m,f auxiliar

instrument /ˈɪnstrəmənt ‖ ˈɪnstrʊmənt/ n [1] (musical ~) instrumento m (musical) [2] (a) (piece of equipment) instrumento m (b)

instruments pl n (Aviat) instrumentos mpl; (Auto) instrumentación f

instrumental /ˈɪnstrəˈmentl ‖ ˌɪnstrʊˈmentl/ adj [1] (serving as a means) **to be ~ IN sth** jugar* un papel decisivo EN algo [2] (Mus) instrumental

instrument panel n (Auto) tablero m de mandos, salpicadero m (Esp); (Aviat) tablero m de mandos

insubordination /ˈɪnsəˈbɔːrdn̩ˈeɪʃən ‖ ˌɪnsəbɔːˈdɪˈneɪʃən/ n insubordinación f

insubstantial /ˈɪnsəbˈstænʃəl ‖ ˌɪnsəbˈstænʃəl/ adj ⟨structure/object⟩ frágil; ⟨evidence/argument⟩ inconsistente

insufferable /ɪnˈsʌfrəbəl/ adj (frml) ⟨person/rudeness⟩ insufrible; ⟨heat/noise⟩ insoportable

insufficient /ˈɪnsəˈfɪʃənt/ adj insuficiente

insular /ˈɪnsələr ‖ ˈɪnsjʊlə(r)/ adj ⟨mentality⟩ cerrado; ⟨person⟩ estrecho de miras

insulate /ˈɪnsəleɪt ‖ ˈɪnsjʊleɪt/ vt aislar*

insulation /ˈɪnsəˈleɪʃən ‖ ˌɪnsjʊˈleɪʃən/ n aislamiento m

insulin /ˈɪnsələn ‖ ˈɪnsjʊlɪn/ n insulina f

insult¹ /ɪnˈsʌlt/ vt insultar

insult² /ˈɪnsʌlt/ n insulto m

insulting /ɪnˈsʌltɪŋ/ adj insultante

insurance /ɪnˈʃʊrəns ‖ ɪnˈʃʊərəns, ɪnˈʃɔːrəns/ n seguro m; **to take out ~** hacerse* un seguro; (before n) **~ company** compañía f de seguros

insure /ɪnˈʃʊr ‖ ɪnˈʃʊə(r), ɪnˈʃɔː(r)/ vt [1] (Fin) asegurar [2] (AmE) ▶ ENSURE

insurer /ɪnˈʃʊrər ‖ ɪnˈʃʊərə(r), ɪnˈʃɔːrə(r)/ n (company) compañía f de seguros; (person) asegurador, -dora m,f

insurgent /ɪnˈsɜːrdʒənt ‖ ɪnˈsɜːdʒənt/ adj (frml) insurgente (frml)

insurmountable /ˈɪnsərˈmaʊntəbəl ‖ ˌɪnsəˈmaʊntəbəl/ adj (frml) ⟨difficulty⟩ insalvable

insurrection /ˈɪnsəˈrekʃən/ n (frml) insurrección f (frml)

intact /ɪn'tækt/ adj ‹usu pred› intacto

intake /'ɪnteɪk/ n **1** (of water, air) entrada f; (of calories, protein) consumo m **2** (Tech) (pipe, vent) toma f (de aire, agua etc)

intangible /ɪn'tændʒəbəl/ adj intangible

integral /'ɪntɪɡrəl/ adj ‹part/feature› integral

integrate /'ɪntəɡreɪt ‖ 'ɪntɪɡreɪt/ vt integrar
■ ~ vi integrarse

integrated /'ɪntəɡreɪtəd ‖ 'ɪntɪɡreɪtɪd/ adj **(a)** ‹system/network› integrado **(b)** (not separate) ‹component/feature› incorporado **(c)** (nonsegregated) no segregacionista

integration /ɪntə'ɡreɪʃən ‖ ɪntɪ'ɡreɪʃən/ n integración f

integrity /ɪn'teɡrəti/ n integridad f

intellect /'ɪntlekt ‖ 'ɪntəlekt/ n intelecto m

intellectual¹ /ɪntə'lektʃuəl/ adj intelectual

intellectual² n intelectual mf

intelligence /ɪn'telədʒəns ‖ ɪn'telɪdʒəns/ n **1** (mental capacity) inteligencia f **2** (Govt, Mil) **(a)** (information) inteligencia f **(b)** (department) servicio m de información

intelligent /ɪn'telədʒənt ‖ ɪn'telɪdʒənt/ adj inteligente

intelligible /ɪn'telədʒəbəl ‖ ɪn'telɪdʒəbəl/ adj inteligible

intemperate /ɪn'tempərət/ adj ‹climate› inclemente, riguroso

intend /ɪn'tend/ vt: no insult was ~ed no fue mi intención ofender; to ~ -ING o to ~ to + INF pensar* + INF; to ~ sb/sth to + INF querer* QUE algn/algo (+ subj)

intense /ɪn'tens/ adj intenso

intensely /ɪn'tensli/ adv ‹as intensifier› ‹moving› profundamente, sumamente; I dislike him ~ siento una profunda antipatía hacia él

intensify /ɪn'tensəfaɪ ‖ ɪn'tensɪfaɪ/ **-fies, -fying, -fied** vt ‹search› intensificar*; ‹efforts› redoblar
■ ~ vi ‹pain› agudizarse*; ‹search› intensificarse*; ‹fighting› recrudecer*

intensity /ɪn'tensəti/ n intensidad f

intensive /ɪn'tensɪv/ adj intensivo

intensive care n cuidados mpl intensivos, terapia f intensiva (Méx, RPl)

intent¹ /ɪn'tent/ adj **(a)** (determined) ‹pred› to be ~ ON sth/-ING estar* decidido or resuelto A + INF **(b)** (attentive, concentrated) ‹expression› de viva atención; ‹look› penetrante, fijo; to be ~ ON sth estar* abstraído EN algo

intent² n propósito m; to all ~s and purposes a efectos prácticos

intention /ɪn'tentʃən ‖ ɪn'tenʃən/ n intención f, I have every ~ of going tengo la firme intención de ir

intentional /ɪn'tentʃnəl ‖ ɪn'tenʃənl/ adj ‹destruction› intencional; ‹insult/cruelty› deliberado

intently /ɪn'tentli/ adv ‹listen› atentamente; he was staring ~ at them tenía la mirada fija en ellos

inter /ɪn'tɜːr ‖ ɪn'tɜː(r)/ vt **-rr-** (frml or liter) inhumar (frml)

interact /ɪntər'ækt/ vi ‹people/organizations› relacionarse

interaction /ɪntər'ækʃən/ n interacción f

interactive /ɪntər'æktɪv/ adj interactivo

intercede /ɪntər'siːd ‖ ɪntə'siːd/ vi interceder

intercept /'ɪntərsept ‖ ɪntə'sept/ vt interceptar; they were ~ed before they reached the building les cerraron el paso antes de llegar al edificio

interchange¹ /'ɪntərtʃeɪndʒ ‖ ɪntə'tʃeɪndʒ/ vt intercambiar

interchange² /'ɪntərtʃeɪndʒ ‖ 'ɪntətʃeɪndʒ/ n **1** (exchange) intercambio m **2** (on road system) enlace m, intercambiador m (Esp)

interchangeable /ɪntər'tʃeɪndʒəbəl ‖ ɪntə'tʃeɪndʒəbəl/ adj intercambiable

intercity /'ɪntərsɪti ‖ ɪntə'sɪti/ adj rápido interurbano

intercom /'ɪntərkɑːm ‖ 'ɪntəkɒm/ n **(a)** (on plane, ship, in office) interfono m **(b)** (at building entrance) (AmE) portero m eléctrico or (Esp) automático, interfón m (Méx), intercomunicador m (Ven)

intercourse /'ɪntərkɔːrs ‖ 'ɪntəkɔːs/ n (sexual ~) coito m (frml), acto m sexual; to have ~ with sb tener* relaciones sexuales con algn

interest¹ /'ɪntrəst/ n **1 (a)** (enthusiasm) interés m; to take (an) ~ in sth/sb interesarse POR algo/algn **(b)** (hobby) interés m **2 (a)** (stake) participación f; he has a number of business ~s abroad tiene varios negocios en el extranjero **(b)** (advantage) ‹often pl› interés m; it was not in our ~(s) to intervene no nos convenía intervenir **3** (Fin) interés m; ‹before n› ~ rate tasa f or (esp Esp) tipo m de interés

interest² vt interesar

interested /'ɪntrəstəd ‖ 'ɪntrəstɪd/ adj interesado; I am ~ in astronomy me interesa la astronomía; ~ party parte f interesada

interesting /'ɪntrəstɪŋ/ adj interesante

interface /'ɪntərfeɪs ‖ 'ɪntəfeɪs/ n (Comput) interface f or m, interfaz f or m, interfase f or m

interfere /ɪntər'fɪr ‖ ɪntə'fɪə(r)/ vi **1** (get involved) to ~ (IN sth) entrometerse (EN algo) **2 (a)** (disrupt) to ~ WITH sth afectar (A) algo **(b)** (tamper) to ~ WITH sth tocar* algo

interference /ɪntər'fɪrəns ‖ ɪntə'fɪərəns/ n **(a)** (meddling) intromisión f **(b)** (Phys, Rad, Telec) interferencia f

interfering /ɪntər'fɪrɪŋ ‖ ɪntə'fɪərɪŋ/ adj entrometido

interim¹ /'ɪntərəm ‖ 'ɪntərɪm/ adj ‹before n› ‹measure› provisional, provisorio (AmS); an ~ period un período intermedio

interim² n: in o during the ~ en el interín or interin

interior¹ /ɪn'tɪriər ‖ ɪn'tɪəriə(r)/ n **1 (a)** (of building) interior m **(b)** (Cin) interior m **2 (a)** (Geog) the ~ el interior **(b)** (Govt) the Ministry/ Department of the I~ el Ministerio/Departamento del Interior

interior² adj **1 (a)** (inside) ‹walls› interior **(b)** (mental) interior **2** (inland) del interior

interior: ~ **decorator** n (painter) pintor, -tora m,f; (designer) interiorista mf, decorador, -dora m,f (de interiores); ~ **design** n interiorismo m

interjection /ɪntər'dʒekʃən ‖ ɪntə'dʒekʃən/ n (Ling) interjección f; (exclamation) exclamación f

interloper /'ɪntərləʊpər ‖'ɪntələʊpə(r)/ n
intruso, -sa m,f

interlude /'ɪntərluːd ‖'ɪntəluːd/ n **1** (intervening
period) intervalo m **2** **(a)** (Theat) (intermission)
entreacto m **(b)** (Mus) interludio m

intermediary /'ɪntər'miːdiəri ‖,ɪntə'miːdiəri/
n (pl **-ries**) (fml) intermediario, -ria m,f

intermediate /'ɪntər'miːdiət ‖,ɪntə'miːdiət/
adj ‹stage/step› intermedio; ‹size/weight/level›
medio; ‹course› de nivel medio or intermedio

intermediate school n (in US) **(a)**
(secondary) escuela donde se cursa el primer ciclo
de la enseñanza secundaria **(b)** (primary) escuela
donde se cursa segundo ciclo de la enseñanza
primaria

interminable /ɪn'tɜːrmənəbəl ‖ɪn'tɜːmɪnəbəl/
adj interminable

intermission /'ɪntər'mɪʃən ‖,ɪntə'mɪʃən/ n
intermedio m

intermittent /'ɪntər'mɪtn̩t ‖,ɪntə'mɪtənt/ adj
intermitente

intern¹ /ɪn'tɜːrn ‖ɪn'tɜːn/ vt recluir*, confinar

intern² /'ɪntɜːrn ‖'ɪntɜːn/ n (AmE) **(a)** (Med)
interno, -na m,f **(b)** (Educ) profesor, -sora m,f en
prácticas

internal /ɪn'tɜːrn̩l ‖ɪn'tɜːn̩l/ adj interno

Internal Revenue Service n (in US) the
~ ~ ~ ≈ Hacienda, ≈ la Dirección General
Impositiva (en RPl), ≈ Impuestos Internos (en
Chi)

international¹ /'ɪntər'næʃnəl ‖,ɪntə'næʃənl̩/
adj internacional

international² n (Sport) **(a)** (event) partido m
internacional **(b)** (player) internacional mf

internationally /'ɪntər'næʃnəli
‖,ɪntə'næʃnəli/ adv ‹expand/trade›
internacionalmente **(b)** ‹famous/known›
mundialmente

International Monetary Fund n the ~
~ ~ el Fondo Monetario Internacional

Internet /'ɪntərnet ‖'ɪntənet/ n the ~ el
Internet

Internet service provider /prə'vaɪdər
‖prə'vaɪdə(r)/ n proveedor m de servicios
Internet

internment /ɪn'tɜːrnmənt ‖ɪn'tɜːnmənt/ n
internamiento m

interpret /ɪn'tɜːrprət ‖ɪn'tɜːprɪt/ vt interpretar
■ ~ vi (Ling) (translate) traducir* ‹oralmente›,
interpretar

interpretation /ɪn'tɜːrprə'teɪʃən
‖ɪn,tɜːprɪ'teɪʃən/ n interpretación f

interpreter /ɪn'tɜːrprətər ‖ɪn'tɜːprɪtə(r)/ n
intérprete mf

interrogate /ɪn'terəgeɪt/ vt interrogar*

interrogation /ɪn'terə'geɪʃən/ n
interrogatorio m

interrogation point n (AmE frml) signo m de
interrogación

interrogative /'ɪntə'rɑːgətɪv ‖,ɪntə'rɒgətɪv/
adj interrogativo

interrupt /'ɪntə'rʌpt/ vt/i interrumpir

interruption /'ɪntə'rʌpʃən/ n interrupción f

intersect /'ɪntər'sekt ‖,ɪntə'sekt/ vi «roads/
paths» cruzarse*

intersection /'ɪntər'sekʃən ‖,ɪntə'sekʃən/ n
(a) (Transp) cruce m **(b)** (Geog, Math) intersección f

intersperse /'ɪntər'spɜːrs ‖,ɪntə'spɜːs/ vt
intercalar

interstate (highway) /'ɪntərsteɪt
‖'ɪntəsteɪt/ n (AmE) carretera f interestatal

intertwine /'ɪntər'twaɪn ‖,ɪntə'twaɪn/ vi
«fingers/plants» entrelazarse*; «paths/
destinies» entrecruzarse*
■ ~ vt ‹fingers› entrelazar*

interval /'ɪntərvəl ‖'ɪntəvəl/ n **1** (time, distance)
intervalo m **2** (pause) (BrE Cin, Mus) intermedio
m; (BrE Theat) entreacto m; (Sport) descanso m,
entretiempo m (Chi) **3** (Mus) intervalo m

intervene /'ɪntər'viːn ‖,ɪntə'viːn/ vi **(a)**
(interpose oneself) intervenir* **(b)** **intervening**
pres p: in the intervening period en el interín or
ínterin

intervention /'ɪntər'ventʃən ‖,ɪntə'venʃən/ n
intervención f

interview¹ /'ɪntərvjuː ‖'ɪntəvjuː/ n entrevista
f

interview² vt entrevistar

interviewee /'ɪntərvjuː'iː ‖,ɪntəvjuː'iː/ n
entrevistado, -da m,f

interviewer /'ɪntərvjuːər ‖'ɪntəvjuːə(r)/ n
entrevistador, -dora m,f

interweave /'ɪntər'wiːv ‖,ɪntə'wiːv/ vt (past
-wove or **-weaved**; past p **-woven** or
-weaved) entretejer; their lives were interwoven
sus vidas estaban inextricablemente unidas

intestate /ɪn'testeɪt/ adj intestado

intestine /ɪn'testən ‖ɪn'testɪn/ n (often pl)
intestino m; the small/large ~ el intestino
delgado/grueso

intimacy /'ɪntəməsi ‖'ɪntɪməsi/ n intimidad f

intimate /'ɪntəmət ‖'ɪntɪmət/ adj ‹friend/
atmosphere› íntimo; ‹talk› de carácter íntimo;
‹knowledge› profundo; to be on ~ terms with sb
ser* íntimo de algn

intimation /'ɪntə'meɪʃən ‖,ɪntɪ'meɪʃən/ n (sign)
indicio m; (inkling) presentimiento m

intimidate /ɪn'tɪmədeɪt ‖ɪn'tɪmɪdeɪt/ vt
intimidar

intimidating /ɪn'tɪmədeɪtɪŋ ‖ɪn'tɪmɪdeɪtɪŋ/
adj intimidante

intimidation /ɪn'tɪmə'deɪʃən ‖ɪn,tɪmɪ'deɪʃən/
n intimidación f

into /'ɪntu, before consonant 'ɪntə/ prep **1** **(a)**
(indicating motion, direction): to walk ~ a building
entrar en or (esp AmL) a un edificio; they helped
him ~ the chair lo ayudaron a sentarse en el
sillón; she sat staring ~ space estaba sentada
mirando al vacío; to translate sth ~ Spanish
traducir* algo al español **(b)** (against): she walked
~ a tree se dio contra un árbol; he drove ~ the
other car chocó con el otro coche
2 (in time, distance): ten minutes ~ the game a los
diez minutos de empezar el partido; they
penetrated deep ~ the jungle entraron en el
corazón de la selva
3 (indicating result of action): we split ~ two groups
nos dividimos en dos grupos; roll the dough ~ a
ball hacer una bola con la masa
4 (involved in) (colloq) they're ~ drugs se drogan;
at two, children are ~ everything a los dos años,
los niños son muy inquietos

intolerable /ɪnˈtɑːlərəbəl ‖ ɪnˈtɒlərəbəl/ *adj*
intolerable

intolerance /ɪnˈtɑːlərəns ‖ ɪnˈtɒlərəns/ *n*
intolerancia *f*

intolerant /ɪnˈtɑːlərənt ‖ ɪnˈtɒlərənt/ *adj*
intolerante

intonation /ˌɪntəˈneɪʃən/ *n* entonación *f*

intone /ɪnˈtəʊn/ *vt* ⟨*psalm/Gloria*⟩ entonar

intoxicated /ɪnˈtɑːksəkeɪtəd ‖ ɪnˈtɒksɪkeɪtɪd/
adj (frml) en estado de embriaguez (frml)

intoxicating /ɪnˈtɑːksəkeɪtɪŋ ‖ ɪnˈtɒksɪkeɪtɪŋ/
adj (frml) ⟨*substance*⟩ estupefaciente; ~ **liquor**
bebida *f* alcohólica

intractable /ɪnˈtræktəbəl/ *adj* (frml) (a)
⟨*temperament*⟩ obstinado; ⟨*child*⟩ incorregible (b)
⟨*problem/dilemma*⟩ inextricable (frml)

intransigent /ɪnˈtrænsədʒənt
‖ ɪnˈtrænsɪdʒənt/ *adj* intransigente

intransitive /ɪnˈtrænsətɪv/ *adj* intransitivo

intrauterine device /ˌɪntrəˈjuːtərən
‖ ˌɪntrəˈjuːtəram/ *n* dispositivo *m* intrauterino; (in
the shape of a coil) espiral *f*

intravenous /ˌɪntrəˈviːnəs/ *adj* intravenoso

intrepid /ɪnˈtrepəd ‖ ɪnˈtrepɪd/ *adj* intrépido

intricacy /ˈɪntrɪkəsi/ *n* (a) (of pattern, embroidery)
lo intrincado (b) **intricacies** *pl* (complexities)
complejidades *fpl*

intricate /ˈɪntrɪkət/ *adj* complicado

intrigue¹ /ˈɪntriːg/ *n* intriga *f*

intrigue² /ɪnˈtriːg/ *vt* intrigar*

intriguing /ɪnˈtriːgɪŋ/ *adj* ⟨*problem/text*⟩
intrigante; ⟨*possibility*⟩ fascinante; ⟨*person*⟩
interesante

intrinsic /ɪnˈtrɪnzɪk/ *adj* intrínseco

introduce /ˈɪntrəˈduːs ‖ ˌɪntrəˈdjuːs/ *vt* **1** (a)
(acquaint) presentar; **allow me to** ~ **myself/my
mother** (frml) permítame que me presente/le
presente a mi madre; **to** ~ **sb TO sb** presentarle a
algn A algn (b) (initiate) **to** ~ **sb TO sth**
introducir* a algo, iniciar a algn EN algo
(c) (present) ⟨*speaker/program*⟩ presentar;
⟨*meeting/article*⟩ iniciar **2** (bring in) ⟨*subject/
custom/legislation*⟩ introducir*; ⟨*product*⟩ lanzar*,
sacar*

introduction /ˌɪntrəˈdʌkʃən/ *n* **1** (a) (to
person) presentación *f* (b) (to activity, experience) ~
TO sth introducción *f* A algo (c) (of speaker,
performer) presentación *f* **2** (of species, practice,
legislation) introducción *f* **3** (insertion, entry) (frml)
introducción *f* **4** (a) (to meeting, lecture)
presentación *f* (b) (in book) introducción *f* (c)
(Mus) introducción *f* **5** (elementary instruction)
introducción *f*, iniciación *f*

introductory /ˌɪntrəˈdʌktəri/ *adj* (a) (opening)
⟨*notes/remarks*⟩ preliminar; ⟨*lecture/chapter*⟩ de
introducción; ⟨*offer*⟩ (Busn) de lanzamiento (b)
(elementary) ⟨*course/lesson*⟩ de introducción

introspective /ˌɪntrəˈspektɪv/ *adj*
introspectivo

introvert /ˈɪntrəvɜːrt ‖ ˈɪntrəvɜːt/ *n*
introvertido, -da *m,f*

introverted /ˈɪntrəvɜːrtəd ‖ ˈɪntrəvɜːtɪd/ *adj*
introvertido

intrude /ɪnˈtruːd/ *vi* (disturb) importunar;
(interfere) inmiscuirse*; **to** ~ **on sb's privacy**
inmiscuirse* en la vida privada de algn

intruder /ɪnˈtruːdər ‖ ɪnˈtruːdə(r)/ *n* intruso, -sa
m,f

intrusion /ɪnˈtruːʒən/ *n* intrusión *f*

intrusive /ɪnˈtruːsɪv/ *adj* (a) ⟨*noise/smell*⟩
molesto (b) ⟨*questioning/reporter*⟩ impertinente

intuition /ˌɪntuˈɪʃən ‖ ˌɪntjuˈɪʃən/ *n* intuición *f*

intuitive /ɪnˈtuːətɪv ‖ ɪnˈtjuːɪtɪv/ *adj* intuitivo

Inuit /ˈɪnuːɪt ‖ ˈɪnjuːɪt/ *n* (*pl* ~ *or* ~**s**) (a)
(person) esquimal *mf* (b) (Ling) esquimal *m*

inundate /ˈɪnʌndeɪt/ *vt* inundar

invade /ɪnˈveɪd/ *vt/i* invadir

invader /ɪnˈveɪdər ‖ ɪnˈveɪdə(r)/ *n* invasor,
-sora *m,f*

invalid¹ /ɪnˈvæləd ‖ ɪnˈvælɪd/ *adj* inválido

invalid² /ˈɪnvəlɪd ‖ ˈɪnvəliːd, ˈɪnvəlɪd/ *n*
inválido, -da *m,f*

invalidate /ɪnˈvælədeɪt ‖ ɪnˈvælɪdeɪt/ *vt* (frml)
invalidar

invalidity /ˌɪnvəˈlɪdəti/ *n* (frml) invalidez *f*

invaluable /ɪnˈvæljuəbəl/ *adj* inapreciable,
invalorable (AmL)

invariable /ɪnˈveriəbəl ‖ ɪnˈveəriəbəl/ *adj*
invariable

invariably /ɪnˈveriəbli ‖ ɪnˈveəriəbli/ *adv*
invariablemente, siempre

invasion /ɪnˈveɪʒən/ *n* invasión *f*

invective /ɪnˈvektɪv/ *n* (a) (abuse) invectivas
fpl (frml) (b) (condemnation) invectiva *f* (frml)

invent /ɪnˈvent/ *vt* inventar

invention /ɪnˈventʃən ‖ ɪnˈvenʃən/ *n* **1** (a)
(device) invento *m* (b) (action) invención *f*
2 (imagination): (**powers of**) ~ inventiva *f*

inventive /ɪnˈventɪv/ *adj* ingenioso

inventor /ɪnˈventər ‖ ɪnˈventə(r)/ *n* inventor,
-tora *m,f*

inventory /ˈɪnvəntɔːri ‖ ˈɪnventri/ *n* (*pl* **-ries**)
inventario *m*

inverse /ˈɪnvɜːrs, ˈɪnvɜːrs ‖ ˌɪnˈvɜːs, ˈɪnvɜːs/ *adj*
(*usu before n*) inverso; **in** ~ **proportion to sth** en
proporción inversa a algo

inversion /ɪnˈvɜːrʒən ‖ ɪnˈvɜːʃən/ *n* inversión *f*

invert /ɪnˈvɜːrt ‖ ɪnˈvɜːt/ *vt* invertir*

invertebrate /ɪnˈvɜːrtəbrət ‖ ɪnˈvɜːtɪbrət/ *n*
invertebrado, -da *m,f*

inverted commas /ɪnˈvɜːrtəd ‖ ɪnˈvɜːtɪd/ *pl*
n (BrE) comillas *fpl*

invest /ɪnˈvest/ *vt* **to** ~ **sth** (**IN sth**) ⟨*money/
time*⟩ invertir* algo (EN algo)
■ ~ *vi* **to** ~ (**IN sth**) invertir* (EN algo)

investigate /ɪnˈvestəgeɪt ‖ ɪnˈvestɪgeɪt/ *vt* (a)
⟨*crime/cause*⟩ investigar*; ⟨*complaint/possibility*⟩
estudiar (b) (do research on) hacer* una
investigación sobre
■ ~ *vi* investigar*

investigation /ɪnˌvestəˈgeɪʃən ‖ ɪnˌvestɪˈgeɪʃən/ n **(a)** (detailed examination) estudio m **(b)** (official, scientific) investigación f

investigator /ɪnˈvestəgeɪtər ‖ ɪnˈvestɪgeɪtə(r)/ n **(a)** (private ∼) investigador privado, investigadora privada m,f **(b)** (official) inspector, -tora m,f

investiture /ɪnˈvestətʃʊr ‖ ɪnˈvestɪtʃə(r)/ n investidura f

investment /ɪnˈvestmənt/ n inversión f

investor /ɪnˈvestər ‖ ɪnˈvestə(r)/ n inversor, -sora m,f, inversionista mf

inveterate /ɪnˈvetərət/ adj (frml) (usu before n) ⟨thief/liar⟩ empedernido

invigorating /ɪnˈvɪgəreɪtɪŋ/ adj ⟨weather/walk⟩ vigorizante; ⟨environment/change⟩ estimulante

invisible /ɪnˈvɪzəbəl/ adj invisible

invitation /ˌɪnvəˈteɪʃən ‖ ˌɪnvɪˈteɪʃən/ n invitación f; **at the ∼ of** invitado por, por invitación de

invite /ɪnˈvaɪt/ vt to ∼ sb (TO sth)/to + INF invitar a algn (A algo)/A + INF or A QUE (+ subj); **to ∼ sb in/out** invitar a algn a pasar/a salir; **his work ∼s comparison with the classics** su obra sugiere comparación con los clásicos

inviting /ɪnˈvaɪtɪŋ/ adj ⟨prospect/offer⟩ atractivo

in vitro /ɪnˈviːtrəʊ/ adj in vitro adj inv

invoice¹ /ˈɪnvɔɪs/ n factura f

invoice² vt to ∼ sb (FOR sth) pasarle A algn factura (POR algo)

invoke /ɪnˈvəʊk/ vt invocar*

involuntary /ɪnˈvɑːlənteri ‖ ɪnˈvɒləntri/ adj involuntario

involve /ɪnˈvɑːlv ‖ ɪnˈvɒlv/ vt [1] **(a)** (entail, comprise) suponer*; **what exactly does your work ∼?** ¿en qué consiste exactamente tu trabajo? **(b)** (affect, concern): **where national security is ∼d …** cuando se trata de la seguridad nacional …; **it's my reputation that's ∼d here** es mi reputación lo que está en juego

[2] **to ∼ sb IN sth/-ING** (implicate) implicar* or involucrar EN algo; (allow to participate) darle* participación a algn EN algo

[3] **involved** past p **(a)** (implicated): **I was ∼d in an accident last year** el año pasado me vi envuelto en un accidente; **several high-ranking officials were ∼d in the affair** había varios oficiales de alto rango implicados en el asunto; **the people you're ∼d with** la gente con la que andas metido **(b) to be ∼d IN sth** (engrossed) estar* absorto EN algo; (busy) estar* ocupado CON algo **(c)** (emotionally): **she doesn't want to get too ∼d with him** no quiere llegar a una relación muy seria con él

involved /ɪnˈvɑːlvd ‖ ɪnˈvɒlvd/ adj enrevesado, complicado

involvement /ɪnˈvɑːlvmənt ‖ ɪnˈvɒlvmənt/ n **(a)** n (entanglement) participación f; **they deny any ∼ in terrorist attacks** niegan estar implicados en ningún ataque terrorista **(b)** (relationship) relación f (sentimental)

inward¹ /ˈɪnwərd ‖ ˈɪnwəd/ adj **(a)** (toward inside) ⟨curve⟩ hacia adentro **(b)** (private, mental) ⟨torment/serenity⟩ interior

inward², (BrE also) **inwards** adv **(a)** (toward inside) ⟨move/bend⟩ hacia adentro; ⟨travel⟩ hacia

el interior (b) (toward mind, spirit): **meditation involves looking ∼** la meditación exige introspección

iodine /ˈaɪədaɪn ‖ ˈaɪədiːn/ n yodo m

ion /ˈaɪən, ˈaɪɑːn ‖ ˈaɪən/ n ión m

iota /aɪˈəʊtə/ n (usu with neg) pizca f, ápice m

IOU n (= **I owe you**) pagaré m

IQ n (= **intelligence quotient**) CI m

IRA n (= **Irish Republican Army**) IRA m

Iran /ɪˈrɑːn, ɪˈræn/ n Irán m

Iranian¹ /ɪˈreɪniən/ adj iraní

Iranian² n iraní mf

Iraq /ɪˈrɑːk, ɪˈræk/ n Irak m

Iraqi¹ /ɪˈrɑːki, ɪˈræki/ adj iraquí

Iraqi² n iraquí mf

irascible /ɪˈræsəbəl/ adj irascible

irate /aɪˈreɪt/ adj airado

ire /aɪr ‖ ˈaɪə(r)/ n (liter) ira f, cólera f

Ireland /ˈaɪrlənd ‖ ˈaɪələnd/ n (the island) Irlanda f; (the Republic) Irlanda f, (el) Eire

iris /ˈaɪrəs ‖ ˈaɪərɪs/ n (Bot) lirio m

Irish¹ /ˈaɪrɪʃ ‖ ˈaɪərɪʃ/ adj irlandés; **the ∼ Sea** el Mar de Irlanda

Irish² n **(a)** (people) (+ pl vb) **the ∼** los irlandeses **(b)** (language) irlandés m

Irish: ∼man /ˈaɪrɪʃmən ‖ ˈaɪərɪʃmən/ n (pl **-men** /-mən/) irlandés m; **∼woman** n irlandesa f

irk /ɜːrk ‖ ɜːk/ vt fastidiar, irritar

iron¹ /ˈaɪərn ‖ ˈaɪən/ n [1] **(a)** (metal) hierro m, fierro m (AmL) **(b)** (in food) hierro m [2] (for clothes) plancha f [3] (golf club) hierro m [4] **irons** pl (fetters) grilletes mpl, grillos mpl

iron² adj **(a)** (made of iron) de hierro **(b)** (strong) ⟨before n⟩ ⟨constitution⟩ de hierro; ⟨will/resolve⟩ férreo, de hierro

iron³ vt/i planchar

■ **iron out** [v + o + adv, v + adv + o] ⟨problems⟩ resolver*; ⟨difficulties⟩ allanar

Iron Curtain n **the ∼ ∼** la cortina de hierro (AmL), el telón de acero (Esp)

ironic /aɪˈrɑːnɪk ‖ aɪˈrɒnɪk/ adj irónico

ironically /aɪˈrɑːnɪkli ‖ aɪˈrɒnɪkli/ adv irónicamente

ironing /ˈaɪərnɪŋ ‖ ˈaɪənɪŋ/ n **to do the ∼** planchar

ironing board n tabla f or (Méx) burro m de planchar

ironmonger /ˈaɪərnˌmɑːŋgər ‖ ˈaɪənˌmʌŋgə(r)/ n (BrE) ferretero, -ra m,f; **at the ∼'s** en la ferretería

irony /ˈaɪrəni/ n (pl **-nies**) ironía f

irrational /ɪˈræʃnəl ‖ ɪˈræʃənl/ adj irracional

irreconcilable /ɪˈrekənˌsaɪləbəl/ adj irreconciliable

irrefutable /ɪˈrefjətəbəl, ˌɪrɪˈfjuː- ‖ ˌɪrɪˈfjuːtəbəl/ adj irrefutable

irregular /ɪˈregjələr ‖ ɪˈregjʊlə(r)/ adj [1] (in shape, positioning, time) irregular [2] (contrary to rules) inadmisible, contrario a las normas [3] (Ling) irregular

irregularity /ɪˌregjəˈlærəti ‖ ɪˌregjʊˈlærəti/ n (pl **-ties**) [1] (in shape, positioning, time) ⋯⟶

irregularidad f [2] (of action) lo inadmisible; **several irregularities** varias contravenciones de las normas

irrelevant /ɪˈreləvənt/ adj ‹fact/detail›
irrelevante; **to be ~ to sth** no tener* relación or no tener* que ver CON algo

irreparable /ɪˈreprəbəl/ adj irreparable

irreplaceable /ɪrɪˈpleɪsəbəl/ adj irreemplazable

irrepressible /ɪrɪˈpresəbəl/ adj ‹laughter› incontenible; ‹desire› irreprimible

irresistible /ɪrɪˈzɪstəbəl/ adj irresistible

irrespective /ɪrɪˈspektɪv/ adv ~ OF sth: ~ of what you say independientemente de lo que usted diga; ~ of age or sex sin distinción de edad o sexo

irresponsible /ɪrɪˈspɒnsəbəl/ ‖ ɪrɪˈspɒnsəbəl/ adj irresponsable

irreverent /ɪˈrevrənt, ɪˈrevərənt/ adj irreverente

irreversible /ɪrɪˈvɜːrsəbəl ‖ ɪrɪˈvɜːsəbəl/ adj ‹decision› irrevocable; ‹process/event› irreversible

irrigate /ˈɪrəgeɪt ‖ ˈɪrɪgeɪt/ vt irrigar*, regar*

irrigation /ɪrəˈgeɪʃən ‖ ɪrɪˈgeɪʃən/ n irrigación f, riego m

irritable /ˈɪrətəbəl ‖ ˈɪrɪtəbəl/ adj
[1] (bad-tempered) ‹person/mood› irritable; ‹reply› irritado [2] (sensitive) ‹skin/scalp› sensible

irritant /ˈɪrətənt ‖ ˈɪrɪtənt/ n (a) (Med) agente m irritante (b) (person, thing) fastidio m

irritate /ˈɪrəteɪt ‖ ˈɪrɪteɪt/ vt irritar

irritated /ˈɪrəteɪtəd ‖ ˈɪrɪteɪtɪd/ adj [1] ‹look/ frown› de impaciencia; **to be ~ WITH sb/ WITH sth** estar* irritado POR algo/CON algn [2] ‹skin/hands› irritado

irritating /ˈɪrəteɪtɪŋ ‖ ˈɪrɪteɪtɪŋ/ adj irritante

irritation /ɪrəˈteɪʃən ‖ ɪrɪˈteɪʃən/ n irritación f

IRS n (in US) = **Internal Revenue Service**

is /ɪz/ 3rd pers sing pres of BE

ISBN n (= **International Standard Book Number**) ISBN m

-ish /ɪʃ/ suff: long~ más bien largo; green~ verdoso; tennish a eso de las diez

Islam /ˈɪzlɑːm, ɪzˈlɑːm/ n el Islam

Islamic /ɪzˈlæmɪk, ɪzˈlɑːmɪk/ adj islámico

island /ˈaɪlənd/ n isla f

islander /ˈaɪləndər ‖ ˈaɪləndə(r)/ n isleño, -ña m,f

isle /aɪl/ n (a) (poet) isla f, ínsula f (liter) (b) (in place names): **the I~ of Wight** la Isla de Wight

Isles of Scilly /ˈaɪlzəvˈsɪli/ pl n **the ~ ~ ~** las islas Scilly or Sorlingas

isn't /ˈɪznt/ = **is not**

isolate /ˈaɪsəleɪt/ vt aislar*

isolated /ˈaɪsəleɪtəd ‖ ˈaɪsəleɪtɪd/ adj aislado

isolation /aɪsəˈleɪʃən/ n aislamiento m

ISP n (= **Internet service provider**) ISP m

Israel /ˈɪzreɪəl/ n Israel m

Israeli¹ /ɪzˈreɪli/ adj israelí

Israeli² n israelí mf

issue¹ /ˈɪʃuː ‖ ˈɪʃuː, ɪsjuː/ n [1] (subject discussed) tema m, cuestión f, asunto m; **to take ~ with sb/ sth** discrepar de or con algn/en or de algo [2] (a) (of documents) expedición f; (of library books)

préstamo m; (of tickets) venta f (b) (of stamps, shares, bank notes) emisión f (c) (of newspaper, magazine) número m

issue² vt (give out) ‹statement/report› hacer* público; ‹instructions› dar*; ‹guidelines› establecer*; ‹tickets/visas› expedir*; ‹library books› prestar; ‹bank notes/stamps/shares› emitir; ‹summons› dictar; **we can ~ you with the necessary documents** le podemos proporcionar los documentos necesarios
■ ~ vi (fml) [1] (result) **to ~ FROM sth** derivar(se) DE algo (fml) [2] (emerge) salir*; «liquid» fluir*

it /ɪt/ pron [1] (replacing noun — as direct object) lo, la; (— as indirect object) le; (— as subject, after prep) gen not translated; **~'s enormous** es enorme; **there's nothing behind ~** no hay nada detrás [2] (introducing person, thing, event): **who is ~?** ¿quién es?; **~'s me** soy yo; **I'll see to ~** yo me encargo (de ello); **~'s his attitude that I don't like** su actitud es lo que no me gusta; **a little higher up ... that's ~!** un poco más arriba ... ¡ahí está! or ¡eso es!; **one more and that's ~** uno más y ya está or se acabó [3] (in impersonal constructions): **~'s raining** está lloviendo; **~'s two o'clock** son las dos; **~ says here that ...** aquí dice que ...; **~ is known that ...** se sabe que ...

Italian¹ /ɪˈtæljən/ adj italiano

Italian² n (a) (person) italiano, -na m,f (b) (language) italiano m

italics /ɪˈtælɪks/ pl n (letra f) cursiva f

Italy /ˈɪtli ‖ ˈɪtəli/ n Italia f

itch¹ /ɪtʃ/ vi [1] (a) ‹scalp/toe› picar* (+ me/te/ le etc) (b) (be impatient, eager) (colloq) **to be ~ing to + INF: he was ~ing to tell her** estaba que se moría por decírselo (fam) [2] «wool/underwear» picar* (cause irritation)

itch² n (a) (irritation) picor m, picazón f (b) (desire) ansia f‡

itchy /ˈɪtʃi/ adj **itchier, itchiest** (a) (feeling irritation): **I've got an ~ nose/scalp** me pica la nariz/la cabeza (b) (causing irritation) ‹garment/ material› que pica

it'd /ˈɪtəd/ (a) = **it had** (b) = **it would**

item /ˈaɪtəm/ n (a) (article) (Busn) artículo m; (in collection) pieza f; (on agenda) punto m: **~s of clothing** prendas fpl de vestir (b) (in newspaper) artículo m; **news ~** noticia f

itemize /ˈaɪtəmaɪz/ vt (break down) detallar; (list) hacer* una lista de

itinerant /aɪˈtɪnərənt/ adj (fml) ‹worker/judge› itinerante (fml); ‹salesman/musician› ambulante

itinerary /aɪˈtɪnəreri ‖ aɪˈtɪnərəri/ n (pl -ries) itinerario m

it'll /ˈɪtl/ = **it will**

its /ɪts/ adj (sing) su; (pl) sus
■ Note The translation su agrees in number with the noun which it modifies; its is translated by su, sus, depending on what follows: its snout/head su hocico/ cabeza; its problems/difficulties sus problemas/ dificultades

it's /ɪts/ (a) = **it is** (b) = **it has**

itself /ɪtˈself/ pron (a) (reflexive): **it has earned ~ a reputation** se ha hecho fama; **another problem**

presented ∼ se presentó otro problema **(b)** (emphatic use): **the town ∼ is small** la ciudad en sí *or* propiamente dicha es pequeña

ITV *n* (in UK) (*no art*) = **Independent Television**

IUD *n* (= **intrauterine device**) DIU *m*

I've /aɪv/ = **I have**

ivory /'aɪvəri/ *n* (*pl* **-ries**) **(a)** (material) marfil *m* **(b)** (color) (color *m*) marfil *m*

Ivory Coast *n* Costa *f* de Marfil

ivy /'aɪvi/ *n* hiedra *f*

Ivy League *n* (AmE) **the ∼ ∼** *grupo de ocho universidades prestigiosas de EEUU*

Jj

J, j /dʒeɪ/ *n* J, j *f*

jab¹ /dʒæb/ *vt* **-bb-**: **I ∼bed myself with the needle** me pinché con la aguja, me piqué con la aguja (Méx); **she ∼bed me with her fork** me clavó con el tenedor

jab² *n* **(a)** (prick) pinchazo *m*; (blow) golpe *m*; (with elbow) codazo *m* **(b)** (in boxing) jab *m*, corto *m* **(c)** (injection) (BrE colloq) inyección *f*

jabber /'dʒæbər ‖ 'dʒæbə(r)/ *vi/t* farfullar

jack /dʒæk/ *n* **(a)** (lifting device) gato *m* **(b)** (socket) enchufe *m* hembra **(c)** (in French pack of cards) jota *f*, valet *m*; (in Spanish pack) sota *f*
■ **jack up** [*v* + *o* + *adv*, *v* + *adv* + *o*] ‹*car*› levantar (*con el gato*)

jackal /'dʒækəl/ *n* chacal *m*

jackdaw /'dʒækdɔː/ *n* grajilla *f*

jacket /'dʒækət ‖ 'dʒækɪt/ *n* **1** (Clothing) chaqueta *f*; (sports ∼) americana *f*, saco *m* (sport) (AmL) **2** (of book) sobrecubierta *f*; (of record) (AmE) funda *f*, carátula *f* **3** (of potato) (BrE): **∼ potatoes** papas *fpl* asadas (*con la cáscara*) (AmL), patatas *fpl* asadas (*con la piel*) (Esp)

jack: ∼hammer *n* martillo *m* neumático; **∼-in-the-box** /'dʒækɪnðəˌbɒks ‖ 'dʒækɪnðəˌbɒks/ *n* caja *f* de sorpresas (*con muñeco a resorte*); **∼knife** *vi* ‹*truck*› plegarse*; **∼ of all trades** /'dʒækəvˌɔːltreɪdz/ *n* (*pl* **∼s of all trades**) hombre *m* or mujer *f* orquesta, manitas *mf* (Esp, Méx fam); **∼pot** *n* (in bingo, lottery) bote *m*, pozo *m*; **∼rabbit** *n*: *tipo de liebre de Norteamérica*

Jacuzzi®, jacuzzi /dʒə'kuːzi/ *n* Jacuzzi® *m*

jade /dʒeɪd/ *n* **(a)** (Min) jade *m* **(b)** (color) verde *m* jade

jaded /'dʒeɪdəd ‖ 'dʒeɪdɪd/ *adj* hastiado

jagged /'dʒægəd ‖ 'dʒægɪd/ *adj* ‹*edge/cut*› irregular; ‹*rock/cliff*› recortado, con picos

jaguar /'dʒægwɑːr ‖ 'dʒægjʊə(r)/ *n* jaguar *m*

jail¹ /dʒeɪl/ *n* cárcel *f*, prisión *f*; **he went to ∼** lo metieron preso

jail² *vt* encarcelar

jailer, jailor /'dʒeɪlər ‖ 'dʒeɪlə(r)/ *n* carcelero, -ra *m,f*

jailhouse /'dʒeɪlhaʊs/ *n* (AmE) cárcel *f*

jam¹ /dʒæm/ *n* **1** (Culin) mermelada *f*, dulce *m* (RPl) **2** (difficult situation) (colloq) aprieto *m*

jam² **-mm-** *vt* **1** **(a)** (cram) **to ∼ sth INTO sth** meter algo a la fuerza EN algo **(b)** (congest, block) ‹*road*› atestar; **the switchboard was ∼med with**

calls la centralita estaba saturada de llamadas **2** (wedge firmly): **he ∼med his foot in the door** metió el pie entre la puerta y el marco **3** (Rad) interferir*
■ **∼** *vi* ‹*brakes*› bloquearse; ‹*machine*› trancarse*; ‹*switch/lock*› trabarse; ‹*gun*› encasquillarse
■ **jam on** [*v* + *o* + *adv*, *v* + *adv* + *o*]: **to ∼ on the brakes** dar* un frenazo

Jamaica /dʒə'meɪkə/ *n* Jamaica *f*

Jamaican /dʒə'meɪkən/ *adj* jamaicano

jamb /dʒæm/ *n* jamba *f*

jam: ∼ jar *n* (BrE) tarro *m* or bote *m* para mermelada; **∼-packed** /'dʒæm'pækt/ *adj* (colloq) repleto, atestado (de gente); **∼ session** *n*: *sesión de un grupo de músicos de jazz o rock que se reúnen para improvisar*

jangle /'dʒæŋgəl/ *vi* hacer* ruido (*metálico*)

janitor /'dʒænətər ‖ 'dʒænɪtə(r)/ *n* conserje *m*

January /'dʒænjueri ‖ 'dʒænjʊəri/ *n* enero *m*

Japan /dʒə'pæn/ *n* (el) Japón *m*

Japanese¹ /'dʒæpə'niːz/ *adj* japonés

Japanese² *n* (*pl* ∼) **(a)** (language) japonés *m* **(b)** (person) japonés, -nesa *m,f*

jar¹ /dʒɑːr ‖ dʒɑː(r)/ *n* **1** (container) tarro *m*, bote *m* **2** (jolt) sacudida *f*

jar² **-rr-** *vi* **(a)** (clash) desentonar **(b)** (irritate): **∼s on my nerves** me crispa los nervios, me enerva
■ **∼** *vt* sacudir

jargon /'dʒɑːrgən ‖ 'dʒɑːgən/ *n* jerga *f*

jarring /'dʒɑːrɪŋ/ *adj* ‹*sound*› discordante

jasmine /'dʒæzmən ‖ 'dʒæsmɪn/ *n* jazmín *m*

jaundice /'dʒɔːndəs ‖ 'dʒɔːndɪs/ *n* ictericia *f*

jaundiced /'dʒɔːndəst ‖ 'dʒɔːndɪst/ *adj* **(a)** (Med) ‹*skin/baby*› ictérico **(b)** ‹*view/opinion*› negativo

jaunt /dʒɔːnt/ *n* excursión *f*

jaunty /'dʒɔːnti/ *adj* **-tier, -tiest** (*usu before n*) ‹*air*› garboso; ‹*tune*› alegre

javelin /'dʒævlən ‖ 'dʒævlɪn/ *n* jabalina *f*

jaw /dʒɔː/ *n* **(a)** (of person, animal) mandíbula *f*; (esp of animal) quijada *f*; **his ∼ dropped** se quedó boquiabierto **(b)** **jaws** *pl* fauces *fpl*

jawbone /'dʒɔːbəʊn/ *n* mandíbula *f*, maxilar *m*; (of an animal) quijada *f*

jay /dʒeɪ/ *n* arrendajo *m*

jay: ~**walk** vi cruzar* la calzada imprudentemente; ~**walker** n peatón m imprudente

jazz /dʒæz/ n (Mus) jazz m
■ **jazz up** [v + o + adv, v + adv + o] (colloq) (a) ⟨music⟩ tocar* con ritmo sincopado (b) ⟨room⟩ alegrar, darle* vida a

jazzy /'dʒæzi/ adj **jazzier, jazziest** 1 (flashy) (colloq) llamativo 2 (Mus) ⟨rhythm⟩ de jazz

jealous /'dʒeləs/ adj (a) ⟨husband/wife⟩ celoso; **to be** ~ estar* celoso, tener* celos (b) (envious) envidioso; **to be** ~ **OF sb** tenerle* envidia A algn

jealousy /'dʒeləsi/ n (pl **-sies**) (a) (fear of rivalry) celos mpl (b) (envy) envidia f

jeans /dʒiːnz/ pl n vaqueros mpl, jeans mpl, bluyines mpl (Andes)

Jeep®, **jeep** /dʒiːp/ n Jeep® m

jeer /dʒɪr ‖dʒɪə(r)/ vi: **to** ~ **AT sth/sb** (boo) abuchear (algo/a algn); (mock) burlarse (DE algo/ algn)

Jehovah /dʒə'həʊvə/ n Jehová

Jehovah's Witness n testigo mf de Jehová

jell /dʒel/ vi ▶ GEL²

Jell-O® /'dʒeləʊ/ n (AmE) gelatina f ⟨con sabor a frutas⟩

jelly /'dʒeli/ n (pl **-lies**) 1 (Culin) (a) (clear jam) jalea f (b) (as dessert) (BrE) gelatina f ⟨con sabor a frutas⟩ 2 (gelatinous substance) gelatina f

jellyfish /'dʒeli,fɪʃ/ n (pl **-fish** or **-fishes**) medusa f, malagua f (Per), aguaviva f (RPl), aguamala f (Col, Méx)

jeopardize /'dʒepərdaɪz ‖'dʒepədaɪz/ vt poner* en peligro, arriesgar* peligrar

jeopardy /'dʒepərdi ‖'dʒepədi/ n: **in** ~ en peligro

jerk¹ /dʒɜːrk ‖dʒɜːk/ vi «leg/arm» hacer* un movimiento brusco; (repeatedly) «legs/arms» agitarse; **the train** ~**ed to a stop** el tren se detuvo con una sacudida
■ ~ vt: **the impact** ~**ed him forward** el impacto lo propulsó hacia adelante

jerk² n 1 (a) (tug) tirón m (b) (sudden movement) sacudida f 2 (contemptible person) (colloq) estúpido, -da m,f, pendejo, -ja m,f (AmL exc CS fam), gilipollas mf (Esp fam), huevón, -ona m,f (Andes, Ven fam)

jerky /'dʒɜːrki ‖'dʒɜːki/ adj **-kier, -kiest** ⟨speech⟩ entrecortado; **it was a** ~ **ride** fuimos (or fueron etc) dando botes por el camino

jerry /'dʒeri/: ~**-built** adj mal construido; ~**can** n bidón m

jersey /'dʒɜːrzi ‖'dʒɜːzi/ n (pl **-seys**) 1 (a) (sports shirt) camiseta f (b) (Tex) jersey m (c) (BrE) ▶ SWEATER 2 **Jersey** (la isla de) Jersey

Jerusalem /dʒə'ruːsələm/ n Jerusalén m

jest /dʒest/ n (arch) broma f, chanza f (arc); **in** ~ en broma

jester /'dʒestər ‖'dʒestə(r)/ n bufón m

Jesuit /'dʒezuɪt ‖'dʒezjʊɪt/ n jesuita m

Jesus /'dʒiːzəs/ n Jesús; ~ **Christ** Jesucristo

jet¹ /dʒet/ n 1 (Aviat) avión m ⟨con motor a reacción⟩ 2 (of water, air, gas) chorro m 3 (Min) azabache m

jet² vi **-tt-** (fly) (colloq) volar*

jet: ~**-black** /'dʒet'blæk/ adj (pred ~ **black**) negro azabache adj inv; ~ **lag** n jet lag m, desfase m horario

jetsam /'dʒetsəm/ n echazón f; see also FLOTSAM

jet set n the ~ ~ el jet set (AmL), la jet set (Esp)

jettison /'dʒetəsən ‖'dʒetɪsən/ vt (Naut) echar por la borda; (Aviat) deshacerse* de

jetty /'dʒeti/ n (pl **-ties**) embarcadero m, malecón m

Jew /dʒuː/ n judío, -día m,f

jewel /'dʒuːəl/ n (gem) piedra f preciosa; (piece of jewelry) alhaja f, joya f; (in watch) rubí m; (sb, sth wonderful) joya f

jeweler, (BrE) **jeweller** /'dʒuːələr ‖'dʒuːələ(r)/ n joyero, -ra m,f; **a** ~**'s** (shop) una joyería

jewelry, (BrE) **jewellery** /'dʒuːəlri/ n joyas fpl, alhajas fpl; (before n) ~ **box** joyero m; ~ **store** (AmE) joyería f

Jewish /'dʒuːɪʃ/ adj judío

jibe /dʒaɪb/ n pulla f

jiffy /'dʒɪfi/ n (colloq) (no pl) segundo m

jig /dʒɪg/ n 1 (dance) giga f 2 (Tech) plantilla f de guía

jiggle /'dʒɪgəl/ vt mover*, sacudir

jigsaw /'dʒɪgsɔː/ n 1 ~ (**puzzle**) rompecabezas m, puzzle m 2 (saw) sierra f de vaivén or de puñal

jilt /dʒɪlt/ vt dejar plantado

jingle¹ /'dʒɪŋgəl/ n 1 (sound) (no pl) tintineo m; (of harness bells) cascabeleo m, tintineo m 2 (Marketing) jingle m (publicitario)

jingle² vi tintinear

jingoism /'dʒɪŋgəʊɪzəm/ n patriotería f, jingoísmo m

jinx¹ /dʒɪŋks/ n: **there's a** ~ **on this project** este proyecto le han echado una maldición

jinx² vt traer* mala suerte a

jitters /'dʒɪtərz ‖'dʒɪtəz/ pl n (colloq): **he got the** ~ se puso nervioso, le dio el tembleque (fam)

jittery /'dʒɪtəri/ adj nervioso

Jnr (BrE) (= **Junior**) (h), Jr.

job /dʒɑːb ‖dʒɒb/ n 1 (a) (occupation, post) trabajo m, empleo m; **is he the right person for the** ~? ¿es la persona idónea para el puesto?; (before n) ~ **creation** creación f de empleo (b) (duty, responsibility): **it's your** ~ **to make the tea** tú eres el encargado de hacer el té; **I'm only doing my** ~ sólo cumplo con mi deber
2 (a) (task, piece of work) trabajo m; (Comput) trabajo m; **you're doing a fine** ~ lo estás haciendo muy bien; **a good** ~ (BrE colloq) menos mal; **it's a good** ~ **I did it yesterday** menos mal que lo hice ayer; **to give sth up as a bad** ~ dejar algo por imposible; **to make the best of a bad** ~

AmC América Central	Arg	Argentina	Cu	Cuba	Per	Perú
AmL América Latina	Bol	Bolivia	Ec	Ecuador	RPI	Río de la Plata
AmS América del Sur	Chi	Chile	Esp	España	Ur	Uruguay
Andes Región andina	CS	Cono Sur	Méx	México	Ven	Venezuela

apechugar* y hacer* lo que se pueda **(b)** (difficult task) (colloq): **I had a (terrible)** ∼ **getting that nail out** me dio mucho trabajo sacar ese clavo

job: **J**∼**centre** n (in UK) agencia f de colocaciones, oficina f de empleo; ∼ **description** n descripción f del puesto; ∼**-hunt** vi (usu in -ing form) buscar* trabajo

jobless /'dʒɑːbləs ‖ 'dʒɒblɪs/ adj (journ) desempleado, en paro (Esp), cesante (Chi)

job: ∼ **lot** n lote m; ∼**share** n puesto m de trabajo compartido (entre dos); ∼ **sharing** /'ʃerɪŋ ‖ 'ʃeərɪŋ/ n sistema m en el cual dos personas comparten un puesto de trabajo

jockey /'dʒɑːki ‖ 'dʒɒki/ n (pl ∼**s**) jockey mf, jinete mf

Jockey shorts® /'dʒɑːki ‖ 'dʒɒki/ pl n (AmE) calzoncillos mpl, calzones mpl (Méx), interiores mpl (Col, Ven)

jockstrap /'dʒɑːkstræp ‖ 'dʒɒkstræp/ n suspensorio m, suspensor m (Per, RPl)

jocular /'dʒɑːkjələr ‖ 'dʒɒkjʊlə(r)/ adj jocoso

jodhpurs /'dʒɑːdpərz ‖ 'dʒɒdpəz/ pl n pantalones mpl de montar, breeches mpl (Col, RPl)

jog¹ /dʒɑːg ‖ dʒɒg/ -**gg**- vt (table) mover*; she ∼**ged his elbow** le dio en el codo; **to** ∼ **sb's memory** refrescarle* la memoria a algn
∎ ∼ vi **(a)** (run) correr **(b)** (Leisure) hacer* footing or jogging; **to go** ∼**ging** salir* a hacer footing or jogging

jog² n (no pl) (Leisure): **to go for a** ∼ hacer* footing or jogging

jogger /'dʒɑːgər ‖ 'dʒɒgə(r)/ n: persona que hace footing

jogging /'dʒɑːgɪŋ ‖ 'dʒɒgɪŋ/ n footing m, jogging m

john /dʒɑːn ‖ dʒɒn/ n **1** (toilet) (AmE colloq) baño m, váter m (Esp fam) **2** **John Doe** (AmE) (Law) persona f indentificada; (colloq) el típico americano

join¹ /dʒɔɪn/ vt **1** (fasten, link) (ropes/wires) unir; (put together) (tables) juntar; **to** ∼ **two things together** unir dos cosas; **to** ∼ **hands** tomarse o (esp Esp) cogerse* de la mano
2 (meet, keep company with): **we're going for a drink, will you** ∼ **us?** vamos a tomar algo ¿nos acompañas?; **you go ahead, I'll** ∼ **you later** ustedes vayan que ya iré yo luego; **may I** ∼ **you?** ¿le importa si me siento aquí?
3 **(a)** (become part of) unirse a, sumarse a; **I** ∼**ed the line** me puse en la cola **(b)** (become member of) (club) hacerse* socio de; (union) afiliarse a; (army) alistarse en; (firm) entrar en or (AmL tb) entrar a
∎ ∼ vi **1** **to** ∼ **(together)** «parts/groups» unirse **2** (merge) «streams» confluir*; «roads» empalmar
∎ **join in** **1** [v + adv] participar, tomar parte **2** [v + adv + o] (celebrations) participar or tomar parte en
∎ **join up** [v + adv] **(a)** (enlist) alistarse **(b)** (fit together) «pieces/parts» encajar **(c)** (team up) «people» unirse

join² n juntura f, unión f

joiner /'dʒɔɪnər ‖ 'dʒɔɪnə(r)/ n carpintero, -ra m,f (de obra)

joint¹ /dʒɔɪnt/ n **1** (Anat) articulación f **2** (Const) (point of joining) unión f, junta f; (in

woodwork) ensambladura f **3** (Culin) trozo m de carne (para asar) **4** (of marijuana) (colloq) porro m (Esp arg), canuto m (Esp arg), toque m (Méx arg), varillo m (Col arg), pito m (Chi arg)

joint² adj (before n) (action) conjunto; ∼ **owner** copropietario, -ria m,f; **it was a** ∼ **effort** fue un trabajo realizado en conjunto

joint account n cuenta f conjunta

jointly /'dʒɔɪntli/ adv (decide/act) conjuntamente

joint: ∼ **stock company** n sociedad f por acciones; ∼ **venture** n empresa f conjunta

joist /dʒɔɪst/ n viga f

joke¹ /dʒəʊk/ n **(a)** (verbal) chiste m; (directed at sb) broma f; **he can't take a** ∼ no sabe aceptar una broma **(b)** (practical ∼) broma f

joke² vi bromear; **you must be joking!** ¡tú debes estar loco!; **I was only joking** lo dije en broma

joker /'dʒəʊkər ‖ 'dʒəʊkə(r)/ n **1** (cards) comodín m **2** (prankster) bromista mf; (contemptible person) (colloq) tipo, -pa m,f (fam)

jokey /'dʒəʊki/ adj ▶ **JOKY**

joky /'dʒəʊki/ adj **jokier, jokiest** jocoso

jolly¹ /'dʒɑːli ‖ 'dʒɒli/ adj -**lier, -liest** (person) jovial; (laugh/tune) alegre

jolly² adv (BrE colloq) (as intensifier): **you were** ∼ **lucky!** ¡qué suerte tuviste!; ∼ **good!** ¡muy bien!

jolly³ vt -**lies, -lying, -lied** (colloq): **to** ∼ **sb along** animar a algn

jolt¹ /dʒəʊlt/ vi (train/bus) dar* or pegar* una sacudida; (repeatedly) dar* tumbos
∎ ∼ vt: **she** ∼**ed his arm** le movió el brazo

jolt² n sacudida f

Jordan /'dʒɔːrdn ‖ 'dʒɔːdn/ n **(a)** (country) Jordania f **(b)** **the** ∼**, the** ∼ **River** (AmE), **the River** ∼ (BrE) el Jordán

Jordanian /dʒɔːrˈdeɪniən ‖ dʒɔːˈdeɪniən/ adj jordano

jostle /'dʒɑːsəl ‖ 'dʒɒsəl/ vt empujar
∎ ∼ vi: **people were jostling trying to get out** la gente se empujaba tratando de salir

jot /dʒɑːt ‖ dʒɒt/ n (no pl, usu with neg): **it doesn't make a** o **one** ∼ **of difference** da exactamente igual
∎ **jot down**: -**tt**- [v + o + adv, v + adv + o] apuntar or anotar (rápidamente)

journal /'dʒɜːrnl ‖ 'dʒɜːnl/ n **(a)** (periodical) revista f, publicación f; (newspaper) periódico m **(b)** (diary) (frml) diario m

journalism /'dʒɜːrnlɪzəm ‖ 'dʒɜːnəlɪzəm/ n periodismo m

journalist /'dʒɜːrnləst ‖ 'dʒɜːnlɪst/ n periodista mf

journey /'dʒɜːrni ‖ 'dʒɜːni/ n (pl -**neys**) viaje m; **to go on** o **to make a** ∼ hacer* un viaje

joust /dʒaʊst/ vi justar

jovial /'dʒəʊviəl/ adj jovial

jowls /dʒaʊlz/ pl n (sometimes sing) parte inferior de los carrillos, que a veces cuelga de la mandíbula

joy /dʒɔɪ/ n **(a)** (emotion) alegría f, dicha f; **to jump for** ∼ saltar de alegría **(b)** (source of pleasure): **she's a** ∼ **to teach** es un verdadero placer or da gusto tenerla como alumna

joyful /'dʒɔɪfəl/ adj (event) feliz; (dance/news) alegre

joyless /'dʒɔɪləs ‖'dʒɔɪlɪs/ adj ⟨occasion⟩ falto de alegría; ⟨existence⟩ sombrío

joyous /'dʒɔɪəs/ adj ⟨expression⟩ de dicha; ⟨occasion⟩ feliz

joy: ~**rider** n: joven que roba un coche para dar una vuelta; ~**stick** n (Aviat) palanca f de mando; (Electron, Comput) mando m, joystick m

Jr (esp AmE) (= **Junior**) (h), Jr.

jubilant /'dʒu:bələnt ‖'dʒu:bɪlənt/ adj ⟨expression⟩ de júbilo (liter); ⟨speech⟩ exultante (liter); **to be** ~ estar* radiante de alegría

jubilee /'dʒu:bəli: ‖'dʒu:bɪli:/ n: **the Queen's silver** ~ el vigésimo quinto aniversario de la reina

Judaism /'dʒu:deɪzəm ‖'dʒu:deɪɪzəm/ n judaísmo m

judge¹ /dʒʌdʒ/ n ① (Law) juez mf, juez, jueza m,f; (of competition) juez mf, (Sport) juez mf ② (appraiser): **he's a good** ~ **of character** es muy buen psicólogo; **let me be the** ~ **of that** eso lo decidiré yo

judge² vt ① (Law) ⟨case/person⟩ juzgar*; ⟨contest⟩ ser* el juez de ② (a) (estimate) ⟨size/speed⟩ calcular (b) (assess) ⟨situation/position⟩ evaluar*; ⟨person⟩ juzgar* (c) (deem) juzgar* ③ (censure, condemn) juzgar*
■ ~ vi juzgar*; **judging by** a juzgar por

judgment, judgement /'dʒʌdʒmənt/ n ① (Law) fallo m, sentencia f, (in arbitration) fallo m; **to pass** ~ **on sth/sb** juzgar* algo/a algn ② (a) (estimation) cálculo m (b) (view) opinión f ③ (a) (sense, discernment): **an error of** ~ una equivocación; **I lent him the money against my better** ~ le presté el dinero sabiendo que era un error

judgmental, judgemental /dʒʌdʒˈmentl̩/ adj ⟨attitude/assessment⟩ sentencioso

judicial /dʒu:ˈdɪʃəl/ adj judicial

judiciary /dʒu:ˈdɪʃiəri ‖dʒu:ˈdɪʃəri/ n (judges) judicatura f, (arm of government) poder m judicial

judicious /dʒu:ˈdɪʃəs/ adj ⟨decision⟩ acertado; ⟨historian⟩ de criterio

judo /'dʒu:dəʊ/ n judo m

jug /dʒʌg/ n (large) jarra f, (for milk, cream) jarrita f

juggernaut /'dʒʌgənɔ:t ‖'dʒʌgənɔ:t/ n (BrE) camión m grande

juggle /'dʒʌgəl/ vi hacer* malabarismos
■ ~ vt hacer* malabarismos con

juggler /'dʒʌglər ‖'dʒʌglə(r)/ n malabarista mf

Jugoslavia /ˈjuːgəʊˈslɑːviə, ˈjuːgəˈslɑːviə/ etc ▶ YUGOSLAVIA etc

jugular /'dʒʌgjələr ‖'dʒʌgjʊlə(r)/ n (vena f) yugular f

juice /dʒu:s/ n (fruit drink) jugo m, zumo m; (from fruit, meat) jugo m; (Physiol) jugo m

juicer /'dʒu:sər ‖'dʒu:sə(r)/ n exprimidor m (gen eléctrico), juguera f (CS)

juicy /'dʒu:si/ adj **-cier, -ciest** (a) (Culin) jugoso (b) (colloq) ⟨gossip/details⟩ sabroso (fam)

jukebox /'dʒu:kbɑ:ks ‖'dʒu:kbɒks/ n máquina f de discos, rocola f (AmL)

July /dʒʊˈlaɪ/ n julio m

jumble¹ /'dʒʌmbəl/ vt ~ (**up**) ⟨cards/pieces⟩ mezclar; **the clothes were all** ~**d up in the drawer** la ropa estaba toda revuelta en el cajón

jumble² n (no pl) (of clothes, papers) revoltijo m; (of facts, data) embrollo m

jumble sale n (BrE) mercadillo de beneficencia donde se venden artículos de segunda mano

jumbo /'dʒʌmbəʊ/ adj (before n) ⟨packet/size⟩ gigante

jumbo (**jet**) n jumbo m

jump¹ /dʒʌmp/ vi ① (a) (leap) saltar; **the horse** ~**ed over the gate** el caballo saltó la verja (b) (move quickly): **I** ~**ed out of bed** me levanté (de la cama) de un salto; **they'll** ~ **at the chance** no van a dejar pasar la oportunidad ② (a) (change, skip) saltar (b) (increase, advance suddenly) subir de un golpe ③ (a) (jerk) saltar (b) (in alarm) sobresaltarse; **you made me** ~! ¡qué susto me diste!
■ ~ vt ① (leap over) ⟨hurdle⟩ saltar, brincar* (Méx); **to** ~ **rope** (AmE) saltar a la cuerda o (Esp tb) a la comba o (Chi) al cordel, brincar* la reata (Méx) ② (a) (spring out of) ⟨rails/tracks⟩ salirse* de (b) (disregard) saltarse; **to** ~ **the lights** pasar el semáforo en rojo, pasarse el alto (Méx); **to** ~ **the line** o (BrE) **queue** colarse* ③ (ambush, attack) (colloq) asaltar, atacar*

jump² n ① (a) (leap) salto m; **I sat up with a** ~ me incorporé sobresaltado (b) (fence) valla f ② (a) (sudden transition) salto m (b) (increase, advance) aumento m

jumper /'dʒʌmpər ‖'dʒʌmpə(r)/ n (a) (dress) (AmE) jumper m or f (AmL), pichi m (Esp) (b) (BrE) ▶ SWEATER

jumper cables pl n (AmE) cables mpl de arranque

jump: ~ **jet** n avión m de despegue vertical; ~ **leads** /liːdz/ pl n (BrE) ▶ JUMPER CABLES; ~ **rope** n (AmE) cuerda f or (Méx) reata f or (Chi) cordel m (de saltar), comba f (Esp); ~**start** vt: hacer arrancar un coche ya sea empujándolo o haciendo un puente; ~ **suit** n mono m, enterito m (RPl)

jumpy /'dʒʌmpi/ adj **-pier, -piest** nervioso

junction /'dʒʌŋkʃən/ n (a) (meeting point — of roads, rails) cruce m; (— of rivers) confluencia f (b) (Elec) empalme m

juncture /'dʒʌŋktʃər ‖'dʒʌŋktʃə(r)/ n coyuntura f, **at this** ~ en este momento

June /dʒu:n/ n junio m

jungle /'dʒʌŋgəl/ n selva f, jungla f

junior¹ /'dʒu:njər ‖'dʒu:niə(r)/ adj ① (a) (lower in rank) ⟨official⟩ subalterno; ⟨position⟩ de subalterno (b) (younger) más joven; **James D. Clark J~** (AmE) James D. Clark, hijo or junior ② (AmE Educ) (before n) de tercer año

junior² n ① (a) (younger person): **he is two years my** ~ tiene dos años menos que yo (b) (person of lower rank) subalterno, -na m,f ② (Educ) (in US) estudiante de tercer año de colegio secundario o universidad; (in UK) alumno de primaria o de los primeros años de secundaria

junior: ~ **college** n (in US) establecimiento universitario donde se estudian los dos primeros años de la carrera; ~ **high** (**school**) n (in US) colegio en el que se imparten los dos o tres primeros años de la enseñanza secundaria; ~ **school** n (in UK) escuela f primaria (para niños de 7 a 11 años)

junk /dʒʌŋk/ n ① (a) (discarded items) trastos mpl (viejos); (before n) ~ **shop** tienda f de viejo

(c) (worthless stuff) (colloq) basura f (fam); (before n) ∼ **mail** propaganda f que se recibe por correo [2] (boat) junco m

junk food n comida f basura, alimento m chatarra (Méx)

junkie /'dʒʌŋki/ n (colloq) yonqui mf (fam), drogadicto, -ta m,f, pichicatero, -ra (CS, Per fam)

junkyard /'dzʌŋkjɑːrd ‖'dʒʌŋkjɑːd/ n depósito m de chatarra, deshuesadero m (Méx)

junta /'hʊntə ‖'dʒʌntə/ n junta f militar

Jupiter /'dʒuːpətər ‖'dʒuːpɪtə(r)/ n Júpiter m

jurisdiction /ˌdʒʊrəs'dɪkʃən ‖ˌdʒʊərɪs'dɪkʃən/ n jurisdicción f

juror /'dʒʊrər ‖'dʒʊərə(r)/ n jurado mf

jury /'dʒʊri ‖'dʒʊəri/ n (pl **-ries**) jurado m

just¹ /dʒʌst/ adj justo

just² adv [1] **(a)** (in recent past): she's ∼ left se acaba de ir, recién se fue (AmL) **(b)** (at the moment): I was ∼ about to leave when he called estaba a punto de salir cuando llamó

[2] **(a)** (barely) justo; I arrived ∼ in time llegué justo a tiempo; I ∼ missed him no lo vi por poco or por apenas unos minutos **(b)** (a little): ∼ above the knee justo or apenas encima de la rodilla

[3] **(a)** (only) solo; she was ∼ three when her father died tenía apenas or solo tres años cuando murió su padre; would you like some more? — ∼ a little, please ¿quieres más? — bueno, un poquito **(b)** (simply): I ∼ stopped by to say hello pasé para saludarte; that's ∼ gossip no son más que chismes; ∼ because he's famous doesn't mean he can be rude (colloq) el hecho de que sea famoso no le da derecho a ser grosero

[4] **(a)** (exactly, precisely): it's ∼ what I wanted es justo or precisamente or exactamente lo que quería; the temperature was ∼ right la

temperatura era la perfecta **(b)** (equally): the desserts were ∼ as good as the rest of the meal los postres estuvieron tan buenos como el resto de la comida; it's ∼ as well you're leaving menos mal que te vas

[5] (emphatic use): I ∼ can't understand it simplemente no lo entiendo; ∼ leave it here déjelo aquí, déjelo aquí nomás (AmL)

justice /'dʒʌstəs ‖'dʒʌstɪs/ n justicia f; to do sb/sth ∼: the photo doesn't do her ∼ la foto no le hace justicia; he couldn't do ∼ to the meal no pudo hacerle honor a la comida; she didn't do herself ∼ in the exam no rindió a la altura de su capacidad en el examen

Justice of the Peace n (pl ∼s ∼ ∼ ∼) juez mf de paz, juez, jueza m,f de paz

justifiable /'dʒʌstəfaɪəbəl ‖'dʒʌstɪfaɪəbəl/ adj justificable

justification /ˌdʒʌstəfə'keɪʃən ‖ˌdʒʌstɪfɪ'keɪʃən/ n justificación f

justified /'dʒʌstəfaɪd ‖'dʒʌstɪfaɪd/ adj justificado

justify /'dʒʌstəfaɪ ‖'dʒʌstɪfaɪ/ vt **-fies, -fying, -fied** justificar*

jut /dʒʌt/ **-tt-** vi sobresalir*
■ **jut out** [v + adv] sobresalir*

jute /dʒuːt/ n yute m

juvenile¹ /'dʒuːvənaɪl, -vənl ‖'dʒuːvənaɪl/ adj **(a)** (Law) (before n) ⟨court⟩ de menores; ⟨delinquent⟩ juvenil **(b)** (childish) (pej) infantil **(c)** ⟨literature⟩ (AmE) infantil y juvenil

juvenile² n (Law) menor mf

juxtapose /'dʒʌkstəpəʊz ‖ˌdʒʌkstə'pəʊz/ vt yuxtaponer*

k

Kk

K, k /keɪ/ n K, k f

K (Comput) (= **kilobyte**) K

kale /keɪl/ n col f rizada

kaleidoscope /kə'laɪdəskəʊp/ n caleidoscopio m

Kampuchea /ˌkæmpuː'tʃiə/ n Kampuchea f

kangaroo /'kæŋgə'ruː/ n (pl **-roos**) canguro m

Kans = **Kansas**

karaoke /'kæri'əʊki/ n karaoke m

karat n (AmE) ▶ CARAT A

karate /kə'rɑːti/ n kárate m, karate m (AmL)

kayak /'kaɪæk/ n kayak m

Kazakhstan /ˌkɑːzɑːk'stɑːn/ n Kazajstán m

kebab /'kəbɑːb ‖kɪ'bæb/ n pincho m, anticucho m (Bol, Chi, Per), brocheta f (Esp, Méx)

keel /kiːl/ n quilla f
■ **keel over** [v + adv] **(a)** (capsize) ⟨ship⟩ volcar(se)* **(b)** (collapse) (colloq) ⟨person⟩ caer* redondo (fam)

keen /kiːn/ adj **-er, -est** [1] (enthusiastic) ⟨photographer⟩ entusiasta; ⟨student⟩ aplicado; he was ∼ to start work tenía muchas ganas de empezar a trabajar; he's ∼ to take part tiene mucho interés en participar; to be ∼ ON sth/sb/-ING (BrE): I'm ∼ on golf me encanta el golf; she's very ∼ on him le gusta muchísimo; they're ∼ on joining the club tienen muchas ganas de hacerse socios del club [2] **(a)** (sharp) ⟨blade⟩ afilado, filoso (AmL), filudo (Chi, Per) **(b)** (acute) ⟨hearing⟩ muy fino; ⟨sight/sense of smell/ intelligence⟩ agudo **(c)** (intense) ⟨competition⟩ muy reñido; ⟨interest⟩ vivo

keep¹ /kiːp/ n [1] (living) sustento m [2] for ∼s (colloq) para siempre [3] (in castle, fortress) torre f del homenaje

keep² (past & past p **kept**) vt [1] **(a)** (not throw away) ⟨receipt/ticket⟩ guardar; (not give back) quedarse con; (not lose) conservar; ∼ the change quédese (con) el cambio **(b)** (look after, reserve) to ∼ sth (FOR sb) guardar(le) algo (A algn) ····▶

2 (store) guardar; **I always ~ a first-aid kit in the car** me gusta tener un botiquín en el coche
3 (reserve for future use) guardar
4 (a) (raise) ⟨*pigs/bees*⟩ criar* **(b)** (manage, run) ⟨*stall/guesthouse*⟩ tener*
5 (a) (support) mantener* **(b)** (maintain): **I've kept a note** *o* **record of everything** he tomado nota de todo
6 (a) (cause to remain, continue) mantener*; **try and ~ it clean** trata de mantenerlo limpio; **the noise kept me awake** el ruido no me dejó dormir **(b)** (detain): **don't let me ~ you** no te quiero entretener; **what kept you?** ¿qué te retuvo?; **they kept her in hospital** la dejaron ingresada *or* (CS, Méx tb) internada
7 (adhere to, fulfill) ⟨*promise/vow*⟩ cumplir; ⟨*secret*⟩ guardar
■ **~** *vi* **1** (remain) mantenerse*; **to ~ fit** mantenerse* en forma; **to ~ awake** mantenerse* despierto; **~ still!** ¡estate quieto!
2 (a) (continue) seguir*; **~ left** siga por la izquierda; **to ~ -ING** seguir* + GER; **to ~ at it** seguir* dandole (fam) **(b)** (repeatedly): **he ~s interfering** está continuamente entrometiéndose; **I ~ forgetting to bring it** nunca me acuerdo de traerlo
3 ⟨*food*⟩ conservarse (fresco)
4 (be in certain state of health) (colloq): **how are you ~ing?** ¿qué tal estás? (fam)
■ **keep away** [*v + adv*] **to ~ away** (FROM sb/sth) no acercarse* (A algn/algo)
■ **keep back**
I [*v + adv*]: **~ back!** ¡atrás!; **~ well back from the edge** mantente bien alejado del borde
II [*v + o + adv, v + adv + o*] **1 (a)** ⟨*crowd/floodwaters*⟩ contener* **(b)** ⟨*tears/sobs*⟩ contener*
2 (not reveal) ⟨*information/facts*⟩ ocultar
■ **keep down** **1** [*v + adv*] (not raise): **~ your head/voice down** no levantes la cabeza/la voz **(b)** ⟨*food*⟩ retener*
2 [*v + o + adv, v + adv + o*] (not allow to increase) ⟨*prices*⟩ mantener* al mismo nivel; ⟨*weeds*⟩ contener*
■ **keep from** [*v + o + prep + o*] **1** (restrain, prevent): **I don't want to ~ you from your work** no quiero distraerte de tu trabajo; **I managed to ~ myself from laughing** pude aguantar la risa
2 (not reveal) ocultar; **he kept vital information from them/us** les/nos ocultó información vital
■ **keep in** [*v + o + adv, v + adv + o*] **(a)** (detain): **the teacher kept me in after school** el maestro me hizo quedar después de clase; **he was kept in for observation** lo dejaron ingresado *or* (CS, Méx tb) internado en observación **(b)** ⟨*anger/feelings*⟩ contener*
■ **keep off** **1** [*v + prep + o*] **(a)** (stay away from) ⟨*land/property*⟩ mantenerse* alejado de; **⑤ keep off the grass** prohibido pisar el césped **(b)** (avoid) ⟨*cigarettes/subject*⟩ evitar
2 [*v + o + prep + o*]: **~ your hands off me!** ¡quítame las manos de encima!
■ **keep on** **1** [*v + adv*] **(a)** (continue) seguir*; **to ~ on -ING** seguir* + GER **(b)** (repeatedly): **I ~ on forgetting to tell him** siempre me olvido de

decírselo; **she kept on interrupting him** lo interrumpía constantemente **(c)** (talk incessantly): **she ~s on at me about my weight** me está siempre encima con que estoy muy gordo
2 [*v + o + adv, v + adv + o*] (continue to employ) no despedir*
3 [*v + o + adv*] (continue to wear): **~ your coat on** no te quites el abrigo
■ **keep out** **1** [*v + adv*] (not enter): **⑤ keep out** prohibido el paso; **~ out of the kitchen** no entres en la cocina
2 [*v + o + adv, v + adv + o*] (prevent from entering, exclude) ⟨*rain/sun*⟩ impedir* que entre
■ **keep out of** [*v + adv + prep + o*] ⟨*danger*⟩ no exponerse* a; ⟨*trouble/argument*⟩ no meterse en
■ **keep to** **1** [*v + prep + o*] **(a)** (adhere to, fulfill) ⟨*plan*⟩ ceñirse* a; ⟨*promise*⟩ cumplir **(b)** (not deviate from) ⟨*path*⟩ seguir* por; ⟨*script*⟩ ceñirse* a **(c)** (stay on): **~ to the right** (Auto) mantenga su derecha
2 [*v + o + prep + o*] (not divulge): **to ~ sth to oneself** guardarse algo
3 [*v + prep + o*] [*v + o + prep + o*]: **to ~ (oneself) to oneself** no ser* muy sociable
■ **keep up**
I [*v + adv*] **1** (not stop) ⟨*rain/noise*⟩ seguir*, continuar*; **to ~ up WITH sth** seguir* *or* continuar* CON algo
2 (a) (maintain pace) **to ~ up WITH sb** seguirle* el ritmo A algn; **he's finding it difficult to ~ up in class** le está resultando difícil mantenerse al nivel de la clase **(b)** (remain informed) **to ~ up WITH sth** mantenerse* al tanto *or* al corriente DE algo
II [*v + o + adv, v + adv + o*] **1** (maintain at present level) mantener*
2 (continue, not stop) ⟨*payments*⟩ mantenerse* al día con; ⟨*friendship*⟩ mantener*
III [*v + o + adv*] **1** ⟨*trousers/socks*⟩ sujetar
2 (prevent from sleeping): **I hope we're not ~ing you up** espero que no te estemos quitando el sueño; **the baby kept me up all night** el niño me tuvo toda la noche en vela

keeper /'ki:pər ‖'ki:pə(r)/ *n* (in zoo) guarda *mf*, cuidador, -dora *m,f*; (in museum) (BrE) conservador, -dora *m,f*

keep-fit /'ki:p'fɪt/ *n* (BrE) gimnasia *f* (de mantenimiento)

keeping /'ki:pɪŋ/ *n* **(a)** (conformity): **in ~ with** ⟨*with law/tradition*⟩ en conformidad con **(b)** (trust, care): **to leave sth in sb's ~** dejar algo al cuidado de algn

keepsake /'ki:pseɪk/ *n* recuerdo *m*

keg /keg/ *n* barril *m*

kennel /'kenl/ *n* **(a)** (AmE) (for boarding) residencia *f* canina; (for breeding) criadero *m* de perros **(b)** (BrE) (hut) casa *f* del perro

kennels /'kenlz/ *n* (*pl* **~**) (BrE) (+ *sing vb*) ▶ KENNEL A

Kenya /'kenjə, 'ki:-/ *n* Kenia *f*

Kenyan /'kenjən, 'ki:-/ *adj* keniano

kept /kept/ *past & past p of* KEEP²

kerb /kɜːrb ‖kɜːb/ *n* (BrE) ▶ CURB¹ 2

AmC	Central America	Arg	Argentina
AmL	Latin America	Bol	Bolivia
AmS	South America	Chi	Chile
Andes	Andean Region	CS	Southern Cone

Cu	Cuba	Per	Peru
Ec	Ecuador	RPI	River Plate Area
Esp	Spain	Ur	Uruguay
Méx	Mexico	Ven	Venezuela

kernel /'kɜːrnl̩ ‖'kɜːnl̩/ *n* (of nut, fruit) almendra *f*; (of corn, wheat) grano *m*

kerosene /'kerəsiːn/ *n* queroseno *m*, kerosene *m*

kestrel /'kestrəl/ *n* cernícalo *m*

ketchup /'ketʃəp ‖'ketʃʌp/ *n* salsa *f* de tomate, ketchup *m*, catsup *m*

kettle /'ketl̩/ *n* pava *f or* (Bol, Ur) caldera *f or* (Andes, Méx) tetera *f*

kettledrum /'ketl̩drʌm/ *n* timbal *m*

key¹ /kiː/ *n* (*pl* **~s**) [1] (for lock) llave *f*; (on can) llave *f*, abridor *m*; (*before n*) **~ ring** llavero *m* [2] **(a)** (to puzzle, code etc) clave *f* **(b)** (to map) explicación *f* de los signos convencionales **(c)** (answers) soluciones *fpl* [3] (crucial element) clave *f*; **patience is the ~** la paciencia es el factor clave *or* la clave [4] (of typewriter, piano) tecla *f*; (of wind instrument) llave *f* [5] (Mus) tono *m*; **to be off ~** no estar* en el tono

key² *adj* ⟨man/question⟩ clave *adj inv*
■ **key in** [*v + o + adv, v + adv + o*] ⟨text/data⟩ teclear

key: ~board *n* teclado *m*; **~hole** *n* ojo *m* de la cerradura; (*before noun*) **~hole surgery** cirugía *f* no invasiva; **~note** *n* (Mus) tónica *f*; (central idea) tónica *f*; **~pad** *n* (Comput, Telec, TV) teclado *m* numérico; **~word** *n* palabra *f* clave

kg (= **kilo(s)** o **kilogram(s)**) Kg.

khaki /'kæki ‖'kɑːki/ *adj* caqui *or* kaki *adj inv*

kibbutz /kɪ'bʊts/ *n* (*pl* **-butzim** /-bʊtsɪm/) kibbutz *m*

kick¹ /kɪk/ *n* [1] (by person) patada *f*, puntapié *m*; (by horse) coz *f* [2] (colloq) (thrill, excitement): **to get a ~ out of doing sth** deleitarse haciendo algo; **just for ~s** nada más que por divertirse

kick² *vi* «*person*» dar* patadas; «*swimmer*» patalear; «*horse*» cocear
■ **~ vt** [1] ⟨ball⟩ patear, darle* una patada *or* un puntapié a; ⟨person⟩ pegarle* una patada a [2] (stop) (colloq) ⟨habit⟩ dejar
■ **kick around,** (BrE also) **kick about** (colloq) [*v + o + adv*] **(a)** (treat badly) maltratar **(b)** ⟨idea⟩ estudiar **(c) to ~ a ball around** pelotear
■ **kick down** [*v + o + adv, v + adv + o*] ⟨door⟩ echar abajo (*a patadas*)
■ **kick off** [1] [*v + adv*] **(a)** (in football): **they ~ off at three** el partido empieza a las tres **(b)** (begin) (colloq) «*person/meeting*» empezar* [2] [*v + adv + o*] (begin) ⟨discussion⟩ iniciar, empezar*
■ **kick out** [*v + o + adv*] echar
■ **kick up** [1] [*v + o + adv, v + adv + o*] ⟨leaves/dust⟩ levantar [2] [*v + adv + o*]: **to ~ up a fuss** *o* **row** armar una bronca (fam); **to ~ up a din** armar un escándalo

kick: ~off *n* (Sport) saque *m or* puntapié *m* inicial, patada *f* de inicio; **~start** *vt* ⟨engine⟩ arrancar* (*con el pedal de arranque*)

kid¹ /kɪd/ *n* [1] (colloq) **(a)** (child) niño, -ña *m,f*, chaval, -vala *m,f* (Esp fam), chavalo, -vala *m,f* (AmC, Méx fam), escuincle, -cla (Méx fam), pibe, -ba *m,f* (RPl fam), cabro, -bra *m,f* (Chi fam) **(b)** (young person) chico, -ca *m,f* [2] **(a)** (goat) cabrito, -ta *m,f*, choto, -ta *m,f* **(b)** (leather) cabritilla *f*

kid² **-dd-** *vi* (colloq) bromear

■ **~ vt (a)** (tease) **to ~ sb** (ABOUT sth) tomarle el pelo a algn (CON algo) **(b)** (deceive) engañar; **don't ~ yourself!** ¡no te hagas ilusiones!

kidnap /'kɪdnæp/ *vt* **-pp-** *or* (AmE) **-p-** secuestrar, raptar

kidnapper, (AmE also) **kidnaper** /'kɪdnæpər ‖'kɪdnæpə(r)/ *n* secuestrador, -dora *m,f*, raptor, -tora *m,f*

kidnapping, (AmE also) **kidnaping** /'kɪdnæpɪŋ/ *n* secuestro *m*, rapto *m*

kidney /'kɪdni/ *n* (*pl* **-neys**) (Anat, Culin) riñón *m*; (*before n*) ⟨disease/stone⟩ renal; **~ machine** riñón *m* artificial

kidney bean *n* frijol *m or* (Esp) judía *f or* (CS) poroto *m* (*con forma de riñón*)

kill¹ /kɪl/ *vt* [1] (cause death of) ⟨person/animal⟩ matar; **she was ~ed in a car crash** se mató *or* murió en un accidente de coche [2] **(a)** (destroy) ⟨hopes⟩ acabar con **(b)** (spoil) ⟨flavor/taste⟩ estropear **(c)** (deaden) ⟨pain⟩ calmar **(d)** (use up): **to ~ time** matar el tiempo
■ **~ vi** matar
■ **kill off** [*v + o + adv, v + adv + o*] matar

kill² *n* **(a)** (act): **he went in for the ~** entró a matar **(b)** (animal, animals killed) presa *f*

killer /'kɪlər ‖'kɪlə(r)/ *n* (person) asesino, -na *m,f*; (*before n*) ⟨shark⟩ asesino; ⟨disease⟩ mortal

killer whale *n* orca *f*

killing /'kɪlɪŋ/ *n* (of person) asesinato *m*; (of animal) matanza *f*; **to make a ~** hacer* un gran negocio, forrarse (fam)

killjoy /'kɪldʒɔɪ/ *n* aguafiestas *mf*

kiln /kɪln/ *n* horno *m*

kilo /'kiːləʊ/ *n* (*pl* **-los**) kilo *m*

kilobyte /'kɪləbaɪt/ *n* kilobyte *m*, kilocteto *m*

kilogram, (BrE also) **kilogramme** /'kɪləgræm/ *n* kilogramo *m*

kilometer, (BrE also) **kilometre** /'kɪləmiːtər ‖kɪ'lɒmɪtə(r), 'kɪləmiːtə(r)/ *n* kilómetro *m*

kilowatt /'kɪləwɑːt ‖'kɪləwɒt/ *n* kilovatio *m*

kilt /kɪlt/ *n* falda *f or* (CS) pollera *f* escocesa

kimono /kə'məʊnəʊ ‖kɪ'məʊnəʊ/ *n* (*pl* **-nos**) kimono *m*, quimono *m*

kin /kɪn/ *n* (+ *pl vb*) familiares *mpl*, parientes *mpl*

kind¹ /kaɪnd/ *n* [1] (sort, type) **(a)** (of things) tipo *m*, clase *f*; **of all ~s** de todo tipo, de toda clase **(b)** (of people) clase *f*, tipo *m* [2] (sth approximating to) especie *f*; **she was overcome by a ~ of yearning** la invadió una especie de añoranza [3] (*in phrases*) **in kind** ⟨pay⟩ en especie; **kind of** (colloq): **he seemed ~ of stupid** parecía como tonto (fam); **of a kind: they served a meal, of a ~** sirvieron una especie de comida, si se le puede llamar así; **they're two of a ~** son tal para cual

kind² *adj* **-er, -est** ⟨offer⟩ amable; **he's very ~ to me** es muy buena persona; **she's always been ~ to me** siempre ha sido muy amable conmigo; **it's very ~ to your skin** no daña la piel; **would you be ~ enough to accompany me?** ¿tendría la amabilidad de acompañarme?

kindergarten /'kɪndər,gɑːrtn̩ ‖'kɪndəgɑːtn̩/ *n* jardín *m* de infancia *or* de niños

kind-hearted /'kaɪnd'hɑːrtəd ‖,kaɪnd'hɑːtɪd/ *adj* de buen corazón

k

kindle /'kɪndl̩/ vt ⟨fire⟩ encender*; ⟨interest⟩ despertar*; ⟨passion⟩ encender*

kindly¹ /'kaɪndli/ adv **1** **(a)** (generously) amablemente **(b)** (adding polite emphasis) (frml): **passengers are ~ requested to ...** se ruega a los pasajeros tengan la amabilidad de ... **2** (favorably): **they didn't take ~ to my suggestions** no recibieron demasiado bien mis sugerencias; **she doesn't take ~ to being contradicted** no le hace ninguna gracia que la contradigan

kindly² adj **-lier, -liest** bondadoso

kindness /'kaɪndnəs ‖ 'kaɪndnɪs/ n **(a)** (quality) ~ **(TO** o **TOWARD sb)** amabilidad f **(PARA CON** algn) **(b)** (act) favor m

kindred /'kɪndrəd ‖ 'kɪndrɪd/ adj (before n) (similar) similar; ~ **spirits** almas fpl gemelas

king /kɪŋ/ n rey m

kingdom /'kɪŋdəm/ n reino m; **the animal ~** el reino animal

king: ~fisher /'kɪŋ͵fɪʃər ‖ 'kɪŋ͵fɪʃə(r)/ n martín m pescador; **~-size, ~-sized** /'kɪŋsaɪzd/ adj ⟨cigarette⟩ extralargo; ⟨bed⟩ de matrimonio (extragrande)

kink /kɪŋk/ n (in rope, wire) vuelta f, curva f; (in hair) onda f

kinky /'kɪŋki/ adj **-kier, -kiest** (colloq) pervertidillo (fam)

kinship /'kɪnʃɪp/ n parentesco m

kiosk /'kiːɑːsk ‖ 'kiːɒsk/ n (stall) quiosco m

kipper /'kɪpər ‖ 'kɪpə(r)/ n arenque m salado y ahumado

Kirghizia /kɪr'giːziə ‖ kiə'gɪziə/, **Kirghizstan** /͵kɪrgiːˈstɑːn ‖ ͵kɪəgɪˈstɑːn/ n Kirguizistán m

kiss¹ /kɪs/ vt ⟨person⟩ besar; **to ~ sb goodbye/ goodnight** darle* un beso de despedida/de buenas noches a algn
■ ~ vi besarse

kiss² n beso m; **to give sb a ~** darle* un beso a algn; **she gave him the ~ of life** le hizo (la) respiración artificial

kit /kɪt/ n **1** **(a)** (set of items): **first-aid ~** botiquín m de primeros auxilios; **tool ~** caja f de herramientas **(b)** (parts for assembly) kit m **2** **(a)** (personal effects) cosas fpl; (Mil) petate m **(b)** (Clothing) (esp BrE) **gym ~** (Sport) equipo m de gimnasia

kitchen /'kɪtʃən ‖ 'kɪtʃɪn/ n cocina f

kitchen garden n huerto m

kite /kaɪt/ n cometa f or (RPl tb) barrilete m or (AmC, Méx) papalote m or (Ven) papagayo m or (Chi) volantín m

kitten /'kɪtn̩/ n gatito, -ta m,f

kitty /'kɪti/ n (pl **-ties**) (colloq) bote m, fondo m común

kiwi /'kiːwiː/ n **(a)** (Zool) kiwi m **(b)** ~ **(fruit)** kiwi m

kleptomaniac /͵kleptə'meɪniæk/ n cleptómano, ·na m,f

klutz /klʌts/ n (AmE colloq) torpe mf, patoso, -sa m,f (Esp fam)

km (= **kilometer(s)** o (BrE) **kilometre(s)**) Km.

knack /næk/ n: **there's a ~ to making omelettes** hacer tortillas tiene su truco or (Méx) su chiste;

I'll never get the ~ of this! ¡nunca le voy a agarrar la onda (AmL fam) or (Esp) coger el tranquillo a esto!

knapsack /'næpsæk/ n mochila f

knave /neɪv/ n **(a)** (rogue) (arch) truhán m (ant) **(b)** (in French pack of cards) jota f; (in Spanish pack) sota f

knead /niːd/ vt (Culin) amasar

knee¹ /niː/ n (Anat, Clothing) rodilla f; **to be on one's ~s** estar* arrodillado; **to go** o **get down on one's ~s** ponerse* de rodillas

knee² vt darle* or pegarle* un rodillazo a

knee: ~cap n rótula f; **~-deep** /'niːˈdiːp/ adj (pred): **the water is ~-deep** el agua llega hasta la(s) rodilla(s); **they were ~-deep in mud** estaban con el barro hasta las rodillas; **~-high** /'niːˈhaɪ/ adj ⟨sock⟩ largo

kneel /niːl/ vi (past & past p **kneeled** or **knelt**) (get down on one's knees) arrodillarse; (be on one's knees) estar* arrodillado; **to ~ down** arrodillarse

knee-length /'niːleŋθ/ adj ⟨sock⟩ largo; ⟨skirt⟩ hasta la rodilla; ⟨boot⟩ alto

knelt /nelt/ past & past p of KNEEL

knew /nuː ‖ njuː/ past of KNOW

knickerbockers /'nɪkərbɑːkərz ‖ 'nɪkəbɒkəz/ pl n pantalones mpl bombachos

knickers /'nɪkərz ‖ 'nɪkəz/ pl n **1** (AmE) ▶ KNICKERBOCKERS **2** (BrE) (undergarment) calzones mpl (AmS), bragas fpl (Esp), pantaletas fpl (AmC, Ven), bombacha f (RPl)

knickknack /'nɪknæk/ n chuchería f

knife¹ /naɪf/ n (pl **knives**) cuchillo m; (penknife) navaja f, cortaplumas m or f; (dagger) puñal m

knife² vt acuchillar

knife: ~ edge n filo m (de cuchillo, navaja etc); **to be on a ~ edge** pender de un hilo; **~-point** n: **he was robbed at ~-point** le robaron amenazándolo con un cuchillo

knight¹ /naɪt/ n **(a)** (Hist) caballero m **(b)** (holder of title) sir m **(c)** (in chess) caballo m

knight² vt conceder el título de sir a

knighthood /'naɪthʊd/ n título m de sir

knit /nɪt/ n (pres p **knitting**; past & past p **knitted** or **knit**) vt **1** **(a)** ⟨sweater⟩ (by hand) hacer*, tejer; (with machine) tejer, tricotar (Esp) **(b)** **knitted** o (esp AmE) **knit** past p ⟨jacket/cuffs⟩ de punto, tejido **2** (join, unite) ⟨bones⟩ soldar*; **a tightly ~ family** una familia muy unida
■ ~ vi (by hand) tejer, hacer* punto or calceta (Esp); (with machine) tejer, tricotar (Esp)

knitting /'nɪtɪŋ/ n **(a)** (piece of work) tejido m, punto m (Esp) **(b)** (activity): **I like ~** me gusta tejer, me gusta hacer* punto or calceta (Esp)

knitting: ~ machine n máquina f de tejer, tricotosa f (Esp); **~ needle** n aguja f de tejer or (Esp) de hacer punto, palillo m (Chi)

knives /naɪvz/ pl of KNIFE¹

knob /nɑːb ‖ nɒb/ n **(a)** (on door) pomo m, perilla f (AmL); (on drawer) tirador m, perilla f (AmL); (on walking stick) puño m; (on radio, TV) botón m **(b)** (lump) bulto m **(c)** (small piece) (esp BrE): **a ~ of butter** un trocito or una nuez de mantequilla

knobbly /'nɑːbli ‖ 'nɒbli/ adj **-lier, -liest** ⟨tree/fingers⟩ nudoso; ⟨knees⟩ huesudo

knock¹ /nɑːk ‖nɒk/ n (sound) golpe m; (blow to head, on door) golpe m

knock² vt [1] (strike, push): **to ~ one's head on/against sth** darse* (un golpe) en la cabeza con/contra algo; **she ~ed the vase off the shelf** tiró el jarrón de la repisa; **they ~ed a large hole in the wall** hicieron un gran boquete en la pared
[2] (criticize) (colloq) criticar*
■ **~ vi (a)** (on door) llamar, golpear (AmL), tocar* (AmL) **(b)** (collide) **to ~ AGAINST/INTO sb/sth** darse* or chocar* CONTRA algn/algo
■ **knock about, knock around** (colloq) [v + o + adv] pegarle* a
■ **knock back** [v + o + adv, v + adv + o] (colloq) ⟨drink⟩ beberse, tomarse
■ **knock down** [v + o + adv, v + adv + o] [1] **(a)** (cause to fall) ⟨door/fence⟩ tirar abajo; ⟨obstacle⟩ derribar; **he ran into her and ~ed her down** chocó con ella y la hizo caer **(b)** «vehicle/driver» atropellar **(c)** (demolish) echar abajo
[2] (colloq) (reduce) ⟨price/charge⟩ rebajar
■ **knock off** [1] [v + adv] [v + prep + o] (stop work) (colloq): **when do you ~ off (work)?** ¿a qué hora sales del trabajo?, ¿hasta qué hora trabajas?; **let's ~ off for lunch** vamos a parar para comer
[2] [v + o + adv, v + adv + o] (stop) (colloq) dejar de; **~ it off, will you!** ¡déjala ya! (fam)
[3] [v + o + adv, v + adv + o] (deduct, eliminate) (colloq) rebajar; **I'll ~ off 25% for you** le hago un descuento del 25%
■ **knock out** [1] [v + o + adv, v + adv + o] (make unconscious) dejar sin sentido, hacer* perder el conocimiento; (in boxing) dejar K.O., noquear; **she hit her head and ~ed herself out** se dio un golpe en la cabeza y perdió el conocimiento
[2] [v + o + adv, v + adv + o] (of competition) eliminar
■ **knock over** [v + o + adv, v + adv + o] **(a)** (cause to fall) tirar **(b)** «vehicle» atropellar
■ **knock up** [v + o + adv, v + adv + o] (colloq) (assemble hurriedly) improvisar

knocker /'nɑːkər ‖'nɒkə(r)/ n aldaba f, llamador m

knocking /'nɑːkɪŋ ‖'nɒkɪŋ/ n **(a)** (noise) (no pl) golpes mpl **(b)** (Auto) golpeteo m, cascabeleo m (AmL)

knock: ~-kneed /'nɑːk'niːd ‖nɒk'niːd/ adj patizambo; **~-on effect** /'nɑːk'ɑːn ‖nɒk'ɒn/ n repercusiones fpl; **~out** n (in boxing) nocaut m, K.O. m (read as: nocaut or (Esp) cao)

knoll /nəʊl/ n loma f, montículo m

knot¹ /nɑːt ‖nɒt/ n [1] (in string, hair, wood) nudo m; (in muscles) nódulo m [2] (measure of speed) nudo m

knot² vt -tt- hacer* un nudo en

know¹ /nəʊ/ (past **knew**; past p **known**) vt [1] **(a)** (have knowledge of, be aware of) saber*; **I don't ~ his name/how old he is** no sé cómo se llama/cuántos años tiene; **it is well ~n that ...** todo el mundo sabe que ...; **to let sb ~ sth** decirle* algo a algn; (warn) avisarle algo a algn; **without our ~ing it** sin saberlo nosotros; **there's no ~ing what he might do** quién sabe qué hará; **I ~ what: let's go skating!** ¡tengo una idea: vayamos a patinar!; **to ~ sth backwards** ⟨part/play⟩

saber* algo al dedillo or al revés y al derecho **(b)** (have skill, ability) **to ~ how to + INF** saber* + INF
[2] (be acquainted with) ⟨person/place⟩ conocer*; **how did they get to ~ each other?** ¿cómo se conocieron?; **to get to ~ sth** ⟨subject/job⟩ familiarizarse* con algo
[3] **(a)** (recognize, identify) reconocer*; **to ~ sth/sb BY sth** reconocer* algo/a algn POR algo **(b)** (distinguish) **to ~ sth/sb FROM sth/sb** distinguir* algo/a algn DE algo/algn
■ **~ vi** saber*; **how do you ~?** ¿cómo lo sabes?; **I ~!** ¡ya sé!, ¡tengo una idea!; **you never ~** nunca se sabe; **I'm not stupid, you ~!** oye, que no soy tonto ¿eh? or ¿sabes?; **did you ~ about John?** ¿sabías lo de John?; **to get to ~ about sth** enterarse de algo; **she knew of their activities** tenía conocimiento or estaba enterada de sus actividades; **not that I ~** of que yo sepa, no; **do you ~ of a good carpenter?** ¿conoces a or sabes de algún carpintero bueno?

know² n: **to be in the ~** estar* enterado

know: ~-all n (BrE) ▶ KNOW-IT-ALL; **~how** n know-how m, conocimientos mpl y experiencia

knowing /'nəʊɪŋ/ adj ⟨smile⟩ de complicidad; **she gave me a ~ look** me miró dándome a entender que ya lo sabía

knowingly /'nəʊɪŋli/ adv **(a)** ⟨smile/nod⟩ de manera cómplice **(b)** (deliberately) ⟨hurt/lie⟩ a sabiendas

know-it-all /'nəʊɪtɔːl/ n (colloq) sabelotodo mf (fam)

knowledge /'nɑːlɪdʒ ‖'nɒlɪdʒ/ n [1] (awareness) conocimiento m; **to the best of my ~** que yo sepa; **it is common ~ that ...** todo el mundo sabe que ... [2] (facts known) saber m; (by particular person) conocimientos mpl

knowledgeable /'nɑːlɪdʒəbəl ‖'nɒlɪdʒəbəl/ adj (about current affairs) entendido; (about given subject) entendido; (in general) culto

known¹ /nəʊn/ past p of KNOW

known² adj ⟨fact⟩ conocido, sabido; **a little-~ artist** un artista poco conocido; **to be ~ AS sth** (have reputation) tener* fama DE algo; **better ~ as ...** más conocido como ...; **for reasons best ~ to herself** por motivos que ella conocerá; **he's better ~ for his work in films** se le conoce mejor por su trabajo cinematográfico

knuckle /'nʌkəl/ n **(a)** (finger joint) nudillo m **(b)** (of pork) codillo m; (of veal) morcillo m, jarrete m
■ **knuckle down** [v + adv] ponerse* a trabajar en serio
■ **knuckle under** [v + adv] ceder*, pasar por el aro

knuckleduster /'nʌkəlˌdʌstər ‖'nʌkəlˌdʌstə(r)/ n (BrE) ▶ BRASS KNUCKLES

koala /kəʊ'ɑːlə/ n **~ (bear)** koala m

kooky /'kuːki/ adj **-kier, -kiest** (AmE colloq) chiflado (fam)

Koran /kə'rɑːn/ n **the ~** el Corán

Korea /kə'riːə/ n Corea f

Korean¹ /kə'riːən/ adj coreano

Korean² n **(a)** (person) coreano, -na m,f **(b)** (language) coreano m

kosher /'kəʊʃər ‖'kəʊʃə(r)/ adj ⟨food/butcher⟩ kosher adj inv

Kosovo /'kɑːsəvəʊ ‖'kɒsəvəʊ/ n Kosovo m

k

kowtow /'kaʊtaʊ/ vi to ~ **TO** sb doblar la cervíz ANTE algn

kph (= **kilometers** o (BrE) **kilometres per hour**) Km/h.

KS = **Kansas**

kung fu /'kʌŋ'fuː/ n kung fu m

Kurd /kɜːrd ‖ kɜːd/ n kurdo, -da m,f

Kurdish /'kɜːrdɪʃ ‖ 'kɜːdɪʃ/ adj kurdo

Kuwait /kə'weɪt ‖ kʊ'weɪt/ n Kuwait m

Kuwaiti /kə'weɪti ‖ kʊ'weɪti/ adj kuwaití

KY, Ky = **Kentucky**

L l

L, l /el/ n L, l f

l (= **liter(s)** or (BrE) **litre(s)**) l.

L (a) (BrE Auto) Ⓢ **L** (= **learner**) L (conductor en aprendizaje) (b) (Clothing) (= **large**) G (talla grande)

la /lɑː/ n (Mus) la m

La = **Louisiana**

LA (a) = **Los Angeles** (b) = **Louisiana**

lab /læb/ n (colloq) laboratorio m

label¹ /'leɪbəl/ n etiqueta f

label² vt, (BrE) **-ll-** (a) ⟨bottle/luggage⟩ ponerle* una etiqueta a (b) (categorize) to ~ sth/sb (AS) sth catalogar* algo/a algn DE algo

labor¹, (BrE) **labour** /'leɪbər ‖ 'leɪbə(r)/ n **1** (a) (work) trabajo m; (before n) ⟨dispute/laws⟩ laboral (b) (workers) mano f de obra **2** **Labour** (in UK) (Pol) (no art, + sing or pl vb) los laboristas, el Partido Laborista **3** (a) (effort) esfuerzos mpl, trabajo m (b) (task) labor f, tarea f **4** (Med) parto m; **to be in** ~ estar* de parto; (before n) ~ **pains** dolores mpl or contracciones fpl del parto

labor², (BrE) **labour** vt: **to** ~ **a point** insistir excesivamente sobre un punto
■ ~ vi (toil) trabajar; **he** ~**ed up the hill** subió trabajosamente or penosamente la cuesta

laboratory /'læbərətɔːri ‖ lə'bɒrətri/ n (pl **-ries**) laboratorio m

Labor Day n Día m del Trabajo or de los trabajadores

labored, (BrE) **laboured** /'leɪbərd ‖ 'leɪbəd/ adj ⟨breathing⟩ dificultoso, fatigoso; ⟨metaphor/joke⟩ forzado, torpe

laborer, (BrE) **labourer** /'leɪbərər ‖ 'leɪbərə(r)/ n peón m; **farm** ~ peón m, trabajador m agrícola

laborious /lə'bɔːriəs/ adj ⟨task/process⟩ laborioso; ⟨style⟩ farragoso

labor union n (AmE) sindicato m

labour etc (BrE) ▶ **LABOR** etc

labrador /'læbrədɔːr ‖ 'læbrədɔː(r)/ n labrador m

labyrinth /'læbərɪnθ/ n laberinto m

lace¹ /leɪs/ n **1** (fabric) encaje m; (as border) puntilla f **2** (shoe~) cordón m (de zapato), agujeta f (Méx), pasador m (Per)

lace² vt **1** ⟨shoes/boots⟩ ponerles* los cordones or (Méx) las agujetas or (Per) los pasadores a **2** (fortify): **he** ~**d my drink with vodka** me echó un chorro de vodka en la bebida

lacerate /'læsəreɪt/ vt lacerar

lack¹ /læk/ n ~ **of** sth falta f or (frml) carencia f DE algo

lack² vt no tener*, carecer* de (frml); **it** ~**s originality** le falta or no tiene originalidad, carece de originalidad (frml)

lacking /'lækɪŋ/ adj (pred) (a) (absent): **the necessary resources are** ~ faltan los recursos necesarios (b) (deficient) **to be** ~ **IN** sth no tener* algo, carecer DE algo (frml)

lackluster, (BrE) **lacklustre** /'læk,lʌstər ‖ 'læk,lʌstə(r)/ adj (a) ⟨eyes⟩ apagado; ⟨hair⟩ opaco (b) (mediocre) ⟨performance/campaign⟩ deslucido; ⟨candidate⟩ mediocre

laconic /lə'kɑːnɪk ‖ lə'kɒnɪk/ adj lacónico

lacquer /'lækər ‖ 'lækə(r)/ n (a) (varnish) laca f (b) (hair ~) laca f or fijador m (para el pelo)

lad /læd/ n muchacho m, chaval m (Esp fam), pibe m (RPI fam), chavo m (Méx, Ven fam), chavalo m (AmC, Méx fam), cabro m (Chi fam)

ladder /'lædər ‖ 'lædə(r)/ n **1** (Const) escalera f (de mano) **2** (in stocking, tights) (BrE) carrera f

laden /'leɪdn/ adj ~ **WITH** sth cargado DE algo

ladies /'leɪdiz/ n (BrE) ▶ **LADIES' ROOM**

ladies' room /'leɪdiz/ n (AmE) baño m or (esp Esp) servicio m de señoras; Ⓢ **Ladies (Room)** Señoras, Damas

ladle /'leɪdl/ n cucharón m

lady /'leɪdi/ n (pl **ladies**) **1** (a) (woman) señora f; **ladies and gentlemen** señoras y señores, damas y caballeros (b) (refined woman) señora f, dama f **2** (noblewoman or wife of a knight) lady f

lady: ~**bug** (AmE), ~**bird** (BrE) n mariquita f, catarina f (Méx), petaca f (Col), chinita f (Chi), San Antonio m (Ur), vaca f de San Antón (Arg); ~**-in-waiting** /'leɪdɪm'weɪtɪŋ/ n (pl **ladies-in-waiting**) dama f de honor; ~**like** adj fino

ladyship /'leɪdiʃɪp/ n: **Her/Your L**~ la señora

lag¹ /læg/ n (interval) lapso m, intervalo m; (delay) retraso m, demora f (esp AmL)

lag² -gg- *vi* to ~ (behind) quedarse atrás; to ~ behind sb/sth ir* a la zaga de algn/algo
■ ~ *vt* ⟨*pipes*⟩ revestir* con aislantes

lager /'lɑːgər ‖ 'lɑːgə(r)/ *n* cerveza *f* (rubia)

lagoon /lə'guːn/ *n* laguna *f*

lah /lɑː/ *n or* (BrE Mus) la *m*

laid /leɪd/ *past & past p of* LAY²

laid-back /'leɪd'bæk/ *adj* (colloq) ⟨*person*⟩ tranquilo y relajado; ⟨*atmosphere*⟩ relajado

lain /leɪn/ *past p of* LIE² II

lair /ler ‖ leə(r)/ *n* guarida *f*

lake /leɪk/ *n* lago *m*

Lake District *n* the ~ ~ el Lake District (*región de lagos al noroeste de Inglaterra*)

lamb /læm/ *n* cordero *m*; (*before n*) ~ **chop** chuleta *f* de cordero

lame¹ /leɪm/ *adj* **1** (in foot, leg) cojo, rengo (AmL); to go ~ quedarse cojo *or* (AmL tb) rengo **2** (weak) ⟨*excuse*⟩ pobre, malo

lame² *vt* lisiar

lament¹ /lə'ment/ *n* lamento *m*

lament² *vt* (a) ⟨*misfortune/failure*⟩ lamentar (b) (liter) ⟨*death/loss*⟩ llorar

lamentable /'læməntəbəl/ *adj* lamentable

lamp /læmp/ *n* lámpara *f*; (Auto) luz *f*

lamplight /'læmplaɪt/ *n* (of table lamp) luz *f* de (la) lámpara; (of streetlamp) luz *f* de(l) farol

lampoon /læm'puːn/ *vt* satirizar*

lamp: ~**post** *n* farol *m*; ~**shade** *n* pantalla *f* (*de lámpara*)

lance¹ /lɑːns ‖ lɑːns/ *n* lanza *f*

lance² *vt* abrir* con lanceta

lancet /'lɑːnsət ‖ 'lɑːnsɪt/ *n* lanceta *f*

land¹ /lænd/ *n* **1** (Geog, Agr) tierra *f*; (*before n*) ⟨*animal/defenses*⟩ de tierra; ~ **reform** reforma *f* agraria **2** (country, realm) (liter) país *m*; (kingdom) reino *m*

land² *vi* **1** (a) (Aerosp, Aviat) aterrizar*; (on the moon) alunizar* (b) (fall) caer* **2** (arrive, end up) (colloq) ir* a parar (fam) **3** (Naut) ⟨*ship*⟩ atracar*; ⟨*traveler/troops*⟩ desembarcar*
■ ~ *vt* **1** (a) (from sea) ⟨*passengers*⟩ desembarcar*; ⟨*cargo*⟩ descargar* (b) (from air) ⟨*plane*⟩ hacer* aterrizar; ⟨*troops*⟩ desembarcar*; ⟨*supplies*⟩ descargar* **2** ⟨*fish*⟩ sacar* del agua; ⟨*contract/job*⟩ conseguir* **3** (burden) (colloq) to ~ sb WITH sth/sb, to ~ sth/sb ON sb endilgarle* algo/a algn a algn (fam)

landing /'lændɪŋ/ *n* **1** (a) (Aerosp, Aviat) aterrizaje *m*; (on moon) alunizaje *m*; (*before n*) ~ **strip** pista *f* de aterrizaje (b) (Mil, Naut) desembarco *m* (of cargo) descarga *f*; (of troops) desembarco *m* **2** (on staircase) rellano *m*, descanso *m* (Col, CS)

land: ~**lady** *n* (a) (of rented dwelling) casera *f* (b) (of small hotel) dueña *f* (c) (BrE) (of pub — owner) dueña *f*; (— manager) encargada *f*, ~**locked** /'lændlɒːkt ‖ 'lændlɒkt/ *adj* sin salida al mar; ~**lord** *n* (a) (of landed estate) terrateniente *m* (b) (of rented dwelling) casero *m*, dueño *m* (c) (BrE) (of pub — owner) dueño *m*; (— manager) encargado *m*; ~**mark** *n* monumento *m or* edificio *m etc*) famoso; ~ **mine** *n* mina *f* (de tierra); ~**owner** *n* terrateniente *mf*; ~**scape** /'lændskeɪp/ *n* paisaje *m*; (*before n*) ~scape **gardener** jardinero,

-ra *m,f* paisajista; ~**slide** *n* (a) (Geog) derrumbamiento *m or* desprendimiento *m* de tierras (b) (Pol) victoria *f* aplastante

lane /leɪn/ *n* **1** (in countryside) camino *m*, sendero *m*; (alleyway) callejón *m* **2** (Transp) (a) (for road traffic) carril *m or* (Chi) pista *f or* (RPI) senda *f*; **bus/bicycle** ~ carril *m* de autobuses/bicicletas (b) (for ships) ruta *f* **3** (in athletics) carril *m* (AmL), calle *f* (Esp)

language /'læŋgwɪdʒ/ *n* **1** (means of communication, style of speech) lenguaje *m*; **bad** ~ palabrotas *fpl* **2** (a) (particular tongue) idioma *m*, lengua *f* (b) (Comput) lenguaje *m*

languid /'læŋgwəd ‖ 'læŋgwɪd/ *adj* lánguido

languish /'læŋgwɪʃ/ *vi* (liter) languidecer*; (in prison) pudrirse*

lank /læŋk/ *adj* lacio

lanky /'læŋki/ *adj* -**kier**, -**kiest** desgarbado

lantern /'læntərn ‖ 'læntən/ *n* farol *m*

Laos /laʊs ‖ 'lɑːɒs, laʊs/ *n* Laos *m*

lap¹ /læp/ *n* **1** (of body) rodillas *fpl* **2** (a) (Sport) vuelta *f* (b) (stage) etapa *f*

lap² -pp- *vt* **1** (Sport) sacarle* una vuelta de ventaja a **2** ⟨*water/milk*⟩ beber a lengüetazos
■ ~ *vi* chapalear; to ~ AGAINST sth lamer *or* besar algo (liter)
■ **lap up** [*v + o + adv, v + adv + o*] beber a lengüetazos

lapel /lə'pel/ *n* solapa *f*

Lapland /'læplænd/ *n* Laponia *f*

lapse¹ /læps/ *n* **1** (fault, error) falla *f*, fallo *m* (Esp) **2** (interval) lapso *m*, período *m*

lapse² *vi* **1** (fall, slip): **standards have** ~d el nivel ha decaído; to ~ **into bad habits** adquirir* malos hábitos **2** (a) (cease) ⟨*project*⟩ cancelarse; ⟨*practice*⟩ perderse* (b) ⟨*membership/contract*⟩ caducar*, vencer* **3** ⟨*time*⟩ transcurrir

laptop /'læptɑːp ‖ 'læptɒp/ *n* (~ computer) laptop *f or* (Esp) *m*

lapwing /'læpwɪŋ/ *n* avefría *f*;

larceny /'lɑːrsəni ‖ 'lɑːsəni/ *n* (in US) robo *m*

larch /lɑːrtʃ ‖ lɑːtʃ/ *n* alerce *m*

lard /lɑːrd ‖ lɑːd/ *n* manteca *f or* (RPI) grasa *f* de cerdo

larder /'lɑːrdər ‖ 'lɑːdə(r)/ *n* despensa *f*

large¹ /lɑːrdʒ ‖ lɑːdʒ/ *adj*
■ **Note** The usual translation of *large*, *grande*, becomes *gran* when it precedes a singular noun.

larger, largest grande; the ~st **collection of stamps in the world** la mayor colección de sellos del mundo

large² *n* **at large** (a) (as a whole) en general; **the public at** ~ el público en general (b) (at liberty): to **be at** ~ andar* suelto

largely /'lɑːrdʒli ‖ 'lɑːdʒli/ *adv* en gran parte

lark /lɑːrk ‖ lɑːk/ *n* alondra *f*

larva /'lɑːrvə ‖ 'lɑːvə/ *n* (*pl* -**vae** /-viː/) larva *f*

laryngitis /ˌlærən'dʒaɪtəs ‖ ˌlærɪn'dʒaɪtɪs/ *n* laringitis *f*

larynx /'lærɪŋks/ *n* (*pl* **larynxes** *or* **larynges** /lə'rɪndʒiːs/) laringe *f*

laser /'leɪzər ‖ 'leɪzə(r)/ *n* láser *m*; (*before n*) ~ **beam** rayo *m* láser; ~ **printer** impresora *f* láser

lash¹ /læʃ/ n ① (eye∼) pestaña f ② (whip) látigo m

lash² vt ① (a) (whip) ⟨person⟩ azotar; ⟨horse⟩ fustigar* (b) (beat against) azotar ② (bind) to ∼ sth/sb TO sth amarrar algo/a algn A algo
■ **lash out** [v + adv (+ prep + o)] atacar*; to ∼ out AT/AGAINST sb (physically) emprenderla a golpes (or patadas etc) CON algn; (verbally) arremeter CONTRA algn

lass /læs/ n (liter or dial) muchacha f

lasso /ˈlæsəʊ, læˈsuː/ ‖læˈsuː/ n (pl **-sos** or **-soes**) lazo m

last¹ /læst ‖lɑːst/ adj ① (a) (in series) último; the ∼ door but one la penúltima puerta; to be ∼ (in race, on arrival) ser* el último (en llegar); to be ∼ to + INF ser* el último en + INF (b) (final, ultimate) ⟨chance/day⟩ último; at the very ∼ minute en el último momento, a última hora (c) (only remaining) último; I'm down to my ∼ few dollars solo me quedan unos pocos dólares ② (previous, most recent) (before n): ∼ Tuesday el martes pasado; in my ∼ letter en mi última carta ③ (least likely): that was the ∼ thing I expected to hear from you es lo que menos me esperaba que me dijeras; that's the ∼ thing I'd do! ¡no se me ocurriría hacer eso!

last² pron ① (a) (in series) último, -ma m,f; the ∼ to + INF el último/la última/los últimos/las últimas EN + INF; the ∼ I remember que lo recuerdo (b) (only remaining): the ∼ of its kind el último de su clase; that's the ∼ of the jam esa es toda la mermelada que queda (c) (in phrases) (liter) at the last al final; to the ∼ hasta el último momento ② (preceding one): the night before ∼ anteanoche, antenoche (AmL); each hill seemed steeper than the ∼ cada colina parecía más empinada que la anterior

last³ adv ① (a) (at the end): I went in ∼ fui el último en entrar; our team finished ∼ nuestro equipo quedó en último lugar (b) (finally): ∼ of all por último; and ∼ but not least y por último, pero no por eso menos importante (c) (in phrases) at last por fin, al fin; at long last por fin, finalmente ② (most recently): she was ∼ seen a year ago la última vez que se la vio fue hace un año; when did you ∼ see him? ¿cuándo fue la última vez que lo viste?

last⁴ vi/t durar

last-ditch /ˈlæstˈdɪtʃ ‖ˈlɑːstˈdɪtʃ/ adj (before n) desesperado

lasting /ˈlæstɪŋ ‖ˈlɑːstɪŋ/ adj duradero

lastly /ˈlæstli ‖ˈlɑːstli/ adv (as linker) por último

last-minute /ˈlæstˈmɪnət ‖ˌlɑːstˈmɪnɪt/ adj (before n) de última hora

latch /lætʃ/ n pasador m, pestillo m; (on lock) seguro m
■ **latch on** [v + adv (+ prep + o)] (understand) (colloq) agarrar or (Esp) coger* la onda; to ∼ on TO sth entender* algo; (realize) darse* cuenta DE algo

late¹ /leɪt/ adj later, latest ① (after correct, scheduled time): the ∼ arrival of the train el retraso en la llegada del tren; to be ∼ «person» llegar* tarde; the train was an hour ∼ el tren llegó con una hora de retraso; you'll be ∼ for work vas a llegar tarde al trabajo ② (a) (after usual time): to have a ∼ night

acostarse* tarde; Spring is ∼ this year la primavera se ha atrasado este año (b) ⟨chrysanthemum/potatoes⟩ tardío ③ (a) (far on in time): it's ∼ es tarde; it's getting ∼ se está haciendo tarde; (before n) ⟨shift/ bus⟩ último; at this ∼ stage a estas alturas; in ∼ April a finales de abril; she's in her ∼ forties tiene cerca de cincuenta años ④ (before n) (deceased) difunto (frml); the ∼ John Doe el difunto John Doe

late² adv later, latest ① (after correct, scheduled time) tarde; the trains are running 20 minutes ∼ los trenes llevan 20 minutos de retraso; better ∼ than never más vale tarde que nunca ② (after usual time) ⟨work/sleep⟩ hasta tarde; ⟨mature⟩ tarde ③ (recently): as ∼ as the thirteenth century aún en el siglo trece; of ∼ últimamente ④ (toward end of period): ∼ in the afternoon a última hora de la tarde; ∼ in the year a finales del año; ∼ in her career hacia el final de su carrera ⑤ (far on in time) tarde; don't leave it too ∼ no lo dejes para muy tarde; we stayed up ∼ nos quedamos levantados hasta tarde

lately /ˈleɪtli/ adv últimamente

latent /ˈleɪtn̩t/ adj latente

later¹ /ˈleɪtər ‖ˈleɪtə(r)/ adj posterior

later² adv después, más tarde; ∼ that day más tarde or posteriormente ese día; not o no ∼ than May 14 a más tardar el 14 de mayo; ∼ on más tarde, después; see you ∼! ¡hasta luego!

lateral /ˈlætərəl/ adj lateral

latest /ˈleɪtəst ‖ˈleɪtɪst/ adj (a) (superl of LATE¹) último (b) (most up to date) (before n) último

latex /ˈleɪteks/ n látex m

lathe /leɪð/ n torno m

lather¹ /ˈlæðər ‖ˈlɑːðə(r), læðə(r)/ n (no pl) espuma

lather² vt enjabonar

Latin¹ /ˈlætɪn ‖ˈlætɪn/ adj latino

Latin² n (a) (language) latín m (b) (person) latino, -na m,f

Latin America n América f Latina, Latinoamérica f

Latin American¹ adj latinoamericano

Latin American² n latinoamericano, -na m,f

latitude /ˈlætətuːd ‖ˈlætɪtjuːd/ n (a) (Geog) latitud f (b) (freedom to choose) libertad f

latter¹ /ˈlætər ‖ˈlætə(r)/ n (pl ∼s) the ∼ este, -ta; (pl) estos, -tas

latter² adj (before n) (a) (second of two) segundo, último (b) (later, last): in the ∼ part of the season hacia el final de la temporada; in his ∼ years (frml) en sus últimos años

lattice /ˈlætəs ‖ˈlætɪs/ n entramado m, enrejado m

Latvia /ˈlætviə/ n Letonia f

Latvian /ˈlætviən/ adj letón m

laugh¹ /læf ‖lɑːf/ n risa f; she's a good ∼ es muy divertida; to do/say sth for a ∼ hacer*/ decir* algo por divertirse; to have a ∼ (about/at sth) reírse* (de algo)

laugh² vi reír(se)*; to burst out ∼ing soltar* una carcajada; to ∼ AT sb/sth reírse* DE algn/ algo

■ **laugh off** [v + o + adv, v + adv + o] tomar a broma

laughing /'læfɪŋ ‖'lɑːfɪŋ/ adj risueño; **this is no ~ matter** no es motivo de risa

laughingstock /'læfɪŋstɑːk ‖'lɑːfɪŋstɒk/ n hazmerreír m; **he made a ~ of his opponent** dejó or puso a su contrincante en ridículo

laughter /'læftər ‖'lɑːftə/ n risas fpl

launch¹ /lɔːntʃ/ vt **1** **(a)** ⟨new vessel⟩ botar; ⟨lifeboat⟩ echar al agua **(b)** ⟨satellite/missile⟩ lanzar; ⟨attack⟩ emprender **2** ⟨product/ campaign⟩ lanzar*; ⟨company⟩ fundar*

launch² n **1** (motorboat) lancha f (a motor) **2** **(a)** (of new vessel) botadura f; (of lifeboat) lanzamiento m (al agua) **(b)** (of rocket, missile) lanzamiento m **3** (of product, campaign) lanzamiento m

launching pad /'lɔːntʃɪŋ/, **launchpad** /'lɔːntʃpæd/ n **(a)** (Aerosp) rampa f de lanzamiento **(b)** (for ideas, career) trampolín m

launder /'lɔːndər ‖'lɔːndə(r)/ vt **(a)** (wash and iron) (frml) lavar y planchar **(b)** ⟨money⟩ blanquear, lavar (AmL)

launderette /'lɔːndəˈret ‖lɔːn'dret/ n lavandería f automática

Laundromat®, **laundromat** /'lɔːndrəmæt/ n (AmE) lavandería f automática

laundry /'lɔːndri/ n (pl **-dries**) **(a)** (commercial) lavandería f, lavadero m (RPl); (in home) lavadero m (b) (dirty clothes) ropa f sucia or para lavar; (washed clothes) ropa f limpia or lavada; (before n) **~ basket** canasto m or cesto m de la ropa sucia

laurel /'lɔːrəl ‖'lɒrəl/ n laurel m

lava /'lɑːvə/ n lava f

lavatory /'lævətɔːri ‖'lævətri/ n (pl **-ries**) **(a)** (room in house) (cuarto m de) baño m **(b)** (public) (often pl) baños mpl, servicios mpl (Esp) **(c)** (receptacle) taza f, inodoro m

lavender /'lævəndər ‖'lævəndə(r)/ n lavanda f, espliego m

lavish¹ /'lævɪʃ/ adj ⟨lifestyle⟩ de derroche; ⟨gift/ meal⟩ espléndido; ⟨production⟩ fastuoso

lavish² vt to ~ sth on sb prodigar(le)* algo A algn

lavishly /'lævɪʃli/ adv ⟨give⟩ con esplendidez; ⟨decorated/illustrated⟩ magníficamente

law /lɔː/ n **(a)** (rule, principle) ley f **(b)** (collectively): **the ~** la ley; **to break the ~** violar or contravenir* or infringir* la ley; **it is against the ~** es ilegal; **under French ~** según la ley francesa; **to lay down the ~** dar* órdenes **(c)** (as field, discipline) derecho m; (profession) abogacía f; (before n) **~ school** facultad f de Derecho

law: **~-abiding** /'lɔːəˌbaɪdɪŋ/ adj respetuoso de la ley; **~ and order** n (+ sing o pl vb) el orden público

lawful /'lɔːfəl/ adj ⟨ruler/heir⟩ legítimo; ⟨contract⟩ válido, legal; ⟨conduct⟩ lícito

lawless /'lɔːləs ‖'lɔːlɪs/ adj ⟨mob⟩ desmandado; ⟨region⟩ anárquico, donde no rige la ley

lawn /lɔːn/ n césped m, pasto m (AmL), grama f (AmC, Ven)

lawnmower /'lɔːnˌməʊər ‖'lɔːnˌməʊə(r)/n máquina f de cortar el césped or (AmL tb) el pasto, cortadora f de césped or (AmL tb) de pasto, cortacésped m (Esp), cortagrama m (AmC, Ven)

lawsuit /'lɔːsuːt/ n juicio m

lawyer /'lɔːjər ‖'lɔːjə(r)/ n abogado, -da m,f

lax /læks/ adj ⟨discipline/supervision⟩ poco estricto; ⟨standards⟩ laxo

laxative /'læksətɪv/ n laxante m

lay¹ /leɪ/ past of LIE² II

lay² (past & past p **laid**) vt **1** (put) poner*; **~ the cloth flat on the table** extiende la tela sobre la mesa

2 (put in position) ⟨bricks/carpet⟩ poner*, colocar*; ⟨cable/pipes⟩ tender*; ⟨mines⟩ sembrar*

3 (prepare) ⟨trap⟩ tender*; ⟨plans⟩ hacer*; **to ~ the table** poner* la mesa

4 (cause to be): **one blow laid him flat on his back** de un golpe quedó tendido de espaldas en el suelo; **to ~ sb low: he was laid low by malaria** estuvo postrado con malaria

5 (Zool): **to ~ eggs** «bird/reptile» poner* huevos; «fish/insects» desovar*

■ ~ vi **1** «hen» poner* huevos

2 (crit) ▶ LIE² II

■ **lay down** [v + o + adv, v + adv + o] **(a)** ⟨tools/ weapons⟩ dejar (a un lado) **(b)** ⟨guidelines/ procedure⟩ establecer*

■ **lay off** [v + adv + o, v + o + adv] (AmE) despedir*; (BrE) suspender temporalmente por falta de trabajo

■ **lay on** [v + adv + o, v + o + adv] ⟨transport/ food⟩ hacerse* cargo de; ⟨entertainment⟩ ofrecer*

■ **lay out** [v + o + adv, v + adv + o] **1** **(a)** ⟨park/ garden⟩ diseñar; ⟨town⟩ hacer* el trazado de; ⟨objects⟩ disponer* **(b)** ⟨page⟩ diseñar

2 (spend) gastar; (invest) invertir*

3 (knock unconscious) dejar sin sentido

4 ⟨dead body⟩ amortajar

lay³ adj (before n) **(a)** (secular) laico; **~ preacher** predicador, -dora m,f seglar **(b)** (not expert): **the ~ reader** el lector profano en la materia

lay-by /'leɪbaɪ/ n (BrE) área f‡ de reposo

layer¹ /'leɪər ‖'leɪə(r)/ n (of dust, paint, snow) capa f; (of rock, sediment) capa f, estrato m

layer² vt: **I had my hair ~ed** me corté el pelo en or (Esp) a capas, me rebajé el pelo (RPl)

lay: **~man** /'leɪmən/ n (pl **-men** /-mən/) (non-expert): **a book written for the ~man** un libro dirigido al gran público; **in ~man's terms** en lenguaje accesible; **~out** n **(a)** (of house) distribución f; (of town, garden) trazado m **(b)** (in magazine, newspaper) diseño m

laze /leɪz/ vi haraganear

lazily /'leɪzəli ‖'leɪzɪli/ adv perezosamente

lazy /'leɪzi/ adj **lazier, laziest** perezoso

lazybones /'leɪzibəʊnz/ n (pl **~**) (colloq) haragán, -gana m,f

lb = **pound(s)**

LCD n = **liquid crystal display**

lead¹ n

I /led/ **1** (metal) plomo m; (before n) **~ poisoning** intoxicación f por plomo; (chronic disease) saturnismo m **2** (in pencil) mina f

II /liːd/ **1** (in competition) (no pl): **to be in/take the ~** llevar/tomar la delantera **2** (example, leadership) (no pl) ejemplo m; **to follow sb's ~** seguir* el ejemplo de algn **3** (clue) pista f **4** **(a)** (for dog) (BrE) correa f **(b)** (Elec) cable m **5** **(a)** (main role) papel m principal **(b)** (Mus) solista mf; (before n) ⟨guitar/singer⟩ principal

lead² /liːd/ (*past & past p* **led**) *vt* **1** (conduct) ⟨*person/animal*⟩ llevar, guiar*; **to ∼ sb to sth/sb** conducir* *or* llevar a algn a algo/ANTE algn; **to ∼ sb away** llevarse a algn; **I was led to believe that ...** me dieron a entender que ...; **he's easily led** se deja llevar fácilmente
2 (head, have charge of) ⟨*discussion*⟩ conducir*; **the expedition was led by Smith** la expedición iba al mando de Smith
3 (a) (be at front of) ⟨*parade/attack*⟩ encabezar* **(b)** (in race, competition) aventajar
4 ⟨*life*⟩ llevar
■ **∼** *vi* **1 to ∼ to sth** ⟨*road/steps*⟩ llevar *or* conducir* *or* dar* a algo; ⟨*door*⟩ dar* A algo
2 (a) (be leader): **you ∼, we'll follow** ve delante *or* (esp AmL) adelante, que te seguimos **(b)** (in race, competition) ir* a la cabeza, puntear (AmL); **they are ∼ing by three goals** van ganando por tres goles
■ **lead on** **1** [*v + adv*]: **∼ on!** ¡adelante! (¡te seguimos!)
2 [*v + o + adv*] (raise false hopes) engañar
■ **lead to** [*v + prep + o*] llevar *or* conducir* a

leaded /ˈledəd ‖ ˈledɪd/ *adj* ⟨*fuel*⟩ con plomo

leader /ˈliːdər ‖ ˈliːdə(r)/ *n* **(a)** (of group, political party) líder *mf*; (of expedition) jefe, -fa *m,f*; (of gang) cabecilla *mf* **(b)** (in race, competition) primero, -ra *m,f*; (in league) líder *m*

leadership /ˈliːdərʃɪp ‖ ˈliːdəʃɪp/ *n* **(a)** (direction, control — of party) liderazgo *m*; (— of country) conducción *f* **(b)** (quality) autoridad *f*, dotes *fpl* de mando **(c)** (leaders) (+ *sing o pl vb*) dirigentes *mpl*

lead-free /ˈledˈfriː/ *adj* ⟨*fuel*⟩ sin plomo

leading /ˈliːdɪŋ/ *adj* (before *n*) **(a)** (principal) ⟨*scientist/playwright*⟩ destacado; ⟨*brand/company*⟩ líder *adj inv* **(b)** (in front) ⟨*runner/horse/driver*⟩ que va a la cabeza

leading: **∼ lady** *n* (Cin) protagonista *f*; (Theat) primera actriz *f*; **∼ light** *n* estrella *f*

leaf /liːf/ *n* (*pl* **leaves**) **1** (of plant) hoja *f*
2 (page, sheet) hoja *f*; **to turn (over) a new ∼** reformarse **3** (of table) ala *f⁺*; (of door, shutter) hoja *f*
■ **leaf through** [*v + prep + o*] hojear

leaflet /ˈliːflət ‖ ˈliːflɪt/ *n* (Print) folleto *m*; (Pol) panfleto *m*

leafy /ˈliːfi/ *adj* **-fier, -fiest** ⟨*boughs*⟩ frondoso; ⟨*lane*⟩ arbolado

league /liːɡ/ *n* **1** (alliance) liga *f*; **to be in ∼ (with sb)** estar* aliado (con algn) **2 (a)** (Sport) liga *f* **(b)** (level, category): **not to be in the same ∼ as sb/sth** no estar* a la misma altura que algn/algo **3** (measure of distance) legua *f*

leak¹ /liːk/ *vi* **(a)** ⟨*bucket/tank*⟩ gotear, perder* (RPI), salirse* (Chi, Méx); ⟨*shoes/tent*⟩ dejar pasar el agua; ⟨*faucet*⟩ gotear; ⟨*pen*⟩ perder* tinta; **the roof is ∼ing** hay una gotera/hay goteras en el techo **(b)** (escape) ⟨*liquid*⟩ escaparse
■ **∼** *vt* **(a)** ⟨*liquid/gas*⟩ perder*, botar (AmL exc RPI) **(b)** ⟨*information*⟩ filtrar

leak² *n* **(a)** (in bucket, boat, pipe) agujero *m*; (in roof) gotera *f* **(b)** (escaping liquid, gas) escape *m* **(c)** (of information) filtración *f*

leakage /ˈliːkɪdʒ/ *n* escape *m*

leaky /ˈliːki/ *adj* **-kier, -kiest** agujereado

lean¹ /liːn/ (*past & past p* **leaned** *or* (BrE also) **leant** /lent/) *vi* **(a)** (bend, incline): **she ∼ed back in her chair** se echó hacia atrás en la silla; **don't ∼ out of the window** no te asomes por la ventana **(b)** (support oneself) apoyarse; **to ∼ against sth** apoyarse CONTRA algo; **to ∼ on sth/sb** apoyarse EN algo/algn
■ **∼** *vt* apoyar

lean² *adj* **(a)** ⟨*person*⟩ delgado; ⟨*animal*⟩ flaco **(b)** ⟨*meat*⟩ magro

leant /lent/ (BrE) *past & past p of* LEAN¹

leap¹ /liːp/ *vi/t* (*past & past p* **leaped** *or* (BrE also) **leapt** /lept/) saltar

leap² *n* salto *m*, brinco *m*; **by ∼s and bounds** a pasos agigantados

leapfrog /ˈliːpfrɔːɡ ‖ ˈliːpfrɒɡ/ *n*: **to play ∼** jugar* a la pídola, brincar* al burro (Méx), jugar* al rango (RPI)

leapt /lept/ (BrE) *past & past p of* LEAP¹

leap year *n* año *m* bisiesto

learn /lɜːrn ‖ lɜːn/ (*past & past p* **learned** *or* (BrE also) **learnt**) *vt* **1 (a)** (gain knowledge of) aprender; **to ∼ to + INF** aprender A + INF **(b)** (memorize) aprender de memoria **2** (become informed about) enterarse de
■ **∼** *vi* **1** (gain knowledge) aprender **2** (become informed) **to ∼ ABOUT O OF sth** enterarse DE algo

learned /ˈlɜːrnəd ‖ ˈlɜːnɪd/ *adj* docto

learner /ˈlɜːrnər ‖ ˈlɜːnə(r)/ *n*: **he's a fast/slow ∼** aprende con mucha rapidez/tiene dificultades de aprendizaje; (before *n*) **∼ (driver)** (esp BrE) persona que está aprendiendo a conducir

learning /ˈlɜːrnɪŋ ‖ ˈlɜːnɪŋ/ *n* **(a)** (knowledge) saber *m*; (education) educación *f*; **a man of ∼** un erudito **(b)** (act) aprendizaje *m*; (before *n*) **∼ difficulties** dificultades *fpl* de aprendizaje

learnt /lɜːrnt ‖ lɜːnt/ (BrE) *past & past p of* LEARN

lease¹ /liːs/ *n* ≈ contrato *m* de arrendamiento; (of real estate) ≈ usufructo *m*

lease² *vt* **(a)** **∼ (out)** (grant use of) arrendar*; ⟨*real estate*⟩ dar* en usufructo **(b)** (hold under lease) arrendar*; ⟨*real estate*⟩ tener* el usufructo de

leasehold /ˈliːshəʊld/ *n* arrendamiento *m*

leash /liːʃ/ *n* correa *f*

least¹ /liːst/ *adj* **1** (*superl* of LITTLE¹ II): **she has the ∼ money** es quien menos dinero tiene **2** (smallest, slightest) más mínimo; **that's the ∼ of my worries** es lo que menos me preocupa

least² *pron* **1** (*superl* of LITTLE²): **to say the ∼** por no decir más; **it's the ∼ I can do** es lo menos que puedo hacer **2** (in adv phrases) **at least** por lo menos; **in the least** en lo más mínimo

least³ adv **1** (superl of LITTLE³): ~ **of all you** tú menos que nadie; **when you** ~ **expect it** cuando menos te lo esperas **2** (before adj, adv) menos

leather /'leðər ‖'leðə(r)/ n cuero m, piel f (Esp, Méx)

leave¹ /li:v/ n **1** (authorized absence) permiso m, licencia f (esp AmL); (Mil) licencia f; **to be/go on** ~ estar*/salir* de permiso or (esp AmL) de licencia **2** (permission) (fml) permiso m **3** (departure) (fml): **to take** ~ **of sb** despedirse* de algn; **have you taken** ~ **of your senses?** ¿te has vuelto loco?

leave² (past & past p **left**) vt **1** (a) (go away from): **she** ~**s home at 6** sale de casa a las 6; **I left her reading a book** la dejé leyendo un libro; **to** ~ **school** dejar el colegio; **she left home at the age of 17** se fue de casa a los 17 años (b) (withdraw from) ⟨profession/organization/politics⟩ dejar **2** (abandon) dejar; **she left her husband for another man** dejó a su marido por otro (hombre) **3** (a) (deposit in specified place) dejar; **to** ~ **sth FOR sb** dejarle algo A algn (b) (not take — deliberately) dejar; (— inadvertently) olvidarse de, dejarse (c) (not eat) ⟨food⟩ dejar **4** (allow, cause to remain) dejar; **please** ~ **the window open** por favor deja la ventana abierta **5** (have as aftereffect) ⟨stain/scar⟩ dejar **6** (a) (not attend to) dejar (b) (not disturb) dejar; ~ **her to finish on her own** déjala terminar sola **7** (entrust): ~ **it to me!** ¡déjalo por mi cuenta!; **we must** ~ **nothing to chance** no debemos dejar nada (librado) al azar **8** (after deduction, elimination): **6 from 10** ~**s 4** si a 10 le quitamos 6, quedan 4; **there isn't much time left** no queda mucho tiempo **9** (bequeath) **to** ~ **sth TO sb/sth** dejar(le) algo A algn/algo

■ ~ vi irse*, marcharse (esp Esp); **the train** ~**s at 5 o'clock** el tren sale a las 5 en punto

■ **leave behind** [v + o + adv, v + adv + o] **(a)** (not take or bring — deliberately) dejar; (— inadvertently) olvidarse de, dejarse (b) ⟨worries/cares⟩ dejar atrás

■ **leave on** [v + o + adv, v + adv + o] **(a)** ⟨light/ machine/television⟩ dejar encendido or (AmL tb) prendido (b) (keep wearing) no quitarse

■ **leave out** **1** [v + o + adv, v + adv + o] [v + o + adv (+ prep + o)] **(a)** (omit) omitir (b) (exclude) excluir* **2** [v + o + adv, v + adv + o] **(a)** (leave outside) dejar fuera or (esp AmL) afuera (b) (not put away) ⟨clothes/toys⟩ no guardar (c) (leave available) dejar preparado

■ **leave over** [v + o + adv, v + adv + o] (usu pass): **tomorrow we can eat what's left over** mañana podemos comer lo que sobre or quede

leaves /li:vz/ pl of LEAF

leaving /'li:vɪŋ/ adj (before n) ⟨present⟩ de despedida; ~ **party** despedida f

Lebanese /'lebə'ni:z/ adj libanés

Lebanon /'lebənɑ:n ‖'lebənən/ n (el) Líbano

lecherous /'letʃərəs/ adj libidinoso

lectern /'lektərn ‖'lektɜ:n/ n atril m; (in church) facistol m

lecture¹ /'lektʃər ‖'lektʃə(r)/ n (public address) conferencia f; (Educ) clase f; (before n) ~ **theater** auditorio m

lecture² vi (Educ) dar* clase, dictar clase (AmL fml), hacer* clase (Chi)

■ ~ vt (scold) sermonear

lecturer /'lektʃərər ‖'lektʃərə(r)/ n **(a)** (speaker) conferenciante mf, conferencista mf (AmL) (b) (esp BrE Educ) profesor universitario, profesora universitaria m,f

led /led/ past & past p of LEAD²

LED n = **light-emitting diode**

ledge /ledʒ/ n **(a)** (on wall) cornisa f; (window ~) (exterior) alféizar m (de la ventana); (interior) repisa f (de la ventana) (b) (on cliff) saliente m or f

ledger /'ledʒər ‖'ledʒə(r)/ n libro m de contabilidad

leech /li:tʃ/ n sanguijuela f

leek /li:k/ n puerro m

leer /lɪr ‖lɪə(r)/ vi **to** ~ **AT sb** lanzarle* una mirada lasciva A algn

leeway /'li:weɪ/ n: **I am given a lot of** ~ me dan mucha libertad de acción; **there isn't much** ~ **in the budget** el presupuesto tiene poco margen de flexibilidad

left¹ /left/ past & past p of LEAVE²

left² n **1** (a) (left side) izquierda f; **on the** ~ a la izquierda; **to drive on the** ~ manejar or (esp Esp) conducir* por la izquierda (b) (left turn): **to make** o (BrE) **take a** ~ girar a la izquierda (c) (Sport) (hand) izquierda f **2** (Pol) **the** ~ la izquierda

left³ adj (before n) izquierdo

left⁴ adv a or hacia la izquierda

left: ~**-hand** adj (before n) de la izquierda; **on the** ~**-hand side** a mano izquierda; ~**-handed** /'left'hændəd ‖,left'hændɪd/ adj ⟨person⟩ zurdo; ⟨tool⟩ para zurdos; ~**-luggage** (office) /'left'lʌɡɪdʒ/ n (BrE) consigna f; ~**-over** adj (before n) sobrante; ~**overs** /'left,əʊvərz ‖'left,əʊvəz/ pl n sobras fpl; ~ **wing** n **(a)** (Pol) (+ sing or pl vb) (ala f) izquierda f (b) (Sport) ala f; izquierda; ~**-wing** /'left'wɪŋ/ adj (Pol) izquierdista; ~**-winger** /'left'wɪŋər ‖,left'wɪŋə(r)/ n (Pol) izquierdista mf

leg /leɡ/ n **1** (Anat) (of person) pierna f; (of animal, bird) pata f; **to pull sb's** ~ (colloq) tomarle el pelo a algn (fam) **2** (a) (Culin) (of lamb, pork) pierna f; (of chicken) pata f, muslo m (b) (Clothing) pierna f; (of chair, table) pata f **3** (stage — of competition, race) manga f; (— of journey) etapa f

legacy /'leɡəsi/ n (pl **-cies**) legado m

legal /'li:ɡəl/ adj **1** (a) (allowed) legal; ⟨tackle/ move⟩ reglamentario (b) (founded upon law) ⟨contract/requirement⟩ legal **2** (relating to legal system, profession) (before n) jurídico; **we will be forced to take** ~ **action** nos veremos obligados a poner el asunto en manos de nuestro(s) abogado(s)

legal holiday n (AmE) día m festivo oficial, feriado m oficial (esp AmL)

legalization /,li:ɡələ'zeɪʃən ‖,li:ɡəlaɪ'zeɪʃən/ n legalización f

legalize /'li:ɡəlaɪz/ vt legalizar*

legally /'li:ɡəli/ adv legalmente

legal tender n moneda f de curso legal

legend /'ledʒənd/ n leyenda f

legendary /'ledʒənderi ‖'ledʒəndri/ adj legendario

leggings /'leɡɪŋz/ pl n **(a)** (pants, trousers) leggings mpl, mallas fpl, calzas fpl (RPl) (b) (for lower leg) polainas fpl

legible /'ledʒəbəl/ adj legible

legion /'li:dʒən/ n legión f

legislate /'ledʒəsleɪt ‖'ledʒɪsleɪt/ vi legislar

legislation /ledʒəs'leɪʃən ‖ledʒɪs'leɪʃən/ n legislación f

legislative /'ledʒəsleɪtɪv ‖'ledʒɪslətɪv/ adj (before n) legislativo

legislator /'ledʒəsleɪtər ‖'ledʒɪsleɪtə(r)/ n legislador, -dora m,f

legislature /'ledʒɪsleɪtʃər ‖'ledʒɪsleɪtʃə(r)/ n asamblea f legislativa

legitimate /lɪ'dʒɪtəmət ‖lɪ'dʒɪtɪmət/ adj legítimo

legitimize /lɪ'dʒɪtəmaɪz ‖lɪ'dʒɪtɪmaɪz/ vt legitimar

legroom /'legru:m, -rʊm/ n espacio m para las piernas

leisure /'li:ʒər ‖'leʒə(r)/ n tiempo m libre; **read it at your ~** léalo cuando le venga bien; (before n) ⟨activity⟩ de tiempo libre; **~ center** (AmE) centro m recreativo; **~ centre** (BrE) centro m deportivo

leisurely /'li:ʒərli ‖'leʒəli/ adj lento, pausado; **at a ~ pace** sin prisas

lemon /'lemən/ n **(a)** (fruit) limón m, limón m francés (Méx, Ven); (before n) **~ squeezer** (BrE) exprimelimones m, exprimidor m; **~ tea** té m con limón **(b)** **(~ tree)** (color) limonero m **(c)** (color) amarillo m limón; (before n) amarillo limón adj inv

lemonade /lemə'neɪd/ n **(a)** (with fresh lemons) limonada f **(b)** (fizzy drink) (BrE) (bebida f) gaseosa f

lemon cheese, lemon curd n crema f de limón (en conserva)

lend /lend/ vt (past & past p **lent**) prestar; **this ~s an air of mystery to the scene** esto le da un aire de misterio a la escena

lender /'lendər ‖'lendə(r)/ n (institution) entidad f crediticia; (person) prestamista mf

length /leŋθ/ n **1** **(a)** (of line, surface) longitud f; (of sleeve, coat) largo m; **it's 5m in ~** mide 5 metros de largo; **he traveled the ~ and breadth of the country** viajó a lo largo y (a lo) ancho del país; **he'd go to any ~s to get what he wants** es capaz de hacer cualquier cosa con tal de obtener lo que se propone **(b)** (of book, list) extensión f **2** **(a)** (duration) (of movie, play) duración f; **after a considerable ~ of time** después de mucho tiempo **(b) at length** (finally) finalmente; (for a long time) extensamente; (in detail) detenidamente; **to talk at ~** hablar largo y tendido **3** (section — of wood, pipe) trozo m; (— of river, road) tramo m **4** **(a)** (in swimming) largo m **(b)** (in horse, dog racing) cuerpo m; (in rowing) largo m

lengthen /'leŋθən/ vt ⟨skirt/novel⟩ alargar*; ⟨line/visit⟩ alargar*

lengthwise /'leŋθwaɪz/, (esp BrE)
lengthways /-weɪz/ adv a lo largo

lengthy /'leŋθi/ adj **-thier -thiest** (long) largo; (tedious) largo y pesado

lenient /'li:nɪənt/ adj ⟨attitude/view⟩ indulgente; ⟨sentence⟩ poco severo

lens /lenz/ n (pl **lenses**) **(a)** (Opt) lente f **(b)** (for magnifying) lupa f **(c)** (in spectacles) cristal m **(d)** ► CONTACT LENS **(e)** (Phot) lente f

lent /lent/ past & past p of LEND

Lent /lent/ n Cuaresma f

lentil /'lentl/ n lenteja f

Leo /'li:əʊ/ n (pl **-os**) **(a)** (sign) (no art) Leo **(b)** (person) Leo or leo mf

leopard /'lepərd ‖'lepəd/ n leopardo m

leotard /'li:ətɑːrd ‖'li:ətɑːd/ n malla f

leper /'lepər ‖'lepə(r)/ n leproso, -sa m,f

leprosy /'leprəsi/ n lepra f

lesbian /'lezbɪən/ n lesbiana f

lesion /'li:ʒən/ n lesión f

less¹ /les/ adj (comp of LITTLE¹ II) menos; **~ and ~ money** cada vez menos dinero

less² pron (comp of LITTLE²) menos; **a sum of ~ than $1,000** una suma inferior a los 1.000 dólares

less³ adv (comp of LITTLE³) menos; **the situation is no ~ serious than it was** la situación sigue siendo tan grave como antes

-less /ləs ‖lɪs/ suff sin; **hat~** sin sombrero

lessen /'lesn/ vt ⟨pain⟩ aliviar; ⟨cost/risk⟩ reducir*
■ ~ vi ⟨noise⟩ disminuir*; ⟨pain⟩ aliviarse; ⟨interest⟩ decrecer*

lesser /'lesər ‖'lesə(r)/ adj (before n) menor; **to a ~ extent** en menor grado

lesson /'lesn/ n **1** (Educ) **(a)** (class) clase f **(b)** (in textbook) lección f **2** (from experience) lección f; **to learn one's ~** aprender la lección

lest /lest/ conj (liter) no sea que (+ subj); **~ we forget** para que no olvidemos

let /let/ (pres p **letting**; past & past p **let**) vt **1** (no pass) **(a)** (allow to) dejar; **he ~ his hair grow** se dejó crecer el pelo; **~ me help you** deja que te ayude; **~ me see** ¿a ver?; **don't ~ me catch you here again!** ¡que no te vuelva a pescar por aquí! **(b)** (cause to, make): **~ me know if there are any problems** avísame si hay algún problema; **he ~ it be known that ...** hizo saber que ... **(c)** to **~ go soltar***; **~ go of my hand!** ¡suéltame la mano!; **to ~ oneself go** (enjoy oneself) soltarse*; (neglect oneself) abandonarse **2** (+ adv compl): **to ~ sth/sb by** o past dejar pasar algo/a algn; **she ~ herself into the house** abrió la puerta y entró en la casa **3** [Used to form 1st pers pl imperative] **~'s go** vamos, vámonos; **~'s ask Chris** vamos a preguntarle a Chris, preguntémosle a Chris; **don't ~'s** o **~'s not argue** no discutamos; **~ us pray** (frml) oremos **4** [Used to form 3rd pers imperative, gen translated by QUE + SUBJ in Spanish] **~ that be a lesson to you** que te sirva de lección; **just ~ them try!** ¡que se atrevan! **5** (rent) (esp BrE) alquilar; **⑤ to let** se alquila
■ **let down** [v + o + adv, v + adv + o] **1** **(a)** (lower) ⟨rope/bucket⟩ bajar **(b)** (lengthen) ⟨skirt⟩ alargar*; (lower) ⟨hem⟩ bajar, sacar **(c)** ⟨tire/balloon⟩ desinflar **2** (disappoint) fallar; **her spelling ~s her down** su ortografía no le hace justicia a su trabajo
■ **let in** [v + o + adv, v + adv + o] dejar entrar
■ **let off**
I **1** **(a)** [v + o + adv] (forgive, not punish) perdonar; **she was ~ off with a reprimand** solo le hicieron una amonestación **(b)** [v + o + adv] [v + o + prep + o] (excuse from) perdonar **2** [v + o + adv] (allow to go) dejar salir

II [v + o + adv, v + adv + o] ⟨fireworks⟩ hacer*
estallar; ⟨rocket/cracker⟩ tirar
■ **let on** [v + adv] [v + adv + o]: **you mustn't ~
on about this to Jim** no le vayas a decir nada de
esto a Jim; **don't ~ on (that) you know me!** no
digas que me conoces
■ **let out**
  I [v + o + adv, v + adv + o] **1** (disclose) ⟨secret⟩
revelar
  2 (rent out) (esp BrE) alquilar
  3 (make wider) ⟨skirt/dress⟩ ensanchar, agrandar
  II [v + o + adv, v + adv + o] [v + o + adv (+ prep
+ o)] (allow to leave) dejar salir; **someone ~ the air
out of my tires** alguien me desinfló los
neumáticos
  III [v + adv + o] ⟨scream/yell⟩ soltar*
■ **let up** [v + adv] ⟨wind/storm⟩ amainar;
«pressure/work» disminuir*

letdown /'letdaʊn/ n decepción f

lethal /'li:θəl/ adj mortal, letal; ⟨weapon⟩
mortífero

lethargic /lə'θɑːrdʒɪk ‖lɪ'θɑːdʒɪk/ adj
aletargado

let's /lets/ (= **let us**) ▸ LET² 3

letter /'letər ‖'letə(r)/ n **1** (written message)
carta f **2** (of alphabet) letra f

letter: ~ bomb n carta f bomba; **~ box** n
buzón m

lettuce /'letəs ‖'letɪs/ n lechuga f

let-up /'letʌp/ n interrupción f

leukemia, (esp BrE) **leukaemia** /luː'kiːmiə/ n
leucemia f

level¹ /'levəl/ n nivel m; **at eye ~** a la altura de
los ojos; **a top-~ meeting** una reunión de or a
alto nivel

level² adj **1** ⟨ground/surface⟩ plano, llano; **a ~
spoonful** una cucharada rasa; **to do one's ~ best**
hacer* todo lo posible **2 (a)** (at same height) **to be
~** (WITH sth) estar* al nivel (DE algo) **(b)** (abreast,
equal): **the two teams were ~ at half-time** al medio
tiempo los dos equipos iban empatados; **to draw
~ with sb** (in a race) alcanzar* a algn **3** (unemotional, calm) desapasionado

level³, (BrE) **-ll-** vt **1 (a)** (make flat) ⟨ground/
surface⟩ nivelar **(b)** (raze) ⟨building/town⟩ arrasar
2 (make equal) igualar **3** (direct) **to ~ sth AT/A
sth** ⟨weapon⟩ apuntarle A algn/A algo CON algo; **to
~ an accusation at sb** acusar a algn
■ **~** vi (be honest) (colloq) **to ~ WITH sb** ser* franco
CON algn
■ **level off** [v + adv] **(a)** «aircraft» nivelarse,
enderezarse* **(b)** «prices/growth/inflation»
estabilizarse*

level: ~ crossing n (BrE) paso m a nivel,
crucero m (Méx); **~-headed** /'levəl'hedəd
‖,levəl'hedɪd/ adj sensato

lever¹ /'levər ‖'liːvə(r)/ n palanca f

lever² vt (+ adv compl): **to ~ sth open** abrir*
algo haciendo palanca

levy¹ /'levi/ vt **levies, levying, levied (a)**
⟨tax/duty⟩ (impose) imponer*; (collect) recaudar **(b)**
⟨fee/charge⟩ cobrar **(c)** ⟨fine⟩ imponer*

levy² n (pl **levies**) **(a)** (raising of tax, contributions):
the strike was funded by a ~ on all members la
huelga se financió mediante el cobro de una
cuota a todos los miembros **(b)** (tax) impuesto m

lewd /luːd ‖ljuːd/ adj **-er, -est** lascivo

liability /ˌlaɪə'bɪləti/ n (pl **-ties**)
1 (responsibility) responsabilidad f **2 liabilities**
pl (debt) (Fin) pasivo m **3** (disadvantage) (no pl):
she's a positive ~ es un verdadero lastre; **the car
turned out to be a ~** el coche terminó dándonos
más problemas que otra cosa

liable /'laɪəbəl/ adj (pred) **1** (responsible)
responsable; **to be ~ FOR sth** ser* responsable DE
algo **2** (likely): **I'm ~ to forget** es probable que me
olvide; **the earlier model was ~ to overheat** el
modelo anterior tenía tendencia a recalentarse

liaise /li'eɪz/ vi (esp BrE) **to ~** (WITH sb) actuar*
de enlace (CON algn); **the departments will ~
closely** los departamentos mantendrán un
estrecho contacto

liaison /li'eɪzɑːn ‖li'eɪzn/ n **1** (coordination)
enlace m **2** (affair) (liter) affaire m

liar /'laɪər ‖'laɪə(r)/ n mentiroso, -sa m,f

libel¹ /'laɪbəl/ n (defamation) difamación f; (where
a crime is implied) calumnia f

libel² vt, (BrE) **-ll-** (defame) difamar; (where a crime
is implied) calumniar

liberal¹ /'lɪbərəl/ adj **1 (a)** (tolerant) ⟨ideas⟩
liberal; ⟨interpretation⟩ libre **(b) Liberal** (Pol)
del Partido Liberal; **L~ Democrat** (in UK)
demócrata mf liberal **2** (generous) generoso

liberal² n **(a)** (progressive thinker) liberal mf **(b)
Liberal** (party member) liberal mf

liberalism /'lɪbərəlɪzəm/ n liberalismo m

liberalize /'lɪbərəlaɪz/ vt liberalizar*

liberally /'lɪbərəli/ adv **(a)** (generously)
generosamente **(b)** (not strictly) libremente

liberate /'lɪbəreɪt/ vt liberar

liberation /ˌlɪbə'reɪʃən/ n liberación f

Liberia /laɪ'bɪriə ‖laɪ'bɪəriə/ n Liberia f

Liberian /laɪ'bɪriən ‖laɪ'bɪəriən/ adj liberiano

liberty /'lɪbərti ‖'lɪbəti/ n (pl **-ties**) libertad f;
I'm not at ~ to tell you no se lo puedo decir; **to
take the ~ of -ING** (esp BrE) tomarse la libertad DE
+ INF

Libra /'liːbrə, 'laɪbrə ‖'liːbrə/ n **(a)** (sign) (no
art) Libra **(b)** (person) Libra or libra mf

librarian /laɪ'breriən ‖laɪ'breəriən/ n
bibliotecario, -ria m,f

library /'laɪbreri ‖'laɪbrəri/ n (pl **-ries**)
biblioteca f

libretto /lə'bretəʊ ‖lɪ'bretəʊ/ n (pl **-tos** or **-ti**
/-tiː/) libreto m

Libya /'lɪbiə/ n Libia f

Libyan /'lɪbiən/ adj libio

lice /laɪs/ pl of LOUSE

license¹, (BrE) **licence** /'laɪsns/ n **1 (a)**
(permit) permiso m; **import/export ~** permiso de
importación/exportación; (before n) **~ number**
(AmE Auto) número m de matrícula or (CS) de
patente; **~ plate** matrícula f, placa f (AmL),
patente f (CS), chapa f (RPl) **(b)** ▸ DRIVER'S
LICENSE **2 (a)** (freedom): **poetic ~** licencia f
poética **(b)** (excessive freedom) (fml) libertinaje m

license² /'laɪsns/ vt otorgarle* un permiso a

licensed /'laɪsnst/ adj ⟨practitioner⟩ autorizado
para ejercer; ⟨premises⟩ (BrE) autorizado para
vender bebidas alcohólicas

licentious /laɪ'sentʃəs ‖laɪ'senʃəs/ adj
licencioso

lichen /'laɪkən, 'lɪtʃən/ n liquen m

lick /lɪk/ vt lamer; ⟨stamp⟩ pasarle la lengua a

licorice, (BrE) **liquorice** /'lɪkərɪʃ, -ɪs/ n
regaliz f, orozuz m

lid /lɪd/ n **1** (of container) tapa f **2** (eye ∼)
párpado m

lie¹ /laɪ/ n (untruth) mentira f; **to tell ∼s** decir*
mentiras, mentir*

lie² vi
I (3rd pers sing pres **lies**; pres p **lying**; past &
past p **lied**) (tell untruths) mentir*
II (3rd pers sing pres **lies**; pres p **lying**; past
lay; past p **lain**) **1** (a) (lie down) echarse,
tenderse* (b) (be in lying position) estar* tendido; **I
lay awake for hours** estuve horas sin poder
dormir (c) (be buried) yacer* (liter); **ⓢ here lies
John Brown** aquí yacen los restos de John Brown
2 (be) «object» estar*; **the snow lay two feet
deep** la nieve tenía dos pies de espesor
3 (be located) «building/city» encontrarse*; **a
group of islands lying off the west coast** un
conjunto de islas situadas cerca de la costa
occidental
4 «problem/difference» radicar*; «answer»
estar*
■ **lie down** [v + adv] (a) (adopt lying position)
echarse, tenderse* (b) (be lying) estar* tendido

lie detector n detector m de mentiras

lieu /lu: ‖lju:/ n (frml): **in ∼ of** en lugar de, en
vez de; **time off in ∼** horas fpl/días mpl libres a
cambio

lieutenant /lu:'tenənt ‖lef'tenənt/ n (a) (in
navy) teniente mf de navío, teniente mf primero
(en Chi) (b) (in other services) teniente mf

life /laɪf/ n (pl **lives**) **1** vida f; **animal/plant ∼**
vida animal/vegetal; **in later ∼** más tarde or más
adelante; **it brings the history of this period to ∼**
hace cobrar vida a este período de la historia; **to
bring sb back to ∼** resucitar a algn; **to come to
∼** «party» animarse; «puppet» cobrar vida; **he
was fighting for his life** se debatía entre la vida y
la muerte; **to have the time of one's ∼** divertirse*
como nunca; **run for your lives!** ¡sálvese quien
pueda!; **to save sb's ∼** salvarle la vida a algn; **to
be the ∼** o (esp BrE) **the ∼ and soul of the party**
ser* el alma de la fiesta; **to live the ∼ of Riley**
darse* la gran vida; **to take one's ∼ in one's
hands** jugarse* la vida; (before n) «member/
president» vitalicio; **his ∼ story** la historia de su
vida
2 (duration — of battery) duración f; (— of agreement)
vigencia f
3 (imprisonment) (colloq) cadena f perpetua

life: **∼ assurance** n (BrE) ▶ INSURANCE; **∼
belt** n (BrE) salvavidas m; **∼boat** n (on ship)
bote m salvavidas; (shore-based) lancha f de
salvamento; **∼ buoy** n salvavidas m; **∼ cycle**
n ciclo m vital; **∼guard** n salvavidas mf,
socorrista mf; **∼ insurance** n seguro m de
vida; **∼ jacket** n chaleco m salvavidas

lifeless /'laɪfləs ‖'laɪflɪs/ adj (dead) sin vida,
inánime (frml), exánime (liter); (unconscious) inerte

life: **∼like** adj verosímil; **∼line** n (rope) cuerda

f de salvamento; **his letters were my ∼line** sus
cartas eran lo único que me mantenía viva;
∼long adj (before n): **a ∼long friend** un amigo
de toda la vida; **∼ preserver** /prɪ'zɜ:rvər
‖prɪ'zɜ:və(r)/ n (AmE) (a) ▶ LIFE BUOY (b) ▶ LIFE
JACKET; **∼ raft** n balsa f salvavidas; **∼ ring** n
(AmE) salvavidas m; **∼saver** /'laɪf‚seɪvər
‖'laɪf‚seɪvə(r)/ n (a) ▶ LIFEGUARD (b) (from bad
situation) salvación f; **∼-saving** adj (before n) que
salva vidas; **∼size** /'laɪf'saɪz/, **∼sized** /-d/ adj
(de) tamaño natural; **∼ span** n (of living creature)
vida f; (of project) duración f; (of equipment) vida f
útil; **∼style** n estilo m de vida; **∼time** n vida
f; **the chance of a ∼time** la oportunidad de su (or
mi etc) vida; (before n) «appointment/post»
vitalicio; **∼time guarantee** garantía f para toda la
vida; **∼ vest** n (AmE) chaleco m salvavidas

lift¹ /lɪft/ n **1** (boost) impulso m **2** (ride): **can I
give you a ∼?** ¿quieres que te lleve or (Per fam)
jale?, ¿quieres que te dé un aventón (Méx) or (Col
fam) una palomita? **3** (elevator) (BrE) ascensor m

lift² vt **1** (raise) levantar **2** (end) ⟨ban/siege⟩
levantar
■ ∼ vi (a) (rise) «curtain» levantarse (b) (clear)
«mist» disiparse
■ **lift off** [v + adv] «rocket» despegar*
■ **lift up** [v + o + adv, v + adv + o] levantar

lift-off /'lɪftɔ:f ‖'lɪftɒf/ n (Aerosp) despegue m

ligament /'lɪgəmənt/ n ligamento m

ligature /'lɪgətʃʊr ‖'lɪgətʃə(r)/ n ligadura f

light¹ /laɪt/ n **1** luz f; **by the ∼ of the moon** a
la luz de la luna; **to come to ∼** salir* a la luz; **to
see the ∼** abrir* los ojos
2 (a) (source of light) luz f; (lamp) lámpara f;
(before n) **∼ switch** interruptor m (b) (of car,
bicycle) luz f (c) (traffic ∼) semáforo m
3 (a) (aspect) (no pl): **to see sth/sb in a good/
bad/new** o **different** ∼ ver* algo/a algn con
buenos/malos/otros ojos (b) **in the ∼ of** o (AmE
also) **in ∼ of** (as prep) a la luz de, en vista de
4 (for igniting): **have you got a ∼?** ¿tienes fuego?;
to set ∼ to sth prenderle fuego a algo

light² adj **-er, -est**
I **1** (not heavy) ligero, liviano (esp AmL); ⟨voice⟩
suave **2** (a) (Meteo) ⟨breeze/wind⟩ suave; **∼ rain**
llovizna f (b) (sparse): **the losses were fairly ∼** las
pérdidas fueron de poca consideración (c) (not
strenuous) ⟨work/duties⟩ ligero, liviano (esp AmL)
3 (not serious) ⟨music/comedy/reading⟩ ligero; **to
make ∼ of sth** quitarle or restarle importancia a
algo
II (a) (pale) ⟨green/brown⟩ claro (b) (bright): **it
gets ∼ very early these days** ahora amanece muy
temprano; **it's already ∼** ya es de día

light³ adv: **to travel ∼** viajar con el mínimo de
equipaje

light⁴ vt **1** (past & past p **lighted** or **lit**) (set
alight) encender* **2** (past & past p **lit**) (illuminate)
iluminar
■ ∼ vi (past & past p **lighted** or **lit**) encenderse*
■ **light up** (past & past p **lit**) **1** [v + adv] (a)
«eyes/face» iluminarse (b) «smoker» encender*

un cigarrillo (*or* un puro *etc*) **2** [*v + o + adv, v + adv + o*] **(a)** ‹*street/square*› iluminar **(b)** ‹*cigar/ pipe*› encender*

light: **~ bulb** *n* ▶ BULB 2; **~ cream** *n* (AmE) crema *f* líquida, nata *f* líquida (Esp); **~-emitting diode** /'daɪəʊd/ *n* diodo *m* emisor de luz

lighten /'laɪtn/ *vt* **1** ‹*load/workload*› aligerar; ‹*responsibility/conscience*› descargar* **2 (a)** ‹*room*› dar* más luz a; ‹*sky*› iluminar **(b)** ‹*color/ hair*› aclarar
■ **~** *vi* **1** «*load/weight*» hacerse* más liviano *or* (esp AmL) liviano, aligerarse **2** «*sky*» despejarse; «*face*» iluminarse; «*atmosphere*» relajarse

lighter /'laɪtər ‖ 'laɪtə(r)/ *n* (cigarette **~**) encendedor *m*, mechero *m* (Esp)

light: **~-fingered** /'laɪt'fɪŋgərd ‖ ˌlaɪt'fɪŋgəd/ *adj* (colloq): **to be ~-fingered** tener* (la) mano larga (fam); **~-hearted** /'laɪt'hɑːrtəd ‖ ˌlaɪt'hɑːtɪd/ *adj* alegre, desenfadado; **~house** *n* faro *m*

lighting /'laɪtɪŋ/ *n* iluminación *f*; (on streets) alumbrado *m*

lightly /'laɪtli/ *adv* **1 (a)** ‹*touch*› suavemente; ‹*snow*› ligeramente **(b)** ‹*grill/beat*› ligeramente **2 (a)** (frivolously) a la ligera **(b)** (not severely): **they were let off ~** los trataron con indulgencia

lightning[1] /'laɪtnɪŋ/ *n*: **a bolt of ~** un relámpago; **a flash of ~** un relámpago; **a streak of ~** un rayo; **like greased ~** como un relámpago; (*before n*) **~ conductor** *o* **rod** pararrayos *m*

lightning[2] *adj* relámpago *adj inv*; **with ~ speed** como un rayo

lightweight[1] /'laɪtweɪt/ *adj* ligero, liviano (esp AmL); ‹*writer/performance*› de poco peso

lightweight[2] *n* (in boxing, wrestling) peso *m* ligero; (minor figure) persona *f* de poco peso

light year *n* año *m* luz

likable /'laɪkəbəl/ *adj* agradable, simpático

like[1] /laɪk/ *vt* **1** (enjoy, be fond of): **I ~ tennis** me gusta el tenis; **she ~s him, but she doesn't love him** le resulta simpático pero no lo quiere; **do as** *o* **what you ~** haz lo que quieras; **I ~ dancing** me gusta bailar; **I don't ~ to mention it, but ...** no me gusta (tener que) decírtelo pero ...
2 (in requests, wishes) querer*; **we would just ~ to say how grateful we are** queríamos decirle lo agradecidos que estamos; **would you ~ a cup of tea?** ¿quieres una taza de té?
■ **~** *vi* querer*; **if you ~** si quieres

like[2] *n* **1** (sth liked): **her/his ~s and dislikes** sus preferencias **2** (similar thing, person) **the ~:** **judges, lawyers and the ~** jueces, abogados y (otra) gente por el estilo; **I've never heard the ~ (of this)** nunca he oído cosa igual

like[3] *adj* (dated *or* frml) parecido

like[4] *prep* **1 (a)** (similar to) como; **what's she ~?** ¿cómo es?; **she's very ~ her mother** se parece mucho a su madre **(b)** (typical of): **that's not ~ her** es muy raro en ella; **it's just ~ you to think of food** ¡típico! *or* ¡cuándo no! ¡tú pensando en comida! **2** (indicating manner): **~ this/that** así; **to run ~ mad** correr como un loco **3** (such as, for example) como

like[5] *conj* (crit) **(a)** (as if): **she looks ~ she knows**

---

what she's doing parece que sabe lo que hace; **they stared at him ~ he was crazy** se quedaron mirándolo como si estuviera loco **(b)** (as, in same way) como

-like /laɪk/ *suff*: **prison~** parecido a una prisión; **snake~** ‹*appearance*› (como) de serpiente; ‹*movement*› serpenteante

likeable *adj* ▶ LIKABLE

likelihood /'laɪklihʊd/ *n* probabilidad *f*, posibilidad *f*; **there is every ~ that she'll agree** es muy probable que acepte

likely[1] /'laɪkli/ *adj* **-lier, -liest (a)** (probable) ‹*outcome/winner*› probable; **it's more than ~ that she's out** lo más seguro es que no esté; **a ~ story!** (iro) ¡cuéntame otra! (iró); **it is ~ to be a tough match** lo más probable es que sea un partido difícil **(b)** (promising): **she's the most ~ applicant** es la candidata con más posibilidades; **this is a ~ place to find a telephone** aquí tiene que haber un teléfono

likely[2] *adv*: **most ~ she'll forget** lo más probable es que se olvide; **not ~!** (colloq) ¡ni hablar! (fam)

liken /'laɪkən/ *vt* **to ~ sth/sb TO sth/sb** comparar algo/a algn CON *or* A algo/algn

likeness /'laɪknəs ‖ 'laɪknɪs/ *n* **(a)** (resemblance) parecido *m* **(b)** (referring to a portrait): **it's a good ~** es un buen retrato

likewise /'laɪkwaɪz/ *adv* **(a)** (in the same way) asimismo **(b)** (the same): **to do ~** hacer* lo mismo

liking /'laɪkɪŋ/ *n* **(a)** (fondness) **~ (FOR sth)** afición *f* (A algo); **to take a ~ to sb/sth** tomarle *or* (esp Esp) cogerle* simpatía a algn/gusto a algo **(b)** (satisfaction) gusto *m*; **to be to sb's ~** ser* del gusto de algn

lilac /'laɪlək/ *n* **(a)** **~ (bush)** lila *f*, lilo *m*; (*before n*) **~ flower** lila *f* **(b)** (color) lila *m*; (*before n*) lila *adj inv*

lilt /lɪlt/ *n* (of song, tune) cadencia *f*; **to speak with a ~** hablar con un tono cantarín

lilting /'lɪltɪŋ/ *adj* ‹*voice*› cantarín, musical; ‹*melody*› cadencioso

lily /'lɪli/ *n* (*pl* **lilies**) (Bot) liliácea *f*; (white **~**) azucena *f*, lirio *m* blanco

lily-of-the-valley /'lɪliəvðə'vælɪ/ *n* (*pl* **lilies-of-the-valley**) lirio *m* de los valles, muguete *m*

limb /lɪm/ *n* **(a)** (Anat) miembro *m*; **to tear sb ~ from ~** despedazar* a algn **(b)** (of tree) rama *f* (*principal*); **to go out on a ~** aventurarse

limber up /'lɪmbər ‖ 'lɪmbə(r)/ [*v + adv*] hacer* ejercicios de calentamiento

lime /laɪm/ *n* **1** (calcium oxide) cal *f* **2 (a)** (fruit) lima *f* **(b)** (tree) limero *m*, lima *f* **(c)** (color) verde *m*; (*before n*) verde lima *adj inv* **3** (linden) (BrE) tilo *m*

lime: **~-green** /'laɪm'griːn/ *adj* (*pred* **~ green**) verde lima *adj inv*; **~light** *n*: **to be in the ~light** estar* en primer plano; **to steal the ~light** acaparar la atención del público

limerick /'lɪmərɪk/ *n*: poema humorístico de cinco versos

limestone /'laɪmstəʊn/ *n* (piedra *f*) caliza *f*

limit[1] /'lɪmət ‖ 'lɪmɪt/ *n* **1 (a)** (boundary) límite ⋯⋗

m **(b)** (furthest extent): **she pushes herself to the ~** se esfuerza al máximo; **that's the ~!** (colloq) ¡es el colmo! (fam) **2** (restriction, maximum) límite *m*

limit² *vt* limitar; **to ~ oneself TO sth/-ING** limitarse A algo/+ INF

limitation /ˌlɪməˈteɪʃən/ /ˌlɪmɪˈteɪʃən/ *n* limitación *f*

limited /ˈlɪmətəd/ /ˈlɪmɪtɪd/ *adj* **(a)** ‹number/ experience/scope› limitado **(b)** (AmE Transp) ‹express/train/bus› semi-directo **(c)** (Busn) ‹liability› limitado; **public ~ company** (BrE) sociedad *f* anónima

limitless /ˈlɪmətləs/ /ˈlɪmɪtlɪs/ *adj* ilimitado, sin límites

limousine /ˈlɪməziːn, ˌlɪməˈziːn/ *n* limusina *f*

limp¹ /lɪmp/ *vi* cojear, renguear (AmL)

limp² *n* cojera *f*, renguera *f* (AmL); **she walks with a ~** cojea *or* (AmL tb) renguea

limp³ *adj* ‹handshake› flojo; ‹lettuce› mustio; ‹hair› lacio y sin vida

limpet /ˈlɪmpət/ /ˈlɪmpɪt/ *n* lapa *f*

linden /ˈlɪndən/ *n* (AmE) tilo *m*

line¹ /laɪn/ *n* **1** **(a)** (mark, trace) línea *f*; (Math) recta *f*; **to be on the ~** (colloq) estar* en peligro, peligrar; (before *n*) ‹drawing› dibujo *m* lineal **(b)** (on face, palm) línea *f*; (wrinkle) arruga *f* **2** **(a)** (boundary, border) línea *f*; **the county/state ~** (AmE) (la línea de) la frontera del condado/estado **(b)** (Sport) línea *f*; (before *n*) **~ judge** juez *mf* de línea **(c)** (contour) línea *f* **3** **(a)** (cable, rope) cuerda *f*; (clothes o washing ~) cuerda (de tender la ropa); (fishing ~) sedal *m*; **power ~** cable *m* eléctrico **(b)** (Telec) línea *f*; **hold the ~, please** no cuelgue *or* (CS tb) no corte, por favor; **it's a very bad ~** se oye muy mal **4** (Transp) **(a)** (company, service) línea *f*; **shipping ~** línea de transportes marítimos **(b)** (Rail) línea *f*; (track) (BrE) vía *f* **5** **(a)** (path) línea *f*; **it was right in my ~ of vision** me obstruía la visual **(b)** (attitude, policy) postura *f*, línea *f*; **to take a hard ~ (with sb/on sth)** adoptar una postura *or* línea dura (con algn/ con respecto a algo) **(c)** (method, style): **~ of inquiry** línea *f* de investigación; **I was thinking of something along the ~s of ...** pensaba en algo del tipo de ... **6** **(a)** (row) fila *f*; (queue) (AmE) cola *f*; **to wait in ~** (AmE) hacer* cola; **to get in ~** (AmE) ponerse* en la cola; **to cut in ~** (AmE) colarse* (fam), brincarse* *or* saltarse la cola (Méx fam); **in/into ~ with sth: the new measures are in ~ with government policy** las nuevas medidas siguen la línea de la política del gobierno; **he needs to be brought into ~** hay que llamarlo al orden **(b)** (series) serie *f*; **he's the latest in a long ~ of radical leaders** es el último de una larga serie de dirigentes radicales **(c)** (succession) línea *f*; **he's next in ~ to the throne** es el siguiente en la línea de sucesión al trono **7** (Mil) línea *f* **8** **(a)** (of text) línea *f*, renglón *m*; (of poem) verso *m*; **to read between the ~s** leer* entre líneas **(b) lines** *pl* (Theat): **to learn one's ~s** aprenderse el papel; **he forgot his ~s** se olvidó de lo que le tocaba decir **(c)** (note): **to drop sb a ~** escribirle* a algn unas líneas

line² *vt* **1** **(a)** ‹skirt/box› forrar **(b)** (form lining along) cubrir* **2** (border): **the avenue is ~d with**

trees la avenida está bordeada de árboles; **crowds ~d the route** cientos de personas estaban alineadas a ambos lados del camino

■ **line up 1** [*v* + *adv*] (form line, row) ponerse* en fila; (queue up) (AmE) hacer* cola **2** [*v* + *o* + *adv*, *v* + *adv* + *o*] **(a)** (form into line) ‹soldiers/prisoners› poner* en fila **(b)** (arrange): **we've a busy program ~d up for you** le tenemos preparada una apretada agenda **(c)** (align) alinear

lineage /ˈlɪnɪdʒ/ *n* linaje *m*

linear /ˈlɪnɪər/ /ˈlɪnɪə(r)/ *adj* lineal

lined /laɪnd/ *adj* **(a)** ‹paper› con renglones *or* (Chi) reglones **(b)** ‹jacket/boots/curtains› forrado **(c)** (Tech) revestido **(d)** ‹face/skin› arrugado

linen /ˈlɪnən/ *n* **1** (cloth) hilo *m*, lino *m* **2** (bed ~) ropa *f* blanca *or* de cama; (table ~) mantelerías *fpl*; (before *n*) **~ basket** canasto *m or* cesto *m* de la ropa sucia

liner /ˈlaɪnər/ /ˈlaɪnə(r)/ *n* **1** (ship) buque *m* (de pasaje *or* pasajeros); (ocean ~) transatlántico *m* **2** **(a)** (lining) forro *m*; (dust)bin ~ (BrE) bolsa *f* de la basura **(b)** (of record) (AmE) funda *f*, carátula *f*

line: ~sman /ˈlaɪnzmən/ *n* (*pl* **-men** /-mən/) (Sport) juez *m* de línea; **~up** *n* **(a)** (Sport) alineación *f*; **the band's original ~up** la integración original del grupo **(b)** (of suspects) (AmE) rueda *f* de identificación *or* de sospechosos

linger /ˈlɪŋgər/ /ˈlɪŋgə(r)/ *vi* **(a)** (delay leaving) quedarse (un rato) **(b)** ~ (**on**) ‹aftertaste/smell› persistir; ‹tradition› perdurar, sobrevivir **(c) lingering** *pres p* persistente, que no desaparece **(d)** (take one's time): **her eyes ~ed on the child** se quedó largo rato mirando al niño; **they ~ed over their coffee** se entretuvieron tomando el café

lingerie /ˈlɑːnʒəreɪ/ /ˈlænʒəri/ *n* lencería *f*

linguist /ˈlɪŋgwəst/ /ˈlɪŋgwɪst/ *n* lingüista *mf*

linguistic /lɪŋˈgwɪstɪk/ *adj* lingüístico

linguistics /lɪŋˈgwɪstɪks/ *n* (+ *sing vb*) lingüística *f*

lining /ˈlaɪnɪŋ/ *n* forro *m*

link¹ /lɪŋk/ *n* **1** **(a)** (in chain) eslabón *m* **(b)** ▶ CUFF LINK **2** **(a)** (connection) conexión *f* **(b)** (tie, bond) vínculo *m*, lazo *m* **(c)** (Telec, Transp) conexión *f*, enlace *m*

link² *vt* **(a)** ‹components› unir; ‹terminals› conectar; **to ~ arms** tomarse *or* (esp Esp) cogerse* del brazo **(b)** ‹buildings/towns› unir, conectar **(c)** ‹facts/events› relacionar

■ **link up 1** [*v* + *adv*] conectar; ‹spacecraft› acoplarse **2** [*v* + *o* + *adv*, *v* + *adv* + *o*] conectar

links /lɪŋks/ *n* (*pl* **~**) (+ *sing o pl vb*) campo *m* de golf (*esp a orillas del mar*)

linkup /ˈlɪŋkʌp/ *n* **(a)** (connection) conexión *f*; (of spacecraft) acoplamiento *m* **(b)** (Rad, TV) conexión *f*, enlace *m*

linoleum /lɪˈnəʊlɪəm/ *n* linóleo *m*

linseed /ˈlɪnsiːd/ *n* linaza *f*; (before *n*) **~ oil** aceite *m* de linaza

lint /lɪnt/ *n* hilas *fpl*

lion /ˈlaɪən/ *n* león *m*

lioness /ˈlaɪənəs/ /ˈlaɪənes/ *n* leona *f*

lion tamer /ˈteɪmər/ /ˈteɪmə(r)/ *n* domador, -dora *m,f* de leones

lip /lɪp/ *n* **(a)** (Anat) labio *m* **(b)** (of cup, tray) borde *m*

lip: ~ **gloss** n brillo m de labias; ~**read** (past & past p -**read** vi /-red/) leer* los labios; ~ **salve** n bálsamo m labial; ~ **service** n: he just pays ~ service to feminism es feminista de los dientes para afuera; ~**stick** n (a) (stick) lápiz m or barra f de labios, lápiz m labial (AmL), pintalabios m (Esp fam) (b) (substance) rouge m

liquefy /'lɪkwəfaɪ ‖'lɪkwɪfaɪ/ -**fies, -fying, -fied** vi licuarse*
■ ~ vt licuar*

liqueur /lɪ'kɜːr ‖li'kjʊə(r)/ n licor m

liquid¹ /'lɪkwəd ‖'lɪkwɪd/ n líquido m

liquid² adj líquido

liquidation /ˌlɪkwə'deɪʃən ‖ˌlɪkwɪ'deɪʃən/ n liquidación f

liquid crystal display n pantalla f de cristal líquido

liquidize /'lɪkwədaɪz ‖'lɪkwɪdaɪz/ vt licuar*

liquidizer /'lɪkwədaɪzər ‖'lɪkwɪdaɪzə(r)/ n (BrE) licuadora f

liquor /'lɪkər ‖'lɪkə(r)/ n alcohol m, bebidas fpl alcohólicas; (before n) ~ **cabinet** (AmE) mueble-bar m

liquorice (BrE) ▶ LICORICE

liquor store n (AmE) ≈ tienda f de vinos y licores, botillería f (Chi)

Lisbon /'lɪzbən/ n Lisboa f

lisp¹ /lɪsp/ n ceceo m

lisp² vi cecear

list¹ /lɪst/ n lista f

list² vt (a) (enumerate) hacer* una lista de; (verbally) enumerar (b) ⟨securities/stocks⟩ cotizar*
■ ~ vi (Naut) escorar

listen /'lɪsn/ vi escuchar; **to** ~ **TO** sth/sb escuchar algo/a algn

listener /'lɪsnər ‖'lɪsnə(r)/ n (a) (Rad) oyente mf, radioyente mf (b) (in conversation): he's a good ~ es una persona que sabe escuchar

listing /'lɪstɪŋ/ n lista f; ~**s magazine** guía f de espectáculos, ≈guía f del ocio (en Esp)

listless /'lɪstləs ‖'lɪstlɪs/ adj (lacking enthusiasm) apático; (lacking energy) lánguido

lit /lɪt/ past & past p of LIGHT⁴

litany /'lɪtəni/ n (pl -**nies**) letanía f

liter, (BrE) **litre** /'liːtər ‖'liːtə(r)/ n litro m

literacy /'lɪtərəsi/ n alfabetismo m

literal /'lɪtərəl/ adj literal

literally /'lɪtərəli/ adv literalmente; I didn't mean it ~ no lo decía en sentido literal

literary /'lɪtəreri ‖'lɪtərəri/ adj literario

literate /'lɪtərət/ adj alfabetizado

literature /'lɪtərətʃʊr ‖'lɪtrətʃə(r)/ n (a) (art) literatura f (b) (promotional material) folletos mpl

lithe /laɪð/ adj **lither, lithest** ágil

lithograph /'lɪθəgræf ‖'lɪθəgrɑːf/ n litografía f

Lithuania /ˌlɪθjuˈeɪniə/ n Lituania f

Lithuanian /ˌlɪθjuˈeɪniən/ adj lituano

litigation /ˌlɪtə'geɪʃən ‖ˌlɪtɪ'geɪʃən/ n litigio m

litmus /'lɪtməs/: ~ **paper** n papel m (de) tornasol; ~ **test** n (Chem) prueba f de acidez or de tornasol

litre /'liːtər ‖'liːtə(r)/ n (BrE) ▶ LITER

litter¹ /'lɪtər ‖'lɪtə(r)/ n **1** (refuse) basura f **2** (offspring) (Zool) camada f, cría f **3** (for horses, cows) lecho m de paja; (for cats) arena f higiénica

litter² vt: newspapers ~ed the floor el suelo estaba cubierto de papeles; **to be** ~**ed WITH** sth estar* lleno DE algo

litter: ~ **bin** n (BrE) papelera f or (AmL tb) papelero m or (Col) caneca f; ~**bug** n: persona que tira basura en lugares públicos; ~ **lout** n (BrE) ▶ ~BUG

little¹ /'lɪtl/ adj
I (comp **littler** /'lɪtlər ‖'lɪtlə(r)/; superl **littlest** /'lɪtləst ‖'lɪtlɪst/) (small, young) pequeño, chico (esp AmL); **a** ~ **while** un ratito; **my** ~ **sister/brother** mi hermanita/hermanito
II (comp **less;** superl **least**) (a) (not much) poco; there is very ~ bread left queda muy poco pan (b) **a little** (some) un poco de

little² pron (comp **less;** superl **least**) (a) (not much) poco, -ca; ~ **by** ~ poco a poco (b) **a little** (some) un poco, algo

little³ adv (comp **less;** superl **least**) poco; ~ **did he know that ...** lo que menos se imaginaba era que ...; **a little** (somewhat) un poco; **I'm feeling a** ~ **tired** estoy algo or un poco cansado

live¹ /lɪv/ vi vivir; she ~**d to be 100** llegó a cumplir 100 años; she had three months to ~ le quedaban tres meses de vida; **where do you** ~? ¿donde vives?; **long** ~ **the king!** ¡viva el rey!; ~ **and let** ~ (set phrase) vive y deja vivir a los demás
■ ~ vt vivir; she ~**s a happy life** lleva una vida feliz, vive feliz; **to** ~ **life to the full** vivir la vida al máximo
■ **live down** [v + o + adv, v + adv + o]: if they see you wearing that, you'll never ~ **it down** si te ven con eso no lo van a olvidar nunca
■ **live for** [v + prep + o]: she ~**s for her work** vive para su trabajo; **I've nothing left to** ~ **for** ya no tengo nada por lo que vivir
■ **live off** [v + prep + o] (a) (be supported by) ⟨family/friends⟩ vivir a costa de; ⟨crime/the land⟩ vivir de (b) (feed on) ⟨fruits/seeds⟩ alimentarse de
■ **live on 1** [v + adv] «memory» seguir* presente; «tradition» seguir* existiendo
2 [v + prep + o] (a) (feed on) alimentarse de (b) (support oneself with): she ~**s on $75 a week** vive con 75 dólares a la semana
■ **live through** [v + prep + o] ⟨war/experience⟩ vivir
■ **live together** [v + adv] (a) (cohabit) vivir juntos (b) (coexist) convivir
■ **live up** [v + o + adv]: **to** ~ **it up** (colloq) darse* la gran vida (fam)
■ **live up to** [v + adv + prep + o]: it didn't ~ **up to its reputation** no estuvo a la altura de su reputación; **they** ~ **up to their name** hacen honor a su nombre

live² /laɪv/ adj **1** (alive) vivo **2** (of current interest) ⟨issue⟩ candente **3** (Rad, TV): the show was ~ el programa era en directo; the program is recorded before a ~ **audience** el programa se graba con público en la sala

live³ /laɪv/ adv ⟨broadcast⟩ en directo

live-in /'lɪvɪn/ adj (before n) ⟨staff⟩ residente; ⟨nanny/maid⟩ con cama, de planta (Méx), puertas adentro (Chi); **she has a** ~ **lover** su amante vive con ella

livelihood /'laɪvlɪhʊd/ n (no pl): farming is their ~ viven de la agricultura; to earn one's ~ ganarse la vida

lively /'laɪvli/ adj -lier, -liest ⟨place/debate⟩ animado; ⟨music⟩ alegre; ⟨account⟩ vívido

liven up /'laɪvən/ **1** [v + adv] animarse **2** [v + o + adv, v + adv + o] animar

liver /'lɪvər ‖ 'lɪvə(r)/ n hígado m; (before n) ⟨transplant⟩ de hígado; ~ disease enfermedad f del hígado

lives /laɪvz/ pl of LIFE

livestock /'laɪvstɑːk ‖ 'laɪvstɒk/ n (+ sing or pl vb) animales mpl (de cría); (cattle) ganado m

livid /'lɪvəd ‖ 'lɪvɪd/ adj **1** (furious) (colloq) furioso **2** ⟨bruise⟩ amoratado; ⟨face⟩ lívido

living¹ /'lɪvɪŋ/ n **1** (livelihood) (no pl): to earn o make one's/a ~ ganarse la vida; to work for a ~ trabajar para vivir; what does he do for a ~? ¿en qué trabaja? **2** (style of life) vida f; (before n) ⟨space/area⟩ destinado a vivienda; ~ standards nivel m de vida

living² adj (before n) vivo

living room n sala f (de estar) , living m (esp AmS), salón m (esp Esp)

lizard /'lɪzərd ‖ 'lɪzəd/ n lagarto m; (wall ~) lagartija f

'll /l/ (a) = **will** (b) = **shall**

llama /'lɑːmə/ n llama f

LLB n = **Bachelor of Laws**

lo /ləʊ/ interj (arch or hum): ~ and behold ¡y quién lo iba a decir!

load¹ /ləʊd/ n **1** (cargo, burden) carga f; four ~s of washing cuatro lavados or (Esp) coladas **2** (often pl) (colloq) (much, many) cantidad f, montón m (fam); the play is a ~ of rubbish la obra es una porquería (fam) **3** (Civil Eng) carga f; ❺ maximum load 15 tons peso máximo: 15 toneladas

load² vt/i cargar*
■ **load up 1** [v + o + adv, v + adv + o] cargar* **2** [v + adv] cargar*

loaded /'ləʊdəd ‖ 'ləʊdɪd/ adj (a) ⟨vehicle/gun/camera⟩ cargado (b) (richly provided) (pred) to be ~ WITH sth estar* repleto DE algo (c) (weighted) ⟨dice⟩ cargado; ⟨question⟩ tendencioso

loaf¹ /ləʊf/ n (pl loaves): a ~ (of bread) un pan; (of French bread) una barra de pan, una flauta (CS); (baked in tin) un pan de molde

loaf² vi (colloq): to ~ (around o about) holgazanear

loan¹ /ləʊn/ n préstamo m

loan² vt prestar

loath /ləʊθ/ adj (pred) to be ~ to + INF resistirse A + INF

loathe /ləʊð/ vt odiar, detestar

loathsome /'ləʊðsəm/ adj repugnante

loaves /ləʊvz/ pl of LOAF¹

lob¹ /lɑːb ‖ lɒb/ vt -bb- lanzar* por lo alto

lob² n globo m, lob m

lobby¹ /'lɑːbi ‖ 'lɒbi/ n (pl -bies) **1** (entrance hall) vestíbulo m; (in theater) foyer m **2** (pressure group) grupo m de presión

lobby² -bies, -bying, -bied vt ejercer* presión sobre
■ ~ vi to ~ FOR sth ejercer* presión para obtener algo

lobe /ləʊb/ n (ear~) lóbulo m (de la oreja)

lobster /'lɑːbstər ‖ 'lɒbstə(r)/ n langosta f, bogavante m (Esp)

local¹ /'ləʊkəl/ adj **1** ⟨dialect/newspaper⟩ local; ⟨council/election⟩ ≈municipal; a ~ call una llamada urbana; he's a ~ man es de aquí (or de allí) **2** (Med) ⟨anesthetic⟩ local; ⟨infection⟩ localizado

local² n (a) (inhabitant): he's not a ~ no es de aquí (or de allí); the ~s say it's true los (vecinos) del lugar dicen que es verdad (b) (pub) (BrE colloq): our ~ el bar de nuestro barrio (or de nuestra zona etc)

locale /ləʊˈkæl ‖ ləʊˈkɑːl/ n escenario m

local government n ≈administración f municipal; (before n) ⟨elections⟩ ≈municipal

locality /ləʊˈkæləti/ n (pl -ties) (frml) localidad f

localize /'ləʊkəlaɪz/ vt localizar*

locally /'ləʊkəli/ adv ⟨live/work⟩ en la zona

locate /'ləʊkeɪt ‖ ləʊˈkeɪt/ vt **1** (find) ⟨fault/leak⟩ localizar*, ubicar* (esp AmL) **2** (position) ⟨building/business⟩ situar*, ubicar* (esp AmL)

location /ləʊˈkeɪʃən/ n **1** (position) posición f, ubicación f (esp AmL) **2** (Cin) lugar m de filmación; we were filming on ~ in Italy estábamos rodando los exteriores en Italia

loch /lɑːk, lɑːx ‖ lɒk, lɒx/ n lago m

lock¹ /lɑːk ‖ lɒk/ n **1** (device) cerradura f, chapa f (AmL) **2** (on canal) esclusa f **3** (of hair) mechón m

lock² vt ⟨door/car⟩ cerrar* (con llave); to ~ sb in a room encerrar* a algn en una habitación
■ **lock in** [v + o + adv, v + adv + o] encerrar*
■ **lock out** [v + o + adv, v + adv + o]: I ~ed myself out (of the house) me quedé afuera sin llaves
■ **lock up** [v + o + adv, v + adv + o] (a) ⟨valuables⟩ guardar bajo llave; ⟨person⟩ encerrar* (b) ⟨house/shop⟩ cerrar* con llave

locker /'lɑːkər ‖ 'lɒkə(r)/ n armario m, locker m (AmL); (at bus, railway station) casilla f (de la) consigna f automática

locker room n (esp AmE) vestuario m

locket /'lɑːkət ‖ 'lɒkɪt/ n relicario m

lock: **~out** n cierre m patronal, paro m patronal (AmL); **~smith** n cerrajero, -ra m,f

locomotive /'ləʊkəˈməʊtɪv/ n locomotora f

locust /'ləʊkəst/ n langosta f

lode /ləʊd/ n veta f, filón m

lodge¹ /lɑːdʒ ‖ lɒdʒ/ n **1** (a) (for gatekeeper) (BrE) casa f del guarda (b) (for porter) portería f (c) (on private estate) pabellón m (d) (at resort) (AmE) hotel m **2** (branch, meeting place) logia f

lodge² *vt* **1** ⟨*appeal*⟩ interponer*; ⟨*complaint*⟩ presentar **2** (deposit) depositar
■ ~ *vi* **1** (become stuck): **the bullet had ~d in his spine** la bala se le había alojado en la columna **2** (live as lodger) alojarse, hospedarse

lodger /ˈlɑːdʒər ‖ˈlɒdʒə(r)/ *n* inquilino, -na *m,f* (*de una habitación en una casa particular*)

lodging /ˈlɑːdʒɪŋ ‖ˈlɒdʒɪŋ/ *n* **(a)** (accommodations) alojamiento *m* **(b) lodgings** *pl* (rented): **to live in ~s** vivir en una habitación alquilada (*or* en una pensión *etc*)

loft /lɔːft ‖lɒft/ *n* (BrE) desván *m*, altillo *m* (esp AmL), zarzo *m* (Col)

loftily /ˈlɔːftəli ‖ˈlɒftɪli/ *adv* con altivez, altaneramente

lofty /ˈlɔːfti ‖ˈlɒfti/ *adj* **-tier, -tiest (a)** (elevated) ⟨*ideals/sentiments*⟩ noble, elevado **(b)** (haughty) altivo, altanero **(c)** (high) (liter) alto, majestuoso (liter)

log¹ /lɔːg ‖lɒg/ *n* **1** (wood) tronco *m*; (as fuel) leño *m*; **to sleep like a ~** dormir* como un tronco (fam) **2** (record) diario *m* **3** (Math) logaritmo *m*

log² **-gg-** *vt* ⟨*speed/position/time*⟩ registrar, anotar; ⟨*call*⟩ registrar
■ **log in, log on** [*v + adv*] (Comput) entrar (al sistema)
■ **log off, log out** [*v + adv*] (Comput) salir* (del sistema)

loganberry /ˈləʊgənˌberi ‖ˈləʊgənbəri/ *n* (*pl* **-ries**) frambuesa *f* de Logan

logarithm /ˈlɔːgərɪðəm ‖ˈlɒgərɪðəm/ *n* logaritmo *m*

logbook /ˈlɔːgbʊk ‖ˈlɒgbʊk/ *n* (register) diario *m*; (Naut) diario *m* de navegación *or* de a bordo; (Aviat) diario *m* de vuelo

loggerheads /ˈlɔːgərhedz ‖ˈlɒgəhedz/ *pl n*: **they were constantly at ~** siempre estaban en desacuerdo

logic /ˈlɑːdʒɪk ‖ˈlɒdʒɪk/ *n* lógica *f*

logical /ˈlɑːdʒɪkəl ‖ˈlɒdʒɪkəl/ *adj* lógico

logistics /ləˈdʒɪstɪks/ *n* **(a)** (Mil) (+ *sing vb*) logística *f* **(b)** (practicalities) (+ *pl vb*) problemas *mpl* logísticos

logo /ˈləʊgəʊ, ˈlɑː- ‖ˈləʊgəʊ/ *n* (*pl* **logos**) logo *m*

loin /lɔɪn/ *n* **(a)** (meat) lomo *m* **(b) loins** *pl* (Anat) (liter) entrañas *fpl* (liter)

loincloth /ˈlɔɪnklɔːθ ‖ˈlɔɪnklɒθ/ *n* taparrabos *m*

loiter /ˈlɔɪtər ‖ˈlɔɪtə(r)/ *vi* perder* el tiempo

lollipop /ˈlɑːlipɑːp ‖ˈlɒlipɒp/ *n* piruleta *f or* (Esp) Chupa Chups®, chupachup(s) *m or* (Andes, Méx) paleta *f or* (RPl) chupetín *m or* (Col) colombina *f or* (Chi, Per) chupete *m*

lolly /ˈlɑːli ‖ˈlɒli/ *n* (*pl* **-lies**) (BrE) (ice ~) paleta *f* (helada) *or* (Esp) polo *m or* (RPl) palito *m or* (CS) chupete *m* helado

London /ˈlʌndən/ *n* Londres *m*; (*before n*) londinense

lone /ləʊn/ *adj* solitario; ⟨*explorer/sailor*⟩ en solitario

loneliness /ˈləʊnlinəs ‖ˈləʊnlinɪs/ *n* soledad *f*

lonely /ˈləʊnli/ *adj* **-lier, -liest (a)** (feeling alone): **to feel ~** sentirse* solo **(b)** (isolated) solitario, aislado

loner /ˈləʊnər ‖ˈləʊnə(r)/ *n*: **she's a bit of a ~** le gusta estar sola

lonesome /ˈləʊnsəm/ *adj* (esp AmE) ▶ LONELY

long¹ /lɔːŋ ‖lɒŋ/ *adj* **longer** /ˈlɔːŋgər ‖ˈlɒŋgə(r)/, **longest** /ˈlɔːŋgəst ‖ˈlɒŋgɪst/ **1** (in space) ⟨*distance/hair/list*⟩ largo; **how ~ do you want the skirt?** ¿cómo quieres la falda de larga?; **the wall is 200 m ~** el muro mide 200 m de largo; **the book is over 300 pages ~** el libro tiene más de 300 páginas **2** (in time) largo; **two months isn't ~ enough** dos meses no son suficientes; **she's been gone a ~ time** hace tiempo que se fue

long² *adv* **-er, -est 1** (in time): **how ~ have you been living here?** ¿cuánto hace que vives aquí?; **people live ~er now** ahora la gente vive más (años); **it won't be ~ before they get here** no tardarán en llegar; **not ~ afterwards** poco después; **not ~ ago** no hace mucho **2 (a)** (*in phrases*) **before long: you'll be an aunt before ~** dentro de poco serás tía; **for long: she wasn't gone for ~** no estuvo fuera mucho tiempo; **no longer, not any longer: I can't stand it any ~er** ya no aguanto más; **they no ~er live here** ya no viven aquí **(b) as long as, so long as** (*as conj*) (for the period) mientras; (providing that) con tal de que (+ *subj*); **for as ~ as I can remember** desde que tengo memoria

long³ *vi* **to ~ to + INF** estar* deseando + INF
■ **long for** [*v + prep + o*] ⟨*mother/friend*⟩ echar de menos, extrañar (esp AmL); **she ~ed for Friday to arrive** estaba deseando que llegara el viernes

long-distance¹ /ˈlɔːŋˈdɪstəns ‖ˌlɒŋˈdɪstəns/ *adj* ⟨*truck driver*⟩ que hace largos recorridos; ⟨*train*⟩ de largo recorrido; ⟨*race/runner*⟩ de fondo; **a ~ telephone call** una llamada de larga distancia, una conferencia (interurbana) (Esp)

long-distance² *adv* (esp AmE): **to call ~** hacer* una llamada de larga distancia, poner* una conferencia (Esp)

longevity /lɑːnˈdʒevəti ‖lɒnˈdʒevəti/ *n* (fml) longevidad *f*

long: ~-haired /ˈlɔːŋˈherd ‖ˌlɒŋˈheəd/ *adj* de pelo largo; **~hand** *n*: **in ~hand** en escritura normal (*no en taquigrafía*); **~-haul** /ˈlɔːŋˈhɔːl ‖ˌlɒŋˈhɔːl/ *adj* (before n) de larga distancia

longing /ˈlɔːŋɪŋ ‖ˈlɒŋɪŋ/ *n* (nostalgia) añoranza *f*; (desire) vivo deseo *m*

longitude /ˈlɑːndʒətuːd ‖ˈlɒŋgɪtjuːd, ˈlɒndʒɪtjuːd/ *n* longitud *f*

long: ~ johns /dʒɑːnz ‖dʒɒnz/ *pl n* calzoncillos *mpl* largos; **~ jump** *n* salto *m* de longitud, salto *m* (en) largo (AmL); **~-lost** /ˈlɔːŋˈlɔːst ‖ˈlɒŋlɒst/ *adj* (before n): **she had a ~-lost uncle in Australia** tenía un tío en Australia a quien había perdido de vista hacía mucho tiempo; **~-playing record** /ˈlɔːŋˈpleɪɪŋ ‖ˈlɒŋˌpleɪŋ/ *n* disco *m* de larga duración; **~-range** /ˈlɔːŋˈreɪndʒ ‖ˈlɒŋreɪndʒ/ *adj* (before n) ⟨*missile*⟩ de largo alcance; ⟨*aircraft*⟩ para vuelos largos; **~-running** /ˈlɔːŋˈrʌnɪŋ ‖ˈlɒŋˌrʌnɪŋ/ *adj* ⟨*musical/farce*⟩ que lleva tiempo en cartelera; ⟨*feud/controversy*⟩ que viene (*or* venía *etc*) de largo; **~shoreman** /ˈlɔːŋˈʃɔːrmən ‖ˈlɒŋˌʃɔːmən/ *n* (*pl* **-men** /-mən/) (AmE) estibador *m*, changador *m* (RPl); **~sighted** /ˈlɔːŋˈsaɪtəd ‖ˌlɒŋˈsaɪtɪd/ *adj* hipermétrope; **~-sleeved** /ˈlɔːŋˈsliːvd ‖ˈlɒŋsliːvd/ *adj* de manga larga; **~standing** /ˈlɔːŋˈstændɪŋ

‖ˌlɒŋ'stændɪŋ/ adj antiguo, que viene (or venía etc) de largo; ∼**-suffering** /'lɔːŋ'sʌfərɪŋ ‖ˌlɒŋ'sʌfərɪŋ/ adj sufrido; ∼**-term** /'lɔːŋ'tɜːrm ‖'lɒŋtɜːm/ adj (usu before n) **(a)** (in the future) ⟨effects/benefits⟩ a largo plazo **(b)** (for a long period) ⟨solution⟩ duradero; ⟨effects⟩ prolongado; ⟨unemployment⟩ de larga duración; ∼ **wave** n onda f larga; ∼**-winded** /'lɔːŋ'wɪndəd ‖ˌlɒŋ'wɪndɪd/ adj ⟨speech/article⟩ denso, prolijo

loo /luː/ n (BrE colloq) baño m (esp AmL), váter m (Esp fam)

look[1] /lʊk/ n **1** (glance) mirada f; **to have** o **take a** ∼ **at sth/sb** echarle un vistazo a algo/algn **2** (search, examination): **have a** ∼ **for my pipe, will you?** mira a ver si me encuentras la pipa, por favor; **do you mind if I take a** ∼ **around?** ¿le importa si echo un vistazo? **3 (a)** (expression) cara f **(b)** (appearance) aire m; **I don't like the** ∼ **of his friend** no me gusta el aspecto or (fam) la pinta de su amigo **(c)** (Clothing) moda f, look m **(d)** ⟨looks pl⟩ (beauty) belleza f; **she was attracted by his good** ∼**s** la atrajo lo guapo or (AmL tb) lo buen mozo que era

look[2] vi **I 1** (see, glance) mirar; **I** ∼**ed around** (behind) me volví a mirar or miré hacia atrás; (all around) miré a mi alrededor; **to** ∼ **away** apartar la vista; **to** ∼ **down** (lower eyes) bajar la vista; (from tower, clifftop) mirar hacia abajo; ∼ **out (of) the window** mira por la ventana; **to** ∼ **up** (raise eyes) levantar la vista; (toward ceiling, sky) mirar hacia arriba; **to** ∼ **on the bright side of sth** ver* el lado bueno or positivo de algo **2** (search, investigate) mirar, buscar* **II** (seem, appear): **he** ∼**s well** tiene buena cara; **he** ∼**s like his father** se parece a su padre; **I wanted to** ∼ **my best** quería estar lo mejor posible ▪ ∼ vt mirar; **to** ∼ **sb up and down** mirar a algn de arriba (a) abajo; ∼ **where you're going!** ¡mira por dónde vas!

▪ **look after** [v + prep + o] **(a)** (care for) ⟨invalid/child/animal⟩ cuidar (de); ⟨guest⟩ atender* **(b)** (keep watch on) cuidar **(c)** (be responsible for) encargarse* de

▪ **look ahead** [v + adv] (in space) mirar hacia adelante; (into the future) mirar hacia el futuro

▪ **look at** [v + prep + o] **1** ⟨person/picture⟩ mirar **2** (consider) considerar; ∼ **at it from my point of view** míralo desde mi punto de vista; **the program** ∼**s at university life** el programa enfoca la vida universitaria **3** (check) ⟨patient/arm⟩ examinar; ⟨car/pump⟩ revisar

▪ **look back** [v + adv] **(a)** (in space) mirar (hacia) atrás **(b)** (into the past): ∼**ing back, it seems foolish** mirándolo ahora, parece una locura; **the program** ∼**s back over the last 20 years** el programa es una retrospectiva de los últimos veinte años

▪ **look down on** [v + adv + prep + o] mirar por encima del hombro a

▪ **look for** [v + prep + o] buscar*

▪ **look forward to** [v + adv + prep + o]: **I'm** ∼**ing forward to my birthday** estoy deseando que llegue mi cumpleaños; **I'm really** ∼**ing forward to the trip** tengo muchas ganas de hacer el viaje; **I** ∼ **forward to hearing from you soon** (Corresp) esperando tener pronto noticias suyas

▪ **look into** [v + prep + o] ⟨matter/case⟩ investigar*; ⟨possibility⟩ estudiar

▪ **look on** [v + adv] mirar

▪ **look out** [v + adv] **(a)** (be careful) tener* cuidado; ∼ **out!** ¡cuidado! **(b)** (overlook) **to** ∼ **out ON** o **OVER sth** dar* a algo

▪ **look out for** [v + adv + prep + o]: ∼ **out for her at the station** fíjate a ver si la ves en la estación; **we were warned to** ∼ **out for thieves** nos advirtieron que tuviéramos cuidado con los ladrones

▪ **look over** [v + adv] ⟨work/contract⟩ revisar; ⟨building⟩ inspeccionar

▪ **look to** [v + prep + o] (rely on): **they are** ∼**ing to you for guidance** esperan que tú los guíes

▪ **look up 1** [v + o + adv, v + adv + o] **(a)** ⟨word⟩ buscar* (en el diccionario) **(b)** ⟨person⟩ ir* a ver **2** [v + adv] (improve) mejorar

▪ **look up to** [v + adv + prep + o] admirar

look-alike /'lʊkəˌlaɪk/ n (colloq) (person) doble mf

looking glass /'lʊkɪŋˌglæs ‖'lʊkɪŋˌglɑːs/ n (dated) espejo m

lookout /'lʊkaʊt/ n **(a)** (watch) (no pl): **to be on the** ∼ **for sth/sb** andar* a la caza de algo/algn **(b)** (person) (Mil) vigía mf

loom[1] /luːm/ n telar m

loom[2] vi **(a)** (be imminent) avecinarse **(b)** (look threatening): **the mountain** ∼**ed high above them** la montaña surgió imponente ante ellos; **the problem** ∼**ed large in his mind** el problema dominaba sus pensamientos

▪ **loom up** [v + adv]: **a figure** ∼**ed up in the darkness** una figura surgió de entre las tinieblas

loop[1] /luːp/ n **1 (a)** (shape) curva f; (in river) meandro m **(b)** (in thread) lazada f **(c)** (in sewing) presilla f **(d)** (Aviat): **to loop the** ∼ rizar* el rizo **2 (a)** (circuit) circuito m cerrado **(b)** (Comput) bucle m

loop[2] vt: ∼ **the wool** haz una lazada con la lana; **I** ∼**ed the dog's lead over the post** enganché la correa del perro en el poste ▪ ∼ vi «road» serpentear

loophole /'luːphəʊl/ n: **a legal** ∼ una laguna jurídica (que se presta a trampas)

loose[1] /luːs/ adj **looser, loosest 1 (a)** (not tight) ⟨garment⟩ suelto **(b)** (not secure) ⟨screw/knot⟩ flojo; ⟨thread/end⟩ suelto; ⟨hair⟩ suelto; **to be at a** ∼ **end** no tener* nada que hacer **(c)** (separate, not packaged) ⟨cigarettes⟩ suelto; ⟨tea/lentils⟩ a granel, suelto; ∼ **change** calderilla f **2** (free) (pred) suelto; **to let** o **set** o **turn sb** ∼ soltar* a algn; **to be on the** ∼ andar* suelto **3** ⟨definition⟩ poco preciso; ⟨translation⟩ libre

loose[2] vt (liter) **(a)** ⟨prisoner⟩ poner* en libertad; ⟨horse⟩ soltar* **(b)** ⟨arrow⟩ lanzar*; ⟨violence/wrath⟩ desatar

loose: ∼**-fitting** /'luːs'fɪtɪŋ/ adj suelto; ⟨clothes⟩ holgado; ∼**-leaf** /'luːs'liːf/ adj ⟨binder⟩ de anillas

loosely /'luːsli/ adv **1** (not tightly) ⟨tie/bandage⟩ sin apretar; **the dress fits** ∼ el vestido no es entallado **2** (not precisely) ⟨define⟩ sin excesivo rigor; ⟨translate⟩ libremente; ∼ **speaking** (indep) (hablando) en términos generales

loosen /'luːsṇ/ vt **(a)** ⟨tooth⟩ aflojar **(b)** ⟨collar/

knot/bolt⟩ aflojar, soltar*; **she ~ed her grip on the steering wheel** dejó de apretar con tanta fuerza el volante
■ ~ *vi* «*knot/bolt*» aflojarse

loot¹ /luːt/ *n* **(a)** (plunder) botín *m* **(b)** (money) (sl) guita *f* (arg), lana *f* (AmL fam), pasta *f* (Esp fam)

loot² *vt/i* saquear

looter /'luːtər ‖'luːtə(r)/ *n* saqueador, -dora *m,f*

looting /'luːtɪŋ/ *n* saqueo *m*

lop /lɑːp ‖lɒp/ *vt* **-pp-** **(a)** ⟨*tree*⟩ podar **(b)** ~ **(off)** ⟨*branch*⟩ cortar

lope /ləʊp/ *vi* ⟨*wolf/dog*⟩ trotar

lopsided /'lɑːp'saɪdəd ‖‚lɒp'saɪdɪd/ *adj* **(a)** (not straight) torcido, chueco (AmL) **(b)** (asymmetric) ⟨*face/smile*⟩ torcido; ⟨*shape*⟩ asimétrico

lord /lɔːrd ‖lɔːd/ *n* **1** **(a)** (nobleman) señor *m*, noble *m* **(b)** **Lord** (in UK) lord *m*; **the (House of) L~s** la cámara de los lores **(c)** **my L~** (addressing judge) (BrE) (su) señoría **2** **Lord** (God): **the L~** el Señor; **the L~'s Prayer** el Padrenuestro

lordship /'lɔːrdʃɪp ‖'lɔːdʃɪp/ *n*: **His/Your L~** (of or to peers, judges) (su) señoría; (of or to bishops) (su) Ilustrísima

lore /lɔːr ‖lɔː(r)/ *n*: **French peasant ~** las tradiciones rurales francesas

lorry /'lɔːri ‖'lɒri/ *n* (*pl* **-ries**) (BrE) camión *m*; (*before n*) ~ **driver** camionero, -ra *m,f*

lose /luːz/ *vt* (*past & past p* **lost**)
I **1** (mislay) perder*
2 (be deprived of) ⟨*sight/territory/right*⟩ perder*; **to ~ one's voice** quedarse afónico
3 (rid oneself of) ⟨*inhibitions*⟩ perder*; **to ~ weight** adelgazar*, perder* peso
4 (cause to lose) costar*; **their hesitation lost them the contract** la falta de decisión les costó *or* les hizo perder el contrato
5 (let pass) ⟨*time/opportunity*⟩ perder*; **my watch ~s three minutes every day** mi reloj (se) atrasa tres minutos por día
II (fail to win) ⟨*game/battle/election*⟩ perder*
■ ~ *vi* **1** **(a)** (be beaten) «*team/contestant/party*» perder*; **they're losing 3-1** van perdiendo 3 a 1; **to ~ TO sb** perder* FRENTE A algn **(b) losing** *pres p* ⟨*team/party*⟩ perdedor
2 (suffer losses) perder*
3 «*watch/clock*» atrasar, atrasarse

loser /'luːzər ‖'luːzə(r)/ *n* perdedor, -dora *m,f*

loss /lɔːs ‖lɒs/ *n* pérdida *f*; **to be a dead ~** (colloq): **this typewriter is a dead ~** esta máquina de escribir no sirve para nada *or* (fam) es una porquería; **to be at a ~**: **I was at a ~ for words** no supe qué decir; **to cut one's ~es** cortar por lo sano; (Fin) reducir* las pérdidas

lost¹ /lɔːst ‖lɒst/ *past & past p of* LOSE

lost² *adj*
I **1** (mislaid, missing) perdido; **to get ~** perderse*, extraviarse* (frml); **get ~!** (sl) ¡vete al diablo! (fam), ¡andá a pasear! (RPl fam) **2** (wasted) ⟨*time*⟩ perdido; ⟨*opportunity*⟩ desperdiciado, perdido; **to be ~ on sb**: **these subtleties are ~ on him** se le escapan estas sutilezas **4** (absorbed) **to be ~ IN sth** estar* ensimismado EN algo; **to be ~ in thought** estar* absorto *or* ensimismado
II (not won) ⟨*battle/election*⟩ perdido

lost: ~ **and found** /'lɔːstən'faʊnd ‖‚lɒstən'faʊnd/ *n* (AmE) objetos *mpl* perdidos; ~ **property** *n* (esp BrE) objetos *mpl* perdidos

lot /lɑːt ‖lɒt/ *n* **1** (large number, quantity) **(a)** (*no pl*): **a ~ of wine** mucho vino; **I've seen a ~ of her recently** la he visto mucho últimamente; **what a ~ of books you've got!** ¡cuántos libros tienes! **(b)** **a ~** (*as adv*) mucho **(c) lots** *pl* (colloq): **how many seats are there left? — lots** ¿cuántos asientos quedan? — muchos *or* (Esp) montones; **~s of people liked it** a mucha gente le gustó **2** **(a)** (group, mass of things) montón *m*, pila *f* **(b)** (group of people) (colloq): **they're a funny ~** son raros, son gente rara; **come on, you ~!** ¡vamos, ustedes *or* (Esp) vosotros! **(c)** **the ~** (esp BrE): **they ate the ~** se lo comieron todo (*or* se las comieron todas *etc*) **3** (at auction) lote *m*

loth /ləʊθ/ *adj* ▶ LOATH

lotion /'ləʊʃən/ *n* loción *f*

lottery /'lɑːtəri ‖'lɒtəri/ *n* (*pl* **-ries**) lotería *f*

lotus /'ləʊtəs/ *n* (*pl* **~es**) loto *m*

loud¹ /laʊd/ *adj* **-er, -est** **(a)** ⟨*noise*⟩ fuerte; **he said it in a ~ voice** lo dijo en voz alta **(b)** (vigorous) ⟨*protests*⟩ enérgico **(c)** (ostentatious) ⟨*color*⟩ llamativo, chillón

loud² *adv* **-er, -est** ⟨*speak*⟩ alto; **she laughed (the) ~est of all** fue la que se rio más fuerte

loudly /'laʊdli/ *adv* **(a)** ⟨*shout*⟩ fuerte; ⟨*speak*⟩ alto, en voz alta **(b)** ⟨*complain*⟩ a voz en grito

loud: ~**mouth** *n* (colloq) gritón, -tona *m,f*; ~**speaker** /'laʊd'spiːkər ‖‚laʊd'spiːkə(r)/ *n* altavoz *m*, altoparlante *m* (AmC)

lounge¹ /laʊndʒ/ *n* (on ship, in hotel) salón *m*; (in house) (BrE) sala *f* (de estar), living *m* (esp AmS), salón *m* (esp Esp)

lounge² *vi*: **to ~ around** *o* **about** no hacer* nada

louse /laʊs/ *n* (*pl* **lice**) (Zool) piojo *m*

lousy /'laʊzi/ *adj* **-sier, -siest** (colloq) ⟨*food/weather*⟩ asqueroso (fam); **a ~ movie** una película malísima

lout /laʊt/ *n* patán *m* (fam), gandalla *m* (Méx fam), jallán *m* (AmC)

louver, (BrE) **louvre** /'luːvər ‖'luːvə(r)/ *n* lama *f*, listón *m* (de persiana); (*before n*) ⟨*door/window*⟩ de lamas, tipo persiana

lovable /'lʌvəbəl/ *adj* adorable, amoroso (AmL)

love¹ /lʌv/ *n* **1** **(a)** (emotional attachment) amor *m*; **to fall/be in ~ with sb/sth** enamorarse/estar* enamorado de algn/algo; **to make ~ to sb** hacer* el amor con algn **(b)** (enthusiasm, interest) ~ **OF sth** amor *m* A *or* POR algo **2** **(a)** (greetings, regards): **give my ~ to your parents** (dale) recuerdos a tus padres (de mi parte) **(b)** (in letters) ~ **from John** *o* ~, **John** un abrazo, John **3** (person loved) amor *m*; (thing loved) pasión *f* **4** (colloq) (*as form of address*) cariño **5** (in tennis) cero *m*

love² *vt* querer*, amar (liter); **I ~ music/reading** me encanta la música/leer; **I'd ~ a cup of tea** una taza de té me vendría de maravilla

loveable *adj* ▶ LOVABLE

loveless /'lʌvləs ‖'lʌvlɪs/ *adj* sin amor

lovely /'lʌvli/ *adj* **-lier, liest** ⟨*appearance*⟩ precioso, lindo (esp AmL); ⟨*person/nature*⟩ encantador, amoroso (AmL); ⟨*meal/taste*⟩ (BrE) riquísimo; **the weather was ~** hacía un tiempo buenísimo

lover /'lʌvər ‖'lʌvə(r)/ n **1** (partner in love) amante mf **2** (fan) ~ **OF sth** amante mf DE algo

loving /'lʌvɪŋ/ adj cariñoso; **with ~ care** con tierno cuidado

lovingly /'lʌvɪŋli/ adv ⟨gaze/whisper⟩ tiernamente; ⟨handwritten/prepared⟩ con amor or cariño; ⟨restored⟩ con el mayor cuidado

low¹ /ləʊ/ adj **-er, -est 1** (in height) bajo; **the dress had a very ~ back** el vestido era muy escotado por la espalda

2 (a) (in volume) ⟨voice⟩ bajo; ⟨sound/whisper⟩ débil; **turn the radio down ~** bájale al radio (AmL exc CS), baja la radio (CS, Esp) **(b)** ⟨key/note/pitch⟩ grave

3 (in intensity, amount, quality) bajo; ⟨proportion⟩ pequeño; **cook on a ~ flame** o **heat** cocinar a fuego lento; **he has a ~ opinion of doctors** no tiene muy buena opinión de los médicos; **a ~ point in his career** un momento bajo en su carrera

4 (in short supply): **stocks are running ~** se están agotando las existencias

low² adv **-er, -est 1** (in height) bajo; **to fly ~** volar* bajo or a poca altura **2** (in volume, pitch) bajo

low³ n punto m más bajo; **relations between the two countries are at an all-time ~** las relaciones entre los dos países nunca han sido peores

low⁴ vi mugir*

low- /ləʊ/ pref: **~priced** de bajo precio; **~income** de bajos ingresos

low: ~alcohol /'ləʊˌælkəhɒːl ‖'ləʊˌælkəhɒl/ adj de baja graduación alcohólica; **~-calorie** /'ləʊˈkæləri/ adj bajo en calorías; **~-class** /'ləʊˈklæs ‖ˌləʊˈklɑːs/ adj ⟨place⟩ de mala muerte (fam); ⟨clientele⟩ de poca categoría; **~-cut** /'ləʊˈkʌt/ adj escotado; **~down** n (colloq): **to give sb the ~down (on sth)** poner* a algn al tanto (de algo)

lower¹ /'ləʊər ‖'ləʊə(r)/ adj **1 (a)** (spatially, numerically) ⟨jaw/lip⟩ inferior; **~ age limit** edad f mínima **(b)** (in rank, importance) inferior, más bajo **(c)** ⟨life form⟩ inferior **2** (Geog) bajo; **the ~ reaches of the Nile** el curso bajo del Nilo

lower² /'ləʊər ‖'ləʊə(r)/ vt **1** ⟨blind/flag⟩ bajar; **he ~ed himself into his chair** se sentó en el sillón **2** ⟨temperature/volume/price/voice⟩ bajar ■ v refl **to ~ oneself** rebajarse

lower: ~ class n (often pl) clase f baja; **~-class** /ˌləʊərˈklæs ‖ˌləʊəˈklɑːs/ adj de clase baja

lowest common denominator /ˌləʊəst ‖ˈləʊɪst/ n (Math) mínimo común denominador m; **a series aimed at the ~ ~ ~** una serie dirigida al público de nivel más bajo

low: ~-fat /'ləʊˈfæt/ adj de bajo contenido graso; **~-flying** /'ləʊˈflaɪɪŋ/ adj ⟨aircraft⟩ que vuela bajo; **~-grade** /'ləʊˈgreɪd/ adj ⟨oil⟩ de baja calidad; ⟨ore⟩ pobre; **~-key** /'ləʊˈkiː/ adj ⟨speech⟩ mesurado; ⟨ceremony⟩ sencillo; **~land** /'ləʊlənd/ adj (before n) de las tierras bajas; (in tropical countries) de tierra caliente; **~lands** /'ləʊləndz/ pl n tierras fpl bajas; (in tropical

countries) tierras fpl calientes; **~-level** /'ləʊˈlevəl/ adj **(a)** ⟨talks⟩ a bajo nivel **(b)** ⟨radiation⟩ de baja intensidad **(c)** (Comput): **~-level language** lenguaje m de bajo nivel

lowly /'ləʊli/ adj **-lier, -liest** humilde

low: ~-lying /'ləʊˈlaɪɪŋ/ adj bajo; **~-necked** /'ləʊˈnekt/ adj escotado; **~-paid** /'ləʊˈpeɪd/ adj mal remunerado; **~-profile** /'ləʊˈprəʊfaɪl/ adj poco prominente; **~-rise** /'ləʊˈraɪz/ adj de poca altura; **~-risk** /'ləʊˈrɪsk/ adj ⟨business⟩ poco arriesgado; ⟨investment⟩ de poco or bajo riesgo; **~ season** n (BrE) temporada f baja

loyal /'lɔɪəl/ adj ⟨friend/customer⟩ fiel; **to be ~ TO sth** ⟨to the state/party⟩ ser* leal A algo; ⟨to one's ideals⟩ ser* fiel A algo; **he is ~ to his friends** es un amigo leal or fiel

loyalist /'lɔɪələst ‖'lɔɪəlɪst/ n partidario, -ria m,f del régimen

loyalty /'lɔɪəlti/ n (pl **-ties**) lealtad f

loyalty card n tarjeta f de cliente (que otorga puntos)

lozenge /'lɑːzɪndʒ ‖'lɒzɪndʒ/ n (Med) pastilla f

LP n (= **long-playing record**) LP m, elepé m

L-plate /'elpleɪt/ n (in UK) placa f de la L or de prácticas (placa que se debe exhibir en el coche cuando se aprende a conducir)

LSD n (= **lysergic acid diethylamide**) LSD m

LST (in US) = **Local Standard Time**

Ltd (= **Limited**) Ltda., S.A.

lubricant /'luːbrɪkənt/ n lubricante m

lubricate /'luːbrɪkeɪt/ vt lubricar*

lucid /'luːsəd ‖'luːsɪd/ adj lúcido

luck /lʌk/ n suerte f; **good ~!** ¡buena suerte!; **a piece** o **stroke of ~** un golpe de suerte; **to be down on one's ~** estar* de mala racha; **to push one's ~** desafiar* a la suerte

luckily /'lʌkəli ‖'lʌkɪli/ adv (indep) por suerte

lucky /'lʌki/ adj **luckier, luckiest (a)** ⟨person⟩ con suerte, suertudo (AmL fam); **he's ~ to be alive** tuvo suerte de no matarse; **~ you!** (colloq) ¡qué suerte (tienes)! **(b)** (fortuitous): **he had a ~ escape** se salvó de milagro; **it was ~ you were there** fue una suerte que estuvieras ahí **(c)** (bringing luck): **~ charm** amuleto m (de la suerte); **seven is my ~ number** el siete es mi número de la suerte

lucrative /'luːkrətɪv/ adj lucrativo

ludicrous /'luːdɪkrəs/ adj ridículo

lug /lʌg/ vt **-gg-** (colloq) arrastrar

luggage /'lʌgɪdʒ/ n equipaje m

luggage: ~ checkroom n (AmE) consigna f (de equipajes); **~ rack** n **(a)** (Rail) rejilla f (portaequipajes) **(b)** (Auto) baca f, parrilla f (Andes)

lugubrious /lʊˈguːbrɪəs/ adj lúgubre

lukewarm /'luːkˈwɔːrm ‖ˌluːkˈwɔːm/ adj **(a)** ⟨water/milk⟩ tibio **(b)** ⟨support/reaction⟩ poco entusiasta

lull¹ /lʌl/ vt **(a)** ⟨baby⟩: **to ~ a baby to sleep**

AmC	América Central	Arg	Argentina
AmL	América Latina	Bol	Bolivia
AmS	América del Sur	Chi	Chile
Andes	Región andina	CS	Cono Sur

Cu	Cuba	Per	Perú
Ec	Ecuador	RPI	Río de la Plata
Esp	España	Ur	Uruguay
Méx	México	Ven	Venezuela

arrullar a un niño hasta dormirlo **(b)** ⟨*fears*⟩
calmar; ⟨*suspicions*⟩ desvanecer **(c)** (deceive): **we
were ~ed into a false sense of security** nos
confiamos demasiado

lull² /lʌl/ n (in activity) período m de calma; (in fighting)
tregua f; (in conversation) pausa f

lullaby /'lʌləbaɪ/ n (pl -**bies**) canción f de cuna

lumbago /lʌm'beɪɡəʊ/ n lumbago m

lumber¹ /'lʌmbər ‖'lʌmbə(r)/ n **(a)** (timber)
(AmE) madera f **(b)** (junk) cachivaches mpl

lumber² vt (colloq) **to ~ sb WITH sth** enjaretarle
algo a algn (fam)
  ■ ~ vi **(a)** (move awkwardly) avanzar* pesadamente
  (b) lumbering pres p ⟨*gait*⟩ torpe

lumber: ~jack n leñador m; **~yard** n (AmE)
almacén m de maderas, barraca f (CS)

luminous /'luːmənəs ‖'luːmɪnəs/ adj luminoso

lump¹ /lʌmp/ n **1** (swelling, protuberance) bulto m;
(as result of knock) chichón m; **a ~ in one's throat**
un nudo en la garganta **2** (piece — of coal, iron,
clay, cheese) trozo m, pedazo m; (— of sugar) terrón
m

lump² vt **(a)** (put up with) (colloq): **to ~ it**
aguantarse (fam); **if you don't like it, (you can) ~
it** si no te gusta, te aguantas **(b)** (place together): **to
~ sth together: you can ~ all those items
together under one heading** todo eso puede ir
junto bajo el mismo epígrafe; **they can't all be
~ed together as reactionaries** no se puede tachar
a todos indiscriminadamente de reaccionarios

lump sum n cantidad f global (*que se paga o
recibe para saldar totalmente una obligación*)

lumpy /'lʌmpi/ adj -**pier, -piest (a)** ⟨*sauce*⟩
lleno de grumos **(b)** ⟨*mattress/cushion*⟩ lleno de
bultos

lunacy /'luːnəsi/ n (pl -**cies**) locura f

lunar /'luːnər ‖'luːnə(r)/ adj lunar

lunatic /'luːnətɪk/ n loco, -ca m,f

lunch /lʌntʃ/ n almuerzo m, comida f (esp Esp,
Méx); **to have ~** almorzar*, comer (esp Esp, Méx)

lunchbox /'lʌntʃbɑːks ‖'lʌntʃbɒks/ n lonchera
f (AmL), fiambrera f (Esp)

luncheon /'lʌntʃən/ n (frml) almuerzo m

lunchtime /'lʌntʃtaɪm/ n hora f de almorzar,
hora f de comer (esp Esp, Méx)

lung /lʌŋ/ n (often pl) pulmón m; (before n) ~
cancer cáncer m de pulmón

lunge¹ /lʌndʒ/ vi embestir*; **to ~ AT sb/sth**
arremeter CONTRA algn/algo

lunge² n arremetida f

lurch¹ /lɜːrtʃ ‖lɜːtʃ/ vi ⟨*vehicle*⟩ dar*
bandazos; «*person*» tambalearse

lurch² n bandazo m; **to leave sb in the ~** (colloq)
dejar a algn plantado

lure /lʊr ‖ljʊə(r), lʊə(r)/ vt atraer*

lurid /'lʊrəd ‖'lʊərɪd/ adj **(a)** (sensational)
⟨*details/imagination*⟩ morboso **(b)** (garish) ⟨*color/
garment*⟩ chillón

lurk /lɜːrk ‖lɜːk/ vi merodear

luscious /'lʌʃəs/ adj **(a)** ⟨*girl*⟩ seductora **(b)**
⟨*scent/sweetness*⟩ exquisito

lush /lʌʃ/ adj -**er**, -**est** ⟨*vegetation*⟩ exuberante

lust¹ /lʌst/ n **(a)** (sexual) lujuria f **(b)** (craving)
deseo m

lust² vi **to ~ AFTER sb** desear a algn; **to ~
AFTER sth** codiciar algo

luster, (BrE) **lustre** /'lʌstər ‖'lʌstə(r)/ n (liter)
lustre m

lustful /'lʌstfəl/ adj lujurioso

lustre /'lʌstər ‖'lʌstə(r)/ n (BrE) ▶ LUSTER

lusty /'lʌsti/ adj -**tier, tiest** sano

Luxembourg, Luxemburg /'lʌksəmbɜːrg
‖'lʌksəmbɜːg/ n Luxemburgo m

luxuriant /lʌɡ'ʒʊriənt ‖lʌɡ'zjʊəriənt/ adj
⟨*vegetation/growth*⟩ exuberante; ⟨*hair*⟩ hermoso y
abundante

luxuriate /lʌɡ'ʒʊrieit ‖lʌɡ'zjʊərieɪt/ vi (revel)
to ~ IN sth deleitarse CON algo

luxurious /lʌɡ'ʒʊriəs ‖lʌɡ'zjʊəriəs/ adj lujoso

luxury /'lʌkʃəri/ n (pl -**ries**) lujo m; (before n)
⟨*car/hotel*⟩ de lujo

lying¹ /'laɪɪŋ/ n mentiras fpl

lying² adj (before n) mentiroso

lymph /lɪmf/ n linfa f; (before n) ~ **gland**
glándula f linfática

lynch /lɪntʃ/ vt linchar

lynx /lɪŋks/ n (pl ~**es** or ~) lince m

lyre /'laɪr ‖'laɪə(r)/ n lira f

lyric /'lɪrɪk/ n **(a)** (poem) poema m lírico **(b)**
lyrics pl n (Mus) letra f

lyrical /'lɪrɪkəl/ adj (Lit) lleno de lirismo

m

Mm

M, m /em/ n M, m f

m (a) (= **million(s)**) m **(b)** (= **meter(s)** o (BrE)
metre(s)) m **(c)** (= **male**) de sexo masculino
(d) (Ling) (= **masculine**) m

M (a) (Clothing) (= **medium**) M, talla f mediana
or (RPl) talle m mediano **(b)** (in UK) (Transp)
(= **motorway**) indicador de autopista

ma /mɑː/ n (colloq) mamá f

MA /'em'eɪ/ n **(a)** = **Master of Arts (b)**
= **Massachusetts**

macabre /məˈkɑːbrə/ adj macabro

macaroni /'mækəˈrəʊni/ n macarrones mpl

mace /meɪs/ n **1** (Art, Hist, Mil) maza f **2** (Culin)
macis f **3 Mace**® (tear gas) (AmE) gas para
defensa personal

Macedonia /'mæsəˈdəʊniə/ n Macedonia f

machete /məˈʃeti, məˈtʃeti/ n machete m

machinations /ˈmækəˈneɪʃənz, ˈmæʃ-
‖ˌmækɪˈneɪʃənz, ˈmæʃ-/ *pl n* (liter) maquinaciones
fpl

machine /məˈʃiːn/ *n* máquina *f*, (washing ∼)
lavadora *f*, máquina *f* (de lavar), lavarropas *m*
(RPl)

machine gun *n* ametralladora *f*

machinery /məˈʃiːnəri/ *n* (machines)
maquinaria *f*; (working parts) mecanismo *m*

macho /ˈmɑːtʃəʊ ‖ˈmætʃəʊ/ *adj* ⟨behavior/
attitude⟩ machista; ⟨image⟩ de macho

macintosh *n* ▶ MACKINTOSH

mackerel /ˈmækrəl/ *n* (*pl* ∼ *or* ∼s) caballa *f*

mackintosh /ˈmækəntəʃ ‖ˈmækɪntɒʃ/ *n*
impermeable *m*

macro /ˈmækrəʊ/ *n* (*pl* **-ros**) (Comput) macro *m*

mad /mæd/ *adj* **-dd-** 1 (a) (insane) loco; **to go**
∼ volverse* loco; **to work/run like** ∼ trabajar/
correr como un loco (b) ⟨rush⟩ loco; **we made a**
∼ **dash for the airport** salimos como locos para el
aeropuerto (c) ⟨scheme/idea⟩ disparatado
2 (angry) (esp AmE) ⟨person⟩ **to be** ∼ ⟨WITH/AT sb⟩
estar* furioso *or* (esp AmL) enojadísimo *or* (esp
Esp) enfadadísimo ⟨CON algn⟩; **to get** ∼ ponerse*
furioso 3 (very enthusiastic) (colloq) ⟨person⟩ **to be** ∼
ABOUT sb estar* loco POR algn; **she's** ∼ **about** *o*
on African music la música africana la vuelve
loca

Madagascar /ˈmædəˈɡæskər
‖ˌmædəˈɡæskə(r)/ *n* Madagascar *m*

madam /ˈmædəm/ *n* (as title) señora *f*

madden /ˈmædn̩/ *vt* (make angry) enfurecer*;
(drive mad) enloquecer*

made¹ /meɪd/ *past & past p of* MAKE¹

made² *adj* (*pred*) (a) (assured of success) **to have
it** ∼ tener* el éxito asegurado (b) (ideally suited):
they were ∼ **for each other** estaban hechos el uno
para el otro

Madeira /məˈdɪrə ‖məˈdɪərə/ *n* Madeira *f*,
Madera *f*

made-to-measure /ˈmeɪdtəˈmeʒər
‖ˌmeɪdtəˈmeʒə(r)/ *adj* (*pred* **made to
measure**) hecho a (la) medida

madly /ˈmædli/ *adv* (a) (frantically) ⟨rush/work⟩
como un loco; ⟨love⟩ locamente (b) (very) (as
intensifier): ∼ **in love** locamente enamorado

madman /ˈmædmən/ *n* (*pl* **-men** /-mən/) loco
m

madness /ˈmædnəs ‖ˈmædnɪs/ *n* locura *f*

Madrid /məˈdrɪd/ *n* Madrid *m*; (before *n*)
madrileño

Mafia /ˈmɑːfiə, ˈmæ- ‖ˈmæfiə/ *n* Mafia *f*

magazine /ˈmæɡəˈziːn/ *n* 1 (a) (Publ) revista
f; (before *n*) ∼ **rack** revistero *m* (b) ∼
(**program**) (Rad, TV) programa *m* de entrevistas
y variedades 2 (on gun — compartment) recámara
f; (— bullet case) cargador *m*

maggot /ˈmæɡət/ *n* gusano *m*

magic¹ /ˈmædʒɪk/ *n* magia *f*

magic² *adj* (a) ⟨power/potion⟩ mágico; ⟨trick⟩
de magia (b) (enchanting) ⟨moment/beauty⟩ mágico

magical /ˈmædʒɪkəl/ *adj* mágico

magician /məˈdʒɪʃən/ *n* (sorcerer) mago *m*;
(conjurer) mago, -ga *m,f*, prestidigitador, -dora *m,f*

magistrate /ˈmædʒəstreɪt ‖ˈmædʒɪstreɪt/ *n* (in
UK) *juez que conoce de faltas y asuntos civiles de
menor importancia*

magnanimous /mæɡˈnænəməs
‖mæɡˈnænɪməs/ *adj* magnánimo

magnesium /mæɡˈniːziəm/ *n* magnesio *m*

magnet /ˈmæɡnət ‖ˈmæɡnɪt/ *n* imán *m*

magnetic /mæɡˈnetɪk/ *adj* magnético;
⟨personality⟩ lleno de magnetismo

magnetism /ˈmæɡnətɪzəm ‖ˈmæɡnɪtɪzəm/ *n*
magnetismo *m*

magnificent /mæɡˈnɪfəsənt ‖mæɡˈnɪfɪsənt/
adj magnífico

magnify /ˈmæɡnəfaɪ ‖ˈmæɡnɪfaɪ/ *vt* **-fies,
-fying, -fied** ⟨image⟩ ampliar*, aumentar de
tamaño; ⟨problem/difficulty⟩ exagerar

magnifying glass /ˈmæɡnəfaɪɪŋ
‖ˈmæɡnɪfaɪɪŋ/ *n* lupa *f*

magnitude /ˈmæɡnətuːd ‖ˈmæɡnɪtjuːd/ *n*
(size) magnitud *f*; (importance) envergadura *f*

magpie /ˈmæɡpaɪ/ *n* urraca *f*, picaza *f*

mahogany /məˈhɑːɡəni ‖məˈhɒɡəni/ *n* caoba *f*

maid /meɪd/ *n* 1 (a) (servant) sirvienta *f*, criada
f, mucama *f* (AmL); (parlor/lady's ∼) (primera)
doncella *f* (b) (in hotel) camarera *f*, mucama *f*
(AmL) (c) (occasional housekeeper) (AmE) señora *f* de
la limpieza, limpiadora *f* 2 (young woman) (arch or
liter) doncella *f* (arc o liter)

maiden¹ /ˈmeɪdn̩/ *n* (arch or liter) doncella *f* (arc
o liter)

maiden² *adj* (before *n*) ⟨flight/speech⟩
inaugural

maiden name *n* apellido *m* de soltera

mail¹ /meɪl/ *n* 1 (a) (system) correo *m*; **by** ∼
por correo (b) (letters, parcels) correspondencia *f*,
correo *m* 2 (armor) malla *f*

mail² *vt* (esp AmE) ⟨letter/parcel⟩ echar al correo;
(drop in mailbox) echar al buzón; **to** ∼ **sth TO sb**
mandarle *or* enviarle* algo por correo A algn

mail: ∼**box** *n* (a) (for receiving mail) (AmE) buzón
m, casillero *m* (Ven) (b) (for sending mail) (AmE)
buzón *m* (de correos) (c) (electronic) buzón *m*; ∼
carrier *n* (AmE) cartero, -ra *m,f*

mailing list /ˈmeɪlɪŋ/ *n* (Marketing) banco *m* or
lista *f* de direcciones

mail: ∼**man** /ˈmeɪlmæn/ *n* (*pl* **-men** /-men/)
(AmE) cartero *m*; ∼ **order** *n* venta *f* por correo;
(before *n*) ∼**-order catalog** catálogo *m* de venta
por correo

maim /meɪm/ *vt* (cripple) lisiar; (mutilate) mutilar

main¹ /meɪn/ *adj* (before *n*, no comp) principal;
the ∼ **thing** lo principal; ∼ **course** plato *m*
principal *or* fuerte; ∼ **street** calle *f* principal

main² *n* (a) (pipe) cañería *f* or tubería *f*
principal; (cable) cable *m* principal (b) (supply) **the**
∼ *o* (BrE) **the** ∼**s** la red de suministro; **to turn the
water/gas off at the** ∼ *o* (BrE) **the** ∼**s** cerrar la
llave (principal) del agua/del gas

main: ∼**frame** *n* unidad *f* central,
computadora *f* or (Esp tb) ordenador *m* central;
∼**land** /ˈmeɪnlənd, -lænd/ *n* **the** ∼**land** *la masa
territorial de un país o continente excluyendo sus
islas*; (before *n*) ∼**land China** (la) China
continental; ∼ **line** *n* (Rail) línea *f* principal

mainly /ˈmeɪnli/ *adv* principalmente

main: ∼ **road** *n* (BrE) carretera *f* principal;

∼stream adj ⟨culture⟩ establecido; **∼stream politics** la política a nivel de los partidos mayoritarios

maintain /meɪnˈteɪn/ vt **1** **(a)** ⟨speed/lead⟩ mantener*; ⟨silence⟩ guardar **(b)** ⟨house/machine⟩ ocuparse del mantenimiento de; ⟨aircraft⟩ mantener* **(c)** ⟨family/dependents⟩ mantener* **2** (claim) mantener*

maintenance /ˈmeɪntnəns ‖ˈmeɪntənəns/ n **1** (repairs) mantenimiento m **2** (money) (BrE Law) pensión f alimenticia

maisonette /ˌmeɪzɪˈnet ‖ˌmeɪzəˈnet/ n (BrE) (apartment) dúplex m; (house) vivienda independiente de dos pisos que forma parte de una casa

maize /meɪz/ n **(a)** (plant) maíz m **(b)** (grains) maíz m, choclo m (CS, Per), elote m (Méx)

majestic /məˈdʒestɪk/ adj majestuoso

majesty /ˈmædʒəsti/ n (pl **-ties**) **(a)** (of appearance, landscape) majestuosidad f **(b)** (as title) **Her/Your M∼** su Majestad

major¹ /ˈmeɪdʒə ‖ˈmeɪdʒə(r)/ adj **1** ⟨change/client⟩ muy importante; ⟨setback⟩ serio; ⟨revision⟩ a fondo **2** (Mus) mayor

major² n **1** (Mil) mayor mf (en AmL), comandante mf (en Esp) **2** (AmE Educ) asignatura f principal

major³ vi (AmE Educ) **to ∼ IN sth** especializarse* **EN** algo

Majorca /məˈjɔːrkə ‖məˈjɔːkə, məˈdʒɔːkə/ n Mallorca f

majority /məˈdʒɔːrəti ‖məˈdʒɒrəti/ n (pl **-ties**) (greater number) (+ sing o pl vb) mayoría f; (before n) ⟨decision/party⟩ mayoritario

major league n (Sport) liga f nacional

make¹ /meɪk/ (past & past p **made**) vt **I** **1** (create, produce) hacer*; **to ∼ a note of sth** anotar algo; **she made the dress out of an old sheet** se hizo el vestido con una sábana vieja; **it's made of wood** es de madera; see also DIFFERENCE, FUSS¹, MESS 1 etc
2 **(a)** (carry out) ⟨repairs/payment/journey⟩ hacer*; **∼ a left** (turn) **here** (AmE) dobla a la izquierda aquí **(b)** ⟨remark/announcement⟩ hacer*

II **1** (cause to) **I'll ∼ you happy** te haré feliz; **that made me sad** eso me entristeció; **the work made me thirsty** el trabajo me dio sed; **what ∼s me angry is ...** lo que me da rabia es ...; **they've made him supervisor** lo han nombrado supervisor; **if nine o'clock is too early, ∼ it later** si las nueve es muy temprano, podemos reunirnos (or encontrarnos etc) más tarde
2 **(a)** (cause to) hacer*; **whatever made you do it?** ¿por qué lo hiciste? **(b)** (compel) obligar* a, hacer*; **she was made to apologize** la obligaron a or la hicieron pedir perdón **(c)** (in phrases) **to make believe: you can't just ∼ believe it never happened** no puedes hacer como si no hubiera sucedido; **to make do** (WITH **sth**) arreglárselas (CON algo)

III **1** **(a)** (constitute, be) ser*; **it would ∼ a nice change** sería un cambio agradable; **they ∼ a nice couple** hacen buena pareja **(b)** (amount to) ser*; **five plus five ∼s ten** cinco y or más cinco son diez
2 (calculate) **I ∼ it 253** (a mí) me da 253; **what time do you ∼ it?** ¿qué hora tienes?

3 **(a)** (understand): **I could ∼ nothing of the message** no entendí el mensaje; **∼ of that what you will** tú saca tus propias conclusiones **(b)** (think) **to ∼ sth OF sb/sth: what did you ∼ of him?** ¿qué te pareció?; **I don't know what to ∼ of it** no sé qué pensar

IV **1** **(a)** (gain, earn) ⟨money⟩ hacer* **(b)** (acquire) ⟨friends⟩ hacer*; **to ∼ a name for oneself** hacerse* un nombre
2 (colloq) (manage to attend, reach): **we just made the 3 o'clock train** llegamos justo a tiempo para el tren de las tres; **to ∼ it: he'll never ∼ it as a doctor** nunca será un buen médico
3 (assure success of): **to ∼ or break sth/sb** ser* el éxito o la ruina de algo/algn

■ **make for** [v + prep + o] **1** (head toward) dirigirse* hacia/a
2 (encourage, promote) contribuir* a

■ **make out**
I [v + o + adv, v + adv + o] **1** **(a)** (discern) ⟨object/outline⟩ distinguir*; (from a distance) divisar; ⟨sound⟩ distinguir*; ⟨writing⟩ descifrar **(b)** (figure out) (colloq) entender*
2 (write) ⟨list/invoice/receipt⟩ hacer*; **∼ the check out to P. Jones** haga el cheque pagadero a P. Jones
II (claim, pretend) [v + adv + o]: **she made out it was her own work** dio a entender que lo había hecho ella misma; **you're not as ill as you ∼ out** no estás tan enfermo como pretendes

■ **make up**
I [v + o + adv, v + adv + o] **1** ⟨story/excuse⟩ inventar
2 (prepare) ⟨prescription/food parcel⟩ preparar; ⟨agenda/list⟩ hacer*
3 **(a)** (complete, add) completar; **she came along to ∼ up the numbers** vino para completar el grupo **(b)** (compensate for): **I'll take the afternoon off, and ∼ up the time later** me tomaré la tarde libre y ya recuperaré el tiempo más tarde
II [v + adv + o] (constitute) formar; **it is made up of three parts** está compuesto de tres partes
III [v + adv, v + o + adv + o] (achieve reconciliation) **to ∼ (it) up** (WITH **sb**) hacer* las paces (CON algn)

make² n marca f

make: ∼-believe n fantasía f; **don't be frightened, it's only ∼-believe** no te asustes, es de mentira; **∼over** n (AmE) maquillaje m; **to have a** ⟨cosmetic⟩ **∼over** maquillarse

maker /ˈmeɪkər ‖ˈmeɪkə(r)/ n fabricante mf

make: ∼shift adj ⟨repair⟩ provisional, provisorio (AmS); ⟨bed⟩ improvisado; **∼up** n **1** (cosmetics) maquillaje m; **to put on one's ∼up** maquillarse, pintarse; (before n) **∼up remover** desmaquillador m; **2** (no pl) (of person) carácter m; **3** (AmE Educ) examen m de recuperación

making /ˈmeɪkɪŋ/ n **(a)** (production, creation): **a book about the ∼ of the TV series** un libro que trata de cómo se hizo la serie de televisión; **this is history in the ∼** esto va a pasar a la historia **(b) makings** pl: **you have the ∼s of a good story there** allí tienes material para una buena historia; **she has the ∼s of a great actress** es una gran actriz en ciernes

maladjusted /ˌmælə'dʒʌstəd ‖ˌmælə'dʒʌstɪd/ adj (Psych) inadaptado

maladjustment /ˌmælə'dʒʌstmənt/ n (Psych) inadaptación f

malaria /mə'leriə ‖mə'leəriə/ n malaria f, paludismo m

Malawi /mə'lɑːwi/ n Malaui m, Malawi m

Malawian /mə'lɑːwiən/ adj malauiano

Malaysia /mə'leɪʒə ‖mə'leɪzɪə/ n Malaisia f; (continental part) Malasia f

Malaysian¹ /mə'leɪʒən ‖mə'leɪzɪən/ adj malaisio; (from continental part) malasio

Malaysian² n malaisio, -sia m,f; (from continental part) malasio, -sia m,f

Maldive Islands /'mɔːldiːv, -daɪv/, **Maldives** /-z/ pl n the ~ ~ las (islas) Maldivas

male¹ /meɪl/ adj ⟨animal/plant⟩ macho; ⟨attitude⟩ masculino; **there were several ~ applicants** se presentaron varios candidatos varones

male² n (animal) macho m; (person) varón m

malevolent /mə'levələnt/ adj ⟨grin⟩ malévolo; ⟨deity⟩ maligno

malformation /ˌmælfɔːr'meɪʃən ‖ˌmælfɔː'meɪʃən/ n deformación f (esp congénita), malformación f

malfunction¹ /'mæl'fʌŋkʃən/ n (a) (defective functioning) mal funcionamiento m (b) (failure) falla f or (Esp) fallo m

malfunction² vi (Med, Tech) fallar, funcionar mal

malice /'mæləs ‖'mælɪs/ n mala intención f

malicious /mə'lɪʃəs/ adj ⟨person/gossip⟩ malicioso; ⟨damage⟩ doloso

malignant /mə'lɪgnənt/ adj maligno

malinger /mə'lɪŋgər ‖mə'lɪŋgə(r)/ vi hacerse* el enfermo

mall /mɔːl ‖mæl, mɔːl/ n (a) (for shopping) centro m comercial (b) (avenue) paseo m

mallet /'mælət ‖'mælɪt/ n mazo m

malnutrition /ˌmælnuː'trɪʃən ‖ˌmælnjuː'trɪʃən/ n desnutrición f

malpractice /'mæl'præktəs ‖ˌmæl'præktɪs/ n mala práctica f (en el ejercicio de la profesión)

malt /mɔːlt/ n (a) (grain) malta f (b) ~ **(whisky)** whisky m de malta

Malta /'mɔːltə/ n Malta f

Maltese¹ /'mɔːl'tiːz/ adj maltés

Maltese² n (pl ~) (a) (person) maltés, -tesa m,f (b) (language) maltés m

mamma /'mæmə ‖'mʌmə/ n ▶ MOMMA

mammal /'mæməl/ n mamífero m

mammoth¹ /'mæməθ/ n mamut m

mammoth² adj ⟨building/cost⟩ gigantesco; ⟨task⟩ de titanes

man¹ /mæn/ n (pl **men** /men/) **1** (a) (adult male) hombre m (b) (husband/boyfriend): **her new ~** su nueva pareja (or su nuevo compañero etc); **to live together as ~ and wife** vivir como marido y mujer (c) (type): **he's a local ~** es del lugar; **he's a family ~** es un padre de familia **2** (a) (person) persona f; **every ~ for himself** (set phrase) sálvese quien pueda (fr hecha) (b) also **Man** (mankind) (no art) el hombre

3 men pl: **the men** (troops) los soldados; (employees) los trabajadores **4** (in chess) pieza f; (in draughts) ficha f **5** (as form of address) (colloq): **hey, ~!** ¡oiga, amigo!, ¡oye, tío (Esp) or (AmL exc CS) mano or (Chi) gallo! (fam), ¡oíme, che! (RPI fam)

man² vt -nn- ⟨switchboard⟩ encargarse* de; ⟨ship⟩ tripular; **soldiers ~ned the barricades** había soldados apostados en las barricadas

manacles /'mænəkəlz/ pl n (for wrists) esposas fpl; (for legs) grillos mpl

manage /'mænɪdʒ/ vt **1** (Busn) ⟨company/bank⟩ dirigir*, administrar, gerenciar (AmL); ⟨staff/team⟩ dirigir*; ⟨land/finances⟩ administrar **2** (handle, cope with) ⟨children⟩ manejar; ⟨household⟩ llevar; **she can't ~ the stairs** no puede subir la escalera **3** (achieve): **he ~d a smile** esbozó una sonrisa forzada; **I can't ~ the meeting** no puedo ir a la reunión; **to ~ to + INF** lograr + INF ■ ~ vi **1** (Busn) dirigir*, administrar **2** (cope): **can I help you? — thank you, I can ~** ¿me permite que la ayude? — gracias, yo puedo sola; **they have to ~ on $300 a week** tienen que arreglarse con 300 dólares a la semana

manageable /'mænɪdʒəbəl/ adj ⟨child/animal/hair⟩ dócil; ⟨task/goal⟩ posible de alcanzar; ⟨size/amount⟩ razonable

management /'mænɪdʒmənt/ n **1** (act) (a) (Busn) dirección f, administración f (b) (handling, control) manejo m **2** (managers) (a) (as group) (no art, + sing o pl vb) directivos mpl; **senior ~** altos cargos mpl (b) (of particular company) dirección f, gerencia f

manager /'mænɪdʒər ‖'mænɪdʒə(r)/ n (Busn) (of company, department) director, -tora m,f, gerente mf; (of store, restaurant) gerente mf, encargado, -da m,f; (of estate, fund) administrador, -dora m,f; (of pop group, boxer) manager mf; (Sport) agente mf; (of soccer) entrenador, -dora m,f, director técnico, directora técnica m,f (AmL)

manageress /'mænɪdʒərəs ‖ˌmænɪdʒə'res/ n (esp BrE) encargada f

managerial /ˌmænə'dʒɪriəl ‖ˌmænɪ'dʒɪərɪəl/ adj directivo, gerencial (AmL)

managing director /'mænədʒɪŋ ‖'mænɪdʒɪŋ/ n (esp BrE) director ejecutivo, directora ejecutiva m,f

mandarin /'mændərən ‖'mændərɪn/ n ~ **(orange)** mandarina f

mandate /'mændeɪt/ n mandato m

mandatory /'mændətɔːri ‖'mændətəri/ adj (fml) obligatorio

mane /meɪn/ n (of horse) crin(es) f(pl); (of lion) melena f

maneuver¹, (BrE) **manoeuvre** /mə'nuːvər ‖mə'nuːvə(r)/ n maniobra f

maneuver², (BrE) **manoeuvre** vt: **they ~ed the piano up the stairs** subieron trabajosamente el piano por la escalera; **she ~ed the car out of the garage** sacó el coche del garaje maniobrando ■ ~ vi «vehicle/driver» maniobrar, hacer* una maniobra; **to have room to** ∼ «*driver*» tener* espacio para maniobrar; «*diplomat*» tener* libertad de acción

manger /'meɪndʒər ‖'meɪndʒə(r)/ *n* pesebre *m*

mangle¹ /'mæŋgəl/ *vt* destrozar*

mangle² *n* rodillo *m* (escurridor)

mango /'mæŋgəʊ/ *n* (*pl* **-goes** *or* **-gos**) mango *m*

mangy /'meɪndʒi/ *adj* **-gier, -giest** ‹*cat*› sarnoso

man: ∼**handle** *vt* (move by hand) mover* a pulso; (treat roughly) maltratar; ∼**hole** *n* registro *m*, pozo *m* de inspección; (into sewer) boca *f* de alcantarilla

manhood /'mænhʊd/ *n* **(a)** (adulthood) madurez *f* **(b)** (virility) hombría *f*

man: ∼**hour** *n* hora *f* hombre; ∼**hunt** *n* persecución *f*

mania /'meɪniə/ *n* (*pl* **-nias**) manía *f*

maniac /'meɪniæk/ *n* maniaco, -ca *m,f*, maníaco, -ca *m,f*

manic /'mænɪk/ *adj* ‹*behavior*› maniaco, maníaco; ‹*activity*› frenético

manic-depressive /'mænɪkdɪ'presɪv/ *n* maniacodepresivo, -va *m,f*

manicure¹ /'mænəkjʊr ‖'mænɪkjʊə(r)/ *n* manicura *f*, manicure *f* (AmL exc RPl)

manicure² *vt* arreglarle las manos *or* las uñas a

manifest¹ /'mænəfest ‖'mænɪfest/ *v refl* (fml) **to** ∼ **itself** «*ghost*» aparecerse*; «*disease/fear*» manifestarse*
  ∎ ∼ *vt* (express) manifestar*

manifest² *adj* manifiesto

manifestation /'mænəfəˈsteɪʃən ‖,mænɪfəˈsteɪʃən/ *n* manifestación *f*; (of ghost) aparición *f*

manifesto /'mænəˈfestəʊ ‖,mænɪˈfestəʊ/ *n* (*pl* **-toes** *or* **-tos**) manifiesto *m*; (for a specific election) (esp BrE) plataforma *f* electoral

manifold¹ /'mænəfəʊld ‖'mænɪfəʊld/ *adj* (fml) múltiples

manifold² *n* colector *m*

manipulate /məˈnɪpjəleɪt ‖məˈnɪpjʊleɪt/ *vt* manipular

manipulative /məˈnɪpjələtɪv ‖məˈnɪpjʊlətɪv/ *adj* manipulador

mankind /mænˈkaɪnd/ *n* humanidad *f*, género *m* humano

manly /'mænli/ *adj* **-lier, -liest** ‹*physique/ pursuits*› varonil, masculino

man-made /'mænˈmeɪd/ *adj* ‹*lake*› artificial; ‹*material*› sintético

manna /'mænə/ *n* maná *m*

manner /'mænər ‖'mænə(r)/ *n* **1** (way, fashion) forma *f*, modo *m*, manera *f*; **in a** ∼ **of speaking** en cierto modo **2** (bearing, demeanor) actitud *f*; **a good telephone** ∼ **is essential** es imprescindible tener buen trato por teléfono **3** (variety) tipo *m*, suerte *f*, clase *f*; **all** ∼ **of things** todo tipo *or* toda suerte *or* toda clase de cosas **4** **manners** *pl* (personal conduct) modales *mpl*, educación *f*

mannerism /'mænərɪzəm/ *n* (peculiarity, habit) peculiaridad *f*; (gesture) gesto *m*

manoeuvre *n/vt/vi* (BrE) ▶ MANEUVER¹,²

manor /'mænər ‖'mænə(r)/ *n* ∼ **(house)** casa *f* solariega

manpower /'mænpaʊər ‖'mænpaʊə(r)/ *n* (workers) personal *m*; (blue-collar) mano *f* de obra

mansion /'mænʃən/ *n* mansión *f*

manslaughter /'mæn,slɔːtər ‖'mæn,slɔːtə(r)/ *n* homicidio *m* sin premeditación

mantelpiece /'mæntlpiːs/ *n* repisa *f* de la chimenea

mantle /'mæntl̩/ *n* **1** (covering) (liter) manto *m* (liter) **2** (Geol) manto *m*, sima *f*

manual¹ /'mænjuəl/ *adj* manual

manual² *n* manual *m*

manufacture¹ /'mænjəˈfæktʃər ‖,mænjʊˈfæktʃə(r)/ *vt* ‹*cars/toys*› fabricar*; ‹*clothes*› confeccionar; ‹*foodstuffs*› elaborar

manufacture² *n* (act) fabricación *f*; (of clothes) confección *f*; (of foodstuffs) elaboración *f*

manufacturer /'mænjəˈfæktʃərər ‖,mænjʊˈfæktʃərə(r)/ *n* fabricante *mf*

manufacturing /'mænjəˈfæktʃərɪŋ ‖,mænjʊˈfæktʃərɪŋ/ *adj* ‹*sector/town*› manufacturero; ‹*output/capacity*› industrial; ∼ **industry** industria *f* manufacturera

manure /məˈnʊr ‖məˈnjʊə(r)/ *n* estiércol *m*

manuscript /'mænjəskrɪpt ‖'mænjʊskrɪpt/ *n* manuscrito *m*

Manx /mæŋks/ *adj* manés, de la isla de Man

many¹ /'meni/ *adj* muchos, -chas; **how** ∼ **plates/cups?** ¿cuántos platos/cuántas tazas?; **I've had as** ∼ **jobs as you** he tenido tantos trabajos como tú; **too** ∼ **problems** demasiados problemas

many² *pron* muchos, -chas; **how** ∼ **of you smoke?** ¿cuántos/cuántas de ustedes fuman?; **would ten be too** ∼? ¿diez serían demasiados?

Maori /'maʊri/ *n* maori *mf*

map¹ /mæp/ *n* (of country, region) mapa *m*; (of town, subway, building) plano *m*

map² **-pp-** *vt* trazar* el mapa de
  ∎ **map out** [*v* + *o* + *adv*, *v* + *adv* + *o*] ‹*itinerary/ holiday*› planear

maple /'meɪpəl/ *n* ∼ **(tree)** arce *m*; (before *n*) ∼ **syrup** jarabe *m* *or* sirope *m* de arce

mar /mɑːr ‖mɑː(r)/ *vt* **-rr-** estropear

marathon /'mærəθən ‖'mærəθən/ *n* maratón *m or f*

marauder /məˈrɔːdər ‖məˈrɔːdə(r)/ *n* (criminal) maleante *mf*; (prowler) merodeador, -dora *m,f*

marble /'mɑːrbəl ‖'mɑːbəl/ *n* **1** (Min) mármol *m* **2** (Games) canica *f or* (AmS) bolita *f*

march¹ /mɑːrtʃ ‖mɑːtʃ/ *n* **1** **(a)** (Mil, Mus) marcha *f* **(b)** (demonstration) marcha *f* (de protesta) **2** (of time) paso *m*; (of science, technology) avance *m*

march² *vi* ‹*troops*› marchar; **when Saddam** ∼**ed on Kuwait** cuando Saddam invadió Kuwait; **she** ∼**ed into the office** entró con paso firme en *or* (esp AmL) a la oficina
  ∎ ∼ *vt* hacer* marchar; **the prisoner was** ∼**ed in** hicieron entrar al prisionero

March /mɑːrtʃ ‖mɑːtʃ/ *n* marzo *m*

mare /mer ‖meə(r)/ *n* yegua *f*

margarine /'mɑːrdʒərən ‖,mɑːdʒəˈriːn/ *n* margarina *f*

margin /'mɑːrdʒən ‖'mɑːdʒɪn/ *n* **1** (on page, typewriter) margen *m* **2** **(a)** (leeway) margen *m* **(b)** ····⊹

(Busn) (of profit) margen m (de ganancia) **3** (fringe — of lake) (*often pl*) margen f; (— of society) margen m

marginal /ˈmɑːrdʒɲəl ‖ˈmɑːdʒɪnl̩/ adj ⟨*difference*⟩ mínimo; ⟨*role*⟩ menor

marginally /ˈmɑːrdʒɲəli ‖ˈmɑːdʒɪnəli/ adv ligeramente

marigold /ˈmærəɡəʊld ‖ˈmærɪɡəʊld/ n caléndula f, maravilla f

marijuana, marihuana /ˈmærəˈwɑːnə, -ˈhwɑː- ‖ˌmæriˈwɑːnə/ n marihuana f

marinade, marinate /ˈmærəneɪd, -eɪt ‖ˈmærɪneɪd, -eɪt/ vt dejar en adobo

marine¹ /məˈriːn/ n also **Marine** (Mil) ≈ infante m de marina

marine² adj (before n) ⟨*biology*⟩ marino; ⟨*engineering*⟩ naval; ⟨*insurance*⟩ marítimo

marital /ˈmærətl̩ ‖ˈmærɪtl̩/ adj ⟨*problems*⟩ matrimonial; ⟨*bliss*⟩ conyugal; ~ **status** estado m civil

marjoram /ˈmɑːrdʒərəm ‖ˈmɑːdʒərəm/ n mejorana f

mark¹ /mɑːrk ‖mɑːk/ n **1** (sign, symbol) marca f; (stain) mancha f; (imprint) huella f; (on body) marca f; **as a** ~ **of respect** en señal de respeto; **to make one's** ~ dejar su impronta
2 (Educ) nota f; (Sport) punto m; **to get a good** ~ sacar* una buena nota
3 (a) (indicator): **the cost has reached the $100,000** ~ el costo ha llegado a los 100.000 dólares; **to overstep the** ~ pasarse de la raya (b) (for race) línea f de salida; **on your** ~**s!** ¡a sus marcas!
4 (target) blanco m; **to be wide of the** ~: **his estimate was wide of the** ~ erró por mucho en su cálculo
5 also **Mark** (type, version) modelo m
6 (Fin) marco m

mark² vt **1** (stain, scar) manchar **2** (indicate) señalar, marcar* **3** ⟨*anniversary*⟩ celebrar; ⟨*beginning*⟩ marcar*, señalar **4** ⟨*exam*⟩ (make corrections in) corregir*; (grade) poner(le)* nota a **5** (BrE Sport) ⟨*opponent*⟩ marcar*
■ **mark down** [$v + o + adv$, $v + adv + o$] (a) (Busn) ⟨*goods*⟩ rebajar (b) (BrE Educ) ⟨*person/ work*⟩ bajarle la nota a
■ **mark out** [$v + o + adv$, $v + adv + o$] (a) ⟨*sports ground*⟩ marcar* (b) (select) señalar (c) (distinguish) distinguir*

marked /mɑːrkt ‖mɑːkt/ adj ⟨*improvement*⟩ marcado; ⟨*contrast*⟩ acusado

marker /ˈmɑːrkər ‖ˈmɑːkə(r)/ n (a) (to show position) indicador m (b) ~ (**pen**) rotulador m

market¹ /ˈmɑːrkət ‖ˈmɑːkɪt/ n mercado m; (street ~) mercado m or mercadillo m or (CS, Per) feria f; **to come on (to) the** ~ salir* a la venta; **we put the house on the** ~ **at $320,000** pusimos la casa en venta en $320.000; (before n) ~ **forces** fuerzas fpl del mercado **2** (Fin) (stock ~) bolsa f (de valores); **to corner the** ~ (**in sth**) hacerse* con el mercado (de algo)

market² vt comercializar*

market garden n (BrE) huerta f

marketing /ˈmɑːrkətɪŋ ‖ˈmɑːkɪtɪŋ/ n marketing m

market: ~**place** n (in town) mercado m, plaza f del mercado; (Busn) mercado m; ~ **research** n estudio m or investigación f de mercado

marking /ˈmɑːrkɪŋ ‖ˈmɑːkɪŋ/ n (a) (on animal, plant) mancha f (b) (manmade) marca f; **road** ~**s** líneas fpl de señalización vial

marksman /ˈmɑːrksmən ‖ˈmɑːksmən/ n (pl **-men** /-mən/) tirador m

marmalade /ˈmɑːrməleɪd ‖ˈmɑːməleɪd/ n mermelada f (*de cítricos*)

maroon¹ /məˈruːn/ adj granate adj inv

maroon² vt (usu pass) ⟨*castaway*⟩ abandonar (*en una isla desierta*)

marquee /mɑːrˈkiː ‖mɑːˈkiː/ n (a) (canopy) (AmE) marquesina f (b) (tent) (BrE) entoldado m

marriage /ˈmærɪdʒ/ n **1** (a) (act) casamiento m, matrimonio m; (before n) ~ **certificate** certificado m de matrimonio (b) (relationship) matrimonio m; **her** ~ **to the poet lasted two years** estuvo dos años casada con el poeta **2** (union) (liter) (no pl) maridaje m, unión f

married /ˈmærid/ adj ⟨*man/woman*⟩ casado; **a** ~ **couple** un matrimonio; **they have been** ~ **for two years** llevan dos años casados; **to get** ~ (**to sb**) casarse (con algn)

marrow /ˈmærəʊ/ n **1** (bone ~) médula f **2** ~ **squash** o (BrE) ~ (Culin) tipo de calabaza alargada y de cáscara verde

marry /ˈmæri/ **-ries, -rying, -ried** vt (a) (get married to) casarse con (b) (perform ceremony) casar (c) (unite, combine) unir
■ ~ vi casarse
■ **marry off** [$v + o + adv$, $v + adv + o$] casar

Mars /mɑːrz ‖mɑːz/ n Marte m

marsh /mɑːrʃ ‖mɑːʃ/ n (often pl) pantano m; (on coast) marisma f

marshal¹ /ˈmɑːrʃəl ‖ˈmɑːʃəl/ n **1** (as title) (Mil) mariscal m **2** (as title) (AmE) (a) (police chief) jefe, -fa m,f de policía (b) (Law) supervisor de los tribunales de un distrito judicial **3** (at public gathering) miembro m del servicio de vigilancia

marshal² vt, (BrE) **-ll-** ⟨*troops/crowd*⟩ reunir*; ⟨*thoughts*⟩ poner* en orden; ⟨*evidence*⟩ reunir*

martial /ˈmɑːrʃəl ‖ˈmɑːʃəl/ adj marcial

martial: ~ **arts** pl n artes fpl marciales; ~ **law** n ley f marcial

martyr /ˈmɑːrtər ‖ˈmɑːtə(r)/ n mártir mf

martyrdom /ˈmɑːrtərdəm ‖ˈmɑːtədəm/ n martirio m

marvel¹ /ˈmɑːrvəl ‖ˈmɑːvəl/ n maravilla f

marvel², (BrE) **-ll-** vi **to** ~ (**AT sth**) maravillarse (DE algo)

marvelous, (BrE) **marvellous** /ˈmɑːrvləs ‖ˈmɑːvələs/ adj maravilloso

Marxism /ˈmɑːrksɪzəm ‖ˈmɑːksɪzəm/ n marxismo m

Marxist¹ /ˈmɑːrksəst ‖ˈmɑːksɪst/ n marxista mf

Marxist² adj marxista

marzipan /ˈmɑːrzəpɑːn ‖ˈmɑːzɪpæn, ˌmɑːzɪˈpæn/ n mazapán m

mascara /mæˈskærə ‖mæˈskɑːrə/ n rímel® m

mascot /ˈmæskɑːt ‖ˈmæskət, -skɒt/ n mascota f

masculine /ˈmæskjələn ‖ˈmæskjʊlm/ adj masculino

mash¹ /mæʃ/ n(BrE colloq) puré m de papas or (Esp) de patatas

mash² vt hacer* puré de, moler* (Chi, Méx), pisar (RPl, Ven), espichar (Col); **~ed potato(es)** puré m de papas or (Esp) de patatas

mask¹ /mæsk ‖mɑːsk/ n (for disguise, ritual) máscara f; (in fencing, ice hockey) careta f; (used by doctors) mascarilla f, barbijo m; (for diving) gafas fpl or anteojos mpl de bucear; (against dust, fumes) mascarilla f

mask² vt (a) (conceal) ocultar (b) (cover) cubrir*

masking tape /'mæskɪŋ ‖'mɑːskɪŋ/ n cinta f adhesiva protectora, cinta f de enmascarar (Col), tirro m (Ven)

masochist /'mæsəkəst ‖'mæsəkɪst/ n masoquista mf

mason /'meɪsn̩/ n (a) (Const) albañil mf; (stone ~) mampostero m (b) also **Mason** (Free~) masón m, francmasón m

masquerade¹ /ˌmæskə'reɪd ‖ˌmɑːskə'reɪd, ˌmæ-/ n mascarada f

masquerade² vi **to ~ AS sb** hacerse* pasar POR algn

mass¹ /mæs/ n **1** (bulk, body) masa f; her hair was a ~ of curls tenía la cabeza cubierta de rizos **2** **masses** pl (a) (great quantity) (BrE colloq): we received ~es of complaints recibimos montones de quejas (fam) (b) the ~es las masas **3** (Phys) masa f **4** also **Mass** (Mus, Relig) misa f

mass² vi «crowd/clouds» concentrarse

mass³ adj (before n) «culture/market» de masas; «hysteria/suicide» colectivo; «protest» masivo; «unemployment» generalizado; **a ~ meeting** una reunión de todo el personal (or el estudiantado etc); **~ transit** (AmE) transporte m público

Mass = Massachusetts

massacre¹ /'mæsəkər ‖'mæsəkə(r)/ vt masacrar

massacre² n matanza f, masacre f

massage¹ /mə'sɑːʒ ‖'mæsɑːʒ/ vt masajear

massage² n masaje m

massive /'mæsɪv/ adj «wall» sólido; «support/task» enorme; «heart attack/overdose» masivo

mass: **~ media** pl n the **~ media** los medios de comunicación (de masas); **~-produce** /'mæsprə'duːs ‖ˌmæsprə'djuːs/ vt fabricar* en serie

mast /mæst ‖mɑːst/ n (a) (Naut) mástil m (b) (flagpole) mástil m (c) (relay ~) antena f repetidora, repetidor m

mastectomy /mæ'stektəmi/ n (pl **-mies**) mastectomía f

master¹ /'mæstər ‖'mɑːstə(r)/ n **1** (of household) señor m, amo m; (of animal) amo m, dueño m; (of servant) amo m, patrón m **2** (expert) **~ OF sth** maestro, -tra m,f DE algo **3** (Educ) (a) (degree) **~'s** (degree) master m, maestría f; **M~ of Arts/Science** poseedor de una maestría en Humanidades/Ciencias f; (b) (BrE) (in secondary school) profesor m **4** (Naut) capitán m **5** (~ copy) (Audio, Comput, Print) original m

master² vt «technique/subject» llegar* a dominar

master³ adj (before n, no comp) (a) (expert): ~ baker/builder maestro m panadero/de obras (b) (main) «switch/key» maestro (c) (original) «tape» original, matriz; **~ plan** plan m general

mastermind¹ /'mæstərmaɪnd ‖'mɑːstəmaɪnd/ n cerebro m

mastermind² vt planear y organizar*

master: **~ of ceremonies** n maestro, -tra m,f de ceremonias; **~piece** n obra f maestra

mastery /'mæstəri ‖'mɑːstəri/ n (a) (expertise, skill) maestría f; (of language, technique) dominio m (b) (control) dominio m

masturbate /'mæstərbeɪt ‖'mæstəbeɪt/ vi masturbarse

mat¹ /mæt/ n (of rushes, straw) estera f, esterilla f; (door ~) felpudo m, tapete m (Col, Méx); (table~) (individual) (mantel m) individual m; (in center of table) salvamanteles m, posafuentes m (CS)

mat² adj (AmE) ▶ MATT

match¹ /mætʃ/ n **1** (for fire) fósforo m, cerilla f (Esp), cerillo m (AmC, Méx) **2** (Sport): **boxing ~** combate m de boxeo; **tennis ~** partido m de tenis; **football ~** (BrE) partido m de fútbol **3** (equal) (no pl): **to be a/no ~ for sb** estar*/no estar* a la altura de algn

match² vt **1** (equal) igualar **2** (a) (correspond to) «description» ajustarse a, corresponder a (b) (harmonize with) hacer* juego con (c) (make correspond, find equivalent for): **~ the words with the pictures** encuentra la palabra que corresponda a cada dibujo; **to be well ~** «competitors» ser* del mismo nivel, ser* muy parejos (esp AmL); «couple» hacer* buena pareja (d) **matching** pres p haciendo juego, a juego (Esp)
■ ~ vi (a) (go together) «clothes/colors» hacer* juego; **a demanding job with a salary to ~** un trabajo que exige mucho con un salario acorde (b) (tally) coincidir

match: **~book** n (AmE) librito m de fósforos or (Esp) de cerillas or (AmC, Méx tb) de cerillos; **~box** n caja f de fósforos or (Esp) de cerillas or (AmC, Méx tb) de cerillos; **~maker** n casamentero, -ra m,f; **~ point** n punto m de partido; **~stick** n (a) ▶ MATCH¹ 1 (b) (stick) palillo m

mate¹ /meɪt/ n **1** (a) (assistant) ayudante mf (b) (Naut) oficial mf de cubierta; **first ~** primer oficial m **2** (a) (Zool) (male) macho m; (female) hembra f (b) (of person) pareja f **3** (BrE colloq) amigo, -ga m,f, cuate, -ta m,f (Méx fam) **4** (check~) (jaque m) mate m

mate² vi aparearse

material¹ /mə'tɪriəl ‖mə'tɪəriəl/ n **1** (a) (used in manufacturing etc) material m (b) **materials** pl (equipment) material m **2** (cloth) tela f, género m, tejido m **3** (a) (for book, show etc) material m (b) (potential, quality): **this is bestseller ~** este es un bestseller en potencia; **she's champion ~** tiene madera de campeona

material² adj material

materialistic /mə'tɪriə'lɪstɪk ‖mə'tɪəriə'lɪstɪk/ adj materialista

materialize /mə'tɪriəlaɪz ‖mə'tɪəriəlaɪz/ vi «object/ghost» aparecer*; «hope/idea» hacerse* realidad

maternal /mə'tɜːrnl̩ ‖mə'tɜːnl̩/ adj (a) (motherly) maternal (b) (on mother's side) (before n) materno

maternity /mə'tɜːrnəti ‖məˈtɜːnəti/ n maternidad f; (before n) ⟨clinic/ward⟩ de obstetricia; ⟨dress/clothes⟩ de embarazada, premamá adj inv (Esp); ⟨pay/leave⟩ por maternidad; ∼ **hospital** maternidad f

math /mæθ/ n (AmE) matemática(s) f(pl)

mathematical /ˈmæθəˈmætɪkəl/ adj matemático

mathematician /ˈmæθəməˈtɪʃən/ n matemático, -ca m,f

mathematics /ˈmæθəˈmætɪks/ n (+ sing vb) matemática(s) f(pl)

maths /mæθs/ n (BrE) (+ sing vb) matemática(s) f(pl)

matinee, matinée /ˈmætn̩ˈeɪ ‖ˈmætɪneɪ/ n (Cin) primera sesión f (de la tarde), matiné(e) f (AmS); (Theat) función f de tarde, matiné(e) f (AmS)

matrices /ˈmeɪtrəsiːz, ˈmæt- ‖ ˈmeɪtrɪsiːz/ pl of MATRIX

matriculate /məˈtrɪkjəleɪt ‖məˈtrɪkjʊleɪt/ vi (frml) matricularse

matrimony /ˈmætrəməʊni ‖ˈmætrɪməni/ n (frml) matrimonio m

matrix /ˈmeɪtrɪks/ n (pl **matrices** or ∼**es**) matriz f

matron /ˈmeɪtrən/ n (a) (dignified woman) matrona f (b) (in prison) (AmE) matrona f (c) (in hospital) (BrE dated) enfermera f jefe or jefa (d) (in school) ≈ enfermera f

matt, (AmE also) **matte, mat** /mæt/ adj mate; **a ∼ finish** un acabado mate

matted /ˈmætəd ‖ˈmætɪd/ adj enmarañado y apelmazado

matter¹ /ˈmætər ‖ˈmætə(r)/ n **1** **(a)** (substance) (Phil, Phys) materia f **(b)** (discharge) (Med) pus m, materia f **(c)** (subject ∼) temática f, tema m **(d)** (written, printed material): **printed ∼** impresos mpl; **reading ∼** material m de lectura **2** **(a)** (question, affair) asunto m, cuestión f; **it's only a ∼ of time** solo es cuestión de tiempo; **that's a ∼ of opinion** eso es discutible **(b)** **matters** pl: **to make ∼s worse** para colmo (de males); **that didn't help ∼s** aquello no ayudó a mejorar la situación **(c)** (in phrases) **as a matter of fact: as a ∼ of fact, I've never been to Spain** la verdad es que nunca he estado en España; **for that matter** en realidad; **no matter** (as interj) no importa; (as conj): **no ∼ how hard I try** por mucho que me esfuerce **3** (problem, trouble): **what's the ∼?** ¿qué pasa?; **what's the ∼ with Jane?** ¿qué le pasa a Jane?

matter² vi importar

matter-of-fact /ˈmætərəvˈfækt/ adj ⟨person⟩ práctico; **he explained it in a very ∼ way** lo explicó con total naturalidad

mattress /ˈmætrəs ‖ˈmætrɪs/ n colchón m

mature¹ /məˈtʊr ‖məˈtjʊə(r)/ adj **(a)** (developed) ⟨animal/tree⟩ adulto; ⟨fruit/artist/ideas⟩ maduro **(b)** (sensible) maduro

mature² vi **(a)** (develop) «plant/animal/person» desarrollarse; «artist/work» madurar; «wine» añejarse **(b)** (become sensible) madurar **(c)** (Fin) «bond/policy» vencer*

maturity /məˈtʊrəti ‖məˈtjʊərəti/ n madurez f

maudlin /ˈmɔːdlən ‖ˈmɔːdlɪn/ adj llorón

maul /mɔːl/ vt atacar* (y herir*)

mausoleum /ˈmɔːsəˈliːəm/ n (pl -**ums**) mausoleo m

mauve /məʊv/ adj malva adj inv

maverick /ˈmævərɪk/ n inconformista mf; (Pol) disidente mf

maxim /ˈmæksəm ‖ˈmæksɪm/ n máxima f

maximize /ˈmæksəmaɪz ‖ˈmæksɪmaɪz/ vt maximizar*

maximum¹ /ˈmæksəməm ‖ˈmæksɪməm/ n máximo m

maximum² adj (before n) máximo

may /meɪ/ v mod (past **might**) **1** (asking, granting permission) poder*; **∼ I smoke?** ¿puedo fumar?; **∼ I have your name and address, please?** ¿quiere darme su nombre y dirección, por favor? **2** (indicating probability) [El grado de probabilidad que indica MAY es mayor que el que expresan MIGHT o COULD]: **we ∼ increase the price** quizás aumentemos el precio; **it ∼ or ∼ not be true** puede o no ser cierto **3** (indicating sth is natural): **you ∼ well ask!** ¡buena pregunta! **4** (conceding): **he ∼ not be clever, but he's very hard-working** no será inteligente, pero es muy trabajador; **that's as ∼ be** puede ser

May /meɪ/ n mayo m

Maybe /ˈmeɪbiː/ adv quizá(s), tal vez; **∼ I'll come later** quizá(s) or tal vez venga luego

May: ∼ Day n el primero de mayo; (in some countries) el día del trabajo; **m∼fly** n efímera f, cachipolla f

mayhem /ˈmeɪhem/ n caos m

mayonnaise /ˈmeɪəˈneɪz, ˈmeɪəneɪz ‖ˈmeɪəˈneɪz/ n mayonesa f, mahonesa f

mayor /ˈmeɪər ‖meə(r)/ n alcalde, -desa m,f, intendente mf (municipal) (RPl)

mayoress /ˈmeɪərəs ‖ˈmeəres/ n (BrE) (female mayor) alcaldesa f, intendente f (RPl); (mayor's wife) alcaldesa f

maze /meɪz/ n laberinto m

MB (= megabyte(s)) Mb.

MBA n = **Master of Business Administration**

MC n = **master of ceremonies**

Md = **Maryland**

me¹ /miː/, weak form /mi/ pron **1** **(a)** (as direct object) me; **she helped ∼** me ayudó; **help ∼** ayúdame **(b)** (as indirect object) me; **he bought ∼ flowers** me compró flores **(c)** (after prep) mí; **for/behind ∼** para mí/detrás de mí; **come with ∼** ven conmigo; **she's older than ∼** es mayor que yo **2** (emphatic use) yo; **it's ∼** soy yo

me² /miː/ n (Mus) mi m

ME ☐1 (Geog) = **Maine** ☐2 = **myalgic encephalomyelitis**

meadow /'medəʊ/ n prado m, pradera f

meager, (BrE) **meagre** /'miːgər ‖'miːgə(r)/ adj ‹portion/salary› escaso; ‹existence› precario

meal /miːl/ n ☐1 (Culin) comida f ☐2 (Agr, Culin) harina f (de avena, maíz etc)

mealtime /'miːltaɪm/ n hora f de comer

mean¹ /miːn/ vt (past & past p **meant**)
☐1 (represent, signify) «word/symbol» significar*, querer* decir; **that ~s trouble** eso quiere decir que va a haber problemas; **does the number 0296 ~ anything to you?** ¿el número 0296 te dice algo?; **fame ~s nothing to her** la fama la tiene sin cuidado
☐2 **(a)** (refer to, intend to say) «person» querer* decir; **what do you ~?** ¿qué quieres decir (con eso)?; **do you know what I ~?** ¿me entiendes?; **I know who you ~** ya sé de quién hablas **(b)** (be serious about) decir* en serio
☐3 (equal, entail) significar*; **that would ~ repainting the kitchen** eso supondría volver a pintar la cocina
☐4 **(a)** (intend): **he didn't ~ (you) any harm** no quiso hacerte daño; **to ~ to + INF: I ~ to succeed** mi intención es triunfar; **I ~ to do it but I forgot** tenía toda la intención de hacerlo pero me olvidé **(b) to be ~t to + INF** (supposed, intended): **you weren't ~t to hear that** no pensaron (or pensé etc) que tú estarías escuchando; **I was never ~t to be a teacher** yo no estoy hecho para enseñar

mean² adj ☐1 (miserly) ‹person› tacaño; ‹portion› mezquino ☐2 **(a)** (unkind, nasty) malo; **it was really ~ of you** fue una maldad (de tu parte) **(b)** (excellent) (esp AmE sl) genial ☐3 (inferior, humble) (liter) humilde; **that's no ~ feat** no es poca cosa ☐4 (Math) ‹before n› medio

mean³ n media f, promedio m; see also MEANS

meander /mi'ændər ‖mi'ændə(r)/ vi «river» serpentear; «person» deambular, vagar*

meaning /'miːnɪŋ/ n significado m

meaningful /'miːnɪŋfəl/ adj ‹look/experience/ relationship› significativo; ‹explanation› con sentido; ‹discussions› positivo

meaningless /'miːnɪŋləs ‖'miːnɪŋlɪs/ adj sin sentido

means /miːnz/ n (pl ~) ☐1 (+ sing vb) **(a)** (method) medio m; **a ~ to an end** un medio para lograr un fin; **~ of transport** medio de transporte; see also WAYS AND MEANS **(b)** (in phrases) **by all means** por supuesto, ¡cómo no! (esp AmL); **by no means, not by any means: we are by no ~ rich** no somos ricos ni mucho menos; **it's not a perfect film by any ~** de ninguna manera es una película perfecta; **by means of** (as prep) por medio de, mediante
☐2 (frml) (+ pl vb) (wealth) medios mpl (económicos); (income) ingresos mpl

means test n: investigación de los ingresos de una persona para determinar si tiene derecho o no a ciertas prestaciones

meant /ment/ past & past p of MEAN¹

meantime /'miːntaɪm/ n: **in the ~** (while sth else happens) mientras tanto, entretanto; (in the intervening period) en el ínterin or interín; **for the ~** por ahora

meanwhile /'miːnhwaɪl ‖'miːnwaɪl/ adv mientras tanto, entretanto

measles /'miːzəlz/ n (+ sing or pl vb) (Med) sarampión m

measure¹ /'meʒər ‖'meʒə(r)/ n ☐1 **(a)** (system) medida f **(b)** (unit) medida f **(c)** (amount) medida f; **with a (certain) ~ of success** con cierto éxito ☐2 (device) medida f ☐3 (step) medida f; **to take ~s to + INF** tomar medidas para + INF ☐4 (AmE Mus) compás m

measure² vt ☐1 ‹length/speed/waist› medir*; ‹weight› pesar ☐2 (assess) calcular; **to ~ sth AGAINST sth** comparar algo CON algo
■ **~** vi medir*
■ **measure out** [v + o + adv, v + adv + o] ‹length› medir*; ‹weight› pesar
■ **measure up** [v + adv] estar* a la altura de las circunstancias; **to ~ up TO sth** estar* a la altura DE algo

measurement /'meʒərmənt ‖'meʒəmənt/ n **(a)** (act) medición f **(b)** (dimension) medida f

measuring /'meʒərɪŋ/: **~ cup**, (BrE) **~ jug** n jarra f graduada; **~ spoon** n cuchara f de medir

meat /miːt/ n **(a)** carne f; (before n) ‹product› cárnico **(b)** (substance) sustancia f

meat: ~ball n albóndiga f, **~loaf** n pan m de carne

meaty /'miːti/ adj **-tier, -tiest** ‹taste/smell› a carne; ‹soup/stew› con mucha carne

Mecca /'mekə/ n **(a)** La Meca **(b)** also **mecca** (center of attraction) meca f

mechanic /mə'kænɪk ‖mɪ'kænɪk/ n mecánico, -ca m,f, see also MECHANICS

mechanical /mə'kænɪkəl ‖mɪ'kænɪkəl/ adj mecánico, maquinal; ‹action/reply› mecánico

mechanics /mə'kænɪks ‖mɪ'kænɪks/ n ☐1 (+ sing vb) (Phys, Mech Eng) mecánica f ☐2 (+ pl vb) **the ~** (practical details) los aspectos prácticos; (mechanical parts) el mecanismo

mechanism /'mekənɪzəm/ n mecanismo m

mechanize /'mekənaɪz/ vt mecanizar*

medal /'medl/ n medalla f

medalist, (BrE) **medallist** /'medləst ‖'medəlɪst/ n medallista mf; **gold/silver ~** medalla mf de oro/plata

medallion /mə'dæljən/ n medallón m

medallist (BrE) ▶ MEDALIST

meddle /'medl/ vi **(a)** (interfere) **to ~ (IN/WITH) sth** meterse or entrometerse (EN algo) **(b)** (tamper) **to ~ WITH sth** toquetear algo

media¹ /'miːdɪə/ n: **the ~** (+ pl or (crit) sing vb) los medios de comunicación

media² pl of MEDIUM² 1, 2

mediaeval /'miːdi'iːvəl, ˌme-‖ˌmedi'iːvəl/ ▶ MEDIEVAL

median¹ /'miːdɪən/ adj (Math) medio

median² n ☐1 (Math) mediana f ☐2 **~ (strip)** (AmE) mediana f, bandejón m (central) (Chi), camellón m (Méx)

mediate /'miːdɪeɪt/ vi mediar

mediator /'miːdɪeɪtər ‖'miːdɪeɪtə(r)/ n mediador, -dora m,f

Medicaid /'medɪkeɪd/ n (in US) organismo y programa estatal de asistencia sanitaria a personas de bajos ingresos

medical¹ /'medɪkəl/ adj ‹care/examination/ insurance› médico; ‹student› de medicina; ~ school facultad f de medicina

medical² n revisión f médica

Medicare /'medɪker ‖'medɪkeə(r)/ n (in US) organismo y programa estatal de asistencia sanitaria a personas mayores de 65 años

medicated /'medəkeɪtəd ‖'medɪkeɪtɪd/ adj medicinal

medication /medə'keɪʃən ‖medɪ'keɪʃən/ n **(a)** (substance) medicamento m **(b)** (drugs) medicación f

medicinal /mə'dɪsɪnəl ‖mɪ'dɪsɪnl/ adj medicinal

medicine /'medəsən ‖'medsən, 'medəsən/ n **1** (substance) medicamento m, medicina f, remedio m (esp AmL) **2** (science) medicina f

medieval /mi:di'i:vəl, 'me- ‖medi'i:vəl/ adj medieval, medioeval

mediocre /mi:di'əʊkər ‖mi:dɪ'əʊkə(r)/ adj mediocre

mediocrity /mi:di'ɑ:krəti ‖mi:dɪ'ɒkrəti/ n (pl **-ties**) **(a)** (quality) mediocridad f **(b)** (person) mediocre mf

meditate /'medəteɪt ‖'medɪteɪt/ vi meditar

meditation /medə'teɪʃən ‖medɪ'teɪʃən/ n meditación f

Mediterranean¹ /medətə'reɪniən ‖medɪtə'reɪniən/ adj mediterráneo

Mediterranean² n the ~ (Sea) el (mar) Mediterráneo

medium¹ /'mi:diəm/ adj **1** (intermediate) ‹size› mediano **2** (Culin) **(a)** ‹steak› a punto, término medio (Méx) **(b)** (as adv): ~ **rare** ‹steak› poco hecho, a la inglesa (Méx); ~ **dry** ‹wine› semi-seco

medium² n **1** (pl **media**) (means, vehicle) medio m **2** (pl **media**) (environment) medio m (ambiente) **3** (middle position) (no pl) punto m medio; **to strike a happy** ~ lograr un término medio **4** (pl **mediums**) (Occult) médium mf

medium: ~**-size** /'mi:diəm'saɪz/, (BrE also) ~**-sized** /-d/ adj ‹book/house› de tamaño mediano; ‹person› de talla media or mediana; ~**-term** /'mi:diəm'tɜ:rm ‖mi:diəm'tɜ:m/ adj (before n) a medio plazo; ~ **wave** n (BrE) (no pl) onda f media

medley /'medli/ n **(a)** (mixture) mezcla f **(b)** (Mus) popurrí m

meek /mi:k/ adj **-er, -est** dócil, sumiso

meet¹ /mi:t/ (past & past p **met**) vt **1 (a)** (encounter) encontrarse* con **(b)** (welcome) recibir; (collect on arrival) ir* a buscar; **she ran to** ~ **me** corrió a mi encuentro **2** (make acquaintance of) conocer*; **pleased to** ~ **you** encantado de conocerlo **3** (come up against, experience) encontrar*; **there's more to this than** ~**s the eye** esto es más complicado de lo que parece **4** ‹demands/wishes/debt› satisfacer*; ‹deadline/ quota/obligation› cumplir con; ‹requirements› reunir*; ‹cost› hacerse* cargo de

■ ~ vi **1 (a)** (encounter each other) encontrarse*; **we arranged to** ~ **at three** quedamos en or (AmL tb) quedamos de encontrarnos a las tres, quedamos a las tres (esp Esp) **(b)** (hold meeting) «club» reunirse*; «heads of state/ministers» entrevistarse **(c)** (make acquaintance) conocerse*; **have you two already met?** ¿ya se conocen? **2** (come into contact): **the vehicles met head on** los vehículos chocaron de frente; **their eyes met** sus miradas se cruzaron

■ **meet up** [v + adv] **to** ~ **up (WITH sb)** encontrarse* (CON algn)

■ **meet with** [v + prep + o] **(a)** ‹opposition/ hostility› ser* recibido con; **she met with an unfortunate accident** le ocurrió un lamentable accidente **(b)** (meet) (AmE) encontrarse* con

meet² n **(a)** (AmE Sport) encuentro m **(b)** (in hunting) partida f (de caza)

meeting /'mi:tɪŋ/ n **1** (assembly) reunión f; **to call/hold a** ~ convocar*/celebrar una reunión; **political** ~ mitin m, mítin m **2** (encounter) encuentro m; (between presidents) entrevista f **3** (BrE Sport) encuentro m

megabyte /'megəbaɪt/ n megabyte m, megaocteto m

megalomaniac /megələʊ'meɪniæk/ n megalómano, -na m,f

megaphone /'megəfəʊn/ n megáfono m

melancholy /'melənkəli ‖'melənkəli/ adj ‹person/mood› melancólico; ‹sound› triste

mellow¹ /'meləʊ/ adj **-er, -est (a)** ‹fruit› maduro; ‹wine› añejo; ‹sound/voice› dulce; ‹light/ color› tenue **(b)** ‹person/mood› apacible

mellow² vt suavizar*

■ ~ vi ‹color/voice› suavizarse*; **he has** ~**ed with age** se le ha suavizado el carácter con los años

melodrama /'melədrɑ:mə/ n melodrama m

melodramatic /melədrə'mætɪk/ adj melodramático

melody /'melədi/ n (pl **-dies**) melodía f

melon /'melən/ n melón m

melt /melt/ vi ‹ice/butter› derretirse*; «metal/ wax» fundirse; «anger» desaparecer*; **they** ~**ed into the crowd** se perdieron en la muchedumbre

■ ~ vt ‹snow/butter› derretir*; **their cries** ~**ed her heart** su llanto la conmovió

■ **melt away** [v + adv] «ice/snow» derretirse*; «mist/fog» levantarse; «fear/suspicion» disiparse; «confidence» desvanecerse*; «resistance/opposition» desaparecer*; **they** ~**ed away into the woods** desaparecieron ocultándose en el bosque

■ **melt down** [v + o + adv, v + adv + o] ‹gold/ coins› fundir

member /'member ‖'membə(r)/ n **1** (of committee, board) miembro mf; (of club) socio, -cia m,f; ~ **of staff** empleado, -da m,f; **a** ~ **of the audience** un espectador; **the offer is open to any** ~ **of the public** la oferta está abierta al público en general; (before n) ~ **states** países mpl miembros **2** (limb) (arch) miembro m

Member: ~ **of Congress** n (in US) miembro mf del Congreso; ~ **of Parliament** n (in UK etc) diputado, -da m,f, parlamentario, -ria m,f

membership /'membərʃɪp ‖'membəʃɪp/ n **(a)** (being a member): ~ **of the club is restricted to residents** solo los residentes pueden hacerse socios del club; **to apply for** ~ solicitar el ingreso en un club (or partido etc); (before n) ~ **card**

carné *m* de socio **(b)** (members) (+ *sing or pl vb*) socios *mpl* (*or* afiliados *mpl etc*); (number of members) número *m* de socios (*or* afiliados *etc*)

membrane /'membreɪn/ *n* membrana *f*

memento /məˈmentəʊ ‖ mɪˈmentəʊ/ *n* (*pl* **-tos** *or* **-toes**) recuerdo *m*

memo /'meməʊ/ *n* (*pl* **-os**) memorándum *m*

memoirs /'memwɑːrz ‖ 'memwɑːz/ *pl n* memorias *fpl*

memorabilia /'memərəˈbɪliə/ *pl n* objetos *mpl* de interés

memorable /'memərəbəl/ *adj* memorable

memorandum /'meməˈrændəm/ *n* (*pl* **-dums** *or* **-da** /-də/) memorándum *m*

memorial¹ /məˈmɔːriəl/ *n* monumento *m*

memorial² *adj* conmemorativo

Memorial Day *n* (in US) el último lunes de mayo, día en que se recuerda a los caídos en la guerra

memorize /'meməraɪz/ *vt* memorizar*

memory /'meməri/ *n* (*pl* **-ries**) ⬚1 **(a)** (faculty) memoria *f* **(b)** (period): the worst storm in living ∼ la peor tormenta que se recuerde ⬚2 **(a)** (recollection) recuerdo *m*; **his** ∼ **will live on** su recuerdo permanecerá vivo **(b)** (remembrance) memoria *f*; **in** ∼ **of sb/sth** a la memoria de algn/en conmemoración de algo ⬚3 (Comput) memoria *f*

men /men/ *pl of* MAN¹

menace /'menəs ‖ 'menɪs/ *n* ⬚1 **(a)** (threatening quality): **the** ∼ **in his voice** el tono amenazador de su voz **(b)** (threat) amenaza *f* ⬚2 (danger) amenaza *f*

menacing /'menəsɪŋ ‖ 'menɪsɪŋ/ *adj* amenazador

menagerie /məˈnædʒəri/ *n* colección *f* de animales salvajes

mend¹ /mend/ *vt* ⟨garment⟩ coser; ⟨shoe/clock/roof⟩ arreglar, reparar; **to** ∼ **one's ways** enmendarse*

■ ∼ *vi* (heal) «injury» curarse; «fracture/bone» soldarse*

mend² *n* remiendo *m*; **to be on the** ∼ (colloq) ir* mejorando

menial /'miːniəl/ *adj* de ínfima importancia

meningitis /'menənˈdʒaɪtəs ‖ ˌmenɪnˈdʒaɪtɪs/ *n* meningitis *f*

menopause /'menəpɔːz/ *n* **the** ∼ la menopausia

men's room *n* (AmE) baño *m* or servicios *mpl* de caballeros

menstruate /'menstrueɪt/ *vi* menstruar*

menswear /'menzwer ‖ 'menzweə(r)/ *n* ropa *f* de caballeros

mental /'mentl/ *adj* (before n) ⟨powers/illness⟩ mental; ⟨hospital/patient⟩ psiquiátrico

mental arithmetic *n* cálculos *mpl* mentales

mentality /men'tæləti/ *n* (*pl* **-ties**) mentalidad *f*

mentally /'mentəli/ *adv* mentalmente; **he's** ∼ **ill/handicapped** es un enfermo mental/un disminuido psíquico

menthol /'menθɒl ‖ 'menθɒl/ *n* mentol *m*; (before n) ⟨cigarettes⟩ mentolado

mentholated /'menθəleɪtəd ‖ 'menθəleɪtɪd/ *adj* mentolado

mention¹ /'mentʃən ‖ 'menʃən/ *vt* mencionar; **I won't** ∼ **any names** no daré nombres; **there's the problem of time, not to** ∼ **the cost** está el problema del tiempo, y no digamos ya el costo; **don't** ∼ **it** (on being thanked) no hay de qué, de nada

mention² *n* mención *f*

mentor /'mentɔːr ‖ 'mentɔː(r)/ *n* (liter) mentor, -tora *m,f* (liter)

menu /'menjuː/ *n* **(a)** (in restaurant) carta *f*, menú *m* (esp AmL) **(b)** (Comput) menú *m*

meow¹ /miˈaʊ/ *n* maullido *m*

meow² *vi* maullar*

MEP *n* (= **Member of the European Parliament**) eurodiputado, -da *m,f*

mercenary /'mɜːrsṇeri ‖ 'mɜːsɪnəri/ *n* (*pl* **-ries**) mercenario, -ria *m,f*

merchandise /'mɜːrtʃəndaɪz ‖ 'mɜːtʃəndaɪz/ *n* mercancía *f*, mercadería *f* (AmS)

merchant /'mɜːrtʃənt ‖ 'mɜːtʃənt/ *n* **(a)** (retailer) comerciante *mf* **(b)** (Hist) mercader *m*

merchant marine, (BrE also) **merchant navy** *n* marina *f* mercante

merciful /'mɜːrsɪfəl ‖ 'mɜːsɪfəl/ *adj* misericordioso

merciless /'mɜːrsɪləs ‖ 'mɜːsɪlɪs/ *adj* despiadado

mercury /'mɜːrkjəri ‖ 'mɜːkjʊri/ *n* mercurio *m*

Mercury /'mɜːrkjəri ‖ 'mɜːkjʊri/ *n* Mercurio *m*

mercy /'mɜːrsi ‖ 'mɜːsi/ *n* (*pl* **-cies**) **(a)** (clemency) misericordia *f*; **to have** ∼ **(on sb)** tener* misericordia (de algn), apiadarse (de algn); **at the** ∼ **of the elements** a merced de los elementos **(b)** (blessing) bendición *f*; **it's a** ∼ **that** ... (colloq) es una suerte que ...; **let's be thankful for small mercies** (set phrase) seamos positivos, podría haber sido peor

mere /mɪr ‖ mɪə(r)/ *adj* (superl **merest**) (before n) simple, mero

merely /'mɪrli ‖ 'mɪəli/ *adv* simplemente

merge /mɜːrdʒ ‖ mɜːdʒ/ *vi* «roads/rivers» confluir*; «colors» fundirse; «companies» fusionarse; **he** ∼**d into the crowd** se perdió entre el gentío

■ ∼ *vt* ⟨companies/organizations⟩ fusionar; ⟨colors⟩ combinar

merger /'mɜːrdʒər ‖ 'mɜːdʒə(r)/ *n* **(a)** (Busn) fusión *f* **(b)** (of organizations etc) fusión *f*

meringue /məˈræŋ/ *n* merengue *m*

merit¹ /'merət ‖ 'merɪt/ *n* mérito *m*; **each case is judged on its (own)** ∼**s** se juzga cada caso individualmente

merit² *vt* merecer*

mermaid /'mɜːrmeɪd ‖ 'mɜːmeɪd/ *n* sirena *f*

merrily /'merəli ‖ 'merɪli/ *adv* **(a)** (joyfully) alegremente **(b)** (unconcernedly) tranquilamente

merriment /'merimənt/ *n* (joy) alegría *f*; (laughter) risas *fpl*

merry /'meri/ *adj* **-rier, -riest** alegre; ∼ **Christmas!** ¡feliz Navidad!, ¡felices Pascuas!

merry-go-round /'merigəʊˌraʊnd/ *n* carrusel *m*, tiovivo *m* (Esp), calesita *f* (Per, RPl)

mesh /meʃ/ *n* malla *f*

mesmerize /'mezməraɪz/ *vt* **(a)** (fascinate) cautivar **(b)** (hypnotize) (dated) hipnotizar*

m

mess /mes/ n ⟦1⟧ **(a)** (no pl) (untidiness) desorden m; **the bedroom was (in) a ~** el dormitorio estaba todo desordenado; **my hair is a ~** (colloq) tengo el pelo hecho un desastre **(b)** (dirt): **what a ~!** ¡qué desastre or (RPl tb) enchastre! (fam); **they made a ~ on the carpet** dejaron la alfombra hecha un asco (fam) ⟦2⟧ (no pl) (confused, troubled state): **the country is (in) a complete ~** la situación del país es caótica; **my life's a ~** mi vida es un desastre; **to make a ~ of sth: you made a real ~ of this job** hiciste muy mal este trabajo ⟦3⟧ (Mil): **officers' ~** casino m or comedor m de oficiales

▪ **mess around,** (BrE also) **mess about** (colloq) [v + adv] **(a)** (misbehave) «children» hacer* travesuras **(b)** (interfere): **stop ~ing around with my things!** ¡deja mis cosas tranquilas!; **don't ~ around with me** no me juegues conmigo

▪ **mess up** [v + o + adv, v + adv + o] **(a)** (make untidy) desordenar **(b)** (make dirty) ensuciar **(c)** (spoil) «plans» estropear

message /'mesɪdʒ/ n mensaje m; **would you like to leave a ~?** ¿quiere dejar algún recado or (esp AmL) mensaje?; ¿quiere dejar algo dicho? (CS); **to get the ~** (colloq) entender*, darse* cuenta

messenger /'mesn̩dʒər ‖ 'mesɪndʒə(r)/ n mensajero, -ra m,f

Messiah /mə'saɪə/ n Mesías m

Messrs /'mesərz ‖ 'mesəz/ pl of **Mr** Sres.

messy /'mesi/ adj **-sier, -siest** (untidy) «room» desordenado; «writing» sucio y descuidado, desprolijo (CS) **(b)** (dirty) sucio; **he's a ~ eater** no sabe comer **(c)** (unpleasant, confused) «business» turbio

met /met/ past & past p of **MEET**[1]

metabolism /mə'tæbəlɪzəm ‖ mə'tæbəlɪzəm/ n metabolismo m

metal /'metl̩/ n (Chem, Metall) metal m; (before n) «box» metálico

metallic /mə'tælɪk/ adj metálico

metamorphosis /metə'mɔːrfəsəs ‖ metə'mɔːfəsɪs/ n (pl **-phoses** /-fəsiːz/) metamorfosis f

metaphor /'metəfɔːr, -fər ‖ 'metəfɔː(r), -fə(r)/ n metáfora f

metaphorical /metə'fɔːrɪkəl ‖ metə'fɒrɪkəl/ adj metafórico

mete /miːt/ ▶ **METE OUT**

meteor /'miːtiər, -ɔːr ‖ 'miːtiə(r), -ɔː(r)/ n meteorito m

meteoric /miːti'ɔːrɪk ‖ miːtɪ'ɒrɪk/ adj «rise/progress» meteórico; **~ rock** piedra f meteórica

meteorite /'miːtiəraɪt/ n meteorito m

meteorology /miːtiə'rɑːlədʒi ‖ miːtiə'rɒlədʒi/ n meteorología f

mete out [v + o + adv, v + adv + o] «fine/punishment» imponer*

meter[1] /'miːtər ‖ 'miːtə(r)/ n ⟦1⟧ **(a)** (measuring device): **gas/electricity/water ~** contador m or (AmL

tb) medidor m de gas/electricidad/agua **(b)** (parking ~) parquímetro m ⟦2⟧ (AmE Mus) compás m ⟦3⟧ (BrE) **metre** (measure) metro m

meter[2] vt medir* (con contador)

methane /'meθeɪn ‖ 'miːθeɪn/ n metano m

method /'meθəd/ n método m

methodical /mə'θɑːdɪkəl ‖ mɪ'θɒdɪkəl/ adj metódico

Methodism /'meθədɪzəm/ n metodismo m

Methodist /'meθədəst ‖ 'meθədɪst/ n metodista mf

methylated spirit(s) /'meθəleɪtəd ‖ 'meθəleɪtɪd/ n (+ sing vb) alcohol m desnaturalizado

meticulous /mə'tɪkjələs ‖ mə'tɪkjʊləs/ adj meticuloso

metre (BrE) ▶ **METER**[1] 3

metric /'metrɪk/ adj métrico

metro /'metrəʊ/ n (pl **-ros**) (Rail, Transp) metro m, subterráneo m (RPl)

metropolitan /metrə'pɑːlətn̩ ‖ metrə'pɒlɪtən/ adj (frml) metropolitano

mettle /'metl̩/ n temple m; **to be on one's ~** estar* dispuesto a dar lo mejor de sí

mew /mjuː/ vi maullar*

Mexican[1] /'meksɪkən/ adj mexicano, mejicano

Mexican[2] n mexicano, -na m,f, mejicano, -na m,f

Mexico /'meksɪkəʊ/ n México m, Méjico m

Mexico City n (ciudad f de) México m or Méjico m

mezzanine /'mezəniːn/ n **(a)** ~ **(floor)** entresuelo m, mezzanine f or m (AmL) **(b)** (AmE Theat) platea f alta

mi /miː/ n (Mus) mi m

MI = **Michigan**

miaow /mi'aʊ/ n/vi ▶ **MEOW**[1,2]

mice /maɪs/ pl of **MOUSE**

Mich = **Michigan**

microbe /'maɪkrəʊb/ n microbio m

microchip /'maɪkrəʊtʃɪp/ n (micro)chip m, pastilla f de silicio

microcomputer /'maɪkrəʊkəm.pjuːtər ‖ maɪkrəʊkəm'pjuːtə(r)/ n microcomputadora f (esp AmL), microordenador m (Esp)

microfilm /'maɪkrəʊfɪlm/ n microfilm m, microfilme m

microlight /'maɪkrəʊlaɪt/ n aeroligero m

microphone /'maɪkrəfəʊn/ n micrófono m

microprocessor /'maɪkrəʊ'prɑːsesər ‖ 'maɪkrəʊ.prəʊsesə(r)/ n microprocesador m

microscope /'maɪkrəskəʊp/ n microscopio m

microscopic /maɪkrə'skɑːpɪk ‖ maɪkrə'skɒpɪk/ adj microscópico, al microscopio

microwave /'maɪkrəʊweɪv, 'maɪkrə-/ n ~ **(oven)** (horno m de) microondas m

AmC Central America	Arg Argentina	Cu Cuba	Per Peru
AmL Latin America	Bol Bolivia	Ec Ecuador	RPl River Plate Area
AmS South America	Chi Chile	Esp Spain	Ur Uruguay
Andes Andean Region	CS Southern Cone	Méx Mexico	Ven Venezuela

mid- /mɪd/ *pref*: in ∼**January** a mediados de enero; ∼**morning** a media mañana; **she was in her** ∼**forties** tenía alrededor de 45 años

midair /'mɪd'er ‖,mɪd'eə(r)/ *n*: in ∼ en el aire

midday /'mɪd'deɪ/ *n* mediodía *m*

middle¹ /'mɪdl/ *n* [1] (of object, place — center) centro *m*, medio *m*; (— half-way line) mitad *f*; **it stood in the** ∼ **of the room** estaba en el centro *or* en (el) medio de la habitación; **in the** ∼ **of nowhere** quién sabe dónde, en el quinto pino (Esp *fam*), donde el diablo perdió el poncho (AmS *fam*) [2] (of period, activity): **in the** ∼ **of the week/January** a mediados de semana/de enero; **it's the** ∼ **of winter** estamos en pleno invierno; **in the** ∼ **of the night** en la mitad de la noche; **I'm in the** ∼ **of a really exciting novel at the moment** en este momento estoy leyendo una novela muy interesante; **I'm in the** ∼ **of cooking dinner** estoy preparando la cena [3] (waist) cintura *f*

middle² *adj* (*before n*): **the** ∼ **house of the three** de las tres, la casa de en medio *or* del medio

middle: ∼**-aged** /'mɪdl'eɪdʒd/ *adj* de mediana edad; **M**∼ **Ages** *pl n* **the M**∼ **Ages** la Edad Media; ∼ **class** *n* (*often pl*) clase *f* media; ∼**-class** /'mɪdl'klæs ‖,mɪdl'klɑːs/ *adj* de clase media; ∼**-distance** /'mɪdl'dɪstəns/ *adj* (*before n*) ⟨*running/race*⟩ de medio fondo; ∼**-distance runner** mediofondista *mf*; **M**∼ **East** *n* **the M**∼ **East** el Oriente Medio, el Medio Oriente; ∼**man** /'mɪdlmæn/ *n* (*pl* **-men** /-men/) intermediario *m*; ∼ **management** *n* mandos *mpl* (inter)medios; ∼ **name** *n* segundo nombre *m*; ∼**-of-the-road** /'mɪdləvðə'rəʊd/ *adj* ⟨*politician/views*⟩ moderado; ⟨*artist*⟩ del montón; ∼ **school** *n* (in US) colegio para niños de 12 a 14 años; (in UK) colegio para niños de 9 a 13 años

midge /mɪdʒ/ *n*: especie de mosquito pequeño

midget /'mɪdʒət ‖'mɪdʒɪt/ *n* enano, -na *m,f* (*de proporciones normales*)

midnight /'mɪdnaɪt/ *n* medianoche *f*

midst /mɪdst/ *n*: **in the** ∼ **of sth** en medio de algo; **in our** ∼ entre nosotros

midsummer /'mɪd'sʌmər ‖,mɪd'sʌmə(r)/ *n* pleno verano *m*; **M**∼**'s Day** el solsticio estival *or* vernal; (in the Northern hemisphere) el día de San Juan

midtown /'mɪd'taʊn/ *n* casco *m*, centro *m*; (*before n*) ⟨*apartment/hotel*⟩ de la periferia del centro

midway /'mɪd'weɪ/ *adv* ⟨*stop*⟩ a mitad de camino; ∼ **through the morning** a media mañana

midweek¹ /'mɪd'wiːk/ *n*: **around** ∼ a mediados de semana; (*before n*) ⟨*concert/flight*⟩ de entre semana

midweek² *adv* entre semana

Midwest /'mɪd'west/ *n* **the** ∼ la región central de los EEUU

midwife /'mɪdwaɪf/ *n* (*pl* **-wives**) partera *f*

midwinter /'mɪd'wɪntər ‖,mɪd'wɪntə(r)/ *n* pleno invierno *m*

might¹ /maɪt/ *v mod* [1] *past of* MAY [2] (a) (asking permission) (esp BrE) podría (*or* podríamos *etc*); ∼ **I make a suggestion?** si se me permite (hacer) una sugerencia … (b) (in suggestions, expressing annoyance, regret) poder*; **you** ∼ **at least listen** al menos podrías escuchar

[3] (indicating possibility) [*La posibilidad que indica* MIGHT *es más remota que la que expresan* MAY *o* COULD]: **somebody** ∼ **have found it** pudiera ser que alguien lo hubiera encontrado; **it** ∼ **(well) have been disastrous if the police hadn't arrived** podría haber sido catastrófico si no hubiera llegado la policía [4] (indicating sth is natural): **he rang to apologize — and well he** ∼! llamó para pedir perdón — ¡era lo menos que podía hacer! [5] (conceding): **the house** ∼ **not be big, but …** la casa no será grande pero …

might² *n* poder *m*

mighty¹ /'maɪti/ *adj* **-tier, -tiest** (a) (powerful) ⟨*empire/ruler*⟩ poderoso; ⟨*kick/blow*⟩ fortísimo (b) (imposing) ⟨*ocean/river*⟩ imponente

mighty² *adv* (colloq) (*as intensifier*) muy

migraine /'maɪɡreɪn ‖'miːɡreɪn, 'maɪ-/ *n* jaqueca *f*, migraña *f*

migrant¹ /'maɪɡrənt/ *n* (a) (Zool) (species) especie *f* migratoria; (bird) ave *f*† migratoria (b) (person) trabajador, -dora *m,f* itinerante

migrant² *adj* (a) (Zool) migratorio (b) (*before n*) ⟨*worker*⟩ itinerante; (foreign) extranjero

migrate /'maɪɡreɪt ‖maɪ'ɡreɪt/ *vi* emigrar

migration /maɪ'ɡreɪʃən/ *n* migración *f*

mike /maɪk/ *n* (colloq) micro *m* (*fam*)

milage *n* ▶ MILEAGE

mild /maɪld/ *adj* **-er, -est** [1] (a) (gentle) ⟨*person*⟩ afable; ⟨*manner/criticism*⟩ suave (b) (not serious or potent) ⟨*attack/form*⟩ ligero, leve; ⟨*discomfort*⟩ ligero [2] ⟨*climate*⟩ templado; ⟨*winter*⟩ no muy frío; **it's very** ∼ **today** hoy no hace nada de frío [3] ⟨*cheese/tobacco/detergent/ sedative*⟩ suave

mildew /'mɪlduː ‖'mɪldjuː/ *n* (on plants) mildeu *m*, mildiu *m*; (on wall, fabric) moho *m*

mildly /'maɪldli/ *adv* (a) (gently) ⟨*rebuke*⟩ suavemente; **to put it** ∼ por no decir algo peor (b) (slightly) ligeramente

mile /maɪl/ *n* milla *f* (*1.609 metros*); **that's** ∼**s away from here** (colloq) eso está lejísimos de aquí; **it sticks** *o* **stands out a** ∼ se ve a la legua

mileage /'maɪlɪdʒ/ *n* [1] (Auto) distancia *f* recorrida (*en millas*), ≈ kilometraje *m* [2] (advantage, profit): **they want to extract maximum** ∼ **from the Pope's visit** quieren explotar al máximo la visita del Papa

mileometer /maɪ'lɑːmətər ‖maɪ'lɒmɪtə(r)/ *n* (BrE) ≈ cuentakilómetros *m*

milestone /'maɪlstəʊn/ *n* (on road) mojón *m*; (significant event) hito *m*, jalón *m*

militant¹ /'mɪlɪtənt/ *adj* militante

militant² *n* militante *mf*

military¹ /'mɪləteri ‖'mɪlɪtri/ *adj* militar; ∼ **academy** (in US) escuela *f* militar; **to do** ∼ **service** hacer* el servicio militar

military² *n* **the** ∼ los militares

military police *n* policía *f* militar

militia /mə'lɪʃə ‖mɪ'lɪʃə/ *n* (+ *sing or pl vb*) milicia *f*

milk¹ /mɪlk/ *n* (a) leche *f*; (*before n*) ⟨*production/bottle*⟩ de leche; ⟨*product*⟩ lácteo; ∼ **chocolate** chocolate *m* con leche (b) (lotion) (BrE) leche *f*

milk² vt (a) ⟨cow/herd⟩ ordeñar (b) (exploit) explotar

milk: ~**man** /'mɪlkmən/ n (pl -**men** /-mən/) lechero m; ~ **shake** n batido m, (leche f) malteada f (AmL), licuado m con leche (AmL)

milky /'mɪlki/ adj -**kier, -kiest** lechoso; ⟨coffee/tea⟩ con mucha leche

Milky Way n the ~ ~ la Vía Láctea

mill¹ /mɪl/ n ① (a) (building, machine) molino m (b) (for pepper etc) molinillo m ② ⟨cotton ~⟩ fábrica f de tejidos de algodón

mill² vt ⟨flour⟩ moler*
■ **mill about, mill around** [v + adv] «crowd» dar* vueltas

millennium /mɪ'leniəm/ n (pl -**niums** or -**nia** /-niə/) milenio m

millennium bug n efecto m dos mil

miller /'mɪlər ‖ 'mɪlə(r)/ n molinero, -ra m,f

milligram /'mɪləɡræm ‖ 'mɪlɪɡræm/ n miligramo m

millimeter, (BrE) millimetre /'mɪlə‚miːtər ‖ 'mɪlimiːtə(r)/ n milímetro m

milliner /'mɪlənər ‖ 'mɪlɪnə(r)/ n sombrerero, -ra m,f de señoras

million /'mɪljən/ n millón m; a ~ people un millón de personas

millionaire /‚mɪljə'ner ‖ ‚mɪljə'neə(r)/ n millonario, -ria m,f

milometer /maɪ'lɒ‚mətər ‖ maɪ'lɒmɪtə(r)/ n ▶ MILEOMETER

mime¹ /maɪm/ n (a) (technique) mímica f (b) ~ (artist) mimo mf (c) (performance) pantomima f

mime² vt imitar, hacer* la mímica de
■ ~ vi hacer* la mímica

mimic /'mɪmɪk/ vt -**ck-** imitar

mince¹ /mɪns/ vt ⟨onions⟩ picar* (en trozos menudos); ⟨meat⟩ moler* or (Esp, RPl) picar*; **not to** ~ ⟨one's⟩ **words** no andar(se)* con rodeos
■ ~ vi caminar con afectación

mince² n (BrE) carne f molida or (Esp, RPl) picada

mincemeat /'mɪnsmiːt/ n picadillo de frutos secos, grasa y especias usado en pastelería

mind¹ /maɪnd/ n ① (a) (Psych) mente f; **to bear** o **keep sth/sb in** ~ tener* algo/a algn en cuenta; **to bring** o **call sth to** ~ recordar(le)* algo (a algn); **to have sth/sb in** ~ tener* algo/a algn en mente; **with that in** ~ pensando en eso; **what's on your** ~? ¿qué es lo que te preocupa?; **that put my** ~ **at rest** con eso me tranquilicé; **put it out of your** ~! ¡no pienses más en eso!; **I can't get him/the thought out of my** ~ no puedo quitármelo de la cabeza; **to read sb's** ~ adivinarle or leerle* el pensamiento a algn (b) (mentality) mentalidad f ② (attention): **my** ~ **was on other things** tenía la cabeza en otras cosas; **he needs something to take his** ~ **off it** necesita algo que lo distraiga ③ (a) (opinion): **to change one's** ~ cambiar de opinión; **to make up one's** ~ decidirse; **to my** ~ a mi parecer (b) (will, intention): **he has a** ~ **of his own** (he is obstinate) es muy empecinado; (he knows his own mind) sabe muy bien lo que quiere; **I've a good** ~ **to complain to the manager** tengo ganas de ir a quejarme al gerente ④ (mental faculties) juicio m, razón f; **to be/go out of one's** ~ estar*/volverse* loco

mind² vt ① (look after) ⟨children⟩ cuidar, cuidar de; ⟨seat/place⟩ guardar; ⟨shop/office⟩ atender* ② (usu in imperative) (a) (be careful about): ~ **your head!** ¡ojo or cuidado con la cabeza!; ~ **(that) you don't forget!** procura no olvidarte (b) (concern oneself about) preocuparse por; **never** ~ **him!** ¡no le hagas caso! ③ (object to) (usu neg or interrog): **I don't** ~ **the noise** no me molesta or no me importa el ruido; **I don't** ~ **him, but I can't stand her** él no me disgusta, pero a ella no la soporto; **I don't** ~ **what you do** me da igual lo que hagas; **would you** ~ **waiting?** ¿le importaría esperar?
■ ~ vi ① (in imperative) (concern oneself) **never** ~ no importa, no te preocupes (or no se preocupen etc); **never you** ~! ¡(a ti) qué te importa! ② (object) (usu neg or interrog): **I don't** ~ me da igual; **do you** ~ **if I open the window?** ¿le importa or le molesta si abro la ventana?; **do you** ~ **if I smoke? — yes, I do** ~! ¿te importa si fumo? — ¡sí que me importa!

-**minded** /'maɪndəd ‖ 'maɪndɪd/ suff: **business**~ con mentalidad para los negocios; **liberal**~ liberal

mindless /'maɪndləs ‖ 'maɪndlɪs/ adj ⟨activity⟩ mecánico; ⟨violence/obedience⟩ ciego

mine¹ /maɪn/ n ① (Min) mina f; **to be a** ~ **of information** ser* una mina de información ② (Mil) mina f

mine² pron
■ **Note** The translation mío reflects the gender and number of the noun it is standing for; mine is translated by el mío, la mía, los míos, las mías, depending on what is being referred to.

(sing) mío, mía; (pl) míos, mías; ~ **is here** el mío/la mía está aquí; **a friend of** ~ un amigo mío; **it's a hobby of** ~ es uno de mis hobbies

mine³ vt ① (Min) ⟨gold/coal⟩ extraer* ② (Mil) minar

minefield /'maɪnfiːld/ n campo m minado

miner /'maɪnər ‖ 'maɪnə(r)/ n minero, -ra m,f

mineral /'mɪnərəl/ n mineral m

mineral water n agua f‡ mineral

mingle /'mɪŋɡəl/ vi (a) «people» mezclarse; (at a party etc) circular (b) «liquids» mezclarse; «sounds» fundirse
■ ~ vt **to** ~ **sth WITH sth** mezclar algo CON algo

miniature¹ /'mɪnɪtʃʊr ‖ 'mɪnɪtʃə(r)/ n miniatura f

miniature² adj (before n) ⟨portrait⟩ en miniatura; ⟨poodle⟩ enano

minibus /'mɪnibʌs/ n microbús m, micro m

minicab /'mɪnikæb/ n (BrE) taxi m (que se pide por teléfono)

minim /'mɪnɪm/ n (BrE) blanca f

minimal /'mɪnəməl ‖ 'mɪnɪməl/ adj mínimo

minimize /'mɪnəmaɪz ‖ 'mɪnɪmaɪz/ vt ⟨risk/cost⟩ reducir* (al mínimo)

minimum¹ /'mɪnəməm ‖ 'mɪnɪməm/ n mínimo m

minimum² adj (before n) mínimo

mining /'maɪnɪŋ/ n minería f; (before n) ⟨company/town⟩ minero

miniskirt /'mɪnɪskɜrt ‖ 'mɪnɪskɜːt/ n minifalda f

minister¹ /ˈmɪnəstər ‖ˈmɪnɪstə(r)/ n **1** (Relig) pastor, -tora m,f, **2** (Pol) ministro, -tra m,f, secretario, -ria m,f (Méx)

minister² vi to ~ TO sb cuidar DE algn

ministry /ˈmɪnəstri ‖ˈmɪnɪstri/ n (pl **-tries**) (Pol) ministerio m, secretaría f (Méx)

mink /mɪŋk/ n (pl ~s or ~) **(a)** (animal) visón m **(b)** (fur) visón m

Minn = **Minnesota**

minor¹ /ˈmaɪnər ‖ˈmaɪnə(r)/ adj **1** (unimportant) ⟨poet/work⟩ menor; ⟨role⟩ secundario; de poca importancia or gravedad **2** (Mus) menor

minor² n **1** (Law) menor mf (de edad) **2** (AmE Educ) asignatura f secundaria

Minorca /məˈnɔːrkə ‖mɪˈnɔːkə/ n Menorca f

minority /məˈnɔːrəti ‖maɪˈnɒrɪti/ n (pl **-ties**) **(a)** (smaller number) (+ sing o pl vb) minoría f; (before n) ⟨group/vote⟩ minoritario **(b)** (in US) (Govt) oposición f

minor league n (in US) (Sport) liga f menor

minstrel /ˈmɪnstrəl/ n trovador m

mint¹ /mɪnt/ n **1** (Bot, Culin) (spear~) menta f (verde) **(b)** (pepper~) menta f, hierbabuena f **(c)** (confection) pastilla f de menta **2** (Fin) casa f de la moneda

mint² vt ⟨coin⟩ acuñar

mint³ adj (before n) ⟨coin/stamp⟩ sin usar; in ~ condition en perfecto estado

minus¹ /ˈmaɪnəs/ n (pl **-nuses** or **-nusses**) **(a)** ~ (sign) (signo m de) menos m **(b)** (disadvantage) (colloq) desventaja f

minus² adj **(a)** (disadvantageous) (colloq) (before n) on the ~ side, ... un factor negativo es que ... **(b)** (negative) (before n) ⟨number⟩ negativo

minus³ prep **(a)** (Math) menos ▶ FOUR¹ **(b)** (without, missing) (colloq) sin

minuscule /ˈmɪnəskjuːl/ adj minúsculo

minute¹ /ˈmɪnət ‖ˈmɪnɪt/ n **1** **(a)** (unit of time) minuto m; (before n) ~ hand minutero m **(b)** (short period) minuto m, momento m **(c)** (instant) minuto m; any ~ (now) de un momento a otro **2** **(a)** (memorandum) acta f **(b)** (of meeting): the ~s el acta

minute² /maɪˈnuːt ‖maɪˈnjuːt/ adj ⟨amount⟩ mínimo; ⟨object⟩ diminuto

miracle /ˈmɪrɪkəl ‖ˈmɪrəkəl/ n milagro m; (before n) ⟨drug/cure⟩ milagroso

miraculous /məˈrækjələs ‖mɪˈrækjʊləs/ adj milagroso

mirage /məˈrɑːʒ ‖ˈmɪrɑːʒ, mɪˈrɑːʒ/ n espejismo m

mirror¹ /ˈmɪrər ‖ˈmɪrə(r)/ n espejo m; (driving ~) (espejo m) retrovisor m

mirror² vt reflejar

mirth /mɜːrθ ‖mɜːθ/ n (liter) regocijo m (liter)

misadventure /ˌmɪsədˈventʃər ‖ˌmɪsədˈventʃə(r)/ n desventura f

misapprehension /ˌmɪsæprɪˈhentʃən ‖ˌmɪsæprɪˈhenʃən/ n (fml) malentendido m

misappropriate /ˌmɪsəˈprəʊprieɪt/ vt malversar

misbehave /ˌmɪsbɪˈheɪv/ vi portarse mal

miscalculation /ˌmɪskælkjəˈleɪʃən ‖ˌmɪskælkjʊˈleɪʃən/ n error m de cálculo

miscarriage /ˈmɪsˈkærɪdʒ/ n **1** (Med) aborto m espontáneo or no provocado; **to have a ~** tener* un aborto **2** a ~ **of justice** una injusticia

miscarry /ˈmɪsˈkæri/ vi **-ries, -rying, -ried** **(a)** (Med) abortar (espontáneamente), tener* un aborto **(b)** (liter) ⟨plan⟩ malograrse (liter)

miscellaneous /ˌmɪsəˈleɪniəs/ adj ⟨collection/ crowd⟩ heterogéneo; ⟨assortment⟩ variado

mischance /ˈmɪsˈtʃæns ‖ˌmɪsˈtʃɑːns/ n infortunio m

mischief /ˈmɪstʃəf ‖ˈmɪstʃɪf/ n **(a)** (naughtiness): **to get up to ~** hacer* travesuras **(b)** (trouble, harm) daño m; **to make ~** causar daños

mischievous /ˈmɪstʃəvəs ‖ˈmɪstʃɪvəs/ adj ⟨child⟩ travieso; ⟨grin⟩ pícaro

misconception /ˌmɪskənˈsepʃən/ n error m

misconduct /ˈmɪsˈkɑːndʌkt ‖ˌmɪsˈkɒndʌkt/ n (fml) mala conducta f

misconstrue /ˌmɪskənˈstruː/ vt (fml) malinterpretar

misdemeanor, (BrE) **misdemeanour** /ˈmɪsdɪˈmiːnər ‖ˌmɪsdɪˈmiːnə(r)/ n (Law) delito m menor

miser /ˈmaɪzər ‖ˈmaɪzə(r)/ n avaro, -ra m,f

miserable /ˈmɪzərəbəl/ adj **1** **(a)** (in low spirits) abatido **(b)** (depressing) ⟨weather⟩ deprimente; ⟨prospect⟩ triste **2** **(a)** (mean-spirited) miserable **(b)** (wretched, poor) mísero **(c)** ⟨episode/failure⟩ lamentable

miserably /ˈmɪzərəbli/ adv **(a)** (unhappily) con abatimiento **(b)** ⟨fail⟩ de manera lamentable

miserly /ˈmaɪzərli ‖ˈmaɪzəli/ adj mezquino

misery /ˈmɪzəri/ n sufrimiento m; **to make sb's life a ~** amargarle* la vida a algn

misfire /ˈmɪsˈfaɪr ‖ˌmɪsˈfaɪə(r)/ vi «gun/engine/ plan» fallar

misfit /ˈmɪsfɪt/ n: **a social ~** un inadaptado social

misfortune /ˌmɪsˈfɔːrtʃən ‖ˌmɪsˈfɔːtʃən, ˌmɪsˈfɔːtʃuːn/ n (fml) desgracia f; **to have the ~ to + INF** tener* la desgracia DE + INF

misgiving /ˈmɪsˈgɪvɪŋ/ n recelo m

misguided /ˈmɪsˈgaɪdəd ‖ˌmɪsˈgaɪdɪd/ adj equivocado

mishandle /ˈmɪsˈhændl/ vt (deal with ineptly) llevar mal

mishap /ˈmɪshæp/ n percance m

mishear /ˈmɪsˈhɪr ‖ˌmɪsˈhɪə(r)/ (past & past p **-heard**) vt/i entender* mal

misinform /ˌmɪsɪnˈfɔːrm ‖ˌmɪsɪnˈfɔːm/ vt (fml) informar mal, malinformar (CS fml)

misinterpret /ˌmɪsɪnˈtɜːrprət ‖ˌmɪsɪnˈtɜːprɪt/ vt ⟨statement/action⟩ interpretar mal; (deliberately) tergiversar

misjudge /ˈmɪsˈdʒʌdʒ/ vt **(a)** (judge unfairly) juzgar* mal **(b)** (miscalculate) calcular mal

mislay /ˈmɪsˈleɪ/ vt (past & past p **-laid**) perder* (momentáneamente)

mislead /ˈmɪsˈliːd/ vt (past & past p **-led**) engañar; ⟨court/parliament⟩ inducir* a error

mismanage /ˈmɪsˈmænɪdʒ/ vt ⟨affair⟩ llevar mal; ⟨company⟩ administrar mal

misogynist /mɪˈsɑːdʒənəst ‖mɪˈsɒdʒɪnɪst/ n misógino m

m

misplace /'mɪs'pleɪs/ *vt* perder*
(*momentáneamente*)

misprint /'mɪsprɪnt/ *n* errata *f*

misrepresent /'mɪsreprɪ'zent/ *vt* ‹*event*›
deformar; ‹*remarks/views*› tergiversar

miss¹ /mɪs/ *n* **1** **Miss** (as title) señorita *f*; **M~**
Jane Smith la señorita Jane Smith; (in
correspondence) Sra Jane Smith **2** (failure to hit)
fallo *m*; **to give sth a ~** (colloq): **I think I'll give**
swimming a ~ this afternoon creo que esta tarde
no voy a ir a nadar

miss² *vt*
I 1 **(a)** (fail to hit): **the bomb ~ed its target** la
bomba no cayó en el blanco; **the bullet just ~ed**
him la bala le pasó rozando **(b)** (overlook, fail to
notice): **you ~ed three mistakes** se te pasaron (por
alto) tres errores; **you can't ~ it** lo va a ver
enseguida, no tiene pérdida (Esp) **(c)** (fail to hear,
understand) no oír*; **he's ~ed the point** no ha
entendido **(d)** ‹*chance*› perder*
2 (fail to catch) ‹*bus/flight*› perder*; **sorry, you've**
just ~ed him lo siento, acaba de irse
3 **(a)** (fail to experience) perderse*; **you didn't ~**
much no te perdiste nada **(b)** (fail to attend)
‹*meeting*› faltar a; ‹*party/show*› perderse*
II (a) (regret absence of) ‹*friend/country/activity*›
echar de menos, extrañar (esp AmL) **(b)** (notice
absence of) echar en falta; **when did you first ~**
the necklace? ¿cuándo echaste en falta el collar?
■ **~** *vi* «*marksman*» errar* el tiro, fallar;
«*bullet*» no dar* en el blanco
■ **miss out 1** [*v + o + adv, v + adv + o*] ‹*line/*
paragraph› saltarse
2 [*v + adv*] **to ~ out ON sth** perderse* algo

Miss = **Mississippi**

misshapen /'mɪs'ʃeɪpən/ *adj* deforme

missile /'mɪsəl ‖ 'mɪsaɪl/ *n* (Mil) misil *m*; (sth
thrown) proyectil *m*

missing /'mɪsɪŋ/ *adj*: **the ~ papers** los papeles
que faltan; **~ person** desaparecido, -da *m,f*; **to be**
~ faltar; **to go ~** (BrE) desaparecer*

mission /'mɪʃən/ *n* misión *f*

missionary /'mɪʃəneri ‖ 'mɪʃənəri/ *n*
misionero, -ra *m,f*

misspent /'mɪs'spent/ *adj* (before n) ‹*money*›
malgastado; ‹*hours*› perdido; **a ~ youth** (set
phrase) una juventud disipada

mist /mɪst/ *n* **(a)** (Meteo) neblina *f*; **sea ~** bruma
f **(b)** (condensation) vaho *m* **(c)** (spray) vaporización
f
■ **mist over** [*v + adv*] «*eyes*» empañarse;
«*glass/mirror*» empañarse
■ **mist up** [*v + adv*] «*glass/mirror*» empañarse

mistake¹ /mə'steɪk ‖ mɪ'steɪk/ *n* error *m*; **to**
make a ~ cometer un error; **by ~** por
equivocación, por error

mistake² *vt* (*past* **-took**; *past p* **-taken**)
confundir; **to ~ sth/sb FOR sth/sb** confundir
algo/a algn CON algo/algn

mistaken /mə'steɪkən ‖ mɪ'steɪkən/ *adj*
‹*impression/idea*› equivocado; **unless I'm (very)**
much ~ si no me equivoco

mistletoe /'mɪsəltəu/ *n* muérdago *m*

mistook /mɪ'stʊk/ *past of* MISTAKE²

mistreat /'mɪs'triːt/ *vt* maltratar

mistress /'mɪstrəs ‖ 'mɪstrɪs/ *n* **(a)** (of dog)
dueña *f*, ama *f*‡; (of servant) señora *f* **(b)** (lover)
amante *f*

mistrust¹ /'mɪs'trʌst/ *vt* desconfiar* de, recelar
de

mistrust² *n* desconfianza *f*, recelo *m*

mistrustful /'mɪs'trʌstfəl/ *adj* desconfiado,
receloso

misty /'mɪsti/ *adj* **-tier, -tiest** ‹*day/morning*›
neblinoso; **it's ~** hay neblina; (it's drizzling) (AmE)
está lloviznando

misunderstand /'mɪsʌndər'stænd
‖ ˌmɪsʌndə'stænd/ (*past & past p* **-stood**) *vt*
‹*idea/instructions*› entender* *or* comprender mal;
‹*remark/motives*› malinterpretar; ‹*artist/work*›
interpretar mal

misunderstanding /'mɪsʌndər'stændɪŋ
‖ ˌmɪsʌndə'stændɪŋ/ *n* malentendido *m*

misunderstood /'mɪsʌndər'stʊd
‖ ˌmɪsʌndə'stʊd/ *past & past p of* MISUNDERSTAND

misuse¹ /'mɪs'juːs/ *n* (of word) mal uso *m*; (of
power) abuso *m*; (of funds) malversación *f*; (of
resources) despilfarro *m*

misuse² /'mɪs'juːz/ *vt* ‹*language/tool*› utilizar*
or emplear mal; ‹*resources*› despilfarrar; ‹*funds*›
malversar

mite /maɪt/ *n* (Zool) ácaro *m*

miter, (BrE) **mitre** /'maɪtər ‖ 'maɪtə(r)/ *n* mitra
f

mitigate /'mɪtəgeɪt ‖ 'mɪtɪgeɪt/ *vt* (frml) **(a)**
(soften, lessen) mitigar* (frml) **(b)** **mitigating** *pres*
p ‹*factor*› atenuante; **mitigating circumstances**
(circunstancias *fpl*) atenuantes *fpl or mpl*

mitre /'maɪtər ‖ 'maɪtə(r)/ *n* (BrE) ▶ MITER

mitt /mɪt/ *n* **(a)** (mitten) mitón *m* **(b)** (in baseball)
manopla *f*, guante *m* (de béisbol)

mitten /'mɪtṇ/ *n* mitón *m*

mix¹ /mɪks/ *n* (mixture, ingredients) mezcla *f*;
cake ~ preparado comercial para hacer pasteles
(b) (Audio) mezcla *f*

mix² *vt* **(a)** ‹*ingredients/paint*› mezclar;
‹*cocktail*› preparar **(b)** (Audio) mezclar
■ **~** *vi* **(a)** (combine) «*substances*» mezclarse **(b)**
(go together) «*foods/colors*» combinar (bien) **(c)**
(socially): **she doesn't ~ well at parties** le cuesta
entablar conversación con la gente en una
reunión; **to ~ WITH sb** tratarse CON algn
■ **mix up**
I [*v + o + adv, v + adv + o*] **1** (throw into confusion)
desordenar **2** (confuse) confundir
II (usu pass) **(a)** (involve) **to get ~ed up IN sth**
meterse EN algo **(b)** (confuse): **to get ~ed up**
confundirse

mixed /mɪkst/ *adj* **(a)** (various) mezclado; **~**
spice mezcla *f* de especias **(b)** (male and female)
‹*sauna/bathing*› mixto **(c)** (ambivalent) ‹*fortunes*›
desigual; **I have ~ feelings about it** no sé muy
bien qué pensar sobre el asunto

mixer /'mɪksər ‖ 'mɪksə(r)/ n (a) (Culin) batidora f (b) (Audio, Cin, TV) (person) operador, -dora m,f de sonido; (machine) mezcladora f (c) (sociable person) persona f sociable (d) (dance) (AmE) baile m (e) (drink) refresco m (para mezclar con alcohol)

mixing bowl /'mɪksɪŋ/ n bol m (grande, para mezclar ingredientes)

mixture /'mɪkstʃər ‖ 'mɪkstʃə(r)/ n mezcla f

mix-up /'mɪksʌp/ n (colloq) lío m (fam)

mm (= **millimeter(s)** o (BrE) **millimetre(s)**) mm.

MN = **Minnesota**

MO = **Missouri**

moan¹ /məʊn/ vi (a) (make sound) «person/ wind» gemir* (b) (complain) (pej) **to ~** (ABOUT sth) quejarse (DE algo)

moan² n (a) (sound) gemido m (b) (complaint) (colloq) (no pl) queja f

moat /məʊt/ n foso m

mob¹ /mɑːb ‖ mɒb/ n turba f; (before n) **~ rule** la ley de la calle

mob² vt **-bb-** atacar* en grupo

mobile¹ /'məʊbəl ‖ 'məʊbaɪl/ adj (a) ‹library/ shop› ambulante (b) (able to move): **we try and get the patient ~ as soon as possible** tratamos de que el paciente recupere su movilidad lo más pronto posible

mobile² n móvil m

mobile: ~ home n trailer m (AmL), caravana f fija (Esp); **~ phone** n (teléfono m) celular m (AmL), (teléfono m) móvil m (Esp)

mobilize /'məʊbəlaɪz ‖ 'məʊbɪlaɪz/ vt movilizar*

mock¹ /mɑːk ‖ mɒk/ vt burlarse de

mock² adj (before n) ‹examination/interview› de práctica; ‹anger/outrage› fingido

mockery /'mɑːkəri ‖ 'mɒkəri/ n (a) (ridicule) burla f (b) (travesty) (no pl) farsa f; **to make a ~ of sth** ridiculizar* algo

mocking /'mɑːkɪŋ ‖ 'mɒkɪŋ/ adj burlón

mod cons /'mɑːd'kɑːnz ‖ ,mɒd'kɒnz/ pl n (= **modern conveniences**) (BrE colloq & journ) comodidades fpl

mode /məʊd/ n **1** (a) (means) medio m; (kind) modo m (b) (operating method) (Comput, Tech) modalidad f **2** (Math) modo m **3** (Clothing) moda f

model¹ /'mɑːdl ‖ 'mɒdl/ n **1** (reproduction) maqueta f, modelo m **2** (paragon, example) modelo m **3** (design) modelo m **4** (person) modelo mf

model², (BrE) **-ll-** vt **1** ‹clay/shape› modelar **2** (base): **their education system was ~ed on that of France** su sistema educativo se inspiró en el francés; **to ~ oneself on sb** tomar a algn como modelo **3** ‹garment›: **she ~s sportswear** es modelo de ropa sport

model³ adj (before n, no comp) **1** (miniature) ‹railway/village› en miniatura **2** (ideal) ‹citizen/ husband/pupil› modelo adj inv; ‹answer› tipo adj inv

modem /'məʊdem/ n módem m

moderate¹ /'mɑːdərət ‖ 'mɒdərət/ adj moderado

moderate² /'mɑːdəreɪt ‖ 'mɒdəreɪt/ vt moderar

moderate³ /'mɑːdərət ‖ 'mɒdərət/ n moderado, -da m,f

moderation /,mɑːdə'reɪʃən ‖ ,mɒdə'reɪʃən/ n moderación f; **drinking is not harmful, in ~** beber no es nocivo, si se hace con moderación

modern /'mɑːdərn ‖ 'mɒdn/ adj moderno

modernization /,mɑːdərnə'zeɪʃən ‖ ,mɒdənər'zeɪʃən/ n modernización f

modernize /'mɑːdərnaɪz ‖ 'mɒdənaɪz/ vt modernizar*

modest /'mɑːdəst ‖ 'mɒdɪst/ adj (a) (not boastful) ‹person/remark› modesto (b) ‹income/gift› modesto; ‹improvement/success› moderado (c) (chaste) pudoroso

modesty /'mɑːdəsti ‖ 'mɒdɪsti/ n (a) (absence of conceit) modestia f (b) (propriety) recato m, pudor m

modicum /'mɑːdɪkəm ‖ 'mɒdɪkəm/ n (no pl) (frml) **a ~ OF sth** un atisbo DE algo (frml), un mínimo DE algo

modification /,mɑːdəfə'keɪʃən ‖ ,mɒdɪfɪ'keɪʃən/ n modificación f

modify /'mɑːdəfaɪ ‖ 'mɒdɪfaɪ/ vt **-fies, -fying, -fied** modificar*

modular /'mɑːdʒələr ‖ 'mɒdjʊlə(r)/ adj ‹design/ furniture› modular; ‹degree/course› dividido en módulos

modulate /'mɑːdʒəleɪt ‖ 'mɒdjʊleɪt/ vt modular

modulation /,mɑːdʒə'leɪʃən ‖ ,mɒdjʊ'leɪʃən/ n modulación f; **frequency ~** frecuencia f modulada

module /'mɑːdʒuːl ‖ 'mɒdjuːl/ n módulo m

Mohammed /məʊ'hæməd ‖ məʊ'hæmɪd/ n Mahoma

moist /mɔɪst/ adj ‹climate/soil› húmedo; ‹cake› no seco

moisten /'mɔɪsn/ vt humedecer*

moisture /'mɔɪstʃər ‖ 'mɔɪstʃə(r)/ n humedad f

moisturize /'mɔɪstʃəraɪz/ vt hidratar

moisturizer /'mɔɪstʃəraɪzər ‖ 'mɔɪstʃəraɪzə(r)/, **moisturizing cream** /'mɔɪstʃəraɪzɪŋ/ n crema f hidratante

molar /'məʊlər ‖ 'məʊlə(r)/ n muela f

molasses /mə'læsəz ‖ mə'læsɪz/ n (+ sing vb) melaza f

mold¹, (BrE) **mould** /məʊld/ n **1** (a) (hollow vessel) molde m (b) (dish) timbal m **2** (fungus) moho m

mold², (BrE) **mould** vt ‹steel/plastic› moldear; ‹character/attitudes› formar

Moldavia /mɑːl'deɪvjə ‖ mɒl'deɪvɪə/ n Moldavia f

Moldova /mɑːl'dəʊvə ‖ mɒl'dəʊvə/ n Moldova f

moldy, (BrE) **mouldy** /'məʊldi/ adj mohoso; **to become** o (BrE) **go ~** enmohecerse*

mole /məʊl/ n **1** (Zool) topo m **2** (on skin) lunar m

molecule /'mɑːlɪkjuːl ‖ 'mɒlɪkjuːl/ n molécula f

molest /mə'lest/ vt (a) (sexually) abusar (sexualmente) de (b) (harass) importunar

mollusk, mollusc /'mɑːləsk ‖ 'mɒləsk/ n molusco m

mollycoddle /'mɑːlikɑːdl̩ ‖ 'mɒlɪkɒdl̩/ vt (colloq & pej) mimar

molt, (BrE) **moult** /məʊlt/ vi «snake» mudar de piel; «bird» mudar de plumas; «dog/cat» pelechar, mudar de pelo

molten /'məʊltən/ adj ‹rock/metal› fundido; ‹lava› líquido

mom /maːm ‖ mɒm/ n (AmE colloq) mamá f (fam)

moment /'məʊmənt/ n momento m; **at the ~** en ese momento; **for the ~** de momento; **to have one's ~s** tener* sus (or mis etc) buenos momentos

momentary /'məʊməntəri ‖ 'məʊməntri/ adj ‹feeling/glimpse› momentáneo

momentous /məʊ'mentəs/ adj ‹occasion/ decision› trascendental; ‹day› memorable

momentum /məʊ'mentəm/ n (pl **-ta** /-tə/ or **-tums**) **(a)** (Phys) momento m **(b)** (speed) velocidad f; **to gather ~** ir* adquiriendo velocidad

momma /'maːmə ‖ 'mɒmə/ n (AmE) (colloq) mamá f (fam)

mommy /'maːmi ‖ 'mɒmi/ n (pl **-mies**) (AmE colloq) mami f (fam), mamita f (fam)

Monaco /'maːnəkəʊ, mə'naː- ‖ 'mɒnəkəʊ/ n Mónaco m

monarch /'maːnərk ‖ 'mɒnək/ n monarca mf

monarchist /'maːnərkəst ‖ 'mɒnəkɪst/ n monárquico, -ca m,f

monarchy /'maːnərki ‖ 'mɒnəki/ n monarquía f

monastery /'maːnəstəri ‖ 'mɒnəstri/ n (pl **-ries**) monasterio m

Monday /'mʌndeɪ, -di/ n **1** (day) lunes m; **on ~** el lunes; **next ~** el próximo lunes or el lunes que viene; **(on) ~s** los lunes; **the ~ after next** el lunes que viene no, el siguiente; **(before in) ~ afternoon/morning** el lunes por la tarde/mañana, la tarde/mañana del lunes **2 Mondays** (as adv) los lunes

monetarism /'maːnətərɪzəm ‖ 'mʌnɪtərɪzəm/ n monetarismo m

monetary /'maːnəteri ‖ 'mʌnɪtəri/ adj monetario

money /'mʌni/ n (pl **-nies** or **-neys**) dinero m; (currency) moneda f, dinero m; **their European operation is making a lot of ~** su operación europea está dando mucho; **to put ~ into sth** invertir* dinero en algo; **~ talks** poderoso caballero es don Dinero

money: ~ belt n faltriquera f, **~box** n alcancía f (AmL), hucha f (Esp); **~lender** n prestamista mf; **~-making** adj lucrativo; **~ order** n ≈ giro m postal; **~ supply** n the **~ supply** la masa monetaria

Mongolia /maːn'gəʊliə ‖ mɒŋ'gəʊliə/ n Mongolia f

Mongolian /maːn'gəʊliən ‖ mɒŋ'gəʊliən/ adj mongol

mongrel /'maːŋgrəl ‖ 'mʌŋgrəl/ n: perro mestizo, chucho, -cha m,f (fam), gozque mf (Col), quiltro, -tra m,f (Chi fam)

monitor¹ /'maːnətər ‖ 'mɒnɪtə(r)/ n **1 (a)** (screen) monitor m **(b)** (for measuring) monitor m **2** (listener) escucha mf **3** (Educ) encargado, -da m,f, monitor, -tora m,f (CS)

monitor² vt **(a)** ‹elections› observar; ‹process/ progress› seguir*; (esp electronically) monitorizar* **(b)** ‹radio station› escuchar

monk /mʌŋk/ n monje m

monkey /'mʌŋki/ n mono, -na m,f

monkey wrench n llave f inglesa; **to throw a ~ in the works** o **the machinery** (AmE) fastidiarlo todo

mono /'maːnəʊ ‖ 'mɒnəʊ/ n (Audio) monofonía f

monochrome /'maːnəkrəʊm ‖ 'mɒnəkrəʊm/ adj ‹picture› monocromático, monocromo

monogamy /məˈnaːgəmi ‖ məˈnɒgəmi/ n monogamía f

monologue, (AmE also) **monolog** /'maːnəlɔːg ‖ 'mɒnəlɒg/ n monólogo m

monopolize /məˈnaːpəlaɪz ‖ məˈnɒpəlaɪz/ vt ‹market/industry› monopolizar*; ‹conversation/ television› acaparar

monopoly /məˈnaːpəli ‖ məˈnɒpəli/ n (pl **-lies**) monopolio m

monosyllable /'maːnəˌsɪləbəl ‖ 'mɒnəsɪləbəl/ n monosílabo m

monotone /'maːnətəʊn ‖ 'mɒnətəʊn/ n tono m monocorde

monotonous /məˈnaːtṇəs ‖ məˈnɒtənəs/ adj monótono

monotony /məˈnaːtṇi ‖ məˈnɒtəni/ n monotonía f

monsoon /maːn'suːn ‖ mɒn'suːn/ n monzón m

monster /'maːnstər ‖ 'mɒnstə(r)/ n monstruo m

monstrous /'maːnstrəs ‖ 'mɒnstrəs/ adj **(a)** (huge) gigantesco **(b)** (shocking) monstruoso

Mont = **Montana**

month /mʌnθ/ n mes m; **$900 a ~** 900 dólares mensuales or por mes or al mes; **in a ~'s time** dentro de un mes

monthly¹ /'mʌnθli/ adj ‹journal/event› mensual; **~ payment** mensualidad f, cuota f mensual (esp AmL)

monthly² adv mensualmente, una vez al or por mes

monthly³ n (pl **-lies**) publicación f mensual

monument /'maːnjəmənt ‖ 'mɒnjʊmənt/ n monumento m

monumental /ˌmaːnjə'mentḷ ‖ ˌmɒnjʊ'mentḷ/ adj monumental

moo /muː/ vi moos, mooing, mooed mugir*

mood /muːd/ n **1 (a)** (state of mind) humor m; **to be in a good/bad ~** estar* de buen/de mal humor; **I'm not in the ~** no tengo ganas; **I'm not in the ~ for dancing** no tengo ganas de bailar **(b)** (atmosphere) atmósfera f **2** (Ling) modo m

moody /'muːdi/ adj **-dier, -diest (a)** (irritable, sulky) de mal humor; (gloomy) deprimido **(b)** (changeable) ‹person› temperamental

moon /muːn/ n luna f; **once in a blue ~** muy de vez en cuando

moonbeam /'muːnbiːm/ n rayo m de luna

moonlight¹ /'muːnlaɪt/ n luz f de la luna

moonlight² vi tener* un segundo empleo; **he ~s as a cab driver** trabaja además como taxista

moon: ~lighting n pluriempleo m; **~lit** adj iluminado por la luna

moor¹ /mʊr ‖mʊə(r), mɔː(r)/ *n* **(a)** (boggy area) llanura *f* anegadiza **(b)** (high exposed area) (esp BrE) páramo *m*; (covered with heather) brezal *m*

moor² *vt* amarrar
■ ~ *vi* echar amarras

mooring /'mʊrɪŋ ‖'mʊərɪŋ, 'mɔːrɪŋ/ *n* **(a)** (place) amarradero *m* **(b) moorings** *pl* (ropes) amarras *fpl*

moose /muːs/ *n* (*pl* **moose**) alce *m* americano *or* de América

mop¹ /mɑːp ‖mɒp/ *n* **(a)** (for floor) trapeador *m* (AmL), fregona *f* (Esp) **(b)** ~ **of hair** mata *f* de pelo

mop² -**pp**- *vt* ‹floor/room› limpiar, trapear (AmL), pasarle la fregona a (Esp); **to** ~ **one's brow** secarse* la frente
■ **mop up** [*v* + *o* + *adv*, *v* + *adv* + *o*] ‹water› secar*; ‹mess› limpiar

mope /məʊp/ *vi* (colloq) estar* deprimido

moped /'məʊped/ *n* ciclomotor *m*

moral¹ /'mɔːrəl ‖'mɒrəl/ *adj* moral

moral² *n* **1** (message) moraleja *f* **2 morals** *pl* (principles) moralidad *f*

morale /məˈræl ‖məˈrɑːl/ *n* moral *f*

morality /məˈræləti/ *n* (*pl* -**ties**) moralidad *f*

morally /'mɔːrəli ‖'mɒrəli/ *adv* moralmente

morbid /'mɔːrbəd ‖'mɔːbɪd/ *adj* morboso

more¹ /mɔːr ‖mɔː(r)/ *adj* más; **there'll be no** ~ **talking** se acabó la charla; **how much** ~ **flour?** ¿cuánta harina más?; **for** ~ **information call** 387351 para mayor información llamar al 38-73-51; ~ **and** ~ **people** cada vez más gente; **I eat** ~ **meat than you** yo como más carne que tú

more² *pron* más; **let's say no** ~ **about it** no hablemos más del asunto; **the** ~ **she eats, the thinner she gets** cuanto más come, más adelgaza; **you eat** ~ **than me** tú comes más que yo

more³ *adv* más; **you watch television** ~ **than I do** tú ves más televisión que yo; ~ **or less** más o menos; **could you please speak** ~ **clearly?** ¿podría hacer el favor de hablar más claro?; ~ **often** con más frecuencia; **I don't eat meat any** ~ ya no como carne

moreover /mɔːrˈəʊvər ‖mɔːˈrəʊvə(r)/ *adv* (frml) (*as linker*) además

morgue /mɔːrg ‖mɔːg/ *n* depósito *m* de cadáveres, morgue *f* (AmL)

Mormon /'mɔːrmən ‖'mɔːmən/ *n* mormón, -mona *m,f*

morning /'mɔːrnɪŋ ‖'mɔːnɪŋ/ *n* **1** (time of day) mañana *f*; **yesterday/tomorrow** ~ ayer/mañana por la mañana *or* (AmL tb) en la mañana *or* (RPl tb) a la mañana *or* de mañana; **we'll do it first thing in the** ~ lo haremos por la mañana a primera hora; **(good)** ~! ¡buenos días!, ¡buen día! (RPl) **2 mornings** (*as adv*) por las mañanas, en las mañanas (AmL), a la *or* de mañana (RPl)

morning: ~ **coat** *n* chaqué *m*, frac *m*; ~ **sickness** *n* náuseas *fpl* (matinales) (*del embarazo*)

Moroccan /məˈrɑːkən ‖məˈrɒkən/ *adj* marroquí

Morocco /məˈrɑːkəʊ ‖məˈrɒkəʊ/ *n* Marruecos *m*

moron /'mɔːrɑːn ‖'mɔːrɒn/ *n* (colloq & pej) imbécil *mf*, tarado, -da *m,f* (fam)

morose /məˈrəʊs/ *adj* taciturno

morphine /'mɔːrfiːn ‖'mɔːfiːn/ *n* morfina *f*

Morse /mɔːrs ‖mɔːs/ *n* morse *m*; **in** ~ **(code)** en (código) morse

morsel /'mɔːrsəl ‖'mɔːsəl/ *n* bocado *m*

mortal¹ /'mɔːrtl ‖'mɔːtl/ *adj* **(a)** (subject to death) mortal **(b)** (liter) ‹blow/injury/sin› mortal

mortal² *n* mortal *mf*

mortality /mɔːrˈtæləti ‖mɔːˈtæləti/ *n* **(a)** (death rate) mortalidad *f* **(b)** (loss of life) mortandad *f* **(c)** (condition) mortalidad *f*

mortar /'mɔːrtər ‖'mɔːtə(r)/ *n* **1** (cement) argamasa *f*, mortero *m* **2** (weapon) mortero *m* **3** (bowl) mortero *m*, molcajete *m* (Méx)

mortgage¹ /'mɔːrgɪdʒ ‖'mɔːgɪdʒ/ *n* (charge) hipoteca *f*; (loan) préstamo *m* hipotecario, hipoteca *f*; **to take out a** ~ **on a property** hipotecar* una propiedad

mortgage² *vt* hipotecar*

mortician /mɔːrˈtɪʃən ‖mɔːˈtɪʃən/ *n* (AmE) (employee) persona que trabaja en una funeraria; (funeral director) director, -tora *m,f* de pompas fúnebres

mortified /'mɔːrtəfaɪd ‖'mɔːtɪfaɪd/ *adj*: **I was** ~ me dio mucha vergüenza, me dio mucha pena (AmL exc CS)

mortuary /'mɔːrtʃʊeri ‖'mɔːtjʊəri/ *n* (*pl* -**ries**) depósito *m* de cadáveres, morgue *f* (AmL)

mosaic /məʊˈzeɪɪk/ *n* mosaico *m*

Moscow /'mɑːskaʊ ‖'mɒskəʊ/ *n* Moscú *m*

Moslem /'mɑːzləm ‖'mɒzləm/ *n/adj* ▶ MUSLIM¹,²

mosque /mɑːsk ‖mɒsk/ *n* mezquita *f*

mosquito /məˈskiːtəʊ ‖mɒsˈkiːtəʊ/ *n* (*pl* -**toes** *or* -**tos**) mosquito *m*, zancudo *m* (AmL)

moss /mɔːs ‖mɒs/ *n* musgo *m*

most¹ /məʊst/ *adj* **(a)** (nearly all) la mayoría de, la mayor parte de; ~ **days** todos los días **(b)** (as superl) más; **who eats (the)** ~ **meat in your family?** ¿quién es el que come más carne de tu familia?

most² *pron* **(a)** (nearly all) la mayoría, la mayor parte; **I read** ~ **of it** lo leí casi todo **(b)** (*as superl*): **she ate the** ~ fue la que más comió; **at (the)** ~ como máximo; **to make the** ~ **of sth** sacar* el mejor provecho posible de algo **(c)** (people) la mayoría

most³ *adv* **1 (a)** (to greatest extent) más; **I enjoyed the last act** ~ **of all** el último acto fue el que más me gustó **(b)** (before adj, adv) más; **which is the** ~ **expensive?** ¿cuál es el más caro? **2** (*as intensifier*): **what happened was** ~ **interesting** lo que sucedió fue de lo más interesante; ~ **likely** muy probablemente **3** (almost) (AmE colloq) casi

mostly /'məʊstli/ *adv*: **her friends are** ~ **students** la mayoría de sus amigos son estudiantes; **the land is** ~ **flat** el terreno es en su mayor parte llano

motel /məʊˈtel/ *n* motel *m*

moth /mɔːθ ‖mɒθ/ *n* mariposa *f* de la luz, palomilla *f*; (clothes ~) polilla *f*

mother¹ /'mʌðər ‖'mʌðə(r)/ *n* madre *f*; (before *n*) ~ **country** madre patria *f*

mother² *vt* mimar

motherhood /'mʌðərhʊd ‖'mʌðəhʊd/ *n* maternidad *f*

Mothering Sunday /ˈmʌðərɪŋ/ n (BrE) ▶
MOTHER'S DAY

mother: ∼**-in-law** n (pl ∼**s-in-law**) suegra f;
∼**land** n patria f

motherly /ˈmʌðərli ‖ˈmʌðəli/ adj maternal

mother: ∼**-of-pearl** /ˈmʌðərəvˈpɜːrl
‖ˌmʌðərəvˈpɜːl/ n nácar m, madreperla f, concha
f nácar (Méx), concha f de perla (Chi); **M**∼**'s Day**
n el día de la Madre (el segundo domingo de mayo
en EEUU y el cuarto domingo de Cuaresma en
GB); **M**∼ **Superior** n Madre f Superiora;
∼**-to-be** /ˈmʌðərtəˈbiː ‖ˌmʌðətəˈbiː/ n (pl
∼**s-to-be**) futura madre f, futura mamá f; ∼
tongue n lengua f materna

motif /məʊˈtiːf/ n (a) (theme) tema m (b) (design)
motivo m

motion[1] /ˈməʊʃən/ n **1** (a) (movement)
movimiento m; **to be in** ∼ estar* en movimiento;
to set o **put sth in** ∼ ‹wheel› poner* algo en
movimiento; ‹project/plan› poner* algo en
marcha (b) (action, gesture) gesto m; **to go through
the** ∼**s**: he went through the ∼s of interviewing
them los entrevistó por pura fórmula **2** (for vote)
moción f

motion[2] vi: she ∼ed to her assistant le hizo
una señal a su ayudante; they ∼ed to us to sit
down nos hicieron señas para que nos
sentáramos

motionless /ˈməʊʃənləs ‖ˈməʊʃənlɪs/ adj
inmóvil

motion picture n película f

motivate /ˈməʊtəveɪt ‖ˈməʊtɪveɪt/ vt motivar

motivation /ˌməʊtəˈveɪʃən ‖ˌməʊtɪˈveɪʃən/ n
(a) (drive) motivación f (b) (motive) motivo m

motive /ˈməʊtɪv/ n motivo m

motley /ˈmɑːtli ‖ˈmɒtli/ adj variopinto

motor[1] /ˈməʊtər ‖ˈməʊtə(r)/ n motor m

motor[2] adj (before n) **1** (Auto, Mech Eng) ‹parts›
de automóvil; ‹mechanic› de automóvil; ∼
show salón m del automóvil; ∼ **vehicle** (vehículo
m) automóvil m (frml) **2** (Physiol) ‹neuron/nerve›
motor [The feminine of MOTOR is MOTRIZ or
MOTORA]

motor: ∼**bike** n moto f; ∼**boat** n lancha f a
motor; ∼**car** n (BrE) automóvil m (frml);
∼**cycle** n motocicleta f; ∼**cyclist** n
motociclista mf, motorista mf

motoring /ˈməʊtərɪŋ/ n automovilismo m

motorist /ˈməʊtərəst ‖ˈməʊtərɪst/ n
automovilista mf, conductor, -tora m,f

motorway /ˈməʊtərweɪ ‖ˈməʊtəweɪ/ n (BrE)
autopista f

mottled /ˈmɑːtld ‖ˈmɒtld/ adj ‹skin›
manchado; ‹marble› veteado

motto /ˈmɑːtəʊ ‖ˈmɒtəʊ/ n (pl **-toes**) (of family,
school) lema m

mould etc (BrE) ▶ MOLD etc

moult vi (BrE) ▶ MOLT

mound /maʊnd/ n (a) (hillock) montículo m (b)
(man-made) túmulo m; **burial** ∼ túmulo funerario
(c) (heap) montón m

mount[1] /maʊnt/ n **1** (mountain) (liter) monte m
2 (Equ) montura f **3** (for machine, gun) soporte m;
(for picture – surround) paspartú m, marialuisa f
(Méx); (– backing) fondo m; (for slide) marco m; (for
stamp) fijasellos m; (for jewel) montura f, engaste m

mount[2] vt **1** (a) ‹horse› montar, montarse en
(b) ‹platform/throne› subir a **2** ‹gun/picture›
montar; ‹stamp/butterfly› fijar; ‹gem› engarzar*,
montar **3** ‹attack/offensive› preparar;
‹campaign/event› organizar*
■ ∼ vi **1** (a) ‹cost/temperature› subir;
‹excitement/alarm› crecer* (b) **mounting** pres
p ‹cost/fears/tension› cada vez mayor, creciente
2 (climb onto horse) montar
■ **mount up** [v + adv] ‹bills› irse* acumulando

mountain /ˈmaʊntn̩ ‖ˈmaʊntɪn/ n (Geog)
montaña f; (before n) ‹stream/path› de montaña;
‹scenery› montañoso; ∼ **range** cordillera f;
(shorter) sierra f

mountain bike n bicicleta f de montaña

mountaineer /ˌmaʊntn̩ˈɪr ‖ˌmaʊntɪˈnɪə(r)/ n
alpinista mf, andinista mf (AmL)

mountaineering /ˌmaʊntn̩ˈɪrɪŋ
‖ˌmaʊntɪˈnɪərɪŋ/ n alpinismo m, andinismo m
(AmL)

mountainous /ˈmaʊntn̩əs ‖ˈmaʊntɪnəs/ adj
montañoso

mountaintop /ˈmaʊntn̩ˌtɑːp ‖ˈmaʊntɪnˌtɒp/ n
cima f or cumbre f (de la montaña)

mounted /ˈmaʊntəd ‖ˈmaʊntɪd/ adj montado:
∼ **police** policía f montada

mourn /mɔːrn ‖mɔːn/ vt ‹loss/tragedy› llorar
■ ∼ vi **to** ∼ **FOR sb** llorar a algn

mourner /ˈmɔːrnər ‖ˈmɔːnə(r)/ n doliente mf

mournful /ˈmɔːrnfəl ‖ˈmɔːnfəl/ adj ‹expression/
glance› de profunda tristeza; ‹sigh/cry› lastimero

mourning /ˈmɔːrnɪŋ ‖ˈmɔːnɪŋ/ n (action, period)
duelo m, luto m; **to be in** ∼ **for sb** estar* de luto
por algn

mouse /maʊs/ n (pl **mice**) **1** (animal) ratón m,
laucha f (CS) **2** (Comput) ratón m; (before n) ∼
mat alfombrilla f para ratón

mousey adj ▶ MOUSY

mousse /muːs/ n (a) (Culin) mousse f or m (b)
(for hair) mousse f

moustache n (BrE) ▶ MUSTACHE

mousy /ˈmaʊsi/ adj **-sier, -siest** ‹hair›
castaño desvaído adj inv

mouth[1] /maʊθ/ n (pl **mouths** /maʊðz/) **1** (of
person, animal) boca f; **down in the** ∼ alicaído; **to
make sb's** ∼ **water**: it made my ∼ **water** se me
hizo agua la boca (or Esp) se me hizo la boca
agua **2** (of bottle) boca f; (of tunnel, cave) entrada f;
(of river) desembocadura f

mouth[2] /maʊð/ vt (silently): **it's him, she** ∼ed
es él —me/le dijo articulando para que le leyera
los labios

mouthful /ˈmaʊθfʊl/ n (of food) bocado m; (of
drink) trago m; (of air) bocanada f

mouth: ∼ **organ** n armónica f; ∼**piece** n
1 (of telephone) micrófono m; (Mus) boquilla f;

2 (spokesperson) portavoz *mf*; **~-to-~**
/'maυθtə'maυθ/ *adj* (*before n*) boca a boca;
~-wash *n* enjuague *m* (bucal); **~-watering**
/'maυθ‚wɔːtərɪŋ/ *adj* delicioso

move¹ /muːv/ *n* **1** (movement) movimiento *m*;
on the ~: **she's always on the ~** siempre está de
un lado para otro **2** (change — of residence)
mudanza *f*, trasteo *m* (Col); (— of premises)
traslado *m* **3** (a) (action, step) paso *m*; (measure)
medida *f*; **what's the next ~?** ¿cuál es el siguiente
paso? **(b)** (in profession, occupation): **it would be a
good career ~** sería un cambio muy provechoso
para mi (*or* su *etc*) carrera profesional **4** (Games)
movimiento *m*; **whose ~ is it?** ¿a quién le toca
mover?

move² *vi* **1** (a) (change place): **he ~d nearer
the fire** se acercó al fuego; **to ~ to a new job**
cambiar de trabajo **(b)** (change location, residence)
mudarse
2 (change position) moverse*
3 (proceed, go): **the vehicle began to ~** el
vehículo se puso en marcha; **the police kept the
crowds moving** la policía hacía circular a la
multitud; **the earth ~s around the sun** la Tierra
gira alrededor del sol; **we ~d to one side** nos
apartamos, nos hicimos a un lado
4 (advance, develop): **events ~d rapidly** los
acontecimientos se desarrollaron rápidamente; **to
~ with the times** mantenerse* al día; **to ~ into
the lead** pasar a ocupar el primer lugar
5 (carry oneself) moverse*
6 (go fast) (colloq) correr
7 (take steps, act): **we must ~ now** tenemos que
actuar ahora; **she ~d quickly to scotch rumors**
inmediatamente tomó medidas para acallar los
rumores
■ **~** *vt* **1** (transfer, shift position of): **~ your chair a
little** corre un poco la silla; **ask him to ~ the
boxes out of the way** dile que quite las cajas de
en medio; **I can't ~ my leg** no puedo mover la
pierna
2 (a) (transport) transportar **(b)** (relocate, transfer)
trasladar **(c)** (change residence, location): **the firm
that ~d us** la compañía que nos hizo la mudanza;
to ~ house (BrE) mudarse de casa
3 (a) (arouse emotionally) conmover*; **to ~ sb to
tears** hacer* llorar a algn de la emoción **(b)**
(prompt) **to ~ sb to + INF: this ~d her to
remonstrate** esto la indujo a protestar
4 (propose) (Adm, Govt) proponer*
■ **move along** **1** [*v + adv*] **(a)** (go further along)
correrse **(b)** (disperse) circular
2 [*v + o + adv*] (cause to disperse) hacer*
circular
■ **move around,** (BrE also) **move about** [*v +
adv*] **(a)** (walk) andar* **(b)** (change residence)
mudarse (*a menudo*); (change job) cambiar de
trabajo (*a menudo*)
■ **move away** [*v + adv*] **(a)** (move house)
mudarse (*de la ciudad, el barrio etc*) **(b)** ▶ MOVE
OFF
■ **move down** **1** [*v + adv*] bajar
2 [*v + o + adv*] bajar
■ **move in** [*v + adv*] **(a)** (set up home) mudarse (*a
una casa etc*); **to ~ in WITH sb** irse* a vivir CON
algn **(b)** (draw closer) acercarse* **(c)** (go into action)
«*police*» intervenir*; (Mil) atacar*
■ **move off** [*v + adv*] «*procession*» ponerse* en
marcha; «*car*» arrancar*
■ **move on**

mouth-to-mouth ⋯▸ much

I [*v + adv*] **1** (walk further) seguir* adelante;
(continue journey) continuar* el viaje
2 (a) (proceed) pasar **(b)** (progress) progresar
II [*v + o + adv*] (cause to disperse) hacer* circular
■ **move out** [*v + adv*] irse* (*de una casa etc*)
■ **move over** [*v + adv*] (make room) correrse
■ **move up** **1** [*v + adv*] **(a)** (rise) subir **(b)** (make
room) correrse
2 [*v + o + adv*] ⟨*picture/shelf*⟩ subir; **they ~d
him up a class** lo pusieron en la clase
inmediatamente superior

movement /'muːvmənt/ *n* **1** (a) (motion)
movimiento *m* **(b) movements** *pl* (activities,
whereabouts) desplazamientos *mpl*, movimientos
mpl **2** (a) (transportation) movimiento *m* **(b)**
(travel) desplazamiento *m* **3** (Art, Pol, Relig)
movimiento *m*

mover /'muːvər ‖'muːvə(r)/ *n* (of furniture,
belongings) (AmE): **a firm of ~s** una compañía de
mudanzas

movie /'muːvi/ *n* (esp AmE) **1** (film) película *f*,
film(e) *m* (period); (*before n*) ⟨*actor/director*⟩ de
cine **2 movies** *pl* (esp AmE) **the ~s** el cine

movie camera *n* (esp AmE) filmadora *f or*
(Esp) tomavistas *m*; (large, professional) cámara *f*
cinematográfica

moving /'muːvɪŋ/ *adj* **1** (emotionally) emotivo,
conmovedor **2** (in motion) (*before n*) **~ part** pieza *f*
movible **3** (AmE) (*before n*) ⟨*van/company*⟩ de
mudanzas

mow /məυ/ *vt* (*past* **mowed**; *past p* **mown** *or*
mowed) ⟨*hay*⟩ segar*; ⟨*lawn*⟩ cortar
■ **mow down** [*v + o + adv, v + adv + o*]
acribillar

mower /'məυər ‖'məυə(r)/ *n* **(a)** (Hort) ▶
LAWNMOWER **(b)** (on farm) segadora *f*

mown /məυn/ *past p of* MOW

Mozambique /‚məυzəm'biːk ‖‚məυzæm'biːk/
n Mozambique *m*

MP *n* **(a)** (in UK) (Govt) = **Member of
Parliament (b)** (= **military police**) PM *f*

mph = **miles per hour**

Mr /'mɪstər ‖'mɪstə(r)/ (= **Mister**) Sr.

Mrs /'mɪsəs ‖'mɪsɪz/ Sra.

Ms /mɪz ‖məz/ ≈ Sra. (*tratamiento que se da a
las mujeres y que no indica su estado civil*)

MS *n* **(a)** *also* **ms** (*pl* **MSS** *or* **mss**)
(= **manuscript**) ms. **(b)** (= **multiple
sclerosis**) E.M. *f* (c) (AmE) = **Master of
Science (d)** = **Mississippi**

MSc *n* (BrE) = **Master of Science**

MST (in US) = **Mountain Standard Time**

Mt (= **Mount**) **~ Rushmore** el monte Rushmore

MT = **Montana**

much¹ /mʌtʃ/ *adj* mucho, -cha; **how ~ coffee/
milk?** ¿cuánto café/cuánta leche?; **I do as ~ work
as anybody** trabajo tanto como cualquiera; **too ~
coffee** demasiado café

much² *pron* mucho, -cha; **do you see ~ of the
Smiths?** ¿ves mucho a los Smith?; **how ~ does it
cost?** ¿cuánto cuesta?; **I've done as ~ as I can** he
hecho todo lo que he podido; **and as ~ again** y
otro tanto; **you've drunk too ~** has bebido
demasiado

much³ *adv* mucho; **I'd very ~ like to meet her**
me gustaría mucho conocerla; **you deserve the** ⋯▸

prize just as ~ as I do te mereces el premio tanto como yo; so ~ the better tanto mejor; you talk too ~ hablas demasiado; this church is ~ the larger of the two de las dos iglesias esta es, con mucho, la más grande; I'm ~ too busy to do it estoy demasiado ocupada para hacerlo

muck /mʌk/ n (dung) estiércol m; (dirt) mugre f
■ **muck out** [v + o + adv, v + adv + o] limpiar

mucus /'mjuːkəs/ n mucosidad f

mud /mʌd/ n barro m, fango m, lodo m; (before n) ⟨brick/hut⟩ de barro, de adobe

muddle¹ /'mʌdl/ n lío m, follón m (Esp fam); to be in a ~ ⟨«papers»⟩ estar* (todo) revuelto; ⟨«person»⟩ estar* liado or hecho un lío (fam)

muddle² vt ▸ MUDDLE UP
■ **muddle up** [v + o + adv, v + adv + o] (a) ⟨papers⟩ entreverar (b) (mix up) confundir (c) (bewilder) confundir; to get ~d up confundirse

muddled /'mʌdld/ adj confuso; to get ~ hacerse* un lío (fam)

muddy /'mʌdi/ adj -dier, -diest ⟨boots/hands/road⟩ lleno or cubierto de barro or de lodo; ⟨water⟩ turbio

mudguard /'mʌdgɑːrd ‖ 'mʌdgɑːd/ n guardabarros m, salpicadera f (Méx), tapabarros m (Chi, Per)

muesli /'mjuːzli, 'muː- ‖ 'mjuːzli/ n (esp BrE) musli m, muesli m

muff¹ /mʌf/ vt (colloq) ⟨shot⟩ errar*; ⟨chance⟩ desperdiciar

muff² n (Clothing) manguito m

muffin /'mʌfən ‖ 'mʌfɪn/ n (AmE) mollete m (bollo dulce hecho con huevos); (BrE) bollo de pan que suele servirse tostado

muffle /'mʌfl/ vt 1 ⟨sound⟩ amortiguar* 2 ~ (up): her face was ~d (up) in a scarf una bufanda casi le tapaba la cara

muffler /'mʌflər ‖ 'mʌflə(r)/ n 1 (scarf) bufanda f 2 (a) (Mus) sordina f (b) (AmE Auto) silenciador m, mofle m (AmC, Méx)

mug¹ /mʌg/ n 1 (cup) taza f ⟨alta y sin platillo⟩, tarro m (Méx, Ven) 2 (gullible person) (BrE colloq) idiota mf 3 (face) (sl) cara f, jeta f (arg), careto m (Esp arg)

mug² vt -gg- atracar*

mugger /'mʌgər ‖ 'mʌgə(r)/ n atracador, -dora m,f

mugging /'mʌgɪŋ/ n atraco m

muggy /'mʌgi/ adj -gier, -giest ⟨weather/day⟩ pesado

mug shot n (colloq) foto f ⟨de archivo policial⟩

Muhammad /mə'hæməd ‖ mə'hæmɪd/ n Mahoma

mulberry /'mʌl.beri ‖ 'mʌlbəri/ n (pl -ries) (tree) morera f, (fruit) mora f ⟨de morera⟩

mule /mjuːl/ n mula f ⟨cruce de burro y yegua⟩; stubborn as a ~ más terco que una mula

mull /mʌl/ vt (a) (Culin): ~ed wine ponche caliente de vino y especias (b) (AmE) ▸ MULL OVER
■ **mull over** [v + o + adv, v + adv + o] reflexionar sobre

multicolored, (BrE) **multi-coloured** /'mʌlti.kʌlərd ‖ ,mʌlti'kʌləd/ adj multicolor

multicultural /,mʌlti'kʌltʃərəl/ adj multicultural

multilevel /'mʌlti'levl/ adj (AmE) de varias plantas, de varios pisos

multinational¹ /'mʌlti'næʃnəl ‖ ,mʌlti'næʃənl/ adj multinacional

multinational² n multinacional f

multiple¹ /'mʌltəpəl ‖ 'mʌltɪpəl/ adj (a) (involving many elements) múltiple (b) (many) múltiples

multiple² n múltiplo m

multiple: ~-choice /'mʌltəpəl'tʃɔɪs ‖ ,mʌltɪpəl'tʃɔɪs/ adj de opción múltiple, tipo test; ~ sclerosis /sklə'rəʊsəs/ n esclerosis f múltiple

multiplication /,mʌltəplə'keɪʃən ‖ ,mʌltɪplɪ'keɪʃən/ n multiplicación f

multiply /'mʌltəplaɪ ‖ 'mʌltɪplaɪ/ -plies, -plying, -plied vt (a) (Math) to ~ sth (by sth) multiplicar* algo (por algo) (b) (increase) multiplicar*
■ ~ vi (a) (Math) multiplicar* (b) (increase, reproduce) multiplicarse*

multipurpose /'mʌlti'pɜːrpəs ‖ ,mʌlti'pɜːpəs/ adj ⟨tool/appliance⟩ multiuso adj inv

multistory, (BrE) **multistorey** /'mʌlti'stɔːri/ adj de varias plantas, de varios pisos

multitude /'mʌltətuːd ‖ 'mʌltɪtjuːd/ n (a) (large number) (frml) (no pl) a ~ of sth: a ~ of problems innumerables or múltiples problemas (b) (crowd) (arch or liter) multitud f

mum /mʌm/ n 1 (mother) (BrE colloq) mamá f (fam) 2 (silence) (colloq): ~'s the word ¡punto en boca! (fam); to keep ~ no decir* ni pío (fam)

mumble /'mʌmbəl/ vi hablar entre dientes
■ ~ vt mascullar

mumbo jumbo /'mʌmbəʊ'dʒʌmbəʊ/ n (pej): religion, he said, was a lot of ~ dijo que la religión no era más que supercherías

mummy /'mʌmi/ n (pl -mies) 1 (mother) (BrE colloq: esp used by children) mami f (fam), mamita f (fam) 2 (Archeol) momia f

mumps /mʌmps/ n paperas fpl

munch /mʌntʃ/ vt/i mascar*

mundane /mʌn'deɪn/ adj ⟨existence⟩ prosaico; ⟨activity⟩ rutinario

municipal /mju'nɪsəpəl ‖ mju'nɪsɪpəl/ adj (usu before n) municipal

munitions /mju'nɪʃənz ‖ mju:'nɪʃənz/ pl n municiones fpl

mural /'mjʊrəl ‖ 'mjʊərəl/ n mural m

murder¹ /'mɜːrdər ‖ 'mɜːdə(r)/ n asesinato m; (Law) homicidio m; to get away with ~: she lets them get away with ~ les permite cualquier cosa

murder² vt (a) (kill) asesinar (b) (ruin) ⟨music/play⟩ destrozar*
■ ~ vi matar

murderer /'mɜːrdərər ‖ 'mɜːdərə(r)/ n asesino, -na m,f

murderous /'mɜːrdərəs ‖ 'mɜːdərəs/ adj ⟨instinct/look⟩ asesino; ⟨individual⟩ de instintos asesinos

murky /'mɜːrki ‖ 'mɜːki/ adj -kier, -kiest ⟨water⟩ turbio; ⟨green/brown⟩ sucio; ⟨past⟩ turbio

murmur¹ /'mɜːrmər ‖ 'mɜːmə(r)/ n murmullo m

murmur² vt murmurar

muscle /'mʌsəl/ n **(a)** (Anat) músculo m **(b)** (power) fuerza f

■ **muscle in** [v + adv] (colloq) meterse por medio (con prepotencia); **a rival company ~d in on their market** una compañía de la competencia se introdujo en su sector del mercado

muscular /'mʌskjələr ǁ'mʌskjʊlə(r)/ adj **(a)** ⟨arms/build⟩ musculoso **(b)** ⟨strain/contraction⟩ muscular

muscular dystrophy /'dɪstrəfi/ n distrofia f muscular

muse¹ /mju:z/ vi **to ~ (on** o **upon sth)** cavilar or reflexionar (sobre algo)

muse², Muse n musa f

museum /mjʊ'zi:əm/ n museo m

mush /mʌʃ/ n papilla f, pasta f

mushroom¹ /'mʌʃrʊm, -ru:m/ n hongo m (esp AmL), seta f (esp Esp), callampa f (Chi); (rounded, white) champiñón m

mushroom² vi «town/population» crecer* rápidamente; «companies/buildings» aparecer* como hongos or (Chi) como callampas, multiplicarse*

mushy /'mʌʃi/ adj **mushier, mushiest** ⟨vegetables/fruit⟩ blando

music /'mju:zɪk/ n **(a)** (art form) música f; **to face the ~** afrontar las consecuencias **(b)** (written notes) partitura f, música f

musical¹ /'mju:zɪkəl/ adj **(a)** (Mus) (before n) ⟨ability/tradition⟩ musical **(b)** (musically gifted) con aptitudes para la música **(c)** (melodious) ⟨voice/laugh⟩ musical

musical² n musical m

musical chairs n (+ sing vb): **to play ~ ~** jugar* a las sillitas

music: ~ box n caja f de música; **~ hall** n **(a)** (entertainment) music hall m, ≈ revista f de variedades **(b)** (building) teatro m de variedades

musician /mjʊ'zɪʃən/ n músico, -ca m,f

musk /mʌsk/ n almizcle m

musket /'mʌskət ǁ'mʌskɪt/ n mosquete m

Muslim¹ /'mʊzləm ǁ'mʊzlɪm/ n musulmán, -mana m,f

Muslim² adj musulmán

muslin /'mʌzlən ǁ'mʌzlɪn/ n muselina f (de algodón)

muss /mʌs/ vt **~ (up)** (AmE colloq) ⟨room⟩ desordenar; **she ~ed her hair** se despeinó

mussel /'mʌsəl/ n mejillón m

must¹ /mʌst, weak form məst/ v mod
☐1☐ (expressing obligation) tener* que or deber: **it ~ be remembered that ...** hay que recordar que ..., tenemos que or debemos recordar que ...; **she ~ not know that I am here** no debe enterarse de que estoy aquí, no se entere de que estoy aquí; **I ~ say, everywhere looks very tidy** tengo que reconocer que está todo muy ordenado
☐2☐ (expressing certainty, supposition) deber (de) or (esp AmL) haber* de; **it ~ be six o'clock** deben (de) ser or (esp AmL) han de ser las seis, serán las seis

must² /mʌst/ n (essential thing, activity): **a car is a ~ here** aquí es indispensable tener coche; **this book is a ~** este es un libro que hay que leer

mustache /'mʌstæʃ/, (BrE) **moustache** /mə'stɑːʃ/ n bigote(s) m(pl); **to grow a ~** dejarse bigote(s) or el bigote

mustard /'mʌstərd ǁ'mʌstəd/ n mostaza f

muster /'mʌstər ǁ'mʌstə(r)/ vt **(a)** (Mil) ⟨soldiers⟩ reunir*, llamar a asamblea **(b)** (succeed in raising) **to ~ (up)** ⟨team/army⟩ lograr formar; **if they can ~ enough support** si logran el apoyo que necesitan

mustn't /'mʌsṇt/ = **must not**

musty /'mʌsti/ adj **-tier, tiest** que huele a humedad or a moho

mutate /'mju:teɪt ǁmju:'teɪt/ vi **(a)** (Biol, Ling) mutar **(b)** (change) (frml) sufrir una transformación/transformaciones

mutation /mju:'teɪʃən/ n **(a)** (Biol, Ling) mutación f **(b)** (change) (frml) transformación f

mute /mju:t/ adj mudo

muted /'mju:təd ǁ'mju:tɪd/ adj ⟨sound⟩ sordo; ⟨voice⟩ apagado; ⟨trumpet⟩ con sordina; ⟨shade⟩ apagado; ⟨protest/reaction⟩ débil

mutilate /'mju:tʃeɪt ǁ'mju:tɪleɪt/ vt mutilar

mutiny¹ /'mju:tṇi ǁ'mju:tɪni/ n (pl **-nies**) **(a)** (instance) motín m, amotinamiento m **(b)** (offense) amotinamiento m

mutiny² vi **-nies, -nying, -nied** amotinarse

mutt /mʌt/ n (AmE colloq) (dog) chucho m (fam), gozque m (Col fam), quiltro m (Chi fam), pichicho m (RPl fam)

mutter /'mʌtər ǁ'mʌtə(r)/ vi hablar entre dientes

■ **~** vt mascullar

mutton /'mʌtṇ/ n carne f de ovino (de más de un año), añojo m (Esp), capón m (RPl)

mutual /'mju:tʃʊəl/ adj **(a)** (reciprocal) mutuo **(b)** (shared, common) (before n) ⟨friend/enemy⟩ común

muzzle /'mʌzəl/ n **(a)** (snout) hocico m **(b)** (for dog) bozal m **(c)** (of gun) boca f

my /maɪ/ adj

■ **Note** The translation *mi* agrees in number with the noun which it modifies; *my* is translated by *mi, mis,* according to what follows: *my father/mother* mi padre/madre; *my books/magazines* mis libros/revistas.

(sing) mi; (pl) mis; **I put ~ hat on** me puse el sombrero; **I broke ~ arm** me rompí el brazo

myalgic encephalomyelitis /maɪˈældʒɪkenˌsefələʊməɪəˈlaɪtəs ǁmaɪˌældʒɪkenˌsefələʊˌmaɪəˈlaɪtɪs/ n encefalomielitis f miálgica

myriad /'mɪriəd/ adj (liter): **the ~ varieties of butterfly** los miles tipos de mariposas

myrrh /mɜːr ǁmɜː(r)/ n mirra f

myself /maɪ'self/ pron **(a)** (reflexive): **I cut/hurt ~** me corté/lastimé; **I was talking to ~** estaba hablando solo/sola; **I was by ~** estaba solo/sola **(b)** (emphatic use) yo mismo, yo misma; **I made it ~** lo hice yo mismo/misma **(c)** (normal self): **I haven't been feeling ~ lately** no me encuentro muy bien últimamente

mysterious /mɪ'strɪəs ǁmɪ'stɪərɪəs/ adj misterioso

mystery /'mɪstəri/ n (pl **-ries**) ☐1☐ **(a)** (puzzle) misterio m **(b)** (quality) misterio m; (before n) ⟨guest/tour⟩ sorpresa adj inv ☐2☐ (Cin, Lit, Theat) película f (or novela f etc) de misterio or de suspenso or (esp Esp) de suspense

mystical /'mɪstɪkəl/ *adj* místico

mystify /'mɪstəfaɪ ‖'mɪstɪfaɪ/ *vt* **-fies, -fying, -fied** desconcertar*

myth /mɪθ/ *n* mito *m*

mythology /mɪ'θɑːlədʒi ‖mɪ'θɒlədʒi/ *n* (*pl* **-gies**) mitología *f*

Nn

N, n /en/ *n* **(a)** (letter) N, n *f* **(b)** (indeterminate number) (Math) (número *m*) n

'n' /ən/ = **and**

N (= **north**) N

NAACP /'endʌbəl'eɪsiː'piː/ *n* (in US) = **National Association for the Advancement of Colored People**

nab /næb/ *vt* **-bb-** (colloq) **(a)** (catch) ‹person› pescar* (fam) **(b)** (snatch) agarrar *or* (esp Esp) coger*

nadir /'neɪdɪr ‖'neɪdɪə(r)/ *n* (Astron) nadir *m*; (lowest point) punto *m* más bajo

nag /næg/ **-gg-** *vt* **(a)** (pester) fastidiar **(b)** (criticize): he's always ∼ging her for being untidy siempre le está encima con que es desordenada
■ ∼ *vi* **1** **(a)** (pester) fastidiar **(b)** (criticize) rezongar* **2 nagging** *pres p* ‹doubt/worry› persistente; ‹husband/wife› rezongón (fam)

nail¹ /neɪl/ *n* **1** (Const) clavo *m*; (smaller) puntilla *f*; **to be as hard as ∼s** ser* muy duro (de corazón) **2** (Anat) uña *f*; (before n) ∼ **polish** *o* (BrE also) **varnish** esmalte *m* de uñas

nail² *vt* **1** (fix) clavar **2** (colloq) (apprehend) agarrar *or* (esp Esp) coger*
■ **nail down** [*v* + *o* + *adv, v* + *adv* + *o*] clavar, asegurar con clavos

nail: ∼**brush** *n* cepillo *m* de uñas; ∼ **clippers** *pl n* cortaúñas *m*; ∼ **file** *n* lima *f* (de uñas)

naive, naïve /naː'iːv, naɪ'iːv/ *adj* ingenuo

naked /'neɪkəd/ *adj* **(a)** (unclothed) desnudo **(b)** ‹sword/blade› desenvainado; **visible/ invisible to the** ∼ **eye** que se puede ver/invisible a simple vista

name¹ /neɪm/ *n* **1** (of person, thing) nombre *m*; (surname) apellido *m*; **what's your** ∼? ¿cómo te llamas?, ¿cómo se llama (Ud)?; **my** ∼ **is John Baker; he knows them all by** ∼ los conoce a todos por su nombre; **in** ∼ **only** solo de nombre; **mentioning no** ∼**s** sin mencionar a nadie; **to call sb** ∼**s** insultar a algn; (before n) ∼ **tag** etiqueta *f* de identificación **2 (a)** (reputation) fama *f*, **to give sb/sth a bad** ∼ darle* mala fama a algn/algo **(b)** (person) figura *f*, (company) nombre *m*; **to drop** ∼**s** mencionar a gente importante (*para darse tono*)

name² *vt* **1** (give name to) ‹company/town› ponerle* (un) nombre a; ‹boat› bautizar*; **a man** ∼**d Smith** un hombre llamado Smith; **they** ∼**d her**

after *o* (AmE also) **for Ann's mother** le pusieron el nombre de la madre de Ann **2** (identify, mention): **police have** ∼**d the suspect** la policía ha dado el nombre del sospechoso; **to** ∼ **but a few** por mencionar a unos pocos; **you** ∼ **it, she's done it** ha hecho de todo lo habido y por haber **3** (appoint) nombrar

nameless /'neɪmləs ‖'neɪmlɪs/ *adj* **1** (not specified) anónimo **2** ‹fear/yearning› indescriptible

namely /'neɪmli/ *adv* (frml) a saber (frml)

namesake /'neɪmseɪk/ *n* tocayo, -ya *m,f*

nanny /'næni/ *n* (*pl* **-nies**) **1** (nursemaid) (esp BrE) niñera *f* **2** (granny) (used to or by children) abuelita *f* (fam) **3** ∼ **goat** cabra *f*

nap /næp/ *n* sueñecito *m* (fam), sueñito *m* (esp AmL fam); (esp in the afternoon) siesta *f*

nape /neɪp/ *n* nuca *f*

napkin /'næpkɪn/ *n* servilleta *f*

nappy /'næpi/ *n* (*pl* **-pies**) (BrE) pañal *m*

narcotic /naːr'kɑːtɪk ‖naː'kɒtɪk/ *n* estupefaciente *m*, narcótico *m*

narrate /'næreɪt ‖nə'reɪt/ *vt* **(a)** (Lit frml) ‹story/ events› narrar **(b)** ‹film/documentary› hacer* el comentario de

narrative¹ /'nærətɪv/ *adj* narrativo

narrative² *n* **(a)** (story) (frml) narración *f* **(b)** (Lit) (narrated part) narración *f*

narrator /'næreɪtər ‖nə'reɪtə(r)/ *n* **(a)** (Lit) narrador, -dora *m,f* **(b)** (Cin, Theat, TV) comentarista *mf*

narrow¹ /'næroʊ/ *adj* **1** **(a)** (not wide) ‹path/ opening/hips› estrecho, angosto (esp AmL) **(b)** (slender) ‹margin› escaso; ‹win/victory› conseguido por un escaso margen; **to have a** ∼ **escape** salvarse de milagro **2** (restricted) ‹range/ view› limitado; ‹attitude/ideas› cerrado

narrow² *vt* **(a)** (reduce width of) ‹range/field› estrechar, angostar (esp AmL) **(b)** (restrict) ‹range/field› restringir*
■ ∼ *vi* **(a)** «road/river/valley» estrecharse, angostarse (esp AmL) **(b)** «options/odds» reducirse*
■ **narrow down** [*v* + *o* + *adv, v* + *adv* + *o*]: **they've** ∼**ed their investigation down to this area** han restringido su investigación a esta área; **we**

~ed it down to only three candidates fuimos descartando candidatos hasta quedar con solo tres

narrowly /'nærəʊli/ adv por poco

narrow-minded /'nærəʊ'maɪndəd ‖,nærəʊ'maɪndɪd/ adj de mentalidad cerrada

NASA /'næsə/ n (in US) (no art) (= **National Aeronautics and Space Administration**) la NASA

nasal /'neɪzəl/ adj (Anat, Ling) nasal; ‹voice/ accent› gangoso, de timbre nasal

nasty /'næsti ‖'nɑːsti/ adj **-tier, -tiest** [1] ‹taste/smell/medicine› asqueroso; ‹habit› feo [2] (spiteful) ‹person› malo [3] (a) (severe) ‹cut/ injury/cough› feo; ‹accident› serio; (stronger) horrible (b) (unpleasant) ‹situation/experience› desagradable

nation /'neɪʃn̩/ n nación f

national¹ /'næʃnəl ‖'næʃənl̩/ adj nacional

national² n ciudadano, -na m,f

national: N~ Health (Service) n (in UK) the N~ Health (Service) servicio de asistencia sanitaria de la Seguridad Social; **N~ Insurance** n (in UK) Seguridad f Social

nationalism /'næʃnəlɪzəm/ n nacionalismo m

nationalist¹ /'næʃnələst ‖'næʃnəlɪst/ adj nacionalista

nationalist² n nacionalista mf

nationality /'næʃə'næləti/ n (pl **-ties**) nacionalidad f; **what's your?, what ~ are you?** ¿de qué nacionalidad eres?

nationalize /'næʃnəlaɪz/ vt nacionalizar*

nationally /'næʃnəli/ adv a escala nacional

national park n parque m nacional

nationwide¹ /'neɪʃənwaɪd/ adj ‹campaign› a escala nacional; ‹appeal› a toda la nación

nationwide² adv ‹distribute/operate› a escala nacional

native¹ /'neɪtɪv/ adj [1] (a) (of or by birth) ‹country/town› natal; ‹customs› nativo; ‹language› materno; **his ~ land** su patria, su tierra natal; **a ~ speaker of ...** un hablante nativo de ... (b) (innate) ‹ability/wit/charm› innato [2] (indigenous) ‹plant/animal› autóctono

native² n (a) (Anthrop) nativo, -va m,f, indígena mf (b) (plant, animal): **the dingo is a ~ of Australia** el dingo es originario de Australia

Native American n indio americano, india americana m,f

nativity /nə'tɪvəti/ n: **The N~** (Relig) la Natividad

NATO /'neɪtəʊ/ n (no art) (= **North Atlantic Treaty Organization**) la OTAN

natural /'nætʃrəl/ adj [1] (as in nature) natural [2] (a) ‹talent/propensity› innato; ‹leader› nato (b) ‹reaction/response› natural; ‹successor› lógico [3] (not forced) ‹warmth/style› natural

natural history n historia f natural

naturalist /'nætʃrələst ‖'nætʃrəlɪst/ n naturalista mf

naturalization /,nætʃrələ'zeɪʃən ‖,nætʃrələr'zeɪʃən/ n naturalización f

naturalized /'nætʃrəlaɪzd/ adj (a) ‹citizen/ American› naturalizado (b) (Bot, Zool) aclimatado

naturally /'nætʃrəli/ adv [1] (a) (inherently)

‹shy/tidy› por naturaleza (b) (unaffectedly) ‹smile/ behave/speak› con naturalidad [2] (without artifice) ‹form/heal› de manera natural [3] (indep) (of course) naturalmente, por supuesto

nature /'neɪtʃər ‖'neɪtʃə(r)/ n [1] (universe, way of things) naturaleza f [2] (a) (of people) carácter m; **by ~** por naturaleza (b) (of things, concepts) naturaleza f

nature reserve n reserva f natural

naturist /'neɪtʃərəst ‖'neɪtʃərɪst/ n (esp BrE) nudista mf; (before n) ‹beach/camp› nudista

naught /nɔːt/ n (esp AmE) cero m

naughty /'nɔːti/ adj **-tier, -tiest** malo, travieso

nausea /'nɔːsiə, -ziə/ n náusea f

nauseating /'nɔːsieɪtɪŋ, 'nɔːz-/ adj ‹violence/ brutality› repugnante; ‹smell› nauseabundo

nauseous /'nɔːʃəs, 'nɔːziəs ‖'nɔːsiəs, nɔːz-/ adj (bilious): **to feel ~** sentir* náuseas

nautical /'nɔːtɪkl̩ ‖'nɔːtɪkəl/ adj náutico, marítimo; **~ mile** milla f marina

naval /'neɪvəl/ adj naval; ‹officer› de marina

nave /neɪv/ n nave f

navel /'neɪvəl/ n ombligo m

navigable /'nævɪgəbəl/ adj navegable

navigate /'nævɪgeɪt ‖'nævɪgeɪt/ vi (a) (Aviat, Naut) navegar* (b) (in car) hacer* de copiloto ■ ~ vt (a) (steer) ‹ship/plane› conducir*, llevar (b) (travel across, along) ‹sea/river› navegar* por

navigation /'nævɪ'geɪʃən ‖,nævɪ'geɪʃən/ n navegación f; (in car) dirección f

navigator /'nævəgeɪtər ‖'nævɪgeɪtə(r)/ n [1] (crew member) (Naut) oficial mf de derrota; (Aviat) navegante mf [2] (explorer) navegante m

navy¹ /'neɪvi/ n (pl **navies**) [1] (Mil, Naut) marina f de guerra [2] **~ (blue)** azul m marino

navy², navy-blue /'neɪvi'bluː/ (pred **navy blue**) adj azul marino adj inv

Nazi¹ /'nɑːtsi/ n nazi mf, nazista mf

Nazi² adj nazi, nazista

NB (= **nota bene**) NB

NBC n (in US) (no art) (= **National Broadcasting Company**) la NBC

NC = **North Carolina**

NCO n = **noncommissioned officer**

ND, N Dak = **North Dakota**

NE (a) (= **northeast**) NE (b) = **Nebraska**

near¹ /nɪr ‖nɪə(r)/ adj **-er, -est** [1] (a) (in position, time) cercano, próximo (b) ‹relative› cercano [2] (virtual) (before n): **there was ~ panic when the alarms sounded** casi se produjo el pánico cuando sonaron las alarmas; **in a state of ~ exhaustion** prácticamente en estado de agotamiento

near² adv **-er, -est** [1] (in position) cerca; **from ~ and far** de todas partes [2] (nearly) casi

near³ prep **-er, -est** (a) (in position) cerca de; **don't go too ~ the fire** no te acerques demasiado al fuego (b) (in time): **we're getting very ~ Christmas** falta muy poco para Navidad (c) (in approximation): **I'd say he's ~er 70 than 60** yo diría que está más cerca de los 70 que de los 60

near⁴ vt acercarse* a; **the project is ~ing completion** el proyecto se está por acabar

near- /nɪr ‖'nɪə(r)/ pref casi

nearby¹ /'nɪrbaɪ ‖nɪə'baɪ/ *adj* cercano

nearby² *adv* cerca

nearly /'nɪrli ‖'nɪəli/ *adv* casi; **she very ~ died** por poco *or* casi se muere

nearsighted /'nɪr'saɪtəd ‖ˌnɪə'saɪtɪd/ *adj* miope, corto de vista

neat /niːt/ *adj* **-er, -est** **1** (tidy, orderly) ⟨*appearance*⟩ arreglado, cuidado, prolijo (RPl); ⟨*person*⟩ pulcro, prolijo (RPl); ⟨*garden*⟩ muy cuidado **2** (good, nice) (AmE colloq) fantástico (fam), padre (Méx fam), chévere (AmL exc CS fam), chulo (Esp fam), encachado (Chi fam) **3** (BrE) ⟨*brandy/ alcohol*⟩ solo

neatly /'niːtli/ *adv* (a) (tidily): **the papers were ~ organized into piles** los papeles estaban cuidadosamente apilados; **she was ~ dressed** iba bien arreglada (b) (snugly): **the table fits ~ into the alcove** la mesa cabe perfectamente en el hueco (c) ⟨*explain/evade*⟩ hábilmente

Neb, Nebr = **Nebraska**

necessarily /'nesə'serəli ‖ˌnesə'sɪrɪli/ *adv* forzosamente, necesariamente

necessary /'nesəseri ‖'nesəsəri/ *adj* necesario

necessitate /nə'sesɪteɪt ‖nɪ'sesɪteɪt/ *vt* (frml) exigir*

necessity /nə'sesəti ‖nɪ'sesəti/ *n* (*pl* **-ties**) **1** (imperative need) (*no pl*) necesidad *f*; **~ FOR sth** necesidad DE algo; **out of ~** por necesidad **2** (necessary item): **the bare necessities** lo indispensable; **a car is a ~ for me** para mí tener coche es una necesidad

neck /nek/ *n* **1** (Anat) (of person) cuello *m*; (of animal) cuello *m*, pescuezo *m*; **they were ~ and ~** iban a la par, iban parejos (esp AmL); **to be up to one's ~ in sth** (colloq): **she's up to her ~ in work** está hasta aquí de trabajo (fam); **they're up to their ~s in debt** deben hasta la camisa (fam) **2** (Clothing) cuello *m*, escote *m*; (measurement) cuello *m* **3** (of pork, beef, lamb) (esp BrE) cuello *m* **4** (of bottle, vase) cuello *m*; (of guitar, violin) mástil *m*; **a ~ of land** un istmo

necklace /'nekləs ‖'neklɪs/ *n* collar *m*

neck: **~line** *n* escote *m*; **~tie** *n* (AmE) corbata *f*

nectar /'nektər ‖'nektə(r)/ *n* néctar *m*

nectarine /'nektəriːn ‖'nektərɪn, -riːn/ *n* nectarina *f*, pelón *m* (RPl), durazno *m* pelado (Chi)

née /neɪ/ *adj* de soltera

need¹ /niːd/ *n* **1** (requirement, necessity) necesidad *f*; **~ FOR sth/to + INF** necesidad DE algo/DE + INF; **there's no ~ to tell her** no hay ninguna necesidad de decírselo; **if ~ be** si hace falta; **the house is badly in ~ of renovation** a la casa le hacen muchísima falta unos arreglos **2** (a) (emergency): **he abandoned them in their hour of ~** los abandonó cuando más falta les hacía (b) (poverty) necesidad *f*; **those in ~** los necesitados

need² *vt* necesitar; **the plants ~ watering** hay que regar las plantas; **to ~ to + INF** tener* QUE + INF

■ *v mod* (*usu with neg or interrog*) (be obliged to): **you ~n't come if you don't want to** no hay necesidad de que vengas si no tienes ganas; **that ~n't mean that ...** eso no significa necesariamente que ...

needle¹ /'niːdl/ *n* (a) (for sewing, on syringe) aguja *f*; (on record player) aguja *f*, púa *f* (RPl); (knitting ~) aguja *f* de tejer *or* (Esp) de hacer punto, palillo *m* (Chi); **to look for a ~ in a haystack** buscar* una aguja en un pajar (b) (on gauge) aguja *f* (c) (Bot) aguja *f*

needle² *vt* pinchar (fam)

needless /'niːdləs ‖'niːdlɪs/ *adj* innecesario; **~ to say, no one asked me** de más está decir que nadie me preguntó

needlework /'niːdlwɜːrk ‖'niːdlwɜːk/ *n* (activity, skill) labores *fpl* de aguja

needn't /'niːdnt/ = **need not**

needy¹ /'niːdi/ *adj* **-dier, -diest** necesitado

needy² *pl n* **the ~** los necesitados

negative¹ /'negətɪv/ *adj* negativo

negative² *n* **1** (a) (word, particle) negación *f* (b) (no) negativa *f* **2** (Phot) negativo *m*

neglect¹ /nɪ'glekt/ *vt* (a) (leave uncared-for) ⟨*family/child*⟩ desatender*; ⟨*house/health*⟩ descuidar (b) (not carry out) ⟨*duty/obligations*⟩ desatender*; ⟨*studies/business*⟩ descuidar

neglect² *n* (lack of care) abandono *m*; (negligence) negligencia *f*

neglected /nɪ'glektəd ‖nɪ'glektɪd/ *adj* ⟨*building/garden*⟩ abandonado, descuidado; ⟨*appearance*⟩ dejado, abandonado

neglectful /nɪ'glektfəl/ *adj* negligente

negligee /'neglɪʒeɪ ‖'neglɪʒeɪ/ *n* negligé *m*

negligence /'neglɪdʒəns/ *n* negligencia *f*

negligent /'neglɪdʒənt/ *adj* negligente

negligible /'neglɪdʒəbəl/ *adj* insignificante

negotiable /nɪ'gəʊʃəbəl/ *adj* (a) (subject to negotiation) ⟨*contract/claim/salary*⟩ negociable (b) (passable) ⟨*road*⟩ transitable; ⟨*obstacle*⟩ superable

negotiate /nɪ'gəʊʃieɪt/ *vi* negociar

■ *vt* **1** (obtain by discussion) ⟨*contract/treaty*⟩ negociar; ⟨*loan*⟩ gestionar **2** (pass, deal with) ⟨*obstacle*⟩ sortear; ⟨*difficulty*⟩ superar

negotiation /nɪ'gəʊʃi'eɪʃən/ *n* (*sometimes pl*) negociación *f*

negotiator /nɪ'gəʊʃieɪtər ‖nɪ'gəʊʃieɪtə(r)/ *n* negociador, -dora *m,f*

Negro /'niːgrəʊ/ *n* (*pl* **Negroes**) (often offensive) negro, -gra *m,f*

neigh /neɪ/ *vi* relinchar

neighbor, (BrE) **neighbour** /'neɪbər ‖'neɪbə(r)/ *n* vecino, -na *m,f*

neighborhood, (BrE) **neighbourhood** /'neɪbərhʊd ‖'neɪbəhʊd/ *n* (a) (residential area) barrio *m*; (before n) ⟨*school/policeman*⟩ del barrio (b) (inhabitants) vecindario *m* (c) (vicinity) zona *f*; **in the ~** en los alrededores

neighboring, (BrE) **neighbouring** /'neɪbərɪŋ/ *adj* ⟨*country*⟩ vecino; **the town and the ~ villages** la ciudad y los pueblos de los alrededores

neither¹ /'niːðər, 'naɪ- ‖'naɪðə(r), 'niːð-/ *conj* **1** **neither ... nor ...** ni ... ni ... **2** (nor) tampoco; **I don't want to go — ~ do I** o (colloq) **me — ~** no quiero ir — yo tampoco *or* ni yo

neither² *adj*: **~ proposal was accepted** no se aceptó ninguna de las (dos) propuestas

neither³ *pron* ninguno, -na

neo- /'niːəʊ/ *pref* neo-

neon /'niːɑːn ‖'niːɒn/ n neón m; (before n) ⟨glow/lighting/sign⟩ de neón

Nepal /nə'pɔːl ‖nɪ'pɔːl/ n Nepal m

Nepalese /ˌnepə'liːz/ adj nepalés

nephew /'nefjuː ‖'nevjuː, 'nef-/ n sobrino m

nepotism /'nepətɪzəm/ n nepotismo m

Neptune /'neptuːn ‖'neptjuːn/ n Neptuno m

nerve /nɜːrv ‖nɜːv/ n **1** (Anat, Bot) nervio m; (before n) ⟨fiber/ending⟩ nervioso **2** **nerves** pl **(a)** (emotional constitution) nervios mpl; **to get on sb's ~s** (colloq) ponerle* los nervios de punta a algn **(b)** (anxiety) nervios mpl **3** **(a)** (resolve) valor m; **to lose one's ~** perder* el valor **(b)** (effrontery) (colloq) (no pl) frescura f (fam); **to have the ~ to + INF** tener* la frescura de + INF (fam)

nerve-racking /'nɜːrˈrækɪŋ ‖'nɜːvˌrækɪŋ/ adj que destroza los nervios

nervous /'nɜːrvəs ‖'nɜːvəs/ adj **1** (apprehensive, tense) nervioso; **to feel/get ~** estar*/ponerse* nervioso; **to make sb ~** poner* nervioso a algn **2** ⟨system/tissue/tension⟩ nervioso; **she's a ~ wreck** (colloq) es un manojo de nervios

nervously /'nɜːrvəsli ‖'nɜːvəsli/ adv nerviosamente

nest¹ /nest/ n nido m

nest² vi anidar

nest egg n (colloq) ahorros mpl

nestle /'nesəl/ vi (snuggle) acurrucarse*; **the village ~s at the foot of the hill** el pueblo está enclavado al pie de la montaña

net¹ /net/ n **1** red f **2** (Sport) red f **3** (fabric) tela f de visillos; (before n) ~ **curtains** visillos mpl

net² vt -tt- **1** (catch) ⟨butterfly⟩ cazar* (con red); ⟨fish⟩ pescar* (con red) **2** (earn) ⟨company/sale⟩ producir*; **he ~ted $50,000** se embolsó 50.000 dólares limpios (fam)

net³ adj ⟨income/profit⟩ neto; ⟨effect/result⟩ global

netball /'netbɔːl/ n (in UK) deporte similar al baloncesto jugado esp por mujeres

Netherlands /'neðərləndz ‖'neðələndz/ n (+ sing or pl vb) **the ~** los Países Bajos

nett adj (BrE) ▶ NET³

netting /'netɪŋ/ n redes fpl; **wire ~** tela f metálica, tejido m metálico (RPl), anjeo m (Col)

nettle /'netl̩/ n ortiga f; (stinging ~) ortiga f (romana)

network¹ /'netwɜːrk ‖'netwɜːk/ n **(a)** (system) red f **(b)** (Elec) red f **(c)** (Rad, TV) cadena f; (before) ~ **television** (in US) emisiones fpl televisivas en cadena

network² vt **1** (BrE Rad, TV) transmitir en cadena **2** (link together) (Comput) interconectar

neuralgia /nʊ'rældʒə ‖njʊə'rældʒə/ n neuralgia f

neurosis /nʊ'rəʊsəs ‖njʊə'rəʊsɪs/ n (pl -roses /-'rəʊsiːz/) neurosis f

neurotic /nʊ'rɑːtɪk ‖njʊə'rɒtɪk/ adj neurótico

neuter¹ /'nuːtər ‖'njuːtə(r)/ adj neutro

neuter² vt castrar

neutral¹ /'nuːtrəl ‖'njuːtrəl/ adj **(a)** (impartial) neutral **(b)** (not bright) ⟨shade/tone⟩ neutro **(c)** (Chem, Elec, Ling) neutro

neutral² n (Auto): **to be in ~** estar* en punto muerto

neutralize /'nuːtrəlaɪz ‖'njuːtrəlaɪz/ vt neutralizar*

neutron /'nuːtrɑːn ‖'njuːtrɒn/ n neutrón m

Nev = **Nevada**

never /'nevər ‖'nevə(r)/ adv nunca; (more emphatic) jamás; **as ~ before** como nunca; **she said she'd call but she ~ did** dijo que llamaría pero no llamó; **this will ~ do!** ¡esto no puede ser!

never: **~-ending** /'nevər'endɪŋ/ adj (pred ~ **ending**) ⟨dispute/saga⟩ interminable; ⟨devotion/supply⟩ inagotable; **~theless** /ˌnevərðə'les ‖ˌnevəðə'les/ adv sin embargo, no obstante (frml)

new¹ /nuː ‖njuː/ adj **-er, -est** nuevo; **after the shower I felt like a ~ man** la ducha me dejó como nuevo

new² adv recién

new: **N~ Age** adj New Age, de la Nueva Era; **~born** /'nuːbɔːrn ‖'njuːbɔːn/ adj recién nacido; **~comer** /'nuːkʌmər ‖'njuːkʌmə(r)/ n recién llegado, -da m,f, **~fangled** /'nuː'fæŋgəld ‖'njuː'fæŋgəld/ adj (before n) (pej) moderno; **~found** /'nuːfaʊnd ‖'njuːfaʊnd/ adj nuevo, recién descubierto

newlyweds /'nuːliwedz ‖'njuːliwedz/ pl n recién casados mpl

news /nuːz ‖njuːz/ n **1** (fresh information): **a piece of ~** una noticia; **I have (some) good/bad ~** tengo buenas/malas noticias **2** (Journ, Rad, TV) noticias fpl; (before n) ~ **bulletin** boletín m informativo

news: **~agent** n (BrE) dueño o empleado de una tienda que vende prensa, caramelos etc; **~caster** n locutor, -tora m,f, presentador, -dora m,f (de un informativo); ~ **flash** (BrE) información f de última hora; ~ **group** n grupo m de noticias; **~letter** n boletín m informativo

newspaper /'nuːz,peɪpər ‖'njuːs,peɪpə(r)/ n periódico m, diario m

news: **~print** n papel m de prensa; **~reel** n noticiario m or (AmL tb) noticiero m (cinematográfico), nodo m (Esp); **~stand** n kiosco m de periódicos

newt /nuːt ‖njuːt/ n tritón m

new: **N~ Year** n Año m Nuevo; **N~ Year's Day** n día m de Año Nuevo; **N~ Year's Eve** n la noche de Fin de Año, la Nochevieja (Esp); **N~ York** /jɔːrk ‖jɔːk/ n Nueva York f; (before n) neoyorquino; **N~ Zealand** /'ziːlənd/ n Nueva Zelanda; (before n) neocelandés

next¹ /nekst/ adj **1** (in time — talking about the future) próximo; (— talking about the past) siguiente; **I'll see you ~ Thursday** nos vemos el jueves que viene or el jueves próximo; **the matter was discussed at the ~ meeting** el asunto se trató en la reunión siguiente; **the week after ~** la semana que viene no, la otra or la siguiente **(b)** (in position) siguiente; **take the ~ turning on the right** tome la próxima or la siguiente a la derecha **(c)** (in sequence): **who's ~?** ¿quién sigue?; **you're the ~ to speak** luego te toca a ti hablar

next² adv **1** **(a)** (then) luego, después **(b)** (now): **what shall we do ~?** ¿y ahora qué hacemos?; **what comes ~?** ¿qué sigue (ahora)?; **whatever ~!** ¡adónde vamos (a ir) a parar!

2 (second): **Tom is the tallest in the class, Bob the ~ tallest** Tom es el más alto de la clase y (a Tom) le sigue Bob; **it's the ~ best thing to champagne** después del champán, es lo mejor que hay

3 next to **(a)** (beside) al lado de; **come and sit ~ to me** ven y siéntate a mi lado **(b)** (compared with) al lado de **(c)** (second): **the ~ to last page** la penúltima página **(d)** (almost, virtually): **I bought it for ~ to nothing** lo compré por poquísimo dinero; **I'll have it ready in ~ to no time** lo termino en un segundo

next: ~ door adv al lado; **~ door TO sb/sth** al lado DE algn/algo; **~door** /'neks'dɔ:r ‖'neks'dɔ:(r)/ adj (before n) de al lado; **~ of kin** n (pl ~ **of kin**) familiar(es) m(pl) más cercano(s)

NH = **New Hampshire**

NHS n (in UK) = **National Health Service**

nib /nɪb/ n plumín m, pluma f

nibble /'nɪbəl/ vt **(a)** (bite) mordisquear **(b)** (eat, pick at) picar*
■ ~ vi **(a)** (bite, gnaw) **to ~ AT/ON sth** mordisquear algo **(b)** (eat) picar*

Nicaragua /'nɪkə'rɑːgwə ‖‚nɪkə'rægjʊə/ n Nicaragua f

Nicaraguan[1] /'nɪkə'rɑːgwən ‖‚nɪkə'rægjʊən/ adj nicaragüense

Nicaraguan[2] n nicaragüense mf

nice /naɪs/ adj **nicer, nicest** **1** **(a)** (kind, amiable) amable; (kind-hearted) bueno; (friendly) simpático; **to be ~ TO sb** ser* amable CON algn **(b)** (attractive, appealing) ⟨place/dress/face⟩ bonito, lindo (esp AmL); ⟨food⟩ bueno, rico; **the soup smells ~** la sopa huele bien **(c)** (enjoyable) ⟨walk/surprise⟩ agradable, lindo (esp AmL)
2 (as intensifier): **I had a ~ hot shower** me di una buena ducha caliente; **her apartment is ~ and sunny** tiene un apartamento muy or de lo más soleado
3 (respectable, decent): **he seemed such a ~ boy** parecía tan buen chico; **it isn't a very ~ area** es un barrio bastante feo

nicely /'naɪsli/ adv **1** **(a)** (amiably) ⟨treat/smile⟩ amablemente **(b)** (politely, respectably) con buenos modales **2** (attractively) ⟨presented/dressed⟩ bien

niceties /'naɪsətiz/ pl n sutilezas fpl

niche /nɪtʃ, niːʃ/ n nicho m, hornacina f

nick[1] /nɪk/ n (in wood) muesca f; (in blade) mella f; **did you cut yourself? — it's just a little ~** ¿te cortaste? — es solo un rasguño; **in the ~ of time** justo a tiempo

nick[2] vt **1** (notch) hacer* una muesca en; **I ~ed myself shaving** me corté al afeitarme **2** (steal) (BrE colloq) afanar (arg), volar* (Méx, Ven fam), robar

nickel /'nɪkəl/ **1** n (Chem, Metall) níquel m
2 (US coin) moneda de cinco centavos

nickname[1] /'nɪkneɪm/ n apodo m; (relating to personal characteristics) mote m

nickname[2] vt apodar

nicotine /'nɪkətiːn/ n nicotina f

nicotine patch n parche m de nicotina

niece /niːs/ n sobrina f

Nigeria /naɪ'dʒɪriə ‖naɪ'dʒɪəriə/ n Nigeria f

Nigerian /naɪ'dʒɪriən ‖naɪ'dʒɪəriən/ adj nigeriano

niggle /'nɪgəl/ vt: **something's niggling him** algo le preocupa

niggling /'nɪglɪŋ/ adj ⟨doubt/worry⟩ constante

night /naɪt/ n **1** noche f; **at ~** por la noche, de noche; **~ and day** día y noche; **last ~** anoche; **the ~ before last** anteanoche, antenoche (AmL); **we stayed (for) the ~** nos quedamos a dormir; **we haven't had a ~ out for ages** hace muchísimo que no salimos por la noche; **good ~** buenas noches; (before n) ⟨flight/patrol⟩ nocturno
2 **nights** (as adv) por las noches

night: ~cap n **(a)** (Clothing) gorro m de dormir **(b)** (drink) bebida alcohólica o caliente tomada antes de acostarse; **~clothes** pl n ropa f de dormir; **~club** n club m nocturno; **~dress** n camisón m; **~fall** n anochecer m; **at ~fall** al anochecer; **~gown** n camisón m

nightingale /'naɪtŋgeɪl ‖'naɪtɪŋgeɪl/ n ruiseñor m

nightlife /'naɪtlaɪf/ n vida f nocturna

nightly[1] /'naɪtli/ adj diario, de todas las noches

nightly[2] adv todas las noches

nightmare /'naɪtmer ‖'naɪtmeə(r)/ n pesadilla f

night: ~ school n clases fpl nocturnas; **~time** n noche f; **~ watchman** n sereno m

nil /nɪl/ n **(a)** (nothing): **its food value is virtually ~** su valor nutritivo es casi nulo **(b)** (BrE Sport) cero m

Nile /naɪl/ n **the ~** el Nilo

nimble /'nɪmbəl/ adj **-bler** /-blər/, **-blest** /-bləst/ ⟨person/step/mind⟩ ágil; ⟨fingers⟩ diestro

nine[1] /naɪn/ n nueve m; see also **FOUR[1]**

nine[2] adj nueve adj inv; **~ times out of ten he's late/right** casi siempre llega tarde/tiene razón

ninefold /'naɪnfəʊld/ adj/adv ▶ -FOLD

nineteen /'naɪn'tiːn/ adj/n diecinueve adj inv/ m; **to talk ~ to the dozen** hablar (hasta) por los codos or como una cotorra (fam); see also **FOUR[1]**

nineteenth[1] /'naɪn'tiːnθ/ adj decimonoveno

nineteenth[2] adv en decimonoveno lugar

nineteenth[3] n (Math) diecinueveavo m; (part) diecinueveava parte f

ninetieth[1] /'naɪntiəθ/ adj nonagésimo

ninetieth[2] adv en nonagésimo lugar

ninetieth[3] n (Math) noventavo m; (part) noventava or nonagésima parte f

nine-to-five /'naɪntə'faɪv/ adj ⟨job/worker⟩ de oficina (con horario de nueve a cinco)

ninety /'naɪnti/ adj/n noventa adj inv/m; see also **FOUR[1]**

ninth[1] /naɪnθ/ adj noveno

ninth[2] adv en noveno lugar

AmC	Central America	Arg	Argentina	Cu	Cuba	Per	Peru
AmL	Latin America	Bol	Bolivia	Ec	Ecuador	RPI	River Plate Area
AmS	South America	Chi	Chile	Esp	Spain	Ur	Uruguay
Andes	Andean Region	CS	Southern Cone	Méx	Mexico	Ven	Venezuela

ninth³ n (Math) noveno m; (part) novena parte f

nip¹ /nɪp/ n **(a)** (pinch) pellizco m; (bite) mordisco m **(b)** (chill): **there's a ∼ in the air** hace bastante fresco

nip² vt **-pp-** (pinch) pellizcar*; (bite) mordisquear

nipple /'nɪpəl/ n **(a)** (on breast — of woman) pezón m; (— of man) tetilla f **(b)** (on bottle) (AmE) tetina f, chupón m (Méx)

nippy /'nɪpi/ adj **-pier, -piest** (colloq) frío; **it's ∼** hace frío

nit /nɪt/ n (Zool) liendre f

nit: ∼pick vi encontrarle* defectos a todo; **∼picking** adj quisquilloso

nitrate /'naɪtreɪt/ n nitrato m

nitrogen /'naɪtrədʒən/ n nitrógeno m

NJ = **New Jersey**

NM, N Mex = **New Mexico**

no¹ /nəʊ/ adj ⒈ **(a)** (+ pl n): **they have ∼ children** no tienen hijos; **the room has ∼ windows** la habitación no tiene ninguna ventana or no tiene ventanas **(b)** (+ uncount n): **there's ∼ food left** no queda nada de comida; **there's ∼ time for that now** no tenemos tiempo para eso ahora; **I'll be finished in ∼ time (at all)** termino enseguida **(c)** (+ sing count n): **this cup has ∼ handle** esta taza no tiene asa; **∼ intelligent person would do that** ninguna persona inteligente haría eso ⒉ (in understatement): **I'm ∼ expert, but ...** no soy ningún experto, pero ...; **she told him what she thought in ∼ uncertain terms** le dijo lo que pensaba muy claramente ⒊ **(a)** (prohibiting, demanding): ☉ **no smoking** prohibido fumar **(b)** (with -ing form): **there's ∼ pleasing some people** no hay manera de complacer a cierta gente; **there'll be ∼ stopping them now** ahora no hay quien los pare

no² adv (before adj or adv): **my house is ∼ larger than yours** mi casa no es más grande que la tuya; **∼ fewer than 200 guests are expected** se espera nada menos que a unos 200 invitados

no³ interj no; **to say ∼** decir* que no; **have you seen John? — ∼, I haven't** ¿has visto a John? — no

no⁴ n (pl **noes**) no m

no⁵ (pl **nos**) (= **number**) nº, Nº

Nobel Prize /nəʊ'bel/ n **the ∼** el Premio Nobel

nobility /nəʊ'bɪləti/ n nobleza f; **the ∼** la nobleza

noble¹ /'nəʊbəl/ adj **nobler** /-blər/, **noblest** /-bləst/ noble

noble² n noble mf

nobleman /'nəʊbəlmən/ n (pl **-men** /-mən/) noble m

nobody¹ /'nəʊˌbɑːdi ‖ 'nəʊbədi/ pron nadie

nobody² n (pl **-dies**): **to be a** (a) **∼** ser* un don nadie

nocturnal /nɑːk'tɜːrn̩ ‖ nɒk'tɜːn̩/ adj nocturno

nod¹ /nɑːd ‖ nɒd/ n: **he greeted her with a ∼** la saludó con un movimiento de cabeza; **to give sb/ sth the ∼** darle* luz verde a algn/algo

nod² **-dd-** vt: **he ∼ded his head (in agreement)** asintió con la cabeza

■ **∼** vi: **she smiled at me and I ∼ed to her** me sonrió y la saludé con la cabeza; **they ∼ded in assent** asintieron con la cabeza

■ **nod off** [v + adv] (colloq) dormirse*

nodule /'nɑːdʒuːl ‖ 'nɒdjuːl/ n nódulo m

no-fly zone /nəʊ'flaɪ/n zona f de exclusión aérea

no-good /'nəʊˈɡʊd/ adj (AmE colloq) maldito (fam)

noise /nɔɪz/ n ruido m

noisily /'nɔɪzəli ‖ 'nɔɪzɪli/ adv ruidosamente

noisy /'nɔɪzi/ adj **-sier, -siest** ⟨machine/office/ street⟩ ruidoso; ⟨person/child/party⟩ bullicioso

nomad /'nəʊmæd/ n nómada mf, nómade mf (CS)

no-man's land /'nəʊmænzlænd/ n tierra f de nadie

nominal /'nɑːmən̩ ‖ 'nɒmɪn̩/ adj **(a)** (in name) nominal **(b)** (token) ⟨fee/rent⟩ simbólico

nominate /'nɑːməneɪt ‖ 'nɒmɪneɪt/ vt **(a)** (propose) **to ∼ sb (FOR sth)** (for a post) proponer* or (AmL tb) postular a algn (PARA algo) **(b)** (appoint, choose) nombrar; ⟨candidate⟩ (AmE Pol) proclamar

nomination /ˌnɑːməˈneɪʃən ‖ ˌnɒmɪˈneɪʃən/ n **(a)** (choice, appointment) nombramiento m; (of candidate) (AmE Pol) proclamación f **(b)** (proposal) propuesta f, postulación f (AmL)

nominee /ˌnɑːməˈniː ‖ ˌnɒmɪˈniː/ n **(a)** (person proposed) candidato, -ta m,f **(b)** (person appointed) persona f nombrada; (candidate) (AmE Pol) candidato, -ta m,f

non- /nɑːn ‖ nɒn/ pref no; **∼swimmers must ...** las personas que no saben nadar deben ...

nonchalant /'nɑːnʃəˈlɑːnt ‖ 'nɒnʃələnt/ adj (casual) despreocupado; (indifferent) indiferente

noncommissioned officer /ˌnɑːnkəˈmɪʃənd ‖ ˌnɒnkəˈmɪʃənd/ n **∼** suboficial mf

noncommittal /ˌnɑːnkəˈmɪtl̩ ‖ ˌnɒnkəˈmɪtl̩/ adj ⟨reply⟩ evasivo

nondescript /'nɑːndɪˈskrɪpt ‖ 'nɒndɪskrɪpt/ adj (not unusual or outstanding) anodino; (dull) insulso

none¹ /nʌn/ pron ⒈ (not any, not one) (referring to count n) ninguno, ninguna; **I tried to get tickets, but there were ∼ left** traté de comprar entradas pero no quedaba ninguna or ni una; **∼ of us know** o **knows her** ninguno de nosotros la conoce ⒉ (no amount or part) (referring to uncount n): **did you buy any milk? there's ∼ left** ¿compraste leche? no hay más

none² adv **(a)** none the (not, in no way) (with comp): **I was ∼ the wiser after his explanation** su explicación no me aclaró nada **(b)** none too (not very) (with adj or adv): **she was ∼ too pleased to see me** no le hizo demasiada gracia verme

nonentity /nɑːˈnentəti ‖ nɒˈnentəti/ n (pl **-ties**) persona f insignificante

nonetheless /ˌnʌnðəˈles/ adv ▶ NEVERTHELESS

non-existent /ˌnɑːnɪɡˈzɪstənt ‖ ˌnɒnɪɡˈzɪstənt/ adj inexistente

nonfiction /ˌnɑːnˈfɪkʃən ‖ ˌnɒnˈfɪkʃən/ n no ficción f (ensayos, biografías, obras de divulgación etc)

no-nonsense /'nəʊˈnɑːnsens ‖ ˈnəʊˈnɒnsəns/ adj (before n) ⟨approach/attitude⟩ sensato

nonplused, nonplussed /nɑːnˈplʌst ‖ˌnɒnˈplʌst/ adj desconcertado

nonprofit /ˈnɑːnˈprɑːfət ‖ˌnɒnˈprɒfɪt/‖, (BrE) **non-profitmaking** /ˈnɑːnˈprɑːfətˌmeɪkɪŋ ‖ˌnɒnˈprɒfɪtmeɪkɪŋ/ adj sin fines lucrativos

nonsense /ˈnɑːnsens ‖ˈnɒnsəns/ n tonterías fpl

nonsensical /nɑːnˈsensɪkəl ‖nɒnˈsensɪkəl/ adj disparatado

nonsmoker /ˈnɑːnˈsməʊkər ‖ˌnɒnˈsməʊkə(r)/ n no fumador, -dora m,f

nonsmoking /nɑːnˈsməʊkɪŋ ‖nɒnˈsməʊkɪŋ/ adj para no fumadores

nonstick /ˈnɑːnˈstɪk ‖nɒnˈstɪk/ adj antiadherente, de teflón®, de tefal®

nonstop /ˈnɑːnˈstɑːp ‖nɒnˈstɒp/ adv **(a)** ⟨work/talk⟩ sin parar **(b)** ⟨sail/fly⟩ sin hacer escalas

noodle /ˈnuːdl̩/ n fideo m

nook /nʊk/ n rincón m; **to search every ~ and cranny** mirar/buscar* hasta en el último rincón

noon /nuːn/ n mediodía m; **at ~** a mediodía

no one pron ▶ NOBODY

noose /nuːs/ n soga f, dogal m

noplace /ˈnəʊpleɪs/ adv (AmE) ▶ NOWHERE[1] 1

nor /nər, nɔːr ‖nɔː(r)/ conj **(a)** neither ... nor ... ▶ NEITHER[1] 1 **(b)** (usu with neg) tampoco

norm /nɔːrm ‖nɔːm/ n norma f

normal /ˈnɔːrməl ‖ˈnɔːməl/ adj normal; **when things get back to ~** cuando todo vuelva a la normalidad

normality /nɔːrˈmæləti ‖nɔːˈmæləti/ n normalidad f

normally /ˈnɔːrməli ‖ˈnɔːməli/ adv normalmente

north[1] /nɔːrθ ‖nɔːθ/ n (point of the compass, direction) norte m; **the ~, the N~** (region) el norte

north[2] adj (before n) norte adj inv, septentrional; ⟨wind⟩ norte adj inv

north[3] adv al norte

north: N~ America n´ Norteamérica f, América f del Norte; **N~ American** adj de América del Norte, norteamericano; **~bound** adj ⟨traffic/train⟩ que va (or iba etc) en dirección norte

northeast[1], Northeast /ˈnɔːrθˈiːst ‖ˌnɔːθˈiːst/ n **the ~** el nor(d)este or Nor(d)este

northeast[2] adj nor(d)este adj inv, del nor(d)este, nororiental

northeast[3] adv hacia el nor(d)este, en dirección nor(d)este

northeasterly /ˈnɔːrθˈiːstərli ‖ˌnɔːθˈiːstəli/ adj ⟨wind⟩ del noreste

northeastern /ˈnɔːrθˈiːstərn ‖ˌnɔːθˈiːstən/ adj nor(d)este adj inv, del nor(d)este, nororiental

northerly /ˈnɔːrðərli ‖ˈnɔːðəli/ adj ⟨wind⟩ del norte; ⟨latitude⟩ norte adj inv; **in a ~ direction** hacia el or en dirección norte

northern /ˈnɔːrðərn ‖ˈnɔːðən/ adj ⟨region/country⟩ del norte, septentrional, norteño, nortino (Chi, Per); **~ England** el norte de Inglaterra; **the ~ states** (in US) los estados del norte

Northern Ireland n Irlanda f del Norte

north: N~ Sea n Mar m del Norte; **N~ Star** n estrella f polar

northward[1] /ˈnɔːrθwərd ‖ˈnɔːθwəd/ adj (before n): **in a ~ direction** en dirección norte, hacia el norte

northward[2], (BrE) **northwards** /-z/ adv hacia el norte

northwest[1], Northwest /ˈnɔːrθˈwest ‖ˌnɔːθˈwest/ n **the ~** el noroeste or Noroeste

northwest[2] adj noroeste adj inv, del noroeste

northwest[3] adv hacia el noroeste, en dirección noroeste

northwesterly /ˈnɔːrθˈwestərli ‖ˌnɔːθˈwestəli/ adj ⟨wind⟩ del noroeste

northwestern /ˈnɔːrθˈwestərn ‖ˌnɔːθˈwestən/ adj noroccidental, noroeste adj inv, del noroeste

Norway /ˈnɔːrweɪ ‖ˈnɔːweɪ/ n Noruega f

Norwegian[1] /nɔːrˈwiːdʒən ‖nɔːˈwiːdʒən/ adj noruego

Norwegian[2] n **(a)** (person) noruego, -ga m,f **(b)** (language) noruego m

nose[1] /nəʊz/ n [1] (of person, animal) nariz f; **to look down one's ~ at sb** mirar a algn por encima del hombro; **to poke o stick one's ~ in** (colloq) meter las narices en algo (fam); **to turn one's ~ up at sth/sb** (colloq) despreciar algo/a algn [2] (of plane, car) parte f delantera, trompa f (RPl)

nose[2] vi (rummage, pry) entrometerse; **to ~ around o about in sth** husmear en algo

nose: ~bleed n hemorragia f nasal (frml); **I've got a ~bleed** me sangra la nariz; **~dive** vi **(a)** (Aviat) «plane/pilot» descender* or bajar en picada or (Esp) en picado **(b)** (drop sharply) «prices» caer* en picada or (Esp) en picado

nosey /ˈnəʊzi/ adj (BrE) ▶ NOSY

no-smoking /ˈnəʊˈsməʊkɪŋ/ adj ⟨compartment/section⟩ para no fumadores

nostalgia /nɑːˈstældʒə ‖nɒˈstældʒə/ n nostalgia f

nostalgic /nɑːˈstældʒɪk ‖nɒˈstældʒɪk/ adj nostálgico

nostril /ˈnɑːstrəl ‖ˈnɒstrɪl/ n ventana f de la nariz

nosy, (BrE also) **nosey** /ˈnəʊzi/ adj **nosier, nosiest** (colloq) ⟨person⟩ entrometido, metiche (AmL fam), metido (AmL fam); ⟨question⟩ impertinente

not /nɑːt ‖nɒt/ adv **(a)** no; **I asked them ~ to tell anyone** les pedí que no se lo dijeran a nadie **(b)** not that (as conj): **I'm going to London, ~ that it's any business of yours** voy a Londres, no es que a ti te importe, pero ... **(c)** (emphatic) ni; **~ a penny more** ni un penique más **(d)** (replacing clause): **I hope ~** espero que no; **are you going to help me or ~?** ¿me vas a ayudar o no?

notable /ˈnəʊtəbəl/ adj ⟨author/actor⟩ distinguido; ⟨success⟩ señalado; ⟨improvement/difference⟩ notable

notably /ˈnəʊtəbli/ adv **(a)** (noticeably) notablemente **(b)** (in particular) particularmente, en particular

notch /nɑːtʃ ‖nɒtʃ/ n (in wood, metal) muesca f, (on belt) agujero m
■ **notch up** [v + adv + o] (colloq) apuntarse

note[1] /nəʊt/ n [1] (record, reminder) nota f; **to**

make a ~ of sth anotar *or* apuntar algo; **to make ~s** hacer* anotaciones; **to take ~s** tomar apuntes *or* notas; **to compare ~s** cambiar impresiones **2** (message): nota *f* **3 (a)** (Mus) nota *f* **(b)** (tone): **I detected a ~ of sarcasm in his voice** percibí un tono de sarcasmo en su voz; **the evening ended on a sad ~** la velada terminó con una nota triste **4** (esp BrE) billete *m* **5** (attention): **take ~ of what he says** toma nota de *or* presta atención a lo que dice

note² *vt* **(a)** (observe, notice) observar **(b)** (record) ⟨information⟩ anotar
■ **note down** [*v + adv + o, v + o + adv*] apuntar

notebook /'nəʊtbʊk/ *n* cuaderno *m*

noted /'nəʊtəd ‖'nəʊtɪd/ *adj* ⟨historian/surgeon⟩ renombrado, de nota

note: **~pad** *n* bloc *m*; **~paper** *n* papel *m* de carta(s)

nothing /'nʌθɪŋ/ *pron* **1** nada; **there's ~ to eat** no hay nada de comer **2** (in phrases) **for nothing: she gave it to me for ~** me lo dio gratis; **it was all for ~** todo fue en vano; **if nothing else** al menos, por lo menos; **nothing but: she's caused ~ but trouble** no ha causado (nada) más que problemas; **nothing like: there's ~ like a shower to freshen you up** no hay (nada) como una ducha para refrescarse; **nothing much: ~ much happened** no pasó gran cosa

notice¹ /'nəʊtəs ‖'nəʊtɪs/ *n* **1 (a)** (written sign) letrero *m* **(b)** (item of information) anuncio *m* **2** (attention): **it has come/been brought to my ~ that ...** (frml) ha llegado a mi conocimiento que .../ se me ha señalado que ... (frml); **she took no ~ of him** no hizo caso; **don't take any ~ of him** no le hagas caso **3 (a)** (notification) aviso *m*; **until further ~** hasta nuevo aviso; **it's impossible to do it at such short ~** es imposible hacerlo a tan corto plazo **(b)** (of termination of employment) preaviso *m*; **I have to give (the company) a month's ~** tengo que dar un mes de preaviso; **to give o hand in one's ~** presentar su (*or* mi *etc*) renuncia

notice² *vt* notar; **nobody ~d him put it in his pocket** nadie lo vio ponérselo en el bolsillo
■ *vi* (realize, observe) darse* cuenta

noticeable /'nəʊtəsəbəl ‖'nəʊtɪsəbəl/ *adj* perceptible

noticeboard /'nəʊtəsbɔːrd ‖'nəʊtɪsbɔːd/ *n* (esp BrE) tablero *m or* (Esp) tablón *m* de anuncios, cartelera *f* (AmL), diario *m* mural (Chi)

notification /ˌnəʊtəfə'keɪʃən ‖ˌnəʊtɪfɪ'keɪʃən/ *n* notificación *f*

notify /'nəʊtəfaɪ ‖'nəʊtɪfaɪ/ *vt* **-fies, -fying, -fied** (inform) informar; (in writing) notificar*; **to ~ sb or sth** comunicarle* algo A algn

notion /'nəʊʃən/ *n* **1** (idea) idea *f* **2** (concept) concepto *m* **3** **notions** *pl* **(a)** (in sewing) artículos *mpl* de mercería **(b)** (AmE): **household/gift ~s** artículos *mpl* para el hogar/de regalo

notorious /nəʊ'tɔːriəs/ *adj* ⟨liar/womanizer/gossip⟩ (bien) conocido; ⟨place⟩ de mala fama

notwithstanding¹ /ˌnɑːtwɪð'stændɪŋ ‖ˌnɒtwɪθ'stændɪŋ/ *prep* (frml) a pesar de, no obstante (frml)

notwithstanding² *adv* (frml) no obstante (frml)

nougat /'nuːgət ‖'nuːgɑː, 'nʌgət/ *n* ≈turrón *m*

nought /nɔːt/ *n* (esp BrE) cero *m*

noun /naʊn/ *n* sustantivo *m*, nombre *m*

nourish /'nɜːrɪʃ ‖'nʌrɪʃ/ *vt* nutrir

nourishing /'nɜːrɪʃɪŋ ‖'nʌrɪʃɪŋ/ *adj* nutritivo

nourishment /'nɜːrɪʃmənt ‖'nʌrɪʃmənt/ *n* alimento *m*

nouveau riche /ˌnuːvəʊ'riːʃ/ *n* (*pl* **~x ~s** /ˌnuːvəʊ'riːʃ/) (pej) nuevo rico, nueva rica *m,f* (pey)

novel¹ /'nɑːvəl ‖'nɒvəl/ *n* novela *f*

novel² *adj* original, novedoso (esp AmL)

novelist /'nɑːvələst ‖'nɒvəlɪst/ *n* novelista *mf*

novelty /'nɑːvəlti ‖'nɒvəlti/ *n* (*pl* **-ties**) **(a)** (newness): **the ~ will soon wear off** pronto dejará de ser novedad *or* (esp AmL) novedoso **(b)** (new thing, situation) novedad *f*

November /nəʊ'vembər ‖nəʊ'vembə(r)/ *n* noviembre *m*

novice /'nɑːvəs ‖'nɒvɪs/ *n* principiante *mf*, novato, -ta *m,f*

now¹ /naʊ/ *adv* **1 (a)** (at this time) ahora; **you can come in ~** ya puedes entrar; **any minute ~** en cualquier momento; **~'s your chance** esta es tu oportunidad **(b)** (at that time): **it was ~ time to say goodbye** había llegado el momento de decir adiós **(c)** (nowadays) hoy en día, actualmente **(d)** (in phrases) **(every) now and then** *o* **again** de vez en cuando; **for now** por ahora **2 (a)** (at once, immediately) ahora (mismo); **it's ~ or never!** ¡ahora o nunca! **(b)** (in phrases) **just now: he's talking to a client just ~** en este momento está hablando con un cliente; **right now** (immediately) ahora mismo, inmediatamente; (at present) ahora mismo, en este momento **3 (a)** (showing length of time) ya; **we've been living here for 40 years ~** ya hace 40 años que vivimos aquí **(b)** (after prep): **between ~ and Friday** de aquí al viernes; **she should be here by ~** ya debería estar aquí; **(up) until** *o* **till ~, up to ~** hasta ahora **4 (a)** (indicating pause, transition): **~, who's next?** bueno ¿(ahora) a quién le toca? **(b)** (emphasizing command, request, warning, advice): **~ look here!** ¡espera un momento! **(c)** (in phrases) **now, now** ¡vamos, vamos!; **now then ...** a ver ...

now² *conj* **~ (that)** ahora que

nowadays /'naʊədeɪz/ *adv* hoy (en) día, actualmente

nowhere¹ /'nəʊhwer ‖'nəʊweə(r)/ *adv* **1**: **where did you go last night? — nowhere** ¿adónde fuiste anoche? — a ningún lado *or* a ninguna parte; **she was ~ to be found/seen** no se la encontraba/se la veía por ningún lado *or* por ninguna parte; **to get ~** no conseguir* nada **2** **nowhere near: Warsaw is ~ near Moscow** Varsovia está lejísimos de Moscú; **I'm ~ near finished** me falta mucho para terminar

nowhere² *pron*: **he had ~ to go** no tenía dónde ir; **the car just appeared from ~** el coche apareció de la nada

noxious /'nɑːkʃəs ‖'nɒkʃəs/ *adj* (frml) nocivo

nozzle /'nɑːzəl ‖'nɒzəl/ *n* (on hose) boca *f*; (on fire extinguisher) boquilla *f*

NSPCC *n* (in UK) (= **National Society for the Prevention of Cruelty to Children**) ≈ Asociación *f* de protección a la infancia

nuance /'nu:ɑ:ns ‖'nju:ɑ:ns/ n matiz m
nuclear /'nu:kliər ‖'nju:kliə(r)/ adj nuclear; ~ power energía f nuclear; ~ power station central f nuclear
nuclear: ~ **family** n familia f nuclear; ~-**powered** /'nu:kliər'paʊərd ‖'nju:kliə'paʊəd/ adj nuclear
nucleus /'nu:kliəs ‖'nju:kliəs/ n (pl -clei /-kliaɪ/) núcleo m
nude[1] /nu:d ‖nju:d/ n (Art) desnudo m; in the ~ desnudo
nude[2] adj desnudo
nudge[1] /nʌdʒ/ vt codear (ligeramente)
nudge[2] n golpe m (suave) con el codo
nudist /'nu:dəst ‖'nju:dɪst/ n nudista mf; (before n) ⟨beach/camp⟩ nudista
nudity /'nu:dəti ‖'nju:dəti/ n desnudez f
nugget /'nʌɡət ‖'nʌɡɪt/ n (Min) pepita f
nuisance /'nu:sns ‖'nju:sns/ n (a) (occurrence, thing): **to be a** ~ ser* una molestia, ser* un incordio (Esp) (b) (person) pesado, -da m,f, incordio m (Esp fam); **he's always making a** ~ **of** himself siempre está dando la lata (fam)
null /nʌl/ adj (Law): **to declare sth** ~ **and void** declarar nulo algo
numb[1] /nʌm/ adj **-er, -est** (with cold) entumecido; **the injection made my gums go** ~ la inyección me durmió las encías
numb[2] vt ⟨cold⟩ entumecer*; ⟨drug⟩ dormir*
number[1] /'nʌmbər ‖'nʌmbə(r)/ n número m; (telephone ~) número de teléfono; **wrong** ~ número equivocado; **student** ~**s** el número de estudiantes; **on a** ~ **of occasions** en varias ocasiones
number[2] vt (a) (assign number to) ⟨houses/pages/items⟩ numerar (b) (amount to): **the spectators** ~**ed 50,000** había (un total de) 50.000 espectadores (c) (count) contar*; **his days are** ~**ed** tiene los días contados
numberplate /'nʌmbərpleɪt'nʌmbəpleɪt/ n (BrE) matrícula f, placa f (AmL), patente f (CS), chapa f (RPl)
numeral /'nu:mərəl ‖'nju:mərəl/ n número m
numerical /nʊ'merɪkəl ‖nju:'merɪkəl/ adj numérico

numerous /'nu:mərəs ‖'nju:mərəs/ adj numeroso
nun /nʌn/ n monja f, religiosa f (frml)
nurse[1] /nɜ:rs ‖nɜ:s/ n (a) (Med) enfermero, -ra m,f (b) (nanny) niñera f
nurse[2] vt [1] (Med) ⟨patient⟩ atender*; **he** ~**d her back to health** la atendió hasta que se repuso [2] (cradle) ⟨baby⟩ arrullar [3] (suckle) ⟨baby⟩ amamantar
nursery /'nɜ:rsri ‖'nɜ:səri/ n (pl -ries) (a) (day ~) guardería f (b) (room in house) cuarto m or habitación f de los niños (c) (Agr, Hort) vivero m
nursery: ~ **rhyme** n canción f infantil; ~ **school** n jardín m de infancia, jardín m infantil (AmL), kindergarten m (AmL); (preschool) pre-escolar m
nursing /'nɜ:rsɪŋ ‖'nɜ:sɪŋ/ n (a) (profession) enfermería f (b) (care) atención f
nursing home n (for the aged) residencia f de ancianos ⟨con mayor nivel de asistencia médica⟩; (for convalescence) clínica f, casa f de reposo or (Ur) de salud
nurture /'nɜ:rtʃər ‖'nɜ:tʃə(r)/ vt ⟨child/person⟩ criar*; ⟨plant/crop⟩ cuidar; ⟨friendship⟩ cultivar
nut /nʌt/ n [1] (Agr, Bot, Culin) fruto m seco ⟨nuez, almendra, avellana etc⟩ [2] (Tech) tuerca f
nut: ~**case** n (colloq) chiflado, -da m,f (fam); ~**crackers** pl n (BrE) cascanueces m
nutmeg /'nʌtmeɡ/ n nuez f moscada
nutrient /'nu:triənt ‖'nju:triənt/ n nutriente m
nutrition /nʊ'trɪʃən ‖nju:'trɪʃən/ n nutrición f
nutritious /nʊ'trɪʃəs ‖nju:'trɪʃəs/ adj nutritivo
nuts /nʌts/ adj (colloq) ⟨pred⟩ chiflado (fam)
nutshell /'nʌtʃel/ n cáscara f de nuez; **in a** ~ en dos or en pocas palabras
nutty /'nʌti/ adj **-tier, -tiest** [1] ⟨taste⟩ a nueces ⟨or almendras etc⟩ [2] (colloq) (eccentric) ⟨professor⟩ chiflado (fam); ⟨idea⟩ de loco
NVQ n (in UK) = **National Vocational Qualification**
NW (= **northwest**) NO
NY = **New York**
nylon /'naɪlɑ:n ‖'naɪlɒn/ n nylon m
nymph /nɪmf/ n (Myth, Zool) ninfa f

Oo

O, o /əʊ/ n O, o f

oaf /əʊf/ n zoquete mf (fam)

oak /əʊk/ n (a) ∼ (**tree**) roble m (b) (wood) roble m

OAP n (BrE) = **old age pensioner**

oar /ɔːr ‖əː(r)/ n remo m

OAS n (= **Organization of American States**) OEA f

oasis /əʊ'eɪsɪs/ n (pl **oases** /əʊ'eɪsiːz/) oasis m

oat /əʊt/ n (a) (plant) avena f (b) **oats** pl (cereal) avena f, copos mpl de avena

oath /əʊθ/ n (pl ∼s /əʊðz/) (a) (promise) juramento m; **under** o (BrE also) **on** ∼ (Law) bajo juramento (b) (curse) (liter) juramento m (liter)

oatmeal /'əʊtmiːl/ n (Culin) (flour) harina f de avena; (flakes) (AmE) avena f (en copos)

obedience /ə'biːdiəns, əʊ-/ n obediencia f

obedient /ə'biːdiənt, əʊ-/ adj obediente

obese /əʊ'biːs/ adj obeso

obesity /əʊ'biːsəti/ n obesidad f

obey /ə'beɪ, əʊ-/ vt/i obedecer*

obituary /ə'bɪtʃuəri ‖ə'bɪtʃʊəri/ n (pl **-ries**) obituario m, nota f necrológica

object¹ /'ɑːbdʒɪkt ‖'ɒbdʒɪkt/ n **1** (a) (thing) objeto m (b) **no** ∼: **money's no** ∼ **for them** el dinero no les preocupa (c) (of actions, feelings) objeto m **2** (aim, purpose) objetivo m **3** (Ling) complemento m

object² /əb'dʒekt/ vi **to** ∼ (**to** sth) oponerse* (A algo); **I** ∼! ¡protesto!; **if you don't** ∼ si no le molesta
■ ∼ vt objetar

objection /əb'dʒekʃən/ n (a) (argument against) objeción f (b) (Law) protesta f; ∼! ¡protesto! (c) (disapproval, dislike): **I have no** ∼ **to her** no tengo nada en contra de ella

objectionable /əb'dʒekʃnəbəl/ adj ⟨attitude/ remark⟩ censurable; ⟨person/tone⟩ desagradable

objective¹ /ɑːb'dʒektɪv ‖əb'dʒektɪv/ adj objetivo

objective² n objetivo m

objectively /ɑːb'dʒektɪvli ‖əb'dʒektɪvli/ adv objetivamente

obligate /'ɑːbləgeɪt ‖'ɒblɪgeɪt/ vt (esp AmE fml) **to** ∼ **sb to** + INF obligar* a algn A + INF; **to be/ feel** ∼**d** (**to** + INF) estar*/sentirse* obligado (A + INF)

obligation /'ɑːblə'geɪʃən ‖'ɒblɪ'geɪʃən/ n obligación f; ∼ **to** + INF obligación DE + INF; **I understand that I am under no** ∼ entiendo que no contraigo ninguna obligación

obligatory /ə'blɪgətɔːri ‖ə'blɪgətri/ adj obligatorio

oblige /ə'blaɪdʒ/ vt **1** (require, compel) **to** ∼ **sb to** + INF obligar* a algn A + INF; **to be** ∼**d to** + INF estar* obligado A + INF **2** (do favor for): **I'd be much** ∼**d if you could help me** le quedaría muy agradecido si pudiera ayudarme

■ ∼ vi: **he's always willing to** ∼ siempre está dispuesto a hacer un favor

obliging /ə'blaɪdʒɪŋ/ adj atento

oblique /ə'bliːk, əʊ- ‖ə'bliːk/ adj ⟨line/angle⟩ oblicuo; ⟨reply/reference⟩ indirecto

obliterate /ə'blɪtəreɪt/ vt (a) (destroy) arrasar (b) (obscure, erase) borrar

oblivion /ə'blɪvɪən/ n (a) (obscurity) olvido m (b) (unconsciousness) inconsciencia f

oblivious /ə'blɪvɪəs/ adj (pred): **she was quite** ∼ **of** o **to her surroundings** estaba totalmente ajena a lo que la rodeaba; ∼ **of** o **to the danger** (unaware of) ignorante del peligro; (not mindful of) haciendo caso omiso del peligro

oblong¹ /'ɑːblɔːŋ ‖'ɒblɒŋ/ adj alargado

oblong² n rectángulo m

obnoxious /ɑːb'nɑːkʃəs ‖əb'nɒkʃəs/ adj detestable

oboe /'əʊbəʊ/ n oboe m

obscene /ɑːb'siːn ‖əb'siːn/ adj obsceno

obscenity /ɑːb'senəti ‖əb'senəti/ n (pl **-ties**) obscenidad f

obscure¹ /əb'skjʊr ‖əb'skjʊə(r)/ adj **obscurer, obscurest** (a) (not easily understood) ⟨meaning⟩ oscuro; ⟨message/reference⟩ críptico (b) (little known) ⟨writer/journal⟩ oscuro

obscure² vt ⟨object/beauty/sun⟩ ocultar; ⟨sky⟩ oscurecer*; ⟨issue⟩ impedir* ver claramente

obscurity /əb'skjʊrəti ‖əb'skjʊərəti/ n (pl **-ties**) oscuridad f

obsequious /əb'siːkwiəs/ adj servil

observant /əb'zɜːrvənt ‖əb'zɜːvənt/ adj observador

observation /'ɑːbzər'veɪʃən ‖'ɒbzə'veɪʃən/ n (all senses) observación f

observatory /əb'zɜːrvətɔːri ‖əb'zɜːvətri/ n (pl **-ries**) observatorio m

observe /əb'zɜːrv ‖əb'zɜːv/ vt **1** (watch, notice) observar; ⟨patient⟩ observar **2** (comment) (liter) observar

observer /əb'zɜːrvər ‖əb'zɜːvə(r)/ n observador, -dora m,f

obsess /əb'ses/ vt obsesionar

obsessed /əb'sest/ adj (pred) obsesionado

obsession /əb'seʃən/ n obsesión f

obsessive /əb'sesɪv/ adj obsesivo

obsolete /'ɑːbsəliːt ‖'ɒbsəliːt/ adj obsoleto

obstacle /'ɑːbstɪkəl ‖'ɒbstəkəl/ n obstáculo m

obstetrics /əb'stetrɪks/ n (+ sing vb) obstetricia f, tocología f

obstinate /'ɑːbstənət ‖'ɒbstɪnət/ adj obstinado

obstinately /'ɑːbstənətli ‖'ɒbstɪnətli/ adv (stubbornly) obstinadamente; (determinedly) tenazmente

obstruct /əb'strʌkt/ vt (a) (block) obstruir* (b) (impede, hinder) ⟨traffic⟩ bloquear (c) (Sport) obstruir*

O

obstruction /əb'strʌkʃən/ n (a) (in traffic, pipeline) obstrucción f; (Med) obstrucción f, oclusión f (b) (Sport) obstrucción f

obtain /əb'teɪn/ vt conseguir*, obtener* (frml)

obtrusive /əb'truːsɪv/ adj ⟨presence/building⟩ demasiado prominente; ⟨noise⟩ molesto; ⟨smell⟩ penetrante

obtuse /ɑːb'tuːs ‖ɒb'tjuːs/ adj [1] (Math) ⟨angle⟩ obtuso [2] (frml) (stupid) obtuso

obvious /'ɑːbviəs ‖'ɒbviəs/ adj (a) (evident) ⟨answer/advantage/difference⟩ obvio (b) (unmistakable) (before n) ⟨candidate/choice⟩ indiscutible

obviously /'ɑːbviəsli ‖'ɒbviəsli/ adv obviamente; they're ~ not coming está visto que no van a venir; the two ideas are ~ not related es evidente que las dos ideas no tienen relación; ~, I'm sad, but what can I do? (indep) como es lógico estoy triste pero ¿qué puedo hacer?

OCAS (= Organization of Central American States) n ODECA f

occasion /ə'keɪʒən/ n ocasión f

occasional /ə'keɪʒnəl ‖ə'keɪʒənl̩/ adj ⟨showers/sunny spells⟩ aislado; I like an o the ~ glass of wine de tanto en tanto me gusta tomarme un vaso de vino

occasionally /ə'keɪʒnəli/ adv de vez en cuando

occult¹ /ə'kʌlt ‖ɒ'kʌlt/ n the ~ las ciencias ocultas

occult² adj ⟨arts/powers⟩ oculto; ⟨ritual⟩ ocultista

occupant /'ɑːkjəpənt ‖'ɒkjʊpənt/ n (of building, room, vehicle) ocupante mf; (tenant) inquilino, -na m,f

occupation /ˌɑːkjə'peɪʃən ‖ˌɒkjʊ'peɪʃən/ n (a) (profession, activity) ocupación f (b) (Mil) ocupación f (c) (of accommodations) ocupación f

occupational /ˌɑːkjə'peɪʃnəl ‖ˌɒkjʊ'peɪʃənl̩/ adj ⟨training⟩ ocupacional; ⟨disease⟩ profesional; it's an ~ hazard son riesgos de la profesión/del oficio

occupational therapy n terapia f ocupacional

occupier /'ɑːkjəpaɪər ‖'ɒkjʊpaɪə(r)/ n (BrE) ocupante mf

occupy /'ɑːkjəpaɪ ‖'ɒkjʊpaɪ/ vt -pies, -pying, -pied ocupar; to keep sb occupied mantener* a algn ocupado

occur /ə'kɜːr ‖ə'kɜː(r)/ vi -rr- [1] (a) (take place) (frml) ⟨event/incident⟩ tener* lugar (frml); ⟨change⟩ producirse* (frml) (b) (appear, be found) ⟨disease/species⟩ darse*, encontrarse* [2] (come to mind) to ~ TO sb (to + INF) ocurrírsele A algn (+ INF)

occurrence /ə'kɜːrəns ‖ə'kʌrəns/ n (a) (event, instance): it is a rare ~ no es algo frecuente (b) (incidence) incidencia f

ocean /'əʊʃən/ n océano m

ocean-going /'əʊʃənˌgəʊɪŋ/ adj ⟨vessel⟩ transatlántico

o'clock /ə'klɑːk ‖ə'klɒk/ adv: it's four ~ son las cuatro; it's one ~ es la una; at ten ~ a las diez

octagon /'ɑːktəgɑːn ‖'ɒktəgən/ n octágono m, octógono m

octane /'ɑːkteɪn ‖'ɒkteɪn/ n octano m

octave /'ɑːktɪv ‖'ɒktɪv/ n (Lit, Mus) octava f

October /ɑːk'təʊbər ‖ɒk'təʊbə(r)/ n octubre m

octopus /'ɑːktəpəs ‖'ɒktəpəs/ n (pl -puses) pulpo m

odd /ɑːd ‖ɒd/ adj -er, -est [1] (strange) raro, extraño [2] (occasional, random) (no comp): she smokes the ~ cigarette se fuma algún o alguno que otro cigarrillo [3] (no comp) (a) (unmatched, single) desparejado, sin pareja; the ~ one out la excepción (b) (Math) ⟨number⟩ impar

oddball /'ɑːdbɔːl ‖'ɒdbɔːl/ n (colloq) bicho m raro (fam)

oddity /'ɑːdəti ‖'ɒdɪti/ n (pl -ties) rareza f

odd-job man /ˌɑːd'dʒɑːbˌmæn ‖ˌɒd'dʒɒbmæn/ n (pl -men /-men/) hombre que hace pequeños trabajos o arreglos

oddly /'ɑːdli ‖'ɒdli/ adv ⟨dress/behave⟩ de una manera rara o extraña

oddment /'ɑːdmənt ‖'ɒdmənt/ n: ~s of fabric o material retazos mpl or (Esp) retales mpl

odds /ɑːdz ‖ɒdz/ pl n [1] (in betting) proporción en que se ofrece pagar una apuesta, que refleja las posibilidades de acierto de la misma [2] (likelihood, chances) probabilidades fpl, posibilidades fpl; the ~ are against her winning tiene pocas probabilidades or posibilidades de ganar; the pilot survived against all (the) ~ aunque parezca increíble, el piloto sobrevivió [3] (variance): those two are always at ~ with each other esos dos siempre están en desacuerdo; that's at ~ with the official version eso no concuerda con la versión oficial

odds and ends /ˌɑːdzən'endz ‖ˌɒdzən'endz/ pl n (colloq) cosas fpl sueltas; (trinkets) chucherías fpl; (junk) cachivaches mpl

odious /'əʊdiəs/ adj (frml) detestable

odometer /əʊ'dɑːmətər ‖ɒ'dɒmɪtə(r), əʊ-/ n (AmE) cuentarrevoluciones m

odor, (BrE) **odour** /'əʊdər ‖'əʊdə(r)/ n olor m; (pleasant) aroma m

of /ɑːv ‖ɒv, weak form əv/ prep [1] (indicating relationship, material, content) de; it's made ~ wood es de madera; a colleague ~ mine/his un colega mío/suyo [2] (descriptive use): a boy ~ ten un niño de diez años; a woman ~ courage una mujer valiente [3] (a) (partitive use): there were eight ~ us éramos ocho; six ~ them survived seis de ellos sobrevivieron (b) (with superl) de; the wisest ~ men el más sabio de los hombres; most ~ all más que nada [4] (a) (indicating date) de; the sixth ~ October el seis de octubre (b) (indicating time): it's ten (minutes) ~ five (AmE) son las cinco menos diez, son diez para las cinco (AmL exc RPl); Jane, his wife ~ six months ... Jane, con la que lleva/llevaba casado seis meses ... [5] (on the part of): it was very kind ~ you fue muy amable de su parte [6] (indicating cause): it's a problem ~ their own making es un problema que ellos mismos se han creado; what did he die ~? ¿de qué murió?

off¹ /ɔːf ‖ɒf/ prep [1] (from) de; she picked it up ~ o (crit) ~ of the floor lo recogió del suelo; he bought it ~ a friend (colloq) se lo compró a un amigo

2 (a) (distant from): **3 ft ~ the ground** a 3 pies del suelo; **just ~ the coast of Florida** a poca distancia de la costa de Florida (b) (leading from): **it's just ~ Oxford Street** está en una bocacalle de Oxford Street; **the bathroom's ~ the bedroom** el baño da al dormitorio **3** (a) (absent from): **I've been ~ work for a week** hace una semana que no voy a trabajar (b) (indicating dislike, abstinence) (BrE): **he's ~ his food** anda sin apetito; **is he ~ drugs now?** ¿ha dejado las drogas?

off² adv **1** (a) (removed): **the lid was ~** la tapa no estaba puesta; **20% ~** 20% de descuento (b) **off and on ▶** ON² 2c **2** (indicating departure): **I must be ~** me tengo que ir **3** (distant): **some way ~** a cierta distancia; **my birthday is a long way ~** falta mucho para mi cumpleaños

off³ adj **1** (pred) (a) (not turned on): **to be ~** «TV/light» estar* apagado (b) (canceled): **the game/wedding is ~** el partido/la boda se ha suspendido; **the deal is ~** ya no hay trato **2** (absent, not on duty) libre; **a day ~** (AmE also **an ~ day**) un día libre **3** (poor, unsatisfactory) (before n) malo; **to have an ~ day** tener* un mal día **4** (Culin) (pred) **to be ~** «meat/fish» estar* malo o pasado; «milk» estar* cortado; «butter/cheese» estar* rancio

off: ~beat adj poco convencional; **~-chance** n: **on the ~-chance** por si acaso; **~-color,** (BrE) **~-colour** /'ɔːfˈkʌlər ‖ˌɒfˈkʌlə(r)/ adj (pred **~ color**) (a) (unwell) (pred): **to feel ~ color** no encontrarse* muy bien (b) (risqué) (esp AmE) «joke» subido de tono; **~-cut** n (of leather, fabric, paper, wood) recorte m; (of meat) resto m

offence /əˈfens/ n (BrE) **▶** OFFENSE

offend /əˈfend/ vt ofender
■ ~ vi (a) (cause displeasure) «person/action/remark» ofender (b) **offending** pres p: **he rewrote it omitting the ~ing paragraph** volvió a escribirlo omitiendo el párrafo que había causado controversia (c) (Law frml) infringir* la ley (or el reglamento etc); (criminally) cometer un delito

offender /əˈfendər ‖əˈfendə(r)/ n (against regulations) infractor, -tora m,f; (criminal) delincuente mf; **young ~** menor mf (que ha cometido un delito)

offense, (BrE) **offence** /əˈfens/ n **1** (breach of law, regulations) infracción f; (criminal ~) delito m **2** (a) (cause of outrage) (no pl) atentado m (b) (resentment, displeasure): **to take ~ at sth** ofenderse or sentirse* ofendido por algo **3** (AmE) also /'ɑːfens/ (a) (attack) ataque m (b) (Sport) (línea f de) ataque m

offensive¹ /əˈfensɪv/ adj **1** «language/gesture» ofensivo; «sight/smell» desagradable **2** (a) «strategy» (b) (AmE Sport) «play/tactics» de ataque

offensive² n ofensiva f

offer¹ /'ɔːfər ‖'ɒfə(r)/ vt **1** (a) (proffer) ofrecer* (b) (show willingness) **to ~ to + INF** ofrecerse* A + INF **2** (put forward) «idea/solution» proponer* **3** (provide) «reward» ofrecer*; «opportunity» brindar
■ ~ vi (show willingness) ofrecerse*

offer² n **1** (a) (proposal — of job, money) oferta f;

(— of help, mediation) ofrecimiento m (b) (bid) oferta f; **\$650 or nearest ~** 650 dólares negociables **2** (bargain, reduced price) oferta f; **on ~** (BrE) (at reduced price) de oferta

offering /'ɔːfərɪŋ ‖'ɒfərɪŋ/ n ofrenda f

offhand¹ /'ɔːfˈhænd ‖ˌɒfˈhænd/ adj: **to say sth in a very ~ way** o manner decir* algo muy a la ligera; **she was very ~ with me** estuvo muy brusca conmigo

offhand² adv así de pronto, en este momento

office /'ɑːfəs ‖'ɒfɪs/ n **1** (a) (room) oficina f, despacho m; (building, set of rooms) oficina f, oficinas fpl; (staff) oficina f; (doctor's ~) (AmE) consultorio m, consulta f; (before n) «work/furniture» de oficina; «block/building» de oficinas; **during ~ hours** en horas de oficina; **~ worker** oficinista mf, empleado, -da m,f de oficina **2** (post, position) cargo m; **he was in ~ for three years** ocupó el cargo durante tres años

officer /'ɑːfəsər ‖'ɒfɪsə(r)/ n (a) (Mil, Naut) oficial mf (b) (police ~) policía mf, agente mf de policía; (as form of address) agente

official¹ /əˈfɪʃəl/ adj oficial

official² n (government ~) funcionario, -ria m,f del Estado or gobierno; (party/union ~) dirigente mf (del partido/sindicato)

officially /əˈfɪʃəli/ adv oficialmente

officiate /əˈfɪʃieɪt/ vi **to ~ AT sth** «at mass/at a wedding» oficiar (EN) o celebrar algo

officious /əˈfɪʃəs/ adj oficioso

offing /'ɔːfɪŋ ‖'ɒfɪŋ/ n: **in the ~** en perspectiva

off: ~ key adv: **to play/sing ~ key** desafinar; **~-licence** n (in UK) ≈ tienda f de vinos y licores, botillería f (Chi); **~ limits** /'lɪməts ‖'lɪmɪts/ adv: **to go/be ~ limits** entrar/estar* en zona prohibida; **~-line** /'ɔːfˈlaɪn ‖ˌɒfˈlaɪn/ adj (pred **~ line**) «storage/printer» autónomo; **~-peak** /'piːk/ adj (before noun) «travel/fare/tariffs» fuera de las horas pico or (Esp) punta; (Elec) fuera de (las) horas pico or (Esp) punta; **~-putting** /'ɔːfˈpʊtɪŋ ‖ˌɒfˈpʊtɪŋ/ adj (BrE) (disagreeable) desagradable; (discouraging) desmoralizador; **~road** adj: **~road vehicle** todoterreno m; **~set** /'ɔːfˈset ‖'ɒfset/ vt (pres **-sets**; pres p **-setting**; past & past p **-set**) compensar; **~shoot** n (a) (of plant, tree) retoño m (b) (of company, organization) filial f; **~shore** /'ɔːfˈʃɔːr ‖ˌɒfˈʃɔː(r)/ adj «oilfield/pipeline» submarino; «exploration/drilling» off-shore adj inv

offside¹ /ˌɔːfˈsaɪd ‖ˌɒfˈsaɪd/ adj (Sport) «player» en fuera de juego o (AmL tb) de lugar

offside² adv (Sport) fuera de juego or (AmL tb) de lugar

off: ~spring n (pl **~spring**) (a) (animal) cría f (b) (hum) (child) hijo, -ja m,f, crío, cría m,f (fam); (children) prole f (fam & hum), críos mpl (fam); **~stage** /'ɔːfˈsteɪdʒ ‖'ɒfˈsteɪdʒ/ adv fuera del escenario; **~-the-peg** /'ɔːfðəˈpeg ‖ˌɒfðəˈpeg/ adj (pred **~ the peg**) (esp BrE) **▶** ~-THE-RACK; **~-the-rack** /'ɔːfðəˈræk ‖ˌɒfðəˈræk/ adj (pred **~ the rack**) (AmE) «suit» de confección; **~-white** /'ɔːfˈhwaɪt ‖ˌɒfˈwaɪt/ adj color hueso adj inv

often /'ɔːfən, 'ɔːftən ‖'ɒfən, 'ɒftən/ adv a menudo; **how ~ do you see her?** ¿con qué frecuencia la ves?

ogle /'əʊgəl/ vt comerse con los ojos

ogre /'əʊgər ‖ 'əʊgə(r)/ n ogro m

oh /əʊ/ interj: ~, **it's you** ah, eres tú; ~ **no, not him again!** ¡ay no, es él otra vez!

OH = **Ohio**

oil¹ /ɔɪl/ n **1 (a)** (petroleum) petróleo m; (before n) ~ **refinery** refinería f de petróleo; ~ **tanker** (ship) petrolero m; (truck) camión m cisterna (para petróleo) **(b)** (lubricant) aceite m **(c)** (fuel) ~ fuel-oil m **2** (Culin) aceite m **3** **oils** pl (paints): **he paints in** ~s pinta al óleo

oil² vt lubricar*, aceitar

oil: ~**can** n aceitera f; ~**cloth** n hule m; ~**field** n yacimiento m petrolífero; ~ **paint** n óleo m; ~ **painting** n óleo m; ~ **rig** n plataforma f petrolífera; (derrick) torre f de perforación; ~ **slick** n marea f negra; ~ **well** n pozo m petrolero

oily /'ɔɪli/ adj **oilier, oiliest** ⟨substance⟩ oleaginoso; ⟨food⟩ aceitoso; ⟨skin/hair⟩ graso (AmL)

ointment /'ɔɪntmənt/ n pomada f

OK¹, okay /əʊ'keɪ/ interj (colloq) ¡bueno!, ¡okey! (esp AmL fam), ¡vale! (Esp fam), ¡vaya (pues)! (AmC)

OK², okay adj (all right) (colloq) ⟨pred⟩: **how are you?** — ~, **thanks** ¿qué tal estás? — bien, gracias; **the job's** ~, **but ...** el trabajo no está mal, pero ...

OK³, okay vt (pres **OK's**; pres p **OK'ing**; past & past p **OK'ed**) (colloq) darle* el visto bueno a

OK⁴, Okla = **Oklahoma**

old /əʊld/ adj **1** (of certain age): **he's 10 years** ~ tiene 10 años; **how** ~ **are you?** ¿cuántos años tienes?; **she's two years** ~**er than me** me lleva dos años

2 (not young) mayor; (less polite) viejo; ~ o ~**er people** los ancianos, las personas mayores or de edad; **to get** o **grow** ~/~**er** envejecer*

3 (a) (not new) ⟨clothes/car/custom⟩ viejo; ⟨city/civilization⟩ antiguo **(b)** (longstanding, familiar) (before n) ⟨friend/enemy/rivalry⟩ viejo; ⟨injury/problem⟩ antiguo

4 (former, previous) (before n) antiguo

5 (colloq) (before n) (as intensifier): **just wear any** ~ **thing** ponte cualquier cosa; **this book is a load of** ~ **rubbish** este libro es una porquería (fam)

old: ~ **age** n vejez f; ~ **age pensioner** n (BrE) pensionista mf (de la tercera edad)

olden /'əʊldən/ adj (liter): **in** ~ **days** o **times** antaño (liter)

old: ~**fashioned** /'əʊld'fæʃənd/ adj (outdated) anticuado; (traditional) tradicional; ~ **people's home** n residencia f de ancianos; ~ **wives' tale** n cuento m de viejas

olive¹ /'ɑːlɪv ‖ 'ɒlɪv/ n **(a)** (Culin) aceituna f; (before n) ~ **oil** aceite m de oliva **(b)** ~ **tree** olivo m

olive² adj color aceituna adj inv; ⟨skin⟩ aceitunado

Olympic /ə'lɪmpɪk/ adj olímpico

Olympic Games pl n **the** ~ los juegos Olímpicos

Olympics /ə'lɪmpɪks/ pl n **the** ~ las Olimpíadas or Olimpiadas

ombudsman /'ɑːmbʊdzmən ‖ 'ɒmbʊdzmən/ n (pl **-men** /-mən/) defensor m del pueblo, ombudsman m

omelet, (BrE) **omelette** /'ɑːmlət ‖ 'ɒmlɪt/ n omelette f or (Esp) tortilla f francesa

omen /'əʊmən/ n presagio m; **it's a good/bad** ~ es un buen/mal augurio

ominous /'ɑːmənəs ‖ 'ɒmɪnəs/ adj: **there was an** ~ **silence** se hizo un silencio que no presagiaba nada bueno; **there are some** ~ **clouds on the horizon** hay nubes que no auguran nada bueno

omission /əʊ'mɪʃən ‖ ə'mɪʃən/ n omisión f

omit /əʊ'mɪt ‖ ə'mɪt/ vt **-tt-** (leave out) omitir; (accidentally) olvidar incluir

omnibus /'ɑːmnɪbəs ‖ 'ɒmnɪbəs/ n (pl **-buses**) **1** (Publ) antología f **2** (Transp dated) ómnibus m (ant exc en Per y RPI)

omnipotent /ɑːm'nɪpətənt ‖ ɒm'nɪpətənt/ adj (fml) omnipotente

omnivorous /ɑːm'nɪvərəs ‖ ɒm'nɪvərəs/ adj omnívoro

on /ɑːn ‖ ɒn/ prep **1 (a)** (indicating position) en; **put it** ~ **the table** ponlo en or sobre la mesa; ~ **the ground** en el suelo; **he hung it** ~ **a hook** lo colgó de un gancho **(b)** (belonging to) de; **the handle** ~ **the cup** el asa de la taza **(c)** (against): **I hit my head** ~ **the shelf** me di con la cabeza contra el estante; **he cut his hand** ~ **the glass** se cortó la mano con el vidrio

2 (a) (of clothing): **it looks better** ~ **you than me** te queda mejor a ti que a mí **(b)** (about one's person): **I didn't have any cash** ~ **me** no llevaba dinero encima

3 (indicating means of transport): **I went** ~ **the bus** fui en autobús; ~ **a bicycle/horse** en bicicleta/a caballo; ~ **foot** a pie

4 (a) (playing instrument) a; **George Smith** ~ **drums** George Smith a la or en la batería **(b)** (Rad, TV): **I heard it** ~ **the radio** lo oí por la radio; **I was** ~ **TV last night** anoche salí por televisión; **the play's** ~ **channel 4** la obra la dan en el canal 4

5 (a) (using equipment): **who's** ~ **the computer?** ¿quién está usando la computadora?; **you've been** ~ **the phone an hour!** ¡hace una hora que estás hablando por teléfono! **(b)** (contactable via): **call us** ~ **800 7777** llámenos al 800 7777

6 (a member of): **she's** ~ **the committee** está en la comisión; ~ **a team** (AmE) en un equipo

7 (indicating time): ~ **Monday** el lunes; ~ **Wednesdays** los miércoles; ~ **-ING** al + INF; ~ **hearing the news** al enterarse de la noticia

8 (about, concerning) sobre

9 (working on, studying): **we're** ~ **page 45** vamos por la página 45; **I'm still** ~ **question 1** todavía estoy con la pregunta número 1

AmC	Central America	Arg	Argentina	Cu	Cuba	Per	Peru
AmL	Latin America	Bol	Bolivia	Ec	Ecuador	RPI	River Plate Area
AmS	South America	Chi	Chile	Esp	Spain	Ur	Uruguay
Andes	Andean Region	CS	Southern Cone	Méx	Mexico	Ven	Venezuela

10 (taking, consuming): **she's ~ antibiotics** está tomando antibióticos; **he's ~ heroin** es heroinómano

11 (talking about income, available funds): **I manage ~ less than that** yo me las arreglo con menos de eso

12 (at the expense of): **this round's ~ me** a esta ronda invito yo

13 (in comparison with): **profits are up ~ last year** los beneficios han aumentado respecto al año pasado

on² *adv* **1** **(a)** (worn): **she had a blue dress ~** llevaba (puesto) un vestido azul; **I had nothing ~** estaba desnudo **(b)** (in place): **the lid's not ~ properly** la tapa no está bien puesta

2 (indicating progression) **(a)** (in space): **further ~** un poco más allá; **go ~ up; I'll follow in a minute** tú ve subiendo que yo ya voy **(b)** (in time, activity): **from then ~** a partir de ese momento; **from now ~** de ahora en adelante **(c)** on and off, off and on: **we still see each other ~ and off** todavía nos vemos de vez en cuando; **it rained ~ and off** *o* **off and ~ all week** estuvo lloviendo y parando toda la semana

on³ *adj* **1** *(pred)* **(a)** (functioning): **to be ~** «*light/ TV/radio*» estar* encendido, estar* prendido (AmL); «*faucet*» estar* abierto; **the electricity/ water isn't ~ yet** la electricidad/el agua todavía no está conectada **(b)** (on duty): **we work four hours ~, four hours off** trabajamos cuatro horas y tenemos otras cuatro de descanso

2 *(pred)* **(a)** (taking place): **there's a lecture ~ in there** hay una conferencia allí; **while the conference is ~** mientras dure el congreso **(b)** (due to take place): **the party's definitely ~ for Friday** la fiesta se celebrará el viernes seguro; **I don't have anything ~ that day** no tengo ningún compromiso ese día **(c)** (being presented): **what's ~ at the Renoir?** (Cin, Rad, Theat, TV) ¿qué dan *o* (Esp tb) ponen en el Renoir?; **the exhibition is still ~** la exposición sigue abierta

3 (indicating agreement, acceptance) (colloq): **you teach me Spanish and I'll teach you French — you're ~!** tú me enseñas español y yo te enseño francés — ¡trato hecho!; **that sort of thing just isn't ~** (esp BrE) ese tipo de cosa no se puede tolerar

once¹ /wʌns/ *adv* **1** **(a)** (one time, on one occasion) una vez; **~ a week** una vez por semana **(b)** (formerly): **a health care system which was ~ the pride of the nation** un sistema de asistencia sanitaria que antes era el orgullo de la nación; **~ upon a time there was ...** érase una vez ...

2 (in phrases) **at once: come here at ~!** ¡ven aquí inmediatamente!; **don't all shout at ~** no griten todos al mismo tiempo; **for once** por una vez; **once again** *o* **once more** otra vez; **once (and) for all** de una vez por todas; **(every) once in a while** de vez en cuando; **once or twice** una o dos veces

once² *conj* una vez que; (with verb omitted) una vez

once- /wʌns/ *pref* otrora (liter)

oncoming /ˈɑːnˌkʌmɪŋ ‖ ˈɒnˌkʌmɪŋ/ *adj* (before n) «*vehicle*» que viene (*or* venía) en dirección contraria

one¹ /wʌn/ *n* **1** **(a)** (number) uno *m*; *see also* FOUR¹ **(b)** (elliptical use): **he's nearly ~** tiene casi un año; **it was interesting in more ways than ~**

fue interesante en más de un sentido/en muchos sentidos **2** (in phrases) **as one: they rose as ~** se pusieron de pie todos a la vez; **for one** por lo pronto; **one by one** uno a *or* por uno

one² *adj* **1** (stating number) un, una; **~ button/ pear** un botón/una pera; **~ window looks out over the park** una de las ventanas da al parque **2** (single): **she was the ~ person I trusted** era la única persona en quien confiaba; **there is not ~ shred of evidence** no existe ni la más mínima prueba; **the ~ and only Frank Sinatra** el incomparable Frank Sinatra **3** (unspecified) un, una; **you must come over ~ evening** tienes que venir una noche **4** (with names): **in the name of ~ John Smith/ Sarah Brown** a nombre de un tal John Smith/una tal Sarah Brown

one³ *pron* **1** (thing): **this ~** este/esta; **that ~** ese/ esa; **which ~?** ¿cuál?; **the ~ on the right/left** el/la de la derecha/izquierda; **the ~s on the table** los/ las que están en la mesa; **the blue ~s** los/las azules; **I want the big ~** quiero el/la grande; **~ of the oldest cities in Europe** una de las ciudades más antiguas de Europa **2** (person): **the ~ on the right's my cousin** el/la de la derecha es mi primo/prima; **I'm not ~ to gossip, but ...** no me gustan los chismes pero ...; **~ after another** *o* **the other** uno tras otro *or* detrás de otro

one⁴ *pron* uno, una; **~ simply never knows** realmente nunca se sabe; **~ another = each other,** ▶ EACH² 2

one: **~-armed** /ˈwʌnˈɑːrmd ‖ ˈwʌnˈɑːmd/ *adj* manco; **~-man** /ˈwʌnˈmæn/ *adj* (before n) «*business*» unipersonal; «*operation*» dirigido por una sola persona; **~-off** /ˈwʌnˈɔːf ‖ ˈwʌnˈɒf/ *n* (BrE colloq): **this payment is strictly a ~-off** este pago es una excepción; **~ on ~** *adv* (AmE) uno a uno; **~-piece** /ˈwʌnpiːs/ *adj* «*swimsuit*» entero

onerous /ˈəʊnərəs/ *adj* «*task*» pesado

one: **~self** /wʌnˈself/ *pron* (frml) (reflexive) se; (after prep) sí mismo; (emphatic use) uno mismo; **to cut ~self** cortarse; **~-sided** /ˈwʌnˈsaɪdəd ‖ ˌwʌnˈsaɪdɪd/ *adj* «*account/version*» parcial; «*game/contest*» desigual; **~-stop shopping** *n* compras *fpl* en un mismo sitio; **~-time** *adj* antiguo; **~-to-~** /ˈwʌntəˈwʌn/ *adj* «*teaching/ attention*» individualizado; «*discussion*» mano a mano; **on a ~-to-~ basis** de uno a uno

one-upmanship /ˈwʌnˈʌpmənʃɪp/ *n* (colloq) arte de colocarse siempre en una situación de superioridad con respecto a uno demás

one-way /ˈwʌnˈweɪ/ *adj* **(a)** «*street*» de sentido único **(b)** (for one journey): **~ or round trip?** ¿ida solo *o* ida y vuelta?, ¿sencillo *o* redondo? (Méx)

ongoing /ˈɑːnˌɡəʊɪŋ ‖ ˈɒnˌɡəʊɪŋ/ *adj*: **the ~ talks** las conversaciones en curso; **the investigations have been ~ for several months** se están llevando a cabo investigaciones desde hace meses

onion /ˈʌnjən/ *n* cebolla *f*

on: **~ line** *adv*: **to edit/work ~ line** (Comput) editar/trabajar en línea; **~-line** /ˈɑːnˈlaɪn ‖ ˌɒnˈlaɪn/ *adj* (pred **~ line**) (Comput) conectado, en línea; **~looker** /ˈɑːnˌlʊkər ‖ ˈɒnˌlʊkə(r)/ *n* espectador, -dora *m,f*

only¹ /ˈəʊnli/ *adv* **(a)** (merely, no more than) solo, solamente; **you'll ~ make matters worse** lo único que vas a lograr es empeorar las cosas **(b)**

···❖

O

(exclusively) solo, solamente, únicamente **(c)** (no longer ago than): **~ last week** the very same problem came up la semana pasada, sin ir más lejos, surgió el mismo problema **(d)** (in phrases) **if only: if ~ I were rich!** ¡ojalá fuera rico!; **if ~ I'd known** si lo hubiera sabido; **only just: they've ~ just arrived** ahora mismo acaban de llegar; **will it fit in? — ~ just** ¿cabrá? — apenas *or* (fam) justito; **not only ... , but also ...** no solo ... , sino también ...

only² *adj* (before n) único; **she's an ~ child** es hija única

only³ *conj* (colloq) pero

-only /'əʊnli/ *suff*: **a men~/women~ session** una sesión solo *or* exclusivamente para hombres/mujeres

on: **~set** *n* (of winter, rains) llegada *f*; (of disease) aparición *f*; **~shore** /'ɑːnʃɔːr ‖ 'ɒnʃɔː(r)/ *adj* **(a)** ⟨*wind*⟩ que sopla desde el mar **(b)** (on land) ⟨*oil terminal/location*⟩ en tierra

onslaught /'ɑːnslɔːt ‖ 'ɒnslɔːt/ *n* ataque *m*

onstage /ɑːn'steɪdʒ ‖ ɒn'steɪdʒ/ *adv*: **to come ~** salir* a escena

onto /'ɑːntu ‖ 'ɒntuː, before consonant 'ɑːntə ‖ 'ɒntə/ *prep* **1** (on): **it fell ~ the table** cayó sobre la mesa; **he climbed ~ the cart** se subió al carro **2** (aware of) (colloq) **the police are ~ her** la policía anda tras ella; **I think we're ~ something big** creo que hemos dado con algo gordo (fam)

onus /'əʊnəs/ *n* (fml) responsabilidad *f*; **the ~ is on him to prove his theory** le corresponde a él probar su teoría

onward¹ /'ɑːnwərd ‖ 'ɒnwəd/ *adj* (before n) hacia adelante

onward², (BrE also) **onwards** /-z/ *adv* (hacia) adelante; **from now ~** de ahora en adelante

ooh /uː/ *interj*: **~, what a beautiful sunset!** ¡ah, qué puesta de sol tan bonita!; **~, that hurt** ¡ay, eso me dolió!

oops /ʊps ‖ uːps/ *interj* (colloq) ¡uy! (fam)

ooze /uːz/ *vi*: **blood ~d from his wound** le salía sangre de la herida; **to ~ WITH sth: the walls were oozing with damp** las paredes rezumaban humedad

■ **~** *vt*: **the wound ~d pus** la herida (le) supuraba; **he ~s charm** irradia simpatía

opal /'əʊpəl/ *n* ópalo *m*

opaque /əʊ'peɪk/ *adj* opaco

OPEC /'əʊpek/ *n* (no art) (= **Organization of Petroleum Exporting Countries**) la OPEC *or* la OPEP

open¹ /'əʊpən/ *adj* **1** **(a)** (not shut, sealed, fastened) abierto; **he pushed the door ~** abrió la puerta de un empujón **(b)** (not folded) ⟨*flower/newspaper/book*⟩ abierto

2 (not enclosed) abierto; **~ prison** cárcel *f* en régimen abierto; **on the ~ seas** en alta mar **3** **(a)** (not covered) ⟨*carriage*⟩ abierto; ⟨*sewer*⟩ a cielo abierto; **an ~ fire** una chimenea, un hogar **(b)** (exposed, vulnerable) **~ TO sth** ⟨*to elements/enemy attack*⟩ expuesto A algo **4** (pred) (ready for business) **to be ~** ⟨*shop/museum*⟩ estar* abierto **5** (unrestricted) ⟨*membership*⟩ abierto al público en general; ⟨*meeting*⟩ a puertas abiertas; ⟨*ticket/reservation*⟩ abierto **6** (not decided): **let's leave things ~ for the time**

being no descartemos ninguna posibilidad de momento; **~ verdict** veredicto que se emite cuando no se puede establecer la causa de la muerte de una persona

7 **(a)** (receptive) abierto; **I'm ~ to suggestions** estoy abierto a todo tipo de sugerencias **(b)** (frank, candid): **to be ~ WITH sb** ser* sincero *or* franco CON algn **8** (not concealed) ⟨*resentment/hostility*⟩ abierto

open² *vt* **1** **(a)** ⟨*door/box/bottle*⟩ abrir*; **to ~ one's mouth/eyes** abrir* la boca/los ojos **(b)** (unfold) ⟨*newspaper/book*⟩ abrir* **2** (clear) ⟨*road/channel*⟩ abrir* **3** (set up, start) ⟨*shop*⟩ abrir* **4** (begin) ⟨*debate/meeting*⟩ abrir*; ⟨*bidding*⟩ iniciar; ⟨*talks*⟩ entablar

■ **~** *vi* **1** **(a)** ⟨*door/window/wound*⟩ abrirse* **(b)** (unfold) ⟨*flower/parachute*⟩ abrirse* **2** (give access) **to ~ ONTO/INTO sth** dar* A algo **3** (for business) **to ~** ⟨*shop/museum*⟩ abrir* **4** (begin) ⟨*play/book*⟩ comenzar*, empezar*

■ **open up**

I [v + o + adv, v + adv + o] abrir*

II [v + adv] **1** (become open) abrirse* **2** (become accessible, available) ⟨*country/market*⟩ abrirse* **3** (start up) ⟨*business/factory/store*⟩ abrir*

open³ *n*: **in the ~** (in open space or country) al aire libre; (Mil) al descubierto; **I feel better now it's all out in the ~** me siento mejor ahora que todo el mundo lo sabe

open: **~ air** *n*: **in the ~ air** al aire libre; **~-and-shut** /'əʊpənən'ʃʌt/ *adj*: **an ~-and-shut case** un caso clarísimo; **~ day** *n* (BrE) día en que un establecimiento educativo, científico etc puede ser visitado por el público; **~-ended** /'əʊpən'endəd ‖ 'əʊpən'endɪd/ *adj* ⟨*contract/lease*⟩ de duración indefinida; ⟨*discussion*⟩ abierto

opener /'əʊpnər ‖ 'əʊpnə(r)/ *n* (for bottle) abridor *m*, abrebotellas *m*, destapador *m* (AmL); (for can) abrelatas *m*

open house *n* **1** (no art): **to keep ~ ~** tener* las puertas siempre abiertas a todos; **2** (AmE) día en que un establecimiento educativo, científico etc puede ser visitado por el público

opening /'əʊpnɪŋ/ *n* **1** (in hedge, fence) abertura *f* **2** (beginning, initial stage) apertura *f* **3** (of exhibition, building) inauguración *f*; (Cin, Theat) estreno *m*; (before n) ⟨*speech*⟩ inaugural; **~ night** noche *f* del estreno **4** (period when open): **hours of ~** (of shop) horario *m* comercial; (of bank, office) horario *m* de atención al público **5** (favorable opportunity) oportunidad *f*

openly /'əʊpənli/ *adv* abiertamente

open: **~-minded** /'əʊpən'maɪndəd ‖ 'əʊpən'maɪndɪd/ *adj* ⟨*person*⟩ de actitud abierta; ⟨*approach*⟩ imparcial; **~-mouthed** /'əʊpən'maʊðd/ *adj* boquiabierto; **~-plan** /'əʊpən'plæn/ *adj* abierto, de planta abierta; **~ university** *n* universidad *f* a distancia, universidad *f* abierta (Méx); **the O~ U~** (in UK) la universidad a distancia del Reino Unido

opera /'ɑːprə ‖ 'ɒprə/ *n* (pl **-ras**) ópera *f*

operate /'ɑːpəreɪt ‖ 'ɒpəreɪt/ *vi* **1** ⟨*machine/mechanism*⟩ funcionar **2** (be applicable) ⟨*rules/laws*⟩ regir* **3** (pursue one's business) ⟨*company/airline/gang*⟩ operar **4** (Med) operar, intervenir* (fml); **to ~ ON sb** (FOR sth) operar A algn (DE algo)

■ ~ *vt* **1** ‹*machine/controls*› manejar **2** (manage, run) ‹*business*› llevar; ‹*bus service*› tener*

operatic /ˌɑːpəˈrætɪk ‖ˌɒpəˈrætɪk/ *adj* operístico

operating /ˈɑːpəreɪtɪŋ ‖ˈɒpəreɪtɪŋ/ *adj* (*before n*) **1** (Busn) ‹*profit/loss/costs*› de explotación **2** (Med): ~ **room** *o* (BrE) **theatre** quirófano *m*, sala *f* de operaciones; ~ **table** mesa *f* de operaciones

operation /ˌɑːpəˈreɪʃən ‖ˌɒpəˈreɪʃən/ *n* **1** (functioning) funcionamiento *m*; **to be in** ~ «*machine*» estar* en funcionamiento; «*system*» regir* **2** (using, running of machine) manejo *m* **3** (activity, series of activities) operación *f* **4** (Med) operación *f*, intervención *f* quirúrgica (fml)

operative /ˈɑːpərətɪv ‖ˈɒpərətɪv/ *adj* **to be** ~ «*rules/measures*» estar* en vigor; **the** ~ **word** la palabra clave

operator /ˈɑːpəreɪtər ‖ˈɒpəreɪtə(r)/ *n* **(a)** (Telec) operador, -dora *m,f*; **(b)** (of equipment) operario, -ria *m,f*; (Comput) operador, -dora *m,f*

ophthalmic optician /ɑːpˈθælmɪk, ɑːf- ‖ ɒfˈθælmɪk/ *n* ≈ oculista *mf*

opinion /əˈpɪnjən/ *n* opinión *f*; **what's your** ~? ¿qué opinas?, ¿qué te parece?; **in my** ~ en mi opinión, a mi parecer; **I'd like a second** ~ me gustaría consultarlo con otro especialista

opinionated /əˈpɪnjəneɪtəd ‖əˈpɪnjə‚neɪtɪd/ *adj* dogmático, aferrado a sus (*or* tus *etc*) opiniones

opinion poll *n* sondeo *m or* encuesta *f* de opinión

opium /ˈəʊpiəm/ *n* opio *m*

opponent /əˈpəʊnənt/ *n* **(a)** (of a regime, policy) opositor, -tora *m,f*; (in debate) adversario, -ria *m,f* **(b)** (Games, Sport) contrincante *mf*, rival *mf*

opportune /ˈɑːpərˌtuːn ‖ˈɒpətjuːn/ *adj* (fml) oportuno

opportunist¹ /ˌɑːpərˈtuːnəst ‖ˌɒpəˈtjuːnɪst/ *n* oportunista *mf*

opportunist², opportunistic /-tuːˈnɪstɪk ‖-tjuː-/ *adj* oportunista

opportunity /ˌɑːpərˈtuːnəti ‖ˌɒpəˈtjuːnəti/ *n* (*pl* **-ties**) oportunidad *f*, ocasión *f*; ~ **to** + INF/OF -ING oportunidad DE + INF; **there was little** ~ **for** sightseeing hubo poco tiempo para hacer turismo

oppose /əˈpəʊz/ *vt* **(a)** (be against) ‹*measure/ policy/actions*› oponerse* a **(b)** (resist) ‹*decision/ plan*› combatir

opposed /əˈpəʊzd/ *adj* **1** (against, in disagreement with) (*pred*) **to be** ~ **TO sth** oponerse* A algo **2** **as opposed to** a diferencia de

opposing /əˈpəʊzɪŋ/ *adj* (*before n*) ‹*viewpoint/ faction/team*› contrario; ‹*army*› enemigo

opposite¹ /ˈɑːpəzət ‖ˈɒpəzɪt/ *adj* **1** (facing) ‹*side/wall/page*› de enfrente **2** (contrary) ‹*opinions/news*› opuesto; **we set off in** ~ **directions** partimos en direcciones opuestas; **it was coming in the** ~ **direction** venía en dirección contraria; **the** ~ **sex** el sexo opuesto

opposite² *adv* enfrente

opposite³ *prep* enfrente de, frente a

opposite⁴ *n*: **the** ~ lo contrario

opposite number *n* homólogo, -ga *m,f*

opposition /ˌɑːpəˈzɪʃən ‖ˌɒpəˈzɪʃən/ *n*

1 (antagonism, resistance) oposición *f* **2** (+ *sing or pl vb*) **(a)** (rivals, competitors) (Busn) competencia *f*; (Sport) adversarios *mpl* **(b)** (Pol) oposición *f*

oppress /əˈpres/ *vt* oprimir

oppression /əˈpreʃən/ *n* (Pol) opresión *f*; (feeling) agobio *m*

oppressive /əˈpresɪv/ *adj* (Pol) opresivo; ‹*heat/ humidity*› agobiante

opt /ɑːpt ‖ɒpt/ *vi* optar; **to** ~ **FOR sth** optar POR algo; **to** ~ **to** + INF optar POR + INF

■ **opt out** [*v* + *adv*] **to** ~ **out** (**OF sth**) decidir no tomar parte (EN algo); (when already involved) dejar de tomar parte (EN algo)

optical /ˈɑːptɪkəl ‖ˈɒptɪkəl/ *adj* óptico

optician /ɑːpˈtɪʃən ‖ɒpˈtɪʃən/ *n* óptico, -ca *m,f*; (esp in UK) ≈ oculista *mf*

optics /ˈɑːptɪks ‖ˈɒptɪks/ *n* (+ *sing vb*) óptica *f*

optimism /ˈɑːptəmɪzəm ‖ˈɒptɪmɪzəm/ *n* optimismo *m*

optimist /ˈɑːptəməst ‖ˈɒptɪmɪst/ *n* optimista *mf*

optimistic /ˌɑːptəˈmɪstɪk ‖ˌɒptɪˈmɪstɪk/ *adj* optimista

optimum /ˈɑːptəməm ‖ˈɒptɪməm/ *adj* (*before n*) óptimo

option /ˈɑːpʃən ‖ˈɒpʃən/ *n* opción *f*; (Educ) (asignatura *f*) optativa *f*

optional /ˈɑːpʃənḷ ‖ˈɒpʃənḷ/ *adj* ‹*accessories/ features*› opcional; ‹*course/subject*› optativo

opulence /ˈɑːpjələns ‖ˈɒpjʊləns/ *n* opulencia *f*

opulent /ˈɑːpjələnt ‖ˈɒpjʊlənt/ *adj* opulento

opus /ˈəʊpəs/ *n* obra *f*; (Mus) opus *m*

or /ər, ɔːr ‖ɔː(r)/ *conj*

■ **Note** The usual translation of *or*, *o*, becomes *u* when it precedes a word beginning with *o* or *ho*.

o; **either … or …** ▸ EITHER¹; **five minutes** ~ **so** unos cinco minutos; **do as I say,** ~ **else!** ¡haz lo que digo o vas a ver!

OR = **Oregon**

oracle /ˈɔːrəkəl ‖ˈɒrəkəl/ *n* oráculo *m*

oral¹ /ˈɔːrəl/ *adj* (*usu before n*) oral

oral² *n* (examen *m*) oral *m*

orange¹ /ˈɑːrɪndʒ ‖ˈɒrɪndʒ/ *n* **(a)** (fruit) naranja *f*; (*before n*) ~ **juice** jugo *m or* (Esp) zumo *m* de naranja **(b)** ~ (**tree**) naranjo *m* **(c)** (color) naranja *m*

orange² *adj* naranja *adj inv*, de color naranja

orangeade /ˌɑːrɪndʒˈeɪd ‖ˌɒrɪndʒˈeɪd/ *n* naranjada *f*

orator /ˈɔːrətər ‖ˈɒrətə(r)/ *n* orador, -dora *m,f*

orbit¹ /ˈɔːrbət ‖ˈɔːbɪt/ *n* órbita *f*

orbit² *vt* girar *or* orbitar alrededor de

■ ~ *vi* orbitar

orchard /ˈɔːrtʃərd ‖ˈɔːtʃəd/ *n* huerto *m* (*de árboles frutales*)

orchestra /ˈɔːrkəstrə ‖ˈɔːkɪstrə/ *n* **1** (Mus) orquesta *f* **2** (AmE Theat) platea *f*, patio *m* de butacas

orchestral /ɔːrˈkestrəl ‖ɔːˈkestrəl/ *adj* ‹*music*› orquestal; ‹*piece*› para orquesta

orchestrate /ˈɔːrkəstreɪt ‖ˈɔːkɪstreɪt/ *vt* orquestar

orchid /ˈɔːrkəd ‖ˈɔːkɪd/ *n* orquídea *f*

ordain /ɔːrˈdeɪn ‖ɔːˈdeɪn/ vt **1** (Relig) ordenar **2 (a)** (decree) (frml) **to ~ THAT** decretar QUE (+ subj) **(b)** (predestine) predestinar

ordeal /ɔːrˈdiːl ‖ɔːˈdiːl/ n terrible experiencia f

order¹ /ˈɔːrdər ‖ˈɔːdə(r)/ n
I 1 (command) orden f; **~ to + INF** orden DE + inf **2** (request, goods requested) pedido m; **the books are on ~** los libros están pedidos; **we make them to ~** los hacemos por encargo; **the waiter took my ~** el camarero tomó nota de lo que quería
II 1 (sequence) orden m; **to put sth in(to) ~** poner* algo en orden **2** (satisfactory condition) orden m; **I'm trying to put my affairs in ~** estoy tratando de poner mis asuntos en orden; **the car was in perfect working ~** el coche funcionaba perfectamente bien **3** (harmony, discipline) orden m; **to keep ~** mantener* el orden **4** (in phrases) **(a)** in order: **are her papers in ~?** ¿tiene los papeles en regla?; **an apology would seem to be in ~** parecería que lo indicado sería disculparse **(b)** in order to para **(c)** in order that para que (+ subj) **(d)** out of order (not in sequence) desordenado; (not working) averiado, descompuesto (AmL); **❺ out of order** no funciona
III 1 (Biol) orden m **2** (of monks, nuns) orden f

order² vt **1 (a)** (command) ordenar; **to ~ sb to + INF** ordenarle a algn QUE (+ subj) **(b)** (Med) mandar **2** (request) pedir*; ‹goods› encargar* **3** (put in order) ordenar
■ **~** vi (in restaurant): **are you ready to ~?** ¿ya han decidido qué van a tomar?

order book n libro m de pedidos

ordered /ˈɔːrdərd ‖ˈɔːdəd/ adj ordenado

orderly¹ /ˈɔːrdərli ‖ˈɔːdəli/ adj **(a)** ‹life/mind› ordenado **(b)** ‹crowd› disciplinado

orderly² n (pl **-lies**) **(a)** (in hospital) camillero m **(b)** (Mil) ordenanza m

ordinal (number) /ˈɔːrdṇəl ‖ˈɔːdɪnəl/ (número m) ordinal m

ordinarily /ˈɔːrdṇˈerəli ‖ˈɔːdənrəli/ adv **(a)** (usually) normalmente **(b)** (averagely) medianamente

ordinary¹ /ˈɔːrdṇeri ‖ˈɔːdənri/ adj **(a)** (average, normal) normal, corriente **(b)** (usual) normal

ordinary² n (average): **out of the ~** fuera de lo común

ore /ɔːr ‖ɔː(r)/ n mena f, mineral m metalífero

Ore, Oreg = Oregon

oregano /əˈregənoʊ ‖ˌɒrɪˈgɑːnəʊ/ n orégano m

organ /ˈɔːrgən ‖ˈɔːgən/ n **1** (Anat) órgano m **2** (Mus) órgano m

organic /ɔːrˈgænɪk ‖ɔːˈgænɪk/ adj orgánico; ‹farming› ecológico; ‹vegetable› biológico, cultivado sin pesticidas ni fertilizantes artificiales

organism /ˈɔːrgənɪzəm ‖ˈɔːgənɪzəm/ n organismo m

organization /ˌɔːrgənəˈzeɪʃən

‖ˌɔːgənaɪˈzeɪʃən/ n **(a)** (group) organización f; (before n) **~ chart** organigrama m **(b)** (organizing) organización f

organize /ˈɔːrgənaɪz ‖ˈɔːgənaɪz/ vt **1** (arrange, set up) organizar* **2** (systematize) ‹ideas/life› ordenar; **to get oneself ~d** organizarse* **3** (Lab Rels) sindicalizar* (esp AmL), sindicar* (esp Esp)

organized /ˈɔːrgənaɪzd ‖ˈɔːgənaɪzd/ adj **1** (methodical) organizado **2** (Lab Rels) sindicalizado (esp AmL), sindicado (esp Esp) **3** ‹crime› organizado

organizer /ˈɔːrgənaɪzər ‖ˈɔːgənaɪzə(r)/ n organizador, -dora m,f

orgasm /ˈɔːrgæzəm ‖ˈɔːgæzəm/ n orgasmo m

orgy /ˈɔːrdʒi ‖ˈɔːdʒi/ n (pl **orgies**) orgía f

orient¹, Orient /ˈɔːriənt/ n **the ~** (el) Oriente

orient² vt (esp AmE) orientar

oriental /ˌɔːriˈentḷ/ adj oriental

orientate /ˈɔːrienteɪt/ vt (esp BrE) ▶ ORIENT²

orientation /ˌɔːrienˈteɪʃən/ n **(a)** (leanings, preference) tendencia f **(b)** (guidance) orientación f

orienteering /ˌɔːrienˈtɪrɪŋ ‖ˌɔːriənˈtɪərɪŋ/ n orientación f

orifice /ˈɔːrəfəs ‖ˈɒrɪfɪs/ n orificio m

origin /ˈɔːrədʒən ‖ˈɒrɪdʒɪn/ n origen m

original¹ /əˈrɪdʒ̣ən̩l/ adj **1** (first) original; **the ~ inhabitants** los primeros habitantes **2 (a)** (not copied) original **(b)** (unusual) original

original² n (document, painting) original m

originality /əˌrɪdʒəˈnæləti/ n originalidad f

originally /əˈrɪdʒən̩li/ adv **(a)** (in the beginning) originariamente **(b)** (unusually) con originalidad

originate /əˈrɪdʒəneɪt ‖əˈrɪdʒɪneɪt/ vi **(a)** (begin) ‹‹custom›› originarse; ‹‹fire›› empezar* **(b)** **to ~ from sth** (develop from) tener* su origen en algo **(c)** (AmE Transp) salir* de

originator /əˈrɪdʒəneɪtər ‖əˈrɪdʒɪneɪtə(r)/ n creador, -dora m,f

Orkney Islands /ˈɔːrkni ‖ˈɔːkni/, **Orkneys** /-z/ pl n (Islas fpl) Órcadas fpl

ornament /ˈɔːrnəmənt ‖ˈɔːnəmənt/ n adorno m

ornamental /ˌɔːrnəˈmentḷ ‖ˌɔːnəˈmentḷ/ adj ornamental

ornate /ɔːrˈneɪt ‖ɔːˈneɪt/ adj ornamentado; (pej) recargado

ornithologist /ˌɔːrnəˈθɑːlədʒəst ‖ˌɔːnɪˈθɒlədʒɪst/ n ornitólogo, -ga m,f

ornithology /ˌɔːrnəˈθɑːlədʒi ‖ˌɔːnɪˈθɒlədʒi/ n ornitología f

orphan¹ /ˈɔːrfən ‖ˈɔːfən/ n huérfano, -na m,f

orphan² vt (usu pass): **she was ~ed at the age of two** quedó huérfana a los dos años

orphanage /ˈɔːrfənɪdʒ ‖ˈɔːfənɪdʒ/ n orfanato m

orthodox /ˈɔːrθədɑːks ‖ˈɔːθədɒks/ adj ortodoxo

orthopedic, (BrE) **orthopaedic** /ˌɔːrθəˈpiːdɪk ‖ˌɔːθəˈpiːdɪk/ adj ortopédico

Oscar /ˈɑːskər ‖ˈɒskə(r)/ n oscar m

oscillate /'ɑːsəleɪt ‖'ɒsɪleɪt/ *vi* (Elec, Phys) oscilar

ostensible /ɑːs'tensəbəl ‖ɒ'stensəbəl/ *adj* aparente

ostensibly /ɑːs'tensəbli ‖ɒ'stensəbli/ *adv* aparentemente

ostentatious /ˌɑːstən'teɪʃəs ‖ˌɒsten'teɪʃəs/ *adj* ostentoso

osteopath /'ɑːstiəpæθ ‖'ɒstiəpæθ/ *n* osteópata *mf*

ostracize /'ɑːstrəsaɪz ‖'ɒstrəsaɪz/ *vt* hacerle* el vacío a

ostrich /'ɑːstrɪtʃ ‖'ɒstrɪtʃ/ *n* avestruz *m*

other¹ /'ʌðər ‖'ʌðə(r)/ *adj* otro, otra; (*pl*) otros, otras; **he doesn't relate easily to ~ people** no se relaciona fácilmente con los demás; **the ~ day** el otro día

other² *pron* (*pl* **others**) **1 (a)** (different, alternative one or ones) otro, otra; ~**s** otros, otras; **I'll think of some excuse or ~** ya me inventaré alguna excusa (u otra); **he was called Richard something or ~** se llamaba Richard no sé cuánto (fam) **(b)** (the remaining one or ones) otro, otra; ~**s** otros, otras; **what do the ~s think?** ¿qué piensan los demás? **(c)** (additional one or ones) otro, otra; ~**s** otros, otras; **answer the first three questions and one ~** conteste las tres primeras preguntas y otra más **2 other than** (apart from) aparte de; (different from) distinto (*or* distinta *etc*) de *or* a; **it was none ~ than Bob** no era ni más ni menos que Bob

other³ *adv*: **somehow or ~** de alguna manera; **somewhere or ~** en algún sitio; **where would you like to live? — anywhere ~ than London** ¿dónde te gustaría vivir? — en cualquier (otro) sitio menos en Londres

otherwise /'ʌðərwaɪz ‖'ʌðəwaɪz/ *adv* **1** (if not) (*as linker*) si no **2** (in other respects) por lo demás **3 (a)** (in a different way): **he could not have done ~** no podía haber hecho otra cosa; **unless ~ agreed, payments ...** a menos que se convenga otra cosa, los pagos ... **(b)** (other, different): **there are many problems, legal and ~** hay muchos problemas, legales y de otro tipo

otter /'ɑːtər ‖'ɒtə(r)/ *n* nutria *f*

ouch /aʊtʃ/ *interj* (colloq) ¡ay!

ought /ɔːt/ *v mod* **~ to + INF** debería (*or* deberías *etc*) + INF, debiera (*or* debieras *etc*) + INF; **she ~ not to have said that** no debería haber dicho eso

ounce /aʊns/ *n* **(a)** (unit) onza *f* (28,35 gramos) **(b)** (small quantity) (*no pl*): **if you had an ~ of decency/sense ...** si tuvieras una pizca de vergüenza/sentido común ...

our /aʊr ‖'aʊə(r)/ *adj*

■ **Note** The translation *nuestro* agrees in number and gender with the noun which it modifies; *our* is translated by *nuestro, nuestra, nuestros, nuestras*, according to what follows: *our father/mother* nuestro padre/nuestra madre; *our books/magazines* nuestros libros/nuestras revistas.

(*sing*) nuestro, -tra; (*pl*) nuestros, -tras; **we were washing ~ hair** nos lavábamos el pelo

ours /aʊrz ‖'aʊəz/ *pron*

■ **Note** The translation *nuestro* reflects the gender and

number of the noun it is standing for; *ours* is translated by *el nuestro, la nuestra, los nuestros, las nuestras*, depending on what is being referred to.

___

(*sing*) nuestro, -tra; (*pl*) nuestros, -tras; **~ is blue** el nuestro/la nuestra es azul; **a friend of ~** un amigo nuestro

ourselves /aʊr'selvz ‖aʊə'selvz, ɑː-/ *pron* **(a)** (reflexive): **we behaved ~** nos portamos bien; **we thought only of ~** solo pensamos en nosotros mismos/nosotras mismas; **we were by ~** estábamos solos/solas **(b)** (emphatic use): **we did it ~** lo hicimos nosotros mismos/nosotras mismas

oust /aʊst/ *vt* ‹rival/leader› desbancar*; ‹government› derrocar*

out¹ /aʊt/ *adv*

I 1 (a) (outside) fuera, afuera (esp AmL) **(b)** (not at home, work): **tell him I'm ~** dile que no estoy; **I was ~ most of the day** estuve (a)fuera casi todo el día; **to eat ~** cenar/comer fuera *or* (esp AmL) afuera; **~ and about: you must get ~ and about more** tienes que salir más **2** (removed): **I'm having my stitches ~ next week** la semana que viene me sacan los puntos **3 (a)** (indicating movement, direction): **~!** ¡fuera!; **s out** salida; **she went over to the window and looked ~** se acercó a la ventana y miró para afuera **(b)** (outstretched, projecting): **the dog had its tongue ~** el perro tenía la lengua fuera *or* (esp AmL) afuera **4** (indicating distance): **~ here in Japan** aquí en Japón; **we live ~ Brampton way** vivimos en la dirección de Brampton **5** (from hospital, jail): **he's been ~ for a month now** ya hace un mes que salió **6** (in phrases) **out for**: **Lewis was ~ for revenge** Lewis quería vengarse; **out to + INF**: **she's ~ to beat the record** está decidida a batir el récord; **they're only ~ to make money** su único objetivo es hacer dinero; *see also* OUT OF

II 1 (a) (displayed, not put away): **are the plates ~ yet?** ¿están puestos ya los platos? **(b)** (in blossom) en flor **(c)** (shining): **when the sun's ~** cuando hay *or* hace sol **2** (published, produced): **a report ~ today points out that ...** un informe publicado hoy señala que ...; **their new album will be ~ by April** sacarán el nuevo disco para abril

out² *adj* **1** (pred) **(a)** (extinguished) **to be ~** ‹fire/light/pipe› estar* apagado **(b)** (unconscious) inconsciente **2** (pred) **(a)** (at an end): **before the month/year is ~** antes de que acabe el mes/año **(b)** (out of fashion) pasado de moda **3** (Sport) **(a)** (eliminated) **to be ~** ‹batter/batsman› quedar out; ‹team› quedar eliminado **(b)** (outside limit) (pred) fuera; **~!** (call) ¡out!

out³ *prep*: **he looked ~ the window** miró (hacia afuera) por la ventana; *see also* OUT OF 1

out: **~-and-~** /'aʊtn'aʊt/ *adj* (as intensifier) ‹villain/liar› consumado; ‹radical/feminist› acérrimo; ‹defeat/disgrace› total; **~back** *n* the **~back** el interior (zona despoblada de Australia); **~bid** /'aʊt'bɪd/ *vt* (pres p **-bidding**; past **-bid**; past p **-bid** *or* (AmE also) **-bidden**) **to ~bid sb** (FOR sth) pujar más que algn (POR algo); **~board** (motor) *n* motor *m* fuera de borda, fueraborda *m*; **~break** *n* (of war) estallido *m*; (of hostilities) comienzo *m*; (of cholera, influenza, violence) brote *m*; **~building** *n* edificación *f* anexa;

···>

~**burst** n (of emotion) arrebato m; ~**cast** n paria mf; ~**come** n (result) resultado m; (consequences) consecuencias fpl; ~**crop** n afloramiento m; ~**cry** n protesta f (enérgica); there was a public ~cry hubo protestas generalizadas; ~**dated** /'aʊt'deɪtəd ‖ ,aʊt'deɪtɪd/ adj ‹style/custom› pasado de moda; ‹idea/theory› anticuado; ~**did** /'aʊt'dɪd/ past of ~DO; ~**distance** /'aʊt'dɪstəns/ vt dejar atrás; ~**do** /'aʊt'duː/ vt (3rd pers sing pres ~**does**; past ~**did**; past p ~**done**) ‹person/team› superar; ‹result/achievement› mejorar; ~**door** /'aʊtdɔːr ‖ 'aʊtdɔː(r)/ adj (before n) ‹clothes› de calle; ‹plants› de exterior; ‹swimming pool› descubierto; ~**doors** /'aʊt'dɔːrz ‖ ,aʊt'dɔːz/ adv al aire libre

outer /'aʊtər ‖ 'aʊtə(r)/ adj (before n) exterior; ~ **space** el espacio sideral

out: ~**fit** n (a) (clothes) conjunto m, tenida f (Chi) (b) (equipment) equipo m; ~**flow** n (of water) desagüe m, flujo m; ~**go** n (AmE) salida f; ~**going** adj [1] (sociable) sociable; [2] ‹president/administration› saliente; ~**goings** pl n (esp BrE) gastos mpl; ~**grow** /'aʊt'grəʊ/ vt (past ~**grew**; past p ~**grown**) he's already ~grown his new shoes los zapatos nuevos ya le han quedado chicos or (Esp) ya se le han quedado pequeños; she's ~grown these toys ya está grande para jugar con esos juguetes; ~**house** n (a) (building) (BrE) edificación f anexa (b) (outdoor privy) (AmE) excusado m exterior

outing /'aʊtɪŋ/ n excursión f

outlandish /aʊt'lændɪʃ/ adj ‹clothes› extravagante; ‹idea/suggestion› descabellado

outlast /'aʊt'læst ‖ ,aʊt'lɑːst/ vt (a) (last longer than) durar más que (b) (survive) sobrevivir a

outlaw¹ /'aʊtlɔː/ n forajido, -da m,f, bandido, -da m,f

outlaw² vt ‹activity/product› prohibir*, declarar ilegal; ‹organization› proscribir*; ‹person› declarar fuera de la ley

out: ~**lay** n desembolso m; ~**let** n [1] (a) (for liquid, gas) salida f (b) (AmE Elec) toma f de corriente, tomacorriente m (AmL); [2] (means of expression): she found an ~let for her feelings encontró una manera de canalizar sus sentimientos; [3] (Busn, Marketing) punto m de venta; retail ~let tienda f al por menor

outline¹ /'aʊtlaɪn/ n [1] (a) (contour) contorno m (b) (shape) perfil m [2] (summary) resumen m; (plan of project, article) esquema m

outline² vt (a) (sketch) ‹shape› bosquejar; ‹map› trazar* (b) (summarize) esbozar*

out: ~**live** /'aʊt'lɪv/ vt sobrevivir a; ~**look** n (a) (attitude) punto m de vista (b) (prospects) perspectivas fpl; ~**lying** adj (before n) ‹villages/islands› alejado; ‹area/hills/suburbs› de la periferia; ~**number** /'aʊt'nʌmbər ‖ ,aʊt'nʌmbə(r)/ vt superar en número a

out of prep [1] (from inside): it fell ~ ~ her hand se le cayó de la mano; (come) ~ ~ there! ¡salgan de ahí!; to look ~ ~ the window mirar (hacia afuera) por la ventana [2] (outside): I was ~ ~ the room for two minutes estuve dos minutos fuera or (AmL tb) afuera de la habitación

[3] (eliminated, excluded): Korea is ~ ~ the tournament Corea ha quedado eliminada; he was left ~ ~ the team no lo incluyeron en el equipo [4] (a) (indicating substance, makeup) de; made ~ ~ steel hecho de acero (b) (indicating motive) por; ~ ~ charity por caridad [5] (from among) de; eight ~ ~ ten people ocho de cada diez personas [6] (indicating lack): we're ~ ~ bread nos hemos quedado sin pan

out: ~**of-date** /'aʊtəv'deɪt/ adj (pred ~ **of date**) ‹ideas/technology› desfasado, perimido (RPl); ‹ticket/check› caducado, vencido (AmL); ‹clothes› pasado de moda; ~**of-the-way** /'aʊtəvðə'weɪ/ adj ‹place› apartado; ~**patient** n paciente externo, -na m,f; ~**post** n (a) (Mil) avanzada f (b) (settlement) puesto m de avanzada; ~**put** n (of factory, writer, artist) producción f; (of worker, machine) rendimiento m; (Comput) salida f; (Elec) salida f

outrage¹ /'aʊtreɪdʒ/ n (a) (cruel act) atrocidad f (b) (scandal) escándalo m (c) (feeling) ~ ⟨AT sth⟩ indignación f ⟨ANTE algo⟩

outrage² vt (a) (offend) indignar (b) (scandalize) escandalizar*

outrageous /aʊt'reɪdʒəs/ adj (a) (scandalous) ‹behavior/state of affairs› vergonzoso; ‹demands/price› escandaloso; how dare you! this is ~! ¡cómo te atreves! ¡esto es intolerable! (b) (unconventional) ‹clothes› extravagante

outran /aʊt'ræn/ past of OUTRUN

outright¹ /'aʊtraɪt/ adj (before n) ‹refusal/opposition› rotundo; ‹hostility› declarado; ‹winner› indiscutido; ‹lie› descarado

outright² adv (a) (completely) ‹refuse/reject› rotundamente; ‹win› indiscutiblemente (b) (directly, frankly) ‹ask/say› abiertamente (c) (instantly) ‹kill› en el acto

out: ~**run** /'aʊt'rʌn/ vt (pres p ~**running**; past ~**ran**; past p ~**run**) dejar atrás; ~**set** n: from the ~set desde el principio; ~**shine** /'aʊt'ʃaɪn/ vt (past & past p ~**shone**) eclipsar

outside¹ /'aʊt'saɪd/ n (exterior part) exterior m; (surface) parte f de fuera or (esp AmL) de afuera; at the (very) ~ como máximo

outside² adv fuera, afuera (esp AmL); to run ~ salir* corriendo

outside³ prep fuera de; it's just ~ London está en las afueras de Londres; it's ~ my responsibilities no está dentro de mis responsabilidades

outside⁴ adj (before n) (a) (exterior, outward) exterior (b) (outdoor) ‹toilet› fuera de la vivienda, exterior (c) (outer) exterior; the ~ lane (Auto) el carril de la izquierda; (in UK etc) el carril de la derecha; (Sport) el carril (AmL) or (Esp) la calle número ocho (or seis etc) (d) (external) ‹interference/pressure› externo

outsider /'aʊt'saɪdər ‖ ,aʊt'saɪdə(r)/ n (a) (person not belonging) persona f de fuera, afuerano, -na m,f (b) (in competition): he was beaten by an ~ fue derrotado por un desconocido (un competidor que se consideraba tenía pocas probabilidades de ganar)

out: ~**size** /'aʊt'saɪz/, (esp AmE) ~**-sized** /-d/ adj (Clothing) de talla or (RPl) talle gigante; (very large) gigantesco; ~**skirts** pl n afueras fpl, alrededores *mpl*; **~smart** /'aʊt'smɑːrt ǁ,aʊt'smɑːt/ *vt* (esp AmE colloq) burlar; **~source** *vt* adquirir* ... de fuentes externas; **~spoken** /'aʊt'spəʊkən/ *adj* directo, franco; **~spread** /'aʊt'spred/ *adj* ‹wings› extendido; **~standing** /aʊt'stændɪŋ/ *adj* **1** (a) (excellent) ‹ability/ beauty› extraordinario; ‹achievement/performer› destacado (b) (prominent) (before n) ‹feature› destacado; **2** ‹debt› pendiente (de pago); **~stay** /'aʊt'steɪ/ *vt*: **I think we've ~stayed our welcome** creo que nos hemos quedado más de la cuenta; **~stretched** /'aʊt'stretʃt/ *adj* extendido; **~strip** /'aʊt'strɪp/ *vt* **-pp-** (run faster than) tomarle la delantera a; (exceed) sobrepasar; **~vote** /'aʊt'vəʊt/ *vt*: **to be ~voted** perder* la votación

outward¹ /'aʊtwərd ǁ'aʊtwəd/ *adj* (before n) (a) ‹appearance› exterior; ‹sign› externo (b) ‹journey/flight› de ida

outward², (BrE also) **outwards** /-z/ *adv* hacia afuera

outwardly /'aʊtwərdli ǁ'aʊtwədli/ *adv* en apariencia

out: **~weigh** /'aʊt'weɪ/ *vt* ser* mayor que; **~wit** /'aʊt'wɪt/ *vt* **-tt-** burlar

oval¹ /'əʊvəl/ *n* óvalo *m*

oval² *adj* ovalado, oval

ovary /'əʊvəri/ *n* (*pl* **-ries**) ovario *m*

ovation /əʊ'veɪʃən/ *n* (frml) ovación *f* (frml); **he got a standing ~** los delegados se pusieron de pie para aplaudirlo

oven /'ʌvən/ *n* horno *m*; (before n) **~ glove** guante *m* para el horno

oven: **~proof** *adj* refractario; **~-ready** /'ʌvən'redi/ *adj* listo para el horno

over¹ /'əʊvər ǁ'əʊvə(r)/ *adv*
I **1** (a) (across): **come ~ here!** ¡ven aquí!; **look ~ there!** ¡mira allí!; **she called me ~** me llamó (desde el otro lado); **he reached ~ and took the money** se estiró y tomó el dinero (b) (overhead) por encima
2 (a) (in another place): **she was sitting ~ there** estaba sentada allí; **how long are you ~ (here) for?** ¿cuánto tiempo te vas a quedar (aquí)? (b) (on other page, TV station etc): **see ~** véase al dorso; **for the latest news, ~ to New York** para las últimas noticias, conectamos ahora con Nueva York (c) (Rad, Telec) corto; **~ and out!** corto y fuera
3 (out of upright position): **to knock sth ~** tirar *or* (AmL exc RPl) botar algo (de un golpe); **to tip sth ~** volcar* algo
II **1** (finished): **the film was ~ by 11 o'clock** la película terminó antes de las 11; **it's all ~ between us** lo nuestro se ha acabado; **to be ~ (and done) with** haber* terminado
2 (remaining): **if you have any material ~** si te sobra tela; **3 into 10 goes 3 and 1 ~** 10 dividido (por) 3 cabe a 3 y sobra 1
3 (a) (as intensifier): **twice/ten times ~** dos/diez veces (b) (again) (AmE) otra vez; **we had to start ~** tuvimos que volver a empezar
4 (more) más
5 (excessively) demasiado
III (in phrases) **1** all over (everywhere) por todas partes; **I'm aching all ~** me duele todo (el cuerpo); **that's her all ~** (colloq) eso es típico de ella

2 (all) over again: **to start (all) ~ again** volver* a empezar (desde cero)
3 over and over (repeatedly) una y otra vez

over² *prep*
I **1** (across): **he jumped ~ the fence** saltó (por encima de) la valla; **they built a bridge ~ the river** construyeron un puente sobre el río; **she peered ~ his shoulder** atisbó por encima de su hombro
2 (above) encima de
3 (covering, on): **snow was falling ~ the countryside** nevaba sobre la campiña; **my room looks out ~ the square** mi habitación da a la plaza; **he put a coat on ~ his pajamas** se puso un abrigo encima del pijama; **she hit me ~ the head with her stick** me dio con el bastón en la cabeza
4 (a) (through, all around): **~ an area of 50km²** en un área de 50km²; **I've been ~ the details with her** he repasado los detalles con ella (b) (referring to experiences, illnesses): **is she ~ her measles yet?** ¿ya se ha repuesto del sarampión?; **we're ~ the worst now** ya hemos pasado lo peor
5 (during, in the course of): **~ the past/next few years** en los últimos/próximos años; **we can discuss it ~ lunch** podemos hablarlo mientras comemos
6 (by the medium of) por; **~ the loudspeaker** por el altavoz
7 (about, on account of): **to cry ~ sth** llorar por algo; **they argued ~ money** discutieron por asuntos de dinero
8 all over: **there are black marks all ~ the floor** hay marcas negras por todo el suelo; **all ~ town** por toda la ciudad
II **1** (a) (more than) más de (b) over and above (in addition to) además de
2 (a) (senior to) por encima de (b) (indicating superiority) sobre; **to have control ~ sb/sth** tener* control sobre algn/algo

over³ *n* (in cricket) over *m* (serie de seis lanzamientos)

over- /'əʊvər ǁ'əʊvə(r)/ *pref* (a) (excessively) demasiado (b) (in deliberate understatement): **she wasn't ~enthusiastic** no demostró mucho entusiasmo que digamos

overact /'əʊvər'ækt/ *vi* sobreactuar*

overall¹ /'əʊvərɔːl/ *adj* (before n) ‹length› total; ‹result/cost› global; **the ~ impression** la impresión general

overall² *n*. **1** (protective garment) (esp BrE) bata *f*
2 overalls *pl* (a) (dungarees) (AmE) overol *m* (AmL), (pantalones *mpl* de) peto *m* (Esp), mameluco *m* (CS) (b) (boiler suit) (BrE) overol *m* (AmL), mono *m* (Esp, Méx)

over: **~arm** *adv* (esp BrE) por encima de la cabeza; **~ate** /'əʊvər'et/ *past of* ~EAT; **~awe** /'əʊvər'ɔː/ *vt* intimidar; **~balance** /'əʊvər'bæləns ǁ,əʊvə'bæləns/ *vi* perder* el equilibrio; **~board** *adv*: **they threw him ~board** lo echaron por la borda; **to go ~board** (colloq — exaggerate) exagerar; (— be excessively enthusiastic, generous) pasarse (fam); **~came** /'əʊvər'keɪm ǁ,əʊvə'keɪm/ *past of* ~COME; **~cast** *adj* ‹sky› cubierto; ‹day› nublado; **it's ~cast** está nublado *or* cubierto; **~charge** /'əʊvər'tʃɑːrdʒ ǁ,əʊvə'tʃɑːdʒ/ *vt* **to ~charge sb** (FOR sth) cobrarle de más a algn (POR algo); **~coat** *n* abrigo *m*, sobretodo *m* (esp RPl); **~come** /'əʊvər'kʌm ǁ,əʊvə'kʌm/ (*past* **-came**; *past p* ⋯⟶

-come vt (a) ⟨opponent⟩ reducir*; ⟨fear⟩ superar; ⟨inhibitions⟩ vencer* (b) (overwhelm) invadir; he was ~come by fatigue lo venció la fatiga; to be ~come WITH sth ⟨with guilt/remorse⟩ sentirse* abrumado POR algo ■ ~ vi: we shall ~come venceremos; ~**crowded** /'əʊvər'kraʊdəd ‖,əʊvə'kraʊdɪd/ adj abarrotado (de gente); ⟨country⟩ superpoblado; ~**crowding** /'əʊvər'kraʊdɪŋ ‖,əʊvə'kraʊdɪŋ/ n: they complained about the ~crowding on the trains se quejaron de lo aborrotados que iban los trenes; the severe ~crowding in our prisons el hacinamiento en nuestras cárceles; ~**do** /'əʊvər'du: ‖,əʊvə'du:/ vt (3rd pers sing pres -does; past -did; past p -done) ⒈ (exaggerate) exagerar; to ~do it (go too far) írsele la mano a algn; (overexert oneself) exigir* demasiado; ⒉ (Culin) cocinar demasiado, recocer*; ~**dose** n sobredosis f; ~**draft** n descubierto m; ~**draw** /'əʊvər'drɔː ‖,əʊvə'drɔː/ vt (past -drew; past p -drawn) (Fin): I'm ~drawn tengo un descubierto; ~**drive** /'əʊvərdraɪv ‖'əʊvədraɪv/ n superdirecta f; ~**due** /'əʊvər'dju: ‖,əʊvə'dju:/ adj: the book is a month ~due el plazo de devolución del libro venció hace un mes; such measures are long ~due tales medidas deberían haberse adoptado mucho antes; ~**eat** /'əʊvər'iːt/ vi (past -ate; past p -eaten) comer demasiado; ~**excited** /'əʊvərɪk'saɪtəd ‖,əʊvərɪk'saɪtɪd/ adj sobreexcitado; ~**feed** /'əʊvər'fiːd ‖,əʊvə'fiːd/ vt (past & past p -fed) sobrealimentar

overflow[1] /'əʊvər'fləʊ ‖,əʊvə'fləʊ/ vi «liquid» derramarse; ⟨bucket/bath/river⟩ desbordarse; the house is ~ing with junk la casa está hasta el techo de cachivaches

overflow[2] /'əʊvərfləʊ ‖'əʊvəfləʊ/ n (a) (excess): we put a bowl there to catch the ~ pusimos un bol para recoger el líquido que se derramaba (b) (outlet) rebosadero m

over: ~**grown** /'əʊvər'grəʊn ‖,əʊvə'grəʊn/ adj (a) ⟨garden⟩ lleno de maleza (b) (too big) demasiado grande; ~**hand** adv (AmE) por encima de la cabeza; ~**hang** /'əʊvər'hæŋ ‖,əʊvə'hæŋ/ (past & past p -hung) vt sobresalir* por encima de ■ ~ vi sobresalir*

overhaul[1] /'əʊvər'hɔːl ‖,əʊvə'hɔːl/ vt revisar

overhaul[2] /'əʊvərhɔːl ‖'əʊvəhɔːl/ n revisión f (general), overjol m (AmC)

overhead[1] /'əʊvər'hed ‖,əʊvə'hed/ adv: the sun was directly ~ el sol caía de pleno; a plane flew ~ pasó un avión

overhead[2] /'əʊvərhed ‖'əʊvəhed/ adj ⟨cable⟩ aéreo; ⟨railway⟩ elevado

overhead[3] /'əʊvərhed ‖'əʊvəhed/ n (AmE) gastos mpl indirectos

over: ~**heads** /'əʊvərhedz ‖'əʊvəhedz/ pl n (BrE) ▶ OVERHEAD[3]; ~**hear** /'əʊvər'hɪr ‖,əʊvə'hɪə(r)/ vt (past & past p -heard) oír* (por casualidad); ~**heat** /'əʊvər'hiːt ‖,əʊvə'hiːt/ vi recalentarse*; ~**hung** past & past p of OVERHANG; ~**joyed** /'əʊvər'dʒɔɪd ‖,əʊvə'dʒɔɪd/ adj encantado; ~**kill** n exageración f; ~**land**

adj/adv por tierra; ~**lap** /'əʊvər'læp ‖,əʊvə'læp/ vi **-pp-** (a) «tiles/planks» estar* montados unos sobre otros, traslaparse (b) «responsibilities» coincidir en parte; ~**leaf** /'əʊvər'liːf ‖,əʊvə'liːf/ adv al dorso; ~**load** /'əʊvər'ləʊd ‖,əʊvə'ləʊd/ vt sobrecargar*; ~**look** /'əʊvər'lʊk ‖,əʊvə'lʊk/ vt ⒈ (a) (not notice) pasar por alto (b) (disregard) disculpar; ⒉ (have view over): a room ~**looking** the sea una habitación con vista al mar or que da al mar

overly /'əʊvərli ‖'əʊvəli/ adv demasiado

overnight[1] /'əʊvər'naɪt ‖,əʊvə'naɪt/ adv (a) (through the night): to stay ~ quedarse a pasar la noche; there had been a heavy fall of snow ~ durante la noche había nevado mucho; soak the chickpeas ~ ponga los garbanzos en remojo la noche anterior (b) (suddenly) ⟨change/disappear⟩ de la noche a la mañana

overnight[2] /'əʊvərnaɪt ‖'əʊvənaɪt/ adj (a) (through the night) ⟨journey⟩ de noche; ⟨stay⟩ de una noche (b) (sudden) ⟨change/success⟩ repentino

over: ~**paid** /'əʊvər'peɪd ‖,əʊvə'peɪd/ adj: she's ~paid le pagan demasiado ~**pass** n paso m elevado, paso m a desnivel (Méx); ~**population** /,əʊvər,pɑːpjə'leɪʃən ‖,əʊvə,pɒpjʊ'leɪʃən/ n superpoblación f, sobrepoblación f (AmL); ~**power** /'əʊvər'paʊər ‖,əʊvə'paʊə(r)/ vt (a) (render helpless) dominar (b) (affect greatly) «smell» marear; «heat» sofocar*; «emotion» abrumar; ~**powering** /'əʊvər'paʊrɪŋ ‖,əʊvə'paʊərɪŋ/ adj (a) ⟨smell⟩ muy fuerte; ⟨heat⟩ aplastante; ⟨desire⟩ irresistible (b) ⟨personality⟩ apabullante; ~**priced** /'əʊvər'praɪst ‖,əʊvə'praɪst/ vt: it's ~priced es caro para lo que es; ~**ran** /'əʊvər'ræn ‖,əʊvə'ræn/ past of ~RUN; ~**rated** /'əʊvər'reɪtəd ‖,əʊvə'reɪtɪʃ/ adj sobrevalorado; ~**reach** /'əʊvər'riːtʃ ‖,əʊvə'riːtʃ/ v refl: to ~reach oneself intentar hacer demasiado; ~**react** /'əʊvərri'ækt ‖,əʊvəri'ækt/ vi reaccionar en forma exagerada; ~**ride** /'əʊvər'raɪd ‖,əʊvə'raɪd/ vt (past -rode; past p -ridden) ⟨decision/recommendation⟩ invalidar; ⟨wishes/advice⟩ hacer* caso omiso de; ~**ripe** /'əʊvər'raɪp ‖,əʊvə'raɪp/ adj demasiado maduro; ~**rode** /'əʊvər'rəʊd ‖,əʊvə'rəʊd/ past of ~RIDE; ~**rule** /'əʊvər'ruːl ‖,əʊvə'ruːl/ vt ⟨decision/verdict⟩ anular; ⟨objection⟩ rechazar*; ~**run** /'əʊvər'rʌn ‖,əʊvə'rʌn/ vt (past -ran; past p -run) (a) (invade, swarm over) invadir; to be ~run WITH sth estar* plagado DE algo (b) (exceed) exceder; ~**saw** /'əʊvər'sɔː ‖,əʊvə'sɔː/ past of OVERSEE

overseas[1] /'əʊvər'siːz ‖,əʊvə'siːz/ adj (before n) ⟨trade⟩ exterior; ⟨investments/branches⟩ en el exterior; ⟨student/visitor⟩ extranjero; ⟨news⟩ del exterior

overseas[2] /'əʊvər'siːz ‖,əʊvə'siːz/ adv ⟨live⟩ en el extranjero; ⟨travel/send⟩ al extranjero

over: ~**see** /'əʊvər'siː ‖,əʊvə'siː/ vt (past -saw; past p -seen) supervisar; ~**seer** /'əʊvər'sɪr, -'siːər ‖'əʊvəsiːə(r)/ n capataz mf; ~**shadow** /'əʊvər'ʃædəʊ ‖,əʊvə'ʃædəʊ/ vt eclipsar; ~**shoot** /'əʊvər'ʃuːt ‖əʊvə'ʃuːt/ vt (past & past p -**shot**) ⟨runway⟩ salirse* de; ⟨turning⟩ pasarse de; ⟨target/budget⟩ exceder; ~**sight** /'əʊvərsaɪt ‖'əʊvəsaɪt/ n descuido m; ~**sleep** /'əʊvər'sliːp ‖əʊvə'sliːp/ vi (past & past p -**slept**) quedarse dormido; ~**spend** /'əʊvər'spend ‖əʊvə'spend/ vi (past & past p -**spent**) gastar más de la cuenta; ~**spill** n excedente m de población; ~**staffed** /'əʊvər'stæft ‖əʊvə'staːft/ adj con exceso de personal or (Esp tb) de plantilla; ~**state** /'əʊvər'steɪt ‖əʊvə'steɪt/ vt exagerar; ~**stay** /'əʊvər'steɪ ‖əʊvə'steɪ/ vt ▶ OUTSTAY; ~**step** /'əʊvər'step ‖əʊvə'step/ vt -**pp**- sobrepasar

overt /əʊ'vɜːrt ‖'əʊvɜːt/ adj ⟨hostility⟩ declarado; ⟨criticism⟩ abierto

over: ~**take** /'əʊvər'teɪk ‖əʊvə'teɪk/ (past -**took**; past p -**taken**) vt (a) (go past) adelantar, rebasar (Méx) (b) (surpass) superar ■ ~ vi (BrE) adelantar, rebasar (Méx); ~**tax** /'əʊvər'tæks ‖əʊvə'tæks/ vt (a) (strain) poner* a prueba (b) (Tax) gravar en exceso (con impuestos); ~**throw** /'əʊvər'θrəʊ ‖əʊvə'θrəʊ/ vt (past -**threw**; past p -**thrown**) ⟨government⟩ derrocar*; ~**time** n 1 (extra work hours) horas fpl extra(s), sobretiempo m (Chi, Per); 2 (AmE Sport) prórroga f; ~**tone** n (suggestion, hint) (usu pl) dejo m, deje m (Esp); ~**took** /'əʊvər'tʊk ‖əʊvə'tʊk/ past of ~TAKE

overture /'əʊvərtʃʊr ‖'əʊvətʃʊə(r)/ n 1 (Mus) obertura f 2 **overtures** pl (approaches) (frml) intento m de acercamiento; (sexual) insinuación f

over: ~**turn** /'əʊvər'tɜːrn ‖əʊvə'tɜːn/ vt (a) (tip over) ⟨table/boat⟩ darle* la vuelta a, dar* vuelta (CS) (b) (depose) ⟨government⟩ derrocar* ■ ~ vi «vehicle» volcar*; ~**weight** /'əʊvər'weɪt ‖əʊvə'weɪt/ adj ⟨person⟩ demasiado gordo; I am 10lb ~**weight** peso 10 libras de más, tengo un sobrepeso de 10 libras (Chi, Méx)

overwhelm /'əʊvər'hwelm ‖əʊvə'welm/ vt (a) (emotionally) abrumar (b) (defeat) aplastar (c) (swamp): they've been ~ed with applications/ complaints han recibido infinidad de solicitudes/ quejas

overwhelming /'əʊvər'hwelmɪŋ ‖əʊvə'welmɪŋ/ adj ⟨grief⟩ inconsolable; ⟨urge⟩ irresistible; ⟨anger⟩ incontenible; ⟨boredom⟩ insoportable; ⟨defeat⟩ aplastante

overwind /'əʊvər'waɪnd ‖əʊvə'waɪnd/ vt (past & past p -**wound** /-waʊnd/) dar* demasiada cuerda a

overwork¹ /'əʊvər'wɜːrk ‖əʊvə'wɜːk/ vt hacer* trabajar demasiado

overwork² n agotamiento m

ovulate /'ɑːvjəleɪt ‖'ɒvjʊleɪt/ vi ovular

ovulation /'ɑːvjə'leɪʃən ‖ɒvjʊ'leɪʃən/ n ovulación f

owe /əʊ/ vt (a) (financially) deber; to ~ sb sth, ~ sth TO sb deberle algo a algn (b) (be obliged to give, do) ⟨explanation/apology/favor⟩ deber

owing /'əʊɪŋ/ adj 1 (pred): the money still ~ el dinero que aún se debe 2 **owing to** (as prep) debido a

owl /aʊl/ n búho m, tecolote m (Méx); (barn ~) lechuza f

own¹ /əʊn/ vt ⟨property⟩ tener*
■ **own up** [v + adv]: no one ~ed up nadie reconoció tener la culpa; no one would ~ up to having left the window open nadie quiso reconocer que había sido quien dejó la ventana abierta

own² adj my/her/your etc ~: in our ~ house en nuestra propia casa; she makes her ~ clothes se hace la ropa ella misma

own³ pron my/her/your etc ~: it isn't a company car, it's her ~ no es un coche de la empresa, es suyo (propio); she wanted a room of her ~ quería una habitación para ella sola; on one's ~ solo; to get one's ~ back (BrE colloq) desquitarse

owner ?/'əʊnər ‖'əʊnə(r)/ n (of house, car) dueño, -ña m,f, propietario, -ria m,f; (of pet) dueño, -ña m,f

ownership /'əʊnərʃɪp ‖'əʊnəʃɪp/ n propiedad f

own goal n autogol m, gol m en contra (CS)

ox /ɑːks ‖ɒks/ n (pl **oxen**) buey m

oxen /'ɑːksən ‖'ɒksən/ pl of ox

oxide /'ɑːksaɪd ‖'ɒksaɪd/ n óxido m

oxtail /'ɑːksteɪl ‖'ɒksteɪl/ n rabo m de buey

oxygen /'ɑːksədʒən ‖'ɒksɪdʒən/ n oxígeno m; (before n) ~ **mask** (Aviat, Med) mascarilla f de oxígeno

oyster /'ɔɪstər ‖'ɔɪstə(r)/ n ostra f, ostión m (Méx)

oz = **ounce(s)**

ozone /'əʊzəʊn/ n (Chem) ozono m; (before n) the ~ **layer** la capa de ozono

P

P, p /piː/ n P, p f

p (in UK) (= **penny/pence**) penique(s) m(pl)

p. (pl **pp.**) (= **page**) pág., p.; **pp. 12-48** págs. 12 a 48

pa¹ /pɑː/ n (colloq) papá m

pa², p.a. /'piː'eɪ/ = **per annum**

PA n (a) /'piː'eɪ/ ~ (**system**) = **public-address system** (b) /piː'eɪ/ (BrE) = **personal assistant** (c) also **Pa** = **Pennsylvania**

pace¹ /peɪs/ n 1 (stride) paso m; to put sb through her/his ~s poner* a algn a prueba 2 (speed) (no pl) ritmo m; to keep ~ with sb ···⋗

seguirle* el ritmo lento a algn; **to set the ~** marcar* la pauta

pace² *vi*: **to ~ up and down** caminar *or* (esp Esp) andar de un lado para otro

pace: **~maker** *n* (Sport) liebre *f*; (Med) marcapasos *m*; **~setter** /'peɪs,setə(r) ||'peɪs,setə(r)/ *n* (Sport) liebre *f*; (pioneer) líder *mf*

Pacific /pə'sɪfɪk/ *n* **the ~ (Ocean)** el (Océano) Pacífico

pacifier /'pæsəfaɪər ||'pæsɪfaɪə(r)/ *n* (AmE) chupete *m*, chupón *m* (AmL exc CS), chupo *m* (Col), chupa *f* (Ven)

pacifism /'pæsəfɪzəm ||'pæsɪfɪzəm/ *n* pacifismo *m*

pacifist /'pæsəfəst ||'pæsɪfɪst/ *n* pacifista *mf*

pacify /'pæsəfaɪ ||'pæsɪfaɪ/ *vt* **-fies, -fying, -fied** (a) (calm, satisfy) apaciguar* (b) (restore to peace) pacificar*

pack¹ /pæk/ *n* **1** (bundle, load) fardo *m*; (rucksack) mochila *f* **2** (a) (package) paquete *m*; (of cigarettes) paquete *m*, cajetilla *f* (b) (of cards) (BrE) baraja *f*, mazo *m* (esp AmL) **3** (a) (of wolves) manada *f*; **a ~ of hounds** (Sport) una jauría (b) (in race) pelotón *m* **4** (a) (of thieves, fools) (pej) partida *f* (pey); **a ~ of lies** una sarta de mentiras

pack² *vt* **1** (a) (Busn) ⟨goods/products⟩ (put into container) envasar*; (make packets with) empaquetar*; (for transport) embalar (b) (put into suitcase, bag): **have you ~ed your toothbrush?** ¿llevas el cepillo de dientes?; **to ~ one's suitcase** hacer* la maleta *or* (RPl) la valija, empacar (AmL); **she takes a ~ed lunch to work** se lleva el almuerzo *or* (esp Esp, Méx) la comida al trabajo

2 (a) (press tightly together): **~ the soil (down) firmly** apisone bien la tierra (b) (cram): **the book is ~ed with useful information** el libro está lleno de información útil; **we ~ed a lot into a short time** hicimos un montón de cosas en poco tiempo fam

■ **~** *vi* (fill suitcase) hacer* la(s) maleta(s) *or* (RPl) la(s) valija(s), empacar* (AmL)

■ **pack in** [*v* + *o* + *adv*, *v* + *adv* + *o*] **1** (quit) (colloq) ⟨job/course⟩ dejar

2 (cram in): **we managed to ~ in 50 people** pudimos meter a 50 personas

■ **pack off** [*v* + *o* + *adv*, *v* + *adv* + *o*] despachar, mandar; **she ~ed the children off to school** mandó a los niños al colegio

■ **pack up 1** [*v* + *adv*] (a) (assemble belongings) liar* el petate, hacer* su itacate (Méx) (b) (stop) (colloq): **let's ~ up for the day** dejémoslo por hoy (c) (break down) (colloq) ⟨motor/radio⟩ dejar de funcionar, descomponerse* (esp AmL), tronarse* (Méx fam)

2 [*v* + *o* + *adv*, *v* + *adv* + *o*] (a) ⟨tools/belongings⟩ recoger* (b) ▶ PACK IN 1

package /'pækɪdʒ/ *n* paquete *m*

package: **~ holiday** (BrE) ▶ ~ VACATION; **~ store** *n* (AmE) tienda *f* de bebidas alcohólicas; **~ tour** *n* viaje *m* organizado (en el que se recorren diferentes localidades); **~ vacation** *n* (AmE) vacaciones *fpl* organizadas

packaging /'pækɪdʒɪŋ/ *n* (a) (packing) embalaje *m* (b) (wrapping) envoltorio *m* (c) (Marketing) presentación *f*

packed /pækt/ *adj* ⟨hall/restaurant⟩ lleno de gente, repleto

packet /'pækət ||'pækɪt/ *n* (esp BrE) paquete *m*; (before *n*) ⟨soup/cake mix⟩ de sobre

packing /'pækɪŋ/ *n* (a) (of luggage): **to do one's ~** hacer* la(s) maleta(s) *or* (RPl) la(s) valija(s), empacar* (AmL) (b) (in factory) embalaje *m*

packing case *n* caja *f* de embalaje

pact /pækt/ *n* pacto *m*

pad¹ /pæd/ *n* **1** (a) (cushioning) almohadilla *f*; **shoulder ~s** hombreras *fpl*; **knee ~s** rodilleras *fpl* **2** (of paper) bloc *m*

pad² *vt* **-dd-** **1** (a) (line) ⟨seat/panel⟩ acolchar, enguatar (Esp) (b) **padded** *past p* ⟨jacket⟩ acolchado, enguatado (Esp); ⟨bra⟩ con relleno; ⟨envelope⟩ acolchado; **~ded cell** celda *f* de aislamiento **2** **~** (out) ⟨essay⟩ rellenar, meter* paja en (fam)

padding /'pædɪŋ/ *n* (material) relleno *m*, guata *f* (Esp); (in essay) paja *f* (fam)

paddle¹ /'pædl/ *n* **1** (oar) zagual *m*, pala *f* **2** (no pl): **to go for a ~** ir* a mojarse los pies

paddle² *vi* **1** (wet feet) mojarse los pies (en la orilla) **2** (a) (in canoe) remar (con pala *or* zagual) (b) (swim) ⟨duck/dog⟩ chapotear

■ **~** *vt* ⟨boat/canoe⟩ llevar (remando con pala *or* zagual)

paddling pool /'pædlɪŋ/ *n* (BrE) (in park) estanque *m*; (inflatable) piscina *f or* (Méx) alberca *f* inflable (para niños)

paddock /'pædək/ *n* prado *m*

paddy /'pædi/ *n* (pl **-dies**) **~ (field)** arrozal *m*

padlock¹ /'pædlɑːk ||'pædlɒk/ *n* candado *m*

padlock² *vt* cerrar* con candado

paediatric *etc* (BrE) ▶ PEDIATRIC *etc*

paedophile *n* (BrE) ▶ PEDOPHILE

pagan¹ /'peɪɡən/ *n* pagano, -na *m,f*

pagan² *adj* pagano

page¹ /peɪdʒ/ *n* **1** (of book, newspaper) página *f*; **on ~ four** en la página cuatro **2** (attendant) paje *m*; (in hotel) botones *m*

page² *vt* (over loudspeaker) llamar por megafonía; (by beeper) llamar por buscapersonas *or* (Méx) bip *or* (Chi) bíper

pageant /'pædʒənt/ *n* (a) (show, ceremony) festividades *fpl* (b) (historical show) espectáculo histórico al aire libre

pageboy /'peɪdʒbɔɪ/ *n* ▶ PAGE¹ 2

pager /'peɪdʒər ||'peɪdʒə(r)/ *n* buscapersonas *m*, bip *m* (Méx), bíper *m* (Chi)

paid¹ /peɪd/ *past & past p of* PAY¹

paid² *adj* ⟨employment⟩ remunerado; ⟨worker⟩ asalariado; ⟨vacation⟩ pagado; ⟨leave⟩ con goce de sueldo

pail /peɪl/ *n* balde *m*, cubo *m* (Esp), cubeta *f* (Méx)

pain /peɪn/ *n* **1** (a) (physical) dolor *m*; **she was in great ~** estaba muy dolorida *or* (AmL tb) adolorida; **to be a ~ in the neck** ser* un pesado (b) (annoying person or thing) (colloq) lata *f* (fam) **2** **pains** *pl* (effort): **that's all you get for your ~s** así se pagan la molestia; **I went to great ~s to explain it to them carefully** puse mucho esmero en explicárselo

painful /'peɪnfəl/ *adj* (a) (physically) doloroso; **it's very ~** duele mucho (b) (mentally) ⟨task⟩ desagradable; ⟨reminder⟩ doloroso

painfully /'peɪnfəli/ adv: she dragged herself ~ along se iba arrastrando con mucho dolor; she's ~ shy es tan tímida que da pena

painkiller /'peɪnˌkɪlər ‖'peɪnˌkɪlə(r)/ n analgésico m

painless /'peɪnləs ‖'peɪnlɪs/ adj (a) (causing no pain) indoloro; ~ childbirth parto m sin dolor (b) (easy, pleasant) (colloq) ⟨method⟩ sencillo

painstaking /'peɪnzˌteɪkɪŋ/ adj ⟨research/ efforts⟩ concienzudo; ⟨person/personality⟩ meticuloso

paint¹ /peɪnt/ n pintura f

paint² vt/i pintar

paint: ~box n caja f de acuarelas; **~brush** n pincel m; (large, for walls) brocha f

painter /'peɪntər ‖'peɪntə(r)/ n (Art, Const) pintor, -tora m,f

painting /'peɪntɪŋ/ n (a) (picture) cuadro m, pintura f (b) (Art) pintura f

paintwork /'peɪntwɜːrk ‖'peɪntwɜːk/ n pintura f

pair /per ‖peə(r)/ n **1** (a) (of shoes, socks, gloves) par m; a ~ of trousers unos pantalones; a ~ of scissors unas tijeras (b) (in cards) pareja f, par m **2** (couple) pareja f

■ **pair up** [v + adv] formar parejas

pajamas, (BrE) **pyjamas** /pə'dʒɑːməz/ pl n pijama m, piyama m or f (AmL)

Pakistan /'pækɪstæn ‖,pɑːkɪ'stɑːn, ,pækɪ-/ n Pakistán m, Paquistán m

Pakistani¹ /'pækɪstæni ‖,pɑːkɪ'stɑːnɪ, ,pækɪ-/ adj pakistaní, paquistaní

Pakistani² n pakistaní mf, paquistaní mf

pal /pæl/ n (colloq) amigo m, compinche m (fam), cuate m (Méx fam)

palace /'pæləs ‖'pælɪs/ n palacio m

palatable /'pælətəbəl/ adj agradable

palate /'pælət/ n paladar m

pale¹ /peɪl/ adj (a) ⟨skin/person⟩ (naturally) blanco; (pallid) pálido (b) ⟨blue/pink⟩ pálido

pale² vi (a) «person» palidecer* (b) (seem minor) to ~ BESIDE O BEFORE sb/sth palidecer* JUNTO A algn/algo

pale³ n: to be beyond the ~ ser* intolerable

Palestine /'pæləstaɪn/ n Palestina f

Palestinian¹ /'pælə'stɪniən/ adj palestino

Palestinian² n palestino, -na m,f

palette /'pælət ‖'pælɪt/ n paleta f

pall¹ /pɔːl/ n: to cast a ~ on o over sth empañar algo

pall² vi hacerse* pesado

pallid /'pæləd ‖'pælɪd/ adj pálido

palm /pɑːm/ n **1** (a) ~ (tree) palmera f (b) (leaf, branch) palma f **2** (Anat) palma f

■ **palm off** [v + o + adv] to ~ sth off ON O ONTO sb encajarle algo a algn (fam); to ~ sb off WITH sth quitarse a algn de encima CON algo

palmistry /'pɑːməstri ‖'pɑːmɪstri/ n quiromancia f

Palm Sunday n Domingo m de Ramos

palpable /'pælpəbəl/ adj (frml) palmario, palpable

palpitate /'pælpəteɪt ‖'pælpɪteɪt/ vi palpitar

palpitation /'pælpə'teɪʃən ‖,pælpɪ'teɪʃən/ n (Med) palpitación f

paltry /'pɔːltri/ adj -trier -triest ⟨sum/ amount⟩ mísero; ⟨excuse⟩ malo

pamper /'pæmpər ‖'pæmpə(r)/ vt mimar

pamphlet /'pæmflət ‖'pæmflɪt/ n (informative) folleto m; (political) panfleto m

pan¹ /pæn/ n **1** (Culin) cacerola f; (large, with two handles) olla f; (small) cacerola f, cazo m (Esp); (frying ~) sartén f **2** (of toilet) (BrE) taza f

pan² vi -nn- **1** (Min): to ~ for gold lavar oro **2** (Cin): the camera ~s across to the two figures la cámara recorre hasta enfocar en las dos figuras

panacea /'pænə'siːə/ n (frml) panacea f

panache /pə'næʃ/ n garbo m

Panama /'pænəmɑː/ n Panamá m; (before n) the ~ Canal el Canal de Panamá

Panamanian¹ /'pænə'meɪniən/ adj panameño

Panamanian² n panameño, -ña m,f

pancake /'pænkeɪk/ n (Culin) crep(e) m, panqueque m (AmL), crepa f (Méx), panqué m (AmC, Col), panqueca f (Ven)

pancreas /'pæŋkriəs/ n páncreas m

panda /'pændə/ n (oso, osa m,f) panda mf

pandemonium /'pændə'məʊniəm/ n pandemonio m, pandemónium m

pander /'pændər ‖'pændə(r)/ vi: to ~ to sb's whims consentirle* los caprichos a algn

pane /peɪn/ n (hoja f de) vidrio m, cristal m (Esp)

panel¹ /'pænl/ n **1** (a) (of door, car body, plane wing) panel m; (of garment) pieza f (b) (instrument ~) tablero m (de instrumentos); (control ~) tablero m (de control) **2** (in discussion, interview) panel m or (Col, Ven) panel m; (in quiz, contest) equipo m; (in exam) mesa f, comisión f (Chi)

panel² vt, (BrE) **-ll-** (a) ⟨room/wall⟩ revestir* con paneles (b) **paneled,** (BrE) **panelled** past p ⟨door⟩ de paneles

pang /pæŋ/ n punzada f; ~s of hunger retorcijones mpl or (Esp) retortijones mpl de hambre

panhandler /'pænˌhændlər ‖'pænˌhændlə(r)/ n (AmE colloq) mendigo m

panic¹ /'pænɪk/ n(fear, anxiety) pánico m; (before n) ~ button botón m de alarma

panic² vi -ck- dejarse llevar por el pánico; don't ~! ¡tranquilo!

panicky /'pæniki/ adj ⟨person⟩ muy nervioso; ⟨behavior/decision⟩ precipitado

panic-stricken /'pænɪkˌstrɪkən/ adj aterrorizado

pannier /'pæniər ‖'pæniə(r)/ n alforja f; (on cycle) maletero m

panorama /'pænə'ræmə ‖,pænə'rɑːmə/ n panorama m

panoramic /'pænə'ræmɪk/ adj panorámico

pansy /'pænzi/ n (pl -sies) (Bot) pensamiento m

pant¹ /pænt/ vi jadear

pant² n jadeo m; see also PANTS

pantheon /'pænθiːɑːn ‖'pænθiən/ n panteón m

panther /'pænθər ‖'pænθə(r)/ n pantera f

panties /'pæntiz/ pl n calzones mpl (AmL), bragas fpl (Esp), pantaletas fpl (Méx, Ven), bombacha f (RPl), calzoneta f (AmC)

pantihose /'pæntihəʊz/ pl n ▶ PANTYHOSE

pantomime /'pæntəmaɪm/ n **(a)** (mime) pantomima f **(b)** (in UK) comedia musical navideña, basada en cuentos de hadas

pantry /'pæntri/ n (pl **-tries**) despensa f

pants /pænts/ pl n [1] (trousers) (AmE) pantalón m, pantalones mpl [2] (underwear) (BrE) **(a)** (men's) calzoncillos mpl, calzones mpl (Méx), interiores mpl (Col, Ven) **(b)** (women's) ▶ PANTIES

pantsuit /'pæntsuːt/, **pants suit** n (AmE) traje m pantalón

pantyhose /'pæntihəʊz/ pl n (AmE) medias fpl, pantimedias fpl (Méx), medias fpl bombacha (RPI) or (Col) pantalón or (Ven) panty

papa n **(a)** /'pɑːpə/ (AmE) papá m **(b)** /pə'pɑː/ (BrE dated) padre m (ant)

paper[1] /'peɪpər ‖'peɪpə(r)/ n [1] **(a)** (material) papel m; (before n) ⟨towel/handkerchief/bag⟩ de papel **(b)** (wrapper) (esp BrE) envoltorio m [2] (newspaper) diario m, periódico m [3] (for journal) trabajo m; (at conference) ponencia f [4] (exam ∼) (BrE) examen m; (part) parte f [5] **papers** pl (documents) documentos mpl

paper[2] vt ⟨wall/room⟩ empapelar or (Méx tb) tapizar*

paper: ∼**back** n libro m en rústica or (Méx) de pasta blanda; ∼**clip** n clip m, sujetapapeles m; ∼**weight** n pisapapeles m; ∼**work** n papeleo m (fam), trabajo m administrativo

paprika /pə'priːkə ‖'pæprɪkə/ n pimentón m dulce, paprika f

Pap smear, Pap test /pæp/ n (AmE) citología f, frotis m, Papanicolau m (AmL)

Papua New Guinea /'pɑːpuə ‖'pæpjʊə/ n Papua Nueva Guinea f

papyrus /pə'paɪrəs/ n (pl **-ruses** or **-ri** /-raɪ/) papiro m

par /pɑːr ‖pɑː(r)/ n [1] **(a)** (equal level) on a ∼: the two athletes are on a ∼ los dos atletas son del mismo nivel; this puts us on a ∼ with workers in other countries esto nos pone en igualdad de condiciones con los trabajadores de otros países **(b)** (accepted standard): your work is below o not up to ∼ tu trabajo no está a la altura de lo que se esperaba; to feel below o under∼ no sentirse* del todo bien [2] (in golf) par m

parable /'pærəbəl/ n parábola f

parachute[1] /'pærəʃuːt/ n paracaídas m

parachute[2] vi saltar en or con paracaídas

parachutist /'pærəʃuːtəst ‖'pærəʃuːtɪst/ n paracaidista mf

parade[1] /pə'reɪd/ n **(a)** (procession) desfile m **(b)** (assembly) (Mil) formación f

parade[2] vt **(a)** (display) ⟨wealth⟩ hacer* ostentación de **(b)** (march, walk) ⟨streets⟩ desfilar por **(c)** (assemble) ⟨troops⟩ hacer* formar ■ ∼ vi **(a)** (march, walk) desfilar **(b)** (assemble) (Mil) formar

paradise /'pærədaɪs/ n **(a)** (heaven) paraíso m **(b)** **Paradise** (Garden of Eden) Paraíso m (Terrenal)

paradox /'pærədɑːks ‖'pærədɒks/ n paradoja f

paraffin /'pærəfən ‖'pærəfɪn/ n **(a)** ∼ **(wax)** parafina f **(b)** ∼ **(oil)** (BrE) queroseno m, kerosene m, parafina f (Chi)

paragliding /'pærə,glaɪdɪŋ/ n parapente m

paragon /'pærəgɑːn ‖'pærəgən/ n: **a** ∼ **of** virtue (set phrase) un dechado de virtudes (fr hecha)

paragraph /'pærəgræf ‖'pærəgrɑːf/ n párrafo m

Paraguay /'pærəgwaɪ/ n Paraguay m

Paraguayan[1] /'pærə'gwaɪən/ adj paraguayo

Paraguayan[2] n paraguayo, -ya m,f

parallel[1] /'pærəlel/ adj paralelo

parallel[2] n [1] (Math) (line) paralela f [2] (similarity) paralelismo m, paralelo m; **without** ∼ sin parangón

parallel[3] vt **-l-** or (BrE also) **-ll-** (frml) ser* análogo or paralelo a

parallel bars pl n (barras fpl) paralelas fpl

paralysis /pə'ræləsəs ‖pə'ræləsɪs/ n (pl **-ses** /-siːz/)(Med) parálisis f

paralyze /'pærəlaɪz/ vt paralizar*

paramedic /'pærə'medɪk/ n: profesional conectado con la medicina, como enfermero, kinesiólogo etc

parameter /pə'ræmətər ‖pə'ræmɪtə(r)/ n parámetro m

paramilitary /'pærə'mɪləteri ‖,pærə'mɪlɪtəri/ adj paramilitar

paramount /'pærəmaʊnt/ adj (frml) primordial

paranoia /'pærə'nɔɪə/ n paranoia f

paranoid /'pærənɔɪd/ adj paranoico

parapet /'pærəpət ‖'pærəpɪt/ n parapeto m

paraphernalia /'pærəfər'neɪljə ‖,pærəfə'neɪliə/ n parafernalia f

paraphrase /'pærəfreɪz/ vt parafrasear

paraplegic /,pærə'pliːdʒɪk/ n parapléjico, -ca m,f

parasailing /'pærəseɪlɪŋ/ n parasailing m

parasite /'pærəsaɪt/ n parásito m

parasol /'pærəsɔːl ‖'pærəsɒl/ n sombrilla f, quitasol m

paratrooper /'pærə,truːpər ‖'pærə,truːpə(r)/ n (Mil) paracaidista mf (del ejército)

parcel /'pɑːrsəl ‖'pɑːsəl/ n (BrE) paquete m

parched /pɑːrtʃt ‖pɑːtʃt/ adj **(a)** (very dry) reseco **(b)** (very thirsty) (colloq) ⟨pred⟩ muerto de sed (fam)

parchment /'pɑːrtʃmənt ‖'pɑːtʃmənt/ n pergamino m

pardon[1] /'pɑːrdn ‖'pɑːdn/ n [1] **(a)** (forgiveness) perdón m **(b)** (as interj): ∼? o (frml) **I beg your** ∼? (requesting repetition) ¿cómo?, ¿mande? (Méx); **I beg your** ∼ (apologizing) perdón [2] (Law) indulto m

pardon[2] vt [1] (forgive) perdonar; ∼ **me!** (apologizing) ¡perdón!; ∼ **me?** (requesting repetition) (esp AmE) ¿cómo? [2] (Law) ⟨offender⟩ indultar

pare /per ‖peə(r)/ vt **(a)** (peel) pelar **(b)** ⟨nails⟩ cortar

■ **pare down** [v + o + adv, v + adv + o] reducir*

parent /'perənt ‖'peərənt/ n: **my/his** ~s mis/ sus padres; **the responsibility of being a** ~ las responsabilidades que conlleva el ser padre/ madre; (before n) ~ **company** sociedad f matriz

parental /pə'rentl/ adj de los padres

parenthesis /pə'renθəsəs ‖pə'renθəsɪs/ n (pl **-theses** /-θəsi:z/) paréntesis m; **in parentheses** entre paréntesis

parenthood /'perənthʊd ‖'peərənthʊd/ n el ser padre/madre

parenting /'perəntɪŋ ‖'peərəntɪŋ/ n crianza f de los hijos

Paris /'pærəs ‖'pærɪs/ n París f

parish /'pærɪʃ/ n 1 (Relig) parroquia f; (before n) ~ **church** parroquia f, iglesia f parroquial 2 (Govt) distrito m

parishioner /pə'rɪʃənər ‖pə'rɪʃənə(r)/ n feligrés, -gresa m,f (de una parroquia)

Parisian /pə'rɪʒən ‖pə'rɪziən/ n parisino, -na m,f, parisiense mf, parisién mf

parity /'pærəti/ n(equality) (frml) igualdad f, paridad f

park¹ /pɑːrk ‖pɑːk/ n parque m; (before n) ~ **bench** banco m or (Méx) banca f (de plaza)

park² vt ⟨car⟩ estacionar (esp AmL), aparcar* (Esp), parquear (AmL)
■ ~ vi (Auto) estacionar (esp AmL), aparcar* (Esp), parquear (AmL), estacionarse (Chi, Méx)

parking /'pɑːrkɪŋ ‖'pɑːkɪŋ/ n estacionamiento m (esp AmL), aparcamiento m (Esp); ⊗ **no parking** prohibido estacionar (esp AmL) or (Esp) aparcar or (AmL) parquear; (before n) **a** ~ **place** o **space** un lugar para estacionar (or aparcar etc); ~ **ticket** multa f (por estacionamiento indebido)

parking: ~ garage n (AmE) estacionamiento m (esp AmL), aparcamiento m (Esp), parking m (Esp); ~ **lot** n (AmE) estacionamiento m (esp AmL), aparcamiento m (Esp), parking m (Esp), parqueadero m (Col); ~ **meter** n parquímetro m

Parkinson's Disease /'pɑːrkənsənz ‖'pɑːkɪnsənz/ n enfermedad f de Parkinson, Parkinson m

parkway /'pɑːrkweɪ ‖'pɑːkweɪ/ n (AmE) carretera f/avenida f ajardinada

parliament /'pɑːrləmənt ‖'pɑːləmənt/ n (a) (assembly) parlamento m (b) **Parliament** (in UK etc) Parlamento m

parliamentary /ˌpɑːrlə'mentəri ‖ˌpɑːlə'mentri/ adj parlamentario

parlor, (BrE) **parlour** /'pɑːrlər ‖'pɑːlə(r)/ n 1 (dated in BrE) (in house) salón m (esp Esp), sala f (de estar) 2 (for business) (AmE) sala f; **ice-cream** ~ heladería f

Parmesan (cheese) /'pɑːrməzɑːn ‖'pɑːmɪzæn/ n (queso m) parmesano m

parochial /pə'rəʊkiəl/ adj (a) (pej) ⟨person/ attitude/outlook⟩ provinciano (b) (Relig) parroquial

parody¹ /'pærədi/ n (pl **-dies**) parodia f

parody² vt **-dies, -dying, -died** parodiar

parole /pə'rəʊl/ n libertad f condicional

paroxysm /'pærəksɪzəm/ n (Med) paroxismo m; **the news sent them into** ~s **of laughter** la noticia los hizo desternillarse de risa

parquet /pɑːr'keɪ ‖'pɑːkeɪ/ n 1 (Const) parqué m, parquet m 2 (AmE Theat) platea f

parrot /'pærət/ n loro m, papagayo m

parry /'pæri/ vt **-ries, -rying, -ried** ⟨blow/ thrust⟩ parar; ⟨attack⟩ rechazar*; ⟨question⟩ eludir

parsley /'pɑːrsli ‖'pɑːsli/ n perejil m

parsnip /'pɑːrsnəp ‖'pɑːsnɪp/ n chirivía f, pastinaca f

parson /'pɑːrsn̩ ‖'pɑːsn̩/ n clérigo m; (vicar) ≈(cura m) párroco m

part¹ /pɑːrt ‖pɑːt/ n 1 (a) (section) parte f (b) (in phrases) **in part** en parte; **for the most part** en su mayor parte; **for my part** por mi parte, por mi lado
2 (component) pieza f; (spare ~) repuesto m or (Méx) refacción f
3 (a) (in play) papel m (b) (role, share) papel m; **she had** o **played a major** ~ **in** ... tuvo or desempeñó un papel fundamental en ...; **to take** ~ **in sth** tomar parte en algo
4 (episode of TV, radio serial) episodio m; (Publ) fascículo m
5 (Mus) (vocal, instrumental line) parte f
6 (in hair) (AmE) raya f, carrera f (Col, Ven), partidura f (Chi)
7 **parts** pl (area): **in/around these** ~s por aquí; **in foreign** ~s en el extranjero

part² vt (separate) separar
■ ~ vi (a) (separate) ⟨lovers⟩ separarse; **they** ~ed **on bad terms** quedaron disgustados (b) ⟨curtains/lips⟩ (open up) abrirse*
■ **part with** [v + prep + o] desprenderse de

part³ adv en parte

part⁴ adj (before n) ⟨payment⟩ parcial

part exchange n (esp BrE): **in** ~ ~ a cuenta or como parte del pago

partial /'pɑːrʃəl ‖'pɑːʃəl/ adj 1 (not complete) parcial 2 (a) (fond) (pred) **to be** ~ **TO sth** tener* debilidad POR algo (b) (biased) (frml) parcial

partially /'pɑːrʃəli ‖'pɑːʃəli/ adv (a) (partly) parcialmente (b) (with bias) con parcialidad

participant /pər'tɪsəpənt, pɑːr- ‖pɑː'tɪsɪpənt/ n participante mf

participate /pər'tɪsəpeɪt, pɑːr- ‖pɑː'tɪsɪpeɪt/ vi **to** ~ (IN sth) participar (EN algo)

participation /pərˌtɪsə'peɪʃən, pɑːr- ‖pɑːˌtɪsɪ'peɪʃən/ n participación f

participle /'pɑːrtəsɪpəl ‖'pɑːtɪsɪpəl/ n participio m

particle /'pɑːrtɪkəl ‖'pɑːtɪkəl/ n partícula f

particular¹ /pər'tɪkjələr ‖pə'tɪkjʊlə(r)/ adj 1 (specific, precise): **this** ~ **one** este en especial; **is there any** ~ **style you'd prefer?** ¿tiene preferencia por algún estilo determinado?; **for no** ~ **reason** por nada en especial 2 (special) ⟨interest/concern⟩ especial 3 (fastidious) (pred) **to be** ~ (ABOUT sth): **she's very** ~ **about what she eats** es muy especial con la comida

particular² n (a) (detail) (frml) (usu pl) detalle m 2 **in particular** en particular

particularly /pər'tɪkjələrli ‖pə'tɪkjʊləli/ adv (a) (specifically) específicamente (b) (especially) particularmente

parting¹ /'pɑːtɪŋ ‖'pɑːtɪŋ/ n **1** (separation) despedida f **2** (in hair) (BrE) raya f, carrera f (Col, Ven), partidura f (Chi)

parting² adj (before n) ‹kiss/words› de despedida

partisan¹ /'pɑːtɪzæn ‖'pɑːtɪzæn/ n (a) (guerrilla) partisano, -na m,f (b) (supporter) partidario, -ria m,f

partisan² adj ‹crowd/decision› partidista

partition¹ /pər'tɪʃən, pɑːr- ‖pɑː'tɪʃən/ n **1** (a) (screen) tabique m, mampara de vidrio or (Esp) de cristal (b) (divider) separador m **2** (of country, territory) división f

partition² vt (a) ‹country/territory› dividir (b) ‹room› dividir con un tabique/con una mampara

partly /'pɑːtli ‖'pɑːtli/ adv en parte

partner¹ /'pɑːtnər ‖'pɑːtnə(r)/ n (a) (in an activity) compañero, -ra m,f; (in dancing, tennis) pareja f (b) (Busn) socio, -cia m,f; ~s in crime cómplices mpl or fpl (c) (in personal relationship) pareja f, compañero, -ra m,f

partner² vt bailar (or jugar* etc) en pareja con

partnership /'pɑːtnərʃɪp ‖'pɑːtnəʃɪp/ n (a) (relationship) asociación f (b) (Busn) sociedad f (collective)

part of speech n (pl ~s or ~) categoría f gramatical

partridge /'pɑːtrɪdʒ ‖'pɑːtrɪdʒ/ n (pl ~s or ~) perdiz f

part-time¹ /'pɑːttaɪm ‖,pɑːt'taɪm/ adj de medio tiempo (AmL), a tiempo parcial (Esp)

part-time² adv de medio tiempo (AmL), a tiempo parcial (Esp)

party¹ /'pɑːti ‖'pɑːti/ n **1** (event) fiesta f; I was invited to a tea ~ me invitaron a un té **2** (Pol) partido m **3** (group) grupo m; (in hunting) partida f **4** (person or body involved) parte f; the guilty/innocent ~ el culpable/inocente

party² vi (esp AmE colloq) (go to parties) ir* a fiestas; (have fun) divertirse*

party line n (Pol) the ~ ~ la línea del partido

pass¹ /pæs ‖pɑːs/ n **1** (document, permit) pase m; (ticket) abono m **2** (Geog) paso m; (narrow) desfiladero m **3** (in test, examination) (BrE) aprobado m **4** (Sport) pase m **5** (sexual advance): to make a ~ at sb intentar besar a algn

pass² vt
I 1 (a) (go by, past) ‹shop/house› pasar por; I ~ed him in the street me crucé con él en la calle (b) (overtake) pasar, rebasar (Méx) **2** (a) (cross, go beyond) ‹limit› pasar; ‹frontier› pasar, cruzar* (b) (surpass) sobrepasar **3** (spend) ‹time› pasar; to ~ the time pasar el rato
II (a) (convey, hand over) to ~ sb sth, to ~ sth TO sb pasarle algo A algn (b) (Sport) ‹ball› pasar **III** (a) (succeed in) ‹exam/test› aprobar*, salvar (Ur) (b) (approve) ‹candidate/work› aprobar* (c) ‹law/motion› aprobar*

■ ~ vi
I 1 (move, travel) pasar **2** (a) (go, move past) pasar; I was just ~ing pasaba por aquí; they ~ed on the stairs se cruzaron en la escalera (b) (overtake) adelantarse, rebasar (Méx) **3** (a) (elapse) «time» pasar (b) (disappear) «feeling/pain» pasarse

4 (be transferred) «title/estate/crown» pasar **5** (decline chance to play) pasar; (as interj) ¡paso! **6** (Sport) to ~ (TO sb) pasar(le) la pelota (or el balón etc) (A algn)
II (a) (be acceptable) pasar (b) (in an exam) aprobar

■ **pass away** [v + adv] (frml & euph) fallecer* (frml)

■ **pass by 1** [v + adv] (go past) pasar **2** [v + o + adv] (not affect): he felt life had ~ed him by sentía que no había vivido

■ **pass down** [v + o + adv, v + adv + o] (often pass) ‹heirloom› pasar; ‹story/tradition› transmitir

■ **pass for** [v + prep + o] pasar por

■ **pass off** [v + o + adv, v + adv + o] (represent falsely) hacer* pasar; she ~ed herself off as a journalist se hizo pasar por periodista

■ **pass on 1** [v + o + adv, v + adv + o] ‹information› pasar; ‹infection› contagiar **2** [v + adv] (a) to ~ on TO sth pasar A algo (b) ▶ PASS AWAY

■ **pass out 1** [v + adv] (become unconscious) desmayarse, perder* el conocimiento **2** [v + o + adv, v + adv + o] (distribute) repartir

■ **pass over 1** [v + adv + o] (omit) ‹fact/detail› pasar por alto **2** [v + o + adv] (disregard for promotion) (usu pass) pasarle por encima a

■ **pass through** (a) [v + adv] pasar; we're just ~ing through estamos solo de paso (b) [v + prep + o] ‹town/area› pasar por

■ **pass up** [v + o + adv, v + adv + o] colloq ‹opportunity› dejar pasar

passable /'pæsəbəl ‖'pɑːsəbəl/ adj (a) (adequate) pasable (b) ‹road/route› transitable

passage /'pæsɪdʒ ‖ n **1** (a) (alleyway) callejón m, pasaje m; (narrow) pasadizo m (b) (corridor) (esp BrE) pasillo m (c) (Anat) conducto m **2** (lapse): the ~ of time el paso del tiempo **3** (voyage) viaje m; (fare) pasaje m **4** (extract) pasaje m

passageway /'pæsɪdʒweɪ/ n pasillo m

passenger /'pæsɪndʒər ‖'pæsɪndʒə(r)/ n pasajero, -ra m,f

passer-by /'pæsər'baɪ ‖,pɑːsə'baɪ/ n (pl **passers-by**) transeúnte mf

passing¹ /'pæsɪŋ ‖'pɑːsɪŋ/ adj (before n) **1** (going past): she hailed a ~ taxi llamó a un taxi que pasaba **2** (a) ‹fad/fashion› pasajero; ‹glance› rápido (b) (casual): it was only a ~ thought simplemente fue algo que se me ocurrió

passing² n in passing al pasar, de pasada

passing lane n (AmE) carril m de adelantamiento

passion /'pæʃən/ n pasión f

passionate /'pæʃənət/ adj ‹love› apasionado; ‹hatred› mortal; ‹admirer› ardiente; ‹speech› vehemente

passionately /'pæʃənətli/ adv ‹love› apasionadamente; ‹believe› fervientemente; ‹desire› ardientemente

passion fruit n granadilla f, maracuyá m, parchita f (Ven)

passive¹ /'pæsɪv/ adj pasivo

passive² n voz f pasiva

pass: ~ **key** n llave f maestra; **P~over** n

Pascua f ⟨judía⟩; **∼port** n pasaporte m; **∼word** n (a) (secret word or phrase) contraseña f (b) (Comput) clave f de acceso

past¹ /pæst ‖pɑːst/ adj **1** (a) (former) anterior; ⟨life⟩ pasado; (old) antiguo (b) (most recent) ⟨week/ month/year⟩ último (c) (finished, gone) (pred): what's ∼ is ∼ lo pasado, pasado **2** (Ling): the ∼ tense el pasado, el pretérito

past² n **1** (a) (former times) pasado m; steam trains are a thing of the ∼ las locomotoras de vapor han pasado a la historia; in the ∼, women ... antes or antiguamente las mujeres ...; that's all in the ∼ eso forma parte del pasado (b) (of person) pasado m; (of place) historia f **2** (Ling) pasado m, pretérito m

past³ prep **1** (a) (by the side of): I go ∼ their house every morning paso por (delante de) su casa todas las mañanas; she walked straight ∼ him pasó de largo por su lado (b) (beyond): it's just ∼ the school queda un poco más allá de la escuela **2** (a) (after) (esp BrE): it's ten ∼ six/half ∼ two son las seis y diez/las dos y media; it was ∼ eleven eran las once pasadas; it's ∼ your bedtime ya deberías estar acostado (b) (older than): I'm ∼ the age/stage when ... ya he pasado la edad/ superado la etapa en que ... **3** (outside, beyond): to be ∼ -ING: I'm ∼ caring ya no me importa; I wouldn't put it ∼ her no me extrañaría que lo hiciera; to be ∼ it (colloq) estar* para el arrastre (fam)

past⁴ adv (a) (with verbs of motion): to fly/cycle/ drive ∼ pasar volando/en bicicleta/en coche; he hurried ∼ pasó a toda prisa (b) (giving time) (esp BrE): it's twenty-five ∼ son y veinticinco

pasta /'pɑːstə ‖'pæstə/ n pasta(s) f(pl)

paste /peɪst/ n (a) (thick mixture) pasta f (b) (glue) engrudo m; (wallpaper ∼) pegamento m, cola f (c) (imitation gem) estrás m

pastel /pæs'tel ‖'pæstl/ n (a) (Art) (crayon) pastel m (b) (pale shade) tono m pastel; (before n) ⟨shades/color⟩ pastel adj inv

pasteurize /'pæstʃəraɪz ‖'pɑːstʃəraɪz/ vt pasteurizar*, pasterizar*

pastille /pæs'tiːl ‖'pæstɪl/ n pastilla f

pastime /'pæstaɪm ‖'pɑːstaɪm/ n pasatiempo m

pastor /'pæstər ‖'pɑːstə(r)/ n pastor, -tora m,f

pastoral /'pæstərəl ‖'pɑːstərəl/ adj (a) ⟨painting/scene⟩ pastoril (b) (Relig) ⟨care/duties⟩ pastoral

pastry /'peɪstri/ n (pl **-tries**) (a) (substance) masa f (b) (cake) pastelito m or (RPl) masa f

pasture¹ /'pæstʃər ‖'pɑːstʃə(r)/ n (a) (grazing land) pastos mpl (b) (grass) pasto m, pastura f

pasture² vt apacentar*, pastar

pasty /'pæsti/ n (pl **-ties**) (esp BrE) empanada f (AmL), empanadilla f (Esp)

pat¹ /pæt/ vt **-tt-** darle* palmaditas a

pat² n **1** (tap) palmadita f; (touch) toque m **2** (of butter) porción f

pat³ adj (pej) ⟨answer⟩ fácil

pat⁴ adv (by heart): to have o know sth down (AmE) o (BrE) off ∼ saberse* algo al dedillo

patch¹ /pætʃ/ n **1** (a) (for mending clothes) remiendo m, parche m; (for reinforcing) refuerzo m; (on knee) rodillera f; (on elbow) codera f (b) (eye ∼) parche m ⟨en el ojo⟩ **2** (a) (area): she slipped on a ∼ of ice/oil resbaló en el hielo/en una mancha de aceite; a damp ∼ una mancha de humedad; to go through a bad o rough o sticky ∼ (BrE) pasar por una mala racha (b) (of land): a ∼ of ground un área de terreno; a vegetable ∼ un huerto (c) (territory) (BrE colloq): my/his ∼ mi/su territorio

patch² vt remendar*, parchar (esp AmL)

■ **patch up** [v + o + adv, v + adv + o] (a) (mend) ⟨roof/furniture⟩ hacerle* un arreglo a ⟨provisionalmente⟩; ⟨clothes⟩ remendar*, parchar (esp AmL); ⟨hole⟩ ponerle* un parche a (b) (resolve, settle): I tried to help ∼ things up betweem them quise ayudar para que hicieran las paces

patchwork /'pætʃwɜːrk ‖'pætʃwɜːk/ n patchwork m, labor f de retazos or (Esp) retales; (before n) ⟨quilt⟩ de patchwork, de retazos or (Esp) retales

patchy /'pætʃi/ adj **-chier**, **-chiest** ⟨paintwork/color⟩ disparejo; ⟨coverage⟩ incompleto; ⟨description⟩ fragmentario; ⟨performance/work⟩ irregular; ∼ fog zonas fpl de niebla

pâté /pɑːˈteɪ ‖'pæteɪ/ n paté m

patent¹ /'pætṇt ‖'peɪtṇt, 'pætṇt/ n patente f

patent² /'pætṇt ‖'peɪtṇt, 'pætṇt/ vt patentar

patent³ adj /'peɪtṇt, 'pæt- ‖'peɪtṇt/ (frml) patente

patent leather /'pætṇt ‖'peɪtṇt, 'pæt-/ n charol m

patently /'peɪtṇtli, 'pæt- ‖'peɪtṇtli/ adv: it's ∼ clear o obvious that ... salta a la vista que ...

paternal /pə'tɜːrnl ‖pə'tɜːnl/ adj (a) (fatherly) ⟨affection⟩ paternal; ⟨pride⟩ de padre; ⟨trait/ inheritance⟩ paterno (b) (on father's side) (before n) por parte de padre

paternity /pə'tɜːrnəti ‖pə'tɜːnəti/ n (frml) paternidad f

path /pæθ ‖pɑːθ/ n (a) (track, walkway) sendero m, senda f (b) (of missile) trayectoria f; (of the sun) recorrido m

pathetic /pə'θetɪk/ adj (a) (pitiful) patético (b) (feeble) (colloq): what a ∼ excuse! ¡qué excusa más pobre!; don't be so ∼ no seas tan pusilánime

pathological /'pæθə'lɑːdʒɪkəl ‖,pæθə'lɒdʒɪkəl/ adj patológico

pathologist /pə'θɑːlədʒəst ‖pə'θɒlədʒɪst/ n patólogo, -ga m,f

pathology /pə'θɑːlədʒi ‖pə'θɒlədʒi/ n patología f

pathos /'peɪθɑːs ‖'peɪθɒs/ n patetismo m

pathway /'pæθweɪ ‖'pɑːθweɪ/ n camino m, sendero m

patience /'peɪʃəns/ n (a) (quality) paciencia f (b) (cards) (BrE) solitario m

patient¹ /'peɪʃənt/ adj paciente; to be ∼ WITH sb tener* paciencia CON algn

patient² n paciente mf

patiently /'peɪʃəntli/ adv pacientemente

patio /'pætiəʊ/ n patio m

patriot /'peɪtriət ‖'pætriət, 'peɪ-/ n patriota mf

patriotic /'peɪtri'ɑːtɪk ‖,pætri'ɒtɪk, 'peɪ-/ adj patriótico

patriotism /'peɪtrɪətɪzəm ‖ 'pætrɪətɪzəm, 'peɪ-/ *n* patriotismo *m*

patrol¹ /pə'trəʊl/ *n* **(a)** (act) patrulla *f*; **to be on ∼** estar* patrullando, estar* de patrulla; *(before n)* **∼ car** coche *m* patrulla, patrullero *m* (RPl), auto *m* patrulla (Chi) **(b)** (group) patrulla *f*

patrol² *vt/i* **-ll-** patrullar

patron /'peɪtrən/ *n* **(a)** (sponsor) patrocinador, -dora *m,f*; **a ∼ of the arts** un mecenas **(b)** (customer) *(frml)* cliente, -ta *m,f*

patronize /'peɪtrənaɪz/ *vt* **1** (condescend to) tratar con condescendencia **2** (frequent) *(frml)* *(shop/hotel)* ser* cliente de; *(theater/cinema)* frecuentar

patronizing /'peɪtrənaɪzɪŋ ‖ 'pætrənaɪzɪŋ/ *adj* condescendiente

patter¹ /'pætər ‖ 'pætə(r)/ *vi* golpetear

patter² *n* **1** (of rain) golpeteo *m* **2** (talk): **he has a good sales ∼** tiene mucha labia para vender

pattern /'pætərn ‖ 'pætən/ *n* **1 (a)** (decoration) diseño *m*, dibujo *m*; (on fabric) diseño *m*, estampado *m* **(b)** (order, arrangement): **it follows the normal ∼** sigue las pautas normales; **the murders all seem to follow a ∼** todos los asesinatos parecen responder al mismo patrón **2 (a)** (model) modelo *m* **(b)** (in dressmaking) patrón *m*, molde *m* (CS) **(c)** (sample) muestra *f*

patterned /'pætərnd ‖ 'pætənd/ *adj* con dibujos; *(fabric)* estampado

paunch /pɔːntʃ/ *n* panza *f* (fam)

pauper /'pɔːpər ‖ 'pɔːpə(r)/ *n* pobre *mf*

pause¹ /pɔːz/ *n* pausa *f*; **without ∼** sin interrupción

pause² *vi* (in speech) hacer* una pausa; (in movement) detenerse*

pave /peɪv/ *vt* (with concrete) pavimentar; (with flagstones) enlosar; (with stones) empedrar*

pavement /'peɪvmənt/ *n* **(a)** (paved area) pavimento *m* **(b)** (beside road) (BrE) ▶ SIDEWALK

pavilion /pə'vɪljən/ *n* **(a)** (tent, stand) pabellón *m* **(b)** (BrE Sport) caseta *f*

paving /'peɪvɪŋ/ *n* pavimento *m*; (of flagstones) enlosado *m*, (of stones) empedrado *m*; *(before n)* **∼ stone** losa *f*

paw¹ /pɔː/ *n* pata *f*

paw² *vt* *(animal)* tocar* con la pata; **to ∼ the ground** *(horse)* piafar

pawn¹ /pɔːn/ *n* **(a)** (in chess) peón *m* **(b)** (manipulated person) títere *m*

pawn² *vt* empeñar

pawnbroker /'pɔːnbrəʊkər ‖ 'pɔːnbrəʊkə(r)/ *n* prestamista *mf*

pay¹ /peɪ/ (*past & past p* **paid**) *vt* **1 (a)** *(tax/rent/sum/debt)* pagar*; **how much did you ∼ for the painting?** ¿cuánto te costó el cuadro? **(b)** *(employee/creditor/tradesperson)* pagarle* a; **to ∼ sb FOR sth** pagarle* algo A algn **2** *(respects)* presentar; *(attention)* prestar
■ **∼** *vi* **1 (a)** *(person)* pagar* **(b)** *(work/activity)* pagarse*; **teaching doesn't ∼ very well** la enseñanza no está muy bien pagada

2 (suffer) **to ∼ for sth** pagar* algo; **he paid for the mistake with his life** el error le costó la vida
■ **∼** *v impers* convenir*
■ **pay back** [*v + o + adv, v + adv + o*] **1** (repay) *(money)* devolver*, regresar (AmL exc CS); *(loan/mortgage)* pagar*; **to ∼ sb back** devolverle *or* (AmL exc CS) regresarle el dinero a algn
2 (take revenge on): **I'll ∼ you back!** ¡ya me las vas a pagar!
■ **pay in** [*v + o + adv, v + adv + o*] (BrE) *(money)* depositar *or* (Esp) ingresar *or* (Col) consignar
■ **pay off** **1** [*v + o + adv, v + adv + o*] *(debt)* cancelar, saldar; *(worker)* liquidarle el sueldo (*or* jornal *etc*) a (al despedirlo)
2 [*v + adv*] (prove worthwhile) valer* la pena; *(gamble)* resultar
■ **pay out** [*v + o + adv, v + adv + o*] pagar*
■ **pay up** [*v + adv*] pagar*

pay² *n* (of manual worker) paga *f*; (of employee) sueldo *m*; **equal ∼** igualdad *f* salarial; *(before n)* **∼ increase** aumento *m* salarial

payable /'peɪəbəl/ *adj* (frml) *(pred)* pagadero; **the rent becomes ∼ on the first of the month** el alquiler vence el primero de mes; **make the check ∼ to ...** extienda el cheque a nombre de ...

pay: ∼check, (BrE) **∼ cheque** *n* cheque *m* del sueldo; (salary) sueldo *m*; **∼day** *n* día *m* de paga

payee /peɪ'iː/ *n* beneficiario, -ria *m,f*

payment /'peɪmənt/ *n* **(a)** (of debt, money, wage) pago *m*; **he received no ∼ for what he did** no recibió remuneración por lo que hizo (frml) **(b)** (installment) plazo *m*, cuota *f* (AmL)

pay: ∼ phone *n* teléfono *m* público, monedero *m* (público) (Ur); **∼roll** *n* (list) nómina *f*, planilla *f* (de sueldos) (AmL), plantilla *f* (Esp) **(b)** (wages) nómina *f*; **∼ slip** *n* nómina *f*, recibo *m* del sueldo

PC¹ *n* **1** = **personal computer** **2** (in UK) = **police constable**

PC² *adj* = **politically correct**

PD *n* (in US) = **Police Department**

PE *n* = **physical education**

pea /piː/ *n* arveja *f or* (Esp) guisante *m or* (AmC, Méx) chícharo *m*

peace /piːs/ *n* **1** paz *f*; **in o at ∼** en paz; *(before n)* para la paz; *(proposal/initiative/treaty)* de paz; *(talks/march/campaign)* por la paz; **the ∼ movement** el movimiento pacifista; **as a ∼ offering** en señal de reconciliación **2** (Law): **to keep the ∼** mantener* el orden **3** (tranquillity) paz *f*; **I went to the library for some ∼ and quiet** me fui a la biblioteca para poder estar tranquilo; **I turned off the gas for my own ∼ of mind** apagué el gas para quedarme tranquilo

peaceful /'piːsfəl/ *adj* **(a)** (calm, quiet) *(place)* tranquilo **(b)** (non-violent) *(protest)* pacífico; **they are a ∼ people** son un pueblo amante de la paz

peacefully /'piːsfəli/ *adv* *(sleep)* plácidamente; *(read/sit)* tranquilamente

peace: ~**keeping** adj (before n): ~keeping forces fuerzas fpl de paz; ~**maker** n conciliador, -dora m,f; ~**time** n época f de paz

peach /piːtʃ/ n durazno m (esp AmL), melocotón m (Esp); (before n) ~ tree duraznero m (esp AmL), melocotonero m (Esp)

peacock /'piːkɑːk ‖'piːkɒk/ n pavo m real

peak¹ /piːk/ n **(a)** (of mountain) cima f, cumbre f; (mountain) pico m; (of cap) visera f **(b)** (highest point): at the ~ of her career en el apogeo de su carrera

peak² adj (before n) **(a)** (maximum) ‹level/power› máximo; to be in ~ condition «athlete/horse» estar* en plena forma **(b)** (busiest): during ~ hours durante las horas de mayor demanda (or consumo etc); ~ rate tarifa f alta

peal /piːl/ n: ~ of bells (sound) repique m de campanas; (set) carillón m; ~s of laughter carcajadas fpl; a ~ of thunder un trueno

peanut /'piːnʌt/ n **(a)** (Agr, Culin) maní m or (Esp) cacahuete m or (Méx) cacahuate m **(b)** **peanuts** pl (small sum) (colloq) una miseria (fam)

peanut butter n mantequilla f de maní or (Esp) de cacahuete or (Méx) de cacahuate, manteca f de maní (RPl)

pear /per ‖peə(r)/ n pera f; ~ (tree) peral m

pearl /pɜːrl ‖pɜːl/ n **(a)** perla f; ~s of wisdom sabias palabras fpl, (iro) joyitas fpl (iró) **(b)** (mother-of-~) nácar m, madreperla f, concha f nácar (Méx), concha f de perla (Chi)

peasant /'peznt/ n campesino, -na m,f

peat /piːt/ n turba f

pebble /'pebəl/ n guijarro m

pecan /pɪ'kæn ‖'piːkən/ n pacana f, nuez f (Méx)

peck¹ /pek/ n **(a)** (of bird) picotazo m **(b)** (kiss) beso m

peck² vt picotear

pecking order /'pekɪŋ/ n jerarquía f

peckish /'pekɪʃ/ adj (esp BrE colloq) (pred) to be o feel ~ tener* un poco de hambre

peculiar /pɪ'kjuːljər ‖pɪ'kjuːliə(r)/ adj **(a)** (strange) raro, extraño **(b)** (particular, exclusive) peculiar, característico

peculiarity /pɪ'kjuːli'ærəti ‖pɪ,kjuːli'ærəti/ n (pl **-ties**) (sth unusual) rasgo m singular; (oddity) rareza f

pedal¹ /'pedl/ n pedal m

pedal² vi, (BrE) **-ll-** pedalear

pedal bin n (BrE) cubo m or (Méx) bote m or (CS) tacho m or (Ven) tobo m or (Col) caneca f de la basura (con pedal)

pedantic /pɪ'dæntɪk/ adj pedante

peddle /'pedl/ vt vender (en las calles o de puerta en puerta); to ~ drugs traficar* con drogas

peddler /'pedlər ‖'pedlə(r)/ n vendedor, -dora ambulante m,f; (in former times) buhonero m; a drug ~ un traficante de drogas

pedestal /'pedəstl ‖'pedɪstl/ n pedestal m

pedestrian¹ /pə'destriən ‖pɪ'destriən/ n peatón, -tona m,f; (before n) ~ crossing cruce m peatonal or de peatones; ~ mall o (BrE) precinct zona f peatonal

pedestrian² adj pedestre

pediatric, (BrE also) **paediatric** /'piːdi'ætrɪk/ adj ‹hospital› pediátrico; ‹specialist› en pediatría

pediatrician, (BrE also) **paediatrician** /'piːdiə'trɪʃən/ n pediatra mf

pedicure /'pedɪkjʊr ‖'pedɪkjʊə(r)/ n: to have a ~ arreglarse/hacerse* arreglar los pies

pedigree /'pedəgri ‖'pedɪgriː/ n **(a)** (ancestry — of animal) pedigrí m; (— of person) linaje m; (before n) ‹bull/dog› de raza **(b)** (certificate, document) pedigrí m

pedlar /'pedlər ‖'pedlə(r)/ n (BrE) ▶ PEDDLER

pedophile, (BrE) **paedophile** /'piːdəfaɪl/ n pedófilo, -la m,f

pee¹ /piː/ vi (past & past p **peed**) (colloq) hacer* pis or pipí (fam), hacer* del uno (Méx, Per fam & euf)

pee² n (colloq) (no pl) pis m (fam), pipí m (fam)

peek¹ /piːk/ vi ~ (AT sth/sb) mirar (algo/a algn) (a hurtadillas), vichar (algo/a algn) (RPl fam)

peek² n to take o have a ~ at sth echar(le) una miradita a algo, vichar algo (RPl fam)

peel¹ /piːl/ vt ‹apple/potato› pelar
■ ~ vi «person» pelarse; «paint» desconcharse; «wallpaper» despegarse*
■ **peel off** ⏵ [v + adv] «wallpaper/label» despegarse*; ‹paint› desconcharse ⏵ [v + o + adv, v + adv + o] ‹stamp/sticker› despegar*; ‹paint/bark› quitar

peel² n (of potato, apple) piel f, cáscara f (esp AmL); (of orange, lemon) cáscara f

peelings /'piːlɪŋz/ pl n cáscaras fpl, peladuras fpl

peep¹ /piːp/ vi **(a)** (watch) espiar*, vichar (RPl fam); (look quickly) mirar (a hurtadillas), vichar (RPl fam) **(b)** (show, stick out) ~ (out) asomar
■ ~ vt (colloq): I ~ed the horn toqué la bocina or el claxon

peep² n ⏵ **(quick or furtive look)** vistazo m; to have a ~ AT sth echarle un vistazo A algo ⏷ (of bird) pío m; (of car horn) pitido m

peephole /'piːphəʊl/ n mirilla f

peer¹ /pɪr ‖pɪə(r)/ n ⏵ **(a)** (equal) par mf **(b)** (contemporary) coetáneo, -nea m,f ⏷ (lord) (in UK) par m

peer² vi: to ~ AT sth/sb (with difficulty) mirar algo/a algn con ojos de miope; (closely) mirar algo/a algn detenidamente

peerage /'pɪrɪdʒ ‖'pɪərɪdʒ/ n the ~ la nobleza

peer group n grupo m paritario (frml)

peeved /piːvd/ adj ‹expression/look› de fastidio; to be o feel ~ estar* molesto

peevish /'piːvɪʃ/ adj ‹remark› desagradable, malhumorado; to be ~ estar* fastidioso

peg¹ /peg/ n ⏵ **(a)** (in ground) estaca f, (on violin, guitar) clavija f; (tent ~) estaquilla f; (on board game) pieza o ficha que encaja en un tablero **(b)** (clothes-~) (BrE) ▶ CLOTHESPIN ⏷ (hook, hanger) colgador m, perchero m, gancho m

peg² vt **-gg-** (attach, secure) sujetar, asegurar (con estaquillas etc)

pejorative /pɪ'dʒɔːrətɪv ‖pɪ'dʒɒrətɪv/ adj peyorativo

Peking /'piːkɪŋ/ n Pekín m

pelican /'pelɪkən/ n pelícano m

pellet /'pelət ‖'pelɪt/ n **(a)** (of bread, paper) bolita f **(b)** (ammunition) perdigón m

pelt¹ /pelt/ vt: **to ~ sb with tomatoes** lanzarle* tomates a algn

■ **~** vi (colloq) ⊡ (rush): **they came ~ing down the hill** bajaron la cuesta (corriendo) a toda velocidad ⊡ (fall heavily): **it was ~ing with rain** llovía a cántaros

pelt² n (animal skin) piel f; (stripped) cuero m

pelvis /'pelvəs ‖'pelvɪs/ n (pl **-vises**) pelvis f

pen /pen/ n ⊡ (fountain **~**) pluma f fuente (AmL); (ballpoint **~**) bolígrafo m, boli m (Esp fam), birome f (RPl), pluma f atómica (Méx), lápiz m de pasta (Chi); (felt **~**) rotulador m ⊡ (Agr) (sheep **~**) redil m; (cattle **~**) corral m

penal /'piːnl/ adj penal

penalize /'piːnlaɪz ‖'piːnəlaɪz/ vt **(a)** (punish) ⟨player⟩ sancionar **(b)** (make punishable, illegal) penalizar*

penalty /'penlti/ n (pl **-ties**) ⊡ (punishment) pena f; (fine) multa f; **to pay the ~** pagar* las consecuencias ⊡ (Sport) (punishment) penalty m; (in US football) castigo m; **~ (kick)** (in soccer) penalty m, penalti m, penal m (AmL), pénal m (Andes); (before n) **~ area** (in soccer) área f; **~** de penalty

penance /'penəns/ n **(a)** (Relig) penitencia f **(b)** (punishment) (hum) castigo m

pence /pens/ n pl of PENNY 1A

penchant /'pentʃənt ‖'pɒnʃɒŋ/ n (frml) **~ (FOR sth)** inclinación f (POR algo)

pencil /'pensəl/ n lápiz m; **in ~** con lápiz

pencil: ~ case n estuche m (para lápices), plumier m (Esp), chuspa f (Col), cartuchera f (RPl); **~ sharpener** n sacapuntas m, tajalápiz m (Col)

pendant /'pendənt/ n colgante m

pending¹ /'pendɪŋ/ adj **(a)** (awaiting action) (pred): **to be ~** estar* pendiente **(b)** (imminent) próximo

pending² prep (frml) en espera de

pendulum /'pendʒələm ‖'pendjʊləm/ n (pl **-lums**) péndulo m

penetrate /'penɪtreɪt ‖'penɪtreɪt/ vt **(a)** ⟨membrane/defenses⟩ penetrar (en); ⟨armor⟩ atravesar*; ⟨enemy lines⟩ adentrarse en; ⟨territory⟩ penetrar en; ⟨organization⟩ infiltrarse en; ⟨market⟩ introducirse* en **(b)** «liquid» penetrar (en)

■ **~** vi **(a)** «arrow/water/light» penetrar **(b)** (sink in mentally): **it took a long time to ~** tardé (or tardó etc) en entenderlo

penetrating /'penɪtreɪtɪŋ ‖'penɪtreɪtɪŋ/ adj penetrante

penetration /penɪ'treɪʃən ‖,penɪ'treɪʃən/ n penetración f

pen friend n (esp BrE) ▶ PEN PAL

penguin /'peŋgwən ‖'peŋgwɪn/ n pingüino m

penicillin /penɪ'sɪlən ‖,penɪ'sɪlɪn/ n penicilina f

peninsula /pə'nɪnsələ ‖pə'nɪnsjʊlə/ n península f

penis /'piːnəs ‖'piːnɪs/ n pene m

penitent /'penətənt ‖'penɪtənt/ adj arrepentido

penitentiary /penə'tentʃəri ‖,penɪ'tenʃəri/ n (pl **-ries**) (AmE) prisión f

penknife /'pennaɪf/ n (pl **-knives**) navaja f

Penn, Penna = **Pennsylvania**

pen name n seudónimo m

penniless /'penɪləs ‖'penɪlɪs/ adj pobre, sin un céntimo

penny /'peni/ n ⊡ (in UK) **(a)** (pl **pence**) penique m **(b)** (pl **pennies**) (coin) penique m ⊡ (pl **pennies**) (cent coin) (in US, Canada) (colloq) (moneda f de un) centavo m

penny-pinching /'peni,pɪntʃɪŋ/ adj cicatero (fam)

pen pal /'penpæl/ n (esp AmE) amigo, -ga m,f por correspondencia

pension /'pentʃən ‖'penʃən/ n pensión f; (retirement **~**) pensión de jubilación

pensioner /'pentʃənər ‖'penʃənə(r)/ n pensionado, -da m,f, pensionista mf; (retired person) jubilado, -da m,f

pensive /'pensɪv/ adj pensativo

pentagon /'pentəgɑːn ‖'pentəgən/ n **(a)** (Math) pentágono m **(b)** (in US) **the Pentagon** el Pentágono

pentathlon /pen'tæθlən/ n pentatlón m

Pentecost /'pentəkɔːst ‖'pentɪkɒst/ n Pentecostés m

penthouse /'penthaʊs/ n penthouse m

pent-up /'pent'ʌp/ adj (pred **pent up**) ⟨emotions⟩ contenido; ⟨energy⟩ acumulado

penultimate /prɪ'nʌltəmət ‖pen'ʌltɪmət/ adj (before n) penúltimo

people¹ /'piːpəl/ n ⊡ (+ pl vb, no art) **(a)** (in general) gente f; **~ say that ...** dicen que ..., se dice que ...; **some ~ don't like it** a algunos no les gusta **(b)** (individuals) personas fpl **(c)** (specific group): **tall/rich ~** la gente alta/rica, los altos/ricos; **young ~** los jóvenes ⊡ **(a)** (inhabitants) (+ pl vb): **the ~ of this country** la gente de este país; **the country and its ~** el país y su(s) gente(s) **(b)** (citizens, nation) (+ pl vb) **the ~** el pueblo **(c)** (race) (+ sing vb) pueblo m

people² vt poblar*

pepper¹ /'pepər ‖'pepə(r)/ n ⊡ (spice) pimienta f; **black/white ~** pimienta negra/blanca ⊡ (capsicum fruit, plant) pimiento m, pimentón m (AmS exc RPl), ají m (RPl); **green ~** pimiento (or pimentón etc) verde; **red ~** pimiento (or pimentón etc) rojo or colorado, ají m morrón (RPl)

pepper² vt (intersperse) **to ~ sth WITH sth** salpicar* algo DE algo

pepper: ~box n (AmE) pimentero m; **~mint** n **(a)** (plant) menta f; (before n) ⟨tea/oil⟩ de menta; ⟨flavor⟩ a menta **(b)** (sweet) caramelo m de menta; **~pot** n (BrE) pimentero m

pep /pep/: **~ talk** n: **he gave them a ~ talk** les habló para levantarles la moral/infundirles ánimo; **~ up: -pp-** [v + o + adv, v + adv + o] (colloq) ⟨person⟩ animar; (physically) darle* energía a

per /pɜːr ‖pɜː(r)/ prep (for each) por; **£10 ~ head** 10 libras por cabeza; **at $25 ~ kilo** a 25 dólares el kilo; **30 miles ~ hour** 30 millas por hora

per: ~ annum /pər'ænəm/ adv al año, por año; **~ capita** /pər'kæpətə ‖pə'kæpɪtə/ adv per cápita

perceive /pər'si:v ‖pə'si:v/ vt **(a)** ‹object/ sound› percibir **(b)** (realize) percatarse de **(c)** (regard) ver*

percent¹, per cent /pər'sent ‖pə'sent/ n (no pl) porcentaje m

percent², per cent adv por ciento

percentage /pər'sentɪdʒ ‖pə'sentɪdʒ/ n porcentaje m

perceptible /pər'septəbəl ‖pə'septəbəl/ adj perceptible

perception /pər'sepʃən ‖pə'sepʃən/ n **(a)** (faculty) percepción f **(b)** (idea) idea f; (image) imagen f **(c)** (insight) perspicacia f

perceptive /pər'septɪv ‖pə'septɪv/ adj perspicaz

perch¹ /pɜːtʃ ‖pɜːtʃ/ n **1** (in birdcage) percha f **2** (pl ~ or ~es) (fish) perca f

perch² vi ‹bird› posarse; **he ~ed on the edge of the table** se sentó en el borde de la mesa

percolate /'pɜːrkəleɪt ‖'pɜːkəleɪt/ vi **(a)** (filter) filtrarse **(b)** (Culin) ‹coffee› hacerse*

percolator /'pɜːrkəleɪtər ‖'pɜːkəleɪtə(r)/ n cafetera f eléctrica

percussion /pər'kʌʃən ‖pə'kʌʃən/ n percusión f

perennial¹ /pə'reniəl/ adj **(a)** (Bot) perenne **(b)** (recurring) perenne, perpetuo

perennial² n planta f perenne or vivaz

perfect¹ /'pɜːrfɪkt ‖'pɜːfɪkt/ adj **1** (flawless, ideal) perfecto; ‹day/opportunity› ideal; **he speaks ~ French** habla francés perfectamente **2** (complete) (before n): **he's a ~ stranger to me** me es totalmente desconocido

perfect² /pər'fekt ‖pə'fekt/ vt perfeccionar

perfect³ /'pɜːrfɪkt ‖'pɜːfɪkt/ n: **the future/ present ~** el futuro/pretérito perfecto; **the past ~** el pluscuamperfecto

perfection /pər'fekʃən ‖pə'fekʃən/ n **(a)** (state, quality) perfección f **(b)** (act) perfeccionamiento m

perfectionist /pər'fekʃənəst ‖pə'fekʃənɪst/ n perfeccionista mf

perfectly /'pɜːrfɪktli ‖'pɜːfɪktli/ adv **1 (a)** (exactly) ‹round/straight› totalmente; ‹fit/match› perfectamente **(b)** (faultlessly, ideally) perfectamente **2** (completely, utterly) ‹safe/ridiculous› totalmente; **he knows ~ well that ...** sabe perfectamente que ...

perforate /'pɜːrfəreɪt ‖'pɜːfəreɪt/ vt perforar

perforation /'pɜːrfə'reɪʃən ‖,pɜːfə'reɪʃən/ n perforación f; **~s** (on sheet of stamps etc) perforado m

perform /pər'fɔːrm ‖pə'fɔːm/ vi **1** (Mus, Theat) ‹actor/comedian› actuar*; ‹singer› cantar; ‹musician› tocar*; ‹dancer› bailar **2** (work, produce results) ‹student/worker› rendir*, trabajar; ‹team/athlete/vehicle› responder; ‹company/stocks› rendir*
■ **~** vt **1** (Mus, Theat) ‹play› representar; ‹symphony› tocar* **2** (carry out, fulfill) ‹function› desempeñar; ‹role› desempeñar; ‹task› ejecutar; ‹experiment› realizar*; ‹ceremony› celebrar; ‹rites› practicar*

performance /pər'fɔːrməns ‖pə'fɔːməns/ n **1** (Cin, Mus, Theat) **(a)** (session) (Theat) representación f, función f; (Cin) función f **(b)** (of symphony, song) interpretación f; (of play)

representación f **(c)** (of actor) interpretación f; (of pianist, tenor) interpretación f; (of entertainer) actuación f **2** (of employee) rendimiento m, desempeño m (AmL); (of student) rendimiento m; (of team, athlete) actuación f, performance f (AmL period); (of machine, vehicle) comportamiento m, performance f (AmL); (of company) resultados mpl

performer /pər'fɔːrmər ‖pə'fɔːmə(r)/ n (Theat, Cin) actor, -triz m,f; (entertainer) artista mf

performing /pər'fɔːrmɪŋ ‖pə'fɔːmɪŋ/ adj (before n) **(a)** (Mus, Theat): **the ~ arts** las artes interpretativas **(b)** ‹seal/dog› amaestrado

perfume¹ /'pɜːrfjuːm ‖'pɜːfjuːm/ n perfume m

perfume² /pər'fjuːm ‖'pɜːfjuːm/ vt perfumar

perfunctory /pər'fʌŋktəri ‖pə'fʌŋktəri/ adj ‹inspection/description› somero; ‹greeting› mecánico

perhaps /pər'hæps ‖pə'hæps/ adv quizá(s), tal vez; **~ they'll come later** tal vez or quizá(s) vengan más tarde

peril /'perəl ‖'perɪl, 'perəl/ n peligro m

perilous /'perələs ‖'perɪləs, 'perələs/ adj peligroso

perimeter /pə'rɪmətər ‖pə'rɪmɪtə(r)/ n perímetro m

period¹ /'pɪriəd ‖'pɪəriəd/ n [the forms PERÍODO and PERIODO are equally acceptable in Spanish where this translation applies] **1 (a)** (interval, length of time) período m; (when specifying a time limit) plazo m; **for a ~ of five hours/12 months** por un espacio de cinco horas/período de 12 meses **(b)** (epoch) época f **2** (menstruation) período m, regla f **3** (in school) hora f (de clase) **4** (in punctuation) (AmE) punto m

period² adj ‹costume/furniture› de época

periodic /ˌpɪri'ɑːdɪk ‖ˌpɪəri'ɒdɪk/ adj periódico

periodical¹ /ˌpɪri'ɑːdɪkəl ‖ˌpɪəri'ɒdɪkəl/ n publicación f periódica

periodical² adj ▶ PERIODIC

peripheral /pə'rɪfərəl ‖pə'rɪfərəl/ adj **(a)** (minor, secondary) secundario **(b)** (Comput) ‹device/unit› periférico

periphery /pə'rɪfəri/ n (pl **-ries**) (frml) (of city) periferia f; (of society) margen m

periscope /'perəskəʊp ‖'perɪskəʊp/ n periscopio m

perish /'perɪʃ/ vi **(a)** (die) (liter) perecer* (liter) **(b)** (decay) ‹rubber/leather› deteriorarse; ‹foodstuffs› echarse a perder

perishable /'perɪʃəbəl/ adj perecedero

perjure /'pɜːrdʒər ‖'pɜːdʒə(r)/ v refl (Law) **to ~ oneself** perjurar(se), cometer perjurio

perjury /'pɜːrdʒəri ‖'pɜːdʒəri/ n perjurio m

perk /pɜːrk ‖pɜːk/ n (colloq) (of job) (beneficio m) extra m; (particular advantage) ventaja f
■ **perk up** [v + adv] ‹person› animarse; ‹business/weather› mejorar

perky /'pɜːrki ‖'pɜːki/ adj **-kier, -kiest** alegre

perm¹ /pɜːrm ‖pɜːm/ n permanente f or (Méx) m

perm² vt: **to have one's hair ~ed** hacerse* la or (Méx) un permanente

permanent¹ /'pɜːrmənənt ‖'pɜːmənənt/ adj permanente; ‹address/job› fijo, permanente; ‹dye/ ink› indeleble

permanent² n (AmE) ▶ PERM¹

p

permanently /'pɜːrmənəntli ‖'pɜːmənəntli/ *adv* ‹work/settle› permanentemente; ‹marked/disfigured› para siempre

permeate /'pɜːrmieɪt ‖'pɜːmieɪt/ *vt* «liquid» calar; «smoke/smell» impregnar

permissible /pər'mɪsəbəl ‖pə'mɪsəbəl/ *adj* (permitted) permisible; (acceptable) tolerable

permission /pər'mɪʃən ‖pə'mɪʃən/ *n* permiso *m*; **she gave me ~** me dio (su) permiso

permissive /pər'mɪsɪv ‖pə'mɪsɪv/ *adj* permisivo

permit¹ /pər'mɪt ‖pə'mɪt/ **-tt-** *vt* permitir; **photography is not ~ted** no se permite tomar fotografías; **to ~ sb to + INF** permitirle a algn que (+ *subj*)
■ **~** *vi:* **weather ~ting** si hace buen tiempo

permit² /'pɜːrmɪt ‖'pɜːmɪt/ *n* permiso *m* (por escrito); **work/residence ~** permiso de trabajo/de residencia; **gun ~** (AmE) licencia *f* de armas

permutation /'pɜːrmjʊ'teɪʃən ‖,pɜːmjʊ'teɪʃən/ *n* (a) (arrangement) variante *f* (b) (Math) permutación *f*

peroxide /pə'rɑːksaɪd ‖pə'rɒksaɪd/ *n* peróxido *m*

perpendicular /'pɜːrpən'dɪkjələr ‖,pɜːpən'dɪkjʊlə(r)/ *adj* (a) (vertical) ‹wall/surface› perpendicular al horizonte (b) (Math) **~ TO sth** perpendicular A algo

perpetrate /'pɜːrpətreɪt ‖'pɜːpɪtreɪt/ *vt* (frml) perpetrar

perpetrator /'pɜːrpətreɪtər ‖'pɜːpɪtreɪtə(r)/ *n* (frml or hum) autor, -tora *m,f* (de un crimen etc)

perpetual /pər'petʃuəl ‖pə'petʃuəl/ *adj* eterno, perpetuo

perpetuate /pər'petʃueɪt ‖pə'petʃuɪt/ *vt* perpetuar*

perplex /pər'pleks ‖pə'pleks/ *vt* dejar perplejo

perplexed /pər'plekst ‖pə'plekst/ *adj* perplejo

per se /pɜːr'seɪ ‖,pɜː'seɪ/ *adv* en sí, per se

persecute /'pɜːrsɪkjuːt ‖'pɜːsɪkjuːt/ *vt* perseguir*

persecution /'pɜːrsɪ'kjuːʃən ‖,pɜːsɪ'kjuːʃən/ *n* persecución *f*

perseverance /'pɜːrsə'vɪrəns ‖,pɜːsɪ'vɪərəns/ *n* perseverancia *f*

persevere /'pɜːrsə'vɪr ‖,pɜːsɪ'vɪə(r)/ *vi* perseverar

Persia /'pɜːrʒə ‖'pɜːʃə/ *n* Persia *f*

Persian /'pɜːrʒən ‖'pɜːʃən/ *adj* persa; **the ~ Gulf** el Golfo Pérsico

persist /pər'sɪst ‖pə'sɪst/ *vi* persistir; **to ~ IN sth/-ING: they ~ed in the belief o in believing that ...** persistieron en la creencia de que ...

persistence /pər'sɪstəns ‖pə'sɪstəns/ *n* perseverancia *f*

persistent /pər'sɪstənt ‖pə'sɪstənt/ *adj* (a) (unceasing) ‹demands/warnings› continuo, constante; ‹cough/fog› persistente; ‹rain› continuo (b) (undaunted) ‹salesman/suitor› insistente

person /'pɜːrsn ‖'pɜːsn/ *n* **1** (*pl* **people** *o* (frml) **persons**) persona *f*; **Sue's the ~ to ask** a quien hay que preguntarle es a Sue; **in ~ en persona 2** (Ling) (*pl* **persons**) persona *f*

personable /'pɜːrsnəbəl ‖'pɜːsnəbəl/ *adj* agradable

personal /'pɜːrsnəl ‖'pɜːsnl/ *adj* **1** (a) (own) ‹experience/preference› personal; ‹property› privado (b) (private) personal; **a ~ call** una llamada particular; **don't ask ~ questions** no hagas preguntas indiscretas (c) (individual) ‹account/loan› personal **2** (a) (in person) ‹appearance› en persona (b) (physical) ‹hygiene› íntimo; ‹appearance› personal (c) (directed against individual): **it's nothing ~, but ...** no tengo nada contra ti (*o* ella *etc*), pero ...

personal: ~ assistant *n* (Busn) secretario, -ria *m,f* personal; **~ computer** *n* computadora *f or* (Esp tb) ordenador *m* personal

personality /'pɜːrsn'æləti ‖,pɜːsə'næləti/ *n* (*pl* **-ties**) personalidad *f*

personally /'pɜːrsnəli ‖'pɜːsnəli/ *adv* personalmente

personal organizer *n* agenda *f* de uso múltiple, Filofax® *m*

personification /pər'sɑːnəfə'keɪʃən ‖pə,sɒnɪfɪ'keɪʃən/ *n* personificación *f*

personify /pər'sɑːnəfaɪ ‖pə'sɒnɪfaɪ/ *vt* **-fies, -fying, -fied** personificar*

personnel /'pɜːrsn'el ‖,pɜːsə'nel/ *n* (a) (staff) (+ *pl vb*) personal *m*; (before n) **~ manager** jefe *m,f* de personal (b) **Personnel** (department) (+ *sing vb*) sección *f* de personal

perspective /pər'spektɪv ‖pə'spektɪv/ *n* perspectiva *f*; **you have to keep things in ~** no tienes que perder de vista la verdadera dimensión de las cosas

Perspex® /'pɜːrspeks ‖'pɜːspeks/ *n* (BrE) acrílico *m*, plexiglás® *m* (Esp)

perspiration /'pɜːrspə'reɪʃən ‖,pɜːspɪ'reɪʃən/ *n* transpiración *f*

perspire /pər'spaɪr ‖pə'spaɪə(r)/ *vi* transpirar

persuade /pər'sweɪd ‖pə'sweɪd/ *vt* ‹person› convencer*, persuadir; **to ~ sb to + INF** convencer* *or* persuadir a algn DE QUE *or* PARA QUE (+ *subj*)

persuasion /pər'sweɪʒən ‖pə'sweɪʒən/ *n* (a) (act) persuasión *f* (b) (Relig) (frml): **people of all ~s** gente de todas las creencias

persuasive /pər'sweɪsɪv ‖pə'sweɪsɪv/ *adj* ‹person/manner› persuasivo; ‹argument› convincente

pert /pɜːrt ‖pɜːt/ *adj* ‹reply› descarado; ‹hat/dress› coqueto

pertinent /'pɜːrtn̩ənt ‖'pɜːtɪnənt/ *adj* (frml) pertinente; **to be ~ TO sth** guardar relación CON algo

perturb /pər'tɜːrb ‖pə'tɜːb/ *vt* (usu pass) perturbar

Peru /pə'ruː/ *n* (el) Perú *m*

peruse /pə'ru:z/ vt (a) (read through) (frml or hum) leer* detenidamente (b) (examine, study) (frml) examinar

Peruvian¹ /pə'ru:viən/ adj peruano

Peruvian² n peruano, -na m,f

pervade /pər'veɪd ‖pə'veɪd/ vt «idea/mood» dominar; «smell» llenar

pervasive /pər'veɪsɪv ‖pə'veɪsɪv/ adj «smell» penetrante; «idea/mood» dominante; «influence» omnipresente

perverse /pər'vɜːrs ‖pə'vɜːs/ adj (stubborn) obstinado; (wayward, contrary) retorcido

perversion /pər'vɜːrʒən ‖pə'vɜːʃən/ n (a) (distortion): **a ~ of justice** una deformación de la justicia (b) (Psych) perversión f

pervert¹ /pər'vɜːrt ‖pə'vɜːt/ vt pervertir*

pervert² /'pɜːrvɜːrt ‖'pɜːvɜːt/ n pervertido, -da m,f

peseta /pə'seɪtə/ n peseta f

pesky /'peski/ adj **-kier, -kiest** (AmE colloq) latoso (fam)

peso /'peɪsəʊ/ n (pl **~s**) peso m

pessimism /'pesəmɪzəm ‖'pesɪmɪzəm/ n pesimismo m

pessimist /'pesəməst ‖'pesɪmɪst/ n pesimista mf

pessimistic /'pesə'mɪstɪk ‖,pesɪ'mɪstɪk/ adj pesimista

pest /pest/ n (a) (Agr, Hort) plaga f (b) (person, thing) (colloq) peste f (fam)

pester /'pestər ‖'pestə(r)/ vt molestar

pesticide /'pestəsaɪd ‖'pestɪsaɪd/ n pesticida m

pestle /'pesəl/ n mano f de mortero

pet¹ /pet/ n (a) (animal) animal m doméstico or de compañía; (before n) **~ food** comida f para animales; **~ shop** ≈ pajarería f (b) (favorite): **he's teacher's ~** es el niño mimado de la maestra

pet² adj (before n) (a) (kept as pet): **his ~ budgie** su periquito (b) (favorite) «subject/theory» favorito; **my ~ hate** lo que más odio

pet³ -tt- vt «animal» acariciar
■ ~ vi acariciarse, manosearse (pey)

petal /'petḷ/ n pétalo m

peter out /'pi:tər ‖[v + adv] «supplies» irse* agotando; «conversation» apagarse*

petition /pə'tɪʃən/ n (a) (written document) petición f (b) (Law) demanda f

pet name n apodo m

petrified /'petrɪfaɪd/ adj (a) (terrified) muerto de miedo (b) (Geol) petrificado

petrochemical /'petrəʊ'kemɪkəl/ n producto m petroquímico; (before n) «industry/plant» petroquímico

petrol /'petrəl/ n (BrE) gasolina f, bencina f (Andes), nafta f (RPl); (before n) **~ pump** surtidor m; **~ station** estación f de servicio, gasolinera f, bomba f (Andes, Ven), estación f de nafta (RPl), bencinera f (Andes), grifo m (Per)

petroleum /pə'trəʊliəm/ n petróleo m; (before n) **~ jelly** vaselina f

petticoat /'petikəʊt/ n (a) (underskirt) enagua f or (Méx) fondo m (b) (slip) (BrE) combinación f, viso m

petty /'peti/ adj **-tier, -tiest** (a) (unimportant) «details» insignificante, nimio; **~ thief** ladronzuelo, -la m,f (b) (small-minded) mezquino

petty cash n caja f chica, dinero m para gastos menores

petulant /'petʃələnt ‖'petjʊlənt/ adj de mal genio

pew /pju:/ n banco m (de iglesia)

pewter /'pju:tər ‖'pju:tə(r)/ n peltre m

PG (= **parental guidance**) menores acompañados

PG-13 (in US) mayores de 13 años o menores acompañados

phantom¹ /'fæntəm/ n (liter) fantasma m

phantom² adj (a) (ghostly) (liter) (before n) «shape» fantasmal; «horseman» fantasma adj inv (b) (imaginary) ilusorio

Pharaoh /'ferəʊ ‖'feərəʊ/ n faraón m

pharmaceutical /'fɑːrmə'su:tɪkəl ‖,fɑːmə'sju:tɪkəl/ adj farmacéutico

pharmacist /'fɑːrməsəst ‖'fɑːməsɪst/ n farmacéutico, -ca m,f, farmaceuta mf (Col, Ven)

pharmacy /'fɑːrməsi ‖'fɑːməsi/ n (pl **-cies**) (a) (discipline) química f farmacéutica, farmacia f (b) (dispensary) farmacia f

phase /feɪz/ n fase f
■ **phase out** [v + o + adv, v + adv + o] «service» retirar paulatinamente; «old model» dejar de producir

PhD n (= **Doctor of Philosophy**) (award) doctorado m; (person) Dr., Dra.

pheasant /'fezṇt/ n (pl **~s** or **~**) faisán m

phenomena /fɪ'nɑːmənə ‖fə'nɒmɪnə/ pl of
<small>PHENOMENON</small>

phenomenal /fɪ'nɑːmənḷ ‖fə'nɒmɪnḷ/ adj (colloq) «success/achievement» espectacular; «strength» increíble

phenomenon /fɪ'nɑːmənɑːn ‖fə'nɒmɪnən/ n (pl **-mena**) fenómeno m

phew /fju:/ interj (colloq) ¡uf!

philanderer /fə'lændərər ‖fɪ'lændərə(r)/ n (pej) mujeriego m (pey)

philanthropic /'fɪlən'θrɑːpɪk ‖,fɪlən'θrɒpɪk/ adj filantrópico

philanthropist /fə'lænθrəpəst ‖fɪ'lænθrəpɪst/ n filántropo, -pa m,f

philately /fə'lætḷi ‖fɪ'lætəli/ n (frml) filatelia f

Philippine /'fɪləpi:n ‖'fɪlɪpi:n/ adj filipino

Philippines /'fɪləpi:nz ‖'fɪlɪpi:nz/ pl n **the ~** (las) Filipinas

philistine /'fɪləsti:n, -aɪn ‖'fɪlɪstaɪn/ n ignorante mf

philosopher /fə'lɑːsəfər ‖fɪ'lɒsəfə(r)/ n filósofo, -fa m,f

philosophic /'fɪlə'sɑːfɪk ‖,fɪlə'sɒfɪk/, **-ical** /-ɪkəl/ adj filosófico; **to be ~ ABOUT sth** tomarse algo con filosofía

philosophy /fə'lɑːsəfi ‖fɪ'lɒsəfi/ n filosofía f

phlegm /flem/ n flema f

phobia /'fəʊbiə/ n fobia f

phoenix /'fi:nɪks/ n Ave f‡ Fénix, fénix m or f

phone¹ /fəʊn/ n teléfono m; **to be on the ~** (be speaking) estar* hablando por teléfono; (subscribe) (BrE) tener* teléfono; (before n) **~ call** llamada f (telefónica); **~ number** (número m de) teléfono m

phone² *vt* ‹*person*› llamar (por teléfono),
telefonear, hablar (Méx); ‹*place/number*› llamar
(por teléfono) a
■ **phone up** [*v* + *adv* + *o*, *v* + *o* + *adv*] llamar,
telefonear

phone: ∼ **book** *n* (colloq) guía *f* (telefónica *or*
de teléfonos) *or* (Col, Méx) directorio *m*; ∼
booth, (BrE) ∼ **box** *n* cabina *f* telefónica;
∼**card** *n* tarjeta *f* telefónica

phonetics /fəˈnetɪks/ *n* (+ *sing vb*) fonética *f*

phoney¹, (AmE also) **phony** /ˈfəʊni/ *adj* **-nier,
-niest** (colloq & pej) falso

phoney², (AmE also) **phony** *n* (*pl* **-neys** *or*
-nies) (colloq & pej) (person) farsante *mf* (fam);
(thing) falsificación *f*

phosphate /ˈfɑːsfeɪt ‖ ˈfɒsfeɪt/ *n* fosfato *m*

phosphorus /ˈfɑːsfərəs ‖ ˈfɒsfərəs/ *n* fósforo *m*

photo /ˈfəʊtəʊ/ *n* (*pl* **-tos**) (colloq) foto *f*; **to take
a** ∼ **(of sb/sth)** sacar(le)* *or* (Esp *tb*) hacer(le)*
una foto (a algn/algo)

photocopier /ˈfəʊtəʊˌkɑːpiər
‖ ˈfəʊtəʊˌkɒpiə(r)/ *n* fotocopiadora *f*

photocopy¹ /ˈfəʊtəʊˌkɑːpi ‖ ˈfəʊtəʊˌkɒpi/ *n* (*pl*
-copies) fotocopia *f*

photocopy² *vt* **-copies, -copying,
-copied** fotocopiar

photo: ∼ **finish** *n* foto(-)finish *f*; **P∼fit®** *n*
(BrE): **P∼fit (picture)** retrato *m* hablado (AmS)
or (Esp) robot *or* (Méx) reconstruido

photogenic /ˌfəʊtəˈdʒenɪk/ *adj* fotogénico

photograph¹ /ˈfəʊtəɡræf ‖ ˈfəʊtəɡrɑːf/ *n*
fotografía *f*, foto *f*; **to take a** ∼ **(of sb/sth)**
sacar(le)* *or* (Esp *tb*) hacer(le)* una foto *or* una
fotografía (a algn/algo)

photograph² *vt* fotografiar*, sacarle* *or* (Esp
tb) hacerle* una foto *or* una fotografía a

photographer /fəˈtɑːɡrəfər ‖ fəˈtɒɡrəfə(r)/ *n*
fotógrafo, -fa *m,f*

photographic /ˌfəʊtəˈɡræfɪk/ *adj* ‹*copy/
evidence/memory*› fotográfico; ‹*shop/equipment*›
de fotografía

photography /fəˈtɑːɡrəfi ‖ fəˈtɒɡrəfi/ *n*
fotografía *f*

photosynthesis /ˌfəʊtəʊˈsɪnθəsəs
‖ ˌfəʊtəʊˈsɪnθəsɪs/ *n* fotosíntesis *f*

phrasal verb /ˈfreɪzl/ *n* verbo *m* con
partícula(s)

phrase¹ /freɪz/ *n* frase *f*

phrase² *vt* expresar

phrase book *n* manual *m* de conversación,
≈ guía *m* de bolsillo para el viajero

physical¹ /ˈfɪzɪkəl/ *adj* **1** (bodily) físico;
‹*illness*› orgánico; ∼ **education** educación *f* física
2 (material) ‹*world*› material

physical² *n* reconocimiento *m* médico

physically /ˈfɪzɪkli/ *adv* ‹*attractive*›
físicamente; ‹*demanding*› desde el punto de vista
físico; **it's** ∼ **impossible** es materialmente
imposible

physical therapist *n* (AmE) ▶
PHYSIOTHERAPIST

physical therapy *n* (AmE) ▶ PHYSIOTHERAPY

physician /fəˈzɪʃən ‖ fɪˈzɪʃən/ *n* (frml) médico,
-ca *m,f*

physicist /ˈfɪzəsəst ‖ ˈfɪzɪsɪst/ *n* físico, -ca *m,f*

physics /ˈfɪzɪks/ *n* (+ *sing vb*) física *f*

physiological /ˌfɪziəˈlɑːdʒɪkəl ‖ ˌfɪziəˈlɒdʒɪkəl/
adj fisiológico

physiology /ˌfɪziˈɑːlədʒi ‖ ˌfɪziˈɒlədʒi/ *n*
fisiología *f*

physiotherapist /ˌfɪziəʊˈθerəpəst
‖ ˌfɪziəʊˈθerəpɪst/ *n* fisioterapeuta *mf*,
kinesiólogo, -ga *m,f*

physiotherapy /ˌfɪziəʊˈθerəpi/ *n* (discipline)
kinesiología *f*; (treatment) fisioterapia *f*,
kinesiterapia *f*

physique /fəˈziːk ‖ fɪˈziːk/ *n* físico *m*

pianist /ˈpiːənəst ‖ ˈpiːənɪst/ *n* pianista *mf*

piano /piˈænəʊ/ *n* (*pl* **-os**) piano *m*

pick¹ /pɪk/ *n* **1** (a) ▶ PICKAX (b) (ice ∼) piolet
m (c) (plectrum) púa *f*, plectro *m*, uñeta *f* (CS),
uña *f* (Méx, Ven) **2** (choice) (*no pl*): **take your** ∼
elige *or* escoge el (*or* los *etc*) que quieras

pick² *vt* **1** (a) (choose, select) ‹*number/color*›
elegir*, escoger*; ‹*team/crew*› seleccionar (b)
(provoke): **to** ∼ **a fight with sb** meterse con algn
2 (gather) ‹*flower*› cortar, coger* (esp Esp); ‹*fruit/
cotton/tea*› recoger, coger* (esp Esp), pizcar*
(Méx)

3 (a) (remove matter from): **to** ∼ **one's nose**
meterse el dedo en la nariz, hurgarse* la nariz;
don't ∼ **your spots** no te toques los granitos; **to**
∼ **sb's pocket** robarle la billetera (*or* las llaves
etc) a algn del bolsillo, bolsear a algn (Mex fam),
carterear a algn (Chi fam) (b) (open) ‹*lock*› abrir*
con una ganzúa (*or* una horquilla *etc*)
■ ∼ *vi* (a): **to** ∼ **and choose** ser exigente (b) (take
bits): **he was** ∼**ing at his dinner** comía desganado
■ **pick on** [*v* + *prep* + *o*] (colloq) meterse con,
agarrársela*) con (AmL fam)
■ **pick out** [*v* + *o* + *adv*, *v* + *adv* + *o*] **1** (choose,
select) elegir*, escoger*
2 (a) (recognize, identify) reconocer* (b) (discern)
distinguir*
■ **pick up**
I [*v* + *o* + *adv*, *v* + *adv* + *o*] **1** (gather off floor,
ground) recoger*; (take) tomar, agarrar (esp AmL),
coger* (esp Esp); (lift up) levantar
2 (learn) ‹*language*› aprender; ‹*habit*› adquirir,
agarrar (esp AmL), coger* (esp Esp)
3 (a) (collect, fetch) recoger* (b) (take on board)
‹*passenger*› recoger* (c) (colloq) ‹*man/woman*›
ligarse* (fam), levantar (AmS fam)
4 (receive) ‹*signal*› captar
II [*v* + *adv* + *o*] (gain) ‹*speed*› agarrar, coger* (esp
Esp)
III [*v* + *o* + *adv*] (a) (revive) reanimar (b) (correct)
corregir*
IV [*v* + *adv*] (improve) «*prices/sales*» subir;
«*economy/business*» repuntar; «*invalid*»
mejorar; «*weather*» mejorar

pickax, (BrE) **pickaxe** /ˈpɪkæks/ *n* pico *m*,
piqueta *f*

picket¹ /ˈpɪkət ‖ ˈpɪkɪt/ *n* (group) piquete *m*;
(*before n*) ∼ **line** piquete *m*

picket² *vt* ‹*factory/workplace*› formar un
piquete frente a, piquetear (esp AmL)

pickings /ˈpɪkɪŋz/ *pl n* (a) (profits) ganancias
fpl (b) (food) sobras *fpl*

pickle¹ /ˈpɪkəl/ *n* (a) (dill ∼) (AmE) pepinillo *m*

en vinagre al eneldo **(b)** ~**s** (vegetables) encurtidos *mpl*, pickles *mpl* (CS) **(c)** (relish) (BrE) *condimento a base de encurtidos en una salsa*

pickle² *vt* conservar en vinagre *or* (Chi tb) en escabeche, encurtir

pick: ~**-me-up** *n* (colloq) estimulante *m*; ~**pocket** *n* carterista *mf*, bolsista *mf* (Méx); ~**up** (**truck**) *n* camioneta *f* (de reparto)

picky /'pɪki/ *adj* **pickier, pickiest** (colloq) quisquilloso

picnic /'pɪknɪk/ *n* picnic *m*; **to go for** *o* **on a** ~ ir* de picnic

pictorial /pɪk'tɔːriəl/ *adj* ⟨representation⟩ pictórico; ⟨account/history⟩ en imágenes; ⟨magazine⟩ ilustrado

picture¹ /'pɪktʃər ‖'pɪktʃə(r)/ *n* **1** **(a)** (illustration) ilustración *f*; (drawing) dibujo *m*; (painting) cuadro *m*, pintura *f*; (print) cuadro *m*, lámina *f*; (portrait) retrato *m* **(b)** (photo) foto *f*; **to take a** ~ **of** sth/sb sacarle* *or* (Esp tb) hacerle* una foto a algo/algn **2** (situation) panorama *m*; **to put** sb **in the** ~ poner* a algn al tanto (de la situación) **3** (idea) idea *f* **4** (TV) imagen *f* **5** (Cin) **(a)** (movie) película *f* **(b)** **pictures** *pl* (cinema) (BrE dated) **the** ~**s** el cine

picture² *vt* imaginarse

picturesque /pɪktʃə'resk/ *adj* pintoresco

pie /paɪ/ *n* (savory) empanada *f*; (sweet) pastel *m*, pay *m* (AmC, Méx)

piece /piːs/ *n* **1** **(a)** (part of sth broken, torn, cut, divided) pedazo *m*, trozo *m*; **she ripped the letter into** ~**s** rompió la carta en pedacitos; **to come** *o* **fall to** ~**s** hacerse* pedazos; **a** ~ **of land** un terreno, una parcela; **in one** ~ (safe) sano y salvo; (unbroken) intacto; **to go to** ~**s** perder* el control; **to pull** sth/sb **to** ~**s** destrozar* algo/a algn; **to say one's** ~ dar* su (*or* mi *etc*) opinión **(b)** (component) pieza *f*, parte *f*; **to take** sth **to** ~**s** desarmar algo **2** (item): **a** ~ **of advice** un consejo; **a** ~ **of furniture** un mueble; **a** ~ **of paper** un papel; **an excellent** ~ **of work** un trabajo excelente; **to give** sb **a** ~ **of one's mind** cantarle las cuarenta a algn **3** **(a)** (Mus): **a** ~ **(of music)** una pieza (de música) **(b)** (Journ) artículo *m* **4** (coin) moneda *f* **5** (in board games) ficha *f*; (in chess) figura *f*

■ piece together [*v* + *o* + *adv*, *v* + *adv* + *o*] ⟨fragments⟩ juntar*; ⟨events/facts⟩ reconstruir*

piecemeal¹ /'piːsmiːl/ *adj* poco sistemático

piecemeal² *adv* (gradually) poco a poco; (unsystematically) de manera poco sistemática

piecework /'piːswɜːrk ‖'piːswɜːk/ *n* trabajo *m* a destajo

pier /pɪr ‖pɪə(r)/ *n* **(a)** (landing place) embarcadero *m*, muelle *m* **(b)** (with amusements) *paseo con juegos y atracciones sobre un muelle*

pierce /pɪrs ‖pɪəs/ *vt* **(a)** (make a hole in) agujerear; (go through) atravesar*; **she's had her ears** ~**d** se ha hecho hacer agujeros en las orejas **(b)** ⟨sound/light⟩ (liter) rasgar* (liter)

piercing /'pɪrsɪŋ ‖'pɪəsɪŋ/ *adj* ⟨eyes/look⟩ penetrante; ⟨scream⟩ desgarrador

piety /'paɪəti/ *n* piedad *f*

pig¹ /pɪg/ *n* **1** (Agr, Zool) cerdo *m*, chancho *m*

(AmL) **2** **(a)** (obnoxious person) (colloq) cerdo, -da *m,f* (fam) **(b)** (glutton) (colloq) glotón, -tona *m,f*, angurriento, -ta *m,f* (CS fam)

pigeon /'pɪdʒən ‖'pɪdʒɪn, 'pɪdʒən/ *n* (Zool) paloma *f*; (Culin) pichón *m*

pigeonhole /'pɪdʒənhəʊl ‖'pɪdʒɪnhəʊl, 'pɪdʒən-/ *n* **(a)** (on wall, desk) casillero *m* **(b)** (category) casilla *f*

piggy /'pɪgi/ *n* (*pl* **-gies**) (used to or by children) cerdito *m*, chanchito *m* (AmL)

piggy: ~**back** *n*: **to give** sb **a** ~**back** llevar a algn a caballo; ~**bank** *n* alcancía *f* (AmL), hucha *f* (Esp) (*en forma de cerdito*)

pigheaded /'pɪg'hedəd ‖'pɪg'hedɪd/ *adj* terco

piglet /'pɪglət ‖'pɪglɪt/ *n* cochinillo *m*, lechón *m*, chanchito *m* (AmL)

pigment /'pɪgmənt/ *n* pigmento *m*

pigmy /'pɪgmi/ *n* ▶ PYGMY

pig: ~**pen** (AmE) ▶ ~STY; ~**sty** *n* pocilga *f*, chiquero *m* (AmL); ~**tail** *n* (bunch) coleta *f*, chape *m* (Chi); (plait) trenza *f*

pike /paɪk/ *n* **(a)** (*pl* ~) (Zool) lucio *m* **(b)** (turn~) (AmE) carretera *f*

pilchard /'pɪltʃərd ‖'pɪltʃəd/ *n* sardina *f* (grande)

pile¹ /paɪl/ *n* **1** (stack, heap) montón *m* **2** (Tex) pelo *m* **3** **piles** *pl* (BrE Med) hemorroides *fpl*, almorranas *fpl*

pile² *vt* amontonar

■ pile in [*v* + *adv*] (colloq) meterse

■ pile into [*v* + *prep* + *o*] (colloq) **(a)** (squeeze into) ⟨car⟩ meterse en **(b)** (attack) arremeter contra **(c)** (crash into) ⟨vehicle⟩ estrellarse contra

■ pile up **1** [*v* + *adv*] (accumulate) amontonarse **2** [*v* + *o* + *adv*, *v* + *adv* + *o*] (form into pile) apilar

pileup /'paɪlʌp/ *n* choque *m* múltiple

pilfering /'pɪlfərɪŋ/ *n* robos *mpl*, hurtos *mpl*

pilgrim /'pɪlgrəm ‖'pɪlgrɪm/ *n* peregrino, -na *m,f*; (before *n*) **the P**~ **Fathers** *los primeros colonizadores de Nueva Inglaterra*

pilgrimage /'pɪlgrəmɪdʒ ‖'pɪlgrɪmɪdʒ/ *n* peregrinación *f*

pill /pɪl/ *n* **(a)** (tablet) pastilla *f*, píldora *f* **(b)** (contraceptive) **the P**~ la píldora (anticonceptiva); **to be on the P**~ tomar la píldora

pillage¹ /'pɪlɪdʒ/ *n* pillaje *m*

pillage² *vt/i* saquear

pillar /'pɪlər ‖'pɪlə(r)/ *n* pilar *m*; **he is a** ~ **of the community** es uno de los pilares *or* baluartes de la comunidad

pillar box *n* (BrE) buzón *m*

pillion¹ /'pɪljən ‖'pɪliən/ *n* (Auto) asiento *m* trasero (*de una moto*)

pillion² *adv* ⟨ride⟩ en el asiento trasero

pillory /'pɪləri/ *n* (*pl* **-ries**) picota *f*

pillow /'pɪləʊ/ *n* almohada *f*

pillowcase /'pɪləʊkeɪs/, (BrE also) **pillow slip** *n* funda *f*, almohadón *m* (Esp)

pilot¹ /'paɪlət/ *n* **1** (Aerosp, Aviat) piloto *mf* **2** (Naut) práctico *mf* (de puerto) **3** (Rad, TV) programa *m* piloto

pilot² *adj* (before *n*) piloto *adj inv*

pilot³ *vt* **1** (Aviat, Naut) pilotar, pilotear (AmL) **2** (test) poner* a prueba

pilot light *n* piloto *m*

pimple /'pɪmpəl/ n grano m, espinilla f (AmL)

pin¹ /pɪn/ n **1** (for cloth, paper) alfiler m **2** (brooch, badge) (AmE) insignia f **3** (a) (on plug) (BrE Elec) clavija f, borne m (b) (peg) (Tech) perno m

pin² -nn- vt **1** (fasten, attach) ‹dress/seam› prender con alfileres; I ~ned the papers together sujeté los papeles con un alfiler; she had ~ned her hopes on getting a scholarship había depositado sus esperanzas en conseguir una beca; they tried to ~ the blame on him trataron de hacerle cargar con la culpa **2** (hold motionless) inmovilizar*

■ **pin down** [v + o + adv, v + adv + o] **1** (prevent from moving): they ~ned him down (se echaron sobre él y) lo inmovilizaron **2** (a) (define) ‹cause/identity› definir; something's wrong with me, but I can't ~ it down algo tengo, pero no sabría decir exactamente qué (b) (force to state position): I managed to ~ him down to a definite date conseguí que se comprometiera para una fecha concreta

PIN /pɪn/ n (= personal identification number) PIN m

pinafore /'pɪnəfɔːr ‖ 'pɪnəfɔː(r)/ n (a) ~ (dress) (sleeveless dress) jumper m or (Esp) pichi m (b) (apron) (BrE) delantal m or (esp Méx) mandil m (con peto) (c) (protective overdress) delantal m

pinball /'pɪnbɔːl/ n (before n) ~ machine flipper m

pincer /'pɪnsər ‖ 'pɪnsə(r)/ n (a) (Zool) pinza f (b) **pincers** pl (tool) tenaza(s) f (pl)

pinch¹ /pɪntʃ/ n (a) (act) pellizco m; in o (BrE) at a ~ si fuera necesario (b) (small quantity) pizca f

pinch² vt **1** ‹person› pellizcar*; ‹shoes› apretar* **2** (BrE colloq) (steal) robar

pinched /pɪntʃt/ adj: faces ~ with grief caras transidas de dolor

pincushion /'pɪnˌkʊʃən/ n alfiletero m

pine¹ /paɪn/ n (a) ~ (tree) pino m; (before n) ~ cone piña f; ~ needle hoja f de pino (b) (wood) (madera f de) pino m

pine² vi estar* triste; to ~ FOR sth suspirar POR algo

■ **pine away** [v + adv] languidecer* de añoranza

pineapple /'paɪnˌæpəl/ n piña f or (esp RPl) ananá f

Ping-Pong®, **ping-pong** /'pɪnpɑːŋ ‖ 'pɪnpɒŋ/ n ping-pong m

pinion /'pɪnjən/ vt ‹person› inmovilizar* (esp sujetándole los brazos)

pink¹ /pɪnk/ adj -er, -est rosa adj inv, rosado m (AmL); ‹cheeks› sonrosado

pink² n rosa m, rosado m (AmL)

pinking shears /'pɪnkɪn/ pl n tijeras fpl dentadas

pin money n dinero para gastos personales

pinnacle /'pɪnɪkəl ‖ 'pɪnəkəl/ n (a) (Archit) pináculo m (b) (mountain peak) cumbre f, cima f

pin: ~point vt ‹position› localizar* or (AmL tb) ubicar* con exactitud; to ~point the causes of the problem establecer* con exactitud cuáles son las causas del problema; ~prick n pinchazo m; ~s and needles pl n hormigueo m; ~stripe, ~striped adj: ~stripe(d) suit traje m oscuro de raya diplomática

pint /paɪnt/ n pinta f (EEUU: 0,47 litros, RU: 0,57 litros)

pinup /'pɪnʌp/ n foto f (de chica atractiva, actor famoso etc); (person) pin-up mf

pioneer¹ /ˌpaɪə'nɪr ‖ ˌpaɪə'nɪə(r)/ n pionero, -ra m,f

pioneer² vt (a) ‹policy› promover*; ‹technique› ser* el primero (or la primera etc) en aplicar (b) (technique) pioneering

pioneering pres p ‹research› pionero

pious /'paɪəs/ adj piadoso; (sanctimonious) beato

pip /pɪp/ n **1** (seed) pepita f **2** (BrE Rad, Telec) pitido m

pipe¹ /paɪp/ n **1** (for liquid, gas) caño m **2** (for tobacco) pipa f **3** (Mus) (a) (wind instrument) caramillo m (b) (of organ) tubo m (c) **pipes** pl gaita f

pipe² vt (transport by pipe) (+ adv compl) llevar (por tuberías, gasoducto, oleoducto)

■ **pipe down** [v + adv] (colloq) (usu in imperative) callarse la boca (fam)

piped music /paɪpt/ n música f ambiental, hilo m musical (Esp)

pipe: ~ dream n quimera f, sueño m guajiro (Méx); ~line n conducto m, ducto m (Méx); it's in the ~line está proyectado

piper /'paɪpər ‖ 'paɪpə(r)/ n gaitero, -ra m,f

piping¹ /'paɪpɪŋ/ n cañería f, tubería f

piping² adv (as intensifier): ~ hot bien caliente

pique¹ /piːk/ n despecho m

pique² vt: he was ~d by her lack of interest se resintió por su falta de interés

piracy /'paɪrəsi/ n piratería f

pirate /'paɪrət/ n (a) (at sea) pirata mf (b) (before n) ‹tape/video/radio station› pirata adj inv

pirouette¹ /ˌpɪru'et/ n giro m; (in ballet) pirueta f

pirouette² vi girar

Pisces /'paɪsiːz/ n (a) (sign) (no art) Piscis (b) (person) Piscis or piscis mf

piss¹ /pɪs/ n (sl) (a) (act) (no pl) meada f (vulg) (b) (urine) meados mpl (vulg)

piss² vi (sl) mear (vulg)

■ **piss off** (sl) **1** [v + adv] (go away) (BrE): ~ off! ¡vete a la mierda! (vulg) **2** [v + o + adv] (anger): it ~es me off me revienta (fam), me encabrona (Esp, Méx vulg)

pissed /pɪst/ adj (sl) (a) (AmE) (fed up) cabreado (fam), encabronado (Esp, Méx vulg), choreado (Chi fam) (b) (drunk) (BrE) como una cuba (fam), tomado (AmL fam)

pistachio /pɪ'stæʃiəʊ/ n ~ (nut) pistacho m, pistache m (Méx)

pistol /'pɪstl/ n pistola f

piston /'pɪstən/ n émbolo m, pistón m

pit¹ /pɪt/ n **1** (hole — in ground) hoyo m; (— for

AmC	Central America	Arg	Argentina	Cu	Cuba	Per	Peru
AmL	Latin America	Bol	Bolivia	Ec	Ecuador	RPI	River Plate Area
AmS	South America	Chi	Chile	Esp	Spain	Ur	Uruguay
Andes	Andean Region	CS	Southern Cone	Méx	Mexico	Ven	Venezuela

burying) fosa *f*; (— as trap) trampa *f*; (**inspection**) ~
(Auto) foso *m or* (RPl) fosa *f* **2** (coalmine) mina *f*
(*de carbón*); (quarry) cantera *f* **3** (orchestra ~) foso
m orquestal *or* de la orquesta **4** **pits** *pl* (the very
worst) (sl) **the ~s** lo peor que hay (fam) **5** (in fruit)
(AmE) hueso *m*, carozo *m* (CS), pepa *f* (Col)

pit² **-tt-** *vt* ‹*surface/metal*› picar*
■ **pit against** [*v + o + prep + o*] enfrentar a; **to
~ oneself against sb** enfrentarse a algn

pitch¹ /pɪtʃ/ *n* **(a)** (level, degree) (*no pl*) punto *m*,
extremo *m* **(b)** (Mus) tono *m* **(c)** (in baseball)
lanzamiento *m* **(d)** (Sport) (playing area) (BrE)
campo *m*, cancha *f* (AmL) **(e)** (position, site) (BrE)
lugar *m*, sitio *m*; (in market, fair) puesto *m* **(f)**
(substance) brea *f*

pitch² *vt* **1** (set up) ‹*tent*› armar, montar;
‹*camp*› montar, hacer* **2** (Sport) ‹*ball*› lanzar*,
pichear **3** (aim, set, address): **she doesn't know at
what level to ~ her talk** no sabe qué nivel darle a
la charla
■ ~ *vi* **(a)** (fall) (+ *adv compl*) caerse* **(b)** (lurch)
‹*ship/plane*› cabecear
■ **pitch in** [*v + adv*] (colloq) arrimar el hombro

pitch-black /ˈpɪtʃˈblæk/, **pitch-dark**
/ˈpɪtʃˈdɑːrk ‖ˌpɪtʃˈdɑːk/ *adj* ‹*night*› (oscuro)
como boca de lobo (fam), muy oscuro; ‹*surface*›
negro como el azabache

pitched battle /pɪtʃt/ *n* batalla *f* campal

pitcher /ˈpɪtʃər ‖ˈpɪtʃə(r)/ *n* **1** (for pouring)
jarra *f*, pichel *m* (AmC); (of clay) (BrE) cántaro *m*
2 (in baseball) lanzador, -dora *m,f*, pítcher *mf*

pitchfork /ˈpɪtʃfɔːrk ‖ˈpɪtʃfɔːk/ *n* horca *f*,
horquilla *f*, horqueta *f* (Chi)

pitfall /ˈpɪtfɔːl/ *n* (difficulty) dificultad *f*; (risk)
riesgo *m*

pith /pɪθ/ *n* tejido blanco fibroso que recubre el
interior de la cáscara de los cítricos

pithy /ˈpɪθi/ *adj* **pithier, pithiest** ‹*remark/
reply*› sucinto *or* conciso y expresivo

pitiful /ˈpɪtɪfəl/ *adj* **(a)** (arousing pity) ‹*cry/moan*›
lastimero, ‹*sight*› lastimoso **(b)** (wretched,
inadequate) lamentable

pittance /ˈpɪtn̩s/ *n* miseria *f*

pituitary gland /pəˈtjuːəteri ‖prˈtjuːɪtəri/ *n*
glándula pituitaria *f*

pity¹ /ˈpɪti/ *n* **1** (*no pl*) (cause of regret) lástima *f*,
pena *f*; **it's a ~** (THAT) es una lástima *or* una
pena QUE (+ *subj*); **what a ~!** ¡qué lástima!, ¡que
pena! **2** (compassion) piedad *f*; **to take ~ on sb/
sth** apiadarse de algn/algo

pity² *vt* **pities, pitying, pitied** tenerle*
lástima a

pivot /ˈpɪvət/ *vi* (Mech Eng) pivotar; **he ~ed on
his heel** giró sobre sus talones

pixie /ˈpɪksi/ *n* (elf) duendecillo *m*; (fairy) hadita
f

pizza /ˈpiːtsə/ *n* pizza *f*

pizzeria /ˌpiːtsəˈriːə/ *n* pizzería *f*

placard /ˈplækɑːrd ‖ˈplækɑːd/ *n* letrero *m*; (at
demonstration) pancarta *f*

placate /ˈpleɪkeɪt ‖pləˈkeɪt/ *vt* apaciguar*

place¹ /pleɪs/ *n* **1** **(a)** (spot, position, area) lugar
m, sitio *m*; **to have friends in high ~s** tener*
amigos influyentes; **all over the ~** por todas
partes; **to fall into ~** aclararse **(b)** (specific location)
lugar *m*; **~ of birth** lugar de nacimiento **(c)** (in

phrases) **in place: to hold sth in ~** sujetar algo;
out of place: to look out of ~ ‹*furniture*› quedar
mal; **to feel out of ~** sentirse* fuera de lugar
2 **(a)** (building, shop, restaurant etc) sitio *m*, lugar
m **(b)** (home): **my/his ~** mi/su casa
3 **(a)** (position, role) lugar *m*; **I wouldn't change
~s with her for anything** no me cambiaría por
ella por nada; **nobody can ever take your ~** nadie
podrá jamás ocupar tu lugar **(b)** **in place of** (*as
prep*) en lugar de **(c)** **to take place** (occur) ocurrir;
‹*meeting/concert/wedding*› tener* lugar
4 **(a)** (seat): **save me a ~** guárdame un asiento
(b) (at table) cubierto *m*; **to lay/set a ~ for sb**
poner* un cubierto para algn
5 (in contest, league) puesto *m*; **your social life will
have to take second ~** tu vida social va a tener
que pasar a un segundo plano
6 (in book, sequence): **you've made me lose my ~**
me has hecho perder la página (*or* la línea *etc*)
por donde iba
7 **(a)** (job) puesto *m* **(b)** (BrE Educ) plaza *f* **(c)**
(on team) puesto *m*
8 (in argument) lugar *m*; **in the first/second ~** en
primer/segundo lugar

place² *vt* **1** (put, position) ‹*object*› poner*;
(carefully, precisely) colocar* **2** (in race): **this victory
~s her among the top three** este triunfo la sitúa
entre las tres primeras **3** **(a)** (find a home, job for)
colocar* ‹*advertisement*› poner*; ‹*phone call*›
pedir*; **we ~d an order with Acme Corp** hicimos
un pedido a Acme Corp **4** (identify) ‹*tune*›
identificar*, ubicar* (AmL); **her face is familiar,
but I can't quite ~ her** su cara me resulta
conocida pero no sé de dónde *or* (AmL tb) pero no
la ubico

placebo /pləˈsiːbəʊ/ *n* (*pl* **~s** *or* **~es**) placebo
m

place mat *n* (mantel *m*) individual *m*

placement /ˈpleɪsmənt/ *n* **(a)** (in employment)
colocación *f* **(b)** (positioning) colocación *f*,
ubicación *f* (esp AmL)

place name *n* topónimo *m*

placenta /pləˈsentə/ *n* (*pl* **~s** *or* **~e** /-tiː/)
placenta *f*

placid /ˈplæsɪd ‖ˈplæsɪd/ *adj* plácido

plagiarism /ˈpleɪdʒərɪzəm/ *n* plagio *m*

plagiarize /ˈpleɪdʒəraɪz/ *vt* plagiar

plague¹ /pleɪg/ *n* **(a)** (disease) peste *f* **(b)** (horde
— of locusts, tourists) plaga *f*

plague² *vt* **(a)** (afflict): **a country ~d by strikes**
un país asolado por constantes huelgas; **~d with
problems** plagado de problemas **(b)** (pester)
acosar

plaice /pleɪs/ *n* (*pl* **~**) platija *f*

plaid /plæd/ *n* (pattern) cuadros *mpl* escoceses;
(material) tela *f* escocesa

plain¹ /pleɪn/ *adj* **-er, -est** **1** **(a)** (unadorned)
‹*decor/cooking/language*› sencillo; ‹*fabric*› liso
(b) (Culin): **~ chocolate** (BrE) chocolate *m* sin
leche; **~ flour** harina *f* común **2** **(a)** (clear) claro;
the reasons are ~ to see las razones saltan a la
vista **(b)** (blunt): **the ~ truth** la pura verdad
3 (not good-looking) feo, poco agraciado

plain² *adv* (as intensifier) totalmente; **that's just
~ stupid** eso es una completa estupidez

plain³ *n* llanura *f*

plain clothes *pl n*: in ～ ～ de civil *or* (Esp tb) de paisano

plainly /'pleɪnli/ *adv* (a) (obviously, visibly) claramente (b) (clearly) ⟨*explain*⟩ claramente; ⟨*remember*⟩ perfectamente (c) (bluntly) ⟨*speak*⟩ claramente (d) ⟨*dress*⟩ con sencillez

plaintiff /'pleɪntəf ‖'pleɪntɪf/ *n* demandante *mf*

plaintive /'pleɪntɪv/ *adj* lastimero

plait¹ /plæt/ *n* trenza *f*

plait² *vt* trenzar*

plan¹ /plæn/ *n* ⟦1⟧ (a) (diagram, map) plano *m* (b) (of book, essay) esquema *m* ⟦2⟧ (arrangement, scheme) plan *m*; do you have any ～s for tonight? ¿tienes algún plan para esta noche?

plan² **-nn-** *vt* ⟨*journey/raid*⟩ planear; ⟨*garden/ house*⟩ diseñar; ⟨*economy/strategies*⟩ planificar*; ⟨*essay*⟩ hacer* un esquema de; ⟨*surprise*⟩ preparar; **as ～ned** según lo planeado; **to ～ to +** INF: where are you ～ning to spend Christmas? ¿dónde tienes pensado pasar las Navidades?
■ ～ *vi*: **to ～ ahead** planear las cosas de antemano
■ **plan on** [*v + prep + o*] (a) (intend) pensar* (b) (expect, count on) contar* con

plane¹ /pleɪn/ *n* ⟦1⟧ (aircraft) avión *m* ⟦2⟧ ～ **(tree)** plátano *m* ⟦3⟧ (tool) cepillo *m* de carpintero; (longer) garlopa *f* ⟦4⟧ (surface) plano *m*

plane² *vt* ⟨*wood/surface*⟩ cepillar

planet /'plænət ‖'plænɪt/ *n* planeta *m*

planetary /'plænətəri ‖'plænɪtəri/ *adj* (*before n*) planetario

plank /plæŋk/ *n* tabla *f*, tablón *m*

plankton /'plæŋktən/ *n* plancton *m*

planned /plænd/ *adj* planeado; ～ **parenthood** (AmE) planificación *f* familiar

planner /'plænər ‖'plænə(r)/ *n* (a) (of project) planificador, -dora *m,f* (b) (town ～) urbanista *mf*

planning /'plænɪŋ/ *n* (a) (of project) planificación *f* (b) (town ～) urbanismo *m*; (*before n*) ～ **permission** (BrE) permiso *m* de obras

plant¹ /plænt ‖plɑ:nt/ *n* ⟦1⟧ (Bot) planta *f* ⟦2⟧ (a) (factory, installation) planta *f* (b) (equipment) maquinaria *f*

plant² *vt* ⟦1⟧ ⟨*flower/trees*⟩ plantar; ⟨*seeds*⟩ sembrar* ⟦2⟧ (place) ⟨*bomb*⟩ colocar*; ⟨*kiss*⟩ dar*, plantar (fam); **she ～ed herself right next to me** se me plantó justo al lado (fam) ⟦3⟧ ⟨*drugs/evidence*⟩ colocar*; ⟨*agent/informer*⟩ infiltrar

plantain /'plæntn̩ ‖'plæntɪn/ *n* plátano *m* grande (*para cocinar*), plátano (Col, Ven), plátano *m* macho (Méx)

plantation /plæn'teɪʃən ‖plæn'teɪʃən, plɑ:n-/ *n* plantación *f*

plaque /plæk/ *n* ⟦1⟧ (tablet) placa *f* ⟦2⟧ (Dent) sarro *m*, placa *f* (dental)

plasma /'plæzmə/ *n* plasma *m*

plaster¹ /'plæstər ‖'plɑ:stə(r)/ *n* ⟦1⟧ (a) (Const) (powder, mixture) yeso *m*; (on walls) revoque *m* (b) ～ **(of Paris)** (AmE) (Med) yeso *m*, escayola *f* (Esp); **to have one's leg in ～** tener* la pierna enyesada *or* (Esp) escayolada ⟦2⟧ (sticking ～) (BrE) ▶ BAND-AID

plaster² *vt* (Const) ⟨*wall/room*⟩ revocar*; ⟨*cracks*⟩ rellenar con yeso

plaster cast *n* (a) (Med) yeso *m* *or* (Esp) escayola *f* (b) (Art) molde *m* de yeso, escayola *f* (Esp)

plastic¹ /'plæstɪk/ *n* plástico *m*; (*before n*) de plástico

plastic² *adj* ⟦1⟧ (artificial) (pej) ⟨*smile/people*⟩ de plástico (pey) ⟦2⟧ (a) (malleable) (Tech) plástico, moldeable (b) (Art) plástico

plastic: ～ **bullet** *n* bala *f* de plástico; ～ **explosive** *n* explosivo *m* plástico, goma dos *f*

Plasticine® /'plæstəsi:n/ *n* plastilina® *f*, plasticina® *f* (CS)

plastic: ～ **surgeon** *n* cirujano plástico, cirujana plástica *m,f* (AmL), especialista *mf* en cirugía estética *or* plástica; ～ **surgery** *n* cirugía *f* estética *or* plástica

plate¹ /pleɪt/ *n* ⟦1⟧ (a) (dish) plato *m* (b) (dishes) vajilla *f* (*de plata u oro*) ⟦2⟧ (of metal) chapa *f*; (thin) lámina *f*; (of glass) placa *f* ⟦3⟧ (a) (Phot) placa *f* (b) (Art, Print) plancha *f* (c) (illustration) ilustración *f*, lámina *f*

plate² *vt* (Metall) **to ～ sth WITH sth** recubrir* algo DE algo

plateau /plæ'təʊ ‖'plætəʊ/ *n* (*pl* **-teaus** *or* **-teaux** /-z/) meseta *f*

platform /'plætfɔrm ‖'plætfɔ:m/ *n* (a) (raised structure) plataforma *f*; (for orator) estrado *m*, tribuna *f* (b) (Rail) andén *m* (c) (Pol) (opportunity to air views) plataforma *f*, tribuna *f*

platinum /'plætnəm ‖'plætɪnəm/ *n* platino *m*

platitude /'plætətu:d ‖'plætɪtju:d/ *n* lugar *m* común

platonic /plə'tɑ:nɪk ‖plə'tɒnɪk/ *adj* platónico

platoon /plə'tu:n/ *n* (Mil) sección *f*

platter /'plætər ‖'plætə(r)/ *n* fuente *f*

platypus /'plætɪpəs/ *n* (*pl* ～**es**) (duck-billed ～) ornitorrinco *m*

plausible /'plɔ:zəbəl/ *adj* ⟨*argument/story*⟩ verosímil; ⟨*liar*⟩ convincente

play¹ /pleɪ/ *n* ⟦1⟧ (a) (recreation) juego *m* (b) (Sport) juego *m* ⟦2⟧ (interplay) juego *m* ⟦3⟧ (slack) (Tech) juego *m* ⟦4⟧ (Theat) obra *f* (de teatro), pieza *f* (teatral), comedia *f* ⟦5⟧ (pun): **a ～ on words** un juego de palabras, un albur (Méx)

play² *vt*
I ⟦1⟧ (a) ⟨*cards/hopscotch*⟩ jugar* a; **to ～ a joke/ trick on sb** hacerle* *or* gastarle una broma/una jugarreta a algn (b) ⟨*football/chess*⟩ jugar* (AmL exc RPI), jugar* a (Esp, RPI)
⟦2⟧ (a) (compete against) ⟨*opponent*⟩ jugar* contra (b) ⟨*card*⟩ tirar, jugar*; ⟨*piece*⟩ mover* (c) (in particular position) jugar* de
II ⟦1⟧ (Theat) (a) ⟨*villain/Hamlet*⟩ representar el papel de; **to ～ the innocent** hacerse* el inocente (b) ⟨*theater/town*⟩ actuar* en
⟦2⟧ (Mus) ⟨*instrument/note/piece*⟩ tocar*
⟦3⟧ (Audio) ⟨*tape/record*⟩ poner*
■ ～ *vi*
I ⟦1⟧ (amuse oneself) «*children*» jugar*; **to ～ AT sth** jugar* A algo
⟦2⟧ (Games, Sport) jugar*
II ⟦1⟧ (Theat) «*cast*» actuar*; «*show*» ser* representado (b) (pretend): **to ～ dead** hacerse* el muerto; *to ～ hard to get* hacerse* el (*or* la *etc*) interesante
⟦2⟧ (Mus) «*musician*» tocar*; **music was ～ing in the background** se escuchaba una música de fondo
■ **play along** ⟦1⟧ [*v + adv*] (cooperate): **I refuse to**

~ **along with him/his schemes** me niego a hacerle el juego/a tener nada que ver con sus enjuagues (fam)
2 [*v* + *o* + *adv*] (deceive, manipulate) manipular
■ **play around** [*v* + *adv*] jugar*, juguetear (fam & pey)
■ **play back** [*v* + *o* + *adv*, *v* + *adv* + *o*] poner* ⟨*una grabación*⟩
■ **play down** [*v* + *o* + *adv*, *v* + *adv* + *o*] ⟨*importance*⟩ minimizar*; ⟨*risk/achievement*⟩ quitarle importancia a
■ **play off** [*v* + *o* + *adv*] oponer*; **to ~ sb off against sb: she ~s her parents off against each other** hace pelear a sus padres para lograr sus propósitos
■ **play up** **1** [*v* + *adv*] (BrE) (cause trouble) colloq) «*child*» dar* guerra (fam); «*car/TV*» no funcionar bien
2 [*v* + *o* + *adv*] (cause trouble) (BrE colloq) «*child*» darle* guerra a (fam); «*shoulder/back*» darle* problemas a (fam)

play: **~back** *n* play-back *m*; **~boy** *n* playboy *m*; **~by-~** /'pleɪbaɪ'pleɪ/ *adj* (AmE Sport) ⟨*before n*⟩ jugada a jugada

player /'pleɪər ‖ 'pleɪə(r)/ *n* **1** (Games, Sport) jugador, -dora *m,f* **2** (Mus) músico *mf*, músico, -ca *m,f*

playful /'pleɪfəl/ *adj* **(a)** (boisterous) juguetón **(b)** (not serious) pícaro

playfully /'pleɪfəli/ *adv* **(a)** (boisterously) juguetonamente **(b)** (humorously) ⟨*remark/slap*⟩ en broma

play: **~ground** *n* (BrE) patio *m* (de recreo); **~group** *n*: grupo de actividades lúdico-educativas para niños de edad preescolar

playing /'pleɪɪŋ/**:** ~ **card** *n* naipe *m*, carta *f*; ~ **field** *n* (BrE) ⟨*often pl*⟩ campo *m* de juego, cancha *f* de deportes (esp AmL)

play: **~mate** *n* compañero, -ra *m,f* de juegos; **~off** *n* desempate *m*; **~pen** *n* corral *m*, parque *m* (Esp); **~room** *n* cuarto *m* de los juguetes; **~thing** *n* juguete *m*; **~time** *n* (*no art*) (BrE) recreo *m*; **~wright** /'pleɪraɪt/ *n* dramaturgo, -ga *m,f*

plaza /'plæzə ‖ 'plɑːzə/ *n* **(a)** (square) plaza *f*; (in front of large building) explanada *f* **(b)** (complex) (AmE) centro *m* comercial

plc, Plc (in UK) (= **public limited company**) ≈S.A.

plea /pliː/ *n* **1** (appeal) (frml) petición *f*; (in supplication) ruego *m* **2** (Law): **to enter a ~ of guilty/not guilty** declararse culpable/inocente

plead /pliːd/ (*past & past p* **pleaded** *or* (AmE also) **pled**) *vt* alegar*; **she's not coming, she ~ed poverty** no viene, dijo que no tenía dinero
■ ~ *vi* **(a)** (implore, beg) suplicar*; **to ~ FOR sth** suplicar* algo; **to ~ WITH sb to + INF** suplicarle* a algn QUE (+ *subj*) **(b)** (Law): **to ~ guilty/not guilty** declararse culpable/inocente

pleasant /'plezn̩t/ *adj* **-er, -est** agradable; ⟨*person*⟩ simpático, agradable

pleasantly /'plezn̩tli/ *adv* ⟨*say/speak*⟩ en tono agradable; ⟨*smile*⟩ con simpatía; **I was ~ surprised by the changes** los cambios me causaron una grata sorpresa

pleasantry /'plezn̩tri/ *n* (*pl* **-ries**) cortesía *f*

please¹ /pliːz/ *interj* por favor; **yes, ~** sí, gracias

please² *vt* (make happy) complacer*; (satisfy) contentar
■ ~ *vi* **(a)** (satisfy): **we do our best to ~** hacemos todo lo posible por complacer al cliente (*or* a todo el mundo *etc*) **(b)** (choose) querer*; **do as you ~** haz lo que quieras
■ *v refl* **to ~ oneself: ~ yourself** haz lo que quieras

pleased /pliːzd/ *adj* (satisfied) satisfecho; (happy) contento; **I'm very ~ for you!** me alegro mucho por ti; **she was very ~ with herself** estaba muy ufana; **I am ~ to inform you that …** (frml) tengo el placer de comunicarle que … (frml); **~ to meet you** encantado (de conocerlo), mucho gusto

pleasing /'pliːzɪŋ/ *adj* **(a)** (pleasant) agradable **(b)** (gratifying) ⟨*news*⟩ grato

pleasurable /'pleʒərəbəl/ *adj* placentero

pleasure /'pleʒər ‖ 'pleʒə(r)/ *n* **1** (happiness, satisfaction) placer *m*; **it's a ~ to listen to her** es un placer escucharla; **it gives me great ~ to introduce …** es un placer para mí presentarles …; **to take ~ in sth** disfrutar con algo **2** (a) (recreation) placer *m*; **I play just for ~** toco sólo porque me gusta **(b)** (source of happiness) placer *m*; **Jane is a real ~ to teach** da gusto darle clases a Jane

pleasure boat *n* (steamer) barco *m* de recreo; (small craft) bote *m* de recreo

pleat /pliːt/ *n* pliegue *m*; (wide) tabla *f*

plectrum /'plektrəm/ *n* (*pl* **-trums** *or* **-tra** /-trə/) púa *f*, plectro *m*, uñeta *f* (CS), uña *f* (Méx, Ven)

pled /pled/ (AmE) *past & past p of* PLEAD

pledge¹ /pledʒ/ *vt* ⟨*support/funds*⟩ prometer

pledge² *n* **(a)** (promise) promesa *f*; **to make a ~ to + INF** prometer + INF **(b)** (of money) cantidad *f* prometida

plentiful /'plentɪfəl/ *adj* abundante

plenty¹ /'plenti/ *n* abundancia *f*

plenty² *pron* **1** **(a)** (large, sufficient number) muchos, -chas **(b)** **plenty of muchos, -chas 2 (a)** (large, sufficient quantity) mucho, -cha; **$50 is ~** 50 dólares es más que suficiente **(b) plenty of** mucho, -cha; **~ of time** tiempo de sobra

plethora /'pleθərə/ *n* (*no pl*) **a ~ OF sth** una plétora DE algo

Plexiglas® /'pleksɪɡlæs ‖ 'pleksɪɡlɑːs/ *n* (AmE) acrílico *m*, plexiglás® *m* (Esp)

pliable /'plaɪəbəl/, **pliant** /'plaɪənt/ *adj* ⟨*material/substance*⟩ maleable; ⟨*person/attitude*⟩ flexible

pliers /'plaɪərz ‖ 'plaɪəz/ *pl n* alicate(s) *m(pl)*, pinza(s) *f(pl)* (Méx, RPl)

plight /plaɪt/ *n* (*no pl*) situación *f* difícil

plimsoll /'plɪmsəl/ *n* (BrE) zapatilla *f* de lona, tenis *m*, playera *f* (Esp)

plinth /plɪnθ/ *n* (of pillar, column) plinto *m*; (of statue) pedestal *m*

plod /plɒd ‖ plɒd/ *vi* **-dd-** **(a)** (walk) caminar lenta y pesadamente **(b)** (work): **she's still ~ding away at her thesis** sigue lidiando con la tesis

plonk¹ /plɑːŋk ‖ plɒŋk/ *vt* (BrE colloq) ▶ PLUNK

plonk² *n* (colloq) vino *m* peleón (fam)

plot¹ /plɑːt ‖ plɒt/ n **1** (conspiracy) complot m **2** (story) argumento m **3** (piece of land) terreno m, solar m, parcela f

plot² -tt- vt **1** (mark out) ⟨curve/graph⟩ trazar*; ⟨position⟩ determinar **2** (plan) ⟨rebellion/revenge⟩ tramar
■ ~ vi to ~ (AGAINST sb) conspirar ⟨CONTRA algn⟩

plotter /'plɑːtər ‖ 'plɒtə(r)/ n **1** (conspirator) conspirador, -dora m,f **2** (Comput, Tech) trazador m de gráficos

plough etc /plaʊ/ (BrE) ▶ PLOW etc

plow¹, (BrE) **plough** /plaʊ/ n (Agr) arado m

plow², (BrE) **plough** vt arar
■ ~ vi arar la tierra

■ **plow back,** (BrE) **plough back** [v + o + adv, v + adv + o] ⟨profits⟩ reinvertir*

■ **plow into,** (BrE) **plough into** [v + prep + o] ⟨vehicle/wall⟩ estrellarse contra

■ **plow through,** (BrE) **plough through** [v + prep + o] ⟨mud/snow⟩ abrirse* camino a través de; I'm still ~ing through the book todavía estoy tratando de leer el libro, pero me cuesta

plowman, (BrE) **ploughman** /'plaʊmən/ n (pl -men /-mən/) labrador m

ploy /plɔɪ/ n treta f

pluck¹ /plʌk/ vt (a) ⟨chicken⟩ desplumar; to ~ one's eyebrows depilarse las cejas (b) ⟨fruit/ flower⟩ arrancar*; to ~ up (the) courage to + INF armarse de valor para + INF (c) (Mus) ⟨string/ guitar⟩ puntear

pluck² n valor m

plucky /'plʌki/ adj **pluckier, pluckiest** valiente

plug¹ /plʌg/ n **1** (stopper) tapón m **2** (Elec) (a) (attached to lead) enchufe m; (socket) toma f de corriente, enchufe m, tomacorriente(s) m (AmL) (b) (spark ~) bujía f

plug² -gg- vt **1** ⟨hole/gap⟩ tapar **2** (promote) ⟨record/book⟩ hacerle* propaganda a
■ **plug in 1** [v + o + adv, v + adv + o] enchufar **2** [v + adv] enchufarse

plughole /'plʌghəʊl/ n (BrE) desagüe m

plum /plʌm/ n ciruela f

plumage /'pluːmɪdʒ/ n plumaje m

plumb¹ /plʌm/ adv (colloq) justo

plumb² vt **1** (fathom) ⟨mystery⟩ dilucidar **2** (Naut) sondar, sondear

plumber /'plʌmər ‖ 'plʌmə(r)/ n plomero, -ra m,f or (AmC, Esp) fontanero, -ra f or (Per) gasfitero, -ra m,f or (Chi) gásfiter mf

plumbing /'plʌmɪŋ/ n (pipes) cañerías fpl, tuberías fpl; (installation) instalación f de agua

plume /pluːm/ n pluma f; (cluster of feathers) penacho m

plummet /'plʌmət ‖ 'plʌmɪt/ vi caer* en picada or (Esp) en picado

plump /plʌmp/ adj -er, -est ⟨person/face⟩ (re)llenito; ⟨chicken/rabbit⟩ gordo
■ **plump for** [v + prep + o] (colloq) decidirse por
■ **plump up** [v + o + adv, v + adv + o] ⟨pillow/ cushion⟩ ahuecar*

plunder¹ /'plʌndər ‖ 'plʌndə(r)/ vt (a) (steal from) ⟨village⟩ saquear (b) (steal) ⟨treasure/wealth⟩ robar

plunder² n (a) (objects) botín m (b) (action) saqueo m

plunge¹ /plʌndʒ/ vt to ~ sth INTO sth (a) (immerse, thrust) ⟨into liquid⟩ sumergir* algo EN algo; she ~d the knife into his heart le hundió el cuchillo en el corazón (b) (into state, condition) sumir algo/a algn EN algo
■ vi **1** (dive) zambullirse*; (fall) caer* **2** (a) (slope downward steeply) ⟨road/path⟩ descender* bruscamente (b) (drop) ⟨price/temperature/ popularity⟩ caer* en picada or (Esp) en picado

plunge² n (in water) zambullida f; to take the ~ (take a risk) arriesgarse*, jugarse* el todo por todo; (get married) casarse, darse* el paso

plunger /'plʌndʒər ‖ 'plʌndʒə(r)/ n (a) (for unblocking drain) desatascador m, chupona f (Esp), destapador m (de caño) (Méx), sopapa f (RPl), sopapo m (Chi), chupa f (Col), goma f (Ven) (b) (in syringe) émbolo m

plunk /plʌŋk/ vt (AmE) poner*, plantificar* (fam)

pluperfect /'pluːpɜːrfɪkt ‖ pluː'pɜːfɪkt/ n pluscuamperfecto m

plural¹ /'plʊrəl ‖ 'plʊərəl/ adj (Ling) en plural

plural² n plural m; in the ~ en plural

plus¹ /plʌs/ n (pl ~es or ~ses) (a) ~ (sign) (signo m de) más m (b) (advantage, bonus) (colloq) ventaja f

plus² adj (a) (advantageous) (colloq) ⟨before n⟩ ⟨point⟩ positivo (b) (and more) ⟨pred⟩: children aged 13 ~ niños de 13 años para arriba

plus³ prep más; ~ the fact that ... aparte de que ...; ▶ FOUR¹

plush /plʌʃ/ adj lujoso

Pluto /'pluːtəʊ/ n Plutón m

plutonium /pluː'təʊniəm/ n plutonio m

ply¹ /plaɪ/ n (pl plies) (a) (of wood) chapa f (b) (of wool, yarn) cabo m; three-~ wool lana f de tres cabos

ply² plies, plying, plied vt (a) (carry out): to ~ one's trade ejercer* su oficio (b) ⟨oar⟩ mover*; ⟨tools⟩ manejar (c) ⟨ship⟩ ⟨sea⟩ navegar* por
■ ~ vi (fml) ⟨ship/plane/bus⟩ hacer* el trayecto
■ **ply with** [v + o + prep + o]: he kept ~ing me with whiskey estaba constantemente sirviéndome whisky

plywood /'plaɪwʊd/ n contrachapado m (tablero en varias capas)

pm (after midday) p.m.; at 2 ~ a las 2 de la tarde, a las 2 p.m.

PM (BrE) n = prime minister

PMS n = premenstrual syndrome

PMT n (BrE) = premenstrual tension

pneumatic drill /nʊ'mætɪk ‖ njuː'mætɪk/ n martillo m neumático

pneumonia /nʊ'məʊnjə ‖ njuː'məʊniə/ n pulmonía f, neumonía f

poach /pəʊtʃ/ *vt* **1** (Culin) ⟨egg⟩ escalfar; ⟨fish⟩ cocer* a fuego lento **2** (steal) ⟨game⟩ cazar* furtivamente; ⟨staff/ideas⟩ robar
■ **~** *vi* (hunt game) cazar* furtivamente

poacher /'pəʊtʃər ‖'pəʊtʃə(r)/ *n* cazador furtivo, cazadora furtiva *m,f*

PO box *n* Apdo. postal, Apdo. de correos, C.C. (CS)

pocket¹ /'pɑːkət ‖'pɒkɪt/ *n* **1** (a) (in garment) bolsillo *m* (b) (on billiard, snooker, pool table) tronera *f* **2** (small area) bolsa *f*; ~s of resistance bolsas *fpl* de resistencia

pocket² *vt* (a) (put in pocket) meterse en el bolsillo (b) (steal, gain) (colloq) embolsarse (fam)

pocket³ *adj* (before n) de bolsillo

pocket: ~book /'pɑːkətbʊk ‖'pɒkɪtbʊk/ *n* (a) (handbag) (AmE) cartera *f or* (Esp) bolso *m or* (Méx) bolsa *f* (b) (wallet) (AmE) cartera *f*, billetera *f* (c) (paperback) (AmE) libro *m* en rústica (d) (notebook) (BrE) cuaderno *m*; ~ **money** *n* (spending money) dinero *m* para gastos personales; (for children) (BrE) dinero *m* de bolsillo, ≈mesada *f* (AmL), domingo *m* (Méx), propina *f* (Per)

pod /pɑːd ‖pɒd/ *n* (of peas, beans) vaina *f*

podiatrist /pə'daɪətrəst ‖pə'daɪətrɪst/ *n* (AmE) pedicuro, -ra *m,f*, podólogo, -ga, *m,f* (frml)

podium /'pəʊdiəm/ *n* estrado *m*

poem /'pəʊəm ‖'pəʊɪm/ *n* poema *m*

poet /'pəʊət ‖'pəʊɪt/ *n* poeta *mf*

poetic /pəʊ'etɪk/ *adj* poético

poet laureate, Poet Laureate /'lɔːriət ‖'lɒriət/ *n* (pl ~s ~) poeta laureado, poeta laureada *m,f*

poetry /'pəʊətri ‖'pəʊɪtri/ *n* poesía *f*

poignant /'pɔɪnjənt/ *adj* ⟨story/moment⟩ conmovedor; ⟨look/plea⟩ patético; ⟨reminder⟩ doloroso

point¹ /pɔɪnt/ *n*
I **1** (a) (dot) punto *m* (b) (decimal ~) ≈coma *f*, punto *m* decimal (AmL) (the point is used instead of the comma in some Latin American countries)
2 (a) (in space) punto *m*; the ~s of the compass los puntos cardinales; the ~ of no return: we've reached the ~ of no return ahora ya no nos podemos echar atrás (b) (on scale) punto *m*; you're right, up to a ~ hasta cierto punto tienes razón
3 (in time) momento *m*; at this ~ in time en este momento; to be on the ~ of -ING estar* a punto de + INF
4 (in contest, exam) punto *m*
II **1** (a) (item, matter) punto *m*; to bring up or raise a ~ plantear una cuestión; to make a ~ of -ING: I'll make a ~ of watching them closely me encargaré de vigilarlos de cerca (b) (argument): yes, that's a ~ sí, ese es un punto interesante; to make a ~: that was a very interesting ~ you made lo que señalaste es muy interesante; all right, you've made your ~! sí, bueno, ya has dicho lo que querías decir; ~ taken de acuerdo
2 (no pl) (central issue, meaning): to come/get to the ~ ir* al grano; she was brief and to the ~ fue breve y concisa; that's beside the ~ eso no tiene nada que ver, eso no viene al caso; the ~ is that ... el hecho es que ...; that's not the ~ no se trata de eso
3 (purpose): what's the ~ of going on? ¿qué

sentido tiene seguir?; there's no ~ o there isn't any ~ (in) feeling sorry for yourself no sirve de nada compadecerse
4 (feature, quality): strong ~ fuerte *m*; bad ~s defectos *mpl*; he has many good ~s tiene muchos puntos a su favor
III **1** (a) (sharp end, tip) punta *f* (b) (promontory) (Geog) punta *f*
2 points *pl* (BrE Rail) agujas *fpl*
3 (socket) (BrE) ⟨electrical o power⟩ ~ toma *f* de corriente, enchufe *m*, tomacorriente *m* (AmL)

point² *vt* (aim, direct) señalar, indicar*; to ~ sth AT sb/sth: he ~ed his finger at me me señaló con el dedo; she ~ed the gun at him le apuntó con la pistola
■ ~ *vi* (a) (with finger, stick etc) señalar; it's rude to ~ es de mala educación señalar con el dedo; to ~ AT/TO sth/sb señalar algo/a algn (b) (call attention) to ~ TO sth señalar algo (c) (indicate) to ~ TO sth ⟨facts/symptoms⟩ indicar* algo
■ **point out** [v + o + adv, v + adv + o] **1** (show) señalar; I'll ~ it/her out to you te lo/la señalaré **2** (make aware of) ⟨problem/advantage⟩ señalar

point: ~ blank *adv* ⟨shoot⟩ a quemarropa; ~**-blank** /'pɔɪnt'blæŋk/ *adj*: at ~-blank range a quemarropa

pointed /'pɔɪntəd ‖'pɔɪntɪd/ *adj* **1** (with a point) ⟨stick/leaf⟩ acabado en punta, puntudo (Andes); ⟨arch⟩ ojival; ⟨chin/nose⟩ puntiagudo, puntudo (Andes); ⟨shoe⟩ de punta, puntudo (Andes); ⟨hat⟩ de pico **2** (deliberate) ⟨remark/comment⟩ mordaz

pointer /'pɔɪntər ‖'pɔɪntə(r)/ *n* **1** (on dial, gage) aguja *f* **2** (clue, signal) pista *f*; ~ TO sth indicador *m* DE algo **3** (tip) idea *f*

pointless /'pɔɪntləs ‖'pɔɪntlɪs/ *adj* ⟨attempt⟩ vano, inútil; ⟨existence⟩ sin sentido; it's ~ arguing with him no tiene sentido discutir con él

point of view *n* (pl ~s ~ ~) punto *m* de vista

poise /pɔɪz/ *n* (a) (bearing) porte *m* (b) (composure) desenvoltura *f*

poised /pɔɪzd/ *adj* **1** (a) (balanced, suspended): ~ in the air suspendido en el aire; they were waiting with pencils ~ esperaban, lápiz en mano (b) (ready) listo **2** (self-assured): she is very ~ tiene mucho aplomo

poison¹ /'pɔɪzn̩/ *n* veneno *m*

poison² *vt* (a) (with poison) envenenar; (make ill) intoxicar*; ⟨river/soil⟩ contaminar (b) (corrupt) ⟨mind/society⟩ corromper; ⟨relationship/atmosphere⟩ dañar

poisoning /'pɔɪzn̩ɪŋ/ *n* envenenamiento *m*

poisonous /'pɔɪzn̩əs/ *adj* venenoso

poison-pen letter /'pɔɪzn̩'pen/ *n* anónimo *m* ponzoñoso

poke¹ /pəʊk/ *vt* (a) (jab): to ~ sb's eye out sacarle* un ojo a algn; she ~d him in the ribs le dio en el costado; (with elbow) le dio un codazo en el costado (b) (thrust): she ~d her head around the door asomó la cabeza por la puerta; he ~d his finger through the crack metió el dedo por la ranura
■ ~ *vi* (project) asomar; her feet were poking out of the sheets los pies le asomaban por entre las sábanas; a few shoots were poking up out of the soil unos cuantos brotes asomaban en la tierra ···⟶

■ **poke about, poke around** [*v* + *adv*]
fisgonear

poke² *n* golpe *m*; (with elbow) codazo *m*

poker /'pəʊkər ‖'pəʊkə(r)/ *n* **1** (for fire)
atizador *m* **2** (game) póker *m*, póquer *m*

poky /'pəʊki/ *adj* **pokier, pokiest** (colloq) **(a)**
(cramped) diminuto **(b)** (slow) (AmE) lerdo

Poland /'pəʊlənd/ *n* Polonia *f*

polar /'pəʊlər ‖'pəʊlə(r)/ *adj* polar

polar bear *n* oso *m* polar

polarize /'pəʊləraɪz/ *vt* polarizar*

pole /pəʊl/ *n* **1** (fixed support) poste *m*; (flag~)
mástil *m*; (tent ~) palo *m* **2** (a) (Geog) polo *m*;
the North/South P~ el Polo Norte/Sur **(b)** (Phys)
polo *m*

Pole *n* polaco, -ca *m,f*

polecat *n* **(a)** (of weasel family) turón *m* **(b)**
(AmE) ▶ SKUNK

polemical /pə'lemɪkəl/ *adj* polémico

pole: ~**star**, (BrE) **P~ Star** *n* estrella *f* polar;
~**-vault** *n* salto *m* con garrocha *or* (Esp) con
pértiga

police¹ /pə'liːs/ *n* (force) (+ *sing or pl vb*) **the** ~
la policía; (before *n*) ⟨escort/patrol⟩ policial; ~ **car**
coche *m* patrulla *or* de policía; ~ **constable** (in
UK) agente *mf*; ~ **department** (in US) distrito *m*
policial; **the** ~ **force** la policía; ~ **officer** agente
mf, policía *mf*; **to have a** ~ **record** estar* fichado
or (CS *tb*) prontuariado

police² *vt* (keep order in) ⟨streets⟩ patrullar;
⟨region/area⟩ mantener* una fuerza policial en

police: ~ **dog** *n* perro *m* policía; ~**man**
/pə'liːsmən/ *n* (*pl* **-men** /-mən/) policía *m*,
agente *m*; ~ **state** *n* estado *m* policía; ~
station *n* comisaría *f*, ~**woman** *n* agente *f*,
policía *f*, mujer *f* policía

policy /'pɑːləsi ‖'pɒləsi/ *n* (*pl* **-cies**) **1 (a)**
(Pol) política *f* **(b)** (standard practice, plan) (Busn)
política *f*; **it is good/bad** ~ es/no es
recomendable **2** (insurance ~) (contract) seguro *m*;
(document) póliza *f* de seguros

policyholder /'pɑːləsiˌhəʊldər
‖'pɒləsiˌhəʊldə(r)/ *n* asegurado, -da *m,f*

polio /'pəʊliəʊ/ *n* polio *f*

poliomyelitis /ˌpəʊliəʊˌmaɪə'laɪtəs
‖ˌpəʊliəʊˌmaɪə'laɪtɪs/ *n* poliomielitis *f*

polish¹ /'pɑːlɪʃ ‖'pɒlɪʃ/ *n* **(a)** (shoe ~) betún *m*,
pomada *f* (RPl), pasta *f* (Chi); (furniture ~) cera *f*
para muebles, lustramuebles *m* (CS); (metal ~)
limpiametales *m*; (floor ~) (esp BrE) abrillantador
m (de suelos); (wax ~) cera *f* (abrillantadora) **(b)**
(sheen) brillo *m* **(c)** (refinement): **he lacks** ~ tiene
que pulir su estilo

polish² *vt* **(a)** ⟨floor/table/car/brass⟩ darle* *or*
sacarle* brillo a; ⟨shoes⟩ limpiar, lustrar (esp
AmL), bolear (Méx), embolar (Col); ⟨lens/mirror⟩
limpiar; ⟨stone⟩ pulir **(b)** (refine) pulir
■ **polish off** [*v* + *o* + *adv*, *v* + *adv* + *o*] (colloq)
⟨food⟩ liquidarse (fam)

Polish¹ /'pəʊlɪʃ/ *adj* polaco

Polish² *n* polaco *m*

polished /'pɑːlɪʃt ‖'pɒlɪʃt/ *adj* **(a)** (shiny)
⟨metal/marble⟩ pulido; ⟨wood⟩ brillante, lustrado
(esp AmL) **(b)** (refined) ⟨manners/accent⟩ refinado;
⟨performance/translation⟩ pulido

polite /pə'laɪt/ *adj* **politer, politest** ⟨manner/

person⟩ cortés; **they were making** ~ **conversation**
conversaban tratando de ser agradables; **it's not**
~ **to shout** gritar es una falta de educación

politely /pə'laɪtli/ *adv* ⟨behave⟩ correctamente;
⟨ask/refuse⟩ con buenos modales

politeness /pə'laɪtnəs ‖pə'laɪtnɪs/ *n* cortesía *f*

political /pə'lɪtɪkəl/ *adj* político

politically correct /pə'lɪtɪkli/ *adj* ⟨term⟩
usado por gente de ideología progresista

politician /ˌpɑːlə'tɪʃən ‖ˌpɒlɪ'tɪʃən/ *n* político,
-ca *m,f*

politics /'pɑːlətɪks ‖'pɒlətɪks/ *n* **1** (+ *sing vb*)
(science, activity) política *f* **2** (+ *pl vb*) (political
relations) política *f*

polka /'pəʊlkə ‖'pɒlkə, 'pəʊlkə/ *n* polca *f*,
polka *f*

polka dot /'pəʊkə, pəʊlkə ‖'pɒlkə, 'pəʊlkə/ *n*
lunar *m*, topo *m* (Esp)

poll¹ /pəʊl/ *n* **1 (a)** (ballot) votación *f* **(b)** (opinion
~) encuesta *f or* sondeo *m* (de opinión) **2 polls**
pl (polling stations) **the** ~**s: to go to the** ~**s** ir* *or*
acudir a las urnas

poll² *vt* (Pol) ⟨votes⟩ (obtain) obtener*; (cast) emitir

pollen /'pɑːlən ‖'pɒlən/ *n* polen *m*

pollinate /'pɑːləneɪt ‖'pɒləneɪt/ *vt* polinizar*

polling /'pəʊlɪŋ/ *n* votación *f*; (before *n*) ~ **place**
o (BrE) **station** centro *m* electoral

pollutant /pə'luːtn̩t/ *n* (agente *m*)
contaminante *m*

pollute /pə'luːt/ *vt* (Ecol) contaminar

pollution /pə'luːʃən/ *n* contaminación *f*

polo /'pəʊləʊ/ *n* polo *m*

polo: ~ **neck** *n* (BrE) **(a)** (style of neck) cuello *m*
alto **(b)** ▶ ~ NECK SWEATER; ~ **neck sweater**
n (BrE) suéter *m* de cuello alto, polera *f* (RPl)

poly- /'pɑːli ‖'pɒli/ *pref* poli-

polyester /'pɑːliˌestər ‖ˌpɒli'estə(r)/ *n*
poliéster *m*

polyethylene /ˌpɑːli'eθəliːn ‖ˌpɒli'eθəliːn/ *n*
(esp AmE) polietileno *m*

polygamy /pə'lɪgəmi/ *n* poligamia *f*

Polynesia /ˌpɑːlə'niːʒə ‖ˌpɒlɪ'niːʒə/ *n* (la)
Polinesia

Polynesian /ˌpɑːlə'niːʒən ‖ˌpɒlɪ'niːʒən/ *adj*
polinesio

polystyrene /ˌpɑːli'staɪriːn ‖ˌpɒli'staɪriːn/ *n*
poliestireno *m*

polythene /'pɑːləθiːn ‖'pɒlɪθiːn/ *n* (BrE)
plástico *m*, polietileno *m* (téc)

pomegranate /'pɑːməgrænət ‖'pɒmɪgrænɪt/
n granada *f*

pomp /pɑːmp ‖pɒmp/ *n* pompa *f*, fausto *m*

pompom /'pɑːmpɑːm ‖'pɒmpɒm/ *n* (on hat)
borla *f*, pompón *m*

pompous /'pɑːmpəs ‖'pɒmpəs/ *adj* pomposo

pond /pɑːnd ‖pɒnd/ *n* (man-made) estanque *m*;
(natural) laguna *f*

ponder /'pɑːndər ‖'pɒndə(r)/ *vt* considerar

ponderous /'pɑːndərəs ‖'pɒndərəs/ *adj*
⟨movement⟩ lento y pesado; ⟨explanation/speech⟩
pesado

pong¹ /pɑːŋ ‖pɒŋ/ *n* (BrE colloq) peste *f* (fam)

pong² *vi* (BrE colloq) apestar (fam)

pontiff /'pɑːntəf ‖'pɒntɪf/ *n* pontífice *m*

pony /ˈpəʊni/ n (pl **ponies**) poni m

ponytail /ˈpəʊniteɪl/ n cola f de caballo

poodle /ˈpuːdl/ n caniche m

pooh-pooh /ˈpuːˈpuː/ vt (colloq) reírse* de

pool¹ /puːl/ n **1** (a) (collection of water) charca f (b) (swimming ∼) piscina f, pileta f (RPI), alberca f (esp Méx) (c) (puddle) charco m **2** (common reserve of money) fondo m común **3** **pools** pl (BrE) ▸ FOOTBALL POOLS **4** (billiards) billar m americano, pool m

pool² vt hacer* un fondo común de

pooped (out) /puːpt/ adj (AmE sl) (pred) reventado (fam)

poor /pɔːr ‖pɔːr, pʊə(r)/ adj **-er, -est** **1** (not wealthy) pobre **2** (unsatisfactory, bad) ‹harvest› pobre, escaso; ‹diet/quality› malo; ‹imitation› burdo **3** (unfortunate) (before n) pobre; **you ∼ thing!** ¡pobrecito!

poorly¹ /ˈpʊrli ‖ˈpɔːli, ˈpʊəli/ adj (pred) (esp BrE) mal

poorly² adv ‹perform/play› mal

pop¹ /pɑːp ‖pɒp/ n **1** (noise): **to go ∼** hacer 'pum'; (burst) reventar* **2** (Mus) música f pop **3** (Culin) gaseosa f **4** (father) (AmE colloq) papá m (fam)

pop² **-pp-** vi **1** «balloon» estallar, reventar(se)*; «cork» saltar; **my ears ∼ped** se me destaparon los oídos

2 (spring) saltar; **his eyes were ∼ping (out of his head)** los ojos se le salían de las órbitas **3** (go casually) (colloq): **to ∼ out** salir* un momento; **he just ∼ped in to say hello** pasó un minuto a saludar

■ ∼ vt **1** (burst) ‹balloon› reventar*, hacer* estallar

2 (put quickly, casually): **she ∼ped her head around the door** asomó la cabeza por la puerta; **∼ it into your pocket** métetelo en el bolsillo

■ **pop up** [v + adv] (colloq) (a) (rise) «toast» saltar; **his head ∼ped up from behind the wall** asomó la cabeza por encima del muro (b) (appear) aparecer*

pop³ adj (a) (popular) ‹sociology/culture› popular; ‹music/singer› (AmE) popular (b) (BrE Mus) pop adj inv

popcorn /ˈpɑːpkɔːrn ‖ˈpɒpkɔːn/ n palomitas fpl (de maíz), cabritas fpl (de maíz) (Chi), pororó m (RPI), maíz m pira or tote (Col)

pope /pəʊp/ n papa m

poplar /ˈpɑːplər ‖ˈpɒplə(r)/ n álamo m (blanco)

poppa /ˈpɑːpə ‖ˈpɒpə/ n (AmE) papá m (fam)

poppy /ˈpɑːpi ‖ˈpɒpi/ n (pl **-pies**) amapola f, adormidera f

Popsicle® /ˈpɑːpsɪkəl ‖ˈpɒpsɪkəl/ n (AmE) paleta f (helada) or (Esp) polo m or (RPI) palito m or (CS) chupete m helado

populace /ˈpɑːpjələs ‖ˈpɒpjʊləs/ n (+ sing o pl vb) **the ∼** (common people) el pueblo; (population) la población

popular /ˈpɑːpjʊlər ‖ˈpɒpjʊlə(r)/ adj **1** (a) (well-liked) popular; **she is ∼ with her students** goza de popularidad entre sus alumnos (b) ‹resort/restaurant› muy frecuentado; ‹brand/product› popular **2** (a) (not highbrow, specialist) ‹music/literature› popular (b) (of populace) ‹feeling› popular; ‹rebellion› del pueblo, popular;

by ∼ demand/request a petición or (AmL tb) a pedido del público (c) (widespread) ‹belief/notion› generalizado

popularity /ˌpɑːpjəˈlærəti ‖ˌpɒpjʊˈlærəti/ n popularidad f

popularize /ˈpɑːpjələraɪz ‖ˈpɒpjʊləraɪz/ vt (a) (make popular) popularizar* (b) (make accessible) divulgar*

populate /ˈpɑːpjəleɪt ‖ˈpɒpjʊleɪt/ vt poblar*

population /ˌpɑːpjəˈleɪʃən ‖ˌpɒpjʊˈleɪʃən/ n población f; (before n) **∼ explosion** explosión f demográfica

porcelain /ˈpɔːrsələn ‖ˈpɔːsəlɪn/ n porcelana f

porch /pɔːrtʃ ‖pɔːtʃ/ n (a) (covered entrance) porche m (b) (veranda) (AmE) porche m, galería f

porcupine /ˈpɔːrkjəpaɪn ‖ˈpɔːkjʊpaɪn/ n puercoespín m

pore /pɔːr ‖pɔː(r)/ n poro m

■ **pore over** [v + prep + o] estudiar minuciosamente

pork /pɔːrk ‖pɔːk/ n (carne f de) cerdo m, (carne f de) puerco m (Méx), chancho m (Chi, Per), marrano m (Col); (before n) **∼ chop** chuleta f de cerdo (or de chancho etc), costilla f de cerdo (RPI)

pornographic /ˌpɔːrnəˈɡræfɪk ‖ˌpɔːnəˈɡræfɪk/ adj pornográfico

pornography /pɔːrˈnɑːɡrəfi ‖pɔːˈnɒɡrəfi/ n pornografía f

porous /ˈpɔːrəs/ adj poroso

porpoise /ˈpɔːrpəs ‖ˈpɔːpəs/ n marsopa f

porridge /ˈpɔːrɪdʒ ‖ˈpɒrɪdʒ/ n avena f (cocida), gachas fpl (de avena) (Esp); (before n) **∼ oats** copos mpl de avena

port¹ /pɔːrt ‖pɔːt/ n **1** (for ships) puerto m; (before n) ‹authority/tax/regulation› portuario **2** (left side) babor m **3** (a) (for loading) (Aviat, Naut) porta f (b) (Comput) puerto m **4** (Culin) oporto m, vino m de Oporto

port² adj (before n) ‹lights› de babor

portable /ˈpɔːrtəbəl ‖ˈpɔːtəbəl/ adj portátil

portcullis /pɔːrtˈkʌləs ‖ˌpɔːtˈkʌlɪs/ n rastrillo m

portend /pɔːrˈtend ‖pɔːˈtend/ vt (liter) augurar

portent /ˈpɔːrtent ‖ˈpɔːtent/ n augurio m, presagio m

porter /ˈpɔːrtər ‖ˈpɔːtə(r)/ n **1** (at station, airport) maletero m, changador m (RPI); (on expedition) porteador m; (in hospital) (BrE) camillero m **2** (in hotel, apartment block) portero m

portfolio /pɔːrtˈfəʊliəʊ ‖pɔːtˈfəʊliəʊ/ n (pl **-lios**) **1** (a) (case) portafolio(s) m (b) (samples of work) carpeta f de trabajos **2** (Pol) cartera f

porthole /ˈpɔːrthəʊl ‖ˈpɔːthəʊl/ n (Naut) ojo m de buey, portilla f

portion /ˈpɔːrʃən ‖ˈpɔːʃən/ n (a) (of food) porción f (esp AmL), ración f (esp Esp) (b) (share, part) parte f

portrait /ˈpɔːrtrət, -treɪt ‖ˈpɔːtrɪt, -treɪt/ n retrato m

portray /pɔːrˈtreɪ ‖pɔːˈtreɪ/ vt (a) (depict) «picture» representar (b) (describe, represent) ‹person/scene› describir*

portrayal /pɔːrˈtreɪəl ‖pɔːˈtreɪəl/ n (Art) representación f; (Lit) descripción f; (Theat) interpretación f

Portugal /ˈpɔːrtʃɪɡəl ‖ˈpɔːtjʊɡl/ n Portugal m

p

Portuguese¹ /ˌpɔːrtʃəˈgiːz ‖ˌpɔːtjʊˈgiːz/ adj portugués

Portuguese² n (pl ~) (a) (language) portugués m (b) (person) portugués, -guesa m,f

pose¹ /pəʊz/ vt ⟨threat⟩ representar; ⟨problem/ question⟩ plantear
■ ~ vi (a) (Art, Phot) posar (b) (put on an act) hacerse* el interesante (c) (pretend to be) to ~ AS sb/sth hacerse* pasar POR algn/algo

pose² n (a) (position of body) pose f, postura f (b) (assumed manner) pose f, afectación f

poser /ˈpəʊzər ‖ˈpəʊzə(r)/ n (a) (question) pregunta f difícil; (problem) dilema m (b) (person) (BrE colloq) ▶ POSEUR

poseur /pəʊˈzɜːr ‖pəʊˈzɜː(r)/ n: he's a real ~ todo en él es pura pose or afectación

posh /pɑːʃ ‖pɒʃ/ adj **-er, -est** (esp BrE colloq) elegante, pijo (Esp fam), posudo (Col fam), pituco (CS fam), cheto (RPl fam), sifrino (Ven fam), popoff (Méx fam)

position¹ /pəˈziʃən/ n ⓵ (a) (location) posición f, ubicación f (esp AmL) (b) (Sport) posición f ⓶ (a) (posture) posición f (b) (stance, point of view) postura f ⓷ (a) (in league) puesto m (b) (job, post) (frml) puesto m ⓸ (situation, circumstances) situación f; I'm not in a ~ to help them no estoy en condiciones de prestarles ayuda

position² vt colocar*, poner*

positive /ˈpɑːzətɪv ‖ˈpɒzətɪv/ adj ⓵ ⟨number/ quantity⟩ positivo; ⟨electrode⟩ positivo; the test was ~ (Med) el análisis dio positivo ⓶ (constructive) ⟨attitude⟩ positivo; ⟨criticism⟩ constructivo ⓷ (definite): there is no ~ evidence no hay pruebas concluyentes ⓸ (absolute) (before n) ⟨disgrace/outrage⟩ auténtico ⓹ (sure) (colloq) (pred): are you sure? — positive ¿estás seguro? — segurísimo

positively /ˈpɑːzətɪvli ‖ˈpɒzətɪvli/ adv ⓵ (constructively): to think ~ ser* positivo; they reacted ~ tuvieron una reacción/respuesta positiva ⓶ (a) (definitely) ⟨prove⟩ de forma concluyente (b) (absolutely) ⟨delighted/furious⟩ verdaderamente

posse /ˈpɑːsi ‖ˈpɒsi/ n (in US) partida f (al mando de un sheriff)

possess /pəˈzes/ vt ⓵ (own) tener*, poseer* (frml) ⓶ (influence) «anger/fear» apoderarse de; whatever can gave ~ed him to say such a thing? ¿qué lo habrá llevado a decir semejante cosa?

possessed /pəˈzest/ adj (pred) to be ~ (by the devil) estar* endemoniado

possession /pəˈzeʃən/ n (a) (sth owned) bien m (b) (ownership) posesión f; (of arms) tenencia f

possessive /pəˈzesɪv/ adj posesivo

possessor /pəˈzesər ‖pəˈzesə(r)/ n dueño, -ña m,f, poseedor, -dora m,f

possibility /ˌpɑːsəˈbɪləti ‖ˌpɒsəˈbɪləti/ n posibilidad f

possible /ˈpɑːsəbəl ‖ˈpɒsəbəl/ adj posible; get here by eight if ~ llega antes de las ocho, si es posible; as little as ~ lo menos posible

possibly /ˈpɑːsəbli ‖ˈpɒsəbli/ adv (a) (conceivably): I couldn't ~ eat any more me es totalmente imposible comer nada más; could you ~ give me a hand with this? ¿sería tan amable de ayudarme con esto? (b) (perhaps) (indep) posiblemente

post¹ /pəʊst/ n ⓵ (pole) poste m ⓶ (mail) (esp BrE) correo m; to send sth by ~ o through the ~ mandar or enviar* algo por correo; it's in the ~ ya ha sido enviado; the first/second ~ (delivery) el primer/segundo reparto; (collection) la primera/ segunda recogida ⓷ (job) puesto m

post² vt ⓵ (a) (position) ⟨policeman/soldier⟩ apostar (b) (send) ⟨employee/diplomat⟩ destinar ⓶ (mail) (esp BrE) ⟨letter/parcel⟩ echar al correo; (drop in postbox) echar al buzón; to ~ sth to sb mandarle or enviarle* algo a algn (por correo)

post- /pəʊst/ pref post-, pos-

postage /ˈpəʊstɪdʒ/ n franqueo m; ~ and handling (AmE), ~ and packing (BrE) gastos mpl de envío

postage: ~ **paid** adv con franqueo pagado; ~ **stamp** n (frml) sello m (de correos), estampilla f (AmL), timbre m (Méx)

postal /ˈpəʊstl/ adj (before n) postal

postal order n (BrE) ≈ giro m postal

post: ~**box** n (BrE) buzón m; ~**card** n tarjeta f postal, postal f; ~**code** n (BrE) código m postal

postdate /ˌpəʊstˈdeɪt/ vt ⟨contract/check⟩ posfechar, diferir* (RPl)

poster /ˈpəʊstər ‖ˈpəʊstə(r)/ n cartel m, póster m

posterity /pɑːˈsterəti ‖pɒˈsterəti/ n posteridad f

postgraduate /ˌpəʊstˈgrædʒuət/ n estudiante mf de postgrado; (before n) ⟨student/research⟩ de postgrado

posthumous /ˈpɑːstʃəməs ‖ˈpɒstjʊməs/ adj póstumo

posting /ˈpəʊstɪŋ/ n destino m

postman /ˈpəʊstmən/ n (pl **-men** /-mən/) (esp BrE) cartero m

postmark¹ /ˈpəʊstmɑːrk ‖ˈpəʊstmɑːk/ n matasellos m

postmark² vt matasellar

postmortem /ˌpəʊstˈmɔːrtəm ‖ˌpəʊstˈmɔːtəm/ n (esp BrE Med) autopsia f

postnatal /ˌpəʊstˈneɪtl/ adj postnatal

post office n oficina f de correos, correo m (AmL), estafeta f de correos (Esp)

postpone /pəʊsˈpəʊn ‖pəʊstˈpəʊn/ vt aplazar*, posponer*, postergar* (esp AmL)

postponement /pəʊsˈpəʊnmənt ‖pəʊstˈpəʊnmənt/ n aplazamiento m, postergación f (esp AmL)

postscript /ˈpəʊstskrɪpt/ n (to letter) postdata f; (to book) epílogo m

posture /ˈpɑːstʃər ‖ˈpɒstʃə(r)/ n postura f

postwar /ˈpəʊstˈwɔːr ‖ˌpəʊstˈwɔː(r)/ adj (before n) de la posguerra

posy /'pəʊzi/ n (pl **posies**) ramillete m

pot¹ /pɑːt ‖pɒt/ n **1** (a) (cooking ∼) olla f; ∼s and pans cacharros mpl (fam), trastes mpl (Méx); to go to ∼ (colloq) echarse a perder (b) (for jam, honey etc) tarro m, bote m (Esp) (c) (tea∼) tetera f; (coffee∼) cafetera f (d) (in pottery) vasija f **2** (flower∼) maceta f, tiesto m (Esp)

pot² vt **-tt-** ⟨plant⟩ plantar (en una maceta)

potash /'pɑːtæʃ ‖'pɒtæʃ/ n potasa f

potassium /pə'tæsiəm/ n potasio m

potato /pə'teɪtəʊ/ n (pl **-toes**) papa f or (Esp) patata f; (before n) ∼ **chips** o (BrE) **crisps** papas fpl or (Esp) patatas fpl fritas; ∼ **peeler** pelapapas m or (Esp) pelapatatas m

potbelly /'pɑːtˌbeli ‖ˌpɒt'beli /n barriga f (fam), panza f (fam), guata f (Chi fam)

potency /'pəʊtnsi/ n **1** (a) (of drink) lo fuerte (b) (sexual ∼) potencia f sexual

potent /'pəʊtnt/ adj **1** ⟨drink/drug/medicine⟩ fuerte **2** (Physiol) potente

potential¹ /pə'tentʃəl ‖pə'tenʃəl/ n (capacity) potencial m; (possibilities) posibilidades fpl

potential² adj (before n) ⟨danger⟩ potencial; ⟨leader⟩ en potencia

potentially /pə'tentʃəli ‖pə'tenʃəli/ adv potencialmente

pot: ∼**hole** n (a) (cave) cueva f subterránea; (hole) sima f (b) (in road) bache m; ∼**holing** /'pɑːtˌhəʊlɪŋ ‖'pɒtˌhəʊlɪŋ/ n (BrE) espeleología f

potion /'pəʊʃən/ n poción f, pócima f

pot: ∼**luck** /'pɑːt'lʌk ‖ˌpɒt'lʌk/ n: to take ∼**luck** conformarse con lo que haya; ∼ **plant** n planta f (cultivada en una maceta), mata f (Col, Ven); ∼**shot** n (Sport) tiro m al azar

potted /'pɑːtəd ‖'pɒtɪd/ adj (before n) (a) ⟨plant⟩ en maceta or tiesto (b) ⟨account/version⟩ resumido

potter¹ /'pɑːtər ‖'pɒtə(r)/ n alfarero, -ra m,f

potter² vi (BrE) (+ adv compl) ▶ PUTTER²

pottery /'pɑːtəri ‖'pɒtəri/ n (pl **-ries**) (a) (vessels) cerámica f (b) (workshop) alfarería f (c) (craft) alfarería f

potty¹ /'pɑːti ‖'pɒti/ n (pl **-ties**) (colloq) orinal m (para niños) (fam), bacinica f (AmL exc RPl), pelela f (CS fam); he's ∼**-trained** ya no usa pañales

potty² adj **-tier, -tiest** (BrE colloq) chiflado (fam)

pouch /paʊtʃ/ n **1** (a) (small bag) bolsa f (b) (for correspondence) (AmE) valija f **2** (Anat, Zool) bolsa f

poultice /'pəʊltəs ‖'pəʊltɪs/ n cataplasma f

poultry /'pəʊltri/ n (a) (birds) (+ pl vb) aves fpl de corral (b) (meat) carne f de ave

pounce /paʊns/ vi saltar; to ∼ ON/UPON sb/sth abalanzarse* SOBRE algn/algo

pound¹ /paʊnd/ n **1** (a) (measure) libra f (454 gramos) **2** (Fin) libra f; (before n) a ∼ **coin** una moneda de (una) libra **3** (enclosure — for cars) depósito m; (— for dogs) perrera f

pound² vt (a) ⟨corn/spices⟩ machacar*; ⟨garlic/chili⟩ majar (b) ⟨table/door⟩ aporrear; the waves ∼ed the wall las olas batían contra el muro
■ ∼ vi (a) (strike, beat) aporrear (b) «heart» palpitar; «sound» retumbar; my head is ∼ing tengo la cabeza a punto de reventar

pour /pɔːr ‖pɔː(r)/ vt (a) (+ adv compl) ⟨liquid⟩ verter*, echar; ⟨salt/powder⟩ echar; he ∼ed the tea down the sink tiró el té por el fregadero (b) ∼ (out) (serve) ⟨drink⟩ servir*
■ ∼ vi (+ adv compl) «blood» manar; «water/sweat» salir*
■ ∼ v impers diluviar, llover* a cántaros
■ **pour out** **1** [v + o + adv, v + adv + o] (a) ▶ POUR vt (b) (emotionally): he ∼ed out his feelings reveló sus sentimientos; she ∼ed her heart out to him se desahogó con él **2** [v + adv] salir*

pouring /'pɔːrɪŋ/ adj: he went out in the ∼ rain salió en medio de una lluvia torrencial

pout /paʊt/ vi hacer* un mohín

poverty /'pɑːvərti ‖'pɒvəti/ n pobreza f

poverty-stricken /'pɑːvərtiˌstrɪkən ‖'pɒvətiˌstrɪkən/ adj pobrísimo

POW n = **prisoner of war**

powder¹ /'paʊdər ‖'paʊdə(r)/ n (a) (control, polvo m (b) (face ∼) polvo(s) m(pl) (de tocador); (before n) ∼ **puff** borla f, cisne m (RPl)

powder² vt **1** (cover) empolvar; to ∼ one's nose retocarse* el maquillaje; (euph) lavarse las manos (euf) **2** **powdered** past p ⟨milk/eggs⟩ en polvo; ∼ed **sugar** (AmE) azúcar m or f glas, azúcar m or f flor (Chi), azúcar m or f impalpable (RPl), azúcar m or f en polvo (Col)

powdery /'paʊdəri/ adj como polvo

power¹ /'paʊər ‖'paʊə(r)/ n **1** (a) (control, influence) poder m; (of country) poderío m, poder m; to be in ∼ estar* en el poder (b) (official authority) poder m; ∼ to + INF poder PARA + INF **2** (a) (nation) potencia f (b) (person, group): the ∼s that be los que mandan; the ∼s of darkness las fuerzas del mal **3** (a) (physical strength, force) fuerza f (b) (of engine, loudspeaker, transmitter) potencia f **4** (a) (ability, capacity): I did everything in my ∼ hice todo lo que estaba en mi(s) mano(s) (b) (specific faculty) (often pl): he lost the ∼ of speech perdió el habla; ∼(s) of **concentration** capacidad f de concentración **5** (a) (Eng, Phys) potencia f; (particular source of energy) energía f (b) (electricity) electricidad f; (before n) ∼ **lines** cables mpl de alta tensión; ∼ **point** (BrE) toma f de corriente, enchufe m, tomacorriente m (AmL) **6** (a lot) (colloq): to do sb a ∼ of good hacerle* a algn mucho bien

power² vt: the plane is ∼ed by four engines el avión está propulsado por cuatro motores

power: ∼**boat** n lancha f de motor, lancha f motora (Esp); ∼ **cut** n apagón m

powerful /'paʊərfəl ‖'paʊəfəl/ adj (a) ⟨country⟩ poderoso (b) ⟨shoulders/arms⟩ fuerte (c) ⟨performance/image⟩ impactante; ⟨argument⟩ poderoso; ⟨incentive⟩ poderoso (d) ⟨engine/weapon/drug⟩ potente; ⟨smell/current⟩ fuerte

powerless /'paʊərləs ‖'paʊəlɪs/ adj impotente; they were ∼ to prevent it no pudieron hacer nada por impedirlo

power: ∼ **of attorney** n (pl ∼s of **attorney**) (Law) poder m (notarial); ∼ **plant** n (AmE) ▶ ∼ STATION; ∼ **station** n central f eléctrica, usina f eléctrica (AmS)

pp. (= **pages**) págs.

PR¹ n (a) = **public relations** (b) = **proportional representation**

PR² = **Puerto Rico**

practicable /'præktɪkəbəl/ adj (a) práctico; **for all ~ purposes** a efectos prácticos (b) (feasible) factible

practical¹ /'præktɪkəl/ adj (a) práctico; **for all ~ purposes** a efectos prácticos (b) (feasible) factible

practical² n (Educ) práctica f

practicality /ˌpræktɪ'kæləti/ n **1** (of scheme/ idea) lo práctico **2 practicalities** pl aspectos mpl prácticos

practical joke n broma f

practically /'præktɪkli/ adv **1** (virtually) casi, prácticamente **2** (in a practical way) ⟨consider/ think⟩ con sentido práctico

practice¹ /'præktəs ‖ 'præktɪs/ n **1** (training, repetition) práctica f; **he's out of ~** le falta práctica; **piano ~** ejercicios mpl de piano; **~ teaching** o (BrE) **teaching ~** prácticas fpl de magisterio; **~ makes perfect** la práctica hace al maestro **2** (a) (carrying out, implementing) práctica f; **to put sth into ~** llevar algo a la práctica; **in ~** en la práctica (b) (exercise of profession) ejercicio m **3** (custom, procedure) costumbre f **4** (Med) consultorio m

practice², (BrE) **practise** vt **1** (rehearse) practicar*; ⟨song/act⟩ ensayar **2** ⟨doctor/ lawyer⟩ ejercer* **3 practicing** pres p (a) ⟨doctor/lawyer⟩ en ejercicio (de su profesión) (b) ⟨Catholic⟩ practicante
■ ~ vi **1** (rehearse, train) practicar* **2** (professionally) ejercer*

practitioner /præk'tɪʃnər ‖ præk'tɪʃnə(r)/ n médico, -ca m,f

pragmatic /præg'mætɪk/ adj pragmático

pragmatism /'prægmətɪzəm/ n pragmatismo m

Prague /prɑːg/ n Praga f

prairie /'preri ‖ 'preəri/ n pradera f; **the ~(s)** (in US) la Pradera

prairie dog n perro m de las praderas

praise¹ /preɪz/ n (a) (credit, applause) elogios mpl; **to sing sth's/sb's ~s** poner* algo/a algn por las nubes (b) (Relig) alabanza f

praise² vt (a) (compliment) elogiar (b) (Relig) alabar

praiseworthy /'preɪzˌwɜːrði ‖ 'preɪzˌwɜːði/ adj digno de elogio

pram /præm/ n (BrE) cochecito m

prance /præns ‖ prɑːns/ vi (a) «horse» brincar* (b) (pej) «person»: **she ~d into the room wearing her new dress** entró meneándose con el vestido nuevo
■ **prance about** [v + adv] brincar*

prank /præŋk/ n broma f; (of child) travesura f

prat /præt/ n (BrE sl) imbécil mf

prattle /'prætl/ vi «adult» cotorrear (fam); «child» balbucear

prawn /prɔːn/ n (large) langostino m, camarón m (AmL); (medium) camarón m (AmL), gamba f (esp Esp), langostino m (CS); (small) camarón m, quisquilla f (Esp)

pray /preɪ/ vi rezar*, orar (frml)

prayer /prer ‖ preə(r)/ n oración f

pre- /priː/ pref (a) (in advance): **~planned** planeado de antemano (b) (before): **a ~dinner drink** una copa antes de cenar

preach /priːtʃ/ vt (a) (Relig) predicar*; ⟨sermon⟩ dar* (b) (advocate) ⟨doctrine/ideas⟩ preconizar*
■ ~ vi predicar*

preacher /'priːtʃər ‖ 'priːtʃə(r)/ n (a) (one who preaches) predicador, -dora m,f (b) (minister) (AmE) pastor, -tora m,f

prearrange /ˌpriːə'reɪndʒ/ vt (a) (arrange in advance) concertar* de antemano (b) **prearranged** past p ⟨meeting⟩ concertado de antemano; ⟨signal/place/time⟩ convenido

precarious /prɪ'keriəs ‖ prɪ'keəriəs/ adj precario

precaution /prɪ'kɔːʃən/ n precaución f; **as a ~** por or como precaución

precautionary /prɪ'kɔːʃəneri ‖ prɪ'kɔːʃənəri/ adj preventivo

precede /prɪ'siːd/ vt (frml) preceder a
■ ~ vi (a) (come before) preceder (b) **preceding** pres p anterior

precedence /'presədəns/ n precedencia f

precedent /'presədənt/ n precedente m; **to set a ~ (for sth)** sentar* precedente (para algo)

precept /'priːsept/ n precepto m

precinct /'priːsɪŋkt/ n **1** (a) (delimited zone) (BrE): **shopping ~** centro m/zona f comercial (b) (AmE) (police district) distrito m policial; (police station) comisaría f (c) (voting district) (AmE) circunscripción f, distrito m electoral **2 precincts** pl (of city) límites mpl; (of cathedral, castle, hospital) recinto m, predio(s) m(pl) (esp AmL)

precious¹ /'preʃəs/ adj **1** (a) (valuable) ⟨jewel/ object⟩ precioso; **~ metal** metal m precioso; **~ stone** piedra f preciosa (b) (dear) querido (c) (iro): **her ~ son** su queridísimo hijo (iró) **2** (affected) preciosista

precious² adv (colloq) (as intensifier): **~ few** muy pocos; **she's done ~ little to help** bien poco ha hecho para ayudar

precipice /'presəpəs ‖ 'presɪpɪs/ n precipicio m

precipitate /prɪ'sɪpəteɪt ‖ prɪ'sɪpɪteɪt/ vt (frml) precipitar

precipitation /prɪˌsɪpə'teɪʃən ‖ prɪˌsɪpɪ'teɪʃən/ n (a) (Meteo) precipitaciones fpl (b) (Chem) precipitación f

precis, précis /preɪ'siː, 'preɪsiː ‖ 'preɪsiː/ n (pl ~ /-z/) resumen m

precise /prɪ'saɪs/ adj (a) (accurate) ⟨calculations/measurements⟩ exacto; ⟨description/ instructions⟩ preciso (b) (specific) preciso; **there were about 60, 59 to be ~** había unos 60, 59 para ser exacto or preciso (c) (meticulous) minucioso

precisely /prɪ'saɪsli/ adv (a) (accurately) ⟨calculate/measure/describe⟩ con precisión (b) (exactly): **we have ~ one hour** tenemos exactamente una hora; **at two o'clock ~** a las dos en punto; **precisely!** ¡exacto!, ¡justamente!

precision /prɪ'sɪʒən/ n precisión f; (before n) ⟨instrument/tool⟩ de precisión

preclude /prɪ'kluːd/ vt (frml) ⟨possibility⟩ excluir*

precocious /prɪ'kəʊʃəs/ adj precoz

793

reconceived ····⫶··· prenatal ···

preconceived /ˈpriːkənˈsiːvd/ *adj* (*before n*) preconcebido

preconception /ˈpriːkənˈsepʃən/ *n* idea *f* preconcebida

precondition /ˈpriːkənˈdɪʃən/ *n* condición *f* previa

precursor /prɪˈkɜːrsər ‖ prɪˈkɜːsə(r)/ *n* (fml) precursor, -sora *m,f*

predate /ˈpriːˈdeɪt/ *vt* (fml) **(a)** (precede) ser* anterior a **(b)** ‹*document/letter*› antedatar (fml)

predator /ˈpredətər ‖ ˈpredətə(r)/ *n* depredador *m*, predador *m*

predatory /ˈpredətəːri ‖ ˈpredətri/ *adj* ‹*animal*› predador, depredador; ‹*person*› rapaz

predecessor /ˈpredəsesər ‖ ˈpriːdɪsesə(r)/ *n* predecesor, -sora *m,f*

predestine /ˈpriːˈdestən ‖ ˌpriːˈdestɪn/ *vt* predestinar

predetermine /ˈpriːdɪˈtɜːrmən ‖ ˌpriːdɪˈtɜːmɪn/ *vt* predeterminar

predicament /prɪˈdɪkəmənt/ *n* aprieto *m*

predicative /prɪˈdɪkətɪv/ *adj* predicativo

predict /prɪˈdɪkt/ *vt* predecir*

predictable /prɪˈdɪktəbəl/ *adj* ‹*result/outcome*› previsible; **you're so ~** siempre sales con lo mismo

predictably /prɪˈdɪktəbli/ *adv* de manera previsible

prediction /prɪˈdɪkʃən/ *n* (forecast) pronóstico *m*, predicción *f*; (prophecy) profecía *f*

predispose /ˈpriːdɪsˈpəʊz/ *vt* (fml) predisponer*

predominance /prɪˈdɑːmənəns ‖ prɪˈdɒmɪnəns/ *n* predominio *m*

predominant /prɪˈdɑːmənənt ‖ prɪˈdɒmɪnənt/ *adj* predominante

predominantly /prɪˈdɑːmənəntli ‖ prɪˈdɒmɪnəntli/ *adv* predominantemente

predominate /prɪˈdɑːməneɪt ‖ prɪˈdɒmɪneɪt/ *vi* predominar

pre-eminent /ˈpriːˈemənənt ‖ ˌpriːˈemɪnənt/ *adj* (fml) preeminente

pre-empt /ˈpriːˈempt/ *vt* ‹*attack/move*› adelantarse a

pre-emptive /ˈpriːˈemptɪv/ *adj* ‹*strike/attack*› preventivo

preen /priːn/ *vt* ‹*feathers*› arreglar con el pico ▪ *v refl* **to ~ oneself** «*bird*» arreglarse las plumas con el pico; «*person*» acicalarse

pre-exist /ˈpriːɪgˈzɪst/ *vi* (fml) **(a)** preexistir **(b) pre-existing** *pres p* preexistente

prefab /ˈpriːfæb/ *n* (colloq) vivienda *f* prefabricada

prefabricated /ˈpriːˈfæbrɪkeɪtəd ‖ ˌpriːˈfæbrɪkeɪtɪd/ *adj* prefabricado

preface /ˈprefɪs/ *n* (to book, speech) prefacio *m*; (to event) prólogo *m*

prefect /ˈpriːfekt/ *n* **1** (BrE Educ) *alumno encargado de la disciplina*, ≈ monitor, -tora *m,f* **2** (official) prefecto *m*

prefer /prɪˈfɜːr ‖ prɪˈfɜː(r)/ *vt* **-rr-** preferir*; **to ~ sth TO sth** preferir* algo A algo; **to ~ to + INF** preferir* + INF

preferable /ˈprefərəbəl/ *adj* preferible

preferably /ˈprefərəbli/ *adv* (*indep*) preferentemente; **I'd like a size 10, ~ in red** quisiera la talla 10, de ser posible en rojo

preference /ˈprefərəns/ *n* preferencia *f*; **~ FOR sth** preferencia POR algo

preferential /ˈprefəˈrentʃəl ‖ ˌprefəˈrenʃəl/ *adj* (*before n*) preferente, preferencial; **to give ~ treatment to sb** dar* trato preferente *or* preferencial a algn

prefix /ˈpriːfɪks/ *n* prefijo *m*

pregnancy /ˈpregnənsi/ *n* (*pl* **-cies**) (of woman) embarazo *m*; (of animal) preñez *f*

pregnant /ˈpregnənt/ *adj* **1** ‹*woman*› embarazada; ‹*cow/mare*› preñada **2** (liter) (meaningful) ‹*pause/silence*› elocuente, preñado de significado (liter)

preheat /ˈpriːˈhiːt/ *vt* precalentar*

prehistoric /ˈpriːhɪˈstɔːrɪk ‖ ˌpriːhɪˈstɒrɪk/ *adj* prehistórico

prejudge /ˈpriːˈdʒʌdʒ/ *vt* prejuzgar*

prejudice¹ /ˈpredʒədəs ‖ ˈpredʒʊdɪs/ *n* prejuicio *m*

prejudice² *vt* **1** (influence) predisponer* **2** (harm) ‹*case/claim*› perjudicar*

prejudiced /ˈpredʒədəst ‖ ˈpredʒʊdɪst/ *adj* lleno de prejuicios, prejuiciado (AmL)

preliminary¹ /prɪˈlɪməneri ‖ prɪˈlɪmɪnəri/ *adj* preliminar

preliminary² *n* (*pl* **-ries**) **(a)** (preamble) prolegómeno *m* **(b) preliminaries** *pl* (Sport) etapa *f* de clasificación previa, preliminares *mpl or fpl*

prelude /ˈpreljuːd/ *n* **(a)** (introduction) ~ (**TO sth**) preludio *m* (DE algo) **(b)** (Mus) preludio *m*

premature /ˈpriːməˈtʊr ‖ ˈpremətjʊə(r)/ *adj* prematuro

prematurely /ˈpriːməˈtʊrli ‖ ˈpremətjʊəli/ *adv* prematuramente

premeditated /ˈpriːˈmedəteɪtəd ‖ ˌpriːˈmedɪteɪtɪd/ *adj* premeditado

premenstrual /ˈpriːˈmenstruəl/ *adj* premenstrual; **~ syndrome/tension** síndrome *m*/tensión *f* premenstrual

premier /prɪˈmɪr ‖ ˈpremɪə(r)/ *n* primer ministro, primera ministra *m,f*, premier *mf*

premiere¹, première /prɪˈmɪr ‖ ˈpremɪeə(r)/ *n* estreno *m*

premiere², première *vt* ‹*play/film*› estrenar ▪ **~** *vi* «*play/film*» estrenarse

premise /ˈpreməs ‖ ˈpremɪs/ *n* **1** (Phil) premisa *f* **2 premises** *pl* (building, site) local *m*; **they've moved to new ~s** se han mudado a un nuevo local (*or* a nuevas oficinas *etc*); **meals are cooked on the ~s** las comidas se preparan en el mismo establecimiento

premium /ˈpriːmiəm/ *n* (Fin) **(a)** (insurance ~) prima *f* (de seguro) **(b)** (surcharge) recargo *m*; **to be at a ~** (in short supply) escasear; (lit: above par) estar* por encima de la par **(c)** (bonus) prima *f*

Premium Bond *n* (in UK) *bono del Estado que permite ganar dinero participando en sorteos mensuales*

premonition /ˈpriːməˈnɪʃən, ˈprem-/ *n* premonición *f*

prenatal /ˈpriːˈneɪtl/ *adj* (esp AmE) ▶ ANTENATAL

preoccupation /priː'ɒkjə'peɪʃən ‖ˌpriːɒkjʊ'peɪʃən/ n [1] (obsession) obsesión f [2] (concern): my main ~ was not to offend my parents mi mayor preocupación/lo que más me importaba era no ofender a mis padres

preoccupied /priː'ɒkjəpaɪd ‖priː'ɒkjʊpaɪd/ adj (absorbed) absorto; (worried) preocupado

preoccupy /priː'ɒkjəpaɪ ‖priː'ɒkjʊpaɪ/ vt -pies, -pying, -pied preocupar

prepaid /'priːpeɪd/ adj ⟨envelope⟩ con franqueo pagado; ⟨advertisement/insertion⟩ pagado por adelantado

preparation /prepə'reɪʃən/ n [1] (a) (act) preparación f (b) **preparations** pl (arrangements) preparativos mpl [2] (substance) preparado m

preparatory /prɪ'pærətəːri ‖prɪ'pærətri/ adj preparatorio

preparatory school n (fml) (a) (in US) colegio secundario privado (b) (in UK) colegio primario privado

prepare /prɪ'per ‖prɪ'peə(r)/ vt preparar ■ ~ vi to ~ (FOR sth) prepararse (PARA algo)

prepared /prɪ'perd ‖prɪ'peəd/ adj (a) (ready in advance) ⟨speech/statement⟩ preparado; I wasn't ~ for this no contaba con esto (b) (willing) ⟨pred⟩ to be ~ to + INF estar* dispuesto A + INF

preposition /prepə'zɪʃən/ n preposición f

prepossessing /'priːpə'zesɪŋ/ adj (fml) (usu neg) atractivo

preposterous /prɪ'pɑːstərəs ‖prɪ'pɒstərəs/ adj absurdo

prep school /prep/ n ▶ PREPARATORY SCHOOL B

prerequisite /'priː'rekwəzət ‖ˌpriː'rekwɪzɪt/ n requisito m esencial

prerogative /prɪ'rɑːgətɪv ‖prɪ'rɒgətɪv/ n prerrogativa f; that's your ~ estás en todo tu derecho

Pres (title) = **President**

Presbyterian¹ /'prezbə'tɪrɪən ‖ˌprezbɪ'tɪərɪən/ n presbiteriano, -na m,f

Presbyterian² adj presbiteriano

preschool¹ /'priː'skuːl/ adj ⟨before n⟩ ⟨child⟩ de edad preescolar; ⟨education⟩ preescolar

preschool² n (AmE) jardín m de infancia, kindergarten m (AmL), jardín m de niños (Méx), jardín m de infantes (RPl), jardín m infantil (Chi)

prescribe /prɪ'skraɪb/ vt (a) ⟨drug⟩ recetar; ⟨rest⟩ recomendar* (b) (order) (fml) prescribir* (fml); ~d reading libros mpl de lectura obligatoria

prescription /prɪ'skrɪpʃən/ n receta f; available on ~ only en venta solamente bajo receta

presence /'prezns/ n presencia f; to make one's ~ felt hacerse* sentir

presence of mind n presencia f de ánimo

present¹ /prɪ'zent/ vt [1] (a) (give, hand over) to ~ sth TO sb entregarle* algo A algn; to ~ sb

WITH sth obsequiar a algn CON algo (fml), obsequiarle algo A algn (esp AmL fml) (b) (confront): we were ~ed with a very difficult situation nos vimos frente a una situación muy difícil [2] ⟨ticket/passport/account/ideas⟩ presentar [3] (Cin, Theat, Rad, TV) presentar [4] (introduce) (fml) presentar

present² /'preznt/ adj [1] (at scene) ⟨pred⟩ to be ~ estar* presente [2] (current) (a) (current) actual; at the ~ time en este momento (b) (Ling): the ~ tense el presente

present³ /'preznt/ n [1] (a) (current time): the ~ el presente; at ~ en este momento (b) (Ling) the ~ el presente [2] (gift) regalo m

presentable /prɪ'zentəbəl/ adj presentable

presentation /'priːzen'teɪʃən, 'prezən'teɪʃən ‖ˌprezən'teɪʃən/ n [1] (of gift, prize) entrega f [2] (a) (of document, bill, proposal) presentación f (b) (display) (Busn) presentación f [3] (manner of presenting) presentación f

present-day /'preznt'deɪ/ adj ⟨before n⟩ actual

presenter /prɪ'zentər ‖prɪ'zentə(r)/ n (BrE) presentador, -dora m,f

presently /'prezntli/ adv (a) (now) en este momento (b) (soon afterwards, in past) pronto (c) (soon, in future) poco después

preservation /'prezər'veɪʃən, ˌprezə'veɪʃən/ n conservación f

preservative /prɪ'zɜːrvətɪv ‖prɪ'zɜːvətɪv/ n conservante m

preserve¹ /prɪ'zɜːrv ‖prɪ'zɜːv/ vt (a) ⟨food/specimen⟩ conservar (b) (Culin) ⟨fruit/vegetables⟩ hacer* conserva de (c) ⟨building/traditions⟩ conservar

preserve² n [1] (a) (exclusive privilege, sphere): to be a male ~ ser* terreno exclusivamente masculino (b) (restricted area): game ~ coto m de caza; wildlife ~ (AmE) reserva f de animales [2] (Culin) (jam, jelly) confitura f, mermelada f

preside /prɪ'zaɪd/ vi presidir; to ~ over a meeting presidir una reunión

presidency /'prezədənsi ‖'prezɪdənsi/ n presidencia f

president /'prezədənt ‖'prezɪdənt/ n (a) (of state, society) presidente, -ta m,f (b) (of bank, corporation) (esp AmE) director, -tora m,f, presidente, -ta m,f (c) (of university) (AmE) rector, -tora m,f

presidential /'prezə'dentʃəl ‖ˌprezɪ'denʃəl/ adj ⟨before n⟩ presidencial

press¹ /pres/ n [1] (newspapers, journalists) prensa f; the ~ la prensa; ⟨before n⟩ ~ agency (BrE) agencia f de prensa; ~ photographer reportero gráfico, reportera gráfica m,f; ~ release comunicado m de prensa [2] (a) (printing ~) prensa f, imprenta f; to go to ~ entrar en prensa (b) (publishing house) editorial f [3] (for pressing — grapes, flowers, machine parts) prensa f; (— trousers) prensa f plancha-pantalones

press² vt [1] (push) ⟨button/doorbell⟩ apretar*; ⟨pedal/footbrake⟩ pisar [2] (a) (squeeze) apretar*

AmC	América Central	Arg	Argentina	Cu	Cuba	Per	Perú
AmL	América Latina	Bol	Bolivia	Ec	Ecuador	RPl	Río de la Plata
AmS	América del Sur	Chi	Chile	Esp	España	Ur	Uruguay
Andes	Región andina	CS	Cono Sur	Méx	México	Ven	Venezuela

(a) (in press) ‹grapes/olives/flowers› prensar **(c)** ‹disk/album› imprimir **(d)** ‹clothes› planchar ▣ **(a)** (put pressure on) presionar **(b)** (pursue): to ∼ **charges against sb** presentar cargos en contra de algn
■ ∼ vi ① (exert pressure): ∼ **firmly** presione con fuerza ② (urge, pressurize) presionar
■ **press on** [v + adv] to ∼ **on** (WITH sth) seguir∼ adelante (CON algo)

press conference n rueda f de prensa

pressed /prest/ adj (pred): to be ∼ **for time** estar∼ or andar∼ escaso de tiempo

pressing /'presɪŋ/ adj ‹engagements/concerns› urgente; ‹need/desire› apremiante

press: ∼ **stud** n (BrE) broche m or botón m de presión (AmL), (cierre m) automático m (Esp); ∼**up** n (BrE) flexión f (de brazos or de pecho), fondo m, lagartija f (Méx)

pressure¹ /'preʃər ‖'preʃə(r)/ n presión f; **to put** ∼ **on sth/sb** hacer∼ presión sobre algo/ presionar a algn; **the** ∼**s of city life** las presiones a las que somete la vida urbana; **I've been under a lot of** ∼ **recently** últimamente he estado muy agobiado

pressure² vt presionar; **to** ∼ **sb to + INF** presionar a algn PARA QUE (+ subj)

pressure: ∼ **cooker** n olla f a presión or (Esp tb) olla f exprés or (Méx) olla f presto; ∼ **group** n grupo m de presión; ∼ **pan** n (AmE) ▶ ∼ COOKER

pressurize /'preʃəraɪz/ vt **(a)** (Aerosp, Aviat) presurizar∗ **(b)** (urge) (BrE) ▶ PRESSURE²

prestige /pre'sti:ʒ/ n prestigio m

prestigious /pre'stɪdʒəs/ adj prestigioso

presumably /prɪ'zu:məbli ‖prɪ'zju:məbli/ adv (indep): **you've taken the necessary steps,** ∼ supongo or me imagino que habrás tomado las medidas pertinentes

presume /prɪ'zu:m ‖prɪ'zju:m/ vt **(a)** (assume) suponer∗; **I** ∼ **so** supongo or me imagino que sí **(b)** (dare) **to** ∼ **to + INF** atreverse A + INF

presumption /prɪ'zʌmpʃən/ n **(a)** (boldness) atrevimiento m **(b)** (assumption) suposición f

presumptuous /prɪ'zʌmptʃəs ‖prɪ'zʌmptʃʊəs/ adj impertinente

presuppose /ˌpri:sə'pəʊz/ vt presuponer∗

pretence n (BrE) ▶ PRETENSE

pretend¹ /prɪ'tend/ vt/i fingir∗

pretend² adj (used to or by children) ‹money/ gun› de mentira (fam)

pretender /prɪ'tendər ‖prɪ'tendə(r)/ n ∼ (TO sth) pretendiente mf (A algo)

pretense, (BrE) **pretence** /'pri:tens, prɪ'tens ‖prɪ'tens/ n: **her air of confidence is a** ∼ ese aire de seguridad suyo es fingido; **let's drop this** ∼! ¡vamos a dejarnos de fingir!; **under false** ∼**s** de manera fraudulenta

pretension /prɪ'tenʃən ‖prɪ'tenʃən/ n (often pl) pretensión f

pretentious /prɪ'tentʃəs ‖prɪ'tenʃəs/ adj ‹person/language/film› pretencioso; ‹house/decor› presuntuoso

pretext /'pri:tekst/ n pretexto m; **on** o **under the** ∼ **of** con el pretexto de

pretty¹ /'prɪti/ adj **-tier, -tiest** bonito, lindo (AmL)

pretty² adv (rather, quite) bastante; (emphatic) bien

prevail /prɪ'veɪl/ vi ① (triumph) «justice/common sense» prevalecer∗; «enemy» imponerse∗ ② (predominate) «attitude/pessimism» preponderar; «situation» reinar

prevailing /prɪ'veɪlɪŋ/ adj (before n) ‹wind› preponderante; ‹trend/view› imperante; ‹uncertainty› reinante

prevalence /'prevələns/ n **(a)** (widespread occurrence) preponderancia f **(b)** (predominance) predominio m

prevalent /'prevələnt/ adj frecuente, corriente; ‹disease› común

prevaricate /prɪ'værəkeɪt ‖prɪ'værɪkeɪt/ vi **(a)** (not answer directly) andarse∗ con rodeos **(b)** (lie) (AmE) mentir∗

prevent /prɪ'vent/ vt **(a)** (hinder) impedir∗; **to** ∼ **sb/sth** (FROM) -ING impedir QUE algn/algo (+ subj) **(b)** (forestall) ‹crime/disease/accident› prevenir∗, evitar

preventative /prɪ'ventətɪv/ adj ▶ PREVENTIVE

prevention /prɪ'ventʃən ‖prɪ'venʃən/ n prevención f

preventive /prɪ'ventɪv/ adj preventivo

preview /'pri:vju:/ n **(a)** (advance showing) preestreno m **(b)** (trailer) avance m, trailer m (Esp), sinopsis f (CS)

previous /'pri:viəs/ adj (earlier) (before n) ‹occasion/attempt/page› anterior; ‹experience/ knowledge› previo; **on the** ∼ **day** el día anterior; **I had a** ∼ **engagement** ya tenía un compromiso

previously /'pri:viəsli/ adv antes

prewar /'pri:'wɔːr ‖ˌpri:'wɔː(r)/ adj de antes de la guerra

prey /preɪ/ n presa f
■ **prey on, prey upon** [v + prep + o] **(a)** ‹animal› (hunt) cazar∗; (feed on) alimentarse de; **it's been** ∼**ing on my mind** me ha estado preocupando **(b)** (exploit) explotar

price¹ /praɪs/ n ① (cost) precio m; **to go up/ down in** ∼ subir/bajar de precio; **to pay a/the** ∼ **for sth** pagar∗ algo caro; (before n) ∼ **list** lista f de precios; **it's out of my** ∼ **range** cuesta más de lo que puedo pagar ② (value) (liter) precio m; **one cannot put a** ∼ **on freedom** la libertad no tiene precio

price² vt **(a)** (fix price of) (often pass): **their products are reasonably** ∼**d** sus productos tienen precios razonables; **they have** ∼**d themselves out of the market** han subido tanto los precios que se han quedado sin compradores (or clientes etc) **(b)** (mark price on) ponerle∗ el precio a

priceless /'praɪsləs ‖'praɪslɪs/ adj inestimable, invalorable (CS)

price tag n etiqueta f (del precio), precio m

pricey, pricy /'praɪsi/ adj **pricier, priciest** (colloq) ‹item› carito (fam); ‹store› carero (fam)

prick¹ /prɪk/ vt ① (pierce, wound) pinchar, picar∗ (Méx); **that** ∼**ed his conscience** eso hizo que le remordiera la conciencia ② -up (ears) «dog» levantar, parar (AmL); **she** ∼**ed up her ears at the mention of France** aguzó el oído or (AmL fam) paró la oreja al oír hablar de Francia
■ ∼ vi pinchar

prick² n **(a)** (act) pinchazo m, piquete m (Méx) **(b)** (mark) agujero m

prickle¹ /'prɪkəl/ n (a) (thorn) espina f (b) (sensation) picor m

prickle² vi «wool» picar*; «beard» pinchar, picar* (Méx); «skin/scalp» picar*

prickly /'prɪkli/ adj **-lier, -liest (a)** (with prickles) ⟨plant⟩ espinoso; ⟨animal⟩ con púas **(b)** (scratchy) ⟨wool⟩ que pica; ⟨beard⟩ que pincha or (Méx) pica

pride¹ /praɪd/ n **1 (a)** (self-respect) orgullo m; false ~ vanidad f; **she takes great ~ in her work** se toma muy en serio su trabajo; **to swallow one's ~** tragarse* el orgullo **(b)** (conceit) orgullo m **2** (source of pride) orgullo m; **she is her mother's ~ and joy** es el orgullo de su madre **3** (of lions) manada f

pride² v refl **to ~ oneself ON sth/-ING** enorgullecerse* DE algo/+ INF

priest /priːst/ n sacerdote m; (parish ~) cura m (párroco), párroco m

priestess /'priːstəs ‖ 'priːstes/ n sacerdotisa f

priesthood /'priːsthʊd/ n **(a)** (office) sacerdocio m **(b)** (clergy) clero m

prig /prɪg/ n mojigato, -ta m,f

prim /prɪm/ adj **-mer, -mest (a)** (prudish) mojigato; (affected) remilgado, repipi (Esp fam); **she's so ~ and proper!** es tan correcta y formal **(b)** (neat) cuidado

prima ballerina /'priːmə/ n primera bailarina f

primaeval adj (BrE) ▶ PRIMEVAL

primarily /praɪ'merəli ‖ 'praɪmərɪli/ adv fundamentalmente

primary /'praɪmeri ‖ 'praɪməri/ adj **1** (principal) ⟨purpose/role/aim⟩ primordial **2 (a)** (first, basic) ⟨source/energy⟩ primario; ⟨industry⟩ de base **(b)** ⟨education⟩ primario

primary: ~ color, (BrE) **colour** n color m primario; **~ school** n escuela f (de enseñanza) primaria

primate n **1** /'praɪmeɪt/ (Zool) primate m **2** /'praɪmeɪt, -ət/ (Relig) primado m

prime¹ /praɪm/ adj (no comp) **(a)** (major) principal **(b)** (first-rate) ⟨example/location⟩ excelente; ⟨cut⟩ de primera (calidad)

prime² n (best time): **to be in one's ~ o in the ~ of life** estar* en la flor de la vida

prime³ vt **(a)** (prepare for painting) ⟨wood/metal⟩ aplicar* una capa de imprimación a; ⟨canvas⟩ preparar **(b)** ⟨pump/gun⟩ cebar **(c)** (brief) preparar

prime minister n primer ministro, primera ministra m,f

primer /'praɪmər ‖ 'praɪmə(r)/ n **1 (a)** (paint) imprimación f **(b)** (explosive) cebo m **2** (textbook) manual m

prime time n horas fpl de máxima audiencia

primeval, (BrE) **primaeval** /praɪ'miːvəl/ adj primigenio

primitive /'prɪmɪtɪv ‖ 'prɪmɪtɪv/ adj primitivo; ⟨urges/instincts⟩ primario

primrose /'prɪmrəʊz/ n primavera f, prímula f

Primus® **(stove)** /'praɪməs/ n hornillo m de queroseno, Primus® m

prince /prɪns/ n príncipe m

princess /'prɪnsəs ‖ 'prɪnses/ n princesa f

principal¹ /'prɪnsəpəl/ adj (before n) principal

principal² n (of school) director, -tora m,f; (of university) rector, -tora m,f

principally /'prɪnsəpli/ adv principalmente

principle /'prɪnsəpəl/ n **1** (basic fact, law) principio m; **in ~** en principio **2** (rule of conduct) principio m; **I never borrow money, on ~** nunca pido dinero prestado, por principio; **it is against my ~s** va contra mis principios

print¹ /prɪnt/ n **1** (Print) **(a)** (lettering) letra f **(b)** (text): **in ~** (published) publicado; (available) a la venta; **out of ~** agotado **2 (a)** (Art, Print) grabado m **(b)** (Phot) copia f **3** (of foot, finger) huella f **4** (fabric) estampado m

print² vt **1 (a)** ⟨letter/text/design⟩ imprimir* **(b)** ⟨fabric⟩ estampar **(c)** (publish) publicar* **(d)** **printed** past p impreso **2** (write clearly) escribir* con letra de imprenta **3** (Phot) ⟨negative⟩ imprimir*

■ ~ vi **(a)** (Print) imprimir* **(b)** (write without joining the letters) escribir* con letra de imprenta or de molde

■ **print out** [v + adv + o, v + o + adv] imprimir*

printer /'prɪntər ‖ 'prɪntə(r)/ n **(a)** (worker) tipógrafo, -fa m,f, impresor, -sora m,f **(b)** (business) imprenta f **(c)** (machine) impresora f

printing /'prɪntɪŋ/ n **(a)** (act, process, result) impresión f **(b)** (quantity printed) edición f **(c)** (trade) imprenta f

printing press n imprenta f, prensa f

print: ~out n listado m; **~ run** n tirada f

prior¹ /'praɪər ‖ 'praɪə(r)/ adj (before n) ⟨knowledge/warning⟩ previo; **I had a ~ engagement** ya tenía un compromiso; **prior to** (as prep) antes de

prior² n prior m

priority /praɪ'ɔːrəti ‖ praɪ'ɒrɪti/ n (pl **-ties**) **(a)** (precedence) prioridad f; **to have/take ~** (over sth) tener* prioridad (sobre algo) **(b)** (important matter, aim): **you have to get your priorities right** tienes que saber decidir qué es lo más importante **(c)** (in traffic) (BrE) preferencia f

priory /'praɪəri/ n (pl **-ries**) priorato m

prise /praɪz/ vt (BrE) ▶ PRIZE³ 2

prism /'prɪzəm/ n prisma m

prison /'prɪzn/ n prisión f, cárcel f; (before n) ⟨system/reform⟩ carcelario, penitenciario; **~ officer** (BrE) funcionario, -ria m,f de prisiones

prison camp n campo m de prisioneros

prisoner /'prɪznər ‖ 'prɪznə(r)/ n **(a)** (captive) prisionero, -ra m,f; **to take sb ~** tomar or (esp Esp) coger* a algn prisionero **(b)** (in jail) preso, -sa m,f **(c)** (person arrested) detenido, -da m,f **(d)** (accused) reo mf, acusado, -da m,f

prisoner of war n (pl **~s ~**) prisionero, -ra m,f de guerra

prissy /'prɪsi/ adj **-sier, -siest** (colloq) remilgado, repipi (Esp fam)

pristine /'prɪstiːn, -taɪn/ adj (frml & liter) inmaculado, prístino (liter)

privacy /'praɪvəsi ‖ 'prɪvəsi/ n privacidad f

private¹ /'praɪvət ‖ 'praɪvɪt/ adj **1 (a)** (confidential) ⟨conversation/matter⟩ privado; ⟨letter⟩ personal **(b)** **in private: she told me in ~** me lo dijo confidencialmente; **can we talk in ~?** ¿podemos hablar en privado? **2** (for own use, in own possession) ⟨road/lesson/

secretary⟩ particular; ⟨*income*⟩ personal; ∼ **property** propiedad *f* privada; ∼ **income** rentas *fpl*
3 **(a)** (not official) ⟨*visit/correspondence*⟩ privado; their ∼ **life** su vida privada **(b)** (unconnected to the state) ⟨*school*⟩ privado, de pago (Esp); ⟨*ward*⟩ reservado; ⟨*patient*⟩ particular; ∼ **enterprise** la empresa privada; **the** ∼ **sector** el sector privado **4** **(a)** ⟨*thoughts/doubts*⟩ íntimo; **it's a** ∼ **joke** es un chiste que los dos entendemos/entienden **(b)** ⟨*person*⟩ reservado

private² *n* soldado *mf* raso

private: ∼ **detective** *n* detective *mf* privado; ∼ **eye** *n* (esp AmE colloq) sabueso *mf*

privately /'praɪvətli ‖ 'praɪvɪtli/ *adv* **1** (in private) en privado **2** (not by state): **she had the operation done** ∼ (BrE) la operaron en una clínica privada; **this land is** ∼ **owned** esta tierra es de particulares

private parts *pl n* (euph & hum) partes *fpl* pudendas (euf & hum)

privation /praɪ'veɪʃən/ *n* (fml) privación *f*

privatization /ˌpraɪvətə'zeɪʃən ‖ ˌpraɪvɪtɑɪ'zeɪʃən/ *n* privatización *f*

privatize /'praɪvətaɪz ‖ 'praɪvɪtaɪz/ *vt* privatizar*

privilege /'prɪvəlɪdʒ/ *n* privilegio *m*

privileged /'prɪvəlɪdʒd/ *adj* **(a)** (having advantages) ⟨*position*⟩ privilegiado **(b)** (honored) ⟨*pred*⟩ **to be** ∼ **to** + INF tener* el privilegio *or* el honor DE + INF

privy /'prɪvi/ *adj* (fml) ⟨*pred*⟩ **to be** ∼ **TO sth** tener* conocimiento DE algo

prize¹ /praɪz/ *n* premio *m*

prize² *adj* (before *n*) premiado

prize³ *vt* **1** (value) valorar (mucho) **2** (BrE) **prise**: **to** ∼ **information out of sb** arrancarle* información a algn; **he** ∼**d the lid off the crate** le arrancó la tapa a la caja haciendo palanca

prize: ∼ **money** *n* premio *m* (*en metálico*); ∼**winner** *n* ganador, -dora *m,f* (*de un premio*)

pro /prəʊ/ *n* **1** (professional) (colloq) profesional *mf* **2** **pros** *pl* (advantages): **the** ∼**s and cons** los pros y los contras

pro- /'prəʊ/ *pref* pro(·)

proactive /prəʊ'æktɪv/ *adj* proactivo

probability /ˌprɑːbə'bɪləti ‖ ˌprɒbə'bɪlɪti/ *n* (*pl* **-ties**) probabilidad *f*

probable /'prɑːbəbəl ‖ 'prɒbəbəl/ *adj* probable; ⟨*reason*⟩ posible

probably /'prɑːbəbli ‖ 'prɒbəbli/ *adv* (indep) probablemente (+ *subj*)

probation /prəʊ'beɪʃən ‖ prə'beɪʃən/ *n* **1** (Law) libertad *f* condicional; **to be on** ∼ estar* en libertad condicional **2** (trial period) período *m* de prueba

probationary /ˌprəʊ'beɪʃənəri ‖ prə'beɪʃənəri/ *adj* ⟨*period*⟩ de prueba

probe¹ /prəʊb/ *vt* **(a)** (physically) sondar **(b)** (investigate) investigar*; ⟨*mind/subconscious*⟩ explorar
■ ∼ *vi* investigar*

probe² *n* **(a)** (Med, Elec) sonda *f* **(b)** (investigation) investigación *f*

probing /'prəʊbɪŋ/ *adj* ⟨*question*⟩ sagaz; ⟨*study*⟩ a fondo

problem /'prɑːbləm ‖ 'prɒbləm/ *n* problema *m*; **no** ∼! (colloq) ¡no hay problema!; **what's the** ∼? ¿qué pasa?; (before *n*) ⟨*family/child*⟩ difícil

problematic /ˌprɑːblə'mætɪk ‖ ˌprɒblə'mætɪk/**, -ical** /-ɪkəl/ *adj* problemático

procedure /prə'siːdʒər ‖ prə'siːdjə(r), prə'siːdʒə(r)/ *n* (practice) procedimiento *m*; (step) trámite *m*

proceed /prəʊ'siːd, prə- ‖ prə'siːd, prəʊ-/ *vi* **(a)** (move forward) (fml) ⟨*person/vehicle*⟩ avanzar* **(b)** (continue) continuar*; **to** ∼ **to** + INF: **she** ∼**ed to tell us why** pasó a explicarnos por qué **(c)** (act) (fml) proceder **(d)** (progress) marchar

proceedings /prəʊ'siːdɪŋz, prə- ‖ *pl n* **(a)** (events): ∼ **began late** la reunión (*or* el acto *etc*) empezó tarde **(b)** (measures) medidas *fpl*; (Law) juicio *m*

proceeds /'prəʊsiːdz/ *pl n*: **the** ∼ (from charity sale, function) lo recaudado

process¹ /'prɑːses, 'prəʊ- ‖ 'prəʊses/ *n* **(a)** (series of actions, changes) proceso *m*; **the** ∼ **of obtaining a permit** el trámite para obtener un permiso; **I am in the** ∼ **of writing to him right now** en este preciso momento le estoy escribiendo **(b)** (method) proceso *m*, procedimiento *m*

process² *vt* ⟨*raw materials/waste*⟩ procesar, tratar; ⟨*film*⟩ revelar; ⟨*applications*⟩ dar* curso a; ⟨*order*⟩ tramitar; ⟨*data*⟩ procesar

process cheese (AmE), **processed cheese** /'prɑːsest ‖ 'prəʊsest/ (BrE) *n* queso *m* fundido

processing /'prɑːsesɪŋ, 'prəʊ- ‖ 'prəʊsesɪŋ/ *n* **(a)** (of materials, waste) tratamiento *m*, procesamiento *m*; (of film) revelado *m* **(b)** (of an order, an application) tramitación *f* **(c)** (Comput) procesamiento *m*

procession /prə'seʃən/ *n* desfile *m*; (Relig) procesión *f*; **a funeral** ∼ un cortejo fúnebre

proclaim /prəʊ'kleɪm, prə- ‖ prə'kleɪm/ *vt* (fml) ⟨*independence*⟩ proclamar; ⟨*love*⟩ declarar

proclamation /ˌprɑːklə'meɪʃən ‖ ˌprɒklə'meɪʃən/ *n* (fml) proclamación *f*

procrastinate /prəʊ'kræstəneɪt ‖ prəʊ'kræstɪneɪt/ *vi* dejar las cosas para más tarde

procreation /ˌprəʊkri'eɪʃən/ *n* (fml) procreación *f*

procure /prə'kjʊr ‖ prə'kjʊə(r)/ *vt* (fml) procurar (fml)

prod¹ /prɑːd ‖ prɒd/ *vt* **-dd-** (with elbow) darle* un codazo a; (with sth sharp) pinchar

prod² *n* (with elbow) codazo *m*; (with sth sharp) pinchazo *m*

prodigal /'prɑːdɪgəl ‖ 'prɒdɪgəl/ *adj* pródigo

prodigious /prə'dɪdʒəs/ *adj* ⟨*amount/cost*⟩ enorme; ⟨*efforts/strength*⟩ prodigioso

prodigy /'prɑːdədʒi ‖ 'prɒdɪdʒi/ *n* (*pl* **-gies**) prodigio *m*; **child** ∼ niño, -ña *m,f* prodigio

produce¹ /prə'duːs ‖ prə'djuːs/ *vt* **1** **(a)** (manufacture, yield) ⟨*cars/cloth*⟩ producir*, fabricar*; ⟨*coal/grain/beef*⟩ producir*; ⟨*fruit*⟩ ⟨*country/region*⟩ producir*; ⟨*tree/bush*⟩ dar*, producir* **(b)** (create, give) ⟨*energy/sound*⟩ producir* **(c)** (cause) ⟨*effect*⟩ surtir, producir* **(d)** (give birth to) ⟨*young*⟩ tener* **2** (show, bring out) ⟨*ticket/document/evidence*⟩ presentar, aportar; ⟨*gun/*

⋯⟩

knife› sacar* **3 (a)** (Cin, TV) producir*; (Theat) ‹*play*› poner* en escena; ‹*show*› montar **(b)** (Rad, Theat) (direct) dirigir*

produce² /ˈprɑːduːs ‖ˈprɒdjuːs/ *n* productos *mpl* (alimenticios)

producer /prəˈduːsər ‖prəˈdjuːsə(r)/ *n* **1** (manufacturer) fabricante *mf* **2 (a)** (Cin, TV, Theat) productor, -tora *m,f* **(b)** (Rad, Theat) (director) director, -tora *m,f*

product /ˈprɑːdəkt ‖ˈprɒdʌkt/ *n* producto *m*

production /prəˈdʌkʃən/ *n* **1 (a)** (manufacture) fabricación *f* **(b)** (output) producción *f* **2** (showing) presentación *f* **3** (staging, version) (Theat, Cin) producción *f* **4 (a)** (act of producing) (Cin, TV) producción *f*; (Theat) puesta *f* en escena **(b)** (direction) (Rad, Theat) dirección *f*

production line *n* cadena *f* de fabricación

productive /prəˈdʌktɪv/ *adj* ‹*land/factory/ mine*› productivo; ‹*meeting*› fructífero

productively /prəˈdʌktɪvli/ *adv* productivamente; **I didn't spend my time very ~** no saqué buen partido del tiempo

productivity /ˌprəʊdʌkˈtɪvəti ‖ˌprɒdʌkˈtɪvəti/ *n* productividad *f*

profane /prəˈfeɪn/ *adj* **(a)** (blasphemous) irreverente **(b)** (secular) profano

profanity /prəˈfænəti/ *n* (*pl* -**ties**) **(a)** (blasphemy, vulgarity) irreverencia *f* **(b)** (swearword) blasfemia *f*

profess /prəˈfes/ *vt* **(a)** (claim) (frml) ‹*desire/ belief*› manifestar*; **he ~ed to be an expert** se preciaba de ser un experto **(b)** (Relig) profesar

profession /prəˈfeʃən/ *n* **1 (a)** (occupation) profesión *f*; **by ~** de profesión **(b)** (members) (*no pl*): **the medical ~** el cuerpo médico; **the teaching ~** la enseñanza **2** (declaration) (frml) profesión *f*

professional¹ /prəˈfeʃnəl ‖prəˈfeʃənl/ *adj* (*before n*) ‹*musician/golfer*› profesional; ‹*soldier*› de carrera; **to take ~ advice** asesorarse con un profesional (*or* un experto, técnico *etc*)

professional² *n* profesional *mf*; (competent person) experto, -ta *m,f*

professionalism /prəˈfeʃnəlɪzəm ‖prəˈfeʃənlɪzəm/ *n* profesionalidad *f*

professionally /prəˈfeʃnəli/ *adv* **(a)** (as livelihood) ‹*sing/act*› profesionalmente **(b)** (by qualified person): **we had the job done ~** hicimos hacer el trabajo por un experto (*or* por un pintor, albañil *etc*) **(c)** (in a professional way) con profesionalidad

professor /prəˈfesər ‖prəˈfesə(r)/ *n* (of the highest academic rank) catedrático, -ca *m,f*; (any university teacher) (AmE) profesor universitario, profesora universitaria *m,f*

proffer /ˈprɑːfər ‖ˈprɒfə(r)/ *vt* (frml) ofrecer*

proficiency /prəˈfɪʃənsi/ *n* competencia *f*

proficient /prəˈfɪʃənt/ *adj* muy competente

profile¹ /ˈprəʊfaɪl/ *n* perfil *m*; **to keep a low ~** tratar de pasar desapercibido

profile² *vt* ‹*situation*› hacer* un esbozo de; **to ~ sb's life** hacer* una reseña biográfica de algn

profit¹ /ˈprɑːfət ‖ˈprɒfɪt/ *n* (Busn, Econ) ganancias *fpl*, utilidades *fpl* (AmL); **to sell sth at a ~** vender algo con ganancia

profit² *vi* **to ~ FROM sth** sacar* provecho DE algo

profitable /ˈprɑːfətəbəl ‖ˈprɒfɪtəbəl/ *adj* **(a)** (Busn) ‹*company/investment/crop*› rentable **(b)** ‹*day/journey*› provechoso

profitably /ˈprɑːfətəbli ‖ˈprɒfɪtəbli/ *adv* **(a)** (Busn) ‹*trade/operate*› de manera rentable; ‹*sell*› con ganancia **(b)** (fruitfully) provechosamente

profiteer /ˌprɑːfəˈtɪr ‖ˌprɒfɪˈtɪə(r)/ *n* especulador, -dora *m,f*

profiteering /ˌprɑːfəˈtɪrɪŋ ‖ˌprɒfɪˈtɪərɪŋ/ *n* especulación *f*

profit-making /ˈprɑːfətˌmeɪkɪŋ ‖ˈprɒfɪtˌmeɪkɪŋ/ *adj* (profitable) rentable; (which aims to make a profit) con fines lucrativos

profound /prəˈfaʊnd/ *adj* **-er, -est** profundo

profoundly /prəˈfaʊndli/ *adv* profundamente

profuse /prəˈfjuːs/ *adj* abundante; ‹*bleeding*› intenso

profusely /prəˈfjuːsli/ *adv* ‹*bleed*› profusamente; ‹*thank*› efusivamente; **he apologized ~** se deshizo en disculpas

profusion /prəˈfjuːʒən/ *n* profusión *f*

prognosis /prɑːgˈnəʊsəs ‖prɒgˈnəʊsɪs/ *n* (*pl* -**ses** /-siːz/) pronóstico *m*

program¹, (BrE) **programme** /ˈprəʊgræm/ *n* **1 (a)** (schedule, plan) programa *m* **(b)** (for concert, performance) programa *m* **(c)** (esp AmE Educ) (course) curso *m* **2** (Rad, TV) programa *m* **3** (Comput) programa *m*

program² *vt* -**mm-** *or* -**m-** **1** (BrE also) **programme (a)** (schedule) ‹*activities*› programar, planear **(b)** (instruct) programar **2** (Comput) programar

programmer, (AmE also) **programer** /ˈprəʊgræmər ‖ˈprəʊgræmə(r)/ *n* (Comput) programador, -dora *m,f*

progress¹ /ˈprɑːgrəs ‖ˈprəʊgres/ *n* **1** (advancement) progreso *m*; (of situation, events) desarrollo *m*; **to make ~** «*pupil*» adelantar, hacer* progresos; «*patient*» mejorar **2 in progress: talks are in ~ between the two parties** los dos partidos están manteniendo conversaciones; **while the examination is in ~** mientras dure el examen **3** (forward movement) avance *m*

progress² /prəˈgres/ *vi* «*work/science/ technology*» progresar; «*patient*» mejorar

progression /prəˈgreʃən/ *n* **(a)** (advance) evolución *f* **(b)** (Math, Mus) progresión *f*

progressive /prəˈgresɪv/ *adj* **1** ‹*attitude/ thinker/measure*› progresista **2** ‹*illness/ deterioration/improvement*› progresivo

prohibit /prəʊˈhɪbɪt ‖prəˈhɪbɪt/ *vt* **(a)** (forbid) prohibir* **(b)** (prevent) impedir*

prohibition /ˌprəʊəˈbɪʃən ‖ˌprəʊhɪˈbɪʃən/ *n* **(a)** prohibición *f* **(b) Prohibition** (in US history) (*no art*) la Ley seca, la Prohibición

AmC	Central America	Arg	Argentina	Cu	Cuba	Per	Peru
AmL	Latin America	Bol	Bolivia	Ec	Ecuador	RPI	River Plate Area
AmS	South America	Chi	Chile	Esp	Spain	Ur	Uruguay
Andes	Andean Region	CS	Southern Cone	Méx	Mexico	Ven	Venezuela

prohibitive /prəʊˈhɪbətɪv ‖ prəˈhɪbətɪv/ *adj* ‹price/cost› prohibitivo

project¹ /ˈprɑːdʒekt ‖ ˈprɒdʒekt/ *n* (a) (scheme) proyecto *m* (b) (Educ) trabajo *m* (c) (housing ∼) (in US) complejo *m* de viviendas subvencionadas

project² /prəˈdʒekt/ *vt* **1** (a) ‹beam/shadow/image› proyectar (b) (convey) ‹personality/image/voice› proyectar **2** (fml) ‹missile› lanzar* **3** (forecast) pronosticar*; ‹costs/trends› hacer* una proyección de; **the ∼ed figure** la cifra prevista

■ ∼ *vi* (jut out) sobresalir*

projection /prəˈdʒekʃən/ *n* **1** (of image, slide) proyección *f* **2** (forecast) proyección *f*, pronóstico *m* **3** (protuberance) saliente *f or m*

projector /prəˈdʒektər ‖ prəˈdʒektə(r)/ *n* proyector *m*

proletarian /ˌprəʊləˈteriən ‖ ˌprəʊləˈteəriən/ *adj* proletario

pro-life *adj* pro-vida

proliferate /prəˈlɪfəreɪt/ *vi* proliferar

prolific /prəˈlɪfɪk/ *adj* prolífico

prologue, (AmE also) **prolog** /ˈprəʊlɔːg ‖ ˈprəʊlɒg/ *n* prólogo *m*

prolong /prəˈlɔːŋ ‖ prəˈlɒŋ/ *vt* prolongar*

prom /prɑːm ‖ prɒm/ *n* (a) (ball) (in US) (colloq) baile *m* del colegio (or de la facultad etc) (b) (esplanade) (BrE colloq) ▸ PROMENADE¹

promenade¹ /ˌprɑːməˈneɪd ‖ ˈprɒmənɑːd/ *n* (at seaside) (esp BrE) paseo *m* marítimo, malecón *m* (AmL), costanera *f* (CS)

promenade² *vi* pasear(se)

prominence /ˈprɑːmənəns ‖ ˈprɒmɪnəns/ *n* (conspicuousness) prominencia *f*; (eminence, importance) importancia *f*

prominent /ˈprɑːmənənt ‖ ˈprɒmɪnənt/ *adj* (a) ‹position› destacado; ‹role/politician› prominente, destacado (b) ‹jaw/nose› prominente

prominently /ˈprɑːmənəntli ‖ ˈprɒmɪnəntli/ *adv*: **it was ∼ displayed** ocupaba un lugar prominente *or* destacado; **he figured ∼ in the negotiations** desempeñó un papel prominente *or* destacado en las negociaciones

promiscuity /ˌprɑːməsˈkjuːəti ‖ ˌprɒmɪˈskjuːəti/ *n* promiscuidad *f*

promiscuous /prəˈmɪskjuəs/ *adj* promiscuo

promise¹ /ˈprɑːməs ‖ ˈprɒmɪs/ *n* **1** (pledge) promesa *f* **2** (potential): **his work showed great** *o* **a lot of ∼** su trabajo prometía mucho

promise² *vt/i* prometer; **to ∼ to +** INF prometer + INF

promising /ˈprɑːməsɪŋ ‖ ˈprɒmɪsɪŋ/ *adj* ‹pupil/writer/career› prometedor; ‹future› halagüeño

promote /prəˈməʊt/ *vt* **1** (a) (raise in rank) ‹employee› ascender* (b) (AmE Educ) promover* **2** (a) (encourage) promover*; ‹growth› estimular (b) (advocate) promover* **3** ‹product/service› promocionar

promoter /prəˈməʊtər ‖ prəˈməʊtə(r)/ *n* (a) (Busn) promotor, -tora *m,f* (b) (Sport) empresario, -ria *m,f*

promotion /prəˈməʊʃən/ *n* **1** (advancement in rank) ascenso *m*; **she got (a) ∼** la ascendieron **2** (a) (of research, peace, trade) promoción *f* (b) (advocacy) promoción *f* **3** (publicity) promoción *f*

promotional /prəˈməʊʃnəl ‖ prəˈməʊʃənl/ *adj* de promoción, promocional

prompt¹ /prɑːmpt ‖ prɒmpt/ *vt* **1** ‹response/outcry› provocar*; **to ∼ sb to +** INF mover* a algn A + INF **2** ‹actor/orator› apuntarle a

prompt² *adj* **-er, -est** rápido

prompt³ *adv* (BrE): **at ten o'clock ∼** a las diez en punto

prompt⁴ *n* (a) (reminder) apunte *m* (b) (Comput) presto *m*

prompter /ˈprɑːmptər ‖ ˈprɒmptə(r)/ *n* apuntador, -dora *m,f*

promptly /ˈprɑːmptli ‖ ˈprɒmptli/ *adv* (a) (on time) puntualmente (b) (speedily) ‹pay/deliver› sin demora (c) (instantly) de inmediato

prone /prəʊn/ *adj* **1** (liable, disposed) ‹pred› **to be ∼ TO sth** ser* propenso A algo; **to be ∼ to +** INF ser* propenso a + INF **2** (face downward) (tendido) boca abajo

prong /prɔːŋ ‖ prɒŋ/ *n* diente *m*

pronoun /ˈprəʊnaʊn/ *n* pronombre *m*

pronounce /prəˈnaʊns/ *vt* (a) ‹sound/word/syllable› pronunciar (b) ‹judgment/sentence› pronunciar (c) (declare) (frml): **the doctor ∼d him dead** el médico dictaminó que estaba muerto

pronounced /prəˈnaʊnst/ *adj* pronunciado

pronouncement /prəˈnaʊnsmənt/ *n* declaración *f*

pronunciation /prəˌnʌnsiˈeɪʃən/ *n* pronunciación *f*

proof¹ /pruːf/ *n* **1** (conclusive evidence) prueba *f* **2** (Print) prueba *f* (de imprenta) **3** (alcoholic strength) graduación *f* alcohólica

proof² *adj* ‹pred› **to be ∼** AGAINST **sth** ser* a prueba DE algo

proof: ∼read (past & past p **-read** /-red/) *vt* *corregir ■ ∼ *vi* corregir* pruebas; **∼reader** *n* corrector, -tora *m,f* de pruebas

prop¹ /prɑːp ‖ prɒp/ *n* **1** (holding up roof etc) puntal *m* **2** (Cin, Theat) accesorio *m*, objeto *m* de utilería *or* (Esp, Méx) del attrezzo

prop² **-pp-** *vt* **to ∼ sth** AGAINST **sth** apoyar algo EN *or* CONTRA algo

■ **prop up** [*v + o + adv, v + adv + o*] (a) (support) ‹wall/building› sostener* (b) (lean) apoyar

propaganda /ˌprɑːpəˈgændə ‖ ˌprɒpəˈgændə/ *n* propaganda *f*

propagate /ˈprɑːpəgeɪt ‖ ˈprɒpəgeɪt/ *vt* propagar*

propel /prəˈpel/ *vt* **-ll-** ‹plane/ship› propulsar

propeller /prəˈpelər ‖ prəˈpelə(r)/ *n* hélice *f*

proper /ˈprɑːpər ‖ ˈprɒpə(r)/ *adj* **1** (before n, no comp) (correct) ‹treatment/procedure› apropiado; ‹pronunciation› correcto **2** (before n, no comp) (genuine) ‹chance› verdadero; ‹meal› como Dios manda; ‹vacation› de verdad **3** (a) ‹behavior/person› correcto (b) (overly decorous) recatado **4** (in the strict sense) (after n) propiamente dicho

properly /ˈprɑːpərli ‖ ˈprɒpəli/ *adv* (a) ‹write/spell/fit› correctamente; ‹work/concentrate/eat› bien (b) (appropriately) apropiadamente

proper name, proper noun *n* nombre *m* propio

property /ˈprɑːpərti ‖ ˈprɒpəti/ *n* (*pl* **-ties**) **1** (possessions) propiedad *f* **2** (a) (buildings, land) ····▸

propiedades *fpl*, bienes *mpl* raíces (frml); (*before n*) ~ **developer** promotor inmobiliario, promotora inmobiliaria *m,f*, ~ **tax** (in US) impuesto *m* sobre la propiedad inmobiliaria **(b)** (building) inmueble *m* (frml); (piece of land) terreno *m*, solar *m*, parcela *f* **3** (quality) propiedad *f*

prophecy /'prɑːfəsi ‖ 'prɒfəsi/ *n* (*pl* **-cies**) profecía *f*

prophesy /'prɑːfəsaɪ ‖ 'prɒfəsaɪ/ *ut* **-sies, -sying, -sied** predecir*; (Relig) profetizar*

prophet /'prɑːfət ‖ 'prɒfɪt/ *n* profeta, -tisa *m,f*

prophetic /prə'fetɪk/ *adj* profético

proportion /prə'pɔːrʃən ‖ prə'pɔːʃən/ *n* **1** (part) (*no pl*) parte *f* **2** (ratio) proporción *f*; **in equal ~s** por partes iguales; **in ~ to sth** en proporción a algo **3** (proper relation) proporción *f*; **let's keep things in ~** no exageremos; **to blow sth up out of all ~** exagerar algo desmesuradamente **4 proportions** *pl* (size) proporciones *fpl*

proportional /prə'pɔːrʃənəl ‖ prə'pɔːʃənl/ *adj* proporcional; ~ **representation** representación *f* proporcional

proportionate /prə'pɔːrʃnət ‖ prə'pɔːʃənət/ *adj* proporcional

proposal /prə'pəʊzəl/ *n* **(a)** (suggestion) propuesta *f* **(b)** (of marriage) proposición *f* matrimonial

propose /prə'pəʊz/ *ut* **1 (a)** (suggest) proponer*; **to ~ -ING/(THAT)** proponer* QUE (+ *subj*) **(b) proposed** *past p*: **the ~d cuts** los recortes que se proponen implementar **(c)** (in meeting) ⟨amendment⟩ proponer*; ⟨motion⟩ presentar **2** (intend) **to ~ to + INF, to ~ -ING** pensar* + INF
■ ~ *vi* **to ~ TO sb** proponerle* matrimonio a algn

proposition[1] /prɑːpə'zɪʃən ‖ prɒpə'zɪʃən/ *n* **1** (suggestion) propuesta *f*; (offer) oferta *f* **2** (prospect): **it's not a viable ~** no es viable

proposition[2] *ut* hacerle* proposiciones deshonestas a (euf)

proprietary /prə'praɪəteri ‖ prə'praɪətri/ *adj* ⟨device/software/drug⟩ de marca registrada

proprietor /prə'praɪətər ‖ prə'praɪətə(r)/ *n* propietario, -ria *m,f*, dueño, -ña *m,f*

propulsion /prə'pʌlʃən/ *n* propulsión *f*

pro rata /'prəʊ'rɑːtə/ *adv* a prorrata

prosaic /prəʊ'zeɪɪk/ *adj* prosaico

proscribe /prəʊ'skraɪb ‖ prə'skraɪb/ *ut* proscribir*

prose /prəʊz/ *n* (Lit) prosa *f*

prosecute /'prɑːsɪkjuːt ‖ 'prɒsɪkjuːt/ *ut* (Law) **to ~ sb FOR sth** procesar a algn POR algo
■ ~ *vi* iniciar procedimiento criminal; **prosecuting attorney** (in US) fiscal *mf*

prosecution /prɑːsɪ'kjuːʃən ‖ prɒsɪ'kjuːʃən/ *n* (Law) **(a)** (bringing to trial) interposición *f* de una acción judicial **(b)** (prosecuting side) **the ~** la acusación

prosecutor /'prɑːsɪkjuːtər ‖ 'prɒsɪkjuːtə(r)/ *n* fiscal *mf*; (in private prosecutions) abogado, -da *m,f* de *or* por la acusación

prospect[1] /'prɑːspekt ‖ 'prɒspekt/ *n* **1 (a)** (possibility) posibilidad *f*; ~ **OF sth** posibilidades *fpl* DE algo **(b)** (situation envisaged) perspectiva *f* **(c)**

prospects *pl* (chances) perspectivas *fpl*; **a job with no ~s** un trabajo sin futuro **2** (potential customer) posible cliente, -ta *m,f*

prospect[2] /'prɑːspekt ‖ prə'spekt/ *vi* **to ~ FOR sth** buscar* algo

prospective /prə'spektɪv/ *adj* (*before n*) ⟨customer⟩ posible; ⟨husband⟩ futuro

prospector /'prɑːspektər ‖ prə'spektə(r)/ *n* prospector, -tora *m,f*, cateador, -dora *m,f* (AmS)

prospectus /prə'spektəs/ *n* (*pl* **~es**) (Educ) folleto *m* informativo

prosper /'prɑːspər ‖ 'prɒspə(r)/ *vi* prosperar

prosperity /prɑːs'perəti ‖ prɒ'sperəti/ *n* prosperidad *f*

prosperous /'prɑːspərəs ‖ 'prɒspərəs/ *adj* próspero

prostate (gland) /'prɑːsteɪt ‖ 'prɒsteɪt/ *n* próstata *f*

prostitute[1] /'prɑːstʌtuːt ‖ 'prɒstɪtjuːt/ *n* prostituta *f*; **male ~** prostituto *m*

prostitute[2] *ut* prostituir*; **to ~ oneself** prostituirse*

prostitution /prɑːstə'tuːʃən ‖ prɒstɪ'tjuːʃən/ *n* prostitución *f*

prostrate /'prɑːstreɪt ‖ 'prɒstreɪt/ *adj* postrado

protagonist /prəʊ'tægənəst ‖ prə'tægənɪst/ *n* (Lit) protagonista *mf*

protect /prə'tekt/ *ut* proteger*

protection /prə'tekʃən/ *n* protección *f*; (*before n*) ~ **racket** chantaje *m* (que se practica a propietarios de comercios)

protectionism /prə'tekʃənɪzəm/ *n* proteccionismo *m*

protective /prə'tektɪv/ *adj* **(a)** ⟨headgear/covering⟩ protector; ⟨clothing⟩ de protección **(b)** ⟨attitude/feelings⟩ protector

protector /prə'tektər ‖ prə'tektə(r)/ *n* protector, -tora *m,f*

protein /'prəʊtiːn/ *n* proteína *f*

protest[1] /'prəʊtest/ *n* **(a)** (expression of disagreement) protesta *f*; **in ~** (against sth) en señal de protesta (contra algo); **under ~** bajo protesta **(b)** (complaint) protesta *f* **(c)** (demonstration) manifestación *f* de protesta

protest[2] /prə'test/ *vi* protestar; **to ~ AGAINST/ ABOUT sth** protestar CONTRA/ACERCA DE algo
■ ~ *ut* **1 (a)** (complain) **to ~ THAT** quejarse DE QUE, protestar QUE **(b)** (object to) (AmE) ⟨decision/action⟩ protestar (contra) **2** (assert) ⟨love⟩ declarar; ⟨innocence/loyalty⟩ hacer* protestas de

Protestant[1] /'prɑːtəstənt ‖ 'prɒtɪstənt/ *n* protestante *mf*

Protestant[2] *adj* protestante

Protestantism /'prɑːtəstəntɪzəm ‖ 'prɒtɪstəntɪzəm/ *n* protestantismo *m*

protester /prə'testər ‖ prə'testə(r)/ *n* manifestante *mf*

protocol /'prəʊtəkɔːl ‖ 'prəʊtəkɒl/ *n* protocolo *m*

prototype /'prəʊtətaɪp/ *n* prototipo *m*

protracted /prə'træktəd ‖ prə'træktɪd/ *adj* prolongado

protrude /prə'truːd/ *vi* (frml) **(a)** ⟨nail/ledge⟩

sobresalir* **(b) protruding** *pres p* ⟨*chin*⟩
prominente; ⟨*teeth*⟩ salido; ⟨*nail*⟩ que sobresale;
protruding eyes ojos *mpl* saltones

proud /praʊd/ *adj* **-er, -est (a)** (pleased)
⟨*parent/winner*⟩ orgulloso; ⟨*smile/moment*⟩ de
orgullo; **to be ∼ OF sb/sth** estar* orgulloso DE
algn/algo **(b)** (having self-respect) ⟨*nation/race*⟩
digno **(c)** (arrogant, haughty) orgulloso

proudly /ˈpraʊdli/ *adv* **(a)** (with pleasure,
satisfaction) con orgullo **(b)** (arrogantly)
orgullosamente

prove /pruːv/ (*past* **proved**; *past p* **proved** or
proven) *vt* ⟨*theory/statement/innocence*⟩
demostrar*; ⟨*loyalty/courage*⟩ demostrar*
■ *v refl* **to ∼ oneself: he was given three months to
∼ himself** le dieron tres meses para que
demostrara su valía; **to ∼ oneself to be sth**
demostrarse* ser algo
■ **∼** *vi* resultar

proven /ˈpruːvən/ *adj* ⟨*experience/ability*⟩
probado; ⟨*method*⟩ de probada eficacia

proverb /ˈprɑːvɜːrb ‖ˈprɒvɜːb/ *n* refrán *m*,
proverbio *m*

proverbial /prəˈvɜːrbiəl ‖prəˈvɜːbiəl/ *adj*
proverbial

provide /prəˈvaɪd/ *vt* (supply) proporcionar;
⟨*accommodation*⟩ dar*; **to ∼ sb WITH sth** proveer*
a algn DE algo
■ **provide for** [*v + prep + o*] **(a)** (support) ⟨*family*⟩
mantener* **(b)** (make arrangements for): **I have to ∼
for my old age** tengo que asegurarme el bienestar
en la vejez

provided /prəˈvaɪdəd ‖prəˈvaɪdɪd/ *conj* **∼
(that)** siempre que (+ *subj*)

providence /ˈprɑːvədəns ‖ˈprɒvɪdəns/ *n* **(a)**
(Relig) providencia *f* **(b)** (fate, chance): **it was sheer
∼ that ...** fue providencial que ...

providing /prəˈvaɪdɪŋ/ *conj* ▶ PROVIDED

province /ˈprɑːvəns ‖ˈprɒvɪns/ *n*
1 (administrative unit) provincia *f* **2** (a) (area of
knowledge, activity) terreno *m* **(b)** (area of responsibility)
competencia *f*

provincial /prəˈvɪntʃəl ‖prəˈvɪnʃəl/ *adj*
1 (Govt) provincial **2** (a) ⟨*town*⟩ de provincia(s)
(b) (pej) ⟨*outlook*⟩ provinciano

provision /prəˈvɪʒən/ *n* **1** (of funding) provisión
f, (of food, supplies) suministro *m* **2** (preparatory
arrangements) previsiones *fpl* **3** (stipulation) (Govt,
Law) disposición *f* **4 provisions** *pl* provisiones
fpl, víveres *mpl*

provisional /prəˈvɪʒnəl ‖prəˈvɪʒənl/ *adj*
provisional, provisorio (AmS)

proviso /prəˈvaɪzəʊ/ *n* (*pl* **-sos**) condición *f*

provocation /ˌprɑːvəˈkeɪʃən ‖ˌprɒvəˈkeɪʃən/
n provocación *f*

provocative /prəˈvɑːkətɪv ‖prəˈvɒkətɪv/ *adj*
1 (causing trouble) provocador **2** (seductive)
provocativo

provoke /prəˈvəʊk/ *vt* **1** ⟨*person/animal*⟩
provocar*; **I was ∼d into hitting him** tanto me
provocó, que le pegué **2** ⟨*argument/revolt/
criticism*⟩ provocar*; ⟨*discussion/debate*⟩ motivar;
⟨*interest/curiosity*⟩ despertar*

prow /praʊ/ *n* proa *f*

prowess /ˈpraʊəs ‖ˈpraʊɪs/ *n* destreza *f*

prowl /praʊl/ *vi* merodear

proximity /prɑːkˈsɪməti ‖prɒkˈsɪməti/ *n* (fml)
proximidad *f*

proxy /ˈprɑːksi ‖ˈprɒksi/ *n* (*pl* **-xies**) **(a)**
(person) representante *mf* **(b)** (authorization) poder
m; **by ∼** por poder *or* (Esp) por poderes

prude /pruːd/ *n* mojigato, -ta *m,f*

prudence /ˈpruːdn̩s/ *n* prudencia *f*

prudent /ˈpruːdn̩t/ *adj* prudente

prudish /ˈpruːdɪʃ/ *adj* mojigato

prune¹ /pruːn/ *n* ciruela *f* pasa *or* (CS) seca

prune² *vt* **(a)** (Hort) podar **(b)** ⟨*costs/workforce*⟩
reducir*

pry /praɪ/ **pries, prying, pried** *vi* curiosear;
to ∼ INTO sth entrometerse EN algo
■ **∼** *vt* (esp AmE) (+ *adv compl*): **she pried the lid
off** levantó la tapa (haciendo palanca)

PS *n* (postscript) P.D.

psalm /sɑːm/ *n* salmo *m*

pseudonym /ˈsuːdn̩ɪm ‖ˈsjuːdənɪm/ *n*
(p)seudónimo *m*

PST (in US) = **Pacific Standard Time**

psychiatric /ˌsaɪkiˈætrɪk/ *adj* (p)siquiátrico

psychiatrist /səˈkaɪətrəst ‖saɪˈkaɪətrɪst/ *n*
(p)siquiatra *mf*

psychiatry /səˈkaɪətri ‖saɪˈkaɪətri/ *n*
(p)siquiatría *f*

psychic /ˈsaɪkɪk/ *adj* **(a)** (Occult)
para(p)sicológico **(b)** (Psych) (p)síquico

psychoanalysis /ˌsaɪkəʊəˈnæləsəs
‖ˌsaɪkəʊəˈnæləsɪs/ *n* (p)sicoanálisis *m*

psychological /ˌsaɪkəˈlɑːdʒɪkəl
‖ˌsaɪkəˈlɒdʒɪkəl/ *adj* (p)sicológico

psychologist /saɪˈkɑːlədʒəst ‖saɪˈkɒlədʒɪst/ *n*
(p)sicólogo, -ga *m,f*

psychology /saɪˈkɑːlədʒi ‖saɪˈkɒlədʒi/ *n* (*pl*
-gies) (p)sicología *f*

psychopath /ˈsaɪkəpæθ ‖ˈsaɪkəʊpæθ/ *n*
(p)sicópata *mf*

psychosis /saɪˈkəʊsəs ‖saɪˈkəʊsɪs/ *n* (*pl* **-ses**
/-siːz/) (p)sicosis *f*

psychosomatic /ˌsaɪkəsəˈmætɪk
‖ˌsaɪkəʊsəˈmætɪk/ *adj* (p)sicosomático

psychotherapy /ˌsaɪkəʊˈθerəpi/ *n*
(p)sicoterapia *f*

psychotic /saɪˈkɑːtɪk ‖saɪˈkɒtɪk/ *adj*
(p)sicótico

PTO (= **please turn over**) sigue al dorso

pub /pʌb/ *n* (BrE) ≈ bar *m*; (before n) **to go on a
∼ crawl** ir* de bar en bar tomando copas

puberty /ˈpjuːbɜːrti ‖ˈpjuːbəti/ *n* pubertad *f*

pubic /ˈpjuːbɪk/ *adj* ⟨*hair*⟩ púbico, pubiano;
⟨*region/bone*⟩ pubiano

public¹ /ˈpʌblɪk/ *adj* público; **it is ∼ knowledge**
es de dominio público; **at ∼ expense** con fondos
públicos; **the ∼ sector** el sector público; **∼
speaking** oratoria *f*

public² *n* (+ *sing* or *pl vb*) **(a)** (people in general)
the ∼ el público **(b)** (audience) público *m* **(c) in
public** en público

public-address system /ˌpʌblɪkəˈdres/ *n*
(sistema *m* de) megafonía *f*, altoparlantes *mpl*
(AmL)

publican /ˈpʌblɪkən/ *n* (BrE) dueño, -ña *m,f* de
un bar

public assistance n (AmE) *ayuda estatal a los sectores más necesitados de la población*; **to be on ~ ~** *recibir ayuda estatal*

publication /ˌpʌbləˈkeɪʃən ‖ ˌpʌblɪˈkeɪʃən/ n *publicación f*

public: ~ health n *salud f* or *sanidad f pública*; **~ holiday** n *fiesta f oficial*, (*día m*) *feriado m* (AmL); **~ house** n (BrE) ≈*bar m*

publicity /pʌbˈlɪsəti/ n *publicidad f*

publicize /ˈpʌbləsaɪz ‖ ˈpʌblɪsaɪz/ vt *hacer* público*

publicly /ˈpʌblɪkli/ adv **(a)** *públicamente* **(b)** (Govt) ⟨*funded/maintained*⟩ *con fondos públicos*

public: ~ relations n *relaciones fpl públicas*; **~ school** n (in US) *escuela f pública*; (in UK) *colegio m privado*; (— boarding school) *internado m privado*; **~ service** n (communal provision) *servicio m público*; **~-spirited** /ˈpʌblɪkˈspɪrətəd ‖ ˌpʌblɪkˈspɪrɪtɪd/ adj *solidario*; **~ transportation** (AmE), **~ transport** (BrE) n *transporte m público*

publish /ˈpʌblɪʃ/ vt **(a)** ⟨*book/newspaper/article*⟩ *publicar** **(b)** (make known) *hacer* público*

publisher /ˈpʌblɪʃər ‖ ˈpʌblɪʃə(r)/ n **(a)** (company) *editorial f* **(b)** (job title) *editor, -tora m,f*

publishing /ˈpʌblɪʃɪŋ/ n *mundo m editorial*; (*before n*) **~ house** *editorial f*

pucker /ˈpʌkər ‖ ˈpʌkə(r)/ vt *fruncir**

pudding /ˈpʊdɪŋ/ n **(a)** (baked, steamed) *budín m, pudín m* **(b)** (dessert) (BrE) *postre m*

puddle /ˈpʌdl̩/ n *charco m*

Puerto Rican¹ /ˈpwertəˈriːkən ‖ ˌpwɜːtəʊˈriːkən/ adj *portorriqueño, puertorriqueño*

Puerto Rican² n *portorriqueño, -ña m,f, puertorriqueño, -ña m,f*

Puerto Rico /ˈpwertəˈriːkəʊ ‖ ˌpwɜːtəʊˈriːkəʊ/ n *Puerto Rico m*

puff¹ /pʌf/ n **(a)** (of wind, air) *ráfaga f*; **a ~ of smoke** *una nube de humo* **(b)** (action) *soplo m*; (on cigarette) *chupada f, pitada f* (AmL), *calada f* (Esp) **(c)** (sound) *resoplido m*

puff² vt **(a)** (blow) *soplar* **(b)** (smoke) ⟨*cigarette/ cigar/pipe*⟩ *dar* chupadas* or (AmL tb) *pitadas* or (Esp tb) *caladas a*
■ ~ vi **1 (a)** (blow) *soplar* **(b)** (smoke) **to ~ ON** o **AT sth** ⟨*on cigarette/cigar/pipe*⟩ *dar* chupadas* or (AmL tb) *pitadas* or (Esp tb) *caladas A algo* **2** (pant) *resoplar*
■ **puff out** [v + o + adv, v + adv + o] ⟨*cheeks*⟩ *inflar, hinchar* (Esp); ⟨*feathers*⟩ *erizar**
■ **puff up** [v + adv] *hincharse*

puffed /pʌft/ adj ⟨*sleeve*⟩ *abombado*

puffed-up /ˈpʌftˈʌp/ adj (pred **puffed up**) **(a)** (swollen) *hinchado* **(b)** (conceited) *engreído*

puffin /ˈpʌfən ‖ ˈpʌfɪn/ n *frailecillo m*

puff paste, (BrE) **puff pastry** n *hojaldre m*

puffy /ˈpʌfi/ adj **-fier, -fiest** *hinchado*

puke /pjuːk/ vi (colloq) *vomitar, devolver**

pull¹ /pʊl/ vt **1 (a)** (draw) *tirar de, jalar* (AmL

exc CS); (drag) *arrastrar* **(b)** (in specified direction) (+ *adv compl*): **he was ~ed from the rubble alive** *lo sacaron vivo de entre los escombros*; **the current ~ed him under** *la corriente lo arrastró al fondo* **2 (a)** (tug) *tirar de, jalar* (AmL exc CS) **(b)** (tear, detach): **he ~ed the toy to bits** *rompió el juguete* **3 (a)** ⟨*tooth*⟩ *sacar** **(b)** ⟨*gun*⟩ *sacar** **4** (colloq) ⟨*crowd/audience*⟩ *atraer** **5** (Med) ⟨*muscle/tendon*⟩ *desgarrarse*
■ ~ vi **1** (drag, tug) *tirar, jalar* (AmL exc CS) **2** «*vehicle*» (move) (+ *adv compl*): **to ~ off the road** *salir* de la carretera*; **to ~ into the station** *entrar en la estación*
■ **pull apart** [v + o + adv] **(a)** (separate) *separar* **(b)** (pull to pieces) *destrozar*, hacer* pedazos*
■ **pull away** [v + adv] **(a)** (free oneself) *soltarse** **(b)** (move off) «*train/bus*» *arrancar**
■ **pull back** [v + adv] **(a)** (retreat) ⟨*troops/ enemy*⟩ *retirarse* **(b)** (withdraw) *echarse atrás*
■ **pull down** [v + o + adv, v + adv + o] **(a)** (lower) ⟨*blind*⟩ *bajar* **(b)** (demolish) ⟨*building*⟩ *echar, tumbar* (Méx)
■ **pull in**
  I [v + o + adv, v + adv + o] **1** (draw in) ⟨*nets/ rope*⟩ *recoger**; ⟨*claws*⟩ *retraer** **2** (attract) ⟨*customers*⟩ *atraer**
  II [v + adv] **1** (arrive) ⟨*train/bus*⟩ *llegar** **2 (a)** (move over) «*ship/car*» *arrimarse* **(b)** (stop) (BrE) «*car/truck*» *parar*
■ **pull off** [v + o + adv, v + adv + o] **1** (remove) ⟨*cover/lid*⟩ *quitar* **2** (achieve) (colloq) *conseguir**
■ **pull out**
  I [v + adv] **1** «*vehicle/driver*» **(a)** (depart) *arrancar** **(b)** (enter traffic): **he ~ed out right in front of me** *se me metió justo delante* **2** (withdraw) «*troops/partner*» *retirarse*
  II [v + o + adv, v + adv + o] **1 (a)** (extract, remove) ⟨*tooth/nail/plug*⟩ *sacar**; ⟨*weeds/page*⟩ *arrancar** **(b)** (produce) ⟨*wallet/gun*⟩ *sacar** **2** (withdraw) ⟨*team/troops*⟩ *retirar*
■ **pull over** [v + adv] «*driver/car*» *hacerse a un lado*; (to stop) *acercarse* a la acera* (or *al arcén etc*) *y parar* **(b)** [v + o + adv] *parar*
■ **pull through** [v + adv] **(a)** (recover) *reponerse** **(b)** (survive) *salir* adelante*
■ **pull together 1** [v + adv] (cooperate) *trabajar codo con codo* **2** [v + o + adv] (control oneself): **to ~ oneself together** *calmarse*
■ **pull up 1** [v + o + adv, v + adv + o] **(a)** (draw up) *levantar, subir*; **to ~ one's socks up** *subirse los calcetines* **(b)** (uproot) ⟨*plant*⟩ *arrancar** **2** [v + o + adv] (reprimand) **to ~ sb up** (ON sth) *regañar or* (CS) *retar a algn* (POR algo) **3** [v + adv] (stop) «*car/driver*» *parar*

pull² n **1** (tug) *tirón m, jalón m* (AmL exc CS) **2 (a)** (pulling force) *fuerza f* **(b)** (influence) *influencia f*

pulley /ˈpʊli/ n (pl **~s**) *polea f*

pull: ~-out n **(a)** (withdrawal) *retirada f* **(b)** (Journ) *suplemento m*; **~over**, (AmE also) **~over sweater** n ▸ SWEATER

AmC	América Central	Arg	Argentina	Cu	Cuba
AmL	América Latina	Bol	Bolivia	Ec	Ecuador
AmS	América del Sur	Chi	Chile	Esp	España
Andes	Región andina	CS	Cono Sur	Méx	México

Per	Perú
RPI	Río de la Plata
Ur	Uruguay
Ven	Venezuela

pulp /pʌlp/ n (a) (of fruit, vegetable) pulpa f, carne f; (of wood, paper) pasta f (de papel) (b) (crushed material) pasta f

pulpit /'pʊlpɪt/ n púlpito m

pulsate /'pʌlseɪt ‖pʌl'seɪt/ vi «heart» latir; «light/current» oscilar

pulse¹ /pʌls/ n ① (a) (Physiol) pulso m; (before n) ~ **rate** número m de pulsaciones (b) (throbbing) cadencia f (c) (Phys) pulsación f ② (Agr, Culin) legumbre f (como los garbanzos, las lentejas etc)

pulse² vi latir

pulverize /'pʌlvəraɪz/ vt pulverizar*

puma /'puːmə ‖'pjuːmə/ n puma m, león m (Chi, Méx)

pummel /'pʌməl/ vt, (BrE) **-ll-** darle* una paliza a

pump¹ /pʌmp/ n ① bomba f; (gasoline o (BrE) petrol ~) surtidor m ② (AmE Clothing) zapato m (de) salón

pump² vt (a) (supply) bombear; **to ~ sth INTO sth** «water/oil» bombear algo A algo (b) (drain) **to ~ sth OUT OF sth** sacar* algo de algo con una bomba; **to ~ sb's stomach out** hacerle* un lavado de estómago a algn (c) (ask) (colloq): **he was ~ing me for information** me estaba tratando de (son)sacar información
■ ~ vi «machine/heart» bombear
■ **pump up** [v + o + adv, v + adv + o] (inflate) «tire» inflar, hinchar (Esp)

pumpkin /'pʌmpkən ‖'pʌmpkɪn/ n calabaza f, zapallo m (CS, Per)

pun /pʌn/ n juego m de palabras, albur m (Méx)

punch¹ /pʌntʃ/ n ① (a) (blow) puñetazo m (b) (vigor) garra f (fam), fuerza f ② (for paper) perforadora f; (for metal, leather) sacabocados m ③ (Culin) (a) ponche m; (before n) ~ **bowl** ponchera f (b) (in US) refresco m de frutas

punch² vt ① (hit) pegarle* a ② (perforate) «ticket» picar*, ponchar (Méx); «leather/metal» perforar; **to ~ a hole in sth** hacerle* un agujero a algo
■ **punch in** [v + adv] (AmE) fichar, marcar* or (Méx) checar* tarjeta (al entrar al trabajo)
■ **punch out** [v + adv] (AmE) fichar, marcar* or (Méx) checar* tarjeta (al salir del trabajo)

punch: ~**-drunk** adj grogui (fam), atontado; ~ **line** n remate m (de un chiste); ~**-up** n (BrE colloq) bronca f (fam)

punctual /'pʌŋktʃuəl ‖'pʌŋktjʊəl, 'pʌŋktʃʊəl/ adj puntual

punctuality /ˌpʌŋktʃu'ælətɪ ‖ˌpʌŋktjʊ'ælətɪ, ˌpʌŋktʃʊ'ælətɪ/ n puntualidad f

punctually /'pʌŋktʃuəlɪ ‖'pʌŋktjʊəlɪ, 'pʌŋktʃʊəlɪ/ adv puntualmente

punctuate /'pʌŋktʃueɪt ‖'pʌŋktjʊeɪt, 'pʌŋktʃʊeɪt/ vt (a) «writing/text» puntuar* (b) (intersperse) salpicar*

punctuation /ˌpʌŋktʃu'eɪʃən ‖ˌpʌŋktjʊ'eɪʃən, ˌpʌŋktʃʊ'eɪʃən/ n puntuación f; (before n) ~ **mark** signo m de puntuación

puncture¹ /'pʌŋktʃər ‖'pʌŋktʃə(r)/ n (in tire, ball) pinchazo m, pinchadura f (AmL), ponchadura f (Méx); **we had a ~ on the way there** pinchamos por el camino, se nos ponchó una llanta en el camino (Méx)

puncture² vt «tire/ball» pinchar, ponchar (Méx)

pungent /'pʌndʒənt/ adj «taste/smell» acre

punish /'pʌnɪʃ/ vt castigar*

punishable /'pʌnɪʃəbəl/ adj punible; ~ **BY sth** penado CON algo

punishing /'pʌnɪʃɪŋ/ adj «schedule/treatment» duro; «pace» agotador, extenuante

punishment /'pʌnɪʃmənt/ n (a) (chastisement) castigo m (b) (rough treatment): **it's taken a lot of ~** ha sido muy maltratado

punk /pʌŋk/ n ① (a) (person) ~ (**rocker**) punk mf, punki mf (b) ~ (**rock**) punk m ② (young hoodlum) (AmE colloq) vándalo, -la m,f, gamberro, -rra m,f (Esp)

punt¹ /pʊnt/ n (Fin) libra f (irlandesa)

punt² /pʌnt/ vi (in boat): **to go ~ing** salir* de paseo en batea

puny /'pjuːnɪ/ adj **punier, puniest** (pej) «person» enclenque; «effort» lastimoso

pup /pʌp/ n cría f; (of dog) cachorro, -rra m,f

pupil /'pjuːpəl ‖'pjuːpɪl/ n ① (Educ) alumno, -na m,f, educando, -da m,f (frml) ② (of eye) pupila f

puppet /'pʌpət ‖'pʌpɪt/ n ① (a) (marionette) marioneta f, títere m (b) (glove puppet) títere m ② (stooge) títere m; (before n) «regime/leader» títere

puppy /'pʌpɪ/ n (pl **-pies**) cachorro, -rra m,f

purchase¹ /'pɜːrtʃəs ‖'pɜːtʃəs/ n (frml) adquisición f (frml)

purchase² vt (frml) adquirir (frml)

purchaser /'pɜːrtʃəsər ‖'pɜːtʃəsə(r)/ n (frml) comprador, -dora m,f

pure /pjʊr ‖pjʊə(r)/ adj **purer, purest** puro

puree, purée /pjʊ'reɪ ‖'pjʊəreɪ/ n puré m; **tomato ~** concentrado m de tomate

purely /'pjʊrlɪ ‖'pjʊəlɪ/ adv «decorative» puramente; ~ **by chance** por pura casualidad

purgatory /'pɜːrgətɔːrɪ ‖'pɜːgətərɪ/ n purgatorio m

purge¹ /pɜːrdʒ ‖pɜːdʒ/ vt (a) (cleanse) purgar* (b) (Pol) «party/government/committee» hacer* una purga en

purge² n (Med, Pol) purga f

purify /'pjʊrəfaɪ ‖'pjʊərɪfaɪ/ vt **-fies, -fying, -fied** purificar*; «water» depurar

purist /'pjʊrəst ‖'pjʊərɪst/ n purista mf

puritan /'pjʊrətn̩ ‖'pjʊərɪtən/ n puritano, -na m,f

puritanical /ˌpjʊrə'tænɪkəl ‖ˌpjʊərɪ'tænɪkəl/ adj puritano

purity /'pjʊrətɪ ‖'pjʊərətɪ/ n pureza f

purl¹ /pɜːrl ‖pɜːl/ n punto m (al or del) revés

purl² vt tejer al or del revés

purple¹ /'pɜːrpəl ‖'pɜːpəl/ adj (bluish) morado; (reddish) púrpura

purple² n (bluish) morado m, violeta m; (reddish) púrpura m

purport /pər'pɔːrt ‖pə'pɔːt/ vt (frml) **to ~ to +** INF pretender + INF

purpose /'pɜːrpəs ‖'pɜːpəs/ n ① (a) (intention, reason) propósito m; **for one's own ~s** por su (or mi etc) propio interés; **the machine is good enough for our ~s** la máquina sirve para lo que nos proponemos hacer con ella; **on ~** a propósito (b) (use): **to serve a (useful) ~** servir* de algo ② (resolution) determinación f

purposeful /ˈpɜːrpəsfəl ‖ˈpɜːpəsfəl/ *adj* ‹*person/stride*› resuelto; ‹*expression*› de determinación

purposely /ˈpɜːrpəsli ‖ˈpɜːpəsli/ *adv* ‹*facetious/hurtful*› deliberadamente; ‹*say/do*› a propósito

purr¹ /pɜːr ‖pɜː(r)/ *vi* ronronear

purr² *n* ronroneo *m*

purse¹ /pɜːrs ‖pɜːs/ *n* **1** (a) (for money) monedero *m*, portamonedas *m* (b) (funds) fondos *mpl* **2** (handbag) (AmE) cartera *f* or (Esp) bolso *m* or (Méx) bolsa *f*

purse² *vt* to ~ one's lips fruncir* la boca

purser /ˈpɜːrsər ‖ˈpɜːsə(r)/ *n* sobrecargo *mf*

pursue /pərˈsuː ‖pəˈsjuː/ *vt* **1** (chase) perseguir*; ‹*pleasure/happiness*› buscar* **2** ‹*policy/course of action*› continuar* con; ‹*research/study*› continuar* con; ‹*profession*› ejercer*

pursuer /pərˈsuːər ‖pəˈsjuːə(r)/ *n* perseguidor, -dora *m,f*

pursuit /pərˈsuːt ‖pəˈsjuːt/ *n* **1** (chase) persecución *f*; she set off in ~ of the thief salió en persecución del ladrón; the ~ of happiness la búsqueda de la felicidad **2** (pastime) actividad *f*

pus /pʌs/ *n* pus *m*

push¹ /pʊʃ/ *n* empujoncito *m*; (violent) empujón *m*; she gave the door a ~ empujó la puerta; at the ~ of a button con solo apretar un botón; at a ~ (colloq): at a ~, I could finish it by Friday si me apuras, podría terminarlo para el viernes

push² *vt* **1** (a) ‹*person/car/table*› empujar; I ~ed the door to o shut cerré la puerta empujándola (b) (press) ‹*button*› apretar* (c) (force): to ~ prices up/down hacer* que suban/ bajen los precios; I tried to ~ the thought to the back of my mind traté de no pensar en ello **2** (put pressure on): you're ~ing him/yourself too hard le/te exiges demasiado; to be ~ed for time/ money (colloq) andar* corto de tiempo/de dinero (fam) **3** (a) (promote) promocionar (b) (sell) (colloq) ‹*drugs*› pasar (fam), transar (CS arg) **4** (approach) (colloq) (*only in -ing form*): to be ~ing forty rondar los cuarenta
■ ~ *vi* **1** (give a push) empujar **2** (apply pressure) presionar
■ **push back** [*v + o + adv, v + adv + o*] (a) (force back) ‹*person/object*› empujar hacia atrás; ‹*crowd/ army*› hacer* retroceder (b) (extend) ‹*limits*› ampliar*
■ **push in** [*v + adv*] colarse* (fam)
■ **push off** [*v + adv*] (a) (in boat) desatracar* (b) (leave, go) (colloq) largarse* (fam)
■ **push on** [*v + adv*] (a) (continue journey) seguir* el viaje (b) (continue working) seguir* adelante
■ **push through** [*v + o + adv, v + adv + o*] ‹*legislation*› hacer* aprobar

push: ~**bike** *n* (BrE) bicicleta *f*; ~**button** *adj* (*before n*) ‹*controls/telephone*› de botones; ~**chair** *n* (BrE) sillita *f* (de paseo), carreola *f* (Méx)

pusher /ˈpʊʃər ‖ˈpʊʃə(r)/ *n* (colloq) camello *mf* (arg), jíbaro *mf* (Col, Ven arg), conecte *m,f* (Mex arg)

push: ~**over** *n*: to be a ~over «*task/game*» ser* pan comido (fam), estar* chupado (Esp fam);

«*person*» ser* un incauto; ~**start** /ˈpʊʃstɑːrt ‖ˌpʊʃˈstɑːt/ *vt* ‹*car*› arrancar* empujando; ~**up** *n* flexión *f* (de brazos *or* de pecho), fondo *m*, lagartija *f* (Méx)

pushy /ˈpʊʃi/ *adj* **pushier, pushiest** (colloq) prepotente

pussy /ˈpʊsi/ (*pl* **-sies**), **pussycat** /ˈpʊsikæt/ *n* (colloq) minino, -na *m,f* (fam), gatito, -ta *m,f* (fam)

put /pʊt/ (*pres p* **putting**; *past & past p* **put**) *vt*
I **1** (place) poner*; (with care, precision etc) colocar*; (inside sth) meter*; he ~ it in his mouth se lo puso en la boca
2 (a) (thrust): he ~ his arms around her la abrazó; she ~ her head out of the window asomó la cabeza por la ventana (b) (Sport) to ~ the shot lanzar* el peso
3 (a) (rank) poner*; she ~s herself first se pone ella primero; he ~s his art before everything else antepone su arte a todo (b) (in competition, league): this victory ~s them in o into the lead con esta victoria pasan a ocupar la delantera
II **1** (cause to be) poner*; the doctor ~ me on a diet el doctor me puso a régimen
2 (make undergo) to ~ sb TO sth: I don't want to ~ you to any trouble no quiero causarle ninguna molestia
III **1** (a) (attribute, assign): I ~ a high value on our friendship valoro mucho nuestra amistad (b) (impose) to ~ sth ON sth/sb: to ~ the blame on sb echarle la culpa a algn; it ~ a great strain on their relationship eso sometió su relación a una gran tensión
2 (a) (invest) to ~ sth INTO sth ‹*money*› invertir* algo EN algo; she had ~ a lot of thought into it lo había pensado mucho (b) (bet, stake) to ~ sth ON sth ‹*money*› apostar* algo A algo (c) (contribute) to ~ sth TOWARD sth contribuir* CON algoA algo
IV **1** (present) ‹*views/case*› exponer*; ‹*proposal*› presentar
2 (write, indicate, mark) poner*
3 (express) decir*; ~ it this way: I wouldn't invite him again no lo volvería a invitar; to ~ sth well/badly expresar algo bien/ mal
■ **put about** [*v + o + adv, v + adv + o*] (colloq) ‹*story/rumor*› hacer* correr
■ **put across** [*v + o + adv, v + adv + o*] ‹*idea/ message*› comunicar*
■ **put aside** [*v + o + adv, v + adv + o*] (a) (lay to one side) dejar a un lado (b) (reserve) ‹*money*› guardar; ‹*goods/time*› reservar (c) ‹*differences*› dejar de lado
■ **put away** [*v + o + adv, v + adv + o*] (a) (put in cupboard, drawer) ‹*dishes/tools/clothes*› guardar (b) (save) ‹*money*› guardar, ahorrar (c) (consume) (colloq) ‹*food/drink*› zamparse (fam) (d) (confine) (colloq) ‹*criminal/lunatic*› encerrar* (e) (destroy) (AmE euph) ‹*animal*› sacrificar* (euf)
■ **put back** [*v + o + adv, v + adv + o*] (a) (replace) volver* a poner (b) (reset) ‹*clocks*› atrasar (c) (delay, retard) ‹*project*› retrasar (d) (postpone) posponer*, aplazar*, postergar* (AmL)
■ **put by** [*v + o + adv, v + adv + o*] ‹*money*› ahorrar
■ **put down**
I [*v + o + adv, v + adv + o*] **1** (a) (set down)

⟨*bag/pen*⟩ dejar; ⟨*telephone*⟩ colgar* **(b)** (lay) ⟨*tiles/carpet*⟩ poner*, colocar* **(c)** (lower) bajar **(d)** ⟨*passenger*⟩ dejar

2 (a) (suppress) ⟨*rebellion*⟩ sofocar* **(b)** (destroy) (BrE euph) ⟨*animal*⟩ sacrificar* (euf)

3 (a) (write down) ⟨*thoughts*⟩ anotar, escribir*; ⟨*name*⟩ poner*, escribir* **(b)** (attribute) to ∼ sth **down** TO sth atribuirle* algo A algo

4 (in part payment) ⟨*sum*⟩ entregar*; ⟨*deposit*⟩ dejar

II [*v + o + adv*] (belittle) rebajar

■ **put forward** [*v + o + adv, v + adv + o*] **1 (a)** ⟨*theory/plan*⟩ presentar; ⟨*suggestion*⟩ hacer* **(b)** ⟨*candidate*⟩ proponer*, postular (AmL)

2 (a) ⟨*clocks*⟩ adelantar **(b)** ⟨*trip/meeting*⟩ adelantar

■ **put in**
I [*v + o + adv, v + adv + o*] **1** (install) ⟨*central heating/shower unit*⟩ poner*, instalar

2 (enter, submit) ⟨*claim/request/tender*⟩ presentar

3 (invest): **how much time can you put in?** ¿cuánto tiempo puedes dedicarle?

4 (insert, add) ⟨*word/chapter/scene*⟩ poner*

II [*v + adv*] **1** (Naut) hacer* escala

2 (apply) to ∼ **in** FOR sth solicitar algo

■ **put off**
I [*v + o + adv, v + adv + o*] **1 (a)** (postpone) ⟨*meeting/visit/decision*⟩ aplazar*, posponer*, postergar* (AmL); **I keep** ∼**ting off going to the dentist** siempre estoy aplazando ir al dentista **(b)** (stall) ⟨*visitor/creditor*⟩: **if Saturday isn't convenient, I can** ∼ **them off** si el sábado no es conveniente, puedo decirles que lo dejen para más adelante

2 (turn off) (BrE) ⟨*light*⟩ apagar*

II [*v + o + adv, v + adv + o*] **1** (discourage): **the thought of the journey** ∼**s me off going to see them** pensar en el viaje me quita las ganas de ir a visitarlos

2 (distract) distraer*; (disconcert) desconcertar*

■ **put on**
I [*v + o + adv, v + adv + o*] **1** ⟨*jacket/sweater*⟩ ponerse*; **to put one's clothes on** vestirse*, ponerse* la ropa; **to** ∼ **one's shoes on** ponerse* los zapatos, calzarse*

2 ⟨*light/radio/oven*⟩ encender*, prender (AmL); ⟨*music*⟩ poner*

3 (gain): **I've** ∼ **on four pounds** he engordado cuatro libras; **to** ∼ **on weight** engordar

4 ⟨*exhibition*⟩ organizar*; ⟨*play/show*⟩ presentar

5 (assume) ⟨*expression*⟩ adoptar; **he's just** ∼**ting it on** está haciendo teatro

II [*v + o + adv*] **1 (a)** (alert) to ∼ **sb on** TO sb: **somebody had** ∼ **the police on to them** alguien había puesto a la policía sobre su pista **(b)** (introduce) to ∼ **sb on** TO sb: **I can** ∼ **you on to someone who ...** puedo ponerte en contacto con una persona que ...

2 (tease) (AmE colloq) tomarle el pelo a (fam)

■ **put out**
I [*v + o + adv, v + adv + o*] **1 (a)** (put outside) ⟨*washing/cat*⟩ sacar* **(b)** (set out) disponer* **(c)** (extend) ⟨*arm/tongue*⟩ sacar* **(d)** (dislocate) dislocarse*, zafarse (Chi, Méx)

2 (a) (extinguish) ⟨*fire/light/cigarette*⟩ apagar* **(b)** (anesthetize) (colloq) dormir*

3 (offend, inconvenience) molestar

4 (a) (issue, publish) ⟨*statement*⟩ publicar* **(b)** (broadcast) transmitir

II [*v + adv*] (Naut) salir*; **to** ∼ **out to sea** hacerse* a la mar

■ **put over (a)** ▶ PUT ACROSS **(b)** (AmE) ▶ PUT OFF I 1A

■ **put past** [*v + o + prep + o*]: **not to** ∼ **it past sb**: **I wouldn't** ∼ **it past her** no me extrañaría nada *or* la creo muy capaz

■ **put through 1** [*v + o + prep + o*] (make undergo) someter a

2 [*v + o + adv, v + adv + o*] (Telec): **to** ∼ **sb through** (TO sb) pasar *or* (AmL) comunicar* *or* (Esp) poner* a algn CON algn

■ **put together** [*v + o + adv, v + adv + o*] **1 (a)** (assemble) armar; ⟨*collection*⟩ reunir* **(b)** (create) ⟨*team*⟩ formar; ⟨*magazine*⟩ producir*; ⟨*meal*⟩ preparar; (quickly) improvisar

2 (combine) juntar, reunir*; **more than everything else** ∼ **together** más que todo lo demás junto

■ **put up**
I [*v + o + adv, v + adv + o*] **1 (a)** ⟨*hotel*⟩ levantar; ⟨*tent*⟩ armar **(b)** ⟨*decorations/curtains/notice*⟩ poner* **(c)** ⟨*umbrella*⟩ abrir* **(d)** ⟨*hand*⟩ levantar

2 ⟨*price/fare*⟩ aumentar

3 ⟨*candidate*⟩ proponer*, postular (AmL)

4 (in accommodation) alojar; **they** ∼ **us up for the night** nos quedamos a dormir en su casa

II [*v + adv + o*] **(a)** (present): **to** ∼ **up resistance/ a struggle/a fight** ofrecer* resistencia (**b**) ⟨*money/ capital*⟩ poner*

III [*v + adv*] (stay) quedarse

■ **put up to** [*v + o + adv + prep + o*]: **somebody must have** ∼ **them up to it** alguien debe haberlos empujado a ello

■ **put up with** [*v + adv + prep + o*] aguantar

put: ∼**-down** *n* (colloq) desprecio *m*; ∼ **out** *adj* (*pred*) **to be** ∼ **out** estar* molesto

putrid /'pjuːtrəd ‖ 'pjuːtrɪd/ *adj* putrefacto, pútrido

putt /pʌt/ *vi* golpear la bola, potear (AmL)
■ ∼ *vt* golpear

putter[1] /'pʌtər ‖ 'pʌtə(r)/ *n* (club) putter *m*

putter[2] *vi* (AmE) (+ *adv compl*): **to** ∼ **around** *o* **about in the garden** entretenerse trabajando en el jardín; **I've been** ∼**ing around the house all day** me he pasado el día haciendo un poco de esto y un poco de aquello en la casa

putting green /'pʌtɪŋ/ *n* putting green *m*

putty /'pʌti/ *n* masilla *f*

puzzle[1] /'pʌzəl/ *n* **(a)** (game,toy) rompecabezas *m*; (riddle) adivinanza *f* **(b)** (mystery) misterio *m*

puzzle[2] *vt*: **one thing** ∼**s me** hay algo que no entiendo

puzzled /'pʌzəld/ *adj* ⟨*expression/tone*⟩ de desconcierto; **I'm** ∼ **about it** me tiene perplejo

PVC *n* PVC *m*

pygmy /'pɪgmi/ *n* (*pl* -**mies**) **(a)** (Anthrop) *also* **Pygmy** pigmeo, -mea *m,f* **(b)** (Zool) (*before n*) enano

pyjamas /pə'dʒɑːməz/ *n* (BrE) ▶ PAJAMAS

pylon /'paɪlɑːn, -lən ‖ 'paɪlɒn, -lən/ *n* torre *f* de alta tensión

pyramid /'pɪrəmɪd/ *n* pirámide *f*

pyre /paɪr ‖ 'paɪə(r)/ *n* pira *f*

p

Pyrenees /ˈpɪrəˈniːz ‖ ˌpɪrəˈniːz/ *pl n* the ~ los Pirineos

Pyrex® /ˈpaɪreks/ *n* pyrex® *m*, arcopal® *m*

python /ˈpaɪθɑːn ‖ ˈpaɪθən/ *n* (serpiente *f*) pitón *f*

Qq

Q, q /kjuː/ *n* Q, q *f*

QC *n* (in UK) (= **Queen's Counsel**) *título conferido a ciertos abogados de prestigio*

QED (= **quod erat demonstrandum**) Q.E.D. (frml), que es lo que había que demostrar

quack¹ /kwæk/ *vi* graznar

quack² *n* (pej) **1** (charlatan) charlatán, -tana *m,f*; (professing medical skill) (~ doctor) curandero, -ra *m,f* **2** (of duck) graznido *m*

quad /kwɑːd ‖ kwɒd/ *n* (colloq) **1** (quadruplet) cuatrillizo, -za *m,f* **2** (of college) ▶ QUADRANGLE 1

quadrangle /ˈkwɑːdræŋgəl ‖ ˈkwɒdræŋgəl/ *n* **1** (BrE Archit) patio *m* interior **2** (Math) ▶ QUADRILATERAL

quadrant /ˈkwɑːdrənt ‖ ˈkwɒdrənt/ *n* cuadrante *m*

quadrilateral /ˌkwɑːdrəˈlætərəl ‖ ˌkwɒdrɪˈlætərəl/ *n* cuadrilátero *m*

quadruped /ˈkwɑːdrʊped ‖ ˈkwɒdrʊped/ *n* cuadrúpedo *m*

quadruple¹ /kwɑːˈdruːpl̩ ‖ ˈkwɒdrʊpl̩/ *adj* cuádruple, cuádruplo

quadruple² /kwɑːˈdruːpl̩ ‖ kwɒˈdruːpl̩/ *vi* cuadruplicarse*

quadruplet /kwɑːˈdruːplət ‖ ˈkwɒdrʊplət/ *n* cuatrillizo, -za *m,f*

quaff /kwɑːf ‖ kwɒf/ *vt* (hum) beberse, zamparse (fam)

quagmire /ˈkwæɡmaɪr, ˈkwɑːɡ- ‖ ˈkwɒɡmaɪə(r), ˈkwæɡ-/ *n* (a) (bog) lodazal *m*, barrial *m* (AmL) (b) (situation) atolladero *m*

quail¹ /kweɪl/ *vi* temblar*; **she ~ed at the idea** la idea le daba pavor

quail² *n* (*pl* **quails** *or* **quail**) codorniz *f*

quaint /kweɪnt/ *adj* **-er, -est** (a) (charming, picturesque) pintoresco (b) (odd) extraño

quake¹ /kweɪk/ *vi* temblar*

quake² *n* (colloq) (earthquake) terremoto *m*

Quaker /ˈkweɪkər ‖ ˈkweɪkə(r)/ *n* cuáquero, -ra *m,f*

qualification /ˌkwɑːləfəˈkeɪʃən ‖ ˌkwɒlɪfɪˈkeɪʃən/ *n* **1** (a) (Educ): **she has a teaching** ~ tiene título de maestra/profesora; **his ~s are very good** está muy bien calificado *or* (Esp) cualificado (b) (skill, necessary attribute) requisito *m* **2** (a) (eligibility) derecho *m* (b) (being accepted) clasificación *f* **3** (reservation) reserva *f*

qualified /ˈkwɑːləfaɪd ‖ ˈkwɒlɪfaɪd/ *adj* (a) (trained) titulado; **to be ~ to + INF** tener* la titulación necesaria PARA + INF (b) (competent) (*pred*) capacitado; **to be ~ to + INF** estar* capacitado PARA + INF (c) (eligible) (*pred*) **to be ~ to + INF** reunir* los requisitos necesarios PARA + INF

qualify /ˈkwɑːləfaɪ ‖ ˈkwɒlɪfaɪ/ **-fies, -fying, -fied** *vt* **1** (equip, entitle): **this degree qualifies you to practice anywhere in Europe** este título te habilita para ejercer en cualquier parte de Europa; **their low income qualifies them for some benefits** sus bajos ingresos les dan derecho a recibir ciertas prestaciones **2** (a) (limit): **I'd like to ~ the statement I made earlier** quisiera matizar lo que expresé anteriormente haciendo algunas salvedades (*or* puntualizaciones *etc*) (b) (Ling) calificar*

■ ~ *vi* (a) (gain professional qualification) titularse, recibirse (AmL) (b) (Sport) clasificarse* (c) (be entitled) **to ~ (FOR sth)** tener* derecho (A algo)

quality /ˈkwɑːləti ‖ ˈkwɒləti/ *n* (*pl* **-ties**) calidad *f*

qualm /kwɑːm/ *n* (*often pl*) (a) (scruple) reparo *m*; **to have no ~s about sth** no tener* ningún reparo en algo (b) (misgiving) duda *f*

quandary /ˈkwɑːndri ‖ ˈkwɒndri/ *n* (*pl* **-ries**) (*usu sing*) dilema *m*

quango /ˈkwæŋɡəʊ/ *n* (*pl* **-gos**) (BrE) (= **quasi-autonomous non-governmental organization**) organismo *m* *or* ente *m* semi-autónomo

quantify /ˈkwɑːntəfaɪ ‖ ˈkwɒntɪfaɪ/ *vt* **-fies, -fying, -fied** cuantificar*

quantity /ˈkwɑːntəti ‖ ˈkwɒntəti/ *n* (*pl* **-ties**) cantidad *f*

quantity surveyor *n*: ingeniero o técnico que se ocupa de mediciones y cálculo de materiales

quarantine¹ /ˈkwɔːrəntiːn ‖ ˈkwɒrəntiːn/ *n* cuarentena *f*

quarantine² *vt* poner* en cuarentena

quarrel¹ /ˈkwɔːrəl ‖ ˈkwɒrəl/ *n* (a) (argument) pelea *f*, riña *f*; **to have a ~ with sb** pelearse con algn (b) (disagreement) discrepancia *f*

quarrel² *vi*, (BrE) **-ll-** (argue) pelearse, discutir

quarrelsome /ˈkwɔːrəlsəm ‖ ˈkwɒrəlsəm/ *adj* peleador, peleón (Esp fam)

AmC	Central America	Arg	Argentina	Cu	Cuba	Per	Peru
AmL	Latin America	Bol	Bolivia	Ec	Ecuador	RPI	River Plate Area
AmS	South America	Chi	Chile	Esp	Spain	Ur	Uruguay
Andes	Andean Region	CS	Southern Cone	Méx	Mexico	Ven	Venezuela

quarry¹ /'kwɔːri ‖'kwɒri/ n (pl **-ries**) **1** (excavation) cantera f **2** (prey) presa f

quarry² vt **-ries, -rying, -ried** ⟨stone/slate⟩ extraer* (de una cantera); ⟨land/hillside⟩ abrir* una cantera en

quart /kwɔːrt ‖kwɔːt/ n cuarto m de galón (EEUU: 0,94 litros, RU: 1,14 litros)

quarter /'kwɔːrtər ‖'kwɔːtə(r)/ n **1** (fourth part) cuarta parte f, cuarto m; **a ~ of a mile** un cuarto de milla **2** (US, Canadian coin) moneda f de 25 centavos **3** **(a)** (in telling time) cuarto m; **a ~ of an hour** un cuarto de hora; **it's a ~ of** o (BrE) **to one** es la una menos cuarto o (AmL exc RPl) un cuarto para la una; **a ~ after** o (BrE) **past one** la una y cuarto **(b)** (three months) trimestre m **4** **(a)** (district of town) barrio m **(b)** (area) parte f; **at close ~s** de cerca **5** **quarters** pl (accommodations): **the servants' ~s** las habitaciones de la servidumbre

quarterfinal /'kwɔːrtər'faɪml ‖,kwɔːtə'faɪnl/ n cuarto m de final

quarterly¹ /'kwɔːrtərli ‖'kwɔːtəli/ adj trimestral

quarterly² adv trimestralmente

quarter note n (AmE) negra f

quartet /kwɔːr'tet ‖kwɔː'tet/ n cuarteto m

quartz /kwɔːrts ‖kwɔːts/ n cuarzo m

quash /'kwɑːʃ ‖kwɒʃ/ vt **(a)** (Law) ⟨verdict/sentence⟩ anular **(b)** (suppress) ⟨revolt⟩ sofocar*; ⟨protest⟩ acallar

quaver¹ /'kweɪvər ‖'kweɪvə(r)/ n **(a)** (in voice) temblor m **(b)** (BrE Mus) corchea f

quaver² vi «voice» (in singing) vibrar; (in speech) temblar*

quay /kiː/ n muelle m

quayside /'kiːsaɪd/ n muelle m

queasy /'kwiːzi/ adj **-sier, -siest** mareado

queen /kwiːn/ n reina f

queen: ~ bee n (Zool) abeja f reina; **~ mother** n reina f madre

queer¹ /kwɪr ‖kwɪə(r)/ adj **1** (odd) raro, extraño **2** (male homosexual) (colloq & sometimes pej) maricón (fam & pey), gay

queer² n (colloq & sometimes pej) maricón m (fam & pey), gay m

quell /kwel/ vt ⟨revolt⟩ sofocar*; ⟨criticism⟩ acallar

quench /kwentʃ/ vt **(a)** ⟨thirst⟩ quitar, saciar (liter) **(b)** ⟨flames⟩ sofocar*

querulous /'kwerələs ‖'kwerʊləs/ adj quejumbroso

query¹ /'kwɪri ‖'kwɪəri/ n (pl **-ries**) (doubt) duda f; (question) pregunta f

query² vt **-ries, -rying, -ried** cuestionar

quest /kwest/ n búsqueda f; **~ FOR sth** búsqueda DE algo

question¹ /'kwestʃən/ n **(a)** (inquiry) pregunta f; **to ask a ~** hacer* una pregunta **(b)** (in quiz, exam) pregunta f **(c)** (issue, problem) cuestión f, asunto m; **the person in ~** la persona en cuestión; **if it's a ~ of money** ... si es cuestión o se trata de dinero ... **(d)** (doubt) duda f; **beyond ~** fuera de duda **(e)** (possibility) posibilidad f; **it is completely out of the ~** es totalmente imposible

question² vt **(a)** ⟨person⟩ hacerle* preguntas a; ⟨suspect/student⟩ interrogar* **(b)** (doubt) ⟨integrity/motives⟩ poner* en duda

questionable /'kwestʃənəbəl/ adj cuestionable

questioner /'kwestʃənər ‖'kwestʃənə(r)/ n interrogador, -dora m,f

questioning¹ /'kwestʃənɪŋ/ adj ⟨expression/voice⟩ inquisidor; ⟨mind⟩ inquisitivo

questioning² n interrogatorio m

question mark n signo m de interrogación

questionnaire /'kwestʃə'neər ‖,kwestʃə'neə(r)/ n cuestionario m

queue¹ /kjuː/ n (BrE) cola f; **to form a ~** hacer* cola; **to jump the ~** colarse* (fam), brincarse* or saltarse la cola (Méx fam)

queue² vi **queues, queueing, queued ~ (up)** (BrE) hacer* cola

quibble¹ /'kwɪbəl/ n objeción f (de poca monta)

quibble² vi hacer* problemas por nimiedades

quick¹ /kwɪk/ adj **quicker, quickest** **(a)** (speedy) ⟨action/movement⟩ rápido; **I'll be as ~ as I can** volveré (or lo haré etc) lo más rápido que pueda; **that was ~!** ¡qué rapidez! **(b)** (before n, no comp) ⟨calculation/question⟩ rápido; ⟨nod⟩ breve; **he'd like a ~ word with you** quiere hablar contigo un momento **(c)** (easily roused): **she has a ~ temper** tiene mucho genio **(d)** (prompt): **he's ~ to take offense** se ofende por lo más mínimo

quick² adv **quicker, quickest** rápido, rápidamente

quick³ n the **~**: **her nails were bitten to the ~** tenía las uñas en carne viva de mordérselas; **to cut sb to the ~** herir* a algn en lo más vivo

quicken /'kwɪkən/ vt acelerar
■ **~** vi acelerarse

quickly /'kwɪkli/ adv **(a)** (speedily) ⟨move/recover⟩ rápidamente, rápido **(b)** (promptly) ⟨understand/reply⟩ pronto

quickness /'kwɪknəs ‖'kwɪknɪs/ n rapidez f

quick: ~sand n (often pl) arenas fpl movedizas; **~-tempered** /'kwɪk'tempərd ‖,kwɪk'tempəd/ adj ⟨person⟩ de genio vivo, irascible; **~-witted** /'kwɪk'wɪtəd ‖,kwɪk'wɪtɪd/ adj agudo

quid /kwɪd/ n (pl **~**) (pound) (BrE colloq) libra f

quiet¹ /'kwaɪət/ adj **1** **(a)** (silent) ⟨street⟩ silencioso; **be ~!** (to one person) ¡cállate!; (to more than one person) ¡callense! or (Esp tb) ¡callaros or callaos!, ¡silencio!; **I kept ~ about the bill** no dije nada de lo de la factura **(b)** (not loud) ⟨engine⟩ silencioso; **he has a very ~ voice** habla muy bajo **(c)** (not boisterous) ⟨manner⟩ tranquilo; **you're very ~ today** hoy estás muy callada **2** **(a)** (peaceful) tranquilo; **they had a ~ wedding** la boda se celebró en la intimidad **(b)** (not busy) ⟨day⟩ tranquilo

quiet² n **(a)** (silence) silencio m **(b)** (peace, tranquility) tranquilidad f

quiet³ (AmE) vt **(a)** (silence) ⟨uproar/protests⟩ acallar; ⟨class⟩ hacer* callar **(b)** (calm) ⟨horse/person⟩ tranquilizar*; ⟨fear/suspicion⟩ disipar
■ **quiet down** (AmE) ▶ QUIET DOWN

quieten /'kwaɪətn/ vt (esp BrE) ▶ QUIET³
■ **quieten down** **1** [v + o + adv, v + adv + o] ····❯

q

⟨*person*⟩ calmar; ⟨*rumors/clamor*⟩ acallar **2** [*v* + *adv*] «*person*» calmarse; (with maturity) sentar* la cabeza; «*rumors*» acallarse

quietly /ˈkwaɪətli/ *adv* **1** (silently, not loudly) ⟨*move*⟩ silenciosamente; ⟨*say/speak*⟩ en voz baja **2 (a)** (peacefully) ⟨*sleep/rest*⟩ tranquilamente **(b)** (unobtrusively) ⟨*dress/mention/slip away*⟩ discretamente

quill /kwɪl/ *n* pluma *f* (de oca *or* ganso)

quilt /kwɪlt/ *n* edredón *m*, acolchado *m* (RPl), cobija *f* (Méx)

quilted /ˈkwɪltəd ‖ ˈkwɪltɪd/ *adj* acolchado, guateado (Esp)

quin /kwɪn/ *n* (BrE colloq) ▶ QUINTUPLET

quince /kwɪns/ *n* membrillo *m*

quint /kwɪnt/ *n* (AmE colloq) ▶ QUINTUPLET

quintessential /ˈkwɪntəˈsentʃəl ‖ ˌkwɪntɪˈsenʃəl/ *adj* (*usu before n*) por excelencia

quintet /kwɪnˈtet/ *n* quinteto *m*

quintuplet /kwɪnˈtuːplət ‖ ˈkwɪntjʊplət/ *n* quintillizo, -za *m,f*, quíntuple *mf* (Chi, Ven)

quip¹ /kwɪp/ *n* ocurrencia *f*, salida *f*

quip² *vt* **-pp-** decir* bromeando

quirk /kwɜrk ‖ kwɜːk/ *n* **(a)** (of circumstance) singularidad *f* **(b)** (of person) rareza *f*

quit /kwɪt/ (*pres p* **quitting**; *past & past p* **quit** *or* **quitted**) *vt* (esp AmE) ⟨*job/habit*⟩ dejar; ⟨*contest*⟩ abandonar; **to ~ -ING** dejar DE + INF
■ **~** *vi* **(a)** (stop) (esp AmE) parar **(b)** (give in) abandonar **(c)** (leave): **notice to ~** notificación *f* de desahucio

quite /kwaɪt/ *adv* **1 (a)** (completely, absolutely) completamente, totalmente; **is this what you wanted? — not ~** ¿es esto lo que buscaba? — no exactamente; **there isn't ~ enough** falta un poquito; **there's nothing ~ like champagne** realmente no hay como el champán; **~ the opposite** todo lo contrario **(b)** (as intensifier): it

makes **~ a difference** hace bastante diferencia; **~ a few of them** muchos de ellos; **that was ~ a game!** ¡fue un partidazo! (fam), ¡fue flor de partido! (CS fam)
2 (fairly) (BrE) bastante; **it's ~ warm today** hoy hace bastante calor; **there were ~ a few** había bastantes, había unos cuantos

quits /kwɪts/ *adj* **to be ~** estar* en paz *or* (AmL) a mano; **to call it ~:** **take the money and call it ~** toma el dinero y dejémoslo de una vez

quiver¹ /ˈkwɪvər ‖ ˈkwɪvə(r)/ *vi* «*person/lips*» temblar*; «*leaves*» agitarse

quiver² *n* **1** (for arrows) carcaj *m*, aljaba *f* **2** (movement) temblor *m*

quiz¹ /kwɪz/ *n* (*pl* **~es**) **(a)** (competition) concurso *m*; (*before n*) **~ show** programa *m* concurso **(b)** (test) (AmE) prueba *f*

quiz² *vt* **-zz- (a)** (question) ⟨*suspect*⟩ interrogar* **(b)** (test) (AmE) ⟨*students*⟩ poner* *or* hacer* una prueba a

quizzical /ˈkwɪzɪkəl/ *adj* socarrón, burlón

quorum /ˈkwɔːrəm/ *n* quórum *m*

quota /ˈkwəʊtə/ *n* (*pl* **~s**) (EC, Econ) cuota *f*

quotation /kwəʊˈteɪʃən/ *n* **1** (passage) cita *f* **2** (estimate) presupuesto *m*

quotation marks *pl n* comillas *fpl*

quote¹ /kwəʊt/ *vt* **1 (a)** ⟨*writer/passage*⟩ citar; ⟨*reference number*⟩ indicar* **(b)** ⟨*example*⟩ dar*; ⟨*instance*⟩ citar **2 (a)** (Busn) ⟨*price*⟩ dar*, ofrecer* **(b)** (Fin) cotizar*
■ **~** *vi* (repeat, recite): **he was quoting from the Bible** citaba de la Biblia; **she said, and I ~** ... dijo, y lo repito textualmente ..., sus palabras textuales fueron ...

quote² *n* (colloq) **1** (passage) cita *f* **2** (estimate) presupuesto *m*

quotient /ˈkwəʊʃənt/ *n* (Math) cociente *m*

Rr

R, r /ɑːr ‖ ɑː(r)/ *n* R, r *f*

R (in US) (Cin) (= **restricted**) menores acompañados

rabbi /ˈræbaɪ/ *n* (*pl* **-bis**) rabino, -na *m,f*, (as title) rabí *mf*

rabbit /ˈræbət ‖ ˈræbɪt/ *n* **(a)** (Zool) conejo, -ja *m,f* **(b)** (meat) conejo *m*

rabble /ˈræbəl/ *n* **(a)** (mob) muchedumbre *f* **(b)** (common people) (pej) **the ~** la chusma (pey)

rabid /ˈræbəd ‖ ˈræbɪd/ *adj* rabioso

rabies /ˈreɪbiːz/ *n* rabia *f*

RAC *n* (in UK) = **Royal Automobile Club**

raccoon /ræˈkuːn ‖ rəˈkuːn/ *n* mapache *m*

race¹ /reɪs/ *n* **1** (contest) carrera *f* **2** (Anthrop) raza *f*; **the human ~** el género humano; (*before n*) **~ relations** *pl n* relaciones *fpl* raciales

race² *vi* **(a)** (rush) (+ *adv compl*): **she ~d down the hill on her bike** bajó la cuesta en bicicleta a

toda velocidad **(b)** (in competition) correr, competir* **(c)** «*pulse/heart*» latir aceleradamente
■ **~** *vt* ⟨*person*⟩ echarle *or* (RPl) jugarle* una carrera a

race: **~course** *n* (stadium) hipódromo *m*; (track) pista *f* (de carreras); **~horse** *n* caballo *m* de carrera(s)

racial /ˈreɪʃəl/ *adj* racial

racially /ˈreɪʃəli/ *adv* ⟨*pure/mixed/motivated/ prejudiced*⟩ racialmente

racing¹ /ˈreɪsɪŋ/ *n* **(a)** (horse ~) carreras *fpl* de caballos **(b)** (sport, pastime) carreras *fpl*

racing² *adj* (*before n*) ⟨*bicycle/car*⟩ de carrera(s)

racism /ˈreɪsɪzəm/ *n* racismo *m*

racist¹ /ˈreɪsəst ‖ ˈreɪsɪst/ *n* racista *mf*

racist² *adj* racista

rack¹ /ræk/ *n* **1** (shelf) estante *m*; (for baggage) rejilla *f*; (clothes ∼) perchero *m*; (drying ∼) tendedero *m* [2] (for torture) potro *m* (de tortura); *to go to* ∼ *and ruin* venirse* abajo

rack² *vt* (shake): **to be** ∼**ed with pain** sufrir dolores atroces; **to be** ∼**ed with guilt** estar* atormentado por el remordimiento

racket /'rækət ‖'rækɪt/ *n* [1] (Sport) raqueta *f* [2] (noise) (colloq) jaleo *m* (fam) [3] (business) (colloq) tinglado *m* (fam)

racketeer /ˌrækə'tɪr ‖ˌrækə'tiə(r)/ *n* mafioso, -sa *m,f*

racquet /'rækət ‖'rækɪt/ *n* ▶ RACKET 1

racy /'reɪsi/ *adj* **racier, raciest** (a) (lively) animado (b) (risqué) ⟨*story/joke*⟩ subido de tono

radar /'reɪdɑːr ‖'reɪdɑː(r)/ *n* radar *m*

radiant /'reɪdiənt/ *adj* ⟨*smile/look*⟩ radiante; ⟨*sun/blue*⟩ resplandeciente

radiate /'reɪdieɪt/ *vt* irradiar

radiation /ˌreɪdi'eɪʃən/ *n* radiación *f*; (*before n*) ∼ **sickness** radiotoxemia *f*

radiator /'reɪdieɪtər ‖'reɪdieɪtə(r)/ *n* radiador *m*

radical /'rædɪkəl/ *adj* radical; ⟨*writer*⟩ de ideas radicales

radically /'rædɪkli/ *adv* radicalmente

radii /'reɪdiaɪ/ *pl of* RADIUS

radio¹ /'reɪdiəʊ/ *n* (*pl* **-os**) (a) (receiver) radio *m* (AmL exc CS), radio *f* (CS, Esp); **I heard it on the** ∼ lo oí por el *or* (CS, Esp) la radio (b) (medium) radio *f*

radio² (*3rd pers sing pres* **radios**; *pres p* **radioing**; *past & past p* **radioed**) *vt* ⟨*person*⟩ llamar por radio; ⟨*message*⟩ transmitir por radio

radio: ∼**active** /ˌreɪdiəʊ'æktɪv/ *adj* radiactivo; ∼**activity** /ˈreɪdiəʊæk'tɪvəti/ *n* radiactividad *f*; ∼**-controlled** /'reɪdiəʊkən'trəʊld/ *adj* teledirigido

radiographer /ˌreɪdi'ɑːɡrəfər ‖ˌreɪdi'ɒɡrəfə(r)/ *n* radiógrafo, -fa *m,f*

radiologist /ˌreɪdi'ɑːlədʒəst ‖ˌreɪdi'ɒlədʒɪst/ *n* radiólogo, -ga *m,f*

radiotherapy /ˌreɪdiəʊ'θerəpi/ *n* radioterapia *f*

radish /'rædɪʃ/ *n* rabanito *m*, rábano *m*

radius /'reɪdiəs/ *n* (*pl* **radiuses** or **radii**) radio *m*

RAF /ˌɑː'reɪ'ef/ (in UK) (= **Royal Air Force**) the ∼ la Fuerza Aérea británica

raffle¹ /'ræfəl/ *n* rifa *f*

raffle² *vt* rifar, sortear

raft /ræft ‖rɑːft/ *n* balsa *f*

rafter /'ræftər ‖'rɑːftə(r)/ *n* viga *f*

rag /ræɡ/ *n* [1] (a) (piece of cloth) trapo *m* (b) **rags** *pl* (tattered clothes) harapos *mpl*, andrajos *mpl*; **dressed in** ∼**s** harapiento, andrajoso [2] (newspaper) (colloq & pej) periodicucho *m* (pey)

ragamuffin /'ræɡəˌmʌfən ‖'ræɡəˌmʌfɪn/ *n* pilluelo, -la *m,f*

rag doll *n* muñeca *f* de trapo

rage¹ /reɪdʒ/ *n* [1] (a) (violent anger) furia *f* (b) (fit of fury): **to be in a** ∼ estar* furioso [2] (fashion) (colloq): **to be (all) the** ∼ hacer* furor

rage² *vi* (a) «*storm/sea*» rugir*; «*fire*» arder

furiosamente (b) «*person*» rabiar (c) **raging** *pres p* ⟨*storm*⟩ rugiente; ⟨*sea*⟩ embravecido; ⟨*headache*⟩ enloquecedor; ⟨*argument*⟩ enconado

ragged /'ræɡəd ‖'ræɡɪd/ *adj* ⟨*clothes/ appearance*⟩ harapiento, andrajoso; ⟨*edge*⟩ irregular

raid¹ /reɪd/ *n* (a) (Mil) asalto *m* (b) (air ∼) bombardeo *m* aéreo (c) (by thieves) atraco *m* (d) (by police) redada *f*, allanamiento *m* (AmL)

raid² *vt* (a) (Mil) asaltar (b) ⟨*bank*⟩ asaltar (c) «*police*» ⟨*house/building*⟩ hacer* una redada en, allanar (AmL)

raider /'reɪdər ‖'reɪdə(r)/ *n* asaltante *mf*

rail /reɪl/ *n* [1] (a) (bar) riel *m* (b) (hand ∼) pasamanos *m* (c) (barrier) baranda *f* [2] (a) (for trains, trams) riel *m*, raíl *m* (Esp) (b) (railroad) ferrocarril *m*; **by** ∼ en *or* por ferrocarril

railing /'reɪlɪŋ/ *n* (*often pl*) reja *f*

rail: ∼**road** *n* (AmE) (a) (system) ferrocarril *m* (b) (track) vía *f* férrea; ∼**way** *n* (BrE) ▶ ∼ROAD

rain¹ /reɪn/ *n* lluvia *f*

rain² *v impers* llover*; **it's** ∼**ing** está lloviendo, llueve

rainbow /'reɪnbəʊ/ *n* arco *m* iris

rain: ∼**coat** *n* impermeable *m*; ∼**drop** *n* gota *f* de lluvia; ∼**fall** *n* precipitaciones *fpl*, lluvia *f*; ∼ **forest** *n* selva *f* tropical (húmeda); ∼**water** *n* agua *f⁺* de lluvia

rainy /'reɪni/ *adj* **-nier, -niest** lluvioso

raise¹ /reɪz/ *vt*

I [1] (a) ⟨*head/hand*⟩ levantar, alzar*; ⟨*eyebrows*⟩ arquear; ⟨*flag*⟩ izar* (b) (make higher) ⟨*shelf/level*⟩ subir [2] (a) (set upright) levantar (b) (erect) ⟨*monument/building*⟩ levantar, erigir* (fml) [3] (a) ⟨*pressure/temperature*⟩ aumentar, elevar; ⟨*price/salary*⟩ subir, aumentar; **to** ∼ **one's voice** levantar la voz (b) ⟨*consciousness*⟩ aumentar

II [1] (a) ⟨*money/funds*⟩ recaudar (b) ⟨*army*⟩ reclutar [2] ⟨*fears/doubt*⟩ suscitar; **he managed to** ∼ **a smile** pudo sonreír; **to** ∼ **the alarm** dar* la alarma [3] ⟨*subject*⟩ sacar*; ⟨*question*⟩ formular; **to** ∼ **an objection** poner* una objeción [4] (a) ⟨*family*⟩ criar* (b) ⟨*cattle*⟩ dedicarse* a la cría de

raise² *n* (AmE) aumento *m* or subida *f* de sueldo

raisin /'reɪzn̩/ *n* (uva *f*) pasa *f*, pasa *f* (de uva)

rake¹ /reɪk/ *n* (tool) rastrillo *m*

rake² *vt* rastrillar

rakish /'reɪkɪʃ/ *adj* (casual, jaunty) desenfadado

rally¹ /'ræli/ *n* (*pl* **-lies**) [1] (mass meeting) concentración *f*, **political** ∼ mitin *m*, mitín *m* [2] (Auto) rally *m* [3] (in tennis, badminton) peloteo *m*

rally² **-lies, -lying, -lied** *vi* [1] (unite) unirse; (gather) congregarse* [2] (a) (recover) «*person*» recuperarse, reponerse* (b) (Fin) «*currency/ price*» repuntar, recuperarse

■ ∼ *vt* [1] ⟨*support/vote*⟩ conseguir* [2] ⟨*strength/ spirits*⟩ recobrar

■ **rally round** [*v + adv*]: **all the neighbors rallied round to help** todos los vecinos se juntaron para ayudar

ram¹ /ræm/ *n* (Zool) carnero *m*

ram² **-mm-** *vt* (a) (force) (+ *adv compl*): **he** ∼**med the stake into the ground** hincó la estaca en la tierra; **he** ∼**med his fist through the door** atravesó la puerta de un puñetazo (b) (crash into) chocar* con; (deliberately) embestir* contra ···⫶

■ **ram home** [v + o + adv, v + adv + o] ‹point/
message› hacer* entender a la fuerza

RAM /ræm/ n (Comput) (= **random access
memory**) RAM f

Ramadan /ˈrɑːmədɑːn ‖ˌræməˈdæn/ n
Ramadán m

ramble¹ /ˈræmbəl/ n paseo m; (BrE Sport)
excursión f ‹a pie›

ramble² vi (a) (walk) pasear; **to go rambling**
(BrE) hacer* excursionismo (b) (in speech, writing)
irse* por las ramas
■ **ramble on** [v + adv] divagar*

rambler /ˈræmblər ‖ˈræmblə(r)/ n
excursionista mf

rambling /ˈræmblɪŋ/ adj (a) ‹essay/lecture› que
se va por las ramas (b) ‹streets› laberíntico; **a ~
old house** una vieja casona llena de recovecos (c)
‹rose› trepador

ramp /ræmp/ n (a) (slope) rampa f, **entrance o
on ~** (AmE) vía f de acceso; **exit o off ~** (AmE) vía
f de salida (b) (on ship, aircraft) (for passengers)
escalerilla f, (for vehicles) rampa f (c) (platform)
elevador m (d) (hump) (BrE) desnivel m

rampage /ˈræmpeɪdʒ/ n: **to be/go on the ~**
empezar* a arrasarlo todo

rampant /ˈræmpənt/ adj ‹inflation› galopante;
‹growth› desenfrenado; ‹crime› endémico

rampart /ˈræmpɑːrt ‖ˈræmpɑːt/ n (bank)
terraplén m; (wall) muralla f

ram: ~ raid n asalto ‹rompiendo el escaparate
con un vehículo›; **~-raid** vt asaltar ‹rompiendo
el escaparate con un vehículo›

ramshackle /ˈræmˌʃækəl/ adj destartalado

ran /ræn/ past of RUN¹

ranch /ræntʃ ‖rɑːntʃ/ n: **cattle ~** finca f
(ganadera), hacienda f (ganadera) (esp AmL),
rancho m ganadero (Méx), estancia f (CS)

rancher /ˈræntʃər ‖ˈrɑːntʃə(r)/ n hacendado,
-da m,f, estanciero, -ra m,f (CS), ranchero, -ra
m,f (Méx); **cattle ~** ganadero, -ra m,f

rancid /ˈrænsɪd/ adj rancio

rancor, (BrE) **rancour** /ˈræŋkər ‖ˈræŋkə(r)/ n
rencor m

rand /rænd/ n (pl **~**) rand m

random /ˈrændəm/ adj (a) ‹testing/choice› al
azar; ‹sample› aleatorio (b) **at random** (as adv) al
azar

rang /ræŋ/ past of RING²

range¹ /reɪndʒ/ n 1 (a) (scope) ámbito m (b)
(Mus) registro m (c) (bracket): **within/out of our
price ~** dentro de/fuera de nuestras posibilidades
2 (a) (variety) gama f (b) (selection) línea f 3 (a)
(of gun, transmitter) alcance m; **at close/long ~** de
cerca/lejos; **to come/be within ~** ponerse*/estar*
a tiro (b) (of vehicle, missile) autonomía f 4 (for
shooting) campo m de tiro 5 (chain) cadena f; **a
mountain ~** una cordillera 6 (stove) cocina f
económica, estufa f (Col, Méx)

range² vi: **their ages ~ from 12 to 20** tienen
entre 12 y 20 años

ranger /ˈreɪndʒər ‖ˈreɪndʒə(r)/ n guarda mf
forestal, guardabosques mf

rank¹ /ræŋk/ n 1 (line) fila f 2 (status)
categoría f; (Mil) grado m, rango m 3 (taxi ~)
(BrE) parada f de taxis, sitio m (Méx)

rank² vt: **he's ~ed fourth** está clasificado cuarto
■ **~** vi (a) (be classed) estar*; **it ~s among the best**
está entre los mejores (b) (hold rank): **to ~ above/
below sb** estar* por encima/por debajo de algn

rank³ adj 1 (before n) (complete) ‹beginner›
absoluto; ‹injustice› flagrante 2 ‹smell› fétido

rank and file n (Mil) (+ pl vb) tropa f; **the ~
~ ~ of the union** las bases del sindicato

rankle /ˈræŋkəl/ vi doler*

ransack /ˈrænsæk/ vt ‹room/drawer›
revolver*; ‹house/premises› (search) registrar (de
arriba a abajo); (pillage) saquear

ransom /ˈrænsəm/ n rescate m; **to hold sb o**
(AmE also) **for ~** exigir* un rescate por algn

rant /rænt/ vi despotricar*

rap¹ /ræp/ n 1 (blow) golpe m 2 **to take the ~
for sth** (esp AmE colloq) cargar* con la culpa de
algo 3 (a) (chat) (colloq) cháchara f (fam) (b)
(Mus) rap m

rap² -**pp**- vi dar* un golpe
■ **~** vt: **he ~ped my knuckles** me pegó en los
nudillos

rape¹ /reɪp/ n 1 (a) (sexual violation) violación f;
(of a minor) estupro m (b) (of the countryside) (liter)
expoliación f (liter) 2 (plant) colza f

rape² vt ‹person› violar

rapid /ˈræpəd ‖ˈræpɪd/ adj rápido

rapidly /ˈræpədli ‖ˈræpɪdli/ adv rápidamente

rapids /ˈræpədz ‖ˈræpɪdz/ pl n rápidos mpl

rapist /ˈreɪpəst ‖ˈreɪpɪst/ n violador, -dora m,f

rapport /ræˈpɔːr ‖ræˈpɔː(r)/ n relación f de
comunicación

rapt /ræpt/ adj (liter) ‹expression/smile›
embelesado

rapture /ˈræptʃər ‖ˈræptʃə(r)/ n éxtasis m,
arrobamiento m (liter)

rapturous /ˈræptʃərəs/ adj ‹applause/welcome›
calurosísimo

rare /rer ‖reə(r)/ adj **rarer** /ˈrerər ‖ˈreərər/,
rarest /ˈrerəst ‖ˈreərɪst/ 1 (a) (uncommon) raro
(b) (liter) ‹talent/beauty› excepcional 2 (Culin)
‹steak› vuelta y vuelta

rarely /ˈrerli ‖ˈreəli/ adv rara vez

raring /ˈrerɪŋ ‖ˈreərɪŋ/ adj: **to be ~ to go**: **he's
~ to go** está que ya no se aguanta

rarity /ˈrerəti ‖ˈreərɪti/ n (pl **-ties**) algo poco
común

rascal /ˈræskəl ‖ˈrɑːskəl/ n granuja mf

rash¹ /ræʃ/ n sarpullido m

rash² adj -**er**, -**est** precipitado

rasher /ˈræʃər ‖ˈræʃə(r)/ n loncha f, lonja f

rashly /ˈræʃli/ adv ‹act› precipitadamente

rasp¹ /ræsp ‖rɑːsp/ n escofina f

rasp² vt ‹wood› raspar, escofinar

raspberry /'ræz,beri ‖'rɑːzbəri/ n (pl **-ries**) frambuesa f

rasping /'ræspɪŋ ‖'rɑːspɪŋ/ adj ⟨sound/voice⟩ áspero

Rastafarian /,ræstə'feriən ‖,ræstə'feəriən/ n rastafari mf

rat /ræt/ n (a) (Zool) rata f; ⟨before n⟩ ∼ **poison** raticida m (b) (person) (colloq) rata f de alcantarilla (fam)

rate¹ /reɪt/ n [1] (a) (speed) velocidad; (rhythm) ritmo m; **at this** ∼ a este paso; **at any** ∼ (at least) por lo menos; (in any case) en todo caso (b) (level, ratio): **birth** ∼ índice m de natalidad; **death** ∼ mortalidad f; ∼ **of inflation** tasa f de inflación; **interest** ∼ tasa f or (esp Esp) tipo m de interés; ∼ **of exchange** tipo m de cambio (c) (price, charge) tarifa f; **that's the going** ∼ eso es lo que se suele pagar [2] (local tax) (formerly, in UK) ⟨often pl⟩ ≈ contribución f (municipal or inmobiliaria)

rate² vt [1] (rank, consider): **I** ∼ **her work very highly** tengo una excelente opinión de su trabajo; **I** ∼ **her as the best woman tennis player** yo la considero la mejor tenista [2] (deserve) merecer*

rather /'ræðər ‖'rɑːðə(r)/ adv [1] (a) (stating preference): **I'd** ∼ **walk than go by bus** prefiero andar a ir en autobús; ∼ **you than me!** ¡menos mal que eres tú y no yo! (b) (more precisely): **or** ∼ o mejor dicho [2] (fairly) bastante; (somewhat) algo

ratification /,rætəfə'keɪʃən ‖,rætɪfɪ'keɪʃən/ n (frml) ratificación f

ratify /'rætəfaɪ ‖'rætɪfaɪ/ vt **-fies, -fying, -fied** (frml) ratificar*

rating /'reɪtɪŋ/ n (a) (evaluation): **credit** ∼ clasificación f crediticia (b) **ratings** pl (Rad, TV) índice m de audiencia

ratio /'reɪʃəʊ, -ʃiəʊ ‖'reɪʃiəʊ/ n (pl **ratios**) proporción f, ratio m (téc); **in a** ∼ **of two to one** en una proporción de dos a uno

ration¹ /'ræʃən/ n (a) (allowance) ración f (b) **rations** pl víveres mpl

ration² vt racionar

rational /'ræʃnəl ‖'ræʃənl/ adj (a) (able to reason) ⟨being⟩ racional (b) (sane, lucid) **to be** ∼ estar* en su (or mi etc) sano juicio (c) (sensible) ⟨suggestion⟩ razonable

rationale /,ræʃə'næl ‖,ræʃə'nɑːl/ n (no pl) base f, razones fpl

rationalize /'ræʃnəlaɪz/ vt racionalizar*

rationally /'ræʃnəli/ adv ⟨think⟩ racionalmente; ⟨behave⟩ con sensatez

rationing /'ræʃənɪŋ/ n racionamiento m

rat run n (Auto) atajo m (para evitar el tráfico de una calle principal en horas punta)

rattle¹ /'rætl/ n [1] (no pl) (noise) ruido m; (of train, carriage) traqueteo m [2] (baby's) ∼ sonajero m, sonaja f (Méx)

rattle² vi (a) (make noise) «chains/bottles/keys» repiquetear; «window/engine» vibrar (b) (move) (+ adv compl) traquetear
■ ∼ vt ⟨keys/chain⟩ hacer* repiquetear; ⟨door/window⟩ «wind» hacer* vibrar
■ **rattle off** [v + o + adv, v + adv + o] recitar
■ **rattle on** [v + adv] hablar or (fam) parlotear sin parar

rattlesnake /'rætlsneɪk/ n serpiente f (de) cascabel, cascabel f

raucous /'rɔːkəs/ adj (loud) estentóreo; (shrill) estridente

raunchy /'rɔːntʃi/ adj **-chier, -chiest** (colloq) ⟨humor⟩ picante; ⟨joke⟩ escabroso

ravage /'rævɪdʒ/ vt (plunder) saquear; **a country** ∼**d by war** un país asolado por la guerra

ravages /'rævɪdʒəz ‖'rævɪdʒɪz/ pl n estragos mpl

rave¹ /reɪv/ vi (a) (talk deliriously) delirar (b) (talk, write enthusiastically): **to** ∼ **about sth** poner* a algo por las nubes (c) (talk angrily) despotricar*

rave² n (colloq) [1] ⟨before n⟩ (full of praise) ∼ **reviews** críticas fpl muy favorables [2] (BrE) (party) fiesta con música acid

raven /'reɪvən/ n cuervo m

ravenous /'rævənəs/ adj hambriento; **to be** ∼ (colloq) tener* un hambre canina (fam)

ravine /rə'viːn/ n barranco m, quebrada f

raving¹ /'reɪvɪŋ/ adj (colloq) ⟨before n, as intensifier⟩: **he's a** ∼ **lunatic** está loco de atar (fam); ⟨as adv⟩ **he's** ∼ **mad** está como una cabra (fam)

raving² n ⟨often pl⟩ desvarío m

ravish /'rævɪʃ/ vt (liter) violar

ravishing /'rævɪʃɪŋ/ adj deslumbrante

raw /rɔː/ adj [1] (a) ⟨meat/vegetables⟩ crudo (b) ⟨silk⟩ crudo; ⟨sugar⟩ sin refinar; ⟨sewage⟩ sin tratar [2] (sore): **my fingers were** ∼ tenía los dedos en carne viva [3] (inexperienced) verde (fam); ⟨recruit⟩ novato

raw material n materia f prima

ray /reɪ/ n [1] (beam) rayo m [2] (Mus) re m [3] (Zool) raya f

rayon /'reɪɒn ‖'reɪɒn/ n rayón m

raze /reɪz/ vt: **to** ∼ **sth** (to the ground) arrasar algo

razor /'reɪzər ‖'reɪzə(r)/ n (a) (safety ∼) cuchilla f or máquina f or maquinilla f de afeitar, rastrillo m (Méx); ⟨before n⟩ ∼ **blade** cuchilla f, hoja f de afeitar (b) (electric) máquina f or maquinilla f de afeitar, máquina f de rasurar (esp Méx)

razzmatazz /'ræzmə'tæz/ n (colloq) bulla f; (publicity) alarde m publicitario

Rd = **Road**

re¹ /reɪ/ n (Mus) re m

re² /riː/ prep con relación a, con referencia a

re- /riː/ pref re-

RE n (BrE) (= **religious education**) religión f

reach¹ /riːtʃ/ n [1] (a) (distance) alcance m (b) (in phrases) **within reach** a mi (or tu etc) alcance; **out of reach** fuera de su (or mi etc) alcance [2] (of river) tramo m

reach² vt [1] (a) (with hand) alcanzar* (b) (extend to) llegar* a [2] ⟨destination/limit/age⟩ llegar* a; ⟨stage/agreement⟩ llegar* a, alcanzar* [3] (contact) ponerse* en contacto con
■ ∼ vi (a) (extend hand, arm): **he** ∼**ed for his gun** echó mano a la pistola; **she** ∼**ed across the table for the salt** agarró or (esp Esp) cogió la sal, que estaba al otro lado de la mesa (b) (stretch far enough) alcanzar*; **I can't** ∼**!** ¡no alcanzo! (c) (extend) extenderse*
■ **reach out** [v + adv] alargar* la mano

react /ri'ækt/ vi reaccionar

reaction /ri'ækʃən/ n reacción f

reactionary /rɪˈækʃənerɪ ‖rɪˈækʃənrɪ/ adj (pej) reaccionario (pey)

reactor /rɪˈæktər ‖rɪˈæktə(r)/ n (nuclear ~) reactor m (nuclear)

read¹ /riːd/ (past & past p **read** /red/) vt
1 (a) ⟨book/map/music/meter⟩ leer* (b) (interpret) ⟨sign/mood/situation⟩ interpretar **2** (a) ⟨sign/notice⟩ decir* (b) (indicate) ⟨thermometer/gauge⟩ marcar*
■ ~ vi leer*
■ **read out** [v + o + adv, v + adv + o] leer* (en voz alta)
■ **read over, read through** [v + o + adv] leer* (por entero)
■ **read up** [v + adv] to ~ **up** (ON sth) estudiar (algo)

read² /red/ adj: to be well ~ ser* muy leído

readable /ˈriːdəbəl/ adj ⟨book/style⟩ ameno; ⟨writing⟩ legible

reader /ˈriːdər ‖ˈriːdə(r)/ n **1** (person) lector, -tora m,f; she's a fast/slow ~ lee muy rápido/lento **2** (Educ, Publ) libro m de lectura

readership /ˈriːdərʃɪp ‖ˈriːdəʃɪp/ n lectores mpl; it has a ~ **of over 10 million** tiene una tirada de 10 millones

readily /ˈredlɪ ‖ˈredɪlɪ/ adv (a) (willingly): she ~ agreed accedió de buena gana (b) (easily) ⟨understand⟩ fácilmente; they are ~ available se pueden conseguir fácilmente

reading /ˈriːdɪŋ/ n **1** (a) (activity, skill) lectura f; (before n) ⟨glasses⟩ para leer; ~ **list** lista f de lecturas recomendadas; ~ **room** sala f de lectura (b) (event): poetry ~ recital m de poesía **2** (on dial, gauge) lectura f

readjust /ˌriːəˈdʒʌst/ vt reajustar
■ ~ vi «person» to ~ (TO sth) readaptarse (A algo)

ready¹ /ˈredɪ/ adj **-dier, -diest** **1** (a) (having completed preparations) (pred) to be ~ estar* listo, estar* pronto (RPl); to be ~ to + INF estar* PARA + INF; to get ~ (prepare oneself) prepararse, aprontarse (CS); (get dressed, made up etc) arreglarse, aprontarse (CS) (b) (mentally prepared) (pred) to be ~ FOR sth/to + INF estar* preparado PARA algo/PARA + INF **2** (willing) dispuesto **3** (easy, available): ~ **money** o **cash** dinero m (en efectivo)

ready² n at the ~ listo

ready³ vt **-dies, -dying, -died** preparar

ready: ~**-made** /ˈredɪˈmeɪd/ adj ⟨suit⟩ de confección; ⟨soup/sauce⟩ preparado; ~**-to-wear** /ˈredɪtəˈwer ‖ˌredɪtəˈweə(r)/ adj (before n) ⟨clothes⟩ de confección

reaffirm /ˌriːəˈfɜːrm ‖ˌriːəˈfɜːm/ vt reiterar, reafirmar

real¹ /riːl, rɪl ‖rɪəl, rɪəl/ adj (a) (actual, not imaginary) real, verdadero (b) (actual, true) (before n) ⟨reason/name⟩ verdadero (c) (genuine, not fake) ⟨fur/leather⟩ auténtico; ⟨gold⟩ de ley (d) (as intensifier) auténtico

real² adv (AmE colloq) (as intensifier) muy

real estate n (esp AmE) bienes mpl raíces or inmuebles, propiedad f inmobiliaria; (before n) ~ **agent** ▶ REALTOR

realism /ˈriːəlɪzəm/ n realismo m

realist /ˈriːələst ‖ˈriːəlɪst/ n realista mf

realistic /ˌriːəˈlɪstɪk ‖ˌrɪəˈlɪstɪk/ adj realista

reality /rɪˈælətɪ/ n (pl **-ties**) realidad f; in ~ en realidad

realization /ˌriːələˈzeɪʃən ‖ˌrɪəlaɪˈzeɪʃən/ n **1** (understanding) comprensión f **2** (of plan) realización f

realize /ˈriːəlaɪz/ vt **1** (a) (become aware of) darse* cuenta de, comprender, caer* en la cuenta de (b) (know, be aware of) saber* **2** (achieve) ⟨ambition⟩ hacer* realidad; ⟨potential⟩ desarrollar
■ ~ vi darse* cuenta

really /ˈriːəlɪ ‖ˈriːəlɪ, ˈrɪəlɪ/ adv (a) (in fact): I ~ did see him! ¡de verdad que lo vi!; **the tomato is** ~ **a fruit** el tomate en realidad es una fruta (b) (as intensifier): it's ~ **good/old** es buenísimo/viejísimo (c) (as interj): (oh,) ~? ¿ah sí?; **really?** (expressing surprise) ¿de verdad?

realm /relm/ n (a) (kingdom) (frml) reino m (b) (sphere) (often pl) mundo m

realtor /ˈriːəltər ‖ˈrɪəltə(r)/ n (AmE) agente inmobiliario, -ria m,f

ream /riːm/ n (Print) resma f

reamer /ˈriːmər ‖ˈriːmə(r)/ n (AmE) exprimelimones m, exprimidor m

reap /riːp/ vt (Agr) cosechar, recoger*; to ~ **the benefits of sth** cosechar los beneficios de algo

reappear /ˌriːəˈpɪr ‖ˌriːəˈpɪə(r)/ vi volver* a aparecer

rear¹ /rɪr ‖rɪə(r)/ n (a) (back part) (no pl) parte f trasera or de atrás (b) (of column, procession) (no pl) the ~ la retaguardia (c) (buttocks) (colloq) trasero m (fam)

rear² adj ⟨window/wheel⟩ de atrás, trasero

rear³ vt ⟨child/cattle⟩ criar*
■ ~ vi ~ (up) «horse» encabritarse

rearguard /ˈrɪrgɑːrd ‖ˈrɪəgɑːd/ n retaguardia f

rearm /ˌriːˈɑːrm ‖ˌriːˈɑːm/ vt rearmar
■ ~ vi rearmarse

rearrange /ˌriːəˈreɪndʒ/ vt (a) ⟨furniture⟩ cambiar de lugar (b) (change time of) ⟨appointment⟩ cambiar la fecha/la hora de

rear-view mirror /ˈrɪrvjuː ‖ˈrɪəvjuː/ n (espejo m) retrovisor m

reason¹ /ˈriːzn/ n **1** (cause) razón f, motivo m; ~ FOR sth razón or motivo DE algo; **I left it there for a** ~ por algo lo dejé ahí **2** (faculty) razón f **3** (good sense): **to listen to** ~ atender* a razones; **it stands to** ~ es lógico

reason² vt pensar*
■ ~ vi razonar, discurrir

reasonable /ˈriːznəbəl/ adj (a) ⟨offer/request/person⟩ razonable (b) ⟨price/sum⟩ razonable, moderado

reasonably /ˈriːznəblɪ/ adv (a) ⟨behave/argue⟩ razonablemente (b) (fairly): I'm ~ **certain** estoy casi seguro

reasoning /ˈriːznɪŋ/ n razonamiento m

reassemble /ˌriːəˈsembəl/ vt (a) ⟨people/group⟩ volver* a reunir, reunir (b) ⟨parts/engine⟩ reensamblar
■ ~ vi «meeting/group» volverse* a reunir, reunirse*

reassurance /ˌriːəˈʃʊərəns ‖ˌriːəˈʃʊərəns, ˌriːəˈʃɔːrəns/ n (a) (feeling): **he drew** ~ **from his wife's words** lo que le dijo su mujer lo confortó *or* lo tranquilizó **(b)** (words, support): **he gave us countless ~s that ...** nos tranquilizó asegurándonos repetidamente que ...

reassure /ˌriːəˈʃʊr ‖ˌriːəˈʃʊə(r), ˌriːəˈʃɔː(r)/ *vt* tranquilizar*

reassuring /ˌriːəˈʃʊrɪŋ ‖ˌriːəˈʃʊərɪŋ, ˌriːəˈʃɔːrɪŋ/ *adj* ⟨voice/manner/answer⟩ tranquilizador; **it's ~ to know that ...** tranquiliza saber que ...

rebate /ˈriːbeɪt/ *n* (repayment) reembolso *m*; (discount) descuento *m*

rebel¹ /ˈrebəl/ *n* rebelde *mf*

rebel² /rɪˈbel/ *vi* **-ll-** rebelarse, sublevarse

rebellion /rɪˈbeljən/ *n* rebelión *f*

rebellious /rɪˈbeljəs/ *adj* rebelde

rebirth /ˈriːˈbɜːrθ ‖ˌriːˈbɜːθ/ *n* renacimiento *m*

reboot /ˌriːˈbuːt/ *vt* (Comput) reiniciar

rebound¹ /ˈriːbaʊnd/ *n*: **she married him on the ~** se casó con él por despecho

rebound² /rɪˈbaʊnd/ *vi* ⟨ball⟩ rebotar

rebuff¹ /rɪˈbʌf/ *n*: **to meet with/receive a ~** ser* rechazado

rebuff² *vt* rechazar*

rebuild /ˈriːˈbɪld/ *vt* (past & past p **rebuilt**) ⟨building/economy⟩ reconstruir*; **he tried to ~ his life** intentó rehacer su vida

rebuke¹ /rɪˈbjuːk/ *vt* reprender

rebuke² *n* reprimenda *f*

rebut /rɪˈbʌt/ *vt* **-tt-** (fml) rebatir

recall¹ /rɪˈkɔːl, ˈriːkɔːl/ *n* **1** (memory) memoria *f*; **to have total ~** tener* una memoria excelente **2** (of goods, ambassador) retirada *f*

recall² /rɪˈkɔːl/ *vt* **1** (remember) recordar* **2** **(a)** ⟨faulty goods⟩ retirar (*del mercado*) **(b)** ⟨ambassador⟩ retirar; (temporarily) llamar; ⟨troops⟩ llamar

recant /rɪˈkænt/ *vi* retractarse; (Relig) abjurar

recap¹ /ˈriːkæp/ *n* (colloq) resumen *m*

recap² /ˈriːˈkæp/ **-pp-** *vt* **1** (summarize) (colloq) resumir, recapitular **2** (AmE Auto) ▶ RETREAD¹
■ ~ *vi* (colloq) resumir

recapitulate /ˌriːkəˈpɪtʃəleɪt ‖ˌriːkəˈpɪtjʊleɪt/ *vt/i* (fml) recapitular, resumir

recapture /ˈriːˈkæptʃər ‖ˌriːˈkæptʃə(r)/ *vt* ⟨convict/animal⟩ capturar; ⟨youth/beauty⟩ recuperar

recede /rɪˈsiːd/ *vi* **(a)** (move back) «tide» retirarse; **to ~ into the distance** perderse en la distancia **(b)** «danger» alejarse; «prospect» desvanecerse* **(c) receding** *pres p* ⟨chin⟩ hundido; **he has a receding hairline** tiene entradas

receipt /rɪˈsiːt/ *n* **(a)** (paper) recibo *m* **(b)** (act) recibo *m*, recepción *f*

receive /rɪˈsiːv/ *vt* **1** **(a)** ⟨letter/award/visit⟩ recibir; ⟨payment⟩ recibir, cobrar, percibir (fml); ⟨stolen goods⟩ comerciar con, reducir* (AmS); ⟨serve/ball⟩ recibir; ⟨injuries⟩ recibir; ⟨blow⟩ recibir **(b)** (react to) ⟨news/idea⟩ recibir **2** (welcome, admit) (fml) ⟨person⟩ recibir, acoger* **3** (Rad, TV) ⟨signal⟩ recibir, captar

receiver /rɪˈsiːvər ‖rɪˈsiːvə(r)/ *n* **1** (Telec) auricular *m* **2** (Rad, TV) receptor *m* **3** (of stolen goods) comerciante *mf* de mercancía robada

receivership /rɪˈsiːvərʃɪp ‖rɪˈsiːvəʃɪp/ *n* **to go into/be in ~** ser* declarado/estar* en suspensión *or* en cesación de pagos

recent /ˈriːsn̩t/ *adj* reciente; **in ~ years/months** en los últimos años/meses; **in the ~ past** en los últimos tiempos

recently /ˈriːsn̩tli/ *adv* recientemente; **until quite ~** hasta hace bien poco

receptacle /rɪˈseptɪkəl/ *n* (fml) recipiente *m*, receptáculo *m*

reception /rɪˈsepʃən/ *n* **(a)** (reaction) (no pl) recibimiento *m*, acogida *f* **(b)** (in hotel, office) (no art) recepción *f*; (before n) ~ **desk** recepción *f* **(c)** (social event) recepción *f* **(d)** (Rad, TV) recepción *f*

receptionist /rɪˈsepʃənəst ‖rɪˈsepʃənɪst/ *n* recepcionista *mf*

receptive /rɪˈseptɪv/ *adj* receptivo

recess /ˈriːses/ *n* **1** **(a)** (of legislative body) receso *m* (AmL), suspensión *f* de actividades (Esp); (of committee etc) intermedio *m* **(b)** (AmE Educ) recreo *m* **2** (alcove) hueco *m*, entrada *f*

recession /rɪˈseʃn̩ ‖rɪˈseʃən/ *n* (Econ) recesión *f*

recharge /ˈriːˈtʃɑːrdʒ ‖ˌriːˈtʃɑːdʒ/ *vt* volver* a cargar, recargar?

rechargeable /ˈriːˈtʃɑːrdʒəbəl ‖ˌriːˈtʃɑːdʒəbəl/ *adj* recargable

recipe /ˈresəpi/ *n* receta *f*; (before n) ~ **book** libro *m* de cocina; (personal) cuaderno *m* de recetas (de cocina)

recipient /rɪˈsɪpiənt/ *n* (fml) (of letter) destinatario, -ria *m,f*; (of an organ) (Med) receptor, -tora *m,f*

reciprocal /rɪˈsɪprəkəl/ *adj* recíproco

reciprocate /rɪˈsɪprəkeɪt/ *vt* corresponder a, reciprocar* (AmL)
■ ~ *vi* corresponder, reciprocar* (AmL)

recital /rɪˈsaɪtl̩/ *n* (Mus) recital *m*

recite /rɪˈsaɪt/ *vt* **(a)** (declaim) ⟨poem⟩ recitar **(b)** (list) ⟨names⟩ enumerar

reckless /ˈrekləs ‖ˈreklɪs/ *adj* imprudente, temerario

reckon /ˈrekən/ *vt* **(a)** (calculate) calcular **(b)** (consider) considerar **(c)** (think) (colloq) creer*; **what do you ~?** ¿tú qué opinas?, ¿y a ti qué te parece?
■ **reckon on** [v + prep + o] contar con

reckoning /ˈrekənɪŋ/ *n* cálculos *mpl*

reclaim /rɪˈkleɪm/ *vt* **(a)** (claim back): **I filled in a form to ~ tax** llené un formulario para que me devolvieran parte de los impuestos; **to ~ one's luggage** (Aviat) recoger* el equipaje; (at left luggage) (pasar) a retirar el equipaje **(b)** (recover) recuperar; **~ed land** terreno *m* ganado al mar

recline /rɪˈklaɪn/ *vi* **(a)** (lean back) recostarse*, reclinarse; (rest) apoyarse **(b)** «chair» reclinarse **(c) reclining** *pres p* ⟨chair/seat⟩ reclinable, abatible; ⟨figure⟩ yacente (liter), recostado

recluse /rɪˈkluːs/ *n* ermitaño, -ña *m,f*

reclusive /rɪˈkluːsɪv/ *adj* dado a recluirse

recognition /ˌrekəɡˈnɪʃən/ *n* reconocimiento *m*; **in ~ of** (fml) en reconocimiento a *or* por (fml)

recognizable /ˈrekəɡnaɪzəbəl/ *adj* reconocible; ⟨difference⟩ apreciable

recognize /ˈrekəɡnaɪz/ *vt* **(a)** ⟨voice/person⟩ reconocer* **(b)** (acknowledge) reconocer*, admitir

r

recoil¹ /rɪˈkɔɪl/ vi (shrink back) retroceder; **to ~ FROM sth** rehuir* algo

recoil² /ˈriːkɔɪl/ n retroceso m

recollect /rekəˈlekt/ vt recordar*

recollection /rekəˈlekʃən/ n recuerdo m

recommend /rekəˈmend/ vt (a) (praise, declare acceptable) recomendar* (b) (advise) **to ~ sth/-ING** aconsejar or recomendar* algo/+ INF; **~ed (retail) price** precio m de venta recomendado

recommendation /rekəmenˈdeɪʃən/ n recomendación f

recompense /ˈrekəmpens/ n (frml) recompensa f

reconcile /ˈrekənsaɪl/ vt (a) (enemies) reconciliar (b) (theories/ideals) conciliar (c) **to become ~d TO sth** resignarse A algo

reconciliation /rekənsɪliˈeɪʃən/ n reconciliación f

recondition /ˈriːkənˈdɪʃən/ vt reacondicionar

reconnaissance /rəˈkɑːnəzəns, -səns ‖rɪˈkɒnɪsəns/ n (Mil) reconocimiento m

reconnoiter, (BrE) **reconnoitre** /ˈriːkəˈnɔɪtər, ˈre- ‖rekəˈnɔɪtə(r)/ vt reconocer*

reconquer /ˈriːˈkɑːŋkər ‖riːˈkɒŋkə(r)/ vt reconquistar

reconsider /ˈriːkənˈsɪdər ‖riːkənˈsɪdə(r)/ vt reconsiderar

reconstruct /ˈriːkənˈstrʌkt/ vt reconstruir*

reconstruction /ˈriːkənˈstrʌkʃən/ n (a) (rebuilding) reconstrucción f (b) (re-creation) reconstitución f

record¹ /ˈrekərd ‖ˈrekɔːd/ n **1** (a) (document) documento m; (of attendances etc) registro m; (file) archivo m; (minutes) acta f; (note) nota f; **medical ~s** historial m médico; **keep a ~ of your expenses** anote sus gastos; **according to our ~s** según nuestros datos (b) (in phrases) **off the record** extraoficialmente; **on record: the hottest summer on ~** el verano más caluroso del que se tienen datos

2 (a) (of performance, behavior): **he has a good academic ~** tiene un buen curriculum académico; **our products have an excellent safety ~** nuestros productos son de probada seguridad (b) (criminal ~) antecedentes mpl (penales)

3 (highest, lowest, best, worst) récord m, marca f

4 (Audio, Mus) disco m; (before n) **~ store** disquería f, tienda f de discos

record² /rɪˈkɔːrd ‖rɪˈkɔːd/ vt **1** (a) (person) (write down) anotar; (in minutes) hacer* constar (b) (register) (instrument) registrar **2** (song/program/album) grabar

record³ /ˈrekərd ‖ˈrekɔːd/ adj (before n, no comp) récord adj inv

record card n ficha f

recorded /rɪˈkɔːrdəd ‖rɪˈkɔːdɪd/ adj (a) (music) grabado (b) (history) escrito, documentado

recorder /rɪˈkɔːrdər ‖rɪˈkɔːdə(r)/ n (Mus) flauta f dulce

recording /rɪˈkɔːrdɪŋ ‖rɪˈkɔːdɪŋ/ n grabación f

record player n tocadiscos m

recount /rɪˈkaʊnt/ vt narrar, contar*

re-count /ˈriːˈkaʊnt/ vt volver* a contar; (votes) hacer* un segundo escrutinio de, recontar*

recoup /rɪˈkuːp/ vt (costs) recuperar; (losses) resarcirse* de

recourse /ˈriːkɔːrs ‖rɪˈkɔːs/ n **to have ~ to sth/sb** recurrir a algo/algn

recover /rɪˈkʌvər ‖rɪˈkʌvə(r)/ vt (a) (consciousness/strength) recuperar, recobrar; (investment/lead) recuperar (b) (retrieve) rescatar ■ ~ vi (a) (person) reponerse*, restablecerse*, recuperarse (b) (economy) recuperarse, repuntar

recovery /rɪˈkʌvəri/ n (pl **-ries**) **1** (a) (return to health) recuperación f, restablecimiento m (b) (of economy) recuperación f **2** (of stolen goods, missing documents) recuperación f; (retrieval) rescate m

re-create /ˈriːkriˈeɪt/ vt recrear

recreation /ˈrekriˈeɪʃən/ n (a) (leisure) esparcimiento m (b) (in school, prison) (BrE) recreo m

recreational /ˈrekriˈeɪʃəl ‖rekriˈeɪʃənl/ adj recreativo; **~ drug** droga f recreativa

recrimination /rɪˈkrɪməˈneɪʃən/ n (often pl) recriminación f

recruit¹ /rɪˈkruːt/ n (Mil) recluta mf

recruit² vt reclutar; (staff) contratar

recruitment /rɪˈkruːtmənt/ n reclutamiento m

rectangle /ˈrektæŋɡəl/ n rectángulo m

rectangular /rekˈtæŋɡjələr ‖rekˈtæŋɡjʊlə(r)/ adj rectangular

rectify /ˈrektəfaɪ ‖ˈrektɪfaɪ/ vt **-fies, -fying, -fied** rectificar*

rector /ˈrektər ‖ˈrektə(r)/ n (a) (Relig) rector, -tora m,f, ≈ párroco m (b) (in US) (Educ) rector, -ra m,f

rectum /ˈrektəm/ n (pl **rectums** or **recta** /ˈrektə/) recto m

recuperate /rɪˈkuːpəreɪt/ vi recuperarse, reponerse*

recuperation /rɪˈkuːpəˈreɪʃən/ n recuperación f, restablecimiento m

recur /rɪˈkɜːr ‖rɪˈkɜː(r)/ vi **-rr-** (a) (phenomenon) volver* a ocurrir or a suceder, repetirse*; (symptom) volver* a presentarse (b) **recurring** pres p recurrente

recurrence /rɪˈkɜːrəns ‖rɪˈkʌrəns/ n (of symptoms) reaparición f; (of incident) repetición f

recurrent /rɪˈkɜːrənt ‖rɪˈkʌrənt/ adj recurrente

recycle /ˈriːˈsaɪkəl/ vt reciclar

recycling /ˈriːˈsaɪklɪŋ/ n reciclaje m

red¹ /red/ adj **redder, reddest** (rose/dress) rojo, colorado; (flag/signal) rojo; (meat) rojo; (wine) tinto; **her eyes were ~** tenía los ojos enrojecidos or rojos

AmC	Central America	Arg	Argentina	Cu	Cuba	Per	Peru
AmL	Latin America	Bol	Bolivia	Ec	Ecuador	RPl	River Plate Area
AmS	South America	Chi	Chile	Esp	Spain	Ur	Uruguay
Andes	Andean Region	CS	Southern Cone	Méx	Mexico	Ven	Venezuela

red² n rojo m, colorado m; **to see ~** ponerse* hecho una furia or un basilisco; **to be in the ~** estar* en números rojos

red: ~ admiral n vanesa f roja; **~ carpet** n: **to roll out the ~ carpet for sb** recibir* a algn con bombos y platillos or (Esp) a bombo y platillo; **R~ Cross** n Cruz f Roja

redden /'redn̩/ vi enrojecerse*

redecorate /ˌriː'dekəreɪt/ vt/i pintar (y empapelar)

redeem /rɪ'diːm/ vt **1** (a) ‹good name› rescatar (b) ‹sinners› redimir (c) **redeeming** pres p: **he has no ~ing features** no tiene ningún punto a su favor **2** (from pawnshop) desempeñar

redefine /ˌriːdɪ'faɪn/ vt redefinir

redemption /rɪ'dempʃən/ n (saving) salvación f; (Relig) redención f

redeploy /ˌriːdɪ'plɔɪ/ vt ‹resources› reorientar; ‹staff› asignar un nuevo destino a, reubicar* (AmL); ‹troops› cambiar la disposición de

redevelop /ˌriːdɪ'veləp/ vt reurbanizar*

red: ~-haired /'red'herd ‖ˌred'heəd/ adj pelirrojo; **~-handed** /'red'hændəd ‖ˌred'hændɪd/ adj: **to catch sb ~-handed** agarrar or (esp Esp) coger* a algn con las manos en la masa; **~head** n pelirrojo, -ja m,f; **~ herring** n (in detective story) pista f falsa; **~-hot** /'red'hɑːt ‖ˌred'hɒt/ adj (pred ~ **hot**) al rojo vivo

redial /ˌriː'daɪl ‖ˌriː'daɪəl/ vi/t, (BrE) **-ll-** volver* a marcar or (AmS tb) a discar

redirect /ˌriːdə'rekt, -daɪ- ‖ˌriːdaɪ'rekt, -də-/ vt (often pass) ‹mail› enviar* a una nueva dirección; ‹traffic› desviar*

rediscover /ˌriːdɪ'skʌvər ‖ˌriːdɪ'skʌvə(r)/ vt redescubrir*, volver* a descubrir

redistribute /ˌriːdɪ'strɪbjət ‖ˌriːdɪ'strɪbjuːt/ vt redistribuir*

red: ~ light n luz f roja, semáforo m en rojo, alto m (Méx); **~-light district** /'red'laɪt/ n zona f de tolerancia, zona f roja (AmL); **~neck** n (in US) (pej) sureño reaccionario de la clase baja rural

redo /ˌriː'duː/ vt (3rd pers sing pres **redoes**; past **redid**; past p **redone**) rehacer*, volver* a hacer

redouble /ˌriː'dʌbəl/ vt ‹efforts› redoblar

red pepper n (capsicum) ▶ PEPPER¹ 2

redraft /ˌriː'dræft ‖ˌriː'drɑːft/ vt volver* a redactar

redress¹ /rɪ'dres/ n reparación f

redress² vt ‹wrong› reparar; ‹imbalance› corregir*

red: R~ Sea n the R~ Sea el Mar Rojo; **~ tape** n (bureaucracy) trámites mpl burocráticos, papeleo m (fam)

reduce /rɪ'duːs ‖rɪ'djuːs/ vt **1** ‹number/amount› reducir*; ‹pressure/speed› disminuir*, reducir*; ‹price/taxes› reducir*, rebajar; ‹pain› aliviar; ❺ **reduce speed now** disminuya la velocidad **2** (break down, simplify) **to ~ sth TO sth** reducir* algo A algo **3** **to ~ sb to tears** hacer* llorar a algn

reduced /rɪ'duːst ‖rɪ'djuːst/ adj reducido

reduction /rɪ'dʌkʃən/ n reducción f; (in prices, charges) rebaja f

redundancy /rɪ'dʌndənsi/ n (pl **-cies**) (BrE Lab Rel) despido m, cese m; (before n) **~ money** o **pay** indemnización f (por despido or cese)

redundant /rɪ'dʌndənt/ adj (a) (superfluous) superfluo (b) (esp BrE Lab Rel): **she was made ~** la despidieron por reducción de planilla or (Esp) de plantilla

reed /riːd/ n (a) (Bot) carrizo m, junco m (b) (Mus) lengüeta f

reeducate /ˌriː'edʒəkeɪt ‖ˌriː'edʒʊkeɪt/ vt reeducar*

reef /riːf/ n (Geog) arrecife m; (seen as hazard) escollo m, arrecife m

reek /riːk/ vi (a) (stink) **to ~ (OF sth)** apestar or heder* (A algo) (b) (have air of) **to ~ OF sth** ‹of corruption/fraud› oler* A algo

reel¹ /riːl/ n (a) (for wire, thread, tape) carrete m (b) (of film) rollo m, carrete m (esp Esp) (c) (fishing) carrete m, carretel m

reel² vi tambalearse; **my head was ~ing** todo me daba vueltas
  ■ **reel in** [v + o + adv, v + adv + o] ‹line› enrollar
  ■ **reel off** [v + o + adv, v + adv + o] recitar de un tirón

reelect /ˌriːə'lekt ‖ˌriːɪ'lekt/ vt reelegir*

reemerge /ˌriːə'mɜːrdʒ ‖ˌriːɪ'mɜːdʒ/ vi (a) (reappear) volver* a salir (b) (regain prominence) resurgir*

reenact /ˌriːə'nækt ‖ˌriːɪ'nækt/ vt ‹historical event› recrear; ‹crime› reconstruir*

reenter /ˌriː'entər ‖ˌriː'entə(r)/ vt volver* a entrar en or (esp AmL) a

reexamine /ˌriːɪg'zæmən ‖ˌriːɪg'zæmɪn/ vt volver* a examinar

ref¹ /ref/ n (colloq) (= **referee**) árbitro, -tra m,f, réferi mf (AmL)

ref² /ref/ (= **reference**) ref.

refectory /rɪ'fektəri/ n (pl **-ries**) comedor m

refer /rɪ'fɜːr ‖rɪ'fɜː(r)/ **-rr-** vt remitir; **to ~ sb to a specialist** (Med) mandar or (AmL) derivar a algn a un especialista
  ■ **refer to** [v + prep + o] (a) (mention) hacer* referencia a, aludir a (b) (allude to) referirse* a (c) ‹dictionary/notes› consultar

referee¹ /ˌrefə'riː/ n **1** (a) (Sport) árbitro, -tra m,f, réferi mf (AmL) (b) (in dispute) árbitro -tra m,f **2** (for job candidate) (BrE): **you need two ~s** necesitas el aval de dos personas

referee² vt/i arbitrar

reference /'refrəns, 'refərəns/ n **1** (allusion) alusión f, referencia f; **with ~ to** con referencia or relación a **2** (a) (consultation) consulta f; (before n) **~ book/library** obra f/biblioteca f de consulta or de referencia (b) (indicator) referencia f; (before n) **~ number** número m de referencia **3** (for job candidate — testimonial) referencia f, informe m; (— person giving testimonial) (AmE): **you need two ~s** necesitas el aval de dos personas

referendum /ˌrefə'rendəm/ n (pl **-dums** or **-da** /-də/) referéndum m, referendo m

refill¹ /'riːfɪl/ n (for pen) repuesto m, recambio m; (for lighter) carga f

refill² /ˌriː'fɪl/ vt volver* a llenar, rellenar

refine /rɪ'faɪn/ vt (a) ‹sugar/oil› refinar (b) (improve) ‹design/style› pulir, perfeccionar

refined /rɪ'faɪnd/ adj (a) ⟨person/manners⟩ refinado, fino (b) ⟨sugar/oil⟩ refinado

refinement /rɪ'faɪnmənt/ n (a) (gentility, elegance) refinamiento m, finura f (b) (improvement) mejora f

refinery /rɪ'faɪnəri/ n (pl **-ries**) refinería f

reflect /rɪ'flekt/ vt reflejar
■ ~ vi **1** (think) to ~ (**ON sth**) reflexionar or meditar (SOBRE algo) **2** «light/heat» reflejarse
■ **reflect on, reflect upon** [v + prep + o] repercutir en; to ~ **badly on sth/sb** perjudicar* algo/a algn

reflection /rɪ'flekʃən/ n **1** (a) (Opt, Phys) reflexión f (b) (image) reflejo m; (of situation, feeling) reflejo m **2** (a) (contemplation) reflexión f; **on** o **upon** ~ ... pensándolo bien ... (b) (comment) observación f

reflector /rɪ'flektər ‖rɪ'flektə(r)/ n (of light, heat) reflector m; (Auto) catafaros m

reflex /'riːfleks/ n reflejo m

reflexive /rɪ'fleksɪv/ adj reflexivo

reform¹ /rɪ'fɔːrm ‖rɪ'fɔːm/ n reforma f

reform² vt reformar

reformation /ˌrefər'meɪʃən ‖ˌrefə'meɪʃən/ n reforma f; **the Reformation** (Relig) la Reforma

reformatory /rɪ'fɔːrmətɔːri ‖rɪ'fɔːmətəri/ n (pl **-ries**) (in US) reformatorio m

refractory /rɪ'freɪn/ vi (fml) to ~ (**FROM sth/-ING**) abstenerse* (DE algo/+ INF)

refrain² n (Lit, Mus) estribillo m

refresh /rɪ'freʃ/ vt refrescar*

refreshing /rɪ'freʃɪŋ/ adj ⟨drink/bath⟩ refrescante; ⟨sleep⟩ reparador; ⟨enthusiasm⟩ reconfortante

refreshments /rɪ'freʃmənts/ pl n refrigerio m

refrigerate /rɪ'frɪdʒəreɪt/ vt refrigerar

refrigerator /rɪ'frɪdʒəreɪtər ‖rɪ'frɪdʒəreɪtə(r)/ n nevera f, refrigerador m, frigorífico m (Esp), heladera f (RPl), refrigeradora f (Col, Per)

refuel /'riː'fjuːəl/, (BrE) **-ll-** vt reabastecer* de combustible
■ ~ vi repostar, reabastecerse* de combustible

refuge /'refjuːdʒ/ n refugio m; to take ~ refugiarse

refugee /ˌrefjuː'dʒiː/ n refugiado, -da m,f; (before n) ~ **camp** campamento m de refugiados

refund¹ /rɪ'fʌnd/ vt ⟨expenses/postage⟩ reembolsar

refund² /'riː'fʌnd/ n reembolso m

refurbish /riː'fɜːrbɪʃ ‖ri'fɜːbɪʃ/ vt renovar*, hacer* reformas en; (restore) restaurar

refusal /rɪ'fjuːzəl/ n (of permission, request) denegación f; (of offer) rechazo m; (to do sth) negativa f

refuse¹ /rɪ'fjuːz/ vt ⟨offer/gift⟩ rechazar*, no aceptar, rehusar*; to ~ to + INF negarse* A + INF
■ ~ vi negarse*

refuse² /'refjuːs/ n residuos mpl

refute /rɪ'fjuːt/ vt refutar, rebatir

regain /rɪ'geɪn, 'riː-/ vt recuperar, recobrar

regal /'riːɡəl/ adj majestuoso, regio

regalia /rɪ'ɡeɪljə ‖rɪ'ɡeɪliə/ pl n ropajes mpl

regard¹ /rɪ'ɡɑːrd ‖rɪ'ɡɑːd/ vt **1** (a) (consider) considerar; **he is very highly** ~ed **within the** profession está muy bien considerado en esa profesión (b) **as regards** en lo que se refiere a, en lo que atañe a **2** (look at) (liter) contemplar

regard² n **1** (a) (esteem): **to have a high** ~ **for sb** tener* muy buena opinión de algn, tener* a algn en gran estima (b) (consideration) consideración f **2** **regards** pl (greeting) saludos mpl, recuerdos mpl **3** (in phrases) **with regard to** (con) respecto a, con relación a, en relación con

regarding /rɪ'ɡɑːrdɪŋ ‖rɪ'ɡɑːdɪŋ/ prep (fml) en lo que concierne or respecta a, en lo que se refiere a

regardless /rɪ'ɡɑːrdləs ‖rɪ'ɡɑːdlɪs/ adv (a) (in spite of everything): **to carry on** ~ seguir* como si no pasara nada or (fam) como si tal cosa (b) **regardless of** (as prep): ~ **of the cost** cueste lo que cueste

regatta /rɪ'ɡætə/ n regata f

regenerate /rɪ'dʒenəreɪt/ vt (revive) revitalizar*; (Biol) regenerar

regent /'riːdʒənt/ n (ruler) regente mf

reggae /'reɡeɪ/ n reggae m

regime, régime /reɪ'ʒiːm/ n (a) (rule) régimen m (b) (system) sistema m

regiment /'redʒəmənt ‖'redʒɪmənt/ n regimiento m

regimental /ˌredʒə'ment ‖ˌredʒɪ'ment‖/ adj (before n) ⟨mascot/band⟩ del regimiento

region /'riːdʒən/ n (a) (Anat, Geog) (area) región f, zona f (b) **in the region of** alrededor de

regional /'riːdʒənl/ adj regional

register¹ /'redʒəstər ‖'redʒɪstə(r)/ n (a) (record, list) registro m; (in school) lista f; **to take** o **call the** ~ (BrE Educ) pasar lista (b) (Mus) registro m

register² vt **1** (record) ⟨death/birth⟩ inscribir*, registrar; ⟨ship/car⟩ matricular **2** (Post) mandar certificado or (Méx) registrado **3** **registered** past p: (a) (Fin, Adm) ~**ed trademark** marca f registrada; ~**ed nurse** enfermero titulado, enfermera titulada m,f (b) (Post) certificado or (Méx) registrado **4** (a) (make known) ⟨complaint⟩ presentar (b) «dial» registrar, marcar*
■ ~ vi **1** (enroll) inscribirse*; (Educ) matricularse, inscribirse*; (at a hotel) registrarse **2** (show, be revealed) ser* detectado **3** (be understood, remembered): **eventually it** ~ed **who he was** al final caí en la cuenta de quién era

registrar /'redʒəstrɑːr ‖ˌredʒɪs'trɑː(r), 'redʒɪstrɑː(r)/ n (a) (Soc Adm) funcionario encargado de llevar los registros de nacimientos, defunciones, etc (b) (in university, college) secretario, -ria m,f de admisiones

registration /ˌredʒə'streɪʃən ‖ˌredʒɪs'treɪʃən/ n (a) (enrollment) inscripción f, matrícula f; (Educ) inscripción f, matriculación f (b) (BrE Educ) (before n) ~ **number** (número m de) matrícula f

registry /'redʒəstri ‖'redʒɪstri/ n (pl **-tries**) registro m; (at university) secretaría f; (at church) ≈ sacristía f

registry office n (in UK) ≈ juzgado m (de paz)

regret¹ /rɪ'ɡret/ vt **-tt-** arrepentirse* de, lamentar; **we** ~ **to inform you that** ... lamentamos comunicarle or informarle que ...

regret² n (sadness) pesar m; (remorse) arrepentimiento m

regretful /rɪˈgretfəl/ adj ‹expression› de pesar

regretfully /rɪˈgretfəli/ adv con pesar; (indep) muy a mi (or nuestro etc) pesar, lamentablemente

regrettable /rɪˈgretəbəl/ adj lamentable

regrettably /rɪˈgretəbli/ adv lamentablemente

regroup /ˈriːˈgruːp/ vi reagruparse

regular¹ /ˈregjələr ‖ˈregjʊlə(r)/ adj **1** (a) ‹pulse› regular; ‹breathing› acompasado; at ∼ intervals (in time) con regularidad; (in space) a intervalos regulares **(b)** ‹customer/reader› habitual, asiduo; a ∼ income una fuente regular de ingresos; on a ∼ basis con regularidad **(c)** (customary) habitual **2** (even, symmetrical) ‹shape› regular **3** (Ling) ‹verb/plural› regular **4** (colloq) (as intensifier) verdadero

regular² n cliente mf habitual, asiduo, -dua m,f

regularity /ˌregjəˈlærəti ‖ˌregjʊˈlærəti/ n regularidad f

regularly /ˈregjələrli ‖ˈregjʊləli/ adv con regularidad, regularmente; (frequently) con frecuencia

regulate /ˈregjəleɪt ‖ˈregjʊleɪt/ vt regular

regulation /ˌregjəˈleɪʃən ‖ˌregjʊˈleɪʃən/ n **1** (rule) norma f, regla f; (before n) ‹dress/haircut› reglamentario **2** (control, adjustment) regulación f

regurgitate /rɪˈgɜːrdʒəteɪt ‖rɪˈgɜːdʒɪteɪt/ vt ‹food› regurgitar; ‹information› repetir* mecánicamente

rehabilitate /ˌriːhəˈbɪləteɪt, ˈriːə-‖ˌriːhəˈbɪlɪteɪt, ˌriːə-/ vt rehabilitar

rehabilitation /ˌriːhəˈbɪləˈteɪʃən, ˈriːə-‖ˌriːhəˌbɪlɪˈteɪʃən, ˌriːə-/ n rehabilitación f

rehearsal /rɪˈhɜːrsəl ‖rɪˈhɜːsəl/ n ensayo m

rehearse /rɪˈhɜːrs ‖rɪˈhɜːs/ vt/i ensayar

reheat /ˈriːˈhiːt/ vt recalentar*

rehouse /ˈriːˈhaʊz/ vt realojar

reign¹ /reɪn/ n reinado m

reign² vi (a) «monarch» reinar **(b)** **reigning** pres p ‹monarch› reinante; ‹champion› actual

reimburse /ˌriːɪmˈbɜːrs ‖ˌriːɪmˈbɜːs/ vt reembolsar

rein /reɪn/ n (Equ) rienda f; to give free ∼ to sb darle* carta blanca a algn

reincarnation /ˌriːɪnkɑːrˈneɪʃən ‖ˌriːɪnkɑːˈneɪʃən/ n reencarnación f

reindeer /ˈreɪndɪr ‖ˈreɪndɪə(r)/ n (pl ∼) reno m

reinforce /ˌriːɪnˈfɔːrs ‖ˌriːɪnˈfɔːs/ vt reforzar*

reinforcement /ˌriːɪnˈfɔːrsmənt ‖ˌriːɪnˈfɔːsmənt/ n **(a)** (strengthening) refuerzo m **(b)** **reinforcements** pl refuerzos mpl

reinstate /ˌriːɪnˈsteɪt/ vt ‹worker› reintegrar, reincorporar; ‹official› restituir* en el cargo

reintegrate /ˌriːˈɪntəgreɪt/ vt reintegrar; they must be ∼d into society es preciso reinsertarlos en la sociedad

reintegration /ˌriːˌɪntəˈgreɪʃən/ n reintegración f; (into society) reinserción f social

reissue /ˈriːˈɪʃuː/ vt ‹book/record› reeditar; ‹document› reexpedir*

reiterate /riːˈɪtəreɪt/ vt (frml) reiterar, repetir*

reject¹ /rɪˈdʒekt/ vt rechazar*

reject² /ˈriːdʒekt/ n (flawed product) artículo m (or producto m etc) defectuoso

rejection /rɪˈdʒekʃən/ n rechazo m; (following job application) respuesta f negativa

rejoice /rɪˈdʒɔɪs/ vi alegrarse mucho, regocijarse (liter)

rejoin /ˈriːˈdʒɔɪn/ vt ‹regiment/team› reincorporarse a; ‹firm› reincorporarse a, reintegrarse a

rejuvenate /rɪˈdʒuːvəneɪt/ vt rejuvenecer*

rekindle /ˈriːˈkɪndl/ vt ‹fire› reavivar; ‹desire› reavivar

relapse¹ /ˈriːlæps/ n recaída f

relapse² /rɪˈlæps/ vi recaer*, tener* or sufrir una recaída

relate /rɪˈleɪt/ vt **1** (link) to ∼ sth TO sth relacionar algo con algo **2** (tell) (frml) ‹story› relatar, referir* (liter)
  ■ ∼ vi **1** (a) (be connected with) to ∼ TO sth estar* relacionado con algo **(b)** relating to (as prep) relativo a, relacionado con **2** (understand, sympathize with) to ∼ TO sb sintonizar* con algn; to ∼ TO sth identificarse* con algo

related /rɪˈleɪtəd ‖rɪˈleɪtɪd/ adj **(a)** (of same family) (pred) to be ∼ (TO sb) ser* pariente (DE algn), estar* emparentado (con algn) **(b)** ‹ideas/questions/subjects› relacionado, afín

relation /rɪˈleɪʃən/ n **1** (relative) pariente mf, pariente, -ta m,f, familiar m **2** (a) (connection) relación f **(b)** in relation to (as prep) en relación con, con relación a **3** **relations** pl relaciones fpl; sexual ∼s relaciones sexuales

relationship /rɪˈleɪʃənʃɪp/ n **1** (between people) relación f **2** (between things, events) relación f **3** (kinship) ∼ (TO sb) parentesco m (con algn)

relative¹ /ˈrelətɪv/ n pariente mf, pariente, -ta m,f, familiar mf

relative² adj **(a)** (comparative): the ∼ merits of los pros y los contras de **(b)** (not absolute) relativo; it's all ∼ (set phrase) todo es relativo (fr hecha) **(c)** relative to (compared to) en comparación con

relatively /ˈrelətɪvli/ adv relativamente

relax /rɪˈlæks/ vi relajarse
  ■ ∼ vt relajar; she ∼ed her grip sujetó con menos fuerza

relaxation /ˌriːlækˈseɪʃən/ n (rest) relax m; (recreation) esparcimiento m, distracción f

relaxed /rɪˈlækst/ adj ‹manner/person› relajado; ‹atmosphere/party› informal

relaxing /rɪˈlæksɪŋ/ adj relajante

relay¹ /ˈriːleɪ/ n **(a)** (team) relevo m; to work in ∼s trabajar en or por relevos **(b)** ∼ (race) (Sport) carrera f de relevos or (AmL) de postas

relay² /ˈriːleɪ, rɪˈleɪ/ vt transmitir

release¹ /rɪˈliːs/ vt **1** ‹prisoner/hostage› poner* en libertad, liberar **2** ‹information› hacer* público; ‹record/book› sacar* (a la venta); ‹movie› estrenar **3** (emit) ‹gas› despedir* **4** ‹brake/clutch› soltar*

release² n **1** (from prison, captivity) puesta f en libertad, liberación f **2** (of record) salida f al mercado; (of movie) estreno m; in o (BrE) on general ∼ en todos los cines

relegate /ˈreləgeɪt ‖ˈrelɪgeɪt/ vt **(a)** (consign, ⋯⇢

demote) relegar* **(b)** (BrE Sport) (*usu pass*): **the team was ~d to the third division** el equipo descendió *or* bajó a tercera división

relent /rɪˈlent/ *vi* «*person*» transigir*, ceder

relentless /rɪˈlentləs ǁrɪˈlentlɪs/ *adj* «*enemy*/*pursuer*» implacable; «*pursuit*» incesante

relentlessly /rɪˈlentləsli ǁrɪˈlentlɪsli/ *adv* implacablemente

relevance /ˈreləvəns/ *n* (connection) relación *f*, (importance) relevancia *f*

relevant /ˈreləvənt/ *adj* «*document*/*facts*» pertinente, relevante

reliability /rɪˌlaɪəˈbɪləti/ *n* (of worker) formalidad *f*, responsabilidad *f*, (of sources) fiabilidad *f*, (of vehicle) fiabilidad *f*

reliable /rɪˈlaɪəbəl/ *adj* **(a)** «*information*/*source*» fidedigno; «*witness*» fiable, confiable (esp AmL) **(b)** «*worker*» responsable, de confianza; «*vehicle*» fiable

reliably /rɪˈlaɪəbli/ *adv*: **I am ~ informed that ...** sé de fuentes fidedignas que ..., sé de buena fuente que ...

reliant /rɪˈlaɪənt/ *adj* (*pred*) **to be ~ on sth/sb** depender DE algo/algn

relic /ˈrelɪk/ *n* reliquia *f*

relief /rɪˈliːf/ *n* **1** (from worry, pain) alivio *m*; **it's a ~ that the rain's stopped at last** menos mal que ha parado de llover **2** (aid) ayuda *f*, auxilio *m* (*de emergencia*); **to be on ~** (AmE) recibir prestaciones de la seguridad social **3** (replacement) relevo *m* **4** (Art, Geog) relieve *m*

relieve /rɪˈliːv/ *vt* **(a)** «*pain*» calmar, aliviar; «*suffering*» mitigar*, aliviar; «*tension*» aliviar; **to ~ sb of his/her duties** relevar a algn de su cargo **(b)** «*town*/*fortress*» liberar **(c)** «*guard*/*driver*» relevar
■ *v refl* **to ~ oneself** (euph) orinar

relieved /rɪˈliːvd/ *adj* aliviado; **to feel ~** sentir* un gran alivio, sentirse* aliviado

religion /rɪˈlɪdʒən/ *n* religión *f*

religious /rɪˈlɪdʒəs/ *adj* religioso

religiously /rɪˈlɪdʒəsli/ *adv* religiosamente

relinquish /rɪˈlɪŋkwɪʃ/ *vt* renunciar a

relish¹ /ˈrelɪʃ/ *vt* «*meal*/*joke*/*success*» saborear; **I don't ~ the prospect of ...** no me entusiasma *or* no me hace ninguna gracia la perspectiva de ...

relish² *n* **1** (Culin) salsa o conserva que se come con carnes **2** (enjoyment): **with ~** «*eat*/*drink*» con gusto, con fruición; «*read*/*listen to*» con placer, con deleite

relive /ˈriːˈlɪv/ *vt* revivir

relocate /ˈriːləʊˈkeɪt/ *vt* trasladar
■ *~ vi* «*company*» trasladarse; «*employee*» mudarse *or* trasladarse de domicilio

reluctance /rɪˈlʌktəns/ *n* renuencia *f* (frml)

reluctant /rɪˈlʌktənt/ *adj* reacio, renuente

reluctantly /rɪˈlʌktəntli/ *adv* a su (*or* mi *etc*) pesar, a regañadientes

rely /rɪˈlaɪ/ *vi* **relies, relying, relied (a)** (have confidence) **to ~ on** *or* **upon sb/sth** contar* CON

algn/algo; **you can ~ on me** puedes contar conmigo; **she can't be relied (up)on to help** no se puede contar con *or* confiar en que vaya a ayudar **(b)** (be dependent) **to ~ on sb/sth FOR sth** depender DE algn/algo (PARA algo)

remain /rɪˈmeɪn/ *vi* **1 (a)** (+ *adj or adv compl*) (continue to be) seguir*, continuar*; **her condition ~s critical** su estado sigue siendo crítico; **he ~ed silent** se mantuvo en silencio **(b)** (stay) quedarse, permanecer* (frml); **to ~ behind** quedarse **2 (a)** (be left) quedar; **what still ~s to be done?** ¿qué queda por hacer?; **that ~s to be seen** eso está por verse **(b)** (remaining) *pres p*: **the ~ing ten pounds** las diez libras restantes *or* que quedan

remainder /rɪˈmeɪndər ǁrɪˈmeɪndə(r)/ *n* **the ~** el resto

remains /rɪˈmeɪnz/ *pl n* restos *mpl*; (of meal) sobras *fpl*, restos *mpl*

remake¹ /ˈriːmeɪk/ *n* nueva versión *f*

remake² /ˈriːˈmeɪk/ *vt* (*past & past p* **remade**) volver* a hacer, rehacer*

remand¹ /rɪˈmænd ǁrɪˈmɑːnd/ *vt*: **to be ~ed on bail** quedar en libertad bajo fianza; **he was ~ed in custody** se decretó su prisión preventiva

remand² *n*: **to be on ~** (in detention) estar* en prisión preventiva

remand centre, remand home *n* (in UK) centro para menores en prisión preventiva

remark¹ /rɪˈmɑːrk ǁrɪˈmɑːk/ *n* comentario *m*, observación *f*

remark² *vi* **to ~ on** *or* **upon sth** hacer* un comentario/comentarios ACERCA DE algo
■ *~ vt* observar, comentar

remarkable /rɪˈmɑːrkəbəl ǁrɪˈmɑːkəbəl/ *adj* «*ability*/*likeness*» notable; «*achievement*» sorprendente; «*coincidence*» extraordinario; «*person*» excepcional

remarkably /rɪˈmɑːrkəbli ǁrɪˈmɑːkəbli/ *adv* **(a)** (surprisingly) sorprendentemente **(b)** (exceptionally) «*stupid*» increíblemente

remarry /ˈriːˈmæri/ *vi* **-ries, -rying, -ried** volver* a casarse

remedial /rɪˈmiːdiəl/ *adj* de recuperación

remedy¹ /ˈremədi/ *n* (*pl* **-dies**) remedio *m*

remedy² *vt* **-dies, -dying, -died** «*mistake*/*situation*» remediar; «*injustice*/*evil*» reparar

remember /rɪˈmembər ǁrɪˈmembə(r)/ *vt* **1** (recall) acordarse* de, recordar*; **I ~ him saying something about ...** me acuerdo de *or* recuerdo que dijo algo de ... **2 (a)** (be mindful of, not forget): **to ~ to + INF** acordarse* DE + INF **(b)** (commemorate) «*dead*» recordar* **(c)** (send regards): **~ me to your mother** dale recuerdos *or* saludos a tu madre (de mi parte)
■ *~ vi* **(a)** (recall) acordarse*, recordar*; **try to ~!** ¡haz memoria! **(b)** (be mindful, not forget) no olvidarse

remembrance /rɪˈmembrəns/ *n* (liter *or* frml) recuerdo *m*, remembranza *f* (liter); **in ~ of sth/sb** en memoria de algo/algn; (*before n*) **R~ Sunday**

AmC	América Central	Arg	Argentina	Cu	Cuba	Per	Perú
AmL	América Latina	Bol	Bolivia	Ec	Ecuador	RPl	Río de la Plata
AmS	América del Sur	Chi	Chile	Esp	España	Ur	Uruguay
Andes	Región andina	CS	Cono Sur	Méx	México	Ven	Venezuela

(in UK) *domingo de noviembre en que se conmemora a los caídos en las dos guerras mundiales*

remind /rɪ'maɪnd/ *vt* recordarle* a; **oh, that ∼s me** ¡ah! por cierto ..., y a propósito ...; **to ∼ sb to + INF** recordarle* A algn QUE (+ *subj*); **he ∼s me of my grandfather** me recuerda a mi abuelo

reminder /rɪ'maɪndər ‖rɪ'maɪndə(r)/ *n* **(a)** **to serve as a ∼ of sth** recordar* algo **(b)** (requesting payment) recordatorio *m* de pago

reminisce /'remə'nɪs ‖,remɪ'nɪs/ *vi* rememorar los viejos tiempos; **to ∼ ABOUT sth** rememorar algo

reminiscences /'remə'nɪsn̩sɪz ‖,remɪ'nɪsn̩sɪz/ *pl n* recuerdos *mpl*, memorias *fpl*

reminiscent /'remə'nɪsn̩t ‖,remɪ'nɪsn̩t/ *adj* (*pred*) **to be ∼ OF sb/sth** recordar* a algn/(a) algo

remiss /rɪ'mɪs/ *adj* (fml) (*pred*) negligente

remission /rɪ'mɪʃən/ *n* remisión *f*

remit /rɪ'mɪt/ *vt* **-tt-** (fml) **1** (send) remitir (fml) **2** (Law) ⟨*sentence*⟩ perdonar, condonar (fml)

remnant /'remnənt/ *n* **(a)** (leftover) **a ∼ of the past** una reliquia del pasado; **the ∼s of a meal** los restos de una comida **(b)** (Tex) retazo *m*, retal *m* (Esp)

remonstrate /'rɪ'mɑːnstreɪt, 'remən- ‖'remənstreɪt/ *vi* protestar, quejarse; **to ∼ with sb about sth** reprocharle algo a algn

remorse /rɪ'mɔːrs ‖rɪ'mɔːs/ *n* remordimiento *m*

remorseful /rɪ'mɔːrsfəl ‖rɪ'mɔːsfəl/ *adj* arrepentido

remorseless /rɪ'mɔːrsləs ‖rɪ'mɔːslɪs/ *adj* despiadado

remote /rɪ'məʊt/ *adj* **-ter, -test** remoto

remote: ∼ control *n* mando *m* a distancia, control *m* remoto; **∼-controlled** /rɪ'məʊtkən'trəʊld/ *adj* (*pred* ∼ **controlled**) ⟨*TV/hi-fi*⟩ con mando a distancia *or* con control remoto; ⟨*model/toy*⟩ de control remoto

remotely /rɪ'məʊtli/ *adv* (at all, in the least) (*usu with neg*) remotamente

remould¹ /'riː'məʊld/ *vt* (BrE Auto) ▶ RETREAD¹

remould² /'riː'məʊld/ *n* (BrE Auto) ▶ RETREAD²

removable /rɪ'muːvəbəl/ *adj* ⟨*hood/lining*⟩ de quita y pon; ⟨*handle/shelf*⟩ desmontable

removal /rɪ'muːvəl/ *n* **1** (of contents) extracción *f*; (of appendix, tonsils) extirpación *f* **2** (of stain, unwanted hair) eliminación *f* **3** **(a)** (moving, taking away) traslado *m* **(b)** (from house to house) (BrE) mudanza *f*

remove /rɪ'muːv/ *vt* **1** **(a)** (take off) quitar, sacar* **(b)** (take out) ⟨*contents*⟩ sacar*; ⟨*tonsils/ appendix*⟩ extirpar (fml); ⟨*bullet*⟩ extraer* (fml) **2** **(a)** (get rid of) ⟨*stain/grease*⟩ quitar; ⟨*unwanted hair*⟩ eliminar **(b)** ⟨*doubt*⟩ disipar; ⟨*threat*⟩ eliminar **3** (take away, move) ⟨*object*⟩ quitar; ⟨*person*⟩ sacar* **4** (dismiss from post, position) destituir*

remover /rɪ'muːvər ‖rɪ'muːvə(r)/ *n* (substance): **makeup ∼** desmaquillador *m*; **nail polish o** (BrE also) **nail varnish ∼** quitaesmalte *m*

remuneration /rɪ'mjuːnə'reɪʃən/ *n* (fml) remuneración *f*

renaissance /'renə'saːns ‖rɪ'neɪsəns/ *n* **(a)** **Renaissance** Renacimiento *m* **(b)** (revival) (liter) renacimiento *m*

rename /'riː'neɪm/ *vt* dar* un nuevo nombre a

render /'rendər ‖'rendə(r)/ *vt* **1** (make): **to ∼ sth useless** hacer* que algo resulte inútil **2** (give, proffer) (fml) ⟨*thanks*⟩ dar*; ⟨*assistance*⟩ prestar; **for services ∼ed** por servicios prestados **3** (translate) traducir*

rendezvous /'rɑːndeɪvuː ‖'rɒndɪvuː, -deɪvuː/ *n* (*pl* ∼ /-z/) (meeting) encuentro *m*, cita *f*; (place) lugar *m* señalado para un encuentro *or* una cita

rendition /ren'dɪʃən/ *n* interpretación *f*

renegade /'renɪgeɪd/ *n* renegado, -da *m,f*

renew /rɪ'nuː ‖rɪ'njuː/ *vt* **(a)** ⟨*hope/promise*⟩ renovar*; ⟨*efforts/friendship*⟩ reanudar; ⟨*library book*⟩ renovar* **(b) renewed** *past p* renovado

renewal /rɪ'nuːəl ‖rɪ'njuːəl/ *n* renovación *f*

renounce /rɪ'naʊns/ *vt* **(a)** (cede) (fml) ⟨*claim/ title*⟩ renunciar a **(b)** (reject) ⟨*religion*⟩ renunciar a

renovate /'renəveɪt/ *vt* renovar*

renovation /'renə'veɪʃən/ *n* renovación *f*

renown /rɪ'naʊn/ *n* renombre *m*, fama *f*

renowned /rɪ'naʊnd/ *adj* de renombre

rent¹ /rent/ *n* **(a)** (for accommodations, office) alquiler *m*, arrendamiento *m*, arriendo *m*, renta *f* (esp Méx) **(b)** (for boat, suit) (esp AmE) alquiler *m*, arriendo *m* (esp Andes), renta *f* (Méx)

rent² *vt* **(a)** (pay for) **to ∼ sth** (FROM sb) alquilarle *or* arrendarle* *or* (Méx tb) rentarle algo (A algn) **(b)** ▶ RENT OUT
■ **rent out** [*v* + *o* + *adv*, *v* + *adv* + *o*] alquilar, arrendar*

rental /'rentl/ *n* **(a)** (act of renting) alquiler *m*, arriendo *m* **(b)** (charge) alquiler *m*, renta *f* (Méx), arriendo *m* (esp Andes)

renunciation /rɪ'nʌnsɪ'eɪʃən/ *n* (fml) **(a)** (of faith) rechazo *m* **(b)** (of claim, right, title) renuncia *f*

reopen /'riː'əʊpən ‖,riː'əʊpən/ *vt* ⟨*book/road*⟩ volver* a abrir; ⟨*negotiations/hostilities*⟩ reanudar; ⟨*criminal case*⟩ reabrir*
■ ∼ *vi* abrir* de nuevo

reorganize /'riː'ɔːrgənaɪz ‖,riː'ɔːgənaɪz/ *vt* reorganizar*

rep /rep/ *n* (sales ∼) representante *mf or* agente *mf* (comercial); **a union ∼** un/una representante *or* (Esp) un/una enlace sindical

repair¹ /rɪ'per ‖rɪ'peə(r)/ *vt* ⟨*machinery/roof*⟩ arreglar, reparar; ⟨*shoes/clothes*⟩ arreglar

repair² *n* arreglo *m*, reparación *f*; **the museum is closed for ∼s** el museo está cerrado por obras; **in a good/bad state of ∼**, **in good/bad ∼** en buen/mal estado

repairer /rɪ'perər ‖rɪ'peərə(r)/ *n* técnico, -ca *m,f*; **watch ∼** relojero, -ra *m,f*

repairman /rɪ'permæn ‖rɪ'peəmæn/ *n* (*pl* **-men** /-men/) técnico *m*

repatriate /'riː'peɪtrieɪt ‖,riː'pætrieɪt/ *vt* repatriar

repay /'riː'peɪ/ *vt* (*past & past p* **repaid**) **(a)** ⟨*money/loan*⟩ devolver*; ⟨*debt*⟩ pagar*, cancelar **(b)** ⟨*kindness/favor*⟩ pagar*, corresponder a

repayment /'riː'peɪmənt/ *n* **(a)** (act of repaying) pago *m* **(b)** (installment) plazo *m*, cuota *f* (AmL)

repeal¹ /rɪ'piːl/ *vt* (Govt, Law) revocar*

repeal² n revocación f

repeat¹ /rɪ'piːt/ vt **1** (a) (say again) repetir*
(b) (divulge) contar* **2** (do again) repetir*
■ v refl to ~ oneself repetirse*
■ ~ vi repetir*

repeat² n repetición f

repeated /rɪ'piːtəd ‖rɪ'piːtɪd/ adj (before n)
‹attempts› repetido, reiterado; ‹requests›
reiterado

repeatedly /rɪ'piːtədli ‖rɪ'piːtɪdli/ adv
repetidamente, reiteradamente

repel /rɪ'pel/ vt **-ll-** (a) ‹enemy/army› repeler;
‹attack› repeler, rechazar* (b) ‹insects› repeler,
ahuyentar (c) (disgust) repeler, repugnar

repellant /rɪ'pelənt/ n: **insect** ~ repelente m
para insectos

repellent /rɪ'pelənt/ adj repelente

repent /rɪ'pent/ vi arrepentirse*

repentance /rɪ'pentn̩s/ n arrepentimiento m

repentant /rɪ'pentn̩t/ adj arrepentido

repercussions /'riːpər'kʌʃənz
‖,riːpə'kʌʃənz/ pl n repercusiones fpl

repertoire /'repərtwɑːr ‖'repətwɑː(r)/ n
repertorio m

repertory /'repərtɔːri ‖'repətəri/ n: **to be/act/
work in** ~ trabajar en una compañía de
repertorio

repetition /'repə'tɪʃən/ n repetición f

repetitious /'repə'tɪʃəs/ adj repetitivo

repetitive /rɪ'petətɪv/ adj repetitivo

repetitive strain injury n lesión f por
fatiga crónica

rephrase /'riː'freɪz/ vt expresar de otra
manera

replace /rɪ'pleɪs/ vt **1** (a) (take the place of)
sustituir*, reemplazar* (b) ‹lost item› reponer*;
‹broken window/battery› cambiar **2** (put back in
its place) ‹poner a poner or colocar; ‹lid› volver*
a poner; ‹receiver› colgar*

replacement /rɪ'pleɪsmənt/ n (a) (act)
sustitución f, reemplazo m (b) (person) sustituto,
-ta m,f (c) (object): **I'll buy you a** ~ te compraré
uno nuevo

replay¹ /'riː'pleɪ/ vt (a) (Sport) ‹game/match›
volver* a jugar, repetir* (b) (Audio, Video) volver*
a poner

replay² /'riː'pleɪ/ n (Sport) repetición f (de la
jugada)

replenish /rɪ'plenɪʃ/ vt ‹stock› reponer*

replete /rɪ'pliːt/ adj (liter) ~ **WITH sth** repleto DE
algo

replica /'replɪkə/ n (pl **-cas**) réplica f,
reproducción f

reply¹ /rɪ'plaɪ/ n (pl **replies**) (spoken, written)
respuesta f, contestación f; **in** ~ **to your letter** en
respuesta a su carta

reply² vi/t **replies, replying, replied**
responder, contestar

report¹ /rɪ'pɔːrt ‖rɪ'pɔːt/ n **1** (a) (account)
informe m; (piece of news) noticia f; (in newspaper)
reportaje m, crónica f (b) (evaluation) informe m,
reporte m (Méx); **medical** ~ parte m médico;
(school) ~ boletín m or (Méx) boleta f de
calificaciones **2** (sound) estallido m

report² vt **1** (a) (relate, announce): **several**

people ~ed seeing the tiger varias personas
dijeron haber visto al tigre; **he is** ~ed **to be very
rich** se dice que es muy rico (b) (Journ) «reporter/
media» informar sobre **2** (a) (notify) ‹accident›
informar de, dar* parte de; ‹crime› denunciar, dar*
parte de, reportar (AmL); **to** ~ **sth** **TO sb** dar* parte
DE algo A algn (b) (denounce) denunciar, reportar
(AmL) ■ ~ vi **1** (Journ) «reporter» informar
2 (present oneself) presentarse, reportarse (AmL);
to ~ **sick** dar* parte de enfermo
■ **report back** [v + adv] (return): **to** ~ **back**
(**to base**) regresar a la base (b) (give report) **to** ~
back (**TO sb**) presentar un informe (A algn)

report card n (AmE Educ) boletín m or (Méx)
boleta f de calificaciones

reported speech /rɪ'pɔːrtəd ‖rɪ'pɔːtɪd/ n
estilo m indirecto

reporter /rɪ'pɔːrtər ‖rɪ'pɔːtə(r)/ n periodista
mf, reportero, -tera m,f

repose /rɪ'pəʊz/ n (liter) reposo m

repossess /'riːpə'zes/ vt ‹car/house› recuperar
la posesión de (por falta de pago)

reprehensible /'reprɪ'hensəbəl/ adj
reprensible

represent /'reprɪ'zent/ vt **1** (a) (stand for)
representar (b) (constitute) representar, constituir*
2 (act as representative for) ‹client› representar
3 (frml) (describe) presentar

representation /'reprɪzen'teɪʃən/ n
representación f

representative¹ /'reprɪ'zentətɪv/ n (a)
representante mf (b) (in US) (Govt) representante
mf, diputado, -da m,f (c) (sales ~) representante
mf or agente mf comercial

representative² adj representativo

repress /rɪ'pres/ vt reprimir

repression /rɪ'preʃən/ n represión f

repressive /rɪ'presɪv/ adj represivo

reprieve¹ /rɪ'priːv/ n (Law) indulto m

reprieve² vt indultar

reprimand¹ /'reprəmænd ‖'reprɪmɑːnd/ n
reprimenda f

reprimand² vt reprender

reprint¹ /'riːprɪnt/ n (Publ) reimpresión f; (Phot)
copia f

reprint² /'riː'prɪnt/ vt (Publ) reimprimir*

reprisal /rɪ'praɪzəl/ n represalia f

reproach¹ /rɪ'prəʊtʃ/ vt to ~ **sb** FOR **-ING**: he
~ed her for not having written to him le reprochó
que no le hubiera escrito

reproach² n reproche m; **above** o **beyond** ~
irreprochable, intachable

reproachful /rɪ'prəʊtʃfəl/ adj (lleno) de
reproche

reproduce /'riːprə'duːs ‖,riːprə'djuːs/ vt
reproducir*
■ ~ vi (Biol) reproducirse*

reproduction /'riːprə'dʌkʃən/ n reproducción
f

reproductive /'riːprə'dʌktɪv/ adj reproductor

reproof /rɪ'pruːf/ n (frml) reprobación f

reprove /rɪ'pruːv/ vt (frml) to ~ **sb** (FOR **sth**)
reprender or (frml) reconvenir* a algn (POR algo)

reptile /'reptl̩, -taɪl ‖'reptaɪl/ n reptil m

republic /rɪ'pʌblɪk/ n república f

republican¹ /rɪ'pʌblɪkən/ adj (a) (of a republic) republicano (b) **Republican** (in US) republicano

republican² n (a) (supporter of republic) republicano, -na m,f (b) **Republican** (in US) republicano, -na m,f

repudiate /rɪ'pju:dɪeɪt/ vt (a) (deny) ⟨accusation⟩ rechazar*, negar* (b) ⟨violence/ family⟩ repudiar

repugnance /rɪ'pʌgnəns/ n repugnancia f

repugnant /rɪ'pʌgnənt/ adj repugnante

repulse /rɪ'pʌls/ vt repeler, rechazar*

repulsion /rɪ'pʌlʃən/ n (fml) repulsión f

repulsive /rɪ'pʌlsɪv/ adj repulsivo, repugnante

reputable /'repjətəbəl ‖ 'repjʊtəbəl/ adj acreditado (fml), reputado (fml)

reputation /ˌrepjə'teɪʃən ‖ ˌrepjʊ'teɪʃən/ n reputación f; good/bad ~ buena/mala reputación or fama; a ~ **FOR** sth fama DE algo

repute /rɪ'pju:t/ n (fml) reputación f, fama f; of ~ de renombre

reputed /rɪ'pju:təd ‖ rɪ'pju:tɪd/ adj presunto, supuesto; she is ~ to be the best in the world está considerada como la mejor del mundo

reputedly /rɪ'pju:tədli ‖ rɪ'pjʊtɪdli/ adv (indep) según se dice or cree

request¹ /rɪ'kwest/ n (a) (polite demand) petición f, pedido m (esp AmL), solicitud f (frml); ~ **FOR** sth petición f or pedido etc) DE algo (b) (for song) petición f, pedido m (esp AmL)

request² vt pedir*, solicitar (frml)

requiem /'rekwɪəm/ n réquiem m

require /rɪ'kwaɪr ‖ rɪ'kwaɪə(r)/ vt ① (a) (need) necesitar; (call for) ⟨patience/dedication⟩ requerir*, exigir* (b) (demand) to ~ sb/sth to + **INF** requerir* que algn/algo (+ subj); I shall do all that is ~d of me haré todo lo que me corresponda ② **required** past p (a) ⟨dose/amount⟩ necesario (b) (compulsory) ⟨reading/viewing⟩ obligado

requirement /rɪ'kwaɪrmənt ‖ rɪ'kwaɪəmənt/ n (a) (usu pl) (need) necesidad f (b) (condition) requisito m

requisite /'rekwəzət ‖ 'rekwɪzɪt/ adj (frml) necesario, requerido

requisition /ˌrekwə'zɪʃən ‖ ˌrekwɪ'zɪʃən/ vt requisar

reroute /ˌri:'ru:t/ vt desviar*

reschedule /ˌri:'skedʒu:l ‖ ˌri:'ʃedju:l/ vt ⟨meeting⟩ cambiar la hora/fecha de

rescind /rɪ'sɪnd/ vt (fml) ⟨contract⟩ rescindir; ⟨order/ruling⟩ revocar*; ⟨law⟩ derogar*

rescue¹ /'reskju:/ n rescate m; they went to his ~ acudieron a socorrerlo (liter), fueron or (liter) acudieron en su auxilio

rescue² vt rescatar, salvar

rescuer /'reskjuər ‖ 'reskju:ə(r)/ n salvador, -dora m,f

research¹ /rɪ'sɜːrtʃ, 'ri:sɜːrtʃ ‖ rɪ'sɜːtʃ/ n investigación f; ~ **INTO/ON** sth investigación **SOBRE** algo

research² vi investigar*

■ ~ vt ⟨causes/problem⟩ investigar*, estudiar; this article is well ~ed este artículo está bien documentado

researcher /rɪ'sɜːrtʃər ‖ rɪ'sɜːtʃə(r)/ n investigador, -dora m,f

resemblance /rɪ'zembləns/ n parecido m, semejanza f; ~ **TO** sb/sth parecido CON algn/algo

resemble /rɪ'zembəl/ vt parecerse* a

resent /rɪ'zent/ vt ⟨person⟩ guardarle rencor a; he ~ed her success le molestaba que ella tuviera éxito; I ~ having to help him me molesta tener que ayudarle

resentful /rɪ'zentfəl/ adj ⟨person⟩ resentido, rencoroso; ⟨air/look⟩ de resentimiento

resentment /rɪ'zentmənt/ n resentimiento m, rencor m

reservation /ˌrezər'veɪʃən ‖ ˌrezə'veɪʃən/ n (a) (booking) reserva f, reservación f (AmL) (b) (doubt, qualification) reserva f; without ~ sin reservas (c) (land) (in US) reserva f, reservación f (AmL)

reserve¹ /rɪ'zɜːrv ‖ rɪ'zɜːv/ n ① (stock) reserva f; to keep sth in ~ ⟨money/food⟩ tener* algo reservado ② (Sport) reserva mf ③ **reserves** pl (Mil) reservas fpl ④ (land) coto m, reserva f ⑤ (self-restraint) reserva f, cautela f

reserve² vt (a) (book) ⟨room/table⟩ reservar (b) (keep, save) reservar, guardar; to ~ (one's) judgment reservarse la opinión

reserved /rɪ'zɜːrvd ‖ rɪ'zɜːvd/ adj reservado

reservoir /'rezərvwɑːr ‖ 'rezəvwɑː(r)/ n embalse m, presa f, represa f (AmS)

reset /ˌri:'set/ vt (pres p **resetting**; past & past p **reset**) (a) ⟨alarm clock⟩ (volver* a) poner*; ⟨counter/dial⟩ volver* a cero (b) (Med) ⟨bone⟩ colocar*

reshuffle /'ri:ʃʌfəl/ n reorganización f; cabinet ~ remodelación f del gabinete

reside /rɪ'zaɪd/ vi (fml) residir (fml)

residence /'rezədəns ‖ 'rezɪdəns/ n ① (a) (in a country) residencia f (b) (in building) (fml) residencia f; to take up ~ instalarse (c) ~ hall (AmE) residencia f universitaria or de estudiantes, colegio m mayor (Esp) ② (home) residencia f

resident¹ /'rezədənt ‖ 'rezɪdənt/ n (a) (in country) residente mf (b) (of district) vecino, -na m,f

resident² adj residente

residential /ˌrezə'dentʃəl ‖ ˌrezɪ'denʃəl/ adj ⟨area/suburb⟩ residencial; ⟨course⟩ con alojamiento para los asistentes

residue /'rezədu: ‖ 'rezɪdju:/ n residuo m

resign /rɪ'zaɪn/ vi renunciar, dimitir; to ~ **FROM** sth renunciar A algo, dimitir algo

■ v refl to ~ oneself (**TO** sth/-**ING**) resignarse (A algo/+ **INF**)

resignation /ˌrezɪg'neɪʃən/ n ① (from job, position) renuncia f, dimisión f ② (acceptance, submission) resignación f

resigned /rɪ'zaɪnd/ adj resignado

resilience /rɪ'zɪljəns ‖ rɪ'zɪliəns/ n (a) (of person) capacidad f de recuperación, resistencia f (b) (of material) elasticidad f

resilient /rɪ'zɪljənt ‖ rɪ'zɪliənt/ adj (a) ⟨person⟩ fuerte, con capacidad de recuperación (b) ⟨material⟩ elástico

resin /'rezn̩ ‖ 'rezɪn/ n resina f

resist /rɪˈzɪst/ vt resistir; ⟨change/plan⟩ oponer* resistencia a; **I can't ~ chocolate** el chocolate me vuelve loco; **to ~ -ING** resistirse A + INF

resistance /rɪˈzɪstəns/ n resistencia f; **the ~** la resistencia

resistant /rɪˈzɪstənt/ adj resistente

resit¹ /ˈriːsɪt/ vt (pres p **resitting**; past & past p **resat** /ˈriːsæt/) (BrE) ⟨examination⟩ volver* a presentarse a

resit² /ˈriːsɪt/ n (BrE): **to do a ~** volver* a examinarse

resolute /ˈrezəluːt/ adj resuelto, decidido

resolution /ˌrezəˈluːʃən/ n **(a)** (decision) determinación f, propósito m; **New Year's ~s** buenos propósitos de Año Nuevo **(b)** (in US, passed by legislature) resolución f

resolve¹ /rɪˈzɑːlv ‖ rɪˈzɒlv/ n resolución f

resolve² vt **(a)** (clear up) ⟨difficulty⟩ resolver*; ⟨differences⟩ saldar, resolver **(b)** (decide) **to ~ (to + INF)** resolver* or decidir (+ INF)

resonance /ˈrezənəns ‖ ˈrezənəns/ n resonancia f

resonant /ˈrezənənt ‖ ˈrezənənt/ adj resonante

resort /rɪˈzɔːrt ‖ rɪˈzɔːt/ n **1** (for vacations) centro m turístico or vacacional; **a seaside ~** un centro turístico costero, un balneario (AmL); **a ski ~** una estación de esquí **2** (recourse) recurso m; **as a/the last ~** como último recurso

■ **resort to** [v + prep + o]: **to ~ to force/violence** recurrir a la fuerza/violencia; **they had to ~ to strike action** no les quedó más remedio que ir a la huelga

resound /rɪˈzaʊnd/ vi retumbar, resonar*

resounding /rɪˈzaʊndɪŋ/ adj (before n) **(a)** ⟨cheers/explosion⟩ retumbante, resonante **(b)** ⟨success/failure⟩ rotundo

resource /ˈriːsɔːrs ‖ rɪˈsɔːs/ n recurso m; **natural/human ~s** recursos naturales/humanos

resourceful /rɪˈsɔːrsfəl ‖ rɪˈsɔːsfəl/ adj de recursos

respect¹ /rɪˈspekt/ n **1 (a)** (esteem) respeto m; **to have ~ for sb** respetar algn **(b)** (consideration) consideración f, respeto m; **~ respects** pl respetos mpl **2 (a)** (way, aspect) sentido m, respecto m; **in this ~** en cuanto a esto, en este sentido **(b)** **with respect to** (fml) (introducing subject) en lo que concierne a (fml); (in relation to) con respecto a

respect² vt respetar

respectable /rɪˈspektəbəl/ adj **1** (socially acceptable) ⟨person/conduct⟩ decente, respetable **2 (a)** (quite large) ⟨amount/salary⟩ respetable **(b)** (reasonably good) ⟨performance/score⟩ digno, aceptable

respected /rɪˈspektəd ‖ rɪˈspektɪd/ adj respetado

respectful /rɪˈspektfəl/ adj respetuoso

respecting /rɪˈspektɪŋ/ prep (fml) en lo que concierne a (fml)

respective /rɪˈspektɪv/ adj (before n) respectivo

respiration /ˌrespəˈreɪʃən ‖ ˌrespɪˈreɪʃən/ n respiración f

respirator /ˈrespəreɪtər ‖ ˈrespɪreɪtə(r)/ n **(a)** (Med) respirador m **(b)** (mask) máscara f de oxígeno

respiratory /ˈrespərətɔːri ‖ rɪˈspɪrətəri/ adj respiratorio

respite /ˈrespət ‖ ˈrespaɪt/ n (no pl) respiro m, descanso m; **without ~** sin respiro

resplendent /rɪˈsplendənt/ adj resplandeciente

respond /rɪˈspɑːnd ‖ rɪˈspɒnd/ vi **(a)** (reply) responder, contestar **(b)** (react) responder, reaccionar

response /rɪˈspɑːns ‖ rɪˈspɒns/ n **(a)** (reply) respuesta f **(b)** (reaction) respuesta f; (to news) reacción f

responsibility /rɪˌspɑːnsəˈbɪləti ‖ rɪˌspɒnsəˈbɪləti/ n (pl **-ties**) **(a)** (task, duty) responsabilidad f **(b)** (authority, accountability) responsabilidad f; **to take ~ for sth** responsabilizarse* or encargarse* de algo **(c)** (liability, blame) responsabilidad f; **they took full ~ for the disaster** aceptaron ser responsables del desastre

responsible /rɪˈspɑːnsəbəl ‖ rɪˈspɒnsəbəl/ adj **(a)** (accountable) (pred) **to be ~ (FOR sth): who's ~?** ¿quién es el responsable?; **a build-up of gas was ~ for the explosion** una acumulación de gas fue la causa de la explosión; **to hold sb ~ for sth** responsabilizar* or hacer* responsable a algn de algo **(b)** (in charge) (pred) **to be ~ FOR sth** ser* responsable DE algo **(c)** (trustworthy) responsable, formal **(d)** (before n) ⟨post⟩ de responsabilidad

responsibly /rɪˈspɑːnsəbli ‖ rɪˈspɒnsɪbli/ adv con responsabilidad, responsablemente

responsive /rɪˈspɑːnsɪv ‖ rɪˈspɒnsɪv/ adj ⟨brakes/engine⟩ sensible; ⟨person/audience⟩ receptivo

rest¹ /rest/ n

I 1 (a) (break) descanso m; **to have a ~** tomarse un descanso **(b)** (relaxation) descanso m, reposo m; **try to get some ~** trata de descansar un poco **2** (motionlessness) **to come to ~** detenerse* **3** (support) apoyo m **4** (Mus) silencio m

II (remainder) **the ~: the ~ of the money** el resto del dinero; **the ~ of the children** los demás niños

rest² vi **1** (relax) descansar **2 (a)** (be supported) **to ~ ON sth** (Const) descansar or apoyarse EN or SOBRE algo **(b)** (be based, depend) **to ~ ON sth** ⟨argument/theory⟩ descansar SOBRE algo **(c)** (stop) **to ~ ON sth/sb** ⟨eyes/gaze⟩ detenerse* SOBRE algo/algn **3** (be responsibility of) **to ~ WITH sb** ⟨responsibility⟩ recaer* SOBRE algn

■ **~ vt 1** (relax) descansar **2** (place for support) apoyar

■ **rest up** [v + adv] (AmE) descansar

rest area n (AmE) área f de reposo

restaurant /ˈrestərɑːnt ‖ ˈrestrɒnt/ n restaurante m, restorán m

restaurant car n (BrE) coche-comedor m, vagón m restaurante

AmC	Central America	Arg	Argentina	Cu	Cuba	Per	Peru
AmL	Latin America	Bol	Bolivia	Ec	Ecuador	RPI	River Plate Area
AmS	South America	Chi	Chile	Esp	Spain	Ur	Uruguay
Andes	Andean Region	CS	Southern Cone	Méx	Mexico	Ven	Venezuela

restful /'restfəl/ adj tranquilo, apacible

restless /'restləs ‖'restlɪs/ adj ⟨person/ manner⟩ inquieto; ⟨waves/wind⟩ (liter) agitado

restoration /'restəreɪʃən/ n **1** **(a)** (of order, peace) restablecimiento m **(b)** (to throne, power) restauración f, reinstauración f **2** (of building, painting) restauración f

restore /rɪ'stɔːr ‖rɪ'stɔː(r)/ vt **1** **(a)** (re-establish) ⟨order/peace⟩ restablecer*; ⟨confidence/health/energy⟩ devolver*; ⟨monarchy/ king⟩ restaurar, reinstaurar **(b)** (give back) (frml) restituir* (frml) **2** ⟨building/painting⟩ restaurar

restrain /rɪ'streɪn/ vt contener*
■ v refl to ~ oneself contenerse*, refrenarse

restrained /rɪ'streɪnd/ adj ⟨person/behavior⟩ moderado, comedido; ⟨colors/style⟩ sobrio

restraint /rɪ'streɪnt/ n **(a)** (self-control) compostura f, circunspección f **(b)** (restriction) limitación f, restricción f

restrict /rɪ'strɪkt/ vt ⟨power/freedom/access⟩ restringir*, limitar; ⟨imports/movements⟩ restringir*

restricted /rɪ'strɪktəd ‖rɪ'strɪktɪd/ adj **(a)** ⟨number/space⟩ limitado **(b)** ⟨information⟩ confidencial; ~ **area** (Mil) zona f restringida

restriction /rɪ'strɪkʃən/ n restricción f

restrictive /rɪ'strɪktɪv/ adj restrictivo

rest room n (AmE) baño m, servicio(s) m(pl)

restructure /ˌriː'strʌktʃər ‖ˌriː'strʌktʃə(r)/ vt reestructurar

rest stop n (AmE) ▷ REST AREA

result¹ /rɪ'zʌlt/ n **1** **(a)** (consequence) resultado m; **the company collapsed, with the ~ that …** la compañía quebró, y como consecuencia … **(b)** (of calculation, exam, contest) resultado m **2** **(a) as a result** (as linker) por consiguiente, por ende (frml) **(b) as a result of** (as prep) a raíz de

result² vi: **to ~ in** traer* como consecuencia, resultar en; **it could ~ in his dismissal** podría ocasionar or acarrear su despido

resultant /rɪ'zʌltənt/, **resulting** /rɪ'zʌltɪŋ/ adj (before n) consiguiente, resultante

resume /rɪ'zuːm ‖rɪ'zjuːm/ vt ⟨work/journey⟩ reanudar
■ ~ vi «negotiations/work» reanudarse, continuar*

resumé /'rezəmeɪ, 'rezə'meɪ ‖'rezjomeɪ/ n **(a)** (summary) resumen m **(b)** (of career) (AmE) currículum m (vitae), historial m personal

resurgence /rɪ'sɜːrdʒəns ‖rɪ'sɜːdʒəns/ n resurgimiento m, renacer m

resurrect /'rezə'rekt/ vt desenterrar*, resucitar

resurrection /'rezə'rekʃən/ n resurrección f

resuscitate /rɪ'sʌsəteɪt ‖rɪ'sʌsɪteɪt/ vt (Med) resucitar

resuscitation /rɪ'sʌsə'teɪʃən ‖rɪˌsʌsɪ'teɪʃən/ n (Med) resucitación f

retail¹ /'riːteɪl/ vt vender al por menor or al detalle
■ ~ vi venderse al por menor

retail² n venta f al por menor or al detalle; (before n) ~ **price** precio m de venta al público, precio m al por menor

retailer /'riːteɪlər ‖'riːteɪlə(r)/ n minorista mf, detallista mf

retail price index n (BrE) índice m de precios al consumo

retain /rɪ'teɪn/ vt ⟨property/money⟩ quedarse con; ⟨authority/power⟩ retener*; ⟨heat⟩ conservar; ⟨moisture/water⟩ retener*; ⟨information⟩ retener*

retake¹ /'riː'teɪk/ vt (past **retook**; past p **retaken**) (Educ) volver* a presentarse a, volver* a presentar

retake² /'riːteɪk/ n (of exam): **to do a ~** volver* a examinarse

retaliate /rɪ'tælieɪt/ vi (Mil) tomar represalias

retaliation /rɪ'tæli'eɪʃən/ n represalias fpl

retarded /rɪ'tɑːrdəd ‖rɪ'tɑːdɪd/ adj (sometimes offensive) retrasado

retch /retʃ/ vi hacer* arcadas

retention /rɪ'tentʃən ‖rɪ'tenʃən/ n retención f

retentive /rɪ'tentɪv/ adj ⟨memory⟩ retentivo

rethink /'riː'θɪŋk/ vt (past & past p **rethought**) reconsiderar, replantearse

reticence /'retəsəns ‖'retɪsəns/ n reticencia f

reticent /'retəsənt ‖'retɪsənt/ adj reticente

retina /'retnə ‖'retɪnə/ n (pl **-nas** or **-nae** /-niː/) retina f

retinue /'retnuː ‖'retɪnjuː/ n séquito m, comitiva f

retire /rɪ'taɪr ‖rɪ'taɪə(r)/ vi **1** (from occupation) jubilarse, retirarse; ⟨soldier/athlete⟩ retirarse **2** **(a)** (retreat, withdraw) (frml) retirarse **(b)** (go to bed) (frml or hum) retirarse a sus (or mis etc) aposentos (frml o hum)

retired /rɪ'taɪrd ‖rɪ'taɪəd/ adj jubilado, retirado

retirement /rɪ'taɪrmənt ‖rɪ'taɪəmənt/ n (from job) jubilación f, retiro m

retiring /rɪ'taɪrɪŋ ‖rɪ'taɪərɪŋ/ adj (shy) retraído

retort¹ /rɪ'tɔːrt ‖rɪ'tɔːt/ vt replicar* (liter), contestar

retort² n réplica f (liter), contestación f

retrace /'riː'treɪs/ vt **to ~ one's steps** volver* sobre sus (or mis etc) pasos

retract /rɪ'trækt/ vt **(a)** ⟨allegation/statement⟩ retirar **(b)** ⟨undercarriage⟩ replegar*, levantar

retrain /'riː'treɪn/ vi hacer* un curso de reciclaje or recapacitación

retread¹ /'riː'tred/ vt (past and past p **~ed**) ⟨tire⟩ recauchutar, recauchar, reencauchar (AmC, Ven)

retread² /'riːtred/ n neumático m recauchutado or recauchado or (AmC, Ven) reencauchado, llanta f vulcanizada (AmL)

retreat¹ /rɪ'triːt/ vi retirarse

retreat² n **1** (Mil) retirada f, repliegue m **2** **(a)** (place) refugio m **(b)** (Relig) retiro m espiritual

retrial /'riː'traɪəl/ n nuevo juicio m

retribution /'retrə'bjuːʃən ‖ˌretrɪ'bjuːʃən/ n castigo m

retrieve /rɪ'triːv/ vt ⟨object/data⟩ recuperar

retriever /rɪ'triːvər ‖rɪ'triːvə(r)/ n perro m cobrador

retrograde /'retrəgreɪd/ adj retrógrado

retrospect /'retrəspekt/ n: **in ~** mirando hacia atrás, en retrospectiva

retrospective¹ /'retrə'spektɪv/ adj retrospectivo

r

retrospective² n (exposición f)
retrospectiva f

return¹ /rɪˈtɜːrn ‖rɪˈtɜːn/ vi (a) (to place)
volver*, regresar; **to ~ TO sth** (to former activity,
state) volver* A algo (b) (reappear) «symptom»
volver* a aparecer; «doubts/suspicions»
resurgir*
■ ~ vt 1 (a) (give back) devolver*, regresar (AmL
exc CS), restituir* (frml) (b) (reciprocate) «affection»
corresponder a; «blow/favor» devolver*; «greeting»
devolver*, corresponder a; **to ~ sb's call**
devolverle* la llamada a algn (c) (Sport) «ball»
devolver* 2 (Law) «verdict» emitir

return² n 1 (a) (to place) regreso m, vuelta f,
retorno m (frml o liter) (b) (reappearance)
reaparición f; **many happy ~s of the day!** ¡que
cumplas muchos más! 2 (to owner) devolución f,
regreso m (AmL) 3 (in phrases) **in ~ (FOR sth)** a
cambio (DE algo) 4 (profit) rendimiento m 5 (tax
~) declaración f (de la renta or de impuestos)
6 (ticket) (BrE) boleto m or (Esp) billete m de ida y
vuelta, boleto m de viaje redondo (Méx)

return³ adj (before n) «journey/flight» de vuelta,
de regreso; «ticket/fare» (BrE) de ida y vuelta, de
viaje redondo (Méx)

returnable /rɪˈtɜːrnəbəl ‖rɪˈtɜːnəbəl/ adj
«deposit» reembolsable, reintegrable; «bottle»
retornable

reunion /riːˈjuːnjən/ n reunión f, reencuentro
m; **a family ~** una reunión familiar

reunite /riːjuˈnaɪt/ vt «family/party» volver* a
unir; **to be ~d with sb** reencontrarse* con algn

reusable /riːˈjuːzəbəl/ adj reutilizable

reuse /riːˈjuːz/ vt reutilizar*, volver* a usar

rev¹ /rev/ n revolución f

rev² vt **-vv- ~ (up)** «engine/car» acelerar (sin
desplazarse)

revalue /riːˈvæljuː/, (AmE also) **revaluate**
/-jueɪt/ vt «currency» revalorizar*, revaluar* (esp
AmL); «house» reevaluar*, revalorar

revamp /riːˈvæmp/ vt «kitchen/interior»
reformar; «image» modernizar*; «image»
cambiar; «organization» modernizar*

reveal /rɪˈviːl/ vt (a) (disclose) revelar, develar
(AmL), desvelar (Esp) (b) (bring to view) dejar ver

revealing /rɪˈviːlɪŋ/ adj revelador

revel /ˈrevəl/ vi, (BrE) **-ll-** (enjoy greatly) **to ~ IN**
sth deleitarse CON o EN algo

revelation /revəˈleɪʃən/ n (a) (disclosure)
revelación f (b) (Bib): **(the Book of) Revelations** el
Apocalipsis

reveler, (BrE) **reveller** /ˈrevələr ‖ˈrevələ(r)/ n
(liter) juerguista mf (fam)

revelry /ˈrevəlri/ n (pl **-ries**) jolgorio m

revenge¹ /rɪˈvendʒ/ n venganza f; **to take ~**
vengarse*, desquitarse

revenge² vt vengar*

revenue /ˈrevənuː ‖ˈrevənjuː/ n (a) (Tax)
rentas fpl públicas (b) **revenues** pl ingresos
mpl

reverberate /rɪˈvɜːrbəreɪt ‖rɪˈvɜːbəreɪt/ vi
retumbar

revere /rɪˈvɪr ‖rɪˈvɪə(r)/ vt (frml) reverenciar
(frml)

reverence /ˈrevrəns, ˈrevərəns/ n reverencia f

Reverend adj (in titles) reverendo

reverent /ˈrevrənt, ˈrevərənt/ adj reverente

reverie /ˈrevəri/ n ensueño m

reversal /rɪˈvɜːrsəl ‖rɪˈvɜːsəl/ n (a) (inversion)
inversión f (b) (of trend, policy) cambio m completo
or total (c) (setback) (frml) revés m

reverse¹ /rɪˈvɜːrs ‖rɪˈvɜːs/ n 1 (of picture,
paper) reverso m, dorso m; (of cloth, garment) revés
m; (of coin) reverso m 2 (no pl) (opposite) **the ~** lo
contrario 3 (a) (gear) (no art) marcha f atrás,
reversa f (Col, Méx) 4 (setback) (frml) revés m

reverse² vt 1 (a) (transpose) «roles/positions»
invertir*; **to ~ the charges** (BrE Telec) llamar a
cobro revertido or (Chi, Méx) por cobrar (b) (invert)
«order/process» invertir* 2 (undo, negate) «policy»
cambiar radicalmente; «trend» invertir* el
sentido de; «ruling» revocar* 3 «vehicle»: **she ~d**
her car around the corner dobló la esquina dando
marcha atrás or (Col, Méx) en reversa
■ ~ vi «vehicle/driver» dar* marcha atrás, meter
reversa (Col, Méx)

reverse³ adj (before n) (a) (backward, opposite)
«movement/direction/trend» contrario, inverso; **in**
~ order en orden inverso (b) (back): **the ~ side**
(of cloth) el revés; (of paper) el reverso, el dorso

reverse-charge call /rɪˈvɜːsˈtʃɑːrdʒ
‖rɪˈvɜːsˈtʃɑːdʒ/ n (BrE) llamada f a cobro
revertido or (Chi, Méx) por cobrar

reversible /rɪˈvɜːrsəbəl ‖rɪˈvɜːsəbəl/ adj
reversible

reversion /rɪˈvɜːrʒən ‖rɪˈvɜːʃən/ n (to former
state, practice) vuelta f, reversión f (frml)

revert /rɪˈvɜːrt ‖rɪˈvɜːt/ vi: **to ~ to** volver a

review¹ /rɪˈvjuː/ n 1 (a) (of book, film) crítica
f, reseña f (b) (report, summary) resumen m, reseña
f 2 (a) (reconsideration) revisión f (b) (for exam)
(AmE) repaso m

review² vt 1 (a) (consider) «situation»
examinar, estudiar (b) (reconsider) «policy/case»
reconsiderar; «salary» reajustar 2 (a)
(summarize) «news/events» resumir, reseñar (b)
«book/play» hacer* (or escribir* etc) la crítica de,
reseñar 3 (for exam) (AmE) repasar

revise /rɪˈvaɪz/ vt (a) (alter) modificar* (b) (for
exam) (BrE) repasar
■ ~ vi (BrE) repasar

revision /rɪˈvɪʒən/ n 1 (a) (alteration)
modificación f (b) (text) edición f corregida 2 (for
exam) (BrE) repaso m

revitalize /riːˈvaɪtəlaɪz/ vt vigorizar*, darle*
vitalidad a; «economy» estimular, reactivar

revival /rɪˈvaɪvəl/ n (renewal, upsurge): **a ~ of**
interest in ... un renovado interés por ...;
economic ~ reactivación f económica; **a religious**
~ un renacer or un renacimiento religioso (b)
(Med) reanimación f

revive /rɪˈvaɪv/ vt (a) (Med) reanimar, resucitar
(b) (revitalize) «economy» reactivar, estimular;
«interest/friendship» hacer* renacer, reavivar (c)
«custom/practice» restablecer*
■ ~ vi «trade» reactivarse, repuntar; «hope/
interest» renacer*, resurgir*; «patient»
reanimarse; «plant» revivir

revoke /rɪˈvəʊk/ vt revocar*

revolt¹ /rɪˈvəʊlt/ n revuelta f, sublevación f

revolt² vi sublevarse
■ ~ vt darle* asco a

revolting /rɪˈvəʊltɪŋ/ adj (nauseating) repugnante; (horrible) (colloq) asqueroso, horrible

revolution /revəˈluːʃən/ n revolución f

revolutionary¹ /revəˈluːʃəneri ‖ˌrevəˈluːʃənəri/ adj revolucionario

revolutionary² n (pl **-ries**) revolucionario, -ria m,f

revolutionize /revəˈluːʃənaɪz/ vt revolucionar

revolve /rɪˈvɑːlv ‖rɪˈvɒlv/ vi (a) (rotate) girar (b) **revolving** pres p ⟨chair/door⟩ giratorio

revolver /rɪˈvɑːlvər ‖rɪˈvɒlvə(r)/ n revólver m

revue /rɪˈvjuː/ n revista f

revulsion /rɪˈvʌlʃən/ n repugnancia f, asco m

reward¹ /rɪˈwɔːrd ‖rɪˈwɔːd/ n recompensa f

reward² vt premiar, recompensar

rewarding /rɪˈwɔːrdɪŋ ‖rɪˈwɔːdɪŋ/ adj gratificante

rewind /riːˈwaɪnd/ vt (past & past p **rewound**) rebobinar

rewire /riːˈwaɪr ‖ˌriːˈwaɪə(r)/ vt ⟨house⟩ renovar* la instalación eléctrica de

reword /riːˈwɜːrd ‖ˌriːˈwɜːd/ vt ⟨question⟩ formular de otra manera; ⟨statement⟩ volver* a redactar

rewound /riːˈwaʊnd/ past & past p of REWIND

rewrite /riːˈraɪt/ vt (past **rewrote**; past p **rewritten**) volver* a escribir or redactar

rhapsody /ˈræpsədi/ n (pl **-dies**) rapsodia f

rhetoric /ˈretərɪk/ n retórica f

rhetorical /rɪˈtɔːrɪkəl ‖rɪˈtɒrɪkəl/ adj retórico

rheumatic /ruːˈmætɪk/ adj reumático

rheumatism /ˈruːmətɪzəm/ n reumatismo m

Rhine /raɪn/ n the ~ el Rin

rhino /ˈraɪnəʊ/ n (pl ~ or ~**s**) rinoceronte m

rhinoceros /raɪˈnɑːsrəs, -sərəs ‖raɪˈnɒsərəs, -srəs/ n (pl **-oses** or ~) rinoceronte m

rhubarb /ˈruːbɑːrb ‖ˈruːbɑːb/ n ruibarbo m

rhyme¹ /raɪm/ n (a) (correspondence of sound) rima f (b) (poem) rima f, poema m

rhyme² vi/t rimar

rhythm /ˈrɪðəm/ n ritmo m

rhythmic /ˈrɪðmɪk/, **-mical** /-mɪkəl/ adj rítmico

RI = **Rhode Island**

rib /rɪb/ n (Anat, Culin) costilla f

ribald /ˈrɪbəld/ adj ⟨comments/humor⟩ procaz, picaresco

ribbed /rɪbd/ adj ⟨neck/sleeves⟩ en punto elástico, en canalé, en resorte (AmC, Col, Méx)

ribbon /ˈrɪbən/ n (a) (strip of fabric) cinta f, listón m (Méx) (b) (as insignia, award) galón m (c) (of typewriter, printer etc) cinta f (d) **ribbons** pl (shreds) jirones mpl

ribcage /ˈrɪbkeɪdʒ/ n caja f torácica

rice /raɪs/ n arroz m; (before n) ~ **pudding** arroz con leche

rice: ~**field** n arrozal m; ~ **paper** n papel m de arroz

rich /rɪtʃ/ adj **-er, -est** ⓵ (a) (wealthy) rico (b) (opulent) ⟨banquet⟩ suntuoso; ⟨furnishings⟩ lujoso, suntuoso (c) (abundant) ⟨harvest/supply⟩ abundante; ⟨reward⟩ generoso; ⟨history/

experience⟩ rico ⓶ (a) ⟨food⟩ con alto contenido de grasas, huevos, azúcar etc (b) ⟨soil⟩ rico; ⟨color⟩ cálido e intenso

riches /ˈrɪtʃəz ‖ˈrɪtʃɪz/ pl n riquezas fpl

richness /ˈrɪtʃnəs ‖ˈrɪtʃnɪs/ n riqueza f

rickety /ˈrɪkəti/ adj desvencijado

rickshaw /ˈrɪkʃɔː/ n: calesa oriental de dos ruedas tirada por un hombre

ricochet /ˈrɪkəʃeɪ/ vi **-chets** /-ʃeɪz/, **-cheting** /-ʃeɪɪŋ/, **-cheted** /-ʃeɪd/ to ~ (OFF sth) rebotar (EN algo)

rid /rɪd/ vt (pres p **ridding**; past & past p **rid**): they ~ **the country of corruption** libraron al país de la corrupción; **to get** ~ **of** ⟨unwanted object⟩ deshacerse* de; ⟨person, cold⟩ quitarse de encima; ⟨smell⟩ quitar

riddance /ˈrɪdns/ n: **good** ~! (colloq) ¡adiós y buen viaje! (fam & iró)

ridden /ˈrɪdn/ past p of RIDE¹

riddle¹ /ˈrɪdl/ n (a) (puzzle) adivinanza f, acertijo m (b) (mystery) enigma m, misterio m

riddle² vt (perforate) (often pass) **to be** ~**d WITH sth**: his body was ~d with bullets lo habían acribillado a balazos; she was ~d with cancer tenía cáncer por todo el cuerpo

ride¹ /raɪd/ (past **rode**; past p **ridden**) vt ⓵ (a) **to** ~ **a horse** montar a caballo; **to** ~ **a bicycle/motorbike** montar or (AmL tb) andar* en bicicleta/moto (b) (AmE) ⟨bus/subway/train⟩ ir* en ⓶ (be carried upon) ⟨waves/wind⟩ dejarse llevar por

■ ~ vi (a) (on horse) montar or (AmL tb) andar* a caballo; **to go riding** ir* a montar or (AmL tb) a andar a caballo (b) (on bicycle, in vehicle) ir*; **we rode into town** fuimos al centro en bicicleta (or en moto etc)

■ **ride out** [v + o + adv, v + adv + o] aguantar, sobrellevar

■ **ride up** [v + adv] subirse

ride² n (on horse, in vehicle etc): let's go for a ~ **on our bikes/in your car** vamos a dar una vuelta or un paseo en bicicleta/en tu coche; **it was a long** ~ fue un viaje largo; **to give sb a** ~ (esp AmE) llevar a algn en coche, darle* un aventón (Méx) or (Col fam) una palomita a algn; **to take sb for a** ~ (colloq) tomarle el pelo a algn (fam)

rider /ˈraɪdər ‖ˈraɪdə(r)/ n ⓵ (a) (on horseback) jinete mf; (on bicycle) ciclista mf; (on motorbike) motociclista mf, motorista mf (b) (of subway, bus) (AmE) pasajero, -ra m,f ⓶ (appended statement) cláusula f adicional; (condition) condición f

ridge /rɪdʒ/ n (of hills) cadena f; (hilltop) cresta f

ridicule¹ /ˈrɪdəkjuːl ‖ˈrɪdɪkjuːl/ n burlas fpl

ridicule² vt ridiculizar*, burlarse de

ridiculous /rɪˈdɪkjələs ‖rɪˈdɪkjʊləs/ adj ridículo

riding /ˈraɪdɪŋ/ n equitación f; (before n) ⟨school/lesson⟩ de equitación; ⟨breeches/boots⟩ de montar

rife /raɪf/ adj ⟨pred⟩ extendido; **disease is** ~ cunden las enfermedades; **corruption is** ~ reina la corrupción

riffraff /ˈrɪfræf/ n (+ sing or pl vb) chusma f

rifle¹ /ˈraɪfəl/ n rifle m, fusil m

rifle² vi to ~ **THROUGH sth** hojear algo

rift /rɪft/ n (a) (in rock) fisura f (b) (within party) escisión f; (between people) distanciamiento m; (between countries) ruptura f

rig[1] /rɪg/ n (oil ~) plataforma f petrolífera or petrolera; (derrick) torre f de perforación

rig[2] **-gg-** vt ⟨election/contest⟩ amañar; ⟨fight⟩ arreglar

■ **rig out** [v + o + adv, v + adv + o] (colloq) equipar

■ **rig up** [v + o + adv, v + adv + o] (set up) instalar

rigging /'rɪgɪŋ/ n (Naut) jarcia(s) f(pl)

right[1] /raɪt/ adj **1** (correct) ⟨answer/ interpretation⟩ correcto; **are we going in the ~ direction?** ¿vamos bien?; **did you press the ~ button?** ¿apretaste el botón que debías?; **do you have the ~ change?** ¿tienes el cambio justo?; **do you have the ~ time?** ¿tienes hora (buena)? **2** (not mistaken): **to be ~** «person» tener* razón, estar* en lo cierto; «clock» estar* bien; **you got two answers ~** acertaste dos respuestas; **to be ~ to + INF** hacer* bien en + INF **3** (good, suitable) adecuado, apropiado; **if the price is ~** si está bien de precio; **just ~** perfecto; **the ~ person for the job** la persona indicada para el puesto **4** (just, moral) (pred) **to be ~** ser* justo **5** (pred) (in order): **to put sth ~** arreglar algo **6** (opposite of left) (before n) ⟨side/ear/shoe⟩ derecho

right[2] adv **1** (correctly, well) bien, correctamente; **nothing goes ~ for them** todo les sale mal, nada les sale bien; ▶ **SERVE**[1] vt 2 **2** (a) (all the way, completely): **the road goes ~ along the coast** la carretera bordea toda la costa; **~ from the start** desde el principio (b) (directly): **it's ~ in front of you** lo tienes allí delante; **he was ~ here/there** estaba aquí mismo/allí mismo; **~ now** ahora mismo (c) (immediately): **~ after lunch** inmediatamente después de comer; **I'll be ~ back** vuelvo enseguida **3** ⟨turn/look⟩ a la derecha

right[3] n **1** (a) (entitlement) derecho m; **~ to sth/ + INF** derecho A algo/+ INF; **the title is his by ~** el título le corresponde a él (b) **rights** pl derechos mpl **2** (what is correct): **to know ~ from wrong** saber* distinguir entre el bien y el mal; **to be in the ~** tener* razón, llevar la razón, estar* en lo cierto; **to put** o **set sth to ~s** (esp BrE) arreglar algo **3** (a) (opposite of left) derecha f; **on the ~** a la derecha; **to drive on the ~** manejar or (Esp) conducir* por la derecha (b) (right turn): **to make** o (BrE) **take a ~** girar a la derecha (c) (Sport) (hand) derecha f **4** (Pol) **the ~** la derecha

right[4] vt (a) (set upright) enderezar* (b) (redress) reparar; **to ~ a wrong** reparar un daño

right[5] interj (colloq) ¡bueno!, ¡vale! (Esp fam)

right: **~ angle** n ángulo m recto; **~ away** adv enseguida

righteous /'raɪtʃəs/ adj (a) ⟨indignation⟩ justificado (b) ⟨person⟩ recto, honrado

rightful /'raɪtfəl/ adj (before n) ⟨owner/heir⟩ legítimo; ⟨share/reward⟩ justo

right: **~-hand** /'raɪt'hænd/ adj (before n) de la derecha; **on the ~-hand side** a la derecha, a mano derecha; **~-handed** /'raɪt'hændəd ‖ ,raɪt'hændɪd/ adj ⟨person⟩ diestro; **~-hand man** /'raɪt'hænd/ n brazo m derecho

rightly /'raɪtli/ adv (a) (correctly, accurately): **if I remember ~** si mal no recuerdo; **I can't ~ say** (colloq) no sabría decir exactamente (b) (justly) con toda la razón; **~ or wrongly** justa o injustamente

right: **~ of way** n (precedence in traffic) preferencia f; **~ on** adj (AmE colloq) (pred): **his analysis was ~ on** su análisis era muy acertado or (fam) daba justo en el clavo; **~-on** /'raɪt'ɒn ‖ ,raɪt'ɒn/ adj (BrE colloq & hum) progre (fam); **~ wing** n (a) (Pol) (ala f♯) derecha f (b) (Sport) ala f♯ derecha; **~-wing** /'raɪt'wɪŋ/ adj derechista; **~-winger** /'raɪt,wɪŋər ‖ 'raɪt,wɪŋə(r)/ n (Pol) derechista mf

rigid /'rɪdʒəd ‖ 'rɪdʒɪd/ adj (a) (stiff) rígido (b) ⟨discipline⟩ estricto; ⟨person/principles⟩ inflexible

rigmarole /'rɪgmərəʊl/ n (colloq) lío m (fam)

rigor, (BrE) **rigour** /'rɪgər ‖ 'rɪgə(r)/ n rigor m

rigor mortis /'rɪgər'mɔːrtəs ‖ ,rɪgə'mɔːtɪs/ n rigidez f cadavérica; **~ ~ had set in** el cuerpo ya estaba rígido

rigorous /'rɪgərəs/ adj riguroso

rigour (BrE) ▶ **RIGOR**

rile /raɪl/ vt (colloq) irritar

rim /rɪm/ n (of cup, bowl) borde m; (of spectacles) montura f, armazón m or f; (of wheel) (Auto) llanta f, rin m (Col, Méx); (of bicycle wheel) aro m

rind /raɪnd/ n (of lemon, orange) cáscara f, corteza f; (of cheese) corteza f; (of bacon) piel f

ring[1] /rɪŋ/ n **1** (a) (on finger) anillo m; (woman's) anillo m, sortija f (b) (circle) círculo m; **to stand in a ~** hacer* un corro, formar un círculo (c) (burner) (BrE) quemador m, hornilla f (AmL exc CS), hornillo m (Esp) **2** (a) (in boxing, wrestling) cuadrilátero m, ring m (b) (in circus) pista f (c) (bull ~) ruedo m **3** (of criminals) red f, banda f **4** (a) (sound of bell) (of phone) timbrazo m; **there was a ~ at the door** sonó el timbre de la puerta (b) (telephone call) (BrE) (no pl): **to give sb a ~** llamar (por teléfono) a algn

ring[2] (past **rang**; past p **rung**) vi **1** (a) (make sound) sonar* (b) (operate bell) «person» tocar* el timbre, llamar al timbre **2** (telephone) (BrE) llamar (por teléfono), telefonear **3** (a) (resound) resonar*; **to ~ true** ser* or sonar* convincente (b) «ears» zumbar

■ **~** vt **1** (a) ⟨bell⟩ tocar* (b) (telephone) ⟨person⟩ (BrE) llamar (por teléfono) **2** (past & past p **ringed**) (a) (surround) cercar*, rodear (b) (with pen, pencil) marcar* con un círculo

■ **ring back** (BrE) **1** [v + adv] volver* a llamar **2** [v + o + adv] (ring again) volver* a llamar; (return call) llamar

■ **ring off** [v + adv] (BrE) colgar*, cortar (CS)

■ **ring out** [v + adv] «*shot/voice*» oírse*, resonar*; «*bells*» sonar*, resonar*

■ **ring up** ⟦1⟧ [v + o + adv, v + adv + o] (BrE) ▶ RING² vt 1B

⟦2⟧ [v + adv] (BrE) ▶ RING² vi 2

ring binder n archivador m, carpeta f de anillos or (Esp) de anillas

ringing /'rɪŋɪŋ/ n (a) (of bell) repique m, toque m (b) (of doorbell, telephone) timbre m (c) (in ears) zumbido m

ringleader /'rɪŋ‚liːdər ‖'rɪŋ‚liːdə(r)/ n cabecilla mf

ringlet /'rɪŋlət/ n tirabuzón m, rizo m

ring road n (BrE) carretera f de circunvalación

rink /rɪŋk/ n (ice ~) pista f de hielo; (skating ~) pista f de patinaje

rinse¹ /rɪns/ vt (a) (wash) ⟨*cutlery/hands*⟩ enjuagar*; ⟨*rice/mushrooms*⟩ lavar (b) (to remove soap) ⟨*clothes/hair*⟩ enjuagar*, aclarar (Esp); ⟨*dishes*⟩ enjuagar*

rinse² n (a) (wash) enjuague m (b) (to remove soap — from clothes) enjuague m, aclarado m (Esp); (— from dishes) enjuague m (c) (tint) tintura f (*no permanente*)

riot¹ /'raɪət/ n (a) (disorder) disturbio m; (mutiny) motín m; **to run ~** «*fans*» descontrolarse, desmadrarse (fam); **she let her imagination run ~** dio rienda suelta a su imaginación; (*before n*) ⟨*gear/shield*⟩ antidisturbios *adj inv*; **the ~ squad** la brigada antidisturbios (b) (profusion): **a ~ of color** un derroche or una profusión de color

riot² vi causar disturbios or desórdenes; «*prisoners*» amotinarse

rioter /'raɪətər ‖'raɪətə(r)/ n alborotador, -dora m,f

rioting /'raɪətɪŋ/ n disturbios mpl

riotous /'raɪətəs/ adj (a) ⟨*crowd/behavior*⟩ descontrolado, desenfrenado (b) ⟨*occasion*⟩ desenfrenado

rip¹ /rɪp/ **-pp-** vt ⟨*cloth*⟩ rasgar*, romper*; ⟨*skirt/trousers*⟩ hacerse* un rasgón en; **she ~ped the letter open** abrió la carta de un rasgón

■ ~ vi rasgarse*

■ **rip off** [v + o + adv, v + adv + o] ⟦1⟧ (remove) arrancar* ⟦2⟧ (sl) (a) (cheat) timar, estafar, tracalear (Méx, Ven fam) (b) (steal) afanar (arg), robar

■ **rip up** [v + o + adv, v + adv + o] romper*, hacer* pedazos

rip² n rasgón m, desgarrón m

RIP (= **rest in peace**) R.I.P.

rip cord n cordón m de apertura

ripe /raɪp/ adj ⟨*fruit*⟩ maduro; ⟨*cheese*⟩ a punto

ripen /'raɪpən/ vi madurar

■ ~ vt hacer* madurar

rip-off /'rɪpɔːf ‖'rɪpɒf/ n (colloq) (con) timo m, estafa f; (theft) robo m; (copy) plagio m

ripple¹ /'rɪpəl/ n (on water) onda f; **a ~ of applause** un breve aplauso

ripple² vi (a) «*water*» rizarse*; «*wheat/grass*» mecerse* (b) «*muscles*» tensarse

■ ~ vt ⟨*muscles*⟩ tensar; **rippling** *pres p* ⟨*muscles*⟩ tensado

rise¹ /raɪz/ n ⟦1⟧ (a) (upward movement — of tide, level) subida f; (— in pitch) elevación f (b) (increase — in prices, interest rates) subida f, aumento m, alza f‡ (frml); (— in pressure, temperature) aumento m,

subida f; (— in number, amount) aumento m (c) (in pay) (BrE) aumento m, incremento m (frml); **a pay ~** un aumento or (frml) un incremento salarial ⟦2⟧ (advance) (to fame, power) ascenso m, ascensión f; (of movement, ideology) surgimiento m; **to give ~ to sth** ⟨*to belief*⟩ dar* origen or lugar a algo; ⟨*to dispute*⟩ ocasionar or causar algo; ⟨*to ideas*⟩ suscitar algo

⟦3⟧ (slope) subida f, cuesta f

rise² (*past* **rose**; *past p* **risen** /'rɪzn/) vi ⟦1⟧ (a) (come, go up) subir; «*sun/moon*» salir*; «*river*» crecer*; «*cake*» subir; **to ~ to the surface** salir* or subir a la superficie (b) (increase) «*price/temperature/pressure*» subir, aumentar; «*wind*» arreciar; «*wage/amount*» aumentar; «*tension*» crecer*, aumentar (c) «*sound*» (become louder) aumentar de volumen; (become higher) subir de tono (d) (improve) «*standard*» mejorar; **their spirits rose** se les levantó el ánimo, se animaron ⟦2⟧ (a) (slope upward) «*ground/land*» elevarse (b) (extend upwards) «*building/hill*» levantarse, alzarse*

⟦3⟧ (a) (stand up) «*person/audience*» (frml) ponerse* de pie, levantarse, pararse (AmL) (b) (out of bed) levantarse

⟦4⟧ (in rank): **she has ~n in my estimation** ha ganado en mi estima

⟦5⟧ (revolt) **to ~** (up) levantarse, alzarse*

⟦6⟧ (originate) «*river*» (frml) nacer*

■ **rise above** [v + prep + o] ⟨*disability*⟩ sobreponerse* a; ⟨*difficulty*⟩ superar

■ **rise to** [v + prep + o] (respond to): **to ~ to the challenge** aceptar el reto; **to ~ to the occasion** estar* a la altura de las circunstancias

rising¹ /'raɪzɪŋ/ n (rebellion) levantamiento m

rising² adj (*before n*) (a) ⟨*tide/level*⟩ creciente; **the ~ sun** el sol naciente (b) (increasing) ⟨*number*⟩ creciente; ⟨*temperature*⟩ creciente, en aumento; ⟨*prices/interest rates*⟩ en alza or en aumento (c) (sloping) en pendiente

rising damp n humedad f (*que sube de los cimientos por las paredes*)

risk¹ /rɪsk/ n riesgo m; **those most at ~ from the disease** los que corren mayor riesgo or peligro de contraer la enfermedad; **at the ~ of -ING** a riesgo de + INF; **to take a ~** correr un riesgo; **to take ~s** arriesgarse, correr riesgos

risk² vt (a) (put in danger) arriesgar*, poner* en peligro (b) (expose oneself to) arriesgarse* a; **to ~ -ING** arriesgarse* A or correr el riesgo DE + INF

risky /'rɪski/ adj **-kier, -kiest** arriesgado, riesgoso (AmL)

risqué /rɪ'skeɪ, 'rɪskeɪ/ adj atrevido, subido de tono

rite /raɪt/ n rito m

ritual¹ /'rɪtʃuəl/ n ritual m

ritual² adj ritual

rival¹ /'raɪvəl/ n rival mf

rival² adj (*before n*) ⟨*company*⟩ rival, competidor

rival³ vt, (BrE) **-ll-**: **his voice ~s that of the lead singer** su voz no tiene nada que envidiarle a la del cantante principal

rivalry /'raɪvəlri/ n (pl **-ries**) rivalidad f, competencia f

river /'rɪvər ‖'rɪvə(r)/ n río m; (*before n*) ⟨*traffic/port*⟩ fluvial; ⟨*mouth/basin*⟩ del río

river: ~bank n ribera f, margen f (*de un río*); ···▸

∼bed n lecho m (de un río); **R∼ Plate** n Río m de la Plata; **∼side** n ribera f, margen f (de un río); (before n) ‹café› a orillas del río

rivet¹ /'rɪvət ‖'rɪvɪt/ n remache m, roblón m

rivet² vt (a) (attach) remachar (b) (fix) (usu pass): my eyes were ∼ed to the screen estaba absorto, con los ojos clavados en la pantalla; their eyes were ∼ed on her no le quitaban los ojos de encima (c) (fascinate) (usu pass) fascinar

riveting /'rɪvətɪŋ/ adj fascinante

Riviera /rɪvi'erə ‖rɪvi'eərə/ n: the (French) ∼ la Costa Azul; the Italian ∼ la Riviera

RN n (in UK) = **Royal Navy**

RNA n (= ribonucleic acid) RNA m, ARN m

road /rəʊd/ n **1** (for vehicles — in town) calle f; (— out of town) carretera f; (— minor) camino m; **by ∼** por carretera, por tierra; (before n) ‹accident› de tráfico or (AmL tb) de tránsito; **∼ safety** seguridad f en la carretera; **∼ sign** señal f vial or de tráfico or (AmL tb) de tránsito; **∼ tax** impuesto m de rodaje
2 (route, way) camino m; **the economy is on the ∼ to recovery** la economía está en vías de recuperación
3 **to be on the road** ‹car› estar* en circulación; **we've been on the ∼ for four days** llevamos cuatro días viajando

road: **∼block** n control m (de carretera); **∼ hog** n (colloq) loco, -ca m,f del volante; **∼ hump** n badén m, tope m (Méx), lomo m de burro (RPl); **∼map** n mapa m de carreteras; **∼ rage** n (Auto) agresión f (provocada por el estrés que supone conducir en condiciones difíciles); **∼side** n borde m de la carretera/del camino; **∼ sweeper** n (person) barrendero, -ra m,f; (machine) barredera f, barredora f; **∼works** pl n (BrE) obras fpl (de vialidad); **∼worthy** adj **-thier, -thiest** apto para circular

roam /rəʊm/ vt vagar* de or deambular por
■ ∼ vi vagar*, errar* (liter)

roar¹ /rɔːr ‖rɔː(r)/ vi «lion/engine» rugir*; «sea/wind/fire» bramar, rugir*; **to ∼ with laughter** reírse* a carcajadas

roar² n (of lion, tiger) rugido m; (of person) rugido m, bramido m; (of thunder) estruendo m; (of traffic, engine, guns) estruendo m; (of crowd) clamor m

roaring /'rɔːrɪŋ/ adj (before n) ‹waves› rugiente; ‹traffic› estruendoso

roast¹ /rəʊst/ adj asado; **∼ beef** rosbif m, rosbeef m

roast² n asado m (al horno)

roast³ vt ‹meat/potatoes› asar; ‹coffee beans› tostar*, torrefaccionar; ‹peanuts› tostar*
■ ∼ vi asarse

roasting /'rəʊstɪŋ/ adj (colloq): it's absolutely ∼ hace un calor que te asas (fam)

rob /rɑːb ‖rɒb/ vt **-bb-** (a) (steal from) ‹person› robarle a; ‹bank› asaltar, atracar*, robar (b) (deprive) **to ∼ sb/sth or sth** privar a algn/algo DE algo

robber /'rɑːbər ‖'rɒbə(r)/ n ladrón, -drona m,f; **bank ∼** atracador, -dora m,f or asaltante mf de bancos

robbery /'rɑːbəri ‖'rɒbəri/ n (pl **-ries**) robo m, asalto m; **bank ∼** asalto m or atraco m a un banco

robe /rəʊb/ n (a) (worn by magistrates) (often pl) toga f (b) (worn in house) bata f, salto m de cama (CS)

robin /'rɑːbən ‖'rɒbɪn/ n (European) petirrojo m; (N. American) ceón m, tordo m norteamericano

robot /'rəʊbɑːt ‖'rəʊbɒt/ n robot m

robust /rəʊ'bʌst/ adj ‹person/animal› robusto; ‹health› resistente, sólido

rock¹ /rɑːk ‖rɒk/ n **1** (substance) roca f **2** (a) (crag, cliff) peñasco m, peñón m (b) (in sea) roca f, escollo m; **on the ∼s** con hielo; **their marriage is on the ∼s** su matrimonio anda muy mal (c) (boulder) roca f (d) (stone) (esp AmE) piedra f **3** (music) rock m

rock² vt (a) (gently) ‹cradle› mecer*; ‹child› acunar (b) (violently) sacudir, estremecer*; «scandal» convulsionar, conmocionar
■ ∼ vi (gently) mecerse*, balancearse

rock: **∼ and roll** n ▶ ROCK'N'ROLL; **∼bottom** /'rɑːk'bɑːtəm ‖rɒk'bɒtəm/ n: **to hit/reach ∼bottom** tocar* fondo; **∼ climbing** /'rɑːk'klaɪmɪŋ ‖'rɒk'klaɪmɪŋ/ n escalada f en roca

rocket¹ /'rɑːkət ‖'rɒkɪt/ n (a) (spacecraft) cohete m espacial (b) (missile) cohete m, misil m; (before n) **∼ launcher** lanzacohetes m, lanzamisiles m

rocket² vi «price» dispararse, ponerse* por las nubes

rock: **∼face** n pared f rocosa; **∼-hard** /'rɑːk'hɑːrd ‖rɒk'hɑːd/ adj (duro) como una piedra

rocking /'rɑːkɪŋ ‖'rɒkɪŋ/: **∼ chair** n mecedora f; **∼ horse** n caballito m mecedor or de balancín

rock'n'roll /'rɑːkən'rəʊl ‖rɒkən'rəʊl/ n rocanrol m, rock and roll m

rocky /'rɑːki ‖'rɒki/ adj **rockier, rockiest** **1** ‹ground› rocoso; ‹path› pedregoso **2** (unsteady) ‹period› de incertidumbre; ‹base› nada sólido, tambaleante

Rocky Mountains pl n: the ∼ ∼ las Montañas Rocallosas or Rocosas

rod /rɑːd ‖rɒd/ n (a) (bar) varilla f, barra f (b) (fishing ∼) caña f (de pescar) (c) (for punishment) vara f

rode /rəʊd/ past of RIDE¹

rodent /'rəʊdnt/ n roedor m

rodeo /'rəʊdiəʊ, rə'deɪəʊ/ n (pl **-os**) rodeo m

roe /rəʊ/ n **1** (of fish) hueva f **2** **∼ deer** corzo, -za m,f

rogue /rəʊg/ n pícaro, -ra m,f, pillo, -lla m,f

roguish /'rəʊgɪʃ/ adj pícaro

role, rôle /rəʊl/ n (a) (Cin, Theat) papel m (b) (function) papel m, rol m; (before n) **∼ model** modelo m de conducta

role-play /'rəʊlpleɪ/ n teatro m improvisado; (Psych) psicodrama m

roll¹ /rəʊl/ n **1** (Culin) (bread) **∼** pancito m or (Esp) panecillo m or (Méx) bolillo m **2** (of paper, wire, fabric) rollo m; (of banknotes) fajo m; **a ∼ of film** un rollo or un carrete (de fotos) **3** (sound — of drum) redoble m; (— of thunder) retumbo m **4** (list) lista f; **to call the ∼** pasar lista

roll² vt **1** (a) (rotate) ‹ball/barrel› rodar* (b) (turn over): **the car ∼ed over three times** el coche dio tres vueltas de campana; **∼ (over) onto your**

back ponte boca arriba, date la vuelta *or* (CS) date vuelta; **to be ~ing in money** o **in it** (colloq) estar* forrado (de oro) (fam) **(c)** (sway) «*ship*» bambolearse

2 (move) (+ *adv compl*): **the car began to ~ down the hill** el coche empezó a deslizarse cuesta abajo; **tears ~ed down his cheeks** las lágrimas le corrían por las mejillas

3 (begin operating) «*camera*» empezar* a rodar

4 (make noise) «*drum*» redoblar; «*thunder*» retumbar

5 rolling *pres p* «*countryside/hills*» ondulado

■ ~ *vt* **1 (a)** ‹*ball/barrel*› hacer* rodar; ‹*dice*› tirar **(b) to ~ one's eyes** poner* los ojos en blanco

2 ‹*cigarette*› liar*; **it ~ed itself into a ball** se hizo un ovillo; **to ~ up one's sleeves** arremangarse

3 ‹*dough/pastry*› estirar

4 (Ling): **to ~ one's 'r's** hacer* vibrar las erres

■ **roll in** [*v + adv*] (arrive in large quantities) llover*

■ **roll on** [*v + adv*] **(a)** (pass) «*time/months*» pasar **(b)** (arrive) (colloq): **~ on vacation time!** ¡que lleguen pronto las vacaciones!

■ **roll out** [*v + o + adv, v + adv + o*] ‹*dough/pastry*› estirar

■ **roll up** [*v + adv*] (arrive) (colloq) aparecer*

roll call *n* **(a)** (calling of roll): **~ is 9 a.m.** pasan lista a las nueve de la mañana **(b)** (list) lista *f*

rolled gold /rəʊld/ *n* metal *m* (en)chapado en oro

roller /ˈrəʊlər ‖ˈrəʊlə(r)/ *n* **1** (for lawn, in machine, for applying paint) rodillo *m* **2** (for hair) rulo *m* **3** (caster) ruedecita *f*, ruedita *f* (esp AmL) **4** (wave) ola *f* grande

roller: R~blade® *n* patín *m* en línea; **~ blind** *n* persiana *f or* cortina *f* de enrollar; **~ coaster** *n* montaña *f* rusa; **~ skate** *n* patín *m* (de ruedas); **~skate** /ˈrəʊlərskeɪt ‖ˈrəʊləskeɪt/ *vi* patinar (*sobre ruedas*)

rolling pin /ˈrəʊlɪŋ/ *n* rodillo *m*, rollo *m* pastelero (Esp)

roll-on /ˈrəʊlɒn ‖ˈrəʊlɒn/*adj* (before n) ‹*deodorant*› de bola

ROM /rɑːm ‖rɒm/ *n* (= **read-only memory**) ROM *f*

Roman¹ /ˈrəʊmən/ *adj* **(a)** (of, from Rome) romano **(b) roman** ‹*numeral*› romano; ‹*alphabet*› latino

Roman² *n* romano, -na *m,f*

Roman Catholic¹ *n* católico, -ca *m,f*

Roman Catholic² *adj* católico

romance /rəˈmæns, ˈrəʊmæns ‖rəʊˈmæns/ *n* **1 (a)** (affair) romance *m*, idilio *m* **(b)** (feeling) romanticismo *m* **2** (Lit) (love story) novela *f* romántica

Romance /rəˈmæns, ˈrəʊmæns ‖rəʊˈmæns/ *adj* ‹*languages*› romance, románico

Romania /rəʊˈmeɪniə/ *n* Rumania *f*, Rumanía *f*

Romanian¹ /rəʊˈmeɪniən/ *adj* rumano

Romanian² *n* **(a)** (language) rumano *m* **(b)** (person) rumano, -na *m,f*

romantic¹ /rəʊˈmæntɪk, rə-/ *adj* romántico

romantic² *n* romántico, -ca *m,f*

romanticize /rəʊˈmæntəsaɪz, rə- ‖rəʊˈmæntɪsaɪz/ *vt* idealizar*

Romany /ˈrɑːməni, ˈrəʊ- ‖ˈrɒməni, ˈrəʊ-/ *n* (*pl* **-nies**) **(a)** (person) gitano, -na *m,f* **(b)** (language) romaní *m*

Rome /rəʊm/ *n* Roma *f*

romp¹ /rɑːmp ‖rɒmp/ *n* **(a)** (frolic) retozo *m* **(b)** (sexual) revolcón *m* (fam)

romp² *vi* (frolic) retozar*

rompers /ˈrɑːmpərz ‖ˈrɒmpəz/ *pl n*, (BrE also) **romper suit** /ˈrɑːmpər ‖ˈrɒmpə(r)/ *n* mameluco *m* (AmL), pelele *m* (Esp)

roof¹ /ruːf/ *n* (*pl* **~s** /ruːfs/) **(a)** (of building) tejado *m*, techo *m* (AmL); (*before n*) **~ garden** terraza *f or* azotea *f* ajardinada **(b)** (of car) techo *m*; (*before n*) **~ rack** baca *f*, portaequipajes *m*, parrilla *f* (AmL) **(c) the ~ of the mouth** el paladar

roof² *vt* techar

roofing /ˈruːfɪŋ/ *n* materiales *mpl* para techar

rooftop /ˈruːftɑːp ‖ˈruːftɒp/ *n* tejado *m*, techo *m* (AmL)

rook /rʊk/ *n* **(a)** (Zool) grajo *m* **(b)** (in chess) torre *f*

rookie /ˈrʊki/ *n* (colloq) **(a)** (novice) novato, -ta *m,f* **(b)** (military recruit) recluta *m*

room /ruːm, rʊm/ *n* **1** (in house, building) habitación *f*, pieza *f* (esp AmL); (bedroom) habitación *f*, dormitorio *m*, cuarto *m*, pieza *f* (esp AmL), recámara *f* (Méx); (for meeting) sala *f*; (*before n*) **~ temperature** temperatura *f* ambiente **2** (space) espacio *m*, lugar *m*; **there's ~ for improvement** se puede mejorar

room: ~ clerk *n* (AmE) recepcionista *mf*; **~mate** *n* (sharing apartment) compañero, -ra *m,f* de apartamento *or* (Esp) de piso; **~ service** *n* servicio *m* a las habitaciones

roomy /ˈruːmi, ˈrʊmi/ *adj* **-mier, -miest** amplio

roost /ruːst/ *vi* posarse (*para pasar la noche*)

rooster /ˈruːstər ‖ˈruːstə(r)/ *n* (esp AmE) gallo *m*

root¹ /ruːt/ *n* **(a)** raíz *f*; **to take ~** «*plant*» echar raíces, arraigar*; «*idea*» arraigarse* **(b) roots** *pl* (background) raíces *fpl*

root² *vi* **1** «*pig*» hozar* **2** (Bot) echar raíces, arraigar*

■ **root for** [*v + prep + o*] (encourage) animar, alentar; (support) apoyar

■ **root out** [*v + o + adv, v + adv + o*] (remove) arrancar* de raíz, erradicar*

root beer *n* refresco hecho con distintas raíces

rooted /ˈruːtəd ‖ˈruːtɪd/ *adj*: **a deeply ~ prejudice** un prejuicio profundamente arraigado; **he stood ~ to the spot** se quedó como clavado donde estaba

rope¹ /rəʊp/ *n* cuerda *f*, soga *f*; (Naut) cabo *m*; **to show sb the ~s: Mike will show you the ~s** Mike te enseñará cómo funciona todo

rope² *vt* **(a)** (tie) atar, amarrar (AmL exc RPl) (*con una cuerda*) **(b)** (lasso) (AmE) ‹*steer/cattle*› enlazar* *or* (Méx) lazar* *or* (CS) lacear

■ **rope in** [*v + o + adv, v + adv + o*] (colloq) (*usu pass*) agarrar (fam)

rope ladder *n* escala *f or* escalera *f* de cuerda *or* de soga

ropey, ropy /ˈrəʊpi/ *adj* **ropier, ropiest** (BrE ···>

colloq ⟨wine⟩ malo, chungo (Esp arg); **I feel a bit ∼** me siento bastante mal, estoy bastante pachucho (Esp fam)

rosary /ˈrəʊzəri/ n (pl **-ries**) rosario m

rose¹ /rəʊz/ past of RISE²

rose² n **1** (Bot) (flower) rosa f; (plant) rosal m; (before n) ∼ **bush** rosal m **2** (on watering can) roseta f

rosé /ˈrəʊzeɪ ‖ rəʊˈzeɪ/ n (vino m) rosado m

rose: ∼**bud** n capullo m or pimpollo m de rosa; ∼**hip** n escaramujo m

rosemary /ˈrəʊzˌmeri ‖ ˈrəʊzməri/ n romero m

rosette /rəʊˈzet/ n escarapela f

roster /ˈrɑːstər ‖ ˈrɒstə(r)/ n (a) (duty ∼) lista f de turnos (b) (list) lista f

rostrum /ˈrɑːstrəm ‖ ˈrɒstrəm/ n (pl **-trums** or **-tra** /-trə/) (for public speaking) tribuna f, estrado m; (for orchestra conductor) podio m

rosy /ˈrəʊzi/ adj **rosier, rosiest** ⟨cheeks⟩ sonrosado; ⟨outlook⟩ halagüeño, optimista

rot¹ /rɑːt ‖ rɒt/ n (Biol) podredumbre f, putrefacción f; **the** ∼ **set in** las cosas empezaron a decaer or a venirse abajo

rot² -tt- vi pudrirse*; **to** ∼ **away** pudrirse* ■ ∼ vt ⟨wood/tree⟩ pudrir*, ⟨teeth⟩ picar*

rota /ˈrəʊtə/ n (BrE) lista f (de turnos)

rotary /ˈrəʊtəri/ adj rotatorio, rotativo

rotate /ˈrəʊteɪt ‖ rəʊˈteɪt/ vi girar, rotar ■ ∼ vt (a) (turn, spin) (hacer*) girar, dar* vueltas a (b) (alternate) ⟨crops⟩ alternar, rotar

rotation /rəʊˈteɪʃən/ n rotación f

rote /rəʊt/ n: **by** ∼ de memoria

rotten /ˈrɑːtn̩ ‖ ˈrɒtn̩/ adj (a) (decayed) podrido; ⟨tooth⟩ picado (b) (bad) (colloq) ⟨weather⟩ horrible; ⟨food⟩ pésimo; **to feel** ∼ (ill) sentirse* mal or pésimo or (Esp fam) fatal

rotund /rəʊˈtʌnd/ adj (hum & euph) voluminoso

rouble /ˈruːbəl/ n (BrE) rublo m

rouge /ruːʒ/ n colorete m

rough¹ /rʌf/ adj **-er, -est** **1** (a) (not smooth) ⟨surface/texture/skin⟩ áspero, rugoso; ⟨cloth⟩ basto; ⟨hands⟩ áspero, basto (b) (uneven) ⟨ground/road⟩ desigual; ⟨terrain⟩ agreste, escabroso (c) ⟨sea⟩ agitado, picado **2** (colloq) (a) (unpleasant, hard) ⟨life⟩ duro (b) (ill): **I feel a bit** ∼ no estoy muy bien, me siento bastante mal **3** (not gentle) brusco; ⟨neighborhood⟩ peligroso **4** (a) (crude, unpolished) tosco, rudo; **a** ∼ **draft** un borrador (b) (approximate) aproximado

rough² adv ⟨sleep⟩ a la intemperie

rough³ vt: **to** ∼ **it** (colloq) pasar sin comodidades

roughage /ˈrʌfɪdʒ/ n fibra f (de los alimentos)

rough-and-ready /ˌrʌfənˈredi/ adj improvisado

roughen /ˈrʌfən/ vt poner* áspero

roughly /ˈrʌfli/ adv (a) (approximately) aproximadamente (b) (not gently) ⟨play⟩ bruscamente, de manera violenta (c) (crudely) toscamente

roughshod /ˈrʌfʃɑːd ‖ ˈrʌfʃɒd/ adv: **to ride** ∼

over sth: he rides ∼ over other people's feelings no tiene la menor consideración para con los sentimientos de los demás; **to ride** ∼ **over sb** llevarse por delante a algn

roulette /ruːˈlet/ n ruleta f

Roumania /ruːˈmeɪniə/ etc ▶ ROMANIA etc

round¹ /raʊnd/ adj redondo

round² n **1** (circle) círculo m, redondel m **2** (a) (series) serie f; ∼ **of talks** ronda f de conversaciones (b) (burst): **let's have a** ∼ **of applause for** … un aplauso para … **3** (Sport, Games) (of tournament, quiz) vuelta f; (in boxing, wrestling) round m, asalto m; (in golf) vuelta f, recorrido m; (in showjumping) recorrido m; (in card games) partida f **4** (a) (of visits) (often pl): **the doctor is off making his** ∼**s** o (BrE) **is on his** ∼**s** el doctor está haciendo visitas a domicilio or visitando pacientes (b) (of watchman) ronda f; (of postman, milkman) (BrE) recorrido m **5** (of drinks) ronda f, vuelta f **6** (shot) disparo m; (bullet) bala f **7** (of bread) (BrE): **a** ∼ **of toast** una tostada or (Méx) un pan tostado; **a** ∼ **of sandwiches** un sándwich **8** (Mus) canon m

round³ vt ⟨corner⟩ doblar ■ **round off** **1** [v + o + adv, v + adv + o] (a) ⟨sharp edge⟩ redondear (b) (end suitably) ⟨day/meal⟩ terminar, rematar (c) ⟨number⟩ redondear **2** [v + adv] concluir*, terminar ■ **round on** [v + prep + o] volverse* contra ■ **round up** [v + o + adv, v + adv + o] ⟨sheep/cattle⟩ rodear; ⟨criminals⟩ hacer* una redada de

round⁴ adv (esp BrE) **1** (a) (in a circle): **we walked all the way** ∼ dimos toda la vuelta; **all year** ∼ durante todo el año (b) (so as to face in different direction): **she spun** ∼ dio media vuelta; see also TURN ROUND (c) (on all sides) alrededor **2** (a) (from one place, person to another): **the curator took us** ∼ el conservador nos mostró or nos enseñó el museo (or la colección etc); **a list was handed** ∼ se hizo circular una lista (b) **all round** (in every respect) en todos los sentidos; (for everybody) a todos

round⁵ prep (esp BrE) **1** (encircling) alrededor de; **the wall** ∼ **the garden** el muro que rodea el jardín; ∼ **the corner** a la vuelta (de la esquina) **2** (a) (in the vicinity of) cerca de, en los alrededores de; **she lives** ∼ **here** vive por aquí (b) (within, through): **he does odd jobs** ∼ **the house** hace arreglitos en la casa; **we had a look** ∼ **the cathedral** (le) echamos un vistazo a la catedral

round- /raʊnd/ pref: ∼**faced** de cara redonda; ∼**shouldered** cargado de espaldas, encorvado

roundabout¹ /ˈraʊndəbaʊt/ n (BrE) (a) ▶ MERRY-GO-ROUND (b) (Transp) rotonda f, glorieta f

roundabout² adj ⟨route⟩ indirecto; **he said it in a very** ∼ **way** lo dijo con muchos rodeos or circunloquios

rounded /ˈraʊndəd ‖ ˈraʊndɪd/ adj redondeado

AmC	Central America	Arg	Argentina	Cu	Cuba	Per	Peru
AmL	Latin America	Bol	Bolivia	Ec	Ecuador	RPI	River Plate Area
AmS	South America	Chí	Chile	Esp	Spain	Ur	Uruguay
Andes	Andean Region	CS	Southern Cone	Méx	Mexico	Ven	Venezuela

rounders ⋯› ruin ⋯

rounders /'raʊndərz ‖'raʊndəz/ n (in UK)
(+ sing vb) juego parecido al béisbol

round: ∼ **table** n mesa f redonda; ∼ **the
clock** adv las 24 horas, día y noche; ∼ **trip** n
(a) (there and back) (viaje m de) ida f y vuelta,
viaje m redondo (Méx) **(b)** (return fare) (AmE) tarifa
f de ida y vuelta or (Méx) de viaje redondo;
(before n) **round-trip ticket** pasaje m or (Esp)
billete m de ida y vuelta, boleto m redondo (Méx);
∼**-up** n **(a)** (of livestock) rodeo m **(b)** (summary)
resumen m

rouse /raʊz/ vt despertar*

rousing /'raʊzɪŋ/ adj ⟨speech⟩ enardecedor

rout¹ /raʊt/ n derrota f aplastante

rout² vt (defeat) derrotar or vencer* de forma
aplastante; (put to flight) poner* en fuga

route /ruːt, raʊt ‖ruːt/ n **(a)** (way) camino m,
ruta f; (of bus) ruta f, recorrido m; **air/sea** ∼ ruta
aérea/marítima **(b)** (highway) (AmE) carretera f

routine¹ /ruː'tiːn/ n **1** (regular pattern) rutina f
2 (of skater, comedian) número m

routine² adj **(a)** (usual) ⟨procedure/inquiries⟩ de
rutina **(b)** (ordinary, dull) rutinario

roving /'rəʊvɪŋ/ adj (before n) errante

row¹ n
I /rəʊ/ **1 (a)** (straight line) hilera f; (of people,
seats) fila f **(b)** (in knitting) vuelta f **2** (succession)
serie f; **four times in a** ∼ cuatro veces seguidas
II /raʊ/ **(a)** (noisy argument) pelea f, riña f; **to have
a** ∼ **with sb** pelearse or reñir* con algn **(b)** (about
a public matter) disputa f **(c)** (noise) (no pl) bulla f
(fam)

row² vt /rəʊ/: **he** ∼**ed the boat towards the
shore** remó hacia la orilla
■ ∼ vi
I /rəʊ/ remar; **to go** ∼**ing** salir* or ir* a remar
II /raʊ/ pelearse, reñir*

rowboat /'rəʊbəʊt/, (BrE) **rowing boat**
/'rəʊɪŋ/ n bote m a remo or de remos

rowdy /'raʊdi/ adj **-dier, -diest** ⟨person⟩
escandaloso, alborotador; (quarrelsome)
pendenciero

row house /'rəʊ/ n (AmE) casa adosada en una
hilera de casas idénticas

rowing /'rəʊɪŋ/ n (Sport) remo m

rowing boat /'rəʊɪŋ/ n (BrE) ▶ ROWBOAT

royal /'rɔɪəl/ adj **(a)** (monarchic) real **(b)**
(magnificent) espléndido, regio

royal: ∼**-blue** /'rɔɪəl'bluː/ adj (pred ∼ **blue**)
azul real adj inv; **R**∼ **Highness** n: **Her/Your
R**∼ **Highness** Su/Vuestra Alteza Real

royalist /'rɔɪəlɪst/ adj monárquico

royalty /'rɔɪəlti/ n (pl **-ties**) **1** (status) realeza
f **2 royalties** mpl derechos mpl de autor,
regalías fpl

rpm (= **revolutions per minute**) r.p.m.

RSI n = **repetitive strain injury**

RSPCA n (in UK) (= **Royal Society for the
Prevention of Cruelty to Animals**)
≈ Asociación f protectora de animales

RSVP (please reply) s.r.c., se ruega contestación

rub /rʌb/ **-bb-** vt **(a)** (with hand, finger) frotar;
(firmly) restregar*; (massage) masajear, friccionar;
to ∼ **one's eyes** restregarse* or refregarse* or
(Méx) tallarse los ojos **(b)** (with a cloth) frotar

■ **rub down** [v + o + adv, v + adv + o] **(a)**
⟨horse⟩ almohazar* **(b)** (using sandpaper) lijar
■ **rub in** [v + o + adv, v + adv + o] ⟨cream/lotion⟩
aplicar* frotando
■ **rub off** [v + o + adv, v + adv + o] ⟨dirt/marks⟩
quitar frotando or restregando or refregando;
(from blackboard) (BrE) borrar
■ **rub out** [v + o + adv, v + adv + o] borrar
■ **rub up** [v + o + adv, v + adv + o]: **to** ∼ **sb up
the wrong way** caerle* mal a algn

rubber /'rʌbər ‖'rʌbə(r)/ n **(a)** (substance) goma
f, caucho m, hule m (Méx); (before n) ∼ **ring**
flotador m **(b)** (eraser) (BrE) goma f (de borrar)

rubber: ∼ **band** n goma f (elástica), gomita f
(RPl); ∼ **bullet** n bala f de goma or caucho; ∼
plant n ficus m, gomero m (CS); ∼ **stamp** n
(device) sello m; (approval) visto m bueno; ∼ **tree**
n árbol m del caucho, hule m (Méx)

rubbery /'rʌbəri/ adj ⟨texture⟩ gomoso;
⟨material⟩ parecido a la goma or al caucho or
(Méx) al hule

rubbish /'rʌbɪʃ/ n **(a)** (refuse) basura f; (before
n) ∼ **bag** bolsa f de la basura; ∼ **bin** (BrE) cubo m
or (CS) tacho m or (Méx) bote m or (Col) caneca f
or (Ven) tobo m de la basura **(b)** (junk) (colloq)
porquerías fpl (fam) **(c)** (nonsense) (colloq) tonterías
fpl

rubble /'rʌbəl/ n escombros mpl

ruble, (BrE) **rouble** /'ruːbəl/ n rublo m

ruby /'ruːbi/ n (pl **rubies**) rubí m

rucksack /'rʌksæk, 'rʊk-/ n mochila f, morral
m

ructions /'rʌkʃənz/ pl n (colloq) jaleo m (fam)

rudder /'rʌdər ‖'rʌdə(r)/ n timón m

ruddy /'rʌdi/ adj **-dier, -diest** ⟨cheeks⟩
rubicundo

rude /ruːd/ adj **(a)** (bad-mannered) ⟨person⟩
maleducado, grosero; ⟨remark⟩ grosero,
descortés; **to be** ∼ **to sb** ser* grosero con algn
(b) (vulgar) (esp BrE) grosero

rudely /'ruːdli/ adv groseramente

rudeness /'ruːdnəs ‖'ruːdnɪs/ n grosería f,
mala educación f

rudimentary /ˌruːdə'mentri ‖ˌruːdɪ'mentri/
adj rudimentario

rudiments /'ruːdəmənts ‖'ruːdɪmənts/ pl n
rudimentos mpl, nociones fpl elementales

rue /ruː/ vt lamentar, arrepentirse* de

rueful /'ruːfəl/ adj atribulado, compungido

ruff /rʌf/ n (collar) gorguera f; (on animal, bird)
collar m

ruffian /'rʌfiən/ n rufián m, villano m

ruffle¹ /'rʌfəl/ n (frill) volante m or (RPl) volado
m or (Chi) vuelo m

ruffle² vt **(a)** ⟨hair⟩ alborotar; ⟨feathers⟩ erizar*;
⟨clothes⟩ arrugar* **(b)** ⟨person⟩ alterar, contrariar

rug /rʌg/ n **(a)** (small carpet) alfombra f,
alfombrilla f, tapete m (Col, Méx) **(b)** (blanket)
manta f de viaje

rugby /'rʌgbi/ n rugby m

rugged /'rʌgəd ‖'rʌgɪd/ adj **(a)** ⟨rocks/coast⟩
escarpado; ⟨terrain⟩ escabroso **(b)** ⟨face⟩ de
facciones duras

ruin¹ /'ruːən ‖'ruːɪn/ n **(a)** (sth ruined) (often pl) ⋯›

ruina *f*; **his career was in ~s** su carrera estaba arruinada **(b)** (cause) (*no pl*) ruina *f*, perdición *f* **(c)** (state) ruina *f*

ruin² *vt* **1** (destroy) ‹*city/building*› destruir*; ‹*career/plans*› arruinar; ‹*person*› (financially) arruinar **2** (spoil) ‹*dress/carpet/toy*› estropear; ‹*party/surprise*› echar a perder, estropear, arruinar

rule¹ /ruːl/ *n* **1** (regulation, principle) regla *f*, norma *f*; **it's against the ~s** está prohibido; **~s and regulations** reglamento *m*; **to work to ~** (Lab Rel) hacer* huelga de celo **2 as a ~** por lo general, generalmente **3** (government) gobierno *m*; (of monarch) reinado *m*; **to be under foreign ~** estar* bajo dominio extranjero

rule² *vt* **1** (govern, control) ‹*country*› gobernar*, administrar; ‹*person*› dominar **2** (pronounce) dictaminar **3** (draw) ‹*line*› trazar* con una regla
■ **~** *vi* **1** (govern) gobernar*; «*monarch*» reinar **2** (pronounce) **to ~** (**ON sth**) fallar *or* resolver* (**EN** algo)
■ **rule out** [*v + o + adv, v + adv + o*] ‹*possibility*› descartar; ‹*course of action*› hacer* imposible

ruler /ˈruːlər ‖ ˈruːlə(r)/ *n* **1** (leader) gobernante *mf*; (sovereign) soberano, -na *m,f* **2** (measure) regla *f*

ruling¹ /ˈruːlɪŋ/ *n* fallo *m*, resolución *f*

ruling² *adj* (*before n*) ‹*monarch*› reinante; **the ~ classes** las clases dirigentes

rum /rʌm/ *n* ron *m*

Rumania /ruːˈmeɪniə/ *etc* ▶ ROMANIA *etc*

rumble¹ /ˈrʌmbəl/ *n* (sound) ruido *m* sordo; (of thunder) estruendo *m*; (of stomach) ruido *m* de tripas (fam)

rumble² *vi* «*guns/drums*» hacer* un ruido sordo; «*thunder*» retumbar; **my stomach's rumbling** me suenan las tripas (fam)

ruminate /ˈruːməneɪt ‖ ˈruːmɪneɪt/ *vi* **(a)** (Zool) rumiar **(b)** (ponder) **to ~ ON/ABOUT sth** cavilar SOBRE algo, rumiar algo

rummage /ˈrʌmɪdʒ/ *vi* hurgar*

rumor¹, (BrE) **rumour** /ˈruːmər ‖ ˈruːmə(r)/ *n* rumor *m*

rumor², (BrE) **rumour** *vt* (*usu pass*) rumorear; **it is ~ed that ...** se rumorea que ...

rump /rʌmp/ *n* **(a)** (Culin) cadera *f*; (*before n*) **~ steak** filete *m* de cadera, churrasco *m* de cuadril (RPl) **(b)** (bottom) (colloq & hum) traste *m* (fam)

rumpus /ˈrʌmpəs/ *n* (*pl* **~es**) lío *m*, escándalo *m*

run¹ /rʌn/ (*pres p* **running**; *past* **ran**; *past p* **run**) *vi*
I **1** correr; **he ran downstairs/indoors** bajó/entró corriendo
2 (colloq) (drive) ir* (*en coche*)
3 (Transp): **the trains ~ every half hour** hay trenes cada media hora
4 (flow) «*water/oil*» correr; **she left the water ~ning** dejó la llave abierta (AmL) *or* (Esp) el grifo abierto; **my nose is ~ning** me gotea la nariz
5 (Pol) «*candidate*» presentarse, postularse (AmL)
II (operate, function): **with the engine ~ning** con el motor encendido *or* en marcha (AmL tb) prendido; **it ~s off batteries** funciona con pilas *or* a pila(s)
III **1** (extend) **(a)** (in space): **the streets ~ parallel**

to each other las calles corren paralelas; **the path ~s across the field** el sendero atraviesa el campo **(b)** «*show*» estar* en cartel
2 (be, stand): **feelings are ~ning high** los ánimos están caldeados; **inflation is ~ning at 4%** la tasa de inflación es del 4%; **it ~s in the family** es de familia **(b)** (become): **stocks are ~ning low** se están agotando las existencias; *see also* DRY¹ 1c
3 (melt, merge) «*paint/makeup*» correrse; «*color*» desteñir*, despintarse (Méx)
■ **~** *vt*
I **1** ‹*race/marathon*› correr, tomar parte en
2 (a) (push, move) pasar **(b)** (drive) ‹*person*› (colloq) llevar (*en coche*)
3 to ~ a bath preparar un baño
4 (a) (extend) ‹*cable/wire*› tender* **(b)** (pass) (hacer*) pasar
II **1** (operate) ‹*engine*› hacer* funcionar; ‹*program*› (Comput) pasar, ejecutar
2 (manage) ‹*business*› dirigir*, llevar
3 ‹*course*› organizar*; ‹*article*› publicar*; ▶ TEMPERATURE B
■ **run about** ▶ RUN AROUND
■ **run across** [*v + prep + o*] **(a)** (meet) ‹*person*› encontrarse* *or* toparse con **(b)** (find) ‹*object*› encontrar*
■ **run after** [*v + prep + o*] (pursue) correr detrás de *or* tras; (romantically) andar* detrás de, perseguir*
■ **run along** [*v + adv*] irse*
■ **run around** [*v + adv*] «*children*» corretear
■ **run away** [*v + adv*] huir*, escaparse, fugarse*; (run off) salir* corriendo; **she ran away from home** se escapó de casa
■ **run away with** [*v + adv + prep + o*] **1 (a)** ‹*race/contest*› ganar fácilmente **(b)** (take over): **she lets her imagination ~ away with her** se deja llevar por la imaginación
2 (elope with) escaparse *or* fugarse* *or* irse* con
■ **run down**
I [*v + o + adv, v + adv + o*] **1** (disparage) (colloq) criticar*, hablar mal de
2 ‹*pedestrian*› atropellar
II [*v + adv*] **(a)** ‹*battery*› (Auto) descargarse* **(b)** «*business/factory*» venirse* abajo **(c)** «*stocks*» agotarse
■ **run in** [*v + o + adv*] (BrE Auto) ‹*car/engine*› hacer* el rodaje de
■ **run into** [*v + prep + o*] **(a)** ‹*vehicle*› chocar* con **(b)** ‹*person/table*› toparse con
■ **run off** **1** [*v + o + adv, v + adv + o*] (produce) ‹*copies*› tirar*; ‹*photocopies*› sacar*
2 [*v + adv*] (depart) salir* corriendo
■ **run off with** [*v + adv + prep + o*] ▶ RUN AWAY WITH 2
■ **run out** [*v + adv*] **(a)** (exhaust supplies): **to ~ out OF sth** quedarse SIN algo **(b)** «*money*» acabarse; «*supplies/stock*» acabarse, agotarse; «*lease/ policy*» vencer*, caducar*
■ **run over** **1** [*v + o + adv, v + adv + o*] ‹*pedestrian*› atropellar
2 [*v + prep + o*] (review) ‹*details/plan*› repasar; (rehearse) ‹*scene*› ensayar
■ **run through** [*v + prep + o*] ▶ RUN OVER 2
■ **run up** **1** [*v + adv + o*] **(a)** ‹*total/debts*› ir* acumulando **(b)** ‹*flag*› izar*
2 [*v + o + adv, v + adv + o*] ‹*dress*› hacer* (*rápidamente*)

■ **run up against** [v + adv + prep + o]
⟨difficulty/obstacle⟩ toparse or tropezar* con

run² n ① (on foot): **to go for a** ~ salir* a correr;
on the ~: **he's on the** ~ está prófugo; **after seven
years on the** ~ después de estar siete años
huyendo de la justicia; **to make a** ~ **for it**
escaparse

② (a) (trip, outing) vuelta f, paseo m (en coche) (b)
(journey): **it's only a short** ~ está muy cerca
③ (a) (sequence): **a** ~ **of good/bad luck** una
racha de buena/mala suerte, una buena/mala
racha (b) (period of time): **in the long** ~ a la larga
④ (heavy demand) ~ **ON** sth: **there's been a** ~ **on
these watches** estos relojes han estado muy
solicitados
⑤ (Cin, Theat) temporada f
⑥ (track) pista f; **ski** ~ pista de esquí
⑦ (in stocking, knitted garment) carrera f
⑧ (in baseball, cricket) carrera f

runaway¹ /'rʌnəweɪ/ n fugitivo, -va m,f
runaway² adj (before n) ⟨slave/prisoner⟩
fugitivo

run: ~**down** n resumen m; ~-**down**
/'rʌn'daʊn/ adj ⟨pred ~ **down**⟩ (a) (tired, sickly)
(usu pred) **to be/feel** ~ **down** estar*/sentirse*
cansado or débil (b) (dilapidated) ⟨district/hotel⟩
venido a menos

rung¹ /rʌŋ/ past p of RING²
rung² n (a) (of ladder, chair) travesaño m (b) (in
career, organization) peldaño m

runner /'rʌnər ‖ 'rʌnə(r)/ n ① (in race, baseball)
corredor, -dora m,f ② (taking messages) mensajero,
-ra m,f ② (a) (on sled) patín m (b) (for drawer) riel
m, guía f

runner: ~ **bean** n (esp BrE) habichuela f (Col)
or (Esp) judía f verde or (Chi) poroto m verde or
(RPl) chaucha f or (Ven) vainita f or (Méx) ejote m;
~-**up** /'rʌnər'ʌp/ n (pl ~**s-up**): **to be** ~-**up**
quedar en segundo lugar or puesto

running¹ /'rʌnɪŋ/ n (a) (exercise): ~ **is a good
form of exercise** correr es muy buen ejercicio;
there are five candidates in the ~ **for the post** hay
cinco candidatos compitiendo or en liza por el
puesto (b) (of machine) funcionamiento m, marcha
f (c) (management) gestión f

running² adj (before n, no comp) ① (a) **to take
a** ~ **jump** saltar tomando carrera or (Esp)
carrerilla (b) (continuous) ⟨joke⟩ continuo; ~ **water**
agua f; corriente ② (discharging) ⟨sore⟩ supurante
running³ adv: **the third day** ~ el tercer día
consecutivo or seguido

running costs pl n (of car) gastos mpl de
mantenimiento m; (of company) costos mpl or (Esp)
costes mpl corrientes

runny /'rʌni/ adj -**nier, -niest** (a) ⟨eyes⟩
lloroso; **I've got a** ~ **nose** me gotea la nariz (b)
⟨sauce⟩ líquido

run-of-the-mill /'rʌnəvðə'mɪl/ adj ⟨pred **run
of the mill**⟩ ⟨job/car⟩ común or normal y
corriente

runt /rʌnt/ n (Agr) animal más pequeño de una
camada

run: ~-**up** n (preparatory period) ~-**up TO** sth
período m previo A algo; ~**way** n (Aviat) pista f;
(at fashion show) (AmE) pasarela f

rupee /ru:'pi:, ru:'pi:/ n rupia f

rupture¹ /'rʌptʃər ‖ 'rʌptʃə(r)/ n ruptura f

rupture² vt romper*

rural /'rʊrəl ‖ 'rʊərəl/ adj rural

ruse /ru:s, ru:z ‖ru:z/ n artimaña f, treta f

rush¹ /rʌʃ/ n ① (a) (haste) (no pl) prisa f, apuro
m (AmL); **I'm in a** ~ tengo prisa, ando or estoy
apurado (AmL) (b) (movement): **a** ~ **of air** una
ráfaga de aire; **there was a** ~ **for the exit** todo el
mundo se precipitó hacia la salida ② (Bot) junco
m

rush² vi (a) (hurry) darse* prisa, apurarse (AmL);
she ~**ed through the first course** se comió el
primer plato a todo correr or a la carrera (b)
(run) (+ adv compl): **he** ~**ed in/out** entró/salió
corriendo; **to** ~ **around** ir* de acá para allá,
correr de un lado para otro (c) (surge, flow): **blood**
~**ed to his face** (from anger) se le subió la sangre a
la cabeza
■ ~ vt (a) ⟨job⟩ hacer* a todo correr or a la
carrera, hacer* deprisa y corriendo; ⟨person⟩
meterle prisa a, apurar (AmL) (b) (take hastily): **she
was** ~**ed to hospital** la llevaron rápidamente al
hospital
■ **rush into** [v + prep + o]: **she** ~**ed into marriage**
se precipitó al casarse; **don't** ~ **into anything** no
te precipites

rush: ~ **hour** n hora f pico (AmL), hora f punta
(Esp); ~ **job** n (colloq) (urgent) trabajo m urgente;
(hastily done): **it was a** ~ **job** se hizo a todo correr
or deprisa y corriendo or a la(s) carrera(s)

rusk /rʌsk/ n galleta f (dura, para bebés)

Russia /'rʌʃə/ n Rusia f

Russian¹ /'rʌʃən/ adj ruso

Russian² n (a) (language) ruso m (b) (person)
ruso, -sa m,f

Russian roulette n ruleta f rusa

rust¹ /rʌst/ n óxido m, herrumbre f, orín m

rust² vi oxidarse, herrumbrarse

rustic /'rʌstɪk/ adj rústico

rustle¹ /'rʌsəl/ vi «leaves» susurrar; «paper»
crujir
■ ~ vt ① «wind» «leaves» hacer* susurrar
② (steal) ⟨cattle/horses⟩ robar

rustle² n (of leaves) susurro m; (of paper) crujido
m; (of silk) frufrú m

rustler /'rʌslər ‖ 'rʌslə(r)/ n ladrón, -drona m,f
de ganado

rustproof /'rʌstpru:f/ adj ⟨surface/metal⟩
inoxidable; ⟨coating⟩ anticorrosivo, antioxidante

rusty /'rʌsti/ adj -**tier, -tiest** oxidado,
herrumbrado; **to get** o (BrE also) **go** ~ oxidarse,
herrumbrarse; **my German is a bit** ~ tengo muy
olvidado el alemán

rut /rʌt/ n ① (groove) surco m, rodada f; **to be in
a** ~ estar* anquilosado; **to get into a** ~
anquilosarse ② (Zool) celo m

rutabaga /'ru:tə'beɪgə ‖,ru:tə'beɪgə/ n (AmE)
nabo m sueco

ruthless /'ru:θləs ‖ 'ru:θlɪs/ adj ⟨person⟩
despiadado; ⟨persecution⟩ implacable, inexorable

Rwanda /rʊ'ændə/ n Ruanda f

Rwandan /rʊ'ændən/ adj ruandés

rye /raɪ/ n (a) (plant, grain) centeno m (b) ~
(**bread**) pan m de centeno

r

Ss

S, s /es/ n S, s f

S (a) (Geog) (= **south**) S **(b)** (Clothing) (= **small**) P

Sabbath /'sæbəθ/ n (Jewish) sábado m; (Christian) domingo m

sabbatical /sə'bætɪkəl/ n (year) año m sabático; (period) período m sabático

saber, (BrE) **sabre** /'seɪbər ‖'seɪbə(r)/ n sable m

sabotage¹ /'sæbətɑːʒ/ n sabotaje m

sabotage² vt sabotear

saboteur /ˌsæbə'tɜːr ‖ˌsæbə'tɜː(r)/ n saboteador, -dora m,f

sabre n (BrE) ▶ SABER

saccharin /'sækərən ‖'sækərɪn/ n sacarina f

sachet /sæ'ʃeɪ ‖'sæʃeɪ/ n (of shampoo, cream) sachet m; (of powder, sugar) (BrE) sobrecito m

sack¹ /sæk/ n **1 (a)** (large bag) saco m **(b)** (paper bag) (AmE) bolsa f (de papel) **2** (dismissal) (BrE colloq): **to give sb the ~** echar a algn (del trabajo), botar a algn (del trabajo) (AmL fam)

sack² vt **1** (dismiss) (BrE colloq) ⟨person/ employee⟩ echar (del trabajo), botar (del trabajo) (AmL fam) **2** (destroy) ⟨town/city⟩ saquear

sacrament /'sækrəmənt/ n sacramento m

sacred /'seɪkrəd ‖'seɪkrɪd/ adj sagrado

sacrifice¹ /'sækrəfaɪs ‖'sækrɪfaɪs/ n **1** (Occult, Relig) **(a)** (practice, act) sacrificio m **(b)** (offering) ofrenda f **2** (giving up) sacrificio m; **to make ~s** sacrificarse*

sacrifice² vt sacrificar*

sacrilege /'sækrəlɪdʒ ‖'sækrɪlɪdʒ/ n sacrilegio m

sad /sæd/ adj -dd- triste; **~ to say** lamentablemente

sadden /'sædn̩/ vt entristecer*

saddle¹ /'sædl̩/ n (on horse) silla f (de montar); (on bicycle) sillín m

saddle² vt **(a)** ~ (up) ⟨horse⟩ ensillar **(b)** (burden) (colloq) **to ~ sb WITH sth** endilgarle* or (esp AmL) encajarle algo A algn

saddle-bag /'sædl̩bæg/ n (on horse) alforja f; (on bicycle) maletero m

sadist /'seɪdəst ‖'seɪdɪst/ n sádico, -ca m,f

sadly /'sædli/ adv **(a)** (sorrowfully) ⟨smile/speak⟩ tristemente, con tristeza **(b)** (regrettably): **you are ~ mistaken** estás totalmente equivocado **(c)** (unfortunately) ⟨indep⟩ lamentablemente

sadness /'sædnəs ‖'sædnɪs/ n tristeza f

sae, SAE n (BrE) (= **stamped, addressed envelope**) ▶ SASE

safari /sə'fɑːri/ n safari m; (before n) ~ **park** safari-park m

safe¹ /seɪf/ adj **safer, safest 1** (secure from danger) seguro; ⟨haven/place⟩ seguro; **you are not ~ here** corres peligro aquí; **keep these documents ~** guarda estos documentos en un lugar seguro; **they're ~** están a salvo; **they were found ~ and well** o ~ **and sound** los encontraron sanos y salvos **2** (not dangerous) ⟨ladder⟩ seguro **3** (not risky) ⟨investment/sex/method⟩ seguro; **to be on the ~ side** por si acaso; **better (to be) ~ than sorry** más vale prevenir que curar

safe² n caja f fuerte, caja f de caudales

safe: ~**-conduct** /'seɪf'kɒndʌkt ‖,seɪf'kɒndʌkt/ n protección f; ~**-deposit (box)** /'seɪfdɪ'pɑːzət ‖'seɪfdɪ'pɒzɪt/ n caja f de seguridad

safeguard¹ /'seɪfgɑːrd ‖'seɪfgɑːd/ n salvaguarda f

safeguard² vt salvaguardar

safe: ~ **house** n piso m franco; ~**keeping** n: **he gave her the watch for ~keeping** le dio el reloj para que lo guardara en lugar seguro or (esp Esp frml) para que lo pusiera a buen recaudo

safely /'seɪfli/ adv **1 (a)** (without mishap, unharmed): **we got home ~** llegamos a casa sin novedad **(b)** (without danger) sin peligro; **drive ~** conduzca con prudencia or cuidado **2** (with certainty) ⟨say/assume⟩ sin temor a equivocarse (or equivocarnos etc)

safety /'seɪfti/ n (pl -**ties**)(security, freedom from risk) seguridad f; (before n) ⟨device/precautions/ regulations⟩ de seguridad

safety: ~ **belt** n cinturón m de seguridad; ~ **catch** (on gun) seguro m; ~ **net** n (for acrobats) red f de seguridad; (protection) protección f; ~ **pin** n imperdible m, gancho m (Andes), alfiler m de gancho (CS, Ven), gancho m de nodriza (Col), seguro m (Méx)

saffron /'sæfrən/ n azafrán m

sag /sæg/ vi -**gg**- **(a)** «beams/ceiling» combarse; «bed» hundirse **(b)** (hang down, droop): ~**ging breasts** pechos mpl caídos

saga /'sɑːgə/ n (Lit) saga f; (long story) historia f, saga f

sage /seɪdʒ/ n **1** (Bot, Culin) salvia f **2** (wise man) sabio m

Sagittarius /'sædʒə'teriəs ‖,sædʒɪ'teəriəs/ n **(a)** (sign) (no art) Sagitario **(b)** (person) Sagitario or sagitario mf, sagitariano, -na m,f

Sahara /sə'hærə ‖sə'hɑːrə/ n **the ~** el Sahara or (Esp) el Sáhara

said /sed/ past & past p of SAY¹

---

sail¹ /seɪl/ n (of ship, boat) vela f; **to set ~** (start journey) zarpar, hacerse* a la mar; «*yacht/ galleon*» hacerse* a la vela

sail² vt «*boat/ship*» gobernar*
■ **~** vi (a) (travel) «*ship/boat*» navegar*; «*person/ passenger*» ir* en barco; **to go ~ing** salir a navegar (b) (depart) «*person/ship*» zarpar, salir*
■ **sail through** [v + prep + o]: **you'll ~ through the exam** aprobarás el examen con los ojos cerrados

sailboat /'seɪlbəʊt/ n (AmE) velero m, barco m de vela

sailing /'seɪlɪŋ/ n (a) (skill) navegación f (b) (Sport) vela f

sailing: ~ boat n (BrE) ▶ SAILBOAT; **~ ship** n velero m, barco m de vela

sailor /'seɪlər ‖'seɪlə(r)/ n (a) (seaman) marinero m (b) (Sport) navegante mf

saint /seɪnt/ n
■ Note Although the usual translation for *saint* as a title is *san* for a man or *santa* for a woman, *santo* is used before *Domingo, Tomás, Tomé,* and *Toríbio.*

(a) (canonized person) santo, -ta m,f (b) **Saint** /seɪnt ‖sənt/ (before name) san, santa

sake /seɪk/ n (a) (benefit, account): **for my/their ~** por mí/ellos; **for your own ~** por tu propio bien (b) (purpose, end): **art for art's ~** el arte por el arte; **for argument's ~** pongamos por caso (c) (in interj phrases): **for goodness' o heaven's ~!** ¡por Dios!; **for God's ~!** ¡por el amor de Dios!

salad /'sæləd/ n ensalada f; (before n) **~ bowl** ensaladera f; **~ dressing** aliño m para ensalada

salad cream n (BrE) aliño para ensalada parecido a la mayonesa

salami /sə'lɑːmi/ n (pl **-mis**) salami or (CS) salame m

salary /'sæləri/ n (pl **-ries**) sueldo m

sale /seɪl/ n **1** (a) (act of selling) venta f (b) (individual transaction) venta f (c) (auction) subasta f, remate m (AmL)
2 (in phrases) **for sale: ❸ for sale** se vende; **on sale** (at reduced price) (AmE): **toys are on ~ this week** esta semana los juguetes están rebajados; (offered for sale) (BrE): **on ~ now at leading stores** ya está a la venta en los principales comercios
3 (clearance) liquidación f; (seasonal reductions) rebajas fpl; (before n) ‹price› de liquidación
4 **sales** (a) pl (volume sold) (sometimes sing) (volumen m de) ventas fpl (b) (department) (+ sing o pl vb) ventas (+ sing vb)

saleroom /'seɪlruːm, -rʊm/ n (BrE) ▶ SALESROOM A

sales /seɪlz/: **~clerk** n (AmE) vendedor, -dora m,f, dependiente, -ta m,f; **~man** /'seɪlzmən/ n (pl **-men** /-mən/) (in shop) vendedor m; (representative) representante m, corredor m (RPl); **~room** n (AmE) (a) (for auctions) sala f de subastas, sala f de remates (AmL) (b) (showroom) salón m de exposición (y ventas); **~ slip** n (AmE) recibo m; **~woman** n (in shop) vendedora f; (representative) representante f, corredora f (RPl)

saliva /sə'laɪvə/ n saliva f

sallow /'sæləʊ/ adj **-er, -est** cetrino

salmon /'sæmən/ n (pl **~**) salmón m

salon /sə'lɑːn ‖'sælɒn/ n (business): **hairdressing ~** peluquería f; **beauty ~** salón m de belleza

saloon /sə'luːn/ n **1** (bar) (AmE) bar m (del Lejano Oeste) **2** **~ (car)** (BrE) sedán m

salt¹ /sɔːlt/ n sal f

salt² vt (a) (put salt on) ‹vegetables/meat› salar, ponerle* or echarle sal a; ‹road› echar sal en (b) **salted** past p salado

salt: ~ cellar n salero m; **~water** adj ‹lake› de agua salada; ‹fish› de mar, de agua salada

salty /'sɔːlti/ adj **-tier, -tiest** salado

salubrious /sə'luːbriəs/ adj (a) (healthy) (frml) saludable, salubre (b) (wholesome) (usu neg): **not a very ~ district** un barrio muy poco recomendable

salutary /'sæljətəri ‖'sæljʊtri/ adj saludable

salute¹ /sə'luːt/ n (a) (gesture) saludo m, venia f (RPl) (b) (firing of guns) salva f (c) (tribute) homenaje m

salute² vt (a) (Mil) ‹officer› saludar (b) (acknowledge, pay tribute) (frml) ‹courage/achievement› rendir* homenaje a
■ **~** vi (Mil) **to ~** (TO sb) hacerle* el saludo or (RPl) la venia (A algn)

Salvadorean¹, Salvadorian /ˌsælvə'dɔːriən/ adj salvadoreño

Salvadorean², Salvadorian n salvadoreño, -ña m,f

salvage /'sælvɪdʒ/ vt rescatar

salvation /sæl'veɪʃən/ n salvación f

Salvation Army n Ejército m de Salvación

salve¹ /sæv ‖sælv/ n (ointment) bálsamo m, ungüento m

salve² vt: **to ~** one's conscience acallar la voz de su (or mi etc) conciencia

Samaritan /sə'mærətn ‖sə'mærɪtn/ n (Bib) samaritano, -na m,f; **the good ~** el buen samaritano

same¹ /seɪm/ adj (before n) mismo, misma; **the ~ address/mistake** la misma dirección/el mismo error; **the two boxes are exactly the ~** las dos cajas son exactamente iguales; **that dress is the ~ as mine** ese vestido es igual al mío; **the ~ thing happened to me** a mí me pasó lo mismo; **on that very ~ day** ese mismísimo día

same² pron (a): **the ~** lo mismo; **have a nice vacation! — ~ to you!** ¡felices vacaciones! — ¡igualmente! (b) **all the same, just the same** igual; (as linker) de todas formas or maneras; **it's all the ~ to me/you/them** me/te/les da lo mismo, me/te/ les da igual

same³ adv: **the ~** igual

sample¹ /'sæmpəl ‖'sɑːmpl/ n muestra f

sample² vt ‹food› degustar

sanatorium /ˌsænə'tɔːriəm/ n (pl **-riums** or **-ria** /-riə/) sanatorio m (para convalecientes)

sanctify /'sæŋktəfaɪ ‖'sæŋktɪfaɪ/ vt **-fies, -fying, -fied** santificar*

sanctimonious /ˌsæŋktə'məʊniəs ‖ˌsæŋktɪ'məʊniəs/ adj (frml) moralista, gazmoño, mojigato

sanction¹ /'sæŋkʃən/ n **1** (authorization) autorización f, sanción f **2** **sanctions** pl (coercive measures) sanciones fpl

sanction² vt ‹act/initiative› sancionar (frml), aprobar*; ‹injustice› consentir*

sanctity /'sæŋktəti/ n (a) (inviolability) inviolabilidad f (b) (holiness) santidad f

sanctuary /'sæŋktʃuери ‖'sæŋktʃuəri/ n (pl **-ries**) (a) (protection, safety) asilo m, refugio m (b) (place of refuge) santuario m

sand¹ /sænd/ n arena f

sand² vt ~ (**down**) ‹wood/furniture› lijar; ‹floor› pulir

sandal /'sændl/ n sandalia f

sand: ~**bank** n banco m de arena; ~**box** n (AmE) cajón m de arena (en parques y jardines); ~**castle** n castillo m de arena; ~**paper** n papel m de lija; ~**pit** n (BrE) ▶ ~BOX; ~**stone** n arenisca f; ~**storm** n tormenta f de arena

sandwich¹ /'sænwɪtʃ ‖'sændwɪdʒ/ n (pl ~**es**) sándwich m, emparedado m, ≈ bocadillo m (Esp)

sandwich² vt (usu pass): I was ~ed between two fat men estaba apretujado entre dos gordos

sandy /'sændi/ adj **-dier, -diest** (a) ‹beach/ path› de arena; ‹soil› arenoso (b) (in color) ‹hair› rubio rojizo adj inv

sane /sein/ adj **saner, sanest** (a) (not mad) cuerdo (b) (sensible) sensato

sang /sæŋ/ past of SING

sanitarium /ˌsænə'teriəm ‖ˌsænɪ'teəriəm/ n (AmE) ▶ SANATORIUM

sanitary /'sænəteri ‖'sænɪtri/ adj (a) (concerning health) (before n) ‹conditions/ regulations› sanitario; ‹inspector› de sanidad (b) (hygienic) higiénico

sanitary napkin, (BrE) **sanitary towel** n compresa f, paño m higiénico

sanitation /ˌsænə'teɪʃən ‖ˌsænɪ'teɪʃən/ n (a) (hygiene) condiciones fpl de salubridad (b) (waste disposal system) servicios mpl sanitarios

sanitize /'sænətaɪz ‖'sænɪtaɪz/ vt (a) (disinfect) desinfectar (b) (make inoffensive) (pej) hacer* potable; **a ~d version** una versión aséptica

sanity /'sænəti/ n (a) (mental health) razón f, cordura f (b) (good sense) sensatez f

sank /sæŋk/ past of SINK¹

Santa Claus /'sæntəklɔːz/ n Papá Noel, San Nicolás, Santa Claus, Viejo m Pascuero (Chi)

sap¹ /sæp/ n savia f

sap² vt **-pp-** minar

sapling /'sæplɪŋ/ n árbol m joven

sapphire /'sæfaɪr ‖'sæfaɪə(r)/ n zafiro m

sarcasm /'sɑːrkæzəm ‖'sɑːkæzəm/ n sarcasmo m

sarcastic /sɑːr'kæstɪk ‖sɑː'kæstɪk/ adj sarcástico

sardine /sɑːr'diːn ‖sɑː'diːn/ n sardina f

sardonic /sɑːr'dɑːnɪk ‖sɑː'dɒnɪk/ adj sardónico

sari /'sɑːri/ n (pl ~**s**) sari m

SASE n (AmE) (= **self-addressed stamped envelope**): I **enclose an** ~ adjunto sobre franqueado (a mi nombre)

sash /sæʃ/ n ① (on dress) faja f; (on uniform — around waist) fajín m; (— over shoulder) banda f ② (of window) marco m

sassy /'sæsi/ adj **-sier, -siest** (AmE colloq) (a) (impertinent) caradura (fam) (b) (brash) ‹hat/style› llamativo y atrevido

sat /sæt/ past & past p of SIT

Satan /'seɪtn/ n Satanás

satanic /sə'tænɪk/ adj satánico

satchel /'sætʃəl/ n cartera f (de colegial)

sate /seɪt/ vt (liter) (usu pass) ‹appetite/lust› saciar (liter)

satellite /'sætlaɪt ‖'sætəlaɪt/ n ① (a) (Aerosp) satélite m (artificial); (before n) ~ **TV** televisión f por or vía satélite (b) (Astron) satélite m ② (dependent body, state) satélite m; (before n) **a ~ town** una ciudad satélite

satin /'sætn ‖'sætɪn/ n satén m, satín m (AmE)

satire /'sætaɪr ‖'sætaɪə(r)/ n sátira f

satirical /sə'tɪrɪkəl/ adj satírico

satirize /'sætəraɪz/ vt satirizar*

satisfaction /ˌsætəs'fækʃən ‖ˌsætɪs'fækʃən/ n satisfacción f

satisfactory /ˌsætəs'fæktri ‖ˌsætɪs'fæktəri/ adj satisfactorio

satisfied /'sætəsfaɪd ‖'sætɪsfaɪd/ adj ‹expression/customer› satisfecho; ‹smile› de satisfacción

satisfy /'sætəsfaɪ ‖'sætɪsfaɪ/ vt **-fies, -fying, -fied** ① (a) (please) satisfacer* (b) (meet) ‹requirements› llenar; ‹demand› satisfacer* ② (convince) (often pass) **to ~ sb OF sth** convencer* a algn DE algo

satisfying /'sætəsfaɪɪŋ ‖'sætɪsfaɪɪŋ/ adj (a) (pleasing) ‹result/job› satisfactorio (b) (filling) ‹meal› que llena

satsuma /sæt'suːmə/ n satsuma f (tipo de mandarina)

saturate /'sætʃəreɪt/ vt ① (drench) empapar ② (fill) ‹market/mind/place› saturar ③ (Chem, Phys) saturar

saturation /ˌsætʃə'reɪʃən/ n ① (Busn, Marketing) saturación f ② (Chem, Phys) saturación f

Saturday /'sætərdeɪ, -di ‖'sætədeɪ, -di/ n sábado m; see also MONDAY

Saturn /'sætərn ‖'sætən/ n Saturno m

sauce /sɔːs/ n salsa f

saucepan /'sɔːspæn ‖'sɔːspən/ n cacerola f, cazo m (Esp); (large) olla f

saucer /'sɔːsər ‖'sɔːsə(r)/ n platillo m

saucy /'sæsi, 'sɔːsi ‖'sɔːsi/ adj **-cier, -ciest** insolente, fresco (fam)

Saudi¹ /'saudi/ adj saudita, saudí

Saudi² n saudita mf, saudí mf

Saudi Arabia /ə'reɪbiə/ n Arabia f Saudita, Arabia f Saudí

sauna /'sɔːnə/ n sauna f, sauna m (AmL)

saunter /'sɔːntər ‖'sɔːntə(r)/ vi pasear; **she ~ed in/out** entró/salió andando despacio

sausage /'sɔːsɪdʒ ‖'sɒsɪdʒ/ n (for cooking) salchicha f; (cold, cured) embutido m

sauté /sɔː'teɪ ‖'səuteɪ/ vt **-tés, -téeing** or **-téing, -téed** or **-téd** saltear

savage¹ /'sævɪdʒ/ adj (a) (fierce, wild) ‹beast/ attack› salvaje; ‹blow› violento (b) (uncivilized) ‹tribe/people› salvaje

savage² n salvaje mf

savage³ vt atacar* salvajemente a

savagely /'sævɪdʒli/ adv salvajemente

savagery /'sævɪdʒri/ n ferocidad f

save¹ /seɪv/ vt ① (a) (preserve) ‹life/person/job› salvar; ‹possessions› rescatar; **firefighters ~d 20 people** bomberos rescataron a 20 personas (b)

(redeem) ⟨soul/sinner⟩ salvar **2 (a)** (be economical with) ⟨money/fuel/space/time⟩ ahorrar **(b)** (spare, avoid) ⟨trouble/expense/embarrassment⟩ ahorrar, evitar **3 (a)** (keep, put aside) guardar; ⟨money⟩ ahorrar; **don't eat it now; ~ it for later** no te lo comas ahora; déjalo para luego; **to ~ one's energy** guardarse las energías **(b)** (Comput) guardar **4** (Sport) ⟨shot/penalty⟩ salvar
■ ~ vi ahorrar
■ **save up** **1** [v + adv] ahorrar **2** [v + o + adv, v + adv + o] ahorrar

save² n parada f

save³ prep (frml) (apart from) ~ **(for)** salvo, excepto

saving¹ /'seɪvɪŋ/ n **(a)** (economy) ahorro m **(b) savings** pl ahorros mpl; (before n) **~s account** cuenta f de ahorros

saving² adj (before n) ▶ GRACE 2c

savings /'seɪvɪŋz/: ~ **and loan** n ~ ~ ~ **(association/company)** (AmE) sociedad f de ahorro y préstamos; ~ **bank** n caja f de ahorros

savior, (BrE) **saviour** /'seɪvjər ‖ 'seɪvjə(r)/ n salvador, -dora m,f

savor¹, (BrE) **savour** /'seɪvər ‖ 'seɪvə(r)/ vt saborear

savor², (BrE) **savour** n (taste) sabor m; (hint, trace) dejo m

savory, (BrE) **savoury** /'seɪvəri/ adj (tasty) sabroso; (wholesome) (usu with neg) limpio

savour vt/n (BrE) ▶ SAVOR¹,²

savoury /'seɪvəri/ adj (BrE) **(a)** ▶ SAVORY² **(b)** (not sweet) salado

saw¹ /'sɔː/ past of SEE

saw² n (manual) sierra f; (— with one handle) serrucho m; (power-driven) sierra f mecánica

saw³ vt (past p sawed or (esp BrE) sawn) (with handsaw) cortar (con serrucho), serruchar (AmL); (with a larger saw) cortar (con sierra), serrar*, aserrar*

sawdust /'sɔːdʌst/ n serrín m, aserrín m (esp AmL)

sawed-off /'sɔːd'ɔːf ‖ 'sɔːdɒf/, (BrE) **sawn-off** /'sɔːnɔːf ‖ 'sɔːnɒf/ adj: ~ **shotgun** escopeta f recortada

sawn /sɔːn/ past p of SAW³

sawn-off adj (BrE) ▶ SAWED-OFF

saxophone /'sæksəfəʊn/ n saxofón m, saxófono m

say¹ /seɪ/ (pres **says** /sez/; past & past p **said** /sed/) vt **1** (utter, express in speech) ⟨word/sentence⟩ decir*; ⟨prayer⟩ rezar*; **I said yes/no** dije que sí/no; **to ~ sth TO sb** decirle* algo A algn; **why didn't you ~ so before?** haberlo dicho antes; **that's to ~** es decir; **to ~ the least** como mínimo; **what have you got to ~ for yourself?** a ver, explícate; ~ **no more** no me digas más; **you can** ~ **that again!** ¡y que lo digas!; **it goes without** ~**ing that ...** huelga decir que ...; **that's easier said than done** del dicho al hecho hay mucho trecho; **no sooner said than done** dicho y hecho; **when all's said and done** al fin y al cabo **2** «watch/dial» marcar* **3** (suppose) (colloq) suponer*; **(let's) ~ that ...** supongamos que ... **4** (allege) decir*; **..., or so he ~s ...**, al menos eso es lo que dice

■ ~ vi decir*; **I'd rather not ~** prefiero no decirlo; **it's hard to ~** es difícil decirlo

say² interj (AmE colloq) ¡oye! (fam)

say³ n (no pl) **(a)** (statement of view): **to have one's** ~ dar* su (or mi etc) opinión **(b)** (power): **I have no ~ in the matter** yo no tengo ni voz ni voto en el asunto

saying /'seɪɪŋ/ n refrán m, dicho m

SC = **South Carolina**

scab /skæb/ n **1** (on wound) costra f **2** (strikebreaker) (pej) esquirol mf (pey), carnero, -ra m,f (RPl fam & pey)

scaffold /'skæfəld, -fəʊld/ n (for execution) patíbulo m, cadalso m

scaffolding /'skæfəldɪŋ, '-fəʊldɪŋ/ n andamiaje m

scald /skɔːld/ vt escaldar

scale¹ /skeɪl/ n **I** **1** (no pl) **(a)** (extent, size) escala f; **on a large/small ~** en gran/pequeña escala **(b)** (of map, diagram) escala f; (before n) ⟨model/drawing⟩ a escala **2** (on measuring instrument) escala f **3** (Mus) escala f **4** (for weighing) (usu pl) balanza f, pesa f; **bathroom ~s** una báscula or pesa (de baño) **II** **1** (on fish) escama f **2** (deposit in kettle, pipes) sarro m

scale² vt ⟨mountain/wall⟩ escalar; ⟨ladder⟩ subir
■ **scale down** [v + o + adv, v + adv + o] ⟨drawing⟩ reducir* (a escala); ⟨operation⟩ recortar

scallion /'skæljən/ n (AmE) **(a)** (young onion) cebolleta f, cebollino m **(b)** (shallot) chalote m, chalota f

scallop /'skæləp/ n vieira f, ostión m (CS)

scalp¹ /skælp/ n (Anat) cuero m cabelludo

scalp² vt: **to ~ sb** arrancarle* la cabellera a algn

scalpel /'skælpəl/ n bisturí m, escalpelo m

scaly /'skeɪli/ adj **-lier, -liest** ⟨skin⟩ escamoso

scamper /'skæmpər ‖ 'skæmpə(r)/ vi corretear; **she ~ed off** se fue correteando

scampi /'skæmpi/ pl n langostinos mpl (gen rebozados)

scan¹ /skæn/ vt **-nn-** **1 (a)** ⟨horizon⟩ escudriñar **(b)** ⟨noticeboard/newspaper⟩ recorrer con la vista; ⟨report⟩ echarle un vistazo a **2** (Med) ⟨body/brain⟩ hacer* un escáner de; (with ultrasound scanner) hacer* una ecografía de

scan² n (Med) escáner m; (ultrasound) ecografía f

scandal /'skændl/ n **(a)** (outrage) escándalo m **(b)** (gossip) chismorreo m

scandalize /'skændlaɪz/ vt escandalizar*

scandalous /'skændləs/ adj escandaloso

Scandinavia /ˌskændə'neɪvɪə ‖ ˌskændɪ'neɪvɪə/ n Escandinavia f

Scandinavian¹ /ˌskændə'neɪvɪən ‖ ˌskændɪ'neɪvɪən/ adj escandinavo

Scandinavian² n escandinavo, -va m,f

scanner /'skænər ‖ 'skænə(r)/ n (Med) escáner m, scanner m

scanty /'skænti/ adj **-tier, -tiest** ⟨information⟩ insuficiente; ⟨meal⟩ poco abundante, frugal; ⟨costume⟩ breve

scapegoat /'skeɪpgəʊt/ n chivo m expiatorio

S

scar¹ /skɑːr ‖skɑː(r)/ n cicatriz f

scar² vt **-rr-:** his face was badly ∼red le quedó una enorme cicatriz en el rostro; she'll be ∼red for life (physically) le va a quedar (la) cicatriz; (emotionally) va a quedar marcada

scarce /skers ‖skeəs/ adj escaso; to be ∼ escasear

scarcely /'skersli ‖'skeəsli/ adv apenas

scarcity /'skersəti ‖'skeəsəti/ n (pl **-ties**) escasez f

scare¹ /sker ‖skeə(r)/ vt asustar
■ **scare away, scare off** [v + o + adv, v + adv + o] espantar

scare² n (a) (fright, shock) susto m (b) (panic) (Journ): bomb ∼ amenaza f de bomba

scarecrow /'skerkrəʊ ‖'skeəkrəʊ/ n espantapájaros m

scared /skerd ‖skeəd/ adj asustado; I'm ∼ tengo miedo; to be ∼ oʀ sth/sb tenerle* miedo ᴀ algo/algn

scarf /skɑːrf ‖skɑːf/ n (pl ∼**s** or **scarves**) (a) (muffler) bufanda f (b) (square) pañuelo m

scarlet /'skɑːrlət ‖'skɑːlət/ adj (rojo) escarlata adj inv

scarlet fever n escarlatina f

scarves /skɑːrvz ‖skɑːvz/ pl of scarf

scathing /'skeɪðɪŋ/ adj mordaz

scatter /'skætər ‖'skætə(r)/ vt ⚊ 1 ⟨salt/grit⟩ esparcir*; ⟨seeds⟩ sembrar* (a voleo) ⚊ 2 (disperse) ⟨crowd/group⟩ dispersar; they are ∼ed all over the country están desperdigados por todo el país
■ ∼ vi ⟨crowd/light⟩ dispersarse

scatterbrained /'skætər'breɪnd ‖'skætəbreɪnd/ adj atolondrado, despistado

scattered /'skætərd ‖'skætəd/ adj (before n) ⟨fighting/applause/outbreak⟩ aislado; ⟨community⟩ diseminado; ∼ showers chubascos mpl aislados

scavenge /'skævəndʒ ‖'skævɪndʒ/ vi to ∼ ꜰoʀ sth escarbar or hurgar* en busca de algo

scavenger /'skævəndʒər ‖'skævɪndʒə(r)/ n (a) (animal, bird) carroñero, -ra m,f (b) (person) persona que busca comida etc hurgando en los desperdicios

scenario /sə'neriəʊ, -'næ- ‖sɪ'nɑːriəʊ/ n (pl **-os**) (a) (Cin, TV) guion m (b) (of future) perspectiva f, escenario m (period)

scene /siːn/ n ⚊ 1 (a) (view, situation) escena f (b) (of incident, crime) escena f; it was the ∼ of violent demonstrations fue el escenario de violentas manifestaciones; to appear on the ∼ aparecer*; to set the ∼ (for sth) situar* la escena (de algo) ⚊ 2 (in play, book etc) escena f ⚊ 3 (stage setting) decorado m; behind the ∼s entre bastidores ⚊ 4 (fuss, row) escena f ⚊ 5 (sphere) ámbito m; it's not my ∼ no es lo mío

scenery /'siːnəri/ n (a) (surroundings) paisaje m (b) (Theat) escenografía f

scenic /'siːnɪk/ adj pintoresco

scent¹ /sent/ n (a) (fragrance) perfume m (b) (perfume) (BrE) perfume m (c) (trail) rastro m; to put o throw sb off the ∼ despistar a algn

scent² vt (a) (sense) ⟨danger/victory⟩ intuir* (b) (perfume) ⟨air/room/skin⟩ perfumar (c) **scented** past p ⟨writing paper⟩ perfumado; ⟨rose⟩ fragante

scepter, (BrE) **sceptre** /'septər ‖'septə(r)/ n cetro m

sceptic etc (BrE) ▶ skeptic etc

sceptre n (BrE) ▶ scepter

schedule¹ /'skedʒuːl ‖'ʃedjuːl/ n ⚊ 1 (plan) programa m; the flight is due to arrive on ∼ el vuelo llegará a la hora prevista; to be ahead of/ behind ∼ estar* adelantado/atrasado con respecto al programa ⚊ 2 (a) (list) lista f (b) (AmE) (timetable — for transport) horario m; (— for classes) horario m (de clases)

schedule² vt (timetable, plan) (usu pass) programar; the conference is ∼d to take place in August la conferencia está planeada para el mes de agosto

scheduled /'skedʒuːld ‖'ʃedjuːld/ adj (before n) (a) (planned) ⟨meeting/visit⟩ previsto, programado (b) ⟨flight/service⟩ regular

scheme¹ /skiːm/ n (plan) plan m; (underhand) ardid m; (plot) confabulación f, conspiración f

scheme² vi intrigar*; (plot) conspirar

scheming¹ /'skiːmɪŋ/ adj intrigante

scheming² n maquinaciones fpl, intrigas fpl

schism /'sɪzəm, 'skɪzəm/ n cisma m

schizophrenia /ˌskɪtsə'friːniə ‖ˌskɪtsə'friːniə/ n esquizofrenia f

schizophrenic /ˌskɪtsə'frenɪk, -'friːnɪk ‖ˌskɪtsəʊ'frenɪk, -fri:nɪk/ adj esquizofrénico

schmaltz /ʃmɔːlts/ n (colloq) sensiblería f

schmaltzy /'ʃmɔːltsi/ adj **-zier, -ziest** (colloq) sensiblero

scholar /'skɑːlər ‖'skɒlə(r)/ n (a) (learned person) erudito, -ta m,f (b) (holder of scholarship) becario, -ria m,f

scholarly /'skɑːlərli ‖'skɒləli/ adj ⟨person⟩ erudito, docto; ⟨attainments⟩ en el campo académico

scholarship /'skɑːlərʃɪp ‖'skɒləʃɪp/ n ⚊ 1 (grant) beca f ⚊ 2 (learning) erudición f

school¹ /skuːl/ n ⚊ 1 (a) (in primary, secondary education) colegio m, escuela f; to go to ∼ ir* al colegio or a la escuela; (before n) ⟨uniform/rules⟩ del colegio; ⟨bus⟩ escolar; ∼ fees cuotas que se pagan en un colegio particular, colegiatura f (Méx); ∼ year año m escolar or lectivo (b) (college, university) (AmE) universidad f (c) (department) facultad f ⚊ 2 (other training establishment) academia f, escuela f ⚊ 3 (of fish) cardumen m, banco m; (of dolphins, whales) grupo m

school² vt ⟨person⟩ instruir*; (train) capacitar

school: ∼**boy** n colegial m, escolar m; ∼**child** n colegial, -giala m,f, escolar mf; ∼**girl** n colegiala f, escolar f

schooling /'skuːlɪŋ/ n educación f, estudios mpl

AmC Central America
AmL Latin America
AmS South America
Andes Andean Region

Arg Argentina
Bol Bolivia
Chi Chile
CS Southern Cone

Cu Cuba
Ec Ecuador
Esp Spain
Méx Mexico

Per Peru
RPI River Plate Area
Ur Uruguay
Ven Venezuela

school: ~-leaver /'liːvər ‖'liːvə(r)/ *n* (BrE)
joven *mf* que termina el colegio; **~master** *n*
(BrE frml) (in primary school) maestro *m*; (in secondary
school) profesor *m*; **~mistress** *n* (BrE frml) (in
primary school) maestra; (in secondary school)
profesora *f*; **~teacher** *n* (in primary school)
maestro, -tra *m,f*; (in secondary school) profesor,
-sora *m,f*

science /'saɪəns/ *n* ciencia *f*

science fiction *n* ciencia ficción *f*

scientific /saɪən'tɪfɪk/ *adj* científico

scientist /'saɪəntəst ‖'saɪəntɪst/ *n* científico,
-ca *m,f*

sci-fi /'saɪfaɪ/ *n* (colloq) ciencia ficción *f*

Scillies /'sɪliz/ *pl n* ▶ ISLES OF SCILLY

scintillating /'sɪntleɪtɪŋ ‖'sɪntɪleɪtɪŋ/ *adj*
‹wit/conversation› chispeante

scissors /'sɪzərz ‖'sɪzəz/ *n* (+ *pl vb*) tijeras *fpl*,
tijera *f*

scoff /skɑːf ‖skɒf/ *vi* to ~ (AT sb/sth) burlarse
(DE algn/algo)
■ ~ *vt* (eat greedily) (BrE colloq) engullirse*

scold /skəʊld/ *vt* reprender, regañar, retar (CS)

scone /skəʊn, skɑːn ‖skɒn, skəʊn/ *n* (in UK)
bollito que se come untado de mantequilla,
mermelada etc, scone *m* (CS), bísquet *m* (Méx)

scoop /skuːp/ *n* **1** (a) (for grain, ice cream) pala *f*
(b) (measure — of ice cream) bola *f* **2** (Journ)
primicia *f*
■ **scoop out** **1** [*v + o + adv, v + adv + o*] ‹flour/
rice/soil› sacar* (con pala, cuchara etc) **2** [*v +
adv + o*] (hollow) ‹hole/tunnel› excavar
■ **scoop up** [*v + o + adv, v + adv + o*] recoger*
(con pala, cuchara etc)

scooter /'skuːtər ‖'skuːtə(r)/ *n* (a) (motor ~)
escúter *m*, Vespa® *f* (b) (toy) patinete *m*

scope /skəʊp/ *n* (of law, regulations) alcance *m*; (of
influence) ámbito *m*; (of investigation) campo *m*

scorch /skɔːrtʃ ‖skɔːtʃ/ *vt* ‹fabric›
chamuscar*; «sun» ‹plant› quemar, abrasar

score¹ /skɔːr ‖skɔː(r)/ *n* **1** (a) (in game): the
final ~ el resultado final; what's the ~? ¿cómo
van? (b) (in competition, test etc) puntuación *f*,
puntaje *m* (AmL) **2** (a) (account): I have no
worries on that ~ en lo que a eso se refiere, no
me preocupo; to have a ~ to settle with sb tener*
que arreglar cuentas con algn (b) (situation)
(colloq): to know the ~ saber cómo son las cosas
3 (Mus) (a) (notation) partitura *f* (b) (music for
show, movie) música *f* **4** (twenty) veintena *f*; there
were ~s of people there había muchísima gente

score² *vt* **1** (a) (Sport) ‹goal› marcar*,
anotar(se) (AmL); you ~ 20 points for that eso te
da *or* (AmL tb) con eso te anotas 20 puntos (b) (in
competition, test) «person» sacar* (c) (win) ‹success›
lograr, conseguir* **2** (cut, mark) ‹surface/paper›
marcar*
■ ~ *vi* (Sport) marcar*, anotar(se) un tanto (AmL)

scoreboard /'skɔːrbɔːrd ‖'skɔːbɔːd/ *n*
marcador *m*

scorn¹ /skɔːrn ‖'skɔːn/ *n* desdén *m*; to pour ~
on sth desdeñar algo

scorn² *vt* (reject, despise) desdeñar

scornful /'skɔːrnfəl ‖'skɔːnfəl/ *adj* desdeñoso;
to be ~ of sth desdeñar algo

Scorpio /'skɔːrpiəʊ ‖'skɔːpiəʊ/ *n* (*pl* **-os**) (a)
(sign) (no art) Escorpio, Escorpión (b) (person)
Escorpio *or* escorpio *mf*, Escorpión *or* escorpión
mf, escorpión, -na *m,f*

scorpion /'skɔːrpiən ‖'skɔːpiən/ *n* escorpión
m, alacrán *m*

Scot /skɑːt ‖skɒt/ *n* escocés, -cesa *m,f*

scotch¹ /skɑːtʃ ‖skɒtʃ/ *vt* ‹plan/efforts› echar
por tierra; ‹rumors› acallar

scotch², Scotch *n* whisky *m* *or* güisqui *m*
(escocés)

Scotch: ~ egg *n*: huevo duro envuelto en
carne de salchicha y rebozado; ~ **tape**® *n* (AmE)
cinta *f* Scotch®, cel(l)o® *m* (Esp), (cinta *f*) durex®
m (AmL)

scot-free /skɑːt'friː ‖,skɒt'friː/ *adj* (pred): to
get away ~ quedar impune

Scotland /'skɑːtlənd ‖'skɒtlənd/ *n* Escocia *f*

Scots /skɑːts ‖skɒts/ *adj* (before n) escocés

Scots: ~man /'skɑːtsmən ‖'skɒtsmən/ *n* (*pl*
-men /-mən/) escocés *m*; **~woman** *n* escocesa
f

Scottish /'skɑːtɪʃ ‖'skɒtɪʃ/ *adj* escocés

scoundrel /'skaʊndrəl/ *n* (dated) sinvergüenza
mf

scour /skaʊr ‖skaʊə(r)/ *vt* **1** (rub hard) fregar*
2 (search thoroughly) registrar

scourge /skɜːrdʒ ‖skɜːdʒ/ *n* azote *m*

scouring powder /'skaʊrɪŋ ‖'skaʊərɪŋ/ *n*
polvo *m* limpiador, limpiador *m* en polvo,
pulidor *m* (RPl)

scout /skaʊt/ *n* **1** (person) explorador, -dora
m,f **2** also **Scout** (boy ~) explorador *m*, (boy)
scout *m*; (girl ~) exploradora *f*, (girl) scout *f*
■ **scout around** [*v + adv*] to ~ around (FOR sth)
buscar* (algo)

scowl¹ /skaʊl/ *n* ceño *m* fruncido

scowl² *vi* fruncir* el ceño; to ~ AT sb mirar a
algn con el ceño fruncido

scrabble /'skræbəl/ *vi* «dog/chicken»
escarbar; he was scrabbling about in the drawers
of the desk estaba hurgando en los cajones del
escritorio

scraggy /'skrægi/ *adj* **-gier, -giest** (a)
(scrawny) esmirriado (b) (tough) ‹meat› duro

scram /skræm/ *vi* **-mm-** (colloq): go on, ~!
¡fuera *or* largo de aquí! (fam)

scramble¹ /'skræmbəl/ *n* (*no pl*) (a) (chaotic
rush): barullo *m*; there was a last-minute ~ for
tickets a último momento hubo una rebatiña
para conseguir entradas (b) (difficult climb) subida *f*
difícil

scramble² *vi* (+ *adv compl*): we ~d through
the bushes nos abrimos paso con dificultad a
través de los arbustos
■ ~ *vt* (a) (mix) mezclar (b) ‹message› codificar*

scrambled egg /'skræmbəld/ *n* (Culin)
huevos *mpl* revueltos

scrap¹ /skræp/ *n* **1** (a) (of paper, cloth, leather)
pedacito *m*, trocito *m* (b) (single bit) (with neg, no
pl): it doesn't make a ~ of difference what you
think lo que tú pienses no importa en lo más
mínimo **2 scraps** *pl* sobras *fpl*, sobros *mpl*
(AmC) **3** (reusable waste) chatarra *f*; (before n) ~
paper papel *m* para borrador

S

scrap² *vt* **-pp- (a)** (abandon) ⟨idea⟩ desechar; ⟨plan⟩ abandonar **(b)** (throw away) tirar a la basura, botar (AmL exc RPl)

scrapbook /'skræpbʊk/ *n* álbum *m* de recortes

scrape¹ /skreɪp/ *n* (colloq) lío *m* (fam)

scrape² *vt* **1 (a)** (rub against) rozar*; (grate against) rascar* **(b)** (damage, graze) ⟨paintwork⟩ rayar; ⟨knee/elbow⟩ rasparse, rasguñarse **2 (a)** (clean) ⟨carrot/potato⟩ pelar; ⟨woodwork⟩ raspar, rascar*; **to ~ sth off** ⟨paint/wallpaper⟩ quitar algo (con una rasqueta/un cuchillo); **~ the mud off your boots** quítales el barro a las botas (con un cuchillo, contra una piedra etc) **(b)** ⟨bowl/pan⟩ fregar*

■ **scrape through** [v + adv] [v + prep + o] ⟨exam⟩ aprobar* raspando or (fam) por los pelos

scraper /'skreɪpər ‖ 'skreɪpə(r)/ *n* (tool) rasqueta *f*, espátula *f*

scrap: **~heap** *n*: **to throw sth on the ~heap** desechar algo; **at 50 he found himself on the ~heap** a los 50 años se vio sin trabajo y sin perspectivas de futuro; **~yard** *n* chatarrería *f*; (for cars) cementerio *m* de automóviles, desguace *m* or (Méx) deshuesadero *m*

scratch¹ /skrætʃ/ *n* **1** rasguño *m*, arañazo *m*; (on paint, record, furniture) rayón *m* **2** (in phrases) **from scratch: to start from ~** empezar* desde cero; **to be up to ~** (colloq) dar* la talla

scratch² *vt* **(a)** ⟨paint/record/furniture⟩ rayar **(b)** (with claws, nails) arañar **(c)** ⟨name/initials⟩ marcar* **(d)** (to relieve itch) rascarse*

■ **~** *vi* **(a)** (damage, wound) arañar **(b)** (to relieve itching) rascarse*

■ **scratch out** [v + o + adv, v + adv + o] **(a)** (gouge): **to ~ sb's eyes out** sacarle* los ojos a algn **(b)** (strike out) ⟨name/sentence⟩ tachar; (on ticket) rascar*

scratch: **~ card** *n* número *m* de la lotería (con sección que se raspa); **~ pad** *n* (AmE) bloc *m* (para borrador o apuntes)

scrawl¹ /skrɔːl/ *n* garabatos *mpl*

scrawl² *vt/i* garabatear

scrawny /'skrɔːni/ *adj* **-nier, -niest** ⟨person⟩ escuálido; ⟨arms/legs⟩ esquelético

scream¹ /skriːm/ *n* grito *m*, chillido *m*; (louder) alarido *m*

scream² *vi* gritar, chillar; « baby » llorar a gritos

■ **~** *vt* (insult) gritar, soltar*; ⟨command⟩ dar* a voces or a gritos

screech¹ /skriːtʃ/ *n* (of terror, pain) alarido *m*; (of joy) chillido *m*; (of brakes) chirrido *m*; (of bird) chillido *m*

screech² *vi* « person/animal » chillar; « brakes/tires » chirriar*

screen¹ /skriːn/ *n* **1** (folding) biombo *m*; (as partition) mampara *f*; (protective, defensive) cortina *f* **2** (Cin, Comput, Phot, TV) pantalla *f*

screen² *vt* **1 (a)** (conceal) ocultar, tapar **(b)** (protect) proteger* **2** ⟨TV program⟩ emitir; ⟨film⟩ proyectar **3** (check, examine) ⟨blood donor⟩ someter a una revisión (médica); ⟨applicants⟩ someter a una investigación de antecedentes

■ **screen off** [v + o + adv, v + adv + o] aislar*, separar (con un biombo o una mampara)

screen: **~ door** *n* puerta *f* mosquitera;

~play *n* guion *m*; **~ saver** /'seɪvər ‖ 'seɪvə(r)/ *n* (Comput) protector *m* de pantalla, salvapantalla *m*; **~ test** *n* prueba *f* (cinematográfica)

screw¹ /skruː/ *n* (Const, Tech) tornillo *m*; **to have a ~ loose** (colloq & hum): **he's/you've got a ~ loose** le/te falta un tornillo (fam & hum)

screw² *vt* (Const, Tech) atornillar; **to ~ sth down** (securely) atornillar (bien) algo; **~ the lid on tight** enrosca bien la tapa

■ **~ up** [v + o + adv, v + adv + o] **1** (tighten) ⟨bolt⟩ apretar* **2** (crumple) ⟨letter/paper⟩ arrugar* **3** (spoil, botch) (sl) fastidiar (fam)

screw: **~ball** *n* (eccentric person) (AmE colloq) excéntrico, -ca *mf*, chiflado, -da *m,f* (fam); **~driver** *n* destornillador *m*, desarmador *m* (Méx), desatornillador *m* (AmC, Chi); **~top** *adj* ⟨bottle⟩ con tapón de rosca; ⟨jar⟩ con tapa de rosca

scribble¹ /'skrɪbəl/ *n* garabato *m*

scribble² *vt* garabatear; **to ~ sth down** anotar algo rápidamente

■ **~** *vi* garabatear

scrimp /skrɪmp/ *vi*: **to ~ on sth** escatimar en algo; **to ~ and save** cuidar mucho el dinero

script /skrɪpt/ *n* **1 (a)** (handwriting) letra *f* **(b)** (style of writing) caligrafía *f* **(c)** (alphabet) escritura *f* **2** (text of film, broadcast) guion *m*

scripture /'skrɪptʃər ‖ 'skrɪptʃə(r)/ *n*: **the (Holy) S~s** las (Sagradas) Escrituras

scriptwriter /'skrɪptˌraɪtər ‖ 'skrɪptˌraɪtə(r)/ *n* guionista *mf*

scroll¹ /skrəʊl/ *n* rollo *m*

scroll² *vi* (Comput): **to ~ up/down** hacer* avanzar/retroceder el texto que aparece en pantalla

scroll bar *n* (Comput) barra *f* de enrollar

scrounge /skraʊndʒ/ (colloq) *vt* **to ~ sth FROM/OFF sb** gorronearle or gorrearle or (RPl) garronearle or (Chi) bolsearle algo a algn (fam)

■ **~** *vi* gorronear or gorrear or (RPl) garronear or (Chi) bolsear (fam)

scrub¹ /skrʌb/ *n* **1** (vegetation) matorrales *mpl* **2** (act) (no pl): **to give sth a good ~** fregar* or (Méx) tallar algo bien (con cepillo); (before *n*) **~ brush** (AmE) cepillo *m* de fregar

scrub² *vt* **-bb-** ⟨floor/table⟩ fregar*; ⟨knees/hands⟩ restregar*

scrubbing brush /'skrʌbɪŋ/ *n* cepillo *m* de fregar

scruff /skrʌf/ *n*: **by the ~ of the neck** por el pescuezo

scruffy /'skrʌfi/ *adj* **-fier, -fiest** (colloq) ⟨person⟩ dejado, desaliñado; **a ~-looking building** un edificio de aspecto destartalado

scrum /skrʌm/, **scrummage** /'skrʌmɪdʒ/ *n* (in rugby) melé *f* (ordenada), scrum *m*

scrumptious /'skrʌmpʃəs/ *adj* (colloq) ⟨meal⟩ para chuparse los dedos (fam)

scruple /'skruːpəl/ *n* (usu pl) escrúpulo *m*

scrupulous /'skruːpjələs ‖ 'skruːpjʊləs/ *adj* escrupuloso

scrupulously /'skruːpjələsli ‖ 'skruːpjʊləsli/ *adv* escrupulosamente; **~ clean** impecable

scrutinize /'skruːtɪnaɪz ‖ 'skruːtɪnaɪz/ *vt* ⟨document⟩ inspeccionar; ⟨face⟩ escudriñar

scrutiny /'skru:tɲi ‖'skru:tɪni/ n (pl **-nies**) examen m

scuba diving /'sku:bə/ n buceo m, submarinismo m

scuff /skʌf/ vt ⟨floor⟩ dejar marcas en; ⟨leather⟩ raspar

scuffle /'skʌfəl/ n refriega f

scullery /'skʌləri/ n (pl **-ries**) habitación anexa a la cocina donde se fregaba, se preparaban las verduras etc

sculpt /skʌlpt/ vt/i esculpir

sculptor /'skʌlptər ‖'skʌlptə(r)/ n escultor, -tora m,f

sculpture¹ /'skʌlptʃər ‖'skʌlptʃə(r)/ n escultura f

sculpture² vt esculpir

scum /skʌm/ n **1** (on liquid) capa f de suciedad **2** (colloq) (people) escoria f; the **~ of the earth** la escoria de la sociedad

scupper /'skʌpər ‖'skʌpə(r)/ vt (BrE) ⟨ship⟩ hundir; ⟨plan/talks⟩ echar por tierra

scurry /'skɜːri ‖'skʌri/ vi: he scurried away o off salió disparado; to **~ around** «mice» corretear

scuttle¹ /'skʌtl/ n (coal **~**) cubo m para el carbón

scuttle² vt ⟨ship⟩ hundir; ⟨plans/talks⟩ echar por tierra

■ **~** vi: the children **~**d away o off los niños se escabulleron rápidamente

scythe /saɪð/ n guadaña f

SD, S Dak = South Dakota

SE (= **southeast**) SE

sea /si:/ n **1** (often pl) (ocean) mar m [The noun MAR is feminine in literary language and in some set idiomatic expressions]; to go/travel by **~** ir*/ viajar en barco; ⟨before n⟩ ⟨route/transport⟩ marítimo; ⟨battle⟩ naval; the **~** breeze la brisa del mar; **~** crossing travesía f **2** (large mass, quantity) (no pl): a **~** of faces una multitud de rostros

sea: **~ anemone** n anémona f or ortiga f de mar; **~bed** n the **~bed** el lecho marino; **~ bird** n ave f‡ marina; **~food** n mariscos mpl, marisco m (Esp); **~front** n paseo m marítimo, malecón m (AmL), costanera f (CS); **~gull** n gaviota f; **~horse** n caballito m de mar

seal¹ /si:l/ n **1** (implement, impression) sello m; he gave the plan his **~ of approval** dio su aprobación al plan **2** (a) (security device) precinto m (b) (airtight closure) cierre m hermético; (on glass jar) aro m de goma **3** (Zool) foca f

seal² vt **1** (a) ⟨envelope/parcel⟩ cerrar*; (with tape) precintar; (with wax) lacrar; my lips are **~ed** (set phrase) soy una tumba (b) ⟨jar/container⟩ cerrar* herméticamente; ⟨tomb/door⟩ precintar; ⟨wood⟩ sellar **2** (affix seal to) ⟨document/treaty⟩ sellar **3** (decide, determine) ⟨victory/outcome⟩ decidir; their fate was **~ed** su destino estaba escrito

■ **seal off** [v + o + adv, v + adv + o] ⟨area/road/ building⟩ acordonar; ⟨exit⟩ cerrar*

sea level n nivel m del mar

sealing wax /'si:lɪŋ/ n lacre m

sea lion n león m marino

seam /si:m/ n **1** (stitching) costura f **2** (of coal, gold) veta f, filón m

seaman /'si:mən/ n (pl **-men** /-mən/) (sailor) marinero m; (officer) marino m

seamy /'si:mi/ adj **-mier, -miest** sórdido

seance /'seɪɑːns/ n sesión f de espiritismo

sear /sɪr ‖sɪə(r)/ vt (a) ⟨flesh⟩ quemar; ⟨meat⟩ (Culin) dorar rápidamente a fuego muy vivo (b) (wither) ⟨heat⟩ secar*, abrasar

search¹ /sɜːrtʃ ‖sɜːtʃ/ vt ⟨building⟩ registrar, esculcar* (AmL exc CS); ⟨person⟩ registrar, cachear, catear (Méx); ⟨luggage⟩ registrar, revisar (AmL), esculcar* (AmL exc CS); ⟨records/files⟩ buscar* en

■ **~** vi buscar*; to **~ FOR** sth/sb buscar* algo/a algn

search² n (a) (hunt, quest) **~** (FOR sth/sb) búsqueda f (DE algo/algn) (b) (of building, pockets) registro m, esculque m (Col, Méx); (of records, documents) inspección f (c) (Comput) búsqueda f

search engine n (Comput) buscador m

searching /'sɜːrtʃɪŋ ‖'sɜːtʃɪŋ/ adj ⟨look⟩ inquisitivo; ⟨question⟩ perspicaz

search: **~light** n reflector m; **~ party** n partida f de rescate

sea: **~scape** /'si:skeɪp/ n marina f; **~shell** n concha f (de mar); **~shore** n orilla f del mar; **~sick** adj mareado; **~sickness** n mareo m (en los viajes por mar); **~side** n costa f, playa f; we spent two weeks at the **~side** pasamos dos semanas en la costa or en la playa

season¹ /'si:zn/ n **1** (division of year) estación f **2** (for specific activity, event, crop) temporada f **3** (in phrases) **in season** (of female animal) en celo; (of fresh food, game): cherries are in **~** es época or temporada de cerezas; **out of season** fuera de temporada

season² vt **1** (Culin) condimentar, sazonar; (with salt and pepper) salpimentar* **2** ⟨wood⟩ secar*, curar

seasonal /'si:zṇəl ‖'si:zənl/ adj ⟨variations/ fluctuations⟩ estacional; ⟨vegetables⟩ del tiempo; ⟨demand⟩ de estación

seasoned /'si:zṇd/ adj **1** (experienced) ⟨troops/ traveler⟩ avezado, experimentado **2** ⟨food⟩ condimentado, sazonado **3** ⟨wood⟩ seco, curado

seasoning /'si:zṇɪŋ/ n (Culin) condimento m, sazón f

season ticket n abono m (de temporada)

seat¹ /si:t/ n **1** (place to sit) asiento m; please have o take a **~** tome asiento, por favor (frml), siéntese, por favor; there aren't any **~s** left (in cinema) no quedan localidades **2** (of chair) asiento m **3** (a) (Govt) escaño m, banca f (RPl), curul m (Col, Méx) (b) (constituency) (BrE) distrito m electoral **4** (center) sede f; the **~ of government** la sede del gobierno

seat² vt (a) ⟨child⟩ sentar*; to remain **~ed** permanecer* sentado (b) (have room for) ⟨auditorium⟩ tener* cabida or capacidad para

seat belt n cinturón m de seguridad

seating /'si:tɪŋ/ n número m de asientos; ⟨before n⟩ **~ capacity** aforo m

sea: **~ urchin** n erizo m de mar; **~water** n ⋯⋙

S

agua f‡ de mar, agua f‡ salada; **~way** n ruta f
marítima; **~weed** n alga f‡ marina; **~worthy**
adj ⟨ship⟩ en condiciones de navegar

secluded /sɪ'klu:dəd ‖sɪ'klu:dɪd/ adj ⟨house/
area⟩ apartado, aislado; ⟨life/existence⟩ solitario

seclusion /sɪ'klu:ʒən/ n aislamiento m

second¹ /'sekənd/ adj **1** segundo; **~ language**
segundo idioma m; **our service is ~ to none**
nuestro servicio es insuperable **2** (elliptical use): **I
leave on the ~ (of the month)** me voy el (día) dos

second² adv (a) (in position, time, order) en
segundo lugar (b) (secondly) en segundo lugar (c)
(with superl): **the ~ highest building** el segundo
edificio en altura

second³ n **1** (of time) segundo m; **it doesn't
take a ~** no lleva ni un segundo; ⟨before n⟩ **~
hand** segundero m **2** (a) **~ (gear)** (Auto) ⟨no
art⟩ segunda f (b) (in competition): **he finished a
good/poor ~** quedó en un honroso/deslucido
segundo lugar **3** (substandard product) artículo m
con defectos de fábrica **4 seconds** pl (second
helping; colloq): **to have ~s** repetir*

second⁴ vt **1** (support) ⟨motion/candidate⟩
secundar **2** /sɪ'kʊnd/ (attach) (BrE) **to ~ sb (TO
sth)** trasladar a algn temporalmente (A algo)

secondary /'sekənderi ‖'sekəndri/ adj **1** (a)
(subordinate) ⟨matter⟩ de interés secundario; ⟨road⟩
secundario (b) (not primary, original) ⟨source⟩ de
segunda mano; ⟨industry⟩ derivado **2** ⟨teacher/
pupils⟩ de enseñanza secundaria

secondary school n instituto m or colegio
m de enseñanza secundaria, liceo m (CS, Ven)

second: ~ best n: **he won't accept ~ best**
solo se conforma con lo mejor; **~ class** adv
⟨travel/go⟩ en segunda (clase); **~-class**
/'sekənd'klɑːs ‖'sekənd'klɑːs/ adj ⟨pred **~
class**⟩ (a) (inferior) ⟨goods/service⟩ de segunda
(clase or categoría), de calidad inferior (b) (Post):
~-class mail (in UK) servicio regular de correos,
que tarda más en llegar a destino que el de
primera clase (c) (in UK) (Transp) ⟨travel/ticket/
compartment⟩ de segunda (clase)

second-hand¹ /'sekənd'hænd/ adj ⟨pred
second hand⟩ ⟨car/clothes⟩ de segunda mano,
usado; ⟨bookstore⟩ de viejo; ⟨shop⟩ de artículos de
segunda mano; ⟨information⟩ de segunda mano

second-hand² adv: **to buy sth ~** comprar
algo de segunda mano

second-in-command /'sekəndɪnkə'mænd
‖,sekəndɪnkə'mɑːnd/ n (pl
seconds-in-command) número dos mf
(persona directamente por debajo de la autoridad
máxima de una organización, departamento etc)

secondly /'sekəndli/ adv (indep) en segundo
lugar

second-rate /'sekənd'reɪt/ adj mediocre

secrecy /'siːkrəsi/ n secreto m

secret¹ /'siːkrət ‖'siːkrɪt/ n secreto m; **in ~** en
secreto; **to make no ~ of sth** no esconder algo

secret² adj secreto

secretarial /'sekrə'teriəl ‖,sekrə'teəriəl/ adj
⟨job⟩ de oficina, de secretaria/secretario; ⟨course⟩
de secretariado

secretary /'sekrəteri ‖'sekrətri/ n (pl **-ries**)
1 (in office, of committee, of society) secretario, -ria
m,f **2** (Govt) ministro, -tra m,f, secretario, -ria
m,f (Méx)

Secretary of State n (pl **Secretaries of
State**) (Govt) (a) (in US) secretario, -ria m,f de
Estado (de los Estados Unidos); (b) (in UK)
ministro, -tra m,f, secretario, -ria m,f (Méx)

secrete /sɪ'kriːt/ vt **1** (Biol, Physiol) segregar*,
secretar **2** (hide) (frml) ocultar

secretive /'siːkrətɪv/ adj reservado

secret: ~ police n policía f secreta; **~
service** n (intelligence service) servicio m secreto

sect /sekt/ n secta f

sectarian /sek'teriən ‖sek'teəriən/ adj ⟨views/
violence⟩ sectario; ⟨schooling/school⟩ confesional

section /'sekʃən/ n **1** (of object, newspaper,
orchestra) sección f; (of machine, piece of furniture)
parte f; (of road) tramo m; (of city, population) sector
m **2** (department) sección f **3** (in geometry, drawing)
sección f

sector /'sektər ‖'sektə(r)/ n sector m

secular /'sekjələr ‖'sekjʊlə(r)/ adj ⟨education⟩
laico; ⟨society/art⟩ secular

secure¹ /sɪ'kjʊr ‖sɪ'kjʊə(r)/ adj **1** (a) (safe)
⟨fortress/hideaway⟩ seguro (b) (emotionally)
⟨childhood/home⟩ estable (c) (assured) ⟨job/
investment⟩ seguro **2** ⟨foothold/shelf⟩ firme;
⟨foundation⟩ sólido

secure² vt **1** (obtain) ⟨job/votes/support⟩
conseguir* **2** (fasten, fix firmly) ⟨door/shelf⟩
asegurar

security /sɪ'kjʊrəti ‖sɪ'kjʊərəti/ n (pl **-ties**)
1 (against crime, espionage etc) seguridad f; ⟨before
n⟩ **~ guard** guarda jurado, guarda jurada m,f **2**
(a) (safety, certainty) seguridad f (b) (protection)
seguro m **3** (Fin) (a) (guarantee) garantía f (b)
securities pl (Fin) valores mpl, títulos mpl

Security Council n the (United Nations) ~
~ el Consejo de Seguridad (de las Naciones
Unidas)

sedan /sɪ'dæn/ n **1** (car) (AmE) sedán m **2** ~
(chair) palanquín m, silla f de manos

sedate¹ /sɪ'deɪt/ adj reposado, tranquilo

sedate² vt (Med) sedar

sedation /sɪ'deɪʃən/ n sedación f; **to be under
~** estar* bajo el efecto de los sedantes

sedative /'sedətɪv/ n sedante m

sediment /'sedəmənt ‖'sedɪmənt/ n (a) (in
wine, coffee) poso m, asiento m (b) (Geol)
sedimento m

seduce /sɪ'duːs ‖sɪ'djuːs/ vt seducir*

seduction /sɪ'dʌkʃən/ n seducción f

seductive /sɪ'dʌktɪv/ adj seductor

see /siː/ (past saw; past p seen) vt **1** (regard,
perceive) ver*; **I can't ~ a thing!** ¡no veo nada!; **I
saw her cross the street** la vi cruzar la calle; **I**

AmC	América Central	Arg	Argentina	Cu	Cuba	Per	Perú
AmL	América Latina	Bol	Bolivia	Ec	Ecuador	RPI	Río de la Plata
AmS	América del Sur	Chi	Chile	Esp	España	Ur	Uruguay
Andes	Región andina	CS	Cono Sur	Méx	México	Ven	Venezuela

thought I was ~ing things pensé que estaba viendo visiones; ~ **page 20** ver página 20; **I don't know what she ~s in him** no sé qué es lo que le ve; **anyone can ~ she's upset** cualquiera se da cuenta de que está disgustada; **the way I ~ it, as I ~ it** a mi modo de ver; **can you ~ him as a teacher?** ¿te lo imaginas de profesor?; **I'll ~ what I can do** veré qué puedo hacer; **that remains to be ~** en eso está por verse
2 (understand) ver*; **do you ~ what I mean?** ¿entiendes?
3 (ensure) **to ~ THAT** asegurarse DE QUE; **~ that it doesn't happen again** que no vuelva a suceder
4 (a) (meet, visit) ver*; **I'm ~ing him on Tuesday** lo voy a ver el martes **(b)** (go out with) (colloq) **salir*** con **(c)** (saying goodbye) (colloq): **~ you!** ¡hasta luego!, ¡hasta la vista!; **~ you later/soon!** ¡hasta luego/pronto!
5 (a) (consult) ⟨doctor/manager⟩ **ver* (b)** (receive) ver*, atender*; **the doctor will ~ you now** el doctor lo verá **or** lo atenderá ahora
6 (escort, accompany) acompañar; **to ~ sb to the door** acompañar a algn a la puerta
■ **~** vi ver*; **~ for yourself!** ¡compruébalo tú mismo!; **as far as I can ~** por lo que ya veo; **I ~** (expressing realization) ya veo; (accepting explanation) entiendo; **let's ~** vamos a ver, veamos; **will it work? — try it and ~** ¿funcionará? — prueba a ver; **~ing is believing** ver para creer
■ **see off** [v + o + adv, v + adv + o] **1** (say goodbye to) despedir*, despedirse* de **2** (get rid of) deshacerse* de
■ **see out** [v + o + adv, v + adv + o] ⟨person⟩ acompañar (hasta la puerta); **I can ~ myself out** no hace falta que me acompañes
■ **see through 1** [v + prep + o] (not be deceived by) calar
2 [v + o + adv] [v + o + prep + o] (last): **make sure this ~s you through** con esto te tienes que alcanzar; **$20 should ~ me through the week** con 20 dólares me alcanza hasta el fin de semana **3** [v + o + adv] (carry to completion) terminar
■ **see to** [v + prep + o] (attend to) ocuparse de

seed /siːd/ n **1** (of plant) semilla f; (of orange, grape) (AmE) pepita f, semilla f; **to go to ~** estar* en decadencia **2** (Sport) cabeza mf de serie, sembrado, -da m,f (Méx)

seedless /'siːdləs ‖'siːdlɪs/ adj sin pepitas or semillas

seedling /'siːdlɪŋ/ n planta f de semillero

seedy /'siːdi/ adj **-dier, -diest** ⟨nightclub/bar⟩ sórdido, de mala muerte (fam), cutre (Esp fam); ⟨appearance⟩ desastrado

seeing /'siːɪŋ/ conj (colloq) **~ (that)** o **~ as** ya que

seek /siːk/ (past & past p **sought**) vt **(a)** (search for) (frml) ⟨person/object⟩ buscar* **(b)** (try to obtain) ⟨work/companionship⟩ buscar*; ⟨solution/explanation⟩ tratar de encontrar **(c)** (request) ⟨approval/help⟩ pedir* **(d)** (try to bring about) (frml) ⟨reconciliation⟩ buscar*
■ **seek out** [v + o + adv, v + adv + o] ⟨person⟩ buscar*; ⟨opinion⟩ pedir*

seem /siːm/ vi parecer*; **strange as it may ~** por raro que parezca; **she ~s to like you** parece que le caes bien; **so it ~s, so it would ~** eso parece, así parece; **I ~ to remember that you …** creo recordar que tú …; **it ~s to me/him/them**

that … me/le/les parece que …; I can't ~ to remember where I put it no logro acordarme de dónde lo puse

seen /siːn/ past p of SEE

seep /siːp/ vi ⟨liquid/moisture⟩ filtrarse

seesaw /'siːsɔː/ n balancín m, subibaja m

seethe /siːð/ vi **(a)** (be agitated) bullir*; **the town was seething with tourists** la ciudad estaba plagada de turistas **(b)** (be angry) estar* furioso; **I was absolutely seething** me hervía la sangre

see-through /'siːθruː/ adj transparente

segment /'segmənt/ n **(a)** (of circle, sphere, line) segmento m **(b)** (of citrus fruit) gajo m; **(c)** (section) sector m

segregate /'segrɪgeɪt/ vt ⟨races/sexes⟩ segregar*; ⟨rival groups⟩ mantener* aparte

segregation /segrɪ'geɪʃən/ n segregación f

seize /siːz/ vt **1** (grab, snatch) ⟨hand/object⟩ agarrar; ⟨opportunity⟩ aprovechar; ⟨power⟩ tomar **2 (a)** (capture) ⟨town/fortress⟩ tomar; ⟨person⟩ detener* **(b)** ⟨assets/property⟩ (confiscate) confiscar*; (impound) embargar*; ⟨cargo/contraband⟩ confiscar*; ⟨drugs/arms⟩ incautar
■ **seize on, seize upon** [v + prep + o] ⟨chance⟩ aprovechar
■ **seize up** [v + adv] ⟨engine⟩ agarrotarse, fundirse (AmL); ⟨muscles⟩ agarrotarse; ⟨traffic⟩ paralizarse*

seizure /'siːʒər ‖'siːʒə(r)/ n **1** (of property, contraband) confiscación f **2** (Med) ataque m

seldom /'seldəm/ adv rara vez, pocas veces

select¹ /sɪ'lekt/ vt ⟨gift/book/wine⟩ elegir*, escoger*; ⟨candidate/team member⟩ seleccionar

select² adj **(a)** (exclusive) ⟨school⟩ de élite; ⟨district⟩ distinguido **(b)** (choice) ⟨fruit/wine⟩ selecto **(c)** (especially chosen) ⟨group⟩ selecto

selection /sɪ'lekʃən/ n **1** (act, thing chosen) selección f **2** (Busn) (of chocolates, buttons, yarns) surtido m; **a wide ~ of new and used cars** una amplia gama de coches nuevos y usados

selective /sɪ'lektɪv/ adj **(a)** ⟨control/recruitment⟩ selectivo; ⟨reporting⟩ parcial **(b)** (discriminating): **he's fairly ~ about who he mixes with** elige or escoge mucho sus amistades

self /self/ n (pl **selves**): **she's her old ~ again** vuelve a ser la de antes; **you're not your usual cheerful ~** no estás tan alegre como de costumbre

self- /self/ pref **(a)** (concerning the self): **~doubt** duda f de sí mismo **(b)** (with no outside agency) auto-; **~financing** autofinanciado

self-: **~-addressed** /'selfə'drest/ adj: con el nombre y la dirección del remitente; **send a ~-addressed envelope to …** envíe un sobre con su nombre y dirección a …; **~-adhesive** /'selfəd'hiːsɪv/ adj autoadhesivo; **~-assured** /'selfə'ʃʊrd ‖selfə'ʃʊəd, ˌselfə'ʃɔːd/ adj seguro de sí mismo; **~-catering** /'selfˈkeɪtərɪŋ/ adj (BrE) ⟨accommodation⟩ equipado con cocina; **~-centered,** (BrE) **~-centred** /'selfˈsentəd ‖ˌself'sentəd/ adj egocéntrico; **~-confessed** /'selfkən'fest/ adj (before n) confeso; **~-confidence** /'selfˈkɑːnfɪdəns ‖ˌself'kɒnfɪdəns/ n confianza f en sí mismo; **~-confident** /'selfˈkɑːnfɪdənt ‖ˌself'kɒnfɪdənt/ adj seguro de sí mismo; **~-conscious** /'selfˈkɑːntʃəs ‖ˌself'kɒnʃəs/ adj **1** (shy,

S

embarrassed) ⟨person/manner⟩ tímido; **to feel ~-conscious** sentirse* cohibido; **2** (unspontaneous, unnatural) (pej) afectado; **~-contained** /ˌselfkənˈteɪnd/ adj **(a)** ⟨flat⟩ (BrE) con cocina y cuarto de baño propios **(b)** ⟨person⟩ independiente; **~-control** /ˈselfkənˈtrəʊl/ n dominio m de sí mismo; **~-defense,** (BrE) **~-defence** /ˈselfdɪˈfens/ n **(a)** (Law): **to act in ~-defense** actuar* en defensa propia **(b)** (fighting technique) defensa f personal; **~-destruct** /ˈselfdɪˈstrʌkt/ vi autodestruirse*; **~-destructive** /ˈselfdɪˈstrʌktɪv/ adj autodestructivo; **~-determination** /ˌselfdɪˌtɜːrməˈneɪʃən ‖ ˌselfdɪˌtɜːmɪˈneɪʃən/ n autodeterminación f; **~-discipline** /ˈselfˈdɪsəplɪn ‖ ˈselfˈdɪsɪplɪn/ n autodisciplina f; **~-employed** /ˈselfɪmˈplɔɪd/ adj autónomo; **~-esteem** /ˈselfɪˈstiːm/ n autoestima f; **~-evident** /ˈselfˈevədənt ‖ ˈselfˈevɪdənt/ adj ⟨truth⟩ manifiesto; ⟨conclusion⟩ evidente; **~-explanatory** /ˈselfɪkˈsplænətəri ‖ ˌselfɪkˈsplænətri/ adj: **the instructions are ~-explanatory** las instrucciones son muy claras; **~-government** /ˈselfˈɡʌvənmənt ‖ ˌselfˈɡʌvənmənt/ n autogobierno m, autonomía f; **~-help** /ˈselfˈhelp/ n autoayuda f; **~-image** /ˈselfˈɪmɪdʒ/ n imagen f de sí mismo; **~-important** /ˈselfɪmˈpɔːrtnt ‖ ˌselfɪmˈpɔːtnt/ adj engreído, presumido; **~-imposed** /ˈselfɪmˈpəʊzd/ adj voluntario, autoimpuesto; **~-indulgent** /ˈselfɪnˈdʌldʒənt/ adj demasiado indulgente consigo mismo; **~-interest** /ˈselfˈɪntrəst ‖ ˌselfˈɪntrɪst/ n interés m (personal)

selfish /ˈselfɪʃ/ adj egoísta

selfishly /ˈselfɪʃli/ adv egoístamente

selfishness /ˈselfɪʃnəs ‖ ˈselfɪʃnɪs/ n egoísmo m

self: ~-made /ˈselfˈmeɪd/ adj (before n) ⟨man/woman⟩ que ha alcanzado su posición gracias a sus propios esfuerzos; **~-pity** /ˈselfˈpɪti/ n autocompasión f; **~-portrait** /ˈselfˈpɔːrtrət ‖ ˌselfˈpɔːtrɪt/ n autorretrato m; **~-preservation** /ˈselfˈprezərˈveɪʃən ‖ ˌselfˈprezəˈveɪʃən/ n: **the instinct of ~-preservation** el instinto de conservación; **~-raising** /ˈselfˈreɪzɪŋ/ adj (BrE) ▶ ~-RISING; **~-reliant** /ˈselfrɪˈlaɪənt/ adj independiente; **~-respect** /ˈselfrɪˈspekt/ n dignidad f, amor m propio; **~-respecting** /ˈselfrɪˈspektɪŋ/ adj (before n): **no ~-respecting editor would work for them** ningún editor que se precie trabajaría para ellos; **~-righteous** /ˈselfˈraɪtʃəs/ adj ⟨person⟩ con pretensiones de superioridad moral; **~-rising** /ˈselfˈraɪzɪŋ/ adj (AmE) ⟨flour⟩ con polvos de hornear (AmL), con levadura (Esp), leudante (RPl); **~-same** adj (before n) mismísimo; **~-satisfied** /ˈselfˈsætəsfaɪd ‖ ˌselfˈsætɪsfaɪd/ adj ufano, satisfecho de sí mismo; ⟨expression/grin⟩ de (auto)suficiencia; **~-service** /ˈselfˈsɜːrvəs ‖ ˈselfˈsɜːvɪs/, (esp AmE) **self-serve** /-ˈsɜːrv/ adj: **~-service restaurant** autoservicio m, self-service m; **~-sufficiency** /ˌselfsəˈfɪʃənsi/ n independencia f, (Econ) autosuficiencia f; **~-sufficient** /ˈselfsəˈfɪʃənt/ adj ⟨person⟩ independiente; ⟨country⟩ autosuficiente; **~-taught** /ˈselfˈtɔːt/ adj autodidacta, autodidacto

sell /sel/ (past & past p **sold**) vt vender; **to ~ sth TO sb, to ~ sb sth** venderle algo A algn; **to ~ sth FOR sth** vender algo EN or POR algo
■ ~ vi **(a)** ⟨person/company⟩ vender **(b)** (be sold) ⟨product⟩ venderse; **to ~ AT/FOR sth** venderse A/POR algo
■ **sell off** [v + o + adv, v + adv + o] vender; (cheaply) liquidar
■ **sell out 1** [v + adv + o] (sell all of) ⟨stock⟩ agotar; ⟨article⟩ agotar las existencias de **2** [v + adv] **(a)** (sell all stock) ⟨shop⟩ **to ~ out (OF sth):** we've o we're sold out of umbrellas los paraguas están agotados, se agotaron los paraguas **(b)** (be sold) ⟨stock/tickets⟩ agotarse **(c)** (be traitor) ⟨leader/artist⟩ venderse

sell-by date /ˈselbaɪ/ n (BrE) fecha f límite de venta

seller /ˈselər ‖ ˈselə(r)/ n vendedor, -dora m,f

selling /ˈselɪŋ/ n ventas fpl; (before n) **~ price** precio m de venta

Sellotape® /ˈseləteɪp/ n (BrE) ▶ SCOTCH TAPE

sell-out /ˈselaʊt/ n **1** (performance) éxito m de taquilla **2** (betrayal) capitulación f

selves /selvz/ pl of SELF

semaphore /ˈseməfɔːr ‖ ˈseməfɔː(r)/ n código m de señales

semblance /ˈsembləns/ n (frml) **~ OF sth** apariencia f DE algo

semen /ˈsiːmən/ n semen m

semester /səˈmestər ‖ sɪˈmestə(r)/ n (in US) semestre m (lectivo)

semi- /ˈsemi, ˈsemaɪ ‖ ˈsemi/ pref semi-

semibreve /ˈsemibriːv/ n (BrE) semibreve f, redonda f

semicircle /ˈsemiˌsɜːrkəl ‖ ˈsemiˌsɜːkəl/ n semicírculo m

semicolon /ˈsemiˈkəʊlən/ n punto y coma m

semiconscious /ˈsemiˈkɑːntʃəs ‖ ˌsemiˈkɒnʃəs/ adj semiconsciente

semidetached /ˈsemidɪˈtætʃt/ adj: **a ~ house** una casa pareada or adosada

semifinal /ˈsemiˈfaɪnl/ n semifinal f

seminar /ˈsemənɑːr ‖ ˈsemɪnɑː(r)/ n seminario m

semiquaver /ˈsemiˌkweɪvər ‖ ˈsemiˌkweɪvə(r)/ n (BrE) semicorchea f

semiskilled /ˈsemiˈskɪld/ adj semicalificado or (Esp) semicualificado

semitone /ˈsemitəʊn/ n semitono m

semitrailer /ˈsemiˌtreɪlər ‖ ˈsemiˌtreɪlə(r)/ n (AmE) camión m con remolque or (CS tb) con acoplado, tráiler m (Esp), trailer m (Méx)

senate /ˈsenət ‖ ˈsenɪt/ n **the Senate** (Govt) el senado or Senado

senator /ˈsenətər ‖ ˈsenətə(r)/ n senador, -dora m,f

send /send/ (past & past p **sent**) vt mandar, enviar*; **to ~ sb to prison** mandar a algn a la cárcel; **the blow sent him reeling** el golpe lo dejó tambaleándose; **she sent everything flying** lo hizo saltar todo por los aires; **to ~ sb to sleep** dormir* a algn
■ **send away 1** [v + o + adv, v + adv + o] **(a)** (dismiss) despachar; **don't ~ me away** no me digas que me vaya **(b)** (send elsewhere) mandar, enviar* **2** [v + adv] ▶ SEND OFF 3

■ **send for** [*v + prep + o*] **(a)** (ask to come) ⟨*doctor/ambulance*⟩ mandar a buscar, mandar llamar (AmL) **(b)** (order) ⟨*catalog/application form*⟩ pedir*; ⟨*books/tapes/clothes*⟩ encargar*

■ **send in** [*v + o + adv, v + adv + o*] **(a)** ⟨*troops*⟩ enviar*, mandar **(b)** (by post) ⟨*entry/coupon/ application*⟩ mandar, enviar* **(c)** (into room) ⟨*person*⟩ hacer* ▸ **him in** hágalo pasar

■ **send off** **1** [*v + o + adv, v + adv + o*] (dispatch) ⟨*letter/parcel/goods*⟩ despachar, mandar; ⟨*person*⟩ mandar

2 [*v + o + adv, v + adv + o*] (BrE Sport) expulsar

3 [*v + adv*] **to ~ off FOR sth: I sent off for a brochure** escribí pidiendo un folleto, mandé pedir un folleto (AmL)

■ **send on** [*v + o + adv, v + adv + o*] ⟨*luggage*⟩ enviar* *or* mandar por adelantado; ⟨*mail*⟩ hacer* seguir

■ **send out** [*v + o + adv, v + adv + o*] **(a)** (emit) ⟨*heat*⟩ despedir*, irradiar; ⟨*signal/radio waves*⟩ emitir **(b)** (on errand) mandar **(c)** ⟨*invitations*⟩ mandar, enviar*

■ **send up** [*v + o + adv, v + adv + o*] **1** (to prison) (AmE) meter preso

2 (satirize) (BrE colloq) parodiar

sender /'sendər ‖'sendə(r)/ *n* remitente *mf*

send: **~-off** *n* (colloq) despedida *f*; **~-up** *n* (esp BrE colloq) parodia *f*

Senegal /'senɪ'gɔːl/ *n* (el) Senegal

Senegalese /'senɪgə'liːz/ *adj* senegalés

senile /'siːnaɪl/ *adj* senil

senile dementia *n* demencia *f* senil

senior[1] /'siːnjər ‖'siːnɪə(r)/ *adj* **(a)** (superior in rank): **a ~ officer in the Army** un oficial de alto rango del Ejército; **~ lecturer** (BrE) ≈ profesor adjunto, profesora adjunta *m,f*; **she's ~ to him** es su superior **(b)** (older): **the ~ members of a club** los socios más antiguos de un club; **Robert King, S~** (esp AmE) Robert King, padre *or* sénior

senior[2] *n* **1** **(a)** (older person): **he's five years my ~** me lleva cinco años **(b)** (person of higher rank) superior *m* **(c)** (AmE) ▶ SENIOR CITIZEN

2 (Educ) estudiante *mf* del último año *or* curso

senior: **~ citizen** *n* persona *f* de la tercera edad; **~ high (school)** *n* (in US) colegio donde se imparten los tres últimos años de la enseñanza secundaria

seniority /siːn'jɔːrəti ‖,siːni'ɒrəti/ *n* **(a)** (in rank) jerarquía *f* **(b)** (in length of service) antigüedad *f*

sensation /sen'seɪʃən/ *n* **1** (feeling, impression) sensación *f* **2** **(a)** (furor) sensación *f* **(b)** (success): **to be a ~ «***play/show***»** ser* todo un éxito

sensational /sen'seɪʃnəl ‖sen'seɪʃənl/ *adj* **(a)** (causing furor) que causa sensación **(b)** (sensationalist) sensacionalista **(c)** (very good) (colloq) sensacional (fam)

sensationalist /sen'seɪʃənələst ‖sen'seɪʃənəlɪst/ *adj* sensacionalista

sense[1] /sens/ *n* **1** **(a)** (physical faculty) sentido *m*; **the ~ of hearing/smell/taste/touch** el (sentido del) oído/olfato/gusto/tacto **(b)** **senses** *pl* (rational state): **to come to one's ~s** entrar en razón

2 **(a)** (impression) (*no pl*) sensación *f* **(b)**

(awareness) sentido *m*; **~ of direction/humor** sentido de la orientación/del humor; **I lost all ~ of time** perdí completamente la noción del tiempo

3 (common ~) sentido *m* común; **she had the (good) ~ to leave her phone number** tuvo la sensatez de dejar su número de teléfono; **I can't make him see ~** no puedo hacerlo entrar en razón

4 **(a)** (meaning) sentido *m*; **in every ~ of the word** en todo sentido **(b)** (aspect, way): **in a ~ they're both correct** en cierto modo ambos tienen razón

5 **to make ~ (a)** (be comprehensible) tener* sentido **(b)** (be sensible): **what he said made a lot of ~** lo que dijo era muy razonable; **to make ~ of sth** entender* algo

sense[2] *vt* **(a)** (be aware of) sentir*, notar **(b)** (detect) (Tech) detectar

senseless /'sensləs ‖'senslɪs/ *adj* **1** (pointless) ⟨*act/destruction*⟩ sin sentido **2** (unconscious) inconsciente

sensible /'sensəbəl/ *adj* ⟨*person/approach*⟩ sensato; ⟨*decision*⟩ prudente; ⟨*clothes/shoes*⟩ cómodo y práctico

sensitive /'sensətɪv/ *adj* **1** **(a)** (emotionally responsive) ⟨*person*⟩ sensible; ⟨*performance*⟩ lleno de sensibilidad **(b)** (touchy) ⟨*person*⟩ susceptible **2** (physically responsive) ⟨*skin/instrument*⟩ sensible **3** (requiring tact) ⟨*topic/issue*⟩ delicado

sensor /'sensər ‖'sensə(r)/ *n* sensor *m*

sensual /'sentʃuəl ‖'senʃʊəl/ *adj* sensual

sensuous /'sentʃuəs ‖'sensjʊəs/ *adj* sensual

sent /sent/ *past & past p of* SEND

sentence[1] /'sentns ‖'sentəns/ *n* **1** (Ling) oración *f*, frase *f* **2** (Law) (judgment) sentencia *f*; (punishment) pena *f*; **to pass ~ (on sb)** dictar *or* pronunciar sentencia (contra algn); **a life ~** una condena a cadena perpetua

sentence[2] *vt* **to ~ sb (TO sth)** condenar *or* sentenciar a algn (A algo)

sentiment /'sentɪmənt/ *n* **(a)** (feeling) sentir *m*, sentimiento *m* **(b)** (view) opinión *f*; **my ~s exactly** *o* **entirely** estoy totalmente de acuerdo

sentimental /'sentɪ'mentl/ *adj* sentimental

sentry /'sentri/ *n* (*pl* **-tries**) centinela *m*

Seoul /səʊl/ *n* Seúl *m*

separate[1] /'sepərət/ *adj* **(a)** (individual) separado **(b)** (physically apart) aparte *adj inv*; **~ FROM sth** separado DE algo **(c)** (distinct, different): **it has three ~ meanings** tiene tres significados distintos; **answer each question on a ~ sheet of paper** conteste cada pregunta en una hoja aparte

separate[2] /'sepəreɪt/ *vt* **(a)** (set apart) separar **(b)** (distinguish) distinguir*; **to ~ sth FROM sth** distinguir* algo DE algo

■ **~** *vi* separarse

separately /'seprətli, 'sepərətli/ *adv* **(a)** (apart) por separado **(b)** (individually) separadamente

separation /'sepə'reɪʃən/ *n* separación *f*

separatism /'seprətɪzəm, 'sepərətɪzəm/ *n* separatismo *m*

separatist /'seprətəst, 'sepə- ‖'sepərətɪst, 'seprə-/ *n* separatista *mf*; ⟨*group/ movement*⟩ separatista

September /sep'tembər ‖sep'tembə(r)/ *n* septiembre *m*, setiembre *m*

S

septic /ˈseptɪk/ *adj* séptico; **to go ~** infectarse

sequel /ˈsiːkwəl/ *n* (a) (Cin, Lit, TV) continuación *f* (b) (later events) secuela *f*

sequence /ˈsiːkwəns/ *n* [1] (order): **the police established the ~ of events** la policía estableció cómo se sucedieron los hechos; **it's better to look at the pictures in ~** es mejor ver las fotos en *or* por orden [2] (a) (series) serie *f* (b) (Math, Mus) secuencia *f* [3] (Cin, TV) secuencia *f*

sequin /ˈsiːkwɪn/ *n* lentejuela *f*

Serb /sɜːb ‖sɜːb/ *adj/n* ▶ SERBIAN[1,2]

Serbia /ˈsɜːrbiə ‖ˈsɜːbiə/ *n* Serbia *f*, Servia *f*

Serbian¹ /ˈsɜːrbiən ‖ˈsɜːbiən/ *adj* serbio, servio

Serbian² *n* serbio, -bia *m,f*, servio, -via *m,f*

Serbo-Croat /ˈsɜːrbəʊˈkrəʊæt ‖ˌsɜːbəʊˈkrəʊæt/ *n* serbocroata *m*

serenade¹ /ˈserəˈneɪd/ *n* serenata *f*

serenade² *vt* darle* (una) serenata a

serene /səˈriːn ‖sɪˈriːn/ *adj* sereno

sergeant /ˈsɑːdʒənt ‖ˈsɑːdʒənt/ *n* sargento *mf*

sergeant major *n* ≈ brigada *mf*

serial /ˈsɪriəl ‖ˈsɪəriəl/ *n* (a) (Rad, TV) serie *f*, serial *m* or (CS) serial *f* (b) (Publ): **it was published as a ~** se publicó por entregas

serialize /ˈsɪriəlaɪz ‖ˈsɪəriəlaɪz/ *vt* serializar*

serial: ~ killer *n* asesino, -na *m,f* en serie; **~ number** *n* número *m* de serie

series /ˈsɪriːz ‖ˈsɪəriːz/ *n* (*pl* **~**) (a) (succession) serie *f* (TV, Rad) serie *f*, serial *m* or (CS) *f* (b) (Math, Rad) serie *f*, serial *m* or (CS) *f*

serious /ˈsɪriəs ‖ˈsɪəriəs/ *adj* [1] (a) (in earnest, sincere) serio; **I'm ~** lo digo en serio (b) (committed) ⟨*before n*⟩ ⟨*student/worker*⟩ dedicado (c) (not lightweight) ⟨*before n*⟩ ⟨*newspaper/play/music*⟩ serio [2] (grave) ⟨*injury/illness*⟩ grave; **I have ~ doubts about him** tengo mis serias dudas acerca de él

seriously /ˈsɪriəsli ‖ˈsɪəriəsli/ *adv* [1] (a) (not frivolously) seriamente; **to take sth/sb ~** tomar(se) algo/a algn en serio (b) (genuinely, sincerely): **you can't ~ mean that** no lo puedes estar diciendo en serio [2] (gravely) ⟨*ill/injured*⟩ gravemente

seriousness /ˈsɪriəsnəs ‖ˈsɪəriəsnɪs/ *n* seriedad *f*; **he said it in all ~** lo dijo muy en serio

sermon /ˈsɜːrmən ‖ˈsɜːmən/ *n* sermón *m*

serpent /ˈsɜːrpənt ‖ˈsɜːpənt/ *n* (liter) sierpe *f* (liter)

serrated /ˈsəreɪtəd ‖səˈreɪtɪd/ *adj* ⟨*edge/knife*⟩ serrado

serum /ˈsɪrəm ‖ˈsɪərəm/ *n* suero *m*

servant /ˈsɜːrvənt ‖ˈsɜːvənt/ *n* criado, -da *m,f*, sirviente, -ta *m,f*

serve¹ /sɜːrv ‖sɜːv/ *vt* [1] (work for) ⟨*God/country*⟩ servir* a
[2] (help, be useful to) servir*; **it ~s no useful purpose** no sirve para nada (útil); **to ~ sb right** (colloq): **it ~s her right!** ¡se lo merece!, ¡le está bien empleado! (Esp)
[3] (a) (Culin) ⟨*food/drink*⟩ servir* (b) (in shop) (BrE) atender*
[4] (Law) ⟨*summons/notice/order*⟩ entregar*

[5] (complete) ⟨*apprenticeship*⟩ hacer*; ⟨*sentence*⟩ cumplir
■ **~** *vi* [1] (a) (be servant) (liter) servir* (b) (in shop) (BrE) atender* (c) (distribute food) servir*
[2] (spend time, do duty): **to ~ in the army** servir* en el ejército
[3] (have effect, function) **to ~ to +** INF servir* PARA + INF
[4] (Sport) sacar*, servir*

serve² *n* servicio *m*, saque *m*

server /ˈsɜːrvər ‖ˈsɜːvə(r)/ *n* [1] (Sport) *jugador que tiene el saque* [2] (Comput) servidor *m*

service¹ /ˈsɜːrvəs ‖ˈsɜːvɪs/ *n* [1] (a) (duty, work) servicio *m* (b) (given by a tool, machine): **you'll get years of ~ from this iron** esta plancha le durará años
[2] (of professional, tradesman, company) servicio *m*; **we no longer require your ~s** ya no precisamos sus servicios
[3] (assistance) servicio *m*; **she has done us all a ~** nos ha hecho a todos un favor *or* servicio; **how can I be of ~ to you?** ¿en qué puedo ayudarlo *or* servirlo?
[4] (organization, system) servicio *m*; **telephone/ postal ~** servicio telefónico/postal
[5] (Mil): **the ~s** las fuerzas armadas
[6] (in shop, restaurant) servicio *m*
[7] (overhaul, maintenance) revisión *f*, servicio *m* (AmL), service *m* (RPI)
[8] (Relig) oficio *m* religioso
[9] (in tennis) servicio *m*, saque *m*
[10] (dinner ~) vajilla *f*

service² *vt* ⟨*car*⟩ hacerle* una revisión *or* (AmL) un servicio a; ⟨*machine/appliance*⟩ hacerle* el mantenimiento a

service: ~ charge *n* (a) (in restaurant) servicio *m* (b) (for maintenance — of apartment) gastos *mpl* comunes *or* (Esp) de comunidad; (— of office) gastos *mpl* de mantenimiento; **~ industry** *n* sector *m* (de) servicios; **~man** /ˈsɜːrvəsmən ‖ˈsɜːvɪsmən/ *n* (*pl* **-men** /-mən/) militar *m*, soldado *m*; **~ station** *n* estación *f* de servicio

serviette /ˈsɜːrviˈet ‖ˌsɜːviˈet/ *n* (BrE) servilleta *f*

serving /ˈsɜːrvɪŋ ‖ˈsɜːvɪŋ/ *n* porción *f*, ración *f*; ⟨*before n*⟩ **~ dish** fuente *f*; **~ spoon** cuchara *f* de servir

session /ˈseʃən/ *n* [1] (Adm, Govt, Law) (single meeting) sesión *f*; **to be in ~** estar* en sesión, estar* sesionando (esp AmL) [2] (period of time) sesión *f*; **a recording ~** una sesión de grabación

set¹ /set/ *n* [1] (of tools, golf clubs, pens, keys) juego *m*; (of books, records) colección *f*; (of stamps) serie *f*, **a matching ~ of sheets and pillowcases** un juego de cama [2] (TV) aparato *m*, televisor *m*; (Rad) aparato *m*, receptor *m* [3] (in tennis, squash) set *m* [4] (a) (Theat) (stage) escenario *m*; (scenery) decorado *m* (b) (Cin) plató *m* [5] (in hairdressing) marcado *m*

set² *adj* [1] (established, prescribed) ⟨*wage/price*⟩ fijo; **there are no ~ times for visiting** no hay

---

AmC Central America	Arg	Argentina	Cu	Cuba	Per	Peru
AmL Latin America	Bol	Bolivia	Ec	Ecuador	RPI	River Plate Area
AmS South America	Chi	Chile	Esp	Spain	Ur	Uruguay
Andes Andean Region	CS	Southern Cone	Méx	Mexico	Ven	Venezuela

horas de visita establecidas; **a ~ phrase** una frase hecha; **we ordered the ~ menu** (BrE) pedimos el menú del día

2 (*pred*) **(a)** (ready, prepared): **to be ~** estar* listo, estar* pronto (RPl) **(b)** (likely, about to) (*journ*) **to be ~ to + INF** llevar camino de + INF **(c)** (determined, resolute): **she's absolutely ~ on that bicycle** está empeñada en que tiene que ser esa bicicleta; **he's dead ~ on going to college** está resuelto a ir a la universidad sea como sea

3 (rigid, inflexible): **to be ~ in one's ways** tener* costumbres muy arraigadas

set³ (*pres p* **setting**; *past & past p* **set**) *vt*
1 (put, place) poner*, colocar*
2 (cause to be, become): **to ~ sb free** poner* en libertad a algn; **to ~ fire to sth, to ~ sth on fire** prenderle fuego a algo
3 (a) (prepare) ⟨*trap*⟩ tender*; ⟨*table*⟩ poner* **(b)** (Med) ⟨*bone*⟩ encajar, componer* (AmL) **(c)** ⟨*hair*⟩ marcar*
4 (adjust) ⟨*oven/alarm clock/watch*⟩ poner*
5 (a) (arrange, agree on) ⟨*date/time*⟩ fijar **(b)** (impose, prescribe) ⟨*target*⟩ establecer* **(c)** (allot) ⟨*task*⟩ asignar; ⟨*homework*⟩ mandar; ⟨*exam/test/ problem*⟩ poner*; ⟨*text*⟩ prescribir* **(d)** (establish) ⟨*precedent*⟩ sentar*; ⟨*record/standard*⟩ establecer*; **to ~ a good example** dar* buen ejemplo
6 (cause to do, start): **she ~ them to work in the garden** los puso a trabajar en el jardín; **to ~ sth going** poner* algo en marcha
7 (*usu pass*) ⟨*book/film*⟩ ambientar; **the novel is ~ in Japan** la novela está ambientada en el Japón
8 (mount, insert) ⟨*gem*⟩ engarzar*, engastar; ⟨*stake*⟩ hincar*, clavar; **the posts are ~ in concrete** los postes están puestos en hormigón
■ ~ *vi* **1** (go down) ⟨*sun/moon*⟩ ponerse*
2 (a) (become solid, rigid) ⟨*jelly*⟩ cuajar(se); ⟨*cement*⟩ fraguar* **(b)** ⟨*bone*⟩ soldarse*
■ **set about** [*v + prep + o*] **(a)** ⟨*task*⟩ (begin) emprender; (tackle) acometer **(b)** **to ~ about -ING** ponerse* a + INF **(c)** (attack) atacar*
■ **set apart** [*v + o + adv*] distinguir*
■ **set aside** [*v + o + adv, v + adv + o*] **(a)** (save, reserve) ⟨*food/goods*⟩ guardar, apartar; ⟨*time*⟩ dejar; ⟨*money*⟩ guardar, ahorrar **(b)** (put to one side, shelve) ⟨*book/project*⟩ dejar (de lado) **(c)** (disregard) ⟨*hostility*⟩ dejar de lado; ⟨*rules/ formality*⟩ prescindir de
■ **set back** [*v + o + adv, v + adv + o*] ⟨*progress*⟩ retrasar, atrasar; ⟨*clock*⟩ atrasar
■ **set in** [*v + adv*] ⟨*infection*⟩ declararse
■ **set off 1** [*v + adv*] (begin journey) salir*
2 [*v + o + adv, v + adv + o*] **(a)** (activate) ⟨*bomb/ mine*⟩ hacer* explotar; ⟨*alarm*⟩ hacer* sonar; ⟨*firework*⟩ lanzar*, tirar **(b)** (enhance) hacer* resaltar
■ **set out 1** [*v + adv*] **(a)** (begin journey) salir* **(b)** (begin, intend): **I didn't ~ out with that intention** no empecé con esa intención; **she had failed in what she had ~ out to achieve** no había logrado lo que se había propuesto
2 [*v + o + adv, v + adv + o*] **(a)** ⟨*argument/ theory*⟩ exponer* **(b)** ⟨*goods*⟩ exponer*; ⟨*chess pieces*⟩ colocar*
■ **set to** [*v + adv*] ponerse* a trabajar
■ **set up** [*v + o + adv, v + adv + o*] **1 (a)** (erect, assemble) ⟨*monument*⟩ levantar; ⟨*machine/tent*⟩

montar, armar; **they ~ up camp near the river** acamparon cerca del río **(b)** (arrange, plan) ⟨*meeting*⟩ convocar* a
2 (institute, found) ⟨*committee/commission*⟩ crear; ⟨*inquiry*⟩ abrir*; ⟨*business*⟩ montar
3 (establish): **she ~ herself up as a photographer** se estableció como fotógrafa
4 (colloq) **(a)** (frame) tenderle* una trampa a **(b)** (rig) arreglar

set: **~back** *n* revés *m*; **~ square** *n* escuadra *f*, (with two equal sides) cartabón *m*

settee /se'tiː/ *n* sofá *m*

setting /'setɪŋ/ *n* **1** (of dial, switch) posición *f*
2 (a) (of novel, movie) escenario *m* **(b)** (surroundings) marco *m*, entorno *m* **(c)** (for gem) engarce *m*, engaste *m*, montura *f* **3** (place ~) cubierto *m*

settle /'setl/ *vt* **1 (a)** ⟨*price/terms/time*⟩ acordar*; **it's all been ~d, we're going to Miami** ya está (todo) decidido, nos vamos a Miami; **that ~s it: I never want to see him again** ya no me cabe duda: no lo quiero volver a ver **(b)** (resolve) ⟨*dispute/differences*⟩ resolver*
2 ⟨*bill/account*⟩ pagar*; ⟨*debt*⟩ saldar, liquidar
3 ⟨*country/region*⟩ colonizar*
4 (make comfortable) ⟨*patient/child*⟩ poner* cómodo
5 (make calm) ⟨*child*⟩ calmar; ⟨*doubts*⟩ disipar; ⟨*stomach*⟩ asentar*
■ ~ *vi* **1** (come to live) establecerse*
2 (become calm) ⟨⟨*person*⟩⟩ tranquilizarse*
3 (a) (make oneself comfortable) ponerse* cómodo **(b)** ⟨⟨*bird*⟩⟩ posarse
4 (a) ⟨⟨*dust*⟩⟩ asentarse*; ⟨⟨*snow*⟩⟩ cuajar **(b)** (sink) ⟨⟨*soil/foundations*⟩⟩ asentarse*; ⟨⟨*sediment*⟩⟩ depositarse
5 (a) (pay) saldar la cuenta (*or* la deuda *etc*) **(b)** (Law): **to ~ out of court** resolver* una disputa extrajudicialmente
■ **settle down 1** [*v + adv*] **(a)** (become calm): **things have ~d down now** las cosas ya se han apaciguado; **~ down please, children** niños, por favor, tranquilos **(b)** (get comfortable): **we ~d down for the night** nos acomodamos para pasar la noche **(c)** (in place, activity): **she's settling down well in her new school** se está adaptando bien a su nueva escuela; **you should get a job and ~ down** deberías conseguirte un trabajo y establecerte *or* echar raíces en algún sitio **(d)** (become more responsible) sentar* (la) cabeza
2 [*v + o + adv*] (make calm) calmar, tranquilizar*
■ **settle for** [*v + prep + o*] conformarse con
■ **settle in** [*v + adv*]: **I'll come and see you when you've ~d in** te vendré a ver cuando estés instalado; **she's settling in well in her new job** se está adaptando bien a su nuevo trabajo
■ **settle into** [*v + prep + o*] ⟨*school/job*⟩ adaptarse a; ⟨*routine*⟩ acostumbrarse a
■ **settle on** [*v + prep + o*] ⟨*date/place*⟩ decidirse por
■ **settle up** [*v + adv*] (colloq) arreglar (las) cuentas

settled /'setld/ *adj* **(a)** (established) ⟨*habits/life*⟩ ordenado; ⟨*order*⟩ estable **(b)** ⟨*weather*⟩ estable

settlement /'setlmənt/ *n* **1** (agreement) acuerdo *m*, convenio *m*; **wage ~** (agreement) convenio *m* (laboral), acuerdo *m* salarial; (increase) aumento *m* (salarial) **2 (a)** (of account, ⸱⸱⸱ᐳ

bill) pago *m*; (of debt) liquidación *f*, satisfacción *f*
(b) (payment) pago *m* **3** (of dispute) resolución *f*
4 (village) asentamiento *m*

settler /'setlər ‖'setlə(r)/ *n* colono, -na *m,f*

set-up /'setʌp/ *n* (colloq) (situation, arrangement)
sistema *f*; (pej) tinglado *m* (fam & pey)

seven /'sevən/ *adj/n* siete *adj inv/m; see also*
FOUR¹

sevenfold /'sevənfəʊld/ *adj/adv* ▶ -FOLD

seventeen /'sevən'tiːn/ *adj/n* diecisiete *adj
inv/m; see also* FOUR¹

seventeenth¹ /'sevən'tiːnθ/ *adj*
decimoséptimo

seventeenth² *adv* en decimoséptimo lugar

seventeenth³ *n* (Math) diecisieteavo *m*; (part)
diecisieteava parte *f*

seventh¹ /'sevənθ/ *adj* séptimo

seventh² *adv* en séptimo lugar

seventh³ *n* (Math) séptimo *m*; (part) séptima
parte *f*

seventieth¹ /'sevəntiəθ/ *adj* septuagésimo

seventieth² *adv* en septuagésimo lugar

seventieth³ *n* (Math) setentavo *m*; (part)
setentava *or* septuagésima parte *f*

seventy /'sevənti/ *adj/n* setenta *adj inv/m; see
also* FOUR¹

sever /'sevər ‖'sevə(r)/ *vt* **(a)** (cut) ‹rope/chain›
cortar; **the saw ~ed his finger** la sierra le cortó
or le amputó el dedo **(b)** (break off)
‹communications› cortar; ‹relations› romper*

several¹ /'sevrəl/ *adj* varios, -rias

several² *pron* varios, varias

severance /'sevərəns/ *n* **(a)** (of relations, links)
ruptura *f* **(b)** (Lab Rel) cese *m*; (before *n*) ~ **pay**
indemnización *f* por cese

severe /sə'vɪr ‖sɪ'vɪə(r)/ *adj* **severer,
severest** **1** **(a)** (strict, harsh) ‹punishment/
judge› severo; ‹discipline› riguroso **(b)** (austere)
‹style/colors› austero **2** **(a)** (serious, bad) ‹illness/
injury› grave; ‹pain› fuerte; ‹winter› severo;
‹weather conditions› muy malo **(b)** (difficult,
rigorous) ‹conditions› estricto

severely /sə'vɪrli ‖sɪ'vɪəli/ *adv* con severidad,
severamente

severity /sə'verəti ‖sɪ'verəti/ *n* severidad *f*; (of
illness, injury) gravedad *f*; (of pain) intensidad *f*

sew /səʊ/ (past **sewed**; past p **sewn** or
sewed) *vt* coser; ‹seam/hem› hacer*; **to ~ sth
on** coser algo
■ ~ *vi* coser
■ **sew up** [*v + o + adv, v + adv + o*] coser

sewage /'suːɪdʒ ‖'suːɪdʒ, 'sjuːɪdʒ/ *n* aguas *fpl*
negras *or* residuales, aguas *fpl* servidas (CS)

sewer /'suːər ‖'suːə(r), 'sjuːə(r)/ *n* **(a)**
(underground) alcantarilla *f*, cloaca *f* **(b)** (drain)
(AmE) boca *f* de (la) alcantarilla, sumidero *m*

sewing /'səʊɪŋ/ *n* costura *f*

sewing machine *n* máquina *f* de coser

sewn /səʊn/ *past p of* SEW

sex /seks/ *n* **1** **(a)** (sexual matters) sexo *m*;
(before *n*) ~ **education** educación *f* sexual; ~
symbol sex symbol *mf* **(b)** (intercourse) relaciones
fpl sexuales **2** **(a)** (gender) sexo *m* **(b)** (men,
women collectively) sexo *m*; (before *n*) ~
discrimination discriminación *f* sexual

sexism /'seksɪzəm/ *n* sexismo *m*

sexist¹ /'seksəst ‖'seksɪst/ *n* sexista *mf*

sexist² *adj* sexista

sextet /seks'tet/ *n* sexteto *m*

sexual /'sekʃuəl/ *adj* sexual

sexuality /'sekʃu'æləti/ *n* sexualidad *f*

sexually /'sekʃuəli/ *adv* sexualmente; **a ~
transmitted disease** una enfermedad de
transmisión sexual

sexy /'seksi/ *adj* **sexier, sexiest** **(a)** (sexually
attractive) sexy **(b)** (erotic) ‹book/film/talk› erótico

sh /ʃ/ *interj* ¡sh!

shabby /'ʃæbi/ *adj* **-bier, -biest** **(a)** ‹carpet/
sofa/jacket› gastado; (threadbare) raído **(b)** (bad,
unfair): **what a ~ way to treat him** qué manera más
fea de tratarlo

shack /ʃæk/ *n* choza *f*, casucha *f*, rancho *m*
(AmL); jacal *m* (Méx), bohío *m* (AmC, Col)

shackles /'ʃækəlz/ *pl n* grilletes *mpl*

shade¹ /ʃeɪd/ *n* **1** (dark place) sombra *f*; **in the
~** a la sombra **2** (over window) (AmE) persiana *f*,
estor *m* (Esp) **3** **(a)** (of color) tono *m* **(b)** (degree of
difference, nuance) matiz *m*

shade² *vt* ‹eyes/face› proteger* del sol/de la luz;
her seat was ~d from the sun su asiento estaba
resguardado del sol

shadow¹ /'ʃædəʊ/ *n* sombra *f*; **she was a ~ of
her former self** no era ni sombra de lo que había
sido; **without a ~ of (a) doubt** sin la más mínima
duda

shadow² *vt* seguir* de cerca a

shadowy /'ʃædəʊi/ *adj* **(a)** (indistinct) ‹form›
impreciso **(b)** (full of shadows) ‹place/forest› oscuro

shady /'ʃeɪdi/ *adj* **-dier, -diest** **(a)** (giving
shade) ‹place/garden› sombreado; ‹tree› que da
mucha sombra **(b)** (disreputable) (colloq) ‹deal/
business› turbio; ‹character› sospechoso

shaft /ʃæft ‖ʃɑːft/ *n* **1** **(a)** (of arrow, spear) asta
f‡, astil *m*; (of hammer, ax) mango *m* **(b)** (of light)
rayo *m* **2** (Mech Eng) eje *m* **3** (of elevator) hueco
m; (of mine) pozo *m*, tiro *m*

shaggy /'ʃægi/ *adj* **-gier, -giest** ‹dog› lanudo,
peludo; ‹beard/hair› enmarañado, greñudo

shake¹ /ʃeɪk/ (past **shook**; past p **shaken**)
vt **1** **(a)** (cause to move, agitate) ‹bottle/cocktail›
agitar; ‹person/building› sacudir; ‹dice› agitar,
revolver* (AmL); **she shook the sand out of the
towel** sacudió la toalla para quitarle la arena; **to
~ hands with sb, to ~ sb's hand** darle* *or*
estrecharle la mano a algn; **they shook hands** se
dieron la mano; **to ~ one's head** negar* con la
cabeza; (meaning yes) (AmE) asentir* con la cabeza
(b) (brandish) ‹sword/stick› agitar; **to ~ one's fist
at sb** amenazar* a algn con el puño
2 **(a)** (undermine, impair) ‹courage/nerve› hacer*
flaquear; ‹faith› debilitar **(b)** (shock, surprise)
‹person› impresionar
■ ~ *vi* **1** (move, tremble) «earth/hand/voice»
temblar*; **he was shaking with fear/cold/rage**
estaba temblando de miedo/frío/rabia
2 (shake hands) (colloq): **they shook on it** sellaron
el acuerdo con un apretón de manos
■ **shake off** [*v + o + adv, v + adv + o*] ‹pursuer/
reporter› deshacerse* de; ‹habit› quitarse; ‹cold›
quitarse de encima
■ **shake up** [*v + o + adv, v + adv + o*] **1** ‹liquid›
agitar

2 (colloq) ⟨*industry/personnel*⟩ reorganizar* totalmente

3 (disturb, shock) (colloq): **he's a bit ~n up** está un poco alterado

shake² *n* **1** (act) sacudida *f*; (violent) sacudida *f* violenta, sacudón *m* (AmL); **he replied with a ~ of the head** contestó negando con la cabeza **2** (milk ~) (AmE) batido *m*, (leche *f*) malteada *f* (AmL), licuado *m* con leche (AmL)

shaken /'ʃeɪkən/ *past p of* SHAKE¹

shaker /'ʃeɪkə(r)/ *n* **(a)** (for cocktails) coctelera *f* **(b)** (for salt) salero *m*; (for pepper) pimentero *m*; (for sugar) azucarero *m* **(c)** (for dice) cubilete *m*, cacho *m* (Andes)

shaky /'ʃeɪki/ *adj* **-kier, -kiest (a)** (trembling) ⟨*hands/voice*⟩ tembloroso; ⟨*writing*⟩ de trazo poco firme **(b)** (unsteady) ⟨*table*⟩ poco firme; ⟨*structure*⟩ tambaleante; ⟨*health*⟩ delicado; ⟨*currency/government*⟩ débil; ⟨*theory/start*⟩ flojo

shale /ʃeɪl/ *n* esquisto *m*, pizarra *f*

shall /ʃæl, *weak forms* ʃl, ʃəl/ *v mod* (*past* **should**) **1** (with 1st person) **(a)** (in statements about the future): **I ~ be very interested to see what happens** tendré mucho interés en ver qué sucede; **we shan't be able to come** (BrE) no podremos venir **(b)** (making suggestions, asking for assent) [*The present tense is used in this type of question in Spanish*] **~ I open the window?** ¿abro la ventana?; **~ we go out tonight?** ¿qué te (*or* le *etc*) parece si salimos esta noche? **2** (with 2nd and 3rd persons) (in commands, promises etc): **they ~ not pass** no pasarán

shallot /ʃə'lɑːt ‖ ʃə'lɒt/ *n* chalote *m*, chalota *f*

shallow /'ʃæləʊ/ *adj* **-er, -est (a)** (not deep) ⟨*water/pond/river*⟩ poco profundo; ⟨*dish*⟩ llano, plano; ⟨*breathing*⟩ superficial **(b)** (superficial) ⟨*person*⟩ superficial

shallows /'ʃæləʊz/ *pl n* bajío *m*

sham¹ /ʃæm/ *n* farsa *f*

sham² *adj* (pej) (*no comp*) fingido

sham³ *vt/i* **-mm-** fingir*

shambles /'ʃæmbəlz/ *n* (+ *sing vb*) caos *m*, desquicio *m* (RPl); (fiasco) desastre *m*

shame¹ /ʃeɪm/ *n* **1** (feeling) vergüenza *f*, pena *f* (AmL exc CS); **~ on you!** ¡qué vergüenza!; **to put sb to ~:** **she's such a good hostess, she puts me to ~** es tan buena anfitriona que me hace sentir culpable **2** (pity) (*no pl*) lástima *f*, pena *f*; **what a ~!** ¡qué lástima!; **it's a ~ you can't go** es una pena que no puedas ir

shame² *vt* avergonzar*, apenar (AmL exc CS); **they ~d us into paying** nos hicieron avergonzarnos de tal manera que al final pagamos

shamefaced /'ʃeɪmˈfeɪst/ *adj* avergonzado

shameful /'ʃeɪmfəl/ *adj* vergonzoso

shameless /'ʃeɪmləs ‖ 'ʃeɪmlɪs/ *adj* ⟨*lie/exploitation*⟩ descarado; ⟨*liar/cheat*⟩ desvergonzado

shampoo¹ /ʃæm'puː/ *n* (*pl* **-poos**) champú *m*

shampoo² *vt* **-poos, -pooing, -pooed** ⟨*hair*⟩ lavar; ⟨*carpet/upholstery*⟩ limpiar

shan't /ʃænt ‖ ʃɑːnt/ = **shall not**

shanty /'ʃænti/ *n* (*pl* **-ties**) **1** (hut) casucha *f*, rancho *m* (AmL), chabola *f* (Esp) **2** (sea ~) (BrE) canción *f* de marineros

shantytown /'ʃæntiˌtaʊn/ *n* barriada *f* (AmL), chabolas *fpl* (Esp), población *f* callampa (Chi), villa *f* miseria (Arg), ciudad *f* perdida (Méx), cantegril *m* (Ur), ranchos *mpl* (Ven)

shape¹ /ʃeɪp/ *n* **1 (a)** (visible form) forma *f*; **it is triangular in ~** tiene forma triangular; **in the ~ of a cross** en forma de cruz; **to take ~** tomar forma **(b)** (general nature, outline) conformación *f*; **the ~ of things to come** lo que nos espera **2** (guise): **assistance in the ~ of food stamps** ayuda consistente en vales canjeables por comida; **I won't tolerate bribery in any ~ or form** no pienso tolerar sobornos de ningún tipo **3** (condition, order): **she's in pretty good/bad ~** está bastante bien/mal (de salud); **to keep in ~** mantenerse* en forma

shape² *vt* **(a)** ⟨*object/material*⟩ darle* forma a **(b)** (influence) ⟨*events*⟩ determinar; ⟨*character/ideas*⟩ formar

■ **~** *vi* «*project*» tomar forma; «*plan*» desarrollarse

■ **shape up** [*v* + *adv*] **(a)** ▶ SHAPE² *vi* **(b)** (improve, pull oneself together) entrar en vereda (fam)

-shaped /ʃeɪpt/ *suff*: **L~/heart~** con *or* en forma de L/corazón

shapeless /'ʃeɪpləs ‖ 'ʃeɪplɪs/ *adj* informe, sin forma

shapely /'ʃeɪpli/ *adj* **-lier, -liest** ⟨*figure*⟩ bien modulado, hermoso; ⟨*legs*⟩ torneado

share¹ /ʃer ‖ ʃeə(r)/ *n* **1** (portion) parte *f*; **she must take her ~ of the blame** debe aceptar que tiene parte de la culpa **2** (Busn, Fin) **(a)** (held by partner) (*no pl*) participación *f* **(b)** (held by shareholder) acción *f*

share² *vt* **1 (a)** (use jointly) to **~ sth** (WITH sb) compartir algo (CON algn) **(b)** (have in common) ⟨*interest/opinion*⟩ compartir; ⟨*characteristics*⟩ tener* en común **2 (a)** (divide) dividir **(b)** (communicate) ⟨*experience/knowledge*⟩ intercambiar

■ **~** *vi* **(a)** (use jointly) compartir; **to ~ and ~ alike** compartir las cosas **(b)** (have a part) **to ~ IN sth** compartir algo, participar DE algo

■ **share out** [*v* + *o* + *adv, v* + *adv* + *o*] repartir, distribuir*

shareholder /'ʃerhəʊldər ‖ 'ʃeəhəʊldə(r)/ *n* accionista *mf*

shark /ʃɑːrk ‖ ʃɑːk/ *n* (Zool) tiburón *m*

sharp¹ /ʃɑːrp ‖ ʃɑːp/ *adj* **-er, -est 1 (a)** ⟨*knife/edge/scissors*⟩ afilado, filoso (AmL), filudo (Chi, Per); ⟨*features*⟩ anguloso; ⟨*pencil*⟩ con punta; **it has a ~ point** es muy puntiagudo **(b)** ⟨*pain*⟩ agudo **(c)** ⟨*wind*⟩ cortante; ⟨*frost*⟩ crudo, fuerte **(d)** ⟨*taste*⟩ ácido **2 (a)** (abrupt, steep) ⟨*bend/angle*⟩ cerrado; ⟨*turn*⟩ brusco; ⟨*rise/fall*⟩ brusco **(b)** (sudden) repentino, súbito **3 (a)** (keen) ⟨*eyesight*⟩ agudo; ⟨*hearing*⟩ fino, agudo **(b)** (acute) ⟨*wit/mind*⟩ agudo **4** (clear, unblurred) ⟨*photo/TV picture*⟩ nítido; ⟨*outline*⟩ definido; ⟨*contrast*⟩ marcado **5** (harsh) ⟨*retort*⟩ cortante; **to have a ~ tongue** ser* muy mordaz, tener* una lengua muy afilada **6** (clever, shrewd) ⟨*person*⟩ listo, astuto; ⟨*move*⟩ astuto **7** (Mus) (referring to key) sostenido; **C ~** do *m* sostenido

sharp² *adv* **1** (exactly): **at six o'clock ~** a las ····≻

S

seis en punto **2** (abruptly): **turn ~ right** gire a la derecha en curva cerrada **3** (Mus) ‹play› demasiado alto

sharp³ n (Mus) sostenido m

sharpen /'ʃɑːrpən ‖'ʃɑːpən/ vt ‹knife/claws› afilar; ‹pencil› sacarle* punta a

sharpener /'ʃɑːrpnər ‖'ʃɑːpnə(r)/ n (knife ~) afilador m; (pencil ~) sacapuntas m

sharply /'ʃɑːrpli ‖'ʃɑːpli/ adv **1** (a) (steeply, abruptly) ‹drop/fall/increase› bruscamente; ‹bend› repentinamente **(b)** (suddenly, swiftly) de repente **2** ‹outlined/defined› claramente, nítidamente **3** (harshly) ‹answer› con dureza

shat /ʃæt/ past & past p of SHIT²

shatter /'ʃætər ‖'ʃætə(r)/ vt ‹window/plate› hacer* añicos or pedazos; ‹health/nerves› destrozar*; ‹confidence/hopes› destruir*; ‹silence› romper*; **she was ~ed by the news** la noticia la dejó destrozada
■ ~ vi hacerse* añicos or pedazos

shave¹ /ʃeɪv/ vt **1** ‹person› afeitar or (esp Méx) rasurar **2** (touch in passing) rozar*
■ ~ vi «person» afeitarse or (esp Méx) rasurarse

shave² n afeitada f or (esp Méx) rasurada f; **to have a ~** afeitarse or (esp Méx) rasurarse; **a close ~** (colloq): **we won in the end, but it was a pretty close ~** al final ganamos, pero por los pelos or por un pelo (fam)

shaven /'ʃeɪvən/ adj ‹head› rapado

shaver /'ʃeɪvər ‖'ʃeɪvə(r)/ n (electric ~) máquina f de afeitar, afeitadora f or (esp Méx) rasuradora f

shaving /'ʃeɪvɪŋ/ n (a) (before n) ‹cream/soap› de afeitar or (esp Méx) de rasurar; **~ brush** brocha f de afeitar **(b) shavings** pl (pieces) virutas fpl

shawl /ʃɔːl/ n chal m

she /ʃiː, weak form ʃi/ pron ella

■ Note Although *ella* is given as the main translation of *she*, it is in practice used only for emphasis, or to avoid ambiguity: *she went to the theater* fue al teatro; *she went to the theater, he went to the cinema* ella fue al teatro y él fue al cine; *she did it* ella lo hizo.

~'s a writer/my sister es escritora/mi hermana; **~ didn't say it, I did** no fue ella quien lo dijo, sino yo

sheaf /ʃiːf/ n (pl **sheaves**) **(a)** (Agr) gavilla f **(b)** (of notes) fajo m; (of arrows) haz m

shear /ʃɪr ‖ʃɪə(r)/ vt (past **sheared**; past p **shorn**) ‹sheep› esquilar

shears /ʃɪrz ‖ʃɪəz/ pl n (for grass, hedge) tijeras fpl; (for shearing sheep) tijeras fpl de esquilar

sheath /ʃiːθ/ n (pl **~s** /ʃiːðz/) (for sword, knife) funda f, vaina f

sheaves /ʃiːvz/ pl of SHEAF

shed¹ /ʃed/ vt (pres p **shedding**; past & past p **shed**) **1** (a) ‹tears/blood› derramar **(b)** ‹leaves/ skin› mudar, ‹clothing› despojarse de (frml) **2** (send out) ‹light› emitir

shed² n **(a)** (hut) cabaña f; (garden ~) cobertizo m **(b)** (larger building) nave f

she'd /ʃiːd/ **(a)** = **she would (b)** = **she had**

sheen /ʃiːn/ n brillo m, lustre m

sheep /ʃiːp/ n (pl ~) oveja f

sheepdog /'ʃiːpdɔːg ‖'ʃiːpdɒg/ n perro m pastor

sheepish /'ʃiːpɪʃ/ adj avergonzado

sheepskin /'ʃiːpskɪn/ n piel f de borrego or de cordero

sheer /ʃɪr ‖ʃɪə(r)/ adj **sheerer, sheerest** **1** (pure, absolute) (as intensifier) puro; **the ~ size of the problem** la mera magnitud del problema **2** (vertical) ‹drop› a pique; ‹cliff› escarpado **3** (fine) ‹stockings/fabric› muy fino

sheet /ʃiːt/ n **1** (on bed) sábana f **2** (of paper) hoja f, (of wrapping paper) pliego m, hoja f; (of stamps) pliego m **3** (a) (of metal) chapa f, plancha f, lámina f; **a ~ of glass** un vidrio **(b)** (of ice) capa f, (before n) **~ lightning** relámpagos mpl difusos

sheet: **~ metal** n metal m en planchas or chapas; **~ music** n partituras fpl

sheik, sheikh /ʃiːk ‖ʃeɪk/ n jeque m

shelf /ʃelf/ n (pl **shelves**) **1** (in cupboard, bookcase) estante m, balda f (Esp); **a set of shelves** unos estantes, una estantería **2** (Geol): **continental ~** plataforma f continental

shell¹ /ʃel/ n **1** (a) (of egg, nut) cáscara f; (of sea mollusk) concha f; (of tortoise, turtle, snail, crustacean) caparazón m or f **(b)** (of building, vehicle) armazón m or f **2** (Mil) proyectil m, obús m

shell² vt **1** (Culin) ‹peas/nuts/eggs› pelar; ‹mussel/clam› quitarle la concha a **2** (Mil) ‹position/troops/city› bombardear

she'll /ʃiːl, weak form ʃɪl/ = **she will**

shell: **~fish** n (pl **~fish**) (creature) marisco m **(b)** (collectively) mariscos mpl, marisco m (Esp); **~shock** n neurosis f de guerra

shelter¹ /'ʃeltər ‖'ʃeltə(r)/ n **1** (building) refugio m **2** (a) (protection): **to take ~** refugiarse **(b)** (accommodations): **they need food and ~** necesitan alimentos y albergue

shelter² vt **(a)** (protect from weather) resguardar **(b)** ‹criminal/fugitive› darle* cobijo a
■ ~ vi **to ~ (FROM sth)** refugiarse or resguardarse (DE algo)

sheltered /'ʃeltərd ‖'ʃeltəd/ adj ‹valley/ harbor› abrigado; ‹life› protegido

shelve /ʃelv/ vt ‹plan/project› archivar

shelves /ʃelvz/ pl of SHELF

shelving /'ʃelvɪŋ/ n estantería f

shepherd /'ʃepərd ‖'ʃepəd/ n pastor m

sherbet /'ʃɜːrbət ‖'ʃɜːbət/ n **(a)** (sorbet) (AmE) sorbete m **(b)** (powder) (BrE) polvos efervescentes con sabor a frutas, sidral® m (Esp)

sheriff /'ʃerəf ‖'ʃerɪf/ n (in US) sheriff mf

sherry /'ʃeri/ n (pl **-ries**) jerez m

she's /ʃiːz, weak form ʃɪz/ **(a)** = **she is (b)** = **she has**

AmC	América Central	Arg	Argentina	Cu	Cuba	Per	Perú
AmL	América Latina	Bol	Bolivia	Ec	Ecuador	RPI	Río de la Plata
AmS	América del Sur	Chi	Chile	Esp	España	Ur	Uruguay
Andes	Región andina	CS	Cono Sur	Méx	México	Ven	Venezuela

shield¹ /ʃiːld/ n **1** (Hist, Mil) escudo m
2 (protective cover on machine) revestimiento m

shield² vt to ~ sth/sb (FROM sb/sth) proteger*
algo/a algn (DE algn/algo)

shift¹ /ʃɪft/ vt **(a)** (change position of) ‹object/
furniture› correr, mover* **(b)** (transfer): they tried
to ~ the responsibility onto us trataron de
cargarnos la responsabilidad
■ ~ vi **1** (change position, direction) «cargo»
correrse; «wind» cambiar; he ~ed uneasily in
his chair se movía intranquilo en la silla; the
focus of attention has ~ed to Europe el foco de
atención ha pasado a Europa **2** (change gear)
(AmE) cambiar de marcha or de velocidad

shift² n **1** (change in position) cambio m **2** (work
period) turno m; to work the day/night ~ hacer* el
turno de día/de noche; (before n) ~ work trabajo
m por turnos **3** (AmE Auto) palanca de cambio
or (Méx) de velocidades

shift key n tecla f de las mayúsculas

shifty /ˈʃɪfti/ adj **-tier, -tiest** ‹expression/eyes›
furtivo; ‹appearance› sospechoso

shilling /ˈʃɪlɪŋ/ n chelín m

shimmer /ˈʃɪmər ‖ ˈʃɪmə(r)/ vi «water/silk»
brillar; «lights» titilar; (in water) rielar (liter)

shin /ʃɪn/ n espinilla f, canilla f

shine¹ /ʃaɪn/ n brillo m

shine² (past & past p **shone**) vi **(a)** (gleam,
glow) «star/sun/eyes» brillar; «metal/shoes»
relucir*, brillar **(b)** (excel) to ~ (AT sth)
destacar(se*) (EN algo)
■ ~ vt (+ adv compl): to ~ a light on sth alumbrar
algo con una luz

shingle /ˈʃɪŋgəl/ n guijarros mpl

shingles /ˈʃɪŋgəlz/ n (Med) (+ sing vb) herpes
m, culebrilla f

shining /ˈʃaɪnɪŋ/ adj ‹eyes› brillante, luminoso;
‹hair/metal› brillante, reluciente

shiny /ˈʃaɪni/ adj **-nier, -niest** ‹hair/fabric/
shoe› brillante; ‹coin› reluciente

ship¹ /ʃɪp/ n barco m, buque m

ship² vt **-pp- (a)** (send by sea) enviar* or mandar
por barco **(b)** (send) enviar*, despachar

ship: ~**building** n construcción f naval;
~**load** n cargamento m

shipment /ˈʃɪpmənt/ n (goods) envío m, remesa
f

shipping /ˈʃɪpɪŋ/ n **(a)** (ships) barcos mpl,
embarcaciones fpl (fml); (before n) ‹lane/route› de
navegación **(b)** (transportation of freight) transporte
m

shipshape /ˈʃɪpʃeɪp/ adj (pred) limpio y
ordenado

shipwreck¹ /ˈʃɪprek/ n naufragio m

shipwreck² vt (usu pass): to be ~ed
naufragar*

shipyard /ˈʃɪpjɑːrd ‖ ˈʃɪpjɑːd/ n (often pl)
astillero m

shirk /ʃɜːrk ‖ ʃɜːk/ vt ‹task/duty› eludir, rehuir*

shirt /ʃɜːrt ‖ ʃɜːt/ n camisa f

shirtsleeve /ˈʃɜːrtsliːv ‖ ˈʃɜːtsliːv/ n manga f
de camisa; in (one's) ~s en mangas de camisa

shit¹ /ʃɪt/ n (vulg) mierda f (vulg)

shit² vi (pres p **shitting**; past & past p **shit** or
shat) (vulg) cagar* (vulg)

shit³ interj (vulg) ¡carajo! (vulg), ¡mierda! (vulg)

shiver¹ /ˈʃɪvər ‖ ˈʃɪvə(r)/ n escalofrío m; the
scream sent ~s o a ~ down my spine el grito me
produjo escalofríos

shiver² vi (with cold) temblar*; (with fear)
temblar*; (with anticipation) estremecerse*

shivery /ˈʃɪvəri/ adj: to feel ~ tener*
escalofríos

shmaltz, shmalz etc ▶ SCHMALTZ etc

shoal /ʃəʊl/ n **1** (of fish) cardumen m, banco m
2 (sandbank) bajío m, banco m de arena

shock¹ /ʃɑːk ‖ ʃɒk/ n **1** (a) (of impact) choque
m; (of earthquake, explosion) sacudida f **(b)** (electric
~) descarga f (eléctrica) **2** (a) (Med) shock m; to
be in (a state of) ~ estar* en estado de shock **(b)**
(distress, surprise) shock m; to get a ~ llevarse un
shock; the news came as a great ~ to us la
noticia nos conmocionó **(c)** (scare) susto m; to get
a ~ llevarse un susto **3** (bushy mass): a ~ of hair
una mata de pelo

shock² vt (stun, appal) horrorizar*; (scandalize)
escandalizar*

shock absorber /əbˈsɔːrbər ‖ əbˈzɔːbə(r)/ n
amortiguador m

shocked /ʃɑːkt ‖ ʃɒkt/ adj **(a)** (appalled)
horrorizado **(b)** (scandalized): I was ~ to hear that
… me indigné cuando me enteré de que …

shocking /ˈʃɑːkɪŋ ‖ ˈʃɒkɪŋ/ adj **(a)** ‹news/
report› espeluznante **(b)** ‹behavior/language›
escandaloso

shock wave n (Phys) onda f expansiva

shod /ʃɑːd ‖ ʃɒd/ past & past p of SHOE²

shoddy /ˈʃɑːdi ‖ ˈʃɒdi/ adj **-dier, -diest**
‹goods/workmanship› de muy mala calidad

shoe¹ /ʃuː/ n **(a)** (Clothing) zapato m; (before n)
~ polish betún m; ~ repairer zapatero, -ra m,f
(b) (for horse) herradura f **(c)** (brake ~) zapata f

shoe² vt (pres **shoes**; pres p **shoeing**; past &
past p **shod**) ‹horse› herrar*

shoe: ~**brush** n cepillo m de los zapatos;
~**horn** n calzador m; ~**lace** n cordón m (de
zapato), agujeta f (Méx), pasador m (Per)

shone /ʃəʊn, ʃɑːn ‖ ʃɒn/ past & past p of SHINE²

shoo¹ /ʃuː/ interj ¡fuera!, ¡úscale! (Méx)

shoo² vt **shoos, shooing, shooed**: I ~ed
the birds off o away espanté a los pájaros

shook /ʃʊk/ past of SHAKE¹

shoot¹ /ʃuːt/ n **1** (Bot) brote m **2** (shooting
expedition) cacería f **3** (Cin) rodaje m

shoot² (past & past p **shot**) vt **1** (a) ‹person/
animal› pegarle* un tiro a; they shot him dead,
they shot him to death (AmE) lo mataron a tiros/
de un tiro; to ~ oneself pegarse* un tiro **(b)**
(hunt) ‹duck/deer› cazar*
2 (fire) ‹bullet› disparar, tirar; ‹arrow/missile›
lanzar*, arrojar; ‹glance› lanzar*
3 (pass swiftly): to ~ the rapids salvar los rápidos
4 (Cin) rodar*
■ ~ vi **1** (a) (fire weapon) disparar; to ~ AT sb/sth
dispararle A algn/A algo **(b)** (hunt) cazar*
2 (move swiftly): she shot past pasó como una
bala (fam); he shot out of his seat saltó del
asiento
3 (Sport) tirar, disparar
■ **shoot down** [v + o + adv, v + adv + o] ‹plane›
derribar, abatir ⸱⸱⸱⟩

S

■ **shoot out** [v + adv] (emerge quickly) salir*
disparado or (fam) como un bólido

■ **shoot up** [v + adv] **(a)** (grow tall) crecer* mucho
(b) (go up quickly) «prices/temperature»
dispararse; «flames» alzarse*

shoot³ interj (AmE colloq) ¡miércoles! (fam & euf)

shooting /ˈʃuːtɪŋ/ n **(a)** (exchange of fire) tiroteo
m, balacera f (AmL); (shots) tiros mpl, disparos
mpl **(b)** (killing) asesinato m

shooting star n estrella f fugaz

shoot-out /ˈʃuːtaʊt/ n tiroteo m, balacera f
(AmL), baleo m (Chi)

shop¹ /ʃɑːp ‖ ʃɒp/ n **(a)** (retail outlet) tienda f,
negocio m (CS), comercio m (frml); **to go to the
~s** ir* de compras **(b)** (business) (colloq): **to talk ~**
hablar del trabajo

shop² -pp- vi hacer* compras; **to go ~ping** ir*
de compras

shopaholic /ˌʃɑːpəˈhɔːlɪk ‖ ˌʃɒpəˈhɒlɪk/ n
(colloq) persona f adicta a las compras

shop: **~ assistant** n (BrE) dependiente, -ta
m,f, (de tienda) (AmL),
vendedor, -dora m,f (CS); **~ floor** n (part of
factory) taller m; (workers) obreros mpl,
trabajadores mpl; (as union members) bases fpl
sindicales; **~keeper** n comerciante mf, tendero,
-ra m,f, **~lifter** /ˈʃɑːpˌlɪftər ‖ ˈʃɒpˌlɪftə(r)/ n
ladrón, -drona m,f (que roba en las tiendas);
~lifting /ˈʃɑːpˌlɪftɪŋ ‖ ˈʃɒpˌlɪftɪŋ/ n hurto m (en
las tiendas)

shopper /ˈʃɑːpər ‖ ˈʃɒpə(r)/ n comprador, -dora
m,f

shopping /ˈʃɑːpɪŋ ‖ ˈʃɒpɪŋ/ n **(a)** (act): **to do
the ~** hacer* la compra or (AmS) las compras,
hacer* el mercado (Col, Ven), hacer* el mandado
(Méx); (before n) (basket) de la compra or (AmS)
las compras **(b)** (purchases) compras fpl

shopping: **~ bag** n **(a)** (given by store) (AmE)
bolsa f (de plástico, papel etc) **(b)** (owned by
customer) (BrE) bolsa f (de la compra or (AmS) de
las compras); **~ cart** n (AmE) carrito m (de la
compra or (AmS) las compras); **~ center**,
(BrE) **~ centre ▶ ~** MALL; **~ list** n lista f de la
compra or (AmS) de las compras or (Col, Ven) del
mercado or (Méx) del mandado; **~ mall** n (esp
AmE) centro m comercial; **~ trolley** n (BrE) **(a)**
▶ ~ CART **(b)** (bag on wheels) carrito m, changuito
m (RPl)

shop: **~-soiled** adj (goods) deteriorado; **~
window** n escaparate m, vitrina f (AmL),
aparador m (AmC, Col, Méx); **~worn** adj (AmE)
(goods) deteriorado

shore /ʃɔːr ‖ ʃɔː(r)/ n **1** **(a)** (of sea, lake) orilla f
(b) (coast) costa f, ribera f **2** (land): **to go on ~**
bajar a tierra (firme)

■ **shore up** [v + o + adv, v + adv + o] apuntalar

shorn /ʃɔːrn ‖ ʃɔːn/ past p of SHEAR

short¹ /ʃɔːrt ‖ ʃɔːt/ adj -er, -est **1** (of length,
height, distance) corto; (person) bajo
2 **(a)** (brief) (visit/trip) corto; **the days are
getting ~er** los días van acortándose; **a ~ time
ago** hace poco (tiempo); **we call him Rob for ~** lo
llamamos Rob para abreviar **(b)** **in short** (briefly)
(as linker) en resumen
3 (brusque) (manner) brusco; **she has a ~ temper**
tiene muy mal genio
4 (inadequate, deficient) escaso; **to be in ~ supply**

escasear; **we're six people ~** todavía nos faltan
seis personas; **(to be) ~ OF sth/sb: we're very ~
of time** estamos muy cortos de tiempo; **they were
~ of staff** no tenían suficiente personal

short² adv **1** (suddenly, abruptly): **he cut ~ his
vacation** interrumpió sus vacaciones; **he stopped
~ when he saw me** se paró en seco cuando me
vio **2** (below target, requirement): **to fall ~** «shell/
arrow» quedarse corto; **we never went ~ of food**
nunca nos faltó la comida

short³ n **1** (Cin) cortometraje m, corto m
2 (drink) (BrE) copa f de bebida alcohólica de las
que se sirven en pequeñas cantidades, como el
whisky o el coñac **3** **shorts** pl **(a)** (short trousers)
shorts mpl, pantalones mpl cortos **(b)** (men's
underwear) (AmE) calzoncillos mpl

short⁴ vi (Elec) hacer* un cortocircuito

■ **short out** (AmE Elec) [v + adv] «fuse»
fundirse; «iron/hairdryer» hacer* (un)
cortocircuito

shortage /ˈʃɔːrtɪdʒ ‖ ˈʃɔːtɪdʒ/ n **~** (OF sth/sb)
falta f or escasez f (DE algo/algn)

short: **~bread** n galleta dulce de mantequilla;
~change /ˌʃɔːrtˈtʃeɪndʒ ‖ ˌʃɔːtˈtʃeɪndʒ/ vt (in
shop): **he ~changed me** me dio mal el cambio or
(AmL tb) el vuelto; **~ circuit** n cortocircuito m;
~circuit /ˌʃɔːrtˈsɜːrkət ‖ ˌʃɔːtˈsɜːkɪt/ vt (Elec)
provocar* un cortocircuito en ■ **~** vi (Elec)
hacer* (un) cortocircuito; **~coming** n defecto
m, deficiencia f; **~crust (pastry)** n (BrE) pasta
f quebradiza (tipo de masa para empanadas,
tartas etc); **~ cut** n atajo m; **there are no ~ cuts
to success** no hay fórmulas mágicas para el éxito

shorten /ˈʃɔːrtn ‖ ˈʃɔːtn/ vt (skirt/sleeves)
acortar; (text/report) acortar, abreviar

short: **~fall** n **~fall** (IN sth) n **: a ~fall of 7% in
revenues** un déficit del 7% en los ingresos;
~haired /ˈʃɔːrtherd ‖ ˈʃɔːtˈheəd/ adj de pelo
corto; **~hand** n taquigrafía f; **~ list** n lista f de
candidatos preseleccionados; **~list** vt
preseleccionar; **~lived** /ˈʃɔːrtˈlɪvd ‖ ˈʃɔːtˈlɪvd/
adj (success/enthusiasm) efímero; (recovery)
pasajero

shortly /ˈʃɔːrtli ‖ ˈʃɔːtli/ adv dentro de poco; **~
before/after midnight** poco antes/después de la
medianoche

short: **~sighted** /ˈʃɔːrtˈsaɪtəd ‖ ˈʃɔːtˈsaɪtɪd/ adj
(a) (esp BrE Med) miope, corto de vista **(b)**
(attitude/policy) corto de miras; **~sleeved**
/ˈʃɔːrtˈsliːvd ‖ ˈʃɔːtˈsliːvd/ adj de manga corta;
~staffed /ˈʃɔːrtˈstæft ‖ ˈʃɔːtˈstɑːft/ adj: **they/we
were ~staffed** les/nos faltaba personal; **~ story**
n cuento m, relato m breve; **~tempered**
/ˈʃɔːrtˈtempərd ‖ ˈʃɔːtˈtempəd/ adj de mal genio;
~term /ˈʃɔːrtˈtɜːrm ‖ ˈʃɔːtˈtɜːm/ adj a corto
plazo; **~wave** /ˈʃɔːrtˈweɪv ‖ ˈʃɔːtˈweɪv/ n onda f
corta

shot¹ /ʃɑːt ‖ ʃɒt/ past & past p of SHOOT²

shot² n **1** **(a)** (from gun, rifle) disparo m, tiro m;
(from cannon) cañonazo m; **she fired three ~s**
disparó tres veces; **she was off like a ~** salió
disparada **(b)** (marksman): **a good/poor ~** un
buen/mal tirador
2 (colloq) (attempt, try): **it costs $50 a ~** son 50
dólares por vez; **I'd love another ~ at it** me
gustaría volver a intentarlo
3 (Phot) foto f, (Cin) toma f
4 (pellets): (lead) **~** perdigones mpl

5 (used in shotput) bala *f*, peso *m* (Esp)
6 (in soccer) disparo *m*, tiro *m*; (in basketball) tiro *m*, tirada *f*; (in golf, tennis) tiro *m*
7 (injection) inyección *f*

shot: ~**gun** *n* escopeta *f*; ~**put** *n* (event) lanzamiento *m* de bala *or* (Esp) de peso

should¹ /ʃʊd/ *past of* SHALL

should² *v mod* **1** (expressing desirability) debería (*or* deberías *etc*), debiera (*or* debieras *etc*); **you ~ have thought of that before** deberías *or* debieras haber pensado en eso antes
2 (indicating probability, logical expectation) debería (*or* deberías *etc*) (de), debiera (*or* debieras *etc*) (de); **it ~ add up to 100** debería (de) *or* debiera (de) dar 100
3 (*with first person only*) **(a)** (conditional use) (BrE fml): **I ~ like to see her** me gustaría verla **(b)** (venturing a guess) (BrE): **I ~ think she must be over 80** yo diría que debe tener más de 80 **(c)** (expressing indignation): **I ~ think so too!** ¡(no) faltaría más!
4 (subjunctive use) (*with all persons*): **it's natural that he ~ want to go with her** es natural que quiera ir con ella; **if you ~ happen to pass a bookshop ...** si pasaras por una librería ...

shoulder¹ /ˈʃəʊldər ‖ ˈʃəʊldə(r)/ *n* **1** (Anat, Clothing) hombro *m* **2** (of road) arcén *m*, berma *f* (Andes), acotamiento *m* (Méx), banquina *f* (RPl), hombrillo *m* (Ven)

shoulder² *vt* ⟨*knapsack*⟩ ponerse* *or* echarse al hombro; ⟨*blame/responsibility*⟩ cargar* con

shoulder: ~ **bag** *n* bolso *m or* (CS) cartera *f or* (Méx) bolsa *f* (*con correa larga para colgar del hombro*); ~ **blade** *n* omóplato *m*; ~-**length** /ˈʃəʊldərˈleŋθ ‖ ˈʃəʊldəˈleŋθ/ *adj*: ~-**length hair** pelo *m* hasta los hombros; ~ **strap** *n* (of garment) tirante *m or* (CS) bretel *m*; (of bag) correa *f*

shouldn't /ˈʃʊdn̩t/ = **should not**

shout¹ /ʃaʊt/ *n* grito *m*

shout² *vi* gritar; **to ~ AT sb** gritarle A algn
■ ~ *vt* gritar
■ **shout out** **1** [*v + o + adv, v + adv + o*] ⟨*answer*⟩ gritar **2** [*v + adv + o*] dar* un grito

shouting /ˈʃaʊtɪŋ/ *n* griterío *m*

shove /ʃʌv/ *vt* **(a)** (push roughly) empujar; **they ~d her out of the way** la quitaron de en medio a empellones *or* a empujones **(b)** (put) (colloq) poner*, meter
■ ~ *vi* empujar

shove² *n* empujón *m*, empellón *m*

shovel¹ /ˈʃʌvəl/ *n* pala *f*

shovel² *vt*, (BrE) **-ll-** ⟨*coal*⟩ palear; ⟨*snow*⟩ espalar

show¹ /ʃəʊ/ (*past* **showed**; *past p* **shown** *or* **showed**) *vt* **1** **(a)** ⟨*photograph/passport*⟩ mostrar*, enseñar; **to ~ sb sth, to ~ sth TO sb** mostrarle* algo a algn **(b)** ⟨*feelings*⟩ demostrar*; ⟨*interest/enthusiasm*⟩ demostrar*, mostrar*; ⟨*courage*⟩ demostrar* (tener); **could you ~ me the way?** ¿me podría indicar el camino? **(c)** (allow to be seen): **this carpet ~s every mark** en esta alfombra se notan todas las marcas; **he's started to ~ his age** se le han empezado a notar los años
2 (record, register) « *barometer/dial/indicator* » marcar*, señalar, indicar*; ⟨*profit/loss*⟩ arrojar

3 **(a)** (demonstrate) ⟨*truth/importance*⟩ demostrar*; **it just goes to ~ how wrong you can be** eso te demuestra lo equivocado que puedes estar **(b)** (teach) enseñar; **I ~ed her how to do it** le enseñé cómo se hacía
4 (by accompanying) (+ *adv compl*): **he ~ed us to our seats** nos llevó hasta nuestros asientos; **to ~ sb in** hacer* pasar a algn; **to ~ sb out** acompañar a algn a la puerta
5 **(a)** (screen) ⟨*movie*⟩ dar*, pasar, poner* (Esp); ⟨*program*⟩ dar*, poner* (Esp); ⟨*slides*⟩ pasar **(b)** (exhibit) ⟨*paintings/sculpture*⟩ exponer*; ⟨*horse/dog*⟩ presentar
■ ~ *vi* **1** (be visible) «*dirt/stain*» verse*; «*emotion/scar*» notarse; **your petticoat is ~ing** se te ve la enagua
2 (be screened) (Cin): **it's ~ing at the Trocadero** la están dando en el Trocadero, la ponen en el Trocadero (Esp)
■ *v refl* **to ~ oneself (a)** (become visible) «*person*» asomarse **(b)** (prove to be) demostrar* ser; (turn out to be) resultar ser
■ **show off** **1** [*v + adv*] lucirse*; **stop ~ing off** déjate de hacer tonterías
2 [*v + o + adv, v + adv + o*] **(a)** (display for admiration) ⟨*car/girlfriend*⟩ lucir*, presumir de (Esp); ⟨*wealth/knowledge*⟩ presumir de **(b)** (display to advantage) ⟨*beauty/complexion*⟩ hacer* resaltar
■ **show up** **1** [*v + o + adv, v + adv + o*] **(a)** (reveal) ⟨*mistake/deception*⟩ poner* de manifiesto (fml) **(b)** (embarrass) ⟨*parents/friends*⟩ hacer* quedar mal
2 [*v + adv*] **(a)** (be visible) «*imperfection*» notarse **(b)** (arrive) (colloq) aparecer* (fam)

show² *n* **1** (exhibition) (Art) exposición *f*; **to be on ~** estar* expuesto; **to put sth on ~** exponer* algo
2 **(a)** (stage production) espectáculo *m*; **to steal the ~** robarse el espectáculo **(b)** (on television, radio) programa *m*
3 (*no pl*) **(a)** (display) muestra *f*, demostración *f*; **a ~ of force** un despliegue de fuerza **(b)** (outward appearance): **I made a ~ of enthusiasm** fingí estar entusiasmado; **their plush office is simply for ~** su elegante oficina es solo para darse tono
4 (colloq) (*no pl*) (activity, organization) asunto *m*; **to run the ~** llevar la voz cantante (fam)

show: ~ **business** (colloq) *n* mundo *m* del espectáculo; ~**case** *n* (cabinet) vitrina *f* **(b)** (for products, ideologies) escaparate *m*; ~**down** *n* enfrentamiento *m*

shower¹ /ˈʃaʊər ‖ ˈʃaʊə(r)/ *n* **1** (in bathroom) ducha *f*, regadera *f* (Méx); **to take a ~** ducharse; (*before n*) ~ **cap** gorro *m* de ducha **2** (Meteo) chaparrón *m*, chubasco *m* **3** (party) (AmE) *fiesta en la que unos invitados obsequian a la homenajeada con motivo de su próxima boda, el nacimiento de su niño etc*

shower² *vt* **(a)** (spray) regar*; **to ~ sb WITH sth** tirarle algo A algn **(b)** (bestow lavishly) **to ~ sb WITH sth**: **he ~ed her with gifts** la llenó de regalos; **the country ~ed him with honors** el país lo colmó de honores
■ ~ *vi* **(a)** (wash) ducharse **(b)** (be sprayed) «*water/leaves/stones*» caer*; «*letters/congratulations/protests*» llover*

show jumping /ˌdʒʌmpɪŋ/ *n* concursos *mpl* hípicos

shown /ʃəʊn/ *past p of* SHOW¹

show: ∼-**off** n (colloq) fanfarrón, -rrona m,f, fantasma mf (Esp fam); ∼**room** n (often pl) salón m de exposición (y ventas)

showy /'ʃəʊi/ adj **showier, showiest** (a) (gaudy) llamativo (b) (attractive) vistoso

shrank /ʃræŋk/ past of SHRINK

shrapnel /'ʃræpnl/ n metralla f

shred¹ /ʃred/ n (of paper, fabric) tira f, trozo m; **not a (single)** ∼ **of evidence** ni una (sola) prueba; **not a** ∼ **of truth** ni pizca de verdad; **to be in** ∼**s** «clothes/fabric» estar* hecho jirones or tiras; «argument/reputation» estar* destrozado

shred² vt -**dd**- cortar en tiras; «documents» destruir*, triturar

shredder /'ʃredər ‖'ʃredə(r)/ n (for paper) trituradora f; (for vegetables) cortadora f

shrew /ʃruː/ n (Zool) musaraña f

shrewd /ʃruːd/ adj -**er**, -**est** «person» astuto; «move/investment/assessment» hábil

shriek¹ /ʃriːk/ n (of delight, terror) grito m, chillido m; (of pain) grito m, alarido m; **we could hear** ∼**s of laughter** oíamos risotadas

shriek² vi/t gritar, chillar

shrift /ʃrɪft/ n: **to give sth short** ∼ «idea/suggestion» desestimar algo de plano; **to give sb short** ∼ echar a algn con cajas destempladas

shrill /ʃrɪl/ adj -**er**, -**est** «whistle/laugh» agudo, estridente; «voice» agudo, chillón

shrimp /ʃrɪmp/ n (pl ∼ or (BrE also) ∼**s**) (large) (AmE) langostino m; (medium) camarón m (AmL), gamba f (esp Esp); (small) (BrE) camarón m, quisquilla f (Esp)

shrine /ʃraɪn/ n (holy place) santuario m; (in out-of-the-way place) ermita f

shrink /ʃrɪŋk/ (past **shrank** or **shrunk**; past p **shrunk** or **shrunken**) vi **1** (diminish in size) «clothes/fabric» encoger(se)*; «meat» achicarse*; «wood» contraerse*; «area/amount» reducirse* **2** (recoil) retroceder; **to** ∼ **back o away from sth/sb** echarse atrás or retroceder ante algo/algn
■ ∼ vt «clothes/fabric» encoger*

shrinkage /'ʃrɪŋkɪdʒ/ n (of clothes, fabric) encogimiento m; (of wood, metal) contracción f

shrivel /'ʃrɪvl/, (BrE) -**ll**- ∼ **(up)** vi «leaf/plant» marchitarse, secarse*; «fruit/vegetables» resecarse* y arrugarse*; «skin» ajarse
■ vt «leaf/plant» secar*, marchitar

shroud¹ /ʃraʊd/ n mortaja f

shroud² vt envolver; **a case** ∼**ed in mystery** (journ) un caso envuelto en un velo de misterio

Shrove Tuesday /ʃrəʊv/ n martes m de Carnaval

shrub /ʃrʌb/ n arbusto m, mata f

shrubbery /'ʃrʌbəri/ n arbustos mpl, matas fpl

shrug¹ /ʃrʌg/ n: **with a** ∼ **(of her shoulders)** encogiéndose de hombros

shrug² -**gg**- vi encogerse* de hombros

■ ∼ vt: **to** ∼ **one's shoulders** encogerse* de hombros
■ **shrug off** [v + o + adv, v + adv + o] «misfortune/disappointment» superar; «criticism» hacer* caso omiso de

shrunk /ʃrʌŋk/ past & past p of SHRINK

shrunken¹ /'ʃrʌŋkən/ past p of SHRINK

shrunken² adj «body» consumido

shudder¹ /'ʃʌdər ‖'ʃʌdə(r)/ vi (a) «person» estremecerse* (b) «bus/train/plane» dar* sacudidas; **to** ∼ **to a halt** pararse abruptamente

shudder² n (a) (of person) estremecimiento m (b) (of vehicle, engine) sacudida f

shuffle /'ʃʌfl/ vt **1 to** ∼ **one's feet** arrastrar los pies **2** «cards/papers» barajar
■ ∼ vi caminar or andar* arrastrando los pies

shun /ʃʌn/ vt -**nn**- «person/society» rechazar*, rehuir*; «publicity/limelight» evitar, rehuir*

shunt /ʃʌnt/ vt (Rail) cambiar de vía

shush¹ /ʃʊʃ/ vt acallar

shush² interj: ∼! ¡chitón!, ¡silencio!

shut¹ /ʃʌt/ (pres p **shutting**; past & past p **shut**) vt **1** (a) «window/book/eyes» cerrar* (b) «store/business» cerrar* **2** (confine) **to** ∼ **sb IN sth** encerrar* a algn EN algo; **he** ∼ **himself in his room** se encerró en su cuarto
■ ∼ vi **1** «door/window» cerrar(se)* **2** (esp BrE) (cease business — for day) cerrar*; (— permanently) cerrar* (sus puertas)
■ **shut down 1** [v + adv] «factory/business» cerrar*; «machinery» apagarse* **2** [v + o + adv, v + adv + o] «factory/business» cerrar*; «machinery» apagar*
■ **shut in** [v + o + adv, v + adv + o] encerrar*
■ **shut off** [v + o + adv, v + adv + o] (a) «water/electricity» cortar; «engine» apagar* (b) (isolate) (often pass) «place/person» aislar*
■ **shut out** [v + o + adv, v + adv + o] (a) «person/animal» dejar (a)fuera; «light/heat» no dejar entrar; **to** ∼ **oneself out** quedarse (a)fuera (b) (AmE Sport) «team/pitcher» ganarle a (sin conceder ni un gol o carrera etc)
■ **shut up 1** [v + o + adv, v + adv + o] (a) (close) «house/office» cerrar*; (confine) «dog» encerrar* **2** [v + o + adv] (silence) (colloq) hacer* callar **3** [v + adv] (a) (close business) cerrar* (b) (stop talking) (colloq) callarse

shut² adj (pred) cerrado

shutdown /'ʃʌtdaʊn/ n (of hospital, college) cierre m; (of power) corte m; (of services) paralización f

shutter /'ʃʌtər ‖'ʃʌtə(r)/ n **1** (on window) postigo m **2** (Phot) obturador m

shuttle¹ /'ʃʌtl/ n **1** (in loom, sewing machine) lanzadera f **2** (a) (Aviat) puente m aéreo; (bus, train service) servicio m (regular) de enlace (b) (space ∼) transbordador m or lanzadera f espacial

shuttle² vi: **to** ∼ **back and forth** ir* y venir*
■ ∼ vt «passengers» transportar, llevar

AmC	Central America	Arg	Argentina	Cu	Cuba	Per	Peru
AmL	Latin America	Bol	Bolivia	Ec	Ecuador	RPl	River Plate Area
AmS	South America	Chi	Chile	Esp	Spain	Ur	Uruguay
Andes	Andean Region	CS	Southern Cone	Méx	Mexico	Ven	Venezuela

shuttlecock /'ʃʌtl̩kɑːk ‖ 'ʃʌtl̩kɒk/ n volante m, plumilla f, rehilete m, gallito m (Col, Méx)

shy¹ /ʃaɪ/ adj **shyer, shyest** ‹person› tímido; ‹animal› huraño

shy² vi **shies, shying, shied** «horse» respingar*

shyly /'ʃaɪli/ adv tímidamente, con timidez

shyness /'ʃaɪnəs ‖ 'ʃaɪnɪs/ n timidez f

Siamese /saɪə'miːz/ n (pl ~) ~ **(cat)** gato m siamés

Siamese twins pl n (hermanos) siameses mpl, (hermanas) siamesas fpl

sibling /'sɪblɪŋ/ n (frml) (brother) hermano m; (sister) hermana f

sick /sɪk/ adj **-er, -est** 1 (ill) enfermo; **to be off** ~ estar* ausente por enfermedad 2 (nauseated) (pred): **to feel** ~ (dizzy, unwell) estar* mareado; (about to vomit) tener* ganas de vomitar; **to be** ~ vomitar; **he makes me** ~ me da asco 3 (a) (disturbed, sickened) (pred): **to be** ~ **with fear/worry** estar* muerto de miedo/preocupación (b) (weary, fed up) **to be** ~ **OF sth/-ING** estar* harto DE algo/+ INF; **I'm** ~ **and tired of hearing that** estoy absolutamente harto de oír eso 4 (gruesome) ‹person/mind› morboso; ‹humor/joke› de muy mal gusto

sick: ~ **bay** n enfermería f; ~**bed** n (liter) lecho m de enfermo (liter)

sicken /'sɪkən/ vt dar* rabia, enfermar (AmL); (stronger) asquear
■ ~ vi (BrE) **to be** ~**ing FOR sth** estar* incubando algo

sickening /'sɪkənɪŋ/ adj (a) (appalling): **it's** ~, **isn't it?** da mucha rabia ¿no?; (stronger) da asco ¿no? (b) ‹smell/sight› nauseabundo

sickle /'sɪkəl/ n hoz f

sick leave n permiso m or (Esp) baja f or (RPl) licencia f por enfermedad

sickly¹ /'sɪkli/ adj **-lier, -liest** (a) ‹complexion/child› enfermizo (b) ‹taste/smell› empalagoso (c) ‹color› horrible, asqueroso

sickly² adv: ~ **sweet** demasiado empalagoso

sickness /'sɪknəs ‖ 'sɪknɪs/ n (a) (disease) (liter) enfermedad f (b) (nausea) náuseas fpl; (vomiting) vómitos mpl

sick pay n salario que se percibe mientras se está con permiso por enfermedad

side¹ /saɪd/ n 1 (surface — of cube, record, coin, piece of paper) lado m, cara f; (— of building, cupboard) lado m, costado m; (— of mountain, hill) ladera f, falda f
2 (boundary, edge): **they were playing by the** ~ **of the pool** estaban jugando junto a or al lado de la piscina
3 (a) (of person) costado m; (of animal) ijada f, ijar m; **Roy stood at her** ~ Roy estaba a su lado; **they sat** ~ **by** ~ estaban sentados uno junto al otro (b) (Culin) **a** ~ **of beef** media res f
4 (contrasted area, part, half) lado m; **from** ~ **to** ~ de un lado al otro; **on the** ~: **he repairs cars on the** ~ arregla coches como trabajo extra
5 (a) (faction): **to take** ~**s** tomar partido; **whose** ~ **are you on?** ¿tú de parte de quién estás? (b) (Sport) equipo m
6 (area, aspect) lado m, aspecto m; **you must**

listen to both ~**s of the story** hay que oír las dos versiones; **it's a little on the short** ~ es un poco corto
■ **side with** [v + prep + o] ponerse* de parte de

side² adj (before n, no comp) (a) ‹door/entrance/wall› lateral; **a** ~ **street** una calle lateral, una lateral (b) (incidental, secondary) ‹issue› secundario (c) (Culin): ~ **dish** acompañamiento m; **a** ~ **salad** una ensalada (como acompañamiento)

side: ~**board** n 1 (piece of furniture) aparador m, seibó m (Ven); 2 ~**boards** pl (BrE) ▶ ~**BURNS**; ~**burns** pl n patillas fpl; ~**car** n sidecar m; ~ **effect** n (of drug, treatment) efecto m secundario; (incidental result) consecuencia f indirecta; ~**kick** n (colloq) adlátere mf; ~**line** n 1 (Sport) línea f de banda; 2 (subsidiary activity) actividad f suplementaria; ~**long** adj (before n) ‹glance› de reojo, de soslayo; ~**saddle** adv a mujeriegas (con las dos piernas hacia el mismo lado); ~**show** n (at fair) puesto m; ~**step** vt **-pp-** ‹blow/opponent› esquivar; ‹problem/question› eludir; ~**track** vt (a) (from subject) hacer* desviar del tema (b) (from purpose): **sorry, I got** ~**tracked** perdón, me entretuve haciendo otra cosa; ~**walk** n (AmE) acera f, banqueta f (Méx), andén m (AmC, Col), vereda f (CS, Per)

sideways¹ /'saɪdweɪz/ adv (a) ‹glance› de reojo, de soslayo; ‹walk› de lado, de costado (b) (with side part forward) de lado

sideways² adj ‹look› de reojo, de soslayo; ‹movement› lateral, de lado

siding /'saɪdɪŋ/ n (Rail) apartadero m

sidle /'saɪdl̩/ vi **to** ~ **up to sb** acercársele* sigilosamente a algn

siege /siːdʒ/ n sitio m; **the city was under** ~ la ciudad estaba sitiada

Sierra Leone /si'erəli'əʊn/ n Sierra Leona f

siesta /si'estə/ n siesta f; **to have a** ~ dormir* or echarse una siesta

sieve¹ /sɪv/ n (Culin) (for flour etc) tamiz m, cedazo m, cernidor m

sieve² vt ‹flour› (BrE) tamizar*, cernir*, cerner*

sift /sɪft/ vt (a) ‹sugar/flour› tamizar*, cernir*, cerner*; (sprinkle) espolvorear (b) ‹facts/evidence› pasar por el tamiz or la criba

sigh¹ /saɪ/ vi suspirar; **he** ~**ed with relief/contentment** suspiró aliviado/satisfecho

sigh² n suspiro m; **she breathed** o **heaved a** ~ **of relief** dio un suspiro de alivio

sight¹ /saɪt/ n 1 (eye~) vista f
2 (range of vision): **to come into** ~ aparecer*; **to lose** ~ **of sth/sb** perder* algo/a algn de vista; **the finishing line was now in** ~ ya se veía la meta; **she watched until they were out of** ~ los siguió con la mirada hasta que los perdió de vista
3 (act of seeing, view) (no pl): **at first** ~ a primera vista; **it was love at first** ~ fue amor a primera vista; **to catch** ~ **of sth/sb** ver* algo/a algn; (in distance) avistar algo/a algn; **to know sb by** ~ conocer* a algn de vista; **to play at** o **by** ~ (Mus) tocar* a primera vista; **I can't stand the** ~ **of him** (colloq) no lo puedo ver (fam)
4 (a) (thing seen): **the sparrow is a familiar** ~ **in our gardens** el gorrión se ve con frecuencia en nuestros jardines; **it's not a pretty** ~ (colloq) no es ···>

muy agradable de ver **(b) sights** pl (famous places): **to see the ~s** visitar los lugares de interés

⑤ **(a)** (of gun) mira f **(b) sights** pl (ambition): **to have sth in one's ~s** tener* la mira puesta en algo

sight² vt ⟨land/ship⟩ divisar; ⟨person/animal⟩ ver*

sighted /'saɪtəd ‖'saɪtɪd/ adj vidente; **he's partially ~** tiene visión parcial

sight: ~read /'saɪtˌriːd/ (past & past p **-read** /-red/) vt/i repentizar*; **~seeing** /'saɪtˌsiːɪŋ/ n: **to go ~seeing** ir* a visitar los lugares de interés; **~seer** /'saɪtˌsiːər/ n turista mf, visitante mf

sign¹ /saɪn/ n ① **(a)** (indication) señal f, indicio m; **it's a ~ of the times** es un indicio de los tiempos que corren **(b)** (omen) presagio m ② (gesture) seña f, señal f ③ **(a)** (notice, board) letrero m, cartel m; (in demonstration) pancarta f **(b)** (road ~) señal f (vial) ④ **(a)** (symbol) símbolo m; (Math) signo m **(b)** (Astrol) signo m

sign² vt **(a)** (write signature on) firmar **(b)** (hire) ⟨actor⟩ contratar; ⟨player⟩ fichar

■ **~** vi firmar

■ **sign for** [v + prep + o] ⟨goods/parcel⟩ firmar el recibo de

■ **sign on** [v + adv] **(a)** (enlist) «recruit» alistarse, enlistarse (AmC, Col, Ven) **(b)** (in UK) (Soc Adm) anotarse para recibir el seguro de desempleo, apuntarse al paro (Esp)

■ **sign up** ① [v + adv] (for a course) inscribirse*, matricularse; (to join the army) alistarse, enlistarse (AmC, Col, Ven) ② [v + o + adv, o + adv + o] ⟨soldiers⟩ reclutar; ⟨player⟩ fichar

signal¹ /'sɪgnl/ n señal f

signal², (BrE) **-ll-** vt señalar

■ **~** vi **(a)** (gesture) **to ~ (to sb)** hacer(le)* señas/una seña (a algn) **(b)** (Auto) señalizar*, poner* el intermitente or (Col, Méx) la direccional or (CS) el señalizador

signature /'sɪgnətʃʊr ‖'sɪgnətʃə(r)/ n ① (written name) firma f ② (Mus): **time ~** compás m, tiempo m

signature tune n (BrE) sintonía f (del programa), cortina f musical (CS)

significance /sɪg'nɪfɪkəns/ n importancia f

significant /sɪg'nɪfɪkənt/ adj **(a)** (important) importante **(b)** (meaningful) ⟨look/smile⟩ expresivo; ⟨fact/remark⟩ significativo

significantly /sɪg'nɪfɪkəntli/ adv considerablemente

signify /'sɪgnəfaɪ ‖'sɪgnɪfaɪ/ vt **-fies, -fying, -fied** significar*

signing /'saɪnɪŋ/ n **(a)** (act of signing) firma f **(b)** (Sport) fichaje m

sign language n lenguaje m gestual

signpost¹ /'saɪnpəʊst/ n señal f, poste m indicador

signpost² vt (BrE Auto) ⟨way/route⟩ señalizar*

Sikh¹ /siːk/ n sij mf

Sikh² adj sij adj inv

silage /'saɪlɪdʒ/ n ensilaje m, ensilado m (forraje fermentado en silos)

silence¹ /'saɪləns/ n silencio m; **in ~** en silencio

silence² vt ⟨cries/voice⟩ acallar; ⟨child/animal⟩ hacer* callar; ⟨opposition/criticism⟩ silenciar

silencer /'saɪlənsər ‖'saɪlənsə(r)/ n **(a)** (on gun) silenciador m **(b)** (on car) (BrE) silenciador m, mofle m (AmC, Méx)

silent /'saɪlənt/ adj **(a)** (noiseless, still) ⟨night/forest⟩ silencioso **(b)** (not speaking) ⟨gesture/protest⟩ mudo; **the 'h' is ~** la hache es muda; **a ~ movie** una película muda

silently /'saɪləntli/ adv **(a)** (noiselessly) ⟨creep/glide/enter⟩ silenciosamente **(b)** (without speaking) ⟨pray/stand/listen⟩ en silencio, calladamente

silent partner n socio, -cia m,f capitalista

silhouette /'sɪluːet/ n silueta f

silicon /'sɪləkən ‖'sɪlɪkən/ n silicio m; (before n) **~ chip** (Comput) pastilla f de silicio

silk /sɪlk/ n seda f

silky /'sɪlki/ **-kier, -kiest** adj ⟨fabric/fur⟩ sedoso

sill /sɪl/ n (window~) alféizar m, antepecho m

silly /'sɪli/ adj **-lier, -liest** ⟨person/idea/mistake⟩ tonto; ⟨name/hat⟩ ridículo

silo /'saɪləʊ/ n (pl **-los**) silo m

silt /sɪlt/ n cieno m, limo m

silver¹ /'sɪlvər ‖'sɪlvə(r)/ n ① (metal) plata f ② **(a)** (household items) platería f, plata f **(b)** (coins) monedas fpl (de plata, aluminio etc)

silver² adj **(a)** (made of silver) de plata **(b)** (in color) plateado **(c)** (representing 25 years) (before n): **~ jubilee** el vigésimo quinto aniversario; **~ wedding** (BrE) bodas fpl de plata

silver: ~ foil n (BrE Culin) papel m de aluminio or de plata; **~plate** /'sɪlvər'pleɪt ‖'sɪlvə'pleɪt/ vt dar*(le) un baño de plata a, platear; **~smith** n platero, -ra m,f, orfebre mf; **~ware** /'sɪlvərweər ‖'sɪlvəweə(r)/ n platería f, plata f

similar /'sɪmələr ‖'sɪmɪlə(r)/ adj similar, parecido, semejante; **to be ~ to sth** parecerse* a algo

similarity /ˌsɪmə'lærəti ‖ˌsɪmɪ'lærəti/ n (pl **-ties**) **(a)** (likeness — between things) similitud f, parecido m, semejanza f; (— between persons) parecido m **(b)** (common feature) semejanza f, similitud f

similarly /'sɪmələrli ‖'sɪmɪləli/ adv **(a)** (in a similar way) de modo parecido or similar **(b)** (equally) igualmente **(c)** (as linker) asimismo

simile /'sɪməli ‖'sɪmɪli/ n símil m

simmer /'sɪmər ‖'sɪmə(r)/ vt/i hervir* a fuego lento

simple /'sɪmpəl/ adj **simpler** /-plər/, **simplest** /-pləst/ ① (uncomplicated) ⟨task/problem⟩ sencillo, simple ② (plain, unpretentious) ⟨dress/food⟩ sencillo, simple ③ **(a)** (unsophisticated, humble) simple **(b)** (backward) simple

simplicity /sɪm'plɪsəti/ n simplicidad f, sencillez f

simplify /'sɪmpləfaɪ ‖'sɪmplɪfaɪ/ vt **-fies, -fying, -fied** simplificar*

simplistic /sɪm'plɪstɪk/ adj simplista

simply /'sɪmpli/ adv ① (only, merely) simplemente, sencillamente ② **(a)** (plainly) con sencillez, sencillamente **(b)** (in simple language) simplemente, sencillamente

simulate /'sɪmjəleɪt ‖'sɪmjʊleɪt/ vt simular

simultaneous /'saıməl'temıəs ‖ˌsıməl'temıəs/ *adj* simultáneo

simultaneously /'saıməl'temıəsli ‖ˌsıməl'temıəsli/ *adv* simultáneamente, a la vez

sin¹ /sın/ *n* pecado *m*

sin² *vi* **-nn-** pecar*

since¹ /sıns/ *conj* [1] (in time) desde que; ~ **coming to London** desde que vino (*or* vine *etc*) a Londres [2] (introducing a reason) ya que; ~ **you can't go, can I have your ticket?** ya que no puedes ir ¿me das tu entrada?

since² *prep* desde; **they've worked there** ~ **1970** han trabajado allí desde 1970; **how long is it** ~ **your operation?** ¿cuánto (tiempo) hace de tu operación?

since³ *adv* desde entonces; **she has lived here ever** ~ desde entonces que vive aquí

sincere /sın'sır ‖sın'sıə(r)/, **sincerer, sincerest** *adj* sincero

sincerely /sın'sırli ‖sın'sıəli/ *adv* sinceramente; ~ **(yours)** *o* (BrE) **yours** ~ (in letters) (saluda) a usted atentamente

sincerity /sın'serəti/ *n* sinceridad *f*

sinew /'sınju:/ *n* tendón *m*; (in meat) nervio *m*

sinful /'sınfəl/ *adj* ‹person› pecador; ‹act› pecaminoso

sing /sıŋ/ (*past* **sang**; *past p* **sung**) *vt/i* cantar
■ **sing along** [*v* + *adv*] **to** ~ **along** (WITH sb) cantar (CON algn)

Singapore /'sıŋɡə'pɔːr ‖ˌsıŋə'pɔː(r)/ *n* Singapur *m*

singe /sındʒ/ *vt* **singes, singeing, singed** chamuscar*

singer /'sıŋər ‖'sıŋə(r)/ *n* cantante *mf*

singing /'sıŋıŋ/ *n* canto *m*; (*before n*) **a good** ~ **voice** una buena voz (para el canto)

single¹ /'sıŋɡəl/ *adj* [1] (just one) (*before n*) solo; **the largest** ~ **shareholder** el mayor accionista individual; **every** ~ **day** todos los días sin excepción; (*with neg*) **not a** ~ **house was left standing** no quedó ni una sola casa en pie [2] (*before n*) **(a)** (for one person) ‹room› individual; ‹bed/sheet› individual, de una plaza (AmL) **(b)** (not double): **in** ~ **file** en fila india **(c)** (BrE Transp) ‹fare/ticket› de ida, sencillo [3] (unmarried) soltero
■ **single out** [*v* + *o* + *adv*, *v* + *adv* + *o*]: **to** ~ sb **out** (select) escoger* a algn en particular; (identify) señalar a algn en particular; **she was** ~d **out for criticism/praise** se la criticó/elogió a ella en particular

single² *n* [1] (Mus) single *m*, (disco *m*) sencillo *m* [2] (ticket) (BrE) boleto *m* *or* (Esp) billete *m* de ida

single: ~**-breasted** /'sıŋɡəl'brestəd ‖ˌsıŋɡəl'brestıd/ *adj* de una fila de botones, derecho (AmL); ~ **cream** *n* (BrE) crema *f* líquida, nata *f* líquida (Esp); ~**-handed** /'sıŋɡəl'hændəd ‖ˌsıŋɡəl'hændıd/ *adv* sin (la) ayuda de nadie; ~ **market** *n* mercado *m* único; ~**-minded** /'sıŋɡəl'maındəd ‖ˌsıŋɡəl'maındıd/ *adj* decidido, resuelto; ~ **parent** *n*: **he's/she's a** ~ **parent** es un padre/una madre que cría a su(s) hijo(s) sin pareja

singles /'sıŋɡəlz/ *pl n* (Sport) individuales *mpl*, singles *mpl* (AmL)

singsong /'sıŋsɔːŋ ‖'sıŋsɒŋ/ *adj* ‹voice/accent› cantarín

singular¹ /'sıŋɡjələr ‖'sıŋɡjʊlə(r)/ *adj* singular

singular² *n* singular *m*; **in the** ~ en singular

sinister /'sınıstər ‖'sınıstə(r)/ *adj* siniestro

sink¹ /sıŋk/ (*past* **sank**; *past p* **sunk**) *vi* [1] **(a)** ‹ship/stone› hundirse **(b)** (subside) **to** ~ (INTO sth) ‹building/foundations› hundirse (EN algo); **he sank back into the chair** se arrellanó en el sillón [2] (fall, drop) ‹water/level› descender*, bajar; ‹price/value› caer* a pique; ‹attendance/output› decaer*; **my heart sank** se me cayó el alma a los pies [3] (degenerate) degradarse; **I'd never** ~ **so low** nunca caería tan bajo
■ ~ *vt* [1] ‹ship› hundir [2] (bury, hide) ‹pipe/cable› enterrar* [3] **(a)** (drive in): **the dog sank its teeth into my thigh** el perro me clavó los dientes en el muslo **(b)** (excavate) ‹shaft› abrir*; ‹well› perforar
■ **sink in** [*v* + *adv*] (colloq): **it finally sank in that ...** finalmente nos dimos cuenta de que ...

sink² *n* **(a)** (in kitchen) fregadero *m*, lavaplatos *m* (Andes) **(b)** (washbasin) (AmE) lavabo *m*, lavamanos *m*, lavatorio *m* (CS), pileta *f* (RPl)

sinner /'sınər ‖'sınə(r)/ *n* pecador, -dora *m,f*

sinus /'saınəs/ *n* (*pl* **-nuses**) seno *m*

sip¹ /sıp/ *vt* **-pp-** sorber, beber *or* tomar a sorbos

sip² *n* sorbo *m*

siphon /'saıfən/ *n* sifón *m*
■ **siphon off** [*v* + *o* + *adv*, *v* + *adv* + *o*] ‹liquid/fuel› sacar* con sifón; ‹money› desviar*

sir /sɜːr ‖sɜː(r)/ *n* [1] **(a)** (as form of address — to male customer) señor, caballero; (— to male teacher) (BrE) profesor, señor **(b)** (Corresp): **Dear Sir** De mi mayor consideración:, Muy señor mío: [2] **Sir** (as title) sir *m*

siren /'saırən/ *n* sirena *f*

sirloin /'sɜːrlɔın ‖'sɜːlɔın/ *n* preciado corte de carne vacuna del cuarto trasero

sirup *n* (AmE) ▶ SYRUP

sister /'sıstər ‖'sıstə(r)/ *n* [1] (sibling) hermana *f*; (*before n*) ‹company› afiliado; ~ **ship** buque *m* gemelo [2] **(a)** (nun) hermana *f*, monja *f* **(b)** (nurse) (BrE) enfermera *f* jefe *or* jefa (a cargo de una o más salas)

sisterhood /'sıstərhʊd ‖'sıstəhʊd/ *n* **(a)** (association of women) asociación *f* de mujeres **(b)** (Relig) congregación *f* **(c)** (sisterly relationship) solidaridad *f* (entre mujeres)

sister-in-law /'sıstərənlɔː ‖'sıstərınlɔː/ *n* (*pl* **sisters-in-law**) cuñada *f*

sisterly /'sıstərli ‖'sıstəli/ *adj* (propio) de hermana

sit /sıt/ (*pres p* **sitting**; *past & past p* **sat**) *vi* [1] **(a)** (sit down) sentarse* **(b)** (be seated) estar* sentado [2] (be in session) ‹committee/court› reunirse* en sesión, sesionar (esp AmL) [3] **sitting** *pres p* ‹figure› sentado
■ ~ *vt* [1] (cause to be seated) ‹person› sentar*; ‹object› poner*, colocar* (*en posición vertical*) [2] (BrE Educ): **to** ~ **an exam** hacer* *or* dar* *or* (CS) rendir* *or* (Méx) tomar un examen, examinarse

···⫶

■ **sit around** [v + adv]: he ~s around all day doing nothing se pasa el día sentado sin hacer nada

■ **sit back** [v + adv] (colloq) recostarse*

■ **sit down** [v + adv] sentarse*

■ **sit in** [v + adv] to ~ in on a class asistir a una clase como oyente (or observador etc)

■ **sit out** [v + o + adv, v + adv + o] **(a)** (wait until end of) ⟨siege⟩ aguantar; **to ~ it out** aguantarse **(b)** (not participate in) ⟨dance⟩ no bailar; ⟨game⟩ no tomar parte en

■ **sit up** [v + adv] **(a)** (in upright position) «person/patient» incorporarse; «dog» sentarse* sobre las patas traseras; **that should make them ~ up and take notice** eso debería alertarlos **(b)** (with straight back) ponerse* derecho, enderezarse* **(c)** (not go to bed): **we sat up talking** nos quedamos (levantados) conversando

sitcom /'sɪtkɑːm ‖'sɪtkɒm/ n (colloq) ▶ SITUATION COMEDY

site /saɪt/ n **(a)** (location) emplazamiento m (frml); (piece of land) terreno m, solar m **(b)** (building ~) obra f **(c)** (archeological ~) yacimiento m (arqueológico) **(d)** (camp~) camping m

sit-in /'sɪtɪn/ n (demonstration) sentada f, sitin m (Méx); (strike) encierro m, ocupación f or toma f (del lugar de trabajo)

sitting /'sɪtɪŋ/ n **(a)** (for meal etc) turno m; **I watched three movies in a single ~** vi tres películas de una sentada (fam) **(b)** (of committee, parliament) sesión f

sitting: **~ duck** n (colloq) presa f fácil, blanco m seguro; **~ room** n (BrE) sala f de estar, living m (esp AmL), salón m (esp Esp)

situate /'sɪtʃueɪt ‖'sɪtʃʊeɪt/ vt (locate) (often pass) ⟨building/town⟩ situar*, ubicar* (esp AmL)

situation /sɪtʃu'eɪʃən ‖,sɪtjʊ'eɪʃən/ n **1** (circumstances, position) situación f **2** (job) (frml) empleo m; **⑨ situations vacant** ofertas de empleo

situation comedy n comedia f (acerca de situaciones de la vida diaria)

sit-up /'sɪtʌp/ n (ejercicio m) abdominal m (levantando el torso del suelo)

six¹ /sɪks/ n seis m; **it's ~ of one and half a dozen of the other** (colloq) (it makes no difference) da lo mismo; (both parties are to blame) los dos tienen parte de la culpa; see also FOUR¹

six² adj seis adj inv

sixteen /sɪks'tiːn/ adj/n dieciséis adj inv/m; see also FOUR¹

sixteenth¹ /sɪks'tiːnθ/ adj decimosexto

sixteenth² adv en decimosexto lugar

sixteenth³ n dieciseisavo m; (part) dieciseisava parte f

sixteenth note n (AmE) semicorchea f

sixth¹ /sɪksθ/ adj sexto

sixth² adv en sexto lugar

sixth³ n (Math) sexto m; (part) sexta parte f, sexto m

sixth: **~ form** n (in UK) los dos últimos años de la enseñanza secundaria; **~ sense** n sexto sentido m

sixtieth¹ /'sɪkstiəθ/ adj sexagésimo

sixtieth² adv en sexagésimo lugar

sixtieth³ n (Math) sesentavo m; (part) sesentava or sexagésima parte f

sixty /'sɪksti/ adj/n sesenta adj inv/m; see also FOUR¹

sizable /'saɪzəbəl/ adj ⟨fortune⟩ considerable; ⟨property⟩ de proporciones considerables

size /saɪz/ n **1** (dimensions) tamaño m; (of problem, task) magnitud f; **what ~ is it?** ¿de qué tamaño es?; **to cut sb down to ~** poner* a algn en su sitio, bajarle los humos a algn (fam) **2** (of clothes) talla f or (RPl) talle m; (of shoes, gloves) número m; **what ~ do you take?** ¿qué talla or (RPl) talle tiene or usa?; **I take (a) ~ 10 in shoes** calzo or (Esp tb) gasto el número 10

■ **size up** [v + o + adv, v + adv + o] (colloq) ⟨problem⟩ evaluar*; **she ~d him up immediately** enseguida lo caló

sizeable adj ▶ SIZABLE

sizzle /'sɪzəl/ vi chisporrotear

skate¹ /skeɪt/ n **1** (ice ~) patín m (para patinaje sobre hielo); (roller ~) patín m (de ruedas) **2** (pl ~ or ~s) (Culin, Zool) raya f

skate² vi patinar

skate: **~board** n monopatín m or (CS, Méx, Ven) patineta f; **~boarding** n deporte m del monopatín or (CS, Méx, Ven) de la patineta

skater /'skeɪtər ‖'skeɪtə(r)/ n patinador, -dora m,f

skating /'skeɪtɪŋ/ n (ice ~) patinaje m sobre hielo; (roller ~) patinaje m sobre ruedas; (before n) **~ rink** pista f de patinaje

skeleton /'skelɪtn ‖'skelɪtn/ n **(a)** (Anat) esqueleto m **(b)** (of building, vehicle) armazón m or f

skeleton key n llave f maestra

skeptic, (BrE) **sceptic** /'skeptɪk/ n escéptico, -ca m,f

skeptical, (BrE) **sceptical** /'skeptɪkəl/ adj ⟨person/attitude⟩ escéptico

skepticism, (BrE) **scepticism** /'skeptɪsɪzəm/ n escepticismo m

sketch¹ /sketʃ/ n **1** (drawing) bosquejo m, esbozo m **2** (Theat, TV) sketch m, apunte m

sketch² vt hacer* un bosquejo de, bosquejar

■ ~ vi hacer* bosquejos or bocetos

sketch: **~book** n cuaderno m de bocetos; **~pad** n bloc m de dibujo

sketchy /'sketʃi/ adj -chier, -chiest ⟨account/treatment⟩ muy superficial; ⟨knowledge⟩ muy básico

skewer /'skjuːər ‖'skjuː:ə(r)/ n pincho m, brocheta f

ski¹ /skiː/ n esquí m

ski² vi skis, skiing, skied esquiar*; **to go ~ing** ir* a esquiar

AmC	América Central	Arg	Argentina	Cu	Cuba	Per	Perú
AmL	América Latina	Bol	Bolivia	Ec	Ecuador	RPI	Río de la Plata
AmS	América del Sur	Chi	Chile	Esp	España	Ur	Uruguay
Andes	Región andina	CS	Cono Sur	Méx	México	Ven	Venezuela

skid¹ /skɪd/ n (Auto) patinazo m, patinada f (AmL)

skid² vi -dd- «car/plane/wheels» patinar; «person» resbalarse; «object» deslizarse*

skier /'skiːər ‖'skiə(r)/ n esquiador, -dora m,f

skiing /'skiːɪŋ/ n esquí m

skilful adj (BrE) ▶ SKILLFUL

skilift /'skiːlɪft/ n telesquí m

skill /skɪl/ n (a) (ability) habilidad f; **technical ~** destreza f (b) (technique): **typing is a very useful ~ to have** saber escribir a máquina es muy útil; **social ~s** don m de gente

skilled /skɪld/ adj «negotiator» hábil; «pilot» diestro; «worker/labor» calificado or (Esp) cualificado; «work» de especialista

skillful, (BrE) **skilful** /'skɪlfəl/ adj «liar/play» hábil; «surgeon/mechanic» diestro; (at sewing, craftwork) habilidoso

skim /skɪm/ -mm- vt **1** (Culin) «milk» descremar, desnatar (Esp); «soup» espumar **2** (a) «water/treetops» pasar casi rozando (b) (throw): **to ~ stones** hacer* cabrillas **3** (read quickly) leer* por encima
■ ~ vi **1** (glide): **the speedboat ~med over the sea** la lancha apenas rozaba la superficie del mar **2** (read quickly) leer* por encima

skim milk, (BrE) **skimmed milk** /skɪmd/ n leche f descremada or (Esp tb) desnatada

skimp /skɪmp/ vi (colloq) **to ~ (on sth)** escatimar (algo)

skimpy /'skɪmpi/ adj **-pier, -piest** «meal/portion» mezquino, pobre; «funds» escaso; «nightdress/bikini» brevísimo

skin¹ /skɪn/ n (a) (of person) piel f; (esp of face; in terms of quality, condition) cutis m, piel f; (in terms of color) tez f, piel f; **to have a thick/thin ~** ser* insensible/muy sensible a las críticas (b) (of animal, bird, fish) piel f (c) (of tomatoes, plums, sausage) piel f; (of potatoes, bananas) piel f, cáscara f (d) (on milk, custard) nata f; (on paint) capa f dura

skin² vt -nn- «animal» despellejar, desollar*

skin: ~**deep** /skɪn'diːp/ adj (pred) superficial; ~**dive** /'skɪndaɪv/ vi hacer* submarinismo, bucear; **to go ~diving** ir* a hacer submarinismo, ir* a bucear; ~**diver** n buzo m, submarinista mf; ~**diving** n submarinismo m, buceo m; ~**head** n cabeza mf rapada

skinny /'skɪni/ adj **-nier, -niest** flaco, flacucho (fam)

skintight /'skɪntaɪt/ adj muy ceñido, muy ajustado

skip¹ /skɪp/ n **1** (jump) brinco m, saltito m **2** (BrE) (container) contenedor m (para escombros, basura etc)

skip² -pp- vi (a) (move lightly and quickly) brincar, dar* saltitos (b) (with rope) (BrE) ▶ vt 2
■ ~ vt **1** (a) (omit) «page/chapter» saltarse (b) (not attend) «class/meeting» faltar a **2** (jump) (AmE): **to ~ rope** saltar a la cuerda or (Esp tb) a la comba

skipper /'skɪpər ‖'skɪpə(r)/ n (colloq) (a) (of boat) patrón, -trona m,f, capitán, -tana m,f; (of plane) capitán, -tana m,f (b) (Sport) (coach) entrenador, -dora m,f; (captain) capitán, -tana m,f

skip rope, (BrE) **skipping rope** /'skɪpɪŋ/ n ▶ JUMP ROPE

skirmish /'skɜːrmɪʃ ‖'skɜːmɪʃ/ n escaramuza f

skirt¹ /skɜːrt ‖skɜːt/ n falda f, pollera f (CS)

skirt² vt (a) (run alongside) bordear (b) ▶ SKIRT AROUND
■ **skirt around**, (BrE also) **skirt round** [v + prep + o] (a) «mountain/lake» bordear (b) «issue/problem» eludir

skittle /skɪtl/ n bolo m

skittles /'skɪtlz/ n (+ sing vb) bolos mpl

skive off /skaɪv/ [v + adv] (BrE colloq) (a) (disappear) escurrir el bulto (fam), escaparse, pirarse (Esp fam) (b) (stay away — from school) hacer* novillos (fam); (— from work) no ir* a trabajar, capear (Chi) or (Col) capar trabajo (fam)

skulk /skʌlk/ vi: **I saw him ~ing in the background** lo vi al fondo, tratando de pasar desapercibido; **to ~ around** merodear

skull /skʌl/ n cráneo m

skullcap /'skʌlkæp/ n casquete m; (Relig) solideo m

skunk /skʌŋk/ n mofeta f, zorrillo m (AmL), zorrino m (CS), mapurite m (AmC, Ven)

sky /skaɪ/ n (pl **skies**) cielo m

sky: ~**diving** n paracaidismo m (en la modalidad de caída libre); ~**high** /'skaɪ'haɪ/ adj: **prices are ~high** los precios están por las nubes; ~**lark** n alondra f; ~**light** n tragaluz m, claraboya f; ~**line** n (a) (horizon) línea f del horizonte m (b) (of city): **the Manhattan ~line** los edificios de Manhattan recortados contra el horizonte; ~**scraper** n rascacielos m

slab /slæb/ n (of stone) losa f; (of concrete) bloque m; (of wood) tabla f; (of cake, bread) pedazo m, trozo m (grueso)

slack¹ /slæk/ adj **-er, -est** **1** (loose) «rope/cable» flojo **2** (lax, negligent) «student» poco aplicado; «piece of work» flojo **3** (not busy) «period» de poca actividad

slack² n: **there's too much ~ in the rope** la cuerda está demasiado floja; **to take up the ~ in sth** tensar algo

slack³ vi (colloq) haraganear, flojear (fam)

slacken /'slækən/ vi (a) (become looser) «rope/wire» aflojarse (b) (diminish) ▶ SLACKEN OFF 1
■ ~ vt (a) (loosen) ▶ SLACKEN OFF 2 (b) (reduce) «speed» reducir*; «pace» aflojar
■ **slacken off** **1** [v + adv] «wind» amainar, aflojar; «student» aflojar el ritmo de trabajo; «speed/rate» disminuir*; «trade/demand» decaer*, disminuir* **2** [v + o + adv, v + adv + o] «rope/wire» aflojar

slacks /slæks/ n pantalones mpl (de sport)

slag /slæg/ n (Metall) escoria f; (Min) escombro m, escoria f; (before n) **~ heap** escorial m, escombrera f

slain /sleɪn/ past p of SLAY

slake /sleɪk/ vt (liter) «thirst» saciar

slalom /'slɑːləm/ n slalom m

slam /slæm/ -mm- vt **1** (a) (close violently): **to ~ the door** dar* un portazo (b) (put with force): **he ~med the book down on the table** tiró el libro sobre la mesa **2** (criticize) (journ) atacar* violentamente
■ ~ vi «door» cerrarse* de un portazo

slander¹ /'slændər ‖'slɑːndə(r)/ n calumnia f, difamación f

slander² vt calumniar, difamar

S

slang /slæŋ/ n argot m

slant¹ /slænt ‖slɑ:nt/ n **1** (slope) inclinación f, (of roof, floor) pendiente f **2** (point of view) enfoque m; (bias) sesgo m

slant² vi (a) inclinarse (b) **slanting** pres p inclinado; ⟨eyes⟩ rasgado

slap¹ /slæp/ vt **-pp-** **1** (hit): to ∼ sb (on face) pegarle* or darle* una bofetada or (AmL tb) una cachetada a algn; (on arm, leg) pegarle* or darle* una palmada a algn **2** (a) (put with force) tirar (b) (put, apply carelessly): he ∼ped some paint on it le dio una mano de pintura rápidamente; she ∼ped on some makeup se maquilló de cualquier manera

slap² n (on face) bofetada f, cachetada f (AmL); (on back, leg) palmada f

slap: ∼**dash** adj ⟨work⟩ chapucero (fam); ∼**stick** n bufonadas fpl; (before n) ∼**stick comedy** astracanada f

slash¹ /slæʃ/ n **1** (cut — on body) cuchillada f, tajo m; (— in tire, cloth) raja f, corte m **2** (oblique) barra f (oblicua)

slash² vt **1** ⟨person/face⟩ acuchillar, tajear (AmL); ⟨tires/coat⟩ rajar; **he** ∼**ed his wrists** se cortó las venas **2** (reduce) ⟨prices/taxes⟩ rebajar drásticamente

slat /slæt/ n (of wood) listón m, tablilla f; (of other material) tira f

slate¹ /sleɪt/ n pizarra f

slate² vt **1** ⟨roof⟩ empizarrar **2** (criticize) ⟨book/film/writer⟩ poner* por los suelos

slaughter¹ /'slɔ:tər ‖'slɔ:tə(r)/ n (of animals) matanza f; (massacre) matanza f, carnicería f

slaughter² vt ⟨animal⟩ matar, carnear (CS); ⟨people⟩ matar salvajemente

slaughterhouse /'slɔ:tərhaʊs ‖'slɔ:təhaʊs/ n matadero m

Slav /slɑ:v/ n eslavo, -va m,f

slave¹ /sleɪv/ n esclavo, -va m,f

slave² vi (colloq): **I've been slaving away all day** he estado trabajando como un negro todo el día (fam)

slave: ∼ **driver** n (colloq) negrero, -ra m,f (fam); ∼ **labor**, (BrE) ∼ **labour** n el trabajo de los esclavos

slaver /'slævər ‖'slævə(r)/ vi babear

slavery /'sleɪvəri/ n esclavitud f

slaw /slɔ:/ n (AmE) ensalada de repollo, zanahoria y cebolla con mayonesa

slay /sleɪ/ vt (past **slew**; past p **slain**) (liter or journ) dar* muerte a

sleazy /'sli:zi/ adj **-zier, -ziest** ⟨district/bar⟩ sórdido; ⟨character/type⟩ de mala pinta

sled¹ /sled/ n (AmE) trineo m

sled² vi **-dd-** (AmE) ir* en trineo

sledge /sledʒ/ n/vi ▶ SLED¹,²

sledgehammer /'sledʒhæmər ‖'sledʒhæmə(r)/ n mazo m, almádena f

sleek /sli:k/ adj **-er, -est** (a) (glossy) ⟨hair/fur⟩ lacio y brillante (b) (well-groomed) acicalado

sleep¹ /sli:p/ n **1** sueño m; **to go to** ∼ dormirse*; **my foot has gone to** ∼ se me ha dormido el pie; **the cat had to be put to** ∼ (euph) hubo que sacrificar al gato (euf); **to talk in one's** ∼ hablar dormido **2** (in eyes) lagañas fpl, legañas fpl

sleep² (past & past p **slept**) vi dormir*
■ ∼ vt: **the hotel** ∼**s 200 guests** el hotel tiene 200 camas
■ **sleep around** [v + adv] (colloq & pej) acostarse* con cualquiera
■ **sleep in** [v + adv] (a) (sleep late) dormir* hasta tarde (b) ⟨servant/nurse⟩ vivir en (la) casa (or hospital etc)
■ **sleep on** [v + prep + o] ⟨decision/problem⟩ consultar con la almohada
■ **sleep through** [v + prep + o]: **he slept through the alarm clock** no oyó el despertador y siguió durmiendo; **she slept through the whole film** durmió durante toda la película
■ **sleep together** [v + adv] (euph) tener* relaciones (sexuales)
■ **sleep with** [v + prep + o] (euph) acostarse* con (euf)

sleeper /'sli:pər ‖'sli:pə(r)/ n **1** (person): **to be a heavy/light** ∼ tener* el sueño pesado/ligero **2** (Rail) (a) (berth) litera f (b) (train) tren m con coches camas or (CS) coches dormitorio **3** (on track) (Rail) durmiente m or (Esp) traviesa f

sleeping /'sli:pɪŋ/: ∼ **bag** n saco m de dormir; ∼ **car** n (Rail) coche m cama, coche m dormitorio (CS); ∼ **partner** n (BrE) socio, -cia m,f capitalista; ∼ **pill**, ∼ **tablet** (BrE) n somnífero m

sleepless /'sli:pləs ‖'sli:plɪs/ adj: **to have a** ∼ **night** pasar la noche en blanco

sleepwalk /'sli:pwɔːk/ vi caminar dormido

sleepy /'sli:pi/ adj **-pier, -piest** ⟨expression⟩ adormilado, somnoliento; **to be/feel** ∼ tener* sueño

sleet /sli:t/ n aguanieve f

sleeve /sli:v/ n (a) (of garment) manga f; **to have sth up one's** ∼ (colloq) tener* algo planeado (b) (of record) (BrE) funda f, carátula f

sleeveless /'sli:vləs ‖'sli:vlɪs/ adj sin mangas

sleigh /sleɪ/ n trineo m

sleight of hand /slaɪt/ n prestidigitación f

slender /'slendər ‖'slendə(r)/ adj **-derer, -derest** (a) ⟨person/figure⟩ delgado, esbelto; ⟨waist/neck⟩ fino, delgado (b) ⟨means⟩ escaso; ⟨majority⟩ estrecho

slept /slept/ past & past p of SLEEP²

sleuth /slu:θ/ n sabueso mf

slew /slu:/ past of SLAY

slice¹ /slaɪs/ n (piece — of bread, cheese) rebanada f; (— of cake) trozo m; (— of lemon, cucumber) rodaja f; (— of meat) tajada f; (— of ham) loncha f, lonja f; (— of melon) raja f

slice² vt ⟨bread⟩ cortar (en rebanadas); ⟨meat⟩ cortar (en tajadas); ⟨cake⟩ cortar (en trozos); ⟨lemon/cucumber⟩ cortar (en rodajas); ⟨ham⟩ cortar (en lonchas)

slick¹ /slɪk/ adj **-er, -est** **1** (a) ⟨book/program⟩ ingenioso pero insustancial (b) ⟨person⟩ (glib) de mucha labia; (clever) hábil; ⟨reply⟩ fácil (c) ⟨performance/production⟩ muy logrado or pulido **2** (slippery) (AmE) ⟨surface⟩ resbaladizo

slick² n (oil ∼) marea f negra

slide¹ /slaɪd/ (past & past p **slid** /slɪd/) vi deslizarse*

■ ~ *vt* (+ *adv compl*): **she slid the book across the table to him** le pasó el libro deslizándolo por la mesa; **to ~ the bolt back** correr el cerrojo

slide² *n* **1** (in playground) tobogán *m* **2** (action — accidental) resbalón *m*, resbalada *f*; (— deliberate) deslizamiento *m* **3** **(a)** (Phot) diapositiva *f*; (*before n*) ~ **projector** proyector *m* de diapositivas **(b)** (for microscope — glass plate) portaobjetos *m*; (— specimen) muestra *f* **4** (for hair) (BrE) ▶ BARRETTE

slide rule *n* regla *f* de cálculo

sliding /'slaɪdɪŋ/: ~ **door** puerta *f* corrediza; ~ **scale** *n* escala *f* móvil

slight¹ /slaɪt/ *adj* **-er, -est** **1** **(a)** ⟨*improvement/accent*⟩ ligero, leve; **she has a ~ temperature** tiene un poco de fiebre; **I haven't the ~est idea** no tengo (ni) la menor idea; **he's not the ~est bit interested** no le interesa en lo más mínimo **(b)** (minimal) ⟨*chance/hope*⟩ escaso **2** (slim) delgado, menudo

slight² *vt* (frml) desairar

slight³ *n* (frml) desaire *m*

slightly /'slaɪtli/ *adv* ligeramente

slim¹ /slɪm/ *adj* **-mm-** ⟨*person/figure*⟩ esbelto, delgado; ⟨*waist*⟩ fino; ⟨*chance*⟩ escaso; ⟨*majority*⟩ estrecho

slim² *vi* **-mm-** **(a)** (become slimmer) adelgazar*, bajar de peso **(b)** (BrE) (diet) hacer* régimen

slime /slaɪm/ *n* (thin mud) limo *m*, cieno *m*; (of snail, slug etc) baba *f*

slimmer /'slɪmər ‖'slɪmə(r)/ *n* (BrE) *persona que está a régimen*

slimy /'slaɪmi/ *adj* **-mier, -miest** **(a)** ⟨*substance/surface*⟩ viscoso **(b)** ⟨*person*⟩ excesivamente obsequioso, falso

sling¹ /slɪŋ/ *n* **(a)** (Med) cabestrillo *m* **(b)** (for carrying a baby) canguro *m* **(c)** (for lifting) eslinga *f*

sling² *vt* (*past & past p* **slung**) (colloq) tirar, lanzar*, aventar* (Col, Méx, Per)

slink /slɪŋk/ *vi* (*past & past p* **slunk**) (+ *adv compl*): **to ~ off** *o* **away** escabullirse*

slip¹ /slɪp/ *n* **1** (slide) resbalón *m*, resbalada *f* (AmL); **to give sb the ~** (colloq) lograr zafarse de algn **2** (mistake) error *m*; **a ~ of the tongue/pen** un lapsus (linguae/cálami) **3** **a ~ of paper** un papelito, un papel **4** (undergarment) (full-length) combinación *f*; (half-length) enagua *f*, fondo *m* (Méx)

slip² **-pp-** *vi* **1** **(a)** (slide, shift position) ⟨*person*⟩ resbalar(se); ⟨*clutch*⟩ patinar; **it just ~ped out of my hands** se me resbaló de las manos **(b)** ⟨*standards/service*⟩ decaer*
2 **(a)** (move unobtrusively) (+ *adv compl*): **he ~ped out the back door** se deslizó por la puerta trasera; **we managed to ~ past the guards** logramos pasar sin que nos vieran las guardias **(b)** (escape, be lost): **to let ~ an opportunity** dejar escapar una oportunidad; **to ~ through one's fingers** escapársele a algn de las manos; **I didn't mean to say that: it just ~ped out** no quería decirlo, pero se me escapó

■ ~ *vt* **1** **(a)** (put unobtrusively) (+ *adv compl*) poner*, meter, deslizar*; **she ~ped a coin into his hand** le pasó disimuladamente una moneda **(b)** (pass) **to ~ sth TO sb** pasarle algo A algn con disimulo
2 **to ~ sb's mind**: **it ~ped my mind** me olvidé, se me olvidó

■ **slip away** ⟨*person/opportunity*⟩ escabullirse*; ⟨*hours/time*⟩ pasar

■ **slip in** [*v + o + adv, v + adv + o*] ⟨*comment/reference*⟩ incluir*

■ **slip off** **1** [*v + o + adv, v + adv + o*] ⟨*clothes/shoes*⟩ quitarse
2 [*v + adv*] escabullirse*

■ **slip on** [*v + o + adv, v + adv + o*] ⟨*clothes/shoes*⟩ ponerse*

■ **slip up** [*v + adv*] equivocarse*

slipped disc /slɪpt/ *n* hernia *f* de disco

slipper /'slɪpər ‖'slɪpə(r)/ *n* zapatilla *f*, pantufla *f* (esp AmL)

slippery /'slɪpəri/ *adj* **(a)** ⟨*surface/soap*⟩ resbaladizo, resbaloso (AmL) **(b)** ⟨*person*⟩ (elusive) escurridizo; (untrustworthy) que no es de fiar

slip: ~**-road** *n* (BrE) vía *f* de acceso; ~**-up** *n* error *m*

slit¹ /slɪt/ *n* (opening) rendija *f*; (cut) raja *f*

slit² *vt* (*pres p* **slitting**; *past & past p* **slit**) cortar, rajar (Méx); **to ~ sb's throat** degollar a algn

slither /'slɪðər ‖'slɪðə(r)/ *vi* ⟨*snake*⟩ deslizarse*

sliver /'slɪvər ‖'slɪvə(r)/ *n* **(a)** (of glass, wood) astilla *f* **(b)** (thin slice) tajada *f* (*or* rodaja *f etc*) fina; *see also* SLICE¹

slob /slɑːb ‖slɒb/ *n* (colloq) vago, -ga *m,f* (fam)

slobber /'slɑːbər ‖'slɒbə(r)/ *vi* babear

slog /slɑːg ‖slɒg/ *n* (colloq) (*no pl*): **we've got a long ~ ahead of us** tenemos un largo y arduo camino por delante

■ **slog away**: **-gg-** [*v + adv*] (BrE colloq) sudar tinta (fam), trabajar duro (esp AmL)

slogan /'sləʊgən/ *n* (Busn) slogan *m*, eslogan *m*; (Pol) lema *m*, consigna *f*

slop /slɑːp ‖slɒp/ *vi* **-pp-** (colloq) (spill) derramarse, volcarse*

slope¹ /sləʊp/ *n* **(a)** (sloping ground) cuesta *f*, pendiente *f*, barranca *f* (RPl) **(b)** (of mountain) ladera *f*, falda *f* **(c)** (for skiing) pista *f* de esquí, cancha *f* de esquí (CS)

slope² *vi*: **to ~ down** ⟨*hill/road*⟩ tener* un declive; **her handwriting ~s backward/forward** tiene la letra inclinada hacia atrás/adelante

sloping /'sləʊpɪŋ/ *adj* ⟨*field/floor*⟩ en declive; ⟨*roof/handwriting*⟩ inclinado

sloppy /'slɑːpi ‖'slɒpi/ *adj* **-pier, -piest** **1** (careless) ⟨*manners/work*⟩ descuidado; ⟨*presentation*⟩ descuidado, desprolijo (CS) **2** ⟨*kiss*⟩ baboso

slosh /slɑːʃ ‖slɒʃ/ *vt* (splash) echar
■ ~ *vi* **to ~ around** *o* **about** ⟨*person*⟩ chapotear; ⟨*liquid*⟩ agitarse haciendo ruido

slot¹ /slɑːt ‖slɒt/ *n* **1** (opening, groove) ranura *f* **2** (Rad, TV) espacio *m*

slot² **-tt-***vt* (insert) **to ~ sth INTO sth** encajar algo EN algo
■ **slot in** **1** [*v + adv*] ⟨*shelf/part*⟩ encajar **2** [*v + o + adv, v + adv + o*] ⟨*component*⟩ hacer* encajar

sloth /sləʊθ/ *n* (Zool) perezoso *m*

slot machine *n* **(a)** (vending machine) distribuidor *m* automático, máquina *f* expendedora **(b)** (for gambling) máquina *f* tragamonedas *or* (Esp tb) tragaperras

slouch /slaʊtʃ/ *vi* **(a)** (droop shoulders) encorvarse; **don't ∼!** ¡ponte derecho! **(b)** (walk) (+ *adv compl*): **he ∼ed out of the room** salió de la habitación arrastrando los pies

Slovak /'sləʊvæk/ *n* **(a)** (person) eslovaco, -ca *m,f* **(b)** (language) eslovaco *m*

Slovakia /sləʊ'vɑːkiːə ‖sləʊ'vækiə/ *n* Eslovaquia *f*

Slovene /'sləʊviːn/ *n* **(a)** (person) esloveno, -na *m,f* **(b)** (language) esloveno *m*

Slovenia /sləʊ'viːnjə/ *n* Eslovenia *f*

slovenly /'slʌvənli/ *adj* **-ier, -liest** ⟨*work*⟩ descuidado; ⟨*person*⟩ desaliñado

slow¹ /sləʊ/ *adj* **-er, -est** **1** ⟨*speed/rate/ reactions*⟩ lento; **to be ∼ to + INF** tardar EN + INF **2 (a)** (not lively) ⟨*novel/plot*⟩ lento **(b)** (stupid) (euph) poco despierto (euf) **3** ⟨*of clock, watch*⟩ ⟨*pred*⟩: **my watch is five minutes ∼** mi reloj está cinco minutos atrasado

slow² *vi*: **the train ∼ed to a stop** el tren fue disminuyendo la velocidad hasta detenerse
■ **∼** *vt*: **bad weather ∼ed their progress** el mal tiempo los retrasó
■ **slow down** **1** [v + adv] **(a)** (go more slowly) ⟨*runner*⟩ aflojar el paso; ⟨*vehicle/driver*⟩ reducir* la velocidad; ⟨*speaker*⟩ hablar más despacio **(b)** (be less active) (colloq) tomarse las cosas con más calma **2** [v + o + adv, v + adv + o] **(a)** ⟨*process*⟩ hacer* más lento **(b)** ⟨*vehicle/ engine*⟩ reducir* la velocidad de
■ **slow up** ▶ SLOW DOWN

slow³ *adv* lentamente, despacio

slowly /'sləʊli/ *adv* lentamente, despacio

slow motion *n* cámara *f* lenta; **in ∼ ∼** en *or* (Esp) a cámara lenta

sludge /slʌdʒ/ *n* lodo *m*, fango *m*

slug /slʌg/ *n* (Zool) babosa *f*

sluggish /'slʌgɪʃ/ *adj* **(a)** (slow-moving) lento; ⟨*stream/river*⟩ de aguas mansas **(b)** ⟨*growth*⟩ lento

sluice /sluːs/ *n* **(a)** (channel) canal *m*, conducto *m* (de esclusa) **(b)** (sluicegate) compuerta *f*

sluicegate /'sluːsgeɪt/ *n* compuerta *f* (de esclusa)

slum /slʌm/ *n* **(a)** (poor urban area) ⟨*often pl*⟩ barrio *m* bajo, barriada *f* (AmL exc CS), barrio *m* de conventillos (CS) **(b)** (filthy place) (colloq & pej) pocilga *f*

slumber¹ /'slʌmbər ‖'slʌmbə(r)/ *n* (liter) ⟨*often pl*⟩ sueño *m*

slumber² *vi* (liter) dormir*

slump¹ /slʌmp/ *n* **(a)** (economic depression) depresión *f* **(b)** (in prices, sales) caída *f or* baja *f* repentina; (in attendance, interest) disminución *f*

slump² *vi* **1** (collapse) (+ *adv compl*) desplomarse; **they found her ∼ed over her desk** la encontraron desplomada sobre su escritorio **2** ⟨*prices/output/sales*⟩ caer* *or* bajar repentinamente

slung /slʌŋ/ *past & past p of* SLING²

slunk /slʌŋk/ *past & past p of* SLINK

slur¹ /slɜːr ‖slɜː(r)/ *n* **1** (insult): **a racist ∼** un comentario racista; **to cast a ∼ on sb** injuriar a algn **2** (Mus) ligado *m*

slur² *vt* **-rr-** **1** (pronounce unclearly): **to ∼ one's words** arrastrar las palabras **2** (Mus) ligar*

slurp /slɜːrp ‖slɜːp/ *vt* sorber (*haciendo ruido*)

slurred /slɜːrd ‖slɜːd/ *adj*: **her speech was ∼** arrastraba las palabras

slush /slʌʃ/ *n* **(a)** (snow) nieve *f* fangosa *or* medio derretida **(b)** (sentimental trash) sensiblería *f*

sly /slaɪ/ *adj* **-er, -est** ⟨*person*⟩ astuto; ⟨*look/ grin*⟩ malicioso; **on the ∼** a hurtadillas

smack¹ /smæk/ *n* manotazo *m*, palmada *f* (AmL)

smack² *vt* **(a)** (slap) ⟨*child*⟩ pegarle* a (con la mano) **(b)** **to ∼ one's lips** relamerse
■ **∼** *vi* **to ∼ OF sth** oler* A algo

smack³ *adv* (colloq): **∼ in the middle** justo en el medio; **he went ∼ into a tree** se dio contra el árbol

small¹ /smɔːl/ *adj* **-er, -est** pequeño, chico (esp AmL); ⟨*sum/price*⟩ módico, reducido; ⟨*mistake/problem*⟩ pequeño, de poca importancia; **to feel ∼** sentirse* insignificante

small² *n* **the ∼ of the back** región baja de la espalda, que corresponde al segmento dorsal de la columna vertebral

small: **∼ ad** *n* (BrE) anuncio *m* (clasificado), aviso *m* (clasificado) (AmL); **∼ change** *n* cambio *m*, (dinero *m*) suelto *m*, sencillo *m* (AmL), feria *f* (Méx fam); **∼ hours** *pl n* **the ∼ hours (of the morning)** la madrugada; **∼-minded** /'smɔːl'maɪndəd ‖,smɔːl'maɪndɪd/ *adj* cerrado, de miras estrechas; **∼pox** /'smɔːlpɒks ‖'smɔːlpɒks/ *n* viruela *f*; **∼ print** *n* (BrE) **the ∼ print** la letra pequeña *or* menuda, la letra chica (esp AmL); **∼ talk** *n* charla *f* sobre temas triviales; **∼-time** /'smɔːl'taɪm/ *adj* de poca monta; **∼-town** /'smɔːl'taʊn/ *adj* pueblerino

smart¹ /smɑːrt ‖smɑːt/ *adj* **-er, -est** **1** (esp BrE) (neat, stylish) ⟨*appearance/dress/hotel/ neighborhood*⟩ elegante **2** (clever, shrewd) ⟨*child*⟩ listo; ⟨*answer*⟩ inteligente **3 (a)** (brisk, prompt) ⟨*pace*⟩ rápido **(b)** (forceful) ⟨*blow/tap*⟩ seco, fuerte

smart² *vi* ⟨*eyes/wound*⟩ escocer*

smarten up /'smɑːrtən ‖'smɑːtən/ **(a)** [v + o + adv, v + adv + o] ⟨*house/town*⟩ arreglar **(b)** [v + adv] ⟨*person*⟩ mejorar su (or mi *etc*) aspecto

smash¹ /smæʃ/ *n* **1 (a)** (sound) estrépito *m*, estruendo *m* **(b)** (collision) (BrE) choque *m* **2 (a)** (blow) golpe *m* **(b)** (Sport) smash *m*, remate *m*, remache *m* **3** (success) (colloq) exitazo *m* (fam)

smash² *vt* **1** (break) ⟨*furniture*⟩ romper*; ⟨*car*⟩ destrozar*; ⟨*glass*⟩ romper*; (into small pieces) hacer* añicos **2** (destroy) ⟨*rebellion*⟩ aplastar; ⟨*drug racket/spy ring*⟩ acabar con **3** (Sport) rematar, remachar
■ **∼** *vi* (shatter) hacerse* pedazos
■ **smash up** [v + o + adv] (colloq) destrozar*

smash: **∼ hit** *n* (colloq) exitazo *m* (fam); **∼up** *n* (colloq) choque *m* violento

smattering /'smætərɪŋ/ n (no pl) nociones fpl

smear¹ /smɪr ‖smɪə(r)/ n **1** (stain) mancha f **2** (slander, slur) calumnia f; (before n) ~ **campaign** campaña f difamatoria **3** (Med) ~ (**test**) citología f, frotis m cervical, Papanicolau m (AmL)

smear² vt **1** to ~ sth ON(TO)/OVER sth ⟨paint/ grease⟩ embadurnar algo de algo; ⟨butter⟩ untar algo con algo **2** (slander, libel) difamar
■ ~ vi «ink/lipstick» correrse

smell¹ /smel/ n **(a)** (odor) olor m **(b)** (sense of smell) olfato m

smell² (past & past p **smelled** or (BrE also) **smelt**) vt **(a)** (sense) oler*; to ~ **gas/ burning** olía a gas/quemado; to ~ **danger** olfatear el peligro **(b)** (sniff at) «person» oler*; «animal» olfatear
■ ~ vi oler*; to ~ **OF** sth oler* A algo

smelling salts /'smelɪŋ/ pl n sales fpl (aromáticas)

smelly /'smeli/ adj **-lier, -liest** que huele mal

smelt¹ /smelt/ (BrE) past & past p of SMELL²

smelt² vt fundir

smile¹ /smaɪl/ n sonrisa f

smile² vi sonreír*; to ~ **AT** sb sonreírle* A algn

smirk¹ /smɜːrk ‖smɜːk/ n sonrisita f (de suficiencia, de complicidad, etc)

smirk² vi sonreírse* (con suficiencia, complicidad etc)

smith /smɪθ/ n herrero, -ra m,f

smithereens /ˌsmɪðə'riːnz/ pl n: to smash sth to ~ hacer* algo pedazos or añicos

smock /smɑːk ‖smɒk/ n **(a)** (of fisherman, artist) blusón m, bata f **(b)** (dress) vestido m amplio

smog /smɑːg ‖smɒg/ n smog m

smoke¹ /sməʊk/ n humo m; to go up in ~ «books/papers» quemarse; «hopes» esfumarse; «ambitions/plans» quedar en agua de borrajas

smoke² vi **1** «person» fumar **2** (give off smoke) echar humo
■ ~ vt **1** ⟨cigarettes/tobacco⟩ fumar; he ~s a pipe fuma en pipa **2** (cure) ⟨fish/cheese⟩ ahumar*

smoke-bomb /'sməʊkbɑːm ‖'sməʊkbɒm/ n bomba f de humo

smoked /sməʊkt/ adj ahumado

smoke detector n detector m de humo

smokeless /'sməʊkləs ‖'sməʊklɪs/ adj ⟨fuel⟩ que arde sin humo; ~ **zone** (in UK) zona donde está prohibido usar combustibles que produzcan humo

smoker /'sməʊkər ‖'sməʊkə(r)/ n fumador, -dora m,f; he's a heavy ~fuma mucho

smoke: ~screen n cortina f de humo; ~ **signal** n señal f de humo

smoking /'sməʊkɪŋ/ n 🚫 no smoking prohibido fumar; to give up ~ dejar de fumar

smoking: ~ car n (AmE) vagón m or (Chi, Méx) carro m de fumadores; ~ **compartment** n compartimento m de fumadores

smoky /'sməʊki/ adj **-kier, -kiest** ⟨fire/ chimney⟩ que echa humo; ⟨room⟩ lleno de humo; ⟨atmosphere⟩ cargado de humo

smolder, (BrE) **smoulder** /'sməʊldər ‖'sməʊldə(r)/ vi ⟨fire⟩ arder (sin llama); «eyes» arder

smooth¹ /smuːð/ adj **-er, -est** **1** **(a)** ⟨texture/stone⟩ liso, suave; ⟨skin⟩ suave, terso; ⟨sea⟩ tranquilo **(b)** (of consistency) ⟨sauce⟩ sin grumos **(c)** (of taste) ⟨wine⟩ suave **2** **(a)** (of movement) ⟨take-off⟩ suave; ⟨flight⟩ cómodo **(b)** (trouble-free) ⟨journey⟩ sin complicaciones **3** **(a)** (easy, polished) ⟨performance⟩ fluido **(b)** (glib, suave) (pej) poco sincero, falso; he's a ~ **talker** tiene mucha labia

smooth² vt **(a)** ⟨dress/sheets/hair⟩ alisar, arreglar **(b)** (polish) pulir
■ **smooth out** [v + o + adv, v + adv + o] **(a)** ⟨sheets/creases⟩ alisar **(b)** ⟨difficulties/problems⟩ allanar
■ **smooth over** [v + o + adv, v + adv + o] ⟨differences⟩ dejar de lado

smoothly /'smuːðli/ adv **1** **(a)** (of movement) ⟨take off/drive⟩ suavemente **(b)** (without problems) sin problemas **2** (glibly, suavely) (pej) ⟨talk⟩ con mucha labia

smother /'smʌðər ‖'smʌðə(r)/ vt **(a)** (stifle) ⟨person⟩ asfixiar, ahogar*; ⟨flames⟩ sofocar* **(b)** (suppress) ⟨yawn/giggle⟩ reprimir **(c)** (cover profusely): she ~ed him with kisses lo cubrió de besos

smoulder vi (BrE) ▶ SMOLDER

smudge¹ /smʌdʒ/ n mancha f

smudge² vt correr; (deliberately) difuminar

smug /smʌg/ adj **-gg-** ⟨expression⟩ de suficiencia, petulante; ⟨person⟩ pagado de sí mismo, petulante

smuggle /'smʌgəl/ vt ⟨tobacco/drugs⟩ contrabandear, pasar de contrabando; I ~d her into my room la hice entrar a mi habitación a escondidas

smuggler /'smʌglər ‖'smʌglə(r)/ n contrabandista mf

smuggling /'smʌglɪŋ/ n contrabando m

snack /snæk/ n tentempié m; to have a ~ comer algo ligero or (esp AmL) liviano, tomar(se) un tentempié

snack bar n bar m, cafetería f

snag¹ /snæg/ n **(a)** (difficulty) inconveniente m, pega f (Esp fam) **(b)** (in fabric, stocking) enganchón m

snag² vt **-gg-** enganchar

snail /sneɪl/ n caracol m; at a ~'s pace a paso de tortuga

snake /sneɪk/ n culebra f, serpiente f; (poisonous) víbora f

snake: ~bite n mordedura f de serpiente; ~ **charmer** /'tʃɑːrmər ‖'tʃɑːmə(r)/ n encantador, -dora m,f de serpientes

snap¹ /snæp/ n **1** (sound) chasquido m **2** ~ (**fastener**) (AmE) (on clothes) broche m or botón m de presión (AmL), (cierre m) automático m (Esp) **3** (photo) (colloq) foto f, instantánea f **4** (Meteo): a cold ~ una ola de frío

snap² **-pp-** vt **1** **(a)** (break) partir **(b)** (cause to make sharp sound): she ~ped the lid/book shut cerró la tapa/el libro de un golpe; ▶ FINGER¹ **2** (utter sharply) decir* bruscamente **3** (photograph) ⟨person/thing⟩ sacarle* una foto a
■ ~ vi **1** (bite) to ~ **AT** sth intentar morder algo **2** **(a)** (break) «twigs/branch» romperse*, quebrarse* (esp AmL); «elastic» romperse* **(b)** (click): to ~ **shut** cerrarse* (con un clic) **3** (speak sharply) hablar con brusquedad   ····⋗

4 (move quickly): to ~ out of it (of depression) animarse; (of lethargy, inertia) espabilarse
∎ **snap up** [v + o + adv, v + adv + o] ⟨offer⟩ no dejar escapar

snap³ adj ⟨decision⟩ precipitado, repentino

snappy /'snæpi/ adj **-pier, -piest (a)** ⟨person⟩ irascible; ⟨retort⟩ brusco **(b)** ⟨pace⟩ (colloq) ágil

snapshot /'snæpʃɑ:t ‖'snæpʃʊt/ n foto f, instantánea f

snare¹ /sner ‖sneə(r)/ n trampa f

snare² vt atrapar

snarl¹ /snɑ:rl ‖snɑ:l/ n gruñido m

snarl² vi/t gruñir*
∎ **snarl up** [v + adv + o] (usu pass) ⟨ball of wool⟩ enmarañar, enredar; ⟨traffic⟩ atascar*

snatch¹ /snætʃ/ vt **1 (a)** (grab) to ~ sth FROM sb arrebatarle algo A algn; she ~ed the letter out of my hand me arrancó la carta de las manos **(b)** (steal) (colloq & journ) robar (arrebatando) **(c)** (kidnap) (journ) secuestrar, raptar **2** (take hurriedly) ⟨opportunity⟩ no dejar pasar

snatch² n **1** (robbery) (BrE journ) robo m **2 (a)** (fragment) fragmento m **(b)** (brief spell) rato m; to sleep in ~es dormir* (de) a ratos

sneak /sni:k/ (past & past p **sneaked** or (AmE also) **snuck**) vt **(a)** (smuggle) (+ adv compl): he ~ed the files out of the office sacó los archivos de la oficina a escondidas; she tried to ~ him in without paying trató de colarlo sin pagar **(b)** (take furtively): to ~ a look at sth/sb mirar algo/a algn con disimulo
∎ ~ vi (+ adv compl): to ~ in entrar a hurtadillas; to ~ away escabullirse*
∎ **sneak up** [v + adv] to ~ up (ON sb) acercarse* sigilosamente (A algn)

sneakers /'sni:kərz ‖'sni:kəz/ pl n zapatillas fpl (de deporte), tenis mpl, playeras fpl (Esp)

sneak: ~ **preview** n (Cin, TV) preestreno m; ~ **thief** n ratero, -ra m,f

sneaky /'sni:ki/ adj **-kier, -kiest** (colloq) ⟨person⟩ artero, taimado; ⟨behavior⟩ solapado

sneer¹ /snɪr ‖snɪə(r)/ vi adoptar un aire despectivo; (with facial expression) hacer* una mueca de desprecio

sneer² n expresión f desdeñosa

sneeze¹ /sni:z/ vi estornudar

sneeze² n estornudo m

snide /snaɪd/ adj insidioso

sniff /snɪf/ vt **(a)** (smell) «person» oler*; «animal» olfatear **(b)** ⟨glue⟩ inhalar, esnifar
∎ ~ vi «animal» husmear, olfatear; «person» sorberse la nariz

sniffer dog /'snɪfər ‖'snɪfə(r)/ n (BrE) perro m rastreador

sniffle /'snɪfəl/ vi (due to cold) sorberse la nariz; (when crying) gimotear

snigger¹ /'snɪgər ‖'snɪgə(r)/ n risilla f, risita f

snigger² vi reírse* (por lo bajo)

snip¹ /snɪp/ n (act) tijeretazo m; (sound) tijereteo m

snip² vt **-pp-** cortar (con tijera)

sniper /'snaɪpər ‖'snaɪpə(r)/ n francotirador, -dora m,f

snippet /'snɪpət ‖'snɪpɪt/ n (of conversation) trozo m; ~s of information (algunos) datos aislados

snivel /'snɪvəl/ vi, (BrE) **-ll-** lloriquear

snob /snɑ:b ‖snɒb/ n (e)snob mf

snobbery /'snɑ:bəri ‖'snɒbəri/ n (e)snobismo m

snobbish /'snɑ:bɪʃ ‖'snɒbɪʃ/ adj (e)snob

snooker /'snʊkər ‖'snu:kə(r)/ n snooker m (modalidad de billar que se juega con 15 bolas rojas y 6 de otro color)

snoop /snu:p/ vi (colloq) husmear, fisgonear

snooper /'snu:pər ‖'snu:pə(r)/ n (colloq) fisgón, -gona m,f

snooze¹ /snu:z/ vi (colloq) dormitar

snooze² n (colloq) sueñecito m (fam), sueñito m (esp AmL fam); to have a ~ echar una cabezada (fam)

snore¹ /snɔ:r ‖snɔ:(r)/ vi roncar*

snore² n ronquido m

snoring /'snɔ:rɪŋ/ n ronquidos mpl

snorkel /'snɔ:rkəl ‖'snɔ:kəl/ n esnórkel m

snort¹ /snɔ:rt ‖snɔ:t/ vi bufar, resoplar
∎ ~ vt (utter) bramar, gruñir*

snort² n bufido m, resoplido m

snout /snaʊt/ n hocico m, morro m

snow¹ /snəʊ/ n **(a)** nieve f **(b)** (snowfall) nevada f

snow² v impers nevar*
∎ **snow in** [v + o + adv]: to be ~ed in estar* aislado por la nieve
∎ **snow under** [v + o + adv]: I'm ~ed under with work estoy agobiada or desbordada de trabajo

snowball¹ /'snəʊbɔ:l/ n (Meteo) bola f de nieve

snowball² vi «problems» agravarse

snow: ~**board** n snowboard m; ~**boarding** n snowboard m; ~**bound** adj bloqueado por la nieve; ~**drift** n: nieve acumulada durante una ventisca; ~**drop** n campanilla f de invierno; ~**flake** n nevada f; ~**flake** n copo m de nieve; ~**man** /'snəʊmæn/ n (pl **-men** /-men/) muñeco m de nieve; ~**plow**, (BrE) ~**plough** n quitanieves m; ~**shoe** n raqueta f; ~**storm** n tormenta f de nieve

snowy /'snəʊi/ adj **snowier, snowiest** nevoso

snub¹ /snʌb/ vt **-bb- (a)** ⟨person⟩ desairar; (ignore) ignorar; (treat coldly) tratar fríamente (CS) **(b)** (reject) ⟨offer⟩ desdeñar, rechazar*

snub² n desaire m

snub³ adj ⟨nose⟩ respingón, respingado (AmL)

snub-nosed /'snʌb'nəʊzd/ adj de nariz respingona or (AmL tb) respingada

snuck /snʌk/ (AmE colloq) past & past p of SNEAK

snuff /snʌf/ n rapé m
∎ **snuff out** [v + o + adv, v + adv + o] ⟨candle⟩ apagar*

snuffbox /'snʌfbɑ:ks ‖'snʌfbɒks/ n caja f de rapé

snug /snʌg/ adj **(a)** (cosy) cómodo y acogedor **(b)** (close-fitting) ceñido, ajustado

snuggle /'snʌgəl/ vi acurrucarse*; he ~d up against her se le arrimó

so¹ /səʊ/ adv **1 (a)** (very) tan; she's ~ tall es tan alta; he did it ~ quickly lo hizo tan rápido; thank you ~ much muchísimas gracias **(b)** so much/many (as adj) tanto, -ta/tantos, -tas; ~

much space/food tanto espacio/tanta comida; ∼ **many things** tantas cosas **(c) so much** (*as pronoun*) tanto; **he eats** ∼ **much** come tanto **2** **or so** más o menos **3** (with clauses of result or purpose) ∼ ... **(that)** tan ... que; **he was** ∼ **rude (that) she slapped him** fue tan grosero, que le dio una bofetada **4 (a)** (thus, in this way): **the street was** ∼ **named because** ... se le puso ese nombre a la calle porque ...; **hold the bat like** ∼ agarra el bate así **(b)** (as stated) así; **that is** ∼ (fml) así es; **if** ∼, **they're lying** si es así or de ser así, están mintiendo **(c) and so on (and so forth)** etcétera (etcétera) **5** (*replacing clause, phrase, word*): **I expect** ∼ me imagino que sí; **I got a bit dirty — ∼ I see** me ensucié un poco — sí, ya veo; **I told you — ∼** ¿no te lo dije? **6** (*with v aux*) **(a)** (also, equally): **Peter agrees and** ∼ **does Bill** Peter está de acuerdo y Bill también **(b)** (indeed): **you promised — ∼ I did!** lo prometiste — ¡es verdad! or ¡tienes razón! **7 (a)** (indicating pause or transition) bueno; ∼ **here we are again** bueno, aquí estamos otra vez **(b)** (querying, eliciting information): ∼ **now what do we do?** ¿y ahora qué hacemos? **(c)** (summarizing, concluding) así que; ∼ **now you know** así que ya sabes **(d)** (expressing surprised reaction) así que, conque; ∼ **that's what he's after!** ¡así que or conque eso es lo que quiere! **(e)** (challenging): ∼ **what?** ¿y qué?

so² *conj* **1** (in clauses of purpose or result) **(a)** so **(that)** (expressing purpose) para que (+ *subj*); (expressing result) así que or de manera que (+ *indic*); **she said it slowly,** ∼ **(that) we'd all understand** lo dijo despacio, para que todos entendiéramos; **she said it slowly,** ∼ **(that) we all understood** lo dijo despacio, así que or de manera que todos entendimos **(b) so as to + INF** para + INF **2** (therefore, consequently) así que, de manera que

so³ *n* (Mus) sol *m*

soak /səʊk/ *vt* **(a)** ⟨*lentils/clothes*⟩ (immerse) poner* en or a remojo; (leave immersed) dejar en or a remojo **(b)** (drench) empapar; **to be ∼ed (to the skin)** estar* empapado, estar* calado hasta los huesos

■ ∼ *vi* **(a)** (lie in liquid): **to leave sth to** ∼ dejar algo en or a remojo **(b)** (penetrate) (+ *adv compl*): **to** ∼ **into/through sth** calar algo

■ **soak up** [*v* + *o* + *adv, v* + *adv* + *o*] ⟨*liquid/information*⟩ absorber; ⟨*sun*⟩ empaparse de

soaking /ˈsəʊkɪŋ/ *adj* empapado; (*as adv*) **it's** ∼ **wet** está empapado

so-and-so /ˈsəʊənsəʊ/ *n* (colloq) (unspecified person) (*no art*) fulano, -na *m,f*

soap /səʊp/ *n* **1** jabón *m*; (*before n*) ∼ **dish** jabonera *f* **2** ▶ SOAP OPERA

soap: ∼**flakes** *pl n* jabón *m* en escamas; ∼ **opera** *n* (TV) telenovela *f*, culebrón *m*; (Rad) radionovela *f*, comedia *f* (AmL); ∼ **powder** *n* (BrE) jabón *m* en polvo, detergente *m* (en polvo); ∼**suds** *pl n* espuma *f* (de jabón)

soapy /ˈsəʊpi/ *adj* **-pier, -piest (a)** ⟨*water*⟩ jabonoso; ⟨*cloth/hands*⟩ enjabonado **(b)** ⟨*smell/taste*⟩ a jabón

soar /sɔːr ‖sɔː(r)/ *vi* **1 (a)** (fly) ⟨*bird/glider*⟩ planear **(b)** (rise) ⟨*bird/kite*⟩ elevarse; ⟨*prices/costs*⟩ dispararse; ⟨*hopes*⟩ aumentar;

⟨*popularity*⟩ aumentar **(c)** (tower) ⟨*skyscraper/mountain*⟩ alzarse* **2 soaring** *pres p* ⟨*inflation*⟩ galopante, de ritmo vertiginoso; ⟨*popularity*⟩ en alza; **caused by** ∼ **temperatures** causado por una subida vertiginosa de las temperaturas

sob¹ /sɑːb ‖sɒb/ *vi* **-bb-** sollozar*

sob² *n* sollozo *m*

sober /ˈsəʊbər ‖ˈsəʊbə(r)/ *adj* **1** (not drunk) sobrio **2 (a)** (serious) ⟨*expression*⟩ grave; ⟨*young man*⟩ serio; ⟨*occasion*⟩ formal **(b)** (subdued) ⟨*dress/colors*⟩ sobrio

■ **sober up 1** [*v* + *adv*]: **he's** ∼**ed up now** ya está sobrio **2** [*v* + *o* + *adv, v* + *adv* + *o*] despejar

sobriety /səʊˈbraɪəti, sə- ‖sə'braɪəti/ *n* seriedad *f*, sensatez *f*; (before ∼) ∼ **test** (AmE) prueba *f* del alcohol or de la alcoholemia

so-called /ˈsəʊˈkɔːld/ *adj* (usu before n) **(a)** (commonly named) (así) llamado **(b)** (indicating skeptical attitude) ⟨*expert*⟩ supuesto, presunto

soccer /ˈsɑːkər ‖ˈsɒkə(r)/ *n* fútbol *m or* (AmC, Méx) futbol *m*

sociable /ˈsəʊʃəbəl/ *adj* sociable

social /ˈsəʊʃəl/ *adj* social; **he has no** ∼ **graces** no sabe cómo comportarse; ∼ **life** vida *f* social

social democrat *n* socialdemócrata *mf*

socialism /ˈsəʊʃəlɪzəm/ *n* socialismo *m*

socialist¹, Socialist /ˈsəʊʃələst ‖ˈsəʊʃəlɪst/ *adj* socialista

socialist², Socialist *n* socialista *mf*

socialize /ˈsəʊʃəlaɪz/ *vi* alternar; (at party) circular

socially /ˈsəʊʃəli/ *adv* **(a)** (relating to the community) ⟨*divisive/useful*⟩ socialmente; ⟨*indep*⟩ desde el punto de vista social **(b)** (in social situations): **it's not** ∼ **acceptable** está mal visto, no se considera correcto

social: ∼ **science** *n* ciencia *f* social; ∼ **security** *n* (BrE) seguridad *f* social; ∼ **service** *n* **(a)** (welfare work) (AmE) asistencia *f* or trabajo *m* social **(b)** (in UK) servicio *m* social; ∼ **work** *n* asistencia *f* social; ∼ **worker** *n* (Soc Adm) asistente, -ta *m,f* social, trabajador, -dora *m,f* social (Méx), visitador, -dora *m,f* social (Chi)

society /səˈsaɪəti/ *n* (*pl* **-ties**) **1 (a)** (community) sociedad *f*; **in polite** ∼ entre la gente educada **(b)** (fashionable elite) (alta) sociedad *f* **2** (association, club) sociedad *f*

sociologist /ˌsəʊsiˈɑːlədʒəst, -ʃi- ‖ˌsəʊsiˈɒlədʒɪst, -ʃi-/ *n* sociólogo, -ga *m,f*

sociology /ˌsəʊsiˈɑːlədʒi, -ʃi- ‖ˌsəʊsiˈɒlədʒi, -ʃi-/ *n* sociología *f*

sociopath /ˈsəʊsiəpæθ, -ʃi-/ *n* (p)sicópata *mf*

sock /sɑːk ‖sɒk/ *n* calcetín *m*, media *f* (AmL)

socket /ˈsɑːkət ‖ˈsɒkɪt/ *n* **(a)** (Anat) (of eye) cuenca *f*, órbita *f*; (of joint) fosa *f*, hueco *m* **(b)** (Elec) (for plug) enchufe *m*, toma *f* de corriente, tomacorriente *m* (AmL) **(c)** (Tech) encaje *m*

sod /sɑːd ‖sɒd/ *n* **1** (piece of turf) tepe *m*, champa *f* (Andes) **2** (BrE vulg) (obnoxious person) cabrón, -brona *m,f* (vulg)

soda /ˈsəʊdə/ *n* **1 (a)** (soda water) soda *f*, agua *f*; de seltz **(b)** (flavored) (AmE) refresco *m*, fresco *m* (AmL) **(c)** (ice-cream soda) (AmE) ice-cream soda *m* (AmL) (*refresco con helado*) **2** (Chem) soda *f*, sosa *f*

soda: ~ **pop** n (AmE) refresco m; ~ **water** n soda f, agua f de seltz

sodden /'sɑːdn̩ ‖'sɒdn̩/ adj empapado

sodium /'səʊdiəm/ n sodio m

sodium bicarbonate n bicarbonato m sódico or de sodio

sofa /'səʊfə/ n sofá m

soft /sɒːft ‖sɒft/ adj **-er, -est** [1] (a) (not hard) blando; ‹metal› maleable; **to go** ~ ablandarse (b) (smooth) ‹fur/fabric/skin› suave [2] (mild, subdued) ‹light/color/music› suave [3] (lenient) blando, indulgente [4] ‹drugs/pornography› blando [5] (Chem) ‹water› blando

soft: ~**ball** n softball m (especie de béisbol que se juega con pelota blanda); ~ **drink** n refresco m (bebida no alcohólica)

soften /'sɒːfən ‖'sɒfn̩/ vt (a) ‹butter/leather› ablandar; ‹skin› suavizar*; ‹light/color› suavizar*; ‹contours› difuminar (b) (mitigate) ‹effect› atenuar*, mitigar*; **to** ~ **the blow** suavizar* el golpe (c) ‹water› ablandar, descalcificar*

■ ~ vi (a) «butter/leather» ablandarse; «skin» suavizarse* (b) (become gentler) ablandarse; (become more moderate) volverse* menos intransigente

■ **soften up** [v + o + adv, v + adv + o] ablandar

softener /'sɒːfnər ‖'sɒfnə(r)/ n (a) (for water) descalcificador m (b) (for fabric) suavizante m

softly /'sɒːftli ‖'sɒftli/ adv (a) (gently) ‹touch› suavemente (b) (quietly) ‹speak› bajito

soft: ~-**spoken** /sɒːft'spəʊkən ‖,sɒft'spəʊkən/ adj de voz suave; ~ **top** n (AmE) (car) descapotable m, convertible m (AmL); (roof) capota f; ~**ware** /'sɒːftweər ‖'sɒftweə(r)/ n software m

soggy /'sɑːgi ‖'sɒgi/ adj **-gier, -giest** ‹ground/grass› empapado; ‹vegetables› pasado

soh /səʊ/ n (Mus) sol m

soil¹ /sɔɪl/ n (a) (earth) tierra f (b) (filth, dirt) (AmE) suciedad f

soil² vt ensuciar

soiled /sɔɪld/ adj ‹linen› sucio; ‹goods› dañado

sol /səʊl ‖sɒl/ n (Mus) sol m

solace /'sɑːləs ‖'sɒlɪs/ n (liter) consuelo m

solar /'səʊlər ‖'səʊlə(r)/ adj solar

solar system n the ~ el sistema solar

sold /səʊld/ past & past p of SELL

solder /'sɑːdər ‖'səʊldə(r)/ vt soldar*

soldier /'səʊldʒər ‖'səʊldʒə(r)/ n soldado mf; (officer) militar mf

■ **soldier on** [v + adv] (BrE colloq) seguir* al pie del cañón

sole¹ /səʊl/ n [1] (of foot) planta f; (of shoe) suela f [2] (fish) (pl ~ or ~s) lenguado m

sole² adj (before n) (a) (only) único (b) (exclusive) ‹rights› exclusivo

sole³ vt (usu pass): **to have one's shoes** ~**d and heeled** hacerles* poner suelas y tacones or (CS, Per) tacos a los zapatos

solely /'səʊlli/ adv (a) (wholly) únicamente, exclusivamente (b) (only, simply) solo, solamente, únicamente

solemn /'sɑːləm ‖'sɒləm/ adj (a) (serious, formal) ‹occasion/silence› solemne (b) (grave) ‹person› serio; ‹face› solemne

sol-fa /sɒl'faː/ n solfa f

solicit /sə'lɪsət ‖sə'lɪsɪt/ vt (frml) ‹information/ help› solicitar (frml)

■ ~ vi «prostitute» ejercer la prostitución callejera (abordando a posibles clientes)

solicitor /sə'lɪsətər ‖sə'lɪsɪtə(r)/ n (a) (in US and in UK) abogado responsable de los asuntos legales de un municipio o de un departamento gubernamental (b) (in UK) abogado, -da m,f (que prepara causas legales y desempeña también funciones de notario)

solid¹ /'sɑːləd ‖'sɒlɪd/ adj **-er, -est** [1] (a) (not liquid or gaseous) sólido (b) (not hollow) ‹rubber ball/ tire› macizo [2] (a) (unbroken) ‹line/row› continuo, ininterrumpido (b) (continuous) (colloq) ‹month/ year› seguido [3] (a) (physically sturdy) ‹furniture/ house› sólido; ‹meal› consistente (b) (substantial) ‹reason› sólido [4] (pure) ‹metal/wood› macizo, puro; ‹rock› vivo

solid² n [1] (Chem, Phys) sólido m [2] **solids** pl (food) alimentos mpl sólidos

solid³ adv: **to be packed/jammed** ~ estar* lleno hasta el tope or hasta los topes

solidarity /'sɑːlə'dærəti ‖,sɒlɪ'dærəti/ n solidaridad f

solidify /sə'lɪdəfaɪ/ vi **-fies, -fying, -fied** solidificarse*

solidly /'sɑːlədli ‖'sɒlɪdli/ adv (a) (sturdily) ‹fixed/grounded› firmemente; ‹made› sólidamente (b) (unanimously) unánimemente

solitaire /'sɑːləˌter ‖'sɒlɪˌteə(r)/ n [1] ~ (diamond) solitario m [2] (Games) solitario m

solitary /'sɑːləteri ‖'sɒlɪtəri/ adj (a) (alone) ‹person/life/place› solitario (b) (single) (before n) solo

solitary confinement n incomunicación f; **he's in** ~ ~ lo han incomunicado

solitude /'sɑːlətuːd ‖'sɒlɪtjuːd/ n soledad f

solo¹ /'səʊləʊ/ n (pl **-los**) solo m

solo² adj (a) (Mus) ‹violin/voices› solista; ‹album› en solitario (b) ‹flight› en solitario

solo³ adv en solitario

soloist /'səʊləʊəst ‖'səʊləʊɪst/ n solista mf

so long interj (colloq) hasta luego, hasta la vista

solstice /'sɑːlstəs ‖'sɒlstɪs/ n solsticio m

soluble /'sɑːljəbəl ‖'sɒljʊbəl/ adj soluble

solution /sə'luːʃən/ n solución f

solve /sɑːlv ‖sɒlv/ vt ‹mystery/equation› resolver*; ‹crossword puzzle› sacar*; ‹crime› esclarecer*; ‹riddle› encontrar* la solución a

solvent¹ /'sɑːlvənt ‖'sɒlvənt/ adj solvente

solvent² n disolvente m, solvente m

Somali /sə'mɑːli/ adj somalí

Somalia /sə'mɑːliə/ n Somalia f

somber, (BrE) **sombre** /'sɑ:mbər ‖'sɒmbə(r)/ *adj* **(a)** (dark) sombrío **(b)** (melancholy) ⟨*mood/ thought*⟩ sombrío; ⟨*music*⟩ lúgubre

some¹ /sʌm, *weak form* səm/ *adj* **1** **(a)** (unstated number or type) (+ *pl n*) unos, unas; **there were ~ children in the park** había unos niños en el parque; **would you like ~ cherries?** ¿quieres (unas) cerezas? **(b)** (unstated quantity or type) (+ *uncount n*): **~ paint fell on my head** me cayó (un poco de) pintura en la cabeza; **would you like ~ coffee?** ¿quieres café?

2 (a, one) (+ *sing count noun*) algún, -guna; **~ day I'll get my revenge** ya me vengaré algún día **3** (particular, not all) (+ *pl n*) algunos, -nas; **I like ~ modern artists** algunos artistas modernos me gustan; **in ~ ways** en cierto modo **4** **(a)** (not many, a few) ⟨*lemons/apples*⟩ algunos, -nas **(b)** (not much, a little) ⟨*meat/rice*⟩ un poco de **5** **(a)** (several, many): **she's been bedridden for ~ years now** hace algunos años que está postrada en cama **(b)** (large amount of): **we've known each other for quite ~ time now** ya hace mucho (tiempo) que nos conocemos **6** (colloq) **(a)** (expressing appreciation): **that's ~ car you've got!** ¡vaya coche que tienes! **(b)** (stressing remarkable, ridiculous nature): **that was ~ exam!** ¡vaya examen! **(c)** (expressing irony): **~ friend you are!** ¡qué buen amigo eres! (iró)

some² *pron* **1** **(a)** (a number of things or people) algunos, -nas **(b)** (an amount): **there's no salt left; we'll have to buy ~** no queda sal; vamos a tener que comprar; **the coffee's ready: would you like ~?** el café está listo: ¿quieres? **2** (certain people) algunos, -nas; **~ say that ...** algunos dicen que ...

some³ *adv* (approximately) unos, unas, alrededor de

somebody¹ /'sʌm.bɑ:di ‖'sʌmbədi/ *pron* alguien; **~'s coming** viene alguien; **who was it? — John** ~ ¿quién era? — John algo *or* John no sé cuánto (fam)

somebody² *n* (*no pl*): **to be ~** ser* alguien

somehow /'sʌmhaʊ/ *adv* **(a)** (by some means) de algún modo, de alguna manera; **~ or other** de algún modo u otro **(b)** (in some way, for some reason): **it isn't the same, ~** no sé por qué, pero no es lo mismo

someone /'sʌmwʌn/ *pron* ▶ SOMEBODY¹

someplace /'sʌmpleɪs/ *adv* (AmE) ▶ SOMEWHERE¹ 1

somersault¹ /'sʌmərsɔ:lt ‖'sʌməsɒlt, -sɔ:lt/ *n* (on ground) voltereta *f*, vuelta *f* (de) carnero (CS); (in air) (salto *m*) mortal *m*

somersault² *vi* (on ground) hacer* volteretas, dar* vueltas (de) carnero (CS); (in air) dar* un (salto) mortal

something /'sʌmθɪŋ/ *pron* **1** algo; **have ~ to eat/drink** come/bebe algo; **it's not ~ to be proud of** no es como para estar orgulloso; **that was ~ I hadn't expected** eso no me lo esperaba; **is it ~ I said?** ¿qué pasa? ¿qué he dicho? **2** **(a)** (in vague statements or approximations): **she's 30 ~** tiene treinta y pico años (fam); **he said it was because of the traffic or ~** dijo que era por el tráfico o qué se yo **(b)** **something like: ~ like 200 spectators** alrededor de *or* unos 200 espectadores **(c)** **something of** (rather): **she's ~ of an eccentric** es algo excéntrica; **it came as ~ of a surprise** me (*or* nos *etc*) sorprendió un poco

3 (sth special): **it was quite ~ for him to reach that position** era todo un logro que él alcanzara esa posición

sometime¹ /'sʌmtaɪm/ *adv* (at unspecified time): **I'll get around to it ~** ya lo haré en algún momento; **we'll have to finish it ~ or another** algún día habrá que terminarlo; **~ next week** un día de la semana que viene

sometime² *adj* (*before n*) (frml) ex, antiguo

sometimes /'sʌmtaɪmz/ *adv* a veces, algunas veces

someway /'sʌmweɪ/ *adv* (AmE) ▶ SOMEHOW

somewhat /'sʌmhwɑ:t ‖'sʌmwɒt/ *adv* algo, un tanto

somewhere¹ /'sʌmhwer ‖'sʌmweə(r)/ *adv* **1** (in, at a place) en algún lado *or* sitio *or* lugar; (to a place) a algún lado *or* sitio *or* lugar; **to get ~** avanzar*, adelantar **2** (in approximations): **~ around $10,000** cerca de *or* alrededor de 10.000 dólares

somewhere² *pron*: **will there be ~ open?** ¿habrá algo (*or* algún sitio *etc*) abierto?; **she's found ~ to live** ha encontrado casa (*or* habitación *etc*)

son /sʌn/ *n* hijo *m*

sonata /sə'nɑ:tə/ *n* (*pl* **-tas**) (Mus) sonata *f*

song /sɔ:ŋ ‖sɒŋ/ *n* **(a)** (piece) canción *f* **(b)** (of bird) canto *m*

song: ~bird *n* pájaro *m* cantor; **~writer** *n* compositor, -tora *m,f* (*de canciones*)

sonic /'sɑ:nɪk ‖'sɒnɪk/ *adj* sónico

son-in-law /'sʌnɪnlɔ:/ *n* (*pl* **sons-in-law**) yerno *m*, hijo *m* político

sonnet /'sɑ:nət ‖'sɒnɪt/ *n* soneto *m*

son of a bitch *n* (*pl* **sons of bitches**) (esp AmE sl) hijo *m* de puta, hijo *m* de la chingada (Méx vulg)

soon /su:n/ *adv* **-er, -est** **1** (shortly, after a while) pronto, dentro de poco; **~ afterward** poco después; **it'll ~ be spring** ya falta poco para (que empiece) la primavera; **~er or later** tarde o temprano **2** **(a)** (early, quickly) pronto; **how ~ can you be here?** ¿cuándo puedes llegar?, ¿qué tan pronto puedes llegar? (AmL); **I finished ~er than I expected** terminé antes de lo que esperaba; **not a minute** *o* **moment too ~** no antes de tiempo; **to speak too ~** hablar antes de tiempo; **as ~ as possible** lo antes posible, cuanto antes; **the ~er the better** cuanto antes mejor **(b)** (*as conj*): **as ~ as** en cuanto, tan pronto como; **as ~ as you've finished, you can go** en cuanto hayas terminado *or* tan pronto como hayas terminado, te puedes ir; **no ~er had we set out than it began to rain** apenas nos habíamos puesto en camino cuando empezó a llover; **no ~er said than done** dicho y hecho **3** (*in phrases*) **as soon ... (as):** **I'd just as ~ stay at home (as go out)** no me importaría quedarme en casa, tanto me da quedarme en casa (como salir)

soot /sʊt/ *n* hollín *m*

soothe /su:ð/ *vt* ⟨*person/nerves*⟩ calmar; ⟨*pain/ cough*⟩ aliviar

soothing /'su:ðɪŋ/ *adj* **(a)** ⟨*voice/words*⟩ tranquilizador; ⟨*music/bath*⟩ relajante **(b)** ⟨*ointment/syrup*⟩ balsámico; ⟨*medicine*⟩ calmante

S

sophisticated /sə'fɪstəkeɪtəd ‖ sə'fɪstɪkeɪtɪd/ *adj* **(a)** ⟨*appearance/person*⟩ sofisticado **(b)** ⟨*machine/technique*⟩ complejo, altamente desarrollado

sophomore /'sɑːfəmɔːr ‖ 'sɒfəmɔː(r)/ *n* (AmE) estudiante *mf* de segundo curso (*en una universidad o colegio secundario estadounidense*)

sopping¹ /'sɑːpɪŋ ‖ 'sɒpɪŋ/ *adj* empapado

sopping² *adv* (*as intensifier*) ∼ **wet** (of people) calado hasta los huesos; (of clothes) chorreando

soprano¹ /sə'prænəʊ ‖ sə'prɑːnəʊ/ *n* (*pl* **-nos**) soprano *mf*

soprano² *adj* ⟨*voice/recorder*⟩ soprano; ⟨*part/ role*⟩ de soprano

sorbet /sɔːr'beɪ, 'sɔːrbət ‖ 'sɔːbeɪ/ *n* sorbete *m*

sorcerer /'sɔːrsərər ‖ 'sɔːsərə(r)/ *n* (liter) hechicero *m*, brujo *m*

sordid /'sɔːrdəd ‖ 'sɔːdɪd/ *adj* **(a)** (base) ⟨*method/ deal*⟩ vergonzoso **(b)** (squalid) ⟨*hotel/conditions*⟩ sórdido

sore¹ /sɔːr ‖ sɔː(r)/ *adj* **sorer** /'sɔːrər ‖ 'sɔːrə(r)/, **sorest** /'sɔːrəst ‖ 'sɔːrɪst/ **(a)** (painful) ⟨*finger/foot*⟩ dolorido; ⟨*eye*⟩ irritado; ⟨*lips*⟩ reseco; **she has a** ∼ **throat** le duele la garganta; *a* ∼ *point/subject* un punto/tema delicado **(b)** (angry) (AmE colloq) **to be** ∼ **AT** *o* **WITH sb** estar* picado CON algn (fam)

sore² *n* llaga *f*, úlcera *f*

sorority /sə'rɔːrəti ‖ sə'rɒrəti/ *n* (*pl* **-ties**) (in US) hermandad *f* femenina de estudiantes (*en universidades norteamericanas*)

sorrow /'sɑːrəʊ ‖ 'sɒrəʊ/ *n* pesar *m*, pena *f*

sorrowful /'sɑːrəʊfəl ‖ 'sɒrəʊfəl/ *adj* afligido, triste

sorry /'sɑːri ‖ 'sɒri/ *adj* **-rier, -riest** **1** (*pred*) **(a)** (grieved, sad): **I'm** ∼ lo siento; **I'm very** ∼, **but I can't help you** lo siento mucho, pero no te puedo ayudar; **to feel** *o* **be** ∼ **FOR sb**: **I feel so** ∼ **for you/him** te/lo compadezco; **to feel** ∼ **for oneself** lamentarse de su (*or* tu *etc*) suerte; **I'm** ∼ **to have to tell you that …** siento tener que decirte que …; **to be** ∼ (**THAT**) sentir* QUE (+ *subj*) **(b)** (apologetic, repentant): **to say** ∼ pedir* perdón, disculparse; **I'm** ∼, **I didn't mean to …** perdóname *o* lo siento *or* disculpa, no fue mi intención …; **I'm very sorry, but I can't help you** lo siento mucho, pero no te puedo ayudar; **to be** ∼ **ABOUT sth** arrepentirse* DE algo; **I'm** ∼ **I didn't make it to your party** siento no haber podido ir a tu fiesta **2** (*as interj*) perdón, lo siento **3** (pitiful, miserable) (*before n*) ⟨*tale*⟩ lamentable; **he was a** ∼ **sight** tenía un aspecto lamentable

sort¹ /sɔːrt ‖ sɔːt/ *n* **1** (kind, type) tipo *m*, clase *f*; **what** ∼ **of car is it?** ¿qué tipo *or* clase de coche es?; **she's not the** ∼ **to let you down** no es de las que te fallan; **a** ∼ **of** *o* ∼ **of a** una especie de; **I didn't say anything of the** ∼ no dije nada semejante

2 (*in phrases*) **sort of** (colloq): **it's** ∼ **of sad to think of him all alone** da como pena pensar que está solo (fam); **do you want to go?** — **well,** ∼ **of** ¿quieres ir? — bueno, en cierto modo sí

sort² *vt* **(a)** (classify) ⟨*papers/letters*⟩ clasificar* **(b)** (mend) arreglar

■ **sort out** [*v* + *o* + *adv*, *v* + *adv* + *o*] **1** **(a)** (put in order) ⟨*books/photos/desk/room*⟩ ordenar; ⟨*finances*⟩ organizar* **(b)** (separate out) separar

2 **(a)** (arrange) (BrE) ⟨*date*⟩ fijar; ⟨*deal*⟩ llegar* a **(b)** (resolve) ⟨*problem/dispute*⟩ solucionar; ⟨*misunderstanding*⟩ aclarar

■ **sort through** [*v* + *prep* + *o*] ⟨*papers/files*⟩ revisar

SOS *n* S.O.S. *m*

so-so /'səʊsəʊ/ *adj* (colloq) así así (fam)

soufflé /su:'fleɪ ‖ 'su:fleɪ/ *n* suflé *m*

sought /sɔːt/ *past & past p of* SEEK

sought-after /'sɔːt,æftər ‖ 'sɔːt,ɑːftə(r)/ *adj* (*pred* **sought after**) ⟨*product*⟩ solicitado, en demanda; ⟨*prize*⟩ codiciado; ⟨*area*⟩ en demanda

soul /səʊl/ *n* **1** (Relig) alma *f*‡ **2** (person): **I won't tell a (living)** ∼ no se lo diré a nadie; **poor old** ∼! ¡pobrecilla!, ¡pobrecita! **3** ∼ **(music)** soul *m*

soul-destroying /'səʊldɪ'strɔɪɪŋ/ *adj* desmoralizador

soulful /'səʊlfəl/ *adj* enternecedor, conmovedor

soul: ∼**mate** *n* alma *f*‡ gemela; ∼**-searching** /'səʊl'sɜːrtʃɪŋ ‖ 'səʊl,sɜːtʃɪŋ/ *n* introspección *f*

sound¹ /saʊnd/ *n* **1** (noise) sonido *m*; (unpleasant, disturbing) ruido *m*; (*before n*) **the** ∼ **barrier** la barrera del sonido; ∼ **effects** efectos *mpl* sonoros **2** (impression conveyed) (colloq) (*no pl*): **I don't like the** ∼ **of that at all** eso no me huele nada bien; **by** *o* **from the** ∼ **of it, everything's going very well** parece que *or* por lo visto todo marcha muy bien

sound² *vi* **1** **(a)** (give impression) sonar*; **you** ∼ **as if** *o* **as though you could do with a rest** me da la impresión de que no te vendría mal un descanso; **that** ∼**s like Susan** eso debe (de) ser Susan **(b)** (seem) parecer*; **how does that** ∼ **to you?** ¿qué te parece?; **it** ∼**s as if** *o* **as though you had a great time** parece que lo pasaste fenomenal **2** (make noise, resound) «*bell/alarm*» sonar*

■ ∼ *vt* ⟨*trumpet/horn*⟩ tocar*, hacer* sonar

■ **sound out** [*v* + *o* + *adv*, *v* + *adv* + *o*] tantear, sondear

sound³ *adj* **-er, -est** **1** **(a)** (healthy) sano; **being of** ∼ **mind** (estando) en pleno uso de sus facultades **(b)** (in good condition) ⟨*basis/foundation*⟩ sólido, firme; ⟨*timber*⟩ en buenas condiciones **2** (valid) ⟨*reasoning/knowledge*⟩ sólido; ⟨*advice/ decision*⟩ sensato

sound⁴ *adv* **-er, -est**: ∼ **asleep** profundamente dormido

sound bite *n* (Journ, Pol) frase *f* corta (*que suena bien en los titulares y en los discursos*)

soundly /'saʊndli/ *adv* **1** ⟨*sleep*⟩ profundamente **2** (solidly, validly) sólidamente

soundproof¹ /'saʊndpru:f/ *adj* insonorizado

soundproof² *vt* insonorizar*

sound: ∼ **system** *n* equipo *m* de sonido; ∼**track** *n* banda *f* sonora

soup /su:p/ *n* sopa *f*; **clear** ∼ caldo *m*, consomé *m*

sour¹ /saʊər ‖ saʊə(r)/ *adj* **sourer, sourest** **(a)** (sharp, acid) ácido, agrio **(b)** (spoiled) ⟨*milk*⟩ agrio, cortado **(c)** (bad-tempered, disagreeable) agrio, avinagrado

sour² *vt* ⟨*relationship/occasion*⟩ amargar*

source /sɔːrs ‖ sɔːs/ *n* **1** (origin, supply) fuente *f*;

(of river) nacimiento *m*; ∼ **of income** fuente de ingresos **2** (providing information) **(a)** (person) (journ) fuente *f* **(b)** (text, document) fuente *f*

sourdough /'saʊərdəʊ ‖'saʊədəʊ/ *n* (AmE) masa *f* fermentada (*para hacer pan*)

south¹ /saʊθ/ *n* (point of the compass, direction) sur *m*; **the** ∼, **the S**∼ (region) el sur

south² *adj* (*before n*) sur *adj inv*, meridional; ⟨*wind*⟩ del sur

south³ *adv* al sur

South Africa *n* Sudáfrica *f*, Suráfrica *f*

South African *adj* sudafricano, surafricano

South America *n* América *f* del Sur *or* del Sud, Sudamérica *f*, Suramérica *f*

South American¹ *adj* sudamericano, suramericano

South American² *n* sudamericano, -na *m,f*, suramericano, -na *m,f*

southbound /'saʊθbaʊnd/ *adj* ⟨*traffic/train*⟩ que va (*or* iba *etc*) hacia el sur *or* en dirección sur

southeast¹, Southeast /'saʊθ'i:st/ *n* **the** ∼ el sudeste *or* Sudeste, el sureste *or* Sureste

southeast² *adj* sudeste *adj inv*, sureste *adj inv*, del sudeste *or* sureste, sudoriental

southeast³ *adv* hacia el sudeste *or* sureste, en dirección sudeste *or* sureste

south: ∼**easterly** /'saʊθ'i:stərli ‖,saʊθ'i:stəli/ *adj* ⟨*wind*⟩ del sudeste *or* sureste; ∼**eastern** /'saʊθ'i:stərn ‖,saʊθ'i:stən/ *adj* sudeste *adj inv*, sureste *adj inv*, del sudeste *or* sureste, sudoriental

southerly /'sʌðərli ‖'sʌðəli/ *adj* ⟨*wind*⟩ del sur; ⟨*latitude*⟩ sur *adj inv*; **in a** ∼ **direction** hacia el sur, en dirección sur

southern /'sʌðərn ‖'sʌðən/ *adj* ⟨*region*⟩ del sur, meridional, sur *adj inv*; ⟨*country*⟩ del sur, meridional; ∼ **Italy** el sur de Italia; **the** ∼ **states** (in US) los estados del sur

southward¹ /'saʊθwərd ‖'saʊθwəd/ *adj* (*before n*): **in a** ∼ **direction** hacia el sur, en dirección sur

southward², (BrE also) **southwards** /-z/ *adv* hacia el sur

southwest¹, Southwest /'saʊθ'west/ *n* **the** ∼ el sudoeste *or* Sudoeste, el suroeste *or* Suroeste

southwest² *adj* sudoeste *adj inv*, suroeste *adj inv*, del sudoeste *or* suroeste

southwest³ *adv* hacia el sudoeste *or* suroeste, en dirección sudoeste *or* suroeste

south: ∼**westerly** /'saʊθ'westərli ‖,saʊθ'westəli/ *adj* ⟨*wind*⟩ del sudoeste *or* suroeste; ∼**western** /'saʊθ'westərn ‖,saʊθ'westən/ *adj* sudoccidental, sudoeste *adj inv*, suroeste *adj inv*, del sudoeste *or* suroeste

souvenir /'su:vənɪr ‖,su:və'nɪə(r)/ *n* recuerdo *m*, souvenir *m*

sovereign¹ /'sɑ:vrən ‖'sɒvrɪn/ *n* **1** (monarch) soberano, -na *m,f* **2** (coin) soberano *m*, libra *f* (de oro)

sovereign² *adj* soberano

sovereignty /'sɑ:vrənti ‖'sɒvrənti/ *n* soberanía *f*

Soviet /'saʊviet, 'sɑ:viət ‖'səʊviət/ *adj* (Hist) soviético

Soviet Union *n* (Hist) **the** ∼ **la** la Unión Soviética

sow¹ /saʊ/ *vt/i* (*past* **sowed**; *past p* **sowed** *or* **sown**) sembrar*

sow² /saʊ/ *n* cerda *f*, puerca *f*

sown /saʊn/ *past p of* sow¹

soy /sɔɪ/, (BrE) **soya** /'sɔɪə/ *n* soya *f* (AmL), soja *f* (Esp)

soy: ∼ **bean,** (BrE) **soya bean** *n* soya *f* (AmL), soja *f* (Esp); ∼ **sauce** *n* salsa *f* de soya (AmL) *or* (Esp) soja

spa /spɑ:/ *n* **(a)** (resort) balneario *m* **(b)** (spring) manantial *m* (*de agua mineral*) **(c)** (health club) (AmE) gimnasio *m*

space¹ /speɪs/ *n* **1** **(a)** (Phys) espacio *m* **(b)** (Aerosp) espacio *m*; (*before n*) ⟨*station/program*⟩ espacial **2** **(a)** (room) espacio *m*, lugar *m* **(b)** (empty area) espacio *m*; **let's clear a** ∼ **for it first** hagámosle (un) sitio primero **3** (of time) (*no pl*) espacio *m*; **in the** ∼ **of one hour** en el espacio *or* lapso de una hora **4** (Print) espacio *m*

space² *vt* ∼ **(out)** espaciar

space: ∼**-age** *adj* ⟨*technology*⟩ futurista, espacial; ∼**craft** *n* (*pl* ∼**craft**) nave *f* espacial; ∼**man** /'speɪsmæn/ *n* (*pl* **-men** /-men/) astronauta *m*, cosmonauta *m*; ∼**ship** *n* nave *f* espacial, astronave *f*

spacing /'speɪsɪŋ/ *n* (Print) espaciado *m*

spacious /'speɪʃəs/ *adj* ⟨*house/room*⟩ amplio, espacioso; ⟨*park*⟩ grande, extenso

spade /speɪd/ *n* **1** (tool) pala *f*; **to call a** ∼ **a** ∼ llamar al pan, pan y al vino, vino **2** (Games) **spades** *pl* (suit) (+ *sing or pl vb*) picas *fpl*

spaghetti /spə'geti/ *n* espaguetis *mpl*, spaghetti *mpl*

Spain /speɪn/ *n* España *f*

span¹ /spæn/ *n* **(a)** (of hand) palmo *m*; (of wing) envergadura *f*; (of bridge, arch) luz *f* **(b)** (part of bridge) arco *m* **(c)** (of time) lapso *m*; ▶ LIFE SPAN

span² *vt* **-nn-** (extend over) abarcar* **(b)** (cross) ⟨*bridge*⟩ ⟨*river*⟩ extenderse* sobre

Spaniard /'spænjərd ‖'spænjəd/ *n* español, -ñola *m,f*

spaniel /'spænjəl/ *n* spaniel *m*

Spanish¹ /'spænɪʃ/ *adj* español; ⟨*language*⟩ castellano, español

Spanish² *n* **(a)** (language) castellano *m*, español *m* **(b)** (people) (+ *pl vb*) **the** ∼ los españoles

Spanish omelet, (BrE) **Spanish omelette** *n* tortilla *f* de papas *or* (Esp) patatas, tortilla *f* española

spank /spæŋk/ *vt* pegarle* (*en las nalgas*)

spanner /'spænər ‖'spænə(r)/ *n* (BrE) (adjustable ∼) llave *f* inglesa; (box ∼) llave *f* de tubo; **to throw a** ∼ **in the works** fastidiarlo todo

spar¹ /spɑ:r ‖spɑ:(r)/ *n* (Naut) palo *m*

spar² *vi* **-rr-** (in boxing) entrenarse; (argue) discutir

spare¹ /sper ‖speə(r)/ *adj* **(a)** (not in use) ⟨*umbrella/pen*⟩ de más; **have you got any** ∼ **paper?** ¿tienes un poco de papel que no te haga falta? **(b)** (*before n*) ⟨*key/cartridge*⟩ de repuesto **(c)** (free) libre; **if you've got a** ∼ **minute** si tienes un minuto (libre)

spare² *n*: **I'll take a** ∼ **just in case** llevaré uno de repuesto por si acaso

spare³ vt 1 (a) (do without): can you ~ your dictionary for a moment? ¿me permites el diccionario un momento, si no lo necesitas?; if you can ~ the time si tienes or dispones de tiempo (b) (give) to ~ (sb) sth: can you ~ me a pound? ¿tienes una libra que me prestes/des?; can you ~ me a few minutes? ¿tienes unos minutos? (c) to spare (as adj): there's food to ~ hay comida de sobra; have you got a few minutes to ~? ¿tienes unos minutos?
2 (a) (keep from using, stint) (usu neg): to ~ no effort no escatimar esfuerzos; to ~ no expense no reparar en gastos (b) (save, relieve) to ~ sb sth ‹trouble/embarrassment› ahorrarle algo a algn (c) (show mercy, consideration toward) perdonar

spare: ~ **part** n repuesto m or (Méx) refacción f; ~ **room** n cuarto m de huéspedes or (Esp) de los invitados, recámara f de visitas (Méx); ~ **time** n tiempo m libre; ~ **tire**, (BrE) ~ **tyre** n rueda f de repuesto or (Esp tb) de recambio, llanta f de refacción (Méx)

sparingly /'speərɪŋli ‖'speərɪŋli/ adv ‹use› con moderación

spark¹ /spaːrk ‖spaːk/ n chispa f

spark² vt, (BrE also) **spark off** ‹rioting/revolution› hacer* estallar; ‹interest› suscitar; ‹criticism› provocar*

sparking plug /'spaːrkɪŋ ‖'spaːkɪŋ/ n (BrE) ▶ SPARK PLUG

sparkle¹ /'spaːrkəl ‖'spaːkəl/ vi «gem/glass» centellear, destellar, brillar; «eyes» brillar

sparkle² n (a) (no pl) (of gem, glass) destello m, brillo m; (of eyes) brillo m (b) (animation) chispa f, brillo m

sparkler /'spaːrklər ‖'spaːklə(r)/ n (firework) luz f de Bengala, bengala f

sparkling /'spaːrklɪŋ ‖'spaːklɪŋ/ adj (a) (shining) ‹gems/stars› centelleante; ‹eyes› chispeante (b) ‹wit/conversation› chispeante (c) (effervescent) ‹wine› espumoso

spark plug n bujía f, chispero m (AmC)

sparrow /'spærəʊ/ n gorrión m

sparse /spaːrs ‖spaːs/ adj ‹population/vegetation/furniture› escaso; ‹beard/hair› ralo

sparsely /'spaːrsli ‖'spaːsli/ adv: the area was ~ populated la zona estaba escasamente poblada; the room is ~ furnished la habitación tiene pocos muebles

spartan /'spaːrtn ‖'spaːtn/ adj espartano

spasm /'spæzəm/ n espasmo m

spasmodic /spæz'maːdɪk ‖spæz'mɒdɪk/ adj (a) ‹growth/activity› irregular (b) (Med) ‹pain/cough› espasmódico

spat /spæt/ past & past p of SPIT²

spate /speɪt/ n racha f, serie f; to be in (full) ~ (BrE) ‹river› estar* crecido

spatial /'speɪʃəl/ adj (before n) espacial

spatter /'spætər ‖'spætə(r)/ vt/i salpicar*

spatula /'spætʃələ ‖'spætjʊlə/ n (a) (Culin) (for turning, serving) pala f (de servir); (for scraping out bowls) espátula f (b) (Pharm, Med) espátula f

spawn¹ /spɔːn/ n (of fish) hueva(s) f(pl); (of frogs) huevas fpl

spawn² vt (journ) generar, producir*
■ ~ vi «frogs/fish» desovar

SPCA n (in US) (= **Society for the Prevention of Cruelty to Animals**) ≈ Asociación f protectora de animales

SPCC n (in US) (= **Society for the Prevention of Cruelty to Children**) ≈ Asociación f de proteccion a la infancia

speak /spiːk/ (past **spoke**; past p **spoken**) vi 1 (a) (say sth) hablar; to ~ TO o (esp AmE) WITH sb hablar CON algn, hablarle A algn; they are not ~ing (to each other) no se hablan; to ~ OF sth/sb/-ING hablar DE algo/algn/+ INF; so to ~ por así decirlo (b) (on telephone): hello, Barbara Mason ~ing ... buenas tardes, habla or (Esp tb) soy Barbara Mason; could I ~ to Mrs Hodges, please? — ~ing! ¿podría hablar con la Sra. Hodges, por favor? — con ella (habla) or (Esp tb) soy yo
2 (make speech) hablar; to ~ ON o ABOUT sth hablar ACERCA DE or SOBRE algo
■ ~ vt (say, declare): nobody spoke a word nadie dijo nada; to ~ one's mind hablar claro; to ~ the truth decir* la verdad (b) ‹language› hablar
■ **speak for** [v + prep + o] hablar por; we'd love to meet him — ~ for yourself! nos encantaría conocerlo — ¡eso lo dirás por ti!; the facts ~ for themselves los hechos son elocuentes
■ **speak out** [v + adv]: to ~ out AGAINST sth denunciar algo
■ **speak up** [v + adv] (a) (speak loudly, clearly) hablar más fuerte or más alto (b) (speak boldly) decir* lo que se piensa; to ~ up FOR sb defender* a algn

speaker /'spiːkər ‖'spiːkə(r)/ n 1 (a) (in public) orador, -dora m,f (b) (of language) hablante m,f (c) (Govt) presidente, -ta m,f 2 (Audio) (a) (loudspeaker) altavoz m, (alto)parlante m (AmS) (b) (of hi-fi) baf(f)le m, parlante m (AmS)

speaking /'spiːkɪŋ/ n (before n): a good ~ voice una voz muy clara (or potente etc); to be on ~ terms with sb estar* en buenas relaciones con algn

-speaking /ˌspiːkɪŋ/ suff -hablante, -parlante; Spanish~ hispanohablante, hispanoparlante; French~ francófono; English~ de habla inglesa

spear¹ /spɪr ‖'spɪə(r)/ n (a) (weapon) lanza f (b) (for fishing) arpón m

spear² vt ‹fish› arponear

spear: ~**head** vt (Mil) encabezar*; ~**mint** n menta f verde

spec /spek/ n: on ~ (colloq) por si acaso

special /'speʃəl/ adj (a) (exceptional) (before n) ‹favor/request› especial (b) (for specific purpose) (before n) ‹arrangements/fund› especial (c) (particular, individual) especial, particular; children with ~ needs (Educ) niños que requieren una atención diferenciada

- -

AmC	Central America	Arg	Argentina	Cu	Cuba	Per	Peru
AmL	Latin America	Bol	Bolivia	Ec	Ecuador	RPI	River Plate Area
AmS	South America	Chi	Chile	Esp	Spain	Ur	Uruguay
Andes	Andean Region	CS	Southern Cone	Méx	Mexico	Ven	Venezuela

special: ~ **delivery** n correo m exprés or expreso; ~ **effects** pl n efectos mpl especiales

specialist /'speʃəlɪst ‖'speʃəlɪst/ n especialista mf; (before n) ⟨knowledge/shop⟩ especializado

speciality /ˌspeʃi'ælətɪ/ n (pl **-ties**) (BrE) ▶ SPECIALTY¹

specialize /'speʃəlaɪz/ vi to ~ (IN sth) especializarse* (EN algo)

specialized /'speʃəlaɪzd/ adj especializado

specially /'speʃəli/ adv (a) (specifically) especialmente, expresamente (b) (especially) ⟨long/difficult⟩ particularmente

specialty¹ /'speʃəlti/ n (pl **-ties**) (AmE) especialidad f

specialty² adj (AmE) (before n: no comp) ⟨merchandise/store⟩ especializado

species /'spiːʃiːz/ n (pl ~) especie f

specific /spɪ'sɪfɪk/ adj (a) (particular, individual) específico; ⟨example⟩ concreto (b) (exact, precise) preciso

specifically /spɪ'sɪfɪkli ‖spə'sɪfɪkli/ adv (a) (explicitly) ⟨state/mention⟩ explícitamente (b) (specially, particularly) ⟨built/designed⟩ específicamente

specification /ˌspesəfə'keɪʃən ‖ˌspesɪfɪ'keɪʃən/ n (often pl) especificación f

specify /'spesəfaɪ ‖'spesɪfaɪ/ vt **-fies, -fying, -fied** especificar*

specimen /'spesəmən ‖'spesɪmən/ n (a) (sample — of rock, plant, tissue) muestra f, espécimen m; (— of blood, urine) muestra f; (— of work, handwriting) muestra f (b) (individual example) ejemplar m, espécimen m

speck /spek/ n (of dust) mota f; (in distance) punto m; (dirt stain) manchita f

speckle /'spekəl/vt (usu pass) motear; **a ~d hen** una gallina pinta or (RPl) bataraza

spectacle /'spektɪkəl ‖'spektəkəl/ n **1** (show, sight) espectáculo m **2** **spectacles** pl gafas fpl, anteojos mpl (esp AmL), lentes mpl (esp AmL)

spectacular /spek'tækjələr ‖spek'tækjʊlə(r)/ adj espectacular

spectator /'spekteɪtər ‖spek'teɪtə(r)/ n espectador, -dora m,f

specter, (BrE) **spectre** /'spektər ‖'spektə(r)/ n (liter) espectro m

spectra /'spektrə/ pl of SPECTRUM

spectre /'spektər/ n (BrE) ▶ SPECTER

spectrum /'spektrəm/ n (pl **-tra**) **1** (Opt, Phys) espectro m **2** (range) espectro m, gama f; **the political ~** el espectro político

speculate /'spekjəlert ‖'spekjʊlert/ vi **1** (Fin) especular **2** (guess, conjecture) **to ~** (ON o ABOUT sth) hacer* conjeturas or especular (SOBRE algo)

speculation /ˌspekjə'leɪʃən ‖ˌspekjʊ'leɪʃən/ n especulación f

speculative /'spekjələtɪv ‖'spekjʊlətɪv/ adj especulativo

sped /sped/ past & past p of SPEED² vi A

speech /spiːtʃ/ n **1** (a) (act, faculty) habla f‡ (b) (manner of speaking) forma f de hablar (c) (language, dialect) habla f‡ **2** (a) (oration) discurso m; **to make a ~** dar* un discurso (b) (Theat) parlamento m

speechless /'spiːtʃləs ‖'spiːtʃlɪs/ adj: **she was ~ with rage** enmudeció de rabia; **I'm ~!** no sé qué decir

speech therapy n foniatría f, logopedia f

speed¹ /spiːd/ n **1** (a) (rate of movement, progress) velocidad f (b) (relative quickness) rapidez f **2** (Phot): **film ~** sensibilidad f de la película; **shutter ~** tiempo m de exposición **3** (gear) velocidad f, marcha f **4** (amphetamine) (sl) anfetas fpl (fam)

speed² vi (a) (past & past p **sped**) (go, pass quickly) (+ adv compl): **to ~ off** o **away** alejarse a toda velocidad; **he sped by** o **past in his new sports car** nos pasó a toda velocidad con su nuevo coche deportivo; **the hours sped by** las horas pasaron volando (b) (past & past p **speeded**) (drive too fast) ir* a velocidad excesiva
■ ~ vt (past & past p **speeded**) (hasten) acelerar
■ **speed up** (past & past p **speeded**) **1** [v + adv] (a) (move faster) ⟨vehicle/driver⟩ acelerar; ⟨walker⟩ apretar* el paso (b) ⟨process/production⟩ acelerarse **2** [v + o + adv, v + adv + o] (a) ⟨vehicle⟩ acelerar (b) ⟨work/production⟩ acelerar

speed: ~**boat** n (lancha f) motora f; ~ **bump** n badén m, guardia m tumbado (Esp), tope m (Méx), policía m acostado (Col), lomo m de burro (RPl), baden m (Chi); ~ **limit** n velocidad f máxima, límite m de velocidad

speedometer /spɪ'dɑːmətər ‖spiː'dɒmɪtə(r)/ n velocímetro m, indicador m de velocidad

speedway /'spiːdweɪ/ n (a) (sport) carreras fpl de motocicletas (b) (AmE Transp) autopista f

speedy /'spiːdi/ adj **-dier, -diest** ⟨reply/delivery⟩ rápido; ⟨solution⟩ pronto, rápido

spell¹ /spel/ n **1** (magic ~) encanto m, hechizo m, encantamiento m; **evil ~** maleficio m; **to cast a ~ over** o **to put a ~ on sth/sb** hechizar* or embrujar algo/a algn **2** (of weather) período m (b) (of work, activity) período m, temporada f; **a bad ~** una mala racha

spell² (past & past p **spelled** or (BrE also) **spelt**) vt **1** (write) escribir*; (orally) deletrear; **how do you ~ Zimbabwe?** ¿cómo se escribe Zimbabwe?; **could you ~ it for me?** ¿me lo deletrea? **2** (mean) significar*; (foretell) anunciar, augurar
■ ~ vi: **he can't ~** tiene mala ortografía
■ **spell out** [v + o + adv, v + adv + o] (a) ⟨word⟩ deletrear (b) (explain) explicar* en detalle

spell: ~**binding** adj ⟨speech/film⟩ fascinante; ~**bound** adj embelesado, maravillado; ~**checker** n (Comput) corrector m ortográfico

spelling /'spelɪŋ/ n (a) (system, ability) ortografía f; **to be good/bad at ~** tener* buena/mala ortografía; (before n) ~ **mistake** falta f de ortografía, error m ortográfico (b) (of a word) grafía f, ortografía f

spelt /spelt/ (BrE) past & past p of SPELL²

spelunking /spɪ'lʌŋkɪŋ/ n (AmE) espeleología f

spend /spend/ vt (past & past p **spent**) **1** (a) ⟨money⟩ gastar (b) (expend) **to ~ sth** (ON sth) dedicar* algo A algo; **don't ~ too long on each question** no le dediquen mucho tiempo a cada pregunta **2** (pass) ⟨period of time⟩ pasar **3** (exhaust) agotar

S

spending /'spendɪŋ/ n gastos mpl; **public ∼** el gasto público; (before n) **∼ power** poder m adquisitivo

spending money n dinero m para gastos personales

spendthrift /'spendθrɪft/ n despilfarrador, -dora m,f

spent /spent/ past & past p of SPEND

sperm /spɜːrm ‖ spɜːm/ n (pl ∼ or ∼s) (a) (seminal liquid) esperma m or f (b) (gamete) espermatozoide m, espermatozoo m

spew /spjuː/ vi (a) «water» salir* a borbotones (b) (vomit) (BrE sl) vomitar, lanzar* (fam)
■ ∼ vt «lava/flames» arrojar

sphere /sfɪr ‖ sfɪə(r)/ n esfera f

spherical /'sfɪrɪkəl ‖ 'sferɪkəl/ adj esférico

Sphinx /sfɪŋks/ n **the ∼** la Esfinge

spice¹ /spaɪs/ n (a) (seasoning) especia f (b) (zest, interest) sabor m

spice² vt (a) (Culin) (often pass) condimentar, sazonar* (b) (add excitement to): **to ∼ up a story** darle* más sabor a un relato

spick-and-span /ˌspɪkən'spæn/ adj (colloq) (pred) limpio y ordenado

spicy /'spaɪsi/ adj -cier, -ciest (a) «sauce/ food» (with spices) con muchas especias; (hot, peppery) picante (b) (racy) «story/account» sabroso; (with sexual connotations) picante

spider /'spaɪdər ‖ 'spaɪdə(r)/ n araña f

spike¹ /spaɪk/ n **1** (pointed object) punta f, púa f, pincho m or (Arg) pinche m; (on track shoes) clavo m or (Chi, Ven) púa f or (Col) carramplón m **2 spikes** pl (running shoes) zapatillas fpl de clavos or (Chi, Ven) de púas or (Col) con carramplones, picos mpl (Méx)

spike² vt **1** (pierce) pinchar, clavar **2** (add sth to) (colloq): **they ∼d his lemonade with vodka** le echaron vodka en la limonada

spiky /'spaɪki/ adj -kier, -kiest (a) (having spikes) con puntas or púas or pinchos (b) (sharp, pointed) puntiagudo, puntudo (Col, CS) (c) «hair» de punta

spill /spɪl/ (past & past p **spilled** or **spilt** /spɪlt/) vt «liquid» derramar, verter*; (knock over) volcar*
■ ∼ vi «liquid» derramarse; **people ∼ed (out) into the streets** la gente se volcó or se echó a las calles
■ **spill over** [v + adv] «container» desbordarse; «liquid» rebosar; «fighting/conflict» extenderse*

spillage /'spɪlɪdʒ/ n vertido m, derrame m

spilt /spɪlt/ past & past p of SPILL

spin¹ /spɪn/ n **1** (on ball) (Sport) efecto m, chanfle m (AmL) **2** (of aircraft) barrena f (b) (Auto) trompo m **3** (ride) (colloq): **to go for a ∼** ir* a dar un paseo en coche (or en moto etc), ir* a dar un garbeo (Esp fam)

spin² (pres p **spinning**; past & past p **spun**) vt **1** «wheel/top» hacer* girar **2** (a) «wool/ cotton» hilar (b) «web» tejer
■ ∼ vi **1** (a) (rotate) «wheel/top» girar; **my head is ∼ning** la cabeza me da vueltas (b) «washing machine» centrifugar* (c) (move rapidly) (+ adv compl): **the car spun out of control** el coche giró fuera de control **2** (Tex) hilar

■ **spin out** [v + o + adv, v + adv + o] «money» estirar; «vacation/story» alargar*, prolongar*

spina bifida /ˌspaɪnə'bɪfədə ‖ ˌspaɪnə'bɪfɪdə/ n espina f bífida

spinach /'spɪnɪtʃ ‖ 'spɪnɪdʒ, -ɪtʃ/ n (Bot) espinaca f; (Culin) espinaca(s) f(pl)

spinal /'spaɪnl/ adj de la columna vertebral

spinal: ∼ column n columna f vertebral; **∼ cord** n médula f espinal

spindle /'spɪndl/ n (a) (Mech Eng) eje m (b) (Tex) huso m

spindly /'spɪndli/ adj -dlier, -dliest «legs» largo y flaco; «plant» alto y débil

spin: ∼ doctor n (esp Pol) portavoz mf (contratado para dar a la prensa, TV, etc, una interpretación favorable de los hechos); **∼ drier** n centrifugadora f (de ropa); **∼-dry** /ˌspɪn'draɪ/ vt -dries, -drying, -dried centrifugar*; **∼ dryer** n ▶ ∼ DRIER

spine /spaɪn/ n **1** (a) (Anat) columna f (vertebral) (b) (of book) lomo m **2** (on animal) púa f; (on plant) espina f

spine-chilling /'spaɪnˌtʃɪlɪŋ/ adj espeluznante

spineless /'spaɪnləs ‖ 'spaɪnlɪs/ adj (a) (cowardly, weak) débil, sin carácter (b) (Zool) invertebrado

spinning /'spɪnɪŋ/ n (Tex) hilado m

spinning wheel n rueca f

spin-off /'spɪnɔːf ‖ 'spɪnɒf/ n (product) producto m derivado; (result) resultado m indirecto

spinster /'spɪnstər ‖ 'spɪnstə(r)/ n soltera f

spiral¹ /'spaɪrəl ‖ 'spaɪərəl/ n (a) (shape, movement) espiral f (b) (of smoke) voluta f, espiral f

spiral² adj «shape» de espiral, acaracolado; **∼ staircase** escalera f de caracol

spiral³ vi, (BrE) -ll- «unemployment» escalar; «prices» dispararse

spire /spaɪr ‖ spaɪə(r)/ n aguja f, chapitel m

spirit /'spɪrət ‖ 'spɪrɪt/ n **1** (a) (life force, soul) espíritu m (b) (Occult) espíritu m **2** (vigor, courage) espíritu m, temple m; **to break sb's ∼** quebrantarle el espíritu a algn **3** (mental attitude, mood) (no pl) espíritu m; **the party/Christmas ∼** el espíritu festivo/navideño **4 spirits** pl (emotional state): **to be in good ∼s** estar* animado; **keep your ∼s up** ¡arriba ese ánimo! **5 spirits** pl (alcohol) bebidas fpl alcohólicas (de alta graduación), licores mpl

spirited /'spɪrətəd ‖ 'spɪrɪtɪd/ adj «horse/child» brioso; «reply» enérgico; «defense» ardiente

spirit level n nivel m (de burbuja or de aire)

spiritual¹ /'spɪrɪtʃuəl ‖ 'spɪrɪtjʊəl/ adj espiritual

spiritual² n (negro ∼) espiritual m (negro)

spiritualism /'spɪrɪtʃuəlɪzəm ‖ 'spɪrɪtjʊəlɪzəm/ n (Occult) espiritismo m; (Phil) espiritualismo m

spit¹ /spɪt/ n **1** (saliva) saliva f **2** (for roasting) asador m (en forma de varilla), espetón m

spit² vi (pres p **spitting**; past & past p **spat** or (AmE esp) **spit**) (a) «person/animal» escupir; **to ∼ at/on sb** escupirle a algn; ▶ IMAGE (b) «fire/ fat» chisporrotear (c) «cat» bufar
■ ∼ vt (past & past p **spat**) «food/blood» escupir

■ ~ v impers (colloq): it's ~ting caen algunas gotas (de lluvia), está chispeando (fam)

■ **spit out** [v + o + adv, v + adv + o] escupir

spite[1] /spaɪt/ n **1** (malice) maldad f; (resentment) rencor m, resentimiento m **2 in spite of** (as prep) a pesar de

spite[2] vt molestar, fastidiar

spiteful /'spaɪtfəl/ adj ⟨remark⟩ malicioso; ⟨person⟩ malo; (resentful) rencoroso

spittle /'spɪtl/ n baba f

splash[1] /splæʃ/ n **1 (a)** (spray) salpicadura f **(b)** (sound): we heard a ~ oímos el ruido de algo al caer al agua **(c)** (paddle, swim) (no pl) chapuzón m **2 (a)** (of milk, paint) (no pl) a ~ un poco **(b)** (mark, patch) salpicadura f, manchón m

splash[2] vt salpicar*; to ~ sth/sb WITH sth salpicar* algo/a algn DE algo
■ ~ vi **(a)** «water/paint» salpicar* **(b)** «person/animal» chapotear

■ **splash out** (BrE colloq) [v + adv] darse* un lujo; to ~ out ON sth gastar(se) un dineral EN algo (fam)

splashguard /'splæʃgɑːrd ‖ 'splæʃgɑːd/ n (AmE) guardabarros m, salpicadera f (Méx), tapabarros m (Chi, Per)

splatter /'splætər ‖ 'splætə(r)/ vt/i ▶ SPATTER

splay /spleɪ/ vt ~ (out) ⟨fingers⟩ abrir*, separar; to ~ one's legs abrirse* de piernas

spleen /spliːn/ n (Anat) bazo m

splendid /'splendəd ‖ 'splendɪd/ adj **(a)** (very good) ⟨idea/opportunity/meal⟩ espléndido **(b)** (imposing) ⟨clothes/building⟩ magnífico; ⟨ceremony⟩ lleno de esplendor

splendor, (BrE) **splendour** /'splendər ‖ 'splendə(r)/ n esplendor m

splice /splaɪs/ vt ~ (together) ⟨ropes⟩ coser; ⟨tape/film⟩ unir

splint /splɪnt/ n tablilla f

splinter[1] /'splɪntər ‖ 'splɪntə(r)/ n (of wood) astilla f; (of glass, bone, metal) esquirla f, astilla f; (before n) ~ **group** grupo m escindido

splinter[2] vi **(a)** (break into pieces) «wood/bone» astillarse **(b)** «political party/society» escindirse
■ ~ vt ⟨wood/bone⟩ astillar

split[1] /splɪt/ n **1 (a)** (in garment, cloth — in seam) descosido m; (— part of design) abertura f, raja f **(b)** (in wood, glass) rajadura f, grieta f **2 (a)** (Pol) escisión f; (Relig) cisma m, escisión f **(b)** (breakup) ruptura f, separación f **3 splits** pl: to do the ~s abrirse* completamente de piernas, hacer* el spagat (Esp)

split[2] adj **1** (damaged) ⟨wood⟩ rajado, partido; ⟨lip⟩ partido **2 (a)** (divided): ~ **personality** doble personalidad f; ~ **shift** horario m (de trabajo) partido **(b)** (in factions) dividido

split[3] (pres p **splitting**; past & past p **split**) vt **1 (a)** (break) ⟨wood/stone⟩ partir; to ~ **the atom** fisionar el átomo **(b)** (burst) ⟨pants/trousers⟩ reventar* **(c)** (divide into factions) ⟨nation/church⟩ dividir
2 (divide, share) ⟨cost/food⟩ dividir
■ ~ vi **1** (crack, burst) «wood/rock» partirse, rajarse; «leather/seam» abrirse*, romperse*; I've got a ~ting headache tengo un dolor de cabeza espantoso
2 «political party/church» dividirse, escindirse
3 (leave) (sl) abrirse* (arg), largarse* (fam)

■ **split away, split off** [v + adv] to ~ away o off FROM sth escindirse or separarse DE algo

■ **split up 1** [v + adv] «couple/band» separarse; «crowd» dispersarse
2 [v + o + adv, v + adv + o] «wrestlers/boxers» separar; ⟨lovers⟩ hacer* que se separen; ~ **them up into groups** divídelos en grupos

split: ~ **end** n (of hair): I've got ~ ends tengo las puntas abiertas or (CS) florecidas, tengo horquillas (Col) or (Méx) orzuela or (Ven) horquetillas; ~-**level** /'splɪt'levəl/ adj ⟨apartment⟩ en dos niveles; ~ **second** n fracción f de segundo; (before n) ~-**second timing** sincronización f perfecta

splutter /'splʌtər ‖ 'splʌtə(r)/ vi **(a)** «fire/fat» chisporrotear; «engine» resoplar **(b)** «person» resoplar; (in anger, embarrassment etc) resollar

spoil /spoɪl/ (past & past p **spoiled** or (BrE also) **spoilt**) vt **1** ⟨party/surprise⟩ echar a perder, estropear; I don't want to ~ your fun but ... no les quiero aguar la fiesta pero ...; it will ~ your appetite te quitará el apetito **2** (overindulge) ⟨child⟩ consentir*, malcriar*; to be ~ed for choice tener* mucho de donde elegir
■ ~ vi **1** «food/meal» echarse a perder, estropearse **2** (be eager) (colloq): to be ~ing for a fight estar* or andar* buscando pelea

spoiled /spoɪld/, (BrE also) **spoilt** /spoɪlt/ adj mimado

spoils /spoɪlz/ pl n botín m

spoilsport /'spoɪlspɔːrt ‖ 'spoɪlspɔːt/ n (colloq) aguafiestas mf (fam)

spoilt[1] /spoɪlt/ (BrE) past & past p of SPOIL

spoilt[2] adj (BrE) ▶ SPOILED

spoke[1] /spəʊk/ n rayo m (de una rueda)

spoke[2] past of SPEAK

spoken[1] /'spəʊkən/ past p of SPEAK

spoken[2] adj (before n) hablado, oral

spokesman /'spəʊksmən/ n (pl -**men** /-mən/) portavoz m, vocero m (esp AmL)

spokesperson /'spəʊks,pɜːrsn ‖ 'spəʊks,pɜːsn/ n portavoz mf, vocero, -ra m,f (esp AmL)

spokeswoman /'spəʊks,wʊmən/ (pl -**women**) n portavoz f, vocera f (esp AmL)

sponge[1] /spʌndʒ/ n **1 (a)** (Zool) esponja f **(b)** (for bath) esponja f **2** (Culin) ~ **(cake)** bizcocho m, bizcochuelo m (CS)

sponge[2] vt pasar una esponja por
■ ~ vi: he lives by sponging on o off his relatives vive a costillas de sus parientes

sponsor[1] /'spɑːnsər ‖ 'spɒnsə(r)/ n **(a)** (of program, show, sporting event) patrocinador, -dora m,f, espónsor mf; (for the arts) mecenas mf **(b)** (for membership): you need two members to act as ~s te tienen que presentar dos socios **(c)** (of bill, motion) proponente mf

sponsor[2] vt **(a)** ⟨event/festival⟩ patrocinar; ⟨research/expedition⟩ subvencionar **(b)** ⟨applicant/application⟩ apoyar **(c)** ⟨bill/motion⟩ (present) presentar, proponer*; (support) apoyar

sponsorship /'spɑːnsərʃɪp ‖ 'spɒnsəʃɪp/ n patrocinio m; (of the arts) mecenazgo m

spontaneous /spɑːn'teɪniəs ‖ spɒn'teɪniəs/ adj espontáneo

S

spontaneously /spɑ:n'temɪəsli ‖spɒn'temɪəsli/ adv espontáneamente

spoof /spu:f/ n (colloq) parodia f, burla f

spooky /'spu:ki/ adj **-kier, -kiest** (colloq) espeluznante

spool /spu:l/ n carrete m, carretel m (AmL)

spoon /spu:n/ n cuchara f, (small) cucharita f

spoonfeed /'spu:nfi:d/ vt (past & past p **-fed**) ⟨baby⟩ darle* de comer en la boca a; **she ~s her students** se lo da todo mascado a sus alumnos

spoonful /'spu:nfʊl/ n (pl **~s** or **spoonsful**) cucharada f, (small) cucharadita f

sporadic /spə'rædɪk/ adj esporádico

sport¹ /spɔ:rt ‖spɔ:t/ n **1** deporte m **2** (person): **to be a good ~** (to be sporting) tener* espíritu deportivo; (to be understanding) ser* comprensivo

sport² vt ⟨clothes/hairstyle⟩ lucir*

sport³ adj (AmE) (a) (Sport) ⟨equipment⟩ de deportes (b) (casual) ⟨clothes⟩ sport adj inv, de sport

sporting /'spɔ:rtɪŋ ‖'spɔ:tɪŋ/ adj **1** (fair) ⟨spirit⟩ deportivo; **it's very ~ of you** es muy amable de tu parte **2** (no comp) (relating to sport) ⟨press/interests⟩ deportivo

sports /spɔ:rts ‖spɔ:ts/ adj (a) (Sport) ⟨page/program⟩ de deportes; **~ complex** polideportivo m (b) (casual) ⟨clothes/shirt⟩ sport adj inv

sports: ~ car n coche m deportivo, carro m sport (AmL exc CS), auto m sport or deportivo (CS); **~man** /'spɔ:rtsmən ‖/'spɔ:tsmən/ n (pl **-men** /-mən/) deportista m

sportsmanship /'spɔ:rtsmənʃɪp ‖'spɔ:tsmənʃɪp/ n espíritu m deportivo

sportswoman /'spɔ:rtswʊmən ‖'spɔ:tswʊmən/ n deportista f

sporty /'spɔ:rti ‖'spɔ:ti/ adj **-tier, -tiest** (a) ⟨person⟩ deportista (b) (Auto) deportivo

spot¹ /spɑ:t ‖spɒt/ n **1** (a) (dot — on material) lunar m, mota f; (— on animal's skin) mancha f (b) (blemish, stain) mancha f (c) (pimple) (BrE) grano m, espinilla f (AmL) **2** (a) (location, place) lugar m, sitio m; **on the ~:** **he had to decide on the ~** tuvo que decidir en ese mismo momento; **they were killed on the ~** los mataron allí mismo; **on-the-~ fine** multa que se paga en el acto (b) (difficult situation): **to be in a** (tight) **~** estar* en apuros **3** (a) (drop) gota f (b) (small amount) (BrE colloq) (no pl): **do you fancy a ~ of supper?** ¿quieres cenar algo?

spot² vt **-tt-** **1** ⟨error⟩ descubrir*; ⟨bargain⟩ encontrar*; **he ~ted her in the crowd** la vio or (AmL tb) la ubicó entre el gentío **2** (mark) (usu pass) manchar

spot check n: control o inspección realizada al azar

spotless /'spɑ:tləs ‖'spɒtlɪs/ adj ⟨clothes⟩ impecable; ⟨house⟩ limpísimo; ⟨reputation/record⟩ intachable

spotlight /'spɑ:tlaɪt ‖'spɒtlaɪt/ n (in theater) foco m; (on building) reflector m

spotted /'spɑ:təd ‖'spɒtɪd/ adj ⟨tie/material⟩ de or a lunares or motas

spotty /'spɑ:ti ‖'spɒti/ adj **-tier, -tiest** (BrE) ⟨skin⟩ lleno de granos; ⟨youth⟩ con la cara llena de granos

spouse /spaʊs/ n (frml or hum) cónyuge mf (frml)

spout¹ /spaʊt/ n (a) (of teapot, kettle) pico m, pitorro m (Esp) (b) (pipe — on gutter) canalón m; (— on fountain, gargoyle) caño m (c) (jet) chorro m

spout² vt ⟨oil/liquid⟩ arrojar or expulsar chorros de
■ **~** vi «liquid» salir* a chorros; «whale» expulsar chorros de agua

sprain¹ /spreɪn/ n esguince m, distensión f

sprain² vt hacerse* un esguince en, distenderse*

sprang /spræŋ/ past of SPRING¹

sprawl¹ /sprɔ:l/ vi «person» sentarse* (or tumbarse etc) de forma poco elegante

sprawl² n (of built-up area) expansión f

spray¹ /spreɪ/ vt (a) ⟨liquid⟩ pulverizar*, aplicar* con atomizador; ⟨paint⟩ aplicar* con pistola pulverizadora (b) ⟨plants⟩ rociar* (con atomizador)

spray² n **1** (a) (fine drops) rocío m (b) (liquid in spray form) espray m; (before n) ⟨deodorant/polish⟩ en aerosol, en espray; en atomizador (c) (implement) rociador m **2** (bunch) ramillete m

spread¹ /spred/ (past & past p **spread**) vt **1** (extend) ⟨arms/legs⟩ extender*; ⟨map/sails/ wings⟩ desplegar*; **you can ~ the cost over five years** se puede pagar el costo a lo largo de cinco años **2** (a) ⟨paint/glue⟩ extender*; ⟨seeds/sand⟩ esparcir*; **to ~ butter on a piece of toast** untar una tostada con mantequilla (b) ⟨knowledge/ news⟩ difundir; ⟨influence⟩ extender*; ⟨rumor⟩ hacer* correr; ⟨disease⟩ propagar*; ⟨fear⟩ sembrar*; ⟨ideas/culture⟩ diseminar
■ **~** vi **1** «disease» propagarse*; «liquid/fire» extenderse*; «ideas/culture» diseminarse; «panic/fear» cundir; «influence/revolt» extenderse* **2** (extend in space, time) extenderse* **3** «paint» extenderse*; «butter» untarse
■ **spread out** [v + adv] (a) (move apart) «troops» desplegarse* (b) (extend) extenderse*

spread² n **1** (diffusion — of disease) propagación f, (— of ideas) difusión f, diseminación f; (— of fire) propagación f **2** (of wings, sails) envergadura f **3** (Culin) (a) (meal) (colloq) festín m, banquete m (b) (paste) pasta para extender sobre pan, tostadas etc **4** (Journ, Print): **it was advertised in a full-page ~** venía anunciado a plana entera

spread: ~-eagled /'spred'i:gəld/ adj con los brazos y piernas abiertos; **~sheet** n hoja f de cálculo; (before n) **~sheet program** hoja f electrónica

spree /spri:/ n: **to go on a shopping ~** ir* de expedición a las tiendas

sprig /sprɪg/ n ramito m

sprightly /'spraɪtli/ adj **-lier, -liest** ⟨person⟩ lleno de brío; ⟨walk/step⟩ ágil

spring¹ /sprɪŋ/ (past **sprang** or (esp AmE) **sprung**; past p **sprung**) vi [1] (leap) saltar; **to ~ into action** entrar en acción [2] (a) (liter) ⟨⟨stream⟩⟩ surgir*, nacer*; ⟨⟨shoots⟩⟩ brotar (b) **to ~ FROM sth** ⟨ideas/doubts⟩ surgir* DE algo; ⟨⟨problem⟩⟩ provenir* DE algo

■ ~ vt (a) (produce suddenly): **to ~ a surprise on sb** darle* una sorpresa a algn (b) **to ~ a leak** empezar* a hacer agua

■ **spring up** [v + adv] ⟨⟨stores/housing estates⟩⟩ surgir*; ⟨⟨plant⟩⟩ brotar; ⟨⟨wind⟩⟩ levantarse

spring² n [1] (season) primavera f; **in (the) ~** en primavera; (before n) ⟨weather/showers⟩ primaveral [2] (Geog) manantial m, fuente f [3] (jump) salto m, brinco m [4] (a) (in watch, toy) resorte m; (in mattress) muelle m, resorte m (AmL) (b) (elasticity) (no pl) elasticidad f

spring: ~**board** n trampolín m; ~**clean** /'sprɪŋ'kliːn/ vi hacer* limpieza general; ~**cleaning** /'sprɪŋ'kliːnɪŋ/ n (no pl) limpieza f general; ~ **onion** n (BrE) cebolleta f, cebollino m; ~**time** n primavera f

springy /'sprɪŋi/ adj **-gier, -giest** ⟨mattress/grass⟩ mullido; ⟨floor⟩ elástico

sprinkle /'sprɪŋkəl/ vt (a) (scatter) **to ~ sth ON sth: to ~ water on the plants** rociar* las plantas con agua; **to ~ sugar on sth** espolvorear algo con azúcar (b) (cover) **to ~ sth WITH sth: ~ the board with flour** espolvoree la tabla con harina

sprinkler /'sprɪŋklər ‖ 'sprɪŋklə(r)/ n (a) (garden ~) aspersor m (b) (for firefighting) (usu pl) rociador m; (before n) ~ **system** sistema m de rociadores

sprint¹ /sprɪnt/ n (a) (fast run) (e)sprint m (b) (short race) (Sport) carrera f corta

sprint² vi (a) (Sport) (e)sprintar (b) (run fast): **I ~ed after him** salí corriendo tras él a toda velocidad

sprout¹ /spraʊt/ vt ⟨leaves/shoots⟩ echar

■ ~ vi ⟨⟨plant⟩⟩ echar retoños, retoñar*; ⟨⟨leaf⟩⟩ brotar, salir*; ⟨⟨seeds⟩⟩ germinar

sprout² n (a) (Brussels ~) col f or (AmS) repollito m de Bruselas (b) (shoot) brote m

spruce¹ /spruːs/ n (tree) picea f, abeto m falso

spruce² adj **sprucer, sprucest** ⟨appearance⟩ cuidado, acicalado; ⟨garden⟩ cuidado, arreglado

■ **spruce up** [v + o + adv, v + adv + o] ⟨garden/room⟩ arreglar

sprung /sprʌŋ/ past p & (esp AmE) past of SPRING¹

spry /spraɪ/ adj **-er, -est** lleno de vida, dinámico

spud /spʌd/ n (colloq) papa f or (Esp) patata f

spun¹ /spʌn/ past & past p of SPIN²

spun² adj ⟨silk/cotton⟩ hilado

spur¹ /spɜːr ‖ spɜː(r)/ n (a) (Equ) espuela f; **on the ~ of the moment** sin pensarlo (b) (stimulus) acicate m

spur² vt **-rr-** (a) (Equ) ⟨horse⟩ espolear (b) ~ (on) ⟨person/team⟩ estimular

spurious /'spjʊriəs ‖ 'spjʊəriəs/ adj ⟨document⟩ falso, espurio; ⟨argument⟩ falaz, espurio

spurn /spɜːrn ‖ spɜːn/ vt desdeñar, rechazar*

spurt¹ /spɜːrt ‖ spɜːt/ n (a) (of speed, activity) racha f; **to put on a ~** acelerar (b) (jet) chorro m

spurt² vi ⟨⟨liquid/steam⟩⟩ salir* a chorros

spy¹ /spaɪ/ n (pl **spies**) espía mf; (before n) ⟨story⟩ de espías, de espionaje; ~ **ring** red f de espionaje

spy² spies, spying, spied vi espiar*; **to ~ ON sb** espiar* a algn

■ ~ vt descubrir*, ver*

sq adj (= square): **220 ~** 220 m²

Sq (= Square) Pza.

squabble /'skwɑːbəl ‖ 'skwɒbəl/ vi pelear(se), reñir*

squad /skwɑːd ‖ skwɒd/ n (a) (Mil) pelotón m; (of workmen) cuadrilla f (b) (of policemen) brigada f; **drug ~** brigada f antidroga (c) (Sport) equipo m

squad car n (AmE) coche m or (AmL tb) auto m patrulla, patrullero m (CS, Per)

squadron /'skwɑːdrən ‖ 'skwɒdrən/ n (Mil, Aviat) escuadrón m; (Naut) escuadra f

squalid /'skwɑːləd ‖ 'skwɒlɪd/ adj (a) (dirty) ⟨existence/house⟩ miserable (b) (sordid) ⟨story/business⟩ sórdido

squall /skwɔːl/ n borrasca f, turbión m

squalor /'skwɑːlər ‖ 'skwɒlə(r)/ n miseria f

squander /'skwɑːndər ‖ 'skwɒndə(r)/ vt ⟨money⟩ despilfarrar; ⟨opportunity⟩ desaprovechar

square¹ /skwer ‖ skweə(r)/ n [1] (a) (shape) cuadrado m; (in fabric design) cuadro m (b) (on chessboard) casilla f, escaque m; (in crossword) casilla f; **to go back to ~ one** volver* a empezar desde cero [2] (in town, city) plaza f [3] (Math) cuadrado m

square² adj **squarer, squarest** [1] (a) ⟨box/table/block⟩ cuadrado; **the room is 15 feet ~** la habitación mide 15 (pies) por 15 (pies) (b) (having right angles) ⟨corner/edges⟩ en ángulo recto (c) ⟨face⟩ cuadrado; ⟨jaw⟩ angular [2] (Math) (before n) ⟨yard/mile⟩ cuadrado [3] (a) (fair, honest): **he'll give you a ~ deal** no te va a engañar (b) (large and wholesome) (before n) ⟨meal⟩ decente

square³ vt [1] (make square) ⟨angle/side⟩ cuadrar [2] (Math) elevar al cuadrado [3] (a) (settle, make even) ⟨debts/accounts⟩ pagar*, saldar (b) (reconcile) ⟨facts/principles⟩ conciliar

■ ~ vi ⟨⟨ideas/arguments⟩⟩ concordar*

■ **square up** [v + adv] (settle debts) (colloq) **to ~ up (WITH sb)** arreglar cuentas (CON algn)

square root n raíz f cuadrada

squash¹ /skwɑːʃ ‖ skwɒʃ/ n [1] (Sport) squash m [2] (drink) (BrE) refresco a base de extractos; **orange ~** naranjada f [3] (Bot, Culin) nombre genérico de varios tipos de calabaza y zapallo

squash² vt [1] (a) (crush) ⟨fruit/insect⟩ aplastar (b) (squeeze): **to ~ sth/sb in** meter algo/a algn (apretando) [2] (suppress, silence) (colloq) ⟨protests/rumors⟩ acallar

■ ~ vi (+ adv compl): **we all ~ed into his study** nos metimos todos en su despacho

squashy /'skwɑːʃi ‖ 'skwɒʃi/ adj **-shier, -shiest** ⟨fruit⟩ blando; ⟨ground⟩ húmedo y mullido

squat¹ /skwɑ:t ‖skwɒt/ vi -tt- **1** (crouch) agacharse, ponerse* en cuclillas **2** (in building, on land) ocupar un inmueble ajeno sin autorización

squat² adj -tt- ‹person› rechoncho y bajo; ‹building/church› achaparrado

squatter /'skwɑ:tər ‖'skwɒtə(r)/ n (in building) ocupante mf ilegal, ocupa or okupa mf (Esp), paracaidista mf (Méx)

squawk¹ /skwɔ:k/ n (of bird) graznido m

squawk² vi «bird» graznar; «person» chillar

squeak¹ /skwi:k/ n (of animal, person) chillido m; (of hinge) chirrido m; (of shoes) crujido m

squeak² vi «animal/person» chillar; «hinge» chirriar*; «shoes» crujir

squeaky /'skwi:ki/ adj -kier, -kiest ‹hinge/ pen› chirriante; ‹voice› chillón, de pito

squeal¹ /skwi:l/ vi (a) (make noise) «person/ animal» chillar; «brakes/tires» chirriar* (b) (inform) (colloq) cantar (fam), chivarse (Esp fam), sapear (Ven fam)

squeal² n (of animal) chillido m; (of person) grito m, chillido m; (of brakes, tires) chirrido m

squeamish /'skwi:mɪʃ/ adj impresionable, aprensivo

squeeze¹ /skwi:z/ n **1** (a) (application of pressure) apretón m; he gave her hand a ~ le dio un apretón de manos (b) (restrictions): a credit ~ una restricción crediticia (c) (hug) apretón m **2** (confined, restricted condition) (colloq) (no pl): it will be a (tight) ~ vamos (or van etc) a estar apretados

squeeze² vt (a) (press) ‹tube/pimple› apretar*, espichar (Col); ‹lemon› exprimir; to ~ a cloth (out) retorcer* un trapo (b) (extract) ‹liquid/juice› extraer*, sacar*; he tried to ~ more money out of them trató de sacarles más dinero (c) (force, fit) meter; I can ~ you in tomorrow morning le puedo hacer un huequito mañana por la mañana ■ ~ vi: he ~d in through the hole se metió por el agujero

squelch /skweltʃ/ vi «shoes/hooves» hacer* un ruido como de succión

squid /skwɪd/ n (pl ~) calamar m

squiggle /'skwɪgəl/ n garabato m

squint¹ /skwɪnt/ n bizquera f, estrabismo m

squint² vi (a) (attempting to see) entrecerrar* los ojos (b) (be cross-eyed) bizquear, torcer* la vista

squire /skwaɪr ‖'skwaɪə(r)/ n (a) (Hist, Mil) escudero m (b) (in UK: landowner) señor m

squirm /skwɜ:rm ‖skwɜ:m/ vi retorcerse*; she ~ed with embarrassment le dio mucha vergüenza, no sabía dónde meterse de la vergüenza

squirrel /'skwɜ:rl ‖'skwɪrəl/ n ardilla f

squirt¹ /skwɜ:rt ‖skwɜ:t/ n **1** (stream) chorrito m **2** (person) (colloq) mequetrefe m (fam)

squirt² vt ‹liquid› echar un chorro de ■ ~ vi «liquid» salir* a chorros

Sr (= **Senior**) Sr.

Sri Lanka /sri:'lɑ:ŋkə, ʃri:- ‖srɪ'læŋkə, ʃrɪ-/ n Sri Lanka m

St (a) (= **Saint**) S(an), Sta.; ~ **Thomas** Sto. Tomás (b) (= **Street**) c/

stab¹ /stæb/ n (a) (with knife) puñalada f,

cuchillada f; to have a ~ at sth intentar algo (b) (sudden sensation): a ~ of pain una punzada de dolor

stab² vt -bb- apuñalar, acuchillar; he had been ~bed to death había muerto apuñalado or acuchillado

stabbing¹ /'stæbɪŋ/ n apuñalamiento m

stabbing² adj ‹pain/sensation› punzante

stability /stə'bɪləti/ n estabilidad f

stabilize /'steɪbəlaɪz/ vt estabilizar* ■ ~ vi estabilizarse*

stable¹ /'steɪbəl/ adj -bler, -blest (a) (firm, steady) estable (b) (Psych) equilibrado

stable² n (often pl) (for horses) caballeriza f, cuadra f; (for other livestock) establo m

staccato /stə'kɑ:təʊ/ adj (Mus) staccato

stack¹ /stæk/ n (a) (pile) montón m, pila f (b) (many, much) (colloq) (often pl) montón m (fam), pila f (AmS fam)

stack² vt ~ (up) amontonar, apilar

stadium /'steɪdiəm/ n (pl -diums or -dia /-diə/) estadio m

staff¹ /stæf ‖stɑ:f/ n **1** (a) (as group) (+ sing o pl vb) personal m; the teaching ~ el personal docente; a member of ~ un empleado (b) (as individuals) (BrE) (pl ~) (+ pl vb) empleados mpl **2** (pl staffs or staves /steɪvz/) (stick) bastón m; (of bishop) báculo m, cayado m **3** (Mus) ▶ STAVE 2

staff² vt proveer* de personal

staffroom /'stæfrʊm, -ru:m ‖'stɑ:fru:m, -rʊm/ n (BrE) sala f de profesores

stag /stæg/ n ciervo m, venado m

stage¹ /steɪdʒ/ n **1** (a) (platform) tablado m; (in theater) escenario m; (before n) ~ door entrada f de artistas (b) (medium, profession) the ~ el teatro; (before n) ~ name nombre m artístico **2** (in development, activity) fase f, etapa f; at some ~ en algún momento

stage² vt **1** (a) ‹event› organizar*, montar; ‹strike/demonstration› hacer*; ‹attack› llevar a cabo; ‹coup› dar* (b) (engineer, arrange) arreglar, orquestar **2** (Theat) ‹play› poner* en escena

stage: ~**coach** n diligencia f; ▶ **fright** n miedo m a salir a escena; ~**hand** n tramoyista mf; ~**manage** vt ‹event› orquestar, arreglar; ~ **manager** n director, -tora m,f de escena

stagger /'stægər ‖'stægə(r)/ vi tambalearse ■ ~ vt **1** (amaze) dejar estupefacto **2** ‹shifts/ payments› escalonar

staggering /'stægərɪŋ/ adj asombroso

stagnant /'stægnənt/ adj estancado

stagnate /'stægneɪt ‖stæg'neɪt/ vi «water/ economy» estancarse*; «person» anquilosarse

stag: ~ **night** n (for men only) ▶ PARTY A; ~ **party** n (a) (before wedding) despedida f de soltero (b) (all-male celebration) fiesta f para hombres, noche f de cuates (Méx)

staid /steɪd/ adj -er, -est serio, formal; ‹clothes› serio, sobrio; (pej) aburrido

stain¹ /steɪn/ n (a) (dirty mark) mancha f (b) (dye) tintura f, tinte m (c) (on character) mancha f

stain² vt (a) ‹clothes/skin› manchar (b) (dye) ‹wood› teñir* ■ ~ vi manchar

stained glass ··◆ stand ···

stained glass /steind/ n vidrio m or cristal m de colores; (before n) ~ ~ **window** vitral m, vidriera f (de colores)

stainless steel /'steinləs ‖'steinlɪs/ n acero m inoxidable

stain remover n quitamanchas m

stair /ster ‖stea(r)/ n **(a) stairs** pl (flight of stairs, stairway) escalera(s) f(pl) **(b)** (single step) escalón m, peldaño m

stair: ~**case,** ~**way** n escalera(s) f(pl); ~**well** n caja f or hueco m or (Méx) cubo m de la escalera

stake¹ /steik/ n **1** (pole) estaca f **2 (a)** (bet) apuesta f; **to be at** ~ estar* en juego **(b)** (interest): **to have a** ~ **in a company** tener* participación or intereses en una compañía

stake² vt **1** (risk) ‹money/reputation› jugarse* **2 (a)** (mark with stakes) marcar* con estacas, estacar*; **the government was quick to** ~ **its claim** el gobierno se apresuró a reclamar su parte **(b)** ‹tree/plant› arrodrigar*

stalactite /stə'læktait ‖'stæləktait/ n estalactita f

stalagmite /stə'lægmait ‖'stæləgmait/ n estalagmita f

stale /steil/ adj **staler, stalest** ‹bread› no fresco; ‹butter/cheese› rancio; ‹beer› pasado; ‹air› viciado; ‹joke› añejo, viejo; ‹ideas› trasnochado

stalemate /'steilmeit/ n (in chess) tablas fpl (por ahogar al rey); **to be at a** ~ estar* en un punto muerto

stalk¹ /stɔːk/ n (of plant) tallo m; (of leaf, flower) pedúnculo m, tallo m; (of fruit) rabillo m

stalk² vt acechar
■ ~ vi: **to** ~ **off** irse* ofendido/indignado

stall¹ /stɔːl/ n **1** (in market) puesto m, tenderete m **2 stalls** pl (in theater, movie house) (BrE) platea f, patio m de butacas **3** (in stable) compartimiento m

stall² vi **1** ‹‹engine/car›› pararse, calarse (Esp), atascarse* (Méx) **2** (play for time) (colloq): **quit** ~**ing** no andes con rodeos or con evasivas
■ ~ vt **1** ‹engine/car› parar, calar (Esp), atascar* (Méx) **2** (delay) (colloq) entretener*

stallion /'stæljən/ n semental m

stalwart /'stɔːlwart ‖'stɔːlwət/ adj ‹supporter› incondicional, fiel

stamina /'stæmənə ‖'stæminə/ n resistencia f

stammer¹ /'stæmər ‖'stæmə(r)/ n tartamudeo m

stammer² vi tartamudear

stamp¹ /stæmp/ n **1** (postage ~) sello m, estampilla f (AmL), timbre m (Méx); (before n) ~ **collecting** filatelia f; ~ **collector** coleccionista mf de sellos (or estampillas etc), filatelista mf **2 (a)** (instrument) sello m **(b)** (printed mark) sello m **3** (character) impronta f; **she left her** ~ **on the institute** dejó su impronta en el instituto

stamp² vt **1** (with foot) ‹ground› dar* una patada en; **to** ~ **one's foot** dar* una patada en el suelo **2** ‹letter/parcel› franquear, ponerle* sellos (or estampillas etc) a, estampillar (AmL), timbrar (Méx); **a** ~**ed addressed envelope** un sobre franqueado or (AmL tb) estampillado or (Méx) timbrado con su dirección **3 (a)** ‹passport/ticket› sellar **(b)** ‹coin› acuñar
■ ~ vi ‹‹person›› dar* patadas en el suelo; ‹‹horse›› piafar; **he** ~**ed on the spider** le dio un pisotón a la araña
■ **stamp out** [v + o + adv, v + adv + o] **(a)** ‹fire› apagar* (con los pies) **(b)** (suppress) ‹resistance› aplastar; ‹rebellion› sofocar*; ‹crime› erradicar*

stampede¹ /stæm'piːd/ n estampida f

stampede² vi salir* en estampida

stance /stæns ‖stɑːns/ n postura f

stand¹ /stænd/ n **1 (a)** (position) lugar m **(b)** (attitude) postura f **(c)** (resistance) resistencia f; **to make a** ~ **against sth** oponer* resistencia a algo **2 (a)** (base) pie m, base f **(b)** (for coats, hats) perchero m **3** (at fair, exhibition) stand m, caseta f; **newspaper** ~ puesto m de periódicos; **a hot-dog** ~ (esp AmE) un puesto de perritos calientes **4** (for spectators) (often pl) tribuna f **5** (witness box) (AmE) estrado m

stand² (past & past p **stood**) vi **1 (a)** (be, remain upright) ‹‹person›› estar* de pie, estar* parado (AmL) **(b)** (rise) levantarse, ponerse* de pie, pararse (AmL); **her hair stood on end** se le pusieron los pelos de punta, se le pararon los pelos (AmL); see also STAND UP **2** (move, take up position) ponerse*, pararse (AmL); ~ **over there** ponte or (AmL) párate allí; **to** ~ **aside** hacerse* a un lado; **to** ~ **on one's head** pararse de cabeza (AmL), hacer* el pino (Esp) **3 (a)** (be situated, located): **a church stood here long ago** hace mucho tiempo aquí había una iglesia; **I won't** ~ **in your way** no seré yo quien te lo impida **(b)** (hold position): **where do you** ~ **on this issue?** ¿cuál es tu posición en cuanto a este problema?; **you never know where you** ~ **with him** con él uno nunca sabe a qué atenerse **(c)** (be mounted, fixed): **a hut** ~**ing on wooden piles** una choza construida sobre pilotes de madera **4 (a)** (stop, remain still) ‹‹person›; **they stood and stared** se quedaron mirando; **time stood still** el tiempo se detuvo **(b)** (Culin) ‹‹batter/water››: **leave to** ~ dejar reposar **(c)** (survive, last): **the tower is still** ~**ing** la torre sigue en pie **5** (remain unchanged, valid) ‹‹law/agreement›› seguir* vigente; **the offer still** ~**s** la oferta sigue en pie **6 (a)** (be currently): **as things** ~ tal (y) como están las cosas **(b)** (be likely to): **to** ~ **to** + INF: **she** ~**s to lose a fortune** puede llegar a perder una fortuna; **what does she** ~ **to gain out of this?** ¿qué es lo que puede ganar con esto? **7** (for office, election) (BrE) presentarse (como candidato)
■ ~ vt **1** (place) poner*; (carefully, precisely) colocar* **2 (a)** (tolerate, bear) (with CAN, CAN'T, WON'T) ‹pain/noise› aguantar, soportar; **I can't** ~ **him** no lo aguanto or soporto; **I can't** ~ **it any longer!** ¡no puedo más!; **she can't** ~ **being interrupted** no soporta que la interrumpan **(b)** (withstand) ‹heat/strain› soportar
■ **stand back** [v + adv] (move away) **to** ~ **back** (FROM sth) apartarse (DE algo)
■ **stand by** **1** [v + adv] **(a)** (remain uninvolved) mantenerse* al margen; **people just stood by and did nothing** la gente estaba allí mirando sin hacer nada **(b)** (be at readiness) ‹‹army/troops›› estar* en estado de alerta **2** [v + prep + o] **(a)** ‹promise› mantener*; ‹decision› atenerse* a **(b)** (support) ‹friend› apoyar ···▷

■ **stand down** [v + adv] (relinquish position) retirarse; (resign) renunciar, dimitir

■ **stand for** [v + prep + o] **(a)** (represent) «*initials/symbol*» significar*; **CTI ~s for ...** CTI son las siglas de ...; **he has betrayed everything he once stood for** ha traicionado todo aquello con lo que solía identificar* **(b)** (put up with) (*usu with neg*) consentir*

■ **stand in** [v + adv] **to ~ in FOR sb** sustituir* a algn

■ **stand out** [v + adv] **(a)** (project) **to ~ out** (FROM sth) sobresalir* (DE algo) **(b)** (be conspicuous, contrast) sobresalir*, destacar(se)*; «*color*» resaltar

■ **stand up** ⊡ [v + adv] **(a)** (get up) ponerse* de pie, levantarse, pararse (AmL) **(b)** (be, remain standing): **~ up straight** ponte derecho **(c)** (endure, withstand wear) resistir; **to ~ up TO sth** ⟨*to cold/ pressure*⟩ resistir *or* soportar algo; *see also* STAND UP TO

⊡ [v + o + adv] **(a)** (set upright) poner* de pie, levantar **(b)** (not keep appointment with) (colloq) dejar plantado a (fam)

■ **stand up for** [v + adv + prep + o] defender*; **I can ~ up for myself** me puedo defender solo

■ **stand up to** [v + adv + prep + o] ⟨*person; threats*⟩ hacerle* frente a; *see also* STAND UP 1C

standard¹ /'stændərd ‖'stændəd/ n ⊡ **(a)** (level) nivel m; (quality) calidad f; **~ of living** nivel m *or* estándar m de vida **(b)** (norm): **she sets very high ~s** exige un estándar *or* nivel muy alto; **the product was below ~** el producto no era de la calidad requerida **(c)** (official measure) estándar m ⊡ **(a)** (yardstick) criterio m, parámetro m **(b) standards** pl (moral principles) principios mpl ⊡ (flag, emblem) estandarte m

standard² adj ⊡ (normal) ⟨*size*⟩ estándar adj inv, normal; ⟨*model*⟩ (Auto) estándar adj inv, de serie; ⟨*procedure*⟩ habitual; ⟨*reaction*⟩ típico; **~ rate** tarifa f normal ⊡ (officially established) ⟨*weight; measure*⟩ estándar adj inv, oficial; **~ time** hora f oficial

standardization /ˌstændərdə'zeɪʃən ‖ˌstændədaɪ'zeɪʃən/ n estandarización f

standardize /'stændərdaɪz ‖'stændədaɪz/ vt estandarizar*

standard lamp n (BrE) lámpara f de pie

standby¹ /'stændbaɪ/ n (pl **-bys**) **(a)** (thing one can turn to): **frozen meals are a useful ~** las comidas congeladas son muy socorridas **(b)** (state of readiness): **to be on ~** «*police/squadron*» estar* en estado de alerta **(c)** (Aviat) stand-by m

standby² adj (before n) **(a)** (ready for emergency) de emergencia; **to be on ~ duty** estar* de guardia **(b)** (Aviat) ⟨*passenger/ticket/fare*⟩ stand-by adj inv

stand-in /'stændɪn/ n suplente mf; (Cin) doble mf

standing¹ /'stændɪŋ/ n **(a)** (position) posición f; (prestige) prestigio m **(b)** (duration): **friends of more than 20 years' ~** amigos desde hace más de 20 años

standing² adj (before n, no comp) **(a)** (permanent) permanente; **~ charge** cuota f fija; (for utilities) cuota f abono; **it's a ~ joke that he never pays for a single drink** tiene fama de no invitar nunca a una copa **(b)** (upright, not seated) ⟨*passenger*⟩ de pie, parado (AmL)

standing order n **(a)** (with bank) (BrE) orden f permanente de pago **(b)** (with supplier) pedido m fijo

stand: **~off** n (AmE) **(a)** (tie, draw) empate m **(b)** (deadlock) callejón m sin salida; **~point** n punto m de vista; **~still** n (no pl): **to be at a ~still** «*traffic*» estar* paralizado; **to come to a ~still** «*vehicle*» parar; «*city/factory*» quedar paralizado

stank /stæŋk/ past of STINK²

staple¹ /'steɪpl/ n ⊡ (for fastening paper, cloth etc) grapa f, ganchito m, corchete m (Chi) ⊡ **(a)** (basic food) alimento m básico **(b)** (principal product) producto m principal

staple² adj ⟨*food/ingredient*⟩ básico; ⟨*industry*⟩ principal; **rice is their ~ diet** se alimentan principalmente a base de arroz

staple³ vt grapar, engrapar (AmL), corchetear (Chi)

stapler /'steɪplər ‖'steɪplə(r)/ n grapadora f, engrapadora f (AmL), corchetera f (Chi)

star¹ /stɑːr ‖stɑː(r)/ n ⊡ (in sky) estrella f; (Astrol, Astron) astro m; (before n) **~ sign** signo m del zodíaco ⊡ (symbol) estrella f; (asterisk) asterisco m; **a four-~ hotel** un hotel de cuatro estrellas; **four-~ petrol** (BrE) gasolina f or (RPl) nafta f súper, bencina f especial (Andes) ⊡ (celebrity) estrella f

star² **-rr-** vt: **the famous film which ~red Bogart and Bergman** la famosa película que tuvo como protagonistas a Bogart y Bergman; **'2005', ~ring Mike Kirnon** '2005', con (la actuación estelar de) Mike Kirnon

■ **~** vi: **to ~ in a film** protagonizar* una película

starboard¹ /'stɑːrbərd ‖'stɑːbəd/ n estribor m

starboard² adj (before n) de estribor

starch /stɑːrtʃ ‖stɑːtʃ/ n **(a)** (in food, for clothes) almidón m **(b)** (starchy food) fécula f, almidón m

starchy /'stɑːrtʃi ‖'stɑːtʃi/ adj **-chier, -chiest** ⟨*diet*⟩ a base de féculas *or* de almidones

stardom /'stɑːrdəm ‖'stɑːdəm/ n estrellato m

stare¹ /ster ‖steə(r)/ vi mirar (*fijamente*); **to ~ AT sth/sb** mirar algo/a algn fijamente

stare² n mirada f (fija)

starfish /'stɑːrfɪʃ ‖'stɑːfɪʃ/ n (pl **-fish**) estrella f de mar

stark¹ /stɑːrk ‖stɑːk/ adj **-er, -est** ⟨*landscape*⟩ agreste; ⟨*truth*⟩ escueto; ⟨*realism*⟩ descarnado

stark² adv: **~ naked** completamente desnudo

starlet /'stɑːrlət ‖'stɑːlɪt/ n starlet(te) f (*joven actriz que aspira al estrellato*)

starling /'stɑːrlɪŋ ‖'stɑːlɪŋ/ n estornino m

starry /'stɑːri/ adj **-rier, -riest** estrellado

starry-eyed /ˌstɑːri'aɪd/ adj **(a)** (full of illusions) ⟨*person*⟩ iluso, soñador **(b)** (dreamy): **she gazed at him all ~** lo miraba arrobada

s

star: S∼s and Stripes n the S∼s and Stripes la bandera de las barras y las estrellas;
 ∼-spangled /'stɑːr,spæŋgəld ‖'stɑːˌspæŋgəld/ adj (liter) ⟨sky/heavens⟩ tachonado de estrellas (liter); **S∼-Spangled Banner** n the S∼-Spangled Banner el himno de las barras y las estrellas (himno nacional de EEUU)

start¹ /stɑːrt ‖stɑːt/ n **1 (a)** (beginning) principio m, comienzo m; from ∼ to finish del principio al fin; **to make a ∼ (ON sth)** empezar* (algo); **to make an early ∼** empezar* temprano; (on a journey) salir* temprano **(b) for a ∼** (as linker) para empezar **2** (Sport) **(a)** (of race) salida f **(b)**, (lead, advantage) ventaja f **3** (jump): **to give sb a ∼** darle* or pegarle* un susto a algn; **I woke up with a ∼** me desperté sobresaltado

start² vt **1** (begin) empezar*, comenzar*; **I ∼ work at eight** empiezo a trabajar a las ocho; **to ∼ -ING, to ∼ to + INF** empezar* A + INF
 2 (cause to begin) ⟨race⟩ dar* comienzo a, largar* (CS, Méx); ⟨fire/epidemic⟩ provocar*; ⟨argument/fight⟩ empezar*; ⟨war⟩ «incident» desencadenar
 3 (establish) ⟨business⟩ abrir*; ⟨organization⟩ fundar
 4 (cause to operate) ⟨engine/dishwasher⟩ encender*, prender (AmL); ⟨car⟩ arrancar*
 ■ ∼ vi
 I 1 (a) (begin) empezar*, comenzar*; **to get ∼ed** empezar*, comenzar*; **to ∼ BY -ING** empezar* POR + INF; **∼ing (from)** next January a partir del próximo mes de enero **(b) to ∼ with** (as linker) primero, para empezar
 2 (originate) empezar*, originarse
 3 (set out) (+ adv compl): **to ∼ back** emprender el regreso; **we ∼ from the hotel at six** salimos del hotel a las seis
 4 (begin to operate) «car» arrancar*
 II (move suddenly) dar* un respingo; (be frightened) asustarse, sobresaltarse
 ■ **start off 1** [v + adv] **(a)** ▶ START OUT A **(b)** (begin moving) arrancar* **(c)** (begin) empezar*
 2 [v + o + adv, v + adv + o] (begin) ⟨discussion/concert⟩ empezar*
 3 [v + o + adv] (get sb started): **I'll do the first one, just to ∼ you off** yo haré el primero, para ayudarte a empezar
 ■ **start out** [v + adv] **(a)** (set out) salir* **(b)** (in life, career) empezar* **(c)** (begin) **to ∼ out (BY) -ING: we ∼ed out (by) thinking it would be easy** empezamos pensando que sería fácil
 ■ **start over** (AmE) [v + adv] [v + o + adv] volver* a empezar
 ■ **start up 1** [v + adv] **(a)** ▶ START vi I 4 **(b)** (begin business) empezar*
 2 [v + o + adv, v + adv + o] **(a)** ⟨engine/car/machinery⟩ arrancar*, poner* en marcha **(b)** ⟨business⟩ montar **(c)** ⟨conversation⟩ entablar; ⟨discussion⟩ empezar*

starter /'stɑːrtər ‖'stɑːtə(r)/ n **1** (Culin) entrada f, primer plato m, entrante m (Esp) **2** (Auto) (∼ motor) motor m de arranque

starting /'stɑːrtɪŋ/: ∼ **line** n línea f de salida; ∼ **point** n ∼ point (FOR sth) punto m de partida (DE/PARA algo)

startle /'stɑːrt‖'stɑːt‖/ vt sobresaltar, asustar

startling /'stɑːrtlɪŋ ‖'stɑːtlɪŋ/ adj **(a)** (surprising) asombroso; ⟨similarity/coincidence⟩ extraordinario **(b)** (alarming) ⟨report/increase⟩ alarmante

starvation /stɑːr'veɪʃən ‖stɑː'veɪʃən/ n hambre f‡, inanición f

starve /stɑːrv ‖stɑːv/ vt **(a)** (deny food) privar de comida a; **I'm ∼d** (AmE colloq) me muero de hambre **(b)** (deprive) **to ∼ sth/sb OF sth** privar algo/a algn DE algo
 ■ ∼ vi (die) morirse* de hambre or de inanición; (feel hungry) pasar hambre; **I'm starving** (BrE colloq) me muero de hambre

starving /'stɑːrvɪŋ ‖'stɑːvɪŋ/ adj hambriento, famélico

stash /stæʃ/ vt ∼ **(away)** (colloq) (hide) esconder; (save) ir* ahorrando

state¹ /steɪt/ n
 I 1 (a) (nation) estado m; (before n) ∼ **visit** visita f oficial **(b)** (division of country) estado m; **the S∼s** los Estados Unidos
 2 (Govt) estado m; (before n) (esp BrE) ⟨control/funding⟩ estatal; ∼ **school** escuela f pública or estatal
 3 (pomp): **to lie in ∼** yacer* en capilla ardiente
 II (condition) estado m; ∼ **of war/emergency** estado de guerra/emergencia; ∼ **of mind** estado de ánimo; **I was in no (fit) ∼ to make a decision** no estaba en condiciones de tomar una decisión; **the kitchen is in a ∼** (colloq) la cocina está hecha un asco (fam)

state² vt «person» ⟨facts/case⟩ exponer*; ⟨problem⟩ plantear; ⟨name/address⟩ (in writing) escribir*; (orally) decir*; «law/document» establecer*; **he ∼d that he had seen her there earlier** afirmó haberla visto antes allí

State Department n (in US) the ∼ ∼ el Departamento de Estado de los EEUU, ≈el Ministerio de Asuntos Exteriores or de Relaciones Exteriores

stately /'steɪtli/ adj **-lier, -liest** majestuoso

stately home n (in UK) casa f solariega

statement /'steɪtmənt/ n **1 (a)** (declaration) declaración f, afirmación f; **official** ∼ comunicado m oficial **(b)** (to police, in court) declaración f
 2 (bank) ∼ estado m or extracto m de cuenta

state: ∼**-of-the-art** /'steɪtəvðiˈɑːrt ‖ˌsteɪtəvðiˈɑːt/ adj último modelo adj inv;
 S∼side, ∼side adv (AmE colloq) en/a/hacia los Estados Unidos

statesman /'steɪtsmən/ n (pl **-men** /-mən/) estadista m, hombre m de estado

static¹ /'stætɪk/ adj **1** ⟨situation⟩ estacionario **2** ⟨electricity⟩ estático

static² n **(a)** (electricity) electricidad f estática **(b)** (interference) estática f

station¹ /'steɪʃən/ n **1 (a)** (Rail) estación f **(b)** (bus ∼) estación f or terminal f de autobuses **2** (place of operations) **research** ∼ centro m de investigación; see also FIRE STATION, POLICE STATION etc **3** (TV) canal m; (Rad) emisora f or (AmL tb) estación f (de radio)

station² vt **(a)** (position) ⟨sentries⟩ apostar* **(b)** (post) (usu pass) ⟨personnel⟩ destinar; ⟨fleet/troops⟩ emplazar*

stationary /'steɪʃənəri ‖'steɪʃənəri/ adj ⟨object/vehicle⟩ estacionario

stationery /'steɪʃənəri ‖'steɪʃənəri/ n **(a)** (writing materials) artículos mpl de papelería or de escritorio **(b)** (writing paper) papel m y sobres mpl de carta

s

station: ~ **house** n (AmE) (a) (police station) comisaría f (b) ▶ FIRE STATION; ~**master** n jefe, -fa m,f de estación; ~ **wagon** n (AmE) ranchera f, (coche m) familiar m, camioneta f (AmL)

statistic /stə'tɪstɪk/ n estadística f; **the ~s show that ...** las estadísticas demuestran que ...

statistical /stə'tɪstɪkəl/ adj estadístico

statistics /stə'tɪstɪks/ n (+ sing vb) estadística f

statue /'stætʃu: ‖'stætʃu:, 'stætʃu:/ n estatua f

stature /'stætʃər ‖'stætʃə(r)/ n (a) (status) talla f (b) (height) (frml) estatura f, talla f

status /'stætəs ‖'steɪtəs/ n (pl -tuses) (a) (category, situation): **the group has no official ~** el grupo no está oficialmente reconocido como tal; **financial ~** situación f económica (b) (social ~) posición f social, estatus m (c) (kudos) estatus m; (before n) ~ **symbol** símbolo m de estatus

status quo /kwəʊ/ n statu quo m

statute /'stætʃu:t ‖'stætju:t, 'stætʃu:t/ n ley f

statutory /'stætʃu:tɔ:ri ‖'stætʃʊtəri, 'stætʃu:təri/ adj (right/obligation) legal; (penalty) establecido por la ley

staunch /stɔ:ntʃ/ adj -er, -est (supporter) incondicional; (Protestant) acérrimo

stave /steɪv/ n [1] (of barrel, hull) duela f [2] (Mus) pentagrama m

■ **stave off** [v + o + adv, v + adv + o] (defeat/ disaster) evitar; (danger) conjurar

staves (a) pl of STAFF[1] 2A (b) pl of STAVE

stay[1] /steɪ/ vi [1] (a) (in specified place, position) quedarse; ~ **there** quédate ahí; **to ~ put** quedarse (b) (in specified state): ~ **still** quédate quieto; **we ~ed friends** seguimos siendo amigos [2] (a) (remain, not leave) quedarse (b) (reside temporarily) quedarse; (in a hotel etc) hospedarse, alojarse, quedarse; **he's ~ing with us over Easter** va a pasar la Semana Santa con nosotros

■ **stay away** [v + adv] **to ~ away FROM sth/sb** no acercarse* A algo/algn

■ **stay in** [v + adv] (remain in position) quedarse en su sitio; (remain indoors) quedarse en casa

■ **stay on** [v + adv] (a) (remain in position) «hat/ top» quedarse en su sitio (b) (at school, in job) quedarse

■ **stay out** [v + adv] (a) (not come home): **to ~ out late** quedarse fuera hasta tarde; **he usually ~s out late** normalmente no vuelve hasta tarde (b) (out of doors) quedarse fuera

■ **stay out of** [v + adv + prep + o] (a) (avoid) (trouble) no meterse en; ~ **out of the sun** quédate a la sombra (b) (not get involved in) (argument) no meterse en

■ **stay up** [v + adv] (a) (not fall or sink) «tent/ pole» sostenerse* (b) (not go to bed) quedarse levantado

stay[2] n [1] (time) estadía f (AmL), estancia f (Esp, Méx); **during her ~ in hospital** mientras estuvo en el hospital [2] (Law): ~ **of execution** suspensión f del cumplimiento de la sentencia

staying power /'steɪɪŋ/ n resistencia f, aguante m

stead /sted/ n: **in sb's ~** (liter) en lugar de algn; **to stand sb in good ~** resultarle muy útil a algn

steadfast /'stedfæst ‖'stedfɑ:st/ adj (liter) (refusal) firme, categórico; (resolve) inquebrantable

steadily /'stedli ‖'stedɪli/ adv (a) (constantly, gradually) (breathe/beat/work) regularmente (b) (incessantly) (rain/work) sin cesar, sin parar (c) (not shaking) (gaze) fijamente; (walk) con paso seguro

steady[1] /'stedi/ adj -dier, -diest [1] (not shaky) (gaze) fijo; (chair/table/ladder) firme, seguro; **with a ~ hand** con pulso firme; **hold the camera ~** no muevas la cámara [2] (a) (constant) (rain/speed/pace) constante; (flow/stream) continuo (b) (regular) (before n) (job) fijo; (income) regular; ~ **boyfriend** novio m; ~ **girlfriend** novia f (c) (dependable) (person/worker) serio, formal

steady[2] vt -dies, -dying, -died (a) (make stable) (table/ladder) (by holding) sujetar (para que no se mueva) (b) (make calm) calmar, tranquilizar*

steak /steɪk/ n (a) bistec m, filete m, churrasco m (CS), bife m (RPl, Bol) (b) (cut) carne f para filete o bistec etc)

steal /sti:l/ (past **stole**; past p **stolen**) vt [1] (object/idea) robar; **to ~ sth FROM sb** robarle algo a algn; **to ~ a glance at sth/sb** (liter) echar una mirada furtiva a algo/algn [2] **stolen** past p (money/property) robado

■ ~ vi [1] robar [2] (go stealthily) (+ adv compl): **to ~ away** o **off** escabullirse*; **they stole into the room** entraron en la habitación a hurtadillas

stealth /stelθ/ n sigilo m

stealthy /'stelθi/ adj -thier, -thiest (movement/departure) furtivo; (footsteps) sigiloso

steam[1] /sti:m/ n vapor m; **to let off ~** desahogarse*; **to run out of ~** perder* ímpetu

steam[2] vt (Culin) (vegetables/rice) cocinar o cocer* al vapor; (pudding) cocinar o cocer* al baño (de) María

■ ~ vi [1] (give off steam) echar vapor; «hot food» humear

■ **steam up** [v + adv] «window/glass» empañarse

steam: ~**boat** n vapor m, barco m de or a vapor; ~ **engine** n (a) (Mech Eng) motor m de or a vapor (b) (esp BrE Rail) locomotora f or máquina f de or a vapor

steamer /'sti:mər ‖'sti:mə(r)/ n [1] (Naut) vapor m, buque m or barco m de or a vapor [2] (cooking vessel) vaporera f

steam: ~**roller** n apisonadora f, aplanadora f (AmL); ~**ship** n ▶ STEAMER 1

steamy /'sti:mi/ adj -mier, -miest (room/ atmosphere) lleno de vapor; (window/glass) empañado

steel[1] /sti:l/ n (Metall) acero m

steel[2] v refl **to ~ oneself FOR sth/to + INF** armarse de valor PARA algo/PARA + INF

steel wool n lana f de acero, virulana® f (Arg), fibra f metálica (Méx)

steely /'sti:li/ adj -lier, -liest (gaze/ expression) duro; (determination) férreo

steep[1] /sti:p/ adj -er, -est [1] (a) (slope) empinado; (drop) brusco; (descent) en picada or (Esp) en picado (b) (large) (increase/decline) considerable [2] (colloq) (prices) alto, excesivo

steep² vt (to soften, clean) remojar; (to flavor) macerar

steeple /'sti:pəl/ n aguja f, campanario m

steeple: ∼**chase** n carrera f de obstáculos; ∼**jack** n: *persona que repara chimeneas, torres etc*

steeply /'sti:pli/ adv (a) ⟨slope/rise/fall⟩ abruptamente (b) ⟨increase/decline⟩ considerablemente

steer¹ /stɪr ‖stɪə(r)/ n (a) (castrated bull) buey m (b) (young bull) novillo m

steer² vt (a) ⟨vehicle/plane⟩ dirigir*, conducir*; ⟨ship⟩ gobernar* (b) (guide) llevar, conducir* ■ ∼ vi (Naut) estar* or ir* al timón; (Auto) ir* al volante; **to** ∼ **clear of sth/sb** evitar algo/a algn

steering /'stɪrɪŋ ‖'stɪərɪŋ/ n dirección f

steering wheel n (Auto) volante m

stem¹ /stem/ n **1** (of plant) tallo m; (of leaf) pecíolo m, peciolo m; (of fruit) pedúnculo m **2** (of glass) pie m

stem² -mm- vt ⟨flow/bleeding⟩ contener*; ⟨outbreak/decline⟩ detener* ■ ∼ vi **to** ∼ **FROM sth** provenir* DE algo

stench /stentʃ/ n fetidez f

stencil¹ /'stensəl ‖'stensɪl/ n (a) (for lettering, decoration) plantilla f, troquel m (b) (for duplicating) stencil m, cliché m (Esp)

stencil² vt, (BrE) -ll- ⟨design/pattern⟩ escribir, dibujar o pintar utilizando una plantilla

stenographer /stə'nɑ:grəfər ‖ste'nɒgrəfə(r)/ n (esp AmE) taquígrafo, -fa m,f, estenógrafo, -fa m,f

stenography /stə'nɑ:grəfi ‖ste'nɒgrəfi/ n (AmE) taquigrafía f, estenografía f

step¹ /step/ n **1** (footstep, pace) paso m; **to take a** ∼ **forward** dar* un paso adelante; **to watch one's** ∼ andarse* con cuidado **2** (a) (of dance) paso m (b) (in marching, walking) paso m; **to be in/out of** ∼ llevar/no llevar el paso **3** (measure) medida f; **to take** ∼**s (to + INF)** tomar medidas (PARA + INF) **4** (on stair) escalón m, peldaño m; (on ladder) travesaño m, escalón m **5** (AmE Mus): **whole** ∼ tono m; **half** ∼ semitono m

step² -pp- vi: would you ∼ inside/outside for a moment? ¿quiere pasar/salir un momento?; **to** ∼ **off a plane** bajarse de un avión; **to** ∼ **IN/ON sth** pisar algo
■ **step aside** [v + adv] hacerse* a un lado
■ **step back** [v + adv] (a) (move back) dar* un paso atrás (b) (become detached) **to** ∼ **back (FROM sth)** distanciarse (DE algo)
■ **step down** [v + adv] (a) (get down) bajar (b) (resign) renunciar, dimitir
■ **step forward** [v + adv] (a) (move forward) dar* un paso adelante (b) (present oneself) ofrecerse*
■ **step in** [v + adv] intervenir*
■ **step up** [v + o + adv, v + adv + o] ⟨production/ campaign⟩ intensificar*; ⟨efforts/security/attacks⟩ redoblar

step: ∼**brother** n hermanastro m; ∼ **by** ∼ adv (one stage at a time) paso a paso; (gradually) poco a poco; ∼**by-**∼ /'stepbaɪ'step/ adj ⟨instructions⟩ detallado, paso a paso; ∼**child** n (son) hijastro m; (daughter) hijastra f; ∼**daughter** n hijastra f; ∼**father** n padrastro m; ∼**ladder** n escalera f de mano or de tijera; ∼**mother** n madrastra f

stepping-stone /'stepɪŋstəʊn/ n: cada una

de las piedras que se colocan para cruzar un arroyo, un pantano etc; **a** ∼ **to success** un peldaño en el camino del éxito

step: ∼**sister** n hermanastra f; ∼**son** n hijastro m

stereo¹ /'steriəʊ/ n (pl -os) (a) (player) estéreo m (b) (sound) estéreo m

stereo² adj estéreo adj inv

stereotype¹ /'steriətaɪp/ n estereotipo m

stereotype² vt catalogar*, estereotipar

sterile /'sterəl ‖'steraɪl/ adj estéril

sterility /stə'rɪləti/ n esterilidad f

sterilize /'sterəlaɪz/ vt esterilizar*

sterling¹ /'stɜːrlɪŋ ‖'stɜːlɪŋ/ n la libra (esterlina)

sterling² adj: **the pound** ∼ la libra esterlina

stern¹ /stɜːrn ‖stɜːn/ n popa f

stern² adj -er, -est severo

steroid /'stɪrɔɪd, 'ste- ‖'stɪərɔɪd, 'ste-/ n esteroide m

stethoscope /'steθəskəʊp/ n estetoscopio m

stevedore /'sti:vədɔːr ‖'sti:vədɔː(r)/ n estibador, -dora m,f

stew¹ /stu: ‖stju:/ n estofado m, guiso m

stew² vt ⟨meat⟩ estofar, guisar; ⟨fruit⟩ hacer* compota de

steward /'stuːərd ‖'stjuːəd/ n **1** (a) (on ship) camarero m (b) (on plane) auxiliar (m) de vuelo, sobrecargo (m), aeromozo m (AmL) **2** (a) (manager of estate) administrador, -dora m,f (b) (at public gatherings) (BrE) *persona encargada de supervisar al público en manifestaciones*

stewardess /'stuːərdəs ‖'stjuːədes/ n (a) (on ship) camarera f (b) (on plane) auxiliar f de vuelo, azafata f, sobrecargo f, aeromoza f (AmL)

stick¹ /stɪk/ n **1** (of wood) palo m, vara f; (twig) ramita f; (for fire) astilla f **2** (a) (walking ∼) bastón m (b) (hockey ∼) palo m **3** (of celery, rhubarb) rama f, penca f; (of dynamite) cartucho m; (of rock, candy) palo m; **a** ∼ **of chalk** una tiza; **a** ∼ **of chewing gum** un chicle **4** **sticks** pl **the** ∼**s** (colloq): **to live out in the** ∼**s** vivir en la Cochinchina or (Esp tb) en las Batuecas

stick² (past & past p **stuck**) vt **1** (attach, glue) pegar* **2** (a) (thrust) ⟨needle/knife/sword⟩ clavar (b) (impale) **to** ∼ **sth ON sth** clavar algo EN algo **3** (put, place) (colloq) poner* **4** (tolerate) (esp BrE colloq) aguantar, soportar ■ ∼ vi **1** (adhere) ⟨⟨glue⟩⟩ pegar*; ⟨⟨food⟩⟩ pegarse*; **to** ∼ **TO sth** pegarse* or (frml) adherirse* A algo; **the two pages have stuck together** las dos páginas se han pegado; **the song stuck in my mind** la canción se me quedó grabada **2** (become jammed) atascarse*; *see also* STUCK²
■ **stick at** [v + prep + o] (colloq) seguir* con; ∼ **at it** sigue así
■ **stick by** [v + prep + o] ⟨friend⟩ no abandonar; ⟨promise⟩ mantener* en pie
■ **stick out 1** [v + adv] (a) (protrude) sobresalir* (b) (be obvious) resaltar; **he really** ∼**s out in a crowd** uno enseguida lo nota en un grupo de gente **2** [v + o + adv, v + adv + o] (stretch out) (colloq) ⟨hand⟩ extender*; ⟨tongue⟩ sacar*
■ **stick to** [v + prep + o] (a) (hold to) ⟨road/path⟩ ···⊱

S

seguir* por; ⟨principles⟩ mantener*; ⟨rules⟩
ceñirse* a, atenerse* a; **I'll ~ to my original plan**
seguiré con mi plan original **(b)** (not digress from)
⟨subject/facts⟩ ceñirse* a **(c)** (restrict oneself to)
limitarse a
■ **stick together** [v + adv] no separarse; (support
each other) mantenerse* unidos
■ **stick up** **1** [v + o + adv, v + adv + o] **(a)** (on
wall) ⟨notice⟩ colocar*, poner* **(b)** (raise) ⟨hand⟩
levantar
2 [v + adv] (project): **something was ~ing up out
of the ground** algo sobresalía del suelo; **her hair
was ~ing up** tenía el pelo de punta, tenía el pelo
parado (AmL)
■ **stick up for** [v + adv + prep + o] ⟨person⟩
sacar* la cara por, defender*; **to ~ up for oneself**
hacerse* valer

sticker /'stɪkər ‖ 'stɪkə(r)/ n (label) etiqueta f,
(with slogan etc) pegatina f, adhesivo m

sticking plaster /'stɪkɪŋ/ n (BrE) **(a)**
(individual strip) curita® f (AmL), tirita® f (Esp) **(b)**
(tape) esparadrapo m, cinta f adhesiva

stick: ~ insect n insecto m palo;
~-in-the-mud n (colloq): **don't be such a
~-in-the-mud** no seas tan rutinario e inflexible

stickler /'stɪklər ‖ 'stɪklə(r)/ n: **he's a ~ for
discipline** insiste mucho en la disciplina

stick: ~-on adj adhesivo; **~ shift** n (AmE) **(a)**
(lever) palanca f de cambio(s) or (Méx) de
velocidades **(b)** (car) coche m (de transmisión)
estándar or manual; **~up** n (colloq) atraco m,
asalto m

sticky /'stɪki/ adj **stickier, stickiest** **1** **(a)**
⟨label⟩ engomado, autoadhesivo; ⟨surface⟩
pegajoso **(b)** ⟨weather⟩ bochornoso **2** (difficult)
(colloq) ⟨problem/issue⟩ peliagudo; ⟨situation⟩
violento

stiff¹ /stɪf/ adj **-er, -est** **1** **(a)** ⟨collar/bristles⟩
duro; ⟨fabric⟩ tieso, duro; ⟨corpse⟩ rígido;
⟨muscles⟩ entumecido, agarrotado; **to have a ~
neck** tener* tortícolis; **I'm ~ after that walk** estoy
dolorido or (esp AmL) adolorido despues de la
caminata **(b)** ⟨paste/dough⟩ consistente; ⟨egg
white⟩ firme **2** ⟨test/climb⟩ difícil, duro;
⟨resistance⟩ férreo; ⟨penalty⟩ fuerte; ⟨breeze/
drink⟩ fuerte **3** ⟨person/manner⟩ estirado; ⟨bow/
smile⟩ forzado

stiff² adv (colloq): **I'm frozen ~** estoy helado
hasta los huesos (fam); **we were bored ~** nos
aburrimos como ostras (fam); **scared ~** muerto de
miedo

stiffen /'stɪfən/ vt **(a)** (with starch) almidonar;
(with fabric underneath) armar **(b)** ~ **(up)** ⟨resolve⟩
fortalecer*
■ ~ vi **(a)** ~ **(up)** (become rigid) «person/muscles/
joint» agarrotarse **(b)** (become firm) endurecerse*
(c) (in manner, reaction) ponerse* tenso

stiffly /'stɪfli/ adv **(a)** ⟨walk/move⟩ rígidamente,
con rigidez **(b)** ⟨greet⟩ fríamente; ⟨bow⟩ con fría
formalidad

stifle /'staɪfəl/ vt **1** (suffocate) (often pass)
⟨person⟩ sofocar* **2** (suppress) ⟨flames⟩ sofocar*;
⟨yawn/anger⟩ contener*; ⟨noise⟩ ahogar*

stifling /'staɪflɪŋ/ adj ⟨heat⟩ sofocante

stigma /'stɪgmə/ n (pl **-mas**) estigma m

stile /staɪl/ n: escalones que permiten pasar por
encima de una cerca

stiletto /stɪ'letəʊ/ n (pl **-tos** or **-toes**) ~
(heel) tacón m de aguja, taco m aguja or alfiler
(CS)

still¹ /stɪl/ adv
■ **Note** Spanish has two words for still: todavía and
aún. Both can go at the beginning or end of the
sentence: I still haven't seen him todavía or aún no lo
he visto or no lo he visto todavía or aún. The
distinction in English between he hasn't arrived yet
and he still hasn't arrived is not expressed verbally in
Spanish. Both can be translated by todavía or aún no
ha llegado, or no ha llegado todavía or aún. The
degree of intensity, surprise, or annoyance is often
expressed by intonation. Note that the verb seguir can
be used to express continuation: I still don't
understand why sigo sin entender por qué; he's still
looking for a job sigue buscando trabajo.

1 (even now, even then) todavía, aún; **there's ~
plenty left** todavía or aún queda mucho; **are we ~
friends?** ¿seguimos siendo amigos?
2 (as intensifier) aún, todavía; **the risk is greater
~** el riesgo es aún or todavía mayor
3 (as linker): **they say it's safe, but I'm ~ scared**
dicen que no hay peligro pero igual or aun así
tengo miedo; **~, it could have been worse** de
todos modos, podría haber sido peor

still² adj **(a)** (motionless) ⟨lake/air⟩ en calma,
quieto, tranquilo; **sit/stand ~** quédate quieto; **her
heart stood ~ for a moment** el corazón se le paró
un momento **(b)** ⟨drink⟩ sin gas, no efervescente

still³ n **1** (Cin, Phot) fotograma m **2** (distillery)
destilería f, (distilling apparatus) alambique m

still: ~born /'stɪl'bɔːrn ‖ 'stɪlbɔːn/ adj nacido
muerto; **~ life** n (pl **lifes**) naturaleza f
muerta

stilt /stɪlt/ n zanco m

stilted /'stɪltəd ‖ 'stɪltɪd/ adj **(a)** ⟨conversation/
manner⟩ forzado **(b)** ⟨language/writing⟩
rebuscado; ⟨acting⟩ acartonado

stimulate /'stɪmjəleɪt ‖ 'stɪmjʊleɪt/ vt
estimular

stimulating /'stɪmjəleɪtɪŋ ‖ 'stɪmjʊleɪtɪŋ/ adj
estimulante

stimulation /ˌstɪmjə'leɪʃən ‖ ˌstɪmjʊ'leɪʃən/ n
estímulo m

stimulus /'stɪmjələs ‖ 'stɪmjʊləs/ n (pl **-li**
/-laɪ/) estímulo m

sting¹ /stɪŋ/ n **1** **(a)** (of bee, wasp) aguijón m
(b) (action, wound) picadura f **2** (no pl) (pain)
escozor m, ardor m (CS)

sting² (past & past p **stung**) vt **1** «bee/
nettle» picar* **2** (cause pain) hacer* escocer,
hacer* arder (CS)

AmC	América Central	Arg	Argentina	Cu	Cuba	Per	Perú
AmL	América Latina	Bol	Bolivia	Ec	Ecuador	RPI	Río de la Plata
AmS	América del Sur	Chi	Chile	Esp	España	Ur	Uruguay
Andes	Región andina	CS	Cono Sur	Méx	México	Ven	Venezuela

■ ~ vi [1] «insect/nettle» picar* [2] (hurt physically) «ointment» hacer* escocer, hacer* arder (CS); «cut» escocer*, arder (CS)

stinging nettle /'stɪŋɪŋ/ n ortiga f

stingy /'stɪndʒi/ adj **-gier -giest** ⟨person⟩ tacaño; ⟨portion⟩ mezquino

stink¹ /stɪŋk/ n (a) (bad smell) hediondez f, mal olor m, peste f (fam) (b) (fuss) (colloq) escándalo m, lío m (fam), follón m (Esp fam); **to make** o **kick up a ~** armar un lío (or un escándalo etc)

stink² vi (past **stank** or **stunk**; past p **stunk**) «person/place/breath» apestar; **the whole business ~s** (colloq) todo el asunto da asco

stink bomb n bomba f fétida

stinking /'stɪŋkɪŋ/ adj (before n) hediondo, fétido, apestoso; **I've got a ~ cold** (colloq) tengo un resfriado espantoso

stint¹ /stɪnt/ n (a) (fixed amount, share): **I've done my ~ for today** hoy ya he hecho mi parte (b) (period) período m; **he did a five-year ~ in the army** pasó (un período de) cinco años en el ejército

stint² vi **to ~ on sth** escatimar algo

stipulate /'stɪpjəleɪt ‖ 'stɪpjʊleɪt/ vt estipular

stipulation /ˌstɪpjə'leɪʃən ‖ ˌstɪpjʊ'leɪʃən/ n condición f, estipulación f

stir¹ /stɜːr ‖ stɜː(r)/ n (a) (action) **to give sth a ~** revolver* or (Esp) remover* algo (b) (excitement) revuelo m, conmoción f

stir² **-rr-** vt [1] (mix) ⟨liquid/mixture⟩ revolver*, remover* (Esp) [2] (a) (move slightly) agitar, mover* (b) (get moving) (colloq) mover* (c) (waken) despertar* [3] (a) (arouse) ⟨imagination⟩ estimular (b) (move, affect) conmover* (c) (provoke, incite) **to ~ sb into action** empujar or incitar a algn a la acción

■ ~ vi (a) (change position) moverse*, agitarse (b) (venture out) moverse*, salir* (c) (wake up) despertarse*; (get up) levantarse

■ **stir up** [v + o + adv, v + adv + o] ⟨mud/waters⟩ revolver*, remover* (Esp); ⟨hatred/unrest/revolt⟩ provocar*; ⟨discontent⟩ promover*; **to ~ up trouble** armar lío (fam)

stir-fry /'stɜːr'fraɪ ‖ 'stɜː'fraɪ/ vt **-fries, -frying, -fried** freír en poco aceite y revolviendo constantemente

stirring /'stɜːrɪŋ/ adj conmovedor

stirrup /'stɜrəp ‖ 'stɪrəp/ n estribo m

stitch¹ /stɪtʃ/ n [1] (a) (in sewing) puntada f (b) (in knitting) punto m (c) (Med) punto m [2] (pain) (no pl) punzada f or (CS) puntada f (en el costado), flato m (Esp)

stitch² vt (a) (sew) coser (b) (embroider) bordar (c) (Med) suturar

stoat /stəʊt/ n armiño m

stock¹ /stɑːk ‖ stɒk/ n [1] (a) (supply) (often pl) reserva f (b) (of shop, business) existencias fpl, estoc m; **we're out of ~ of green ones** las verdes se han agotado; **to take ~ of sth** hacer* un balance de algo

[2] (Fin) (a) (shares) acciones fpl, valores mpl; (government securities) bonos mpl or papel m del Estado (b) **~s and bonds** o (BrE) **~s and shares** acciones fpl

[3] (livestock) ganado m

[4] (descent) linaje m, estirpe f

[5] (Culin) caldo m

[6] **stocks** pl (Hist) **the ~s** el cepo

[7] (Am Theat) repertorio m

stock² vt [1] (Busn) vender [2] (fill) ⟨store⟩ surtir, abastecer*; ⟨larder/freezer⟩ llenar

■ **stock up** [v + adv] abastecerse*; (Busn) hacer* un estoc; **we'd better ~ up on coffee before it goes up** más vale que compremos bastante café antes de que suba

stock³ adj (before n) ⟨size⟩ estándar adj inv; ⟨model⟩ de serie

stock: **~broker** n corredor, -dora m,f de valores or de Bolsa, agente mf de Bolsa; **~ company** n (AmE) (a) (Fin) sociedad f anónima (b) (Theat) compañía f de repertorio; **~ cube** n cubito m de caldo; **~ exchange** n bolsa f (de valores), Bolsa f; **~holder** n accionista mf

Stockholm /'stɑːkhəʊlm ‖ 'stɒkhəʊm/ n Estocolmo

stocking /'stɑːkɪŋ ‖ 'stɒkɪŋ/ n media f

stock-in-trade /'stɑːkɪn'treɪd ‖ ˌstɒkɪn'treɪd/ n especialidad f

stockist /'stɑːkəst ‖ 'stɒkɪst/ n (BrE) proveedor, -dora m,f, distribuidor, -dora m,f

stock market n mercado m de valores, mercado m (bursátil)

stockpile¹ /'stɑːkpaɪl ‖ 'stɒkpaɪl/ n reservas fpl

stockpile² vt almacenar

stock: **~room** n almacén m, depósito m, bodega f (Méx); **~-still** /'stɑːk'stɪl ‖ ˌstɒk'stɪl/ adj inmóvil; **~taking** /'stɑːkˌteɪkɪŋ ‖ 'stɒkˌteɪkɪŋ/ n (esp BrE Busn): **Ⓢ closed for stocktaking** cerrado por inventario

stocky /'stɑːki ‖ 'stɒki/ adj **stockier, stockiest** bajo y fornido

stockyard /'stɑːkjɑːrd ‖ 'stɒkjɑːd/ n (AmE) corral m

stodgy /'stɑːdʒi ‖ 'stɒdʒi/ adj **-dgier, -dgiest** (BrE) ⟨food⟩ feculento, pesado

stoical /'stəʊɪkəl/ adj estoico

stoke /stəʊk/ vt echarle carbón (or leña etc) a

stole¹ /stəʊl/ past of STEAL

stole² n estola f

stolen /'stəʊlən/ past p of STEAL

stolid /'stɑːləd ‖ 'stɒlɪd/ adj impasible

stomach¹ /'stʌmək/ n (a) (organ) estómago m; **on an empty ~** con el estómago vacío, en ayunas (b) (belly) barriga f (fam), panza f (fam)

stomach² vt (usu neg) ⟨insults/insolence/person⟩ soportar, aguantar

stomach: **~ache** n dolor m de estómago; (in lower abdomen) dolor m de barriga or (frml) de vientre; **~ pump** n bomba f estomacal

stomp /stɑːmp ‖ stɒmp/ vi (+ adv compl): **to ~ in/out** entrar/salir* pisando fuerte

stone¹ /stəʊn/ n [1] (substance, piece) piedra f [2] (a) (gem) piedra f (b) (in kidney) cálculo m, piedra f (c) (of fruit) hueso m, cuesco m [3] (pl ~ or ~s) (in UK) unidad de peso equivalente a 14 libras o 6,35kg

stone² vt apedrear, lapidar

stone: **S~ Age** n Edad f de Piedra; **~-cold** /'stəʊn'kəʊld/ adj (colloq) helado

stoned /stəʊnd/ adj (colloq) (usu pred) (from ···⟶

drugs) volado, pacheco (Méx), colocado (Esp fam); **to get ~** volarse*, ponerse* pacheco (Méx), colocarse* (Esp fam)

stone: **~-deaf** /'stəʊn'def/ adj (colloq) sordo como una tapia (fam); **~mason** n picapedrero m, cantero m; **~wall** /'stəʊn'wɔːl/ vi (be evasive) andarse* con evasivas; (be obstructive) utilizar* tácticas obstruccionistas

stony /'stəʊni/ adj **-nier, -niest** [1] ⟨ground/ path⟩ pedregoso [2] ⟨look/person⟩ frío, glacial; ⟨silence⟩ sepulcral

stood /stʊd/ past & past p of STAND[2]

stool /stuːl/ n taburete m, banco m

stoop¹ /stuːp/ vi [1] (have a stoop): **he ~s a little** es un poco cargado de espaldas or encorvado [2] (bend over) agacharse [3] (demean oneself): **how could he ~ so low?** ¿cómo pudo llegar tan bajo?; **to ~ TO sth** rebajarse a algo

stoop² n (no pl): **she walks with a ~** camina encorvada

stop¹ /stɑːp ‖stɒp/ n [1] (halt): **to come to a ~** ⟨vehicle/aircraft⟩ detenerse*; ⟨production/ conversation⟩ interrumpirse; **to put a ~ to sth** ⟨to mischief/malpractice⟩ poner* fin a algo [2] (a) (break on journey) parada f (b) (stopping place) parada f, paradero m (AmL exc RPl)

stop² **-pp-** vt [1] (a) (halt) ⟨taxi/bus⟩ parar; ⟨person⟩ parar, detener* (b) (switch off) ⟨machine/ engine⟩ parar

[2] (a) (bring to an end, interrupt) ⟨decline/inflation⟩ detener*, parar; ⟨discussion/abuse⟩ poner* fin a, acabar con; **~ that noise!** ¡deja de hacer ruido! (b) (cease): **~ what you're doing and listen to me** deja lo que estás haciendo y escúchame; **~ it!** ¡basta ya!; **to ~ -ING** dejar DE + INF

[3] (prevent): **what's ~ping you?** ¿qué te lo impide?; **I had to tell him, I couldn't ~ myself** tuve que decírselo, no pude contenerme; **to ~ sb (FROM) -ING** (esp BrE) impedirle* a algn + INF, impedir* QUE algn (+ subj); **to ~ sth happening** impedir* que ocurra algo

[4] (cancel, withhold) ⟨subscription⟩ cancelar; ⟨payment⟩ suspender

[5] (block) ⟨hole⟩ tapar; ⟨gap⟩ rellenar

[6] (parry) ⟨blow/punch⟩ parar, detener*

■ **~** vi [1] (a) (halt) ⟨vehicle/driver⟩ parar, detenerse*; **~ or I'll shoot!** ¡alto o disparo! (b) (interrupt journey) ⟨train/bus⟩ parar (c) (cease operating) ⟨watch/clock/machine⟩ pararse

[2] (a) (cease): **the rain has ~ped** ha dejado or parado de llover, ya no llueve; **the pain/bleeding has ~ped** ya no le (or me etc) duele/sale sangre (b) (interrupt activity) parar; **I didn't ~ to think** no me detuve a pensar

[3] (colloq) (stay) quedarse

■ **stop by** [v + adv] [v + prep o]: **I ~ped by (at) the store for some milk** pasé por la tienda para comprar leche

■ **stop off** [v + adv]: **I ~ped off at home to change** pasé por casa para cambiarme; **we ~ped off in San Juan for a few hours** paramos unas horas en San Juan

■ **stop over** [v + adv] (a) (overnight) hacer* noche (b) (Aviat) ⟨plane⟩ hacer* escala

■ **stop up** [v + o + adv, v + adv + o] (fill) ⟨hole/ crack⟩ tapar, rellenar

stop: **~gap** n recurso m provisional or (AmS tb) provisorio; **~over** n (break in journey) parada f; (Aviat) escala f

stoppage /'stɑːpɪdʒ ‖'stɒpɪdʒ/ n [1] (a) (in play, production) interrupción f (b) (strike) huelga f, paro m (AmL) (c) (cancellation) suspensión f [2] (blockage) obstrucción f

stopper /'stɑːpər ‖'stɒpə(r)/ n tapón m

stopping train /'stɑːpɪŋ ‖'stɒpɪŋ/ n (BrE) tren con parada en todas las estaciones

stop: **~ press** n noticias fpl de última hora; **~watch** n cronómetro m

storage /'stɔːrɪdʒ/ n (a) (of goods) depósito m, almacenamiento m, almacenaje m; (before n) **~ space** lugar m or espacio m para guardar cosas (b) (Comput) almacenamiento m

store¹ /stɔːr ‖stɔː(r)/ n [1] (a) (stock, supply) reserva f, provisión f; **in ~: there's a surprise in ~ for her** la espera una sorpresa; **who knows what the future has in ~?** ¿quién sabe lo que nos deparará el futuro?; **to set great/little ~ by sth** dar* mucho/poco valor a algo (b) **stores** pl (Mil, Naut) pertrechos mpl [2] (warehouse, storage place) (often pl) almacén m, depósito m, bodega f (Méx) [3] (a) (shop) (esp AmE) tienda f (b) (department **~**) grandes almacenes mpl, tienda f

store² vt (a) (keep) ⟨food/drink/supplies⟩ guardar; (Busn) almacenar; ⟨information⟩ almacenar; ⟨electricity⟩ acumular (b) (Comput) ⟨data/program⟩ almacenar

■ **store up** [v + o + adv, v + adv + o] (a) ⟨supplies⟩ almacenar (b) ⟨resentment⟩ ir* acumulando

store: **~house** n (a) (warehouse) almacén m, depósito m, bodega f (Méx) (b) (source) mina f; **~keeper** n tendero, -ra m,f; **~room** n almacén m, depósito m, bodega f (Méx); (for food) despensa f

storey /'stɔːri/ n (BrE) ▶ STORY II

stork /stɔːrk ‖stɔːk/ n cigüeña f

storm¹ /stɔːrm ‖stɔːm/ n [1] (Meteo) tormenta f, **a ~ at sea** una tempestad; **to take sth by ~** ⟨city/fortress⟩ tomar algo por asalto; **she took New York's audiences by ~** cautivó al público neoyorquino [2] (of protest) ola f, tempestad f

storm² vi [1] (move violently) (+ adv compl): **she ~ed into the office** irrumpió en la oficina [2] (express anger) despotricar*, vociferar

■ **~** vt ⟨city/fortress⟩ tomar por asalto; ⟨house⟩ irrumpir en

stormy /'stɔːrmi ‖'stɔːmi/ adj **-mier, -miest** (a) (Meteo) tormentoso; ⟨sea⟩ tempestuoso (b) (turbulent) ⟨relationship⟩ tempestuoso

story /'stɔːri/ n (pl **-ries**) I [1] (a) (account) historia f, relato m; (genre) cuento m; **to cut a long ~ short** en pocas palabras (b) (anecdote) anécdota f [2] (plot) argumento m, trama f [3] (Journ) artículo m [4] (lie) (colloq) cuento m (fam), mentira f II (BrE) storey (of building) piso m, planta f

story: **~book** n libro m de cuentos; **~ line** n argumento m; **~teller** n narrador, -dora m,f

stout¹ /staʊt/ adj **-er, -est** ⟨person/figure⟩ robusto, corpulento; ⟨door⟩ sólido

stout² n cerveza f negra

stove /stəʊv/ n (a) (for cooking) cocina f, estufa f (Col, Méx) (b) (for warmth) estufa f

stow /stəʊ/ vt (put away) guardar, poner*; (hide) esconder; (Naut) estibar
■ **stow away** [v + adv] viajar de polizón
stowaway /'stəʊəˌweɪ/ n polizón mf

straddle /'strædl/ vt ‹horse› sentarse* a horcajadas sobre; **he ~d the chair** se sentó a caballo or a horcajadas en la silla

straggle /'strægəl/ vi [1] (spread untidily) «plant» crecer* desordenadamente [2] (lag behind, fall away) rezagarse*

straggler /'stræglər ‖'stræglə(r)/ n rezagado, -da m,f

straggly /'strægli/ adj **-glier, -gliest** ‹hair› desordenado, desgreñado; ‹beard› descuidado

straight¹ /streɪt/ adj **-er, -est** [1] (a) (not curved or wavy) recto; ‹hair› lacio, liso [b] (level, upright, vertical) (pred) **to be ~** estar* derecho; **is my tie ~?** ¿tengo la corbata derecha or bien puesta?
[2] (in order) (pred): **I have to put my room ~** tengo que ordenar mi cuarto; **let's get this ~** a ver si nos entendemos; **to set the record ~** dejar las cosas en claro
[3] (a) (direct, clear) ‹denial/refusal› rotundo, categórico (b) (unmixed) ‹gin/vodka› solo
[4] (honest, frank) ‹question› directo; ‹answer› claro
[5] (successive): **he won in ~ sets** (Sport) ganó sin conceder or sin perder ningún set; **she's had five ~ wins** ha ganado cinco veces seguidas
[6] (a) (serious) ‹play/actor› dramático, serio (b) (conventional) (colloq) convencional (c) (heterosexual) (colloq) heterosexual

straight² adv [1] (a) (in a straight line) ‹walk› en línea recta; **she looked ~ ahead** miró al frente; **the truck was coming ~ at me** el camión venía derecho hacia mí; **he made ~ for the bar** se fue derecho al bar; **keep ~ on until you come to the lights** sigue derecho hasta llegar al semáforo (b) (erect) ‹sit/stand› derecho; **sit up ~** ponte derecho
[2] (a) (directly) directamente; **I came ~ home from work** vine directamente or derecho a casa después del trabajo (b) (immediately): **~ after dinner** inmediatamente después de cenar; **I'll bring it ~ back** enseguida te lo devuelvo; **I'll come ~ to the point** iré derecho al grano; **~ away** ▶ STRAIGHTAWAY
[3] (colloq) (frankly) con franqueza; **she told him ~ out** se lo dijo sin rodeos
[4] (clearly) ‹see/think› con claridad

straight: ~ and narrow n the **~ and narrow** el buen camino, el camino recto; **~away** /'streɪtəˌweɪ/, **~ away** adv enseguida, inmediatamente

straighten /'streɪtn̩/ vt (a) ‹nail/wire/picture› enderezar*; ‹hair› alisar; **he ~ed his tie** se enderezó la corbata (b) (tidy) ‹room/papers› arreglar, ordenar
■ **straighten out** [v + o + adv, v + adv + o] ‹confusion/misunderstanding› aclarar; ‹problem› resolver*
■ **straighten up** [1] [v + o + adv, v + adv + o] (tidy) ‹room/papers› ordenar, arreglar; ‹bed› arreglar [2] [v + adv] (stand up straight) ponerse* derecho

straight: ~faced /'streɪtˈfeɪst/ adj: **he said it completely ~faced** lo dijo muy serio; **~forward** /'streɪtˈfɔːrwərd ‖ˌstreɪtˈfɔːwəd/ adj (a) (honest,

frank) ‹person/answer› franco (b) (uncomplicated) ‹problem/question› sencillo; **~jacket** n ▶ STRAITJACKET

strain¹ /streɪn/ n [1] (tension) tensión f; (pressure) presión f; **it puts ~ on the spine** ejerce presión sobre la columna vertebral; **the incident put a ~ on Franco-German relations** las relaciones franco-alemanas se volvieron tirantes a raíz del incidente [2] (Med) (resulting from wrench, twist) torcedura f; (on a muscle) esguince m [3] **strains** pl (tune): **the ~s of** el sonido de; **to the ~s of the violin** al son del violín [4] (a) (type — of plant) variedad f; (— of virus) cepa f; (— of animal) raza f (b) (streak) (no pl) veta f

strain² vt [1] (exert): **to ~ one's eyes/voice** forzar* la vista/voz; **he ~ed every muscle to lift the weight** usó todas sus fuerzas para levantar el peso [2] (a) (overburden) ‹beam/support› ejercer* demasiada presión sobre (b) (injure): **to ~ one's back** hacerse* daño en la espalda; **to ~ a muscle** hacerse* un esguince (c) (overtax, stretch) ‹relations› someter a demasiada tensión; ‹patience› poner* a prueba [3] (filter) filtrar; (Culin) colar*; ‹vegetables/rice› escurrir
■ **~** vi: **to ~ AT sth** tirar DE algo; **to ~ to + INF** hacer* un gran esfuerzo PARA + INF

strained /streɪnd/ adj [1] (tense) ‹relations/ atmosphere› tenso, tirante; ‹expression› tenso, crispado; ‹voice› forzado [2] (Med) **a ~ muscle** un esguince

strainer /'streɪnər ‖'streɪnə(r)/ n (Culin) colador m

strait /streɪt/ n [1] (Geog) (often pl) estrecho m [2] **straits** pl (difficulties, difficult position): **to be in dire ~s** estar* en grandes apuros

strait: ~jacket n camisa f de fuerza, chaleco m de fuerza (CS); **~laced** /'streɪtˈleɪst/ adj puritano

strand¹ /strænd/ n (of rope, string) ramal m; (of thread, wool) hebra f; (of wire) filamento m; **a ~ of hair** un pelo

strand² vt (usu pass): **to be ~ed** «ship» quedar encallado; «whale» quedar varado; **they left me ~ed** me abandonaron a mi suerte, me dejaron tirado or (AmL exc RPl) botado (fam)

strange /streɪndʒ/ adj **stranger, strangest** [1] (odd) raro, extraño; **it is ~ (THAT)** es raro QUE (+ subj) [2] (a) (unfamiliar, unaccustomed) ‹faces/ handwriting› desconocido (b) (alien) (liter): **in a ~ land** en tierras extrañas

strangely /'streɪndʒli/ adv ‹behave/act› de una manera rara or extraña; **~ enough** (indep) aunque parezca mentira

stranger /'streɪndʒər ‖'streɪndʒə(r)/ n desconocido, -da m,f; (from another place) forastero, -ra m,f; **I'm a ~ here myself** yo tampoco soy de aquí

strangle /'stræŋgəl/ vt (a) ‹person› estrangular (b) **strangled** past p ‹cry/voice› ahogado

stranglehold /'stræŋgəlˌhəʊld/ n (a) (Sport) llave f al cuello (b) (absolute control) poder m, dominio m

strap¹ /stræp/ n (a) (of leather) correa f; (of canvas) asa f‡ (b) (shoulder ~) tirante m, bretel m (CS)

strap² vt **-pp-** (tie) atar or sujetar con una correa, amarrar con una correa (AmL exc RPl)

S

strapless /'stræpləs ‖'stræplɪs/ adj sin tirantes, sin breteles (CS)

strapping /'stræpɪŋ/ adj robusto, fornido

Strasbourg /'stra:sbʊrg ‖'stræzbɜ:g/ n Estrasburgo m

strata /'streɪtə, 'strætə ‖'stra:tə, 'streɪtə/ pl of STRATUM

stratagem /'strætədʒəm/ n estratagema f

strategic /strə'ti:dʒɪk/ adj estratégico

strategy /'strætədʒi/ n (pl **-gies**) estrategia f

stratify /'strætəfaɪ ‖'streɪtɪfaɪ/ vt **-fies, -fying, -fied** (usu pass) estratificar*

stratum /'streɪtəm, 'stræ- ‖'stra:təm, 'streɪ-/ n (pl **-ta**) estrato m

straw /strɔ:/ n (a) (material, single stem) paja f; **to be the last o final ~** ser* el colmo; **to clutch o grasp at ~s** aferrarse desesperadamente a una esperanza (b) (for drinking) pajita f, paja f, caña f (Esp), pitillo m (Col), popote m (Méx)

strawberry /'strɔ:.beri ‖'strɔ:bəri/ n (pl **-ries**) fresa f, frutilla f (Bol, CS); (large) fresón m

stray¹ /streɪ/ vi (a) (wander away) apartarse, alejarse; (get lost) extraviarse*, perderse* (b) (digress) apartarse, desviarse*

stray² adj (a) ⟨dog⟩ (ownerless) callejero; (lost) perdido; ⟨sheep⟩ descarriado (b) (random, scattered) ⟨bullet⟩ perdido; ⟨hair⟩ suelto

stray³ n (ownerless animal) perro m/gato m callejero; (lost animal) perro m/gato m perdido

streak¹ /stri:k/ n ① (a) (line, band) lista f, raya f; (in hair) reflejo m, mechón m; (in marble) veta f; (of ore) veta f, filón m (b) (in personality) veta f ② (spell) racha f; **to be on a winning ~** tener* una buena racha

streak² vi (+ adv compl): **to ~ past** pasar como una centella
■ **~** vt: **tears ~ed her face** tenía el rostro surcado de lágrimas; **to have one's hair ~ed** hacerse* mechas or reflejos or (RPl) claritos or (Méx) luces or (Chi) visos (en el pelo)

streaky /'stri:ki/ adj **-kier, -kiest** (a) (uneven) ⟨paint⟩ no uniforme, disparejo (AmL) (b) (BrE Culin): **~ bacon** tocino m or (Esp) bacon m or (RPl) panceta f

stream¹ /stri:m/ n ① (a) (small river) arroyo m, riachuelo m (b) (current) corriente f ② (flow): **a thin ~ of water** un chorrito de agua; **a ~ of abuse** una sarta de insultos; **there is a continuous ~ of traffic** pasan vehículos continuamente

stream² vi ① (flow) (+ adv compl): **blood ~ed from the wound** salía or manaba mucha sangre de la herida; **tears were ~ing down her cheeks** lloraba a lágrima viva; **the sunlight was ~ing in through the window** el sol entraba a raudales por la ventana; **I've got a ~ing cold** tengo un resfriado muy fuerte ② (wave) ⟨flag/hair⟩ ondear
■ **~** vt (BrE Educ) dividir (a los alumnos) en grupos según su aptitud para una asignatura

streamer /'stri:mər ‖'stri:mə(r)/ n (a) (banner) banderín m (b) (of paper) serpentina f

stream: ~line vt ⟨car/plane⟩ hacer* más aerodinámico el diseño de, aerodinamizar*; ⟨organization/production⟩ racionalizar*; **~lined** adj ⟨car/plane⟩ aerodinámico; ⟨methods/production⟩ racionalizado

street /stri:t/ n calle f; **it's on o (BrE) in Elm S~** queda en la calle Elm; (before n) ⟨musician/theater⟩ callejero; **~ corner** esquina f; **~ map o plan** plano m de la ciudad, callejero m (Esp); **~ market** mercado m al aire libre, feria f (CS)

street: ~car n (AmE) tranvía m; **~ cleaner** n (AmE) barrendero, -ra m,f; **~ lamp** n farol m; **~ level** n: **at ~ level** a nivel de la calle; **~ light** n ▶ ~ LAMP; **~ sweeper** n (person) barrendero, -ra m,f; (machine) (máquina f) barredora f

strength /streŋθ/ n ① (of persons) (a) (physical energy) fuerza(s) f(pl); (health) fortaleza f física; **to get one's ~ back** recobrar las fuerzas (b) (emotional, mental) fortaleza f ② (of economy, currency) solidez f ③ (a) (of materials) resistencia f; (of wind, current) fuerza f; (of drug, solution) concentración f; (of alcoholic drink) graduación f (b) (of sound, light) potencia f; (of emotions) intensidad f (c) (of argument, evidence) lo convincente; (of protests) lo enérgico ④ (strong point) virtud f, punto m fuerte ⑤ (force in numbers): **their fans were there in ~** sus hinchas estaban allí en bloque or en masa

strengthen /'streŋθən/ vt ⟨muscle/limb⟩ fortalecer*; ⟨wall/furniture/glass⟩ reforzar*; ⟨support⟩ aumentar
■ **~** vi «limb/muscle» fortalecerse*; «opposition/support» aumentar

strenuous /'strenjuəs/ adj (a) ⟨activity⟩ agotador (b) ⟨denial⟩ vigoroso; ⟨opposition⟩ tenaz

stress¹ /stres/ n ① (a) (tension) tensión f; (Med) estrés m, tensión f; **she's under a lot of ~** está sometida a muchas presiones (b) (Phys, Tech) tensión f ② (a) (emphasis) énfasis m, hincapié m (b) (Ling, Lit) acento m (tónico)

stress² vt (a) (emphasize) poner* énfasis or hacer* hincapié en, enfatizar* (b) (Ling) acentuar*

stressful /'stresfəl/ adj ⟨life/job⟩ estresante

stretch¹ /stretʃ/ vt ① ⟨arm/leg⟩ estirar, extender*; ⟨wing⟩ extender*, desplegar* ② ⟨sheet/canvas⟩ extender* ③ (eke out) ⟨money/resources⟩ estirar ④ (a) (make demands on) exigirle* a; **she's not being ~ed at school** en el colegio no le exigen de acuerdo a su capacidad (b) (strain): **our resources are ~ed to the limit** nuestros recursos están empleados al máximo ⑤ ⟨truth/meaning⟩ forzar*; ⟨rules⟩ apartarse un poco de
■ **~** vi ① «person» estirarse; (when sleepy) desperezarse*

2 (a) (reach, extend) «*sea/influence/power*» extenderse* (b) (in time): **to ~ over a period** alargarse* *or* prolongarse* durante un período
3 (a) (be elastic) «*elastic/rope*» estirarse (b) (become loose, longer) «*garment*» estirarse
4 (be enough) «*money/resources/supply*» alcanzar*, llegar*

■ *v refl* **to ~ oneself** (physically) estirarse; (when sleepy) desperezarse*

■ **stretch out** **1** [*v + o + adv, v + adv + o*] (extend) estirar
2 [*v + adv*] (a) (lie full length) tenderse* (b) (extend — in space) extenderse*; (— in time) alargarse*

stretch² *n* **1** (act of stretching) (*no pl*): **to have a ~** estirarse; (when sleepy) desperezarse* **2** (a) (expanse — of road, river) tramo *m*, trecho *m* (b) (period) período *m*; **at a ~** (without a break) sin parar **3** (elasticity) elasticidad *f*

stretch³ *adj* (*before n, no comp*) «*fabric/pants*» elástico; **~ limo** (colloq) limusina *f* (*grande*)

stretcher /'stretʃər ‖'stretʃə(r)/ *n* (Med) camilla *f*

stretch marks *pl n* estrías *fpl*

stretchy /'stretʃi/ *adj* **-chier, -chiest** elástico

strew /struː/ *vt* (*past* **strewn** /struːn/ *past p* **strewn** *or* **strewed** /-d/) «*gravel/seeds*» esparcir*; «*objects*» (untidily) desparramar

stricken /'strɪkən/ *adj* (a) (afflicted) ~ **WITH sth: a country ~ with famine** un país asolado por el hambre; **I was suddenly ~ with remorse** de pronto me empezó a remorder la conciencia (b) «*vessel*» siniestrado (frml), dañado; «*area*» damnificado, afectado

strict /strɪkt/ *adj* **-er, -est** (a) (severe) estricto, severo (b) (rigorous) «*vegetarian*» estricto, riguroso (c) (exact) (*before n*) estricto, riguroso; **in the ~ sense of the word** en el sentido estricto *or* riguroso de la palabra (d) (complete) (*before n*) absoluto; **in ~est secrecy** en el más absoluto secreto

strictly /'strɪktli/ *adv* (a) (severely) con severidad, severamente, rigurosamente (b) (rigorously): **smoking is ~ prohibited** fumar está terminantemente prohibido; **~ speaking** (*indep*) en rigor, en sentido estricto (c) (exactly) totalmente; **that's not ~ true** eso no es totalmente cierto (d) (exclusively) exclusivamente; **this is ~ between ourselves** que quede entre nosotros

stride¹ /straɪd/ *vi* (*past* **strode**; *past p* **stridden** /'strɪdn/) (+ *adv compl*): **he strode across the room** cruzó la habitación a grandes zancadas

stride² *n* zancada *f*, tranco *m*; **to take sth in one's ~** tomarse algo con calma

strident /'straɪdnt/ *adj* estridente

strife /straɪf/ *n* (journ *or* frml) conflictos *mpl*; (armed) luchas *fpl*

strike¹ /straɪk/ *vt* (*past & past p* **struck**) *vt*
1 (a) (hit) «*person*» pegarle* a, golpear; «*blow*» dar*, pegar*; «*key*» pulsar (b) (collide with, fall on) «*vehicle*» chocar* *or* dar* contra; «*stone/ball*» pegar* *or* dar* contra; «*lightning/bullet*» alcanzar*; **I struck my head on the beam** me di (un golpe) en la cabeza contra la viga; **he was struck by lightning** le cayó un rayo
2 (a) (cause to become): **to be struck blind/dumb**

quedarse ciego/mudo; **to ~ sb dead** matar a algn (b) (introduce): **to ~ fear into sb** infundirle miedo a algn
3 (a) (occur to) ocurrirse (+ *me/te/le etc*); **it ~s me (that)** ... me da la impresión de que ..., se me ocurre que ... (b) (impress) parecerle* a; **it ~s me as odd** me parece raro; **I was struck by his changed appearance** me llamó la atención lo cambiado que estaba
4 «*oil/gold*» encontrar*, dar* con
5 «*match/light*» encender*
6 (a) (Mus) «*note*» dar* (b) «*clock*» dar*; **the clock struck five** el reloj dio las cinco
7 (enter into, arrive at): **to ~ a deal** llegar* a un acuerdo, cerrar* un trato; **to ~ a balance between** ... encontrar* el justo equilibrio entre ...
8 (adopt) «*pose/attitude*» adoptar
9 (delete) suprimir; **his name was struck off the register** se borró su nombre del registro; *see also* STRIKE OFF

■ **~** *vi* **1** (hit) «*person*» golpear; «*lightning*» caer*
2 (a) (attack) atacar* (b) (happen suddenly) «*illness/misfortune*» sobrevenir*; «*disaster*» ocurrir
3 (withdraw labor) hacer* huelga, declararse en huelga *or* (esp AmL) en paro
4 «*clock*» dar* la hora

■ **strike back** [*v + adv*] (Mil) contraatacar*; **he struck back at his critics** devolvió el golpe a sus detractores

■ **strike down** [*v + o + adv, v + adv + o*] (liter): **she was struck down with cholera** fue abatida por el cólera (liter)

■ **strike off** [*v + o + adv, v + adv + o*] (a) (delete) tachar (b) (disqualify) (BrE) «*doctor/lawyer*» prohibirle* el ejercicio de la profesión a

■ **strike out**
I [*v + adv*] **to ~ out** (AT sb/sth) arremeter (CONTRA algn/algo)
II [*v + o + adv, v + adv + o*] (remove from list) tachar

■ **strike up** **1** [*v + adv + o*] (a) (begin) «*conversation*» entablar; «*friendship*» trabar, entablar (b) (start to play) «*tune*» empezar* a tocar **2** [*v + adv*] «*band*» empezar* a tocar

strike² *n* **1** (stoppage) huelga *f*, paro *m* (esp AmL); **to be on ~** estar* en *or* de huelga, estar* en *or* de paro (esp AmL); **to come out** *o* **go (out) on ~** ir* a la huelga, declararse en huelga, ir* al paro (esp AmL), declararse en paro (esp AmL); **hunger ~** huelga de hambre **2** (find) descubrimiento *m* **3** (attack) ataque *m*

strikebreaker /'straɪkˌbreɪkər ‖'straɪkˌbreɪkə(r)/ *n* rompehuelgas *mf*

striker /'straɪkər ‖'straɪkə(r)/ *n* **1** (Lab Rel) huelguista *mf* **2** (in soccer) artillero, -ra *m,f*, ariete *mf*

striking /'straɪkɪŋ/ *adj* «*resemblance/similarity*» sorprendente, asombroso; «*color*» llamativo; **a ~ woman** una mujer muy atractiva

string¹ /strɪŋ/ *n* **1** (a) (cord, length of cord) cordel *m*, bramante *m* (Esp), mecate *m* (AmC, Méx, Ven), pita *f* (Andes), cáñamo *m* (Andes), piolín *m* (RPl) (b) (on apron) cinta *f*; (on puppet) hilo *m*; **no ~s attached** sin compromisos, sin condiciones **2** (a) (on instrument) cuerda *f* (b) (on racket) cuerda *f* (c) **strings** *pl* (Mus) cuerdas *fpl* **3** (a) (set — of pearls, beads) sarta *f*, hilo *m*; (— of ⋯

onions, garlic) ristra f **(b)** (series — of people)
sucesión f; (— of vehicles) fila f; (— of events) serie
f; (— of curses, complaints, lies) sarta f

string² (*past & past p* **strung**) *vt* ☐ (suspend)
colgar* ☐ ⟨*guitar/racket/bow*⟩ encordar*,
ponerle* (las) cuerdas a; ⟨*beads/pearls*⟩ ensartar,
enhebrar
■ **string along** (colloq) [*v + o + adv*] (mislead)
tomarle el pelo a (fam) ⟨*dando esperanzas falsas*⟩
■ **string together** [*v + o + adv, v + adv + o*]
⟨*thoughts*⟩ coordinar, hilar; **she could barely ~ a
sentence together** apenas podía hilar una frase

string bean *n* ▶ RUNNER BEAN

stringed /strɪŋd/ *adj* ⟨*instrument*⟩ de cuerda

stringent /'strɪndʒənt/ *adj* riguroso, estricto

strip¹ /strɪp/ **-pp-** *vt* ☐ **(a)** (remove covering from)
⟨*bed*⟩ deshacer*, quitar la ropa de; ⟨*wood/
furniture*⟩ quitarle la pintura (*or* el barniz *etc*) a,
decapar; **to ~ sb** (naked) desnudar a algn **(b)**
(remove contents from) ⟨*room/house*⟩ vaciar*
☐ (Auto, Tech) ~ (**down**) desmontar
■ ~ *vi* desnudarse, desvestirse*
■ **strip off** [*v + o + adv, v + adv + o*] ⟨*wallpaper/
paint*⟩ quitar; ⟨*leaves*⟩ arrancar*

strip² *n* ☐ **(a)** (of leather, cloth, paper) tira f; (of metal)
tira f, cinta f; (of land) franja f ☐ (BrE Sport) (*no
pl*) equipo m

strip cartoon *n* (BrE) historieta f, tira f
cómica

stripe /straɪp/ *n* raya f, lista f

striped /straɪpt/ *adj* a *or* de rayas, rayado,
listado

strip: ~ **lighting** *n* (BrE) luz f fluorescente;
~**-search** /'strɪp'sɜ:rtʃ ‖'strɪp,sɜ:tʃ/ *vt* hacer*
desnudar y registrar

strive /straɪv/ *vi* (*past* **strove** *or* **strived**;
past p **striven** /'strɪvən/) **to ~** FOR *o* AFTER sth
luchar *or* esforzarse* por alcanzar algo; **to ~ to +**
INF esforzarse* POR + INF

strobe (light) /strəʊb/ *n* luz f estroboscópica

strode /strəʊd/ *past of* STRIDE¹

stroke¹ /strəʊk/ *n* ☐ (Sport) **(a)** (in ball games)
golpe m **(b)** (in swimming — movement) brazada f;
(— style) estilo m **(c)** (in rowing — movement) palada
f, remada f
☐ **(a)** (blow) golpe m **(b)** (of clock) campanada f
☐ **(a)** (of thin brush) pincelada f; (of thick brush)
brochazo m; (of pen, pencil) trazo m **(b)** (oblique,
slash) barra f, diagonal f
☐ **(a)** (action, feat) golpe m; **not to do a ~ of work**
no hacer* absolutamente nada **(b)** (instance): **a ~
of luck** un golpe de suerte
☐ (Med) ataque m de apoplejía, derrame m
cerebral
☐ (caress) caricia f

stroke² *vt* acariciar

stroll¹ /strəʊl/ *vi* pasear(se), dar* un paseo

stroll² *n* paseo m; **to have** *o* **go for a ~** dar* un
paseo

stroller /'strəʊlər ‖'strəʊlə(r)/ *n* ☐ (person)
paseante *mf* ☐ (pushchair) (esp AmE) sillita f (de
paseo), cochecito m, carreola f (Méx)

strong¹ /strɔːŋ ‖strɒŋ/ *adj* **stronger**
/'strɔːŋgər ‖'strɒŋgə(r)/, **strongest** /'strɔːŋgəst
‖'strɒŋgɪst/ ☐ **(a)** (physically powerful) ⟨*person/*

⟨*arm*⟩ fuerte **(b)** (healthy, sound) ⟨*heart/lungs*⟩
fuerte, sano; ⟨*constitution*⟩ robusto **(c)** (firm)
⟨*character/leader*⟩ fuerte
☐ **(a)** (solid) ⟨*material/construction*⟩ fuerte **(b)**
(powerful) ⟨*army/economy*⟩ fuerte **(c)** ⟨*current/
wind*⟩ fuerte
☐ **(a)** (deeply held) ⟨*views/faith/support*⟩ firme **(b)**
(forceful) ⟨*protest*⟩ enérgico; ⟨*argument/evidence*⟩
de peso
☐ (definite) **(a)** ⟨*tendency/resemblance*⟩ marcado;
⟨*candidate*⟩ con muchas posibilidades **(b)**
⟨*features*⟩ marcado
☐ (good) ⟨*team*⟩ fuerte; ⟨*cast*⟩ sólido; ~ **point**
punto m fuerte; **she's a ~ swimmer** es una buena
nadadora
☐ **(a)** (concentrated) ⟨*color/light*⟩ fuerte, intenso;
⟨*tea/coffee*⟩ cargado; ⟨*solution*⟩ concentrado **(b)**
(pungent) ⟨*smell/flavor*⟩ fuerte **(c)** (unacceptable)
⟨*language*⟩ fuerte
☐ (in number) (*no comp*): **an army ten thousand ~**
un ejército de diez mil hombres

strong² *adv*: **to be going ~** «*car/machine*»
marchar bien; «*organization*» ir* *or* marchar
viento en popa; **he's still going ~** «*old person*»
sigue (estando) en plena forma

strong: ~**box** *n* caja f fuerte *or* de caudales;
~**hold** *n* (fortress) fortaleza f, bastión m; (center of
support) bastión m, baluarte m

strongly /'strɔːŋli ‖'strɒŋli/ *adv* ☐ **(a)**
(powerfully) fuerte, con fuerza **(b)** (sturdily) ⟨*made/
welded*⟩ sólidamente ☐ **(a)** (deeply, ardently)
totalmente; **it's something I feel very ~ about** es
algo que me parece sumamente importante **(b)**
(forcefully) ⟨*protest/criticize*⟩ enérgicamente; **I ~
advise you not to sell** te recomiendo con
insistencia que no vendas

strong: ~ **room** *n* cámara f acorazada;
~**-willed** /'strɔːŋ'wɪld ‖,strɒŋ'wɪld/ *adj*
(determined) tenaz; (obstinate) terco, tozudo

strove /strəʊv/ *past of* STRIVE

struck /strʌk/ *past & past p of* STRIKE¹

structural /'strʌktʃərəl/ *adj* estructural

structure¹ /'strʌktʃər ‖'strʌktʃə(r)/ *n* **(a)**
(composition, organization) estructura f **(b)** (thing
constructed) construcción f

structure² *vt* estructurar

struggle¹ /'strʌgəl/ *n* **(a)** (against opponent)
lucha f; (physical) refriega f; **to put up a ~** luchar,
oponer* resistencia **(b)** (against difficulties) lucha f;
it's a ~ to make ends meet cuesta mucho llegar a
fin de mes

struggle² *vi* ☐ **(a)** (thrash around) forcejear **(b)**
(contend, strive) luchar; **she had to ~ to support
her family** tuvo que luchar para mantener a su
familia; **to ~** ⟨AGAINST/WITH sth⟩ luchar (CONTRA
algo); **to ~** FOR sth luchar POR algo **(c)** (be in
difficulties) pasar apuros ☐ (move with difficulty) (+
adv compl): **he ~d up the hill** subió penosamente
la cuesta; **he ~d to his feet** se levantó con gran
dificultad

strum /strʌm/ *vt* **-mm-** ⟨*guitar/tune*⟩ rasguear

strung /strʌŋ/ *past & past p of* STRING²

strut¹ /strʌt/ *vi* **-tt-** (+ *adv compl*): **to ~ around**
o **about** pavonearse

strut² *n* (Const) tornapunta f, puntal m

stub¹ /stʌb/ *n* **(a)** (of candle, pencil) cabo m; (of

889

stub ···> stupor ···

cigarette) colilla f, pucho m (AmL fam) **(b)** (of check) talón m (AmL), matriz f (Esp); (of ticket) contraseña f, resguardo m (Esp)

stub² -bb- vt: to ~ one's toe darse* en el dedo (del pie)

■ **stub out** [v + o + adv, v + adv + o] ‹cigarette› apagar*

stubble /'stʌbəl/ n **(a)** (Agr) rastrojo m **(b)** (of beard): **he had three days' ~ on his chin** tenía una barba de tres días

stubborn /'stʌbərn ‖'stʌbən/ adj **(a)** ‹person/ nature› (obstinate) terco, testarudo; (resolute) tenaz, tesonero; ‹refusal/insistence› pertinaz **(b)** ‹cold/ weeds› pertinaz, persistente; ‹stain› rebelde

stuck¹ /stʌk/ past & past p of STICK²

stuck² adj ‹pred› (unable to move): **the drawer is ~** el cajón se ha atascado; **the door is ~** la puerta se ha atrancado; **she's ~ at home with the kids all day** está todo el día metida en la casa con los niños **(b)** (at a loss) atascado; **I got ~ on the second question** me quedé atascado en la segunda pregunta **(c)** (burdened) (colloq): **I was ~ with the bill** me tocó pagar la cuenta, me cargaron el muerto (fam); **I got ~ with Bob all evening** tuve que aguantar a Bob toda la noche

stuck-up /'stʌk'ʌp/ adj (colloq) estirado (fam)

stud¹ /stʌd/ n **1** **(a)** (nail, knob) tachuela f **(b)** (earring) arete m or (Esp) pendiente m (en forma de bolita) **(c)** (for collar, shirtfront) gemelo m (para cuello o pechera de camisa) **2** (male animal) semental m

stud² vt -dd- (usu pass) (with studs) tachonar; **the sky was ~ded with stars** el cielo estaba tachonado de estrellas (liter)

student /'stuːdn̩t ‖'stjuːdn̩t/ n (at university) estudiante mf; (at school) (esp AmE) alumno, -na m,f; **a medical ~** un/una estudiante de medicina; (before n) **~ driver** (AmE) persona que está aprendiendo a conducir; **~ nurse** estudiante mf de enfermería

student union n (association) asociación f de estudiantes; (building) centro estudiantil en el campus

studio /'stuːdiəʊ ‖'stjuːdiəʊ/ n **(a)** (Art, Mus, Phot) estudio m **(b)** (Cin, Rad, TV) estudio m **(c)** **~ (apartment** o (BrE also) **flat)** estudio m

studious /'stuːdiəs ‖'stjuːdiəs/ adj estudioso, aplicado

study¹ /'stʌdi/ n (pl **-dies**) **1** (act, process of learning) estudio m **2** **studies** pl **(a)** (work of student) estudios mpl **(b)** (academic discipline): **business studies** empresariado m or (Esp) empresariales fpl; **social studies** estudios vinculados a las relaciones sociales que comprenden cursos de historia, sociología y otras asignaturas afines **3** (room) estudio m **4** (investigation, examination) estudio m **5** (Art, Liter, Mus) estudio m

study² -dies, -dying, -died vt **(a)** (at school, university) estudiar **(b)** (investigate, research into) estudiar **(c)** (examine, scrutinize) estudiar

■ **~** vi estudiar; **she's ~ing to be a doctor/lawyer** estudia medicina/derecho

stuff¹ /stʌf/ n **1** (colloq) **(a)** (substance, matter): **what's this ~ called?** ¿cómo se llama esto or (fam) esta cosa? **(b)** (miscellaneous items) cosas fpl; (personal items) cosas fpl, bártulos mpl; (junk,

rubbish) cachivaches mpl; **and ~ like that** y cosas de esas; **what sort of ~ does he write?** ¿qué tipo de cosa(s) escribe? **2** (nonsense, excuse) (colloq): **surely you don't believe all that ~ he tells you?** tú no te creerás todo lo que te cuenta ¿no?

stuff² vt **1** **(a)** (fill) ‹quilt/mattress/toy› rellenar; ‹hole› tapar; **the drawer was ~ed with clothes** el cajón estaba atiborrado de ropa; **to ~ oneself/ one's face** (colloq) darse* un atracón (fam), ponerse* morado or ciego (Esp fam) **(b)** (Culin) rellenar **(c)** (in taxidermy) disecar* **2** **(a)** (thrust) **to ~ sth INTO sth** meter algo EN algo **(b)** (put) (colloq) poner*

stuffed /stʌft/ adj **(a)** (in taxidermy) disecado; (toy) de peluche **(b)** ‹pepper/tomatoes› relleno

stuffing /'stʌfɪŋ/ n relleno m

stuffy /'stʌfi/ adj -fier, -fiest **1** **(a)** ‹air› viciado; **it's ~ in here** está muy cargado el ambiente **(b)** ‹nose› tapado **2** (staid) (colloq) ‹person› acartonado, estirado (fam); ‹organization› convencional

stumble /'stʌmbəl/ vi **(a)** (trip) tropezar*, dar* un traspié **(b)** (in speech) atrancarse*; **he ~d over the long words** se atrancaba la lengua con las palabras largas

■ **stumble across** ▶ STUMBLE ON

■ **stumble on, stumble upon** [v + prep + o] dar* con, encontrar*

stumbling block /'stʌmblɪŋ/ n escollo m

stump¹ /stʌmp/ n (of tree) tocón m, cepa f; (of limb) muñón m; (of pencil, candle) cabo m

stump² vt (colloq) (often pass): **the problem has me ~ed** el problema me tiene perplejo; **to be ~ed for an answer** no saber qué contestar

stun /stʌn/ vt -nn- **(a)** (make unconscious) dejar sin sentido; (daze) aturdir **(b)** (amaze) dejar atónito or (fam) helado; (shock) dejar anonadado

stung /stʌŋ/ past & past p of STING²

stunk /stʌŋk/ past p of STINK²

stunned /stʌnd/ adj **(a)** (unconscious) sin sentido; (dazed) aturdido **(b)** (shocked, amazed) ‹expression› de asombro; **he was ~ when they told me** se quedó atónito or (fam) helado cuando se lo dijeron

stunning /'stʌnɪŋ/ adj ‹success/performance› sensacional; ‹person/dress› despampanante

stunt¹ /stʌnt/ n **1** (feat of daring) proeza f; **she does all her own ~s** (Cin, TV) hace todas las escenas peligrosas ella misma; (before n) **~ man/ woman** especialista mf **2** (hoax, trick) truco m, maniobra f; (publicity **~**) ardid m publicitario

stunt² vt detener*, atrofiar

stunted /'stʌntəd ‖'stʌntɪd/ adj ‹growth/ development› atrofiado; ‹tree/body› raquítico

stupefy /'stuːpəfaɪ ‖'stjuːpɪfaɪ/ vt -fies, -fying, -fied (usu pass) dejar estupefacto

stupendous /stuː'pendəs ‖stjuː'pendəs/ adj (colloq) ‹effort/strength› tremendo; ‹success› formidable

stupid /'stuːpəd ‖'stjuːpɪd/ adj (foolish) tonto (fam); (unintelligent) estúpido

stupidity /stuː'pɪdəti ‖stjuː'pɪdəti/ n estupidez f, tontería f

stupor /'stuːpər ‖'stjuːpə(r)/ n (Med) estupor m; (lethargy) aletargamiento m; **in a drunken ~** en un sopor etílico (frml o hum)

S

sturdy /'stɜːrdi ‖'stɜːdi/ adj **-dier, -diest** ⟨build/legs/figure⟩ robusto, macizo; ⟨furniture/bicycle⟩ sólido y resistente

stutter¹ /'stʌtər ‖'stʌtə(r)/ n tartamudeo m

stutter² vi tartamudear
■ ~ vt balbucear, decir* tartamudeando

St Valentine's Day ▶ VALENTINE'S DAY

sty /staɪ/ n (pl **sties**) **(a)** (pig~) pocilga f, chiquero m (AmL) **(b)** ▶ STYE

stye /staɪ/ n (pl **sties** or **styes**) orzuelo m

style /staɪl/ n **1** **(a)** (manner of acting) estilo m; telling lies is not my ~ decir mentiras no va conmigo **(b)** (Art, Lit, Mus) estilo m **2** ⟨elegance⟩ estilo m; **to live/travel in** ~ vivir/viajar a lo grande **3** **(a)** (type, model) diseño m, modelo m **(b)** (fashion) moda f; **to be in** ~ estar* de moda **(c)** (hair ~) peinado m

-style /staɪl/ suff: American~ al estilo americano, a la americana

stylish /'staɪlɪʃ/ adj ⟨furniture/clothes/decor⟩ con mucho estilo; ⟨person⟩ con clase or estilo, estiloso (AmL fam); ⟨resort/restaurant⟩ elegante

stylist /'staɪlɪst ‖'staɪlɪst/ n (hair ~) estilista mf

stylistic /staɪ'lɪstɪk/ adj estilístico

stylized /'staɪlaɪzd/ adj estilizado

stylus /'staɪləs/ n (pl **-li** or **-luses**) aguja f, púa f (RPI)

Styrofoam® /'staɪrəfəʊm/ n (AmE) espuma f de poliestireno

suave /swɑːv/ adj suaver, suavest ⟨voice⟩ engolado; ⟨man⟩ elegante y desenvuelto

sub /sʌb/ n (colloq) **(a)** (substitute) suplente mf, sustituto, -ta m,f **(b)** (submarine) submarino m **(c)** **subs** pl (subscription) cuota f

subconscious¹ /'sʌb'kɑːntʃəs ‖,sʌb'kɒnʃəs/ adj subconsciente

subconscious² n the ~ el subconsciente

subcontract /,sʌb'kɑːntrækt ‖,sʌbkən'trækt/ vt subcontratar

subcontractor /sʌb'kɑːntræktər ‖,sʌbkən'træktə(r)/ n subcontratista mf

subdivide /'sʌbdəvaɪd ‖,sʌbdɪ'vaɪd/ vt subdividir

subdivision /'sʌbdəvɪʒən ‖,sʌbdɪ'vɪʒən/ n subdivisión f

subdue /səb'duː ‖səb'djuː/ vt **(a)** (bring under control) ⟨person⟩ someter, dominar **(b)** (vanquish) (liter) sojuzgar* (liter)

subdued /səb'duːd ‖səb'djuːd/ adj ⟨lighting/color⟩ tenue, apagado; ⟨person/atmosphere⟩ apagado

subheading /'sʌb,hedɪŋ/ n subtítulo m

subject¹ /'sʌbdʒɪkt/ n **1** (topic) tema m; **to change the** ~ cambiar de tema **2** (discipline) asignatura f, materia f (esp AmL), ramo m (Chi) **3** (Pol) súbdito, -ta m,f **4** (Ling) sujeto m

subject² /'sʌbdʒɪkt/ adj **1** (owing obedience) ⟨people/nation⟩ sometido **2** **(a)** (liable, prone) **to be** ~ **TO** sth ⟨to change/delay⟩ estar* sujeto A algo,

ser* susceptible DE algo; ⟨to flooding⟩ estar* expuesto A algo **(b)** (conditional upon) **to be** ~ **TO** sth estar* sujeto A algo

subject³ /səb'dʒekt/ vt **to** ~ sth/sb **TO** sth someter algo/a algn A algo

subject index n índice m de materias

subjective /səb'dʒektɪv/ adj subjetivo

subject matter n (theme) tema m; (content) contenido m

subjugate /'sʌbdʒəgeɪt ‖'sʌbdʒʊgeɪt/ vt subyugar*

subjunctive¹ /səb'dʒʌŋktɪv/ n subjuntivo m

subjunctive² adj subjuntivo

sublet /'sʌb'let/ vt/i ⟨pres p **-letting**; past & past p **-let**⟩ subarrendar*

sublime /sə'blaɪm/ adj sublime

submachine gun /'sʌbmə'ʃiːn/ n metralleta f

submarine /'sʌbməriːn/ n submarino m

submerge /səb'mɜːrdʒ ‖səb'mɜːdʒ/ vt **(a)** (cover, flood) sumergir* **(b)** (plunge) **to** ~ sth **IN** sth sumergir* algo EN algo
■ ~ vi sumergirse*

submission /səb'mɪʃən/ n **1** (surrender) sumisión f **2** (plan, proposal) propuesta f

submissive /səb'mɪsɪv/ adj sumiso

submit /səb'mɪt/ **-tt-** vt **1** ⟨claim/report/application⟩ presentar **2** (subject) **to** ~ sb **TO** sth someter a algn A algo **3** (contend) sostener*
■ ~ vi rendirse*

subnormal /'sʌb'nɔːrməl ‖,sʌb'nɔːməl/ adj por debajo de lo normal; ⟨person⟩ retrasado, subnormal

subordinate¹ /sə'bɔːrdṇət ‖sə'bɔːdɪnət/ adj subordinado

subordinate² n subordinado, -da m,f

subscribe /səb'skraɪb/ vi **1** (buy) **to** ~ (**TO** sth) ⟨to magazine/newspaper⟩ suscribirse* (A algo) **2** (support) **to** ~ **TO** sth suscribir* algo (frml); **I** ~ **to the view that** ... yo soy de la opinión de que ...

subscriber /səb'skraɪbər ‖səb'skraɪbə(r)/ n (to paper, magazine) suscriptor, -tora m,f

subscription /səb'skrɪpʃən/ n **(a)** (to magazine) suscripción f; (for theatrical events) abono m **(b)** (membership fees) (BrE) cuota f

subsequent /'sʌbsɪkwənt/ adj (before n) posterior, subsiguiente

subsequently /'sʌbsɪkwəntli/ adv posteriormente

subservient /səb'sɜːrviənt ‖səb'sɜːviənt/ adj servil

subside /səb'saɪd/ vi **1** «land/road/foundations» hundirse **2** (abate) «storm/wind» amainar; «floods/swelling» decrecer*, bajar; «excitement» decaer*; «anger» calmarse, pasarse

subsidence /səb'saɪdṇs, 'sʌbsədṇs ‖səb'saɪdṇs, 'sʌbsɪdəns/ n hundimiento m

AmC	América Central	Arg	Argentina	Cu	Cuba
AmL	América Latina	Bol	Bolivia	Ec	Ecuador
AmS	América del Sur	Chi	Chile	Esp	España
Andes	Región andina	CS	Cono Sur	Méx	México

Per	Perú
RPI	Río de la Plata
Ur	Uruguay
Ven	Venezuela

subsidiary¹ /səb'sɪdieri ‖səb'sɪdiəri/ *adj* ‹*role/interest*› secundario; **~ subject** materia *f* complementaria

subsidiary² *n* (*pl* **-ries**) (Busn) filial *f*

subsidize /'sʌbsədaɪz ‖'sʌbsɪdaɪz/ *vt* subvencionar, subsidiar (AmL)

subsidy /'sʌbsədi ‖'sʌbsɪdi/ *n* (*pl* **-dies**) subvención *f*, subsidio *m*

subsist /səb'sɪst/ *vi* subsistir

subsistence /səb'sɪstəns/ *n* subsistencia *f*; (*before n*) ‹*farming*› de subsistencia; **~ wage** sueldo *m* de hambre; **to live at ~ level** vivir con lo justo para subsistir

substance /'sʌbstəns/ *n* **1** (type of matter) sustancia *f* **2 (a)** (solid quality, content) sustancia *f*; (of book) enjundia *f*, sustancia *f* **(b)** (foundation) fundamento *m* **(c) in ~** en lo esencial

substandard /'sʌb'stændərd ‖,sʌb'stændəd/ *adj* ‹*goods/clothes*› de calidad inferior

substantial /səb'stæntʃəl ‖səb'stænʃəl/ *adj* **1 (a)** ‹*amount/income/loan*› considerable, importante **(b)** ‹*changes/difference*› sustancial; ‹*contribution*› importante **2 (a)** (sturdy, solid) ‹*furniture/building*› sólido **(b)** (nourishing, filling) ‹*meal*› sustancioso

substantiate /səb'stæntʃieɪt ‖səb'stænʃieɪt/ *vt* ‹*rumors/story/statement*› confirmar, corroborar; **can you ~ these accusations?** ¿puede probar estas acusaciones?

substation /'sʌbsteɪʃən/ *n* (AmE) estafeta *f* de correos

substitute¹ /'sʌbstətut ‖'sʌbstɪtjuːt/ *n* **(a)** (thing) **~** (**for** sth) sucedáneo *m* (**de** algo); **sugar ~** sucedáneo *m* del azúcar; **there's no ~ for experience** nada puede sustituir a la experiencia **(b)** (person) sustituto, -ta *m,f*, reemplazo *m*, suplente *mf*

substitute² *vt* sustituir*, reemplazar*

substitute teacher *n* (AmE) (profesor, -sora *m,f*) suplente *mf*

substitution /'sʌbstə'tuːʃən ‖,sʌbstɪ'tjuːʃən/ *n* sustitución *f*

subterfuge /'sʌbtərfjuːdʒ ‖'sʌbtəfjuːdʒ/ *n* subterfugio *m*

subterranean /'sʌbtə'reɪmiən/ *adj* subterráneo

subtitle¹ /'sʌb,taɪtl/ *n* subtítulo *m*

subtitle² *vt* (*usu pass*) subtitular

subtle /'sʌtl/ *adj* **subtler** /'sʌtlər ‖'sʌtlə(r)/, **subtlest** /'sʌtləst ‖'sʌtlɪst/ **(a)** (delicate, elusive) ‹*fragrance*› sutil **(b)** (not obvious) ‹*difference/ distinction/hint*› sutil; ‹*change*› imperceptible **(c)** (tactful) (colloq) delicado

subtlety /'sʌtlti/ *n* (*pl* **-ties**) **(a)** (delicacy, elusiveness) sutileza *f* **(b)** (tact, finesse) delicadeza *f*; **to lack ~** ser* poco delicado

subtly /'sʌtli/ *adv* **(a)** (delicately, elusively) sutilmente **(b)** (tactfully) con delicadeza

subtotal /'sʌbtəʊtl/ *n* subtotal *m*, total *m* parcial

subtract /səb'trækt/ *vt* **to ~** sth (**from** sth) restar algo (**de** algo)

subtraction /səb'trækʃən/ *n* resta *f*, sustracción *f* (frml)

suburb /'sʌbɜːrb ‖'sʌbɜːb/ *n* barrio *m* or (Méx)

colonia *f* residencial de las afueras; **the ~s** los barrios periféricos *or* de las afueras (de la ciudad)

suburban /sə'bɜːrbən ‖sə'bɜːbən/ *adj* ‹*area*› suburbano; ‹*shopping mall*› de las afueras

suburbia /sə'bɜːrbiə ‖sə'bɜːbiə/ *n* zonas *residenciales de las afueras de una ciudad*

subversive /səb'vɜːrsɪv ‖səb'vɜːsɪv/ *adj* subversivo

subway /'sʌbweɪ/ *n* **1** (AmE Rail) metro *m*, subterráneo *m* (RPl) **2** (BrE) (for pedestrians) pasaje *m* subterráneo

succeed /sək'siːd/ *vi* **1** (have success) «*plan*» dar* resultado, surtir efecto; **she tried to persuade him, but did not ~** intentó convencerlo pero no lo consiguió; **he's ~ed in all that he's done** ha tenido éxito en todo lo que ha hecho; **to ~ in life** triunfar en la vida; **he finally ~ed in passing the exam** al final logró aprobar el examen **2 to ~** (**to** sth): **he ~ed to the throne** subió al trono; **to ~ to a title** heredar un título ■ **~** *vt* suceder; **who ~ed him?** ¿quién lo sucedió?

succeeding /sək'siːdɪŋ/ *adj* (*before n*) subsiguiente

success /sək'ses/ *n* éxito *m*; **to be a ~** ser* un éxito; **without ~** sin (ningún) éxito

successful /sək'sesfəl/ *adj* ‹*person*› de éxito, exitoso (AmL); **the ~ applicant for the job** el candidato que obtenga el puesto; **to be ~ in life** triunfar en la vida

successfully /sək'sesfəli/ *adv* satisfactoriamente

succession /sək'seʃən/ *n* **1 (a)** (act of following) sucesión *f*; **for 6 years in ~** durante seis años consecutivos; **in rapid ~** uno tras otro **(b)** (series) sucesión *f* **2** (to office, rank) sucesión *f*

successive /sək'sesɪv/ *adj* (*before n*) consecutivo

successor /sək'sesər ‖sək'sesə(r)/ *n* sucesor, -sora *m,f*

succinct /sək'sɪŋkt/ *adj* sucinto, conciso

succulent /'sʌkjələnt ‖'sʌkjʊlənt/ *adj* suculento

succumb /sə'kʌm/ *vi* **to ~** (**to** sth) sucumbir (**a** algo)

such¹ /sʌtʃ/ *adj* **1 (a)** (emphasizing degree, extent) tal (+ *noun*); tan (+ *adj*); **I woke up with ~ a headache** me levanté con tal dolor de cabeza ...; **I've got ~ a lot of work to do** tengo tanto (trabajo) que hacer; **I've never heard ~ nonsense** nunca he oído semejante estupidez **(b)** (*with clauses of result or purpose*) **such ... (that)** tal/tan ... que **(c)** (*in comparisons*) **such ... as** tan ... como

2 (a) (of this, that kind) tal; **~ children are known as ...** a dichos *or* a tales niños se los conoce como ...; **there's no ~ thing as the perfect crime** el crimen perfecto no existe; **I said no ~ thing!** ¡yo no dije tal cosa! **(b)** (unspecified) tal; **the letter tells you to go to ~ a house on ~ a date** la carta te dice que vayas a tal casa en tal fecha

such² *pron* **1 (a)** (of the indicated kind) tal; **~ were her last words** fueron sus últimas palabras **(b) such as** como; **many modern inventions, ~ as radar ...** muchos inventos modernos, (tales) como el radar ... **(c) as such** como tal/tales **2** (indicating lack of quantity, quality): ⋯ ⃗ the evidence, ~ as it is, seems to ... las pocas pruebas que hay parecen ... **3** (of such a kind, extent, degree) **such that** tal ... que

such: ~-and-~ *adj* tal (o cual); **we were told to get ~-and-~ a book** nos dijeron que compráramos tal (o cual) libro; **~-like** *pron* (colloq) (of things) cosas por el estilo; (of people) gente por el estilo

suck /sʌk/ *vt* **(a)** «*person*» ‹*thumb/candy*› chupar; ‹*liquid*› (through a straw) sorber; «*vacuum cleaner*» aspirar; «*pump*» succionar, aspirar; «*insect*» ‹*blood/nectar*› chupar **(b)** (pull, draw) (+ *adv compl*) arrastrar; **she was ~ed under by the current** la corriente se la tragó
■ ~ *vi* **1** «*person*» chupar; **to ~ AT/ON sth** chupar algo **2** (be objectionable) (AmE sl): **the movie really ~s** la película es una mierda (vulg)
■ **suck in** [*v + o + adv, v + adv + o*] ‹*air/breath*› tomar

sucker /'sʌkər ‖ 'sʌkə(r)/ *n* **1** (colloq) (fool) (pej) imbécil *mf*; **to be a ~ for punishment** ser* un masoquista **2** (suction device — on animal, plant) ventosa *f*; (— made of rubber) (BrE) ventosa *f* **3** (Bot) (shoot) chupón *m*, mamón *m*

suckle /'sʌkəl/ *vt* amamantar, darle* de mamar a
■ ~ *vi* mamar

suction /'sʌkʃən/ *n* succión *f*; (before *n*) ~ **cup** ventosa *f*

Sudan /suː'dɑːn/ *n* (the) ~ (el) Sudán

Sudanese /suːdn̩'iːz ‖ suːdə'niːz/ *adj* sudanés

sudden /'sʌdn̩/ *adj* **(a)** (rushed) repentino, súbito; (unexpected) imprevisto, inesperado; **all of a ~** de repente, de pronto **(b)** (abrupt) ‹*movement*› brusco

suddenly /'sʌdn̩li/ *adv* **(a)** (unexpectedly) de repente, de pronto **(b)** (abruptly) bruscamente

suds /sʌdz/ *pl n* espuma *f* de jabón

sue /suː ‖ suː, sjuː/ *vt* **to ~ sb (FOR sth)** demandar a algn (POR algo)
■ ~ *vi* (Law) entablar una demanda, poner* pleito (Esp)

suede /sweɪd/ *n* ante *m*, gamuza *f*

suet /'suːət ‖ 'suːɪt, 'suːɪt/ *n* sebo *m*, grasa *f* de pella

suffer /'sʌfər ‖ 'sʌfə(r)/ *vt* **(a)** (undergo) ‹*injury/damage/loss*› sufrir; ‹*pain*› padecer*, sufrir **(b)** (endure) aguantar, tolerar
■ ~ *vi* **(a)** (experience pain, difficulty) sufrir **(b)** (be affected, deteriorate) «*health/eyesight*» resentirse*; «*business/relationship*» verse* afectado, resentirse* **(c)** (be afflicted) **to ~ FROM sth** sufrir *or* (frml) padecer* DE algo

sufferer /'sʌfərər ‖ 'sʌfərə(r)/ *n* ~**s from arthritis, arthritis ~s** quienes sufren de artritis, los artríticos

suffering /'sʌfərɪŋ/ *n* sufrimiento *m*

suffice /sə'faɪs/ *vi* (frml) bastar, ser* suficiente

sufficient /sə'fɪʃənt/ *adj* suficiente, bastante

sufficiently /sə'fɪʃəntli/ *adv* lo suficientemente

suffix /'sʌfɪks/ *n* sufijo *m*

suffocate /'sʌfəkeɪt/ *vt* asfixiar, ahogar*
■ ~ *vi* asfixiarse*, ahogarse*

suffocating /'sʌfəkeɪtɪŋ/ *adj* ‹*smoke/routine*› asfixiante; ‹*heat*› sofocante

suffocation /sʌfə'keɪʃən/ *n* asfixia *f*

suffrage /'sʌfrɪdʒ/ *n* sufragio *m*

sugar /'ʃʊɡər ‖ 'ʃʊɡə(r)/ *n* azúcar *m or f*; (before *n*) ~ **bowl** azucarero *m*, azucarera *f* (esp AmL); ~ **cube** *o* **lump** terrón *m* de azúcar

sugar: ~ beet *n* remolacha *f* azucarera *or* (Méx) betabel *m* blanco; ~ **cane** *n* caña *f* de azúcar

sugary /'ʃʊɡəri/ *adj* **(a)** ‹*drink/taste*› dulce, azucarado **(b)** ‹*tones/smile*› meloso, almibarado

suggest /səg'dʒest ‖ sə'dʒest/ *vt* **1 (a)** (propose) sugerir*; **to ~ sth TO sb** sugerirle* algo A algn; **to ~ -ING** sugerir* + INF, sugerir* QUE (+ *subj*); **to ~ TO sb THAT** sugerirle* a algn QUE (+ *subj*) **(b)** (offer for consideration): **can you ~ a possible source for this rumor?** ¿se le ocurre quién puede haber empezado este rumor? **(c)** (imply, insinuate) insinuar*; **are you ~ing (that) my son is a thief?** ¿insinúa usted que mi hijo es un ladrón? **2** (indicate, point to) indicar* **3** (evoke, bring to mind) sugerir*

suggestion /səg'dʒestʃən ‖ sə'dʒestʃən/ *n* **1 (a)** (proposal) sugerencia *f*; **to make a ~** hacer* una sugerencia; **have you any ~s for speeding up the process?** ¿se le ocurre algo para acelerar el proceso? **(b)** (explanation, theory) teoría *f* **(c)** (insinuation) insinuación *f* **2** (indication, hint) indicio *m* **3** (Psych) sugestión *f*

suggestive /səg'dʒestɪv ‖ sə'dʒestɪv/ *adj* **1** ‹*gesture/laugh*› insinuante, provocativo **2** (pred) **to be ~ OF sth (a)** (indicative) parecer* indicar algo **(b)** (reminiscent) hacer* pensar EN algo, evocar* algo

suicidal /suːə'saɪdl̩ ‖ suːɪ'saɪdl̩, sjuː-/ *adj* suicida

suicide /'suːəsaɪd ‖ 'suːɪsaɪd, 'sjuː-/ *n* (act) suicidio *m*; **to commit ~** suicidarse*; (before *n*) ‹*attempt/pact*› de suicidio; ‹*mission/bombing*› suicida; ~ **note** carta *f* de despedida de un suicida

suit¹ /suːt ‖ suːt, sjuːt/ *n* **1** (Clothing) (male) traje *m*, terno (AmS); (female) traje *m* (de chaqueta), traje *m* sastre **2** (Law) juicio *m*, pleito *m* **3** (in cards) palo *m*; **to follow ~** seguir* su (*or* nuestro *etc*) ejemplo

suit² *vt* **1** (be convenient to, please) venirle* bien a, convenirle* a; **to ~ oneself** hacer* lo que uno quiere; ~ **yourself!** ¡haz lo que quieras! **2 (a)** (be appropriate, good for): **the job doesn't ~ him** el trabajo no es para él *or* no le va **(b)** (look good on) «*hairstyle/dress*» quedarle *or* (esp Esp) irle* bien a; *see also* SUITED **(c)** (adapt) **to ~ sth TO sth/sb** adaptar algo A algo/algn

suitable /'suːtəbəl ‖ 'suːtəbəl, 'sjuː-/ *adj* **(a)** (appropriate) apropiado, adecuado; **(to be) ~ FOR sb/sth/-ING** (ser*) apropiado *or* adecuado PARA algn/algo/+ INF **(b)** (acceptable, proper) apropiado **(c)** (convenient) conveniente

suitably /'suːtəbli ‖ 'suːtəbli, 'sjuː-/ *adv* ‹*qualified*› adecuadamente; ‹*dressed/equipped*› apropiadamente

suitcase /'suːtkeɪs ‖ 'suːtkeɪs, 'sjuː-/ *n* maleta *f*, valija *f* (RPl), petaca *f* (Méx)

suite /swiːt/ *n* **(a)** (of rooms) suite *f* **(b)** (of furniture) juego *m* **(c)** (Mus) suite *f*

suited /'suːtəd ‖ 'suːtɪd, 'sjuː-/ *adj* (pred) **to be ~ TO sth** «*thing*» ser* apropiado *or* adecuado PARA algo; **I'm not ∼ to this type of work** no sirvo para este tipo de trabajo; **they are very well ∼ (to each other)** están hechos el uno para el otro

suitor /'suːtər ‖'suːtə(r), 'sjuː-/ n (dated) pretendiente m

sulfur, (BrE) **sulphur** /'sʌlfər ‖'sʌlfə(r)/ n azufre m

sulk /sʌlk/ vi enfurruñarse

sulky /'sʌlki/ adj **-kier, -kiest** ⟨child⟩ con tendencia a enfurruñarse; ⟨look/reply⟩ malhumorado

sullen /'sʌlən/ adj hosco, huraño

sultan /'sʌltn̩/ n sultán m

sultana /sʌl'tænə ‖sʌl'tɑːnə/ n (Culin) pasa f sultana or de Esmirna

sultry /'sʌltri/ adj **-trier, -triest (a)** ⟨climate/day⟩ bochornoso **(b)** ⟨voice/smile/person⟩ seductor

sum /sʌm/ n **1** (calculation — in general) cuenta f; (— addition) suma f, adición f (frml) **2** (total, aggregate) suma f, total m **3** (of money) suma f or cantidad f (de dinero)

■ **sum up: -mm- 1** [v + o + adv, v + adv + o] **(a)** (summarize) ⟨discussion/report⟩ resumir **(b)** (assess) ⟨person⟩ catalogar*; **she quickly ∼med up the situation** enseguida se hizo una composición de lugar **2** [v + adv] **(a)** (summarize) recapitular; **to ∼ up** (as linker) resumiendo, en resumen **(b)** (Law) recapitular

summarize /'sʌməraɪz/ vt resumir

summary¹ /'sʌməri/ n (pl **-ries**) resumen m

summary² adj ⟨dismissal⟩ inmediato; ⟨trial/judgment⟩ sumario

summer /'sʌmər ‖'sʌmə(r)/ n verano m; **in (the) ∼** en (el) verano; (before n) ⟨weather/clothes/vacation⟩ de verano; **∼ camp** (in US) colonia f de vacaciones

summer: ∼house n cenador m; **∼ school** n (in US) clases fpl de verano (gen de repaso); (in UK) curso m de verano; **∼time** n verano m, estío m (liter); **∼ time** n (BrE) horario m de verano

summery /'sʌməri/ adj veraniego, de verano

summing-up /'sʌmɪŋ'ʌp/ n (pl **summings-up**) recapitulación f

summit /'sʌmət ‖'sʌmɪt/ n **1** (of mountain, career) cumbre f, cima f **2** ∼ **(conference)** (conferencia f) cumbre f

summon /'sʌmən/ vt **(a)** (send for) ⟨servant/waiter⟩ llamar, mandar llamar (AmL); ⟨police/doctor⟩ llamar; ⟨help/reinforcements⟩ pedir*; ⟨meeting/parliament⟩ convocar* **(b)** (Law) ⟨witness/defendant⟩ citar, emplazar* **(c)** ▶ SUMMON UP

■ **summon up** [v + adv + o] **(a)** (gather): **he ∼ed up the courage to ask her** se armó de valor para preguntárselo; **I couldn't even ∼ up the strength to get up the stairs** ni siquiera pude reunir fuerzas para subir la escalera **(b)** (call up) ⟨thoughts/memories⟩ evocar*

summons¹ /'sʌmənz/ n (pl **-monses**) **(a)** (Law) citación f, citatorio m (Méx) **(b)** (for help etc) llamamiento m, llamado m (AmL)

summons² vt (Law) citar, emplazar*

sumptuous /'sʌmptʃuəs ‖'sʌmptjʊəs/ adj ⟨fabric/color⟩ suntuoso; ⟨mansion/decor⟩ lujoso

sun¹ /sʌn/ n sol m; **under the ∼: I've tried everything under the ∼** he probado de todo

sun² v refl **-nn-**: **to ∼ oneself** tomar el sol or (CS tb) tomar sol, asolearse (AmL)

sun: ∼bathe vi tomar el sol or (CS tb) tomar sol, asolearse (AmL); **∼beam** n rayo m de sol; **∼bed** n cama f solar; **∼block** n filtro m solar; **∼burn** n quemadura f de sol; **∼burned** /'sʌnbɜːrnd ‖'sʌnbɜːnd/, (BrE also) **∼burnt** /'sʌnbɜːrnt ‖'sʌnbɜːnt/ adj **(a)** (painfully) quemado por el sol **(b)** (brown) bronceado, tostado, quemado (AmL), moreno (Esp), asoleado (Méx)

sundae /'sʌndeɪ/ n sundae m (helado con fruta, crema, jarabe etc)

Sunday /'sʌndeɪ, -di/ n domingo m; (before n) **∼ school** sesiones dominicales de catequesis para niños; see also MONDAY

sun: ∼dial n reloj m de sol; **∼down** n (no art) puesta f de(l) sol; **∼dress** n vestido m de tirantes, solera f (CS)

sundries /'sʌndriz/ pl n **(a)** (goods) artículos mpl diversos **(b)** (expenses) gastos mpl varios

sundry¹ /'sʌndri/ adj varios, diversos

sundry² pron: **all and ∼** todos sin excepción, todo el mundo

sunflower /'sʌnflaʊr ‖'sʌnflaʊə(r)/ n girasol m; (before n) **∼ oil** aceite m de girasol; **∼ seed** semilla f de girasol, pipa f (Esp)

sung /sʌŋ/ past p of SING

sunglasses /'sʌnˌɡlæsəz ‖'sʌnˌɡlɑːsɪz/ pl n gafas fpl or (esp AmL) lentes mpl or anteojos mpl de sol

sunk¹ /sʌŋk/ past p of SINK

sunk² adj (pred) **(a)** (in trouble) (colloq) **to be ∼** estar* perdido **(b)** (immersed) **to be ∼ IN sth** ⟨in depression/gloom⟩ estar* sumido EN algo (liter)

sunken /'sʌŋkən/ adj **(a)** (before n) ⟨ship/treasure⟩ hundido, sumergido **(b)** (before n) ⟨garden/patio⟩ a nivel más bajo **(c)** (hollow) ⟨eyes/cheeks⟩ hundido

sun: ∼ lamp n lámpara f de rayos ultravioletas; **∼light** n sol m, luz f del sol; **∼lit** adj soleado

sunny /'sʌni/ adj **-nier, -niest (a)** ⟨day⟩ de sol; ⟨room/garden⟩ soleado; **it's ∼ today** hoy hace sol **(b)** (good-humored) alegre

sun: ∼rise n salida f del sol; **∼roof** n techo m corredizo; **∼screen** n filtro m solar; **∼set** n puesta f de(l) sol; **at ∼set** al atardecer, a la caída de la tarde; **∼shine** n sol m; **∼spot** n **(a)** (Astron) mancha f solar **(b)** (resort) (colloq) lugar de veraneo con mucho sol; **∼stroke** n insolación f; **∼tan** n bronceado m, moreno m (Esp); **to get a ∼tan** broncearse, tostarse*, quemarse (AmL); (before n) ⟨lotion⟩ bronceador; **∼trap** n: lugar muy soleado y resguardado

super /'suːpər ‖'suːpə(r)/ adj (colloq) genial (fam), súper adj inv (fam)

superb /suː'pɜːrb ‖suː'pɜːb/ adj magnífico, espléndido

superbug /'suːpərbʌɡ ‖'suːpəbʌɡ/ n microbio m multiresistente

supercilious /ˌsuːpər'sɪliəs ‖ˌsuːpə'sɪliəs/ adj desdeñoso

superficial /ˌsuːpər'fɪʃəl ‖ˌsuːpə'fɪʃəl/ adj superficial

superfluous /suː'pɜːrfluəs ‖suː'pɜːfluəs/ adj superfluo

S

superglue[1] /'su:pərglu: ‖'su:pəglu:/ n cola f de contacto, superglue m (Esp)

superglue[2] vt pegar* con cola de contacto, pegar* con superglue (Esp)

superhighway /'su:pər'haɪweɪ ‖'su:pə,haɪweɪ/ n (a) (AmE Auto) autopista f (b) (Comput): **the information** ~ la autopista de la comunicación

superhuman /'su:pər'hju:mən ‖,su:pə'hju:mən/ adj sobrehumano

superimpose /'su:pərɪm'pəʊz/ vt superponer*

superintend /'su:pərɪn'tend/ vt supervisar

superintendent /'su:pərɪn'tendənt/ n (a) (person in charge — of maintenance, hostel, swimming pool) encargado, -da m,f; (— of building) (AmE) portero, -ra m,f; (— of institution) director, -tora m,f (b) (police officer) (in US) superintendente mf (jefe de un departamento de policía); (in UK) comisario, -ria m,f de policía

superior[1] /sʊ'prɪər ‖su:'pɪərɪə(r)/ adj **1** (a) (better) **to be** ~ (**TO sth/sb**) ser* superior (A algo/algn), ser* mejor (QUE algo/algn) (b) (above average) (workmanship/writer) de gran calidad **2** (arrogant) (tone/smile) de superioridad; **he's so** ~ se da unos aires de superioridad **3** (rank) superior; **his** ~ **officer** su superior

superior[2] n superior m

superiority /sʊ'pɪrɪ'ɔ:rəti ‖su:,pɪərɪ'ɒrəti/ n superioridad f

superlative[1] /sʊ'pɜ:rlətɪv ‖su:'pɜ:lətɪv/ adj inigualable, excepcional

superlative[2] n superlativo m

superman /'su:pərmæn ‖'su:pəmæn/ n (pl **-men** /-men/) superhombre m

supermarket /'su:pər,mɑ:rkət ‖'su:pə,mɑ:kɪt/ n supermercado m, autoservicio m

supernatural /'su:pər'nætʃərəl ‖,su:pə'nætʃərəl/ adj sobrenatural

superpower /'su:pərpaʊər ‖'su:pəpaʊə(r)/ n superpotencia f

supersede /'su:pər'si:d ‖,su:pə'si:d/ vt (often pass) reemplazar*, sustituir*

supersonic /'su:pər'sɑ:nɪk ‖,su:pə'sɒnɪk/ adj supersónico

superstar /'su:pərstɑ:r ‖'su:pəstɑ:(r)/ n superestrella f, gran estrella f

superstition /'su:pər'stɪʃən ‖,su:pə'stɪʃən/ n superstición f

superstitious /'su:pər'stɪʃəs ‖,su:pə'stɪʃəs/ adj supersticioso

superstore /'su:pərstɔ:r ‖'su:pəstɔ:(r)/ n (BrE) hipermercado m

supervise /'su:pərvaɪz ‖'su:pəvaɪz/ vt (a) (project/staff) supervisar (b) (watch over) vigilar

supervision /'su:pər'vɪʒən ‖,su:pə'vɪʒən/ n supervisión f

supervisor /'su:pərvaɪzər ‖'su:pəvaɪzə(r)/ n supervisor, -sora m,f

supper /'sʌpər ‖'sʌpə(r)/ n cena f (ligera), comida f (ligera) (esp AmL); **to have** ~ cenar, comer (esp AmL)

supplant /sə'plænt ‖sə'plɑ:nt/ vt sustituir*, reemplazar*

supple /'sʌpəl/ adj **-pler** /-plər ‖-plə(r)/, **-plest** /-pləst ‖-plɪst/ (body/fingers) ágil; (leather) fino y flexible, suave

supplement[1] /'sʌpləmənt ‖'sʌplɪmənt/ n **1** (addition to diet, income) complemento m **2** (a) (additional part published separately) suplemento m (b) (section of newspaper — separate) suplemento m; (— inserted) separata f

supplement[2] /'sʌpləmənt ‖'sʌplɪment/ vt (diet/income) complementar; (report) completar

supplementary /'sʌplə'mentəri ‖,sʌplɪ'mentəri/ adj suplementario

supplier /sə'plaɪər ‖sə'plaɪə(r)/ n (Busn) proveedor, -dora m,f, abastecedor, -dora m,f

supply[1] /sə'plaɪ/ n (pl **-plies**) **1** (provision) suministro m; **the water/electricity** ~ el suministro de agua/electricidad; **the law of** ~ **and demand** la ley de la oferta y la demanda **2** (stock, store): **food supplies are running low** se están agotando las provisiones or los víveres or (Mil) los pertrechos; **we only have a month's** ~ **of coal left** solo nos queda carbón para un mes; (Busn) las existencias de carbón solo van a durar un mes; **to be in short** ~ escasear

supply[2] vt **-plies, -plying, -plied** **1** (a) (provide, furnish) (electricity/gas) suministrar; (goods) suministrar, abastecer* or proveer* de; (evidence/information) proporcionar, facilitar (b) (retailer/manufacturer) abastecer*; **to** ~ **sb WITH sth** (with equipment) proveer* a algn DE algo; (Busn) abastecer* a algn DE algo, suministrarle algo A algn; (with information) facilitarle or proporcionarle algo A algn **2** (meet) (fml) (demand/need) satisfacer*

supply teacher n (BrE) (profesor, -sora m,f) suplente mf

support[1] /sə'pɔ:rt ‖sə'pɔ:t/ vt **1** (hold up) (bridge/structure) sostener*; **the chair couldn't** ~ **his weight** la silla no pudo aguantar or resistir su peso **2** (a) (maintain, sustain) (family) mantener*; **to** ~ **oneself** ganarse la vida (b) (Comput) admitir **3** (a) (back) (cause/motion) apoyar; **what team do you** ~? ¿de qué equipo eres (hincha)? (b) (back up) apoyar **4** (corroborate) (theory) respaldar, confirmar

support[2] n **1** (a) (of structure) soporte m (b) (physical): **to lean on sb for** ~ apoyarse en algn (para sostenerse) **2** (a) (financial) ayuda f (económica), apoyo m (económico) (b) (person) sostén m **3** (backing, encouragement) apoyo m **4** (Mil) apoyo m, refuerzo m **5** **in support of** (as prep) en apoyo de

support band n grupo m telonero

supporter /sə'pɔ:rtər ‖sə'pɔ:tə(r)/ n (a) (adherent) partidario, -ria m,f (b) (Sport) hincha mf

supporting /səˈpɔːrtɪŋ ‖ səˈpɔːtɪŋ/ adj (before n) ⟨role/actor⟩ secundario; ~ act número m telonero

supportive /səˈpɔːrtɪv ‖ səˈpɔːtɪv/ adj: she's been very ~ me (or lo etc) ha apoyado mucho

suppose /səˈpəʊz/ vt **1 (a)** (assume, imagine) suponer*, imaginarse; ~ he phones and you're not in ¿y si llama y tú no estás?; I ~ so supongo or me imagino que sí; I ~ not supongo que no or no creo **(b)** (believe, think) creer*; what do you ~ he'll do? ¿tú qué crees que hará? **2 to be supposed to + INF (a)** (indicating obligation, expectation): I'm ~d to start work at nine se supone que tengo que empezar a trabajar a las nueve; aren't you ~d to be at home? ¿tú no tendrías que estar en casa? **(b)** (indicating intention): what's that ~d to be? ¿y eso qué se supone que es?; what's that ~d to mean? ¿y qué quieres (or quieren etc) decir con eso, (si se puede saber)? **(c)** (indicating general opinion): it's ~d to be a very interesting book dicen que es un libro muy interesante

supposing /səˈpəʊzɪŋ/ conj **(a)** (expressing hypothesis) suponiendo que; ~ she agrees, will they let us go? suponiendo que ella esté de acuerdo ¿nos dejarán ir? **(b)** (introducing suggestion) ¿y si ... ?

supposition /ˌsʌpəˈzɪʃən/ n suposición f

suppress /səˈpres/ vt **(a)** ⟨anger/laughter⟩ contener*; ⟨feelings⟩ reprimir **(b)** ⟨facts/evidence/ truth⟩ ocultar **(c)** ⟨revolt⟩ sofocar*; ⟨organization⟩ suprimir

suppression /səˈpreʃən/ n **(a)** (of feelings) represión f **(b)** (of evidence) ocultación f **(c)** (of revolt) represión f

supremacy /səˈpreməsi ‖ suːˈpreməsi, sjuː-/ n supremacía f

supreme /suːˈpriːm ‖ suːˈpriːm, sjuː-/ adj supremo

Supreme Court n the ~ ~ el Tribunal Supremo or (esp AmL) la Corte Suprema (de Justicia)

surcharge /ˈsɜːrtʃɑːrdʒ ‖ ˈsɜːtʃɑːdʒ/ n recargo m

sure¹ /ʃʊr ‖ ʃʊə(r), ʃɔː(r)/ adj surer, surest **1** (convinced) (pred) seguro; to be ~ ABOUT sth estar* seguro DE algo; I'm not ~ I agree with you no sé si estoy de acuerdo contigo; I'm not ~ who/ why/what ... no sé muy bien quién/por qué/qué ...; to be ~ OF sth/sb estar* seguro DE algo/algn; I want to be ~ of getting there on time quiero asegurarme de que voy a llegar a tiempo; to be ~ of oneself (convinced one is right) estar* seguro; (self-confident) ser* seguro de sí mismo **2** (certain): one thing is ~: he's lying lo que está claro or lo que es seguro es que está mintiendo; it's ~ to rain seguro que llueve; to make ~ of sth asegurarse de algo; make ~ (that) you're not late no vayas a llegar tarde **3** (accurate, reliable) ⟨remedy/method⟩ seguro; ⟨judgment/aim⟩ certero; ⟨indication⟩ claro; ⟨ground⟩ seguro **4** (in phrases) for sure: we don't know anything for ~ no sabemos nada seguro or con seguridad; we'll win for ~ seguro que ganamos; to be sure (admittedly) (indep) por cierto

sure² adv **1** (colloq) (as intensifier): she ~ is clever, she's ~ clever ¡qué lista es!, ¡si será lista!;

do you like it? — I ~ do! ¿te gusta? — ¡ya lo creo! **2** (of course) por supuesto, claro **3 sure enough** efectivamente, en efecto

sure: ~**fire** adj (before n) ⟨method⟩ segurísimo, infalible; ~**footed** /ˈʃʊrˈfʊtəd ‖ ˌʃʊəˈfʊtɪd, ˌʃɔːˈfʊtɪd/ adj ⟨goat/cat⟩ de pie firme

surely /ˈʃʊrli ‖ ˈʃʊəli, ˈʃɔːli/ adv **(a)** (expressing conviction): ~ the real problem is ... el verdadero problema, digo yo or me parece a mí, es ...; ~ she doesn't mean that! ¡no puede ser que lo diga en serio! **(b)** (expressing uncertainty): he must be mistaken, ~? tiene que estar equivocado ¿no? **(c)** (expressing disbelief): ~ you don't believe that! ¡no te creerás eso!; ~ not! ¡no es posible! or ¡no puede ser! **2** (undoubtedly, certainly) seguramente, sin duda **3** (gladly, willingly) por supuesto, desde luego

surf¹ /sɜːrf ‖ sɜːf/ n **(a)** (waves) olas fpl (rompientes); (swell) oleaje m **(b)** (foam) espuma f

surf² vi hacer* surf or surfing ■ ~ vt (Comput) explorar, navegar* en

surface¹ /ˈsɜːrfəs ‖ ˈsɜːfəs/ n **1 (a)** (of solid, land) superficie f; (before n) ⟨wound/mark⟩ superficial; ⟨resemblance⟩ superficial **(b)** (of liquid, sea) superficie f **(c) on the surface** (superficially) en apariencia **2** (Math) ~ (area) superficie f, área f‡

surface² vi «diver/submarine» salir* a la superficie; «problems/difficulties» aflorar, aparecer* ■ ~ vt ⟨road⟩ revestir*, recubrir*; (with asphalt) asfaltar

surfboard /ˈsɜːrfbɔːrd ‖ ˈsɜːfbɔːd/ n tabla f de surf or de surfing

surfeit /ˈsɜːrfɪt ‖ ˈsɜːfɪt/ n (liter) a ~ OF sth un exceso or (liter) una plétora DE algo

surfer /ˈsɜːrfər ‖ ˈsɜːfə(r)/ n surfista mf

surfing /ˈsɜːrfɪŋ ‖ ˈsɜːfɪŋ/ n surf m, surfing m

surge¹ /sɜːrdʒ ‖ sɜːdʒ/ n (in demand, sales) aumento m; a ~ of people una oleada de gente; we felt a new ~ of hope sentimos renacer nuestras esperanzas

surge² vi «wave» levantarse; «sea» hincharse; the crowd ~d out through the gates la gente salió en tropel por las puertas; anger/ hatred ~d up inside her la ira/el odio la invadió; to ~ ahead of sb adelantársele a algn

surgeon /ˈsɜːrdʒən ‖ ˈsɜːdʒən/ n cirujano, -na m,f

surgery /ˈsɜːrdʒəri ‖ ˈsɜːdʒəri/ n (pl -ries) **1** (science) cirugía f **2** (BrE) **(a)** (room) consultorio m, consulta f **(b)** (consultation period of doctor) consulta f; (before n) ⟨times/hours⟩ de consulta

surgical /ˈsɜːrdʒɪkəl ‖ ˈsɜːdʒɪkəl/ adj ⟨instruments/treatment⟩ quirúrgico; ⟨stocking/ appliance⟩ ortopédico

surgical spirit n (BrE) alcohol m (de 90°)

surly /ˈsɜːrli ‖ ˈsɜːli/ adj -lier, -liest hosco

surmise /sərˈmaɪz ‖ səˈmaɪz/ vt (frml) conjeturar (frml)

surmount /sərˈmaʊnt ‖ səˈmaʊnt/ vt superar

surname /ˈsɜːrneɪm ‖ ˈsɜːneɪm/ n apellido m

surpass /sərˈpæs ‖ səˈpɑːs/ vt superar

surplus¹ /ˈsɜːrpləs ‖ ˈsɜːpləs/ n (pl ~es) (of produce, stock) excedente m; (of funds) superávit m

S

surplus² *adj* ⟨*goods/stocks*⟩ excedente

surprise¹ /səˈpraɪz/ *n* sorpresa *f*; **to my ~** para mi sorpresa; **to take sb by ~** sorprender a algn, pillar *or* (esp Esp) coger* a algn desprevenido; (*before n*) ⟨*gift/visit/attack*⟩ sorpresa *adj inv*

surprise² *vt* **(a)** (astonish) sorprender **(b)** (catch unawares) sorprender, pillar *or* agarrar *or* (esp Esp) coger* desprevenido

surprised /səˈpraɪzd/ *adj* ⟨*look*⟩ sorprendido, de sorpresa; **I was so ~** me quedé tan sorprendido; **I'm ~ about** *o* **at that** eso me sorprende mucho; **I'm ~ (THAT)** ... me sorprende *or* me extraña QUE ... (+ *subj*)

surprising /səˈpraɪzɪŋ/ *adj* sorprendente

surprisingly /səˈpraɪzɪŋli/ *adv* **(a)** ⟨*quiet/near/good*⟩ sorprendentemente **(b)** (*indep*): **~, she feels no resentment** no está resentida, lo cual es sorprendente

surreal /səˈriːəl/ *adj* surrealista

surrealism /səˈriːəlɪzəm/ *n* surrealismo *m*

surrealist /səˈriːələst ‖səˈriːəlɪst/ *n* surrealista *mf*; (*before n*) ⟨*painter/poem*⟩ surrealista

surrender¹ /səˈrendər ‖səˈrendə(r)/ *vt* **(a)** (Mil) rendir*, entregar* **(b)** (frml) ⟨*document/ticket*⟩ entregar* **(c)** (relinquish) ⟨*right/claim*⟩ renunciar a ■ ~ *vi* rendirse*; **to ~ TO sb** entregarse* a algn

surrender² *n* **(a)** (capitulation) rendición *f*, capitulación *f* **(b)** (frml) (*no pl*) (of passport, document) entrega *f*

surreptitious /ˌsʌrəpˈtɪʃəs/ *adj* furtivo, subrepticio

surrogate¹ /ˈsʌrəgət/ *n* (frml) sustituto *m*

surrogate² *adj* ⟨*material*⟩ sucedáneo; **~ mother** madre *f* suplente *or* de alquiler

surround¹ /səˈraʊnd/ *vt* **(a)** (encircle) ⟨*place/person*⟩ rodear; **the house is ~ed by trees** la casa está rodeada de árboles **(b)** (Mil) rodear, cercar*

surround² *n* marco *m*

surrounding /səˈraʊndɪŋ/ *adj* (*before n*) ⟨*countryside/area*⟩ de alrededor

surroundings /səˈraʊndɪŋz/ *pl n* **(a)** (of town, village) alrededores *mpl* **(b)** (environment) ambiente *m*

surveillance /sərˈveɪləns ‖səˈveɪləns/ *n* vigilancia *f*

survey¹ /ˈsɜːrveɪ ‖ˈsɜːveɪ/ *n* **1** **(a)** (of land) inspección *f*, reconocimiento *m*; (for mapping) medición *f* **(b)** (of building) inspección *f*, peritaje *m*, peritación *f*, (written report) informe *m* del perito, peritaje *m*, peritación *f* **2** (overall view) visión *f* general **3** (investigation) estudio *m*; (poll) encuesta *f*, sondeo *m*

survey² /sərˈveɪ ‖səˈveɪ/ *vt* **1** **(a)** ⟨*land/region*⟩ (measure) medir*; (inspect) inspeccionar, reconocer* **(b)** ⟨*building*⟩ inspeccionar, llevar a cabo un peritaje de **2** **(a)** (look at) contemplar, mirar **(b)** (view, consider) ⟨*situation/plan/prospects*⟩ examinar, analizar* **3** (question) ⟨*group*⟩ encuestar, hacer* un sondeo de

surveyor /sərˈveɪər ‖səˈveɪə(r)/ *n* **(a)** (of land) agrimensor, -sora *m,f*, topógrafo, -fa *m,f* **(b)** (of building) perito, -ta *m,f*

survival /sərˈvaɪvəl ‖səˈvaɪvəl/ *n* (continued existence) sobrevivencia *f*, supervivencia *f*

survive /sərˈvaɪv ‖səˈvaɪv/ *vi* sobrevivir; **her last surviving descendant** su último descendiente vivo; **I can just ~ on \$100 a week** con 100 dólares semanales apenas me alcanza para vivir ■ ~ *vt* **1** ⟨*accident/crash*⟩ salir* con vida de; ⟨*war/earthquake*⟩ sobrevivir a; ⟨*experience*⟩ superar* **2** (outlive) ⟨*person*⟩ sobrevivir

survivor /sərˈvaɪvər ‖səˈvaɪvə(r)/ *n* superviviente *mf*, sobreviviente *mf*

susceptible /səˈseptəbəl/ *adj* **~ TO sth** ⟨*to colds/infections*⟩ propenso A algo; **he's ~ to a bit of flattery** se le puede persuadir halagándolo

suspect¹ /səˈspekt/ *vt* **1** **(a)** (believe guilty) ⟨*person*⟩ sospechar de; **we ~ him of lying** sospechamos que miente **(b)** (doubt, mistrust) ⟨*sincerity/probity*⟩ dudar de, tener* dudas acerca de **2** **(a)** (believe to exist): **they ~ nothing** no sospechan nada; **arson is not ~ed** no existen sospechas de que el incendio haya sido provocado **(b) suspected** *past p*: **a ~ed fracture** una posible fractura; **the ~ed murderer** el presunto asesino **3** (think probable) **to ~ (THAT)** imaginarse QUE

suspect² /ˈsʌspekt/ *n* sospechoso, -sa *m,f*

suspect³ /ˈsʌspekt/ *adj* ⟨*package/behavior*⟩ sospechoso; ⟨*document/evidence*⟩ de dudosa autenticidad

suspend /səˈspend/ *vt* **1** ⟨*payment/work*⟩ suspender **2** (debar, ban) suspender; ⟨*student*⟩ expulsar temporalmente, suspender (AmL) **3** (hang) ⟨*often pass*⟩ suspender

suspended sentence *n*: pena de prisión que no se cumple a menos que el delincuente reincida

suspenders /səˈspendərz ‖səˈspendəz/ *pl n* (*sometimes sing*) **1** (braces) (AmE) tirantes *mpl or* (RPl) tiradores *mpl or* (Chi) suspensores *mpl or* (Col) cargaderas *fpl* **2** (for stockings, socks) (BrE) ligas *fpl*

suspense /səˈspens/ *n* (in literary work, movie) suspenso *m or* (Esp) suspense *m*; **to keep sb in ~** mantener* a algn sobre ascuas

suspension /səˈspenʃən/ *n* **1** (cessation) suspensión *f* **2** (banning, withdrawal) suspensión *f*; (of student) expulsión *f* temporaria, suspensión *f* (AmL) **3** (hanging, being hung) suspensión *f* **4** (Auto) suspensión *f*

suspension: ~ bridge *n* puente *m* colgante; **~ points** *pl n* (AmE) puntos *mpl* suspensivos

suspicion /səˈspɪʃən/ *n* (belief) sospecha *f*; (mistrust) desconfianza *f*, recelo *m*; **he's under ~** está bajo sospecha

suspicious /səˈspɪʃəs/ *adj* **(a)** (mistrustful) desconfiado, suspicaz; **to be ~ OF/ABOUT sb/sth** desconfiar* DE algn/algo **(b)** (arousing suspicion) ⟨*actions/movements*⟩ sospechoso

suspiciously /səˈspɪʃəsli/ *adv* **(a)** (mistrustfully) ⟨*regard/watch*⟩ con desconfianza, con recelo **(b)** (arousing suspicion) ⟨*act*⟩ sospechosamente

sustain /səˈsteɪn/ *vt* **(a)** ⟨*life*⟩ preservar, sustentar; ⟨*hope/interest*⟩ mantener*; ⟨*pretense/conversation*⟩ mantener*; ⟨*effort*⟩ sostener* **(b)** (suffer) ⟨*injury/loss/defeat*⟩ sufrir

sustainable /səˈsteɪnəbəl/ *adj* sostenible

sustained /səˈsteɪnd/ *adj* ⟨*efforts*⟩ sostenido

sustenance /ˈsʌstənəns/ *n* alimento *m*, sustento *m*

SW (= **southwest**) SO

swab¹ /swɑːb ‖swɒb/ n **(a)** (of cotton, gauze) hisopo m húmedo **(b)** (specimen) muestra f, frotis m

swab² vt **-bb-** to ~ (**down**) ⟨*deck*⟩ lavar, limpiar

swagger /'swægər ‖'swægə(r)/ vi caminar or andar* con aire arrogante

Swahili /swɑːˈhiːli ‖swəˈhiːli/ n swahili m, suajili m

swallow¹ /'swɑːləʊ ‖'swɒləʊ/ n ⌊1⌋ (Zool) golondrina f ⌊2⌋ (gulp) trago m

swallow² vt ⌊1⌋ ⟨*food/drink*⟩ tragar* ⌊2⌋ ⟨*insult/taunts*⟩ tragarse*; **that's a bit hard to ~** eso no hay quien se lo trague (fam) ⌊3⌋ ▶ SWALLOW UP
■ ~ vi tragar*
■ **swallow up** [v + o + adv, v + adv + o] **(a)** (use up) ⟨*money/time*⟩ consumir, tragarse* (fam), comerse (fam) **(b)** (cause to disappear) tragarse*

swam /swæm/ past of SWIM¹

swamp¹ /swɑːmp ‖swɒmp/ n pantano m, ciénaga f; (of sea water) marisma f, ciénaga f

swamp² vt **(a)** (with water) ⟨*land*⟩ anegar*, inundar **(b)** (overwhelm) (*often pass*): they were ~ed by offers of help los abrumaron con ofertas de ayuda; I'm absolutely ~ed with work estoy inundada de trabajo

swan /swɑːn ‖swɒn/ n cisne m

swanky /'swæŋki/ adj **-kier, -kiest** (colloq) **(a)** (boastful) (pej) ⟨*person*⟩ fanfarrón (fam) **(b)** (classy) chic adj inv, pijo (Esp fam), pituco (CS fam), posudo (Col fam), popoff adj inv (Méx fam)

swap¹ /swɑːp ‖swɒp/ n (colloq) cambio m, trueque m

swap² vt **-pp-** ⟨*possessions/ideas*⟩ intercambiar; to ~ **sth FOR sth** cambiar algo POR algo

swarm¹ /swɔːrm ‖swɔːm/ n enjambre m

swarm² vi «*bees*» enjambrar; the flies ~ed around the meat las moscas revoloteaban alrededor de la carne; the beaches were ~ing with tourists las playas eran un hormiguero de turistas

swarthy /'swɔːrði ‖'swɔːði/ adj **-thier, -thiest** moreno

swastika /'swɑːstɪkə ‖'swɒstɪkə/ n svástica f, esvástica f, suástica f, cruz f gamada

swat /swɑːt ‖swɒt/ vt **-tt-** ⟨*insect*⟩ matar (con matamoscas, periódico etc)

sway¹ /sweɪ/ n to hold ~ «*ideas*» prevalecer*; «*leader*» ejercer* dominio

sway² vi «*branch/tree*» balancearse; (gently) mecerse*; «*tower/building*» bambolearse
■ ~ vt ⌊1⌋ (influence) ⟨*person/crowd*⟩ influir* en ⌊2⌋ (move) ⟨*hips*⟩ menear, bambolear

swear /swer ‖sweə(r)/ (*past* **swore**; *past p* **sworn**) vt ⟨*allegiance/fidelity/revenge*⟩ jurar; I could have sworn I left it there hubiera jurado que lo dejé ahí
■ ~ vi **(a)** (vow) jurar; but I couldn't ~ to it pero no podría jurarlo **(b)** (curse) decir* palabrotas, soltar* tacos (Esp fam), mentar* madres (Méx fam); to ~ AT sb insultar a algn (*usando palabrotas*)
■ **swear by** [v + prep + o] ⟨*gadget*⟩ ser* un entusiasta de; ⟨*remedy*⟩ tenerle* una fe ciega a
■ **swear in** [v + o + adv, v + adv + o] ⟨*jury/witness/president*⟩ tomarle juramento a, juramentar

swearword /'swerwɜːrd ‖'sweəwɜːd/ n palabrota f, mala palabra f, taco m (Esp)

sweat¹ /swet/ n (perspiration) sudor m, transpiración f; I broke out in a cold ~ me vino un sudor frío

sweat² vi (*past & past p* **sweated** or (AmE also) **sweat**) sudar, transpirar

sweater /'swetər ‖'swetə(r)/ n suéter m, pulóver m, jersey m (Esp), chompa f (Per)

sweat: ~**shirt** n sudadera f, camiseta f gruesa; ~**shop** n: fábrica donde se explota a los trabajadores; ~**suit** n (AmE) equipo m (de deportes), chándal m (Esp), pants mpl (Méx)

sweaty /'sweti/ adj **-tier, -tiest** sudado, transpirado

swede /swiːd/ n (esp BrE) nabo m sueco

Swede /swiːd/ n sueco, -ca m,f

Sweden /'swiːdn/ n Suecia f

Swedish¹ /'swiːdɪʃ/ adj sueco

Swedish² n **(a)** (language) sueco m **(b)** (people) (+ pl vb) the ~ los suecos

sweep¹ /swiːp/ n ⌊1⌋ **(a)** (movement): with a ~ of his arm con un amplio movimiento del brazo **(b)** (curve — of road, river) curva f **(c)** (range) (no pl) alcance m, extensión f ⌊2⌋ (chimney ~) deshollinador, -dora m,f

sweep² (*past & pp* **swept**) vt ⌊1⌋ **(a)** (clean) ⟨*floor/path*⟩ barrer; ⟨*chimney*⟩ deshollinar **(b)** (remove) ⟨*leaves/dirt*⟩ barrer; ⟨*mines*⟩ barrer; to ~ **sth under the rug** o (BrE) **carpet** correr un velo sobre algo
⌊2⌋ (touch lightly, brush) ⟨*surface*⟩ rozar*
⌊3⌋ **(a)** (pass over, across) «*storm*» azotar, barrer; the epidemic is ~ing the country la epidemia se extiende como un reguero de pólvora por el país **(b)** (remove by force) ⟨*sea/tide*⟩ arrastrar
⌊4⌋ **(a)** (scan) recorrer **(b)** (search) ⟨*area*⟩ peinar
■ ~ vi ⌊1⌋ (+ adv compl) (move proudly): she swept into the room entró majestuosamente en la habitación
⌊2⌋ (+ adv compl) **(a)** (spread): fire swept through the hotel el fuego se propagó por todo el hotel **(b)** (extend): the path ~s down to the road el sendero baja describiendo una curva hasta la carretera
■ **sweep aside** [v + o + adv, v + adv + o] ⟨*object*⟩ apartar; ⟨*opposition/doubts*⟩ desechar
■ **sweep away** [v + o + adv, v + adv + o] **(a)** (carry away) ⟨*flood/storm*⟩ arrastrar **(b)** (abolish) erradicar*
■ **sweep up** ⌊1⌋ [v + adv] (clear up) barrer, limpiar
⌊2⌋ [v + o + adv, v + adv + o] **(a)** (clear up) ⟨*dust/leaves*⟩ barrer y recoger* **(b)** (gather up) ⟨*belongings/bags*⟩ recoger*

sweeper /'swiːpər ‖'swiːpə(r)/ n **(a)** (road~) barrendero, -ra m,f, barredor, -dora m,f (Per) **(b)** (carpet ~) cepillo m mecánico

sweeping /'swiːpɪŋ/ adj **(a)** ⟨*movement*⟩ amplio; ⟨*gesture*⟩ dramático, histriónico **(b)** (indiscriminate) (pej): that's rather a ~ statement, isn't it? ¿no estás generalizando demasiado? **(c)** (far-reaching) ⟨*reforms/changes*⟩ radical; ⟨*powers*⟩ amplio

sweet¹ /swiːt/ adj **-er, -est** ⌊1⌋ ⟨*taste*⟩ dulce ⌊2⌋ ⟨*wine/sherry*⟩ dulce ⌊3⌋ (fresh, wholesome) ⟨*smell*⟩ agradable ⌊4⌋ **(a)** (pleasant, gratifying) ⟨*sounds/voice/music*⟩ dulce, melodioso **(b)** (kind, lovable) ⟨*nature*⟩ ···⟶

S

temper/smile) dulce; **she's a very ~ person** es un encanto (de persona); **it was very ~ of her to offer** fue un detalle que se ofreciese **(c)** (attractive) ‹*baby/puppy*› rico (fam), mono (fam), amoroso (AmL fam)

sweet² *n* **1** (item of confectionery) (BrE) caramelo *m or* (AmL exc RPl) dulce *m* **2** (dessert) (BrE) postre *m* **3 sweets** *pl* (sugary food) (AmE) dulces *mpl*

sweet: ~-and-sour /'swiːtn̩'saʊr ‖,swiːtn̩'saʊə(r)/ *adj* (before n) agridulce; **~corn** *n* maíz *m* tierno, elote *m* (Méx), choclo *m* (AmS), jojoto *m* (Ven)

sweeten /'swiːtn̩/ *vt* **(a)** ‹*drink/dish*› endulzar* **(b)** ‹*air/breath*› refrescar*

sweetener /'swiːtn̩ər ‖'swiːtn̩ə(r)/ *n* (Culin) endulzante *m*; (artificial) edulcorante *m*

sweet: ~heart /'swiːthɑːrt ‖'swiːthɑːt/ *n* **(a)** (lover, darling) novio, -via *m,f*, enamorado, -da *m,f* **(b)** (colloq) (as form of address) (mi) amor; **~ potato** *n* boniato *m*, batata *f*, camote *m* (Andes, Méx); **~shop** *n* (BrE) tienda *f* de golosinas; **~-talk** *vt* (colloq) engatusar (fam), camelar (Esp fam)

swell¹ /swel/ (past p **swollen** *or* (AmE esp) **swelled**) *vi* **1** ‹*wood/sails/ankles*› hincharse; ‹*river/stream*› crecer*, subir **2** (increase) ‹*population/crowd*› crecer*, aumentar
■ **~** *vt* **1** (increase in size) ‹*body/joint/features*› hinchar; ‹*sails*› hinchar; ‹*river*› hacer* crecer *or* subir **2** (increase in number, volume) ‹*population/ total/funds*› aumentar
■ **swell up** [*v + adv*] hincharse

swell² *n* **(a)** (of sea) oleaje *m* **(b)** (surge, movement) oleada *f*

swell³ *adj* (fine, excellent) (AmE colloq) fenomenal (fam), bárbaro (fam)

swelling /'swelɪŋ/ *n* hinchazón *f*

sweltering /'sweltərɪŋ/ *adj* sofocante

swept /swept/ past & past p of SWEEP²

swerve /swɜːrv ‖swɜːv/ *vi* ‹*vehicle/driver/ horse*› virar bruscamente

swift¹ /swift/ *adj* **-er, -est** ‹*runner/movement/ animal*› veloz, rápido; ‹*reply/reaction/denial*› rápido

swift² *n* vencejo *m*

swiftly /'swiftli/ *adv* (rapidly) rápidamente con rapidez; (promptly) con prontitud *or* rapidez

swig¹ /swig/ *n* (colloq) trago *m*

swig² *vt* **-gg-** (colloq) tomar, beber

swill¹ /swil/ *n* comida *f* para cerdos

swill² *vt* **1** (wash, rinse) to **~ sth out** ‹*cups/pans*› lavar/enjuagar* algo **2** (drink) (colloq & pej) ‹*beer*› tomar *or* beber (a grandes tragos)

swim¹ /swim/ (pres p **swimming**; past **swam**; past p **swum**) *vi* **1** ‹*person/animal/ fish*› nadar; **to go ~ming** ir* a nadar; **he swam across the river** cruzó el río nadando *or* a nado **2** (be immersed, overflowing) (usu in -ing form) to **~**

IN **sth** nadar *or* flotar EN algo **3** (of blurred, confused perceptions) dar* vueltas; **my head was ~ming** la cabeza me daba vueltas
■ **~** *vt* ‹*length*› nadar, hacer*; ‹*river*› cruzar* a nado

swim² *n*: **to go for a ~** ir* a nadar; **to have a ~** nadar, bañarse, darse* un baño

swimmer /'swimər ‖'swimə(r)/ *n* nadador, -dora *m,f*

swimming /'swimiŋ/ *n* natación *f*; (before n) **~ cap** gorro *m or* gorra *f* (de baño)

swimming: ~ bath *n*, **~ baths** *pl n* (BrE) piscina *f* cubierta, alberca *f* techada (Méx), pileta *f* cubierta (RPl); **~ costume** *n* (BrE) ▸ SWIMSUIT; **~ pool** *n* piscina *f*, alberca *f* (Méx), pileta *f* (RPl); **~ trunks** *pl n* ▸ TRUNK 4

swimsuit /'swimsuːt ‖'swimsuːt, -sjuːt/ *n* traje *m* de baño, bañador *m* (Esp), malla *f* (de baño) (RPl)

swindle¹ /'swindl̩/ *n* estafa *f*, timo *m* (fam)

swindle² *vt* estafar, timar

swindler /'swindlər ‖'swindlə(r)/ *n* estafador, -dora *m,f*, timador, -dora *m,f*

swine /swain/ *n* **(a)** (pl **~**) (pig, hog) cerdo *m* **(b)** (pl **~s**) (contemptible person) (colloq) cerdo, -da *m,f* (fam), canalla *mf*

swing¹ /swiŋ/ (past & past p **swung**) *vi* **1** (hang, dangle) balancearse; (on a swing) columpiarse *or* (RPl) hamacarse*; ‹*pendulum*› oscilar **2 (a)** (move on pivot) mecerse*; **the door swung open/shut** la puerta se abrió/se cerró **(b)** (turn) girar *or* doblar (describiendo una curva); **the ball swung away** la pelota salió desviada **3** (shift, change) ‹*opinion/mood*› cambiar, oscilar
■ **~** *vt* **1** (move to and fro) ‹*arms/legs*› balancear; ‹*object on rope*› hacer* oscilar; **to ~ one's hips** contonearse, contonear *or* menear las caderas **2** (wave, brandish) ‹*club/hammer*› blandir **3** (shift) ‹*vote*› inclinar
■ **swing around**, (BrE also) **swing round 1** [*v + adv*] ‹*vehicle*› dar* un viraje, girar *or* virar (en redondo); **she swung around to face me** giró sobre sus talones para darme la cara **2** [*v + o + adv*] ‹*car/boat*› hacer* girar en redondo

swing² *n* **1 (a)** (movement) oscilación *f*, vaivén *m* **(b)** (blow, stroke) golpe *m*; (in golf, boxing) swing *m*; **to take a ~ at sb/sth** intentar darle a algn/ algo **2 (a)** (shift) cambio *m*; **a ~ in public opinion** un cambio en la opinión pública **(b)** (Pol) viraje *m* **3 (a)** (rhythm, vitality): **to be in full ~** estar* en pleno desarrollo; **the party was in full ~** la fiesta estaba ya muy animada; **to get into the ~ of sth** agarrarle el ritmo *or* (Esp) cogerle* el tranquillo a algo **(b)** (Mus) swing *m* **4** (Leisure) columpio *m or* (RPl) hamaca *f*

swing: ~ bin *n* cubo *m or* (CS) tacho *m or* (Méx) bote *m or* (Col) caneca *f or* (Ven) tobo *m* de la basura (con tapa de vaivén); **~ bridge** *n* puente *m* giratorio; **~ door** *n* puerta *f* (de) vaivén

---

swinging door /'swɪŋɪŋ/ n (AmE) ▶ SWING DOOR

swipe¹ /swaɪp/ n (colloq) golpe m

swipe² vt (colloq) **1** (hit) darle* (un golpe) a **2** (steal) afanarse (arg), volarse* (Méx fam)

swipe card n tarjeta f de plástico con banda magnética

swirl¹ /swɜːrl ‖swɜːl/ n (of water, dust, people) remolino m; (of smoke) voluta f, espiral f

swirl² vi «water/dust/paper» arremolinarse; «dancers/skirts» girar

swish /swɪʃ/ n (a) (of cane) silbido m (b) (of water) rumor m, susurro m (c) (of skirt) frufrú m

Swiss¹ /swɪs/ adj suizo

Swiss² n (pl ~) suizo, -za m,f

switch¹ /swɪtʃ/ vt **1** (a) (change) cambiar de; to ~ channels cambiar de canal; my appointment has been ~ed to Tuesday me cambiaron la cita al martes (b) (exchange) ⟨suitcases/roles⟩ intercambiar
2 (shunt) (AmE Rail) cambiar de vía
■ ~ vi cambiar; I ~ed to Channel Four cambié al Canal Cuatro; we've ~ed from electricity to gas hemos empezado a usar gas en lugar de electricidad
■ **switch off** **1** [v + o + adv, v + adv + o] ⟨light/ TV/heating⟩ apagar*; ⟨gas/electricity/water⟩ cortar, desconectar
2 [v + adv] «light/machine/heating» apagarse*
■ **switch on** **1** [v + o + adv, v + adv + o] (esp BrE) ⟨light/heating/television⟩ encender*, prender (AmL)
2 [v + adv] «light/heating/machine» encenderse*, prenderse (AmL)
■ **switch over** [v + adv] (a) (change) to ~ over TO sth cambiar A algo (b) (change channels) cambiar de canal (c) (exchange positions, roles) cambiar

switch² n **1** (a) (Elec) interruptor m, llave f (de encendido/de la luz) (b) (AmE Rail) agujas fpl **2** (exchange) intercambio m, trueque m

switchboard n centralita f, conmutador m (AmL); (before n) ~ **operator** telefonista mf

Switzerland /'swɪtsərlənd ‖'swɪtsələnd/ n Suiza f

swivel /'swɪvəl/, (BrE) **-ll-** vi girar
■ ~ vt hacer* girar

swivel chair n silla f giratoria

swollen¹ /'swəʊlən/ past p of SWELL¹

swollen² adj ⟨ankle/knee/joints⟩ hinchado; ⟨gland⟩ inflamado; ~ **with pride** henchido de orgullo; the river was ~ el río iba crecido

swoon /swuːn/ vi (a) (show rapture) to ~ (OVER sb) derretirse* (POR algn) (b) (faint) (arch or liter) desvanecerse*

swoop¹ /swuːp/ vi «bird of prey» abatirse; «police» llevar a cabo una redada

swoop² n (of bird, aircraft) descenso m en picada or (Esp) en picado; (by police) redada f; **in one fell** ~ de una sola vez, de un tirón (fam)

swop /swɒp ‖swɒp/ vt/n ▶ SWAP¹,²

sword /sɔːrd ‖sɔːd/ n espada f

sword: ~fish n (pl ~fish or ~fishes) pez m espada; **~sman** /'sɔːrdzmən ‖'sɔːdzmən/ n (pl **-men** /-mən/) espadachín m, espada m

swore /swɔːr ‖swɔː(r)/ past of SWEAR

sworn¹ /swɔːrn ‖swɔːn/ past p of SWEAR

sworn² adj (before n) **1** ⟨enemy⟩ declarado, acérrimo **2** ⟨statement⟩ jurado

swot¹ /swɑːt ‖swɒt/ n (BrE colloq & pej) matado, -da m,f or (Col) pilo, -la m,f or (Chi) mateo, -tea m,f or (Per) chancón, -cona m,f or (RPl) traga mf or (Esp) empollón, -llona m,f (fam & pey)

swot² vi **-tt-** (BrE colloq) estudiar como loco (fam), empollar (Esp fam), matearse (Chi fam), chancar* (Per arg), tragar* (RPl fam)

swum /swʌm/ past p of SWIM¹

swung /swʌŋ/ past & past p of SWING¹

sycamore /'sɪkəmɔːr ‖'sɪkəmɔː(r)/ n ~ (**maple**) plátano m (falso), sicómoro m, sicomoro m

sycophantic /ˌsɪkə'fæntɪk/ adj adulador

syllable /'sɪləbəl/ n sílaba f

syllabus /'sɪləbəs/ n (pl **-buses**) plan m de estudios; (of a particular subject) programa m

symbol /'sɪmbəl/ n símbolo m

symbolic /sɪm'bɑːlɪk ‖sɪm'bɒlɪk/ adj simbólico; **to be** ~ **OF sth** simbolizar* algo

symbolism /'sɪmbəlɪzəm/ n simbolismo m

symbolize /'sɪmbəlaɪz/ vt simbolizar*

symmetrical /sə'metrɪkəl ‖sɪ'metrɪkəl/ adj simétrico

symmetry /'sɪmətri/ n simetría f

sympathetic /ˌsɪmpə'θetɪk/ adj
1 (understanding) comprensivo; he was most ~ to o toward me when my wife died me dio todo su apoyo y comprensión cuando murió mi mujer
2 (approving) ⟨response/view⟩ favorable; ⟨audience⟩ bien dispuesto, receptivo

sympathetically /ˌsɪmpə'θetɪkli/ adv (a) (with understanding) ⟨listen/consider/respond⟩ con comprensión (b) (showing pity) con compasión

sympathize /'sɪmpəθaɪz/ vi (a) (commiserate): I ~ **with him** lo compadezco (b) (understand) to ~ (WITH sth/sb) comprender or entender* (algo/a algn)

sympathizer /'sɪmpəθaɪzər ‖'sɪmpəθaɪzə(r)/ n simpatizante mf, partidario, -ria m,f

sympathy /'sɪmpəθi/ n (pl **-thies**) **1** (a) (pity) compasión f, lástima f (b) (condolences) (often pl): **you have my deepest** ~ lo acompaño en el sentimiento (fr hecha), mi más sentido pésame (fr hecha) **2** (a) (support, approval): **to come out in** ~ **with sb** (Lab Rel) declararse en huelga en solidaridad con algn (b) **sympathies** pl (loyalty, leanings) simpatías fpl

symphony /'sɪmfəni/ n (pl **-nies**) sinfonía f; (before n) ~ **orchestra** orquesta f sinfónica

symptom /'sɪmptəm/ n síntoma m

symptomatic /ˌsɪmptə'mætɪk/ adj ~ (OF sth) sintomático (DE algo)

synagogue /'sɪnəgɑːg ‖'sɪnəgɒg/ n sinagoga f

synchronize /'sɪŋkrənaɪz/ vt sincronizar*

syndicate /'sɪndəkət ‖'sɪndɪkət/ n (a) (group, cartel) agrupación f; **a crime** ~ una organización mafiosa (b) (in US) (Journ, TV) agencia f de distribución periodística

syndrome /'sɪndrəʊm/ n síndrome m

synonymous /sə'nɑːnəməs ‖sɪ'nɒnɪməs/ adj ⟨terms/phrases⟩ sinónimo; ⟨ideas⟩ análogo; **to be** ~ **WITH sth** ser* sinónimo DE algo

S

synopsis /sə'nɑ:psəs ‖sɪ'nɒpsɪs/ n (pl **-opses** /-si:z/) sinopsis f

syntax /'sɪntæks/ n sintaxis f

synthesis /'sɪnθəsəs ‖'sɪnθəsɪs/ n (pl **-theses** /-θəsi:z/) síntesis f

synthesize /'sɪnθəsaɪz/ vt sintetizar*

synthesizer /'sɪnθəsaɪzər ‖'sɪnθəsaɪzə(r)/ n sintetizador m

synthetic¹ /sɪn'θetɪk/ adj sintético

synthetic² n fibra f sintética, tejido m sintético

syphilis /'sɪfələs ‖'sɪfɪlɪs/ n sífilis f

syphon n/vt /'saɪfən/ ▶ SIPHON

Syria /'sɪriə/ n Siria f

Syrian /'sɪriən/ adj sirio

syringe /sə'rɪndʒ ‖sɪ'rɪndʒ/ n jeringa f, jeringuilla f

syrup /'sɜːrəp, 'sɪ- ‖'sɪrəp/ n **(a)** (Culin) (sugar solution) almíbar m; (with other ingredients) jarabe m, sirope m **(b)** (medicine) jarabe m

system /'sɪstəm/ n **1** (ordered structure) sistema m, método m **2 (a)** (technical, mechanical) sistema m **(b)** (Comput) sistema m **3** (Anat, Physiol): **the digestive** ~ el aparato digestivo; **the nervous** ~ el sistema nervioso; **to get sth out of one's** ~ desahogarse* **4** (establishment, status quo): **the** ~ el sistema

systematic /sɪstə'mætɪk/ adj sistemático

systematically /sɪstə'mætɪkli/ adv sistemáticamente

systems analyst n analista mf de sistemas

Tt

T, t /tiː/ n T, t f

tab /tæb/ n **1 (a)** (flap) lengüeta f **(b)** (label on clothing) etiqueta f **2** (account, bill) (colloq) cuenta f; **to keep** ~**s on sth/sb** tener* algo/a algn controlado **3** (on typewriter, word processor) tabulador m

tabby /'tæbi/ (pl **-bies**), **tabby cat** n gato atigrado, gata atigrada m,f

tab key n tecla f de tabulación

table /'teɪbəl/ n **1** (piece of furniture) mesa f; (before n) ~ **football** (BrE) futbolín m, taca-taca m (Chi), metegol m (Arg), futbolito m (Ur); ~ **mat** (mantelito m) individual m **2** (list) tabla f; **multiplication** o (used by children) **times** ~**s** tablas de multiplicar

table: ~**cloth** n mantel m; ~**spoon** n (utensil) cuchara f grande or de servir; (measure) cucharada f (grande)

tablet /'tæblət ‖'tæblɪt/ n **(a)** (pill) pastilla f, comprimido m **(b)** (commemorative, of stone) lápida f

table tennis n ping-pong m, tenis m de mesa

tabloid /'tæblɔɪd/ n tabloide m (formato de periódicos utilizado por la prensa popular)

taboo /tə'buː/ adj tabú adj inv

tabulate /'tæbjələt ‖'tæbjʊleɪt/ vt tabular

tacit /'tæsət ‖'tæsɪt/ adj tácito

taciturn /'tæsətɜːrn ‖'tæsɪtɜːn/ adj taciturno

tack¹ /tæk/ n **(a)** (nail) tachuela f **(b)** (Naut) bordada f **(c)** (stitch) (BrE) puntada f; (seam) hilván m **(d)** (Equ) arreos mpl, aperos mpl (AmL)

tack² vt **1** (nail) ⟨carpet⟩ ~ **down** clavar con tachuelas **2** (stitch) (BrE) hilvanar
■ ~ vi (Naut) dar* bordadas
■ **tack on** [v + o + adv, v + adv + o] agregar*, añadir

tackle¹ /'tækəl/ n **1** (equipment): **sports** ~ equipo m de deporte; **fishing** ~ aparejo m or

avíos mpl de pesca **2** (Sport) (in rugby, US football) placaje m, tacle m (AmL); (in soccer) entrada f fuerte **3** (Naut) aparejo m, polea f

tackle² vt **1 (a)** (come to grips with) ⟨problem⟩ enfrentar, abordar; ⟨subject⟩ tratar; ⟨task⟩ abordar **(b)** (confront) ⟨intruder/colleague⟩ enfrentar, enfrentarse con **2** (Sport) (in rugby, US football) placar*, taclear (AmL); (in soccer) entrarle a

tacky /'tæki/ adj **tackier, tackiest** **1** (cheap, tawdry) chabacano, hortera (Esp fam), naco (Méx fam), lobo (Col fam), rasca (Chi fam), mersa (RPl fam) **2** (sticky) pegajoso

tact /tækt/ n tacto m

tactful /'tæktfəl/ adj ⟨person⟩ de mucho tacto; ⟨question/reply⟩ diplomático

tactfully /'tæktfəli/ adv con mucho tacto

tactic /'tæktɪk/ n táctica f

tactical /'tæktɪkəl/ adj táctico

tactics /'tæktɪks/ n (Mil) (+ sing or pl vb) táctica f

tactless /'tæktləs ‖'tæktlɪs/ adj poco diplomático

tadpole /'tædpəʊl/ n renacuajo m

Tadzhikistan /tɑːˌdʒɪkɪ'stɑːn/ n Tayiquistán m

taffeta /'tæfətə ‖'tæfɪtə/ n tafetán m

taffy /'tæfi/ n (AmE) caramelo m masticable

tag /tæg/ n **1** (label) etiqueta f (atada) **2** (Ling) coletilla f; (before n) ~ **question** coletilla f, coletilla interrogativa
■ **tag on: -gg-** [v + o + adv, v + adv + o] agregar*, añadir

Tahiti /tə'hiːti/ n Tahití m

tail¹ /teɪl/ n **(a)** (of horse, fish, bird) cola f; (of dog, pig) rabo m, cola f **(b)** (of plane, kite) cola f; (of shirt, coat) faldón m; see also TAILS 1

tail² vt (follow) ⟨suspect⟩ seguir*
■ **tail off** [v + adv] **(a)** «demand» disminuir*, mermar **(b)** «sound/words» apagarse*

tail: ∼**back** n (BrE) caravana f, cola f (*debido a un embotellamiento*); ∼**coat** n frac m; ∼ **end** n: **the** ∼ **end** (of film, concert) el final, los últimos minutos; (of procession) la cola; ∼**light** n luz f trasera

tailor¹ /ˈteɪlər ‖ ˈteɪlə(r)/ n sastre m

tailor² vt **1** (Clothing) **(a)** (make) confeccionar **(b) tailored** past p (*before* n) (fitted) entallado; (lined, structured etc) armado **2** (adapt) adaptar

tailor-made /ˈteɪlərˈmeɪd ‖ ˌteɪləˈmeɪd/ adj **(a)** (*suit*) hecho a (la) medida **(b)** (*product/plan*) a la medida de sus (*or* nuestras *etc*) necesidades

tailpipe /ˈteɪlpaɪp/ n (AmE Auto) tubo m or (RPI) caño m de escape

tails /teɪlz/ n **1** (tailcoat) (+ pl vb) frac m **2** (on coin) (+ sing vb) cruz f, sello m (Andes, Ven), sol m (Méx), ceca f (Arg)

taint /teɪnt/ vt **(a)** (*meat/water*) contaminar **(b)** (*name/reputation*) mancillar (liter), deshonrar

Taiwan /ˈtaɪˈwɑːn/ n Taiwan m

take¹ /teɪk/ (past **took**; past p **taken**) vt

I (carry, lead, drive) llevar; ∼ **an umbrella** lleva un paraguas

II 1 (a) (*train/plane/bus/taxi/elevator*) tomar, coger* (esp Esp) **(b)** (*road/turning*) tomar, agarrar (esp AmL), coger* (esp Esp); ∼ **a left** (turn) (BrE) dobla a la izquierda **(c)** (*bend*) tomar, coger* (esp Esp); (*fence*) saltar
2 (a) (grasp, seize) tomar, agarrar (esp AmL), coger* (esp Esp); (*opportunity*) aprovechar; **she took the knife from him** le quitó el cuchillo **(b)** (take charge of): **may I** ∼ **your coat?** ¿me permite el abrigo? **(c)** (occupy): ∼ **a seat** siéntese, tome asiento (frml); **this chair is** ∼n esta silla está ocupada
3 (remove, steal) (*wallet/purse*) llevarse
4 to be ∼n ill caer* enfermo
5 (a) (capture) (*town/position*) tomar; (*pawn/piece*) comer **(b)** (win) (*prize/title*) llevarse, hacerse* con; (*game/set*) ganar **(c)** (receive as profit) hacer*, sacar*
6 (*medicine/drugs*) tomar; **I don't** ∼ **sugar in my coffee** no le pongo azúcar al café
7 (a) (buy, order) llevar(se); **I'll** ∼ **this pair** (me) llevo este par **(b)** (rent) alquilar, coger* (Esp)

III 1 (of time) «*job/task*» llevar; «*process*» tardar; «*person/letter*» tardar, demorar(se) (AmL); **the flight** ∼s **two hours** el vuelo dura dos horas; **it took me a long time to do it** me llevó mucho tiempo hacerlo
2 (need): **it** ∼s **courage to do a thing like that** hay que tener *or* hace falta valor para hacer algo así; **it took four men to lift it** se necesitaron cuatro hombres para levantarlo
3 (a) (wear): **what size shoes do you** ∼? ¿qué número calzas?; **she** ∼s **a 14** usa la talla *or* (RPI) el talle 14 **(b)** (Ling) construirse* con, regir*

IV 1 (accept) (*money/bribes/job*) aceptar; **do you** ∼ **checks?** ¿aceptan cheques?; ∼ **it from me** hazme caso
2 (a) (hold, accommodate): **it** ∼s/**will** ∼ **42 liters** tiene una capacidad de 42 litros; **we can** ∼ **up to 50 passengers** tenemos cabida para un máximo de 50 pasajeros **(b)** (*patients/pupils*) admitir, tomar
3 (a) (withstand, suffer) (*strain/weight*) aguantar; (*beating*) recibir **(b)** (tolerate, endure) aguantar; **he**

can't ∼ **a joke** no sabe aceptar una broma **(c)** (bear): **she's** ∼n **it very badly/well** lo lleva muy mal/bien; *see also* HEART 2, 3
4 (a) (understand, interpret) tomarse; **don't** ∼ **it personally** no te lo tomes como algo personal; **I** ∼ **it you didn't like him much** por lo que veo no te cayó muy bien **(b)** (consider) (*in imperative*) mirar; ∼ **Japan, for example** mira el caso del Japón, por ejemplo

V 1 (*steps/measures*) tomar; (*exercise*) hacer*; **to** ∼ **a step forward** dar* un paso adelante
2 (Educ) **(a)** (teach) (BrE) darle* clase a **(b)** (learn) (*subject*) estudiar, hacer*; (*course*) hacer*; **to** ∼ **an exam** hacer* *or* dar* *or* (CS) rendir* *or* (Méx) tomar un examen, examinarse (Esp)
3 (a) (record) (*measurements/temperature*) tomar **(b)** (write down) (*notes*) tomar
4 (adopt): **he** ∼s **the view that ...** opina que ..., es de la opinión de que ...; *see also* LIKING A, OFFENSE 2B, SHAPE¹ 1A *etc*

■ ∼ vi **(a)** «*cutting*» prender **(b)** «*dye*» agarrar (esp AmL), coger* (esp Esp)
■ **take aback** [v + o + adv] (*usu pass*) sorprender
■ **take after** [v + prep + o] salir* a, parecerse* a; **he** ∼s **after his father** salió a su padre, se parece a su padre
■ **take along** [v + o + adv, v + adv + o] llevar
■ **take apart** [v + o + adv] **(a)** (dismantle) desmontar **(b)** (show weakness of) (*argument*) desbaratar
■ **take around,** (BrE) **take round** [v + o + prep + o] (*house/estate*) mostrar*, enseñar (esp Esp)
■ **take aside** [v + o + adv] llevar aparte *or* a un lado

■ **take away**
I [v + o + adv, v + adv + o] **(a)** (carry, lead away) (*person/object*) llevarse **(b)** (remove, confiscate) (*possession*) quitar; **to** ∼ **sth away FROM sb** quitarle algo A algn **(c)** (erase, obliterate): **this will** ∼ **the pain away** con esto se te pasará el dolor; **this will** ∼ **the taste away** esto te quitará el sabor de la boca
II [v + adv + o] (BrE) (*food*) llevar
■ **take back** **1** [v + o + adv, v + adv + o] **(a)** (return) devolver* **(b)** (repossess) llevarse **(c)** (accept back): **she wouldn't** ∼ **back the money she'd lent me** no quiso que le devolviera el dinero que me había prestado **(d)** (withdraw, retract) (*statement*) retirar
2 [v + o + adv] (in time): **it** ∼s **me back to my childhood** me transporta a mi niñez
■ **take down** [v + o + adv, v + adv + o] **(a)** (*decorations/notice*) quitar **(b)** (dismantle) desmontar **(c)** (*name/address*) apuntar, anotar
■ **take home** [v + adv + o]: **she** ∼s **home less than £600** su sueldo neto *or* líquido es de menos de 600 libras

■ **take in**
I [v + o + adv, v + adv + o] **1** (move indoors) meter (dentro), entrar (esp AmS)
2 (give home to) (*orphan*) recoger*; (*lodger*) alojar
3 (grasp) (*information*) asimilar
4 (make narrower) (*dress/waist*) meterle *or* tomarle a
II [v + o + adv] (deceive) engañar
III [v + adv + o] **(a)** (include) (*areas/topics*) incluir*, abarcar* **(b)** (visit) visitar, incluir* (*en el recorrido*) ···▸

■ **take off**

I [v + o + adv, v + adv + o] [v + o + prep + o]
1 (detach, remove) quitar, sacar*; **to ~ off one's clothes** quitarse or (esp AmL) sacarse* la ropa
2 (a) (cut off) cortar **(b)** (deduct) descontar*
3 (have free): **she's ~n the morning off (from) work** se ha tomado la mañana libre
II [v + adv] **(a)** «aircraft/pilot» despegar*, decolar (AmL); «flight» salir* **(b)** (succeed) «career» tomar vuelo **(c)** (depart) largarse* (fam), irse*
III [v + o + adv] [v + o + prep + o] **1** (remove) quitar, sacar*; **~ your hands off me!** ¡quítame las manos de encima!
2 (take away from) (colloq) quitar, sacar* (CS)

■ **take on** **1** [v + o + adv, v + adv + o] **(a)** (employ) «staff» contratar, tomar (esp AmL) **(b)** (undertake) «work» encargarse* de, hacerse* cargo de; «responsibility» asumir **(c)** (tackle) «opponent» enfrentarse a
2 [v + adv + o] (acquire) «expression» adoptar; «appearance» adquirir*

■ **take out**

I [v + o + adv, v + adv + o] **1 (a)** (remove physically) sacar*; **to ~ it out of sb** «fight/race» dejar a algn rendido **(b)** (exclude) eliminar **(c)** (transport) sacar* **(d)** (AmE) «food» llevar
2 (withdraw) «money» sacar*
3 (produce) «gun/wallet» sacar*
II [v + o + adv, v + adv + o] **(a)** (extract) «tooth/appendix» sacar* **(b)** (obtain) «insurance/permit» sacar*
III [v + o + adv] (accompany, conduct): **he'd like to ~ her out** le gustaría invitarla a salir; **she took me out to dinner** me invitó a cenar

■ **take out on** [v + o + adv + prep + o]: **to ~ it out on sb** desquitarse con algn

■ **take over** **1** [v + adv] **(a)** (assume control) «political party» asumir el poder; **he will ~ over as managing director** asumirá el cargo de director ejecutivo; **to ~ over FROM sb** sustituir* a algn; (in shift work) relevar a algn **(b)** (seize control) hacerse* con el poder
2 [v + o + adv, v + adv + o] «responsibility/role» asumir; «job» hacerse* cargo de; «company» absorber

■ **take round** (BrE) ► TAKE AROUND

■ **take to** [v + prep + o] **(a)** (develop liking for): **she took to teaching immediately** enseguida le tomó gusto a la enseñanza; **I didn't ~ to him** no me cayó muy bien **(b)** (form habit of): **to ~ to drink** darse* a la bebida; **to ~ to -ING** darle* a algn POR + INF

■ **take up**

I [v + o + adv, v + adv + o] **1 (a)** (pick up) tomar **(b)** (accept) «offer/challenge» aceptar **(c)** (adopt) «cause» hacer* suyo (or mío etc) **(d)** (begin): **he's ~n up pottery** ha empezado a hacer cerámica
2 (lift) «carpet/floorboards» levantar
3 (a) (continue) «story» seguir*, continuar*; «conversation» reanudar **(b)** «issue/point» tratar; (pursue) volver* a
4 (shorten) «skirt» acortar; «hem» subir

II [v + adv + o] **1** (use up) «time» llevar; «space» ocupar
2 (move into) «position» tomar

■ **take up on** [v + o + adv + prep + o] **(a)** (take person at word): **I may well ~ you up on that** a lo mejor te tomo la palabra or te acepto el ofrecimiento **(b)** (challenge): **I must ~ you up on that** sobre eso discrepo con usted

take² n (Cin) toma f

takeaway¹ /'teɪkəweɪ/ adj (BrE) «meal/pizza» para llevar; «restaurant» de comida para llevar

takeaway² n (BrE) **(a)** (restaurant) restaurante m de comida para llevar **(b)** (meal) comida f preparada

take-home pay /'teɪkhəʊm/ n sueldo m neto

taken¹ /'teɪkən/ past p of TAKE¹

taken² adj (pred) **to be ~ WITH sth/sb: I was quite ~ with him** me cayó muy bien; **they were very ~ with the house** quedaron encantados con la casa

takeoff /'teɪkɔːf ‖ 'teɪkɒf/ n **(a)** (Aviat) despegue m, decolaje m (AmL) **(b)** (imitation) (colloq) parodia f

takeout¹ /'teɪkaʊt/ adj (AmE) «meal» para llevar; «restaurant» de comida para llevar

takeout² n (AmE) comida f preparada

takeover /'teɪkəʊvər ‖ 'teɪkəʊvə(r)/ n **(a)** (Govt) toma f del poder **(b)** (Busn) absorción f, adquisición f (de una empresa por otra); (before n) **~ bid** oferta f pública de adquisición or de compra, OPA f

takings /'teɪkɪŋz/ n pl (BrE Busn) recaudación f; (at box office) taquilla f, entrada f

talc /tælk/ n polvos mpl de talco, talco m (AmL)

talcum powder /'tælkəm/ n polvos mpl de talco

tale /teɪl/ n cuento m, relato m; **to tell ~s** contar* chismes or cuentos

talent /'tælənt/ n **(a)** (aptitude, skill) talento m **(b)** (talented people) gente f con talento

talented /'tæləntəd ‖ 'tæləntɪd/ adj talentoso, de talento

talisman /'tæləsmən ‖ 'tælɪzmən/ n (pl ~s) talismán m

talk¹ /tɔːk/ vi **1** (speak) hablar; (converse) hablar, platicar* (esp AmC, Méx); **to ~ ABOUT sb/ sth** hablar DE algn/algo; **to ~ OF sth/-ING** hablar DE algo/DE + INF; **to ~ TO sb** hablar CON algn; **he was ~ing to Jane** estaba hablando con Jane; **are you ~ing to me?** ¿me hablas a mí?; **we're not ~ing to each other** no nos hablamos; **to ~ WITH sb** hablar CON algn
2 (a) (have discussion) hablar; **we need to ~** tenemos que hablar; **to ~ ABOUT sth** discutir algo **(b)** (give talk) **to ~ ABOUT/ON sth** hablar DE/ SOBRE algo

■ ~ vt **1** (speak) (colloq): **to ~ business** hablar de negocios; **don't ~ nonsense!** ¡no digas tonterías!
2 (argue, persuade) **to ~ sb INTO/OUT OF sth/-ING** convencer* a algn DE QUE/DE QUE NO (+ subj)

■ **talk down to** [v + adv + prep + o] hablarle en tono condescendiente a

■ **talk over** [v + o + adv, v + adv + o] discutir

talk² n **1** **(a)** (conversation) conversación f; **I had a long ~ with him** estuve hablando or (AmC, Méx tb) platicando un rato largo con él **(b)** (lecture) charla f **(c) talks** pl (negotiations) conversaciones fpl **2** (words) (colloq & pej) palabrería f (fam & pey)

talkative /'tɔːkətɪv/ adj conversador, hablador

talker /'tɔːkər ‖'tɔːkə(r)/ n hablador, -dora m,f

talking /'tɔːkɪŋ/: **~ point** n tema m de conversación; **~-to** n (pl **-tos**) (colloq): **to give sb a good ~-to** leerle* la cartilla a algn (fam)

talk show n programa m de entrevistas

tall /tɔːl/ adj **-er, -est** alto; **how ~ are you?** ¿cuánto mides?; **he's nearly 6 feet ~** mide casi 6 pies

tall story, tall tale n cuento m chino (fam)

tally¹ /'tælɪ/ n (pl **-lies**) cuenta f

tally² vi **-lies, -lying, -lied** coincidir, cuadrar

Talmud /'tælmʊd/ n the ~ el Talmud

talon /'tælən/ n garra f

tambourine /tæmbə'riːn/ n pandereta f

tame¹ /teɪm/ adj **tamer, tamest** **(a)** ⟨animal⟩ (by nature) manso, dócil; (tamed) domado, domesticado **(b)** (unexciting) ⟨show/story⟩ insulso, insípido

tame² vt ⟨wild animal⟩ domar; ⟨stray⟩ domesticar*

Tamil /'tæmɪl ‖'tæmɪl/ n **(a)** (person) tamil mf, tamul mf **(b)** (language) tamul m

tamper with /'tæmpər ‖'tæmpə(r)/ v + o + adv, v + adv + o ⟨engine/controls⟩ tocar*; ⟨figures⟩ alterar

tampon /'tæmpɒːn ‖'tæmpɒn/ n tampón m

tan¹ /tæn/ **-nn-** vt **1** ⟨leather/hide⟩ curtir **2** ⟨sun⟩ ⟨body/skin⟩ broncear, tostar*
■ ~ vi broncearse, quemarse (AmL)

tan² n (on skin) bronceado m, moreno m (esp Esp)

tan³ adj habano

tandem /'tændəm/ n tándem m

tang /tæŋ/ n (strong taste) sabor m fuerte; (sharp taste) acidez f; (smell) olor m penetrante

tangent /'tændʒənt/ n tangente f; **to go o fly off at o on a ~** irse* por las ramas

tangerine /tændʒə'riːn/ n mandarina f, tangerina f

tangible /'tændʒəbəl/ adj tangible

tangle¹ /'tæŋgəl/ vt enredar, enmarañar; **to get ~d (up)** enredarse
■ **tangle up** [v + o + adv, v + adv + o] enredar, enmarañar

tangle² n (of threads, hair) enredo m, maraña f, embrollo m; (of weeds) maraña f

tangled /'tæŋgəld/ adj enredado

tango /'tæŋgəʊ/ n (pl **-gos**) tango m

tank /tæŋk/ n **1** (for liquid, gas) depósito m, tanque m; (on trucks, rail wagons) cisterna f; (Auto) tanque m, depósito m **2** (Mil) tanque m, carro m de combate

tankard /'tæŋkərd ‖'tæŋkəd/ n jarra f

tanker /'tæŋkər ‖'tæŋkə(r)/ n **(a)** (ship) buque m cisterna or tanque **(b)** (truck) camión m cisterna

tanned /tænd/ adj bronceado, moreno

Tannoy® /'tænɔɪ/ n (BrE) sistema m de megafonía

tantalizing /'tæntlaɪzɪŋ ‖'tæntəlaɪzɪŋ/ adj tentador

tantamount /'tæntəmaʊnt/ adj **to be ~ to sth** equivaler* a algo

tantrum /'tæntrəm/ n berrinche m, rabieta f; **Jack had o threw a ~** a Jack le dio un berrinche, Jack hizo un berrinche (Méx)

Tanzania /tænzə'niːə/ n Tanzania f, Tanzanía f

Tanzanian /tænzə'niːən/ adj tanzano

tap¹ /tæp/ n **1** **(a)** (for water) (BrE) llave f or (Esp) grifo m or (RPI) canilla f or (Per) caño m or (AmC) paja f or (AmC, Ven) chorro m **(b)** (gas ~) llave f del gas **(c)** (on barrel) espita f **2** (light blow) toque m, golpecito m **3** ▶ TAP DANCING

tap² **-pp-** vt **1** (strike lightly) dar* un toque or golpecito en **2** **(a)** ⟨tree⟩ sangrar **(b)** ⟨resources/ reserves⟩ explotar **3** ⟨telephone⟩ intervenir*, pinchar (fam); ⟨conversation⟩ interceptar
■ ~ vi **(a)** (strike lightly) **to ~ AT/ON sth** dar* toques or golpecitos EN algo **(b)** (make tapping sound) dar* golpecitos, tamborilear

tap dancing n claqué m

tape¹ /teɪp/ n **1** **(a)** (of paper, cloth) cinta f **(b)** (adhesive) cinta f adhesiva; (Med) esparadrapo m; see also MASKING TAPE, SCOTCH TAPE® etc **(c)** (Sport) cinta f de llegada **(d)** ▶ TAPE MEASURE **2** (Audio, Comput, Video) cinta f

tape² vt (record) grabar

tape: ~ deck n platina f, pletina f; **~ measure** n cinta f métrica, metro m

taper vi afilarse, estrecharse
■ ~ vt afilar, estrechar
■ **taper off** [v + adv] **(a)** «enthusiasm» decaer*; «demand/sales» disminuir* **(b)** ▶ TAPER vi

tape: ~-record /'teɪprɪkɔːrd ‖'teɪprɪkɔːd/ vt grabar; **~ recorder** n grabador m, grabadora f; (for cassette format) grabador m, grabadora f, casete m (Esp)

tapestry /'tæpəstrɪ/ n (pl **-tries**) **(a)** (wall hanging) tapiz m **(b)** (art form) tapicería f

tapeworm /'teɪpwɜːrm ‖'teɪpwɜːm/ n (lombriz f) solitaria f, tenia f

tar¹ /tɑːr ‖tɑː(r)/ n alquitrán m

tar² vt **-rr-** ⟨road/fence⟩ alquitranar; ⟨roof⟩ impermeabilizar* (con alquitrán)

target¹ /'tɑːrgət ‖'tɑːgɪt/ n **1** **(a)** (thing aimed at) blanco m; (Mil) objetivo m; (board) (Sport) diana f **(b)** (of criticism) blanco m **2** (objective, goal) objetivo m; **to be on ~** ir* de acuerdo a lo previsto (or al plan de trabajo etc); (before n) ⟨date/figure⟩ fijado; ⟨market⟩ objetivo adj inv

target² vt **(a)** (select as target): **the company is ~ing the small investor** la empresa está intentando captar al pequeño inversor **(b)** (direct) ⟨advertising⟩ dirigir*; **to ~ benefits at those most in need** concentrar la ayuda a los más necesitados

target practice n prácticas fpl del tiro

tariff /'tærəf ‖'tærɪf/ n **1** (price list) (BrE) tarifa f **2** (Tax) arancel m (aduanero)

tarmac /'tɑːrmæk ‖'tɑːmæk/ n **(a) tarmac®** (AmE) (tar mixture) asfalto m **(b)** (surface — in airport, racetrack) pista f, (— on road) asfalto m

Tarmac® n (BrE) ▶ TARMAC A

tarnish /ˈtɑːrnɪʃ ‖ ˈtɑːnɪʃ/ vt (a) ⟨silver⟩ deslustrar (b) ⟨reputation/name⟩ empañar

tarot card /ˈtærəʊ/ n carta f de tarot

tarpaulin /tɑːrˈpɔːlən ‖ tɑːˈpɔːlɪn/ n (a) (sheet) lona f (b) (material) lona f impermeabilizada

tarragon /ˈtærəgən/ n estragón m

tart¹ /tɑːrt ‖ tɑːt/ n **1** (Culin) (large) tarta f; (individual) tartaleta f **2** (promiscuous woman) (colloq) fulana f (fam), puta f (vulg)

tart² adj (a) ⟨taste/apple⟩ ácido, agrio (b) ⟨remark⟩ cortante, áspero

tartan /ˈtɑːrtn̩ ‖ ˈtɑːtn̩/ n (a) (cloth) tela f escocesa or de cuadros escoceses (b) (pattern) tartán m

tartar /ˈtɑːrtər ‖ ˈtɑːtə(r)/ n (Dent) sarro m

task /tæsk ‖ tɑːsk/ n tarea f; **to take sb to ~** llamarle la atención or leerle* la cartilla a algn

tassel /ˈtæsəl/ n borla f

taste¹ /teɪst/ n **1** (a) (flavor) sabor m, gusto m (b) (sense) gusto m **2** (no pl) (sample, small amount): **can I have a ~ of your ice cream?** ¿me dejas probar tu helado?; **we got a ~ of what was to come** fue un anticipo de lo que nos esperaba **3** (liking) gusto m; **to be to one's ~** ser* de su (or mi etc) gusto **4** (judgment) gusto m; **in good/bad ~ de** buen/mal gusto

taste² vt (a) (test flavor of) ⟨food/wine⟩ probar* (b) (test quality of) ⟨food⟩ degustar; ⟨wine⟩ catar (c) (perceive flavor): **you can ~ the sherry in it** sabe a jerez, le siento gusto a jerez (AmL) (d) (experience) ⟨freedom⟩ conocer*
■ ~ vi saber*; **to ~ of sth** saber* A algo

taste bud n papila f gustativa

tasteful /ˈteɪstfəl/ adj de buen gusto

tastefully /ˈteɪstfəli/ adv con (buen) gusto

tasteless /ˈteɪstləs ‖ ˈteɪstlɪs/ adj (a) (flavorless) insípido, soso, desabrido (b) (in bad taste) de mal gusto

tasty /ˈteɪsti/ adj **-tier, -tiest** sabroso, apetitoso

tattered /ˈtætərd ‖ ˈtætəd/ adj ⟨clothes⟩ hecho jirones; ⟨pride/image⟩ destrozado

tatters /ˈtætərz ‖ ˈtætəz/ pl n: **to be in ~** ⟨clothes⟩ estar* hecho jirones

tattoo¹ /tæˈtuː/ n (pl **-toos**) **1** (picture) tatuaje m **2** (display) espectáculo militar con música

tattoo² vt **-toos, -tooing, -tooed** tatuar*

tatty /ˈtæti/ adj **-tier, -tiest** (BrE colloq) ⟨clothes/shoes⟩ gastado, estropeado; ⟨furniture⟩ estropeado

taught /tɔːt/ past & past p of TEACH

taunt¹ /tɔːnt/ vt provocar* mediante burlas

taunt² n (insult) insulto m; (jibe) pulla f

Taurus /ˈtɔːrəs/ n (a) (sign) (no art) Tauro (b) (person) Tauro or tauro mf, taurino -na m,f

taut /tɔːt/ adj ⟨rope/sail⟩ tenso, tirante; ⟨skin⟩ tirante

tavern /ˈtævərn ‖ ˈtævən/ n taberna f

tawdry /ˈtɔːdri/ adj ⟨jewelry/decorations⟩ de oropel; ⟨decor⟩ de mal gusto

tawny /ˈtɔːni/ adj **-nier, -niest** leonado, pardo rojizo adj inv

tawny owl n cárabo m, antillo m

tax¹ /tæks/ n (individual charge) impuesto m, tributo m (fml); (in general) impuestos mpl; (before n) **the ~ year** (in UK) el año or ejercicio fiscal

tax² vt **1** ⟨company/goods/earnings⟩ gravar; **we're being ~ed too highly** nos están cobrando demasiado en impuestos **2** (strain) ⟨resources/health⟩ poner* a prueba

taxable /ˈtæksəbəl/ adj ⟨goods⟩ sujeto a impuestos; **~ income** ingresos mpl gravables, ≈ base f imponible

taxation /tækˈseɪʃən/ n (taxes) impuestos mpl, cargas fpl fiscales; (system) sistema m or régimen m tributario or fiscal

tax: ~ collector n recaudador, -dora m,f de impuestos; **~ evasion** n evasión f fiscal or de impuestos; (large scale) fraude m fiscal; **~-free** /ˈtæksˈfriː/ adj libre de impuestos; **~ haven** n paraíso m fiscal

taxi¹ /ˈtæksi/ n (pl **~s**) taxi m; (before n) **~ driver** taxista mf

taxi² vi **taxies, taxiing** or **taxying, taxied** (Aviat) rodar* por la pista de despegue/de aterrizaje, carretear (AmL)

taxidermy /ˈtæksədɜːrmi ‖ ˈtæksɪˌdɜːmi/ n taxidermia f

taxing /ˈtæksɪŋ/ adj ⟨problem⟩ difícil, complicado; ⟨job⟩ (mentally) que exige mucho

tax: ~man /ˈtæksmæn/ (pl **-men** /-men/) n (colloq) **the ~man** Hacienda f, el fisco; **~payer** /ˈpeɪər ‖ ˈpeɪə(r)/ n contribuyente mf; **~ return** n declaración f de la renta or (esp AmL) de impuestos

TB n = tuberculosis

tbs, tbsp = tablespoon(s)

te /tiː/ n (BrE Mus) si m

tea /tiː/ n **1** (drink, leaves, plant) té m **2** (meal) (a) (in the afternoon) té m, merienda f (b) (evening) (BrE) cena f, comida f (AmL)

tea bag n bolsita f de té

teach /tiːtʃ/ (past & past p **taught**) vt ⟨subject⟩ dar* clases de, enseñar; ⟨course⟩ dar*, impartir (fml); **to ~ sb to + INF** enseñarle a algn a + INF; **who ~es you?** ¿quién te da clase?; **to ~ school** (AmE) dar* clase(s) en un colegio
■ ~ vi dar* clase(s)

teacher /ˈtiːtʃər ‖ ˈtiːtʃə(r)/ n profesor, -sora m,f, docente mf (fml), enseñante mf (period); (primary school ~) maestro, -tra m,f

teacher: ~s college n (AmE) (for primary education) escuela f normal; (for secondary education) instituto m de profesorado; **~ training** n formación f pedagógica or de profesorado; (before n) **~ training college** (BrE) ▶ ~S COLLEGE

tea chest n caja f de embalaje (utilizada en mudanzas)

teaching /ˈtiːtʃɪŋ/ n **1** (profession) enseñanza f, docencia f **2** (doctrine) (often pl) enseñanza f

teaching practice n (BrE) práctica f docente

tea: ~ cloth n (BrE) ▶ TEA TOWEL; **~ cozy, cosy** (BrE) n cubretetera m; **~cup** n taza f de té

teak /tiːk/ n (madera f de) teca f

tealeaf /ˈtiːliːf/ n (pl **-leaves**) hoja f de té

team /tiːm/ n (a) (of players, workers) equipo m; *(before n)* **it was a ~ effort** fue un trabajo de equipo (b) (of horses) tiro m; (of oxen) yunta f

team: ~**mate** n compañero, -ra m,f de equipo; ~ **spirit** n espíritu m de equipo

teamster /'tiːmstər ‖ 'tiːmstə(r)/ n (AmE) camionero, -ra m,f

teamwork /'tiːmwɜːrk ‖ 'tiːmwɜːk/ n trabajo m or labor f de equipo

tea: ~ **party** n té m; ~**pot** n tetera f

tear[1] n ⟦1⟧ /tɪr ‖ tɪə(r)/ lágrima f; **to be in ~s** estar* llorando ⟦2⟧ /ter ‖ teə(r)/ rotura f; (rip, slash) desgarrón m, rasgón m; *see also* WEAR[1] 1B

tear[2] /ter ‖ teə(r)/ *(past* **tore**; *past p* **torn**) vt (a) ⟨cloth/paper⟩ romper*, rasgar*; **I tore** **the letter** abrí la carta *(rasgando el sobre)*; **to ~ sth to pieces** o **bits** o **shreds** ⟨cloth/paper⟩ hacer* algo pedazos; ⟨play/essay⟩ hacer* algo pedazos or trizas or (fam) polvo; ⟨argument⟩ echar algo por tierra (b) (divide) *(usu pass)* dividir; **he was torn** **between ... and ...** se debatía entre ... y ... (c) (remove forcibly) **to ~ sth FROM sth** arrancar* algo DE algo

■ ~ vi ⟦1⟧ ⟨cloth/paper⟩ romperse*, rasgarse* ⟦2⟧ (rush) (+ adv compl): **to ~ along** ir* a toda velocidad

■ **tear apart** [v + o + adv] desgarrar

■ **tear down** [v + o + adv, v + adv + o] tirar abajo

■ **tear off** [v + o + adv, v + adv + o] arrancar*

■ **tear out** [v + o + adv, v + adv + o] arrancar*

■ **tear up** [v + o + adv, v + adv + o] romper*

teardrop /'tɪrdrɑːp ‖ 'tɪədrɒp/ n lágrima f

tearful /'tɪrfəl ‖ 'tɪəfəl/ adj ⟨look/expression⟩ lloroso; ⟨farewell⟩ triste, emotivo

tear gas /'tɪrgæs ‖ 'tɪəgæs/ n gas m lacrimógeno

tearoom /'tiːruːm, -rʊm/ n salón m de té

tease /tiːz/ vt tomarle el pelo a (fam); (cruelly) burlarse or reírse de

tea: ~ **service,** ~ **set** n juego m de té; ~**shop** n (esp BrE) ▶ TEAROOM; ~**spoon** n (a) (spoon) cucharita f, cucharilla f (b) (quantity) cucharadita f; ~ **strainer** n colador m *(pequeño)*

teat /tiːt/ n (a) (Zool) tetilla f (b) (of feeding bottle) (BrE) ▶ NIPPLE B

tea: ~**time** n (of afternoon snack) la hora del té, ≈ la hora de merendar; (of evening meal) (BrE) la hora de cenar or (AmL tb) de comer; ~ **towel** n (BrE) paño m or trapo m de cocina

technical /'teknɪkəl/ adj técnico

technical college n (in UK) escuela f politécnica, ≈ instituto m de formación profesional *(en Esp)*

technicality /teknɪ'kæləti/ n *(pl* **-ties)** (detail) detalle m técnico

technically /'teknɪkli/ adv técnicamente; *(indep)* desde el punto de vista técnico

technician /tek'nɪʃən/ n técnico mf, técnico, -ca m,f

technique /tek'niːk/ n técnica f

technological /teknə'lɑːdʒɪkəl ‖ teknə'lɒdʒɪkəl/ adj tecnológico

technology /tek'nɑːlədʒi ‖ tek'nɒlədʒi/ n *(pl* **-gies)** tecnología f

teddy bear /'tedi/ n osito m de peluche

tedious /'tiːdiəs/ adj tedioso

tedium /'tiːdiəm/ n tedio m

teem /tiːm/ vi **to ~ WITH sth: the forest is ~ing** **with birds** el bosque está repleto de pájaros; **the** **streets were ~ing with people** las calles hervían de gente

teenage /'tiːneɪdʒ/ adj ⟨girl/boy⟩ adolescente; ⟨fashions⟩ juvenil, para adolescentes

teenager /'tiːneɪdʒər ‖ 'tiːneɪdʒə(r)/ n adolescente mf

teens /tiːnz/ pl n adolescencia f

tee shirt /tiː/ n ▶ T-SHIRT

teeter /'tiːtər ‖ 'tiːtə(r)/ vi ⟨person⟩ tambalearse

teeth /tiːθ/ pl of TOOTH

teethe /tiːð/ vi: **she's teething** le están saliendo los dientes

teething troubles /'tiːðɪŋ/pl n problemas mpl iniciales

teetotal /'tiː'təʊtl/ adj abstemio

teetotaler, (BrE) **teetotaller** /'tiː'təʊtlər ‖ tiː'təʊtlə(r)/ n abstemio, -mia m,f

TEFL /'tefəl/ n (BrE) (= **teaching English as** **a foreign language**) enseñanza del inglés como lengua extranjera

tel (= **telephone number**) Tel., fono m (CS)

telebanking /'teli,bæŋkɪŋ/ n telebanca f

telecommunications /'telikə'mjuːnə'keɪʃənz ‖ telikə,mjuːnɪ'keɪʃənz/ n telecomunicaciones fpl

telegram /'teləgræm ‖ 'telɪgræm/ n telegrama m

telegraph /'teləgræf ‖ 'telɪgrɑːf/ n (a) (method) telégrafo m; *(before n)* ⟨wire/cable⟩ telegráfico; ~ **pole** poste m telegráfico (b) (message) telegrama m, despacho m telegráfico

telemarketing /'teli,mɑːrkətɪŋ ‖ 'teli,mɑːkɪtɪŋ/ n telemarketing m, teletienda f

telepathic /telə'pæθɪk ‖ telɪ'pæθɪk/ adj ⟨message⟩ telepático; ⟨person⟩ con telepatía, telépata

telepathy /tə'lepəθi/ n telepatía f

telephone[1] /'teləfəʊn ‖ 'telɪfəʊn/ n teléfono m; *(before n)* ⟨message/line⟩ telefónico; ~ **number** (número m de) teléfono m; ~ **operator** telefonista mf; *see also* PHONE[1]

telephone[2] vt telefonear, llamar por teléfono a

telephone: ~ **booth,** (BrE) ~ **box** n cabina f telefónica or de teléfonos; ~ **directory** n guía f telefónica or de teléfonos; ~ **exchange** n central f telefónica or de teléfonos

telephonist /tə'lefənəst ‖ tə'lefənɪst/ n (BrE) telefonista mf

telesales /'teliseɪlz/ pl n televentas fpl

telescope /'teləskəʊp ‖ 'telɪskəʊp/ n telescopio m

telescopic /telə'skɑːpɪk ‖ telɪs'kɒpɪk/ adj telescópico

teleshopping /'teli,ʃɑːpɪŋ ‖ 'teli,ʃɒpɪŋ/ n compra(s) f(pl) por teléfono

teletext /'telitekst/ n teletex(to) m, videotex(to) m

televise /'teləvaɪz ‖ 'telɪvaɪz/ vt televisar

television /'telɪvɪʒən ‖'telɪvɪʒən/ n (a) (medium, industry) televisión f; on ~ en or por (la) televisión; (before n) ~ **licence** (in UK) impuesto y licencia que debe obtenerse para poder usar un receptor de televisión (b) ~ (**set**) televisor m

telex /'teleks/ n télex m

tell /tel/ (past & past p **told**) vt **1** (inform, reveal) decir*; he was told that ... le dijeron que ...; could you ~ me the way to the station? ¿me podría decir cómo se llega a la estación? **2** (recount, relate) ⟨joke/story⟩ contar*; she's told me all about you me ha hablado mucho de ti; ~ us about Lima cuéntanos cómo es Lima (or qué tal se fue en Lima etc) **3** (instruct, warn) decir*; to ~ sb to + INF decirle* a algn QUE (+ subj) **4** (a) (ascertain, know): I could ~ from her voice that ... noté por la voz que ...; to ~ the time decir la hora (b) (distinguish) to ~ sth/sb (FROM sth/sb) distinguir* algo/a algn (DE algo/algn); I can't ~ the difference yo no veo or no noto ninguna diferencia **5** : all told en total
■ ~ vi **1** (reveal): promise you won't ~? ¿prometes que no se lo vas a contar or decir a nadie?; to ~ on sb (TO sb) (colloq) acusar a algn (A or CON algn) **2** (know) saber*; you never can ~ nunca se sabe **3** (count, have an effect): her age is beginning to ~ se le está empezando a notar la edad
■ **tell apart** [v + o + adv] distinguir*
■ **tell off** [v + o + adv, v + adv + o] (colloq) regañar, reñir* (esp Esp), retar (CS), resondrar (Per), rezongar* (AmC, Ur)

teller /'telər ‖'telə(r)/ n (in bank) cajero, -ra m,f

telling /'telɪŋ/ adj ⟨sign/remark⟩ revelador

telltale¹ /'telteɪl/ adj (before n) revelador

telltale² n (person) (colloq) soplón, -plona m,f (fam), acusete mf (fam)

temp /temp/ n empleado, -da m,f eventual or temporal

temper¹ /'tempər ‖'tempə(r)/ n (a) (no pl) (mood) humor m; (temperament, disposition) carácter m, genio m; (rage): to have a bad ~ tener* mal genio (b) (rage): to be in a ~ estar* furioso or hecho una furia (c) (composure): to lose one's ~ perder* los estribos

temper² vt (a) (moderate) ⟨criticism⟩ atenuar* (b) (Metall) templar

temperament /'temprəmənt/ n temperamento m

temperamental /temprə'mentl/ adj ⟨person⟩ temperamental

temperance /'tempərəns/ n (a) (moderation) (frml) templanza f, moderación f (b) (alcohol avoidance) abstinencia f de bebidas; (before n) ⟨movement⟩ antialcohólico

temperate /'tempərət/ adj templado

temperature /'temprətʃər ‖'temprətʃə(r)/ n (a) (Phys) temperatura f (b) (Med) (reading on thermometer) temperatura f; (abnormally high reading)

fiebre f, temperatura f (CS); to have o run a ~ tener* fiebre or (CS) temperatura; to take sb's ~ tomarle la temperatura a algn

tempest /'tempəst ‖'tempɪst/ n (liter) tempestad f (liter)

tempestuous /tem'pestʃuəs ‖tem'pestjʊəs/ adj ⟨relationship⟩ tempestuoso (b) ⟨sea⟩ (liter) tempestuoso (liter)

temple /'tempəl/ n **1** (Relig) templo m **2** (Anat) sien f

tempo /'tempəʊ/ n (pl **-pos** or **-pi** /-pi/) ritmo m; (Mus) tempo m

temporal /'tempərəl/ adj temporal

temporarily /'tempə'rerəli ‖'tempərərɪli/ adj temporalmente, temporariamente (AmL)

temporary /'tempəreri ‖'temprəri/ adj ⟨accommodation/arrangement⟩ temporal, provisional; ⟨job/work/worker⟩ eventual, temporal

tempt /tempt/ vt (often pass) tentar*

temptation /temp'teɪʃən/ n tentación f

tempting /'temptɪŋ/ adj tentador

ten¹ /ten/ n diez m; see also FOUR¹

ten² adj diez adj inv

tenable /'tenəbəl/ adj defendible

tenacious /tə'neɪʃəs ‖tɪ'neɪʃəs/ adj tenaz

tenacity /tə'næsəti ‖tɪ'næsəti/ n tenacidad f

tenancy /'tenənsi/ n (pl **-cies**) (holding, possession) tenencia f

tenant /'tenənt/ n inquilino, -na m,f, arrendatario, -ria m,f

tend /tend/ vi **1** (have tendency, be inclined) tender*; to ~ to + INF tender* A + INF **2** (attend) to ~ TO sth/sb ocuparse DE algo/algn
■ ~ vt ⟨sheep⟩ cuidar (de), ocuparse de; ⟨victims⟩ cuidar (de), atender*; ⟨garden/grave⟩ ocuparse de

tendency /'tendənsi/ n (pl **-cies**) tendencia f; (Med) propensión f, tendencia f

tender¹ /'tendər ‖'tendə(r)/ adj (a) (sensitive) ⟨spot⟩ sensible; ⟨age⟩ tierno (b) ⟨meat⟩ tierno (c) (loving) tierno

tender² n (a) (Busn) (offer) propuesta f, oferta f (b) (legal ~) moneda f de curso legal

tender³ vt (frml) ⟨resignation⟩ presentar, ofrecer*

tenderize /'tendəraɪz/ vt ⟨meat⟩ ablandar

tenderly /'tendərli ‖'tendəli/ adv tiernamente, con ternura

tendon /'tendən/ n tendón m

tendril /'tendrəl/ n zarcillo m

tenet /'tenət ‖'tenɪt/ n principio m

tenfold /'tenfəʊld/ adj/adv ▶ -FOLD

Tenn = **Tennessee**

tennis /'tenəs ‖'tenɪs/ n tenis m; (before n) ~ **court** cancha f or (esp Esp) pista f de tenis; ~ **player** tenista mf; ~ **racket** raqueta f de tenis

tenor¹ /'tenər ‖'tenə(r)/ n **1** (Mus) tenor m **2** (frml) (sense) tenor m

tenor² adj (before n) ⟨voice⟩ de tenor; ⟨saxophone⟩ tenor

ten: ~**pin bowling** n (BrE) ▶ ~**PINS**; ~**pins** n (+ sing vb) (AmE) bolos mpl, bowling m

tense¹ /tens/ adj (a) ⟨situation/person⟩ tenso (b) (taut) tenso, tirante

tense² vt ⟨muscles⟩ poner* tenso, tensar
■ **tense up** [v + adv] (colloq) ponerse* tenso

tense³ n (Ling) tiempo m

tension /'tentʃən ‖'tenʃən/ n **1** (a) (of situation) tensión f, tirantez f (b) (felt by person) tensión f (c) (between two parties) conflicto m **2** (tautness) tensión f **3** (Elec) tensión f

tent /tent/ n tienda f (de campaña), carpa f (AmL)

tentacle /'tentɪkəl ‖'tentəkəl/ n tentáculo m

tentative /'tentətɪv/ adj (a) ⟨plan⟩ provisional, provisorio (AmS); ⟨offer⟩ tentativo (b) ⟨person⟩ indeciso

tenterhooks /'tentərhʊks ‖'tentəhʊks/ pl n: **to be on** ~ estar* en o sobre ascuas

tenth¹ /tenθ/ adj décimo

tenth² adv en décimo lugar

tenth³ n (Math) décimo m; (part) décima parte f

tenuous /'tenjuəs/ adj ⟨claim⟩ poco fundado; ⟨link⟩ indirecto

tenure /'tenjər ‖'tenjə(r)/ n (a) (of property, land) tenencia f (b) (period of office) ejercicio m, ocupación f

tepid /'tepəd ‖'tepɪd/ adj tibio

term¹ /tɜːrm ‖tɜːm/ n
I **1** (word) término m **2** (a) (period) período m, periodo m; ~ **of** o (AmE also) **in office** mandato m; **in the short/long** ~ a corto/largo plazo (b) (Educ) trimestre m
II terms pl **1** (conditions) condiciones fpl; **to come to** ~**s with sth** aceptar algo **2** (relations): **to be on good/bad** ~**s with sb** estar* en buenas/malas relaciones con algn **3** (a) (sense): **in financial** ~**s** desde el punto de vista financiero; **in real** ~**s** en términos reales (b) **in terms of: in** ~**s of efficiency** en cuanto a eficiencia

term² vt calificar* de

terminal¹ /'tɜːrmənl ‖'tɜːmɪnl/ adj ⟨illness⟩ terminal; ⟨patient⟩ (en fase) terminal, desahuciado

terminal² n (a) (Transp) (at airport) terminal f; **bus** ~ terminal f de autobuses (b) (Comput) terminal m (c) (Elec) terminal m

terminally /'tɜːrmənəli ‖'tɜːmɪnəli/ adv: **he's** ~ **ill** está en fase terminal, está desahuciado

terminate /'tɜːrmɪneɪt ‖'tɜːmɪneɪt/ vt (fml) ⟨relationship⟩ poner* fin a; ⟨contract⟩ poner* término a; ⟨employee⟩ (AmE) despedir*, cesar (frml or period); ⟨pregnancy⟩ interrumpir
■ ~ vi «lease/relationship» terminarse; **this train** ~**s here** este es el final del recorrido de este tren

termination /ˌtɜːrmə'neɪʃən ‖ˌtɜːmɪ'neɪʃən/ n (a) (of contract) (frml) terminación f (b) (Med): ~ **of pregnancy** interrupción f del embarazo

terminology /ˌtɜːrmə'nɑːlədʒi ‖ˌtɜːmɪ'nɒlədʒi/ n (pl **-gies**) terminología f

terminus /'tɜːrmənəs ‖'tɜːmɪnəs/ n (pl **-nuses** or **-ni** /-niː, -naɪ ‖-naɪ/) (of buses) terminal f, (of trains) estación f terminal

termite /'tɜːrmaɪt ‖'tɜːmaɪt/ n termita f

terrace /'terəs ‖'terəs, 'terɪs/ n (a) (patio) terraza f (b) (balcony) (AmE) terraza f (c) (on hillside) terraza f (d) (row of houses) (BrE) hilera de casas adosadas

terraced /'terəst ‖'terəst, 'terɪst/ adj (a) ⟨hillside/slope⟩ en terrazas or bancales (b) ⟨house⟩ (BrE) adosado (en una hilera de casas uniformes)

terrain /te'reɪn/ n terreno m

terrestrial /tə'restriəl/ adj terrestre

terrible /'terəbl/ adj espantoso, atroz

terribly /'terəbli/ adv ⟨suffer⟩ terriblemente; ⟨sing/act⟩ terriblemente mal

terrier /'teriər ‖'teriə(r)/ n terrier mf

terrific /tə'rɪfɪk/ adj (a) (enormous) (colloq) tremendo, increíble; ⟨argument⟩ espantoso (b) (very good) (colloq) estupendo, genial (fam)

terrified /'terəfaɪd ‖'terɪfaɪd/ adj ⟨crowd⟩ aterrorizado, aterrado; **to be** ~ **of sth/sb** tenerle* terror or pánico a algo/algn

terrify /'terəfaɪ ‖'terɪfaɪ/ vt **-fies, -fying, -fied** aterrorizar*

terrifying /'terəfaɪŋ ‖'terɪfaɪŋ/ adj aterrador

territorial /ˌterə'tɔːriəl ‖ˌterɪ'tɔːriəl/ adj territorial

territory /'terətɔːri ‖'terɪtəri, -tri/ n (pl **-ries**) territorio m

terror /'terər ‖'terə(r)/ n terror m; **they fled in** ~ huyeron aterrorizados or despavoridos

terrorism /'terərɪzəm/ n terrorismo m

terrorist /'terərəst ‖'terərɪst/ n terrorista mf

terrorize /'terəraɪz/ vt aterrorizar*, tener* atemorizado

terse /tɜːrs ‖tɜːs/ adj seco, lacónico

test¹ /test/ n (a) (Educ) prueba f, (multiple-choice type) test m (b) (of machine, drug) prueba f; (before n) ⟨run/flight⟩ experimental, de prueba (c) (of blood, urine) análisis m; (for hearing, eyes) examen m

test² vt (a) ⟨student/class⟩ examinar, hacerle* una prueba a; ⟨knowledge/skill⟩ evaluar* (b) ⟨product⟩ probar*, poner* a prueba (c) ⟨friendship/endurance⟩ poner* a prueba (d) ⟨blood/urine⟩ analizar*; ⟨sight/hearing⟩ examinar; ⟨hypothesis⟩ comprobar*

testament /'testəmənt/ n **1** (will) testamento m **2 Testament** (Bib): **the Old/New T**~ el Antiguo/Nuevo Testamento

test: ~ **case** n: caso que sienta jurisprudencia; ~ **drive** n (Auto) prueba f de circulación en carretera

testicle /'testɪkəl/ n testículo m

testify /'testəfaɪ ‖'testɪfaɪ/ vi **-fies, -fying, -fied** (Law frml) prestar declaración, testificar*; **to** ~ **to sth** declarar o testificar* algo

testimonial /ˌtestə'məʊniəl ‖ˌtestɪ'məʊniəl/ n recomendación f

testimony /'testəməʊni ‖'testɪməni/ n (pl **-nies**) (Law) declaración f, testimonio m

testing¹ /'testɪŋ/ n pruebas fpl

testing² adj duro, arduo

test: ~ **match** n (Sport) partido m internacional; ~ **paper** n (Educ) examen m, prueba f; ~ **pilot** n piloto mf de pruebas; ~ **tube** n probeta f, tubo m de ensayo; (before n) ~-**tube baby** niño, -ña m,f probeta

tetanus /ˈtetnəs/ n tétano(s) m

tether¹ /ˈteðər ‖ˈteðə(r)/ n soga f

tether² vt atar, amarrar

Tex = **Texas**

text /tekst/ n texto m

textbook /ˈtekstbʊk/ n libro m de texto

textile /ˈtekstaɪl/ n textil m

textual /ˈtekstʃuəl ‖ˈtekstjʊəl/ adj textual

texture /ˈtekstʃər ‖ˈtekstʃə(r)/ n textura f

Thai¹ /taɪ/ adj tailandés

Thai² n (a) (person) tailandés, -desa m,f (b) (language) tailandés m

Thailand /ˈtaɪlænd/ n Tailandia f

Thames /temz/ n the ~ el Támesis

than¹ /ðæn, weak form ðən/ conj (a) (in comparisons) que; (with quantity) de; **I'm feeling better ~ I was** me siento mejor que antes; **more ~ $25** más de 25 dólares; **the situation is worse ~ we thought** la situación es peor de lo que pensábamos (b) (with alternatives): **I'd rather walk ~ go by bus** prefiero ir a pie a tomar el autobús (c) (when) cuando; **no sooner had I sat down ~ the bell rang** apenas me había sentado cuando sonó el timbre

than² prep (in comparisons) que; (with quantity) de

thank /θæŋk/ vt **to ~ sb (FOR sth)** darle* las gracias a algn (POR algo), agradecerle* (algo) a algn; **~ God/heaven(s)** menos mal, gracias a Dios; see also THANK YOU

thankful /ˈθæŋkfəl/ adj ‹look/smile› de agradecimiento, agradecido

thankfully /ˈθæŋkfəli/ adv (indep) menos mal, gracias a Dios

thankless /ˈθæŋkləs ‖ˈθæŋklɪs/ adj ingrato

thanks /θæŋks/ pl n (a) (expression of gratitude) agradecimiento m (b) (as interj) ~! ¡gracias!; ~ **very much** o **a lot!** ¡muchas gracias!; **many ~** muchas gracias (c) **thanks to** gracias a

Thanksgiving (Day) /ˈθæŋksˈgɪvɪŋ/ n (in US) el día de Acción de Gracias

thank you interj ¡gracias!; ~ ~ **very much** muchas gracias; **to say ~ ~** dar* las gracias; ~ ~ **for coming/your help** gracias por venir/tu ayuda

that¹ /ðæt/ pron **1** (pl **those**) (demonstrative) ese, esa; (neuter) eso; **those** esos, esas; (to refer to sth more distant or to the remote past) aquel, aquélla; (neuter) aquello; **those** aquellos, aquellas; **~'s wonderful!** ¡es maravilloso!; **those who have been less fortunate** los que no han tenido tanta suerte **2** (in phrases) **at that** (moreover) además; (thereupon): **at ~ they all burst out laughing** al oír (or ver etc) eso, todos se echaron a reír; **that is** es decir; **that's it:** ~'s **it for today** eso es todo por hoy; **now lift your left arm:** ~'s **it!** ahora levanta el brazo izquierdo ¡eso es! or ¡ahí está!; ~'s **it: I've had enough!** ¡ya acabó! ¡ya no aguanto más! **3** /ðæt, strong form ðæt/ (relative) que; **it wasn't Helen (~) you saw** no fue a Helen a quien viste, no fue a Helen que viste (AmL)

that² /ðæt/ adj (pl **those**) ese, esa; **those** esos, esas; (to refer to sth more distant, to the remote past) aquel, aquella; **those** aquellos, aquellas

that³ /ðət, strong form ðæt/ conj que; **she said (~) ... dijo que ...; the news ~ our team had won** la noticia de que nuestro equipo había ganado

that⁴ /ðæt/ adv tan; **he can't be all ~ stupid** no es posible que sea tan tonto

thatched /θætʃt/ adj ‹roof› de paja (or de juncos etc)or (AmS) de quincha; ‹cottage› con el tejado de paja (or de juncos etc), quinchado (AmS)

thaw¹ /θɔː/ vi «snow/ice» derretirse*, fundirse; «frozen food» descongelarse; «relations» hacerse* más cordial
■ ~ vt ‹frozen food› descongelar

thaw² n (Meteo, Pol) deshielo m

the¹ /before vowel ði, ðɪ; before consonant ðə, strong form ðiː/ def art **1** (sing) el, la; (pl) los, las **2** (a) (with names): **Henry ~ First** Enrique primero; ~ **Smiths** los Smith (b) (in abstractions, generalizations) (+ sing vb): ~ **impossible** lo imposible; ~ **young** los jóvenes **3** (per): **they sell it by ~ square foot** lo venden por pie cuadrado; **I get paid by ~ hour** me pagan por hora

the² /before vowel ði; before consonant ðə/ adv (+ comp) (as conj) cuanto; ~ **more you have,** ~ **more you want** cuanto más tienes, más quieres; ~ **sooner,** ~ **better** cuanto antes, mejor

theater, (BrE) **theatre** /ˈθiːətər ‖ˈθɪətə(r)/ n **1** (a) (building) teatro m (b) (theatrical world) **the ~** el teatro **2** (movie ~) (AmE) cine m

theatrical /θiˈætrɪkəl/ adj teatral

theft /θeft/ n robo m

their /ðer ‖ðeəz/ adj
■ **Note** The translation su agrees in number with the noun which it modifies; their is translated by su, sus, depending on what follows: their father/mother su padre/madre; their books/magazines sus libros/revistas.

(a) (sing) su; (pl) sus; **he cut off ~ heads** les cortó la cabeza (b) (belonging to indefinite person) (sing) su; (pl) sus; **whoever called didn't leave ~ number** la persona que ha llamado no dejó su teléfono

theirs /ðerz ‖ðeəz/ pron
■ **Note** The translation suyo reflects the gender and number of the noun it is standing for; theirs is translated by el suyo, la suya, los suyos, las suyas, depending on what is being referred to.

(sing) suyo, -ya; (pl) suyos, -yas; ~ **is blue** el suyo/la suya or el/la de ellos es azul; **a friend of ~** un amigo suyo or de ellos

them /ðem, weak form ðəm/ pron **1** (a) (as direct object) los, las; (referring to people) los or (Esp tb) les, las; **where did you buy ~?** ¿dónde los/las compraste?; **he has two sons, do you know ~?** tiene dos hijos ¿los or (Esp tb) les conoces? (b) (as indirect object) les; (with direct object pronoun present) se; **I lent ~ some money** les presté dinero (c) (after preposition) ellos, ellas **2** (emphatic use) ellos, ellas; **that'll be ~** deben de ser ellos **3** (indefinite person): **if anyone calls, tell ~ that ...** si llama alguien, dile que ...

theme /θiːm/ n tema m; (before n) ~ **park** parque m temático; ~ **song** tema m musical; (of TV program) (AmE) música f de un programa

themselves /ðəmˈselvz/ pron (a) (reflexive): **they bought ~ a new car** se compraron otro coche; **they only think of ~** solo piensan en sí mismos; **they were by ~** estaban solos/solas **(b)** (emphatic) ellos mismos, ellas mismas **(c)** (normal selves): **the children aren't ~** los niños no son los de siempre **(d)** (indefinite person or persons): **if anyone's interested they can find out for ~** si a alguien le interesa, puede averiguarlo por sí mismo

then¹ /ðen/ *adv* **1 (a)** (at that time) entonces **(b)** (in those days) en aquel entonces **2** (*after prep*): **by ~** para entonces; **from ~ on** a partir de ese momento, desde entonces; (**up**) **until** *o* **till ~** hasta entonces **3 (a)** (next, afterward) después, luego **(b)** (in those circumstances) entonces **(c)** (besides, in addition) además **4** (in that case) entonces; **you do it, ~!** ¡hazlo tú, entonces! **5** then again (*as linker*) también

then² *adj* (*before n*) entonces; **the ~ leader** el entonces líder

theologian /ˌθɪəˈləʊdʒən/ *n* teólogo, -ga *m,f*

theological /ˌθɪəˈlɒdʒɪkəl ‖ˌθɪəˈlɒdʒɪkəl/ *adj* teológico

theology /θɪˈɒlədʒi ‖θɪˈɒlədʒi/ *n* (*pl* **-gies**) teología *f*

theorem /ˈθɪərəm/ *n* teorema *m*

theoretical /ˌθɪəˈretɪkəl/ *adj* teórico

theorize /ˈθɪəraɪz/ *vi* especular, teorizar*

theory /ˈθɪəri/ *n* (*pl* **-ries**) teoría *f*

therapeutic /ˌθerəˈpjuːtɪk/ *adj* terapéutico

therapist /ˈθerəpəst ‖ˈθerəpɪst/ *n* terapeuta *mf*

therapy /ˈθerəpi/ *n* (*pl* **-pies**) terapia *f*

there¹ /ðer ‖ðeə(r)/ *adv* **1 (a)** (close to person being addressed) ahí; (further away) allí, ahí (esp AmL); (less precise, further) allá; **up/down ~** ahí arriba/abajo **(b)** there and then ⟨decide⟩ en ese mismo momento; **they mended it for me ~ and then** me lo arreglaron en el acto **2** (calling attention to sth): **~ you are** (giving sth) aquí tiene; **~ go my chances of promotion!** ¡adiós ascenso! **3** (present): **all his friends were ~** estaban todos sus amigos; **is Tony ~?** ¿está Tony?; **who's ~?** (at the door) ¿quién es?; (in the dark) ¿quién anda ahí? **4** (*as interj*) **~! that's the last of the boxes** ¡listo! esa es la última caja; **~, ~, don't cry!** vamos, no llores

there² /ðer, *weak form* ðər ‖ðeə(r), *weak form* ðə(r)/ *pron*: **there is/are** hay; **there was** había/ hubo; **there will be** habrá

there: ~about /ˈðerəbaʊt ‖ˈðeərəbaʊt/ *adv* (AmE) ▶ ~ABOUTS; **~abouts** /ˈðerəbaʊts ‖ˈðeərəbaʊts/ *adv* **(a)** (near that figure, time) por ahí **(b)** (in that vicinity) por allí; **~after** /ðerˈæftər ‖ðeərˈɑːftə(r)/ *adv* (frml) a partir de entonces; **~by** /ˈðerˈbaɪ ‖ðeəˈbaɪ, ˈðeəbaɪ/ *adv* (frml) de ese modo, así; **~fore** /ˈðerfɔːr ‖ˈðeəfɔː(r)/ *adv* por lo tanto, por consiguiente

there's /ðerz, *weak form* ðərz ‖ðeəz, *weak form* ðəz/ **(a)** = **there is (b)** = **there has**

thermal /ˈθɜːrməl ‖ˈθɜːməl/ *adj* **(a)** ⟨stream/ bath⟩ termal **(b)** ⟨underwear/glove⟩ térmico

thermometer /θərˈmɑːmətər ‖θəˈmɒmɪtə(r)/ *n* termómetro *m*

Thermos® (**flask**) /ˈθɜːrməs ‖ˈθɜːməs/, (AmE also) **thermos** (**bottle**) *n* termo *m*

thermostat /ˈθɜːrməstæt ‖ˈθɜːməstæt/ *n* termostato *m*

thesaurus /θɪˈsɔːrəs/ *n* (*pl* **-ruses** *or* **-ri** /-raɪ/) diccionario *m* ideológico *or* de ideas afines, tesauro *m*

these /ðiːz/ *pl of* THIS¹,²

thesis /ˈθiːsəs ‖ˈθiːsɪs/ *n* (*pl* **-ses** /-siːz/) tesis *f*, (shorter) tesina *f*

they /ðeɪ/ *pron*

■ **Note** Although *ellos* and *ellas* are given as translations of *they*, they are in practice used only for emphasis, or to avoid ambiguity: *they went to the theater* fueron al teatro; **they** *did it* ellos or ellas lo hicieron.

(a) (*pl of* he, she, it) ellos, ellas **(b)** (indefinite person or persons): **~'ve dug up the road** han levantado la calle

they'd /ðeɪd/ **(a)** = **they would (b)** = **they had**

they'll /ðeɪl/ = **they will**

they're /ðer, *weak form* ðər ‖ðeə(r), *weak form* ðə(r)/ = **they are**

they've /ðeɪv/ = **they have**

thick /θɪk/ *adj* **-er, -est** **1 (a)** ⟨layer/book/ sweater⟩ grueso, gordo (fam); ⟨line⟩ grueso; **it's 5cm ~** tiene 5cm de espesor *or* de grosor **(b)** ⟨sauce/paint⟩ espeso **(c)** ⟨fog/smoke⟩ espeso, denso; ⟨fur⟩ tupido; ⟨beard/eyebrows⟩ poblado; **through ~ and thin** tanto en las duras como en las maduras **2** (colloq) (stupid) burro (fam), corto (fam)

thicken /ˈθɪkən/ *vt* ⟨sauce/paint⟩ espesar

■ **~** *vi* «sauce/paint» espesar(se); «fog» hacerse* más espeso *or* denso

thicket /ˈθɪkət ‖ˈθɪkɪt/ *n* matorral *m*

thickly /ˈθɪkli/ *adv* **(a)** (in a thick layer): **spread the jam ~** pon una capa gruesa de mermelada **(b)** (densely) ⟨populated⟩ densamente

thickness /ˈθɪknəs ‖ˈθɪknɪs/ *n* (of fabric, wire) grosor *m*; (of paper, wood, wall) espesor *m*, grosor *m*

thick: ~set /ˈθɪkˈset/ *adj* fornido; **~-skinned** /ˈθɪkˈskɪnd/ *adj* insensible

thief /θiːf/ *n* (*pl* **thieves** /θiːvz/) ladrón, -drona *m,f*

thigh /θaɪ/ *n* muslo *m*

thimble /ˈθɪmbəl/ *n* dedal *m*

thin¹ /θɪn/ *adj* **-nn-** **1 (a)** ⟨layer/slice⟩ delgado, fino **(b)** ⟨person⟩ delgado, flaco; ⟨waist⟩ delgado **2 (a)** ⟨soup/sauce⟩ claro, poco espeso **(b)** ⟨hair⟩ ralo

thin² *vt* **-nn-** ⟨paint⟩ diluir*, rebajar*; ⟨sauce⟩ aclarar, hacer* más espeso

■ **~** *vi*: **his hair is ~ning** está perdiendo pelo

thing /θɪŋ/ *n* **1** (physical object) cosa *f* **2** (non-material) cosa *f*; **the same ~ happened to me** a mí me pasó lo mismo; **it's a good ~** (that) … menos mal que …; **the last ~ I expected** lo que menos me imaginaba; **he hadn't done a ~** no había hecho absolutamente nada; **it's just one of those ~s** son cosas que pasan **3** (affair, matter) asunto *m*; **I'm fed up with the whole ~** estoy harto del asunto **4** the thing **(a)** (that which, what) lo que **(b)** (what is needed): **I've got just the ~ for you** tengo exactamente lo que necesitas *or* lo que te hace falta **(c)** (crucial point, factor): **the ~ is, …** resulta que *or* el caso es que *or* lo que pasa es que … **5** things *pl* **(a)** (belongings, equipment) cosas *fpl*

(b) (matters, the situation) cosas *fpl*; if ~s don't improve si las cosas no mejoran; how's ~s? (colloq) ¿qué tal? (fam)

6 (person, creature): you poor ~! ¡pobrecito!; you lucky ~! ¡qué suerte tienes!

7 (preference, fad) (colloq): it's not my ~ no es lo mío

8 (in expressions of time): first ~ (in the morning) a primera hora (de la mañana)

thingamabob /'θɪŋəmɑːb ‖'θɪŋəməbɒb/, **thingamajig** /-dʒɪg/ *n* (colloq) cosa *f*, chisme *m* (Esp, Méx fam), coso *m* (AmS fam), vaina *f* (Col, Per, Ven fam)

think /θɪŋk/ (*past & past p* thought) *vi* **1** (use one's mind) pensar*; to ~ ABOUT sth pensar* EN algo; (consider) pensar* algo; to ~ OF sth/sb pensar* EN algo/algn; I hadn't thought of that no se me había ocurrido eso

2 (intend, plan) to ~ OF -ING pensar* + INF

3 **(a)** (find, come up with): can you ~ of anything better? ¿se te ocurre algo mejor? **(b)** (remember) to ~ OF sth acordarse* DE algo; I can't ~ of his name no me puedo acordar de su nombre

4 (have opinion): to ~ highly of sb tener* muy buena opinión de algn; he ~s a lot of you te aprecia mucho

■ ~ *vt* **1** (reflect, ponder) pensar*; ~ what that would cost piensa (en) lo que costaría; that's wrong, I thought to myself eso está mal — pensé para mí *or* para mis adentros; I didn't ~ to look there no se me ocurrió mirar allí

2 **(a)** (suppose, imagine, expect) pensar*; I thought you knew pensé que lo sabías; I can't ~ why he refused no me explico por qué se negó **(b)** (indicating intention): we thought we'd eat out tonight esta noche tenemos pensado salir a cenar

3 (believe) creer*; I ~ so creo que sí *or* me parece que sí; I don't think so creo que no *or* me parece que no; I thought as much ya me lo parecía *or* ya me lo imaginaba

■ **think ahead** [*v + adv*]: you have to ~ ahead hay que ser previsor

■ **think back** [*v + adv*] (reflect) recordar*; ~ back haz memoria; to ~ back TO sth recordar* algo, acordarse* DE algo

■ **think out** [*v + o + adv*, *v + adv + o*] pensar *or* planear cuidadosamente; a well thought-out proposal una propuesta bien elaborada

■ **think over** [*v + o + adv*] pensar*

■ **think through** [*v + o + adv*, *v + adv + o*] ⟨project⟩ planear detenidamente; ⟨idea⟩ considerar detenidamente

■ **think up** [*v + o + adv*, *v + adv + o*] ⟨excuse⟩ inventar; ⟨slogan⟩ idear

thinker /'θɪŋkər ‖'θɪŋkə(r)/ *n* pensador, -dora *m,f*

thinking /'θɪŋkɪŋ/ *n* ideas *fpl*, pensamiento *m*; to my (way of) ~ a mi modo de ver, en mi opinión; good ~! ¡buena idea!

think tank *n* gabinete *m* estratégico

thinly /'θɪnli/ *adv* **(a)** ⟨slice⟩ en rebanadas finas **(b)** (sparsely): ~ populated poco poblado

thinner /'θɪnər ‖'θɪnə(r)/ *n* disolvente *m*, diluyente *m*

third¹ /θɜːrd ‖θɜːd/ *adj* tercero

■ **Note** The usual translation of *third*, *tercero*, becomes *tercer* when it precedes a masculine singular noun.

third² *adv* **(a)** (in position, time, order) en tercer lugar **(b)** (thirdly) en tercer lugar **(c)** (*with superl*): the ~ highest mountain la tercera montaña en altura

third³ *n* **1** **(a)** (Math) tercio *m* **(b)** (part) tercera parte *f*, tercio *m* **(c)** (Mus) tercera *f* **2** ~ **(gear)** (Auto) (*no art*) tercera *f*

third-class /'θɜːrd'klæs ‖,θɜːd'klɑːs/ *adj* (*pred* ~ **class**) **(a)** (inferior) de tercera **(b)** ⟨mail⟩ (in US) de franqueo económico

thirdly /'θɜːrdli ‖'θɜːdli/ *adv* (*indep*) en tercer lugar

third: ~ **party insurance** *n* seguro *m* contra terceros; **T~ World** *n* the T~ World el Tercer Mundo; (*before n*) ⟨nation⟩ tercermundista

thirst /θɜːrst ‖θɜːst/ *n* sed *f*

thirsty /'θɜːrsti ‖'θɜːsti/ *adj* **-tier, -tiest** ⟨person/animal⟩ que tiene sed; to be ~ tener* sed

thirteen /'θɜːr'tiːn ‖,θɜː'tiːn/ *adj/n* trece *adj inv/m*; *see also* FOUR¹

thirteenth¹ /'θɜːr'tiːnθ ‖,θɜː'tiːnθ/ *adj* decimotercero; (before masculine singular nouns) decimotercer

thirteenth² *adv* en decimotercer lugar

thirteenth³ *n* (Math) treceavo *m*; (part) treceava parte *f*

thirtieth¹ /'θɜːrtiəθ ‖'θɜːtiəθ/ *adj* trigésimo

thirtieth² *adv* en trigésimo lugar

thirtieth³ *n* (Math) treintavo *m*; (part) treintava *or* trigésima parte *f*

thirty /'θɜːrti ‖'θɜːti/ *adj/n* treinta *adj inv/m*; *see also* FOUR¹

this¹ /ðɪs/ *pron* (*pl* these) este, -ta; (*neuter*) esto; these estos, -tas; what is ~? ¿qué es esto?; ~ is John (on photo) este es John; (introducing) te presento a John; is ~ where you work? ¿aquí es donde trabajas?; ~ is Jack Smith (on telephone) habla Jack Smith, soy Jack Smith

this² *adj* (*pl* these) este, -ta; (*pl*) estos, -tas; look at ~ tree/house mira este árbol/esta casa; I like these ones me gustan estos/estas

this³ *adv*: it's ~ big es así de grande; now we've come ~ far … ya que hemos venido hasta aquí …

thistle /'θɪsəl/ *n* cardo *m*

thong /θɔːŋ ‖θɒŋ/ *n* **(a)** (leather strip) correa *f* **(b)** (sandal) (AmE) chancla *f*, chancleta *f*

thorn /θɔːrn ‖θɔːn/ *n* espina *f*

thorny /'θɔːrni ‖'θɔːni/ *adj* **-nier, -niest** ⟨plant⟩ espinoso; ⟨problem/issue⟩ espinoso, peliagudo

thorough /'θɜːrəʊ ‖'θʌrə/ *adj* ⟨person⟩ concienzudo, cuidadoso; ⟨search/investigation⟩ riguroso

---

thoroughbred /'θɜ:rəbred ‖'θʌrəbred/ adj
⟨horse⟩ de pura sangre, de raza

thoroughfare /'θɜrəˈfer ‖'θʌrəfeə(r)/ n (a)
(street) (liter) calle f, vía f (b) (public road) vía f
pública

thoroughly /'θɜ:rəʊli ‖'θʌrəli/ adv (a) ⟨wash/
clean⟩ a fondo, a conciencia; ⟨research⟩
rigurosamente; ⟨examine⟩ minuciosamente (b)
(completely) ⟨understand⟩ perfectamente; **we ~
enjoyed ourselves** nos divertimos muchísimo

those /ðəʊz/ pl of THAT adj, pron 1

though¹ /ðəʊ/ conj aunque

though² adv: **it's easy, ~, to understand their
feelings** sin embargo, es fácil comprender sus
sentimientos; **the course is difficult; it's
interesting, ~** el curso es difícil, pero es
interesante

thought¹ /θɔ:t/ past & past p of THINK¹

thought² n 1 (a) (intellectual activity)
pensamiento m (b) (deliberation): **after much ~** tras
mucho pensarlo 2 (a) (reflection) pensamiento m;
what are your ~s on the matter? ¿tú qué opinas
al respecto?; **on second ~(s)** pensándolo bien (b)
(idea) idea f; **I've just had a ~** se me acaba de
ocurrir una idea; **the ~ never even entered my
head** ni se me pasó por la cabeza

thoughtful /'θɔ:tfəl/ adj (a) (kind) atento,
amable; (considerate) considerado (b) (pensive)
pensativo, meditabundo

thoughtfully /'θɔ:tfəli/ adv pensativamente

thoughtless /'θɔ:tləs ‖'θɔ:tlɪs/ adj
desconsiderado

thought-provoking /'θɔ:tprə,vəʊkɪŋ/ adj
que hace pensar or reflexionar

thousand /'θaʊzṇd/ n mil m

thousandth¹ /'θaʊzəndθ/ adj milésimo

thousandth² adv en milésimo lugar

thousandth³ n (Math) milésimo m; (part)
milésima parte f

thrash /θræʃ/ vt golpear; (as punishment) azotar;
darle* una paliza a
■ ~ vi: ~ **(around** o **about)** revolverse*,
retorcerse*; (in mud, water) revolcarse*
■ **thrash out** [v + o + adv, v + adv + o]
⟨problem⟩ discutir, tratar de resolver

thrashing /'θræʃɪŋ/ n paliza f, zurra f

thread¹ /θred/ n (a) (filament) hilo m; (of plot,
conversation) hilo m (b) (of screw) rosca f, filete m

thread² vt ⟨needle⟩ enhebrar; ⟨bead⟩ ensartar

threadbare /'θredber ‖'θredbeə(r)/ adj
gastado, raído

threat /θret/ n amenaza f; **to be under ~** ⟨way
of life⟩ verse* amenazado; ⟨factory⟩ estar* bajo
amenaza de cierre

threaten /'θretṇ/ vt (a) ⟨person/stability⟩
amenazar*; **to ~ sb WITH sth** amenazar* a algn
CON algo (b) (give warning of) ⟨action/violence⟩
amenazar* con
■ ~ vi amenazar*

threatening /'θretṇɪŋ/ adj amenazador

three /θri:/ adj/n tres adj inv/m; see also FOUR¹

three: **~-dimensional** /'θri:də'mentʃṇəl, -daɪ-
‖,θri:daɪ'menʃən̩l, -dɪ-/ adj tridimensional;
~fold adj/adv ▶ -FOLD; **~-piece** /'θri:'pi:s/ adj

(before n): **~-piece suit** traje m con chaleco, terno
m; **~-piece suite** juego m de living (de sofá y dos
sillones) (AmL), tresillo m (Esp)

three-quarters¹ /'θri:'kwɔːrtərz
‖,θri:'kwɔ:təz/ pron las tres cuartas partes

three-quarters² adv: **it's ~ full** contiene el
75% or las tres cuartas partes de su capacidad

threshold /'θreʃhəʊld/ n (a) (doorway) umbral
m; **to be on the ~ of sth** estar* en el umbral or a
las puertas de algo (b) (of pain) umbral m

threw /θru:/ past of THROW¹

thrift /θrɪft/ n economía f, ahorro m; (before n)
~ shop (esp AmE) tienda que vende artículos de
segunda mano con fines benéficos

thrifty /'θrɪfti/ adj **-tier, -tiest** económico,
ahorrativo

thrill¹ /θrɪl/ n (excitement) emoción f; **it was a real
~** fue verdaderamente emocionante

thrill² vt emocionar

thrilled /θrɪld/ adj (pred) **to be ~ (ABOUT/WITH
sth)** estar* contentísimo or (fam) chocho (CON
algo); **to be ~ to + INF: she was really ~ to meet
him** le encantó or (Esp tb) le hizo muchísima
ilusión conocerlo

thriller /'θrɪlər ‖'θrɪlə(r)/ n novela f/película f
de misterio or de suspenso or (Esp) de suspense

thrilling /'θrɪlɪŋ/ adj emocionante

thrive /θraɪv/ vi (past **thrived** or (liter)
throve; past p **thrived**) ⟨business/town⟩
prosperar; ⟨plant⟩ crecer* con fuerza

thriving /'θraɪvɪŋ/ adj (before n) ⟨business/
town⟩ próspero

throat /θrəʊt/ n garganta f; (neck) cuello m

throb /θrɑ:b ‖θrɒb/ vi **-bb-** (a) ⟨heart/pulse⟩
latir con fuerza; ⟨engine⟩ vibrar (b) (with pain):
his leg was ~bing tenía un dolor punzante en la
pierna

throes /θrəʊz/ pl n (death ~) agonía f; **to be in
one's death ~** agonizar*, estar agonizando

thrombosis /θrɑ:m'bəʊsəs ‖θrɒm'bəʊsɪs/ n
(pl **-ses** /-si:z/) trombosis f

throne /θrəʊn/ n trono m

throng /θrɔːŋ ‖θrɒŋ/ n muchedumbre f

throttle¹ /'θrɑ:tl̩ ‖'θrɒtl̩/ vt ahogar*,
estrangular

throttle² n (a) (Auto) acelerador m (que se
acciona con la mano) (b) (pedal) acelerador m

through¹ /θru:/ prep 1 (from one side to the
other) por; **it went right ~ the wall** atravesó la
pared de lado a lado; **to hear sth ~ sth** oír* algo
a través de algo; **we drove ~ Munich** atravesamos
Munich (en coche) (b) (past, beyond) **to be ~ sth**
haber* pasado algo
2 (a) (in time): **we worked ~ the night**
trabajamos durante toda la noche; **half-way ~ his
speech** en medio de su discurso; **~ the centuries**
a través de los siglos (b) (until and including) (AmE):
Tuesday ~ Thursday de martes a jueves; **October
~ December** desde octubre hasta diciembre
inclusive
3 (by): **she spoke ~ an interpreter** habló a través
de un intérprete; **I heard about it ~ a friend** me
enteré a través de or por un amigo

through² adv 1 (from one side to the other): **it
sped ~ without stopping** pasó a toda velocidad
sin parar; **the red paint shows ~** se nota la

    ···⟩

pintura roja que hay debajo; *see also* GET, PULL, PUT *etc* THROUGH **2** (completely): **wet ~** mojado hasta los huesos

through³ *adj* **1** (Transp) (*before n*) ⟨*train/route*⟩ directo; **~ traffic** tráfico *m* de paso; **☉ no through road** calle sin salida **2** (finished) (colloq) (*pred*): **to be ~ WITH sb/sth** haber* terminado CON algn/algo

throughout¹ /θruːˈaʊt/ *prep* **1** (all over): **~ Europe** en toda Europa **2** (in time): **~ the weekend** (durante) todo el fin de semana; **~ his career** a lo largo de toda su carrera

throughout² *adv* (a) ⟨*decorated/carpeted*⟩ totalmente (b) (in time) desde el principio hasta el fin

throughway /ˈθruːweɪ/ *n* (AmE) autopista *f*

throve /θrəʊv/ *past of* THRIVE

throw¹ /θrəʊ/ (*past* **threw**; *past p* **thrown**) *vt* **1** (a) ⟨*ball/stone*⟩ tirar, aventar* (Col, Méx, Per); ⟨*grenade/javelin*⟩ lanzar* (b) ⟨*dice*⟩ echar, tirar **2** (send, propel) (+ *adv compl*): **to ~ sb into jail** meter a algn preso or en la cárcel; **to ~ oneself into a task** meterse de lleno en una tarea **3** «*horse*» ⟨*rider*⟩ desmontar, tirar **4** (disconcert) desconcertar* **5** (have, hold) ⟨*party*⟩ hacer*, dar*

■ **throw away** [*v + o + adv, v + adv + o*] (a) (discard) ⟨*can/paper*⟩ tirar (a la basura), botar (a la basura) (AmL exc RPl) (b) (waste) ⟨*money*⟩ tirar, botar (AmL exc RPl)

■ **throw back** [*v + o + adv, v + adv + o*] (a) ⟨*ball*⟩ devolver* (b) (pull back) ⟨*curtains*⟩ (des)correr; ⟨*bedclothes*⟩ echar atrás

■ **throw off** [*v + o + adv, v + adv + o*] (a) ⟨*jacket/hat*⟩ quitarse ⟨*rápidamente*⟩ (b) ⟨*illness/habit*⟩ quitarse; ⟨*pursuer*⟩ despistar

■ **throw out** [*v + o + adv, v + adv + o*] (a) (discard) tirar (a la basura), botar (a la basura) (AmL exc RPl) (b) ⟨*bill/proposal*⟩ rechazar (c) ⟨*person*⟩ echar

■ **throw together** [*v + o + adv, v + adv + o*] ⟨*meal/plan*⟩ improvisar

■ **throw up**
   I [*v + adv + o*] **1** (raise) ⟨*hands*⟩ levantar or alzar* ⟨*rápidamente*⟩
   2 (bring to light) ⟨*facts*⟩ revelar (la existencia de)
   II [*v + adv*] (vomit) (colloq) devolver*, arrojar

throw² *n* **1** (a) (of ball) tiro *m*; (of javelin, discus) lanzamiento *m* (b) (of dice) tirada *f*, lance *m* **2** (AmE) (bedspread) cubrecama *m* (b) (shawl) chal (*m*), echarpe (*m*)

thrown /θrəʊn/ *past p of* THROW¹

thrush /θrʌʃ/ *n* **1** (bird) tordo *m*, zorzal *m* **2** (Med) aftas *fpl*

thrust¹ /θrʌst/ *vt* (*past & past p* **thrust**) (push) empujar; (push out) sacar*; **to ~ out one's chest** sacar* pecho; **she ~ the book at me** me tendió el libro bruscamente; **he ~ his hands into his pockets** se metió las manos en los bolsillos; **to ~ sth INTO sth** ⟨*knife/sword*⟩ clavar algo EN algo

thrust² *n* **1** (a) (with sword) estocada *f* (b) (push) empujón *m* (c) (attack, advance) ofensiva *f* **2** (impetus) empuje *m*, fuerza *f*

thruway /ˈθruːweɪ/ *n* (AmE) autopista *f*

thud /θʌd/ *n* ruido *m* sordo

thug /θʌɡ/ *n* matón *m*

thumb¹ /θʌm/ *n* pulgar *m*

thumb² *vt* : **I ~ed a lift home** me fui a casa a dedo (fam)

thumbtack /ˈθʌmtæk/ *n* (AmE) tachuela *f*, chinche *m* (Andes), chinche *f* (AmC, Méx, RPl), chincheta *f* (Esp)

thump¹ /θʌmp/ *n* (sound, blow) golpazo *m*

thump² *vt* golpear

thunder¹ /ˈθʌndər ‖ˈθʌndə(r)/ *n* (a) (Meteo) truenos *mpl* (b) (*no pl*) (sound — of traffic) estruendo *m*

thunder² *vi* (move loudly): **the train ~ed through the station** el tren pasó por la estación con gran estruendo
   ■ **~** *vt* (shout): **get out! he ~ed** —¡fuera de aquí! — bramó *or* rugió

thunder: ~bolt *n* rayo *m*; **~storm** *n* tormenta *f* eléctrica

thundery /ˈθʌndəri/ *adj* tormentoso

Thursday /ˈθɜːrzdeɪ, -di ‖ˈθɜːzdeɪ, -di/ *n* jueves *m*; *see also* MONDAY

thus /ðʌs/ *adv* **1** (in this way) (frml) así, de este modo **2** (consequently) (*as linker*) por lo tanto, por consiguiente (frml)

thwart /θwɔːrt ‖θwɔːt/ *vt* ⟨*plan/attempt*⟩ frustrar

thyme /taɪm/ *n* tomillo *m*

thyroid (gland) /ˈθaɪrɔɪd/ *n* tiroides *f*, glándula *f* tiroidea

ti /tiː/ *n* (Mus) si *m*

tiara /tiˈɑːrə/ *n* diadema *f*

Tibet /tɪˈbet/ *n* el Tíbet

Tibetan¹ /tɪˈbetn̩/ *adj* tibetano

Tibetan² *n* (a) (person) tibetano, -na *m,f* (b) (language) tibetano *m*

tic /tɪk/ *n* tic *m*

tick¹ /tɪk/ *n* **1** (sound) tic *m* **2** (Zool) garrapata *f* **3** (mark) (BrE) marca *f*, tic *m*, palomita *f* (Méx), visto *m* (Esp)

tick² *vi* «*clock/watch*» hacer* tictac
   ■ **~** *vt* (BrE) marcar* ⟨*con un visto or una palomita etc*⟩
   ■ **tick over** [*v + adv*] «*engine*» marchar al ralentí

ticket /ˈtɪkət ‖ˈtɪkɪt/ *n* **1** (for bus, train) boleto *m* or (Esp) billete *m*; (for plane) pasaje *m* or (Esp) billete *m*; (for theater, museum) entrada *f*; (for baggage, coat) ticket *m*; (*before n*) **~ collector** revisor, -sora *m,f*; **~ office** (Transp) mostrador *m* (*or* ventanilla *f etc*) de venta de pasajes (*or* billetes *etc*); (Theat) taquilla *f*, boletería *f* (AmL) **2** (label) etiqueta *f*

tickle /ˈtɪkəl/ *vt* hacerle* cosquillas a
   ■ **~** *vi* «*wool/beard*» picar*

ticklish /ˈtɪklɪʃ/ *adj*: **to be ~** tener* cosquillas, ser* cosquilloso *or* (Méx) cosquilludo

tidal /ˈtaɪdl̩/ *adj* con régimen de marea

tidal wave *n* maremoto *m*

tidbit /ˈtɪdbɪt/ *n* (AmE) ▶ TITBIT

tide /taɪd/ *n* **1** (Geog) marea *f*; **the ~ is in/out** la marea está alta/baja; **high/low ~** marea alta/baja **2** (movement) corriente *f*; (of violence) oleada *f*
   ■ **tide over** [*v + o + adv*]: **this should ~ us over until next month** nos arreglaremos con esto hasta el próximo mes

tidily /ˈtaɪdl̩i ‖ˈtaɪdɪli/ *adv* ordenadamente, prolijamente (RPl)

tidiness /'taɪdɪnəs ‖'taɪdɪnɪs/ n orden m, prolijidad f (RPl)

tidy¹ /'taɪdi/ adj **tidier, tidiest** ordenado, prolijo (RPl)

tidy² **tidies, tidying, tidied** vt arreglar, ordenar

■ **tidy up** ⎡1⎤ [v + o + adv, v + adv + o] ⟨room/desk⟩ ordenar, arreglar; ⟨toys⟩ ordenar, recoger* ⎡2⎤ [v + adv] ordenar

tie¹ /taɪ/ n ⎡1⎤ (Clothing) corbata f ⎡2⎤ **(a)** (bond) lazo m, vínculo m **(b)** (obligation, constraint) atadura f; **family ~s** obligaciones fpl familiares ⎡3⎤ (Sport) (equal score) empate m

tie² **ties, tying, tied** vt ⎡1⎤ **(a)** (make) ⟨knot/bow⟩ hacer* **(b)** (fasten) atar, amarrar (AmL exc RPl) ⎡2⎤ (restrict) ⟨person⟩ atar ⎡3⎤ (Games, Sport) ⟨game⟩ empatar

■ **~** vi ⎡1⎤ (fasten) atarse ⎡2⎤ (draw) «teams» empatar

■ **tie in** [v + adv] **to ~ in (WITH** sth) concordar* or cuadrar (CON algo)

■ **tie up** [v + o + adv, v + adv + o] **(a)** ⟨parcel/animal⟩ atar, amarrar (AmL exc RPl) **(b) to be ~d up** (busy) estar* ocupado **(c) to be ~d up WITH** sth (connected) estar* ligado A or relacionado CON algo

tie: ~break n ▶ **~BREAKER** A; **~breaker** n **(a)** (in tennis) muerte f súbita **(b)** (in quiz game) pregunta f de desempate; **~pin** n alfiler m de corbata

tier /tɪr ‖tɪə(r)/ n **(a)** (layer) hilera f superpuesta **(b)** (of cake) piso m **(c)** (in hierarchy) escalón m

tiger /'taɪgər ‖'taɪgə(r)/ n (pl **~s** or **~**) tigre m

tight¹ /taɪt/ adj **-er, -est** ⎡1⎤ **(a)** (fitting closely) ⟨dress/skirt⟩ ajustado, ceñido; (if uncomfortable) apretado **(b)** ⟨knot⟩ apretado **(c)** (stiff) ⟨screw/lid⟩ apretado, duro **(d)** ⟨schedule⟩ apretado; ⟨budget⟩ limitado ⎡2⎤ (strict) ⟨security/control⟩ estricto ⎡3⎤ (taut) ⟨cord/thread⟩ tirante, tenso ⎡4⎤ (colloq) **(a)** (mean) ▶ **TIGHTFISTED** **(b)** (drunk) ⟨pred⟩ borracho, como una cuba (fam)

tight² adv: **hold ~!** ¡agárrate bien or fuerte!; **screw the lid on ~** aprieta bien el tapón; **sleep ~!** ¡que duermas bien!

tighten /'taɪtn̩/ vt **(a)** ⟨nut/bolt/knot⟩ apretar*; ⟨rope⟩ tensar; **to ~ one's belt** apretarse* el cinturón **(b)** ⟨regulations⟩ hacer* más estricto or rígido

■ **tighten up** [v + o + adv, v + adv + o] ⟨laws/rules⟩ hacer* más estricto; **to ~ up security** reforzar* las medidas de seguridad

tight: ~fisted /'taɪt'fɪstəd ‖,taɪt'fɪstɪd/ adj (colloq) agarrado (fam), amarrete (AmS fam); **~fitting** /'taɪt'fɪtɪŋ/ adj ⟨jeans⟩ ajustado, ceñido

tightly /'taɪtli/ adv ⟨hold/grip⟩ fuerte; **~ fastened** fuertemente atado

tightrope /'taɪtrəʊp/ n cuerda f floja; (before n) **~ walker** funámbulo, -la m,f, equilibrista mf

tights /taɪts/ pl n **(a)** (for ballet etc) malla(s) f(pl), leotardo(s) m(pl) **(b)** (BrE) ▶ **PANTYHOSE**

tile¹ /taɪl/ n **(a)** (for floor) baldosa f, losa f; (for wall) azulejo m **(b)** (for roof) teja f

tile² vt ⟨floor⟩ embaldosar; ⟨wall⟩ revestir* de azulejos, azulejar, alicatar (Esp); ⟨roof⟩ tejar

till¹ /tɪl/ conj/prep ▶ **UNTIL**[1,2]

till² n caja f (registradora)

till³ vt cultivar, labrar

tiller /'tɪlər ‖'tɪlə(r)/ n (Naut) caña f or barra f del timón

tilt¹ /tɪlt/ vt inclinar

■ **~** vi inclinarse

tilt² n inclinación f

timber /'tɪmbər ‖'tɪmbə(r)/ n **(a)** (material) madera f (para construcción) **(b)** (trees) árboles mpl (madereros) **(c)** (beam) viga f, madero m

time¹ /taɪm/ n

I ⎡1⎤ (past, present, future) tiempo m; **at this point o moment in ~** en este momento, en el momento presente; (before n) ⟨travel⟩ en el tiempo; **~ machine** máquina f del tiempo

⎡2⎤ (time available, necessary for sth) tiempo m; **to make ~ for sth** hacer(se)* or encontrar* tiempo para algo; **just take your ~** tómate todo el tiempo que necesites or quieras

⎡3⎤ (no pl) (period — of days, months, years) tiempo m; (— of hours) rato m; **that was a long ~ ago** eso fue hace mucho (tiempo); **in an hour's/ten years' ~** dentro de una hora/diez años; **for the ~ being** por el momento, de momento

⎡4⎤ (in phrases) **all the time** (constantly) constantemente; (the whole period) todo el tiempo; **in time** (early enough) a tiempo; (eventually) con el tiempo; **in good time** con tiempo; **in no time** (at all) rapidísimo, en un abrir y cerrar de ojos

⎡5⎤ (with respect to work): **to take** o (BrE also) **have ~ off** tomarse tiempo libre

⎡6⎤ (epoch, age) (often pl) época f, tiempo m; **in former ~s** antiguamente; **in ~s to come** en el futuro, en tiempos venideros; **to be behind the ~s** ser* anticuado, estar* desfasado

II ⎡1⎤ **(a)** (by clock) hora f; **what ~ is it?** o **what's the ~?** ¿qué hora es? **(b)** (of event) hora f; **we have to arrange a ~ for the next meeting** tenemos que fijar una fecha y hora para la próxima reunión; **it's ~ you left** o **you were leaving** es hora de que te vayas

⎡2⎤ (point in time): **at this ~ of (the) year** en esta época del año; **at this ~ of night** a estas horas de la noche; **at all ~s** siempre; **it'll be dark by the ~ we get there** (para) cuando lleguemos ya estará oscuro

⎡3⎤ (instance, occasion) vez f; **let's try one more ~** probemos otra vez or una vez más; **nine ~s out of ten** en el noventa por ciento de los casos

⎡4⎤ (in phrases) **about time: it's about ~ someone told him** ya es hora or ya va siendo hora de que alguien se lo diga; **about ~ (too)!** ¡ya era hora!; **at a time:** **four at a ~** de cuatro en cuatro, de a cuatro (AmL); **I can only do one thing at a ~** solo puedo hacer una cosa a la or por vez; **at the same time** (simultaneously) al mismo tiempo; (however) (as linker) al mismo tiempo, de todas formas; **at times** a veces; **every** o **each time** (as conj) (whenever) cada vez; **from time to time** de vez en cuando; **on time** (on schedule): **the buses never run on ~** los autobuses casi nunca pasan a su hora or puntualmente; **she's never on ~** nunca llega temprano, siempre llega tarde

⎡5⎤ (experience): **to have a good/bad/hard ~** pasarlo bien/mal/muy mal; **have a good ~!** ¡que te diviertas (or que se diviertan etc)!, ¡que lo pases (or pasen etc) bien!

⎡6⎤ (Mus) compás m; (before n) **~ signature** llave f de tiempo

⎡7⎤ **times** pl (Math): **it's four ~s bigger** es cuatro veces más grande

time² vt (Sport) cronometrar; **I've ~d how long it takes me** he calculado cuánto tiempo me lleva

time: ~ bomb n bomba f de tiempo or de relojería; **~-consuming** /kən'suːmɪŋ/ adj que lleva mucho tiempo; **~keeper** n (a) (Sport) cronometrador, -dora m,f (b) (worker) (BrE): **to be a good/bad ~keeper** ser* puntual/impuntual

timeless /'taɪmləs ‖ 'taɪmlɪs/ adj (liter) eterno

time limit n plazo m

timely /'taɪmli/ adj **-lier, -liest** oportuno

timer /'taɪmər ‖ 'taɪmə(r)/ n temporizador m; (of oven, video etc) reloj m (automático)

times /taɪmz/ prep: **3 ~ 4 is 12** 3 (multiplicado) por 4 son 12; ▶ FOUR¹

time: ~saving adj que ahorra tiempo; **~scale** n escala f de tiempo; **~share** n (property) multipropiedad f; **~sheet** n hoja f de asistencia; **~table** n (a) (Transp) horario m (b) (esp BrE Educ) horario m (c) (schedule, programme) agenda f

timid /'tɪməd ‖ 'tɪmɪd/ adj tímido; ‹animal› huraño

timidly /'tɪmədli ‖ 'tɪmɪdli/ adv tímidamente, con timidez

timing /'taɪmɪŋ/ n (choice of time): **the ~ of the action was disastrous** la acción fue de lo más inoportuna; **that was good ~: we've just arrived** calculaste muy bien el tiempo: acabamos de llegar

tin /tɪn/ n **1** (a) (metal) estaño m (b) (tinplate) (hoja)lata f; (before n) ‹soldier› de plomo **2** (can) (esp BrE) lata f or (Esp tb) bote m (de conservas, bebidas etc)

tinfoil /'tɪnfɔɪl/ n (made of tin) papel m de estaño; (made of aluminium) papel m de aluminio

tinge¹ /tɪndʒ/ n (a) (of color) tinte m, matiz m (b) (hint, trace) dejo m, matiz m

tinge² vt (usu pass) (color) **to be ~d WITH sth** estar* matizado DE algo

tingle /'tɪŋɡəl/ vi: **it makes your skin ~** te hace sentir un cosquilleo or hormigueo en la piel

tingling /'tɪŋɡlɪŋ/ n cosquilleo m, hormigueo m

tinker /'tɪŋkər ‖ 'tɪŋkə(r)/ vi **to ~ WITH sth** hacerle* pequeños ajustes A algo; (pej) juguetear CON algo

tinkle vi «bell/glass» tintinear

tinned /tɪnd/ adj (BrE) enlatado, en or de lata

tin: ~ opener n (BrE) abrelatas m; **~plate** n hojalata f

tint¹ /tɪnt/ n (a) (of color) tinte m, matiz m; (color) tono m (b) (for hair) tintura f, tinte m

tint² vt teñir*

tinted /'tɪntəd ‖ 'tɪntɪd/ adj ‹glass› coloreado; ‹lenses› con un tinte; ‹hair› teñido

tiny /'taɪni/ adj **tinier, tiniest** minúsculo, diminuto

tip¹ /tɪp/ n **1** (end, extremity) punta f; (of stick, umbrella) contera f, regatón m; (filter ~) filtro m; **to be standing on the ~s of one's toes** estar* de

puntillas or (CS) en puntas de pie; **on the ~ of one's tongue** en la punta de la lengua **2** (helpful hint) consejo m (práctico) **3** (gratuity) propina f **4** (BrE) (rubbish dump) vertedero m (de basuras)

tip² **-pp-** vt **1** (give gratuity to) darle* (una) propina a **2** (a) (tilt) inclinar (b) (pour, throw) tirar

■ **tip off** [v + o + adv, v + adv + o] ‹police/criminal› avisar(le a), pasarle el dato a (CS), darle* un chivatazo a (Esp fam)

■ **tip over** **1** [v + o + adv, v + adv + o] volcar* **2** [v + adv] caerse*

tipped /tɪpt/ adj ‹cigarette› con filtro

tiptoe¹ /'tɪptəʊ/ vi **-toes, -toeing, -toed** caminar or (esp Esp) andar* de puntillas

tiptoe² n: **on ~** de puntillas

tiptop /'tɪp'tɑːp ‖ ,tɪp'tɒp/ adj de primera, excelente; **in ~ condition** en excelente estado

tirade /taɪ'reɪd/ n diatriba f

tire¹ /taɪr ‖ 'taɪə(r)/ vt cansar

■ **~** vi (a) (become weary) cansarse (b) (become bored) **to ~ OF sth/sb/-ING** cansarse DE algo/algn/+ INF

■ **tire out** [v + o + adv, v + adv + o] agotar

tire², (BrE) **tyre** /taɪr ‖ 'taɪə(r)/ n neumático m, llanta f (AmL)

tired /taɪrd ‖ 'taɪəd/ adj (a) (weary) cansado; **to get ~** cansarse (b) (fed up) **to be ~ OF sth/sb/-ING** estar* cansado DE algo/algn /+ INF

tiredness /'taɪrdnəs ‖ 'taɪədnɪs/ n cansancio m

tireless /'taɪrləs ‖ 'taɪəlɪs/ adj ‹person› infatigable, incansable; ‹patience/efforts› inagotable

tiresome /'taɪrsəm ‖ 'taɪəsəm/ adj ‹person› pesado; ‹task› tedioso

tiring /'taɪrɪŋ ‖ 'taɪərɪŋ/ adj cansador (AmS), cansado (AmC, Esp, Méx)

tissue /'tɪʃuː ‖ 'tɪʃuː, 'tɪsjuː/ n **1** (Anat, Bot) tejido m **2** (a) (paper handkerchief) pañuelo m de papel, Kleenex® m (b) (~ paper) papel m de seda

tit /tɪt/ n **1** (Zool) paro m **2** (sl) (breast) teta f (fam)

titbit /'tɪtbɪt/ n (a) (of food) exquisitez f (b) (of gossip) chisme m

tit for tat /tæt/ n: **it was ~ ~ ~** fue ojo por ojo, diente por diente

title /'taɪtl/ n **1** (of creative work) título m **2** (a) (status) tratamiento m (como Sr, Sra, Dr etc) (b) (noble rank) título m (nobiliario or de nobleza) (c) (Sport) título m **3** (Law) (right of ownership) derecho m

title: ~ deed n (usu pl) título m de propiedad; **~holder** n campeón, -peona m,f, **~ page** n portada f, carátula f

titter /'tɪtər ‖ 'tɪtə(r)/ vi reírse* disimuladamente

tittle-tattle /'tɪtl,tætl/ n (colloq) chismes mpl

titular /'tɪtʃələr ‖ 'tɪtjʊlə(r)/ adj nominal

T-junction /'tiː,dʒʌŋkʃən/ n (BrE) cruce m (en forma de T)

TN = Tennessee

to¹ /tuː, *weak form* tə/ *prep* **1** **(a)** (indicating destination) a; **you can wear it ~ the wedding** puedes ponértelo para la boda **(b)** (indicating direction) hacia; **move a little ~ the right** córrete un poco hacia la derecha **(c)** (indicating position) a; **~ the left/right of sth** a la izquierda/derecha de algo **2** **(a)** (as far as) hasta; **she can count ~ 10** sabe contar hasta 10 **(b)** (until) hasta; **I can't stay ~ the end** no puedo quedarme hasta el final; *see also* FROM 5 **3** **(a)** (showing indirect object): **give it ~ me** dámelo; **I gave it ~ Rachel** se lo di a Rachel; **what did you say ~ him/them?** ¿qué le/les dijiste?; **I was talking ~ myself** estaba hablando solo **(b)** (in dedications): **~ Paul with love from Jane** para Paul, con cariño de Jane **4** (indicating proportion, relation): **how many ounces are there ~ the pound?** ¿cuántas onzas hay en una libra?; **Barcelona won by two goals ~ one** Barcelona ganó por dos (goles) a uno; **there's a 10 ~ 1 chance** o 1 ... hay una probabilidad de uno en 10 de ... **5** (producing): **~ my horror ...** para mi horror ... **6** (indicating belonging) de; **the key ~ the front door** la llave de la puerta principal **7** (telling time) (BrE): **ten ~ three** las tres menos diez, diez para las tres (AmL exc RPl)

to² /tə/ (*in infinitives*) **1** **(a)** **~ sing/fear/leave** cantar/temer/partir **(b)** (in order to) para; **I do it ~ save money** lo hago para ahorrar dinero **2** (*after adj or n*): **it's easy ~ do** es fácil de hacer; **you're too young ~ drink wine** eres demasiado joven para beber vino; **she was the first ~ arrive** fue la primera en llegar; **she has a lot ~ do** tiene mucho que hacer

to³ /tuː/ *adv* (shut): **I pulled the door ~** cerré la puerta

toad /təʊd/ *n* sapo *m*

toadstool /ˈtəʊdstuːl/ *n* hongo *m* (*no comestible*)

to and fro /frəʊ/ *adv* de un lado a otro

toast¹ /təʊst/ *n* **1** (bread) tostadas *fpl*, pan *m* tostado; **a piece of ~** una tostada *or* (Chi, Méx) un pan tostado; (*before n*): **~ rack** portatostadas *m* **2** (tribute) brindis *m*; **we drank a ~ to him** brindamos por él

toast² *vt* **1** (Culin) tostar* **2** (drink tribute to) ⟨*person/success*⟩ brindar por

toaster /ˈtəʊstər ‖ ˈtəʊstə(r)/ *n* tostadora *f* (eléctrica), tostador *m*

tobacco /təˈbækəʊ/ *n* (*pl* **-cos** *or* **-coes**) tabaco *m*

tobacconist /təˈbækənəst ‖ təˈbækənɪst/ *n*: *expendedor de tabaco, cigarrillos y artículos para el fumador*, ≈estanquero, -ra *m,f* (en Esp); **~'s** (shop) tabaquería *f*, tienda *f* de artículos para fumador, ≈estanco *m* (en Esp)

-to-be /təˈbiː/ *suff*: **father~/husband~** futuro padre/esposo

toboggan /təˈbɑːgən ‖ təˈbɒgən/ *n* trineo *m*, tobogán *m*

today¹ /təˈdeɪ/ *adv* **(a)** (this day) hoy **(b)** (nowadays) hoy (en) día, actualmente

today² *n* (*no art*) **(a)** (this day) hoy *adv*; (**as from ~** a partir de hoy *or* del día de hoy **(b)** (present age) hoy *adv*, hoy (en) día

toddler /ˈtɑːdlər ‖ ˈtɒdlə(r)/ *n* niño pequeño, niña pequeña *m,f* (*entre un año y dos años y medio de edad*)

to-do /təˈduː/ *n* (colloq) (*no pl*) lío *m*, jaleo *m*

toe¹ /təʊ/ *n* dedo *m* (*del pie*); **big ~** dedo *m* gordo (del pie); **to be on one's ~s** estar* *or* mantenerse* alerta

toe² *vt*: **to ~ the line** acatar la disciplina

toenail *n* uña *f* (*del pie*)

toffee /ˈtɑːfi ‖ ˈtɒfi/ *n* toffee *m* (*golosina hecha con azúcar y mantequilla*)

toffee-nosed /ˈtɑːfiˈnəʊzd ‖ ˈtɒfiˌnəʊzd/ *adj* (BrE colloq) estirado (fam)

tofu /ˈtəʊfuː/ *n* tofu *m*, queso *m* de soya (AmL) *or* (Esp) soja

toga /ˈtəʊgə/ *n* toga *f*

together /təˈgeðər ‖ təˈgeðə(r)/ *adv* **(a)**: **they went ~** fueron juntos/juntas; **we left them alone ~** los dejamos solos a los dos; **all ~ now!** ¡todos (juntos *or* a la vez)! **(b)** **together with** junto con

toil¹ /tɔɪl/ *n* (liter) trabajo *m* duro

toil² *vi* (liter) trabajar duro

toilet /ˈtɔɪlət ‖ ˈtɔɪlɪt/ *n* **1** (room) baño *m* (esp AmL), servicio *m* (esp Esp), váter *m* (Esp); (bowl) water *m* *or* (Esp) váter *m*, inodoro *m*; (*before n*): **~ paper** papel *m* higiénico; **~ roll** rollo *m* de papel higiénico **2** (washing and dressing) (*before n*): **~ soap** jabón *m* de tocador; **~ water** agua *f*‡ de colonia

toiletries /ˈtɔɪlətriz ‖ ˈtɔɪlɪtriz/ *pl n* artículos *mpl* de tocador *or* de perfumería

token¹ /ˈtəʊkən/ *n* **1** (expression, indication): **a small ~ of gratitude** un pequeño obsequio como muestra *or* prueba de agradecimiento; **as a ~ of respect** en señal de respeto; **by the same ~** de igual modo **2** **(a)** (coin) ficha *f* **(b)** (voucher) (BrE) vale *m*; (given as present) vale *m*, cheque-regalo *m*

token² *adj* (*before n, no comp*) ⟨*fine/gesture*⟩ simbólico

told /təʊld/ *past & past p of* TELL

tolerable /ˈtɑːlərəbəl ‖ ˈtɒlərəbəl/ *adj* **(a)** (endurable) tolerable **(b)** (passable) pasable

tolerance /ˈtɑːlərəns ‖ ˈtɒlərəns/ *n* tolerancia *f*

tolerant /ˈtɑːlərənt ‖ ˈtɒlərənt/ *adj* tolerante

tolerate /ˈtɑːləreɪt ‖ ˈtɒləreɪt/ *vt* **(a)** ⟨*attitude/behavior*⟩ tolerar **(b)** ⟨*person/pain/noise*⟩ soportar, aguantar

toleration /ˌtɑːləˈreɪʃən ‖ ˌtɒləˈreɪʃən/ *n* tolerancia *f*

toll¹ /təʊl/ *n* **(a)** (Transp) peaje *m*, cuota *f* (Méx); (*before n*): **~ call** (AmE) llamada *f* interurbana, conferencia *f* (Esp); **~ road** carretera *f* de peaje *or* (Méx) de cuota **(b)** (cost, damage): **the climate took a ~ on his health** el clima le afectó la salud

toll² *vi* tocar*, doblar

toll: **~booth** *n* cabina *f* de peaje; **~bridge** *n* puente *m* de peaje *or* (Méx) de cuota; **~free** /ˈtəʊlˈfriː/ *adj* (AmE) gratuito

tomato /təˈmeɪtəʊ ‖ təˈmɑːtəʊ/ *n* (*pl* **-toes**) tomate *m* *or* (Méx) jitomate *m*

tomb /tuːm/ *n* tumba *f*, sepulcro *m*

tomboy /ˈtɑːmbɔɪ ‖ ˈtɒmbɔɪ/ *n* niña *f* poco femenina, machona *f* (RPl), machetona *f* (Méx), varonera *f* (Arg)

tombstone /ˈtuːmstəʊn/ *n* lápida *f*

tomcat /'tɑ:mkæt ‖'tɒmkæt/ n gato m (macho)

tome /təʊm/ n (hum) libro m, librote m

tomorrow¹ /tə'mɔ:rəʊ, tə'mɑ:rəʊ ‖tə'mɒrəʊ/ adv mañana; ~ **morning** mañana por la mañana, mañana en la mañana (AmL); **the day after** ~ pasado mañana

tomorrow² n (no art) (a) (day after today) mañana adv (b) (future) mañana m

tom-tom /'tɑ:mtɑ:m ‖'tɒmtɒm/ n tam-tam m

ton /tʌn/ n **1** (unit of weight) tonelada f (EEUU: 907kg., RU: 1.016kg.); **this suitcase weighs a** ~ (colloq) esta maleta pesa una tonelada (fam) **2** (large amount) (colloq) (usually pl): ~**s of people/ work** montones mpl de gente/trabajo (fam)

tone¹ /təʊn/ n **1** (a) (quality of sound, voice) tono m (b) **tones** pl (sound) sonido m; (voice) voz f (c) (Telec) señal f (sonora) **2** (shade) tono m, tonalidad f **3** (a) (mood, style) tono m (b) (standard, level) nivel m **4** (Mus) (interval) tono m

tone² vt (muscles/skin) tonificar*
■ **tone down** [v + o + adv, v + adv + o] (language) moderar; (color) atenuar*

tone-deaf /'təʊn'def/ adj: **to be** ~ no tener* oído (musical)

tongs /tɑ:ŋz, tɔ:ŋz ‖tɒŋz/ pl n tenacillas fpl

tongue /tʌŋ/ n (a) (Anat) lengua f; **to say sth** ~ **in cheek** decir* algo medio burlándose or medio en broma (b) (language) lengua f

tongue: ~**-tied** /taɪd/ adj tímido, cohibido; ~ **twister** n trabalenguas m

tonic /'tɑ:nɪk ‖'tɒnɪk/ n (a) (pick-me-up) tónico m (b) ~ (**water**) (agua f‡) tónica f

tonight¹ /tə'naɪt/ adv esta noche

tonight² n (no art) esta noche f

tonne /tʌn/ n tonelada f (métrica)

tonsil /'tɑ:nsəl ‖'tɒnsəl/ n amígdala f

tonsillitis /ˌtɑ:nsə'laɪtəs ‖ˌtɒnsɪ'laɪtɪs/ n amigdalitis f

too /tu:/ adv **1** (excessively) demasiado; **there were** ~ **many people/cars** había demasiada gente/demasiados coches; **that's** ~ **difficult for her to understand** es demasiado difícil para que lo entienda **2** (as well) también **3** (very) muy; **I'm not** ~ **sure** no estoy muy seguro

took /tʊk/ past of TAKE¹

tool /tu:l/ n (instrument) instrumento m; (workman's etc) herramienta f; **garden** ~**s** herramientas fpl or utensilios mpl de jardinería

tool: ~**bar** n (Comput) barra f de herramientas; ~**box** n caja f de herramientas; ~**kit** n juego m de herramientas; ~**shed** n cobertizo m (para herramientas)

toot¹ /tu:t/ n bocinazo m

toot² vi (driver) tocar* la bocina or el claxon, pitar
■ ~ vt (car horn) tocar*

tooth /tu:θ/ n (pl **teeth**) (a) (of person, animal) diente m; (molar) muela f; **front teeth** dientes mpl de adelante; **back teeth** muelas fpl; **to grit one's teeth** aguantarse; (lit) apretar* los dientes; **to have a sweet** ~ ser* goloso; **to lie through one's teeth** mentir* descaradamente; (before n) ~ **decay** caries f dental (b) (of zip, saw, gear) diente m; (of comb) púa f, diente m

tooth: ~**ache** n dolor m de muelas; ~**brush** n cepillo m de dientes; ~**paste** n dentífrico m,

pasta f dentífrica or de dientes; ~**pick** n palillo m (de dientes), escarbadientes m, mondadientes m

top¹ /tɑ:p ‖tɒp/ n **1** (a) (highest part) parte f superior or de arriba; (of mountain) cima f, cumbre f; (of tree) copa f; (of page) parte f superior; **from** ~ **to bottom** de arriba abajo; **at the** ~ **of one's voice** a voz en cuello or en grito, a grito pelado (fam) (b) (BrE) (of road) final m **2** (highest rank, position): **she came** ~ **of the class** sacó la mejor nota de la clase; **at the** ~ **of the league** (Dep) a la cabeza de la liga **3** (table) ~ tablero m **4** (Clothing): **a blue** ~ una blusa (or un suéter or un top etc) azul **5 on top** (as adv) encima, arriba; **to come out on** ~ salir* ganando **6 on top of** (as prep) encima de; **and on** ~ **of it all** o **on** ~ **of all that,** ... y encima or para colmo, ... **7** (of jar, box) tapa f, tapón m (Esp); (of pen) capuchón m; **to blow one's** ~ (colloq) explotar (fam) **8** (spinning ~) trompo m, peonza f

top² adj (before n) **1** (a) (layer/shelf) de arriba, superior; (note) más alto; **on the** ~ **floor** en el último piso; **the** ~ **left-hand corner of the page** la esquina superior izquierda de la página (b) (speed/temperature) máximo, tope **2** (a) (best): **to be** ~ **quality** ser* de primera calidad; **the service is** ~ **class** el servicio es de primera (b) (in ranked order): **our** ~ **priority** nuestra prioridad absoluta (c) (leading, senior) (scientists/chefs) más destacado; **the** ~ **jobs** los mejores puestos

top³ -pp- vt **1** (exceed, surpass) superar; **to** ~ **it all** para coronarlo, para colmo **2** (cover) ~**ped with cheese** con queso por encima
■ **top up** [v + o + adv, v + adv + o] (glass) llenar; (battery) (Auto) cargar*; (income) suplementar

topaz /'təʊpæz/ n topacio m

top: ~ **hat** n sombrero m de copa; ~**-heavy** /'tɑ:p'hevi ‖ˌtɒp'hevi/ adj (structure) inestable (por ser muy pesado en su parte superior)

topic /'tɑ:pɪk ‖'tɒpɪk/ n tema m

topical /'tɑ:pɪkəl ‖'tɒpɪkəl/ adj de interés actual, de actualidad

topless /'tɑ:pləs ‖'tɒplɪs/ adj topless

top-level /'tɑ:p'levəl ‖ˌtɒp'levəl/ adj (before n) (talks) de alto nivel

topography /tə'pɑ:grəfi ‖tə'pɒgrəfi/ n topografía f

topping /'tɑ:pɪŋ ‖'tɒpɪŋ/ n: **ice-cream with chocolate** ~ helado con (salsa de) chocolate por encima

topple /'tɑ:pəl ‖'tɒpəl/ vi caerse*
■ ~ vt (a) (government/dictator) derrocar*, derribar (b) (overturn) volcar*

top: ~**-ranking** /'tɑ:p'ræŋkɪŋ ‖ˌtɒp'ræŋkɪŋ/ adj (before n) de alto nivel; ~**-secret** /'tɑ:p'si:krət ‖ˌtɒp'si:krɪt/ adj (pred ~ **secret**) secreto, reservado; ~**soil** n capa superior del suelo

topsy-turvy /'tɑ:psi'tɜ:rvi ‖ˌtɒpsi'tɜ:vi/ adj (colloq) (room) desordenado, patas (para) arriba (fam)

Torah /'tɔ:rə/ n **the** ~ la or el Torá

torch /tɔːrtʃ ‖ tɔːtʃ/ *n* **(a)** (flame) antorcha *f*, tea *f* **(b)** (electric) (BrE) linterna *f*

torchlight /'tɔːrtʃlaɪt ‖ 'tɔːtʃlaɪt/ *n*: **by ~** a la luz de la(s) antorcha(s); (*before n*) ⟨*procession*⟩ con antorchas

tore /tɔːr ‖ tɔː(r)/ *past of* TEAR²

torment¹ /'tɔːrment ‖ 'tɔːment/ *n* tormento *m*

torment² /tɔːr'ment ‖ tɔː'ment/ *vt* atormentar, torturar; (tease) martirizar*

torn /tɔːrn ‖ tɔːn/ *past p of* TEAR²

tornado /tɔːr'neɪdəʊ ‖ tɔː'neɪdəʊ/ *n* (*pl* **-does** *or* **-dos**) tornado *m*

torpedo¹ /tɔːr'piːdəʊ ‖ tɔː'piːdəʊ/ *n* (*pl* **-does**) (Mil) torpedo *m*

torpedo² *vt* **-does, -doing, -doed** torpedear

torpor /'tɔːrpər ‖ 'tɔːpə(r)/ *n* (frml) letargo *m*, sopor *m*

torrent /'tɔːrənt ‖ 'tɒrənt/ *n* torrente *m*

torrential /tɔː'rentʃəl ‖ tə'renʃəl/ *adj* torrencial

torrid /'tɔːrəd ‖ 'tɒrɪd/ *adj* ⟨*heat*⟩ tórrido; ⟨*affair*⟩ apasionado

torso /'tɔːrsəʊ ‖ 'tɔːsəʊ/ *n* (*pl* **-sos**) torso *m*

tortoise /'tɔːrtəs ‖ 'tɔːtəs/ *n* tortuga *f*

tortoiseshell¹ /'tɔːrtəʃel, -təsʃel ‖ 'tɔːtəsʃel, 'tɔːtəʃəl/ *n* (material) carey *m*, concha *f*

tortoiseshell² *adj* (color) de color carey; ⟨*cat*⟩ pardo

tortuous /'tɔːrtʃuəs ‖ 'tɔːtjuəs/ *adj* tortuoso, sinuoso

torture¹ /'tɔːrtʃər ‖ 'tɔːtʃə(r)/ *n* tortura *f*

torture² *vt* ⟨*person/animal*⟩ torturar; **she was ~d by doubts** las dudas la atormentaban

Tory /'tɔːri/ *n* (*pl* **Tories**) (in UK) tory *mf*

toss¹ /tɔːs ‖ tɒs/ *n* **(a)** (throw) lanzamiento *m*; **with a ~ of his head** con un movimiento brusco de la cabeza **(b)** (of coin): **to win/lose the ~** ganar/perder* jugándoselo a cara o cruz (*or* sello *etc*)

toss² *vt* **(a)** (throw) ⟨*ball*⟩ tirar, lanzar*, aventar* (Col, Méx, Per); ⟨*pancake*⟩ darle* la vuelta a (*lanzándolo al aire*); **let's ~ a coin** echémoslo a cara o cruz *or* (Andes, Ven) a cara o sello *or* (Arg) a cara o ceca *or* (Méx) a águila o sol **(b)** (agitate) ⟨*boat*⟩ sacudir, zarandear **(c)** ⟨*salad*⟩ mezclar
■ **~** *vi* ⟨*boat*⟩ dar* bandazos; **to ~ and turn** dar* vueltas (*in the cama*)

tot /tɑːt ‖ tɒt/ *n* **(a)** (young child) pequeño, -ña *m,f*, chiquito, -ta *m,f* (esp AmL) **(b)** (of alcohol) copita *f*
■ **tot up: -tt-** [*v + o + adv, v + adv + o*] (colloq) sumar

total¹ /'təʊtl/ *adj* total; ⟨*failure*⟩ rotundo

total² *n* total *m*

total³ *vt*, (BrE) **-ll- (a)** (amount to) ascender* *or* elevarse a un total de **(b)** (add up) totalizar*

totalitarian /təʊ'tælə'teriən ‖ ˌtəʊtælɪ'teəriən/ *adj* totalitario

totally /'təʊtli ‖ 'təʊtəli/ *adv* totalmente, completamente

tote /təʊt/ *vt* (esp AmE colloq) ⟨*weapons*⟩ llevar

totem pole /'təʊtəm/ *n* tótem *m*

totter /'tɑːtər ‖ 'təʊtə(r)/ *vi* tambalearse

touch¹ /tʌtʃ/ *n* **1 (a)** (sense) tacto *m* **(b)** (physical contact): **at the ~ of a button** con solo tocar un botón **2** (small amount, degree — of humor, irony) dejo *m*, toque *m*; (— of paint) toque *m*; (— of

salt) pizca *f* **3** (detail) detalle *m*; **to add** *o* **put the final** *o* **finishing ~es to sth** darle* los últimos toques a algo **4** (communication): **to get/keep** *o* **stay in ~ with sb** ponerse*/mantenerse* en contacto con algn; **I lost ~ with her** perdí el contacto *or* ella

touch² *vt* **1 (a)** (be in physical contact with) tocar*; **my feet don't ~ the bottom** (of pool) no hago pie, no toco fondo **(b)** (brush, graze) rozar*, tocar*

2 (a) (affect, concern) afectar **(b)** (move emotionally): **he was ~ed by her kindness** su amabilidad lo enterneció *or* le llegó al alma; **I was very ~ed** me emocioné
■ **~** *vi* **(a)** (with finger, hand) tocar* **(b)** ⟨*hands*⟩ rozarse*; ⟨*wires*⟩ tocarse*
■ **touch down** [*v + adv*] (on land) aterrizar*, tomar tierra; (on moon) alunizar*
■ **touch on** [*v + prep + o*] ⟨*subject*⟩ tocar*, mencionar
■ **touch up** [*v + o + adv, v + adv + o*] ⟨*photograph/painting*⟩ retocar*

touch: ~-and-go /ˈtʌtʃənˈɡəʊ/ *adj*: **I passed the exam, but it was ~-and-go** aprobé el examen, pero por poco; **how is the patient? — it's ~-and-go at the moment** ¿cómo está el paciente? — en situación crítica; **~down** *n* (on land) aterrizaje *m*; (on moon) alunizaje *m*

touching /'tʌtʃɪŋ/ *adj* enternecedor, conmovedor

touch: ~line *n* línea *f* de banda; **~-type** *vi* mecanografiar* al tacto

touchy /'tʌtʃi/ *adj* **-chier, -chiest** ⟨*person*⟩ susceptible; ⟨*subject*⟩ delicado

tough /tʌf/ *adj* **-er, -est 1 (a)** (strong, hard-wearing) ⟨*fabric/clothing*⟩ resistente, fuerte **(b)** ⟨*meat*⟩ duro **2** ⟨*person*⟩ **(a)** (resilient) fuerte **(b)** (aggressive, violent) bravucón **3 (a)** (strict) ⟨*boss/teacher*⟩ severo; ⟨*policy/discipline*⟩ duro **(b)** ⟨*exam/decision*⟩ difícil

toughen /'tʌfən/ **~ (up)** *vt* **(a)** ⟨*muscles*⟩ endurecer*; ⟨*material*⟩ hacer* más fuerte *or* resistente **(b)** ⟨*person*⟩ hacer* más fuerte

toupee /tuː'peɪ ‖ 'tuːpeɪ/ *n* peluquín *m*, tupé *m*

tour¹ /tʊr ‖ tʊə(r), tɔː(r)/ *n* **(a)** (by bus, car) viaje *m*, gira *f*; (of castle, museum) visita *f*; (of town) visita *f* turística, recorrido *m* turístico; (*before n*) **~ guide** guía *mf* de turismo *or* (Méx) de turistas **(b)** (official visit) (to country, region) gira *f*, viaje *m*; (of factory, hospital) visita *f* **(c)** (Mus, Sport, Theat) gira *f*, tournée *f*; **to be/go on ~** estar*/ir* de gira

tour² *vt* **(a)** ⟨*country/area*⟩ recorrer, viajar por **(b)** (visit officially) visitar **(c)** (Mus, Sport, Theat) ir* de gira *or* hacer* una gira por

tourism /'tʊrɪzəm ‖ 'tʊərɪzəm, 'tɔːr-/ *n* turismo *m*

tourist /'tʊrəst ‖ 'tʊərɪst, 'tɔːr-/ *n* turista *mf*; (*before n*) **~ guide** (book) guía *f* turística; (person) guía *mf* de turismo *or* (Méx) de turistas; **the ~ industry** el turismo, la industria del turismo; **~ office** oficina *f* de (información y) turismo

tournament /'tʊrnəmənt ‖ 'tɔːnəmənt/ *n* torneo *m*

tourniquet /'tʊrnɪkət ‖ 'tʊənɪkeɪ/ *n* torniquete *m*

tousled /'taʊzəld/ *adj* despeinado, alborotado

tout /taʊt/ vi: to ~ for customers andar* a la caza de clientes

tow¹ /təʊ/ n remolque m; **to give sb a** ~ remolcar* a algn

tow² vt remolcar*, llevar a remolque; **they** ~**ed the car away** se llevaron el coche a remolque

toward /tɔːrd ‖ tə'wɔːd/, (esp BrE) **towards** /tɔːrdz ‖ tə'wɔːdz/ prep **1** (in the direction of) hacia **2** (as contribution): **she gave us $100** ~ **it** nos dio 100 dólares como contribución **3** (regarding) para con, hacia; **your attitude** ~ **them** tu actitud para con or hacia ellos

towel¹ /'taʊəl/ n toalla f; (before n) ~ **bar** o (BrE) **rail** toallero m (de barra)

towel² vt, (BrE) **-ll-** secar* con toalla

toweling, (BrE) **towelling** /'taʊəlɪŋ/ n (tela f de) toalla f, felpa f

tower /'taʊər ‖ 'taʊə(r)/ n torre f
■ **tower above, tower over** [v + prep + o] ‹building› descollar* sobre; ‹person› destacar* sobre

tower block n (BrE) (residential) edificio m or bloque m de apartamentos or (AmL tb) de departamentos or (Esp tb) de pisos, torre f

towering /'taʊərɪŋ/ adj (before n) **(a)** ‹building› altísimo **(b)** ‹genius› destacado

town /taʊn/ n (in general) ciudad f, (smaller) pueblo m, población f; **to go to** ~ on sth tirar la casa por la ventana; (before n) ~ **center** o (BrE) **centre** centro m de la ciudad

town: ~ **clerk** n (in US) funcionario encargado de llevar los registros de nacimientos, defunciones etc; ~ **council** n (in UK) ayuntamiento m, municipio m, municipalidad f; ~ **crier** /'kraɪər ‖ 'kraɪə(r)/ n pregonero m; ~ **hall** n ayuntamiento m, municipio m; ~ **planner** n urbanista mf; ~ **planning** n urbanismo m

township /'taʊnʃɪp/ n **(a)** (in US) (Govt) municipio m, municipalidad m, ayuntamiento m **(b)** (in South Africa) distrito m segregado

tow: ~ **path** n camino m de sirga; ~**rope** n (Naut) sirga f, (Auto) cuerda f or cable m de remolque; ~ **truck** n grúa f

toxic /'tɑːksɪk ‖ 'tɒksɪk/ adj tóxico

toxin /'tɑːksən ‖ 'tɒksɪn/ n toxina f

toy¹ /tɔɪ/ n juguete m
■ **toy with** [v + prep + o] ‹pen/food› juguetear con; ‹idea/possibility› darle* vueltas a

toy² adj **(a)** ‹car/gun› de juguete **(b)** (miniature) enano

toyshop /'tɔɪʃɑːp ‖ 'tɔɪʃɒp/ n juguetería f

trace¹ /treɪs/ n **(a)** (indication) señal f, indicio m, rastro m **(b)** (small amount): ~**s of poison** rastros de veneno

trace² vt **1** **(a)** ‹criminal/witness› localizar*, ubicar* (AmL) **(b)** ‹fault/malfunction› descubrir* **2** **(a)** (on tracing paper) calcar* **(b)** ‹line/outline› trazar*

tracing paper /'treɪsɪŋ/ n papel m de calco or de calcar

track¹ /træk/ n **1** (mark) pista f, huellas fpl; **to**

throw sb off the ~ despistar a algn; **to keep/lose** ~ **of the conversation** seguir*/perder* el hilo de la conversación; **I lost all** ~ **of the time** no me di cuenta de la hora
2 **(a)** (road, path) camino m, sendero m **(b)** to be **on the right/wrong** ~ estar* bien/mal encaminado, ir* por buen/mal camino
3 (race ~) pista f; (before n) ~ **events** atletismo m en pista
4 (track events) (AmE) atletismo m en pista
5 (Rail) **(a)** (way) vía f (férrea) **(b)** (rails etc) vías fpl
6 (song, piece of music) tema m, pieza f

track² vt seguirle* la pista a, rastrear
■ **track down** [v + o + adv, v + adv + o] ‹criminal/lost object› localizar*

trackball /'trækbɔːl/ n (Comput) ratón m de bola

tracker /'trækər ‖ 'trækə(r)/ n rastreador, -dora m,f; (before n) ~ **dog** perro m rastreador

tracking /'trækɪŋ/ n (AmE Educ) división del alumnado en grupos de acuerdo al nivel académico

track: ~ **record** n historial m, antecedentes mpl; ~**suit** n equipo m (de deportes), chándal m (Esp), pants mpl (Méx), buzo m (Chi, Per), sudadera f (Col)

tract /trækt/ n **1** (of land, sea) extensión f **2** (Anat) tracto m **3** (short treatise) tratado m breve

traction /'trækʃən/ n **(a)** (Mech Eng, Med) tracción f **(b)** (grip) agarre m, adherencia f

tractor /'træktər ‖ 'træktə(r)/ n (Agr) tractor m

trade¹ /treɪd/ n **(a)** (buying, selling) comercio m **(b)** (business, industry) industria f **(c)** (skilled occupation) oficio m **(d)** (people in particular trade): **the** ~ el gremio

trade² vi (buy, sell) comerciar
■ ~ vt ‹blows/insults› intercambiar; **to** ~ **sth FOR sth** cambiar or canjear algo POR algo
■ **trade in** [v + o + adv, v + adv + o] entregar* como parte del pago

trade: ~**mark** n **(a)** (symbol, name) marca f (de fábrica) **(b)** (distinctive characteristic) sello m característico; ~ **name** n nombre m comercial

trader /'treɪdər ‖ 'treɪdə(r)/ n comerciante mf

trade: ~ **secret** n secreto m comercial; ~**sman** /'treɪdzmən/ n (pl **-men** /-mən/) **(a)** (shopkeeper) (dated) comerciante m, tendero m **(b)** (deliveryman) proveedor m; ~ **union** n sindicato m, gremio m (CS, Per); (before n) ‹leader› sindical, sindicalista, gremial (AmL)

trading /'treɪdɪŋ/ n **(a)** (in goods) comercio m, actividad f or movimiento m comercial **(b)** (on stock exchange) contratación f, operaciones fpl (bursátiles)

tradition /trə'dɪʃən/ n tradición f

traditional /trə'dɪʃnəl ‖ trə'dɪʃənl/ adj tradicional

traffic /'træfɪk/ n **1** (vehicles) tráfico m,

circulación f, tránsito m (esp AmL) **2** (goods, people transported) tránsito m **3** (trafficking) tráfico m

■ **traffic in**: -**ck**- [v + prep + o] traficar* en

traffic: ~ **calming** /'kɑːmɪŋ/ n (before n): ~ **calming measures** medidas fpl para reducir la velocidad del tráfico; ~ **circle** n (AmE) rotonda f, glorieta f; ~ **island** n isla f peatonal; ~ **jam** n embotellamiento m, atasco m

trafficker /'træfɪkər ‖'træfɪkə(r)/ n traficante mf

traffic: ~ **light** n (often pl) semáforo m; ~ **warden** n (in UK) persona que controla el estacionamiento de vehículos en las ciudades

tragedy /'trædʒədi/ n (pl -**dies**) tragedia f

tragic /'trædʒɪk/ adj trágico

tragicomedy /ˌtrædʒɪ'kɑːmədi ‖ˌtrædʒɪ'kɒmədi/ n tragicomedia f

trail¹ /treɪl/ n (a) (left by animal, person) huellas fpl, rastro m; **to be on the** ~ **of sb/sth** seguir* la pista de algn/algo, seguirle* la pista a algn/algo (b) (path) sendero m, senda f

trail² vt **1** (drag) arrastrar **2** (follow) seguir* la pista de, seguirle* la pista a, rastrear
■ ~ vi **1** (drag) arrastrar **2** (lag behind) ir* a la zaga **3** «plant» trepar

■ **trail away, trail off** [v + adv] irse* apagando

trailer /'treɪlər ‖'treɪlə(r)/ n **1** (a) (for boats, equipment) remolque m (b) (house ~) (AmE) caravana f, tráiler m (AmL), casa f rodante (CS, Ven), cámper f (Chi, Méx), rulot f (Esp) **2** (Cin, TV) avance(s) m(pl) or (Esp tb) tráiler m or (CS) sinopsis f

train¹ /treɪn/ n **1** (Rail) tren m; (before n) ~ **driver** (BrE) maquinista mf; ~ **set** ferrocarril m de juguete **2** (a) (of servants) séquito m (b) (of events) serie f; **to lose one's** ~ **of thought** perder* el hilo (de las ideas) **3** (of dress, robe) cola f

train² vt **1** (a) (instruct) «athlete» entrenar; «soldier» adiestrar; «animal» (to perform tricks etc) amaestrar, adiestrar; «employee» capacitar; «teacher» formar (b) «voice/ear» educar* (c) «plant» guiar* **2** (aim) **to** ~ **sth on sth/sb** «gun» apuntarle A algo/algn con algo
■ ~ vi (a) «nurse/musician» estudiar (b) (Sport) entrenar(se)

trained /treɪnd/ adj (a) «worker» calificado (esp AmL), cualificado (Esp); «teacher» titulado, diplomado; **a highly** ~ **army** un ejército muy bien adiestrado (b) «dog» entrenado (c) «voice» educado

trainee /treɪ'niː/ n (a) (in a trade) aprendiz, -diza m,f; (before n) ~ **manager** empleado que está haciendo prácticas de gerencia (b) (AmE Mil) recluta mf

trainer /'treɪnər ‖'treɪnə(r)/ n **1** (of athletes) entrenador, -dora m,f; (of performing animals) amaestrador, -dora m,f, adiestrador, -dora m,f **2** (training shoe) (BrE colloq) zapatilla f de deporte, tenis m

training /'treɪnɪŋ/ n (a) (instruction) capacitación f (b) (Sport) entrenamiento m

traipse /treɪps/ vi (colloq) (+ adv compl): **I** ~**d all over town** me pateé (fam) toda la ciudad

trait /treɪt/ n rasgo m

traitor /'treɪtər ‖'treɪtə(r)/ n traidor, -dora m,f

tram /træm/ n (BrE Transp) tranvía m

tramp¹ /træmp/ vi (+ adv compl) **to** ~ (**along**) caminar or marchar (pesadamente)

tramp² n vagabundo, -da m,f

trample /'træmpəl/ vt pisotear; **they were** ~**d to death** murieron aplastados
■ ~ vi **to** ~ **on sth** pisotear algo

trampoline /'træmpəliːn/ n trampolín m, cama f elástica

trance /træns ‖trɑːns/ n trance m

tranquil /'træŋkwəl ‖'træŋkwɪl/ adj tranquilo

tranquillity, (BrE) **tranquillity** /træŋ'kwɪləti/ n (of place, atmosphere) paz f, tranquilidad f; (of person) calma f, serenidad f

tranquilize, (BrE) **tranquillize** /'træŋkwəlaɪz ‖'træŋkwɪlaɪz/ vt sedar, dar* un sedante a

tranquilizer, (BrE) **tranquillizer** /'træŋkwəlaɪzər ‖'træŋkwɪlaɪzə(r)/ n sedante m, tranquilizante m

transaction /trænz'ækʃən/ n transacción f, operación f

transatlantic /'trænzət'læntɪk/ adj transatlántico

transcend /træn'send/ vt (fml) (a) (go beyond) «boundaries» ir* más allá de, trascender* (b) (overcome) superar

transcribe /træn'skraɪb/ vt transcribir*

transcript /'trænskrɪpt/ n transcripción f

transcription /træn'skrɪpʃən/ n transcripción f

transfer¹ /træns'fɜːr ‖ træns'fɜː(r)/ vt -**rr**- (a) «funds/account» transferir*, traspasar, transmitir (c) «call» pasar (d) «employee/prisoner» trasladar; «player» (esp BrE) traspasar

transfer² /'trænsfɜːr ‖'trænsfɜː(r)/ n **1** (a) (Fin, Law) transferencia f (b) (of employee) traslado m; (of player) (esp BrE) traspaso m (c) (of passengers) transbordo m **2** (design) calcomanía f

transferable /træns'fɜːrəbəl/ adj transferible; **not** ~ intransferible

transferal /træns'fɜːrəl/ n (AmE) ▶ TRANSFER² 1 A, B

transfix /træns'fɪks/ vt (usu pass) paralizar*

transform /træns'fɔːrm ‖træns'fɔːm/ vt transformar

transformation /'trænsfər'meɪʃən ‖ˌtrænsfə'meɪʃən/ n transformación f

transformer /træns'fɔːrmər ‖træns'fɔːmə(r)/ n transformador m

transfusion /træns'fjuːʒən/ n transfusión f

transgress /træns'gres ‖trænz'gres/ vt (fml) (a) «law» transgredir (fml) (b) (go beyond) exceder, sobrepasar
■ ~ vi pecar*

transient /'trænziənt, 'trænʃənt ‖'trænziənt/ adj pasajero, fugaz

transistor /træn'zɪstər, -'sɪstər ‖træn'zɪstə(r), -'sɪstə(r)/ n (a) (Electron) transistor m (b) (~ radio) (esp BrE) transistor m, radio f or (AmL exc CS) radio m a transistores

transit /'trænsət, -zət ‖'trænzɪt, -sɪt/ n tránsito m; **passengers in** ~ pasajeros mpl en or de tránsito; **it was lost in** ~ se perdió en el viaje

transition /træn'zɪʃən/ n transición f

transitional /træn'zɪʃnəl ‖træn'zɪʃənḷ/ *adj* ⟨*stage/period*⟩ de transición

transitive /'trænsətɪv/ *adj* transitivo

translate /træns'leɪt/ *vt/i* traducir*

translation /træns'leɪʃən/ *n* traducción *f*

translator /træns'leɪtər ‖træns'leɪtə(r)/ *n* traductor, -tora *m,f*

transmission /trænz'mɪʃən/ *n* transmisión *f*

transmit /trænz'mɪt/ *vt* **-tt-** transmitir

transmitter /'trænzmɪtər ‖trænz'mɪtə(r)/ *n* transmisor *m*

transparency /træns'pærənsi/ *n* (*pl* **-cies**) (Phot) transparencia *f*, diapositiva *f*

transparent /træns'pærənt/ *adj* transparente

transpire /træn'spaɪr ‖træn'spaɪə(r)/ *vi* ① (a) (become apparent): it **~d that** ... resultó que ... (b) (happen) ocurrir, suceder ② (Biol, Bot) transpirar

transplant¹ /træns'plænt ‖træns'plɑːnt/ *vt* (Hort, Med) trasplantar

transplant² /'trænsplænt ‖'trænsplɑːnt/ *n* (Med) trasplante *m*

transport¹ /'trænspɔːrt ‖'trænspɔːt/ *n* transporte *m*

transport² /træns'pɔːrt ‖træns'pɔːt/ *vt* transportar

transportation /'trænspərteɪʃən ‖,trænspɔː'teɪʃən/ *n* transporte *m*

transpose /træns'pəʊz/ *vt* trasponer*, transponer*

transvestite /trænz'vestaɪt/ *n* travestido *m*, travesti *m*, travestí *m*

trap¹ /træp/ *n* trampa *f*

trap² *vt* **-pp-** (a) ⟨*animal*⟩ cazar* (con trampa) (b) (cut off, catch) (*often pass*) atrapar; **he was ~ped in the car** quedó atrapado en el coche

trapdoor, trap door /træp'dɔːr ‖'træpdɔː(r)/ trampilla *f*

trapeze /træ'piːz, trə- ‖trə'piːz/ *n* trapecio *m*

trapper /'træpər ‖'træpə(r)/ *n* trampero, -ra *m,f*

trappings /'træpɪŋz/ *pl n* (a) (paraphernalia): **all the ~ of success** los símbolos del éxito (b) (of horse) arreos *mpl*, jaeces *mpl*

trash¹ /træʃ/ *n* (a) (refuse) (AmE) basura *f*; (*before n*) **~ bag** bolsa *f* de la basura; **~ can** cubo *m or* (CS, Per) tacho *m or* (Méx) bote *m or* (Col) caneca *f or* (Ven) tobo *m* de la basura (b) (worthless stuff) basura *f* (c) (worthless people) (AmE colloq) escoria *f*

trash² *vt* (AmE) (a) (dispose of) botar (a la basura), tirar (a la basura) (AmL exc RPl), tirar (a la basura) (Esp, RPl) (b) (criticize) (colloq) ⟨*movie/book*⟩ poner* por los suelos *or* por el suelo; ⟨*person*⟩ despellejar (fam)

trashman /'træʃmæn/ *n* (*pl* **-men** /-men/) (AmE) basurero *m*

trashy /'træʃi/ *adj* **-shier, -shiest** ⟨*souvenir*⟩ barato, de porquería (fam); ⟨*movie/magazine*⟩ malo

trauma /'trɔːmə/ *n* (*pl* **-mas**) trauma *m*

traumatic /trɔː'mætɪk/ *adj* traumático, traumatizante

travel¹ /'trævəl/, (BrE) **-ll-** *vi* ① (make journey) viajar ② (move, go) «*vehicle*» desplazarse*, ir*; «*light/waves*» propagarse*

■ **~** *vt* ⟨*country/world*⟩ viajar por, recorrer; ⟨*road/distance*⟩ recorrer

travel² *n* (*before n*) ⟨*company/brochure*⟩ de viajes

travel: ~ agency *n* agencia *f* de viajes; **~ agent** *n* agente *mf* de viajes; **~ agent's** agencia *f* de viajes

traveler, (BrE) **-ll-** /'trævlər ‖'trævlə(r)/ *n* (a) viajero, -ra *m,f* (b) (itinerant person) (BrE) persona que ha adoptado el estilo de vida errante de los gitanos

traveler's check, (BrE) **traveller's cheque** *n* cheque *m* de viaje *or* de viajero

traveling¹, (BrE) **-ll-** /'trævlɪŋ/ *n* (*before n*) **~ expenses** gastos *mpl* de viaje

traveling², (BrE) **-ll-** *adj* (a) ⟨*clothes/companion*⟩ de viaje (b) (itinerant) ambulante; **~ salesman** viajante *m*

travel: ~-sick /'trævəlsɪk/ *adj* (BrE) mareado; **to get ~** marearse; **~ sickness** *n* (BrE) mareo *m*; (*before n*) ⟨*pills*⟩ para el mareo

trawl /trɔːl/ *vi* hacer* pesca de arrastre

trawler /'trɔːlər ‖'trɔːlə(r)/ *n* barca *f* pesquera (utilizada para hacer pesca de arrastre), bou *m*

tray /treɪ/ *n* bandeja *f*

treacherous /'tretʃərəs/ *adj* ⟨*person*⟩ traicionero, traidor; ⟨*sea/current*⟩ traicionero

treachery /'tretʃəri/ *n* (*pl* **-ries**) traición *f*

treacle /'triːkəl/ *n* (esp BrE) melaza *f*

tread¹ /tred/ (*past* **trod**; *past p* **trodden** *or* **trod**) *vi* pisar; **to ~ in sth** pisar algo; **to ~ carefully** *o* **warily** andarse* con cuidado *or* con pie(s) de plomo

■ **~** *vt*: **she trod the earth down** apisonó la tierra; **to ~ grapes** pisar uvas; **to ~ water** flotar (en posición vertical)

■ **tread on** [*v* + *prep* + *o*] (esp BrE) pisar

tread² *n* ① (step, footfall) paso *m*; (steps) pasos *mpl* ② (on tire) banda *f* de rodamiento

treadle /'tredḷ/ *n* pedal *m*

treason /'triːzn/ *n* traición *f*

treasure¹ /'treʒər ‖'treʒə(r)/ *n* (a) (hoard of wealth) tesoros *mpl* (b) (sth valuable, prized) tesoro *m*; (*before n*) **~ hunt** (Games) búsqueda *f* del tesoro

treasure² *vt* (a) (value greatly): **thank you for the book, I shall always ~ it** gracias por el libro, lo guardaré como algo muy especial (b) ⟨*possession*⟩ preciado

treasured *adj* ⟨*possession*⟩ preciado

treasurer /'treʒərər ‖'treʒərə(r)/ *n* tesorero, -ra *m,f*

treasury /'treʒəri/ *n* (*pl* **-ries**) (a) (public funds) erario *m*, tesoro *m* (b) **the Treasury** *o* **the treasury** el fisco, la hacienda pública, el tesoro (público); **Department of the T~** (in US) Departamento *m* del Tesoro (de los Estados Unidos), ≈ ministerio *m* de Hacienda

treat¹ /triːt/ *vt* (a) (+ *adv compl*) ⟨*person/animal*⟩ tratar; **you seem to ~ this whole thing as a joke** pareces tomarte a broma todo esto (b) ⟨*process*⟩ tratar (c) (deal with) (frml) ⟨*subject*⟩ tratar (d) (Med) ⟨*patient/disease*⟩ tratar (e) (entertain)*: **I'm ~ing you** te invito yo; **I ~ed myself to a new dress** me di el gusto de comprarme un vestido nuevo

treat² n gusto m; **I bought myself an ice cream as o for a ~** me compré un helado para darme (un) gusto

treatise /'tri:təs ‖'tri:tɪs, -ɪz/ n tratado m

treatment /'tri:tmənt/ n **(a)** (of person, animal, object) trato m; (of subject) tratamiento m **(b)** (of waste) tratamiento m **(c)** (Med) tratamiento m

treaty /'tri:ti/ n (pl **-ties**) tratado m

treble¹ /'trebəl/ n **(a)** (singer) tiple mf; (voice) voz f de tiple **(b)** (Audio) agudos mpl

treble² vt triplicar*
■ ~ vi triplicarse*

treble³ adj **1** (threefold) triple **2** (before n) (Mus) de tiple o soprano

treble clef n clave f de sol

tree /tri:/ n árbol m; (before n) ~ **trunk** tronco m

tree: **~-lined** adj (before n) bordeado de árboles, arbolado; **~-top** n copa f de árbol

trek¹ /trek/ n (hike) caminata f; **it's quite a ~ to the shops** hay un buen paseo hasta llegar a las tiendas

trek² vi **-kk-** caminar; **to go ~king** hacer* senderismo

trellis /'treləs ‖'trelɪs/ n enrejado m, espaldera f

tremble /'trembəl/ vi temblar*

tremendous /trɪ'mendəs/ adj **(a)** (great, huge) tremendo **(b)** (very good) formidable

tremendously /trɪ'mendəsli/ adv tremendamente

tremor /'tremər ‖'tremə(r)/ n **(a)** (quiver) temblor m **(b)** (earth ~) temblor m (de tierra), seísmo m, sismo m (AmL)

trench /trentʃ/ n zanja f; (Mil) trinchera f

trench coat n trinchera f

trend /trend/ n **(a)** (pattern, tendency) tendencia f **(b)** (fashion) moda f

trendy /'trendi/ adj **-dier, -diest** moderno

trepidation /trepə'deɪʃən ‖,trepɪ'deɪʃən/ n (fml) (fear) temor m (fml); (anxiety) inquietud f

trespass /'trespəs/ vi (Law) entrar sin autorización en propiedad ajena

trespasser /'trespəsər ‖'trespəsə(r)/ n intruso, -sa m,f; ⊖ **trespassers will be prosecuted** ≈ prohibido el paso

tress /tres/ n (liter) **(a)** (lock of hair) mechón m **(b)** **tresses** pl (hair) cabellera f (liter), cabellos mpl

trestle /'tresəl/ n caballete m

trial¹ /'traɪəl/ n **1** (Law) **(a)** (court hearing) proceso m, juicio m **(b)** (judgment) juicio m; **a fair ~** un juicio imparcial; **to be on ~ for murder** estar* siendo procesado por asesinato **2** (test) prueba f; **clinical ~** ensayo m clínico; **on ~** a prueba; **by ~ and error** por ensayo y error **3** (trouble) **~s and tribulations** tribulaciones fpl **4** (Sport) (usu pl) prueba f de selección

trial² adj (period/flight) de prueba; **~ offer** oferta f especial (para promover un producto nuevo); **~ run** prueba f

triangle /'traɪæŋgəl/ n (Math, Mus) triángulo m

triangular /traɪ'æŋgjələr ‖traɪ'æŋgjʊlə(r)/ adj triangular

tribal /'traɪbəl/ adj tribal

tribe /traɪb/ n tribu f

tribesman /'traɪbzmən/ n (pl **-men** /-mən/) miembro m de una tribu

tribunal /traɪ'bju:nl/ n (court) tribunal m

tributary /'trɪbjətəri ‖'trɪbjʊtəri/ n (pl **-ries**) afluente m, río m tributario

tribute /'trɪbju:t/ n **1** (acknowledgment) homenaje m, tributo m; **to pay ~ to sb/sth** rendir* homenaje or (AmL tb) tributo a algn/algo **2** (payment) tributo m

triceps /'traɪseps/ n (pl ~) tríceps m

trick¹ /trɪk/ n **1 (a)** (ruse) trampa f, ardid m; (before n) ~ **photography** trucaje m; **a ~ question** una pregunta con trampa **(b)** (prank, joke) broma f, jugarreta f **2** (feat, skilful act) truco m; **to do card ~s** hacer* trucos con las cartas **3** (in card games) baza f

trick² vt engañar

trickle¹ /'trɪkəl/ vi (+ adv compl) **(a)** ‹liquid›: **sweat ~d down his forehead** le corrían gotas de sudor por la frente **(b)** (arrive, go): **letters are still trickling in** todavía se está recibiendo alguna que otra carta

trickle² n hilo m

trickster /'trɪkstər ‖'trɪkstə(r)/ n embaucador, -dora m,f

tricky /'trɪki/ adj **trickier, trickiest (a)** (difficult) ‹task/problem› difícil, peliagudo, que tiene sus bemoles **(b)** (sensitive) ‹matter/problem› delicado

tricycle /'traɪsɪkəl/ n triciclo m

trifle /'traɪfəl/ n **1 (a)** (trivial thing) nimiedad f **(b)** (small amount) (no pl) insignificancia f **2** (Culin) postre de bizcocho, jerez, crema y frutas
■ **trifle with** [v + prep + o] jugar* con

trifling /'traɪflɪŋ/ adj insignificante, sin importancia

trigger¹ /'trɪgər ‖'trɪgə(r)/ n gatillo m

trigger² vt ~ **(off)** ‹reaction/response› provocar*

trill /trɪl/ n **(a)** (in music, of birdsong) trino m **(b)** (Ling) vibración f

trilogy /'trɪlədʒi/ n (pl **-gies**) trilogía f

trim¹ /trɪm/ adj **-mm- (a)** (slim) esbelto, estilizado **(b)** (neat) ‹uniform/suit› elegante

trim² n **1** (good condition): **to be in (good) ~** estar* en buen estado or en buenas condiciones **2** (cut) recorte m

trim³ vt **-mm- 1** (cut) recortar **2** (decorate): **~med with velvet** con adornos de terciopelo; (round edge) ribeteado de terciopelo

trimester /traɪ'mestər ‖traɪ'mestə(r)/ n (AmE) trimestre m

trimming /'trɪmɪŋ/ n **1** (on clothes) adorno m; (along edges) ribete m **2** **trimmings** pl (offcuts) recortes mpl

Trinidad /'trɪnədæd ‖'trɪnɪdæd/ n Trinidad f; ~ **and Tobago** Trinidad y Tobago

Trinity /'trɪnəti/ n **the (Holy) ~** la (Santísima) Trinidad

trinket /'trɪŋkət ‖'trɪŋkɪt/ n chuchería f, baratija f

trio /'tri:əʊ/ n trío m

trip¹ /trɪp/ n **1** (journey) viaje m; (excursion) excursión f; (outing) salida f; **she's going on a ~** ····⟫

to Japan se va de viaje al Japón; **a ~ to the zoo** una visita al zoológico ⚹2⚹ (stumble, fall) tropezón *m*, traspié *m*

trip² -pp- *vi* tropezar*
■ **~** *vt* (**up**) hacerle* una zancadilla a
■ **trip over** [*v* + *adv*] tropezar* y caerse*

tripe /traɪp/ *n* (**a**) (Culin) mondongo *m* (AmS), callos *mpl* (Esp), pancita *f* (Méx) (**b**) (nonsense) (colloq) paparruchas *fpl* (fam)

triple¹ /'trɪpəl/ *adj* triple

triple² *adv*: **~ the amount** el triple

triple³ *vt* triplicar*
■ **~** *vi* triplicarse*

triple jump *n* triple salto *m* (de longitud)

triplet /'trɪplət ‖'trɪplɪt/ *n* trillizo, -za *m,f*

triplicate /'trɪpləkət ‖'trɪplɪkət/ *n*: **in ~** por triplicado

tripod /'traɪpɑːd ‖'traɪpɒd/ *n* trípode *m*

trite /traɪt/ *adj* **triter, tritest** trillado

triumph¹ /'traɪəmf ‖'traɪʌmf/ *n* triunfo *m*

triumph² *vi* triunfar

triumphal /traɪ'ʌmfəl/ *adj* triunfal

triumphant /traɪ'ʌmfənt/ *adj* ⟨troops/team⟩ triunfador; ⟨moment/entry⟩ triunfal; ⟨smile⟩ de triunfo, triunfal

trivia /'trɪviə/ *pl n* trivialidades *fpl*, nimiedades *fpl*

trivial /'trɪviəl/ *adj* ⟨events/concerns⟩ trivial; ⟨sum/details⟩ insignificante, nimio

triviality /trɪvi'æləti/ *n* (*pl* **-ties**) trivialidad *f*

trivialize /'trɪviəlaɪz/ *vt* trivializar*

trod /trɑːd ‖trɒd/ *past and past p of* TREAD¹

trodden /'trɑːdn̩ ‖'trɒdn̩/ *past p of* TREAD¹

trolley /'trɑːli ‖'trɒli/ *n* ⚹1⚹ (**a**) (**~ bus**) trolebús *m* (**b**) (**~ car**) tranvía *m* ⚹2⚹ (BrE) (for food, drink) carrito *m*, mesa *f* rodante; (at airport, in supermarket, in hospital) carrito *m*

trombone /trɑːm'bəʊn ‖trɒm'bəʊn/ *n* trombón *m*

troop¹ /truːp/ *n* ⚹1⚹ (unit) compañía *f*; (of cavalry) escuadrón *m* ⚹2⚹ **troops** *pl*: **our ~s** nuestras tropas; **500 ~s** 500 soldados

troop² *vi* (+ *adv compl*): **to ~ in/out** entrar/ salir* en tropel *or* en masa

trooper /'truːpər ‖'truːpə(r)/ *n* (**a**) (cavalryman) soldado *m* de caballería (**b**) (state police officer) (AmE) agente *mf*

trophy /'trəʊfi/ *n* (*pl* **-phies**) trofeo *m*

tropic /'trɑːpɪk ‖'trɒpɪk/ *n* (**a**) (line) trópico *m*; **the T~ of Cancer/Capricorn** el trópico de Cáncer/ Capricornio (**b**) **tropics** *pl* (area) **the ~s** el trópico

tropical /'trɑːpɪkəl ‖'trɒpɪkəl/ *adj* tropical

trot¹ /trɑːt ‖trɒt/ *n* (*no pl*) trote *m*; **on the ~** (BrE colloq): **four nights on the ~** cuatro noches seguidas

trot² -tt- *vi* trotar
■ **trot out** [*v* + *o* + *adv*, *v* + *adv* + *o*] ⟨excuses/ clichés⟩ salir* con; ⟨facts⟩ recitar de memoria

trouble¹ /'trʌbəl/ *n* ⚹1⚹ (problems, difficulties) problemas *mpl*; (particular problem) problema *m*; **to get into ~** meterse en problemas *or* en líos; **to have ~ with sb/sth** tener* problemas con algn/ algo; **what's the ~?** ¿qué pasa?
⚹2⚹ (effort) molestia *f*; **I don't want to put you to any ~** no quiero ocasionarle ninguna molestia; **to go to the ~ of doing sth, to take the ~ to do sth** molestarse en hacer algo
⚹3⚹ (strife, unrest) (*often pl*): **the ~s in Northern Ireland** los disturbios de Irlanda del Norte; **to look for ~** buscar* camorra; (*before n*) **~ spot** punto *m* conflictivo

trouble² *vt* (**a**) (worry) preocupar (**b**) (bother) molestar; **I'm sorry to ~ you** perdone *or* disculpe la molestia

troubled /'trʌbəld/ *adj* (**a**) ⟨person⟩ preocupado, atribulado; ⟨look⟩ de preocupación (**b**) (strife-torn) (journ) aquejado de problemas

trouble: **~maker** *n* alborotador, -dora *m,f*; **~shooter** /'ʃuːtər ‖'ʃuːtə(r)/ *n* (within company) persona *que se envía a resolver problemas, crisis etc*; (mediator) mediador, -dora *m,f*

troublesome /'trʌbəlsəm/ *adj* problemático

trough /trɔːf ‖trɒf/ *n* ⚹1⚹ (for water) abrevadero *m*, bebedero *m*; (for feed) comedero *m* ⚹2⚹ (Geog) hoya *f*, depresión *f*

troupe /truːp/ *n* (Theat) compañía *f* teatral; (in circus) troupe *f*

trousers /'traʊzərz ‖'traʊzəz/ *pl n* pantalón *m*, pantalones *mpl*; **a pair of ~** un pantalón, unos pantalones, un par de pantalones

trouser suit *n* (BrE) traje *m* pantalón, traje *m* de chaqueta y pantalón

trousseau /'truːsəʊ/ *n* (*pl* **-x** *or* **-s** /-z/) ajuar *m*

trout /traʊt/ *n* (*pl* **trout** *or* Zool **trouts**) trucha *f*

trowel /'traʊəl/ *n* (Const) paleta *f*, llana *f*; (for gardening) desplantador *m*, palita *f*

truancy /'truːənsi/ *n* ausentismo *m or* (Esp) absentismo *m* escolar

truant /'truːənt/ *n*: **to play ~** faltar a clase, hacer* novillos *or* (Méx) irse* de pinta *or* (RPl) hacerse* la rata *or* la rabona *or* (Per) la vaca *or* (Chi) hacer* la cimarra *or* (Col) capar clase (fam)

truce /truːs/ *n* tregua *f*

truck /trʌk/ *n* ⚹1⚹ (**a**) (vehicle) camión *m*; (*before n*) **~ driver** camionero, -ra *m,f* (**b**) (BrE Rail) furgón *m*, vagón *m* ⚹2⚹ (vegetables, fruit) (AmE) productos *mpl* de la huerta; (*before n*) **~ farm** huerta *f*

trucker /'trʌkər ‖'trʌkə(r)/ *n* (AmE) camionero, -ra *m,f*, transportista *mf*

trucking /'trʌkɪŋ/ *n* (AmE) transporte *m* por carretera

truculent /'trʌkjələnt ‖'trʌkjʊlənt/ *adj* malhumorado y agresivo

trudge /trʌdʒ/ *vi* caminar con dificultad

true¹ /truː/ *adj* **truer, truest** ⚹1⚹ (**a**) (consistent with fact, reality) ⟨story⟩ verídico; **to be ~** ser* cierto, ser* verdad; **to come ~** hacerse* realidad; **to hold ~** ser* válido **(b)** (accurate) ⟨before n⟩ ⟨account⟩ verídico **2** (real, actual, genuine) ⟨before n⟩ ⟨purpose/courage⟩ verdadero; ⟨friend⟩ auténtico, de verdad; **~ north** el norte geográfico; **it's ~ love** es amor de verdad **3** (faithful) fiel; **~ TO sth/sb** fiel A algo/algn **4** (Tech) ⟨pred⟩: **to be ~** ⟨wall⟩ estar* a plomo; ⟨beam⟩ estar* a nivel

true² n: **to be out of ~** no estar* a plomo

true: **~-life** /'truː.laɪf/ adj (journ) ⟨before n⟩ ⟨story⟩ verídico; **~-to-life** /'truːtə'laɪf/ adj ⟨pred ~ to life⟩ ⟨novel/film⟩ realista; ⟨situation⟩ verosímil

truffle /'trʌfəl/ n trufa f

truly /'truːli/ adv verdaderamente, realmente; ⟨grateful⟩ sinceramente, verdaderamente; **yours ~** (Corresp) cordiales saludos

trump /trʌmp/ n **(a) ~** ⟨card⟩ (Games) triunfo m; (resource, weapon) baza f **(b) trumps** pl (suit) triunfo m

trumped-up /'trʌmpt'ʌp/ adj ⟨before n⟩ falso, fabricado

trumpet /'trʌmpət ‖'trʌmpɪt/ n trompeta f

trumpeter /'trʌmpətər ‖'trʌmpɪtə(r)/ n trompetista mf, trompeta mf

truncheon /'trʌntʃən/ n (esp BrE) porra f, cachiporra f

trunk /trʌŋk/ n **1 (a)** (of tree) tronco m **(b)** (torso) tronco m **2** (of elephant) trompa f **3 (a)** (box) baúl m **(b)** (of car) (AmE) maletero m **4 trunks** pl (Clothing) (for swimming) traje m de baño or (Esp tb) bañador m ⟨de hombre⟩

truss /trʌs/ vt atar

■ **truss up** [v + o + adv, v + adv + o] atar

trust¹ /trʌst/ n **1 (a)** (confidence, faith) confianza f **(b)** (responsibility): **a position of ~** un puesto de confianza or responsabilidad **2** (Fin) **(a)** (money, property) fondo m de inversiones **(b)** (institution) fundación f **(c)** (custody) (Law) fideicomiso m

trust² vt **1** (have confidence in) ⟨person⟩ confiar* en, tener* confianza en; (in negative sentences) fiarse* de; **he can't be ~ed** no es de fiar; **to ~ sb WITH sth** confiarle* algo A algn **2** (hope, assume) (fml) esperar

■ **~** vi **to ~ IN sb/sth** confiar* or tener* confianza EN algn/algo

trusted /'trʌstəd ‖'trʌstɪd/ adj ⟨before n⟩ leal, de confianza

trustee /trʌs'tiː/ n **(a)** (of money, property) fideicomisario, -ria m,f, fiduciario, -ria m,f **(b)** (of institution) miembro m del consejo de administración

trust fund n fondo m fiduciario or de fideicomiso

trusting /'trʌstɪŋ/ adj confiado

trustworthy /'trʌst,wɜːrði ‖'trʌst,wɜːði/ adj ⟨colleague/child⟩ digno de confianza; ⟨account/witness⟩ fidedigno

truth /truːθ/ n (pl **~s** /truːðz/) **(a)** verdad f; (of account, story) veracidad f **(b)** (fact) verdad f

truthful /'truːθfəl/ adj ⟨person⟩ que dice la verdad, veraz; ⟨answer⟩ veraz

try¹ /traɪ/ n (pl **tries**) **1** (attempt) intento m, tentativa f **2** (in rugby) ensayo m

try² **tries, trying, tried** vt **1 (a)** (attempt) intentar; **to ~ to + INF** tratar DE + INF, intentar +

INF; **~ not to forget** procura no olvidarte **(b)** (attempt to operate): **he tried all the windows** probó a abrir todas las ventanas **2 (a)** ⟨product/technique/food⟩ probar*; **~ some** pruébalo, prueba un poquito **(b)** (have recourse to): **I'll ~ his work number** voy a probar a llamarlo al trabajo **3** (test, strain) ⟨courage/patience⟩ poner* a prueba **4** **to ~ one's luck at sth** probar* suerte con algo **5** (Law) ⟨person⟩ procesar, juzgar*; **to ~ sb FOR sth** juzgar* a algn POR algo

■ **~** vi (make attempt) intentar, probar; (make effort) esforzarse*; **you must ~ harder** tienes que esforzarte más

■ **try on** [v + o + adv, v + adv + o] probarse*

■ **try out** [v + o + adv, v + adv + o] ⟨product/method⟩ probar*; ⟨employee/player⟩ probar*, poner* a prueba; **to ~ sth out ON sb** probar* algo CON algn

trying /'traɪɪŋ/ adj ⟨day/experience⟩ duro

tsar /zɑːr ‖zɑː(r)/ n zar m

T-shirt /'tiːʃɜːrt ‖'tiːʃɜːt/ n camiseta f

tsp = **teaspoon(s)**

tub /tʌb/ n **(a)** (for holding liquids) cuba f; (for washing clothes) tina f **(b)** (bath~) bañera f, tina f (AmL) **(c)** (for ice cream) envase m ⟨gen de plástico⟩, tarrina f (Esp)

tuba /'tuːbə ‖'tjuːbə/ n tuba f

tubby /'tʌbi/ adj **-bier, -biest** (colloq) rechoncho (fam)

tube /tuːb ‖tjuːb/ n **1** (pipe, container) tubo m **2** (television) (esp AmE colloq): **the ~** la tele (fam) **3** (BrE Transp colloq): **the ~** el metro, el subte (Arg)

tuber /'tuːbər ‖'tjuːbə(r)/ n (Bot) tubérculo m

tuberculosis /tʊˌbɜːrkjəˈləʊsəs ‖tjʊˌbɜːkjʊˈləʊsɪs/ n tuberculosis f

tubing /'tuːbɪŋ ‖'tjuːbɪŋ/ n tubería f

tubular /'tuːbjələr ‖'tjuːbjʊlə(r)/ adj tubular

TUC n (in UK) = **Trades Union Congress**

tuck¹ /tʌk/ n (fold, pleat) jareta f, alforza f (CS)

tuck² vt meter; **he ~ed the blanket under the mattress** metió bien la manta debajo del colchón

■ **tuck in** **1** [v + adv] (eat) (colloq) ponerse* a comer, atacar* (fam) **2** [v + o + adv, v + adv + o] **(a)** ⟨sheet⟩ meter; **~ your shirt in** métete la camisa por dentro (de los pantalones) **(b)** ⟨child⟩ arropar

■ **tuck up** [v + o + adv] **to ~ sb up** (in bed) arropar a algn (en la cama)

tuckered out /'tʌkərd ‖'tʌkəd/ adj (AmE colloq) ⟨pred⟩ molido (fam), hecho polvo (fam)

Tuesday /'tuːzdeɪ, -di ‖'tjuːzdeɪ, -di/ n martes m; see also MONDAY

tuft /tʌft/ n **(a)** (of hair) mechón m; (on top of head) copete m **(b)** (of grass) mata f

tug¹ /tʌg/ **-gg-** vt tirar de, jalar (de) (AmL exc CS)

■ **~** vi **to ~ AT sth** tirar DE algo, jalar (DE) algo (AmL exc CS)

tug² n **1** (pull) tirón m, jalón m (AmL exc CS) **2** (Naut) remolcador m

tug of war n: juego de tira y afloja con una cuerda

tuition /tʊˈɪʃən ‖tjuːˈɪʃən/ n **(a)** (instruction) (fml) **~** ⟨IN sth⟩ clases fpl ⟨DE algo⟩; **private ~** clases fpl particulares **(b)** (fees) matrícula f

tulip /'tu:ləp ‖'tju:lɪp/ n tulipán m

tumble¹ /'tʌmbəl/ n (fall) caída f

tumble² vi **1** (fall) caerse* **2** (roll, turn) «acrobat» dar* volteretas

tumble: ~down adj (before n) en ruinas; **~dryer** /'tʌmbəl'draɪər ‖'tʌmbəl,draɪə(r)/ n secadora f

tumbler /'tʌmblər ‖'tʌmblə(r)/ n (glass) vaso m (de lados rectos)

tummy /'tʌmi/ n (pl **-mies**) (used to or by children) barriga f (fam), pancita f (fam), tripita f (fam)

tumor, (BrE) **tumour** /'tu:mər ‖'tju:mə(r)/ n tumor m

tumult /'tu:mʌlt ‖'tju:mʌlt/ n tumulto m

tumultuous /tʊ'mʌltʃuəs ‖tjʊ'mʌltjʊəs/ adj «applause» apoteósico; «protest» tumultuoso

tuna /'tu:nə ‖'tju:nə/ n (pl **~** or **~s**) atún m

tundra /'tʌndrə/ n tundra f

tune¹ /tu:n ‖tju:n/ n (a) (melody) melodía f; (piece) canción f, tonada f; **to change one's ~** cambiar de parecer (b) (correct pitch): **to be in/out of ~** estar* afinado/desafinado

tune² vt (a) (Mus) afinar (b) (Auto) poner* a punto, afinar (c) (Rad, TV) sintonizar*
■ **tune in** [v + adv] **to ~ in to sth** sintonizar* (con) algo

tuneful /'tu:nfəl ‖'tju:nfəl/ adj melódico

tuner /'tu:nər ‖'tju:nə(r)/ n (a) (piano **~**) (Mus) afinador, -dora m,f de pianos (b) (Rad) sintonizador m

tunic /'tu:nɪk ‖'tju:nɪk/ n (a) (of military uniform) guerrera f (b) (in ancient Rome) túnica f

tuning fork /'tu:nɪŋ ‖'tju:nɪŋ/ n diapasón m

Tunisia /tu:'ni:ʒə ‖tju:'nɪzɪə/ n Túnez m

Tunisian /tu:'ni:ʒən ‖tju:'nɪzɪən/ adj tunecino

tunnel¹ /'tʌnl/ n túnel m; (in mine) galería f, socavón m

tunnel², (BrE) vi **-ll-** abrir* or hacer* un túnel

turban /'tɜ:rbən ‖'tɜ:bən/ n turbante m

turbid /'tɜ:rbəd ‖'tɜ:bɪd/ adj turbio

turbine /'tɜ:rbən, -baɪn ‖'tɜ:baɪn/ n turbina f

turbo /'tɜ:rbəʊ ‖'tɜ:bəʊ/ n turbocompresor m, turbo m

turbulence /'tɜ:rbjələns ‖'tɜ:bjʊləns/ n turbulencia f

turbulent /'tɜ:rbjələnt ‖'tɜ:bjʊlənt/ adj turbulento

tureen /tjʊ'ri:n, tə- ‖tjʊə'ri:n/ n sopera f

turf¹ /tɜ:rf ‖tɜ:f/ n (pl **~s** or **turves**) (a) (grass) césped m (b) (square of grass) (esp BrE) tepe m

turf² vt «garden» encespedar, colocar* tepes en

turgid /'tɜ:rdʒəd ‖'tɜ:dʒɪd/ adj «prose» ampuloso

Turk /tɜ:rk ‖tɜ:k/ n turco, -ca m,f

turkey /'tɜ:rki ‖'tɜ:ki/ n (pl **~s**) pavo m, guajolote m (Méx)

Turkey /'tɜ:rki ‖'tɜ:ki/ n Turquía f

Turkish¹ /'tɜ:rkɪʃ ‖'tɜ:kɪʃ/ adj turco

Turkish² n turco m

Turkish: ~ bath n baño m turco; **~ delight** n delicia f turca (dulce gelatinoso recubierto de azúcar)

Turkmenistan /,tɜ:rkmenɪ'stɑ:n ‖,tɜ:kmenɪ'stɑ:n/ n Turkmenistán m

turmeric /'tɜ:rmərɪk ‖'tɜ:mərɪk/ n cúrcuma f

turmoil /'tɜ:rmɔɪl ‖'tɜ:mɔɪl/ n confusión f

turn¹ /tɜ:rn ‖tɜ:n/ n **1** (a) (rotation) vuelta f; the meat was done to a ~ la carne estaba hecha a la perfección, la carne estaba en su punto justo (b) (change of direction) vuelta f, giro m (c) (bend) curva f (d) (change, alteration): this dramatic ~ of events este dramático giro de los acontecimientos; **to take a ~ for the better** empezar* a mejorar; **to take a ~ for the worse** empeorar, ponerse* peor; **the ~ of the century** el final del siglo (y el principio del siguiente)
2 (place in sequence): **whose ~ is it?** ¿a quién le toca?; **I think it's my ~** creo que me toca (el turno) a mí; **to take ~s** o **to take it in ~(s)** turnarse
3 (service): **to do sb a good ~** hacerle* un favor a algn
4 (bout of illness): **he had a funny ~** le dio un ataque (or un mareo etc)

turn² vt **1** (rotate) «knob/wheel/key» (hacer*) girar
2 (change position, direction of) «head» volver*, voltear (AmL exc RPl); **she ~ed her back on them** les volvió or les dio la espalda, les volteó la espalda (AmL exc RPl); **the nurse ~ed her onto her side** la enfermera la puso de lado;
3 (reverse) «mattress/omelette» darle* la vuelta a, voltear (AmL exc CS), dar* vuelta (CS); «page» pasar, volver*, dar* vuelta (CS)
4 (a) (go around) «corner» dar* la vuelta a, dar* vuelta (CS) (b) (pass): **she's just ~ed 16** acaba de cumplir (los) 16
5 (change, transform) volver*; **to ~ sth TO/INTO sth** transformar or convertir* algo EN algo
6 (shape — on lathe) tornear; (— on potter's wheel) hacer*
■ **~** vi **1** (rotate) «handle/wheel» girar, dar* vuelta(s)
2 (a) (to face in different direction) «person» volverse*, darse* la vuelta, voltearse (AmL exc CS), darse* vuelta (CS); «car» dar* la vuelta, dar* vuelta (CS); **he ~ed onto his side** se volvió or se puso de lado (b) (change course, direction): **to ~ into a side street** meterse en una calle lateral; **to ~ left/right** girar or doblar or torcer* a la izquierda/derecha (c) (curve) «road/river» torcer*
3 (a) (focus on): **to ~ to another subject** pasar a otro tema; **his mind ~ed to thoughts of escape** se puso a pensar en escaparse (b) (have recourse to): **to ~ to sb** (for protection, advice) recurrir a algn; **to ~ to drink** darse* a la bebida
4 (a) (become): **his face ~ed red** se le puso la cara colorada; **her hair had ~ed gray** había encanecido (b) (be transformed) **to ~ INTO/TO sth** convertirse* EN algo (c) (change) «luck/weather/tide» cambiar (d) (go sour) «milk» agriarse*
5 (when reading): **~ to page 19** vayan a la página 19
■ **turn against** [v + o + prep + o]: **she ~ed them against me** los puso en mi contra
■ **turn around,** (BrE also) **turn round 1** [v + adv] darse* la vuelta, volverse*, voltearse (AmL exc CS), darse* vuelta (CS)
2 [v + o + adv] darle* la vuelta a, voltear (AmL exc CS), dar* vuelta (CS)

■ **turn aside** [*v* + *adv*] darse* la vuelta, voltearse (AmL exc CS), darse* vuelta (CS)

■ **turn away** [1] [*v* + *adv*] apartarse
[2] [*v* + *o* + *adv*, *v* + *adv* + *o*] **(a)** ‹*head/face*› volver*, voltear (AmL exc RPl), dar* vuelta (CS); **he ~ed his eyes away** apartó la mirada **(b)** (send away) ‹*business*› no aceptar; **the doorman ~ed them away** el portero no los dejó entrar

■ **turn back** [1] [*v* + *adv*] (go back) volver*, regresar
[2] [*v* + *o* + *adv*, *v* + *adv* + *o*]: **he was ~ed back at the border** en la frontera lo hicieron regresar

■ **turn down** [*v* + *o* + *adv*, *v* + *adv* + *o*] **(a)** (fold back) doblar **(b)** (diminish) ‹*heating/volume/ temperature*› bajar **(c)** (reject) ‹*offer/candidate*› rechazar*

■ **turn in** [1] [*v* + *adv*] (go to bed) (colloq) acostarse*
[2] [*v* + *o* + *adv*, *v* + *adv* + *o*] (hand in, over) entregar*

■ **turn off** [1] [*v* + *o* + *adv*, *v* + *adv* + *o*] ‹*light/ radio/heating*› apagar*; ‹*faucet*› cerrar*; ‹*water*› cortar
[2] [*v* + *adv*] **(a)** (from road) doblar **(b)** (switch off) apagarse*

■ **turn on** [1] [*v* + *o* + *adv*, *v* + *adv* + *o*] **(a)** ‹*light/television/oven*› encender*, prender (AmL); ‹*faucet*› abrir* **(b)** (excite) (colloq) gustar; (sexually) excitar
[2] [*v* + *prep* + *o*] (attack) atacar*

■ **turn out** [1] [*v* + *o* + *adv*, *v* + *adv* + *o*] **(a)** (switch off) ‹*light*› apagar* **(b)** (empty) ‹*pockets/ cupboard*› vaciar*
[2] [*v* + *adv* + *o*] (produce) sacar*
[3] [*v* + *o* + *adv*, *v* + *adv* + *o*] (force to leave) echar
[4] [*v* + *adv*] **(a)** (attend): **several thousand ~ed out to welcome the Pope** varios miles de personas acudieron *or* fueron/vinieron a recibir al Papa **(b)** (result, prove): **everything ~ed out well** todo salió bien

■ **turn over** [1] [*v* + *o* + *adv*] **(a)** (flip, reverse) darle* la vuelta a, voltear (AmL exc CS), dar* vuelta (CS); ‹*soil*› remover*; ‹*idea*› darle* vueltas a **(b)** (Auto) ‹*engine*› hacer* funcionar
[2] [*v* + *o* + *adv*, *v* + *adv* + *o*] (hand over) entregar*
[3] [*v* + *adv* + *o*] ‹*page*› pasar, volver*, dar* vuelta (CS)
[4] [*v* + *adv*] (onto other side) darse* la vuelta, darse* vuelta (CS); «*car*» volcarse*

■ **turn round** (esp BrE) ▸ TURN AROUND

■ **turn up** [1] [*v* + *o* + *adv*, *v* + *adv* + *o*] **(a)** ‹*collar*› levantarse, subirse **(b)** (shorten) ‹*trousers*› acortar; ‹*hem*› subir **(c)** (increase) ‹*oven/volume*› subir; ‹*radio*› subir el volumen de
[2] [*v* + *adv*] (colloq) **(a)** (be found) «*sth lost*» aparecer* **(b)** (arrive) (BrE) llegar*; **she didn't ~ up** no apareció

turn: **~about, ~around** *n* giro *m*, cambio *m*; **~coat** *n* renegado, -da *m,f*

turned-up /'tɜːrnd'ʌp ‖ ˌtɜːnd'ʌp/ *adj* ‹*nose*› respingón, respingado (AmL)

turning /'tɜːrnɪŋ ‖ 'tɜːnɪŋ/ *n* (in town) bocacalle *f*; **we've missed the ~** nos hemos pasado la calle (*or* carretera *etc*)

turning point *n* momento *m* decisivo *or* crucial

turnip /'tɜːrnəp ‖ 'tɜːnɪp/ *n* nabo *m*

turn: **~out** *n* (at election) número *m* de votantes; (at public spectacle) número *m* de asistentes;

~over *n* [1] **(a)** (volume of business, sales) facturación *f* **(b)** (of stock) rotación *f* **(c)** (of staff) movimiento *m* [2] (Culin) empanada *f* (esp AmL), empanadilla *f* (esp Esp); **~pike** *n* (AmE) autopista *f* de peaje *or* (Méx) de cuota; **~ signal** *n* (AmE) intermitente *m* direccional *f* (Col, Méx), señalizador *m* (de viraje) (Chi); **~stile** *n* torniquete *m*; **~table** *n* (Audio) (platter) plato *m*; (deck) platina *f*, tornamesa *f or m* (AmL); **~up** *n* **(a)** (hem) dobladillo *m* **(b)** (on trousers) (BrE) vuelta *f or* (RPl) botamanga *f or* (Chi) bastilla *f or* (Méx) valenciana *f*

turpentine /'tɜːrpəntaɪn ‖ 'tɜːpəntaɪn/ *n* aguarrás *m*, trementina *f*

turquoise /'tɜːrkwɔɪz ‖ 'tɜːkwɔɪz/ *adj* (azul) turquesa *adj inv*

turret /'tɜːrət ‖ 'tʌrɪt/ *n* torrecilla *f*

turtle /'tɜːrt̬l ‖ 'tɜːtl/ *n* **(a)** (marine reptile) tortuga *f* marina *or* de mar **(b)** (tortoise) tortuga *f*

turtleneck /'tɜːrt̬lnek ‖ 'tɜːtlnek/ *n* **(a)** **~ (collar)** cuello *m* alto **(b)** **~ (sweater)** suéter *m* de cuello vuelto

turves /tɜːrvz ‖ tɜːvz/ *pl of* TURF[1]

tusk /tʌsk/ *n* colmillo *m*

tussle /'tʌsəl/ *n* pelea *f*, lucha *f*

tut /tʌt/ *vi* **-tt-** chasquear la lengua

tutor /'tuːtər ‖ 'tjuːtə(r)/ *n* profesor, -sora *m,f* particular

tutorial /tuːˈtɔːriəl ‖ tjuːˈtɔːriəl/ *n*: clase *f* individual o con un pequeño número de estudiantes

tutu /'tuːtuː/ *n* (*pl* **~s**) tutú *m*

tuxedo /tʌkˈsiːdəʊ/ *n* (*pl* **-dos** *or* **-does**) (AmE) esmoquin *m*, smoking *m*

TV *n* (= television) televisión *f*, tele *f* (fam), TV *f*

twang /twæŋ/ *n* (of guitar) tañido *m*; (of voice, accent): **his voice has a nasal ~** tiene la voz gangosa

tweak /twiːk/ *vt* pellizcar* (*retorciendo*)

twee /twiː/ *adj* (BrE) cursi

tweed /twiːd/ *n* (Tex) tweed *m*

tweet /twiːt/ *vi* piar*, gorjear

tweezers /'twiːzərz ‖ 'twiːzəz/ *pl n* pinza(s) *f(pl)*

twelfth[1] /twelfθ/ *adj* duodécimo

twelfth[2] *adv* en duodécimo lugar

twelfth[3] *n* (Math) doceavo *m*; (part) doceava parte *f*

Twelfth Night *n* Noche *f* de Reyes

twelve /twelv/ *adj/n* doce *adj inv/m*; **~ (o'clock)** midnight/noon las doce de la noche/del mediodía; *see also* FOUR[1]

twentieth[1] /'twentiəθ/ *adj* vigésimo

twentieth[2] *adv* en vigésimo lugar

twentieth[3] *n* (Math) veinteavo *m*; (part) veinteava *or* vigésima parte *f*

twenty /'twenti/ *adj/n* veinte *adj inv/m*; *see also* FOUR[1]

twenty-first[1] /'twenti'fɜːrst ‖ ˌtwenti'fɜːst/ *adj* vigesimoprimero

twenty-first[2] *adv* en vigesimoprimer lugar

twice /twaɪs/ *adv* dos veces; **~ a year** dos veces por año; **to think ~** pensarlo* dos veces; **~ three is six** dos por tres es (igual a) seis; **I've got ~ as many as you** yo tengo el doble que tú

twiddle /'twɪdl/ *vt* (hacer*) girar ⋯▸

■ ~ *vi* to ~ WITH sth juguetear CON algo

twig /twɪg/ *n* ramita *f*

twilight /'twaɪlaɪt/ *n* **(a)** (dusk) crepúsculo *m* **(b)** (half-light) penumbra *f* **(c)** (period of decline) (liter) crepúsculo *m* (liter)

twin¹ /twɪn/ *n* mellizo, -za *m,f*, gemelo, -la *m,f* (esp Esp); **identical ~s** gemelos idénticos *or* (téc) univitelinos, gemelos (AmL)

twin² *adj* **(a)** ‹brother/sister› mellizo, gemelo (esp Esp) **(b)** (paired): ~ **beds** camas *fpl* gemelas

twin³ *vt* **-nn-** (BrE) (*usu pass*) **to be ~ned** WITH sth estar* hermanado CON algo

twine¹ /twaɪn/ *n* cordel *m*, bramante *m* (Esp), cáñamo *m* (Andes), mecate *m* (AmC, Méx, Ven)

twine² *vi* to ~ AROUND sth enroscarse* ALREDEDOR DE algo

twinge /twɪndʒ/ *n* (of pain) punzada *f*, puntada *f* (CS); (of remorse) puntada *f*

twinkle¹ /'twɪŋkəl/ *n* **(a)** (of lights, stars) centelleo *m*, titilar *m* **(b)** (in eye) brillo *m*

twinkle² *vi* **(a)** «light/star» titilar, centellear **(b)** «eyes» brillar

twinkling /'twɪŋklɪŋ/ *n*: **in the ~ of an eye** en un abrir y cerrar de ojos

twirl /twɜːrl ‖ twɜːl/ *vt* ‹cane/baton› (hacer*) girar
■ ~ *vi* «baton» girar; **to ~ around** girar

twist¹ /twɪst/ *vt* **1** **(a)** (screw, coil) retorcer*; **to ~ sth** AROUND **sth** enrollar *or* enroscar* algo ALREDEDOR DE algo **(b)** (turn) ‹handle/knob› girar **2** **(a)** (distort) retorcer* **(b)** (sprain) torcer* **(c)** (alter, pervert) ‹words› tergiversar; ‹meaning› torcer*
■ ~ *vi* **(a)** (wind, coil) «rope/wire» enrollarse, enroscarse*; «road/river» serpentear **(b)** (turn, rotate) girar

twist² *n* **1** **(a)** (bend — in wire, rope) vuelta *f*, onda *f*; (— in road) recodo *m*, vuelta *f* **(b)** (turning movement) giro *m* **(c)** **a ~ of lemon** una rodajita de limón (retorcida) **2** (in story, events) giro *m* inesperado **3** (dance) twist *m*

twisted /'twɪstɪd/ *adj* retorcido

twister /'twɪstər ‖ 'twɪstə(r)/ *n* (AmE colloq) tornado *m*

twit /twɪt/ *n* (BrE colloq) imbécil *mf*

twitch¹ /twɪtʃ/ *vi* «tail/nose» moverse*

twitch² *n* tic *m*

twitter /'twɪtər ‖ 'twɪtə(r)/ *vi* **(a)** «birds» gorjear **(b)** «person» parlotear, cotorrear (fam)

two¹ /tuː/ *n* dos *m*; ~ **by** ~ (liter) de dos en dos, de a dos (AmL); **to put ~ and ~ together** atar cabos; *see also* FOUR¹

two² *adj* dos *adj inv*

two: ~**-bit** *adj* (AmE) (before *n*) (colloq) de tres al

cuarto (fam); ~**-dimensional** /'tuːdə'mentʃnəl, -daɪ- ‖ ,tuːdɪ'menʃən̩l, -daɪ-/ *adj* bidimensional; ~**-edged** /'tuː'edʒd/ *adj* de doble filo; ~**-faced** /'tuː'feɪst/ *adj* (colloq) falso, doble (Andes, Ven fam); ~**fold** *adj/adv* ▶ -FOLD; ~**pence** /'tʌpəns/ *n* dos peniques *mpl*; ~**-piece** *adj* ‹swimsuit› de dos piezas; ~**-piece suit** traje *m or* (Col) vestido *m* de dos piezas, ambo *m* (CS); ~**-seater** /'tuː'siːtər ‖ 'tuː'siːtə(r)/ *n* biplaza

twosome /'tuːsəm/ *n* (pair) pareja *f*

two: ~**-time** *vt* (colloq) (be unfaithful to) ponerle* *or* meterle los cuernos a (fam); (double-cross) engañar; ~**-tone** *adj* de dos tonos; ~**-way** /'tuː'weɪ/ *adj* ‹traffic/street› de doble sentido *or* dirección; ‹agreement› bilateral; ~**-way radio** aparato *m* emisor y receptor

TX = **Texas**

tycoon /taɪ'kuːn/ *n* magnate *mf*

tympani /'tɪmpəni/ *pl n* timbales *mpl*

type¹ /taɪp/ *n* **1** **(a)** (sort, kind) tipo *m*; **it's a ~ of ...** (in descriptions, definitions) es una especie de ... **(b)** (typical example) tipo *m*, ejemplo *m* típico; (stereotype) estereotipo *m* **2** (Print) (characters) tipo *m* (de imprenta)

type² *vt/i* escribir* a máquina, tipear (AmS)

type: ~**cast** *vt* (past & past p **-cast**) ‹actor› encasillar (en cierto tipo de papel); ~**face** *n* tipo *m* (de), (tipo *m* de) caracteres *mpl*, (tipo *m* de) letra *f*; ~**script** *n* texto *m* mecanografiado, manuscrito *m* (de una obra, novela etc); ~**set** *vt* (pres *p* **-setting**; past & past *p* **-set**) componer*; ~**setter** /'taɪpsetər ‖ 'taɪpsetə(r)/ *n* (person) cajista *mf*, componedor, -dora *m,f*; ~**write** (past **-wrote**; past *p* **-written**) *vt* (usu pass) escribir* a máquina, mecanografiar*; ~**writer** *n* máquina *f* de escribir

typhoid (fever) /'taɪfɔɪd/ *n* (fiebre *f*) tifoidea

7typhoon /taɪ'fuːn/ *n* tifón *m*

typical /'tɪpɪkəl/ *adj* típico

typically /'tɪpɪkli/ *adv* típicamente

typify /'tɪpəfaɪ ‖ 'tɪpɪfaɪ/ *vt* **-fies, -fying, -fied** tipificar*

typing /'taɪpɪŋ/ *n* mecanografía *f*, (before *n*) ‹error› de máquina; ‹lesson› de mecanografía

typist /'taɪpəst ‖ 'taɪpɪst/ *n* mecanógrafo, -fa *m,f*, dactilógrafo, -fa *m,f*

typography /taɪ'pɑːgrəfi ‖ taɪ'pɒgrəfi/ *n* tipografía *f*

tyrannical /tə'rænɪkəl ‖ tɪ'rænɪkəl/ *adj* tiránico

tyranny /'tɪrəni/ *n* tiranía *f*

tyrant /'taɪrənt/ *n* tirano, -na *m,f*

tyre /taɪr ‖ 'taɪə(r)/ *n* (BrE) ▶ TIRE²

Uu

U, u /juː/ n U, u f

U (in UK) (Cin) (= **universal**) apta para todo público (AmL), todos los públicos (Esp)

U, u /juː/ n U, u f

ubiquitous /juːˈbɪkwətəs ‖juːˈbɪkwɪtəs/ adj omnipresente (frml), ubicuo (liter)

udder /ˈʌdər ‖ˈʌdə(r)/ n ubre f

UFO n (= **unidentified flying object**) ovni m, OVNI m

Uganda /juːˈgændə/ n Uganda f

Ugandan /juːˈgændən/ adj ugandés

ugly /ˈʌgli/ adj **uglier, ugliest** feo

UHT adj (BrE) (= **ultra high temperature**) UHT, UAT (AmL), uperizado (Esp)

UK n (= **United Kingdom**) RU m

Ukraine /juːˈkreɪn/ n Ucrania f

Ukrainian¹ /juːˈkreɪniən/ adj ucraniano, ucranio

Ukrainian² n (a) (person) ucraniano, -na m,f, ucranio, -nia m,f (b) (language) ucraniano m, ucranio m

ulcer /ˈʌlsər ‖ˈʌlsə(r)/ n (internal) úlcera f; (external) llaga f; **a mouth** ∼ una llaga en la boca

ulterior /ʌlˈtɪriər ‖ʌlˈtɪəriə(r)/ adj oculto; ∼ **motive** segunda intención f, motivo m oculto

ultimata /ˈʌltəˈmeɪtə ‖ˌʌltɪˈmeɪtə/ pl of **ULTIMATUM**

ultimate¹ /ˈʌltəmət ‖ˈʌltɪmət/ adj **1** (eventual) ⟨aim/destination⟩ final **2 (a)** (utmost, supreme) ⟨sacrifice⟩ máximo, supremo **(b)** (most sophisticated) (journ): **the** ∼ **sound system** lo último en sistemas de sonido, el no va más en sistemas de sonido (fam)

ultimate² n: **the** ∼ **in sth** lo último en algo, el no va más en algo (fam)

ultimately /ˈʌltəmətli ‖ˈʌltɪmətli/ adv **(a)** (finally) en última instancia **(b)** (in the long run) a la larga

ultimatum /ˈʌltəˈmeɪtəm ‖ˌʌltɪˈmeɪtəm/ n (pl **-tums** or **-ta**) ultimátum m

ultra- /ˈʌltrə/ pref ultra-, super- (fam)

ultrasonic /ˈʌltrəˈsɑːnɪk ‖ˌʌltrəˈsɒnɪk/ adj ultrasónico

ultrasound /ˈʌltrəsaʊnd/ n **(a)** (Phys) ultrasonido m **(b)** (Med) ecografía f

ultraviolet /ˈʌltrəˈvaɪələt/ adj ultravioleta adj inv

umbilical cord /əmˈbɪlɪkəl ‖ʌmˈbɪlɪkəl/ n cordón m umbilical

umbrage /ˈʌmbrɪdʒ/ n: **to take** ∼ (AT sth) ofenderse or sentirse* agraviado (POR algo)

umbrella /ʌmˈbrelə/ n (pl **-las**) paraguas m

umpire /ˈʌmpaɪr ‖ˈʌmpaɪə(r)/ n árbitro, -tra m,f; (in baseball) umpire mf

umpteen /ˈʌmpˈtiːn/ adj (colloq) tropecientos (fam), miles or un millón de

umpteenth /ˈʌmpˈtiːnθ/ adj (colloq) enésimo; **for the** ∼ **time** por enésima vez

un- /ʌn/ pref in-, des-, no, sin, poco; see individual words

UN n (= **United Nations**) ONU f

unable /ʌnˈeɪbəl/ adj (pred) **to be** ∼ **to** + INF no poder* + INF

unabridged /ˈʌnəˈbrɪdʒd/ adj íntegro

unacceptable /ˈʌnəkˈseptəbəl/ adj ⟨conduct/ standard⟩ inaceptable, inadmisible; ⟨terms/ conditions⟩ inadmisible

unaccompanied /ˈʌnəˈkʌmpənid/ adj **(a)** ⟨luggage⟩ no acompañado; ⟨person⟩ solo **(b)** (Mus) ⟨singing⟩ sin acompañamiento; ⟨instrument⟩ solo

unaccounted for /ˈʌnəˈkaʊntəd ‖ˌʌnəˈkaʊntɪd/ adj (pred): **the rest of the money is** ∼ ∼ no se han dado explicaciones sobre qué sucedió con el resto del dinero; **the others are still** ∼ ∼ los otros siguen su aparecer

unaccustomed /ˈʌnəˈkʌstəmd/ adj **(a)** (unusual) desacostumbrado, poco habitual **(b)** (unused) **to be** ∼ **TO sth**/**-ING** no estar* acostumbrado A algo/+ INF

unadventurous /ˈʌnədˈventʃərəs/ adj poco atrevido or audaz

unaffected /ˈʌnəˈfektəd ‖ˌʌnəˈfektɪd/ adj **(a)** (sincere, natural) ⟨person⟩ natural, sencillo **(b)** (not damaged, hurt) no afectado

unaided /ʌnˈeɪdəd ‖ʌnˈeɪdɪd/ adj sin ayuda

unambitious /ˈʌnæmˈbɪʃəs/ adj poco ambicioso

unanimous /juːˈnænəməs ‖juːˈnænɪməs/ adj unánime

unanimously /juːˈnænəməsli ‖juːˈnænɪməsli/ adv ⟨vote/state⟩ unánimemente; ⟨elect⟩ por unanimidad

unanswered /ʌnˈænsərd ‖ʌnˈɑːnsəd/ adj ⟨question/letter⟩ sin contestar

unappetizing /ʌnˈæpətaɪzɪŋ/ adj ⟨dish/smell⟩ poco apetitoso; ⟨prospect⟩ poco apetecible

unappreciative /ˈʌnəˈpriːʃətɪv/ adj ⟨person⟩ ingrato, desagradecido

unapproachable /ˈʌnəˈprəʊtʃəbəl/ adj ⟨person⟩ inabordable, poco accesible or asequible

unarmed /ʌnˈɑːrmd ‖ʌnˈɑːmd/ adj ⟨person⟩ desarmado; ⟨combat⟩ sin armas

unassisted /ˈʌnəˈsɪstəd ‖ˌʌnəˈsɪstɪd/ adj sin ayuda

unassuming /ˈʌnəˈsuːmɪŋ ‖ˌʌnəˈsjuːmɪŋ/ adj sencillo, sin pretensiones

unattached /ˈʌnəˈtætʃt/ adj **(a)** (not affiliated) independiente **(b)** (not married) sin ataduras

unattended /ˈʌnəˈtendəd ‖ˌʌnəˈtendɪd/ adj (usu pred) **(a)** (unwatched, unsupervised): **to leave sb** ∼ dejar a algn solo; **don't leave your luggage** ∼ vigile su equipaje en todo momento **(b)** (not dealt with) desatendido

unattractive /ˈʌnəˈtræktɪv/ adj poco atractivo

unauthorized /ˌʌnˈɔːθəraɪzd/ adj no autorizado

unavailable /ˌʌnəˈveɪləbəl/ adj: that number is ~ ese número está desconectado (or averiado etc); he is ~ for comment no desea hacer ningún comentario

unavoidable /ˌʌnəˈvɔɪdəbəl/ adj inevitable

unavoidably /ˌʌnəˈvɔɪdəbli/ adv: I was ~ delayed no pude evitar llegar retrasado

unaware /ˌʌnəˈwer ‖ ˌʌnəˈweə(r)/ adj (a) (not conscious) (pred) to be ~ OF sth ignorar algo, no ser* consciente DE algo (b) (naive): politically ~ sin conciencia política

unawares /ˌʌnəˈwerz ‖ ˌʌnəˈweəz/ adv: to catch o take sb ~ agarrar or (esp Esp) coger* a algn desprevenido

unbalanced /ˌʌnˈbælənst/ adj (a) ‹diet/composition› desequilibrado (b) (mentally) desequilibrado, trastornado

unbearable /ˌʌnˈberəbəl ‖ ˌʌnˈbeərəbəl/ adj insoportable, inaguantable

unbeatable /ˌʌnˈbiːtəbəl/ adj ‹team› invencible; ‹quality/value› insuperable; ‹price› imbatible

unbeaten /ˌʌnˈbiːtn̩/ adj ‹champion/army› invicto; ‹record› insuperado

unbeknown /ˌʌnbɪˈnəʊn/, **unbeknownst** /-ˈnəʊnst/ adv (liter): ~ to me/her sin saberlo yo/ella

unbelievable /ˌʌnbəˈliːvəbəl ‖ ˌʌnbɪˈliːvəbəl/ adj increíble

unbelievably /ˌʌnbəˈliːvəbli ‖ ˌʌnbɪˈliːvəbli/ adv increíblemente

unbelieving /ˌʌnbəˈliːvɪŋ ‖ ˌʌnbɪˈliːvɪŋ/ adj ‹smile/look› de incredulidad

unbending /ˌʌnˈbendɪŋ/ adj ‹person/attitude› inflexible; ‹determination› firme

unbiased /ˌʌnˈbaɪəst/ adj imparcial, objetivo

unblock /ˌʌnˈblɑːk ‖ ˌʌnˈblɒk/ vt desatascar*, destapar (AmL)

unbolt /ˌʌnˈbəʊlt/ vt ‹gate/door› descorrer el pestillo or cerrojo de

unborn /ˌʌnˈbɔːrn ‖ ˌʌnˈbɔːn/ adj ‹child› que todavía no ha nacido

unbreakable /ˌʌnˈbreɪkəbəl/ adj irrompible

unbridled /ˌʌnˈbraɪdl̩d/ adj desenfrenado

unbroken /ˌʌnˈbrəʊkən/ adj intacto, en perfecto estado; ‹silence/run› ininterrumpido

unbuckle /ˌʌnˈbʌkəl/ vt desabrochar

unbutton /ˌʌnˈbʌtn̩/ vt desabotonar, desabrochar

uncalled-for /ˌʌnˈkɔːldfɔːr ‖ ˌʌnˈkɔːldfɔː(r)/ adj ‹criticism/remark› fuera de lugar

uncanny /ˌʌnˈkæni/ adj raro, extraño

uncaring /ˌʌnˈkerɪŋ ‖ ˌʌnˈkeərɪŋ/ adj indiferente

unceremonious /ˌʌnˈserəˈməʊniəs ‖ ˌʌnˌserɪˈməʊniəs/ adj brusco, poco ceremonioso

uncertain /ˌʌnˈsɜːrtn̩ ‖ ˌʌnˈsɜːtn̩/ adj **1** (a) (unsure) (pred) to be ~ ABOUT/OF sth no estar* seguro DE algo (b) (hesitant) vacilante **2** ‹prospects/future› incierto **3** (vague): in no ~ terms muy claramente, inequívocamente

uncertainty /ˌʌnˈsɜːrtn̩ti ‖ ˌʌnˈsɜːtn̩ti/ n incertidumbre f

unchanged /ˌʌnˈtʃeɪndʒd/ adj (usu pred): she was quite ~ no había cambiado para nada; the ceremony has remained ~ for centuries la ceremonia se ha celebrado de la misma forma durante siglos

uncharacteristic /ˌʌnˌkærəktəˈrɪstɪk/ adj desacostumbrado, insusitado

uncharitable /ˌʌnˈtʃærətəbəl ‖ ˌʌnˈtʃærɪtəbəl/ adj ‹act/remark› poco caritativo

unchecked /ˌʌnˈtʃekt/ adj libre, sin obstáculos

uncivilized /ˌʌnˈsɪvəlaɪzd ‖ ˌʌnˈsɪvɪlaɪzd/ adj incivilizado

uncle /ˈʌŋkəl/ n tío m

unclean /ˌʌnˈkliːn/ adj impuro

unclear /ˌʌnˈklɪr ‖ ˌʌnˈklɪə(r)/ adj poco claro, confuso; he was ~ about his reasons for doing it no dio una explicación muy clara de sus motivos

uncoil /ˌʌnˈkɔɪl/ vi desenroscarse*

uncomfortable /ˌʌnˈkʌmfərtəbəl ‖ ˌʌnˈkʌmftəbəl/ adj incómodo

uncommon /ˌʌnˈkɑːmən ‖ ˌʌnˈkɒmən/ adj poco común or frecuente

uncommunicative /ˌʌnkəˈmjuːnəkeɪtɪv ‖ ˌʌnkəˈmjuːnɪkətɪv/ adj poco comunicativo

uncomplaining /ˌʌnkəmˈpleɪnɪŋ/ adj resignado

uncomplicated /ˌʌnˈkɑːmpləkeɪtəd ‖ ˌʌnˈkɒmplɪkeɪtɪd/ adj sin complicaciones; ‹character/style› poco complicado

uncompromising /ˌʌnˈkɑːmprəmaɪzɪŋ ‖ ˌʌnˈkɒmprəmaɪzɪŋ/ adj inflexible, intransigente

unconcerned /ˌʌnkənˈsɜːrnd ‖ ˌʌnkənˈsɜːnd/ adj indiferente

unconditional /ˌʌnkənˈdɪʃənəl ‖ ˌʌnkənˈdɪʃənl̩/ adj incondicional

unconnected /ˌʌnkəˈnektəd ‖ ˌʌnkəˈnektɪd/ adj (unrelated) sin conexión; these incidents are completely ~ estos incidentes no guardan ninguna relación (entre sí)

unconscious¹ /ˌʌnˈkɑːntʃəs ‖ ˌʌnˈkɒnʃəs/ **1** (Med) inconsciente **2** (unaware) (pred) to be ~ OF sth no ser* consciente DE algo **3** (Psych) inconsciente

unconscious² n the ~ el inconsciente

unconsciously /ˌʌnˈkɑːntʃəsli ‖ ˌʌnˈkɒnʃəsli/ adv inconscientemente

uncontested /ˌʌnkənˈtestəd ‖ ˌʌnkənˈtestɪd/ adj ‹will› no impugnado; ‹leader› indiscutible

uncontrollable /ˌʌnkənˈtrəʊləbəl/ adj ‹trembling› incontrolable; ‹urge› irresistible, irrefrenable; ‹laughter› incontenible

uncontrolled /ˌʌnkənˈtrəʊld/ adj incontrolado

unconventional /ˌʌnkənˈventʃənəl ‖ ˌʌnkənˈvenʃənl̩/ adj poco convencional

unconvinced /ˌʌnkənˈvɪnst/ adj: I'm still ~ aún no estoy muy convencida

unconvincing /ˌʌnkənˈvɪnsɪŋ/ adj poco convincente

uncoordinated /ˌʌnkəʊˈɔːrdn̩eɪtəd ‖ ˌʌnkəʊˈɔːdɪneɪtɪd/ adj ‹person› falto de coordinación; ‹movements› no coordinado

uncork /ˌʌnˈkɔːrk ‖ ˌʌnˈkɔːk/ vt descorchar

uncorroborated /'ʌnkə'rɑːbəreɪtəd ‖ ʌnkə'rɒbəreɪtɪd/ adj no confirmado, no corroborado

uncouth /ʌn'kuːθ/ adj zafio, burdo

uncover /ʌn'kʌvər ‖ ʌn'kʌvə(r)/ vt **(a)** (remove covering of) destapar **(b)** (expose) ⟨scandal/plot⟩ revelar, sacar* a la luz

unctuous /'ʌŋktʃuəs ‖ 'ʌŋktjuəs/ adj empalagoso

uncultivated /ʌn'kʌltəveɪtəd ‖ ʌn'kʌltɪveɪtɪd/ adj ⟨land/mind⟩ sin cultivar

uncurl /ʌn'kɜːrl ‖ ʌn'kɜːl/ vt desenrollar ■ ~ vi «snake» desenroscarse*

uncut /ʌn'kʌt/ adj ⒈ **(a)** ⟨grass/hedge⟩ sin cortar **(b)** ⟨diamond/gem⟩ sin tallar, en bruto; ⟨stone/marble⟩ sin labrar ⒉ (unabridged) íntegro, completo

undamaged /ʌn'dæmɪdʒd/ adj intacto

undaunted /ʌn'dɔːntəd ‖ ʌn'dɔːntɪd/ adj impertérrito

undecided /ʌndɪ'saɪdəd ‖ ʌndɪ'saɪdɪd/ adj **(a)** (wavering) (usu pred) indeciso **(b)** ⟨matter⟩ pendiente, no resuelto

undefeated /ʌndɪ'fiːtəd ‖ ʌndɪ'fiːtɪd/ adj invicto

undemanding /ʌndɪ'mændɪŋ ‖ ʌndɪ'mɑːndɪŋ/ adj ⟨job⟩ cómodo, que exige poco; ⟨person⟩ poco exigente

undeniable /ʌndɪ'naɪəbəl/ adj innegable

undeniably /ʌndɪ'naɪəbli/ adv sin lugar a dudas

under¹ /'ʌndər ‖ 'ʌndə(r)/ prep **(a)** (beneath) debajo de, abajo de (AmL) **(b)** (less than) menos de **(c)** ⟨name/heading⟩ bajo **(d)** ⟨government/ authority⟩ bajo; **he has 20 people** ~ **him** tiene 20 personas a su mando **(e)** (according to) según

under² adv ⒈ (less) menos; **it will cost $10 or** ~ costará 10 dólares como mucho ⒉ (under water): **they pushed him** ~ lo empujaron debajo del agua

under- /'ʌndər/ pref **(a)** (below, lower): **the** ~**mentioned** los abajo mencionados **(b)** (less than proper): **they are** ~**represented on the committee** no tienen la representación que les corresponde en la comisión **(c)** (of lesser rank) sub-; ~**manager** subgerente m

under: ~**age** /'ʌndər'eɪdʒ/ adj (before n) ⟨person⟩ menor de edad; ~**arm** adj (before n) (Sport) sin levantar el brazo por encima del hombro; ~**carriage** n tren m de aterrizaje; ~**charge** /'ʌndər'tʃɑːrdʒ ‖ ʌndə'tʃɑːdʒ/ vt cobrarle de menos a; ~**coat,** (AmE also) ~**coating** n ⒈ **(a)** (paint) pintura f base **(b)** (coating) primera mano f de pintura; ⒉ (AmE Auto) tratamiento m anticorrosivo del chasis; ~**cover** /'ʌndər'kʌvər ‖ ʌndə'kʌvə(r)/ adj secreto; ~**current** n **(a)** (of discontent) trasfondo m, corriente f subyacente **(b)** (of water) contracorriente f; ~**cut** /'ʌndər'kʌt ‖ ʌndə'kʌt/ vt (pres p -**cutting;** past & past p -**cut**) ⟨competitor⟩ vender más barato que; ~**developed** /ʌndərdɪ'veləpt ‖ ʌndədɪ'veləpt/ adj poco desarrollado; ⟨nation⟩ subdesarrollado; ~**done** /'ʌndər'dʌn ‖ ʌndə'dʌn/ adj ⟨meat⟩ poco cocido, poco hecho (Esp); ~**estimate** /'ʌndər'estəmeɪt ‖ ʌndər'estɪmeɪt/ vt **(a)** (guess too low): **they** ~**estimated the cost** calcularon el costo en menos de lo que correspondía **(b)**

(underrate) subestimar; ~**fed** /'ʌndər'fed ‖ ʌndə'fed/ adj subalimentado; ~**foot** /'ʌndər'fut ‖ ʌndə'fut/ adv debajo de los pies; ~**go** /'ʌndər'gəʊ ‖ ʌndə'gəʊ/ vt (3rd pers sing pres -**goes;** pres p -**going;** past -**went;** past p -**gone**) ⟨change/hardship⟩ sufrir; **he is** ~**going treatment** está en tratamiento; ~**graduate** /'ʌndər'grædʒuət ‖ ʌndə'grædʒuət/ n estudiante universitario, -ria m,f (de licenciatura); (before n) ⟨course/student⟩ universitario

underground¹ /'ʌndərgraʊnd ‖ 'ʌndəgraʊnd/ adj (before n) subterráneo; ⟨organization⟩ clandestino

underground² /'ʌndər'graʊnd ‖ ʌndə'graʊnd/ adv bajo tierra

underground³ /'ʌndər'graʊnd ‖ ʌndə'graʊnd/ n ⒈ also **Underground** (BrE Transp) metro m, subterráneo m (RPl) ⒉ (secret organization) movimiento m clandestino

under: ~**growth** n maleza f, monte m bajo; ~**hand** /'ʌndər'hænd ‖ ʌndə'hænd/, ~**handed** /'ʌndər'hændəd ‖ ʌndə'hændɪd/ adj ⟨person⟩ solapado; ⟨method/dealings⟩ poco limpio; ~**lie** /'ʌndər'laɪ ‖ ʌndə'laɪ/ vt (3rd pers sing pres -**lies;** pres p -**lying;** past -**lay;** past p -**lain**) subyacer* a; ~**line** vt subrayar; ~**lying** /'ʌndər'laɪɪŋ ‖ ʌndə'laɪɪŋ/ adj (before n) subyacente; ~**manned** /'ʌndər'mænd ‖ ʌndə'mænd/ adj ⟨factory⟩ con personal or con mano de obra insuficiente; ~**mine** /'ʌndər'maɪn ‖ ʌndə'maɪn/ vt ⟨health/strength⟩ minar; ⟨authority⟩ quitar

underneath¹ /'ʌndər'niːθ ‖ ʌndə'niːθ/ prep debajo de, abajo de (AmL)

underneath² adv debajo, abajo; ⟨dig/crawl⟩ por debajo, por abajo

under: ~**nourished** /'ʌndər'nɜːrɪʃt ‖ ʌndə'nʌrɪʃt/ adj desnutrido; ~**paid** /'ʌndər'peɪd ‖ ʌndə'peɪd/ adj mal pagado; ~**pants** pl n calzoncillos mpl, calzones mpl (Méx); ~**pass** n (for traffic) paso m inferior; pedestrian ~**pass** pasaje m subterráneo; ~**privileged** /'ʌndər'prɪvəlɪdʒd ‖ ʌndə'prɪvəlɪdʒd/ adj desfavorecido; ~**rate** /'ʌndər'reɪt ‖ ʌndə'reɪt/ vt ⟨ability/opponent⟩ subestimar **(b)** ~**rated** past p ⟨writer/play⟩ no debidamente apreciado or valorado; ~**secretary** /'ʌndər'sekrəteri ‖ ʌndə'sekrətri/ n subsecretario, -ria m,f; ~**sell** vt (past & past p -**sold**) ⟨competitor⟩ vender más barato que; ~**shirt** n (AmE) camiseta f (interior); ~**shorts** pl n (AmE) calzoncillos mpl (en forma de pantalón corto); ~**side** n parte f inferior or de abajo; ~**skirt** n enagua(s) f(pl), viso m, fondo m (Méx); ~**sold** /'ʌndər'səʊld ‖ ʌndə'səʊld/ past and past p of UNDERSELL; ~**staffed** /'ʌndər'stæft ‖ ʌndə'stɑːft/ adj: **to be** ~**staffed** estar* muy escaso or falto de personal

understand /'ʌndər'stænd ‖ ʌndə'stænd/ (past & past p -**stood**) vt ⒈ **(a)** (grasp meaning of) entender* **(b)** (sympathize, empathize with) comprender, entender* ⒉ (believe, infer): **I** ~ **you play tennis** tengo entendido que juega al tenis ■ ~ vi entender*, comprender

understandable /'ʌndər'stændəbəl ‖ ʌndə'stændəbəl/ adj comprensible

understanding¹ /'ʌndər'stændɪŋ ‖ ʌndə'stændɪŋ/ n ⒈ **(a)** (grasp) entendimiento ⋯⟩

m (b) (interpretation) interpretación *f* (c) (sympathy) comprensión *f* **2** (agreement, arrangement) acuerdo *m*; **we had an ~ that …** habíamos convenido que … **3** **on the ~ that** bien entendido que

understanding² *adj* comprensivo

understatement /'ʌndər'steɪtmənt ‖'ʌndəsteɪtmənt/ *n*: **to say it wasn't well attended is an ~** decir que no estuvo muy concurrido es quedarse corto

understood¹ /'ʌndər'stʊd ‖,ʌndə'stʊd/ *past & past p of* UNDERSTAND

understood² *adj* (assumed): **expenses will be paid, that's ~** se sobreentiende que nos (*or* les *etc*) pagarán los gastos

under: **~study** *n* suplente *mf*, sobresaliente *mf*; **~take** /'ʌndər'teɪk ‖,ʌndə'teɪk/ *vt* (*past* **-took**; *past p* **-taken**) (a) (*responsibility*) asumir; (*obligation*) contraer*; (*task*) emprender (b) **to ~take to + INF** comprometerse A + INF; **~taker** /'ʌndər'teɪkər ‖'ʌndə,teɪkə(r)/ *n* ▶ MORTICIAN; **~taking** /'ʌndər'teɪkɪŋ ‖,ʌndə'teɪkɪŋ/ *n* (a) (task) empresa *f*, tarea *f* (b) (promise) promesa *f*; **~tone** *n* (a) (low voice): **to speak in an ~tone** hablar en voz baja (b) (hint) trasfondo *m*; **~took** /'ʌndər'tʊk ‖,ʌndə'tʊk/ *past of* ~TAKE; **~value** /'ʌndər'vælju: ‖,ʌndə'vælju:/ *vt* (*goods*) subvalorar; (*person/skill*) subvalorar

underwater¹ /'ʌndər'wɔ:tər ‖,ʌndə'wɔ:tə(r)/ *adj* submarino

underwater² *adv* debajo del agua

under: **~wear** *n* ropa *f* interior; **~weight** /'ʌndər'weɪt ‖,ʌndə'weɪt/ *adj* (*person/baby*) de peso más bajo que el normal; **~went** /'ʌndər'went ‖,ʌndə'went/ *past of* UNDERGO; **~world** *n* (a) (Myth) **the U~world** el infierno, el averno (liter) (b) (criminals): **the ~world** el hampa, los bajos fondos; **~write** /'ʌndər'raɪt ‖,ʌndə'raɪt/ *vt* (*past* **-wrote**; *past p* **-written**) (a) (in insurance) asegurar (b) (guarantee financially) (*project/venture*) financiar

undeserving /'ʌndɪ'zɜ:rvɪŋ ‖,ʌndɪ'zɜ:vɪŋ/ *adj* (*person*) de poco mérito; (*cause*) poco meritorio

undesirable /'ʌndɪ'zaɪrəbəl ‖,ʌndɪ'zaɪərəbəl/ *adj* (*consequence*) no deseado; (*person*) indeseable

undeveloped /'ʌndɪ'veləpt/ *adj* (*resources/region*) sin explotar

undid /'ʌn'dɪd/ *past of* UNDO

undignified /'ʌn'dɪgnəfaɪd ‖'ʌn'dɪgnɪfaɪd/ *adj* (a) (lacking modesty) indecoroso (b) (inappropriate to status) poco digno

undisciplined /'ʌn'dɪsəplənd ‖,ʌn'dɪsɪplɪnd/ *adj* indisciplinado

undiscovered /'ʌndɪs'kʌvərd ‖,ʌndɪs'kʌvəd/ *adj* (not found) no descubierto; (unknown) desconocido

undisguised /'ʌndɪs'gaɪzd/ *adj* manifiesto, abierto

undisputed /'ʌndɪ'spju:təd ‖,ʌndɪ'spju:tɪd/ *adj* (*champion/leader*) indiscutido; (*facts*) innegable

undivided /'ʌndɪ'vaɪdəd ‖,ʌndɪ'vaɪdɪd/ *adj*: **you have my ~ attention** tienes toda mi atención

undo /'ʌn'du:/ *vt* (*3rd pers sing pres* **-does**; *pres p* **-doing**; *past* **-did**; *past p* **-done**) (*button/ jacket*) desabrochar; (*zipper*) abrir*; (*knot/parcel*) desatar, deshacer*; (*shoelaces*) desatar, desamarrar (AmL exc RPl)

undone /'ʌn'dʌn/ *adj* (*pred*) (a) (unfastened) desatado, desamarrado (AmL exc RPl) (b) (not started) sin empezar; (unfinished) sin terminar

undoubtedly /ʌn'daʊtədli ‖ʌn'daʊtɪdli/ *adv* indudablemente, sin duda

undress /'ʌn'dres/ *vt* desvestir*, desnudar; **to get ~ed** desvestirse*, desnudarse

undue /'ʌn'du: ‖'ʌn'dju:/ *adj* (before n) excesivo, demasiado

unduly /'ʌn'du:li ‖'ʌn'dju:li/ *adv* excesivamente, demasiado

unearth /'ʌn'ɜ:rθ ‖'ʌn'ɜ:θ/ *vt* (a) (*remains*) desenterrar* (b) (*fact/document*) descubrir*

unearthly /'ʌn'ɜ:rθli ‖'ʌn'ɜ:θli/ *adj* **-lier, -liest** sobrenatural; **at this ~ hour** a estas horas (intempestivas)

unease /'ʌn'i:z/ *n* (nervousness) inquietud *f*; (tension, discontent) malestar *m*

uneasy /'ʌn'i:zi/ *adj* **-sier, -siest** (a) (anxious, troubled) inquieto, preocupado (b) (awkward, constrained) (*laugh/silence*) incómodo, molesto

uneconomical /'ʌn'ekə'nɑ:mɪkl, -'i:kə- ‖,ʌn,i:kə'nɒmɪkəl, -,ek-/ *adj* poco económico

uneducated /'ʌn'edʒəkeɪtəd ‖,ʌn'edʒʊkeɪtɪd/ *adj* sin educación, inculto

unemotional /'ʌnɪ'məʊʃnəl ‖,ʌnɪ'məʊʃənl/ *adj* (*person*) indiferente; (*account/report*) objetivo

unemployable /'ʌnɪm'plɔɪəbəl/ *adj* inempleable

unemployed /'ʌnɪm'plɔɪd/ *adj* (*person*) desempleado, parado (Esp), en paro (Esp), cesante (Chi)

unemployment /'ʌnɪm'plɔɪmənt/ *n* (being out of work) desempleo *m*, paro *m* (Esp), cesantía *f* (Chi); (before n) **~ benefit** *o* (AmE also) **compensation** subsidio *m* de desempleo, paro *m* (Esp), subsidio *m* de desempleo

unending /'ʌn'endɪŋ/ *adj* interminable, sin fin

unenthusiastic /'ʌnɪn'θu:zi'æstɪk ‖,ʌnɪmθju:zi'æstɪk/ *adj* poco entusiasta

unenviable /'ʌn'enviəbəl/ *adj* nada envidiable

unequal /'ʌn'i:kwəl/ *adj* desigual

UNESCO /ju:'neskəʊ/ *n* (*no art*) (= **United Nations Educational, Scientific and Cultural Organization**) la UNESCO

unethical /ʌn'eθɪkəl/ *adj* inmoral, poco ético

uneven /'ʌn'i:vən/ *adj* **1** (a) (not straight) torcido (b) (not level) (*surface*) desigual, irregular, disparejo (AmL); (*ground*) desnivelado, desigual, disparejo (AmL) **2** (*color/paint*) poco uniforme, disparejo (AmL) **3** (unequal) (*widths/lengths/contest*) desigual

uneventful /ˌʌnɪˈventfəl/ *adj* ⟨*journey*⟩ sin incidentes; ⟨*day*⟩ tranquilo; ⟨*life*⟩ sin acontecimientos de nota

unexciting /ˌʌnɪkˈsaɪtɪŋ/ *adj* ⟨*prospect/job*⟩ poco estimulante; ⟨*food*⟩ insulso, poco apetitoso

unexpected /ˌʌnɪkˈspektəd ‖ ˌʌnɪkˈspektɪd/ *adj* ⟨*reaction/visitor*⟩ inesperado; ⟨*result/delay*⟩ imprevisto

unexpectedly /ˌʌnɪkˈspektədli ‖ ˌʌnɪkˈspektɪdli/ *adv* ⟨*arrive*⟩ de improviso; ⟨*happen*⟩ de forma imprevista

unexploded /ˌʌnɪkˈspləʊdəd/ *adj* sin detonar

unexplored /ˌʌnɪkˈsplɔːrd ‖ ˌʌnɪksˈplɔːd/ *adj* inexplorado

unfailing /ʌnˈfeɪlɪŋ/ *adj* ⟨*optimism*⟩ indefectible, a toda prueba; ⟨*interest/support*⟩ constante

unfair /ʌnˈfer ‖ ʌnˈfeə(r)/ *adj* ⟨*treatment/ decision*⟩ injusto; ⟨*competition*⟩ desleal; ⟨*dismissal*⟩ improcedente, injustificado; **it was ∼ of him to blame you** fue injusto que te echara la culpa a ti

unfairly /ʌnˈferli ‖ ʌnˈfeəli/ *adv* injustamente

unfaithful /ʌnˈfeɪθfəl/ *adj* ⟨*spouse/lover*⟩ infiel; ⟨*follower*⟩ desleal

unfamiliar /ˌʌnfəˈmɪljər ‖ ˌʌnfəˈmɪlɪə(r)/ *adj* ⟨*face/surroundings*⟩ desconocido, nuevo

unfashionable /ʌnˈfæʃnəbəl/ *adj* fuera de moda

unfasten /ʌnˈfæsn̩ ‖ ʌnˈfɑːsn̩/ *vt* ⟨*seat belt/ button*⟩ desabrochar; ⟨*knot*⟩ deshacer*, desatar

unfavorable, (BrE) **unfavourable** /ʌnˈfeɪvrəbəl/ *adj* desfavorable

unfinished /ʌnˈfɪnɪʃt/ *adj* sin terminar, inacabado

unfit /ʌnˈfɪt/ *adj* **(a)** (unsuitable) ⟨*mother*⟩ inepto, incapaz; **he was ∼ for the job** no estaba capacitado para el trabajo; **∼ for human consumption** no apto para el consumo **(b)** (physically): **I'm ∼** no estoy en forma, estoy fuera de forma

unflagging /ʌnˈflægɪŋ/ *adj* ⟨*energy/ enthusiasm*⟩ inagotable; ⟨*interest*⟩ sostenido

unflattering /ʌnˈflætərɪŋ/ *adj* ⟨*remark/ description*⟩ poco halagüeño; ⟨*dress*⟩ poco favorecedor

unfold /ʌnˈfəʊld/ *vt* ⟨*tablecloth/map*⟩ desdoblar, extender*; ⟨*wings*⟩ desplegar*
■ **∼** *vi* **(a)** «*flower/leaf*» abrirse*; «*wings*» desplegarse* **(b)** «*story/events*» desarrollarse; «*scene*» extenderse*

unforeseen /ˌʌnfɔːˈrsiːn ‖ ˌʌnfɔːˈsiːn/ *adj* imprevisto

unforgettable /ˌʌnfərˈgetəbəl ‖ ˌʌnfəˈgetəbəl/ *adj* inolvidable

unforgivable /ˌʌnfərˈgɪvəbəl ‖ ˌʌnfəˈgɪvəbəl/ *adj* imperdonable

unfortunate /ʌnˈfɔːrtʃnət ‖ ʌnˈfɔːtʃənət/ *adj* desafortunado; **he has been very ∼** ha tenido muy mala suerte

unfortunately /ʌnˈfɔːrtʃnətli ‖ ʌnˈfɔːtʃənətli/ *adv* (indep) lamentablemente, desafortunadamente; (stronger) desgraciadamente, por desgracia

unfounded /ʌnˈfaʊndəd ‖ ʌnˈfaʊndɪd/ *adj* infundado

unfriendly /ʌnˈfrendli/ *adj* **-lier, -liest** poco amistoso; (stronger) antipático

unfulfilled /ˌʌnfʊlˈfɪld/ *adj* ⟨*ambition/hope*⟩ frustrado; ⟨*prophecy*⟩ no cumplido

unfurl /ʌnˈfɜːrl ‖ ʌnˈfɜːl/ *vt* desplegar*

unfurnished /ʌnˈfɜːrnɪʃt ‖ ʌnˈfɜːnɪʃt/ *adj* sin amueblar

ungainly /ʌnˈgeɪnli/ *adj* desgarbado

ungracious /ʌnˈgreɪʃəs/ *adj* descortés

ungrateful /ʌnˈgreɪtfəl/ *adj* desagradecido, ingrato, malagradecido

unguarded /ʌnˈgɑːrdəd ‖ ʌnˈgɑːdɪd/ *adj* (incautious): **in an ∼ moment** en un momento de descuido

unhappily /ʌnˈhæpəli ‖ ʌnˈhæpɪli/ *adv* **(a)** ⟨*sigh*⟩ tristemente, con tristeza **(b)** (unfortunately) (indep) lamentablemente

unhappiness /ʌnˈhæpinəs ‖ ʌnˈhæpinɪs/ *n* infelicidad *f*; (stronger) desdicha *f*; (sadness) tristeza *f*

unhappy /ʌnˈhæpi/ *adj* **-pier, -piest** **(a)** (sad) ⟨*childhood*⟩ infeliz; (stronger) desgraciado, desdichado **(b)** (worried) ⟨*pred*⟩: **I was ∼ about the children being left alone** me preocupaba *or* inquietaba que los niños se quedaran solos **(c)** (discontented) ⟨*pred*⟩ **to be ∼ ABOUT sth** no estar* contento CON algo

unharmed /ʌnˈhɑːrmd ‖ ʌnˈhɑːmd/ *adj*: **he escaped ∼** salió *or* resultó ileso

unhealthy /ʌnˈhelθi/ *adj* **-thier, -thiest** **(a)** ⟨*person*⟩ de mala salud; ⟨*complexion*⟩ enfermizo; ⟨*climate*⟩ poco saludable, insalubre, malsano **(b)** ⟨*interest/obsession*⟩ malsano

unheard of /ʌnˈhɜːrdɑːv ‖ ʌnˈhɜːdɒv/ *adj* insólito

unhelpful /ʌnˈhelpfəl/ *adj* ⟨*assistant/secretary*⟩ poco servicial; **he was most ∼** no se mostró nada dispuesto a ayudar

unhinge /ʌnˈhɪndʒ/ *vt* ⟨*person/mind*⟩ trastornar

unhurt /ʌnˈhɜːrt ‖ ʌnˈhɜːt/ *adj* ileso; **to escape ∼** salir* *or* resultar ileso

unhygienic /ˌʌnhaɪˈdʒiːnɪk/ *adj* antihigiénico

UNICEF /ˈjuːnɪsef/ *n* (no art) (= **United Nations International Children's Emergency Fund**) UNICEF *m or f*

unicorn /ˈjuːnəkɔːrn ‖ ˈjuːnɪkɔːn/ *n* unicornio *m*

unidentified /ˌʌnaɪˈdentəfaɪd ‖ ˌʌnaɪˈdentɪfaɪd/ *adj* no identificado; **∼ flying object** objeto *m* volador *or* (Esp) volante no identificado

unification /ˌjuːnəfəˈkeɪʃən ‖ ˌjuːnɪfɪˈkeɪʃən/ *n* unificación *f*

uniform[1] /ˈjuːnəfɔːrm ‖ ˈjuːnɪfɔːm/ *n* uniforme *m*

uniform[2] *adj* ⟨*color/length*⟩ uniforme; ⟨*temperature/speed*⟩ constante

uniformity /ˌjuːnəˈfɔːrməti ‖ ˌjuːnɪˈfɔːməti/ *n* uniformidad *f*

unify /ˈjuːnəfaɪ ‖ ˈjuːnɪfaɪ/ *vt* **-fies, -fying, -fied** unir

unilateral /ˌjuːnɪˈlætərəl/ *adj* unilateral

unimaginable /ˌʌnəˈmædʒənəbəl ‖ ˌʌnɪˈmædʒɪnəbəl/ *adj* inimaginable

u

unimaginative /ˌʌnəˈmædʒənətɪv ‖ˌʌnɪˈmædʒmətɪv/ adj ⟨person⟩ poco imaginativo; ⟨story/design⟩ falto de imaginación

unimportant /ˌʌnɪmˈpɔːrtn̩t ‖ˌʌnɪmˈpɔːtn̩t/ adj ⟨matter/detail⟩ sin importancia

uninhabited /ˌʌnɪnˈhæbətəd ‖ˌʌnɪnˈhæbɪtɪd/ adj ⟨house⟩ deshabitado; ⟨region/island⟩ despoblado

uninhibited /ˌʌnɪnˈhɪbətəd ‖ˌʌnɪnˈhɪbɪtɪd/ adj desinhibido, desenfadado

unintelligent /ˌʌnɪnˈtelədʒənt ‖ˌʌnɪnˈtelɪdʒənt/ adj poco inteligente

unintelligible /ˌʌnɪnˈtelədʒəbəl ‖ˌʌnɪnˈtelɪdʒəbəl/ adj ininteligible

unintentional /ˌʌnɪnˈtentʃn̩əl ‖ˌʌnɪnˈtenʃən̩/ adj involuntario, no deliberado

unintentionally /ˌʌnɪnˈtentʃn̩əli ‖ˌʌnɪnˈtenʃn̩əli/ adv involuntariamente, sin querer

uninterested /ʌnˈɪntrəstəd ‖ʌnˈɪntrestɪd/ adj indiferente

uninteresting /ʌnˈɪntrəstɪŋ/ adj ⟨topic⟩ sin interés; ⟨person⟩ poco interesante

uninvited /ˌʌnɪnˈvaɪtəd ‖ˌʌnɪnˈvaɪtɪd/ adj: they came ~ vinieron sin que nadie los invitara

uninviting /ˌʌnɪnˈvaɪtɪŋ/ adj ⟨appearance⟩ poco atractivo; ⟨food⟩ poco apetitoso

union /ˈjuːnjən/ n **1** (act, state) unión f **2** (Lab Rel) sindicato m, gremio m (CS, Per); (before n) ⟨official/movement⟩ sindical, gremial (CS, Per); ~ card carné m de afiliado **3** (at college, university) asociación f or federación f de estudiantes

unionize /ˈjuːnjənaɪz / vt sindicalizar* (esp AmL), sindicar* (esp Esp)

Union Jack n bandera f del Reino Unido

unique /juˈniːk/ adj ⟨no comp⟩ único

unisex /ˈjuːnəseks ‖ˈjuːnɪseks/ adj unisex adj inv

unison /ˈjuːnəsən ‖ˈjuːnɪsən/ n: in ~ al unísono

unit /ˈjuːnət ‖ˈjuːnɪt/ n **1** (a) (item) (Busn) unidad f (b) (of furniture) módulo m **2** (group) (Mil) unidad f **3** (of measurement) unidad f **4** (Educ) (in course) módulo m

unite /juˈnaɪt ‖juːˈnaɪt/ vt unir
■ ~ vi unirse

united /juˈnaɪtəd ‖juːˈnaɪtɪd/ adj unido

united: U~ Arab Emirates /ˈemɪrəts ‖ˈemɪərəts/ pl n the U~ Arab Emirates los Emiratos Árabes Unidos; **U~ Kingdom** n the U~ Kingdom el Reino Unido; **U~ Nations (Organization)** n (+ sing o pl vb) the U~ Nations (organization) (la Organización de) las Naciones Unidas; **U~ States** n (usu + sing vb) the U~ States los Estados Unidos; **U~ States of America** n (usu + sing vb) the U~ States of America los Estados Unidos de América

unity /ˈjuːnəti/ n (pl **-ties**) unidad f

universal /ˌjuːnəˈvɜːrsəl ‖ˌjuːnɪˈvɜːsəl/ adj (a) (general) general (b) (worldwide) universal (c) (all-purpose, versatile) ⟨adaptor⟩ universal

universally /ˌjuːnəˈvɜːrsəli ‖ˌjuːnɪˈvɜːsəli/ adv ⟨known/admired⟩ mundialmente, universalmente

universe /ˈjuːnəvɜːrs ‖ˈjuːnɪvɜːs/ n universo m

university /ˌjuːnəˈvɜːrsəti ‖ˌjuːnɪˈvɜːsəti/ n (pl **-ties**) universidad f; (before n) ⟨town/life⟩ universitario

unjust /ʌnˈdʒʌst/ adj injusto

unjustified /ʌnˈdʒʌstəfaɪd ‖ʌnˈdʒʌstɪfaɪd/ adj injustificado

unkempt /ʌnˈkempt/ adj (frml) ⟨appearance⟩ descuidado, desarreglado; ⟨hair⟩ despeinado

unkind /ʌnˈkaɪnd/ adj **-er, -est** (unpleasant) poco amable; (cruel) cruel, malo; ⟨remark⟩ hiriente

unknown[1] /ʌnˈnəʊn/ adj desconocido

unknown[2] n (a) (phenomenon) the ~ lo desconocido (b) (person) desconocida, -da m,f

unknown[3] adv: ~ to her sin ella saberlo

unlawful /ʌnˈlɔːfəl/ adj ⟨conduct⟩ ilegal; ⟨possession⟩ ilícito

unleaded /ʌnˈledəd ‖ʌnˈledɪd/ adj sin plomo

unleash /ʌnˈliːʃ/ vt ⟨dog⟩ soltar*, desatar; ⟨anger/imagination⟩ dar(le)* rienda suelta a; ⟨war⟩ desencadenar

unless /ʌnˈles, ən-/ conj a no ser que (+ subj), a menos que (+ subj)

unlike /ʌnˈlaɪk/ prep (a) (not similar to) diferente or distinto de (b) (untypical of): it's ~ you to be so optimistic tú no sueles ser tan optimista (c) (in contrast to) a diferencia de

unlikely /ʌnˈlaɪkli/ adj **-lier, liest** (a) (improbable) ⟨outcome/victory⟩ improbable, poco probable (b) (far-fetched) ⟨story/explanation⟩ inverosímil (c) (odd, unexpected) insólito

unlimited /ʌnˈlɪmətəd ‖ʌnˈlɪmɪtɪd/ adj ilimitado

unlined /ʌnˈlaɪnd/ adj (a) ⟨paper⟩ sin pautar (b) ⟨dress/jacket⟩ sin forro

unlisted /ʌnˈlɪstəd ‖ʌnˈlɪstɪd/ adj (AmE Telec) que no figura en la guía telefónica

unlit /ʌnˈlɪt/ adj ⟨road⟩ sin luz, sin alumbrado

unload /ʌnˈləʊd/ vt/i descargar*

unlock /ʌnˈlɑːk ‖ʌnˈlɒk/ vt abrir* (algo que está cerrado con llave)

unlucky /ʌnˈlʌki/ adj **unluckier, unluckiest** ⟨person⟩ sin suerte, desafortunado; ⟨day⟩ funesto, de mala suerte; ⟨object⟩ que trae mala suerte; **to be ~** tener* mala suerte

unmanageable /ʌnˈmænɪdʒəbəl/ adj ⟨child/horse⟩ rebelde; ⟨hair⟩ rebelde

unmanned /ʌnˈmænd/ adj ⟨vehicle/rocket⟩ sin tripulación; ⟨space flight⟩ no tripulado

unmarried /ʌnˈmærid/ adj soltero

unmask /ʌnˈmæsk ‖ʌnˈmɑːsk/ vt desenmascarar

unmentionable /ʌnˈmentʃn̩əbəl ‖ʌnˈmenʃənəbəl/ adj inmencionable, innombrable

unmistakable /ˌʌnməˈsteɪkəbəl ‖ˌʌnmɪˈsteɪkəbəl/ adj inconfundible; ⟨proof⟩ inequívoco

unnamed /ʌnˈneɪmd/ adj no identificado

unnatural /ʌnˈnætʃərəl/ adj (a) (unusual) poco natural or normal (b) (awkward, affected) ⟨smile⟩ poco natural (c) (against nature) (frml) antinatural

unnecessarily /ˌʌnnesəˈserəli ‖ˌʌnnesəˈserɪli, ˌʌnˈnesəserɪli/ adv innecesariamente

unnecessary /ʌn'nesəseri ‖ʌn'nesəsəri/ *adj* innecesario

unnerve /ʌn'nɜːrv ‖ʌn'nɜːv/ *vt* poner* nervioso, turbar (liter)

unnerving /ʌn'nɜːrvɪŋ ‖ʌn'nɜːvɪŋ/ *adj* desconcertante, que pone nervioso

unnoticed /ʌn'nəʊtəst ‖ʌn'nəʊtɪst/ *adj* (*pred*): **to go ~** pasar desapercibido *or* inadvertido

unobtainable /ˌʌnəb'teməbəl/ *adj* imposible de conseguir

unobtrusive /ˌʌnəb'truːsɪv/ *adj* discreto

unoccupied /ʌn'ɑːkjəpaɪd ‖ʌn'ɒkjʊpaɪd/ *adj* **(a)** ⟨*seat/toilet*⟩ desocupado, libre; ⟨*house*⟩ deshabitado, desocupado **(b)** (Mil) no ocupado

unofficial /ˌʌnə'fɪʃəl/ *adj* no oficial

unofficially /ˌʌnə'fɪʃəli/ *adv* extraoficialmente

unopened /ʌn'əʊpənd/ *adj* sin abrir

unopposed /ˌʌnə'pəʊzd/ *adj* sin oposición

unoriginal /ˌʌnə'rɪdʒənl/ *adj* poco original, sin originalidad

unorthodox /ʌn'ɔːrθədɑːks ‖ʌn'ɔːθədɒks/ *adj* poco ortodoxo

unpack /ʌn'pæk/ *vt* ⟨*bags*⟩ sacar* las cosas de, desempacar* (AmL); ⟨*suitcase*⟩ deshacer*, desempacar* (AmL)

■ **~** *vi* deshacer* las maletas, desempacar* (AmL)

unpaid /ʌn'peɪd/ *adj* ⟨*work*⟩ no retribuido, no remunerado; ⟨*leave*⟩ sin sueldo; ⟨*debt*⟩ pendiente, no liquidado

unpalatable /ʌn'pælətəbəl/ *adj* **(a)** ⟨*food/ drink*⟩ de sabor desagradable **(b)** ⟨*fact/truth*⟩ desagradable, difícil de digerir

unparalleled /ʌn'pærəleld/ *adj* ⟨*success/ achievement*⟩ sin paralelo, sin parangón; ⟨*disaster*⟩ sin precedentes; ⟨*beauty*⟩ incomparable

unperturbed /ˌʌnpər'tɜːrbd ‖ˌʌnpə'tɜːbd/ *adj* impasible, impertérrito; **she carried on ~** siguió sin inmutarse

unpleasant /ʌn'pleznt/ *adj* desagradable

unplug /ʌn'plʌg/ *vt* **-gg-** desenchufar, desconectar

unpopular /ʌn'pɑːpjələr ‖ʌn'pɒpjʊlə(r)/ *adj* impopular; **he is ~ with everybody** le cae muy mal a todo el mundo

unprecedented /ʌn'presədentəd ‖ʌn'presɪdentɪd/ *adj* ⟨*success/hostility*⟩ sin precedentes; ⟨*decision*⟩ inaudito

unpredictable /ˌʌnprɪ'dɪktəbəl/ *adj* ⟨*result/ weather*⟩ imprevisible; **she's very ~** nunca se sabe cómo va a reaccionar

unprepared /ˌʌnprɪ'perd ‖ˌʌnprɪ'peəd/ *adj* **(a)** (not ready) (*pred*) **to be ~** no estar* preparado **(b)** (not expecting) (*pred*) **to be ~ FOR sth** no esperar algo

unprepossessing /ˌʌnpriːpə'zesɪŋ/ *adj* poco atractivo

unprincipled /ʌn'prɪnsəpəld/ *adj* sin escrúpulos *or* principios

unproductive /ˌʌnprə'dʌktɪv/ *adj* ⟨*meeting*⟩ infructuoso

unprofessional /ˌʌnprə'feʃnəl ‖ˌʌnprə'feʃənl/ *adj* poco profesional

unprofitable /ʌn'prɑːfətəbəl ‖ʌn'prɒfɪtəbəl/ *adj* no rentable

unprotected /ˌʌnprə'tektəd ‖ˌʌnprə'tektɪd/ *adj* sin protección; ⟨*sex*⟩ sin el uso de preservativos

unproven /ʌn'pruːvən/ *adj* ⟨*theory*⟩ (que está) por demostrar *or* probar

unpublished /ʌn'pʌblɪʃt/ *adj* inédito, no publicado

unpunished /ʌn'pʌnɪʃt/ *adj*: **to go ~** «*person*» quedar sin castigo; «*crime*» quedar impune

unqualified /ʌn'kwɑːləfaɪd ‖ʌn'kwɒlɪfaɪd/ *adj* **1** (complete, total) ⟨*approval*⟩ incondicional; ⟨*disaster*⟩ absoluto; ⟨*success/failure*⟩ rotundo **2** (without qualifications) ⟨*teacher/nurse*⟩ sin titulación *or* título, no titulado; ⟨*staff*⟩ no calificado *or* (Esp) cualificado

unquestionable /ʌn'kwestʃənəbəl/ *adj* ⟨*sincerity/loyalty*⟩ incuestionable, innegable

unquestioning /ʌn'kwestʃənɪŋ/ *adj* ⟨*obedience/faith*⟩ ciego; ⟨*loyalty*⟩ incondicional

unravel /ʌn'rævəl/ *vt*, (BrE) **-ll-** **(a)** ⟨*threads/ string*⟩ desenredar **(b)** ⟨*mystery*⟩ desentrañar

unreadable /ʌn'riːdəbəl/ *adj* **(a)** ⟨*handwriting*⟩ ilegible **(b)** ⟨*novel*⟩ muy difícil de leer

unrealistic /ˌʌnriːə'lɪstɪk ‖ˌʌnriə'lɪstɪk/ *adj* ⟨*expectations*⟩ poco realista; **it's ~ to expect that** no es realista esperar eso

unreasonable /ʌn'riːznəbəl/ *adj* ⟨*person*⟩ poco razonable, irrazonable; ⟨*demand/price*⟩ excesivo, poco razonable

unrecognizable /ʌn'rekəgnaɪzəbəl/ *adj* irreconocible

unrefined /ˌʌnrɪ'faɪnd/ *adj* ⟨*flour/sugar*⟩ sin refinar, no refinado; ⟨*gold*⟩ en estado bruto; ⟨*person*⟩ poco refinado; **~ oil** crudo *m*

unrelated /ˌʌnrɪ'leɪtəd ‖ˌʌnrɪ'leɪtɪd/ *adj* ⟨*facts/ events*⟩ no relacionados (entre sí)

unreliable /ˌʌnrɪ'laɪəbəl/ *adj* ⟨*person*⟩ informal; ⟨*information*⟩ poco fidedigno; ⟨*weather*⟩ variable

unrepeatable /ˌʌnrɪ'piːtəbəl/ *adj* irrepetible

unrepentant /ˌʌnrɪ'pentnt/ *adj* impenitente

unreported /ˌʌnrɪ'pɔːrtəd ‖ˌʌnrɪ'pɔːtɪd/ *adj* ⟨*crime*⟩ no denunciado

unrepresentative /ˌʌnreprə'zentətɪv/ *adj* poco representativo

unrequited /ˌʌnrɪ'kwaɪtəd ‖ˌʌnrɪ'kwaɪtɪd/ *adj* ⟨*love*⟩ no correspondido

unresolved /ˌʌnrɪ'zɑːlvd ‖ˌʌnrɪ'zɒlvd/ *adj* no resuelto

unresponsive /ˌʌnrɪ'spɑːnsɪv ‖ˌʌnrɪ'spɒnsɪv/ *adj* ⟨*audience/expression*⟩ indiferente; ⟨*pupil*⟩ que no responde

unrest /ʌn'rest/ *n* (Pol) descontento *m*, malestar *m*; (active) disturbios *mpl*

unrestricted /ˌʌnrɪ'strɪktəd ‖ˌʌnrɪ'strɪktɪd/ *adj* ilimitado

unrewarded /ˌʌnrɪ'wɔːrdəd ‖ˌʌnrɪ'wɔːdɪd/ *adj* no recompensado

unripe /ʌn'raɪp/ *adj* verde, que no está maduro

unrivaled, (BrE) **unrivalled** /ʌn'raɪvəld/ *adj* incomparable, inigualable

unroll /ʌn'rəʊl/ *vt* desenrollar

unruffled /ʌn'rʌfəld/ *adj* **(a)** (undisturbed) ⟨*manner*⟩ sereno **(b)** (smooth) liso

u

unruly /ʌnˈruːli/ adj **-lier, -liest** (class) indisciplinado, difícil de controlar; (conduct) rebelde; (child) revoltoso

unsafe /ʌnˈseɪf/ adj inseguro

unsaid /ʌnˈsed/ adj: **to leave sth ~** callar(se) algo, no decir* algo

unsalted /ʌnˈsɔːltəd ‖ ʌnˈsɔːltɪd/ adj sin sal

unsatisfactory /ʌnˈsætəsˈfæktri ‖ ʌnsætɪsˈfæktəri/ adj insatisfactorio; (explanation) poco convincente

unsatisfying /ʌnˈsætəsfaɪŋ ‖ ʌnˈsætɪsfaɪŋ/ adj (meal) que no llena or satisface; (job) poco gratificante; (ending) decepcionante

unsavory, (BrE) **unsavoury** /ʌnˈseɪvəri/ adj desagradable

unscathed /ʌnˈskeɪðd/ adj (pred) (unhurt) ileso; (of reputation etc) indemne

unscented /ʌnˈsentəd ‖ ʌnˈsentɪd/ adj sin perfume

unscheduled /ʌnˈskedʒuːld ‖ ʌnˈʃedjuːld/ adj no programado, no previsto

unscientific /ʌnˈsaɪənˈtɪfɪk/ adj falto de rigor científico

unscrew /ʌnˈskruː/ vt (screw/panel) destornillar, desatornillar; (lid) desenroscar*

unscrupulous /ʌnˈskruːpjələs ‖ ʌnˈskruːpjuləs/ adj inescrupuloso

unseat /ʌnˈsiːt/ vt (a) (rider) desmontar (b) (government) derribar

unseen /ʌnˈsiːn/ adj (a) (invisible) (danger/obstacle) oculto (b) (unnoticed) sin ser visto

unselfish /ʌnˈselfɪʃ/ adj (person) nada egoísta; (act) desinteresado

unsentimental /ʌnˈsentəˈmentl ‖ ʌnsentɪˈmentl/ adj (person/outlook) poco sentimental

unsettle /ʌnˈsetl/ vt (plans) alterar; (situation) desestabilizar*; **the question clearly ~d him** la pregunta lo desconcertó visiblemente

unsettled /ʌnˈsetld/ adj 1 (a) (troubled) (period) agitado; (childhood) poco estable (b) (weather) inestable 2 (undecided) (issue/dispute) pendiente (de resolución), sin resolver; (future) incierto

unsettling /ʌnˈsetlɪŋ/ adj inquietante; (effect) desestabilizador

unshakable, unshakeable /ʌnˈʃeɪkəbəl/ adj inquebrantable

unshaven /ʌnˈʃeɪvən/ adj sin afeitar, sin rasurar (esp Méx)

unsightly /ʌnˈsaɪtli/ adj **-lier, -liest** feo, antiestético

unsigned /ʌnˈsaɪnd/ adj sin firmar

unskilled /ʌnˈskɪld/ adj (worker) no calificado or (Esp) cualificado; (work) no especializado

unsociable /ʌnˈsəʊʃəbəl/ adj insociable, poco sociable

unsold /ʌnˈsəʊld/ adj no vendido

unsolicited /ʌnsəˈlɪsətəd ‖ ʌnsəˈlɪsɪtɪd/ adj que no se ha pedido or solicitado

unsolved /ʌnˈsɑːlvd ‖ ʌnˈsɒlvd/ adj no resuelto

unsophisticated /ʌnsəˈfɪstəkeɪtəd ‖ ʌnsəˈfɪstɪkeɪtɪd/ adj (person) sencillo; (tastes/technology) simple, poco sofisticado

unspeakable /ʌnˈspiːkəbəl/ adj (evil) incalificable, atroz; (joy) indescriptible

unspecified /ʌnˈspesəfaɪd ‖ ʌnˈspesɪfaɪd/ adj no especificado

unspoiled /ʌnˈspɔɪld/, (BrE also) **unspoilt** /ʌnˈspɔɪlt/ adj (countryside) que conserva su belleza natural

unspoken /ʌnˈspəʊkən/ adj (agreement) tácito; (wish) no expresado

unstable /ʌnˈsteɪbəl/ adj inestable; (prices) variable

unsteadily /ʌnˈstedli ‖ ʌnˈstedɪli/ adv de modo inseguro or vacilante

unsteady /ʌnˈstedi/ adj (chair/ladder) inestable, poco firme; (walk/step) vacilante, inseguro

unstick /ʌnˈstɪk/ vt (past & past p **unstuck**) despegar*, quitar

unstuck /ʌnˈstʌk/ adj despegado; **to come ~** despegarse*

unsuccessful /ʌnsəkˈsesfəl/ adj (attempt) infructuoso, fallido; **they were ~ in their attempt** fracasaron en su intento

unsuccessfully /ʌnsəkˈsesfəli/ adv en vano, sin éxito

unsuitable /ʌnˈsuːtəbəl/ adj (clothing) poco apropiado or adecuado; (candidate) poco idóneo; (time) inconveniente

unsuited /ʌnˈsuːtəd ‖ ʌnˈsuːtɪd/ adj (pred) **she is ~ to this work** no sirve para este trabajo; **they are completely ~** son totalmente incompatibles

unsure /ʌnˈʃʊr ‖ ʌnˈʃʊə(r), ʌnˈʃɔː(r)/ adj inseguro, indeciso; **to be ~ of oneself** estar* or sentirse* inseguro de sí mismo

unsurpassed /ʌnsərˈpæst ‖ ʌnsəˈpɑːst/ adj (beauty/mastery) sin igual, sin par (liter)

unsuspecting /ʌnsəˈspektɪŋ/ adj desprevenido; **to be ~** no sospechar nada

unsweetened /ʌnˈswiːtɪnd/ adj (without sugar) sin azúcar; (without sweeteners) sin edulcorantes

unsympathetic /ʌnˈsɪmpəˈθetɪk/ adj (a) (showing no sympathy) (person/attitude) indiferente, poco comprensivo (b) (unfavorable) (account) adverso, desfavorable; **she was ~ to our cause** no veía nuestra causa con simpatía

unsystematic /ʌnsɪstəˈmætɪk/ adj poco sistemático

untamed /ʌnˈteɪmd/ adj (animal) sin domar; (wilderness/forests) virgen, agreste

untangle /ʌnˈtæŋɡəl/ vt desenredar, desenmarañar; (mystery) desentrañar

untapped /ʌnˈtæpt/ adj sin explotar

untenable /ʌnˈtenəbəl/ adj (fml) insostenible

untended /ʌnˈtendəd ‖ ʌnˈtendɪd/ adj (garden) descuidado; (patient) desatendido

AmC	Central America	Arg	Argentina	Cu	Cuba
AmL	Latin America	Bol	Bolivia	Ec	Ecuador
AmS	South America	Chi	Chile	Esp	Spain
Andes	Andean Region	CS	Southern Cone	Méx	Mexico

Per	Peru
RPI	River Plate Area
Ur	Uruguay
Ven	Venezuela

unthinkable /ʌn'θɪŋkəbəl/ *adj* inconcebible, inimaginable

untidy /ʌn'taɪdi/ *adj* **-dier, -diest** ‹*room/desk/ person*› desordenado; ‹*appearance*› descuidado, desprolijo (RPl); ‹*writing/schoolwork*› descuidado, desprolijo (RPl)

untie /ʌn'taɪ/ *vt* **unties, untying, untied** ‹*knot*› desatar; ‹*shoelaces*› desatar, desamarrar (AmL exc RPl); ‹*animal*› soltar*, desatar, desamarrar (AmL exc RPl)

until¹ /ʌn'tɪl, ən'tɪl/ *conj* hasta que

■ **Note** When used as a conjunction in positive sentences expressing the future, *until* is translated by *hasta que* + subjunctive: *we'll stay here until Carol comes back* nos quedaremos aquí hasta que llegue Carol. In negative sentences *no* is used optionally before the verb: *he won't be satisfied until they give him his money back* no estará satisfecho hasta que (no) le devuelvan su dinero.

until² *prep* hasta

untimely /ʌn'taɪmli/ *adj* **(a)** ‹*death/end*› prematuro **(b)** ‹*arrival*› inoportuno, intempestivo

untold /ʌn'təʊld/ *adj* ‹*before n*› ‹*wealth/sums*› incalculable; ‹*misery/pleasures*› indecible, inenarrable

untouched /ʌn'tʌtʃt/ *adj* **(a)** (not handled) intacto, sin tocar; **he left his food ~** no probó la comida **(b)** (safe, unharmed) intacto

untoward /ʌn'tɔːrd , ˌʌntə'wɔːrd ‖ʌntə'wɔːd/ *adj* (frml) perjudicial, adverso; **I hope nothing ~ has happened** espero que no haya pasado nada (que haya que lamentar)

untrained /ʌn'treɪnd/ *adj* falto de formación *or* capacitación; ‹*teacher*› sin título; **to the ~ eye/ ear ...** para (el ojo/oído de) quien no es experto ...

untreated /ʌn'triːtəd ‖ʌn'triːtɪd/ *adj* ‹*sewage/ waste*› sin tratar *or* procesar

untried /ʌn'traɪd/ *adj* **(a)** (not tested) ‹*method*› no probado **(b)** (Law) ‹*case*› no sometido a juicio

untroubled /ʌn'trʌbəld/ *adj* tranquilo

untrue /ʌn'truː/ *adj* falso; **it is ~ (to say) that ...** es falso *or* no es cierto que ...

untrustworthy /ʌn'trʌst,wɜːrði ‖ʌn'trʌst,wɜːði/ *adj* ‹*person*› de poca confianza; ‹*source*› poco fidedigno

untruthful /ʌn'truːθfəl/ *adj* ‹*account/answer*› falso; ‹*person*› falso, mentiroso

unusual /ʌn'juːʒuəl/ *adj* poco corriente *or* común, fuera de lo corriente *or* común, inusual; **with ~ frankness** con inusitada *or* insólita franqueza; **did you notice anything ~ about him?** ¿le notaste algo raro *or* fuera de lo normal?

unusually /ʌn'juːʒuəli/ *adv* excepcionalmente, inusitadamente; **she was ~ talkative** estaba más conversadora que de costumbre

unveil /ʌn'veɪl/ *vt* descubrir*, develar (AmL)

unwanted /ʌn'wɔːntəd ‖ʌn'wɒntɪd/ *adj* ‹*pregnancy/child*› no deseado; ‹*object*› superfluo

unwarranted /ʌn'wɔːrəntəd ‖ʌn'wɒrəntɪd/ *adj* injustificado

unwavering /ʌn'weɪvərɪŋ/ *adj* ‹*loyalty/belief*› inquebrantable; ‹*determination*› férreo

unwelcome /ʌn'welkəm/ *adj* ‹*visit*› inoportuno; ‹*guest*› inoportuno, poco grato; ‹*news*› poco grato

unwell /ʌn'wel/ *adj* mal

unwholesome /ʌn'həʊlsəm/ *adj* ‹*diet/ climate*› poco sano *or* saludable; ‹*smell/person*› desagradable

unwieldy /ʌn'wiːldi/ *adj* **-dier, -diest** pesado y difícil de manejar

unwilling /ʌn'wɪlɪŋ/ *adj* mal dispuesto; **to be ~ to + INF** no querer* + INF, no estar* dispuesto a + INF

unwillingly /ʌn'wɪlɪŋli/ *adv* de mala gana, a regañadientes

unwind /ʌn'waɪnd/ (*past & past p* **unwound** /ʌn'waʊnd/) *vt* desenrollar
■ **~** *vi* (colloq) relajarse

unwise /ʌn'waɪz/ *adj* poco prudente *or* sensato; **it would be ~ of you to do that** hacer eso no sería sensato

unwitting /ʌn'wɪtɪŋ/ *adj* involuntario

unwittingly /ʌn'wɪtɪŋli/ *adv* sin ser consciente (de ello), sin darse* cuenta

unworthy /ʌn'wɜːrði ‖ʌn'wɜːði/ *adj* **-thier, -thiest** indigno; **to be ~ to + INF** no ser* digno DE + INF

unwound /ʌn'waʊnd/ *past & past p of* UNWIND

unwrap /ʌn'ræp/ *vt* **-pp-** desenvolver*

unwritten /ʌn'rɪtn/ *adj* ‹*rule*› no escrito; ‹*agreement*› verbal, de palabra

unyielding /ʌn'jiːldɪŋ/ *adj* ‹*person*› inflexible; ‹*opposition*› implacable

up¹ /ʌp/ *adv*
I **1** (in upward direction): **~ a bit ... left a bit** un poco más arriba ... un poco a la izquierda; **we saw them on the way ~** los vimos cuando subíamos; **from the waist ~** desde la cintura para arriba
2 **(a)** (of position) arriba; **~ here/there** aquí/allí arriba; **300ft ~** a una altura de 300 pies **(b)** (upstairs, on upper floor): **I'll be ~ in a minute** subiré en un minuto **(c)** (raised): **with the blinds ~** con las persianas levantadas *or* subidas; **face ~** boca arriba
3 **(a)** (upright): **the nurse helped him ~** la enfermera lo ayudó a sentarse **(b)** (out of bed): **they're not ~ yet** todavía no se han levantado
4 (of numbers, intensity): **she had the volume ~ high** tenía el volumen muy alto; **from $25/the age of 11 ~** a partir de 25 dólares/de los 11 años
5 (at or to another place): **the path ~ to the house** el sendero hasta la casa
6 (in position, erected): **is the tent ~?** ¿ya han armado la tienda *or* (AmL) la carpa?; **the shelves are ~** los estantes están colocados *or* puestos
7 (going on) (colloq): **what's ~ with you?** ¿a ti qué te pasa?; **what's ~?** (what's the matter?) ¿qué pasa?; (as greeting) (AmE) ¿qué hay? (colloq)
8 (finished): **your time is ~** se te ha acabado el tiempo
9 (Sport) (ahead in competition): **they're two goals ~** van ganando por dos goles; **to be one ~ on sb** tener* una ventaja sobre algn
II (*in phrases*) **1** **up against (a)** (next to) contra **(b)** (confronted by): **you don't know what you're ~ against** no sabes a lo que se enfrentas
2 **up and down (a)** (vertically): **to jump ~ and down** dar* saltos; **to look sb ~ and down** mirar a algn de arriba abajo **(b)** (back and forth) de arriba abajo ⋯⊹

3 up till o until hasta
III up to **1** (as far as, as much as) hasta; **~ to here/now** hasta aquí/ahora
2 (a) (equal to): **it isn't ~ to the usual standard** no es del alto nivel al que estamos acostumbrados; ▶ COME UP TO B (b) (capable of): **she's not ~ to the job** no tiene las condiciones necesarias para el trabajo; **I'm not ~ to going out** no me siente con fuerzas (como) para salir
3 (depending on): **that's ~ to you** eso depende de ti; **it's not ~ to me to decide** no me corresponde a mí decidir
4 to be **~ to sth** (colloq): **they're ~ to something** (planning) están tramando algo, se traen algo entre manos; (doing) están haciendo algo; **what have you been ~ to lately?** ¿en qué has andado últimamente?

up² prep **1** (a) (in upward direction): **to go ~ the stairs/hill** subir la escalera/colina (b) (at higher level): **80ft ~ the cliff** a 80 pies del pie del acantilado **2** (a) (along): **to go ~ the river** ir* por el río; **she walked ~ and down the room** iba de un lado a otro de la habitación (b) (further along): **it's just ~ the road** está un poco más allá or adelante

up³ n: **~s and downs** (of life) vicisitudes fpl; (of marriage) altibajos mpl

up: ~-and-coming /'ʌpən'kʌmɪŋ/ adj (before n): **an ~-and-coming actor** un actor que promete; **~beat** adj (colloq) optimista; **~braid** /ʌp'breɪd/ vt (fml) reprender, reconvenir* (frml); **~bringing** /'ʌp.brɪŋɪŋ/ n (no pl) educación f; **~coming** /'ʌp'kʌmɪŋ/ adj (before n) próximo, que se acerca

update¹ /ʌp'deɪt/ vt poner* al día
update² /'ʌpdeɪt/ n: **to give sb an ~ on sth** poner* a algn al corriente or al tanto de algo

up: ~end /ʌp'end/ vt poner* vertical, parar (AmL); **~front** /'ʌp'frʌnt/ adv por adelantado; **~grade** vt (a) ⟨employee⟩ elevar de categoría; ⟨job⟩ elevar la categoría de (b) (improve) ⟨facilities⟩ mejorar

upheaval /ʌp'hi:vəl/ n trastorno m; (social, political) agitación f

up: ~held /ʌp'held/ past & past p of ~HOLD; **~hill** /'ʌp'hɪl/ adv cuesta arriba, en subida; **~hold** /ʌp'həʊld/ vt (past & past p ~held) (a) ⟨tradition⟩ conservar; ⟨principle⟩ mantener* (b) (Law) ⟨decision/verdict⟩ confirmar

upholster /ʌp'həʊlstər ‖ʌp'həʊlstə(r)/ vt tapizar*

upholstery /ʌp'həʊlstəri/ n (a) (stuffing, springs) relleno m; (covers) tapizado m (b) (craft, trade) tapicería f

up: ~keep n (running, maintenance) mantenimiento m; (costs) gastos mpl de mantenimiento; **~lift** /ʌp'lɪft/ vt elevar; **~lifting** /ʌp'lɪftɪŋ/ adj (spiritually) que eleva el espíritu; (emotionally) que levanta el ánimo; **~load** /ʌp'ləʊd/ vt (Comput) cargar*, subir

upmarket¹ /'ʌp'mɑ:rkət ‖ʌp'mɑ:kɪt/ adj de categoría, para gente pudiente
upmarket² adv: **to go ~** subir de categoría

upon /ə'pɑ:n ‖ə'pɒn/ prep (frml) (a) (on) sobre; **~ -ING** al + INF (b) (indicating large numbers): **thousands ~ thousands** miles y miles

upper /'ʌpər ‖'ʌpə(r)/ adj (before n) **1** (a) (spatially, numerically) superior; ⟨lip⟩ superior, de arriba (b) (in rank, importance) superior, más elevado **2** (Geog) alto; **the U~ Danube** el alto Danubio

upper: ~ class n clase f alta; **~-class** /'ʌpər'klæs ‖ʌpə'klɑ:s/ adj de clase alta; **~most** adj más alto

upright /'ʌpraɪt/ adj (a) ⟨post/position⟩ vertical; **to place/stand sth ~** colocar*/poner* algo de pie or vertical (b) ⟨citizen⟩ recto

up: ~rising n levantamiento m, alzamiento m; **~river** /ʌp'rɪvər ‖ʌp'rɪvə(r)/ adv río arriba; **~roar** n (noise, chaos) tumulto m, alboroto m; (outcry) protesta f airada; **~root** /ʌp'ru:t/ vt ⟨plant⟩ arrancar* de raíz, desarraigar* (téc); ⟨person⟩ desarraigar*

upset¹ /'ʌp'set/ adj **1** (unhappy, hurt) disgustado; (distressed) alterado; (offended) ofendido; (disappointed) desilusionado **2** (Med): **I have an ~ stomach** estoy or ando mal del estómago, estoy descompuesto (del estómago) (esp AmL)

upset² /'ʌp'set/ vt (pres p upsetting; past & past p upset) **1** (hurt) disgustar; (distress) alterar, afectar; (offend) ofender **2** (make ill): **it ~s my stomach** me cae mal, me sienta mal (al estómago) **3** ⟨plans/calculations⟩ desbaratar, trastornar

upset³ /'ʌpset/ n **1** (a) (upheaval) trastorno m (b) (emotional trouble) disgusto m **2** (Med): **to have a stomach ~** estar* mal or (esp AmL) descompuesto del estómago

upshot /'ʌpʃɑ:t ‖'ʌpʃɒt/ n: **the ~ of it all is that ...** lo que resulta de todo esto es que ...

upside down /'ʌpsaɪd/ adj al revés (con la parte de arriba abajo); **to turn sth ~** poner* algo boca abajo; ⟨theory/world⟩ revolucionar algo

upstage /'ʌp'steɪdʒ/ vt eclipsar

upstairs /'ʌp'sterz ‖ʌp'steəz/ adv arriba; **to go ~** subir

up: ~start n advenedizo, -za m,f; **~state** /'ʌp'steɪt/ adv (AmE): **he lives ~state** vive en el norte del estado (fuera de la capital); **~stream** /'ʌp'stri:m/ adv río or corriente arriba; **~surge** n ⟨of/in violence⟩ recrudecimiento m; ⟨in demand⟩ aumento m; **~take** n **to be quick on the ~take** agarrar or (esp Esp) coger* las cosas al vuelo; **~tight** /'ʌp'taɪt/ adj (colloq) nervioso, tenso; **~-to-date** /'ʌptə'deɪt/ adj (pred ~ to date) al día, actualizado

uptown¹ /'ʌp'taʊn/ adj (AmE) que va hacia el norte/hacia el distrito residencial (de la ciudad)
uptown² adv (AmE): **they live/went ~** viven en/ fueron hacia el norte/hacia el distrito residencial de la ciudad

up: ~turn n (in demand, production) repunte m, mejora f; **~turned** /'ʌp'tɜ:rnd ‖'ʌptɜ:nd/ adj ⟨nose⟩ respingón, respingado (AmL); ⟨table⟩ boca abajo, patas arriba; ⟨car/crate⟩ volcado

upward¹ /'ʌpwərd ‖'ʌpwəd/ adj (before n) ⟨direction⟩ hacia arriba; ⟨movement⟩ ascendente; ⟨tendency⟩ al alza

upward², (esp BrE) **upwards** /-z/ adv ⟨climb/ look⟩ hacia arriba; **face ~** boca arriba

upwardly mobile /'ʌpwərdli ‖'ʌpwədli/ adj de movilidad social ascendente

uranium /jʊ'reɪniəm/ n uranio m
Uranus /'jʊərənəs, jʊə'reɪnəs/ n Urano m

urban /'ɜːrbən ‖'ɜːbən/ adj urbano

urbane /ɜːr'beɪn ‖ɜː'beɪn/ adj (fml) fino y cortés, urbano (fml)

urchin /'ɜːrtʃən ‖'ɜːtʃɪn/ n golfillo, -lla m,f; pilluelo, -la m,f

Urdu /'ʊrduː ‖'ʊədu:/ n urdu m

urge[1] /ɜːrdʒ ‖ɜːdʒ/ n (wish, whim) ganas fpl; (creative, sexual) impulso m

urge[2] vt instar (fml); (entreat) pedir* con insistencia; **to ~ sb to + INF** instar a algn A QUE (+ subj) (fml), pedirle* A algn con insistencia QUE (+ subj)
■ **urge on** [v + o + adv] animar, alentar*; ⟨horse⟩ espolear

urgency /'ɜːrdʒənsi ‖'ɜːdʒənsi/ n urgencia f

urgent /'ɜːrdʒənt ‖'ɜːdʒənt/ adj ⟨matter/case⟩ urgente; ⟨tone⟩ apremiante

urgently /'ɜːrdʒəntli ‖'ɜːdʒəntli/ adv urgentemente, con urgencia

urinal /'jʊrənl ‖jʊə'raɪnl/ n (place) urinario m; (receptacle) orinal m

urinate /'jʊrəneɪt ‖'jʊərɪneɪt/ vi (fml) orinar

urine /'jʊrən ‖'jʊərɪn/ n orina f

urn /ɜːrn ‖ɜːn/ n (a) (vase) urna f (b) (for ashes) urna f funeraria (c) (for tea, coffee) recipiente grande para hacer o mantener caliente té, café etc

Uruguay /'jʊrəgwaɪ ‖'jʊərəgwaɪ/ n Uruguay m

Uruguayan[1] /'jʊrə'gwaɪən ‖ˌjʊərə'gwaɪən/ adj uruguayo

Uruguayan[2] n uruguayo, -ya m,f

us /ʌs, weak form əs/ pron [1] (a) (as direct object) nos; **they helped ~** nos ayudaron (b) (as indirect object) nos; **he gave ~ the book** nos dio el libro; **he gave it to ~** nos lo dio (c) (after preposition) nosotros, -tras; **there were four of ~** éramos cuatro [2] (emphatic use) nosotros, -tras; **it was ~** fuimos nosotros

US n (+ sing vb) EEUU, EE UU, EE.UU.

USA n (a) (= **United States of America**) EEUU, EE UU, EE.UU. (b) (= **United States Army**) ejército m estadounidense or de los EEUU

usable, useable /'juːzəbəl/ adj utilizable

USAF n (= **United States Air Force**) la Fuerza Aérea de los EEUU

usage /'juːsɪdʒ/ n (Ling) uso m

use[1] /juːs/ n [1] (of machine, substance, method, word) uso m, empleo m, utilización f; **to be in ~** «machine» estar* funcionando or en funcionamiento; «word» emplearse, usarse; **to make ~ of sth** usar algo, hacer* uso de algo; **to put sth to good ~** hacer* buen uso de algo [2] (application, function) uso m [3] (usefulness): **to be of ~ to sb** serle* útil or de utilidad a algn, servirle* a algn; **these scissors aren't much ~** estas tijeras no sirven para nada; **it's no ~** es inútil, no hay manera, no hay caso (AmL); **what's the ~ (of -ING)?** ¿de qué sirve (+ INF)?, ¿qué sentido tiene (+ INF)? [4] (right to use): **to have the ~ of sb's car** poder* usar el coche de algn

use[2] /juːz/ vt [1] (a) (for task, purpose) usar; **to ~ sth AS sth** usar algo DE or COMO algo (b) (avail oneself of) ⟨service/facilities⟩ utilizar*, usar, hacer*

uso de; **may I ~ your phone?** ¿puedo hacer una llamada or llamar por teléfono?; **may I ~ your toilet?** ¿puedo pasar or ir al baño? [2] (do with) (colloq): **I could ~ a drink** no me vendría mal un trago [3] (consume) ⟨food/fuel⟩ consumir, usar [4] (manipulate, exploit) (pej) utilizar*, usar (esp AmL)
■ ~ v mod /juːs/ (in neg, interrog sentences): **I didn't ~ to visit them very often** no solía visitarlos muy a menudo; **where did you ~ to live?** ¿dónde vivías?; see also USED[2]
■ **use up** [v + o + adv, v + adv + o] ⟨supplies/strength⟩ agotar, consumir; ⟨leftovers⟩ usar

useable adj ▶ USABLE

used[1] adj [1] /juːzd/ ⟨needle/stamp/car⟩ usado [2] /juːst/ (accustomed) (pred) **to be ~ TO sth/-ING** estar* acostumbrado a algo/+ INF; **to get ~ TO sth/-ING** acostumbrarse A algo/+ INF

used[2] /juːst/ v mod (indicating former state, habit) (only in past) ~ **to (+ INF)**: **there ~ to be** (antes) había; **I ~ to work in that shop** (antes) trabajaba en esa tienda; see also USE[2] v mod

useful /'juːsfəl/ adj útil; **to come in ~** (BrE) ser* útil, venir* bien

useless /'juːsləs ‖'juːslɪs/ adj (a) (ineffective) inútil; **these scissors are ~** estas tijeras no sirven para nada (b) (not capable) (colloq) ⟨person⟩ inútil, negado (fam)

user /'juːzər ‖'juːzə(r)/ n usuario, -ria m,f; **drug ~** consumidor, -dora m,f de drogas

user-friendly /'juːzər'frendli ‖ˌjuːzə'frendli/ adj fácil de usar or de utilizar

usher[1] /'ʌʃər ‖'ʌʃə(r)/ n (a) (Cin, Theat) acomodador, -dora m,f (b) (at wedding) persona allegada a los novios que se encarga de recibir y sentar a los invitados en la iglesia

usher[2] vt: **to ~ sb to her/his seat** conducir* a algn hasta su asiento; **he ~ed her into the room** la hizo pasar a la habitación
■ **usher in** [v + o + adv, v + adv + o] ⟨person⟩ hacer* pasar; ⟨new era⟩ marcar* el comienzo de

usherette /'ʌʃə'ret/ n acomodadora f

USN n = **United States Navy**

USS = **United States ship**

USSR n (= **Union of Soviet Socialist Republics**) URSS f

usual /'juːʒuəl/ adj ⟨method/response⟩ acostumbrado, habitual, usual; ⟨time/place⟩ de siempre, de costumbre; ⟨clothes⟩ de costumbre; **as ~** como de costumbre

usually /'juːʒuəli/ adv normalmente, usualmente; **what do you ~ do in the evenings?** ¿qué sueles hacer por las noches?

usurp /jʊ'sɜːrp ‖ju:'zɜːp/ vt (fml) usurpar

UT = **Utah**

utensil /ju:'tensəl ‖ju:'tensɪl/ n utensilio m

uterus /'juːtərəs/ n (pl **-teri** /-təraɪ/ or **-teruses**) útero m, matriz f

utility /ju:'tɪləti/ n (pl **-ties**) (public service ~) empresa f de servicio público

utility room n: cuarto para lavar y planchar

utilize /'juːtlaɪz ‖'juːtɪlaɪz/ vt (fml) utilizar*

utmost[1] /'ʌtməʊst/ adj (before n) mayor, sumo; **with the ~ care** con el mayor cuidado, con sumo cuidado; **of the ~ importance** de suma importancia

u

utmost² *n*: to do one's ~ (to (+ INF)) esforzarse* al máximo *or* hacer* todo lo posible (PARA + INF)

utopia, Utopia /juːˈtəʊpiə/ *n* (*pl* **-as**) utopía *f*

utter¹ /ˈʌtər ‖ˈʌtə(r)/ *adj* (*as intensifier*) completo, total

utter² *vt* ⟨*word*⟩ decir*, pronunciar; ⟨*cry*⟩ dar*

utterly /ˈʌtərli ‖ˈʌtəli/ *adv* (*as intensifier*) completamente, totalmente

U-turn /ˈjuːtɜːrn ‖ˈjuːtɜːn/ *n* cambio *m* de sentido; **to make** (AmE) *o* (BrE) **do a** ~ cambiar de sentido

Uzbekistan /ˈʊzbekɪˈstɑːn/ *n* Uzbekistán *m*

Vv

V, v /viː/ *n* V, v *f*

v [1] ▸ vs [2] (*pl* **vv**) (Bib, Lit) = **verse** [3] (colloq) (= **very**) muy

V (Elec) (= **volt(s)**) V (*read as: voltio(s)*)

VA *n* = **Virginia**

vacancy /ˈveɪkənsi/ *n* (*pl* **-cies**) **(a)** (*job*) vacante *f*; ⊙ **vacancies** ofertas de trabajo **(b)** (in hotel) habitación *f* libre

vacant /ˈveɪkənt/ *adj* [1] **(a)** ⟨*building/premises*⟩ desocupado **(b)** ⟨*post*⟩ vacante **(c)** ⟨*room*⟩ disponible, libre; ⟨*seat/space*⟩ libre [2] (blank) ⟨*look/expression*⟩ ausente

vacate /ˈveɪkeɪt ‖verˈkeɪt, və-/ *vt* (fml) ⟨*building*⟩ desocupar, desalojar; ⟨*seat/room*⟩ dejar libre; ⟨*job/post*⟩ abandonar, dejar

vacation¹ /verˈkeɪʃən/ *n* (esp AmE) (from work) vacaciones *fpl*, licencia *f* (Col, Méx, RPl); (from studies) vacaciones *fpl*; **to go/be on** ~ irse*/estar* de vacaciones

vacation² *vi* (AmE) pasar las vacaciones, vacacionar (Méx)

vacationer /verˈkeɪʃnər ‖vəˈkeɪʃənə(r)/, **vacationist** /-ʃnəst ‖-ʃənɪst/ *n* (AmE) turista *mf*; (in summer) veraneante *mf*

vaccinate /ˈvæksəneɪt ‖ˈvæksɪneɪt/ *vt* vacunar

vaccination /ˈvæksəˈneɪʃən ‖ˌvæksɪˈneɪʃən/ *n* vacunación *f*

vaccine /vækˈsiːn ‖ˈvæksiːn/ *n* vacuna *f*

vacillate /ˈvæsəleɪt/ *vi* (hesitate) vacilar; (sway) oscilar

vacuum¹ /ˈvækjuəm, -juːm/ *n* vacío *m*; (*before n*) ~ **pump** bomba *f* neumática

vacuum² *vi* pasar la aspiradora, aspirar (AmL)

vacuum: ~ **bottle** *n* (AmE) termo *m*; ~ **cleaner** *n* aspiradora *f*; ~ **flask** *n* termo *m*

vagabond /ˈvægəbɑːnd ‖ˈvægəbɒnd/ *n* vagabundo, -da *m,f*

vagina /vəˈdʒaɪnə/ *n* vagina *f*

vagrant /ˈveɪɡrənt/ *n* vagabundo, -da *m,f*

vague /veɪɡ/ *adj* **vaguer, vaguest** (a) (imprecise, unclear) ⟨*term/wording/concept*⟩ impreciso, vago **(b)** (indistinct) ⟨*outline*⟩ borroso **(c)** (absentminded) ⟨*expression*⟩ distraído; ⟨*person*⟩ distraído, despistado

vaguely /ˈveɪɡli/ *adv* **(a)** (in imprecise, unclear way) ⟨*explain/remember*⟩ vagamente; ⟨*answer/define*⟩ con vaguedad *or* imprecisión; ⟨*suspicious/ridiculous*⟩ ligeramente; **he looks** ~ **like his father** tiene un ligero parecido con *or* a su padre **(b)** (absentmindedly) distraídamente

vain /veɪn/ *adj* **-er, -est** [1] (self-admiring) vanidoso [2] (*before n, no comp*) **(a)** ⟨*attempt*⟩ vano; ⟨*hope/belief*⟩ vano **(b)** ⟨*promise/words*⟩ vano **(c) in vain** en vano, vanamente

vainly /ˈveɪnli/ *adv* (uselessly) en vano, vanamente

valentine /ˈvæləntaɪn/ *n* **(a)** (card) tarjeta de tono humorístico y/o amoroso que se envía anónimamente el día de San Valentín **(b)** *also* **Valentine** (person) enamorado, -da *m,f*

Valentine's Day /ˈvæləntaɪnz/ *n* el día de San Valentín, el día de los enamorados

valet /ˈvælət, ˈvæleɪ ‖ˈvæleɪ, ˈvælɪt/ *n* **(a)** (servant) ayuda *m* de cámara **(b)** (in hotel) mozo *m* de hotel

valiant /ˈvæljənt/ *adj* ⟨*hero/deed*⟩ valiente, valeroso; ⟨*attempt*⟩ valeroso

valid /ˈvæləd ‖ˈvælɪd/ *adj* válido

validate /ˈvælədeɪt ‖ˈvælɪdeɪt/ *vt* **(a)** (fml) ⟨*theory*⟩ dar* validez a, validar (fml) **(b)** (Law) ⟨*contract/document*⟩ validar

valley /ˈvæli/ *n* (*pl* **-leys**) valle *m*

valor, (BrE) **valour** /ˈvælər ‖ˈvælə(r)/ *n* (fml *o* liter) valor *m*, valentía *f*

valuable /ˈvæljuəbəl/ *adj* valioso; ⟨*time*⟩ precioso

valuables /ˈvæljuəbəlz/ *pl n* objetos *mpl* de valor

valuation /ˈvæljuˈeɪʃən/ *n* valoración *f*, tasación *f*, avalúo *m* (AmL)

value¹ /ˈvæljuː/ *n* [1] (worth) valor *m* [2] **values** (standards) valores *mpl*

value² *vt* **(a)** (Fin) ⟨*assets/property*⟩ tasar, valorar, avaluar* (AmL) **(b)** (regard highly) ⟨*friendship/advice*⟩ valorar, apreciar; ⟨*freedom/privacy*⟩ valorar

AmC	América Central	Arg	Argentina	Cu	Cuba	Per	Perú
AmL	América Latina	Bol	Bolivia	Ec	Ecuador	RPl	Río de la Plata
AmS	América del Sur	Chi	Chile	Esp	España	Ur	Uruguay
Andes	Región andina	CS	Cono Sur	Méx	México	Ven	Venezuela

value-added tax /'vælju:'ædəd
  ‖,vælju:'ædɪd/ *n* impuesto *m* al valor agregado
  or (Esp) sobre el valor añadido

valve /vælv/ *n* válvula *f*; (on musical instrument)
  pistón *m*

vampire /'væmpaɪr ‖'væmpaɪə(r)/ *n* vampiro
  m

van /væn/ *n* **(a)** (Auto) furgoneta *f*, camioneta *f*
  (b) (BrE Rail) furgón *m*

vandal /'vændl/ *n* vándalo *m*

vandalism /'vændlɪzəm/ *n* vandalismo *m*

vandalize /'vændlaɪz/ *vt* destrozar*

vanguard /'vænɡɑːrd ‖'vænɡɑːd/ *n*
  vanguardia *f*

vanilla /və'nɪlə/ *n* vainilla *f*

vanish /'vænɪʃ/ *vi* desaparecer*

vanity /'vænəti/ *n* (*pl* **-ties**) **(a)** (about
  appearance) vanidad *f* **(b)** (pride) orgullo *m*,
  vanidad *f*

vanity case *n* neceser *m*

vanquish /'væŋkwɪʃ/ *vt* (liter) vencer*

vantage point /'væntɪdʒ ‖'vɑːntɪdʒ/ *n*
  posición *f* ventajosa; (for view) mirador *m*

vapor, (BrE) **vapour** /'veɪpər ‖'veɪpə(r)/ *n* (on
  glass) vaho *m*; (steam) vapor *m*

vaporize /'veɪpəraɪz/ *vi* evaporarse,
  vaporizarse*

vapour *n* (BrE) ▶ VAPOR

variable /'veriəbəl ‖'veəriəbəl/ *adj* variable

variance /'veriəns ‖'veəriəns/ *n*: **to be at ∼
  with sth** no estar* de acuerdo con algo, discrepar
  de algo

variant /'veriənt ‖'veəriənt/ *n* variante *f*

variation /'veri'eɪʃən ‖,veəri'eɪʃən/ *n*
  variación *f*

varicose veins /'værəkəʊs ‖'værɪkəʊs/ *pl n*
  varices *fpl*, várices *fpl* (esp AmL)

varied /'verid ‖'veərid/ *adj* variado

variegated /'verɪɡeɪtəd ‖'veərɪɡeɪtɪd/ *adj*
  abigarrado, multicolor

variety /və'raɪəti/ *n* (*pl* **-ties**) **(a)** (diversity)
  variedad *f*, diversidad *f* **(b)** (assortment) ∼ **of** sth:
  it comes in a ∼ **of shades** viene en varios colores
  (c) (sort) clase *f*

variety show *n* espectáculo *m* de variedades

various /'veriəs ‖'veəriəs/ *adj* **(a)** (several)
  (*before n, no comp*) varios **(b)** (different, diverse)
  diferentes, diversos

varnish¹ /'vɑːrnɪʃ ‖'vɑːnɪʃ/ *n* barniz *m*; (for
  nails) (BrE) esmalte *m*

varnish² *vt* barnizar*; **to ∼ one's nails** (BrE)
  pintarse las uñas

vary /'veri ‖'veəri/, **varies, varying, varied**
  vi **(a)** (change, fluctuate) variar*; **the temperature
  varies between … la** temperatura oscila entre …
  (b) (differ) «*standards/prices*» variar*
  ■ ∼ *vt* variar*; «*diet*» dar* variedad a

vase /veɪs, veɪz ‖vɑːz/ *n* (for flowers) florero *m*;
  (ornament) jarrón *m*

vasectomy /və'sektəmi/ *n* (*pl* **-mies**)
  vasectomía *f*

Vaseline® /'væsəliːn/ *n* vaselina *f*

vast /væst ‖vɑːst/ *adj* ⟨*size/wealth*⟩ inmenso,
  enorme; ⟨*area*⟩ vasto, extenso; ⟨*knowledge*⟩ vasto

vastly /'væstli ‖'vɑːstli/ *adv* infinitamente

vat /væt/ *n* cuba *f*, tanque *m*

VAT *n* (= **value-added tax**) IVA *m*

Vatican /'vætɪkən/ *n* **the ∼** el Vaticano

Vatican City *n* Ciudad *f* del Vaticano

vault¹ /vɔːlt/ *n* **1 (a)** (strongroom) cámara *f*
  acorazada, bóveda *f* de seguridad (AmL) **(b)** (crypt)
  cripta *f* **2** (Archit) bóveda *f*

vault² *vi/t* saltar (*apoyándose en algo*)

VCR *n* = **videocassette recorder**

VD *n* = **venereal disease**

VDT *n* (esp AmE) = **visual display terminal**

VDU *n* = **visual display unit**

've /əv/ = **have**

veal /viːl/ *n* ternera *f* (*de animal muy joven y de
  carne pálida*)

VE-Day /'viː'iːdeɪ/ *n*: *día de la victoria aliada en
  Europa en la segunda guerra mundial*

veer /vɪr ‖vɪə(r)/ *vi* «*vehicle/horse*» dar* un
  viraje, virar; «*wind*» cambiar de dirección; **the
  road ∼s to the left** el camino tuerce *or* se desvía
  hacia la izquierda

vegan /'viːɡən/ *n* vegetariano estricto,
  vegetariana estricta *m,f*

vegetable /'vedʒtəbəl/ *n* **(a)** (Culin) verdura *f*;
  fresh/frozen/canned ∼s verdura fresca/
  congelada/enlatada **(b)** (plant) vegetal *m*; (*before
  n*) ⟨*oil/fats*⟩ vegetal

vegetarian¹ /'vedʒə'teriən ‖,vedʒɪ'teəriən/ *n*
  vegetariano, -na *m,f*

vegetarian² *adj* vegetariano

vegetate /'vedʒəteɪt ‖'vedʒɪteɪt/ *vi* vegetar

vegetation /'vedʒə'teɪʃən ‖,vedʒɪ'teɪʃən/ *n*
  vegetación *f*

vehement /'viːəmənt/ *adj* vehemente

vehemently /'viːəməntli/ *adv* con
  vehemencia, vehementemente

vehicle /'viːəkəl/ *n* vehículo *m*

veil¹ /veɪl/ *n* velo *m*

veil² *vt* (cover with a veil): **to ∼ one's face** taparse
  or cubrirse* con un velo, velarse (liter)

veiled /veɪld/ *adj* ⟨*threat/insult*⟩ velado

vein /veɪn/ *n* **1** (Anat, Bot, Zool) vena *f* **2 (a)** (of
  ore, mineral) veta *f*, filón *m*, vena *f* **(b)** (in marble)
  veta *f* **3** (*no pl*) (mood, style) vena *f*

velocity /və'lɑːsəti ‖və'lɒsəti/ *n* (*pl* **-ties**)
  velocidad *f*

velvet /'velvət ‖'velvɪt/ *n* terciopelo *m*

vendetta /ven'detə/ *n* vendetta *f*

vending machine /'vendɪŋ/ *n* máquina *f*
  expendedora

vendor /'vendər ‖'vendə(r)/ *n* (Busn, Law)
  vendedor, -dora *m,f*

veneer /və'nɪr ‖vɪ'nɪə(r)/ *n* (of wood, gold)
  enchapado *m*, chapa *f*

venerate /'venəreɪt/ *vt* venerar, reverenciar

venereal disease /və'nɪriəl ‖və'nɪəriəl/ *n*
  enfermedad *f* venérea

Venetian blind /və'niːʃən/ *n* persiana *f*
  veneciana *or* de lamas

Venezuela /'venə'zweɪlə ‖,venɪ'zweɪlə/ *n*
  Venezuela *f*

Venezuelan¹ /'venə'zweɪlən ‖,venɪ'zweɪlən/
  adj venezolano

Venezuelan² *n* venezolano, -na *m,f*

V

vengeance /'vendʒəns/ n venganza f; **with a ~** (colloq) de verdad or con ganas

vengeful /'vendʒfəl/ adj vengativo

venison /'venəsən ‖'venɪsən/ n (carne f de) venado m

venom /'venəm/ n (a) (Zool) veneno m (b) (malice) ponzoña f, veneno m

venomous /'venəməs/ adj ⟨snake/spider⟩ venenoso; ⟨look/words⟩ ponzoñoso

vent¹ /vent/ n (a) (in building, tunnel) (conducto m de) ventilación f; (in chimney, furnace) tiro m (b) (air ~) (shaft) respiradero m; (grille) rejilla f de ventilación

vent² vt descargar*; **she ~ed her anger on the children** descargó su ira sobre los niños

ventilate /'ventleɪt ‖'ventɪleɪt/ vt ventilar

ventilation /,vent'leɪʃən ‖,ventɪ'leɪʃən/ n ventilación f; (system) sistema m de ventilación

ventilator /'ventleɪtər ‖'ventɪleɪtə(r)/ n (Med) respirador m (artificial)

ventriloquist /ven'trɪləkwəst ‖ven'trɪləkwɪst/ n ventrílocuo, -cua m,f

venture¹ /'ventʃər ‖'ventʃə(r)/ n (Busn) empresa f

venture² vi atreverse; **to ~ out** (atreverse a) salir*
■ **~** vt ⟨opinion/guess⟩ aventurar

venue /'venju:/ n (for concert) lugar m de actuación; (for conference, Olympics) sede f

Venus /'vi:nəs/ n Venus m

veranda, verandah /və'rændə/ n galería f

verb /vɜːrb ‖vɜːb/ n verbo m

verbal /'vɜːrbəl ‖'vɜːbəl/ adj verbal

verbatim /vər'beɪtəm ‖vɜː'beɪtɪm/ adv al pie de la letra

verbose /vər'bəʊs ‖vɜː'bəʊs/ adj ampuloso, verboso

verdict /'vɜːrdɪkt ‖'vɜːdɪkt/ n (a) (Law) veredicto m (b) (opinion) opinión f

verge /vɜːrdʒ ‖vɜːdʒ/ n ❶ (a) (border) (BrE) borde m (b) **to be on the ~ of tears** estar* al borde de las lágrimas; **to be on the ~ of -ING** estar* a punto de + INF ❷ (of road) (BrE) arcén m
■ **verge on** [v + prep + o] rayar en

verification /'verəfə'keɪʃən ‖,verɪfɪ'keɪʃən/ n (a) (confirmation) confirmación f (b) (checking) verificación f

verify /'verəfaɪ ‖'verɪfaɪ/ vt **-fies, -fying, -fied** (a) (confirm) confirmar (b) (check) ⟨fact/ statement⟩ verificar*

veritable /'verətəbəl ‖'verɪtəbəl/ adj (frml or hum) auténtico, verdadero

vermin /'vɜːrmən ‖'vɜːmɪn/ n (pl ~) (animals) alimañas fpl; (insects) bichos mpl

vernacular /vər'nækjələr ‖və'nækjʊlə(r)/ n (native language) lengua f vernácula; (local speech) habla f‡ local

verruca /və'ru:kə/ n verruga f

versatile /'vɜːrsət‖'vɜːsətaɪl/ adj ⟨person⟩ polifacético, versátil; ⟨tool⟩ versátil; ⟨mind⟩ flexible

versatility /'vɜːrsə'tɪləti ‖,vɜːsə'tɪləti/ n versatilidad f

verse /vɜːrs ‖vɜːs/ n ❶ (poetry) verso m ❷ (a) (short poem) verso m, rima f (b) (stanza) estrofa f (c) (in Bible) versículo m

versed /vɜːrst ‖vɜːst/ adj ⟨pred⟩: **to be well ~ in sth** ser* muy versado en algo

version /'vɜːrʒən ‖'vɜːʃən/ n versión f

versus /'vɜːrsəs ‖'vɜːsəs/ prep (Law) contra; (Sport) contra, versus

vertebra /'vɜːrtəbrə ‖'vɜːtəbrə/ n (pl **-bras** or **-brae** /-breɪ/) vértebra f

vertebrate /'vɜːrtəbrət ‖'vɜːtɪbrət/ n vertebrado m

vertical /'vɜːrtɪkəl ‖'vɜːtɪkəl/ adj vertical

vertigo /'vɜːrtɪgəʊ ‖'vɜːtɪgəʊ/ n vértigo m

verve¹ /vɜːrv ‖vɜːv/ n brío m

very¹ /'veri/ adv (a) (extremely) muy; **she's ~ tall** es muy alta; (more emphatic) es altísima; **it was ~ hot** hacía mucho calor (b) (in phrases) **very much** ⟨like/enjoy⟩ mucho; **thank you ~ much** muchas gracias (c) (emphatic): **the ~ next day** precisamente al día siguiente; **at the ~ least** como mínimo

very² adj (before n) (a) (exact, precise) mismo; **for that ~ reason** por esa misma razón, por eso mismo (b) (actual) mismo; **its ~ existence is threatened** su misma existencia se halla amenazada (c) (mere, sheer) solo, mero; **the ~ mention of her name** la sola or mera mención de su nombre

vespers /'vespərz ‖'vespəz/ pl n vísperas fpl

vessel /'vesəl/ n ❶ (Naut frml) navío m (frml), nave f (liter) ❷ (receptacle) (frml) recipiente m; (drinking ~) vasija f ❸ (Anat, Bot) vaso m

vest /vest/ n (a) (waistcoat) (AmE) chaleco m (b) (undergarment) (BrE) camiseta f

vested interest /'vestəd ‖'vestɪd/ n **to have a ~ ~ in -ING/sth** tener* gran interés en + INF/ algo

vestige /'vestɪdʒ/ n vestigio m

vestry /'vestri/ n (pl **-tries**) sacristía f

vet¹ /vet/ n ❶ (veterinarian) veterinario, -ria m,f ❷ (veteran) (AmE colloq) veterano, -na m,f

vet² vt **-tt-** ⟨applicant⟩ someter a investigación; ⟨application⟩ examinar

veteran /'vetərən/ n (a) (of war) veterano, -na m,f de guerra (b) (experienced person) veterano, -na m,f

veteran: ~ car n (BrE) coche m antiguo (fabricado antes de 1919); **V~s Day** /'vetərənz/ n (in US) día m del Armisticio

veterinarian /'vetərə'neriən ‖,vetərɪ'neəriən/ n (AmE) médico veterinario, médica veterinaria m,f

veterinary /'vetərəneri ‖'vetrɪnəri/ adj veterinario; **~ surgeon** (BrE frml) médico veterinario, médica veterinaria m,f

veto¹ /'vi:təʊ/ n (pl **vetoes**) veto m

veto² vt **vetoes, vetoing, vetoed** vetar

vex /veks/ vt (a) (annoy) irritar, sacar* de quicio (b) (worry, puzzle) desconcertar*

vexed /vekst/ adj (a) (annoyed) ⟨expression/tone⟩ irritado; **to be ~** estar* enojado (esp AmL), estar* enfadado (esp Esp) (b) (worried, puzzled) desconcertado

VHF (= very high frequency) VHF

via /ˈvaɪə, ˈviːə ‖ ˈvaɪə/ prep **(a)** (by way of) vía **(b)** (by means of) a través de

viable /ˈvaɪəbəl/ adj viable

viaduct /ˈvaɪədʌkt/ n viaducto m

vibrant /ˈvaɪbrənt/ adj **(a)** ‹color› vibrante; ‹atmosphere› efervescente **(b)** (resonant) ‹voice› vibrante

vibrate /ˈvaɪbreɪt ‖ vaɪˈbreɪt/ vi vibrar

vibration /vaɪˈbreɪʃən/ n vibración f

vicar /ˈvɪkər ‖ ˈvɪkə(r)/ n párroco m

vicarage /ˈvɪkərɪdʒ/ n vicaría f, casa f del párroco

vicarious /vɪˈkeriəs ‖ vɪˈkeəriəs/ adj indirecto

vice /vaɪs/ n **1** (wickedness) vicio m **2** (BrE) ▶ VISE

vice- /ˈvaɪs/ pref vice-

vice: ∼ president n vicepresidente, -ta m,f; **∼ versa** /ˈvaɪsiˈvɜːrsə, ˈvaɪsˈvɜːrsə ‖ ˌvaɪsiˈvɜːsə, ˌvaɪsˈvɜːsə/ adv viceversa

vicinity /vɪˈsɪnəti/ n (fml) inmediaciones fpl

vicious /ˈvɪʃəs/ adj **(a)** (savage, violent) ‹dog› fiero; ‹criminal› despiadado; ‹attack› feroz, salvaje; ‹crime› atroz **(b)** (malicious) ‹rumor› malicioso

vicious circle n círculo m vicioso

viciously /ˈvɪʃəsli/ adv brutalmente, ferozmente

victim /ˈvɪktəm ‖ ˈvɪktɪm/ n víctima f; the flood ∼s los damnificados por las inundaciones

victimize /ˈvɪktəmaɪz ‖ ˈvɪktɪmaɪz/ vt victimizar*

victor /ˈvɪktər ‖ ˈvɪktə(r)/ n vencedor, -dora m,f

Victorian /vɪkˈtɔːriən/ adj victoriano

victorious /vɪkˈtɔːriəs/ adj ‹army› victorioso; ‹team› vencedor

victory /ˈvɪktəri/ n (pl -ries) victoria f, triunfo m; (Mil) victoria f

video¹ /ˈvɪdiəʊ/ n (pl videos) video m or (Esp) vídeo m; (before n) ∼ **camera** videocámara f; ∼ **recorder** aparato m de video or (Esp) vídeo

video² vt **videoes, videoing, videoed** grabar

video: ∼cassette /ˈvɪdiəʊkəˈset/ n videocasete m; (before n) ∼**cassette recorder** magnetoscopio m, video m or (Esp) vídeo m; ∼ **game** n videojuego m

Vienna /viˈenə/ n Viena f

Vietnam /ˌviːetˈnɑːm, -næm ‖ vjetˈnæm/ n Vietnam m

Vietnamese¹ /ˌviːetnəˈmiːz ‖ ˌvɪetnəˈmiːz/ adj vietnamita

Vietnamese² n (pl ∼) **(a)** (person) vietnamita mf **(b)** (language) vietnamita m

view¹ /vjuː/ n **1** **(a)** (sight) vista f; in full ∼ of **sb** a la vista de algn **(b)** (range of vision): we had a good ∼ of the stage veíamos muy bien el escenario **2** (scene, vista) vista f **3** (opinion, attitude) opinión f, parecer m; in my ∼ en mi opinión, a mi modo de ver **4** (plan, intention): with a ∼ to -ING con vistas A + INF **5** (in phrases) in view of en vista de; on view: to be on ∼ (to the public) exponerse* (al público)

view² vt **(a)** ‹sights/scene› ver*, mirar **(b)** (inspect) ‹property› ver* **(c)** (regard) ver*, considerar

viewer /ˈvjuːər ‖ ˈvjuːə(r)/ n **(a)** (person) telespectador, -dora m,f, televidente mf **(b)** (for slides) visionadora f

view: ∼finder /ˈvjuːfaɪndər ‖ ˈvjuːfaɪndə(r)/ n visor m; ∼**point** n punto m de vista

vigil /ˈvɪdʒəl ‖ ˈvɪdʒɪl/ n **(a)** (watch) (liter or journ) vela f; to keep a ∼ over sth velar sobre algo **(b)** (Relig) vigilia f

vigilance /ˈvɪdʒələns ‖ ˈvɪdʒɪləns/ n vigilancia f

vigilant /ˈvɪdʒələnt ‖ ˈvɪdʒɪlənt/ adj alerta, vigilante

vigilante /ˌvɪdʒəˈlænti ‖ ˌvɪdʒɪˈlænti/ n vigilante, -ta m,f

vigor, (BrE) **vigour** /ˈvɪɡər ‖ ˈvɪɡə(r)/ n vigor m

vigorous /ˈvɪɡərəs/ adj enérgico; ‹growth› vigoroso

vigorously /ˈvɪɡərəsli/ adv enérgicamente; ‹deny› rotundamente

vigour n (BrE) ▶ VIGOR

Viking /ˈvaɪkɪŋ/ n vikingo, -ga m,f

vile /vaɪl/ adj **viler, vilest (a)** (despicable) (liter) vil (liter) **(b)** (colloq) ‹taste/food› vomitivo (fam), asqueroso; ‹color/weather› horrible

villa /ˈvɪlə/ n **(a)** (Hist) villa f **(b)** (holiday house) chalet m

village /ˈvɪlɪdʒ/ n (large) pueblo m; (small) aldea f

villager /ˈvɪlədʒər ‖ ˈvɪlɪdʒə(r)/ n (of large village) vecino, -na m,f or habitante mf del pueblo; (of small village) aldeano, -na m,f

villain /ˈvɪlən/ n **(a)** (in fiction) villano, -na m,f **(b)** (criminal) (BrE sl) maleante mf

vinaigrette /ˈvɪnɪˈɡret/ n vinagreta f

vindicate /ˈvɪndəkeɪt ‖ ˈvɪndɪkeɪt/ vt (fml) (justify) ‹action› justificar*; ‹assertion› confirmar; ‹right› reivindicar*

vindictive /vɪnˈdɪktɪv/ adj vengativo

vine /vaɪn/ n (grape∼) (on ground) vid f; (climbing) parra f

vinegar /ˈvɪnɪɡər ‖ ˈvɪnɪɡə(r)/ n vinagre m

vineyard /ˈvɪnjərd, -jɑːrd ‖ ˈvɪnjəd, -jɑːd/ n viñedo m, viña f

vintage¹ /ˈvɪntɪdʒ/ n **(a)** (wine, year) cosecha f **(b)** (harvest, season) vendimia f

vintage² adj (before n, no comp) **(a)** ‹wine› añejo **(b)** (outstanding) ‹year/performance› excelente

vintage car n (esp BrE) coche m antiguo (fabricado entre 1919 y 1930)

vinyl /ˈvaɪnl/ n vinilo m

viola /viˈəʊlə/ n (Mus) viola f

violate /ˈvaɪəleɪt/ vt **1** ‹agreement/rights› violar; ‹ban› desobedecer* **2** ‹shrine/grave› profanar

violation /ˌvaɪəˈleɪʃən/ n violación f

violence /ˈvaɪələns/ n violencia f

violent /ˈvaɪələnt/ adj **(a)** ‹person/behavior› violento **(b)** (strong, forceful) ‹storm/explosion› violento, fuerte; he has a ∼ temper tiene muy mal genio

violently /ˈvaɪələntli/ adv violentamente

violet /ˈvaɪələt/ n **(a)** (Bot) violeta f **(b)** (color) violeta m; (before n) violeta adj inv

violin /ˌvaɪəˈlɪn/ n violín m

V

violinist /ˈvaɪəˈlɪnəst ‖ˌvaɪəˈlɪnɪst/ *n* violinista *mf*

VIP *n* (colloq) (= **very important person**) VIP *mf*

viper /ˈvaɪpər ‖ˈvaɪpə(r)/ *n* víbora *f*

virgin[1] /ˈvɜːrdʒən ‖ˈvɜːdʒɪn/ *n* virgen *f*

virgin[2] *adj* ⟨*forest*⟩ virgen; ⟨*snow*⟩ intacto

virginity /vərˈdʒɪnəti ‖vəˈdʒɪnɪti/ *n* virginidad *f*; **to lose one's ∼** perder* la virginidad

Virgo /ˈvɜːrɡəʊ ‖ˈvɜːɡəʊ/ *n* (*pl* **-gos**) **(a)** (sign) (*no art*) Virgo *or* virgo *mf* **(b)** (person) Virgo *or* virgo *mf*

virile /ˈvɪrəl ‖ˈvɪraɪl/ *adj* viril

virtual /ˈvɜːrtʃuəl ‖ˈvɜːtjʊəl, ˈvɜːtʃʊəl/ *adj* (*before n*) **1** (near total): **traffic is at a ∼ standstill** el tráfico está prácticamente paralizado **2** (Comput, Opt) virtual

virtually /ˈvɜːrtʃuəli ‖ˈvɜːtjʊəli, ˈvɜːtʃʊəli/ *adv* prácticamente, casi

virtue /ˈvɜːrtʃuː ‖ˈvɜːtjuː, ˈvɜːtʃuː/ *n* **(a)** (moral excellence) virtud *f* **(b)** (advantage) ventaja *f* **(c)** **by virtue of** (*as prep*) en virtud de

virtuoso /ˌvɜːrtʃuˈəʊsəʊ ‖ˌvɜːtjʊˈəʊsəʊ, ˌvɜːtʃʊˈəʊsəʊ/ *n* (*pl* **-sos** *or* **-si** /-siː/) virtuoso, -sa *m,f*

virtuous /ˈvɜːrtʃuəs ‖ˈvɜːtjʊəs, ˈvɜːtʃʊəs/ *adj* virtuoso

virulent /ˈvɪrələnt, ˈvɪrjə- ‖ˈvɪrʊlənt, ˈvɪrjʊ-/ *adj* virulento

virus /ˈvaɪrəs ‖ˈvaɪərəs/ *n* (*pl* **∼es**) (Med, Comput) virus *m*

virus checker *n* (Comput) programa *m* antivirus

visa /ˈviːzə/ *n* (*pl* **-s**) visado *m*, visa *f* (AmL)

vis-à-vis /ˈviːzəˈviː ‖ˌviːzɑːˈviː/ *prep* con respecto a, respecto de

viscose /ˈvɪskəʊs/ *n* viscosilla *f*

viscount /ˈvaɪkaʊnt/ *n* vizconde *m*

viscous /ˈvɪskəs/ *adj* viscoso

vise, (BrE) **vice** /vaɪs/ *n* torno *m or* tornillo *m* de banco

visibility /ˌvɪzəˈbɪləti/ *n* visibilidad *f*

visible /ˈvɪzəbəl/ *adj* visible; ⟨*sign/ improvement*⟩ evidente

visibly /ˈvɪzəbli/ *adv* visiblemente

vision /ˈvɪʒən/ *n* **1** **(a)** (faculty of sight) visión *f*, vista *f* **(b)** (visibility) visibilidad *f* **2** (imagination, foresight) visión *f* (de futuro) **3** (dreamlike revelation) visión *f*

visionary /ˈvɪʒəneri ‖ˈvɪʒənri/ *n* (*pl* **-ries**) visionario, -ria *m,f*

visit[1] /ˈvɪzət ‖ˈvɪzɪt/ *n* visita *f*; **to pay a ∼ to sb** hacerle* una visita a algn

visit[2] *vt* visitar

■ ∼ *vi* hacer* una visita; (stay) estar* de visita

visitor /ˈvɪzətər ‖ˈvɪzɪtə(r)/ *n* (to museum, town etc) visitante *mf*; (to person's home) visita *f*

visitor center *n* (AmE) centro *m* de informaciones

visor /ˈvaɪzər ‖ˈvaɪzə(r)/ *n* visera *f*

vista /ˈvɪstə/ *n* vista *f*

visual /ˈvɪʒuəl/ *adj* visual; **∼ display unit** pantalla *f*, monitor *m*

visualize /ˈvɪʒuəlaɪz/ *vt* **(a)** (picture mentally) imaginarse, visualizar* **(b)** (expect) prever*

vital /ˈvaɪtl/ *adj* **(a)** (essential) esencial, fundamental **(b)** ⟨*factor/issue*⟩ decisivo, de vital importancia **(c)** ⟨*organ/function*⟩ vital

vitality /vaɪˈtæləti/ *n* vitalidad *f*

vitamin /ˈvaɪtəmən, ˈvɪtəmɪn, ˈvaɪt-/ *n* vitamina *f*; (*before n*) **∼ pill** *o* **tablet** vitamina *f*

vivacious /vəˈveɪʃəs ‖vɪˈveɪʃəs/ *adj* vivaz

vivid /ˈvɪvəd ‖ˈvɪvɪd/ *adj* **(a)** ⟨*color*⟩ vivo **(b)** ⟨*account/dream*⟩ vívido **(c)** ⟨*imagination*⟩ rico

vividly /ˈvɪvədli ‖ˈvɪvɪdli/ *adv* **(a)** ⟨*colored*⟩ vistosamente **(b)** ⟨*describe*⟩ vívidamente, gráficamente

vivisection /ˈvɪvəˈsekʃən ‖ˌvɪvɪˈsekʃən/ *n* vivisección *f*

vixen /ˈvɪksən/ *n* (Zool) zorra *f*, raposa *f*

viz /vɪz/ *adv* a saber

VJ-Day /ˈviːˈdʒeɪdeɪ/ *n*: *día de la victoria aliada sobre el Japón*

V-neck /ˈviːnek/, (BrE also) **V-necked** /ˈviːnekt/ *adj* de escote *or* cuello en pico, de escote en V

vocabulary /vəʊˈkæbjələri ‖vəʊˈkæbjʊləri/ *n* (*pl* **-ries**) vocabulario *m*

vocal /ˈvəʊkəl/ *adj* vocal

vocal cords *pl n* cuerdas *fpl* vocales

vocalist /ˈvəʊkələst ‖ˈvəʊkəlɪst/ *n* cantante *mf*

vocation /vəʊˈkeɪʃən/ *n* vocación *f*

vodka /ˈvɑːdkə ‖ˈvɒdkə/ *n* vodka *m*

vogue /vəʊɡ/ *n* moda *f*

voice[1] /vɔɪs/ *n* voz *f*

voice[2] *vt* expresar

voice mail *n* audiomensajería *f*, correo *m* de voz

void[1] /vɔɪd/ *n* vacío *m*

void[2] *adj* **1** (liter) (*pred*) **to be ∼ of** sth estar* desprovisto de algo **2** (Law) nulo, inválido

vol (*pl* **vols**) (= **volume**) vol., t.

volatile /ˈvɑːlətl ‖ˈvɒlətaɪl/ *adj* **(a)** (Chem) volátil **(b)** ⟨*person/personality*⟩ imprevisible **(c)** ⟨*situation*⟩ volátil

volcanic /vɑːlˈkænɪk ‖vɒlˈkænɪk/ *adj* volcánico

volcano /vɑːlˈkeɪnəʊ ‖vɒlˈkeɪnəʊ/ *n* (*pl* **-noes** *or* **-nos**) volcán *m*

volition /vəʊˈlɪʃən ‖vəˈlɪʃən/ *n* (fml) volición *f* (frml); **of one's own ∼** por voluntad propia, (de) motu proprio

volley[1] /ˈvɑːli ‖ˈvɒli/ *n* **1** (of shots) descarga *f* (cerrada) **2** (Sport) volea *f*

volley[2] *vt/i* volear

volleyball /ˈvɑːlibɔːl ‖ˈvɒlibɔːl/ *n* vóleibol *m*, balonvolea *m*

volt /vəʊlt/ *n* voltio *m*

voltage /ˈvəʊltɪdʒ/ *n* voltaje *m*

volume ⋯⊹ wail ⋯

volume /'vɑːljuːm ‖'vɒljuːm/ *n* **1** (Phys) (of a body) volumen *m*; (of container) capacidad *f* **2** (amount) cantidad *f*, volumen *m*; (of business, trade) volumen *m* **3** (of sound) volumen *m* **4** (book) tomo *m*, volumen *m*

voluminous /və'luːmənəs ‖və'luːmɪnəs/ *adj* **(a)** ⟨blouse/skirt⟩ amplísimo **(b)** ⟨correspondence⟩ voluminoso

voluntarily /'vɑːlən'terəli ‖'vɒləntrɪli/ *adv* voluntariamente, por voluntad propia

voluntary /'vɑːləntri ‖'vɒləntri/ *adj* **1** (unforced) voluntario; ~ **redundancy** (BrE) baja *f* incentivada **2** (unpaid) ⟨work⟩ voluntario; ⟨organization⟩ de beneficencia

volunteer¹ /'vɑːlən'tɪr ‖,vɒlən'tɪər/ *n* voluntario, -ria *m,f*

volunteer² *vt* ofrecer*
■ ~ *vi* ofrecerse*; **to** ~ **to** + INF ofrecerse* A + INF

voluptuous /və'lʌptʃuəs/ *adj* voluptuoso

vomit¹ /'vɑːmət ‖'vɒmɪt/ *vi/t* vomitar

vomit² *n* vómito *m*

voodoo /'vuːduː/ *n* vudú *m*

voracious /vɔː'reɪʃəs ‖və'reɪʃəs/ *adj* voraz

vote¹ /vəʊt/ *n* **1** **(a)** (ballot cast) voto *m* **(b)** (right to vote) **the** ~ el sufragio, el derecho de *or* al voto **2** (act) votación *f*; **to take a** ~ **on sth** someter algo a votación

vote² *vi* votar; **to** ~ **FOR sb** votar POR *or* A algn; **to** ~ **ON sth** someter algo a votación; **to** ~ **FOR/ AGAINST sth** votar A FAVOR DE/EN CONTRA DE algo

■ ~ *vt* **1** **(a)** (support, choose) votar por, votar **(b)** (elect) elegir* por votación **2** (decide) **to** ~ **to** + INF votar POR + INF
■ **vote in** [*v* + *o* + *adv*, *v* + *adv* + *o*] elegir* (*por votación*)

voter /'vəʊtər ‖'vəʊtə(r)/ *n* votante *mf*

voting /'vəʊtɪŋ/ *n* votación *f*

vouch /vaʊtʃ/ *vi* **to** ~ **FOR sb** responder POR algn

voucher /'vaʊtʃər ‖'vaʊtʃə(r)/ *n* (cash substitute) vale *m*

vow¹ /vaʊ/ *n* voto *m*, promesa *f*

vow² *vt* jurar, hacer* voto de (frml)

vowel /'vaʊəl/ *n* vocal *f*

voyage /'vɔɪɪdʒ/ *n* viaje *m*; (overseas) travesía *f*

voyager /'vɔɪədʒər ‖'vɔɪɪdʒə(r)/ *n* (liter) viajero, -ra *m,f*; (by sea) navegante *mf*

voyeur /vwɑː'jɜːr, 'vɔɪ- ‖vwɑː'jɜː(r), 'vɔɪ-/ *n* voyeur *mf*

vs = **versus**

VT, Vt = **Vermont**

vulgar /'vʌlɡər ‖'vʌlɡə(r)/ *adj* **(a)** (coarse) ⟨person/remark⟩ grosero, ordinario, vulgar **(b)** (tasteless) de mal gusto, ordinario

vulgarity /vʌl'ɡærəti/ *n* **(a)** (coarseness) ordinariez *f*, grosería *f*, vulgaridad *f* **(b)** (tastelessness) mal gusto *m*, chabacanería *f*

vulnerable /'vʌlnərəbəl/ *adj* vulnerable

vulture /'vʌltʃər ‖'vʌltʃə(r)/ *n* buitre *m*; (turkey ~) gallinazo *m*, zopilote *m* (AmC, Méx)

vv = **verses**

W w

W, w /'dʌbəljuː/ *n* W, w *f*

W (a) (Elec) (= **watt(s)**) W **(b)** (Geog) (= **west**) O

WA = **Washington**

wad /wɑːd ‖wɒd/ *n* (roll, bundle — of bills, notes) fajo *m*; (— of papers) montón *m*, tambache *m* (Méx); (— tied together) lío *m*

waddle /'wɑːdl̩ ‖'wɒdl̩/ *vi* «*person*» caminar *or* andar* como un pato; «*duck*» caminar balanceándose

wade /weɪd/ *vi* caminar (*por el agua, barro etc*)
■ **wade through** [*v* + *prep* + *o*] (colloq) leerse* (*algo difícil, largo, aburrido etc*)

wader /'weɪdər ‖'weɪdə(r)/ *n* **(a)** (Zool) ave *f*‡ zancuda **(b)** **waders** *pl* (Clothing) botas *fpl* de pescador

wading pool /'weɪdɪŋ/ *n* (AmE) piscina *f or* (Méx) alberca *f* inflable (*para niños*)

wafer /'weɪfər ‖'weɪfə(r)/ *n* **(a)** (Culin) galleta *f* de barquillo, oblea *f* **(b)** (Relig) hostia *f*

wafer-thin /'weɪfər'θɪn ‖,weɪfə'θɪn/ *adj* finísimo

waffle¹ /'wɑːfəl ‖'wɒfəl/ *n* **1** (Culin) wafle *m* (AmL), gofre *m* (Esp) **2** (nonsense) (BrE pej) palabrería *f*; (in essay, exam) paja *f* (fam)

waffle² *vi* (esp BrE) hablar sin decir nada; (in essay, exam) meter paja (fam), payar (RPl)

waft /wɑːft ‖'wɒft/ *vi* (+ *adv compl*): **the smell of coffee that** ~**ed from the kitchen** el olor a café que venía de la cocina

wag /wæɡ/ **-gg-** *vt* ⟨*tail*⟩ menear
■ ~ *vi* ⟨*tail*⟩ menearse, moverse*

wage¹ /weɪdʒ/ *n* (rate of pay) sueldo *m*; **wages** (actual money) sueldo *m*, paga *f*

wage² *vt*: **to** ~ **war** hacer* la guerra

wager¹ /'weɪdʒər ‖'weɪdʒə(r)/ *n* apuesta *f*

wager² *vt* apostar*

waggon *n* (BrE) ▶ WAGON

wagon /'wæɡən/ *n* **1** (drawn by animals) carro *m*; (covered) carromato *m* **2** **(a)** (delivery truck) (AmE) furgoneta *f or* camioneta *f* de reparto **(b)** (BrE Rail) vagón *m* de mercancías

waif /weɪf/ *n* (liter) persona *o* animal sin hogar

wail¹ /weɪl/ *vi* «*person*» llorar; «*siren/ bagpipes*» gemir*; «*wind*» aullar*

wail² *n* gemido *m*

waist /weɪst/ n (of body) cintura f; (of garment) talle m

waist: ~**band** n pretina f, cinturilla f; ~**coat** n (esp BrE) chaleco m; ~**line** n (of garment) talle m; (of body) cintura f

wait¹ /weɪt/ vi **1** esperar; **we'll have to ~ and see** habrá que esperar a ver qué pasa; **I can't ~ to see his face** me muero de ganas de ver la cara que pone; **to ~ FOR sth/sb** esperar algo/a algn; **to ~ FOR sb/sth to + INF** esperar (A) QUE algn/algo (+ subj)
2 (serve) **to ~ ON sb** atender* a algn

■ ~ vt **1** (await) esperar; **you have to ~ your turn** tienes que esperar (a) que te toque
2 (serve): **to ~ table** (AmE) servir* a la mesa

■ **wait up** [v + adv] (not go to bed) **to ~ up** (FOR sb) esperar (A algn) levantado

wait² n (no pl) espera f; **to lie in ~ for sb/sth** estar* al acecho de algn/algo

waiter /'weɪtər ‖'weɪtə(r)/ n camarero m, mesero m (AmL), mozo m (Col, CS), mesonero m (Ven)

waiting /'weɪtɪŋ/: ~ **list** n lista f de espera; ~ **room** n sala f de espera

waitress /'weɪtrəs ‖'weɪtrɪs/ n camarera f, mesera f (AmL), moza f (Col, CS), mesonera f (Ven)

waive /weɪv/ vt (frml) **(a)** (not apply) ⟨rule⟩ no aplicar*; ⟨condition⟩ no exigir* **(b)** (renounce) ⟨right/privilege⟩ renunciar a

wake¹ /weɪk/ (past **woke**; past p **woken**) vt despertar*; see also WAKE UP 1

■ ~ vi despertar*, despertarse*

■ **wake up 1** [v + o + adv, v + adv + o] despertar* **2** [v + adv] (become awake) despertarse*; ~ **up!** ¡despiértate!; (pay attention) ¡espabílate!, ¡despabílate!; **to ~ up TO sth** ⟨to danger/fact⟩ darse* cuenta DE algo

wake² n **1** (of ship) estela f; **the hurricane left a trail of destruction in its ~** el huracán dejó una estela de destrucción a su paso **2** (for dead person) velatorio m

Wales /weɪlz/ n (el país de) Gales

walk¹ /wɔːk/ vi **1** (go by foot) caminar, andar* (esp Esp); (in a leisurely way) pasear; **he ~ed down/up the steps** bajó/subió los peldaños; **to ~ in/out** entrar/salir*; **to ~ up to sb** acercarse* a algn
2 (not use bus, car, etc) ir* a pie

■ ~ vt **1** (go along) ⟨hills/path⟩ recorrer
2 (a) (take for walk) ⟨dog⟩ pasear, sacar* a pasear **(b)** (accompany) acompañar

■ **walk away** [v + adv] alejarse

■ **walk into** [v + prep + o] **(a)** (enter) ⟨room/building⟩ entrar en, entrar a (AmL) **(b)** (fall into) ⟨trap⟩ caer* en **(c)** (collide with) darse* contra

■ **walk off 1** [v + adv] (go away) irse*, marcharse (esp Esp)
2 [v + o + adv, v + adv + o]: **we went out to ~ off our lunch** salimos a dar un paseo para bajar la comida

■ **walk out** [v + adv] (Lab Rel) abandonar el trabajo (como media reivindicatoria)

■ **walk out on** [v + adv + prep + o] ⟨lover/family⟩ dejar, abandonar

■ **walk over** [v + prep + o] (colloq): **don't let him ~ all over you** no te dejes pisotear (por él)

walk² n **1** (leisurely) paseo m; (long) caminata f; **to go for a ~** ir* a pasear or a dar un paseo, ir* a caminar (esp AmL); **it's five minutes' o a**

five-minute ~ from here está a cinco minutos de aquí a pie **2** (path) (esp AmE) camino m **3** (gait) manera f de caminar or andar; see also WALK OF LIFE

walker /'wɔːkər ‖'wɔːkə(r)/ n **(a)** (sb that walks): **to be a fast/slow ~** caminar or andar* rápido/despacio **(b)** (hiker) excursionista f

walkie-talkie /'wɔːkiˈtɔːki/ n walkie-talkie m

walk-in /'wɔːkɪn/ adj: ~ **closet** vestidor m

walking¹ /'wɔːkɪŋ/ n: **I do a lot of ~** yo camino or ando mucho; (before n) ⟨tour⟩ a pie; **is it within ~ distance?** ¿se puede ir a pie?

walking² adj: **she's a ~ encyclopedia** (hum) es una enciclopedia ambulante (hum); **he's a ~ miracle** vive de milagro

walking stick n bastón m

Walkman® /'wɔːkmən/ n (pl -**mans** /-mənz/) walkman® m

walk: ~ of life n: **people from all ~s of life** gente de todas las profesiones y condiciones sociales; ~-**on** n (before n) ~-**on part** (Theat) papel m de figurante; (Cin) papel m de extra; ~**out** n (from talks, meeting) retirada en señal de protesta; (strike) abandono del trabajo como medida reivindicatoria; ~**over** n (victory by default) walkover m (victoria por la no comparecencia del contrincante); (easy victory) (colloq) paseo m (fam); ~**way** n (bridge) puente m, pasarela f; (passageway) pasillo m; (path) sendero m

wall /wɔːl/ n **1 (a)** (freestanding) muro m; (of castle, city) muralla f; **garden ~** tapia f, muro m **(b)** (barrier) barrera f; **a ~ of fire** una barrera de fuego **2** (of building, room) pared f, muralla f (Chi); (before n) ~ **chart** gráfico m mural; ~ **painting** mural m **3** (of stomach, artery) pared f

■ **wall off** [v + o + adv, v + adv + o] separar con un muro or una pared or una tapia

■ **wall up** [v + o + adv, v + adv + o] ⟨doorway/window⟩ tapiar; ⟨person/body⟩ emparedar

walled /wɔːld/ adj ⟨city⟩ amurallado; ⟨garden⟩ tapiado

wallet /'wɑːlət ‖'wɒlɪt/ n **(a)** (for money) cartera f, billetera f **(b)** (folder) carpeta f

wallflower /'wɔːlflaʊr ‖'wɔːlflaʊə(r)/ n **1** (Bot) alhelí m **2** (person) (colloq): **she was always a ~** nunca la sacaban a bailar, siempre planchaba (Bol, CS fam), siempre comía pavo (Col fam)

wallop /'wɑːləp ‖'wɒləp/ vt (colloq) darle* una paliza a

wallow /'wɑːləʊ ‖'wɒləʊ/ vi **(a)** (bathe) ⟨animal⟩ revolcarse* **(b)** (delight): **to ~ in self-pity** regodearse en la autocompasión

wall: ~paper n papel m pintado, tapiz m de empapelar (Méx, Ven); **W~ Street** n Wall Street (centro financiero de los EEUU); ~-**to-~ carpet** /'wɔːltəˈwɔːl/ n alfombra f de pared a pared, moqueta f (Esp), moquette f (RPl)

walnut /'wɔːlnʌt/ n **1 (a)** (nut) nuez f, nuez f de Castilla (Méx) **(b)** ~ (**tree**) nogal m **(c)** (wood) nogal m

walrus /'wɔːlrəs/ n (pl -**es** or ~) morsa f

waltz¹ /wɔːls, wɒːlts/ n vals m

waltz² vi valsar, valsear

wan /wɑːn ‖wɒn/ adj **(a)** (pallid) ⟨face/complexion⟩ pálido **(b)** ⟨smile⟩ lánguido

wand /wɑːnd ‖wɒnd/ n (of sorcerer, conjurer)
varita f mágica

wander¹ /'wɑːndər ‖'wɒndə(r)/ vi (a) (+ adv
compl) (walk — in a leisurely way) pasear; (—
aimlessly) deambular, vagar* (b) (stray): don't let
the children ~ away from the car no dejes que los
niños se alejen del coche; don't let your mind ~!
¡no te distraigas!

wander² n (esp BrE) (no pl) vuelta f, paseo m

wanderer /'wɑːndərər ‖'wɒndərə(r)/ n
trotamundos mf

wanderings /'wɑːndərɪŋz ‖'wɒndərɪŋz/ pl n
correrías fpl

wanderlust /'wɑːndərlʌst ‖'wɒndələst/ n
ansias fpl de conocer mundo

wane¹ /weɪn/ vi (a) «moon» menguar* (b)
«interest/popularity» decaer*, disminuir* (c)
waning pres p «moon» menguante; «interest/
popularity/influence» decreciente

wane² n: to be on the ~ «moon» estar*
menguando; «popularity» estar* decayendo or
disminuyendo

wangle /'wæŋɡəl/ vt (colloq) agenciarse (fam)

want¹ /wɒnt ‖wɒnt/ vt **1** (a) (require, desire)
querer*; to ~ to + INF querer* + INF; to ~ sb/sth
to + INF querer* QUE alguien/algo + (subj) (b)
«police» buscar*; ⑤ wanted se busca (c) (as price
for sth) pedir* (d) «person» (sexually) desear
2 (need) necesitar; ⑤ gardener wanted se
necesita or se precisa jardinero; you ~ to see a
doctor tienes que ver a un médico.
■ ~ vi (lack) (frml) (usu with neg): you/they will ~
for nothing no te/les faltará nada

want² n **1** (requirement, need) necesidad f
2 (lack, absence) falta f, carencia f (frml); for ~ of
sth a falta de algo; for ~ of a better word por así
decirlo **3** (destitution, penury) miseria f

wanted /'wɒntəd ‖'wɒntɪd/ adj «criminal/
terrorist» buscado (por la policía); see also
WANT¹ 1B

wanton /'wɒntn̩ ‖'wɒntən/ adj (a) (willful) sin
sentido, gratuito (b) (licentious) licencioso

war /wɔːr ‖wɔː(r)/ n guerra f; to be at ~ with
sb/sth estar* en guerra con algn/algo; the ~ on
crime la lucha contra la delincuencia; (before n)
~ memorial monumento m a los caídos

warble /'wɔːrbəl ‖'wɔːbəl/ vi trinar, gorjear

ward /wɔːrd ‖wɔːd/ n **1** (in hospital) sala f
2 (person) pupilo, -la m,f
■ **ward off** [v + adv + o] «attack» rechazar*;
«blow» desviar*; «danger» conjurar; «illness»
protegerse* contra

warden /'wɔːrdn̩ ‖'wɔːdn̩/ n (of castle, museum)
guardián, -diana m,f; (of hostel, home) encargado,
-da m,f; (of university, college) rector, -tora m,f;
(church~) coadjutor m; (fire ~) (AmE) encargado,
-da m,f de la lucha contra incendios; (game ~)
guardabosque(s) mf; (of prison) (AmE) director,
-tora m,f (de una cárcel)

warder /'wɔːrdər ‖'wɔːdə(r)/ n (BrE) celador,
-dora m,f (de una cárcel)

wardrobe /'wɔːrdrəʊb ‖'wɔːdrəʊb/ n (a)
(clothes cupboard) armario m, ropero m (esp AmL)
(b) (set of clothes) guardarropa m, vestuario m

warehouse /'werhaʊs ‖'weəhaʊs/ n depósito
m, almacén m, bodega f (Chi, Col, Méx)

wares /werz ‖weəz/ pl n mercancía(s) f(pl),
mercadería(s) f(pl) (AmS)

war: ~fare n guerra f; ~head n cabeza f,
ojiva f

warily /'werəli ‖'weərɪli/ adv con cautela,
cautelosamente

warlike /'wɔːrlaɪk ‖'wɔːlaɪk/ adj guerrero

warm¹ /wɔːrm ‖wɔːm/ adj **-er, -est**
1 «water/day» tibio, templado; «climate/wind»
cálido; the ~est room in the house la habitación
más caliente de la casa; I'm lovely and ~ now
estoy muy calentito ahora; ~ clothes ropa f de
abrigo or (RPl, Ven tb) abrigada or (Andes, Méx tb)
abrigadora; to get ~ «person» entrar en calor,
calentarse*; «room» calentarse* **2** (a)
(affectionate, cordial) «person» cariñoso; «welcome»
caluroso (b) «color/atmosphere» cálido **3** (fresh)
«scent/trail» reciente, fresco

warm² vt calentar*
■ ~ vi (a) (become hotter) calentarse* (b) (become
affectionate) to ~ TO o TOWARD sb: we soon ~ed to
o toward her pronto se ganó nuestra simpatía
■ **warm over** [v + o + adv, v + adv + o] (AmE
Culin) calentar*
■ **warm up 1** [v + adv] (a) (become warmer)
«place/food» calentarse*; «person» entrar en
calor (b) «engine/apparatus» calentarse* (c)
(become lively) «party/match» animarse (d) (for
action) «athlete» hacer* ejercicios de
calentamiento **2** [v + o + adv, v + adv + o] (a)
(heat) «food/place» calentar* (b) «engine/
apparatus» calentar* (c) (make lively) animar

warm: ~-blooded /'wɔːrm'blʌdəd
‖,wɔːm'blʌdɪd/ adj (Zool) de sangre caliente;
~-hearted /'wɔːrm'hɑːrtəd ‖,wɔːm'hɑːtɪd/ adj
afectuoso

warmly /'wɔːrmli ‖'wɔːmli/ adv «congratulate/
welcome» calurosamente; «smile» afectuosamente

warmth /wɔːrmθ ‖wɔːmθ/ n (a) (heat) calor m
(b) (of welcome) lo caluroso (c) (of color, atmosphere)
calidez f

warm-up /'wɔːrmʌp ‖'wɔːmʌp/ n (exercise)
ejercicio m de calentamiento; (practice)
(pre)calentamiento m

warn /wɔːrn ‖wɔːn/ vt (a) (admonish) advertir*;
we had been ~ed not to go nos habían advertido
que no fuéramos (b) (inform, advise) avisar,
advertir*; we were ~ed against swimming in the
river nos advirtieron que era peligroso nadar en
el río

warning /'wɔːrnɪŋ ‖'wɔːnɪŋ/ n (a) (advice, threat)
advertencia f (b) (prior notice) aviso m; they
arrived without ~ llegaron sin avisar or sin
previo aviso

warp /wɔːrp ‖wɔːp/ vt «wood/metal» alabear*

warped /wɔːrpt ‖wɔːpt/ adj «timber/metal»
alabeado; «record» combado; «mind/sense of
humor» retorcido

warplane /'wɔːrpleɪn ‖'wɔːpleɪn/ n avión m de
combate

warrant¹ /'wɒrənt ‖'wɒrənt/ n (written
authorization) (Law) orden f judicial; (search ~)
orden f de registro or (AmL tb) de allanamiento; to
have a ~ for sb's arrest tener* una orden de
arresto contra algn

warrant² vt **1** (justify) justificar* **2** (guarantee)
(often pass) garantizar*

warranty /'wɔːrənti ‖'wɒrənti/ n (pl **-ties**) garantía f

warren /'wɔːrən ‖'wɒrən/ n (Zool) madriguera f (de conejos), conejera f

warring /'wɔːrɪŋ/ adj (before n) ⟨countries/tribes⟩ en guerra; ⟨factions⟩ enfrentado

warrior /'wɔːrjər ‖'wɒriə(r)/ n guerrero, -ra m,f

Warsaw /'wɔːrsɔː ‖'wɔːsɔː/ n Varsovia f

warship /'wɔːrʃɪp ‖'wɔːʃɪp/ n buque m de guerra

wart /wɔːrt ‖wɔːt/ n verruga f

war: ~**time** n: in ~**time** en tiempo de guerra; ~**torn** adj devastado por la guerra

wary /'weri ‖'weəri/ adj **warier, wariest** cauteloso; **to be** ~ **OF** sb/sth no fiarse* DE algn/algo

was /wɑːz, weak form wəz ‖wɒz, weak form wəz/ past of BE

wash¹ /wɔːʃ ‖wɒʃ/ n [1] **(a)** (act): **to have a** ~ lavarse; **I'll give the car a** ~ voy a lavar el coche, voy a darle una lavada al coche (AmL) **(b)** (in washing machine) lavado m; **your shirt is in the** ~ tu camisa está lavándose [2] (left by boat, plane) estela f

wash² vt [1] (clean) ⟨shirt/car/fruit⟩ lavar; ⟨floor⟩ fregar*, lavar (esp AmL); **to** ~ **one's face/hair** lavarse la cara/la cabeza or el pelo; **to** ~ **the dishes** fregar* or lavar los platos
[2] (carry away) (+ adv compl): **the body had been** ~**ed ashore by the tide** la corriente había arrastrado el cuerpo hasta la orilla; see also WASH AWAY, WASH UP
■ ~ vi **(a)** (clean oneself) lavarse **(b)** (do dishes) lavar, fregar* **(c)** (do laundry) ⟨washing machine/person⟩ lavar (la ropa), hacer* la colada (Esp)
■ **wash away** [v + o + adv, v + adv + o] **(a)** (carry away) llevarse **(b)** (cleanse) ⟨dirt⟩ quitar (lavando)
■ **wash down** [v + o + adv, v + adv + o] **(a)** (clean) ⟨paintwork/wall⟩ lavar **(b)** (accompany) (colloq): **a plate of pasta** ~**ed down with the local wine** un plato de pasta acompañado del vino de la región
■ **wash out** [1] [v + o + adv, v + adv + o] ⟨sink/cloth⟩ (clean) lavar; (rinse) enjuagar*
[2] [v + adv] (disappear): **the stain will** ~ **out la** mancha saldrá or se quitará al lavarlo
■ **wash up** [1] [v + adv] **(a)** (wash oneself) (AmE) lavarse **(b)** (wash dishes) (BrE) lavar los platos, fregar* (los platos)
[2] [v + o + adv, v + adv + o] **(a)** (deposit) (usu pass) **to be** ~**ed up** ⟨body/wreckage⟩ ser* traído por la corriente **(b)** ⟨dishes⟩ (BrE) lavar, fregar*

Wash = Washington

washable /'wɔːʃəbəl ‖'wɒʃəbəl/ adj lavable

wash: ~**basin** n (BrE) ▶ ~BOWL; ~**bowl** n (AmE) **(a)** (in modern bathroom) lavabo m, lavamanos m, lavatorio m (CS), pileta f (RPI) **(b)** (bowl) palangana f, jofaina f, lavatorio m (Chi, Per); ~**cloth** n (AmE) toallita f (para lavarse), ≈ manopla f

washed-out /wɔːʃt'aʊt ‖,wɒʃt'aʊt/ adj (pred **washed out**) **(a)** ⟨fabric⟩ descolorido; ⟨color⟩ pálido, lavado (RPI fam) **(b)** (exhausted) rendido

washer /'wɔːʃər ‖'wɒʃə(r)/ n [1] (Tech) (ring) arandela f; (— on faucet) arandela f, junta f, suela f universal, cuerito m (CS fam), empaque m (Col, Ven) [2] ▶ WASHING MACHINE

washing /'wɔːʃɪŋ ‖'wɒʃɪŋ/ n **(a)** (laundry — dirty) ropa f para lavar; (— clean) ropa f lavada; **to do the** ~ lavar la ropa, hacer* la colada (Esp) **(b)** (act) lavado m

washing: ~ **line** n (BrE) cuerda f para tender la ropa; ~ **machine** n máquina f de lavar, lavadora f, lavarropas m (RPI); ~ **powder** n (esp BrE) jabón m en polvo, detergente m; ~**-up** /'wɔːʃɪŋ'ʌp ‖,wɒʃɪŋ'ʌp/ n (BrE): **to do the** ~**-up** lavar los platos, fregar* (los platos); (before n) ~**-up liquid** lavavajillas m

wash: ~**out** n (failure) (colloq) desastre m (fam); ~**room** n baño(s) m(pl), servicios mpl (esp Esp)

wasn't /'wɑːznt ‖'wɒznt/ = **was not**

wasp /wɑːsp ‖wɒsp/ n avispa f

WASP /wɑːsp ‖wɒsp/ n (esp AmE) (= **white Anglo-Saxon Protestant**) persona de la clase privilegiada de los EEUU, blanca, anglosajona y protestante

waspish /'wɑːspɪʃ ‖'wɒspɪʃ/ adj sardónico

wastage /'weɪstɪdʒ/ n: **there is too much** ~ **of raw material** se desperdicia demasiada materia prima; **natural** ~ (of workforce) bajas fpl vegetativas

waste¹ /weɪst/ n [1] (of fuel, materials) desperdicio m; **a** ~ **of time** una pérdida de tiempo; **it's a** ~ **of money** es tirar el dinero; **to go to** ~ ⟨⟨talent⟩⟩ desperdiciarse; ⟨⟨food⟩⟩ echarse a perder [2] **(a)** (refuse) residuos mpl **(b)** (surplus matter) material m sobrante [3] **wastes** (pl): **the deserted** ~**s of Antarctica** las desiertas inmensidades de la Antártica

waste² vt [1] ⟨talents/efforts⟩ desperdiciar; ⟨money/electricity⟩ despilfarrar; ⟨food⟩ tirar; ⟨time⟩ perder*; ⟨space⟩ desaprovechar
[2] **wasted** past p **(a)** (misused, futile) ⟨time/money⟩ perdido; ⟨opportunity/space⟩ desperdiciado; ⟨effort⟩ inútil **(b)** (shrunken) ⟨body⟩ debilitado; ⟨limb⟩ atrofiado
■ **waste away** [v + adv] ⟨⟨person/body⟩⟩ consumirse; ⟨⟨muscle⟩⟩ atrofiarse

waste³ adj [1] ⟨ground⟩ (barren) yermo; (not cultivated) baldío; **to lay** ~ **(to) sth** arrasar algo [2] ⟨material/matter⟩ de desecho

waste: ~**basket** n (esp AmE) ▶ WASTE-PAPER BASKET; ~ **disposal unit** n triturador m or trituradora f de desperdicios

wasteful /'weɪstfəl/ adj ⟨person⟩ despilfarrador; ⟨method⟩ poco económico

waste: ~**land** n (often pl) (barren land) páramo m, tierra f yerma or baldía; (uncultivated land) erial m; ~ **paper** n papel m sobrante; ~**-paper basket**, ~**-paper bin** /'weɪst'peɪpər ‖,weɪst'peɪpə(r)/ n papelera f, papelero m (CS); ~ **pipe** n tubo m de desagüe

watch¹ /wɑːtʃ ‖wɒtʃ/ n **1** (timepiece) reloj *m* (*de pulsera/de bolsillo*); (*before n*) ~ **band** o (BrE) **strap** correa *f* de reloj **2** (observation) vigilancia *f*; **to keep** ~ hacer* guardia **3** **(a)** (period of time) guardia *f* **(b)** (individual) guardia *mf*; (group) guardia *f*

watch² *vt* **1** ⟨*person/expression*⟩ observar; ⟨*movie/game*⟩ mirar; **to** ~ **television** ver* televisión; **we** ~**ed the sun go down** miramos la puesta de sol

2 **(a)** (keep under observation) ⟨*suspect/house*⟩ vigilar **(b)** (look after) ⟨*luggage/children*⟩ cuidar **(c)** ⟨pay attention to⟩ mirar (con atención) **3** (be careful of) ⟨*diet/weight*⟩ vigilar, tener* cuidado con; ~ **it!** (colloq) ¡cuidado!

■ ~ *vi* (look on) mirar

■ **watch out** [*v + adv*] **(a)** (be careful) tener* cuidado; ~ **out!** ¡(ten) cuidado!, ¡ojo! (fam), ¡abusado! (Méx fam) **(b)** (look carefully) estarse* atento; ~ **out for spelling mistakes** estáte atento por si hay faltas de ortografía

■ **watch over** [*v + prep + o*] ⟨*patient/child*⟩ cuidar (de); ⟨*safety/interests*⟩ velar por

watchdog /ˈwɑːtʃdɔːg ‖ˈwɒtʃdɒg/ n (dog) perro *m* guardián; (group) organismo *m* de control

watchful /ˈwɑːtʃfəl ‖ˈwɒtʃfəl/ adj vigilante

watch: ~**maker** n relojero, -ra *m,f*; ~**man** /ˈwɑːtʃmən ‖ˈwɒtʃmən/ n (*pl* -**men** /mən/) vigilante *m*; ~**tower** n atalaya *f*, torre *f* de vigilancia

water¹ /ˈwɔːtər ‖ˈwɔːtə(r)/ n **1** agua *f*⃰; **to be lie under** ~ estar*/quedar inundado; **high/low** ~ marea *f* alta/baja; **to pass** ~ (frml & euph) orinar, hacer* aguas menores (euph); **to hold** ~ tenerse* en pie; (*before n*) ⟨*bird/plant*⟩ acuático; ~ **sports** deportes *mpl* acuáticos **2** **waters** *pl* (of sea, river) aguas *fpl*

water² *vi*: her eyes began to ~ empezaron a llorarle los ojos; **his mouth** ~**ed** se le hizo agua la boca (AmL), se le hizo la boca agua (Esp)

■ ~ *vt* ⟨*plant/garden/land*⟩ regar*; ⟨*livestock*⟩ dar* de beber a

■ **water down** [*v + o + adv, v + adv + o*] ⟨*liquid/mixture*⟩ diluir*; ⟨*wine/beer*⟩ aguar

water: ~**bed** n cama *f* de agua; ~ **bottle** n cantimplora *f*; ~**color**, (BrE) ~**colour** n acuarela *f*; ~**cress** n berro *m*; ~**fall** n cascada *f*, salto *m* de agua; (large) catarata *f*; ~**front** n (beside lake, river) zona *f* de una ciudad que bordea un lago o río; (docks) (esp AmE) muelles *mpl*

watering can /ˈwɔːtərɪŋ/ n regadera *f*

water: ~ **lily** n nenúfar *m*; ~**logged** /ˈwɔːtərlɔːgd ‖ˈwɔːtəlɒgd/ adj ⟨*land/soil*⟩ anegado, inundado; ⟨*shoes*⟩ empapado; ~**mark** n filigrana *f*; ~**melon** n sandía *f*; ~ **mill** n molino *m* de agua; ~ **parting** n (AmE) ▶ WATERSHED A

waterproof¹ /ˈwɔːtərpruːf ‖ˈwɔːtəpruːf/ adj ⟨*fabric*⟩ impermeable; ⟨*mascara*⟩ a prueba de agua; ⟨*watch*⟩ sumergible

waterproof² n (esp BrE) prenda *f* impermeable

waterproof³ *vt* impermeabilizar*

water: ~-**resistant** adj impermeabilizado, hidrófugo; ~**shed** n (Geog) **(a)** (divide) (línea *f*) divisoria *f* de aguas **(b)** (drainage basin) cuenca *f*; ~-**ski** *vi* -**skis**, -**skiing**, -**skied** hacer* esquí acuático; ~-**skiing** n esquí *m* acuático; ~ **table** n nivel *m* freático; ~**tight**

adj ⟨*seal/container*⟩ hermético; ⟨*boat*⟩ estanco; ⟨*argument*⟩ irrebatible, sin fisuras; ⟨*alibi*⟩ a toda prueba; ~**way** n (river) vía *f* fluvial; (canal) vía *f* or canal *m* navegable; ~ **wheel** n (for driving machinery) rueda *f* hidráulica; (for raising water) noria *f*; ~ **wings** *pl* n flotadores *mpl* (*que se colocan en los brazos*)

watery /ˈwɔːtəri/ adj **(a)** (of, like water) acuoso **(b)** ⟨*beer/gravy*⟩ aguado **(c)** ⟨*eyes*⟩ lloroso

watt /wɑːt ‖wɒt/ n vatio *m*

wave¹ /weɪv/ n **1** **(a)** (of water) ola *f* **(b)** (in hair) onda *f* **(c)** (Phys) onda *f* **2** (surge, movement) oleada *f* **3** (gesture): **she gave them a** ~ les hizo adiós/los saludó con la mano

wave² *vt* **1** **(a)** (shake, swing) ⟨*handkerchief/flag*⟩ agitar; **to** ~ **sth around** agitar algo; **she** ~**d goodbye to him** le hizo adiós con la mano **(b)** (direct) (+ *adv compl*): **the policeman** ~**d us on** el policía nos hizo señas para *or* de que siguiéramos adelante **2** (curl) ⟨*hair*⟩ marcar*, ondular

■ ~ *vi* **1** (signal): **he** ~**d when he saw us** nos saludó con la mano al vernos; **to** ~ **AT** *o* **TO sb** (to say goodbye) hacerle* adiós A algn con la mano; (in greeting) saludar a algn con la mano **2** (sway, flutter) «*corn/trees*» agitarse; «*flag*» ondear

■ **wave aside** [*v + o + adv, v + adv + o*] **(a)** (with hand): **he** ~**d me aside** me hizo señas para que me hiciera a un lado **(b)** ⟨*arguments/attempts*⟩ rechazar*

wave: ~**band** n banda *f* de frecuencia; ~**length** n longitud *f* de onda

waver /ˈweɪvər ‖ˈweɪvə(r)/ *vi* **1** (falter) «*person*» flaquear; «*faith*» tambalearse **2** (indecisive) titubear

wavy /ˈweɪvi/ adj **wavier, waviest** ondulado

wax¹ /wæks/ n cera *f*; (ear~) cera *f* (de los oídos), cerumen *m*; (sealing ~) lacre *m*

wax² *vt* **(a)** (treat with wax) ⟨*floor/table/skis*⟩ encerar **(b)** (to remove hair) depilar con cera

■ ~ *vi* «*moon*» crecer*; **his popularity** ~**ed and waned** su popularidad sufrió muchos altibajos

waxworks /ˈwækswɜːrks ‖ˈwækswɜːks/ n (*pl* ~**works**) (+ *sing or pl vb*) museo *m* de cera

way¹ /weɪ/ n

I **1** **(a)** (route) camino *m*; **the** ~ **back** el camino de vuelta; **the** ~ **in/out** la entrada/salida; **it's difficult to find one's** ~ **around this town** es difícil orientarse en esta ciudad; **can you find your** ~ **there by yourself?** ¿sabes ir solo?; **I can drop the package off on my** ~ de paso puedo dejar el paquete; **which** ~ **did you come?** ¿por dónde viniste?; **which** ~ **did he go?** ¿por dónde fue?; (following sb) ¿por dónde se fue?; **could you tell me the** ~ **to the city center?** ¿me podría decir por dónde se va al centro (de la ciudad)?; **on my** ~ **to work** de camino al trabajo; **the doctor is on her** ~ la doctora ya va para allí/viene para aquí; **I'll tell you on the** ~ te lo cuento por el camino; **I don't know the** ~ **up/down** no sé por dónde se sube/se baja; **to lead the** ~ ir* delante; **to lose one's** ~ perderse*; **there is no** ~ **around it** no hay otra solución; **to go out of one's** ~ (make a detour) desviarse* del camino; (make special effort): **they went out of their** ~ **to be helpful** se desvivieron por ayudar **(b)** (road, path) camino *m*, senda *f* ···❖

2 (passage, space): **to be/get in the ~** estorbar; **to stand in the ~: they stood in our ~** nos impidieron el paso; **I couldn't see it, she was standing in my ~** no podía verlo, ella me tapaba (la vista); **I won't stand in your ~** no seré yo quien te lo impida; **(get) out of the ~!** ¡hazte a un lado!; **to move sth out of the ~** quitar algo de en medio; **to keep out of sb's ~** rehuir* a algn **3** (direction): **it's that ~** es en esa dirección, es por ahí; **this ~!** ¡por aquí!; **we didn't know which ~ to go** no sabíamos por dónde ir; **this ~ and that** de un lado a otro; **we're both going the same ~** vamos por el mismo lado; **look the other ~!** ¡mira para otro lado!; **whichever ~ you look at it, it's a disaster** es un desastre, lo mires por donde lo mires; **the other ~ around** al revés; **which ~ up should it be?** ¿cuál es la parte de arriba?; **to split sth three ~s** dividir algo en tres partes; **every which ~** (AmE) para todos lados; **to go sb's ~: are you going my ~?** ¿vas en mi misma dirección?; **the decision went our ~** se decidió en nuestro favor; **~ to go!** (AmE colloq) ¡así se hace! **4** (distance) (no pl): **there's only a short ~ to go now** ya falta poco para llegar; **it's a long ~ from here to Rio** Río queda muy lejos de aquí; **he's come a long ~** ha venido de muy lejos; **we've come a long ~ since those days** hemos evolucionado mucho desde entonces; **a little goes a long ~** un poco cunde or (AmL tb) rinde mucho; **we had to walk all the ~ up** tuvimos que subir a pie hasta arriba

II **1** (method, means) forma f, manera f, modo m; **there's no ~ of crossing the border without a passport** es imposible cruzar la frontera sin pasaporte; **it doesn't matter to me one ~ or the other** me da igual una cosa u otra; **all right, we'll do it your ~** muy bien, lo haremos a tu manera; **to do sth the hard/easy ~** hacer* algo de manera difícil/fácil; **to have it both ~s** quererlo* todo, querer* la chancha y los cinco reales or los veinte (RPl fam); **you can't have it both ~s** tienes que elegir entre una cosa u otra **2** (manner) manera f, modo m, forma f; **in a subtle ~** de manera or modo or forma sutil; **he's in a bad ~** está muy mal; **that's the ~ it goes** así son las cosas, así es la vida; **it looks that ~** así or eso parece; **this ~ it's better for everyone** así es mejor para todos; **the ~ I see it** tal y como yo lo veo; **to have a ~ with ...: to have a ~ with children/animals** saber* cómo tratar a los niños/tener* mano con los animales; **to have a ~ with words** tener* mucha facilidad de palabra **3** **(a)** (custom, characteristic): **the ~s of our people** las costumbres de nuestro pueblo; **he has a ~ of making people feel at ease** sabe hacer que la gente se sienta cómoda; **to be set in one's ~s** estar* muy acostumbrado a hacer las cosas de cierta manera **(b)** (wish, will): **to get/have one's (own) ~** salirse* con la suya (or mía etc) **4** (feature, respect) sentido m, aspecto m; **in a ~, it's like losing an old friend** de alguna manera or en cierta forma es como perder a un viejo amigo; **our product is in no ~ inferior to theirs** nuestro producto no es de ninguna manera inferior al suyo

III (in phrases) **1** **by the way** (indep) a propósito, por cierto

2 **by way of** (as prep) **(a)** (via) vía, pasando por **(b)** (to serve as) a modo or manera de

3 **in the way of** (as regards) (as prep): **don't expect too much in the ~ of help** en cuanto a ayuda, no esperes mucho

4 **no way** (colloq): **no ~ is he going to do it** de ninguna manera lo va a hacer (fam); **no ~!** ¡ni hablar! (fam)

5 **to give way** **(a)** (break, collapse) «ice/rope/cable» romperse*; «floor» hundirse **(b)** (succumb, give in) **to give ~ to sth** «to threats/blackmail» ceder A or ANTE algo **(c)** (BrE Transp) **to give ~ (to sb/sth)** ceder el paso (A algn/algo) **(d)** (be replaced, superseded by) **to give ~ to sth** dejar or dar* paso A algo

6 **under way: to get under ~** ponerse* en marcha; **an investigation is under ~** se está llevando a cabo una investigación

way² adv (colloq): **~ back in February** allá por febrero; **~ behind** muy por detrás; **they were ~ out in their calculations** se equivocaron en mucho en los cálculos; **~ past midnight** mucho después de la medianoche; **~ and away** (as intensifier) (AmE) con mucho, lejos (AmL fam)

way: **~·lay** /'weɪleɪ/ vt (past & past p **~·laid**) abordar; **~·out** /'weɪaʊt/ adj (pred ~ **out**) (colloq) ultramoderno, estrambótico (fam); **~s and means** pl n **~s and means** (OF + -ING) métodos mpl (DE + INF)

we /wiː, weak form wi/ pron

■ **Note** Although pron nosotros and nosotras are given as translations of we, in practice they are used only for emphasis: we went to the theater fuimos al teatro; we did it nosotros or nosotras lo hicimos.

nosotros, -tras; **~ English** nosotros los ingleses

weak /wiːk/ adj **-er, -est** **1** **(a)** «person/muscles/economy» débil; «structure» poco sólido, endeble; «handshake» flojo; **to have a ~ heart** sufrir del corazón; **to grow ~** debilitarse **(b)** (ineffectual) «character/leader» débil **2** **(a)** (not competent) «student/performance» flojo **(b)** (not convincing) «argument/excuse» poco convincente **3** (diluted) «coffee/tea» poco cargado; «beer» suave; «solution» diluido

weaken /'wiːkən/ vt debilitar

■ ~ vi «person/animal» (physically) debilitarse; «resolve» flaquear; «power» debilitarse; (relent) ceder

weakling /'wiːklɪŋ/ n alfeñique m

weakly /'wiːkli/ adv «say» con voz débil; **he struggled ~ and then gave in** se rindió sin apenas oponer resistencia

weakness /'wiːknəs ‖ 'wiːknɪs/ n **1** **(a)** (of body, defenses) debilidad f; (of structure, material) falta f de solidez, endeblez f; (of argument) pobreza f **(b)** (ineffectualness) falta f de carácter **2** **(a)** (weak point — in structure, policy) punto m débil; (— in character) flaqueza f, punto m débil **(b)** (liking) debilidad f; **to have a ~ for sth** tener* debilidad por algo

weak-willed /'wiːkwɪld/ adj «person» de poca (fuerza de) voluntad; **to be ~** tener* poca fuerza de voluntad

weal /wiːl/ n verdugón m (de un golpe dado con una cuerda, correa etc)

wealth /welθ/ n **1** riqueza f **2** (large quantity): **a ~ of sth** abundancia f de algo

wealthy /'welθi/ adj **-thier, -thiest** «person/family» adinerado, rico; «nation/area» rico

wean /wiːn/ *vt* ‹*baby/young*› destetar; **to ~ sb OFF sth: we ~ed him off drugs** conseguimos que dejara las drogas, conseguimos desengancharle de las drogas (Esp)

weapon /'wepən/ *n* arma *f*‡

weaponry /'wepənri/ *n* armamento *m*

wear¹ /wer ‖weə(r)/ *n* [1] (a) (use): **I've had a lot of ~ out of these shoes** les he dado mucho uso a estos zapatos; **carpets that stand hard ~** alfombras que resisten el uso constante (b) (damage) desgaste *m*; **~ and tear** uso *m or* desgaste natural [2] (a) (wearing of clothes): **clothes for evening ~** ropa para la noche (b) (clothing) ropa *f*; **children's ~** ropa de niños

wear² (*past* **wore**; *past p* **worn**) *vt* [1] (a) (at specific moment) ‹*clothes/jewelry/watch/makeup*› llevar; ‹*glasses*› llevar (puesto), usar; ‹*green/ black*› vestir* de; **what perfume are you ~ing?** ¿qué perfume llevas? (b) (usually) ‹*clothes*› usar, ponerse*, ‹*glasses*› llevar, usar; ‹*makeup/ perfume/earrings*› usar; **he ~s size 44 shoes** calza (el) 44; **she ~s her hair in a ponytail** se peina con cola de caballo [2] (through use): **the step had been worn smooth** el peldaño se había alisado con el uso; **she's worn holes in the soles** se le han agujereado las suelas
■ **~** *vi* [1] (through use) ‹*collar/carpet/brakes*› gastarse; **to ~ thin** (lit: through use) ‹*cloth/metal*› gastarse; ‹*joke*› perder* la gracia [2] (last) (+ *adv compl*) durar; **to ~ well** ‹*cloth/ clothes*› durar mucho; ‹*person*› conservarse bien

■ **wear away** [1] [*v + o + adv, v + adv + o*] (erode) ‹*rock*› desgastar; ‹*pattern/inscription*› borrar
[2] [*v + adv*] (become eroded) ‹*rock*› desgastarse; ‹*inscription*› borrarse

■ **wear down** [1] [*v + o + adv, v + adv + o*] (a) (by friction) ‹*heel/pencil*› gastar (b) (weaken) ‹*resistance*› menoscabar; ‹*person*› agotar
[2] [*v + adv*] ‹*heel/tread*› gastarse

■ **wear off** [*v + adv*] (a) (be removed) ‹*paint*› quitarse (b) (disappear) ‹*distress/numbness*› pasarse

■ **wear on** [*v + adv*] ‹*winter/years*› pasar (lentamente); ‹*meeting/drought*› continuar*

■ **wear out** [1] [*v + o + adv, v + adv + o*] (a) (through use) ‹*shoes/carpet/batteries*› gastar (b) (exhaust) ‹*person*› agotar
[2] [*v + adv*] (through use) ‹*shoes/towel/batteries*› gastarse

■ **wear through** [*v + adv*] (get hole in) ‹*soles/ cloth*› agujerearse

wearily /'wɪrəli ‖'wɪərɪli/ *adv* ‹*walk/move*› cansinamente; **he sighed ~** suspiró cansado

weary¹ /'wɪri ‖'wɪəri/ *adj* **-rier, -riest** ‹*person/legs*› cansado; ‹*sigh*› de cansancio; **to be ~ OF sth/-ING** estar* cansado *or* harto DE algo/+ INF

weary² *vt* **-ries, -rying, -ried** (a) (tire) cansar (b) (annoy) hartar, cansar

weasel /'wiːzəl/ *n* (Zool) comadreja *f*

weather¹ /'weðər ‖'weðə(r)/ *n* tiempo *m*; **what's the ~ like?** ¿cómo está el tiempo?, ¿qué tiempo hace?; **you can't go out in this ~** no puedes salir con este tiempo; (*before n*) ‹*map/ chart*› meteorológico; **~ forecast** pronóstico *m* del tiempo

weather² *vt* (a) (wear) ‹*rocks*› erosionar; ‹*surface*› desgastar; ‹*skin/face*› curtir (b) ‹*wood*› secar*
■ **~** *vi* «*rock*» erosionarse; «*surface*» desgastarse

weather: **~beaten** *adj* ‹*face/sailor*› curtido; ‹*walls/rocks*› azotado por los elementos; **~cock** *n* veleta *f*

weathered /'weðərd ‖'weðəd/ *adj* ‹*rocks/ brick/stone*› erosionado (*por la acción de los elementos*); ‹*wood*› curado

weather: **~man** /'weðərmæn ‖'weðəmæn/ *n* (*pl* **-men** /-men/) hombre que transmite el pronóstico del tiempo por radio o televisión; **~proof** *adj* impermeable; **~ vane** /veɪn/ *n* veleta *f*

weave /wiːv/ *vt* (*past* **wove**; *past p* **woven**) (a) ‹*cloth/mat*› tejer (*en telar*); ‹*basket/web*› tejer; ‹*story/plot*› tejer (b) (thread together) ‹*threads/ branches/straw*› entretejer
■ **~** *vi* [1] (*past* **wove**; *past p* **woven**) (make cloth, baskets) tejer [2] (*past* **wove** *or* **weaved**; *past p* **woven** *or* **weaved**) «*road*» serpentear; «*person*» zigzaguear

weaver /'wiːvər ‖'wiːvə(r)/ *n* tejedor, -dora *m,f*

weaving /'wiːvɪŋ/ *n* (of cloth) tejido *m*

web /web/ *n* (a) (spider's ~) telaraña *f*; **a ~ of intrigue** una red de intriga (b) (Comput): **World Wide ~** telaraña *f* mundial

webbed /webd/ *adj* palmeado

web: **W~ page** *n* (Comput) página *f* web; **W~ site** *n* (Comput) sitio *m* web

wed /wed/ *vt* (*past & past p* **wedded** *or* **wed**) (marry) (dated *or* journ) ‹*man/woman*› casarse con

we'd /wiːd/ (a) = **we had** (b) = **we would**

wedding /'wedɪŋ/ *n* (a) (ceremony) boda *f*, casamiento *m*, matrimonio *m* (AmS exc RPl); **to have a church/civil** (AmE) *o* (BrE) **registry-office ~** casarse por la iglesia *or* (RPl) por iglesia/por lo civil *or* (Per, RPl, Ven) por civil *or* (Chi, Méx) por lo civil; (*before n*) **~ dress** vestido *m or* traje *m* de novia; **~ ring** alianza *f*, anillo *m* de boda, argolla *f* (de matrimonio) (Chi) (b) (anniversary): **silver/ golden ~** bodas *fpl* de plata/oro

wedge¹ /wedʒ/ *n* (a) (for securing) cuña *f* (b) (for splitting) cuña *f* (c) (shape): **a ~ of cake** un trozo grande de pastel

wedge² *vt* (a) (secure): **to ~ a door open** ponerle* una cuña a una puerta para que no se cierre (b) (squeeze) meter (*a presión*)

Wednesday /'wenzdeɪ, -di/ *n* miércoles *m*; *see also* MONDAY

wee¹ /wiː/ *adj* (small) (esp Scot, IrE) pequeño, chico (esp AmL); **in the ~ small hours** *o* (AmE also) **the ~ hours** a las altas horas de la madrugada

wee² *n* (BrE colloq): **to have** *o* **do a ~** hacer* pis *or* pipí (fam), hacer* del uno (Méx, Per fam)

weed¹ /wiːd/ *n* (a) (Hort) hierbajo *m*, mala hierba *f*, yuyo *m* (RPl), maleza *f* (AmL) (b) (aquatic growth) algas *fpl*

weed² *vt* deshierbar, desherbar*, desmalezar* (AmL), sacar* los yuyos de (RPl)
■ **weed out** [*v + o + adv, v + adv + o*] (a) (Hort) quitar (b) ‹*errors/items*› eliminar; ‹*applicants*› eliminar

weedkiller /'wiːdˌkɪlər ‖'wiːdˌkɪlə(r)/ *n* herbicida *m*

W

weedy /'wi:di/ *adj* **-dier, -diest (a)** (lanky) (AmE) larguirucho (fam) **(b)** (feeble, puny) (BrE colloq) enclenque

week /wi:k/ *n* **(a)** (7 days) semana *f*; **once a ~** una vez por semana *or* a la semana; **we get paid by the ~** nos pagan por semana; **(on) Tuesday ~** *o* (BrE also) **a ~ on Tuesday** el martes que viene no, el otro; **she arrived a ~ (ago)** yesterday ayer hizo una semana que llegó **(b)** (working days): **I never go out in** *o* **during the ~** nunca salgo los días de semana

week: **~day** *n* día *m* de semana; **~end** /'wi:kend ‖wi:k'end/ *n* fin *m* de semana; **what are you doing on** *o* **during the ~?** ¿qué vas a hacer el fin de semana?

weekly¹ /'wi:kli/ *adj* semanal

weekly² *adv* semanalmente; **we get paid ~** nos pagan por semana

weekly³ *n* (*pl* **weeklies**) semanario *m*

weep /wi:p/ *vi* (*past & past p* **wept**) **(a)** (cry) llorar **2** (exude liquid) «*wound/eye*» supurar

weeping willow /'wi:pɪŋ/ *n* sauce *m* llorón

weepy /'wi:pi/ *adj* **-pier, -piest** (colloq) **1 (a)** «*person*»: **to feel ~** tener* ganas de llorar **(b)** «*film/play*» que hace llorar, cebollento (Chi fam) **2** «*eye*» lloroso

weigh /weɪ/ *vt* **1** «*person/load/food*» pesar; **to ~ oneself** pesarse **2** (consider) «*factors/arguments/evidence*» sopesar; **to ~ one's words** medir* sus (*or* mis *etc*) palabras

■ **~** *vi* **2** (measure in weight) «*person/load/food*» pesar; **how much** *or* **what do you ~?** ¿cuánto pesas?; **your inexperience will ~ against you** tu falta de experiencia será un factor en tu contra

■ **weigh down** [*v + o + adv, v + adv + o*] **(a)** (impose weight on): **the bag was ~ing me down** la bolsa me pesaba mucho; **trees ~ed down with fruit** árboles cargados de fruta **(b)** (depress) abrumar **(c)** ▶ WEIGHT DOWN

■ **weigh on** [*v + prep + o*]: **it still ~ed heavily on her conscience** todavía sentía un gran cargo de conciencia; **it's been ~ing heavily on my mind** me ha estado preocupando

■ **weigh out** [*v + o + adv, v + adv + o*] pesar

■ **weigh up** [*v + o + adv, v + adv + o*] «*situation*» considerar; «*pros and cons*» sopesar; «*person*» evaluar*

weight¹ /weɪt/ *n* **1** (mass, heaviness) peso *m*; **the bag is 5kg in ~** la bolsa pesa 5kg; **you mustn't lift heavy ~s** no debe levantar cosas pesadas; **that has taken a ~ off my mind** eso me ha sacado un peso de encima; **to pull one's ~:** **John isn't pulling his ~** John no trabaja como debería **2** (importance, value) peso *m* **3 (a)** (unit) peso *m*; **~s and measures** pesos y medidas **(b)** (for scales, clocks) pesa *f* **(c)** (Sport) pesa *f*; (*before n*) **~ training** entrenamiento *m* con pesas

weight² *vt* (make heavier) darle* peso a; «*fishing net*» lastrar

■ **weight down** [*v + o + adv, v + adv + o*] **(a)** «*tarpaulin/papers*» sujetar con algo pesado **(b)** «*body*» (to make it sink) ponerle* un lastre a

weightless /'weɪtləs ‖'weɪtlɪs/ *adj* ingrávido

weight: **~lifter** /'weɪt,lɪftər ‖'weɪt,lɪftə(r)/ *n* levantador, -dora *m,f* de pesas, pesista *mf* (Andes), halterófilo, -la *m,f*; **~lifting** /'weɪt,lɪftɪŋ/ *n* levantamiento *m* de pesas, halterofilia *f*

weighty /'weɪti/ *adj* **-tier, -tiest** «*argument*» de peso; «*matter*» importante

weir /wɪr ‖wɪə(r)/ *n* presa *f*

weird /wɪrd ‖wɪəd/ *adj* **-er, -est (a)** (strange) (colloq) raro, extraño **(b)** (unearthly) «*apparition/ figure*» misterioso

welcome¹ /'welkəm/ *interj* bienvenido

welcome² *adj* **(a)** (gladly received) «*guest*» bienvenido; «*change/news*» grato **(b)** (freely permitted): **you're ~ to use the phone** el teléfono está a tu disposición; **you're ~ to these books** puedes llevarte estos libros, si quieres **(c)** (responding to thanks): **you're ~!** ¡de nada!, ¡no hay de qué!

welcome³ *vt* (greet) darle* la bienvenida a; (receive): **we would ~ any advice you can give us** le agradeceríamos cualquier consejo que pudiera darnos

welcome⁴ *n* bienvenida *f*

welcoming /'welkəmɪŋ/ *adj* «*ceremony/ delegation*» de bienvenida **(b)** «*smile/hug*» acogedor; **the little bar looked very ~** el barcito parecía muy acogedor

weld /weld/ *vt/i* soldar*

welfare /'welfer ‖'welfeə(r)/ *n* **1** (well-being) bienestar *m* **2** (Soc Adm) **(a)** (assistance) asistencia *f* social **(b)** (payment) (AmE) prestaciones *fpl* sociales

welfare state *n* estado *m* de bienestar

well¹ /wel/ *adv* (*comp* **better**; *superl* **best**) **1** (to high standard, satisfactorily) «*sing/write/work*» bien; **he's doing very ~** le van muy bien las cosas; **~ done!** ¡así se hace!, ¡muy bien!; **to go ~** «*performance/operation*» salir* bien **2** (thoroughly) «*wash/dry/know*» bien; **it was ~ worth the effort** realmente valió la pena; **~ and truly** (colloq): **he was ~ and truly drunk** estaba pero bien borracho **3 (a)** (considerably) (*no comp*) bastante; **until ~ into the next century** hasta bien entrado el siglo que viene **(b)** (with justification): **you may ~ ask!** ¡muy buena pregunta!; **she couldn't very ~ ask** ¿cómo iba a negarlo? **4** (advantageously) «*marry*» bien; **to do ~ to + INF** hacer* bien *en* + INF, deber *en* + INF; **to do ~ out of sth** salir* bien parado de algo **5** (*in phrases*) **(a)** as well (in addition) también **(b)** as well as (in addition to) además de **(c)** may/might as well: **now you've told him, you may** *o* **might as ~ give it to him!** ahora que se lo has dicho dáselo ¿total?

well² *adj* (*comp* **better**; *superl* **best**) **1** (healthy) bien; **how are you? — I'm very ~, thank you** ¿cómo estás? — muy bien, gracias; **get**

∼ soon! ¡que te mejores! **2** (pleasing, satisfactory) bien; **it's all very ∼ for him to talk, but ...** él podrá decir todo lo que quiera pero ... **3** **as well: it would be as ∼ to keep this quiet** mejor no decir nada de esto; **it's just as ∼ I've got some money with me** menos mal que llevo dinero encima

well³ interj **1** **(a)** (introducing/continuing topic, sentence) bueno, bien **(b)** (expressing hesitation): **do you like it? — well ...** ¿te gusta? — pues or (esp AmL) este ... **2** **(a)** (expressing surprise): **∼, ∼, ∼! look who's here!** ¡vaya, vaya! ¡mira quién está aquí! **(b)** (expressing indignation) bueno **(c)** (dismissively) ¡bah! **(d)** (expressing resignation) bueno **3** (expressing expectation): **∼? who won?** bueno ¿y quién ganó?

well⁴ n (for water, oil, gas) pozo m
■ **well up** [v + adv] «water» brotar, manar; **tears ∼ed up in his eyes** los ojos se le llenaron de lágrimas

well- /wel/ pref bien

we'll /wiːl/ = **we will**

well: ∼-balanced /'wel'bælənst/ adj (pred ∼ **balanced**) «person» equilibrado; «diet» equilibrado, balanceado; **∼-behaved** /'welbɪ'heɪvd/ adj (pred ∼ **behaved**) «child» que se porta bien, bueno; «dog» obediente; **∼-being** /'wel'biːɪŋ/ n bienestar m; **∼-disposed** /'weldɪ'spəʊzd/ adj (pred ∼ **disposed**) dispuesto a colaborar (or ayudar etc); **∼-done** /'wel'dʌn/ adj (pred ∼ **done**) (Culin) bien cocido or (Esp) muy hecho; **∼-dressed** /'wel'drest/ adj (pred ∼ **dressed**) bien vestido; **∼-educated** /'wel'edʒəkeɪtəd ǁ,wel'edʒʊkeɪtɪd/ adj (pred ∼ **educated**) culto; **∼-founded** /'wel'faʊndəd ǁ,wel'faʊndɪd/ adj (pred ∼ **founded**) bien fundado; **∼-groomed** /'wel'gruːmd/ adj (pred ∼ **groomed**) «person» bien arreglado; «hair» bien peinado; «horse/garden» bien cuidado; **∼-informed** /'welɪn'fɔːrmd ǁ,welɪn'fɔːmd/ adj bien informado

wellington (boot) /'welɪŋtən/ n **(a)** (short boot) (AmE) botín m, bota f (corta) **(b)** (gumboot) (BrE) bota f de goma or de agua or de lluvia, catiusca f (Esp)

well: ∼-kept /'wel'kept/ adj (pred ∼ **kept**) **(a)** «house/lawns» bien cuidado **(b)** «secret» bien guardado; **∼-known** /'wel'nəʊn/ adj (pred ∼ **known**) «person» conocido, famoso; **it is ∼ known that ...** es bien sabido que ...; **∼-mannered** /'wel'mænərd ǁ,wel'mænəd/ adj (pred ∼ **mannered**) de buenos modales, educado; **∼-meaning** /'wel'miːnɪŋ/ adj (pred ∼ **meaning**) «person» bienintencionado; **he's ∼ meaning, but ...** no lo hace con la mejor intención, pero ...; **∼-off** /'wel'ɔːf ǁ,wel'ɒf/ adj (pred ∼ **off**) adinerado; **∼-read** /'wel'red/ adj (pred ∼ **read**) culto; **∼-to-do** /'weltə'duː/ adj «businessman/family» adinerado; **∼-wisher** /'wel,wɪʃər ǁ,wel,wɪʃə(r)/ n: **she received lots of cards from ∼-wishers** recibió muchas tarjetas en que le deseaban una pronta recuperación (or mucha felicidad etc); **∼-worn** /'wel'wɔːrn ǁ,wel'wɔːn/ adj (pred ∼ **worn**) «coat/carpet» muy gastado; «phrase» muy trillado

Welsh¹ /welʃ/ adj galés

Welsh² n **(a)** (language) galés m **(b)** (people) (+ pl vb) **the ∼** los galeses

Welshman /'welʃmən/ n (pl **-men** /-mən/) galés m

welt /welt/ n (weal) verdugón m

went /went/ past of GO¹

wept /wept/ past & past p of WEEP

were /wɜːr ǁ wɜː(r), weak form wər ǁ wə(r)/ **(a)** 2nd pers sing past ind of BE **(b)** 1st, 2nd & 3rd pers pl past ind of BE **(c)** subjunctive of BE

we're /wɪr ǁ wɪə(r)/ = **we are**

weren't /wɜːrnt ǁ wɜːnt/ = **were not**

west¹ /west/ n **1** (point of the compass, direction) oeste m; **the ∼, the W∼** (region) el oeste **2** **the West** (the Occident) (el) Occidente m; (Pol, Hist) el Oeste

west² adj (before n) oeste adj inv, occidental; «wind» del oeste

west³ adv al oeste

westbound /'westbaʊnd/ adj que va (or iba etc) hacia el or en dirección oeste

westerly /'westərli ǁ'westəli/ adj «wind» del oeste; **in a ∼ direction** hacia el oeste, en dirección oeste

western¹ /'westərn ǁ'westən/ adj **(a)** (Geog) oeste adj inv, del oeste, occidental; **the ∼ areas of the country** las zonas oeste or occidentales del país **(b)** (occidental) (Geog, Pol) occidental

western² n western m, película f (or novela f etc) del Oeste or de vaqueros

Westerner, westerner /'westərnər ǁ'westənə(r)/ n occidental mf

westernized /'westərnaɪzd ǁ'westənaɪzd/ adj occidentalizado

west: W∼ Indian adj antillano; (in UK) afroantillano; **W∼ Indies** /'ɪndiz/ pl n **the W∼ Indies** las Antillas

westward¹ /'westwərd ǁ'westwəd/ adj (before n): **in a ∼ direction** hacia el oeste, en dirección oeste

westward², (BrE) **westwards** /-z/ adv hacia el oeste

wet¹ /wet/ adj **-tt-** **(a)** (moist) «floor/grass/clothes» mojado; (damp) húmedo; «concrete/plaster» blando; **☉ wet paint** pintura fresca or (Esp tb) ojo, pinta; **to get ∼** mojarse **(b)** (rainy) «weather/day» lluvioso

wet² vt (pres p **wetting**; past & past p **wet** or **wetted**) mojar; (dampen) humedecer*; **to ∼ the bed** mojar la cama; **to ∼ oneself** orinarse, hacerse* pipí (encima) (fam)

wet: ∼ blanket n (colloq) aguafiestas mf (fam); **∼ suit** n traje m de neopreno or de neopreno

we've /wiːv/ = **we have**

whack¹ /hwæk ǁ wæk/ n (blow) golpe m; (sound) ¡zas!

whack² vt golpear, aporrear; «person» pegarle* a

whale /hweɪl ǁ weɪl/ n **1** (pl **∼s** or **∼**) (Zool) ballena f **2** (colloq) (as intensifier): **we had a ∼ of a time** lo pasamos bomba or genial (fam)

wharf /hwɔːrf ǁ wɔːf/ n (pl **wharves** /hwɔːrvz ǁ wɔːvz/) muelle m, embarcadero m

what¹ /hwɑːt ǁ wɒt/ pron **1** (in questions) qué; **∼'s that?** ¿qué es eso?; **∼'s the problem?** ¿cuál es el problema?; **∼'s 'I don't understand' in Russian?** ¿cómo se dice 'no entiendo' en ruso? **2** (in phrases) **or what?** (colloq) ¿o qué?; **so what?** ⋯⋟

W

¿y qué?; **what about: but ~ about the children?** y los niños ¿qué?; **you know Julie's boyfriend? —** **yes, ~ about him?** ¿conoces al novio de Julie? — sí ¿por qué?; **what ... for: ~'s this button for?** ¿para qué es este botón?; **~ are you complaining for?** ¿por qué te quejas?; **what if: ~ if she finds out?** ¿y si se entera?; **what's-her/-his-name** (colloq): **go and ask ~'s-her-name next door** ve y pregúntale a la de al lado ¿cómo se llama? **3 (a)** (in indirect speech) qué; **she knows ~ to do** ella sabe qué hacer; **I still don't know ~'s ~ in the office** aún no sé cómo funcionan las cosas en la oficina; **(I'll) tell you ~, ...** mira, ... **(b)** (relative use) lo que; **they did ~ they could** hicieron lo que pudieron

what² adj **1 (a)** (in questions) qué; **~ color are the walls?** ¿de qué color son las paredes? **(b)** (in indirect speech) qué; **she didn't know ~ color to choose** no sabía qué color elegir **2** (in exclamations) qué; **~ a surprise!** ¡qué sorpresa!; **~ a lot of people!** ¡cuánta gente!

whatever¹ /hwɑːˈtevər ‖ wɒtˈevə(r)/ pron **1** (in questions, exclamations) qué; **~ is she doing?** ¿qué (es lo que) está haciendo? **2 (a)** (no matter what): **~ you do, don't laugh!** hagas lo que hagas ¡no te vayas a reír!; **he talked about percentiles, ~ they are** habló de percentiles, que no tengo ni idea de qué son **(b)** (all that): **they let him do ~ he likes** lo dejan hacer todo lo que quiere; **~ you say** lo que tú digas, como quieras

whatever² adj (a) (no matter what): **don't give up, ~ doubts you may have** no renuncies, tengas las dudas que tengas; **all people, of ~ race or creed** todos, cualquiera sea su raza o credo **(b)** (any): **~ changes are necessary** los cambios que sean necesarios

whatever³ adv (as intensifier): **none/nothing ~** ninguno/nada en absoluto

wheat /hwiːt ‖ wiːt/ n trigo m

wheatgerm /ˈhwiːtdʒɜːrm ‖ ˈwiːtdʒɜːm/ n germen m de trigo

wheedle /ˈhwiːdl̩ ‖ ˈwiːdl̩/ vt **to ~ sth OUT OF sb** sonsacarle* algo a algn

wheel¹ /hwiːl ‖ wiːl/ n **1 (a)** (of vehicle) rueda f **(b)** (potter's ~) torno m **2** (steering ~ — of car) volante m; (— of ship) timón m; **at the ~ — (of car)** al volante; (of ship) al timón

wheel² vt ‹bicycle/wheelchair› empujar; ‹person› llevar (en silla de ruedas etc)
■ ~ vi **(a)** (turn suddenly) **~ (around** o (BrE) **round)** «person» girar sobre sus (or mis etc) talones **(b)** (circle) dar* vueltas; «birds» revolotear

wheel: ~barrow n carretilla f, **~chair** n silla f de ruedas; **~ clamp** n cepo m

wheeling and dealing /ˈhwiːlɪŋənˈdiːlɪŋ ‖ ˌwiːlɪŋənˈdiːlɪŋ/ n (colloq) tejemanejes mpl (fam)

wheeze /hwiːz ‖ wiːz/ vi «person» respirar con dificultad (produciendo un sonido sibilante como los asmáticos); «machine» resollar*

when¹ /hwen ‖ wen/ adv
■ **Note** When used as a conjunction in sentences expressing the future, *when* is translated by *cuando* + subjunctive: *we'll speak to Carol when she gets back* hablaremos con Carol cuando vuelva.

1 (in questions, indirect questions) cuándo; **that was ~ I realized that ...** fue entonces cuando *or* (esp AmL tb) que me di cuenta de que ...; **say ~!** di

cuándo **2** (as relative): **the year ~ we got married** el año en que nos casamos; **in December, ~ we were on holiday** en diciembre, cuando estábamos de vacaciones

when² conj **1 (a)** (temporal sense) cuando; **I'll ask him ~ I see him** se lo preguntaré cuando lo vea **(b)** (if) si, cuando **2 (a)** (since, considering that) si, cuando **(b)** (although) cuando; **he said he was 18 ~ in fact he's only 15** dijo que tenía 18 años cuando en realidad solo tiene 15

when³ pron cuándo; **~ do you have to be in London by?** ¿para cuándo tienes que estar en Londres?

whenever /hwenˈevər ‖ wenˈevə(r)/ conj **(a)** (every time that) siempre que; **~ I hear that song I think of Spain** siempre que *or* cada vez que escucho esa canción, me acuerdo de España **(b)** (at whatever time): **we'll go ~ you're ready** saldremos cuando estés listo

where¹ /hwer ‖ weə(r)/ adv dónde; (indicating direction) adónde, dónde; **~'s Lewes?** ¿dónde está Lewes?; **~ are you taking me?** ¿(a)dónde me llevan?; **~ are you from?** ¿de dónde eres?

where² conj **(a)** donde; (indicating direction) adonde, donde **(b)** (in cases where) cuando; **~ appropriate** cuando *or* allí donde sea apropiado

whereabouts¹ /ˈhwerəbaʊts ‖ ˌweərəˈbaʊts/ adv: **~ in Austria do you live?** ¿en qué parte de Austria vives?

whereabouts² /ˈhwerəbaʊts ‖ ˈweərəbaʊts/ n (+ sing or pl vb) paradero m

whereas /hwerˈæz ‖ ˌweərˈæz/ conj mientras que

whereby /hwerˈbaɪ ‖ weəˈbaɪ/ pron (frml): **a system ~ payments are made automatically** un sistema por *or* según el cual los pagos se efectúan automáticamente

wherever¹ /hwerˈevər ‖ weərˈevə(r)/ adv **(a)** (in questions) dónde **(b)** (no matter where) (colloq) en cualquier parte *or* lado

wherever² conj: **you can use your card ~ you see this sign** puede usar su tarjeta (en cualquier establecimiento) donde vea este símbolo; **~ he goes, I'll go too** vaya donde vaya, yo iré tambien; **you can sit ~ you like** puedes sentarte donde quieras

wherewithal /ˈhwerwɪðɔːl ‖ ˈweəwɪðɔːl/ n the **~** los medios; **we don't have the ~ to do this** no tenemos los recursos para hacer esto

whet /hwet ‖ wet/ vt **-tt-** ‹interest/curiosity› estimular; **the walk ~ted our appetites** la caminata nos abrió el apetito

whether /ˈhweðər ‖ ˈweðə(r)/ conj: **tell me ~ you need us or not** *o* **~ or not you need us** dime si nos necesitas o no; **I doubt ~ he knew** dudo que lo supiera; **~ you like it or not** te guste o no te guste

whey /hwei ‖ wei/ n suero m (de la leche)

which¹ /hwɪtʃ ‖ wɪtʃ/ pron **1 (a)** (in questions) (sing) cuál; (pl) cuáles **(b)** (in indirect use) cuál; **I can never remember ~ is ~** nunca recuerdo cuál es cuál **2** (as relative): **the parcel ~ arrived this morning** el paquete que llegó esta mañana; **the newspaper in ~ the article appeared** el diario en el que *or* en el cual apareció el artículo

which² adj **1** (in questions) (sing) qué, cuál; (pl)

qué, cuáles **2** (as relative): **we arrived at two, by ~ time they had gone** llegamos a las dos y para entonces ya se habían ido; **in ~ case** en cuyo caso

whichever¹ /hwɪtʃˈevər ‖wɪtʃˈevə(r)/ *pron* **(a)** (no matter which): **there are several options, but ~ you choose ...** hay varias opciones, pero elijas la que elijas *or* cualquiera que elijas ... **(b)** (the one, ones that): **buy ~ is cheaper** compra el que sea más barato

whichever² *adj* **(a)** (no matter which): **~ party is in power** sea cual sea *or* cualquiera que sea el partido que esté en el poder **(b)** (any that): **you can write about ~ subject you know best** puedes escribir sobre el tema que mejor conozcas, sea cual sea *or* fuere

while¹ /hwaɪl ‖waɪl/ *conj* **1** (in time) mientras; **they don't drink ~ on duty** no beben cuando están de guardia **2** (though) aunque **3** (whereas) mientras que

▪ **while away** [*v + adv + o, v + o + adv*]: **we had a game of chess to ~ away the time** jugamos una partida de ajedrez para pasar el rato

while² *n*: **wait a ~** (a few days, weeks) espera un tiempo; (a few minutes, hours) espera un rato; (a very short period) espera un ratito *or* un momentito; **it's been a good ~ since we had any rain** hace bastante (tiempo) que no llueve; **he was here a little ~ ago** hace un ratito estaba aquí; **(every) once in a ~** de vez en cuando

whilst /hwaɪlst ‖waɪlst/ *conj* (BrE) ▶ WHILE¹

whim /hwɪm ‖wɪm/ *n* capricho *m*

whimper¹ /ˈhwɪmpər ‖ˈwɪmpə(r)/ *vi* gimotear

whimper² *n* quejido *m*

whimsical /ˈhwɪmzɪkəl ‖ˈwɪmzɪkəl/ *adj* ⟨person⟩ caprichoso; ⟨mood⟩ voluble

whine¹ /hwaɪn ‖waɪn/ *vi* **(a)** ⟨dog⟩ aullar*; ⟨person⟩ gemir*; ⟨child⟩ lloriquear **(b)** (complain) (pej) quejarse

whine² *n* (of dog) aullido *m*; (of person) quejido *m*; (of engine) chirrido *m*; (of bullet) silbido *m*

whinny /ˈhwɪni ‖ˈwɪni/ *vi* (3rd pers sing pres **whinnies**; *pres p* **whinnying**; *past & past p* **whinnied**) ⟨horse⟩ relinchar

whip¹ /hwɪp ‖wɪp/ *n* (in horse riding) fusta *f*, fuete *m* (AmL exc CS); (of tamer) látigo *m*; (for punishment) azote *m*

whip² **-pp-** *vt* **1** **(a)** (lash) ⟨horse⟩ pegarle* a (con la fusta), fustigar*; ⟨person⟩ azotar; ⟨child⟩ darle* una paliza a **(b)** (beat) ⟨egg whites⟩ batir; ⟨cream⟩ batir *or* (Esp) montar; **~ped cream** crema *f* batida *or* (Esp) nata *f* montada **2** (take quickly) (+ adv compl): **she ~ped out her notebook** sacó rápidamente la libreta

▪ **whip up** [*v + o + adv, v + adv + o*] **1** **(a)** (arouse) ⟨trouble/unrest⟩ provocar*; ⟨hatred⟩ fomentar; ⟨support⟩ conseguir* **(b)** (incite) ⟨crowd⟩ incitar **(c)** ⟨wind⟩ ⟨sea/waves⟩ agitar; ⟨dust⟩ levantar **2** **(a)** (beat, whisk) ⟨egg whites⟩ batir; ⟨cream⟩ batir, montar (Esp) **(b)** (prepare hurriedly) (colloq) ⟨meal⟩ improvisar

whip: **~lash injury** *n* (Med) traumatismo *m* cervical; **~round** *n* (BrE colloq) colecta *f*, vaca *f* (AmL fam)

whir, (BrE) **whirr** /hwɜːr ‖wɜː(r)/ *vi* **-rr-** ⟨machine/propellers⟩ runrunear, zumbar

whirl¹ /hwɜːrl ‖wɜːl/ *vi* **(a)** (spin) ⟨person⟩ girar, dar* vueltas; ⟨leaves/dust⟩ arremolinarse **(b)** (move fast) (+ adv compl): **he ~ed around** se dio media vuelta rápidamente

▪ **~** *vt* (+ adv compl) hacer* girar

whirl² *n* (turn) giro *m*, vuelta *f*; (of dust) remolino *m*; **my head was in a ~** la cabeza me daba vueltas

whirl: **~pool** *n* vorágine *f*, remolino *m*; **~wind** *n* torbellino *m*; (before n) **a ~wind romance** un idilio arrollador

whirr /hwɜːr ‖wɜː(r)/ *vi* (BrE) ▶ WHIR

whisk¹ /hwɪsk ‖wɪsk/ *vt* **1** (Culin) batir **2** (convey quickly) (+ adv compl): **she was ~ed off to a meeting** se la llevaron a una reunión a toda prisa; **he ~ed away the plates** retiró los platos rápidamente

whisk² *n* (Culin) batidor *m*

whisker /ˈhwɪskər ‖ˈwɪskə(r)/ *n* **1** **(a)** (single hair) pelo *m* (de la barba) **(b)** (narrow margin) (no pl) pelo *m* **2** **whiskers** *pl* (of animal) bigotes *mpl*

whiskey /ˈhwɪski ‖ˈwɪski/ *n* (pl **-keys**) whisky *m*, güisqui *m* (esp americano o irlandés)

whisky /ˈhwɪski ‖ˈwɪski/ *n* (pl **-kies**) whisky *m*, güisqui *m* (esp escocés)

whisper¹ /ˈhwɪspər ‖ˈwɪspə(r)/ *vi* **(a)** ⟨person⟩ cuchichear **(b)** (liter) ⟨wind/leaves⟩ susurrar (liter)

▪ **~** *vt* ⟨remark/words⟩ susurrar

whisper² *n* **(a)** (soft voice) susurro *m*; **yes, he said in a ~** —sí —susurró **(b)** (rumor) rumor *m*

whistle¹ /ˈhwɪsəl ‖ˈwɪsəl/ *vi* ⟨person/kettle/wind⟩ silbar; (loudly) chiflar; ⟨referee⟩ pitar; ⟨train⟩ pitar

▪ **~** *vt* ⟨tune⟩ silbar

whistle² *n* **(a)** (instrument) silbato *m*, pito *m* **(b)** (sound — made with mouth) silbido *m*; (loud) chiflido *m*; (— made by referee's whistle) silbato *m*, pitido *m*; (— of kettle, wind, bullet) silbido *m*

white¹ /hwaɪt ‖waɪt/ *adj* **-er, -est** **(a)** ⟨paint/cat/bread/wine/chocolate⟩ blanco; ⟨coffee/tea⟩ con leche; **she had a ~ wedding** se casó de blanco; **he went ~** se puso blanco **(b)** (Caucasian) blanco

white² *n* **1** (color) blanco *m* **2** *also* **White** (person) blanco, -ca *m,f* **3** **(a)** (of egg) clara *f* **(b)** (of eye) blanco *m*

white: **~bait** *n* morralla *f*, chanquetes *mpl* (Esp), cornalitos *mpl* (Arg), majuga *f* (Ur); **~collar** /ˈhwaɪtˈkɑːlər ‖ˌwaɪtˈkɒlə(r)/ *adj* ⟨worker/job⟩ no manual; (clerical) de oficina; **~ elephant** *n* (building, project) elefante *m* blanco; (object) objeto superfluo; **~ gasoline, ~ gas** *n* (AmE) gasolina *f* or (Andes) bencina *f* or (RPl) nafta *f* sin plomo; **~hot** /ˈhwaɪtˈhɑːt ‖ˌwaɪtˈhɒt/ *adj* ⟨metal⟩ al rojo blanco; **W~ House** *n* the W~ House la Casa Blanca; **~ lie** *n* mentira *f* piadosa

whiten /ˈhwaɪtn ‖ˈwaɪtn/ *vt* blanquear

white: **~ sauce** *n* salsa *f* blanca *or* bechamel; **~ spirit** *n* (BrE) espíritu *m* de petróleo (usado como sustituto del aguarrás)

whitewash¹ /ˈhwaɪtwɔːʃ ‖ˈwaɪtwɒʃ/ *n* **1** (Const) cal *f* **2** (defeat) (colloq) paliza *f* (fam)

whitewash² *vt* ⟨wall/building⟩ blanquear, encalar, enjalbegar*

whiting /ˈhwaɪtɪŋ ‖ˈwaɪtɪŋ/ *n* (pl **~s** or **~**) pescadilla *f*

W

Whitsun /'hwɪtsən ‖'wɪtsən/ n (esp BrE)
Pentecostés f

whittle /'hwɪtl̩ ‖'wɪtl̩/ vt tallar

■ **whittle away** [v + o + adv, v + adv + o]
⟨funds/resources⟩ ir* mermando; ⟨influence⟩ ir*
reduciendo; ⟨rights⟩ ir* menoscabando

■ **whittle down** [v + o + adv, v + adv + o]
⟨expenses⟩ recortar*; ⟨applicants⟩ reducir* el
numero de

whiz, whizz /hwɪz ‖wɪz/ vi **-zz-** (+ adv compl):
to ~ by «bullet/arrow/car» pasar zumbando; I
~zed through my homework hice los deberes
zumbando or a toda velocidad

whiz kid, whizz kid n (colloq) lince m (fam)

who /huː/ pron **1** (a) (in questions) (sing) quién;
(pl) quiénes; ~ are you writing to? ¿a quién le
estás escribiendo? (b) (in indirect questions) I
don't know ~ you're talking about no sé de quién
estás hablando **2** (as relative): the boy ~ won the
prize el chico que ganó el premio; there are
blankets for those ~ want them hay mantas para
quienes quieran

WHO n (= **World Health Organization**)
OMS f

who'd /huːd/ (a) = **who had** (b) = **who
would**

whodunit, whodunnit /huː'dʌnət
‖ˌhuː'dʌnɪt/ n (colloq) novela f policíaca

whoever /huː'evər ‖huː'evə(r)/ pron (a) (no
matter who): she's not coming in here, ~ she is
aquí no entra, quien quiera que sea; ~ you ask
se lo preguntes a quien se lo preguntes (b) (the
one, ones who): ~ did this must be insane
quienquiera que haya hecho esto debe (de) estar
loco; I'll invite ~ I like voy a invitar a quien (se)
me dé la gana (c) (in questions) quién

whole¹ /həʊl/ adj **1** (entire) (before n):
there's a ~ bottle left queda una botella entera;
the ~ truth toda la verdad; I'm fed up with the ~
affair estoy harto del asunto **2** (pred) (in one
piece) entero

whole² n (a) (integral unit) todo m; the ~ of sth:
a threat to the ~ of mankind una amenaza para
toda la humanidad (b) (in phrases) as a whole:
this will affect Europe as a ~ esto va a afectar a
Europa en su totalidad; on the whole (indep) en
general

wholehearted /ˈhəʊlˈhɑːrtəd ‖ˌhəʊlˈhɑːtɪd/
adj ⟨approval⟩ sin reservas; ⟨support⟩
incondicional

wholeheartedly /ˈhəʊlˈhɑːrtədli
‖ˌhəʊlˈhɑːtɪdli/ adv ⟨approve/support⟩ sin
reservas

whole: ~**meal** adj (BrE) integral; ▶ **note** n
(AmE) semibreve f, redonda f

wholesale¹ /'həʊlseɪl/ adj (a) (Busn) (before n)
al por mayor (b) ⟨destruction/slaughter⟩
sistemático

wholesale² adv (a) (Busn) ⟨buy/sell⟩ al por
mayor (b) (on a large scale) de modo general

wholesaler /'həʊlseɪlər ‖'həʊlseɪlə(r)/ n
mayorista mf

wholesome /'həʊlsəm/ adj (a) (healthy) ⟨food/
climate⟩ sano (b) (morally good) ⟨image⟩ de persona
sana

wholewheat /'həʊlhwiːt ‖'həʊlwiːt/ adj
integral

who'll /huːl/ = **who will**

wholly /'həʊlli/ adv totalmente

whom /huːm/ pron (frml) (a) (in questions): ~ did
you visit? ¿a quién visitaste? (b) (as relative): the
cousin ~ I mentioned earlier el primo que or a
quien mencioné antes; the girls, both of ~ could
dance las chicas, que ambas sabían bailar

whooping cough /'huːpɪŋ/ n tos f convulsa
or convulsiva

whoops /hwʊps ‖wʊps/ interj ¡ay!, ¡epa! (AmS
fam), ¡híjole! (Méx fam)

whore /hɔːr ‖hɔː(r)/ n (pej) puta f (vulg & pey)

who's /huːz/ (a) = **who is** (b) = **who has**

whose¹ /huːz/ pron (sing) de quién; (pl) de
quiénes

whose² adj (a) (in questions) (sing) de quién;
(pl) de quiénes (b) (as relative) (sing) cuyo; (pl)
cuyos

who've /huːv/ = **who have**

why¹ /hwaɪ ‖waɪ/ adv por qué; ~ not? ¿por
qué no?; ~ don't you apply for the post? ¿por qué
no solicitas el puesto?; this is ~ the attempt failed
fue por esto que el intento fracasó; the reason ~
he couldn't attend la razón por la cual no pudo
asistir

why² interj ¡vaya!

why³ n porqué m

WI = **Wisconsin**

wick /wɪk/ n mecha f

wicked /'wɪkəd ‖'wɪkɪd/ adj **-er, -est** (a) (evil)
⟨person⟩ malvado, malo; ⟨thought⟩ malo; ⟨lie⟩
infame (b) (vicious) ⟨blow⟩ malintencionado (c)
(mischievous) ⟨grin/laugh⟩ travieso

wicker /'wɪkər ‖'wɪkə(r)/ n mimbre m

wickerwork /'wɪkərwɜːrk ‖'wɪkəwɜːk/ n (a)
(articles) artículos mpl de mimbre (b) ▶ **WICKER**

wicket /'wɪkət ‖'wɪkɪt/ n **1** (in cricket) (stumps
and bails) palos mpl **2** (window) (AmE) ventanilla f

wide¹ /waɪd/ adj **wider, widest 1** (in
dimension) ⟨river/feet/trousers⟩ ancho; ⟨gap⟩
grande; ⟨desert/ocean⟩ vasto; it's two meters ~
tiene or mide dos metros de ancho **2** (in extent,
range) ⟨experience/powers/area⟩ amplio; a ~
variety of things una gran variedad de cosas
3 (off target) ⟨ball/shot⟩ desviado; ~ or sth lejos
DE algo; ▶ **MARK¹** 4

wide² adv **wider, widest** ~ apart: with your
feet ~ apart con los pies bien separados; ~
awake: to be ~ awake estar* completamente
espabilado or despierto; open ~! abra bien la
boca; ~ open: you left the door ~ open dejaste la
puerta abierta de par en par

wide-angle lens /'waɪdˈæŋɡəl/ n
granangular m

widely /'waɪdli/ adv (a) (extensively): she is very

w

~ traveled ha viajado mucho; **it was ~ publicized** se le dio mucha publicidad **(b)** (commonly): **a ~ held view** una opinión muy extendida **(c)** (to a large degree) ‹vary› mucho

widen /'waɪdn̩/ vt ‹road/entrance› ensanchar; ‹range/debate/scope› ampliar*
■ ~ vi «road/tunnel» ensancharse

wide: ~-ranging /'waɪd'reɪndʒɪŋ/ adj ‹powers/curriculum› amplio; ‹interests› variado; ‹effects› de gran alcance; **~-screen** /'waɪd'skriːn/ adj para pantalla ancha; **~spread** adj ‹custom/belief› extendido

widget /'wɪdʒət ‖'wɪdʒɪt/ n (colloq) aparato m, artilugio m, chisme m (Esp fam)

widow¹ /'wɪdəʊ/ n viuda f

widow² vt: to be ~ed enviudar, quedar viudo

widower /'wɪdəʊə(r)/ n viudo m

width /wɪdθ/ n **(a)** (measurement) ancho m, anchura f; **what ~ is the cloth?** ¿qué ancho tiene la tela? **(b)** (in swimming pool) ancho m

wield /wiːld/ vt ‹sword› blandir*; ‹power/authority› ejercer*

wife /waɪf/ n (pl **wives**) esposa f, mujer f

wig /wɪg/ n peluca f

wiggle /'wɪgəl/ vt ‹toes› mover*; ‹hips› contonear

wild¹ /waɪld/ adj **-er, -est** **1** **(a)** ‹animal› salvaje; ‹plant/flower› silvestre; ‹vegetation› agreste **(b)** (uncivilized) ‹tribe› salvaje **(c)** (desolate) ‹country› agreste
2 **(a)** (unruly) ‹party/lifestyle› desenfrenado **(b)** (random, uncontrolled) ‹attempt› desesperado; **a ~ guess** una conjetura hecha totalmente al azar **(c)** ‹allegation/exaggeration› absurdo
3 **(a)** (violent) (liter) ‹sea/waters› embravecido, proceloso (liter); ‹wind› fuertísimo, furioso (liter) **(b)** (frantic) ‹excitement/dancing› desenfrenado; ‹shouting› desaforado; ‹appearance/stare› de loco; **her perfume was driving him ~** su perfume lo estaba enloqueciendo **(c)** (enthusiastic) (colloq) (pred): **to be ~ ABOUT sth: I'm not ~ about the idea** la idea no me enloquece **(d)** (angry) (colloq) (pred): **it makes me ~** me saca de quicio

wild² adv: **these flowers grow ~** estas flores son silvestres; **to run ~: these kids have been allowed to run ~** a estos niños los han criado como salvajes; **the garden has run ~** la maleza ha invadido el jardín

wild³ n **the ~: an opportunity to observe these animals in the ~** una oportunidad de observar estos animales en libertad

wild: ~ boar n jabalí m; **~ card** n (Comput) comodín m; **~cat** /'waɪldkæt/ n (pl **~cats** or **~cat**) (European) gato m montés; (bobcat) (esp AmE) lince m

wilderness /'wɪldərnəs ‖'wɪldənɪs/ n **(a)** (wasteland) páramo m; (jungle) jungla f **(b)** (undeveloped land) (AmE) parque m natural

wild: ~fire n (AmE) fuego m arrasador; **to spread like ~fire** (also BrE) extenderse* como un reguero de pólvora; **~-goose chase** /'waɪld'guːs/ n: **I'm not going into town again on another ~-goose chase** no pienso ir otra vez al centro a perder el tiempo para nada; **~life** n fauna f y flora f

wildly /'waɪldli/ adv **1** **(a)** (frantically) ‹kick/struggle/rush› como (un) loco **(b)** (violently) ‹rage/blow› con furia **2** **(a)** (in undisciplined fashion) ‹live› desordenadamente **(b)** (haphazardly, randomly) ‹shoot/guess› a lo loco **3** (extremely): **~ funny** comiquísimo; **~ inaccurate estimates** cálculos absolutamente errados

Wild West n the ~ ~ el Lejano Oeste; (before n) ‹adventure/story› del oeste

wiles /waɪlz/ pl n artimañas fpl

wilful adj (BrE) ▶ WILLFUL

will¹ /wɪl/ v mod
■ **Note** When translating will into Spanish, the future tense is not always the first option. Ir + a + infinitive is common in Latin American countries. For examples, see the entry below.

(past **would**) ['LL **es la contracción de** WILL, WON'T **de** WILL NOT **y** 'LL'VE **de** WILL HAVE]
1 (talking about the future): **he'll come on Friday** vendrá el viernes, va a venir el viernes; **he said he would come on Friday** dijo que vendría o iba a venir el viernes; **at the end of this month, he'll have been working here for a year** este fin de mes hará un año que trabaja aquí; **I won't let you down** no te fallaré
2 **(a)** (expressing willingness): **~ o would you do me a favor?** ¿quieres hacerme un favor?; **she won't tell us what happened** no nos quiere decir qué pasó **(b)** (in orders, invitations): **be quiet, ~ you!** cállate, ¿quieres?; **~ you have a drink?** ¿quieres tomar algo?
3 (expressing conjecture): **won't they be having lunch now?** ¿no estarán comiendo ahora?; **that would have been in 1947** eso debe (de) haber sido en 1947
4 **(a)** (indicating habit, characteristic): **I'll watch anything on television** yo soy capaz de mirar cualquier cosa en la televisión; **he'd get drunk every Saturday** se emborrachaba todos los sábados **(b)** (indicating capability): **this door won't shut** esta puerta no cierra or no quiere cerrar
■ ~ vt (past & past p **willed**) **1** **(a)** (urge, try to cause): **I was ~ing her to get the answer right** estaba deseando con todas mis fuerzas que diera la respuesta correcta **(b)** (desire, ordain) (frml) «God» disponer*, querer*
2 (bequeath) legar*

will² n **1** **(a)** (faculty) voluntad f **(b)** (willpower) voluntad f; **to lose the ~ to live** perder* las ansias de vivir **(c)** (desire, intention) voluntad f; **patients may come and go at ~** los pacientes pueden entrar y salir a voluntad; ▶ FREE WILL **2** (testament) testamento m

willful, (BrE) **wilful** /'wɪlfəl/ adj **1** (deliberate) ‹misconduct/neglect› intencionado; ‹damage› causado con premeditación **2** (obstinate) ‹person› terco

willing /'wɪlɪŋ/ adj **(a)** (eager, compliant) (before n) ‹servant/worker› servicial **(b)** (inclined) (pred): **to be ~ to + INF** estar* dispuesto A + INF

willingly /'wɪlɪŋli/ adv (gladly) con gusto; (readily, freely) por voluntad propia

willingness /'wɪlɪŋnəs ‖'wɪlɪŋnɪs/ n buena voluntad f, buena disposición f

willow /'wɪləʊ/ n sauce m

willpower /'wɪlpaʊər ‖'wɪlpaʊə(r)/ n (fuerza f de) voluntad f

W

willy-nilly /ˈwɪliˈnɪli/ *adv* **(a)** (haphazardly) de cualquier manera **(b)** (like it or not) sea como sea

wilt /wɪlt/ *vi* «*plant/flower*» ponerse* mustio, marchitarse

wily /ˈwaɪli/ *adj* **wilier, wiliest** astuto

win¹ /wɪn/ (*pres p* **winning**; *past & past p* **won**) *vt* **1** (gain) ‹*prize/title*› ganar; ‹*support*› conseguir*; ‹*fame/recognition/affection*› ganarse; ‹*scholarship/promotion/contract*› conseguir* **2** (be victorious in) ‹*war/race/bet/election*› ganar
■ ~ *vi* ganar
■ **win over,** (BrE also) **win round** [*v + o + adv, v + adv + o*] conquistarse a

win² *n* victoria *f*, triunfo *m*

wince /wɪns/ *vi* hacer* un gesto de dolor; (shudder) estremecerse*

winch¹ /wɪntʃ/ *n* cabrestante *m*, torno *m*

winch² *vt*: *levantar con un torno o cabrestante*

wind¹ /wɪnd/ *n* **1** (Meteo) viento *m*; **to get ~ of sth** enterarse de algo; (*before n*) ~ **power** energía *f* eólica **2** (in bowels) gases *mpl* **3** (breath) aliento *m* **4** (Mus): **the ~** los instrumentos de viento; (*before n*) ~ **instrument** instrumento *m* de viento

wind² *vt*
I /wɪnd/ **(a)** «*exertion*» dejar sin aliento; «*blow*» cortarle la respiración a **(b)** ‹*baby*› sacarle* el aire a (fam)
II /waɪnd/ (*past & past p* **wound** /waʊnd/) **1** (coil) ‹*yarn/wool*› ovillar; **to ~ sth AROUND** *o* (esp BrE) **ROUND sth** enroscar* algo ALREDEDOR DE algo; **to ~ sth into a ball** hacer* un ovillo con algo; **to ~ the film on** (hacer*) correr la película **2** **(a)** (turn) ‹*handle*› hacer* girar, darle* vueltas a; ‹*clock/watch*› darle* cuerda a **(b)** (hoist, pull) levantar
■ ~ *vi* /waɪnd/ (*past & past p* **wound** /waʊnd/) **(a)** «*river/road*» serpentear **(b) winding** *pres p* ‹*river/road*› sinuoso, serpenteante
■ **wind down** **1** [*v + o + adv, v + adv + o*] ‹*window*› (Auto) bajar; ‹*production/trade*› reducir* paulatinamente
2 [*v + adv*] (colloq) relajarse
■ **wind up** **1** [*v + o + adv, v + adv + o*] **(a)** (tighten spring) ‹*watch/toy*› darle* cuerda a **(b)** (bring to conclusion) ‹*meeting/speech*› cerrar* **(c)** (close down) ‹*company*› cerrar*, liquidar
2 [*v + o + adv*] (colloq) (make angry) torear, darle* manija a (RPl fam); (tease) tomarle el pelo a (fam)
3 [*v + adv*] **(a)** (end up, find oneself) (colloq) terminar, acabar **(b)** (conclude) «*speaker*» concluir*, terminar

wind /wɪnd/: ~**fall** *n* **(a)** (fruit) *fruta caída del árbol* **(b)** (unexpected benefit): **the $100 prize was a nice little ~fall** el premio de 100 dólares le (*or me etc*) cayó como llovido del cielo; ~**mill** *n* molino *m* de viento

window /ˈwɪndəʊ/ *n* **1** **(a)** (of building) ventana *f*; (of car) ventanilla *f*; (of shop) vitrina *f* (AmL), vidriera *f* (AmL), escaparate *m* (esp Esp); **to fly/go out (of) the ~** «*plans*» venirse* abajo, desbaratarse; «*hopes*» desvanecerse* **(b)** (sales counter) ventanilla *f* **2** (Comput) ventana *f*, recuadro *m*

window: ~ **box** *n* jardinera *f*; ~ **cleaner** *n* (product) limpiacristales *m*, limpiavidrios *m* (esp AmL); (person) limpiacristales *mf*, limpiavidrios *mf* (esp AmL); ~ **dressing** *n* (in shop) vitrinismo *m* (AmL), vidrierismo *m* (AmL), escaparatismo *m*

(esp Esp); ~ **ledge** *n* alféizar *m or* repisa *f* de la ventana; ~**pane** *n* vidrio *m or* (Esp) cristal *m* (de una ventana); ~ **seat** *n* (in train, plane) asiento *m* junto a la ventanilla; ~**shop** *vi* **-pp-**: **to go ~-shopping** ir* a mirar vitrinas *or* vidrieras *or* (esp Esp) escaparates; ~**sill** *n* alféizar *m or* repisa *f* de la ventana

wind /wɪnd/: ~**pipe** *n* tráquea *f*; ~**screen** *n* (BrE) ▶ ~**SHIELD**; ~**shield** *n* (AmE) parabrisas *m*; (*before n*) ~**shield wiper** limpiaparabrisas *m*, limpiador *m* (Méx); ~**surfer** *n* (person) tablista *mf*, surfista *mf*; (board) tabla *f* de windsurf; ~**surfing** *n* windsurf *m*, windsurfing *m*, surf *m* a vela; ~**swept** *adj* ‹*beach/plain*› azotado por el viento; ‹*person*› despeinado; ‹*hair*› alborotado

windy /ˈwɪndi/ *adj* **-dier, -diest** ‹*day/ weather*› ventoso, de viento; **it's ~** hace viento

wine /waɪn/ *n* **(a)** (beverage) vino *m*; (*before n*) ~ **cellar** bodega *f*; ~ **list** carta *f* de vinos; ~ **rack** botellero *m*; ~ **waiter** sommelier *m*, sumiller *m* **(b)** (color) rojo *m* granate; (*before n*) rojo granate *adj inv*

wine: ~ **and dine** *vt* agasajar (*con una comida*); ~ **bar** *n* bar *m* (especializado en vinos); ~ **glass** *n* copa *f* de vino; ~**growing** *n* viticultura *f*; (*before n*) ‹*area/region*› vinícola; ‹*country*› productor de vino; ~**tasting** /ˈwaɪnˌteɪstɪŋ/ *n* **(a)** (act, skill) cata *f or* catadura *f* de vinos **(b)** (event) degustación *f* de vinos

wing /wɪŋ/ *n* **1** (Zool) ala *f* ‡ **2** (Aviat) ala *f* ‡ **3** (BrE Auto) guardabarros *m or* (Méx) salpicadera *f or* (Chi, Per) tapabarros *m* **4** (Pol) ala *f* ‡ **5** (of building) ala *f* ‡ **6** **wings** *pl* (Theat) **the ~s** los bastidores

wingspan /ˈwɪŋspæn/ *n* envergadura *f*

wink¹ /wɪŋk/ *n* guiño *m*, guiñada *f*; **to give sb a ~** guiñarle el ojo a algn; **not to get a ~ of sleep** no pegar* (el *or* un) ojo

wink² *vi* **(a)** «*person*» guiñar el ojo **(b)** (flash) «*light*» parpadear

winner /ˈwɪnər ‖ ˈwɪnə(r)/ *n* ganador, -dora *m,f*

winning /ˈwɪnɪŋ/ *adj* **(a)** (victorious) ‹*candidate/team*› ganador; ‹*goal/shot*› de la victoria **(b)** (appealing) ‹*smile/personality*› encantador

winning post *n* (poste *m* de) llegada *f*

winnings /ˈwɪnɪŋz/ *pl n* ganancias *fpl* (*obtenidas en el juego*)

winter /ˈwɪntər ‖ ˈwɪntə(r)/ *n* invierno *m*; **in (the) ~** en invierno; (*before n*) ‹*weather*› invernal; ~ **sports** deportes *mpl* de invierno

wintertime /ˈwɪntərtaɪm ‖ ˈwɪntətaɪm/ *n* invierno *m*

wintry /ˈwɪntri/ *adj* **-trier, -triest** invernal

wipe¹ /waɪp/ *n* **(a)** (action): **give the table a ~ with a damp cloth** pásale un trapo húmedo a la mesa **(b)** (cloth) toallita *f*

wipe² *vt* ‹*floor/table*› limpiar, pasarle un trapo a; ‹*dishes*› secar*; ~ **your nose** límpiate la nariz
■ ~ *vi* (dry dishes) secar*
■ **wipe away** [*v + o + adv, v + adv + o*] ‹*tears*› secar*; ‹*memory*› borrar
■ **wipe off** [*v + o + adv, v + adv + o*] **(a)** (remove) ‹*mud/oil*› limpiar **(b)** (erase) ‹*recording*› borrar
■ **wipe out** [*v + o + adv, v + adv + o*] **(a)** (clean) limpiar, pasarle un trapo a **(b)** (destroy, eradicate)

W

⟨species/population⟩ exterminar; ⟨resistance⟩ acabar con; ⟨disease⟩ erradicar*; ⟨army⟩ aniquilar **(c)** (erase) ⟨writing/memory⟩ borrar
■ **wipe up** [v + o + adv, v + adv + o] limpiar

wire¹ /waɪr ‖'waɪə(r)/ n **1 (a)** (metal strand) alambre m; (before n) ∼ **fence** alambrada f, alambrado m (AmL) **(b)** (fencing, mesh) alambrada f, alambrado m (AmL) **(c)** (finishing line) (AmE): the ∼ la línea de llegada, la meta **2 (a)** (Elec, Telec) cable m **(b)** (telegram) (colloq) telegrama m

wire² vt (Elec): to be ∼**d** to sth estar* conectado a algo

wire: ∼ **cutters** /'kʌtərz ‖'kʌtəz/ pl n cortaalambres m, pinzas fpl de corte (Méx); (large) cizalla(s) f(pl); ∼**walker** n (AmE) equilibrista mf, funámbulo, -la m,f; ∼ **wool** n ▶ STEEL WOOL

wiring /'waɪrɪŋ ‖'waɪərɪŋ/ n (Elec) cableado m, instalación f eléctrica

wiry /'waɪri ‖'waɪəri/ adj **wirier, wiriest (a)** ⟨person⟩ enjuto y nervudo **(b)** ⟨hair⟩ áspero

Wis = **Wisconsin**

wisdom /'wɪzdəm/ n sabiduría f

wisdom tooth n muela f del juicio

wise /waɪz/ adj **wiser, wisest (a)** (prudent) ⟨person⟩ prudente; ⟨choice/decision⟩ acertado **(b)** (learned, experienced) sabio; **to be none the ∼r.** I'm none the ∼r sigo sin entender **(c)** (aware) (colloq) **to be ∼ TO sth/sb:** I'm ∼ to him/his tricks lo conozco muy bien/le conozco las mañas
■ **wise up** (colloq) [v + adv] (d)espabilarse, avivarse (AmL fam), apiolarse (RPl fam)

-wise /waɪz/ suff **(a)** (with reference to): **price**∼/ **weather**∼ en lo que respecta al precio/tiempo **(b)** (in particular way): **length**∼ a lo largo

wisecrack n broma f, chiste m

wisely /'waɪzli/ adv sabiamente

wish¹ /wɪʃ/ n **(a)** (desire) deseo m; **to make a ∼** pedir* un deseo; **they got married against my ∼es** se casaron en contra de mi voluntad **(b)** **wishes** pl (greetings): **give your mother my best** ∼**es** dale a tu madre muchos recuerdos de mi parte, cariños a tu madre (AmL); **best** ∼**es, Jack** saludos or un abrazo de Jack

wish² vt **(a)** (desire fervently) desear; **to ∼ sth ON sb** desearle algo A algn; **I ∼ I were rich** ¡ojalá fuera rico!; **she** ∼**ed she hadn't told him** lamentó habérselo dicho; **I ∼ you wouldn't say things like that** me disgusta mucho que digas esas cosas **(b)** (want) (frml) desear (frml) **(c)** (want for sb) desear; ∼ **me luck!** ¡deséame suerte!; **to ∼ sb good night** darle* las buenas noches a algn
■ ∼ vi **(a)** (make magic wish) pedir* un deseo **(b)** (want, desire): **if you ∼** como quieras

wishful thinking /'wɪʃfəl/ n: **do you know for sure that they're leaving or is it just ∼ ∼?** ¿sabes a ciencia cierta que se van o es simplemente lo que tú querrías?

wisp /wɪsp/ n (of smoke) voluta f; (of hair) mechón m

wispy /'wɪspi/ adj **-pier, -piest** ⟨cloud⟩ tenue; ⟨hair⟩ ralo

wistful /'wɪstfəl/ adj ⟨smile/thought⟩ nostálgico

wit /wɪt/ n **1 (a)** (often pl) (intelligence) inteligencia f; (ingenuity) ingenio m; **to be at one's** ∼**s' end** estar* desesperado **2** (humor) ingenio m

witch /wɪtʃ/ n bruja f

witch: ∼**craft** n brujería f, hechicería f; ∼ **doctor** n hechicero m, brujo m

with /wɪð, wɪθ/ prep

■ **Note** When the translation con is followed by the pronouns mi, ti, and si, it combines with them to form conmigo, contigo, and consigo: **come with me** ven conmigo; **take it with you** llévalo contigo; **he had his dog with him** tenía el perro consigo

1 (a) (in the company of) con; **she went ∼ him/ them/me/you** fue con él/con ellos/conmigo/ contigo **(b)** (member, employee, client etc of) en; **I've been banking ∼ them for years** hace años que tengo cuenta en ese banco **2** (in descriptions): **the shirt is black ∼ white stripes** la camisa es negra a or con rayas blancas; **the man ∼ the beard** el hombre de barba; **a tall woman ∼ long hair** una mujer alta con el pelo largo or de pelo largo; **he is married, ∼ three children** está casado y tiene tres hijos **3 (a)** (indicating manner) con; **the proposal was greeted ∼ derision** la propuesta fue recibida con burlas **(b)** (by means of, using) con; **she ate it ∼ her fingers** lo comió con la mano **(c)** (as a result of): **trembling ∼ fright** temblando de miedo

withdraw /wɪð'drɔː/ (past **-drew;** past p **-drawn**) vt **1 (a)** (recall, remove) ⟨troops/ representative⟩ retirar; ⟨hand/arm⟩ retirar; ⟨coin/ note⟩ retirar de la circulación; ⟨product⟩ retirar de la venta **(b)** ⟨money/cash⟩ retirar, sacar* **2 (a)** (cancel, discontinue) ⟨support/funding⟩ retirar; ⟨permission⟩ cancelar; **they threatened to** ∼ **their labor** amenazaron con ir a la huelga **(b)** (rescind) ⟨application/charges⟩ retirar; ⟨demand⟩ renunciar a **(c)** (retract) ⟨statement/allegation⟩ retirar
■ ∼ vi **(a)** «troops/competitor/candidate» retirarse **(b)** (socially) recluirse*; (psychologically) retraerse*

withdrawal /wɪð'drɔːəl/ n **1** (of troops, team, representative) retirada f; (of coinage) retirada f de la circulación; (of product) retirada f de la venta **2** (of support, funding) retirada f, retiro m (AmL); (of application, nomination, competitor) retirada f **3** (Psych) retraimiento m **4** (of cash) retirada f, retiro m (AmL) **5** (from drugs) abandono m; (before n) ∼ **symptoms** síndrome m de abstinencia

withdrawn¹ /wɪð'drɔːn/ past p of WITHDRAW

withdrawn² adj retraído

withdrew /wɪð'druː/ past of WITHDRAW

wither /'wɪðər ‖'wɪðə(r)/ vi «plant/flower» marchitarse; «limb» atrofiarse

withered /'wɪðərd ‖'wɪðəd/ adj ⟨plant/flower⟩ marchito, mustio; ⟨limb⟩ atrofiado

withering /'wɪðərɪŋ/ adj **(a)** ⟨heat⟩ abrasador **(b)** ⟨look⟩ fulminante

withhold /wɪð'həʊld ‖wɪð'həʊld/ vt (past & past p **-held**) ⟨payment/funds⟩ retener*; ⟨truth⟩ ocultar; ⟨consent⟩ negar*; ⟨information⟩ no revelar

within¹ /wɪð'ɪn/ prep **1** (inside) dentro de; ∼ **a radius of 20 miles** en un radio de 20 millas **2** (indicating nearness) a; **we were ∼ 150m of the summit** estábamos a 150m de la cumbre **3** (in less than): ∼ **the time allotted** dentro del tiempo establecido; **they'll be here ∼ an hour** estarán aquí en menos de una hora

within² adv (arch or liter) dentro

W

without /wɪð'aʊt/ *prep* sin; do it ∼ cheating hazlo sin hacer trampas

withstand /wɪð'stænd/ *vt* ⟨*past & past p* **-stood**⟩ ⟨*attack*⟩ resistir; ⟨*heat/pain*⟩ soportar

witness¹ /'wɪtnəs ‖'wɪtnɪs/ *n* **1** (person) testigo *mf*; (*before n*) ∼ **stand** *o* (BrE) **box** estrado *m* **2** (testimony, evidence) to be ∼ to sth ser* testimonio DE algo

witness² *vt* (a) (observe) ⟨*change/event*⟩ ser* testigo de; ⟨*crime/accident*⟩ presenciar (b) (authenticate) (Law) ⟨*signature*⟩ atestiguar*; ⟨*will*⟩ atestiguar* la firma de

witticism /'wɪtəsɪzəm ‖'wɪtɪsɪzəm/ *n* agudeza *f*; (in conversation) salida *f*

witty /'wɪti/ *adj* **-tier, -tiest** ⟨*person*⟩ ingenioso; (funny) gracioso; ⟨*answer/remark*⟩ ingenioso

wives /waɪvz/ *pl of* WIFE

wizard /'wɪzərd ‖'wɪzəd/ *n* mago *m*, brujo *m*

wizened /'wɪznd/ *adj* (wrinkled) arrugado; (withered) marchito

wk = **week**

wobble /'wɑːbəl ‖'wɒbəl/ *vi* (a) (tremble) «*jelly*» temblar* (b) (sway, waver) «*cyclist*» bambolearse; «*wheel*» bailar; «*chair*» tambalearse

wobbly /'wɑːbli ‖'wɒbli/ *adj* **-blier, -bliest** (a) ⟨*voice*⟩ tembloroso (b) ⟨*wheel/tooth*⟩ flojo; ⟨*table/chair*⟩ poco firme, que se tambalea; my legs are ∼ me tiemblan las piernas

woe /wəʊ/ *n* (a) (sorrow) congoja *f* (liter), aflicción *f*, ∼ betide you if you lose it! ¡pobre de ti *or* ay de ti si lo pierdes! (b) **woes** *pl* (afflictions) males *mpl*

woeful /'wəʊfəl/ *adj* (a) (deplorable) ⟨*neglect/ignorance*⟩ lamentable (b) (sorrowful) (liter) ⟨*person*⟩ acongojado (liter); ⟨*expression*⟩ desconsolado

woke /wəʊk/ *past of* WAKE¹

woken /'wəʊkən/ *past p of* WAKE¹

wolf¹ /wʊlf/ *n* ⟨*pl* **wolves**⟩ (Zool) lobo *m*

wolf² *vt* ∼ (down) devorar(se)

wolves /wʊlvz/ *pl of* WOLF¹

woman /'wʊmən/ *n* ⟨*pl* **women**⟩ mujer *f*; (*before n*) a ∼ **lawyer** una abogada; a ∼ **friend of mine** una amiga mía

womanizer /'wʊmənaɪzər ‖'wʊmənaɪzə(r)/ *n* mujeriego *m*

womanly /'wʊmənli/ *adj* femenino

womb /wuːm/ *n* útero *m*, matriz *f*

women /'wɪmɪn/ *pl of* WOMAN

women's room *n* (AmE) baño *m or* (Esp) servicios *mpl* de damas *or* señoras

won /wʌn/ *past & past p of* WIN¹

wonder¹ /'wʌndər ‖'wʌndə(r)/ *n* **1** (awe, curiosity) asombro *m* **2** (marvel, miracle) maravilla *f*; no ∼ you feel tired! ¡no me extraña que estés cansado!

wonder² *vi* (a) (ponder, speculate): why do you ask? — oh, I was just ∼ing ¿por qué preguntas? — por nada (b) (marvel, be surprised) maravillarse; I ∼ at your patience me maravilla la paciencia que tienes

■ ∼ *vt* (a) (ask oneself) preguntarse; I ∼ if *o* whether he'll be there me pregunto si estará (b) (be amazed): I ∼ (that) she didn't fire you on the spot me sorprende que no te haya echado inmediatamente

wonder³ *adj* (*before n*) ⟨*drug/cure*⟩ milagroso

wonderful /'wʌndərfəl ‖'wʌndəfəl/ *adj* maravilloso

wonderfully /'wʌndərfli ‖'wʌndəfəli/ *adv* maravillosamente, de maravilla

wont /wɑːnt ‖wəʊnt/ *n* (liter or hum) costumbre *f*; as is her ∼ como tiene por costumbre

won't /wəʊnt/ = **will not**

woo /wuː/ *vt* ⟨*woman*⟩ cortejar; ⟨*customers/investors*⟩ atraer*; ⟨*voters*⟩ buscar* el apoyo de

wood /wʊd/ *n* **1** (material) madera *f*; (firewood) leña *f* **2** (wooded area) (*often pl*) bosque *m* **3** (in golf) palo *m* de madera

wooded /'wʊdəd ‖'wʊdɪd/ *adj* boscoso

wooden /'wʊdn/ *adj* (a) (made of wood) de madera; ∼ **leg** pata *f* de palo (fam) (b) (stiff) ⟨*expression*⟩ rígido; ⟨*performance*⟩ acartonado

wood: ∼**land** /'wʊdlənd/ *n* (*often pl*) bosque *m*; ∼**louse** *n* (*pl* **-lice**) cochinilla *f*, chanchito *m* (Andes, CS fam); ∼**pecker** /'wʊd,pekə(r) ‖'wʊd,pekə(r)/ *n* pájaro *m* carpintero, pico *m* (barreno *or* carpintero); ∼ **pigeon** *n* paloma *f* torcaz; ∼**pile** *n* (AmE) montón *m* de leña; ∼**shed** *n* leñera *f*; ∼**wind** /'wʊdwɪnd/ *n* (*pl* ∼**wind** *or* ∼**winds**) the ∼**wind(s)** los instrumentos de viento de madera; ∼**work** *n* (a) (wooden fittings) carpintería *f* (b) (BrE) ▶ ∼WORKING; ∼**working** *n* (AmE) (carpentry) carpintería *f*; (cabinet making) ebanistería *f*; (craftwork) artesanía *f* en madera; ∼**worm** *n* (*pl* ∼**worm**) (a) (larva) carcoma *f* (b) (infestation): the table's full of ∼**worm** la mesa está llena de carcoma *or* está toda carcomida

woody /'wʊdi/ *adj* **-dier, -diest** leñoso

woof *n* /wʊf/ (colloq) ladrido *m*; ∼ ∼! ¡guau guau!

wool /wʊl/ *n* lana *f*

woolen, (BrE) **woollen** /'wʊlən/ *adj* de lana

woolens, (BrE) **woollens** /'wʊlənz/ *pl n* (Clothes) prendas *fpl* de lana

wooly, (BrE) **woolly** /'wʊli/ *adj* **-lier, -liest** (a) ⟨*hat/sweater*⟩ de lana (b) (unclear) ⟨*thinking/argument*⟩ vago, impreciso

word¹ /wɜːrd ‖wɜːd/ *n* **1** (term, expression) palabra *f*, what's the German ∼ for 'dog'? ¿cómo se dice 'perro' en alemán?; in other ∼s (introducing a reformulation) es decir; to be lost for ∼s no encontrar* palabras

2 (thing said) palabra *f*; a ∼ of advice un consejo; I can't hear a ∼ you're saying no te oigo nada; I don't believe a ∼ of it no me lo creo; by ∼ of mouth: the news spread by ∼ of mouth la noticia se fue transmitiendo de boca en boca; the last ∼:

AmC	Central America	Arg	Argentina	Cu	Cuba	Per	Peru
AmL	Latin America	Bol	Bolivia	Ec	Ecuador	RPI	River Plate Area
AmS	South America	Chi	Chile	Esp	Spain	Ur	Uruguay
Andes	Andean Region	CS	Southern Cone	Méx	Mexico	Ven	Venezuela

W

to have the last ∼ tener* la última palabra; **the last** ∼ **in computers** tiene la última palabra en computadoras; *to eat one's* ∼**s: I was forced to eat my** ∼**s** me tuve que tragar lo que había dicho; *to have a* ∼ *with sb about sth* hablar con algn de *or* sobre algo; *to have* ∼**s** *with sb* tener* unas palabras con algn; ▶ MINCE[1]

3 (assurance) (*no pl*) palabra *f*; **to keep/give one's** ∼ cumplir/dar* su (*or* mi *etc*) palabra; **you can take my** ∼ **for it** te lo aseguro; *to take sb at her/ his* ∼ tomarle la palabra a algn

4 (a) (news, message): **there is still no** ∼ **of survivors** todavía no se sabe si hay supervivientes; ∼ **has it that ...** corre la noticia *or* el rumor de que ... (b) (instruction): **if you need a hand just say the** ∼ si quieres que te ayude no tienes más que pedirlo; **to give the** ∼ **(to** + INF) dar* la orden (de + INF)

5 words *pl* (a) (lyrics) letra *f* (b) (Theat): **he forgot his** ∼**s** se le olvidó lo que tenía que decir

word² *vt* ⟨document/letter⟩ redactar; ⟨question⟩ formular

word for word *adv* ⟨repeat/copy⟩ palabra por palabra; ⟨translate⟩ literalmente

wording /'wɜːrdɪŋ ‖ 'wɜːdɪŋ/ *n* (of paragraph, letter) redacción *f*; (of question) formulación *f*

word: ∼ **processing** *n* tratamiento *m or* procesamiento *m* de textos; ∼ **processor** /'prɑːsesər, 'prəʊ- ‖ 'prəʊsesə(r)/ *n* procesador *m* de textos

wordy /'wɜːrdi ‖ 'wɜːdi/ *adj* **-dier, -diest** verboso

wore /wɔːr ‖ wɔː(r)/ *past of* WEAR²

work¹ /wɜːrk ‖ wɜːk/ *n* **1** (labor, tasks) trabajo *m*; **she put a lot of** ∼ **into it** puso mucho esfuerzo en ello; **it's hard** ∼ **digging** cavar es muy duro **2** (employment) trabajo *m*; **to go to** ∼ ir* a trabajar *or* al trabajo **3** (*in phrases*) **at work: he's at** ∼ está en el trabajo, está en la oficina (*or* la fábrica *etc*); **they were hard at** ∼ estaban muy ocupados trabajando; **off work: she was off** ∼ **for a month after the accident** después del accidente estuvo un mes sin trabajar; **he took a day off** ∼ se tomó un día libre; **out of work: to be out of** ∼ estar* sin trabajo *or* desocupado *or* desempleado *or* (Chi tb) cesante, estar* parado (Esp); (*before n*) **out-of-work** desocupado, desempleado, parado (Esp), cesante (Chi) **4** (a) (product, single item) obra *f*; **a** ∼ **of art** una obra de arte (b) (output) trabajo *m*; **a piece of** ∼ un trabajo; **it was the** ∼ **of a professional** era obra de un profesional; *see also* WORKS

work² *vi* **1** «person» trabajar; **I** ∼ **as a receptionist** trabajo de recepcionista; **to** ∼ **hard** trabajar mucho *or* duro; **to** ∼ FOR **sb** trabajar PARA algn; **to** ∼ **in oils** pintar al óleo, trabajar con óleos; **he's** ∼**ing on his car** está arreglando el coche; **scientists are** ∼**ing on a cure to** los científicos están intentando encontrar una cura; **to** ∼ UNDER **sb** trabajar bajo la dirección de algn **2** (a) (operate, function) «machine/system» funcionar; «drug/person» actuar*; **it** ∼**s both ways: you have to make an effort too, you know: it** ∼**s both ways** tú también tienes que hacer el esfuerzo, ¿sabes? funciona igual *or* (esp AmL)

parejo para los dos (b) (have required effect) «drug/ plan/method» surtir efecto; **try it, it might** ∼ pruébalo, quizás resulte

■ ∼ *vt* **1** (a) (force to work) hacer* trabajar; **to** ∼ **oneself to death** matarse trabajando (b) (exploit) ⟨land/soil⟩ trabajar; ⟨mine⟩ explotar (c) ⟨nightclubs/casinos⟩ trabajar en (d) (pay for by working): **he** ∼**ed his passage to Australia** se costeó el pasaje a Australia trabajando en el barco

2 (cause to operate): **do you know how to** ∼ **the machine?** ¿sabes manejar la máquina?; **this lever** ∼**s the sprinkler system** esta palanca acciona el sistema de riego

3 (a) (move gradually, manipulate) (+ *adv compl*): ∼ **the brush into the corners** mete bien el cepillo en los rincones; *to* ∼ *one's way*: **we** ∼**ed our way toward the exit** nos abrimos camino hacia la salida; **she** ∼**ed her way to the top of her profession** trabajó hasta llegar a la cima de su profesión (b) (shape, fashion) ⟨clay/metal⟩ trabajar; ⟨dough⟩ sobar

4 (a) (*past & past p* **worked** *or* **wrought**) (bring about) ⟨miracle⟩ hacer*; *see also* WROUGHT (b) (arrange) (colloq) arreglar

■ **work off** [*v* + *o* + *adv*, *v* + *adv* + *o*] (a) (get rid of): **you can** ∼ **off a few kilos in the gym** puede rebajar algunos kilos en el gimnasio (b) ⟨debt⟩ amortizar*, pagar* (*trabajando*)

■ **work out**
I [*v* + *adv*] **1** (a) (turn out) salir*, resultar; **it** ∼**s out at $75 a head** sale (a) 75 dólares por cabeza (b) (be successful) «plan» salir* bien **2** (train, exercise) (Sport) hacer* ejercicio
II [*v* + *o* + *adv*, *v* + *adv* + *o*] **1** (a) (solve) ⟨sum⟩ hacer*; ⟨riddle/puzzle⟩ resolver* (b) (find, calculate) ⟨percentage/probability⟩ calcular; **have you** ∼**ed out the answer?** ¿lo has resuelto? (c) (understand) entender*
2 (devise, determine) ⟨solution/procedure⟩ idear; ⟨plan⟩ elaborar

■ **work up** [*v* + *o* + *adv*, *v* + *adv* + *o*] (a) (stimulate): **they had** ∼**ed up an appetite** se les había abierto el apetito; **I couldn't** ∼ **up much enthusiasm** no me entusiasmaba demasiado (b) (excite, arouse): **she gets very** ∼**ed up about it** se pone como loca; **they had been** ∼**ed up into a frenzy** los habían puesto frenéticos, los habían exaltado

workable /'wɜːrkəbəl ‖ 'wɜːkəbəl/ *adj* ⟨arrangement/solution⟩ factible

work: ∼**bench** *n* banco *m* de trabajo; ∼**day** *n* (a) (part of day) jornada *f* laboral (b) (weekday) día *m* hábil *or* laborable *or* laboral *or* de trabajo

worker /'wɜːrkər ‖ 'wɜːkə(r)/ *n* (a) trabajador, -dora *m,f*; **he's a good/slow** ∼ trabaja bien/ lentamente (b) (ant, bee) obrera *f*

work: ∼ **experience** *n* experiencia *f* laboral; ∼ **force** *n* (of nation) población *f* activa; (of company) personal *m*, plantilla *f* (Esp)

working /'wɜːrkɪŋ ‖ 'wɜːkɪŋ/ *adj* (*before n*) **1** (a) ⟨mother/parent⟩ que trabaja; ∼ **population** población *f* activa (b) ⟨hours/conditions⟩ de trabajo; **we have a good** ∼ **relationship** trabajamos muy bien juntos **2** (a) (capable of operating): **it's in perfect** ∼ **order** funciona perfectamente (b) (suitable for working with) ⟨hypothesis⟩ de trabajo; **I have a** ∼ **knowledge of Russian** tengo conocimientos básicos de ruso

W

working: ~ **class** n (sometimes pl) the ~ class(es) la clase obrera or trabajadora; ~**-class** /'wɜːrkɪŋˈklæs ‖ˌwɜːkɪŋˈklɑːs/ adj ⟨person⟩ de clase obrera or trabajadora; ⟨area⟩ obrero; ~ **day** n (a) (weekday) día m hábil or laborable or laboral or de trabajo **(b)** ▶ WORKDAY A; ~ **party** n equipo m de trabajo

workings /'wɜːrkɪŋz ‖'wɜːkɪŋz/ pl n (of machine) funcionamiento m

work: ~**load** n (volumen m de) trabajo m; ~**man** /'wɜːrkmən ‖'wɜːkmən/ n (pl **-men** /-mən/) obrero m

workmanlike /'wɜːrkmənlaɪk ‖'wɜːkmənlaɪk/ adj eficiente, profesional

workmanship /'wɜːrkmənʃɪp ‖'wɜːkmənʃɪp/ n (of craftsman) trabajo m; (of object) factura f

work: ~**out** n sesión f de ejercicios or gimnasia; ~**place** n lugar m de trabajo

works /wɜːrks ‖wɜːks/ n **1** (actions) (liter) (+ pl vb) obras fpl **2** (engineering operations) (+ pl vb) obras fpl; **road** ~ obras viales **3** (factory) (+ sing or pl vb) fábrica f **4** (mechanism) (+ pl vb) mecanismo m

work: ~**shop** n taller m; ~**station** n (Comput) terminal m de trabajo; ~**surface** n (a) (area) superficie f de trabajo **(b)** ▶ ~TOP; ~**top** n encimera f, mesada f (RPl)

world /wɜːrld ‖wɜːld/ n **1** (earth) mundo m; **the longest bridge in the** ~ el puente más largo del mundo; **to see the** ~ ver* mundo; **(it's a) small** ~! el mundo es un pañuelo, ¡qué pequeño or (AmL) chico es el mundo!; **to be out of this** ~ «food/music» ser* increíble; **to have the best of both** ~s tener* todas las ventajas; (before n) ⟨economy/peace⟩ mundial; ⟨politics/trade⟩ internacional **2** (a) (people generally) mundo m; **what is the** ~ **coming to?** ¿adónde vamos a ir a parar? **(b)** (society): **they've gone up in the** ~ han prosperado mucho (or hecho fortuna etc); **a woman/man of the** ~ una mujer/un hombre de mundo **3** (specific period, group) mundo m; **the art** ~ el mundo del arte **4** (as intensifier): **we are** ~s **apart** no tenemos nada que ver; **it did her a** ~ **of good** le hizo la mar de bien; **he thinks the** ~ **of her** tiene un altísimo concepto de ella; **to have all the time in the** ~ tener* todo el tiempo del mundo; **without a care in the** ~ sin ninguna preocupación **5** (Relig): **this/the other** ~ este/el otro mundo

world: W~ **Bank** n the W~ Bank el Banco Mundial; ~ **champion** n campeón, -peona m,f mundial; W~ **Cup** n the W~ Cup el Mundial, la Copa del Mundo; ~**famous** /'wɜːrldˈfeɪməs ‖ˌwɜːldˈfeɪməs/ adj mundialmente famoso

worldly /'wɜːrldli ‖'wɜːldli/ adj (a) ⟨goods⟩ material; ⟨desires⟩ mundano **(b)** ⟨person⟩ de mucho mundo; ⟨manner/charm⟩ sofisticado

worldly-wise /'wɜːrldliˈwaɪz ‖ˌwɜːldliˈwaɪz/ adj de mucho mundo

world: ~ **record** n récord m or marca f mundial; W~ **Series** n (in US baseball) the W~ Series la Serie Mundial, el campeonato mundial de béisbol; W~ **War** n guerra f mundial; **the First/Second W~ War, W~ War I/II** la primera/ segunda Guerra Mundial

worldwide¹ /'wɜːrldˈwaɪd ‖ˌwɜːldˈwaɪd/ adj mundial

worldwide² adv ⟨travel⟩ por todo el mundo

World Wide Web n telaraña f mundial

worm¹ /wɜːrm ‖wɜːm/ n (a) (earth~) gusano m, lombriz f (de tierra) **(b)** (maggot) gusano m **(c)** **worms** pl (Med) lombrices fpl

worm² vt (Vet Sci) ⟨dog/cat⟩ desparasitar

worn¹ /wɔːrn ‖wɔːn/ past p of WEAR²

worn² adj ⟨tire/clothes⟩ gastado; ⟨carpet⟩ raído; ⟨flagstones/steps⟩ desgastado

worn-out /'wɔːrnˈaʊt ‖ˌwɔːnˈaʊt/ adj (pred **worn out**) (a) ⟨shoes/clothes⟩ muy gastado **(b)** (exhausted) rendido

worried /'wɜːrid ‖'wʌrɪd/ adj ⟨look/voice⟩ de preocupación; ⟨person⟩ preocupado; **to get** ~ preocuparse, inquietarse; **to be** ~ ABOUT sb/sth estar* preocupado POR algn/algo

worrier /'wɜːriər ‖'wʌrɪə(r)/ n: **she's such a** ~ se preocupa or se angustia tanto por todo

worry¹ /'wɜːri ‖'wʌri/ n (pl **-ries**) preocupación f

worry² **-ries, -rying, -ried** vt **1** (trouble) preocupar, inquietar **2** «dog» ⟨sheep⟩ acosar ■ ~ vi preocuparse, inquietarse; **to** ~ ABOUT sth/ sb preocuparse POR algo/algn

worrying /'wɜːriɪŋ ‖'wʌrɪɪŋ/ adj inquietante, preocupante

worse¹ /wɜːrs ‖wɜːs/ adj (comp of BAD¹) peor; **to get** ~ empeorar; (sicker) ponerse* peor; **things are getting** ~ **and** ~ las cosas van de mal en peor; **to make things** ~, **it started snowing** por si fuera poco, empezó a nevar

worse² adv (comp of BADLY) peor

worse³ n the ~ el (or la etc) peor; **a change for the** ~ un cambio para mal

worsen /'wɜːrsn ‖'wɜːsn/ vi/t empeorar

worse-off /'wɜːrsˈɔːf ‖ˌwɜːsˈɒf/ adj (pred **worse off**) (a) (financially) en peor posición económica **(b)** (emotionally, physically) (pred) peor

worship¹ /'wɜːrʃəp ‖'wɜːʃɪp/ n **1** (Relig) culto m, adoración f **2** **Worship** (as title): **Your/His W~** (of magistrate) Su Señoría; (of mayor) el señor alcalde

worship² vt, (BrE) **-pp-** ⟨God⟩ adorar; ⟨success/ wealth⟩ rendir* culto a; ⟨hero⟩ idolatrar

worshipper /'wɜːrʃəpər ‖'wɜːʃɪpə(r)/ n (Relig) fiel m

worst¹ /wɜːrst ‖wɜːst/ adj (superl of BAD¹) peor; **he's the** ~ **student in the class** es el peor alumno de la clase; ~ **of all** lo peor de todo

worst² adv (superl of BADLY): **she did (the)** ~ **(of all)** in both exams le fue peor que a nadie en los dos exámenes

worst³ n **1** the ~ (a) (+ sing vb) lo peor; **his sister brings out the** ~ **in him** cuando está con su hermana está peor que nunca; **if (the)** ~ **comes to (the)** ~ en el peor de los casos **(b)** (+ pl vb) los peores **2** (a) **at worst** en el peor de los casos **(b)** **at her/his/its worst: I'm at my** ~ **in the morning** la mañana es mi peor momento del día; **this is racism at its** ~ esto es racismo de la peor especie

worth¹ /wɜːrθ ‖wɜːθ/ adj (pred) (a) (equal in value to) **to be** ~ valer*; **it cost 300 dólares, but it was** ~ **the money** costó $300, pero valió la pena; **goods** ~ **£5,000 were stolen** robaron mercancías por valor de 5.000 libras; **this is my opinion, for what it's** ~ esta es mi opinión, si es que a alguien le interesa **(b)** (worthy of): **it's ~ a try** vale la pena intentarlo; **that's ~ knowing** es bueno saberlo; **don't argue with them, it isn't ~** it no discutas con ellos, no vale *or* no merece la pena

worth² *n* **(a)** (equivalent): **$2,000 dollars' ~ of furniture** muebles por valor de 2.000 dólares; **I've had my money's ~ out of this car** le he sacado mucho jugo a este coche (fam) **(b)** (of thing) valor *m*; (of person) valía *f*

worthless /'wɜːrθləs ‖'wɜːθlɪs/ *adj* ⟨object⟩ sin ningún valor; ⟨person⟩ despreciable; **to be ~** no tener* ningún valor, no valer* nada

worthwhile /'wɜːrθ·θ'hwaɪl ‖wɜːθːθ'waɪl/ *adj* ⟨enterprise/project⟩ que vale la pena

worthy /'wɜːrði ‖'wɜːði/ *adj* **-thier, -thiest** **1** (appropriate, equal) ⟨opponent/successor⟩ digno; **to be ~ OF sth/sb** ser* digno DE algo/algn **2** (good, estimable) ⟨person⟩ respetable; **a ~ cause** una buena causa

would /wʊd/ *v mod*

■ **Note** When *would* + a verb in English is used to form the conditional tense, it is translated by the conditional tense in Spanish. When *would* + a verb in English is used to express habitual activity in the past, it is translated by the imperfect tense in Spanish. For examples of both, see the entry below.

['D *es la contracción de* WOULD, WOULDN'T *de* WOULD NOT *y* 'D'VE *de* WOULD HAVE] **1** *past of* WILL¹

2 (in conditional sentences): **I ~ if I could** lo haría si pudiera; **if I had known, I ~n't have come** si lo hubiera sabido no habría *or* no hubiera venido **3** (expressing wishes): **I wish you'd stop pestering me!** ¡deja de fastidiarme por Dios! **4** (in requests, invitations): **~ you type this for me please?** ¿me haría el favor de pasar esto a máquina?; **~ you like to come with us? — I'd love to** ¿quieres venir con nosotros? — me encantaría

would-be /'wʊdbiː/ *adj* (before n): **a ~ star/ poet** un aspirante a estrella/poeta

wouldn't /'wʊdn̩t/ = **would not**

would've /'wʊdəv/ = **would have**

wound¹ /wuːnd/ *n* herida *f*

wound² /wuːnd/ *vt/i* herir*

wound³ /waʊnd/ *past & past p of* WIND² *vt* II, *vi*

wounded /'wuːndəd ‖'wuːndɪd/ *adj* ⟨soldier/ animal/pride⟩ herido; ⟨look/tone⟩ dolido

wove /wəʊv/ *past of* WEAVE

woven /'wəʊvən/ *past p of* WEAVE

WP *n* **(a)** = **word processor** **(b)** = **word processing**

wpm (= **words per minute**) palabras por minuto

wrangle¹ /'ræŋgəl/ *vi* discutir, reñir*

wrangle² *n* altercado *m*, riña *f*

wrap¹ /ræp/ **-pp-** *vt* **(a)** (cover) ⟨parcel/gift⟩ envolver* **(b)** (wind, entwine): **she ~ped a shawl about her** se envolvió en un chal

■ **wrap up** **1** [*v + o + adv, v + adv + o*] **(a)** ▶ WRAP¹ *vt A* **(b)** (complete) (colloq) ⟨order/sale⟩ conseguir*; ⟨deal⟩ cerrar* **(c)** (conclude) (colloq) ⟨meeting⟩ dar* fin a **(d)** (engross) (colloq) **to be ~ped up IN sth: she's totally ~ped up in her work** no piensa más que en su trabajo, vive para su trabajo **2** [*v + adv*] (dress warmly) abrigarse*

wrap² *n* **(a)** (shawl) chal *m*, pañoleta *f* **(b)** (robe) (AmE) bata *f*, salto *m* de cama (CS)

wraparound /'ræpə·raʊnd/ *adj* ⟨skirt/dress⟩ cruzado

wrapper /'ræpər ‖'ræpə(r)/ *n* envoltorio *m*, envoltura *f*

wrapping /'ræpɪŋ/ *n* envoltorio *m*, envoltura *f*

wrapping paper *n* (plain) papel *m* de envolver; (decorative) papel *m* de regalo

wrath /ræθ ‖rɒθ/ *n* (liter) cólera *f*, ira *f*

wreak /riːk/ *vt* (liter) ⟨destruction/chaos⟩ sembrar* (liter); **to ~ havoc** causar estragos

wreath /riːθ/ *n* corona *f*

wreck¹ /rek/ *n* **1** (ship) restos *mpl* del naufragio; (vehicle) restos *mpl* del avión (*or* tren *etc*) siniestrado **2** (sth, sb ruined): **the attack left him a physical ~** el ataque lo dejó hecho una ruina; **he's a nervous ~** tiene los nervios destrozados

wreck² *vt* **(a)** ⟨ship⟩ provocar* el naufragio de; ⟨train⟩ hacer* descarrilar; ⟨car⟩ destrozar* **(b)** (damage) destrozar* **(c)** (demolish) (AmE) ⟨house/ building⟩ demoler* **(d)** (spoil, ruin) ⟨plans/chances⟩ echar por tierra; ⟨marriage/happiness⟩ destrozar*

wreckage /'rekɪdʒ/ *n* (of plane, car, ship) restos *mpl*; (of house) ruinas *fpl*

wrecker /'rekər ‖'rekə(r)/ *n* (AmE) **(a)** (demolition worker) obrero *m* de demolición *or* derribo **(b)** (car dismantler) desguazador *m or* (Méx) deshuesador *m*

wren /ren/ *n* (Zool) carrizo *m*

wrench¹ /rentʃ/ *vt* **(a)** (pull) arrancar*; **to ~ oneself away** soltarse* de un tirón *or* (AmL exc CS) de un jalón **(b)** (sprain) ⟨muscle⟩ desgarrarse; ⟨joint⟩ dislocarse*

wrench² *n* **1** **(a)** (twist, pull) tirón *m*, jalón *m* (AmL exc CS) **(b)** (emotional pain) dolor *m* (*causado por una separación*) **2** (adjustable ~) llave *f* inglesa; *see also* MONKEY WRENCH

wrest /rest/ *vt* **to ~ sth FROM sb** arrancarle* algo A algn

wrestle /'resəl/ *vi* **(a)** (Sport) luchar **(b)** (grapple) **to ~ WITH sb** forcejear CON algn; **to ~ WITH sth** batallar CON algo

wrestler /'reslər ‖'reslə(r)/ *n* luchador, -dora *m,f*

wrestling /'reslɪŋ/ *n* lucha *f*

wretch /retʃ/ *n* (liter) **(a)** (unfortunate person) desdichado, -da *m,f*, infeliz *mf* **(b)** (despicable person) desgraciado, -da *m,f*

wretched /'retʃəd ‖'retʃɪd/ *adj* **(a)** (abject, pitiable) ⟨existence/creature⟩ desdichado **(b)** (very bad) (colloq) ⟨weather⟩ horrible; **to feel ~** sentirse* muy mal

wriggle /'rɪgəl/ *vi* (move) retorcerse*; **the children ~d in their seats** los niños se movían inquietos en sus asientos

■ **wriggle out of** [*v + adv + prep + o*] ⟨dress/ jeans⟩ quitarse (*con dificultad*); **don't try to ~ out of it!** ¡no trates de escabullirte!

wring /rɪŋ/ (*past & past p* **wrung**) *vt* **1** **(a)** ⟨cloth/garment⟩ escurrir, retorcer* **(b)** **to ~ sth FROM/OUT OF sb** ⟨confession/information⟩ arrancarle* algo A algn **2** ⟨neck⟩ retorcer*

W

■ **wring out** [v + o + adv, v + adv + o] **1** ⟨*cloth/swimsuit*⟩ retorcer*, escurrir **2** ⟨*water*⟩ escurrir; ⟨*truth/money*⟩ sacar*

wrinkle¹ /ˈrɪŋkəl/ n arruga f

wrinkle² vi ⟨⟨*skin/garment*⟩⟩ arrugarse*

wrinkled /ˈrɪŋkəld/ adj arrugado

wrinkly /ˈrɪŋkli/ adj **-klier, -kliest** (colloq) arrugado

wrist /rɪst/ n (Anat) muñeca f

wrist: **~band** n (bracelet) pulsera f; (strap) correa f; (sweatband) muñequera f; **~watch** n reloj m (de) pulsera

writ /rɪt/ n (Law) orden f or mandato m judicial

write /raɪt/ (past **wrote**; past p **written**) vt **(a)** (put in writing) escribir*; **I wrote him a letter** le escribí una carta; **to ~ sb a check** o (BrE) **cheque** extender* or hacerle* un cheque a algn **(b)** (write letter to) (AmE) escribirle* a

■ **~** vi escribir*; **to ~ TO sb** escribirle* A algn

■ **write back** [v + adv] **to ~ back** (TO sb) contestar(le A algn)

■ **write down** [v + o + adv, v + adv + o] anotar

■ **write off** **1** [v + adv] **to ~ off FOR sth: she wrote off for a form** escribió pidiendo que le mandaran un formulario

2 [v + o + adv, v + adv + o] **(a)** (consider beyond repair) ⟨*vehicle*⟩ declarar siniestro total **(b)** (damage beyond repair) (BrE) destrozar* **(c)** (consider a failure, disregard) ⟨*marriage/project*⟩ dar* por perdido **(d)** ⟨*debt*⟩ cancelar

■ **write out** [v + o + adv, v + adv + o] **(a)** (write fully, copy) escribir* **(b)** (complete, fill out) ⟨*prescription*⟩ escribir*; ⟨*check/receipt*⟩ hacer*, extender* (frml)

■ **write up** [v + o + adv, v + adv + o] ⟨*report/notes*⟩ pasar en or (Esp) a limpio; ⟨*experiment*⟩ redactar un informe sobre

write-off /ˈraɪtɔːf ‖ˈraɪtɒf/ n: **the car was a ~** el coche fue declarado un siniestro total

writer /ˈraɪtər ‖ˈraɪtə(r)/ n (author) escritor, -tora m,f; **the ~ of the letter** el autor de la carta; **~'s cramp** calambre m ⟨*que da por escribir mucho*⟩

write-up /ˈraɪtʌp/ n (colloq) (review) crítica f, reseña f; (report) artículo m

writhe /raɪð/ vi ⟨⟨*snake*⟩⟩ retorcerse*; **to ~ in agony** retorcerse* de dolor

writing /ˈraɪtɪŋ/ n **(a)** (script) escritura f **(b)** (written material): **the ~'s rather blurred** la letra está algo borrosa; **in ~** por escrito; **(before n) ~ desk** escritorio m; **~ pad** bloc m; **~ paper** papel m de carta **(c)** (BrE) (handwriting) letra f **(d)** (act of composing): **~ takes up a lot of my time** paso mucho tiempo escribiendo **(e)** (written composition) literatura f **(f) writings** pl: **the ~s of Swift** la obra de Swift

written¹ /ˈrɪtn/ past p of WRITE

written² adj ⟨*examination/language*⟩ escrito; **~ permission** permiso m por escrito

wrong¹ /rɔːŋ ‖rɒŋ/ adj **1 (a)** (incorrect, inappropriate) ⟨*answer*⟩ equivocado, incorrecto; **you've given me the ~ change** se ha equivocado al darme el cambio; **we've taken the ~ bus** nos hemos equivocado de autobús; **he went in the ~ direction** tomó or (esp Esp) cogió para dónde no debía; **I did it the ~ way** lo hice mal; **this is the ~ time to mention the subject** este no es (el) momento oportuno para mencionar el tema; **she always says the ~ thing** siempre dice lo que no debe; **the picture is the ~ way up** el cuadro está al revés; **you've got your T-shirt on the ~ way round** llevas la camiseta al or del revés; **I'm the ~ person to ask** no soy la persona indicada para contestar esa pregunta **(b)** (mistaken) ⟨*pred*⟩ **to be ~** estar* equivocado; **I was ~ about her** la había juzgado mal

2 (morally): **stealing is ~** robar está mal; **you were ~ to shout at her like that** no debiste haberle gritado así, estuviste mal en gritarle así; **I haven't done anything ~** no he hecho nada malo; **what's ~ with that?** ¿qué hay de malo en eso?

3 (amiss) ⟨*pred*⟩: **what's ~?** ¿qué pasa?; **there's something ~ with her/with the lock** algo le pasa/algo le pasa a la cerradura; **there's nothing ~ with your heart** su corazón está perfectamente bien

wrong² adv ⟨*answer*⟩ mal, incorrectamente; **I did it all ~** lo hice todo mal; **to go ~** ⟨⟨*machinery*⟩⟩ estropearse, descomponerse* (AmL); ⟨⟨*plans*⟩⟩ salir* mal, fallar

wrong³ n **(a)** (immoral action) mal m; (injustice) injusticia f; **in her eyes he can do no ~** para ella, es incapaz de hacer nada malo; **to be in the ~** estar* equivocado **(b)** (Law) agravio m

wrong⁴ vt (frml): **she had been ~ed by her family** su familia había sido muy injusta con ella

wrong: **~doer** /ˈrɔːŋduːər ‖ˈrɒŋduːə(r)/ n malhechor, -chora m,f; **~doing** n: **she was punished for her ~** la castigaron por sus fechorías

wrongful /ˈrɔːŋfəl ‖ˈrɒŋfəl/ adj ⟨*accusation/punishment*⟩ injusto

wrongly /ˈrɔːŋli ‖ˈrɒŋli/ adv ⟨*spell/pronounce*⟩ mal, incorrectamente; ⟨*believe/assume*⟩ equivocadamente; ⟨*accuse*⟩ injustamente

wrote /rəʊt/ past of WRITE

wrought /rɔːt/ (past & past p of WORK² vt 4A) (frml or liter): **the devastation ~ by the war** los estragos causados por la guerra

wrought iron n hierro m forjado

wrung /rʌŋ/ past & past p of WRING

wry /raɪ/ adj **wrier, wriest** ⟨*smile/laugh/joke*⟩ irónico; **to make a ~ face** torcer* el gesto

WV, W Va = West Virginia

WWW n (= World Wide Web) WWW

WY, Wyo = Wyoming

AmC	América Central	Arg	Argentina	Cu	Cuba
AmL	América Latina	Bol	Bolivia	Ec	Ecuador
AmS	América del Sur	Chi	Chile	Esp	España
Andes	Región andina	CS	Cono Sur	Méx	México

Per	Perú
RPI	Río de la Plata
Ur	Uruguay
Ven	Venezuela

Xx

X, x /eks/ *n* **(a)** (letter) X, x *f* **(b)** (Cin) (in US) prohibida para menores de 18 años

xenophobia /ˌzenəˈfəʊbiə/ *n* xenofobia *f*

xenophobic /ˌzenəˈfəʊbɪk/ *adj* xenófobo

xerox /ˈzɪrɑːks, ˈze-/ ‖ /ˈzɪərɒks/ *vt* fotocopiar, xerografiar*

XL = **extra large**

Xmas /ˈkrɪsməs, ˈeksməs/ *n* Navidad *f*

X-rated /ˈeksˈreɪtəd/ ‖ /ˌeksˈreɪtɪd/ *adj* (BrE) ⟨*film*⟩ solo para adultos, clasificado X (Esp)

X-ray¹, x-ray /ˈeksreɪ/ *n* **(a)** (ray) rayo *m* X **(b)** (photograph) radiografía *f*; **I had a chest ∼** me hicieron *or* me sacaron una radiografía de tórax

X-ray², x-ray *vt* hacer* *or* sacar* una radiografía de

xylophone /ˈzaɪləfəʊn/ *n* xilofón *m*, xilófono *m*

Yy

Y, y /waɪ/ *n* Y, y *f*

yacht /jɑːt/ ‖ /jɒt/ *n* **(a)** (sailing boat — large) velero *m*, yate *m*; (— small) balandro *m*; (*before n*) ∼ **club** club *m* náutico; ∼ **race** regata *f* **(b)** (pleasure cruiser) yate *m*

yachting /ˈjɑːtɪŋ/ ‖ /ˈjɒtɪŋ/ *n* navegación *f* a vela

yak /jæk/ *n* yac *m*, yak *m*

yam /jæm/ *n* **(a)** (plant, vegetable) ñame *m* **(b)** (AmE) ▶ SWEET POTATO

yank /jæŋk/ *vt* tirar de, jalar de (AmL exc CS)

Yank /jæŋk/ *n* (BrE colloq & often pej) ▶ YANKEE C

Yankee /ˈjæŋki/ *n* **(a)** (Hist) yanqui *mf* **(b)** (sb from Northern US) (AmE colloq) norteño, -ña *m,f* **(c)** (US citizen) (colloq: in BrE often pej) yanqui *mf* (fam & pey), gringo, -ga *m,f* (fam & pey)

yap¹ /jæp/ *vi* **-pp-** ladrar (*con ladridos agudos*)

yap² *n* ladrido *m* (*agudo*)

yard /jɑːrd/ ‖ /jɑːd/ *n* **1 (a)** (of school, prison) patio *m* **(b)** (of house) (BrE) patio *m*; (garden) (AmE) jardín *m* **(c)** (stock∼) corral *m* **2** (boat∼, ship∼) astillero *m* **3** (measure) yarda *f* (*0,91m*)

yardstick /ˈjɑːrdstɪk/ ‖ /ˈjɑːdstɪk/ *n* criterio *m*

yarn /jɑːrn/ ‖ /jɑːn/ *n* **1** (Tex) hilo *m* **2** (tale) (colloq) historia *f*

yawn¹ /jɔːn/ *vi* bostezar*

yawn² *n* bostezo *m*

yawning /ˈjɔːnɪŋ/ *adj* (*before n*) enorme

yd (*pl* **yd** *or* **yds**) = **yard**

yeah /jeə/ *interj* (colloq) sí

year /jɪr/ ‖ /jɪə(r)/ *n* **1** (period of time) año *m*; **all (the) ∼ round** todo el año; **by the ∼ 2000** para el año 2000; **over the ∼s I've grown accustomed to it** con el tiempo *or* con los años me he ido acostumbrando; **∼ after ∼/∼ in, ∼ out** año tras año; **I'm 12 ∼s old** tengo doce años **2** **years** *pl* (a long time): **I haven't seen him for ∼s** hace años que no lo veo; **∼s ago, there was a church here** años atrás, aquí había una iglesia **3** (Educ) curso *m*, año *m*

-year /jɪr/ ‖ /jɪə(r)/ *suff*: **a third∼ student** un estudiante de tercer año *or* de tercero

yearly¹ /ˈjɪrli/ ‖ /ˈjɪəli/ *adj* anual; **on a ∼ basis** cada año

yearly² *adv* cada año; **twice ∼** dos veces al *or* por año

yearn /jɜːrn/ ‖ /jɜːn/ *vi* **to ∼ to +** INF anhelar + INF; **to ∼ FOR sth** añorar algo

yearning /ˈjɜːrnɪŋ/ ‖ /ˈjɜːnɪŋ/ *n* ∼ FOR sth/to + INF anhelo *m* *or* ansia *f*; DE algo/+ INF

-year-old /jər'əʊld/ ‖ /jɪərˈəʊld/ *suff*: **a thirty-two∼ woman** una mujer de treinta y dos años; **a six∼** un niño/una niña de seis años

yeast /jiːst/ *n* levadura *f*

yell¹ /jel/ *vi/t* gritar

yell² *n* grito *m*

yellow¹ /ˈjeləʊ/ *adj* amarillo; ⟨*hair*⟩ muy rubio *or* (Méx) güero *or* (Col) mono *or* (Ven) catire; ⟨*traffic light*⟩ (AmE) amarillo, ámbar *adj inv*

yellow² *n* **(a)** (color) amarillo *m* **(b)** (signal) (AmE) luz *f* amarilla

yellow³ *vi* ponerse* amarillo

yellow: ∼ **fever** *n* fiebre *f* amarilla; ∼ **pages,** (BrE) ∼ **Pages**® *pl n* páginas *fpl* amarillas

yelp¹ /jelp/ *vi* dar* un gañido *or* aullido

yelp² *n* gañido *m*, aullido *m*

Yemen /ˈjemən/ *n* Yemen *m*

yen /jen/ *n* **1** (longing) (colloq) (*no pl*) **to have a ∼ to +** INF morirse* de ganas DE + INF (fam) **2** (*pl* ∼) (Fin) yen *m*

yes¹ /jes/ *interj* sí; **are you ready? — ∼, I am** ¿estás listo? — sí; **you didn't tell me — ∼, I did!** no me lo dijiste — ¡sí que te lo dije!

yes² *n* (*pl* ∼**es**) sí *m*

yes-man /ˈjesmæn/ *n* (*pl* **-men** /-men/) (pej): **he's a ∼** es de los que dicen amén a todo

yesterday¹ /ˈjestərdeɪ, -di/ ‖ /ˈjestədeɪ, -di/ *adv* ⋯✦

ayer; ~ **morning** ayer por la mañana, ayer en la mañana (AmL), ayer a la mañana *or* de mañana (RPl)

yesterday² *n*: ~ **was a busy day** ayer fue un día de mucha actividad; **the day before** ~ anteayer

yet¹ /jet/ *adv* [1] **(a)** (up to this or that time, till now) (*with neg*) todavía, aún; **I haven't eaten** *o* (AmE also) **I didn't eat** ~ todavía *or* aún no he comido, todavía no comí (RPl); **as** ~ aún, todavía **(b)** (now, so soon) (*with neg*) todavía **(c)** (thus far) (*after superl*): **it's his best book** ~ es el mejor libro que ha escrito hasta ahora [2] (by now, already) (*with interrog*) ya; **has she decided** *o* (AmE also) **did she decide** ~? ¿ya se ha decidido?, ¿ya se decidió? (AmL) [3] (still) todavía, aún [4] (eventually, in spite of everything): **we may win** ~ todavía podemos ganar [5] (*as intensifier*) **(a)** (even) (*with comp*) aún, todavía; **the story becomes** ~ **more complicated** el cuento se complica aún *or* todavía más **(b)** (in addition, besides): ~ **more problems** más problemas aún; **we had to go back** ~ **again** tuvimos que volver otra vez más (aún) [6] (but, nevertheless) (*as linker*) sin embargo

yet² *conj* pero

yew /juː/ *n* tejo *m*

Yiddish /'jɪdɪʃ/ *n* yídish *m*, yiddish *m*

yield¹ /jiːld/ *vt* [1] (surrender) ceder; **to** ~ **one's right of way** (AmE Transp) ceder el paso [2] ‹*crop/fruit/mineral/oil*› producir*; ‹*results*› dar*
■ ~ *vi* [1] **(a)** (give way) ceder **(b)** (give priority): **⊙ yield** (AmE) ceda el paso [2] ‹‹*ground/ice*›› ceder

yield² *n* rendimiento *m*

YMCA *n* (= **Young Men's Christian Association**) YMCA *f*, Asociación *f* Cristiana de Jóvenes

yodel /'jəʊdl/ *vi*, (BrE) **-ll-** cantar al estilo tirolés

yoga /'jəʊɡə/ *n* yoga *m*

yoghurt, yoghourt, yogurt /'jəʊɡərt ‖'jɒɡət/ *n* yogur *m*, yoghourt *m*

yoke¹ /jəʊk/ *n* **(a)** (for oxen, horses) yugo *m* **(b)** (burden, bondage) yugo *m*

yoke² *vt* ‹*oxen*› uncir*

yokel /'jəʊkəl/ *n* (pej *or* hum) pueblerino, -na *m,f or* (Méx) indio, -dia *m,f or* (Col) montañero, -ra *m,f or* (RPl) pajuerano, -na *m,f or* (Chi) huaso, -sa *m,f* (pey *o* hum)

yolk /jəʊk/ *n* yema *f* (de huevo)

yonder /'jɑːndər ‖'jɒndə(r)/ *adv* (poet *or* dial) allá

you /juː/ *pron* [1] (sing) **(a)** (as subject — familiar) tú, vos (AmC, RPl); (— formal) usted; ~ **liar!** ¡mentiroso! **(b)** (as direct object — familiar) te; (— formal, masculine) lo, le (Esp); (— formal, feminine) la **(c)** (as indirect object — familiar) te; (— formal) le; (— with direct object pronoun present) se; **I told** ~ te dije/ le dije; **I gave it to** ~ te lo di/se lo di **(d)** (after prep — familiar) ti, vos (AmC, RPl); (— formal) usted [2] (pl) **(a)** (as subject, after preposition — familiar) ustedes (AmL), vosotros, -tras (Esp); (— formal) ustedes; **be quiet,** ~ **two** ustedes dos: ¡cállense!, vosotros dos: ¡callaos! (Esp) **(b)** (as direct object — familiar) los, las (AmL), os (Esp); (— formal, masculine)

los, les (Esp); (— formal, feminine) las **(c)** (as indirect object — familiar) les (AmL), os (Esp); (— formal) les; (— with direct object pronoun present) se; **I gave** ~ **the book** les *or* (Esp tb) os di el libro; **I gave it to** ~ se *or* (Esp tb) os lo di

[3] (one) **(a)** (as subject): ~ **can't do that here** aquí no se puede hacer eso, aquí uno no puede hacer eso, no puedes hacer eso aquí (Esp) **(b)** (as direct object): **people stop** ~ **in the street and ask for money** la gente lo para a uno en la calle y le pide dinero, la gente te para en la calle y te pide dinero (Esp) **(c)** (as indirect object): **they can cause** ~ **a lot of trouble** le pueden a uno crear muchos problemas, te pueden crear muchos problemas (Esp)

you'd /juːd/ **(a)** = **you had (b)** = **you would**

you'll /juːl/ = **you will**

young¹ /jʌŋ/ *adj* **younger** /'jʌŋɡər ‖'jʌŋɡə(r)/, **youngest** /'jʌŋɡəst ‖'jʌŋɡɪst/ **(a)** ‹*animal/ person*› joven; **I have a** ~**er brother** tengo un hermano menor; **she is four years** ~**er than me** tiene cuatro años menos que yo; **a** ~ **man/woman** un/una joven; **a** ~ **lady** una señorita, una chica joven; ~ **people** la gente joven, los jóvenes, la juventud; **to marry** ~ casarse joven **(b)** ‹*appearance/manner/complexion*› juvenil

young² *pl n* (animals) crías *fpl*

youngster /'jʌŋstər ‖'jʌŋstə(r)/ *n* chico, -ca *m,f*

your /jʊr, *weak form* jər ‖jɔː(r), *weak form* jʊə(r)/ *adj*
■ **Note** The translations *tu* and *su* agree in number with the noun which they modify; they appear as *tu, tus, su, sus*, depending on what follows: *your father/ mother* tu padre/madre *or* su padre/madre; *your books/magazines* tus libros/revistas *or* sus libros/ revistas.The translation *vuestro* agrees in number and gender with the noun which it modifies; it appears as *vuestro, vuestra, vuestros, vuestras*, depending on what follows: *your father/mother* vuestro padre/ vuestra madre; *your books/magazines* vuestros libros/ vuestras revistas.

(a) (belonging to one person) (*sing, familiar*) tu; (*pl, familiar*) tus; (*sing, formal*) su; (*pl, formal*) sus; **wash** ~ **hands** lávate/lávese las manos **(b)** (belonging to more than one person) (*sing, familiar*) su (AmL), vuestro, -tra (Esp); (*pl, familiar*) sus (AmL), vuestros, -tras (Esp); (*sing, formal*) su; (*pl, formal*) sus; **put** ~ **shoes on** pónganse *or* (Esp) pone/o/nse los zapatos **(c)** (one's): **if** ~ **name begins with A** ... si tu/su nombre empieza con A ...; **you have to take** ~ **shoes off in a mosque** hay que quitarse los zapatos en una mezquita

you're /jʊər ‖jʊə(r), jɔː(r)/ = **you are**

yours /jʊrz ‖jɔːz/ *pron*
■ **Note** The three translations of *yours* reflects the gender and number of the noun they are standing for; *yours* is translated by *tuyo, tuya, tuyos, tuyas, suyo, suya, suyos, suyas, vuestro, vuestra, vuestros, vuestras*, depending on the meaning being translated, and what is being referred to.

(a) (belonging to one person) (*sing, familiar*) tuyo, -ya; (*pl, familiar*) tuyos, -yas; (*sing, formal*) suyo, -ya; (*pl, formal*) suyos, -yas; ~ **is here** el tuyo/la tuya/el suyo/la suya está aquí; **a friend of** ~ un amigo tuyo/suyo **(b)** (belonging to more than one person) (*sing, formal*) suyo, -ya; (*pl, formal*) suyos, -yas; (*sing, familiar*) suyo, -ya (AmL), vuestro, -tra (Esp); (*pl, familiar*) suyos, -yas (AmL), vuestros, -tras (Esp); **∼ are here, children** los suyos *or* los de ustedes están aquí, niños (AmL), los vuestros están aquí, niños (Esp); **is he a friend of ∼?** ¿es amigo de ustedes *or* suyo *or* (Esp) vuestro? **(c)** (Corresp): **∼, Daniel** un abrazo, Daniel

yourself /jər'self ‖jɔː'self/ *pron* **(a)** (reflexive): **describe ∼** (formal) descríbase; (familiar) descríbete; **stop thinking about ∼** (formal) deje de pensar en sí mismo; (familiar) deja de pensar en ti mismo; **by ∼** solo/sola **(b)** (emphatic use) (formal) usted mismo, usted misma; (familiar) tú mismo, tú misma; **you're a musician ∼, I hear** usted también es *or* (*familiar*) tú también eres músico, tengo entendido **(c)** (normal self): **just be ∼** compórtate con naturalidad; **you're not ∼ today** hoy no eres el/la de siempre **(d)** (oneself) uno mismo, una misma

yourselves /jər'selvz ‖jɔː'selvz/ *pron* **(a)** (reflexive): **behave ∼!** ¡pórtense bien! (AmL), ¡porta(r)os bien! (Esp); **by ∼** solos/solas **(b)** (emphatic use) (formal) ustedes mismos/mismas; (familiar) ustedes mismos/mismas *or* (Esp) vosotros mismos/vosotras mismas **(c)** (normal selves): **just be ∼** compórtense *or* (Esp) comporta(r)os con naturalidad

youth /juːθ/ *n* (*pl* **youths** /juːðz/) **1** (early life) juventud *f* **2** (young people) (+ *sing or pl vb*) juventud *f*; (*before n*) ⟨*movement/orchestra*⟩ juvenil; **∼ club** club *m* de jóvenes **3** (young man) (frml) joven *m*

youthful /'juːθfəl/ *adj* ⟨*enthusiasm/manner*⟩ juvenil; ⟨*folly/ignorance*⟩ de juventud

youth hostel *n* albergue *m* juvenil *or* de la juventud

you've /juːv/ = **you have**

yowl /jaʊl/ *vi* «*person*» dar* alaridos; «*dog*» aullar*; «*cat*» maullar*

yo-yo /'jəʊjəʊ/ *n* yo-yo *m*

yr (*pl* **yrs**) = **year**

Yugoslav /'juːgəʊslɑːv ‖'juːgəslɑːv/ *adj/n* ▶ YUGOSLAVIAN[1,2]

Yugoslavia /'juːgəʊslɑːviə ‖'jʊgə'slɑːviə/ *n* (Hist) Yugoslavia *f*

Yugoslavian[1] /'juːgəʊslɑːviən ‖'jʊgə'slɑːviən/ *adj* (Hist) yugoslavo

Yugoslavian[2] *n* (Hist) yugoslavo, -va *m,f*

yuppie, yuppy /'jʌpi/ *n* (*pl* **-pies**) (colloq) yuppy *mf* (fam)

YWCA *n* (= **Young Women's Christian Association**) YWCA *f*, Asociación *f* de Jóvenes Cristianas

Zz

Z, z /ziː ‖zed/ *n* Z, z *f*

Zaire /zɑːir ‖zɑː'iə(r)/ *n* Zaire *m*

Zairean /zɑː'iriən ‖zɑː'iəriən/ *adj* zaireño

Zambia /'zæmbiə/ *n* Zambia *f*

Zambian /'zæmbiən ‖'zæmbiən/ *adj* zambiano

zany /'zeɪni/ *adj* **zanier, zaniest** (colloq) ⟨*person*⟩ chiflado (fam); ⟨*adventure*⟩ loco

zap /zæp/ *vt* **-pp- (a)** (defeat, blast) (colloq) liquidar (fam) **(b)** (Comput) eliminar, borrar

zeal /ziːl/ *n* (Pol, Relig) fervor *m*, celo *m*

zealot /'zelət/ *n* (fanatic) fanático, -ca *m,f*

zealous /'zeləs/ *adj* ⟨*follower*⟩ ferviente; ⟨*worker*⟩ que pone gran celo en su trabajo

zebra /'ziːbrə ‖'zebrə, ziː-/ *n* (*pl* **-bras** *or* **-bra**) cebra *f*

zebra crossing *n* (BrE) paso *m* de cebra

zee /ziː/, (BrE) **zed** /zed/ *n* zeta *f*

zenith /'ziːnəθ ‖'zenɪθ/ *n* (Astron) cenit *m*, zenit *m*; **at the ∼ of her popularity** en el cenit *or* el apogeo de su popularidad

zero[1] /'zɪrəʊ, 'ziː- ‖'zɪərəʊ/ *n* (*pl* **zeros** *or* **zeroes**) cero *m*; **the temperature fell below ∼** la temperatura bajó de los cero grados; (*before n*) **∼ hour** hora *f* cero

zero[2] *adj* cero *adj inv*; **∼ degrees centigrade** cero grados centígrados

zest /zest/ *n* entusiasmo *m*

zigzag[1] /'zɪgzæg/ *n* zigzag *m*

zigzag[2] *vi* **-gg-** zigzaguear

zilch /zɪltʃ/ *n* (sl) nada de nada

Zimbabwe /zɪm'bɑːbwi, -weɪ/ *n* Zimbabwe *m*, Zimbabue *m*

Zimbabwean /zɪm'bɑːbwiən/ *adj* zimbabuense, de Zimbabwe

zinc /zɪŋk/ *n* cinc *m*, zinc *m*

Zionism /'zaɪənɪzəm/ *n* sionismo *m*

Zionist /'zaɪənɪst ‖'zaɪənɪst/ *adj* sionista

zip[1] /zɪp/ *n* **1** (vigor) (colloq) garra *f* (fam) **2** (fastener) (BrE) ▶ ZIPPER[1]

zip[2] **-pp-** *vt* ⟨*pocket/bag*⟩ cerrar* la cremallera (*or* el cierre *etc*) de ∎ **∼** *vi* **1** (with zipper): **the suitcase ∼s open/shut** la maleta se abre/cierra con cremallera (*or* cierre *etc*) **2** (move fast) (colloq): **we ∼ped through the work** (nos) despachamos el trabajo en un santiamén (fam) ∎ **zip up** [*v* + *o* + *adv, v* + *adv* + *o*] ⟨*bag*⟩ cerrar*

zip: **∼ code** *n* (AmE) código *m* postal; **∼ fastener** *n* (BrE) ▶ ZIPPER[1]; **∼-on** *adj* (*before n*) ⟨*hood/lining*⟩ que se puede quitar, desmontable

zipper[1] /'zɪpər ‖'zɪpə(r)/ *n* (AmE) cremallera *f*, cierre *m* (AmL), zíper *m* (AmC, Méx, Ven), cierre *m* relámpago (RPl) *or* (Chi) eclair

zipper[2] *vt* (AmE) ▶ ZIP[2] *vt*

zodiac /'zəʊdiæk/ *n* **the ∼** el zódiaco *or* zodiaco

zombie /'zɑːmbi ‖'zɒmbi/ *n* zombie *mf*

zone /zəʊn/ n **(a)** (area) zona f; time ∼ huso m horario **(b)** (AmE) distrito m

zoo /zuː/ n (pl **zoos**) zoológico m, zoo m (esp Esp)

zoologist /zəʊˈɑːlədʒəst ‖zəʊˈɒlədʒɪst, zuː/ n zoólogo, -ga m,f

zoology /zəʊˈɑːlədʒi ‖zəʊˈɒlədʒi, zuː/ n zoología f

zoom¹ /zuːm/ n **1** (sound) (no pl) zumbido m **2** ∼ **(lens)** (Cin, Phot, TV) teleobjetivo m, zoom m

zoom² vi (move fast) (colloq) (+ adv compl): to ∼ along/past ir*/pasar zumbando (fam)
∎ **zoom in** [v + adv] to ∼ in (ON sth/sb) hacer* un zoom in (SOBRE algo/algn) (*acercar rápidamente una imagen usando un teleobjetivo*)

zucchini /zʊˈkiːni/ n (pl ∼ or ∼**s**) (AmE) calabacín m, calabacita f (Méx), zapallito m (largo or italiano) (CS)

Zulu¹ /ˈzuːluː/ adj zulú

Zulu² n **(a)** (person) zulú mf **(b)** (language) zulú m

Contents

Glossary of grammatical terms

Abbreviation A shortened form of a word or phrase: **Mr** = **Sr.**

Absolute use The use of a transitive verb without an expressed object, as in: **I didn't** *realize*

Active In the active form the subject of the verb performs the action: **Pedro** *kisses* **Ana** = **Pedro** *besa* **a Ana**

Adjective A word describing a noun: **a** *red* **pencil** = **un lápiz** *rojo*; *my* **house** = *mi* **casa**

Adverb A word that describes or changes the meaning of a verb, an adjective, or another adverb: **he ran** *quickly* = **corrió** *rápidamente*; *very* **pretty** = *muy* **bonito**; **she sings** *very* **badly** = **canta** *muy* **mal**

Apocope The omission of the final sound of a word, as in Spanish **algún** (alguno), **tan** (tanto)

Article The definite article, **the** = **el/la/los/las**, and indefinite article, **a/an** = **un/una**

Attributive An adjective or noun is attributive when it is used directly before a noun: **a** *good* **wine** = **un** *buen* **vino**; *business* **hours** = **horas** *de oficina*

Auxiliary verb A verb used with another verb to form compound tenses, as English **be**, **do**, and **have**: **I** *have* **eaten** = *he* **comido**; **he** *was* **sleeping** = *estaba* **durmiendo**

Cardinal number A whole number representing a quantity: **one/two/three** = **uno/dos/tres**

Clause A self-contained section of a sentence that contains a subject and a verb

Collective noun A noun that is singular in form but refers to a group of individual persons or things, e.g. **royalty, government**

Collocate A word that regularly occurs with another; in Spanish, **libro** is a typical collocate of the verb **leer**.

Comparative The form of an adjective or adverb that makes it "more": **smaller** = **más pequeño**; **better** = **mejor**

Compound An adjective, noun, or verb formed from two or more separate words: **self-confident** (self + confident) = **seguro de sí mismo**; **airmail** (air + mail) = **correo aéreo**; **outdo** (out + do) = **superar**

Conditional tense A tense of a verb that expresses what might happen if something else occurred: **he would go** = **iría**

Conjugation Variation of the form of a verb to show tense, person, mood, etc

Conjunction A word used to join clauses together: **and** = **y**; **because** = **porque**

Countable noun A noun that can form a plural and, in the singular, can be used with the indefinite article, e.g. **a book, two books**

Consonant All the letters of the alphabet other than **a, e, i, o, u**

Definite article: **the** = **el/la/los/las**

Demonstrative adjective An adjective indicating the person or thing referred to: *this* **table** = *esta* **mesa**

Demonstrative pronoun A pronoun indicating the person or thing referred to: *this* **is my sister** = *ésta* **es mi hermana**

Direct object The noun or pronoun directly affected by the verb: **I bought** *a book* = **compré** *un libro*

Direct speech A speaker's actual words or the use of these in writing: **he said:** *be quiet!* = **dijo:** *¡cállense!*

Elliptical Having a word or words omitted, especially where the sense can be guessed from the context

Ending Letters added to the stem of a word to show a change in function

Feminine One of the genders in Spanish, applied to nouns, pronouns, adjectives, and articles: **la casa blanca** = **the white house**; **ella** = **she**

Future tense The tense of a verb that refers to something that will happen in the future: **he** *will arrive* **late** = *llegará* **tarde**

Gender Spanish nouns, pronouns, adjectives, and articles almost all fall into two genders, masculine and feminine; in addition, Spanish uses the neuter pronouns **esto, eso,** and **aquello**, and the neuter article **lo**

Gerund The part of a verb used in Spanish to form continuous tenses: **muriendo** = **dying**; **cantando** = **singing**

Imperative A form of a verb that expresses a command: **come here!** = **¡ven aquí!**

Imperfect tense The tense of a verb that refers to an uncompleted or a habitual action in the past: **the children** *were playing* = **los niños** *jugaban*; **I** *went/used to go* **there every Monday** = *iba* **allí todos los lunes**

Impersonal verb A verb in English used only with **it**: **it is raining** = **está lloviendo**

Indefinite article: **a/an** = **un/una**

Indefinite pronoun A pronoun that does not identify a specific person or object: **one, something**

Indicative form The form of a verb used when making a statement of fact or asking questions of fact in various tenses: **I'm not hungry** = **no tengo hambre**

Indirect object The noun or pronoun indirectly affected by the verb, at which the direct object is aimed: **I wrote a letter *to my mother* = *le* escribí una carta *a mi madre***

Indirect speech A report of what someone has said which does not reproduce the exact words: **she said that they had gone out = dijo que habían salido; he told me to be quiet = me dijo que me callara**

Infinitive The basic form of a verb: **to sing = cantar**

Inflect To change the ending or form of a word to show its tense or its grammatical relation to other words: **gone** and **went** are inflected forms of **to go**

Interjection A sound, word, or remark expressing a strong feeling such as anger, fear, or joy, or attracting attention: **¡ouch! = ¡ay!; good heavens! = ¡Dios mío!**

Interrogative An adjective, adverb, or pronoun that asks a question: **what? = ¿qué?; how much? = ¿cuánto?; who? = ¿quién?**

Intransitive verb A verb that does not have a direct object: **he died suddenly = murió repentinamente**

Invariable noun A noun that has the same form in the plural as the singular: **sheep, species**

Irregular verb A verb that does not follow one of the set patterns and has its own individual forms, e.g. English **to be**, Spanish **ser**

Masculine One of the genders in Spanish applied to nouns, pronouns, adjectives, and articles: **el perro negro = the black dog; él= he**

Modal verb A verb that is used with another verb to express necessity or possibility, e.g. **might, should, will**

Mood A category of verb use, expressing fact (indicative), command (imperative), or wish or conditionality (subjunctive)

Negative expressing refusal or denial

Neuter One of the genders in Spanish, used only in the pronouns **esto, eso,** and **aquello,** and the article **lo**

Noun A word that names a person or a thing

Number The state of being either singular or plural

Object The word or words naming the person or thing acted upon by a verb or preposition: **John studies *geography* = John estudia *geografía***

Ordinal number A number that shows a person's or thing's position in a series: **first = primero**

Part of speech A grammatical term for the function of a word; noun, verb, adjective, etc, are parts of speech.

Passive In the passive form the subject of the verb experiences the action rather than performs it – common in English, but not in Spanish: **Ana *is kissed by* Pedro = Ana *es besada por* Pedro**

Past participle The part of a verb used to form past tenses: **she had *gone* = había *ido***

Perfect tense The tense of the verb that refers to an event that has taken place in a period of time that includes the present: **I have eaten = he comido**

Person Any of the three groups of personal pronouns and forms taken by verbs; the **first person** (e.g. I/yo) refers to the person(s) speaking, the **second person** (e.g. you/tú) refers to the person(s) spoken to; the **third person** (e.g. he/él) refers to the persons spoken about

Personal pronoun A pronoun that refers to a person or thing: **I/he/she = yo/él/ella**

Phrasal verb A verb in English combined with a preposition or an adverb to have a particular meaning: **run away = huir; go past = pasar**

Phrase A self-contained section of a sentence that does not contain a full verb

Pluperfect tense The tense of a verb that refers to something that happened before a particular point in the past: **he had left = había salido**

Plural Of nouns etc, referring to more than one: **the houses = las casas**

Possessive adjective An adjective that shows possession, belonging to someone or something: **my/your = mi/tu**

Possessive pronoun A pronoun that shows possession, belonging to someone or something: **mine/yours = mío/tuyo**

Postpositive Placed after the word to which it relates, such as "in stock" in the phrase **items in stock**

Predicative An adjective is predicative when it comes after a verb such as **be** or **become**: **she is beautiful = es hermosa**

Prefix A letter or group of letters added to the beginning of a word to change its meaning: ***im*possible = *im*posible, *un*lucky =*des*afortunado**

Preposition A word that stands in front of a noun or pronoun, relating it to the rest of the sentence: **with = con; without = sin**

Present participle The part of a verb that in English ends in –ing, and is used in forming continuous tenses: **doing = haciendo**

Present tense The tense of a verb that refers to something happening now: **I open the door = *abro* la puerta**

Preterite tense A simple tense referring to a completed action in the past: **I *did* it yesterday = lo *hice* ayer**

Pronominal verb A Spanish verb conjugated using the pronouns **me, te, se, nos,** and **os,** in which the pronoun refers to the subject of the verb: **(yo) me equivoqué = I was wrong.** A subgroup of these verbs are **Reflexive verbs**

Pronoun A word that stands instead of a noun: **he/she = él/ella; someone = alguien; mine = el mío/la mía**

Proper noun A name of a person, place, institution, etc, in English written with a capital letter at the start: **Spain, the Atlantic, London, Juan, Madrid** are all proper nouns.

Reflexive pronoun A pronoun that refers back to the subject of the clause in which it is used: **myself = me; themselves = se**

Reflexive verb A verb whose object is the same as its subject; in Spanish, it is used with a reflexive pronoun: **he washed himself = se lavó**

Regular verb A verb that follows a set pattern in its different forms

Relative pronoun A pronoun that introduces a subordinate clause, relating to a person or thing mentioned in the main clause: **the man *who* visited us = el hombre *que* nos visitó**

Reported speech Another name for **Indirect speech**

Sentence A sequence of words, with a subject and a verb, that can stand on their own to make a statement, ask a question, or give a command

Singular Of nouns etc, referring to just one: **the house = la casa**

Stem The part of a word to which endings are added: **care** is the stem of **careful** and **careless;** in Spanish **cuidado** is the stem of **cuidadoso.**

Subject In a clause or sentence, the noun or pronoun that causes the action of the verb: *John* studies geography = *John* estudia geografía

Subjunctive A verb form that is used to express wishes or conditionality: **long *live* the King! = ¡*viva* el Rey!; if** it *was* or *were* possible = si *fuera* posible

Subordinate clause A clause which adds information to the main clause of a sentence but cannot be used as a sentence by itself, e.g. **she answered the phone *when it rang***

Suffix A letter or group of letters joined to the end of a word to make another word, e.g. **quick*ly* = rápida*mente***

Superlative The form of an adjective or adverb that makes it "most": **the smallest = la más pequeña; the best = el mejor**

Syllable A division of a word that contains a vowel sound that is pronounced as a single unit: **bala** has two syllables, *ba-la*

Tense The form of a verb that tells when the action takes place: present, future, imperfect, perfect, pluperfect are all tenses.

Transitive verb A verb that is used with a direct object: **she *read* the book = *leyó* el libro**

Uncountable noun A noun that cannot form a plural in ordinary usage and is not used with the indefinite article: **china, luggage**

Verb A word or group of words that describes an action: **the children *are playing* = los niños *están jugando***

Vowel One of the following letters: **a, e, i, o, u**

Spanish verb tables

1 Guide to Verb Tables

Every Spanish verb entry in the dictionary is cross-referred to one of the conjugation models shown in the following tables. The reference is given in square brackets immediately after the headword.

All the simple tenses are shown for **hablar** [A1], **meter** [E1], and **partir** [I1], the conjugation models for regular -**ar**, -**er**, and -**ir** verbs. For other verbs only the irregular tenses are given.

Compound tenses are not listed in the tables. The perfect tenses are formed with the relevant tense of the auxiliary **haber** and the past participle:

- Le *he hablado* de ti
- Lamento que *se haya ofendido*
- El profesor nos *había visto*
- Cuando *hubo terminado* de hablar, ...

- Para entonces ya *habremos terminado*
- Si lo *hubiera sabido, habría llamado*

The continuous tenses are formed with the relevant tense of the auxiliary **estar** and the present participle:

- *Estoy estudiando* el problema
- Cuando llegó, *estábamos cerrando*
- *Estuvieron esperando* mucho tiempo
- ¿*Han estado hablando* de mí?

Other verbs such as **andar**, **ir**, and **venir** can also be used as auxiliaries to express different nuances of meaning:

- *Andaba diciendo* que ...
- A medida que lo *fui conociendo*...
- ¿Por qué no *te vas vistiendo?*
- Hace mucho tiempo que te lo *vengo diciendo*

2 Verbs ending in -ar

A1 hablar

gerundio (gerund)	participio pasado (past participle)	indicativo (indicative)			
hablando	hablado	*presente (present)*	*imperfecto (imperfect)*	*pretérito indefinido (past simple)*	*futuro (future)*
		hablo	hablaba	hablé	hablaré
		hablas	hablabas	hablaste	hablarás
		habla	hablaba	habló	hablará
		hablamos	hablábamos	hablamos	hablaremos
		habláis	hablabais	hablasteis	hablaréis
		hablan	hablaban	hablaron	hablarán

condicional (conditional)	subjuntivo (subjunctive)			imperativo (imperative)
	presente (present)	*imperfecto (imperfect)*	*futuro (future)*	
hablaría	hable	hablara*	hablare	
hablarías	hables	hablaras	hablares	habla
hablaría	hable	hablara	hablare	hable
hablaríamos	hablemos	habláramos	habláremos	hablemos
hablaríais	habléis	hablarais	hablareis	hablad
hablarían	hablen	hablaran	hablaren	hablen

* all –**ar** verbs have an alternative form in which the –**ara** is replaced by –**ase**, e.g. hablase, hablases, hablase, hablásemos, hablaseis, hablasen

· ·

2 Verbs ending in -ar continued

A2 sacar

indicativo	subjuntivo	imperativo
pretérito indefinido	presente	
saqué	saque	
sacaste	saques	saca
sacó	saque	saque
sacamos	saquemos	saquemos
sacasteis	saquéis	sacad
sacaron	saquen	saquen

A3 pagar

indicativo	subjuntivo	imperativo
pretérito indefinido	presente	
pagué	pague	
pagaste	pagues	paga
pagó	pague	pague
pagamos	paguemos	paguemos
pagasteis	paguéis	pagad
pagaron	paguen	paguen

A4 cazar

indicativo	subjuntivo	imperativo
pretérito indefinido	presente	
cacé	cace	
cazaste	caces	caza
cazó	cace	cace
cazamos	cacemos	cacemos
cazasteis	cacéis	cazad
cazaron	cacen	cacen

A5 pensar

indicativo		subjuntivo	imperativo
presente	pretérito indefinido	presente	
pienso	pensé, etc	piense	
piensas		pienses	piensa
piensa		piense	piense
pensamos		pensemos	pensemos
pensáis		penséis	pensad
piensan		piensen	piensen

A6 empezar

indicativo		subjuntivo	imperativo
presente	pretérito indefinido	presente	
empiezo	empecé	empiece	
empiezas	empezaste	empieces	empieza
empieza	empezó	empiece	empiece
empezamos	empezamos	empecemos	empecemos
empezáis	empezasteis	empecéis	empezad
empiezan	empezaron	empiecen	empiecen

A7 regar

indicativo		subjuntivo	imperativo
presente	pretérito indefinido	presente	
riego	regué	riegue	
riegas	regaste	riegues	riega
riega	regó	riegue	riegue
regamos	regamos	reguemos	reguemos
regáis	regasteis	reguéis	regad
riegan	regaron	rieguen	rieguen

A8 rogar

indicativo		subjuntivo	imperativo
presente	pretérito indefinido	presente	
ruego	rogué	ruegue	
ruegas	rogaste	ruegues	ruega
ruega	rogó	ruegue	ruegue
rogamos	rogamos	roguemos	roguemos
rogáis	rogasteis	roguéis	rogad
ruegan	rogaron	rueguen	rueguen

A9 volcar

indicativo		subjuntivo	imperativo
presente	pretérito indefinido	presente	
vuelco	volqué	vuelque	
vuelcas	volcaste	vuelques	vuelca
vuelca	volcó	vuelque	vuelque
volcamos	volcamos	volquemos	volquemos
volcáis	volcasteis	volquéis	volcad
vuelcan	volcaron	vuelquen	vuelquen

A10 contar

indicativo		subjuntivo	imperativo
presente	pretérito indefinido	presente	
cuento	conté, etc	cuente	
cuentas		cuentes	cuenta
cuenta		cuente	cuente
contamos		contemos	contemos
contáis		contéis	contad
cuentan		cuenten	cuenten

A11 forzar

indicativo		subjuntivo	imperativo
presente	pretérito indefinido	presente	
fuerzo	forcé	fuerce	
fuerzas	forzaste	fuerces	fuerza
fuerza	forzó	fuerce	fuerce
forzamos	forzamos	forcemos	forcemos
forzáis	forzasteis	forcéis	forzad
fuerzan	forzaron	fuercen	fuercen

2 Verbs ending in -ar continued

A12 degollar

indicativo presente	pretérito indefinido	subjuntivo presente	imperativo
degüello	degollé, etc	degüelle	
degüellas		degüelles	degüella
degüella		degüelle	degüelle
degollamos		degollemos	degollemos
degolláis		degolléis	degollad
degüellan		degüellen	degüellen

A13 avergonzar

indicativo presente	pretérito indefinido	subjuntivo presente	imperativo
avergüenzo	avergoncé	avergüence	
avergüenzas	avergonzaste	avergüences	avergüenza
avergüenza	avergonzó	avergüence	avergüence
avergonzamos	avergonzamos	avergoncemos	avergoncemos
avergonzáis	avergonzasteis	avergoncéis	avergonzad
avergüenzan	avergonzaron	avergüencen	avergüencen

A14 desosar

indicativo presente	pretérito indefinido	subjuntivo presente	imperativo
deshueso	desosé, etc	deshuese	
deshuesas		deshueses	deshuesa
deshuesa		deshuese	deshuese
desosamos		desosemos	desosemos
desosáis		desoséis	desosad
deshuesan		deshuesen	deshuesen

A15 jugar

indicativo presente	pretérito indefinido	subjuntivo presente	imperativo
juego	jugué	juegue	
juegas	jugaste	juegues	juega
juega	jugó	juegue	juegue
jugamos	jugamos	juguemos	juguemos
jugáis	jugasteis	juguéis	jugad
juegan	jugaron	jueguen	jueguen

A16 averiguar

indicativo pretérito indefinido	subjuntivo presente	imperativo
averigüé	averigüe	
averiguaste	averigües	averigua
averiguó	averigüe	averigüe
averiguamos	averigüemos	averigüemos
averiguasteis	averigüéis	averiguad
averiguaron	averigüen	averigüen

A17 vaciar

indicativo presente	pretérito indefinido	subjuntivo presente	imperativo
vacío	vacié, etc	vacíe	
vacías		vacíes	vacía
vacía		vacíe	vacíe
vaciamos		vaciemos	vaciemos
vaciáis		vaciéis	vaciad
vacían		vacíen	vacíen

A18 actuar

indicativo presente	pretérito indefinido	subjuntivo presente	imperativo
actúo	actué, etc	actúe	
actúas		actúes	actúa
actúa		actúe	actúe
actuamos		actuemos	actuemos
actuáis		actuéis	actuad
actúan		actúen	actúen

A19 aislar

indicativo presente	pretérito indefinido	subjuntivo presente	imperativo
aíslo	aislé, etc	aísle	
aíslas		aísles	aísla
aísla		aísle	aísle
aislamos		aislemos	aislemos
aisláis		aisléis	aislad
aíslan		aíslen	aíslen

A20 ahincar

indicativo presente	pretérito indefinido	subjuntivo presente	imperativo
ahínco	ahinqué	ahínque	
ahíncas	ahincaste	ahínques	ahínca
ahínca	ahincó	ahínque	ahínque
ahincamos	ahincamos	ahinquemos	ahinquemos
ahincáis	ahincasteis	ahinquéis	ahincad
ahíncan	ahincaron	ahínquen	ahínquen

A21 arcaizar

indicativo presente	pretérito indefinido	subjuntivo presente	imperativo
arcaízo	arcaicé	arcaíce	
arcaízas	arcaizaste	arcaíces	arcaíza
arcaíza	arcaizó	arcaíce	arcaíce
arcaizamos	arcaizamos	arcaicemos	arcaicemos
arcaizáis	arcaizasteis	arcaicéis	arcaizad
arcaízan	arcaizaron	arcaícen	arcaícen

2 Verbs ending in -ar continued

A22 cabrahigar

indicativo presente	pretérito indefinido	subjuntivo presente	imperativo
cabrahigo	cabrahigué	cabrahígue	
cabrahígas	cabrahigaste	cabrahígues	cabrahíga
cabrahíga	cabrahigó	cabrahígue	cabrahígue
cabrahigamos	cabrahigamos	cabrahiguemos	cabrahiguemos
cabrahigáis	cabrahigasteis	cabrahiguéis	cabrahigad
cabrahígan	cabrahigaron	cabrahíguen	cabrahíguen

A23 aunar

indicativo presente	pretérito indefinido	subjuntivo presente	imperativo
aúno	auné, etc	aúne	
aúnas		aúnes	aúna
aúna		aúne	aúne
aunamos		aunemos	aunemos
aunáis		aunéis	aunad
aúnan		aúnen	aúnen

A24 andar

indicativo pretérito indefinido	subjuntivo imperfecto
anduve	anduviera
anduviste	anduvieras
anduvo	anduviera
anduvimos	anduviéramos
anduvisteis	anduvierais
anduvieron	anduvieran

A25 dar

indicativo presente	pretérito indefinido	subjuntivo presente	imperfecto
doy	di	dé	diera
das	diste	des	dieras
da	dio	dé	diera
damos	dimos	demos	diéramos
dais	disteis	deis	dierais
dan	dieron	den	dieran

A26 errar

indicativo presente	subjuntivo presente	imperativo
yerro	yerre	
yerras	yerres	yerra
yerra	yerre	yerre
erramos	erremos	erremos
erráis	erréis	errad
yerran	yerren	yerren

A27 estar

gerundio	participio pasado	indicativo presente	imperfecto	pretérito indefinido	futuro
estando	estado	estoy	estaba	estuve	estaré
		estás	estabas	estuviste	estarás
		está	estaba	estuvo	estará
		estamos	estábamos	estuvimos	estaremos
		estáis	estabais	estuvisteis	estaréis
		están	estaban	estuvieron	estarán

condicional	subjuntivo presente	imperfecto	imperativo
estaría	esté	estuviera	
estarías	estés	estuvieras	está
estaría	esté	estuviera	esté
estaríamos	estemos	estuviéramos	estemos
estaríais	estéis	estuvierais	estad
estarían	estén	estuvieran	estén

. . . .

3 Verbs ending in -er

E1 meter

gerundio (gerund)	participio pasado (past participle)	indicativo (indicative)			
metiendo	metido	*presente (present)*	*imperfecto (imperfect)*	*pretérito indefinido (past simple)*	*futuro (future)*
		meto	metía	metí	meteré
		metes	metías	metiste	meterás
		mete	metía	metió	meterá
		metemos	metíamos	metimos	meteremos
		metéis	metíais	metisteis	meteréis
		meten	metían	metieron	meterán

condicional (conditional)	subjuntivo (subjunctive)			imperativo (imperative)
	presente (present)	*imperfecto (imperfect)*	*futuro (future)*	
metería	meta	metiera*	metiere	
meterías	metas	metieras	metieres	mete
metería	meta	metiera	metiere	meta
meteríamos	metamos	metiéramos	metiéremos	metamos
meteríais	metáis	metierais	metiereis	meted
meterían	metan	metieran	metieren	metan

* all **–er** verbs have an alternative form in which **–era** is replaced by **–ese**, e.g. met**iese**, met**ieses**, met**iese**, met**iésemos**, met**ieseis**, met**iesen**

E2 vencer

indicativo		subjuntivo	imperativo
presente	*pretérito indefinido*	*presente*	
venzo	vencí, etc	venza	
vences		venzas	vence
vence		venza	venza
vencemos		venzamos	venzamos
vencéis		venzáis	venced
vencen		venzan	venzan

E3 conocer

indicativo		subjuntivo	imperativo
presente	*pretérito indefinido*	*presente*	
conozco	conocí, etc	conozca	
conoces		conozcas	conoce
conoce		conozca	conozca
conocemos		conozcamos	conozcamos
conocéis		conozcáis	conoced
conocen		conozcan	conozcan

• •

3 Verbs ending in -er continued

E4 placer

indicativo		subjuntivo			imperativo
presente	pretérito indefinido	presente	imperfecto	futuro	
plazco	plací	plazca	placiera	placiere	
places	placiste	plazcas	placieras	placieres	place
place	plació[1]	plazca[3]	placiera[4]	placiere[5]	plazca
placemos	placimos	plazcamos	placiéramos	placiéremos	plazcamos
placéis	placisteis	plazcáis	placierais	placiereis	placed
placen	placieron[2]	plazcan	placieran	placieren	plazcan

alternative forms, applicable only to the verb 'placer':
[1]plugo; [2]pluguieron; [3]plega or plegue; [4]pluguiera or pluguiese; [5]pluguiere.

E5 yacer

indicativo		subjuntivo	imperativo
presente	pretérito indefinido	presente	
yazco[1]	yací, etc	yazca[2]	
yaces		yazcas	yace[3]
yace		yazca	yazca
yacemos		yazcamos	yazcamos
yacéis		yazcáis	yaced
yacen		yazcan	yazcan

[1]alternative forms: yazgo or yago; [2]alternative conjugations: yazga, yazgas, etc or yaga, yagas, etc.
[3]alternative conjugations: yaz, yazga or yaga, yazgamos or yagamos, yaced, yazgan or yagan.

E6 coger

indicativo		subjuntivo	imperativo
presente	pretérito indefinido	presente	
cojo	cogí, etc	coja	
coges		cojas	coge
coge		coja	coja
cogemos		cojamos	cojamos
cogéis		cojáis	coged
cogen		cojan	cojan

E7 atañer

gerundio	indicativo	subjuntivo
	pretérito indefinido	imperfecto
atañendo	atañí	atañera
	atañiste	atañeras
	atañó	atañera
	atañimos	atañéramos
	atañisteis	atañerais
	atañeron	atañeran

E8 entender

indicativo		subjuntivo	imperativo
presente	pretérito indefinido	presente	
entiendo	entendí	entienda	
entiendes	entendiste	entiendas	entiende
entiende	entendió	entienda	entienda
entendemos	entendimos	entendamos	entendamos
entendéis	entendisteis	entendáis	entended
entienden	entendieron	entiendan	entiendan

E9 mover

indicativo		subjuntivo	imperativo
presente	pretérito indefinido	presente	
muevo	moví, etc	mueva	
mueves		muevas	mueve
mueve		mueva	mueva
movemos		movamos	movamos
movéis		mováis	moved
mueven		muevan	muevan

3 Verbs ending in -er continued

E10 torcer

indicativo		subjuntivo	imperativo
presente	pretérito indefinido	presente	
tuerzo	torcí, etc	tuerza	
tuerces		tuerzas	tuerce
tuerce		tuerza	tuerza
torcemos		torzamos	torzamos
torcéis		torzáis	torced
tuercen		tuerzan	tuerzan

E11 volver

participio pasado	indicativo		subjuntivo	imperativo
	presente	pretérito indefinido	presente	
vuelto	vuelvo	volví, etc	vuelva	
	vuelves		vuelvas	vuelve
	vuelve		vuelva	vuelva
	volvemos		volvamos	volvamos
	volvéis		volváis	volved
	vuelven		vuelvan	vuelvan

E12 oler

indicativo		subjuntivo	imperativo
presente	pretérito indefinido	presente	
huelo	olí, etc	huela	
hueles		huelas	huele
huele		huela	huela
olemos		olamos	olamos
oléis		oláis	oled
huelen		huelan	huelan

E13 leer

gerundio	indicativo	subjuntivo
	pretérito indefinido	imperfecto
leyendo	leí	leyera
	leíste	leyeras
	leyó	leyera
	leímos	leyéramos
	leísteis	leyerais
	leyeron	leyeran

E14 proveer

participio pasado	indicativo	subjuntivo
	pretérito indefinido	imperfecto
provisto	proveí	proveyera
	proveíste	proveyeras
	proveyó	proveyera
	proveímos	proveyéramos
	proveísteis	proveyerais
	proveyeron	proveyeran

. . . .

3 Verbs ending in -er continued

E15 caber

indicativo				condicional	subjuntivo		imperativo
presente	imperfecto	pretérito indefinido	futuro		presente	imperfecto	
quepo	cabía	cupe	cabré	cabría	quepa	cupiera	
cabes	cabías	cupiste	cabrás	cabrías	quepas	cupieras	cabe
cabe	cabía	cupo	cabrá	cabría	quepa	cupiera	quepa
cabemos	cabíamos	cupimos	cabremos	cabríamos	quepamos	cupiéramos	quepamos
cabéis	cabíais	cupisteis	cabréis	cabríais	quepáis	cupierais	cabed
caben	cabían	cupieron	cabrán	cabrían	quepan	cupieran	quepan

E16 caer

gerundio	participio pasado	indicativo			subjuntivo		imperativo
		presente	imperfecto	pretérito indefinido	presente	imperfecto	
cayendo	caído	caigo	caía	caí	caiga	cayera	
		caes	caías	caíste	caigas	cayeras	cae
		cae	caía	cayó	caiga	cayera	caiga
		caemos	caíamos	caímos	caigamos	cayéramos	caigamos
		caéis	caíais	caísteis	caigáis	cayerais	caed
		caen	caían	cayeron	caigan	cayeran	caigan

E17 haber

indicativo				condicional	subjuntivo		imperativo
presente	imperfecto	pretérito indefinido	futuro		presente	imperfecto	
he	había	hube	habré	habría	haya	hubiera	
has	habías	hubiste	habrás	habrías	hayas	hubieras	he
ha	había	hubo	habrá	habría	haya	hubiera	haya
hemos	habíamos	hubimos	habremos	habríamos	hayamos	hubiéramos	hayamos
habéis	habíais	hubisteis	habréis	habríais	hayáis	hubierais	habed
han	habían	hubieron	habrán	habrían	hayan	hubieran	hayan

E18 hacer

participio pasado	indicativo			condicional	subjuntivo		imperativo
	presente	pretérito indefinido	futuro		presente	imperfecto	
hecho	hago	hice	haré	haría	haga	hiciera	
	haces	hiciste	harás	harías	hagas	hicieras	haz
	hace	hizo	hará	haría	haga	hiciera	haga
	hacemos	hicimos	haremos	haríamos	hagamos	hiciéramos	hagamos
	hacéis	hicisteis	haréis	haríais	hagáis	hicierais	haced
	hacen	hicieron	harán	harían	hagan	hicieran	hagan

- -

3 Verbs ending in -er continued

E19 rehacer

participio pasado	indicativo			condicional	subjuntivo		imperativo
	presente	*pretérito indefinido*	*futuro*		*presente*	*imperfecto*	
rehecho	rehago	rehíce	reharé	reharía	rehaga	rehiciera	
	rehaces	rehiciste	reharás	reharías	rehagas	rehicieras	rehaz
	rehace	rehízo	rehará	reharía	rehaga	rehiciera	rehaga
	rehacemos	rehicimos	reharemos	reharíamos	rehagamos	rehiciéramos	rehagamos
	rehacéis	rehicisteis	reharéis	reharíais	rehagáis	rehicierais	rehaced
	rehacen	rehicieron	reharán	reharían	rehagan	rehicieran	rehagan

E20 satisfacer

indicativo			condicional	subjuntivo		imperativo
presente	*pretérito indefinido*	*futuro*		*presente*	*imperfecto*	
satisfago	satisfice	satisfaré	satisfaría	satisfaga	satisficiera	
satisfaces	satisficiste	satisfarás	satisfarías	satisfagas	satisficieras	satisfaz[1]
satisface	satisfizo	satisfará	satisfaría	satisfaga	satisficiera	satisfaga
satisfacemos	satisficimos	satisfaremos	satisfaríamos	satisfagamos	satisficiéramos	satisfagamos
satisfacéis	satisficisteis	satisfaréis	satisfaríais	satisfagáis	satisficierais	satisfaced
satisfacen	satisficieron	satisfarán	satisfarían	satisfagan	satisficieran	satisfagan

[1]alternative form: satisface

E21 poder

gerundio	participio pasado
pudiendo	podido

indicativo			condicional	subjuntivo		imperativo
presente	*pretérito indefinido*	*futuro*		*presente*	*imperfecto*	
puedo	pude	podré	podría	pueda	pudiera	
puedes	pudiste	podrás	podrías	puedas	pudieras	puede
puede	pudo	podrá	podría	pueda	pudiera	pueda
podemos	pudimos	podremos	podríamos	podamos	pudiéramos	podamos
podéis	pudisteis	podréis	podríais	podáis	pudierais	poded
pueden	pudieron	podrán	podrían	puedan	pudieran	puedan

E22 poner

participio pasado	indicativo			condicional	subjuntivo		imperativo
	presente	*pretérito indefinido*	*futuro*		*presente*	*imperfecto*	
puesto	pongo	puse	pondré	pondría	ponga	pusiera	
	pones	pusiste	pondrás	pondrías	pongas	pusieras	pon
	pone	puso	pondrá	pondría	ponga	pusiera	ponga
	ponemos	pusimos	pondremos	pondríamos	pongamos	pusiéramos	pongamos
	ponéis	pusisteis	pondréis	pondríais	pongáis	pusierais	poned
	ponen	pusieron	pondrán	pondrían	pongan	pusieran	pongan

3 Verbs ending in -er continued

E23 traer

gerundio	participio pasado	indicativo		subjuntivo		imperativo
		presente	pretérito indefinido	presente	imperfecto	
trayendo	traído	traigo	traje	traiga	trajera	
		traes	trajiste	traigas	trajeras	trae
		trae	trajo	traiga	trajera	traiga
		traemos	trajimos	traigamos	trajéramos	traigamos
		traéis	trajisteis	traigáis	trajerais	traed
		traen	trajeron	traigan	trajeran	traigan

E24 querer

indicativo				condicional	subjuntivo		imperativo
presente	imperfecto	pretérito indefinido	futuro		presente	imperfecto	
quiero	quería	quise	querré	querría	quiera	quisiera	
quieres	querías	quisiste	querrás	querrías	quieras	quisieras	quiere
quiere	quería	quiso	querrá	querría	quiera	quisiera	quiera
queremos	queríamos	quisimos	querremos	querríamos	queramos	quisiéramos	queramos
queréis	queríais	quisisteis	querréis	querríais	queráis	quisierais	quered
quieren	querían	quisieron	querrán	querrían	quieran	quisieran	quieran

E25 saber

indicativo			condicional	subjuntivo		imperativo
presente	pretérito indefinido	futuro		presente	imperfecto	
sé	supe	sabré	sabría	sepa	supiera	
sabes	supiste	sabrás	sabrías	sepas	supieras	sabe
sabe	supo	sabrá	sabría	sepa	supiera	sepa
sabemos	supimos	sabremos	sabríamos	sepamos	supiéramos	sepamos
sabéis	supisteis	sabréis	sabríais	sepáis	supierais	sabed
saben	supieron	sabrán	sabrían	sepan	supieran	sepan

E26 ser

gerundio	participio pasado	indicativo			
		presente	imperfecto	pretérito indefinido	futuro
siendo	sido	soy	era	fui	seré
		eres	eras	fuiste	serás
		es	era	fue	será
		somos	éramos	fuimos	seremos
		sois	erais	fuisteis	seréis
		son	eran	fueron	serán

condicional	subjuntivo			imperativo
	presente	imperfecto	futuro	
sería	sea	fuera	fuere	
serías	seas	fueras	fueres	sé
sería	sea	fuera	fuere	sea
seríamos	seamos	fuéramos	fuéremos	seamos
seríais	seáis	fuerais	fuereis	sed
serían	sean	fueran	fueren	sean

• •

3 Verbs ending in -er continued

E27 tener

indicativo			condicional	subjuntivo		imperativo
presente	pretérito indefinido	futuro		presente	imperfecto	
tengo	tuve	tendré	tendría	tenga	tuviera	
tienes	tuviste	tendrás	tendrías	tengas	tuvieras	ten
tiene	tuvo	tendrá	tendría	tenga	tuviera	tenga
tenemos	tuvimos	tendremos	tendríamos	tengamos	tuviéramos	tengamos
tenéis	tuvisteis	tendréis	tendríais	tengáis	tuvierais	tened
tienen	tuvieron	tendrán	tendrían	tengan	tuvieran	tengan

E28 valer

indicativo			condicional	subjuntivo		imperativo
presente	pretérito indefinido	futuro		presente	imperfecto	
valgo	valí	valdré	valdría	valga	valiera	
vales	valiste	valdrás	valdrías	valgas	valieras	vale
vale	valió	valdrá	valdría	valga	valiera	valga
valemos	valimos	valdremos	valdríamos	valgamos	valiéramos	valgamos
valéis	valisteis	valdréis	valdríais	valgáis	valierais	valed
valen	valieron	valdrán	valdrían	valgan	valieran	valgan

E29 ver

participio pasado	indicativo			subjuntivo	imperativo
	presente	imperfecto	pretérito indefinido	presente	
visto	veo	veía	vi	vea	
	ves	veías	viste	veas	ve
	ve	veía	vio	vea	vea
	vemos	veíamos	vimos	veamos	veamos
	veis	veíais	visteis	veáis	ved
	ven	veían	vieron	vean	vean

E30 romper

participio pasado

roto

E31 verter

gerundio	indicativo		subjuntivo	imperativo
	presente	pretérito indefinido	imperfecto	
vertiendo[1]	vierto	vertí	vertiera[4]	
	viertes	vertiste	vertieras	vierte
	vierte	vertió[2]	vertiera	vierta
	vertemos	vertimos	vertiéramos	vertamos
	vertéis	vertisteis	vertierais	verted
	vierten	vertieron[3]	vertieran	viertan

alternative forms: [1]virtiendo; [2]virtió; [3]virtieron; [4]virtiera, virtieras, etc.

4 Verbs ending in -ir

I1 partir

gerundio (gerund)	participio pasado (past participle)	indicativo (indicative)			
		presente (present)	*imperfecto (imperfect)*	*pretérito indefinido (past simple)*	*futuro (future)*
partiendo	partido	parto	partía	partí	partiré
		partes	partías	partiste	partirás
		parte	partía	partió	partirá
		partimos	partíamos	partimos	partiremos
		partís	partíais	partisteis	partiréis
		parten	partían	partieron	partirán

condicional (conditional)	subjuntivo (subjunctive)			imperativo (imperative)
	presente (present)	*imperfecto (imperfect)*	*futuro (future)*	
partiría	parta	partiera*	partiere	
partirías	partas	partieras	partieres	parte
partiría	parta	partiera	partiere	parta
partiríamos	partamos	partiéramos	partiéremos	partamos
partiríais	partáis	partierais	partiereis	partid
partirían	partan	partieran	partieren	partan

* all -**ir** verbs have an alternative form in which -**era** is replaced by -**ese**, e.g. partiese, partieses, partiese, partiésemos, partieseis, partiesen

I2 distinguir

indicativo		subjuntivo	imperativo
presente	*pretérito indefinido*	*presente*	
distingo	distinguí,	distinga	
distingues	etc	distingas	distingue
distingue		distinga	distinga
distinguimos		distingamos	distingamos
distinguís		distingáis	distinguid
distinguen		distingan	distingan

I3 delinquir

indicativo		subjuntivo	imperativo
presente	*pretérito indefinido*	*presente*	
delinco	delinquí,	delinca	
delinques	etc	delincas	delinque
delinque		delinca	delinca
delinquimos		delincamos	delincamos
delinquís		delincáis	delinquid
delinquen		delincan	delincan

I4 zurcir

indicativo		subjuntivo	imperativo
presente	*pretérito indefinido*	*presente*	
zurzo	zurcí, etc	zurza	
zurces		zurzas	zurce
zurce		zurza	zurza
zurcimos		zurzamos	zurzamos
zurcís		zurzáis	zurcid
zurcen		zurzan	zurzan

I5 lucir

indicativo		subjuntivo	imperativo
presente	*pretérito indefinido*	*presente*	
luzco	lucí, etc	luzca	
luces		luzcas	luce
luce		luzca	luzca
lucimos		luzcamos	luzcamos
lucís		luzcáis	lucid
lucen		luzcan	luzcan

4 Verbs ending in -ir continued

I6 reducir

indicativo		subjuntivo		imperativo
presente	pretérito indefinido	presente	imperfecto	
reduzco	reduje	reduzca	redujera	
reduces	redujiste	reduzcas	redujeras	reduce
reduce	redujo	reduzca	redujera	reduzca
reducimos	redujimos	reduzcamos	redujéramos	reduzcamos
reducís	redujisteis	reduzcáis	redujerais	reducid
reducen	redujeron	reduzcan	redujeran	reduzcan

I7 dirigir

indicativo		subjuntivo	imperativo
presente	pretérito indefinido	presente	
dirijo	dirigí, etc	dirija	
diriges		dirijas	dirige
dirige		dirija	dirija
dirigimos		dirijamos	dirijamos
dirigís		dirijáis	dirigid
dirigen		dirijan	dirijan

I8 regir

indicativo		subjuntivo	imperativo
presente	pretérito indefinido	presente	
rijo	regí, etc	rija	
riges		rijas	rige
rige		rija	rija
regimos		rijamos	rijamos
regís		rijáis	regid
rigen		rijan	rijan

I9 gruñir

gerundio	indicativo	subjuntivo
	pretérito indefinido	imperfecto
gruñendo	gruñí	gruñera
	gruñiste	gruñeras
	gruñó	gruñera
	gruñimos	gruñéramos
	gruñisteis	gruñerais
	gruñeron	gruñeran

I10 asir

indicativo		subjuntivo	imperativo
presente	pretérito indefinido	presente	
asgo	así, etc	asga	
ases		asgas	ase
ase		asga	asga
asimos		asgamos	asgamos
asís		asgáis	asid
asen		asgan	asgan

I11 sentir

gerundio	participio pasado	indicativo		subjuntivo		imperativo
		presente	pretérito indefinido	presente	imperfecto	
sintiendo	sentido	siento	sentí	sienta	sintiera	
		sientes	sentiste	sientas	sintieras	siente
		siente	sintió	sienta	sintiera	sienta
		sentimos	sentimos	sintamos	sintiéramos	sintamos
		sentís	sentisteis	sintáis	sintierais	sentid
		sienten	sintieron	sientan	sintieran	sientan

I12 concernir

indicativo		subjuntivo	imperativo
presente	pretérito indefinido	presente	
concierno	concerní,	concierna	
conciernes	etc	conciernas	concierne
concierne		concierna	concierna
concernimos		concernamos	concernamos
concernís		concernáis	concernid
conciernen		conciernan	conciernan

I13 adquirir

indicativo		subjuntivo	imperativo
presente	pretérito indefinido	presente	
adquiero	adquirí, etc	adquiera	
adquieres		adquieras	adquiere
adquiere		adquiera	adquiera
adquirimos		adquiramos	adquiramos
adquirís		adquiráis	adquirid
adquieren		adquieran	adquieran

4 Verbs ending in -ir continued

I14 pedir

gerundio	participio pasado	indicativo		subjuntivo		imperativo
		presente	*pretérito indefinido*	*presente*	*imperfecto*	
pidiendo	pedido	pido	pedí	pida	pidiera	
		pides	pediste	pidas	pidieras	pide
		pide	pidió	pida	pidiera	pida
		pedimos	pedimos	pidamos	pidiéramos	pidamos
		pedís	pedisteis	pidáis	pidierais	pedid
		piden	pidieron	pidas	pidieran	pidan

I15 ceñir

gerundio	participio pasado	indicativo			subjuntivo		imperativo
		presente	*imperfecto*	*pretérito indefinido*	*presente*	*imperfecto*	
ciñendo	ceñido	ciño	ceñía	ceñí	ciña	ciñera	
		ciñes	ceñías	ceñiste	ciñas	ciñeras	ciñe
		ciñe	ceñía	ciñó	ciña	ciñera	ciña
		ceñimos	ceñíamos	ceñimos	ciñamos	ciñéramos	ciñamos
		ceñís	ceñíais	ceñisteis	ciñáis	ciñerais	ceñid
		ciñen	ceñían	ciñeron	ciñan	ciñeran	ciñan

I16 dormir

gerundio	participio pasado	indicativo		subjuntivo		imperativo
		presente	*pretérito indefinido*	*presente*	*imperfecto*	
durmiendo	dormido	duermo	dormí	duerma	durmiera	
		duermes	dormiste	duermas	durmieras	duerme
		duerme	durmió	duerma	durmiera	duerma
		dormimos	dormimos	durmamos	durmiéramos	durmamos
		dormís	dormisteis	durmáis	durmierais	dormid
		duermen	durmieron	duerman	durmieran	duerman

I17 embaír

gerundio	indicativo	subjuntivo
	pretérito indefinido	*imperfecto*
embayendo	embaí	embayera
	embaíste	embayeras
	embayó	embayera
	embaímos	embayéramos
	embaísteis	embayerais
	embayeron	embayeran

Spanish verb tables

4 Verbs ending in -ir continued

I18 reír

gerundio	participio pasado
riendo	reído

indicativo				condicional	subjuntivo		imperativo
presente	imperfecto	pretérito indefinido	futuro		presente	imperfecto	
río	reía	reí	reiré	reiría	ría	riera	
ríes	reías	reíste	reirás	reirías	rías	rieras	ríe
ríe	reía	rio	reirá	reiría	ría	riera	ría
reímos	reíamos	reímos	reiremos	reiríamos	riamos	riéramos	riamos
reís	reíais	reísteis	reiréis	reiríais	riáis	rierais	reíd
ríen	reían	rieron	reirán	reirían	rían	rieran	rían

I19 argüir

gerundio	participio pasado	indicativo				subjuntivo		imperativo
		presente	imperfecto	pretérito indefinido		presente	imperfecto	
arguyendo	argüido	arguyo	argüía, etc	argüí		arguya	arguyera	
		arguyes		argüiste		arguyas	arguyeras	arguye
		arguye		arguyó		arguya	arguyera	arguya
		argüimos		argüimos		arguyamos	arguyéramos	arguyamos
		argüís		argüisteis		arguyáis	arguyerais	argüid
		arguyen		arguyeron		arguyan	arguyeran	arguyan

I20 huir

gerundio	participio pasado	indicativo				subjuntivo		imperativo
		presente	imperfecto	pretérito indefinido		presente	imperfecto	
huyendo	huido	huyo	huía, etc	huí		huya	huyera	
		huyes		huiste		huyas	huyeras	huye
		huye		huyó		huya	huyera	huya
		huimos		huimos		huyamos	huyéramos	huyamos
		huís		huisteis		huyáis	huyerais	huid
		huyen		huyeron		huyan	huyeran	huyan

I21 rehuir

indicativo		subjuntivo	imperativo
presente	pretérito indefinido	presente	
rehúyo	rehuí, etc	rehúya	
rehúyes		rehúyas	rehúye
rehúye		rehúya	rehúya
rehuimos		rehuyamos	rehuyamos
rehuís		rehuyáis	rehuid
rehúyen		rehúyan	rehúyan

I22 prohibir

indicativo		subjuntivo	imperativo
presente	pretérito indefinido	presente	
prohíbo	prohibí, etc	prohíba	
prohíbes		prohíbas	prohíbe
prohíbe		prohíba	prohíba
prohibimos		prohibamos	prohibamos
prohibís		prohibáis	prohibid
prohíben		prohíban	prohíban

4 Verbs ending in -ir continued

I23 reunir

indicativo		subjuntivo	imperativo
presente	pretérito indefinido	presente	
reúno	reuní, etc	reúna	
reúnes		reúnas	reúne
reúne		reúna	reúna
reunimos		reunamos	reunamos
reunís		reunáis	reunid
reúnen		reúnan	reúnan

I24 decir

gerundio	participio pasado
diciendo	dicho

indicativo				condicional	subjuntivo		imperativo
presente	imperfecto	pretérito indefinido	futuro		presente	imperfecto	
digo	decía	dije	diré	diría	diga	dijera	
dices	decías	dijiste	dirás	dirías	digas	dijeras	di
dice	decía	dijo	dirá	diría	diga	dijera	diga
decimos	decíamos	dijimos	diremos	diríamos	digamos	dijéramos	digamos
decís	decíais	dijisteis	diréis	diríais	digáis	dijerais	decid
dicen	decían	dijeron	dirán	dirían	digan	dijeran	digan

I25 bendecir

gerundio	participio pasado
bendiciendo	bendecido

indicativo			condicional	subjuntivo		imperativo
presente	pretérito indefinido	futuro		presente	imperfecto	
bendigo	bendije	bendeciré	bendeciría	bendiga	bendijera	
bendices	bendijiste	bendecirás	bendecirías	bendigas	bendijeras	bendice
bendice	bendijo	bendecirá	bendeciría	bendiga	bendijera	bendiga
bendecimos	bendijimos	bendeciremos	bendeciríamos	bendigamos	bendijéramos	bendigamos
bendecís	bendijisteis	bendeciréis	bendeciríais	bendigáis	bendijerais	bendecid
bendicen	bendijeron	bendecirán	bendecirían	bendigan	bendijeran	bendigan

I26 erguir

gerundio	indicativo		subjuntivo		imperativo
	presente	pretérito indefinido	presente	imperfecto	
irguiendo	yergo[1]	erguí	yerga[2]	irguiera	
	yergues	erguiste	yergas	irguieras	yergue[3]
	yergue	irguió	yerga	irguiera	yerga
	erguimos	erguimos	yergamos	irguiéramos	yergamos
	erguís	erguisteis	yergáis	irguierais	erguid
	yerguen	irguieron	yergan	irguieran	yergan

[1]alternative conjugation: irgo, irgues, irgue, erguimos, erguís, irguen; [2]alternative conjugation: irga, irgas, irga, irgamos, irgáis, irgan; [3]alternative conjugation: irgue, irga, irgamos, erguid, irgan.

. . . .

4 *Verbs ending in -ir continued*

I27 ir

gerundio	participio pasado	indicativo			
		presente	*imperfecto*	*pretérito indefinido*	*futuro*
yendo	ido	voy	iba	fui	iré
		vas	ibas	fuiste	irás
		va	iba	fue	irá
		vamos	íbamos	fuimos	iremos
		vais	ibais	fuisteis	iréis
		van	iban	fueron	irán

condicional	subjuntivo			imperativo
	presente	*imperfecto*	*futuro*	
iría	vaya	fuera	fuere	
irías	vayas	fueras	fueres	ve
iría	vaya	fuera	fuere	vaya
iríamos	vayamos	fuéramos	fuéremos	vayamos
iríais	vayáis	fuerais	fuereis	id
irían	vayan	fueran	fueren	vayan

I28 oír

gerundio	participio pasado
oyendo	oído

indicativo				condicional	subjuntivo		imperativo
presente	*imperfecto*	*pretérito*	*futuro*		*presente*	*imperfecto*	*indefinido*
oigo	oía	oí	oiré	oiría	oiga	oyera	
oyes	oías	oíste	oirás	oirías	oigas	oyeras	oye
oye	oía	oyó	oirá	oiría	oiga	oyera	oiga
oímos	oíamos	oímos	oiremos	oiríamos	oigamos	oyéramos	oigamos
oís	oíais	oísteis	oiréis	oiríais	oigáis	oyerais	oid
oyen	oían	oyeron	oirán	oirían	oigan	oyeran	oigan

I29 salir

indicativo			condicional	subjuntivo		imperativo
presente	*pretérito indefinido*	*futuro*		*presente*	*imperfecto*	
salgo	salí, etc	saldré	saldría	salga	saliera	
sales		saldrás	saldrías	salgas	salieras	sal
sale		saldrá	saldría	salga	saliera	salga
salimos		saldremos	saldríamos	salgamos	saliéramos	salgamos
salís		saldréis	saldríais	salgáis	salierais	salid
salen		saldrán	saldrían	salgan	salieran	salgan

I30 seguir

indicativo		subjuntivo		imperativo
presente	*pretérito indefinido*	*presente*	*imperfecto*	
sigo	seguí	siga	siguiera	
sigues	seguiste	sigas	siguieras	sigue
sigue	siguió	siga	siguiera	siga
seguimos	seguimos	sigamos	siguiéramos	sigamos
seguís	seguisteis	sigáis	siguierais	seguid
siguen	siguieron	sigan	siguieran	sigan

4 Verbs ending in -ir continued

I31 venir

gerundio	indicativo			condicional	subjuntivo		imperativo
	presente	pretérito indefinido	futuro		presente	imperfecto	
viniendo	vengo	vine	vendré	vendría	venga	viniera	
	vienes	viniste	vendrás	vendrías	vengas	vinieras	ven
	viene	vino	vendrá	vendría	venga	viniera	venga
	venimos	vinimos	vendremos	vendríamos	vengamos	viniéramos	vengamos
	venís	vinisteis	vendréis	vendríais	vengáis	vinierais	venid
	vienen	vinieron	vendrán	vendrían	vengan	vinieran	vengan

I32 abolir

This is a regular verb but in the present indicative it is only used in the first and second person plural.

I33 abrir

participio pasado

abierto

I34 escribir

participio pasado

escrito

I35 freír

gerundio	participio pasado	indicativo		subjuntivo		imperativo
		presente	pretérito indefinido	presente	imperfecto	
friendo	frito	frío	freí	fría	friera	
		fríes	freíste	frías	frieras	fríe
		fríe	frió	fría	friera	fría
		freímos	freímos	friamos	friéramos	friamos
		freís	freísteis	friáis	frierais	freíd
		fríen	frieron	frían	frieran	frían

I36 imprimir

participio pasado

impreso

I37 morir

gerundio	participio pasado	indicativo		subjuntivo	
		presente	pretérito indefinido	presente	imperfecto
muriendo	muerto	muero	morí	muera	muriera
		mueres	moriste	mueras	murieras
		muere	murió	muera	muriera
		morimos	morimos	muramos	muriéramos
		morís	moristeis	muráis	murierais
		mueren	murieron	mueran	murieran

I38 pudrir

infinitivo	participio pasado
pudrir, podrir	podrido

All other forms are regular and are derived from the infinitive pudrir e.g. pudro, pudres, etc.

Summary of Spanish grammar

1 Nouns

All Spanish nouns are either masculine or feminine in gender, including nouns referring to objects or ideas. For this reason every Spanish noun mentioned in both sides of the dictionary is accompanied by gender information, shown in italics, *m* for masculine and *f* for feminine. Some nouns can be both masculine and feminine and this is indicated by the abbreviation *mf*, e.g. **belga** *mf* Belgian. Some nouns vary in gender according to region, e.g. **radio** (= radio) is masculine in most of Latin America and feminine in Spain. This information is also given in both sides of the dictionary. The following general rules will help to determine the gender of many nouns:

The following nouns are masculine:

- Male humans and male animals: **el hombre** *man*, **el muchacho** *boy*, **el toro** *bull*, **el león** *lion*, **el gallo** *cockerel*

- Nouns ending in **-o**: **el libro** *book*, **el rollo** *roll*, **el bolígrafo** *ball-point pen*. Exceptions: **la mano** *hand*, **la foto** *photo*, **la moto** *motor-bike*

- Nouns ending in **-aje**: **el viaje** *journey*, **el equipaje** *luggage*

- Nouns ending in a stressed vowel (i.e. an accented vowel): **el tisú** *tissue*, **el menú** *menu*, **el sofá** *sofa*

- Days of the week and months: **el lunes** *Monday*, **los domingos** *Sundays*, **un diciembre frío** *a cold December*

The following nouns are feminine:

- Female humans and female animals: **la mujer** *woman*, **la actriz** *actress*, **la vaca** *cow*, **la gallina** *chicken*

- Nouns ending in **-a** (but see 'Gender problems' below for words ending in **-ma**): **la casa** *house*, **la comida** *meal*, **la camiseta** *tee-shirt*. Exceptions: **el día** *day*, **el mapa** *map*, **el planeta** *planet*, **el tranvía** *tramway*

- Nouns ending in **-ción**: **la nación** *nation*, **la calefacción** *heating*, **la elección** *election*

- Nouns ending in **-dad**, **-tad**, **-tud**, or **-is**; **la ciudad** *city*, **la libertad** *liberty*, **la actitud** *attitude*, **la crisis** *crisis*, **la apendicitis** *appendicitis*. Exceptions: **el análisis** *analysis*, **el tenis** *tennis*

Gender problems

- Some common nouns ending in **-ma** are masculine, e.g. **el programa** *programme*, **el diagrama** *diagram*, **el clima** *climate*, **el problema** *problem*

■ Some nouns change their meaning according to their gender: **el corte** *cut*, but **la corte** *court* (i.e. the royal court), **el margen** *margin*, but **la margen** *river-bank*, **el orden** *order, sequence*, but **la orden** *order, command*

Plurals of nouns

The plural indicates more than one of a thing, and, as in English, it usually ends in -s in Spanish. The two most important ways of making Spanish plurals are:

■ If a noun ends in a vowel (**a**, **e**, **i**, **o**, or **u**), add -s: **la casa-las casas** *house-houses*, **el hombre-los hombres** *man-men*, **el taxi-los taxis** *taxi-taxis*, **el tisú-los tisús** *tissue-tissues*.

■ If a noun ends in a consonant (any letter except a vowel), add -es: **el corredor-los corredores** *runner-runners*, **el español-los españoles** *Spaniard-Spaniards*, **el inglés-los ingleses** *English person-English people*. Note: If the last consonant of a singular noun is **z**, the plural ends in -ces; **la voz-las voces** *voice-voices*.

Exception: If the singular already ends in -s and the last vowel in the word does not have an accent, the plural is the same as the singular: **el martes-los martes** *Tuesday-Tuesdays*, **la crisis-las crisis** *crisis-crises*.

2 Adjectives

2.1 Simple adjectives

Spanish adjectives are different from English ones in two ways:

■ They usually come after the noun: **un libro interesante** *an interesting book*, **el pan blanco** *white bread*, **las camisas azules** *blue shirts*. But some, like **grande** *big* or **pequeño** *small*, often come before the noun: **un gran escritor** *a great writer*, **un pequeño problema** *a small problem*.

■ They agree with the noun or pronoun they describe. This means that if the noun is plural the adjective in Spanish must also be plural, and if the noun is feminine the adjective must also be feminine, if it has a variant feminine form

un hombre delgado	**una mujer delgada**	**un coche nuevo**	**tres coches nuevos**
a thin man	*a thin woman*	*a new car*	*three new cars*
hombres delgados	**mujeres delgadas**	**una camisa nueva**	**camisas nuevas**
thin men	*thin women*	*a new shirt*	*new shirts*

. . . .

The following adjectives agree in both number and gender:

■ Adjectives that end in **-o**. Add **-s** for the plural, change the **-o** to **-a** for the feminine: **el pañuelo blanco-los pañuelos blancos** *white handkerchief-white handkerchiefs*, **la bandera blanca-las banderas blancas** *white flag-white flags*.

■ Adjectives that end in **-és**. Add **-a** for the feminine, and **-es** for the masculine plural. Note that the accent is no longer required, because the ending changes the stress pattern. **El vino francés-los vinos franceses** *French wine-French wines*, **la bebida francesa-las bebidas francesas** *French drink-French drinks*. Exceptions: **cortés** *polite* and **descortés** *impolite*. These have no separate feminine form, and the plural is **corteses/descorteses**.

■ Most adjectives ending in **-n**. Add **-a** for the feminine, and **-es** for the masculine plural: **alemán-alemana-alemanes-alemanas** *German*. Exception: **marrón** (masculine and feminine) *brown*, plural **marrones** (masculine and feminine.)

■ **Español-española-españoles-españolas** *Spanish*, **andaluz-andaluza-andaluces-andaluzas** *Andalusian*.

All adjectives ending in **-dor** add **-a** to show the feminine: **tranquilizador-tranquilizadora-tranquilizadores-tranquilizadoras** *soothing*.

The rest do not have a separate feminine form. Those ending in a vowel (usually **-e**) simply add **-s** for the plural; those ending in anything else add **-es**. If the singular ends in **-z**, the plural ends in **-ces**:

Singular masculine & fem.	Plural masculine & fem.	Meaning
grande	grandes	*big*
difícil	difíciles	*difficult*
superior	superiores	*superior/higher*
feroz	feroces	*ferocious*

2.2 Shortened adjectives

A few adjectives have a short form used immediately before a noun. The most important are:

		Short form	When used
grande	*big*	gran	before all singular nouns
cualquiera	*any*	cualquier	before all singular nouns
bueno	*good*	buen	before singular masculine nouns
malo	*bad*	mal	before singular masculine nouns
primero	*first*	primer	before singular masculine nouns
tercero	*third*	tercer	before singular masculine nouns

Compare **un buen libro** *a good book* and **una buena respuesta** *a good answer*.

• •

2.3 Comparison of adjectives

The comparative form of the adjective (the -er form in English as in: *large,
larger*) is expressed in Spanish by putting **más** *more*, or **menos** *less* in front
of the adjective: **Luis es más/menos alto que ella** *Luis is taller/less tall
than her*.

To indicate the superlative form of the adjective (in English: *most...* or
least... of three or more things), put **el más/el menos** (or **la más/la menos,
los más/los menos, las más/las menos**, according to gender) before the
adjective:

> **pero ella es la más alta de todos** *but she is the tallest of all*.

Note: the following two very common exceptions:

		singular	plural	
bueno/buen	*good*	mejor	mejores	*better/best*
malo/mal	bad	peor	peores	*worse/worst*

Example:

> **San Miguel es una de las mejores cervezas españolas**
> *San Miguel is one of the best Spanish beers.*

• •

3 The definite and indefinite articles: el & la, un & una

These words vary in Spanish according to whether their noun is masculine
or feminine, singular or plural:

	Singular	Plural	English equivalent
MASCULINE	el	los	the
FEMININE	la	las	

	Singular	Plural	
MASCULINE	un	unos	a *or* an
FEMININE	una	unas	

They are used in more or less the same way as their English equivalents:

> **el hombre compró una camisa y la mujer compró unos zapatos y un sombrero**
> *the man bought a shirt, and the woman bought a pair of shoes and a hat.*

Unos/unas means *some*, a *few* before plural nouns: **unos euros** *a few euros*,
unas muchachas *some girls*. They mean *a pair of* before things that come in
pairs like shoes or gloves (**unos guantes** = *a pair of gloves*).

But note the following points

- ■ Always use **el** and **un** before nouns that begin with **a-** or **ha-** when the **a** is
  stressed, even though these words may be feminine: **el agua** *water*, **el/un
  arma** *weapon*, **el hambre** *hunger*. These are all feminine nouns and their
  adjectives take feminine endings; their plurals are **las aguas, las armas,**
  etc.

- **De** + **el** (*of the*) is shortened to **del**: **el coche del profesor** *the teacher's car*. **A** + **el** (*to the*) is shortened to **al**: **doy el libro al profesor** *I give the book to the teacher*.

- Spanish uses the definite article for nouns that refer to things in general: *doctors say apples are good for children* means doctors, apples, and children in general. In Spanish this is: **los médicos dicen que las manzanas son buenas para los niños**. In the same way *el* **amor** = *love*, *la* **libertad** = *freedom*, *la* **justicia** = *justice*.

- The indefinite article **un/una** is not used in Spanish before professions or occupations: **es profesora** = *she is* a *teacher*, **soy estudiante** = *I am* a *student*.

4 Demonstratives

Demonstrative adjectives and pronouns are used to point out people and things. In Spanish the words for *this* and *that*, *this one* and *that one* must agree in number and gender with the following noun. Note that in Spanish there are two words for *that*, **ese/esa**, **aquel/aquella**. **aquel/aquella** refers to something distant or relatively distant from the speaker:

	Singular	Plural	
MASCULINE	**este**	**estos**	*this/these* **or** *this one/these ones*
FEMININE	**esta**	**estas**	
MASCULINE	**ese**	**esos**	*that/those* **or** *that one/those ones*
FEMININE	**esa**	**esas**	
MASCULINE	**aquel**	**aquellos**	*that/those over there* **or** *that one/*
FEMININE	**aquella**	**aquellas**	*those ones over there*

- When these words are used as pronouns, i.e. to mean *this one* or *that one*, they are usually written with an accent. **¿ves estos dos coches? éste es amarillo y ése es rojo** *do you see these two cars? this one is yellow and that one is red*. However, the Spanish *Real Academia de la Lengua* (Royal Academy of the (Spanish) Language) has ruled that these accents are no longer necessary, so follow your course book or your teacher's advice on this point.

- When these words do not refer to any noun in particular, a genderless form must be used, **esto**, **eso**, or **aquello**: **esto es terrible** *this is terrible*, **no quiero hablar de eso** *I don't want to talk about that*. (**éste es terrible** means *this one is terrible* and would refer to something masculine. **no quiero hablar de ésa** means *I don't want to talk about that girl/woman* or some other feminine noun.)

. . . .

5 Possessives

5.1 Possessive Adjectives

In Spanish the possessive adjectives (= my, your, his, her, our, their) agree in number with the thing possessed, not with the person that possesses it. Examples: **mi mano** *my hand* and **mis manos** *my hands*, **tu libro** *your book* and **tus libros** *your books*. Only **nuestro** and **vuestro** have special feminine forms: **nuestra casa** *our house*, **vuestras amigas** *your female friends*. Note: Spanish has no separate words for *his*, *her*, or *their*: **su/sus** cover all these meanings:

Singular	Plural	
mi	mis	*my*
tu	tus	*your* (when speaking to a friend or relative)
su	sus	*his/her/their/your* (use **su** for *your* when using the **usted** form)
nuestro	nuestros	*our* (before masculine nouns)
nuestra	nuestras	*our* (before feminine nouns)
vuestro	vuestros	*your* (before masculine nouns)
vuestra	vuestras	*your* (before feminine nouns)

- **Vuestro** is used in Spain when speaking to more than one friend or relative. Latin Americans never use **vuestro** and always use **su** for *your* when speaking to more than one person.

- Spanish does not use these words with parts of the body or clothes.
  levanta la mano *put up your hand*   **ponte la camisa** *put on your shirt*.

5.2 Possessive Pronouns

In Spanish the possessive pronouns (= mine, your, his, hers, ours, theirs) agree in gender and number with the noun that they refer to:

MASC.	mío	míos	*mine*
FEM.	mía	mías	
MASC.	tuyo	tuyos	*yours* (familiar form)
FEM.	tuya	tuyas	
MASC.	suyo	suyos	*his/hers/theirs/yours* (polite form)
FEM.	suya	suyas	
MASC.	nuestro	nuestros	*ours*
FEM.	nuestra	nuestras	
MASC.	vuestro	vuestros	*yours*
FEM.	vuestra	vuestras	

- **Vuestro** is used in Spain when speaking informally to more than one person. Latin Americans never use **vuestro** and always use **su** for *your* when speaking to more than one person.

- Examples: **este abrigo es mío/tuyo** *this coat is mine/yours*, **estas llaves son suyas** *these keys are his/hers/yours/theirs*, **esta dirección es nuestra** *this address is ours*. After a preposition (see page 999) the article **el** or **la** must be used: **no vamos en tu coche, vamos en *el* mío** *we're not going in your car, we're going in mine*.

6 Personal pronouns

6.1 Me, you, it, us etc

Personal pronouns replace nouns, as in *'John saw Jill and John spoke to Jill'*. We normally say: *John saw Jill and he spoke to her*. *He* and *her* are the personal pronouns. The most important Spanish personal pronouns are the ones used to translate *me, him, her, us, them* in sentences like *John saw me, Anne bought it, Jenny met them*. These are the 'direct object pronouns' and they stand for the person or thing to whom something is done or happens:

me *me*	**nos** *us*
te *you* (familiar form)	**os** *you* (familiar form)
lo *him, you* (male polite form), or *it*	**los** *them* (masculine), or *you* (male polite form)
la *her, you* (female polite form), or *it*	**las** *them* (feminine), or *you* (female polite form)

■ Note: in Spain, **le** is used for *him/you* (male) instead of **lo**, but **lo** must be used for *it* when it refers to a masculine thing like a book (**el libro**). Latin Americans use only **lo**. Both forms are considered correct, so follow your teacher or course book on this point.

■ **Os** is not used in Latin America. Latin Americans say **los** for males, **las** for females.

■ Personal pronouns come directly before verbs: **me ve** *he/she sees me*, **los veo** *I see them*. However, they are joined to the end of infinitives, gerunds, and imperatives (see below): **quiero verla** *I want to see her*, **estoy haciéndolo** *I'm doing it*, **cómpralo** *buy it*.

6.2 To me, to you, to him, etc

The same forms as above are used: **me da cien euros** *he gives 100 euros to me*, **te manda una carta** *he sends a letter to you*, **nos dicen todo** *they tell everything to us*. These forms are the 'indirect object pronouns'.

Note: There are two indirect object forms, **le** and **les**. **Le** means *to him, to her*, or *to you* (speaking formally). **Les** means *to them* and also *to you* when speaking formally: *le* **dije** *I said to him* or *to her* or *to you* (one person), **les dije** *I said to them* or *to you* (two or more people).

6.3 Order of pronouns

These pronouns can be combined, but the order is indirect object first, then direct object, i.e.

me or **te** or **nos** or **os** first   then **lo**, **la**, **los**, or **las**

Examples: **me lo dan** *they give it to me*, **te lo dicen** *they say it to you*, **nos los mandan** *they send them to us*.

■ The rule of two L's. It is an important rule of Spanish that when **le** or **les** is followed by **lo**, **la**, **los**, or **las**, the **le** or **les** becomes **se**. In other words, two pronouns beginning with L can never stand side-by-side: **se lo doy** *I give it to him/to her/to you*, not 'le lo doy'.

6.4 Subject pronouns

The equivalents of *I, you, he, she, we, they* exist in Spanish, but are not often used, because they are explicit in verb endings: **hablo** already means *I speak*, **vas** means *you go*, **compramos** means *we buy*. In nearly all situations the use of the personal pronouns as in, **yo hablo**, **tú vas**, **nosotros compramos**, is to be avoided, because they are unnecessary. But they are needed sometimes, and their forms are as follows:

yo *I*	**nosotros** (males) *we*,
	nosotras (females) *we*
tú *you* (familiar form)	**vosotros** (to two or more males) *you*,
	vosotras (two or more females) *you*
usted *you* (formal form)	**ustedes** *you* (formal form)
él *he*	**ellos** *they* (males)
ella *she*	**ellas** *they* (females)

■ These words are used: (a) to contrast one person with another: **yo trabajo en casa y ella va a la oficina** *I work at home and she goes to the office.* (b) when there is no following verb: —¿**quién lo hizo?** —*Yo* 'Who did it?' 'I did.'

■ **Vosotros** and **vosotras** are not used in Latin America, where they always say **ustedes** to two or more persons.

■ **Tú** (note the accent) and **vosotros** or **vosotras** are the familiar forms used for people you know well (and anyone of your own age group if you are young), relatives, animals, and children. Nowadays Spaniards use them more and more even to complete strangers as a way of being friendly, but you must use **usted**, **ustedes** to people you do not know well, strangers, officials, policemen, etc.

■ **Usted** and **ustedes** are followed by third-person verb forms (i.e. the forms used for *he* and *they*): **usted habla** = *you speak*, **ustedes hablan** *you* (more than one) *speak*.

6.5 *mí* and *ti*

These are forms meaning *me* and *you* (familiar form) that are used after certain prepositions, e.g. after **de** *of/about*, **contra** *against*, **para** *for*, **por** *because of/on behalf of*, **sin** *without*: **hablamos de ti** *we're talking about you*, **esto es para mí** *this is for me*.

Note: When **con** + **mí** or **con** + **ti** are used together, the words **conmigo** *with me*, and **contigo** *with you* (familiar form) must be used: **Miguel va conmigo** *Miguel is going with me*.

7 Hay: There is; there are

There is and *there are* are both **hay** in Spanish: **hay lobos en España** *there are wolves in Spain*, **no hay pan** *there is no bread*.

There was and *there were* are **había** (never habían): **había lobos en Inglaterra** *there were* (or *there used to be*) *wolves in England*. For completed events in the past Spanish uses **hubo**: **hubo una explosión/un accidente** *there was an explosion/accident*. *There will be* is **habrá**.

8 Ser & estar: to be

Spanish has two important verbs for the English *to be*: **ser** and **estar**. Both are irregular and their forms are given on pages 980 and 974 respectively.

8.1 Ser

Generally **ser** is used to convey the idea of inherent qualities and is used in the following situations: When stating the origin of someone or something:

Es de California.	*He's* or *She's* or *It's from California.*
Es americano.	*He's American.*

When stating the material from which something is made:

Es de plata.	*It's made of silver.*

When stating ownership:

Son de Alfonso.	*They belong to Alfonso.*

When describing someone's characteristics:

Es un señor muy simpático.	*He's a very nice man.*
Es muy aburrido.	*He's very boring.*

When stating one's occupation:

Es abogada.	*She's a lawyer.*
Es aduanero.	*He's a customs officer.*

When expressing identity:

Soy Juan Muñoz.	*I'm Juan Muñoz.*
¿Es usted la Señora Sánchez?	*Are you Mrs Sánchez?*

8.2 Estar

As a general rule **estar** is used in the following circumstances: To indicate location:

Está en la esquina.	*It's on the corner.*
Están en el jardín.	*They're in the garden.*
Está de viaje.	*She's away on a trip.*

To indicate the condition or state something or someone is in:

Las sábanas estaban sucias.	*The sheets were dirty.*
Estaba enferma.	*She was ill.*
Estoy aburrido.	*I'm bored.*
Está enamorado de ella.	*He's in love with her.*
Estaba furiosa.	*She was furious.*
Estoy de muy buen humor.	*I'm in a very good mood.*

8.3 Exceptions and anomalies

Ser is used with the following adjectives: **rico** *rich, wealthy*; **pobre** *poor*; **feliz** *happy*; **desgraciado** *unfortunate*.

Son muy ricos.	*They are very wealthy.*
Somos felices.	*We are happy.*

Marital status. Both verbs can be used in this context. **Ser** is used in formal contexts regarding marital status:

¿Es usted casado o soltero?	*Are you married or single?*
Está casado con mi prima.	*He's married to my cousin.*
Mis padres están divorciados.	*My parents are divorced.*

Ser is used when specifying where an event takes place:

¿Dónde es la fiesta?	*Where is the party?*
La reunión es a las diez.	*The meeting is at ten.*

Ser is used when telling the time:

Es la una.	*It's one o'clock.*
Son las tres.	*It's three o'clock.*

Estar is used with **muerto** *dead* and **vivo** *alive*:

Ya estaba muerta.	*She was already dead.*
Aún está vivo.	*He's still alive.*

- -

9 Question words: how, what, which, when etc

These are written with an accent:

¿cómo? *how?*	**¿cuánto?** *how much?, how many?*	**¿qué?** *what?*
¿cuál? *which?*	**¿de quién?** *whose?*	**¿quién?** *who?*
¿cuándo? *when?*	**¿por qué?** *why?*	

¿Cuál? and **¿quién?** become **¿cuáles?** and **¿quiénes?** when they refer to more than one thing or person: **¿quiénes son?** *who are they?*, **¿cuáles quieres?** *which ones do you want?* **¿Cuánto?** agrees in number and gender with what it refers to: **¿cuánto dinero?** *how much money?*, **¿cuántos clavos?** *how many nails?*, **¿cuántas chicas?** *how many girls?*

- Note: the accented form is used in indirect questions, i.e. when there is no question mark in the sentence: **no sé cuál prefiero** *I don't know which I prefer.*

- Note: the meaning of these words changes when no accent is used: **como** = *as* or *like* (**habla como un niño** = *he talks like a little boy*), **porque** (one word) = *because*, **que** = *that* as in **dice que está enfermo** *he says that he is ill.*

10 Prepositions

These are words placed before nouns and pronouns to link them to the meaning of the rest of the sentence. In general they are used in more or less the same way as their English equivalents except that:

■ **a** basically means *to*, not *at*, which is usually **en** in Spanish: **en la estación** = *in the station* or *at the station*. *At the bus-stop* is **en la parada de autobús**, *at the traffic-lights* is **en el semáforo**. **A** means *at* only when movement is involved, as in **tiró una flecha *al* blanco** *he fired an arrow at the target*.

■ **personal a**: The use of **a** before personal objects of verbs is very important in Spanish. Note carefully the difference between these two sentences: **vi tu casa** *I saw your house*, and **vi *a* tu madre** *I saw your mother*. The **a** is necessary in the second example because the thing seen was a human being. So: **no conozco *a* María** *I don't know María* and **admiro *al* profesor** *I admire the teacher*, but **no conozco la ciudad** *I don't know the city*.

■ **para** and **por**: **para** means *for*, as in **este dinero es para ti** *this money is for you*. **Por** means, among other things, *because of*: **lo hago por amor, no por dinero** *I do it for love not for money* (it really means *because of love, because of money*), **lo hice para ti** = *I made it for you*, **lo hice por ti** = *I did it because of you*. **Para** and **por** have many shades of meaning, which are exemplified at their entries in the Spanish-English section of the dictionary.

11 Verbs

Transitive and intransitive verbs

Verbs may be transitive, i.e. they take a direct object, or they may be intransitive, i.e. they do not take a direct object. In the sentence: *he kicks the ball*, *kicks* is the transitive verb, and the direct object is *ball*. In the sentence: *he is sleeping*, the verb *is sleeping* is intransitive as there is no object. Spanish verbs are also transitive and intransitive and this is information is shown by the abbreviations *vt* for 'verb transitive' and *vi* for 'verb intransitive'. It is important not to use transitive verbs intransitively and vice versa.

Reflexive verbs

These are verbs which have a personal pronoun object which is the same as the subject of the verb, e.g. *I shave myself*. Reflexive verbs are very common in Spanish and are listed in the dictionary with the infinitive followed by **se**, e.g. **lavarse** = *to wash oneself*. Note that in the third person, singular and plural, all genders, the reflexive pronoun is **se**. The following are the most important uses of reflexive verbs in Spanish

- If more than one human or animal is performing the action, it often shows that they are doing the action to one another: **se escriben mucho** *they write to one another a lot.*

- Sometimes the reflexive form is the only form used, as in **me atrevo** *I dare*, or **te arrepientes** *you regret* (having done something).

- If no human agent is involved, then the verb often has to be understood as a 'passive', as the translation shows: **este libro se publicó en Argentina** *this book was published in Argentina*, **se dijeron muchas cosas en la reunión** *many things were said in the meeting.*

- The reflexive form of many verbs alters or intensifies the meaning of the basic verb: **ir** = *to go*, **irse** = *to go away*; **caer** = *to fall*, **caerse** = *to fall over.*

12 Tenses of verbs

12.1 The present tense

English has two ways of describing present actions: compare *I smoke*, which describes a habit, and *I'm smoking*, which shows that you are smoking right now. Spanish is very similar in this respect: **fumo** = *I smoke*, **estoy fumando** = *I am smoking* (right now). However, the second of these forms is used less than in English and the simple form, **fumo**, can be used for both meanings:

—¿Qué haces? —Fumo	*'What are you doing?' 'I'm smoking'*
Hablan mucho	*They talk a lot* or *They are talking a lot*
Vamos al cine	*We go to the movies* or *We're going to the movies*

See 12.6 for the use of the present tense with a future meaning.

12.2 The past tenses

In English there are several different verb forms that can be used to describe events that happened in the past. Compare *I did it, I have done it, I was doing it*, and *I had done it*. Spanish also has several ways of describing past events:

(a) The past simple tense (also referred to as the 'pretérito indefinido' in the verb tables): **hablé** *I spoke*, **llegaron** *they arrived*, **compraste** *you bought.*

(b) The imperfect tense (also referred to as the 'imperfecto' in the verb tables): **hablaba** *I was speaking* or *I used to speak*, **llegaban** *they were arriving* or *they used to arrive*, **comprabas** *you were buying* or *you used to buy.*

(c) The perfect tense: **he hablado** *I have spoken*, **han llegado** *they have arrived*, **has comprado** *you have bought.*

(d) The pluperfect tense: **había hablado** *I had spoken*, **habían llegado** *they had arrived*, **habías comprado** *you had bought.*

• •

The two commonest past tenses in Spanish are the past simple and the imperfect.

12.3 The past simple and the imperfect tenses compared

The past simple is used to describe actions that took place *once* or a *specific number* of times in the past:

Ayer compré una nueva impresora	*Yesterday I bought a new printer*
Ganó la lotería	*He/She won the lottery*
Fue presidente durante tres años	*He was President for three years*
Estuve enfermo hace tres meses	*I was ill three months ago*

The imperfect is used to describe actions, events or processes that were not yet finished at the time we are talking about:

Miguel fumaba demasiado	*Miguel was smoking too much/*
	Miguel used to smoke too much
Mi hermana iba mucho a la disco	*My sister used to go/was going to the disco a lot*
Roberto era alto y moreno	*Roberto was tall and dark*

If an event happened once or a specific number of times the past simple tense is used, regardless of how long it went on for: **los dinosaurios reinaron sobre la tierra durante millones de años** *dinosaurs reigned on earth for millions of years* (it only happened once), **ocurrió más de mil veces** *it happened more than a thousand times* (but it happened a specific number of times). The imperfect must be used when an event is described that was interrupted by another event: **yo dormía cuando empezó la tormenta** *I was sleeping when the storm started*.

12.4 The perfect tense

This tense is formed in Spanish with the present tense of **haber**, and the past participle of the verb, which in Spanish usually ends with **-ado**, **-ido**, or **-isto**, see verb tables pages 971–988. As a rule, whenever you say '*I have been*', '*she has done*', '*we have seen*', etc. in English, you use the parallel tense in Spanish: **he sido, ha hecho, hemos visto**.

Nunca he bebido vodka	*I have never drunk vodka*
He estado tres veces en Chicago	*I've been in Chicago three times*
¿Has visto La guerra de las galaxias?	*Have you seen Star Wars?*

Many Latin Americans replace this tense by the past simple tense described earlier: **nunca bebí vodka, estuve tres veces en Chicago, ¿viste La guerra de las galaxias?** If your teacher is Latin American, imitate him or her on this point.

Note: If you study Peninsular Spanish you will notice a big difference between English and Spanish: the latter often uses the perfect tense for any event that has happened since midnight: **esta mañana me he duchado, he desayunado, he cogido el metro y he llegado aquí a las nueve** *this morning I had a shower, I had breakfast, I took the metro, and I got here at nine o'clock*.

. . . .

12.5 The pluperfect tense

This is almost exactly equivalent to the English tense formed with *had*: *I had seen*, *they had eaten*, **había visto**, **habían comido**. It is used in both languages to show that an event finished before another past event happened: **mamá ya se había ido cuando llegué a casa** *mother had already gone when I got home*, **yo iba a mandarles una tarjeta, pero mi hermano ya lo había hecho** *I was going to send them a card, but my brother had already done it*.

12.6 The future

There are several ways in English and Spanish of talking about future events:

(a) *We're going to arrive tomorrow*   **Vamos a llegar mañana**
    (ir + infinitive)

(b) *We are arriving tomorrow*   **Llegamos mañana**
    (present tense)

(c) *We will arrive tomorrow*   **Llegaremos mañana**
    (future tense)

The first two are more or less the same in both languages. Model (c) involves learning the forms of the future tense, see **hablar** [A1], **meter** [E1] and **partir** [I1] in the verb tables, and is normally used where English uses *will*. It is used above all in promises and forecasts as in **te pagaré el dinero mañana** *I will pay you the money tomorrow*, and **el viernes hará buen tiempo** *the weather will be fine on Friday*.

12.7 The conditional tense

This tense, whose forms are given in the Spanish verb tables at **hablar** [A1], **meter** [E1] and **partir** [I1], is used to talk of an event that *would* happen: **estarías más guapa con el pelo recogido** *you would be more attractive with your hair up*, **en ese caso te costaría menos** *in that case it would cost you less*.

12.8 The imperative

The imperative is used to give orders or to ask someone to do something. The forms of the verb used vary:

■ When addressing one person using the familiar form of *you*, the imperative is formed by dropping the -**s** from the **tú** form of the present tense: **das** = *you give*, so *give* is **da**; similarly **hablas** > **habla** *speak*, **comes** > **come** *eat*. There are eight important exceptions:

decir *to say* **di**	**poner** *to put* **pon**	**tener** *to have* **ten**
hacer *to make* **haz**	**salir** *to go out* **sal**	**venir** *to come* **ven**
ir *to go* **ve**	**ser** *to be* **sé**	

- When addressing one person formally the **usted** form is used, which is the same as the *present subjunctive* form for *he/she*. To speak formally to more than one person the **ustedes** form is used, which is the *they* form of the present subjunctive. These forms are given in the Spanish verb tables, beginning on page 971. Examples: ¡**venga!** *come!*, ¡**conteste!** *answer!*, ¡**vengan!** (plural) *come!*, ¡**contesten!** *answer!* (plural)

- In Spain, when talking informally to more than one person, the **vosotros** form of the imperative is used. This is formed by replacing the -**r** of the infinitive form (the form by which verbs are listed in dictionaries) by -**d**. There are no important exceptions: ¡**venid!** *come!*, ¡**contestad!** *answer!*, ¡**dad!** *give!* This form is never used in Latin America, where the formal **ustedes** form is used instead.

- To tell someone not to do something, the present subjunctive of the verb is used: ¡**no vengas!** (tú), ¡**no venga!** (usted), ¡**no vengan!** (ustedes), ¡**no vengáis!** (vosotros). These all mean *don't come!*, but the form varies in Spanish according to whether you are speaking to one or more people and whether you are using the informal or formal options.

- If we need to add pronouns, for example to translate *give it to her*, *sell me them*, these are added to the end of the imperative. In these examples **lo** and **los** refer to a masculine noun like **libro**, **libros** *book(s)*. Note the accents:

familiar to 1 person	formal to to 1 person	to 2 + people	to 2+ people: (familiar Spain)	
dámelo	**démelo**	**dénmelo**	**dádmelo**	= *give it to me*
mándanoslos	**mándenoslos**	**mándennoslos**	**mandádnoslos**	= *send them to us*

But if the order is negative (i.e. it has **no** in front of it), the pronouns come before the present subjunctive of the verb:

no me lo des	**no me lo dé**	**no me lo den**	**no me lo deis**	= *don't give it to me*

. . . .

13 The gerund (-ando, -iendo forms of verbs)

This form of the Spanish verb always ends in -**ando** or -**iendo** and it never changes. It is used:

- With the verb **estar** to stress the fact that an action is actually going on right now, or was in the middle of happening: **estoy comiendo** *I'm eating* (right now), **estabas durmiendo** *you were* (in the middle of) *sleeping*. It is never used for actions in the future: **voy a Madrid mañana** *I'm going to Madrid tomorrow*.

- To show that another action happens at the same time as the main action: **entré silbando** *I went in whistling*, **María salió llorando de la clase** *María came out of the classroom crying*.

Summary of Spanish grammar

. . . .

14 The subjunctive

The subjunctive is very important in Spanish. The forms of the present subjunctive are given in the Spanish verb tables, beginning on page 971. The present subjunctive is used:

■ To give negative orders, i.e. to tell someone *not* to do something: see section 12.8 on the imperative.

■ In a sentence consisting of a present-tense *negative verb* + **que** + *another verb*, the second verb is in the subjunctive: compare **creo que está enferma** *I think that she is ill* and **no creo que esté enferma** *I don't think that she is ill*.

■ After the present tense of verbs **querer** *want* or **esperar** *hope* + **que**: **quiero que vengas a mi casa** *I want you to come to my house*, **espero que ganes** *I hope you win*. But if the person doing the wanting is the same person that is going to perform the action of the second verb, the infinitive (-**r** form) must be used for the second verb: **quiero ir a mi casa** *I want to go to my house*, **espero ganar** *I hope I'll win/I hope to win*.

■ After emotional reactions followed by **que**: **es una pena que no trabajes más** *it's a shame that you don't work more*, **estoy muy contento de que no haya llovido** *I'm very pleased that it hasn't rained* (**haya** is the present subjunctive of **haber**).

■ After certain words, when the action following them still has not happened. The most important of these are **cuando** *when*, **en cuanto** or **apenas** *as soon as*: **te daré el dinero cuando llegues** *I'll give you the money when you arrive*, **te llamaré apenas encuentre mi agenda** *I'll ring you as soon as I find my diary*.

■ Always after these words: **antes de que** *before*, **para que** *in order to*, **sin que** *without*, **con tal de que** *provided that*: **llegaremos antes de que salga el tren** *we'll arrive before the train leaves*, **te doy el dinero con tal de que me lo devuelvas** *I'll give you the money provided that you give it back to me*.

Índice

Glosario de términos gramaticales

Abreviatura Representación de una palabra de una manera más corta por una o varias de sus letras: **Sr. = Mr**

Acento Mayor énfasis al pronunciar una determinada sílaba dentro de una palabra y representación gráfica (tilde) de dicho énfasis: ca*sa; café*

Adjetivo Palabra que califica o determina a un sustantivo: **un lápiz *rojo* = a *red* pencil, *mi* casa = *my* house**

Adverbio Palabra que modifica a un verbo, a un adjetivo o a otro adverbio: **corrió *rápidamente* = he ran *quickly*; *muy* bonito = *very* pretty; canta *muy* mal = she sings *very* badly**

Agente El que ejecuta la acción del verbo: *el perro* ladra = *the dog* barks; fue descubierta por *Colón* = it was discovered by *Columbus*

Aguda Tratándose de palabras, que llevan el acento en la última sílaba: infor*mar*, re*vés*, ca*mión*

Apócope Pérdida o supresión de uno o más sonidos al final de una palabra: **algún** (alguno), **tan** (tanto)

Artículo Palabra que va antepuesta al sustantivo e indica su género y su número

Artículo definido Es el que se antepone a un sustantivo que ya nos es conocido: **el/la/los/las = the**

Artículo indefinido Es el que se antepone a un sustantivo que no conocemos de antemano: **un/una = a/an**

Aumentativo Palabra formada con un sufijo que indica aumento: grand*ote;* cabez*azo;* simpl*ón*

Cardinal Tratándose de números, que expresan la cantidad entera de elementos de un conjunto: **ocho/nueve/diez = eight/nine/ten**

Comparativo Adjetivo, adverbio o conjunción que expresa una comparación. De superioridad: **más ... (que) = more ... (than)**. De inferioridad: **menos ... (que) = less ... (than)**. De igualdad: **tan/tanto ... como = as ... as**

Complemento directo Ver **Objeto directo**

Complemento indirecto Ver **Objeto indirecto**

Complemento circunstancial Completa el significado de un verbo, expresando una circunstancia de la acción: compré un libro *ayer* = I bought a book *yesterday*

Condicional Tiempo verbal que expresa una acción como posible si algo ocurre: iría = he/she/it would go; comeríamos = we would eat

Concordancia Correspondencia del género y el número de un adjetivo con los de un sustantivo y del número y la persona del verbo con el sujeto de una oración: ga**to** neg**ro**; **los** niñ**os** español**es**; mi marido y yo habla**mos** inglés; Pedro y Juan gana**ron**

Conjugación Serie ordenada de las formas que toma un verbo para expresar modo, tiempo, número y persona y cada uno de los tres tipos de verbos en que se dividen, según la terminación del infinitivo: **-ar, -er, -ir**

Conjunción Palabra que une dos oraciones o dos elementos de una oración: **y = and; porque = because**

Contracción Unión de dos palabras en una sola: **al** (a + el); **del** (de + el)

Demostrativo Tratándose de adjetivos y pronombres, que muestran o señalan algo o a alguien: *esta* mesa = *this* table; *ésta* es mi hermana = *this* is my sister

Diéresis Signo que indica que debe pronunciarse la vocal 'u' de las sílabas 'güe' y 'güi': ci**güe**ña; pin**güi**no

Diminutivo Palabra que se forma con un sufijo que indica menor tamaño, poca importancia o valor afectivo: perr*ito*; doctor*cillo*; abuel*ita*

Esdrújula Palabra que lleva el acento (tilde) en la antepenúltima sílaba: *tráfico*

Estilo directo El que consiste en narrar lo que se ha dicho citando textualmente las palabras del hablante: me dijo: ¡cállate! = he said: be quiet!

Estilo indirecto El que consiste en narrar lo que se ha dicho sin citar textualmente las palabras del hablante: me dijo que me callara = he told me to be quiet

Femenino Género que se aplica a los seres del sexo femenino y el que se atribuye a las cosas por la terminación (-a) o por el uso: la mujer; la perra; la página; la cruz

Frase Unidad dentro de una oración, que tiene sentido y que no tiene verbo

Futuro Tiempo verbal que sitúa la acción en un momento futuro: llegará tarde = he will arrive late

Género Una de las tres categorías gramaticales de los sustantivos, adjetivos, artículos y pronombres: masculino, femenino y neutro

Gentilicio Expresa el lugar de origen o la nacionalidad: londinense = Londoner; español = Spanish

Gerundio Forma verbal que presenta la acción en proceso de ejecución. En español acaba en -ando o -iendo: habl*ando*; com*iendo* y en inglés en -ing: speak*ing*

Grave Tratándose de palabras, que llevan el acento en la penúltima sílaba: *examen; débil*

Imperativo Modo verbal que expresa una orden, un mandato o una petición: ¡ven aquí! = come here!

Imperfecto Tiempo verbal que indica una acción pasada sin que se dé idea de su comienzo o final o una acción pasada habitual: **los niños jugaban = the children were playing; iba allí todos los lunes = I used to go/I went there every Monday**

Indicativo Modo verbal en el que la acción del verbo se considera como un hecho sin aportar otro tipo de matices: **no tengo hambre = I'm not hungry**

Infinitivo Forma no personal del verbo que se construye añadiendo la terminación -ar, -er, -ir, a la raíz: cant*ar* = to sing

Interjección Palabra o expresión exclamativa que expresa una impresión repentina de sorpresa, dolor, alegría, ira etc. o que sirve para llamar la atención: ¡caramba! = good heavens!; ¡ay! = ouch!

Interrogativo Adjetivo, adverbio o pronombre que pregunta algo o acerca de alguien: ¿qué? = what?; ¿cuánto? = how much?; ¿quién? = who?

Locución Combinación fija de dos o más palabras cuyo sentido no es el resultado de la suma de los significados de sus miembros. Equivale con frecuencia a un adjetivo, un adverbio o una preposición: de balde = for free

Masculino Género que se aplica a los seres del sexo masculino y el que se atribuye a las cosas por su terminación (-o) o por el uso: el hombre; el perro; el pelo; el árbol

Modo Conjunto de determinadas formas de un verbo que manifiesta la actitud del hablante respecto de lo que está diciendo, diferente según se trate del modo indicativo, modo subjuntivo o modo imperativo.

Negativo Que contiene un adverbio de negación

Neutro Uno de los tres géneros del español, que no es ni masculino ni femenino: **eso es lo bueno de esto = that's the good thing about this**

Nombre Ver **Sustantivo**

Nombre propio Es el que se aplica a una persona, lugar, institución, etc., y se escribe con mayúscula: **Juan, España, London**

No numerable Se aplica a los sustantivos que no se pueden contar y por lo tanto no se usan en plural: **tristeza = sadness; solidaridad = solidarity**

Numerable Se aplica a los sustantivos que se pueden contar, o sea, que se pueden usar en singular o en plural: **una, dos, tres casas** etc. = one, two, three houses etc

Número Indica si un elemento es singular o plural

Objeto Palabra o conjunto de palabras que designa a la persona, el animal o la cosa sobre la que recae la acción del verbo

Objeto directo Es aquel sobre el que recae directamente la acción del verbo: **compré un libro = I bought a book**

Objeto indirecto Es aquel sobre el que recae indirectamente la acción del verbo: **le escribí una carta a mi madre = I wrote a letter to my mother**

Oración Conjunto de palabras que tiene un sentido gramatical completo, con sujeto y predicado y que se puede comprender sin necesidad de otras explicaciones o referencias.

Oración subordinada es la que depende de la principal, a la que completa o determina: **quiero que estudies = I want you to study**

Ordinal Tratándose de números, que indican el orden o la colocación en una serie, como **primero = first; quinto = fifth; undécimo = eleventh**

Parte de la oración Cada uno de los términos gramaticales con los que se designa la función que una palabra desempeña en una oración: sustantivo, verbo, adjetivo, etc., son todos partes de la oración

Participio pasado Parte del verbo que se utiliza para formar tiempos compuestos, expresando una acción acabada, Se utiliza también como adjetivo: **he terminado = I have finished; un producto terminado = a finished product**

Pasiva Ver **Voz pasiva**

Pasiva refleja Oración con significado pasivo que se forma con el pronombre 'se' y el verbo en tercera persona en voz activa y sin agente expreso: **se construyeron muchas casas = many houses were built**

Persona Cualquiera de los tres grupos de pronombres personales y de las formas verbales que designan al individuo que habla o primera persona (p.ej. **yo/I**); al individuo al que se habla o segunda persona (p.ej. **tú** o **Ud/you**); al individuo del cual se habla o tercera persona (p.ej. **él** o **ella/he** o **she**)

Plural Número de los sustantivos, adjetivos etc., cuando se refieren a más de una cosa o persona: **las casas = the houses**

Posesivo Tratándose de pronombres (p.ej. **mío/tuyo = mine/yours**) o de adjetivos (p.ej. **mi/tu = my/your**), que indican pertenencia o posesión

Glosario de términos gramaticales

Predicado Parte de la oración que dice algo del sujeto y cuyo núcleo es el verbo: **Ana** *estudia mucho* = Ana *studies a lot*

Prefijo Letra o grupo de letras que se antepone a una palabra y que modifica su sentido: *i*legible; *ante*sala

Preposición Palabra invariable que establece una relación entre otras dos palabras en una oración: **con** = with; **sin** = without

Presente Tiempo verbal que indica que algo sucede en el momento en que se habla: *abro* la puerta = *I open* the door

Pretérito Tiempo verbal que indica que la acción ya ha ocurrido o pertenece al pasado.

Pretérito imperfecto ver **Imperfecto**

Pretérito indefinido Tiempo simple que indica una acción pasada completa y acabada: **se despertó** = he woke up

Pretérito perfecto Tiempo compuesto que indica que una acción, comenzada en el pasado, dura hasta el presente o tiene efectos todavía o bien que sucedió inmediatamente antes del momento presente: **he aprendido mucho/ha salido** = I have learnt a lot/he has gone out

Pretérito pluscuamperfecto Tiempo compuesto que indica una acción pasada y terminada, anterior a otra también pasada: **se había marchado** = he had left

Pronombre Palabra que sustituye o determina a un sustantivo o nombre: p.ej. **él/ella** = he/she; **alguien** = someone; **el mío/la mía** = mine

Pronombre personal Es el que se refiere a una persona o a una cosa: p.ej. **yo/tú/usted** etc.= I/you etc; **me/te** = me/you etc.

Pronombre reflexivo Es el que representa al sujeto y es parte de un verbo pronominal: **me/te/se/nos/os/se**

Pronombre relativo Es el que representa en una oración subordinada a una persona o a una cosa mencionada en la principal: **el hombre** *que* **nos visitó** = the man *who* visited us

Raíz Parte de una palabra que es común a todas las de la misma familia: *com*- es la raíz de *com*eré y *com*ida

Singular Número de los sustantivos, adjetivos etc., cuando se refieren a una sola persona o cosa: **la casa** = the house

Sintagma Sección, dentro de una oración, que constituye una unidad aislable

Sobresdrújula Tratándose de palabras, que llevan el acento en la sílaba anterior a la antepenúltima: *tí*ramelo

Subjuntivo Modo verbal que expresa idea de duda, posibilidad, deseo etc., y que se usa especialmente en oraciones subordinadas: **espero que** *venga* = I hope he will come; **si** *fuera* **posible** = if it *was* o *were* possible

Sufijo Letra o grupo de letras que se añade a una palabra o a su raíz para formar otra palabra:

cafe*tera*; fru*tería*; cas*ita*

Sujeto Palabra o conjunto de palabras que disigna a la persona, el animal o la cosa que realiza la acción del verbo: *Inés* **estudia geografía** = *Inés* studies geography; **el mío corre más rápido** = *mine* runs faster

Superlativo Grado máximo de significación de un adjetivo o de un adverbio: **la casa más pequeña de la calle** = the smallest house in the street; **muchísimo** = very much

Sustantivo Palabra que nombra a las personas o a las cosas materiales e inmateriales: **silla** = chair

Sustantivo colectivo Es el que en singular se refiere a un conjunto, p.ej: **ejército, rebaño**

Sustantivo compuesto Es el que está formado de dos palabras, p.ej: **aeropuerto (aero + puerto)** = airport

Terminación Letra o conjunto de letras que siguen a la raíz de un vocablo para formar tiempos verbales, el plural de los sustantivos, diminutivos, etc.

Verbo Palabra o conjunto de palabra que describe una acción o un estado: **Los niños están jugando** = the children are playing

Verbo auxiliar Es el que se une a otro para formar los tiempos compuestos o para expresar distintos matices, p.ej.: **haber, estar, poder: he comido** = I *have* eaten

Verbo impersonal Es el que no admite sujeto, p.ej.: **llover: está lloviendo** = it is raining

Verbo intransitivo Es el que no tiene complemento u objeto directo: **murió repentinamente** = he died suddenly

Verbo irregular Es el que no sigue un modelo sistemático, sino que tiene su propias formas individuales de conjugación

Verbo pronominal Es el que se conjuga en todas sus formas con los pronombres **me/te/se/os/se**, p.ej. **equivocarse**

Verbo reflexivo Es el verbo pronominal que expresa una acción que es realizada y recibida por su propio sujeto: **se lavó** = he washed himself

Verbo recíproco Es el verbo pronominal cuya acción se intercambia entre dos o más sujetos y recae sobre todos ellos, p.ej. **besarse: Pedro y Ana se besaron** = Pedro and Ana kissed each other

Verbo regular Es aquél cuya conjugación se ajusta a la de los verbos que se toman como modelo

Voz activa Indica que el sujeto del verbo es el agente de la acción: **Pedro** *besa* **a Ana** = Pedro *kisses* Ana

Voz pasiva Indica que el sujeto recibe la acción del verbo y el agente se introduce por la preposición "por", no es muy usual en español: **Ana** *es besada* **por Pedro**

Los verbos irregulares ingleses

Las formas irregulares que solo se usan en algunas acepciones se indican con un asterisco (e.g. *abode).

La información completa acerca del uso, la pronunciación, etc., de cada verbo se encontrará en el artículo correspondiente.

infinitive/ infinitivo	past tense/ pretérito	past participle/ participio pasado	infinitive/ infinitivo	past tense/ pretérito	past participle/ participio pasado
abide	abided, *abode	abided, *abode	deal	dealt	dealt
arise	arose	arisen	dig	dug	dug
awake	awoke	awoken	dive	dived, (AmE also) dove	dived
be	was/were	been			
bear	bore	borne	do	did	done
beat	beat	beaten	draw	drew	drawn
become	became	become	dream	dreamed, (BrE also) dreamt	dreamed, (BrE also) dreamt
befall	befell	befallen			
beget	begot, (arch) begat	begotten			
begin	began	begun	drink	drank	drunk
behold	beheld	beheld	drive	drove	driven
bend	bent	bent	dwell	dwelt, dwelled	dwelt, dwelled
beseech	beseeched, besought	beseeched, besought	eat	ate	eaten
			fall	fell	fallen
beset	beset	beset	feed	fed	fed
bet	bet	bet	feel	felt	felt
bid	*bade, bid	*bidden, bid	fight	fought	fought
bind	bound	bound	find	found	found
bite	bit	bitten	flee	fled	fled
bleed	bled	bled	fling	flung	flung
bless	blessed	blessed, (arch) blest	floodlight	floodlit	floodlit
			fly	flew	flown
blow	blew	blown, *blowed	forbid	forbade, forbad	forbidden
break	broke	broken	forecast	forecast, forecasted	forecast, forecasted
breed	bred	bred			
bring	brought	brought	foresee	foresaw	foreseen
broadcast	broadcast	broadcast	foretell	foretold	foretold
browbeat	browbeat	browbeaten	forget	forgot	forgotten
build	built	built	forgive	forgave	forgiven
burn	burned, burnt	burned, burnt	forsake	forsook	forsaken
bust	busted, (BrE also) bust	busted, (BrE also) bust	freeze	froze	frozen
			get	got	got, (AmE also) gotten
buy	bought	bought	give	gave	given
cast	cast	cast	go	went	gone
catch	caught	caught	grind	ground	ground
choose	chose	chosen	grow	grew	grown
cling	clung	clung	hang	*hung, *hanged	*hung, *hanged
come	came	come	have	had	had
cost	*cost, *costed	*cost, *costed	hear	heard	heard
creep	crept	crept	hew	hewed	hewn, hewed
crow	crowed	crowed	hide	hid	hidden, (arch) hid
cut	cut	cut			

infinitive/ infinitivo	past tense/ pretérito	past participle/ participio pasado	infinitive/ infinitivo	past tense/ pretérito	past participle/ participio pasado
hit	hit	hit	outshine	outshone	outshone
hold	held	held	overbid	overbid	overbid
hurt	hurt	hurt	overcome	overcame	overcome
inlay	inlaid	inlaid	overdo	overdid	overdone
input	input, inputted	input, inputted	overdraw	overdrew	overdrawn
interweave	interwove, interweaved	interwoven, interweaved	overeat	overate	overeaten
			overfly	overflew	overflown
keep	kept	kept	overhang	overhung	overhung
kneel	kneeled, knelt	kneeled, knelt	overhear	overheard	overheard
knit	knitted, *knit	knitted, *knit	overlay	overlaid	overlaid
know	knew	known	overlie	overlay	overlain
lay	laid	laid	overpay	overpaid	overpaid
lead	led	led	override	overrode	overridden
lean	leaned, (BrE also) leant	leaned, (BrE also) leant	overrun	overran	overrun
			oversee	oversaw	overseen
			overshoot	overshot	overshot
leap	leaped, (BrE also) leapt	leaped, (BrE also) leapt	oversleep	overslept	overslept
			overtake	overtook	overtaken
			overthrow	overthrew	overthrown
learn	learned, (BrE also) learnt	learned, (BrE also) learnt	partake	partook	partaken
			pay	paid	paid
leave	left	left	plead	pleaded, (AmE also) pled	pleaded, (AmE also) pled
lend	lent	lent			
let	let	let	prove	proved	proved, proven
lie (yacer etc)	lay	lain	put	put	put
light	lighted, lit	lighted, lit	quit	quit, quitted	quit, quitted
lose	lost	lost	read /riːd/	read /red/	read /red/
make	made	made	rend	rent	rent
mean	meant	meant	rid	rid	rid
meet	met	met	ride	rode	ridden
miscast	miscast	miscast	ring	rang	rung
misdeal	misdealt	misdealt	rise	rose	risen
mishear	misheard	misheard	run	ran	run
mishit	mishit	mishit	saw	sawed	sawed, (esp BrE) sawn
mislay	mislaid	mislaid			
mislead	misled	misled	say	said	said
misread /ˌmɪsˈriːd/	misread /ˌmɪsˈred/	misread /ˌmɪsˈred/	see	saw	seen
			seek	sought	sought
misspell	misspelled, (BrE also) misspelt	misspelled, (BrE also) misspelt	sell	sold	sold
			send	sent	sent
			set	set	set
misspend	misspent	misspent	sew	sewed	sewn, sewed
mistake	mistook	mistaken	shake	shook	shaken
misunderstand	misunderstood	misunderstood	shear	sheared	*shorn, *sheared
mow	mowed	mown, mowed			
outbid	outbid	outbid, (AmE also) outbidden	shed	shed	shed
			shine	*shone, *shined	*shone, *shined
			shit	shit, shat	shit, shat
outdo	outdid	outdone	shoe	shod	shod
outfight	outfought	outfought	shoot	shot	shot
outgrow	outgrew	outgrown	show	showed	shown, showed
output	output, outputted	output, outputted	shrink	shrank, shrunk	shrunk, shrunken
outrun	outran	outrun	shut	shut	shut
outsell	outsold	outsold	sing	sang	sung
			sink	sank	sunk

Los verbos irregulares ingleses

infinitive/ infinitivo	past tense/ pretérito	past participle/ participio pasado	infinitive/ infinitivo	past tense/ pretérito	past participle/ participio pasado
sit	sat	sat	swim	swam	swum
slay	slew	slain	swing	swung	swung
sleep	slept	slept	take	took	taken
slide	slid	slid	teach	taught	taught
sling	slung	slung	tear	tore	torn
slink	slunk	slunk	tell	told	told
slit	slit	slit	think	thought	thought
smell	smelled, (BrE also) smelt	smelled, (BrE also) smelt	thrive	thrived, (liter) throve	thrived, (arch) thriven
sow	sowed	sowed, sown	throw	threw	thrown
speak	spoke	spoken	thrust	thrust	thrust
speed	*sped, *speeded	*sped, *speeded	tread	trod	trodden, trod
spell	spelled, (BrE also) spelt	spelled, (BrE also) spelt	typecast	typecast	typecast
			typeset	typeset	typeset
spend	spent	spent	typewrite	typewrote	typewritten
spill	spilled, spilt	spilled, spilt	undercut	undercut	undercut
spin	spun, (arch) span	spun	undergo	underwent	undergone
			underlie	underlay	underlain
spit	spat, (esp AmE) spit	spat, (esp AmE) spit	undersell	undersold	undersold
			understand	understood	understood
split	split	split	undertake	undertook	undertaken
spoil	spoiled, (BrE also) spoilt	spoiled, (BrE also) spoilt	undo	undid	undone
			unstick	unstuck	unstuck
			unwind	unwound	unwound
spread	spread	spread	uphold	upheld	upheld
spring	sprang, (AmE also) sprung	sprung	upset	upset	upset
			wake	woke	woken
			waylay	waylaid	waylaid
			wear	wore	worn
stand	stood	stood	weave	wove, *weaved	woven, *weaved
steal	stole	stolen	wed	wedded, wed	wedded, wed
stick	stuck	stuck	weep	wept	wept
sting	stung	stung	wet	wet, wetted	wet, wetted
stink	stank, stunk	stunk	win	won	won
strew	strewed	strewn, strewed	wind (dar cuerda, etc.)	wound	wound
stride	strode	stridden			
strike	struck	struck	withdraw	withdrew	withdrawn
string	strung	strung	withhold	withheld	withheld
strive	strove	striven	withstand	withstood	withstood
sublet	sublet	sublet	work	worked, *wrought	worked, *wrought
swear	swore	sworn			
sweat	sweated, (AmE also) sweat	sweated, (AmE also) sweat	wring	wrung	wrung
			write	wrote	written
sweep	swept	swept			
swell	swelled	swollen, (esp AmE) swelled			

Resumen de la gramática inglesa

1 El artículo

1.1 El artículo indeterminado

El artículo indeterminado es **a** si la palabra que sigue empieza con una consonante. Nótese que el sonido de la *u* inicial de *union* no es vocálico (/juː/).

a ball una pelota **a girl** una niña **a union** una unión

Es *an* delante de una vocal o de *h* muda:

an apple una manzana **an hour** una hora

Nótese el uso del artículo en los siguientes casos:

con profesiones

She is a doctor. Es médico. **He is an engineer.** Es ingeniero.

después de una preposición:

She works as a tour guide.
Trabaja de guía turística.

Anna has gone out without an umbrella.
Ana ha salido sin paraguas.

con sentido genérico:

A hare is larger than a rabbit.
La liebre es más grande que el conejo.

1.2 El artículo determinado

El artículo determinado es *the*, tanto para el singular como para el plural:

the cat	**the cats**	**the frog**	**the frogs**
el gato	los gatos	la rana	las ranas

El artículo determinado no se usa por lo general en los siguientes casos:

con instituciones:

I don't go to church.
No voy a la iglesia.

He's starting school next week.
Empieza el colegio la próxima semana.

Cuando se hace referencia al edificio, el sustantivo va acompañado del artículo: **Turn right at the school** (= Al llegar al colegio, gire a la derecha).

con los nombres de las comidas:

Breakfast is at 8.30.
El desayuno es a las 8.30.

Dinner is ready!
¡La cena está lista!

para referirse a cosas abstractas:

Hatred is a destructive force.
El odio es una fuerza destructora.

The book is on English grammar.
Es un libro de gramática inglesa.

delante de las estaciones del año:

Spring is here!
¡Ha llegado la primavera!

It's like winter today.
Hoy hace de invierno.

con los nombres de calles, parques, etc.:

a concert in Central Park
un concierto en Central Park

I work in Bath Street
Trabajo en la calle Bath

Los nombres de ríos y océanos y nombres geográficos plurales van acompañados por regla general del artículo determinado:

the Thames   **the Pacific**   **the Alps**
el Támesis   el Pacífico   los Alpes

2 El plural

El plural de los sustantivos se indica por lo general añadiendo una -s al final de la palabra:

dog, dogs (= perros)   **tape, tapes** (= cintas)

-es se añade a las palabras que terminan en -s, -x, -ch o -sh:

dress, dresses (= vestidos)   **box, boxes** (= cajas)
hatch, hatches (= cubiertas)   **splash, splashes** (= salpicaduras)

Los nombres que terminan en consonante + y: **baby, babies** (= bebés)
Los nombres que terminan en vocal + y: **volley, volleys** (= voleas)
Los nombres que terminan en -o a veces añaden -s, a veces -es:

potato, potatoes (= patatas)   **hero, heroes** (= héroes)
tomato, tomatoes (= tomates)   **zero, zeros** (= ceros)

El plural de los nombres que terminan en -f(e) es de dos tipos:

life, lives (= vidas)   **dwarf, dwarfs/dwarves** (= enanos)   **roof, roofs/rooves** (= tejados)

Plurales irregulares frecuentes:

child, children (= niños)   **foot, feet** (= pies)   **man, men** (= hombres)
mouse, mice (= ratones)   **tooth, teeth** (= dientes)   **woman, women** (= mujeres)

3 El femenino

El inglés tiene un número relativamente bajo de palabras con forma femenina. Algunos ejemplos de sustantivos femeninos son: **actress** (= actriz); **widow** (= viuda); **heiress** (= heredera). Pero normalmente el sustantivo no especifica el género: **cousin** (= primo o prima); **friend** (= amigo o amiga); **doctor** (= médico o médica). Si es necesario especificar el sexo de la persona a la que nos estamos refiriendo, hay que decir por ejemplo, **a male student** (= un estudiante), **a woman doctor** (= una médica).

4 El genitivo sajón

Las reglas de uso del genitivo son las siguientes:

-'s se añade a los nombres que están en singular:

the boy's book (= el libro del niño)

el apóstrofo solo (') se añade a los nombres que están en plural y terminan en -*s*:

the boys' room (= la habitación de los niños)
the boys' books (= los libros de los niños)

Si el plural de un nombre no termina en -*s*, el genitivo se forma añadiendo -'*s*:

the children's toys (= los juguetes de los niños)

Los nombres propios que terminan en -s, pueden formar el genitivo de las dos maneras -'*s* y *s*':

Keats's poetry o **Keats' poetry** (= la poesía de Keats).

El genitivo se usa sobre todo con nombres de personas, animales (especialmente domésticos) y países: **Andrew's house** (= la casa de Andrew), **the lion's den** (= la guarida del león), **America's foreign policy** (= la política exterior de Estados Unidos).

Debe tenerse en cuenta los siguientes usos del genitivo:

We're going to Anne's. Vamos a casa de Anne.
I got it at the baker's/the chemist's. Lo compré en la panadería/farmacia.

En inglés coloquial es frecuente el uso del "genitivo doble":

He's a friend of my brother's. Es un amigo de mi hermano.

5 El adjetivo

Los adjetivos ingleses tienen sólo una forma, no concuerdan ni en género ni en número con el sustantivo al que modifican:

an old man   **three old women**
un anciano   tres ancianas

5.1 Posición del adjetivo

El adjetivo generalmente va delante del sustantivo: **a long story** (= una historia larga) o después del verbo: **this story is long** (= esta historia es larga).

Algunos adjetivos sólo pueden preceder al sustantivo que modifican y no constituir el predicado de una oración. Estos adjetivos van precedidos por el indicador (*before n*), véanse **adoptive**, **laico -ca**.

5.2 Grados del adjetivo

Hay tres grados de intensidad: el grado positivo, el comparativo y el superlativo.

Los adjetivos de una sílaba forman el comparativo añadiendo -(*e*)*r* y el superlativo añadiendo -(*e*)*st*:

dull aburrido   **duller** más aburrido   **dullest** el más aburrido
big grande   **bigger** más grande   **biggest** el más grande
nice amable   **nicer** más amable   **nicest** el más amable

Nótese que si el adjetivo termina en consonante sencilla, se dobla la

• •

consonante final.

Los adjetivos de tres sílabas forman el comparativo usando **more** y el superlativo usando **most**:

generous generoso   **more generous**   **most generous**

Lo dicho se aplica también a algunos adjetivos de dos sílabas, p. ej. **useful** útil.

Sin embargo, no existe una regla para los adjetivos de dos sílabas, aunque se suele añadir -*er*, -*est* para formar el comparativo y superlativo respectivamente de los adjetivos que terminan en -*y*, -*le*, -*ow*, -*er*.

Ejemplos:

pretty bonito   **prettier**   **prettiest**

(Nótese que la -*y* se sustituye por -*ie*-)

narrow estrecho	**narrower**	**narrowest**
curious curioso	**more curious**	**most curious**

Para el gerundio y el participio pasado, se usa **more/most**:

boring aburrido	**more boring**	**most boring**
bored aburrido	**more bored**	**most bored**

Most se puede usar como sinónimo de "very" (= muy): **That was a most interesting story** (= Esa fue una historia muy interesante).

Algunos adjetivos de uso frecuente tienen comparativos y superlativos irregulares:

bad malo	**worse** peor	**worst** pésimo, el peor
good bueno	**better** mejor	**best** óptimo, el mejor
little poco	**less** menos	**least** el menos
many/much mucho	**more** más	**most** el más
far lejos	**farther/further**	**farthest/furthest**
old[1] viejo	**elder**	**eldest** (se usa sólo para personas)

[1]La forma regular (*old*, *older*, *oldest* = viejo, más viejo, el más viejo) se usa tanto para personas como para cosas.

Las comparaciones de inferioridad se forman usando **less/least**:

expensive caro   **less expensive** menos caro   **least expensive** el menos caro

5.3 Los adjetivos posesivos

Los adjetivos posesivos son:

my mi, mis, mío, mía, míos, mías	**our** nuestro, nuestra, nuestros, nuestras
your tu, tus, tuyo, tuya, tuyos, tuyas	**your** vuestro, vuestra, vuestros, vuestras
his, her, its su, sus, suyo, suya, suyos, suyas	**their** su, sus, suyo, suya, suyos, suyas

Concuerdan con el poseedor y no con la cosa poseída:

his mother su madre (= la madre del niño)
her mother su madre (= la madre de la niña)
their mother su madre (= la madre de los niños, o de las niñas, o de los niños y de las niñas)

Tienen la misma forma para los nombres en singular y en plural:

my cat mi gato   **my boots** mis botas

. . . .

6 El adverbio

Muchos adverbios se forman añadiendo el sufijo *-ly* al adjetivo: **sad**, **sadly**
triste, tristemente; **brave**, **bravely** valiente, valientemente; **careful**,
carefully cuidado, cuidadosamente

Los adverbios pueden modificar los adjetivos:

The job was *extremely* dangerous. El trabajo era muy peligroso.

los verbos:

He finished *quickly*. Terminó enseguida.

u otros adverbios:

***very* quickly** muy rápido

Nótese que se producen algunos cambios ortográficos y fonéticos: **ready**,
readily listo, fácilmente; **true**, **truly** verdadero, verdaderamente; **due**, **duly**
debido, debidamente; **whole**, **wholly** entero, enteramente.

Algunos adverbios comunes tienen la misma forma que el adjetivo
correspondiente; por ejemplo **back** atrás, **early** pronto, **far** lejos, **fast**
rápidamente, **left** a la izquierda, **little** poco, **more** más, **much** mucho, **only**
solamente, **right** correctamente, a la derecha, **still** todavía, **straight** en
línea recta, directamente, **well** bien, **wrong** incorrectamente, mal.
Ejemplos:

a wrong answer (adjetivo) una respuesta incorrecta	**He did it wrong.** (adverbio) Lo hizo mal
an early summer un verano temprano	**Summer has arrived early.** El verano ha llegado pronto.
a straight road una carretera recta	**He came straight to the point.** Fue directamente al grano.

. . . .

7 Los pronombres

7.1 Los pronombres personales

Sujeto	Complemento
I yo	**me** me
you tú, usted	**you** te
he él	**him** le
she ella	**her** la, le
one uno, una	**one** uno, una
it ello	**it** lo
we nosotros, nosotras	**us** nos
you vosotros, vosotras, ustedes	**you** os
they ellos, ellas	**them** los, las, les

Nótese que el pronombre personal sujeto **I** siempre se escribe con
mayúscula.

El pronombre nunca se puede omitir en inglés cuando tiene función de
sujeto, por consiguiente, la traducción del español de *voy* es **I go**, de *vamos*
we go.

Los pronombres complemento se usan como complemento directo:

Mary loves *him*. Mary lo quiere.

como complemento indirecto:

John gave it to *me*. John me lo dio (a mí).

y después de una preposición:

The book is from *her*. El libro es de su parte.

7.1.1 Otros usos de los pronombres personales

he y she

Estos pronombres se usan para referirse a animales, sobre todo a los domésticos:

Poor Whiskers, we had to take him to the vet's.
Pobrecito Whiskers, tuvimos que llevarlo al veterinario.

it

Se usa en construcciones impersonales:

It's sunny.	**It's hard to know what to do.**	**It looks as though they were right.**
Hace sol.	Es difícil saber qué hacer.	Parece que tenían razón.

En expresiones de tiempo y de distancia en el espacio:

It's five o'clock.	**It's January the sixth.**	**How far is it to Edinburgh?**
Son las cinco.	Es el seis de enero.	¿A qué distancia está Edimburgo?

Nótese que *it's* es la contracción de *it is*, y por consiguiente sigue el modelo de otras contracciones como: *he's, she's, isn't, wasn't* etc. No debe confundirse con el pronombre posesivo *its*, que sigue el modelo de los otros posesivos: *his, hers, ours, yours, theirs*.

you

Para referirse a una persona, el inglés no distingue entre el pronombre *tú* y el pronombre de cortesía *usted*, ambos se traducen por *you*.

You se usa a menudo en sentido genérico, para referirse a la gente en general:

You never know.	**You can't buy cars like that any more.**
Nunca se sabe.	Ya no se pueden comprar coches así.

they

Se usa para referirse a una persona o a un grupo de personas desconocidas, especialmente dotados de cierto poder, autoridad o habilidad:

They don't make cars like that any more.	**You'll have to get them to repair it.**
Ya no fabrican coches así.	Tendrás que decirles que lo arreglen.
They will have to find the murderer first.	
Primero tendrán que encontrar al asesino.	

En lugar de *he* o *she* (él o ella):

The person appointed will be answerable to the director. They (= he/she) **will be responsible for …**
La persona que nombren tendrá que rendir cuentas al director. Será responsable de …

Para referirse a los pronombres indefinidos *somebody, someone* alguien; *anybody, anyone* alguien; *everybody, everyone* todos; *nobody, no one* nadie:

If anyone has seen my pen, will they please tell me.

Si alguien ha visto mi pluma, por favor que me lo diga.

one

One equivale al pronombre genérico *you*, pero es más formal:

One needs to get a clearer picture of what one wants.
Uno necesita tener una idea más clara de lo que quiere.

7.2 Pronombres reflexivos

myself me	**ourselves** nos
yourself te	**yourselves** os
himself, herself, itself, oneself se	**themselves** se

Los pronombres reflexivos tienen varias funciones, ejemplos:

He burned himself badly. (complemento directo)
Se quemó gravemente.

I always buy myself a Christmas present. (complemento indirecto)
Siempre me compro un regalo de Navidad.

She talks to herself. (después de preposición)
Habla sola, habla consigo misma.

Do it yourself. (enfático)
Hazlo tú mismo.

7.3 Pronombres posesivos

mine el mío, la mía, los míos, las mías
yours el tuyo, la tuya, los tuyos, las tuyas
his, hers, its el suyo, la suya, los suyos, las suyas
ours el nuestro, la nuestra, los nuestros, las nuestras
yours el vuestro, la vuestra, los vuestros, las vuestras
theirs el suyo, la suya, los suyos, las suyas

Los pronombres posesivos concuerdan con el poseedor y no con la cosa poseída:

Whose book is this? – It's hers. ¿De quién es este libro? – Es suyo/Es de ella.
Whose shoes are these? – They are hers. ¿De quién son estos zapatos? – Son suyos/Son de ella.
Whose car is that? – It's theirs. ¿De quién es ese coche? – Es suyo/Es de ellos.

8 Los adjetivos y los pronombres interrogativos

who quién, quiénes	**which** cuál, cuáles, qué
whom a quién, a quiénes	**whose** de quién, de quiénes
what qué	

who se usa para personas como sujeto: **Who is it?** ¿Quién es?

whom se usa para personas como complemento:

To whom did you send the letter? **Whom did you see?**
¿A quién enviaste la carta? ¿A quién viste?

Whom se considera muy formal y se suele sustituir por **who**:

Who did you send the letter to? **Who did you see?**
¿A quién enviaste la carta? ¿A quién viste?

whose es la forma genitiva de *who*:

· ·

Whose are these?
¿De quién/de quiénes son éstos?

Whose socks are these?
¿De quién son estos calcetines?

which puede referirse a personas o a cosas. Se usa como sujeto:

Which of you are going?
¿Cuál *or* quién de ustedes va a ir?

Which is bigger?
¿Cuál es más grande?

y como complemento:

Which of the singers/pictures do you prefer?
De los cuadros/cantantes ¿cuál prefieres?/¿Qué cantante/cuadro prefieres?

Which dress should I wear?
¿Qué vestido me pongo?

what se usa sólo para cosas. Puede desempeñar la función de sujeto:

What is this?
¿Qué es esto?

What type of bird is that?
¿Qué clase de pájaro es ése?

y de complemento:

What are you going to do?
¿Qué vas a hacer?

What sort of books do you like?
¿Qué tipo de libros te gustan?

· ·

9 Los pronombres relativos

Los pronombres relativos hacen referencia normalmente a un antecedente.
En **She phoned the man who had contacted her** (= Llamó por teléfono al
señor que la había llamado), el pronombre relativo *who* (= que) se refiere a
the man (= al señor).

antecedente	sujeto	complemento
PERSONA	**who/that** que, quien	**whom/who/that** que, quien
COSA	**which/that** que	**which/that** que

9.1 Who, that

9.1.1 Para personas: con función de sujeto

who es el pronombre relativo que se usa generalmente en este caso; también
se puede usar *that*:

There is a prize for the student who/that gets the highest marks.
Hay un premio para el estudiante que saque las mejores notas.

9.1.2 Para personas: con función de complemento

The man who/that/whom she met that night was a spy.
El hombre que conoció aquella noche era un espía.

Whom se considera muy formal y se suele sustituir por **who** o **that**.

El pronombre relativo se suele omitir cuando tiene función de complemento:

The man (who/that) she met last night was a spy.
El hombre que conoció ayer por la noche era un espía.

9.2 Which, that

9.2.1 Para cosas: con función de sujeto

The book, which is on the table, was a present.
El libro que está encima de la mesa fue un regalo.

● ●

John gave me the book which/that is on the table.
John me regaló el libro que está encima de la mesa.

9.2.2 Para cosas: con función de complemento

His latest film, which we went to see last week, is excellent.
Su última película, que fuimos a ver la semana pasada, es fenomenal.

The film which/that we went to see last week was excellent.
La película que fuimos a ver la semana pasada es fenomenal.

Nótese que en el último ejemplo también se puede omitir el pronombre relativo:

The film (which/that) we went to see last week was excellent.

9.3 Whose

Whose es la forma genitiva:

This is the boy whose dog has been killed.
Este es el niño al que le mataron el perro.

Nótese que *who's* es la contracción de *who is*, y no debe confundirse con el pronombre relativo *whose*.

● ●

10 Los adjetivos y los pronombres indefinidos

10.1 Some, any

Como adjetivos, se usan con sustantivos plurales o no contables:

Take some boxes.
Coge unas cajas.

Have some butter.
Toma mantequilla.

Do you have any nails?
¿Tienes clavos?

Have you any jam?
¿Tienes mermelada?

Como pronombres, sustituyen a los sustantivos plurales o no contables:

We haven't got any. No tenemos.

10.2 Some

Some (adjetivo y pronombre) se usa en: Frases afirmativas:

He bought some.
Compró algunos/algunas.

He bought some jam.
Compró mermelada.

He bought some screws.
Compró tornillos.

Preguntas cuando se espera una respuesta afirmativa:

Can you lend me some money? ¿Puedes prestarme dinero?

Para ofrecer o solicitar algo:

Would you like some?
¿Quieres?

Could you buy some onions for me?
¿Podrías comprarme cebollas?

10.3 Any

Any (adjetivo y pronombre) se usa en: Frases negativas:

I haven't got any brothers or sisters. No tengo hermanos.

Preguntas:

Do you have any bananas?
¿Tiene plátanos?

Do you have any sugar?
¿Tienes azúcar?

• •

Los compuestos con *any* y *some* se usan de forma similar. Ejemplos:

I saw something very strange today.	**I met someone who knows you.**
Hoy he visto algo muy extraño.	Me encontré con alguien que te conoce.
We didn't see anything interesting.	**Did you meet anyone you knew?**
No vimos nada interesante.	¿Te encontraste con alguien conocido?

• •

11 El verbo

11.1 El infinitivo constituye la raíz o forma básica del verbo. La forma completa del infinitivo incluye también *to*: *to live* vivir, *to die* morir, etc. Los verbos irregulares más comunes se dan en la página 1009–1011. Los verbos regulares se conjugan de la forma siguiente:

Infinitivo	want	love[1]	stop[2]	prefer[3]
GERUNDIO/ PARTICIPIO PRESENTE	wanting	loving	stopping	preferring
PRETÉRITO/ PARTICIPIO PASADO	wanted	loved	stopped	preferred

1 Infinitivos que terminan en -*e*
2 Infinitivos de una sílaba que terminan en vocal + consonante sencilla
3 Infinitivos que terminan en vocal con acento tónico + consonante sencilla

El gerundio se usa con función nominal:

I don't like swimming.	**Dancing is fun.**
No me gusta la natación.	Bailar es divertido.

11.2 Los tiempos verbales

11.2.1 Presente

Los verbos *to be* y *to have*:

to be ser o estar	**to have** tener
I am soy o estoy	**I have** tengo
you are eres o estás	**you have** tienes
he/she/it is es o está	**he/she/it has** tiene
we are somos o estamos	**we have** tenemos
you are sois o estáis	**you have** tenéis
they are son o están	**they have** tienen

Para formar el presente de los demás verbos se utiliza el infinitivo sin *to* para todas las personas excepto para la tercera persona del singular que se forma añadiendo al infinitivo sin *to* la desinencia -*s*:

to want (= querer): **I want, you want, he/she/it wants, we want, you want, they want**
to love (= amar): **I love, you love, he/she/it loves, we love, you love, they love**

La tercera persona del singular del presente de los verbos terminados en -*ch*, -*sh*, -*x* o -*ss* se forma añadiendo al infinitivo sin *to* la desinencia -*es*:

to watch mirar: **he/she/it watches**	**to kiss** besar: **he/she/it kisses**
to wish desear: **he/she/it wishes**	**to fix** arreglar: **he/she/it fixes**
to witness ser testigo de: **he/she/it witnesses**	

El presente se usa para expresar algo que es siempre cierto o que sucede regularmente y para enunciar hechos:

He takes the 8 o'clock train to work.   I work in publishing.
Coge el tren de las 8 para ir al trabajo.   Trabajo en una casa editorial.

11.2.2 Pretérito

Tiene la misma forma para todas las personas, tanto para el singular como
para el plural:

I/you/he/she/it/we/you/they wanted

Se usa para referirse a hechos que tuvieron lugar en el pasado, a menudo va
acompañado de expresiones adverbiales que especifican un momento o una
fecha concretos:

He flew to America last week. La semana pasada se fue a América en avión.

11.2.3 Pretérito perfecto

Se forma con el presente del verbo *to have* (= haber) y el participio pasado del
verbo que se conjuga:

I/you have loved, he/she/it has loved, we/you/they have loved

Se usa para referirse a acciones pasadas o acontecimientos que tienen
alguna relación con el momento presente. Se puede ver la diferencia entre el
pretérito perfecto y el pretérito comparando las frases siguientes:

Have you seen Peter this morning?
¿Has visto a Peter esta mañana? (es aún por la mañana)
Did you see Peter this morning?
¿Viste a Peter por la mañana? (es por la tarde o noche)

Obsérvese el uso siguiente del pretérito perfecto y del pretérito:

I have lived in Glasgow for three years.
Vivo en Glasgow desde hace tres años.
I lived in Glasgow for three years.
Viví en Glasgow durante tres años. (y ahora no)

11.2.4 Pretérito pluscuamperfecto

Se forma con el pasado del verbo *to have* (= haber) y el participio pasado del
verbo que se conjuga:

I/you/he/she/it/we/you/they had wanted

Se usa para referirse a acciones o acontecimientos pasados cuya
terminación es anterior a la de otra acción también pasada y completa:

She had already left home when I arrived. Cuando llegué, ya había salido de casa.

11.2.5 Las formas perifrásticas

Las formas perifrásticas se forman con el verbo *to be* (= ser), en el tiempo y la
persona requeridos, y el gerundio del verbo que se conjuga.

Presente continuo

I am singing estoy cantando, you are singing, etc.

Se usa para referirse a algo que está sucediendo en el momento de hablar o a
algo que está en proceso, aunque no esté sucediendo precisamente cuando se
habla:

What are you doing? – I'm trying to fix the television.
¿Qué estás haciendo? – Estoy tratando de arreglar la televisión.

. . . .

He always interrupts when I'm reading to the children.
Siempre me interrumpe cuando estoy leyendo a los niños.

Pasado continuo

I was singing estaba cantando, **you were singing**, etc.

Se usa para referirse a acciones que se desarrollaban en un determinado momento en el pasado:

He rushed into my office while I was talking to the manager.
Entró a toda prisa en mi despacho mientras yo estaba hablando con el director.

Los otros tiempos verbales también tienen formas continuas: *I have been living*; *I had been living*; *I will be living*

Obsérvese el uso siguiente del pretérito perfecto en la forma continua:

I have been living in Glasgow for three years. Llevo tres años viviendo en Glasgow.

11.2.6 El futuro

En inglés hay varias formas de expresar el futuro.

11.2.6.1 Will/shall

Will se puede utilizar con todas las personas; *shall* sólo se utiliza con la primera persona del singular y del plural:

I will/shall go iré	**we will/shall go** iremos
you will go irás	**you will go** iréis
he/she/it will go irá	**they will go** irán

Will y las formas negativas *will not* y *shall not* se pueden contraer:

You'll be angry.	**We won't/shan't stay long.**
Te enfadarás.	No estaremos mucho tiempo.

11.2.6.2 Going to

Esta forma se suele usar para expresar una intención o para predecir algo que va a ocurrir:

I'm going to go to Richmond tomorrow. Mañana voy a Richmond.

Going to es intercambiable con *will*:

The boss is going to be/will be furious when he hears.
El jefe se va a poner furioso cuando se entere.

11.2.6.3 El Presente

Se puede usar para expresar algo que ocurrirá en un momento determinado:

When does term end? ¿Cuándo termina el trimestre?

Se usa de forma parecida a *going to* para expresar una intención:

I'm spending Christmas in Paris. Pasaré las Navidades en París.

11.3 El imperativo

Se forma con el infinitivo sin *to*. El imperativo se usa para dar órdenes:

Be quiet! ¡Cállate!   **Shut the door!** ¡Cierra la puerta!

La forma negativa se hace con *don't*:

Don't forget to phone Alan! ¡No os olvidéis de llamar a Alan!

Let's se usa con la primera persona del plural para formular propuestas:

Let's go. Vamos.   **Don't let's go.** No vamos.   **Let's not go.** No vamos.

Resumen de la gramática inglesa

12 La forma interrogativa

12.1 La forma interrogativa de las oraciones en presente y en pasado simple necesitan utilizar el verbo *to do*, y tiene que concordar con el sujeto de la oración:

Do you live here?	**Did you live here?**
¿Vives aquí?	¿Viviste aquí?

Si la oración tiene un verbo auxiliar (*have*, *be*) o modal, la forma interrogativa se hace invirtiendo el verbo y el sujeto:

Are they going to get married?	**Have they seen us?**	**Can John come at eight?**
¿Se van a casar?	¿Nos han visto?	¿John puede venir a las ocho?

Con los pronombres interrogativos, las formas son las siguientes:

Who came?	**Who fed the cat?**
¿Quién vino?	¿Quién le dio de comer al gato?
What have they done to you?	**What shall we write about?**
¿Qué te han hecho?	¿Sobre qué vamos a escribir?

12.2 Las coletillas interrrogativas

Se trata de preguntas cortas, que se añaden al final de una oración para solicitar confirmación de lo que se ha dicho. Si la oración es afirmativa, va seguida de una coletilla interrogativa negativa:

You smoke, don't you?
Fumas ¿no?

Nótese el auxiliar *don't* que sustituye en la coletilla interrogativa al verbo **smoke**.

Si la oración es negativa, va seguida de una coletilla interrogativa afirmativa:

You don't smoke, do you?	**She doesn't mind, does she?**
No fumas ¿verdad?	No le importa ¿verdad?

Si la oración tiene un verbo auxiliar o modal, es éste el que se repite en la coletilla:

You aren't going, are you?	**You will come, won't you?**
No vas a ir ¿verdad?	Vendrás/Vas a venir ¿no?
You shouldn't say that, should you?	
No deberías decir eso ¿verdad?	

12.3 Las respuestas cortas

En las respuestas cortas, no es necesario repetir la forma completa del verbo principal; se puede simplemente repetir el verbo auxiliar (*be*, *have*, *do*) o modal que aparece en la pregunta:

Do you like fish? – Yes, I do./No, I don't.	**Can you drive? – Yes, I can./No, I can't.**
¿Te gusta el pescado? – Sí./No.	¿Sabes conducir? – Sí./No.

13 Las oraciones negativas

Las oraciones negativas se forman con el verbo auxiliar *do* concordando con

. . . .

el sujeto + *not*. Las contracciones son *don't* y *doesn't* para el presente y *didn't* para el pasado:

They do not/don't understand English.
No entienden el inglés.

We did not/didn't go anywhere yesterday.
Ayer no fuimos a ninguna parte.

. . . .

14 Los verbos auxiliares modales

can, could; may, might; shall, should; will, would; must; ought

Los verbos modales son invariables: **I can, you can, he can**, etc.

Los verbos modales forman las interrogaciones invirtiendo el orden del sujeto y del verbo: **Can I go now?** (= ¿Puedo ir ahora?).

La contracción de *will* y *shall* es *'ll*:

I'll be going (= Iré).

La contracción de *would* es *'d*: **I'd like a cup of tea** (= Me gustaría tomar un té.)

Los verbos modales en la forma negativa utilizan *not* (*would not, might not,* etc.). Es especial la forma negativa de **can: cannot**.

Las contracciones negativas son: **can't, couldn't; mightn't; shan't, shouldn't; won't, wouldn't; mustn't; oughtn't**. (*Mayn't* no es muy frecuente).

14.1 can

Sus significados incluyen: autorización:

Can I leave the table?
¿Puedo levantarme de la mesa?

I can have another sweet, daddy said so.
Puedo tomar otro caramelo, lo dijo papá.

aptitud:

He can count to a hundred.
Sabe contar hasta cien.

Can he drive?
¿Sabe conducir?

posibilidad:

Accidents can happen.
Puede haber accidentes.

peticiones:

Can you open the door for me please?
¿Me puedes abrir la puerta, por favor?

14.1.1 could

Could es el pasado de *can*. Sus significados incluyen: autorizaciones, aptitudes, posibilidades, peticiones, expresadas en el pasado:

Daddy said I could have another sweet.
Papá dijo que podía tomar otro caramelo.

By the time he was three, he could count to a hundred.
A los tres años ya sabía contar hasta cien.

She asked if he could open the door for her.
Preguntó si le podía abrir la puerta.

· ·

peticiones formales en el presente:

Could I leave a message please? ¿Podría dejar un recado, por favor?

posibilidad expresada en el presente:

I don't know where John is; I suppose he could be at Anne's.
No se dónde está John; supongo que estará en casa de Anne.

indignación/reproche:

You could have warned me!
¡Podías haberme avisado!

14.2 may

Sus significados incluyen: autorizaciones y peticiones formales:

May I use your telephone please?
¿Puedo usar su teléfono, por favor?

You may not leave the examination hall until I give the sign.
No pueden salir del aula de examen hasta que les haga la seña.

posibilidad:

We may get an extra day's holiday.
Puede que tengamos un día más de vacaciones.

They may have left.
Puede que se hayan ido.

14.2.1 might

Sus significados incluyen: posibilidad:

We might get a pay rise.
A lo mejor nos suben el sueldo. (es poco probable)

Se usa también en pasado:

He was afraid he might have missed the train.
Temía que quizá había perdido el tren.

(*Might* se diferencia de *may* en que a menudo la posibilidad que expresa es más remota que la que expresa *may*.)

autorizaciones y peticiones formales:

Do you think I might have another whisky?
¿Crees que podría tomar otro whisky?

indignación/reproche:

You might have phoned!
¡Podías haber llamado!

14.3 shall

Para ver cómo se expresa el futuro con *shall*, véase 11.2.6.1. *Shall* se puede usar para expresar: peticiones o consejos:

Where shall we put the shopping?
¿Dónde ponemos la compra?

propuestas o sugerencias:

Shall we meet outside the station?
¿Qué te parece si nos vemos en la entrada de la estación?

14.3.1 should

Should es el pasado de *shall*; y también se utiliza para expresar:

• •

obligación:

You shouldn't tell lies.
No deberías decir mentiras.

What do you think we should do?
¿Qué crees que deberíamos hacer?

probabilidad:

Once this job is finished, we should have more spare time.
Una vez que terminemos este trabajo, deberíamos tener más tiempo libre.

They should be there by now.
Ya deberían estar allí.

14.4 will

Para ver cómo se expresa el futuro con *will*, véase 11.2.6.1. **Will** también se puede utilizar para expresar: un comportamiento típico o una característica innata:

Hot air will rise.
El aire caliente asciende.

The stadium will seat 4,000 people.
El estadio tendrá un aforo de 4.000 personas.

voluntad, deseo, consentimiento:

Will you see to the post for me?
¿Quieres ocuparte tú de la correspondencia?

I'll do what I can to help him.
Haré lo que pueda para ayudarle.

para ofrecer algo:

Will you have another slice of cake?
¿Quieres tomar otro trozo de tarta?

algo muy probable o una deducción:

There's someone at the door, that will be Ken.
Llaman a la puerta, debe ser Ken.

14.4.1 would

Would es el pasado de *will*. También se puede utilizar para expresar:

el «futuro en el pasado», o una intención pasada:

He told me he would do it immediately.
Me dijo que lo haría inmediatamente.

They said they wouldn't wait for me.
Dijeron que no me esperarían.

una costumbre/rutina en el pasado:

He would always get up at 6 a.m.
Solía levantarse siempre a la seis de la mañana.

14.5 must

Sus significados incluyen: obligación:

You must make sure you lock up.
Tienes que asegurarte de cerrar con llave.

I must check whether my neighbour is all right.
Tengo que ver si mi vecino está bien.

probabilidad:

They must be there by now.
Ya deben de estar allí.

You must have been annoyed by the decision.
La decisión te debió de sentar fatal.

14.6 ought

Sus significados incluyen: obligación:

You ought to be leaving.
Deberías marcharte.

They ought to send him away.
Deberían decirle que se fuera.

probabilidad, expectativa:

> **They ought to be there by now.**
> Ya tendrían que estar allí.

> **Two kilos of potatoes. That ought to be enough.**
> Dos kilos de patatas. Con eso debería ser suficiente.

15 Los verbos con partículas

Muchos verbos se pueden combinar con preposiciones y adverbios para formar los llamados verbos con partículas (Phrasal verbs). La partícula cambia, en la mayoría de los casos, el significado del verbo. Además las partículas pueden colocarse en posiciones distintas dentro de la frase. En este diccionario todos los verbos con partículas están precedidos del símbolo ■ , p. ej. ■ **take off**.

La posición que dichas partículas ocupan en la frase aparece en la información entre corchetes [...]. Véase el verbo, **take**[1] /teik/ *vt*:

■ **take after** [*v* + *prep* + *o*] salir a, parecerse a; **he ~s after his father** se parece a su padre.

En este caso la información entre corchetes [...] nos indica que la única posición posible de la partícula es *verb* + *preposition* + *object* como aparece en el ejemplo: **he ~s after his father**.

Sin embargo, en la entrada siguiente sacada del diccionario, la partícula puede colocarse en dos posiciones distintas sin alterar el significado:

■ **take off** [*v* + *o* + *adv*, *v* + *adv* + *o*] quitar, sacar; ...

> **He took his boots off./ He took off his boots.** Se quitó las botas.

No obstante, cuando el complemento directo es un pronombre, la única posición posible del pronombre es entre el verbo y la partícula:

> **He took them off.** Se las quitó. (**them** = **his boots**; las = las botas)

Nótese, como claramente indica el diccionario, que en **take off** = despegar, la colocación es [*v* + *adv*] y en este caso la única posición posible de *off*, es a continuación del verbo:

> **The plane took off.** El avión despegó.

16 La voz pasiva

El uso de la voz pasiva en inglés es mucho más frecuente que en español. Se forma con el verbo *to be* y el participio pasado del verbo que se conjuga.

> **The walls were built in the seventeenth century.**
> Se construyeron las murallas en el siglo diecisiete.

> **My car is being repaired.**
> Me están arreglando el coche.